THE FOOTBALL ENCYCLOPEDIA

Other Books Authored by Sports Products Inc.

PRO FOOTBALL: THE EARLY YEARS
THE SPORTS ENCYCLOPEDIA: BASEBALL
THE SPORTS ENCYCLOPEDIA: PRO BASKETBALL
THE SCRAPBOOK HISTORY OF BASEBALL
THE SCRAPBOOK HISTORY OF PRO FOOTBALL
THE ALL-SPORTS WORLD RECORD BOOK
THE WORLD SERIES
THE WORLD BOOK OF ODDS
MONDAY MORNING QUARTERBACK
THE COMPLETE ALL-TIME BASEBALL REGISTER
THE COMPLETE ALL-TIME PRO FOOTBALL REGISTER
THE UNIVERSITY OF MICHIGAN FOOTBALL SCRAPBOOK
THE NOTRE DAME FOOTBALL SCRAPBOOK
THE OHIO STATE FOOTBALL SCRAPBOOK
PRO FOOTBALL WEEKLY'S 1980 ALMANAC
PRO FOOTBALL WEEKLY'S 1981 ALMANAC
BEAT THE SPREAD 1982
THE PRO FOOTBALL BETTOR'S COMPANION

THE FOOTBALL ENCYCLOPEDIA

The Complete History of Professional Football from 1892 to the Present

DAVID S. NEFT,
RICHARD M. COHEN
and
RICK KORCH

Editorial Consultants:
Bob Carroll and John G. Hogrogian

St. Martin's Press
New York

 For information, address St. Martin's Press, 175 Fifth Avenue, New York, N.Y. 10010.

Library of Congress Cataloging-in-Publication Data

Neft, David S.

The football encyclopedia : the complete history of professional football, from 1892 to the present / David S. Neft and Richard M. Cohen.

p. cm.

ISBN 0-312-11435-4

1. Football—United States—History. 2. National Football League—History. 3. Football—United States—Statistics. 4. National Football League—Statistics. I. Cohen, Richard M., 1938- . II. Title.

GV954.N44 1990

796.332'64'0973—dc20 90-36872

CIP

10 9 8 7 6 5 4 3 2 1

Contents

1960-1969 FROM 12 TO 26 318

1970-1979 Big Dollars — Big Problems 493

1980-1993 New Challenges, New Triumphs 699

Preface and Acknowledgments

This is the most comprehensive football encyclopedia ever published. The authors first created *The Football Encyclopedia* in 1974 as the *Sports Encyclopedia: Pro Football.* Years of intensive research have taken place since that first edition and the result is this book, the most complete history of pro football available anywhere. Many corrections and much new information have been found since those earlier editions. For the pro football period 1920-32, there are some gaps in information and the authors are continuing to research out this new information. You, the reader, can help. If you find any new facts or corrections, please send them to us (at the address below) so that future editions can be corrected and updated.

Although the National Football League was basically founded in 1920, the main body of statistical material was not available until 1933. The year 1933 also signalled the standardization of schedules, divisional play and the first official postseason championship games.

The authors have endeavored to recreate the 1920-1932 period as best as possible. For the first time anywhere, lthis book includes scores and dates for each game played during this period. Much of the statistical material (also newly created) has been culled through play-by-plays available in newspapers at the time.

In an effort to keep this material as complete as possible, we hope readers will send all further information and corrections to the address listed at the end of the acknowledgements.

The authors have taken the liberty of arranging the material into various periods (1920-1932, 1933-1945 and 1946-1959). The 1933-1945 period covers the years when professional football became organizationally cohesive and instilled public confidence. Then, in 1946, the All-American Football Conference came upon the scene and, although surviving only four years before a merger with the N.F.L. took place, it served to bolster the "pro game" in cities which were previously unsuitable. The advent of the American Football league in 1960 accounts for the next period (appearing in *Pro Football: The Modern Era*).

It is because of this division that the opportunity is available for fans to now gauge football history in a greater perspective. In each period, the authors have included a wealth of statistical matter and text in a year-by-year format. Additionally, there are register sections, championship games, single-season and lifetime leaders, as well as a host of other featured material, all of which serves to make *Pro Football: The Early Years* the most complete book of its kind.

For the authors, who could not have undertaken this project alone, there are many individuals and former professional players to thank whose assistance was necessary in helping make this book a reality. Their contributions are extensive and range from supplying demographic information to some of the color as it actually took place on the field. To these individuals, the authors express their appreciation that finally there is a book where you can "go and look it up."

Chief consultant in the preparation of the written manuscripts
Jordan A. Deutsch, John G. Hogrogian, Bob Carroll

Director of research and coordinator for earlier editions —
Roland T. Johnson

Special consultants —
Jim Campbell, John G. Hogrogian, Michael Neft, Richard H. Bozzone, Shawn Gray

Pro Football Hall of Fame —
Joe Horrigan, Curator-Director of Research Information, who made available not only his facilities, but also his endless knowledge, time, and cooperation in seeing this book to its fruition.
Don Smith, Public Relations Director
Pete Fierle, Research Associate

Stan Grosshandler —
An independent contributor who coordinated and served as liaison with many of the following former professional football players and their families:

John Alexander	Chuck Bednarik	Lo Boutwell
Hal Broda	Jack Christiansen	Dutch Clark
Charlie Conerly	Jack Cronin	Ernie Cuneo
Ed Danowski	Art DeCarlo	Art Donovan
Benny Friedman	Jon Garnjost	Mrs. Edward Glick
Buckets Goldenberg	Otto Graham	Kinkey Haines
Eddie Halicki	George Halas	Pat Harder
Mrs. Lester Hearden	Mel Hein	Clarke Hinkle
Crazylegs Hirsch	Dick Hoerner	Mack Hummon
Henry Jordan	Don Kindt	Joe Kopcha
Dante Lavelli	Marion Motley	Jim Mutscheller
Ernie Nevers	Ray Novotny	Curley Oden
Glen Presnell	Neil Rengel	William K. Ringwalt
Johnny Sisk	Hank Soar	Ken Strong
Y.A. Tittle	Emlen Tunnell	Ralph Vince
Alex Wojciechowicz	Mrs. Charles Zunker	

Elias Sports Bureau —
Seymour Siwoff
Steve Hirdt

Independent Contributors —

Bob Allen	Hub Arkush	Bob Barnett
Mel Bashore	Richard Brown	Joel Bussert
Bill Carle	Stan Carlson	Tom Cooper
John Crelli	David Daugherty	Bob Davids
Bill Dolbier	Mike Gage	Jim Gallagher
Bob Gill	Bill Himmelman	Lawrence M. Hoff
W. Lloyd Johnson	Joe Junod	Bob Kirlin
Jay Langhammer	Joe Lawler	Charles LeChorchick
Tod Maher	Ron McKenzie	Nancy McKinnon
Mark Maltby	Richard Musterer	Bob Pence
Frank Phelps	Ray Queen	Libby Rehm
Marvin Scade	Jack Selzer	Irwin D. Shapiro
Tod Spieker	Frank M. Swain	George W. Treece
Lance Trusty	Chuck Wasserstrom	Jim Whalen
Karl Wolf	Randy Wooden	

Professional Football Researchers Association (PFRA) — Whose members' research have provided much of the statistical and historical data.

Typesetting — Land Systems, Geri-Ann Israel

The Notre Dame Int'l Sports and Games Research Collections
Jethrow Kyles, Curator
Herb Juliano (Curator-1982)
Rita Erskine

National Baseball Hall of Fame — Bill Deane, Ken Fetterman

National Archives and Records Service, General Services Administration — Carmelita S. Ryan, Scientific, Economic and Natural Resources Branch, Civil Archives Division

Univ. of Akron — John V. Miller, Jr., Director of Archival Services; Ken McDonald, former SID
Univ. of Alabama — Mrs. Gunetta R. Rich, Special Collections Library
Alfred Univ. — Norma Higgins, Archivist
Allegheny College Library
Amherst College — Anne Ostendarp, Archives Assistant
Arizona State Univ. — Jeannette Frantz, University Archives
Univ. of Arizona — David P. Robrock, Peter Steere, Roger Myers, Manuscript Librarians, Special Collections
Univ. of Arkansas — Tony Wappel, Special Collections
Auburn Univ. — David Rosenblatt, Records Manager; Pamela R. Pedersen, Office of Alumni Development; Beverly S. Powers, Reference Assistant
Austin College — Martha Cox, Archivist
Baldwin-Wallace College — Eloise Tressel, Secretary, Athletic Archives
Baylor Univ. — Ellen Brown, Texas Collection
Beloit College — Joseph Kobylka, Alumni Director
Bethany (West Virginia) — Marilyn Shaver, Archivist
Boston College — Reid Oslin, Asst. Athletic Director for Sports Publicity; Prof. Richard J. Schrader, Dept. of English; Mary M. Hawes, Transcript Coordinator; Amy Felker, Asst. Archivist
Boston Univ. — Amy Shepardson, Special Collections Library
Bradley Univ. — Sherri Schneider, Special Collections Asst.; Ruth Jass, Registrar
Brown Univ. — Martha L. Mitchell, University Archivist, Gayle Lynch, Archives Assistant
Bucknell Univ. — Bradley Tufts, Asst. Director of Athletics-PR, courtesy of the Bucknell University Archives; Doris Dysinger
Butler Univ. — Gisela Terrell, Rare Books and Special Collections Librarian
Univ. of California-Berkeley — William M. Roberts, University Archivist
Calif. Polytechnic State Univ. — Ken Kenyon, University Archives
Canisius College — Robert J. Nelson S.J., Archivist; John D. Garvey, S.J., Director of Archives
Carleton College — Mark A. Greene, Archivist
Carnegie-Mellon Univ. — Mary C. Schall, University Libraries
Carroll College — Jean Olsen, Registar's Office; Jame E. Van Ess, Archivist
Case Western Reserve Univ. — Bob Psuik, Assistant Archivist
Catawba College — Brian Morrison, SID
Catholic University — Anthony Zitto, Archivist, Mullen Library; Lynn Conway, Assistant to the Archivist
Centenary College Library
Univ. of Central Arkansas — Tony Sitz, Registrar; Tom W. Dillard, Director, Torreyson Library
Central College (Kans.) — Linda Green, Alumni Director
Central Michigan Univ. — Evelyn Leasher, Public Services Librarian
Central Missouri State Univ. — Nancy E. Littlejohn, Special Collections Librarian
Centre College — Robert Glass-Archivist, Grace Doherty Library
Univ. of Chicago — Caroline Coven, Archives and Manuscripts Assistant
City College of New York — Barbara Dunlap, Archives and Special Collections
Colgate Univ. — Bob Connell, Sports Information Office
Colorado State Univ. — Steve Dahl, Registrar's Office
Columbia Univ. — Curtis Pires, Office of Sports Publicity
Connecticut College Library
Univ. of Connecticut — Randall Jimerson, Archivist; Joanna Oudin, Assistant Archivist
Cornell College — Anne Secor, Archivist, Berta Ringold, Circulation Supervisor-Cole Library
Cornell Univ. — Kathleen Jacklin, Archivist; Roberta M. Moudry, Archives Assistant
Dartmouth College — Kenneth C. Cramer, Archivist
Davidson College Library
Davis & Elkins College — Beth Guye Kittle, Director of Alumni Relations
Denison Univ. — Mrs. Florence Hoffman, Archivist; Larry R. Murdock, Registrar
DePaul Univ. — Eileen Ward, Mary Zimmerman
DePauw Univ. — Virginia Brann, Archivist; Roy O. West, Library
Univ. of Detroit — Rev. Edward J. Dowling S.J. Archives; Andy Glatzman, Asst. SID
Dickinson College — Archivist
Drake Univ. — J. Elias Jones, Bibliographer and Archivist
Duquense Univ. — Fr. Richard Wersing, Archivist
Earlham College — Sara Beth Terrell, Archivist
East Central Univ. (Okla.) — Dava Albertson, Secretary to Dept. of Athletics
Emporia State Univ. — James Meyer, Asst. to the President for Development and University Relations
Findley College — John C. Hutson, Asst. to the President

Fordham Univ. — Rev. Edward Dunn, S.J., Archivist; Stephen Bordas, Registrar
Franklin College — Mary Alice Medlicott, Archivist
Geneva College — W. Lee Troup, Director of Public Relations
Georgetown Univ. — Jon Reynolds, University Archives
George Washington Univ. Library
Univ. of Georgia — Robert M. Willingham, Jr., Curator — Rare Books and Manuscripts; Roy Gatchell, Athletic Association
Georgia Inst. of Technology Library
Grinnell College — Anne Kintner, College Archivist
Grove City College — Cindy Wallheim, Secretary-Public Relations Dept.; John W. Cole, Registrar
Gustavus Adolphus College — Edi Thorstensson, Archivist
Hamline Univ. — Muriel McEachern, Archivist; Thelma Boeder, Consulting Archivist
Hampden-Sydney College — Alan Zoellner, Reference Librarian
Harvard Univ. — Harley P. Holden (Curator) and John Trepasso, Univ. Archives
Haskell Indian J.C. — Milton S. Overby, Director-Learning Resources Center
Heidelberg College — Carl G. Klopfenstein (Prof. Emeritus of History), Director of Archives; Cindy Murphy, Assistant to the Registrar
Hobart and William Smith Colleges — Cahrles P. Boswell, Registrar
College of the Holy Cross — Rev. Eugene J. Harrington S.J., Archivist; Arlene Long and Cynthia Medina, Assistants to the Archivist
Univ. of Idaho — M.E. Telin, Director of Admissions and Registrar
Univ. of Illinois — William Maher, University Archives; Robert T. Chapel, Archives Technical Assistant
Indiana Univ. — J. William Baus, Asst. Archivist; Elisabeth R. Olesskar and Bryan Young — University Archives
Iowa State Univ. — Laura S. Kline, Special Collections Librarian
Univ. of Iowa — Earl M. Rogers, Curator of Archives
John Carroll Univ. Library
Kalamazoo College — Thomas M. Myers, Director of Public Relations
Kansas State Univ. — Denise Wells, Registrar's Office
Univ. of Kansas — John M. Nugent, University Archives
Univ. of Kentucky — Frank B. Stanger, Jr., Archivist
Kenyon College — Thomas B. Greenslade, Archivist
Knox College — Lynn Harlan, Curator — Archives and Manuscript Collections
Lafayette College — Albert W. Gendebein, Archivist, Diane Windham Shaw, Archivist
Lake Forest College — Martha Briggs, Assistant Librarian
Lawrence Univ. — Ms. Kathy Isaacson, Reference Librarian
Lebanon Valley College — Bruce S. Correll, Registrar
Lehigh Univ. — Miss Georgia E. Raynor, Special Collections, Linderman Library
Loras College — Michael D. Gibson, Archives
Univ. of Louisville — Thomas L. Owen, Asst. Director — University Archives and Record Center
Loyola Univ. of Chicago — Brother Michael Grace S.J. Archivist
Luther College — Duane W. Fenstermann, Head of Technical Services
Macalester College — Harry Drake, Archivist
Manchester College — Amy L. Taylor, Sports Information Dept.
Marietta College — Ms. Jody Pannier, Special Collections, Dawes Library
Marquette Univ. — John LeDoux, Archivist, Charles Elston, Archives, Memorial Library and Ms. Terry Margherita
Marshall Univ. — Mrs. Teal, Archivist
Miami Univ. (Ohio) Library
Univ. of Michigan — Matt Louis, SID Office
Michigan State Univ. — Larry Ziewacz, Professor
Middlebury Colleg — Robert Buckeye, Special Collections
Millikin Univ. — Reggie Syrcle, University Relations Director
Univ. of Minnesota — Penny Krosch, Archivist
Univ. of Mississippi — Kenneth L. Wooten, Registrar
Univ. of Missouri — Ms. D.J. Wade, Reference Specialist
Univ. of Missouri-Rolla — Wayne M. Bledsoe, Archivist and Professor of History
Montana State Univ. — Jean Smith, Archivist
Univ. of Montana — Dale L. Johnson, Archivist; Alita Phelps, Transcript Clerk; Dave Guffey, SID
Moorhead State Univ. Library
Morningside College — Candace Davies
Mount Union College — Alan Aldinger, SID
Muhlenberg College — Dr. Ralph S. Graber, Professor of English
Univ. of Nebraska — Lynn R. Beidrick,-Porn, Asst. University Archives; Jane Jameson, Records Dept.-Alumni Assoc.; Ted Pfeifer, Director, Registration and Records
Univ. of Nevada-Reno — Karen Gash, Archivist
Univ. of New Hampshire — Betty Aldrich, Transcript Office
Univ. of New Mexico — Jim Acosta, Associate Registrar
New York Univ. — Rohinie Munzel, N.Y.U. Archives; Peter Braunstein, Archival Assistant
Univ. Of North Carolina — Michael G. Martin, Jr., University Archivist
North Carolina State Univ. Library
North Dakota State Univ. — George Ellis, SID
NE Missouri State Univ. — Judith May, Special Collections
Northwestern Univ. — Patrick M. Quinn, Archivist; Kevin Leonard, University Archives
Univ. of Notre Dame — Daniel H. Winicur, Registrar
Oglethorpe Univ. — Polly Perry, Alumni Director; Earle J. Moore Sr., Retired Coach
Ohio Northern Univ. — Robert L. Allen, Jr., Chemistry Dept.
Ohio State Univ. — Raimund E. Goerler, University Archivist
Ohio Univ. — Sheppard Black, Archives and Special Collections; Frank Morgan, SID; Karen Jones, Registrar's Office
Ohio Wesleyan Univ. — Pam Howard, Reference Librarian-Beeghly Library; Sabrina Pollock, Registrar's Office
Univ. of Oklahoma — Ms. Johnnie Williams, Graduate Assistant-Academic Records
Oklahoma City Univ. — Larry McAlister, Sports Information Office
Oklahoma State Univ. — Heather Lloyd, Reference Librarian; Kayla Barrett, Assistant Librarian for University Archives
Oregon State Univ. — Georgia Scott, Asst. Archivist; Hal Cowan, SID
Univ. of Oregon — Keith Richard, University Archivist
Ottawa Univ. — Annabelle Pence, Registrar
Otterbein College — John Berker
Univ. of Pennsylvania — Mandy Erickson, Administrative Aide-Sports Information Dept.
Pennsylvania State Univ. Library
Phillips Univ. — Nancy Smith, Asst. to the Registrar; Betty Ragsdell, Cataloguing Reference Librarian
Univ. of Pittsburgh Library
Princeton Univ. — Nicholas Donatiello, SID; Earl Coleman, Archivist
Providence College — Jane M. Jackson, Asst. Archivist; Teena Sullivan, Archives
Purdue Univ. — Linda Tye, Special Collections, Purdue Univ. Li-

braries
Univ. of Redlands Library
Univ. of Rhode Island — David C. Masyln, Head Special Collections; Inter-Library loan dept.; and Richard Gelles, Dean
Ripon College — William R. Brandt, College Archivist
Univ. of Rochester — Karl Kabelac, Manuscripts Librarian-Dept. of Rare Books and Special Collections
Rose-Hulman Institute of Technology — Bob Goldring, SID; Dale Long, SID; John Robson, Archivist
Rutgers Univ. — Ruth Simmons, Edward Skipworth and Susan Avallone, Special Collections and Archives; Kenneth J. Iuso, Registrar
St. Ambrose College — Corinne Potter
St. Bonaventure Univ. — Malcolm V.T. Wallace, Archivist; Lorraine Welsh, Assistant Archivist
St. Cloud State — Keith J. Rauch, Director of Records and Registration; Judy Nielson, Transcript Clerk
St. Edward's Univ.— Ms. Inez Nira, Archivist
St. John's Univ. (Minn.) — Vincent Tegeder, Archivist
St. John's Univ. (N.Y.) — Frank Ralaniello, Asst. SID
Sr. Lawrence Univ. — Ms. Lynn Case Ekfelt, University Archivist
St. Mary's College of California — Brother L. Dennis, F.S.C. Archivist
St. Mary's College (Minn.) — Brother Paul J. Ostendorf, Head Librarian and Archivist; Brother Richard Gerlach
St. Olaf College — Joan R. Olson, Archivist
College of St. Thomas — John Davenport, Special Collections Librarian
Samford University — Shirley L. Hutchens, Special Collections Dept.
Univ. of Santa Clara — Julie O'Keefe, Asst. Archivist
Univ. of South Dakota Library
Univ. of Southern California — Paul Christopher, University Archivist
Southern Methodist Univ. — Lee Milazzo, Office of University Archives; P.J. Hunter, Certification Specialist; John Underwood, Assistant Basketball Coach
Southwest Texas State Univ. — Iris T. Schumann, Acting Archivist; Jennifer B. Patterson, Special Collections Assistant
Springfield College — Gerald F. Davis, Library Director; Ms. Marjorie Fish
Swarthmore College — Archivist
Syracuse Univ. — Amy Doherty, Archivist; Mary O'Brien, Asst. Archivist; Carolyn Davis, Manuscript Librarian; Ann Atwater; Cindy L. Curtis, Certification Administrator, Office of the Registrar
Temple Univ. — Carol Ann Harris, Bibliographic Assistant, Templana Collection, Paley Library
Univ. of Tennessee-Chattanooga — Harold Wilkes, Bill Prince
Univ. of Tennessee — H.D. (Bud) Ford, Asst. SID
Texas A&M Univ. — Charles R. Schultz, University Archivist
Texas Chistian Univ. — Archivist
University of Texas — William H. Richter, Asst. Archivist-Public Service
Thiel College — John R. Hauser, Alumni Director; Dr. Paul Mueller, Archivist
Univ. of Toledo Library
Trinity College (Conn.) — Peter Knapp, Archivist
Tufts Univ. — Robert Johnson-Lally, Asst. Archivist; Mildred S. Eastwood, Registrar, A&S
Univ. of Tulsa — Toby Murray, Archivist
U.S. Military Academy — Kenneth W. Rapp, Asst. Archivist; Robert Schnare, Special Collections Division
U.S. Naval Academy — Mrs. Jane H. Price, Asst. Archivist
Ursinus College — James R. Rue, Archivist
Univ. of Utah — Clint Bailey, University Archivist
Valparaiso Univ. — Daniel R. Gahl, Archivist
Vanderbilt Univ. — Sara J. Harwell, Library Asst., Special Collections
Univ. of Vermont — David J. Blow, Asst. Archivist
Villanova Univ. — Mrs. Kathyrn L. Abraham, Archivist
Univ. of Virginia — Michael Plunkett, Asst. Curator of Manuscripts; Jane Desjardins, Sports Information Office
Virginia Military Institute — Archivist
Wabash College — Max Servies, Athletic Director
Wake Forest Univ. — John R. Woodward, Director, Baptist Historical Collection
Washburn Univ. of Topeka — Charlene S. Hurt, Director of Library and Media Services
Washington College (Md.) — F.W. Dumschott
Washington & Jefferson College — David W. Kraueter, Reference Librarian
Washington & Lee Univ. — Lisa M. Hamric, Special Collections Asst.
Washington State Univ. — Terry Abraham, Manuscripts-Archives Librarian
Waynesburg Colege — Janice Brunazi, Teresa Verango; Mrs. Evalyn Black, Assistant Registrar
Western Kentucky Univ. — Helen L. Knight , University Archives
Western Maryland College — Winifred S. Dulany, Asst. Archivist
Westminster College (Pa.) — Archivist
West Virginia Univ. — John Antonik, Associate SID, Bille Leach, Records Officer
Whittier College — Mrs. Ann Topjon, Reference Librarian and Betty Kenworthy, Registrar
Wichita State Univ. — Kayla Barrett, Graduate Asst., Dept. of Special Collections
College of William and Mary — Laura F. Parrish, Asst. College Archivist; Jeff. Nygaard, Assistant SID
William Jewell College — Iva Lea Durocher, Alumni Office
Williams College — Karen D. Drickamer, Curator-Williamsiana Collection; Catherine Curvin
Wilmington College — Ina E. Kelley, Archivist/Curator
Univ. of Wisconsin — Debra Gansen, Office of the Registrar; personnel at the Sports Information Department; Daniel C. Markel, Assistant Archivist; David M. Sieden, Assistant Archivist
Univ. of Wisconsin-Eau Claire — Richard L. Pifer, University Archivist
Univ. of Wisconsin-LaCrosse — Edwin L. Hill, Special Collection, Murphy Library; Alumni Association
Univ. of Wisconsin-Milwaukee — Allan Kovan, University Archivist
Univ. of Wisconsin-Oshkosh — Eva Peterson, Library Services Assistant
Univ. of Wisconsin-Stevens Point — Ray Stroik, Assistant Archivist
Wittenberg Univ. — Ms. Regina Entorf, Archivist; Kathy Schulz, Reference Librarian
College of Wooster — Lowell W. Coolidge, Archivist
Xavier Univ. (Ohio) — Ben Benedict, Office of Sports Information; Doris R. Wolf, Assistant Registrar
Yale Univ. — Patricia Bodak Stark, Principal Reference Archivist

The author's wives (a special thanks for once again displaying their faith, cooperation and patience throughout the project) —

Naomi Neft, Nancy Cohen and Jacquie Korch

Since such a book of this magnitude will include errors, the authors would appreciate, for the purpose of keeping future editions as accurate and complete as possible, if the readers will send any corrections and additions to St. Martins Press.

Codes And Explanations

In each section of the book, unfamiliar abbreviations, and bold facing may be shown. The following, by section, is an explanation of this matter:

Yearly Sections

Age — The age shown for each player is as of Sept. 1 of that year.

Traded Players — From 1933 through 1959, shown only on the team which the player played for most, along with a "from or to" reference.

Bold Facing — Indicates league leaders.

Team Name Line — Shown alongside the name of each team is the team Won-Lost-Tied record and the head coaches.

Home Team Indication — In a team's game-by-game scores, certain opponents appear in upper case. This means that the opponent played at the team's home park.

Opponent's Score — In a team's game-by-game scores the opponent's score always appears in the right hand column.

Rosters — Attempts to include, in a year, only those who actually played in a league game. The limitations of data, however, may have accidentally included men who did not get into a league game.

Position Abbreviations — Applies to all sections. If a man played more than one position, the listing is in order of amount played at each position. For the period 1920-1932, only offense positions are shown.

BB — Blocking back (Quarterback)
C — Center
DB — Defensive back
DE — Defensive end
DG — Defensive guard
DT — Defensive tackle
NT — Nose tackle
FB — Fullback
FL — Flanker
G — Offensive and defensive guard
HB — Halfback
K — Punter or place kicker (and did not play any other position in a particular year)
LB — Linebacker
OG — Offensive guard
OE — Offensive end
OT — Offensive tackle
QB — Quarterback
T — Offensive and defensive tackle
TB — Tailback
TE — Tight end
WB — Wingback
WR — Wide receiver

Note: To see how these positions line up in the formation, see Formation Diagrams on pages 285-288.

Career Interruptions — Fully explained, but only covers a full year or career end interruption.

Team Abbreviations — (Applies to all sections)

Akr — Akron
Atl — Atlanta
Bal — Baltimore
Bkn — Brooklyn
Bos — Boston
Buf — Buffalo
Can — Canton
ChiB — Chicago Bears and Chicago Staleys
ChicC — Chicago Cardinals
ChiT — Chicago Tigers
Cin — Cincinnati
Cle — Cleveland
Col — Columbus
C-T — Chicago Cardinals-Pittsburgh Steelers (merged
C-S — Cincinnati Reds and St. Louis Gunners
Dal — Dallas
Day — Dayton
Dec — Decatur
Den — Denver
Det — Detroit
Dul — Duluth
Eva — Evansville
Fra — Frankford
GB — Green Bay
Ham — Hammond
Har — Hartford
Hou — Houston
KC — Kansas City
Ken — Kenosha
LA — Los Angeles
Lou — Louisville
Mia — Miami
Mil — Milwaukee
Min — Minnesota or Minneapolis
Mun — Muncie
NE — New England
NO — New Orleans
Nwk — Newark
NYB — New York Bulldogs
NYG — New York Giants
NYJ — New York Jets
NYT — New York Titans
NYY — New York Yankees
Oak — Oakland
Oor — Oorang (Marion, Ohio)
Ora — Orange
Phi — Philadelphia
Pit — Pittsburgh
P-P — Philadelphia Eagles-Pittsburgh Steelers (merged)
Port — Portsmouth
Pott — Pottsville
Prov — Providence
Rac — Racine
RI — Rock Island
Roch — Rochester
SD — San Diego
SF — San Francisco
SI — Staten Island
StL — St. Louis
Was — Washington

Championship Section

Giveaways — Passes that were intercepted and fumbles lost.

Takeaways — Passes intercepted and opposing fumbles recovered.

Takeaways — Passes intercepted and opposing fumbles recovered.

Note: These two categories apply to team statistics only.

TAP — Indicates Tackled Attempting to Pass.

Register Sections

Players have been assigned to the various register sections according to what time period they played in most. The only exception to this is that anybody who played mostly before 1933 but overlapped his career beyond 1933, would appear in the 1933-45 Period Register Sections.

Register sections, for 1920-32, 1933-45 and 1946-59, are divided into an alphabetical register, and then into various statistical registers. In the alphabetical register, alongside each man's name are one or more reference numbers (1, 2, 3, 4, 5). These reference numbers are to serve as guides as where to find the player's statistical record (if there is no reference number it means the player did not have enough minimum statistics to rate a ranking). The following are the reference numbers and their identification:

1 Passing
2 Rushing and receiving
3 Punt returns and kickoff returns
4 Punting
5 Kicking

The register sections are broken down into three periods, 1920-32, 1933-45, 1946-59.

Some of the unfamiliar information which appears in each alphabetical register is as follows:

Last name, Use name (name player was known as), nicknames which appear in parenthesis ( ):
Bailey, Howard (Screeno)

Weight — Average weight for career.

HC — Indicates, for year or years, that the player was a head coach.

PC — Indicates, for year or years, that the player was a head coach while actively playing.

* — next to a college indicates that the player attended the college after the start of his pro football career.

League Abbreviations — A (American Football League), AA (All-American Football Conference).

Other Major League Sports — Certain players also played professional basketball or major league baseball. The basketball information is indicated with the league in abbreviations: NBL—National Basketball League, NBA—National Basketball Association, BAA—Basketball Association of America, ABL—American Basketball League.

Career Interruptions — If an abbreviation other than a league follows the year played, it means that a full year was missed or a career end be- of certain prevailing reasons. The codes and explanations follow:

AA	— Injured in automobile accident
AJ	— Arm injury
BA	— Broken arm
BC	— Broken collarbone
BG	— Broken finger
BH	— Broken bone in hand
BL	— Broken leg
BN	— Broken ankle
BQ	— Broken neck
BW	— Broken or dislocated wrist
CFL	— Played in Canadian Football League
CJ	— Concussion
DR	— Suspended for drug use
EJ	— Elbow injury
FJ	— Foot or heel injury
GJ	— Groin injury
HJ	— Hand injury
HO	— Holdout
IJ	— Eye injury
IL	— Illness
JJ	— Injury (type of injury unknown)
KJ	— Knee injury
LJ	— Leg or thigh injury (including Achilles' tendon)
MS	— Military service
NJ	— Ankle injury
PJ	— Hip injury
RJ	— Finger injury
SJ	— Shoulder injury or shoulder separation
SL	— Suspended by commissioner
TJ	— Stomach or abdomen injury
USFL	— Played in USFL
VR	— Voluntarily retired
WFL	— Played in World Football League
XJ	— Back injury

How To Read The 1920-1932 Statistical Tables

The tables opposite each team roster represent a meticulous reconstruction from all available newspaper acounts or other available sources. Some game stories contain complete play-by-play accounts; others give only highlights.

Five statistical categories are given for each player who made any statistical mark: rushing, passing, receiving, punting and punt returns. Each category is subdivided into complete games, wherein are totalled all those games for which complete statistics were recoverable, and incomplete games, wherein are totalled those games for which only partial statistics could be gleaned.

Reading, from left to right, rushing statistics, under complete games: G equals games for which complete statistics are known in which the individual player appeared, Att equals his rushing attempts in those games, Yds equals yards gained rushing, Avg equals average yards per rushing attempt, and TD equals rushing touchdowns. Under incomplete games, G equals games in which the player appeared for which only partial statistics are known, Att, Yds and TD figures are given to the extent known. No Avg is given because such a figure is invalid where only partial information is available.

The same format is used for the other four categories. Passing, complete games: G = games, Comp = passes completed, Att = passes attempted, % = completion percentage, Yds = yards gained, Y/A = yards gained per pass attempt, TD = touchdown passes, and Int = passes intercepted; incomplete games use the same symbols but % and Y/A are not given because partial information yields misleading figures.

Receiving: G = games, Rec = passes received, Avg = average gained per pass reception, TD = touchdown passes received.

Punting: G = games, No = number of punts attempted, Avg = average yards per punt.

Punt returns: G = games, No = number of punts returned, Yds = yards returned, Avg = average yards returned, TD = touchdown returns.

At the bottom of each table are given those team and opponent statistics that have been recoverable from complete games only.

Two other statistical records should be noted. Interceptions (Int) and points scored (Pts) are given in the roster section after the height (Ht), weight (Wt) and Age of the appropriate player. These are cumulative for all games played played by the team. Also cumulative are the kicking statistics given alongside the standings and scoring leaders accompanying each article. FG = field goals made, FGA - field goals attempted and Pct = percentage of field goals made; PAT = points after touchdown made, Att = attempts and Pct = percentage.

1892-1919
From Heffelfinger to Thorpe: Pro Football Before the NFL

In the early 1890's, one New York City athletic club gave its football players a shining gold watch as a "trophy" after each game. The player then took the watch to a designated shop and pawned it for $20. Later, he met a member of the club and sold him the pawn ticket for another $20. After the next game, the player again received his trophy — the same gold watch! All this subterfuge was so the player and the club could avoid the wrath of the Amateur Athletic Union which could punish violators of the amateur code by banning then from competition with "honest" A.A.U. members. Amateurism was the ideal but winning teams increased club membership. Some clubs used trophies to lure good players. Others offered jobs. In Pittsburgh, the Allegheny Athletic Association did it with money. On November 12, 1892, Pudge Heffelfinger, thrice Yale All-America guard, became the first known pro footballer by going to Pittsburgh to play for the AAA against archrival Pittsburgh AC. Two of his friends got twice expenses but Heffelfinger was secretly handed $500. He earned it by jarring loose a fumble, recovering the ball, and running it into the endzone to win the game.

That touchdown counted only four points. Football emphasized kicking. A field goal counted five points. A goal after touchdown was worth two but had to be kicked from the five-yard line, straight out from where the touchdown was scored; if this angle was too acute, the team could punt the ball out and kick from where the punt was caught. Fortunately, the nearly-round football lent itself to dropkicking. Other movement on the 110-yard field was slow going. Forward passes were illegal and a team had only three downs to gain five yards for a first down. No particular numbers of players had to be on the line of scrimmage and everyone could be moving when the ball was snapped. As a consequence, offenses consisted of flying-wedge-type, mass and momentum plays. Pads of any kind were few, but players went the whole game — 90 minutes — or were carried off the field. Referees, paid by the host team, usually acceded willingly to the demands of rabid home-town fans.

A week after the "Heffelfinger game", the AAA paid former Princeton end Sport Donnelly, one of Heffelfinger's friends, $250 to play against Washington & Jefferson. Despite the presence of the second known pro, the Three A's lost. In 1893, the AAA paid Pete Wright, James Van Cleve and Ollie Rafferty $50 each per game. Donnelly also stayed on, but was paid to coach; he played for free. Other Pittsburgh teams began hiring players, but the Three A's had a headstart and dominated local football for two years. All payments were secret but rumors spread. When the A.A.U. started to investigate, the Three A's decided to lie low and not field a team in 1895.

Meanwhile, 30 miles southeast of Pittsburgh, the Greensburg AA hired husky Lawson Fiscus, a bruiser who'd put in one season at Princeton, for $20 a game in 1894. Greensburg's natural rival, nearby Latrobe, put a team organized by newspaperman Dave Berry on the field in 1895 but found itself without a quarterback for its first game. Berry hired 18-year-old John Brallier for $10 and expenses. In leading his new teammates to a 12-0 win over Jeannette, Brallier honestly believed himself to be the first professional. Years later, before other evidence surfaced, that claim was accepted. The NFL even game him a lifetime pass. Fans at these early contests approached hysteria, charging games with life-and-death significance. They often piled out of a park and into the town center in a boisterous and electric mob. The courthouse steeple in Latrobe had to be straightened on its base after one particularly spirited crowd finished celebrating a victory.

A new Pittsburgh team, the Duquesne Country and Athletic Club (DC&AC), took up football in 1895, announcing it would use only amateur players. Good intentions lasted only four games. Then, before meeting the Pittsburgh AC, they began hiring stars. Soon they were the "most pro" team in town and the most popular, turning a $4,000 profit in 1895. In the fall of 1896, the Allegheny AA learned it would soon be banned by the A.A.U. for its earlier use of pros. They decided to go all the way, importing a team of stars, including Heffelfinger, Donnelly and Penn's George Brooke. On consecutive days the picked team easily defeated the Pittsburgh AC and DC&AC, then accepted most of the money in the Three A's treasury and went home.

Games had been shortened to a mere 70 minutes in 1894. In 1897 the value of a touchdown increased to five points and the still difficult goal-after went down to a point. The DC&AC payroll rose out of sight in 1898 because they'd contracted for so many players returning from the Spanish-American War. Steel magnate William C. Temple took over the payroll to become the first individual team owner. Temple is best known as donator of baseball's Temple Cup which went to the National League's playoff winner in the '90's. His DC&AC football team had everything but competition, rolling undefeated through two seasons. other steelmen soon wanted their own teams. In 1900 A.C. Dinkey pirated most of the DC&AC players to his Homestead Library & Athletic Club (HLAC) with offers of higher salaries. For another two years the same players reigned supreme.

Baseball entered pro football in 1902 when the Athletics and Phillies both organized teams in Philadelphia and Pittsburgh Pirates owner Barney Dreyfuss backed a team made up mostly of former DC&AC/HLAC players. The three Pennsylvania clubs modestly termed themselves the National Football League and installed Dave Berry as league president. New York Giants pitcher Christy Mathewson played fullback for Pittsburgh. The Athletics' team was managed by Connie Mack and listed Rube Waddell on its roster, mostly to keep the eccentric lefty under Mack's control. On November 21st, the Athletics won the first night football game 39-0 over Kanaweola AC at Elmira, N.Y., but just which team won the league championship was up for debate. Both the Athletics and Pittsburgh claimed the title. The dispute continued until no one cared anymore. Meanwhile, players from the two Philadelphia teams joined to play as "New York" in an indoor World Series, an invitational tournament held over New Years in New York's Madison Square Garden. Surprisingly, the Syracuse AC won with a team featuring Pop Warner at guard.

Pro football faded In Pittsburgh after 1902, but 60 miles to the north, oil-rich Franklin, Pa. formed the ultimate all-star team for its 1903 game with rival Oil City. They hired so many outstanding players that Oil City refused to play. Nevertheless, Franklin took on the best area teams and then went on to sweep the second (and last) New York Indoor World Series, finishing the season undefeated, untied, and unscored upon.

Ohio picked up the pro football torch in 1903 when the Massillon Tigers hired four veteran pros from Pittsburgh to help them win the state football championship from Akron. The next year saw at least eight Ohio teams playing players on a more or less regular basis. When speedy halfback Charles Follis signed with the Shelby AC, he became the first black pro. Talk about forming a pro league began but quickly ended when

Massillon annihilated everyone in sight. In 1905 the Canton Bulldogs were formed, primarily to beat Massillon. The two cities, both within Stark County, were traditional rivals. Each scrambled to hire the best players in the country. Salaries soared. Before their big meeting, Canton secured Michigan's All-America halfback Willie Heston for a reported $600. The star proved a bust, gaining only a few yards against a stacked defense. The 14-4 win gave Massillon a third-straight Ohio championship.

An appalling number of football deaths and serious injuries, regularly reported in the nation's newspapers, brought moves to outlaw the sport in 1906. Rulemakers defused the criticism by legalizing the forward pass, providing a nuetral zone along the scrimmage line, requiring 10 yards in three downs for a first down, and insisting at least six players be on the line of scrimmage at the snap. All these changes tended to reduce the use of mass plays, the main cause of injuries.

Canton and Massillon feverishly signed stars for their 1906 games. The Bulldogs were temporarily the toast of Ohio when they handed the Tigers their first loss in three years 10-5. However, Massillon kept its championship with a 13-6 win in the rematch. Then things turned ugly. Betting was furious on the games, and a Massillon newspaper charged Canton coach Blondy Wallace with throwing the second game. Canton insisted Massillon simply wanted to cripple the Bulldogs financially by destroying the gate for their remaining games with Latrobe. Massillon couldn't prove its charge but the stands were virtually empty for the Canton-Latrobe game and the Bulldogs couldn't pay their players. Legend has it that the fix scandal killed big-time pro football in Ohio for years; in fact, both Canton and Massillon had spent themselves broke. For several years, teams of local athletes with only a rare imported star fought Ohio's pro football wars. By 1912, renewed public enthusiasm called for large-scale pro football again.

The game had changed. Passing had been legal for six years, though rarely used except in situations of despair. Touchdowns now counted for six points, field goals for three. The field had shrunk slightly to 100 yards, and the offense now had four downs in which to gain 10 yards. A rule prohibited substituted players from re-entering the game in the same half. The ball still resembled a watermelon, making passing a risky tactic. Teams usually lined up in the basic T-formation, with the standard play a snap to the quarterback and handoff to a back ploughing up the middle.

Ohio teams again drew collegiate stars to their lineups with either straight salaries or profit shares. No restrictions existed on hiring players, and collegians played under aliases to preserve their amateur status as well as jumping from team to team to take the best weekly offer. The Columbus Panhandles reported facing Knute Rockne six times in six weeks in six different uniforms. Despite facing instabilities, the professional football resurgance in Ohio flourished and reached a peak in 1915. Toledo, Youngstown, Akron and Dayton all had strong teams. The colorful Columbus Panhandles boasted the six Nesser brothers in their lineup. Massillon had a new Tiger team.

Canton pulled a coup by signing Jim Thorpe for $250 a game. A former star halfback for the Carlisle Indian School, the big Indian had become nationally famous for his decathlon victory in the 1912 Olympic Games and the subsequent loss of his medals when it was discovered he'd previously played a summer of professional baseball. Thorpe was a natural star, despite flaunting every training rule. A brilliant open-field runner and unmatched power runner, he could pass, dropkick, placekick and punt in superior fashion. His jarring tackles struck fear in opponents. Although he did not always play at peak effort, Thorpe was pro football's first glamorous drawing card, the first player whose name preceded his team's on a placard. Before he joined the Bulldogs, Canton was averaging 1,200 paying fans per game; 8,000 showed up for his debut against Massillon. The Tigers held him in check for the first game, but in the rematch he kicked a pair of field goals for a 6-0 victory.

With the enthusiasm and profits at a new high, top Ohio teams hired droves of All-Americans in 1916. Canton's colossal line averaged 213 pounds and allowed only seven points in 10 games. At Massillon, the Tigers held the Bulldogs to a scoreless tie before 10,000 fans, but Canton took its revenge with a 24-0 slaughter in the rematch at home. Canton's newspapers proclaimed the Bulldogs as world champions. The claim was repeated in 1917, although the Bulldogs and Tigers split their two games. By then, pro football was taking a back seat to the Great War, and Uncle Sam was snapping up players and fans to fill his own roster. In the face of the national war effort, pro football ground to a virtual halt in 1918.

Post-collegiate football, though, received a boost when the Great Lakes Naval Training Station team brought together many of the nation's best players. George Halas held down an end position while Jimmy Conzelman and Paddy Driscoll started in the backfield. The powerhouse rolled into the Rose Bowl and emerged victorious, showing what post-graduates could produce.

With peace restored in Europe, 1919 brought a resumption of the football war in Ohio. Most of the old teams returned and many new ones began play. Although a movement was afoot for organization of some sort, all of the teams still existed as freelance operations. Canton hired Carlisle grads Joe Guyon and Pete Calac to join Thorpe in the backfield and Guy Chamberlain to play end. Halas, out of the Navy, signed with the Hammond Pros in Indiana. An early black star, cat-quick Fritz Pollard from Brown University, sparked Akron's team.

In Wisconsin Curly Lambeau organized the Green Bay Packers with backing by the Indian Packing Company. At the end of a 10-1 season, the players split the profits and received $16.75 each. For more established teams, the general pay scale provided $50 to $75 a game for stars and less for the always unsung linemen. Thorpe's pay remained exceptional. Equipment was primitive, with helmets optional.

Thorpe led the Bulldogs to a pair of victories over Massillon in an undefeated Canton season. In the finale, the Tigers hired 45 top players, mostly to keep them out of Bulldog uniforms. Thopre was nursing a lame back, but he was still Thorpe. With the game a scoreless deadlock in the third quarter, he put a 40-yard placekick through the uprights to give Canton the lead. Massillon came roaring back. Only moments later, the Tigers kicker tried for a field goal from 45 yards out, but the ball bounced harmlessly out of bounds at the 15. Canton was still in desparate straights — bogged deep in its own territory, pursued by relentless Tigers, and with more than a quarter to go.

Thorpe was equal to the task. He stood at his own five-yard line, ignored his sore back and smashed an enormous punt. The wind caught the ball and sailed it high over the outstretched hands of the frantic Tigers safety man. When it finally stopped rolling, it was across the Massillon goalline 95 yards away! The game was as good as over; Massillon was finished. Thorpe trotted off the field, having kicked Canton to yet another championship.

Although Thorpe's heroics closed out a free-wheeling and courageous era, there was much more in store for pro football when the American professional Football Association hoisted its colors in 1920.

1920-1932
Surviving With A Different Game

The National Football League was born and spent its formative years during one of America's eccentric eras. With the world safe for democracy, the country discarded its serious war face and replaced it with a grinning harlequin contenance of sometimes mindless exuberence. Prosperity fueled the celebration. Those who couldn't yet celebrate the prosperity could celebrate the expectation of gaining it. The stock market went up and up like an August thermometer. Americans believed — or hoped themselves into believing — that it would never come down. But, just in case the good-times bubble might someday burst, they were all going to get their partying in first. The age wallowed in flappers, Lucky Lindy, bathtub gin, jazz, Scott and Zelda, the Charleston, flaming youth, Valentino, speakeasies, and sports of all sorts.

As never before, sport captured the public's fancy. In the words of historian Preston Slosson, "next to the sport of business, Americans enjoyed the business of sport." By 1928, almost a fourth of the national income was being spent on leisure activities. Much of that went to purchase tickets, as people flocked to arenas in record numbers. Heroes were the stuff that legends and profits were made of. Babe Ruth, Jack Dempsey, Helen Wills, Bobby Jones, Rogers Hornsby, Gene Tunney and a whole pantheon of greats made it a truly Golden Age.

Football had its demigod in Red Grange. Althought the Galloping Ghost earned his adulation as a breakaway halfback for the University of Illinois, it was in professional football that he made his most lasting impact on American sport. Not only did he make play-for-pay almost respectable when he enrolled in its ranks, but, more important, he made it news. Grange may not have been the best player in pro football at the time, but he was surely the most significant.

Despite its increased interest in pro football, the public tolerated the surprising amount of incomplete and even inaccurate information. Much that was important never saw the light of day. Dr. Harry March's *Pro Football" It's "Ups" and "Downs"*, the first attempt at a history of the game, was not published until 1934. It proved lively, readable, opinionated, and often just plain wrong. Not until pro football was being beamed into the nation's living rooms on the family television did serious historians concern themselves with the NFL's beginnings.

The founding fathers of the NFL were not particularly good at recordkeeping; they were too busy trying to construct a lasting sports organization. The final standings from the first few years were highly inaccurate, and the winter meetings were often marked by disputes over the league championship. Individual statistics were not kept by the NFL until 1932. Press guides and yearbooks did not exist, and there is hardly any newsreel film left of the games. Photographs of games tantalize us with frames of action, but cannot tell us of the pace of a game or what it was like to watch.

Much of what we know about the early years of pro football comes from the newspapers of the day. The big-city papers, such as the *Chicago Tribune* and *New York Times*, covered many sports and crowded their pro football reports into a short column. Many small-town papers, however, such as the *Canton Repository* and the *Rock Island Argus*, ran long stories every day of the week. Monday's edition covered the games in great detail and on other days they reported printed play-by-play accounts of games. The *Green Bay Press Gazette* topped off every season starting in 1923 with a poll of league officials, coaches and writers to choose an all-NFL team.

Let's take an imaginary trip to an early NFL game. We can get a pretty good seat for a dollar. If we're in Chicago's Wrigley Field, the crowd of 10,000 or so leaves the park two-thirds empty. If we're in Dayton's Triangle Park, a mere 4,000 pack the bleachers. Our fellow spectators are wildly partisan but their cheers are spontaneous; no scantily clad cheerleaders choreograph yells. We see no signs or banners or outrageous costumes. These fans came to see the game, not to be seen.

The field, the familiar 100 yards marked in five-yard segments, is real grass or, more likely, real dust. It has no hashmarks. Not until 1933 will the ball be brought toward the center of the field when a play ends near or over the sideline. The goalposts, two capital H's, stand on the goallines. In 1927, they'll be moved to the endzone line for a five-year experiment.

When the teams take the field, we note that each squad has only 16 players. Color-blind fans will have trouble telling the teams apart; the uniforms show little individuality except for jersey hue. Each player wears high-top shoes with permanent rectangular cleats. Trousers of light canvas have thigh pads made of fibre and some padding around the high waist to protect the back and kidneys. The fading jerseys may have numbers sewn on, but the practice is not yet standard. It's hard to believe the flimsy shoulder pads that barely make a bulge around a player's neck can absorb much of a shock. The same may be said for the helmets, feeble leather baskets worn by only some of the players. For the next 20 years, no rule will make helmets mandatory.

Instead of a whole herd of zebras, only three officials govern our game — an umpire, a referee and a linesman. There will be fewer penalties and more arguments. Even from our seat in the bleachers we see the leather ball is fat with rounded ends. It's difficult to pass but easily dropkicked. By the end of this era, the ball will start to slim down, making passing easier, but driving dropkicking into extinction.

After a perfunctory coin flip at the center of the field, one player kneels holding the ball at the 40 yard line while a teammate kicks off. We won't be very far into the first quarter before we discern a number of basic differences between 1920's play and a modern contest. Some differences are obvious, but perhaps the most important are less so.

First of all, it's one-platoon football with everyone playing both offense and defense. No specialists here! After 1922, a player withdrawn from the game in the first half was allowed to return in the second half, but one withdrawn during the second half could not return. Despite the strict rule, substitutes run on occasionally so that hardly anyone goes the full 60 minutes. However, the regulars will plays at least three grueling quarters. A few adjustments help them get through the ordeal. Although signals are called at the line of scrimmage rather than in a huddle, a little more time is taken between plays. Linemen tend to lean in their blocks when a play is run to the other side. Nevertheless, the very duration of play puts a premium on endurance and mitigates against elephantine players. Most linemen are slightly over 200 pounds; backs are considerably smaller.

A few teams are still using the old-fashioned T with few frills, but the majority line up in the single wing or the Notre Dame box, formations geared to power running. Defenses naturally favor six- and sometimes seven-man lines. Regardless, both offense and defense are so tight that on most plays when the ball is snapped, 22 men converge into a single indistinguishable pile-up. After the dust clears, we can see the ball has magically advanced a few yards.

Passing is a secondary tactic, but not as rare as legend would have us believe. With the fat ball, completing one out of four passes is acceptable, one out of three marvelous. Rules still handcuff the aerial game. Until 1933, any forward pass has to be thrown from at least five yards behind the line of scrimmage. Until 1934, an incompleted pass into the endzone is an automatic touchback and gives the ball to the opponent. 1926 is a very bad years for passers; one rule gives the ball to the other team if an ineligible receiver even touches the ball. Worse, another new rule penalizes a team five yards for two incomplete passes in one set of downs. Other factors crippling passing attacks are a lack of practice time, small squads that cannot sustain the constant running required, and a coaching philosophy that is generally timid.

Every time a play ends near the sideline or out of bounds, the next plays starts there. The team is virtually forced to waste a down moving the ball to the center of the gridiron. The short punt formation is popular on third and long, however, because then the tailback has an option. If the safety goes deep, throw a short pass; if he stays in, punt the ball over his head. This accounts, in part, for the many gargantuan punts of the era.

Punting is the key to the most important difference between the modern game and our 1920's contest. An amazing number of kicks are on third down because the whole philosophy is defensive. Field position is all. The way to victory is not to possess the ball, but to give it to your opponent deep in his territory and let him make s mistake. Outpunt your opponent and you'll keep him bottled up near his own goalline. Sooner or later, he'll drop the ball. Then, with only 10 or 15 yards to go for a touchdown, you have a 50-50 chance of scoring. To really dismantle your opponent, block his punt. Most high-scoring games involve several blocked kicks. In Muncie's only 1920 game, Rock Island blocked three of the Flyers' punts in the first quarter and went on to win 45-0.

With defense so emphasized, low-scoring games predominate. Only seven teams had a season scoring average of over 20 points a game during the first 13 years of the NFL. A modern fan might soon tire of the seemingly endless succession of dusty plunges and punts. A modern fan expects action and plenty of it. That view might bewilder a 1920's fan. What, he might ask, is the point of scoring so readily and then allowing your opponent to do the same? Should a victory turn simply on which team has the ball last? The joy of a big play is diluted when big plays are the norm. How can we savor such a climatic moment when another will fall fast on its heels?

During the 1920's, pro games were taking place all over the country. The many strong teams in Ohio and Illinois formed the core of the American Professional Football Association. This league, founed in 1920, changed its name to the National Football League two years later. At first, the league was made up only of Midwestern clubs. In the East, independent teams played in Pennsylvania, New Jersey, New England and sporadically in New York City. When the NFL started expanding in the East in 1924 and 1925, it took in the Frankford Yellowjackets, Pottsville Maroons and Providence Steam Roller. The West Coast was too far away to participate in the NFL, but, after an exhibition game featuring Red Grange drew 75,000 fans in Los Angeles in January 1926, pro football on the Pacific Coast flourished and developed a strong regional league that survived until the NFL came to California after World War II.

The NFL in the 1920's ran a loose operation. In 1920, the league had no schedule, no standings, an impotent administration nominally led by Jim Thorpe, and little distinction between teams in the league and outside the league. In 1921, Joe Carr became president and gave the league some administrative skill. Although the league began keeping standings that year, it continued to allow teams to arrange their own schedules with only a few restrictions. Some teams played about 15 games per year, other less than half that number.

Owning an NFL franchise generally required a healthy income from other quarters to support the losses of running a football team. Three big-city teams survived the early period of insecurity to play today. George Halas and Dutch Sternaman operated the Chicago Bears as partners from 1922 until 1932 when Halas brought complete control of the team. Chris O'Brien owned the Chicago Cardinals from their beginnings before the start of the NFL until he sold the team to Dr. David Jones in 1929. Tim Mara organized the New York Giants in 1925 and gave the NFL a strong franchise in the media capital of the country. The small-town teams were usually bankrolled by a local sports enthusiast; notable among these stalwarts were Ralph Hay of Canton, Walter Flanigan of Rock Island, Carl Storck of Dayton, Doc Young of Hammond and Leo Lyons of Rochester. The only small-town team still in existence, the Green Bay Packers, were managed by Curly Lambeau but owned by a public corporation starting in 1923. Some players owned the teams on which they played, such as Halas and Sternaman in Chicago, Lambeau in Green Bay in 1922, Ollie Kraehe in St. Louis in 1923, Pete Henry in Canton in 1925, and Jimmy Conzelman in Detroit in 1925-26. As early as 1927, the league began to reduce its number of small-town teams (and small crowds). The Depression accelerated and finalized that process. No longer could local small-town businessmen afford the luxury of backin a team. Neither could the hard-pressed team owners in major cities afford weaklings as league members. By 1932 the league had a compact membership of eight, half the clubs located on the East Coast.

The average player on an NFL team of this era was paid about $100 to $150 per game. Star players received a little more. Two extraordinary salaries that we know of are Paddy Driscoll's $300 per game from the Cardinals in 1920 and Wildcat Wilson's $600 per game from Providence in 1929. Benny Friedman received the first big annual salary. He came to terms with the Giants for $10,000 for the 1929 season. For their money, most players attended short daily practices, although some who had out-of-town jobs joined their teams only on weekends. Pro football was essentially a part-time job for nearly every player; higher pay and higher status could be found as an assistant coach at a college. Many fine players preferred to play for independent teams rather than NFL clubs so they could pursue permanent careers in small towns or distant areas. As a conseqience, most NFL careers were short. Even the biggest stars of the day seldom played as many as a half-dozen seasons.

The fame of some star players had come down to us in legends, with few films or statistics to give us a hint of their real skills. Jim Thorpe was the NFL's outstanding attraction in the early 1920's although he was clearly past his peak. Red Grange brought his great fame from the University of Illinois into the NFL in 1925, and even inspired the rival American Football League to operate in 1926. The Pro Football Hall of Fame has recognized other greats from the early years: backs Johnny Blood (McNally), Curly Lambeau, Ernie Nevers, Jimmy Conzelman, Paddy Driscoll, Joe Guyon and Ken Strong; ends George Halas, Guy Chamberlin, Red Badgro and Ray Flaherty; and interior linemen Pete Henry, Cal Hubbard, Ed Healey, Mike Michalske, George Trafton, Walt Kiesling and Steve Owem. But the Hall has not recognized other players who appear to have been just as great: backs like Benny Friedman, Verne Lewellen, Tony Latone and Fritz Pollard, and linemen like Lavie Dilweg, Gus Sonnenberg, Swede Youngstrom, Duke Slater and Bull Behman. The fame of these men has faded, much like the old newspapers which reported their feats at the time.

One group of playes had no counterpart in major-league baseball. A handfull of black players competed in the NFL throughout the early years until an unofficial color ban started in 1934, lasting until after World War II. Paul Robeson, the famous black singer, played with Akron and Milwaukee in 1921-22. Fritz Pollard starred for the undefeated Akron Pros of 1920 and played through 1926. Slater excelled as a tackle for Rock Island, Milwaukee and the Chicago Cardinals from 1922 through 1931. Some of the other black players of the 1920's were Inky Williams, Sol Butler, Bobby Marshall, John Shelbourne and Dick Hudson. Joe Lillard and Ray Kemp played in the NFL in 1933, but then NFL then became all white until the late 1940's, when prosperity, television, new rules and the influx of new black talent completely changed the face of the game.

1920 A.P.F.A. A Most Uncertain Venture

While Warren G. Harding pressed his presidential campaign with calls for a return to normalcy, George Halas was wooing players for a football team sponsored by the A.E. Staley company of Decatur, Illinois. It was Staley himself who hired Halas to play for the company baseball team and to run the football team — a move designed more to advertise the Staley Starchworks than to capitalize on the growing interest in professional football. The 25-year-old Halas brought admirable credentials to his new job; he had been a baseball and football player at the University of Illinois, had played pro baseball and had a cup of coffee with the New York Yankees, had played with the famous Great Lakes Naval Training Station football team during the War, and had played for the strong Hammond Pros in 1919. To help Halas recruit players, Staley provided his young coach with fine package deals to offer prospective players: a year-round job with the starch company plus a share of the gate receipts. But it was Staley's promise to allow two hours of daily practice on company time that sold many serious players.

With such generous inducements, Halas brought top-notch players to his team. He himself played one end and Guy Chamberlin left the Canton Bulldogs to play the other end. Former Notre Damer George Trafton signed on as center. Former Great Lakes players rejoining Halas in Decatur were halfback Jimmy Conzelman, tackle Hugh Blacklock and guard Jerry Jones. One of Halas' teammates at Illinois, Dutch Sternaman, came to play halfback. More strong players signed up, making the Decatur Staleys the best advertisement a starch factory could desire. With his team assembled, Halas began contacting existing pro teams to schedule games for the 1920 season. It was one of these contacts — with Ralph Hay, manager of the Canton Bulldogs — which grew into a scheme beyond Halas' wildest dreams. Hay told Halas of plans to organize a league that autumn. An preliminary meeting on August 20 led to a formal organizational conference in Canton on September 17.

The leaders of the 10 clubs gathered in Hay's Hupmobile showroom on that muggy and historic evening, sitting on running boards and refreshed by beer hung in buckets over fenders. Represented were the Staleys, the Bulldogs, the Akron Pros, the Dayton Triangles, the Cleveland Tigers, the Rock Island Independents, the Chicago Cardinals, the Hammond Pros, the Muncie Flyers and the Rochester Jeffersons. An Akron businessman who was trying to organize the Massillon Tigers for the season also showed up, but his plans and financing were so tenuous that he was not invited into the conference. With no one to back the team financially, the legendary Tigers died just as pro football took its first steps into big-league organization.

The pro football magnates who did represent viable teams talked long and hard that night and created the American Professional Football Association. Two general principles were endorsed by all present. To win the good will of college football, all teams pledged to keep hands off undergraduates who still had eligibility remaining. The founders, seeing the necessity for consistent team images, also agreed not to tamper with players on other teams — a move which enabled fans to recognize the teams from week to week. There were no special pro playing rules for APFA members; they followed the same rules as colleges. A new one for

1920 decreed extra points and should be kicked from directly in front of the goalposts instead of straight out from where the touchdown was scored.

Jim Thorpe was named APFA president, not for his administrative ability, but for his famous name. Big Jim continued to coach and play for Canton while his name adorned the league letterhead. Stan Cofall, player-coach for Cleveland, was named vice president, and A.F. Ranney, one of the owners of the Akron Pros, was named secretary and treasurer. To give the organization an air of substance, an admission fee of $100 was announced; however, according to Halas, "I can testify that no money changed hands."

The APFA did not resemble a league as we know it today, but was more like a professional association whose sole functions were memberships and articulation of some general principles. Perhaps the best modern-day analogy would be a weak form of the NCAA. As can be imagined, the league office had no influence on anybody. It set no schedules, leaving each team to arrange its own slate. Some of the teams arranged a good portion of their games against teams that were not APFA members but traditional local rivals. Although a trophy was donated to the league as an award for the championship team, no official standings were kept. The standings on page 15 were collected from newspaper accounts of every game between APFA teams; football fans never saw any such standings in the morning paper. The mentality of the time awarded championships on the basis of head-to-head competition; if you beat the club that had a claim on being champion, you could call yourself champion. Because most APFA teams played teams mainly within their own area, fans in different regions had different ideas about who the champion was.

The popular idea of a championship race was not limited to the 10 teams who attented the APFA meeting in Canton. Fans knew who the best pro teams were and would pay to see them, regardless of whether they belonged to the APFA or not. Four other teams this year had popular reputations as major teams and played enough games against the official APFA members that they were considered a part of the 1920 league season — the Buffalo All-Americans, Chicago Tigers, Columbus Panhandles and Detroit Heralds.

Several of the official league teams, however, stood a step below the others in playing strength and organizational ability. They were not a factor in the popular races for "the championship." The Rochester Jeffersons lost one game to Buffalo and played none against official APFA members. The Muncie Flyers were destroyed 45-0 by Rock Island in their first game, then disbanded. The Hammond Pros had lost most of their players from the strong 1919 squad and could not compete with the powers. "Unofficials" Columbus and Detroit simply had weak teams stocked with over-age sandlotters.

Leaving these weaklings aside, nine teams made up the major pro football powers. These teams generally formed circuits within their states. Rock Island, Decatur and the two Chicago teams played most of their games among themselves. Similarly, Canton, Akron, Cleveland and Dayton furnished the opposition for each other most of the time. Buffalo played host to several Ohio teams during 1920.

The Ohio sector was pro football's most famous, due to the battles between the Canton Bulldogs and the Massillon Tigers over the past several seasons. But Massillon no longer had a team and Canton had a squad not up to its previous standard. Thorpe was 33-years old and planned to devote more of his time to coaching the Bulldogs from the sideline. For most of the season, he held himself out of contests unless he was needed in the second half. In spots, however, he could still shine. In Dayton, on October 25, the Bulldogs trailed the Triangles 20-14 in the second half. In the game since early in the third period, Thorpe dropkicked a 45-yard field goal in that quarter, then placekicked another 35-yarder with about a minute left in the game to bring his team back to a 20-20 tie. The Bulldogs had other stars in backs Pete Calac and Joe Guyon, veteran tackle Cub Buck and rookie tackle Wilbur "Pete" Henry. Buck and Henry were two of the biggest and best linemen in pro ball.

The Akron Pros turned out to be more than a match for Canton. The Pros had a breakaway wingback in black star Fritz Pollard and a passing and plunging tailback in Rip King. The Pros held daily practices, a routine many teams did not have and, despite having only two regular linemen, Alf Cobb and Bob Nash, weighing over 200 pounds, they allowed only seven points all year. They went into Canton on October 31 and shocked 10,000 spectators by whipping the Bulldogs 10-0. On Thanksgiving Day in Akron, they repeated the feat on a muddy field, winning 7-0 in front of 6,000 fans. The Pros had an undisputed claim to the championship, at least in Ohio.

The Pros did not play any Illinois team during the body of the season. In that state, the Staleys had a clear claim as the best. The Rock Island Independents, the state's top 1919 team, suffered a string of injuries which left them subpar for their final league game, a 21-0 trouncing by the Dayton Triangles. Several of those injuries came in two meetings with the Staleys in Rock Island, resulting in a 7-0 Decatur victory and a scoreless tie. Both matches were brutally fought, with several players knocked out of action. The crowds at small Douglas Park were so angry, particularly at Halas and Trafton, that the players were not sure they could leave the ballpark in complete safety.

The Staleys emerged from Rock Island with no losses, but did suffer one setback in Chicago at the hands of the Cardinals. The Cardinals were known about town as the Racine Cardinals, named after the street on which their home field, Normal Park, was located. They were paying Paddy Driscoll the extraordinary amount of $300 per game and, in return, they received perhaps the best all-around player in the game. The Cards were thin in talent aside from Driscoll, but they edged the Staleys 7-6 in Chicago on November 28. One week later, the teams met again, and this time the Staleys came out on top, 10-0. The other Chicago club, the Tigers, had big-name players such as Guil Falcon, Milt Ghee and Emmett Keefe, but never came together in a winning blend.

In New York, the Buffalo All-Americans had been inviting Ohio teams to play in November. They had been beaten by Canton 3-0 on November 21, but still ranked as the best in their part of the pro football world. Regulars Tommy Hughitt, Ockie Anderson, Lud Wray, Lou Little and Swede Youngstrom were all stars as undergraduates. Wray and Little would become prominent college coaches. Youngstrom was a master at blocking kicks.

In a move to claim the national championship, the Buffalo team invited Canton and Akron to play them on the weekend of December 4-5. Buffalo and Canton met on Saturday in the Polo Grounds in new York before about 15,000 curious fans. They saw Thorpe kick one field goal and also break away for a 45-yard run which did not lead to a score. They key play of the game came late in the third quarter when Youngstrom blocked a Thorpe punt and carried it 15 yards for a touchdown when Wray blocked Thorpe out of the way. The game ended 7-3 in favor of Buffalo. The victorious players immediately jumped on a northbound train, arriving in Buffalo in time for Sunday's game with Akron. Despite the travel, the All-Americans held Buffalo to a scoreless tie. On the basis of that weekend, Buffalo claimed part of the championship.

One week later, the Akron team took on another club from out of the state, the Staleys. Playing in Chicago, the two teams battled to a scoreless standstill. Halas broke a league rule by luring Paddy Driscoll into a Staley uniform for this game. Nevertheless, he claimed a part of the championship because of this game. The Pros had their own claim, which looks the best on paper today because they alone went through the season without a loss.

In early December, Bruce Copeland, sports editor of the *Rock Island Argus*, chose an all-pro team from what he called the "big eight" of pro teams: Akron, Dayton, Decatur, Rock Island, Chicago Cardinals, Canton, Chicago Tigers and Cleveland, in that order. Although he ignored Buffalo and revealed a definite Rock Island bias, his choices constitute the first all-league team. His first-team lineup: ends Guy Chamberlin, Decatur, and Oke Smith, Rock Island; tackles Pete Henry, Canton, and Hugh Blacklock, Decatur. guards Fred Denfield and Dewey Lyle, Rock Island; center George Trafton, Decatur; quarterback Paddy Driscoll, Chicago Cardinals; halfbacks Eddie Novak, Rock Island and Fritz Pollard, Akron; and fullback Rip King, Akron.

1920 STANDINGS

	W	L	T	Pct.	Pts.	Opp. Pts.	Avg. Pts.	Opp. Avg.
Akron Pros	6	0	3	1.000	95	7	11	1
Decatur Staleys	5	1	2	.833	67	14	8	2
Buffalo All-Americans	4	1	1	.800	74	19	12	3
Rock Island Independents	4	2	1	.667	98	35	14	5
Dayton Triangles	4	2	2	.667	127	47	16	6
Chicago Cardinals	3	2	1	.600	34	26	6	4
Canton Bulldogs	4	3	1	.571	72	44	9	6
Detroit Heralds	1	3	0	.250	6	61	2	15
Cleveland Tigers	1	4	2	.200	14	46	2	7
Chicago Tigers	1	5	1	.167	22	63	3	9
Rochester Jeffersons (R)	0	1	0	.000	6	17	6	17
Muncie Flyers (R)	0	1	0	.000	0	45	0	45
Hammond Pros (R)	0	3	0	.000	7	98	2	33
Columbus Panhandles (R)	0	5	0	.000	7	107	1	21

(R) — played only road games

Scoring Leaders

Bacon	Day	32
Wyman	RI	30
Pollard	Akr	24
Smith	Buf	24
Calac	Can	18
Chicken	RI	18
Kuehl	RI	18
McCormick	Akr	18
Nash	Akr-Buf	18
Partlow	Day	18
Reese	Day	18
Sacksteder	Day	18
Driscoll	ChiC-Dec	16
Sternaman	Dec	16
Copley	Akr	15
Ursella	Akr	14
Weldon	Buf	14
Anderson	Buf	13
Halas	Dec	12
Kinderdine	Day	12
Koehler	Dec	12
Sachs	ChiC	12

KICKING

		FG	Att	Pct			PAT	Att	Pct
Sternaman	Dec	3	6	50	Copley	Akr	12	13	92
Thorpe	Can	3	9	33	Kinderdine	Day	12	14	86
Laird	Roch-Buf	2	2	100	Feeney	Can	8	8	100
Feeney	Can	1	1	100	Blacklock	Dec	6	7	86
Roudebush	Day	1	1	100	Weldon	Buf	5	5	100
Conzelman	Dec	1	2	50	Ursella	RI	5	6	83
Ursella	RI	1	2	50	Driscoll	ChiC-Dec	4	5	80
Weldon	Buf	1	3	33	Hughitt	Buf	3	3	100
Barrett	ChiT	1	5	20	Nichols	RI	3	3	100
Copley	Akr	1	NA		Marshall	RI	3	5	60
Anderson	Buf	0	1	0	Abrell	Day	2	2	100
Bacon	Day	0	1	0	Bacon	Day	2	2	100
Blacklock	Dec	0	1	0	Pierotti	Akr-Cle	2	2	100
Driscoll	ChiC-Dec	0	1	0	Anderson	Buf	1	1	100
Koehler	Dec	0	1	0	Kolls	Ham-ChiC	1	1	100
Nichols	RI	0	1	0	Kuehner	Col	1	1	100
Webber	RI	0	1	0	Mathews	ChiT	1	1	100
Crawford	Akr	0	2	0	Sternaman	Dec	1	1	100
F. Nesser	Col	0	2	0	Horning	Det	0	1	0
Devlin	Cle	0	3	0	Miller	Buf	0	1	0
Guyon	Can	0	4	0	Ghee	ChiC	0	2	0

AKRON PROS 6-0-3 Elgie Tobin

Regulars

Use Name	Pos.	Hgt.	Wgt.	Age	Int.	Pts.
Scotty Bierce	E	5'9	160	23	1	
Bob Nash	E-T	6'1	205	27		18
Charlie Copley	T	5'9	190	32	1	15
Pike Johnson	T	5'11	185	23	2	6
Alf Cobb	G-T	5'11	210	26		
Tommy Tomlin	G	5'10	195	26		
Russ Bailey	C	5'11	183	20	2	
Harry Harris	BB	5'9	175	24	2	6
Rip King	TB	6'1	195	22		
Fritz Pollard	WB-TB	5'7	165	26	1	24
Frank McCormick	FB	5'11	190	25	3	18

Substitutes

Use Name	Pos.	Hgt.	Wgt.	Age	Int.	Pts.
Al Nesser	E	6'	195	27		
Frank Moran (from HAM)	T	6'4	285	29		
Budge Garrett	G-E	5'9	200	27	1	
Al Pierotti (to CLE)	C	5'10	195	24		
Elgie Tobin	BB	5'9	160	35	1	
TuffyConn (from CLE)	WB-FB	5'6	155	25		
Ken Crawford	FB-WB	5'11	175	21		

Substitutes

Use Name	Pos.	Hgt.	Wgt.	Age	Int.	Pts.
Fred Sweetland	WB-FB	5'10	175	25		6
Buck Miles	FB	6'2	195	31		

Scores of each game

Date	Pts.	Opponent	Pts.
Oct. 10	37	COLUMBUS	0
Oct. 24	7	CLEVELAND	0
Oct. 31	10	Canton	0
Nov. 14	7	Cleveland	7
Nov. 21	13	DAYTON	0
Nov. 25	7	CANTON	0
Nov. 28	14	Dayton	0
Dec. 5	0	Bufalo	0
Dec. 12	0	Decatur (at Chicago)	0

DECATUR STALEYS 5-1-2 George Halas

Regulars

Use Name	Pos.	Hgt.	Wgt.	Age	Int.	Pts.
George Halas	E	6'	182	25	1	12
Guy Chamberlin	E	6'2	190	26	1	
Burt Ingwersen	T	5'11	180	22		
Hugh Blacklock	T	6'	220	29		6
Jerry Jones	G	6'1	205	26		
Ross Petty	G	6'1	180	27		
George Trafton	C	6'2	215	23	1	
Pard Pearce	QB	5'5	150	23		6
Dutch Sternaman	HB	5'8	165	25	3	16
Jimmy Conzelman	HB	6'	170	22	1	9
Bob Koehler	FB	5'11	185	26		12

Substitutes

Use Name	Pos.	Hgt.	Wgt.	Age	Int.	Pts.
Andy Feichtinger	E	5'10	170	22		
Walt May	G	6'1	205	23		
Hub Shoemake	G	6'	186	21		
Jake Mintun	C	5'11	185	26		
Chuck Dressen	QB	5'6	145	21		
Paddy Driscoll (fr. ChiC)	HB	5'8	155	25		
Jake Lanum	HB-FB	6'	190	23		6
Kile MacWherter	FB	5'9	210	28		

Substitutes

Use Name	Pos.	Hgt.	Wgt.	Age	Int.	Pts.
Emmett Keefe (from ChiT)	G	5'10	195	27		
Henry Shank	HB	5'8	160	24		

Scores of each game

Date	Pts.	Opponent	Pts.
Oct. 17	7	Rock Island	0
Oct. 24	10	Chic. Tigers	0
Nov. 7	0	Rock Island	0
Nov. 21	28	HAMMOND	7
Nov. 25	6	Chic. Tigers	0
Nov. 28	6	Chic. Cards	7
Dec. 5	10	Chic. Cards	0
Dec. 12	0	AKRON (at Chicago)	0

BUFFALO ALL AMERICANS 4-1-1 Tommy Hughitt

Regulars

Use Name	Pos.	Hgt.	Wgt.	Age	Int.	Pts.
Heinie Miller	E	5'10	185	26		
Murray Shelton	E	6'1	175	27		
Lou Little	T	6'	205	26		
Tiny Thornhill (from CLE)	T	5'11	185	27		
Bill Brace	G	6'1"	180	24		6
Swede Youngstrom	G	6'1	182	23		6
Lud Wray	C	6'	180	26		
Tommy Hughitt	BB	5'8	150	27		9
Ockie Anderson	TB-BB	5'9	165	26	1	13
Bodie Weldon	WB-TB	5'7	165	25	1	14
Pat Smith	FB	6'	195	25	1	24

Substitutes

Use Name	Pos.	Hgt.	Wgt.	Age	Int.	Pts.
Shirley Brick	E	5'8	165	22		
Butch Spagna (from CLE)	T	6'	210	23		
Jack Beckett	T	6'1	200	28		
Johnny Scott	TB	5'10	172	25		
Earl Potteiger	WB	5'7	170	29		
Buck Gavin	FB-TB-WB	5'10	175	25		

Substitutes

Use Name	Pos.	Hgt.	Wgt.	Age	Int.	Pts.
Barney Lepper	T	5'10	185	24		
Jim Laird (from ROCH)	WB	6'	185	22		

Scores of each game

Date	Pts.	Opponent	Pts.
Oct. 31	17	ROCHESTER	6
Nov. 14	43	COLUMBUS	7
Nov. 21	0	CANTON	3
Nov. 28	7	CLEVELAND	0
Dec. 4	7	Canton (at New York)	3
Dec. 5	0	AKRON	0

ROCK ISLAND INDEPENDENTS 4-2-1 Rube Ursella

Regulars

Use Name	Pos.	Hgt.	Wgt.	Age	Int.	Pts.
Bobby Marshall	E	6'2	190	40	1	3
Oke Smith	E-FB-WB	6'2	185	25		
Ed Shaw	T-FB	6'1	190	25		
Ed Healey	T-G	6'1	195	25		
Dewey Lyle	G-T	5'11	190	29		
Pudge Wyland	G	5'10	180	29		
Freeman Fitzgerald	C-G	6'	195	28		
Sid Nichols	BB	5'7	177	25		9
Fred Chicken	TB	5'10	185	31	2	18
Eddie Novak	WB-TB	5'9	175	23		
Arnie Wyman	FB	5'11	172	25	1	30

Substitutes

Use Name	Pos.	Hgt.	Wgt.	Age	Int.	Pts.
Frank Garden	E	5'11	185	22		
Speed Riddell	E	5'10	185	24		
Walt Buland	T	6'1	215	28		
Polly Koch	T-G	5'11	180	24		
Fred Denfield	T-G	6'	195	23		
Charlie Mockmore	G	5'11	190	28		
Harry Gunderson	C	6'2	200	32		
Rube Ursella	BB	5'9	170	30		14
Waddy Kuehl	TB-WB-BB	5'9	165	28	2	18
Frank Jordan	WB		168	22		
Jerry Mansfield	FB-E-WB-TB	5'8	160	26		6

Substitutes

Use Name	Pos.	Hgt.	Wgt.	Age	Int.	Pts.
Harry Webber	BB-E		170	27		
Paddy Quinn	FB	5'7	170	30		

Scores of each game

Date	Pts.	Opponent	Pts.
Oct. 3	45	MUNCIE	0
Oct. 10	26	HAMMOND	0
Oct. 17	0	DECATUR	7
Oct. 24	7	CHIC. CARDS	0
Oct. 31	20	CHIC. TIGERS	7
Nov. 7	0	DECATUR	0
Nov. 14	0	DAYTON	21

DAYTON TRIANGLES 4-2-2 Bud Talbott

Regulars

Use Name	Pos.	Hgt.	Wgt.	Age	Int.	Pts.
Dave Reese	E	6'	170	27		18
Dutch Thiele	E	6'1	195	27		
Harry Cutler	T	6'2	190	30		
Ed Sauer	T	5'10	230	22		
Larry Dellinger	G	5'11	200	27		
Chuck Winston	G	6'1	185	30		
Hobby Kinderdine	C	5'11	180	29	1	12
Al Mahrt	BB	5'11	168	26		6
Norb Sacksteder	TB-WB	5'9	172	24		18
Frank Bacon	WB	5'11	180	26	2	32
Lou Partlow	FB	6'1	185	27	2	18

Substitutes

Use Name	Pos.	Hgt.	Wgt.	Age	Int.	Pts.
Chuck Helvie (from MUN)	E	5'8	180	28		
Lee Fenner	E-WB	5'10	170	24		
Earl Hauser	T-E	6'1	190	22		
RussHathaway (from MUN)	T	5'11	225	24		
Doc Davis (from MUN)	G-T	5'9	200	31		
Guy Early	G	6'3	210	27		
Glenn Tidd	G-C	5'11	202	26		
Dick Abrell	BB-WB	5'10	172	28		8
George Roudebush	TB-FB	5'10	180	26		9
Pesty Lentz	FB-TB	5'10	175	23		6
Fritz Slackford	FB	6'	180	26		

Substitutes

Use Name	Pos.	Hgt.	Wgt.	Age	Int.	Pts.
Max Broadhurst	T	6'	220	34		
Tiny Turner	G	6'	190	25		
Earl Stoecklein	G	6'2	205	23		
Bill Clark	G-C	5'11	194	29		

Scores of each game

Date	Pts.	Opponent	Pts.
Oct. 3	14	COLUMBUS	0
Oct. 10	0	CLEVELAND	0
Oct. 17	44	HAMMOND	0
Oct. 24	20	CANTON	20
Nov. 14	21	Rock Island	0
Nov. 21	0	Akron	13
Nov. 25	28	DETROIT	0
Nov. 28	0	AKRON	14

CHICAGO CARDINALS 3-2-1 Paddy Driscoll

Regulars

Use Name	Pos.	Hgt.	Wgt.	Age	Int.	Pts.
Lenny Sachs	E	5'8	175	23		12
Paul Florence	E	6'1	185	20		
Fred Gillies	T	6'3	215	24		
Willie Brennan	T	6'	210	26		
Leo Chappell	G	6'2	205	21		6
Clyde Zoia	G	5'7	175	24		
Bill Whalen	C	5'7	165	19		
Bernie Halstrom	BB-FB	5'9	160	25		
Paddy Driscoll (to DEC)	TB	5'8	155	25		16
Harry Curran	WB-BB	5'10	180	26		
Nick McInerney	FB-WB	6'2	195	24		

Substitutes

Use Name	Pos.	Hgt.	Wgt.	Age	Int.	Pts.
Paul LaRosa	E	5'11	175	29		
Red O'Connor	E	5'8	170			
George Knight	T		180	21		
Joe Carey	T-G	6'2	195	24		
Charlie Knight	C	6'2	200	20		
Bill Clark	C-G	6'1	190			
Louie Kolls (to HAM)	C	6'1	185	27		
Egan	WB		175			
Len Charpier	FB	5'10	235	23		

Substitutes

Use Name	Pos.	Hgt.	Wgt.	Age	Int.	Pts.
Pete Schultz	FB		185			

Scores of each game

Date	Pts.	Opponent	Pts.
Oct. 10	0	Chic. Tigers	0
Oct. 24	0	Rock Island	7
Oct. 31	21	DETROIT	0
Nov. 7	6	Chic. Tigers	3
Nov. 28	7	DECATUR	6
Dec. 5	0	DECATUR	10

CANTON BULLDOGS 4-3-1 Jim Thorpe

Regulars

Use Name	Pos.	Hgt.	Wgt.	Age	Int.	Pts.
Bunny Corcoran	E	5'11	185	25		
Tom Whelan	E	5'10	180	26		
Cub Buck	T	6'	255	28	1	
Pete Henry	T	5'11	240	22	2	6
Dan O'Connor	G	6'2	210	26		
Cap Edwards	G	6'	205	32		
Al Feeney	C	5'11	185	27		11
Tex Grigg	BB	5'11	180	29	1	6
Jim Thorpe	TB	6'1	200	33	1	9
Joe Guyon	WB-TB	5'10	195	27	2	6
Pete Calac	FB	5'10	190	28	2	18

Substitutes

Use Name	Pos.	Hgt.	Wgt.	Age	Int.	Pts.
Bob Higgins	E	5'10	195	26		6
Bull Lowe	E	5'11	180	25		
Harrie Dadmun	G	6'	235	26		
John Kellison	G	6'	210	33		
Dutch Speck	G-C	5'10	220	34		
Johnny Gilroy (to CLE)	BB	5'10	175	24		
Lou Smyth	TB	6'1	190	21		
Ike Martin	WB-FB	5'11	190	33		6

Substitutes

Use Name	Pos.	Hgt.	Wgt.	Age	Int.	Pts.
Larry Green	E	6'	180	26		
Ralph Meadow	E	6'2	195			
DocHagerty (from & to CLE)	G	6'	205	25		
John Hendren	TB	5'9	175	23		

Scores of each game

Date	Pts.	Opponent	Pts.
Oct. 17	7	CLEVELAND	0
Oct. 24	20	Dayton	20
Oct. 31	0	AKRON	10
Nov. 7	18	Cleveland	0
Nov. 14	21	CHIC. TIGERS	0
Nov. 21	3	Buffalo	0
Nov. 25	0	Akron	7
Dec. 4	3	Buffalo (at New York)	7

NAME	RUSHING Complete Games					RUSHING Incom. Games				PASSING Complete Games								PASSING Incom. Games						RECEIVING Complete Games					RECEIVING Incom. Games				PUNTING Comp. Games			PUNTING Incom. Games			PUNT RETURNS Complete Games					PUNT RETURNS Incom. Games			
	G	Att.	Yds.	Avg.	TD	G	Att.	Yds.	TD	G	Com.	Att.	%	Yds.	Y/A	TD	Int.	G	Com.	Att.	Yds.	TD	Int.	G	Rec.	Yds	Avg.	TD	G	Rec.	Yds.	TD	G	No.	Avg.	G	No.	Avg.	G	No.	Yds.	Avg.	TD	G	No.	Yds.	TD
AKRON																																															
Pollard	5	65	141	2.2		4	4	64	2	6	1	2	50	6	3.0			3						6	4	84	21.0	1	3	2	50								5	23	256	11.1		4			
McCormick	5	55	114	2.1		4	10	48	2															6	1	15	15.0	1	3	1	25																
King	5	53	93	1.8		4	2	0		6	19	42	45	267	6.4	3	4	3	2	2	33												6	75	38.0	3			5					4	1	15	
Harris	5	18	41	2.3		4	2	35	1	6								2	1	2	50																		5	1	10	10.0		4	1	30	
Conn (2)	2	2	5	2.5		1																		3	1	2	2.0																				
Sweetland						2	1	5	1																																						
Bierce	5	1	1	1.0		3																		6	6	54	9.0		2																		
Crawford	1	2	-2	-1.0		4				2								3	1	1	25																										
Nash																								4	2	36	18.0	1	3	1	8																
Copley																								6	3	34	11.3		3																		
Johnson																								6					3	1	20																
Nesser																								6	2	28	14.0		3																		
Team	5	196	393	2.0		4				6	20	44	45	273	6.2	3	4	3															6	75	38.0	3			5	24	266	11.1		4			
Opp.	5	143	301	2.1		4				6	26	79	33	362	4.6		12	3															6	76	36.7	3			5	15	123	8.2		4			
DECATUR																																															
Sternaman	5	46	274	6.0	1	3				5	0	6	0				4	3						5	2	19	9.5		3				5	6	32.0	3			5	5	35	7.0		3			
Conzelman	4	35	182	5.2	1	3				4	8	20	40	138	6.9	2	1	3															4	27	37.3	3											
Pearce	5	20	103	5.2	1	3				5	0	2	0				1	3						5	1	9	9.0		3										5	18	230	12.8		3			
Driscoll (2)	1	13	58	4.5						1	2	7	29	44	6.3		2																1	7	37.7												
Koehler	4	19	52	2.7		3	1	2	1																																						
Lanum	4	14	51	3.6	1	3																																									
Shank	2	8	32	4.0																																											
Dressen	1	5	19	3.8																				1	2	21	10.5												1	3	67	22.3					
Chamberlin	5	5	11	2.2		3																		5	2	57	28.5																				
MacWherter	1	1	2	2.0																																											
Halas																								5	3	76	25.3	2																			
Shoemake																																	2	3	41.0	2											
Team	5	166	784	4.7	4	3				5	10	35	29	182	5.2	2	8	3															5	43	63.9	3			5	26	332	12.8		3			
Opp.	5	204	549	2.7		3				5	13	49	27	162	3.3	1	10	3															5	50	37.1	3			5	19	146	7.7		3			
BUFFALO																																															
Anderson	1	5	7	1.4		5	14	179	2	3	5	16	31	102	6.4		2	3	3	7	62		2																1	4	35	8.8		5			
Smith	1	6	10	1.7		5	18	71	4																																						
Hughitt	1	2	2	1.0		5	12	55	1	3	1	5	20	20	4.0			3	6	7	95		1	3	1	5	5.0		3				1			5	1	20.0									
Gavin	1					4	10	45																																							
Weldon	1	4	11	2.8		4	7	31	1																																						
Laird (2)						1	3	14																					1	1	20					1	2	42.5									
Potteiger	1					1	1	3																																							
Shelton																								3	2	27	13.5		3	8	137																
Miller																								3	3	90	30.0		3																		
Youngstrom																																	1	12	27.9	5	4	36									
Team	1	17	30	1.8		5				3	6	21	29	122	5.8		2	3															1	12	27.9	5			1	4	35	8.8		5			
Opp.	1	29	94	3.2		5				3	3	10	30	14	1.4		1	3															1	10	39.0	5			1	6	68	11.3		5			
ROCK ISLAND																																															
Chicken	5	73	227	3.1	3																			5	1	6	6.0																				
Novak	6	62	223	3.6																				6	2	6	3.0						6	15	38.5												
Nichols	6	32	218	6.8	1					6	4	6	67	60	10.0	1								6	2	26	13.0												6	9	95	10.6					
Wyman	6	43	194	4.5	1					6	9	30	30	123	4.1	2	5							6	2	28	14.0	1					6	12	43.5				6	1	4	4.0					
Kuehl	7	55	124	2.3	2					7	1	2	50	1	0.1									7	1	15	15.0	1											7	6	95	15.8					
Ursella	5	11	72	6.5	1					5	2	3	67	22	7.3																		5	3	18.3				5	8	39	4.9					
Mansfield	6	19	55	2.9																				6	2	30	15.0	1																			
Jordan	1	9	45	5.0																																											
Webber	2	6	45	7.5						2	0	5	0				1							2	1	18	18.0						2	10	37.5												
Quinn	1	3	9	3.0																																											
Smith	7	3	4	1.3						7	0	1	0				1							7	3	43	14.3																				
Marshall																								7	2	34	17.0												7	1	22	22.0					
Team	7	316	1216	3.8	8					7	16	47	34	206	4.4	3	7																7	40	38.2				7	25	255	10.2					
Opp.	7	193	587	3.0	3					7	23	59	39	294	5.0	2	7																7	54	35.1				7	18	214	11.9					
DAYTON																																															
Bacon	2	19	91	4.8	1	6	5	55	2	4	7	14	50	68	4.9		1	4	1	1	10			3	6	78	13.0		5	2	63	1	3	27	37.5	5			2					6	1	60	1
Pertlow	2	5	21	4.2		6	13	79	3															3					5	1	22																
Sacksteder	2	3	5	1.7		6	4	29																3					5	3	70	3							2					5	3	131	
Abrell	1	2	1	0.5		4	2	19	1	1								4	0	1			1																								
Mahrt	2	4	11	2.8		6	1	1	1	4	20	44	45	381	8.6	3		4	8	10	210	4	2	3	3	28	9.3		5	1	10		3	1	4.0	5											
Slackford	2	5	3	0.6		3																		3	1	15	15.0	2											2	2	5	2.5		3			
Roudebush	2	4	-3	-0.7		6	1	2		4	6	15	40	73	4.9		3	4	3	3	57	1		3	3	65	21.7	1	5																		
Thiele																								3	4	84	21.0		5	4	97																
Reese																								3	7	135	19.3	2	5	1	35	1															
Fenner																								2	1	12	12.0		5	1	15																
Helvie (2)																								1	1	12	12.0		2																		
Team	2	42	129	3.1	1	6				4	33	73	45	522	7.2	3	4	4															3	28	36.5	5			2	2	5	2.5		6			
Opp.	2	78	210	2.7		6				4	13	35	37	255	7.3	2	4	4															3	25	42.8	5			2	3	18	6.0		6			
CHICAGO CARDINALS																																															
Driscoll (1)	1	17	46	2.7		5	5	142	2	1	3	7	43	31	4.4			5															1	9	45.3	5	1	50.0	1	1	24	24.0		5	1	20	
McInerney	1	10	26	2.6		4																																									
Curran	1	5	14	2.8		5																		1	2	21	10.5		5																		
Halstrom	1	5	12	2.4		5				1	0	1	0					5																													
Charpier						1	1	12																																							
Florence	1	1	7	7.0		5																		1	1	10	10.0		5																		
Team	1	38	105	2.8		5				1	3	8	38	31	3.9			5															1	9	45.3	5			1	1	24	24.0		5			
Opp.	1	45	228	5.1		5				1	2	4	50	28	7.0	1		5															1	10	38.6	5			1	6	72	12.0		5			
CANTON																																															
Calac	4	66	138	2.1	1	4	20	105	2	7	1	1	100	8	8.0			1						5					3	1	6																
Guyon	4	56	96	1.7		4	7	28	1	7	5	19	26	89	4.7		2	1						5	3	79	26.3		3				5	41	38.0	3	3	41.7	4	5	73	14.6		4			
Martin	3	23	60	2.6	1	2	10	40		5	1	4	25	12	3.0		1																														
Thorpe	4	14	68	4.9		2	4	14		5	8	23	35	159	6.9		5	1	0	1			1										3	9	37.6	3	2	17.5	3	2	21	10.5		3	1	50	
Smyth	3	15	16	1.1		3	6	21		5	1	4	25	9	2.3		1																						3	1	5	5.0		3			
Grigg	3	6	14	2.3		4	2	17	1	6	2	4	50	13	3.3			1						4	2	40	20.0		3				4			3	1	49	3	4	59	14.8		4			
Hendren						1	2	23																																							
Gilroy (1)	2	1	3	3.0		2				4	0	7	0				1																						2	3	34	11.3		2			
Whalen																								5	3	57	19.0		2																		
Corcoran																								5	3	40	13.3		2				5	1	35.0	2											
Higgins																								1	1	22	22.0		1				1	7	32.4	1											
Lowe																								3	1	21	21.0		3																		
O'Connor																								4	1	2	2.0		2																		
Team	4	177	363	2.1	2	4				7	18	62	29	290	4.7		10	1															5	58	37.2	3			4	15	192	12.8		4			
Opp.	4	137	141	1.0		4				7	28	68	41	444	6.5	2	8	1															5	62	33.0	3			4	14	149	10.6		4			

DETROIT HERALDS 1-3-0 Bill Marshall

Regulars

Use Name	Pos.	Hgt.	Wgt.	Age	Int.	Pts.
Ray Whipple	E	5'9	170	26		
Fitzgerald	E		150	24	1	6
Steamer Horning	T	6'	190	27		
Hugh Lowery	T	6'	220	28		
Clarence Applegran	G	6'2	200	26		
Charlie Guy	G-C	6'	170	23		
Gil Runkel	C-G		210	29		
Perce Wilson	BB		150	30		
Jimmy Kelly	TB	5'9	160	28		
Bo Hanley	WB	5'7	150	32		
Pat Dunne	FB		182	32		

Substitutes

Use Name	Pos.	Hgt.	Wgt.	Age	Int.	Pts.
Birdie Maher	E	5'8	180	29		
Tom Dickinson	E	5'8	175	23		
Chris Bentz	T	6'4	215	28		
Don Straw	T-G	5'11	210	23		
Moose Gardner	G	6'1	210	26		
Bill Joyce	BB	5'8	180	23		
Jacobs	TB					
Marshall Jones (from HAM)	WB	5'11	165	25		
Ty Krentler	FB-TB		160	25		

Substitutes

Use Name	Pos.	Hgt.	Wgt.	Age	Int.	Pts.
Bill Finsterwald	WB	5'9	165	26		
Wood	FB					

Scores of each game

Date	Pts.	Opponent	Pts.
Oct. 17	0	Chic. Tigers	12
Oct. 24	6	COLUMBUS	0
Oct. 31	0	Chic. Cards	21
Nov. 25	0	Dayton	28

CLEVELAND TIGERS 1-4-2 Stan Cofall Al Pierotti

Regulars

Use Name	Pos.	Hgt.	Wgt.	Age	Int.	Pts.
Bert Baston	E	6'1	170	25		
Harry Baujan	E	5'8	170	26		
Tiny Thornhill (to BUF)	T-G	5'11	185	27		
Red Pearlman	T-G	6'	195	22		
Tom Gormley	G	5'11	225	31		
Doc Haggerty (to & from CAN)	G	6'	205	25		
Al Pierotti (from AKR)	C-BB	5'10	195	24		2
Mark Devlin	BB	5'10	180	25		
George Brickley	TB-BB	5'10	190	26		6
Tuffy Conn (to AKR)	WB-TB	5'6	155	25	1	6
Carl Cramer	FB-WB-TB	5'11	180	21		

Substitutes

Use Name	Pos.	Hgt.	Wgt.	Age	Int.	Pts.
Ray Trowbridge	E	6'	170	24		
Phil Marshall	E	5'8	165	25		
George Kerr	T	6'1	200	27		
Butch Spagna (to BUF)	T	6'	210	23		
Ed O'Hearn	G-T	5'7	185	21		
Jake Stahl	G	5'11	185	27		
Al Wesbecher	C-T	5'10	190	27		
Jim Bryant	BB-WB	5'6	156	26		
Stan Cofall	TB-BB	5'11	190	26		
Sandy Hastings	WB-FB-TB	5'8	178	25		
Dinger Doane	FB	5'10	190	25		

Substitutes

Use Name	Pos.	Hgt.	Wgt.	Age	Int.	Pts.
Pat Herron	E	5'10	170	26		
Herb Sies	T	6'1	203	27		
Frank Rydzewski (to & from ChiT, to HAM)	C	6'1	220	27		
Johnny Gilroy (from CAN)	BB	5'10	175	24		
Joey Mattern	TB		155	27		
Moon Ducote	WB-TB	5'11	190	23		
Leo Petree	FB-WB		200	27		

Scores of each game

Date	Pts.	Opponent	Pts.
Oct. 10	0	Dayton	0
Oct. 17	0	Canton	7
Oct. 24	0	Akron	7
Oct. 31	7	COLUMBUS	0
Nov. 7	0	CANTON	18
Nov. 14	7	AKRON	7
Nov. 28	0	Buffalo	7

CHICAGO TIGERS 1-5-1 Guil Falcon

Regulars

Use Name	Pos.	Hgt.	Wgt.	Age	Int.	Pts.
John Bosdett	E			24		
Oscar Knop	E-WB	6'	185	25		6
Neil Mathews	T	6'	200	26		1
Frank Rydzewski (from CLE to & from HAM)	T	6'1	220	27		
Emmett Keefe (to DEC)	G	5'10	195	27		
Garland Buckeye	G	6'	235	22		
Shorty Des Jardien	C	6'4	210	27	2	
Milt Ghee	BB	5'7	167	27		
Dunc Annan	TB	5'10	175	25		6
Grover Malone	WB-FB	5'8	185	24		
Guil Falcon (to & from HAM)	FB	5'10	220	27		

Substitutes

Use Name	Pos.	Hgt.	Wgt.	Age	Int.	Pts.
Jack Meagher	E	5'10	178	24		
Jock Mumgavin	E	5'10	175	26		
Lew Reeve	T	5'10	193	29		
Sid Bennett	T	5'10	192	25		
Dick Pierce	G	5'11	185	24		
Walter Voight	G-C	5'8	200	25		
Johnny Barrett	TB-E-WB	5'9	195	25	1	3
Ben Derr	WB	5'10	180	28		
Al Eissler	FB			23		6

Substitutes

Use Name	Pos.	Hgt.	Wgt.	Age	Int.	Pts.
Pete Volz	G		190	23		
Dick Falcon	G	5'9	175	24		
Ralph Capron	WB	5'11	165	30		

Scores of each game

Date	Pts.	Opponent	Pts.
Oct. 10	0	CHIC. CARDS	0
Oct. 17	12	DETROIT	0
Oct. 24	0	DECATUR	10
Oct. 31	7	Rock Island	20
Nov. 7	3	CHIC. CARDS	6
Nov. 14	0	Canton	21
Nov. 25	0	DECATUR	6

ROCHESTER JEFFERSONS 0-1-0 Jack Forsyth

Regulars

Use Name	Pos.	Hgt.	Wgt.	Age	Int.	Pts.
Hal Clark	E	5'10	185	26		
Darby Lowery	E	6'	182	28		
Lou Usher	T	6'2	230	22		
Bart Carroll	T	5'11	180	26		
Art Webb	G	5'10	210	27		
Hank Smith	G	6'1	184	27		
Joe Bachmaier	C	5'9	175	24		
Red Quigley	BB	5'9	155	24		
Elmer Oliphant	TB	5'7	175	28		
Mike Purdy	WB	5'10	178	25		
Jim Laird (to BUF)	FB	6'	185	22		6

Substitutes

Use Name	Pos.	Hgt.	Wgt.	Age	Int.	Pts.
Vern Thomas	E		155	23		
Jimmy Woods	G	5'9	190	26		
Ben Clime	G	5'11	190	28		
Bob Argus	TB-WB	5'10	190	26		
Dutch Irwin	WB	5'7	170	31		

Scores of each game

Date	Pts.	Opponent	Pts.
Oct. 31	6	Buffalo	17

MUNCIE FLYERS 0-1-0 Ken Huffine

Regulars

Use Name	Pos.	Hgt.	Wgt.	Age	Int.	Pts.
Jess Reno	E	5'9	165	29		
Spencer Pope	E	5'10	170	27		
Bobby Berns	T	6'1	200	24		
Doc Davis (to DAY)	T	5'9	200	31		
Ernie Hole	G			19		
Wilfred Smith	G	6'4	200	21		
Owen Floyd	C	6'	195	23		
Cooney Checkaye	BB	5'9	185	27		
Mickey Hole	TB	5'9	180	28		
Cliff Baldwin	WB	5'10	172	20		
Ken Huffine	FB	6'3	208	22	1	

Substitutes

Use Name	Pos.	Hgt.	Wgt.	Age	Int.	Pts.
Chuck Helvie (to DAY)	E	5'8	180	28		
Russ Hathaway (to DAY)	G	5'11	225	24		
Archie Erehart	WB	5'8	165	26		

Scores of each game

Date	Pts.	Opponent	Pts.
Oct. 3	0	Rock Island	45

HAMMOND PROS 0-3-0 Hank Gillo

Regulars

Use Name	Pos.	Hgt.	Wgt.	Age	Int.	Pts.
Carroll Johnson	E	5'9	165	26		
Dutch Kohl	E			26		
Mose Bashaw	T	5'9	200	32		
Frank Seliger	T		200	29		
Davis	G		185			
Russ Oltz	G	6'	200	21		
Frank Moran (to AKR)	C	6'4	285	29		
Klinks Meyers	BB			26		
Robert Specht	TB	5'9	170			
Ward	WB					
Hank Gillo	FB-WB-TB	5'10	195	25		

Substitutes

Use Name	Pos.	Hgt.	Wgt.	Age	Int.	Pts.
Max Hicks	E		175	26		
Mace Roberts	E	6'	185	23		
Frank Rydzewski (from CLE, from & to ChiT)	T	6'1	220	27		
Walt Sechrist	G	6'	250	23		
Brunswick	G	5'10	182			
Louie Kolls (from ChiC)	C	6'1	185	27		1
Wally Hess	BB	5'9	165	25		6
Marshall Jones (to DET)	TB	5'11	165	25		
Joe Pliska	WB	5'10	185	29		
Guil Falcon (from & to ChiT)	FB	5'10	220	27		

Substitutes

Use Name	Pos.	Hgt.	Wgt.	Age	Int.	Pts.
Tony Catalano	G			25		
Lew Skinner	G-C			21		
Jim Talbott	BB			27		
Wilbur Henderson	FB		195	22		

Scores of each game

Date	Pts.	Opponent	Pts.
Oct. 10	0	Rock Island	26
Oct. 17	0	Dayton	44
Nov. 21	7	Decatur	28

COLUMBUS PANHANDLES 0-5-0 Ted Nesser

Regulars

Use Name	Pos.	Hgt.	Wgt.	Age	Int.	Pts.
Homer Ruh	E	5'10	175	24		6
Jim Flower	E	6'1	190	24		
Oscar Kuehner	T	6'	200	31		1
Joe Mulbarger	T	5'9	215	25		
Frank Lone Star	G-T	5'11	200	33		
Oscar Wolford	G	6'	188	23		
Will Waite	C	6'2	200	27		
Hal Gaulke	BB	5'8	175	26		
Lee Snoots	TB	5'9	185	28		
John Schneider	WB	5'10	180	26		
Frank Nesser	FB-T	6'1	238	31		

Substitutes

Use Name	Pos.	Hgt.	Wgt.	Age	Int.	Pts.
Ted Nesser	T-G	5'10	230	37		
Phil Nesser	G	6'	225	39		
Babe Houck	G	6'	275	23		
Howard Yerges	TB	5'9	155	24		
Wilkie Moody	WB-TB-FB	5'7	175	23		
John Davis	FB-WB-TB-BB		155	24		

Substitutes

Use Name	Pos.	Hgt.	Wgt.	Age	Int.	Pts.
Hi Brigham	G	5'11	185	28		
Charlie Essman	G	6'	220	38		
Beckwith	TB		150	25		

Scores of each game

Date	Pts.	Opponent	Pts.
Oct. 3	0	Dayton	14
Oct. 10	0	Akron	37
Oct. 24	0	Detroit	6
Oct. 31	0	Cleveland	7
Nov. 14	7	Buffalo	43

RUSHING

NAME	Complete Games G	Att.	Yds.	Avg.	TD	Incom. Games G	Att.	Yds.	TD
DETROIT									
Horning									
Team						4			
Opp.						4			
CLEVELAND									
Conn (1)	1	5	12	2.4		5	5	29	
Doane						4	1	11	
Pierotti (2)						4	2	10	
Brickley						4	2	8	1
Petrie						2	1	5	
Cramer	1	4	0	0.0		5	1	4	
Cofall	1	6	3	0.5		2			
Hastings	1	2	0	0.0		2			
Bryant	1	1	-13	-13.0		2			
Devlin									
Ducote									
Baujan									
Baston									
Team	1	18	2	0.1		6			
Opp.	1	49	168	3.4	1	6			
CHICAGO TIGERS									
G. Falcon (1,3)	3	38	95	2.4		4			
Barnett	3	15	46	3.1		3			
Annan	3	19	21	1.1	1	4			
Malone	3	11	12	1.1		3			
Ghee	3	11	12	1.1		4			
Derr	1	5	9	1.8		1			
Eiseler						2	1	3	1
Knop									
Meagher									
Bosdett									
Des Jardien									
Team	3	100	195	2.0	1	4			
Opp.	3	123	434	3.5	5	4			
ROCHESTER									
Argus						1	2	3	
Quigley						1	1	-3	
Oliphant									
Team						1			
Opp.						1			
MUNCIE									
M. Hole	1	10	13	1.3					
Huffine	1	7	8	1.1					
Checkaye	1	2	2	1.0					
Baldwin	1	3	-1	-0.3					
Pope									
Team	1	22	22	1.0					
Opp.	1	43	186	4.3	3				
HAMMOND									
Specht	1	3	1	0.3		2	1	12	
Gillo	1	7	12	1.7		2			
Meyers	1	4	5	1.3		1			
Roberts	1	1	2	2.0		1			
Ward	1	4	0	0.0		1			
Hess									
Team	2	62	164	2.6		1			
Opp.	2	110	505	4.6	4	1			
COLUMBUS									
Moody						4	2	7	
Schneider						4	1	3	
Gaulke						5	1	2	
F. Nesser						5	1	1	
Flower									
Davis									
Ruh									
Team						5			
Opp.						5			

PASSING

NAME	Complete Games G	Com.	Att.	%	Yds.	Y/A	TD	Int.	Incom. Games G	Com.	Att.	Yds.	TD	Int.
DETROIT														
Horning														
Team									4					
Opp.									4					
CLEVELAND														
Conn (1)														
Doane														
Pierotti (2)	2	2	5	40	11	2.2		1	3	1	1	35		
Brickley														
Petrie														
Cramer														
Cofall														
Hastings	1								3	1	1	22		
Bryant	1	0	1	0				1	2					
Devlin	1	2	6	33	36	6.0			2	1	1	53	1	
Ducote	1	1	3	33	27	9.0								
Baujan														
Baston														
Team	3	5	15	33	74	4.9		2	4					
Opp.	2	5	13	38	42	3.2		1	5					
CHICAGO TIGERS														
G. Falcon (1,3)	3	1	1	100	11	11.0			4					
Barnett	3	7	23	30	87	3.8		2	3					
Annan	3	1	1	100	4	4.0			4					
Malone														
Ghee	3	6	19	32	86	4.5		4	4	0	1			
Derr														
Eiseler														
Knop														
Meagher														
Bosdett														
Des Jardien														
Team	3	15	44	34	188	4.3		6	4					
Opp.	3	4	16	25	66	4.1		3	4					
ROCHESTER														
Argus														
Quigley														
Oliphant	1	0	2	0										
Team	1	0	2	0										
Opp.	1	4	8	50	97	12.1								
MUNCIE														
M. Hole	1	1	1	100	1	1.0								
Huffine	1	0	1	0				1						
Checkaye	1	1	3	33	11	3.7								
Baldwin	1	1	2	50	5	2.5								
Pope														
Team	1	3	7	43	17	2.4		1						
Opp.	1	1	5	20	1	0.2		1						
HAMMOND														
Specht	2	6	19	32	83	4.4	1	5	1	0	1			1
Gillo	2	1	4	25	14	3.5		2	1					
Meyers														
Roberts														
Ward														
Hess														
Team	2	7	23	30	97	4.2	1	7	1					
Opp.	2	14	29	48	237	8.2	4	3	1					
COLUMBUS														
Moody														
Schneider														
Gaulke														
F. Nesser									5	5	6	135	1	1
Flower														
Davis														
Ruh														
Team									5					
Opp.									5					

RECEIVING

NAME	Complete Games G	Rec.	Yds	Avg.	TD	Incom. Games G	Rec.	Yds.	TD
DETROIT									
Horning									
Team									
Opp.									
CLEVELAND									
Conn (1)						5	2	75	1
Doane									
Pierotti (2)									
Brickley									
Petrie									
Cramer									
Cofall									
Hastings									
Bryant									
Devlin									
Ducote									
Baujan	2	1	3	3.0		4	2	62	
Baston	2	1	8	8.0		5			
Team									
Opp.									
CHICAGO TIGERS									
G. Falcon (1,3)									
Barnett	3	2	11	5.5		3			
Annan	3	1	13	13.0		4			
Malone									
Ghee	3	2	24	12.0		4			
Derr	1	2	28	14.0		1			
Eiseler									
Knop	3	4	40	10.0		4			
Meagher	1	3	40	13.3		3			
Bosdett	3	1	32	32.0		3			
Des Jardien									
Team									
Opp.									
ROCHESTER									
Argus									
Quigley									
Oliphant									
Team									
Opp.									
MUNCIE									
M. Hole									
Huffine	1	1	1	1.0					
Checkaye	1	1	5	5.0					
Baldwin									
Pope	1	1	11	11.0					
Team									
Opp.									
HAMMOND									
Specht									
Gillo	2	1	18	18.0		1			
Meyers	1	3	33	11.0		1			
Roberts	2	1	14	14.0					
Ward									
Hess	1	2	32	16.0	1				
Team									
Opp.									
COLUMBUS									
Moody									
Schneider									
Gaulke						5	2	55	
F. Nesser									
Flower						5	1	40	
Davis						4	1	30	
Ruh						5	1	10	1
Team									
Opp.									

PUNTING / PUNT RETURNS

NAME	Punting Comp. Games G	No.	Avg.	Punting Incom. Games G	No.	Avg.	Punt Returns Complete Games G	No.	Yds.	Avg.	TD	Punt Returns Incom. Games G	No.	Yds.	TD
DETROIT															
Horning				4	3	0.0									
Team				4								4			
Opp.				4								4			
CLEVELAND															
Conn (1)															
Doane															
Pierotti (2)															
Brickley															
Petrie															
Cramer															
Cofall	1	10	28.7	2											
Hastings															
Bryant							1	2	10	5.0		2			
Devlin															
Ducote	1	8	36.9												
Baujan															
Baston															
Team	2	18	32.3	5			1	2	10	5.0		6			
Opp.	2	14	34.9	5			1	5	65	13.0		6			
CHICAGO TIGERS															
G. Falcon (1,3)							3	1	9	9.0		4			
Barnett	3	29	32.1	3	2	19.5									
Annan							3	1	11	11.0		4			
Malone															
Ghee							3	3	17	5.7		4	1	6	
Derr															
Eiseler															
Knop															
Meagher															
Bosdett															
Des Jardien	3	4	36.3												
Team	3	33	32.6	4			3	5	37	7.4		4			
Opp.	3	28	37.7	4			3	13	175	13.5		4			
ROCHESTER															
Argus															
Quigley															
Oliphant															
Team				1								1			
Opp.				1								1			
MUNCIE															
M. Hole															
Huffine	1	5	15.2												
Checkaye	1	3	43.7												
Baldwin															
Pope															
Team	1	8	25.9				1	0							
Opp.	1	3	37.7				1	3	37	12.3					
HAMMOND															
Specht															
Gillo	2	1	45.0	1											
Meyers															
Roberts															
Ward	1	5	43.2	1											
Hess	1	9	36.2												
Team	2	15	39.1	1								3			
Opp.	2	7	36.1	1								3			
COLUMBUS															
Moody															
Schneider															
Gaulke															
F. Nesser															
Flower															
Davis															
Ruh															
Team				5								5			
Opp.				5								5			

1921 A.P.F.A.
Halas Wins His First

The first order of business when the American Professional Football Association members met in Akron in April of 1921 was to award the 1920 championship and trophy to the Akron Pros. The principle thus established — that the league champion would be designated by the league and not the subject of individual clubs' claims — would be tested several times during the 1920s. With that piece of business out of the way, the managers began serious consideration of how they might continue as an organization for another season.

Realizing that Jim Thorpe could run with the ball better than he could run a league, the managers installed Joe Carr as president of a reorganized association. Long years as the manager of the Columbus Panhandles, plus extensive experience as a minor-league baseball executive, furnished the spectacled Carr with the administrative skills Thorpe lacked. Although personally a gentle man, Carr governed pro football sternly through its formative years until his death in 1939.

Carr's office issued standings this season, but they were highly erratic, including some non-league games with weak clubs and excluding some league games, without apparent pattern. Additionally, those teams that did not play at least six games against APFA opponents were dropped from the standings altogether. All non-league games have been removed from the standings that appear on page 20 and all league games and 21 league members have been included, but this "purification" does not change the relative standings of the leading teams from the official standings.

League membership rose to 21 by admitting teams from Green Bay, Minneapolis, Cincinnati, Evansville, Louisville, Tonawanda, Washington and New York. Toledo was also issued a membership for a team to be run by Thorpe and baseball great Roger Bresnahan, but the team never materialized. The Philadelphia Quakers were about to be issued a membership when their manager withdrew his request. The Quakers, who played on Saturday because of Pennsylvania Blue Laws, used many of the same players who appeared for the Buffalo All-Americans on Sundays, and the APFA had passed a rule that a player could not play for more than one team in a week. Thirteen of the original 1920 APFA members returned for another season; the only casualty from the first season was the Chicago Tigers.

But the death of the Tigers did not leave the Chicago Cardinals as the only APFA team in town. A business recession had prompted the Staley Starchworks to Decatur to drop its pro football team, and A.E. Staley, the company's president, suggested to George Halas that he reestablish the club in Chicago. Halas accepted the offer and was aided by $5,000 which Staley gave him in return for retaining the Staley name for one season. Looking to save on a salary and to cut his risks in half, Halas made halfback Dutch Sternaman his partner in the new Chicago Staleys. After signing a lease to use Cubs Park (later renamed Wrigley Field), the two young partners persuaded Guy Chamberlin, George Trafton, Hugh Blacklock and Pard Pearce to join them from the old Decatur squad as the core of the new team. Since neither owner expected the team to turn a profit the first year (it lost $71.63), Halas worked as a car salesman and Sternaman worked in a gas station.

Despite the financial insecurity, the Staleys nevertheless retained a place among the league powers with the Akrons Pros and the Buffalo All-Americans, the leading clubs of 1920. Akron still had backfield aces Fritz Pollard and Rip King and strong linemen like Al Nesser and Pike Johnson, and added veteran help in fullback Carl Cramer from Cleveland and end Jim Flower from Columbus. Paul Robeson also joined the Pros. In addition to being a fine two-way end, Robeson was attending Columbia University Law School at the time and would soon become famous as a singer and actor. He later became a Marxist who would suffer in the McCarthy era of the 1950s. Buffalo also had back the core of its 1920 squad, and added wingback Elmer Oliphant, a famous All-American from

1921 STANDINGS

	W	L	T	Pct.	Pts.	Opp. Pts.	Avg. Pts.	Opp. Avg.
Chicago Staleys (Bears)	9	1	1	.900	128	53	12	5
Buffalo All-Americans	9	1	2	.900	211	29	18	3
Akron Pros	8	3	1	.727	148	31	12	3
Canton Bulldogs	5	2	3	.714	106	55	11	6
Rock Island Independents	4	2	1	.667	65	30	9	4
Green Bay Packers	3	2	1	.600	70	55	12	9
Evansville Crimson Giants	3	2	0	.600	87	46	17	9
Dayton Triangles	4	4	1	.500	96	67	11	9
Chicago Cardinals	3	3	2	.500	54	53	7	7
Washington Senators	*2	2	0	.500	21	28	7	9
Cleveland Tigers	3	5	0	.375	95	58	12	7
Rochester Jeffersons	2	*4	0	.333	85	76	17	15
Hammond Pros (R)	1	3	1	.250	17	45	3	9
Minneapolis Marines	1	3	0	.250	37	41	9	10
Cincinnati Celts (R)	1	3	0	.250	14	117	5	29
Detroit Panthers	1	5	1	.167	19	109	3	16
Columbus Panhandles	1	8	0	.111	47	222	5	25
Tonawanda Kardex (R)	0	1	0	.000	0	45	0	45
Louisville Brecks	0	2	0	.000	0	27	0	13
Muncie Flyers	0	2	0	.000	0	28	0	14
New York Brickley's Giants	0	2	0	.000	0	72	0	36

(R) — played only road games
* — includes one forfeit

Scoring Leaders

Oliphant	Buf	47
Anderson	Buf	42
Pollard	Akr	42
Bacon	Day	36
Laird	Buf-Roch-Can	36
Sternaman	ChiS	36
Boynton	Roch-Was	32
Cramer	Akr	31
Scott	Buf	30
Henderson	Eva	29
Guyon	Cle-Was-Cle	28
Lambeau	GB	28
Wenig	RI	26
Driscoll	ChiC	25
Hathaway	Day	24
Stinchcomb	ChiS	24
Berry	Roch	20
Hughitt	Buf	20
Calac	Cle-Was-Cle	18
Chamberlin	ChiC	18
Fausch	Eva	18
Halas	ChiS	18
McCormick	Akr-Cin	18
Miller	Buf	18
Smith	Buf	18

KICKING

		FG	Att	Pct
Sternaman	ChiS	5	12	42
Oliphant	Buf	5	15	33
Hathaway	Day	4	6	67
Lambeau	GB	3	12	25
Berry	Roch	2	2	100
E. Ruh	Col	2	5	40
Sheeks	Akr	2	6	33
R. Horween	ChiC	1	1	100
Boynton	Roch-Was	1	2	50
Mathys	Ham	1	2	50
Thorpe	Cle	1	2	50
Driscoll	ChiC	1	4	25
Ursella	Min	1	4	25
West	Can	1	4	25
Conzelman	RI	1	7	14
DeGree	Det	1	NA	
Bondurant	Eva	0	1	0
Bower	Cle	0	1	0
Brawley	NY-Cle	0	1	0
Brindley	RI	0	1	0
Cramer	Akr	0	1	0
Harley	ChiS	0	1	0
Henderson	Eva	0	1	0
Henry	Can	0	1	0
Jones	Ham	0	1	0
Killinger	Can	0	1	0
F. Nesser	Col	0	1	0
Nichols	RI	0	1	0
Risley	Ham	0	1	0
Sampson	Min	0	1	0
Wenig	RI	0	1	0
Feeney	Can	0	2	0
A. Horween	ChiC	0	2	0
Scott	Buf	0	3	0

		PAT	Att	Pct
Oliphant	Buf	26	26	100
Hathaway	Day	12	12	100
Boynton	Roch-Was	11	12	92
Guyon	Cle-Was-Cle	10	11	91
Copley	Akr	10	13	77
Sternaman	ChiS	9	14	64
Wenig	RI	8	9	89
Lambeau	GB	7	9	78
Feeney	Can	6	6	100
Bondurant	Eva	6	7	86
Henderson	Eva	5	5	100
Ursella	Min	4	4	100
Driscoll	ChiC	4	5	80
West	Can	4	6	67
King	Akr	3	4	75
Berry	Roch	2	2	100
Higgins	Can	2	2	100
Hughitt	Buf	2	2	100
Koehler	ChiC	2	2	100
Risley	Ham	2	2	100
Thorpe	Cle	2	2	100
Voss	Det-Buf	2	2	100
Blacklock	ChiS	2	3	67
Bliss	Col	1	1	100
Lewis	Cin	1	1	100
Morrow	Can	1	1	100
Munns	Cin	1	1	100
Sheeks	Akr	1	1	100
L. Tobin	Akr	1	1	100
Cramer	Akr	1	2	50
F. Nesser	Col	1	2	50
E. Ruh	Col	1	3	33
Sampson	Min	0	1	0
Zeller	Eva	0	1	0

CHICAGO STALEYS (BEARS) 9-1-1 George Halas

Regulars

Use Name	Pos.	Hgt.	Wgt.	Age	Int.	Pts.
Guy Chamberlin	E	6'2	190	27	1	18
George Halas	E	6'	182	26		18
Hugh Blacklock	T	6'	220	30		2
Ralph Scott	T	6'2	234	23		6
Russ Smith	G	5'10	220	25		
Tarzan Taylor	G	5'11	170	26		
George Trafton	C	6'2	230	24	1	
Pard Pearce	QB	5'5	150	24		12
Dutch Sternaman	HB	5'8	170	26		36
Chic Harley	HB	5'8	165	25		
Ken Huffine	FB	6'3	208	23		12

Substitutes

Use Name	Pos.	Hgt.	Wgt.	Age	Int.	Pts.
Harry Englund	E-HB	6'	185	21		
Lou Usher (from ROCH & HAM)	G-T	6'2	235	23		
Dick Barker (to RI)	G	5'9	180	24		
Jake Mintun	C	5'11	188	27		
Jake Lanum	HB	6'	190	24	2	
Pete Stinchcomb	HB-QB	5'8	152	26		24
George Bolan	FB-HB	5'11	200	24	1	

Scores of each game

Date	Pts.	Opponent	Pts.
Oct. 10	14	ROCK ISLAND (at Decatur)	10
Oct. 16	16	ROCHESTER	13
Oct. 23	7	DAYTON	0
Nov. 6	20	DETROIT	9
Nov. 13	3	ROCK ISLAND	0
Nov. 20	22	CLEVELAND	7
Nov. 24	6	BUFFALO	7
Nov. 27	20	GREEN BAY	0
Dec. 4	10	BUFFALO	7
Dec. 11	10	CANTON	0
Dec. 18	0	CHIC. CARDS	0

BUFFALO ALL AMERICANS 9-1-2 Tommy Hughitt

Regulars

Use Name	Pos.	Hgt.	Wgt.	Age	Int.	Pts.
Heinie Miller	E	5'10	185	27		18
Luke Urban	E	5'8	165	23		6
Bob Nash	T-E	6'1	205	28	1	6
Lou Little	T	6'	205	27		
Swede Youngstrom (to CAN)	G	6'1	182	24		6
Bill Brace	G	6'	180	25		
Lud Wray	C	6'	180	27		
Tommy Hughitt	BB	5'8	155	28	4	20
Ockie Anderson	TB-WB	5'9	165	27	1	42
Elmer Oliphant	WB-TB	5'7	175	29	4	47
Pat Smith	FB	6'	195	26		18

Substitutes

Use Name	Pos.	Hgt.	Wgt.	Age	Int.	Pts.
John Sullivan	E		170			
Tillie Voss (from DET)	E-T	6'3	204	24		
Steamer Horning (from DET)	T	6'	195	28		6
Bill Ward	T-G	6'	212	23		6
Moose Gardner (from DET)	G	6'1	220	27		
Herb Stein	G	6'	185	23		
Charlie Guy (from DET)	C	6'	170	24	2	
Johnny Scott	BB-TB-WB-FB	5'10	175	26	1	30
Carl Beck	TB-FB-WB-T	5'11	180	21		
Waddy Kuehl (from DET)	WB	5'9	165	29		6
Jim Laird (to ROCH & CAN)	FB	6'	190	23		
Eddie Usher	E	5'11	190	23		
Butch Spagna	T-G	6'	210	24		
Jack O'Hearn	WB	5'10	180	28		
Andy Hillhouse	WB	6'2	190	24		

Scores of each game

Date	Pts.	Opponent	Pts.
Oct. 2	17	HAMMOND	0
Oct. 9	38	COLUMBUS	0
Oct. 16	55	NEW YORK	0
Oct. 23	28	ROCHESTER	0
Oct. 30	21	DETROIT	0
Nov. 6	10	CLEVELAND	6
Nov. 13	0	AKRON	0
Nov. 20	7	CANTON	7
Nov. 24	7	Chic. Staleys	6
Nov. 27	7	DAYTON	0
Dec. 3	14	AKRON	0
Dec. 4	7	Chic. Staleys	10

Army. A brilliant runner, Oliphant also had the most productive toe in the league as he tied for the most field goals with five and successfully booted 26 of 26 extra point tries. Tommy Hughitt, Ockie Anderson and Swede Youngstrom shone particularly bright among the returning players. The Staleys added new help in rookie halfbacks Pete Stinchcomb and Chic Harley out of Ohio State.

All three powers cruised through their early games without obstacle. Akron opened the season against Columbus in a game which is memorable only because Al Nesser played against his five brothers and his nephew — seven Nessers in one game. In fact, Columbus player-coach Ted Nesser spent this season snapping the ball to his tailback son, Charlie. In other early-season news, former Staley halfback Jimmy Conzelman took over as Rock Island coach after tackle Frank Coughlin proved so ineffective as a player in the first few games that he lost respect as a coach. Conzelman, who had been holding down a regular spot in the Independents' backfield, learned of his promotion to coach in the midst of a game when a substitute trotted on the field with the news.

On November 13, after six easy wins and a tough 3-0 victory over Canton, Akron travelled to Buffalo and battled the All-Americans to a scoreless tie. Meanwhile, the Staleys were beating Conzelman's Rock Islanders 3-0 in Cubs Park on a Sternaman field goal.

One week later, Akron's unbeaten streak, which had started with their first game in 1920, ended in Dayton. The Triangles marshalled a fine defensive effort to shut out the Pros and scored on a field goal by guard Dale Sies. Buffalo was held to a tie for the second week in a row, finishing its contest with the Canton Bulldogs at 7-7. The Bulldogs were rebuilding this season, replacing many of their veterans with younger players. Jim Thorpe, after his Toledo plans fell through, went to Cleveland to head up the Tigers and took Joe Guyon and Pete Calac along with him. Thorpe's season in Cleveland was pretty much of a washout, as he suffered broken ribs on October 23 in a game against Cincinnati and missed practically the rest of the campaign. But, even though the Bulldogs were not the power of old, Buffalo was lucky to get past Canton with a tie. The All-Americans were forced to play with a patched-together line. A few days before the game, word finally arrived at the league office that many of Buffalo's best players were performing on Saturdays for the Philadelphia Quakers in violation of the league rule against playing for two teams in the same week. With the impotent administration of the year before, nothing would have been done, but Carr moved quickly to test the power of his office. He ordered the practice to cease, in effect letting the players choose to play for one team or the other. Linemen Heinie Miller, Lou Little, Butch Spagna, Lud Wray and reserve back Johnny Scott blamed the Buffalo management for blowing the whistle, and they stayed with the Quakers. Only by hiring several players from the Detroit Panthers, who ended their season early, was Buffalo able to put a representative team on the field. Although the immediate effect was weaken the All-Americans, the more important result was to show that the league actually had an administration that would enforce its rules. While Buffalo was tied and Akron lost, the Staleys beat the Thorpe-less Cleveland Tigers 22-7 in Chicago.

Four days later, on Thanksgiving Day, the Akron slide continued. The Canton Bulldogs held the Pros to only one first down all day, with Pete Henry particularly rushing Rip King's passes in a 14-0 Canton victory. Shutout in three straight games and beaten in two of them, the Pros suddenly had fallen out of contention. The two unbeaten contenders met in Wrigley Field, The Staleys took the opening kickoff and drove the length of the field against Buffalo, with a short plunge by Sternaman capping the drive. Sternaman missed the extra point, making the Chicago lead 6-0. The All-Americans toughened up against the Staleys after that opening drive and captured momentum in the third quarter by holding for four downs after the Staleys had a first down on the five-yard line. A long pass from Hughitt to Waddy Kuehl broke the Chicago defense for a touchdown and Hughitt's kick gave Buffalo a 7-6 lead. In the fourth quarter, two Hughitt interceptions ended Chicago drives. The 7-6 final score gave the Staleys their first loss and put the All-Americans in charge of the championship race.

The Staleys regained their confidence on Sunday, November 27, by whipping the Green Bay Packers 20-0. The Packers were sponsored by the Acme Packing Company and were coached by Curly Lambeau, star tailback and briefly a player at Notre Dame. The Packers came into the APFA after two years of independent ball, using mostly Wisconsin players and a few Notre Dame cronies of Lambeau. The best player of the lot was tackle Cub Buck, a Wisconsin native who left the Canton Bulldogs to play at home. Buffalo stayed undefeated by beating Dayton 7-0 at home.

The All-Americans had their biggest challenge of the season the next weekend, December 3-4, when they entertained Akron on Saturday, then traveled to Chicago for a rematch with the Staleys. For the fourth straight game, Akron failed to score, dropping a 14-0 decision to the front-running Buffalo squad. After an all-night train ride, the All-Americans squared off against the Staleys in Wrigley Field for the second time in 11 days. Guy Chamberlin picked off an errant Buffalo pass in the first quarter and sprinted 70 yard with it to the endzone. Buffalo evened the score at 7-7 in the second quarter when Swede Youngstrom blocked Ken Huffine's punt and Steamer Horning recovered the ball for a touchdown. Later in the quarter, Sternaman booted a 20-yard field goal to put Chicago ahead 10-7. A scoreless second half left the Staleys winners, and a 10-0 victory over Canton and a scoreless tie with the Cardinals in the next two weeks gave the Staleys the same percentage as the All-Americans.

Buffalo claimed that the rematch with the Staleys was merely a post-season game, and that they had won the championship on Thanksgiving Day. The Staleys scoffed at the idea of a post-season game, pointing out that the league had set no end-date for its season. They claimed the championship with the argument that they had won the second, and therefore decisive, game between the two. Claim what they might, the principle had been decided the previous season that the league champion would be designated at the annual league meeting. After much discussion, the league sided with the Staleys. George Halas had his first pro football championship.

NAME	RUSHING Complete Games					Incom. Games			
	G	Att.	Yds.	Avg.	TD	G	Att.	Yds.	TD
CHICAGO STALEYS									
Sternaman	3	33	167	5.1		8	2	39	2
Stinchcomb	3	14	94	6.7	1	8	3	86	3
Harley	2	14	22	1.6		7	3	63	
Huffine	3	27	79	2.9	1	7	1	5	1
Bolan	2	22	54	2.5		3			
Pearce	3	9	18	2.0	1	8			
Lanum	3	13	5	0.4		5			
Halas									
Chamberlin									
Team	3	132	439	3.3	3	9			
Opp.	3	93	243	2.6		9			
BUFFALO									
Oliphant	1	8	27	3.4		9	14	140	1
Smith	1	5	7	1.4		10	29	131	3
Anderson	1	5	-8	-1.6		10	16	114	5
Hughitt	1	6	15	2.5		11	19	80	1
Scott	1	1	-5	-5.0		6	14	72	2
Laird (1)						1	1	37	
Beck						6	5	17	
Miller									
Urban									
Youngstrom									
Kuehl (2)									
Nash									
Voss (2)									
Wray									
Team	1	25	36	1.4		11			
Opp.	1	34	75	2.2		11			

NAME	PASSING Complete Games								Incom. Games					
	G	Com.	Att.	%	Yds.	Y/A	TD	Int	G	Com.	Att.	Yds.	TD	Int
CHICAGO STALEYS														
Sternaman	3	2	5	40	46	9.2			8	1	1	10	1	
Stinchcomb														
Harley	2	5	9	56	70	7.8	2		7	3	4	50	1	
Huffine	3	2	5	40	38	7.6		1	7	4	4	95	1	
Bolan														
Pearce	3	2	5	40	54	10.8		1	8					
Lanum														
Halas														
Chamberlin														
Team	3	11	24	46	208	8.7	2	2	9					
Opp.	3	13	34	38	239	7.0	1	4	9					
BUFFALO														
Oliphant	1	2	7	29	24	3.4			9	10	13	168	7	
Smith														
Anderson	1	2	9	22	30	3.3			10	10	20	178	1	4
Hughitt	1	0	2	0					11	4	8	88	2	1
Scott	1	2	5	40	29	5.8			6	2	2	43	1	
Laird (1)														
Beck														
Miller														
Urban														
Youngstrom														
Kuehl (2)														
Nash														
Voss (2)														
Wray														
Team	2	16	38	42	244	6.4	1	1	10					
Opp.	2	7	36	19	106	2.9		1	10					

NAME	RECEIVING Complete Games					Incom. Games			
	G	Rec.	Yds.	Avg.	TD	G	Rec.	Yds.	TD
CHICAGO STALEYS									
Sternaman	3	3	61	20.3		8	1	20	
Stinchcomb	3	1	27	27.0		8	2	43	
Harley									
Huffine									
Bolan									
Pearce									
Lanum									
Halas	3	6	78	13.0	2	8	2	35	1
Chamberlin	3	1	42	42.0		8	3	57	2
Team									
Opp.									
BUFFALO									
Oliphant	1	1	15	15.0		9			
Smith	1	1	16	16.0		10	1	20	
Anderson	1	1	14	14.0		10	2	35	1
Hughitt	2	13	148	11.4	1	10	3	25	1
Scott	1	1	15	15.0		6	2	40	2
Laird (1)									
Beck									
Miller	1					6	5	111	3
Urban	1					11	5	108	1
Youngstrom	1					11	2	23	1
Kuehl (2)						2	1	40	1
Nash	1					10	1	30	
Voss (2)						4	1	15	
Wray	1	1	15	15.0		6			
Team									
Opp.									

NAME	PUNTING Comp. Games			Incom. Games			PUNT RETURNS Complete Games					Incom. Games			
	G	No.	Avg.	G	No.	Avg.	G	Rec.	Yds.	Avg.	TD	G	Rec.	Yds.	TD
CHICAGO STALEYS															
Sternaman															
Stinchcomb							3	2	27	13.5		8	3	95	
Harley	2	2	37.0	7											
Huffine	3	6	34.5	7	2	0.0									
Bolan	2	6	22.3	2											
Pearce							3	3	15	4.0		8			
Lanum	3	7	27.9	5											
Halas															
Chamberlin															
Team	3	21	29.0	9			3	5	42	8.4		9			
Opp.	3	18	31.1	9			3	5	62	12.4		9			
BUFFALO															
Oliphant															
Smith															
Anderson												11	2	53	1
Hughitt				12	2	15.0									
Scott															
Laird (1)															
Beck															
Miller															
Urban															
Youngstrom															
Kuehl (2)															
Nash															
Voss (2)															
Wray															
Team	1	18	32.8	11								12			
Opp.	1	16	39.7	11								12			

Regulars							Substitutes							Substitutes							Scores of each game			
Use Name	Pos.	Hgt.	Wgt.	Age	Int.	Pts.	Use Name	Pos.	Hgt.	Wgt.	Age	Int.	Pts.	Use Name	Pos.	Hgt.	Wgt.	Age	Int.	Pts.	Date	Pts.	Opponent	Pts.
AKRON PROS 8-3-1 Fritz Pollard and Elgie Tobin																								
Scotty Bierce	E	5'9	165	24		12	Roy Ratekin	E	5'10	180	21			Bunny Corcoran (from & to CLE)	E	5'11	185	26			Sep. 25	14	COLUMBUS	0
Paul Robeson	E-T	6'3	218	23	1		Jim Flower	E-G	6'1	190	25										Oct. 2	41	CINCINNATI	0
Charlie Copley	T	5'9	190	33		10															Oct. 9	23	Chic. Cards	0
Pike Johnson	T-G	5'11	185	24			Read	G-T		190											Oct.16	20	Detroit	0
Al Nesser	G-E	6'	195	28		6	Alf Cobb	G	5'11	210	27										Oct. 23	3	Canton	0
Leo Tobin	G	5'9	220	30		1	Tommy Tomlin (from HAM)	G	5'10	195	27										Oct. 30	19	ROCHESTER	0
Russ Bailey	C	5'11	175	21	1																Nov. 6	21	Columbus	0
Paul Sheeks	BB	5'8	170	31		13	Elgie Tobin	BB	5'9	160	36			Bruno Haas (from & to CLE)	BB	5'10	180	30			Nov. 13	0	Buffalo	0
Rip King	TB	6'1	195	24	2	15	Marshall Jones	WB-TB-FB	5'11	165	26										Nov. 20	0	Dayton	3
Fritz Pollard	WB	5'7	165	26		42	Marty Beck	FB-WB-BB	5'9	175	21										Nov. 24	0	CANTON	14
Carl Cramer	FB-TB	5'11	180	23	1	31	Frank McCormick (to CIN)	FB	5'11	190	26		18								Dec. 3	0	Buffalo	14
																					Dec. 4	7	Chic. Cards	0
CANTON BULLDOGS 5-2-3 Cap Edwards Bob Higgins																								
Bird Carroll	E	5'8	185	25		6	Red Steele	E	6'	176	24										Oct. 9	7	HAMMOND	7
Bob Higgins	E	5'10	195	27	1	14	Inky Williams (from & to HAM)	E	5'11	170	24										Oct. 16	14	Dayton	14
Pete Henry	T	5'11	245	23																	Oct. 23	0	AKRON	3
Belf West	T	6'2	200	25	1	7															Nov. 6	14	DAYTON	0
John Kellison	G	6'	210	34			Cap Edwards	G	6'	205	33			Paul Griffiths	G	5'8	190	23			Nov. 13	7	Cleveland	0
Duke Osborn	G	5'10	185	24			Swede Youngstrom (from BUF)	G	6'1	182	24			Ed Sauer (from & to DAY)	G	5'10	235	23			Nov. 20	7	Buffalo	7
Al Feeney	C	5'11	185	28		6	Dutch Speck	G-C-T	5'10	220	35			Larry Conover	C	5'10	190	27			Nov. 24	14	Akron	0
Fido Kempton	BB	5'8	155	28			Harry Robb	BB-WB	5'10	180	24	1	6	Marv Smith	TB	5'11	185	23			Nov. 27	15	Washington	0
Tex Grigg	TB-BB	5'11	185	30	2	6	Lou Smyth	TB-FB-WB	6'1	195	22		12	Glenn Killinger	TB	5'9	160	22			Dec. 11	0	Chic. Staleys	10
Charlie Way	WB	5'8	143	23	3	6	Fritz Slackford	WB-FB-E	6'	180	27	1	12	Jim Morrow	WB	5'10	170	25	3	7	Dec. 18	28	Washington	14
Guil Falcon (from HAM)	FB	5'10	220	28	1	12	Jim Laird (from BUF & ROCH)	FB	6'	190	23	1	12											
ROCK ISLAND INDEPENDENTS 4-2-1 Frank Coughlin, Jimmy Conzelman																								
Oke Smith	E	6'2	185	26			Dave Hayes (to GB)	E	5'8	165	24		6								Oct. 2	0	DETROIT	0
Obe Wenig	E-BB	5'10	190	25		26	Bud Menefee	E	6'	185	23										Oct. 10	10	Chic. Staleys	14
Brick Travis	T	6'1	200	24			Frank Coughlin (to DET & GB)	T	6'3	220	25												(at Decatur)	
Ed Healey	T-G-E	6'1	200	26		6	Walt Buland	T	6'1	215	29										Oct. 16	14	Chic. Cards	7
Emmett Keefe (to GB)	G	5'10	195	28			Dick Barker (from ChiS)	G	5'9	180	24										Oct. 23	14	Detroit	0
Dewey Lyle	G	5'11	195	30			Hal Hanson	G-C-T	6'1	190	25										Oct. 30	13	Green Bay	3
Jug Earp	C	6'	220	24			Freeman Fitzgerald	C	6'	195	29										Nov. 6	14	MINNEAPOLIS	3
Jimmy Conzelman	BB-TB	6'	170	23		15	Sid Nichols	BB	5'7	177	26	2	6	Walt Brindley	BB-TB	5'8	150	26			Nov. 13	0	Chic. Staleys	3
Eddie Novak	TB-WB	5'9	175	24	1	6	Jerry Johnson	WB-TB	5'11	195	26			John Hasbrouck	WB-E-FB	6'	190	26						
Lane Bridgeford	WB-FB	5'10	180	23			Grover Malone (to GB)	WB	5'8	185	25	1		(from ROCH)										
Buck Gavin (from DET)	FB	5'10	175	26	1		Viv Vanderloo	FB	5'10	190	23			Eddie Duggan	FB	6'	200	28						
														Jerry Mansfield	FB	5'8	160	27						
														Paddy Quinn	FB	5'7	170	31						
GREEN BAY PACKERS 3-2-1 Curly Lambeau																								
Billy DuMoe	E	5'10	175	23	3	12	Cowboy Wheeler	E	5'9	180	23			Herm Martell	E	5'8	155	20			Oct. 23	7	MINNEAPOLIS	6
Dave Hayes (from RI)	E	5'8	165	24			Nate Abrams	E	5'4	145	23	1	6								Oct. 30	3	ROCK ISLAND	13
Cub Buck	T	6'	255	29																	Nov. 6	43	EVANSVILLE	6
Frank Coughlin (from RI & DET)	T	6'3	220	25																	Nov. 13	14	HAMMOND	7
Joe Carey	G	6'2	195	25			Sammy Powers	G-T	5'10	170	20	1		Warren Smith	G		175	26			Nov. 20	3	Chic. Cards	3
Milt Wilson	G	5'10	200				Jim Cook	G	6'3	220	32			Marty Zoll	G	5'8	185	21			Nov. 27	0	Chic. Staleys	20
Jab Murray	C-T	6'1	215	28	1		Fee Klaus	C	5'9	190	19			Emmett Keefe (from RI)	G	5'10	195	28						
Norm Barry (from ChiC)	BB	5'10	170	23	2	6	Adolph Kliebhan	BB			24													
Curly Lambeau	TB	5'10	185	23	2	28																		
Grover Malone (from RI)	HB-TB	5'8	185	25	2		Buff Wagner	HB-BB-FB	5'9	165	24			Wally Ladrow	HB	5'9	180	25						
Art Schmaehl	FB	5'8	170	27	1	12	Tubby Howard	FB-BB	5'10	210	27		6	Ray McLean	FB-BB	5'7	155	23						
EVANSVILLE CRIMSON GIANTS 3-2-0 Frank Fausch																								
Earl Goldsmith	E		182	27		6	Doc Gorman	E			28										Oct. 2	21	LOUISVILLE	0
Chuck O'Neil	E-BB	5'10	180	23			Chief Mullen	E-BB		165	27										Oct. 9	14	MUNCIE	0
Bourbon Bondurant	T-E	6'1	202	23		6	Red Jackson (to HAM)	T	6'	200	24			John McDonald	T	6'	195	21			Oct. 16	0	HAMMOND	3
Adolph Spiegel	T-G	5'11	190	23			Tubby Rohsenberger	T			24			Leon Winternheimer	T	6'1	240				Nov. 6	6	Green Bay	43
Alec Fishman	G-FB	5'11	218	23		6	Vince Lensing	G-T	6'	200	20			Louie Fritsch	G		240	41			Nov. 27	48	CINCINNATI	0
Bill Garnjost	G-C	5'10	190	28			Mark Ingle	G			30													
Joe Windbiele	C	6'1	220	24			Dick Spain	C	5'8	180	28													
Menz Lindsey	BB-TB	5'6	165	23		12																		
Herb Henderson	TB	5'11	170	22		29																		
Travis Williams	WB	6'	200	29		6	Jerry Zeller	WB-BB	5'11	170	23		6	Earl Warweg	WB	5'6	145	29						
Frank Fausch	FB	6'3	250	26	1	18																		
DAYTON TRIANGLES 4-4-1 Bud Talbott																								
Dave Reese	E	6'	175	28		6	Lee Fenner	E	5'10	170	25										Oct. 2	42	COLUMBUS	13
Dutch Thiele	E	6'1	195	28	2	6															Oct. 9	7	Detroit	10
Russ Hathaway	T	5'11	225	25		24	Jake Stahl (to CLE)	T	5'11	185	28										Oct. 16	14	CANTON	14
Ed Sauer (to & from CAN)	T	5'10	235	23	1		Chalmers Tschappatt	T	5'11	180	25										Oct. 23	0	Chic. Staleys	7
Art Sampson	G	6'1	206	24			Larry Dellinger	G-T	5'11	200	28										Oct. 30	3	CLEVELAND	2
Herb Sies	G	6'1	203	26																	Nov. 6	0	Canton	14
Hobby Kinderdine	C	5'11	180	30			Glenn Tidd	C-T-G	5'11	202	27										Nov. 13	27	DETROIT	0
Al Mahrt	BB-TB	5'11	168	27	1	6	Fay Abbott	BB-TB-WB	5'8	170	26		6								Nov. 20	3	AKRON	0
Frank Bacon	TB	5'11	180	27	1	36	Art Haley	TB	5'10	170	25			Wilkie Moody	WB	5'7	175	24			Nov. 27	0	Buffalo	7
Gus Redman (from MUN)	WB	5'11	170	25	1		Nelson Rupp	WB-FB	5'10	180	30			Frank Sillin	WB	5'11	175	18						
Lou Partlow	FB-WB	6'1	185	28	1	6	George Roudebush	FB-TB	5'10	180	27		6	John Miller	FB	6'	188	28						
CHICAGO CARDINALS 3-3-2 Paddy Driscoll																								
Lenny Sachs	E	5'8	175	24		6	Paul LaRosa	E	5'11	175	30										Oct. 2	20	MINNEAPOLIS	0
Red O'Connor	E	5'8	170				John Marquardt	E			33		6								Oct. 9	0	AKRON	23
Fred Gillies	T	6'3	215	25																	Oct. 16	7	ROCK ISLAND	14
Nick McInerney	T	6'2	195	25																	Oct. 23	17	COLUMBUS	6
Clyde Zoia	G	5'7	175	25			Walter Voight (from HAM)	G	5'8	200	26			Leo Chappell	G	6'2	205	22			Nov. 6	7	HAMMOND	0
Willie Brennan	G	6'	210	27			Garland Buckeye	G-C	6'	235	23										Nov. 20	3	GREEN BAY	3
Frank Rydzewski	C-T	6'1	220	28			Charlie Knight	C-T	6'2	200	21										Dec. 4	0	AKRON	7
Bernie Halstrom	BB-WB	5'9	160	26			Norm Barry (to GB)	BB	5'10	170	23			Egan	BB		175				Dec. 18	0	Chic. Staleys	0
Paddy Driscoll	TB	5'8	160	26	2	25	Arnie Horween	BB	5'11	200	23			Earl Potteiger	WB	5'7	170	30						
Pete Steger	WB-BB			24			John Scanlon	WB		185	21		6	Harry Curran	WB	5'10	180	27						
Bob Koehler	FB	5'11	185	27		8	Ralph Horween	FB-WB	5'10	200	25		3	Ping Rodie	FB			24						

NAME	RUSHING Complete Games G	Att.	Yds.	Avg.	TD	RUSHING Incom. Games G	Att.	Yds.	TD	PASSING Complete Games G	Com.	Att.	%	Yds.	Y/A	TD	Int.	PASSING Incom. Games G	Com.	Att.	Yds.	TD	Int.
AKRON																							
Pollard	4	45	134	3.0	3	8	13	131	3	5	1	4	25	12	3.0	1		7					
Cramer	4	45	155	3.4	1	7	7	98	3	3								6	3	3	83		
King	4	27	29	1.1	1	7	6	25	1	5	23	76	30	331	4.4	1	4	6	10	16	202	2	5
McCormick (1)	1	7	28	4.0	1	1	5	23	2														
Sheeks	4	8	44	5.5		8	2	0		5	1	8	13	14	1.8			7					
Jones	2	5	33	6.6	5																		
Beck	2	5	23	4.6	6																		
Haas	1	3	4	1.3																			
Tobin	3	1	-5	-5.0	5																		
Bierce																							
Flower																							
Ratekin																							
Robeson																							
Team	4	146	445	3.0	6	8				5	25	88	28	359	4.1	2	4	7					
Opp.	3	114	270	2.4	2	9				5	16	59	27	190	3.2		6	7					
CANTON																							
Grigg	2	21	74	3.5		5	9	57		4	5	23	22	91	4.0	1		3	7	12	108	1	2
Falcon (2)	2	33	114	3.5		5	7	24	2														
Robb						5	3	77															
Laird (3)						1	4	54	2														
Henry	3	10	34	3.4		7	1	12															
Slackford	3	10	12	1.2	1	7	4	32	1														
Way	3	13	4	0.3		3	1	9		4	1	3	33	8	2.7		1	2					
West	3	7	16	2.3		7				5	1	2	50	6	3.0		1	5					
Smyth	3	13	28	2.2	1	3	2	3	1	4								2	3	3	38	1	
Kempton	3	10	21	2.1		3				4	5	16	31	55	3.4		2	2	0	2	0		2
Killinger																		1	2	2	31	1	
Smith										1	1	5	20	23	4.6								
Higgins																							
Morrow																							
Carroll																							
Team	3	117	303	2.6	2	7				5	13	49	27	183	3.7	1	4	5					
Opp.	3	94	199	2.1	1	7				5	26	82	32	352	4.3	1	11	5					
ROCK ISLAND																							
Novak	7	66	225	3.4						7	2	6	33	31	5.2	1							
Conzelman	7	57	161	2.8	1					7	21	53	40	324	6.1	2	8						
Bridgeford	5	36	133	3.7						5	0	1	0										
Nichols	7	35	128	3.7	1					7	3	7	43	42	6.0		1						
Gavin (2)	3	30	80	2.7																			
Wenig	7	18	48	2.7						7	2	8	25	26	3.3		1						
Vanderloo	3	16	41	2.6																			
Johnson	2	16	40	2.5																			
Duggan	3	14	21	1.5																			
Brindley	2	3	12	4.0						2	1	2	50	16	8.0								
Mansfield	1	6	7	1.2																			
Malone (1)	3	12	2	0.2																			
Hasbrouck (2)	3	1	1	1.0																			
Hayes (1)																							
Smith																							
Travis																							
Team	7	310	899	2.9	2					7	29	77	38	439	5.7	3	10						
Opp.	7	277	589	2.1	1					7	29	82	35	400	4.9	1	5						
GREEN BAY																							
Schmael	4	34	93	2.7		2	12	47	2														
Lambeau	4	24	64	2.7	1	2	5	32	1	4	15	49	31	268	5.5	1	6	2	3	9	93		2
Barry (2)	4	23	33	1.4		1	5	31	1														
Malone (2)	4	24	28	1.2		2	3	9															
Howard	2	3	1	0.3		2	2	15	1														
McLean	1					2	1	12															
Wagner	3	4	6	1.5		1																	
Buck										4	0	1	0					2					
Hayes (2)																							
DuMoe																							
Wilson																							
Team	4	112	225	2.0	1	2				4	15	50	30	268	5.4	1	6	2					
Opp.	4	164	637	3.9	4	2				4	7	28	25	143	5.1	1	8	2					
EVANSVILLE																							
Henderson						4	4	90	4									4	2	2	35		
Fausch						4	4	18	3														
Lindsey						5	2	12	2									5	2	5	25		3
Williams						3	1	5	1														
Fishman						5	1	5	1														
O'Neil																		5	1	2	50	1	1
Zeller																							
Team						5												5					
Opp.						5												5					
DAYTON																							
Bacon	2	22	70	3.2	1	7	12	79	4	3								6	1	3	20		
Partlow	2	19	41	2.2		4	12	37	1	2								4	1	1	15	1	
Rupp	1	8	15	1.9		4	2	16															
Redmond (2)	1	6	14	2.3		4	5	8		2								3	2	2	9		
Abbott	2	4	2	0.5		7	3	16		3	0	3	0				2	6	4	4	98		
Mahrt	2	4	4	1.0		5				3	22	52	42	332	6.4	1	6	4	7	11	120	1	1
Roudebush	2	1	0	0.0		7	4	3	1	3								6	3	4	37	2	
Thiele																							
Reese																							
Fanner																							
Team	2	64	146	2.3	1	7				3	22	55	40	332	6.0	1	8	6					
Opp.	2	68	179	2.6		7				3	8	27	30	103	3.8		2	6					
CHICAGO CARDINALS																							
Driscoll	2	23	59	2.6		6	4	100	2	2	9	35	26	152	4.3		4	6	5	5	68	1	
Koehler	2	24	47	2.0		6	1	15	1	2								6	1	1	15	1	
Halstrom	2	10	23	2.3		3																	
R. Horween	1	8	22	2.8		1				1	0	1	0					1					
Bodie	1	5	7	1.4																			
Scanlon	1					2	1	5	1														
Steger	2	7	4	0.6		4																	
Barry (1)	1	1	-2	-2.0		2																	
Sachs																							
Marquardt																							
O'Connor																							
Team	2	78	160	2.1		6				2	9	36	25	152	4.2		4	6					
Opp.	2	77	171	2.2		6				2	8	22	36	100	4.5	1	2	6					

NAME	RECEIVING Complete Games G	Rec.	Yds	Avg.	TD	RECEIVING Incom. Games G	Rec.	Yds.	TD	PUNTING Comp. Games G	No.	Avg.	PUNTING Incom. Games G	No.	Avg.	PUNT RETURNS Complete Games G	No.	Yds.	Avg.	TD	PUNT RETURNS Incom. Games G	No.	Yds.	TD
AKRON																								
Pollard	3	4	36	9.0		9	1	9	1							1	6	56	9.3		11	1	24	
Cramer	3					8	4	80	1															
King										5	53	40.2	6	2	14.5									
McCormick (1)																								
Sheeks	3					9	1	35	1							1					11	2	37	
Jones																								
Beck																								
Haas																								
Tobin																								
Bierce	3	4	76	19.0		9	11	209	1															
Flower	1					8	1	37																
Ratekin						4	1	19																
Robeson	3	1	2	2.0		5																		
Team										5	53	40.2	7			1	6	56	4.3		11			
Opp.										5	59	37.5	7			1	0				11			
CANTON																								
Grigg	4	1	15	15.0		3																		
Falcon (2)																								
Robb	1					4	3	38	1															
Laird (3)																								
Henry																								
Slackford	5	1	23	23.0		5	2	23																
Way	4	4	52	13.0	1	2										2	1	8	8.0		4			
West										3	5	34.0	7											
Smyth	4	1	15	15.0		2	1	20		2	3	32.3	4											
Kempton	4	2	26	13.0		2				3	9	34.1	3			2	3	30	10.0		4			
Killinger																								
Smith																								
Higgins	5	4	52	13.0		4	4	71	1	3	14	36.4	6	1	70.0									
Morrow	2					3	2	15																
Carroll	3					3	1	30	1															
Team										3	31	35.0	7			2	4	38	9.5		8			
Opp.										3	31	36.8	7			2	10	81	8.1		8			
ROCK ISLAND																								
Novak																7	1	15	15.0					
Conzelman										7	7	37.0				7	13	123	9.5					
Bridgeford	5	1	38	38.0																				
Nichols	7	1	8	8.0												7	2	9	4.5					
Gavin (2)	3	2	3	1.5																				
Wenig	7	13	242	18.6	2					7	45	33.2												
Vanderloo	3	1	8	8.0																				
Johnson										2	6	28.2												
Duggan																								
Brindley																2	1	6	6.0					
Mansfield																								
Malone (1)	3	2	20	10.0																				
Hasbrouck (2)																								
Hayes (1)	3	6	94	15.7	1																			
Smith	7	2	25	12.5																				
Travis	5	1	1	1.0																				
Team										7	58	33.1				7	17	153	9.0					
Opp.										7	70	32.5				7	10	136	13.6	1				
GREEN BAY																								
Schmael																								
Lambeau										4	4	35.3	2	2	32.5	4	9	109	12.1		2	1	5	
Barry (2)	4	4	36	9.0		1																		
Malone (2)	4	2	9	4.5		2	1	35																
Howard																								
McLean																								
Wagner	3					1	1	21																
Buck	4	1	8	8.0		2				4	25	31.6	2	2	37.5									
Hayes (2)	4	5	92	18.4		2																		
DuMoe	4	3	123	41.0	1	2	1	37																
Wilson										4	3	30.3												
Team										4	32	32.0	2			4	9	109	12.1		2			
Opp.										4	32	34.5	2			4	7	87	12.4		2			
EVANSVILLE																								
Henderson													4	1	85.0									
Fausch													4	4	23.8									
Lindsey																								
Williams																								
Fishman																								
O'Neil						5	4	60																
Zeller						4	1	50	1															
Team													5								5			
Opp.													5								5			
DAYTON																								
Bacon	2	4	28	7.0		7	5	48	1	2	4	34.8	7	1	9.0	2	2	10	5.0		7	3	70	
Partlow	2	1	5	5.0		4	1	35																
Rupp										1	1	35.0	4			1	3	20	6.7		4			
Redmond (2)	1					4	1	20		1	13	32.2	4	3	31.3									
Abbott						7	2	19	1	2	4	37.8	7	1	0.0	2					7	1	40	
Mahrt	2					5	3	45	1															
Roudebush	2	1	40	4.0		7	1	39																
Thiele	2	6	123	20.5	1	5	2	24																
Reese	2	3	39	13.0		7	3	69	1															
Fanner	2	1	35	35.0		6																		
Team										2	22	33.8	7			2	5	30	6.0		7			
Opp.										2	20	33.7	7			2	6	56	9.3		7			
CHICAGO CARDINALS																								
Driscoll										2	12	36.4	6			2	8	154	19.3	1	6			
Koehler										2	4	36.0	6											
Halstrom	2	1	13	13.0		3																		
R. Horween																								
Bodie																								
Scanlon	1	1	8	8.0		2																		
Steger	2	1	17	17.0		4	1	15																
Barry (1)																								
Sachs	2	3	73	24.3		6	3	35	1															
Marquardt	1	2	33	16.5		2	1	33	1															
O'Connor	2	1	8	8.0		3	1	10																
Team										2	16	36.3	6			2	8	154	19.3	1	6			
Opp.										2	21	31.9	6			2	9	91	10.1		6			

WASHINGTON SENATORS 2-2-0 Jack Hegerty

Regulars

Use Name	Pos.	Hgt.	Wgt.	Age	Int.	Pts.
Gordon Patterson	E		165	21		
Don McCarthy	E	5'10	172	24		
Dan Ahern	T	6'2	200	23		
Metz Smeach	T	6'3	195	26		
Tom Gormley (from NY)	G-T	5'11	225	32		
Cy McDonald	G	6'1	197	24		
Billy Crouch	C	6'1	187	22		
Bullets Watson	BB		174	28		6
Benny Boynton (from ROCH)	TB	5'9	165	22		9
Johnny Hudson	WB-FB	5'9	170	22		6
Gene Vidal	FB	5'10	170	26		

Substitutes

Use Name	Pos.	Hgt.	Wgt.	Age	Int.	Pts.
Sam Kaplan	E		166	22		
Patsy Gerardi	E		165	29		
Red Litkus	T-E		187	27		
Buff Turner	T-G		188	30		
Sam Turner	G		195	19		
Ed Van Meter	G	6'1	212	22		
Dutch Leighty	BB-TB	5'11	168	25		
Joe Guyon (from, to CLE)	WB-TB-FB	5'10	195	28		
George Beyers	WB		168			
Pete Calac (from & to CLE)	FB	5'10	195	28		
Joe Coster	T	5'10	175	25		
Alec Anderson	G	5'8	166	28		
Pong Unitas	G		180	25		
Mickey Livers	FB	5'10	175	25		
Johnny Gilroy	TB	5'10	175	25		
Johnny Bleier	WB-BB		160	29		
Jack Sullivan	FB		170	29		
Perry Dowrick	FB		172	27		

Scores of each game

Date	Pts.	Opponent	Pts.
Nov. 27	0	CANTON	15
Dec. 4	1	ROCHESTER (forfeit)	0
Dec. 11	7	CLEVELAND	0
Dec. 18	14	CANTON	28

CLEVELAND TIGERS 3-5-0 Jim Thorpe

Regulars

Use Name	Pos.	Hgt.	Wgt.	Age	Int.	Pts.
Bunny Corcoran (to & from AKR)	E	5'11	185	26		6
Tom Whelan	E-C-G	5'10	180	27		6
Bull Lowe	T	5'11	180	26		
Dan O'Connor	T-G	6'2	210	27		
Red Pearlman	G-T	6'	195	23		
Joe Murphy	G	5'9	215	24		
George Tandy	C	6'1	210	28		
Milt Ghee	BB-TB	5'7	167	28		12
Joe Guyon (to & from WAS)	TB-WB	5'10	195	28	2	28
Bruno Haas (to & from AKR)	WB-BB	5'10	180	30		6
Pete Calac (to & from WAS)	FB	5'10	195	29		18

Substitutes

Use Name	Pos.	Hgt.	Wgt.	Age	Int.	Pts.
Harry Baujan	E	5'8	170	27		
Moore	T					
Jake Stahl (from DAY)	G	5'11	185	28		
Ed Brawley (from NY)	G	5'9	175	26		
Fat Waldsmith	C	5'9	225	29		
Phil Bower	BB-WB	5'8	160	27		
Jim Thorpe	TB	6'1	200	34	1	11
Patterson	BB-G					
John Hendren	FB-WB	5'9	175	24		6

Scores of each game

Date	Pts.	Opponent	Pts.
Oct. 16	35	COLUMBUS	9
Oct. 23	28	CINCINNATI	0
Oct. 30	2	Dayton	3
Nov. 6	6	Buffalo	10
Nov. 13	0	CANTON	7
Nov. 20	7	Chic. Staleys	22
Dec. 3	17	New York	0
Dec. 11	0	Washington	7

ROCHESTER JEFFERSONS 2-4-0 Jack Forsyth

Regulars

Use Name	Pos.	Hgt.	Wgt.	Age	Int.	Pts.
Ray Witter	E	5'10	175	24		
Darby Lowery	E	6'	190	29		
Jim Barron	T	6'	195	28	1	
Carl Thomas	T	5'10	185	24		
Frank Morrissey	G-T	6'1	202	22		
Hank Smith	G-C	6'1	187	28		
Doc Alexander	C	5'11	205	23		
Jerry Noonan (to NY)	BB-E	6'1	182	21		12
Benny Boynton (to WAS)	TB-BB	5'9	165	22		23
Bob Argus	WB	5'10	192	27	1	
Jim Laird (fr. BUF, to CAN)	FB	6'	190	23		24

Substitutes

Use Name	Pos.	Hgt.	Wgt.	Age	Int.	Pts.
Spin Roy	E	6'	175	24		
Joe DuMoe	E	5'9	178	26		
Jimmy Woods	G-T	5'9	195	27		
Frank Whitcomb	G-T	6'3	217	24		
Jim Dufft (to NY)	G	6'6	250	25		
Joe Bachmaier	G-C-E	5'9	175	25		
Howard Berry	TB-WB	5'11	165	26	3	20
Billy Rafter	WB	5'6	155	26		
John Hasbrouck (to RI)	FB-WB	6'	190	26		
Ben Clime	E-WB	5'11	190	29		
Earl Ettenhaus	G			19		
Lou Usher (to Ham & ChiS)	G	6'2	235	23		

Scores of each game

Date	Pts.	Opponent	Pts.
Oct. 16	13	Chic. Staleys	16
Oct. 23	0	Buffalo	28
Oct. 30	0	Akron	19
Nov. 6	45	TONAWANDA	0
Nov. 20	27	COLUMBUS	13
Dec. 4	0	Washington (forfeit)	1

HAMMOND PROS 1-3-1 Max Hicks

Regulars

Use Name	Pos.	Hgt.	Wgt.	Age	Int.	Pts.
Carl Hanke	E	6'	190	23		6
Inky Williams (to & from CAN)	E	5'11	170	24		
Dave Tallant	T	6'1	205	24		
Elliot Risley	T	6'	205	25		2
Russ Oltz	G	6'	205	22		
George Hartong	G	6'	210	25		6
Jack Depler	C	5'10	220	22		
Charlie Mathys	BB	5'7	165	24		3
Wally Hess	TB-BB	5'9	170	26		
Oscar Knop	WB-E	6'	185	26		
Dick King	FB-WB	5'8	175	28		

Substitutes

Use Name	Pos.	Hgt.	Wgt.	Age	Int.	Pts.
Mace Roberts	E	6'	185	24		
Max Hicks	E		175	27		
Lou Usher (from ROCH, to ChiS)	T	6'2	235	23		
Red Jackson (from EVA)	T	6'	200	24		
Frank Seliger	G		200	30		
Tommy Tomlin (to AKR)	G	5'10	195	27		
Walter Voight (to ChiC)	C-G-BB	5'8	200	26		
Ken Crawford (to CIN)	BB	5'11	180	22		
Ben Derr	TB-WB	5'10	180	29		
Joe Pliska	WB	5'10	185	30		
Hank Gillo	FB	5'10	195	26	1	
Jones	TB					
Rice	WB					
Guil Falcon (to CAN)	FB	5'10	220	28		

Scores of each game

Date	Pts.	Opponent	Pts.
Oct. 2	0	Buffalo	17
Oct. 9	7	Canton	7
Oct. 16	3	Evansville	0
Nov. 6	0	Chic. Cards	7
Nov. 13	7	Green Bay	14

MINNEAPOLIS MARINES 1-3-0 Rube Ursella

Regulars

Use Name	Pos.	Hgt.	Wgt.	Age	Int.	Pts.
Oscar Christianson	E	5'10	178	22		6
Sheepy Redeen	E		185	30		
Harold Erickson	T		195	27		
Mike Palmer	T	5'10	203	31		
Dutch Gaustad	G		210	31		
Rudy Tersch	G		195	26		
Harry Gunderson	C	6'2	205	33		
Rube Ursella	BB	5'9	170	31		7
Ben Dvorak	TB	5'10	170	24		12
Doc Regnier	WB		170	25	2	
Eber Sampson	FB	6'	190	26		12

Substitutes

Use Name	Pos.	Hgt.	Wgt.	Age	Int.	Pts.
Charlie Jonasen	E			30		
Einar Cleve	E-TB	5'9	175	25		
John Norbeck	G-BB		195	24		
George Kramer	G	6'2	240	26		
Bill Irgens	BB-WB	5'8	175	38		

Scores of each game

Date	Pts.	Opponent	Pts.
Oct. 2	0	Chic. Cards	20
Oct. 23	6	Green Bay	7
Oct. 30	28	COLUMBUS	0
Nov. 6	3	Rock Island	14

CINCINNATI CELTS 1-3-0 Bill Doherty

Regulars

Use Name	Pos.	Hgt.	Wgt.	Age	Int.	Pts.
Earl Hauser	E	6'1	190	23		6
Pete Volz	E		190	24		
Art Lewis	T	6'1		30		1
Walt Schupp	T-G	6'	185	25	1	
Dane Dasstling	G-T	6'	190	27		
Ferris Beekley	G-BB	5'8	185	24		
Bill Doherty	C	5'11	190	38		
Ken Crawford (from HAM)	BB	5'11	180	22		
George Munns	TB	5'9	170	23		1
Shiner Knab	WB-FB-BB	6'1	190	29		
Tommy McMahon	FB	5'11	200	30		

Substitutes

Use Name	Pos.	Hgt.	Wgt.	Age	Int.	Pts.
Melvin	E-WB	6'1	185			6
Fred Day	T	6'2	195	25		
Lynch	G					
Henry Orth	G	6'	180	22		
Guy Early	G-FB	6'3	210	28		
Ohmer	WB					
Dave Thompson	WB	5'10	215	23		
Frank McCormick (from AKR)	FB	5'11	190	26		

Scores of each game

Date	Pts.	Opponent	Pts.
Oct. 2	0	Akron	41
Oct. 16	14	Muncie	0
Oct. 23	0	Cleveland	28
Nov. 27	0	Evansville	48

DETROIT TIGERS 1-5-1 Bill Marshall

Regulars

Use Name	Pos.	Hgt.	Wgt.	Age	Int.	Pts.
Walt Clago	E	6'	195	22		
Tillie Voss (to BUF)	E-T	6'3	204	24		8
Steamer Horning (to BUF))	T	6'	195	28		
Cy DeGree	T-G	6'1	210	23		3
Moose Gardner (to BUF)	G	6'1	220	27		
Charlie Carman	G	5'10	215	24		
Charley Guy (to BUF)	C	6'	170	24	1	
Bill Stobbs	BB	5'7	165	25	1	
Norb Sacksteder	TB	5'9	172	25		
Waddy Kuehl (to BUF)	WB-FB	5'9	165	29	1	6
Jerry DaPrato	FB	5'10	180	28		

Substitutes

Use Name	Pos.	Hgt.	Wgt.	Age	Int.	Pts.
Vic Whitmarsh	E	5'11	190	25		
Frank Coughlin (from RI, to GB)	T	6'3	220	25	1	
Don Straw	G	5'11	210	24		
Pryor Williams	G-C	6'1	226	27		
Earl Kreiger	TB	5'11	185	25		
Eddie Moegel	WB	5'9	186	24		
Buck Gavin (to RI)	FB	6'	175	26		
Butch Brandau	TB-FB-WB		192	23		
Blake Miller	WB-E	5'10	170	28		
Pat Dunne	FB		182	33		

Scores of each game

Date	Pts.	Opponent	Pts.
Oct. 2	0	Rock Island	0
Oct. 9	10	DAYTON	7
Oct. 16	0	AKRON	20
Oct. 23	0	ROCK ISLAND	14
Oct. 30	0	Buffalo	21
Nov. 6	9	Chic. Staleys	20
Nov. 13	0	Dayton	27

COLUMBUS PANHANDLES 1-8-0 Ted Nesser

Regulars

Use Name	Pos.	Hgt.	Wgt.	Age	Int.	Pts.
Homer Ruh	E	5'10	175	25		6
Morris Glassman	E	5'10	166	21		
Joe Mulbarger	T	5'9	215	26		6
Oscar Kuehner	T-G-E	6'	200	32		
Oscar Wolford	G	6'	188	24	1	12
Babe Houck	G	6'	275	24		
Ted Nesser	C	5'10	230	38		
Harry Bliss	BB-TB-WB	5'8	155	23		1
Charlie Nesser	TB	6'2	195	19		
Emmett Ruh	WB-E	5'8	168	28		13
Frank Nesser	FB-G	6'1	238	32		7

Substitutes

Use Name	Pos.	Hgt.	Wgt.	Age	Int.	Pts.
Ted Hopkins	E-T	5'9	180	30		
Fred Nesser	T-E-FB	6'5	250	33		
Phil Nesser	T-G-WB	6'	225	40		
Will Waite	G-T-WB-FB	6'2	200	28		
Ted Murtha	G-FB	5'11	205	20		
Hal Gaulke	BB-E	5'8	175	27		
Walt Rogers	WB	5'9	215	28		
John Nesser	G-T	5'11	195	45		
Al Shook	G			23		

Scores of each game

Date	Pts.	Opponent	Pts.
Sep. 25	0	Akron	14
Oct. 2	13	Dayton	42
Oct. 9	0	Buffalo	38
Oct. 16	9	Cleveland	35
Oct. 23	6	Chic. Cards	17
Oct. 30	0	Minneapolis	28
Nov. 6	0	AKRON	21
Nov. 20	13	Rochester	27
Dec. 4	6	Louisville	0

NAME	RUSHING									PASSING													
	Complete Games					Incom. Games				Complete Games								Incom. Games					
	G	Att.	Yds.	Avg.	TD	G	Att.	Yds.	TD	G	Com.	Att.	%	Yds.	Y/A	TD	Int.	G	Com.	Att.	Yds.	TD	Int.
WASHINGTON																							
Boynton (2)						2	3	28	1									2	7	10	194	4	3
Walson						2	1	20															
Gilroy																		1	1	2	25		
Vidal																							
Patterson																							
Hudson																							
Team						3												3					
Opp.						3												3					
CLEVELAND																							
Guyon (1,3)	1	13	27	2.1		7	12	156	2	1	0	4	0					7	7	10	189	1	2
Thorpe						5	6	116	1									5	2	5	45	1	
Haas (1,3)	1	13	41	3.2		7	6	2															
Bower	1	8	33	4.1		4	1	6		1								4	0	1			1
Calac (1,3)	1	5	9	1.8		7	6	23	3														
Patterson						2	5	29															
Ghee	1					4	4	15	2	1	2	4	50	12	3.0		1	4	3	3	85	1	
Hendren	1	1	0	0.0		4	1	3	1														
Corcoran (1,3)																							
Whalen																							
Team	1	40	110	2.8		7				1	2	8	25	12	1.5		1	7					
Opp.	1	29	47	1.6		7				1	4	15	27	66	4.4			7					
ROCHESTER																							
Boyton (1)						3	9	130	2	1	0	5	0				1	2	6	6	132	3	1
Laird (2)						5	6	22	3														
Noonan						5	1	8		1	0	1	0										
Argus						4	1	-2															
Thomas										1	0	1	0				1	5	0	1			1
Berry																							
Lowery																							
Clime																							
Team						5				2	2	18	11	30	1.7		2	3					
Opp.						5				2	16	27	59	270	10.0	1		3					
HAMMOND																							
Gillo						1	6	26										1	0	1			1
Derr						4	3	19															
King						5	5	15															
Mathys						5	3	15										5	2	4	35		
Williams (1,3)						5	3	15															
Hess						4	4	9										4	0	2			2
Knop																							
Team						5												5					
Opp.						5												5					
MINNEAPOLIS																							
Sampson	1	24	56	2.3		3	5	53	2	1	2	8	25	26	3.3			3	1	2	20		1
Dvorak	1	13	25	1.9		3	3	24	2														
Ursella	1	10	33	3.3		3																	
Regnier	1	6	6	1.0		3	1	10															
Christianson	1	1	1	1.0		3	1	5	1														
Palmer	1	2	5	2.5		3																	
Redeen	1	1	3	3.0		3																	
Cleve																							
Team	1	57	129	2.3		3				1	2	8	25		3.3			3					
Opp.	1	38	109	2.9		3				1	5	12	42	120	10.0	1	2	3					
CINCINNATI																							
Munns						4	1	15										4	5	5	72	2	
Knab						4	2	8															
Hauser																							
Volz																							
Shriner																							
Melvin																							
Team						4												4					
Opp.	1	53	270	5.1	6	3												4					
DETROIT																							
Stobbs	2	12	60	5.0		5				2	3	7	43	30	4.3		1	5					
DaPrato	2	22	30	1.4		4				2								4	1	3	35		
Sacksteder	2	13	23	1.8		5				2	1	2	50	6	3.0			5					
Kuehl (1)	2	14	12	0.9		4	1	5	1	2	2	3	67	16	5.3			4					
Miller	1	1	12	12.0		2																	
Krieger	2	2	5	2.5		3	1	4															
Gavin (1)	1	2	0	0.0		2	1	4															
Moegel	1	2	-1	-0.5		3																	
DeGree										2								5	0	1			
Voss (1)																							
Horning (1)																							
Team	2	68	141	2.1		5				3	12	25	48	127	5.1		1	4					
Opp.	2	106	269	2.5		5				3	17	43	40	218	5.1	2	4	4					
COLUMBUS																							
F. Nesser						9	1	5	1									9	6	9	210	3	1
E. Ruh						7	1	1															
Hopkins																							
Bliss																							
Mulbarger																							
H. Ruh																							
Team						9												9					
Opp.						9												9					

NAME	RECEIVING									PUNTING						PUNT RETURNS								
	Complete Games					Incom. Games				Comp. Games			Incom. Games			Complete Games					Incom. Games			
	G	Rec.	Yds	Avg.	TD	G	Rec.	Yds.	TD	G	No.	Avg.	G	No.	Avg.	G	No.	Yds.	Avg.	TD	G	No.	Yds.	TD
WASHINGTON																								
Boynton (2)																								
Walson						2	1	70	1															
Gilroy																								
Vidal						1	4	85																
Patterson						3	2	34																
Hudson						3	1	30	1															
Team													3								3			
Opp.													3								3			
CLEVELAND																								
Guyon (1,3)	1					7	1	20		1	11	31.7	7	1	45.0									
Thorpe						5	2	48																
Haas (1,3)						7	2	73	1							1	2	18	9.0		7			
Bower																								
Calac (1,3)	1					7	1	23																
Patterson																								
Ghee																								
Hendren																								
Corcoran (1,3)	1	1	11	11.0		7	4	100	1															
Whalen	1					7	2	55	1															
Team										1	11	31.7	7			1	2	18	9.0		7			
Opp.										1	13	32.2	7			1	1	5	5.0		7			
ROCHESTER																								
Boyton (1)																								
Laird (2)	1					4	1	30	1				5	2	30.0									
Noonan	1					4	4	87	2															
Argus																								
Thomas																								
Berry	1					4	1	30	1				4	4	18.8									
Lowery						3	1	30																
Clime						1	1	15																
Team										1	12	44.0	4								5			
Opp.										1	6	42.5	4								5			
HAMMOND																								
Gillo																								
Derr													4	7	31.7									
King																								
Mathys																								
Williams (1,3)						5	1	10																
Hess																								
Knop						5	1	25																
Team													5								5			
Opp.													5								5			
MINNEAPOLIS																								
Sampson										1			3	1	40.0									
Dvorak																								
Ursella										1	8	29.8	3			1	1	7	7.0		3			
Regnier																								
Christianson	1					3	1	20																
Palmer																								
Redeen																								
Cleve	1	2	26	13.0		2																		
Team										1	8	29.8	3			1	1	7	7.0		3			
Opp.										1	8	25.1	3			1	3	14	4.7		3			
CINCINNATI																								
Munns																								
Knab																								
Hauser						4	2	34	1															
Volz						4	1	17																
Shriner						1	1	15																
Melvin						3	1	6	1															
Team													4								4			
Opp.													4								4			
DETROIT																								
Stobbs	2	2	16	8.0		5																		
DaPrato																								
Sacksteder																								
Kuehl (1)	2	2	12	6.0		4										2	1	2	2.0		4			
Miller																								
Krieger																								
Gavin (1)																								
Moegel	1	1	6	6.0		3																		
DeGree										3	32	35.4	4	2	21.0									
Voss (1)	2	1	18	18.0		4	1	35																
Horning (1)										3			4	1	0.0									
Team										3	32	35.4	4			2	1	2	2.0		5			
Opp.										3	23	42.7	4			2	4	44	11.0		5			
COLUMBUS																								
F. Nesser													9	8	45.0									
E. Ruh						7	1	35	1															
Hopkins						3	1	40																
Bliss						9	1	35																
Mulbarger						8	1	25	1															
H. Ruh						7	1	20	1															
Team													9								9			
Opp.													9								9			

Regulars							Substitutes							Substitutes							Scores of each game			
Use Name	Pos.	Hgt.	Wgt.	Age	Int.	Pts.	Use Name	Pos.	Hgt.	Wgt.	Age	Int.	Pts.	Use Name	Pos.	Hgt.	Wgt.	Age	Int.	Pts.	Date	Pts.	Opponent	Pts.
TONAWANDA KARDEX 0-1-0 Tam Rose																								
Art Goarke	E	5'6	165	26																	Nov. 6	0	Rochester	45
Bill Sanborn	E			22																				
Charlie Tallman	T			25																				
George Kuhrt	T	5'11	185	25			Fred Brumm	T-C			33													
Buck MacDonald (to NY)	G	5'10	180	26			Clarence Hosmer	G	5'10	205	30													
Rudy Kraft	G-C	5'10	190	24																				
Red Werder	C			26			Backnor	C																
Frank Primeau	BB	5'11	170	26			Cassidy	BB																
Tam Rose	TB	5'11	170	32																				
Bill Meisner	WB	5'11	185	28																				
Tom McLaughlin	FB	5'10	185	32																				
LOUISVILLE BRECKS 0-2-0 Austin Higgins																								
Bill Netherton	E			23			Howard Newland	E			29										Oct. 2	0	Evansville	21
Herb Gruber	E	5'9	155	19																	Dec. 4	0	COLUMBUS	6
Tom Ferguson	T			27			Fatty Harris	T			37													
Harper Card	T	6'1	180	18			Hubert Wiggs	T	5'8	180	25			Ted Moser	T	5'9	195	24						
Gene Wiggs	G			21			H. Lewis	G	5'8	175	25			Bill Howser	G			21						
Austin Brunklacher	G		193	23			Howie Stith	G			25													
Austin Higgins	C	5'9	165	23																				
Chase Boldt	BB	5'7	145	21																				
Jimmy Van Dyke	TB	5'7	140	22			Red Chenoweth	TB	5'6	150	28													
Joe Martin	WB			26			Joe Engelhard	WB	5'11	185	22													
Jim Irwin	FB	5'7	165	24			Karl Hower	FB			19													
MUNCIE FLYERS 0-2-0 Cooney Checkaye																								
Chuck Helvie	E	5'8	180	29			Pete Slone	E	5'8	180	24										Oct. 9	0	Evansville	14
Mac McIndoo	E			24																	Oct. 16	0	CINCINNATI	14
Wilfred Smith	T	6'4	200	22																				
Mike Yount	T	6'1	205	27																				
Ken Fulton	G			22			Ray MacMurray	G			32													
Ernie Hole	G			20																				
Owen Floyd	C	6'	195	24																				
Cooney Checkaye	BB	5'9	185	28																				
Gus Redman (to DAY)	TB-BB	5'11	170	25			Kellogg	TB																
Cliff Baldwin	WB-BB	5'10	172	21																				
Mickey Hole	FB-WB	5'9	180	29			Doc Ladorum	FB																
NEW YORK BRICKLEY'S GIANTS 0-2-0 Charlie Brickley																								
Joe Dusossoit	E	5'11	185	25			Paul Meyers	E	5'11	170	26										Oct. 16	0	Buffalo	55
Ray Trowbridge	E	6'	170	25			Johnny Nagle	E	5'9	175	28										Dec. 3	0	CLEVELAND	17
Ed O'Hearn	T	5'7	185	22			George Kerr	T	6'1	200	28													
Tom Gormley (to WAS)	T	5'11	225	32			Jim Dufft (from ROCH)	T	6'6	250	25			Con O'Brien	T	6'2	195	23						
Frank Leavitt	G		240	28			Harrie Dadmun	G-T	6'	235	27			Buck MacDonald (from TON)	G	5'10	180	26						
Al Maginnes	G-C	6'1	188	24			Doc Haggerty	G	6'	205	26			George Kane	G	5'9	195	30						
Al Pierotti	C	5'10	200	25			Ed Brawley (to CLE)	G	5'9	175	26													
Mark Devlin	BB	5'10	180	26			Jerry Noonan (from ROCH)	BB	6'1	182	22			Jimmy Jemail	BB	5'6	165	27						
Dave Maginnes	TB	5'10	165	26																				
Mike Purdy	WB	5'10	180	26			Fred Sweetland	WB	5'10	175	26													
George Brickley	FB	5'10	190	27	1		Dinger Doane	FB	5'10	190	26			Joe Bernstein	FB	6'	210	27						

1922 N.F.L.
The Second Coming of Canton

Although George Halas won his first league championship in 1921, he did not actually own the franchise. His Staley club was still the property of starchmaker A.E. Staley of Decatur. Halas and his partner, Dutch Sternaman, were the managers, although their profits or losses went in and out of their own pockets. Then Chic Harley's brother Bill, a veteran Chicago promoter, applied to the league for the Windy City franchise. Halas and Sternaman immediately asked for one of their own to replace the Staleys. Clouding the issue was the fact that Chic Harley had come to the Staleys in 1921 through a deal arranged by his brother that guaranteed a percentage of the profits to Chic. This transaction, Bill Harley contended, gave him a part interest in the Staleys. The league waited until it received a statement from A.E. Staley on what arrangements he'd made with Halas the year before, then granted Halas and Sternaman their franchise.

In addition to playing a good game of football, Halas proved to have a magic touch when it came to giving names. To create a relationship with the baseball Chicago Cubs in the public mind, he changed the Staleys to the Chicago Bears. Also, at his suggestion, the league itself was rechristened the National Football League. Befitting its new name, the league put itself on firmer financial footing by voting that each team post a $1,000 forfeit fee. One-third of the 1921 teams were unable or unwilling to come up with that much money and, although some continued to play football, they were no longer league members. Gone were New York, Washington, Tonawanda, Cleveland, Muncie, Cincinnati and Detroit. Seven new cities were awarded franchises, but three — Youngstown, New Haven and Philadelphia — were stillborn and played no football in 1922. Four new teams actually made it to the field: the Toledo Maroons, under Bill Harley as sort of a consolation prize; the Milwaukee Badgers, featuring Fritz Pollard, Paul Robeson and tackle John Alexander, who stood up and moved off the line on defense to become ther first modern outside linebacker; the Racine Legion, starring fullback and kicker Hank Gillo, whose 52 points led the league in scoring this season; and the Oorang Indians, perhaps the most colorful team in NFL history.

The Oorang Indians, sponsored by a dog kennel, were based in Marion, Ohio, but played all their games on the road. They had a roster made up entirely of native American Indians, led by Jim Thorpe. Now 35-years old and slipping as a player, he put himself into the action only in the second part of the season. On occasion, his team could do well, as in an October 8 victory over Columbus in which both Joe Guyon and fullback Eagle Feather each rushed for over 100 yards. But, more often, the Indians played poorly and sometimes they were embarassing. One newspaper headlined, "Thorpe's Indians Loaf!" after Akron massacred them 62-0 on October 29. It was all one to owner Walter Lingo, who really didn't like football and sponsored the team strictly as an advertisement for his mail-order airedale puppy business. The Indians put on a good show, running on the field in war bonnets, celebrating touchdowns with war dances and performing all sorts of tricks and stunts with the airdales before games and at halftime.

But, with the new names and images, and old and honorable pro football name returned to the top after a few seasons in the pack. The Canton Bulldogs unloaded most of their mediocre 1921 squad and hired Guy Chamberlin to take charge of the rebuilding. An exceptional two-way end for the Staleys the past two seasons, Chamberlin began his coaching career with an outstanding forward line. In addition to himself, he had superb linemen in tackles Pete Henry and Link Lyman and guard Duke Osborn. Both Henry and Lyman were big, quick, and future Hall of Famers.

The Canton backfield, however, looked weak at the start of the season. After experimenting with a few combinations, including himself at

NAME	RUSHING Complete Games G	Att.	Yds.	Avg.	TD	RUSHING Incom. Games G	Att.	Yds.	TD	PASSING Complete Games G	Com.	Att.	%	Yds.	Y/A	TD	Int	PASSING Incom Games G	Com.	Att.	Yds.	TD	Int
TONAWANDA	- no statistics																						
LOUISVILLE																							
Gruber						2	1	-10															
Irwin																		1	1	1	27		
Martin																							
Team						2												2					
Opp.						2												2					
MUNCIE																							
Redmond										1	1	6	17	13	2.2		2	1					
M. Hole																							
Team						2				1	1	6	17	13	2.2		2	1					
Opp.						2												2					
NEW YORK																							
Doane																		1	0	1			1
Team						2												2					
Opp.						2												2					

NAME	RECEIVING Complete Games G	Rec.	Yds.	Avg.	TD	RECEIVING Incom. Games G	Rec.	Yds.	TD	PUNTING Comp. Games G	No.	Avg.	PUNTING Incom. Games G	No.	Avg.	PUNT RETURNS Complete Games G	Rec.	Yds.	Avg.	TD	PUNT RETURNS Incom. Games G	Rec.	Yds.	TD
TONAWANDA																								
LOUISVILLE																								
Gruber						2	1	27																
Irwin																								
Martin																					1	1	20	
Team													2								2			
Opp.													2								2			
MUNCIE																								
Redmond																								
M. Hole	1	1	13	13.0		1																		
Team													2								2			
Opp.													2								2			
NEW YORK																								
Doane																								
Team													2								2			
Opp.													2								2			

wingback, Chamberlin settled upon rookie Wooky Roberts from Navy as his blocking back, converted tackle Ed Shaw into a fullback, and used second-year man Harry Robb as his wingback and journeyman Norb Sacksteder as his tailback. Later in the season, Chamberlin added backfield strength in veterans Tex Griggs and Lou Smyth and rookie Doc Elliott. This essentially undistinguished group of backs combined with the strong line to form a granite-hard defense and a steady ground-oriented attack.

After beating the weak Louisville Brecks 38-0 to open the season, the Bulldogs were held to a scoreless tie by the Dayton Triangles, raising doubts as to the championship caliber of the team. On October 15, the Bulldogs got back on track with a 14-0 win over the Oorang Indians. The big play for the Bulldogs was a punt return touchdown by Norb Sacksteder. The first hard test of the season for the Bulldogs came a week later when they traveled to Akron to take on the Pros. A power in the league for the past two years, the Pros had a greatly changed squad due to the departure of player-coaches Elgie Tobin and Fritz Pollard. The Bulldogs made it four shutouts in a row by blanking the Pros 22-0, holding them to no first downs. Sacksteder, who had played for Dayton and Detroit the past two seasons, threw a touchdown pass and broke loose for a 38-yard touchdown run.

A trip to Cubs Park in Chicago was next on the agenda for the Bulldogs. The undefeated Bears had their old stars like Halas, Hugh Blacklock, Pete Stinchcomb and Dutch Sternaman, but also had new help in quarterback Joey Sternaman, the co-owner's kid brother, halfback Laurie Walquist from Illinois and tough guard Hunk Anderson from Notre Dame. In his later career as a coach, Anderson would be responsible for a number of innovations; he ad-libbed one this this season when he created the reverse cross-body block to deal with a difficult Akron end. The Bulldogs launched a first quarter drive against the Bears which ended in a touchdown plunge by Shaw, but which covered most of its yardage on passes to Bird Carroll by Sacksteder, enjoying his third starring performance in a row. Shaw's extra point made the score 7-0. The Bears made no headway against the Canton defense until the fourth quarter when Walquist's passes spurred a drive that culminated in Joey Sternaman plunging for the score. A new rule for 1922 allowed teams to try for the extra point with a run or pass, but the Bears elected to go with Joey Sternaman's usually reliable dropkicking. However, the Bulldogs put on a heavy rush causing him to miss. The Bears had no more scoring opportunities, giving Canton a final 7-6 verdict.

Canton fans sensed a championship down the road but their spirits were dampened on November 5, when Toledo held the Bulldogs to a scoreless draw in Canton. A week later, the Bulldogs struggled before a Shaw field goal gave them a win over visiting Buffalo. With only Canton, Toledo and the Chicago Cardinals still unbeaten, the Bulldogs headed to Chicago to take on the Cards in Comiskey Park. The Cards featured backs Arnie Horween, a Harvard grad and future coach at his alma mater, and Paddy Driscoll, who set a new league high with eight field goals in 1922. But the team had risen on the shoulders of an improved line that included Fred Gillies, Willis Brennan, Nick McInerney and Garland Buckeye. Although the Cardinals could not penetrate beyond Canton's 25-yard line, they also held Canton scoreless until the fourth quarter when Sacksteder scored on a 35-yard pass from Smyth. The 7-0 Bulldog win knocked the Cardinals from the unbeaten ranks. A week later, the Cards and Bulldogs met again in Canton. Chicago led 3-0 in the fourth quarter and appeared on the way to an upset. Then Chamberlin took personal charge and turned the contest around. He blocked a punt deep in Chicago territory, leading to a Roberts touchdown a few plays later. When the Cardinals got the ball back, Chamberlin picked off a Chicago pass by Johnny Mohardt and returned it 20 yards for a touchdown. Then, on the first play after the kickoff, Mohardt again passed and Chamberlin again intercepted, carrying the ball 15 yards into the endzone to cap an amazing defensive sequence.

Four days later, on Thanksgiving Day, Chamberlin continued producing points with defense. In the first quarter against Akron, he blocked a punt and returned it 10 yards for a touchdown; the Bulldogs went on to a 14-0 victory before their hometown fans. On Sunday, a large crowd turned out to see the Bulldogs tackle Milwaukee. Fritz Pollard was sidelined with an injury, but the Badgers had the famous Bo McMillin, star of the 1919 Centre College team, and Jimmy Conzelman. On October 15, while playing Rock Island against Evansville, Conzelman scored five rushing touchdowns as Rock Island set an NFL record with nine rushing touchdowns. That helped Conzelman set an odd record of his own, as he led the league in rushing touchdowns with seven and passing touchdowns with a modest three. Neither McMillin nor Conzelman had any luck against Canton on December 3, as the Bulldogs romped 40-6, with six points coming on a fake field goal in which Chamberlin took the snap as holder and sprinted around the surprised Badgers. That same day, the Bears whipped Toledo 22-0, leaving Canton the only undefeated team. To cap their championship, the Bulldogs smothered Toledo 19-0 the next week to end at 10-0-2.

Despite good crowds at Canton's Lakeside Park, the small capacity combined with high salaries for some players to lose money for owner Ralph Hay. In contrast, the Chicago Bears turned a modest $1,476.92 for Halas and Sternaman. To the north, the Green Bay Packers were plagued by bad weather and poor attendance. The Green Bay franchise had been revoked after 1921 because the Packers had used college players under assumed names. Curly Lambeau scraped together enough money to get to Cleveland for the league meeting and purchased a new Green Bay franchise. Then the weather during the season drove Lambeau into insolvency and local businessmen had to come to the rescue. Realizing the value of the team for civic pride and advertisement, the merchants arranged for a $2,500 loan, and then a public non-profit corporation was set up to run the Packers. For five dollars, a Green Bay citizen could buy a share of the team and get a season's pass thrown in. The townfolk snapped up the shares and the Packers had $5,000 in the bank by the time the 1923 season arrived.

In mid-December, George Halas picked what was apparently the second-ever NFL team. His choices, as they appeared in several midwest newspapers: ends Guy Chamberlin, Canton, and Luke Urban, Buffalo; tackles Pete Henry, Canton, and Hugh Blacklock, Bears; guards Herb Stein, Toledo, and Ed Healey, Bears; center Joe Alexander, Rochester; quarterback Tommy Hughitt, Buffalo; halfbacks Paddy Driscoll, Cardinals, and Pete Stinchcomb, Bears; and fullback Rip King, Akron.

1922 STANDINGS

	W	L	T	Pct.	Pts.	Opp. Pts.	Avg. Pts.	Opp. Avg.
Canton Bulldogs	10	0	2	1.000	184	15	15	1
Chicago Bears	9	3	0	.750	123	44	10	4
Chicago Cardinals	8	3	0	.727	96	50	9	5
Toledo Maroons	5	2	2	.714	94	59	10	7
Rock Island Independents	4	2	1	.667	154	27	22	4
Racine Legion	6	4	1	.600	122	56	11	5
Dayton Triangles	4	3	1	.571	80	62	10	8
Green Bay Packers	4	3	3	.571	70	54	7	5
Buffalo All-Americans	5	4	1	.556	87	41	9	4
Akron Pros	3	5	2	.375	146	95	15	10
Milwaukee Badgers	2	4	3	.333	51	71	6	8
Oorang Indians (Marion, O.)	3	6	0	.333	69	190	8	21
Minneapolis Marines	1	3	0	.250	19	40	5	109
Louisville Brecks	1	3	0	.250	13	140	3	35
Rochester Jeffersons	0	4	1	.000	13	76	3	15
Hammond Pros (R)	0	5	1	.000	0	69	0	12
Evansville Crimson Giants	0	3	0	.000	6	88	2	29
Columbus Panhandles	0	8	0	.000	24	174	3	22

(R) — played only road games

Scoring Leaders

Gillo	Rac	52
Conzelman	RI-Mil	48
Chamberlin	Can	42
D. Sternaman	ChiB	41
Driscoll	ChiC	40
Shaw	Can	38
Cramer	Akr	36
Gavin	RI-Buf	36
Guyon	Oor	33
J. Sternaman	ChiB	32
Annan	Tol	31
Lauer	RI-GB	30
A. Horween	ChiC	27
Lambeau	GB	30
Laird	Buf	24
LeJeune	Akr	24
Sacksteder	Can	24
King	Akr	21
Pollard	Mil	20
Kuehl	Buf	19
Foster	Rac	18
Huffine	Day	18
Robb	Can	18
Stinchcomb	ChiB	18
Thorpe	Oor	18
Voss	RI-Akr	18

KICKING

		FG	Att	Pct
Driscoll	ChiC	8	13	62
Gillo	Rac	6	13	46
D. Sternaman	ChiB	6	11	55
R. Horween	ChiC	3	5	60
Sheeks	Akr	3		NA
Hathaway	Day & Can	2	6	33
Conzelman	RI-Mil	2	7	29
Morrissey	Buf	2	7	29
Shaw	Can	2	9	22
Henry	Can	2	12	17
Fenner	Day	1	1	100
A. Horween	ChiC	1	1	100
R. Stein	Tol	1	1	100
Kreinheder	Akr	1	2	50
Mathys	GB	1	2	50
Johnson	RI	1	5	20
Lambeau	GB	1	6	17
Buck	GB	1	10	10
Brindley	RI	0	1	0
Fausch	Eva	0	1	0
Garrett	Mil	0	1	0
Hughitt	Buf	0	1	0
J. Sternaman	ChiB	0	1	0
Purdy	Mil	0	2	0
E. Ruh	Col	0	2	0
Sies	Day	0	2	0
Watson	Tol	0	2	0
Pollard	Mil	0	5	0
Bowser	Can	0	6	0

		PAT	Att	Pct			PAT	Att	Pct
Hathaway	Day & Can	9	10	90	Kreinheder	Akr	1	1	100
Shaw	Can	8	10	80	Langhoff	Rac	1	1	100
Morrissey	Buf	8	11	73	Myers	Tol	1	1	100
Sheeks	Akr	8	12	67	Carroll	Can	1	2	50
Johnson	RI	6	8	75	Lauer	RI-GB	1	2	50
Voss	RI-Akr	6	9	67	Steele	Roch-Akr	1	2	50
D. Sternaman	ChiB	5	9	56	Van Dyke	Lou	1	2	50
Driscoll	ChiC	4	7	57	Copley	Akr-Mil	1	3	33
Gillo	Rac	4	7	57	Irgens	Min	1	3	33
Henry	Can	4	9	44	J. Murray	GB-Rac	1	4	25
King	Akr	3	3	100	Brindley	RI	0	1	0
Buck	GB	3	4	75	Fausch	Eva	0	1	0
Lambeau	GB	3	4	75	Hayes	Rac	0	1	0
Watson	Tol	3	4	75	Purdy	Mil	0	1	0
R. Horween	ChiC	2	2	100	Rapp	Col	0	1	0
Pollard	Mil	2	2	100	Snoots	Col	0	1	0
J. Sternaman	ChiB	2	3	67	Conzelman	RI-Mil	0	2	0
Bowser	Can	2	4	50	Horning	Tol	0	2	0
Guyon	Oor	2	4	50	E. Ruh	Col	0	2	0
R. Stein	Tol	2	4	50	Thorpe	Oor	0	2	0

CANTON BULLDOGS 10-0-2 Guy Chamberlin

Regulars

Use Name	Pos.	Hgt.	Wgt.	Age	Int.	Pts.
Bird Carroll	E	5'8	185	26	1	7
Guy Chamberlin	E-WB	6'2	190	28	5	42
Pete Henry	T	5'11	245	24	2	10
Link Lyman	T	6'2	225	23		
Tarzan Taylor	G	5'11	175	27		
Duke Osborn	G	5'10	185	25	2	
Dutch Speck	C-G	5'10	220	36		
Wooky Roberts	BB	5'7	160	24	6	6
Norb Sacksteder	TB-WB	5'9	172	26	5	24
Harry Robb	WB-BB-TB	5'10	180	25	2	18
Doc Elliott	FB	5'10	200	22		12

Substitutes

Use Name	Pos.	Hgt.	Wgt.	Age	Int.	Pts.
Jim Kendrick (to TOL)	E	6'	190	29		
Dan Batchellor	T	6'3	225	27		
Russ Hathaway (from, to & from DAY)	T	5'11	225	26		
Fat Waldsmith	G-C	5'9	225	30		
Cap Murrah	C	5'10	205	21		
Lou Smyth	TB	6'1	200	23		6
Johnny McQuade	WB-BB	5'10	176	27	1	
Ed Shaw	FB-WB-T-G	6'1	210	27	2	38
Arda Bowser	FB-WB-TB	6'2	210	23		14
Tex Grigg	WB	5'11	185	31		
Candy Miller (to RAC)	FB	6'3	215	25		6

Scores of each game

Date	Pts.	Opponent	Pts.
Oct. 1	38	LOUISVILLE	0
Oct. 8	0	Dayton	0
Oct. 15	14	OORANG	0
Oct. 22	22	Akron	0
Oct. 29	7	Chic. Bears	6
Nov. 5	0	TOLEDO	0
Nov. 12	3	BUFFALO	0
Nov. 19	7	Chic. Cards	0
Nov. 26	20	CHIC. CARDS	3
Nov. 30	14	AKRON	0
Dec. 3	40	MILWAUKEE	6
Dec. 10	19	Toledo	0

CHICAGO BEARS 9-3-0 George Halas

Regulars

Use Name	Pos.	Hgt.	Wgt.	Age	Int.	Pts.
George Halas	E	6'	182	27		14
Hec Garvey	E-T	6'1	228	22		
Hugh Blacklock	T	6'	220	31		
Ralph Scott	T	6'2	234	24		
Hunk Anderson	G	5'11	190	23		
Russ Smith	G-C	5'10	220	26		
Ojay Larson	C	6'1	198	24	1	
Joey Sternaman	QB	5'6	150	22	4	32
Dutch Sternaman	HB	5'8	175	27	2	41
Pete Stinchcomb	HB	5'8	155	27		18
George Bolan	FB	5'11	204	25		12

Substitutes

Use Name	Pos.	Hgt.	Wgt.	Age	Int.	Pts.
Carl Hanke (to HAM)	E	6'	190	24		
Harry Englund (to EVA)	E	6'	185	22		
Ed Healey (from RI)	G-T	6'1	205	27		
Bourbon Bondurant (to EVA)	G	6'1	202	24		
Joe LaFleur	G-FB	6'	220	26		
Pard Pearce	QB	5'5	150	25		6
Jake Lanum	HB-FB	6'	190	25	1	
Laurie Walquist	HB-FB	5'8	165	24	1	

Scores of each game

Date	Pts.	Opponent	Pts.
Oct. 1	6	Racine	0
Oct. 8	10	Rock Island	6
Oct. 15	7	ROCHESTER	0
Oct. 22	7	BUFFALO	0
Oct. 29	6	CANTON	7
Nov. 5	9	DAYTON	0
Nov. 12	33	OORANG	6
Nov. 19	3	ROCK ISLAND	0
Nov. 26	20	AKRON	10
Nov. 30	0	Chic. Cards	6
Dec. 3	22	TOLEDO	0
Dec. 10	0	Chic. Cards	9

CHICAGO CARDINALS 8-3-0 Paddy Driscoll

Regulars

Use Name	Pos.	Hgt.	Wgt.	Age	Int.	Pts.
Egan	E		175			
Eddie Anderson (from ROCH)	E	5'10	170	21	2	
Fred Gillies	T	6'3	215	26		
Swede Rundquist	T	6'2	210	27		
Willie Brennan	G	6'	210	28		
Garland Buckeye	G	6'	235	24		
Nick McInerney	C	6'2	200	26		
Arnie Horween	BB	5'11	205	24		27
Paddy Driscoll	TB	5'8	160	27	2	40
Johnny Mohardt	WB-TB	5'10	165	24	1	6
Bob Koehler	FB	5'11	185	28	1	12

Substitutes

Use Name	Pos.	Hgt.	Wgt.	Age	Int.	Pts.
Red O'Connor	E	5'8	170			
Lenny Sachs	E	5'8	175	25	1	
John Leonard	T	6'2	200	26		
Clyde Zoia	G	5'7	175	26		
Bill Whalen	C-T	5'7	165	21		
Johnny Bryan	WB-BB-FB	5'8	165	25		
Ralph Horween	FB-TB-BB-WB	5'10	200	26	1	11

Scores of each game

Date	Pts.	Opponent	Pts.
Oct. 1	3	MILWAUKEE	0
Oct. 15	16	GREEN BAY	3
Oct. 22	3	MINNEAPOLIS	0
Oct. 29	37	COLUMBUS	6
Nov. 5	9	BUFFALO	7
Nov. 12	7	AKRON	0
Nov. 19	0	CANTON	7
Nov. 26	3	Canton	20
Nov. 30	6	CHIC. BEARS	0
Dec. 3	3	DAYTON	7
Dec. 10	9	CHIC. BEARS	0

TOLEDO MAROONS 5-2-2 Guil Falcon

Regulars

Use Name	Pos.	Hgt.	Wgt.	Age	Int.	Pts.
Truck Myers	E	6'	170	25	1	1
Mac White	E	6'	175	32		
Steamer Horning	T	6'	200	29		6
Russ Stein	T	6'1	210	26		5
Cap Edwards	G-T	6'	205	34		
Herb Stein	G-C	6'	185	24	2	
Marty Conrad	C	6'1	225	27		
Bob Phelan	BB-WB-FB	5'11	185	24	2	12
Rat Watson	TB-BB	5'10	180	23	1	9
Dunc Annan	WB-TB-BB	5'10	175	27	2	31
Guil Falcon	FB-BB	5'10	220	29	1	6

Substitutes

Use Name	Pos.	Hgt.	Wgt.	Age	Int.	Pts.
Gus King	E	5'11	180	25		
Dwight Peabody	E	5'11	170	28		
John Kellison	T	6'	210	35		
Tex Kelly	G-E-T	6'3	220	23		
Reno Jones	G	6'	195	25		
Hippo Gozdowski	FB-C-G			25		12
Jimmy Simpson	BB-TB	5'10	160	24		
Red Roberts	TB-G	6'1	235	22		
Tubby Rousch	WB-G		170	24		6
Leo Petree	FB-BB-TB		200	29		6
Festus Tierney (from HAM)	G	6'1	195	23		
Al Burgin	G	6'	200	28		
Tom Holleran	BB	5'7	170	25		
Jim Kendrick (from CAN)	TB-E-FB	6'	190	29	1	
John Tanner	WB	5'5	165	22		
Chuck O'Neil (to EVA)	FB	5'10	180	24		
Buck Saunders	BB	6'1	190	30		

Scores of each game

Date	Pts.	Opponent	Pts.
Oct. 1	15	EVANSVILLE	0
Oct. 8	12	MILWAUKEE	12
Oct. 15	14	HAMMOND	0
Oct. 22	7	Racine	0
Oct. 29	39	LOUISVILLE	0
Nov. 5	0	Canton	0
Nov. 26	7	COLUMBUS	6
Dec. 3	0	Chic. Bears	22
Dec 10	0	CANTON	19

NAME	RUSHING									PASSING													
	Complete Games					Incom. Games				Complete Games								Incom. Games					
	G	Att.	Yds.	Avg.	TD	G	Att.	Yds.	TD	G	Com.	Att.	%	Yds.	Y/A	TD	Int.	G	Com.	Att.	Yds.	TD	Int.
CANTON																							
Robb	6	47	170	3.6	2	3	11	51	1	8	3	10	30	25	2.5		2	1					
Elliott	5	51	178	3.5	1	2	8	24	1	6	1	1	100	26	26.0			1					
Roberts	7	43	120	2.8	1	4	10	68		10	6	25	24	125	5.0	1	7	1					
Chamberlin	7	15	143	9.5	2	5	3	27	1														
Shaw	7	33	128	3.9	2	5	9	26	2	10	2	5	40	47	9.4		1	2					
Sackstededer	6	26	79	3.0		5	9	70	2	9	7	24	29	133	5.5	1	4	2	1	1	12		
Henry	7	13	67	5.2		5	2	12		10	0	4	0				2	2					
Smyth	3	23	76	3.3	1	2	1	2		4	14	39	36	282	7.2		9	1	1	1	35	1	
Bowser	2	8	9	1.1		3	7	57	2														
Grigg	3	4	12	3.0		1	2	22		4	0	1	0										
McQuade	3	8	25	3.1		2																	
Lyman	7	3	10	3.3		5	1	13															
Miller (1)	2	4	9	2.3		1	1	10	1														
Carroll																							
Kendrick (1)																							
Team	7	278	1026	3.7	9	5				10	33	109	30	638	5.9	2	25	2					
Opp.	7	146	332	2.3		5				10	32	145	22	539	3.7	1	27	2					
CHICAGO BEARS																							
D. Sternaman	3	44	147	3.3		8	10	108	3	4	1	3	33	20	6.7			7					
Stinchcomb	3	26	106	4.1	1	9	4	30	2														
J. Sternaman	3	16	33	2.1		9	7	72	4	4	2	8	25	41	5.1		2	8	2	2	26		
Walquist	3	9	23	2.6		9	7	51		4	10	27	37	124	4.6		3	8	11	17	137	1	5
Bolan	3	7	21	3.0		7	4	12	2														
LaFleur	3	14	46	3.3		7																	
Pearce	1	6	5	0.8		7	2	13	1	2	1	3	33	35	11.7			6	1	1	15	1	
Lanum	3	12	3	3.2		9																	
Halas	3					9	2	6	1	4	0	1						8					
Garvey																							
Englund																							
Team	3	133	419	3.2	1	9				4	14	42	33	220	5.2		5	9					
Opp.	3	92	212	2.3		9				4	11	32	34	152	4.8		7	9					
CHICAGO CARDINALS																							
Driscoll	1	10	14	1.4		10	5	99		1	0	3	0				1	10	1	4	30	1	
Mohardt	1	9	19	2.1		9	5	55		1	0	5	0				2	9	3	4	82	1	
A. Horween	1	4	14	3.5		10	9	57	4	1	1	5	20	30	6.0		1	10	2	2	61	1	
Koehler	1	2	4	2.0		9	7	34	2														
R. Horween	1	1	2	2.0		8																	
Bryan																							
Team	1	26	53	2.0		10				1	1	13	8	30	2.3		4	10					
Opp.	1	20	51	2.6	1	10				1	4	10	40	76	7.6		2	10					
TOLEDO																							
Watson	2	18	98	5.4		5	6	52	1	2	8	31	26	99	3.2		11	5	9	9	179	2	
Falcon	2	17	49	2.9	1	7	8	47	0														
Annan	2	3	15	5.0		7	3	47	2	3	0	1	0					6					
Petree	1					4	2	33	1														
Phelan	2	8	17	2.1		6	4	4	2														
Tanner						2	4	20															
Gozdowski	1					1	2	11	2														
Rousch	1	1	2	2.0		4	1	3	1														
O'Neil (1)	1	1	2	2.0																			
Kendrick (2)										1	2	16	13	45	2.8		2	1					
Simpson										1								2	2	4	54		1
Roberts										1	0	2											
Peabody										2								5	1	1	35		
Holleran																		1	1	1	5		1
Myers																							
King																							
White																							
Horning																							
Team	2	48	183	3.8	1	7				3	10	50	20	144	2.9		13	6					
Opp.	2	74	263	3.6		7				3	8	39	21	212	5.4	1	7	6					

NAME	RECEIVING									PUNTING						PUNT RETURNS								
	Complete Games					Incom. Games				Comp. Games			Incom. Games			Complete Games					Incom. Games			
	G	Rec.	Yds	Avg.	TD	G	Rec.	Yds.	TD	G	No.	Avg.	G	No.	Avg.	G	No.	Yds.	Avg.	TD	G	No.	Yds.	TD
CANTON																								
Robb	8	3	49	16.3		1										6	10	124	12.4		3			
Elliott																								
Roberts	10	2	44	22.0		1				7	72	34.1	4	5	38.2	7	10	124	12.4		4	1	14	
Chamberlin	10	10	258	25.8	1	2																		
Shaw	10	1	13	13.0		2																		
Sackstededer	9	1	12	12.0		2	1	35	1							6	11	217	19.7	1	5	4	38	
Henry																								
Smyth																								
Bowser																								
Grigg										3	4	39.3	1			3					1	1	15	
McQuade	4	1	17	17.0		1																		
Lyman	10	3	48	16.0		2																		
Miller (1)																								
Carroll	10	10	179	17.9	1	2																		
Kendrick (1)	3	2	18	9.0		1	1	12																
Team										7	76	34.3	5			7	31	462	15.0	1	5			
Opp.										7	93	32.5	5			7	14	133	9.5		5			
CHICAGO BEARS																								
D. Sternaman	4	2	21	10.5		7																		
Stinchcomb	4	2	28	14.0		8				3	2	14.0	9			3					9	2	33	
J. Sternaman	4	2	19	9.5		8	3	33	1	3	6	31.7	9			3	6	78	13.0		9			
Walquist										3	5	37.2	9	1	45.0	3	1	11	11.0		9			
Bolan										3	4	30.0	7											
LaFleur										3	1	41.0	7											
Pearce	2	2	40	20.0		6	1	9																
Lanum										3	4	22.3	9											
Halas	4	3	49	16.3		8	7	101	1															
Garvey	4	3	63	21.0		8	2	23		3	1	37.0	9											
Englund	3					8	1	12																
Team										3	24	29.7	9			3	7	89	12.7		9			
Opp.										3	19	34.4	9			3	7	109	15.6		9			
CHICAGO CARDINALS																								
Driscoll	1	1	30	30.0		10	4	124	2	1	13	40.6	10	1	35.0	1					10	1	10	
Mohardt	1					9	2	49	1							1	2	17	8.5		9			
A. Horween										1	3	30.7	10											
Koehler																								
R. Horween										1			8	1	30.0									
Bryan										1	1	0.0	9											
Team										1	17	36.5	10			1	2	17	8.5		10			
Opp.										1	16	35.4	10			1	4	34	8.5		10			
TOLEDO																								
Watson																2	1	18	18.0		5	1	15	
Falcon										2	7	27.9	7											
Annan	3	1	1	1.0		6	4	92	2															
Petree	2					3	1	20																
Phelan	3	2	24	12.0		5																		
Tanner	1	2	45	22.5		1																		
Gozdowski																								
Rousch																								
O'Neil (1)																								
Kendrick (2)													2	4	29.8									
Simpson																								
Roberts																								
Peabody	2	1	7	7.0		5																		
Holleran																								
Myers	3	4	67	16.8		6	1	12																
King	1					2	4	109																
White	2					5	2	25																
Horning	3					6	1	15	1	2	10	23.6	7											
Team										2	17	25.4	7			2	1	18	18.0					
Opp.										2	14	35.2	7			2	7	107	15.3					

ROCK ISLAND INDEPENDENTS 4-2-1 Jimmy Conzelman

Regulars

Use Name	Pos.	Hgt.	Wgt.	Age	Int.	Pts.
Walt Clago	E	6'	195	23	1	
Tillie Voss (to AKR)	E	6'3	204	25	1	18
Ed Healey (to ChiB)	T	6'1	205	27		
Duke Slater (to MIL)	T	6'1	215	23		
Dewey Lyle (to GB)	G-T-E	5'11	200	31		
Jerry Jones	G	6'1	205	28		
Louie Kolls	C	6'1	205	29		
Mike Casteel	BB-TB-WB	5'11	175	26		6
Jimmy Conzelman (to MIL)	TB-BB	6'	170	24	2	48
Dutch Lauer (to GB)	WB-TB	5'10	180	26	1	31
Buck Gavin (to BUF)	FB	5'10	180	27	3	30

Substitutes

Use Name	Pos.	Hgt.	Wgt.	Age	Int.	Pts.
Obe Wenig	E	5'10	190	26		
Emmitt Keefe (to MIL)	G	5'10	195	29		
Jug Earp (to GB)	C	6'	220	25		
Walt Brindley	BB	5'8	155	27		
Eddie Usher (to GB)	WB-TB	5'11	192	24	1	6
Jerry Johnson (to RAC)	WB-BB-FB	5'11	195	27		
Lane Bridgeford	FB-BB-TB	5'10	180	24		15

Substitutes

Use Name	Pos.	Hgt.	Wgt.	Age	Int.	Pts.
Ollie Kraehe	C-G	5'10	180	24		
Eddie Novak	WB	5'9	175	25		

Scores of each game

Date	Pts.	Opponent	Pts.
Oct. 1	19	GREEN BAY	14
Oct. 8	6	CHIC. BEARS	10
Oct. 15	60	EVANSVILLE	0
Oct. 22	26	ROCHESTER	0
Oct. 29	0	Green Bay	0
Nov. 12	43	DAYTON	0
Nov. 19	0	Chic. Bears	3

RACINE LEGION 6-4-1 Babe Ruetz

Regulars

Use Name	Pos.	Hgt.	Wgt.	Age	Int.	Pts.
Fritz Roessler	E	6'	185	24		6
Norb Hayes	E-FB	5'11	175	25		
Candy Miller (from CAN)	T-E	6'3	215	24		
Bull Braman	T	5'11	215	25		
Bud Gorman	G-T		225	26		
Jab Murray (from GB)	G-C	6'1	220	29	1	1
Jake Mintun	C	5'11	190	28	1	
Chuck Dressen	BB	5'6	145	23		12
Al Elliott	TB	5'9	175	27	1	12
Irv Langhoff	WB	5'8	155	25		8
Hank Gillo	FB	5'10	195	27	1	52

Substitutes

Use Name	Pos.	Hgt.	Wgt.	Age	Int.	Pts.
Fritz Heinisch	E	5'10	170	22		
Elmer Rhenstrom	E	5'10	185	27		
Don Murry	T	6'2	190	22		
Frank Linnan	T	6'2	198	23		
George McGill	G	5'10	180	24		
Jack Hueller	G	5'10	200	24		
Vin Shekleton	C	5'8	165	26		
Moxie Dalton	BB-FB	5'6	165	27	1	
Bob Foster	TB-WB-G-T	5'10	190	35		18
Wally Sieb	WB	5'10	175	23		13

Substitutes

Use Name	Pos.	Hgt.	Wgt.	Age	Int.	Pts.
George Berry (to HAM)	T	5'11	195	22		
Buddy Baumann	T-G	6'1	190	22		
Whitey Woodin (to GB)	T-G	5'10	205	27		
Karl George	G	5'11	175	30		
Norm Glockson	G	6'2	230	28		
Dud Pearson	BB	5'9	165	26		
Jerry Johnson (from RI)	TB-WB	5'11	195	27		

Scores of each game

Date	Pts.	Opponent	Pts.
Oct. 1	0	CHIC. BEARS	6
Oct. 8	10	Green Bay	6
Oct. 15	0	Milwaukee	20
Oct. 22	0	TOLEDO	7
Oct. 29	9	ROCHESTER	0
Nov. 5	57	LOUISVILLE	0
Nov. 11	34	COLUMBUS	0
Nov. 19	3	GREEN BAY	3
Nov. 26	6	HAMMOND	0
Nov. 30	3	MILWAUKEE	0
Dec. 3	0	Green Bay (at Milwaukee)	14

DAYTON TRIANGLES 4-3-1 Carl Storck

Regulars

Use Name	Pos.	Hgt.	Wgt.	Age	Int.	Pts.
Dave Reese	E	6'	180	29	1	
Dutch Thiele	E	6'1	195	29		6
Ed Sauer (to & from AKR)	T	5'10	235	24		
Russ Hathaway (to, from & to CAN)	T	5'11	225	26	1	16
Bobby Berns	G	6'1	200	26		
Herb Sies	G	6'1	203	29		
Hobby Kinderdine	C	5'11	180	31		
Al Mahrt	BB	5'11	168	28		6
Frank Bacon	TB-WB	5'11	180	28		6
Jiggs Ullery	WB-FB	6'	200	25		6
Ken Huffine	FB	6'3	208	24	1	18

Substitutes

Use Name	Pos.	Hgt.	Wgt.	Age	Int.	Pts.
Lee Fenner	E	5'10	170	26		3
Larry Delinger	G	5'11	208	29		
Bruno Haas	G	5'10	180	31		
Glenn Tidd	C-WB	5'11	202	28		
Fay Abbott	BB-TB	5'8	175	27		
Gus Redman	TB-FB	5'11	170	26		6
Tip O'Neill	WB	5'10	170	23		6
Lou Partlow	FB-TB	6'1	185	29		6

Scores of each game

Date	Pts.	Opponent	Pts.
Oct. 1	36	OORANG	0
Oct. 8	0	CANTON	0
Oct. 15	17	MINNEAPOLIS	0
Oct. 22	20	HAMMOND	0
Oct. 29	0	BUFFALO	7
Nov. 5	0	Chic. Bears	9
Nov. 12	0	Rock Island	43
Dec. 3	7	Chic. Cards	3

GREEN BAY PACKERS 4-3-3 Curly Lambeau

Regulars

Use Name	Pos.	Hgt.	Wgt.	Age	Int.	Pts.
Cowboy Wheeler	E	5'9	180	24		
Dave Hayes	E	5'8	165	25		
Cub Buck	T	6'	255	30		6
Jug Earp (from RI)	T	6'	220	25		
Whitey Woodin (from RAC)	G	5'10	208	27	1	
Moose Gardner	G	6'1	220	28		
Wally Niemann	C	5'10	180	28	1	
Charlie Mathys	BB	5'7	165	25		15
Curly Lambeau	TB	5'10	185	24		30
Eddie Usher (from RI)	HB-TB	5'11	192	24	1	6
Stan Mills	FB-HB	5'9	180	28		

Substitutes

Use Name	Pos.	Hgt.	Wgt.	Age	Int.	Pts.
Tubby Howard	E	5'10	210	28		
Pat Dunnigan	E	5'10	195	28		
Jab Murray (to RAC)	T-E	6'1	220	29		
Peaches Nadolney	G-T	5'11	210	23		
Pahl Davis	G-E-FB	5'10	185	25		
Dewey Lyle (from RI)	G-E	5'11	200	31		
Joe Secord	C		190	25		
Dutch Lauer (from RI)	FB-BB	5'10	180	26		
Eddie Glick	TB-HB-BB	5'8	165	22	2	
Tommy Cronin	HB	5'9	170	26		6
Gus Gardella	FB		190	27		

Substitutes

Use Name	Pos.	Hgt.	Wgt.	Age	Int.	Pts.
Rex Smith	E	6'	195	26		
Rip Owens	G	5'10	220	27		
Carl Zoll	G	5'9	215	23		
Doc Regnier	HB		170	26		
Biff Taugher	FB	5'10	185	27		6

Scores of each game

Date	Pts.	Opponent	Pts.
Oct. 1	14	Rock Island	19
Oct. 8	6	RACINE	10
Oct. 15	3	Chic. Cards	16
Oct. 22	0	Milwaukee	0
Oct. 29	0	ROCK ISLAND	0
Nov. 5	3	COLUMBUS	0
Nov. 12	14	MINNEAPOLIS	6
Nov. 19	3	Racine	3
Nov. 26	13	MILWAUKEE	0
Dec. 3	14	Racine (at Milwaukee)	0

BUFFALO ALL AMERICANS 5-4-1 Tommy Hughitt

Regulars

Use Name	Pos.	Hgt.	Wgt.	Age	Int.	Pts.
Luke Urban	E	5'8	165	24		
Gus Goetz	E-T	6'	189	25		
Frank Morrissey	T	6'1	202	23		14
Carl Thomas	T-BB	5'10	195	25	1	6
Swede Youngstrom	G-E	6'1	185	25	1	
Bill Brace	G	6'	180	26		
Charlie Guy	C	6'	170	25	1	
Tommy Hughitt	BB-TB	5'8	160	29	1	12
Ockie Anderson	TB-BB	5'9	165	28	2	6
Waddy Kuehl	WB-E	5'9	165	30	3	19
Jim Laird	FB	6'	190	24	1	24

Substitutes

Use Name	Pos.	Hgt.	Wgt.	Age	Int.	Pts.
Bob Nash	E	6'1	205	29		
Mike Wilson (to ROCH)	E	5'10	165	25		
Herb Dieter	G-T-E	6'1	195	26		
Glenn Knack	G			19		
Bill Kibler	TB			26		
Johnny Scott	WB	5'10	176	27		
Buck Gavin (from RI)	FB-TB	5'10	180	27	1	6

Substitutes

Use Name	Pos.	Hgt.	Wgt.	Age	Int.	Pts.
Frank Spellacy	E			21		
Jim Morrow	TB	5'10	170	26		
Bob Rawlings	FB-TB-WB					

Scores of each game

Date	Pts.	Opponent	Pts.
Oct. 1	7	HAMMOND	0
Oct. 15	19	COLUMBUS	0
Oct. 22	0	Chic. Bears	7
Oct. 29	7	Dayton	0
Nov. 5	7	Chic. Cards	9
Nov. 12	0	Canton	3
Nov. 19	3	AKRON	3
Nov. 26	7	OORANG	19
Nov. 30	21	Rochester	0
Dec. 3	16	AKRON	0

AKRON PROS 3-5-2 Untz Brewer Paul Sheeks

Regulars

Use Name	Pos.	Hgt.	Wgt.	Age	Int.	Pts.
Red Daum	E-BB-WB	5'7	158	23	2	12
Bunny Corcoran	E-TB	5'11	185	27		
Bob Spiers	T	5'11	190	27		
Al Jolley	T	6'2	195	22		
Al Nesser	G-E	6'	195	29	3	6
Ray Neal	G-T	5'9	205	24		
Jim Flower	C-G	6'1	195	26		
Paul Sheeks	BB-TB	5'8	175	32		17
Rip King	TB	6'1	205	25	1	21
Untz Brewer	WB-TB	5'6	160	26	3	6
Carl Cramer	FB-TB	5'11	185	24	2	36

Substitutes

Use Name	Pos.	Hgt.	Wgt.	Age	Int.	Pts.
Scotty Bierce	E	5'9	160	25		12
Tillie Voss (from RI)	E-T	6'3	204	25		
Ed Sauer (from & to DAY)	T	5'10	235	24		
Charlie Copley (to MIL)	T	5'9	194	34		
Walt LeJeune	G-FB	6'	210	22	1	24
Leo McCausland	G-C-T-E	6'	195	27		
Walt Krienheder	C-BB	6'2	204	22		4
Cliff Steele (from ROCH)	BB	5'8	150	24		
Marty Beck	WB	5'9	175	22		
Joe Mills	WB	6'3	212	24	2	7

Scores of each game

Date	Pts.	Opponent	Pts.
Oct. 1	36	COLUMBUS	0
Oct. 12	13	ROCHESTER	13
Oct. 22	0	CANTON	22
Oct. 29	62	OORANG	0
Nov. 5	22	HAMMOND	0
Nov. 12	0	Chic. Cards	7
Nov. 19	3	Buffalo	3
Nov. 26	10	Chic. Bears	20
Nov. 30	0	Canton	14
Dec. 3	0	Buffalo	16

NAME	RUSHING									PASSING													
	Complete Games					Incom. Games				Complete Games								Incom. Games					
	G	Att.	Yds.	Avg.	TD	G	Att.	Yds.	TD	G	Com.	Att.	%	Yds.	Y/A	TD	Int.	G	Com.	Att.	Yds.	TD	Int.
ROCK ISLAND																							
Conzelman (1)	6	61	290	4.8	7	1				6	27	53	51	399	7.5	2	7	1					
Gavin (1)	6	63	231	3.7	5	1																	
Casteel	5	27	210	7.8	1	1				5	5	9	56	95	10.6		1						
Lauer (1)	6	53	147	2.8	4	1				6	1	1	100	15	15.0			1					
Usher (1)	4	30	140	4.7	1	1				4	1	1	100	13	13.0			1					
Johnson (1)	4	32	76	2.4	1	1																	
Bridgeford	3	16	64	4.0																			
Brindley	2	2	3	1.5		1				2	0	1	0										
Novak	1	3	-11	-3.7																			
Voss (1)																							
Wenig																							
Clago																							
Team	6	287	1150	4.0	19	1				6	34	65	52	522	8.0	2	8	1					
Opp.	6	159	338	2.1	3	1				6	20	60	33	278	4.6		9	1					
RACINE																							
Elliott	8	81	360	4.4	1	3	4	59	1	8	6	17	35	69	4.1		1	3	1	2	8		1
Gillo	8	102	372	3.6	3	3	9	42	2	8	1	4	25	7	1.8		1	3					
Langhoff	8	60	251	4.2		3	11	59	1	8	0	2	0					3	1	1	22		
Foster	7	23	87	3.8	1	3	10	90	2	7	0	1	0					3					
Dressen	5	38	173	4.6	1	2	4	50	1	5	10	20	50	57	2.9	1	4	2	3	3	48		
Johnson (2)	3	33	94	2.8						3	0	1	0										
Hayes	8	8	18	2.3		3	5	37															
Sieb	1	2	9	4.5		1	5	38	2														
Roessler	8	3	27	9.0		3																	
Dalton	3	9	21	2.3		1	1	0		3	5	12	42	55	4.6		1	1					
Rhenstrom	5	1	11	11.0		1																	
Pearson	3	3	5	1.7		1				3	0	2	0					1					
J. Murray (2)	6	1	4	4.0		2																	
D. Murry	3	1	1	1.0		1																	
McGill																							
Team	8	366	1433	3.9	6	3				8	22	59	37	188	3.2	1	7	3					
Opp.	8	294	927	3.2	2	3				8	31	94	33	433	4.6	1	12	3					
DAYTON																							
Partlow	3	28	76	2.7		3	8	36	1														
Bacon	2	8	25	3.1		4	2	72	1	2	1	2	50	12	6.0			4	3	3	62	1	
Huffine	3	20	39	2.0		5	6	28	3	3								5	1	1	15		
O'Neil	2					2	3	34	1														
Mahrt	3	6	6	1.0		5	2	16		3	11	39	28	123	3.2		5	5	3	8	65	1	1
Ullery	2	11	13	1.2		5	2	8		2	1	1	100	20	20.0			5	2	2	45		
Redman	1					2	2	13	1	1								2	1	1	25		
Abbott										2	1	2	50	16	8.0			4					
Thiele																							
Reese																							
Fenner																							
Team	3	73	159	2.2		5				3	14	44	32	171	3.9		5	5					
Opp.	3	118	322	2.7	4	5				3	12	21	57	191	9.1	2	1	5					
GREEN BAY																							
Lambeau	3	50	131	2.6		5	10	72	3	3	21	46	46	354	7.7	1	4	5	5	9	115	1	
Glick	2					4	2	50															
Mills	1	18	43	2.4		7																	
Cronin	2	18	36	2.0	1	3																	
Usher (2)	1	16	26	1.6	1	4	1	2															
Lauer (2)	1	12	20	1.7		1																	
Mathys	3	3	14	4.7		7																	
Niemann	1					7	1	9															
Buck	3	1	6	6.0		7				3	0	1	0					7					
Gardella	1	5	6	1.2		6	1	1															
Taugher	2	4	2	0.5	1																		
Wheeler																							
Smith																							
Dunnigan																							
Howard																							
Regnier																							
Team	3	127	284	2.2	3	7				3	21	47	45	354	7.5	1	4	8					
Opp.	3	131	399	3.0	2	7				3	14	29	48	158	5.4	1	4	8					
BUFFALO																							
Hughitt	2	13	15	1.2		8	23	128	2	3	4	10	40	39	3.9	1	1	7	5	7	85	1	1
Kuehl	2	12	76	6.3		8	13	60	2	3								7	1	1	10	1	
Laird	2	24	44	1.8		8	15	82	3	3	1	1	100	76	76.0			7	0	1			1
Anderson	2	22	57	2.6		5	5	38		3	6	18	33	80	4.4			4	4	5	63		1
Gavin (2)						3	5	45	1														
Kibler						2	3	12															
Urban	2					7	1	7															
Rawlings						6	1	6															
Scott																		1	1	1	36		
Youngstrom										3								7	1	1	15		
Nash																							
Goetz																							
Team	2	71	192	2.7		8				3	11	29	38	195	6.7	1	1	7					
Opp.	2	109	390	3.6		8				3	13	35	37	193	5.5		7	7					
AKRON																							
Cramer	2	19	70	3.7	2	8	23	134	4	4	1	4	25	3	0.8			6	1	1	50		
Mills	2	12	32	2.7	1	5	5	57		3								4	1	3	25		2
Brewer	1	4	-6	-1.5		7	8	91	1														
King	1	12	59	4.9	2	5	4	23		3	12	26	46	247	9.5	1	2	3	2	5	41	1	
Sheeks	2	8	50	6.3		7	4	10		4	3	9	33	36	4.0		1	5	3	5	28		1
Daum	2	1	35	35.0		7	1	-6		3								6	1	1	35	1	
LeJeune	2	4	13	3.3	2	6	2	8	1														
Steele (2)						4	1	10															
Corcoran	1					8	1	0		3								6	1	1	15	1	
Bierce																							
Nesser																							
Flower																							
Team	2	60	253	4.2	7	8				4	16	39	41	286	7.3	1	3	6					
Opp.	2	28	170	3.5	1	8				4	13	36	36	202	5.6	1	9	6					

NAME	RECEIVING									PUNTING						PUNT RETURNS								
	Complete Games					Incom. Games				Comp. Games			Incom. Games			Complete Games					Incom. Games			
	G	Rec.	Yds	Avg.	TD	G	Rec.	Yds.	TD	G	No.	Avg.	G	No.	Avg.	G	No.	Yds.	Avg.	TD	G	No.	Yds.	TD
ROCK ISLAND																								
Conzelman (1)	6	1	30	30.0		1				6	11	38.0	1			6	6	83	13.8		1			
Gavin (1)																								
Casteel	5	1	25	25.0		1										5	1	25	25.0		1			
Lauer (1)	6	5	34	6.8	1	1				6	2	36.5	1			6	3	33	11.0		1			
Usher (1)																								
Johnson (1)	4	3	27	9.0		1				4	8	33.5	1											
Bridgeford																								
Brindley																2	1	10	10.0		1			
Novak	1	1	2	2.0						1	3	38.0												
Voss (1)	6	10	204	20.4	1	1																		
Wenig	5	9	170	18.9		1																		
Clago	6	4	30	7.5																				
Team										6	24	36.4	1			6	11	151	13.7		1			
Opp.										6	43	29.3	1			6	4	53	13.3		1			
RACINE																								
Elliott	8	6	53	8.8		3																		
Gillo	8					3	1	8		8	4	38.3	3	1	34.0	8	2	42	21.0		3			
Langhoff	8	7	75	10.7		3				8	18	35.1	3	1	29.0									
Foster										7	1	28.0	3			8	8	92	11.5		3			
Dressen										5	1	53.0	2			7	1	5	5.0		3			
Johnson (2)	3	4	33	8.3						3	20	30.4				5	10	161	16.1		2	2	87	
Hayes	8	1	12	12.0		3																		
Sieb	1					1	1	22																
Roessler	8	4	15	3.8	1	3	3	48																
Dalton										4	2	31.0	1											
Rhenstrom																								
Pearson										3	8	29.8	1			3	1	15	15.0		1			
J. Murray (2)																								
D. Murry																								
McGill										2	2	41.0	1											
Team										8	56	33.1	3			8	22	315	14.3		3			
Opp.										8	70	35.6	3			8	9	146	16.2		3			
DAYTON																								
Partlow																								
Bacon	2	2	36	18.0		4	1	15		2	2	30.5	4			2	2	32	16.0		4			
Huffine	3	5	44	8.8		5				3	9	34.2	5	1	45.0									
O'Neil																								
Mahrt	3	2	28	14.0		5	2	42	1															
Ullery																								
Redman	1					2	1	15		1	9	34.0	2											
Abbott	2					4	1	15		2	7	37.9	4			2	1	5	5.0		4			
Thiele	3					4	4	100	1															
Reese	3	3	38	12.7		5	1	25																
Fenner	2	2	25	12.5		4																		
Team										3	27	34.6	5			3	3	37	12.3		5			
Opp.										3	25	34.8	5			3	5	60	12.0		5			
GREEN BAY																								
Lambeau										3	1	55.0	5											
Glick	2	2	38	19.0		4																		
Mills	1					7	1	40																
Cronin	2	3	32	10.7		3																		
Usher (2)																								
Lauer (2)	1	1	15	15.0		1																		
Mathys	3	8	171	21.4	1	7	3	65	1							3	2	27	13.5		7			
Niemann																								
Buck										3	21	38.6	7	6	38.8									
Gardella																								
Taugher																								
Wheeler	3	4	60	15.0		6																		
Smith	1	1	17	17.0		1																		
Dunnigan	2	1	12	12.0																				
Howard	1					7	1	10																
Regnier	2	1	9	9.0		3																		
Team										3	22	39.4	7			3	2	27	13.5		7			
Opp.										3	25	38.2	7			3	6	83	13.8		7			
BUFFALO																								
Hughitt	3	2	18	9.0		7				2	15	34.1	8	2	10.0	2	1	12	12.0		8	2	15	
Kuehl	3	1	18	18.0		7	1	30	1															
Laird	3	1	20	20.0		7	1	10	1	2	9	36.8	8	1	45.0	2	1	4	4.0		8			
Anderson	3	1	13	13.0	1	4										2	3	22	7.3		5	5	150	
Gavin (2)																								
Kibler																								
Urban	3	4	105	26.3		6	4	98																
Rawlings	1					5	1	8																
Scott																								
Youngstrom	3	1	6	6.0		7	2	18																
Nash						2	2	30																
Goetz	3					4	1	15																
Team										2	24	35.1	8			2	5	38	7.6		8			
Opp.										2	24	37.4	8			2	5	58	11.6		8			
AKRON																								
Cramer	4	4	78	19.5		6																		
Mills	3	4	63	15.8		4																		
Brewer										1	18	31.3	7			1	3	30	10.0		8			
King													6	13	41.3						6	1	10	
Sheeks	4	1	8	8.0		5				1			8	2	16.5									
Daum	3	4	98	24.5	1	6																		
LeJeune	3					5	1	16	1	1			7	2	9.0									
Steele (2)	2					2	4	53					4	1	0.0									
Corcoran	3					6	1	50																
Bierce	4					6	2	50	2															
Nesser	4	1	20	20.0		5	1	25																
Flower	4	2	19	9.5		6																		
Team										1	18	31.3	9			1	3	30	10.0		9			
Opp.										1	12	35.7	9			1	12	124	10.3		9			

MILWAUKEE BADGERS 2-4-3 Budge Garrett Jimmy Conzelman

Regulars

Use Name	Pos.	Hgt.	Wgt.	Age	Int.	Pts.
Paul Robeson	E	6'3	220	24		12
Budge Garrett	E-G-BB	5'9	200	29		
John Alexander	T-E	6'4	220	25		
Art Webb	T	5'10	210	29		
Jim Dufft	G	6'6	250	26		
Tommy Tomlin	G	5'10	198	28		
Al Pierotti	C	5'10	200	26		
Mike Purdy	BB-WB	5'10	180	27	1	6
Fritz Pollard	TB-WB	5'7	165	27		20
Dick King (to ROCH)	WB-FB	5'8	175	29		
Dinger Doane	FB	5'10	190	27		6

Substitutes

Use Name	Pos.	Hgt.	Wgt.	Age	Int.	Pts.
Collins	E					
Ward Meese	E	5'10	175	20		
CharlieCopley (from AKR)	T-E	5'9	194	34		1
Duke Slater (from RI)	T	6'1	215	23		
Emmett Keefe (from RI)	G	5'10	195	29		
Mickey Fallon	G-E	5'9	175	24		
Bo McMillin	BB-TB	5'9	155	27		6
JimmyConzelman (from RI)	TB	6'	170	24	1	
Earl Potteiger	WB	5'7	170	31	1	
Norris Armstrong	FB	5'10	165	23		

Substitutes

Use Name	Pos.	Hgt.	Wgt.	Age	Int.	Pts.
Moose Cochran	E	6'	195			
Sid Bennett	G	5'10	192	27		
George Mooney	WB-BB-E	5'8	160	26		
George Seasholtz	TB-WB	5'8	185	23		
Al Greene	WB	5'8	165	22		
Steve Sullivan (to EVA & HAM)	WB-E	5'9	180	24		
Ben Winkelman	E	6'1	190	23		
Lyle Bigbee	E-WB	6'	180	29		
Norm Barry	WB	5'10	170	24		
Frank Jordan	WB		168			

Scores of each game

Date	Pts.	Opponent	Pts.
Oct. 1	0	Chic. Cards	3
Oct. 8	12	Toledo	12
Oct. 15	20	RACINE	0
Oct. 22	0	GREEN BAY	0
Oct. 29	0	HAMMOND	0
Nov. 19	13	OORANG	0
Nov. 26	0	Green Bay	13
Nov. 30	0	Racine	3
Dec. 3	6	Canton	40

OORANG INDIANS (Marion, Ohio) 3-6-0 Jim Thorpe

Regulars

Use Name	Pos.	Hgt.	Wgt.	Age	Int.	Pts.
Stilwell Sanooke	E-WB	5'8	175	30		
Pete Calac	E-FB-TB	5'10	195	30		
Nick Lassa	T-G-E	5'10	205	25	1	
Ted St. Germaine	T-C-G	6'2	250	37		
Bob Hill	G	5'11	190	32		
Elmer Busch	G-C	5'10	210	32	1	
Bill Winneshick	C-G	5'8	190	28		
Lo Boutwell	BB	5'7	185	29		
Jim Thorpe	TB	6'1	200	35		18
Joe Guyon	TB-WB-BB-FB	5'10	195	29	3	33
Eagle Feather	FB-BB-T	6'	220			6

Substitutes

Use Name	Pos.	Hgt.	Wgt.	Age	Int.	Pts.
Asa Walker	E	5'11	180	27		
Dick Deer Slayer	E		190			
Big Bear	E-T	6'4	215			
War Eagle	T-G		195			
Ted Lone Wolf	G-T-WB	6'2	202			
Xavier Downwind	C-T-E	6'	200	28		
Ed Nason	E-WB	5'8	185	23		
Reggie Attache	WB-FB	5'9	195			

Substitutes

Use Name	Pos.	Hgt.	Wgt.	Age	Int.	Pts.
E. Bobadash	E					
Joe Little Twig	E-T	5'11	190	29		
Baptiste Thunder	T	5'10	215			
Fred Broker	T	5'9	175	29		

Scores of each game

Date	Pts.	Opponent	Pts.
Oct. 1	0	Dayton	36
Oct. 8	20	COLUMBUS	6
Oct. 15	0	Canton	14
Oct. 29	0	Akron	62
Nov. 5	6	Minneapolis	13
Nov. 12	6	Chic. Bears	33
Nov. 19	0	Milwaukee	13
Nov. 26	19	Buffalo	7
Nov. 30	18	Columbus	6

MINNEAPOLIS MARINES 1-3-0 Russell Tollefson

Regulars

Use Name	Pos.	Hgt.	Wgt.	Age	Int.	Pts.
Paul Flinn	E	6'	180	26		
Oscar Christianson	E-TB	5'10	185	23	1	
Harold Erickson	T		195	28		
Rudy Tersch	T		195	27		
Dutch Gaustad	G		210	32		
George Kramer	G	6'2	240	27		
Harry Mehre	C	6'1	190	20		
Bill Irgens	BB-E	5'8	175	39		1
Marty Norton	TB	5'6	175	19		12
Einar Cleve	WB	5'9	175	26		6
Eber Sampson	FB	6'	200	27		

Substitutes

Use Name	Pos.	Hgt.	Wgt.	Age	Int.	Pts.
Ren Kraft	E	5'11	170	27		
Shorty Des Jadien	E	6'4	210	29		
Otto Townsend	G-T		190			
Harry Gunderson	G	6'2	205	34		
Louie Mohs	G	6'2	220	29		
John Madigan	C	6'	185	23		
Joey Mattern	BB		155	29		
Sam Mason	FB	5'8	170	23		

Scores of each game

Date	Pts.	Opponent	Pts.
Oct. 15	0	Dayton	17
Oct. 22	0	Chic. Cards	3
Nov. 5	13	OORANG	6
Nov. 12	6	Green Bay	14

LOUISVILLE BRECKS 1-3-0 Hubert Wiggs

Regulars

Use Name	Pos.	Hgt.	Wgt.	Age	Int.	Pts.
Herb Gruber	E	5'9	155	20		
Bill Netherton	E			24		
Harper Card	T	6'1	185	19		
Dick Gibson	T	6'	185	20		
Bo Otto	G-T		182	20		
Austin Brunklacher	G		193	24		
Austin Higgins	C	5'9	168	24		
Chase Boldt	BB-E-FB	5'7	145	22		6
Jimmy Van Dyke	TB	5'7	140	23		7
Bob Padan	WB-TB		165	29		
Jim Irwin	FB	5'7	165	25		

Substitutes

Use Name	Pos.	Hgt.	Wgt.	Age	Int.	Pts.
Ed Gregg	E	5'6	135	25		
Max MacCollum	E	5'9	165	23		
Charlie Lanham	T		170	27		
Hubert Wiggs	T-FB	5'8	185	26		
John Olmstead	G	5'11	180	25		
George Wanless	G	5'8	160	24		
Salem Ford	TB-BB	5'7	150	26		
Eddie Meeks	WB	5'7	155	25		
Loe Jansing	FB-WB		175	31		

Substitutes

Use Name	Pos.	Hgt.	Wgt.	Age	Int.	Pts.
Wilfred Smith	T-BB	6'4	200	23		
Brian McGrath	G		245	21		
Joe Engelhard	TB	5'11	185	23		

Scores of each game

Date	Pts.	Opponent	Pts.
Oct. 1	0	Canton	38
Oct. 29	0	Toledo	39
Nov. 5	0	Racine	57
Nov. 12	13	EVANSVILLE	6

ROCHESTER JEFFERSONS 0-4-1 Doc Alexander

Regulars

Use Name	Pos.	Hgt.	Wgt.	Age	Int.	Pts.
EddieAnderson (to ChiC)	E	5'10	170	21		
Spin Roy	E	6'	175	25		6
Frank Matteo	T	5'11	190	26		
Hank Smith	T-C	6'1	190	29	1	
John Dooley	G-T	6'1	220	24		
Tiny Thompson	G	5'10	233	23		
Doc Alexander	C	5'11	210	24		
Larry Weltman	BB-TB	5'11	175	23		
Chet Wynne	TB-FB	6'	180	23	1	
Bob Argus	WB-FB	5'10	192	28		6
Dick King (from MIL)	FB	5'8	175	29		

Substitutes

Use Name	Pos.	Hgt.	Wgt.	Age	Int.	Pts.
Paul Meyers	E	5'11	170	27		
Hal Clark	E-BB	5'10	195	28		
Harry Robertson	T	5'10	185	26		
Darby Lowery	T-G-E	6'	200	30		
Joe Bachmaier	G-T	5'9	175	26		
Cliff Steele (to AKR)	BB	5'8	150	24		1
Ralph Henricus	TB	6'	175	26		
Herm Sawyer	WB-BB	5'8	170	23		
Ray Witter	TB	5'10	185	25		

Substitutes

Use Name	Pos.	Hgt.	Wgt.	Age	Int.	Pts.
Eddie Bentz	E			30		
Jimmy Woods	T	5'9	195	28		
Benny Boynton	BB	5'9	170	23		
Walt French	TB	5'7	155	23		
Chris Lehrer	WB		185	28		
Mike Wilson (from BUF)	BB	5'10	165	25		

Scores of each game

Date	Pts.	Opponent	Pts.
Oct. 12	13	Akron	13
Oct. 15	0	Chic. Bears	7
Oct. 22	0	Rock Island	26
Oct. 29	0	Racine	9
Nov. 30	0	BUFFALO	21

HAMMOND PROS 0-5-1 Wally Hess

Regulars

Use Name	Pos.	Hgt.	Wgt.	Age	Int.	Pts.
Inky Williams	E	5'11	175	25		
Ed Carman	E-T	5'11	190	28		
Dave Tallant	T	6'1	205	25		
GeorgeBerry (from RAC)	T-G	5'11	195	22		
Festus Tierney (to TOL)	G	6'1	195	23		
Paul Leatherman	G	5'9	200	25		
Frank Rydzewski	C-T	6'1	220	29		
Lloyd Cearing	BB-TB		185	21		
Wally Hess	TB-BB	5'9	175	27		
Bill Giaver	WB-TB	5'9	190	24		
John Shelbourne	FB	5'11	200	26		

Substitutes

Use Name	Pos.	Hgt.	Wgt.	Age	Int.	Pts.
Carl Hanke (from ChiB)	E	6'	190	24		
Dutch Kohl	E			28		
Elliot Risley	T	6'	205	26		
Mace Roberts	T-G	6'	185	25		
Willert	C					
Bill Singleton	G	5'9	190	25		
Tony LaBissoniere	C	5'9	185	25		
Teddy Besta	BB			26		
Steve Sullivan (from MIL & EVA)	TB	5'9	180	24		
Anderson	WB					
Oscar Knop	WB-FB	6'	185	27		

Scores of each game

Date	Pts.	Opponent	Pts.
Oct. 1	0	Buffalo	7
Oct. 15	0	Toledo	14
Oct. 22	0	Dayton	20
Oct. 29	0	Milwaukee	0
Nov. 5	0	Akron	22
Nov. 26	0	Racine	6

EVANSVILLE CRIMSON GIANTS 0-3-0 Frank Fausch

Regulars

Use Name	Pos.	Hgt.	Wgt.	Age	Int.	Pts.
Bill Slyker	E	6'1	180	23		6
Jess Reno	E	5'9	165	31		
Bourbon Bondurant (from ChiB)	T	6'1	202	24		
Travis Williams	T	6'	200	30		
Tiny Ladson	G		254	26		
Leon Winternheimer	G	6'1	240			
Dick Spain	C-T	5'8	180	29		
Spencer Rork	BB-WB	5'9	160	26		
Steve Sullivan (from MIL, to HAM)	TB	5'9	180	24		
Earl Goldsmith	WB-E		182	28		
Frank Fausch	FB	6'3	250	27		

Substitutes

Use Name	Pos.	Hgt.	Wgt.	Age	Int.	Pts.
Lew Skinner	T			23		
Adolph Spiegel	T	5'11	190	24		
Joe Sanders	G-E	5'10	250	21		
Winnie Denton	G	6'1	200	25		
Slats Dalrymple	C	6'2	210	26		
Pete Wathen	BB-E	5'10	175	19		
Pete Lauer	TB	5'6	150	24		
Chuck O'Neil (from TOL)	WB	5'10	180	24		

Substitutes

Use Name	Pos.	Hgt.	Wgt.	Age	Int.	Pts.
Vic Endress	BB			19		
Walker Whitehead	TB	6'	180	20		

Scores of each game

Date	Pts.	Opponent	Pts.
Oct. 1	0	Toledo	15
Oct. 15	0	Rock Island	60
Nov. 12	6	Louisville	13

COLUMBUS PANHANDLES 0-8-0 Herb Dell

Regulars

Use Name	Pos.	Hgt.	Wgt.	Age	Int.	Pts.
Homer Ruh	E	5'10	180	26		
Morris Glassman	E	5'10	166	22		
Joe Mulbarger	T	5'9	215	27		
Bob Karch	T	6'1	220	27		
John Conley	G-T	5'11	200	32		
Mark Stevenson	G-C		196	29		
Oscar Wolford	C-G-E	6'	188	25		
Hal Gaulke	BB	5'8	175	28		
Lee Snoots	TB-FB	5'9	185	30	1	
Bob Rapp	WB-TB	5'8	156	24	1	6
Frank Nesser	G-FB	6'1	240	33	1	6

Substitutes

Use Name	Pos.	Hgt.	Wgt.	Age	Int.	Pts.
Ted Hopkins	E-T	5'9	180	31		
Gene Carroll	E-T-G	5'10	190	24		
Jack Beckett	T	6'1	200	30		
Chuck Carney	T-G	6'1	190	22		
Andy Gump	G		210			
Doc Davis	G	5'9	200	33		
Don Wiper	BB	5'10	150	22		
Paul Ziegler	FB-TB-WB	5'10	185	23		
Emmett Ruh	WB	5'8	168	29	1	6
Walt Rogers	FB	5'9	215	29		

Substitutes

Use Name	Pos.	Hgt.	Wgt.	Age	Int.	Pts.
Burl Atcheson	E			20		
Earl Kreiger	E-FB	5'11	185	26	1	
Pete Schultz	FB		188			

Scores of each game

Date	Pts.	Opponent	Pts.
Oct. 1	0	Akron	36
Oct. 8	6	Oorang	20
Oct. 15	0	Buffalo	19
Oct. 29	6	Chic. Cards	37
Nov. 5	6	Green Bay	3
Nov. 11	0	Racine	34
Nov. 26	6	Toledo	7
Nov. 30	6	OORANG	18

NAME	RUSHING									PASSING													
	Complete Games					Incom. Games				Complete Games								Incom. Games					
	G	Att.	Yds.	Avg.	TD	G	Att.	Yds.	TD	G	Com.	Att.	%	Yds.	Y/A	TD	Int.	G	Com.	Att.	Yds.	TD	Int.
MILWAUKEE																							
Conzelman (2)	2	27	104	3.9		1	1	6		2	8	26	31	75	2.9	1	1	1	0	1			1
Pollard	1	7	12	1.7		6	12	62	3	1								6	2	6	22		1
Doane	2	11	17	1.5		7	6	11	1	2								7	1	1	0		
Purdy	2	6	7	1.2		7	5	30		2								7	2	3	32		
Monney	2	2	4	2.0		3																	
Collins	2	1	3	3.0		1																	
McMillin	1	4	-1	-0.2		1	1	2		1	4	12	33	44	3.7		2	1	2	2	41	1	
King (1)						4	2	1															
Robeson																							
Green																							
Fallon																							
Alexander																							
Seasholtz																							
Pierotti																							
Team	2	58	146	2.5		7				2	12	38	32	119	3.1	1	3	7					
Opp.	2	92	362	3.9	6	7				2	8	20	40	147	7.4		2	7					
OORANG																							
Guyon	3	33	214	6.5	2	6	2	7	1	3	5	15	33	101	6.7		4	6	2	2	53		
Eagle Feather	2	18	108	6.0	1	5																	
Calac	3	3	6	2.0		6	5	83	2														
Thorpe						4	11	83	3									4	7	7	148	1	
Attache	3	18	56	3.1		4																	
Sanooke	3	4	4	1.0		6																	
Team	3	76	388	5.1	3	6				3	5	15	33	101	6.7		4	6					
Opp.	3	102	478	4.7	9	6				3	14	28	50	289	10.3	1	3	6					
MINNEAPOLIS																							
Norton						3	6	106	2														
Sampson						3	1	5															
Christianson						4	1	5															
Cleve						4	1	4															
Mason						2	1	4															
Irgens																		4	1	1	40	1	
Team						4												4					
Opp.						4												4					
LOUISVILLE																							
Padan						3	1	8															
Boldt						4	2	7	1														
Van Dyke						3	1	6	1														
Team						4												4					
Opp.						4												4					
ROCHESTER																							
King (2)	2	16	35	2.2		1	3	45															
Wynne	2	20	78	3.9						2	5	15	33	78	5.2		3						
Argus	2	13	27	2.1		3	4	16	1														
Anderson (1)	2	1	0	0.0		1																	
Wilson (2)	1	1	0	0.0		1																	
Weltman	1	2	-4	-2.0		3				1								4	2	2	50	1	
Witter																		1	0	1			
Lowery																							
Roy																							
Bentz																							
Meyers																							
Team	2	53	136	2.6		3				2	5	15	33	78	5.2		3	3					
Opp.	2	122	502	4.1	4	3				2	8	15	53	96	6.4		2	3					
HAMMOND																							
Sullivan (3)	1	7	19	2.7		1				1	1	12	8	6	0.5		4	1					
Shelbourne	1	10	16	1.6		5																	
Cearing	1	2	2	1.0		5				1	0	3	0				1	5					
Hess																							
Team	1	19	37	1.9		5				1	1	15	7	6	0.4		5	5					
Opp.	1	65	233	3.6		5				1	6	10	60	32	3.2	1	1	5					
EVANSVILLE																							
Sullivan (2)	1	9	12	1.3																			
Rork	1	1	0	0.0		1																	
Fausch	1	2	-6	-3.0		2				1	3	7	43	52	7.4		2	2	1	1	15	1	
Sanders																							
Slyker																							
Bondurant																							
Team	1	12	6	0.5		2				1	3	7	43	52	7.4		2	2					
Opp.	1	66	396	6.0	9	2				1	6	11	55	119	10.8			2					
COLUMBUS																							
Rapp	2	7	42	6.0		5	1	16	1	2								5	1	1	10		
Nesser	2	13	26	2.0		6	2	23		2	1	3	33	23	7.7		1	6	3	6	60		2
Wiper	1	4	40	10.0		1																	
Rogers	1	4	25	6.3		2																	
Snoots	2	10	28	2.8		5	2	-8	1	2	1	6	17	33	5.5		1	5	1	1	45	1	
E. Ruh	2	7	16	2.3	1	5																	
Gaulke	1	5	16	3.2		6				1								6	2	2	60		
Krieger	1	2	9	4.5		3																	
Glassman										2								4	1	1	6		
H. Ruh																							
Hopkins																							
Gump																							
Team	2	52	202	3.9	1	6				2	2	9	22	56	6.2		2	6					
Opp.	2	101	692	6.9	8	6				2	4	11	36	43	3.9		2	6					

NAME	RECEIVING									PUNTING						PUNT RETURNS								
	Complete Games					Incom. Games				Comp. Games			Incom. Games			Complete Games					Incom. Games			
	G	Rec.	Yds	Avg.	TD	G	Rec.	Yds.	TD	G	No.	Avg.	G	No.	Avg.	G	No.	Yds.	Avg.	TD	G	No.	Yds.	TD
MILWAUKEE																								
Conzelman (2)	2	1	3	3.0		1				2	21	30.6	1	1	0.0	2	4	49	12.3		1			
Pollard	1					6	2	43								1					6	2	22	
Doane	2	1	23	23.0		7	1	15																
Purdy																								
Monney	2	2	16	8.0		3																		
Collins	2	1	8	8.0		1																		
McMillin	1	3	42	14.0	1	1																		
King (1)																								
Robeson	1	2	9	4.5		6	3	63	1															
Green						2	1	12																
Fallon	2	1	10	10.0		5																		
Alexander	1	1	8	8.0		7																		
Seasholtz						4	1	0																
Pierotti										2	2	53.5	7											
Team										2	23	32.6	7			2	4	49	12.3		7			
Opp.										2	19	31.0	7			2	7	110	15.7		7			
OORANG																								
Guyon	3					6	5	113	1	2	14	37.2	7	3	5.0									
Eagle Feather	2					5	1	30																
Calac	3	4	81	20.3		6	2	35																
Thorpe																								
Attache																								
Sanooke	3	1	20	20.0		6	1	23																
Team										2	14	37.2	7								9			
Opp.										2	6	44.8	7								9			
MINNEAPOLIS																								
Norton																								
Sampson																								
Christianson																								
Cleve						4	1	40	1															
Mason																								
Irgens																								
Team													4								4			
Opp.													4								4			
LOUISVILLE																								
Padan													4	2	35.0									
Boldt																								
Van Dyke																								
Team													4								4			
Opp.													4								4			
ROCHESTER																								
King (2)																								
Wynne										2	16	35.8												
Argus																								
Anderson (1)	2	3	57	19.0		1																		
Wilson (2)																								
Weltman																								
Witter																								
Lowery	1					4	1	30																
Roy						4	1	20	1															
Bentz	1	1	15	15.0																				
Meyers	1	1	6	6.0												1	1	5	5.0					
Team										2	16	35.8	3			2	1	5	5.0		3			
Opp.										2	6	22.2				2	6	67	11.2		3			
HAMMOND																								
Sullivan (3)										1	13	34.6	1			1					1			
Shelbourne																								
Cearing	1	1	6	6.0		5				1			5	1	45.0									
Hess										1			5	4	19.3									
Team										1	13	34.6	5			1	0				5			
Opp.										1	8	29.5	5			1	2	15	7.5		5			
EVANSVILLE																								
Sullivan (2)	1	1	27	27.0						1	7	24.9				1	1	15	15.0					
Rork																								
Fausch																								
Sanders	1	1	20	20.0		1																		
Slyker						1	1	15	1															
Bondurant	1	1	5	5.0		2																		
Team										1	7	24.9	2			1	1	15	15.0		2			
Opp.										1	1	51.0	2			1	1	25	25.0		2			
COLUMBUS																								
Rapp																								
Nesser	2					6	1	45	1	2	10	32.1	6			1	1	30	30.0					
Wiper						1	1	20																
Rogers										1	1	34.0	2											
Snoots	2					5	1	15																
E. Ruh	2	1	23	23.0		5																		
Gaulke	1					6	1	25																
Krieger																								
Glassman																								
H. Ruh	2	1	33	33.0		5	2	58																
Hopkins	2					2	1	12																
Gump	1					2	1	6																
Team										2	11	32.3	6			1	1	30	30.0		7			
Opp.										2	8	36.9	6			1	4	54	13.5		7			

1923 N.F.L.
Another Year Without A Loss

The National Football League began showing the signs of real stability in 1923. Of the 18 teams of the previous season, only Evansville failed to answer the starting gun. Three new teams in Duluth, St. Louis and Cleveland brought league membership up to 20. As soon as the new members were safely ensconced on the roll, they voted with the old members to raise the franchise fee to $500 and upped league dues to $140 per year. After all, they had to pay Joe Carr's salary and, with a raise, the league president was all the way up to $1,000 a year — about the same as an average tackle could earn in a season. Carr. re-elected again with no opposition, led a movement to put some boundaries on the championship race. A beginning date for the 1923 season was placed at September 30, although no ending date was set. Additionally, to be considered for the league championship, a team had to play at least seven games with at least seven different clubs. Teams still arranged their own schedules, but their slates became more varied and weak teams were better able to schedule lucrative games with some of the stronger clubs. Seven teams — Duluth, Rock Island, Minneapolis, St. Louis, Akron, Louisville and Rochester — did not fulfill the criteria to be eligible for the championship in 1923, but that was academic because the most visible sign of stability was the dominance of the Canton Bulldogs.

With an unbeaten season behind them, the Bulldogs looked even stronger this year. Star linemen Guy Chamberlin, Pete Henry, Link Lyman and Duke Osborn had rookie help in guard Rudy Comstock and center Larry Conover. The makeshift backfield of 1922 was gone, replaced by a mixture of veteran and youthful talent. Lou Smyth took charge at tailback and repeated Jimmy Conzelman's 1922 feat of leading the league in both rushing and passing touchdowns. It has never been done since. Canton's fullback position was shared by rookie Ben Jones and second-year man Doc Elliott. Harry Robb switched to blocking back and alternated with Wooky Roberts, and Tex Grigg, a veteran of the Thorpe years, returned to the starting lineup at wingback. This unit added depth and flexibility to the offense, with Smyth's passing giving the attack a new dimension. As coach, Chamberlin had a valuable new asset when the husky Pete Henry blossomed into a fine dropkicker and punter; the big tackle led the NFL in extra points and was second in field goals.

The Bulldogs marched to a second straight undefeated championship, three times whipping unbeaten challengers in games on the road. After three shutout victories at home, the Bulldogs faced their first big challenge by playing the Bears in Wrigley Field on October 21. George Halas had strengthened his squad by obtaining tackle Ed Healey, a future Hall of Famer, from Rock Island during the previous season. Nevertheless, the Bears had dropped a 3-0 decision to the Independents in Rock Island to open the season. Three weeks later, the Bears were looking to bring the Bulldogs back into the pack. Both clubs played stellar defense in a scoreless first half. In the second half, Smyth began passing the ball more often and moved the Bulldogs close to allow two Henry field goals in the final quarter for a 6-0 triumph. In addition to losing the final game, the Bears also lost tackle Hugh Blacklock for the season with a broken leg.

The Bulldogs followed up by beating Akron 7-3 the next week. The Pros had a weak squad, but were on their way to an upset until Henry put them deep in a hole with an 85-yard punt. Canton took Akron's poor return punt and drove for the winning touchdown. On November 4, the Bulldogs encountered their second serious obstacle of the campaign, a game against the Chicago Cardinals in Comiskey Park. The Cardinals came into the contest at 5-0, having allowed only three points in those games. Paddy Driscoll handed the coaching duties over to Arnie Horween this year, but both men continued to shine in the Chicago backfield. Driscoll led the NFL in scoring with 78 points and topped everyone in field goals with 10. Before 6,000 fans huddled in a rainstorm, Driscoll put the Cardinals ahead 3-0 in the first quarter with a 47-yard dropkick. The Bulldogs bogged down on offense until the final period when Smyth completed several passes and capped a drive with a short plunge into the endzone. Henry's extra point made the score 7-3, and the final gun sounded without any further scoring.

With both Chicago teams knocked into the ranks of the beaten, the Bulldogs barely avoided that fate themselves on November 11 at Buffalo. The lackluster All-Americans had the Bulldogs beaten 3-0 with about one

1923 STANDINGS

	W	L	T	Pct.	Pts.	Opp. Pts.	Avg. Pts.	Opp. Avg.
Canton Bulldogs	11	0	1	1.000	246	19	21	2
Chicago Bears	9	2	2	.818	130	42	10	3
Green Bay Packers	7	2	1	.778	85	34	9	3
Milwaukee Badgers	7	2	4	.778	107	56	8	4
Cleveland Indians	3	1	3	.750	52	49	7	7
Chicago Cardinals	8	4	0	.667	161	56	13	5
Duluth Kelleys	4	3	0	.571	35	33	5	5
Columbus Tigers	5	4	1	.555	119	35	12	4
Buffalo All-Americans	5	4	3	556	94	43	8	4
Racine Legion	4	4	2	.500	86	76	9	8
Toledo Maroons	3	3	2	.500	41	66	5	8
Rock Island Independents	2	3	3	.400	84	62	11	8
Minneapolis Marines	2	5	2	.286	48	81	5	9
St. Louis All-Stars	1	4	2	.200	14	39	2	6
Hammond Pros	1	5	1	.167	14	59	2	8
Dayton Triangles	1	6	1	.143	16	95	2	12
Akron Pros	1	6	0	.143	25	74	4	11
Oorang Indians (Marion,O.)(R)	1	10	0	.091	50	257	5	23
Louisville Brecks	0	3	0	.000	0	90	0	30
Rochester Jeffersons	0	4	0	.000	6	141	2	35

(R) — played only road games

Scoring Leaders

Driscoll	ChiC	78
Henry	Can	59
D. Sternaman	ChiB	52
Winkelman	Mil	45
Gillo	Rac	44
Smyth	Can	42
Tehell	Col	37
Elliott	Can	36
Jones	Can	36
J. Sternaman	Dul-ChiB	34
Morrissey	Buf	31
Rapp	Col	30
Conzelman	Mil	26
Bryan	ChiB	24
Giaver	RI	24
Grigg	Can	24
Kuehl	RI	24
Buck	GB	23

KICKING

		FG	Att	Pct			FG	Att	Pct
Driscoll	ChiC	10	14	71	Brenkert	Akr	0	1	0
Henry	Can	9	25	36	Casey	StL	0	1	0
Gillo	Rac	8	20	40	Crangle	ChiC	0	1	0
Morrissey	Buf	8	18	44	DeClerk	RI	0	1	0
J. Sternaman	Dul-ChiB	6	12	50	Fetz	ChiB	0	1	0
Winkelman	Mil	6	16	38	Mathys	GB	0	1	0
Buck	GB	6	16	38	Roberts	Akr	0	1	0
D. Sternaman	ChiB	5	20	25	Scott	Buf	0	1	0
Tebell	Col	4	14	29	Sheard	Roch	0	1	0
Hathaway	Day	3	5	60	Simpson	StL	0	1	0
Kaplan	Min	3	7	43	Winters	Col	0	2	0
Sies	RI	3	10	30	Goebel	Col	0	2	0
A. Horween	ChiC	2	2	100	Hill	Tol	0	2	0
Keck	Cle	2	3	67	Larson	Ham	0	2	0
McNamara	Tol	1	1	100	King	StL	0	3	0
Hughitt	Buf	1	2	50	Milton	StL	0	3	0
Michaels	Akr	1	3	33	Sonnenberg	Col-Buf	0	3	0
Jim Thorpe	Oor	1	8	13	Lambeau	GB	0	4	0
					Conzelman	Mil	0	10	0

		PAT	Att	Pct			PAT	Att	Pct
Henry	Can	25	30	83	Conover	Can	1	1	100
Winkelman	Mil	9	10	90	Hathaway	Day	1	1	100
Gillo	Rac	8	9	89	Hendrian	Akr-Can	1	1	100
Sies	RI	8	10	80	Pollard	Ham	1	1	100
Morrissey	Buf	7	9	78	Robinson	Ham	1	1	100
Tebell	Col	7	11	64	Scott	ChiB	1	1	100
D. Sternaman	ChiB	7	12	58	Voss	Tol	1	1	100
Driscoll	ChiC	6	7	86	Keck	Cle	1	2	50
Buck	GB	5	8	63	King	ChiC	1	2	50
J. Sternman	Dul-ChiB	4	6	67	Roby	Cle	1	2	50
A. Horween	ChiC	3	4	75	Watson	Tol	1	2	50
Kaplan	Min	3	6	50	Crangle	ChiC	1	3	33
Goebel	Col	2	2	100	McLemore	Oor	1	3	33
King	StL	2	2	100	Brenkert	Akr	0	1	0
Weaver	Col	2	2	100	Earpe	GB	0	1	0
Conzelman	Mil	2	3	67	Hughitt	Buf	0	1	0
Tanner	Cle	2	3	67	Lambeau	GB	0	1	0
					Little Twig	Oor	0	1	0
					Sonnenberg	Col	0	1	0
					Welsh	Roch	0	1	0

CANTON BULLDOGS 11-0-1 Guy Chamberlin

Regulars

UseName	Pos.	Hgt.	Wgt.	Age	Int.	Pts.
Bird Carroll	E	5'8	185	27		13
Guy Chamberlin	E	6'2	190	29	1	12
Pete Henry	T	5'11	245	25		58
Link Lyman	T	6'2	225	24		6
Rudy Comstock	G	5'10	205	22		
Duke Osborn	G	5'10	190	26		
Larry Conover	C	5'10	190	29	6	
Harry Robb	BB-TB	5'10	185	26	2	6
Lou Smyth	TB	6'1	200	24	6	42
Tex Grigg	WB-TB	5'11	190	32	2	24
Ben Jones	FB	5'11	200	23	2	36

Substitutes

UseName	Pos.	Hgt.	Wgt.	Age	Int.	Pts.
Vern Mullen	E	6'	185	23	1	
Joe Williams	G-E	6'	235	25	1	
Russ Smith (to MIL)	G	5'10	220	27		
Ben Shaw	G	5'10	190	29		
Dutch Speck	C-G	5'10	220	37		
Wooky Roberts	BB	5'7	160	25	2	6
Ben Roderick (to BUF)	WB-TB	5'9	175	23		
Dutch Hendrian (from AKR)	WB-FB	5'9	180	26		6
Doc Elliott	FB	5'10	210	23	1	36

Scores of each game

Date	Pts.	Opponent	Pts.
Sep. 30	17	HAMMOND	0
Oct. 7	37	LOUISVILLE	0
Oct. 14	30	DAYTON	0
Oct. 21	6	Chic. Bears	0
Oct. 28	7	AKRON	3
Nov. 4	7	Chic. Cards	3
Nov. 11	3	Buffalo	3
Nov. 18	41	OORANG	0
Nov. 25	46	Cleveland	10
Nov. 29	28	TOLEDO	0
Dec. 2	14	BUFFALO	0
Dec. 9	10	Columbus	0

CHICAGO BEARS 9-2-2 George Halas

Regulars

UseName	Pos.	Hgt.	Wgt.	Age	Int.	Pts.
George Halas	E	6'	182	28	2	6
Duke Hanny	E	6'	195	25	2	6
Ralph Scott	T	6'2	234	25		1
Ed Healey	T-G	6'1	210	28		
Hec Garvey	G-E	6'1	228	23		
Hunk Anderson (to & from CLE)	G-C	5'11	190	24		
George Trafton	C	6'2	230	26	2	
Johnny Bryan	QB-HB	5'8	165	26	4	24
Dutch Sternaman	HB	5'8	180	28	1	52
Jake Lanum	HB	6'	190	26		6
Oscar Knop (from HAM)	FB	6'	190	28	4	12

Substitutes

UseName	Pos.	Hgt.	Wgt.	Age	Int.	Pts.
Jim Flaherty	E-HB		198	27		
Hugh Blacklock	T	6'	220	32		
Lou Usher (from HAM)	T-G	6'2	245	25		
Joe LaFleur	G-FB-C-HB	6'	224	27	1	
Frank Rydzewski (to HAM)	C	6'1	220	30		
Joey Sternaman (from DUL)	QB	5'6	150	23	1	17
Gus Fetz	HB		158	23		6
George Bolan	FB-HB	5'11	204	26	2	

Scores of each game

Date	Pts.	Opponent	Pts.
Sep. 30	0	Rock Island	3
Oct. 7	3	Racine	0
Oct. 14	3	Green Bay	0
Oct. 21	0	CANTON	6
Oct. 28	18	BUFFALO	3
Nov. 4	26	OORANG	0
Nov. 11	20	AKRON	6
Nov. 18	7	ROCK ISLAND	3
Nov. 25	14	HAMMOND	7
Nov. 29	3	CHIC. CARDS	0
Dec. 2	0	MILWAUKEE	0
Dec. 9	29	ROCK ISLAND	7
Dec. 16	7	MILWAUKEE	7

minute left to play. Tommy Hughitt attempted a punt from deep in his own territory but it was blocked by Henry. The tackle then drove a dropkick through the crossbars as the clock wound down to salvage a 3-3 tie, the only time Canton did not win this season.

After that close call, the Bulldogs bore down and massacred the Oorang Indians 41-0 at Canton on November 18. The next week brought the Canton squad face to face with the only other undefeated team, the Cleveland Indians. Former Bulldog Cap Edwards coached the newly formed Indians and built a strong defense which kept the team alive despite an anemic offense. After six games, the Indians had three victories and three ties; they posted shutouts in their first five games, but won only two of them, the other three being scoreless ties. In their sixth contest, with center Guy intercepting four passes (a league record), they could still only defeat a very ordinary Columbus team 9-3. The caliber of opponent which Cleveland had faced was generally weak and, if the Indians stood on a par with the Bulldogs, it was only on paper. The Bulldogs destroyed the Cleveland defense and coasted to a decisive 46-10 romp. Elliot ran for three touchdowns and Smyth for two to lead the scoring. The sole consolation for Cleveland was John Kyle's touchdown run, the only touchdown scored on the Bulldogs all season.

The rest of the way to the championship was easy. The Bulldogs entertained the Toledo Maroons, last year's unexpected contender, on Thanksgiving Day and whipped them 28-0. After shutout victories over Buffalo and Columbus, Chamberlin and the Bulldogs could relax with their second straight title.

Two strong contenders from Wisconsin never played the Bulldogs, but had records good enough to rank third and fourth in the league. The Green Bay Packers jumped to a 7-2-1 record using a passing attack built around Curly Lambeau and a strong line geaturing giant tackles Cub Buck and Jug Earpe. The Packers hosted the Bears for the first time ever on October 13 and dropped a hard-fought 3-0 game before a record crowd of 5,000. The only other Green Bay loss of the year came on October 28 when the Racine Legion, another Wisconsin club, capitalized on three Shorty Barr touchdown passes to post a 24-3 upset. The *Green Bay Press Gazette* published play-by-play accounts of all the Packers' games this season, from which we can get out first statistical look at a complete season for an NFL team of this period. The Packers, who passed more often than most NFL teams, threw about once to every three rushes. Although Lambeau was regarded as one of the top passers in the league, he still completed only 36 percent of his tosses, and he had 17 of his 118 attempts intercepted while only three went for touchdowns. Short passes into the endzone were generally avoided, of course, because of the rule that turned the ball over to the opponent on an endzone incompletion. Cub Buck completed 8 of 11 passes throwing from punt formation as a surprise play. Blocking back Charlie Mathys caught half of the Packers' completions, an amazing-for-the-time total of 33. In addition to the season records, the play-by-plays reveal two exceptional performances. On November 4, playing in a sea of mud at St. Louis, Buck made 19 punts (the official NFL record record is 14) for 687 yards and booted a 28-yard field goal for the only points in the Packers' 3-0 win. One week later, at Racine, the Packers neutralized Shorty Barr's passes by staying on the ground themselves and controlling the football. They made 70 rushing attempts (the NFL record is 72), with three backs carrying more than 20 times each, on their way to a 16-0 victory.

The Packers were joined in their move into contender status by the Milwaukee Badgers. In their second NFL season, the Badgers converted a strong defense into a 7-2-3 record. Coach Jimmy Conzelman saw his team twice lose to the Packers, yet tie the Bears and beat the Cardinals in Chicago on back-to-back Sundays in December. Although the Badgers would relapse into mediocrity after this season, the Packers would not have a losing season for 10 years.

Plenty of losing went on at the bottom of the standings. The Louisville Brecks played three games and lost all three by shutouts. The Rochester Jeffersons lost all four of their league games, including 60-0 to the Cardinals on October 7 and 56-0 to Rock Island a week later. Somewhat sad visitors to the depths were the Oorang Indians. Jim Thorpe played the entire schedule at tailback until missing the final two games with an ankle injury, but his flickering flame could not ignite any drive in the Indian squad. The team dragged through nine straight losses, scoring only 12 points. Most embarassing were a 57-0 beating at Buffalo on October 21 and a 41-0 drubbing by the Bulldogs in front of Thorpe's former hometown fans in Canton. With Joe Guyon signing on for the final four games of the season, things gradually improved. The Cardinals handed the team its 10th straight defeat but had to battle to take a 22-19 decision from the aroused Indians in Chicago on December 2 and, one week later, the Indians ended their schedule with a 12-0 victory over the even more pitiful Louisville Brecks. Thorpe's major impact on the record books this season came in a game against the Bears on November 4. With the Indians on the verge of a touchdown, Thorpe fumbled a bad snap which George Halas scooped up on the two-yard line and carried 98 yards for a touchdown, a record return spurred by Thorpe's furious pursuit every step of the way.

The *Green Bay Press Gazette* conducted its first poll to select an all-NFL team after this season. The team was chosen by a panel of sportswriters from most of the league cities. Eventually, the selectors would include coaches and league officials. In 1931, the league would legitimize the *Press Gazette* poll by making it the official all-league team. The selections for the 1923 season were: ends Inky Williams, Hammond, and Gus Tebell, Columbus; tackles Ed Healey, Bears, and Pete Henry, Canton; guards Swede Youngstrom, Buffalo, and Bub Weller, St. Louis; center Harry Mehre, Minneapolis; quarterback Paddy Driscoll, Cardinals; halfbacks Jim Thorpe, Oorang, and Al Michaels, Akron; and fullback Doc Elliot, Canton. Coaches Guy Chamberlin of Canton, Jimmy Conzelman of Milwaukee and Curly Lambeau of Green Bay were all named to the second team.

NAME	RUSHING									PASSING													
	Complete Games					Incom. Games				Complete Games								Incom. Games					
	G	Att.	Yds.	Avg.	TD	G	Att.	Yds.	TD	G	Com.	Att.	%	Yds.	Y/A	TD	Int	G	Com.	Att.	Yds.	TD	Int
CANTON																							
Grigg	7	60	282	4.7	1	5	18	157	2	11	11	43	26	177	4.1	1	7	1					
Smyth	7	61	240	3.9	6	5	26	158	1	11	25	101	25	559	5.5	6	12	1	2	2	35		
Robb	7	66	314	4.8	1	4	9	75		10	4	10	40	28	2.8		2	1					
Jones	7	66	252	3.8	6	5	20	83		11	1	2	50	26	13.0								
Elliott	4	37	148	4.0	5	5	15	95	1														
Roderick (1)	1	5	5	1.0		3	12	101															
Roberts	5	6	15	2.5		3	2	23	1														
Henry	7	2	11	5.5		5	3	18		11	1	6	17	18	3.0		1	1					
Hendrian (2)	4	8	27	3.4	1					4	0	1	0										
Lyman	7					5	3	8															
Chamberlin	7	1	1	1.0		5	2	5															
Carroll	5					4	1	-1															
Mullen																							
Team	7	313	1300	4.2	20	5				11	41	162	25	803	5.0	7	22	1					
Opp.	7	180	306	1.7	1	5				11	40	166	24	470	2.8		25	1					
CHICAGO BEARS																							
Bryan	5	46	172	3.7	2	8	6	84	2	5	12	34	35	187	5.5		6	8	11	13	173	2	
D. Sternaman	4	44	126	2.9	1	8	14	91	3	4	1	4	25	7	1.8		2	8					
J. Sternaman (2)	1	15	54	3.6	1	3	9	99	1	1	0	1	0					3	1	2	13		1
Bolan	5	37	93	2.5		6	2	18															
Lanum	4	28	67	2.4		6	2	9	1														
Knop	2	18	36	2.0		7	3	12	1														
LaFleur	4	9	21	2.3		6																	
Hanny	4	4	12	3.0		8																	
Fetz	3	3	10	3.3		6	1	3	1														
Halas	5	2	7	3.5		8																	
Trafton										5								8	1	1	15		
Garvey																							
Team	5	206	598	2.9	4	8				5	13	39	33	194	5.0		8	8					
Opp.	5	129	338	2.6		8				5	35	92	38	378	4.1	1	13	8					

NAME	RECEIVING									PUNTING						PUNT RETURNS								
	Complete Games					Incom. Games				Comp. Games			Incom. Games			Complete Games					Incom. Games			
	G	Rec.	Yds.	Avg.	TD	G	Rec.	Yds.	TD	G	No.	Avg.	G	No.	Avg.	G	Rec.	Yds.	Avg.	TD	G	Rec.	Yds.	TD
CANTON																								
Grigg	10	3	33	11.0	1	2	2	35								7	1	20	20.0		5			
Smyth	10	1	18	18.0		2										7	2	18	9.0		5			
Robb	9	0	8			2										7	12	140	11.7		4			
Jones	10	1	2	2.0		2				7	1	43.0	5											
Elliott																								
Roderick (1)	4	1	40	40.0						1			3	1	19.0	1					3	1	15	
Roberts	8	6	86	14.3						5	11	35.8	3	3	29.0	5	8	116	14.5		3			
Henry	10	1	32	32.0	1	2				7	47	39.1	5	4	43.5									
Hendrian (2)																								
Lyman	10	2	77	38.5	1	2																		
Chamberlin	10	13	340	26.2	2	2																		
Carroll	8	9	127	14.1	2	1	1	6																
Mullen	3	1	8	8.0		1																		
Team										7	59	38.6	5			7	23	294	12.8		5			
Opp.										7	74	34.4	5			7	8	103	12.9		5			
CHICAGO BEARS																								
Bryan	5	1	7	7.0		8				5	2	40.5	8			5	1	2	2.0		8			
D. Sternaman	4	3	46	15.3		8	4	55	1	4	2	20.0	8			4	5	43	8.6		8			
J. Sternaman (2)	1					3	1	10								1	1	6	6.0		3			
Bolan										5	1	30.0	6											
Lanum										4	7	36.1	6											
Knop																								
LaFleur										4	4	28.8	6											
Hanny	4	1	18	18.0		8	3	70	1	4	23	34.4	8											
Fetz	3					6	2	33		3	1	35.0	6			3	1	2	2.0		6			
Halas	5	6	78	13.0		8	3	33								5	2	7	3.5		8			
Trafton	5	1	10	10.0		8																		
Garvey	5	1	35	35.0		8																		
Team										5	40	33.6	8			5	10	60	6.0		8			
Opp.										5	40	33.8	8			5	12	156	13.0		8			

GREEN BAY PACKERS 7-2-1 Curly Lambeau

Regulars

Use Name	Pos.	Hgt.	Wgt.	Age	Int.	Pts.
Cowboy Wheeler	E	5'9	180	25	1	6
Norb Hayes	E	5'11	175	26	2	
Cub Buck	T	6'	265	31	3	23
Jug Earp	T-C	6'	225	26		
Whitey Woodin	G	5'10	205	28		
Moose Gardner	G	6'1	220	29		
Wally Niemann	C	5'10	180	29	2	
Charlie Mathys	BB	5'7	165	26	4	6
Curly Lambeau	TB	5'10	185	25	4	18
Myrt Basing	HB-TB	5'9	180	22	3	12
Buck Gavin	FB-TB	5'10	180	28	1	

Substitutes

Use Name	Pos.	Hgt.	Wgt.	Age	Int.	Pts.
Wes Leaper	E	5'11	175	27		
Jack Gray (from StL)	E		175			
Jab Murray	E-T	6'1	220	30	1	
Dewey Lyle	G-E-T	5'11	200	32		
Stan Mills	HB-FB-TB	5'9	180	29	1	18
Hal Hansen	FB	5'10	200	30		

Scores of each game

Date	Pts.	Opponent	Pts.
Sep. 30	12	MINNEAPOLIS	0
Oct. 7	0	ST. LOUIS	0
Oct. 14	0	CHIC. BEARS	3
Oct. 21	12	MILWAUKEE	0
Oct. 28	3	RACINE	24
Nov. 4	3	St. Louis	0
Nov. 11	16	Racine	0
Nov. 18	10	Milwaukee	7
Nov. 25	10	DULUTH	0
Nov. 29	19	HAMMOND	0

MILWAUKEE BADGERS 7-2-4 Jimmy Conzelman

Regulars

Use Name	Pos.	Hgt.	Wgt.	Age	Int.	Pts.
Lenny Sachs	E	5'8	175	26	1	6
Ben Winkelman	E-WB-BB	6'1	190	24	1	45
Russ Blailock	T	5'10	225	21	1	6
Ad Wenke	T	6'4	220	25		
John Underwood	G	6'3	265	23	1	
Russ Smith (from CAN)	G	5'10	220	27	1	
Ojay Larson	C	6'1	198	25		
Marv Mattox	BB-G	5'9	175	23		
Jimmy Conzelman	TB-BB	6'	170	25	3	26
Hal Erickson	WB-FB	5'9	190	24		6
Dinger Doane	FB	5'10	190	28	1	12

Substitutes

Use Name	Pos.	Hgt.	Wgt.	Age	Int.	Pts.
George Mooney	E-BB-FB	5'8	165	27	1	
Dick Reichle	E	6'	185	26		
Roy Vassau	T	6'	220	29		
Chet Widerquist	T	6'1	220	27		
Larry McGinnis	G-E	6'1	210	25	1	
Peaches Nadolney	G	5'10	210	24		
Al Pierotti (to & from RAC)	C	5'10	200	27		
Jim Turner	BB	5'8	165	24		6
Bo McMillin (from CLE)	TB	5'9	155	28		
Frank Jordan	WB		168	25		
Johnny Milton (to StL)	E	5'8	175	24		
Jim Dooley	G	6'	210	27		
Bill Strickland	G		190	24		
Ed Rate	BB	5'9	170	24		

Scores of each game

Date	Pts.	Opponent	Pts.
Sep. 30	13	OORANG	2
Oct. 7	0	COLUMBUS	0
Oct. 14	7	RACINE	7
Oct. 21	0	Green Bay	12
Oct. 28	6	ST. LOUIS	0
Nov. 4	14	Rock Island	3
Nov. 11	6	DULUTH	3
Nov. 18	7	GREEN BAY	10
Nov. 24	17	St. Louis	0
Nov. 29	16	Racine	0
Dec. 2	0	Chic. Bears	0
Dec. 9	14	Chic. Cards	12
Dec. 16	7	Chic. Bears	7

CLEVELAND INDIANS 3-1-3 Cap Edwards

Regulars

Use Name	Pos.	Hgt.	Wgt.	Age	Int.	Pts.
Scotty Bierce (to BUF)	E	5'9	165	26		12
Joe Work	E	5'10	177	23		
Rosey Rosatti	T	6'	210	27		
Iolas Huffman	T-G	5'11	225	25		
Ed Johns	G	6'	175	23		
Ralph Vince	G	5'8	175	23		
Charlie Guy	C	6'	170	26	6	
Pete Bahan (to BUF)	BB	5'9	165	25	2	
Doug Roby	TB	5'10	190	25	3	7
Deke Edler	WB	5'9	170	25		6
Johnny Kyle	FB	5'9	214	24		6

Substitutes

Use Name	Pos.	Hgt.	Wgt.	Age	Int.	Pts.
Frank Garden	E	5'11	190	25		
Truck Myers	E	6'	175	26		
Stan Keck	T-G	5'11	205	25		7
Cap Edwards	T-G	6'	210	35		
Hal Ebersole	G	6'3	190	23		
Hunk Anderson (from & to ChiB)	G	5'11	190	24	1	
John Tanner	BB-WB	5'5	165	23	1	8
Sol Weinberg	TB	5'10	165	27		
Frank Civiletto	WB	5'9	180	26		
Dick Wolf	FB-WB	5'8	160	23		6
Joe Setron	G	5'9	195	22		
Pete Stinchcomb (from COL)	WB	5'8	155	28		
Lou Partlow (from & to DAY)	FB-WB	6'1	170	30		
Bo McMillin (to MIL)	WB	5'9	155	28		
Arda Bowser	FB	6'2	210	24		

Scores of each game

Date	Pts.	Opponent	Pts.
Oct. 7	0	Rock Island	0
Oct. 21	6	ST. LOUIS	0
Oct. 28	27	OORANG	0
Nov. 4	0	BUFFALO	0
Nov. 11	0	DAYTON	0
Nov. 18	9	COLUMBUS	3
Nov. 25	10	CANTON	46

CHICAGO CARDINALS 8-4-0 Arnie Horween

Regulars

Use Name	Pos.	Hgt.	Wgt.	Age	Int.	Pts.
Roger Kiley	E	6'	180	22		6
Eddie Anderson	E	5'10	175	22		6
Sully Montgomery	T	6'3	210	22	1	
Fred Gillies	T	6'3	215	27		
Willie Brennan	G-T	6'	210	29		
Clyde Zoia	G	5'7	175	27		
Nick McInerney	C	6'2	200	27		
Paddy Driscoll	TB-BB	5'8	160	28	2	78
Johnny Mohardt	TB-WB	5'10	165	25	1	6
Ralph Horween	WB-BB-FB	5'10	200	27		12
Bob Koehler	FB-WB	5'11	185	29		6

Substitutes

Use Name	Pos.	Hgt.	Wgt.	Age	Int.	Pts.
Egan	E		175			
John Leonard	T	6'2	200	27		
Wilfred Smith (to & from & to HAM)	G-T-E	6'4	200	24		
Garland Buckeye	G	6'	235	25		
Bill Whalen	C-G	5'7	165	22		
Arnie Horween	BB-FB-T	5'11	210	25	1	9
Rip King	TB-WB-FB	6'1	205	26		7
Art Folz	BB-TB-WB	5'7	155	20		7
Jack Crangle	FB-WB	6'1	200	24	1	18

Scores of each game

Date	Pts.	Opponent	Pts.
Sep. 30	3	BUFFALO	0
Oct. 7	60	ROCHESTER	0
Oct. 14	19	AKRON	0
Oct. 21	9	MINNEAPOLIS	0
Oct. 28	13	DAYTON	3
Nov. 4	3	CANTON	7
Nov. 11	6	HAMMOND	0
Nov. 18	10	DULUTH	0
Nov. 25	4	RACINE	10
Nov. 29	0	Chic. Bears	3
Dec. 2	22	OORANG	19
Dec. 9	12	MILWAUKEE	14

DULUTH KELLEYS 4-3-0 Joey Sternaman

Regulars

Use Name	Pos.	Hgt.	Wgt.	Age	Int.	Pts.
Joe Rooney	E	6'	175	25		6
Dick O'Donnell	E	6'	180	23		6
Art Johnson	T	5'11	185	27		
Howard Kieley	T	5'8	200	30		
Doc Williams	G	6'7	215	25		
Bill Stein	G	6'	190	24		
John Madigan	C	6'	185	24	1	
Joey Sternaman (to ChiB)	BB	5'6	150	23	1	17
Wally Gilbert	WB	6'1	180	22	1	6
Russ Method	WB	5'10	185	26		
Ken Harris	FB	6'	190	29		

Substitutes

Use Name	Pos.	Hgt.	Wgt.	Age	Int.	Pts.
Ike Haaven	E-G	6'2	192	28		
Roddy Dunn	T	5'10	200	28		
Red Morse	G	5'10	198	24		
Bill Rooney	WB-FB	6'2	190	27		
Mickey McDonnell	WB	5'8	150	19	1	

Scores of each game

Date	Pts.	Opponent	Pts.
Sep. 30	10	AKRON	7
Oct. 7	10	Minneapolis	0
Oct. 21	3	HAMMOND	0
Oct. 28	9	MINNEAPOLIS	0
Nov. 11	3	Milwaukee	6
Nov. 18	0	Chic. Cards	10
Nov. 25	0	Green Bay	10

COLUMBUS TIGERS 5-4-1 Pete Stinchcomb Gus Tebell

Regulars

Use Name	Pos.	Hgt.	Wgt.	Age	Int.	Pts.
Paul Goebel	E	6'3	190	22		8
Gus Tebell	E	5'10	170	25		37
Joe Mulbarger	T	5'9	225	28		
Gus Sonnenberg (to & from BUF)	T-FB	5'6	194	25		6
Andy Nemecek	G-T-C	6'4	210	27		
Jack Sack	G	6'2	195	24		
Red Weaver	C	5'10	185	26	2	2
Lee Snoots	BB-WB-TB-FB	5'9	185	31		6
Sonny Winters	TB	5'9	155	25		18
Bob Rapp	WB	5'8	160	25	1	30
Wilmer Isabel	FB-WB	6'	175	23	1	12

Substitutes

Use Name	Pos.	Hgt.	Wgt.	Age	Int.	Pts.
Homer Ruh	E-BB-FB-WB	5'10	180	27		
Gus Goetz	T	6'	190	26		
Bill Passuelo	G-T	6'2	230	25		
Ray Hanson	G-C	5'11	190	30		
Jack Heldt	C	5'9	200	23	1	
Elliott Bonowitz	BB-T-G	6'1	190	20		
Harry Randolph	BB	5'11	195	23		
Pete Stinchcomb (to CLE)	WB-TB	5'8	160	28		

Walt Rogers — knee injury

Scores of each game

Date	Pts.	Opponent	Pts.
Sep. 30	6	Dayton	7
Oct. 7	0	Milwaukee	0
Oct. 14	0	BUFFALO	3
Oct. 21	34	LOUISVILLE	0
Oct. 28	3	Toledo	0
Nov. 11	16	TOLEDO	0
Nov. 18	3	Cleveland	9
Nov. 25	27	OORANG	3
Dec. 2	30	DAYTON	0
Dec. 9	0	CANTON	10

BUFFALO ALL AMERICANS 5-4-3 Tommy Hughitt

Regulars

Use Name	Pos.	Hgt.	Wgt.	Age	Int.	Pts.
Glen Carberry	E	6'	190	27		
Luke Urban	E-BB	5'8	165	25	1	6
Bob Nash	T-E	6'1	205	30		
Mike Gulian	T	6'	205	23		
Frank Morrissey	G-T	6'1	202	24		31
Swede Youngstrom	G	6'1	186	26		
Frank Culver	C	5'11	175	26		
Tommy Hughitt	BB	5'8	165	30	3	9
Tom Holleran	TB	5'7	170	26		12
Mike Trainor	WB-BB-TB	5'9	165	23	5	12
Vince Mulvey	FB		155	31	1	

Substitutes

Use Name	Pos.	Hgt.	Wgt.	Age	Int.	Pts.
Scotty Bierce (from CLE)	E	5'9	165	26		6
Gus Sonnenberg (from & to COL)	T	5'6	194	25		
Carl Thomas	T-FB-G	5'10	195	26		
Tex Kelly	G-T	6'3	220	24		
Elmer McCormick	C-G-WB	5'7	220	25	1	
Jack Flavin	FB	5'11	175	23		12
Ben Roderick (from CAN)	TB	5'9	175	24	1	
John Mahoney	WB-FB-E	6'1	183	23		
Roy Martineau	FB-T-G	6'	205	23		6
Pete Bahan (from CLE)	TB-FB	5'9	165	25		1
Johnny Scott	TB	5'10	178	28		
Bill Edgar (to AKR)	FB-WB-TB	6'2	185	24		
Pat Smith	FB	6'	205	28		
Bunny Corcoran	WB	5'11	185	28		
Fritz Foster (to ROCH)	FB	5'11	185	24		
Gil Gregory	FB	5'11	165	25		

Scores of each game

Date	Pts.	Opponent	Pts.
Sep. 30	0	Chic. Cards	3
Oct. 7	9	AKRON	0
Oct. 14	3	Columbus	0
Oct. 21	57	OORANG	0
Oct. 28	3	Chic. Bears	18
Nov. 4	0	Cleveland	0
Nov. 11	3	CANTON	3
Nov. 18	3	DAYTON	0
Nov. 25	3	TOLEDO	3
Nov. 29	0	Akron	2
Dec. 1	13	Rochester	0
Dec. 2	0	Canton	14

RUSHING

NAME	Complete Games G	Att.	Yds.	Avg.	TD	Incom. Games G	Att.	Yds.	TD
GREEN BAY									
Lambeau	10	133	416	3.1	1				
Gavin	9	110	331	3.0					
Basing	9	84	221	2.6	2				
Mills	9	77	132	1.7	1				
Hansen	1	14	48	3.4					
Mathys	10	6	22	3.7	1				
Buck	10	1	5	5.0					
Wheeler									
Leaper									
Murray									
Team	10	425	1175	2.8	5				
Opp.	10	255	548	2.1	1				
MILWAUKEE									
Conzelman	4	34	125	3.7	1	9	20	63	2
Doane	2	19	46	2.4	1	8	11	74	1
Erickson	2	19	44	2.3	1	9	5	47	
Winkelman	4	29	63	2.2	1	9	1	1	
Blailock	4	3	42	14.0	1	8			
McMillin (2)						3	2	36	
Mooney	3	5	27	5.4		5	2	7	
Mattox									
Sachs									
Turner									
Strickland									
Pierotti									
Team	4	109	347	3.2	5	9			
Opp.	4	152	407	2.7		9			
CLEVELAND									
Kyle	2	23	87	3.8	1	5	9	30	
Bahan (1)	2	3	2	0.7		5	4	39	
Tanner	2	13	29	2.2		4	3	10	
Edler	2					3	3	37	1
Roby	2	19	22	1.2		5	8	9	
Stinchcomb (2)	1	6	23	3.8					
Wolf	1	2	5	2.5		4	2	13	1
Bowser						3	2	13	
Partlow (2)	1	1	1	1.0					
Civiletto	1	1	0	0.0		3			
Weinberg									
Bierce									
Team	2	68	169	2.5	1	5			
Opp.	2	81	56	4.4	7	5			
CHICAGO CARDINALS									
Driscoll	3	38	100	2.6		7	12	267	6
Crangle	3	29	79	2.7	1	6	3	8	2
Mohardt	3	24	48	2.0		7	3	30	1
Koehler	3	12	14	1.2		8	3	31	1
R. Horween	3	2	4	2.0		9	2	15	2
A. Horween	2	11	13	1.2		9	1	5	
King	3	2	4	2.0		8	1	10	1
McInerney	3	1	8	8.0		8			
Folz						4	1	2	1
Anderson									
Kiley									
Team	3	119	270	2.3	1	9			
Opp.	3	129	323	2.5	2	9			
DULUTH									
B. Rooney	2	12	31	2.6		3			
Harris	2	13	25	1.9		4			
Gilbert	2	7	10	1.4		5	2	10	1
McDonnell	1	4	20	5.0					
Method	2	15	17	1.1		5			
J. Sternaman (1)	2	1	0	0.0					
Rooney						5	1	5	
Team	2	52	103	2.0		5			
Opp.	2	75	179	2.4	1	5			
COLUMBUS									
Rapp	2	9	10	1.1		8	10	179	2
Stinchcomb (1)	1	8	42	5.3		6	5	42	
Snoots	2	5	9	1.8		8	3	58	1
Winters	2	10	21	2.1	1	8	6	33	1
Ruh	2	1	28	28.0		6			
Isabel	2	7	20	2.9		8	3	7	2
Sonnenberg (1,3)	2					8	4	17	1
Goebel	2	1	-2	-2.0		8	1	12	
Tebell									
Team	2	41	128	3.1	1	8			
Opp.	2	57	158	2.8	2	8			
BUFFALO									
Hughitt	1	7	8	1.1		11	25	83	1
Trainor	1	2	6	3.0		11	10	72	1
Holleran						5	15	71	2
Flavin						1	6	51	2
Roderick (2)	1	8	-4	-0.5		3	8	40	
Martineau	1					4	4	12	1
Foster (1)						1	3	9	
Mahoney	1					6	3	8	
Urban	1					10	1	5	
Thomas	1	4	4	1.0		9			
Mulvey						3	1	0	
Scott									
Gregory									
Carberry									
Team	1	21	14	0.7		11			
Opp.	1	48	179	3.7	2	11			

PASSING

NAME	Complete Games G	Com.	Att.	%	Yds.	Y/A	TD	Int.	Incom. Games G	Com.	Att.	Yds.	TD	Int.
GREEN BAY														
Lambeau	10	43	118	36	752	6.4	3	17						
Gavin														
Basing	9	8	22	36	126	5.7		6						
Mills	9	0	3	0										
Hansen	1	1	1	100	4	4.0								
Mathys	10	6	12	50	148	12.3	2	1						
Buck	10	8	11	73	99	9.0		1						
Wheeler														
Leaper														
Murray														
Team	10	66	167	40	1129	6.8	5	25						
Opp.	10	50	130	38	570	4.4	3	22						
MILWAUKEE														
Conzelman	4	30	64	47	345	5.4		7	9	19	27	300	2	5
Doane														
Erickson														
Winkelman	4	2	2	100	25	12.5			9	1	1	12		
Blailock														
McMillin (2)									3	2	2	100	1	
Mooney														
Mattox	3	1	3	33	29	9.7		1	2					
Sachs														
Turner														
Strickland														
Pierotti														
Team	4	33	69	48	399	5.8		8	9					
Opp.	4	16	57	28	288	5.1	2	8	9					
CLEVELAND														
Kyle	2								5	1	2	15		
Bahan (1)	2	0	1	0					5	1	2	16	1	1
Tanner	2	0	1	0					4	0	1			1
Edler														
Roby	2	4	23	17	49	2.1		4	5	5	5	91	3	
Stinchcomb (2)														
Wolf														
Bowser														
Partlow (2)														
Civiletto														
Weinberg									2	1	1	37		
Bierce														
Team	2	4	25	16	49	2.0		4	5					
Opp.	2	13	35	37	106	3.0		5	5					
CHICAGO CARDINALS														
Driscoll	3	3	11	27	76	6.9		2	7	2	2	60	1	
Crangle	3	1	1	100	33	33.0			6					
Mohardt	3	4	17	24	30	1.8		2	7	5	6	110	1	
Koehler														
R. Horween														
A. Horween	2	0	4	0					9	2	4	25	1	2
King	3	0	2	0				1	8	0	1			1
McInerney														
Folz														
Anderson														
Kiley														
Team	3	8	35	23	139	4.0		5	9					
Opp.	3	14	31	45	179	5.8		3	9					
DULUTH														
B. Rooney														
Harris	2	6	24	25	81	3.4		4	4	3	4	90	2	1
Gilbert														
McDonnell														
Method														
J. Sternaman (1)														
Rooney	2	2	3	67	14	4.7		1	5					
Team	2	8	27	30	95	3.5		5	5					
Opp.	2	8	53	35	164	7.1	1	4	5					
COLUMBUS														
Rapp														
Stinchcomb (1)														
Snoots														
Winters	3	10	27	37	108	4.0		5	7	22	30	487	5	2
Ruh														
Isabel	3	9	20	45	95	4.8		3	7	2	3	35	1	
Sonnenberg (1,3)														
Goebel	3	1	2	50	32	16.0			7	1	3	45	1	
Tebell														
Team	3	20	49	41	235	4.8		8	7					
Opp.	3	5	29	17	59	2.0		4	7					
BUFFALO														
Hughitt	3	8	24	33	90	3.8		8	9	8	14	109	1	4
Trainor	2								10	1	1	5		
Holleran	1								4	0	1			
Flavin									1	1	2	5		
Roderick (2)														
Martineau														
Foster (1)														
Mahoney														
Urban														
Thomas														
Mulvey														
Scott									2	2	2	20		
Gregory	1	1	2	50	35	17.5								
Carberry														
Team	3	9	26	35	125	4.8		8	9					
Opp.	3	9	54	17	118	2.2		11	9					

RECEIVING

NAME	Complete Games G	Rec.	Yds	Avg.	TD	Incom. Games G	Rec.	Yds.	TD
GREEN BAY									
Lambeau	10	13	217	16.7	2				
Gavin									
Basing	9	5	88	17.6					
Mills	9	5	127	25.4	2				
Hansen									
Mathys	10	33	494	15.0					
Buck									
Wheeler	10	7	145	20.7	1				
Leaper	2	2	30	15.0					
Murray	9	1	28	28.0					
Team									
Opp.									
MILWAUKEE									
Conzelman	4	3	54	18.0		9	2	62	1
Doane	2	1	12	12.0		8			
Erickson	2	3	25	8.3		9	8	155	
Winkelman	4	9	132	14.7		9	3	100	1
Blailock									
McMillin (2)						3	1	28	
Mooney	3	1	17	17.0		5	1	20	
Mattox	3	3	34	11.3		2			
Sachs	4	8	85	10.6		9	5	99	1
Turner	1	3	20	6.7		2			
Strickland						2	2	38	
Pierotti	1	2	20	10.0		3			
Team									
Opp.									
CLEVELAND									
Kyle									
Bahan (1)	2	3	42	14.0		5	2	32	
Tanner	2					4	2	55	1
Edler									
Roby	2					5	2	31	1
Stinchcomb (2)									
Wolf									
Bowser									
Partlow (2)									
Civiletto									
Weinberg									
Bierce	2	1	7	7.0		5	2	41	2
Team									
Opp.									
CHICAGO CARDINALS									
Driscoll	3	4	53	13.3		7	2	45	1
Crangle									
Mohardt	3					7	1	20	
Koehler									
R. Horween	2					9	1	15	
A. Horween									
King									
McInerney									
Folz									
Anderson	3	4	86	21.5		8	3	50	1
Kiley	3					8	2	65	1
Team									
Opp.									
DULUTH									
B. Rooney									
Harris									
Gilbert	2	1	4	4.0		5			
McDonnell	2					5	2	75	1
Method	2	2	11	5.5		5			
J. Sternaman (1)	2	1	10	10.0		5			
Rooney	2	4	70	17.5		5	1	15	1
Team									
Opp.									
COLUMBUS									
Rapp	3	2	25	12.5		8	5	216	3
Stinchcomb (1)	2	3	21	7.0		6	1	45	
Snoots	2	1	10	10.0		8	2	25	
Winters	2					8	1	20	1
Ruh									
Isabel									
Sonnenberg (1,3)									
Goebel	3	4	57	14.3		7	6	77	1
Tebell	3	10	122	12.2		7	10	184	2
Team									
Opp.									
BUFFALO									
Hughitt	2					10	1	5	1
Trainor	2					10	4	54	
Holleran	1	1	35	35.0		4	3	42	
Flavin									
Roderick (2)	1	1	2	2.0		3			
Martineau									
Foster (1)									
Mahoney									
Urban	2	3	21	7.0		9	3	23	
Thomas									
Mulvey									
Scott									
Gregory									
Carberry	2					8	1	15	
Team									
Opp.									

PUNTING / PUNT RETURNS

NAME	Punting Comp. Games G	No.	Avg.	Punting Incom. Games G	No.	Avg.	Punt Returns Complete Games G	No.	Yds.	Avg.	TD	Punt Returns Incom. Games G	No.	Yds.	TD
GREEN BAY															
Lambeau	10	1	35.0				10	9	68	7.6					
Gavin															
Basing							9	1	3	3.0					
Mills							9	1	7	7.0					
Hansen															
Mathys							10	15	153	10.2					
Buck	10	88	36.9												
Wheeler															
Leaper															
Murray															
Team	10	89	36.9				10	26	231	8.9					
Opp.	10	112	35.3				10	12	132	11.0					
MILWAUKEE															
Conzelman	4	31	35.5	9	1	45.0	4	2	8	4.0		9	2	50	
Doane															
Erickson							2	2	24	12.0		9	1	55	
Winkelman	4			9	3	38.3									
Blailock															
McMillin (2)															
Mooney															
Mattox															
Sachs															
Turner															
Strickland															
Pierotti															
Team	4	21	35.5	9			4	4	32	8.0		9			
Opp.	4	33	35.2	9			4	5	56	11.2		9			
CLEVELAND															
Kyle	2			5	6	32.3									
Bahan (1)															
Tanner							2	3	21	7.0		4	2	43	
Edler															
Roby	2	19	35.6	5			2					5	1	10	
Stinchcomb (2)															
Wolf															
Bowser															
Partlow (2)															
Civiletto															
Weinberg															
Bierce															
Team	2	19	35.6	5			2	3	21	7.0		5			
Opp.	2	17	32.6	5			2	10	158	15.8		5			
CHICAGO CARDINALS															
Driscoll	3	30	42.5	7			3	5	31	6.2		7			
Crangle	3	2	40.0	6			3	2	23	11.5		6			
Mohardt							3	2	23	11.5		7			
Koehler															
R. Horween															
A. Horween	2	1	33.0	9											
King															
McInerney															
Folz															
Anderson															
Kiley															
Team	3	33	42.1	9			3	9	77	8.6		9			
Opp.	3	39	32.7	9			3	3	33	11.0		9			
DULUTH															
B. Rooney															
Harris	2	17	33.0	4											
Gilbert	2	4	31.0	5											
McDonnell															
Method															
J. Sternaman (1)	2	3	38.0	5			2	1	10	10.0		5			
Rooney															
Team	2	24	33.3	5			2	1	10	10.0		5			
Opp.	2	18	40.8	5			2	7	62	8.9		5			
COLUMBUS															
Rapp							2	2	21	10.5		8			
Stinchcomb (1)															
Snoots															
Winters	2	5	35.0	8			2	2	25	12.5		8			
Ruh															
Isabel	2	10	31.5	8											
Sonnenberg (1,3)	2	4	37.0	8											
Goebel							2					8	1	40	
Tebell															
Team	2	19	33.6	8			2	4	46	11.5		8			
Opp.	2	28	34.3	8			2	4	45	11.3		8			
BUFFALO															
Hughitt	1	7	31.0	11	8	30.9	1	1	3	3.0		11			
Trainor							1					11	3	75	
Holleran															
Flavin				1	3	49.3									
Roderick (2)	1	4	33.8	3	3	11.7	1	1	15	15.0		3			
Martineau															
Foster (1)															
Mahoney															
Urban							1					10	1	20	
Thomas															
Mulvey															
Scott															
Gregory															
Carberry															
Team	2	24	32.0	10			1	2	18	9.0		11			
Opp.	2	20	38.1	10			1	5	41	8.2		11			

RACINE LEGION 4-4-2 Babe Ruetz

Regulars

Use Name	Pos.	Hgt.	Wgt.	Age	Int.	Pts.
Paul Meyers	E	5'11	170	28		6
Dick Halladay	E-WB	6'	175	22	4	6
Bull Braman	T	5'11	215	26	1	
Len Smith	T	5'11	195	26		
Bud Gorman	G		225	27		
George Hartong	G	6'	210	27		
Jake Mintun	C	5'11	190	29	1	
Milt Romney	BB-TB-WB-FB	5'8	167	24	3	6
Shorty Barr	TB-BB	5'8	195	27	3	6
Al Elliott	WB	5'9	175	28	6	12
Hank Gillo	FB	5'10	195	28		44

Substitutes

Use Name	Pos.	Hgt.	Wgt.	Age	Int.	Pts.
Fritz Roessler	E	6'1	190	25		
Candy Miller	E-T	6'3	215	25		
Howie Stark	T	6'	210	26		
Bob Foster	T-BB-G	5'10	190	36		
Bill McCaw	G-E	6'2	192	25		
Jack Hueller	G	5'10	200	25		
Chuck Dressen	BB	5'6	150	24		
Irv Langhoff	BB-TB-WB	5'8	160	26		
Rollie Williams	WB-BB	5'8	170	25		6
Fritz Heinisch	E-BB	5'10	170	23		
A.C. Bauer	T	6'2	210			
Al Pierotti (from & to MIL)	G	5'10	200	27		
Jimmy Baxter	WB	5'7	175	31		

Scores of each game

Date	Pts.	Opponent	Pts.
Sep. 30	7	TOLEDO	7
Oct. 7	0	CHIC. BEARS	3
Oct. 14	7	Milwaukee	7
Oct. 21	9	AKRON	7
Oct. 28	24	Green Bay	3
Nov. 4	6	Minneapolis	13
Nov. 11	0	GREEN BAY	16
Nov. 25	10	Chic. Cards	4
Nov. 29	0	MILWAUKEE	16
Dec. 2	23	MINNEAPOLIS	0

TOLEDO MAROONS 3-3-2 Guil Falcon

Regulars

Use Name	Pos.	Hgt.	Wgt.	Age	Int.	Pts.
Si Seyfrit	E	5'10	170	30		6
Mac White	E-WB	6'	180	33	1	
Tillie Voss	T-E	6'3	204	26		7
Steamer Horning	T	6'	200	30	1	
Tom McNamara	G-FB	5'10	210	26		3
Jerry Jones	G	6'	205	29		
Marty Conrad	C	6'1	235	28		
Francis Fitzgerald	BB	5'10	185	27		
Cowboy Hill	TB	5'8	180	24	3	18
Dutch Lauer	WB-FB	5'10	180	27		
Dutch Strauss	FB-WB	5'10	205	26	1	

Substitutes

Use Name	Pos.	Hgt.	Wgt.	Age	Int.	Pts.
Chuck O'Neil	E	5'10	180	25		
Don Batchellor	T	6'3	225	28		
Ben Hunt	T	5'9	185	22		
Joe Gillis	G-T	5'8	210	27		
Rat Watson	BB-WB-TB	5'10	180	24		1
Cliff Jetmore	WB			28		
Heinie Kirkgard	WB		165	24		
Guil Falcon	FB	5'10	220	30		

Scores of each game

Date	Pts.	Opponent	Pts.
Sep. 30	7	Racine	7
Oct. 7	7	OORANG	0
Oct. 21	6	DAYTON	3
Oct. 28	0	COLUMBUS	3
Nov. 11	0	Columbus	16
Nov. 24	12	Rochester	6
Nov. 25	3	Buffalo	3
Nov. 29	0	Canton	28

ROCK ISLAND INDEPENDENTS 2-3-3 Herb Sies

Regulars

Use Name	Pos.	Hgt.	Wgt.	Age	Int.	Pts.
Mike Wilson	E	5'10	168	26	2	6
Max Kadesky	E	5'11	175	22	3	
Fod Cotton	T	6'1	195	22		
Duke Slater	T	6'1	215	24		
George Thompson	G-T	6'1	210	23		
Herb Sies	G-BB	6'	203	30	1	17
Frank DeClerk	C	5'9	187	24	2	
Johnny Armstrong	BB	5'8	170	29	3	12
Waddy Kuehl	TB-WB	5'9	165	31	1	24
Bill Giaver	WB-TB	5'9	190	25	1	24
Bob Phelan	FB-TB	5'11	185	25		24

Substitutes

Use Name	Pos.	Hgt.	Wgt.	Age	Int.	Pts.
Harry Webber	E		175	30		
Hank Smith (from ROCH)	G	6'1	190	30		
Joe Bernstein	G-FB-T	6'	210	29		
played as Joe Burten						
Louie Kolls	C-G-E	6'1	205	30		
Charlie Lungren	BB-WB	5'8	158	29	1	
Walt Lowe	FB-WB-TB	5'11	180	24	1	
Sol Butler (to HAM)	WB-TB	5'8	180	26	1	
Alex Gorgal	FB-WB	5'9	180	23	1	

Scores of each game

Date	Pts.	Opponent	Pts.
Sep. 30	3	CHIC. BEARS	0
Oct. 7	0	CLEVELAND	0
Oct. 14	56	ROCHESTER	0
Nov. 4	3	MILWAUKEE	14
Nov. 11	6	Minneapolis	6
Nov. 18	3	Chic. Bears	7
Nov. 25	6	MINNEAPOLIS	6
Dec. 9	7	Chic. Bears	29

MINNEAPOLIS MARINES 2-5-2 Harry Mehre

Regulars

Use Name	Pos.	Hgt.	Wgt.	Age	Int.	Pts.
Paul Flinn	E	6'	180	27		
Louie Mohs	E-T	6'2	220	30		6
Rudy Tersch	T		195	28		6
Adrian Baril	T	5'11	210	25		
Dutch Gaustad	G		215	33		
Festus Tierney	G	6'1	195	24	1	
Harry Mehre	C	6'1	190	21	1	
Einar Cleve	BB	5'9	175	27	1	6
Ave Kaplan	TB	5'7	165	23	1	18
Louie Pahl	WB	5'8	185	26	1	6
Eber Sampson	FB	6'	200	28		6

Substitutes

Use Name	Pos.	Hgt.	Wgt.	Age	Int.	Pts.
Oscar Christianson	E	5'10	190	24		
George Kramer	T-G-BB	6'2	240	28	1	
Bob Fosdick	G	5'10	225	27		
Hal Hanson	C	6'1	190	27		
Bill Irgens	TB-BB	5'8	175	40		
Danny Coughlin	WB	5'9	175	26		
Dick Hudson	FB		180			

Scores of each game

Date	Pts.	Opponent	Pts.
Sep. 30	0	Green Bay	12
Oct. 7	0	DULUTH	10
Oct. 14	23	OORANG	0
Oct. 21	0	Chic. Cards	9
Oct. 28	0	Duluth	9
Nov. 4	13	RACINE	6
Nov. 11	6	ROCK ISLAND	6
Nov. 25	6	Rock Island	6
Dec. 2	0	Racine	23

ST. LOUIS ALL-STARS 1-4-2 Ollie Kraehe

Regulars

Use Name	Pos.	Hgt.	Wgt.	Age	Int.	Pts.
Ward Meese	E	5'10	175	21		
Johnny Milton (from MIL)	E	5'8	175	24	2	
Brick Travis	T	6'1	210	26		
Bub Weller	T	6'4	200	21		
Ollie Kraehe	G-E	5'10	180	25		
Roy Andrews	G	6'	220	26		
Walt Kreinheder	C	6'2	204	23	1	
Eber Simpson	QB	5'8	170	28	5	
Orville Siegfried	HB	5'10	160	24	2	
Pete Casey	HB		180	27		12
Dick King	FB	5'8	175	30	1	2

Substitutes

Use Name	Pos.	Hgt.	Wgt.	Age	Int.	Pts.
Jack Gray (to GB)	E		175		1	
Jim Finnegan	E-QB	5'8	160	22		
Hal Wilder	G	5'10	190	29		
George Meinhardt	G-C	5'9	200	25		
Cap Murrah	G-C	5'10	215	22		
John Cardwell	HB	5'9	170	30		
Lee Wykoff	FB-HB	6'1	195	25		
Ernie Winburn	E	5'11	175	26		

Scores of each game

Date	Pts.	Opponent	Pts.
Oct. 7	0	Green Bay	0
Oct. 14	0	HAMMOND	0
Oct. 21	0	Cleveland	6
Oct. 28	0	Milwaukee	6
Nov. 4	0	GREEN BAY	3
Nov. 11	14	OORANG	7
Nov. 24	0	MILWAUKEE	17

HAMMOND PROS 1-5-1 Wally Hess

Regulars

Use Name	Pos.	Hgt.	Wgt.	Age	Int.	Pts.
Inky Williams	E	5'11	175	26		6
Carl Hanke	E	6'	190	26		
Dave Tallant	T	6'1	205	26		
Lou Usher (to ChiB)	T	6'2	245	25		
Bill Kovacsy	G			22		
George Berry	G	5'11	200	23		
Russ Oltz	C-FB-T	6'	210	24		
Ed Robinson	BB	5'9	155	19		7
Wally Hess	TB	5'9	175	28		
Lloyd Cearing	WB-BB		185	22		
Oscar Knop (to ChiB)	FB	6'	290	28		

Substitutes

Use Name	Pos.	Hgt.	Wgt.	Age	Int.	Pts.
Elliot Risley	T	6'	205	27		
Wilfred Smith	G-E	6'4	200	24		
(from, to & from ChicC)						
Ed Seibert	G-E	5'10	195	26	1	
Frank Rydzewski (from ChiB)	C-T	6'1	220	30	1	
Fritz Pollard	BB-WB	5'7	165	28		1
Steve Sullivan	WB-TB	5'9	180	25	1	
Sol Butler (from RI)	WB	5'8	180	26		
John Detwiler	FB	5'8	190	31		
Swede Larson	BB					
Dunc Annan	FB-WB-TB	5'10	180	28		

Scores of each game

Date	Pts.	Opponent	Pts.
Sep. 30	0	Canton	17
Oct. 7	7	DAYTON	0
Oct. 14	0	St. Louis	0
Oct. 21	0	Duluth	3
Nov. 11	0	Chic. Cards	6
Nov. 25	7	Chic. Bears	14
Nov. 29	0	Green Bay	19

DAYTON TRIANGLES 1-6-1 Carl Storck

Regulars

Use Name	Pos.	Hgt.	Wgt.	Age	Int.	Pts.
Dave Reese	E	6'	180	30	1	
Dutch Thiele	E	6'1	195	30		
Russ Hathaway	T	5'11	235	27		10
Ed Sauer	T	5'10	240	25		
Bobby Berns	G	6'1	200	27		
Larry Dellinger	G	5'11	208	30		
Hobby Kinderdine	C	5'11	180	32		
Fay Abbott	BB	5'8	180	28		6
Lou Partlow (to & from CLE)	TB	6'1	185	30		
Frank Bacon (to & from AKR)	WB	5'11	183	29	1	
Ken Huffine	FB	6'3	208	25		

Substitutes

Use Name	Pos.	Hgt.	Wgt.	Age	Int.	Pts.
Lee Fenner	E	5'10	170	27		
Al Jolley (to OOR)	G	6'2	200	23		
John Beasley	G			26		
Glenn Tidd	G-C-T	5'11	202	29		
Earl Burgner	BB-WB	5'6	165	23		
Walt Kinderdine	FB-WB-T			24		
Ken Crawford	FB	5'11	190	24		

Scores of each game

Date	Pts.	Opponent	Pts.
Sep. 30	7	COLUMBUS	6
Oct. 7	0	Hammond	7
Oct. 14	0	Canton	30
Oct. 21	3	Toledo	6
Oct. 28	3	Chic. Cards	13
Nov. 11	0	Cleveland	0
Nov. 18	0	Buffalo	3
Dec. 2	3	Columbus	30

NAME	RUSHING									PASSING													
	Complete Games					Incom. Games				Complete Games								Incom. Games					
	G	Att.	Yds.	Avg.	TD	G	Att.	Yds.	TD	G	Com.	Att.	%	Yds.	Y/A	TD	Int.	G	Com.	Att.	Yds.	TD	Int.
RACINE																							
Gillo	6	71	287	4.0	2	4	9	26															
Barr	6	37	96	2.6	1	4	3	28		6	30	69	43	412	6.0	4	8	4	5	17	84	1	1
Elliott	6	36	57	1.6		4	6	35		6	1	3	33	10	3.3			4					
Williams	2	11	75	6.8	1																		
Langhoff	2	18	46	2.6		2	3	28		2								2	1	1	40		
Romney	4	22	47	2.1		4	3	1		4	2	8	25	13	1.6		1	4					
Baxter	1	2	11	5.5																			
Foster	6	3	2	0.7		3																	
Heinisch	4	2	2	1.0		3																	
Dressen	1	3	1	0.3																			
Halladay	4	2	-1	-0.5		3																	
Meyers																							
Roessler																							
Miller																							
Hueller																							
Team	6	207	623	3.0	4	4				6	33	80	41	435	5.4	4	9	4					
Opp.	6	259	791	3.1	3	4				6	32	102	31	511	5.0		17	4					
TOLEDO																							
Hill	2	15	48	3.2		6	16	72	3	2	3	11	27	33	3.0		2	6	3	12	117		2
Watson	1	7	26	3.7		4	3	21		1	1	7	14	11	1.6		1	4					
Strauss	2	15	26	1.7		4	1	9															
Lauer	1	10	11	1.1		6	8	13		1								6	3	3	47	1	
Voss	2	1	15	15.0		6																	
Falcon						2	3	12															
Fitzgerald	1					6	2	9															
White	2					6	1	8															
Kirkgard	1	2	3	1.5		4	1	0															
Horning	2	2	2	1.0		6																	
McNamara										2	0	1	0					6					
Seyfrit																							
Conrad																							
Team	2	52	131	2.5	1	6				3	6	32	19	70	2.2		5	5					
Opp.	2	83	340	4.1	4	6				3	18	39	46	262	6.7	1	7	5					
ROCK ISLAND																							
Phelan	7	56	190	3.4						7	1	4	25	5	1.3		1						
Giaver	7	37	148	4.0	4					7	0	1	0										
Armstrong	8	56	140	2.5	2					8	75	171	44	778	4.5	3	17						
Kuehl	8	57	129	2.3	2					8	5	6	83	76	12.7								
Gorgal	5	20	57	2.9						5	1	2	50	3	1.5								
Butler (1)	3	13	56	4.3						3	0	1	0										
Lungren	4	22	43	2.0						4	2	3	67	22	7.3		1						
Lowe	5	8	23	2.9						5	0	1	0				1						
Bernstein	5	4	10	2.5																			
Wilson																							
Kadesky																							
Slater																							
Kolls																							
Sies																							
DeClerk																							
Team	8	273	796	2.9	8					8	84	189	44	884	4.7	3	20						
Opp.	8	325	746	2.3	6					8	26	83	31	345	4.2		17						
MINNEAPOLIS																							
Hudson	2	40	98	2.5		1																	
Pahl	4	29	67	2.3	1	4	2	12															
Kaplan	4	35	31	0.9		4	2	32		4	11	40	28	152	3.8		12	4	3	3	68	2	
Coughlin	1	12	43	3.6		1																	
Cleve	4	26	37	1.4		4				4	0	3	0					4					
Sampson	2	15	29	1.9		5	2	7	1	2	2	5	40	30	6.0		2	5					
Irgens										1								4	2	2	55	1	
Mohs																							
Flinn																							
Kramer																							
Team	4	157	305	1.9	1	5				4	13	48	27	182	3.8		14	5					
Opp.	4	182	616	3.4	7	5				4	24	56	43	286	5.1		6	5					
ST. LOUIS																							
King	3	27	96	3.6		4	3	17		4	0	2	0					3					
Siegfried	3	24	38	1.6		4	4	32															
Wykoff	2	6	26	4.3		1																	
Cardwell						2	3	25															
Casey	3	18	10	0.6		4	1	5															
Simpson	3	4	11	2.8		4				4	12	32	38	156	4.9	1	8	3	8	19	145		4
Milton (2)	2	1	10	10.0		4																	
Finnegan	1	1	0	0.0		1																	
Gray (1)																							
Weller																							
Team	3	81	191	2.4		4				4	12	34	35	156	4.6	1	8	3					
Opp.	3	110	357	3.2	2	4				4	30	68	44	427	6.3	1	10	3					
HAMMOND																							
Annan						2	6	50															
Oltz	1	6	21	3.5		6																	
Sullivan						4	1	20															
Cearing	1	5	6	1.2		6	1	10															
Hess	1	5	8	1.6		6	1	4		1	1	6	17	2	0.3		2	6	0	1			1
Robinson	1	1	0	0.0		2																	
Selbert																							
Pollard																							
Team	1	17	35	2.1		6				2	1	15	7	2	0.1		4	6					
Opp.	1	37	109	2.9	1	6				2	16	36	44	277	7.7	4	3	6					
DAYTON																							
Partlow (1,3)	1	11	25	2.3		7	8	49															
Bacon (1,3)	1	10	52	5.2		7	1	12		2	0	2	0				1	6	1	1	18		
W. Kinderdine						5	1	30															
Huffine	2	3	11	3.7		6	5	8		2	0	1	0					6	0	1			1
Abbott	1	6	8	1.3	1	7	2	3		2	1	11	9	10	0.9		2	6	1	1	45		
Crawford	1	1	5	5.0																			
Reese																							
Team	1	30	95	3.2	1	7				3	1	17	6	10	0.6		3	5					
Opp.	1	22	70	3.2	1	7				2	5	18	28	79	4.4		1	6					

NAME	RECEIVING									PUNTING						PUNT RETURNS								
	Complete Games					Incom. Games				Comp. Games			Incom. Games			Complete Games					Incom. Games			
	G	Rec.	Yds	Avg.	TD	G	Rec.	Yds.	TD	G	No.	Avg.	G	No.	Avg.	G	No.	Yds.	Avg.	TD	G	No.	Yds.	TD
RACINE																								
Gillo										6	3	31.7	4											
Barr	6	2	16	8.0		4	1	40		6	37	33.8	4	3	45.3	6	9	80	8.9		4	3	33	
Elliott	6	14	168	12.0	2	4				6	2	28.0	4			6	1	5	5.0		4			
Williams																2	6	95	15.8					
Langhoff	2	2	50	25.0		2				2	4	21.5	2			2	2	34	17.0		2	2	26	
Romney	4	2	16	8.0	1	4				4	7	29.0	4											
Baxter																								
Foster	6	1	7	7.0		3																		
Heinisch																								
Dressen																								
Halladay	4	8	129	16.1	1	3	4	70								4	1	7	7.0		3			
Meyers	5	2	-2	-1.0		4	1	14	1															
Roessler	5	1	46	46.0		2																		
Miller	4	1	5	5.0		2																		
Hueller																5	1	16	16.0		4			
Team										6	53	31.9	4			6	20	237	11.9		4			
Opp.										6	54	33.4	4			6	11	83	7.5		4			
TOLEDO																								
Hill	2	1	11	11.0		6										2					6	3	84	
Watson																								
Strauss	2	1	2	2.0		4	1	5																
Lauer	1					6	1	5		1	2	32.0	6											
Voss	2	1	23	23.0		6	4	88																
Falcon																								
Fitzgerald	1	1	8	8.0		6	1	13																
White																								
Kirkgard	1					4	1	6																
Horning										2	2	25.5	6	1	30.0									
McNamara										2	11	23.7	6	1	55.0									
Seyfrit	2					6	3	47	1															
Conrad										2	7	34.3	6											
Team										2	22	28.0	6			2	0				6			
Opp.										2	16	31.4	6			2	8	67	8.4		6			
ROCK ISLAND																								
Phelan	7	1	18	18.0						7	20	26.7												
Giaver	7	14	141	10.1						7	15	32.8												
Armstrong	8	4	45	11.3						8	6	23.5				8	17	212	12.5					
Kuehl	8	27	257	9.5	2											8	4	28	7.0					
Gorgal																								
Butler (1)	3	7	48	6.9																				
Lungren	4	3	19	6.3																				
Lowe																								
Bernstein																								
Wilson	8	13	200	15.4	1																			
Kadesky	8	12	121	10.1																				
Slater	8	1	16	16.0																				
Kolls	6	1	10	10.0																				
Sies	8	1	9	9.0																				
DeClerk										6	16	37.4												
Team										8	57	30.9				8	21	240	11.4					
Opp.										8	62	33.5				8	18	148	8.2					
MINNEAPOLIS																								
Hudson																								
Pahl																								
Kaplan	3					5	1	25	1	4	36	32.1	4			4	8	82	10.3		4			
Coughlin	1	1	15	15.0		1																		
Cleve	3	1	22	22.0		5	1	35	1															
Sampson										2	3	42.0	5											
Irgens																								
Mohs	3	2	30	15.0		6	3	78	1															
Flinn	3	3	42	14.0		5	1	15																
Kramer	2					5	1	7																
Team										4	39	32.8	5			4	8	82	10.3		5			
Opp.										4	28	34.3	5			4	17	167	9.8		5			
ST. LOUIS																								
King	3	1	5	5.0		4				3	3	39.3	4											
Siegfried	3	1	0	0.0		4										3	1	10	10.0		4			
Wykoff										2	6	26.7	1											
Cardwell						2	1	20																
Casey	3					4	1	42	1	3	29	41.3	4	4	50.0									
Simpson										3	4	30.8	4	1	0.0	3	3	35	11.7		4			
Milton (2)	2	2	8	4.0		4	6	110																
Finnegan	1					1	1	12																
Gray (1)	1					2	3	35																
Weller	3	1	50	50.0		4				3	1	24.0	4											
Team										3	43	37.7	4			3	4	45	11.3		4			
Opp.										3	36	36.6	4			3	9	70	7.8		4			
HAMMOND																								
Annan																								
Oltz										1			6	4	8.8									
Sullivan																								
Cearing																1	2	14	7.0		6			
Hess										1	11	32.0	6	2	44.0									
Robinson																1	2	40	20.0		6	1	65	1
Selbert	1	1	2	2.0		1																		
Pollard													2	1	42.0									
Team										1	11	32.0	6			1	4	54	13.5		6			
Opp.										1	7	41.1	6			1	4	42	10.5		6			
DAYTON																								
Partlow (1,3)																								
Bacon (1,3)	2	1	10	10.0		6				1	8	33.0	7	6	22.5	1	2	20	10.0		7	1	10	
W. Kinderdine																								
Huffine	2					6	1	18																
Abbott										1	3	22.7	7											
Crawford										1	2	35.5												
Reese	2					6	1	45																
Team										1	13	31.0	7			1	2	20	10.0		7			
Opp.										1	9	35.9	7			1	1	15	15.0		7			

Regulars							Substitutes							Substitutes							Scores of each game			
UseName	Pos.	Hgt.	Wgt.	Age	Int.	Pts.	UseName	Pos.	Hgt.	Wgt.	Age	Int.	Pts.	UseName	Pos.	Hgt.	Wgt.	Age	Int.	Pts.	Date	Pts.	Opponent	Pts.
AKRON PROS 1-6-0 Dutch Hendrian, Carl Cramer																								
Red Daum	E	5'7	160	24			Grover Malone	E	5'8	185	27										Sep. 30	7	Duluth	10
Al Nesser	E-G	6'	195	30	1	6	Red Roberts	E	6'1	235	23										Oct. 7	0	Buffalo	9
Jim Flower	T-E-C	6'1	195	27			George Brown	T			29										Oct. 14	0	Chic. Cards	19
Wilson	T-G-TB						Hugh Sprinkle	T-G	6'2	220	26										Oct. 21	7	Racine	9
Dutch Wallace	G-T	6'	205	27			Les Scott	G-T	5'10	205	24			Charlie Stewart	G	5'9	160	33			Oct. 28	3	Canton	7
Walt LeJeune	G-C	6'	230	23			Bill Edgar (from BUF)	G	6'2	185	24			Isham Hardy	G			24			Nov. 11	6	Chic. Bears	20
Joe Mills	C-T	6'3	212	25	1																Nov. 29	2	BUFFALO	0
Dutch Hendrian (to CAN)	BB	5'9	180	26		1																		
Al Michaels	TB	6'	190	23		3	Frank Bacon (from & to DAY)	WB	5'11	183	29													
Wayne Brenkert	WB-BB	5'10	170	25		12	Art Haley	WB	5'10	180	27													
Carl Cramer	FB-WB	5'11	185	25			Ed Shaw	FB	6'1	210	28													
OORANG INDIANS (Marion, Ohio) 1-10-0 Jim Thorpe																								
Ed Nason	E-WB	5'8	185	24			Arrowhead	E	5'7	160			12	Joe Pappio	E	6'	183	20			Sep. 30	2	Milwaukee	13
Joe Little Twig	E-T	5'11	185	30		1	Woodchuck Welmas	E	5'7	170	30			Peter Black Bear	E	6'	190	23			Oct. 7	0	Toledo	7
Ted Buffalo	T-E-G	6'	190	22		6	Big Bear	T-E	6'4	215											Oct. 14	0	Minneapolis	23
Bill Newashe	T	5'11	200	33			Al Jolley (from DAY)	T	6'2	200	23										Oct. 21	0	Buffalo	57
Stan Powell	G	5'11	185	33			Ted Lone Wolf	G	6'2	212											Oct. 28	0	Cleveland	27
Jack Thorpe	G-C-T-WB	6'	210	24			Xavier Downwind	G	6'	200	29										Nov. 4	0	Chic. Bears	26
Nick Lassa	C-G-T	5'10	205	26			Napoleon Barrel	C-BB	5'8	200	37										Nov. 11	7	St. Louis	14
Emmett McLemore	BB	5'7	160	23		8	Lo Boutwell	BB-WB-FB	5'7	190	30	1									Nov. 18.	0	Canton	41
Jim Thorpe	TB	6'1	200	36	1	3	Joe Guyon	TB-WB	5'10	195	30	1	12								Nov. 25	3	Columbus	27
Pete Calac	FB-WB-E-T-TB	5'10	200	31		6	Chim Lingrel	WB-FB	6'2	200	24			Gray Horse	WB-G	5'8	190				Dec. 2	19	Chic. Cards	22
Eagle Feather	FB	6'	220																		Dec. 9	19	Louisville	0
LOUISVILLE BRECKS 0-3-0 Jim Kendrick																								
Herb Gruber	E	5'9	155	21			John Quast	E	5'10	165	23										Oct. 7	0	Canton	37
Bob White	E		150	20			Austin Higgins	E	5'9	168	25										Oct. 21	0	Columbus	34
Bob Karch	T	6'1	220	28			Charlie Lanham	T		170	28										Dec. 9	0	OORANG	19
Dick Gibson	T-G	6'	190	21			Al Espie	T			22													
John Olmstead	G	5'11	180	26																				
Austin Brunklacher	G		193	25			Russ Meredith	G	5'11	200	26													
Bo Otto	C		182	21																				
Chase Boldt	BB	5'7	145	23			Jimmy Van Dyke	BB	5'7	140	24			Patsy Giugliano	BB	5'4	140	22						
Jim Kendrick	TB-E-T	6'	195	30			John Rowan	TB-BB	5'8	165	27													
Earl Reiser	WB		160	24			Salem Ford	WB	5'7	150	27			George Wanless	WB-E	5'8	160	25						
Hubert Wiggs	FB	5'8	185	27																				
ROCHESTER JEFFERSONS 0-4-0 Leo Lyons																								
Spin Roy	E	6'	175	26			Hugh Bancroft	E			29										Oct. 7	0	Chic. Cards	60
Hal Clark	E	5'10	195	29		6															Oct. 14	0	Rock Island	56
Frank Matteo	T	5'11	195	27																	Nov. 24	6	TOLEDO	12
Darby Lowery	T-G	6'	210	31																	Dec. 1	0	BUFFALO	13
Jim Leonard	G-T	6'	205	24			Joe McShea	G	5'8	185	23			Cy Kasper	G	5'10	170	27						
Jim Welsh	G	5'11	240	21			Joe Bachmaier	G-C	5'9	175	27			Red Emslie	G			25						
Hank Smith (to RI)	C	6'1	190	30			Jimmy Woods	C-T-G	5'9	200	29													
Mike Gavagan	BB	5'10	180	24			Jerry Noonan	BB	6'1	190	24			Will Anderson	BB	5'10	175	26						
Shag Sheard	TB	5'11	175	24	1		Ray Witter	BB-C-G	5'10	190	26			Fritz Foster (from BUF)	BB	5'11	185	24						
Bob Argus	WB	5'10	192	29	1																			
Leo Peyton	FB	5'11	190		1		Gordon Wallace	FB	5'10	170	24													

1924 N.F.L.
The Calendar Calls The Turn

Near the end of the league meeting in Chicago in July, Bears co-owner Dutch Sternaman moved that the 1924 NFL season begin on September 27 and close on November 30 and that the championship standings be decided on a percentage basis of all games between league teams played between those dates. Sternaman's motion carried and a few months later he would live to regret it. Several important things took place at that July meeting and at an earlier January get-together: Joe Carr was re-elected league president as usual; the Frankford Yellowjackets and Kansas City Blues were added as new members; the Toledo franchise shifted to Kenosha; and serious consideration was given to dividing the league into eastern and western divisions and having the league draw up schedules. None, however, brought so much confusion to the season of 1924 as Sternaman's proposal.

But what Sam Deutsch did to the Canton Bulldogs in August ran a close second in the confusion sweepstakes. Although undefeated on the field for two years, the Bulldogs were dying financially. The small capacity of Lakeside Park made it impossible for the team to break even. Ralph Hay had turned the Bulldogs over to a group of local businessmen after the 1922 season but, after 1923, they were ready to throw in the towel. Meanwhile, in Cleveland, Deutsch desparately wanted a championship team but recognized that his 1923 Indians were not it. His solution was to buy the Canton Bulldogs for $1,500, thus giving him two NFL franchises. Then he switched the pick of his Canton players to his Cleveland roster, renamed his Indians the Bulldogs, and left the Canton franchise — which he hoped to sell back to Canton — inactive for 1924.

Not all of the Canton players made the trek north to Cleveland. Pete Henry, Harry Robb and Larry Conover signed with the Pottsville Maroons, an independent team in the Pennsylvania coal-mining region. Lou Smyth and Tex Grigg also chose to play freelance ball in the anthracite circuit, but did join the Rochester Jeffersons for one game late in the NFL season. But coach Guy Chamberlin still had enough talent on hand to fashion a strong team, one which excelled on offense more than on defense. Joining Chamberlin from the 1923 squad were Link Lyman, Duke Osborn, Rudy Comstock, Wooky Roberts, Ben Jones and Doc Elliott. Key additions were rookies Hoge Workman and Dave Noble, who furnished passing ability and speed in the backfield. With a few holdovers from the 1923 Indians, Chamberlin had a team capable of winning Mr. Deutsch his championship.

Two clubs put up strong challenges for the title, the Chicago Bears and the Frankford Yellowjackets. The Bears, second-place finishers in the past two seasons, added big rookie guard Jim McMillin to an already strong team. The Sternaman brothers, Dutch and Joey, spearheaded the backfield, while the line overflowed with such stars as George Trafton, Hunk Anderson, Ed Healey, Hugh Blacklock and Ralph Scott. The Bears were a known factor; the Yellowjackets were an unproven team in their first NFL season. An independent team for several years, the Yellowjackets bore the name of a suburb of Philadelphia and played home games in both small Frankford Stadium and large Shibe Park, home of baseball's Philadelphia Athletics. The Yellowjackets gave the NFL its first solid East Coast station, an expansion which would continue with the addition of more eastern teams the next year. Because of Pennsylvania Blue Laws prohibiting spectator sports on Sunday, the Yellowjackets played home games practically every Saturday and road games almost every Sunday. Year after year, the Yellowjackets played the most games of any NFL team. They featured many graduates of Eastern schools: backs Tex Hamer from Penn and John Storer from Lehigh; and linemen Bull Behman from Dickinson, Jim Welsh from Colgate, Herb Stein from Pittsburgh, Mike Gulian from Brown and Russ Stein from Washington & Jefferson. This team would set an NFL record of 39 rushing touchdowns during the season, with Hamer getting a dozen.

On September 21, the Chicago Bears lost 5-0 to the Packers, but did not have to put the result in their loss column because the official season did not begin until September 27. But, a week later, in their official opener, the Bears could muster only a scoreless tie at Rock Island. The Independents signed Jim Thorpe to play tailback and he responded

NAME	RUSHING Complete Games					RUSHING Incom. Games				PASSING Complete Games								PASSING Incom. Games					
	G	Att.	Yds.	Avg.	TD	G	Att.	Yds.	TD	G	Com.	Att.	%	Yds.	Y/A	TD	Int.	G	Com.	Att.	Yds.	TD	Int.
AKRON																							
Hendrian (1)	1	15	24	1.6		4	3	14		1	4	5	80	23	4.6		2	4	1	3	45		1
Brenkert	1					6	6	29	2														
Cramer	1	7	12	1.7		6	2	9															
Michaels	1	10	8	0.8		6	1	5		1	6	10	60	81	8.1			6	1	3	40		
Shaw (2)	1	10	7	0.7		1																	
Bacon (2)						1	1	5															
Wilson										1								4	2	2	34		
Daum																							
Flower																							
Nesser																							
Wallace																							
Team	1	42	51	1.2		6				2	12	26	46	120	4.6		2	5					
Opp.	1	32	88	2.8	1	6				2	6	26	23	124	4.8		1	5					
OORANG																							
Jim Thorpe	1	7	20	2.9		8	8	34		2	14	35	40	188	5.4	1	4	7	6	8	95		2
Guyon	1	6	9	1.5		3	4	29	1	2	9	22	41	110	5.0	1	1	2					
Calac						10	4	36	1														
Lingrel						6	2	5															
McLemore						9	2	6		1								8	1	1	15	1	
Welmas																							
Arrowhead																							
Little Twig																							
Eagle Feather																							
Team	1	13	29	2.2		10				3	24	59	41	309	5.2	2	5	8					
Opp.	1	54	293	5.4	4	10				3	14	36	39	251	7.0	2	2	8					
LOUISVILLE																							
Kendrick						3	4	7		2	5	37	14	104	2.8		1	1					
Rowan						3	1	1		2	0	8	0					1					
Boldt																		2	1	2	45		
Espie																							
Reiser																							
Gruber																							
Team						3				2	5	45	11	104	2.3		1	1					
Opp.						3				2	13	38	34	294	7.7	4	1	1					
ROCHESTER																							
Sheard	1	10	14	1.4		3	4	104		1	2	12	17	46	3.8		4	3	4	4	52	1	
Peyton	1	8	27	3.4		1																	
Argus	1	11	5	0.5		3	1	7															
Gavagan										1	1	2	50	8	4.0		1	1					
Clark																							
Roy																							
Wallace																		1	0	1			
Foster																							
Bancroft																							
Team	1	29	46	1.6		3				1	3	14	21	54	3.9		5	3					
Opp.	1	45	202	4.5	6	3				1	22	36	61	306	8.5	2	4	3					

NAME	RECEIVING Complete Games					RECEIVING Incom. Games				PUNTING Comp. Games			PUNTING Incom. Games			PUNT RETURNS Complete Games					PUNT RETURNS Incom. Games			
	G	Rec.	Yds	Avg.	TD	G	Rec.	Yds.	TD	G	No.	Avg.	G	No.	Avg.	G	No.	Yds.	Avg.	TD	G	No.	Yds.	TD
AKRON																								
Hendrian (1)	1	1	7	7.0		4				1			4	3	37.7									
Brenkert	1					6	1	16																
Cramer	1	2	21	10.5		6																		
Michaels	1	4	23	5.8		6				2	22	38.5	6			1	1	45	45.0		6	2	40	
Shaw (2)																								
Bacon (2)																								
Wilson																								
Daum	1	2	41	20.5		6	1	40																
Flower	1	1	12	12.0		6	1	18																
Nesser	1					6	1	45																
Wallace													5	1	20.0									
Team										2	22	38.5	5			1	1	45	45.0		6			
Opp.										2	22	34.6	5			1	0				6			
OORANG																								
Jim Thorpe	1	1	11	11.0		8				1	9	31.8	8	8	31.8									
Guyon	1	4	66	16.5		3				2	10	37.0	2											
Calac						10	3	55																
Lingrel																								
McLemore						9	5	87	1															
Welmas						4	2	35																
Arrowhead						4	2	29	2															
Little Twig	1					10	1	15																
Eagle Feather	1	1	5	5.0																				
Team										2	19	34.5	9			1	0				10			
Opp.										2	12	28.3	9			1	7	99	14.1		10			
LOUISVILLE																								
Kendrick										1	8	25.0												
Rowan						3	1	45																
Boldt																								
Espie						1	1	45																
Reiser						2	1	12																
Gruber						3	1	12																
Team										1	8	25.0	2								3			
Opp.										1	10	37.0	2								3			
ROCHESTER																								
Sheard										1	12	28.6	3											
Peyton	1	1	21	21.0		1																		
Argus																								
Gavagan																								
Clark	1					3	2	22	1															
Roy	1	1	25	25.0		3																		
Wallace						2	1	10																
Foster						1	1	20																
Bancroft	1	1	8	8.0		1																		
Team										1	12	28.6	3			1	0				3			
Opp.										1	0		3			1	1	35	35.0		3			

with his best football in several seasons. Rock Island itself had a shot at the title, but suffered a key loss in Kansas City on October 26. That day their star tackle Duke Slater had to stay on the bench because the home team refused to allow a black man to play.

On October 5, the Bears went to Cleveland to open the season for the Bulldogs. In a hard-fought battle, the Bulldogs edged the Bears 16-14. Meanwhile, in Dayton, the Yellowjackets lost their first NFL road game 19-7 to the Triangles. The Bulldogs pulled further ahead the next week. On Sunday, October 11, they came to Frankford and salvaged a 3-3 tie on a Workman dropkick late in the final quarter. On Sunday, the Yellowjackets had no league game, the Bears tied the Racine Legion 10-10 and the Bulldogs beat Akron 29-14. Cleveland continued winning games impressively. The Bears and Yellowjackets, in hot pursuit, met each other on October 26 before 12,000 fans in Wrigley Field. Frankford led 3-0 after the first quarter, but the rest of the day belonged to the Bears who stormed to a 33-3 romp.

The next key confrontation came on November 16 when the Yellowjackets came to Cleveland. Frankford led 6-0 at halftime on two Jim Welsh field goals and a 48-yard run by tiny Charlie Way set up a Tex Hamer touchdown in the fourth quarter. The Bulldogs fought back with a touchdown of their own but fell short in a 12-7 decision, the first loss ever for a Guy Chamberlin-coached team. At Chicago, the Bears were tied, 'for the fourth time in 1924, 3-3 by Racine. Both the Yellowjackets and the Bears added three more victories before November ended while the Bulldogs had two, including a 53-10 Thanksgiving Day win over Milwaukee played at Canton. The game, in which the Bulldogs racked up a record 25 rushing first downs, added to the confusion in fans' minds as to whether the team was a relocated Canton club or a re-fortified Cleveland team. Canton fans would have been disappointed to learn that their old Bulldogs franchise sat inactive all through the season.

The season officially ended on November 30 as the league had decided back in July. Based on percentage, Cleveland was first with a 7-1-1 record, the Bears were second at 6-1-4, and Frankford stood third with 11-2-1. The Duluth Kelleys had the fourth-highest percentage but were not eligible for the championship, having played only six games. Had everyone stopped playing right then, the 1924 championship would have been cut and dried. But, of course, teams that saw a chance to pull in good gate receipts continued to schedule games.

The most important of these post-season games took place on December 7 in Chicago. The Bears invited the Bulldogs to Wrigley Field for what Chicago newspapers trumpeted as a championship game. Cleveland regarded the game as an exhibition. Given the mind-set of the two teams, the result was predictable. The Bears led by a slim 7-0 score early in the fourth quarter, then blew the game into a 23-0 rout in the final 10 minutes.

Regarding themselves as champions, the Bears continued their post-season play. The next Saturday, they took on the Yellowjackets before a full house of 15,000 spectators in Frankford. Jim Welsh scored on a placekick from around midfield in the first half, but Joey Sternaman's dropkick from the 20-yard line in the third quarter broke a 10-10 tie and stood up for a 13-10 Chicago victory. After beating the best in the East, the Bears rode an overnight train back to Chicago to face their interstate rivals, the Rock Island Independents. The two teams had played to 0-0 and 3-3 ties earlier this season, but the third meeting went to the Independents by a score of 7-6. Joey Sternaman scored the touchdown for the Bears with two minutes left in the game but missed the extra point.

Chicago newspapers awarded the Bears the title on the basis of their December 7 "championship game" victory over Cleveland and their 8-2-4 record (no one seemed to notice that the record was 8-3-4 if *all* exhibitions were counted). But, at the January league meeting, the NFL declared its championship in accord with its own rules rather than the newspapers'. Cleveland, with an .875 percentage on November 30, was clearly the winner. As for the "championship game" part of the Chicago argument, it was pointed out that the league had established no such thing and individual clubs had no right to arrange one on their own. Guy Chamberlin had his third championship in a row and Sam Deutsch had his first; it took him only two teams to do it.

Complete play-by-plays from the *Green Bay Press Gazette* show that Curly Lambeau became the first passer to gain over 1,000 yards in a season, with 1,094 in 11 games. Additionally, although only partial information exists, Tex Hamer may well have rushed for more than a thousand. We can verify 789 yards, but figures from 12 of his 14 games are incomplete.

Despite their heroics, Lambeau and Hamer could only make the second team on the *Green Bay Press Gazette* annual all-NFL poll. The first team selections: ends Joe Little Twig, Rock Island, and Tillie Voss, Green Bay; tackles Ed Healey, Bears, and Boni Petcoff, Columbus; guards Swede Youngstrom, Buffalo, and Stan Muirhead, Dayton; center George Trafton, Bears; quarterback Joey Sternaman, Bears (the NFL scoring and field goal leader); halfbacks Charlie Way, Frankford, and Benny Boynton, Buffalo; and fullback Doc Elliott, Cleveland.

1924 STANDINGS

	W	L	T	Pct.	Pts.	Opp. Pts.	Avg. Pts.	Opp. Avg.
Cleveland Bulldogs	7	1	1	.875	229	60	25	7
Chicago Bears	6	1	4	.857	136	55	12	5
Frankford Yellow Jackets	11	2	1	.846	326	109	23	8
Duluth Kelleys	5	1	0	.833	56	16	9	3
Rock Island Independents	5	2	2	.714	88	38	10	4
Green Bay Packers	7	4	0	.636	108	38	10	3
Racine Legion	4	3	3	.571	69	47	7	5
Chicago Cardinals	5	4	1	.556	90	67	9	7
Buffalo Bisons	6	5	0	.545	120	140	11	13
Columbus Tigers	4	4	0	.500	91	68	11	9
Hammond Pros (R)	2	2	1	.500	18	45	4	9
Milwaukee Badgers	5	8	0	.385	142	188	11	14
Akron Pros	2	6	0	.250	59	132	7	17
Dayton Triangles	2	6	0	.250	45	148	6	19
Kansas City Blues	2	7	0	.222	46	124	5	14
Kenosha Maroons	0	4	1	.000	12	117	2	23
Minneapolis Marines	0	6	0	.000	14	108	2	18
Rochester Jeffersons	0	7	0	.000	7	156	1	22

(R) — played only road games

Scoring Leaders

J. Sternaman	ChiB	75
Hamer	Fra	72
Boynton	Roch-Buf	59
Gillo	Rac	48
Storer	Fra	48
Dunn	Mil	47
Gavin	RI	42
Elliott	Cle	40
Welsh	Fra	38
Noble	Cle	36
Driscoll	ChiC	34
Rapp	Col	30
Sullivan	Fra	30
Voss	GB	30
Corgan	KC	26
Jones	Cle	25
Lyman	Cle	25
Roberts	Cle	25
Workman	Cle	25

KICKING

		FG	Att	Pct
J. Sternaman	ChiB	9	18	50
Gillo	Rac	8	20	40
Dunn	Mil	7	11	64
Welsh	Fra	7	16	44
Driscoll	ChiC	7	23	30
Boynton	Roch-Buf	4	7	57
Gilbert	Duluth	3	5	60
Buck	GB	3	11	27
Workman	Cle	3	NA	
Finn	Fra	2	4	50
Morrissey	Buf-Mil	2	4	50
Thorpe	RI	2	6	33
Cramer	Akr	1	1	100
Elliott	Rac	1	1	100
Hathaway	Day	1	1	100
Tebell	Col	1	1	100
Ursella	RI	1	1	100
Winters	Col	1	1	100
Sies	Day	1	2	50
Winkelman	Mil	1	2	50

		FG	Att	Pct
Hogan	Akr	1	3	33
Hendrian	GB	1	3	33
Schell	Col	1	4	25
DeWitz	KC	1	4	25
Lambeau	GB	1	5	20
R. Stein	Fra	1	6	17
D. Sternaman	ChiB	1	6	17
Andrews	KC	1	7	14
Elliott	Cle	1	NA	
Corgan	KC	0	1	0
Feist	Buf	0	1	0
A. Horween	ChiC	0	1	0
Kaw	Buf	0	1	0
Kraus	Buf	0	1	0
Nemecek	Col	0	1	0
Sheard	Roch	0	1	0
Whalen	ChiC	0	1	0
Woodin	GB	0	1	0
Hamer	Fra	0	1	0
Barr	Rac	0	2	0
Method	Dul	0	4	0

		PAT	Att	Pct
Welsh	Fra	17	22	77
Workman	Cle	16	21	76
Dunn	Mil	14	17	82
J. Sternaman	ChiB	12	13	92
R. Stein	Fra	12	19	63
Boynton	Roch-Buf	11	14	79
Buck	GB	8	12	67
Driscoll	ChiC	7	9	78
Gillo	Rac	6	6	100
Winters	Col	5	8	63
Ursella	RI	4	5	80
Tebell	Col	3	3	100
Hathaway	Day	3	5	60
Gilbert	Dul	3	6	50
Finn	Fra	2	2	100
O. Smith	Cle	2	2	100
D. Sternaman	ChiB	2	2	100
Wallace	Akr	2	2	100
Corgan	KC	2	3	67
Hogan	Akr	2	3	67
Armstrong	RI	1	1	100

		PAT	Att	Pct
Burt	Buf	1	1	100
DeWitz	KC	1	1	100
Jones	Cle	1	1	100
Lyman	Cle	1	1	100
McCarthy	RI	1	1	100
Novak	Min	1	1	100
Simon	Min	1	1	100
Andrews	KC	1	2	50
Elliott	Cle	1	2	50
Sechrist	Akr	1	2	50
Roberts	Cle	1	3	33
Thorpe	RI	1	4	25
Hendrian	GB	0	1	0
Hogue	Akr	0	1	0
A. Horween	ChiC	0	1	0
Kolls	RI	0	1	0
Rapp	Col	0	1	0
Seasholtz	Ken	0	1	0
Simpson	Ken	0	1	0
Fortune	Ham	0	1	0
Hess	Ham	0	2	0

CLEVELAND BULLDOGS 7-1-1 Guy Chamberlin

Regulars: UseName	Pos.	Hgt.	Wgt.	Age	Int	Pts.
Guy Chamberlin	E	6'2"	195	30		12
Joe Work	E-WB	5'10"	177	24		6
Link Lyman	T	6'2"	230	25		25
Olin Smith	T-G	6'1"	230	24		8
Rudy Comstock	G	5'10"	210	23		
Jerry Jones	G	6'1"	205	30		
Duke Osborn	C	5'10"	190	27	1	
Wooky Roberts	BB-TB	5'7"	160	26	1	25
Hoge Workman	TB	5'11"	170	24	2	25
Dave Noble	WB	6'2"	195	24	1	36
Doc Elliott	FB-TB-WB	5'10"	210	22		40

Substitutes: UseName	Pos.	Hgt.	Wgt.	Age	Int	Pts.
Scotty Bierce	E	5'9"	165	27		
Charlie Honaker	E	5'11"	185	24		
Stan Muirhead (to DAY)	T	6	180	22		
Cap Edwards	T-G	6'	210	36	1	
Chalmers Ault	G	5'9"	195	24		
Hal Burt	G	5'10"	175	25		
Russ Smith (from MIL)	G-C	5'10"	225	28		
John Tanner	FB-TB	5'5"	165	24		12
Dick Wolf	WB-BB	5'8"	160	24		12
Doc Elliott	FB-WB	5'11"	205	24		25

Date	Pts.	Opponent	Pts.
Oct. 5	16	CHIC. BEARS	14
Oct. 11	3	Frankford	3
Oct. 12	29	AKRON	14
Oct. 26	59	ROCHESTER	0
Nov. 2	35	DAYTON	0
Nov. 9	20	Akron	7
Nov. 16	7	FRANKFORD	12
Nov. 23	7	COLUMBUS	0
Nov. 27	53	MILWAUKEE (at Canton)	10

CHICAGO BEARS 6-1-4 George Halas

Regulars: UseName	Pos.	Hgt.	Wgt.	Age	Int	Pts.
George Halas	E	6'	182	29	1	
Duke Hanny	E-T	6'	195	26	2	6
Ed Healey	T	6'1"	210	29		
Hugh Blacklock	T	6'	220	33		
Jim McMillen	G	6'1"	215	21	1	
Hunk Anderson	G	5'11"	192	25		
George Trafton	C	6'2"	235	27	3	
Joey Sternaman	QB	5'6"	150	24	1	75
Dutch Sternaman	HB	5'8"	180	29	1	23
Jim Kendrick	HB	6'	195	31	1	
Oscar Knop	FB	6'	195	29	3	6

Substitutes: UseName	Pos.	Hgt.	Wgt.	Age	Int	Pts.
Vern Mullen	E	6'	185	24	1	
Harry O'Connell	T	6'1"	190	20		
Ralph Scott	T	6'2"	234	26		
Joe LaFleur	G-C	6'	224	28		
Johnny Bryan	HB-QB	5'8"	165	27		18
Laurie Walquist	HB	5'8"	165	26	1	6
Jake Lanum	FB-HB	6'	190	27		
Oscar Johnson	FB	5'10"	195	23		
George Bolan	FB	5'11"	204	27		

Date	Pts.	Opponent	Pts.
Sep. 28	0	Rock Island	0
Oct. 5	14	Cleveland	16
Oct. 12	10	RACINE	10
Oct. 19	6	CHIC. CARDS	0
Oct. 26	33	FRANKFORD	3
Nov. 2	3	ROCK ISLAND	3
Nov. 9	12	COLUMBUS	6
Nov. 16	3	RACINE	3
Nov. 23	3	GREEN BAY	0
Nov. 27	21	Chic. Cards	0
Nov. 30	31	MILWAUKEE	14

FRANKFORD YELLOWJACKETS 11-2-1 Punk Berryman

Regulars: UseName	Pos.	Hgt.	Wgt.	Age	Int	Pts.
Milt O'Connell	E	6'	175	23		6
Whitey Thomas	E	5'10"	170	29		
Mike Gulian	T	6'	205	24	1	
Russ Stein	T-C	6'1"	210	28	2	15
Butch Spagna	G	6'	215	25		6
Jim Welsh	G-C	5'11"	250	22		38
Herb Stein	G	6'	185	26	3	
Les Haws	BB	5'8"	164	24	3	24
Jack Storer	TB	5'10"	163	23	4	48
Charlie Way	WB	5'8"	145	26		24
Tex Hamer	FB	6'1"	190	22	2	72

Substitutes: UseName	Pos.	Hgt.	Wgt.	Age	Int	Pts.
Eddie O'Doyle	E	5'9"	175	26		12
Bull Behman	T-G	5'10"	210	24		
Bill Hoffman	G	5'10"	220	22		
Al Bedner	G	5'10"	190	26		
Bob Jamieson	C	6'	195	22		
Jack Finn	BB-WB-TB-FB	5'7"	172	23	1	20
Bill Kellogg	TB-FB	5'10"	175	27		18
George Sullivan	WB-TB-FB	5'9"	170	27	1	30
Harry Dayhoff	WB-FB-TB-BB	5'9"	170	28		12

Date	Pts.	Opponent	Pts.
Sep. 27	21	ROCHESTER	0
Oct. 4	31	KENOSHA	6
Oct. 5	7	Dayton	19
Oct. 11	3	CLEVELAND	3
Oct. 18	23	COLUMBUS	7
Oct. 26	3	Chic. Bears	33
Nov. 1	23	AKRON	0
Nov. 2	24	Buffalo	0
Nov. 8	42	KANSAS CITY	7
Nov. 15	39	MINNEAPOLIS	7
Nov. 16	12	Cleveland	7
Nov. 22	21	MILWAUKEE	6
Nov. 27	32	DAYTON	7
Nov. 29	45	BUFFALO	7

DULUTH KELLEYS 5-1-0 Dewey Scanlon

Regulars: UseName	Pos.	Hgt.	Wgt.	Age	Int	Pts.
Joe Rooney	E	6'	173	26	1	6
Jack Underwood	E	6'	190	27		12
Howard Kieley	T	5'8"	210	31		
Art Johnson	T-G	5'11"	190	28		
Bill Stein	G	6'	190	25		
Doc Williams	G	6'7"	215	26		
Leif Strand	C	6'	210	25		
Cobb Rooney	BB	6'	185	24		
Wally Gilbert	TB	6'1"	180	23	4	18
Russ Method	WB	5'10"	190	27	1	6
Bill Rooney	FB	6'2"	195	28		12

Substitutes: UseName	Pos.	Hgt.	Wgt.	Age	Int	Pts.
Eddie Bratt	E		190	26		
Jim Sanford	T	5'8"	195	25		
Oke Carlson	T	6'	210	26		
Bill O'Toole	G			26		
Art Engstrom	G	5'9"	185	27		
Herb Clow	FB	5'4"	180	24		
Doc Kelley	TB-WB	5'10"	170	22	1	
Allen MacDonald	WB-FB	5'10"	170	27		
Roy Vexall	FB		190	22		

Date	Pts.	Opponent	Pts.
Sept. 28	6	GREEN BAY	3
Oct. 5	3	Minneapolis	0
Oct. 26	32	KENOSHA	0
Nov. 2	6	Minneapolis	0
Nov. 9	0	Green Bay	13
Nov. 23	9	Rock Island	0

ROCK ISLAND INDEPENDENTS 5-2-2 Johnny Armstrong

Regulars: UseName	Pos.	Hgt.	Wgt.	Age	Int	Pts.
Fred Thompson	E	5'11"	180	29	1	
Joe Little Twig	E-T	5'11"	180	31		6
Ned Scott	T	6'	200	23		
Duke Slater	T	6'1"	215	25		
George Thompson	G	6'1"	210	24	1	
Joe Kraker	G	6'1"	190	28		
Louie Kolls	C-E	6'1"	205	31		
Johnny Armstrong	BB	5'8"	170	30	1	7
Jim Thorpe	TB	6'1"	200	37	1	7
Rube Ursella	WB-BB	5'9"	170	34	1	13
Buck Gavin	FB	5'10"	180	29	1	42

Substitutes: UseName	Pos.	Hgt.	Wgt.	Age	Int	Pts.
Mike Wilson	E	5'10"	168	27	1	6
Vince McCarthy	WB-BB-E	5'10"	155	24		7
Walt Buland (from GB)	G-T	6'1"	215	32		
Basil Stanley	G	5'9"	195	28		
Joe Bernstein	G	6'	210	30 — played as Joe Burten		
Frank DeClerk	C	5'9"	187	25	1	
Wes Bradshaw	WB-BB-TB	5'8"	175	25		
Joe Guyon	WB-E	5'10"	185	31	1	
Bob Phelan	WB-FB	5'11"	185	26		
Bill Ashbaugh	FB	5'10"	175	24		

Date	Pts.	Opponent	Pts.
Sep. 28	0	Chic. Bears	0
Oct. 5	9	RACINE	0
Oct. 12	26	HAMMOND	0
Oct. 19	20	DAYTON	0
Oct. 26	7	Kansas City	23
Nov. 2	3	Chic. Bears	3
Nov. 9	6	Racine	3
Nov. 16	17	KANSAS CITY	0
Nov. 23	0	DULUTH	9

GREEN BAY PACKERS 7-4-0 Curly Lambeau

Regulars: UseName	Pos.	Hgt.	Wgt.	Age	Int	Pts.
Dick O'Donnell	E	6'	185	24		
Tillie Voss	E	6'3"	204	27	8	30
Cub Buck	T	6'	265	32		17
Rosey Rosatti	T	6'	212	28		
Whitey Woodin	G	5'10"	208	29	1	
Moose Gardner	G	6'1"	220	30		
Jug Earp	C-T	6'	235	27		
Charlie Mathys	BB	5'7"	165	27	2	12
Curly Lambeau	TB	5'10"	185	26	5	10
Myrt Basing	HB-E	5'9"	190	23	2	
Dutch Hendrian	FB	5'9"	180	27	2	21

Substitutes: UseName	Pos.	Hgt.	Wgt.	Age	Int	Pts.
Jab Murray	E	6'1"	220	31	1	
Dukes Duford	E-BB-HB	5'10"	165	25	1	
Walt Buland (to RI)	T	6'1"	215	32		
Wally Niemann	C	5'10"	180	30		
Les Hearden	HB	5'8"	165	22	2	6
Verne Lewellen	HB-TB	6'1"	180	22		12
Eddie Usher (to KC)	HB	5'11"	195	26		

Date	Pts.	Opponent	Pts.
Sept. 28	3	Duluth	6
Oct. 5	0	Chic. Cards	3
Oct. 12	16	KANSAS CITY	0
Oct. 19	17	MILWAUKEE	0
Oct. 26	19	MINNEAPOLIS	0
Nov. 2	6	RACINE	3
Nov. 9	13	DULUTH	0
Nov. 16	17	Milwaukee	10
Nov. 23	0	Chic. Bears	3
Nov. 27	17	Kansas City	6
Nov. 30	0	Racine	7

RACINE LEGION 4-3-3 Babe Ruetz

Regulars: UseName	Pos.	Hgt.	Wgt.	Age	Int	Pts.
Dick Halladay	E	6'	175	23	3	6
Kibo Brumm	E-G	6'	182	26		
Don Murry	T	6'2"	190	24		
Len Smith	T	5'11"	195	27		
Al Bentzin	G	6'	188	22		
Ralph King	G	6'	250	24		
Jake Mintun	C	5'11"	190	30	1	
Milt Romney	BB	5'8"	167	25	3	6
Al Elliott	TB	5'9"	175	29	3	9
Bill Giaver	WB-TB	5'9"	190	26	1	
Hank Gillo	FB	5'10"	195	29		48

Substitutes: UseName	Pos.	Hgt.	Wgt.	Age	Int	Pts.
Fritz Roessler	E	6'1"	190	26		
Jack Hueller	G	5'10"	200	26		
Riley	G	5'11"	195	22		
Johnny Mohardt	TB-WB	5'10"	168	26	4	
Chuck Palmer	WB	5'10"	185	23		
Shorty Barr	FB-TB-BB	5'8"	195	28	1	
Harrison Croft	G-T	6'1"	190	25		
Dick Hanley	WB	5'10"	175	29		
John Thomas (played as John Webster)	FB	6'1"	188	24		

Date	Pts.	Opponent	Pts.
Sep. 28	10	HAMMOND	0
Oct. 5	0	Rock Island	9
Oct. 12	10	Chic. Bears	10
Oct. 19	13	KANSAS CITY	3
Oct. 26	10	Milwaukee	0
Nov. 2	3	Green Bay	6
Nov. 9	3	ROCK ISLAND	6
Nov. 16	3	Chic. Bears	3
Nov. 23	10	Chic. Cards	10
Nov. 30	7	GREEN BAY	0

NAME	RUSHING Complete Games G	Att.	Yds.	Avg.	TD	RUSHING Incom. Games G	Att.	Yds.	TD	PASSING Complete Games G	Com.	Att.	%	Yds.	Y/A	TD	Int.	PASSING Incom. Games G	Com.	Att.	Yds.	TD	Int.
CLEVELAND																							
Elliott						7	9	82	6														
Noble						9	5	55	4														
Wolf						6	3	23	1														
Workman						9	5	15										9	17	26	462	9	7
Jones						8	3	10	3														
Tanner						2	2	7	2														
Roberts						9	1	5	1									9	3	4	61	2	1
Chamberlin																							
Work																							
Lyman																							
Bierce																							
Team						9												9					
Opp.						9												9					
CHICAGO BEARS																							
J. Sternaman	2	18	48	2.7		9	26	208	4	2	0	3	0					9	1	1	8	1	
Knop	2	19	46	2.4		9	22	86	1														
Walquist	1	17	62	3.6		8	9	41	1	1	1	0	3	0			2	8	4	4	103	1	
D. Sternaman	2	11	17	1.5		9	24	76	3														
Bryan	2	3	1	0.3		9	9	60	2	2	1	8	13	23	2.9			9	3	3	100		
Kendrick	2	17	44	2.6		7				2	1	14	7	20	1.4		1	7	2	2	72		
Lanum	1	1	0	0.0		6	6	36		1								6	1	1	15		
Hanny	2	2	-6	-3.0		9				2	1	2	50	15	7.5			9					
Mullen																							
Team	2	88	212	2.4		9				2	3	30	10	58	1.9		3	9					
Opp.	2	62	108	1.7		9				2	7	28	25	94	3.4		8	9					
FRANKFORD																							
Hamer	2	30	151	5.0	1	12	73	638	11	3	5	10	50	79	7.9	2	1	11	17	35	344	2	11
Haws	2	23	196	8.5		11	38	307	3	3	1	2	50	39	19.5			10	2	2	28		
Way	2	17	93	5.5	1	11	28	378	3														
Storer	2	21	86	4.1	2	12	32	232	5	3	2	3	67	59	19.7	1		11	3	3	81		
Sullivan	1	3	36	12.0	1	5	18	252	4														
Dayhoff	2	4	17	4.3		9	13	105	2	3								8	2	4	22		1
Kellogg						4	8	60	3														
Finn	2	3	10	3.3	1	7	8	40	1														
O'Connell																							
Doyle																							
Thomas																							
Behman																							
Team	2	101	589	5.8	6	12				3	8	15	53	177	11.8	3	1	11					
Opp.	2	48	70	1.5		12				2	8	30	27	217	7.2	1	3	12					
DULUTH																							
C. Rooney	2	5	16	3.2		4	5	80		2	4	15	27	46	3.1	1	1	4	4	7	45	1	
Method	2	19	27	1.4		3	6	41	1														
Kelley	2	13	42	3.2		3	5	21															
B. Rooney	2	14	43	3.1		4	3	16															
Gilbert	1	7	15	2.1		4	6	40		1	5	20	25	56	2.8		4	4	3	6	71	2	2
MacDonald	3	12	67	5.6		3	1	10															
Vexall						2	5	23															
Clow						1	1	2															
Underwood																							
J. Rooney																							
Team	2	60	155	2.6		4				2	9	35	26	102	2.9	1	5	4					
Opp.	2	69	202	2.9		4				2	18	41	44	291	7.1	2	5	4					
ROCK ISLAND																							
Gavin	3	21	55	2.6		6	28	119	7														
Armstrong	3	19	46	2.4	1	6	7	53		3	2	9	22	20	2.2	1	2	6	13	20	242		1
Thorpe	3	26	37	1.4		6	10	59		3	2	6	33	18	3.0			6	4	5	90	1	1
Bradshaw	3	11	24	2.2		4	7	60		3	1	4	25	10	2.5		1	4					
Ursella	3	5	10	2.0		5	5	17															
Slater	2	1	19	19.0		6																	
Guyon	2	5	16	3.2		1	1	1															
Ashbaugh						1	1	4															
McCarthy						2	1	2															
Wilson																							
F. Thompson																							
Phelan																							
Team	3	88	207	2.4	1	6				3	5	19	26	48	2.5	1	3	6					
Opp.	3	155	498	3.2	2	6				3	15	44	34	191	4.3	1	6	6					
GREEN BAY																							
Lambeau	11	132	457	3.5						11	75	179	42	1094	6.1	8	29						
Hendrian	11	118	315	2.7	3					11	3	5	60	43	8.6								
Basing	11	87	229	2.6						11	1	6	17	8	1.3								
Lewellen	8	52	121	2.3	2					8	4	8	50	74	9.3								
Hearden	2	9	42	4.7																			
Duford	3	6	14	2.3																			
Usher (1)	1	1	2	2.0																			
Mathys	11	5	-1	-2.0						11	1	1	100	16	16.0								
Buck										11	8	20	40	213	10.7	1	2						
Voss																							
O'Donnell																							
Team	11	410	1179	2.9	5					11	92	219	42	1448	6.6	9	31						
Opp.	11	364	852	2.3	2					11	54	164	33	750	4.6	2	24						
RACINE																							
Gillo	4	63	233	3.7	1	6	43	245	2	4	0	1	0					6					
Elliott	3	14	46	3.3		4	15	127	1	3								4	2	7	35	1	1
Mohardt	4	27	81	3.0		4	22	63		4	4	8	50	46	5.8	1	1	4	3	7	32		1
Giaver	4	37	85	2.3		6	19	16		4	1	1	100	12	2.0			6					
Romney	4	9	38	4.2		6	13	28		4	5	11	45	75	6.8			6	4	4	91		
Barr	4	23	53	2.3		5	2	4		4	17	37	46	213	5.8		5	5	4	6	49		2
Palmer						3	7	15										3	1	1	25		
Murry	4	2	8	4.0		6																	
Thomas						2	3	3															
Halladay																							
Brumm																							
Roessler																							
Team	4	175	544	3.1		6				4	27	58	47	346	6.0	1	6	6					
Opp.	4	125	364	2.9	1	6				4	15	47	32	226	4.8	1	11	6					

NAME	RECEIVING Complete Games G	Rec.	Yds	Avg.	TD	RECEIVING Incom. Games G	Rec.	Yds.	TD	PUNTING Comp. Games G	No.	Avg.	PUNTING Incom. Games G	No.	Avg.	PUNT RETURNS Complete Games G	No.	Yds.	Avg.	TD	PUNT RETURNS Incom. Games G	No.	Yds.	TD
CLEVELAND																								
Elliott																								
Noble						9	6	139	2															
Wolf						6	1	25	1															
Workman													9	10	42.2									
Jones						8	2	34	1															
Tanner																								
Roberts						9	4	106	3				9	2	0.0						9	2	20	
Chamberlin						9	3	83	2															
Work						8	2	36	1															
Lyman						9	1	50	1															
Bierce						4	1	50																
Team													9								9			
Opp.													9								9			
CHICAGO BEARS																								
J. Sternaman	2	1	20	20.0		9	2	75	1							2	10	98	9.8		9	6	147	1
Knop	2	1	15	15.0		9																		
Walquist										1	2	35.0	8											
D. Sternaman	2					9	3	68																
Bryan	2					9	1	8	1							2	1	15	15.0		9			
Kendrick										2	5	36.6	7											
Lanum																								
Hanny	2	1	23	23.0		9	3	112		2	15	36.2	9	17	46.2									
Mullen	2					9	1	15																
Team										2	22	36.2	9			2	11	113	10.3		9			
Opp.										2	23	36.7	9			2	7	60	8.6		9			
FRANKFORD																								
Hamer	3					11	3	37		2	9	45.0	12	11	37.0									
Haws	3	2	59	29.5		10	8	148								2					11	2	25	
Way	3					10	1	40								2	3	35	11.7		11	4	86	
Storer	3					11	4	82	1	2	2	9.5	12	5	32.0									
Sullivan	1					5	2	22								1					5	5	60	
Dayhoff	3	1	12	12.0		8																		
Kellogg													4	1	0.0									
Finn	3					6	1	35		2			7	1	37.0									
O'Connell	3	2	22	11.0		10	3	87	1															
Doyle	2	2	45	22.5	2	8																		
Thomas	3					11	2	24																
Behman	3	1	39	39.0		11																		
Team										2	11	38.5	12			2	3	35	11.7		12			
Opp.										2	15	34.7	12			2	3	65	21.7		12			
DULUTH																								
C. Rooney	2	1	10	10.0		4										2	1	10	10.0		4	1	35	
Method	2					3	1	9		2	4	39.5	3											
Kelley										2	6	33.7	3											
B. Rooney	2	4	46	11.5		4	4	91	2							2					4	1	15	
Gilbert	1	1	5	5.0		4				1	12	38.6	4			1	2	26	13.0		4			
MacDonald																								
Vexall																					2	1	15	
Clow																								
Underwood	2	1	22	22.0	1	4	2	16	1															
J. Rooney	2	2	19	9.5		4																		
Team										2	22	37.4	4			2	3	36	12.0		4			
Opp.										2	17	36.6	4			2	5	40	8.0		4			
ROCK ISLAND																								
Gavin	3	1	9	9.0		6	1	10																
Armstrong	3					6	2	35								3	5	47	9.4		6	2	30	
Thorpe	3	1	18	18.0		6	2	57		3	30	38.2	6	3	34.0									
Bradshaw	3	1	9	9.0		4	1	7								3	2	7	3.5		4			
Ursella	3	1	2	2.0	1	5	2	28		3			5	1	59.0									
Slater																								
Guyon	2					1	1	7																
Ashbaugh																								
McCarthy																					2	1	10	
Wilson	3					5	5	126	1															
F. Thompson	3	1	10	10.0		6	1	30																
Phelan	1					5	2	32																
Team										3	30	38.2	6			3	7	5.4	7.7		6			
Opp.										3	22	33.9	6			3	13	186	14.3		6			
GREEN BAY																								
Lambeau	11	7	112	16.0	1					11	2	28.5				11	17	180	10.6					
Hendrian	11	19	201	10.6												11	6	38	6.3					
Basing	11	7	68	9.7																				
Lewellen	8	3	43	14.3																				
Hearden	2	3	34	11.3	1																			
Duford																1	1	30	30.0					
Usher (1)	1	1	12	12.0																				
Mathys	11	30	579	19.3	2											11	18	155	8.6					
Buck										11	82	38.7												
Voss	11	17	337	19.8	5																			
O'Donnell	9	5	62	12.4																				
Team										11	84	38.5				11	42	403	9.6					
Opp.										11	118	36.6				11	15	173	11.5					
RACINE																								
Gillo	4	1	11	11.0		6																		
Elliott	3	1	20	20.0		4	3	7								3					4	1	8	
Mohardt	4	10	113	11.3		4										4					4	1	20	
Giaver	4	4	62	15.5		6	1	10								4	1	12	12.0		6	1	52	
Romney	4	4	53	13.3	1	6	3	67		4	4	35.0	6	1	13.0									
Barr	4					5	1	45								4	1	15	15.0		5			
Palmer																								
Murry										4	33	35.7	6	17	33.5									
Thomas																								
Halladay	4	4	68	17.0		6	3	66	1															
Brumm	3	3	19	6.3		6																		
Roessler	1					2	2	37																
Team										4	37	35.6				4	2	27	13.5		6			
Opp.										4	30	40.4				4	7	63	9.0		6			

CHICAGO CARDINALS 5-4-1 Arnie Horween

Regulars Use Name	Pos.	Hgt.	Wgt.	Age	Int.	Pts.
Eddie Anderson	E	5'10	175	23		
Carl Hanke	E	6'	190	26		12
Fred Gillies	T	6'3	215	28		
Wilfred Smith	T	6'4	205	25		
Willie Brennan	G-T	6'	215	30		6
Garland Buckeye	G	6'	245	26	1	
Nick McInerney	C-T	6'2	202	28		
Arnie Horween	BB	5'11	210	26		
Paddy Driscoll	TB-BB	5'8	160	29		34
John Hurlburt	WB	6'	175	25		18
Bob Koehler	FB	5'11	185	30	1	6

Substitutes Use Name	Pos.	Hgt.	Wgt.	Age	Int.	Pts.
Paul McNulty	E	6'	175	22		
Red O'Connor	E	5'8	175			
Munger	T					
Bill Ryan (from ROCH)	T	5'11	190	22		
George Hartong	T-G-C	6'	210	28	2	
Charlie Clark	G	5'10	205	26		
Bill Whalen	C	5'7	165	23		
Art Folz	BB-TB-WB	5'7	160	21		6
Rip King	TB	6'1	205	27	1	
Bill McElwain	WB	5'10	170	21		
Fred DeStefano	FB-WB-BB		195	24		6

Date	Pts.	Opponent	Pts.
Sep. 28	17	MILWAUKEE	7
Oct. 5	3	GREEN BAY	0
Oct. 12	13	MINNEAPOLIS	0
Oct. 19	0	Chic. Bears	6
Oct. 26	3	HAMMOND	6
Nov. 2	8	MILWAUKEE	17
Nov. 9	23	DAYTON	0
Nov. 16	13	AKRON	0
Nov. 23	10	RACINE	10
Nov. 27	0	CHIC. BEARS	21

BUFFALO BISONS 6-5-0 Tommy Hughitt

Regulars Use Name	Pos.	Hgt.	Wgt.	Age	Int.	Pts.
Len Watters	E	5'10	185	26		6
Chick Guarnieri	E	5'10	175	25	2	12
Lou Feist	T-E	6'1	200	21		
Iolas Huffman	T-G	5'11	230	26		
Harry Collins	G	5'11	190	24		
Swede Youngstrom	G-T-C	6'1	190	27		
Frank Culver (from ROCH)	C	5'11	175	27	1	
Benny Boynton (from ROCH)	BB-TB-WB	5'9	175	25	2	59
Eddie Kaw	TB	5'11	185	27		12
Mike Trainor	WB	5'9	165	24	1	6
Pete Calac	FB-E-T	5'10	200	32	1	12

Substitutes Use Name	Pos.	Hgt.	Wgt.	Age	Int.	Pts.
Glen Carberry	E	6'	190	28		
Frank Morrissey (to MIL)	T	6'1	205	25		6
Babe Kraus	T-G	6'2	220	24		
Glenn Knack	G			21		
Jim Ailinger	G	5'11	185	23		
Elmer McCormick	C	5'7	220	26	1	
Tommy Hughitt	BB-WB-E	5'8	165	31	1	
Ken Jones	WB-E	6'3	185	26		
Jack Flavin	FB	5'11	175	24	1	
Tally Mitchell	T-G-C	6'1	180	27		
Russ Burt	WB	5'8	170	23		7
Gil Gregory	WB-FB	5'11	165	26		

Date	Pts.	Opponent	Pts.
Oct. 5	13	COLUMBUS	0
Oct. 12	0	DAYTON	7
Oct. 19	26	ROCHESTER	0
Oct. 26	17	AKRON	13
Nov. 2	0	FRANKFORD	24
Nov. 9	27	KENOSHA	0
Nov. 16	14	DAYTON	6
Nov. 22	16	Rochester	0
Nov. 23	0	MILWAUKEE	23
Nov. 27	0	Akron	22
Nov. 29	7	Frankford	45

COLUMBUS TIGERS 4-4-0 Red Weaver

Regulars Use Name	Pos.	Hgt.	Wgt.	Age	Int.	Pts.
Homer Ruh	E	5'10	180	28	1	
Paul Goebel	E	6'3	200	23		18
Walt Ellis	T	5'11	225	25		
Boni Petcoff	T	5'10	218	24		
Joe Mulbarger	G	5'9	225	29		
Earl Duvall	G	6'1	205	25	1	
Andy Nemecek	C	6'4	210	28		
Wilmer Isabel	BB-WB	6'	175	24		
Sonny Winters	TB	5'9	155	26	1	14
Bob Rapp	WB	5'8	160	26	1	30
Buddy Tynes	FB-BB	6'	185	22	1	12

Substitutes Use Name	Pos.	Hgt.	Wgt.	Age	Int.	Pts.
Gus Tebell	E	5'10	170	26		6
Oscar Wolford	E-G	6'	188	27		
Johnnie Layport	G	5'9	170	23		
Joe Mantell	G					
Herb Stock	BB-FB	6'	182	24		
Neil Halleck	BB-WB			22		
Herb Schell	WB-FB-TB		185	22		9
Wilkie Moody	BB-T-G	5'7	180	27		

Date	Pts.	Opponent	Pts.
Oct. 5	0	Buffalo	13
Oct. 12	15	Rochester	7
Oct. 18	7	Frankford	23
Oct. 26	17	Dayton	6
Nov. 2	30	AKRON	0
Nov. 9	6	Chic. Bears	12
Nov. 16	16	ROCHESTER	0
Nov. 23	0	Cleveland	7

HAMMOND PROS 2-2-1 Wally Hess

Regulars Use Name	Pos.	Hgt.	Wgt.	Age	Int.	Pts.
Si Syefrit	E	5'10	170	31		
Mace Roberts	E-G	6'	185	27		
Ray Neal	T-G	5'9	210	26		
Russ Oltz	T-G-C	6'	215	25		
George Berry (to AKR)	G-T	5'11	205	24		
Bill Fortune	G	5'11	218	26		
Frank Rydzewski	C	6'1	220	31		
Rat Watson (to KC)	BB	5'10	180	25		
Sol Butler (to AKR)	TB	5'8	180	27		6
Dunc Annan	WB-FB-E	5'10	180	28		
Guil Falcon	FB	5'10	220	31		12

Substitutes Use Name	Pos.	Hgt.	Wgt.	Age	Int.	Pts.
Lenny Sachs (from MIL)	E	5'8	175	27		
Inky Williams (to DAY)	E	5'11	175	27		
Lou Usher (to KEN & MIL)	T	6'2	245	26		
Dick Stahlman (from & to KC, to KEN, to AKR)	T	6'2	220	22		
Wally Hess	BB	5'9	180	29		
Ed Robinson	TB-WB	5'9	155	20		
Teddy Besta	WB			28		
John Detwiler	FB	5'8	190	32		
Steve Sullivan (from KC)	E	5'9	180	26		
Dave Tallant	T	6'1	205	27		

Date	Pts.	Opponent	Pts.
Sep. 28	0	Racine	10
Oct. 12	0	Rock Island	26
Oct. 19	6	Kenosha	6
Oct. 26	6	Chic. Cards	3
Nov. 2	6	Kansas City	0

MILWAUKEE BADGERS 5-8-0 Hal Erickson

Regulars Use Name	Pos.	Hgt.	Wgt.	Age	Int.	Pts.
Evar Swanson	E	5'9	165	21	2	18
Clem Neacy	E	6'3	205	26		12
Bub Weller	T	6'4	220	22		
Chet Widerquist	T	6'1	220	28		
Lou Usher (from HAM & KEN)	G	6'2	245	26		
Walt LeJeune	G-C	6'	235	24		
Ojay Larson	C	6'1	198	26		
Red Dunn	BB	5'11	170	22	2	47
Jimmy Conzelman	TB-BB	6'	170	26	5	6
Ben Winkelman	WB-E-FB	6'1	190	25		15
Dinger Doane	FB	5'10	190	29		24

Substitutes Use Name	Pos.	Hgt.	Wgt.	Age	Int.	Pts.
Lenny Sachs (to HAM)	E	5'8	175	27		
Al Pierotti	T-G	5'10	200	28		
Frank Morrissey (from BUF)	G	6'1	205	25		
Peaches Nadolney	G	5'11	212	25		
Larry McGinnis	C-G	6'1	210	26		
Hal Erickson	WB-FB	5'9	190	25	1	18
George Mooney	FB-WB-E-TB	5'8	165	28		
Bob Foster	G	5'10	195	37		
Russ Smith (to CLE)	G	5'10	225	28		

Date	Pts.	Opponent	Pts.
Sep. 28	7	Chic. Cards	17
Oct. 5	3	KANSAS CITY	0
Oct. 12	21	KENOSHA	0
Oct. 19	0	Green Bay	17
Oct. 26	0	RACINE	10
Nov. 2	17	Chic. Cards	8
Nov. 9	28	MINNEAPOLIS	7
Nov. 11	3	Kansas City	7
Nov. 16	10	GREEN BAY	17
Nov. 22	6	Frankford	21
Nov. 23	23	Buffalo	0
Nov. 27	10	Cleveland (at Canton)	53
Nov. 30	14	Chic. Bears	31

AKRON PROS 2-6-0 Jim Flower

Regulars Use Name	Pos.	Hgt.	Wgt.	Age	Int.	Pts.
Red Daum	E	5'7	165	25		
Stan Mills	E	5'9	180	30	1	6
Hugh Sprinkle	T	6'2	205	27		
Jim Flower	T-C	6'1	195	28		
Al Nesser	G-E	6'	195	31		
Dutch Wallace	G-C	6'	205	28		2
John Barrett	C-E	5'6	170	25		6
Wayne Brenkert	BB-TB-WB	5'10	170	26		18
Al Michaels	TB	6'	190	24	1	6
Paul Hogan	WB-BB-FB	5'8	170	25		5
Carl Cramer	FB-WB	5'11	185	26	1	9

Substitutes Use Name	Pos.	Hgt.	Wgt.	Age	Int.	Pts.
Joe Mills	E-G	6'3	212	26		
Dick Stahlman (from KEN & HAM & KC & KEN)	T	6'2	220	22		
George Berry (from HAM)	G-T	5'11	205	24		
Harry Newman	G-T	5'6	150	27		
Carl Cardarelli	C			28		
Jimmy Robertson	BB-WB-TB	5'8	160	23		
Sol Butler (from HAM)	WB	5'8	180	27		6
Giff Zimmerman	WB	5'10	180	24		
Marty Beck	WB	5'9	175	24		
Walt Sechrist	G	6'	260	27	1	
Wilson	G					
Dutch Speck	G	5'10	220	38		
Frank Hogue	BB-WB			25		

Date	Pts.	Opponent	Pts.
Oct. 5	3	Rochester	0
Oct. 12	14	Cleveland	29
Oct. 26	13	Buffalo	17
Nov. 1	0	Frankford	23
Nov. 2	0	Columbus	30
Nov. 9	7	CLEVELAND	20
Nov. 16	0	Chic. Cards	13
Nov. 27	22	BUFFALO	0

DAYTON TRIANGLES 2-6-0 Carl Storck

Regulars Use Name	Pos.	Hgt.	Wgt.	Age	Int.	Pts.
Lee Fenner	E	5'10	170	28		6
Frank Bacon	E-WB	5'11	183	30		6
Russ Hathaway	T	5'11	245	28		6
Ed Sauer	T	5'10	245	26		
Elliott Bonowitz	G-E	6'1	190	21		
Stan Muirhead (from CLE)	G	6'	180	22		
Hobby Kinderdine	C	5'11	180	33		
Gus Redman	BB-WB-TB	5'11	170	28		
Armin Mahrt	TB	5'11	178	26		6
Lou Partlow	WB-FB-TB	6'1	185	31	4	12
Ken Huffine	FB	6'3	208	26	1	

Substitutes Use Name	Pos.	Hgt.	Wgt.	Age	Int.	Pts.
Inky Williams (from HAM)	E	5'11	175	27		
Bobby Berns	G	6'1	200	28		
Dick Egan	G			20		
Herb Sies	G	6'1	203	31		3
Glenn Tidd	C-G	5'11	202	30	1	6
Fay Abbott	BB-E	5'8	180	29	1	
Waddy Kuehl	WB	5'9	165	32		
Walt Kinderdine	WB			25		
Harry Kinderdine	G	6'	195	31		
Dick Faust	G	6'1	200	22		

Date	Pts.	Opponent	Pts.
Oct. 5	19	FRANKFORD	7
Oct. 12	7	Buffalo	0
Oct. 19	0	Rock Island	20
Oct. 26	6	COLUMBUS	17
Nov. 2	0	Cleveland	35
Nov. 9	0	Chic. Cards	23
Nov. 16	6	Buffalo	14
Nov. 27	7	Frankford	32

KANSAS CITY BLUES 2-7-0 Roy Andrews

Regulars Use Name	Pos.	Hgt.	Wgt.	Age	Int.	Pts.
Dutch Webber	E	6'2	185	22	1	
Johnny Milton	E-BB-WB	5'8	175	25	1	
Henry Bassett	T	6'2	215	25		
Jimmy Krueger	T	5'10	180	23		
Steve Owen	G-T	5'10	220	26		
Jay Berquist	G	6'3	220	22		
Carl Peterson	C	5'11	175	23		
Chuck Corgan	E-BB-TB	6'	180	21	1	26
Cowboy Hill	TB	5'8	175	25		
Rufe DeWitz	WB-TB	5'9	175	24		4
Dutch Strauss	FB	5'10	205	27		6

Substitutes Use Name	Pos.	Hgt.	Wgt.	Age	Int.	Pts.
Ralph Wiedich	T	6'1	205	22		
Roy Andrews	T-G-BB-TB	6'	220	27		4
Ivan Quinn	G			25		
Milt Rehnquist	G-C	6'	220	27		
Emmett McLemore	BB	5'7	165	24		
Lew Lane	TB-WB-BB	5'10	180	26	2	
Eddie Usher (from GB)	WB-FB-TB	5'11	195	26		
Charlie Hill	FB-WB	6'	180	23		6
Dick Sears	T	5'10	185	25		
Dick Stahlman (from KEN, to HAM & KEN & AKR)	T	6'2	220	22		
Bob Choate	G	6'1	225	30		
Rat Watson (from HAM)	TB	5'10	180	25		
Steve Sullivan (to HAM)	TB	5'9	180	26		
Jim Bradshaw	WB	5'6	150	26		

Date	Pts.	Opponent	Pts.
Oct. 5	0	Milwaukee	3
Oct. 12	0	Green Bay	16
Oct. 19	2	Racine	13
Oct. 26	23	ROCK ISLAND	7
Nov. 2	0	HAMMOND	6
Nov. 8	7	Frankford	42
Nov. 11	7	MILWAUKEE	3
Nov. 16	0	Rock Island	17
Nov. 27	6	GREEN BAY	17

NAME	RUSHING Complete Games					RUSHING Incom. Games			
	G	Att.	Yds.	Avg.	TD	G	Att.	Yds.	TD
CHICAGO CARDINALS									
Driscoll	1	17	68	4.0		9	14	144	1
Folz	1	3	16	5.3		8	7	149	1
Koehler	1	17	40	2.4		9	10	81	1
Hurlburt	1	3	5	1.7		8	6	74	2
King	1	7	23	3.3		1			
McElwain						3	1	15	
DeStefano						4	4	11	1
A. Horween									
Anderson									
Hanke									
Gillies									
Team	1	47	152	3.2		9			
Opp.	1	31	95	3.1		9			
BUFFALO									
Calac						11	19	87	2
Boynton (2)						9	11	72	2
Kaw	1	7	9	1.3		10	5	35	
Hughitt						11	6	31	
Trainor						11	3	16	
Flavin						2	7	13	
Guarnieri									
Watters									
Burt									
Carberry									
Team						11			
Opp.						11			
COLUMBUS									
Rapp	1	1	40	40.0		7	8	99	
Tynes						8	19	98	1
Stock						7	3	31	
Winters						8	5	20	1
Halleck						6	1	5	
Schell						5	1	1	1
Isabel						7	1	0	
Goebel									
Team						8			
Opp.						8			
HAMMOND									
Falcon						5	4	28	2
Watson (1)						3	1	22	
Butler (1)						5	3	3	1
Williams (1)						3	1	0	
Annan						5	1	0	
Team						5			
Opp.						5			
MILWAUKEE									
Doane	2	19	32	1.7		9	18	114	4
Dunn	2	18	36	2.0		11	9	65	2
Conzelman	2	13	13	1.0		11	4	30	
Erickson	1	5	9	1.8		3	2	10	
Winkelman	2	5	4	0.8	1	11			
Swanson									
Neacy									
Mooney									
Team	2	60	94	1.6	1	11			
Opp.	2	103	330	3.2	2	11			
AKRON									
Brenkert						8	10	129	3
Cramer						8	10	63	1
Michaels						7	8	58	1
Hogan						6	4	13	
Butler (2)						1	1	13	1
Flower						8	1	5	
Robertson									
Daum									
Zimmerman									
S. Mills									
Team						8			
Opp.						8			
DAYTON									
Partlow						8	7	90	1
Huffine						7	12	80	
Mahrt						7	9	61	1
W. Kinderedine						4	2	8	
Abbott						7	2	6	
Kuehl	1	0	0			2	1	5	
Bacon						8	2	3	
Redman									
Fenner									
Team						8			
Opp.						8			
KANSAS CITY									
Ch. Hill	5	20	24	6.2	1	2	4	40	
DeWitz	5	45	155	3.4		4			
Co. Hill	4	50	135	2.7		1			
Corgan	5	11	54	4.9	1	4			
Watson (2)	1	9	24	2.7					
Strauss	3	16	32	2.0	1	4			
Usher (2)	3	10	12	1.2		3			
Lane	2	9	11	1.2		3			
McLemore	3	4	2	0.5		1			
Andrews	5	2	1	0.5		3			
Webber	5	1	0	0.0		4			
Milton	5	1	-1	-0.2		3			
Team	5	178	549	3.1	3	4			
Opp.	5	192	765	4.0	6	4			

NAME	PASSING Complete Games								PASSING Incom. Games					
	G	Com.	Att.	%	Yds.	Y/A	TD	Int.	G	Com.	Att.	Yds.	TD	Int.
CHICAGO CARDINALS														
Driscoll	1	0	3	0					9	14	19	303	2	3
Hurlburt	1								8	1	1	30		
King	1	2	5	40	14	2.8			1	0	1			
A. Horween									7	1	1	55		
Team	1	2	8	25	14	1.8			9					
Opp.	1	12	30	40	217	9.2		3	9					
BUFFALO														
Boynton (2)									9	23	30	365	6	2
Kaw									11	12	14	213	4	2
Hughitt									11	1	1	21		
Guarnieri									11	2	3	45		1
Team	1	2	14	28	28	2.0			10					
Opp.	2	20	26	77	381	14.7	3	2	9					
COLUMBUS														
Stock									7	1	1	15		
Winters									8	30	41	616	8	8
Team									8					
Opp.									8					
HAMMOND														
Watson (1)									3	4	5	64		
Butler (1)									5	2	4	15		1
Team									5					
Opp.									5					
MILWAUKEE														
Dunn	5	36	73	49	565	7.7	4	8	8	15	24	309	2	3
Conzelman	5	8	19	42	61	3.2		4	8	10	14	251	3	2
Winkelman	5	0	1	0				1	8					
Team	5	44	93	47	626	6.7	4	13	8					
Opp.	4	19	64	30	332	5.2	2	5	9					
AKRON														
Brenkert									8	1	1	18		
Michaels									7	10	15	192		4
Hogan									6	1	3	10		2
Robertson									8	3	4	45		1
Team									8					
Opp.									8					
DAYTON														
Partlow									8	3	3	45		
Mahrt									7	2	3	33		1
Bacon									8	0	1			
Redman									6	5	6	83	1	
Team									8					
Opp.									8					
KANSAS CITY														
DeWitz	5	3	5	60	60	12.0	1		4	1	1	20		
Co. Hill	5	9	19	47	120	6.3		5	1					
Corgan	5	1	6	17	5	0.8		2	4	1	1	15		
Watson (2)	1	0	2	0										
Strauss	3	4	12	33	81	6.8		2	4	0	1			1
Lane	2	2	2	100	65	32.5			3					
Andrews	5	4	14	29	144	10.3	1	1	3					
Webber	5	0	1	0				1	4					
Milton	5	0	2	0					3					
Team	7	31	93	33	577	6.2	2	14	2					
Opp.	7	45	92	49	564	6.1	4	12	2					

NAME	RECEIVING Complete Games					RECEIVING Incom. Games			
	G	Rec.	Yds	Avg.	TD	G	Rec.	Yds.	TD
CHICAGO CARDINALS									
Driscoll	1	2	14	7.0		9	1	55	
Folz	1					8	1	30	
Koehler	1					9	2	30	
Hurlburt	1					8	5	107	1
McElwain						3	2	38	
A. Horween						7	1	13	
Anderson	1					8	2	70	
Hanke	1					8	1	30	1
Gillies	1					9	1	15	
BUFFALO									
Boynton (2)						9	12	184	3
Kaw						11	5	46	2
Hughitt						11	2	33	
Trainor						11	4	76	1
Guarnieri						11	8	127	2
Watters						9	4	112	1
Burt						1	2	60	1
Carberry						2	1	6	
COLUMBUS									
Rapp	1	1	22	22.0		7	10	294	5
Tynes						8	3	40	1
Schell						5	1	15	
Goebel						8	13	207	2
HAMMOND									
Butler (1)						5	2	21	
Williams (1)						3	3	38	
Annan						5	1	20	
MILWAUKEE									
Doane	3					8	1	13	
Dunn	3	1	0	0.0		10			
Conzelman	3	7	102	14.6		10	2	55	
Erickson	1	4	25	6.3		3			
Winkelman	3	4	61	15.3	1	10	3	56	
Swanson	2	11	218	19.8	1	7	7	166	2
Neacy	3	4	66	16.5	1	10	9	185	1
Mooney	2	1	10	10.0		3			
AKRON									
Brenkert						8	5	52	
Cramer						8	1	25	
Hogan						6	3	72	
Robertson						8	1	18	
Daum						8	3	53	
Zimmerman						2	1	35	
S. Mills						5	1	10	
DAYTON									
Huffine						7	3	45	
Kuehl						3	2	24	
Bacon						8	1	10	
Fenner						7	4	82	1
KANSAS CITY									
DeWitz	5	3	70	23.3		4	1	15	
Co. Hill	4	2	25	12.5		1			
Corgan	5	10	247	24.7	2	4	1	20	
Strauss	3	1	15	15.0		4			
Usher (2)	3	1	50	50.0		3			
Lane	2	1	12	12.0		3			
McLemore	3	2	30	15.0		1			
Webber	5	3	26	8.7		4			

NAME	PUNTING Comp. Games			PUNTING Incom. Games			PUNT RETURNS Complete Games					PUNT RETURNS Incom. Games			
	G	No.	Avg.	G	No.	Avg.	G	No.	Yds.	Avg.	TD	G	No.	Yds.	TD
CHICAGO CARDINALS															
Driscoll	1	12	43.5	9	7	35.9	1	3	18	6.0		9	2	60	
Team	1	12	43.5	9			1	3	18	6.0		9			
Opp.	1	7	37.0	9			1	6	43	7.2		9			
BUFFALO															
Boynton (2)				9	3	18.7						9	2	88	1
Kaw				11	2	0.0									
Flavin				2	1	0.0									
Guarnieri				11	10	42.7									
Team				11								11			
Opp.				11								11			
COLUMBUS															
Winters				8	3	46.7						8	1	4	
Team				8								8			
Opp.				8								8			
HAMMOND															
Falcon				5	1	43.0									
Team				5								5			
Opp.				5								5			
MILWAUKEE															
Doane	3			8	4	31.3									
Dunn	3	27	32.9	10	4	35.3	2	4	45	11.3		11	1	55	
Conzelman							2	1	1	1.0		11			
Team	3	27	32.9	10			2	5	46	9.2		11			
Opp.	3	24	35.4	10			2	9	78	8.7		11			
AKRON															
Cramer				7	2	28.5									
Hogan				6	4	24.5									
Robertson												8	2	66	
Team				8								8			
Opp.				8								8			
DAYTON															
Partlow				8	1	0.0									
Huffine				7	6	34.0									
Team				8								8			
Opp.				8								8			
KANSAS CITY															
Ch. Hill	5	3	24.3	2											
DeWitz	5	2	22.0	4											
Co. Hill	4	7	39.9	1			4	1	8	8.0		1			
Corgan							5	6	171	28.5		4			
Strauss	3	11	34.5	4											
Usher (2)							3	1	5	5.0		3			
Lane	2	2	47.5	3											
Andrews	5	5	29.8	3											
Webber	5	3	44.3	4											
Team	6	39	33.7	3			5	8	184	23.0		4			
Opp.	6	39	36.7	3			5	7	72	10.3		4			

KENOSHA MAROONS 0-4-1 Earl Potteiger and Bo Hanley

Regulars

UseName	Pos.	Hgt.	Wgt.	Age	Int.	Pts.
Walt Cassidy	E	5'10	200	24		
Fritz Heinisch	E	5'10	175	24		
Pep Hurst	T	6'1	195	22		
Lou Usher (from HAM to MIL)	T-C	6'2	245	26	1	
Dick Stahlman (to HAM, to & from KC, to AKR)	G-T	6'2	220	22		
George Dahlgren	G	5'10	200	37		
Marty Conrad	C	6'1	250	29		
Jimmy Simpson	BB-TB	5'10	160	26	1	
Dick Vick	TB	5'9	165	22	1	
Marv Wood	WB-FB-E	6'1	195	23		
George Seasholtz	FB	5'8	185	25	1	12

Substitutes

UseName	Pos.	Hgt.	Wgt.	Age	Int.	Pts.
Swede Erickson	E		215			
Egan	E		175			
Ray Oberbroekling	T	5'8	198	25		
Bud Gorman	G-T		225	28		
Clete Patterson	G	5'10	205	22		
Pard Pearce	BB	5'5	150	27		
Earl Potteiger	WB-BB-TB-E	5'7	170	33		
Jimmy Baxter	WB-E	5'7	175	32		
Whitey Wolter	WB-BB	5'10	170	23		
Irv Carlson	WB-TB	5'8	170	28		

Scores of each game

Date	Pts.	Opponent	Pts.
Oct. 4	6	Frankford	31
Oct. 12	0	Milwaukee	21
Oct. 19	6	HAMMOND	6
Oct. 26	0	Duluth	32
Nov. 9	0	Buffalo	27

MINNEAPOLIS MARINES 0-6-0 Joe Brandy

Regulars

UseName	Pos.	Hgt.	Wgt.	Age	Int.	Pts.
Oscar Christianson	E	5'10	190	25		
Louie Mohs	E	6'2	220	31		
Les Scott	T-E	5'10	205	25		
Pat Dunnigan	T	5'10	215	30		
George Kramer	G-T	6'2	240	29		
Festus Tierney	G	6'1	200	25		
John Madigan	C	6'	185	25	1	
Bill Houle	BB	5'8	175	23		
Marty Norton	TB-WB	5'6	175	21	3	12
Eddie Novak	WB	5'9	175	27	1	1
John Simons	FB-E	5'11	200	24	1	1

Substitutes

UseName	Pos.	Hgt.	Wgt.	Age	Int.	Pts.
Fred Putzier	E-WB	5'9	174	25		
Adrian Baril	T-G	5'11	210	26		
Beanie Eberts	G-T-BB	5'11	198	23		
Ed Johns	G	6'	175	24		
Tom Hogan	C-E-G	6'2	200	26		
Einar Cleve	WB-TB-BB	5'9	175	28	1	
Louis Pahl	FB-WB	5'8	185	27		

Scores of each game

Date	Pts.	Opponent	Pts.
Oct. 5	0	Duluth	3
Oct. 12	0	Chic. Cards	13
Oct. 26	0	Green Bay	19
Nov. 2	0	DULUTH	6
Nov. 9	7	Milwaukee	28
Nov. 15	7	Frankford	39

ROCHESTER JEFFERSONS 0-7-0 Jerry Noonan

Regulars

UseName	Pos.	Hgt.	Wgt.	Age	Int.	Pts.
Spin Roy	E	6'	175	27	1	
Hal Clark	E	5'10	195	30		
John Dooley	T-G	6'1	225	26		
Frank Matteo	T-G	5'11	195	28		
Darby Lowery	G	6'	215	32		
Roy Martineau	G-T-C	6'	210	26		
Hank Smith	C	6'1	190	31		
Leo Peyton	BB	5'11	190		1	
Shag Sheard	TB-BB	5'11	175	25		1
Jerry Noonan	WB-BB	6'1	195	25		6
Bob Argus	FB-WB	5'10	195	30		

Substitutes

UseName	Pos.	Hgt.	Wgt.	Age	Int.	Pts.
Reeves Baysinger	E	6'	180	23		
Frank Culver (to BUF)	E	5'11	175	27		
Doc Alexander	T	5'11	220	26		
Johnny Coaker	T-G			22		
Red Pearlman	G-T	6'	195	26		
Joe Bachmaier	G	5'9	175	28		
Jimmy Woods	C-T-G	5'9	200	30		
Fritz Foster	BB-FB	5'11	185	25		
Tex Grigg	TB	5'11	195	33		
Lou Smyth	WB	6'1	205	25		
Will Anderson	FB-TB	5'10	173	27		
Bob Nash	T	6'1	205	31		
Bill Ryan (to ChiC)	T	5'11	190	22		
Elmer Volgenau	G	6'2	190	24		
Gordon Wallace	C	5'10	170	25		
Billy Rafter	BB-FB	5'6	155	29		
Benny Boynton (to BUF)	TB	5'9	175	25		
Nielson	WB					
Clem Nugent	FB-WB	5'9	155	24		

Scores of each game

Date	Pts.	Opponent	Pts.
Sep. 27	0	Frankford	21
Oct. 5	0	AKRON	3
Oct. 12	7	COLUMBUS	15
Oct. 19	0	Buffalo	26
Oct. 26	0	Cleveland	59
Nov. 16	0	Columbus	16
Nov. 22	0	BUFFALO	16

1925 N.F.L.
Galloping Out of Obscurity

Even though the Four Horsemen of Notre Dame graduated, college football still held the sporting spotlight in the autumn. The national press treated pro football like a raggedy stepchild while trumpeting the exploits of such teams as Dartmouth and the University of Washington. Although Washington's Wildcat Wilson and Stanford's Ernie Nevers achieved national reputations for their running, no football player could approach the fame of the Galloping Ghost — Red Grange of the University of Illinois.

Grange attained a standing next to Babe Ruth and Jack Dempsey on the sports pedestal by slipping and dodging to touchdowns by the bushel. The shy redhead carried only 175 pounds, but he more than made up for his lack of bulk with quick changes of speed and sharp cuts that left frusrated tacklers embracing his jet stream. His No. 77 disappearing downfield brought thousands to their feet cheering, not only in football stadiums, but in movie houses which carried newsreels of his previous week's performance. With all the deserved publicity and fanfare, it was only inevitable that by the time autumn 1925 arrived, Grange was the hottest sports property around. Speculation grew over what Grange would do with his newfound fame. Most of his friends and the public advised him to go into acting or business and to avoid the dirty, profane world of pro football. When Grange finally revealed his choice, it wasn't a popular one, and suddenly America's red-headed golden boy was working at the dirtiest game in town.

But Grange figured that the most honest way to capitalize on his football fame was to play football. With C.C. Pyle, his fast-talking agent, conducting night-and-day secret negotiations with the Chicago Bears, Grange signed a professional contract with that team shortly after his final college game. In return for a healthy share of the gate receipts, Grange agreed to join the Bears for the remainder of their schedule and a post-season barnstorming tour.

The public loudly proclaimed distain over the betrayal of their folk hero, blaming the pros as well as Grange. Colleges were incensed at the pros for signing Grange before he graduated, and fans cursed him for becoming comtaminated with an unnatural professionalism. Grange himself shrugged off the criticism, openly admitting his desire was to make big money before his glittering name was forgotten. As far as the NFL was concerned, all the adjectives in the world couldn't harm it. The league had finally gotten into the headlines and the scorn was not nearly as large as the publicity.

Grange made his pro debut on Thanksgiving Day as the Bears hosted the Chicago Cardinals. A standing-room-only crowd of 36,000 watched Grange pick up only 40 yards on the ground. Popular Paddy Driscoll, the Cardinals' great triple-threat, heard himself booed for perhaps the only time in his career in Chicago for carefully placing his punts out of Grange's reach. But the strategy paid off in a scoreless tie and moral victory for the Cardinals. Three days later, the Ghost galloped to 75 yards in 14 carries as the Bears beat the Columbus Tigers 14-13 in a Chicago snowstorm.

To turn Grange's reputation into dollars, the Bears set out on a tour that listed an exhausting eight games in 12 days; five of the contests were league games, three were exhibition games against non-league teams. The first stop was St. Louis were Red ran for four touchdowns against a hastily gathered squad of semi-pros and NFL players. Three days later, the Frankford Yellowjackets hosted the Bears in Philadelphia before a crowd of 35,000 eager to see some Grange magic. Heavy rain and deep mud ruled out any long runs, but Grange did score both touchdowns in a 14-7 Chicago victory. Immediately after that contest, the Bears piled onto a train heading for New York. The next day, Sunday, December 6, pro football won its spurs in New York City. The New York Giants had played most of their first year in virtual seclusion, but fans mobbed the ticket windows to see the legendary Grange. The 73,000 paying customers at the Polo Grounds set a record for pro football and saved Giants owner Tim Mara from a red-ink bath in his first year running the team. The tired Bears took the field in the same wet uniforms they had worn in Philadelphia. On the other hand, the Giants ran into action in spotless outfits, ready to put their best foot forward before the massive audience. Grange acted as a decoy for most of the game as Joey Sternaman, brother of the Bears' half-owner, broke away for a pair of touchdowns. The customers got their money's worth, though, when late in the contest, Grange intercepted a Giants pass and trotted untouched for a touchdown to cap the 19-7 triumph for the Bears.

As the tour progressed, all the Bears were dragging, nursing various wounds. Grange himself had been kicked in the neck in the New York game and was exhausted by the tarvel and demands of reporters. A listless Grange appeared before crowds in Washington, Boston and Pittsburgh before finally sitting out a game in Detroit due to a badly swollen arm. The Bears ended the tour by hosting the Giants in a rematch at Chicago, and Grange played briefly before his hometown fans with only one arm at his disposal. Although the Giants won 9-0, the crowd applauded the local hero to the end.

Grange earned over $50,000 from the tour, and agent Pyle brought home the same amount. After a week off, the Bears set off on a second tour, playing nine games in the South and West until the end of January. Grange's financial success convinced some other college players to turn pro immediately, and he met some of them on this post-season tour. On January 2, the Bears beat a quickly assembled team led by Ernie Nevers in Jacksonville; despite the presence of the two stars, the attendance was

NAME	Rushing Complete Games G	Att	Yds	Avg	TD	Rushing Incom Games G	Att	Yds	TD	Passing Complete Games G	Com	Att	%	Yds	Y/A	TD	Int	Passing Incom Games G	Com	Att	Yds	TD	Int
KENOSHA																							
Wood						4	3	15															
Seasholtz						5	5	18	1														
Carlson						2	1	1															
Vick						5	1	0										5	13	20	185	1	5
Simpson																		4	4	5	95		1
Cassidy																							
Potteiger																							
Dahlgren																							
Wolters																							
Team						5												5					
Opp.						5												5					
MINNEAPOLIS																							
Norton	1	1	8	8.0		5	3	26	2	1								5	5	5	69		
Cleve	1	5	2	0.4		3				1	0	2	0				2	3					
Pahl	1	1	0	0.0		2	2	12		1								2	1	1	15		
Simon	1	3	-4	-1.3		5																	
Novak	1	2	-7	-3.5		4																	
Houle										1	4	14	29	41	2.9		2	5	5	7	102		
Eberts										1	0	5	0				1	2					
Mohs																							
Team	1	12	-1	-0.1		5				1	4	21	19	41	2.0		5	5					
Opp.	1	43	135	3.1	2	5				1	12	25	48	163	6.5	1	4	5					
ROCHESTER																							
Sheard	1	7	6	0.9		6	5	56		1	1	4	25	8	2.0		1	6	6	10	96		1
Grigg						1	2	15										1	2	2	35		
Smyth						1	2	12															
Nielson						1	1	10															
Argus	1	7	4	0.6		6	2	3															
Boynton (1)	1	9	3	0.3						1	3	10	30	65	6.5		1						
Anderson						3	1	2															
Noonan	1					4	1	1	1									1	3	4	65		1
Roy																							
Clark																							
Team	1	23	13	0.6		6				1	4	14	29	73	5.2		2	6					
Opp.	1	50	274	5.5	2	6				1	1	3	33	30	10.0	1	1	6					

NAME	Receiving Complete Games G	Rec	Yds	Avg	TD	Receiving Incom Games G	Rec	Yds	TD	Punting Comp. Games G	No	Avg	Punting Incom Games G	No	Avg	Punt Returns Complete Games G	Rec	Yds	Avg	TD	Punt Returns Incom Games G	Rec	Yds	TD
KENOSHA																								
Wood						4	2	30					4	5	37.2									
Seasholtz						5	3	80	1				5	1	20.0									
Carlson																								
Vick																					5	1	20	
Simpson																								
Cassidy						5	5	60																
Potteiger						4	2	50																
Dahlgren													4	4	28.5									
Wolters													3	1	37.0									
Team													5								5			
Opp.													5								5			
MINNEAPOLIS																								
Norton	1	2	11	5.5		5				1			5	4	27.5									
Cleve	1					3	3	53																
Pahl																								
Simon	1	1	25	25.0		5	1	15																
Novak	1	1	5	5.0		4	2	30		1	1	35.0	4			1					4	1	35	
Houle										1	11	38.0	5	1	35.0									
Eberts																								
Mohs						5	5	88																
Team										1	12	37.8	5			1	0				5			
Opp.										1	4	38.3	5			1	11	146	13.3		5			
ROCHESTER																								
Sheard	1					6	1	5		1	8	38.0	6	1	40.0									
Grigg																								
Smyth						1	1	10																
Nielson																								
Argus																								
Boynton (1)										1	2	33.5				1	1	20	20.0					
Anderson																								
Noonan	1	2	55	27.5		4	4	55																
Roy	1	1	10	10.0		6	1	31																
Clark	1	1	8	8.0		6	1	30																
Team										1	10	37.1	6			1	1	20	20.0		6			
Opp.										1	7	41.1	6			1	2	10	5.0		6			

disappointing. In Los Angeles, however, a record 75,000 people showed up on January 16 to see Grange score two touchdowns in a victory over the Los Angeles Tigers, led by Wildcat Wilson. When it was all over, Grange had played 18 pro games in less than three months.

The NFL that profited from Grange and his press had 20 teams, an increase of two over 1924. The midwest clubs of Racine, Kenosha and Minneapolis dropped out. In their place, the league took in the Providence Steam Roller and the Pottsville Maroons, both strong independent teams for several years. The Giants gave New York its first successful big-league pro football team. A Detroit franchise was granted to Jimmy Conzelman, who was owner, coach and blocking back. Sam Deutsch, owner of two franchises, sold his inactive Canton franchise back to Canton for $3,000. Star tackle Pete Henry and Link Lyman returned to Canton to lead a mediocre squad. In addition to Lyman, guard Rudy Comstock and fullback Ben Jones left Cleveland for Canton, and Guy Chamberlin moved on to Frankford as player-coach. The 1924 champion Cleveland team was reduced to also-ran status. Jim Thorpe was cut by the New York Giants after three games and took his aging legs to Rock Island to finish the season.

The league championship race, this year extended from September 20 to December 20, went relatively unnoticed in the publicity over Red Grange. Four teams emerged as contenders. Frankford depended on a strong line led by Chamberlin at end and Bull Behman at tackle. They won nine of their first 10 games before losing to the Bears 19-0 on November 8. They rebounded to upset Pottsville 20-0 the next Saturday, but then they collapsed, losing to Cleveland and Providence on successive days.

The Detroit Panthers were the NFL's top defensive club. Behind Conzelman, end Tillie Voss and tackle Gus Sonnenburg, they posted eight shutouts in 12 games and had a shot at the title until Rock Island upset them 6-3 on Thanksgiving Day in Detroit.

The Chicago Cardinals had an early version of the "dream backfield" with Red Dunn, Paddy Driscoll, Hal Erickson and Bob Koehler. Alhough this quartet was light, averaging only 176 pounds, they had great speed and versatility. Driscoll's 11 field goals more than doubled the output of any other player in the league; on October 11, in a 19-9 victory over Columbus, he kicked four field goals, one for 50 yards. It was the second 50-yarder in the NFL in 1925; two weeks earlier, Phil White hit one for Kansas City, his only three-pointer all season.

The Pottsville Maroons scored 20 or more points in nine of their 12 games, a rarity in this era of low-scoring games. They did it mostly with a crushing running attack featuring Tony Latone, Barney Wentz, Hoot Flanagan and Walt French. Jack Ernst was effective as an occasional passer, mostly to Charlie Berry, who caught more than 30 passes on the season. Berry also placekicked field goals and extra points and led the league with 74 points. In addition, he was a major league baseball catcher and would have a long career as an American League umpire.

In the showdown game of the year, the Maroons took their 9-2-0 record to Chicago to play the 9-1-1 Cardinals on December 6, the same day Grange was packing the Polo Grounds. The Maroons ground out three touchdowns by running and held Driscoll in check to score a 21-7 victory which seemingly wrapped up the title for Pottsville. Several newspapers were quick to award the championship to the Maroons, ignoring the fact that the season still had two weeks to run and almost anything could happen.

Cardinals owner Chris O'Brien immediately arranged for two games to improve his team's percentage, one against the Milwaukee Badgers on Thursday and one against the Hammond Pros on Saturday. Both these clubs had disbanded for the season but regrouped for one more payday in exchange for being cannon fodder for the Cardinals. O'Brien seemed more intent on inflating his team's record to justify a spot on the Grange tour than to outflank Pottsville. The Cardinals beat Milwaukee 59-0 in a farce of a game with short quarters and no admission charged to spectators. They also beat Hammond 13-0 two days later.

That same Saturday, December 12, Pottsville outflanked itself. The Maroons scheduled an exhibition game against an all-star team of former Notre Dame players, including the Four Horsemen, in Shibe Park in Philadelphia. Frankford, with a game scheduled the same day at Frankford Stadium, protested because its territorial rights were being invaded. NFL president Joe Carr agreed and ordered Pottsville to cancel the game under pain of suspension. The Maroons claimed the league office had given earlier verbal permission and went ahead with the game, beating the ex-Notre Damers 9-6.

Carr immediately suspended the Pottsville franchise and cancelled its scheduled Sunday game with Providence. Red Grange's arm injury ruined any chance for Chris O'Brien's hoped-for Cardinals-Bears game and his team closed up for the season with an 11-2-1 record, slightly btter than Pottsville's 10-2-0. To this day, old-timers in Pottsville complain about the two extra Cardinals games but, in fact, the Cardinals didn't need them. As soon as they were suspended, the Maroons lost their eligibility for the championship.

At the league meeting in January, O'Brien declined to accept the championship, but the league records quite properly carry the Cardinals on its books as champions. Carr did, however, levy penalties in connection with the ridiculous Cardinals-Milwaukee game of December 10. The Badgers had put a skeleton crew on the field, including four Chicago high school players and, for this, Carr fined the Badgers $500 and ordered the owner to sell the franchise. Cardinals back Art Folz was banned from the NFL for life for arranging the use of the high schoolers from his alma mater. O'Brien was also fined, even though he had no knowledge of the make-up of the Badger team. The league also took this time to reaffirm its policy of good will toward the colleges by ruling that no college player could be signed before his class had graduated. Why not? With Grange in the fold, the Pros didn't need to bother the colleges for at least another 10 years.

Despite his impact on the league, Grange did not make the all-NFL team annually selected in a poll by the *Green Bay Press Gazette*. The first-team selections: ends Charlie Berry, Pottsville, and Ed Lynch, Rochester; tackles Ed Healey, Bears, and Gus Sonnenberg, Detroit; guards Art Carney, New York, and Jim McMillin, Bears; center Ralph Claypool, Cardinals; quarterback Joey Sternaman, Bears; halfbacks Paddy Driscoll, Cardinals, and Dave Noble, Cleveland; and fullback Jack McBride, New York.

CHICAGO CARDINALS 11-2-1 Norm Barry

Regulars

UseName	Pos.	Hgt.	Wgt.	Age	Int.	Pts.
Eddie Anderson	E	5'10	175	24		6
Herb Blumer	E-T	6'1	200	25		12
Fred Gillies	T	6'3	220	29		
Buck Evans	T	5'11	204	25		6
Willie Brennan	G	6'	220	31		
Jerry Lunz	G	6'3	210	22		
Ralph Claypool	C	5'11	195	26		
Red Dunn	BB	5'11	170	23	2	29
Paddy Driscoll	TB	5'8	160	30	2	67
Hal Erickson	WB-FB	5'9	190	26	4	42
Bob Koehler	FB	5'11	185	31	1	24

Substitutes

UseName	Pos.	Hgt.	Wgt.	Age	Int.	Pts.
Lenny Sachs (from HAM)	E	5'8	175	28		
Nick McInerney	E-C-G-T	6'2	202	29		
Bub Weller	T	6'4	218	23		
Wilfred Smith	G-E-C	6'4	210	26	1	
Ike Mahoney	BB-WB	6'	165	23	1	6
Jim Tays	TB-FB-WB-BB	5'8	165	26		6
John Hurlburt	WB-BB	6'	175	26		
Fred DeStefano	FB		195	25		
Paul McNulty	E	6'	175	23	1	6
Evar Swanson (from RI)	E	5'9	165	22		
Art Folz	BB-TB-WB	5'7	160	22		24
Mickey McDonnell (from DUL)	WB	5'8	150	21		

Scores of each game

Date	Pts.	Opponent	Pts.
Sep. 27	6	HAMMOND	10
Oct. 4	34	MILWAUKEE	0
Oct. 11	19	COLUMBUS	9
Oct. 18	20	KANSAS CITY	7
Oct. 25	9	CHIC. BEARS	0
Nov. 1	10	DULUTH	6
Nov. 8	9	GREEN BAY	6
Nov. 15	23	BUFFALO	6
Nov. 22	14	DAYTON	0
Nov. 26	0	Chic. Bears	0
Nov. 29	7	ROCK ISLAND	0
Dec. 6	7	POTTSVILLE	21
Dec. 10	59	MILWAUKEE	0
Dec. 12	13	HAMMOND	0

POTTSVILLE MAROONS 10-2-0 Dick Rauch

Regulars

UseName	Pos.	Hgt.	Wgt.	Age	Int.	Pts.
Charlie Berry	E	6'	185	22	3	74
Frank Bucher	E	5'11	190	24		12
Russ Hathaway	T	5'11	245	29	1	
Russ Stein	T	6'1	210	29		
Frank Racis	G	6'	200	27		
Duke Osborn	G	5'10	190	28	1	
Herb Stein	C	6'	185	27	4	
Jack Ernst	BB	5'11	175	25	2	19
Hoot Flanagan	TB	6'	168	24	6	42
Tony Latone	WB-TB-FB	5'11	190	28	3	48
Barney Wentz	FB	5'11	200	22	3	31

Substitutes

UseName	Pos.	Hgt.	Wgt.	Age	Int.	Pts.
Eddie Doyle	E	5'9	175	27		6
Ed Sauer (from & to DAY)	T	5'10	260	27		
Clarence Beck	T-G	5'11	200	30		
Dick Rauch	G	5'9	178	32		
Denny Hughes	C	5'11	185	25	1	2
Walt French	WB-TB-BB	5'7	155	26	2	30
Armin Mahrt (from, to & from DAY)	TB-WB	5'11	184	27		6
Fungy Lebengood	WB	5'11	175	23		
Harry Dayhoff	WB	5'9	170	29		
Bob Millman	WB	5'11	175	22	1	

Scores of each game

Date	Pts.	Opponent	Pts.
Sep. 27	28	BUFFALO	0
Oct. 4	0	PROVIDENCE	6
Oct. 11	28	CANTON	0
Oct. 18	34	Providence	0
Nov. 1	20	COLUMBUS	0
Nov. 8	21	AKRON	0
Nov. 14	0	Frankford	20
Nov. 15	14	ROCHESTER	6
Nov. 22	24	CLEVELAND	6
Nov. 26	31	GREEN BAY	0
Nov. 29	49	FRANKFORD	0
Dec. 6	21	Chic. Cards	7

DETROIT TIGERS 8-2-2 Jimmy Conzelman

Regulars

UseName	Pos.	Hgt.	Wgt.	Age	Int.	Pts.
Vivian Hultman	E	5'8	175	22		6
Tillie Voss	E	6'3	204	28		
Tom Hogan	T-G-E	6'2	200	27		
Gus Sonnenberg	T	5'6	194	27		27
Tom McNamara	G	5'10	210	28		
Jack Fleischman	G	5'6	185	24		
Ernie Vick	C	5'11	185	25		
Jimmy Conzelman	BB-TB	6'	172	27	7	18
Dick Vick	TB-BB	5'9	165	23		
Al Hadden	WB-FB	5'9	183	25		24
Dinger Doane	FB	5'10	190	30	1	30

Substitutes

UseName	Pos.	Hgt.	Wgt.	Age	Int.	Pts.
Bill Bucher	E	5'10	180	22		
Walt Ellis (from COL)	T	5'11	225	26		
By Wimberly	T-G	6'2	200	32		
Russ Smith (to ChiB)	G	5'10	220	29		
Al Crook	C-G-T	5'10	190	27		
Dutch Lauer	BB-WB-E	5'10	185	29		
Dutch Marion	FB	5'9	180	23		24

Scores of each game

Date	Pts.	Opponent	Pts.
Sep. 27	7	COLUMBUS	0
Oct. 4	0	CHIC. BEARS	0
Oct. 11	3	FRANKFORD	0
Oct. 18	6	DAYTON	0
Oct. 25	0	AKRON	0
Nov. 1	26	HAMMOND	6
Nov. 8	21	MILWAUKEE	0
Nov. 11	22	CLEVELAND	13
Nov. 15	0	Chic. Bears	14
Nov. 22	20	ROCHESTER	0
Nov. 26	3	ROCK ISLAND	6
Dec. 12	21	CHIC. BEARS	0

NEW YORK GIANTS 8-4-0 Bob Folwell

Regulars

UseName	Pos.	Hgt.	Wgt.	Age	Int.	Pts.
Paul Jappe	E	6'1	195	27	1	
Lynn Bomar	E	6'1	210	24	1	18
Century Milstead	T	6'1	213	25		
Babe Parnell	T	6'3	205	23		
Tommy Tomlin	G-T	5'10	198	31		
Art Carney	G	6'2	230	25	1	
Doc Alexander	C	5'11	220	27	1	6
Dutch Hendrian (from RI)	BB-WB	5'9	185	28	2	22
Jack McBride	TB-FB	5'11	185	23	3	25
Hinkey Haines	WB-BB	5'10	170	26	1	18
Heinie Benkert	FB-WB	5'9	165	24	1	

Substitutes

UseName	Pos.	Hgt.	Wgt.	Age	Int.	Pts.
Bob Nash	E	6'1	205	32		
Owen Reynolds	E-BB	6'3	212	25		
Ed McGinley	T	5'11	185	25		
Al Bedner	T-G	5'10	190	27		
Swede Nordstrom	G-T	6'2	240	28		
Joe Williams	G-T-FB	6'	235	27		6
Larry Walbridge	C	5'7	200	27		
Matt Brennan	BB-TB-WB	6'1	195	27	1	3
Jim Thorpe (to RI)	TB	6'1	200	38		
Bill Rooney (from DUL)	WB-FB	6'2	195	29		6
Phil White (from KC)	TB-FB	6'2	210	25	1	8
Mike Palm	BB-WB	5'10	170	25	1	
Jim Frugone	TB-BB	5'10	165	27		
Tommy Myers	WB-BB	5'8	170	24		
Earl Potteiger	BB	5'7	170	34		
Cowboy Hill (from KC)	TB-WB	5'8	175	26		
Bill Kenyon	BB	5'9	180	26	1	
Tom Moran	BB	5'8	175	27		

Scores of each game

Date	Pts.	Opponent	Pts.
Oct. 11	0	Providence	14
Oct. 17	3	Frankford	5
Oct. 18	0	FRANKFORD	14
Nov. 1	19	CLEVELAND	0
Nov. 3	7	BUFFALO	0
Nov. 8	19	COLUMBUS	0
Nov. 11	13	ROCHESTER	0
Nov. 15	13	PROVIDENCE	12
Nov. 22	9	KANSAS CITY	3
Nov. 29	23	DAYTON	0
Dec. 6	7	CHIC. BEARS	19
Dec. 13	9	Chic. Bears	0

AKRON PROS 4-2-2 George Berry, Fritz Pollard

Regulars

UseName	Pos.	Hgt.	Wgt.	Age	Int.	Pts.
Scotty Bierce	E	5'9	170	28	2	
Obie Newman	E	6'2	195	25		7
Cy Caldwell	T	6'1	210	26		5
Dick Stahlman	T	6'2	220	23		
Russ Blailock	G-T	5'10	235	23		5
Al Nesser (to CLE)	G	6'	195	32		
John Barrett	C	5'6	170	26		
Jimmy Robertson	BB	5'8	160	24	1	12
Fritz Pollard (from HAM, to PROV)	TB-BB-WB	5'7	165	31	2	12
Dunc Annan (from & to HAM)	WB-FB	5'10	180	30	2	6
Guil Falcon (from HAM, to ROCH)	FB-BB-G	5'10	220	32		

Substitutes

UseName	Pos.	Hgt.	Wgt.	Age	Int.	Pts.
Red Daum	E	5'7	170	26		6
Fred Bissell	E	6'1	180	22		
Chase Clements (to CLE)	T	6'2	205	23		
Jim Flower	T	6'1	195	29		
Marty Conrad	G-E	6'1	250	30		
George Berry	G-T	5'11	208	25	1	6
Joe Mills	C-G-T	6'3	212	27		
Fanny Neihaus	TB	6'	170	23	1	6
Carl Cramer	FB	5'11	187	27	1	
Fritz Henry	G		190	29		

Scores of each game

Date	Pts.	Opponent	Pts.
Sep. 27	7	CLEVELAND	0
Oct. 4	14	KANSAS CITY	7
Oct. 11	0	Buffalo	0
Oct. 18	20	Canton	3
Oct. 25	0	Detroit	0
Nov. 1	17	DAYTON	3
Nov. 7	7	Frankford	17
Nov. 8	0	Pottsville	21

FRANKFORD YELLOW JACKETS 13-7-0 Guy Chamberlin

Regulars

UseName	Pos.	Hgt.	Wgt.	Age	Int.	Pts.
Rae Crowther	E	5'11	175	22	1	18
Guy Chamberlin	E	6'2	193	31	1	12
Link Lyman (from CAN)	T	6'2	225	26		
Bull Behman	T-C	5'10	210	25	3	39
Bill Hoffman	G	5'10	225	23		
Butch Spagna	G	6'	220	28		
Bill Springsteen	C	6'	190	24	1	
Two Bits Homan	BB	5'5	144	23	4	12
Hust Stockton	TB-FB	5'11	190	23	2	
Bob Fitzke	WB	5'11	195	25	2	6
Tex Hamer	FB-WB-TB	6'1	190	23	8	45

Substitutes

UseName	Pos.	Hgt.	Wgt.	Age	Int.	Pts.
Bull Lowe (from PROV)	E	5'11	180	30		
Charlie Cartin	E-T-C-G	5'10	195	23	1	6
Art Harms	T	6'1	200	23		
Walt Sechrist (to CLE)	T-G	6'	260	28		
Red Seidelson	G-T	6'1	200	24		
Jim Welsh	G-T	5'11	250	23	1	
Elmer McCormick (from BUF)	G-C	5'7	220	27		
Les Haws	BB-WB-TB	5'8	165	25		6
George Sullivan	TB-WB	5'9	170	28	1	18
Doc Bruder (from BUF)	WB-FB-BB	5'11	178	23	1	2
Ben Jones (from CAN)	FB-WB	5'11	205	25		12
Clark Craig	E	5'9	180	23		
Milt O'Connell	E	6'	175	23		
Jug Earp (from & to GB)	T	6'	240	28		
Walt LeJeune (from, to, from GB)	T	6'	240	25		
Saville Crowther	G-T	6'1	220	24		
Frank Wilsbach	G	6'2	215	21		
Stan Burnham	TB-BB-WB-E	5'10	175	28		
Lou Smyth (from ROCH)	TB	6'1	205	26		12
Alex Clement	WB	5'10	170	21	2	

Scores of each game

Date	Pts.	Opponent	Pts.
Sep. 26	27	BUFFALO	7
Oct. 3	7	PROVIDENCE	0
Oct. 10	12	CANTON	7
Oct. 11	0	Detroit	3
Oct. 17	5	NEW YORK	3
Oct. 18	14	New York	0
Oct. 24	3	DAYTON	0
Oct. 31	19	COLUMBUS	0
Nov. 1	12	Buffalo	3
Nov. 7	17	AKRON	7
Nov. 8	0	Chic. Bears	19
Nov. 14	20	POTTSVILLE	0
Nov. 21	0	CLEVELAND	14
Nov. 22	7	Providence	20
Nov. 28	13	GREEN BAY	7
Nov. 29	0	Pottsville	49
Dec. 5	7	CHIC. BEARS	14
Dec. 12	0	CLEVELAND	3
Dec. 13	14	Providence	6
Dec. 20	13	Cleveland	7

RUSHING

NAME	Complete Games G	Att.	Yds.	Avg.	TD	Incom. Games G	Att.	Yds.	TD
CHICAGO CARDINALS									
Driscoll	4	41	77	1.9		9	7	139	4
Erickson	4	38	100	2.6	1	10	9	54	1
Koehler	4	42	91	2.2	1	8	9	37	3
Mahoney	3	15	37	2.5		4	5	39	
Dunn	2	14	32	2.3		8	7	41	3
Folz						5	2	12	2
Tays	1	9	-1	-0.1		8			
Weller	1	1	-1	-0.1		2			
Blumer									
Anderson									
Swanson (2)									
Smith									
McDonnell (2)									
Team	4	160	335	2.1	2	10			
Opp.	4	163	488	3.0	3	10			
POTTSVILLE									
Wentz	11	162	628	3.9	4	1	8	28	1
Latone	11	138	540	3.9	5	1	12	53	2
Flanagan	9	136	495	3.6	3	1	8	30	2
French	8	59	319	5.4	3	1	2	30	
Ernst	11	33	126	3.8	2	1			
Mahrt	2	10	77	7.7	1				
Millman	2	12	38	3.2					
Lebengood	5	12	26	2.2					
Dayhoff	1	5	1	0.2					
Berry									
Bucher									
Doyle									
H. Stein									
Team	11	567	2250	4.0	18	1			
Opp.	11	245	496	2.0	2	1			
DETROIT									
Conzelman	1	5	52	10.4		11	3	36	
Marion	1	8	35	4.4		9	13	42	4
Sonnenberg	2	2	45	22.5		10	2	32	
Doane	1	12	33	2.8	1	10	14	41	4
Hadden	1	4	7	1.8	1	11	4	8	
D. Vick	1	3	12	4.0		10			
Lauer						11	2	1	
Hultman									
Voss									
Team	1	33	159	4.8	2	11			
Opp.	1	16	78	4.9		11			
NEW YORK									
McBride	1	11	36	3.3		11	24	157	2
Benkert	1	2	7	3.5		10	17	131	
Haines	1	9	35	3.9		11	9	49	2
Potteiger						2	3	34	
White (2)						3	8	25	3
Hendrian (2)	1	2	0	0.0		9	5	25	
Brennan	1	4	23	5.8		5			
Rooney (2)						7	3	32	1
Bomar	1	1	4	4.0		11	2	15	
Jappe						11	2	28	
Thorpe (1)	1	3	6	2.0		2	3	5	
Nash	1	1	9	9.0		2			
Williams	1					9	1	2	1
Parnell									
Frugone									
Kenyon									
Palm									
Team	1	33	120	3.6		11			
Opp.	1	30	63	2.1		11			
AKRON									
Pollard (2)	1	5	1	0.2		7	14	112	2
Annan (2)	1	1	1	1.0		7	13	51	1
Neihaus	1	2	1	0.5		6	2	30	1
Falcon (2)	1	10	18	1.8		7	2	1	
Cramer						4	3	11	
Robertson	1	10	1	0.1		7	2	9	1
Newman									
Daum									
Nesser									
Bissell									
Team	1	28	22	0.8		7			
Opp.	1	49	199	4.1	2	7			
FRANKFORD									
Hamer	8	103	280	2.7	4	11	29	120	1
Sullivan	7	31	110	3.5		9	28	90	2
Haws	4	28	114	4.1		8	10	77	1
Fitzke	6	51	95	1.9	1	10	14	94	
Stockton	6	36	132	3.7		8	14	41	
Jones (2)	3	9	26	2.9		2	14	46	1
Bruder (2)	4	12	32	2.7		1	6	23	
Homan	7	6	19	3.2		9	10	30	
Smyth (2)	1					2	14	45	2
Clement	1	5	21	4.2		3			
Chamberlin	5	2	12	6.0		9			
R. Crowther									
Lowe (2)									
Cartin									
Spagna									
Behman									
Team	8	283	841	3.0	5	12			
Opp.	8	278	872	3.1	4	12			

PASSING

NAME	Complete Games G	Com.	Att.	%	Yds.	Y/A	TD	Int.	Incom. Games G	Com.	Att.	Yds.	TD	Int.
CHICAGO CARDINALS														
Driscoll	4	1	5	20	12	2.4		2	9					
Erickson	4	1	2	50	8	4.0			10					
Mahoney	3	2	7	29	19	2.7		2	4	3	3	42		
Dunn	2	18	54	33	227	4.2	1	7	8	13	14	235	8	1
Team	5	29	79	37	364	4.6	1	11	9					
Opp.	5	12	43	28	139	3.2		8	9					
POTTSVILLE														
Wentz	11	1	2	50	18	9.0			1					
Latone	11	4	7	57	27	3.9			1	1	1	10		
Flanagan	9	5	13	38	41	3.2	1		1					
French	8	2	9	22	47	5.2		2	1					
Ernst	11	58	125	46	693	5.5	8	12	1	3	5	21		1
Millman	2	0	1	0										
Lebengood	5	1	3	33	12	4.0			1					
Dayhoff	1	1	2	50	20	10.0								
Team	11	72	162	44	858	5.3	9	14	1					
Opp.	11	65	196	33	930	4.7	3	26	1					
DETROIT														
Conzelman	3	6	11	55	49	4.5			9	6	7	74		1
Doane	3	2	4	50	17	4.3			8					
D. Vick	2	12	26	46	192	7.4	1	4	9	13	16	310	6	3
Team	3	20	41	49	258	6.3	1	5	9					
Opp.	3	6	24	25	62	2.6		6	9					
NEW YORK														
McBride	3	8	15	53	122	8.1		2	9	25	33	528	6	3
Benkert	3	0	2	0				1	8					
Haines	4								8	2	3	17		
White (2)	1	1	5	20	25	5.0			2					
Hendrian (2)	2								8	3	4	44		1
Brennan	1								5	0	1			1
Thorpe (1)	1								2	0	2			
Parnell	3	0	1	0					8					
Team	3	9	23	39	147	6.4		3	9					
Opp.	2	12	31	39	130	4.2		3	10					
AKRON														
Pollard (2)	3	15	29	52	231	8.0	2	3	5	1	2	25	1	
Neihaus	2	2	17	12	18	1.1		1	5	1	1	35		
Falcon (2)	2								6	0	1			
Robertson	2								6	2	4	37		2
Team	2	6	26	23	117	4.5	2	2	6					
Opp.	2	10	28	36	168	6.0	1	5	6					
FRANKFORD														
Hamer	9	16	46	35	183	4.0		6	10	7	13	153	1	2
Sullivan	8								8	2	5	25		
Haws	5								7	1	1	19		
Fitzke	7								9	1	1	20		
Stockton	7	35	75	47	632	8.4	4	7	7	9	18	254	3	7
Homan	8	2	7	29	46	6.6		2	8					
Smyth (2)	1	0	1	0					2	3	5	42		
Team	10	55	137	40	891	6.5	4	18	10					
Opp.	9	34	79	43	567	7.3	6	11	11					

RECEIVING

NAME	Complete Games G	Rec.	Yds	Avg.	TD	Incom. Games G	Rec.	Yds.	TD
CHICAGO CARDINALS									
Driscoll	4	7	91	13.0		9	2	17	
Erickson	4	1	21	21.0		10	7	130	4
Mahoney	3	2	31	15.5		4	1	20	1
Dunn	2	1	8	8.0		8			
Folz						5	1	15	1
Tays	1	1	12	12.0		8	1	30	
Blumer	2	2	30	15.0		8	2	35	2
Anderson	4	4	51	12.8	1	9			
Swanson (2)	1					1	2	30	
Smith	3	2	15	7.5		10			
McDonnell (2)	1	2	7	3.5		1			
POTTSVILLE									
Wentz	11	5	12	2.4		1			
Latone	11	1	6	6.0		1	1	6	
Flanagan	9	2	20	10.0		1			
French	8	4	90	22.5	2	1			
Ernst	11	7	64	9.1		1	1	10	
Millman	2	1	28	28.0					
Lebengood	5	2	14	7.0					
Berry	9	31	349	11.3	4	1	2	15	
Bucher	9	13	194	14.9	2				
Doyle	8	6	81	13.5	1				
DETROIT									
Conzelman	3	7	67	9.6		9	3	119	3
Doane	3	1	8	8.0		8	1	15	
Hadden	3	7	111	15.9	1	9	5	103	2
D. Vick	2	2	15	7.5		9			
Lauer	2					9	1	25	
Hultman	3					8	7	96	1
Voss	3	3	57	19.0		7	2	25	
NEW YORK									
Haines	4	2	45	22.5		8	7	171	1
Hendrian (2)	2					8	4	89	2
Rooney (2)	1					6	1	12	
Bomar	3	7	102	14.6		9	12	250	3
Jappe	3					9	6	67	
AKRON									
Pollard (2)	2	1	5	5.0		6	1	7	
Annan (2)	2	1	14	14.0		6	1	20	
Falcon (2)	2					6	1	35	
Robertson	2	1	55	55.0	1	6			
Newman	2	2	25	12.5	1	6	1	25	
Daum						5	2	55	1
Nesser	2	1	18	18.0		4			
Bissell	2					6	1	5	
FRANKFORD									
Hamer	8	2	27	13.5		11	3	51	
Sullivan	7	4	100	25.0		9	1	10	
Haws	4	1	22	22.0	1	8			
Fitzke	6	8	114	14.3		10	1	15	
Stockton	6	2	15	7.5		8			
Jones (2)	3	1	45	45.0	1	2			
Bruder (2)	4	3	42	14.0		1	1	17	
Homan	7	1	48	48.0		9	5	141	1
Chamberlin	5	1	15	15.0		9	6	141	1
R. Crowther	7	9	93	10.3		12	8	210	3
Lowe (2)	5	4	67	16.8		3	2	19	
Cartin	6	1	24	24.0	1	7	1	18	
Spagna	5	1	6	6.0		2			

PUNTING

NAME	Comp. Games G	No.	Avg.	Incom. Games G	No.	Avg.
CHICAGO CARDINALS						
Driscoll	3	24	36.5	10		
Mahoney	2	1	43.0	5		
Dunn	2	4	24.5	8		
Team	3	29	35.0	11		
Opp.	3	30	36.6	11		
POTTSVILLE						
French	8	9	34.8	1		
Ernst	11	56	35.0	1	5	40.8
Millman	2	1	35.0			
Dayhoff	1	2	42.5			
Team	11	68	35.2	1		
Opp.	11	103	35.0	1		
DETROIT						
Sonnenberg	1	9	40.8	11	1	10.0
Doane	1			10	1	52.0
Team	1	9	40.8	11		
Opp.	1	13	35.5	11		
NEW YORK						
McBride	1	9	39.2	11		
Hendrian (2)	1	2	31.5	9		
Brennan	1			5	1	40.0
Thorpe (1)	1	2	19.0	2	4	22.8
Parnell	1			10	3	38.3
Frugone	1			2	1	55.0
Kenyon				1	1	60.0
Team	1	14	36.4	11		
Opp.	1	9	38.3	11		
AKRON						
Newman	1	11	27.3	7	4	29.0
Team	1	11	27.3	7		
Opp.	1	6	31.7	7		
FRANKFORD						
Hamer	8	65	33.5	11	36	32.4
Fitzke	6	8	40.5	10	7	24.1
Bruder (2)	4			1	3	47.3
Homan	7	1	22.0	9		
Behman	6	2	40.0	10		
Team	8	76	34.2	12		
Opp.	8	87	33.8	12		

PUNT RETURNS

NAME	Complete Games G	No.	Yds.	Avg.	TD	Incom. Games G	No.	Yds.	TD
CHICAGO CARDINALS									
Driscoll	3	6	75	12.5		10			
Mahoney	2	1	12	12.0		5			
Dunn	2	1	5	5.0		8			
Team	3	8	92	11.5		11			
Opp.	3	8	207	25.9		11			
POTTSVILLE									
Wentz	11	1	40	40.0		1			
Latone	11	1	9	9.0		1			
Flanagan	9	2	20	10.0		1			
French	8	6	173	28.8		1			
Ernst	11	26	363	14.0	1	1	1	7	
H. Stein	11	1	5	5.0		1			
Team	11	37	610	16.5	1	1			
Opp.	11	10	98	9.8		1			
DETROIT									
Conzelman	1	1	6	6.0		11	1	30	
Hadden	1	1	10	10.0		11	1	12	
D. Vick	1	1	7	7.0		10			
Team	1	3	23	7.7		11			
Opp.	1	2	25	12.5		11			
NEW YORK									
Benkert	1					10	1	10	
Haines	2	3	37	12.3		10	3	22	
Hendrian (2)	1	1	5	5.0		9			
Palm						2	1	10	
Team	1	3	15	5.0		11			
Opp.	1	5	53	10.6		11			
AKRON									
Robertson	1					7	2	50	
Team	1	0				7			
Opp.	1	0				7			
FRANKFORD									
Hamer	8	4	42	10.5		11			
Sullivan	7	3	40	13.3		9	2	20	
Fitzke	6	1	21	21.0		10			
Homan	7	13	160	12.3		9	2	75	1
Clement	1					3	1	55	
Team	8	21	263	12.5		12			
Opp.	8	19	176	9.3		12			

CHICAGO BEARS 9-5-3 George Halas

Regulars

Use Name	Pos.	Hgt.	Wgt.	Age	Int.	Pts.
George Halas	E	6'	182	30	2	
Duke Hanny	E	6'	195	27	2	6
Ed Healey	T	6'1	210	30		
Don Murry	T	6'2	190	25		6
Jim McMillen	G	6'1	215	22		
Bill Fleckenstein	G	6'1	200	21		
George Trafton	C	6'2	235	28	6	
Joey Sternaman	QB	5'6	150	25	1	62
Red Grange	HB	5'11	175	22	2	18
Laurie Walquist	HB	5'8	165	27	1	18
Oscar Knop	FB-QB-E	6'	195	30	2	12

Substitutes

Use Name	Pos.	Hgt.	Wgt.	Age	Int.	Pts.
Vern Mullen	E	6'	185	25		
Hugh Blacklock	T	6'	220	34		
Ralph Scott	T-G	6'2	234	27		
Mush Crawford	G	6'	195	26		
Hunk Anderson	G-C	5'11	192	26		
Russ Smith (from DET)	C	5'10	220	29		
Dutch Sternaman	HB-FB	5'8	180	30		6
Johnny Mohardt	HB	5'10	168	27	2	6
Buck White	FB	6'	195	24		18
Ralph King	C-G	6'	250	25		
Milt Romney	HB-QB	5'8	167	26	1	
Johnny Bryan (to & from MIL)	HB	5'8	170	28	1	6
Earl Britton	FB	6'	208	22	1	

Bill McElwain — ankle injury

Scores of each game

Date	Pts.	Opponent	Pts.
Sep. 20	0	Rock Island	0
Sep. 27	10	Green Bay	14
Oct. 4	0	Detroit	0
Oct. 11	28	HAMMOND	7
Oct. 18	7	CLEVELAND	0
Oct. 25	0	Chic. Cards	9
Nov. 1	6	ROCK ISLAND	0
Nov. 8	19	FRANKFORD	0
Nov. 15	14	DETROIT	0
Nov. 22	21	GREEN BAY	0
Nov. 26	0	CHIC. CARDS	0
Nov. 29	14	COLUMBUS	13
Dec. 5	14	Frankford	7
Dec. 6	19	New York	7
Dec. 9	6	Providence (at Boston)	9
Dec. 12	0	Detroit	21
Dec. 13	0	NEW YORK	9

ROCK ISLAND INDEPENDENTS 5-3-3 Rube Ursella

Regulars

Use Name	Pos.	Hgt.	Wgt.	Age	Int.	Pts.
Joe Rooney	E	6'	173	27	1	6
Joe Little Twig	E	5'11	180	32	1	6
Duke Slater	T	6'1	215	26		
Chet Widerquist	T-G	6'1	220	29	1	
Lyle Burton	G-T	6'1	195	25		
George Thompson	G	6'1	210	25		
Louie Kolls	C-E	6'1	205	32		
Johnny Armstrong	BB	5'8	175	31	4	31
Roddy Lamb	TB-BB	5'6	162	26	2	27
Rube Ursella	TB-BB-WB-FB	5'9	175	35	3	12
Eddie Novak	FB-WB	5'9	175	28	1	6

Substitutes

Use Name	Pos.	Hgt.	Wgt.	Age	Int.	Pts.
Evar Swanson (to ChiC)	E	5'9	165	22	1	
Ed Herman	E	5'10	175	23		
Fod Cotton	T	6'1	195	24		
Paul Anderson	G	6'	200	24		
George Dahlgren (from HAM)	G	5'10	200	38		
Frank DeClerck	C	5'9	192	26		
Jim Thorpe (from NYG)	TB-BB	6'1	200	37		
Vince McCarthy	WB	5'10	155	25		12
Buck Gavin	FB	5'10	180	30		
Les Belding	E-WB	5'11	195	26		
Jim Kendrick (from HAM & BUF & ROCH)	E	6'	195	32		
Dutch Hendrian (to NYG)	WB-TB	5'9	185	28		
Harry Hall	WB	5'11	160	22		
Chuck Hill	WB-FB	5'8	190	21	1	

Scores of each game

Date	Pts.	Opponent	Pts.
Sep. 20	0	CHIC. BEARS	0
Sep. 27	0	DAYTON	0
Oct. 4	3	GREEN BAY	0
Oct. 11	12	Duluth	0
Oct. 18	0	Green Bay	20
Oct. 25	3	KANSAS CITY	3
Nov. 1	0	Chic. Bears	6
Nov. 15	35	KANSAS CITY	12
Nov. 22	40	MILWAUKEE	7
Nov. 26	6	Detroit	3
Nov. 29	0	Chic. Cards	7

GREEN BAY PACKERS 8-5-0 Curly Lambeau

Regulars

Use Name	Pos.	Hgt.	Wgt.	Age	Int.	Pts.
Dick O'Donnell	E	6'	190	25		6
George Vergara	E	6'1	190	24		
Cub Buck	T	6'	260	33	2	8
Jug Earp (to & from FRA)	T-C	6'	240	28	1	
George Abramson	G-T	5'7	198	22	1	8
Whitey Woodin	G	5'10	208	30		
Ojay Larson	C	6'1	198	27	7	
Charlie Mathys	BB	5'7	165	28	4	
Curly Lambeau	TB-BB	5'10	185	27	2	8
Marty Norton	HB	5'6	175	22	3	36
Myrt Basing	FB-HB	5'9	192	24	6	36

Substitutes

Use Name	Pos.	Hgt.	Wgt.	Age	Int.	Pts.
Elmer Wilkins	E	5'9	175	24		
Moose Gardner	G	6'1	240	31		6
Walt LeJeune (to & from & to FRA)	G-T	6'	224	25	1	
Jim Crowley (to PROV)	TB-HB	5'9	165	22		6
Verne Lewellen	TB-HB-BB	6'1	180	23		25
Eddie Kotal	HB-TB-BB-E	5'8	165	23	1	6
Jack Harris	FB-HB-E	5'11	190	23	5	6

Scores of each game

Date	Pts.	Opponent	Pts.
Sep. 20	14	HAMMOND	0
Sep. 27	14	CHIC. BEARS	10
Oct. 4	0	Rock Island	3
Oct. 11	31	MILWAUKEE	0
Oct. 18	20	ROCK ISLAND	0
Oct. 25	33	ROCHESTER	13
Nov. 1	6	Milwaukee	0
Nov. 8	6	Chic. Cards	9
Nov. 15	7	DAYTON	0
Nov. 22	0	Chic. Bears	21
Nov. 26	0	Pottsville	31
Nov. 28	7	Frankford	13
Dec. 6	13	Providence	10

PROVIDENCE STEAM ROLLER 6-5-1 Archie Golembeski

Regulars

Use Name	Pos.	Hgt.	Wgt.	Age	Int.	Pts.
Red Maloney	E	5'11	180	23		19
Franny Garvey	E	6'1	175	25	2	12
Mike Gulian	T	6'	205	25		
Joe Kozlowsky	T	5'10	188	24		
Archie Golembeski	G-E-BB	5'10	185	25	3	12
Nate Share	G	6'1	210	22		
Dolph Eckstein	C	5'10	185	23	1	
Curly Oden	BB	5'6	160	26	1	
Cy Wentworth	TB	5'8	155	21	6	18
Al McIntosh	WB	5'9	180	22	3	
Jim Laird	FB-G-WB	6'	195	27	1	29

Substitutes

Use Name	Pos.	Hgt.	Wgt.	Age	Int.	Pts.
Bull Lowe (to FRA)	E	5'11	180	30		
Hugh McGoldrick	T-E	5'10	180	24		
John Spellman	T-FB-E	5'10	195	26		6
Sam Young	G-T	6'2	190	22		
Bert Shurtleff	G	5'11	190	28		
Pard Pearce	BB	5'5	150	28		
Fritz Pollard (from HAM & AKR)	TB-WB	5'7	165	31		
Fred Sweet	WB-FB-TB-E	5'10	165	24		7
Dutch Connor	FB	6'	190	30		2
Fred Sheehan	G	6'2	210	22		
Speed Braney	G	6'	188	33		
Spike Staff	G	6'	210	33		
Ching Hammill	BB	5'7	158	23		
Hop Riopel	TB-WB	5'8	165	24		2
Chick Burke	WB	5'9	166	24		1
John Pohlman	FB-WB	5'9	178	22		
Jim Crowley (from GB)	TB	5'9	165	22		
Don Miller	WB	5'11	170	23		
John Thomas	FB	6'1	188	25		

Scores of each game

Date	Pts.	Opponent	Pts.
Oct. 3	0	Frankford	7
Oct. 4	6	Pottsville	0
Oct. 11	14	NEW YORK	0
Oct. 18	0	POTTSVILLE	34
Nov. 1	17	ROCHESTER	0
Nov. 8	10	BUFFALO	0
Nov. 15	12	New York	13
Nov. 22	20	FRANKFORD	7
Nov. 29	7	CLEVELAND	7
Dec. 6	10	GREEN BAY	13
Dec. 9	9	CHIC. BEARS (at Boston)	6
Dec. 13	6	FRANKFORD	14

CANTON BULLDOGS 4-4-0 Harry Robb

Regulars

Use Name	Pos.	Hgt.	Wgt.	Age	Int.	Pts.
Bird Carroll	E	5'8	185	29		
Lou Merrilat	E	5'9	165	33	1	
Link Lyman (to FRA)	T	6'2	225	26		
Pete Henry	T	5'11	245	27	1	8
Rudy Comstock	G-T	5'10	210	24		
Willie Flattery	G	6'	220	23		
Wade McRoberts	C	6'	210	24		
Harry Robb	BB	5'10	190	28	1	18
Paul Hogan	TB	5'8	170	26	1	
Ben Jones (to FRA)	WB-FB	5'11	205	25		12
Pete Calac	FB-WB	5'10	205	33		

Substitutes

Use Name	Pos.	Hgt.	Wgt.	Age	Int.	Pts.
Dutch Strasser	E			24		
Chick Guarnieri	E	5'10	175	26		
Rip Kyle	T-G	6'	240	24		
Dick Schuster	G	6'1	185	25		
Dutch Speck	G-C	5'10	220	39		
Frank Culver	C-E	5'11	175	28	1	
Norb Sacksteder	BB	5'9	175	29		
Giff Zimmerman	TB-WB	5'10	180	25	2	12
Ruel Redinger	WB-TB-BB	5'10	185	28		
Ray Brenner	WB	5'5	145	27		
Bill Fleming	WB	5'11	165	22		

Scores of each game

Date	Pts.	Opponent	Pts.
Sep. 27	14	ROCHESTER	7
Oct. 4	14	DAYTON	0
Oct. 10	7	Frankford	12
Oct. 11	0	Pottsville	28
Oct. 18	3	AKRON	20
Nov. 8	6	CLEVELAND	0
Nov. 22	6	COLUMBUS	0
Dec. 6	0	Cleveland	6

CLEVELAND BULLDOGS 5-8-1 Cap Edwards

Regulars

Use Name	Pos.	Hgt.	Wgt.	Age	Int.	Pts.
Ed Loucks	E	5'9	180	29		
Inky Williams (from HAM)	E	5'11	175	28		
Hugh Sprinkle	T	6'2	220	28		
Russ Meredith	T-G	5'11	200	28	1	
Al Nesser (from AKR)	G-E	6'	195	32	2	6
Ralph Vince	G	5'8	175	25	2	
Larry Conover	C	5'10	190	31		
Dick Wolf	BB-WB	5'8	160	25	1	6
Al Michaels	TB	6'	190	25	1	
Dave Noble	WB	6'2	195	25	3	36
Doc Elliott	FB	5'10	210	25	4	27

Substitutes

Use Name	Pos.	Hgt.	Wgt.	Age	Int.	Pts.
Dutch Webber (from KC)	E	6'2	187	23		
George Baldwin	E-T	5'11	190	23		
Bob Spiers	T	5'11	195	30		
Alf Cobb	T-G	5'11	210	31		
Milt Rehnquist (from KC)	G-C	6'	220	28		
Dutch Wallace	G	6'	210	29		
Walt Kreinheder	C-G	6'2	215	25		
Wooky Roberts	BB	5'7	160	27		
Nick Nardacci	TB-WB	5'10	160	22		
Ray Norton	WB			25		
Gene Stringer	FB-TB-BB-WB-E	6'	200	22		
Paul Suchy	E		188	21		
Herb Bauer	E	5'10	190	18		
Glan Carberry	E	6'	190	29		
Frank Garden	E	5'11	190	27		
Maury Segal	E			23		
Joe Work	E	5'10	177	25		
Truck Myers	T	6'	185	28		
Walt Sechrist (from FRA)	T	6'	260	28		
Karl Broadley	G	6'4	250	29		
Swede Youngstrom (from BUF)	G	6'1	190	28		
Carl Cardarelli	C			29		
Obie Bristow (from KC)	TB	6'2	210	23		
Gus Eckberg	FB	5'9	180	24		
Chase Clements (from AKR)	T	6'2	205	23		
Chalmers Ault	T	5'9	195	25		
Phil Brannon	T	6'	200	27		
Steve Owen (from KC)	T	5'10	225	29		
Rudy Kutler	G	5'9	190	23		

Scores of each game

Date	Pts.	Opponent	Pts.
Sep. 27	0	Akron	7
Oct. 4	3	COLUMBUS	0
Oct. 11	16	KANSAS CITY	13
Oct. 18	0	Chic. Bears	7
Nov. 1	0	New York	19
Nov. 8	0	Canton	6
Nov. 11	13	Detroit	22
Nov. 21	14	Frankford	0
Nov. 22	6	Pottsville	24
Nov. 26	0	Kansas City (at Hartford)	17
Nov. 29	7	Providence	7
Dec. 6	6	CANTON	0
Dec. 12	3	Frankford	0
Dec. 20	7	FRANKFORD	13

KANSAS CITY BLUES 2-5-1 Roy Andrews

Regulars

Use Name	Pos.	Hgt.	Wgt.	Age	Int.	Pts.
Lyle Munn	E	6'	185	23	1	
Dutch Webber (to CLE)	E	6'2	187	23		
Alvie Thompson	T	6'3	210	24		
Steve Owen (to CLE)	T	5'10	225	27		
Dosey Howard	G	6'	225	24		
Milt Rehnquist (to CLE)	G	6'	220	28	1	
Jake Mintun	C	5'11	195	31		
Al Bloodgood	BB	5'8	155	23		7
Charlie Hill	WB	6'	180	25		25
Cowboy Hill (to NYG)	WB-FB	5'8	175	26		6
Phil White (to NYG)	FB	6'2	210	25	2	16

Substitutes

Use Name	Pos.	Hgt.	Wgt.	Age	Int.	Pts.
Joe Milam	G-E-T	5'11	180	26		
Roy Andrews	G-BB-WB-T	6'	230	28		4
Jim Palermo	G-C	5'9	180	23		
Chuck Corgan	BB	6'	185	22		6
Joe Guyon	WB	5'10	195	32		
Bill Ashbaugh	WB	5'10	175	24		
Obie Bristow (to CLE)	WB-FB	6'2	210	23	2	

Scores of each game

Date	Pts.	Opponent	Pts.
Sep. 27	3	Duluth	0
Oct. 4	7	Akron	14
Oct. 11	13	Cleveland	16
Oct. 18	7	Chic. Cards	20
Oct. 25	3	Rock Island	3
Nov. 15	12	Rock Island	35
Nov. 22	3	New York	9
Nov. 26	17	Cleveland (at Hartford)	0

NAME	RUSHING									PASSING													
	Complete Games					Incom. Games				Complete Games								Incom. Games					
	G	Att.	Yds.	Avg.	TD	G	Att.	Yds.	TD	G	Com.	Att.	%	Yds.	Y/A	TD	Int.	G	Com.	Att.	Yds.	TD	Int.
CHICAGO BEARS																							
Walquist	7	61	303	3.3	1	9	12	91	1	7	4	10	40	25	2.5		1	9	5	7	107		1
J. Sternaman	8	59	140	2.4		9	14	92	5	8	13	32	41	196	6.1	2	5	9	4	6	74	1	1
Grange	5	55	203	3.7	2					4	3	12	25	54	4.5		2	1	1	1	38	1	
Mohardt	7	55	162	2.9		7	1	18		7	2	10	20	43	4.3	1	4	7					
Knop	8	26	93	3.6		9	4	35	1														
D. Sternaman	8	27	73	2.7		9	4	23	1														
Bryan (1,3)	4	21	93	4.4		2				4	1	5	20	25	5.0		1	2	1	2	20		1
White	3	2	3	1.5		7	5	46	3														
Romney	7	23	35	1.5		7	2	13															
Britton	3	6	19	3.2		2				3	6	11	55	57	5.2		2	2					
Hanny	8	2	6	3.0		9	1	12															
Healey	8	1	2	2.0		9																	
Mullen																							
Halas																							
Blacklock																							
Heckenstein																							
Team	9	334	928	2.8	3	8				12	44	132	33	593	4.5	4	22	5					
Opp.	9	337	976	2.9	3	8				12	39	117	33	563	4.8	3	19	5					
ROCK ISLAND																							
Lamb	8	88	378	4.3	1	1	1	6	1	8	9	22	41	157	7.1	3	2	1					
Novak	10	100	300	3.0	1	1																	
Gavin	5	63	214	3.4																			
Armstrong	10	42	171	4.1		1				10	23	52	44	347	6.7	3	6	1					
Ursella	10	29	52	1.8		1				10	4	9	44	71	7.9		2	1					
McCarthy	3	7	37	5.3	1	1				3	1	5	20	21	4.2	1		1					
Thorpe (2)	2	2	17	8.5																			
Hendrian (1)	1	3	6	2.0						1	0	2	0					1					
Ch. Hill	1	1	2	2.0																			
Swanson (1)	2	2	-6	-3.0																			
Little Twig																							
Rooney																							
Belding																							
Team	10	337	1171	3.5	3	1				10	37	90	41	596	6.6	7	11	1					
Opp.	10	315	930	3.0	4	1				10	29	101	29	408	4.0	2	14	1					
GREEN BAY																							
Basing	13	149	430	2.9	4					13	2	9	22	17	1.9		2						
Norton	10	95	244	2.6	1					10	1	2	50	21	10.5								
Lambeau	11	74	224	3.0						11	47	121	39	711	5.9	5	7						
Lewellen	10	73	211	2.9	1					10	7	26	27	69	2.7		4						
Harris	11	62	147	2.4	1					11	1	3	33	12	4.0		1						
Kotal	5	21	44	2.1						5	0	2	0				2						
Mathys	12	14	20	1.4						12	9	21	43	98	4.7	6	2						
Crowley (1)	2	5	9	1.8						2	5	12	42	47	3.9		1						
Buck										12	4	7	57	42	6.0								
O'Donnell																							
Vergara																							
Team	13	493	1329	2.7	7					13	76	203	37	1017	5.0	11	19						
Opp.	13	480	1034	2.2	5					13	63	186	34	857	4.6	7	33						
PROVIDENCE																							
Wentworth	4	33	98	3.9	1	8	34	174	1	4	3	12	25	50	4.2		3	8	7	21	145		5
Laird	4	43	124	2.0	1	7	31	88	2	4	0	3	0				1	7					
McIntosh	3	7	5	0.7		6	28	114															
Pollard (3)	3	15	27	1.8		1	5	25		3	0	1	0				1	1	0	1			
Maloney	4	1	0	0.0		8	1	35		4	1	2	50	10	5.0		1	8	2	2	65		
Oden	3	5	28	5.6		5	5	-1		3	0	2	0				1	5	3	6	56		2
Sweet	3					5	12	26		3	2	4	50	45	11.3			5	1	2	29		
Spellman	2					8	8	20															
Miller	1	13	16	1.2																			
Burke	1	2	2	1.0		4	7	10															
Pearce	3	1	0	0.0		5	2	12		3	2	5	40	8	1.6			5	0	1			1
Connor	1	3	5	1.7		3	6	-1		1								3	1	1	28		
Crowley (2)	1	5	3	0.6						1	1	2	50	5	2.5								
Riopel	1	2	7	3.5		3	5	-6		1								3	1	1	11		
Hammill						1	2	-2										1	1	3	8		
Golembeski										4								7	1	1	1		
Garvey																							
Team	4	130	315	2.4	2	8				4	9	31	29	118	3.8		7	8					
Opp.	4	127	370	2.9		8				5	41	102	40	619	6.1	4	13	7					
CANTON																							
Jones (1)	1	2	1	0.5		5	40	146	2														
Calac	1	1	2	2.0		6	16	51															
Robb	1	2	2	1.0		7	17	46		5								3	0	2			1
Zimmerman	1					5	12	41	1	4	2	5	40	14	2.8		2	2					
Redinger	1	1	5	5.0		6	9	26		4								3	0	1			
Hogan	1	2	3	1.5		5	6	19		3	7	20	35	111	5.6	2	5	3	3	5	52	1	
Brenner						2	2	12															
Henry	1					5	2	2		3	5	11	45	79	7.2	1	2	3	3	5	64		2
Strasser										2								1	0	1			
Carroll																							
Team	1	8	13	1.6		7				6	21	55	38	323	5.9	3	14	2					
Opp.	1	60	245	4.1	3	7				6	20	69	29	293	4.2	3	6	2					
CLEVELAND																							
Noble	3	38	88	2.8		10	15	145	3	4	0	1	0				1	9	1	1	33		
Elliott	4	40	73	1.8		10	19	83	2	4	5	13	38	98	7.5		1	10	3	7	54	1	2
Michaels	3	23	69	3.0		11	8	48		4	17	46	37	290	6.3	2	7	10	19	25	340	1	2
Stringer	2	9	33	3.7		8																	
Wolf	3	4	5	1.3		1	2	1															
Nesser	3					4	1	1															
Roberts																		2	1	1	16		
Wallace										2	0	1	0					8					
Bristow																		1	0	1			1
Baldwin																							
Segal																							
Williams (2)																							
Webber (2)																							
Wallace																							
Team	3	87	227	2.6		11				4	22	61	36	388	6.4	2	9	10					
Opp.	3	123	452	3.7	2	11				4	20	52	38	250	4.8	1	6	10					
KANSAS CITY																							
Ch. Hill	2	17	60	3.5	1	6	1	5	1														
Co. Hill (1)	2	8	32	4.0		6	4	24	1	2	1	1	100	6	6.0			6	2	3	65		1
White (1)	2	14	36	2.6		6	3	14		2	10	30	33	204	6.8	1	4	6	10	10	162	1	
Bristow (1)	2	10	18	1.8		6	1	0		2	1	3	33	5	1.7			6	3	3	86	2	
Bloodgood						5	2	40		1	0	1	0					5					
Corgan																							
Munn																							
Webber (1)																							
Milam																							
Team	2	49	146	3.0	1	6				2	12	35	34	215	6.1	1	4	6					
Opp.	2	66	296	4.5	1	6				3	17	26	65	284	10.9	3	2	5					

NAME	RECEIVING									PUNTING						PUNT RETURNS								
	Complete Games					Incom. Games				Comp. Games			Incom. Games			Complete Games					Incom. Games			
	G	Rec.	Yds	Avg.	TD	G	Rec.	Yds.	TD	G	No.	Avg.	G	No.	Avg.	G	No.	Yds.	Avg.	TD	G	No.	Yds.	TD
CHICAGO BEARS																								
Walquist	7	1	10	10.0		9	2	52	1															
J. Sternaman	8	5	57	11.4	1	9	3	57		7	3	43.7	10			7	20	200	10.0		10			
Grange	5	4	54	13.5												5	8	90	11.3					
Mohardt	7	5	82	16.4		7	1	20	1							6	6	78	13.0		8			
Knop	8	3	48	16.0	1	9										7	1	10	10.0		10			
D. Sternaman	8	2	11	5.5		9	1	22		7	2	40.0	10											
Bryan (1,3)	4	2	46	23.5	1	2				4	1	44.0	2											
White										3	5	27.4	7			3	1	20	20.0		7			
Romney																								
Britton										3	6	31.3	2			3	1	1	1.0		2			
Hanny	8	3	49	16.3		9	1	16		7	55	35.3	10	1	46.0									
Healey	8	1	3	3.0		9				7	1	27.0	10											
Mullen	7	2	26	13.0		9	3	58																
Halas	8	1	16	16.0		9				7	2	35.0	10											
Blacklock	3	1	20	20.0																				
Heckenstein										2	1	41.0	1											
Team										7	76	35.1	10			7	31	325	10.5		10			
Opp.										7	82	36.2	10			7	18	233	12.9		10			
ROCK ISLAND																								
Lamb	8	9	73	8.1	1	1										8	18	286	15.9	1	1			
Novak										9	7	37.0	2											
Gavin																								
Armstrong	10	7	108	15.4	3	1										9	6	65	10.8		2			
Ursella	10	5	61	12.2						9	55	36.4	2											
McCarthy	3	4	114	28.5	1																			
Thorpe (2)										2	5	33.4												
Hendrian (1)	1	1	14	14.0																				
Ch. Hill																								
Swanson (1)	2	2	38	19.0																				
Little Twig	10	7	140	20.0	1																			
Rooney	9	2	48	24.0	1	1																		
Belding										1	8	41.4												
Team										9	75	36.8	2			9	24	351	14.6	1	2			
Opp.										9	73	36.7	2			9	31	371	12.0		2			
GREEN BAY																								
Basing	13	5	126	25.2	2					13	5	38.8				13	3	15	5.0					
Norton	10	11	177	16.1	4											10	2	21	10.5					
Lambeau	11	5	39	7.8						11	1	50.0				11	2	14	7.0					
Lewellen	10	9	144	16.0	3					10	91	35.4				10	1	5	5.0					
Harris	11	9	68	7.6																				
Kotal	5	10	114	11.4												5	7	46	6.6					
Mathys	12	14	180	12.9						12	1	43.0				12	23	248	10.8					
Crowley (1)	2	5	33	6.6	1					2	4	30.0												
Buck										12	42	33.2												
O'Donnell	12	6	104	17.3	1																			
Vergara	12	2	32	16.0																				
Team										13	144	34.9				13	38	349	9.2					
Opp.										13	134	34.7				13	37	381	10.3					
PROVIDENCE																								
Wentworth	4					8	4	63		4	3	41.3	8	3	44.3	4	3	65	21.7		8	5	130	
Laird	4	1	17	17.0		7				4	1	42.0	7											
McIntosh	3	1	3	3.0		6	4	103																
Pollard (3)																3					1	1	40	
Maloney	4	1	5	5.0		8	3	77		5	36	37.1	7	20	40.0									
Oden	3	1	23	23.0		5	1	4								3	9	138	15.3		5	4	55	
Sweet	3					5	1	13		3			5	3	33.0									
Spellman	2					8	1	6																
Miller																								
Burke	1					4	1	11																
Pearce	3	1	27	27.0		5										3	1	8	8.0		5			
Connor										1	16	39.9	3	8	34.3									
Crowley (2)																								
Riopel																1	3	38	12.7		3			
Hammill						1	2	66					1	2	35.0									
Golembeski																								
Garvey	4	4	43	10.8		5																		
Team										4	48	37.1	8			4	16	249	15.6		8			
Opp.										4	48	36.0	8			4	11	113	10.3		8			
CANTON																								
Jones (1)	4					2	1	24																
Calac						3	1	20																
Robb	5	9	145	16.1	2	3	3	50	1															
Zimmerman	4	2	17	8.5	1	2										1					5	1	18	
Redinger																								
Hogan	3					3	1	22		1	11	37.0	5	2	32.5	1					5	1	25	
Brenner																								
Henry	3	1	17	17.0		3				1	4	33.5	5	12	30.4									
Strasser																								
Carroll	5	2	25	12.5		2																		
Team										1	15	36.1	7			1	0				7			
Opp.										1	5	42.8	7			1	10	129	12.9		7			
CLEVELAND																								
Noble	4	8	220	27.5	2	9	7	128	1	3	1	37.0	10			3	1	18	18.0		10			
Elliott						10	3	37		3			11	3	37.3									
Michaels	4	1	11	11.0		10				3	6	31.7	11	1	60.0	3	7	78	11.1		11	2	70	
Stringer										2	1	35.0	8											
Wolf	4	7	84	12.0		10	12	220	1							3					11	1	52	
Nesser																								
Roberts																					2	1	19	
Wallace																								
Bristow																								
Baldwin	3	3	35	11.7		6	1	17																
Segal	2	2	28	14.0		3																		
Williams (2)	3	1	10	10.0		6	2	41																
Webber (2)										2	21	35.7	2											
Wallace										2			8	4	40.0									
Team										3	29	34.9	11			3	8	96	12.0		11			
Opp.										3	24	33.4	11			3	12	188	15.7	1	11			
KANSAS CITY																								
Ch. Hill	2	3	26	8.7		6	3	37	2															
Co. Hill (1)																2	1	9	9.0		6			
White (1)	2	1	5	5.0		6	1	55	1	2	8	42.6	6	1	55.0	2	1	25	25.0		6			
Bristow (1)	2	2	22	11.0		6	3	8		2	2	39.0	6											
Bloodgood	1					5	3	107																
Corgan	2	5	148	29.6	1											2	3	33	11.0					
Munn	2	1	14	14.0		5	2	47																
Webber (1)	2					6	2	25																
Milam	2					5	1	34																
Team										2	10	41.9	6			2	5	67	13.4		6			
Opp.										2	10	36.2	6			2	4	45	11.3		6			

HAMMOND PROS 1-4-0 Fritz Pollard Doc Young

Regulars

UseName	Pos.	Hgt.	Wgt.	Age	Int	Pts.
Inky Williams (to CLE)	E	5'11"	175	28		
Harry Curzon (to & from BUF)	E-BB	6'	195	29		
Ed Carman (to & from BUF)	T	5'11"	208	31		1
Ray Neal	T	5'9"	215	27		6
Bill Fortune	G	5'11"	218	27		
George Dahlgren (to RI)	G	5'10"	200	38		
Russ Oltz	C-G	6'	220	26		
Ed Robinson	BB-WB	5'9"	155	21	1	6
Wally Hess	TB-FB	5'9	180	30	1	6
Dick Hudson	WB-FB		183			
Bill Giaver	FB-WB-BB	5'9"	190	27		

Substitutes

UseName	Pos.	Hgt.	Wgt.	Age	Int	Pts.
Lenny Sachs (to ChiC)	E	5'8	175	28		
McDonald	E-G		165			
Dave Tallant	T	6'1"	205	28		
Merle Hunter	G-T		185	19		
Frank Rydzewski (to MIL)	G	6'1"	220	32		
Ken Crawford	C	5'11"	195	26		
Jim Kendrick (to BUF, ROCH, RI)	BB-TB	6'	195	32		4
Rip King	TB	6'1"	205	28		
Dunc Annan (to & from AKR)	WB-TB	5'10"	180	29		
Rat Watson	FB-WB	5'10"	180	26		
Ward Meese	E	5'10"	175	23		
Wop Drumstead	G		185	26		
Glen Magnuson	G-C	5'11"	225	26		
Sol Butler	TB-FB	5'8"	180	28		
Fritz Pollard (to AKR & PROV)	WB	5'7"	165	31		
Guil Falcon (to AKR & ROCH)	FB	5'10"	220	32		

Scores of Each Game

Date	Pts.	Opponent	Pts.
Sep. 20	0	Green Bay	14
Sep. 27	10	Chic. Cards	6
Oct. 11	7	Chic. Bears	28
Nov. 1	6	Detroit	26
Dec. 12	0	Chic. Cards	13

BUFFALO BISONS 1-6-2 Walt Koppisch

Regulars

UseName	Pos.	Hgt.	Wgt.	Age	Int	Pts.
Jim Noble	E	6'1"	190	23		
Harry Curzon (from & to HAM)	E	6'	195	29		6
Norm Harvey	T	6'	190	28		
Chase Van Dyne	T	6'1"	194	24		
Chet Gay	G-T	6'	210	25		
Swede Youngstrom (to CLE)	G	6'1"	190	28		
Max Reed	C-G	5'8"	185	23		
Wally Foster	BB	5'10"	165	22	2	1
Jim Kendrick (from HAM, to ROCH & RI)	TB	6'	195	32		14
Walt Koppisch	WB-TB-FB	5'10"	180	23		
Floyd Christman	FB-WB	5'11"	180	22		6

Substitutes

UseName	Pos.	Hgt.	Wgt.	Age	Int	Pts.
Lou Feist	E	6'1"	200	22		
Milo Gwosden	E-WB	6'	185	26	1	
Ed Carman (from & to HAM)	T	5'11"	208	31		
Ben Barber	T-G	6'3"	235	21		
Eddie Fisher	G	5'11"	210	24		
Elmer McCormick (to FRA)	G-C	5'7"	220	27		
Russ Burt	WB	5'8"	170	24		
Doc Bruder (to FRA)	WB-FB	5'11"	178	23		6
Darrell Fisher	WB-FB	5'11"	190	22	1	
Jimmy Kennedy	WB	5'9"	160	24		
Les Asplundh	FB	6'3"	213	24		

Scores of Each Game

Date	Pts.	Opponent	Pts.
Sep. 26	7	Frankford	27
Sep. 27	0	Pottsville	28
Oct. 4	0	ROCHESTER	0
Oct. 11	0	AKRON	0
Oct. 18	17	COLUMBUS	6
Nov. 1	3	FRANKFORD	12
Nov. 3	0	New York	7
Nov. 8	0	Providence	10
Nov. 15	6	Chic. Cards	23

DULUTH KELLEYS 0-3-0 Dewey Scanlon

Regulars

UseName	Pos.	Hgt.	Wgt.	Age	Int	Pts.
Bobby Marshall	E	6'2"	200	45	1	
Jack Underwood	E	6'	195	28		
Art Johnson	T	5'11"	190	29		
Oke Carlson	T-G	6'	205	27		
Fred Denfield	G-T	5'9"	200	28		
Doc Williams	G	6'7"	220	27		
Bill Stein	C	6'	190	26		
Cobb Rooney	BB-E	6'	185	25		
Wally Gilbert	TB	6'1"	180	24		
Mickey McDonnell (to ChiC)	WB	5'8"	150	21		6
Bill Rooney (to NYG)	FB	6'2"	195	29		

Substitutes

UseName	Pos.	Hgt.	Wgt.	Age	Int	Pts.
Charlie Black	E	5'9"	160	24		
Rex Tobin	E			26		
Porky Rundquist	T	5'10"	220	31		
Howard Kieley	T	5'8"	210	32		
Mike Koziak	G	5'9"	185	32		
Wally O'Neill	E-G-T	6'	195	23		
Doc Kelley	TB	5'10"	170	23		
Roy Vexall	FB		190	23		
Russ Method	FB-WB-BB	5'10"	195	28		

Scores of Each Game

Date	Pts.	Opponent	Pts.
Sep. 27	0	KANSAS CITY	3
Oct. 11	0	ROCK ISLAND	12
Nov. 1	6	Chic. Cards	10

ROCHESTER JEFFERSONS 0-6-1 Tex Grigg

Regulars

UseName	Pos.	Hgt.	Wgt.	Age	Int	Pts.
Hal Clark	E	5'10"	195	31		
Ed Lynch	E	5'11"	185	28		
John Dooley	T	6'1"	225	27		
Frank Matteo	T	5'11"	195	29		
Roy Martineau	G	6'	215	25		
Darby Lowery	G	6'	220	33		
Hank Smith	C	6'1"	190	32		
Tex Grigg	BB	5'11"	195	34	1	2
Lou Smyth (to FRA)	TB	6'1"	205	26	3	
Shag Sheard	WB	5'11"	180	26	1	12
Bill Kellogg	FB	5'10"	180	28		12

Substitutes

UseName	Pos.	Hgt.	Wgt.	Age	Int	Pts.
Spin Roy	E	6'	175	28		
Dave Ziff	E-G	6'	195	23		
Tex Kelly	T-C	6'3"	220			
Roy Mackert	C-T	6'2"	202	31		
Jim Kendrick (from HAM & BUF, to RI)	WB	6'	195	32		
Bob Argus	FB-WB	5'10"	195	31		
Jake Hoffman	FB-WB	5'8"	170	30		
Ham Connors	E		190	27		
Gene Bedford	E	5'9"	165	28		
Guil Falcon (from HAM & AKR)	FB	5'10"	220	32		

Scores of Each Game

Date	Pts.	Opponent	Pts.
Sep. 27	7	Canton	14
Oct. 4	0	Buffao	0
Oct. 25	13	Green Bay	33
Nov. 1	0	Providence	17
Nov. 11	0	New York	13
Nov. 15	6	Pottsville	14
Nov. 22	0	Detroit	20

MILWAUKEE BADGERS 0-6-0 Johnny Bryan

Regulars

UseName	Pos.	Hgt.	Wgt.	Age	Int	Pts.
Cleam Neacy	E	6'3"	205	27	2	6
Fritz Roessler	E	6'1"	190	27		
Kibo Brumm	T-E-G	6'	182	27		
Pat Dunnigan	T	5'10"	215	31		
Festus Tierney	G	6'1"	200	26		
Peaches Nadolney	G	5'11"	212	26		
Barney Traynor	C	6'1"	190	25		
Shorty Barr	BB	5'8"	200	29		
Johnny Bryan (from & to ChiB)	TB	5'8"	170	28		
Johnny Blood	WB	6'1"	185	21	2	
Sam Mason	FB	5'8"	180	26		1

Substitutes

UseName	Pos.	Hgt.	Wgt.	Age	Int	Pts.
Bill Ryan	T	5'11"	190	23		
Adrian Baril	T	5'11"	210	27		
Heinie Miller	G	5'10"	185	31		
Frank Rydzewski (from HAM)	G-T-C	6'1"	220	32		
Bill Thompson	C		182	18		
Darroll DeLaPorte	BB			21		
Jack Daniels	TB		135	18		
Chuck Reichow	FB-BB	5'9"	183	24	2	
Hank Gillo	FB-BB	5'10"	195	30		
Westey	G					
John Fahay	G	6'	188	23		
Charlie Richardson	BB		143	17		
Jim Snyder	TB		162	16		

Scores of Each Game

Date	Pts.	Opponent	Pts.
Oct. 4	0	Chic. Cards	34
Oct. 11	0	Green Bay	31
Nov. 1	0	GREEN BAY	6
Nov. 8	0	Detroit	21
Nov. 22	7	Rock Island	40
Dec. 10	0	Chic. Cards	59

DAYTON TRIANGLES 0-7-1 Carl Storck

Regulars

UseName	Pos.	Hgt.	Wgt.	Age	Int	Pts.
Lee Fenner	E	5'10"	170	29		
Gene Mayl	E	6'2"	198	23		
Clarence Drayer	T	6'4"	225	24		
Ed Sauer (to & from POTT)	T	5'10"	260	27		
Al Graham	G	6'	200	19		
Elliott Bonowitz	G	6'1"	190	22		
Hobby Kinderdine	C	5'11"	185	34		
Fay Abbott	BB	5'8"	180	30	2	3
Armin Mahrt (to, from, to Pott)	TB	5'11"	184	27		
Frank Bacon	WB	5'11"	185	31		
Ken Huffine	FB-T-G	6'3"	208	27	1	

Substitutes

UseName	Pos.	Hgt.	Wgt.	Age	Int	Pts.
John Mahrt	E	5'9"	180	25		
Bill Knecht	T	6'	188	26		
Johnnie Layport	G	5'9"	170	24		
Zip Joseph	G-WB-FB	6'2"	170	22		
Charlie Guy	G-C-BB	6'	170	28		
Dick Dobeleit	WB-TB-BB	5'4"	155	22		
Russ Young	FB	6'	190	22		
John Gabler	G			19		
Walt Kinderdine	WB			26		
Lou Partlow	FB	6'1"	185	32		

Scores of Each Game

Date	Pts.	Opponent	Pts.
Sep. 27	0	Rock Island	0
Oct. 4	0	Canton	14
Oct. 18	0	Detroit	6
Oct. 24	0	Frankford	3
Nov. 1	3	Akron	17
Nov. 15	0	Green Bay	7
Nov. 22	0	Chic. Cards	14
Nov. 29	0	New York	23

COLUMBUS TIGERS 0-9-0 Red Weaver

Regulars

UseName	Pos.	Hgt.	Wgt.	Age	Int	Pts.
Paul Goebel	E	6'3"	200	24		
Homer Ruh	E-WB	5'10"	180	29		
Boni Petcoff	T	5'10"	220	25		
Walt Ellis (to DET)	T	5'11"	225	26		
Joe Mulbarger	G	5'9"	225	30		
George Rohleder	G-FB-TB	5'11"	205	26		10
Andy Nemecek	C	6'4"	210	29	3	
Bob Rapp	BB-TB-WB	5'8"	160	27	2	12
Paul Lynch	TB	6'1"	190	24		
Buddy Tynes	WB-FB	6'	185	23	2	6
Frank Nesser	FB-G	6'1"	255	36		

Substitutes

UseName	Pos.	Hgt.	Wgt.	Age	Int	Pts.
Gale Bullman	E	6'	182	23		
Herb Davis	E-WB-BB	5'10"	175	26		
Earl Duvall	G-E	6'	210	26		
Tom Long	G	6'	205	26		
Jim Regan	BB		172			
Wilkie Moody	WB	5'7"	185	28		
Ray Eichenlaub	FB	6'	225	33		
Lee Snoots	WB	5'9"	185	33		
Dom Albanese	FB-E			19		

Scores of Each Game

Date	Pts.	Opponent	Pts.
Sep. 27	0	Detroit	7
Oct. 4	0	Cleveland	3
Oct. 11	9	Chic. Cards	19
Oct. 18	6	Buffalo	17
Oct. 31	0	Frankford	19
Nov. 1	0	Pottsville	20
Nov. 8	0	New York	19
Nov. 22	0	Canton	6
Nov. 29	13	Chic. Bears	14

1925 STANDINGS

	W	L	T	Pct.	Pts.	Opp. Pts.	Avg. Pts.	Opp. Avg.
Chicago Cardinals	11	2	1	.846	230	65	16	5
Pottsville Maroons	10	2	0	.833	270	45	23	4
Detroit Panthers	8	2	2	.800	129	39	11	3
New York Giants	8	4	0	.667	122	67	10	6
Akron Pros	4	2	2	.667	65	51	8	6
Frankford Yellow Jackets	13	7	0	.650	190	169	10	8
Chicago Bears	9	5	3	.643	158	96	9	6
Rock Island Independents	5	3	3	.625	99	58	9	5
Green Bay Packers	8	5	0	.615	151	110	12	8
Providence Steam Roller	6	5	1	.545	111	101	9	8
Canton Bulldogs	4	4	0	.500	50	73	6	9
Cleveland Bulldogs	5	8	1	.385	75	135	5	10
Kansas City Cowboys	2	5	1	.286	65	97	8	12
Hammond Pros (R)	1	4	0	.200	23	87	5	17
Buffalo Bisons	1	6	2	.143	33	113	4	12
Duluth Kelleys	0	3	0	.000	6	25	2	8
Rochester Jeffersons (R)	0	6	1	.000	26	111	4	16
Milwaukee Badgers	0	6	0	.000	7	191	1	32
Dayton Triangles	0	7	1	.000	3	84	0	11
Columbus Tigers (R)	0	9	0	.000	28	124	3	14

(R) — played only road games

Scoring Leaders

Berry	Pott	74
Driscoll	ChiC	67
J. Sternaman	ChiB	62
Latone	Pott	48
Hamer	Fra	45
Flanagan	Pott	42
Erickson	ChiC	42
Behman	Fra	39
Basing	GB	36
Norton	GB	36
Noble	Cle	36
White	KC-NYG	34
Armstrong	RI	31
Wentz	Pott	31
Doane	Det	30
French	Pott	30
Dunn	ChiC	29
Laird	Prov	29
Elliott	Cle	27
Sonnenberg	Det	27
Lamb	RI	27

KICKING

		FG	Att	Pct
Driscoll	ChiC	11	19	58
Sonnenberg	Det	5	10	50
Behman	Fra	5	14	36
Elliott	Cle	3	4	75
Maloney	Prov	3	6	50
Laird	Prov	3	7	43
Ursella	RI	3	7	43
Hendrian	RI-NYG	3	8	38
Berry	Pott	3	9	33
Kendrick	Ham-Buf-Roch-RI	3	9	33
Rohleder	Col	3	15	20
J. Sternaman	ChiB	3	20	15
Bloodgood	KC	2	4	50
McBride	NYG	2	4	50
Abramson	GB	2	6	33
Sweet	Prov	2	6	33
Andrews	KC	1	1	100
Brennan	NYG	1	1	100
Abbott	Day	1	2	50
Henry	Can	1	3	33
Lambeau	GB	1	3	33
Blailock	Akr	1	4	25
White	KC-NYG	1	8	13
22 players tied		0	1	0
Fitzke	Fra	0	2	0
Wallace	Cle	0	2	0
Hamer	Fra	0	4	0
Welsh	Fra	0	12	0

		PAT	Att	Pct
Berry	Pott	29	34	85
J. Sternaman	ChiB	17	21	81
Sonnenberg	Det	12	17	71
Behman	Fra	12	18	67
Driscoll	ChiC	10	13	77
Dunn	ChiC	9	13	69
Buck	GB	8	11	73
McBride	NYG	7	12	58
Elliott	Cle	6	9	67
Henry	Can	5	5	100
Lambeau	GB	5	5	100
Caldwell	Akr	5	6	83
Maloney	Prov	4	5	80
Hamer	Fra	3	3	100
Kendrick	Ham-Buf-Roch-RI	3	4	75
Blailock	Akr	2	2	100
Bruder	Buf-Fra	2	2	100
Hughes	Pott	2	2	100
Laird	Prov	2	2	100
Abramson	GB	2	3	67
Connors	Prov	2	3	67
Grigg	Roch	2	3	67
Ursella	RI	2	4	50

		PAT	Att	Pct
Andrews	KC	1	1	100
Bloodgood	KC	1	1	100
Ernst	Pott	1	1	100
Foster	Buf	1	1	100
Ch. Hill	KC-RI-KC	1	1	100
Lamb	RI	1	1	100
Lewellen	GB	1	1	100
Mahoney	ChiC	1	1	100
Mason	Mil	1	1	100
Newman	Akr	1	1	100
Sweet	Prov	1	1	100
Wentz	Pott	1	1	100
Carman	Ham-Buf-Ham	1	2	50
Hendrian	RI-NYG	1	3	33
Rohleder	Col	1	3	33
White	KC-NYG	1	4	25
Armstrong	RI	1	6	17
Fitzke	Fra	0	1	0
McDonnell	Dul-ChiC	0	1	0
Palm	NYG	0	1	0
Smyth	Roch-Fra	0	1	0
Widerquist	RI	0	1	0
Hogan	Can	0	2	0

NAME	RUSHING Complete Games					RUSHING Incom. Games				PASSING Complete Games								PASSING Incom. Games					
	G	Att.	Yds.	Avg.	TD	G	Att.	Yds.	TD	G	Com.	Att.	%	Yds.	Y/A	TD	Int.	G	Com.	Att.	Yds.	TD	Int.
HAMMOND																							
Annan (1,3)	1	8	18	2.3		1				1	0	2	0					1					
Falcon (1)	1	5	14	2.8																			
Watson						2	1	10															
Pollard (1)	1	2	5	2.5																			
Hess	1	2	3	1.5		4				1	0	1	0					4	1	1	23	1	
Robinson	1	3	1	0.3		4																	
Kendrick	1	2	0	0.0		1				1	2	17	12	12	0.7		1	1					
Curzon (1,3)										1								3	1	1	50	1	
King																		2	0	3			1
Team	1	22	41	1.9		4				1	2	20	10	12	0.6		1	4					
Opp.	1	47	129	2.7	1	4				1	8	21	38	90	4.3	1	1	4					
BUFFALO																							
Bruder (1)	1	7	33	4.7		5	6	87	1														
Kendrick (2)						7	13	25	1									7	6	15	223	1	5
Christman	2	3	5	1.7		7	8	12															
Koppisch	2	10	-1	-0.1		4	6	16		2	2	6	33	33	5.5		2	4					
Foster	2	1	2	2.0		7	2	10		2	2	4	50	35	8.8	1	1	7					
D. Fisher	1	2	0	0.0		4	4	5															
Asplundh	1	2	-5	-2.5						1	0	2	0					2					
Noble																							
Curzon (2)																							
Kennedy																							
Team	2	18	1	0.1		7				2	4	12	33	68	5.7	1	5	7					
Opp.	2	91	364	4.0	5	7				2	10	25	40	130	5.2	2	2	7					
DULUTH																							
McDonnell (1)	1	7	50	7.1		2	1	35		1	0	1	0					2					
Gilbert	1	3	30	10.0		1	1	3		1	1	7	14	1	0.1		2	1	1	2	25	1	
C. Rooney						2	5	25															
Method	1	5	6	1.2		2	6	27															
Kelly	1	1	-5	-5.0		2	7	25		1	0	1	0					2					
B. Rooney	1	1	1	1.0		1				1								1	1	1	9		
Black																							
Team	1	17	82	4.8		2				1	1	9	11	1	0.1		2	2					
Opp.	1	50	136	2.7		2				1	7	9	78	99	11.0	2	1	2					
ROCHESTER																							
Kellogg	1	21	51	2.4	1	4	5	16															
Grigg	2	17	65	3.8		5	1	2		3	5	16	31	86	5.4		1	4	3	6	65		1
Sheard	2	9	7	0.8		5	8	43		3	1	4	25	25	6.3			4					
Smyth (1)	2	10	15	1.5		5	10	24		3	18	49	37	314	6.4	3	6	4	3	10	65		2
Argus	2	10	11	1.1		3	5	8															
Hoffman	1	5	11	2.2		3	3	8		2	1	2	50	5	2.5			2					
Lynch	2	1	15	15.0		4																	
Bedford																							
Clark																							
Connors																							
Team	2	73	175	2.4	1	5				3	25	71	35	430	6.1	3	7	4					
Opp.	2	88	308	3.5	2	5				3	21	36	58	296	8.2	4	4	4					
MILWAUKEE																							
Gillo	1	4	35	8.8		1																	
Bryan (2)	3	20	27	1.4		2				3	3	12	25	29	2.4		3	2					
Blood	3	11	16	1.5		3																	
Mason	3	4	7	1.8		3				3	3	7	43	30	4.3		1	3					
Reichow	1	2	6	3.0		1																	
Brumm	3	1	1	0.0		2																	
Barr	2	9	-3	-0.3		2				2	9	26	35	84	3.2		8	2	0	1			
DeLaPorte										1	0	1	0										
Neacy																							
Roessler																							
Team	3	51	89	1.7		3				3	15	46	33	143	3.1		12	3					
Opp.	3	146	630	4.3	5	3				3	18	45	40	348	7.7	4	3	3					
DAYTON																							
Mahrt (2,4)	3	21	16	0.8		5	1	60		4	1	7	14	9	1.3		2	4					
Dobeleit	2	18	27	1.5		4	3	41		2	0	2	0					4					
Abbott	3	15	28	1.9		5	1	-5		4	3	14	21	38	2.7		3	4	2	2	37		
Partlow	2	6	17	2.8		1																	
Bacon	1	5	15	3.0		5				2	0	1	0					4	0	2			2
Huffine	3	5	13	2.6		5				4	1	2	50	9	4.5			4					
Young	1	5	1	0.2		3				1	0	1	0										
Joseph										1								4	0	1			1
Mayl																							
Fenner																							
Kinderdine																							
Guy																							
Team	3	75	117	1.6		5				5	6	38	16	77	2.0		7	3					
Opp.	3	99	277	2.8	1	5				5	26	67	39	314	4.7	1	6	3					
COLUMBUS																							
Nesser	1	6	19	3.2		5	6	35		2	1	9	11	12	1.3			4	8	13	93		4
Rapp	1	4	-1	-0.2		8	7	54	1														
Tynes	1	1	0	0.0		8	10	30	1														
Davis	1					3	1	18															
Ruh	1					7	1	7															
Rohleder	1					8	1	0															
Lynch	1	4	-8	-2.0		6	1	0		2	0	6	0					5	4	11	105		4
Albanese										1								2	1	1	65	1	
Goebel																							
Bullman																							
Team	1	15	12	0.8		7				2	1	15	7	12	0.8			6					
Opp	1	44	235	5.3	2	7				2	7	19	07	72	3.8	2	4	6					

NAME	RECEIVING Complete Games					RECEIVING Incom. Games				PUNTING Comp. Games			PUNTING Incom. Games			PUNT RETURNS Complete Games					PUNT RETURNS Incom. Games			
	G	Rec.	Yds	Avg.	TD	G	Rec.	Yds.	TD	G	No.	Avg.	G	No.	Avg.	G	No.	Yds.	Avg.	TD	G	No.	Yds.	TD
HAMMOND																								
Annan (1,3)	1	1	8	8.0		1																		
Falcon (1)																								
Watson																								
Pollard (1)																								
Hess	1					4	1	50	1	1	2	51.5	4											
Robinson	1	1	4	4.0		4	1	23	1															
Kendrick										1	8	32.3	1											
Curzon (1,3)																								
King																								
Team										1	10	36.1	4			1	0				4			
Opp.										1	9	33.7	4			1	5	33	6.6		4			
BUFFALO																								
Bruder (1)																								
Kendrick (2)													7	10	32.0									
Christman	2	1	25	25.0	1	7				2	2	34.5	7											
Koppisch										2	8	35.6	4											
Foster	2	1	18	18.0		7	3	111		2	2	30.0	7											
D. Fisher	1	1	10	10.0		4				1	1	15.0	4			1					4	1	20	
Asplundh										1	2	36.5												
Noble	2					7	2	62																
Curzon (2)						5	1	50	1															
Kennedy	1	1	15	15.0																				
Team										2	15	33.5	7			2	0				7			
Opp.										2	11	34.9	7			2	2	28	14.0		7			
DULUTH																								
McDonnell (1)	1					2	2	34	1							1	3	65	21.7		2	1	10	
Gilbert										1	5	37.2	1			1	1	15	15.0		1			
C. Rooney																								
Method																								
Kelly										1	3	29.0	2			1	1	15	15.0		2			
B. Rooney																								
Black	1	1	1	1.0		1																		
Team										1	8	34.1	2			1	5	95	19.0		2			
Opp.										1	8	37.3	2			1	3	15	5.0		2			
ROCHESTER																								
Kellogg	2	3	30	10.0	1	3																		
Grigg	3	1	27	27.0		4										2	1	5	5.0		5			
Sheard	3	6	118	19.7	2	4	2	53		2	10	40.2	5	8	18.1									
Smyth (1)	3	3	70	23.3		4																		
Argus																								
Hoffman																								
Lynch	2	6	78	13.0		4	1	33		2	5	31.4	4	2	37.5									
Bedford	1	4	73	18.3		1	3	44																
Clark	2	1	22	22.0		3				1			4	1	28.0									
Connors	1	1	12	12.0																				
Team										2	15	37.3	5			2	1	5	5.0		5			
Opp.										2	12	32.6	5			2	7	126	18.0		5			
MILWAUKEE																								
Gillo										1	2	37.5	1											
Bryan (2)	3	7	63	9.0		3				3	1	35.0	2			3	2	8	4.0		2			
Blood	3	1	5	5.0		3				3	12	32.4	3			3	1	5	5.0		3			
Mason										3	7	37.1	3											
Reichow																								
Brumm	3	1	15	15.0		2																		
Barr	2	1	4	4.0		2				2	3	40.7	2			2	2	6	3.0		2			
DeLaPorte																								
Neacy	3	3	42	14.0		3																		
Roessler	3	2	14	7.0		3																		
Team										3	25	35.2	3			3	5	19	3.8		3			
Opp.										3	24	34.5	3			3	14	227	16.2	1	3			
DAYTON																								
Mahrt (2,4)										2	2	39.5	6											
Dobeleit	2	1	14	14.0		4										1	3	17	5.7		5			
Abbott										2	22	32.4	6	6	29.7									
Partlow																								
Bacon	2	1	15	15.0		4				1	4	33.3	5											
Huffine										3	1	29.0	5											
Young																								
Joseph													5	1	29.0									
Mayl	4					4	2	37																
Fenner	4	2	18	9.0		4																		
Kinderdine	1	1	9	9.0		1																		
Guy										1	1	47.0												
Team										2	16	34.3	6			2	3	17	5.7		6			
Opp.										2	14	35.1	6			2	9	78	8.7		6			
COLUMBUS																								
Nesser										1	5	27.8	5	1	0.0									
Rapp	2	1	12	12.0		2																		
Tynes																								
Davis	2					7	9	213	1							1					8	2	70	
Ruh																								
Rohleder																								
Lynch	2					5	1	10		1	4	29.3	6			1	1	5	5.0		6			
Albanese																								
Goebel	1					7	3	40																
Bullman													3	1	25.0									
Team										1	9	28.4	8			1	1	5	5.0		8			
Opp										1	6	26.5	8			1	2	50	25.0		8			

1926 A.F.L.
Grange's Showcase

C.C. Pyle quickly became a familiar face around the NFL, but not a particularly popular one. Commonly called "Cash and Carry", Pyle had driven a hard bargain as Red Grange's agent in negotiating a contract with the Chicago Bears the year before. At the NFL's meeting in February, Pyle flabbergasted the league by requesting a New York franchise for Grange and himself. He'd already taken a five-year lease on Yankee Stadium. New York Giants owner Tim Mara absolutely refused to go along with such an idea. He'd taken a personal dislike for Pyle, but his objection was more of a more practical nature: Pyle and Grange were muscling in on his territory. Ironically, Pyle chose to ask for his New York franchise at the same meeting at which the league ratified president Joe Carr's action in December of suspending the Pottsville franchise for violating Frankford's territorial rights. When the league backed Mara and turned down Pyle, he announced the formation of the American Football League, a new circuit whose main attraction would be Red Grange of the New York Yankees.

Nine clubs made up the new league. In addition to New Yok, New teams were placed in Philadelphia, Newark, Brooklyn, Boston, Chicago and Cleveland. Completing the new league were the Rock Island Independents, which jumped to the AFL from the NFL, and a road team nominally representing Los Angeles. With former Princeton athlete Bill Edwards as league president, the AFL prepared to compete with the seven-year-old NFL.

The new league did have a promising array of star players, mostly young glamour backs recently graduated from college. The New York team had Grange and Eddie Tryon on Colgate; Brooklyn had Harry Stuhldreher of the Four Horsemen of Notre Dame; Los Angeles had Wildcat Wilson of Washington; Newark had Doug Wycoff from Georgia Tech; and Philadelphia had Al Kreuz from Penn. Some NFL veterans also jumped to the new league. In addition to the entire Rock Island squad, seven members of the 1925 Cleveland Bulldogs jumped to the new AFL Cleveland team. Joey Sternaman, brother of Chicago Bears co-owner Dutch Sternaman, was induced to go into direct competition with his brother as owner, coach and quarterback of the Chicago Bulls. Philadelphia signed former Frankford tackle Bull Behman and ex-New York Giants tackle Century Milstead, giving them by far the strongest line in the new league.

But all the promises vanished in the autumn of one rainy Sunday after another. Although Grange continued to draw fans, the other AFL clubs didn't. From the start, there were rumors that the money backing several teams came from Pyle and Grange. Wherever it came from, it was going away rapidly. At the end of October, Newark and Cleveland folded. The Brooklyn team folded in early November and was merged into the rival NFL franchise in that borough. Next, Boston quit playing. Rock Island, which had become a road team after its first three games, gave up in mid-November. At the end of the schedule in December, only New York, Philadelphia, Chicago and Wilson's traveling Los Angeles squad were still playing.

The championship came down to a pair of games between New York and the Philadelphia Quakers. The Yankees had stressed offense, with Grange, Tyron, who finished as the league's top scorer, and George Pease, who led the AFL in passing touchdowns. Altogether, the Yankees scored over 200 points, more than twice as many as any other league team.By contrast, the Quakers were practically punchless. At times their entire offense consisted of Al Kreuz field goals. But the Quaker line had held opponents to less than a touchdown a game. On Thanksgiving Day, before 22,000 fans in Yankee Stadium, the Quakers beat New York 13-10. Grange injured his hip in the contest and had to sit out the rematch two days later in Philadelphia's Shibe Park, when the Quakers triumphed again 13-6 before another crowd of 22,000 fans, The Yankees went on a post-season tour of the South and West in a vain effort to recapture the magic of last winter's Grange tour, but the rest of the AFL — what was left of it — meekly folded its tattered tent. In its final move, the champion Quakers met the NFL's New York Giants, a seventh-place team, in a snowstorm on December 12 at the Polo Grounds. Before 5,000 shivering spectators, the Quakers were soundly thrashed 31-0.

STANDINGS

	W	L	T	Pct.	Pts.	Opp. Pts.	Avg. Pts.	Opp. Avg.
Philadelphia Quakers	8	2	0	.800	93	52	9	5
New York Yankees	10	5	0	.667	212	82	14	5
Cleveland Panthers	3	2	0	.600	62	46	12	9
Los Angeles Wildcats (R)	6	6	2	.500	105	83	8	6
Chicago Bulls	5	6	3	.455	88	69	6	5
Boston Bulldogs	2	4	0	.333	20	81	3	13
Rock Island Independents	2	6	1	.250	21	126	2	14
Brooklyn Horsemen	1	3	0	.250	25	68	6	17
Newark Bears	0	3	2	.000	7	26	1	5

(R) — played only road games

Scoring

Tryon	NYY	72
Sternaman	Chi	52
Grange	NYY	50
Kreuz	Phi	34
Noble	Cle	31
W. Wilson	LA	25
Mohardt	Chi	24
Ford	Phi	18
Fry	NYY	18
Dinsmore	Phi	17
Bross	LA	14
Coglizer	NYY	12
Cunningham	Cle	12
Maloney	NYY	12
Marks	NYY	12
D. Morrison	LA	12
Pease	NYY	12
Way	Phi	12
Elliott	Cle-Phi	12
Reed	LA	10
Lawson	LA	9
Bradshaw	RI	7
Illman	LA	7

Rushing TD's

Tryon	NYY	6
Grange	NYY	4
Mohardt	Chi	4
Noble	Cle	4
W. Wilson	LA	4
Sternaman	Chi	3
D. Morrison	LA	2
Armstrong	RI	1
Bradshaw	LA	1
Britton	Bkn	1
Cronin	Bos	1
Ford	Phi	1
Fry	NYY	1
Goebel	NYY	1
Illman	LA	1
Kreuz	Phi	1
Marks	NYY	1
Norton	RI	1
Pease	NYY	1
Way	Phi	1
White	Chi	1
Wycoff	Nwk	1

Receiving TD's

Grange	NYY	3
Cunningham	Cle	2
Maloney	NYY	2
Tryon	NYY	2
Baker	NYY	1
Bolger	Bkn	1
Bradshaw	RI	1
Bross	LA	1
Flaherty	LA	1
Ford	Phi	1
Harrison	Bkn	1
Hubert	NYY	1
Killinger	Phi	1
Marks	NYY	1
R. Morrison	LA	1
Noble	Cle	1
Otte	NYY	1
Pease	NYY	1
Romey	Chi	1
Tully	Phi	1
Vesser	LA	1
Way	Phi	1
Wolf	Cle	1

TD Passes

Pease	NYY	7
Michaels	Cle	4
W. Wilson	LA	4
Grange	NYY	2
Scott	Phi	2
Stuhldreher	Bkn	2
Baker	NYY	1
Britton	Bkn	1
Dinsmore	Phi	1
Hubert	NYY	1
Kaplan	RI	1
Killinger	Phi	1
Marks	NYY	1
Sternaman	Chi	1

Field Goals

Sternaman	Chi	9
Kreuz	Phi	8
Dinsmore	Phi	3
Elliott	Cle-Phi	2
Lawson	LA	2
Reed	LA	2
Tryon	NYY	2
Coglizer	NYY	1
Etelman	Bos	1
Gehrke	Bos	1
G. Roberts	Cle	1

PAT's		PAT	Att	Pct
Tryon	NYY	12	16	75
Coglizer	NYY	9	10	90
Sternaman	Chi	7	9	78
Elliott	Cle-Phi	4	5	80
Reed	LA	4	5	80
Kreuz	Phi	4	7	57
Lawson	LA	3	3	100
Bross	LA	2	2	100
Dinsmore	Phi	2	2	100
Grange	NYY	2	2	100
Kaplan	RI	2	2	100
Bradshaw	RI	1	1	100
Gehrke	Bos	1	1	100
Illman	LA	1	1	100
McGlone	Bos	1	1	100
Noble	Cle	1	1	100
W. Wilson	LA	1	1	100
Wycoff	Nwk	1	1	100
Stuhldreher	Bkn	1	2	50
Hubert	NYY	0	1	0
Marks	NYY	0	1	0
Wolf	Cle	0	1	0
Drews	Bkn	0	2	0

PHILADELPHIA QUAKERS 8-2-0 Bob Folwell

Regulars

UseName	Pos.	Hgt.	Wgt.	Age	Pts.	College
Whitey Thomas	E	5'10	170	31		Penn State
George Tully	E	5'10"	180	22	6	Dartmouth
Century Milstead	T	6'1"	213	26		Wabash, Yale
Bull Behman	T	5'10"	210	26		Dickinson
Bill Coleman	G	6'	200	24		Pennsylvania
Butch Spagna	G	6'	220	29		Brown, Lehigh
Karl Robinson	C	5'10"	180	23		Pennsylvania
Johnny Scott	BB	5'10"	180	31		Lafayette
George Sullivan	TB	5'9"	170	29		Pennsylvania
Adrian Ford	WB-E	5'10"	190	22	18	Lafayette
Al Kreuz	FB	5'9"	190	28	34	Western Michigan, Pennsylvania

Substitutes

UseName	Pos.	Hgt.	Wgt.	Age	Pts.	College
Knute Johnson	E	6'1"	185	26		Muhlenberg
Joe Kostos	E	5'8"	170	30		Bucknell
Jerry Fay	T-G-E	6'4"	220	28		Grove City
Charlie Cartin	T-C	5'10"	195	24		Holy Cross
Saville Crowther	G	6'1"	220	25		Colgate
Bob Dinsmore	BB-TB-WB-FB	5'8"	165	24	17	Princeton
Doc Elliott (from CLE)	TB-FB	5'10"	210	26		Lafayette
Bob Beattie	WB-E	6'3"	230	23		Princeton
Les Aplundh	FB-BB-WB	6'3"	213	25		Swarthmore
Joe Marhefka	TB	5'6"	150	24		Penn State, Lafayette
Glenn Killinger (from NYG)	TB	5'9"	164	27	6	Penn State
Charlie Way	WB-TB-BB	5'8"	145	28	12	Penn State
Lou "Red" Gebhardt	WB	5'11"	175	23		Lafayette

Scores of each game

Date	Pts.	Opponent	Pts.
Oct. 2	9	CHICAGO	3
Oct. 9	3	LOS ANGELES	0
Oct. 16	9	NEWARK	0
Oct. 23	9	ROCK ISLAND	0
Oct. 30	0	NEW YORK	23
Nov. 6	24	ROCK ISLAND	0
Nov. 14	0	Chicago	3
Nov. 20	13	LOS ANGELES	7
Nov. 25	13	New York	10
Nov. 27	13	NEW YORK	6

NEW YORK YANKEES 10-5-0 Ralph Scott

Regulars

UseName	Pos.	Hgt.	Wgt.	Age	Pts.	College
Paul Goebel	E	6'3"	204	25	6	Michigan
Red Maloney	E-WB	5'11"	180	24	12	Dartmouth
Frank Kearney	T	6'	193	22		Cornell
Dick Hall	T	6'2"	220	23		Butler, Illinois
Bill Oliver	G	5'11"	180	24		Alabama
Paul Minick	G	6'	195	26		Iowa
Hal Griffen	C	6'1"	243	24		Iowa
George Pease	BB	5'8"	185	23	12	Columbia
Red Grange	TB-BB	5'11"	178	23	50	Illinois
Eddie Tryon	WB	5'8"	180	26	72	Colgate
Pooley "Papa" Hubert	FB	5'11"	187	25	6	Alabama

Substitutes

UseName	Pos.	Hgt.	Wgt.	Age	Pts.	College
Art Coglizer	E	5'11"	180	23	12	Missouri
Lowell Otte	E-T	6'2"	180	22	6	Iowa
Gus Goetz	T	6'	215	29		Michigan
Ralph Scott	T-G	6'2"	235	28		Wisconsin
Leo "Tiny" Kriz	G-T	6'1"	205	23		Iowa, George Washington
Mike Michalske	G-T	6'	200	23		Penn State
Steve Schimititisch	C-G	6'	195	23		Columbia
Bullet Baker	TB-BB-FB	5'8"	175	26	6	Southern California
Larry Marks	WB-E	5'11"	185	23	12	Indiana
Harry Fry	FB-WB	5'10"	190	23	18	Iowa
Hec Garvey (from HAR, BKN-AFL, BKN-NFL)	G	6'1"	235	26		Notre Dame

Scores of each game

Date	Pts.	Opponent	Pts.
Sep. 26	0	Cleveland	10
Oct. 3	26	Rock Island	0
Oct. 9	13	Boston	0
Oct. 17	0	Chicago	14
Oct. 24	6	LOS ANGELES	0
Oct. 30	23	Philadelphia	0
Nov. 2	35	ROCK ISLAND	0
Nov. 7	21	BROOKLYN	13
Nov. 8	28	LOS ANGELES (at Toronto)	0
Nov. 14	24	BOSTON	0
Nov. 21	6	LOS ANGELES	16
Nov. 25	10	PHILADELPHIA	13
Nov. 27	6	Philadelphia	13
Nov. 28	7	CHICAGO	0
Dec. 12	7	Chicago	3

CLEVELAND PANTHERS 3-2-0 Ray Watts

Regulars

UseName	Pos.	Hgt.	Wgt.	Age	Pts.	College
Eddie "Red" Kregenow	E	5'8"	170	26		Akron
Cookie Cunningham	E	6'3"	210	21	12	Ohio State
Red Roberts	T	6'3"	235	26		Centre
Myles Evans	T		185	24		Ohio Wesleyan
Al Nesser *	G-E	6'	195	33		none
Jack Sack (to CAN)	G	6'2"	190	27		Pittsburgh
Red Weaver	C	5'10"	185	29		Centre
Dick Wolf	BB	5'8"	160	26	6	Miami-Ohio
Al Michaels	TB	6'	190	26		Heidelberg, Ohio State
Dave Noble	WB-FB	6'2"	195	26	31	Nebraska
Doc Elliott (to PHI)	FB	5'10"	210	26	10	Lafayette

* (from & to AKR, to NYG)

Substitutes

UseName	Pos.	Hgt.	Wgt.	Age	Pts.	College
Norty "Mope" Behm	E-FB	5'7"	150	25		Iowa State
Dean	T					
Bob Spiers	T-G	5'11"	195	31		Ohio State
John Otterbacher	G		190	25		Ohio State
Ralph Vince	G	5'8"	175	26		Washington & Jefferson
Al Thornburg	C	5'10"	170	25		Iowa State
Jay Winters	BB	5'8"	145	22		Ohio Wesleyan
Billy Gribben	TB	5'7"	160	24		Case Reserve
Guy Roberts (to CAN)	FB-WB-BB	5'8"	180	26	3	Dayton
Leo Virant	G	5'11"	195	23		Iowa State

Scores of each game

Date	Pts.	Opponent	Pts.
Sep. 26	10	NEW YORK	0
Oct. 3	17	LOS ANGELES	14
Oct. 17	23	ROCK ISLAND	7
Oct. 24	12	Chicago	19
Oct. 31	0	LOS ANGELES	6

LOS ANGELES WILDCATS 6-6-2 Jim Clark

Regulars

UseName	Pos.	Hgt.	Wgt.	Age	Pts.	College
Ray Flaherty	E	6'	185	22	6	Gonzaga
Jim Lawson	E	5'11"	190	24	9	Stanford
Harry Shipkey	T	6'2"	205	24		Stanford
Walden Erickson	T	6'1"	205	24		Washington
Nick Busch	G	5'10"	181	28		Gonzaga
Abe Wilson	G	5'10"	190	26		Washington
Chal Walters	C	5'9"	190	26		Washington
Mal Bross	BB-TB-WB	5'9"	170	21	14	Gonzaga
Wildcat Wilson	TB	5'11"	200	25	25	Washington
Ram Morrison	WB-T	5'11"	180	26	6	Oklahoma
Ted Bucklin	FB-BB	6'	190	26		Idaho

Substitutes

UseName	Pos.	Hgt.	Wgt.	Age	Pts.	College
John Vesser	E	6'	180	25	6	Idaho
Dick Reed	E-T	6'	180	25	10	Oregon
Charlie Johnston	T-G	6'	190	25		Stanford
Dana Carey	G	6'2"	200	23		California
Ed McRae	G	5'7"	186	24		Washington
Ray Stephens	C	5'11"	190	23		Idaho
Jim Bradshaw	BB	5'6"	150	28	6	Illinois, Nevada
Ted Illman	WB-TB-BB	6'	190	23	7	Montana
Duke Morrison	FB-WB	6'	180	29	12	California

Scores of each game

Date	Pts.	Opponent	Pts.
Sep. 26	3	Rock Island	7
Oct. 3	14	Cleveland	17
Oct. 9	0	Philadelphia	3
Oct. 10	23	Brooklyn	0
Oct. 16	21	Boston	0
Oct. 17	7	Newark	0
Oct. 24	0	New York	6
Oct. 31	6	Cleveland	0
Nov. 7	3	Chicago	3
Nov. 8	0	New York (at Toronto)	28
Nov. 20	7	Philadelphia	13
Nov. 21	16	New York	6
Nov. 25	0	Chicago	0
Dec. 5	5	Chicago	0

CHICAGO BULLS 5-6-3 Joey Sternaman

Regulars

UseName	Pos.	Hgt.	Wgt.	Age	Pts.	College
Eddie Anderson	E	5'10"	180	25		Notre Dame
Dick Romey	E	6'1"	186	21	6	Iowa
Aubrey Goodman	T-E	6'3"	225	22		Baylor, Chicago
John McMullan	T	6'2"	250	23		Notre Dame
Garland Buckeye	G	6'	245	28		none
Red Mahan (from FRA)	G	5'10"	212	24		West Virginia
Ojay Larson	C	6'1"	200	28		Notre Dame
Joey Sternaman	BB	5'6"	155	26	52	Illinois
Johnny Mohardt	TB	5'10"	168	28	24	Notre Dame
Red Strader	WB-FB	5'9"	200	21		St. Mary's
Buck White	FB	6'	195	25	6	Howard Payne, Valparaiso

Substitutes

UseName	Pos.	Hgt.	Wgt.	Age	Pts.	College
John Fahay (to RAC)	E	6'	188	24		St. Thomas, Marquette
Fred Graham (from FRA, to & from PROV)	E	6'	175	22		Indiana State, West Virginia
Dick Stahlman (from RI)	T-G	6'2"	220	24		DePaul, Northwestern
Mush Crawford	G-T	6'	200	27		Beloit, Lake Forest, Illinois
Swede Swenson	G	6'1"	205	28		Chicago, Dartmouth
Harry Hall	BB-TB	5'11"	170	23		Chicago, Illinois
Jim Tays	TB	5'8"	175	27		Penn State, Chicago
Sam Whiteman	WB-TB-FB	5'9"	195	24		Missouri
Ward Connell (from ChiC)	WB-E	5'10"	173	27		Notre Dame
Jack Boyle	E		195	22		Loras
Hal Blackwood	G	6'2"	250	28		Chicago, Northwestern
Doss Richerson	G-E-T	6'1"	225	25		Missouri
Bill Giaver (to LOU)	WB	5'9"	190	28		Georgia Tech

Scores of each game

Date	Pts.	Opponent	Pts.
Sep. 26	7	Newark	7
Oct. 2	3	Philadelphia	9
Oct. 3	7	Brooklyn	12
Oct. 10	3	Rock Island	7
Oct. 17	14	NEW YORK	0
Oct. 24	19	CLEVELAND	12
Oct. 31	23	BOSTON	0
Nov. 7	3	LOS ANGELES	3
Nov. 14	3	PHILADELPHIA	0
Nov. 21	3	ROCK ISLAND	0
Nov. 25	0	LOS ANGELES	0
Nov. 28	0	New York	7
Dec. 5	0	LOS ANGELES	5
Dec. 12	3	NEW YORK	7

BOSTON BULLDOGS 2-4-0 Herb Treat

Regulars

UseName	Pos.	Hgt.	Wgt.	Age	Pts.	College
Bull Lowe (to FRA)	E	5'11"	180	31		Fordham, Lafayette
Charlie Morrison	E-G		185	26	6	none
Herb Treat	T	6'	190	25		Boston, College, Princeton
Tom O'Brien	T	5'9"	210	21		Boston College
Ned Coleman	G-E	5'10"	180	24		Holy Cross
Ray Paten	G	5'10"	190	26		Boston College
Al Pierotti	C	5'10"	200	30		Washington & Lee
Joe McGlone (from PROV)	BB	5'7"	150	31		Harvard
Bill Cronin	TB	5'10"	180	25	6	Boston College
Jim Wallis	WB-BB-FB	5'10"	180	23		Holy Cross
Oscar Johnson	FB-WB	5'10"	200	25		Vermont

Substitutes

UseName	Pos.	Hgt.	Wgt.	Age	Pts.	College
Bill Murphy	E-G	5'11"	200	22		Boston U.
Zeke "Pete" Surabian	T	5'10"	195	22		Williams
Bill Stephens	T-G-C	6'	185	23		Bucknell
Art McManus (from NWK)	G	6'	190	22		Boston College
Art Ray	G	6'	190	24		Holy Cross
Francis Smith	C-E	5'10"	198	23		Holy Cross
Carl Eltelman (to PROV)	BB-WB	5'8"	160	26	3	Tufts
Ralph Gilroy	TB-FB-E	5'9"	175	26		Princeton
Erwin Gehrke	WB-FB-BB	6'1"	190	28	4	Harvard
Phil Corrigan	BB-FB-WB	5'7"	160	28		Boston College
Vern Hagenbuckle (to PROV)	G	5'8"	185	25		Dartmouth
Johnny Gilroy	TB-WB	5'10"	175	30		Georgetown

Scores of each game

Date	Pts.	Opponent	Pts.
Oct. 3	3	Newark	0
Oct. 9	0	NEW YORK	13
Oct. 16	0	LOS ANGELES	21
Oct. 17	17	Brooklyn	0
Oct. 31	0	Chicago	23
Nov. 14	0	New York	24

ROCK ISLAND INDEPENDENTS 2-6-1 Johnny Armstrong

Regulars

UseName	Pos.	Hgt.	Wgt.	Age	Pts.	College
Homer "Bear" Walker	E	5'10"	175	23		Baylor
Mike Wilson	E	5'10"	168	29		Lehigh
Dick Stahlman (to ChiA)	T	6'2"	220	24		DePaul, Northwestern
Duke Slater (to ChiC)	T	6'1"	215	27		Iowa
Bug Hartzog	G-T	5'11"	195	25		Baylor
Chet Widerquist (to ChiC)	G	6'1"	220	30		Northwestern, Wash. & Lee
Riley Biggs (to NYG)	C-G	6'2"	230	26		Baylor
Johnny Armstrong	BB	5'8"	175	22	6	Dubuque
Wes Bradshaw (to BUF)	TB-BB	5'8"	175	27	7	Baylor
Vince McCarthy	WB	5'10"	155	26		St. Viator
Eddie Novak	FB-BB	5'9"	175	29		none

Substitutes

UseName	Pos.	Hgt.	Wgt.	Age	Pts.	College
Frank Coyle	E	5'9"	175	26		Detroit
Bill Scarpino	E	5'11"	175	28		Des Moines
Ken Truckenmiller	G	6'1"	190	22		Cornell College
Ralph Wiedich	C-G	6'1"	205	24		Emporia State
Louie Kolls	C	6'1"	205	33		St. Ambrose
Ave Kaplan	TB-WB-BB	5'7"	165	26	2	Hamline
Marty Norton	TB-WB	5'6"	175	23	6	none
Ray "Red" Rohrabaugh	WB-TB-FB	5'11"	190	25		Franklin (Ind.)
Chuck Hill	FB-E	5'8"	190	22		Iowa State
Elmer Layden (to BKN-AFL)	FB	5'11"	180	23		Notre Dame
Frank Urban	E	6'	190	26		M.I.T.

Scores of each game

Date	Pts.	Opponent	Pts.
Sep. 26	7	LOS ANGELES	3
Oct. 3	0	NEW YORK	26
Oct. 10	7	CHICAGO	3
Oct. 17	7	Cleveland	23
Oct. 23	0	Philadelphia	9
Oct. 24	0	Newark	0
Nov. 2	0	New York	35
Nov. 6	0	Philadelphia	24
Nov. 21	0	Chicago	3

BROOKLYN HORSEMEN 1-3-0 Eddie McNeeley

Regulars

UseName	Pos.	Hgt.	Wgt.	Age	Pts.	College
Ed Harrison *	E	6'	178	23	6	Boston College
Ed Hunsinger	E	5'11"	175	26		Notre Dame
Nate Share	T	6'1"	210	23		Tufts
Hec Garvey (from HAR, *, to NYY)	T	6'1"	235	26		Notre Dame
Red Howard *	G	5'11"	192	25		New Hamp., Princeton
Tarzan Taylor *	G	5'11"	173	31		Ohio State
Sheldon Pollock	C	6'	200	21		Lafayette
Harry Stuhldreher *	BB	5'7"	165	24	1	Notre Dame
Jim Frugone	TB-WB	5'10"	165	28		Syracuse
Dave Sehres	WB-G	5'8"	160	26		N.Y.U.
Earl Britton *	FB-TB	6'3"	210	23	6	Illinois

* — to Brooklyn NFL

Substitutes

UseName	Pos.	Hgt.	Wgt.	Age	Pts.	College
Shep Bingham	E	6'	180	23		Yale
Ted Drews *	E	6'	180	23		Princeton
Bill Koslick	T		190	26		none
Leo Prendergast	T-C	5'8"	170	25		Lafayette
Swede Olsen	G					none
Jack Sheehy	G-C			27		N.Y.U.
Paul Brennan	C-G	5'10"	180	23		Fordham
Jim Fitzgerald	BB	5'5"	150	23		St. John's (N.Y.)
Ray Smith	TB-WB-BB	5'8"	170	26		Lebanon Valley
Jim Bolger	WB-TB	6'	175	23	6	St. Mary's, St. Bonaventure
Elmer Layden (from RI)	FB	5'11"	180	23		Notre Dame
Charlie Hummell	T	5'9"	190	28		Lafayette
Bob Nicholes	T	6'1"	205	27		Oglethorpe
George Baldwin	G	5'11"	190	24		Virginia
Ted Plumridge *	C	6'2"	205	24		Colgate, St. John's (N.Y.)
Jim Flaherty	WB		198	30	6	Georgetown

Scores of each game

Date	Pts.	Opponent	Pts.
Oct. 3	12	CHICAGO	7
Oct. 10	0	LOS ANGELES	23
Oct. 17	0	BOSTON	17
Nov. 7	13	New York	21

NEWARK BEARS 0-3-2 Hal Hansen (Newark Demons for game of Oct. 24)

Regulars

UseName	Pos.	Hgt.	Wgt.	Age	Pts.	College
Sammy Stein	E	6'	190	21		none
Silvio Tursi	E	5'7"	165	25		Muhlenberg
Bob Rives	T-E	6'1"	200	22		Vanderbilt
Cy Williams	T	6'	200	24		Florida
Dom Manella	G	5'7"	205	34		none
Goldie Goldstein	G	6'2"	210	23		Florida
John Murray	C	6'	180	21		Georgia Tech
Jim Brewster	BB	5'10"	170	25		Georgia Tech
Doug Wycoff	TB	6'	190	22	7	Georgia Tech
Adrian "Sparky" Maurer	WB	5'10"	170	25		Oglethorpe
Ike Williams	FB-BB	5'10"	180	23		Georgia Tech

Substitutes

UseName	Pos.	Hgt.	Wgt.	Age	Pts.	College
Ken King	E	5'10"	175	25		Kentucky
Eddie Black	E	5'10"	175	21		Muhlenberg
Carl Davis	T	6'	194	23		West Virginia
Russ Clark	G-T	5'11"	190	22		Muhlenberg
Art McManus (to BOS)	G	6'	190	23		Boston College
George Kerr	G	6'1"	233	33		Catholic
Orin Rice	C-G	6'	165	22		Syracuse, Muhlenberg
Vaughn Connelly	FB-TB	5'8"	170	24		Georgia Tech
Ark Newton	WB	5'10"	185	26		Florida
Hal Hansen	FB-E	5'10"	200	33		Minnesota

Scores of each game

Date	Pts.	Opponent	Pts.
Sep. 26	7	CHICAGO	7
Oct. 3	0	BOSTON	3
Oct. 16	0	Philadelphia	9
Oct. 17	0	LOS ANGELES	7
Oct. 24	0	ROCK ISLAND	0

1926 N.F.L.
Nevers' Traveling Circus

The NFL bloated to 22 teams in 1926 to face the upstart American Football League. When word came that the new league was courting Pottsville, suspended for encroaching Frankford's territorial rights near the close of the 1925 season, the NFL moved to reinstate the Maroons with only moderate fines. The older league had already lost charter member Rock Island to the AFL, but Pottsville's Maroons were a far more powerful commodity, certainly one of the two or three best teams in pro football. Although Rochester, Minneapolis and Cleveland all decided they couldn't make it to the starting blocks and suspended operations for 1926, Hartford, Brooklyn and a traveling Los Angeles team took their places. Former league members Racine, Duluth and Louisville (playing as another road team out of Chicago) came back in, putting league memberships at a number that would stand as a record until 1970. The team roster maximum was increased to 18. The NFL seemed ready to accomodate any team or player if, in doing so, they could deprive the AFL, but most of the new baggage was dead weight.

If the AFL died of financial woes, the NFL was seriously afllicted with the same illness, suffering through bad weather and competition with the rival league. There was head-to-head competition in New York, Brooklyn, Philadelphia and Chicago. The Giants lost $40,000 fighting Red Grange in ballparks within view of each other. In Chicago, the champion Cardinals were thrown back on their heels by the AFL Bulls. The new team leased Comiskey Park, forcing the Cards into smaller Normal Field, and made a lucrative offer to Paddy Driscoll to jump leagues. Cardinals owner Chris O'Brien couldn't meet the offer, so he sold Driscoll to the Bears, who could and did match the offer. Without Driscoll, the Cardinals fell out of contention and would not challenge for the title again until after World War II.

The Bears, on the other hand, strengthened themselves considerably by adding Driscoll, who finished as the NFL scoring leader with 86 points and field goal leader with 12. Other important additions were veteran tackle Link Lyman and rookies Bill Senn and Bill Buckler. When blended with such veterans as George Trafton and Ed Healey, the newcomers gave George Halas a strong squad which had an undefeated 11-0-2 mark through the end of November.

Hot on the tail of the Bears were the Pottsville Maroons and the

1926 STANDINGS

	W	L	T	Pct.	Pts.	Opp. Pts.	Avg. Pts.	Opp. Avg.
Frankford Yellow Jackets	14	1	2	.933	236	49	14	3
Chicago Bears	12	1	3	.923	216	63	14	4
Pottsville Maroons	10	2	2	.833	155	29	11	2
Kansas City Cowboys	8	3	0	.727	76	53	7	5
Green Bay Packers	7	3	3	.700	151	61	12	5
Los Angeles Buccaneers (R)	6	3	1	.667	67	57	7	6
New York Giants	8	4	1	.667	147	51	11	4
Duluth Eskimos	6	5	3	.545	113	81	8	6
Buffalo Rangers	4	4	2	.500	53	62	5	6
Chicago Cardinals	5	6	1	.455	74	98	6	8
Providence Steam Roller	5	7	1	.417	99	103	7	8
Detroit Panthers	4	6	2	.400	107	60	9	5
Hartford Blues	3	7	0	.300	57	99	6	10
Brooklyn Lions	3	8	0	.273	60	150	5	14
Milwaukee Badgers	2	7	0	.222	41	66	5	7
Akron Indians	1	4	3	.200	23	89	3	11
Dayton Triangles	1	4	1	.200	15	82	3	14
Racine Tornadoes	1	4	0	.200	8	92	2	18
Columbus Tigers	1	6	0	.143	26	93	4	13
Canton Bulldogs	1	9	3	.100	46	161	4	12
Hammond Pros	0	4	0	.000	3	56	1	14
Louisville Colonels (R)	0	4	0	.000	0	108	0	27

(R) — played only road games

Scoring Leaders

Driscoll	ChiB	86
Nevers	Dul	71
Wentz	Pott	60
Oden	Prov	60
Jones	Fra	54
McBride	NYG	48
Bloodgood	KC	47
Senn	ChiB	45
Lewellen	GB	42
Haines	NYG	36
Sonnenberg	Det	34
Moran	Fra	33
Budd	Fra	30
Welsh	Pott	30
Thomas	Bkn	25
Romney	ChiB	25
Hanny	ChiB	24
Lidberg	GB	24
Imlay	LA	24
Latone	Pott	24
Maul	LA	21
Purdy	GB	20
Bruder	Fra	19

KICKING

		FG	Att	Pct
Driscoll	ChiB	12	30	40
Sonnenberg	Det	9	20	45
Bloodgood	KC	8	22	36
Budd	Fra	6	20	30
Welsh	Pott	5	27	19
Dunn	ChiC	4	6	67
Nevers	Dul	4	21	19
Curtin	Mil-Rac	2	2	100
Purdy	GB	2	7	29
Maul	LA	2	10	20
Radzevich	Har	1	1	100
Sternaman	ChiB	1	1	100
Weir	Fra	1	1	100
Beckley	Day	1	2	50
Brennan	Bkn	1	2	50
Rohleder	Akr	1	3	33
Sechrist	Ham-Akr-Ham	1	3	33
Wentworth	Prov	1	3	33
Perrin	Har	1	4	25
McBride	NYG	1	10	10
22 players with		0	1	0
8 players with		0	2	0
Abbott	Day	0	3	0
Hogan	NYG-Fra	0	5	0
Henry	Can	0	7	0

		PAT	Att	Pct
McBride	NYG	15	15	100
Welsh	Pott	15	17	88
Purdy	GB	14	14	100
Driscoll	ChiB	14	18	78
Budd	Fra	12	18	67
Nevers	Dul	11	15	73
Sonnenberg	Det	7	9	78
Hogan	NYG-Fra	5	5	100
Bloodgood	KC	5	6	83
Lambeau	GB	4	5	80
Kendrick	Buf	4	7	57
Hathaway	Pott	3	3	100
Henry	Can	3	3	100
Perrin	Har	3	3	100
Senn	ChiB	3	3	100
Hamer	Fra	3	4	75
Dunn	ChiC	3	5	60
Maul	LA	3	5	60
Moran	Fra	3	5	60
Keefer	Prov	3	6	50
Radzevich	Har	2	2	100
Reichle	Col	2	2	100
Sternaman	ChiB	2	2	100
Weir	Fra	2	2	100

		PAT	Att	Pct
Ashmore	Mil	2	3	67
Newmeyer	LA	2	3	67
Rohleder	Akr	2	3	67
Wentworth	Prov	2	3	67
Brennan	Bkn	2	6	33
Andrews	KC	1	1	100
Bruder	Fra	1	1	100
Buckler	ChiB	1	1	100
Conzelman	Det	1	1	100
Curtin	Mil-Rac	1	1	100
Golembeski	Prov	1	1	100
Lamb	ChiC	1	1	100
H. Robb	Can	1	1	100
Swanson	ChiC	1	1	100
Woodin	GB	1	1	100
Gillo	Rac	0	1	0
Grigg	NYG	0	1	0
Imlay	LA	0	1	0
Mahoney	ChiC	0	1	0
Murphy	Mil	0	1	0
Palm	NYG	0	1	0
Thorpe	Can	0	1	0
Woods	Col	0	1	0
Beckley	Day	0	2	0

FRANKFORD YELLOWJACKETS 14-1-2 Guy Chamberlin

Regulars

UseName	Pos.	Hgt.	Wgt.	Age	Int	Pts.
Rae Crowther	E	5'11"	175	23	1	
Guy Chamberlin	E	6'2"	190	32	4	6
Daddy Potts	T	6'1"	235	28		
Johnny Budd	T-G	5'11"	242	27		30
Bill Hoffman	G	5'10"	235	24		
Rudy Comstock	G	5'10"	210	25		
Max Reed	C	5'8"	185	24	2	6
Ben Jones	BB-FB	5'11"	206	26	2	54
Hust Stockton	TB-FB	5'11"	190	24	4	33
Hap Moran	WB-TB-BB	6'1"	190	25	2	15
Tex Hamer	FB-WB-TB	6'1"	190	24	7	12

Substitutes

UseName	Pos.	Hgt.	Wgt.	Age	Int	Pts.
Fred Graham (to PROV & ChiA)	E	6'	175	22		
Bill Springsteen	E-C	6'	200	25	2	
Joe Carpe	T-E-WB	6'	190	23		
Ed Weir	T	5'10"	192	23	1	5
Swede Youngstrom	G-T	6'1"	190	29	1	12
Red Mahan (to ChiA)	G	5'10"	212	24		
Two Bits Homan	BB	5'5"	144	24	2	18
Lou Smythe (to HAR & PROV)	TB	6'1"	205	27	1	
Doc Bruder	WB-TB-BB	5'11"	178	24	1	19
Ned Wilcox	WB-FB	5'11"	185	22	2	18
Bull Lowe (from BOS)	E	5'11"	180	31		
Wooky Roberts	BB	5'7"	160	28	1	6
Bob Books	TB-FB	5'11"	190	24		
Paul Hogan (from NYG)	WB-BB	5'8"	170	27		2
Leo Douglass (to, from BKN)	FB-WB	5'11"	190	25		

Scores of Each Game

Date	Pts.	Opponent	Pts.
Sep. 25	6	AKRON	6
Oct. 2	13	HARTFORD	0
Oct. 3	10	Hartford	0
Oct. 9	30	BUFFALO	0
Oct. 16	6	NEW YORK	0
Oct. 17	6	New York	0
Oct. 23	17	CANTON	0
Oct. 30	6	PROVIDENCE	7
Oct. 31	6	Providence	3
Nov. 6	33	CHIC. CARDS	7
Nov. 13	10	DULUTH	0
Nov. 20	35	DAYTON	0
Nov. 25	20	GREEN BAY	14
Nov. 27	7	DETROIT	6
Dec. 4	7	CHIC. BEARS	6
Dec. 11	24	PROVIDENCE	0
Dec. 18	0	POTTSVILLE	0

CHICAGO BEARS 12-1-3 George Halas

Regulars

UseName	Pos.	Hgt.	Wgt.	Age	Int	Pts.
George Halas	E	6'	182	31		
Duke Hanny	E-FB	6'	195	28	1	24
Ed Healey	T-E	6'1"	210	31		
Don Murry	T-E	6'2"	190	26		
Bill Buckler	G	6'	220	25		1
Jim McMillen	G	6'1"	215	23		
George Trafton	C	6'2"	235	29	3	
Milt Romney	QB-HB	5'8"	167	27	3	25
Paddy Driscoll	HB	5'8"	165	31	2	86
Bill Senn	HB-FB	6'	167	21		45
Oscar Knop	FB	6'	195	31	2	6

Substitutes

UseName	Pos.	Hgt.	Wgt.	Age	Int	Pts.
Cliff Lemon	E	5'10"	190	24		
Verne Mullen	E-HB	6'	185	26		6
Link Lyman	T	6'2"	225	27		
Buck Evans	T-G	5'11"	205	26		
Bill Fleckenstein	C-G-E	6'1"	200	22		
Johnny Bryan (from MIL)	HB-QB	5'8"	175	29		
Laurie Walquist	HB	5'8"	170	28	2	12
Dutch Sternaman	FB-HB-QB	5'8"	180	31		11

Scores of Each Game

Date	Pts.	Opponent	Pts.
Sep. 19	10	Milwaukee	7
Sep. 26	6	Green Bay	6
Oct. 3	10	Detroit	7
Oct. 10	7	NEW YORK	0
Oct. 17	16	CHIC. CARDS	0
Oct. 24	24	DULUTH	6
Oct. 31	17	AKRON	0
No.v 7	34	LOUISVILLE	0
Nov. 11	10	Chic. Cards	0
Nov. 14	10	MILWAUKEE	7
Nov. 21	19	GREEN BAY	13
Nov. 25	0	CHIC. CARDS	0
Nov. 28	35	CANTON	0
Dec. 4	6	Frankford	7
Dec. 12	9	POTTSVILLE	7
Dec. 19	3	GREEN BAY	3

POTTSVILLE MAROONS 10-2-2 Dick Rauch

Regulars

UseName	Pos.	Hgt.	Wgt.	Age	Int	Pts.
Charlie Berry	E	6'	185	23	1	18
George Kenneally	E	6'	180	24		
Frank Racis	T	6'	200	28		6
Russ Hathaway	T-G	5'11"	250	30		3
Jim Welsh	G-T	5'11"	260	24		30
Duke Osborn	G	5'10"	190	29	2	
Herb Stein	C	6'	185	28	3	
Jack Ernst	BB	5'11"	175	26	2	6
Jesse Brown	TB	5'10"	180	23	5	
Hoot Flanagan	WB	6'	170	25	1	
Barney Wentz	FB	5'11"	200	25	6	60

Substitutes

UseName	Pos.	Hgt.	Wgt.	Age	Int	Pts.
Aaron Oliker	E	5'11"	170	22		
Frank Bucher	E	5'11"	190	25		
Zeke Wissinger	T	6'	195	22		
Heinie Jawish	T-G	5'8"	210	26		
Frank Youngfleish	C	5'9"	190	30	3	
Bob Millman	WB-BB	5'11"	175	23		6
Tony Latone	TB-WB-FB	5'11"	190	29	5	24
Heinie Benkert	WB-TB	5'9"	170	25	1	
Fanny Neihaus	WB	6'	168	24		

Scores of Each Game

Date	Pts.	Opponent	Pts.
Oct. 3	3	COLUMBUS	0
Oct. 10	24	DAYTON	6
Oct. 16	21	Brooklyn	0
Oct. 17	14	BROOKLYN	0
Oct. 24	0	Providence	14
Oct. 31	14	BUFFALO	0
Nov. 7	34	AKRON	0
Nov. 11	10	LOS ANGELES	0
Nov. 14	13	DULUTH	0
Nov. 21	7	HAMMOND	0
Nov. 25	8	PRIVIDENCE	0
Nov. 28	0	Buffalo	0
Dec. 12	7	Chic. Bears	9
Dec. 18	0	Frankford	0

Frankford Yellowjackets. The Maroons entered December with a 10-1-1 record and a devastating ground attack. With virtually the same team as the year before, Pottsville combined its powerful grind-it-out attack with a staunch defense that would post 11 shutouts by season's end. The Yellowjackets, 12-1-1 at the end of November, had strengthened themselves over last season's squad, despite the defection of star tackle Bull Behman to the AFL. Coach Guy Chamberlin had convinced his former Canton teammates Rudy Comstock and Ben Jones to join the team. He also obtained guard Swede Youngstrom from Buffalo and added rookie help in tackle Johnny Budd and back Hap Moran. The Yellowjackets had a potent offense which featured the passing of Hust Stockman and the running of fullback Tex Hamer, both holdovers from last year. Hamer was a real ballhawk on defense, and his seven interceptions gave him 15 for the 1925-26 span.

The Yellowjackets hosted the unbeaten Bears on Saturday, December 4 at Shibe Park. The crowd of 10,000 paled in comparison with the 22,000 fans who saw the Philadelphia Quakers beat the New York Yankees in the same park the week before for the AFL title. Neither club could launch a sustained drive through three scoreless periods. With five minutes left in the game, however, Bill Senn broke away for a 62-yard run to put Chicago ahead 6-0; Chamberlin blocked Driscoll's extra point try, just as he had blocked a field goal attempt in the third quarter. Taking the ball after the kickoff on their own 25-yard line, the Yellowjackets pressed forward with a last-chance drive, relying on key pass completions by Stockton to Rae Crowther. With a minute and a half left, Stockton hit Two Bits Homan in the endzone with a 27-yard touchdown pass. Tex Hamer's extra point attempt gave Frankford a 7-6 victory and first place. When the Yellowjackets beat Providence and the Bears beat Pottsville the next weekend, Frankford had an NFL title to match the AFL title won by the Quakers.

Far from the pennant race was the team that would become an NFL legend, the Duluth Eskimos. Rookie fullback Ernie Nevers from Stanford was the centerpiece of the Eskimos and the league. A big, blonde, handsome fullback in the double-wing formation, Nevers could crash the line like a truck, pass accurately, was a top-notch field goal kicker, and played relentless defense at linebacker. To his fellow players, however, he was most outstanding for his all-consuming desire for victory — a passion which kept him in the lineup even when battered and hurt. He first achieved national fame in the 1925 Rose Bowl when he returned to Stanford's lineup after being laid up for most of the season with two broken ankles to put on a great one-man show against Notre Dame's Four Horsemen.

The NFL countered on Nevers' name to draw people as much as the AFL counted on Grange. Like Kansas City, Los Angeles and Louisville, the Duluth team was destined to play most of its games in larger cities away from home. The Eskimos hit the road on September 20 and did not return home until February 5, after playing 29 league and exhibition games in most of the NFL cities and on the West Coast.

Owner Ole Haugsrud agreed to pay Nevers $15,000 plus a percentage of the larger gates. Future Hall of Famers Walt Kiesling and Johnny Blood were on the team, but with the bad weather and some disappointing attendances, Haugsrud had little money to hire other top players. For most of the tour, the Eskimos carried no more than 15 players, making them truly "The Iron Men from the North," as columnist Grantland Rice dubbed them. Nevers played all but 29 minutes of the tour, and his play topped whatever Red Grange offered as a pro. He ranked second in the NFL in scoring and almost single-handedly led a very ordinary squad to a respectable 6-5-3 mark. He also spearheaded a defensive backfield that did not give up a passing touchdown all season.

In Milwaukee on October 31, doctors advised him to sit out the game when abdominal pains indicated a possible case of appendicitis. But, when the Eskimos fell behind 6-0, Nevers put himself into the lineup, threw a 40-yard touchdown pass and kicked the extra point for a 7-6 Duluth victory. It was no slight of the team's home city that the team was usually billed as the Nevers Eskimos. With Red Grange in a rival league and 39-year-old Jim Thorpe playing a sad, injury-spoiled campaign with the Canton Bulldogs, Nevers gave the NFL a needed heroic image and some gate pull in a season of rain and red ink.

The fourth annual *Green Bay Press Gazette* all-NFL poll, with selectors from 17 different NFL cities, gave Nevers 17 votes for the fullback position. Other first team selections were ends Brick Muller (playing his only NFL season), Los Angeles, and Charlie Berry, Pottsville; tackles Ed Healey, Bears, and Walt Ellis, Cardinals; guards Gus Sonnenberg, Detroit, and Johnny Budd, Frankford; center Clyde Smith, Kansas City; quarterback Tut Imlay, Los Angeles; and halfbacks scoring leader Paddy Driscoll, Bears, and Verne Lewellen, Green Bay, who topped off his fine all-around play with nine pass interceptions and a 40.6 punting average on 116 boots.

NAME	RUSHING									PASSING													
	Complete Games					Incom. Games				Complete Games								Incom. Games					
	G	Att.	Yds.	Avg.	TD	G	Att.	Yds.	TD	G	Com.	Att.	%	Yds.	Y/A	TD	Int	G	Com.	Att.	Yds.	TD	Int
FRANKFORD																							
Hamer	3	34	125	3.7	1	14	62	308	1	4	2	4	50	30	7.5			13	4	6	62		2
Stockton	3	23	79	3.4		14	41	267	2	4	14	33	42	245	7.4	2	3	13	22	46	574	3	11
Moran	3	27	58	2.1		10	27	206	4	3	2	4	50	27	6.8			10	1	1	18		
Bruder	2	10	42	42.0		11	28	209	2	3								10	1	2	25		
Wilcox	2	19	76	4.0		10	11	90	2	3								9	1	1	17		
Jones	3	12	34	2.8	1	11	26	99	6	3	5	9	56	80	8.0		1	11	0	1			1
Homan	3	8	16	2.0		4	4	17	1														
Smyth (1)						4	4	32										4	3	7	67		1
Douglass (2)						2	5	26															
Books						4	3	17										4	1	1	35		
Hoffman	3	2	3	1.5		13																	
Roberts						6	1	2										6	1	2	37		
Hogan (2)	1	1	0	0.0		2																	
Chamberlin																							
Crowther																							
Springsteen																							
Youngstrom																							
Team	3	136	433	3.2	2	14				4	23	50	46	392	7.6	2	4	13					
Opp.	3	106	213	2.0	1	14				4	16	59	27	293	5.0	1	10	13					
CHICAGO BEARS																							
Senn	3	14	5	0.4		12	23	422	7	4	0	1	0				1	11	1	1	14		
Driscoll	4	49	122	2.5	1	12	13	107	3	5	12	39	31	294	7.5	1	7	11	18	18	521	5	
Knop	4	37	85	2.3		9	3	14	1														
Romney	4	4	6	1.5		12	10	91	3														
Walquist	4	28	37	1.3		11	3	6	1	5	3	8	38	55	6.9	1		10	1	1	12	1	
Sternaman	3	6	8	1.3		11	6	13															
Bryan (2)	2	7	5	0.7		1	1	6		2	0	1	0					1					
Mullen	4	1	0	0.0		12																	
Hanny																							
Halas																							
Team	4	146	268	1.8	1	12				5	15	49	31	349	7.1	2	8	11					
Opp.	4	134	281	2.1	3	12				5	23	70	33	359	5.1		7	11					
POTTSVILLE																							
Wentz	14	220	727	3.3	10																		
Latone	12	144	578	4.0	4					12	2	3	67	28	9.3								
Brown	14	119	298	2.5						14	15	37	41	251	6.8	3	4						
Benkert	8	64	243	3.8																			
Millman	7	79	205	2.6																			
Flanagan	8	41	104	2.5																			
Neihaus	4	25	83	3.3																			
Ernst	14	30	61	2.0						14	65	163	40	729	4.5	1	21						
Berry																							
Kenneally																							
Bucher																							
Stein																							
Team	14	722	2299	3.2	14					14	82	203	40	1008	5.0	4	25						
Opp.	14	374	842	2.3	2					14	36	144	25	481	3.3	1	29						

NAME	RECEIVING									PUNTING						PUNT RETURNS								
	Complete Games					Incom. Games				Comp. Games			Incom. Games			Complete Games					Incom. Games			
	G	Rec.	Yds.	Avg.	TD	G	Rec.	Yds.	TD	G	No.	Avg.	G	No.	Avg.	G	Rec.	Yds.	Avg.	TD	G	Rec.	Yds.	TD
FRANKFORD																								
Hamer	4	3	55	18.3		13	4	119		3	21	31.6	14	46	36.3	3					14	6	34	
Stockton	4	1	2	2.0		13	1	18		3	4	20.8	14	1	35.0	3	1	15	15.0		14			
Moran	3	8	111	13.9		10	5	144	1	3	1	34.0	10	2	37.5	3	4	29	7.3		10			
Bruder	3	1	6	6.0		10	4	104		2	1	31.0	11	1	0.0	2					11	2	40	1
Wilcox	3	1	15	15.0		9				2	6	34.3	10	5	34.2									
Jones	3					11	4	87	1															
Homan	4	3	70	23.3	2	3				3	1	40.0	4			3	4	35	8.8		4	6	91	
Smyth (1)																					4	1	33	
Douglass (2)																								
Books																								
Hoffman																								
Roberts						6	2	79	1												6	5	26	
Hogan (2)																								
Chamberlin	4	2	50	25.0		13	6	141																
Crowther	3	4	73	18.3		11	2	30																
Springsteen	4					13	3	53																
Youngstrom	4					12	1	30																
Team										3	34	31.1	14			3	9	79	8.8		14			
Opp.										3	35	38.6	14			3	7	58	8.3		14			
CHICAGO BEARS																								
Senn	4	4	97	24.3		11	2	50								3	4	37	9.3		12	1	10	
Driscoll	5	3	55	18.3	1	11				4	60	37.2	12	8	52.5	4	9	108	12.0		12	4	80	
Knop	5					8	2	31																
Romney	5					11	7	189	1															
Walquist	5	1	30	30.0		10	1	16	1															
Sternaman																								
Bryan (2)	2	1	25	25.0		1																		
Mullen	5					11	2	70	1															
Hanny	5	4	113	28.3	1	11	3	127	3	4			12	1	34.0									
Halas	5	2	29	14.5		10	1	36																
Team										4	60	37.2	12			4	13	145	11.2		12			
Opp.										4	54	40.8	12			4	14	200	14.3		12			
POTTSVILLE																								
Wentz	14	1	14	14.0																				
Latone	12	4	49	12.3																				
Brown	14	9	126	14.0						14	94	37.7				14	2	25	12.5					
Benkert	8	1	6	6.0																				
Millman	7	7	97	13.9	1											7	1	10	10.0					
Flanagan	8	6	76	12.7												8	1	10	10.0					
Neihaus	4	3	27	9.0																				
Ernst	14	4	62	15.5	1					14	13	28.1				14	41	453	11.0					
Berry	10	29	330	11.4	2																			
Kenneally	11	11	146	13.3																				
Bucher	13	7	75	10.7																				
Stein																10	1	5	5.0					
Team										14	107	36.6				14	46	503	10.9					
Opp.										14	147	32.6				14	31	352	11.4	1				

KANSAS CITY COWBOYS 8-3-0 Roy Andrews

Regulars Use Name	Pos.	Hgt.	Wgt.	Age	Int.	Pts.
Lyle Munn	E	6'	185	24	2	6
Proc Randels	E	6'	180	26		
Bill Owen	T	6'	200	22		
Tom Cobb	T	5'11	250	22		
Milt Rehnquist	G-T	6'	225	29		
Jay Berquist	G	6'3	235	24		
Clyde Smith	C	5'11	180	22		
Obie Bristow	BB-FB-TB	6'2	210	24	3	
Al Bloodgood	TB	5'8	155	24		47
Charlie Hill	WB-BB-TB-FB	6'	190	25		6
Glen Spears	FB-WB-E	5'10	185	26	1	6

Substitutes Use Name	Pos.	Hgt.	Wgt.	Age	Int.	Pts.
Dutch Webber (from HAR & NYG)	E	6'2	190	24		
Alvie Thompson	T-G	6'3	210	25		
Dosey Howard	G	6'	225	25		
Jim Palermo	G	5'9	180	24		
Joe Westoupal	C	6'3	200	23		
Roy Andrews	BB-G-T-E	6'	230	29		1
Chuck Corgan (from HAR)	BB-WB	6'	185	23		
Rufe DeWitz	WB-BB	5'9	175	26		6
Swede Hummel (to PROV)	FB-WB		195	24		

Substitutes Use Name	Pos.	Hgt.	Wgt.	Age	Int.	Pts.
Jim Jacquith	BB	5'9	175	27		
Tommy Murphy (from COL)	BB	5'10	187	26		

Date	Pts.	Opponent	Pts.
Sep. 19	0	Duluth	7
Oct. 10	0	Detroit	10
Oct. 16	9	Columbus	0
Oct. 24	0	New York	13
Oct. 31	7	Hartford	2
Nov. 7	10	Brooklyn	9
Nov. 14	22	Providence	0
Nov. 21	2	Buffalo	0
Nov. 28	7	Chic. Cards	2
Dec. 5	7	LOS ANGELES	3
Dec. 12	12	DULUTH	7

GREEN BAY PACKERS 7-3-3 Curly Lambeau

Regulars Use Name	Pos.	Hgt.	Wgt.	Age	Int.	Pts.
Dick Flaherty	E	5'10	200	26		12
Dick O'Donnell	E	6'	190	26		12
Rosey Rosatti	T	6'	215	30		
Tiny Cahoon	T	6'2	234	26		
Whitey Woodin	G	5'10	208	31	1	1
Moose Gardner	G	6'1	224	32		
Jug Earp	C	6'	240	29	3	
Pid Purdy	BB	5'6	145	22	3	20
Curly Lambeau	TB-BB-E	5'10	185	28	3	4
Verne Lewellen	HB-TB	6'1	180	24	9	42
Cully Lidberg	FB	5'9	195	26	3	24

Substitutes Use Name	Pos.	Hgt.	Wgt.	Age	Int.	Pts.
Jack Harris	E-HB	5'11	190	24	2	12
Myrt Basing	E-HB-FB	5'9	192	25	1	6
Hec Cyre	T-G-E	6'2	215	24		
Wes Carlson	G-T	6'1	210	25		
Walt McGaw	G		195	26		
Adolph Bieberstein (from RAC)	G	5'10	205	23		
Walt LeJeune	C-G-T	6'	242	26		
Charlie Mathys	BB	5'7	165	29		6
Eddie Kotal	TB-HB	5'8	165	24	2	12
Jack McAuliffe	HB-TB	5'7	155	25		
Rex Enright	FB	5'10	200	25	2	6

Date	Pts.	Opponent	Pts.
Sep. 19	21	DETROIT	0
Sep. 26	6	CHIC. BEARS	6
Oct. 3	0	DULUTH	0
Oct. 10	7	CHIC. CARDS	13
Oct. 17	7	MILWAUKEE	0
Oct. 24	35	RACINE	0
Oct. 31	3	Chic. Cards	0
Nov. 7	21	Milwaukee	0
Nov. 14	14	LOUISVILLE	0
Nov. 21	13	Chic. Bears	19
Nov. 25	14	Frankford	20
Nov. 28	7	Detroit	0
Dec. 19	3	Chic. Bears	3

LOS ANGELES BUCCANEERS 6-3-1 Tut Imlay and Brick Muller

Regulars Use Name	Pos.	Hgt.	Wgt.	Age	Int.	Pts.
Guy Hufford	E	5'11	185	25		
Brick Muller	E	6'2	195	25		6
John Thurman	T	6'1	225	26	1	
Don Newmeyer	T	6'2	205	24		2
Jack Nolan	G	5'10	185	26		
Don Thompson	G	6'2	205	22	1	12
Jack McArthur	C	5'11	200	22	1	
Bull Finch	BB-FB	5'8	180	33	1	
Tut Imlay	TB	5'8	165	24		24
Ellery White	WB-FB		175			
Tuffy Maul	FB	5'11	200	24	1	21

Substitutes Use Name	Pos.	Hgt.	Wgt.	Age	Int.	Pts.
Pete Schaffnit	E-BB-WB-FB	5'11	180	24	1	
Fred Beach	G		180	29		
Juddy Ash	G	6'2	205	26		
Artie Sandberg	BB-WB		190	26		
Al Young	WB-FB-TB-BB-E	5'10	180	24		
Ben Bangs	WB	5'10	180	32		
Bill Gutteron	BB	5'5	155	26		

Date	Pts.	Opponent	Pts.
Sep. 26	0	Chic. Cards	15
Oct. 3	6	Milwaukee	0
Oct. 17	16	Canton	13
Oct. 24	0	Buffalo	0
Nov. 7	7	Providence	6
Nov. 11	0	Pottsville	10
Nov. 14	6	New York	0
Nov. 21	20	Brooklyn	0
Nov. 25	9	Detroit	6
Dec. 5	3	Kansas City	7

NEW YORK GIANTS 8-4-1 Doc Alexander

Regulars Use Name	Pos.	Hgt.	Wgt.	Age	Int.	Pts.
Tillie Voss	E	6'3	205	29		
Lynn Bomar	E	6'1	200	25		12
John Alexander	T-E	6'4	248	29		6
Steve Owen	T	5'10	225	28		
Joe Williams	G	6'	245	28	1	
Doc Alexander	G-C-T-E	5'11	220	28	1	12
Mickey Murtagh	C-E-G	6'1	190	22		
Tex Grigg	BB-TB	5'11	195	35		
Jack McBride	TB	5'11	185	24	2	48
Walt Koppisch	WB-FB	5'10	180	24		
Hinkey Haines	FB	5'10	170	27	4	36

Substitutes Use Name	Pos.	Hgt.	Wgt.	Age	Int.	Pts.
Dutch Webber (from HAR, to KC)	E	6'2	190	24		
Art Carney	E-G	6'1	200	22	1	
Babe Parnell	T	6'3	205	24		
Art Harms	T	6'1	200	24		
Al Nesser (from AKR & CLE)	G	6'	195	33		
Tommy Tomlin	G	5'10	198	32		
Riley Biggs (from RI)	C	6'2	230	26		
Mike Palm	BB	5'10	170	26		
Cowboy Hill	TB-WB-BB	5'8	175	27	1	12
Paul Hogan (to FRA)	WB-FB-BB	5'8	170	27	1	3
Jack Hagerty	FB-WB-BB	5'9	165	23		12

Substitutes Use Name	Pos.	Hgt.	Wgt.	Age	Int.	Pts.
Earl Potteiger	E-BB	5'7	170	35		
Al Bedner	G	5'10	195	28		
Art Stevenson (to BKN)	C	6'	190	28		
Glenn Killinger (to PHI)	TB	5'9	164	27		
Kid Hill	FB	5'11	185	22		

Date	Pts.	Opponent	Pts.
Sep. 26	21	Hartford	0
Oct. 3	7	Providence	6
Oct. 10	0	Chic. Bears	7
Oct. 16	0	Frankford	6
Oct. 17	0	FRANKFORD	6
Oct. 24	13	KANSAS CITY	0
Nov. 2	7	CANTON	7
Nov. 7	20	CHIC. CARDS	0
Nov. 11	14	DULUTH	13
Nov. 14	0	LOS ANGELES	6
Nov. 21	21	PROVIDENCE	0
Nov. 25	17	Brooklyn	0
Nov. 28	27	BROOKLYN	0

DULUTH ESKIMOS 6-5-3 Dewey Scanlon

Regulars Use Name	Pos.	Hgt.	Wgt.	Age	Int.	Pts.
Jack Underwood	E	6'	200	28		6
Joe Rooney	E-T	6'	180	29	3	6
Art Johnson	T	5'11	190	30		
Walt Kiesling	T-G	6'2	243	23		
Doc Williams	G	6'7	222	28	1	
Jimmy Manion	G-C	5'9	180	21		
Bill Stein	C-G	6'	190	26		
Cobb Rooney	BB-WB	6'	185	26	3	6
Paul Fitzgibbon	WB-BB	5'8	175	23	2	6
Johnny Blood	WB-FB	6'1	185	22	2	12
Ernie Nevers	FB	6'	205	23	7	71

Substitutes Use Name	Pos.	Hgt.	Wgt.	Age	Int.	Pts.
Fritz Heinisch (from RAC)	E	5'10	176	26		
Jock Murray	E-G	6'1	210	22		
Ray Suess	T-E		204	23		
Chuck Gayer	T	5'11	205	25		
Oke Carlson	G-C	6'	203	28		
Porky Rundquist	G-C	5'10	220	32		
Jim Murphy (from RAC)	C-WB	6'	187	21		
Louie Larson	BB-E-WB-FB		168	28		
Doc Kelley	WB	5'10	170	24		
Russ Method	WB-BB-E	5'10	195	29	2	6

Substitutes Use Name	Pos.	Hgt.	Wgt.	Age	Int.	Pts.
Walt Buland	T	6'1	225	34		
Hew Sullivan	G		195	28		
Red Quam	BB		165	30		
Dewey Scanlon	WB	5'9	192	27		
Wally Gilbert	WB	6'1	180	25		

Date	Pts.	Opponent	Pts.
Sep. 19	7	KANSAS CITY	0
Oct. 3	0	Green Bay	0
Oct. 10	26	Hammond	0
Oct. 17	21	Racine	0
Oct. 24	6	Chic. Bears	24
Oct. 31	7	Milwaukee	6
Nov. 7	0	Detroit	0
Nov. 11	13	New York	14
Nov. 13	0	Frankford	10
Nov. 14	0	Pottsville	13
Nov. 21	10	Canton	2
Nov. 27	16	Hartford	0
Nov. 28	0	Providence	0
Dec. 12	7	Kansas City	12

BUFFALO RANGERS 4-4-2 Jim Kendrick

Regulars Use Name	Pos.	Hgt.	Wgt.	Age	Int.	Pts.
Neely Allison	E	6'	190	24	2	6
Roy Guffey	E-T	6'	194	24		6
Firpo Wilcox	T	6'	220	23	1	
Les Caywood	T	6'	230	21		
Joe Wilson	G	5'11	185	24		
Barlow Irvin	G	5'10	225	22		
George Kirk	C	6'	205	27		
Elmeer Slough	BB-WB	5'8	160	23	3	12
Jim Kendrick	TB	6'	200	33	2	16
Mule Wilson	WB-TB	5'11	185	24	1	
Ben Hobson	FB	5'10	190	24	2	6

Substitutes Use Name	Pos.	Hgt.	Wgt.	Age	Int.	Pts.
Al Swain	E	6'1	190	26		6
Lou Feist	E-FB	6'1	200	23		
died Nov. 12, 1926 - meningitis						
Firpo McGilbra	T-G	6'1	210	20		
Cop Weathers	G	5'9	230	28		
Ted Schwarzer	G-C	5'11	190	24		
Van Edmondson	C	5'10	210	27		
Ralph Pittman	BB-WB	5'10	200	26		
Dom Dimmick	WB	5'8	160	23		
Bill Vaughn	FB-WB-BB	5'10	192	24	1	

Substitutes Use Name	Pos.	Hgt.	Wgt.	Age	Int.	Pts.
Roger Nairan	E-WB	5'11	185	24		
George Nix	G	5'11	195	31		
Tex Kelly	G	6'3	220	27		
Wes Bradshaw (from RI)	BB	5'8	175	27		
Roger Powell	WB		180	32		

Date	Pts.	Opponent	Pts.
Sep. 26	7	AKRON	0
Oct. 3	0	DAYTON	3
Oct. 9	0	Frankford	30
Oct. 17	7	Dayton	6
Oct. 24	0	LOS ANGELES	0
Oct. 31	0	Pottsville	14
Nov. 7	26	COLUMBUS	0
Nov. 14	13	Hartford	7
Nov. 21	0	KANSAS CITY	2
Nov. 28	0	POTTSVILLE	0

CHICAGO CARDINALS 5-6-1 Norm Barry

Regulars Use Name	Pos.	Hgt.	Wgt.	Age	Int.	Pts.
Herb Blumer	E	6'1	190	26		
Nick McInerney	E-C-WB-FB	6'2	205	30		
Bub Weller	T-E	6'4	222	24		
Walt Ellis	T	5'11	225	27		
Willie Brennan	G-T	6'	220	32		
Jerry Lunz	G	6'3	210	23		6
Ralph Claypool	C	5'11	190	27	1	
Red Dunn	BB-TB	5'11	170	24	1	15
Roddy Lamb	TB-WB	5'6	160	27	2	7
Hal Erickson	WB	5'9	190	27		6
Bob Koehler	FB	5'11	185	32		

Substitutes Use Name	Pos.	Hgt.	Wgt.	Age	Int.	Pts.
Jim Woodruff	E	6'3	210	23		
Evar Swanson	E-WB-BB	5'9	170	23		1
Duke Slater (from RI)	T	6'1	215	27		
Fred Gillies	T	6'3	215	30		
Ed Greene	G-E	5'11	185	25		
Howard Kieley	G	5'8	210	33		
Ike Mahoney	BB-E	6'	165	24	1	12
Mickey McDonnell	TB-WB-BB	5'8	155	22		12
Bill McElwain	WB-TB-BB	5'10	170	23	2	6
Gene Francis	FB	5'10	190	23	1	6

Substitutes Use Name	Pos.	Hgt.	Wgt.	Age	Int.	Pts.
Mel Stuessy	T	5'9	180	25		
Chet Widerquist (from RI)	G	6'1	220	30		
Tom Hogan	G	6'2	200	28		
Ward Connell (to ChiA)	FB-TB	5'10	173	27		

Date	Pts.	Opponent	Pts.
Sep. 19	14	COLUMBUS	0
Sep. 26	15	LOS ANGELES	0
Oct. 3	20	RACINE	0
Oct. 10	13	Green Bay	7
Oct. 17	0	Chic. Bears	16
Oct. 24	3	Milwaukee	2
Oct. 31	0	GREEN BAY	3
Nov. 6	7	Frankford	33
Nov. 7	0	New York	20
Nov. 11	0	CHIC. BEARS	10
Nov. 25	0	Chic. Bears	0
Nov. 28	2	KANSAS CITY	7

NAME	RUSHING									PASSING													
	Complete Games					Incom. Games				Complete Games								Incom. Games					
	G	Att.	Yds.	Avg.	TD	G	Att.	Yds.	TD	G	Com.	Att.	%	Yds.	Y/A	TD	Int.	G	Com.	Att.	Yds.	TD	Int.
KANSAS CITY																							
Bloodgood	1	17	72	4.2		10	11	128	2	1	2	8	25	43	5.4		2	10	2	2	34		
DeWitz						8	2	78	1														
Spears	1	6	10	1.7		9	5	35															
Hill	1	1	2	2.0		9	3	19	1	1								9	1	1	2	1	
Bristow						8	3	21										8	2	5	17		
Corgan (2)						1	1	16															
Hummel (1)	1	4	5	1.3		4																	
Andrews	1	1	4	4.0		7				1	0	5	0					7					
Team	1	29	93	3.2		10				3	8	37	22	96	2.6		5	8					
Opp.	1	39	143	3.7		10				4	15	56	27	140	2.5		11	7					
GREEN BAY																							
Lewellen	13	83	275	3.3	3					13	11	27	41	156	5.8		5						
Enright	10	84	259	3.1	1					10	0	2	0										
Lidberg	11	104	235	2.3	4					11	2	3	67	18	6.0								
Kotal	10	65	196	3.0	1					10	6	16	38	93	5.8	1							
Lambeau	12	44	112	2.5						12	30	80	38	504	6.3	3	5						
McAuliffe	8	42	66	1.6						8	5	10	50	72	7.2	1	1						
Harris	10	40	66	1.7	2																		
Purdy	11	27	64	2.4						11	21	67	31	383	5.7	1	12						
Basing	5	10	27	2.7	1					5	0	1	0					1					
Mathys	4	6	14	2.3						4	4	9	44	67	7.4	2	2						
Flaherty	12	1	3	3.0																			
Woodin	13	1	0	0.0																			
O'Donnell																							
Cahoon																							
Team	13	507	1317	2.6	12					13	79	215	37	1293	6.0	8	26						
Opp.	13	472	863	1.8	2					13	69	198	35	1056	5.3	4	29						
LOS ANGELES																							
Imlay	1	15	72	4.8		9	14	153	3	4	5	10	50	34	3.4		1	6	3	3	97	1	
Maul	1	11	29	2.6		9	23	75	2	4	8	14	57	134	9.6	1	1	6	0	2			1
White	1	14	39	2.8		7	6	39		4	1	1	100	21	21.0								
Muller	1					9	8	64		6	4	12	33	95	7.9		1	4	0	2			2
Sanberg						5	7	24															
Young						7	5	14															
Schaffnit										3	0	1	0					6					
Gutterson																		2	0	1			
Hufford																							
Team	1	40	140	3.5		9				5	20	46	43	321	7.0	1	5	5					
Opp.	1	47	133	2.8		9				5	23	45	51	357	7.9	1	7	5					
NEW YORK																							
Haines	1	14	75	5.4		11	43	458	5	1	0	1	0				1	11	2	3	20		1
McBride	1	14	50	3.6		12	49	325	5	1	1	5	20	22	4.4		3	12	17	29	273	3	7
Hagerty	1	6	32	5.3		9	19	182	1	1								9	1	2	7		1
Koppisch	1	2	1	0.5		8	15	159		1								8	2	2	53	1	
Hill	1					9	10	57	2														
Hogan (1)	1					9	6	26															
Palm						1	2	9	1														
Grigg	1					11	1	9		1	0	1	0				1	11	3	4	46		1
Parnell										1	1	2	50	39	19.5			3					
Killinger																		1	1	1	10		
Bornar																							
Voss																							
Murtagh																							
Carney																							
Team						13				1	2	9	22	61	6.8		5	12					
Opp.						13				1	3	6	50	47	7.8			12					
DULUTH																							
Nevers	5	77	245	3.2	1	9	45	261	7	10	55	145	38	725	5.0	1	19	4	12	14	188	2	1
Blood	5	32	55	1.7		8	6	45	1	9	0	7	0				2	4					
Fitzgibbon	5	31	72	2.3	1	9	3	27															
C. Rooney	5	14	51	3.6		9	4	18		10								4	0	1			1
Method	5	18	31	1.7		7	1	3															
Kelley	3	6	12	2.0		2																	
Larson	2	3	1	0.3		5	1	0		5	0	1	0					2					
Gilbert																							
J. Rooney																							
Underwood																							
Murray																							
Team	5	181	467	2.6	2	9				10	55	153	36	725	4.7	1	21	4					
Opp.	5	211	585	2.8	1	9				7	30	109	28	346	3.2		20	7					
BUFFALO																							
Hobson	2	18	42	2.3		7	12	54	1														
Wilson	2	11	23	2.1		7	10	72		3								6	0	3			1
Kendrick	2	9	12	1.3		8	14	48	2	3	22	55	40	365	6.6	3	4	7	16	24	330	2	5
Vaughn	2	1	1	1.0		8	3	44															
Pittman	1					4	1	20															
Slough	2	8	5	0.6		6	1	4															
Guffey																							
Allison																							
Dimmick																							
Swain																							
Feist																							
Team	2	47	83	1.8		8				3	27	64	42	424	6.6	3	4	7					
Opp.	2	109	358	3.3	2	8				2	6	22	27	54	2.5		3	8					
CHICAGO CARDINALS																							
Lamb	3	44	157	3.6	1	7	6	91		3	3	4	75	51	12.8			7					
McDonnell	3	18	76	4.2	1	8	1	4															
Erickson	2	18	67	3.7		9	2	10															
Dunn	2	17	50	2.9		9	2	18		2	10	25	40	137	5.5	1	2	9	12	21	209	1	6
Mahoney	3	9	42	4.7		8	3	25	1	3	2	3	67	19	6.3		1	8	1	1	2		
Koehler	3	27	38	1.4		7	5	26															
Francis	3	10	29	2.9		8																	
McInerney	3	3	11	3.7		8				3	1	1	100	20	20.0			8					
McElwain	3	3	9	3.0	1	5				3	0	2	0				1	5	1	1	35		
Connell	1	1	7	7.0		1	1	0															
Weller	3	1	0	0.0		9				3	1	1	100	18	18.0			9					
Swanson																							
Team	3	151	486	3.2	3	9				3	17	36	47	245	6.8	1	4	9					
Opp.	3	97	218	2.2	1	9				3	11	37	30	166	4.5		3	9					

NAME	RECEIVING									PUNTING						PUNT RETURNS								
	Complete Games					Incom. Games				Comp. Games			Incom. Games			Complete Games					Incom. Games			
	G	Rec.	Yds	Avg.	TD	G	Rec.	Yds.	TD	G	No.	Avg.	G	No.	Avg.	G	No.	Yds.	Avg.	TD	G	No.	Yds.	TD
KANSAS CITY																								
Bloodgood	1					10	2	17	1	3	27	32.6	8	2	11.5	1	4	91	22.8		10			
DeWitz																								
Spears	1	1	35	35.0		9	1	20																
Hill	1	1	8	8.0		9																		
Bristow										2			6	2	45.0									
Corgan (2)																								
Hummel (1)	1					4	1	14																
Andrews	1					7	1	2																
Team										3	27	32.6	8			1	4	91	22.8		10			
Opp.										3	26	33.1	8			1	2	43	21.5		10			
GREEN BAY																								
Lewellen	13	21	299	14.2	3					13	116	40.6												
Enright																								
Lidberg	11	5	66	13.2																				
Kotal	10	6	72	12.0	1											10	4	42	10.5					
Lambeau	12	5	86	17.2						12	2	32.5												
McAuliffe	8	6	96	16.0						8	12	35.5				8	2	12	6.0					
Harris	10	9	168	18.7																				
Purdy	11	5	61	12.2						11	11	36.3				11	29	323	11.1					
Basing	4	2	17	8.5																				
Mathys																4	6	55	9.2					
Flaherty	12	11	270	24.5	2																			
Woodin																								
O'Donnell	11	8	150	18.8	2																			
Cahoon	11	1	8	8.0																				
Team										13	141	39.7				13	41	432	10.5					
Opp.										13	165	35.1				13	39	384	9.8					
LOS ANGELES																								
Imlay	4	8	175	21.9	1	6										2	13	152	11.7		8	3	82	
Maul										1			9	1	35.0									
White																								
Muller	4	5	72	14.4		6	3	97																
Sanberg																								
Young																								
Schaffnit	3	3	13	4.3		6				1	5	29.2	8	2	30.5									
Gutterson																								
Hufford	4	2	24	12.0		6																		
Team										2	17	30.8	8			2	13	152	11.7		8			
Opp.										2	25	30.9	8			1	1	2	2.0		9			
NEW YORK																								
Haines	1	1	39	39.0		11	5	108	1												12	4	50	
McBride													13	3	29.0									
Hagerty						10	3	52	1				10	2	43.5						10	1	2	
Koppisch													9	2	42.5									
Hill																								
Hogan (1)													10	9	46.3									
Palm						1	1	17																
Grigg	1	1	22	22.0		11	1	7													12	1	5	
Parnell																								
Killinger																								
Bornar						8	8	101	2															
Voss	1					11	6	100																
Murtagh	1					10	1	16																
Carney	1					7	1	8																
Team													13								13			
Opp.													13								13			
DULUTH																								
Nevers										6	40	35.9	8	8	26.9									
Blood	5	6	98	16.3	1	8	3	50		6	1	14.0	7			5	1	12	12.0		8			
Fitzgibbon	5	1	5	5.0		9	1	23								5	6	71	11.8		9			
C. Rooney	5	1	5	5.0		9	5	138	1							5	4	77	19.3		9	1	13	
Method	5	5	79	15.8		7	1	21								5	1	8	8.0		7			
Kelley	3	1	5	5.0		2	1	15																
Larson	2	1	5	5.0		5				3	3	31.0	4											
Gilbert						3	6	86		1	9	30.9	2											
J. Rooney	4	2	28	14.0		9	2	37	1															
Underwood	3	2	1	0.5		9	2	36																
Murray	4	3	6	2.0		3																		
Team										6	53	34.3	8			5	12	168	14.0		9			
Opp.										6	50	32.6	8			5	20	256	12.8		9			
BUFFALO																								
Hobson	2					7	2	55																
Wilson	2					7	3	76		2			7	2	38.0									
Kendrick										2	20	35.3	8	11	39.5									
Vaughn	2	1	4	4.0		8	2	43		2			8	1	42.0									
Pittman										1			4	1	31.0									
Slough	2	1	7	7.0		6	3	100	2							2	2	35	17.5		6	1	20	
Guffey	2	3	44	14.7		7	5	90	1															
Allison	2	1	15	15.0		7	5	70	1															
Dimmick						1	2	18																
Swain						2	1	38	1															
Feist						5	1	12																
Team										2	20	35.3	8			2	2	35	17.5		8			
Opp.										2	19	35.8	8			2	6	35	5.8		8			
CHICAGO CARDINALS																								
Lamb	3	3	60	20.0		7	1	5								3	1	15	15.0		7			
McDonnell	3	4	100	25.0	1	8																		
Erickson	2	3	26	8.7		9	5	97	1															
Dunn	2	2	15	7.5		9	2	37		2	23	33.6	9	9	28.2	2	7	74	10.6		9	1	45	
Mahoney	3	1	4	4.0		8	3	62		3	1	13.0	8	1	0.0	3	2	41	20.5		8			
Koehler																								
Francis																								
McInerney										3	1	48.0	8											
McElwain	3	1	5	3.0		5				3	1	37.0	5											
Connell	1	1	18	18.0		1																		
Weller										3	4	36.3	9											
Swanson	1	2	19	9.5		6	3	45		1			6	1	40.0									
Team										3	30	33.8	9			3	10	130	13.0		9			
Opp.										3	36	39.3	9			3	3	28	9.3					

PROVIDENCE STEAM ROLLER 5-7-1 Jim Laird

Regulars

Use Name	Pos.	Hgt.	Wgt.	Age	Int.	Pts.
Franny Garvey	E	6'1	175	26		1
Archie Golembeski	E	5'10	185	26		7
Joe Kozlowsky	T-E	5'10	190	25	1	
Mike Gulian	T	6'	205	26		
Jack Donahue	G-T	6'2	230	21		
Sam Young	G-E	6'2	190	23		
Dolph Eckstein	C	5'10	180	24	1	
Curly Oden	BB	5'6	160	27	1	60
Jack Keefer	TB	5'9	165	26	3	15
Waddy MacPhee	WB-TB	5'8	160	26		
Jim Laird	FB	6'	195	28	1	

Substitutes

Use Name	Pos.	Hgt.	Wgt.	Age	Int.	Pts.
Pinky Lester	E	5'6	160	26	1	
Jim Stifler	E-WB	5'10	175	25		
John Spellman	T-WB-FB	5'10	195	27		
Joe Koplow	T	6'3	235	25		
Speed Braney	G-T	6'	188	34		
Bull Wesley	G-FB	6'1	190	24		
Bob Scott	C-G-T		195	31		
Joe McGlone (to BOS)	BB	5'7	150	31		
Lou Smyth (from FRA and HAR)	TB-FB-WB	6'1	205	27	4	
Cy Wentworth	WB-TB-FB	5'8	155	22		6
Fred Sweet	WB-FB-TB-BB	5'10	165	25		
Johnny Talbot	E	6'2	182	25		
Vern Hagenbuckle (from BOS)	E	5'8	185	25		
Fred Graham (from FRA, to ChiA)	E	6'	175	22		
Ed McCrillis	G	6'	205	23		
Seneca Samson	BB	5'8	160	27		
Jim Manning (to HAR)	TB	5'11	195	25		
Swede Hummel (from KC)	WB		195	24	3	
Dutch Forst	FB	5'8	195	35		
Jack Triggs	FB	6'	200	23		
Al McIntosh	WB	5'9	180	23		
Carl Etelman (from BOS)	WB	5'8	160	26		
Frank Seyboth	WB			22		

Scores of each game

Date	Pts.	Opponent	Pts.
Sep. 26	13	BROOKLYN	0
Oct. 3	6	NEW YORK	7
Oct. 10	19	COLUMBUS	0
Oct. 24	14	POTTSVILLE	0
Oct. 30	7	Frankford	6
Oct. 31	3	FRANKFORD	6
Nov. 7	6	LOS ANGELES	7
Nov. 11	21	CANTON	2
Nov. 14	0	KANSAS CITY	22
Nov. 21	0	New York	21
Nov. 25	0	Pottsville	8
Nov. 28	0	DULUTH	0
Dec. 11	0	Frankford	24

DETROIT PANTHERS 4-6-2 Jimmy Conzelman

Regulars

Use Name	Pos.	Hgt.	Wgt.	Age	Int.	Pts.
Ed Lynch (to & from HAR)	E	5'11	190	29		
Dutch Lauer	E-WB	5'10	185	30		6
Tom Edwards	T	5'11	185	26		
Gus Sonnenberg	T	5'6	194	28	1	34
Jack Fleischman	G	5'6	180	25		
Tom McNamara	G	5'10	210	29		
John Barrett	C	5'6	170	27		6
Jimmy Conzelman	BB-TB-WB	6'	180	28	2	13
Eddie Scharer	TB-BB	5'6	165	24	1	6
Bruce Gregory	WB	5'10	170	23	7	12
Dinger Doane	FB-E	5'10	190	31		18

Substitutes

Use Name	Pos.	Hgt.	Wgt.	Age	Int.	Pts.
Charlie Grube	E	5'10	175	22		
Vivian Hultman	E-G	5'8	180	23		6
Norm Harvey	T-E	6'	190	29		
John Cameron	G-T		175	24		
Al Crook	C	5'10	190	28	1	
Dick Vick (to CAN)	BB	5'9	170	24		
Al Hadden	TB-WB	5'9	185	26	1	6
McDonald	WB					
Dutch Marion	FB	5'9	180	24		

Scores of each game

Date	Pts.	Opponent	Pts.
Sep. 19	0	Green Bay	21
Sep. 26	0	Milwaukee	6
Oct. 3	7	CHIC. BEARS	10
Oct. 10	10	KANSAS CITY	0
Oct. 17	47	LOUISVILLE	0
Oct. 24	25	AKRON	0
Oct. 31	6	CANTON	0
Nov. 7	0	DULUTH	0
Nov. 14	0	DAYTON	0
Nov. 25	6	LOS ANGELES	9
Nov. 27	6	Frankford	7
Nov. 28	0	GREEN BAY	7

HARTFORD BLUES 3-7-0 Jack Keogh

Regulars

Use Name	Pos.	Hgt.	Wgt.	Age	Int.	Pts.
Grattan O'Connell	E	5'11	185	24	1	6
Dutch Webber (to NYG & KC)	E-TB	6'2	190	24		
Mule Werwaiss	T-G		235	22		
Ralph Nichols	T-G	6'	210	27		
Furlong Flynn	G-T	6'	210	24		
Ed Keenan	G	6'4	320	31		
Red O'Neill	C	5'10	190	24	1	6
Chuck Corgan (to KC)	BB-WB	6'	185	23		
Jim Manning (from PROV)	TB-FB	5'11	195	25		18
Ed McEvoy	WB	5'11	190	22	1	
Lou Smyth (from FRA, to PROV)	FB	6'1	205	27	1	6

Substitutes

Use Name	Pos.	Hgt.	Wgt.	Age	Int.	Pts.
Lefty Jamerson	E	6'1	195	26		
Jake Friedman	E			30		
Ernie McCann	T-E-G	5'11	188	24		
Hec Garvey (to BKN & AFL)	T-G	6'1	235	26		
Jack Bonadies	G-T		208	33		
Dilly Dally	G					
Denny Gildea	C-T-G	5'9	190	27		
Vic Radzevich	BB-G-FB	5'10	165	23	1	5
Jim Foley	TB-WB-BB	5'8	165	23	2	
Enid Thomas	WB-BB-TB	5'8	170	24	1	
Henry Zehrer	FB-WB		175	20		
Ed Lynch (from & to DET)	E	5'11	190	29		
Rocky Segretta	E			27		
Stan Sieracki	T	6'1	192	22		
Frank O'Connor	T	6'	210	26		
Dick Noble	G	5'11	178	23		
Jim Donlan	G			26		
Elmer McCormick	G-C	5'7	220	28		
Jack Perrin	BB	5'9	160	28		6
Dimp Halloran	TB	5'8	175	30		
Hite Brian	WB-TB	6'	180	23		6
Eddie Barnikow	FB			28		
Joe Santone	G		180	32		
Harry McMahon	BB	5'7	150	22		
Ken Simendinger	WB	5'10	175	27		
John Harris	FB-BB		196	28		

Scores of each game

Date	Pts.	Opponent	Pts.
Sep. 26	0	NEW YORK	21
Oct. 2	0	Frankford	13
Oct. 3	0	FRANKFORD	10
Oct. 10	0	Brooklyn	6
Oct. 24	16	BROOKLYN	6
Oct. 31	2	KANSAS CITY	7
Nov. 7	16	CANTON	7
Nov. 14	7	BUFFALO	13
Nov. 21	16	DAYTON	0
Nov. 27	0	DULUTH	16

BROOKLYN LIONS 3-8-0 Punk Berryman (including 0-3-0 as BROOKLYN HORSEMEN)

Regulars

Use Name	Pos.	Hgt.	Wgt.	Age	Int.	Pts.
Owen Reynolds	E	6'3	212	26		
Dave Ziff	E	6'	195	24		
Paul Jappe	T-E	6'1	195	28	1	
Jim Yeager	T-G	6'1	230	23		
Charlie Weber	G-T	6'1	203	35		
Bob Morris	G	5'10	200	22		
Bill Stephens	C	5'8	185	21	1	
Matt Brennan	BB-TB	6'1	195	28	1	11
Rex Thomas	TB-WB	5'9	175	25	4	25
Herm Bagby	WB-TB	5'9	175	23	2	18
George Snell	FB-WB	5'10	185	29		6

Substitutes

Use Name	Pos.	Hgt.	Wgt.	Age	Int.	Pts.
Ted Drews*	E	6'	180	23		
Ed Harrison*	E	6'	178	23		
Hugh Blacklock	T-C	6'	218	35		
Dick McGrath	T-C	5'10	190	28		
Quentin Reynolds	G-T	6'1	205	24		
Red Howard*	G	5'11	192	25		
Ted Plumridge*	C	6'2	205	24		
Al Leith	BB-WB	5'9	175	23		
Harry Stuhldreher*	TB	5'7	165	24	1	
Bill Rooney	WB-BB	6'2	194	30		
Earl Britton*	FB	6'	210	23		6
Jim Sheldon	E	5'11	180	24		
Ed Reagan	T			21		
Tarzan Taylor*	G	5'11	173	31		
Jim Bond	G	5'9	200	31		
Art Stevenson (from NYG)	C	6'	190	28		
Tommy Myers	BB	5'8	170	25	1	
Chief Toorock	WB	5'9	180	24		
Dutch Connor	WB	6'	190	31		
Leo Douglass (from & to FRA)	FB-TB	5'11	190	25		
Swede Nordstrom	G-T	6'2	235	29	1	
Stan Kobolinski	C	5'8	170	22		
Hec Garvey (from HAR & * & to NYY)	C	6'1	235	26		

* - from Brooklyn Horsemen American Football League team

Scores of each game

Date	Pts.	Opponent	Pts.
Sep. 26	0	Providence	13
Oct. 10	6	HARTFORD	0
Oct. 16	0	POTTSVILLE	21
Oct. 17	0	Pottsville	14
Oct. 23	20	COLUMBUS	12
Oct. 24	6	Hartford	16
Nov. 7	9	KANSAS CITY	10
Nov. 14	19	CANTON	0
Nov. 21	0	LOS ANGELES	20
Nov. 25	0	NEW YORK	17
Nov. 28	0	New York	27

MILWAUKEE BADGERS 2-7-0 Johnny Bryan

Regulars

Use Name	Pos.	Hgt.	Wgt.	Age	Int.	Pts.
Lavie Dilweg	E	6'3	195	23	2	
Clem Neacy	E	6'3	205	28	1	
Oxie Lane	T	6'4	220	23		
Marion Ashmore	T	6'	210	23		2
Stan Kuick	G	5'10	192	22		
Pat Dunnigan	G	5'10	215	32		
Joe Burks	C	5'10	171	27		
Stone Hallquist	BB-HB-TB	5'9	168	24		
Johnny Heimsch	TB-HB	5'10	175	24		18
Johnny Bryan (to ChiB)	HB-BB	5'8	175	29		6
Howie Slater	FB	5'10	186	23	2	6

Substitutes

Use Name	Pos.	Hgt.	Wgt.	Age	Int.	Pts.
Frank Hertz	E	5'10	185	23		
Chet Gay	T-G-C	6'	220	26		
Steve Douglas	G-T		200			
Don Curtin (to RAC)	BB	5'8	155	24		7
Tom Murphy	TB-HB	5'8	165	26	1	
Ossie Orwoll	HB	5'11	165	25		
Fred Abel	BB-FB	5'10	170	23		
Clarke Fischer	HB	5'8	165	26		

Scores of each game

Date	Pts.	Opponent	Pts.
Sep. 19	7	CHIC. BEARS	10
Sep. 26	6	DETROIT	0
Oct. 3	0	LOS ANGELES	6
Oct. 10	13	Racine	2
Oct. 17	0	Green Bay	7
Oct. 24	2	CHIC. CARDS	3
Oct. 31	6	DULUTH	7
Nov. 7	0	GREEN BAY	21
Nov. 14	7	Chic. Bears	10

AKRON INDIANS 1-4-3 Al Nesser and Fritz Pollard and Rube Ursella

Regulars

Use Name	Pos.	Hgt.	Wgt.	Age	Int.	Pts.
Fred Bissell	E	6'1	180	23	1	
Red Daum	E	5'7	170	27		
Cy Caldwell	T	6'1	210	27		
Ralph Chase*	T	6'3	220	23		
Nat McCombs	G-E-C	5'11	227	21		6
Red Seidelson	G	6'1	204	25		
George Berry*	C	5'11	208	26	1	
Hal Wendler*	BB	5'10	175	24		
Fritz Pollard	TB-BB	5'7	165	32		
Obie Newman*	WB-TB	6'2	203	26	1	
Carl Cramer	FB	5'11	187	28		

Substitutes

Use Name	Pos.	Hgt.	Wgt.	Age	Int.	Pts.
Joe Little Twig (from CAN)	E	5'11	180	33		
Alvro Casey	T	6'	215	23		
George Rohleder	T-G	5'11	220	27		5
Al Nesser (to CLE & NYG)	G	6'	195	33		
Dutch Wallace (from CAN)	G	6'	200	30		
Joe Mills	C-G-BB	6'3	212	28		
Hal Griggs	BB-TB	5'10	170	25		12
Dunc Annan (from HAM)	TB-WB	5'10	180	31		
Rube Ursella*	WB-BB-TB-FB	5'9	170	36		
Marty Beck	FB	5'9	175	26		
Isham Hardy	G			27		

Scores of each game

Date	Pts.	Opponent	Pts.
Sep. 25	6	Frankford	6
Sep. 26	0	Buffalo	7
Oct. 3	17	HAMMOND	0
Oct. 10	0	CANTON	0
Oct. 24	0	Detroit	25
Oct. 31	0	Chic. Bears	17
Nov. 7	0	Pottsville	34
Nov. 25	0	Canton	0

DAYTON TRIANGLES 1-4-1 Carl Storck

Regulars

Use Name	Pos.	Hgt.	Wgt.	Age	Int.	Pts.
Lee Fenner	E	5'10	170	30		
Gene Mayl	E	6'2	198	24		12
Johnnie Becker	T-G-E-WB	5'11	205	23		
Ed Sauer	T	5'10	280	28		
Al Graham	G	6'	205	20	1	
Peck Reiter	G	5'9	195	27		
Hobby Kinderdine	C	5'11	185	35		
Art Beckley	BB	5'10	180	25	1	3
Lou Mahrt	TB	5'11	178	22	3	
Dick Dobeleit	WB	5'4	155	23		
Fay Abbott	FB	5'8	185	31		

Substitutes

Use Name	Pos.	Hgt.	Wgt.	Age	Int.	Pts.
Mack Hummon	E	5'11	180	25		
Johnnie Layport	T	5'9	170	25		
Eric Calhoun	T-G	5'9	210	26		
Jack Brown	G-C	6'	190	23		
Armin Mahrt	BB-WB-E	5'11	185	28		
Lou Partlow	TB-FB-BB	6'1	185	33		

Scores of each game

Date	Pts.	Opponent	Pts.
Oct. 3	3	Buffalo	0
Oct. 10	6	Pottsville	24
Oct. 17	6	BUFFALO	7
Nov. 14	0	Detroit	0
Nov. 20	0	Frankford	35
Nov. 21	0	Hartford	16

NAME	Rushing Complete G	Att.	Yds.	Avg.	TD	Rushing Incom. G	Att.	Yds.	TD	Passing Complete G	Com.	Att.	%	Yds.	Y/A	TD	Int.	Passing Incom. G	Com.	Att.	Yds.	TD	Int.	Receiving Complete G	Rec.	Yds	Avg.	TD	Receiving Incom. G	Rec.	Yds.	TD	Punting Comp. G	No.	Avg.	Punting Incom. G	No.	Avg.	Punt Returns Complete G	No.	Yds.	Avg.	TD	Punt Returns Incom. G	No.	Yds.	TD
PROVIDENCE																																															
Keefer	3	30	88	2.9	1	8	6	102	1	3	3	8	38	31	3.9		2	8	1	2	12	1		3	7	82	11.7		8				1	7	34.1	10	1	37.0	2	4	47	11.8		9			
Oden	4	19	43	2.3	2	9	12	116	4	4	8	15	53	96	6.4		3	9	1	10	15		4	4	4	33	8.3	1	9										3	8	159	19.9	1	10	5	228	1
Wentworth	2	7	18	2.6		6	4	35		2	1	1	100	2	2.0	1		6															1	1	32.0	7	1	10.0									
Laird	3	18	25	1.4		6	6	16		4								5	0	3			2										2	13	32.6	7	4	24.5									
MacPhee	2	5	20	4.0		8				4	0	2	0				1	6															2	1	35.0	9											
Sweet	1	2	2	1.0		8	1	12																																							
Forst						2	4	13																																							
Spellman	4	6	11	1.8		8																																									
Smyth (3)	1	1	3	3.0		2	1	3		1	0	1	0				1	2																													
Hummel (2)	1	2	1	0.5		3																																									
Garvey																								3	1	14	14.0		7	1	15																
Golembeski																								3					6	1	12	1															
Wesley																																	1			6	3	36.3									
Etelman																																				1	1	32.0									
Team	2	40	47	1.2	1	11				6	18	54	33	207	3.8	1	11	7															2	22	33.2	11			3	12	206	17.2	1	10			
Opp.	2	105	279	2.7		11				5	32	81	40	310	3.8	1	8	8															2	16	31.1	11			3	12	115	9.6		10			
DETROIT																																															
Sonnenberg	2	4	-7	-1.7		10	4	113																									2	17	39.1	10	4	45.5									
Doane	2	17	16	0.9		10	14	61	2																								2	10	36.9	10											
Marion	2	10	9	0.9		10	7	25																2					10	1	20																
Scharer	2	7	-1	-0.1		10	2	7	1	2	10	27	37	93	3.4		4	10	11	12	193	6		2					10	3	57		2			10	1	17.0	2	6	52	8.7		10			
Gregory	2	9	6	0.7		10	2	2		2	1	1	100	5	5.0			10						2	4	46	11.5		10	4	108	2							2	1	7	7.0		10			
Hadden	2	7	-1	-0.1		10	2	8		2	1	2	50	4	2.0			10						2	3	25	8.3		10	2	46	1															
Conzelman	2	1	0	0.0		10	2	9	1	2	1	4	25	5	1.3			10	4	6	70			2	5	23	4.6		10	3	28	1															
Vick (1)										1	1	8	13	16	2.0		1	5	2	3	30																										
Lynch (2)										2	1	1	100	7	7.0			10						2	2	31	15.5		10	1	7																
Lauer																								2					8	2	20	1															
Hultman																								2	1	5	5.0		8	1	7	1															
Team	2	55	22	0.4		10				2	15	43	35	130	3.0		5	10															2	27	38.3	10			2	7	59	8.4		10			
Opp.	2	81	217	2.7	1	10				2	18	34	53	254	7.5	3	4	10															2	23	39.4	10			2	8	64	8.0		10			
HARTFORD																																															
Foley						9	25	135										9	4	6	71		2						9	3	40													9	3	33	
Manning (2)						6	23	112	2									6	3	5	59								6	5	86	1															
Smyth (2)						5	6	23	1									5	10	22	233	1	4																					5	1	20	
Perrin						6	4	19										6	2	2	17								6	1	34													6	2	40	
McEvoy						7	8	11																					7	3	31					7	2	26.5						7	2	5	
Zehrer						7	1	11																																							
McMahon						2	1	8																					2	2	52																
Corgan (1)						7	1	7										7	1	3	30								7	10	228																
Thomas						7	2	5																					7	1	15																
Radzevich						8	1	5										8	9	14	147	1	1																								
Harris						2	2	2																																							
Bernikow						2	2	1																																							
Webber (1)																		8	2	4	28		2													8	6	32.5									
O'Connell																													10	3	44																
Brian																													4	2	43	1				4	2	27.5									
Lynch (1,3)																													1	1	12																
Simendinger																																				2	1	66.0									
Team						10												10																		10								10			
Opp.						10				1	11	16	69	157	9.8			9																		10								10			
BROOKLYN																																															
Thomas	2	18	36	2.0		8	9	101	3	2	1	3	33	8	2.7			8	4	4	84			3	4	110	27.5		7	2	55	1							2					8	2	45	
Bagby	2	17	42	2.5		6	6	45		2								6	1	1	11			2	5	116	23.2		6	4	119	1	2	2	24.0	6											
Snell	2	13	23	1.8		9	5	21	1	2	1	4	25	31	7.8			9	1	1	17			2					9	2	26		2	15	33.6	9			2	1	5	5.0		9			
Rooney	2	7	16	2.3		5	1	8																2	1	8	8.0		5																		
Stuhldreher						1	2	20																																							
Brennan	1					9	2	15	1	1	5	14	36	85	6.1		1	8	5	7	183	1	1	1					9	1	11		1	2	42.0	9			1	1	6	6.0		9			
Toorock	1	1	0	0.0		1																																									
Leith																								2	1	0	0.0		5																		
Britton																																				3	2	32.0									
Team	2	56	117	2.1		9				2	7	21	33	124	5.9		1	9															2	19	33.5	0			2	2	11	5.5		9			
Opp.	2	100	302	3.0	5	9				2	11	21	52	174	8.3		4	9															2	6	47.3	9			2	8	146	18.3		9			
MILWAUKEE																																															
Heimsch	3	43	112	2.6	1	6	2	32	2	3	10	33	30	119	3.6		9	6	2	2	28			3	2	18	9.0		6				3	11	32.8	6	1	50.0									
Slater	3	33	72	2.2		6	1	9																									3	1	38.0	6											
Bryan (1)	3	16	45	2.8	1	6	4	9		3	3	10	30	21	2.1		1	6	1	1	30			3	2	23	11.5		6				3	1	32.0	6			3	0	3			6			
Murphy	3	9	22	2.4		5				3	5	6	83	98	16.3		1	5															3	20	39.7	5	7	25.4	3	5	46	9.2		5			
Hallquist	3	3	15	5.0		6				3	1	2	50	15	7.5		1	6						3	2	34	17.0		6	1	30		3	3	23.0	6			3	1	3	3.0		6			
Abol	1	2	5	2.5		2																																	1	1	2	2.0		2			
Orwoll	2	3	4	1.3		1				2	1	3	33	22	7.3		1	1						2	1	15	15.0		1																		
Curtin (1)																		3	5	6	102																										
Dilweg										3	0	1	0				1	6						3	7	126	18.0		6	5	95																
Neacy																								3	5	52	10.4		6	2	35																
Ashmore																								3	1	7	7.0		6																		
Team	3	109	273	2.5	2	6				3	20	55	36	275	5.0		4	6															3	36	35.9	6			3	7	54	7.7		6			
Opp.	3	119	334	2.8	3	6				3	19	52	37	320	6.2	1	2	6															3	32	36.3	6			3	13	140	10.8		6			
AKRON																																															
Griggs						5	9	134	2									5	1	1	25															5	2	34.5									
Ursella (1,3)	1	9	12	1.3		7	2	30		1	0	1	0					7																													
Pollard						4	10	25										4	4	5	70	1																						4	3	22	
Wendler (1,3)	1	1	0	0.0		6	4	23																1	1	20	20.0		6				1	4	39.5	6											
Cramer	1	5	7	1.4		5	4	1																1					7	1	12		1			7	2	30.0									
Annan (2)	1	6	6	1.0		3				1	0	2	0				1	3																													
Newman (1,3)	1	3	4	1.3		7	1	0		1	2	12	17	25	2.1		2	7						1					7	1	10		1	9	34.3	7	10	29.3	1	2	15	7.5		7			
Mills	1	1	1	1.0		5																																									
Daum	1	1	-2	-2.0		7																		1					7	1	9																
Bissell																								1	1	5	5.0		7	1	25																
Big Twig																								1					7	1	39	1															
Cardwell																																	1			6	1	2.0									
Team	1	26	28	1.1		7				2	2	22	9	25	1.1		5	6															1	13	35.9	7			1	2	15	7.5		7			
Opp.	1	56	292	5.2	3	7				2	12	34	35	127	3.7	1	2	6															1	7	35.0	7			1	5	46	9.2		7			
DAYTON																																															
Abbott	1	8	26	3.3		5	1	12		1								5	0	1			1	1	2	35	17.5		5				1	7	17.9	5	3	35.7									
Dobeleit	1	5	4	0.8		5	1	20																									1			5	4	21.3									
A. Mahrt	1	1	15	15.0		3																																									
L. Mahrt	1	6	6	1.0		5	1	8		1	8	18	44	101	5.6	1	4	5	4	6	76	1	1										1			5	1	9.0	1					5	1	20	
Partlow						4	2	13																																							
Beckley	1	6	7	1.2		5																											1			5	2	32.0									
Mayl	1	1	0	0.0		3																		1	3	33	11.0	1	3	1	15	1															
Hummon																													5	3	61																
Fenner																								1	3	33	11.0		5																		
Team	1	27	58	2.1		5				1	8	18	44	101	5.6	1	4	5															1	7	17.9	5			1	0				5			
Opp.	1	47	181	3.9	2	5				1	6	12	50	118	9.8	1	2	5															1	2	46.0	5			1	0				5			

RACINE TORNADOES 1-4-0 Shorty Barr Wally McIlwain

Regulars: Use Name	Pos.	Hgt.	Wgt.	Age	Int.	Pts.
Barney Mathews	E	5'8	185	23		
Jim Murphy (to DUL)	E-WB-C	6'	187	21		
Dick Hardy	T	5'10	210	22		
Fred Hobscheid	T-G	5'11	215	22		
George Bernard	G-T					
Adolph Bieberstein (to GB)	G	5'10	205	23		
Jake Mintun	C	5'11	196	32		
Shorty Barr	BB-TB-FB	5'8	205	30	2	
Graham Kernwein	TB	5'11	175	21	1	
Wally McIlwain	WB	5'9	173	23	5	
Chuck Reichow	FB-TB	5'9	183	25	4	

Substitutes: Use Name	Pos.	Hgt.	Wgt.	Age	Int.	Pts.
John Fahay (from ChiA)	E	6'	188	24		
Fritz Heinisch (to DUL)	E-WB	5'10	176	26		
Ed Sparr	T	6'	210	28		
Frank Linnan	T	6'2	205	27		
George Glennie	G-E-T	6'2	185	24		
Kibo Brumm	G-C	6'	182	28		
Roy Longstreet	C	5'11	185	25		
Gil Sterr	BB	5'6	150	26	3	
Champ Boettcher	FB-TB-BB	5'10	193	25		
Jim Oldham	E-WB-BB-FB-T	5'10	183	21		6
Hank Gillo	FB	5'10	180	31		
George Burnside	BB	5'9	160	27		
Don Curtin (from MIL)	BB	5'8	155	24		

Date	Pts.	Opponent	Pts.
Sep. 26	6	HAMMOND	3
Oct. 3	0	Chic. Cards	20
Oct. 10	2	MILWAUKEE	13
Oct. 17	0	DULUTH	21
Oct. 24	0	Green Bay	35

COLUMBUS TIGERS 1-6-0 Jack Heldt

Regulars: Use Name	Pos.	Hgt.	Wgt.	Age	Int.	Pts.
Flop Gorrill	E	5'11	178	23		6
Ike Nonnemaker	E-BB	5'8	172	25		
Bill Berrehsem	T-E	5'10	195	23	1	
John Conley	T	5'11	210	36		
Joe Mulbarger	G	5'9	225	31		
Jack Heldt	G-C	5'9	215	26		
Lou Reichel	C	5'11	180	24		2
Tommy Murphy (to KC)	BB	5'10	187	26		
Pete Barnum	TB-FB	5'10	195	25	1	6
Bob Rapp	WB-BB-TB	5'8	160	28	1	
Jim Bertoglio	FB-WB	5'9	187	21	1	6

Substitutes: Use Name	Pos.	Hgt.	Wgt.	Age	Int.	Pts.
Earl Plank	E		178	21		
Harley Pearce	E-TB-BB-WB	5'10	180	25		6
Boni Petcoff	T	5'10	230	26		
Earl Duvall	T-G	6'	225	27		
Frank Nesser	G-T-FB	6'1	260	37		
Len Johnson	BB			24		
Flash Woods	WB	6'	180	24		
Herb Davis	WB-BB	5'10	175	27		

Date	Pts.	Opponent	Pts.
Sep. 19	0	Chic. Cards	14
Sep. 26	14	Canton	2
Oct. 3	0	Pottsville	3
Oct. 10	0	Providence	19
Oct. 16	0	KANSAS CITY	9
Oct. 23	12	Brooklyn	20
Nov. 7	0	Buffalo	26

CANTON BULLDOGS 1-9-3 Pete Henry and Harry Robb

Regulars: Use Name	Pos.	Hgt.	Wgt.	Age	Int.	Pts.
Russ Stein	E	6'1	210	30		
Cliff Marker	E-BB-FB-TB	5'10	190	23	2	6
Don Nelson (from HAM)	T	6'1	210	23		
Pete Henry	T	5'11	245	28		3
John Nichols	G-T	6'	200	22		
Willie Flattery	G-E	6'	220	24		
Rip Kyle	C-T	6'	240	25	2	
Harry Robb	BB-TB-WB	5'10	190	29		13
Jim Thorpe	TB-E-FB	6'1	200	39	1	12
Ben Roderick	WB-FB	5'9	175	27	2	
Pete Calac	FB	5'10	210	34		

Substitutes: Use Name	Pos.	Hgt.	Wgt.	Age	Int.	Pts.
Joe Little Twig (to AKR)	E	5'11	180	33		
Stan Robb	E	6'	185	25		6
Art Deibel	T-G	6'3	235	30		
Dutch Wallace (to AKR)	G	6'	210	30	1	
Dutch Speck	G-C	5'10	220	40		
Wade McRoberts	C	6'	210	25		
Dick Vick (from DET)	TB	5'9	170	24		
Sam Babcock	WB-FB-BB	5'6	168	24		
Sol Butler (to HAM)	FB-WB-BB-TB	5'8	185	29		
Harold Zerbe	E		165	25		
Jack Sack (from CLE)	G	6'2	190	27		
Frank Seeds	WB		170			
Guy Roberts (from CLE)	WB	5'8	180	26		
Hook Comer	FB		180	26		

Date	Pts.	Opponent	Pts.
Sep. 26	2	COLUMBUS	14
Oct. 3	13	LOUISVILLE	0
Oct. 10	0	Akron	0
Oct. 17	13	LOS ANGELES	16
Oct. 23	0	Frankford	17
Oct. 31	0	Detroit	6
Nov. 2	7	New York	7
Nov. 7	7	Hartford	16
Nov. 11	2	Providence	21
Nov. 14	0	Brooklyn	19
Nov. 21	2	DULUTH	10
Nov. 25	0	AKRON	0
Nov. 28	0	Chic. Bears	35

HAMMOND PROS 0-4-0 Doc Young

Regulars: Use Name	Pos.	Hgt.	Wgt.	Age	Int.	Pts.
Inky Williams	E	5'11	175	29		
Ray Hahn	E	5'10	190	28		
George Dahlgren	T	5'10	200	39		
Lou Usher	T	6'2	245	28		
Russ Smith	G-T	5'10	220	30		
Walt Sechrist (to & from LOU)	G	6'	260	29		3
Frank Rydzewski	C-G	6'1	220	33		
Dick Hudson	BB		183			
Harry Curzon (to & from LOU)	TB-E	6'	195	30		
Dunc Annan (to AKR)	WB	5'10	180	30		
Buck Gavin	FB	5'10	185	31		

Substitutes: Use Name	Pos.	Hgt.	Wgt.	Age	Int.	Pts.
Gene Bedford	E	5'9	165	29	1	
Ralph Chase*	T	6'3	220	23		
George Fisher	T	6'	200	25		
Ray Neal	G-T	5'9	215	28		
George Berry*	G	5'11	208	26		
Don Nelson (to CAN)	C	6'1	210	23		
Hal Wendler*	BB	5'10	175	24		
Rube Ursella*	TB	5'9	170	36		
Obie Newman*	WB	6'2	203	26		
Sol Butler (from CAN)	FB	5'8	185	29	1	
Merle Hunter	T		185	20		
Nagida	BB		180			
Ed Robinson (to LOU)	BB	5'9	155	22		
Lee Carr	WB-BB					
McKetes	BB				1	

Date	Pts.	Opponent	Pts.
Sep. 26	3	Racine	6
Oct. 3	0	Akron	17
Oct. 10	0	DULUTH	26
Nov. 21	0	Pottsville	7

LOUISVILLE COLONELS 0-4-0 Lenny Sachs

Regulars: Use Name	Pos.	Hgt.	Wgt.	Age	Int.	Pts.
Lenny Sachs	E	5'8	180	29		
Ray Bush	E	5'8	180	24	1	
Vee Green	T	6'	195	25		
Gartfield Leaf	T	6'1	195	24		
Bill McCaw	G	6'2	195	28		
Dan Bernoske	G	5'10	190	21		
Ed Berwick	C-E	6'	185	21	1	
Chuck Palmer	BB	5'10	185	25	1	
Pete Stinchcomb	TB	5'8	160	31		
Ed Robinson (from HAM)	WB	5'9	155	22		
Lou Metzger	FB-WB	5'9	170	22		

Substitutes: Use Name	Pos.	Hgt.	Wgt.	Age	Int.	Pts.
Harry Curzon (from & to HAM)	E	6'	195	30		
Al Gansberg	E-T	5'11	187	24		
Bill Flannigan	T		210	25		
John McDonald	T-G	6'	195	26		
Walt Sechrist (from & to HAM)	G	6'	260	29		
Pete Vainowski	G			23		
Larry Jackson	C-TB		185	21		
Bill Giaver (from ChiA)	TB	5'9	190	28	1	
Gerry Sherry	FB					
Gene Golsen	FB-TB	5'11	188	24	1	
Steve Hanson	E	6'2	192	24		
Jim Eiden	T	5'8	185	24		
Omensky	G					
Tom Golsen	G	5'11	175	24		
George Slagle	G			28		
John Scanlon	TB		185	26		
Glenn Greenwood	FB	5'10	185	30		

Date	Pts.	Opponent	Pts.
Oct. 3	0	Canton	13
Oct. 17	0	Detroit	47
Nov. 7	0	Chic. Bears	34
Nov. 14	0	Green Bay	14

*Played for Akron through November 7th, then played for Hammond on November 21st, and played again for Akron on November 25th.

1927 N.F.L.
New York Loses A Ghost And Gains A Crown

The red ink bath taken by the NFL in 1926 caused the league to reevaluate its lineup for 1927. Needed was a more compact circuit, fewer weak franchises and a more concentrated player pool. At a special meeting called in April to consider proposals for reorganization, the shakiest franchises were given the option of retiring from the league or suspending operations until the franchise could be sold. Any franchise not sold or reactivated by July 7, 1928, would be cancelled. Out by this shotgun eviction went 12 teams, including original members Canton, Akron, Hammond and Columbus. Ten holdovers and two new members faced 1927 with high hopes.

One of the new teams was the New York Yankees, sole survivors of the AFL. New York Giants owner Tim Mara had obtained the 1926 Brooklyn NFL franchise in payment of debts. He leased the franchise to C.C. Pyle and Red Grange, but severely limited the number of Yankee home games. Thirteen of the 16 Yankee games were booked on the road as a way to show off the famous Grange. Joining the Yankees on the road were the Duluth Eskimos, who showcased the almost-equally famous Ernie Nevers. The league fathers beamed at the thought of Grange and Nevers hyping the gate in most of the NFL cities.

But the Yankees and Eskimos didn't reach the high expectations of the other owners. After three road victories, the Yankees took on the Chicago Bears before 30,000 at Wrigley Field. Late in a 12-0 Chicago victory, Grange was tackled by George Trafton and suffered knee damage. He stayed on crutches for a few weeks and, while he missed only three games, he was never again the breakaway runner of legend; Eddie Tryon picked up some of the slack in the Yankee backfield, but, nevertheless, the team was an artistic and financial disappointment.

An even bigger artistic disappointment was the Duluth squad. With the other teams stronger this year, the Eskimos could win only one game with their thin talent. Despite stacked defenses, Nevers still shone. On October 3, he led the Eskimos to their only victory by passing for 305 yards and four touchdowns against Pottsville. His running, passing, kicking and defense were superior all season, but, try as he could, Nevers simply could not win by himself.

Field goal and extra point kicks were made more difficult this year by placing the goalposts on the backline of the endzone, but an odd rule change aided punters. If a team indicated it intended to punt when the line of scrimmage was within its own five-yard line, the ball would be moved up 10 yards; then, after the return, the 10 yards was added back on.

With all the players made available by the franchise bloodletting, most of the remaining teams were stronger. The biggest winners were the New York Giants, who captured their first league title in their third season. The Giants had a chilling defense, posting 10 shutouts in 13 contests and allowing a total of only 20 points. New coach Earl Potteiger had a wealth of talent gathered from various sources. The star backs were Hinkey Haines, a colorful breakaway runner, and NFL scoring leader Jack McBride, a crafty tailback who could both pass and run skillfully. The line had stars in tough holdover Steve Owen, AFL refugee Century Milstead and rookie Cal Hubbard, at 235 pounds the NFL's largest offensive end and one of its quickest front defenders, playing end, tackle and linebacker. Hubbard tied the defense together and launched a sterling career.

Twice in the season's first four weeks, the Giants played the

NAME	Rushing Complete Games G	Att.	Yds.	Avg.	TD	Rushing Incom. Games G	Att.	Yds.	TD	Passing Complete Games G	Com.	Att.	%	Yds.	Y/A	TD	Int.	Passing Incom. Games G	Com.	Att.	Yds.	TD	Int.
RACINE																							
Reichow	5	58	123	2.1						5	5	15	33	58	3.9		4						
Kernwein	5	34	73	2.1						5	5	14	36	40	2.9		1						
Boettcher	4	26	63	2.4						4	3	11	27	74	6.7		1						
Gillo	4	10	36	3.6																			
McIlwain	5	29	33	1.1						5	3	10	30	19	1.9								
Oldham	5	2	20	10.0						5	0	1	0				1						
Sterr	3	10	16	1.6						3	0	1	0										
Barr	3	4	16	4.0						3	8	30	27	86	2.9	1							
Murphy (1)																							
Mathews																							
Glennie																							
Burnside																							
Team	5	173	380	2.2						5	24	82	29	277	3.4	1	7						
Opp.	5	228	713	3.1	10					5	32	85	38	492	5.8	3	15						
COLUMBUS																							
Rapp	2	25	66	2.6		4				2								4	1	1	42	1	
Barnum	2	10	16	1.6		4				2	2	16	13	20	1.3		3	4	0	1			1
Pearce	1	5	10	2.0		6	1	1	1	2	0	2	0				1	5					
Bertoglio	1	1	0	0.0		6	2	5	1														
Woods						2	1	2															
Nesser										2	1	8	13	22	2.8			5	2	4	55		2
Gorrill																							
Reichie																							
Team	1	12	17	1.4		6				3	6	30	20	97	3.2		4	4					
Opp.	1	73	273	3.7		6				3	23	53	43	204	3.8		5	4					
CANTON																							
H. Robb						13	15	90	2	1								12	6	9	104		1
Thorpe						9	12	46	2	1	4	6	67	60	10.0			8	5	11	70		2
Butler (1)						9	5	19		1								8	3	5	33		
Marker						12	5	16		1								11	4	6	4		
Henry						13	2	9		1								12	2	3	26		1
Roderick						11	8	8															
Calac						10	2	5															
Comer						1	1	0															
Seeds						1	1	-7															
Vick (2)																		7	7	14	138	1	2
Roberts																		3	1	1	12		
Babcock																		7	0	1			1
S. Robb																							
Little Twig																							
Stein																							
Wallace																							
Team						13				5	25	76	33	293	3.9		9	8					
Opp.						13				5	21	57	37	368	6.5	1	9	8					
HAMMOND																							
Annan	1	15	35	2.3		2	2	15		1								2	4	4	35		
Curzon (1,3)	2	6	15	2.5		2				2	1	12	8	35	2.9		4	2	1	2	5		
Gavin	1	7	14	2.0		2																	
Ursella (2)	1	14	11	0.8						1	0	2	0				1						
Williams	1	4	8	2.0		2																	
Newman (2)	1	3	3	1.0						1	0	1	0										
Sechrist (1,3)	2	2	3	1.5		2																	
Butler (2)	1	9	1	0.1						1	1	4	25	9	2.3		1						
Hudson	1	5	1	0.2		1																	
Wendler (2)	1	2	1	0.5						1	0	2	0				1						
McKetes										1	0	1	0				1						
Team	2	67	92	1.4		2				2	2	22	9	44	2.0		8	2					
Opp.	2	100	271	2.7		2				2	13	32	41	134	4.2	2	3	2					
LOUISVILLE																							
Metzger	1	8	13	1.6		2																	
G. Golsen	1	1	5	5.0		2																	
Robinson (2)	1	5	0	0.0		3																	
Palmer	1	2	0	0.0		3				2	7	28	25	78	2.8		5	2					
Giaver	1	6	-9	-1.5		1				1								1	0	1			1
Sachs																							
Eiden																							
Stinchcomb																							
Team	1	22	9	0.4		3				2	7	28	25	78	2.8		5	2					
Opp.	1	54	131	2.4	1	3				2	7	30	23	131	4.4	1	5	2					

NAME	Receiving Complete Games G	Rec.	Yds	Avg.	TD	Receiving Incom. Games G	Rec.	Yds.	TD	Punting Comp. Games G	No.	Avg.	Punting Incom. Games G	No.	Avg.	Punt Returns Complete Games G	No.	Yds.	Avg.	TD	Punt Returns Incom. Games G	No.	Yds.	TD
RACINE																								
Reichow	5	5	33	6.6						5	10	30.0				5	3	24	8.0					
Kernwein	5	1	30	30.0						5	25	31.6												
Boettcher																								
Gillo	4	1	2	2.0																				
McIlwain	5	5	53	10.6						5	14	31.3				5	1	8	8.0					
Oldham	5	4	23	5.8	1																			
Sterr	3	3	39	13.0												3	4	35	8.8					
Barr										3	7	37.0												
Murphy (1)	5	3	75	25.0																				
Mathews	5	1	12	12.0																				
Glennie	5	1	10	10.0																				
Burnside																2	1	5	5.0					
Team										5	56	31.9				5	9	72	8.0					
Opp.										5	37	35.9				5	12	136	11.3					
COLUMBUS																								
Rapp	2	2	20	10.0		4										1	1	5	5.0		5	1	30	
Barnum										1	7	24.6	5	2	0.5									
Pearce	2	1	22	22.0		5				1	3	37.7	6											
Bertoglio																								
Woods						2	1	25					2	1	32.0									
Nesser																								
Gorrill	2					5	2	76	1															
Reichie										1	1	36.0	6											
Team										1	11	29.2	6			1	1	5	5.0		6			
Opp.										1	2	32.0	6			2	12	158	13.2		5			
CANTON																								
H. Robb	1	1	8	8.0		12	12	143													13	1	6	
Thorpe													9	4	33.8						9	1	20	
Butler (1)																					9	2	53	
Marker	1					11	5	49					12	2	52.5									
Henry	1	1	2	2.0		12																		
Roderick	1	1	25	25.0		10	1	20																
Calac	1					9	3	62					10	2	27.5									
Comer																								
Seeds																								
Vick (2)						7	2	47																
Roberts																								
Babcock													8	1	10.0									
S. Robb						3	3	90	1															
Little Twig						6	2	12																
Stein	1	1	25	25.0		7																		
Wallace													7	4	30.3									
Team													13								13			
Opp.													13								13			
HAMMOND																								
Annan	1					2	1	5		1	4	39.5	2			1	1	25	25.0		2			
Curzon (1,3)										2	3	41.3	2											
Gavin																								
Ursella (2)										1	1	30.0				1	2	10	5.0					
Williams	1	1	35	35.0		2										1	2	7	3.5		2			
Newman (2)										1	10	36.1				1	1	5	5.0					
Sechrist (1,3)										2	2	27.5	2											
Butler (2)																1	1	4	4.0					
Hudson	2	4	35	8.8												1	1	3	3.0		1			
Wendler (2)	1	1	9	9.0												1	2	10	5.0					
McKetes																								
Team										2	20	36.4	2			2	10	64	6.4		2			
Opp.										2	22	35.2	2			2	7	66	9.4		2			
LOUISVILLE																								
Metzger	1	1	19	19.0		3																		
G. Golsen										1	2	29.0	2											
Robinson (2)																1	1	10	10.0		3			
Palmer																								
Giaver	1	2	13	6.5		1				1	10	23.2	1			1	1	20	20.0		1			
Sachs	1	1	20	20.0		3																		
Eiden	1	1	20	20.0																				
Stinchcomb													3	1	0.0									
Team										1	12	24.2	3			1	2	30	15.0		3			
Opp.										1	8	35.9	3			1	2	12	6.0		3			

Cleveland Bulldogs, a newly organized team stocked with many players from last year's Kansas City team. The key to the Bulldogs was rookie tailback Benny Friedman, a multi-talented All-American fresh out of Michigan. He often startled fans and coaches by calling for passes on first down, a daring move according to the wisdom of the era. But Friedman had the arm to do it. His 12 touchdown passes and more than 1,700 yards gained passing made him by far the best passer the NFL had ever seen and helped Cleveland become 1927's top scoring machine. The Bulldogs used defense to hold the Giants to a scoreless tie in Cleveland on October 2, then beat the New Yorkers 6-0 at the Polo Grounds on October 16. The Bulldogs would go on to a successful season on the field with less success at the ticket window despite Friedman's well-known name.

The Giants rebounded from their defeat to whip Frankford 13-0 and 27-0 in a home-and-away series the next weekend. The Yellowjackets, defending NFL champions, had almost a completely new squad. Coach Guy Chamberlin had moved on to lead the Chicago Cardinals, taking a few key players along. Frankford rebuilt with young talent, players who would need time to develop. The young team lost its opener to the weak Dayton Triangles and went on to a losing season. Chamberlin, meanwhile, could not lift the Cardinals from their losing ways and retired from professional football after the season.

The Giants went on after their double victory over Frankford to beat Pottsville 16-0, Duluth 21-0 and Providence 25-0. While the Maroons were on the decline due to several key retirements, Providence was on the rise this year after picking up Wildcat Wilson from the AFL and Jimmy Conzelman and Gus Sonnenberg from the defunct Detroit franchise.

With five straight shutouts behind them, the Giants beat the Cardinals 28-7 in the Polo Grounds on November 20. That win ran the New York record to 8-1-1. The same day, the Chicago Bears upped their record to 7-1-1 by beating Green Bay 14-6. The loss dampened the title hopes of the Packers, who had added key players in Lavie Dilweg, Red Dunn and Claude Perry. The Bears were in position to tie the Giants by beating the Cards on Thanksgiving Day and then take first place with a win over the Giants on Sunday.

The Cards upset the Bears on Thanksgiving 3-0. The Bears could still tie for first by beating the Giants. A sparse crowd of 15,000 fans in the Polo Grounds saw a superb football game. Both clubs hit hard from the opening gun and hit harder as the game went on and the stakes rose. The New York line and the Bears' line, which featured veterans George Trafton, Jim McMillin, Bill Buckler, Link Lyman and Ed Healey, battled to a standstill in the first half. The Bears had taken the opening kickoff and driven to a first down on the New York five-yard line, but the Giants held on downs. With the scoreboard still clear in the third quarter, the Giants drove 60 yards, mostly on the ground, to a touchdown, with McBride going over from the two, but then missing the extra point. A few minutes later, the Giants again drove downfield and scored on a McBride plunge. The Bears scored late in the final period on a pass from Laurie Walquist to Joey Sternaman, but it was too little too late. The Giants won 13-6 in what Steve Owen called "the toughest, roughest football game I ever played." After that battle, the road to the championship was clear coasting.

The *Green Bay Press Gazette* all-NFL poll: ends Lavie Dilweg, Green Bay, and Cal Hubbard, Giants; tackles Gus Sonnenberg, Providence, and Ed Weir, Frankford; guards Mike Michalske, Yankees, and Steve Owen, Giants; center Clyde Smith, Cleveland; quarterback Benny Friedman, Cleveland; halfbacks Verne Lewellen, Green Bay, and Paddy Driscoll, Bears; and fullback Ernie Nevers, Duluth.

1927 STANDINGS

	W	L	T	Pct	Pts.	Opp. Pts.	Avg. Pts.	Opp. Avg.
New York Giants	11	1	1	.917	197	20	15	2
Green Bay Packers	7	2	1	.778	113	43	11	4
Chicago Bears	9	3	2	.750	149	98	11	7
Cleveland Bulldogs	8	4	1	.667	209	107	16	8
Providence Steam Roller	8	5	1	.615	105	88	8	6
New York Yankees	7	8	1	.467	142	174	9	11
Frankford Yellow Jackets	6	9	3	.400	152	166	8	9
Pottsville Maroons	5	8	0	.385	80	163	6	13
Chicago Cardinals	3	7	1	.300	69	134	6	12
Dayton Triangles	1	6	1	.143	15	57	2	7
Duluth Eskimos (R)	1	8	0	.111	68	134	8	15
Buffalo Bisons	0	5	0	.000	8	123	2	25

(R) — played only road games

Scoring Leaders

McBride	NYG	57
Bloodgood	Cle	45
Tryon	NYY	44
Driscoll	ChiB	43
Mercer	Fra	39
Haines	NYG	36
Senn	ChiB	36
Wilson	NYG	36
Nevers	Dul	31
Lewellen	GB-NYY	30
Simmons	Cle	30
Moran	Fra-ChiC	27
Fry	NYY	25
Wiberg	Cle	25
Conzelman	Prov	24
Enright	GB	24
Flaherty	NYY	24
Wilson	Prov	24

KICKING

		FG	Att	Pct
Mercer	Fra	5	9	56
Moran	Fra-ChiC	3	4	75
Sonnenberg	Prov	3	11	27
McBride	NYG	2	8	25
Henry	NYG-Pott	2	8	25
Driscoll	ChiB	2	10	20
Bloodgood	Cle	1	1	100
Wentz	Pott	1	1	100
Moynihan	Fra	1	2	50
Swanson	ChiC	1	2	50
Purdy	GB	1	3	33
Britton	Day-Fra	1	7	14
Achui	Day	0	1	0
Friedman	Cle	0	1	0
Nevers	Dul	0	1	0
Tryon	NYY	0	1	0
Carr	Buf-Pott	0	2	0
Dunn	GB	0	2	0
Weller	ChiC	0	3	0

		PAT	Att	Pct
McBride	NYG	15	22	68
Friedman	Cle	11	17	65
Tryon	NYY	8	13	62
Neverε	Dul	7	9	78
Sonnenberg	Prov	7	10	70
Driscoll	ChiB	7	14	50
Dunn	GB	7	14	50
Mercer	Fra	6	9	67
Moran	Fra-ChiC	6	10	60
Bloodgood	Cle	6	11	55
J. Sternaman	ChiB	4	6	67
Pritchard	Prov	3	4	75
Swanson	ChiC	2	3	67
Weller	ChiC	2	5	40
Wentz	Pott	2	5	40

		PAT	Att	Pct
E. Weir	Fra	1	1	100
Fry	NYY	1	2	50
White	NYG	1	2	50
Molenda	NYY	1	3	33
Purdy	GB	1	3	33
Wycoff	NYG	1	3	33
Henry	NYG-Pott	1	6	17
Baker	NYY	0	1	0
Flaherty	NYY	0	1	0
Hathaway	Buf	0	1	0
Senn	ChiB	0	1	0
Slater	ChiC	0	1	0
Britton	Day-Fra	0	2	0
Marks	NYY	0	2	0

NEW YORK GIANTS 11-1-1 Earl Potteiger

Regulars

UseName	Pos.	Hgt.	Wgt.	Age	Int	Pts.
Chuck Corgan	E	6'	180	24	1	
Cal Hubbard	E-T	6'4"	235	26	2	
Century Milstead	T	6'1"	213	27		
Steve Owen	T-G	5'10"	226	29		
Hec Garvey	G	6'1"	240	27	1	
Al Nesser	G-C	6'	196	34		
Mickey Murtagh	C-G	6'1"	186	23	1	
Doug Wycoff	BB-FB-TB	6'	190	23	2	19
Jack McBride	TB	5'11"	187	25	4	57
Hinkey Haines	WB-FB-TB	5'10"	170	28		36
Mule Wilson	FB-BB-TB	5'11"	185	25	3	36

Substitutes

UseName	Pos.	Hgt.	Wgt.	Age	Int	Pts.
Jim Kendrick	E	6'	205	34	1	
Paul Jappe	E-G	6'1"	195	29		
Pete Henry (to POTT)	T	5'11"	245	29		
Dick Stahlman	T-E-G	6'2"	220	25		
Doc Alexander	G-E	5'11"	240	29	1	6
Babe Parnell	G	6'3"	205	25		
Riley Biggs	C	6'2"	230	27		
Joe Guyon	BB-T-G-TB	5'10"	195	34		
Phil White	BB-TB-FB	6'2"	210	27	6	19
Tut Imlay	WB-BB	5'8"	165	26		
Jack Haggerty	WB-FB	5'9"	160	24	3	18
Cliff Marker (to FRA)	E	5'10"	190	24		
Art Harms	T	6'1"	200	25		
Red Howard	G	5'11"	192	26		
Les Caywood (from POTT, to CLE)	G	6'	230	22		
Earl Potteiger	BB-E	5'7"	170	36		

Scores of Each Game

Date	Pts.	Opponent	Pts.
Sep. 25	8	Providence	0
Oct. 2	0	Cleveland	0
Oct. 9	19	Pottsville	0
Oct. 16	0	CLEVELAND	6
Oct. 22	13	Frankford	0
Oct. 23	27	FRANKFORD	0
Oct. 30	16	POTTSVILLE	0
Nov. 6	21	DULUTH	0
Nov. 8	25	PROVIDENCE	0
Nov. 20	28	CHIC. CARDS	7
Nov. 27	13	CHIC. BEARS	7
Dec. 4	14	N.Y. YANKEES	0
Dec. 11	13	N.Y. Yankees	0

GREEN BAY PACKERS 7-2-1 Curly Lambeau

Regulars

UseName	Pos.	Hgt.	Wgt.	Age	Int	Pts.
Lavie Dilweg	E	6'3"	195	24	2	12
Dick O'Donnell	E	6'	195	27	1	
Rosey Rosatti	T	6'	210	31		
Tiny Cahoon	T	6'2"	230	27		6
Bruce Jones	G	6'1"	215	22		
Whitey Woodin	G	5'10"	210	32		
Jug Earp (to NYY)	C	6'	235	30	2	
Red Dunn	BB-TB	5'11"	175	25	4	13
Curly Lambeau	TB-FB	5'10"	185	29	4	12
Verne Lewellen (to NYY)	HB-TB	6'1"	180	25	3	30
Rex Enright	FB	5'10"	195	26	2	24

Substitutes

UseName	Pos.	Hgt.	Wgt.	Age	Int	Pts.
George Tuttle	E	5'11"	180	22		
Claude Perry	T-G-E	6'1"	210	25		
Red Smith	G-E	5'10"	190	23	2	
Frank Mayer	G-T	5'11"	215	25	1	
Boob Darling	C	5'11"	195	23		
Pid Purdy	BB	5'6"	145	23		10
Tom Hearden	HB-TB-BB	5'9"	175	22		6
Eddie Kotal	HB	5'8"	175	25	1	
Myrt Basing	FB	5'9"	200	26		
Mal Bross	HB	5'9"	170	22		
Gib Skeate	FB	5'10"	190	26		

Cully Lidberg — Voluntarily Retired
Dick Flaherty — Knee Injury

Scores of Each Game

Date	Pts.	Opponent	Pts.
Sep. 18	14	DAYTON	0
Sep. 25	12	CLEVELAND	7
Oct. 2	6	CHIC. BEARS	7
Oct. 9	20	DULUTH	0
Oct. 16	13	N.Y. YANKEES	0
Oct. 23	13	N.Y. YANKEES	0
Nov. 6	6	Chic. Cards	6
Nov. 13	6	DAYTON	0
Nov. 20	6	Chic. Bears	14
Nov. 24	17	Frankford	9

CHICAGO BEARS 9-3-2 George Halas

Regulars

UseName	Pos.	Hgt.	Wgt.	Age	Int	Pts.
Tillie Voss	E	6'3"	204	30		
Duke Hanny	E	6'	196	29	1	
Ed Healey	T	6'1"	210	32		
Link Lyman	T	6'2"	224	28		
Bill Buckler	G	6'	215	26		
Jim McMillen	G	6'1"	215	24		
George Trafton	C	6'2"	230	30		
Joey Sternaman	QB	5'6"	158	27		16
Paddy Driscoll	HB	5'8"	175	32		43
Bill Senn	HB-FB	6'	180	22		36
Buck White	FB	6'	195	26	2	12

Substitutes

UseName	Pos.	Hgt.	Wgt.	Age	Int	Pts.
George Halas	E	6'	182	32	1	18
Don Murry	E-T	6'2"	192	27		
Buck Evans	T	5'11"	198	27		
Bill Fleckenstein	G	6'1"	205	23		
Ernie Vick	C	5'10"	185	27		
Milt Romney	QB-HB	5'8"	166	28		6
Dutch Sternaman	HB-FB	5'8"	184	32		
Laurie Walquist	HB	5'8"	170	29	1	6
Oscar Knop	FB	6'	196	32	1	6
Chuck Kassel (to FRA)	E	6'1"	190	23		
Clem Neacy (to DUL)	E	6'3"	205	29		
Johnny Bryan	QB	5'8"	178	30		

Scores of Each Game

Date	Pts.	Opponent	Pts.
Sep. 25	9	Chic. Cards	0
Oct. 2	7	Green Bay	6
Oct. 16	12	N.Y. YANKEES	0
Oct. 23	14	CLEVELAND	12
Oct. 30	14	DAYTON	6
Nov. 6	0	PROVIDENCE	0
Nov. 8	6	N.Y. Yankees	26
Nov. 13	30	POTTSVILLE	12
Nov. 20	14	GREEN BAY	6
Nov. 24	0	CHIC. CARDS	3
Nov. 27	7	N.Y. Giants	13
Dec. 3	0	Frankford	0
Dec. 4	9	FRANKFORD	0
Dec. 11	27	DULUTH	14

CLEVELAND BULLDOGS 8-4-1 Roy Andrews

Regulars

UseName	Pos.	Hgt.	Wgt.	Age	Int	Pts.
Lyle Munn	E	6'	185	25	1	
Carl Bacchus	E	6'	200	23		18
Tom Cobb	T	5'11"	250	23		
Bill Owen	T-G	6'	200	23		
Dosey Howard	G	6'	225	26		
Milt Rehnquist	G-C	6'	225	30		
Clyde Smith	C	5'10"	182	23	2	
Ossie Wilberg	BB-FB-G-E	5'11"	210	22	1	25
Benny Friedman	TB	5'10"	180	22	2	23
Jim Simmons	WB-FB	6'	186	25	1	30
Tiny Feather	FB-BB	6'	190	24		

Substitutes

UseName	Pos.	Hgt.	Wgt.	Age	Int	Pts.
Proc Randels	E	6'	180	27		12
Cookie Cunningham	E	6'3"	210	22		
Jerry Krysl	T	5'11"	200	22		
Les Caywood (from POTT, NYG)	T	6'	230	22		
Roy Andrews	T-G-E	6'	230	30		
Harry McGee	G	6'1"	198	22		
Herb DeWitz	BB-WB-TB	5'9"	165	27		18
Al Bloodgood	TB-BB-WB	5'8"	155	25	1	45
Rex Thomas	WB-FB	5'9"	170	26	1	18
Herm Bagby	FB-BB	5'9"	175	24		
Hal Broda	E	6'1"	180	22		
Dutch Webber	E-BB	6'2"	190	25		
Gordon Peery	BB	5'10"	155	23		
Frank Kelley	WB	5'10"	165	27	1	
Dick Wolf	WB	5'8"	160	27		

Scores of Each Game

Date	Pts.	Opponent	Pts.
Sep. 25	7	Green Bay	12
Oct. 2	0	N.Y. GIANTS	0
Oct. 9	7	N.Y. Yankees (at Detroit)	13
Oct. 16	6	N.Y. Giants	0
Oct. 23	12	Chic. Bears	14
Oct. 30	21	DULUTH	20
Nov. 6	15	N.Y. YANKEES	0
Nov. 12	0	Frankford	22
Nov. 13	37	FRANKFORD	0
Nov. 20	22	Providence	0
Nov. 24	30	N.Y. Yankees	19
Nov. 27	32	Chic. Cards	7
Dec. 3	20	DULUTH	0

PROVIDENCE STEAMROLLER 8-5-1 Jimmy Conzelman

Regulars

UseName	Pos.	Hgt.	Wgt.	Age	Int	Pts.
Ed Lynch	E	5'11"	190	30		6
John Spellman	E-T	5'10"	200	28	1	
Gus Sonnenberg	T	5'6"	195	29		16
Joe Kozlowsky	T-G	5'10"	195	26		
Jack Fleischman	G	5'6"	185	26	1	
Jim Laird	G	6'	195	29	4	
Al Pierotti	C-G	5'10"	200	31		
Jimmy Conzelman	BB-E	6'	180	29	2	24
Wildcat Wilson	TB	5'11"	200	26	4	24
Al Hadden	WB-FB	5'9"	185	27	1	
Bill Pritchard	FB	5'10"	185	25		9

Substitutes

UseName	Pos.	Hgt.	Wgt.	Age	Int	Pts.
Jim Stifler	E	5'10"	175	26		
Bull Lowe	E	5'11"	180	32		
Mike Gulian	T	6'	205	27		
Orland Smith	T-G	5'11"	215	21		
Sam Young	G	6'2"	190	24		
Bull Wesley	C-G	6'1"	190	25	3	
Curly Oden	BB-WB-TB	5'6"	160	28	3	12
Jack Cronin	WB-TB-FB	5'11"	175	24	2	
Bill Cronin	WB-FB	5'10"	180	26	1	
Dinger Doane (from POTT)	FB	5'10"	190	32		
Grattan O'Connell	E	5'11"	185	25		
Dave Mishel	TB-WB-BB	5'9"	180	22		
Les Young	FB	6'1"	190	22		

Scores of Each Game

Date	Pts.	Opponent	Pts.
Sep. 25	0	N.Y. GIANTS	8
Oct. 2	5	BUFFALO	0
Oct. 16	3	POTTSVILLE	6
Oct. 23	7	DAYTON	0
Oct. 29	20	Frankford	7
Oct. 30	14	FRANKFORD	0
Nov. 6	0	Chic. Bears	0
Nov. 8	0	N.Y. Giants	25
Nov. 13	13	DULUTH	7
Nov. 20	0	CLEVELAND	22
Nov. 24	0	Pottsville	6
Nov. 27	14	N.Y. YANKEES	7
Dec. 3	9	N.Y. Yankees (at Syracuse)	0
Dec. 4	20	POTTSVILLE	0

NAME	RUSHING									PASSING														RECEIVING									PUNTING						PUNT RETURNS								
	Complete Games					Incom. Games				Complete Games								Incom. Games						Complete Games					Incom. Games				Comp. Games			Incom. Games			Complete Games					Incom. Games			
	G	Att.	Yds.	Avg.	TD	G	Att.	Yds.	TD	G	Com.	Att.	%	Yds.	Y/A	TD	Int	G	Com.	Att.	Yds.	TD	Int	G	Rec.	Yds.	Avg.	TD	G	Rec.	Yds.	TD	G	No.	Avg.	G	No.	Avg.	G	Rec.	Yds.	Avg.	TD	G	Rec.	Yds.	TD
NEW YORK GIANTS																																															
McBride	3	42	171	4.1	1	9	26	179	5	5	22	47	47	357	7.6	2	6	7	12	13	253	5											2	1	61.0	10											
Haines	3	13	69	5.3		10	8	103	1	6	1	3	33	15	5.0		1	7	1	1	29			4	3	42	14.0		9	7	133	4	2	2	24.0	11			2					11	3	102	1
Wycoff	3	12	36	3.0		8	9	69	2	4	2	3	67	38	12.7		1	7	0	1			1										2	16	43.9	9	1	65.0									
Hagerty	3	19	60	3.2	1	9	4	43																4	2	20	10.0		8	3	67	1							2	3	26	8.7		10	3	88	1
Wilson	3	11	32	2.9	1	10	11	51	2															4					9	2	117	2	2	1	42.0	11			2	1	15	15.0		11			
White	3	5	15	3.0	1	9	5	30	2	6	1	7	14	15	2.1			6															2	4	41.0	10	7	26.4									
Imlay	2	8	41	5.1		5																		3	3	48	16.0		4										1	5	65	13.0		6			
Guyon	2	1	5	5.0		5	1	5																3	2	29	14.5		4																		
Corgan																								4	7	80	11.4		7	3	49																
Hubbard																								4					6	1	30																
Garvey																								3	1	25	25.0		5																		
Kendrick																								3	1	15	15.0		5																		
Team	3	111	429	3.9	4	10				6	26	60	43	425	7.1	2	8	7															2	24	42.4	11			2	9	106	11.8		11			
Opp.	3	98	200	2.0		10				6	40	104	38	556	5.3		21	7															2	30	35.4	11			2	9	102	11.3		11			
GREEN BAY																																															
Lewellen (1)	9	91	305	3.4	5	1				10	11	30	37	160	5.3		4							9	15	246	16.4		1	1	25		10	99	38.4				10	3	25	8.3					
Lambeau	9	64	231	3.6	2	1				10	26	54	48	417	7.7	1	4							9	6	121	20.2		1																		
Enright	8	75	164	2.2	2	1																		8	3	52	17.3	1	1	1	20	1															
Dunn	9	42	149	3.5		1				10	32	85	38	556	6.5	3	7							9	11	162	14.7	1	1				10	5	22.4				10	21	166	7.9					
Kotal	7	49	140	2.9	1	1				8	6	11	55	92	8.4									7	10	204	20.4		1																		
Hearden	3	8	29	3.6		1																																									
Skeate	2	6	12	2.0																																											
Basing	3	5	9	1.8																																											
Purdy	5	6	5	0.8	1	1				6	3	5	60	44	8.8									5	1	10	10.0		1				6	2	40.0				6	7	90	12.9					
Bross	2	1	2	2						2	1	1	100	9	9.0																																
Dilweg																								9	14	199	14.2		1	2	55	1															
O'Donnell																								9	6	74	12.3																				
Perry																								8	1	13	13.0		1																		
Team	9	347	1046	3.0	11	1				10	79	186	42	1278	6.9	4	15																10	106	37.7				10	31	281	9.1					
Opp.	10	334	690	2.1	2					10	42	133	32	692	5.2	4	24																10	120	34.6				10	31	375	12.1					
CHICAGO BEARS																																															
Driscoll	4	45	108	2.4	1	10	28	329	4	5	5	22	23	125	5.7	2	4	9	3	8	72	1											4	36	37.5	10	5	37.6	3					1	1	12	
Senn	4	44	251	5.7	3	9	13	98	2	4	0	1	0					9						4	4	83	20.8	1	9				4	3	34.0	9											
White	4	27	86	3.2		9	9	25	2																																						
Walquist	4	21	48	2.3		10	2	7		5	1	7	14	18	2.6		1	9	3	6	45	1		4	1	15	15.0		10	1	15	1															
Romney	4	1	1	1.0		10	3	46	1	5	1	1	100	27	27.0			9																													
Knop	3	16	31	1.9		7	2	4																3					7	1	18	1															
J. Sternaman	4	13	23	1.8		10	3	12	1	5	2	9	22	32	3.6		3	9	3	6	66	1	2	4					10	1	10	1							3	5	66	13.2		1	2	25	
D. Sternaman	2	1	2	2.0		3	1	30																																							
Halas																								3	2	51	25.5	1	7	2	62																
Voss																								3	2	53	26.5		8	2	43																
Hanny																																	4	5	31.0	10											
Team	4	168	550	3.3	4	11				7	23	77	30	374	4.9	2	18	7															4	44	36.5	10			3	5	66	13.2		11			
Opp.	4	120	347	2.9	3	10				6	37	88	42	626	7.1	1	8	8															4	41	37.2	10			4	9	77	8.6		10			
CLEVELAND																																															
Friedman	2	9	43	4.8	1	11	13	114	1	11	87	196	44	1565	8.0	10	11	2	9	9	156	2		5	1	20	20.0		8				2	9	37.1	11			1					12	4	100	
Thomas	1	5	3	0.6		12	9	101	1	7	0	1	0					6						5	7	172	24.6	1	8	3	58	1															
Simmons	2	21	77	3.7		10	9	27	5															4	2	32	16.0		8	1	13																
Kelley						7	7	50	2															2					5	4	84	1															
Bloodgood	1					9	5	26	4	6	1	8	13	12	1.7		2	4	1	1	25			5	4	88	22.0	1	5	2	41		2	11	34.5	8			1	1	2	2.0		9	2	37	
DeWitz	1	6	17	2.8		12	1	2	1															5					8	1	30	1															
Feather	1	9	12	1.3		10	2	5		6	1	3	33	20	6.7			5	0	1			1	5	5	52	10.4		6	1	35																
Bagby	1	3	12	4.0		4																																									
Wiberg						10	4	5	1	6	1	4	25	3	0.8		2	4						4	2	35	17.5		6	9	144	2															
Peery	1	3	5	1.7		3																		2					2	3	20		1	4	41.8	3											
Bacchus																								3	1	22	22.0		7	4	136	3															
Cunningham																								2	1	12	12.0		3	3	46																
Randels																								3	1	15	15.0		3	1	52	1															
Munn																								5	2	48	24.0		5																		
Broda																								1	1	17	17.0		2																		
Owen																								5	1	15	15.0		8																		
Webber																								1	1	12	12.0		2																		
Team	1	33	56	1.7		12				11	91	214	43	1625	7.6	10	16	4															2	24	36.7	11			1	1	2	2.0		12			
Opp.	2	81	329	4.1	1	11				6	41	120	34	561	4.7	1	7	7															2	29	35.8	11			2	17	221	13.0		11			
PROVIDENCE																																															
Oden	4	32	199	6.2	1	9	18	208		7	3	11	27	47	4.3		1	6	6	13	133	1	1	7	9	100	11.1		6	1	11								3	7	70	10.0		10	3	124	1
Wilson	5	45	113	2.5	3	9	31	149	1	7	40	66	61	544	8.2	3	5	7	11	23	238	1	6	7					7	1	27		4	32	38.9	10	20	30.8	3					11	1	15	
Pritchard	3	23	71	3.1		9	19	90	1															6					6	3	35																
J. Cronin	3	10	30	3.0		9	5	36		6	0	2	0					6	2	2	28			6					6	1	19		3	7	33.6	9	4	19.0	2					10	3	105	1
Hadden	4	30	36	1.2		6	7	20																6	3	26	8.7		4										3					7	1	19	
Mishel	1	2	2	1.0		3	3	28		3	6	15	40	71	4.7		1	1																					2					2	1	20	
Doane (2)	2	9	24	2.7		3	2	2																																							
Sonnenberg	4	2	18	9.0		10																											4	6	28.3	10											
B. Cronin	3	7	14	2.0		6	2	-1																5	2	12	6.0		4	2	50	1															
Conzelman	4	7	13	1.9		10	2	3	1	7	2	5	40	14	2.8			7	0	1				7	25	286	11.4	2	7	9	192	1	7	5	42.8	7											
Spellman	4	1	4	4.0		10																		7	1	18	18.0		7																		
Lowe										6	0	1	0					5						6	4	111	27.8		5	2	65		2	1	54.0	9											
Lynch																								6	7	123	17.6	1	5																		
Team	4	165	523	3.2	4	10				7	51	100	51	676	6.8	3	7	7															4	51	37.6	10			3	7	70	10.0		11			
Opp.	5	180	478	2.7	2	9				7	58	136	43	872	6.4	3	6	7															4	54	31.6	10			4	19	233	12.3		10			

NEW YORK YANKEES 7-8-1 Ralph Scott

Regulars

Use Name	Pos.	Hgt.	Wgt.	Age	Int.	Pts.
Ray Flaherty	E	6'	185	23		24
Red Badgro	E	6'	190	24		6
Norm Harvey (from BUF)	T	6'	200	30		
Dick Hall	T-G	6'2	220	24		
Mike Michalske	G-T-BB	6'	200	24	1	
Bill Oliver	G	5'11	180	25		
Jack McArthur (from BUF)	C	5'11	210	23		
Wild Bill Kelly	BB-TB-WB	5'10	180	22		18
Red Grange	TB-BB	5'11	178	24	1	6
Eddie Tryon	WB-TB	5'8	180	27	3	44
Wes Fry	FB-BB-TB	5'10	190	24	8	25

Substitutes

Use Name	Pos.	Hgt.	Wgt.	Age	Int.	Pts.
Red Maloney	E-WB	5'11	180	25		6
Jim Lawson	E	5'11	190	25		
Ralph Scott	T	6'2	240	29		
Mush Crawford	T-G	6'	205	28		
Forrest Olson	G-FB	6'	205	24		
Fritz Kramer	G-BB	6'	230	24	1	
Ray Stephens	C-G	5'11	190	24		
Bullet Baker	TB-BB-WB	5'8	175	27	1	6
Verne Lewellen (from GB)	WB-TB-FB	6'1	180	25		
Larry Marks	WB-TB-FB	5'11	185	24		
Bo Molenda	FB	5'10	200	22	1	7
John Bayley	T	5'11	180	23		
Bob Beattie	T	6'3	230	24		
Jug Earp (from GB)	T	6'	235	30		
Louie Kolls	C	6'1	210	34		

Scores of each game

Date	Pts.	Opponent	Pts.
Oct. 2	6	Dayton	3
Oct. 9	13	Cleveland (at Detroit)	7
Oct. 12	19	Buffalo	8
Oct. 16	0	Chic. Bears	12
Oct. 23	0	Green Bay	13
Oct. 30	7	Chic. Cards	6
Nov. 6	0	Cleveland	15
Nov. 8	26	CHIC. BEARS	6
Nov. 11	19	Pottsville	12
Nov. 13	20	CHIC. CARDS	6
Nov. 24	19	CLEVELAND	30
Nov. 27	7	Providence	14
Dec. 3	0	Providence (at Syracuse)	9
Dec. 4	0	N.Y. Giants	14
Dec. 10	6	Frankford	6
Dec. 11	0	N.Y. GIANTS	13

FRANKFORD YELLOW JACKETS 6-9-3 Charley Moran Swede Youngstrom Charley Rogers, Russ Daugherity and Ed Weir

Regulars

Use Name	Pos.	Hgt.	Wgt.	Age	Int.	Pts.
Chuck Kassel (from ChiB)	E	6'1	190	23		12
Joe Weir	E	5'11	185	22	1	
Ed Weir	T-E	5'10	192	24	2	1
Bull Behman	T	5'10	218	27		
Rudy Comstock	G	5'10	210	26		
Babe Connaughton	G	6'2	285	22	4	
Max Reed	C	5'8	185	25		
Two Bits Homan	BB	5'5	144	25		12
Ken Mercer	TB-BB-WB-FB	5'11	180	24	4	39
Charley Rogers	WB-BB-TB	5'10	162	23	7	18
Ned Wilcox	FB-WB-TB	5'11	185	23	2	12

Substitutes

Use Name	Pos.	Hgt.	Wgt.	Age	Int.	Pts.
Frank McGrath	E	5'11	193	23		
Tony Kostos	E-T	5'11	190	22	1	
John Filak	T-G	6'	190	23		
Swede Youngstrom	T-G	6'1	190	30		
Joey Maxwell	C-E	6'2	190	22		
Dick Moynihan	BB-FB	5'8	160	24	2	3
Hap Moran (to ChiC)	TB	6'1	190	26	3	21
Paul Fitzgibbon	WB-BB	5'8	175	24	5	
Earl Britton (from DAY)	FB	6'	210	24	5	
Cliff Marker (from NYG)	E	5'10	190	24		
Carl Davis	E-T-C-G	6'	194	24		
Pots Clarke (to DUL)	T	5'7	180	26		
Sully Montgomery	T-C	6'3	215	26		
Pete Richards	C	5'10	190	22		
Bill Donohue	BB-WB-FB	5'9	165	23		12
Tex Hamer	FB-WB-TB	6'1	192	25		
Adrian Ford (from POTT)	WB-BB-FB-E	5'10	190	23		12
Lou Molinet	FB	5'11	195	22	1	6
Chris Cortemeglia	WB	6'	210	23		
Tex Grigg	WB	5'11	195	36		
Russ Daugherity	WB	5'10	175	25		
Tom Leary	E	6'	180	24		
George Tully	E	5'10	180	23		

Scores of each game

Date	Pts.	Opponent	Pts.
Sep. 24	3	DAYTON	6
Oct. 8	0	DAYTON	0
Oct. 15	54	BUFFALO	0
Oct. 16	23	Buffalo	0
Oct. 22	0	N.Y. GIANTS	13
Oct. 23	0	N.Y. Giants	27
Oct. 29	7	PROVIDENCE	20
Oct. 30	0	Providence	14
Nov. 5	10	POTTSVILLE	0
Nov. 6	0	Pottsville	9
Nov. 12	22	CLEVELAND	0
Nov. 13	0	Cleveland	37
Nov. 19	12	CHIC. CARDS	8
Nov. 24	9	GREEN BAY	17
Nov. 26	6	DULUTH	0
Dec. 3	0	CHIC. BEARS	0
Dec. 4	0	Chic. Bears	9
Dec. 10	6	N.Y. YANKEES	6

POTTSVILLE MAROONS 5-8-0 Dick Rauch

Regulars

Use Name	Pos.	Hgt.	Wgt.	Age	Int.	Pts.
George Kenneally	E	6'	185	25		6
Vern Mullen (from ChiC)	E	6'	190	27	2	
Walden Erickson	T	6'1	205	25		
Pete Henry (from NYG)	T	5'11	245	29		7
Johnny Budd	G-T	5'11	245	28		
Frank Racis	G-T	6'	200	29		6
Frank Youngfleish	C-G	5'9	190	31	1	
Jack Ernst	BB-WB	5'11	175	27	2	
Frank Kirkleski	TB	5'10	175	23	2	12
Tony Latone	WB-FB-TB	5'11	195	30	4	
Barney Wentz	FB	5'11	206	26		17

Substitutes

Use Name	Pos.	Hgt.	Wgt.	Age	Int.	Pts.
Adrian Ford (to FRA)	E	5'10	190	23		
Vivian Hultman	E	5'8	175	24		6
Joe Carpe	T-E-C	6'	195	24		
Les Caywood (to NYG & CLE)	T	6'	230	22		
Walt LeJeune	T-G	6'	242	27		
Duke Osborn	G-C	5'10	185	30	1	
John Barrett	C	5'6	170	27		
Eddie Scharer	BB-WB-TB	5'6	165	25	2	
Harlan Carr (from BUF)	TB-WB	5'10	165	24	2	12
Dinty Moore	WB-BB	5'8	160	23	1	12
Dinger Doane (to PROV)	FB-G	5'10	190	32		
Jack Underwood (to BUF)	E	6'	200	30		
Emil Mayer	E	6'	190	24		
Nick Farina	C	5'10	195	23		
Paul Rebseaman	C	6'	188	22		1
Guy Roberts	WB-TB-FB	5'8	170	27		1
Bob Millman	WB	5'11	180	24		

Scores of each game

Date	Pts.	Opponent	Pts.
Sep. 25	22	BUFFALO	0
Oct. 2	7	Chic. Cards	19
Oct. 9	0	N.Y. GIANTS	19
Oct. 16	6	Providence	3
Oct. 23	0	DULUTH	27
Oct. 30	0	N.Y. Giants	16
Nov. 5	0	Frankford	10
Nov. 6	9	FRANKFORD	0
Nov. 11	12	N.Y. YANKEES	19
Nov. 13	12	Chic. Bears	30
Nov. 20	6	DULUTH	0
Nov. 24	6	PROVIDENCE	0
Dec. 4	0	Providence	20

CHICAGO CARDINALS 3-7-1 Guy Chamberlin

Regulars

Use Name	Pos.	Hgt.	Wgt.	Age	Int.	Pts.
John Vesser	E	6'	185	26	1	6
Evar Swanson	E	5'9	172	24		5
Bub Weller	T-E	6'4	225	25		8
Duke Slater	T	6'1	215	28		
Nick McInerney	G	6'2	205	31		
Willie Brennan	G	6'	215	33		
Bill Springsteen	C-E	6'	190	26	2	
Ben Jones	BB-FB	5'11	200	27		12
Hal Erickson	TB-FB-WB	5'9	190	28	1	
Mickey McDonnell	WB-TB	5'8	160	23	1	
Ted Bucklin	FB	6'	190	27	1	6

Substitutes

Use Name	Pos.	Hgt.	Wgt.	Age	Int.	Pts.
Vern Mullen (to ChiC)	E	6'	190	27		
Guy Chamberlin	E	6'2	190	33		
Walt Ellis	T	5'11	220	28		
Herb Blumer	T-E-G-C	6'1	190	27		
Swede Hummel	G		195	25		
Tim Waldron	G-C		195	24		
Ralph Claypool	C	5'11	190	28		
Ike Mahoney	BB-WB	6'	175	25	2	
Hap Moran (from FRA)	TB-WB	6'1	190	26	1	6
Roddy Lamb	WB-TB-BB	5'6	165	28	1	6
Red Strader	TB-FB-WB	5'9	200	22		6
Aubrey Goodman	T	6'3	225	23		
Jay Berquist	G	6'3	235	25		
Paul Hogan	TB-BB	5'8	170	28		6
Ray Risvold	WB-FB		170	25		
Rollin Roach	FB-WB	5'6	145	24	1	6

Scores of each game

Date	Pts.	Opponent	Pts.
Sep. 25	0	CHIC. BEARS	9
Oct. 2	19	POTTSVILLE	7
Oct. 9	7	DAYTON	0
Oct. 16	0	Green Bay	13
Oct. 30	6	N.Y. YANKEES	7
Nov. 6	6	GREEN BAY	6
Nov. 13	6	N.Y. Yankees	20
Nov. 19	8	Frankford	12
Nov. 20	7	N.Y. Giants	28
Nov. 24	3	Chic. Bears	0
Nov. 27	7	CLEVELAND	32

DAYTON TRIANGLES 1-6-1 Lou Mahrt

Regulars

Use Name	Pos.	Hgt.	Wgt.	Age	Int.	Pts.
Lee Fenner	E	5'10	170	31	1	
Red Joseph	E	6'3	180	24		
Johnnie Becker	T	5'11	205	24		
Bill Belanich	T	6'	205	24		6
Ebby DeWeese	G	6'	190	21	1	
Al Graham	G	6'	210	21		6
Hobby Kinderdine	C	5'11	185	36	1	
Jim Tays	BB	5'8	175	28		
Lou Partlow	TB	6'1	185	34		
Sneeze Achui	WB-TB	5'8	170	25		
Earl Britton (to FRA)	FB	6'	210	24	1	3

Substitutes

Use Name	Pos.	Hgt.	Wgt.	Age	Int.	Pts.
Sam Hippa	E	5'11	165	26		
Zip Joseph	E-C	6'2	170	24		
Ed Seibert	T	5'10	190	24		
Peck Reiter	G-E	5'9	195	28		
Corl Zimmerman	G-T	6'	185	28		
Jack Brown	C	6'	190	24		
Lou Mahrt	TB	5'11	178	23		
Fay Abbott	TB-WB-FB-BB	5'8	185	32	2	
Frank Sillin	WB-TB-BB	5'11	175	24	1	
Augie Cabrinha	WB-BB	5'9	170	25		

Scores of each game

Date	Pts.	Opponent	Pts.
Sep. 18	0	Green Bay	14
Sep. 24	6	Frankford	3
Oct. 2	3	N.Y. YANKEES	6
Oct. 8	0	Frankford	0
Oct. 9	0	Chic. Cards	7
Oct. 23	0	Providence	7
Oct. 30	6	Chic. Bears	14
Nov. 13	0	Green Bay	6

DULUTH ESKIMOS 1-8-0 Ernie Nevers

Regulars

Use Name	Pos.	Hgt.	Wgt.	Age	Int.	Pts.
Joe Rooney	E	6'	178	29	2	18
Fritz Cronin	E-G	5'11	182	24		
Jack McCarthy	T		186			
Marion Ashmore	T-G	6'	216	24	1	
Ray Suess	G-T		204	24		
Walt Kiesling	G-T	6'2	254	24		
Bill Rooney	C-G	6'2	197	31	5	
Cobb Rooney	BB	6'	185	27	2	6
Johnny Blood	WB-BB	6'1	193	23	1	6
Russ Method	WB-BB	5'10	194	30	1	6
Ernie Nevers	FB	6'	204	24	3	31

Substitutes

Use Name	Pos.	Hgt.	Wgt.	Age	Int.	Pts.
Clem Neacy (from ChiB)	E-T	6'3	205	29	2	
Shanley	T		214			
Chick Lang	G		195	26		
Jimmy Manion	G	5'9	175	22		
Bill Stein	C-T	6'	190	28		
Bill McNelis	WB	5'11	177	24		
Pots Clarke (from FRA)	WB	5'7	180	26		
Bunny Belden	WB-E-FB	5'8	170	26		

Scores of each game

Date	Pts.	Opponent	Pts.
Oct. 9	0	Green Bay	20
Oct. 23	27	Pottsville	0
Oct. 30	20	Cleveland	21
Nov. 6	0	N.Y. Giants	21
Nov. 13	7	Providence	13
Nov. 20	0	Pottsville	6
Nov. 26	0	Frankford	6
Dec. 3	0	Cleveland	20
Dec. 11	14	Chic. Bears	27

BUFFALO BISONS 0-5-0 Dim Batterson

Regulars

Use Name	Pos.	Hgt.	Wgt.	Age	Int.	Pts.
Lowell Otte	E	6'2	180	23		
Jack Underwood (from POTT)	E	6'	200	30		
Norm Harvey (to NYY)	T	6'	200	30		
Barlow Irvin	T	5'10	225	23		
Paul Minick	G	6'	195	27		
Frank McConnell	G	6'	195	27		
Jack McArthur (to NYY)	C	5'11	210	23		
Ben Hobson	BB-WB	5'10	190	25		
Harlan Carr (to POTT)	TB	5'10	165	24		6
Ben Roderick	WB	5'9	175	28		
Charlie Van Horn	FB-TB	6'2	185	25		

Substitutes

Use Name	Pos.	Hgt.	Wgt.	Age	Int.	Pts.
Ralph White	E	5'9	175	24		
Spin Roy	E	6'	175	30	1	
Russ Hathaway	T-G	5'11	250	31		
Ed Doyle	G-C-T			21		
Rat Watson	BB-E	5'10	185	28		
Orrin Vedder	FB	5'7	165	28		
Karl Bohren	WB-FB	5'8	180	25		
Ken Hauser	FB	6'1	218	28		
Neely Allison	E	6'	190	25		
George Snell	BB	5'10	185	30		
Pinky Thompson	WB					
Joe Willson	FB	5'11	185	25		

Scores of each game

Date	Pts.	Opponent	Pts.
Sep. 25	0	Pottsville	22
Oct. 2	0	Providence	5
Oct. 12	8	N.Y. YANKEES	19
Oct. 15	0	Frankford	54
Oct. 16	0	FRANKFORD	23

NAME	Rushing Complete Games					Rushing Incom. Games				Passing Complete Games								Passing Incom. Games						Receiving Complete Games					Receiving Incom. Games				Punting Comp. Games			Punting Incom. Games			Punt Returns Complete Games					Punt Returns Incom. Games			
	G	Att.	Yds.	Avg.	TD	G	Att.	Yds.	TD	G	Com.	Att.	%	Yds.	Y/A	TD	Int.	G	Com.	Att.	Yds.	TD	Int.	G	Rec.	Yds	Avg.	TD	G	Rec.	Yds.	TD	G	No.	Avg.	G	No.	Avg.	G	No.	Yds.	Avg.	TD	G	No.	Yds.	TD
NEW YORK YANKEES																																															
Tryon	2	15	38	2.5		12	16	97	2	3	1	8	13	23	2.9		1	11	4	6	61		1	3	4	111	27.8	1	11	4	75	1	2	3	24.7	12			2	1	10	10.0		12	1	10	
Grange	3	4	0	0.0		12	25	127	1	3	4	8	50	85	10.6			10	7	13	121		4	3	2	35	17.5		10	3	42																
Kelly	2	4	21	5.3		10	4	52	3	2	3	11	27	110	10.0	2	2	10	7	7	145	3		2					10	1	15								2	2	20	10.0		10			
Fry	2	5	26	5.2		13	11	39	3	3	1	5	20	45	9.0	1	2	12	2	4	43		2	3	1	15	15.0		12	2	40																
Baker	2	18	34	1.9		12	5	27	1	2	3	11	27	66	6.0		2	12	2	5	55	1	2	2	1	14	14.0		12	2	40		2			12	2	58.0	2	3	25	8.3		12	1	10	
Molenda	2	14	29	2.1		8	5	31																2	1	46	46.0	1	8																		
Marks	2	17	45	2.6		11				3	0	2	0					10	1	1	4	4		3	1	30	30.0		10	1	17		2	9	31.3	11	1	25.0									
Lewellen						3	7	24										3	4	6	77	1	2						3	1	28					3	4	48.5									
Michalske	1					13	3	11																																							
Flaherty																								3	1	20	20.0		10	7	126	4	2	3	28.0	11	7	36.1									
Maloney																								3	1	20	20.0		10	1	25	1	2	3	24.7	12											
Badgro																								3	1	50	50.0	1	9																		
Kramer																																	2	1	34.0	8											
Team	2	73	193	2.6		14				5	20	73	27	450	6.2	3	16	11															2	19	30.1	14			2	6	55	9.2		14			
Opp.	2	96	368	3.8	3	14				5	24	59	41	324	5.5	1	12	11															2	18	38.4	14			2	0				14			
FRANKFORD																																															
Rogers	13	120	508	4.2	2	5				10	1	3	33	22	7.3		1	8						12	38	541	14.2	1	6										9	41	564	13.8		9	3	56	
Mercer	12	103	338	3.3	3	5	1	30		10	43	99	43	565	5.7	3	10	7	10	26	197	1	6										9	41	36.1	8	4	28.5	9	2	38	19.0		8			
Wilcox	10	50	165	3.3	2	4	3	14		7	7	19	37	84	4.4		2	7	1	4	19		1	9	6	117	19.5		5	1	15																
Moran (1)	4	28	108	3.9		2	4	17	1	2	3	13	23	19	1.5		2	4	8	15	147		3	3	1	55	55.0		3	1	12		1	12	41.2	5	13	37.7									
Fitzgibbon	9	28	107	3.8		2	1	6																8	4	26	6.5		3										5	1	23	23.0		6	1	15	
Moynihan	7	23	79	3.4		2				5	13	25	52	161	6.4		2	4	1	2	10			6	9	90	10.0		3	4	83								3	3	40	13.3		6	1	5	
Molinet	6	15	67	4.5		3	2	6	1	5	1	2	50	4	2.0			4	2	2	31			5	2	17	8.5		4																		
Britton (2)	5	25	60	2.4		1				4	5	14	36	51	3.6		3	2						5	1	21	21.0		1	1	15		4	50	37.3	2											
Homan	11	16	55	3.4		5	2	4	1	8								8	1	1	12			10	9	221	24.6	1	6	2	33								7	2	34	17.0		9	5	85	
Ford (2)	7	16	50	3.2	2	2																		7	1	8	8.0		2																		
Donohue	5	9	39	4.3	1	3																		4	2	28	14.0	1	4										2	5	62	12.4		6	2	54	
Hamer	4	9	20	2.2		1				3	3	6	50	10	1.7			2						3	1	14	14.0		2				3	7	37.7	2			3	2	26	13.0		2			
Cortemeglia	2	2	10	5.0																																											
E. Weir	13	2	8	4.0		5																		12	1	8	8.0		6										9	1	26	26.0		9			
Daugherity	1	2	7	3.5		1																																									
McGrath	8	1	4	4.0		4																		7	9	50	5.6		5	1	15																
J. Weir	9	1	1	1.0		3																		8	3	59	19.7		4																		
Kassel (2)																								8	3	78	26.0	1	2																		
Kostos																								7	2	16	8.0																				
Behman																								8					3	1	21																
Marker (2)																								1	1	8	8.0		1																		
Team	13	450	1626	3.6	10	5				15	107	284	38	1372	4.8	4	31	4															9	110	37.3	9			9	57	813	14.3		9			
Opp.	7	224	707	3.2	5	11				11	89	197	45	1338	6.8	6	17	7															9	109	38.0	9			2	9	92	10.2		16			
POTTSVILLE																																															
Latone	12	136	407	3.0						12	1	2	50	10	5.0									12	6	140	23.3																				
Kirkleski	12	146	350	2.4	1					12	42	116	36	730	6.3	3	17							12	5	49	9.8						11	95	33.6	1	2	35.0	11	12	99	8.3		1			
Wentz	12	113	333	2.9	2					12	0	3	0											12	4	50	12.5						11	8	36.5	1			11	1	33	33.0		1			
Carr (2)	5	28	105	3.8	1					5	2	7	29	42	6.0									5	2	28	14.0	1					5	17	33.7				5	1	-5	-5.0					
Moore	7	30	60	2.0	1					7	3	8	38	27	3.4		1							7	7	140	20.0	1					6	3	41.0	1			6	13	177	13.6					
Scharer	11	10	35	3.5						11	3	9	33	58	6.4		4							11	2	30	15.0												10	7	75	10.7		1			
Roberts	8	3	9	3.0						8	1	3	33	23	7.7		1							8	3	38	12.7						7	15	29.2	1			7	3	23	7.7		1			
Doane (1)	2	7	7	1.0																																											
Ernst	12	12	5	0.4						12	15	41	37	222	6.0	1	7							12	9	183	20.3						11	1	30.0	1			11	1	11	11.0		1			
Millman	3	3	-1	-0.3																				3	1	10	10.0																				
Kenneally																								13	19	308	16.2	1																			
Hultman																								9	4	73	18.3	1																			
Mullen (2)																								8	4	34	8.5																				
Ford (1)																								2	1	29	29.0																				
Team	13	488	1310	2.7	5					13	67	189	35	1112	5.9	4	31																12	139	33.4	1			10	38	413	10.9		1			
Opp.	13	520	1512	2.9	10					13	77	181	43	1175	6.5	8	19																12	134	36.4	1			12	29	374	12.9					
CHICAGO CARDINALS																																															
Jones	4	29	74	2.6	2	5	1	2		4	3	12	25	36	3.0		3	5	2	2	31			4	6	79	13.2		5	3	46		4	1	30.0	5											
Lamb	3	21	73	3.5		6	1	2	1	3	5	12	42	39	3.3		1	6	1	1	25			3	2	22	11.0		6	1	54		3	1	45.0	6			2	3	35	11.7		7			
McDonnell	3	22	45	2.0		6	2	17		3	3	8	38	60	7.5	1	1	6	2	2	21																		2	5	77	15.4		7	2	90	
Erickson	3	11	52	4.7		5				3	2	4	50	10	2.5		1	5	1	1	14			3	3	20	6.7		5				3	7	33.9	5											
Roach	1	15	27	1.8	1					1	0	1	0											1	2	16	8.0						1	1	33.0				1	1	10	10.0					
Bucklin	3	26	25	1.0		6	1	1	1															3	3	25	8.3		6				3	1	50.0	6											
Moran (2)	2	17	25	1.5		2	1	1	1	2	3	7	43	40	5.7			2						2	1	9	9.0		2				2	1	0.0	2											
Risvold	1	7	13	1.9		6	1	11																																							
Mahoney	3	8	20	2.5		6				3	2	4	50	21	5.3			6	3	3	101	1		3					6	2	36								2	2	11	5.5		7			
Strader	2	6	13	2.2		4	3	4	1	2	2	4	50	14	3.5		1	4	1	1	25			2					4	1	22								2					4	1	15	
Hogan	1	7	17	2.4	1																												1	3	30.3												
Hummel	2					6	2	4																																							
Swanson	1	1	0	0.0		6				2								5	2	2	36			2	1	10	10.0		5	2	49		2	28	37.1	5			1					6	1	40	
Weller										4	2	2	100	32	16.0			7						4	2	42	21.0	1	7				4	11	36.9	7											
Vesser																								4	1	12	12.0		7	2	37	1															
Chamberlin																								2	1	17	17.0		4																		
Blumer																																	3	2	22.5	6											
Team	4	170	384	2.3	4	7				4	22	54	41	252	4.7	1	7	7															4	56	35.3	7			3	11	133	12.1		8			
Opp.	4	141	403	2.9	3	7				5	32	95	34	502	5.3	1	15	6															4	49	37.3	7			4	17	164	9.6		7			
DAYTON																																															
Achul	2	17	-4	-0.2		5	4	22																2	2	17	8.5		5										2	2	14	7.0		5	2	50	
Tays	1	9	14	1.6		6	6	2		1	0	2	0				1	6	1	4	16		3										1			6	1	37.0	1	1	3	3.0		6	1	12	
Mahrt	1	5	12	2.4		1				1	9	18	50	76	4.2		2	1	1	1	35												1	1	29.0	1											
Abbott	1	4	-1	-0.2		6	3	13																									1	9	30.4	6	3	38.3	1					6	1	34	
Britton (1)	2	3	10	3.3		6				2	2	7	29	42	6.0		1	6	1	6	7		4										2	13	33.8	6	12	38.8									
Partlow						5	1	8																																							
Sillin	2	10	7	0.7		5																		2	3	53	17.7		5																		
Cabrinha	1	3	-1	-0.3		2																																									
R. Joseph																								2	5	38	7.6		6	2	23																
Fenner																								1	1	10	10.0		5																		
Team	2	51	37	0.7		6				2	11	27	41	118	4.4		4	6															2	23	32.3	6			2	3	17	5.7		6			
Opp.	2	81	241	3.0	3	6				2	5	22	23	89	4.0		1	6															2	23	32.7	6			2	4	32	8.0		6			
DULUTH																																															
Nevers	5	71	247	3.5	1	4	12	59	3	9	89	197	45	1362	6.9	5	17																5	48	36.5	4	2	44.0	3	1	6	6.0		6			
Blood	5	40	120	3.0		4	1	30		9	1	4	25	22	5.5									4	17	297	17.5		5	4	74	1	5	9	30.8	4			3	3	22	7.3		6			
C. Rooney	5	21	61	2.9		3	1	11	1															4	10	118	11.8		4	9	181								3	2	14	7.0		5			
Clark (2)	5	18	21	1.1		1																		4	2	25	12.5		2										3	3	39	13.0		3	1	12	
Method	5	5	21	4.2		3																		4	4	54	13.5	1	4																		
Belden	3	2	4	2.0		3				6	1	2	50	10	5.0									3	2	17	8.5		3	2	24																
J. Rooney																								4	6	151	25.2	3	5																		
Team	5	157	474	3.0	1	5				9	91	230	45	1394	6.9	5	17																5	57	35.6	4			3	9	81	9.0		6			
Opp.	4	163	525	3.2	2	5				7	49	130	38	800	6.2	5	20	2															4	39	36.2	5			4	22	228	10.4		5			
Hobson	1	11	13	1.2		4	1	1																																							
Carr (1)	1	15	8	0.5		4	5	3	1	1	2	10	20	16	1.6		2	4	3	16	50		7										1	10	41.6	4	15	32.3	1	3	54	18.0		4			
Hauser	1	3	11	3.7		1																																									
Roderick						3	2	5																												3	1	45.0									
Watson																								1	2	16	8.0		1																		
Van Horn																													4	1	26																
Roy																													3	1	15																
Underwood (2)																													3	1	9																
Team	1	29	32	1.1		4				1	2	10	20	16	1.6		2	4															1	10	41.6	4			1	3	54	18.0		4			
Opp.	1	52	135	2.6	1	4				1	7	16	44	110	6.9	2	3	4															1	11	43.0	4			1	4	57	14.3		4			

1928 N.F.L.
Steamrolled By Providence

The 1928 pennant would fly over a 10,000-seat, oval set of bleachers that had been built to house bicycle races in Providence, Rhode Island. The Cycledome had no lockerroom for visiting teams, whose players had to dress and shower in their hotel. The home team was jammed into a lockerroom built to house two bicycle racers. The wooden cycle track ran within a few yards of each sideline, making sideline plays real adventures. At one end of the field, the track cut across the endzone five yards beyond the goalline. Despite its flaws, this was home for the NFL's toughest defensive squad and surprise champs, the Providence Steam Roller. Jimmy Conzelman coached the club and also played blocking back for four games until he ripped up his knee. The Steam Roller had a nationally known star in tailback Wildcat Wilson, a 1925 All-American from Washington who ran powerfully, passed well and excelled as a cornerback. Curly Oden, a local favorite from Brown University, furnished a breakaway threat as a kick returner and pass receiver. The line was the heart of the team and featured two professional wrestlers, Gus Sonnenberg and John Spellman, neither of whom wore helmets. The key additions, center Clyde Smith and guard Milt Rehnquist, came from the Cleveland Bulldogs, who folded after last season. This bunch enjoyed an 8-1-2 season, allowed opponents only 42 points, and did not give up a single rushing touchdown all season.

The Steam Roller's road to the top was paved with the early-season stumblings of last season's top three teams. The New York Giants, the 1927 champions, opened the season with two victories, then lost 13-0 to the Chicago Bears and 28-0 to the new Detroit Wolverines to fall off the pace. Complacency plagued the Giants, as did a nagging backfield problem. Hinkey Haines had retired after last season, and heralded rookie Bruce Caldwell from Yale was a bust. Haines returned after the loss to the Bears, but the momentum had already slipped away. The Green Bay Packers began their season with a loss to the Frankford Yellowjackets, a tie with the Bears and a loss to the Giants, all at home, to fatally hurt their title hopes. The Bears, with several key players growing old, were 2-0-1 but then lost to the Packers and Wolverines at home.

With these favorites slow out of the gate, the leading clubs at the start of November were Providence, Frankford and Detroit. The Steam Roller had a 4-1 record, having lost to Frankford and beaten only lesser teams. The Yellowjackets also had a 4-1 mark, with impressive victories over Providence and Green Bay offset only by a 13-0 loss at home to the New York Yankees. Like Providence, Frankford relied on a strong defense, anchored by tackle Bull Behman and rookie fullback Wally Diehl from Bucknell. The new Detroit Wolverines were the early sensation of the league, beating the Yankees 35-12, the Giants 28-0 and the Bears 6-0. The Wolverines signed many players from the defunct Cleveland Bulldogs. They featured fullback Tiny Feather, ends Carl Bacchus and Lyle Munn, and center Joe Westoupal, but the key to their success was tailback Benny Friedman, the league's top offensive force. In his second NFL season, Friedman led the circuit in scoring with 55 points, was the top passer with well over a thousand yards, and, although we lack complete records, may have been the foremost rusher.

After their first three victories, the Wolverines began November with a three-game, two-week Eastern trip. On Saturday, November 3, they were trounced 25-7 by the Yellowjackets on a muddy field in Frankford. An overnight train ride brought the weary Wolverines to their Sunday date in Providence, which the Steam Roller won 7-0. The next Sunday, the Giants held the Wolverines to a 19-19 tie and, despite winning every game the rest of the way, Detroit never regained first place. And, despite the team's offensive fireworks, they couldn't make a go of it at the gate. When they closed up shop after only one NFL season, their 7-2-1 mark gave the Wolverines the best lifetime percentage (.778) of any team in NFL history.

More teams were using the forward pass as an integral part of the offense. Correspondingly, the number of interceptions soared. The Green Bay Packers, who threw more passes than anyone else, also intercepted the most. Their 39 grabs of enemy tosses were led by Eddie Kotal's 10.

1928 STANDINGS

	W	L	T	Pct.	Pts.	Opp. Pts.	Avg. Pts.	Opp. Avg.
Providence Steam Roller	8	1	2	.889	128	42	12	4
Frankford Yellow Jackets	11	3	2	.786	175	84	11	5
Detroit Wolverines	7	2	1	.778	189	76	19	8
Green Bay Packers	6	4	3	.600	120	92	9	7
Chicago Bears	7	5	1	.583	182	85	14	7
New York Giants	4	7	2	.364	79	136	6	10
New York Yankees	4	8	1	.333	103	179	8	14
Pottsville Maroons	2	8	0	.200	74	134	7	13
Chicago Cardinals	1	5	0	.167	7	107	1	18
Dayton Traingles (R)	0	7	0	.000	9	131	1	19

(R) — played only night games

Scoring Leaders

Friedman	Det	55
Lewellen	GB	54
Welch	NYY	48
Feather	Det	42
Mercer	Fra	38
Senn	ChiB	37
Diehl	Fra	30
Haines	NYG	30
W. Wilson	Prov	30
Sternaman	ChiB	30
Oden	Prov	27

KICKING

		FG	Att	Pct
O'Boyle	GB	3	6	50
Abbott	Day	1	1	100
Caldwell	NYG	1	2	50
Roepke	Fra	1	2	50
Sonnenberg	Prov	1	8	13
Budd	Pott	0	1	0
Grube	NYY	0	1	0
Moran	Pott-NYG	0	1	0
McBride	NYG	0	2	0
Molenda	NYY-GB	0	2	0
Oden	Prov	0	2	0
Mercer	Fra	0	3	0
Driscoll	ChiB	0	4	0

		PAT	Att	Pct
Friedman	Det	19	26	73
Driscoll	ChiB	8	11	73
O'Boyle	GB	8	14	57
Sternaman	ChiB	6	8	75
Sonnenberg	Prov	6	10	60
Budd	Pott	3	6	50
Molenda	NYY-GB	3	7	43
Henry	Pott	2	3	67
Oden	Prov	2	4	50
McBride	NYG	2	5	40
Smith	NYY	2	7	29
Mercer	Fra	2	12	17
Eckhardt	NYG	1	1	100
Grant	ChiC	1	1	100

		PAT	Att	Pct
Grube	NYY	1	1	100
Pritchard	NYY	1	1	100
Scharer	Det	1	1	100
Wiberg	Det	1	1	100
Dunn	GB	1	2	50
Elkins	Fra	1	2	50
Weir	Fra	1	2	50
Roepke	Fra	1	3	33
Wilson	NYG	1	3	33
Senn	ChiB	1	4	25

Abbot-Day, Behman-Fra, Bloodgood-NYG, Ernst-Pott, Flaherty-NYG-NYY, Hadden-Prov, Haines-NYG, Moran-Pott-NYG, Rogers-Fra, Romney-ChiB all 0-1.

PROVIDENCE STEAM ROLLER 8-1-2 Jimmy Conzelman

Regulars

UseName	Pos.	Hgt.	Wgt.	Age	Int	Pts.
Duke Hanny	E	6'	200	30	1	6
John Spellman	E-T	5'10"	200	29	1	
Perry Jackson	T	6'1"	200	25		
Gus Sonnenberg	T-TB	5'6"	200	30		10
Jack Fleischman	G	5'6"	185	27		
Milt Rehnquist	G-C	6'	230	31	2	
Clyde Smith	C	5'10"	182	24		
Curly Oden	BB-WB	5'6"	160	29	1	27
Wildcat Wilson	TB	5'11"	200	27	4	30
Jim Simmons	WB-TB	6'	186	26		
Al Hadden (from ChiB)	FB-TB	5'9"	190	28		

Substitutes

UseName	Pos.	Hgt.	Wgt.	Age	Int	Pts.
Norm Harvey	E	6'	200	31		
Orland Smith	T	5'11"	215	22		
Abe Wilson	G	5'10"	192	28	1	
Jim Laird	G	6'	200	30	2	
Jimmy Conzelman	BB	6'	180	30		13
Jack Cronin	WB-TB-E	5"11"	175	25	2	18
Pop Williams	FB-WB	6'	205	22	1	24
Bill Cronin	FB-WB-E-BB	5'10"	180	27		

Scores of Each Game

Date	Pts.	Opponent	Pts.
Sep. 30	20	N.Y. YANKEES	7
Oct. 7	6	FRANKFORD	10
Oct. 14	28	DAYTON	0
Oct. 21	12	N.Y. Yankees	6
Oct. 28	13	POTTSVILLE	6
Nov. 4	7	DETROIT	0
Nov. 17	6	Frankford	6
Nov. 18	6	FRANKFORD	0
Nov. 25	16	N.Y. GIANTS	0
Nov. 29	7	Pottsville	0
Dec. 2	7	GREEN BAY	7

FRANKFORD YELLOWJACKETS 11-3-2 Ed Weir

Regulars

UseName	Pos.	Hgt.	Wgt.	Age	Int	Pts.
Chuck Kassel	E	6'1"	190	24	1	6
Tony Kostos	E-C	5'11"	190	23	3	2
Bull Behman	T	5'10"	210	28		
Bub Weller	T	6'4"	238	26	1	
Hal Hanson	G	6'1"	205	23		
Rudy Comstock	G	5'10"	210	27		
Joey Maxwell	C	6'2"	195	23	2	
Ken Mercer	BB-TB	5'11"	180	25	2	38
Charley Rogers	TB	5'10"	163	24	1	18
Arnie Oehlrich	WB	5'11"	185	22	5	12
Wally Diehl	FB	6'	192	24	5	30

Substitutes

UseName	Pos.	Hgt.	Wgt.	Age	Int	Pts.
E.A. Dobrey	E	5'11"	175			
Carl Waite	E-WB	5'9"	205	26	2	6
Ed Weir	T-E	5'10"	192	25	1	7
Jack Filak	T-G	6'	190	24		
Roger Mahoney	C-G-E	6'	195	22	3	
Two Bits Homan	BB	5'5"	144	26		6
John Roepke	TB-WB	5'11"	175	22	1	10
Chief Elkins	FB-TB-WB-E	5'11"	190	23	3	13
Hust Stockton	FB-TB	5'11"	195	26	4	24

Babe Connaughton — injured in fire May 24, 1928

Scores of Each Game

Date	Pts.	Opponent	Pts.
Sep. 23	19	Green Bay	9
Sep. 29	6	DAYTON	0
Oct. 7	10	Providence	6
Oct. 13	0	N.Y. YANKEES	13
Oct. 20	13	DAYTON	9
Nov. 3	25	DETROIT	7
Nov. 4	0	N.Y. Giants	0
Nov. 10	19	POTTSVILLE	0
Nov. 11	24	Pottsville	0
Nov. 17	6	PROVIDENCE	6
Nov. 18	0	Providence	6
Nov. 24	19	CHIC. CARDS	0
Nov. 29	2	GREEN BAY	0
Dec. 2	6	Chic. Bears	28
Dec. 8	7	N.Y. GIANTS	0
Dec. 15	19	CHIC. BEARS	0

DETROIT WOLVERINES 7-2-1 Roy Andrews

Regulars

UseName	Pos.	Hgt.	Wgt.	Age	Int	Pts.
Lyle Munn	E	6'	190	26		
Carl Bacchus	E	6'	210	24		24
Tom Cobb	T	5'11"	250	24		
Bill Owen	T	6'	210	24		
Les Caywood	G-T	6'	240	23	1	
Dosey Howard	G	6'	225	27		
Joe Westoupal	C	6'3"	210	25		
Ossie Wiberg	BB	5'11"	210	23	1	13
Benny Friedman	TB	5'10"	185	23	2	55
Len Sedbrook	WB-TB	5'10"	175	23	3	24
Tiny Feather	FB	6'	195	25	2	42

Substitutes

UseName	Pos.	Hgt.	Wgt.	Age	Int	Pts.
Proc Randels	E	6'	180	28		6
Ludwig Bachor	T	6'	215	27		
Chet Widerquist (from, to ChiC)	G-T	6'1"	220	32		
Ernie Vick (from ChiB)	G-T	5'10"	195	28		
John Barrett	C-T	5'6"	170	29		
Eddie Scharer	TB-BB-WB	5'6"	165	26		1
Rex Thomas	WB-FB	5'9"	175	27	1	12
Pete Jackson	FB-BB-WB	5'10"	200	24	1	12

Scores of Each Game

Date	Pts.	Opponent	Pts.
Oct. 14	35	N.Y. Yankees	12
Oct. 21	28	N.Y. GIANTS	0
Oct. 28	6	Chic. Bears	0
Nov. 3	7	Frankford	25
Nov. 4	0	Providence	7
Nov. 11	19	N.Y. Giants	19
Nov. 18	13	N.Y. YANKEES	0
Nov. 25	14	Chic. Bears	7
Nov. 29	33	DAYTON	0
Dec. 9	34	N.Y. Yankees	6

On November 10 at Pottsville, the ball changed hands constantly. Pottsville picked off eight Frankford Yellowjacket passes, including seven from Hust Stockton. Meanwhile, the Yellowjackets intercepted four Maroon passes, for a total of 12 in the game. Although out-intercepted, Frankford won 19-0.

The next key confrontations in the championship race came on the weekend of November 17-18, when the Yellowjackets and Steam Roller played a home-and-away series. A full house of 15,000 spectators saw two defensive clubs pit strength against strength on Saturday. The Yellowjackets scored on a blocked punt in the third quarter, missing the extra point for a 6-0 lead. Late in the fourth quarter a poor punt gave Providence good field position, and Wildcat Wilson's plunge capped a scoring drive. Oden missed the extra point and the game ended 6-6. The teams reassembled in Providence the next day before an overflow crowd of 11,000 in the Cycledome, and a 46-yard pass play from Wilson to Oden was the only score in a bruising 6-0 Providence victory.

One week later, the Giants came to Providence. The defending champions had a 4-3-2 record and a decidedly mediocre tone to their play despite consistently fine work from linemen Cal Hubbard and Steve Owen. The Steam Roller won 16-0 and the Giants went on to lose their three remaining games to finish 4-7-2. The Providence players had three days off before playing Thanksgiving Day in Pottsville against the Maroons. Although fielding a weakened squad not even close to the strength of the 1925 team, the Maroons still featured fine backs in Tony Latone and ex-Duluth Eskimo Johnny Blood. They were coming off a surprise 26-0 crushing of the Green Bay Packers on Sunday in a snowstorm. With the field a muddy mess, the Steam Roller won the game 7-0, using only 11 men until wingback Jack Cronin had to leave the game with a broken nose late in the fourth quarter.

After two days of rest, the Steam Roller took on the Packers in Providence. The Packers featured Verne Lewellen, a fine runner and defender as well as the NFL's best punter, averaging 41.1 yards on 136 boots in 1928. He had just been elected district attorney of Brown County (which includes Green Bay). Lewellen and Red Dunn shared the Green Bay passing chores; halfback Eddie Kotal and Lavie Dilweg, the league's best all-around end, were the top receivers. Both teams scored on third quarter passes, but the Steam Roller had a chance to win in the final period with the score tied 7-7. The 1927 placement of the goalposts on the backline of the endzone had made field goals comparatively rare — only seven were kicked all season — but, when Providence stood fourth-and-three on the Green Bay six-yard line, Gus Sonnenberg lined up for a placekick. Green Bay fullback Harry O'Boyle drove through the line and blocked the kick. The Steam Roller had to settle for a tie, bu it turned out that was all they needed. In Chicago, the Yellowjackets were suffering a 28-6 beating at the hands of the Bears. Paddy Driscoll recalled his youth with a touchdown pass, a touchdown run, a 48-yard sprint to set up another touchdown, and three extra points by dropkick. With this loss, the Yellowjackets were eliminated and the Steam Roller crowned champion for 1928.

A review of this season must note the absence of several famous faces. Ernie Nevers spent his summer piching for the St. Louis Browns and then decided to accept an offer to be an asistant coach with Pop Warner at Stanford; the Duluth Eskimos had no reason to exist without him and promptly suspended operations. Joining Nevers on the sideline were Red Grange and Eddie Tryon, the glamor backs of the New York Yankees. Grange's bad knee kept him off the field, while Tryon decided to play for Orange, an independent team. The NFL public also had a brief encore from Jim Thorpe, who played a few minutes for the Chicago Cardinals in their 34-0 loss to the Bears on Thanksgiving Day. The *Associated Press* reported, "In his forties and muscle-bound, Thorpe was a mere shadow of his former self." Grange and Nevers would return to uniform, but this was Thorpe's final appearance.

The *Green Bay Press Gazette* annual all-NFL poll chose Clyde Smith of Providence at center. Smith, who played only three seasons in the NFL, had the unusual record of being named all-league center in the poll all three seasons for three different teams. Other selections were: ends Lavie Dilweg, Green Bay, and Ray Flaherty, Yankees; tackles Bill Owen (Steve's brother), Detroit, and Bull Behman, Frankford; guards Mike Michalske, Yankees, and Jim McMillin, Bears; quarterback Benny Friedman, Detroit; halfbacks Wildcat Wilson, Providence, and Verne Lewellen, Green Bay; and fullback Wally Diehl, Frankford. Gus Sonnenberg, Milt Rehnquist and Curly Oden, all of Providence, were named to the second team.

NAME	RUSHING Complete Games					RUSHING Incom. Games				PASSING Complete Games								PASSING Incom. Games					
	G	Att.	Yds.	Avg.	TD	G	Att.	Yds.	TD	G	Com.	Att.	%	Yds.	Y/A	TD	Int	G	Com.	Att.	Yds.	TD	Int.
PROVIDENCE																							
W. Wilson	7	89	445	5.0	4	4	5	26	1	10	52	136	38	851	6.3	5	19	1	3	7	69		2
Hadden (2)	6	59	130	2.2		3	6	30															
J. Cronin	6	38	127	3.3	3	2				8	0	1	0										
Williams	2	5	40	8.0		5	13	60	3														
Oden	6	90	74	3.2		5	4	11	1	9	1	4	25	15	3.8			2	0	1			
Simmons	5	19	44	2.3		3	4	31															
B. Cronin	5	10	25	2.5		4	5	3															
Sonnenberg	7	3	14	4.7		4	1	10		9	0	1	0					2	1	1	19	1	
Conzelman										2	1	4	25	10	2.5			2	0	1			
Hanny																							
Harvey																							
Team	6	220	809	3.7	5	5				9	45	128	35	724	5.7	5	19	2					
Opp.	4	114	329	2.3		7				8	52	153	34	693	4.5	1	14	3					
FRANKFORD																							
Diehl	9	121	475	3.9	3	5	8	94		12	21	62	4	216	3.5	3	7	2					
Rogers	9	90	373	4.1	1	4	3	64		12	4	14	29	67	4.8		4	2					
Mercer	9	51	187	3.7	2	5	14	72	3	12	26	69	38	322	4.7	4	7	2	13	21	203	1	4
Stockton	9	66	249	3.8	3	4				11	23	67	34	371	5.5		17	2					
Elkins	7	43	150	3.5		3	3	17		8	3	7	43	45	6.4		2	2					
Roepke	5	19	59	3.1	1	5	1	8		8	4	11	36	85	7.7	1	2	2					
Oehlrich	11	29	55	1.9		5	2	10															
Homan	8	8	31	3.9		3	2	19		9	1	1	100	11	11.0			2					
Waite	6	5	22	4.4		2																	
Kostos																							
Kassel																							
Weir																							
Mahoney																							
Behman																							
Team	11	432	1601	3.7	10	5				14	82	231	35	1117	4.8	8	39	2					
Opp.	12	319	908	2.8	2	4				14	98	271	36	1420	5.2	4	39	2					
DETROIT																							
Friedman	3	38	335	8.8	1	7	32	240	5	8	66	140	47	1144	8.2	7	11	2	11	15	204	3	4
Feather	1	10	41	4.1		9	16	66	5														
Sedbrook	1	3	17	5.7		8	5	80	1														
Thomas	1					9	4	33	1	8	1	2	50	30	15.0	1		2	1	1	35	1	
Jackson	1	2	7	3.5		4	3	14	2														
Wiberg	1	1	1	1.0		9	1	10		8	1	2	50	14	7.0			2	0	1			1
Scharer	1	2	6	3.0		6				0	5	17	29	79	4.6		2	1	2	2	27		
Bacchus																							
Munn																							
Randels																							
Team	1	27	119	4.4		9				8	73	162	45	1267	7.8	8	13	2					
Opp.	1	45	226	5.0	1	9				4	16	49	33	205	4.2	2	5	6					

NAME	RECEIVING Complete Games					RECEIVING Incom. Games				PUNTING Comp. Games			PUNTING Incom. Games			PUNT RETURNS Complete Games					PUNT RETURNS Incom. Games			
	G	Rec.	Yds	Avg.	TD	G	Rec.	Yds.	TD	G	No.	Avg.	G	No.	Avg.	G	No.	Yds.	Avg.	TD	G	No.	Yds.	TD
PROVIDENCE																								
W. Wilson										4	40	37.3	7	4	52.0	5					6	1	36	
Hadden (2)	6	2	23	11.5		3																		
J. Cronin	6	1	17	17.0		2				4	1	49.0	4	4	45.5									
Williams	2					5	2	41	1															
Oden	6	15	279	18.6	3	5	4	75		4	1	16.0	7			5	17	288	16.9		6	3	77	
Simmons	5					3	2	34																
B. Cronin	5	1	20	20.0		4										4	4	48	12.0		5			
Sonnenberg										4	4	28.8	7											
Conzelman						4	9	132	2															
Hanny	6	5	116	23.2		5																		
Harvey	5					4	4	107																
Team										4	46	36.3	7			5	21	336	16.0		6			
Opp.										4	43	39.7	7			4	13	139	10.7		7			
FRANKFORD																								
Diehl	10	6	76	12.3		4	1	10	1	11	88	33.9	3	4	23.8	10	3	36	12.0		4			
Rogers	10	10	131	13.1	2	3										10	43	528	12.3		3			
Mercer	10	4	40	10.0		4	2	28		11	19	34.2	3	2	25.0	10	2	43	21.5		4			
Stockton																9	1	34	34.0		4			
Elkins	8	1	12	12.0		2				7	14	40.2	3	2	40.0	7	2	26	13.0		3			
Roepke	6					4	2	69		6	18	37.6	4	1	25.0									
Oehlrich	12	18	234	13.0	2	4	3	34								12	4	37	9.3		4			
Homan	9	6	139	23.2		2	1	35	1							8	20	281	14.1		3	4	52	
Waite	8	2	28	14.0	1																			
Kostos	12	11	119	10.8		4	4	64								12	1	10	10.0		4			
Kassel	10	7	108	15.4	1	4	2	26								11	1	10	10.0		3			
Weir	11	1	27	27.0		3																		
Mahoney	10	1	10	10.0		4																		
Behman										12	2	37.5	4											
Team										12	141	35.1	4			12	77	1005	13.1		4			
Opp.										12	152	36.2	4			12	58	752	13.0		4			
DETROIT																								
Friedman	1	1	14	14.0		9				1	1	44.0	9			2	4	44	11.0		8	3	71	
Feather	1					9	6	121	2															
Sedbrook	1	6	124	20.7	1	8	6	141	1															
Thomas	1					9	9	170	1															
Jackson						5	1	11																
Wiberg	1	1	15	15.0		9	8	148	2	1	6	34.0	9	3	28.3	1	2	19	9.5		9			
Scharer	1					6	1	20								1	1	7	7.0		6			
Bacchus						9	9	234	4							1	2	44	22.0		8			
Munn	1					9	3	69																
Randels	1	2	30	15.0		9	2	45	1															
Team										1	7	35.4	9			1	5	70	14.0		9			
Opp.										1	9	32.3	9			1	7	100	14.3		9			

GREEN BAY PACKERS 6-4-3 Curly Lambeau

Regulars

UseName	Pos.	Hgt.	Wgt.	Age	Int.	Pts.
Lavie Dilweg	E	6'3	200	25	5	
Dick O'Donnell	E	6'	195	28	3	6
Marion Ashmore	T-E	6'	220	25		
Tiny Cahoon	T	6'2	238	28		
Bruce Jones	G	6'1	220	23	1	6
Jim Bowdoin	G	6'1	218	22		
Jug Earp	C-T	6'	235	31		
Red Dunn	BB	5'11	185	26	2	1
Verne Lewellen	TB-BB	6'1	187	26	4	54
Eddie Kotal	HB-TB	5'8	175	26	10	18
Harry O'Boyle	FB	5'9	175	23	3	23

Substitutes

UseName	Pos.	Hgt.	Wgt.	Age	Int.	Pts.
Tom Nash	E	6'3	210	22	3	
Dutch Webber	E	6'2	190	26	1	
Claude Perry	T	6'1	202	26		
Whitey Woodin	G	5'10	214	33		
Paul Minick	G	6'1	200	28	1	
Boob Darling	C	5'11	205	24		
Curly Lambeau	BB-FB-TB-E	5'10	195	30	1	
Larry Marks	HB-TB-FB	5'11	185	25	2	12
Bullet Baker	HB-BB-FB	5'8	175	28	2	
Bo Molenda (from NYY)	FB	5'10	200	23	2	

Cully Lidberg — Voluntarily Retired

Substitutes

UseName	Pos.	Hgt.	Wgt.	Age	Int.	Pts.
Hal Griffen	C	6'1	248	26		
Tom Hearden	HB	5'9	180	23		
Slick Lollar	FB	5'11	200	22		

Scores of each game

Date	Pts.	Opponent	Pts.
Sep. 23	9	FRANKFORD	19
Sep. 30	12	CHIC. BEARS	12
Oct. 7	0	N.Y. GIANTS	6
Oct. 14	20	CHIC. CARDS	0
Oct. 21	16	Chic. Bears	6
Oct. 28	17	DAYTON	0
Nov. 4	26	POTTSVILLE	14
Nov. 11	0	N.Y. YANKEES	0
Nov. 18	7	N.Y. Giants	0
Nov. 25	0	Pottsville	26
Nov. 29	0	Frankford	2
Dec. 2	7	Providence	7
Dec. 9	6	Chic. Bears	0

CHICAGO BEARS 7-5-1 George Halas

Regulars

UseName	Pos.	Hgt.	Wgt.	Age	Int.	Pts.
Ted Drews	E	6'	190	25		1
Tillie Voss	E	6'3	210	31		6
Don Murry	T	6'2	192	28	1	
Link Lyman	T	6'2	220	29	1	
Jim McMillen	G	6'1	217	25		
Bill Buckler	G-C	6'	215	27		
George Trafton	C	6'2	227	31	3	
Joey Sternaman	QB	5'6	155	28	1	30
Paddy Driscoll	HB	5'8	175	33	1	20
Laurie Walquist	HB	5'8	170	30	3	12
Buck White	FB	6'	195	27		18

Substitutes

UseName	Pos.	Hgt.	Wgt.	Age	Int.	Pts.
Roy Carlson	E	5'9	175	23	1	6
John Wallace	E	6'	180	23	1	6
Buck Evans	T-G	5'11	200	28		
Ed Kailina	T-G	6'	205	27		
Bill Fleckenstein	G-C	6'1	210	24	1	6
Ernie Vick (to DET)	C	5'10	195	28		
Milt Romney	QB	5'8	160	29		13
Dick Sturtridge	HB	5'8	170	24		19
Bill Senn	HB	6'	180	23	2	37
Elmer Wynne	FB	6'1	190	27	1	

Substitutes

UseName	Pos.	Hgt.	Wgt.	Age	Int.	Pts.
Reggie Russell	E		190			
George Halas	E	6'	182	33		6
Al Hadden (to PROV)	HB	5'9	190	28		

Scores of each game

Date	Pts.	Opponent	Pts.
Sep. 23	15	Chic. Cards	0
Sep. 30	12	Green Bay	12
Oct. 14	13	N.Y. GIANTS	0
Oct. 21	6	GREEN BAY	16
Oct. 28	0	DETROIT	6
Nov. 4	27	N.Y. YANKEES	0
Nov. 11	27	DAYTON	0
Nov. 18	13	POTTSVILLE	6
Nov. 25	7	DETROIT	14
Nov. 29	34	CHIC. CARDS	0
Dec. 2	28	FRANKFORD	6
Dec. 9	0	GREEN BAY	6
Dec. 15	0	Frankford	19

NEW YORK GIANTS 4-7-2 Earl Potteiger

Regulars

UseName	Pos.	Hgt.	Wgt.	Age	Int.	Pts.
Neely Allison	E	6'	190	26	1	
Cal Hubbard	E-C	6'4	255	27	2	
Rosey Rosatti	T	6'	210	32		
Steve Owen	T-G	5'10	240	30		
Paul Jappe	G-E	6'1	195	30		
Hec Garvey	G	6'1	240	28		
Mickey Murtagh	C-G	6'1	190	25		
Hinkey Haines	BB-TB-FB	5'10	170	29		30
Jack McBride	TB	5'11	185	26	1	8
Mule Wilson	WB	5'11	195	26	5	7
Ox Eckhardt	FB-WB	6'1	190	26	1	13

Substitutes

UseName	Pos.	Hgt.	Wgt.	Age	Int.	Pts.
Ray Flaherty (to NYY)	E	6'	193	24		
Red Smith (to NYY)	E	5'10	188	24		
Century Milstead	T	6'1	213	28	1	
John Holman	T			26		
Al Nesser	G	6'	196	35		
Bug Hartzog	G-T-C	5'11	195	27		
Bull Wesley	C-T	6'1	190	26	1	
Jack Hagerty	BB-WB-TB	5'9	160	25	2	
Bruce Caldwell	TB-FB	6'	190	22	2	9
Earl Potteiger	BB-E-WB	5'7	170	37	2	
Tony Plansky	FB-BB-WB	6'2	205	28		6

Chuck Corgan - died of cancer, June 13, 1928

Substitutes

UseName	Pos.	Hgt.	Wgt.	Age	Int.	Pts.
Paul Schuette	G	6'	215	22		
Babe Parnell	G	6'3	205	26		
Max Reed	C	5'8	185	26		
Al Bloodgood	BB	5'8	150	26		6
Hap Moran (from POTT)	TB	6'1	190	27		

Scores of each game

Date	Pts.	Opponent	Pts.
Sep. 30	12	Pottsville	6
Oct. 7	6	Green Bay	0
Oct. 14	0	Chic. Bears	13
Oct. 21	0	Detroit	28
Oct. 28	10	N.Y. Yankees	7
Nov. 4	0	FRANKFORD	0
Nov. 6	13	POTTSVILLE	7
Nov. 11	19	DETROIT	19
Nov. 18	0	GREEN BAY	7
Nov. 25	0	Providence	16
Dec. 2	13	N.Y. YANKEES	19
Dec. 8	0	Frankford	7
Dec. 16	6	N.Y. Yankees	7

NEW YORK YANKEES 4-8-1 Dick Rauch

Regulars

UseName	Pos.	Hgt.	Wgt.	Age	Int.	Pts.
Ray Flaherty (from NYG)	E	6'	193	24	3	6
Frank Grube	E	5'9	180	23	1	1
Ed Gallagher	T	6'1	205	25		
Harvey Levy	T-G	5'10	212	26		
Murrell Hogue	G-T	6'1	215	26	1	
Mike Michalske	G	6'	200	25		
Jack McArthur	C	5'11	210	24		
Red Smith (from NYG)	BB-TB-FB-E	5'10	188	24	2	48
Wild Bill Kelly	TB	5'10	185	23	1	12
Gibby Welch	WB-TB-BB	5'11	176	23	8	20
Bo Molenda (to GB)	FB	5'10	200	23	1	3

Substitutes

UseName	Pos.	Hgt.	Wgt.	Age	Int.	Pts.
Red Badgro	E	6'	190	25		
Frank McGrath	E	5'11	190	24		
Joe McClain	T	6'	200	23		
Hec Cyre	T-G	6'2	215	26		
Dick Rauch	C-G	5'9	178	35		
Jack Ernst (from POTT)	BB	5'11	185	28		
Cobb Rooney	TB-WB-FB	6'	185	28		
Sam Salemi	WB	5'9	180	25	1	6
Bill Pritchard	FB-BB-WB	5'10	185	26	2	7

Substitutes

UseName	Pos.	Hgt.	Wgt.	Age	Int.	Pts.
John Colahan	T	6'3	212	23		
Frank Racis (from POTT)	T	6'	200	30		
Art Stevenson	C	6'	190	30		

Scores of each game

Date	Pts.	Opponent	Pts.
Sep. 30	7	Providence	20
Oct. 7	7	Pottsville	9
Oct. 13	13	Frankford	0
Oct. 14	12	DETROIT	35
Oct. 21	6	PROVIDENCE	12
Oct. 28	7	N.Y. GIANTS	10
Nov. 4	0	Chic. Bears	27
Nov. 11	0	Green Bay	0
Nov. 18	0	Detroit	13
Nov. 25	19	CHIC. CARDS	19
Dec. 2	19	N.Y. Giants	13
Dec. 9	6	DETROIT	34
Dec. 16	7	N.Y. GIANTS	6

POTTSVILLE MAROONS 2-8-0 Pete Henry

Regulars

UseName	Pos.	Hgt.	Wgt.	Age	Int.	Pts.
Joe Rooney	E	6'	185	30	1	6
George Kenneally	E	6'	190	26		6
Pete Henry	T	5'11	250	30		2
Johnny Budd	T	5'11	250	29		3
Frank Racis (to NYY)	G-E	6'	200	30		
Walt Kiesling	G-T	6'2	250	25		
Herb Stein	C-G	6'	190	30	2	
Jack Ernst (to NYY)	BB	5'11	185	28	1	12
Hap Moran (to NYG)	TB-WB	6'1	190	27	3	
Johnny Blood	WB-TB-FB	6'1	190	24	4	19
Tony Latone	FB-WB	5'11	200	31	6	18

Substitutes

UseName	Pos.	Hgt.	Wgt.	Age	Int.	Pts.
Earl Goodwin	E	6'1	195	24		
Joe Carpe	T-E	6'	200	25		
Duke Osborn	G-C	5'10	190	31	2	
Merl Goodwin	WB-BB-E	6'1	195	24	2	
Will Norman	WB-TB	6'	175	23	2	6
Barney Wentz	FB	5'11	210	27	1	

Scores of each game

Date	Pts.	Opponent	Pts.
Sep. 30	6	N.Y. GIANTS	12
Oct. 7	9	N.Y. YANKEES	7
Oct. 28	6	Providence	13
Nov. 4	14	Green Bay	26
Nov. 6	7	N.Y. Giants	13
Nov. 10	0	Frankford	19
Nov. 11	0	FRANKFORD	24
Nov. 18	6	Chic. Bears	13
Nov. 25	26	GREEN BAY	0
Nov. 29	0	PROVIDENCE	7

CHICAGO CARDINALS 1-5-0 Fred Gillies

Regulars

UseName	Pos.	Hgt.	Wgt.	Age	Int.	Pts.
Clem Neacy	E	6'3	203	30		
Herb Blumer	E-C-T	6'1	195	28		
Chet Widerquist (to & from DET)	T	6'1	220	32		
Duke Slater	T	6'1	215	29		
Joe Davidson	G	6'	200	25		
Charlie Strack	G	6'	215	26		
Ralph Claypool	C	5'11	190	29		
Ducky Grant	BB	5'11	175	25	1	
Mickey McDonnell	TB	5'8	160	24	1	1
Hal Erickson	WB-TB	5'9	190	29	2	6
Ben Jones	FB	5'11	197	28	1	

Substitutes

UseName	Pos.	Hgt.	Wgt.	Age	Int.	Pts.
Don Yeisley	E	6'1	185	23		
Bill Springsteen	E-C	6'	190	27	2	
Fred Gillies	T	6'3	210	32		
Hal Bradley	G		185	23		
Bill Stein	G	6'	190	29		
Paul Fitzgibbon	WB-BB-TB	5'8	175	25		
Ray Risvold	WB-BB-TB		170	26		
Ike Mahoney	WB-E	6'	178	26		
Ted Illman	FB-BB	6'	190	25		

Substitutes

UseName	Pos.	Hgt.	Wgt.	Age	Int.	Pts.
Ed Allen	E	5'8	175	27		
Jim Thorpe	E	6'1	210	41		
Homer Bliss	G	5'11	195	24		
Ray Marelli	G	5'10	190	27		
Lyons Killiher	G			25		
Jim Murphy	BB	6'	180	23		
Harry Curzon	FB	6'	195	32		

Scores of each game

Date	Pts.	Opponent	Pts.
Sep. 23	0	CHIC. BEARS	15
Oct. 7	7	DAYTON	0
Oct. 14	0	Green Bay	20
Nov. 24	0	Frankford	19
Nov. 25	0	N.Y. Yankees	19
Nov. 29	0	Chic. Bears	34

DAYTON TRIANGLES 0-7-0 Fay Abbott

Regulars

UseName	Pos.	Hgt.	Wgt.	Age	Int.	Pts.
Sam Hippa	E	5'11	165	27		
Carl Mankat	E	6'3	210	24		
Johnnie Becker	T-E	5'11	210	25		
Bill Belanich	T-E	6'	205	25		
Al Graham	G	6'	210	22		
Jim Spencer	G	6'	200	26		
Hobby Kinderdine	C	5'11	185	37		
Art Matsu	BB-WB	5'7	168	24	2	
Win Charles	TB-BB	5'9	160	24		
Clair Cook	WB	5'9	170	19		
Earl Britton	FB	6'	215	25	2	

Substitutes

UseName	Pos.	Hgt.	Wgt.	Age	Int.	Pts.
Mack Hummon	E	5'11	180	28		
Dick Faust	T-E-G	6'1	205	26		
Aubrey Strosnider	T	6'1	205	24		
Ed Seibert	G	5'10	190	25		
Corl Zimmerman	G	6'	185	29		
Jack Brown	C-T-G	6'	190	25		
Fay Abbott	BB-WB-FB	5'8	185	33		3
Jack Keefer	TB	5'9	178	28		
Frank Sillin	WB	5'11	180	25		6

Substitutes

UseName	Pos.	Hgt.	Wgt.	Age	Int.	Pts.
Ebby DeWeese	BB	6'	185	22		
Sneeze Achui	WB-TB-E-BB	5'8	168	26		
Clarence Graham	WB-BB					

Scores of each game

Date	Pts.	Opponent	Pts.
Sep. 29	0	Frankford	6
Oct. 7	0	Chic. Cards	7
Oct. 14	0	Providence	28
Oct. 20	9	Frankford	13
Oct. 28	0	Green Bay	17
Nov. 11	0	Chic. Bears	27
Nov. 29	0	Detroit	33

NAME	Rushing Complete Games G	Att.	Yds.	Avg.	TD	Rushing Incom. Games G	Att.	Yds.	TD	Passing Complete Games G	Com.	Att.	%	Yds.	Y/A	TD	Int.
GREEN BAY																	
Lewellen	13	106	349	3.3	6					13	29	87	33	402	4.6	1	10
Kotal	12	102	298	2.9	2					12	16	29	55	178	6.1	1	2
O'Boyle	13	86	270	3.1	1												
Marks	11	47	142	3.0						11	3	5	60	36	7.2		
Molenda (2)	4	33	123	3.7						4	1	2	50	7	3.5		
Dunn	12	51	97	1.9						12	45	123	37	700	5.7	4	12
Baker	11	52	64	1.2						11	0	4	0				2
Lambeau	8	10	14	1.4						8	11	30	37	149	5.0	1	3
Lollar	3	4	8	2.0													
Dilweg																	
O'Donnell																	
Webber																	
Nash																	
Team	13	491	1365	2.8	9					13	105	280	38	1472	5.3	7	29
Opp.	13	523	1383	2.6	6					13	51	186	27	775	4.2	6	39
CHICAGO BEARS																	
White	4	63	153	2.4		9	18	86	3	5	2	3	67	26	8.7		
Driscoll	4	17	45	2.6		8	23	136	2	5	9	36	25	193	5.4		6
Walquist	3	14	13	0.9		9	9	80	2	4	1	10	10	40	4.0		4
Sternaman	4	13	44	3.4	2	9	9	48	2	5	1	4	25	8	2.0		1
Senn	4	31	37	1.2		8	7	31	1	5	1	7	14	26	3.7		1
Sturtridge	3	5	3	0.6		7	4	62		3	0	1	0				
Wynne	3	18	39	2.2		7											
Hadden (1)	1	3	8	2.7													
Rommey	3	6	7	1.2	1					4	3	9	33	25	2.8	1	1
Voss																	
Wallace																	
Carlson																	
Halas																	
Murry																	
Team	4	170	349	2.1	3	9				5	17	70	24	318	4.5	1	13
Opp.	4	151	398	2.6	2	9				6	37	96	39	600	6.3	3	10
NEW YORK GIANTS																	
Wilson	4	40	124	3.1	1	9	8	56		5	0	2	0				
Eckhardt	3	18	47	2.6		8	6	79	2	4	2	11	18	19	1.7		3
Haines	1	9	36	4.0		8	12	79	4	2	0	1	0				
Caldwell	6	30	56	1.9		4	4	37	1	5							
McBride	3	23	40	1.7		6	7	42	1	4	16	35	46	162	4.6		4
Plansky	2	5	14	2.8	1												
Potteiger	3	3	11	3.7		4											
Allison	4	1	5	5.0		9											
Hagerty	6	4	3	0.8		7				5	2	4	50	15	3.8		1
Bloodgood	2	1	0	0.0		3											
Moran (2)																	
Hubbard																	
Team	4	122	334	2.7	2	9				5	19	54	35	196	3.6		8
Opp.	5	212	680	3.2	3	8				7	37	110	34	513	4.7	2	11
NEW YORK YANKEES																	
Welch	3	41	127	3.1		10	12	100	1	5	13	30	43	234	7.8	1	5
Smith	1	7	14	2.0		9	14	105	3	3							
Molenda (1)	3	38	102	2.7		5	1	-3		5	3	6	50	42	7.0		1
Kelly	3	15	26	1.7	1	9	6	54		4	21	48	44	441	9.2	2	7
Pritchard	3	11	14	1.3		10	3	14									
Flaherty (2)	2	1	0	0.0		9											
Salemi	1	2	-1	-0.5		4				3	1	2	50	10	5.0		1
Grube										5	1	2	50	5	2.5		
Gallagher																	
McClain																	
Team	3	115	284	2.5	1	10				6	41	103	40	754	7.3	3	14
Opp.	3	116	368	3.2		10				5	37	97	38	530	5.5	2	6
POTTSVILLE																	
Latone	9	164	482	2.9	2	1	2	8	1	9	3	6	50	24	4.0	1	1
Moran (1)	9	78	207	2.7		1				9	22	59	37	324	5.5	3	6
Blood	9	43	153	3.6		1				9	6	18	33	72	4.0		5
Ernst (1)	9	24	73	3.0		1				9	28	77	36	457	5.9	3	8
Kenneally	8	11	61	5.5		1											
Norman	9	35	59	1.7		1				9	0	2	0				1
Rooney	9	2	31	15.5		1				9	0	1	0				
M. Goodwin	4	4	18	4.5													
Wentz	2	5	12	2.4													
Racis	9	1	10	10.0		1											
Henry										6	0	1	0				1
E. Goodwin																	
Budd																	
Team	9	367	1106	3.0	2	1				9	59	164	36	877	5.3	7	22
Opp.	9	325	990	3.0	10	1				9	66	150	44	1107	7.4	7	23
CHICAGO CARDINALS																	
McDonnell	2	19	29	1.5		4	1	30		2	2	5	40	30	6.0		
Erickson	2	12	44	3.7		4				2	0	1	0				1
Fitzgibbon	2	8	38	4.8		4											
Mahoney	2	5	11	2.2		3	1	25		2	2	3	67	31	10.3		1
Grant	2	8	27	3.4		4				2	5	18	28	66	3.7		3
Jones	2	11	21	1.9		3				2	0	4	0				
Illman	2	1	4	4.0		3											
Neacy																	
Risvold																	
Murphy																	
Springsteen																	
Team	2	64	174	2.7		4				2	9	31		127	4.1		6
Opp.	2	75	327	4.4	4	4				2	14	36	39	198	5.5	1	6
DAYTON																	
Charles	2	14	20	1.4		3	1	20		3	1	6	17	3	0.5		
Cook	1	1	20	20.0		3											
Achui	1	6	9	1.5		3				2	0	1	0				
Britton	3	8	2	0.3		4				4	7	27	26	75	2.8		4
DeWeese	1	2	2	1.0													
Matsu	1	1	0	0.0	1	3				3	1	8	13	5	0.6		1
Sillin	2	4	-13	-3.2	1	2											
Keefer										1	4	5	80	60	12.0		1
Mankat																	
Belanich																	
Hummon																	
Team	3	36	40	1.1	1	4				4	13	47	28	143	3.0		6
Opp.	3	136	570	4.2	5	4				4	28	74	38	431	5.8	3	8

NAME	Passing Incom. Games G	Com.	Att.	Yds.	TD	Int.	Receiving Complete Games G	Rec.	Yds	Avg.	TD	Receiving Incom. Games G	Rec.	Yds.	TD
GREEN BAY															
Lewellen							13	13	169	13.0	3				
Kotal							12	28	508	18.1	1				
O'Boyle							13	1	8	8.0					
Marks							11	8	108	13.5	2				
Molenda (2)							4	1	20	20.0					
Dunn							12	15	184	12.3					
Baker							11	4	30	7.5					
Lambeau							8	4	48	12.0					
Lollar															
Dilweg							12	18	203	11.3					
O'Donnell							13	9	162	18.0	1				
Webber							3	2	19	9.5					
Nash							8	2	13	6.5					
Team															
Opp.															
CHICAGO BEARS															
White	8	1	1	9			5					8	3	34	
Driscoll	7	5	8	72	2		5	2	48	24.0		7	4	61	
Walquist	8	2	3	38	1		4					8	3	25	
Sternaman	8	11	12	236	3		5	1	47	47.0		8	2	32	
Senn	7	4	4	135	3		5	4	40	10.0	1	7	6	190	3
Sturtridge	7	2	2	20	1		3					7	3	64	2
Wynne															
Hadden (1)															
Rommey	7						4	2	32	16.0		7	1	25	1
Voss							5	3	55	18.3		8	1	10	1
Wallace							5	2	16	8.0		7	1	50	1
Carlson							4	1	27	27.0		6	1	9	1
Halas							2	1	27	27.0	1	2			
Murry							4	1	26	26.0		8			
Team	8														
Opp.	7														
NEW YORK GIANTS															
Wilson	9						4	4	36	9.0		9	4	73	
Eckhardt	7	3	3	62			3					8	1	15	
Haines	7	4	6	52		2	2	2	21	10.5		7			
Caldwell	5	1	4	12			3					7	2	35	
McBride	5	6	11	102		4									
Plansky															
Potteiger															
Allison							4	2	17	8.5		9	3	55	
Hagerty	6						4	3	41	13.7		7	3	52	
Bloodgood															
Moran (2)	1	0	4			4									
Hubbard							4	3	25	8.3		9	3	33	
Team	8														
Opp.	6														
NEW YORK YANKEES															
Welch	8	2	3	74			3	4	87	21.8		10	13	292	6
Smith	7	1	3	40		1	2					8	1	25	
Molenda (1)	3	1	1	15	1		3	2	30	15.0		5	4	108	
Kelly	8	14	22	337	5	3									
Pritchard							3	2	25	12.5		10	2	69	1
Flaherty (2)							2	1	36	36.0		9	6	148	1
Salemi	2						2	3	66	22.0	1	3			
Grube	8						3	1	12	12.0		10	1	16	
Gallagher							3	1	40	40.0		8			
McClain															
Team	7														
Opp.	8														
POTTSVILLE															
Latone	1						9	3	31	10.3		1			
Moran (1)	1						9	7	68	9.7		1			
Blood	1						9	14	194	13.9	2	1			
Ernst (1)	1						9	11	206	18.7	2	1			
Kenneally							8	4	43	10.8	1	1			
Norman	1						9	5	57	11.4	1	1			
Rooney	1						9	5	94	18.8	1	1			
M. Goodwin							4	2	7	3.5					
Wentz															
Racis							9	6	150	25.0		1			
Henry	1														
E. Goodwin							7	2	27	13.5		1			
Budd															
Team	1														
Opp.	1														
CHICAGO CARDINALS															
McDonnell	4						1					5	3	51	
Erickson	4														
Fitzgibbon															
Mahoney	3						1	2	34	17.0		4			
Grant	4														
Jones	3														
Illman															
Neacy							1					5	1	24	
Risvold															
Murphy															
Springsteen															
Team	4														
Opp.	4														
DAYTON															
Charles	2						3	3	19	6.3		2			
Cook							3	2	46	23.0		2			
Achui	2														
Britton	3														
DeWeese															
Matsu	3	0	1				3	2	16	8.0		3			
Sillin							2	2	10	5.0		2			
Keefer															
Mankat							3	2	22	11.0		3			
Belanich							4	1	25	25.0		3			
Hummon							2	1	5	5.0		2			
Team															
Opp.	3														

NAME	Punting Comp. Games G	No.	Avg.	Punting Incom. Games G	No.	Avg.	Punt Returns Complete Games G	No.	Yds.	Avg.	TD	Punt Returns Incom. Games G	No.	Yds.	TD
GREEN BAY															
Lewellen	13	136	41.1												
Kotal							12	2	17	8.5					
O'Boyle															
Marks	11	10	25.6				11	1	20	20.0					
Molenda (2)	4	1	60.0												
Dunn	12	4	27.5				12	36	268	7.4					
Baker							11	1	15	15.0					
Lambeau	8	1	49.0												
Lollar															
Dilweg															
O'Donnell															
Webber															
Nash															
Team	13	152	39.9				13	40	320	8.0					
Opp.	13	171	35.7				13	43	574	13.3	1				
CHICAGO BEARS															
White	4	5	33.4	9											
Driscoll	4	33	38.7	8	12	40.3	4	2	26	13.0		8			
Walquist	3			9	4	34.8									
Sternaman							4	10	98	9.8		9			
Senn	4	6	44.3				4	2	19	9.5		8	1	68	1
Sturtridge							3	1	80	80.0	1	8			
Wynne															
Hadden (1)															
Rommey							3	1	5	5.0		8			
Voss															
Wallace															
Carlson															
Halas															
Murry															
Team	4	44	38.9	9			4	16	228	14.3	1	9			
Opp.	4	46	38.9	9			4	11	66	6.0		9			
NEW YORK GIANTS															
Wilson	4	26	34.0	9	2	12.0									
Eckhardt	3	26	34.4	8	2	31.0	3	1	5	5.0		8			
Haines	1	1	29.0	8			1					8	5	171	1
Caldwell	4	1	0.0	6			4					6	1	20	
McBride	2	7	40.0	4	1	60.0									
Plansky															
Potteiger															
Allison															
Hagerty							4	8	140	17.5		7	1	39	
Bloodgood	2	1	30.0	3			2	2	105	52.5	1	3			
Moran (2)															
Hubbard															
Team	5	79	35.8	8			4	12	275	22.9	1	9			
Opp.	5	73	37.2	8			4	19	199	10.5		9			
NEW YORK YANKEES															
Welch	3	2	35.0	10			3	6	73	12.2		10	1	5	
Smith	1			9	1	0.0									
Molenda (1)	3	3	32.7	5											
Kelly							3	3	53	17.7		9			
Pritchard															
Flaherty (2)	2	19	32.9	9	1	0.0									
Salemi															
Grube	3	13	27.8	10											
Gallagher															
McClain							3	1	25	25.0		4			
Team	3	37	31.2	10			3	10	151	15.1		10			
Opp.	3	29	39.9	10			3	6	74	12.3		10			
POTTSVILLE															
Latone															
Moran (1)	9	47	35.2	1											
Blood	9	31	36.7	1			9	4	40	10.0		1			
Ernst (1)	9	3	37.7	1			9	14	105	7.5		1			
Kenneally															
Norman															
Rooney															
M. Goodwin															
Wentz															
Racis															
Henry															
E. Goodwin															
Budd	9	2	36.5												
Team	9	83	35.9	1			9	18	145	8.1		1			
Opp.	9	81	35.6	1			9	26	399	15.3	1	1			
CHICAGO CARDINALS															
McDonnell	2	1	34.0	4			2	2	40	20.0		4			
Erickson															
Fitzgibbon															
Mahoney															
Grant	2	23	34.0	4	4	0.0	2	2	17	8.5		4			
Jones							2	1	11	11.0		3			
Illman															
Neacy															
Risvold	1	1	31.0	2											
Murphy	1	1	24.0												
Springsteen							2	1	10	10.0		2			
Team	2	26	33.5	4			2	6	78	13.0		4			
Opp.	2	21	40.1	4			2	6	84	14.0		4			
DAYTON															
Charles							2	6	105	17.5		3			
Cook							2	2	17	0.5		3			
Achui							1	4	10	2.5		3			
Britton	3	49	35.2	4											
DeWeese															
Matsu							3	2	27	13.5					
Sillin															
Keefer															
Mankat															
Belanich							3	1	10	10.0		4			
Hummon															
Team	3	49	35.2	4			3	15	169	11.3		4			
Opp.	3	37	32.4	4			3	24	270	11.3		4			

1929 N.F.L.
The Giants Take The Air; The Packers Take The Title

By signing three veteran players of all-star rank, Curly Lambeau turned a good Green Bay Packers team into an NFL powerhouse. His timing was perfect. Just when the Depression was making ownership of an NFL franchise a shaky proposition at best and ownership in a small town almost suicidal, Lambeau made the Packers one of the league's best attractions. In the next few years, as the Depression deepened, every small town NFL team would go under except Green Bay. Although the town owned the team as a public corporation, it was Lambeau, who had founded the team in 1919 and salvaged its NFL franchise in 1922, who brought the Packers intact through the nation's most devastating economic crisis. Today, the fans who jam Lambeau Field each game owe their thanks to him.

The three newcomers — Cal Hubbard, Mike Michalske and Johnny Blood — blended perfectly with talented holdovers like tailback Verne Lewellen, the NFL's best punter, blocking back Red Dunn, all-NFL end Lavie Dilweg, fullback Bo Molenda and center Jug Earp. Together, they formed a versatile offensive unit and the league's most impressive defense. Three Packer runners, Lewellen, Blood and Molenda, rushed for more than 400 yards each, as the line prospered from the presence of 250-pound Hubbard and cat-quick Michalske. Big Cal had requested a trade to Green Bay after two years with the New York Giants. Michalske signed as a free agent after the New York Yankees folded over the summer. Both were fine blockers and, on defense, they made the Packers nearly impregnable. Green Bay matched its 1928 total of 39 pass interceptions and allowed only three touchdowns to its opponents all season.

The third newcomer was one of pro football's most colorful characters. His real name was John McNally but, early in his career, while on his way to earn some secret cash with a semi-pro team, he picked up a pseudonym from a movie marquee. The theatre was playing the Valentino film *Blood and Sand*, and Johnny McNally became forever after Johnny Blood. He'd put in four years with weak NFL teams before coming to Green Bay, a club with which he could showcase his talents. Blood could outsprint most other players, was a slashing inside runner, caught passes better than any back in the league, and was a first-rate cornerback and punter. In addition, he led the league in times fined. He ignored training rules and curfews, but his ability was so great that Lambeau, who was now primarily a bench coach, had to put up with him.

The Packers were not the only team to improve with new talent. Owner Tim Mara of the New York Giants purchased the entire squad of the Detroit Wolverines, the third place team in 1928 but also the third 1928 team to fold. The combination of the best of the Giants and Wolverine squads gave New York a good defense and the best offense in the league. Benny Friedman, the main reason Mara swung the deal, shone as a passer, runner, kicker and gate attraction, making the Giants a profitable enterprise after losing about $40,000 in last season's disastrous campaign. His high salary of $10,000 seemed well worth the expense, for his famous name and exciting skills may have saved the New York franchise from extinction. Easily the best passer in football, Friedman's throws gobbled up more than 1,500 yards and his 20 touchdown passes would not be topped until 1942. The players accompanying Friedman from Detroit were backs Tiny Feather and Led Sedbrook, center Joe Westoupal and tackle Bill Owen, whose older brother Steve had been with the Giants for several years. A key holdover was Tony Plansky, a talented track and field athlete from Georgetown who bounced back from a injury-spoiled 1928 rookie season to become, next to Friedman, the chief New York runner. Friedman's favorite passing targets were Sedbrook and end Ray Flaherty, a refugee from the Yankees.

Both the Giants and the Packers raced through the first two months of the season without a loss. The Packers won their first five games, all at home, by allowing their opponents a total of four points on two safeties. Next came four victories on the road in the midwest, in which the Packers finally gave up two touchdowns. Their only close call came in a fumble-filled performance against the Chicago Cardinals before 10,000 fans at Comiskey Park. Leading by 7-0 midway through the final quarter, the Packers let a long Cardinal pass slip by them for a touchdown. Only an extra point try wide of the crossbar kept Chicago from a tie.

1929 STANDINGS

	W	L	T	Pct.	Pts.	Opp. Pts.	Avg. Pts.	Opp. Avg.
Green Bay Packers	12	0	1	1.000	198	22	15	2
New York Giants	13	1	1	.929	312	86	21	6
Frankford Yellow Jackets	10	4	5	.714	139	128	7	7
Chicago Cardinals	6	6	1	.500	154	83	12	6
Boston Bulldogs	4	4	0	.500	98	73	12	9
Staten Island Stapletons	3	4	3	.429	89	65	9	7
Providence Steam Roller	4	6	2	.400	107	117	9	10
Orange Tornadoes	3	5	4	.375	35	90	3	7
Chicago Bears	4	9	2	.308	119	227	8	15
Buffalo Bisons	1	7	1	.125	48	142	5	16
Minneapolis Redjackets	1	9	0	.100	48	185	5	19
Dayton Triangles (R)	0	6	0	.000	7	136	1	23

(R) — played only road games

Scoring Leaders

Nevers	ChiC	85
Sedbrook	NYG	66
Plansky	NYG	62
Latone	Bos	54
Flaherty	NYG	49
Lewellen	GB	48
Halicki	Fra	45
Williams	Prov	42
Strong	SI	39
Diehl	Fra	36
Welch	Prov	36
Friedman	NYG	32
Blood	GB	30
Moran	NYG	30

KICKING

		FG	Att	Pct
Weimer	Buf	3	7	43
Mercer	Fra	2	3	67
Plansky	NYG	2	3	67
Dunn	GB	2	4	50
Erickson	Min	1	1	100
Holmer	ChiB	1	1	100
Elkins	ChiC	1	2	50
McCormick	Ora	1	3	33
Nevers	ChiC	1	4	25
Halicki	Fra	1	5	20

Blood-GB, Driscoll-ChiB, Ernst-Bos, Friedman-NYG, McCormick-Ora, Waite-Ora all 0-1
McBride-Prov, Molenda-GB, Nydahl-Min, Strong-SI all 0-2

		PAT	Att	Pct
Friedman	NYG	20	31	65
Dunn	GB	11	20	55
Nevers	ChiC	10	19	53
Strong	SI	9	12	75
Sternaman	ChiB	8	11	73
Wentworth	Bos	6	8	75
Halicki	Fra	6	9	67
McBride	Prov	6	9	67
Mercer	Fra	6	9	67
Jennings	Prov	4	5	80
Driscoll	ChiB	3	4	75
Molenda	GB	3	5	60
Weimer	Buf	3	5	60
Nydahl	Min	2	4	50
Plansky	NYG	2	9	22

		PAT	Att	Pct
Duffy	Day	1	1	100
Hanny	Prov	1	1	100
Erickson	Min	1	2	50
Ernst	Bos	1	4	25
Behman	Fra	0	1	0
Blood	GB	0	1	0
Elkins	ChiC	0	1	0
Hamas	Ora	0	1	0
Holmer	ChiB	0	1	0
Maloney	Bos	0	1	0
Stockton	Prov-Bos	0	1	0
Ursella	Min	0	1	0
Williams	Prov	0	1	0
Moran	NYG	0	4	0

GREEN BAY PACKERS 12-0-1 Curly Lambeau

Regulars

UseName	Pos.	Hgt.	Wgt.	Age	Int	Pts.
Lavie Dilweg	E	6'3"	202	26	7	18
Tom Nash	E	6'3"	210	23	2	6
Cal Hubbard	T-E	6'4"	250	28		
Bill Kern	T	6'	187	22	1	
Jim Bowdoin	G	6'1"	220	23		
Mike Michalske	G	6'	209	26		
Jug Earp	C	6'	245	32	2	
Red Dunn	BB	5'11"	178	27	4	17
Verne Lewellen	TB-HB	6'1"	180	27	2	48
Eddie Kotal	HB-TB	5'8"	177	27	4	18
Bo Molenda	FB	5'10"	207	24	5	21

Substitutes

UseName	Pos.	Hgt.	Wgt.	Age	Int	Pts.
Dick O'Donnell	E	6'	196	29	2	
Marion Ashmore	T	6'1"	212	26		
Claude Perry	T-G	6'1"	205	27		
Paul Minick	G	6'	190	29		
Whitey Woodin	G	5'10"	206	34		
Boob Darling	C	5'11"	216	25		
Red Smith	BB	5'10"	190	25		
Johnny Blood	TB-BB-HB	6'1"	185	25	6	30
Hurdis McCrary	HB-FB-TB	6'	213	25	1	24
Cully Lidberg	FB	5'9"	188	29	2	12

Al Bloodgood — Broken Ankle

Substitutes

UseName	Pos.	Hgt.	Wgt.	Age	Int	Pts.
Tiny Cahoon	T	6'2"	238	29		
Billy Young	G	5'10"	210	31		
Jack Evans	BB	5'9"	175	23		
Curly Lambeau	TB	5'10"	195	31		
Don Hill (to ChiC)	HB	5'10"	175	24		
Bullet Baker (to ChiC)	HB	5'8"	177	29		
Dave Zuidmulder	TB	5'10"	166	23	1	

Scores of Each Game

Date	Pts.	Opponent	Pts.
Sep. 22	9	DAYTON	0
Sep. 29	23	CHIC. BEARS	0
Oct. 6	9	CHIC. CARDS	2
Oct. 13	14	FRANKFORD	2
Oct. 20	24	MINNEAPOLIS	0
Oct. 27	7	Chic. Cards	6
Nov. 3	16	Minneapolis	6
Nov. 10	14	Chic. Bears	0
Nov. 17	12	Chic. Cards	0
Nov. 24	20	New York	6
Nov. 28	0	Frankford	0
Dec. 1	25	Providence	0
Dec. 8	25	Chic. Bears	0

NEW YORK GIANTS 13-1-1 Roy Andrews

Regulars

UseName	Pos.	Hgt.	Wgt.	Age	Int	Pts.
Lyle Munn	E	6'	190	27	1	1
Ray Flaherty	E	6'	195	25	2	49
Bill Owen	T	6'	210	25		
Steve Owen	T	5'10"	235	31		
Danny McMullen	G-T	5'8"	230	23		
Les Caywood	G	6'	230	24		
Joe Westoupal	C	6'3"	200	26	2	
Tiny Feather	BB-FB	6'	190	26	4	18
Benny Friedman	TB	5'10"	185	24	4	32
Len Sedbrook	WB-FB	5'10"	175	24	1	66
Tony Plansky	FB	6'2"	205	29	2	62

Substitutes

UseName	Pos.	Hgt.	Wgt.	Age	Int	Pts.
Glenn Campbell	E	5'11"	185	25		6
Babe Lyon	T	6'2"	235	22		
Saul Mielziner	T-G	6'1"	250	24		
Cliff Ashburn	G-T-E	5'11"	190	23		
Dosey Howard	G-T	6'	225	28		
Mickey Murtagh	C-BB	6'1"	190	25		6
Hap Moran	BB-WB-FB-TB	6'1"	190	28	3	30
Jack Hagerty	TB-WB-FB-BB	5'9"	165	26		18
Snitz Snyder	WB-FB-BB	5'8"	190	24		18
Mule Wilson	FB-WB	5'11"	190	27	3	6

Substitutes

UseName	Pos.	Hgt.	Wgt.	Age	Int	Pts.
Orin Rice	BB-C	6'	165	25		

Scores of Each Game

Date	Pts.	Opponent	Pts.
Sep. 29	0	Orange	0
Oct. 6	7	Providence	0
Oct. 13	19	STATEN ISLAND	9
Oct. 20	32	FRANKFORD	0
Oct. 27	19	PROVIDENCE	0
Nov. 3	26	Chic. Bears	14
Nov. 5	45	Buffalo	6
Nov. 10	22	ORANGE	0
Nov. 17	34	CHIC. BEARS	0
Nov. 24	6	GREEN BAY	20
Nov. 28	21	Staten Island	7
Dec. 1	24	CHIC. CARDS	21
Dec. 7	12	Frankford	0
Dec. 8	13	FRANKFORD	0
Dec. 15	14	Chic. Beears	9

The Giants, meanwhile, had opened their season with a scoreless tie with the Orange Tornadoes, a new member of the league from a small city outside Newark, New Jersey. After that slow beginning, Friedman got the offense in gear and the Giants reeled off eight straight victories. Two of those wins were shutouts over the Providence Steam Roller, who dropped from champions to also-rans with the retirement of key players Curly Oden, Gus Sonnenberg and Clyde Smith and the lackluster play of tailback Wildcat Wilson. The most impressive New York victory of the string was a 32-0 trouncing of the Frankford Yellowjackets on October 20 in the Polo Grounds. The Yellowjackets had their usual tough squad, but they could not beat either the Giants or Packers in five meetings this year. Nevertheless, they had a solid star in fullback Wally Diehl, who gained more than 500 yards rushing on offense and intercepted seven passes on defense.

The season's showdown came on November 24 in the Polo Grounds when the 8-0-1 Giants faced the 9-0-0 Packers before an audience of 25,000 fans. The Packers did no have the services of key backs Red Dunn and Eddie Kotal, who had been injured in the November 10 victory over the Bears. Hubbard and Michalske led a Green Bay pass rush which gave Benny Friedman little time to set up. Verne Lewellen consistently boomed 60-yard punts to keep the Giants in poor field position and Johnny Blood set up the first Green Bay touchdown with a fumble recovery and scored the final one with a short run. The Packers triumphed by a score of 20-6 and played practically the entire game with 11 players. Guard Jim Bowdoin had to leave the field with an injury in the final minute of play.

Neither team lost any of its remaining games. The Packers played a scoreless tie at Frankford on Thanksgiving Day, then routed Providence and the Bears to wrap up the season as undefeated champs, the first since 1923. A welcoming party of 20,000 fans danced and caroused all night in freezing temperatures when the Packers arrived home by train on December 9.

A highlight of the Packers' season was their three victories over their arch-rivals, the Chicago Bears. After six games, the Bears stood at 4-4-1, but their final eight contests resulted in seven losses and a tie. It was the Bears' first losing season. Part of the problem was that the Bear had too many past-their-prime regulars, but even more destructive was the trouble at the top. The team's co-owners, George Halas and Dutch Sternaman, had differing opinions about how to run the offense. The result was that the offense didn't run at all. On the bright side, Halas coaxed Red Grange back into uniform to share a halfback slot with Paddy Driscoll who was playing his final season. Prompted back into action by stock market losses, Grange played well, rushing for 552 yards, but he was no longer the breakaway runner of old.

One of the league's pioneers called it quits in July before the season began. Chris O'Brien sold the Chicago Cardinals to Dr. David Jones for $25,000. The Cardinals had never recovered from the AFL war in 1926. Jones tried hard to bring them back to major-league caliber. They became the first NFL team to go to an out-of-town training camp when he sent them to Coldwater, Michigan. He also moved the team back to Comiskey Park. Then he hired former Duluth owner Ole Haugsrud as manager and his partner Dewey Scanlon as coach. The key to this was that, although Haugsrud had sold his Duluth franchise to Orange, New Jersey, several of the Duluth players were under personal contract to Haugsrud, the most important being Ernie Nevers. And Nevers, like Grange, was returning to the NFL. The big blonde fullback missed the Cardinals' first two games of the season because he was playing baseball, and then he needed a few games to gel with his teammates. Once they got together as a unit, the Cards won three of their last four games. In the annual Thanksgiving Day meeting with the Bears, Nevers scored a record 40 points by running for six touchdowns (another record) and kicking four extra points as the Cardinals won 40-6. That performance helped Nevers win the league scoring championship with 85 points, a mark that would hold until 1940.

Another versatile back was Ken Strong, a rookie out of New York University, who signed with the new Staten Island Stapletons. A strong runner and accurate placekicker, Strong signed for $5,000 plus a rent-free apartment. Strong, who rushed for 527 yards, and player-coach Doug Wycoff gave the Stapes a strong running attack, but their inability to come up with an accurate passer kept their offense from scoring many points.

The Stapes were one of five new clubs that swelled league membership to 12 teams. They operated on the old 1926 Brooklyn franchise which they obtained from Tim Mara after C.C. Pyle had returned it to him. Although the same franchise was involved, the 1926 Brooklyn Lions, the 1927-28 New York Yankees and 1929 Staten Island Stapletons were different teams. The Stapes, for example, had been a strong independent outfit for several years before they joined the NFL. Tim Mara, who at one point owned three franchises counting the Detroit Wolverines, was concerned only with protecting his territorial rights and made no attempt to influence the Stapleton owners in the running of their team. If he had, Ken Strong would have joined Benny Friedman in the 1929 Giants backfield.

Of other new clubs, the Orange Tornadoes, another strong former independent, operated the one-time Duluth franchise. The Boston Bulldogs were actually the Pottsville Maroons relocated. The Buffalo franchise, which had sat out 1928, rejoined the league with a weak entry named the Bisons. The Minneapolis Redjackets, under the same management of the ill-fated Marines of 1921-24, joined the league primarily as a vehicle for Herb Joesting, the popular All-American fullback from Minnesota. Of these new members, Buffalo and Boston would fold after one season. Also going out of business after this year were the Dayton Triangles, charter members of the league who lost all six games this season and scored only seven points.

For more than a decade, college games had been controlled by four officials. In 1929, the NFL finally added the fourth man, the field judge, to the crew. Another important rule change declared a fumble when the ball hit a member of the receiving team but that it was dead if touched by a member of the punting team. And, in an effort to control fighting, the penalty for such an offense was placed at 15 yards or half the distance to the offender's goalline, whichever was greater. No one recorded the number of fights during the season, but one game in October saw a 40-yard penalty stepped off.

The *Green Bay Press Gazette* all-NFL poll: ends Lavie Dilweg, Green Bay, and Ray Flaherty, Giants; tackles Bull Behman, Frankford, and Bob Beattie, Orange; guards Mike Michalske, Green Bay, and Milt Rehnquist, Providence; center Joe Westoupal, Giants; quarterback Benny Friedman, Giants; halfbacks Verne Lewellen, Green Bay, and Tony Plansky, Giants; and fullback Ernie Nevers, Cardinals.

NAME	RUSHING Complete Games					RUSHING Incom. Games				PASSING Complete Games								PASSING Incom. Games					
	G	Att.	Yds.	Avg.	TD	G	Att.	Yds.	TD	G	Com.	Att.	%	Yds.	Y/A	TD	Int	G	Com.	Att.	Yds	TD	Int
GREEN BAY																							
Blood	12	104	406	3.9	2					12	16	30	53	271	9.0	1	1						
Lewellen	13	86	405	4.7	6					13	21	56	38	501	8.9	4	5						
Molenda	12	138	401	2.9	3					12	4	9	44	63	7	1	1						
Lidberg	10	82	213	2.6	2																		
Kotal	11	81	201	2.5						11	11	29	38	118	4.1		3						
McCrary	13	67	166	2.5	1					13	4	8	50	44	5.5	1							
Dunn	11	13	25	1.9						11	34	87	39	479	5.5	5	8						
Baker (1)	2	6	17	2.8						2	0	1	0										
Smith	5	5	10	2.0						5	0	1	0				1						
Lambeau	1	3	9	3.0						1	2	5	40	36	7.2		1						
Hill (1)	3	6	8	1.3																			
Evans										3	0	1	0				1						
Dilweg																							
Nash																							
O'Donnell																							
Team	13	591	1861	3.1	14					13	92	227	41	1512	6.7	12	21						
Opp.	13	414	875	2.1	1					13	62	208	30	896	4.3	2	39						
NEW YORK																							
Friedman	4	44	161	3.7	1	11	28	246	1	9	53	117	45	985	8.4	13	7	6	31	39	092	7	3
Plansky	3	20	75	3.8	1	8	17	161	7	6	4	10	40	74	7.4			5	6	8	110	2	
Sedbrook	4	11	62	5.6		11	9	75	4														
Feather	4	25	60	2.4		11	7	22	1	9	0	4	0				1	6					
Hagerty	4	10	52	5.2		10				8	4	12	33	70	5.8	1	1	6					
Wilson	3	6	2	0.3		6	2	47	1														
Moran	4	14	45	3.2		10				8	3	11	27	60	5.5	1	2	6	2	2	73	1	
Snyder	2	22	40	1.8		10	2	5	2	7	0	4	0					5					
Murtagh	4					9	1	33	1														
Flaherty																							
Campbell																							
Munn																							
Team	4	152	497	3.3	2	11				9	64	158	41	1189	7.5	15	11	6					
Opp.	4	150	408	2.7	4	11				8	30	123	24	446	3.6	1	24	7					

NAME	RECEIVING Complete Games					RECEIVING Incom. Games				PUNTING Comp. Games			PUNTING Incom. Games			PUNT RETURNS Complete Games					PUNT RETURNS Incom. Games			
	G	Rec.	Yds.	Avg.	TD	G	Rec.	Yds.	TD	G	No.	Avg.	G	No.	Avg.	G	Rec	Yds.	Avg.	TD	G	Rec	Yds	TD
GREEN BAY																								
Blood	12	12	218	18.2	2					12	46	39.5				12	7	156	22.3	1				
Lewellen	13	8	97	12.1	1					13	85	41.9				13	1	18	18.0					
Molenda	12	5	56	11.2																				
Lidberg	10	2	20	10.0												10	1	10	10.0					
Kotal	11	20	297	14.9	3											11	2	15	7.5					
McCrary	13	6	160	26.7	2					13	2	28.5				13	1	13	13.0					
Dunn	11	8	111	13.9						11	2	43.0				11	41	406	9.9					
Baker (1)																2	1	4	4.0					
Smith																								
Lambeau																								
Hill (1)																								
Evans																3	2	15	7.5					
Dilweg	13	25	429	17.2	3																			
Nash	10	4	86	21.5	1																			
O'Donnell	10	2	38	19.0																				
Team										13	135	40.9				13	56	637	11.4	1				
Opp.										13	153	36.7				13	29	347	12.0					
NEW YORK																								
Friedman										4	1	35.0	11			4	8	88	11.0		11			
Plansky	4	1	16	16.0	1	7	3	65		3	11	38.3	8											
Sedbrook	6	8	164	20.5	2	9	11	230	4															
Feather	6	4	131	32.8	1	9	4	121		4	5	26.8	11											
Hagerty	6	9	133	14.7	1	8	2	47	1							4	2	25	12.5		10	1	49	
Wilson	4					5	2	38		3	2	20.0	6											
Moran	6	7	96	13.7	5	8				4	15	35.7	11	1	0.0									
Snyder	4	3	71	23.7	1	8	1	15																
Murtagh																								
Flaherty	6	7	165	23.6	2	9	11	284	6															
Campbell	6	3	69	23.0	1	9	2	50																
Munn	6	2	63	21.0		9	1	15																
Team										5	44	35.3	10			4	10	113	11.3		11			
Opp.										5	49	35.8	10			4	11	120	11.0		11			

FRANKFORD YELLOW JACKETS 10-4-5 Bull Behman

Regulars

Use Name	Pos.	Hgt.	Wgt.	Age	Int.	Pts.
George Barna	E	6'1	198	21	2	6
Tony Kostos	E	5'11	195	24	3	6
Harry Malcolm	T	6'	195	23		
Bull Behman	T	5'10	210	29	1	
Hal Hanson	G	6'1	205	24		
Rudy Comstock	G	5'10	210	28		
Roger Mahoney	C-G	6'	200	23	1	
Two Bits Homan	BB-WB	5'5	144	27	3	12
Ken Mercer	TB	5'11	190	26	1	18
Arnie Oehlrich	WB-BB	5'11	195	23	4	6
Wally Diehl	FB	6'	200	25	7	36

Substitutes

Use Name	Pos.	Hgt.	Wgt.	Age	Int.	Pts.
Marty Kostos	E-BB-WB	5'11	185	27		
Joey Maxwell	E-C	6'2	205	24	1	
Bill Capps	T	6'1	230	25		
Jack Filak	T-G	6'	190	25		
Johnny Thompson	G	5'10	215	23		
Ted James	G-C	6'2	190	23		
Wild Bill Kelly	BB-TB-WB	5'10	190	24	2	6
Mike Wilson	WB-TB-FB	5'10	175	24	2	
Charley Rogers	WB-TB	5'11	185	25	1	
Eddie Halicki	FB-WB-TB	5'9	185	23	5	45
Al Maglisceau	T-G	6'1	210	25		
Chief Elkins (from ChiC)	FB-WB-BB	5'11	190	24	1	

Scores of each game

Date	Pts.	Opponent	Pts.
Sep. 28	14	DAYTON	7
Oct. 5	19	BUFFALO	0
Oct. 6	13	Buffalo	0
Oct. 13	2	Green Bay	14
Oct. 19	6	ORANGE	6
Oct. 20	0	New York	32
Oct. 26	6	STATEN ISLAND	6
Oct. 27	3	Staten Island	0
Nov. 2	8	CHIC. CARDS	0
Nov. 9	7	PROVIDENCE	0
Nov. 10	7	Providence	6
Nov. 16	20	CHIC. BEARS	14
Nov. 17	0	Orange	0
Nov. 23	24	MINNEAPOLIS	0
Nov. 28	0	GREEN BAY	0
Dec. 1	0	Chic. Bears	0
Dec. 7	0	NEW YORK	12
Dec. 8	0	New York	31
Dec. 14	10	ORANGE	0

CHICAGO CARDINALS 6-6-1 Dewey Scanlon

Regulars

Use Name	Pos.	Hgt.	Wgt.	Age	Int.	Pts.
Pat Dowling	E		185	25		
Chuck Kassel	E	6'1	190	25		12
Jess Tinsley	T-E	6'	198	20		
Duke Slater	T	6'1	215	30	1	6
Herb Blumer	G	6'1	210	29		
Walt Kiesling	G	6'2	243	26		
Ojay Larson (from ChiB)	C	6'1	200	30	3	
Russ Method	BB-WB	5'10	195	32		
Cobb Rooney	WB-BB	6'	185	29	1	18
Mickey McDonnell	WB	5'8	165	25	4	12
Ernie Nevers	FB	6'	204	26	4	85

Substitutes

Use Name	Pos.	Hgt.	Wgt.	Age	Int.	Pts.
Chick Lang	E-G		195	28		
Jack Williams	T-E-G	6'	200	25		
Murrell Hogue	T-G	6'1	205	27		
Jack Underwood	G	6'	195	32		
Bill Stein	G	6'	190	30		
Bill Rooney	C	6'2	195	33	1	
Eddie Butts	BB-WB		190	26		
Don Hill (from GB)	WB-C	5'10	175	24	1	6
Chief Elkins (to FRA)	WB	5'11	190	24		3
Gene Rose	WB-FB-BB	5'8	173	25	1	6
Bullet Baker (from GB)	BB	5'8	177	29		
Louie Larson	WB-BB		168	31		
Earl Britton	FB-BB	6'	215	26		

Scores of each game

Date	Pts.	Opponent	Pts.
Sep. 29	9	Buffalo	3
Oct. 6	2	Green Bay	9
Oct. 13	7	Minneapolis	14
Oct. 20	0	Chic. Bears	0
Oct. 27	6	GREEN BAY	7
Nov. 2	0	Frankford	8
Nov. 6	16	Providence	0
Nov. 10	8	MINNEAPOLIS	0
Nov. 17	0	GREEN BAY	12
Nov. 24	19	DAYTON	0
Nov. 28	40	CHIC. BEARS	6
Dec. 1	21	New York	24
Dec. 8	26	Orange	0

BOSTON BULLDOGS 4-4-0 Dick Rauch

Regulars

Use Name	Pos.	Hgt.	Wgt.	Age	Int.	Pts.
Red Maloney	E	5'11	180	27		
George Kenneally	E	6'	190	27		1
Joe Carpe	T	6'	200	26		
Joe Kozlowsky	T	5'10	210	28		
Ed McCrillis	G	6'	205	26		
Frank Racis	G	6'	200	31	1	
Al Pierotti	C	5'10	200	33	1	
Jack Ernst	BB	5'11	185	29		1
Hust Stockton (from PROV)	TB	5'11	195	27	3	6
Paul Kittredge	HB-BB-TB	5'10	170	25	2	12
Tony Latone	FB	5'11	200	32	2	54

Substitutes

Use Name	Pos.	Hgt.	Wgt.	Age	Int.	Pts.
Thurston Towle	E	5'10	172	24		
Bill Howell	E	5'11	175	25		
Arnie Shockley	T	6'2	220	24		
Bill Connor	G-T	6'1	240	30		
Roy Scholl	G	5'8	205	25		
Dick Rauch	G	5'9	178	36		
Bert Shurtleff	C	5'10	190	32		
Cy Wentworth	BB-HB	5'8	165	25		
Ed Lawrence	TB-HB-FB	5'8	170	24		
Al Miller	HB-FB-BB	5'11	210	25	1	
Red Marston	BB	5'9	170	22		

Scores of each game

Date	Pts.	Opponent	Pts.
Oct. 6	0	Orange	7
Oct. 13	41	DAYTON	0
Oct. 20	13	ORANGE	19
Oct. 27	14	BUFFALO (at Pottsville)	6
Oct. 29	6	ORANGE (at Pottsville)	0
Nov. 10	6	Staten Island	14
Nov. 17	12	BUFFALO	7
Nov. 24	6	Providence	20

STATEN ISLAND STAPLETONS 3-4-3 Doug Wycoff

Regulars

Use Name	Pos.	Hgt.	Wgt.	Age	Int.	Pts.
Tom Leary	E	6'	180	26	3	12
Sammy Stein	E	6'	190	24		6
Bing Miller	T	6'1	180	25		
Cy Williams	T	6'	200	27		
Walt Godwin	G	5'7	205	29		
John Bunyan	G	5'10	215	23		
Harry McGee	C	6'1	198	24	1	
Hinkey Haines	BB-TB	5'10	170	30	3	12
Ken Strong	TB-FB	6'	200	23	2	39
Frank Briante	HB-BB-TB-FB	5'10	185	23	2	6
Doug Wycoff	FB-TB	6'	202	25	3	12

Substitutes

Use Name	Pos.	Hgt.	Wgt.	Age	Int.	Pts.
Tom Lomasney	E	6'	180	23		
Ollie Satenstein	G-E-T	6'	200	23		
Louie Pessolano	T-G-E	6'	215	22		
Dave Skudin	G-E	5'11	195	24		
Jack Lord	G-T	6'	195	25		
Bob Dunn	C-T	6'1	200	24		
Mike Riordan	BB-E-HB-FB	5'11	195	23	1	
Paul Kuczo	TB-BB	5'9	165	26	1	
Ike Williams	HB	5'10	180	26	5	
Hersh Martin	FB-HB-BB	5'11	180	23		
Jack Shapiro	BB	5'2	126	23		

Scores of each game

Date	Pts.	Opponent	Pts.
Oct. 6	12	DAYTON	0
Oct. 13	9	New York	19
Oct. 26	6	Frankford	6
Oct. 27	0	FRANKFORD	3
Nov. 3	0	ORANGE	0
Nov. 5	7	PROVIDENCE	7
Nov. 10	14	BOSTON	6
Nov. 24	34	MINNEAPOLIS	0
Nov. 28	7	NEW YORK	21
Dec. 1	0	Orange	3

PROVIDENCE STEAM ROLLER 4-6-2 Jimmy Conzelman

Regulars

Use Name	Pos.	Hgt.	Wgt.	Age	Int.	Pts.
Duke Hanny	E-T	6'	200	31		1
John Spellman	E-T	5'10	205	30		
Warren McGuirk	T	5'11	200	23		
Orland Smith	T-G	5'11	215	23		
Jack Fleischman	G	5'6	185	28		
Abe Wilson	G	5'10	192	29		
Milt Rehnquist	C	6'	230	32		
Gibby Welch	BB-WB	5'11	180	24	3	36
Wildcat Wilson	TB	5'11	200	28		6
Pop Williams	WB-TB-FB	6'	205	23		42
Jack McBride	FB-TB	5'11	185	27	2	6

Substitutes

Use Name	Pos.	Hgt.	Wgt.	Age	Int.	Pts.
Bill Cronin	E-FB-WB	5'10	185	28		
Perry Jackson	T-E	6'1	200	26		
Norm Harvey	T-C-E-G	6'	198	32		
Hec Garvey	G-T	6'1	240	29		
Archie Golembeski	G-C	5'10	186	29	1	
Lou Jennings	C	6'3	220	25	1	4
Jimmy Conzelman	BB-E-WB	6'	185	31	3	6
Hust Stockton (to BOS)	FB	5'11	195	27		
Jack Cronin	WB-TB-BB-E	5'11	180	26		6
Al Hadden	FB-E-WB	5'9	180	29		

Curly Oden - Voluntarily Retired
Gus Sonnenberg - Retired to be Professional Wrestler

Scores of each game

Date	Pts.	Opponent	Pts.
Sep. 29	41	DAYTON	0
Oct. 6	0	NEW YORK	7
Oct. 13	7	ORANGE	0
Oct. 20	7	BUFFALO	7
Oct. 27	0	New York	19
Nov. 5	7	Staten Island	7
Nov. 6	0	CHIC. CARDS	16
Nov. 9	0	Frankford	7
Nov. 10	6	FRANKFORD	6
Nov. 17	19	MINNEAPOLIS	16
Nov. 24	20	BOSTON	6
Dec. 1	0	GREEN BAY	25

ORANGE TORNADOES 3-5-4 Jack Depler

Regulars

Use Name	Pos.	Hgt.	Wgt.	Age	Int.	Pts.
Paul Longua	E	5'10	175	26		6
Johnny Tomaini	E	6'	185	27		1
Bill Feaster	T	6'	205	25	1	
Bob Beattie	T	6'3	230	26		
Andy Salata	G	5'10	190	25		
Ernie Cuneo	G	5'9	192	24		
Ted Mitchell	C	5'10	195	24	4	
George Pease	BB-TB	5'8	185	26	2	6
Frank Kirkleski	TB-BB	5'10	175	25	2	12
Carl Waite	WB-FB-BB-T-G	5'9	205	27	1	6
Steve Hamas	FB-WB	6'	195	22	1	

Substitutes

Use Name	Pos.	Hgt.	Wgt.	Age	Int.	Pts.
Phil Scott	E			23		
Leon Johnson	E	5'11	185	22		
Ed Lynch	T	5'11	195	32		
Bill Clarkin	T-G	5'10	210	29		
Tom Kerrigan	G	6'2	200	23		
Jack McArthur	G-C	5'11	215	25		
Ralph Barkman	BB-WB-TB	5'8	165	22	1	1
Charlie Van Horn	TB-WB	6'2	185	27		
Heinie Benkert	WB-BB	5'9	170	28	2	
Felix McCormick	FB-G-TB	5'7	185	24		3
Ray Wagner	E	5'10	170	27		
Tex Kelly	T	6'3	220	30		
Jack Depler	T	5'10	220	30		
John Lott	T			23		
Bob Dwyer	WB	5'9	160	24		
Ernie Hambacher	FB-TB	5'8	170	22	1	

Scores of each game

Date	Pts.	Opponent	Pts.
Sep. 29	0	NEW YORK	0
Oct. 6	7	BOSTON	0
Oct. 13	0	Providence	7
Oct. 19	6	Frankford	6
Oct. 20	19	Boston	13
Oct. 29	0	Boston (at Pottsville)	6
Nov. 3	0	Staten Island	0
Nov. 10	0	New York	22
Nov. 17	0	FRANKFORD	0
Dec. 1	3	STATEN ISLAND	0
Dec. 8	0	CHIC. CARDS	26
Dec. 14	0	Frankford	10

CHICAGO BEARS 4-9-2 George Halas

Regulars

Use Name	Pos.	Hgt.	Wgt.	Age	Int.	Pts.
Gardie Grange	E	6'	165	22		12
Luke Johnsos	E	6'2	190	23		18
Don Murry	T	6'2	190	29		
Packie Nelson	T	5'11	205	22		
Bill Fleckenstein	G-E	6'1	210	25		
Zuck Carlson	G	6'	200	24		
George Trafton	C	6'2	230	32	1	
Joey Sternaman	QB	5'6	150	29		8
Red Grange	HB	5'11	185	26	1	13
Laurie Walquist	HB-QB	5'8	164	31		18
Walt Holmer	FB	6'	180	26		3

Substitutes

Use Name	Pos.	Hgt.	Wgt.	Age	Int.	Pts.
Cookie Cunningham	E	6'3	210	24		
Ted Richards	E	5'9	174	27		
Ralph Maillard	T	6'2	190	23		
Sod Ryan	T	6'2	200	23		
Joe Kopcha	G-T	6'	205	23		
Bull Polisky	G-T	6'	225	28		
Bert Pearson	C-G	6'	195	24		
Shorty Elness	HB-QB	5'8	166	23		
Paddy Driscoll	HB-QB	5'8	175	34	1	9
Bill Senn	HB	6'	174	24		24
Buck White	FB	6'	195	28	3	12
Buck Evans	T-G	5'11	212	29		
Harvey Long	T-G	6'	195	24		
Harry Richman	G	5'11	186	22		
Ojay Larson (to ChiC)	C	6'1	200	30		
Dick Sturtridge	HB	5'8	172	25		
Tom Hearden	HB	5'9	180	24		

Scores of each game

Date	Pts.	Opponent	Pts.
Sep. 22	19	Minneapolis (at Madison, Wis.)	6
Sep. 29	0	Green Bay	23
Oct. 6	7	Minneapolis	6
Oct. 13	16	Buffalo	0
Oct. 20	0	CHIC. CARDS	0
Oct. 27	27	MINNEAPOLIS	0
Nov. 3	14	NEW YORK	26
Nov. 10	0	GREEN BAY	14
Nov. 16	14	Frankford	20
Nov. 17	0	New York	34
Nov. 24	7	BUFFALO	19
Nov. 28	6	Chic. Cards	40
Dec. 1	0	FRANKFORD	0
Dec. 8	0	GREEN BAY	25
Dec. 15	9	NEW YORK	14

NAME	RUSHING Complete Games					RUSHING Incom. Games				PASSING Complete Games								PASSING Incom. Games					
	G	Att.	Yds.	Avg.	TD	G	Att.	Yds.	TD	G	Com.	Att.	%	Yds.	Y/A	TD	Int.	G	Com.	Att.	Yds.	TD	Int.
FRANKFORD																							
Diehl	12	123	520	4.2	6	6	2	18		13	12	49	24	191	3.9	1	8	5	0	1			1
Halicki	12	103	362	3.5	2	5	3	25	1	13	1	1	1	2	2.0			4					
Mercer	9	66	221	3.3		4	1	1		10	33	110	30	429	3.9	2	19	3	2	2	50	1	
Wilson	12	59	197	3.3		6				13	8	14	57	97	6.9		3	5	1	1	51		
Kelly	12	43	129	3.0	1	5	1	4		13	31	103	30	482	4.7	3	9	4	12	20	195	1	
Oehlrich	11	37	95	2.6		6																	
Elkins (2)	5	15	37	2.5		2																	
Homan	12	7	21	3.0		5	2	9		13	2	8	25	12	1.5		2	4					
Rogers	4	5	15	3.0		3																	
T. Rostos																							
Barna																							
Maxwell																							
Behman																							
M. Kostos																							
Malcolm																							
Filak																							
Team	13	458	1597	3.5	9	6				14	87	285	31	1213	4.3	6	41	5					
Opp.	12	362	1079	3.0	3	7				14	62	232	27	973	4.2	7	45	5					
CHICAGO CARDINALS																							
Nevers	3	68	230	3.4	1	8	23	148	11	4	25	67	37	360	5.4	2	6	7	11	15	281	4	2
McDonnell	3	27	17	0.6		10	12	127															
C. Rooney	2	17	39	2.3		9	5	75	1	4	2	6	33	9	1.5			7					
Rose	3	15	40	2.7		10	6	46	1	5	2	6	33	15	2.5		3	8	0	1			1
Butts						7	3	25															
Elkins (1)	1	9	12	1.3		1	3	11		1	1	1	100	5	5.0			1					
Hill (2)	2	4	-6	-1.5		9	2	28															
Britton	1	5	6	1.2		1				1	1	5	20	6	1.2		1	1					
Method	2	3	4	1.3		8																	
Kassel																							
Dowling																							
Team	3	125	240	1.9	1	10				5	31	85	36	395	4.6	2	10	8					
Opp.	4	167	446	2.7	3	9				4	30	69	43	536	7.8	2	6	9					
BOSTON																							
Latone	2	41	132	3.2	2	6	40	165	7	2	0	1	0					6					
Miller	1	15	66	4.4		6	7	40		2	0	1	0				1	5					
Stockton (2)	2	13	34	2.6		6	13	30	1	2	5	17	29	74	4.4		3	6	8	10	181	2	1
Kittredge	2	19	33	1.7		5	1	1	1	2	1	3	33	2	0.7		2	5					
Wentworth						6	4	31															
Ernst	2	2	2	1.0		5	2	7		2	3	9	33	46	5.1		2	5	1	3	11		1
Lawrence	1	2	-3	-1.5		5																	
Maloney										2	0	1	0					6					
Kenneally																							
Team	2	92	264	2.9	2	6				2	9	31	29	122	3.9		7	6					
Opp.	2	68	288	4.2	2	6				2	8	19	42	54	2.8		4	6					
STATEN ISLAND																							
Strong	10	115	527	4.6	4					10	24	71	34	291	4.1		15						
Wycoff	9	98	274	2.8	2					9	13	35	37	203	5.8	2	6						
Briante	9	66	141	2.1	1					9	1	1	100	0	0.0								
Haines	4	16	65	4.1	2					4	4	9	44	53	5.9	1	2						
Riordan	9	22	29	1.3																			
I. Williams	6	11	24	2.2																			
Kuczo	4	13	22	1.7						4	1	4	25	6	1.5		2						
Shapiro	1	2	7	3.5																			
Martin	8	15	-6	-0.4																			
Leary																							
Stein																							
Team	10	358	1083	3.0	9					10	42	120	36	553	4.6	3	25						
Opp.	10	350	981	2.8	3					10	55	150	37	758	5.1	5	22						
PROVIDENCE																							
Wilson	3	23	99	4.3		9	36	239	1	6	14	50	28	279	5.6	1	5	6	10	16	221	2	3
Williams	3	25	86	3.1	1	9	20	106	5														
Welch	3	18	40	2.2		9	13	113	2	6	0	7	0				2	6	2	4	20		1
McBride	3	23	45	2.0		9	12	38		6	11	30	37	144	4.8	1	3	6	3	3	58	1	
J. Cronin	3	16	17	1.1		9	7	16	1														
B. Cronin	2	5	17	3.4		8	4	15															
Hadden	2	6	10	1.7		7	5	13		4								5	1	1	9		
Stockton (1)										1	2	6	33	75	12.5	1							
Conzelman																							
McGuirk																							
Hanny																							
Team	3	116	314	2.7	1	9				6	27	93	29	498	5.4	3	10	6					
Opp.	3	128	427	3.3	3	9				5	36	93	39	474	5.1	1	10	7					
ORANGE																							
Waite	5	40	103	2.6		7	12	43	1	6	4	12	33	50	4.2		2	6	1	1	10		
Kirkleski	5	38	80	2.1	1	7	9	41		6	11	30	37	103	3.4		1	6	6	8	153	1	
Barkman	3	12	60	5.0		5	1	10		4	1	1	100	3	3.0			4					
Pease	4	13	50	3.8		6	1	5		5	4	16	25	47	2.9		1	5	6	7	118	2	1
Harnas	5	8	20	2.5		7	4	11		6	1	2	50	20	10.0			6					
McCormick	4	11	28	2.5		6				5	1	3	33	4	1.3		2	5					
Van Horn	1	6	18	3.0		3	1	-3		1	0	1	0				1	3					
Benkert	3	9	14	1.6		5																	
Hambacher	1	6	8	1.3		2				1	0	4	0				1	2					
Tomaini	5	2	6	3.0		6																	
Longua	4					7	1	0															
Scott																							
Wagner																							
McArthur																							
Beattie																							
Team	5	145	387	2.7	1	7				6	22	69	32	227	3.3		8	6					
Opp.	5	193	532	2.8	2	7				6	31	94	33	415	4.4	1	12	6					
CHICAGO BEARS																							
R. Grange	14	130	552	4.2	2					4	3	5	60	49	9.8	1	1	10	1	4	15	1	1
Walquist	4	28	67	2.4		9	6	70	3	4	12	23	52	113	4.9		2	9	3	6	50		
Driscoll	4	20	106	5.3		10	3	19	1	4	4	15	27	99	6.6		1	10	0	1			1
Holmer	4	18	42	2.3		11	6	26		4	6	32	10	100	3.1	2	13	11	7	12	214	3	2
Senn	4	11	11	1.0		11	2	29	1	4	1	3	33	39	13.0		1	11					
White	3	9	21	2.3		7	4	13	2	3								7	1	1	10		
Sternaman	4	10	11	1.1		11	4	9		4	2	6	33	36	6.0		3	11	1	1	18		
Ellness	1	2	9	4.5		3				1	0	1	0					3					
Johnsos																							
G. Grange																							
Team	4	114	315	2.8		11				6	41	127	32	654	5.1	2	28	9					
Opp.	4	171	644	3.8	5	11				5	34	85	40	560	6.6	6	3	10					

NAME	RECEIVING Complete Games					RECEIVING Incom. Games				PUNTING Comp. Games			PUNTING Incom. Games			PUNT RETURNS Complete Games					PUNT RETURNS Incom. Games			
	G	Rec.	Yds	Avg.	TD	G	Rec.	Yds.	TD	G	No.	Avg.	G	No.	Avg.	G	No.	Yds.	Avg.	TD	G	No.	Yds.	TD
FRANKFORD																								
Diehl	12	3	31	10.3		6				13	88	35.8	5	2	20.0	11	3	39	13.0		7			
Halicki	12	14	191	13.6	2	5	2	55	1															
Mercer	9	3	17	5.7	1	4				10	18	34.9	3			9	1	6	6.0		4			
Wilson	12	4	64	16.0		6										11	2	25	12.5		7			
Kelly	12	8	87	10.9		5	1	51		13	2	34.0	4	1	0.0	11	11	141	12.8		6			
Oehlrich	11	16	217	13.6		6	2	46	1							10	4	40	10.0		7			
Elkins (2)										5	19	32.6	2	2	34.5									
Homan	12	7	131	18.7	2	5										12	31	439	14.2		5			
Rogers	4	5	60	12.0		3				5	12	32.2	2			4	7	107	15.3		3			
T. Rostos	13	18	299	16.6	1	6	2	45								12	1	7	7.0		7			
Barna	11	5	71	14.2		6	2	38								10	3	29	9.7		7			
Maxwell	10	2	33	16.5		2																		
Behman										14	12	34.3	4											
M. Kostos																5	1	7	7.0		2			
Malcolm																9	1	6	6.0		5			
Filak																10	1	4	4.0		4			
Team										14	151	34.8	5			12	66	850	12.9		7			
Opp.										10	119	35.9	9			9	42	541	12.9		10			
CHICAGO CARDINALS																								
Nevers										2	24	38.7	9	2	17.0									
McDonnell	4	7	79	11.3		9	3	62	1							3	4	48	12.0		10	3	107	1
C. Rooney	3	7	82	11.7		8	5	97	2							2	1	5	5.0		9			
Rose	4	1	5	5.0		9																		
Butts																								
Elkins (1)										1	11	31.1	1											
Hill (2)	3					8	1	75	1															
Britton										1	3	31.7	1											
Method																								
Kassel	4	5	64	12.8	1	9	4	105	1															
Dowling	4	1	21	21.0		9	1	21																
Team										3	38	35.9	10			3	5	53	10.6		10			
Opp.										3	30	39.1	10			3	16	201	12.6		10			
BOSTON																								
Latone	2					6	2	12																
Miller																								
Stockton (2)	2	2	40	20.0		6																		
Kittredge	2	2	14	7.0		5				2	2	43.5	5			2	1	8	8.0		5	1	35	
Wentworth						6	4	126	2				6	5	31.2						6	2	72	1
Ernst	2	3	43	14.3		5	1	30		2	2	39.0	5			2	5	86	17.2		5			
Lawrence																								
Maloney	2					6	1	14		2	8	32.5	6	2	40.5									
Kenneally	2	2	25	12.5		6	1	10																
Team										2	12	35.4	6			2	6	94	15.7		6			
Opp.										2	14	40.2	6			2	1	5	5.0		6			
STATEN ISLAND																								
Strong	10	2	-2	-1.0						10	75	35.9				10	12	197	16.4	1				
Wycoff	9	5	47	9.4						9	18	33.4				9	3	40	13.3					
Briante	9	4	51	12.8																				
Haines	4	3	36	12.0												4	3	47	15.7					
Riordan	9	5	51	10.2																				
I. Williams	6	2	3	1.5																				
Kuczo										4	1	20.0				4	3	53	17.7					
Shapiro																1	1	12	12.0					
Martin	8	8	112	14.0												8	2	23	11.5					
Leary	10	8	140	17.5	2																			
Stein	9	6	115	19.2	1																			
Team										10	94	35.3				10	24	372	15.5	1				
Opp.										10	88	36.3				10	18	229	12.7					
PROVIDENCE																								
Wilson										3	30	38.1	9			3	1	22	22.0		9			
Williams	6	2	16	8.0		6	1	32	1							3					9	1	24	
Welch	6	11	267	24.3	3	6	4	67	1	3	2	16.5	9			3	7	87	12.4		9	3	65	
McBride																								
J. Cronin	6	1	15	15.0		6	1	41		3	9	33.1	9	2	31.0	3	1	13	13.0		9			
B. Cronin	5	3	64	21.3		5	1	49																
Hadden																								
Stockton (1)																								
Conzelman	5	9	123	13.7		4	8	103	1							3	1	22	22.0		6			
McGuirk	6					6	1	14																
Hanny	5	1	13	13.0		6																		
Team										3	41	36.0	9			3	10	144	14.4		9			
Opp.										3	31	38.3	9			3	16	318	19.9	2	9			
ORANGE																								
Waite	6	4	28	7.0		6				5	1	34.0	7											
Kirkleski	6	1	6	6.0		6	3	27	1	5	19	37.1	7			5	4	37	9.3		7			
Barkman	4	1	0	0.0		4																		
Pease	5	3	42	14.0		5	2	44	1	4	4	33.8	6			4	3	38	12.7		6	2	70	
Harnas	6	2	17	8.5		6	2	55																
McCormick	5	1	3	3.0		5																		
Van Horn	1	1	2	2.0		3	1	7		1	7	32.4	3			1	1	18	18.0		3			
Benkert										3	2	47.5	5			3	1	10	10.0		5			
Hambacher										1	6	26.2	2			1	1	18	18.0		2			
Tomaini	5	3	41	13.7		6	2	44																
Longua	5	2	32	16.0		6	1	52	1	4	5	37.4	7	2	0.0									
Scott	4	1	11	11.0		4	2	52																
Wagner	1	1	20	20.0																				
McArthur	4	1	19	19.0		6				4	1	39.0	6											
Beattie	6	1	6	6.0		5																		
Team										5	45	35.1	7			5	10	121	12.1		7			
Opp.										5	36	32.6	7			5	15	193	12.9		7			
CHICAGO BEARS																								
R. Grange	4	6	66	11.0		10	2	53								3					11	1	13	
Walquist	4	2	43	21.5		9	1	18								4	2	16	8.0		9			
Driscoll	4	1	16	16.0		10	1	10		4	24	38.8	10	1	32.0									
Holmer										4	25	39.0	11											
Senn	4	2	68	34.0		11	4	85	2							4	5	74	14.8		11			
White	3	2	13	6.5		7	1	14																
Sternaman	4	2	46	23.0		11										4	9	111	12.3		11	2	46	
Ellness																								
Johnsos	4	11	150	13.6	2	11	3	44	1															
G. Grange	4	3	31	10.3		10	3	123	2															
Team										4	49	38.9	11			4	16	201	12.6		11			
Opp.										4	53	39.0	11			4	17	157	9.2		11			

Regulars							Substitutes							Substitutes							Scores of each game			
UseName	Pos.	Hgt.	Wgt.	Age	Int.	Pts.	UseName	Pos.	Hgt.	Wgt.	Age	Int.	Pts.	UseName	Pos.	Hgt.	Wgt.	Age	Int.	Pts.	Date	Pts.	Opponent	Pts.
BUFFALO BISONS 1-7-1 Al Jolley																								
Tillie Voss (from DAY)	E	6'3	225	32			Earl Plank	E		173	24										Sep. 29	3	CHIC. CARDS	9
Herb Bizer	E-FB	5'11	205	23	1		Jim Woodruff	E-T-TB	6'3	210	26	1									Oct. 5	0	Frankford	19
Walt Brewster	T	6'1	195	25																	Oct. 6	0	FRANKFORD	13
Al Jolley	T	6'2	225	29			Henry Myles	T-G-E	6'	190	26										Oct. 13	0	CHIC. BEARS	16
Frank Glassman	G-T	6'	210	19			Ed Comstock	G-T	6'2	205	25										Oct. 20	7	Providence	7
Nat McCombs	G-T	5'11	225	24																	Oct. 27	6	Boston	14
Art Dorfman	C	5'10	210	22																			(at Pottsville)	
Cassy Ryan	BB-WB	5'6	160	24		12	Stan Rosen	BB-TB	5'6	155	23										Nov. 5	6	NEW YORK	45
Chuck Weimer	TB-BB	5'9	175	24		18	Jesse Rodriguez	TB	5'7	160	26										Nov. 17	7	Boston	12
Swede Hagberg	WB-E-C-FB	6'4	215	22	3	18	Red Shurtcliffe	WB-TB		160	22			Bob Rapp	WB	5'8	160	31			Nov. 24	19	Chic. Bears	7
Bob Mahan	FB-WB	5'9	180	25	1		Ulysses Comier	WB-FB	5'10	195	24													
MINNEAPOLIS REDJACKETS 1-9-0 Herb Joesting																								
Ken Haycraft	E	6'	175	22		12	John Fahay	BB-E-G	6'	190	27										Sep. 22	6	Chic. Bears	19
Bob Lundell	E	6'4	215	22			Lee Wilson	E-WB	5'11	182	24												(at Madison, Wis.)	
Chief Franta	T	6'1	220	24																	Oct. 6	6	CHIC. BEARS	7
Chet Widerquist	T	6'1	215	33			Al Maeder	T	5'9	185	23										Oct. 13	14	CHIC. CARDS	7
Joe Chrape	G-T		210	20	1																Oct. 20	0	Green Bay	24
Fritz Lovin	G		182	35		6	Tom Mehelich	G		195	23										Oct. 27	0	Chic. Bears	27
Sam Young	C-G	6'2	195	26			Ben Oas	C-BB	6'	195	27			Al Gautsch	C-G		190	29			Nov. 3	6	GREEN BAY	16
Henry Willegalle	BB-HB-FB	5'11	190	28			Artie Sandberg	BB		194	29										Nov. 10	0	Chic. Cards	8
Mally Nydahl	TB-HB	5'11	163	22	3	14	LaDue Lurth	TB	5'8	160	24										Nov. 17	16	Providence	19
Hal Erickson	HB-TB-FB	5'9	200	30		4	Rube Ursella	HB-BB-TB	5'9	175	39										Nov. 23	0	Frankford	24
Herb Joesting	FB	6'2	190	24	1	12	Jack O'Brien	BB	5'10	170	30										Nov. 24	0	Staten Island	34
DAYTON TRIANGLES 0-6-0 Fay Abbott																								
Lee Fenner	E	5'10	170	33	1		John Wallace	E	6'	180	24										Sep. 22	0	Green Bay	9
Roy Carlson	E-G	5'9	180	24			John Depner	E			22										Sep. 28	7	Frankford	14
Dick Faust	T	6'1	220	27			Johnnie Becker	T	5'11	210	26			Tillie Voss (to BUF)	T	6'3	225	32			Sep. 29	0	Providence	41
Carl Mankat	T-G-E	6'3	205	25			Bill Belanich	T	6'	205	26	1		John Kauffman	T-G			22			Oct. 6	0	Staten Island	12
Al Graham	G	6'	210	23		6	Ed Tolley	G	5'8	175	29										Oct. 13	0	Boston	41
Jim Spencer	G	6'	210	27			Corl Zimmerman	G	6'	185	30										Nov. 24	0	Chic. Cards	19
Hobby Kinderdine	C	5'11	185	38			Jack Brown	C-G	6'	195	26	1												
Bob Haas	BB-WB			23			Frank Sillin	BB-WB-TB-FB	5'11	185	26													
Steve Buchanan	TB-BB	5'8	160	26	3		John Singleton	TB-WB	5'11	175	32													
John Brewer	WB	6'	185	23			Lou Partlow	FB	6'1	185	36													
Elmer Wynne	FB	6'	195	28			Pat Duffy	FB-TB-BB-WB	5'10	185	22		1	Fay Abbott	FB	5'8	190	34						

1930 N.F.L.
Nagurski's Debut and Rockne's Lesson

Constant bickering over the team's direction between Chicago Bears' co-owners George Halas and Dutch Sternaman had pointed the team in the direction of the NFL cellar. A new slate was in order. They resolved their differences by agreeing that neither would coach the team. In effect, they fired themselves, vowing to attend to their front-office knitting. Sternaman would sell his interest to Halas after the 1932 season and leave pro football for good. Halas would go on and on.

For a new coach, the Bears tapped Ralph Jones, the head man at Lake Forest (Ill.) Academy and a leading proponent of the T-formation. While other pro teams lined up in the single wing, double wing or Notre Dame box, the Bears under Jones continued to use their basic T but with new refinements such as split ends and a man in motion in the backfield.

With the refined T opening up the Bears offense with more passes and end runs, coach Jones climbed out on a limb by promising a championship within three years. In the general housecleaning, veteran center George Trafton was let go, considered washed up at 33. He surprised everyone by showing up in training camp and winning back his position. To go with veterans like Trafton, Red Grange and Link Lyman, Jones had a large contingent of rookies, featuring Bronko Nagurski, who came out of the University of Minnesota as a legendary All-American, both at fullback and tackle. He stood 6'2" and carried 216 pounds and, running with his head down like a battering ram, he quickly became the league's top power runner. Such was his play that teammate Red Grange, who had the good fortune to face Nagurski only in practice, was led to comment, "When you hit him, it was like getting an electrical shock. If you hit him above the ankles, you were likely to get yourself killed." With Nagurski's muscle and Jones' strategic innovations leading the way, the Bears bounced back from a dismal 1929 season to finish 9-4-1 this year, with five straight victories ending the campaign on a high note.

Late in 1930, just after the college season had ended, Halas signed Notre Dame's popular fullback Jumpin' Joe Savoldi, in a move reminiscent of Halas' 1925 signing of Grange. League president Joe Carr immediately slapped Halas with a $1,000 fine for signing a player before his college class had graduated. Halas pointed out that Savoldi had been expelled from school for being secretly married, but the fine stuck. Jumpin' Joe played only three games for the Bears and then retired. He had run well but had no chance to dislodging Nagurski as the regular.

But, improved as the Bears were, the Green Bay Packers and New York Giants still stood far above the other teams as the class of the NFL. The Packers had essentially the same veteran squad that went undefeated last year. Cal Hubbard, Mike Michalske and Lavie Dilweg anchored the line, while the deep backfield featured Red Dunn, Johnny Blood, Verne Lewellen, Hurdis McCrary and Bo Molenda. The Giants pivoted once again around tailback Benny Friedman, who topped a thousand yards in passing yardgae for the fourth straight year. Favorite target Ray Flaherty had retired for a year to coach at Gonzaga, his alma mater, but the Giants exchanged one Hall of Fame end for another by luring Red Badgro back to pro football. After playing for the 1927-28 New York Yankees, Badgro had devoted himself to baseball for two seasons. Rookie help for the Giants came in tackle Len Grant, guard Butch Gibson and Dale Burnett, a versatile back who grabbed eight interceptions during 1930.

After two easy victories, the Giants travelled to Green Bay on October 5 and dropped a 14-7 decision. Then they rebounded to rip through eight straight wins. On October 16, the Giants played the first Polo Grounds night pro footbal game, beating the Chicago Cardinals 25-12. Governor Al Smith was among the 15,000 in attendance. The Cards had won the first NFL night game on November 6, 1929 at Providence and, now, less than a year later, games under lights were becoming a regular occurence. New teams Portsmouth and Newark scheduled several each. The Orange Tornadoes had moved to Newark this season. With the aid of mid-week games night games, they managed to jam 12 games into six-and-a-half weeks, employ 44 different men in their lineup (the roster limit was up to 20 for this year), win only once, and plummet into last place. At the end of October, they quit. The Portsmouth Spartans, who flew in the face of the prevailing NFL trend away from small-town teams, had a more respectable first season, largely due to a strong running attack led by wingback Chuck Bennett's 744 yards.

By November 10, the Packers had an 8-0 record and the Giants a 10-1 mark, flawed only by the loss at Green Bay. On November 16, both clubs were upset. Led by Ernie Nevers' running and defense, the Chicago

NAME	RUSHING Complete Games G	Att.	Yds.	Avg.	TD	RUSHING Incom. Games G	Att.	Yds.	TD	PASSING Complete Games G	Com.	Att.	%	Yds.	Y/A	TD	Int.	PASSING Incom. Games G	Com.	Att.	Yds.	TD	Int.
BUFFALO																							
Ryan	1	2	4	2.0		8	13	91		1	0	1	0				1	8	3	5	35		
Weimer	1	12	27	2.3		8	7	33	1	1	0	4	0				2	8	8	13	187	3	4
Rosen	1	3	22	7.3		7	1	2		1	0	1	0				1	7	1	3	16		1
Bizer	1	8	18	2.3		8	1	1															
Mahan						8	4	14															
Shurtcliffe						4	2	13															
Rodriguez	1	5	13	2.6		4																	
Hagberg	1					8	3	7		1								8	1	1	8		
Glassman	1	1	2	2.0		8																	
Woodruff																		6	2	3	70	1	
Voss																							
Team	1	31	86	2.8		8				1	0	6	0				4	8					
Opp.	1	36	161	4.5	2	8				1	15	30	50	164	5.5	1	2	8					
MINNEAPOLIS																							
Nydahl	4	22	67	3.0		6	18	171	2	5	4	9	44	52	5.8			5	4	5	66		
Joesting	4	29	95	3.3	1	6	23	115	1	5	11	27	41	135	5.0	2	2	5	3	5	70		1
Erickson	4	34	26	0.8		6	15	78		5	7	17	41	99	5.8		2	5	1	1	20		
Ursella	4	18	41	2.3		4	2	6		5	1	3	33	17	5.7		1	3					
Oas	3	4	14	3.5		4				3	1	4	25	9	2.3		2	4					
Lundell	4	1	4	4.0		6				5	0	1	0				1	5					
O'Brien	1	1	2	2.0																			
Willegalle	4	1	-1	-1.0		5																	
Haycraft																							
Wilson	5					4	1	0															
Sandberg																							
Team	4	110	248	2.3	1	6				5	24	61	39	312	5.1	2	8	5					
Opp.	4	173	717	4.1	8	6				5	31	64	48	602	9.4	5	3	5					
DAYTON																							
Buchanan	3	20	63	3.2		3	1	7		3	5	23	22	66	2.9		5	3	0	1			1
Graham	1	1	13	13.0		2																	
Haas	2	7	10	1.4		3																	
Sillin	3	3	4	1.3		2				3	0	1	0					2					
Singleton	2	3	3	1.0		3				2	1	5	20	28	5.6		1	3	0	1			1
Wynne	3	12	5	0.4		2				3	0	4	0				2	2					
Duffy	3	10	1	0.1		2				3	1	5	20	6	1.2		1	2					
Brewer	3	1	0	0.0		3				3	0	3	0				1	3					
Carlson																							
Wallace																							
Team	3	57	99	1.7		3				3	7	41	17	100	2.4		10	3					
Opp.	3	137	433	3.2	3	3				3	14	54	26	185	3.4	2	7	3					

NAME	RECEIVING Complete Games G	Rec.	Yds	Avg.	TD	RECEIVING Incom. Games G	Rec.	Yds.	TD	PUNTING Comp. Games G	No.	Avg.	PUNTING Incom. Games G	No.	Avg.	PUNT RETURNS Complete Games G	No.	Yds.	Avg.	TD	PUNT RETURNS Incom. Games G	No.	Yds.	TD
BUFFALO																								
Ryan						9	3	60	1												9	2	27	
Weimer													9	2	0.0						9	1	15	
Rosen																								
Bizer																								
Mahan																								
Shurtcliffe						4	1	5																
Rodriguez																								
Hagberg						9	8	191	3				9	3	48.3									
Glassman																								
Woodruff																								
Voss						8	3	60					9								9			
Team										1	8	35.8	8			1	5	60	12.0		8			
Opp.																								
MINNEAPOLIS																								
Nydahl	5	3	27	9.0		5				4	8	32.2	6			3	4	50	12.5		7	1	15	
Joesting																3					7	1	30	
Erickson	5	1	6	6.0		5	1	15		4	6	32.8	6											
Ursella	5	2	17	8.5		3				3			5	1	20.0									
Oas																								
Lundell	5	6	67	11.2		5	2	30		4	21	33.4	6	2	27.5									
O'Brien																								
Willegalle	5	2	41	20.5		4																		
Haycraft	5	7	106	15.1	2	5	2	53																
Wilson	5	3	48	16.0		4	2	40																
Sandberg						3	1	18																
Team										4	33	33.1	6			3	4	50	12.5		7			
Opp.										4	30	34.9	6			4	17	206	12.1		6			
DAYTON																								
Buchanan										2	19	35.3	4	1	34.0									
Graham																								
Haas	2	3	26	8.7		3																		
Sillin	3	1	8	8.0		2																		
Singleton	2	1	30	30.0		3				1	1	45.0	4											
Wynne																								
Duffy																								
Brewer																								
Carlson	3	1	28	28.0		3																		
Wallace	2	1	8	8.0		2																		
Team										2	20	35.8	4			2	0				4			
Opp.										3	32	37.2	3			3	18	239	13.3		3			

Cardinals handed the Packers a 13-6 loss, their first setback in 22 games. The same day, the Bears beat the Giants 12-0 in New York. One week later, on November 23, the Packers came to the Polo Grounds in the game expected to settle the championship. A crowd of 45,000 showed up, drawn by the important match and the professional debut of Chris Cagle, the famous star back of last season's Army team. Cagle's belated entry into pro ball was unspectacular, but the Giants delighted the audience by whipping the Packers 13-6. A long pass from Friedman to Badgro scored one New York touchdown, and an 84-yard run by Hap Moran set up Friedman's one-yard plunge for the winning margin. The Giants' 11-2 record dumped the Packers at 8-2 into second place on percentage.

Four days later, the Giants climbed right back out of the driver's seat by losing 7-6 to the Staten Island Stapletons in a Thanksgiving Day contest. A full house of 12,000 jammed tiny Thompson Stadium to witness player-coach Doug Wycoff, a 29 percent passer on the season, complete two long passes and cap the scoring drive with a short run. Ken Strong, developing into a complete star in his second season, kicked the extra point which the Giants had missed earlier to give the Stapes a lead they never relinquished. The Packers, meanwhile, crushed the Frankford Yellowjackets 25-7. The Yellowjackets fell completely apart this season and, starting November 8, the Yellowjackets and Minneapolis Redjackets, another weak club, pooled players on days when only one team was scheduled. NFL president Carr closed his eyes to this maneuver in the interest of improved competition.

On November 30, the race ended. The Packers beat the Stapes 37-7 on Staten Island while the Giants were upset at home by the Brooklyn Dodgers 7-6. The Dodgers were another new team, having acquired the Dayton Triangles franchise after the 1929 season. They managed a winning record in their first season, mostly through the efforts of Giants castoff Jack McBride, who led the league in scoring with 56 points. He scored all of the Dodgers' points in the Giants' fourth loss. Benny Friedman missed the game with a leg injury, but the New Yorkers had no alibi for three losses in four games at the key stretch of the race. The slump cost coach Roy Andrews his job. Friedman and Steve Owen split duties for the Giants' last two games.

The Giants beat Frankford the next Saturday and Brooklyn on Sunday while the Packers lost on Sunday to the Bears, but the title was already in hand for Curly Lambeau's squad. On Sunday, December 14, the Packers tied the Portsmouth Spartans 6-6 to clinch the championship over the Giants, who had no league game that day. The Packers finished at 10-3-1, the Giants at 13-4-0, with Green Bay champions by four percentage points.

But while the Giants had no league game on December 14, they did play a game with great significance for pro football in New York. With the Great Depression growing worse, the Giants agreed to meet an all-star team of Notre Dame graduates in the Polo Grounds, with all proceeds going to the New York Unemployment Fund.

Knute Rockne coached the Notre Dame squad, which included the Four Horsemen and other more recent graduates. Rockne and much of the public held pro football in low regard and expected an easy Notre Dame victory.

Benny Friedman and the Giants, however, found the game a great opportunity to convince Rockne and the public of the quality of pro ball. Before a crowd of 55,000, Friedman led the Giants to a pair of quick touchdowns while allowing the Notre Dame players not even a first down. Even though most of the New York regulars sat out the second half, the final score was a one-sided 22-0. The Giants profited from the enormous publicity the press gave the contest and no longer would the public shrug off the pros as clumsy goons. More importantly, the New York Unemplyment Fund collected more than $100,000.

Less publicized at the time, the Chicago Bears defeated the Cardinals 9-7 in a charity exhibition game played indoors at Chicago Stadium, the first indoor game since 1903. The truncated 80-yard field was covered with a six-inch layer of dirt. Two years later, the same setting would be used for one of the most significant games of the era.

The *Green Bay Press Gazette* annual NFL team, selected by a poll of sports writers, team officials and coaches, and game officials, showed six future Hall of Famers on the first team. The choices were ends Lavie Dilweg, Green Bay, and Luke Johnsos, Bears; tackles Jap Douds, Providence and Portsmouth, and Link Lyman, Bears; guards Mike Michalske, Green Bay, and Walt Kiesling, Cardinals; center Swede Hagberg, Brooklyn; quarterback Benny Friedman, Giants; halfbacks Red Grange, Bears, and Ken Strong, Stapletons; and fullback Ernie Nevers, Cardinals.

All top pro players were not in the NFL. Most excellent players preferred to play with the independent teams because of full-time jobs. Soem strong independents, such as the Stapletons and the Portsmouth Spartans, eventually joined the NFL, but others, equally strong, continued to play independently. NFL teams often played mid-week or post-season exhibition games with these independents, and some of the wildcatters were quite competitive. None, however, matched the Ironton (Ohio) Tanks' 1930 achievements. The Tanks and Portsmouth Spartans had been strong independent rivals for many years. When the Spartans joined the NFL, they kept the Tanks on their schedule. The Tanks, coached by Greasy Neale and led on the field by former Nebraska star Glenn Presnell, managed one victory in three 1930 meetings with the Spartans. But, late in the season, they caught the New York Giants between strides and beat them 14-13. On November 23 at Cincinnati, they humiliated the Chicago Bears 26-13, with Presnell scoring two touchdowns, one on an 88-yard run. Sadly, it was a last hurrah for the Yanks; the Depression would wipe them out before the 1931 season began. But other independents would survive through the 1930s, bringing often quite respectable pro football to places that might otherwise have not seen it.

GREEN BAY PACKERS 10-3-1 Curly Lambeau

Regulars

UseName	Pos.	Hgt.	Wgt.	Age	Int	Pts.
Lavie Dilweg	E	6'3"	205	27	6	18
Tom Nash	E	6'3"	210	24		6
Cal Hubbard	T-E	6'4"	250	29	1	6
Bill Kern	T	6'	187	23		
Jim Bowdoin	G	6'1"	234	24		
Mike Michalske	G-T	6'	210	27	2	
Boob Darling	C	5'11"	210	26	2	
Red Dunn	BB	5'11"	180	28	4	14
Verne Lewellen	TB-HB-BB	6'1"	184	28	1	54
Johnny Blood	HB-TB	6'1"	186	26	4	30
Bo Molenda	FB	5'10"	215	25	4	22

Substitutes

UseName	Pos.	Hgt.	Wgt.	Age	Int	Pts.
Dick O'Donnell	E	6'	193	30		
Ken Radick	E-T	5'10"	210	23		
Claude Perry	T	6'1"	212	28		
Red Sleight	T	6'2"	220	23		
Whitey Woodin	G	5'10"	210	35		
Merle Zuver	G-C	6'1"	198	24		
Jug Earp	C-T-G	6'	240	33		
Arnie Herber	BB-TB	5'11"	195	20	2	6
Dave Zuidmulder	TB	5'10"	175	24		
Wuert Engelmann	HB	6'3"	190	22	1	18
Hurdis McCrary	FB-HB	6'	207	26	2	36

Substitutes

UseName	Pos.	Hgt.	Wgt.	Age	Int	Pts.
Ken Haycraft (from MIN)	E	6'	180	23		
Duke Hanny (to PORT)	T	6'	215	32		
Chief Franta (from MIN)	G	6'1"	220	25		
Al Bloodgood	BB	5'8"	152	28		
Oran Pape (from MIN)	TB	5'11"	180	26	1	
Paul Fitzgibbon	HB-BB-TB	5'8"	174	27	2	18
Cully Lidberg	FB	5'9"	190	30		6
Mule Wilson (from NYG & SI)	HB	5'11"	190	28		

Scores of Each Game

Date	Pts.	Opponent	
Sep. 21	14	CHIC. CARDS	0
Sep. 28	7	CHIC. BEARS	0
Oct. 5	14	NEW YORK	7
Oct. 12	27	FRANKFORD	12
Oct. 19	13	Minneapolis	0
Oct. 26	19	MINNEAPOLIS	0
Nov. 2	47	PORTSMOUTH	13
Nov. 9	13	Chic. Bears	12
Nov. 16	6	Chic. Cards	13
Nov. 23	6	New York	13
Nov. 27	25	Frankford	7
Nov. 30	37	Staten Island	7
Dec. 7	0	Chic. Bears	21
Dec. 14	6	Portsmouth	6

NEW YORK GIANTS 13-4-0 Roy Andrews, Benny Friedman and Steve Owen

Regulars

UseName	Pos.	Hgt.	Wgt.	Age	Int	Pts.
Red Badgro	E	6'	190	27		18
Glenn Campbell	E	5'11"	190	26		24
Bill Owen	T	6'	205	26		
Steve Owen	T-G	5'10"	235	32		
Rudy Comstock	G	5'10"	210	29		
Les Caywood	G	6'	230	25	2	6
Joe Westoupal	C	6'3"	200	27	1	
Tiny Feather	BB-FB	6'	196	27	5	6
Benny Friedman	TB	5'10"	183	25	3	49
Len Sedbrook	WB-TB	5'10"	175	25	2	48
Ossie Widberg	FB-WB-BB	5'11"	205	25	1	30

Substitutes

UseName	Pos.	Hgt.	Wgt.	Age	Int	Pts.
Hal Hilpert	E	5'9"	185	22		
Len Grant	T	6'3"	235	24		
Dick Stahlman	T-G	6'2"	220	28		
Butch Gibson	G-T	5'9"	200	26		
Dosey Howard	G	6'	225	29		6
Mickey Murtagh	C-E-BB	6'1"	190	26		
Hap Moran	TB-BB-WB-FB-E	6'1"	190	29		27
Jack Hagerty	TB-WB	5'9"	163	27		30
Mule Wilson (to SI, GB)	WB-FB-BB	5'11"	190	28		24
Dale Burnett	FB-WB-BB	6'1"	190	21	8	40

Ray Flaherty — Retired to coach college football

Substitutes

UseName	Pos.	Hgt.	Wgt.	Age	Int	Pts.
Saul Mielziner	G-C	6'1"	240	25	1	
Chris Cagle	TB-FB	5'10"	175	25		

Scores of Each Game

Date	Pts.	Opponent	
Sep. 17	32	Newark	0
Sep. 28	27	Providence	7
Oct. 5	7	Green Bay	14
Oct. 12	12	Chic. Bears	0
Oct. 16	25	CHIC. CARDS	12
Oct. 19	53	FRANKFORD	0
Oct. 26	25	PROVIDENCE	0
Oct. 30	34	NEWARK	7
Nov. 2	9	STATEN ISLAND	7
Nov. 5	19	Portsmouth	6
Nov. 9	13	Chic. Cards	7
Nov. 16	0	CHIC. BEARS	12
Nov. 23	13	GREEN BAY	6
Nov. 27	6	Staten Island	7
Nov. 30	6	BROOKLYN	7
Dec. 6	14	Frankford	6
Dec. 7	13	Brooklyn	0

CHICAGO BEARS 9-4-1 Ralph Jones

Regulars

UseName	Pos.	Hgt.	Wgt.	Age	Int	Pts.
Gardie Grange	E	6'	175	23		1
Luke Johnsos	E	6'2"	190	24	1	28
Don Murry	T	6'2"	188	30		
Link Lyman	T	6'2"	240	31		
Zuck Carlson	G	6'	200	25		
Danny McMullen	G	5'8"	225	24		
George Trafton	C	6'2"	232	33	2	
Carl Brumbaugh	QB	5'10"	160	22		7
Red Grange	HB	5'11"	192	27	3	49
Joe Lintzenich	HB-FB	5'11"	183	22		
Bronko Nagurski	FB-T	6'2"	216	21	1	30

Substitutes

UseName	Pos.	Hgt.	Wgt.	Age	Int	Pts.
Hoot Drury	E	6'4"	185	24	1	
Bill Fleckenstein (to PORT)	E	6'1"	213	26		
Larry Steinbach	T	6'	210	26		
Frank Pauley	T	6'1"	270	26		
Paul Schuette	G	6'	218	24		
Babe Frump	G	6'	225	29		
Bert Pearson	C-G	6'	200	25	1	
Joey Sternaman	QB	5'6"	148	30		11
Walt Holmer	HB	6'	180	27	1	18
Bill Senn	HB	6'	178	25	2	6
Dick Nesbitt	FB-HB	6'	196	22	1	6

Joe Kopcha — Retired to attend Medical School

Substitutes

UseName	Pos.	Hgt.	Wgt.	Age	Int	Pts.
Laurie Walquist	HB-QB	5'8"	163	32	2	7
Joe Savoldi	FB	5'11"	194	22		6
Stub Blackman	FB	5'11"	195	23		

Scores of Each Game

Date	Pts.	Opponent	
Sep. 21	0	BROOKLYN	0
Sep. 28	0	Green Bay	7
Oct. 5	20	Minneapolis	0
Oct. 12	0	NEW YORK	12
Oct. 19	32	Chic. Cards	6
Oct. 22	6	Portsmouth	7
Oct. 26	13	FRANKFORD	7
Nov. 2	20	MINNEAPOLIS	7
Nov. 9	12	GREEN BAY	13
Nov. 16	12	New York	0
Nov. 22	13	Frankford	6
Nov. 27	6	CHIC. CARDS	0
Nov. 30	14	PORTSMOUTH	6
Dec. 7	21	GREEN BAY	0

BROOKLYN DODGERS 7-4-1 Jack Depler

Regulars

UseName	Pos.	Hgt.	Wgt.	Age	Int	Pts.
Mike Stramiello	E	6'1"	192	23		12
Bob Mahan	E-HB	5'9"	175	26		
Hoot Haines	T	6'	205	23		
Stu Worden	T-G	6'	210	20		
Hec Garvey	G-T	6'1"	230	30		
Bob Gillson	G	6'	210	23		
Swede Hagberg	C-T-FB-BB	6'4"	222	23	2	6
Izzy Yablok	BB-TB	5'10"	172	22	1	
Wild Bill Kelly	TB-BB	5'10"	182	25	4	6
Rex Thomas	HB	5'9"	175	29	1	31
Jack McBride	FB-TB	5'11"	190	28	3	56

Substitutes

UseName	Pos.	Hgt.	Wgt.	Age	Int	Pts.
Johnny Tomaini (from NWK)	E	6'	195	28		
Earl Plank	E		170	25		
Jim Mooney (from NWK)	T-E	5'11"	200	22		
Al Jolley	T	6'2"	235	30		
Ernie Cuneo	G	5'9"	192	25		
Ed Comstock	G	6'2"	210	26		
Skippy Scheib	C	6'2"	210	25		
Algy Clark	BB-TB-FB-E	6'	180	26		
Chuck Weimer	TB-HB	5'9"	175	25	1	13
Stumpy Thomason	HB-FB	5'7"	190	24	1	24
Horse Hagerty	FB-TB	5'10"	185	24		

Substitutes

UseName	Pos.	Hgt.	Wgt.	Age	Int	Pts.
Fred Getz	E	6'1"	192	21		
Matt Kelsch	E	5'11"	190	23		
John Lott	T			24		
Hal Stotsbery	T	6'1"	235	24		
Mal Bleeker	G-C-E	6'	205	23		
Dick Crowl	C-G	5'10"	185	22		
Jim Schuber	HB	5'8"	160	26		
Ben Greenberg	TB	5'9"	170	23		
Jim Miller	HB	5'11"	195	23		6
Ev Rowan	FB-HB	6'1"	197	27		
Jack McArthur (from NWK, PROV & FRA)	C-G-T	5'11"	220	26		

Scores of Each Game

Date	Pts.	Opponent	
Sep. 21	0	Chic. Bears	0
Sep. 24	0	Portsmouth	12
Oct. 5	20	Staten Island	0
Oct. 12	32	NEWARK	0
Oct. 18	14	Frankford	7
Oct. 19	14	Newark	0
Nov. 2	0	Providence	3
Nov. 9	34	MINNEAPOLIS	0
Nov. 23	0	STATEN ISLAND	6
Nov. 27	33	PROVIDENCE	12
Nov. 30	7	New York	6
Dec. 7	0	New York	13

PROVIDENCE STEAM ROLLER 6-4-1 Jimmy Conzelman

Regulars

UseName	Pos.	Hgt.	Wgt.	Age	Int	Pts.
Al Rose	E	6'3"	200	23	1	
John Spellman	E	5'10"	205	31		
Perry Jackson	T	6'1"	205	27		
Warren McGuirk	T	5'11"	200	24		
Frank Racis	G	6'	200	32	1	6
Milt Rehnquist	G	6'	235	33		
Ray Smith	C	5'10"	180	22		
Curly Oden	BB	5'6"	165	31		1
Frosty Peters (to PORT)	TB-BB	5'10"	183	26	4	25
Pop Williams	WB-TB	6'	205	24	2	12
Tony Latone	FB	5'11"	195	33	2	18

Substitutes

UseName	Pos.	Hgt.	Wgt.	Age	Int	Pts.
Herm Young	E	5'11"	178	24		6
Ted Kucharski	E	6'1"	185	22		
Jap Douds (to PORT)	T	5'10"	215	25		
Joe Kozlowsky	T-G	5'10"	210	29		
Weldon Gentry	G	5'10"	195	23		
Al Graham (to PORT)	G	6'	210	24		
Herb Eschbach	C	6'	190	23		
Butch Meeker	BB-TB	5'3"	140	26	3	16
Tony Holm	TB-FB	6'1"	215	22		
Jack Cronin	WB-FB-TB	5'11"	180	27	1	
Al Hadden	FB-WB	5'9"	185	30		

Substitutes

UseName	Pos.	Hgt.	Wgt.	Age	Int	Pts.
Dutch Webber (to NWK)	E	6'2"	195	28		
Gus Sonnenberg	T	5'6"	200	32		
Jack McArthur (from NWK, to FRA & BKN)	C	5'11"	220	26		
Bud Edwards	WB-FB-TB	5'11"	190	24		6

Scores of Each Game

Date	Pts.	Opponent	
Sep. 28	7	NEW YORK	27
Oct. 1	14	FRANKFORD	0
Oct. 5	14	NEWARK	0
Oct. 12	9	CHIC. CARDS	7
Oct. 19	7	STATEN ISLAND	6
Oct. 26	0	New York	25
Nov. 2	3	BROOKLYN	0
Nov. 8	7	Frankford	20
Nov. 9	7	FRANKFORD	7
Nov. 23	10	MINNEAPOLIS	0
Nov. 27	12	Brooklyn	33

STATEN ISLAND STAPLETONS 5-5-2 Doug Wycoff

Regulars

UseName	Pos.	Hgt.	Wgt.	Age	Int	Pts.
Sammy Stein	E	6'	190	25		6
Bob Lundell (from MIN)	E	6'4"	215	23	2	6
Bing Miller	T	6'1"	188	26		
Cy Williams	T	6'	200	28	1	
Ollie Satenstein	G	6'	200	24	1	
John Bunyan	G-C	5'10"	215	24	1	
Jim Fitzgerald	C	5'11"	215	23		
Ralph Buckley	BB-HB	5'8"	175	23	3	6
Doug Wycoff	TB-FB	6'	205	26	2	24
Beryl Follet	HB-TB	5'9"	165	27	1	
Ken Strong	FB-TB	6'	200	24	3	53

Substitutes

UseName	Pos.	Hgt.	Wgt.	Age	Int	Pts.
Julie Archoska	E	5'11"	180	25		
Harry Kloppenburg	E-G	6'1"	210	23	2	
John Demmy	T		190	26		
Firpo Wilcox	T	6'	220	27		
Fred Brown	G	6'2"	195	24		
Dave Myers	G-BB	5'11"	183	23	1	
Herb Rapp	C	6'	195	25		
Snitz Snyder	BB-FB-HB	5'8"	190	25	1	
Jim Tays (from NWK)	HB-FB-TB	5'8"	180	31		
Mule Wilson (from NYG to GB)	HB-FB	5'11"	190	28		

Substitutes

UseName	Pos.	Hgt.	Wgt.	Age	Int	Pts.
Jim Nicely	T	5'9"	185	35		
Willie Halpern	G-T	5'11"	220	24		
Henry	G-C					
Bill Wexler	C	5'9"	170	25		
Bernie Finn (from NWK)	BB-HB-TB	5'10"	180	22		
Ed Lawrence	HB-E	5'8"	170	25		

Scores of Each Game

Date	Pts.	Opponent	
Sep. 21	12	NEWARK	6
Sep. 27	3	Frankford	7
Sep. 28	21	FRANKFORD	0
Oct. 1	7	Newark	7
Oct. 5	6	BROOKLYN	20
Oct. 19	6	Providence	7
Oct. 26	6	Newark	0
Nov. 2	7	New York	9
Nov. 9	13	PORTSMOUTH	13
Nov. 23	6	Brooklyn	0
Nov. 27	7	NEW YORK	6
Nov. 30	7	GREEN BAY	37

1930 STANDINGS

	W	L	T	Pct.	Pts.	Opp. Pts.	Avg. Pts.	Opp. Avg.
Green Bay Packers	10	3	1	.769	234	111	17	8
New York Giants	13	4	0	.765	308	98	18	6
Chicago Bears	9	4	1	.692	169	71	12	[illegible]
Brooklyn Dodgers	7	4	1	.636	154	59	13	5
Providence Steam Roller	6	4	1	.600	90	125	8	11
Staten Island Stapletons	5	5	2	.500	95	112	8	9
Chicago Cardinals	5	6	2	.455	128	132	10	10
Portsmouth Spartans	5	6	3	.455	176	161	13	12
Frankford Yellow Jackets	4	13	1	.235	113	321	6	18
Minneapolis Redjackets	1	7	1	.125	27	165	3	18
Newark Tornadoes	1	10	1	.091	51	190	4	16

Scoring Leaders

McBride	Bkn	56
Lewellen	GB	54
Strong	SI	53
Friedman	NYG	49
R. Grange	ChiB	49
Nevers	ChiC	48
Sedbrook	NYG	48
Bennett	Port	42
McLain	Port	42
Burnett	NYG	40
McCrary	GB	36
Thomas	Bkn	31
Blood	GB	30
Hagerty	NYG	30
Nagurski	ChiB	30
Wiberg	NYG	30
Halicki	Fra-Min	29
Johnsos	ChiB	28
Moran	NYG	27

KICKING

		FG	Att	Pct
Peters	Prov-Port	2	9	22
Meeker	Prov	1	1	100
Friedman	NYG	1	2	50
Nevers	ChiC	1	2	50
Strong	SI	1	4	25
Bleeker	Bkn	0	1	0
Burnett	Bkn	0	1	0
Clancy	Nwk	0	1	0
Feather	NYG	0	1	0
Glasgow	Port	0	1	0
G. Grange	ChiB	0	1	0
Halicki	Fra-Min	0	1	0
Holmer	ChiB	0	1	0
McBride	Bkn	0	1	0
Molenda	GB	0	1	0
Mooney	Nwk-Bkn	0	1	0
Moran	NYG	0	1	0
Pharmer	*	0	1	0
Sternaman	ChiB	0	2	0
Wiberg	NYG	0	3	0
Jennings	Port	0	4	0

		PAT	Att	Pct
Dunn	GB	14	24	58
Lewis	Port	10	13	77
Friedman	NYG	10	23	43
Nevers	ChiC	9	14	64
McBride	Bkn	8	9	89
Strong	SI	8	14	57
Peters	Prov-Port	7	8	88
Stramiello	Bkn	6	7	86
Wiberg	NYG	6	8	75
Pharmer	*	6	9	67
Halicki	Fra-Min	5	6	83
Sternaman	ChiB	5	9	56
Johnsos	ChiB	4	4	100
Burnett	NYG	4	6	67
Glasgow	Port	4	6	67
Molenda	GB	4	7	57
Moran	NYG	3	4	75
Mooney	Nwk-Bkn	2	5	40
Meeker	Prov	1	1	100
Rose	ChiC	1	1	100
Smith	Nwk	1	1	100

		PAT	Att	Pct
Tackwell	Fra-Min	1	1	100
Bogue	ChiC	1	2	50
Nydahl	*	1	2	50
Thomas	Bkn	1	2	50
Walquist	ChiB	1	2	50
G. Grange	ChiB	1	3	33
Oden	Prov	1	3	33
Weimer	Bkn	1	3	33
Cagle	NYG	0	1	0
Eby	Port	0	1	0
Feaster	Nwk	0	1	0
Lintzenich	ChiB	0	1	0
McCormick	Nwk	0	1	0
Savoldi	ChiB	0	1	0
Holmer	ChiB	0	2	0
Jennings	Port	0	2	0
Maple	ChiC	0	2	0
Rengel	Fra	0	2	0
Herber	GB	0	3	0
McLain	Port	0	4	0

RUSHING

NAME	Complete Games					Incom. Games			
	G	Att.	Yds.	Avg.	TD	G	Att.	Yds.	TD
GREEN BAY									
Molenda	12	146	458	3.1	2	1	1	1	1
Lewellen	13	118	405	3.4	7	1	1	6	1
McCrary	13	84	351	4.2	4	1			
Blood	9	78	232	3.0		1			
Herber	9	32	135	4.2		1			
Engelmann	8	27	98	3.6		1	1	33	1
Dunn	12	10	82	8.2		1			
Lidberg	5	25	68	2.7	1				
Fitzgibbon	8	21	57	2.7	1	1			
Zuidmulder	4	9	53	5.9					
Pape (2)	2	6	19	3.2					
Bloodgood	3	2	0	0.0					
Dilweg									
Nash									
O'Donnell									
Hubbard									
Team	13	558	1958	3.5	15	1			
Opp.	13	480	1706	3.6	7	1			
NEW YORK									
Friedman	5	68	177	2.6	2	10	22	209	4
Sedbrook	4	7	21	3.0	1	12	18	306	4
Moran	5	18	139	7.7	1	11	12	99	3
Burnett	4	26	86	3.3		10	16	125	4
Cagle	2	24	71	3.0		2			
Wiberg	5	22	38	1.7		12	8	29	4
Feather	5	20	44	2.2	1	10	3	12	
Hagerty	2	1	2	2.0		10	6	45	2
Wilson (1)	2					8	6	35	1
Badgro	5	4	4	1.0		12			
Campbell									
Gibson									
Grant									
Howard									
Team	5	190	582	3.1	5	12			
Opp.	5	208	581	2.8	2	12			
CHICAGO BEARS									
R. Grange	6	58	287	4.9	3	8	19	183	3
Nagurski	6	51	254	5.0		7	12	77	5
Lintzenich	5	27	99	3.7		8	7	80	
Brumbaugh	6	34	115	3.4		8	9	43	1
Senn	5	26	64	2.5		6	3	84	1
Holmer	5	7	23	3.3		7	10	79	2
Sternaman	3	7	62	8.9	1	6	2	28	
Nesbitt	3	16	88	5.5	1	5			
Walquist	4	10	49	4.9	1	6	5	34	
Savoldi	2	10	32	3.2		1	3	24	1
Johnsos									
Drury									
G. Grange									
Fleckenstein (1)									
Team	6	246	1073	4.4	6	8			
Opp.	6	250	974	3.9	4	9			
BROOKLYN									
McBride	3	57	231	4.1	3	8	15	105	5
Thomas	2	24	155	6.5		4	3	27	
Weimer	3	20	109	5.5		8	2	11	
Thomason	1	17	44	2.6		5	9	58	3
Kelly	3	16	65	4.1		8	5	18	1
Yablok	2	16	61	3.8		5	3	7	
Hagerty	2	16	32	2.0		5	3	15	
Clark									
Stramiello									
Mahan									
Miller									
Comstock									
Hagberg									
Plank									
Mooney (2)									
Team	4	212	787	3.7	3	8			
Opp.	4	136	419	3.1	2	8			
PROVIDENCE									
Latone	3	46	223	4.8	2	8	21	60	1
Williams	3	27	89	3.3		8	25	79	2
Meeker	4	21	69	3.3		7	4	7	
Cronin	3	13	63	4.8		7	2	3	
Peters (1)	3	17	46	2.7	1	6	4	18	
Edwards	1	6	36	6.0		8			
Hadden	3	3	5	1.7		6	1	2	
Holm	1	2	5	2.5		2			
Oden	2	2	0	0.0		8	1	4	
Spellman									
Rose									
Kucharski									
Young									
Racis									
Team	4	170	552	3.2	3	7			
Opp.	3	119	427	3.6	2	8			
STATEN ISLAND									
Strong	10	90	369	4.1	1	2	5	100	1
Wycoff	10	124	383	3.1	4	2	2	22	
Follet	8	43	106	2.5		2	1	14	
Snyder	9	28	92	3.3		2	1	4	
Finn (2)	3	18	54	3.0		1			
Wilson (2)	2	19	50	2.6		1	1	-3	
Tays (2)	3	10	22	2.2					
Buckley	6	16	6	0.4		1	1	8	
Lawrence	3	5	10	2.0		1			
Myers	5	1	-10	-10.0		1			
Stein									
Kloppenburg									
Lundell (2)									
Team	10	354	1082	3.1	5	2			
Opp.	10	409	1218	3.0	6	2			

PASSING

NAME	Complete Games								Incom. Games					
	G	Com.	Att.	%	Yds.	Y/A	TD	Int.	G	Com.	Att.	Yds.	TD	Int.
GREEN BAY														
Molenda	12	0	3	0					1					
Lewellen	13	28	71	39	497	7.0	3	8	1					
McCrary														
Blood	9	4	11	36	52	4.7		2	1					
Herber	9	8	28	29	165	5.9	2	3	1	2	2	40	1	
Engelmann														
Dunn	12	34	74	46	672	9.1	9	7	1	9	9	153	2	
Lidberg														
Fitzgibbon	8	1	3	33	34	11.3			1					
Zuidmulder	4	0	1	0										
Pape (2)														
Bloodgood														
Dilweg														
Nash														
O'Donnell														
Hubbard														
Team	13	75	191	39	1420	7.4	14	20	1					
Opp.	13	46	174	26	796	4.6	9	30	1					
NEW YORK														
Friedman	9	56	105	53	922	8.8	10	7	6	15	19	324	3	2
Sedbrook	7	1	3	33	8	2.7			9	1	2	22		1
Moran	8	8	14	57	162	11.6	2	2	8	1	1	14		
Burnett	6	1	2	50	40	20.0			8					
Cagle	2	1	5	20	12	2.4			2					
Wiberg	8	7	16	44	173	10.8			9	2	2	32		
Feather														
Hagerty	5	1	2	50	26	13.0			7	2	2	40		
Wilson (1)														
Badgro	8								9	2	2	25	1	
Campbell	8	1	1	100	10	10.0			9					
Gibson	7	0	1	0					7					
Grant														
Howard														
Team	9	76	149	51	1353	9.1	12	9	8					
Opp.	7	45	137	33	758	5.5	3	21	10					
CHICAGO BEARS														
R. Grange	6	6	14	43	118	8.4	3	1	8	2	2	46		
Nagurski														
Lintzenich	5	2	7	29	16	2.3			8					
Brumbaugh	6	8	19	42	77	4.1		3	8	0	1			1
Senn														
Holmer	5	3	11	27	43	3.9		3	7	2	2	62		
Sternaman	3	1	7	14	3	0.4	1		6	6	7	89	1	
Nesbitt														
Walquist	4	1	4	25	19	4.8			6	2	2	37	1	
Savoldi														
Johnsos														
Drury														
G. Grange														
Fleckenstein (1)														
Team	7	28	86	33	371	4.3	4	12	7					
Opp.	7	31	88	35	372	4.2	2	13	7					
BROOKLYN														
McBride	3	6	16	38	55	3.4			8	12	14	201	2	1
Thomas	3	1	2	50	31	15.5		1	3					
Weimer	4	1	1	100	5	5.0			7					
Thomason														
Kelly	4	11	29	38	110	3.8	1	4	7	9	12	248	6	2
Yablok	3	2	6	33	20	3.3	1							
Hagerty														
Clark														
Stramiello														
Mahan														
Miller														
Comstock														
Hagberg														
Plank														
Mooney (2)														
Team	4	21	54	39	221	4.1	2	5	8					
Opp.	4	21	70	30	323	4.6	1	11	8					
PROVIDENCE														
Latone	2	0	1	0					9	0	1			
Williams														
Meeker	2	1	6	17	1	0.2		1	9	2	2	15		
Cronin														
Peters (1)	2	3	29	10	27	0.9		4	7	13	16	170	1	1
Edwards														
Hadden														
Holm	1	0	1	0				1	2	2	2	25		
Oden	1								9	9	11	179	1	2
Spellman														
Rose														
Kucharski														
Young														
Racis														
Team	3	12	57	21	204	3.6		9	8					
Opp.	3	12	54	22	145	2.7	1	6	8					
STATEN ISLAND														
Strong	10	15	47	32	193	4.1	2	5	2	1	2	12		1
Wycoff	10	40	136	29	625	4.6	4	14	2	1	7	64	1	1
Follet														
Snyder														
Finn (2)														
Wilson (2)														
Tays (2)														
Buckley														
Lawrence														
Myers														
Stein														
Kloppenburg														
Lundell (2)														
Team	10	55	183	30	818	4.5	6	19	2					
Opp.	10	53	161	33	657	4.1	3	19	2					

RECEIVING

NAME	Complete Games					Incom. Games			
	G	Rec.	Yds	Avg.	TD	G	Rec.	Yds.	TD
GREEN BAY									
Molenda									
Lewellen	13	8	143	17.9	1	1	2	30	
McCrary	13	3	100	33.3	2	1	1	30	
Blood	9	22	410	18.6	4	1	4	81	1
Herber	9	1	13	13.0	1	1			
Engelmann	8	3	67	22.3	2	1	1	16	
Dunn	12	5	60	12.0		1			
Lidberg									
Fitzgibbon	8	3	57	19.0	1	1	1	20	1
Zuidmulder									
Pape (2)									
Bloodgood	3	2	17	8.5					
Dilweg	12	16	291	18.2	2				
Nash	12	8	184	23.0	1				
O'Donnell	9	4	78	19.5		1	1	10	
Hubbard	13					1	1	6	1
Team									
Opp.									
NEW YORK									
Friedman									
Sedbrook	6	4	58	14.5	1	10	4	60	1
Moran	7	7	144	20.6		9			
Burnett	5	6	95	15.8		9	4	87	2
Cagle	3	3	12	4.0		1			
Wiberg	7	5	95	19.0		10	1	20	
Feather	6	2	49	24.5		9	2	28	
Hagerty	4	3	86	28.7	1	8	3	84	2
Wilson (1)	4	3	61	20.3		6	4	126	3
Badgro	7	3	65	21.7	1	10	4	55	2
Campbell	7	8	151	18.9		10	9	226	2
Gibson									
Grant	4					8	1	34	
Howard	7					9	1	10	1
Team									
Opp.									
CHICAGO BEARS									
R. Grange	6	4	32	8.0		8	3	69	2
Nagurski									
Lintzenich	5	1	19	19.0		8	1	18	
Brumbaugh	6	1	9	9.0		8			
Senn	5	1	5	5.0		6			
Holmer	5	1	19	19.0		7	1	10	
Sternaman									
Nesbitt									
Walquist	4	1	5	5.0		6	1	10	
Savoldi									
Johnsos	6	8	128	16.0	4	8	1	28	
Drury	6	3	49	16.3		8	3	74	
G. Grange	5	1	10	10.0		7	1	15	
Fleckenstein (1)	1					2	1	10	
Team									
Opp.									
BROOKLYN									
McBride									
Thomas	3	5	78	15.6	2	3	3	66	3
Weimer	4	2	7	3.5		7	6	119	2
Thomason	1	1	6	6.0		5	3	50	1
Kelly	4	4	33	8.3		7	1	8	
Yablok	3	6	55	9.2		4			
Hagerty									
Clark	3	1	3	3.0		7	4	87	
Stramiello	4	1	31	31.0		8	1	40	1
Mahan	3					8	2	31	
Miller						4	1	48	1
Comstock	2	1	8	8.0		4			
Hagberg									
Plank									
Mooney (2)									
Team									
Opp.									
PROVIDENCE									
Latone	3	1	5	5.0		8	1	13	
Williams	3	1	16	16.0		8	2	15	
Meeker	3	2	20	10.0	1	8			
Cronin	3	1	9	9.0		7	1	37	
Peters (1)	3	1	1	1.0		6	2	47	
Edwards	1					8	2	40	1
Hadden									
Holm									
Oden	2					8	1	12	
Spellman	3					8	6	106	
Rose	3	1	7	7.0		8	3	35	
Kucharski	2					6	2	50	
Young	1					2	1	4	1
Racis									
Team									
Opp.									
STATEN ISLAND									
Strong	10	12	202	16.8	4	2	1	64	1
Wycoff	10					2	1	12	
Follet	8	9	133	14.8		2			
Snyder	9	4	27	6.8		2			
Finn (2)	3	7	80	11.4		1			
Wilson (2)	2	2	17	8.5		1			
Tays (2)	3	4	55	13.8					
Buckley	6	4	94	23.5	1	1			
Lawrence									
Myers									
Stein	10	8	135	16.9	1	2			
Kloppenburg	7	3	43	14.3		2			
Lundell (2)	5	2	32	16.0		1			
Team									
Opp.									

PUNTING / PUNT RETURNS

NAME	PUNTING Comp. Games			PUNTING Incom. Games			PUNT RETURNS Complete Games					PUNT RETURNS Incom. Games			
	G	No.	Avg.	G	No.	Avg.	G	No.	Yds.	Avg.	TD	G	No.	Yds.	TD
GREEN BAY															
Molenda															
Lewellen	13	89	40.5	1			13	1	6	6.0		1			
McCrary															
Blood	9	18	36.3	1			9	1	15	15.0		1			
Herber	9	17	42.4	1			9	10	82	8.2		1			
Engelmann															
Dunn	12	2	24.5	1			12	18	150	8.3		1			
Lidberg															
Fitzgibbon															
Zuidmulder							4	1	10	10.0					
Pape (2)															
Bloodgood							3	1	10	10.0					
Dilweg							12	1	10	10.0					
Nash															
O'Donnell															
Hubbard															
Team	13	126	39.9	1			13	33	283	8.6		1			
Opp.	13	113	38.8	1			13	40	526	13.2		1			
NEW YORK															
Friedman	5			12	1	50.0	5	8	107	13.4		10	1	5	
Sedbrook															
Moran	5	4	32.0	11											
Burnett	4	17	34.1	10	1	65.0	4	1	10	10.0		10			
Cagle							2	1	4	4.0		2			
Wiberg	5	21	38.0	12	2	34.0									
Feather															
Hagerty	2	3	52.7	10			2	2	12	6.0		10			
Wilson (1)															
Badgro															
Campbell															
Gibson															
Grant															
Howard															
Team	5	45	37.0	12			5	12	133	11.1		12			
Opp.	5	51	35.3	12			5	13	146	11.2		12			
CHICAGO BEARS															
R. Grange															
Nagurski	6	1	44.0	7											
Lintzenich	5	27	47.9	8	2	70.0	4	1	11	11.0		9			
Brumbaugh	6	2	26.0	8			5	13	125	9.6		9	2	49	
Senn	5	16	39.0	6											
Holmer	5	9	34.3	7											
Sternaman							3	6	84	14.0		6	1	15	
Nesbitt	3	3	37.0	5											
Walquist															
Savoldi															
Johnsos	6	1	29.0												
Drury															
G. Grange															
Fleckenstein (1)															
Team	6	59	42.0	8			5	20	220	11.0		9			
Opp.	6	67	39.5	8			6	19	250	13.2					
BROOKLYN															
McBride															
Thomas															
Weimer	4	12	29.3	7			3	2	14	7.0		8	1	26	
Thomason							1					5	1	13	
Kelly	4	1	30.0	7			3	3	14	4.7		8			
Yablok							3	2	9	4.5		4			
Hagerty															
Clark															
Stramiello	4	1	36.0	8											
Mahan															
Miller															
Comstock															
Hagberg	4	27	36.9	8	2	31.5									
Plank	4	1	27.0	3											
Mooney (2)				3	2	37.0									
Team	4	42	34.3	8			3	7	37	5.3		9			
Opp.	4	41	37.8	8			4	20	227	11.4		8			
PROVIDENCE															
Latone															
Williams															
Meeker							2	8	149	18.6		9	3	63	
Cronin	2			8	1	30.0									
Peters (1)	2	24	42.0	7	1	26.0	1					8	1	25	
Edwards															
Hadden															
Holm							1					2	2	58	
Oden							2					8	1	20	
Spellman															
Rose															
Kucharski															
Young															
Racis							2	1	6	6.0		9			
Team	2	24	42.0	9			2	9	155	17.2		9			
Opp.	2	25	35.5	9			2	7	60	8.6		9			
STATEN ISLAND															
Strong	10	39	36.6	2			10	32	379	11.8		2	1	10	
Wycoff	10	56	36.4	2											
Follet	8			2	1	8.0	7	2	25	12.5		2			
Snyder															
Finn (2)															
Wilson (2)							2	1	15	15.0		1			
Tays (2)							2	2	10	5.0		1			
Buckley															
Lawrence							3	2	39	19.5		1			
Myers															
Stein															
Kloppenburg															
Lundell (2)															
Team	10	95	36.5	2			9	39	468	12.0		3			
Opp.	10	102	36.2	2			10	25	257	10.3		2			

CHICAGO CARDINALS 5-6-2 Ernie Nevers

Regulars

Use Name	Pos.	Hgt.	Wgt.	Age	Int.	Pts.
Chuck Kassel	E	6'1	190	26		
George Kenneally	E	6'	195	28	1	
Jess Tinsley	T	6'	198	21		
Duke Slater	T	6'1	215	31		
Herb Blumer	G-E	6'1	210	30		
Walt Kiesling	G	6'2	243	27		
Mickey Erickson	C	6'2	205	23	1	
Cobb Rooney	BB-WB	6'	185	30	1	6
Bunny Belden	WB-BB	5'8	175	29	1	18
Gene Rose	WB-FB	5'8	170	26	2	25
Ernie Nevers	FB	6'	203	27	2	48

Substitutes

Use Name	Pos.	Hgt.	Wgt.	Age	Int.	Pts.
John Vesser	E	6'	190	29		
Jake Williams	T-E	6'	208	26		
Lou Gordon	T-G	6'5	210	22	1	
Phil Handler	G	6'	208	22		
Buck Weaver (to PORT)	G	6'4	235	23		
Clare Randolph	C-G	6'2	190	23		
Bullet Baker	BB-WB	5'8	180	30	1	
Bill Boyd	WB-BB	5'11	170	23	1	12
Mickey McDonnell	WB	5'8	175	26	1	
Mack Flenniken	FB-WB-BB	6'1	200	24	1	18
Joe Pappio	G-T-BB	6'	195	27		
Fred Failing	G	5'11	200	26		
Charlie Diehl	G	6'	205	24		
Howie Maple	WB	5'7	175	27		
George Bogue (to NWK)	WB-FB	6'	210	24	1	

Scores of each game

Date	Pts.	Opponent	Pts.
Sep. 21	0	Green Bay	14
Sep. 28	7	Minneapolis	7
Oct. 5	0	Portsmouth	0
Oct. 8	13	Newark	0
Oct. 12	7	Providence	9
Oct. 16	12	New York	25
Oct. 19	6	CHIC. BEARS	32
Oct. 25	34	Frankford	7
Oct. 26	23	PORTSMOUTH	13
Nov. 2	6	FRANKFORD	0
Nov. 9	7	NEW YORK	13
Nov. 16	13	GREEN BAY	6
Nov. 27	0	Chic. Bears	6

PORTSMOUTH SPARTANS 5-6-3 Hal Griffen

Regulars

Use Name	Pos.	Hgt.	Wgt.	Age	Int.	Pts.
Red Joseph	E	6'3	190	27	2	6
Bill Fleckenstein (from ChiB)	E-G-T	6'1	213	26	2	
Dud Harris	T	6'2	240	26		
Babe Lyon	T	6'2	240	23		
Ebby DeWeese	G	6'	190	24		
Fred Roberts	G	6'1	200	23		
Bull Wesley	C-G	6'1	190	28	1	
Father Lumpkin	BB-FB-TB	6'2	210	22	3	18
Bill Glassgow	TB	5'10	190	22	1	28
Chuck Bennett	WB	5'9	190	23	1	42
Chief McLain	FB-BB-TB	6'3	230	25	2	42

Substitutes

Use Name	Pos.	Hgt.	Wgt.	Age	Int.	Pts.
Chuck Braidwood	E	6'	195	26		
Lou Jennings	E	6'3	240	26	1	
Vin Schleusner	T	6'3	225	22		6
Jap Douds (from PROV)	T	5'10	215	25		
Al Graham (from PROV)	G	6'	210	24		
Ernie Meyer	G	6'2	200	26	1	
Dick Brown	C	6'1	220	23		
Cy Kahl	BB-WB-FB	6'1	195	24	4	
Ray Novotny	TB-WB-BB	5'10	162	22	1	6
Byron Eby	TB-WB	6'	185	25	1	6
Tiny Lewis	FB-WB-BB	6'2	210	23	1	22
Lee Fenner	E	5'10	180	34		
Koester Christensen	E	5'10	195	25		
Emil Mayer	E-T	6'	190	27	1	
George Hastings	T	6'2	190	24		
Ron Shearer	T	6'	195	24		
Spider Johnson	T	6'4	210	22		
Sod Ryan	T	6'2	210	24		
Hal Griffen	T	6'1	250	28		
Duke Hanny (from GB)	T-G	6'	215	32		
Buck Weaver (from ChiC)	G	6'4	235	23		
Walt Ambrose	G	5'11	210	25		
Caroll Ringwalt	G	6'	210	22		
Gene Smith (from FRA)	C-G	5'9	190	24	1	
Aaron Grant	C	6'2	285	24		
Frosty Peters (from PROV)	TB	5'10	183	26		

Scores of each game

Date	Pts.	Opponent	Pts.
Sep. 14	13	NEWARK	6
Sep. 24	12	BROOKLYN	0
Oct. 5	0	CHIC. CARDS	0
Oct. 8	39	FRANKFORD	7
Oct. 12	0	Minneapolis	13
Oct. 22	7	CHIC. BEARS	6
Oct. 26	13	Chic. Cards	23
Nov. 2	13	Green Bay	47
Nov. 5	6	NEW YORK	19
Nov. 9	13	Staten Island	13
Nov. 15	6	Frankford	7
Nov. 30	6	Chic. Bears	14
Dec. 7	42	MINNEAPOLIS	0
Dec. 14	6	GREEN BAY	6

FRANKFORD YELLOW JACKETS 4-13-1 Bull Behman George Gibson

Regulars

Use Name	Pos.	Hgt.	Wgt.	Age	Int.	Pts.
Bob Tanner	E-T	6'	190	22	3	12
Tony Kostos*	E-C-G	5'11	190	25		7
Ray Richards	T-E	6'1	218	24		
Gordon Watkins*	T	6'1	210	23		
Hal Hanson (to & from MIN)	G-T	6'1	205	25		
Potsy Jones*	G	5'11	208	20		
Charlie Havens	C	5'10	205	24	1	
Clyde Crabtree (to & from MIN)	BB-TB-WB	5'8	160	22	1	12
Eddie Halicki (to MIN)	TB-FB-WB	5'9	185	24	2	30
Kelly Rodriguez*	WB-TB-FB	5'10	180	24		6
Herb Joesting*	FB	6'2	192	25	1	12

Substitutes

Use Name	Pos.	Hgt.	Wgt.	Age	Int.	Pts.
Lee Wilson*	E	5'11	185	25		
Cookie Tackwell (to MIN)	E-T-G	6'2	215	23	1	7
Bull Behman	T	5'10	215	30		
Bill Capps (to MIN)	T-G	6'1	235	26		
George Gibson*	G	6'	210	24		
Clyde Van Sickle	G	6'1	210	22		
Nate Barrager*	C	6'	210	23	1	
Two Bits Homan	BB	5'5	148	28		
Art Pharmer*	TB-BB	5'10	186	22	1	4
Royce Goodbread (to MIN)	WB	5'11	203	22		6
Neil Rengel	FB	5'9	205	24		
Tony Steponovich*	E	5'10	185	23		
Jack Hutton	E-WB	6'1	192	24		
Johnny Ward*	T	6'2	215	23		
Tony Panaccion	T	6'1	212	21		
Gene Smith (to PORT)	G	5'9	190	24		
Roger Mahoney (to MIN)	G-C	6'	220	24		
Mally Nydahl*	BB-TB	5'11	162	23		12
Jack Ernst	TB-BB	5'11	185	30		6
Jim Pederson*	WB	5'9	185	22	1	
Wally Diehl	FB	6'	220	26		
Ken Provincial	E	6'2	190	25		
Eddie Bollinger	T	6'1	215	24		
Jerry Lunz	T	6'3	210	28		
Harvey Long	T	6'	200	25		
Jack McArthur (from NWK & PROV, to BKN)	T	5'11	220	26		
Ed Wall	BB	5'9	170	24		
Ab Wright	TB	6'1	190	24		
Herman Seborg*	WB-BB	5'11	190	23		
Johnny Shultz	WB-FB	6'1	189	22		

Scores of each game

Date	Pts.	Opponent	Pts.
Sep. 24	13	Newark	6
Sep. 27	7	STATEN ISLAND	3
Sep. 28	0	Staten Island	21
Oct. 1	0	Providence	14
Oct. 4	0	NEWARK	19
Oct. 8	7	Portsmouth	39
Oct. 12	12	Green Bay	27
Oct. 18	7	BROOKLYN	14
Oct. 19	0	New York	53
Oct. 25	7	CHIC. CARDS	34
Oct. 26	7	Chic. Bears	13
Nov. 2	0	Chic. Cards	6
Nov. 8	20	PROVIDENCE	7
Nov. 9	7	Providence	7
Nov. 15	7	PORTSMOUTH	6
Nov. 22	6	CHIC. BEARS	13
Nov. 27	7	GREEN BAY	25
Dec. 6	6	NEW YORK	14

MINNEAPOLIS REDJACKETS 1-7-1 George Gibson

Regulars

Use Name	Pos.	Hgt.	Wgt.	Age	Int.	Pts.
Lee Wilson*	E	5'11	185	25		
Tony Steponovich*	E-G	5'10	185	23		
Chief Franta (to GB)	T	6'1	220	25	1	
Johnny Ward*	T	6'2	215	23		
George Gibson*	G	6'	210	24		
Potsy Jones*	G	5'11	208	20		
Nate Barrager*	C	6'	210	23		
Jim Pederson*	BB	5'9	185	22	2	
Art Pharmer*	TB	5'10	186	22	1	8
Oran Pape (to GB)	HB	5'11	180	26		12
Herb Joesting*	FB	6'2	192	25		6

Substitutes

Use Name	Pos.	Hgt.	Wgt.	Age	Int.	Pts.
Ken Haycraft (to GB)	E	6'	180	23		
Bob Lundell (to SI)	E	6'4	215	23		
Gordon Watkins*	T	6'1	210	23		
Ted Nemzek	T		205	24		
Sam Young	G	6'2	195	27		
Hal Hanson (from & to FRA)	G	6'1	205	25		
Jack Corcoran	C-G		180	24		
Herman Seborg*	BB-G	5'11	190	23	1	
Mally Nydahl*	TB-HB	5'11	162	23		1
Verne Miller	HB	5'8	152	22		
Eddie Halicki (from FRA)	TB	5'9	185	24		
Tony Kostos*	E	5'11	190	25		
Cookie Tackwell (from FRA)	E-T	6'2	215	23		
Bill Capps (from FRA)	T	6'1	235	26		
Hal Truesdell	T	6'	200	23		
Murrell Hogue	T	6'1	205	28		
Roger Mahoney (from FRA)	G	6'	220	24		
Ike Kakela	C	6'	220	25		
Kelly Rodriguez*	HB-BB	5'10	180	24		
Hal Erickson	HB-TB-T	5'9	200	31	1	
Clyde Crabtree (from & to FRA)	HB	5'8	150	22		
Royce Goodbread (from FRA)	HB	5'11	203	22		

Scores of each game

Date	Pts.	Opponent	Pts.
Sep. 28	7	CHIC. CARDS	7
Oct. 5	0	CHIC. BEARS	20
Oct. 12	13	PORTSMOUTH	0
Oct. 19	0	GREEN BAY	13
Oct. 26	0	Green Bay	19
Nov. 2	7	Chic. Bears	20
Nov. 9	0	Brooklyn	34
Nov. 23	0	Providence	10
Dec. 7	0	Portsmouth	42

** - After the games of November 2, these men played for both Frankford and Minneapolis. For example, Minneapolis head coach Gibson and star fullback Joesting played in all Minneapolis games through November 2, then played for Frankford November 8, Minneapolis on November 9, Frankford on November 15 and 22, Minneapolis on November 23, Frankford on November 27 and December 6, and Minneapolis on December 7. This was possible because Frankford, due to Pennsylvania Sunday "Blue Laws," played their home games on Saturday.

NEWARK TORNADOES 1-10-1 Al McCall, Jack Fish, Andy Salata

Regulars

Use Name	Pos.	Hgt.	Wgt.	Age	Int.	Pts.
Tom Leary	E	6'	180	27	2	12
Johnny Tomaini (to BKN)	E	6'	195	28		6
Jim Mooney (to BKN)	T-G-BB	5'11	200	22		2
Bill Feaster	T-C	6'	205	26		
Bud Ellor	G-E	6'2	205	24		6
Andy Salata	G	5'10	186	26		
Ted Mitchell	C	5'10	195	25	2	
Bernie Finn (to SI)	BB-WB-TB	5'10	180	22		
Frank Kirkleski	TB-BB	5'10	175	26		6
Teddy Andrulewicz	WB	5'11	175	25	1	6
Nick Borelli	FB-WB-TB-BB	5'10	175	25		

Substitutes

Use Name	Pos.	Hgt.	Wgt.	Age	Int.	Pts.
Paul Longua	E	5'10	175	27		
Dutch Webber (from PROV)	E	6'2	195	28		
Erwin Woerner	T	6'1	200	24		
Bob Beattie	T	6'3	230	27		
Sam Cordovano	G	5'11	185	23		
Tom Kerrigan	G	6'2	200	24		
Joe Davidson	C-G	6'	200	27	1	
Red Smith	BB-TB-FB-WB	5'10	190	26		1
Frank 3riante	TB-FB-WB	5'10	185	24	2	6
Carl Waite	WB-BB-E-TB	5'9	205	28	1	6
Hersh Martin	FB-WB	5'11	180	24	1	
Henry Myles	E	6'	190	27		
Ray Wagner	E	5'10	170	28		
John Law	T	5'9	180	22		
John Dibb	T	6'	200	24		
Pete Bove	G	5'10	187	23		
Bruck Jones	G	6'1	220	25		
Harry McGee	C	6'1	198	25		
Ken Hauser	BB-FB	6'1	230	31		
Tony Manfreda	WB-TB	5'8	172	26		
Heinie Benkert	WB-TB	5'9	170	29		
Felix McCormick	FB	5'7	185	25		
Phil Brennan	E	5'11	165	27		
Les Grace	E	5'11	200	25		
Don Smith	G					
Paul Liston	G	5'11	185	27		
Bill Connor	G	6'1	240	31		
Jack McArthur (to PROV, FRA, BKN)	G	5'11	220	26		
Paul Frank	BB		200	23		
Stu Clancy	FB	5'10	175	24	1	
George Bogue (from ChiC)	FB-WB	6'	210	24	1	
Sam Sebo	FB-WB	5'7	165	24		
Jim Tays (to SI)	FB	5'8	180	31		

Scores of each game

Date	Pts.	Opponent	Pts.
Sep. 14	6	Portsmouth	13
Sep. 17	0	NEW YORK	32
Sep. 21	6	Staten Island	12
Sep. 24	6	FRANKFORD	13
Oct. 1	7	STATEN ISLAND	7
Oct. 4	19	Frankford	0
Oct. 5	0	Providence	14
Oct. 8	0	CHIC. CARDS	13
Oct. 12	0	Brooklyn	32
Oct. 19	0	BROOKLYN	14
Oct. 26	0	STATEN ISLAND	6
Oct. 29	7	New York	34

NAME	RUSHING Complete Games G	Att.	Yds.	Avg.	TD	RUSHING Incom. Games G	Att.	Yds.	TD	PASSING Complete Games G	Com.	Att.	%	Yds.	Y/A	TD	Int	PASSING Incom. Games G	Com.	Att.	Yds.	TD	Int
CHICAGO CARDINALS																							
Nevers	5	73	270	3.7	5	6	8	56	1	5	20	43	47	324	7.5	3	6	6	5	12	123	2	3
Rose	5	28	212	7.6	1	7	4	12	2	5								7	3	3	57		
Belden	5	28	132	4.7	1	7	5	35		5								7	1	2	43		1
Boyd	4	19	68	3.6		8	4	47	1	4	0	1	0					8					
Flenniken	4	18	51	2.8		6	9	44	3	4	2	7	29	47	6.7		2	6	2	5	46		2
Maple	3	17	76	4.5		5	1	7															
McDonnell	3	12	39	3.3		5	1	10															
C. Rooney	4	13	33	2.5		6				4	0	1	0					6					
Bogue (1)	1	2	0	0.0		3	1	13		1	0	3	0				1	3					
Baker	5	2	5	2.5		5																	
Kassel																							
Kenneally																							
Vesser																							
Team	5	212	886	4.2	7	8				5	22	55	40	371	6.7	3	9	8					
Opp.	5	180	707	3.9	4	8				5	20	59	34	283	4.8	2	13	8					
PORTSMOUTH																							
Bennett	13	140	744	5.3	5	1	1	0		14	5	11	45	40	3.6		1						
Lumpkin	13	129	548	4.2	3	1	2	14		14	10	39	26	133	3.4	3	9						
McLain	13	95	466	4.9	4	1				14	1	8	13	29	3.6		2						
Glassgow	11	93	441	4.7	3	1	4	37		12	13	53	25	192	3.6	1	8						
Lewis	12	37	214	5.8	2	1																	
Novotny	10	26	143	5.5	1	1				11	9	16	56	155	9.7	1	1						
Kahl	10	6	13	2.2		1				11	0	4	0				2						
Peters (2)	3	6	9	1.5						3	3	15	20	55	3.7		2						
Ely	2	5	7	1.4						3	1	2	50	9	4.5	1	1						
Braidwood																							
Fleckenstein (2)																							
Joseph																							
Jennings																							
Mayer																							
Team	13	537	2585	4.8	18	1				14	42	148	28	613	4.1	6	26						
Opp.	12	497	1882	3.8	14	2				13	67	170	39	840	4.9	8	25						
FRANKFORD																							
Joesting*	4	65	376	5.8	1	1	3	5	1	4	0	2	0				1	1					
Pharmer*	4	48	227	4.7		1				4	7	19	37	74	3.9	1	5	1	0	2			
Crabtree (1,3)	10	39	149	3.8	1	4	2	15		12	10	32	31	103	3.2		5	2	0	1			1
Halicki(1)	8	52	129	2.5	1	5	8	30	2	9	5	17	29	46	2.7	1	3	4					
Nydahl*	3	31	148	4.8	2	1	1	6		3	1	7	14	3	0.4		2	1					
Rodriguez*	7	30	87	2.9		6	4	18		9	12	41	29	94	2.3	1	9	4					
Goodbread(1)	7	21	42	2.0		6	4	25															
Rengel	5	27	47	1.7		6	1	6		7	23	63	37	304	4.8		10	4	1	1	40	1	
Ernst	5	12	41	3.4		3				6	14	39	36	178	4.6	1	6	2	0	2			2
Pederson*	3	5	25	5.0		1				3	0	2	0				1	1					
Shultz	5	11	21	1.9		1				5	1	2	50	28	14.0	1		1					
Diehl	3	9	16	1.8		3	1	4		4	1	13	8	13	1.0		2	2	2	2	55	1	
Wall	1	2	20	10.0																			
Homan	8	5	13	2.6		6				10	0	3	0				1	4					
Wright	2	2	5	2.5		2				3	10	32	31	121	3.8	1	5	1					
Kostos*																							
Tackwell (1)																							
Wilson*																							
Tanner																							
Watkins																							
Team	11	359	1346	3.7	5	7				13	84	272	31	964	3.5	6	50	5					
Opp.	11	426	2026	4.8	15	7				12	84	199	42	1208	6.1	16	17	6					
MINNEAPOLIS																							
Joesting*	4	54	221	4.1	1	5	4	54		4	0	4	0					5					
Pape (1)	3	21	135	6.4	1	3	1	78	1	3	0	4	0				1	3					
Nydahl*	4	24	72	3.0		5	6	105		4	0	14	0				5	5	1	5	12		4
Halicki (2)	1	9	43	4.8																			
Miller	2	8	13	1.6		3																	
Pharmer*	3	15	10	0.7		5	1	2	1	3	0	9	0				2	5	1	1	15		
Erickson	1	7	11	1.6		3				1	0	1	0				1	3					
Rodriguez*	1	8	5	0.6		1				1	1	1	100	16	16.0			1					
Pederson*	4	1	-2	-2.0		3				4	0	2	0				1	3					
Wilson*																							
Lundell (1)																							
Team	4	147	508	3.5	2	5				4	1	35	3	16	0.5		10	5					
Opp.	4	190	885	4.7	9	5				4	16	53	30	291	5.5	2	6	5					
NEWARK																							
Kirkleski	3	17	28	1.6		9	4	24	1	3	10	25	40	117	4.7	1	1	9	5	10	92	2	5
Briante	1	3	7	2.3		3	3	37															
Borelli	3	7	14	2.0		8	5	13		3	5	7	71	38	5.4			7	0	1			1
Benkert	1	12	27	2.3		4																	
Finn (1)	2	3	6	2.0		8	2	12		2								8	1	1	22		
Smith	2	10	15	1.5		5	1	-3		2	8	19	42	70	3.7		3	5	1	1	15		
Manfreda						2	1	12															
Andrulewicz	3	7	10	1.4		8																	
Waite	2	3	5	1.7		5	1	5															
Bogue (2)	1	5	9	1.8		2				1	0	1	0				1	2					
Frank	1	3	5	1.7		2																	
Clancy						1	2	4															
Hauser	1	2	2	1.0		4																	
McCormick	1	2	2	1.0		2																	
Martin	2	5	1	0.2		5																	
Tomaini (1)																							
Grace																							
Mooney (1)																							
Team	3	79	131	1.7		9				4	29	69	42	291	4.2	1	6	8					
Opp.	4	152	626	4.1	2	8				4	22	68	32	349	5.1	3	11	8					

NAME	RECEIVING Complete Games G	Rec.	Yds.	Avg.	TD	RECEIVING Incom. Games G	Rec.	Yds.	TD	PUNTING Comp. Games G	No.	Avg.	PUNTING Incom. Games G	No.	Avg.	PUNT RETURNS Complete Games G	Rec.	Yds.	Avg.	TD	PUNT RETURNS Incom. Games G	Rec.	Yds.	TD
CHICAGO CARDINALS																								
Nevers										5	18	36.9	6											
Rose	5	2	39	19.5	1	7				5	1	0.0	7											
Belden	5	3	34	11.3	1	7	3	91	1	5	15	34.7	7			4	3	29	9.7		8	1	15	
Boyd	4	2	22	11.0		8	2	35	1	4	4	43.3	8	2	26.0	4	3	29	9.7		8			
Flenniken																								
Maple																								
McDonnell	3	2	18	9.0		5										3	2	11	5.5		5			
C. Rooney	4	5	131	26.2	1	6																		
Bogue (1)																								
Baker	5	3	6	2.0		5	1	16																
Kassel	5	3	64	21.3		8	3	80																
Kenneally	5	2	47	23.5		6																		
Vesser	2					7	2	47																
Team										5	38	35.7	8			4	8	69	8.6		9			
Opp.										5	38	35.8	8			5	11	106	9.7		8			
PORTSMOUTH																								
Bennett	14	2	12	6.0	1											13	4	49	12.3		1			
Lumpkin	14	7	93	13.3												13	6	71	11.8		1			
McLain	14	7	97	13.9	3					12	22	31.8	2	2	45.5									
Glassgow	12	1	18	18.0						10	26	36.5	2			11	14	151	10.8		1			
Lewis	13	4	50	12.5						11	23	36.0	2	2	24.5	12	1	8	8.0		1			
Novotny	11	1	29	29.0						9	2	29.5	2											
Kahl	11	5	37	7.4																				
Peters (2)										3	11	41.1				3	4	122	30.5					
Ely	3	1	68	68.0	1											2	1	16	16.0		1			
Braidwood	10	4	89	22.3																				
Fleckenstein (2)	10	3	43	14.3																				
Joseph	12	3	41	13.7	1																			
Jennings	9	3	23	7.7						7	17	35.3	2	2	43.0	8	1	5	5.0		1			
Mayer	10	1	13	13.0																				
Team										14	129	35.5				13	31	422	13.6		1			
Opp.										14	118	39.7				12	29	341	11.8		2			
FRANKFORD																								
Joesting*																4	2	22	11.0		1			
Pharmer*										4	30	36.2	1			4	6	111	18.5		1			
Crabtree (1,3)	9	9	81	9.0		5	1	40	1	10	6	37.3	4			10	6	79	13.2		4	1	30	
Halicki(1)	8	5	79	15.8	1	5				8	1	29.0	5			8	3	41	13.7		5			
Nydahl*																3	8	189	23.6		1			
Rodriguez*	6	4	27	6.8	1	7				7	22	40.0	6	1	74.0	8	2	41	20.5		6			
Goodbread(1)	8	6	115	19.2		5	1	35	1							7					6	1	16	
Rengel										5	2	29.5	6			5	2	25	12.5		6			
Ernst	6	8	62	7.8	1	2				5	17	33.8	3			5	1	35	35.0		3			
Pederson*										3	1	29.0	1			3	2	29	14.5		1			
Shultz	5	6	74	12.3		1																		
Diehl										3	7	28.4	3			3	3	28	9.3		3			
Wall	1	1	6	6.0																				
Homan	8	5	48	9.6		6										8	12	165	13.8		6	1	22	
Wright	2	2	39	19.5		2																		
Kostos*	10	9	129	14.3	1	6																		
Tackwell (1)	8	8	108	13.5	1	8				9	2	30.0	7											
Wilson*	3	3	49	16.3		2																		
Tanner	7	1	11	11.0	1	5	1	20																
Watkins																5	1	14	14.0		3			
Team										11	88	35.7	7			11	48	779	16.2		7			
Opp.										11	103	38.0	7			5	11	114	10.4		13			
MINNEAPOLIS																								
Joesting*																								
Pape (1)																3	4	40	10.0		3			
Nydahl*	4	1	16	16.0		5				4	2	50.0	5											
Halicki (2)																								
Miller	2					3	1	15		2	1	30.0	3											
Pharmer*										3	20	33.4	5	1	28.0									
Erickson																								
Rodriguez*										1	11	40.6	1											
Pederson*										4	10	42.2	3											
Wilson*	3					5	1	12																
Lundell (1)										2	2	40.5	2											
Team										4	46	38.0	5			4	4	40	10.0		5			
Opp.										4	39	40.1	5			5	20	322	16.1		4			
NEWARK																								
Kirkleski	2	3	24	8.0		10				4	4	33.5	8			2	1	6	6.0		10			
Briante										1	1	43.0	3											
Borelli	2	1	21	21.0		8	1	22								2	1	35	35.0		8			
Benkert																								
Finn (1)	2					9	1	10																
Smith																								
Manfreda																								
Andrulewicz	2	3	37	12.3	1	9																		
Waite	1	1	18	18.0		6	1	7	1															
Bogue (2)	1	1	12	12.0		2																		
Frank																								
Clancy																								
Hauser																								
McCormick																								
Martin	2	2	5	2.5		5	1	15																
Tomaini (1)	2					10	2	60	1															
Grace						2	1	15																
Mooney (1)										4	40	44.3	8	2	75.0									
Team										4	45	43.3	8			2	2	41	20.5		10			
Opp.										4	40	35.5	8			3	18	298	16.6		9			

1931 N.F.L.
The Pack Holds Three of a Kind

Few people were surprised to see the Green Bay Packers win their third straight NFL championship this year. Curly Lambeau had time-tested stars: Verne Lewellen, Johnny Blood, Red Dunn, Cal Hubbard, Mike Michalske and Lavie Dilweg. To the returnees, Lambeau added veteran help in linemen Dick Stahlman and Rudy Comstock from the New York Giants and promising rookies Hank Bruder, Roger Grove and Milt Gantenbein. The Pack excelled both on offense and defense; their 291 points for the season were more than 100 better than any other NFL team, and the 87 points they allowed ranked as the league's second best. For the fourth year in a row they intercepted at least 30 passes. If an injury to Lewellen weakened the backfield in October and November, the acquisition of center Nate Barrager from Frankford at the end of October made the line even stronger.

The toughest challenger to the Packers this season was the Portsmouth Spartans. Potsy Clark took over as coach and turned last year's eighth-place finisher into a title contender with a slew of new talent. Rookies Dutch Clark and Glenn Presnell juiced up the backfield, while George Christensen, Ox Emerson, Maury Bodenger and Bill McKalip strengthened the front line. Clark was the gem of the fine bunch. Coming from Colorado College, he set the league on its ear with his dodging, jackrabbit-like open field running, his leadership on the field, his flawless play at safety and his fine dropkicking. The Spartans alos picked up center Clare Randolph from the Chicago Cardinals and had two solid second-year men in tackle Jap Douds and blocking back Father Lumpkin.

At the end of October, the Spartans were 8-0 and the Packers 7-0. Back in the pack with a 3-3 record were the New York Giants, strong runners-up to Green Bay the past two seasons. Benny Friedman had retired to become an assistant coach at Yale. Friedman had averaged better than a touchdown pass per game since joining the NFL and, shorn of his talents, the New York defense sputtered. Many of the veterans who had come with him to New York from Detroit also left the team. The Giants, however, signed a blue-chip rookie in center Mel Hein. Ironically, Hein wrote to three NFL teams asking for a tryout before the Giants offered him $150 per game. In a 15-year career, Hein would not miss a game. New York also had Chris Cagle from the start of the season, but a season-opening road trip turned out disastrously, with consecutive losses to the Spartans, Packers and Chicago Bears.

Giants fan took heart when Friedman ended his retirement to lead New York to a 14-0 upset victory over Portsmouth in the Polo Grounds on November 1. The Packers beat the Bears that day and the Staten Island

1931 STANDINGS

	W	L	T	Pct.	Pts.	Opp. Pts.	Avg. Pts.	Opp. Avg.
Green Bay Packers	12	2	0	.857	291	87	21	6
Portsmouth Spartans	11	3	0	.786	175	77	13	6
Chicago Bears	8	5	0	.615	145	92	11	7
Chicago Cardinals	5	4	0	.556	120	128	13	14
New York Giants	7	6	1	.538	154	100	11	7
Providence Steam Roller	4	4	3	.500	78	127	7	12
Staten Island Stapletons	4	6	1	.400	79	118	7	11
Cleveland Indians	2	8	0	.200	45	137	5	14
Brooklyn Dodgers	1	12	0	.143	64	199	5	14
Frankford Yellow Jackets	1	6	1	.143	13	99	2	12

Scoring Leaders

Blood	GB	84
Nevers	ChiC	66
Clark	Port	60
Strong	SI	53
R. Grange	ChiB	42
Lewellen	GB	36
Presnell	Port	35
Moran	NYG	35
Kitzmiller	NYG	27
Woodruff	Prov	25
Dilweg	GB	25
Engelmann	GB	24
Vokaty	Cle	24
McKalip	Port	24
Molenda	GB	21

KICKING

		FG	Att	Pct
Strong	SI	2	2	100
Johnsos	ChiB	1	1	100
Presnell	Port	1	1	100
Moran	NYG	1	3	33
Nevers	ChiC	1	3	33
McBride	Bkn	0	1	0
Molenda	GB	0	1	0
Mooney	Bkn	0	1	0
Workman	Cle	0	1	0
Kitzmiller	NYG	0	3	0
Clark	Port	0	4	0

		PAT	Att	Pct
Nevers	ChiC	15	17	88
Dunn	GB	15	20	75
Moran	NYG	8	9	89
Presnell	Port	7	14	50
Clark	Port	6	10	60
Strong	SI	5	10	50
Shelley	Port-Prov	4	6	67
Johnsos	ChiB	4	10	40
Kitzmiller	NYG	3	5	60
Tackwell	Fra-ChiB	3	5	60
Woodin	GB	3	5	60
Molenda	GB	3	8	38
Smith	NYG	2	4	50
Workman	Cle	2	4	50
Grove	GB	2	5	40
Peters	Bkn	2	6	33
G. Grange	ChiB	1	1	100
Mooney	Bkn	1	1	100
Senn	ChiB	1	1	100
McBride	Bkn	1	2	50
Mishel	Cle	1	2	50
Fitzgibbon	GB	1	3	33
Meeker	Prov	1	3	33
Alford	Port	0	1	0
Clark	Cle	0	1	0
Pape	Prov	0	1	0
Parkinson	SI	0	1	0
Saunders	GB	0	1	0
Buckler	ChiB	0	2	0

GREEN BAY PACKERS 12-2-0 Curly Lambeau

Regulars

Use Name	Pos.	Hgt.	Wgt.	Age	Int	Pts.
Lavie Dilweg	E	6'3"	202	28	5	25
Tom Nash	E	6'3"	210	25		6
Cal Hubbard	T-E	6'4"	250	30	1	
Dick Stahlman	T	6'2"	220	29		
Rudy Comstock	G	5'10"	210	30		
Mike Michalske	G	6'	210	28	2	6
Nate Barrager (from FRA)	C-G	6'	215	24		
Red Dunn	BB	5'11"	175	29		15
Hank Bruder	TB	6'	190	23		18
Johnny Blood	HB-TB	6'1"	187	27	6	84
Bo Molenda	FB	5'10"	208	26	4	21

Substitutes

Use Name	Pos.	Hgt.	Wgt.	Age	Int	Pts.
Frank Baker	E	6'2"	182	22		6
Milt Gantenbein	E	6'	200	21	3	6
Claude Perry (to BKN)	T	6'1"	212	29		
Red Sleight	T	6'2"	223	24		
Jim Bowdoin	G	6'1"	230	25		
Whitey Woodin	G	5'10"	210	36	1	9
Waldo Don Carlos	C	6'2"	190	21		
Paul Fitzgibbon	BB	5'8"	172	28		1
Verne Lewellen	TB-HB	6'1"	185	29	2	36
Wuert Engelmann	HB	6'3"	185	23	2	24
Hurdis McCrary	FB	6'	205	27	2	6
Ken Radick (to BKN)	E	5'10	210	24		
Ray Jenison	T	6'3"	198	21		
Jug Earp	C-T	6'	238	34	2	
Boob Darling	C	5'11"	206	27		
Roger Grove	BB	6'	175	23	3	2
Mule Wilson	TB	5'11"	190	29	4	12
Bill Davenport	HB		187	24		
Russ Saunders	FB	5'9"	190	25		6
Arnie Herber	TB-BB	5'11"	195	21		6
Dave Zuidmulder	TB	5'10	184	25		
Swede Johnston	FB	5'10"	186	21		

Scores of Each Game

Date	Pts.	Opponent	Pts.
Sep. 13	26	CLEVELAND	0
Sep. 20	32	BROOKLYN	6
Sep. 27	7	CHIC. BEARS	0
Oct. 4	27	NEW YORK	7
Oct. 11	26	CHIC. CARDS	7
Oct. 18	15	FRANKFORD	0
Oct. 25	48	PROVIDENCE	20
Nov. 1	6	Chic. Bears	2
Nov. 8	26	STATEN ISLAND	0
Nov. 15	13	Chic. Cards	21
Nov. 22	14	New York	10
Nov. 26	38	Providence	7
Nov. 29	7	Brooklyn	0
Nov. 6	6	Chic. Bears	7

PORTSMOUTH SPARTANS 11-3-0 Potsy Clark

Regulars

Use Name	Pos.	Hgt.	Wgt.	Age	Int	Pts.
Harry Ebding	E	5'11"	200	24	1	
Bill McKalip	E	6'1"	195	23		24
George Christensen	T	6'2"	220	21	1	
Jap Douds	T	5'10"	210	26		
Maury Bodenger	G	5'10"	225	22		
Ox Emerson	G	5'11"	197	23	1	
Clare Randolph	C	6'2"	200	24	3	
Father Lumpkin	BB-FB	6'2"	210	23	3	6
Dutch Clark	TB	6'	192	24	3	60
Gene Alford	WB	5'9"'	180	25		12
Tony Holm	FB-BB	6'1"	225	23	1	12

Substitutes

Use Name	Pos.	Hgt.	Wgt.	Age	Int	Pts.
Louie Long	E	6'	185	22	1	6
Buster Mitchell	E-T	6'	195	25		
Dale Waters (to CLE)	T	6'2"	205	22		
Vin Schleusner	T	6'3"	225	23		
Bob Armstrong	G-T-C	5'11"	212	22	1	
Fred Roberts	G	6'1"	195	24	2	
John Wager	C-G	5'11"	200	27	3	
John Cavosie	BB-WB-FB	6'	207	23	1	
Glenn Presnell	TB-WB-FB	5'10"	200	26	4	35
Stud Stennett	WB-BB-FB	6'	198	25		
Elmer Schwartz	FB-WB	6'	210	24	2	18
Les Peterson	E-T	6'3"	204	21		
George Hastings	T	6'2"	190	25		
Biff Lee (to CLE)	G	6'	218	23		
Dutch Miller	C	6'1"	212	25		
Cy Kahl	BB	6'1"	194	25		
Deck Shelley (to PROV)	WB	5'11"	190	25		
Chuck Bennett	WB	5'9"	190	24		
Chief McLain (to SI)	FB	6'3"	220	26		

Scores of Each Game

Date	Pts.	Opponent	Pts.
Sep. 13	14	BROOKLYN	0
Sep. 23	13	CHIC. CARDS	3
Sep. 30	14	NEW YORK	6
Oct. 7	6	CLEVELAND	0
Oct. 15	19	FRANKFORD	0
Oct. 18	19	Brooklyn	0
Oct. 25	20	Staten Island	7
Oct. 31	14	Frankford	0
Nov. 1	0	New York	14
Nov. 8	6	Chic. Bears	9
Nov. 11	14	STATEN ISLAND	12
Nov. 15	14	CLEVELAND (at Cincinnati)	6
Nov. 22	19	Chic. Cards	20
Nov. 29	3	CHIC. BEARS	0

CHICAGO BEARS 8-5-0 Ralph Jones

Regulars

Use Name	Pos.	Hgt.	Wgt.	Age	Int	Pts.
Gardie Grange	E	6'	178	24		7
Luke Johnsos	E	6'2"	195	25		13
Link Lyman	T	6'2"	252	32	1	6
Lloyd Burdick	T	6'4"	240	22		
Zuck Carlson	G	6'	210	26		
Bill Buckler	G	6'	232	30		
Bert Pearson	C	6'	208	26		
Carl Brumbaugh	QB	5'10"	165	23	2	6
Red Grange	HB	5'11"	185	28	1	42
Joe Lintzenich	HB	5'1"	190	23	5	12
Bronko Nagurski	FB	6'2"	222	22		12

Substitutes

Use Name	Pos.	Hgt.	Wgt.	Age	Int	Pts.
Hoot Drury	E	6'4"	193	25	1	6
Cookie Tackwell (from FRA)	T-E	6'2"	215	24		2
Jesse Hibbs	T	6'	195	25		
Don Murry	T-G	6'2"	195	31		
Paul Schuette	G	6'	223	25		
Danny McMullen	G	5'8"	226	25		
George Trafton	C	6'2"	232	34	4	
Laurie Walquist	QB	5'8"	168	33	1	
Keith Molesworth	HB	5'9"	165	25	1	6
Dick Nesbitt	HB	6'	202	23	2	12
Hero Joesting (from FRA)	FB	6'2"	195	26		6
Gus Mastrogany	E	6'	180	23		
Latham Flanagan (to ChiC)	E	6'2"	185	24		
Babe Lyon (to CLE)	T	6'2"	240	24		
Larry Steinbach (to ChiC)	T	6'	220	27		
Denny Myers	G	6'1"	206	24		
Eddie Kawal	C	6'2"	200	21		
Bud Edwards (to PROV)	HB	5'11"	190	25		
Bill Senn (to BKN)	HB	6'	180	26		7
Leo Jensvold (to CLE)	HB	5'8"	173	23		
Paul Franklin	FB-HB	6'2"	194	25		6

Joe Savoldi — Retired to be Professional Wrestler
Joe Kopcha — Retired to attend Medical School

Scores of Each Game

Date	Pts.	Opponent	Pts.
Sep. 18	21	CLEVELAND	0
Sep. 27	0	Green Bay	7
Oct. 11	6	NEW YORK	0
Oct. 18	26	CHIC. CARDS	13
Oct. 25	12	FRANKFORD	13
Nov. 1	2	GREEN BAY	6
Nov. 8	9	PORTSMOUTH	6
Nov. 15	12	New York	6
Nov. 22	26	Brooklyn	0
Nov. 26	18	CHIC. CARDS	7
Nov. 29	0	Portsmouth	3
Dec. 6	7	GREEN BAY	6
Dec. 13	6	NEW YORK	25

Stapletons the next week to run their mark to 9-0. The Spartans lost the the Bears 9-6 to fall further off the pace and the Giants continued their resurgence with a 13-0 victory over the Frankford Yellowjackets. All three title hopefuls reversed directions on November 15. The Giants' comeback ended with a 12-6 loss to the Bears, whose own title hopes were thwarted by a series of annoying injuries. The Packers were beaten by the Chicago Cardinals 21-13 in Chicago. For the second straight year, an outstanding performance by Ernie Nevers handed Green Bay its first loss. The Packers finished the day only half a game ahead of the Spartans.

The Packers made their annual visit to the Polo Grounds the next week, taking a 14-10 decision in front of 40,000 spectators. A Dunn-to-Bruder touchdown pass brought Green Bay from behind in the fourth quarter and the Packers had to choke off a late Giants drive within the Green Bay 20-yard line. In Chicago, meanwhile, Ernie Nevers led the Cardinals to a second straight upset, a 20-19 triumph over Portsmouth which put a crimp in the Spartans' title hopes. The Spartans won their next game. The Packers beat Providence and Brooklyn before being edged 7-6 by the Bears in Chicago on December 6. Green Bay stood 12-2 and the Spartans were 11-3, but Portsmouth could tie for the title with a victory over the Packers in a game they said they had scheduled for December 13 at Portsmouth. To their surprise, Green Bay refused to play. The game, they explained, was not on the official league schedule but had only been tentatively scheduled after the official schedule was drawn. As such, either party had a right to cancel it. NFL president Joe Carr agreed with the Packers, giving Green Bay its third straight championship.

The Bears finished third at 8-5 and the Cardinals closed with a rush, winning five of their last six, to take fourth place with a 5-4 record. The Giants hobbled home fifth under new coach Steve Owen with a 7-6-1 record.

These top five clubs monopolized the first official all-NFL team. Actually, the honor 11 was chosen as the ninth annual *Green Bay Press Gazette* poll, and its "official" status was only conferred later. However, the *Press Gazette* poll, which included the selections of sportswriters, team officials, coaches and game officials, had been regarded as more or less the last word for several seasons. The first choices for 1931 blended youth with stars who had shone in the 1920s. In the backfield were Dutch Clark, Ernie Nevers, Red Grange and Johnny Blood. Clark led the NFL with nine rushing touchdowns, while Blood led with 11 receiving touchdowns and 84 points scored. Nevers, who would retire from pro football this summer after being the heart and soul of the Cardinals for three years, ranked high in nearly every offensive category. Grange was no longer the quick breakaway runner who had fired imaginations in the mid-1920s and put pro football in the headlines for the first time in 1925; he had matured into a solid two-way halfback, a fine defensive cornerback and a versatile man-in-motion in the Chicago Bears T-formation. Selected for the honor roll on the line were ends Red Badgro of the Giants and Lavie Dilweg, Green Bay; tackles George Christensen, Portsmouth, and Cal Hubbard, Green Bay; guards Butch Gibson, Giants, and Mike Michalske, Green Bay; and center Frank McNally, Cardinals. McNally and Christensen were rookies, Gibson was a second-year man, Badgro was a seasoned end, and Michalske, Hubbard and Dilweg were veteran pillars of the three-time champion Packers.

None of these all-stars played for teams in the bottom half of the standings, where a losing season often combined with the deepening Depression to put a team into desperate financial trouble. After last season, Newark and Minneapolis had folded. The league put a new franchise for 1931 in Cleveland, the fourth NFL franchise since 1920. It was hoped that if the team prospered, the league could find financial backing. It didn't, and they didn't. The new Cleveland team went the way of its earlier brethren — out of business, its one season an artistic and financial disaster. With the team's end came the end of 38-year-old Al Nesser's career. The last member of the famous Nesser clan to play pro football, Al had first joined a major pro team in 1910 with the legendary Columbus Panhandles. The Frankford Yellowjackets didn't wait for the end of the season to fold. Beset by hard times both on the field and at the gate, the Yellowjackets called it quits on November 10, ending a franchise that had been one of the most successful over the last eight years. Also giving up the ghost after the season was the Providence Steam Roller, champions in 1928 but casualties of the sick economy of the 1930s.

NAME	RUSHING Complete Games					RUSHING Incom Games				PASSING Complete Games								PASSING Incom Games					
	G	Att.	Yds.	Avg.	TD	G	Att.	Yds.	TD	G	Com.	Att.	%	Yds	Y/A	TD	Int	G	Com.	Att.	Yds.	TD	Int
GREEN BAY																							
Molenda	14	100	425	4.3	3					14	16	47	34	342	7.3	4	6						
McCrary	12	79	353	4.5	1																		
Wilson	12	58	316	5.4	2					12	3	11	27	81	7.4	1	1						
Bruder	13	66	264	4.0	1					13	2	9	22	36	4.0	1	1						
Engelmann	14	41	252	6.1	1																		
Saunders	9	59	248	4.2	1					9	7	30	23	109	3.6	1	5						
Blood	14	63	195	3.1	2					14	7	19	37	153	8.1	1	2						
Lewellen	7	43	177	4.1	6					7	3	10	30	34	3.4		1						
Fitzgibbon	11	9	36	4.0						11	7	17	41	142	8.4	3	3						
Grove	14	7	33	4.7						14	6	16	38	95	5.9	2	3						
Davenport	2	8	20	2.5																			
Herber	3	9	11	1.2	1					3	5	11	45	78	7.1								
Johnston	2	2	7	3.5																			
Dunn	12	1	0	0.0						12	17	31	55	399	12.9	8	2						
Dilweg																							
Nash																							
Gantenbein																							
Sleight																							
Baker																							
Radick (1)																							
Team	14	545	2337	4.3	18					14	73	201	36	1469	7.3	21	24						
Opp.	14	513	1333	2.6	5					14	76	222	34	1041	4.7	6	37						
PORTSMOUTH																							
Presnell	14	138	518	3.8	3					14	37	90	41	651	7.3	5	9						
Clark	11	89	430	4.8	9					11	21	53	40	231	4.4	1	8						
Holm	14	100	329	3.3	1					14	2	13	15	34	2.6		2						
Schwartz	12	61	221	3.6	2																		
Cavosie	13	52	186	3.6						13	3	8	38	37	4.6								
Alford	14	49	183	3.7	1					14	0	1	0										
Lumpkin	14	49	129	2.6	1					14	0	1	0										
Shelley (1)	2	3	8	2.7																			
McLain (1)	1	3	6	2.0																			
Stennett	10	3	3	1.0						10	2	6	33	34	5.7								
McKalip																							
Ebding																							
Long																							
Mitchell																							
Peterson																							
Team	14	547	2013	3.7	17					14	65	172	38	987	5.7	6	19						
Opp.	14	461	1422	3.1	7					14	53	148	36	649	4.4	2	28						
CHICAGO BEARS																							
R. Grange	12	111	599	5.4	5	1				5	4	12	33	63	5.3		3	8	5	5	95	1	
Nesbitt	12	75	372	5.0		1	7	35	1	5	1	3	33	18	6.0		1	8	2	2	45	1	
Nagurski	9	70	401	5.1	2	1				4	2	2	100	32	16.0			6					
Lintzenich	11	65	268	4.1						5	0	2	0				1	6	4	5	49	2	
Molesworth	10	45	196	4.4	1	1	2	5		4	3	8	38	62	7.8		1	7	1	1	45	1	
Brumbaugh	11	59	148	2.5	1	1				5	3	15	20	60	4.0	1	3	7	6	6	117	1	
Joesting (2)	5	29	136	4.7	1	1				2	0	1	0					4					
Franklin	11	19	101	5.3	1	1				4	0	1	0					8					
Walquist	9	25	68	2.7		1				5	1	17	6	3	0.2		4	6	2	4	45		
Senn (1)						1	2	14															
Jensvold (1)						1	1	6	1														
Johnsos																							
G. Grange																							
Drury																							
Team	12	510	2309	4.5	12	1				5	14	61	23	238	3.9	1	13	8					
Opp.	5	195	646	3.3	1	8				5	19	62	31	241	3.9	2	10	8					

NAME	RECEIVING Complete Games					RECEIVING Incom. Games				PUNTING Comp. Games			PUNTING Incom. Games		
	G	Rec.	Yds.	Avg.	TD	G	Rec.	Yds.	TD	G	No.	Avg.	G	No.	Avg.
GREEN BAY															
Molenda															
McCrary															
Wilson	12	2	-4	-2.0						12	14	34.5			
Bruder	13	5	108	21.6	2					13	6	38.7			
Engelmann	14	9	221	24.6	2										
Saunders															
Blood	14	22	490	22.3	11					14	55	37.3			
Lewellen	7	1	14	14.0						7	26	39.5			
Fitzgibbon	11	3	61	20.3											
Grove	14	5	81	16.2						14	18	34.2			
Davenport															
Herber										3	7	44.1			
Johnston															
Dunn	12	5	41	8.2											
Dilweg	14	7	201	28.7	4										
Nash	13	6	122	20.3											
Gantenbein	14	3	49	16.3	1										
Sleight	13	2	39	19.5											
Baker	2	2	31	15.5											
Radick (1)	1	1	15	15.0											
Team										14	126	37.4			
Opp.										14	129	37.0			
PORTSMOUTH															
Presnell	14	5	30	6.0						12	8	38.8	2		
Clark	11	6	75	12.5						9	53	36.3	2	3	40.3
Holm	14	2	20	10.0	1					12	29	34.7	2		
Schwartz															
Cavosie	13	1	9	9.0						12	20	38.3	1		
Alford	14	11	147	13.4	1					12	6	26.8	2		
Lumpkin	14	7	56	8.0											
Shelley (1)	2	1	7	7.0						1	6	36.8	1	1	0.0
McLain (1)															
Stennett										8	3	26.0	2		
McKalip	14	12	266	22.2	4										
Ebding	14	11	190	17.3											
Long	13	4	44	11.0											
Mitchell	13	3	86	28.7											
Peterson	10	2	57	28.5											
Team										14	146	35.6			
Opp.										14	158	36.7			
CHICAGO BEARS															
R. Grange	5	1	20	20.0		8	6	86	?						
Nesbitt	5	1	18	18.0		8				12	39	41.1	1		
Nagurski															
Lintzenich	5	4	67	16.8	1	6	4	82	1	11	46	34.8			
Molesworth	4					7	1	10							
Brumbaugh	5	1	16	16.0		7				5	2	38.5	7		
Joesting (2)															
Franklin															
Walquist	4	1	19	19.0		6									
Senn (1)															
Jensvold (1)															
Johnsos	5	4	58	14.5		8	6	133	1						
G. Grange	5	2	40	20.0		7	1	24	1						
Drury	4					6	2	61	1						
Team										12	87	37.7	1		
Opp.										5	58	36.1	8		

NAME	PUNT RETURNS Complete Games					PUNT RETURNS Incom. Games			
	G	Rec.	Yds.	Avg.	TD	G	Rec.	Yds.	TD
GREEN BAY									
Molenda	14	1	6	6.0					
McCrary									
Wilson									
Bruder									
Engelmann									
Saunders	9	11	111	10.1					
Blood	14	2	17	8.5					
Lewellen									
Fitzgibbon	11	13	104	8.0					
Grove	14	15	141	9.4					
Davenport									
Herber	3	3	26	8.7					
Johnston									
Dunn	12	6	34	5.7					
Dilweg									
Nash	13	1	10	10.0					
Gantenbein	14	1	5	5.0					
Sleight									
Baker									
Radick (1)									
Team	14	53	454	8.6					
Opp.	14	31	317	10.2					
PORTSMOUTH									
Presnell	13	25	407	16.3	1	1			
Clark	10	23	299	13.0		1			
Holm									
Schwartz									
Cavosie									
Alford	13	1	25	25.0		1			
Lumpkin	13	2	16	8.0		1			
Shelley (1)									
McLain (1)									
Stennett									
McKalip									
Ebding									
Long									
Mitchell									
Peterson									
Team	13	51	747	14.6	1	1			
Opp.	12	34	419	12.3	1	2			
CHICAGO BEARS									
R. Grange									
Nesbitt									
Nagurski									
Lintzenich	5	1	5	5.0		6			
Molesworth	4	6	40	6.7		7			
Brumbaugh	5	10	90	9.0		7			
Joesting (2)									
Franklin									
Walquist									
Senn (1)									
Jensvold (1)									
Johnsos									
G. Grange									
Drury									
Team	5	17	135	7.9		8			
Opp.	5	16	163	10.2		8			

CHICAGO CARDINALS 5-4-0 Roy Andrews and Ernie Nevers

Regulars: Use Name	Pos.	Hgt.	Wgt.	Age	Int.	Pts.
Chuck Kassel	E	6'1	190	27		12
Milan Creighton	E	6'	190	23		12
Jake Williams	T	6'	208	27		
Duke Slater	T	6'1	215	32		
Charlie Diehl	G	6'	205	25		
Walt Kiesling	G	6'2	243	28	1	
Frank McNally	C	6'1	205	24		
Irv Hill	BB	6'1	205	23	1	
Walt Holmer	WB-FB	6'	190	28		
Bunny Belden	WB	5'8	175	30	2	12
Ernie Nevers	FB	6'	205	28	2	66

Substitutes: Use Name	Pos.	Hgt.	Wgt.	Age	Int.	Pts.
Latham Flanagan (from ChiB)	E	6'2	185	24		
George Rogge	E	6'	183	23	1	6
Jess Tinsley	T	6'	200	22	1	
Tom Cobb	T-G	5'11	250	27		
Phil Handler	G	6'	210	23	1	
Jesse Shaw	G	6'1	198	24	1	
Mickey Erickson	C	6'2	210	24		
Les Malloy	BB-WB	6'	200	22		6
Bill Glassgow	WB	5'10	190	23		
Gene Rose	WB	5'8	172	27	1	6

Substitutes: Use Name	Pos.	Hgt.	Wgt.	Age	Int.	Pts.
John Vesser	E	6'	190	30		
Lou Gordon (to BKN)	T	6'5	220	23		
Larry Steinbach (from ChiB)	T	6'	220	27		
Les Caywood (to NYG)	G	6'	230	26		
Ike Mahoney	BB	6'	180	29		
Bill Boyd	WB	5'11	180	24		

Date	Pts.	Opponent	Pts.
Sep. 23	3	Portsmouth	13
Oct. 11	7	Green Bay	26
Oct. 18	13	Chic. Bears	26
Nov. 1	14	Brooklyn	7
Nov. 8	14	Cleveland	6
Nov. 15	21	GREEN BAY	13
Nov. 22	20	PORTSMOUTH	19
Nov. 26	7	Chic. Bears	18
Nov. 28	21	CLEVELAND	0

NEW YORK GIANTS 7-6-1 Steve Owen

Regulars: Use Name	Pos.	Hgt.	Wgt.	Age	Int.	Pts.
Ray Flaherty	E	6'	190	27	1	12
Red Badgro	E	6'	190	28		
Bill Owen	T	6'	205	27		
Len Grant	T	6'3	235	25		
Les Caywood (from ChiC)	G	6'	230	26		
Butch Gibson	G	5'9	200	27		
Mel Hein	C	6'2	205	22	1	
Doug Wycoff	BB	6'	205	27	3	12
Benny Friedman	TB	5'10	185	26	1	12
Dale Burnett	WB	6'1	190	22	2	18
Dutch Kitzmiller	FB	5'11	170	27	1	27

Substitutes: Use Name	Pos.	Hgt.	Wgt.	Age	Int.	Pts.
Glenn Campbell	E	5'11	205	27	1	12
Sammy Stein	E-T	6'	200	26	1	
Corrie Artman	T-G	6'2	240	24		
Steve Owen	T	5'10	245	33		
Harvey Sark	G	5'10	210	24		
Milt Rehnquist (from PROV)	G	6'	240	34		
Mickey Murtagh	C-G	6'1	190	27	1	
Ted Bucklin	BB-G	6'	210	28		
Red Smith	TB-BB-G	5'10	200	27	1	2
Hap Moran	WB-TB-FB-BB	6'1	190	30	2	35
Chris Cagle	FB	5'10	170	26		6

Substitutes: Use Name	Pos.	Hgt.	Wgt.	Age	Int.	Pts.
George Munday (from CLE)	T	6'2	210	23		
Marion Broadstone	T-G	6'2	210	25		
Tiny Feather (from SI)	BB	6'	200	28		
Mack Flenniken	TB	6'1	200	25		6
Ray Schwab	BB		210	23		
Len Sedbrook	FB-WB-BB-TB	5'10	170	26	1	12

Date	Pts.	Opponent	Pts.
Sep. 27	14	Providence	6
Sep. 30	6	Portsmouth	14
Oct. 4	7	Green Bay	27
Oct. 11	0	Chic. Bears	6
Oct. 18	7	STATEN ISLAND	0
Oct. 25	27	BROOKLYN	0
Nov. 1	14	PORTSMOUTH	0
Nov. 8	13	FRANKFORD	0
Nov. 15	6	CHIC. BEARS	12
Nov. 22	10	GREEN BAY	14
Nov. 26	6	Staten Island	9
Nov. 29	0	PROVIDENCE	0
Dec. 6	19	Brooklyn	6
Dec. 13	25	Chic. Bears	6

PROVIDENCE STEAM ROLLER 4-4-3 Ed Robinson

Regulars: Use Name	Pos.	Hgt.	Wgt.	Age	Int.	Pts.
Al Rose	E	6'3	200	24		18
John Spellman	E	5'10	205	32		
Joe Schein	T	5'10	212	22		
Tex Irvin	T-FB	6'	205	24		
Al Graham	G	6'	215	25		
Alec Sofish	G	6'2	200	23		
Ray Smith	C	5'10	285	23	3	
Curly Oden	BB	5'6	170	32		6
Deck Shelley (from PORT)	TB	5'11	190	25		4
Oran Pape	WB	5'11	180	27	5	18
Lee Woodruff	FB	6'	204	22	1	25

Substitutes: Use Name	Pos.	Hgt.	Wgt.	Age	Int.	Pts.
George Pyne	T	5'11	218	21		
Jack McArthur	T-G-C-E	5'11	210	27		
Weldon Gentry	G	5'10	195	24		
Milt Rehnquist (to NYG)	G	6'	240	34		
Herb Eschbach	C	6'	190	24		
Herb Titmas	BB	5'8	185	24		6
Lew Pope	TB-WB	6'	195	23		
Pop Williams	WB-TB	6'	210	25	1	
Bud Edwards (from ChiB)	FB-WB-E	5'11	190	25		

Gus Sonnenberg - Retired to be Professional Wrestler

Substitutes: Use Name	Pos.	Hgt.	Wgt.	Age	Int.	Pts.
Butch Meeker	BB-TB	5'3	145	27	1	1
Royce Goodbread	TB	5'10	210	23		
Sky August	TB-WB	5'11	180	27		
Fred DaGata	FB	5'10	187	23		

Date	Pts.	Opponent	Pts.
Sep. 27	6	NEW YORK	14
Oct. 4	0	FRANKFORD	0
Oct. 10	6	Frankford	0
Oct. 18	6	CLEVELAND	13
Oct. 25	20	Green Bay	48
Nov. 1	7	Staten Island	7
Nov. 8	7	BROOKLYN	0
Nov. 15	6	STATEN ISLAND	0
Nov. 21	13	CLEVELAND	7
Nov. 26	7	GREEN BAY	38
Nov. 29	0	New York	0

STATEN ISLAND STAPLETONS 4-6-1 Hinkey Haines Marty Brill

Regulars: Use Name	Pos.	Hgt.	Wgt.	Age	Int.	Pts.
Bob Barabee	E	5'9	190	26		
Cookie Cunningham	E-HB	6'3	210	26	2	
Al Kanya	T-E	6'	200	23	2	6
Bing Miller	T	6'1	195	27		
Hec Garvey	G-T-C	6'1	230	31	1	
Ollie Satenstein	G-C	6'	200	25		
Herb Rapp	C	6'	195	26		
Izzy Yablok (from BKN)	BB-TB	5'10	172	23	1	
Ken Strong	TB	6'	210	25	4	53
Stu Clancy	HB-TB	5'10	190	25	3	6
Doc Parkinson	FB-HB	6'1	205	24	1	

Substitutes: Use Name	Pos.	Hgt.	Wgt.	Age	Int.	Pts.
Charley Marshall	E	6'	190	24		
Ed Comstock	T	6'2	210	27		
John Demmy	T		190	27		
Jim Laird	G-T	6'	210	33		
Erk Taylor	G-T	6'2	210	23		
Jim Fitzgerald	C	5'11	215	24		
Bullet Baker	BB-TB	5'8	185	31		
Beryl Follet	TB-HB	5'9	165	28		
Tiny Feather (to NYG)	HB-E-FB	6'	200	28	3	
Chief McLain (from PORT)	FB	6'3	200	26	1	12

Substitutes: Use Name	Pos.	Hgt.	Wgt.	Age	Int.	Pts.
Hoot Haines (from BKN)	T-G	6'	205	24		
Henry Obst	G	5'11	190	23		
Les Hart	BB	5'11	180	23		
Hinkey Haines	BB-TB	5'10	170	32		
Irv Constantine	HB	5'9	200	24		

Date	Pts.	Opponent	Pts.
Oct. 4	9	BROOKLYN	7
Oct. 11	6	Brooklyn	18
Oct. 18	0	New York	7
Oct. 25	7	PORTSMOUTH	20
Nov. 1	7	PROVIDENCE	7
Nov. 4	13	BROOKLYN	0
Nov. 8	0	Green Bay	26
Nov. 11	12	Portsmouth	14
Nov. 15	0	Providence	6
Nov. 22	16	CLEVELAND	7
Nov. 26	9	NEW YORK	6

CLEVELAND INDIANS 2-8-0 Al Cornsweet and Hoge Workman

Regulars: Use Name	Pos.	Hgt.	Wgt.	Age	Int.	Pts.
John Hurley	E	6'3	192	24		
Al Nesser	E-G-T	6'	195	38		
Ernie Jessen	T	6'1	250	26		
Babe Lyon (from ChiB)	T-G	6'2	240	24		
Merle Hutson	G-T	6'	210	23		
Biff Lee (from PORT)	G	6'	218	23		
Hank Critchfield	C	5'10	207	26	1	
Dave Mishel	QB	5'9	178	26		1
Chuck Weimer	HB-QB	5'9	185	26		
Ray Novotny	HB-QB	5'10	164	23	1	
Otto Vokaty	FB	6'1	190	22	1	24

Substitutes: Use Name	Pos.	Hgt.	Wgt.	Age	Int.	Pts.
Chuck Braidwood	E	6'	195	27	1	
Dale Waters (from PORT)	E-T-HB	6'2	205	22		
Al Jolley	T	6'2	235	31		
George Munday (to NYG)	T	6'2	210	23		
Mike Gregory	G	5'11	215	26		
Dave Cullen	G	5'10	230	26		
Stu MacMillan	C-G	5'9	175	23		
Hoge Workman	QB	5'11	175	31	1	2
Algy Clark	HB	6'	190	27		12
Leo Jensvold (from ChiB)	HB	5'8	173	23		
Al Cornsweet	FB	5'7	180	25		

Substitutes: Use Name	Pos.	Hgt.	Wgt.	Age	Int.	Pts.
Red Joseph	E	6'3	190	28		
Jim Tarr	E	6'2	190	24		
Don Ridler	T	6'	210	24		
Hoot Herrin	C-G	5'10	208	27		
Drip Wilson	C					
Tiny Lewis	FB	6'2	210	24		
Howie Kriss	HB	5'9	175	24		
Carl Pignatelli	HB-FB	6'	210	23		
Doc Elliott	FB	5'10	215	31		6
Fred Danziger	FB	5'11	175	25		
Buck Lamme	E	6'2	180	26		

Date	Pts.	Opponent	Pts.
Sep. 13	0	Green Bay	26
Sep. 18	0	Chic. Bears	21
Sep. 26	6	BROOKLYN	0
Oct. 7	0	Portsmouth	6
Oct. 18	13	Providence	6
Nov. 8	6	CHIC. CARDS	14
Nov. 15	6	Portsmouth (at Cincinnati)	14
Nov. 21	7	Providence	13
Nov. 22	7	Staten Island	16
Nov. 28	0	Chic. Cards	21

BROOKLYN DODGERS 2-12-0 Jack Depler

Regulars: Use Name	Pos.	Hgt.	Wgt.	Age	Int.	Pts.
Dick O'Donnell	E	6'	188	31		6
Mike Stramiello	E	6'1	195	24	1	6
Lou Lubratovich	T	6'2	233	24		
Jim Mooney	T-G	5'11	205	23		1
Ted Fulton	G-T	6'	210	25		
Bob Gillson	G	6'	205	24		
Red Bultman	C	6'2	200	24	1	
Izzy Yablok (to SI)	BB	5'10	172	23	1	
Jack McBride	TB	5'11	184	29	1	19
Joe Vance	WB-FB	6'1	180	25	1	12
Stumpy Thomason	FB-BB-WB-TB	5'7	185	25		6

Substitutes: Use Name	Pos.	Hgt.	Wgt.	Age	Int.	Pts.
Jerry Nemecek	E	6'	185	24		6
Johnny Tomaini	E-T	6'	195	29		
Claude Perry (from GB)	T	6'1	215	29		
Lou Gordon (from ChiC)	T-E-G	6'5	220	23		
Dave Myers	G-WB	5'11	183	24		
Marv Jonas	G	5'11	186	22		
Saul Mielziner	C-G	6'1	243	26		
Frosty Peters	BB-TB-WB	5'10	183	27	1	2
Bill Senn (from ChiB)	WB-TB-BB-FB	6'	180	26		
Rex Thomas	WB	5'9	175	30		6
Swede Hanson	FB-WB	6'1	185	23		

Substitutes: Use Name	Pos.	Hgt.	Wgt.	Age	Int.	Pts.
Ray Wagner	E	5'10	176	29		
Harry Kloppenburg	E	6'1	210	24		
Gordon Watkins	T-G	6'1	230	24		
Hoot Haines (to SI)	T-G	6'	205	24	1	
Ken Radick (from GB)	G-T	5'10	210	24		
Bill Fleckenstein (from FRA)	G-C	5'10	215	27		
Frank Abruzzino	BB-G-E-C	6'	195	23	1	
Frank Kirkleski	TB-BB	5'10	180	26		
Johnny Scalzi	BB-TB-WB	5'7	168	24	1	
Warner Mizell (to FRA)	FB-TB-WB	5'10	188	23		
Megs Apsit (from FRA)	WB-BB	5'11	195	23		
Tommy Dowler	WB	5'8	160	23		

Date	Pts.	Opponent	Pts.
Sep. 13	0	Portsmouth	14
Sep. 20	6	Green Bay	32
Sep. 26	0	Cleveland	6
Oct. 2	20	Frankford	0
Oct. 4	7	Staten Island	9
Oct. 11	18	STATEN ISLAND	6
Oct. 18	0	PORTSMOUTH	19
Oct. 25	0	New York	27
Nov. 1	7	CHIC. CARDS	14
Nov. 4	0	Staten Island	13
Nov. 8	0	Providence	7
Nov. 22	0	CHIC. BEARS	26
Nov. 29	0	GREEN BAY	7
Dec. 6	6	NEW YORK	19

FRANKFORD YELLOW JACKETS 1-6-1 Bull Behman

Regulars: Use Name	Pos.	Hgt.	Wgt.	Age	Int.	Pts.
Tom Leary	E	6'	182	28		
Lee Wilson	E	5'11	185	26		
Frank Racis	T	6'	200	33		
Bull Behman	T	5'10	225	31		
Potsy Jones	G	5'11	208	21		
Herman Seborg	G	5'11	200	24		
Nate Barrager (to GB)	C	6'	215	24	1	
Mort Kaer	BB-TB	5'11	167	28	1	6
Justin Brumbaugh	TB-BB	6'	205	26	2	
Jim Pederson	WB-BB	5'9	187	23		
Herb Joesting (to ChiB)	FB-TB	6'2	195	26		6

Substitutes: Use Name	Pos.	Hgt.	Wgt.	Age	Int.	Pts.
Tony Kostos	E	5'11	190	26		
Bill Fleckenstein (to BKN)	E-G	6'1	215	27		
Cookie Tackwell (to ChiB)	T	6'2	215	24		1
Art Koeninger	T-C	6'1	200	24		
Carroll Ringwalt	C-G	6'	210	23	1	
Megs Apsit (to BKN)	BB-WB	5'11	195	23		
Mally Nydahl	TB-WB	5'11	165	24		
Mickey McDonnell	WB-BB	5'8	170	27	3	
Art Pharmer	FB	5'10	186	23		

Substitutes: Use Name	Pos.	Hgt.	Wgt.	Age	Int.	Pts.
Jim Magner	TB-BB	6'	165	28		
Warner Mizell (from BKN)	WB	5'10	188	23		

Date	Pts.	Opponent	Pts.
Oct. 2	0	BROOKLYN	20
Oct. 4	0	Providence	0
Oct. 10	0	PROVIDENCE	6
Oct. 15	0	Portsmouth	19
Oct. 18	0	Green Bay	15
Oct. 25	13	Chic. Bears	12
Oct. 31	0	PORTSMOUTH	14
Nov. 8	0	New York	13

RUSHING

NAME	Complete Games G	Att.	Yds.	Avg.	TD	Incom. Games G	Att.	Yds.	TD
CHICAGO CARDINALS									
Nevers	4	96	300	3.1	2	5	29	111	6
Belden	3	21	109	5.2	1	5	1	2	1
Rose	4	25	73	2.9	1	4	1	6	
Holmer	4	23	45	2.0		5	2	25	
Glassgow	4	14	31	2.2		5			
Hill	4	3	13	4.3		5			
Malloy	4	1	0	0.0		4			
Boyd	2	1	-3	-3.0		2			
Creighton									
Kassel									
Rogge									
Team	4	184	568	3.1	4	5			
Opp.	4	144	654	4.5	4	5			
NEW YORK									
Friedman	3	48	188	3.9	1	5	18	135	1
Kitzmiller	6	49	114	2.3	1	8	14	48	3
Cagle	7	39	72	1.8		7	6	82	1
Smith	4	19	142	7.5		5	1	10	
Wycoff	7	47	104	2.2	1	5	4	29	
Moran	6	45	116	2.6	1	8	2	9	1
Burnett	6	19	61	3.2		8	4	29	1
Sedbrook	4	5	4	0.8	1	7	2	18	1
Flenniken	2	6	11	1.8		2	1	1	1
Bucklin	3	1	0	0.0		2			
Feather (3)									
Flaherty									
Badgro									
Campbell									
Stein									
Team	6	270	788	2.9	5	8			
Opp.	6	220	779	3.5	6	8			
PROVIDENCE									
Shelley (2)	4	47	117	2.5		4	11	76	
Pape	4	36	69	1.9	1	7	11	111	
Woodruff	4	21	71	3.4	2	7	15	49	2
Edwards (2)	3	16	26	1.6		6	4	31	
Meeker	4	2	34	17.0		5	4	11	
August	2					5	4	36	
Pope	2	5	1	0.2		6	1	20	
Goodbread	1	1	2	2.0		3	1	18	
Williams	2	2	0	0.0		6	2	6	
Titmas	4	1	1	1.0		7	1	4	
Oden	4	1	3	3.0		7			
Rose									
Spellman									
Team	4	132	324	2.5	3	7			
Opp.	4	138	531	3.8	5	7			
STATEN ISLAND									
Strong	11	100	348	3.5	6				
Parkinson	11	93	275	3.0					
Clancy	11	64	222	3.5	1				
Yablok (2)	7	33	110	3.3					
McLain (2)	9	55	102	1.9					
Baker	9	27	51	1.9					
Hart	5	10	43	4.3					
Haines	2	7	23	3.3					
Feather (1)	10	11	9	0.8					
Follet	2	2	-1	-0.5					
Cunningham									
Barrabee									
Marshall									
Team	11	402	1182	2.9	7				
Opp.	11	468	1441	3.1	11				
CLEVELAND									
Vokaty	4	38	155	4.1	1	4	8	46	3
Novotny	4	19	64	3.4		6			
Waters (2)	3	11	16	1.5		3			
Weimer	3	5	14	2.8		4			
Joseph						1	1	14	
Workman	4	5	5	1.0		5	2	5	
Clark	4	9	8	0.9	1	4	1	0	
Pignatelli	3	4	7	1.8		4			
Jensvold (2)	2	3	3	1.0		5			
Mishel	3	5	2	0.4		3			
Elliott						2	1	1	1
Kriss	1	2	-12	-6.0		1			
Nesser									
Braidwood									
Team	4	101	262	2.6	2	6			
Opp.	4	175	718	4.1	6	6			
BROOKLYN									
McBride	7	81	185	2.3	2	6	1	65	1
Thomason	6	34	75	2.2		7	1	25	
Vance	6	26	82	3.1	2	5			
Hanson	5	25	48	1.9		6			
Senn (2)	4	25	25	1.0		5			
Yablok (1)	5	15	22	1.5		1			
Mizell (1)	3	2	1	0.5		2	1	10	
Scalzi	4	7	8	1.1		3			
Apsit (2)	1	1	5	5.0		2			
Dowler	2	6	4	0.7					
Mooney	7	1	2	2.0		7			
Kirkleski	1	1	-1	-1.0		2			
Peters	5	2	-2	-1.0		4			
Nemecek									
Thomas									
O'Donnell									
Stramiello									
Team	7	226	454	2.0	4	7			
Opp.	7	288	895	3.1	10	7			
FRANKFORD									
Brumbaugh	3	36	155	4.3		5	1	0	
Joesting (1)	3	31	84	2.7		5	4	14	1
McDonnell	1	13	40	3.1		2			
Kaer	3	16	27	1.7		5	3	1	
Nydahl	1	1	2	2.0		3	1	10	
Mizell (2)	1	2	3	1.5		2			
Pederson	3	3	2	0.7		5			
Wilson									
Leary									
Fleckenstein									
Kostos									
Apsit (2)									
Team	3	102	313	3.1		5			
Opp.	3	112	439	3.9	6	5			

PASSING

NAME	Complete Games G	Com.	Att.	%	Yds.	Y/A	TD	Int	Incom. Games G	Com.	Att.	Yds.	TD	Int
CHICAGO CARDINALS														
Nevers	5	30	66	45	414	6.3	3	3	4	10	14	235	3	4
Rose	5	1	2	50	4	4			3					
Holmer	5	0	2	0					4					
Team	5	31	70	44	418	6.0	3	3	4					
Opp.	5	35	80	44	499	6.2	4	12	4					
NEW YORK														
Friedman	5	29	52	56	422	8.1		3	3	13	16	307	3	1
Kitzmiller	7	3	10	30	25	2.5		4	7					
Cagle	7	1	4	25	6	1.5	1		7					
Smith	4	3	7	43	37	5.3		1	5	4	6	79	1	2
Wycoff	7	1	8	17	13	2.2		2	5	0	1			1
Moran	7	2	6	33	65	10.8		1	7	2	2	48		
Burnett	7	0	1	0				1	7					
Flenniken	2	9	19	47	122	6.4		1	2	1	1	15	1	
Feather (3)	1	1	1	100	7	7.0	1		1					
Team	7	46	96	48	643	6.7	2	12	7					
Opp.	6	18	60	30	268	4.5	3	8	8					
PROVIDENCE														
Shelley (2)	6	30	91	33	555	6.1	3	12	2	2	4	31		1
Pape	6	1	1	100	6	6.0			5					
August	2	0	2	0					5	1	1	27		
Pope	4	1	5	20	27	5.4		1	4	1	2	7		
Williams	4								4	0	1			
Titmas	6	5	7	71	29	4.1			5	0	1			1
Oden	6	5	12	42	51	4.3		1	5	7	9	96	1	1
Rose	6								5	1	1	16	1	
Team	6	42	118	36	668	5.7	3	14	5					
Opp.	5	23	70	33	482	6.9	9	9	6					
STATEN ISLAND														
Strong	11	9	29	31	118	4.1	1	7						
Parkinson	11	6	12	50	39	3.3		1						
Clancy	11	1	10	10	27	2.7		3						
Yablok (2)	7	2	10	20	28	2.8		5						
Baker	9	2	5	40	51	10.2	1	1						
Hart	5	4	10	40	49	4.9		3						
Haines	2	1	3	33	6	2.0		2						
Feather (1)	10	2	2	100	12	6.0								
Follet	2	0	1	0										
Cunningham	10	0	3	0										
Team	11	27	85	32	330	3.9	2	22						
Opp.	11	65	181	36	957	5.3	4	18						
CLEVELAND														
Novotny	5	1	6	17	10	1.7		2	5	0	1			1
Weimer	4	1	1	100	36	36.0			3					
Workman	5	13	39	33	104	2.7		4	4	2	6	58		
Mishel	4	14	28	50	166	5.9	1	2	2					
Team	7	46	104	44	511	4.9	1	10	3					
Opp.	7	42	108	39	719	6.7	3	5	3					
BROOKLYN														
McBride	7	12	39	31	133	3.4		8	6	5	11	175	2	5
Hanson	5	0	1	0					6					
Senn (2)	4	2	4	50	7	1.8			5					
Yablok (1)	5	1	3	33	8	2.7			1					
Mizell (1)	3	3	8	38	26	3.3		2	2					
Scalzi	4	6	15	40	86	5.7		1	3	1	1	10	1	
Mooney	7	2	3	67	24	8.0			7					
Peters	5	13	34	38	136	4.0		3	4	1	1	35	1	
Team	8	43	116	37	437	3.8		14	6					
Opp.	9	34	77	44	546	7.1	4	6	5					
FRANKFORD														
Brumbaugh	3	1	8	13	7	0.9			5	1	1	25		
Joesting (1)	3	2	4	50	21	5.3		1	5					
McDonnell	1	1	4	25	16	4.0			2					
Kaer	3	4	22	18	58	2.6		5	5	1	2	11		1
Nydahl	1	0	1	0				1	3	1	2	15		1
Team	3	8	39	21	102	2.6		7	5					
Opp.	3	15	34	44	276	8.1	1	5	5					

RECEIVING

NAME	Complete Games G	Rec.	Yds.	Avg.	TD	Incom. Games G	Rec.	Yds.	TD
CHICAGO CARDINALS									
Belden	3	3	17	5.7		5			
Rose	3	2	8	4.0		5	1	30	
Glassgow	3	1	8	8.0		6			
Hill	3	3	27	9.0		6	1	15	
Malloy	3					5	1	44	1
Boyd	1					3	1	48	
Creighton	3	5	82	16.4	1	6	7	139	1
Kassel	3	4	55	13.8	1	6	1	23	1
Rogge	2	1	53	53.0	1	4			
NEW YORK									
Kitzmiller	6	1	12	12.0		8	5	94	
Cagle	6	4	46	11.5		8	4	70	
Wycoff	6	2	17	8.5		6	2	34	
Moran	6	5	103	20.6	1	8	3	49	1
Burnett	6	4	49	12.3		8	3	57	2
Sedbrook	4	1	6	6.0		7			
Feather (3)						2	1	25	
Flaherty	6	6	168	28.0		8	3	113	1
Badgro	6	6	79	13.2		7	1	12	
Campbell	6	3	38	12.7		8	2	45	2
Stein	5					3	1	19	
PROVIDENCE									
Pape	6	9	93	10.3	2	5	2	67	
Woodruff	6	3	23	7.7		5			
Edwards (2)	4	2	31	15.5		5	2	19	
August	2	1	0	0.0		5	1	7	
Pope	4	1	9	9.0		4			
Titmas	6	3	76	25.3		5	1	16	1
Oden	6	7	147	21.0		5			
Rose	6	9	184	20.4	1	5	6	68	1
Spellman	6	7	105	15 0		5			
STATEN ISLAND									
Strong	11	5	50	10.0					
Parkinson	11	2	16	8.0					
Clancy	11	3	46	15.3					
Yablok (2)	7	1	5	5.0					
McLain (2)	9	2	72	36.0	2				
Baker	9	2	19	9.5					
Haines	2	1	16	16.0					
Feather (1)	10	4	40	10.0					
Cunningham	10	2	21	10.5					
Barrabee	10	3	25	8.3					
Marshall	10	2	20	10.0					
CLEVELAND									
Vokaty	4	5	56	11.2		4	1	6	
Novotny	4	5	71	14.2		6	1	39	
Weimer	3	1	2	2.0		4	2	50	
Joseph						1	1	15	
Clark	4	2	13	6.5		4	1	2	1
Pignatelli	3	2	12	6.0		4			
Jensvold (2)	2	2	13	6.5		5			
Mishel	3	1	10	10.0		3			
Nesser	4	2	22	11.0		5			
Braidwood	4	2	21	10.5		4			
BROOKLYN									
McBride	7	2	24	12.0		6			
Thomason	6	9	91	10.1		7	1	35	1
Vance	6	6	72	12.0		5			
Hanson	5	4	5	1.3		6	1	40	
Senn (2)	4	5	76	15.2		5			
Mizell (1)	3	1	10	10.0		2			
Scalzi	4	2	5	2.5		3			
Peters	5	2	50	25.0		4			
Nemecek	5	5	43	8.6		4	1	25	1
Thomas	3					5	3	110	1
O'Donnell	5	1	36	36.0		6	1	10	1
Stramiello	7	2	8	4.0		6			
FRANKFORD									
Brumbaugh	3	1	16	16.0		5			
Joesting (1)	3					5	1	25	
Kaer	3	1	10	10.0		5			
Pederson	3	1	11	11.0		5			
Wilson	2	2	25	12.5		3	2	26	
Leary	3	1	18	18.0		4			
Fleckenstein	3	1	15	15.0		3			
Kostos	2	1	7	7.0		4			

PUNTING / PUNT RETURNS

NAME	Punting Comp. Games G	No.	Avg.	Punting Incom. Games G	No.	Avg.	Punt Returns Complete Games G	Rec.	Yds.	Avg.	TD	Punt Returns Incom. Games G	Rec.	Yds.	TD
CHICAGO CARDINALS															
Nevers	4	30	34.4	5											
Belden							3					5	1	40	
Holmer	4	2	39.0	5											
Glassgow							3	1	25	25.0		6			
Team	4	32	34.7	5			3	1	25	25.0		6			
Opp.	4	28	32.8	5			4	14	207	14.8	1	5			
NEW YORK															
Friedman	3	2	28.0	5			3	4	54	13.5		5			
Kitzmiller	5	15	37.7	9	2	17.0	6	11	114	10.4		8	3	87	
Cagle	5	1	48.0	9			6	4	27	6.8		8	1	30	
Wycoff	5	18	36.9	7	4	16.3									
Moran	5	14	37.0	9			6	2	13	6.5		8			
Burnett	5	1	49.0	9											
Team	6	62	36.8	8			6	21	208	9.9		8			
Opp.	6	69	38.9	8			5	18	184	10.2		9			
PROVIDENCE															
Shelley (2)	4	36	37.2	4											
Pape							4	5	96	19.2		7			
Edwards (2)	3	1	29.0	6			3	1	10	10.0		6			
Meeker							4	2	10	5.0		5			
Pope	2			7	1	0.0									
Williams	2	1	17.0	6	1	10.0									
Oden							4	6	149	24.8	1	7	1	28	
Team	4	38	36.4	7			4	14	265	18.9	1	7			
Opp.	4	38	37.7	7			4	23	223	9.7		7			
STATEN ISLAND															
Strong	11	76	40.9				11	36	428	11.9	1				
Parkinson	11	7	31.1												
Clancy	11	29	37.5												
Yablok (2)							7	8	85	10.6					
Baker							9	6	70	11.7					
Hart	5	1	40.0												
Haines							2	1	3	3.0					
Follet							2	1	6	6.0					
Team	11	113	39.5				11	52	592	11.4	1				
Opp.	11	112	37.9				11	33	490	14.8	1				
CLEVELAND															
Novotny	3	8	28.6	7			4	2	17	8.5		6			
Waters (2)							3	1	8	8.0		3			
Weimer	2	5	43.6	5											
Workman	3	18	40.8	6	1	45.0	4	2	11	5.5		5			
Mishel	2	1	46.0	4											
Kriss							1	2	55	27.5		1			
Team	4	44	38.5	6			4	7	91	13.0		6			
Opp.	4	40	35.5	6			4	14	164	11.7		6			
BROOKLYN															
Thomason	6	3	45.0	7			6	1	20	20.0		7			
Vance	6	1	0.0	5			6					5	1	30	
Hanson	5	7	35.9	6											
Senn (2)	4	12	38.3	5			4	5	70	14.0		5	1	25	
Yablok (1)							5	1	15	15.0		1			
Mizell (1)	3	3	37.3												
Scalzi	4	2	42.5	3			4	3	35	11.7		3			
Mooney	7	35	40.1	7	1	0.0									
Peters	5	14	44.5	4			5	4	48	12.0		4			
Team	7	77	39.8	7			7	14	188	13.4		7			
Opp.	7	69	40.3	7			7	38	447	11.8		7			
FRANKFORD															
Brumbaugh	3	4	31.5	5											
McDonnell	1	2	32.0	2			1	1	12	12.0		2			
Kaer	3	1	52.0	5			3	5	55	11.0		5	1	84	1
Nydahl	1	1	37.0	3											
Mizell (2)	1	4	27.3	2			1	1	5	5.0		2			
Pederson	3	27	32.0	5			3	1	2	2.0		5			
Apsit (2)	1	1	0.0	5											
Team	3	40	31.3	5			3	8	74	9.3		5			
Opp.	3	37	35.1	5			3	17	165	9.7		5			

1932 N.F.L.
The 60-Yard Circus

When the National Football League reached its 13th year in 1932, it had come a long way from its humble beginnings in a Canton, Ohio automobile showroom, but it still had a long way to go. Pro football was still a very distant second to the college game in popularity. The problems were obvious. Too many championship races had seen either runaways by one or two clubs while the rest of the league maneuvered to stay out of last place, or had been embroiled in controversy when it came time to award the championship, or both. Too many franchises teetered on the brink of financial oblivion, lending an air of instability to the entire league. Worst of all, the product needed refurbishing. There were too many dull, low-scoring games. In 1931, half of the league's teams averaged a single touchdown plus extra point or less per game. The NFL played under virtually the same rules as college football, but the perception of the two games by the fans was different: college football, awash in ancient rivalries and hoopla, was exciting; pro football, with its low scores, was not. The only major change in the rules for 1932, a substitution change allowing a replaced player to return in a subsequent quarter, had no effect on the lack of scoring. In 1932, NFL games averaged only 16.4 points for both teams, the lowest per game record since 1926. Ironically, at a time when the NFL showed the least offense in years, the league decided to keep official statistics.

The 1932 season began as a continuation of previous seasons, but before it ended, it pointed the way toward solving some of the problems besetting pro football. In midseason, the Green Bay Packers looked like a sure bet to win their fourth straight NFL championship. On the eve of their annual trip east, they had won seven games, including victories of 15-10 over the Portsmouth Spartans and 2-0 over the Chicago Bears, and had been held to a scoreless tie by the Bears. The unbeaten Pack flexed its defensive muscle, posting five shutouts in the eight games. The rival Spartans and Bears had no losses other than those with the Packers, but both teams had won fewer games and had been tied more often. After the games of November 6, the Packers were 7-0-1, the Spartans were 4-1-2 and the Bears an incredible 2-1-4, including three straight scoreless ties to open the season. The Packers would meet the relatively weak clubs in Boston, New York, Brooklyn and Staten Island, then end the season with key games in Portsmouth and Chicago.

Curly Lambeau traveled east with a squad that had undergone key changes. The veteran line featuring Cal Hubbard, Mike Michalske, Lavie Dilweg and Nate Barrager was unchanged, but the backfield had an injection of youth. After two years of inactivity on the bench, Arnie Herber won the starting job at tailback with long-range passing that more than offset his lack of speed afoot. By the end of the season, he would rank as the league's leading passer. Powerful rookie Clarke Hinkle from Bucknell settled in for a long run as the Green Bay fullback. Second-year men Hank Bruder and Roger Grove also saw increased playing time in the backfield. Of the veteran Packer backs, Johnny Blood still played most of the time, but Verne Lewellen and Hurdis McCrary slipped into reserve status, Red Dunn retired, and Bo Molenda was traded to New York. With the changes, the Packers kept winning.

The road trip began with a 21-0 victory over the Boston Braves on November 13. George Preston Marshall and two partners organized the Braves this season, presumably having purchased the Newark 1931 franchise, but a $46,000 loss this season left Marshall the sole owner for the future. The Braves could not match the Packers, but they did have a respectable club, including rookie Cliff Battles, whose open-field running gave him the NFL rushing leadership. While the Braves and Packers

1932 STANDINGS

	W	L	T	Pct.	Pts.	Opp. Pts.	Avg. Pts.	Opp. Avg.
Chicago Bears*	7	1	6	.875	160	44	11	3
Green Bay Packers	10	3	1	.769	152	63	11	5
Portsmouth Spartans*	6	2	4	.750	116	71	10	6
Boston Braves	4	4	2	.500	55	79	6	8
New York Giants	4	6	2	.400	93	113	8	9
Brooklyn Dodgers	3	9	0	.250	63	131	5	11
Chicago Cardinals	2	6	2	.250	72	114	7	11
Staten Island Stapletons	2	7	3	.222	77	143	6	14

Chicago Bears defeated Portsmouth in post-season playoff to break the tie for the championship. The result of this game was included in the regular season standings and statistics.

Scoring Leaders

Clark	Port	55
Grange	ChiB	42
Flaherty	NYG	30
Grossman	Bkn	30
Johnsos	ChiB	26
Nagurski	ChiB	24
Battles	Bos	24
Blood	GB	24
Bruder	GB	24
Cagle	NYG	24
Grove	GB	23
Hill	ChiC	22
Hinkle	GB	19

KICKING

		FG	Att	Pct
Clark	Port	3	4	75
Wilson	SI	1	1	100
Engbretsen	ChiB	1	2	50
Friedman	Bkn	1	2	50
Cronin	Bkn	0	1	0
Frahm	SI	0	1	0
Hagerty	NYG	0	1	0
Johnsos	ChiB	0	1	0
Molenda	GB-NYG	0	1	0
Presnell	Port	0	1	0
Hughes	Bos	0	2	0
Strong	SI	0	3	0
Tackwell	ChiB	0	3	0

		PAT	Att	Pct
Clark	Port	10	15	67
Engbretsen	ChiB	10	15	67
O'Boyle	GB	7	10	70
Grove	GB	5	6	83
Hughes	Bos	5	6	83
Friedman	Bkn	5	7	71
Hill	ChiC	4	4	100
Tackwell	ChiB	3	3	100
Wilson	SI	3	3	100
Molenda	GB-NYG	3	5	60
Strong	SI	3	5	60
Johnsos	ChiB	2	2	100
Lillard	ChiC	2	2	100
Frahm	SI	2	3	67
Hagerty	NYG	2	4	50
Holmer	ChiC	2	4	50
Moran	NYG	2	4	50
Buckler	ChiB	1	1	100
Presnell	Port	1	1	100
Wiberg	Bkn	1	1	100
Hinkle	GB	1	5	20
Battles	Bos	0	1	0
R. Grange	ChiB	0	1	0
McBride	Bkn-NY	0	1	0
Roberts	Bos-SI	0	1	0

CHICAGO BEARS 7-1-6 Ralph Jones

Regulars

Use Name	Pos.	Hgt.	Wgt.	Age	Int	Pts.
Bill Hewitt	E	5'9"	190	22	2	6
Luke Johnsos	E	6'2"	195	26	1	26
Lloyd Burdick	T	6'4"	248	23	1	
Tiny Engebretsen	T	6'1"	225	22		13
Joe Kopcha	G	6'	220	26		
Zuck Carlson	G	6'	210	27		
Ookie Miller	C	6'	210	22	1	
Keith Molesworth	QB	5'9"	160	26	2	18
Red Grange	HB	5'11"	185	29		42
Dick Nesbitt	HB	6'	206	24	1	12
Bronko Nagurski	FB	6'2"	217	23	2	24

Substitutes

Use Name	Pos.	Hgt.	Wgt.	Age	Int	Pts.
Cookie Tackwell	E	6'2"	216	25		3
Don Murry	T	6'2"	195	32		
Harold Ely (to BKN)	T-G	6'2"	275	22		
Bill Buckler	G-T	6'	230	31		1
Gil Bergerson	G	6'6"	240	22		
George Trafton	C	6'2"	228	35		
Carl Brumbaugh	QB	5'10"	166	24	1	
George Corbett	HB-QB	5'9"	180	24	2	7
Johnny Sisk	HB	6'2"	198	25		
Herb Joesting	FB	6'2"	200	27	1	

Substitutes

Use Name	Pos.	Hgt.	Wgt.	Age	Int	Pts.
Al Culver (to GB)	T	6'2"	212	24		
Paul Schuette (to BOS)	G	6'	223	26		
Bert Pearson	C-G-T	6'	208	27		
Bernie Leahy	HB	5'11"	185	24		
Al Moore	HB	5'9"	170	24		
John Doehring	HB	6'	212	22		6
Paul Franklin	FB-E	6'2"	194	26	2	
Jim Pederson	HB	5'9"	187	24		

Scores of Each Game

Date	Pts.	Opponent	Pts.
Sep. 25	0	Green Bay	0
Oct. 2	0	Staten Island	0
Oct. 9	0	Chic. Cards	0
Oct. 16	0	GREEN BAY	2
Oct. 23	27	STATEN ISLAND	7
Oct. 30	7	Boston	7
Nov. 6	28	New York	8
Nov. 13	13	PORTSMOUTH	13
Nov. 20	20	BROOKLYN	0
Nov. 24	34	CHIC. CARDS	0
Nov. 27	7	Portsmouth	7
Dec. 4	6	NEW YORK	0
Dec. 11	9	GREEN BAY	0
Dec. 18	9	PORTSMOUTH (playoff)	0

GREEN BAY PACKERS 10-3-1 Curly Lambeau

Regulars

Use Name	Pos.	Hgt.	Wgt.	Age	Int	Pts.
Lavie Dilweg	E	6'3"	202	29		1
Milt Gantenbein	E	6'	200	22		
Dick Stahlman	T	6'2"	215	30		
Cal Hubbard	T	6'4"	255	31		
Rudy Comstock	G	5'10"	208	31		
Mike Michalske	G	6'	215	29		8
Nate Barrager	C	6'	215	25		
Roger Grove	BB	6'	180	24	3	23
Arnie Herber	TB	5'11"	205	22	6	12
Johnny Blood	HB-BB-TB	6'1"	195	28	6	24
Clarke Hinkle	FB	5'11"	205	22	4	19

Substitutes

Use Name	Pos.	Hgt.	Wgt.	Age	Int	Pts.
Al Rose	E	6'3"	200	25	1	12
Tom Nash	E	6'3"	204	26	1	2
Claude Perry	T	6'1"	210	30		
Jug Earp	T-C	6'	257	35		
Clyde Van Sickle	G	6'1"	224	24		
Joe Zeller	G	6'1"	198	24	1	
Red Bultman	C-T	6'2"	200	25		
Harry O'Boyle	BB	5'9"	180	27	1	7
Verne Lewellen	TB-HB-BB	6'1"	178	30	1	6
Hank Bruder	HB-TB	6'	199	24		24
Hurdis McCrary	FB	6'	206	28	2	6

Boob Darling — shoulder injury

Substitutes

Use Name	Pos.	Hgt.	Wgt.	Age	Int	Pts.
Les Peterson (to & from SI)	E-T	6'3"	212	22		
Al Culver (from ChiB)	T	6'2"	212	24		
Megs Apsit	BB-HB	5'11"	200	24		
Paul Fitzgibbon	BB	5'8"	183	29		
Deck Shelley (to ChiC)	HB	5'11"	192	26		
Wuert Engelmann	HB	6'3"	195	24	2	6
Bo Molenda (to NYG)	FB	5'10"	215	27		

Scores of Each Game

Date	Pts.	Opponent	Pts.
Sep. 18	15	CHIC. CARDS	7
Sep. 25	0	CHIC. BEARS	0
Oct. 2	13	NEW YORK	0
Oct. 9	15	PORTSMOUTH	10
Oct. 16	2	Chic. Bears	0
Oct. 23	13	BROOKLYN	0
Oct. 30	26	STATEN ISLAND	0
Nov. 6	19	Chic. Cards	9
Nov. 13	21	Boston	0
Nov. 20	0	New York	6
Nov. 24	7	Brooklyn	0
Nov. 27	21	Staten Island	3
Dec. 4	0	Portsmouth	19
Dec. 11	0	Chic. Bears	9

met in Boston, the Bears and Spartans, true to habit, fought to a 13-13 tie in Chicago.

One week later, the Packers made their annual pilgrimage to the Polo Grounds. The Giants had a different look from the powerhouse squads of 1929 and 1930. Benny Friedman had moved across the East River to play with the Brooklyn Dodgers after Giants owner Tim Mara turned down his bid for part ownership in the club. The Giants relied on Chris Cagle as their main running threat and selling point in advertisements, and reacquired Jack McBride from the Dodgers to do the bulk of the passing. Without Friedman, the Giants shuffled into the game 2-5-1. Before 30,000 fans, however, the Giants smothered the Packers offense and built a McBride-to-Ray Flaherty touchdown pass in the first half into a 6-0 upset. The Bears and Spartans both won their games; the three contenders each had one defeat, but the Packers had won eight, the Spartans five and the Bears three.

The Packers finished the eastern swing without further trouble, beating the Dodgers 7-0 in Ebbets Field on Thanksgiving Day and the Staten Island Stapletons 21-3 three days later in tiny Thompson Stadium. The Bears, meanwhile, beat the Cardinals, much weakened without the retired Ernie Nevers, 34-0 on Thanksgiving and met the Spartans on Sunday in a rematch which, of course, ended in a 7-7 tie.

The Spartans hosted the Packers on December 4 and, in a couple hours, the Green Bay dynasty was over. The Packers offense went to pieces, with a passing record of one completion in 16 attempts. The Spartans used 11 men all the way, with Dutch Clark, Father Lumpkin, rookie Ace Gutowsky, George Christensen, Glenn Presnell and their teammates emerged with a 9-0 victory to knock the Packers out of the race and assure Portsmouth of at least a tie for the championship. At Wrigley Field that same afternoon, the Bears beat the Giants 6-0 to stay half a game behind the Spartans. The Giants, finishing fifth in an eight-team league with a 4-6-2 mark, badly needed some new blood, but coach Steve Owen would stay on to supervise the rejuvenation.

On December 11, while the Spartans were idle, the Bears and Packers closed the seasons in a heavy snowstorm in Chicago. The Green Bay offense continued its slump against the Bears, who scored all their points in the fourth quarter for a 9-0 victory. That left the regular schedule in a deadlock for first place between the 6-1-6 Bears and the 6-1-4 Spartans. The league office arranged for a playoff meeting one week later in Chicago. An irony was that because the game would count in the season standings, the loser of the playoff for the championship would drop into third place.

But the week was a weather disaster in Chicago. Bitter cold and heavy snow made football impossible in the city. George Halas, remembering that the Bears and Cardinals had played a charity exhibition indoors at Chicago Stadium in 1930, suggested that as a site for the game. When it was still snowing by Friday, the Spartans had little choice but to agree. The Stadium could accomodate a field only 45 yards wide and 80 yards long. With two half-moon endzones, only 60 yards were left between the goallines. Because a circus was scheduled there a few days later, a six-inch layer of dirt covered the floor. A few special rules had to be put in. Kickoffs were to be made from the 10-yard line. Because a solid fence surrounded the field a few feet from each sideline, the ball was moved in 10 yards following an out-of-bounds (normally, teams started play right at the sideline), but, with the loss of down. Touchbacks were returned to the 10-yard line. And no field goals were permitted.

In this innovative setting, coach Ralph Jones had his entire squad ready to go, featuring Bronko Nagurski, Red Grange, quarterback Keith Molesworth, end Luke Johnsos, guard Zuck Carlson and rookie Bill Hewitt, a colorful end from Michigan whose blonde hair became his trademark as he played most of his career without a helmet. Portsmouth coach Potsy Clark, however, was at a severe disadvantage, since Dutch Clark had already contracted to begin work as a basketball coach at Colorado College and could not make it back for the game. Clark, the NFL scoring leader for 1932, was the key man in the Spartan offense.

For three quarters, neither club scored, giving the 12,000 spectators expectations of yet another tie. But Chicago's Dick Nesbitt intercepted a Gutowsky pass in the fourth quarter and returned it 10 yards before he was run out of bounds at the Spartan seven. The ball, as per the special rule, was brought in 10 yards toward the center of the field, costing the Bears a down. On second and third downs, Bronko Nagurski gained six and lost one, making it fourth and goal from the two. Nagurski took a handoff, faked a dive into the line, retreated a few steps and fired a pass to Grange in the endzone. The league rules said that a pass had to be thrown from at least five yards behind the line of scrimmage, and the Spartans complained that Nagurski had not retreated far enough, if at all, before passing. The officials disagreed and allowed the score. A few moments later, the Bears added a safety and went on to a 9-0 triumph. It was their second league title and made good coach Jones' promise of a championship within three years.

Although the *Portsmouth Times* called it "a sham battle on a Tom Thumb gridiron," the game had more significance than its effect on the immediate standings. The idea of bringing the ball in on a sideline play instead of wasting a down running to the center of the field was appealing and opened up play. The dispute over how many yards Nagurski had been behind the line of scrimmage when he threw the pass led naturally to the suggestion that such restrictions be taken off passers. Most important, the public liked the idea of an end-of-season playoff to settle the championship. The next year, 1933, would see many changes.

The official all-NFL team honored ends Luke Johnsos, Bears, and Ray Flaherty, Giants; tackles Cal Hubbard, Green Bay, and Turk Edwards, Boston; guards Zuck Carlson, Bears, and Walt Kiesling, Cardinals; center Nate Barrager, Green Bay; quarterback Dutch Clark, Portsmouth; halfbacks Arnie Herber, Green Bay, and Father Lumpkin, Portsmouth; and fullback Bronko Nagurski, Bears.

NAME	RUSHING Complete Games G	Att.	Yds.	Avg.	TD	Incom. Games G	Att.	Yds.	TD
CHICAGO BEARS									
Nagurski	14	109	486	4.5	4				
Grange	12	77	232	3.0	3				
Nesbitt	6	44	137	3.1		8	15	84	2
Molesworth	6	27	93	3.4	1	8	8	50	1
Corbett	4	26	110	4.2		8	3	9	
Sisk	6	10	28	2.8		7	2	53	
Hewitt	6					7	1	28	1
Doehring	3	5	16	3.2		4	4	7	1
Joesting	2	6	20	3.3		2			
Franklin	3	4	6	1.5		5	1	2	
Moore	1	2	5	2.5		1			
Brumbaugh	6	8	-5	-0.6		7	1	-7	
Tackwell									
Johnsos									
Team	6	221	769	3.5	3	8			
Opp.	6	246	828	3.4	2	8			
GREEN BAY									
Hinkle	13	113	451	4.0	3				
Bruder	14	86	248	2.9	2				
Herber	14	81	211	2.6	1				
McCrary	11	46	154	3.3	1				
Engelmann	14	38	151	4.0					
Blood	13	49	136	2.8					
Lewellen	14	48	132	2.8					
Grove	13	15	23	1.5					
O'Boyle	11	7	13	1.9					
Shelley (1)	2	3	12	4.0					
Molenda (1)	2	5	8	1.6					
Apsit	2	4	6	1.5					
Fitzgibbon	4	2	-1	-0.5					
Dilweg									
Nash									
Rose									
Gantenbein									
Peterson (1,3)									
Team	14	497	1544	3.1	7				
Opp.	14	534	1374	2.6	4				

NAME	PASSING Complete Games G	Com.	Att.	%	Yds.	Y/A	TD	Int	Incom. Games G	Com	Att	Yds.	TD	Int
CHICAGO BEARS														
Nagurski	7	7	17	41	61	3.6	1	2	7	3	3	62	2	
Grange	5	5	12	42	93	7.8			7	1	1	23		
Nesbitt	7	1	6	17	4	0.7		3	7	0	1			1
Molesworth	14	22	54	41	475	8.8	3	6						
Corbett	5	1	1	100	49	49.0			7					
Sisk	7	0	2	0					6					
Hewitt														
Doehring	4	5	19	26	117	4.5	1	4	3	2	3	83	1	
Joesting	2	0	1	0					2	1	1	23		
Franklin														
Moore														
Brumbaugh	7	1	1	100	34	34.0			6	2	2	23		
Tackwell	5	0	1	0					6					
Johnsos														
Team	7	28	88	32	421	4.8	2	13	7					
Opp.	7	21	82	26	269	3.3	1	9	7					
GREEN BAY														
Hinkle	13	1	4	25	19	4.8								
Bruder	14	3	15	20	65	4.3		1						
Herber	14	44	110	40	774	7.0	9	6						
McCrary														
Engelmann														
Blood	13	0	8	0				2						
Lewellen	14	4	14	29	110	7.9		5						
Grove	13	0	5	0										
O'Boyle	11	1	5	20	7	1.4		1						
Shelley (1)	2	0	1	0				1						
Molenda (1)														
Apsit														
Fitzgibbon	4	1	3	33	14	4.7								
Dilweg														
Nash														
Rose														
Gantenbein														
Peterson (1,3)														
Team	14	54	165	33	989	6.0	9	16						
Opp.	14	69	206	33	845	4.1	3	28						

NAME	RECEIVING Complete Games G	Rec.	Yds.	Avg.	TD	Incom. Games G	Rec.	Yds.	TD
CHICAGO BEARS									
Nagurski	14	6	67	11.2					
Grange	12	15	228	15.2	4				
Nesbitt	7	3	20	6.7		7			
Molesworth	7	2	20	10.0		7	1	1	1
Corbett	5	3	18	6.0		7	5	114	1
Sisk	7	2	45	22.5		6	1	23	
Hewitt	7	2	21	10.5		6	4	111	
Doehring									
Joesting									
Franklin									
Moore									
Brumbaugh	7	4	129	32.3		6			
Tackwell									
Johnsos	14	24	321	13.4	2				
Team									
Opp.									
GREEN BAY									
Hinkle									
Bruder	14	8	161	20.1	2				
Herber	14	2	39	19.5					
McCrary									
Engelmann	14	2	62	31.0					
Blood	13	19	326	17.2	3				
Lewellen	14	2	27	13.5	1				
Grove	13	6	110	18.3	3				
O'Boyle									
Shelley (1)									
Molenda (1)									
Apsit									
Fitzgibbon	4	1	22	22.0					
Dilweg	14	7	120	17.1					
Nash	10	2	40	20.0					
Rose	13	2	33	16.5					
Gantenbein	9	2	19	9.5					
Peterson (1,3)	9	1	30	30.0					
Team									
Opp.									

NAME	PUNTING Comp. Games G	No.	Avg.	Incom. Games G	No.	Avg.	PUNT RETURNS Complete Games G	Rec.	Yds	Avg.	TD	Incom. Games G	Rec.	Yds.	TD
CHICAGO BEARS															
Nagurski	6	2	39.5	8											
Grange															
Nesbitt	6	44	37.7	8	1	0.0	6	1	5	5.0		8			
Molesworth	6	25	31.5	8	2	22.0	6	21	205	9.8		8	7	118	
Corbett	4	1	40.0	8											
Sisk															
Hewitt															
Doehring	3	3	31.3	4											
Joesting															
Franklin															
Moore															
Brumbaugh							6	8	71	8.9		7			
Tackwell															
Johnsos															
Team	7	86	36.4	7			6	30	281	9.4		8			
Opp.	7	94	35.7	7			6	32	322	10.1		8			
GREEN BAY															
Hinkle	13	45	34.5												
Bruder	14	8	38.1				14	1	5	5.0					
Herber	14	72	38.5				14	27	253	9.4					
McCrary							11	1	7	7.0					
Engelmann															
Blood	13	4	22.0				13	6	68	11.3					
Lewellen	14	35	33.9												
Grove	13	1	24.0				13	29	260	9.0					
O'Boyle															
Shelley (1)	2	1	25.0												
Molenda (1)															
Apsit															
Fitzgibbon							4	2	13	6.5					
Dilweg															
Nash															
Rose															
Gantenbein															
Peterson (1,3)															
Team	14	166	35.9				14	66	606	9.2					
Opp.	14	167	34.1				14	47	418	8.9					

PORTSMOUTH SPARTANS 6-2-4 Potsy Clark

Regulars Use Name	Pos.	Hgt.	Wgt.	Age	Int.	Pts.
Bill McKalip	E	6'1	193	24		
Harry Ebding	E	5'11	204	25	1	6
George Christensen	T	6'2	237	22		
Bob Armstrong	T	5'11	230	23		
Maury Bodenger	G	5'10	210	23	1	
Ox Emerson	G	5'11	200	24	1	
Clare Randolph	C-E	6'2	206	25	1	
Father Lumpkin	BB-FB	6'2	212	24	2	6
Dutch Clark	TB	6'	193	25	6	55
Glenn Presnell	TB-WB	5'10	198	27	5	13
Ace Gutowsky	FB	5'11	195	23		18

Substitutes Use Name	Pos.	Hgt.	Wgt.	Age	Int.	Pts.
Buster Mitchell	E-T	6'	203	26		
Dave Ribble	T	6'1	220	25		
Amby Rascher	T-G	6'2	210	23		
Danny McMullen	G	5'8	242	26		
John Wager	G-C-T	5'11	203	28	1	
Ray Davis	C-T-G	6'1	198	25		
Mule Wilson	WB-BB	5'11	200	30		
Gene Alford	WB	5'9	184	26	1	
John Cavosie	FB-BB-WB	6'	205	24	4	18

Substitutes Use Name	Pos.	Hgt.	Wgt.	Age	Int.	Pts.
Fred Roberts	G	6'1	205	25		
Hal Griffen	C-T	6'1	245	30		

Date	Pts.	Opponent	Pts.
Sep. 25	7	NEW YORK	0
Oct 2	7	CHIC. CARDS	7
Oct 9	10	Green Bay	15
Oct 16	7	Staten Island	7
Oct 20	13	Staten Island	6
Oct. 30	6	New York	0
Nov. 6	17	Brooklyn	7
Nov. 13	13	Chic. Bears	13
Nov. 20	10	BOSTON	0
Nov. 27	7	CHIC. BEARS	7
Dec. 4	19	GREEN BAY	0
Dec. 18	0	Chic. Bears (playoff)	9

BOSTON BRAVES 4-4-2 Lud Wray

Regulars Use Name	Pos.	Hgt.	Wgt.	Age	Int.	Pts.
Paul Collins	E	6'1	195	24		
George Kenneally	E-G	6'	190	30		
Turk Edwards	T	6'2	230	24		6
Jim MacMurdo	T-G	6'1	205	21		
Joe Kresky	G-T	6'	210	24		
George Hurley	G	6'	200	23		
Mickey Erickson	C	6'2	210	25		
Honolulu Hughes	BB-TB	5'10	195	25		5
Cliff Battles	TB	6'1	190	22	1	24
Ernie Pinckert	WB	6'	200	24	2	
Jim Musick	FB	5'11	205	22	2	6

Substitutes Use Name	Pos.	Hgt.	Wgt.	Age	Int.	Pts.
Nip Felber	E	6'2	190	23		
John Spellman	E-G-T	5'10	205	33	1	
Dale Waters	T	6'2	215	23		
Russ Peterson	T	6'3	216	23		
Paul Schuette (from ChiB)	G	6'	223	26		
Milt Rehnquist	G	6'1	240	35		
Tony Siano	C	5'8	170	25	1	
Algy Clark	BB-WB	6'	190	28	2	6
Oran Pape (to SI)	TB-BB	5'11	180	28	1	6
Lee Woodruff	WB-FB	6'	200	23		
Jack Roberts (to SI)	FB	6'	210	23		

Substitutes Use Name	Pos.	Hgt.	Wgt.	Age	Int.	Pts.
Kermit Schmidt	E	6'	200	23		
Basil Wilkerson (to SI)	E-T	6'	215	25		
Corrie Artman	T-G	6'2	240	25		
Curly Oden	BB	5'6	165	33		
Reggie Rust	TB-BB	6'2	210	23		
Ed Westfall	TB	5'9	165	23	1	
Tony Plansky	BB	6'2	216	32		

Date	Pts.	Opponent	Pts.
Oct 2	0	BROOKLYN	14
Oct 9	14	NEW YORK	6
Oct 16	0	CHIC. CARDS	9
Oct 23	0	New York	0
Oct 30	7	CHIC. BEARS	7
Nov. 6	19	STATEN ISLAND	6
Nov. 13	0	GREEN BAY	21
Nov. 20	0	Portsmouth	10
Nov. 27	8	Chic. Cards	6
Dec. 4	7	Brooklyn	0

NEW YORK GIANTS 4-6-2 Steve Owen

Regulars Use Name	Pos.	Hgt.	Wgt.	Age	Int.	Pts.
Ray Flaherty	E	6'	187	28		30
Red Badgro	E	6'	190	29	1	
Bill Owen	T	6'	210	28		
Len Grant	T	6'3	235	26	1	
Butch Gibson	G	5'9	205	28		
Potsy Jones	G	5'11	210	22		6
Mel Hein	C	6'2	205	23	3	
Bo Molenda (from GB)	BB-FB	5'10	215	27	2	3
Jack McBride (from BKN)	TB	5'11	190	30	1	6
Dale Burnett	WB	6'1	185	23	1	6
Chris Cagle	FB-TB	5'10	175	27	1	24

Substitutes Use Name	Pos.	Hgt.	Wgt.	Age	Int.	Pts.
Dick Powell	E	6'2	210	28		
Glenn Campbell	E	5'11	198	28		
Tex Irvin	T	6'	230	25		
George Munday	T	6'2	210	24		
Les Caywood (to BKN)	G	6'	230	27		
Jim Bowdoin (from BKN)	G	6'1	225	26		
Mickey Murtagh	C-T	6'1	190	28		
Lee Mulleneaux	BB	6'2	210	25		
Jack Hagerty	TB-FB	5'9	170	29	1	2
Hap Moran	TB-FB-WB-BB	6'1	190	31	1	8
Tiny Feather	FB-BB-WB	6'	197	26		

Substitutes Use Name	Pos.	Hgt.	Wgt.	Age	Int.	Pts.
Mush Dubofsky	G	5'10	210	23		
Otto Vokaty	BB-FB-TB	6'1	190	23		
Shipwreck Kelly	TB-WB	6'2	185	25		
Hoge Workman	BB-WB	5'11	175	32		
Stu Clancy (from SI)	FB	5'10	195	26	1	6

Date	Pts.	Opponent	Pts.
Sep. 25	0	Portsmouth	7
Oct. 2	0	Green Bay	13
Oct. 9	6	Boston	14
Oct. 16	20	BROOKLYN	12
Oct. 23	0	BOSTON	0
Oct. 30	0	PORTSMOUTH	6
Nov. 6	8	CHIC. BEARS	28
Nov. 13	27	STATEN ISLAND	7
Nov. 20	6	GREEN BAY	0
Nov. 24	13	Staten Island	13
Nov. 27	13	Brooklyn	7
Dec. 4	0	Chic. Bears	6

BROOKLYN DODGERS 3-9-0 Benny Friedman

Regulars Use Name	Pos.	Hgt.	Wgt.	Age	Int.	Pts.
Paul Riblett	E	5'10	181	24	1	6
Ev Rowan	E	6'1	197	29		
Babe Lyon	T	6'2	230	25		
Lou Lubratovich	T	6'2	230	25	1	
Bruce Jones	G-E	6'1	215	27		
Stu Worden	G-C	6'	204	22		
Saul Mielziner	C	6'1	245	27		
Bull Karcis	BB	5'9	220	23	1	6
Benny Friedman	TB	5'10	183	27	4	8
Ollie Sansen	HB-BB-FB	6'1	190	24		6
Jack Grossman	FB-TB	6'1	195	22		30

Substitutes Use Name	Pos.	Hgt.	Wgt.	Age	Int.	Pts.
Frank McNeil	E	6'	185	22		
Bill Raffel	E	5'11	195	25		
Harold Ely (from ChiB)	T	6'2	275	22		
Don Greenshields	T	6'1	188	27		
Herman Hickman	G	5'10	240	20		
Jim Bowdoin (to NYG)	G	6'1	225	26		
John Ambrose	C	6'	185	22	1	
Jack McBride (to NYG)	TB-FB	5'11	190	30		
Ray Novotny	TB-HB-BB	5'10	170	24	2	
Ossie Wiberg	HB-BB	5'11	205	27		1
Stumpy Thomason	FB-HB	5'7	185	26		6

Substitutes Use Name	Pos.	Hgt.	Wgt.	Age	Int.	Pts.
Jerry Cronin	E	6'	198	22		
Mike Stramiello (to SI)	E	6'1	197	25		
Cy Williams	T	6'	200	31		
Ted Fulton	G	6'	197	26		
Les Caywood (from NYG)	G	6'	230	27		
John Bunyan (from SI)	G	5'10	215	26		
Jess Eberdt	C	6'2	215	26		
Buck Halperin	TB	5'11	200	22		
Bud Toscani (to ChiC)	HB	5'8	168	23		
Pop Williams	HB	6'	210	26		
Sammy Stein	E	6'	203	27		

Date	Pts.	Opponent	Pts.
Sep. 25	7	Staten Island	0
Oct 2	14	Boston	7
Oct 9	6	STATEN ISLAND	7
Oct 16	12	New York	20
Oct 23	0	Green Bay	13
Oct 30	7	Chic. Cards	27
Nov. 6	7	PORTSMOUTH	17
Nov. 13	3	CHIC. CARDS	0
Nov. 20	0	Chic. Bears	20
Nov. 24	0	GREEN BAY	7
Nov. 27	7	NEW YORK	13
Dec. 4	0	BOSTON	7

CHICAGO CARDINALS 2-6-2 Jack Chevigny

Regulars Use Name	Pos.	Hgt.	Wgt.	Age	Int.	Pts.
Chuck Kassel	E	6'1	190	28	2	6
Milan Creighton	E	6'	185	24		
Jess Tinsley	T	6'	205	23		
Jake Williams	T-C	6'	208	28	1	
Al Graham	G	6'	218	26		
Walt Kiesling	G	6'2	245	29		
Tim Moynihan	C	6'1	205	25		12
Butch Simas	BB	5'10	185	23	1	
Walt Holmer	TB-WB	6'	190	29		8
Abe Martin	WB-FB-BB	6'	185	23	2	12
Irv Hill	FB	6'1	205	24		22

Substitutes Use Name	Pos.	Hgt.	Wgt.	Age	Int.	Pts.
Chuck Braidwood	E	6'	195	28		
George Rogge	E	6'	190	24		
Lou Gordon	T	6'5	220	24		
Jap Douds	T-C	5'10	215	27		
Larry Steinbach	G	6'	212	28		
Phil Handler	G-C	6'	210	24		
Frank McNally	C	6'1	205	25		2
Les Malloy	BB-WB-TB	6'	200	23		
Joe Lillard	TB	6'	185	26	2	2
Bucky Moore	WB	5'11	185	26	1	6
Tony Holm	FB	6'1	210	24		

Substitutes Use Name	Pos.	Hgt.	Wgt.	Age	Int.	Pts.
Joe Crakes	E	6'1	205	23		
Ken Wendt	G	6'	195	24		
Bernie Finn (from SI)	BB	5'10	180	24		
Deck Shelley (from GB)	TB	5'11	192	26		
Bud Toscani (from BKN)	WB	5'8	168	23		
Elmer Schwartz	FB	6'	212	25		
Frosty Peters	BB	5'10	183	28		
Stud Stennett	TB	6'	190	26		
Gene Rose	WB	5'8	172	28		
Doc Ledbetter (from SI)	FB	5'10	190	24	1	
Carmen Scardine	WB			22		
Ed Risk	FB	5'11	180	24		

Date	Pts.	Opponent	Pts.
Sep. 18	7	Green Bay	15
Oct. 2	7	Portsmouth	7
Oct. 9	0	CHIC. BEARS	0
Oct. 16	9	Boston	0
Oct. 30	27	BROOKLYN	7
Nov. 6	9	GREEN BAY	19
Nov. 13	0	Brooklyn	3
Nov. 20	7	Staten Island	21
Nov. 24	0	Chic. Bears	34
Nov. 27	6	BOSTON	8

STATEN ISLAND STAPLETONS 2-7-3 Hal Hanson

Regulars Use Name	Pos.	Hgt.	Wgt.	Age	Int.	Pts.
Les Maynard	E	6'3	210	21	1	
Charley Marshall	E	6'	195	25		
Jim Kamp	T	6'	210	23		
Leo Raskowski	T	6'3	220	26	1	
Ollie Satenstein	G-E	6'	235	26		
Rosie Grant	G-C	5'10	195	23		
Art Koeninger	C	6'1	200	25	1	
Bob Campiglio	BB-TB	6'	180	24	1	18
Ken Strong	TB	6'	202	26	1	15
Dick Frahm	WB	5'10	195	26	3	2
Doug Wycoff	FB	6'	210	28	2	6

Substitutes Use Name	Pos.	Hgt.	Wgt.	Age	Int.	Pts.
Mike Stramiello (from BKN)	E	6'1	197	25		
Al Teeter	E	6'1	202	24		
Al Kanya	T-E	6'	200	24	1	
Basil Wilkerson (from BOS)	T-E	6'	215	25		
George Demas	G	6'	198	25		
John Bunyan (to BKN)	G	5'10	215	26		
Marne Intrieri	G-C	5'8	250	24		
Grassy Hinton	BB-TB	6'	185	25	2	6
Stu Clancy (to NYG)	TB-FB	5'10	195	26		
Stu Wilson	WB-TB-E	6'2	209	27	1	12
Doc Ledbetter (to ChiC)	FB-WB	5'10	190	24	1	12

Substitutes Use Name	Pos.	Hgt.	Wgt.	Age	Int.	Pts.
Les Peterson (from & to GB)	E	6'3	212	22		
Harry Fry	E	6'3	210	24	1	
Rick Concannon	T	6'	215	23		
Art Schiebel	T	6'	220	24		
Harry McGee	G	6'1	198	27		
Vic Reuter	C	6'	215	24		
Bernie Finn (to ChiC)	BB	5'10	180	24		
Swede Hanson	TB	6'1	185	24		6
Oran Pape (from BOS)	TB	5'11	180	28		
Jack Roberts (from BOS)	FB	6'	210	23		
Ray Schwab	E		210	24		
Jack Norris	E	6'3	185	25		

Date	Pts.	Opponent	Pts.
Sep. 25	0	BROOKLYN	7
Oct. 2	0	CHIC. BEARS	0
Oct. 9	7	Brooklyn	6
Oct. 16	7	PORTSMOUTH	7
Oct. 20	6	PORTSMOUTH	13
Oct. 23	7	Chic. Bears	27
Oct. 30	0	Green Bay	26
Nov. 6	6	Boston	19
Nov. 13	7	New York	27
Nov. 20	21	CHIC. CARDS	7
Nov. 24	13	NEW YORK	13
Nov. 27	3	GREEN BAY	21

Rushing and Passing

NAME	Rushing Complete Games G	Att.	Yds.	Avg.	TD	Rushing Incom. Games G	Att.	Yds.	TD	Passing Complete Games G	Com.	Att.	%	Yds.	Y/A	TD	Int	Passing Incom. Games G	Com.	Att.	Yds.	TD	Int
PORTSMOUTH																							
Clark	11	149	546	3.7	3					11	15	53	28	244	4.6	2	9						
Gutowsky	7	90	335	3.7	3	1	4	15		7	3	5	60	24	4.8		1	1	0	1			1
Cavosie	10	95	280	2.9	2	1	1	6		10	10	24	42	219	9.1	2	2	1					
Presnell	11	74	231	3.1	1	1	2	16		11	21	56	38	290	5.2	2	5	1	0	2			1
Lumpkin	11	34	99	2.9		1																	
Alford	10	22	54	2.5																			
Wilson	9	1	-1	-1.0		1																	
Ebding																							
McKalip																							
Mitchell																							
Team	11	465	1544	3.3	9	1				12	51	152	34	806	5.3	6	22						
Opp.	11	428	1327	3.1	6	1				12	42	160	26	594	3.7	1	24						
BOSTON																							
Battles	8	148	576	3.9	3					3	2	14	14	24	1.7		2	5	1	1	26		
Musick	10	77	343	4.5	1																		
Rust	2	17	47	2.8		3				2	2	4	50	30	7.5		1	3					
Pinckert	3	9	39	4.3		6	2	5		3	0	1	0				1	6					
Pape (1)	2	3	33	11.0		2	2	5		2	1	11	9	5	0.6		3	2	1	1	6		
Roberts (1)	2	5	31	6.2		3																	
Westfall	1	4	16	4.0		1				1	0	4	0				1	1					
Hughes	3	5	12	2.4		7	1	1		3	2	10	20	47	7.7			7	5	6	81	1	1
Plansky																		7	1	2	15		
Felber																							
Clark																							
Collins																							
Team	3	143	527	3.7	2	7				3	7	44	16	106	2.4		8	7					
Opp.	3	107	332	3.1	2	7				3	19	47	40	327	7.0	3	6	7					
NEW YORK																							
McBride (2)	6	84	302	3.6	1					6	36	74	49	463	6.3	6	9						
Moran	6	58	133	2.3		5	1	71	1	6	10	25	40	63	2.5		3	5	0	1			1
Kelly	3	39	152	3.9		2	3	-4		2	2	5	40	21	4.2			2	1	1	30		
Cagle	5	41	122	3.0		5	7	25	1	5	2	2	100	4	2.0			5	2	4	48		
Clancy (2)	1	4	21	5.3		2	10	93															
Molenda (2)	4	19	48	2.5		6				4	2	4	50	18	4.5	1	1	6	0	2			1
Burnett	6	15	5	0.3		6	2	28		6	2	4	50	6	1.5			6					
Vokaty	3	10	32	3.2		3																	
Feather	4	10	6	0.6		5				4								5	1	1	12		
Hagerty	1	3	2	0.7		3				1	8	14	57	101	7.2			3	6	7	122	2	
Campbell	6	1	0	0.0		4																	
Mulleneaux	3	1	0	0.0		3																	
Workman										1	0	2	0										
Flaherty																							
Badgro																							
Team	6	219	584	2.7	1	6				6	39	84	46	427	5.1	4	8	6					
Opp.	6	246	836	3.4	5	6				7	23	83	28	401	4.8	3	10	5					
BROOKLYN																							
Grossman	5	59	249	4.2	1	7	10	69	1	5	8	15	53	74	4.9		1	7	2	3	78		1
Friedman	5	40	130	3.3		6	3	48		7	21	68	31	283	4.2	4	8	4	4	9	77	1	1
Thomason	5	36	134	3.7		5				5	0	3	0				1	5					
Sansen	4	19	68	3.6		6	2	1	1														
Karcis	4	13	45	3.5	1	7	2	5		4	0	1	0				1	7					
Wiberg	3	17	40	2.4		3				3	1	3	33	19	6.3		1	3					
Toscani (1)	2	10	25	2.5		2				2	0	1	0				1	2					
McBride (1)	2	2	21	10.5		1																	
Riblett	5	3	9	3.0		6	1	-2															
Novotny	4	2	1	0.5		6				4	0	2	0					6	5	6	74		
McNeil	3	1	-1	-1.0		4																	
Rowan	5	1	-5	-5.0		6																	
Jones																							
Raffel																							
Team	5	203	716	3.5	2	7				6	29	94	31	402	4.3	2	15	6					
Opp.	5	195	596	3.1	3	7				5	17	43	40	383	8.9	2	5	7					
CHICAGO CARDINALS																							
Hill	3	24	37	1.5	1	4	9	77	2														
Holmer	4	26	62	2.4		6	8	49	1	4	13	31	42	203	6.5	1	2	6	2	5	78	1	2
Martin	4	14	25	1.8		5	3	54	1														
Lillard	3	15	22	1.5		4	3	35		3	5	15	33	50	3.3		2	4	1	2	12		1
Moore	2	9	14	1.6		2	4	13	1	2	1	2	50	15	7.5			2					
Malloy	2	8	13	1.6		6				2	1	1	100	10	10.0			6	0	1			1
Toscani (2)	1	4	12	3.0		2																	
Scardine	1	1	10	10.0																			
Holm	4	14	9	0.6		4																	
Simas	4	1	1	1.0		4																	
Ledbetter (2)						2	1	0															
Stennett	1	9	-1	-0.1						1	3	8	38	49	6.1		3						
McNally	2	1	-1	-1.0		5																	
Rose										1	1	1	100	6	6.0								
Kassel																							
Creighton																							
Rogge																							
Team	4	126	203	1.6	1	6				4	24	58	41	333	5.7	1	7	6					
Opp.	4	150	453	3.0	4	6				4	19	61	31	347	5.7	3	7	6					
STATEN ISLAND																							
Campiglio	10	93	366	3.9	2	1	3	18		10	6	15	40	54	3.6		1	1					
Wycoff	11	125	346	2.8	1	1				11	6	28	21	79	2.8		2	1	1	1	13		
Strong	10	91	308	3.4	2	1	1	1		10	4	19	21	82	4.3	1	1	1					
Hanson	3	43	147	3.4	1					3	2	13	15	33	2.5		2						
Ledbetter (1)	7	30	77	2.6	2	1	2	0															
Clancy (1)	8	31	67	2.2		1				8	4	24	17	60	2.5		3	1					
Hinton	11	23	53	2.3		1	2	7	1	11	4	15	27	119	7.9		3	1	1	1	10		
Roberts (2)	3	11	45	4.1																			
Pape (2)	2	6	22	3.7						2	1	7	14	26	3.7	1	2						
Wilson	10	6	10	1.7		1				10	1	9	11	33	3.7		3	1					
Finn (1)	1	2	3	1.5						1	1	1	100	8	8.0								
Frahm	8	4	0	0.0		1																	
Peterson (2)	5	1	0	0.0																			
Maynard																							
Team	11	466	1444	3.1	8	1				11	29	131	22	494	3.8	2	17	1					
Opp.	11	433	1595	3.7	7	1				11	51	134	39	800	6.0	8	16	1					

Receiving, Punting and Punt Returns

NAME	Receiving Complete Games G	Rec.	Yds.	Avg.	TD	Receiving Incom. Games G	Rec.	Yds.	TD	Punting Comp. Games G	No.	Avg.	Punting Incom. Games G	No.	Avg.	Punt Returns Complete Games G	Rec.	Yds.	Avg.	TD	Punt Returns Incom. Games G	Rec.	Yds.	TD
PORTSMOUTH																								
Clark	11	16	216	13.5	3					11	68	36.2				11	30	321	10.7					
Gutowsky																7	1	5	5.0		1			
Cavosie										10	27	33.0	1			10	1	20	20.0		1			
Presnell	11	4	55	13.8	1	1				11	1	49.0	1			11	7	79	11.3		1			
Lumpkin	11	6	92	15.3	1	1																		
Alford	10	1	1	1.0																				
Wilson										9	17	40.1	1											
Ebding	11	13	226	17.4	1	1																		
McKalip	11	5	120	24.0		1																		
Mitchell	9	4	67	16.8		1																		
Team										12	124	36.7				11	39	425	10.9		1			
Opp.										12	129	35.2				11	44	375	8.5		1			
BOSTON																								
Battles	8	4	70	17.5	1					3	3	39.7	5	1	55.0	3	6	33	5.5		5	1	30	
Musick																								
Rust	2	1	18	18.0		3				2	1	43.0	3			2	1	5	5.0		3			
Pinckert	3	2	15	7.5		6	1	6								3	1	5	5.0		6			
Pape (1)																					2	1	30	
Roberts (1)																								
Westfall										1	3	39.3	1											
Hughes	3	1	14	14.0		7	2	41		3	19	35.9	7	4	29.3									
Plansky																								
Felber	3					7	3	47																
Clark	3	2	30	15.0		6																		
Collins										3	1	17.0	7											
Team										3	27	36.3	7			3	8	43	5.4		7			
Opp.										3	32	33.8	7			3	12	87	7.3		7			
NEW YORK																								
McBride (2)																								
Moran	6	6	83	13.8		5	1	10		6	12	36.8	5			6	5	32	6.4		5			
Kelly	2	3	20	6.7		2				2	5	24.8	2											
Cagle	5	2	47	23.5	1	5	2	72	1	5			5	1	35.0	5	5	96	19.2	1	5			
Clancy (2)	1					2	1	2	1	1	2	32.0	2											
Molenda (2)	4					6	1	12		4	1	33.0	6											
Burnett	6	3	51	17.0	1	6	2	25		6	9	39.7	6	2	17.5									
Vokaty	3	2	-1	-0.5		3	1	10																
Feather	4	4	16	4.0		5	1	16																
Hagerty										1	5	31.8	3			1	4	14	3.5		3	1	15	
Campbell	6	5	28	5.6		4	1	2																
Mulleneaux																								
Workman										1	3	25.7												
Flaherty	6	13	183	14.1	2	6	9	162	3	6	28	36.6	6											
Badgro	6	1	0	0.0		6	3	61																
Team										6	65	35.1	6			6	14	142	10.1		6			
Opp.										6	55	36.1	6			6	29	293	10.1		6			
BROOKLYN																								
Grossman	6	4	35	8.8	1	6	5	77	2	5	19	38.6	7	2	5.0	5	6	57	9.5		7	1	14	
Friedman	6	4	51	12.8		5				5	10	31.5	6			5	7	108	15.4		6			
Thomason	6	1	10	10.0		4	1	32	1							5	1	5	5.0		5			
Sansen	5	1	15	15.0		5																		
Karcis																								
Wiberg	4	1	15	15.0		2				3	7	33.9	3											
Toscani (1)																								
McBride (1)																								
Riblett	6	9	142	15.8	1	5	1	11																
Novotny	5	3	78	26.0		5				4	7	37.1	6	1	0.0	4	2	9	4.5		6			
McNeil	4	3	18	6.0		3																		
Rowan	6	2	31	15.5		5	1	34																
Jones	6					6	1	8																
Raffel	1	1	-3	-3.0		3																		
Team										5	43	35.9	7			5	16	179	11.2		7			
Opp.										5	45	38.2	7			5	16	189	11.8		7			
CHICAGO CARDINALS																								
Hill	3	5	48	9.6		4																		
Holmer										4	19	37.6	6	2	15.5									
Martin	4					5	1	63	1															
Lillard	3	1	10	10.0		4				3	11	34.0	4	1	55.0	3	6	29	4.8		4	2	92	
Moore	2	1	11	11.0		2																		
Malloy	2	1	29	29.0		6																		
Toscani (2)																								
Scardine	1	1	5	5.0																				
Holm	4	1	3	3.0		4				4	3	29.3	4											
Simas	4					4	1	15								4	3	22	7.3		4			
Ledbetter (2)																								
Stennett	1	1	6	6.0						1	7	26.0												
McNally																								
Rose																1	3	30	10.0					
Kassel	4	5	96	19.2	1	6																		
Creighton	4	4	62	15.5		6	1	12																
Rogge	4	4	63	15.8		6																		
Team										4	40	34.0	6			4	12	81	6.8		6			
Opp.										4	37	35.8	6			4	17	163	9.6		6			
STATEN ISLAND																								
Campiglio	10	4	85	21.3	1	1										10	19	165	8.7		1			
Wycoff										11	13	33.8	1											
Strong	10	4	66	16.5		1	2	23		10	31	36.8	1			10	7	98	14.0		1			
Hanson										3	1	34.0				3	1	19	19.0					
Ledbetter (1)	7	1	6	6.0		1																		
Clancy (1)										8	11	32.5	1			8	1	12	12.0		1			
Hinton	11	6	120	20.0		1				11	32	29.5	1			11	17	183	10.8		1			
Roberts (2)																								
Pape (2)																								
Wilson	10	8	94	11.8	1	1				10	15	33.5	1			10	1	2	2.0		1			
Finn (1)																1	1	12	12.0					
Frahm	8	3	25	8.3		1										8	1	4	4.0		1			
Peterson (2)	5	1	28	28.0																				
Maynard	7	2	70	35.0		1																		
Team										11	103	33.2	1			11	48	495	10.3		1			
Opp.										11	94	37.4	1			11	38	405	10.7	1	1			

UseName(Nicknames)-Positions	TeambyYear	See Section	Hgt	Wgt	College	Int	Pts
Abbott, Fay (Hack)BB-QB-FB-TB-WB-E	21-27PC 28-29Day	12 4	5'8"	182	Syracuse	6	24
Abel, Fred (Abie) BB-FB	26Mil		5'10"	170	Washington		6
Abrams, Nate E	21GB		5'4"	145	none	1	
Abramson, George G-T	25GB, 26KJ		5'7"	198	Minnesota	1	8
Abrell, Dick BB-WB	20Day		5'10"	172	Purdue		8
Achui, Walter (Sneeze, Chink) WB-TB-E-BB	27-28Day	2	5'8"	169	Hawaii, Dayton		
Ahern, Dan T	21Was		6'2"	200	Georgetown		
Ailinger, Jim G	24 Buf		5'11"	185	Buffalo State		
Albanese, Dom BB-E-FB	25Col				none		
Alexander, Doc (Goliath) C-G-T-E	21PC22,24Roch 25,PC26,27NYG		5'11"	220	Syracuse	3	24
Alexander, John T-E	22Mil 26NYG		6'4"	234	Rutgers, Fordham		6
Allen, Ed E	28ChiC		5'8"	175	Creighton		
Allison, Neely E	26-27Buf 28NYG	6	6'	190	Texas A&M	3	6
Ambrose, John (Whitey) C	32BKN		6'	185	Catholic	1	
Ambrose, Walt G	30Port		5'11"	210	Carroll (Wis.)		
Anderson, Alec G	21Was		5'8"	166	Boston College, Holy Cross, Georgetown		
Anderson WB	22Ham						
Anderson, Eddie E	22Roch 22-25ChiC 26AFL	6	5'10"	176	Notre Dame	2	12
Anderson, Hunk G-C	22-23ChiB23Cle23-25,HC42-45ChiB		5'11"	191	Notre Dame	2	12
Anderson, Ockie TB-BB-WB	20-22Buf	12	5'9"	165	Colgate	4	61
Anderson, Paul (Andy) G	25RI		6'	200	Illinois		
Anderson, Will FB-BB-TB	23-24Roch		5'10"	173	Syracuse		
Andrews, Roy (Bull) G-BB-T-E-TB-WB	23StL PC24-26KC PC27Cle HC28Det HC29-30NYG HC31ChiC	5	6'	226	Pittsburg State	1	9
Andrulewicz, Teddy WB	30Nwk		5'11"	175	Villanova	1	6
Annan, Dunc WB-TB-FB-BB-T	20ChiT 22Tol 23-25Ham 25Akr 25-26Ham 26Akr	2 6	5'10"	178	Brown, Chicago	4	43
Applegran, Clarence G	20Det		6'2"	200	Illinois		
Archoska, Julie E	30SI		5'11"	180	Syracuse		
Argus, Bob WB-FB-TB-BB	20-25Roch	2	5'10"	193	none	2	6
Armstrong, Bob T-G-C	31-32Port		5'11"	221	Missouri	1	
Armstrong, Johnny BB	23,PC24,25RI PC26AFL	123 6	5'8"	173	Dubuque	8	50
Armstrong, Norris (Army) FB	22Mil		5'10"	165	Centre		
Arrowhead E	23Oor		5'7"	160	none		12
Ash, Juddy G	26LA		6'2"	205	Oregon State		
Ashbaugh, Bill FB-WB	24RI 25KC		5'10"	175	Pittsburgh		
Ashburn, Cliff G-T-E	29NYG		5'11"	190	Nebraska		
Ashmore, Marion (Bert) T-G-E	26Mil 27Dul 28-29GB		6'	215	Gonzaga	1	2
Asplundh, Les FB	25Buf 26AFL		6'3"	213	Swarthmore		
Atcheson Burl E	22Col				none		
Attache, ReggieWB-FB(also known as Laughing Gas)	22Oor		5'9"	195	Sherman Indian		
August, Sky TB-WB	31Prov		5'10"	180	Villanova		
Ault, Chalmers T-G	24-25Cle		5'9"	195	West. Va. Wesleyan		
Babcock, Sam WB-FB-BB	26Can		5'6"	168	Syracuse		
Bacchus, Carl E	27Cle 28Det	6	6'	205	Missouri		42
Bachmaier, Joe (Buck) G-C-T-E	20-24Roch		5'9	175	none		
Bachor, Ludwig (Rip, Elmo) T	28Det		6'	215	Detroit		
Backnor C	21Ton						
Bacon, Frank WB-TB-E	20-23Day 23Akr 23-25Day	12 4 6	5'11"	182	Wabash	4	74
Bagby, Herm WB-TB-FB-BB	26Bkn 27Cle	2	5'9"	175	Arkansas	2	18
Bahan, Pete BB-TB-FB	23Cle 23Buf		5'9"	165	Notre Dame, Detroit	3	
Bailey, Russ C	20-21Akr		5'11"	183	West Virginia	3	
Baker, Bullet (Ironsides, Snowy) BB-HB-WB-TB-FB	26AFL 27NYY 28-29GB 29-30ChiC 31SI	12 6	5'8"	178	Southern Calif.	4	6
Baker, Frank E	31GB		6'2"	182	Northwestern		6
Baldwin, Cliff (Kip) WB-BB	20-21Mun		5'10"	172	none		
Baldwin, George E-T	25Cle 26AFL		5'11"	190	Virginia		
Bancroft, Hugh E	23Roch				none		
Bangs, Ben (Biff) WB	26LA		5'10"	180	Washington State		
Barabee, Bob E	31SI		5'9"	190	N.Y.U.		
Barber, Ben T-G	25Buf		6'3"	235	V.M.I.		
Baril, Adrian (Barrel) T-G	23-24Min 25Mil		5'11"	210	St. Thomas		
Barker, Dick G	21ChiB 21RI		5'9"	180	Iowa State		
Barkman, Ralph (Mose) BB-WB-TB	29Ora		5'8"	165	Schuylkill	1	1
Barna, George E	29Fra		6'1"	198	Hobart	2	6
Barnikow, Eddie FB	26Har				none		
Barnum, Pete TB-FB	26Col		5'10"	195	West Virginia	1	6
Barr, Shorty BB-TB-FB	23-24Rac 25Mil PC26Rac	12 4	5'8"	199	Wisconsin	6	6
Barrel, Napoleon C-BB	23Oor		5'8"	200	Carlisle		
Barrett, John (Bunny) C-T-E	24-25Akr 26Det 27Pott 28Det		5'6"	170	Detroit		12
Barrett, Johnny TB-E-WB	20ChiT	4	5'9"	195	Washington & Lee	1	3
Barron, Jim (Botchy) T	21Roch		6'	195	Georgetown	1	6
Barry, Norm BB-WB	21ChiC 21GB 22Mil HC25-26ChiC	2	5'10"	170	Notre Dame	2	6
Bashaw, Mose T	20Ham		5'9"	200	none		
Basing, Myrt (Biff) HB-FB-E-TB	23-27GB	12	5'9"	190	Lawrence	12	54
Bassett, Henry T	24KC		6'2"	215	Nebraska		
Baston, Bert E	20Cle		6'1"	170	Minnesota		
Batchellor, Don T	22Can 23Tol		6'3"	225	Ohio Northern, Grove City		
Batterson, Dim	HC27Buf						
Bauer, A.C. T	23Rac		6'2"	210	none		
Bauer, Herb E	25Cle		5'10"	190	Baldwin-Wallace*		
Baujan, Harry E	20-21Cle		5'8"	170	Notre Dame		
Baumann, Buddy T-G	22Rac		6'1"	190	none		
Baxter, Jimmy WB-E	23Rac 24Ken		5'7"	175	none		
Bayley, John T	27NYY		5'11"	180	Syracuse		
Baysinger, Reeves E	24Roch		6'	180	Syracuse		
Beach, Fred G	26LA			180	California		
Beasley, John G	23Day				Earlham		
Beattie, Bob T	26AFL 27NYY 29Ora 30Nwk		6'3"	230	Princeton		
Beck, Carl TB-FB-WB-T	21Buf		5'11"	180	Bucknell, Lafayette, West Virginia		
Beck, Clarence T-G	25Pott		5'11"	200	Penn State		
Beck, Marty WB-FB-BB-TB	21-22,24,26Akr		5'9"	175	none		
Becker, Johnnie T-E-G-WB	26-29Day		5'11"	208	Denison		
Beckett, Jack T	20Buf 22Col		6'1"	200	Oregon		
Beckley, Art BB-WB	26Day		5'10"	180	Michigan State	1	3
Beckwith TB	20Col				none		
Bedford, Gene (Blink) E	25Roch 26Ham 25 played major league baseball		5'9"	165	Centre, S.M.U.	1	
Bedner, Al G-T	24Fra 25-26NYG		5'10"	193	Lafayette		
Beekley, Ferris G-BB	21Cin		5'8"	185	Miami-Ohio		

UseName(Nicknames)-Positions	TeambyYear	See Section	Hgt	Wgt	College	Int	Pts
Behman, Bull T-G-C	24-25Fra 26AFL 27-2,PC29-31Fra	5	5'10"	214	Lebanon Valley, Dickinson	4	39
Belanich, Bill T-E	27-29Day		6'	205	Dayton	1	6
Belden, Bunny WB-BB-E-FB	27Dul 30-31ChiC	2 6	5'8"	173	none	3	30
Belding, Les E-WB	25RI		5'11"	195	Upper Iowa, Iowa		
Benkert, Heinie WB-TB-BB	25NYG 29Pott 29Oor 30Nwk	2	5'9"	168	Rutgers	4	
Bennett, Sid T-G	20ChiT 22Mil		5'10"	192	Northwestern		
Bentz, Chris T	20Det		6'4"	215	Montana		
Bentz, Eddie E	22 Roch				none		
Bentzin, Al (Mike) G	24Rac		6'	188	Marquette		
Bernard, George G-T	26Rac				none		
Bernoske, Dan G	26Lou		5'10"	190	Indiana		
Berns, Bobby G-T	20Mun 22-24Day		6'1"	200	Purdue		
Bernstein, Joe G-FB-T	21NY 23-24RI 23-24 played as Joe Burten		6'	210	Louisiana State		
Berquist, Jay G	24,26KC 27ChiC		6'3"	230	Nebraska		
Berrehsem, Bill T-E	26Col		5'10"	195	Washington & Jeff.	1	
Berry, Charlie E	25-26Pott 25,28-36,38 played major league baseball	56	6'	185	Lafayette	4	92
Berry, George G-T-C	22Rac 22-24Ham 24,PC25,26Akr 26Ham 26Akr		5'11"	208	none	2	6
Berry, Howard (Nig) TB-WB	21Roch 21-22 played major league baseball		5'11"	165	Muhlenberg, Pennsylvania	3	20
Berryman, Punk	HC24Fra HC26Bkn				Penn State		
Bertoglio, Jim FB-WB	26Col		5'9"	187	Creighton	1	6
Berwick, Ed C-E	26Lou		6'	185	Loyola (Chic.)	1	
Besta, Teddy WB-BB	22,24Ham				none		
Beyers, George WB	21Was			163	none		
Bieberstein, Adolph G	26Rac 26GB		5'10"	205	Wisconsin		
Bierce, Scotty E	20-22Akr 23Cle 23Buf 24Cle 25Akr	6	5'9"	164	Akron	3	42
Big Bear T-E	22-23Oor		6'4"	215	none		
Bigbee, Lyle (Al) E	22Mil 20-21 played major league baseball		6'	180	Oregon		
Biggs, Riley C	26AFL 26-27NYG		6'2"	230	Baylor		
Bissell, Fred (Monk, Doc) E	25-26Akr		6'1"	180	Fordham	1	
Bizer, Herb E-FB	29Buf		5'11"	205	Carroll (Wis.)	1	
Black, Charlie E	25Dul		5'9"	160	Kansas		
Black Bear, Peter E (also known as Bear Behind)	23Oor		6'	190	none		
Blacklock, Hugh T-C-G	20Dec 21-25ChiB 26Bkn	5	6'	220	Michigan State	1	13
Blackman, Stub FB	30ChiB		5'11"	195	Tulsa		
Blailock, Russ T-G	23Mil 25Akr		5'10"	230	Baylor		6
Bleeker, Mal G-C	30Bkn		6'	205	Columbia		
Bleier, Johnny WB-BB	21Was			160	none		
Bliss, Harry BB-TB-WB	21Col		5'8"	155	Ohio State		1
Bliss, Homer G	28ChiC		5'11"	195	Washington & Jeff.		
Bloodgood, Al BB-TB-WB	25-26KC 27Cle 28NYG 29BN 30GB	2 456	5'8"	153	DePauw, Nebraska	1	105
Bobadash, E. E	22Oor				none		
Bodie, Ping FB	21ChiC				none		
Boettcher, Champ FB-TB-BB	26Rac	2	5'10"	193	Lawrence		
Bogue, George FB-WB	30ChiC 30Nwk		6'	210	Stanford	1	1
Bohren, Karl (Jake) WB-FB	27Buf		5'8"	180	Pittsburgh		
Bolan, George FB-HB	21-24ChiB	2	5'11"	203	Purdue	3	12
Boldt, Chase BB-E-FB	21-23Lou		5'7"	145	none		
Bollinger, Eddie T	30Fra		6'1"	215	Bucknell		
Bomar, Lynn E	25-26NYG	6	6'1"	210	Vanderbilt	1	30
Bonadies, Jack G-T	26Har			208	none		
Bond, Jim G	26Bkn		5'9"	200	Pittsburgh		
Bondurant, Bourbon (Sandy) T-E-G	21Eva 22ChiB 22Eva		6'1"	202	DePauw		6
Bonowitz, Elliott G-BB-T-E	23Col 24-25Day		6'1"	190	Wilmington		
Books, Bob TB-FB	26Fra		5'11"	190	Dickinson		
Borelli, Nick FB-WB-TB-BB	30Nwk		5'10"	175	Muhlenberg		
Bosdett, John E	20ChiT				none		
Boutwell, Lo BB-WB-FB (also known as Little Cyclone)	22-23Oor		5'7"	188	Carlisle	1	
Bove, Pete G	30Nwk		5'10"	187	Holy Cross		
Bower, Phil BB-WB	21Cle		5'8"	160	Dartmouth		
Bowser, Arda FB-WB-TB	22Can 23Cle	5	6'2"	210	Bethany (W.Va.) Bucknell		14
Boyd, Bill WB-BB	30-31ChiC		5'11"	175	Westminster (Mo.)	1	12
Boynton, Benny (The Purple Streak) TB-BB-WB	21Roch 21Was 22-24Roch 24Buf	12 56	5'9"	170	Williams	2	91
Brace, Bill (Bus) G-C	20-22Buf		6'	180	Brown		6
Bradley, Hal G	28ChiC			185	none		
Bradshaw, Jim (Rabbit) WB	24KC 26AFL		5'6"	150	Illinois, Nev.-Reno		
Bradshaw, Wes BB-WB-TB	24RI 26AFL 26Buf		5'8"	175	Trinity (Texas), Baylor	1	
Braman, Bull T	22-23Rac		5'11"	215	Yale		
Brandau, Butch TB-FB-WB	21Det			192	none		
Brandy, Joe	HC24Min				Notre Dame		
Braney, Speed (born Joseph Breheney) G-T	25-26Prov		6'	188	Syracuse, Fordham		
Brannon, Phil T	25Cle		6'	200	Holy Cross		
Bratt, Eddie E	24Dul			190	none		
Brawley, Ed G	21NY 21Cle		5'9"	175	Holy Cross		
Brenkert, Wayne TB-BB-WB	23-24Akr	2	5'10"	170	Washington & Jeff.		30
Brennan, Matt BB-TB	25NYG 26Bkn	1	6'1"	195	Villanova, Fordham, Lafayette	2	14
Brennan, Phil E	30Nwk		5'11"	165	Loyola (Chic.)		
Brennan, Willie G-T	20-27ChiC		6'	214	none		6
Brenner, Ray WB	25Can		5'5"	145	none		
Brewer, Untz WB-TB	PC22Akr		5'6"	160	Maryland	3	6
Brewer, John WB	29Day		6'	185	Georgia Tech		
Brewster, Walt T	29Buf		6'1"	195	West Virginia		
Brian, Hite (born Harold Brian Hite) WB-TB	26Har		6'	180	Grove City		6
Briante, Frank (Bullet) TB-FB-HB-BB-WB	29SI 30Nwk	2	5'10"	185	N.Y.U.	4	12
Brick, Shirley E	20Buf		5'8"	165	Rice		
Brickley, Charlie	HC21NY 13 played major league baseball				Harvard		
Brickley, George TB-FB-BB	20Cle 21NY		5'10"	190	Trinity (Conn.)	1	6
Birdgeford, Lane FB-WB-BB-TB	21-22RI	2	5'10"	180	Knox		
Brigham, Hi G	20Col		5'11"	185	Ohio State		
Brill, Marty	HC31SI				Pennsylvania, Notre Dame		
Brindley, Walt BB-TB	21-22RI		5'8"	153	Drake		
Bristow, Obie FB-BB-TB-WB	25KC 25Cle 26KC		6'2"	210	Central St.-Okla., Oklahoma	4	
Britton, Earl FB-BB	25ChiB 26AFL 26Bkn 27Day 27Fra 28Day 29ChiC	12 45	6'	212	Illinois	9	3

UseName(Nicknames)-Positions	Team by Year	See Section	Hgt	Wgt	College	Int	Pts
Broadley, Karl G	25Cle		6'4"	250	Bethany (W. Va.)		
Broadhurst, Max T	20Day		6'	220	none		
Broadstone, Marion T-G	31NYG		6'2"	210	Nebraska		
Broda, Hal E	27Cle		6'1"	180	Brown		
Broker, Fred T	22Oor		5'9"	175	Carlisle		
Bross, Mal HB	26AFL 27GB		5'9"	170	Gonzaga		
Brown, Dick C	30Port		6'1"	220	Iowa		
Brown, Fred G	30SI		6'2"	195	N.Y.U.		
Brown, George T	23Akr				none		
Brown, Jack C-G-T	26-29Day		6'	191	Dayton	1	
Brown, Jesse TB	26Pott	12 4	5'10"	180	Pittsburgh	5	
Bruder, Doc (Woods) WB-TB-BB-FB	25Buf 25-26Fra	2	5'11"	178	Pittsburgh, West Virginia	2	27
Brumbaugh, Justin TB-BB	31Fra	2	6'	205	Bucknell	2	
Brumm, Fred T-C	21Ton				none		
Brumm, Kibo E-G-T-C	24Rac 25Mil 26Rac		6'	182	Wisconsin		
Brunklacher, Austin G	21-23Lou			193	none		
Brunswick G	20Ham		5'10"	182	none		
Bryan, Johnny (Red) HB-QB-TB-WB-BB-FB	22ChiC 23-25ChiB PC25Mil 25ChiB PC26Mil 26-27ChiB	12 6	5'8"	170	Dartmouth, Chicago	5	54
Bryant, Jim BB-WB	20Cle		5'6"	156	Pennsylvania		
Buchanan, Steve TB-BB	29Day		5'8"	160	Miami-Ohio	3	
Bucher, Bill E	25Det		5'10"	180	Clarkson		
Bucher, Frank (Butcher) E	25-26Pott	6	5'11"	190	Detroit		12
Buck, Cub T	20Can 21-25GB	1 45	6'	259	Wisconsin	6	54
Buckeye, Garland (Gob) G-C	20ChiT 21-24ChiC 26AFL 18,25-28 played major league baseball		6'	238	none	1	
Buckley, Ralph BB-HB	30SI		5'8"	175	Fordham	3	6
Bucklin, Ted FB-BB-G	26AFL 27ChiC 31NYG	2	6'	197	Idaho	1	6
Budd, Johnny T-G	26Fra 27-28Pott	5	5'11"	246	Lafayette		39
Buffalo, Ted T-E-G	23Oor		6'	190	Haskell Indian		6
Buland, Walt (Big Boy) T-G	20-21RI 24GB 24RI 26Dul		6'1"	218	none		
Bullman, Gale E	25Col		6'	182	Marietta, West Va. Wesleyan		
Bunyan, John (Bunny, Moose) G-C	29-30,32SI 32Bkn		5'10"	215	N.Y.U.	1	
Burgin, Al G	22Tol		6'	200	none		
Burgner, Earl (Puss) BB-WB	23Day		5'6"	165	Wittenberg		
Burke, Chick WB	25Prov		5'9"	165	Dartmouth	1	
Burks, Joe (Flyweight) C	26Mil		5'10"	171	Washington State		
Burnham, Stan TB-BB	25Fra		5'10"	175	Harvard		
Burnside, George BB	26Rac		5'9"	160	Wisconsin, South Dakota		
Burt, Hal G	24Cle		5'10"	175	Kansas		
Burt, Russ (Peanuts) WB-FB	24-25Buf		5'8"	170	Canisius		7
Burton, Lyle (Liz) G-T	25RI		6'1"	195	DePauw		
Busch, Elmer (Pete) G-C	22Oor		5'10"	210	Sherman Indian, Carlisle	1	
Bush, Ray E	26Lou		5'8"	180	Loyola (Chic.)	1	
Butler, Sol WB-TB-FB-BB	23RI 23-24Ham 24Akr 25Ham 26Can 26Ham	2	5'8"	181	Dubuque	2	12
Butts, Eddie BB-WB	29ChiC			190	Chico State		
Cabrinha, Augie WB-BB	27Day		5'9"	170	Dayton		
Cahoon, Tiny T	26-29GB		6'2"	235	Montana, Gonzaga		6
Calac, Pete FB-E-WB-TB-T	20Can 21Cle 21Was 21Cle 22-23Oor 24Buf 25-26Can	2 6	5'10"	199	Sherman Indian, Carlisle, West Va. Wesleyan	3	60
Caldwell, Bruce TB-FB	28NYG 28,32 played major league baseball	2	6'	190	Brown, Yale	2	9
Caldwell, Cy T	25-26Akr		6'1"	210	Baldwin-Wallace, Notre Dame		5
Calhoun, Eric (Enoch) T-G	26Day		5'9"	210	Denison		
Cameron, John G-T	26Det			175	Kalamazoo, Central Michigan		
Capps, Bill T-G	29-30Fra 30Min		6'1"	233	EC Oklahoma		
Capron, Ralph WB	20ChiT 12-13 played major league baseball		5'11"	165	Minnesota		
Carberry, Glen (Judge) E	23-24 Buf 25Cle		6'	190	Army, Notre Dame		
Card, Harper T	21 22Lou		6'1"	183	none		
Cardarelli, Carl (Squash) C	24Akr 25Cle				none		
Cardwell, John HB	23StL		5'9"	170	none		
Carey, Joe G-T	20ChiC 21GB		6'2"	195	Illinois Tech		
Carlson, Irv WB-TB	24Ken		5'8"	170	St. John's-Minn., Wisconsin		
Carlson, Oke T-G-C	24-26Dul		6'	206	none		
Carlson, Roy E-G	28ChiB 29Day		5'9"	178	Bradley	1	6
Carlson, Wes (Brute) G-T	26GB		6'1"	210	Detroit		
Carman, Charlie (Chili) G	21Det		5'10"	215	Vanderbilt		
Carmen, Ed (Zeb) T-E	22,25Ham 25Buf 25Ham		5'11"	199	Purdue		1
Carney, Art G-E	25-26NYG		6'2"	230	Navy	2	
Carney, Chuck T-G	22Col		6'1"	190	Illinois		
Carr, Harlan (Whippet) TB-WB	27Buf 27Pott	12 4	5'10"	165	Syracuse	2	18
Carr, Lee WB-BB	26Ham				none		
Carroll, Bart T	20Roch		5'11"	180	Colgate		
Carroll, Bird E	21-23,25Can	6	5'8"	185	Washington & Jeff.	1	26
Carroll, Gene E-T-G	22Col		5'10"	190	Marietta		
Cartin, Charlie E-T-C-G	25Fra 26AFL		5'10"	195	Holy Cross	1	6
Casey, Alvro T (also known as Running Wolf)	26Akr		6'	215	Haskell Indian, Northeastern Okla.		
Casey, Pete HB	23StL	4		180	none		12
Cassidy, Walt E	24Ken		5'10"	200	Detroit		
Cassidy BB	21Tol				none		
Casteel, Mike BB-TB-WB	22RI	2	5'11"	175	Kalamazoo		6
Catalano, Tony G	20Ham						
Cearing, Lloyd BB-WB-TB	22-23Ham			185	Valparaiso		
Chamberlin, Guy (Champ) E-WB	20Dec 21ChiB PC22-23Can PC24Cle PC25-26Fra PC27ChiC	23	6'2"	191	Neb. Wesleyan, Nebraska	13	102
Chappell, Leo G (born Leonidas Shappell)	20-21ChiC		6'2"	205	none		6
Charles, Win TB-BB	28Day		5'9"	160	William & Mary		
Charpier, Len (Tank) FB	20ChiC		5'10"	235	Illinois		
Chase, Ralph T	26Akr 26Ham 26Akr		6'3"	220	Pittsburgh		
Checkaye, Cooney BB	20,PC21Mun		5'9"	185	none		
Chenoweth, Red TB	21Lou		5'6"	150	West Virginia		
Chevigny, Jack	HC32ChiC				Notre Dame		
Chicken, Fred TB	20RI	2	5'10"	185	none	2	18
Choate, Bob G	24KC		6'1"	225	Haskell Indian		
Chrape, Joe G-T	29Min			210	Hibbing C.C.	1	
Christensen, Koester E	30Port		5'10"	195	Michigan State		
Christianson, Oscar (Bully) E-TB	21-24Min		5'10"	186	none	1	6
Christman, Floyd WB-TB	25Buf		5'11"	180	Thiel		6
Civiletto, Frank (Civy) WB	23Cle		5'9"	180	Case Reserve, Springfield		
Clago, Walt E	21Det 22RI		6'	195	Detroit	1	
Clark, Bill G-C	20Day		5'11"	194	none		
Clark, Bill C-G	20ChiC		6'1"	190	none		

UseName(Nicknames)-Positions	Team by Year	See Section	Hgt	Wgt	College	Int	Pts
Clark, Charlie G	24ChiC		5'10"	205	Harvard		
Clark, Hal (Fuss, Butch) E-BB	20,22-25Roch		5'10"	195	none		6
Clarke, Pots WB-T	27Fra 27Dul		5'7"	180	Nevada-Reno		
Clarkin, Bill T-G	29Ora		5'10"	210	none		
Claypool, Ralph C	25-28ChiC		5'11"	191	Purdue	1	
Clement, Alex WB	25Fra		5'10"	170	Williams	2	
Clements, Chase T	25Akr		6'2"	205	Washington & Jeff.		
Cleve, Einar WB-BB-TB-E	21-24Min		5'9"	175	none	2	12
Clime, Ben G-E-WB	20-21Roch		5'11"	190	Swarthmore		
Clow, Herb FB	24Dul		5'4"	180	Wis.-Superior		
Coaker, Johnny T-G	24Roch				none		
Cobb, Alf (Ty) G-T	20-21Akr 25Cle		5'11"	210	Syracuse		
Cobb, Tom T-G	26KC 27Cle 28Det 31ChiC		5'11"	250	St. John's (N.Y.)		
Cochran, Moose E	22Mil		6'	195	none		
Cofall, Stan TB-BB	PC20Cle		5'11"	190	Notre Dame		
Colahan, John T	28NYY		6'3"	212	Colorado Mines		
Collins E	22Mil				none		
Collins, Harry G	24Buf		5'11"	190	Canisius		
Comer, Hook FB	26Can			180	none		
Comier, Ulysses WB-FB	29Buf		5'10"	195	none		
Comstock, Ed (Ellie) G-T	29Buf 30Bkn 31SI		6'2"	208	West Va. Wesleyan, Washington-St.L.		
Conley, John (Zip) T-G	22,26Col		5'11"	205	none		
Conn, Tuffy WB-TB-FB	20Cle 20Akr		5'6"	155	Oregon State	1	
Connaughton, Babe (Pud, Gunboat) G	27Fra 28JF		6'2"	285	Georgetown	4	
Connell, Ward (Doc) FB	26ChiC 26AFL		5'10"	173	Notre Dame		
Connor, Bill G-T	29Bos 30Nwk		6'1"	240	Providence, Catholic		
Connor, Dutch FB-WB	25Prov 26Bkn		6'	190	New Hampshire		2
Connors, Ham E	25Roch			190	none		
Conover, Larry (The Atlantic City Airedale) C	21,23Can 25Cle		5'10"	190	Penn State	6	1
Conrad, Marty C-G-E	22-23Tol 24Ken 25Akr		6'1"	240	Kalamazoo		
Constantine, Irv (Murphy) HB	31SI		5'9"	200	Syracuse		
Conzelman, Jimmy BB-TB-HB-E-WB	20Dec PC21-22RI PC22-23,24Mil PC25-26Det PC27-29,HC30Prov HC40-42ChiC 43-45MS HC46-48ChiC 26-27Player-Coach in A.B.L.	123456	6'	175	Washington-St.L.	25	178
Cook, Clair WB	28Day		5'9"	170	none		
Cook, Jim G	21GB		6'3"	220	Notre Dame		
Copley, Charlie T-E	20-22Akr 22Mil	5	5'9"	191	Muhlenberg, Missouri-Rolla	1	26
Corcoran, Bunny (Buddy) E-WB-TB	20Can 21Akr 21Cle 21-22Akr 23Buf		5'11"	184	Georgetown, Fordham		6
Corcoran, Jack C-G	30Min			180	St.Thomas, St. Louis		
Cordovano, Sam G	30Nwk		5'11"	185	Georgetown		
Corgan, Chuck BB-E-WB-TB	24-25KC 26Har 27NYG 25,27 played major league baseball died June 13, 1928 - cancer	6	6'	183	Arkansas	3	32
Cornsweet, Al FB	PC31Cle		5'7"	180	Brown		
Cortemeglia, Chris WB	27Fra		6'	210	S.M.U.		
Coster, Joe T	21Was		5'10"	175	Western Maryland, Maryland		
Cotton, Fod T	23,25RI		6'1"	195	Notre Dame		
Coughlin, Danny WB	23Min		5'9"	175	St. Thomas, Notre Dame		
Coughlin, Frank T	PC21RI 21Det 21GB		6'3"	220	Notre Dame	1	
Crabtree, Clyde (Cannonball) BB-WB-HB	30Fra 30Min 30Fra	12 6	5'8"	160	Northwestern, Florida	1	12
Craig, Clark E	25Fra		5'9"	180	Pennsylvania		
Cramer, Carl (Curly) FB-WB-TB	20Cle 21-22,PC23,24-26Akr	2 6	5'11"	184	Hamline	5	76
Crangle, Jack FB-WB	23ChiC	2	6'1"	200	Illinois	1	18
Crawford, Ken FB-BB-WB-C	20Akr 21Ham 21Cin 23Day		5'11"	185	Miami-Ohio		
Crawford, Mush G-T	25ChiB 26AFL 27NYY		6'	200	Beloit, Lake Forest, Illinois		
Critchfield, Hank (Biff) C	31Cle		5'10"	207	Wooster	1	
Croft, Harrison G-T	24Rac		6'1"	190	Wis.-Platteville		
Cronin, Bill FB-WB-E-BB	26AFL 27-29Prov		5'10"	182	Boston College	1	
Cronin, Fritz E-G	27Dul		5'11"	185	St. Mary's (Minn.)		
Cronin, Jack WB-TB-FB-BB-E	27-30Prov	2 4	5'11"	178	Boston College	5	
Cronin, Jerry E	32Bkn		6'	198	Rutgers		
Cronin, Tommy (Paddy) HB	22GB		5'9"	170	Loras, Marquette		
Crook, Al C-G-T	25-26Det		5'10"	190	Washington & Jeff.	1	
Crouch, Billy C	21Was		6'1"	187	Davidson		
Crowl, Dick G-C	30Bkn		5'10"	185	Rutgers		
Crowley, Jim (Sleepy Jim) TB-HB	25GB 25Prov HC47ChiAA		5'9"	165	Notre Dame		6
Crowther, Rae E	25-26Fra	6	5'11"	175	Penn State, Colgate	2	18
Crowther, Saville G-T	25Fra 26AFL		6'1"	220	Penn State, Colgate		
Cullen, Dave (Jack) G	31Cle		5'10"	230	Geneva		
Culver, Al T	32ChiB 32GB		6'2"	212	Notre Dame	1	
Culver, Frank C-E	23Buf 24Roch 24Buf 25Can		5'11"	175	Syracuse	2	
Cuneo, Ernie G	29Ora 30Bkn		5'9"	192	Columbia		
Cunningham, Cookie E	26AFL 27Cle 29ChiB 31SI 26-31 played in the A.B.L., 37-38 player-coach in the N.B.L.		6'3"	210	Ohio State	2	
Curran, Harry WB-BB	20-21ChiC		5'10"	180	none		
Curtin, Don (Red) BB	26Mil 26Rac		5'8"	155	Marquette		7
Curzon, Harry E-TB-BB-FB	25Ham 25Buf 25-26Ham 26Lou 26Ham 28ChiC		6'	195	none		6
Cutler, Harry (King) T	20Day		6'2"	190	none		
Cyre, Hec T-G-E	26GB 28NYY		6'2"	215	Gonzaga		
Dadmun, Harrie (Hal) G-T	20Can 21NY		6'	235	Tufts, Harvard		
DeGata, Fred FB	31Prov		5'10"	187	Providence		
Dahlgren, George (Swede) G-T	24Ken 25Ham 25RI 26Ham		5'10"	200	Beloit		
Dally, Dilly G	26Har				none		
Dalrymple, Slats C	22Eva		6'2"	210	Indiana, Wabash		
Dalton, Moxie (Jack, Leather) BB-FB	22Rac		5'6"	165	Carroll (Wis.), Loras	1	
Daniels, Jack TB	25Mil			135	none		
Danziger, Fred FB	31Cle		5'11"	175	Michigan State		
DaPrato, Jerry FB	21Det		5'10"	180	Michigan State		
Darling, Boob C	29-31GB 32SJ		5'11"	206	Wisconsin, Ripon, Beloit	2	
Dasstling, Dane G-T	21Cin		6'	190	none		
Daugherity, Russ (Pug) WB	PC27Fra		5'10"	175	Illinois		
Daum, Red E-BB-WB	22-26Akr	6	5'7"	165	Akron	2	18
Davenport, Bill HB	31GB			187	Hardin-Simmons		
Davidson, Joe G-C	28ChiC 30Nwk		6'	200	Colgate, Oklahoma State	1	
Davis, Carl E-T-C-G	26AFL 27Fra		6'	194	Michigan, West Virginia		
Davis, Doc G-T	20Mun 20Day 22Col		5'9"	200	Indiana		
Davis, Herb WB-E-BB	25-26Col		5'10"	175	Xavier-Ohio		
Davis G	20Ham			185	Chicago		

UseName(Nicknames)-Positions	TeambyYear	See Section	Hgt	Wgt	College	Int	Pts
Davis, John FB-WB-TB-BB	20Col			155	none		
Davis, Pahl G-E-FB	22GB		5'10"	185	Marquette		
Day, Fred T	21Cin		6'2"	195	Ohio Wesleyan		
Dayhoff, Harry WB-FB-TB-BB	24Fra 25Pott	2	5'8"	170	Bucknell		12
DeClerk, Frank C	23-25RI		5'9"	189	St. Ambrose	3	
Deer Slayer, Dick E	22Oor			190	none		
DeGree, Cy T-G	21Det	4	6'1"	210	Notre Dame		3
Deibel, Art T-G	26Can		6'3"	235	Lafayette		
DeLaPorte, Darroll BB	25Mil				none		
Dell, Herb	HC22Col						
Dellinger, Larry G-T	20-23Day		5'11"	204	none		
Demmy (born Demyanovich), John T	30-31SI			190	none		
Denfield, Fred G-T	20RI 25Dul		6'	198	Navy		
Denton, Winnie G	22Eva		6'1"	200	DePauw		
Depler, Jack (Fat) C-T	21Ham PC29Ora HC30-31Bkn		5'10"	220	Illinois		
Depner, John E	29Day				none		
Derr, Bob WB-TB	20ChiT 21Ham		5'10"	180	Pennsylvania		
DesJardien, Shorty C-E	20ChiT 22Min		6'4"	210	Chicago	2	
	16 played major league baseball						
DeStefano, Fred FB-WB-BB	24-25ChiC			195	Northwestern		6
Detwiler, John FB-WB	23-24Ham		5'8"	190	Kansas		
Devlin, Mark (Spoke) BB	20Cle 21NY		5'10"	180	Holy Cross		
DeWeese, Ebby G-BB	27-28Day 30Port		6'	188	none	1	
DeWitz, Herb WB-BB	27Cle		5'9"	165	Nebraska		12
DeWitz, Rufe WB-TB	24,26KC	2	5'9"	175	Nebraska	1	10
Dibb, John T	30Nwk		6'	200	Army		
Dickinson, Tom E	20Det		5'8"	175	Syracuse		
Diehl, Wally FB	28-30Fra	12 4 6	6'	204	Bucknell	12	66
Dieter, Herb G-T-E	22Buf		6'1"	195	Pennsylvania		
Dimmick, Don WB	26Buf		5'8"	160	Hobart		
Doane, Dinger FB-WB-G-E	20Cle 21NY 22-24Mil	2	5'10"	190	Tufts	2	90
	25-26Det 27Pott 27Prov						
Dobeleit, Dick WB-TB-BB-FB	25-26Day	2	5'4"	155	Ohio State		
Dobrey, E.A. E	28Fra		5'11"	175	none		
Doherty, Bill C	PC21Cin		5'11"	190	none		
Donahue, Jack (Jiggs) G-T	26Prov		6'2"	230	Boston College		
Don Carlos, Waldo C	31GB		6'2"	190	Drake		
Donlan, Jim G	26Har				none		
Donohue, Bill BB-WB-FB	27Fra		5'9"	165	Carnegie-Mellon		12
Dooley, Jim G	23Mil		6'	210	Notre Dame		
Dooley, John T-G	22,24-25Roch		6'1"	224	Syracuse, Bucknell		
Dorfman, Art C	29Buf		5'10"	210	Boston U.		
Douglas, Steve G-T	26Mil			200	none		
Douglass, Leo FB-TB	26Bkn 26Fra 26Bkn		5'11"	190	Lehigh, Vermont		
Dowler, Tommy (Flash) WB	31Bkn		5'8"	160	Colgate		
Dowling, Pat (Smoke Screen) E	29ChiC			185	DePaul		
Downwind, Xavier (Chief) C-G-T-E	22-23Oor		6'	200	Carlisle		
(also known as Red Fang)							
Dowrick, Perry FB	21Was			172	none		
Doyle, Ed (E.J.) G-C-T	27Buf				Canisius		
Doyle, Eddie E	24Fra 25Pott		5'9"	175	Army		18
Drayer, Clarence (Shorty) T	25Day		6'4"	235	Illinois		
Dressen, Chuck (Dynamite) BB-QB	20Dec 22-23Rac	2	5'6"	147	none		15
	25,31,33 played major league baseball						
	34-37,52-53,55-57,60-61,63-66 managed in						
	major league baseball						
Drews, Ted E	26AFL 26Bkn 28ChiB		6'	185	Princeton		1
Driscoll, Paddy TB-HB-BB-QB	PC20ChiC 20Dec	123456	5'8"	165	Northwestern	12	418
	PC21-22,23-25ChiC 26-29,HC42-45,HC56-57ChiB						
	17 played major league baseball						
Drumstead (born Drumstadt), Wop G	25Ham			185	none		
Drury, Hoot E	30-31ChiB		6'4"	189	St. Louis	2	6
Dubofsky, Mush G	32NYG		5'10"	210	Georgetown		
Ducote, Moon (Duke) WB-TB	20Cle		5'11"	190	Auburn		
Dufft, Jim G-T	21Roch 21NY 22Mil		6'6"	250	Rutgers, Fordham		
Duffy, Pat FB-TB-BB-WB	29Day		5'10"	185	Dayton		1
Duford, Dukes E-BB-HB	24GB		5'10"	165	Marquette	1	
Duggan, Eddie FB	21RI		6'	200	Notre Dame		
DuMoe, Billy E	21GB		5'10"	175	none	3	12
DuMoe, Joe (Stub) E	21Roch		5'9"	178	Syracuse, Fordham		
					Lafayette		
Dunn, Bob (Baron) C-T	29SI		6'1"	200	N.Y.U.		
Dunn, Red BB-TB	24Mil 25-26ChiC 27-31GB	123456	5'11"	175	Marquette	19	148
Dunn, Roddy T	23Dul		5'10"	200	Syracuse		
Dunne, Pat FB	20-21Det			182	none		
Dunnigan, Pat T-G-E	22GB 24Min 25-26Mil		5'10"	210	Minnesota		
Dusossoit, Joe E	21Was		5'11"	185	Dartmouth		
Duvall, Earl (Mooney) G-T-E	24-26Col		6'	213	Ohio U.	1	
Dvorak, Ben TB	21Min		5'10"	170	Minnesota		12
Dwyer, Bob WB	29Ora		5'9"	160	Georgetown		
Eagle Feather FB-BB-T (also played as Pierce)	22-23Oor	2	6'	220	none		6
Early, Guy G-FB	20Day 21Cin		6'3"	210	Miami-Ohio		
Earp, Jug (Jugger) C-T-G	21-22RI 22-25GB 25Fra		6'	236	Monmouth	10	
	25-27GB 27NYY 28-32GB						
Eberdt, Jess C	32Bkn		6'2"	215	Alabama		
Ebersole, Hal G	23Cle		6'3"	190	Cornell		
Eberts, Beanie G-T-BB	24Min		5'11"	198	Catholic		
Eby, Byron TB-WB	30Port		6'	185	Ohio State	1	6
Eckberg, Gus FB	25Cle		5'9"	180	Minnesota,		
					West Virginia		
Eckhardt, Ox FB-WB	28NYG	4	6'1"	190	Texas	1	13
	32,36 played major league baseball						
Eckstein, Dolph C	25-26Prov		5'10"	185	Brown	2	
Edgar, Bill G-FB-WB-TB	23Buf 23Akr		6'2"	185	Washington & Jeff.,		
					Pittsburgh, Bucknell		
Edler, Deke WB	23Cle		5'9"	170	Ohio Wesleyan		6
Edmonson, Van (Gus) C	26Buf		5'10"	210	Oklahoma		
Edwards, Bud FB-WB-HB-TB-E	30Prov 31ChiB 31Prov	2	5'11"	190	Brown		6
Edwards, Cap (Horse) G-T	20,PC21Can 22Tol		6'	207	Notre Dame	1	
	PC23,24HC25Cle						
Edwards, Tom T	26Det		5'11"	185	Central Michigan,		
					Michigan		
Egan, Dick G	24Day				Wilmington		
Egan E-WB-BB	20-23ChiC 24Ken			175	DePaul		
Eichenlaub, Ray FB	25Col		6'	225	Notre Dame		
Eiden, Jim T	26Lou		5'8"	185	none		
Eissler, Al FB	20ChiT				none		6
Elliott, Al (Rowdy) TB-WB	22-24Rac	12 6	5'9"	175	Wisconsin	13	33
	19 played major league baseball as Robert Allen						
Eliott, Doc FB-TB-WB	22-23Can 24-25Cle 26AFL 31Cle	2 5	5'10"	209	Lafayette	5	121
Ellis, Walt (Speed) T	24-25Col 25Det 26-27ChiC		5'11"	224	Detroit		
Ellor, Bud G-E	30Nwk		6'2"	205	Bucknell		6
Elness, Shorty HB-QB	29ChiB		5'8"	166	Bradley		

UseName(Nicknames)-Positions	TeambyYear	See Section	Hgt	Wgt	College	Int	Pts
Emslie, Red G	23Roch				none		
Endress, Vic BB	22Eva				none		
Engelhard, Joe TB-WB	21-22Lou		5'11"	185	Rose-Hulman Tech		
Englund, Harry (Skin) E-HB	21-22ChiB		6'	185	none		
Engstrom, Art G	24Dul		5'9"	185	Chicago, Kansas		
Enright, Rex FB	26-27GB	2	5'10"	198	Notre Dame	4	30
Erehart, Archie WB	20Mun		5'8"	165	Indiana		
Erickson, Hal (Swede, Bull) WB-TB-FB-BB-HB-T	23PC24Mil	12 6	5'9"	193	St. Olaf,	10	82
	25-28Chi 29-30Min				Washington & Jeff.		
Erickson, Harold T	21-22Min			195	none		
Erickson, Mickey C	30-31ChiC 32Bos		6'2"	208	Northwestern	1	
Erickson, Swede E	24Ken			215	none		
Erickson, Walden T	26AFL 27Pott		6'1"	205	Washington		
Ernst, Jack BB-TB-WB	25-28Pott 28NYY 29Bos 30Fra	1234 6	5'11"	180	Lafayette	7	44
Eschbach, Herb C	30-31Prov		6'	190	Penn State		
Espie, Al T	23Lou				none		
Essman, Charlie G	20Col		6'	220	Christian Bros.		
Etelman, Carl (Midget) WB	26AFL 26Prov		5'8"	160	Boston U., Harvard,		
					Tufts		
Ettenhaus, Earl G	21Roch				none		
Evans, Buck T-G	25-29ChiB		5'11"	204	Marquette, Harvard		
Evans, Jack BB	29GB		5'9"	175	California		
Fahay, John (Big Jawn) E-BB-G	25Mil 26AFL 26Rac 29Min		6'	189	St. Thomas,		
					Marquette		
Failing, Fred G	30ChiC		5'11"	200	Central Michigan		
Falcon, Dick G	20ChiT		5'9"	175	none		
Falcon, Guil (Hawk) FB-BB	PC20ChiT 20Ham PC20ChiT	2	5'10"	220	none	2	30
	21Ham 21Can PC22-23Tol 24-25Ham 25Akr 25Roch						
Fallon, Mickey G-E	22Mil		5'9"	175	Muhlenberg,		
					Syracuse		
Farina, Nick C	27Pott		5'10"	195	Villanova		
Fausch, Frank (Whitey, Fox) FB	PC21-22Eva		6'3"	250	Kalamazoo	1	18
Faust, Dick T-G-E	24,28-29Day		6'1"	208	Otterbein		
Feaster, Bill (Vin) T-C	29Ora 30Nwk		6'	205	Fordham	1	
Feeney, Al C	20-21Can	5	5'11"	185	Notre Dame		17
Feichtinger, Andy E	20Dec		5'10"	170	none		
Feist, Lou E-T-FB died Nov. 12, 1926 - meningitis	24-26Buf		6'1"	200	Columbia, Canisius		
Fenner, Lee E-WB	20-27,29Day 30Port	6	5'10"	171	none	2	9
Ferguson, Tom T	21Lou				none		
Fetz, Gus HB	23ChiB			158	none		6
Filak, Jack T-G	27-29Fra		6'	190	Penn State		
Finch, Bull BB-FB	26LA		5'8"	180	Whittier	1	
Finn, Bernie (Barney) BB-WB-TB-HB	30Nwk 30,32SI 32ChiC	2	5'10"	180	Holy Cross		
Finn, Jack BB-WB-TB-FB	24Fra		5'7"	172	Villanova	1	20
Finnegan, Jim E-QB	23StL		5'8"	160	St. Louis		
Finsterwald, Bill (Jube, Wild Bill) WB	20Det		5'9"	165	Ohio U., Syracuse	1	
Fischer, Clarke HB	26Mil		5'8"	165	Marquette,		
					Campion, Catholic		
Fish, Jack	HC30Nwk						
Fisher, Darrell TB-FB	25Buf		5'11"	190	Iowa	1	
Fisher, Eddie G	25Buf		5'11"	210	Columbia		
Fisher, George T	26Ham		6'	200	Indiana		
Fishman, Alec G-FB	21Eva		5'11"	218	none		6
Fitzgerald E	20Det			150	none		6
Fitzgerald, Francis (France) BB	23Tol		5'10"	185	Detroit		
Fitzgerald, Freeman C-G	20-21RI		6'	195	Notre Dame		
Fitzgerald, Jim C	30-31SI		5'11"	215	Holy Cross		
Fitzgibbon, Paul BB-WB-HB-TB	26Dul 27Fra 28ChiC	2 6	5'8"	176	Creighton	9	25
Fitzke, Bob WB	25Fra	2	5'11"	195	Wyoming, Idaho	2	6
	24 played major league baseball						
Flaherty, Dick (Red) E	26GB 27KJ	6	5'10"	200	Marquette		12
Flaherty, Jim E-HB-WB	23ChiB 26AFL			198	Georgetown		
Flanagan, Hoot TB-WB	25-26Pott	2	6'	169	West Va. Wesleyan,	7	42
					Pittsburgh		
Flanagan, Latham (Pete) E	31ChiB 31ChiC		6'2"	185	Carnegie-Mellon		
Flannigan, Bill T	26Lou			210	none		
Flattery, Willie (Pud) G-E	25-26Can		6'	220	Wooster		
Flavin, Jack FB	23-24Buf		5'11"	175	Georgetown	1	12
Fleckenstein, Bill G-E-C-T	25-30ChiB 30Port 31Fra 31Bkn		6'1"	208	Carleton, Iowa	3	6
Fleishman, Jack (Butter) G	25-26Det 27-29Prov		5'6"	184	Pudue	1	
Fleming, Bill WB	25Can		5'11"	165	Mt. Union		
Flenniken, Mack FB-TB-WB-BB	30ChiC 31NYG	12	6'1"	200	Geneva	1	24
Flinn, Paul E	22-23Min		6'	180	Minnesota		
Florence, Paul E	20ChiC		6'1"	185	Loyola (Chic.)		
	26 played major league baseball				Georgetown*		
Flower, Jim T-E-C-G	20Col 21-23,PC24,25-Akr		6'1"	193	Ohio State		
	20 — played as Reeves						
Floyd, Owen (Slivers) C	20-21Mun		6'	195	Rose-Hulman Tech		
Flynn, Furlong G-T	26Har		6'	210	Cornell		
Foley, Jim (Shrimp) TB-WB-FB	26Har	2	5'8"	165	Syracuse	2	
Follet, Beryl HB-TB	30-31SI	2	5'9"	165	N.Y.U.	1	
Folwell, Bob	HC25NYG HC26AFL				Pennsylvania		
Folz, Art BB-TB-WB	23-25ChiC	2	5'7"	158	Chicago		38
Ford, Adrian BB-WB-E-FB	26AFL 27Pott 27Fra		5'10"	190	Lafayette		12
Ford, Salem WB-TB-BB	22-23 Lou		5'7"	150	Louisville		
Forst, Dutch FB	26Prov		5'8"	195	Villanova		
Forsyth, Jack	HC20-21Roch				Rochester		
Fortune, Bill G	24-25Ham		5'11"	218	Michigan		
Fosdick, Bob G	23Min		5'10"	225	Iowa		
Foster, Bob TB-G-T-BB-WB	22-23Rac 24Mil	2	5'10"	192	none		18
Foster, Fritz FB-BB	23Buf 23-24Roch		5'11"	185	Syracuse		
Foster, Wally BB	25Buf		5'10"	165	Bucknell	2	1
Francis, Gene FB	26ChiC		5'10"	190	Chicago	1	6
Frank, Paul BB	30Nwk			200	Waynesburg		
Franta, Chief T-G	29-30Min 30GB		6'1"	220	St. Thomas	1	
French, Walt (Fritz) WB-TB-BB	22Roch 25Pott	2	5'7"	155	Rutgers, Army	2	30
	23,25-29 played major league baseball						
Friedman, Jake E	26Har				none		
Fritsch, Louie G	21Eva			240	Georgetown		
Frugone, Jim (Babe) TB	25NYG 26AFL		5'10"	165	Syracuse		
Frump, Babe G	30ChiB		6'	225	Ohio Wesleyan		
Fry, Harry E	32SI		6'3"	210	Bucknell	1	
Fry, Wes (Cowboy) FB-BB-TB	26AFL 27NYY		5'10"	190	Iowa	8	25
Fulton, Ken G	21Mun						
Fulton, Ted (Curly) G-T	31-32Bkn		6'	196	Oglethorpe		
Gabler, John G	25Day				none		
Gallagher, Ed T	28NYY		6'1"	205	Washington & Jeff.		
Gansberg, Al E-T	26Lou		5'11"	187	Miami-Ohio		
Gardella, Gus (Siki, Hope) FB	22GB			190	none		
Garden, Frank E	20RI 23,25Cle		5'11"	188	none		

UseName(Nicknames)-Positions	Team by Year	See Section	Hgt	Wgt	College	Int	Pts
Gardner, Moose G	20-21Det 21Buf 22-26GB		6'1"	220	Wisconsin		6
Garnjost, Bill (Sherm) G-C	21Eva		5'10"	190	Columbia		
Garrett, Budge E-G-FB	20Akr PC22Mil		5'9"	200	Rutgers	1	
Garvey, Franny E	25-26Prov		6'1"	175	Holy Cross	2	13
Garvey, Hec (Stretch) G-T-E-C	22-23ChiB 26Har 26AFL		6'1"	234	Notre Dame	2	
	26Bkn 26AFL 27-28NYG 29Prov 30Bkn 30SI						
Gaulke, Hal BB-E	20-22Col		5'8"	175	none		
Gaustad, Dutch (Heavy) G	21-23Min			212	none		
Gautsch, Al C-G	29Min			190	Wis.-LaCrosse		
Gavagan, Mike BB	23Roch		5'10"	180	St. Bonaventure*		
Gavin, Buck FB-TB-WB	20Buf 21Det 21-22RI 22Buf	2	5'10"	179	none	7	78
	23GB 24-25RI 26Ham						
Gay, Chet T-G-C	25Buf 26Mil		6'	215	Minnesota		
Gayer, Chuck T	26Dul		5'11"	205	St. Mary's (Minn.),		
					Creighton		
Gentry, Weldon (Cash, Spot) G	30-31Prov		5'10"	195	Oklahoma		
George, Karl G	22Rac		5'11"	175	Carroll (Wis.),		
					Loras		
Gerardi, Patsy E	21Was			165	none		
Getz, Fred E	30Bkn		6'1"	192	Tenn.-Chattanooga		
Ghee, Milt BB-TB	20ChiT 21Cle	1	5'7"	167	Dartmouth		12
Giaver, Bill WB-TB-FB-BB	22Ham 23RI 24Rac 25Ham	2 4 6	5'9"	190	Georgia Tech	3	24
	26AFL 26Lou						
Gibson, Dick T-G	22-23Lou		6'	188	Centre		
Gibson, George G	PC30Min and PC30Fra		6'	210	Minnesota		
Gilbert, Wally TB-WB	23-26Dul	12 45	6'1"	180	Valparaiso	5	24
	28-32 played major league baseball						
Gildea, Denny C-T-G	26Har		5'9"	190	Holy Cross		
Gillies, Fred (Boo) T	20-26PCChiC		6'3"	215	Cornell		
Gillis, Joe G-T	23Tol		5'8"	210	Detroit		
Gillo, Hank FB-WB-BB-TB	PC20,21Ham 22-24Rac	2 5	5'10"	195	Colgate	3	146
	25Mil 26Rac						
Gillson, Bob G	30-31Bkn		6'	208	Colgate	1	
Gilroy, Johnny BB-TB	20Can 20Cle 21Was 26AFL		5'10"	175	Georgetown		
Giuglano, Patsy (Jule) BB	23Lou		5'4"	140	Louisville		
Glassgow, Bill TB-WB	30Port 31ChiC	12	5'10"	190	Iowa	1	12
Glassman, Frank G-T	29Buf		6'	210	Wilmington		
Glassman, Morris E	21-22Col		5'10"	166	none		
Glennie, George G-E-T	26Rac		5'7"	185	Ripon		
Glick, Eddie TB-HB-BB	22GB		5'8"	165	Lawrence,	2	
					Marquette		
Glockson, Norm G 14 played major league baseball	22Rac		6'2"	230	none		
Goarke, Art E	21Ton		5'6"	165	none		
Godwin, Walt G	29SI		5'7"	205	Georgia Tech		
Goebel, Paul E	23-25Col 26AFL	6	6'3"	199	Michigan		26
Goetz, Gus T-E	22Buf 23Col 26AFL		6'	190	Michigan		
Goldsmith, Earl E-WB	21-22Eva			182	Indiana		6
Golembeski, Archie E-G-C-BB	PC25,26,29Prov		5'10"	182	Holy Cross	4	19
Golsen, Gene FB-TB	26Lou		5'11"	188	Georgetown	1	
Golsen, Tom G	26Lou		5'11"	175	Georgetown		
Goodbread, Royce WB-HB-TB	30Fra 30Min 31Prov	2	5'11"	207	Florida		6
Goodman, Aubrey T	26AFL 27ChiC		6'3"	225	Baylor, Chicago		
Goodwin, Earl E	28Pott		6'1"	195	West Texas State,		
					Bucknell		
Goodwin, Merl WB-BB-E	28Pott		6'1"	195	West Texas State,		
					Bucknell	2	
Gorgal, Alex FB-WB	23RI		5'9"	180	none	1	
Gorman, Doc E	21Eva				St. Louis		
Gorman, Bud G-T	22-23Rac 24Ken			225	none		
Gormley, Tom G-T	20Cle 21NY 21Was		5'11"	225	Villanova, Ursinus,		
					Catholic,		
					Georgetown		
Gorrill, Flop E	26Col		5'11"	178	Ohio State		6
Gozdowski, Hippo FB-G-C	22Tol				none		12
Grace, Les (Red) E	30Nwk		5'11"	200	Temple		
Graham, Clarence WB-BB	28Day				none		
Graham, Fred E	26Fra 26AFL 26Prov 26AFL		6'	175	Indiana State,		
					West Virginia		
Grange, Gardie E	29-31ChiB	6	6'	173	Illinois		6
Grant, Aaron (Heavy) C	30Port		6'2"	285	Tenn.-Chattanooga		
Grant, Ducky BB	28ChiC	4	5'11"	175	St. Mary's	1	
Gray, Jack (Dolly) E (not real name)	23StL 23GB			175	none		
Gray Horse WB-G	23Oor		5'8"	190	none		
Green, Larry E	20Can		6'	180	Georgetown		
Green, Vee T	26Lou		6'	195	Illinois		
Greenberg, Ben FB-TB	30Bkn		5'9"	170	Rutgers		
Greene, Al WB	22Mil		5'8"	165	none		
Greene, Ed (Babe) G-E	26ChiC		5'11"	185	Loyola (Chic.)		
Greenwood, Glenn FB	26Lou		5'10"	185	Iowa		
Gregg, Ed E	22Lou		5'6"	135	Kentucky		
Gregory, Bruce WB 25-26 played in the A.B.L.	26Det		5'10"	170	Michigan	7	12
Gregory, Gil FB-WB	23-24Buf		5'11"	165	Williams		
Gregory, Mike G	31Cle		5'11"	215	Denison		
Griffen, Hal (Tubby) C-T	26AFL 28GB PC30,32Port		6'1"	247	Iowa		
Griffiths, Paul G	21Can		5'8"	190	Penn State		
Grigg, Tex (Ranger) BB-TB-WB	20-23Can 24,PC25Roch	12 6	5'11"	191	Austin	6	38
	26NYG 27Fra						
Griggs, Hal BB-TB	26Akr	2	5'10"	170	Butler		12
Grube, Charlie E	26Det		5'10"	175	Michigan		
Grube, Frank E	28NYY		5'9"	180	Lafayette	1	1
	31-36,41 played major league baseball						
Gruber, Herb E	21-23Lou		5'9"	155	Kentucky		
Guarnieri, Chick E	24Buf 25Can		5'10"	175	Niagara, Canisius,	2	12
Guffey, Roy E-T	26Buf		6'	194	Oklahoma		
Gulian, Mike (Doggie) T	23Buf 24Fra 25-27Prov		6'	205	Brown	1	
Gump, Andy G	22Col			210	none		
Gunderson, Harry C-G	20RI 21-22Min		6'2"	203	Iowa		
Gutteron, Bill (Little Giant) BB	26LA		5'5"	155	Nevada-Reno		
Guy, Charlie (Boots) C-G-BB	20-21Det 21-22Buf 23Cle		6'	170	Washington & Jeff.	10	
	25Day						
Guyon, Joe TB-WB-BB-FB-E-T-G	20Can 21Cle 21Was	12 456	5'10"	195	Carlisle,	9	79
	21Cle 22-23Oor 24RI 25KC 27NYG				Georgia Tech		
Gwosden, Milo E	25Buf		6'	185	Pittsburgh	1	
Haas, Bob BB-WB	29Day				none		
Haas, Bruno WB-BB-G	21Akr 21Cle 21Akr 22Day		5'10"	180	Worcester Tech		6
	15 played major league baseball						
Haaven Ike E-G	23Dul		6'2"	192	Hamline		
Hadden, Al WB-FB-TB-HB-E	25-26Det 27Prov	2 6	5'9"	186	Washington & Jeff.	3	30
	28ChiB 28-30Prov						
Hagberg, Swede C-WB-FB-T-E-BB	29Buf 30Bkn	4	6'4"	219	West Virginia		
Hagenbuckle, Vern (Hookey) E	26AFL 26Prov		5'8"	185	Dartmouth		
Hagerty, Horse FB-TB	30Bkn		5'10"	185	Iowa		
Hagerty, Jack (Black Jack) TB-WB-BB-FB	26-30,32NYG	123 6	5'9"	164	Georgetown	6	80
Haggerty, Doc G	20Cle 20Can 20Cle 21NY		6'	205	Tufts		
Hahn, Ray E	26Ham		5'10"	190	Kansas State		

UseName(Nicknames)-Positions	Team by Year	See Section	Hgt	Wgt	College	Int	Pts
Haines, Hinkey TB-BB-FB-WB	25-28NYG 29PC,31SI	12 6	5'10"	170	Lebanon Valley,	8	132
	23 played major league baseball				Penn State		
Haines, Hoot (Red) T-G-E	30-31Bkn 31SI		6'	205	Colgate	1	
Halas, George (Papa Bear) E	PC20Cle PC21-28,HC29ChiB	6	6'	182	Illinois	7	74
	HC33-42ChiB43-45MS HC46-55,HC58-67ChiB						
	19 played major league baseball						
Haley, Art TB-WB	21Day 23Akr		5'10"	175	Akron		
Halicki, Eddie TB-FB-WB-HB	29-30Fra 30Min	2 56	5'9"	185	Bucknell	7	75
Hall, Dick T-G	26AFL 27NYY		6'2"	220	Butler, Illinois		
Hall, Harry (Swede) BB	25RI 26AFL		5'11"	165	Chicago, Illinois		
Halladay, Dick (Death) E-WB	23-24Rac	6	6'	175	Chicago	7	12
Halleck, Neil BB-WB	24Col				none		
Halloran, Dimp TB	26Har		5'8"	175	Boston College,		
					Fordham		
Hallquist, Stone HB-TB	26Mil		5'9"	168	Middlebury		
Halperin, Buck TB	32Bkn		5'11"	200	none		
Halpern, Willie G-T	30SI		5'11"	220	C.C.N.Y.		
Halstrom, Bernie BB-WB-FB	20-21ChiC		5'9"	160	Illinois		
Hamas, Steve FB-WB	29Ora		6'	195	Penn State	1	
Hambacher, Ernie FB-TB	29Ora		5'8"	170	Bucknell	1	
Hamer, Tex FB-WB-TB	24-27Fra	12 456	6'1"	191	Pennsylvania	17	132
Hammill, Ching BB died Nov. 25, 1925	25Prov		5'7"	158	Villanova,		
					Connecticut,		
					Georgetown		
Hanke, Carl E	21Ham 22ChiB 22-23Ham 24ChiC		6'	190	Minnesota		18
Hanley, Bo WB	20Det HC24Ken		5'7"	150	Marquette		
Hanley, Dick WB	24Rac HC46ChiAA		5'10"	175	Washington,		
					Washington State		
Hanny, Duke E-T-G-FB	23-27ChiB 28-29Prov 30GB 30Port	4 6	6'	199	Indiana	9	49
Hansen, Hal (King Hal) FB	23GB PC26AFL		5'10"	200	Minnesota		
Hanson, Hal G-T	28-30Fra 30Min 30Fra HC32SI		6'1"	205	Minnesota		
Hanson, Hal G-C-T	21RI 23Min		6'1"	190	South Dakota		
Hanson, Ray G-C-T	23Col		5'11"	190	Ohio State,		
					Ohio Wesleyan		
Hanson, Steve E	26Lou		6'2"	193	Carthage		
Hardy, Dick T	26Rac		5'10"	210	Boston College		
Hardy, Isham G	23,26Akr				William & Mary		
Harley, Chic HB	21ChiB 22IL		5'8"	165	Ohio State		
Harms, Art T	25Fra 26-27NYG		6'1"	200	Vermont		
Harris, Dud T	30Port		6'2"	240	Ohio State, Marietta		
Harris, Fatty T	21Lou				none		
Harris, Harry BB	20Akr		5'9"	175	W. Va. Wesleyan,		
					West Virginia	2	6
Harris, Jack FB-E-HB	25-26GB	2 6	5'11"	190	Wisconsin	7	18
Harris, John (Soldier) FB-BB	26Har			196	none		
Harris, Ken (Bunk) FB	23Dul	1	6'	190	Syracuse, Columbia		
Harrison, Ed E	26AFL 26Bkn		6'	178	Boston College		
Hart. Les BB	31SI		5'11"	180	Colgate		
Hartong, George G-T-C	21Ham 23Rac 24ChiC		6'	210	Chicago	2	
Hartzog, Bug G-T-C	26AFL 28NYG		5'11"	195	Baylor		
Harvey, Norm T-E-C-G	25Buf 26Det 27Buf 27NYY		6'	196	Detroit		
	28-29Prov						
Hasbrouck, John (Ziggy) WB-FB-E	21Roch 21RI		6'	190	Rutgers		
Hastings, George T	30-31Port		6'2"	190	Ohio U.		
Hastings, Sandy WB-BB-TB	20Cle		5'8"	178	Pittsburgh		
Hathaway, Russ T-G	20Mun 20-22Day 22Can 22-24Day	5	5'11"	238	Indiana	2	58
	25-26Pott 27Buf						
Hauser, Earl E-T	20Day 21Cin		6'1"	190	Miami-Ohio		6
Hauser, Ken (One Round, Truck) FB-BB	27Buf 30Nwk		6'1"	224	none	1	
Havens, Charlie C	30Fra		5'10"	205	Western Maryland	1	
Haws, Les (old Pepper Box) BB-TB	24-25Fra	2 6	5'8"	165	Dartmouth	3	30
Haycraft, Ken E	29-30Min 30GB		6'	178	Minnesota		12
Hayes, Dave E	21RI 21-22GB	6	5'8"	165	Notre Dame		6
Hayes, Norb (Butts) E-FB	22Rac 23GB		5'11"	175	Marquette	4	
Healey, Ed T-G-E	20-21RI 22-27ChiB		6'1"	207	Dartmouth		0
Hearden, Les HB	24GB		5'8"	165	Marquette,	2	6
					St. Ambrose		
Hearden, Tom (Red) HB-TB-BB	27-28GB 29ChiB		5'9"	178	Notre Dame		
Hegerty, Jack	HC21Was				Holy Cross,		
					Georgetown		
Heimsch, Johnny TB-HB	26Mil	12	5'10"	175	Marquette		18
Heinisch, Fritz E-WB-BB	22-23Rac 24Ken 26Rac 26Dul		5'10"	173	none		
Heldt, Jack C-G	23,PC26Col		5'9"	208	Iowa	1	
Helvie, Chuck (Stump) E	20Mun 20Day 21Mun		5'8"	180	none		
Henderson, Herb (Buzz) TB	21Eva		5'11"	170	Ohio State		29
Henderson, Wilbur HB	20Ham			195			
Hendren, John FB-TB-WB	20Can 21Cle		5'9"	175	Bucknell		6
Hendrian, Dutch WB-FB-BB-TB	PC23Akr 23Can 24GB	12 56	5'9"	182	DePauw, Detroit,	4	50
	25RI 25NYG				Pittsburgh,		
					Princeton		
Hanricus, Ralph TB	22Roch		6"	175	none		
Henry G-C	30SI				none		
Henry, Fritz G	25Akr			190	none		
Henry, Pete (Fats) T	20-23,25,PC26Can 27NYG	12 45	5'11"	245	Washington & Jeff.	5	94
	27PC,28Pott						
Herman, Ed (Red) E	25RI		5'10"	175	Northwestern		
Herrin, Hoot C-G	31Cle		5'10"	208	St. Mary's		
Herron, Pat E	20Cle		5'10"	170	Pittsburgh		
Hertz, Frank E	26Mil		5'10"	185	Carroll (Wis.)		
Hess, Wally TB-BB-FB	20-21,PC22-24,25Ham	4	5'9"	174	Indiana	1	12
Hibbs, Jesse T	31ChiB		6'	195	Southern Calif.		
Hicks, Max E	20,PC21Ham			175	Geneva		
Higgins, Austin C-E	PC21,22-23Lou		5'9"	168	none		
Higgins, Bob E	20,PC21Can		5'10"	195	Penn State	1	20
Hill, Bob G (also known as War Horse)	22Oor		5'11"	190	Carlisle		
Hill Charlie (Chub) WB-FB-BB-TB	24-26KC	2	6'	183	Baker	1	37
Hill, Chuck WB-FB	25RI 26AFL		5'8"	190	Iowa State		
Hill, Cowboy (Dutch) TB-WB-BB	23Tol 24-25KC 25-26NYG	12	5'8"	176	Oklahoma	3	36
Hill, Don WB-HB-C	29GB 29ChiC		5'10"	175	Stanford	1	6
Hill, Kid (Bozo) T	26NYG		5'11"	185	Amherst		
Hillhouse, Andy WB	21Buf		6'2"	190	Brown		
Hinton, Grassy BB-TB	32SI	2 4	6'	185	Texas Christian	2	6
Hippa, Sam E	27-28Day		5'11"	165	Dayton		
Hobscheid, Fred T-G	26Rac		5'11"	215	Chicago		
Hobson, Ben FB-BB-WB	26-27Buf	2	5'10"	190	none	4	6
Hoffman, Bill G	24-26Fra		5'10"	227	Lehigh		
Hoffman, Jake FB	25Roch		5'8"	170	none		
Hogan, Paul (Midge) WB-TB-BB-FB	24Akr 25Can 26NYG	1 45	5'8"	170	Notre Dame,	2	16
	26Fra 27ChiC				Niagara,		
					Washington & Jeff.,		
					Detroit		
Hogan, Tom T-C-G-E	24Min 25Det 26ChiC		6'2"	200	Detroit		
Hogue, Frank BB-WB	24Akr				none		

UseName(Nicknames)-Positions	Team by Year	See Section	Hgt	Wgt	College	Int	Pts
Hogue, Murrell T-G	28NYY 29ChiC 30Min		6'1"	208	Centenary	1	
Hole, Ernie (Sarp) G	20-21Mun				none		
Hole, Mickey TB-FB-WB	20-21Mun		5'9"	180	none		
Holleran, Tom (Speed) TB-BB	22Tol 23Buf		5'7"	170	Pittsburgh		12
Holman, John T	28NYG						
Homan, Two Bits (Babe) BB	25-30Fra	23 6	5'5"	145	Lebanon Valley	9	60
Honaker, Charlie E	24Cle		5'11"	185	Ohio State		
Hopkins, Ted E-T	21-22Col		5'9"	180	none		
Horning, Steamer T	20-21Det 21Buf 22-23Tol		6'	196	Colgate	1	12
Horween (born Horowitz), Arnie BB-FB-TB (often played as McMahon)	21-22ChiC PC23-24ChiC	2 5	5'11"	206	Harvard	2	36
Horween (born Horowtiz), Ralph FB-WB-BB-TB	21-23ChiC (often played as McMahon)		5'10"	206	Harvard	1	23
Hosmer, Clarence G	21Ton		5'10"	205	none		
Houck, Babe G	20-21Col		6'	275	none		
Houle, Bill BB	24Min		5'8"	175	St. Thomas		
Howard, Dosey G-T	24-26KC 27Cle 28Det 29-30NYG		6'	225	Marietta		6
Howard, Red G	26AFL 26Bkn 27NYG		5'11"	192	New Hampshire, Princeton		
Howard, Tubby E-FB-BB	21-22GB		5'10"	210	Ripon, Wisconsin, Indiana		6
Howell, Bill E	29Bos		5'11"	175	Catholic		
Hower, Karl FB	21Lou				none		
Howser, Bill G	21Lou				none		
Hudson, Dick (Super Six) FB-WB-BB	23Min 25-26Ham	2		182	none		
Hudson, Johnnie WB-FB	21Was		5'9"	170	N. Carolina State		6
Hueller, Jack G	22-24Rac		5'10"	200	none		
Huffine, Ken FB-T-G	PC20Mun 21ChiB 22-25Day	2 4 6	6'3"	208	Purdue	4	30
Huffman, Iolas T-G	23Cle 24Buf		5'11"	228	Ohio State		
Hufford, Guy (Huf) E	26LA		5'11"	185	California		
Hughes, Denny (Dinty) C	25Pott		5'11"	185	George Washington	1	2
Hughes, Honolulu (Hula-Hula, Hank) BB-TB	32Bos		5'10"	195	Oregon State		5
Hughitt, Tommy (Tiny) BB-TB-WB-E	PC20-24Buf	12 4 6	5'8"	159	Michigan	9	50
Hultman, Vivian E-G	25-26Det 27Pott	6	5'8"	178	Michigan State		18
Hummel, Swede WB-FB-G	26KC 26Prov 27ChiC			195	Lombard	4	
Hummon, Mack (Mousie) E	26,28Day		5'11"	180	Wittenberg		
Hunt, Ben T	23Tol		5'9"	185	Alabama		
Hunter, Merle T-G	25-26Ham			185	none		
Hurlburt, John WB-BB	24-25ChiC		6'	175	Chicago		
Hurley, John E	31Cle		6'3"	192	Washington State		
Hurst, Pep T	24Ken		6'1"	195	none		
Hutson, Merle G-T	31Cle		6'	210	Heidelberg		
Hutton, Jack (Diz) E-WB	30Fra		6'1"	192	Purdue		
Illman, Ted FB-BB	26AFL 28ChiC		6'	190	Montana		
Imlay, Tut TB-WB-BB	PC26LA 27NYG	2 6	5'8"	165	California		24
Ingle, Mark G	21Eva				none		
Ingwersen, Burt T	20Dec		5'11"	180	Illinois		
Irgens, Bill BB-WB-TB-E	21-23Min		5'8"	175	none		
Irvin, Barlow (Bones) G-T	26-27Buf		5'10"	225	Texas A&M		
Irwin, Dutch WB	20Roch		5'7"	170	Mercer		
Irwin, Jim FB	21-22Lou		5'7"	165	none		
Isabel, Wilmer FB-BB-WB	23-24Col		6'	175	Ohio State	1	12
Jackson, Larry C-TB	26Lou			185	Loyola (Chic.)		
Jackson, Perry (born Artha Shockley) T-E	28-30Prov		6'1"	202	Southwestern Okla.		
Jackson, Pete FB-BB-WB	28Det		5'10"	200	Missouri	1	12
Jackson, Red T	21Eva 21Ham		6'	200	Chicago		
Jacobs TB	20Det				none		
Jacquith, Jim BB	26KC		5'9"	175	Coll. of Emporia		
Jamerson, Lefty E	26Har		6'1"	195	Arkansas		
	24 played major league baseball						
James, Ted G-C	29Fra		6'2"	190	Nebraska		
Jamieson, Bob C	24Fra		6'	195	Franklin & Marshall		
Jansing, Lou FB	22Lou			175	none		
Jappe, Paul E-G-T	25NYG 26Bkn 27-28NYG		6'1"	195	Syracuse	2	
Jawish, Heinie (Hy) T-G	26Pott		5'8"	210	George Washington, Georgetown		
Jemail, Jimmy BB	21NY		5'6"	165	Brown		
Jenison, Ray T	31GB		6'3"	198	S. Dakota State		
Jennings, Lou C-E	29Prov 30Port	5	6'3"	230	Haskell Indian, Centenary	2	4
Jensvold, Leo HB	31ChiB 31Cle		5'8"	173	Iowa		
Jessen, Ernie T	31Cle		6'1"	250	Iowa		
Jetmore, Cliff WB	23Tol				none		
Joesting, Herb FB-TB (The Owatonna Thunderbolt)	PC29Min 30Min and 30Fra 31Fra 31-32ChiB	12	6'2"	194	Minnesota	3	42
Johns, Ed G	23Cle 24Min		6'	175	Michigan State, Michigan		
Johnson, Art T-G	23-26Dul		5'11"	189	Fordham		
Johnson, Carroll E	20Ham		5'9"	165	Northwestern		
Johnson, Jerry WB-TB-FB-BB	21-22RI 22Rac	2 5	5'11"	195	Morningside		15
Johnson, Len BB	26Col				Syracuse		
Johnson, Leon E	29Ora		5'11"	185			
Johnson, Oscar (Swede) FB-WB	24ChiB 26BosA		5'10"	195	Vermont		
Johnson, Pike T-G	20-21Akr		5'11"	185	Washington & Lee	2	6
Johnson, Spider T	30Port		6'4"	210	Tenn.-Chattanooga		
Johnston, Swede FB	31GB		5'10"	190	Lawrence		
Jolley, Al (Rocky) T	22Akr 23Day 23Oor PC29Buf 30Bkn 31Cle HC33Cin		6'2"	220	Marietta, Tulsa, Kansas State		
Jonas, Marv G	31Bkn		5'11"	186	Utah		
Jonasen, Charlie E	21Min				none		
Jones, Ben FB-BB-WB	23Can 24Cle 25Can 25-26Fra 27-28ChiC	12 6	5'11"	202	Grove City	5	151
Jones TB	21Ham				none		
Jones, Jerry G	20Dec 22RI 23Tol 24Cle		6'1"	205	Notre Dame		
Jones, Ken WB-E	24Buf		6'3"	185	Franklin & Marshall		
Jones, Marshall (Deacon) WB-TB-FB	20Ham 20Det 21Akr		5'11"	165	North Dakota		
Jones, Ralph	HC30-32ChiB				Wabash		
Jones, Reno G	22Tol		6'	195	Cornell		
Jordan, Frank WB	20RI 23Mil			168	none		
Joseph, Red (Chal) E	27Day 30Port 31Cle	6	6'3"	187	Miami-Ohio, Ohio State	2	
Joseph, Zip E-G-C-WB-FB	25,27Day		6'2"	170	Miami-Ohio		
Joyce, Bill BB	20Det		5'8"	180	Holy Cross		
Kadesky, Max E	23RI	6	5'11"	175	Iowa	3	
Kaer, Mort (Devil May) BB-TB	31Fra		5'11"	167	Southern Calif.	1	6
Kahl, Cy BB-WB-FB-TB	30-31Port		6'1"	195	North Dakota	4	
Kakela, Ike C	30Min		6'	220	Minnesota		
Kailina, Ed T-G	28ChiB		6'	205	SW Texas State		

UseName(Nicknames)-Positions	Team by Year	See Section	Hgt	Wgt	College	Int	Pts
Kane, George G	21NY		5'9"	195	Fordham		
Kanya, Al T-E	31-32SI		6'	200	Syracuse	3	6
Kaplan, Ave TB	23Min 26AFL	12 4	5'7"	165	Hamline	1	18
Kaplan, Sam E	21Was			166	Lehigh		
Karch, Bob T	22Col 23Lou		6'1"	220	Ohio State		
Kasper, Cy G-FB	23Roch		5'10"	170	Notre Dame		
Kauffman, John T-G	29Day				none		
Kaw, Eddie TB	24Buf		5'11"	185	Cornell		12
Keck, Stan T-G	23Cle		5'11"	205	Princeton		7
Keefe, Emmett G	20ChiT 20Dec 21RI 21GB 22RI 22Mil		5'10"	195	Notre Dame		
Keefer, Jack TB	26Prov 28Day	2	5'9"	172	Michigan, Brown	3	15
Keenan, Ed G	26Har		6'4"	320	Washington (Md.)		
Kelley, Doc (The Superior Tooth Carpenter) TB-WB	24-26Dul	2	5'10"	170	Northwestern	1	
Kelley, Frank WB	27Cle		5'10"	165	S. Dakota State	1	18
Kellison, John G-T	20-21Can 22Tol		6'	210	West Va. Wesleyan		
Kellogg, Bill FB-TB	24Fra 25Roch	2	5'10"	178	Syracuse		30
Kellogg TB	21Mun						
Kelly, Jimmy TB	20Det		5'9"	160	St. Louis, Detroit		
Kelly, Tex (Clancy) G-T-C-E	22Tol 23Buf 25Roch 26Buf 29Ora		6'3"	220	none		
Kelly, Wild Bill TB-BB-WB	27-28NYY 29Fra 30Bkn	12 6	5'10"	184	Montana	7	42
Kelsch, Matt E	30Bkn		5'11"	190	Iowa		
Kempton, Fido B	21Can		5'8"	155	Yale		
Kendrick, Jim E-TB-HB-WB-FB-T	22Can 22Tol PC23Lou 24ChiB 25Ham 25Buf 25Roch 25RI 26Buf 27NYG	12 45	6'	197	Texas A&M	5	34
Kennedy, Jimmy FB	25Buf		5'9"	160	Boston College, Holy Cross		
Kenyon, Bill TB	25NYG		5'9"	180	Georgetown	1	
Keogh, Jack	HC26Har				Pennsylvania		
Kern, Bill T	29-30GB		6'	187	Pittsburgh	1	
Kernwein, Graham TB	26Rac	2 4	5'11"	175	Chicago	1	
Kerr, George (Doc) T-G	20Cle 21NY 26AFL		6'1"	211	Catholic		
Kerrigan, Tom G	29Ora 30Nwk		6'2"	200	Columbia		
Kibler, Bill TB	22Buf				none		
Kieley, Howard T-G	23-25Dul 26ChiC		5'8"	208	none		
Kiley, Roger (Rodge) E	23ChiC		6'	180	Notre Dame		6
Killiher, Lyons G	28ChiC				none		
Killinger, Glenn TB	21Can 26NYG 26AFL		5'9"	162	Penn State		
Kinderdine, Hobby C	20-29Day	5	5'11"	183	none	2	12
Kinderdine, Shine G	24Day		6'	195	none		
Kinderdine, Walt (Babe) WB-FB-TB	23-25Day				none		
King, Dick FB-WB	21Ham 22Mil 22Roch 23StL	2	5'8"	175	Harvard		2
King, Gus E	22Tol		5'11"	180	Centre		
King, Ralph (Bud) G-C	24Rac 25ChiB		6'	250	Chicago		
King, Rip TB-WB-FB	20-22Akr 23-24ChiC 25Ham	12 4	6'1"	202	West Virginia	6	43
Kirk, George C	26Buf		6'	205	Baylor		
Kirkgard, Heinie WB	23Tol			165	none		
Kirkleski, Frank TB-BB	27Pott 29Ora 30Nwk 31Bkn	12 4 6	5'10"	179	Lafayette	4	30
Kittredge, Paul HB-BB-TB	29Bos		5'10"	170	Holy Cross	2	12
Kitzmiller, Dutch FB	31NYG	2	5'11"	170	Army, Oregon	1	27
Klaus, Fee C	21GB		5'9"	190	none		
Kliebhan, Adolph BB	21GB				none		
Knab, Shiner WB-FB-BB	21Cin		6'1"	190	none		
Knack, Glenn G	22,24Buf				none		
Knecht, Bill T	25Day		6'	188	Xavier-Ohio		
Knight, Charlie C-T	20-21ChiC		6'2"	200	Northwestern		
Knight, George T	20ChiC			180	Loyola (Chic.)		
Knop, Oscar FB-WB-E-QB	20ChiT 21-23Ham 23-27ChiB	2 6	6'	191	Illinois	12	48
Kobolinski, Stan C	267Bkn		5'8"	170	Boston College		
Koch, Polly T-G	20RI		5'11"	180	Wisconsin		
Koehler, Bob FB-WB	20Dec 21-26ChiC	2	5'11"	185	Northwestern	2	68
Kohl, Dutch E	20,22Ham				none		
Kolls, Louie C-E-G	20ChiC 20Ham 22-25RI 26AFL 27NYY		6'1"	203	St. Ambrose		
Koplow, Joe (Tarzan) T	26Prov		6'3"	235	Boston U.		
Koppisch, Walt TB-WB-FB	PC25Buf 26NYG	2	5'10"	180	Columbia		
Kostos, Marty E-WB-BB	29Far		5'11"	185	Schuylkill		
Kostos, Tony E-C-G-T	27-29Fra 30Fra and 30Min 31Fra	6	5'11"	191	Bucknell	7	15
Kotal, Eddie (The Lawrence Flash) HB-TB-BB-E	25-29GB	12 6	5'8"	170	Illinois, Lawrence	18	60
Kovacsy, Bill G	23Ham				Illinois		
Koziak, Mike G	25Dul		5'9"	185	none		
Kozlowsky, Joe T-G-E	25-27Prov 29Bos 30Prov		5'10"	199	Boston College	1	
Kraehe, Ollie G-C-E	22RI PC23StL		5'10"	180	Washington-St.L.		
Kraft, Ren (Dolly) E	22Min		5'11"	170	Illinois		
Kraft, Rudy G-C	21Ton		5'10"	190	Penn State		
Kraker, Joe G	24RI		6'1"	190	Saskatchewan		
Kramer, Fritz G-BB	27NYY		6'	230	Washington State	1	
Kramer, George G-T	21-24Min		6'2"	240	none	1	
Kraus, Babe T-G	24Buf		6'2"	220	Colgate, Hobart		
Krieger, Earl (Irish) TB-E-FB	21Det 22Col		5'11"	185	Ohio U.	1	
Kreinheder, Walt C-G-BB	22Akr 23StL 25Cle		6'2"	208	Michigan	1	4
Krentler, Ty FB-TB	20Det			160	Detroit		
Kriss, Howie (The Buckeye Bullet) HB	31Cle		5'9"	175	Ohio State		
Krueger, Jimmy T	24KC		5'10"	180	Drake		
Krysl, Jerry T	27Cle		5'11"	200	Kansas State		
Kucharski, Ted E	30Prov		6'1"	185	Holy Cross		
Kuczo, Paul TB-BB	29SI		5'9"	165	Virginia	1	
Kuehl, Waddy (Babe) WB-TB-E-FB-BB	20RI 21Det 21-22Buf 23RI 24Day	2 6	5'9"	165	Dubuque	7	73
Kuehner, Oscar T-G-E	20-21Col		6'	200	none		
Kuhrt, George T	21Ton		5'11"	185	none		
Kuick, Stan G	26Mil		5'10"	192	Beloit		
Kutler, Rudy G	25Cle		5'9"	190	Ohio State		
Kyle, Johnny FB	23Cle	2	5'9"	214	Indiana		6
Kyle, Rip C-T-G	25-26Can		6'	240	Gettysburg	2	
LaBissoniere, Tony C	22Ham		5'9"	185	St. Thomas, Michigan		
Ladorum, Doc FB	21Mun				none		
Ladrow, Wally HB	21GB		5'9"	180	none		
Ladson, Tiny G	22Eva				none		
LaFleur, Joe (Frenchy) G-FB-C-HB	22-24ChiB		6'	223	St. Norbert	1	

UseName(Nicknames)-Positions	Team by Year	See Section	Hgt	Wgt	College	Int	Pts
Laird, Jim FB-G-WB-T	20Roch 20-21Buf 21Roch 21Can 22Buf 25,PC26,27-29Prov 31SI	2 45	6'	194	Colgate	9	83
Lambeau, Curly TB-BB-FB-E	PC21-29,HC30-49 GB HC50-51ChiC HC52-54Was	123 56	5'10"	187	Wisconsin, Notre Dame	21	110
Lamme, Buck E	31Cle 37-38 played in the N.B.L.		6'2"	180	Ohio Wesleyan		
Lane, Lew TB-WB-BB	24KC		5'10"	180	St. Mary's (Kan.)	2	
Lane, Oxie T	26Mil		6'4"	220	Marquette		
Lang, Chick (Cowboy) G-E	27Dul 29Chi			195	none		
Langhoff, Irv (Oofie) WB-BB-TB	22-23Rac	2	5'8"	158	Marquette		8
Lanham, Charlie T	22-23Lou			170	none		
Lanum, Jake HB-FB	20Dec 21-24ChiB	2	6'	190	Illinois, Millikin	3	12
LaRosa, Paul E	20-21ChiC		5'11"	175	none		
Larson, Louie WB-BB-E-FB	26Dul 29ChiC			168	none	3	
Larson, Ojay C	22ChiB 23-24Mil 25GB 26AFL 29ChiB 29ChiC		6'1"	199	Notre Dame		8
Larson, Swede BB	23Ham				none		
Lassa, Nick T-G-C-E (also known as Long Time Sleep)	22-23Oor		5'10"	205	Carlisle, Haskell Indian	1	
Latone, Tony FB-WB-TB	25-28Pott 29Bos 30Prov	12 6	5'11"	195	none	22	162
Lauer, Dutch (Hal) WB-BB-E-FB-TB	22RI 22GB 23Tol 25-26Det	2	5'10"	183	Detroit	1	37
Lauer, Pete TB	22Eva		5'6"	150	Iowa		
Law, John T	30Nwk		5'9"	180	Notre Dame		
Lawrence, Ed HB-TB-FB-E	29Bos 30SI		5'8"	170	Brown		
Lawson, Jim E-WB	26AFL 27NYY		5'11"	190	Stanford		
Layport, Johnnie G-T	24Col 25-26Day		5'9"	170	Wooster		
Leaf, Garfield (Gar, Sock) T	26Lou		6'1"	195	Lake Forest, Syracuse		
Leahy, Bernie HB	32ChiB		5'11"	185	Notre Dame		
Leaper, Wes E	23GB		5'11"	175	Wisconsin		
Leary, Tom E	27Fra 29SI 30Nwk 31Fra		6'	180	Fordham	5	24
Leatherman, Paul G	22Ham		5'9"	200	Chicago		
Leavitt, Frank (Soldier) G	21NY			240	none		
Lebengood, Fungy WB	25Pott		5'11"	175	Villanova		
Lehrer, Chris WB	22Roch			185	none		
Leighty, Dutch BB-TB	21Was		5'11"	168	Georgetown		
Leith, Al BB-WB	26Bkn		5'9"	175	Pennsylvania		
LeJeune, Walt G-C-T-WB-FB (often played as Walt Jean)	22-23Akr 24Mil 25GB 25Fra 25GB 25Fra 26GB 27Pott		6'	233	Heidelberg, Bethany (W. Va.)	2	24
Lemon, Cliff E	26ChiB		5'10"	190	Centre		
Lensing, Vince G-T	21Eva		6'	200	Gen. Motors Inst.		
Lentz, Pesty FB-TB	20Day		5'10"	175	Wittenberg		6
Leonard, Jim G-T	23Roch		6'	205	Colgate		
Leonard, John T	22-23ChiC		6'2"	200	Indiana		
Lepper, Barney T	20Buf		5'10"	185	none		
Lester, Pinky E	26Prov		5'6"	160	none	1	
Levy, Harvey T-G	28NYY		5'10"	212	Syracuse		
Lewellen, Verne (Lew) TB-HB-BB-WB	24-27GB 27NYY 28-32GB	12 4 6	6'1"	182	Nebraska	22	307
Lewis, Art T	21Cin		6'1"		none		1
Lewis, H. G	21Lou		5'8"	175	none		
Lewis, Tiny FB-WB-BB	30Port 31Cle	2 45	6'2"	210	Northwestern	1	
Lidberg, Cully (Swede) FB	26GB 27-28VR 29-30GB	2	5'9"	191	Hamline, Minnesota	5	42
Lindsey, Menz (Flash) BB-TB	21Eva		5'6"	165	Wabash		
Lingrel, Chim WB-FB (also known as Tomahawk)	23Oor		6'2"	200	Miami-Ohio		
Linnan, Frank T	22,26Rac		6'2"	202	Marquette		
Lintzenich, Joe HB-FB	30-31ChiB	2 4	5'11"	187	St. Louis	5	12
Liston, Paul G	30Nwk		5'11"	185	Georgetown		
Litkus, Red T-E	21Was			187	none		
Little, Lou T (born Luigi Piccolo)	20-21Buf		6'	205	Vermont, Pennsylvania		
Little Twig, Joe E-T	22-23Oor 24-25RI 26Can 26Akr	6	5'11"	183	Carlisle	1	13
Livers, Mickey FB	21Was		5'10"	175	Georgetown		
Lollar, Slick FB	28GB		5'11"	200	Samford		
Lomasney, Tom E-BB	29SI		6'	180	Villanova		
Lone Star, Frank G-T	20Col		5'11"	200	Carlisle		
Lone Wolf, Ted G-T-WB	22-23Oor		6'2"	207	none		
Long, Harvey T-G	29ChiB 30Fra		6'	198	Detroit		
Long, Louie E	31Port		6'	185	S.M.U.	1	6
Long, Tom G	25Col		6'	205	Ohio State		
Longstreet, Roy (Shorty) C	26Rac		5'11"	185	Iowa State		
Longua, Paul E	29Ora 30Nwk		5'10"	175	Villanova		6
Lord, Jack G-T	29SI		6'	195	Rutgers		
Lott, John T	29Ora 30Bkn				none		
Loucks, Ed E	25Cle		5'9"	180	Washington & Jeff.		
Lovin, Fritz G	29Min			182	none		
Lowe, Bull (Bulger) E-T	20Can 21Cle 25Prov 25Fra 26AFL 26Fra 27Prov	6	5'11"	180	Lafayette, Fordham		
Lowe, Walt FB-WB-TB	23RI		5'10"	180	Dubuque	1	
Lowery, Darby G-E-T	20-25Roch		6'	203	none		
Lowery, Hugh (Huge) T	20Det		6'	220	Indiana, Franklin (Ind.)		
Lundell, Bob (Gloom) E	29-30Min 30SI	6	6'4"	215	Gustavus Adolphus	2	6
Lungren, Charlie (Babe) BB-WB	23RI		5'8"	158	Swarthmore	1	
Lunz, Jerry G-T	25-26ChiC 30Fra		6'3"	210	Marquette		6
Lurth, LaDue TB	29Min		5'8"	160	Gustavus Adolphus		
Lyle, Dewey G-T-E	20-22RI 22-23GB		5'11"	196	Minnesota		
Lynch, Ed (Ace) E-T	25Roch 26Det 26Har 26Det 27Prov 25-27 played in the A.B.L. 29Ora	6	5'11"	190	Catholic		6
Lynch G	21Cin				none		
Lynch, Paul (Deac) WB-BB	25Col		6'1"	190	Ohio Northern		
Lyons, Leo	HC23Roch				none		
MacCullom, Max (Red) E	22Lou		5'11"	165	Centre		
MacDonald, Allen WB-FB	24Dul		5'10"	170	none		
MacDonald, Buck G	21Ton 21NY		5'10"	180	Lehigh		
Mackert, Roy C-T	25Roch		6'2"	202	Lebanon Valley, Maryland		
MacMillan, Stu C-G	31Cle		5'9"	175	North Dakota		
MacMurray, Ray G	21Mun				none		
MacPhee, Waddy WB-TB	26Prov 22 played major league baseball		5'8"	160	Brooklyn, Princeton		
MacWherter, Kile FB	20Dec		5'9"	210	Millikin, Bethany (W. Va.)*		
Madigan, John C	22Min 23Dul 24Min		6'	185	St. Mary's (Minn.), St. Thomas	2	
Maeder, Al T	29Min		5'9"	185	Minnesota		
Maginnes, Al G-C	21NY		6'1"	188	Lehigh		
Maginnes, Dave TB	21NY		5'10"	165	Lehigh		
Maglisceau, Al T-G	29Fra		6'1"	210	Geneva		
Magner, Jim TB-BB	31Fra		6'	165	Widener, North Carolina		
Magnuson, Glen (Ole) G-C	25Ham		5'11"	225	Northwestern		
Mahan, Bob FB-E-WB-HB	29Buf 30Bkn		5'9"	178	Washington-St.L.	1	
Mahan, Red G	26Fra 26AFL		5'10"	212	West Virginia		
Maher, Birdie E	20Det		5'8"	180	Detroit		
Mahoney, Ike BB-WB-E	25-28,31ChiC 25-28 played in the A.B.L.	12 6	6'	173	Creighton	4	18
Mahoney, John (Buck) WB-FB-E	23Buf		6'	183	Canisius		
Mahoney, Roger C-G-E	28-30Fra 30Min		6'	205	Penn State	4	
Mahrt, Al (Marty) BB	20-22Day	1	5'11"	168	Dayton	1	18
Mahrt, Armin TB-BB-WB-E	24-25Day 25Pott 25Day 25Pott 26Day	2	5'11"	182	Dayton, West Virginia		12
Mahrt, John E	25Day		5'9"	180	Dayton		
Mahrt, Lou TB	26,PC27Day	1	5'11"	178	Dayton	3	
Maillard, Ralph (Mal) T	29ChiB		6'2"	190	Creighton		
Malcolm, Harry T	29Fra		6'	195	Washington & Jeff.		
Malone, Grover (Molly) WB-HB-E-TB-FB	20ChiT 21RI 21GB 23Akr	2	5'8"	175	Notre Dame	3	
Maloney, Red E	25Prov 26AFL 27NYY 29Bos	45	5'11"	180	Dartmouth		25
Manfreda, Tony WB-TB	30Nwk		5'8"	172	Holy Cross		
Manion, Jimmy (Skipper) G-C	26-27Dul		5'9"	178	St. Thomas		
Mankat, Carl E-T-G	28-29Day		6'3"	208	Colgate		
Manning, Jim (Joe) TB-FB	26Prov 26Har		5'11"	195	Fordham		18
Mansfield, Jerry FB-E-WB-TB	20-21RI	2	5'8"	160	none		6
Mantell, Joe G	24Col				none		
Maple, Howie WB	32 played major league baseball 30ChiC		5'7"	175	Oregon State		
Marelli, Roy G	28ChiC		5'10"	190	Notre Dame		
Marion, Dutch FB	25-26Det	2	5'9"	180	Washington & Jeff., Michigan		24
Marker, Cliff E-BB-FB-TB	26Can 27NYG 27Fra		5'10"	190	Washington State		6
Marks, Larry WB-HB-TB-FB	26AFL 27NYY 28GB	2 6	5'11"	185	Indiana	2	12
Marquardt, John (Rube) E	21ChiC				Illinois		6
Marshall, Billy	HC20-21Det						
Marshall, Bobby (Rube) E	20RI 25Dul		6'2"	195	Minnesota	2	3
Marshall, Charley E	31-32SI		6'	193	N.Y.U.		
Marshall, Phil E	20Cle		5'8"	165	Carnegie-Mellon		
Marston, Red BB	29Bos		5'9"	170	Boston U.		
Martell, Herm E	21GB		5'8"	155	none		
Martin, Abe WB-FB-BB	32ChiC		6'	185	Southern Illinois	2	12
Martin, Hersh (Jack) FB-WB-HB-BB	29SI 30Nwk	6	5'11"	180	none	1	
Martin, Ike WB-FB	20Can	2	5'11"	190	William Jewell		
Martin, Joe WB	21Lou				none		
Martineau, Roy G-T-FB-C	23Buf 24-25Roch		6'	210	Buffalo, Syracuse		
Mason, Sam FB	22Min 25Mil		5'8"	175	V.M.I.		
Mastrogany, Gus E	31ChiB		6'	180	Iowa		
Mathews, Barney E	26Rac		5'8"	185	Northwestern		
Mathews, Neil T	20ChiT		6'	200	Pennsylvania		1
Mathys, Charlie BB	21Ham 22-26GB	123 6	5'7"	165	Ripon, Indiana	10	36
Matsu, Art (Matty) BB	28Day		5'7"	168	William & Mary	2	
Matteo, Frank (Patsy) T-G	22-25Roch		5'11"	194	Syracuse		
Mattern, Joey BB-TB	20Cle 22Min			155	Minnesota		
Mattox, Marv (Monk) BB-G	23Mil		5'9"	175	Washington & Lee		
Maul, Tuffy FB	26LA	2	5'11"	200	St. Mary's	1	21
Maxwell, Joey C-E	27-29Fra		6'2"	197	Notre Dame	3	
May, Walt (Red) G	20Dec		6'1"	205	none		
Mayer, Emil (Puss) E-T	27Pott 30Port		6'1"	190	Bethany (W. Va.), Catholic		
Mayer, Frank G-T	27GB		5'11"	215	Iowa State, Notre Dame		
Mayl, Gene E	25-26Day		6'2"	198	Notre Dame		
Maynard, Les E	32SI		6'3"	210	Coast Guard, Rider	1	
McArthur, Jack C-T-G-E	26LA 27Buf 27-28NYY 29Ora 30Nwk 30Prov 30Fra 30Bkn 31Prov		5'11"	211	St. Mary's		
McAuliffe, Jack HB-TB	26GB	2	5'7"	155	Beloit		
McCall, Al	HC30Nwk						
McCann, Ernie T-E-G	26Har		5'11"	188	Penn State		
McCarthy, Don E	21Was		5'10"	172	Lehigh		
McCarthy, Jack T	27Dul			186	California		
McCarthy, Vince WB-BB-E	24-25RI 26AFL		5'10"	155	St. Viator		19
McCausland, Leo (Mac) C-G-T-E	22Akr		6'	195	Detroit		
McCaw, Bill (Bud) G-E	23Rac 26Lou		6'2"	194	Indiana		
McClain, Joe T	28NYY		6'	200	St. John's (N.Y.), Canisius		
McCombs, Nat (Spiecha) G-E-T-C (also known as Chief Big Twig)	26Akr 29Buf		5'11"	226	Haskell Indian		6
McConnell, Frank G	27Buf		6'	195	Georgia Tech		
McCormick, Elmer G-C-T-WB	23-25Buf 25Fra 26Har		5'7"	220	Detroit, Canisius	2	
McCormick, Felix FB-G-TB	20Ora 30Nwk		5'7"	185	Bucknell		3
McCormick, Frank FB	20-21Akr 21Cin	2	5'11"	190	South Dakota	3	36
McCrillis, Ed G	26Prov 29Bos		6'	205	Brown		
McDonald WB	26Det						
McDonald E-G	25Ham			165			
McDonald, Cy G	21Was		6'1"	197	none		
McDonald, John T-G	21Eva 26Lou		6'	195	Lawrence		
McDonnell, Mickey WB-TB-BB	23,25Dul 25-30ChiC 31Fra	2 6	5'8"	159	none	11	31
McElwain, Bill WB-TB-BB	24ChiC 25NJ 26ChiC		5'10"	170	Northwestern	2	6
McEvoy, Ed WB	26Har		5'11"	190	Spring Hill	1	
McGaw, Walt G	26GB			195	Beloit		
McGee, Harry C-G	27Cle 29SI 30Nwk 32SI		6'1"	198	Kansas State	1	
McGilbra, Firpo T-G	26Buf		6'1"	210	Haskell Indian		
McGill, George (Mickey) G	22Rac		5'10"	180	Marquette		
McGinley, Ed T	25NYG		5'11"	185	Pennsylvania		
McGinnis, Larry G-E-C	23-24Mil		6'1"	210	Marquette	1	
McGlone, Joe BB	26Prov 26AFL		5'7"	150	Harvard		
McGoldrick, Hugh T-E	25Prov		5'10"	180	Lehigh		
McGrath, Brian G	22Lou			245	none		
McGrath, Dick T-C	26Bkn		5'10"	190	Holy Cross		
McGrath, Frank E	27Fra 28NYY	6	5'11"	192	Georgetown		
McGuirk, Warren T	29-30Prov		5'11"	200	Boston College		
McIlwain, Wally WB	PC26Rac		5'9"	173	Illinois	5	
McIndoo, Mac E	21Mun				none		
McInerney, Nick (Bull) C-T-E-G-FB-WB	20-27ChiC		6'2"	201	none		
McIntosh, Al (Chick) WB	25-26Prov	2	5'9"	180	Rhode Island	3	
McKetes BB	26Ham				none	1	
McLain, Chief FB-BB-TB	30-31Port 31SI	2	6'3"	225	Haskell Indian, Iowa	3	24
McLaughlin, Tom FB	21Ton		5'10"	185	Notre Dame		
McLean, Ray (Toody) FB-BB	21GB		5'7"	155	none		
McLemore, Emmett BB (also known as Red Fox)	23Oor 24KC		5'7"	163	Haskell Indian, Pittsburg State		8

UseName(Nicknames)-Positions	TeambyYear	See Section	Hgt	Wgt	College	Int	Pts
McMahon, Harry (Shorty) BB	26Har		5'7"	150	Holy Cross		
McMahon, Tommy (Gig) FB	21Cin		5'11"	200	Denison		
McMillen, Jim (Mac) G	24-28ChiB		6'1"	215	Illinois	1	
McMillin, Bo TB-BB	22Mil 22Cle 23Mil HC48-50Det HC51Phi		5'9"	155	Centre		6
McMullen, Danny (Wild Man) G	29NYG 30-31ChiB 32Port		5'8"	231	Nebraska		
McNamara, Tom G-FB	25-26Det		5'10"	210	Tufts, Detroit		3
McNeil, Frank E	32Bkn		6'	185	Washington & Jeff.		
McNelis, Bill WB	27Dul		5'11"	177	St. Mary's (Minn.)		
McNulty, Paul E	24-25ChiC		6'	175	Notre Dame	1	6
McQuade, Johnny WB-BB	22Can		5'10"	176	Georgetown	1	
McRoberts, Wade C	25-26Can		6'	210	Westminster (Pa.)		
McShea, Joe G	23Roch		5'8"	185	Rochester		
Meadow, Ralph E	20Can		6'2"	195	none		
Meagher, Jack E	20ChiT HC46MiaAA		5'10"	178	Notre Dame		
Meeker, Butch (Shorty) BB-TB	30-31Prov	2	5'3"	143	Washington State	4	17
Meeks, Eddie WB	22Lou		5'7"	155	Louisville		
Meese, Ward E	22Mil 23StL 24-25Ham		5'10"	175	Wabash		
Mehelich, Tom G-C	29Min			195	St. Mary's (Minn.)		
Mehre, Harry (Red) C	22,PC23Min		6'1"	190	Notre Dame	1	
Meinhardt, George C-G	23StL		5'9"	200	St. Louis		
Meisner, Bill WB	21Ton		5'11"	185	Syracuse		
Melvin E-WB	21Cin		6'1"	185	none		6
Menefee, Bud E	21RI		6'	185	Morningside		
Mercer, Ken TB-BB-WB-FB	27-29Fra	12 45	5'11"	183	Simpson	7	95
Meredith, Russ G-T	23Lou 25Cle		5'11"	200	West Virginia	1	
Merillat, Lou E	25Can		5'9"	165	Illinois Tech, Army	1	
Method, Russ (Cuss) WB-BB-FB-E	23-27Dul 29ChiC	2 6	5'10"	192	none	4	18
Metzger, Lou FB-WB	26Lou		5'9"	170	Georgetown	1	
Meyer, Ernie (Puss, Egg) G	30Port		6'2"	200	Geneva		
Meyers, Klinks BB	20Ham				none		
Meyers, Paul (Chief) E	21NY 22Roch 23Rac		5'11"	170	Wis.-Milwaukee, Wisconsin		6
Michaels, Al TB	23-24Akr 25Cle 26AFL	12	6'	190	Heidelberg, Ohio State	2	9
Milam, Joe G-E-T	25KC		5'11"	180	Phillips		
Miles, Buck FB	20Akr		6'2"	195	Washington & Lee		
Miller, Al (Truck) HB-FB-BB	29Bos	2	5'11"	210	Harvard	1	
Miller, Bing T	29-31SI		6'1"	188	N.Y.U.		
Miller, Blake WB-E	21Det		5'10"	170	Michigan State		
Miller, Candy E-T	22Can 22-23Rac		6'3"	215	Purdue		6
Miller, Don WB	25Prov		5'11"	170	Notre Dame		
Miller, Dutch C	31Port		6'1"	212	Wittenberg		
Miller, Heinie E-G	20-21Buf 25Mil		5'10"	185	Pennsylvania		18
Miller, Jim HB	30Bkn		5'11"	195	West Va. Wesleyan		6
Miller, John FB	21Day		6'	188	Notre Dame		
Miller, Verne HB	30Min		5'8"	152	St. Mary's (Minn.)		
Millman, Bob WB-BB	26-27Pott	2	5'11"	178	Lafayette	1	6
Mills, Joe C-G-WB-E-T-BB	22-26Akr		6'3"	212	Carnegie-Mellon	4	7
Mills, Stan FB-HB-E	22-23GB 24Akr	2	5'9"	180	Penn State	1	24
Milstead, Century (Wally) T	25NYG 26AFL 27-28NYG		6'1"	213	Wabash, Yale		
Milton, Johnny E-WB-BB	23Mil 23StL 24KC		5'8"	175	Southern Calif.	3	
Minick, Paul G-E	26AFL 27Buf 28-29GB		6'	197	Iowa	1	
Mintun, Jake C	20Dec 21ChiB 22-24Rac 25KC 26Rac		5'11"	191	none	3	
Mishel, Dave TB-QB-WB-FB	27Prov 31Cle	1	5'9"	179	Brown		1
Mitchell, Tally T-C-G	24Buf		6'1"	180	Thiel		
Mitchell, Ted C	20Ora 30Nwk		5'10"	195	Bucknell	6	
Mizell, Warner WB-FB-TB	31Bkn 31Fra		5'10"	188	Georgia Tech		
Mockmore, Charlie G	20RI		5'11"	192	Iowa		
Moegel, Eddie WB	21Det		5'9"	186	Detroit		
Mohardt, Johnny TB-WB-HB 22 played major league baseball	22-23ChiC 24Rac 25ChiB 26AFL	12 6	5'10"	167	Notre Dame	8	12
Mohs, Louie (Big) E-G-T	22-24Min	6	6'2"	220	St. Thomas		6
Molinet, Lou FB	27Fra		5'11"	195	Cornell	1	6
Montgomery, Sully T-C	23ChiC 27Fra		6'3"	213	Centre		6
Moody, Wilkie WB-BB-TB-T-FB-G	20Col 21Day 24-25Col		5'7"	179	Denison		6
Mooney, George WB-E-BB-FB-TB	22-24Mil		5'8"	163	none	1	
Moore, Al HB	32ChiB		5'9"	170	Northwestern		
Moore, Dinty WB-BB	27Pott	2	5'8"	160	Lafayette	1	12
Moore T	21Cle						
Moran, Charley (Uncle Charley) 03,08 played major league baseball	HC27Fra				Bethel (Ky.)		
Moran, Frank C-T	20Ham 20Akr		6'4"	285	none		
Moran, Tom BB	25NYG		5'8"	175	Centre		
Morris, Bob G	26Bkn		5'10"	200	Cornell		
Morrissey, Frank T-G	21Roch 22-24Buf 24Mil	5	6'1"	203	Boston College		51
Morrow, Jim TB-WB-BB	21Can 22Buf		5'10"	170	Pittsburgh	3	7
Morse, Red G	23Dul		5'10"	198	none		
Moser, Ted (Doc) G	21Lou		5'9"	195	none		
Moynihan, Dick BB-FB	27Fra	1	5'8"	160	Villanova	2	3
Muirhead, Stan G-T	24Cle 24Day		6'	180	Michigan		
Mulbarger, Joe (Dutch, Tiny) T-G	20-26Col		5'9"	221	none		6
Mullen, Chief WB	21Eva			165	Haskell Indian		
Mullen, Vern (Moon) E-HB	23Can 24-26ChiB 27ChiC 27Pott	6	6'	186	Illinois	4	6
Muller, Brick E	PC26LA		6'2"	195	California	6	
Mulvey, Vince FB	23Buf			155	Syracuse	1	
Mumgavin, Jock E	20ChiT		5'10"	175	Wisconsin		
Munger T	24ChiC						
Munn, Lyle (Doc) E	25-26KC 27Cle 28Det 29NYG	6	6'	186	Kansas State	5	7
Munns, George (Yats) TB	21Cin		5'9"	170	Miami-Ohio		1
Murphy, Jim WB-E-C-BB	26Rac 26Dul 28ChiC		6'	184	St. Thomas		
Murphy, Joe (Cuddy) G	21Cle		5'9"	215	Harvard, Dartmouth		
Murphy, Tom TB-HB	26Mil	4	5'8"	165	Wis.-Superior	1	
Murphy, Tommy BB	26KC 6Col		5'10"	187	St. Mary's (Kan.)		
Murrah, Cap C-G	22Can 23StL		5'10"	210	Texas A&M		
Murray, Jab T-E-G-C	21-22GB 22Rac 23-24GB		6'3"	219	Marquette	4	1
Murray, Jock E-G	26Dul		6'1"	210	St. Thomas		
Murry, Don T-E-G	22,24Rac 25-32ChiB	4	6'2"	191	Wisconsin	1	6
Murtagh, Mickey C-G-E-BB-T	26-32NYG		6'1"	189	Georgetown	2	6
Murtha, Ted G-FB	21Col		5'11"	205	none		
Myers, Dave G-BB-WB	30SI 31Bkn		5'11"	183	N.Y.U.	1	
Myers, Denny G	31ChiB		6'1"	206	Iowa		
Myers, Tommy BB-WB	25NYG 26Bkn		5'8"	170	Fordham	1	
Myers, Truck E-T	22Tol 23,25Cle		6'	177	Ohio State	1	1
Myles, Henry E-T-G	29Buf 30Nwk		6'	190	Hampden-Sydney		
Nadolney, Peaches G-T	22GB 23-25Mil		5'11"	211	Notre Dame		
Nagida BB	26Ham			180	none		
Nagle, Johnny E	21NY		5'9"	175	none		
Nairan, Roger E-WB	26Buf		5'11"	185	Trinity (Texas)		
Nardacci, Nick TB-WB	25Cle		5'10"	160	West Virginia		
Nash, Bob (Nasty) T-E	20Akr 21-23Buf 24Roch 25NYG		6'1"	205	Cornell, Rutgers	1	24
Nason, Ed E-WB (also known as Running Deer)	22-23Oor		5'8"	185	none		
Neacy, Clem E-T	24-26Mil 27ChiB 27Dul 28ChiC	6	6'3"	206	Wis.-Milwaukee, Colgate	5	18
Neal, Ray (Gaumy) T-G	22Akr 24-26Ham		5'9"	211	Wabash, Washington & Jeff.		6
Neihaus, Fanny WB-BB	25Akr 26Pott	2	6'	170	Washington & Jeff.	1	6
Nelson, Don T-C	26Ham 26Can		6'1"	210	Ohio Wesleyan		
Nelson, Packie T	29ChiB		5'11"	205	Illinois		
Nemecek, Andy C-G-T	23-25Col		6'4"	210	Ohio State		
Nemecek, Jerry E	31Bkn		6'	185	N.Y.U.		6
Nemzek, Ted T	30Min			205	Moorhead State		
Nesser, Al (Nappy, Whitey, Old Pig Iron) G-E-C	20-25Akr 25Cle PC26Akr 26AFL PC26Akr 26-28NYG 31Cle		6'	195	none	6	24
Nesser, Charlie TB	21Col		6'2"	195	none		
Nesser, Frank FB-G-T	20-22,25-26Col	12	6'1"	246	none		13
Nesser, Fred T-E-FB	21Col		6'5"	250	none		
Nesser, John (The Wolf) G-T	21Col		5'11"	195	none		
Nesser, Phil G-T-WB	20-21Col		6'	225	none		
Nesser, Ted C-T-G	PC20-21Col		5'10"	230	none		
Netherton, Bill E	21-22Lou				none		
Nevers, Ernie FB 26-28 played major league baseball	PC26-27Dul 28VR 29,PC30-31ChiC HC39ChiC	12 45	6'	204	Stanford	18	301
Newashe, Bill T	23Oor		5'11"	200	Carlisle		
Newland, Howard E	21Lou				none		
Newman, Harry G-T	24Akr		5'6"	150	none		
Newman, Obie WB-E-TB	25-26Akr 26Ham 26Akr	4	6'2"	199	Carnegie-Mellon	1	7
Newmeyer, Don T	26LA		6'2"	205	California		2
Nicely, Jim T	30SI		5'9"	185	Gettysburg		
Nichols, John G-T	26Can		6'	200	Ohio State		
Nichols, Ralph T-G	26Har		6'	210	Kansas State		
Nichols, Sid BB	20-21RI	2	5'7"	177	Illinois	2	15
Nielson WB	24Roch				none		
Niemann, Wally C	22-24GB		5'11"	180	Michigan	3	
Nix, George (Chief) G	26Buf		5'11"	195	Haskell Indian		
Noble, Dave (Big Moose) WB	24-25Cle 26AFL	2 6	6'2"	195	Wisconsin, Nebraska	4	72
Noble, Dick G	26Har		5'11"	178	Trinity (Conn.)		
Noble, Jim E	25Buf		6'1"	190	Syracuse		
Nolan, Jack G	26LA		5'10"	185	Santa Clara		
Nonnemaker (born Nonenmacher), Ike E-BB	26Col		5'8"	172	none		
Noonan, Jerry BB-WB-E	21Roch 21NY 23,PC24Roch	6	6'1"	189	Notre Dame, Fordham		18
Norbeck, John G-BB	21Min			195	none		
Nordstrom, Swede (Tiny) G-T	25NYG 26Bkn		6'2"	238	Trinity (Conn.)	1	
Norman, Will (Toad) WB-TB	28Pott	2	6'	175	Washington & Jeff.	2	6
Norris, Jack E	32SI		6'3"	185	Western Maryland, Maryland		
Norton, Marty TB-HB-WB	22,24Min 25GB 26AFL	2 6	5'6"	175	none	6	60
Norton, Ray (Nick) WB	25Cle				none		
Novak, Eddie (Five Yards) WB-TB-FB	20-22RI 24Min 25RI 26AFL	2	5'9"	175	none	3	13
Novotny, Ray TB-HB-WB-BB-QB	30Port 31Cle 32Bkn	12 6	5'10"	165	Ashland	2	6
Nugent, Clem FB-WB	24Roch		5'9"	155	Iowa		
Nydahl, Mally TB-HB-BB-WB	29Min 30Min and 30Fra 31Fra	12	5'11"	163	Minnesota	3	27
Oas, Ben C-BB	29Min		6'	195	St. Mary's (Minn.)		
Oberbroekling, Ray T	24Ken		5'8"	198	Loras		
O'Brien, Con T	21NY		6'2"	195	Boston College		
O'Brien, Jack BB	29Min		5'10"	170	Minnesota		
O'Connell, Grattan E	26Har 27Prov		5'11"	185	Boston College	1	6
O'Connell, Harry T	24ChiB		6'1"	190	none		
O'Connell, Milt E	24-25Fra		6'	175	Lafayette		6
O'Connor, Dan G-T	20Can 21Cle		6'2"	210	Georgetown		
O'Connor, Frank T	26Har		6'	210	Holy Cross		
O'Connor, Red E	20-22,24ChiC		5'8"	171	DePaul		
Oden, Curly (Swede) BB-WB-TB	25-28Prov 29VR 30-31Prov 32Bos	123 6	5'6"	162	Brown	6	106
O'Donnell, Dick E	23Dul 24-30GB 31Bkn	2 6	6'	190	none	6	36
Oehlrich, Arnie WB-BB	28-29Fra	6	5'11"	190	Nebraska	9	18
O'Hearn, Ed G-T	20Cle 21NY		5'7"	185	Boston College, Lehigh		
O'Hearn, Jack WB	21Buf		5'10"	180	Cornell		
Ohmer WB	21Cin				none		
Oldham, Jim (Brute, Red) E-WB-BB-FB-T	26Rac		5'10"	183	Arizona		6
Oliker, Aaron E	26Pott		5'11"	170	West Virginia		
Oliphant, Elmer (Ollie) WB-TB	20Roch 21Buf	12 5	5'7"	175	Purdue, Army	4	47
Oliver, Bill (Country) G	26AFL 27NYY		5'11"	180	Alabama		
Olmstead, John G	22-23Lou		5'11"	180	Purdue		
Olson, Forrest (Tiny) G-FB	27NYY		6'	205	Iowa		
Oltz, Russ (Fat) C-G-T-FB	20-21,23-25Ham		6'	210	Illinois		6
Omensky G	26Lou				none		
O'Neil, Chuck E-WB-BB-FB	21Eva 22Tol 22Eva 23Tol		5'10"	180	Phillips	1	
O'Neill, Red C	26Har		5'10"	190	Connecticut	1	6
O'Neill, Tip (Jerry) WB	22Day		5'10"	170	St. Norbert, Detroit		6
O'Neill, Wally E-G-T	25Dul		6'	195	Wis.-Superior		
Orth, Henry G	21Cin		6'	180	Miami-Ohio		
Orwoll, Ossie HB 28-29 played major league baseball	26Mil		5'11"	165	Luther		
Osborn, Duke (Osey) G-C	21-23Can 24Cle 25-28Pott		5'10"	188	Penn State	9	
O'Toole, Bill G	24Dul				none		
Otto, Bo C-G-T	22-23Lou			182	none		
Otte, Lowell E	26AFL 27Buf		6'2"	180	Iowa		
Owens, Rip (Brick) G	22GB		5'10"	220	Nebraska, Lawrence		
Padan, Bob WB-TB	22Lou			165	Ohio State, Otterbein		
Pahl, Louie WB-FB	23-24Min	2	5'8"	185	none	1	6
Palermo, Jim G-C	25-26KC		5'9"	180	Missouri		
Palmer, Chuck BB-WB	24Rac 26Lou	1	5'10"	185	Northwestern	1	
Palmer, Mike T	21Min		5'10"	203	none		
Panaccion, Tony (Toots) T	30Fra		6'1"	212	Penn State		
Pape, Oran TB-WB-HB-BB	30Min 30GB 31Prov 32Bos 32SI	12 6	5'11"	180	Iowa	7	36

UseName(Nicknames)-Positions	Team by Year	See Section	Hgt	Wgt	College	Int	Pts
Pappio, Joe G-E-T-BB	23Oor 30ChiC		6'	189	Haskell Indian*		
Parkinson, Doc (Pug) FB-HB	31SI	2	6'1"	205	Pittsburgh	1	
Parnell, Babe T-G	25-28NYG		6'3"	205	Colgate, Allegheny		
Partlow, Lou FB-TB-WB-BB	20-23Day 23Cle 23-27,29Day	2	6'1"	185	none	7	42
Passuelo, Bill G-T	23Col		6'2"	230	none		
Patterson BB-G	21Cle				none		
Patterson, Clete G	24Ken		5'10"	205	Ohio U.		
Patterson, Gordon E	21Was			165	none		
Pauley, Frank (Heavy) T	30ChiB		6'1"	270	Washington & Jeff.		
Peabody, Dwight E	22Tol		5'11"	170	Ohio State		
Pearce, Harley (Jumbo) E-TB-BB-WB	26Col		5'10"	180	Ohio Wesleyan		6
Pearce, Pard QB-BB	20Dec 21-22ChiB 24Ken 25Prov	2	5'5"	150	Pennsylvania		24
Pearlman, Red G-T	20-21Cle 24Roch		6'	195	Pittsburgh		
Pearson, Dud BB	22Rac		5'9"	165	Notre Dame		
Pease, George BB-TB	26AFL 29Ora		5'8"	185	Columbia	2	6
Pederson, Jim WB-BB-HB	30Min and 30FRa 31Fra 32ChiB	4	5'9"	186	Augsburg	3	
Peery, Gordon (Skeet) BB	27Cle		5'10"	155	Oklahoma State		
Perrin, Jack BB 21 played major league baseball	26Har		5'9"	160	Michigan		6
Pessolano, Louie (Bon Gi, Pess) T-G-E	29SI		6'	215	Villanova		
Petcoff, Boni T	24-26Col		5'10"	223	Ohio State		
Peters, Frosty TB-BB-WB	30Prov 30Port 31Bkn 32ChiC	12 45	5'10"	183	Montana, Illinois	5	27
Peterson, Carl C	24KC		5'11"	175	Nebraska		
Peterson, Russ T	32Bos		6'3"	216	Montana		
Petree, Leo FB-WB-BB-TB	20Cle 22Tol			200	NE Missouri St.		12
Petty, Ross G	20Dec		6'1"	180	Illinois		
Peyton, Leo \BB-FB	23-24Roch		5'11"	190	none	3	
Phamer, Art TB-FB-BB	30Min and 30Fra 31Fra	12 4	5'10"	186	Minnesota	2	12
Phelan, Bob FB-WB-BB-TB	22Tol 23-24RI	2	5'11"	185	Notre Dame	2	12
Pierce, Dick G	20ChiT		5'11"	185	Michigan		
Pierotti, Al C-G-T-BB 20-21 played major league baseball	20Akr PC20Cle 21NY 23Mil 23Rac 23-24Mil 26AFL 27Prov 29Bos		5'10"	199	Washington & Lee	1	2
Pignatelli, Carl HB-FB	31Cle		6'	210	Iowa		
Pittman, Ralph (Bullet) BB-WB (played as Paxton)	26Buf		5'10"	200	Baylor		
Plank, Earl E	26Col 29Buf 30Bkn			174	none		
Plansky, Tony FB-BB-WB	28-29NYG 32Bos	12 5	6'2"	209	Georgetown	2	68
Pliska, Joe BB	20-21Ham		5'10"	185	Notre Dame		
Plumridge, Ted C	26AFL 26Bkn		6'2"	205	Colgate, St. John's (N.Y.)		
Pohlman, John FB	25Prov		5'9"	178	Brown		
Polisky, Bull G-T	29ChiB		6'	225	St. Edward's, Notre Dame		
Pollard, Fritz WB-TB-BB	20,PC21Akr 22Mil 23,PC25Ham PC25Akr 25Prov PC26Akr	123 6	5'7"	165	Bates, Brown	3	99
Pope, Spencer E	20Mun		5'10"	170	Indiana		
Potteiger, Earl WB-BB-E-FB	20Buf 21ChiC 22Mil PC24Ken 25-26,PC27-28NYG		5'7"	170	Ursinus	3	
Potts, Daddy T	26Fra		6'1"	235	Clemson		
Powell, Roger WB	26Buf			180	Texas A&M		
Powell,Stan(Possum)G(also known as Wrinkle Meat)	23Oor		5'11"	185	Carlisle, Haskell Indian	2	
Powers, Sammy G-T	21GB		5'10"	179	none		
Primeau, Frank BB	21Ton		5'11"	170	none		
Pritchard, Bill FB-WB-BB	27Prov 28NYY	2	5'10"	185	Penn State	2	16
Provincial, Ken E	30Fra		6'2"	190	Georgetown		
Purdy, Mike WB-BB	20Roch 21NY 22Mil		5'10"	179	Brown	1	6
Purdy, Pid BB 26-29 played major league baseball	26-27GB	123 5	5'6"	145	Beloit	3	30
Putzier, Fred E-WB	24Min		5'9"	174	St. Olaf		
Pyne, George T	31Prov		5'11"	218	Holy Cross		
Quam, Red BB	26Dul			165	none		
Quast, John E	23Lou		5'10"	165	Purdue		
Quigley, Red BB	20Roch		5'9"	155	none		
Quinn, Ivan G	24KC				Carroll (Wis.)		
Quinn, Paddy FB	20-21RI		5'7"	170	none		
Racis, Frank (Hercules) G-T-E	25-28Pott 28NYY 29Bos 30Prov 31Fra		6'	200	none	2	
Radick, Ken (Fat) E-G-T	30-31GB 31Bkn		5'10"	210	Indiana, Marquette		
Radzevich, Vic BB-G-FB	26Har		5'10"	165	Connecticut	1	5
Raffel, Bill E	32Bkn		5'11"	185	Pennsylvania		
Rafter, Billy BB-WB-FB	21,24Roch		5'6"	155	Syracuse		
Randels, Proc E	26KC 27Cle 28Det		6'	180	Kansas State		18
Randolph, Harry BB	23Col		5'11"	195	Bethany (W.Va.)		
Rapp, Bob (Goldie) WB-BB-TB	22-26Col 29Buf	2 6	5'8"	159	none	6	78
Rapp, Herb (Hub) C	30-31SI		6'	195	Xavier-Ohio		
Rascher, Andy T-G	32Port		6'2"	210	Indiana		
Rate, Ed (Speedy, Pete) BB	23Mil		5'9"	170	Purdue		
Ratekin, Roy E	21Akr		5'10"	180	Colorado State		
Rauch, Dick G-C	PC25,HC26-27Pott PC28NYY PC29Bos		5'9"	178	Penn State		
Rawlings, Bob FB-TB-WB	22Buf				none		
Read G-T	21Akr			190	none		
Reagan, Ed T	26Bkn				none		
Rebseaman, Paul C	27Pott		6'	188	Centenary	1	
Redeen, Sheepy E	21Min			185	none		
Redinger, Ruel (Pete) WB-TB-BB	25Can		5'10"	185	Penn State, Colgate		
Redman, Gus TB-WB-BB-FB	21Mun 21-22,24Day		5'11"	170	none	1	6
Reed, Max C-G	25Buf 26-27Fra 28NYG		5'8"	185	Bucknell	2	6
Reese, Dave E	20-23Day	6	6'	176	Denison	2	24
Reeve, Lew T	20ChiT		5'10"	193	Iowa State		
Regan, Jim BB	25Col			172	Still		
Regnier, Doc WB-HB	22GB			170	Minnesota	2	
Rehnquist, Milt G-C-T	24-25KC 25Cle 26KC 27Cle 28-31Prov 31NYG 32Bos		6'	229	Bethany (Kan.)	3	
Reichel, Lou C	26Col		5'11"	180	Butler		2
Reichle, Dick E 22-23 played major league baseball	23Mil		6'	185	Illinois		
Reichow, Chuck FB-TB-BB	25Mil 26Rac	2	5'9"	183	St. Thomas	6	
Reiser, Earl WB	23Lou			160	none		
Reiter, Peck G-E	26-27Day		5'9"	195	Miami-Ohio, Marietta		
Rengel, Neil FB	30Fra	12	5'9"	205	St. Cloud State, Minnesota, Davis & Elkins		
Reno, Jess E	20Mun 22Eva		5'9"	165	none		
Reuter, Vic C	32SI		6'	215	Lafayette		
Reynolds, Owen E-FB	25NYG 26Bkn		6'3"	212	Georgia		
Reynolds, Quentin (Red) G-T	26Bkn		6'1"	205	Brown		
Rhenstrom, Elmer (Swede) E	22Rac		5'10"	185	Beloit		
Rice, Orin (Bill) C-G-BB	26AFL 29NYG		6'	165	Syracuse, Muhlenberg		

UseName(Nicknames)-Positions	Team by Year	See Section	Hgt	Wgt	College	Int	Pts
Rice WB	21Ham				none		
Richards, Ted E	29ChiB		5'9"	174	Illinois		
Richards, Pete C	27Fra		5'10"	190	Swarthmore		
Richardson, Charlie BB	25Mil			143	none		
Richman, Harry G	29ChiB		5'11"	186	Illinois		
Riddell, Speed E	20RI		5'10"	185	Nebraska		
Ridler, Don T	31Cle		6'	210	Michigan State		
Riley G	24Rac		5'11"	195	none		
Ringwalt, Carroll C-G	30Port 31Fra		6'	210	Indiana	1	
Riopel, Hop TB	25Prov		5'8"	165	Holy Cross	2	
Riordan, Mike (Iron Mike) BB-E-HB-FB	29SI		5'11"	195	N.Y.U.	1	
Risk, Ed FB	32ChiC		5'11"	180	Purdue		
Risley, Elliot T	21-23Ham		6'	205	Indiana		
Risvold, Ray WB-BB-FB-TB	27-28ChiC			170	none		
Roach, Rollin FB-WB	27ChiC		5'6"	145	Texas Christian	1	
Robb, Harry BB-WB-TB	21-23,PC25-26Can	12 6	5'10"	185	Penn State, Columbia	6	61
Robb, Stan E	26Can		6'	185	Centre		6
Roberts, Fred G	30-32Port		6'1"	200	Iowa	2	
Roberts, Guy (Zeke) WB-TB-FB	26AFL 26Can 27Pott		5'8"	175	Iowa State	1	
Roberts, Mace E-G-T	20-22,24Ham		6'	185	none		
Roberts, Red E-TB-G	22Tol 23Akr 26AFL		6'1"	235	Centre		
Roberts, Wooky BB-TB	22-23Can 24-25Cle 26Fra	1234 6	5'7"	160	Colgate, Navy	10	43
Robertson, Harry T	22Roch		5'10"	185	Syracuse		
Robertson, Jimmy BB-WB-TB	24-25Akr		5'8"	160	Carnegie-Mellon	1	12
Robeson, Paul E-T	21Akr 22Mil		6'3"	219	Rutgers	1	12
Robinson, Ed BB-WB-TB	23-26Ham 26Lou		5'9"	155	none	1	13
Robinson, Ed	HC31Prov				Brown		
Roby, Doug TB	23Cle	12	5'10"	190	Phillips, Michigan	3	7
Roderick, Ben WB-TB-FB	23Can 23Buf 26Can 27Buf	2	5'9"	175	Wooster, Boston College, Columbia	4	
Rodriguez, Jesse TB	29Buf		5'7"	160	Salem		
Rodriguez, Kelly WB-HB-TB-BB-FB	30Fra and 30Min	12 4	5'10"	180	West Va. Wesleyan		
Roepke, John TB-WB	28Fra		5'11"	175	Penn State	1	10
Roessler, Fritz E	22-24Rac 25Mil	6	6'1"	189	North Central Coll., Marquette		6
Rogers, Charley TB-WB-BB (The Camden Comet)	PC27,28-29Fra	23 6	5'10"	167	Pennsylvania	9	36
Rogers, Walt FB-WB	21-22Col 23KJ		5'9"	215	Christian Bros., Ohio U.		
Rohleder, George G-T-FB	25Col 26Akr	5	5'11"	213	Wittenberg		15
Rohsenberger, Tubby T	21Eva				Wisconsin		
Romney, Milt QB-HB-BB-TB-WB-FB	23-24Rac 25-28ChiB	12 6	5'8"	166	Utah, Chicago	10	56
Rooney, Bill FB-WB-C-BB-G	23-25Dul 25NYG 26Bkn 27Dul 29ChiC	2 6	6'2"	194	none	6	18
Rooney, Cobb BB-WB-TB-E-FB	24-27Dul 28NYY 29-30ChiC	12 6	6'	185	none	7	36
Rooney, Joe E-T	23-24Dul 25RI 26-27Dul 28Pott	6	6'	177	none	2	48
Rork, Spencer BB-WB	22Eva		5'9"	160	Kentucky		
Rosatti, Rosey T	23Cle 24,26-27GB 28NYG		6'	211	Northern Michigan, Michigan		
Rose, Gene WB-FB-BB	29-32ChiC	2	5'8"	172	Wisconsin	4	37
Rose, Tam TB	PC21Ton		5'11"	170	Syracuse		
Rosen, Stan (Tex) BB-TB	29Buf		5'6"	155	Rutgers		
Roudebush, George TB-FB	20-21Day	1	5'10"	180	Denison		15
Rousch, Tubby WB-G	22Tol			170	Toledo		
Rowan, John TB-BB	23Lou		5'8"	165	none		
Roy, Spin E	21-25Roch 27Buf		6'	175	none	2	6
Ruetz, Babe	HC22-24Rac				none		
Ruh, Emmett WB-E	21-22Col	5	5'8"	168	Davis & Elkins	1	19
Ruh, Homer (Hank) E-WB-BB-FB	20-25Col		5'10"	178	none	2	6
Rundquist, Porky T-G-C	25-26Dul		5'10"	220	Michigan Tech		
Rundquist, Swede T	22ChiC		6'2"	210	Illinois		
Runkel, Gil C-G	20Det			210	none		
Rupp, Nelson (Nocky) WB-FB	21Day		5'10"	180	Denison		
Russell, Reggie E	28ChiB			190	none		
Rust, Reggie TB-BB	32Bos		6'2"	210	Oregon State		
Ryan, Bill T	24Roch 24ChiC 25Mil		5'11"	190	Fordham		
Ryan, Cassy BB-WB	29Buf		5'6"	160	West Virginia		12
Ryan, Sod T	29ChiB 30Port		6'2"	205	Detroit		
Rydzewski, Frank C-T-G	20Cle 20ChiT 20Ham 20ChiT 21ChiC 22Ham 23ChiB 23-25Ham 25Mil 26Ham		6'1"	220	Notre Dame	1	
Sachs, Lenny E 25-26 played in the A.B.L.	20-22ChiC 23-24Mil 24-25Ham 25ChiC PC26Lou	6	5'8"	176	Loyola (Chic.), DePaul	2	24
Sack (born Sacklowski), Jack G	23Col 26AFL 26Can		6'2"	195	Pittsburgh		
Sacksteder, Norb TB-WB-BB	20Day 21Det 22,25Can	12	5'9"	173	Dayton, Christian Bros.	5	42
St. Germaine, Ted T-C-G	22Oor		6'2	250	Carlisle, Howard		
Salata, Andy G	20Ora PC30Nwk		5'10"	188	Pittsburgh		
Salemi, Sam (Smoke) WB	28NYY		5'9"	180	Columbia, St. John's (N.Y.), Canisius	1	6
Sampson, Art G	21Day		6'1"	206	none		
Sampson, Eber FB	21-23Min	2	6'	197	none		18
Samson, Seneca BB	26Prov		5'8"	160	Brown		
Sanborn, Bill E	21Ton				none		
Sandberg, Artie (Swede) BB-WB	26LA 29Min			192	none		
Sanders, Joe G-E	22Eva		5'10"	250	Ky. Wesleyan		
Sanford, Jim T	24Dul		5'8"	195	Lehigh		
Sanooke, Stilwell E-WB	22Oor		5'8"	175	Carlisle		
Santone, Joe G	26Har			180	none		
Sauer, Ed (Tubby) T-G	20-21Day 21Can 21-22Day 22Akr 22-25Day 25Pott 25-26Day		5'10"	246	Miami-Ohio	1	
Saunders, Buck BB	22Tol		6'1"	190	California		
Saunders, Russ (Racehorse) FB	31GB	12	5'9"	190	Southern Calif.		6
Savoldi, Joe (Jumping Joe) FB	30ChiB 31RW		5'11"	194	Notre Dame		6
Sawyer, Herm WB-BB	22Roch		5'8"	170	Syracuse		
Scalzi, Johnny BB-TB-WB 31 played major league baseball	31Bkn		5'7"	168	Georgetown	1	
Scanlon, Dewey WB	HC24-25,PC26Dul HC29ChiC		5'9"	192	Valparaiso		
Scanlon, John TB-WB	21ChiC 26Lou			185	DePaul		6
Scardine, Carmen WB	32ChiC				none		
Schaffnit, Pete E-BB-WB-FB	26LA		5'11"	180	California	1	
Scharer, Eddie TB-BB-WB	27Pott 28Det	1	5'6"	165	Detroit, Notre Dame	3	7
Scheib, Skippy C	30Bkn		6'2"	210	West Va. Wesleyan, Washington-St.L.		
Schein, Joe T	31Prov		5'10"	212	Brown		
Schell, Herb WB-FB-TB	24Col			185	Ohio State		9
Schiebel, Art T	32SI		6'	220	Colgate		

UseName(Nicknames)-Positions	Team by Year	See Section	Hgt	Wgt	College	Int	Pts
Schleusner, Vin (Slice) T	30-31Port		6'3"	225	Iowa		6
Schmael, Art FB	21GB	2	5'8"	170	none	1	12
Schneider, John (Pop) WB	20Col		5'10"	180	none		
Scholl, Roy G	29Bos		5'8"	205	Lehigh		
Schuber, Jim HB	30Bkn		5'8"	160	Navy		
Schuette, Paul G	28NYG 30-32ChiB 32Bos		6'	220	Wisconsin		
Schultz, Pete FB	20ChiC 22Col			187	none		
Schupp, Walt T-G	21Cin		6'	185	Miami-Ohio	1	
Schuster, Dick G	25Can		6'1"	185	Dayton, Penn State		
Schwab, Ray BB-E	31NYG 32SI			210	Oklahoma City		
Schwarzer, Ted G-C	26Buf		5'11"	190	Centenary		
Scott, Bob C-G-T	26Prov			195	none		
Scott, Johnny TB-WB-BB-FB	20-23Buf 26AFL		5'10"	176	Lafayette	1	30
Scott, Les T-G-E	23Akr 24Min		5'10"	205	Hamline		
Scott, Ned T	24RI		6'	200	Monmouth		
Scott, Phil E	29Ora				none		
Scott, Ralph T-G	21-25ChiB 26AFL PC27NYY		6'2"	235	Wisconsin		
Sears, Dick T	24KC		5'10"	185	Kansas State		
Seasholtz, George (Dutch) FB-TB-WB	22Mil 24Ken		5'8"	185	Lafayette	1	12
Sebo, Sam FB-WB	30Nwk		5'7"	165	Syracuse		
Seborg, Herman (Porky) G-BB-WB	30Min and 30Fra 31Fra		5'11"	195	Western Michigan	1	
Sechrist, Walt (Covered Wagon) G-T	20Ham 24Akr 25Fra 25Cle 26Ham 26Lou 26Ham		6'	258	none		4
Secord, Joe C	22GB			190	none		
Sedbrook, Len (Twinkle) WB-FB-TB-BB	28Det 29-31NYG	2 6	5'10"	174	Phillips	7	150
Seeds, Frank (Slippery) WB	26Can			170	none		
Segal, Maury E	25Cle				none		
Segretta, Rocky (born Rocco Segrito) E	26Har				none		
Seibert, Ed G-E	23Ham		5'10"	195	West Virginia	1	
Seibert, Ed T-G	27-28Day		5'10"	190	Otterbein		
Seidelson, Red G-T	25Fra 26Akr		6'1"	202	Pittsburgh		
Seliger, Frank G-T	20-21Ham			200	none		
Setron, Joe G	23Cle		5'9"	195	West Virginia		
Seyboth, Frank WB	26Prov				none		
Seyfrit, Si E	23Tol 24Ham		5'10"	170	Notre Dame		6
Shank, Henry HB	20Dec		5'8"	160	none		
Shanley T	27Dul			214	none		
Shapiro, Jack (Soapy) BB	29SI		5'2"	126	N.Y.U.		
Share, Nate G	25Prov 26AFL		6'1"	210	Tufts		
Shaw, Ben G	23Can		5'10"	190	none		
Shaw, Ed FB-T-WB-G	20RI 22Can 23Akr	2 5	6'1"	203	Nebraska	2	38
Shaw, Jesse G	31ChiC		6'1"	198	Southern Calif.	1	
Sheard, Shag TB-WB	23-25Roch	12 4	5'11"	177	St. Lawrence	2	13
Shearer, Ron T	30Port		6'	195	Drake		
Sheehan, Fred G	25Prov		6'2"	210	Georgetown		
Sheeks, Paul (Pepper) BB	21,PC22Akr; 37-41 head coach in the N.B.L.	5	5'8"	173	Dakota Wesleyan, South Dakota		30
Shekleton, Vin C	22Rac		5'8"	165	Colgate, Marquette		
Shelbourne, John FB	22Ham		5'11"	200	Dartmouth		
Sheldon, Jim E	26Bkn		5'11"	180	Brown		
Shelley, Deck TB-WB-HB	31Port 31Prov 32GB 32ChiC	12 4	5'11"	191	Texas		
Shelton, Murray E	20Buf	6	6'1"	175	Cornell		
Sherry, Gerry FB	26Lou						
Shockley (born Parnel Jackson), Arnie T	29Bos		6'2"	220	Southwestern Okla.		
Shoemake, Hub (Birdie) G	20Dec		6'	186	Lake Forest, Illinois, Bethany (W. Va.)		
Shook, Al G	21Col				none		
Shultz, Johnny (Shebo) WB-FB	30Fra		6'1"	189	Temple		
Shurtcliffe, Red WB-TB	29Buf			160	Marietta		
Shurtleff, Burt (Scrappy) C-G	25Prov 29Bos		5'11"	190	Brown		
Sieb, Wally WB	22Rac		5'10"	175	Ripon		13
Siegfried, Orville HB	23StL	2	5'10"	170	Washington & Jeff.	2	
Sieracki, Stan T	26Har		6'1"	192	Pennsylvania		
Sies, Herb G-T-BB	20Cle 21-22Day PC23RI 24Day	5	6'1"	203	Pittsburgh	1	23
Sillin (born Sillen), Frank WB-TB-BB-FB	21,27-29Day		5'11"	179	Western Maryland*	1	6
Simendinger, Ken (Cy) WB	26Har		5'10"	175	Lehigh, Holy Cross		
Simmons, Jim (Jinks) WB-FB-TB	27Cle 28Prov	2	6'	186	Southwestern Okla.	1	30
Simons, John (Jack) FB-E	24Min		5'11"	200	Hamline	1	1
Simpson, Eber QB	23StL	1	5'8"	170	Wisconsin		
Simpson, Jimmy BB-TB	22Tol 24Ken		5'10"	160	Detroit	6	
Singleton, Bill G	22Ham		5'9"	190	Washington-St.L.		
Singleton, John TB-WB	29Day; 22 played major league baseball		5'11"	175	none		
Skeate, Gib FB	27GB		5'10"	190	Gonzaga		
Skinner, Lew G-C-T	20Ham 22Eva				none		
Skudin, Dave G-E	29SI		5'11"	195	N.Y.U.		
Slackford, Fritz FB-WB-E	20Day 21Can		6'	180	Notre Dame	1	12
Slagle, George G	26Lou				none		
Slater, Duke T	22RI 22Mil 23-25RI 26AFL 26-31ChiC		6'1"	215	Iowa	1	6
Slater, Howie (Dukes) FB	26Mil	2	5'10"	186	Washington State	2	6
Sleight, Red T	30-31GB		6'2"	226	Purdue		
Slone, Pete E	21Mun		5'8"	180	none		
Slough, Elmer (Ben, Peanuts) BB-WB	26Buf		5'8"	160	Oklahoma	3	12
Slyker, Bill E	22Eva		6'1"	180	Ohio State		6
Smeach, Metz T	21Was		6'3"	195	Georgetown		
Smith, Clyde C	26KC 27Cle 28Prov		5'10"	181	Missouri	2	
Smith, Don G	30Nwk				none		
Smith, Gene G-C	30Fra 30Port		5'9"	190	Georgia		
Smith, Hank C-G-T	20-23Roch 23RI 24-25Roch		6'1"	189	none	1	
Smith, Len (Fat) T	23-24Rac		5'11"	195	Wisconsin		
Smith, Marv TB	21Can		5'11"	185	Purdue		
Smith, Oke E-FB-WB	20-21RI		6'2"	185	Drake		
Smith, Olin T-G	24Cle		6'1"	230	Ohio Wesleyan		8
Smith, Orland T-G	27-29Prov		5'11"	215	Brown		
Smith, Pat FB	20-21,23Buf	2	6'	198	Michigan	1	42
Smith, Red BB-G-TB-FB-E-WB	27GB 28NYG 28NYY 29GB 30Nwk 31NYG; 27 played major league baseball	12 5	5'10"	192	Notre Dame	5	23
Smith, Rex E	22GB		6'	195	Beloit		
Smith, Russ G-C	21-22ChiB 23Can 23-24Mil 24Cle 25Det 25ChiB 26Ham		5'10"	220	Illinois	1	
Smith, Warren G	21GB			175	Western Michigan		
Smith, Wilfred T-G-E-C-BB	20-21Mun 22Lou 23ChiC 23Ham 23ChiC 23Ham 24-25ChiC		6'4"	203	DePauw	1	
Smyth, Lou (Hammer) TB-FB-WB	20-23Can 24-25Roch 25-26Fra 26Har 26Prov	12	6'1"	200	Texas, Centre	15	78
Snell, George FB-BB-WB	26Bkn 27Buf		5'10"	185	Penn State		6
Snoots, Lee (Bullet) TB-BB-WB-FB	20,22-23,25Col		5'9"	185	none		12
Snyder, Jim TB	25Mil			162	none		
Snyder, Snitz BB-FB-WB-HB	29NYG 30SI	2	5'8"	190	Maryland	1	18
Snofish, Alec G	31Prov		6'2"	200	Grove City		
Sonnenberg, Gus (Dynamite, Iron Duke) T-FB-TB	23Col 23Buf 23Col 25-26Det 27-28Prov 29RW 30Prov 31RW	2 45	5'6"	196	Dartmouth, Detroit	1	93
Spagna, Butch G-T	20Cle 20-21Buf 24-25Fra 26AFL		6'	215	Brown, Lehigh		6
Spain, Dick C-T	21-22Eva		5'8"	180	none		
Sparr, Ed T	26Rac		6'	210	Carroll (Wis.)		
Spears, Glen (Farmer) FB-WB-E	26KC		5'10"	185	Drake		
Specht, Robert TB	20Ham		5'9"	170	none		
Speck, Dutch G-C-T	20-23Can 24Akr 25-26Can		5'10"	220	none		
Spellacy, Frank E	22Buf				none		
Spellman, John (Jack) E-T-FB-WB-G	25-31Prov 32Bos	6	5'10"	201	Brown	3	6
Spencer, Jim G	28-29Day		6'	205	Dayton		
Spiegel, Adolph T-G	21-22Eva		5'11"	190	Campion		
Spiers, Bob T	22Akr 25Cle 26AFL		5'11"	193	Ohio State		
Springsteen, Bill (Kid) C-E	25-26Fra 27-28ChiC		6'	193	Lehigh	7	
Sprinkle, Hugh T-G	23-24Akr 25Cle		6'2"	220	Missouri, Carnegie-Mellon		
Staff, Spike G	25Prov		6'	210	Brown		
Stahl, Jake G-T	20Cle 21Day 21Cle		5'11"	185	Pittsburgh		
Stanley, Basil (B.L.) G	24RI		5'9"	195	Wabash, Notre Dame, Illinois, St. Mary's		
Stark, Howie T	23Rac		6'	210	Wisconsin		
Steele, Cliff BB	22Roch 22Akr		5'8"	150	Syracuse, Fordham		1
Steele, Red E	21Can		6'	176	Harvard		
Steger, Pete WB-BB	21ChiC				none		
Stein, Bill (Red) G-C-T	23-27Dul 28-29ChiC		6'	190	Fordham		
Stein, Herb C-G	21Buf 22Tol 24Fra 25-26,28Pott		6'1"	186	Pittsburgh	14	
Stein, Russ T-E-C	22Tol 24Fra 25Pott 26Can	5	6'1"	210	Washington & Jeff.	2	20
Stein, Sammy E-T	26AFL 29-30SI 31NYG 32Bkn	6	6'	195	none		12
Stennett, Stud TB-WB-FB-BB	31Port 32ChiC		6'	194	St. Mary's		
Stephens, Bill C	26Bkn		5'8"	185	Brown	1	
Stephens, Ray C-G	26AFL 27NYY		5'11"	190	Idaho		
Steponovich, Tony E-G	30Min and 30Fra		5'10"	185	Southern Calif.		
Sternaman, Dutch HB-FB-QB	20Dec 21-27ChiB	2 56	5'8"	176	Illinois	7	185
Sternaman, Joey QB-BB	22ChiB PC23Dul 23-25ChiB PC26AFL 27-30ChiB	123 56	5'6"	152	Illinois	9	268
Sterr, Gill (Pee Wee) BB	26Rac		5'6"	150	Carroll (Wis.)	3	
Stevenson, Art C	26NYG 26Bkn 28NYY		6'	190	Fordham		
Stevenson, Mark G-C	22Col			196	Lafayette		
Stewart, Charlie G	23Akr		5'9"	160	Colgate		
Stifler, Jim E-WB	26-27Prov		5'10"	175	Brown		
Stinchcomb, Pete HB-WB-TB-QB	21-22ChiB 23Col 23Cle 26Lou		5'8"	157	Ohio State		42
Stith, Howie G	21Lou				none		
Stobbs, Bill BB	21Det		5'7"	165	Washington & Jeff.	1	
Stock, Herb BB-FB	24Col		6'	182	Kenyon		
Stockton, Hust FB-TB	25-26,28Fra 29Prov 29Bos	12	5'11"	193	Gonzaga	13	42
Stoecklein, Earl G	20Day		6'2"	205	none		
Storck, Carl (Scummy)	HC22-26Day				none		
Storer, Jack TB	24Fra	2	5'10"	163	Lehigh	4	48
Stotsbery, Hal T	30Bkn		6'1"	235	Xavier-Ohio		
Strack, Charlie G	28ChiC		6'	215	Colgate, Oklahoma State		
Strader, Red TB-FB-WB	26AFL 27ChiC HC48-49NY-AA HC50-51NYY HC55SF		5'9"	200	St. Mary's		6
Strand, Leif C	24Dul		6'	210	Fordham, Minnesota*		
Strasser, Dutch E	25Can				Findlay*		
Strauss, Dutch FB-WB	23Tol 24KC	2	5'10"	205	Phillips	1	6
Straw, Don G-T	20-21Det		5'11"	210	Washington & Jeff.		
Strickland, Bill G	23Mil			190	Lombard		
Stringer, Gene FB-TB-BB-WB-E	25Cle		6'	200	John Carroll		
Strosnider, Aubrey (Ad) T	29Day		6'1"	205	Dayton		
Stuessy, Mel T	26ChiC		5'9"	180	St. Edward's		
Stuhldreher, Harry TB	26AFL 26Bkn		5'7"	165	Notre Dame	1	
Sturtridge, Dick HB	28-29ChiB		5'8"	171	DePauw		19
Suchy, Paul E	25Cle			188	none		
Suess, Ray T-G-E	26-27Dul			204	none		
Sullivan, George TB-WB-BB	24-25Fra 26AFL	2	5'9"	170	Pennsylvania	2	48
Sullivan, Hew (Red) G	26Dul			195	none		
Sullivan, Jack FB	21Was			170	N. Carolina State		
Sullivan, John (Torchy) E	21Buf			170	none		
Sullivan, Steve (Paddy) TB-WB-E	22Mil 22Eva 22-23Ham 24KC 24Ham		5'9"	180	Montana	1	
Swain, Al (Judge) E	26Buf		6'1"	190	Trinity (Texas)		6
Swanson, Evar E-WB-BB	24Mil 25RI 25--27ChiC; 29-30,32-34 played major league baseball	4 6	5'9"	168	Lombard	3	24
Sweet, Fred WB-FB-TB-BB	25-26Prov		5'10"	165	Brown		7
Sweetland, Fred (Buck) WB-FB	20Akr 21NY		5'10"	175	Washington & Lee, Fordham		6
Talbot, Johnny E	26Prov		6'2"	182	Brown		
Talbott, Bud	HC20-21Day				Yale		
Talbott, Jim BB	20Ham				North Dakota		
Tallant, Dave T	21-25Ham		6'1"	205	Muskingum, Grove City		
Tallman, Charlie T	21Ton				none		
Tandy, George (Yank) C	21Cle		6'1"	190	North Carolina		
Tanner, Bob E-T	30Fra		6'	190	Minnesota	3	12
Tanner, John (Shorty, Hump) WB-FB-BB-TB	22Tol 23-24Cle		5'5"	165	Centre	1	20
Tarr, Jim E	31Cle		6'2"	190	Missouri		
Taugher, Biff (Doc) FB	22GB		5'10"	185	Carroll (Wis.), Marquette		6
Taylor, Erk (Babe) G-T	31SI		6'2"	210	Auburn		
Taylor, Tarzan G	21ChiB 22Can 26AFL 26Bkn		5'11"	173	Ohio State		
Tays, Jim WB-FB-BB-HB	25ChiC 26AFL 27Day 30Nwk 30SI	2	5'8"	174	Chicago, Penn State		6
Tebell, Gus E	PC23,24Col	56	5'10"	170	Wisconsin		43
Teeter, Al E	32SI		6'1"	202	Minnesota		
Tersch, Rudy T-G	21-23Min			195	none		6
Thiele, Dutch E	20-23Day	6	6'1"	195	Denison	2	12
Thomas, Carl (Whitey) T-BB-FB-G	21Roch 22-23Buf		5'10"	195	Pennsylvania		
Thomas, Enid WB-BB-TB	26Har		5'8"	170	Pennsylvania	1	6
Thomas, John FB (played in 24 as John Webster)	24Rac 25Prov		6'1"	188	Jamestown, Chicago		
Thomas, Rex WB-FB-TB-HB	26Bkn 27Cle 28Det 30-31Bkn	2 6	5'9"	174	Tulsa, St. John's (N.Y.)	7	92
Thomas, Vern E	20Roch			155	none		
Thomas, Whitey E	24Fra 26AFL		5'10"	170	Penn State		

UseName(Nicknames)-Positions	TeambyYear	See Section	Hgt	Wgt	College	Int	Pts
Thompson, Alvie T-G	25-26KC		6'3"	210	Lombard, Nebraska		
Thompson, Bill C	25Mil			182	none		
Thompson, Dave (Chubby) WB	21Cin		5'10"	215	Denison		
Thompson, Don (Tommy) G	26LA		6'2"	205	Redlands	1	12
Thompson, Fred E	24RI		5'11"	180	Nebraska	1	
Thompson, George G-T	23-25RI		6'1"	210	Iowa	1	
Thompson, Johnny G	29Fra		5'10"	215	Lafayette		
Thompson, Pinky WB	27Buf				none		
Thompson, Tiny G	22Roch		5'10"	233	Syracuse		
Thornhill, Tiny T-G	20Cle 20Buf		5'11"	185	Pittsburgh		
Thorpe, Jack G-C-T-WB (also known as Deadeye)	23Oor		6'	210	none		
Thorpe, Jim TB-E-FB (also known as (Bright Path) 13-15,17-19 played major league baseball	PC20Can PC21Cle PC22-23Oor 24RI 25NYG 25RI 26Can 28ChiC	123 5	6'1"	201	Carlisle	6	57
Thunder, Baptiste T	22Oor		5'10"	215	none		
Thurman, John (Hackle) T	26LA		6'1"	225	Pennsylvania	1	
Tidd, Glenn C-G-T-WB	20-24Day		5'11"	202	none	1	12
Tierney, Festus G-T	22Ham 22Tol 23-24Min 25Mil		6'1"	198	Minnesota	1	
Titmas, Herb BB	31Prov		5'8"	185	Syracuse		6
Tobin, Elgie (Yegg) BB	PC20-21Akr		5'9"	160	Penn State	1	
Tobin, Leo G	21Akr		5'9"	220	Grove City		1
Tobin, Rex E	25Dul				none		
Tollefson, Russell	HC22Min				Minnesota		
Tolley, Ed G	29Day		5'8"	175	none		
Tomaini, Johnny (Biff) E-T	20Ora 30Nwk 30-31Bkn		6'	192	Georgetown		7
Tomlin, Tommy (Dowie, J.T.) G-T	20Akr 21Ham 21Akr 22Mil 25-26NYG		5'10"	196	Syracuse		
Toorock, Chief WB	26Bkn		5'9"	180	N.Y.U.		
Toscani, Bud WB-HB	32Bkn 32ChiC		5'8"	168	St. Mary's		
Towle, Thurston E	29Bos		5'10"	172	Brown		
Townsend, Otto G-T	22Min			190	none		
Trafton, George (Cyclone, Beast) C	20Dec 21,23-32ChiB		6'2"	230	Notre Dame	26	
Travis, Brick T	21RI 23StL		6'1"	205	Tarkio, Missouri		
Trainor, Mike WB-BB-TB	23-24Buf		5'9"	165	Canisius	6	24
Traynor, Barney C	25Mil		6'1"	190	Colgate		
Triggs, Jack FB	26Prov		6'	200	Providence		
Trowbridge, Ray E	20Cle 21NY		5'10"	170	Boston College, Purdue		
Truesdell, Hal T	30Min		6'	200	Hamline		
Tryon, Eddie (Cannonball) WB-TB	26AFL 27NYY	2 5	5'8"	180	Colgate	3	44
Tschappatt, Chalmers T	21Day		5'11"	180	West Va. Wesleyan		
Tully, George E	26AFL 27Fra		5'10"	180	Dartmouth		
Turner, Biff T-G	21Was			188	none		
Turner, Jim (Buddy) WB	23Mil		5'8"	165	Northwestern		6
Turner, Sam (Bumps) G	21Was			195	none		
Turner, Tiny G	20Day		6'	190	Ohio State		
Tuttle, George E	27GB		5'11"	180	Minnesota		
Tynes, Buddy (Cowboy) FB-TB-BB-WB	24-25Col	2	6'	185	Texas	3	18
Ullery, Jiggs WB-FB	22Day		6'	200	Penn State		
Underwood, Jack E-G-C	24-26Dul 27Pott 27Buf 29ChiC		6'	196	none		18
Underwood, John (Big Heavy) G	23Mil		6'3"	265	Rice	1	
Unitas, Pong G	21Was			180	none		
Urban, Luke E-BB 27-28 played major league baseball	21-23Buf	6	5'8"	165	Boston College	1	12
Ursella, Rube BB-WB-TB-FB	PC20RI PC21Min 24PC25RI 26Akr PC26Ham 26Akr 29Min	2 456	5'9"	172	none	4	38
Usher, Eddie WB-HB-TB-FB-E	21Buf 22RI 22,24GB 24KC	2	5'11"	192	Michigan	3	12
Usher, Lou T-G-C	20-21Roch 21Ham 21ChiB 23Ham 23ChiB 24Ham 24Ken 24Mil 26Ham		6'2"	240	Syracuse	1	
Vainowski, Pete G	26Lou				none		
Vance, Joe WB-FB 35-38 played major league baseball	31Bkn	2	6'1"	180	SW Texas State, Texas	1	12
Vanderloo, Viv FB	21RI		5'10"	190	Iowa State		
Van Dyke, Jimmy (Slim Jimmy) TB-BB	21-23Lou		5'7"	140	none		
Van Dyne, Chase T	25Buf		6'1"	194	Missouri		
Van Horn, Charlie TB-FB-WB	29Ora		6'2"	185	Washington & Lee		
Van Meter, Ed G	21Was		6'1"	212	none		
Vassau, Roy (Tiny) T	23Mil		6'	220	St. Thomas		
Vaughn, Bill FB-WB-BB	26Buf		5'10"	192	S.M.U.		
Vedder, Orrin FB	27Buf		5'7"	165	none		
Vergara, George (Zip) E	25GB		6'1"	190	Fordham, Notre Dame		
Vesser, John E	26AFL 27,30-31ChiC		6'	186	Idaho	1	6
Vexall, Roy FB	24-25Dul			190	none		
Vick, Dick (Dutch) TB-BB	24Ken 25-26Det 26Can	1	5'9"	167	Washington & Jeff.	1	
Vick, Ernie C-G-T 22,24-26 played major league baseball	25Det 27-28ChiB 28Det		5'10"	190	Michigan		
Vidal, Gene FB	21Was		5'10"	170	Nebraska, South Dakota, Army		
Vince, Ralph G	23,25Cle 26AFL		5'8"	175	Washington & Jeff	2	
Voight, Walter G-C-BB	20ChiT 21Ham 21ChiC		5'8"	200	none		
Volgenau, Elmer G	24Roch		6'2"	190	Colgate		
Volz, Pete (The Caveman) E-G	20ChiT 21Cin			190	Northwestern		
Voss, Tillie E-T	21Det 21Buf 22RI 22Akr 23Tol 24GB 25Det 25-30 played in the A.B.L. 26NYG 27-28ChiB 29Day 29Buf	56	6'3"	207	Detroit	9	69
Wagner, Buff HB-FB-BB	21GB		5'9"	165	Carroll (Wis.)		
Wagner, Ray E	29Ora 30Nwk 31Bkn		5'10"	172	Columbia		
Waite, Carl WB-E-BB-FB-T-G-TB	28Fra 29Ora 30Nwk	2	5'9"	205	Rutgers, Georgetown	3	18
Waite, Will G-C-T-WB-FB	20-21Col		6'2"	200	none		
Walbridge, Larry C	25NYG		5'7"	200	Lafayette, Fordham		
Waldron, Tim (Pinky) G-C	27ChiC			195	Gonzaga		
Waldsmith, Fat C-G	21Cle 22Can		5'9"	225	Akron		
Walker, Asa E (also known as White Cloud)	22Oor		5'11"	180	Carlisle		
Wall (born Waleski), Ed BB	30Fra		5'9"	170	Allegheny, Grove City		
Wallace, Dutch G-C-T	23-24Akr 25Cle 26Can 26Akr		6'	208	none	1	2
Wallace, Gordon FB-C	23-24Roch		5'10"	170	Rochester		
Wallace, John E	28ChiB 29Day		6'	180	Notre Dame	1	6
Walquist, Laurie (Larry) HB-QB-FB 25-26 played in the A.B.L.	22,24-31ChiB	12 6	5'8"	167	Illinois	12	79
Walson, Bullets BB	21Was			174	none		6
Wanless, George WB-E-G	22-23Lou		5'8"	160	none		
Ward, Bill T-G	21Buf		6'	212	Pennsylvania		6
Ward, Johnny T	30Min and 30Fra		6'2"	215	Southern Calif.		
Ward WB (not real name)	20Ham						
War Eagle T-G	22Oor			195	none		
Warweg, Earl WB	21Lou		5'6"	145	none		

UseName(Nicknames)-Positions	TeambyYear	See Section	Hgt	Wgt	College	Int	Pts
Wathen, Pete BB-E	22Eva		5'10"	175	Kentucky		
Watkins, Gordon (Coot) T-G	30Fra and 30Min 31Bkn		6'1"	220	Georgia Tech		
Watson, Rat BB-TB-WB-FB-E	22-23Tol 24Ham 24KC 25Ham 27Buf	12	5'10"	181	Southwestern (Tex.), Texas	1	10
Watters, Len (Cupid) E	24Buf		5'10"	185	Springfield		6
Way, Charlie (Pie) WB	21Can 24Fra 26AFL	2	5'8"	144	Penn State	3	30
Weathers, Cop G	26Buf		5'9"	230	Baylor		
Weaver, Buck G	30ChiC 30Port		6'4"	235	Chicago		
Weaver, Red C	23,HC24-25Col PC26AFL		5'10"	185	Centre	2	2
Webb, Art T-G	20Roch 22Mil		5'10"	210	none		
Webber, Dutch (Cowboy) E-BB-TB	24-25KC 25Cle 26Har 26NYG 26KC 27Cle 28GB 30Prov 30Nwk	4	6'2"	190	Kansas State	2	
Webber, Harry E-BB	20,23RI			173	Morningside		
Weber, Charlie G-T	26Bkn		6'1"	203	Colgate		
Weimer, Chuck (Dutch) TB-HB-BB	29Buf 30Bkn 31Cle	12 5	5'9"	178	Wilmington	1	31
Weinberg, Sol TB	23Cle		5'10"	165	Case Reserve		
Weir, Ed T-E	26,PC27,28Fra		5'10"	192	Nebraska	4	15
Weir, Joe E	27Fra		5'11"	185	Nebraska	1	
Welch, Gibby WB-BB-TB	28NYY 29Prov	12 6	5'11"	178	Pittsburgh	11	84
Weldon, Bodie WB-TB	20Buf		5'7"	165	Lafayette	1	14
Weller, Bub T-E	23StL 24Mil 25-27ChiC 28Fra		6'4"	224	Nebraska	1	8
Welmas, Woodchuck E	23Oor		5'7"	170	Carlisle		
Welsh, Jim G-T-C	23Roch 24-25Fra 26Pott	5	5'11"	250	Colgate	1	68
Weltman, Larry BB-TB	22Roch		5'11"	175	Syracuse		
Wendler, Hal (Windy) BB	26Akr 26Ham 26Akr		5'10"	175	Ohio State		
Wendt, Ken G	32ChiC		6'	195	Marquette		
Wenig, Obe E-BB	21-22RI	56	5'10"	190	Morningside		26
Wenke, Ad T	23Mil		6'4"	220	Nebraska		
Wentworth, Cy TB-WB-BB-FB-HB	25-26Prov 29Bos	12 5	5'8"	160	New Hampshire	6	48
Wentz, Barney (The Shenandoah Councilman) FB	25-28Pott	2 6	5'11"	204	Penn State	10	108
Werder, Red (Bus) C	21Ton				Dayton		
Werwaiss, Mule T-G	26Har			235	none		
Wesbecher, Al C-T	20Cle		5'10"	190	Washington & Jeff.		
Wesley, Bull (Rat) C-G-T-FB	26-27Prov 28NYG 30Port		6'1"	190	Alabama	5	
West, Belf (Hi) T	21Can	5	6'2"	200	Colgate	1	2
Westey G	25Mil				none		
Westoupal, Joe C	26KC 28Det 29-30NYG		6'3"	203	Nebraska	3	
Wexler, Bill C	30SI		5'9"	170	N.Y.U.		
Whalen, Bill C-T-G	20,22-24ChiC		5'7"	165	none		
Wheeler, Cowboy E	21-23GB	6	5'9"	180	Ripon	1	6
Whelan, Tom E-C-G 20 played major league baseball	20Can 21Cle		5'10"	180	Notre Dame, Dartmouth, Georgetown		6
Whipple, Ray E	20Det		5'9"	170	Notre Dame		
Whitcomb, Frank G-T	21Roch		6'3"	217	Syracuse		
White, Bob E	23Lou			150	none		
White, Buck FB	25ChiB 26AFL 27-29ChiB	2	6'	195	Howard Payne, Valparaiso	5	60
White, Ellery WB-FB	26LA			175	none		
White, Mac E-WB	22-23Tol		6'	178	Marietta	1	
White, Phil (Doc) FB-BB-WB-TB	25KC 25,27NYG	12 5	6'2"	210	Oklahoma	4	53
White, Ralph E	27Buf		5'9"	175	N.Y.U.		
Whitehead, Walker TB	22Eva		6'	180	none		
Whitmarsh, Vic E	21Det		5'11"	190	Syracuse		
Widerquist, Chet T-G	23-24Mil 25RI 26AFL 26,28ChiC 28Det 28ChiC 29Min		6'1"	219	Northwestern, Washington & Jeff.	1	
Wiedich, Ralph T	24KC 26AFL		6'1"	205	Emporia State		
Wiggs, Gene G	21Lou				none		
Wiggs, Hubert FB-T	21,PC22,23Lou		5'8"	183	Vanderbilt		
Wilcox, Firpo T	26Buf 30SI		6'	220	Oklahoma	1	
Wilcox, Ned FB-WB-TB	26-27Fra	2	5'11"	185	Swarthmore	4	30
Wilder, Hal G	23StL		5'10"	190	Nebraska		
Wilkins, Elmer (Swede) E	25GB		5'9"	175	Indiana		
Willegalle, Henry BB-HB-FB	29Min		5'11"	190	Carleton		
Willert C	22Ham				none		
Williams, Cy T	29-30SI 32Bkn		6'	200	Florida	1	
Williams, Doc G	23-26Dul		6'7"	218	St. Cloud State	1	
Williams, Ike HB	29SI		5'10"	180	Georgia Tech	5	
Williams, Inky E	21Ham 21Can 21-24Ham 24Day 25Ham 25Cle 26Ham		5'11"	174	Brown		
Williams, Joe G-E-FB	23Can 25-26NYG		6'	238	Lafayette	2	6
Williams, Pop WB-FB-TB-HB	28-31Prov 32Bkn	2	6'	207	Connecticut	4	78
Williams, Pryor (Pig Iron) G-C	21Det		6'1"	226	Vanderbilt		
Williams, Rollie WB-BB	23Rac		5'8"	170	Wisconsin		6
Williams, Travis (Bull) WB-T	21-22Eva		6'	200	Indiana		6
Willson, Joe G-FB	26-27Buf		5'11"	185	Pennsylvania		
Wilsbach, Frank G	25Fra		6'2"	215	Bucknell		
Wilson T-G-TB	23-24Akr						
Wilson, Abe G	26AFL 28-29Prov		5'10"	192	Washington	1	
Wilson, Drip C	31Cle				none		
Wilson, Lee E-WB	29Min 30Min and 30Fra 31Fra	6	5'11"	184	Cornell College		
Wilson, Mike WB-TB-FB	29Fra	2	5'11"	185	Lafayette	2	
Wilson, Mike E-BB 21 played major league baseball	22Buf 22Roch 23-24RI 26AFL	6	5'10"	167	Lehigh	3	12
Wilson, Milt G	21GB		5'10"	200	Wis.-Oshkosh*		
Wilson, Perce (Shorty) BB	20Det			150	none		
Wilson, Stu WB-TB-E	32SI		6'2"	209	Washington & Jeff.	1	12
Wilson, Wildcat TB	26AFL 27-29Prov	12 4	5'11"	200	Washington	8	60
Wimberly, By T-G	25Det		6'2"	200	Washington & Jeff.		
Winburn, Ernie E	23StL		5'11"	175	Cent. Missouri St.		
Windbiel, Joe C	21Eva		6'1"	220	Dayton		
Winkelman, Ben E-WB-FB-TB	22-24Mil	2 56	6'1"	190	Arkansas	1	60
Winneshick, Bill C	22Oor		5'8"	190	Carlisle		
Winston, Chuck G	20Day		6'1"	185	Purdue		
Winternheimer, Leon G-T	21-22Eva		6'1"	240	none		
Winters, Sonny TB	23-24Col	1 5	5'9"	155	Ohio Wesleyan	1	32
Wiper, Don BB	22Col		5'10"	150	Ohio State		
Wissinger, Zeke T	26Pott		6'	195	Pittsburgh		
Witter, Ray E-TB-BB-G-C	21-23Roch		5'10"	183	Syracuse, Alfred*		
Woerner, Erwin T	30Nwk		5'8"	200	Bucknell		
Wolf, Dick WB-BB-FB	23-25Cle 26AFL 27Cle	6	5'8"	160	Miami-Ohio	1	18
Wolford, Oscar G-C-E	20-22,24Col		6'	188	none	1	12
Wolter, Whitey WB-BB	24Ken		5'10"	170	Wis.-Milwaukee		
Wood FB	20Det				none		
Wood, Marv (Sam) WB-FB-E	24Ken		6'1"	195	California		
Woodin, Whitey G-T	22Rac 22-31GB		5'10"	208	Marquette	4	10

UseName(Nicknames)-Positions	Team by Year	See Section	Hgt	Wgt	College	Int	Pts
Woodruff, Jim E	26ChiC		6'3"	210	none	1	
Woods, Flash (Nig) WB	26Col		6'	180	Butler		
Woods, Jimmy G-T-C	20-24Roch		5'9"	196	none		
Work, Joe E-WB	23-25Cle		5'10"	177	Miami-Ohio		6
Workman, Hoge (Sonny) TB-QB-BB-WB	24,PC31Cle	1 45	5'11"	173	Ohio State	3	27
24 played major league baseball	32NYG						
Wray, Lud C	20-21Buf HC32Bos HC33-37Phi		6'	180	Pennsylvania		
Wright, Ab TB	30Fra		6'1"	190	Oklahoma State		
35,44 played major league baseball							
Wykoff, Lee FB-HB	23StL		6'1"	195	Washburn		
Wyland, Pudge G	20RI		5'10"	180	Iowa		
Wyman, Arnie FB	20RI	12	5'11"	172	Minnesota	1	30
Wynne, Chet TB-FB	22Roch		6'	180	Notre Dame	1	
Wynne, Elmer FB	28ChiB 29Day	2	6'1"	193	Notre Dame	1	
Yablok, Izzy (Indian) BB-TB	30-31Bkn 31SI	2	5'10"	172	Colgate	3	
Yeager, Jim (Dutch) T-G	26Bkn		6'1"	230	Lehigh		
Yeisley, Don E	28ChiC		6'1"	185	Chicago		
Yerges, Howard TB (played as Littleboy)	20Col		5'9"	155	Ohio State		
Young, Al WB-FB-TB-BB-E	26LA		5'10"	180	California		
Young, Billy G	29GB		5'10"	210	Ohio State		
Young, Doc	HC25-26Ham				Indiana Medical		
Young, Herm E	30Prov		5'11"	178	Detroit		6
Young, Les FB	27Prov		6'1"	190	Macalester, North Dakota		
Young, Russ FB	25Day		6'	190	Dayton		
31 played major league baseball							
Young, Sam G-C-T-E	25-27Prov 29-30Min		6'2"	192	Macalester, North Dakota		
Youngfleish, Frank (Yank) C-G	26-27Pott		5'9"	190	Villanova	4	
Youngstrom, Swede G-T-E-C	20-21Buf 21Can 22-25Buf 25Cle 26PC 27Fra		6'1"	187	Dartmouth	2	24
Yount, Mike T	21Mun		6'1"	205	Franklin (Ind.)		
Zehrer, Henry (Zip) FB-WB	26Har			175	none		
Zeller, Jerry WB-BB	21Eva		5'11"	170	Purdue, Illinois		
Zerbe, Harold E	26Can			165	none		
Ziegler, Paul FB-TB-WB	22Col		5'10"	185	none		
Ziff, Dave E	25Roch 26Bkn		6'	195	Syracuse, Carson-Newman		
Zimmerman, Corl G-T	27-29Day		6'	185	Mt. Union		
Zimmerman, Giff WB-TB	24Akr 25Can		5'10"	180	Syracuse	2	12
Zoia, Clyde G	20-23ChiC		5'7"	175	Notre Dame		
Zoll, Carl G	22GB		5'9"	215	none		
Zoll, Marty G	21GB		5'8"	185	none		
Zuidmulder, Dave TB	29-31GB		5'10"	175	St. Ambrose, Georgetown	1	
Zuver, Merle G-C	30GB		6'1"	198	Nebraska		

Note: All the positions listed in this section are offensive positions. Since there was no free substitution during this period, all these men played defense. The following defense position normally correspond to the listed offense positions:

DE with E	LB with C
DT with T	LB with FB
DG or LB with G	DB with all backs except FB

This register does not include positions, interceptions or points from the 1926AFL.

* - As asterisk next to the name of a college indicates that the player attended the college after the start of his pro football career.

Lifetime Statistics — 1920-1932 Players Section 1 — PASSING
(All men with 25 or more passing attempts or 10 or more completions)

		Complete Games								Incomplete Games					
Name	Years	G	Att	Cmp	Pct	Yds	Y/Att	TD	Int	G	Att	Cmp	Yds	TD	Int
Fay Abbott	21-29	16	30	5	17	64	2.1	0	7	41	8	7	180	0	1
Ockie Anderson	20-22	7	43	13	30	212	4.9	0	3	17	32	17	303	1	7
Johnny Armstrong	23-25	21	232	100	43	1145	4.9	7	25	7	20	13	242	0	1
Frank Bacon	20-25	13	17	8	47	80	4.7	0	2	33	11	6	110	1	2
Bullet Baker	27-31	30	21	5	24	117	5.6	1	5	20	5	2	55	1	2
Shorty Barr	23-26	15	162	64	40	795	4.9	5	21	11	24	9	133	1	3
Myrt Basing	23-27	41	38	11	29	151	4.0	0	9						
Cliff Battles	32-34	13	31	5	16	53	1.7	0	7	19	6	1	26	0	4
	35-37		107	36	34	476	4.4	1							
Johnny Blood	25-34	88	101	35	35	583	5.8	2	14	14	1	0	0	0	1
	35-39		64	24	38	299	4.7	2							
Benny Boynton	21-22,24	2	15	3	20	65	4.3	0	2	14	46	36	691	13	5
Matt Brennan	25-26	2	14	5	36	85	6.1	0	1	13	8	5	183	1	2
Earl Britton	25-29	14	64	21	33	231	3.6	0	11	17	6	1	7	0	4
Jesse Brown	26	14	37	15	41	251	6.8	3	4						
Hank Bruder	31-34	49	39	11	28	147	3.8	1	3						
	35-40		7	1	14	17	2.4	0	2						
Carl Brumbaugh	30-34	34	73	20	30	403	5.5	4	9	31	15	12	226	2	2
	36-38		50	15	30	252	5.0	6	6						
Johnny Bryan	22-27	21	70	20	29	285	4.1	0	10	37	19	16	323	2	1
Cub Buck	20-25	47	40	20	50	354	8.9	1	3	10	0	0	0	0	0
Chris Cagle	30-34	25	100	39	39	472	4.7	1	9	23	14	9	218	3	2
Harlan Carr	27	6	17	4	24	58	3.4	0	3	4	16	3	50	0	7
John Cavosie	31-33	26	44	14	32	271	6.2	2	2	7	0	0	0	0	0
Stu Clancy (35)	30-34	34	34	5	15	87	2.6	0	6	10	1	1	30	0	0
Dutch Clark	31-32,34	34	155	59	38	858	5.5	3	20						
	35-38		148	74	50	852	5.8	8							
Jimmy Conzelman	20-29	47	259	112	43	1420	5.5	7	28	54	57	39	785	5	9
George Corbett	32-34	14	6	3	50	95	15.8	1	0	11	4	1	20	0	1
	35-38		22	8	36	96	4.4	0	4						
Clyde Crabtree	30	12	32	10	31	103	3.2	0	5	3	1	0	0	0	1
Wally Diehl	28-30	29	124	34	27	420	3.4	4	17	9	3	2	55	1	1
John Doehring	32-34	8	35	9	26	207	5.9	2	5	9	14	5	142	2	3
	35-37		23	11	48	249	10.8	4	0						
Charlie Dressen	20,22-23	7	20	10	50	57	2.9	1	4	2	3	3	48	0	0
Paddy Driscoll	20-29	32	183	48	26	1026	5.6	3	28	83	65	48	1126	13	4
Red Dunn	24-31	66	552	226	41	3735	6.8	35	53	26	68	49	906	13	10
Al Elliott	22-24	17	20	7	35	79	4.0	0	1	11	9	3	43	1	2
Doc Elliott	22-25,31	18	14	6	43	124	8.9	0	1	19	8	4	64	1	2
Hal Erickson	23-30	20	25	10	40	117	4.7	0	5	48	2	2	34	0	0
Jack Ernst	25-30	54	454	183	40	2325	5.1	14	56	10	10	4	32	0	4
Mack Flenniken	30-31	6	26	11	42	169	6.5	0	3	8	13	6	138	3	3
Benny Friedman	27-34	56	758	354	47	5918	7.8	49	54	24	112	86	1775	19	13
Milt Ghee	20-21	4	23	8	35	98	4.3	0	5	8	4	3	85	1	0
Wally Gilbert	23-26	7	27	6	22	57	2.1	0	6	10	8	4	96	3	2
Bill Glassgow	30-31	17	53	13	25	192	3.6	1	8	4	0	0	0	0	0
Red Grange	25,27,29-34	45	101	34	33	590	5.7	7	16	52	32	21	431	3	5
Tex Grigg	20-27	30	88	23	26	367	4.2	2	8	21	24	15	254	1	4
Jack Grossman	32, 34	5	15	8	53	74	4.9	0	1	18	5	4	135	1	1
	35-36		35	9	26	149	4.3	2							
Roger Grove	31-34	52	26	10	38	120	4.6	2	3						
	35		0	0	.	0	.	0	0						
Ace Gutowsky	32-34	12	23	11	48	140	6.1	1	3	19	3	1	13	0	1
	35-39		38	12	32	192	5.1	3	6						
Joe Guyon	20-25,27	19	60	19	32	300	5.0	1	7	22	12	9	242	1	2
Jack Hagerty	26-30,32	26	32	15	47	212	6.6	1	2	37	11	9	169	2	1
Hinkey Haines	25-2931	19	17	6	35	74	4.4	1	6	33	13	9	118	0	3
Tex Hamer	24-27	19	66	26	39	302	4.6	2	7	36	54	28	559	3	15
Swede Hanson	31-34	12	28	6	21	82	2.9	0	6	22	4	1	15		2
	35-38		18	1	6	23	1.3	0	3						
Ken Harris	23	2	24	6	25	81	3.4	0	4	4	3	4	90	2	1
Johnny Heimsch	26	3	33	10	30	119	3.6	0	9	6	2	2	28	0	0
Dutch Hendrian	23-25	19	13	7	54	66	5.1	0	1	12	7	4	89	0	2
Pete Henry	20-23,25-28	51	22	6	27	97	4.4	1	6	29	8	5	90	0	3
Arnie Herber	30-34	49	389	150	39	2634	6.8	23	32	1	2	2	40	1	0
	35-4044-45		832	352	42	5939	7.1	58	65						
Cowboy Hill	23-26	8	31	13	42	159	5.1	0	6	25	15	10	182	0	3
Clarke Hinkle	32-34	38	49	18	37	225	4.6	0	6						
	35-41		7	4	57	59	8.4	0	0						
Paul Hogan	24-27	6	20	7	35	111	5.6	2	5	20	8	4	62	1	2
Tony Holm	30-33	28	66	18	27	440	6.7	2	16	6	2	2	25	0	0
Walt Holmer	29-33	18	76	22	29	346	4.6	3	18	37	20	12	384	4	4
Tommy Hughitt	20-24	10	41	13	32	149	3.6	1	9	41	37	24	398	4	7
Herb Joesting	29-32	20	39	13	33	156	4.0	2	4	22	5	3	70	0	1
Ben Jones	23-28	27	27	9	33	142	5.3	0	4	32	3	2	31	0	1
Ave Kaplan	23	4	40	11	28	152	3.8	0	12	4	3	3	68	2	0
Eddie Kaw	24									11	14	12	213	4	2
Wild Bill Kelly	27-30	23	191	66	35	1143	6.0	8	22	29	61	42	925	15	5
Jim Kendrick	22-27	17	139	32	23	546	3.9	3	9	30	41	24	625	3	10
Rip King	20-25	18	151	56	37	859	5.7	5	11	23	28	14	276	3	7
Frank Kirkleski	27, 29-31	22	171	63	37	950	5.6	4	19	17	18	11	245	3	5
Eddie Kotal	25-29	46	87	39	45	481	5.5	2	7						
Roddy Lamb	25-27,33	14	38	17	45	247	6.5	3	3	18	1	1	25	0	0
Curly Lambeau	21-29	70	682	270	40	4285	6.3	23	76	7	18	8	208	1	2
Tony Latone	25-30	48	20	10	50	89	4.5	1	1	17	2	1	10	0	0
Verne Lewellen	24-32	101	329	118	36	2003	6.1	8	42	4	6	4	77	1	2
Joe Lillard	32-33	10	63	20	32	308	4.9	1	9	8	3	1	12	0	1
Father Lumpkin	30-34	41	40	10	25	133	3.3	3	9	20	0	0	0	0	0
	35-37		0	0	-	0	-	0	0						
Ike Mahoney	25-28,31	12	17	8	47	90	5.3	0	4	21	7	7	145	1	0
Al Mahrt	20-22	10	135	53	39	836	6.2	4	11	13	29	18	395	6	4
Lou Mahrt	26-27	2	36	17	47	177	4.9	1	6	6	7	5	111	1	1
Charlie Mathys	21-26	40	43	20	47	329	7.7	10	5	12	4	2	35	0	0
Jack McBride	25-34	42	268	117	44	1546	5.8	12	35	62	114	81	1595	19	20
Ken Mercer	27-29	32	278	102	37	1315	4.7	9	36	12	49	25	450	3	10
Al Michaels	23-25	5	56	23	41	371	6.6	2	9	23	43	30	572	1	6
Dave Mishel	27-31	7	43	20	47	237	5.5	1	3	3	0	0	0	0	0
Johnny Mohardt	22-25	15	40	10	25	119	3.0	2	9	27	17	11	224	2	1
Bo Molenda	27-34	59	71	26	37	472	6.6	5	9	27	4	2	23	1	1
	35		0	0	-	0	-	0	0						
Keith Molesworth	31-34	44	148	57	39	1183	8.0	12	15	7	1	1	45	1	0
	35-37		73	29	40	458	6.3	6							
Hap Moran	26-33	49	140	53	38	760	5.4	6	16	49	26	14	300	1	8
Dick Moynihan	27	5	25	13	52	161	6.4	0	2	4	2	1	10	0	0
Jim Musick	32-33	11	47	11	23	207	4.4	0	14	11	3	3	56	0	0
	35-36		2	1	50	9	4.5	0							
Bronko Nagurski	30-34	33	30	14	47	141	4.7	3	4	30	10	9	222	2	0
	35-37,43		10	2	20	43	4.3	2	2						
Frank Nesser	20-22,25-26	6	20	3	15	57	2.9	0	1	29	38	24	553	4	10
Ernie Nevers	26-27,29-31	33	518	219	42	3185	6.1	14	51	21	55	38	827	11	10
Ray Novotny	30-32	10	24	10	42	165	6.9	1	3	11	7	5	74	0	1
Mally Nydahl	29-31	13	31	5	16	55	1.8	0	8	14	12	6	93	0	5
Curly Oden	25-28,30-32	30	44	17	39	209	4.8	0	6	36	50	26	429	3	10
Elmer Oliphant	20-21	2	9	2	22	24	2.7	0	0	9	13	10	168	7	0
Chuck Palmer	24,26	2	28	7	25	78	2.8	0	5	5	1	1	25	0	0
Oran Pape	30-32	15	23	3	13	25	1.1	1	6	10	1	1	6	0	0
George Pease	29	5	16	4	25	47	2.9	0	1	5	7	6	118	2	1
Frosty Peters	30-32	11	78	19	24	218	2.8	0	9	11	17	14	205	2	0
Art Pharmer	30-31	7	28	7	25	74	2.6	1	7	8	3	1	15	0	0
Tony Plansky	28-29,32	9	11	4	36	74	6.7	0	0	15	10	7	125	2	0
Fritz Pollard	20-23,25-26	19	36	17	47	249	6.9	3	4	28	14	7	117	2	1
Lew Pope	31,33-34	6	17	6	35	83	4.9	0	4	20	8	4	47	0	1
Glenn Presnell	31-34	49	328	118	36	1951	5.9	14	35	1	2	0	0	0	1
	35-36		81	30	37	414	5.1	2							
Pid Purdy	26-27	17	72	24	33	427	5.9	1	2						
Neil Rengel	30	7	63	23	37	304	4.8	0	10	4	1	1	40	1	0
Harry Robb	21-23,25-26	25	20	7	35	53	2.7	0	4	21	11	6	104	0	2
Wooky Roberts	22-26	18	25	6	24	125	5.0	1	7	18	7	5	114	2	1
Doug Roby	23	2	23	4	17	49	2.1	0	4	5	5	5	91	3	0
Kelly Rodriguez	30	10	42	13	31	110	2.6	1	9	5	0	0	0	0	0
Milt Romney	23-28	27	29	11	38	140	4.8	1	2	45	4	4	91	0	0
Cobb Rooney	24-30	30	22	6	27	55	2.5	1	1	24	8	4	45	1	1
George Roudebush	20-21	7	15	6	40	73	4.9	0	3	10	7	6	94	3	0
Norb Sacksteder	20-22,25	15	26	8	31	139	5.3	1	4	12	1	1	12	0	0
Russ Saunders	31	9	30	7	23	109	3.6	1	5						
Eddie Scharer	26-28	19	53	18	34	230	4.3	0	10	11	14	13	220	6	0
Shag Sheard	23-25	5	20	4	20	79	4.0	0	5	13	14	10	148	1	1
Deck Shelley	31-32	10	92	30	33	555	6.0	3	13	4	4	2	31	0	1
Eber Simpson	23	4	32	12	38	156	4.9	1	8	3	19	8	145	0	4
Red Smith	27-31	19	27	11	41	107	4.0	0	5	17	10	6	134	1	3
Lou Smyth	20-26	29	195	58	30	1164	6.0	9	29	23	50	25	515	3	7
Joey Sternaman	22-25,27-30	34	73	23	32	330	4.5	3	15	68	37	20	530	7	4
Hust Stockton	25-26,28-29	25	198	79	40	1397	7.1	7	30	28	74	39	1009	8	19
Ken Strong	29-34	59	190	65	34	856	4.5	5	23	12	6	5	169	2	1
	35, 39, 44-47		3	0	0	0	0.0	0	0						
Jim Thorpe	20-26, 28	14	70	28	40	425	6.1	1	9	33	39	24	448	3	6
Dick Vick	24-26	3	34	13	38	208	6.1	1	5	26	53	35	663	8	10
Laurie Walquist	22, 24-31	40	109	33	30	397	3.6	1	17	71	50	33	574	5	7
Rat Watson	22-25,27	5	40	9	23	110	2.8	0	12	15	14	13	243	2	0
Chuck Weimer	29-31	9	6	2	33	41	6.8	0	2	18	13	8	187	3	4
Gibby Welch	28-29	11	37	13	35	234	6.3	1	7	14	7	4	94	0	1
Cy Wentworth	25-26,29	6	13	4	31	52	4.0	1	3	20	21	7	145	0	5
Phil White	25, 27	9	42	12	29	239	5.7	1	4	14	10	10	162	1	0
Ossie Wiberg	27-28,30,32-33	26	25	10	40	209	8.4	2	3	18	3	2	32	0	1
Wildcat Wilson	27-29	23	252	106	42	1674	6.6	9	29	14	46	24	528	3	11
Sonny Winters	23-24	3	27	10	37	108	4.0	0	5	15	71	52	1197	13	10
Hoge Workman	24, 31-32	6	41	13	32	104	2.5	0	4	13	32	19	520	9	7
Ab Wright	30	3	32	10	31	121	3.8	1	5	1	0	0	0	0	0
Doug Wycoff	27,29-32,34	43	213	65	31	987	4.6	6	25	25	15	5	143	2	5
Arnie Wyman	20	6	30	9	30	123	4.1	2	5						

The figure (35) in parentheses indicates that no 1935 passing data are available for that player.

		Complete Games					Inc. Games			
Name	Years	G	Att	Yds	Avg	TD	G	Att	Yds	TD
Fay Abbott	21-29	12	37	63	1.7	1	45	12	45	0
Walter Achui	27-28	3	23	5	0.2	0	8	4	22	0
Gene Alford	31-34	29	81	259	3.2	1	9	2	11	0
Ockie Anderson	20-22	4	32	56	1.8	0	20	35	328	7
Dunc Annan	20,22-26	9	52	96	1.8	1	31	25	163	3
Bob Argus	20-25	6	41	47	1.1	0	20	15	35	1
Johnny Armstrong	23-25	21	117	357	3.1	3	7	7	53	0
Frank Bacon	20-25	8	64	253	4.0	2	38	23	226	7
Herm Bagby	26-27	3	20	54	2.7	0	10	6	45	0
Bullet Baker	27-31	30	105	171	1.6	0	20	5	27	1
Shorty Barr	23-26	15	73	162	2.2	1	11	5	32	0
Norm Barry	21	5	24	31	1.4	0	3	5	31	1
Myrt Basing	23-27	41	335	916	2.7	7				
Cliff Battles	32-34	32	397	1824	4.6	13				
	35-37		476	1789	3.8	11				
Bunny Belden	27, 30-31	11	51	245	4.8	2	15	6	37	1
Heinie Benkert	25-26,29-30	13	87	291	3.3	0	19	17	131	0
Chuck Bennett	30-31,33	14	140	744	5.3	5	3	1	0	0
Johnny Blood	25-34	80	433	1354	3.1	4	22	9	90	1
	35-39		85	202	2.4	0				
Al Bloodgood	25-28,30	8	20	72	3.6	0	27	18	194	6
Champ Boettcher	26	4	26	63	2.4	0				
George Bolan	21-23	10	66	168	2.5	0	16	6	30	2
Benny Boynton	21-22,24	1	9	3	0.3	0	15	23	230	5
Wayne Brenkert	23-24	1	0	0	-	0	14	16	158	5
Frank Briante	29-30	10	69	148	2.1	1	3	3	37	0
Lane Bridgeford	21-22	8	52	197	3.8	0				
Earl Britton	25-29	14	47	97	2.1	0	17	0	0	0
Jesse Brown	26	14	119	298	2.5	0				
Doc Bruder	25-26	7	29	107	3.7		17	40	319	3
Hank Bruder	31-34	49	267	901	3.4	7				
	35-40		65	213	3.3	1				
Carl Brumbaugh	30-34	49	137	308	2.4	1	16	10	36	1
	36-38		25	-19	-0.8	1				
Justin Brumbaugh	31	3	36	155	4.3	0	5	1	0	0
Johnny Bryan	22-27	21	113	343	3.0	3	37	20	159	4
Ted Bucklin	27,31	6	27	25	0.9	0	8	1	1	1
Dale Burnett	30-34	41	81	194	2.4	0	24	22	182	5
	35-39		24	20	0.8	0				
Sol Butler	23-26	5	22	57	2.6	0	19	9	35	2
Chris Cagle	30-34	14	104	265	2.6	0	34	23	168	2
Pete Calac	20-26	9	75	155	2.1	1	55	72	390	10
Bruce Caldwell	28	6	30	56	1.9	0	4	4	37	1
Bob Campiglio	32-33	10	93	366	3.9	2	6	3	18	0
Harlan Carr	27	6	43	113	2.6	1	4	5	3	1
Mike Casteel	22	5	27	210	7.8	1	1	0	0	0
John Cavosie	31-33	26	148	467	3.2	3	7	1	6	0
Guy Chamberlin	20-27	32	23	167	7.3	2	57	5	32	1
Fred Chicken	20	5	73	227	3.1	3				
Stu Clancy (35)	30-34	40	157	536	3.4	4	4	12	97	0
Dutch Clark	31-32,34	34	360	1739	4.8	20				
	35-38		346	1533	4.4	16				
Jimmy Conzelman	20-29	35	240	940	3.9	10	66	32	147	4
George Corbett (35)	32-34	18	81	283	3.5	0	8	3	9	0
	36-38		20	74	3.7	0				
Clyde Crabtree	30	10	39	149	3.8	1	5	2	15	0
Carl Cramer	20-26	10	80	244	3.1	3	45	50	270	8
Jack Crangle	23	3	29	79	2.7	1	6	3	8	2
Bill Cronin	27-29	10	22	56	2.5	0	18	11	17	0
Jack Cronin	27-30	15	77	237	3.1	3	27	14	55	1
Harry Dayhoff	24-25	3	9	18	2.0	0	9	13	105	2
Rufe DeWitz	24,26	5	45	155	3.4	0	12	2	78	1
Wally Diehl	28-30	24	253	1011	4.0	9	14	11	116	0
Dinger Doane	20-27	13	94	175	1.9	2	52	66	314	12
Dick Dobeleit	25-26	3	23	31	1.3	0	9	4	61	0
John Doehring	32-34	13	24	100	4.2	0	4	4	7	1
	35-37		30	128	4.3	0				
Charlie Dressen	20,22-23	7	46	193	4.2	1	2	4	50	1
Paddy Driscoll	20-29	29	290	803	2.8	2	86	114	1484	25
Red Dunn	24-31	62	166	471	2.8	0	30	18	124	5
Eagle Feather	22-23	2	18	108	6.0	1	15	0	0	0
Ox Eckhardt	28	3	18	47	2.4	0	8	6	79	2
Bud Edwards	30-31	4	22	62	2.8	0	15	4	31	0
Chief Elkins	28-29,33	15	67	199	3.0	0	5	6	28	0
Al Elliott	22-24	17	131	463	3.5	1	11	25	221	2
Doc Elliott	22-25,31	13	128	399	3.1	6	26	52	285	11
Wuert Engelmann	30-33	45	129	558	4.3	1	1	1	33	1
Rex Enright	26-27	18	159	423	2.7	3	1	0	0	0
Hal Erickson	23-30	19	144	353	2.5	2	49	33	199	1
Jack Ernst	25-30	53	113	308	2.7	2	11	2	7	0
Guil Falcon	20-25	9	104	290	2.8	1	33	24	112	4
Tiny Feather	27-34	34	87	178	2.0	1	51	28	105	6
Bernie Finn	30,32	7	23	63	2.7	0	11	2	12	0
Paul Fitzgibbon	26-28,30-32	39	99	309	3.1	2	16	4	33	0
Bob Fitzke	25	6	51	95	1.9	1	10	14	94	0
Hoot Flanagan	25-26	17	177	599	3.4	3	1	8	30	2
Mack Flenniken	30-31	6	24	62	2.6	0	8	10	45	4
Jim Foley	26						9	25	135	0
Beryl Follet	30-31	10	45	105	2.3	0	2	1	14	0
Art Folz	23-25	1	3	16	5.3	0	17	10	163	4
Bob Foster	22-24	13	26	89	3.4	1	8	10	90	2
Walt French	22,25	9	59	319	5.4	3	1	2	30	0
Benny Friedman	27-34	23	252	1068	4.2	6	57	128	1061	12
Buck Gavin	20-26	29	296	925	3.1	5	18	44	213	8
Bill Giaver	22-26	13	80	224	2.8	4	15	19	16	0
Wally Gilbert	23-26	4	17	55	3.2	0	13	9	53	1
Hank Gillo	20-26	24	257	975	3.8	6	17	67	339	4
Bill Glassgow	30-31	15	107	472	4.4	3	6	4	37	0
Royce Goodbread	30-31	8	22	44	2.0	0	10	5	43	0
Red Grange	25,27,29-34	78	546	2306	4.2	17	19	44	310	4
Tex Grigg	20-27	18	108	447	4.1	1	33	33	279	3
Hal Griggs	26						5	9	134	2
Jack Grossman	32,34	5	59	249	4.2	1	18	11	101	1
	35-36		67	208	3.1	2				
Roger Grove (35)	31-34	52	75	283	3.8	1				
Ace Gutowsky	32-34	30	333	1243	3.7	9	1	4	15	0
	35-39		608	2129	3.5	11				
Joe Guyon	20-25,27	13	114	367	3.2	2	28	27	226	5
Al Hadden	25-30	19	112	195	1.7	1	43	25	81	0
Jack Hagerty	26-30,32	15	43	151	3.5	1	48	29	270	3
Hinkey Haines	25-29,31	12	68	303	4.5	2	40	72	689	12
Eddie Halicki	20-30	21	164	534	3.3	3	10	11	55	3
Tex Hamer	24-27	17	176	576	3.3	6	38	164	1066	13
Swedie Hanson	31-34	28	346	1519	4.4	11	6	0	0	0
	35-38		229	677	3.0	2				
Jack Harris	25-26	21	102	213	2.1	3				
Les Haws	24-25	6	51	310	6.1	0	19	48	384	4
Johnny Heimsch	26	3	43	110	2.6	0	6	2	32	2
Dutch Hendrian	23-25	18	146	372	2.5	4	14	8	39	0
Pete Henry	20-23,25-28	37	25	112	4.5	0	43	10	53	0
Arnie Herber	30-34	49	196	546	2.8	2	1	0	0	0
	35-40,44-45		87	-143	-1.6	1				
Charlie Hill	24-26	8	38	186	4.9	2	17	8	64	2
Cowboy Hill	23-26	9	73	215	2.9	0	24	30	153	6
Irv Hill	31-33	8	27	50	1.9	1	9	9	77	2
Clarke Hinkle	32-34	38	400	1254	3.2	7				
	35-41		792	2742	3.5	27				
Grassy Hinton	32	11	23	53	2.3	0	1	2	7	1
Ben Hobson	26-27	3	29	55	1.9	0	11	13	55	1
Paul Hogan	24-27	4	10	20	2.0	1	22	16	58	0
Tony Holm	30-32	19	116	343	3.0	1	15	5	5	0
Walt Holmer	29-33	17	74	172	2.3	0	38	28	185	4
Two Bits Homan	25-30	49	50	155	3.1	0	32	20	79	2
Arnie Horween	21-24	3	15	27	1.8	0	29	10	62	4
Dick Hudson	23,25-26	3	45	99	2.2	0	5	0	0	0
Ken Huffine	20-25	12	62	150	2.4	1	30	24	21	4
Tommy Hughitt	20-24	5	28	40	1.4	0	46	85	377	5
Tut Imlay	26-27	3	23	113	4.9	0	14	14	153	3
Herb Joesting	29-32	22	214	932	4.4	4	20	34	188	3
Jerry Johnson	21-22	9	81	210	2.6	1				
Ben Jones	23-28	20	129	408	3.2	9	39	104	386	12
Ave Kaplan	23	4	35	31	0.9	0	4	2	32	0
Bull Karcis	32-34	4	13	45	3.5	1	26	14	63	0
	35-39,43		417	1301	3.1	10				
Jack Keefer	26, 28	3	30	88	2.9	1	11	6	102	1
Doc Kelley	24-26	6	20	49	2.5	0	7	12	46	0
Bill Kellogg	24-25	1	21	51	2.4	1	8	13	37	3
Shipwreck Kelly	32-34	3	39	152	3.9	0	21	23	120	3
	37		16	29	1.8	0				
Wild Bill Kelly	26-30	20	78	241	3.1	2	32	16	128	4
Jim Kendrick	22-27	9	28	56	2.0	0	38	31	80	3
Graham Kernwein	26	5	34	73	2.1	0				
Dick King	21-23	5	43	131	3.0	0	14	13	78	0
Rip King	20-25	14	101	208	2.1	3	27	13	58	2
Frank Kirkleski	27,29-31	21	202	457	2.3	1	18	13	65	1
Dutch Kitzmiller	31	6	49	114	2.3	1	8	14	48	3
Oscar Knop	20-27	22	116	291	2.5	0	58	34	151	4
Bob Koehler	20-26	18	143	286	2.0	1	50	36	226	9
Walt Koppisch	25-26	2	12	0	0.0	0	12	21	175	0
Eddie Kotal	25-29	45	318	879	2.8	4	1	0	0	0
Waddy Kuehl	20-24	20	138	341	2.5	4	16	15	70	3
John Kyle	23	2	23	87	3.8	1	5	9	30	0
Jim Laird	20-22,25-28,31	25	85	193	2.3	1	45	66	313	10
Roddy Lamb	25-27,33	14	153	608	4.0	2	19	10	108	2
Curly Lambeau	21-29	69	534	1658	3.1	4	8	15	104	4
Irv Langhoff	22-23	10	78	297	3.8	0	5	14	87	1
Ralph Lanum	20-24	15	68	161	2.4	1	29	8	45	1
Tony Latone	25-30	49	669	2362	3.5	15	16	75	286	11
Dutch Lauer	22-23,25-26	8	75	178	2.4	4	19	10	14	0
Doc Ledbetter	32-33	7	30	77	2.6	2	10	4	-1	0
Verne Lewellen	24-32	100	700	2380	3.4	36	5	8	30	1
Tiny Lewis	30-31	12	37	214	5,8	2	1	0	0	0
Cully Lidberg	26,29-30	26	211	516	2.4	7				
Joe Lillard	32-33	8	85	246	2.9	0	10	10	59	1
Joe Lintzenich	30-31	16	92	367	4.0	0	8	7	80	0
Father Lumpkin (35)	30-34	42	216	785	3.6	4	21	9	76	2
	36-37		11	29	2.6	0				
Ike Mahoney	25-28,31	12	37	110	3.0	0	21	9	89	1
Armin Mahrt	24-26	6	32	108	3.4	1	15	10	121	1
Grover Malone	20-21,23	10	47	42	0.9	0	7	3	9	0
Jerry Mansfield	20-21	7	25	62	2.5	0				
Dutch Marion	25-26	3	18	44	2.4	0	19	20	67	4
Larry Marks	27-28	13	64	187	2.9	0	11	0	0	0
Ike Martin	20	3	23	60	2.6	1	2	10	40	0
Charlie Mathys	21-26	40	34	69	2.0	1	12	3	15	0
Tuffy Maul	26	1	11	29	2.6	0	9	23	75	2
Jack McAuliffe	26	8	42	66	1.6	0				
Jack McBride	25-34	42	374	1182	3.2	7	62	134	911	19
Frank McCormick	20-21	6	62	142	2.3	0	6	15	71	4
Hurdis McCrary	29-33	41	282	1033	3.7	7	1	0	0	0
Mickey McDonnell	23,25-31	18	122	316	2.6	1	38	18	223	0
Wally McIlwain	26	5	29	33	1.1	0				
Al McIntosh	25-26	4	7	5	0.7	0	7	28	114	0
Chief McLain	30-31	23	153	574	3.8	4	1	0	0	0
Butch Meeker	30-31	8	23	103	4.5	0	13	8	18	0
Ken Mercer	27-29	30	220	746	3.4	5	14	16	103	3
Russ Method	23-27,29	17	65	106	1.6	0	28	13	71	1
Al Michaels	23-25	4	33	77	2.3	0	24	17	111	1
Al Miller	29	1	15	66	4.4	0	6	7	40	0
Bob Millman	25-27	12	95	242	2.5	0				
Stan Mills	22-24	10	95	175	1.8	1	12	0	0	0
Johnny Mohardt	22-25	15	115	310	2.7	0	27	31	166	0
Bo Molenda (35)	27-34	79	598	1896	3.2	11	20	7	29	1
Keith Molesworth	31-34	42	192	570	3.0	3	9	10	55	1
	35-37		139	614	4.4	5				
Dinty Moore	27	7	30	60	2.0	1				
Hap Moran	26-33	48	296	859	2.9	2	50	47	403	11
Jim Musick	32-33	22	250	1152	4.6	6				
	35-36		66	188	2.8	2				
Bronko Nagurski	30-34	55	490	2260	4.6	14	8	12	77	5
	35-37,43		248	1093	4.4	6				
Fanny Neihaus	25-26	5	27	84	3.1	0				
Dick Nesbitt	30-34	23	143	621	4.3	2	31	34	198	3
Frank Nesser	20-22,25-26	5	19	45	2.4	0	30	10	64	1
Ernie Nevers	26-27,29-31	22	385	1292	3.4	10	32	117	635	28
Sid Nichols	20-21	13	67	346	5.2	2				
Dave Noble	24-25	3	32	88	2.8	0	19	20	200	7
Will Norman	28	9	35	59	1.7	0	1	0	0	0
Marty Norton	22,24-25	11	96	252	2.6	1	8	9	132	4
Eddie Novak	20-22,24-25	25	233	730	3.1	1	5	0	0	0
Ray Novotny	30-32	18	47	208	4.4	1	13	0	0	0
Mally Nydahl	29-31	12	78	289	3.7	2	15	26	292	2
Harry O'Boyle	28,32-33	24	93	283	3.0	1	2	0	0	0
Curly Oden	25-28,30-32	23	68	349	5.1	3	43	40	338	5
Arnie Oehlrich	28-29	22	66	150	2.3	0	11	2	10	0
Elmer Oliphant	20-21	1	8	27	3.4	0	10	14	140	1
Lou Pahl	23-24	5	30	67	2.2	1	6	4	24	0
Oran Pape	30-32	13	72	278	3.9	2	12	14	194	1
Doc Parkinson	31	11	93	275	3.0	0				
Lou Partlow	20-27,29	11	70	181	2.6	0	39	51	312	6
Pard Pearce	20-22,24-25	12	36	126	3.5	2	25	4	25	1
Frosty Peters	30-32	12	25	53	2.1	0	10	4	18	0
Art Pharmer	30-31	7	63	237	3.8	0	8	1	2	0
Bob Phelan	22-24	10	64	207	3.2	0	11	4	4	2
Ernie Pinckert (35)	32-34	5	26	87	3.3	0	27	11	43	1
	36-40		28	114	4.1	0				
Tony Plansky	28-29,32	5	25	89	3.6	2	19	17	161	7
Fritz Pollard	20-23,25-26	15	139	320	2.3	3	32	58	394	10
Lew Pope	31,33-34	4	19	25	1.3	0	22	6	123	1
Glenn Presnell	31-34	49	446	1696	3.8	17	1	2	16	0
	35-36		120	407	3.6	1				
Bill Pritchard	27-28	6	34	85	2.5	0	19	22	104	1
Pid Purdy	26-27	16	33	69	2.1	1	1	0	0	0
Bob Rapp	22-26,29	8	46	157	3.4	0	35	25	350	4
Charlie Reichow	25-26	6	60	129	2.2	0	1	0	0	0
Neil Rengel	30	5	27	47	1.7	0	6	1	6	0
Harry Robb	21-23,25-26	14	115	486	4.2	3	32	55	339	3
Jack Roberts	32-34	9	41	140	3.4	0	15	3	22	1
Wooky Roberts	22-26	12	49	135	2.8	1	24	14	98	2
Doug Roby	23	2	19	22	1.2	0	5	8	9	0
Ben Roderick	23,26-27	2	13	1	0.1	0	20	30	154	0
Kelly Rodriguez	30	8	38	92	2.4	0	7	4	18	0
Charley Rogers	27-29	26	215	896	4.2	3	12	3	64	0
Milt Romney	23-28	25	61	125	2.0	1	47	30	182	4
Bill Rooney	23-27,29	13	33	90	2.7	0	32	8	60	1
Cobb Rooney	24-30	19	70	200	2.9	0	35	19	203	2
Gene Rose	29-32	13	68	325	4.8	2	21	11	64	3
Norb Sacksteder	20-22,25	11	42	107	2.5	0	16	13	99	2
Eber Sampson	21-23	3	39	85	2.2	0	11	8	65	3
Ollie Sansen (35)	32-34	4	19	68	3.6	0	27	6	10	2
Russ Saunders	31	9	59	248	4.2	1				
Art Schmaehl	21	4	34	93	2.7	0	2	12	47	2
Elmer Schwartz	31-33	12	61	221	3.6	2	13	0	0	0
Len Sedbrook	28-31	13	26	104	4.0	2	38	34	479	10
Bill Senn	26-31,33-34	25	152	394	2.6	3	55	50	678	13
Ed Shaw	20,22-23	15	43	135	3.1	2	7	9	26	2
Paul Sheeks	21-22	6	16	94	5.9	0	15	6	10	0
Shag Sheard	23-25	4	26	27	1.0	0	14	17	203	0
Deck Shelley	31-32	8	53	137	2.6	0	6	11	76	0
Orville Siegfried	23	3	24	38	1.6	0	4	4	32	0
Jim Simmons	27-28	7	40	121	3.0	0	13	13	58	5
Johnny Sisk	32-34	27	103	403	3.9	2	7	2	53	0
	35-36		79	385	4.9	1				
Howie Slater	26	3	33	72	2.2	0	6	1	9	0
Pat Smith	20-21,23	2	11	17	1.5	0	16	47	202	7
Red Smith	27-31	17	41	181	4.4	0	19	16	112	3
Lou Smyth	20-26	20	123	378	3.1	8	32	72	323	5
Snitz Snyder	29-30	11	50	132	2.6	0	12	3	9	2
Gus Sonnenberg	23,25-28,30	18	11	70	6.4	0	42	11	172	1
Dutch Sternaman	20-27	30	212	814	3.8	2	59	61	380	13
Joey Sternaman	22-25,27-30	31	152	415	2.7	4	71	75	573	17
Pete Stinchcomb	21-23,26	8	54	265	4.9	2	26	12	158	5
Hust Stockton	25-26,28-29	20	138	494	3.6	3	33	68	338	3
Jack Storer	24	2	21	86	4.1	2	12	32	232	5
Dutch Strauss	23-24	5	31	58	1.9	1	8	1	9	0
Ken Strong	29-34	68	612	2376	3.8	21	3	6	101	1
	35,39,44-47		49	150	3.1	1				
George Sullivan	24-25	8	34	146	4.3	1	14	46	342	6
Jim Tays	25,27,30	6	28	35	1.3	0	14	6	2	0
Rex Thomas	26-28,30-31	9	50	194	3.9	0	38	25	262	5
Stumpy Thomason (35)	30-34	12	87	253	2.9	0	34	13	102	3
	36		109	333	3.1	0				
Jim Thorpe	20-26,28	11	52	148	2.8	0	36	54	357	6
Eddie Tryon	27	2	15	38	2.5	0	12	16	97	2
Buddy Tynes	24-25	1	1	0	0.0	0	16	29	128	2
Rube Ursella	20-21,24-26,29	25	96	231	2.4	1	20	9	53	0
Eddie Usher	21-22,24	9	57	180	3.2	2	9	1	2	0
Joe Vance	31	6	26	82	3.1	2	5	0	0	0
Otto Vokaty	31-34	8	55	216	3.9	1	11	8	46	3
Carl Waite	28-30	13	48	130	2.7	0	14	13	48	1
Laurie Walquist	22,24-31	39	213	570	2.7	2	72	53	380	8
Rat Watson	22-25,27	5	34	148	4.4	0	15	11	105	1
Charlie Way	21,24	5	30	97	3.2	1	14	29	387	3
Chuck Weimer	29-31	7	37	150	4.1	0	20	9	44	1
Gibby Welch	28-29	6	59	167	2.8	0	19	25	313	3
Cy Wentworth	25-26,29	6	40	116	2.9	1	20	42	240	1
Barney Wentz	25-28	39	500	1700	3.4	16	1	8	28	1
Buck White	25,27-29	14	101	263	2.6	0	32	36	170	10
Phil White	25,27	5	19	51	2.7	1	18	16	69	5
Ossie Wiberg	27-28,30,32-33	10	40	79	2.0	0	34	13	44	5
Ned Wilcox	26-27	12	69	241	3.5	2	14	14	104	0
Pop Williams	28-32	10	59	215	3.6	1	29	60	251	10
Mike Wilson	29	12	59	197	3.3	0	6	0	0	0
Mule Wilson	26-33	40	149	551	3.7	4	44	38	258	4
Wildcat Wilson	27-29	15	157	657	4.2	7	22	72	414	3
Ben Winkelman	22-24	7	34	67	2.0	2	20	1	1	0
Lee Woodruff	31-33	7	21	71	3.4	2	19	17	65	3
Doug Wycoff	27,29-32,34	40	414	1186	2.9	8	27	35	205	3
Arnie Wyman	20	6	43	194	4.5	1				
Elmer Wynne	28-29	6	30	44	1.5	0	9	0	0	0
Izzy Yablok	30-31	14	64	193	3.0	0	6	3	7	0

Lifetime Statistics — 1920-1932 Players Section 6 — RECEIVING
(All men with 10 or more receptions)

Name	Years	Complete Games					Inc. Games			
		G	Rec	Yds	Avg	TD	G	Rec	Yds	TD
Gene Alford	31-34	32	18	222	12.3	1	6	1	64	1
Neely Allison	26-28	7	3	32	10.7	0	17	8	125	1
Eddie Anderson	22-25	11	11	194	17.6	1	32	5	120	1
Dunc Annan	20,22-26	11	4	36	9.0	0	29	7	137	2
Johnny Armstrong	23-25	21	11	153	13.9	3	7	2	35	0
Carl Bacchus	27-28	3	1	22	22.0	0	16	13	370	7
Frank Bacon	20-25	11	14	167	11.9	0	35	9	136	2
Red Badgro (35)	27-28,30-34	40	40	656	16.4	4	33	8	128	2
	36		3	59	19.7	0				
Bullet Baker	27-31	30	11	82	7.5	0	20	3	56	0
Myrt Basing	23-27	41	17	280	16.5	2				
Cliff Battles	32-34	32	20	350	17.5	1				
	35-37		17	206	12.1	2				
Bunny Belden	27,30-31	11	7	65	9.3	1	15	5	115	1
Charlie Berry	25-26	19	60	679	11.3	6	1	2	15	0
Scotty Bierce	20-25	18	11	137	12.5	0	33	16	350	5
Johnny Blood	25-34	79	123	2224	18.2	26	23	11	205	2
	35-39		44	724	16.5	9				
Al Bloodgood	25-28,30	12	6	105	17.5	1	23	7	165	1
Lynn Bomar	25-26	2	7	102	14.6	0	17	20	351	5
Benny Boynton	21-22,24	1					15	12	184	3
Hank Bruder (35)	31-34	49	22	463	21.0	5				
	36-40		14	153	10.9	1				
Carl Brumbaugh	30-34	35	13	284	21.8	2	30	2	35	0
	36-38		6	62	10.3	2				
Johnny Bryan	22-27	21	13	165	12.7	1	37	1	8	1
Frank Bucher	25-26	22	20	269	13.5	2	1	0	0	0
Dale Burnett	30-34	42	36	588	16.3	7	23	9	169	4
	35-39		59	797	13.5	11				
Chris Cagle	30-34	14	9	105	11.7	1	34	7	151	1
Pete Calac	20-26	14	4	81	20.3	0	50	11	201	0
Glen Campbell (35)	29-33	29	19	286	15.1	1	40	20	401	5
Bird Carroll	21-23,25	26	21	331	15.8	3	8	2	36	1
Guy Chamberlin	20-27	39	30	779	26.0	3	50	18	422	5
Algy Clark	30-34	15	7	64	9.1	0	33	6	115	1
Dutch Clark	31-32,34	34	29	363	12.5	3				
	35-38		12	162	13.5	0				
Jimmy Conzelman	20-29	43	58	688	11.9	2	58	36	691	9
George Corbett	32-34	14	5	25	5.0	0	11	5	114	1
	35-38		6	84	14.0	1				
Chuck Corgan	24-27	11	22	475	21.6	3	19	14	297	0
Clyde Crabtree	30	8	9	81	9.0	0	7	1	40	1
Carl Cramer	20-26	12	6	99	16.5	0	43	6	117	1
Milan Creighton	31-34	16	14	218	15.6	1	24	11	210	1
	36-37		0	0	-	0				
Rae Crowther	25-26	10	13	166	12.8	0	23	10	240	3
Red Daum	22-26	5	6	139	23.2	1	32	7	157	1
Wally Diehl	28-30	26	9	105	11.7	0	12	1	10	1
Lavie Dilweg	26-34	100	119	1903	16.0	11	7	7	150	1
Paddy Driscoll	20-29	32	20	307	15.4	1	83	14	312	3
Red Dunn	24-31	63	48	581	12.1	1	29	2	37	0
Harry Ebding	31-34	45	38	728	19.2	3	5	4	58	0
	35-37		23	411	17.9	5				
Al Elliott	22-24	17	21	241	11.5	2	11	3	7	0
Wuert Engelmann	30-33	45	17	433	25.5	5	1	1	16	0
Hal Erickson	20-00	10	15	120	8.2	0	40	26	532	8
Jack Ernst	25-30	54	42	620	14.8	4	10	2	40	0
Tiny Feather	27-34	36	22	326	14.8	1	50	16	357	2
Lee Fenner	20-27,29-30	18	10	133	13.3	0	41	5	97	1
Paul Fitzgibbon	26-28,30-32	37	12	171	14.3	1	18	2	43	1
Dick Flaherty	26	12	11	270	24.5	2				
Ray Flaherty (35)	27-29,31-34	48	53	968	18.3	5	42	36	838	15
Milt Gantenbein	31-34	45	26	461	17.7	2				
	35-40		59	936	15.9	6				
Bill Giaver	22-26	12	20	216	10.8	0	16	1	10	0
Paul Goebel	23-25	4	4	57	14.3	0	22	22	324	3
Gardie Grange	29-31	14	6	81	13.5	0	24	5	162	3
Red Grange	25,27,29-34	61	38	570	15.0	6	36	14	250	4
Tex Grigg	20-27	26	8	137	17.1	1	25	3	42	0
Jack Grossman (35)	32,34	17	14	193	13.8	2	6	5	77	2
	36		0	0	-	0				
Roger Grove (35)	31-34	52	37	542	14.6	6				
Joe Guyon	20-25,27	15	9	174	19.3	0	26	7	140	1
Al Hadden	25-30	25	15	185	12.3	1	37	7	149	3
Jack Hagerty	26-30,32	19	17	280	16.5	2	44	14	302	5
Hinkey Haines	25-29,31	17	12	199	16.6	0	35	19	412	6
George Halas	20-28	37	24	404	16.8	6	64	15	267	2
Eddie Halicki	29-30	21	19	270	14.2	3	10	2	55	1
Dick Halladay	23-24	8	12	197	16.4	1	9	7	136	1
Tex Hamer	24-27	18	6	96	16.0	0	37	10	207	0
Duke Hanny	23-30	40	15	332	22.1	1	58	10	325	4
Swede Hanson (35)	31-34	15	12	139	11.6	2	19	7	118	0
	36-38		4	35	8.8	0				
Jack Harris	25-26	21	18	236	13.1	0				
Les Haws	24-25	7	3	81	27.0	1	18	8	148	0
Dave Hayes	21-22	7	11	146	13.3	1	9	0	0	0
Dutch Hendrian	23-25	19	21	222	10.6	0	12	4	89	2
Arnie Herber	30-34	49	5	74	14.8	1	1	0	0	0
	35-40,44-45		6	102	17.0	2				
Bill Hewitt	32-34	33	29	446	15.9	7	6	4	111	0
	35-39,43		71	1137	16.0	16				
Clarke Hinkle	32-34	38	15	167	11.1	1				
	35-41		32	394	12.3	8				
Two Bits Homan	25-30	50	31	657	21.2	5	31	8	209	2
Ken Huffine	20-25	11	6	45	7.5	0	31	4	63	0
Tommy Hughitt	20-24	10	16	171	10.7	1	40	6	63	1
Vivian Hultman	25-27	14	5	78	15.6	1	16	8	103	2
Tut Imlay	26-27	7	11	223	20.3	1	10	0	0	0
Luke Johnsos	29-34	48	63	926	14.7	13	27	10	205	2
	35-36		24	419	17.5	6				
Ben Jones	23-28	25	8	125	15.6	0	34	10	191	2
Red Joseph	27,30-31	14	8	79	9.9	1	7	3	38	0
Max Kadesky	23	8	12	121	10.1	0				
Bull Karcis	32-34	4	0	0	-	0	26	0	0	0
	35-39, 43		16	148	9.3	0				
Chuck Kassel	27-33	37	27	465	17.2	5	42	10	234	2
Shipwreck Kelly	32-34	12	25	266	10.6	3	11	0	0	0
	37		1	7	7.0	0				
Wild Bill Kelly	27-30	20	12	120	10.0	0	32	3	74	0
George Kennealy (35)	26-30,32-34	49	40	593	14.8	2	32	3	23	0
Frank Kirkleski	27,29-31	21	9	79	8.8	0	18	3	27	1
Oscar Knop	20-27	24	8	103	12.9	1	57	4	74	1
Tony Kostos	27-31	45	41	570	13.9	2	21	6	109	0
Eddie Kotal	25-29	45	74	1195	16.1	5	1	0	0	0
Waddy Kuehl	20-24	20	31	302	9.7	3	16	4	94	2
Roddy Lamb	25-27	14	14	155	11.1	1	18	2	59	0
Curly Lambeau	21-29	69	40	623	15.6	3	8	0	0	0
Tony Latone	25-30	49	15	231	15.4	0	16	4	31	0
Verne Lewellen	24-32	100	80	1182	14.8	12	5	4	83	0
Joe Lintzenich	30-31	10	5	86	17.2	1	14	5	100	1
Joe Little Twig	22-26	15	7	140	20.0	1	22	3	27	0
Bull Lowe	20-21,25-27	15	9	199	22.1	0	19	4	84	0
Father Lumpkin (35)	30-34	50	28	380	13.6	2	14	3	32	0
	36-37		6	34	5.7	0				
Bob Lundell	29-30	12	8	99	12.4	0	8	2	30	0
Ed Lynch	25-27,29	10	15	232	15.5	1	20	3	52	0
Ike Mahoney	25-28,31	10	5	69	13.8	0	23	6	118	1
Larry Marks	27-28	14	9	138	15.3	0	10	1	17	0
Hersh Martin	29-30	10	10	117	11.7	0	5	1	15	0
Charlie Mathys	21-26	40	87	1441	16.6	3	12	3	65	1
Hurdis McCrary	29-33	41	9	260	28.9	4	1	1	30	0
Mickey McDonnell	23,25-31	17	15	204	13.6	1	39	8	147	2
Frank McGrath	27-28	9	9	50	5.6	0	14	1	15	0
Bill McKalip	31-32,34	29	19	398	20.9	4	10	4	91	0
	36		1	10	10.0	0				
Russ Method	23-27,29	17	11	144	13.1	1	28	2	30	0
Buster Mitchell (35)	31-34	27	7	153	21.9	0	16	0	0	0
	36-37		10	125	12.5	1				
Johnny Mohardt	22-25	15	15	195	13.0	0	27	4	89	2
Louie Mohs	22-24	3	2	30	15.0	0	12	8	166	1
Bo Molenda (35)	27-34	69	13	222	17.1	1	30	5	120	0
Keith Molesworth	31-34	28	7	99	14.1	1	23	3	51	1
	35-37		20	321	16.1	0				
Hap Moran	26-33	46	45	783	17.4	7	52	10	215	2
Dick Moynihan	27	6	9	90	10.0	0	3	4	83	0
Verne Mullen	23-27	25	7	68	9.7	0	31	6	143	1
Lyle Munn	25-29	15	6	125	20.8	0	38	6	121	0
Bronko Nagurski	30-34	50	10	122	12.2	0	3	0	0	0
	35-37,43		1	12	12.0	0				
Tom Nash	28-34	53	22	445	20.2	2	12	6	145	2
Clem Neacy	24-28	14	12	160	13.3	1	27	12	244	1
Dave Noble	24-25	4	8	220	27.5	2	18	13	277	3
Jerry Noonan	21,23-24	2	2	55	27.5	0	9	8	142	2
Marty Norton	22,24-25	11	13	188	14.5	4	8	0	0	0
Ray Novotny	30-32	20	9	178	19.8	0	11	1	39	0
Curly Oden	25-28,30-32	28	36	582	16.2	4	38	7	102	0
Dick O'Donnell	23-31	80	41	704	17.2	4	12	4	95	2
Arnie Oehlrich	28-29	23	34	451	13.3	2	10	5	80	1
Oran Pape	30-32	15	9	93	10.3	2	10	2	67	0
Les Peterson	31-34	44	26	443	17.0	0				
Ernie Pinckert	32-34	15	5	68	13.6	0	18	2	36	0
	35-40		21	269	12.8	1				
Fritz Pollard	20-23,25-26	16	9	125	13.9	1	31	6	109	1
Glenn Presnell (35)	31-34	36	10	100	10.0	1	14	0	0	0
	36		0	0	-	0				
Bob Rapp	22-26,29	9	4	52	13.0	0	34	24	723	9
Dave Reese	20-23	10	13	210	16.2	2	23	6	174	2
Paul Riblett	32-34	16	21	314	15.0	2	16	4	98	1
	35-37		10	135	13.5	1				
Harry Robb	21-23,25-26	24	13	210	16.2	2	22	18	231	2
Wooky Roberts	22-26	18	8	130	16.3	0	18	6	185	4
Fritz Roessler	22-25	17	7	75	10.7	1	10	5	85	0
Charley Rogers	27-29	26	53	732	13.8	3	12	0	0	0
Milt Romney	23-28	25	8	101	12.6	2	47	11	281	2
Bill Rooney	23-27,29	14	5	54	10.8	0	31	5	103	2
Cobb Rooney	24-30	20	24	346	14.4	1	34	20	416	3
Joe Rooney	23-28	30	21	410	19.5	5	25	3	52	2
Al Rose	30-34	44	23	380	16.9	4	13	9	103	1
	35-36		8	91	11.4	0				
Len Sachs	20-26	9	12	178	14.8	0	37	8	134	2
Len Sedbrook	28-31	17	19	352	18.5	4	34	21	431	6
Bill Senn	26-31,33-34	27	20	369	18.5	2	53	12	325	5
Murray Shelton	20	3	2	27	13.5	0	3	8	137	0
John Spellman	25-32	34	8	123	15.4	0	4	7	112	0
Sammy Stein	29-32	24	14	250	17.9	2	5	1	19	0
Dutch Sternaman	20-27	31	12	158	13.2	0	58	9	165	1
Joey Sternaman	22-25,27-30	33	12	199	16.6	1	69	12	217	3
Ken Strong (35)	29-34	68	39	594	15.2	6	3	3	87	1
	39,44-47		0	0	-	0				
Evar Swanson	24-27	8	16	285	17.8	1	19	14	290	2
Cookie Tackwell	30-34	13	10	139	13.9	0	21	3	40	0
Gus Tebell	23-24	3	10	122	12.2	0	8	10	184	2
Dutch Thiele	20-23	10	10	207	20.7	1	20	10	221	1
Rex Thomas	26-28,30-31	15	16	360	22.5	3	32	24	559	7
Stumpy Thomason (35)	30-34	12	10	97	9.7	0	33	5	117	2
	36		0	0	-	0				
Luke Urban	21-23	6	7	126	18.0	0	26	12	229	1
Rube Ursella	20-21,24-26,29	26	8	80	10.0	1	19	2	28	0
Tillie Voss	21-29	35	37	747	20.2	6	51	20	376	1
Laurie Walquist	22,24-31	38	7	122	17.4	0	73	9	136	3
Chuck Weimer	29-31	7	3	9	3.0	0	20	8	169	2
Gibby Welch	28-29	9	15	354	23.6	1	16	17	359	7
Obe Wenig	21-22	12	22	412	18.7	2	1	0	0	0
Barney Wentz	25-28	39	10	76	7.6	0	1	0	0	0
Cowboy Wheeler	21-23	14	11	205	18.6	1	8	0	0	0
Ossie Wiberg	27-38,30,32-33	17	9	160	17.8	0	27	18	312	4
Lee Wilson	29-31	13	8	122	15.3	0	14	5	78	0
Mike Wilson	22-24	11	13	200	15.4	1	5	5	126	1
Mule Wilson	26-33	44	11	110	10.0	0	40	15	430	5
Ben Winkelman	22-24	8	13	193	14.8	1	19	6	156	1
Dick Wolf	23-25,27	6	7	84	12.0	0	20	13	245	2
Doug Wycoff	27,29-32,34	41	7	64	9.1	0	27	3	46	0

The figure (35) in parentheses indicates that no 1935 data are available for that player.

Lifetime Statistics — 1920-1932 Players

Section 3 — PUNT RETURNS

(All men with 25 or more punt returns)

Name	Years	Complete Games G	No	Yds	Avg	TD	Inc. Games G	No	Yds	TD
Johnny Armstrong	23-25	20	28	324	11.6	0	8	2	30	0
Cliff Battles (35-37)	32-34	8	27	240	8.9	0	23	9	231	0
Johnny Blood (35-39)	25-34	78	27	359	13.3	1	24	0	0	0
Carl Brumbaugh (36-38)	30-34	21	33	299	9.1	0	44	4	87	0
Dutch Clark (35-38)	31-32,34	22	54	625	11.6	0	12	1	22	0
Jimmy Conzelman	20-29	34	28	292	10.4	0	67	3	80	0
Paddy Driscoll	20-29	27	34	436	12.8	1	88	9	182	0
Red Dunn	24-31	63	134	1148	8.6	0	29	2	100	0
Benny Friedman	27-34	20	31	401	12.9	0	60	8	176	0
Roger Grove (35)	31-34	48	76	729	9.6	0	4	0	0	0
Jack Hagerty	26-30,32	13	19	217	11.4	0	50	7	193	1
Arnie Herber (35-40)	30-34	45	52	502	9.7	0	5	0	0	0
	44-45		0							
Two Bits Homan	25-30	45	82	1114	13.6	0	36	18	325	1
Curly Lambeau	21-29	70	37	371	10.0	0	7	1	5	0
Charlie Mathys	21-26	40	64	638	10.0	0	12	0	0	0
Keith Molesworth (35-37)	31-34	15	37	433	11.7	0	36	9	179	0
Curly Oden	25-28,30-32	20	47	804	17.1	2	46	17	532	2
Fritz Pollard	20-23,25-26	13	29	312	10.8	0	34	7	108	0
Glenn Presnell (35-36)	31-34	28	43	629	14.6	1	22	8	162	0
Pid Purdy	26-27	17	36	413	11.5	0				
Wooky Roberts	22-26	12	18	240	13.3	0	24	9	79	0
Charley Rogers	27-29	23	91	1199	13.2	0	15	3	56	0
Joey Sternaman	22-25,27-30	29	68	751	11.0	0	73	11	233	1
Ken Strong(35)	29-34,39,44-47	45	88	1108	12.6	2	26	3	73	0

Section 4 — PUNTING

(All men with 25 or more punts)

Names	Years	Complete Games G	No	Avg	Inc. Games G	No	Avg
Fay Abbott	21-29	11	52	30.7	46	13	30.8
Frank Bacon	20-25	9	45	35.9	37	8	19.3
Shorty Barr	23-26	14	47	34.7	12	3	45.3
Johnny Barrett	20	3	29	32.1	3	2	19.5
Cliff Battles (35-37)	32-34	5	45	41.4	19	10	45.5
Johnny Blood (35-38)	25-34	81	179	36.6	21	0	-
	39		0	-			
Al Bloodgood	25-28,30	11	39	33.1	24	2	11.5
Earl Britton	25-29	13	121	35.6	18	14	37.8
Jesse Brown	26	14	94	37.7			
Hank Bruder (35-38)	31-34	49	37	37.8			
	39-40		0	-			
Cub Buck	20-25	45	258	36.5	12	8	38.5
Dale Burnett (35-38)	30-34	20	28	36.5	44	3	33.3
	39		0	-			
Harlan Carr	27	6	27	36.6	4	15	32.3
Al Casey	23	3	29	41.3	4	4	50.0
John Cavosie	31-33	25	60	35.3	8	2	52.5
Stu Clancy (35)	30-34	25	42	36.0	19	0	-
Dutch Clark (35-38)	31-32,34	22	123	36.1	12	6	20.2
Jimmy Conzelman	20-29	38	102	35.7	63	2	22.5
Jack Cronin	27-30	12	17	34.2	30	11	31.8
Cy DeGree	21	3	32	35.4	4	2	21.0
Wally Diehl	28-30	27	183	34.6	11	6	22.5
Paddy Driscoll	20-29	28	260	38.8	87	35	41.7
Red Dunn	24-31	64	67	31.6	28	13	30.4
Ox Eckhardt	28	3	26	34.4	8	2	31.0
Chief Elkins	28-29,33	14	45	34.6	6	5	38.8
Ray Flaherty (35)	27-29,31-34	24	50	34.7	66	9	28.1
Bill Giaver	22-26	13	25	29.0	15	0	-
Wally Gilbert	23-26	5	30	35.0	12	0	-
Ducky Grant	28	2	23	34.0	4	4	0.0
Joe Guyon	20-25,27	13	76	36.8	28	7	26.4
Swede Hagberg	29-30	4	27	36.9	17	5	41.6
Tex Hamer	24-27	16	102	34.4	39	93	34.9
Duke Hanny	23-30	34	98	35.0	64	19	45.5
Swede Hanson (35-38)	31-34	12	23	35.1	22	3	0.0
Pete Henry	20-23,25-28	36	51	38.7	44	16	33.7
Arnie Herber	30-34	49	166	38.1	1	0	-
	39-40,44-45		39	40.0			
Wally Hess	20-25	4	22	35.5	23	6	27.5
Clarke Hinkle (35-38)	32-34	38	192	35.4			
	39-41		87	40.9			
Grassy Hinton	32	11	32	29.5	1	0	-
Paul Hogan	24-27	3	14	35.6	23	15	38.7
Tony Holm	30-33	17	32	34.2	17	0	-
Walt Holmer	29-33	17	55	37.8	38	2	15.5
Ken Huffine	20-25	12	21	29.5	30	9	27.7
Tommy Hughitt	20-24	4	22	33.1	46	13	24.4
Jerry Johnson	21-22	9	34	30.7	1	0	-
Ave Kaplan	23	4	36	32.1	4	0	-
Jim Kendrick	22-27	10	41	32.9	37	25	34.9
Graham Kernwein	26	5	25	31.6			
Rip King	20-25	15	128	38.9	26	15	37.7
Frank Kirkleski	27,29-31	21	118	34.2	18	2	35.0
Jim Laird	20-22,25-28,31	23	23	34.7	47	9	32.0
Verne Lewellen	24-32	101	677	39.4	4	4	48.5
Tiny Lewis	30-31	11	23	36.0	2	2	23.5
Joe Lintzenich	30-31	16	73	39.6	8	2	70.0
Bob Lundell	29-30	11	23	34.0	9	2	27.5
Red Maloney	25,27,29	9	47	36.0	24	22	40.0
Ken Mercer	27-29	30	78	35.3	14	6	27.3
Al Michaels	23-25	5	28	37.0	23	3	39.0
Keith Molesworth (35-37)	31-34	15	51	35.2	36	5	32.2
Jim Mooney	30-31,33-34	14	105	42.8	30	9	35.6
Hap Moran	26-33	37	108	35.8	61	17	35.4
Tom Murphy	26	3	20	39.7	5	7	25.4
Don Murry	22,24-32	40	33	35.7	73	17	33.5
Dick Nesbitt	30-34	23	93	39.6	31	4	34.8
Ernie Nevers	26-27,29-31	22	160	36.3	32	12	28.1
Obie Newman	25-26	3	30	32.3	14	14	29.2
Eddie Novak	20-22,24-25	24	26	37.9	6	0	-
Jim Pederson	30-32	10	38	34.6	10	0	-
Frosty Peters	30-32	11	49	42.5	11	0	-
Art Pharmer	30-31	7	50	35.1	8	1	28.0
Wooky Roberts	22-26	12	83	34.3	24	10	27.8
Kelly Rodriguez	30	8	33	40.2	7	1	74.0
Bill Senn	26-31,33-34	24	37	39.6	56	1	0.0
Shag Sheard	23-25	4	30	35.0	13	9	20.6
Deck Shelley	31-32	7	43	36.9	7	1	0.0
Gus Sonnenberg	23,25-28,30	14	40	36.6	46	5	38.4
Ken Strong (35)	29-34	47	268	38.5	24	11	39.6
	39, 44-47		6	53.2			
Evar Swanson	24-27	8	28	37.1	19	1	40.0
Jim Thorpe	20-26,28	10	55	35.9	37	21	29.4
Rube Ursella	20-21,24-26,29	23	67	34.7	22	2	39.5
Dutch Webber	24-28	10	24	36.8	25	6	32.5
Obe Wenig	21-22	12	45	33.2	1	0	-
Ossie Wiberg	27-28,30,32-33	10	34	36.4	34	5	30.6
Mule Wilson	26-33	39	64	35.8	45	4	25.0
Wildcat Wilson	27-29	11	102	38.0	26	24	34.7
Hoge Workman	24,31-32	4	21	38.6	15	11	42.5
Doug Wycoff	27,29-32,34	40	121	36.8	28	5	26.0

Section 5 — KICKING

(All men with 10 or more PAT ar Field Goal Attempts)

Name	Years	PAT	PAT Att	PAT Pct	FG	FG Att	FG Pct
Roy Andrews	23-27	3	4	75	2	8	25
Bull Behman	24-25,27-31	12	20	60	5	14	36
Charlie Berry	25-26	29	34	85	3	9	33
Hugh Blacklock	20-26	8	10	80	0	1	0
Al Bloodgood	25-28,30	12	19	63	11	27	41
Arda Bowser	22-23	2	4	50	0	6	0
Benny Boynton	21-22,24	22	26	85	5	9	56
Earl Britton	25-29	0	2	0	1	8	13
Cub Buck	20-25	24	35	69	10	38	26
Johnny Budd	26-28	15	24	63	6	21	29
Algy Clark	30-32	0	1	0	0	0	-
	33-34	3	4	75	5		
Dutch Clark	31-32,34,38	32	46	70	9	23	39
	35-37	40	51	78	6		
Jimmy Conzelman	20-29	3	5	60	4	27	15
Charlie Copley	20-22	23	29	79	1		
Paddy Driscoll	20-29	67	93	72	51	119	43
Red Dunn	24-31	74	115	64	13	23	57
Doc Elliott	22-25,31	7	11	64	4		
Tiny Engebretsen	32,38-41	45	51	88	9	22	41
	33-37	8	9	89	7		
Benny Friedman	27-34	71	110	65	2	8	25
Wally Gilbert	23-26	3	6	50	3	6	50
Hank Gillo	20-26	18	23	78	22	54	41
Roger Grove	31-35	16	22	73	0	1	0
Joe Guyon	20-25,27	12	15	80	0	4	0
Eddie Halicki	29-30	11	15	73	1	5	20
Tex Hamer	24-27	6	7	86	0	7	0
Russ Hathaway	20-27	28	32	88	10	18	56
Dutch Hendrian	23-25	2	5	40	4	11	36
Pete Henry	20-23,25-28	40	56	71	14	56	25
Clarke Hinkle	32-34,38-41	20	26	77	24	66	36
	35-37	9	10	90	4		
Paul Hogan	24-27	7	10	70	1	9	11
Arnie Horween	21-24	3	5	60	3	6	50
Lou Jennings	29-30	4	7	57	0	4	0
Jerry Johnson	21-22	6	8	75	1	5	20
Luke Johnsos	29-36	10	16	63	1	2	50
Ave Kaplan	23	3	6	50	3	7	43
Jim Kendrick	22-27	7	11	64	3	11	27
Hobby Kinderdine	20-29	12	14	86			
Jim Laird	20-22 25-28,31	2	2	100	5	10	50
Curly Lambeau	21-29	19	24	79	6	32	19
Tiny Lewis	30-31	10	13	77			
Red Maloney	25,27,29	4	6	67	3	6	50
Tuffy Maul	26	3	5	60	2	10	20
Jack McBride	25-34	61	82	74	5	28	18
Ken Mercer	27-29	14	30	47	7	13	54
Bo Molenda	27-32	17	35	49	0	7	0
	33-35	2	2	100	0		
Hap Moran	26-33	22	35	63	4	9	44
Frank Morrissey	21-24	15	20	75	12	29	41
Jim Musick	32-33,35-36	13	15	87	1	4	25
Ernie Nevers	26-27,29-31	52	74	70	7	31	23
Harry O'Boyle	28,32-33	15	24	63	3	6	50
Elmer Oliphant	20-21	26	26	100	5	15	33
Frosty Peters	30-32	9	14	64	2	9	22
Tony Plansky	28-29,32	2	9	22	2	3	67
Glenn Pressnell	31-34	28	40	70	10	27	37
	35-36	10	12	83	5		
Pid Purdy	26-27	15	17	88	3	9	33
George Rohleder	25-26	3	6	50	4	19	21
Emmett Ruh	21-22	1	5	20	2	7	29
Bill Senn	26-31,33-34	5	9	56	1	1	100
Ed Shaw	20,22-23	8	10	80	2	9	22
Paul Sheeks	21-22	9	13	69	5		
Dale Sies	20-24	8	10	80	4	14	29
Red Smith	27-31	5	12	42	0	0	-
Gus Sonnenberg	23,25-28,30	32	47	68	18	52	35
Russ Stein	22,24-26	14	23	61	2	8	25
Dutch Sternaman	20-27	26	40	65	21	57	37
Joey Sternaman	22-25,27-30	58	77	75	18	54	33
Ken Strong	29-34,39,44-47	156	176	89	34	81	42
	35	11	12	92	4		
Cookie Tackwell	30-34	7	9	78	0	4	0
Gus Tebell	23-24	10	14	71	5	15	33
Jim Thorpe	20-26,28	3	9	33	7	28	25
Eddie Tryon	27	8	13	62	0	1	0
Rube Ursella	20-21,24-26,29	15	20	75	6	15	40
Tillie Voss	21-29	9	12	75	0	0	-
Chuck Weimer	29-31	4	8	50	3	7	43
Jim Welsh	23-26	32	40	80	12	55	22
Obe Wenig	21-22	8	9	89	0	1	0
Cy Wentworth	25-26,29	8	11	73	1	3	33
Belf West	21	4	6	67	1	4	25
Phil White	25,27	2	6	33	1	8	13
Ossie Wiberg	27-38,30,32-33	8	10	80	0	3	0
Ben Winkelman	22-24	9	10	90	7	19	39
Sonny Winters	23-24	5	8	63	1	2	50
Hoge Workman	24,31-32	18	25	72	3		

The figures in parentheses indicate years between 1934 and 1940 for which no data are available for that player.

1933—1945

1933-1945
Divide, Bring in the Goal Posts and Conquer

While President Franklin D. Roosevelt was driving his New Deal legislation through Congress in early 1933, George Halas and George Preston Marshall were ushing in a new deal of their own. NFL president Joe Carr presided over league meetings in February and July in which Halas, the strong-willed owner of the Chicago Bears, and Marshall, the equally stubborn owner of the Boston Redskins, led the club owners in adopting some needed innovations in their game and league.

One change in the playing rules brought the goalposts back to the goallines where they had been stationed until 1927. The 10-yard difference brought a spectacular increase in the number of field goals tried and made. In 1932, Portsmouth's Dutch Clark led the NFL with a mere three successful boots, and only three other players managed even a single three-pointer. In 1933, with the posts moved closer, Jack Manders, Glenn Presnell and Ken Strong each registered five succesful kicks. The league total jumped from six to 36. More important, the number of tie games dropped from 10 (including six involving the Chicago Bears) to only five. The "kiss-your-sister" frustration of tie games had brought extensive criticism in 1932, particularly in Green Bay where the Packers had won more games than any other NFL team but lost the championship to the oft-tied Bears on winning percentage.

An even more important rule change opened up the passing game by permitting throws from anywhere behind the line of scrimmage instead of the mandatory, but difficult to enforce, distance of at least five yards back. At the league meeting, Portsmouth coach Potsy Clark, remembering the controversial pass that sank his Spartans in the special 1932 playoff, grumbled, "Nagurski will pass from anywhere, so we might as well make it legal!" Clark, Halas, Curly Lambeau, Steve Owen and the league's other coaches quickly learned to use the less restrictive rule to create clever, razzle-dazzle offenses featuring forward passing as a major weapon. For the first time, professional football had more wide-open fan appeal than the college game.

Less spectacular, but equally important in opening up the game, was the rule that moved the ball 10 yards in from the sidelines on any play within five yards of the out-of-bounds line. No longer forced to waste a down just to bring the ball back to the center of the field, offenses could concentrate on the main order of business — getting the ball into the endzone.

All three of these changes could be traced in one way or another to the playoff game arranged at the end of the 1932 season to break the first place tie between the Chicago Bears and Portsmouth. The idea of a regularly-scheduled game between the winners of a two-division NFL had been fermenting for years and the success of the '32 playoff showed that the time was ripe. The division of the league into Eastern and Western divisions in 1933 spurred interest in the pro game which was struggling against the financial hardships of the Depression as well as the overwhelming emphasis put on college football by the media and fans. With two divisional races, more teams could now entertain title hopes into autumn, while the NFL championship game at the end of the season paralleled baseball's World Series and won big headlines in the newspapers. It didn't hurt that the second championship game produced one of the most famous comebacks in pro football history — the so-called "Sneakers Game" in which the Giants used basketball shoes to rally against the Bears.

The changes as the NFL entered its 14th season were both revolutionary and much needed. The Depression hurt all areas of American life, sports included. Pro football, less established in the country's heart than the college brand or professional baseball, suffered more than either of these long-time favorites. The National Football League had been shrinking since the start of the Depression, hitting a low of eight teams in 1932, but membership swelled to 10 clubs in 1933 when Pittsburgh, Philadelphia and Cincinnati joined after Staten Island folded. The league roll call stayed relatively stable through the rest of the 1930s, in sharp contrast to the constant franchise changes of the '20s. The only changes after 1933 were the folding of the Cincinnati team in 1934, the transfer of Portsmouth to Detroit in 1934, the shift of Boston to Washington in 1937, and the admittance of the Cleveland Rams in 1937.

With the small, steady number of clubs, league meetings were lively affairs where the tight circle of financially-pressed owners heatedly thrashed out at all proposals. Halas and Marshall, who loved to spar verbally with each other, were the main idea men of the organization. Two other steady owners of the 1930s were Bert Bell of Philadelphia, who doubled as his team's coach, general manager, publicity man and ticket salesman, and Pittsburgh's Art Rooney, who reportedly founded his team with the winnings from a big day at the racetrack. He always denied that, but admitted to having some extremely pleasant experiences following the horses. Rooney and Bell entered the NFL when a change in Pennsylvania law permitted football games to be played on Sundays. Both often served as pacifiers in the volatile discussions between Halas and Marshall. Green Bay's Curly Lambeau represented that club although the team was now municipally owned. New York's Tim Mara, who started his team in 1925 with the statement that "an exclusive franchise for anything in New York is worth $500 (which was the admission fee at the time)," had an important voice in league affairs because of the necessity of maintaining a strong franchise in New York. Charles Bidwell bought the Chicago Cardinals in late 1933 after several years of close association with Halas and the Bears. He immediately began rebuilding the long moribund Cardinals, a task that ironically came to fruition only after his death in 1947. Detroit's Dick Richards, an egocentric radio tycoon, often bombarded his coaches with suggestions and arguments. Brooklyn's Dan Topping, who would later own the New York Yankees baseball team, had less success with his football Dodgers.

The game that these gentlemen presided over was gradually changing even before the rules changes of 1933. Pro football in the 1920s was primarily a running game. With the exceptions of Benny Friedman's teams and Lambeau's Packers, most teams used passes only in desperation. However, several outstanding passers entered pro football in the 1930s. Green Bay's Arnie Herber was the top thrower of the first half of the decade, famed for his long-distance tosses. In 1937, Sammy Baugh, still considered by many to tbe the best passer ever in the NFL, arrived in Washington. Other fine passers of the period included New York's Harry Newman and Ed Danowski, Green Bay's Cecil Isbell and Bob Monnett, Brooklyn's Ace Parker, Detroit's Dutch Clark and Glenn Presnell, Philadelphia's Davey O'Brien, the Bears' Bernie Masterson, and Parker Hall of Cleveland. Nevertheless, the player most influential in advancing the passing game was not a thrower but a catcher. Slim Don Hutson of Green Bay, an end with a sprinter's speed, was football's first modern wide receiver. He practically invented the position by creating moves and fakes that still leave modern players gasping when they see films of him in action. For years he was the NFL's top offensive threat.

Almost all of the league and divisional titles in the 1930s went to the Packers, Bears, Giants and Redskins, with the other clubs perrenial runners-up. Starting in 1940, however, the Chicago Bears rode roughshod over the rest of the competition with one of the greatest pro football teams ever assembled. With limited substitution the rule of the day and most players required to play both offense and defense, the Bears had a roster deep in talent at all positions. Many of their third-team players would have started for any other team in the league. But, in addition to superior personnel, the Bears had a tactical advantage over their rivals. Aided by football genius Clark Shaughnessy, Halas had installed the modern T-formation offense with the Bears. With an intelligent and talented quarterback in Sid Luckman to make it go, the Bears' T attack confused opponents with quick-opening running plays and a variety of passing plays. Although their colorful nickname of "The Monsters of the Midway" suggested a brute force image, the Bears were often outweighed by such teams as the Giants and Redskins. It was their T-formation that often made them seem unstoppable. After the Bears crushed the Redskins 73-0 in the 1940 championship game, most of the NFL teams shifted from the single wing and similar formations to the T by the mid-1940s. By 1950, only the Pittsburgh Steelers still attacked from the old-fashioned single wing.

Other innovations changed the face of pro football in the 1930s. The football, which had been slimming down from the fat bladder it had originally been, reached its modern shape in 1933. The new ball was much easier to pass but practically impossible to drop-kick. When Detroit's Dutch Clark drop-kicked a three-pointer early in 1938, the NFL saw the last of this famous kicking mode. Colorful uniforms and halftime entertainment became common fare, with the Redskins marching band the best show on the field. A rule making helmets mandatory was passed late in the decade, much to the disgust of such iconoclasts as end Bill Hewitt. Black players, never too common in the 1920s, disappeared completely behind an unspoken color bar. After Joe Lillard of the Cardinals and Ray Kemp of Pittsburgh played in 1933, no black man entered the NFL until after World War II.

From 1936 through 1941, the New York Giants annually played a collection of NFL all-stars, an early version of the Pro Bowl. Even higher in fan appeal, starting in 1934, the defending NFL championship team met a collection of college all-stars in a preseason game for charity. Although the College All-Star game was bandoned after 1976, in part because of the dominance of the pro teams, the collegians gave a good acount of themselves in the early years, winning two and tying two of the first five games. Each time the college kids did well, anti-pro critics would crow about a triumph of "spirit" over the play-for-pay approach. More discerning observers pointed out the fact that the collegians, with four-deep rosters, were able to keep fresh players in the game against the limited manpower of the pros. Once the pros enlarged their rosters, they began to regularly trounce "spirit."

The player limit for each team had been raised to 20 in 1930. In 1935 it went up to 24, and the following year to 25. In 1938, it was placed at 30. Finally, in 1940, it was raised to 33, allowing three-deep teams and a good deal of specialization. Although there was a cutback during World War II, the magic 33 was restored as soon as the fighting ended and more players became available.

One of the most important innovations was the draft of college players begun in 1936. With the weaker teams in the league picking first, the draft eliminated bidding over All-Americans and gave the weak teams a fighting chance to build up. Philadelphia's Bert Bell is usually given credit for the idea. The Eagles made halfback Jay Berwanger of the University of Chicago their first pick in the initial draft, but Berwanger, who was also the first Heisman Trophy winner, chose to go into business rather than engage in the shaky proposition of pro football. More and more big-name college players were turning pro, however, with Davey O'Brien and Whizzer White especially famous players signed to big NFL contracts.

As the 1930s turned into the 1940s, the personnel at the top of the league changed. Joe Carr died in 1939 and Elmer Layden, one of the Four Horsemen of Notre Dame, was named Commissioner in 1941. In 1940, Dan Reeves bought the Rams and Fred Mandel purchased the Lions. In a complicated deal that same year, Alexis Thompson became head of the Eagles and Bert Bell became Art Rooney's partner in Pittsburgh. Hugh (Shorty) Ray took over as supervisor of officials and consultant on rule changes in 1938, and his long service to the league until his death in 1956 earned him election to the Pro Football Hall of Fame in 1966.

Through all the changes, the NFL survived. Attendance was modest, but the league outlasted two upstart competitors, the American Football League of 1936-37 and another league of the same name that operated in 1940-41.

But World War II almost put an end to the NFL. Starting in 1942, the military draft took away so many players that the league considered shutting down for the duration. Although it was a near thing, the league persisted with over-age and draft-deferred men and with a truncated array of teams. The Rams went into mothballs for the 1943 season, the Steelers merged with the Eagles in 1943 and with the Cardinals in 1944, and Brooklyn went out of action in 1945. The Boston Yanks, however, came into the league in 1944 and fleshed out the league roster a bit. Attendance fell off during the war years as most star players were away in the service and other more pressing matters captured the attention of Americans on the home front. But the end of the war would bring a flood of top talent into the game, a spiraling boom in the nation's economy, and an incredible skyrocketing in the affairs of the game which had struggled through the first 50 years of its existence.

NEW YORK GIANTS 11-3-0 Steve Owen

Scores of Each Game		
23	Pittsbsurgh	2
7	Portsmouth	17
10	Green Bay	7
20	Boston	21
56	PHILADELPHIA	0
21	BROOKLYN	7
10	Chic. Bears	14
13	PORTSMOUTH	10
7	BOSTON	0
3	CHIC. BEARS	0
17	GREEN BAY	6
10	Brooklyn	0
27	PITTSBURGH	3
20	Philadelphia	14

Use Name	Pos.	Hgt.	Wgt.	Age	Int	Pts.
Mel Hein	C-LB	6'2"	200	24	4	
Len Grant	T	6'3"	235	27		
Tex Irvin	T-G	6'	230	26		6
(1 reception for 15 yard touchdown)						
Bill Morgan	T	6'2"	226	23		
Bill Owen	T	6'	210	29		
John Cannella	G-C-LB	6'1"	198	25		
Butch Gibson	G	5'9"	205	29		
Potsy Jones	G	5'11"	210	23		
Dick Marsh	G	6'2"	200	27		
Steve Owen	G	5'10"	260	35		
Hank Reese	G-C-LB	5'11"	210	23	1	
Ollie Satenstein	G-C	6'	230	27		

The Giants became the class of the new Eastern Division by signing two new backs. Rookie Harry Newman came out of Michigan to lead the NFL in four passing categories, while Ken Strong joined the Giants after the Staten Island club left the league. Strong balanced the pasing attack with powerful running and accurate placekicking and punting. Coach Steve Owen also had some of the league's best linemen in Mel Hein, Red Badgro, Ray Flaherty, Glen Campbell, Len Grant and Butch Gibson. Blessed with depth, the Giants split two games with the Bears during the regular season, shutting them out 3-0 on November 19 in the Polo Grounds. They won they last seven games, including a key victory over Brooklyn to wrap up the first Eastern Division title.

BROOKLYN DODGERS 5-4-1 Cap McEwen

Scores of Each Game		
0	CHIC. BEARS	10
27	CINCINNATI	0
7	New York	21
7	CHIC. CARDS	0
3	PITTSBURGH	3
32	Pittsburgh	0
3	Chic. Cards	0
14	BOSTON	0
0	NEW YORK	10
0	Cincinnati	10

Use Name	Pos.	Hgt.	Wgt.	Age	Int	Pts.
George Chalmers	C-LB	6'	196	24		
Doc Morrison	C-LB	5'11"	210	24	2	
Harold Ely	T	6'2"	270	23		
Don Greenshields	T	6'1"	190	28		
Lou Lubratovich	T	6'2"	230	26	2	
Saul Mielziner	T	6'1"	245	28		
(1 PAT attempt)						
Ralph Wright	T	6'	230	25		
Herman Hickman	G	5'10"	248	21		8
(2 PAT's in 3 arrempts, 2 field goals)						
Bruce Jones	G	6'1"	222	28		
Hughie Rhea	G	6'3"	225	23		
Stu Worden	G	6'	210	23		

Two young backs for the New York Giants, Shipwreck Kelly and Chris Cagle, pooled their resources and purchased the Brooklyn franchise over the summer for $25,000. The new owners hired Cap McEwen as head coach, but freely dispensed their own instructions to the other players. Even with the confusion, the Dodgers put together a midseason hot streak to challenge for first place. Individual heroics came from co-owner and receiver Kelly, passer Benny Friedman and guard Herman Hickman. With first place at stake, the Dodgers dropped a 10-0 decision to the Giants on Thanksgiving Day before 28,000 fans in Ebbets Field.

BOSTON REDSKINS 5-5-2 Lone Star Dietz

Scores of Each Game		
7	Green Bay	7
0	Chic. Bears	7
21	Pittsburgh	6
21	NEW YORK	20
0	PORTSMOUTH	13
10	CHIC. CARDS	0
14	PITTSBURGH	16
10	CHIC. BEARS	0
0	New York	7
20	GREEN BAY	7
0	Brooklyn	14
0	Chic. Cards	0

Use Name	Pos.	Hgt.	Wgt.	Age	Int	Pts.
Orien Crow	C-LB	6'	220	20		
Chief Johnson	C-LB	6'3"	205	24		
David Ward	DE-OE	5'10"	195	26		
Hal Cherne	T-G	6'	230	26		
Turk Edwards	T	6'2"	235	25		
Marne Intrieri	T-OE-DE	5'8"	250	25		
Jack Riley	T	6'2"	230	23		
John Scafide	T	6'	210	23		
George Hurley	G	6'	200	24		
Jim Kamp	G	6'	210	24		
Jim MacMurdo	G-T	6'1"	210	22		
Mike Steponovich	G	5'9"	205	24		
Dale Waters	G-OE-DE	6'2"	215	24		

When his partners bailed out, George Preston Marshall became the sole owner of the money-losing Boston franchise. He renamed the team the Redskins, hired Lone Star Dietz, an Indian, as head coach, and moved the team to Fenway Park. Strong on defense, the Redskins ran the ball well, but had no passing game worthy of mention. Fullback Jim Musick led the league in rushing with 809 yards while tailback Cliff Battles ranked second with 737 yards. Battles ran for 161 of those yards on October 8 in a 21-20 victory over the Giants. Of the linemen, Turk Edwards earned praise as one of the best tackles in the league and George Hurley ranked high at guard. The high point of the season was a 10-0 upset victory over the undefeated Bears before 22,820 hometown fans on November 5.

PHILADELPHIA EAGLES 3-5-1 Lud Wray

Scores of Each Game		
0	New York	56
0	PORTSMOUTH	25
9	Green Bay	35
6	Cincinnati	0
3	CHIC. BEARS	3
25	PITTSBURGH	6
20	CINCINNATI	3
0	GREEN BAY	10
14	NEW YORK	20

Use Name	Pos.	Hgt.	Wgt.	Age	Int	Pts.
Art Koeninger	C-LB	6'1"	205	26		
Bull Lipski	C-LB	5'11"	200	24	1	
Ray Smith	C-LB	5'10"	220	25	2	
Howie Auer	T	6'1"	205	25		
Joe Carpe	T	6'	220	30		
Paul Cuba	T	6'	215	26		
Bob Gonya	T	6'2"	210	23		
Tex Leyendecker	T-C-LB	6'1"	235	23		
Larry Steinbach (from ChiC)	T	6'	212	32		
Guy Turnbow	T-OE-DE	6'2"	217	25		3
(1 field goal)						
Joe Kresky	G	6'	210	25		
Red Leathers	G	5'11"	198	24		
Roy Lechthaler	G	5'10"	198	24		
Henry Obst	G	5'11"	192	25		
Diddie Wilson	G-OE-DE	5'10"	198	22		
Jim Zyntell (from NY)	G	6'1"	200	23		

Bert Bell, a wealthy football fanatic and future NFL commissioner, purchased a Philadelphia franchise when the Pennsylvania law forbidding Sunday sports was about to be repealed. Bell handled all the front-office duties while Lud Wray left Boston to coach the team. The Giants welcomed the Eagles into the league with a 56-0 thrashing, and Wray's men suffered 25-0 and 35-9 drubbings in their next two games. Surprisingly, the Eagles won three and tied one of the next four contests. On the first Sunday of legalized sports in the state, the Eagles shocked 17,850 fans in Baker Bowl by tying the Bears 3-3 on a fourth quarter field goal by Guy Turnbow. On a squad of rookies and veteran castoffs, the star was fullback Swede Hanson, a third-year pro from Temple who ran for 519 yards.

PITTSBURGH PIRATES 3-6-2 Jap Douds

Scores of Each Game		
2	NEW YORK	23
14	CHIC. CARDS	13
6	BOSTON	21
17	CINCINNATI	3
0	Green Bay	47
0	Cincinnati	0
16	Boston	14
3	Brooklyn	3
0	BROOKLYN	32
6	Philadelphia	25
3	New York	27

Use Name	Pos.	Hgt.	Wgt.	Age	Int	Pts.
Mose Lantz	C-LB	5'11"	185	29		
Cap Oehler	C-LB	6'	200	22	5	
Corrie Artman	T	6'2"	240	26		
Sam Cooper	T	6'	200	24		
Jap Douds	T-BB-LB	5'10"	225	28	1	
Tiny Engbretsen (to ChiC, G)	T	6'1"	225	23		3
(1 field goal)						
Ray Kemp	T	6'1"	215	25		
Leo Raskowski (from BKN)	T	6'3"	220	27		
Don Rhodes	T	6'2"	225	24		
John Burleson	G-T	6'2"	237	24		
(from PORT, T, to CIN, T)						
Larry Critchfield	G	5'11"	195	25		
Nick DeCarbo	G	5'9"	185	27		
Clarence Janacek	G	6'	200	22		
Jim Letsinger	G	5'10"	190	22		

After running a semi-pro team for several years, 32-year-old Art Rooney organized the football Pirates and brought the NFL into Pittsburgh. The new law legalizing Sunday sports in Pennsylvania wouldn't go into effect until November 12, so the Pirates opened the season with four home games on Wednesday nights at Forbes Field. Coached by Jap Douds, the Pirates threw a lot of passes on offense, but struggled to put points on the scoreboard. Opponents had far less trouble scoring against the Pirates. Center Cap Oehler and ends Ray Tesser and Paul Moss won praise for their line play, but the most colorful Pirate was 37-year-old Mose Kelsch. Used mostly as a placekick specialist, the bald, chubby Kelsch enjoyed a moment of NFL glory by drilling a last-second field goal on November 5 to tie Brooklyn 3-3.

TEAM TOTALS	YARDS GAINED	OPP. YARDS	PASS ATT.	PASS COMP.	COMP. PCT.	TOTAL POINTS	RUSH TD	PASS TD	OTHER TD	PAT	FG	SAF	OPP. PTS.
NEW YORK	2970	2529	180	74	41.1	244	15	15	3	28	6	0	101
BROOKLYN	2207	1754	169	79	46.7	93	4	7	2	9	2	0	54
BOSTON	2823	2525	113	34	30.1	103	12	1	1	13	2	0	97
PHILADELPHIA	1786	2236	149	41	27.5	77	6	4	1	6	1	1	158
PITTSBURGH	1887	2761	195	61	31.3	67	4	3	1	5	4	1	208

UseName-Backs&Ends	Pos.	Age	Hgt	Wgt	Pts	Int	RUSHING				PASSING								RECEIVING				PUNTING		KICKING						PUNTRETURNS				KICKOFFRETURNS			
							No.	Yds.	Avg	TD	Att	Comp	%	Yds	Yd/Att	TD	Int-%	RK	No.	Yds.	Avg	TD	No.	Avg	Pat	Att	%	FG	Att	%	No.	Yds.	Avg	TD	No.	Yds.	Avg	TD
NEW YORK GIANTS																																						
Harry Newman	TB-DB	23	5'8"	175	32	5	139	452	3.3	3	136	53	39	973	7.2	11	17-13	4				1			5	8	63	1										
Stu Clancy	TB-FB-DB	27	5'10"	190	18	1	41	166	4.0	3																												
Ken Strong	FB-DB	27	6'	198	59	5	108	386	3.6	2						2			7	146	21	2			14	15	93	5										
Kink Richards	FB-TB-DB	22	5'11"	190	43		41	277	6.8	4												3			1	1	100											
Jack McBride	FB-TB-DB	31	5'11"	185	6		33	87	2.6	0						2									6	6	100											
Dale Burnett	WB-DB	24	6'1	185	30	4	17	36	2.1	0									12	211	18	4																
Hap Moran	WB-FB-DB	32	6'1"	190	7	1	11	28	2.5	0												1			1	1	100	(Reception)										
Bo Molenda	BB-LB	28	5'10"	220	18	3	77	203	2.6	3																												
Max Krause	BB-LB	24	5'10"	197	7		33	61	1.8	0												1			1	1	100	(Reception)										
Ray Flaherty	OE-DE	29	6'	187															11	187	17	0																
Red Badgro	OE-DE	30	6'	190	12	1													9	176	20	1																
Glenn Campbell	OE-DE	29	5'11"	204	6																	1																
Tiny Feather	OE-WB-BB DE-DB-LB	30	6'	200		1	2	4	2.0	0																												
Joe Zapaustas	OE-DE	23	6'	198																																		
Tony Rovinski	OE-DE	24	5'9"	195																																		
BROOKLYN DODGERS																																						
Benny Friedman	TB-DB	28	5'10"	182	6	1					80	42	53	597	7.5	5	7- 9	1							6	6	100							2				
Chris Cagle	TB-WB-DB	28	5'10"	170		3					74	31	42	385	5.2	2	9-12	7																				
Ollie Sansen	WB-BB-OE-DB LB-DE	25	6'1"	187	6					1																												
Stumpy Thomason	WB-BB-DB-LB	27	5'7"	190		1																																
Dick Richards	WB-DB	25	6'	194																																		
Shipwreck Kelly	WB-DB	26	6'2"	185	43	1				2									22	246	11	3			1	1	100											
Ben Douglas	WB-DB	24	6'	185	6	2																1																
Bull Karcis	BB-LB	24	5'9"	225																																		
Dick Fishel	BB-WB-TB-LB-DB	23	5'9"	190	6					1																												
Les Peterson	OE-DE	23	6'3"	205															13	170	13	0																
Paul Riblett	OE-DE	25	5'10"	184	6														12	172	14	1																
Tom Nash	OE-DE	27	6'3"	205	12																	2			0	1	0											
Van Rayburn	OE-DE	22	6'1"	180																																		
John Lyons	OE-DE	21	6'1"	185																																		
Harry Kloppenburg	OE-DE	26	6'1"	210																																		
BOSTON REDSKINS																																						
Jim Musick	FB-DB	23	5'11"	205	44	1	173	809	4.7	5															11	12	92	1										
Walt Holmer (to PIT, TB, BB, DB)	FB-WB-DB	30	6'	185	6					1																												
Roy Horstmann	FB-WB-DB	22	6'	185		1																																
Cliff Battles	WB-DB	23	6'1"	198	27	4	146	737	5.0	4									11	185	17	0						1						1				
Ernie Pinckert	WB-DB	25	6'	195	6	6																																
Bob Campiglio	WB-DB	25	6'1"	185																																		
Rabbit Weller	WB-DB	29	5'6"	150	13					2															1	1	100											
Irv Hill	WB-OE-DB-DE	25	6'1"	210																																		
Megs Apsit	BB-LB	25	5'11"	205		1																																
Benny LaPresta	BB-LB	24	5'9"	185	1																				1	1	100											
Ike Frankian	OE-DE	26	5'11"	210	6																	1																
Paul Collins	OE-DE	25	6'1"	195																																		
Steve Hokuf	OE-BB-FB-DE-LB-DB	22	6'	195		1																																
PHILADELPHIA EAGLES																																						
Red Davis	TB-DB	25	5'11"	195	9					1						1									3	5	60											
Lee Woodruff	TB-FB-HB-DB-LB	24	6'	202	12	1				1																												
Nick Prisco	TB-DB	24	5'8"	193																																		
Swede Hanson	FB-LB	25	6'1"	192	24	3	131	519	4.0	3												1																
Jodie Whire	FB-LB	23	6'1"	185																																		
Jack Roberts	HB-DB	24	6'	210	6	2				1																												
Reb Russell (from NY, BB-LB)	HB-FB-DB-LB	27	6'1"	195		1																			0	1	0											
Rick Lackman	HB-TB-DB	21	5'11"	185		1																																
Red Kirkman	BB-TB-DB	27	6'1"	195	8						73	22	30	354	4.8	2	13-18	10				1			2	3	67											
Dick Thornton	BB-DB	25	5'8"	165																																		
Harry O'Boyle	BB-DB	28	5'9"	180																																		
Porter Lainhart	BB-DB	25	6'	180																																		
Joe Carter	OE-DE	23	6'1"	202	13																	2			1	2	50											
George Kenneally	OE-DE	31	6'	192																																		
Dick Fencl	OE-DE	23	5'10"	160																																		
Ev Rowan	OE-DE	30	6'1"	197																																		
Nip Felber	OE-DE	24	6'2"	190																																		
PITTSBURGH PIRATES																																						
Angie Brovelli	TB-BB-DB	23	6'	190	14					2															2	3	67											
Ed Westfall (from BOS, TB-BB-DB)	TB-DB	24	5'9"	175	13					1						1						1			1	1	100											
Harp Vaughn	TB-HB-BB-DB	28	5'7"	150	6					1																												
Bill Tanguay	TB-DB	23	6'	190												1																						
Tommy Whalen	TB-DB	23	5'8"	165																																		
Tony Holm	FB-LB	25	6'1"	215							52	16	31	406	7.8	2	13-25	8																				
Marty Kottler	FB-BB-LB-DB	23	5'9"	180	6	1																																
Jimmy Clark	HB-FB-DB	24	5'9"	170		2																																
Elmer Schwartz	HB-FB-DB-LB	26	6'	215																																		
Bucky Moore	HB-DB	27	5'11"	185																																		
Frank Hood	HB-BB-DB	25	6'	235																																		
Mose Kelsch	HB-FB-DB-LB	37	5'10"	225	11																				2	3	67	3										
George Shaffer	BB-DB	23	6'	190																																		
Ray Tesser	OE-DE	23	6'2"	200															14	274	20	0																
Paul Moss	OE-DE	24	6'2"	200	12														18	383	21	2																
Bill Sortet	OE-DE	21	6'1"	185																																		
Ted Dailey	OE-DE	23	5'9"	170																																		
Gil Robinson	OE-DE	22	6'	180																																		

1933 N.F.L. WEST

CHICAGO BEARS 10-2-1 George Halas

Scores of Each Game		
14	Green Bay	7
7	BOSTON	0
10	Brooklyn	0
12	Chic. Cards	9
10	GREEN BAY	7
14	NEW YORK	10
0	Boston	10
3	Philadelphia	3
0	New York	3
17	PORTSMOUTH	14
22	CHIC. CARDS	6
17	Portsmouth	7
7	GREEN BAY	6

Use Name	Pos.	Hgt.	Wgt.	Age	Int	Pts.
Ookie Miller	C-LB	6'	210	23		
Bert Pearson	C-LB	6'	208	28		
Dick Smith (from BOS)	C-LB	6'2"	225	21		
Link Lyman	T	6'2"	252	34		
George Musso	T	6'2"	257	23		
Ray Richards	T-G	6'1"	225	27		
Dick Stahlman	T	6'2"	216	31		
Bill Buckler	G-T-OE-DE	6'	230	32		
Zuck Carlson	G-C-LB	6'	210	28	1	
Joe Kopcha	G	6'	220	27		

After three years off the field, George Halas returned to the sidelines as coach of the Bears and the defending champions responded by ripping off six straight victories to start the season. The Bears slumped in November on their Eastern trip, losing to Boston and New York and tying Philadelphia. They rebounded to win their last four games, including two showdown matches with the Portsmouth Spartans. In winning the new Western Division title, the Bears allowed two touchdowns in only one game all year. On offense, the Bears used Bronko Nagurski's power running to set up a versatile passing attack. The broad foundation of the team was a strong line featuring Bill Hewitt, Joe Kopcha, Zuck Carlson, Ookie Miller, Link Lyman and rookie George Musso.

PORTSMOUTH SPARTANS 6-5-0 Potsy Clark

21	CINCINNATI	0
17	NEW YORK	7
7	CHIC. CARDS	6
0	Green Bay	17
13	Boston	0
25	Philadelphia	0
10	New York	13
7	GREEN BAY	0
7	Cincinnati	10
14	Chic. Bears	17
7	CHIC. BEARS	17

Use Name	Pos.	Hgt.	Wgt.	Age	Int	Pts.
Clare Randolph	C-LB	6'2"	210	26	1	
John Wager	C-G-LB	5'11"	207	29	1	
Ben Boswell	T	6'	245	23		
George Christensen	T	6'2"	242	23		
Earl Elser	T	6'1"	230	21		
Harry Thayer	T-G	6'1"	215	26		
Maury Bodenger	G	5'10"	210	24	1	
Jim Bowdoin	G	6'1"	225	27		
Ray Davis	G	6'1"	198	26		
Ox Emerson	G-C-LB	5'11"	205	25		

Voluntarily retired — Dutch Clark

The Spartans lost the NFL's leading scorer when Dutch Clark quit to become athletic director at the Colorado School of Mines, but veteran back Glenn Presnell stepped into the vacuum and won another scoring crown for Portsmouth. Working behind a good line featuring Harry Ebding, George Christensen and Ox Emerson, Presnell led the Spartans to six triumphs in their first eight games. On November 26, the Spartans met the Bears in Chicago's Soldier Field in a showdown for first place. Portsmouth went ahead 14-10 on a fourth quarter touchdown by speedy Ernie Caddel but, with less than four minutes remaining, Bronko Nagurski rumbled 24 yards for a 17-14 Chicago victory. One week later, the Bears won 17-7 in Portsmouth to end the race. The Spartans were also losing a long battle to stay afloat financially, as the players missed several paydays.

GREEN BAY PACKERS 5-7-1 Curly Lambeau

7	BOSTON	7
7	CHIC. BEARS	14
7	NEW YORK	10
17	PORTSMOUTH	0
47	PITTSBURGH	0
7	Chic. Bears	10
35	PHILADELPHIA	9
14	Chic. Cards	6
0	Portsmouth	7
7	Boston	20
6	New York	17
10	Philadelphia	0
6	Chic. Bears	7

Use Name	Pos.	Hgt.	Wgt.	Age	Int	Pts.
Larry Bettencourt	C-LB	5'11"	205	27		
Red Bultman	C-LB	6'2"	202	26	1	
Al Sarafiny	C-LB	5'11"	235	27	1	
Paul Young	C-LB	6'4"	195	24	1	
Cal Hubbard	T	6'4"	265	32	1	
Joe Kurth	T	6'1"	202	22		
Claude Perry	T	6'1"	210	31		
Jess Quatse (to PIT)	T	5'11"	230	26		
Rudy Comstock	G	5'10"	208	32		
Lon Evans	G-T	6'2"	225	21		
Norm Greeney	G	5'11"	215	23		
Mike Michalske	G	6'	210	30	1	
Clyde Van Sickle	G	6'1"	225	25		

Voluntarily retired — Nate Barrager

The once-perennial champions continued their slump from the end of 1932. They opened the season by tying Boston, then lost to the Bears and Giants. The Packers never regained their championship form and finished with a losing record for the first time ever. Particularly galling to coach Curly Lambeau was losing all three contests with the Bears. Cal Hubbard, Mike Michalske and Clarke Hinkle all played first-rate ball, but the squad as a whole failed to show any fire. The retirement of all-pro center Nate Barrager hurt the line. The club also suffered financially when a fan fell out of temporary bleachers at City Stadium and sued the team for $5,000. A major civic effort by local businessmen bailed the team out of financial chaos and reorganized them on a firm basis.

CINCINNATI REDS 3-6-1 Al Jolley, Mike Palm

0	Portsmouth	21
0	CHIC. CARDS	3
3	Pittsburgh	17
0	Brooklyn	27
0	PITTSBURGH	0
0	PHILADELPHIA	6
12	Chic. Cards	9
10	PORTSMOUTH	7
3	Philadelphia	20
10	BROOKLYN	0

Use Name	Pos.	Hgt.	Wgt.	Age	Int	Pts.
Frank Abruzzino	C-OE BB-WB-LB-DE-DB	6'	190	25	1	
Mil Berner	C-LB	6'2"	204	27		
John Rogers	C-LB	5'8"	205	23	1	
Lloyd Burdick	T	6'4"	257	24		
Sonny Doell	T	6'	200	26		
Leo Draveling	T	6'2"	210	26		
George Munday	T	6'2"	215	25		
Tom Blondin	G	6'	195	22		
Les Caywood	G	6'	230	28		
Rosie Grant	G	5'10"	198	24		
Biff Lee (1 field goal)	G	6'	225	25		3

One of three expansion teams, the Reds scored a grand total of three points in their first six games. They lost five of those games and played one scoreless tie. The Reds then suddenly developed some offense and won three of their last four games. On November 19, the Portsmouth Spartans came to Cincinnati trailing the first-place Bears by only half a game. The Reds turned two Spartan fumbles into a Red Corzine touchdown and a Biff Lee field goal in the second quarter and held on to take a 10-7 upset victory. In the season finale, they shut out Brooklyn 10-0 in Crosley Field. In the fourth quarter of that game, 5-foot 6-inch Gil LeFebvre broke a 98-yard punt return for the game's only touchdown. The Reds made progress on the field as the season wore on, but attendance stayed sparse all year.

CHICAGO CARDINALS 1-9-1 Paul Schissler

13	Pittsburgh	14
6	Portsmouth	7
3	Cincinnati	0
9	CHIC. BEARS	12
0	Boston	10
0	Brooklyn	7
6	GREEN BAY	14
9	CINCINNATI	12
0	BROOKLYN	3
6	CHIC. BEARS	22
0	BOSTON	0

Use Name	Pos.	Hgt.	Wgt.	Age	Int	Pts.
Frank McNally	C-T-G-LB	6'1"	205	26	1	6
Tim Moynihan	C-G-LB	6'1"	204	26	1	
Tommy Yarr	C-LB	5'10"	205	25	1	
Lou Gordon	T	6'5"	220	25		
Jess Tinsley	T	6'	204	24	1	
Jake Williams	T	6'	205	29		
Gil Bergerson (from ChiB)	G	6'6"	245	23	1	
Herb Blumer	G	6'1"	200	33		
Al Graham	G	6'	218	27		
Phil Handler	G	6'	218	25		
Walt Kiesling	G-T	6'2"	245	30		
Dave Ribble	G	6'1"	225	26		

The Cardinals hit rock bottom by finishing with the worst record in a league with three expansion teams. New coach Paul Schissler had a pair of quality linemen in Lou Gordon and Frank McNally, but his roster had few other first-class players. Most of the backfield spark came from tailback Joe Lillard, one of two black players in the NFL. Cursed with a lack of offense, the Cards dropped both of their meetings with the rival Bears. They lost 12-9 at Wrigley Field on October 15 despite a 50-yard touchdown run by Lillard, and were trounced 22-6 at Soldier Field on Thanksgiving Day. With attendance down, team owner Dr. David Jones sold the team in midseason to Charles Bidwill, who would remain at the head of the Cardinals organization until his death in 1947.

TEAM TOTALS	YARDS GAINED	OPP. YARDS	PASS ATT.	PASS COMP.	COMP. PCT.	TOTAL POINTS	RUSH TD	PASS TD	OTHER TD	PAT	FG	SAF	OPP. PTS.
CHICAGO BEARS	3029	2326	210	71	33.8	133	3	11	2	15	6	2	82
PORTSMOUTH	2710	1983	170	65	38.2	128	10	6	0	14	6	0	87
GREEN BAY	2758	1929	209	88	42.1	170	15	6	3	20	2	0	107
CINCINNATI	1206	2319	101	24	23.8	38	2	0	1	3	5	1	110
CHICAGO CARDS	1508	2308	141	37	26.2	52	3	2	2	2	2	1	101

							RUSHING				PASSING								RECEIVING				PUNTING		KICKING						PUNT RETURNS				KICKOFF RETURNS			
UseName- Backs&Ends	Pos.	Age	Hgt	Wgt	Pts	Int	No.	Yds.	Avg	TD	Att	Comp	%	Yds	Yd/Att	TD	Int-%	RK	No.	Yds.	Avg	TD	No.	Avg	Pat	Att	%	FG	Att	%	No.	Yds.	Avg	TD	No.	Yds.	Avg	TD
CHICAGO BEARS																																						
Keith Molesworth	QB-HB-DB	27	5'9"	160	6	1	60	145	2.4	0	50	19	38	421	8.4	4	4- 8	2				1																
Carl Brumbaugh	QB-DB	25	5'10"	165		2	19	41	2.2	0						1																						
Bronko Nagurski	FB-LB	24	6'2"	217	7	2	128	533	4.2	1									1	23	23	0			1	1	100											
Red Grange	HB-DB	30	6'	185	6	2	79	297	3.8	1						2			3	74	25	0																
Johnny Sisk	HB-LB	26	6'2"	198	6	3	52	219	4.2	1																												
Jack Manders	FB-HB-LB	24	6'	202	32	2	65	244	3.8	0															14	14	100	6										
Gene Ronzani	HB-LB	24	5'9"	200	6		26	91	3.5	0												1																
John Doehring	HB-LB	23	6'	212			12	68	5.7	0						1																						
George Corbett	HB-QB-DB	25	5'9"	180			25	54	2.2	0																												
Paul Franklin	FB-OE-LB-DE	27	6'2"	205																																		
Bill Hewitt	OE-DE	23	5'9"	190	18											3			16	274	17	2																
Bill Karr	OE-DE	22	6'1"	194	24	1													8	184	23	3																
Luke Johnsos	OE-DE	27	6'2"	195	18														10	175	18	3																
Joe Zeller	G-OE-DE	25	6'1"	205	6	3																1																
PORTSMOUTH SPARTANS																																						
Glenn Presnell	TB-DB	28	5'10"	190	63	5	118	522	4.4	6	125	47	38	774	6.2	5	12-10	6							12	14	86	5										
Elmer Schaake	FB-WB-TB-LB-DB	22	5'11"	207	6	2	125	412	3.3	0												1																
Ace Gutowsky	FB-TB-LB-DB	24	5'11"	200	7	2	103	385	3.7	1						1									1	1	100											
Ernie Caddel	WB-DB	22	6'2"	198	24		74	286	3.9	2												2																
Gene Alford	WB-BB-DB	27	5'9"	184	6																	1																
Mule Wilson	WB-FB-DB-LB	31	5'11"	203		1																																
Father Lumpkin	BB-DB	25	6'2"	213	12	2				1												1																
Harry Ebding	OE-DE	26	5'11"	207																																		
John Cavosie	OE-FB-BB-DE-LB-DB-T	25	6'	207	10	1																1			1	1	100											
John Schneller	OE-DE	21	6'2"	200																																		
Buster Mitchell	T-OE-DE	27	6'	210																																		
Ramey Hunter	OE-DE	23	6'	178																																		
GREEN BAY PACKERS																																						
Arnie Herber	TB-HB-DB	23	5'11"	200	1	4	49	125	2.6	0	125	51	41	818	6.5	4	11- 9	5	2	22	11	0	50	35.9	1	1	100				6	83	13.8	0				
Bob Monnett	TB-HB-DB	23	5'9"	188	34	1	108	412	3.8	3	44	19	43	279	6.3	3	2- 5	3	4	78	20	0			9	10	90	0	1	0	25	356	14.2	1				
Clarke Hinkle	FB-HB-LB-DB	23	5'11"	200	24	3	145	419	2.9	3	29	10	34	152	5.2	0	5-17	9	5	44	9	0	83	35.8				2	7	29								
Buckets Goldenberg	FB-LB	22	5'10"	220	42	3	56	209	3.7	4									7	47	7	1									1	30	30.0	1				
Hurdis McCrary	FB-LB	29	6'	204			6	9	1.5	0																												
Hank Bruder	TB-HB-DB	25	6'	194	18	3	74	274	3.7	3	9	4	44	23	2.6		0- 0		3	94	31	0	5	39.4				0	1	0								
Wuert Engelmann	HB-TB-BB-FB-DB-LB	26	6'3"	195	12	4	23	57	2.5	0									3	83	28	1			0	1	0											
Buster Mott	HB-FB-DB-LB	24	5'8"	190			5	12	2.4	0																												
Roger Grove	BB-DB	25	6'	188	8	5	3	1	0.3	0									18	235	13	0	2	31.0	8	9	89	0	1	0	30	305	10.2	0				
Johnny Blood	BB-HB-DB	29	6'1"	190	19	1	13	41	3.2	0	4	1	25	13	3.3		0- 0		10	206	21	3	3	42.7	1	1	100	(reception)			2	24	12.0	0				
Lavie Dilweg	OE-DE	30	6'3"	202															18	200	11	0																
Milt Gantenbein	OE-DE	23	6'	200	6														7	143	20	1																
Al Rose	OE-DE	26	6'3"	204	6														6	92	15	1																
Ben Smith	OE-DE	22	6'3"	205															2	41	21	0																
CINCINNATI REDS																																						
Lew Pope	TB-WB-FB-DB-LB	25	6'	195	6	1				1																												
Gil LeFebvre	TB-WB-DB	23	5'6"	157	6																																	
Jim Bausch (from ChiC, FB-LB)	TB-DB	27	6'1"	200																																		
Blake Workman	TB-DB	23	5'11"	185																																		
Seaman Squyers	TB-DB	23	6'3"	200																																		
Bill Senn	TB-DB	28	6'	185																																		
Red Corzine	FB-LB	24	6'	210	6	2				1																												
Ossie Wiberg	FB-LB	28	5'11"	207																																		
Lee Mulleneaux	WB-FB-BB-DB-LB	26	6'2"	215																																		
Mike Palm	WB-BB-DB	33	5'10"	172																																		
Chief Elkins	WB-DB	28	5'11"	190		1																	1	34														
Algy Clark	BB-DB	29	6'	190	15	3																			3	3	100											
Don Moses	BB-DB	26	5'11"	185																																		
Joe Crakes	OE-DE	24	6'1"	205																																		
Jim Mooney	OE-DE	25	5'11"	197																																		
Cookie Tackwell (from ChiB)	OE-DE	26	6'2"	212																																		
Chuck Braidwood	OE-DE	29	6'	210																																		
Kermit Schmidt	OE-WB-DE-DB	24	6'	200																																		
Hal Hilpert	OE-DE	25	5'9"	190																																		
Dick Powell	OE-DE	29	6'2"	220																																		
CHICAGO CARDINALS																																						
Joe Lillard	TB-DB	27	6'	185	19	1				1						1									1	4	25	2						1				
Mike Koken	TB-BB-DB	23	5'11"	180	1											1																						
Cliff Hansen	TB-FB-DB-LB	23	6'1"	190		1																																
Curley Hinchman	FB-LB	26	5'10"	190																																		
Dick Nesbitt (from ChiB, HB-LB)	FB-LB	25	6'	206	6	2				1															1	2	50											
Doc Ledbetter	FB-LB	25	5'10"	190																																		
Otto Vokaty	FB-LB	24	6'1"	195																																		
Hal Moe	WB-DB	24	5'10"	182	12	1																																
Howie Tipton	WB-TB-BB-OE-G-DB-DE	22	5'11"	185	6					1																												
Les Malloy	BB-DB	24	6'	200		1																																
Roddy Lamb	BB-TB-DB	34	5'6"	160																		2																
Chuck Bennett	BB-DB	26	5'9"	198																																		
Butch Simas	BB-DB	24	5'10"	185																																		
Milan Creighton	OE-DE	25	6'	185																																		
Dave Nisbet	OE-DE	23	6'1"	180																																		
Chuck Kassel	OE-DE	29	6'1"	195		1																																
George Hogge	OE-DE	25	6'	185																																		

NEW YORK GIANTS 8-5-0 Steve Owen

Scores of Each Game		
0	Detroit	9
6	Green Bay	20
14	Pittsburgh	12
16	Boston	13
14	BROOKLYN	0
17	PITTSBURGH	7
17	PHILADELPHIA	0
7	Chic. Bears	27
17	GREEN BAY	3
9	CHIC. BEARS	10
3	BOSTON	0
27	Brooklyn	0
0	Philadelphia	6

Use Name	Pos.	Hgt.	Wgt.	Age	Int	Pts.
Mel Hein (2 receptions for 15 yds.)	C-LB	6'2"	218	25	1	
Johnny Dell Isola	C-LB	5'11"	205	22	1	
Illness — Glenn Campbell						
Knuckles Boyle	T	5'11"	232	25		
Len Grant	T	6'3"	225	28		
Tex Irvin	T	6'	230	27		
Bill Morgan	T	6'2"	230	24		
Bill Owen	T	6'	220	30		
Babe Scheuer	T	6'3"	240	22		
Bob Bellinger	G	5'11"	212	21		
John Cannella (to BKN)	G-T	6'1"	200	26		
Butch Gibson	G	5'9"	208	30		
Potsy Jones	G	5'11"	210	24		
Hank Reese	G-LB	5'11"	210	24		

After losing in Detroit and Green Bay, the Giants whipped five straight Eastern Division opponents. A strong defense and balanced offense brought New York a repeat divisional crown. The superior line featured all-pros Mel Hein, Butch Gibson, Potsy Jones, Bill Morgan and Red Badgro. In the backfield, Ken Strong enjoyed his best season, excelling as a kicker, runner, blocker and tackler. Harry Newman also shone, blending accurate passing, dangerous kick returning and reliable defensive work. Newman's season ended prematurely on November 18 when he suffered two broken vertabrae in a 10-9 loss to the Bears at the Polo Grounds. Rookie Ed Danowski replaced Newman and played well for the final three games of the regular season.

BOSTON REDSKINS 6-6-0 Lone Star Dietz

Scores of Each Game		
7	Pittsburgh	0
6	Brooklyn	10
13	NEW YORK	16
39	PITTSBURGH	0
0	Detroit	24
6	PHILADELPHIA	0
9	CHIC. CARDS	0
0	GREEN BAY	10
0	CHIC. BEARS	21
14	Philadelphia	7
0	New York	3
13	BROOKLYN	3

Use Name	Pos.	Hgt.	Wgt.	Age	Int	Pts.
Frank Bausch	C-LB	6'3"	215	26	2	
Orien Crow	C-LB	6'	220	21		
Ben Boswell	T	6'	245	24		
Turk Edwards	T	6'2"	250	26	1	
Gail O'Brien	T	6'1"	220	22		
Steve Sinko	T-G	6'3"	230	23		
Rick Concannon	G	6'	220	25		
Marne Intrieri	G	5'8"	250	26		
Les Olsson	G	6'	220	25		
Frank Walton	G	5'11"	215	22		

Despite some talented rookies, the Redskins couldn't improve their break-even mark. They beat the smaller fry of the league, but lost every meeting with the Giants, Bears and Lions. The offense revolved around the speed of Cliff Battles and the power of rookie Hal McPhail, who replaced season-long holdout Jim Musick. Surrounded with a platoon of first-year players, tackle Turk Edwards remained one of the NFL's best linemen. The Redskins had a chance to move into a tie for first place on November 25, but they lost a 3-0 battle to the Giants in New York. Attendance at Fenway Park was modest, with a crowd of 26,000 to see the Bears the biggest.

BROOKLYN DODGERS 4-7-0 Cap McEwen

Scores of Each Game		
10	BOSTON	6
7	CHIC. BEARS	21
0	New York	14
0	Detroit	28
21	PITTSBURGH	3
0	CHIC. CARDS	21
10	Philadelphia	7
10	Pittsburgh	0
0	PHILADELPHIA	13
0	NEW YORK	27
3	Boston	13

Use Name	Pos.	Hgt.	Wgt.	Age	Int	Pts.
Doc Morrison	C-LB	5'11"	210	25		
Tony Siano	C-LB	5'8"	172	27		
Harold Ely	T	6'2"	260	24		
Tiny Engebretsen (to GB, G)	T	6'1"	225	24		
Bruce Jones	T-G	6'1"	220	29		
Lou Lubratovich	T	6'2"	228	27		
Saul Mielziner	T-G-C-LB	6'1"	245	29		
Jim Bowdoin	G	6'1"	225	28		
Chuck Brodnicki	G	6'2"	225	23		
George Demas	G	6'	190	27		
Herman Hickman	G	5'10"	250	22		
Stu Worden	G	6'	210	24		

During the summer, Chris Cagle sold his 50 percent share of the Dodgers to Dan Topping, a future owner of the New York Yankees baseball team. Topping and co-owner Shipwreck Kelly brought back most of last year's squad, but Benny Freidman retired to coach the City College of New York team. Cagle, Kelly and rookie Cliff Montgomery all tried Friedman's tailback slot but failed to ignite the offense. Another rookie, Ralph Kercheval from Kentucky, made the grade at wingback, placekicker and punter, scoring every Brooklyn point in the last six games of the season. Unfortunately, four of those games wound up in defeat, including a 27-0 trouncing by the Giants in Ebbets Field on Thanksgiving Day, a debacle which Friedman's return to uniform could not prevent.

PHILADELPHIA EAGLES 4-7-0 Lud Wray

Scores of Each Game		
6	Green Bay	19
17	Pittsburgh	0
7	PITTSBURGH	9
0	DETROIT	10
0	Boston	6
0	New York	17
64	CINCINNATI	0
7	BROOKLYN	10
7	BOSTON	14
13	Brooklyn	0
6	NEW YORK	3

Use Name	Pos.	Hgt.	Wgt.	Age	Int	Pts.
Chuck Hajek (1 PAT in 1 attempt)	C-LB-G	6'1"	210	23	1	1
Bull Lipski	C-LB	5'11"	200	24	2	
Paul Cuba	T	6'	210	26		
Jim MacMurdo	T	6'1"	210	23		
Guy Turnbow	T	6'2"	217	26		
Vince Zizak	T	5'8"	208	25		
Joe Kresky	G	6'	220	26		
Barnes Milam	G-T		190	28		
Phil Poth	G	5'11"	195	23		
Diddie Willson	G	5'10"	195	23	2	
Jim Zyntell	G	6'1"	200	24		

On November 6, a Philadelphia audience watched in shock as the Eagles destroyed the Cincinnati Reds 64-0. The surprise was heightened by the Eagles' failure to score a point in their previous three games. Coach Lud Wray coaxed tough performances out of his low-talent squad, managing to stay close in almost all the games and to win four of them. Two Eagles ranked high in the league's final offensive statistics. Fullback Swede Hanson ran for 805 yards, second in the league, while end Joe Carter ranked second among pass receivers with 16 catches. Aside from the Cincinnati massacre, the Eagles' best moments came at the tail end of the season. On November 25, they whipped the Dodgers 13-0 in Brooklyn. One week later, they hosted the Giants and beat the Eastern champs 13-3.

PITTSBURGH PIRATES 2-10-0 Luby DiMelio

Scores of Each Game		
13	CINCINNATI	0
0	BOSTON	7
0	PHILADELPHIA	17
12	NEW YORK	14
9	Philadelphia	7
0	CHIC. BEARS	28
0	Boston	39
7	New York	1.
3	Brooklyn	21
7	Detroit	40
0	St. Louis	6
0	BROOKLYN	10

Use Name	Pos.	Hgt.	Wgt.	Age	Int	Pts.
Ben Ciccone	C-LB	5'10"	193	24		
Cap Oehler	C-LB	6'	206	23	3	
John Dempsey (from PHI)	T	6'2"	225	23		
Armand Niccolai (1 PAT in 2 attempts, 3 field goals)	T	6'2"	220	22		10
Jess Quatse	T	5'11"	218	26		
Jap Douds	G-T	5'10"	216	29		
Norm Greeney	G-T	5'11"	210	24		
Zvonimir Kvaternick	G	5'11"	210	23		
Basilio Marchi	G	6'2"	215	25		
Dave Ribble	G	6'1"	212	27		
Bull Snyder	G-T	6'2"	230	22		
Henry Weinberg	G	5'7"	190	23		

Team owner Art Rooney made lots of changes, but the Pirates still finished last in the Eastern Division. Rooney hired Luby DiMelio as coach, signed a lot of rookies and purchased four players from the Green Bay Packers. The best of the freshmen were tailback Warren Heller and end Joe Skladany from Pitt, and tackle Armand Niccolai from Duquesne. Johnny Blood had the biggest reputation of the ex-Packers, but injuries ruined his season. Two other Green Bay alumni, end Ben Smith and tackle Jess Quatse, won starting positions. Of the returning players, center Cap Oehler provided consistent high-quality play. But, with all this new talent, the offense produced few points and the Pirates lost their last seven games to finish 2-10-0.

TEAM TOTALS	YARDS GAINED	OPP. YARDS	PASS ATT.	PASS COMP.	COMP. PCT.	TOTAL POINTS	RUSH TD	PASS TD	OTHER TD	PAT	FG	SAF	OPP. PTS.
NEW YORK	2775	2342	184	80	43.5	147	11	6	1	16	7	1	107
BOSTON	3351	2606	152	44	28.9	107	10	4	2	8	1	0	94
BROOKLYN	1481	2687	161	43	26.7	61	1	5	1	7	4	0	153
PHILADELPHIA	2554	2237	163	47	28.8	127	11	7	1	10	1	0	85
PITTSBURGH	2527	3304	182	58	31.9	51	2	4	0	3	4	0	206

							RUSHING				PASSING								RECEIVING				PUNTING		KICKING						PUNT RETURNS				KICKOFF RETURNS			
UseName-Backs&Ends	Pos.	Age	Hgt	Wgt	Pts	Int	No.	Yds.	Avg	TD	Att	Comp	%	Yds	Yd/Att	TD	Int-%	RK	No.	Yds.	Avg	TD	No.	Avg	Pat	Att	%	FG	Att	%	No.	Yds.	Avg	TD	No.	Yds.	Avg	TD
NEW YORK GIANTS																																						
Harry Newman	TB-DB	24	5'8"	180	37	1	129	527	4.1	3	104	43	41	591	5.7	1	8- 8	4	4	55	14	0			4	4	100	3										1
Ed Danowski	TB-WB-DB	22	6'1"	200			95	307	3.2	0	40	17	43	278	7.0	2	4- 10																					
Wee Willie Smith	TB-FB-DB	24	5'6"	148	12		45	232	5.2	2	12	4	33	62	5.2	1	1- 50		2	32	16	0																
Jack McBride	TB-DB	32	5'11"	185	1		4	14	3.5	0	3	3	100	39	13.0	1	0 0								1	1	100											
Ken Strong	FB-DB	28	6'	202	56	3	108	438	4.1	6	23	12	52	159	6.9	1	2- 9		9	132	15	0			8	9	89	4	11	36								
Kink Richards	FB-DB	23	5'11"	195	13	1	52	182	3.5	0	1	1	100	10	0.0	0	0- 0		7	85	12	2			1	1	100											
Dale Burnett	WB-DB	25	6'1"	186	12	3	4	6	1.5	0									11	182	17	2																
Harry Stafford	WB-DB	24	5'11"	205			4	4	1.0	0									3	43	14	0																
Stu Clancy	WB-TB-DB	28	5'10"	195			17	60	3.5	0																												
John Norby (to PHI, HB, DB to C-S)	WB-DB	23	6'	195															1	6	6	0																
Bo Molenda	BB-LB	29	5'10"	213	2	2	28	99	3.5	0									4	70	18	0			2	2	100											
Max Krause	BB-LB	25	5'10"	206			26	69	2.7	0									1	4	4	0																
Red Badgro	OE-DE	31	6'	190	6	1					1	0	0						20	286	14	1																
Ray Flaherty	OE-DE	30	6'	190	6	1													14	209	15	1																
Ike Frankian	OE-DE	27	5'11"	207		1													2	20	10	0																
BOSTON REDSKINS																																						
Hal McPhail	FB-DB	22	6'1"	230	22	4				1															4	6	67											
Doug Wycoff	FB-BB-DB-LB	30	6'	225	6	1				1						1																						
Cliff Battles	WB-DB	24	6'1"	195	43	3	103	511	5.0	6									5	95	19	1			1	3	33											
Ted Wright	WB-DB	20	6'	185	8					1															2	4	50											
Ernie Pinckert	WB-DB-BB-LB	26	6'	190	6	4				1																												
Pug Rentner	WB-TB-DB	23	6'1"	195	6	3																1																
Steve Hokuf	BB-LB-OE-DE	23	6'	200	4	2					51	13	25	203	4.0	3	10-20	7							1	2	50	1										
Arnie Arenz	BB-LB	23	6'1"	215																																		
Charley Malone	OE-DE	24	6'4"	200	12														11	121	11	2																
Paul Collins	OE-DE	26	6'1"	200																																		
Flavio Tosi	OE-DE	22	6'1"	190																																		
Chief Johnson	OE-DE-C-LB	25	6'3"	225																																		
BROOKLYN DODGERS																																						
Chris Cagle	TB-WB-DB	29	5'10"	177												3																						
Shipwreck Kelly	TB-DB	27	6'2"	195	6	1				1																												
Cliff Montgomery	TB-DB	23	5'9"	165												1																						
Benny Friedman	TB-DB	29	5'10"	182																																		
Jack Grossman	WB-TB-DB	24	6'1"	195	12	1										1			10	158	16	1												1				
Ollie Sansen	WB-DB	26	6'1"	195																																		
Ralph Kercheval	WB-DB	23	6'1"	195	36	1																3			6	6	100	4										
Dick Fishel	WB-DB	24	5'9"	190																																		
Bull Karcis	BB-LB	25	5'9"	220		1																																
Dick Nesbitt	BB-LB-WB-DB	26	6'	210																																		
Stumpy Thomason	BB-LB	28	5'7"	195																																		
Paul Riblett	OE-DE	26	5'10"	182	7																	1			1	1	100	(reception)										
Wayland Becker (from ChiB)	OE-DE	23	6'	200		1													1	18	18	0																
Doc Cronkhite	OE-DE	23	6'5"	210		1																																
Harry Kloppenburg	OE-DE	27	6'1"	210																																		
Phil Peterson	OE-DE	28	5'11"	195																																		
Tom Nash	OE-DE	28	6'3"	205																																		
Mike Stramiello	OE-DE	27	6'1"	207																																		
Joe Hugret	OE-DE	24	6'2"	105																																		
PHILADELPHIA EAGLES																																						
Ed Matesic	TB-DB	23	6'1"	195	7	1					60	20	33	272	4.5	2	5- 8	3							1	2	50											
Rick Lackman	TB-HB-DB	22	5'11"	186																																		
Dan Barnhart	TB-DB	22	6'	200												1																						
Swede Hanson	FB-LB	26	6'1"	192	48	4	147	805	5.5	7												1																
Ed Storm	FB-HB-TB-BB-DB-LB	26	6'1"	195	12					2																												
Reds Weiner	FB-LB-BB-DB	23	5'9"	180	6	1										2									3	4	75	1	2	50								
Lorne Johnson	FB-LB	24	6'2"	195																					0	1	0											
Swede Ellstrom (from BOS, FB-DB)	HB-DB	26	6'1"	200	6					1						1																						
Jack Knapper	HB-DB	24	6'3"	190		1	6	9	1.5		4	0	0				2- 50																					
Red Kirkman	BB-TB-DB	28	6'1"	195	11											1							2	30.5														
Jim Leonard	BB-HB-DB	24	6'	204	6					1												1			5	7	71											
Joe Carter	OE-DE	24	6'1"	203	24														16	238	15	4																
George Kenneally	OE-DE	32	6'	192																																		
Joe Pilconis	OE-DE	22	6'1"	192		1																																
Bob Gonya	T-OE-DE	24	6'2"	205	6																	1																
Len Gudd	OE-DE	23	6'3"	220																																		
PITTSBURGH PIRATES																																						
Warren Heller	TB-DB	23	5'11"	195	6	3	131	543	4.1	1	112	31	28	511	4.6	2	15-13	6																				
Harp Vaughan	TB-BB-HB-DB	29	5'7"	150		3					39	14	36	272	7.0	2	5-13																					
Jimmy Clark	FB-HB-DB	25	5'9"	177	6																	1																
Angie Brovelli	FB-HB-LB-DB	24	6'	195	6					1																												
Mose Kelsch	FB-LB	38	5'10"	220	5		3	12	4.0	0															2	4	50	1										
Pete Rajkovich	FB-LB	23	5'10"	190																																		
Jack Roberts (from PHI, HB)	FB-LB-BB-DB	25	6'	220																																		
Alex Rado	HB-DB	23	6'1"	200		1																																
Johnny Blood	HB-DB	30	6'1"	188		1																																
Jim Levey	HB-DB	27	5'10"	156																																		
George Kavel (to PHI)	HB-DB	24	5'11"	170																																		
Silvio Zaninelli	BB-FB-LB-DB	20	5'10"	204		2																																
Buster Mott (from C-S)	BB-DB	25	5'8"	195																																		
Harry Marker	BB-DB	23	5'6"	155																																		
Ben Smith	OE-DE	23	6'3"	210															12	190	16	0																
Joe Skladany	OE-DE	23	5'10"	210	12														10	246	25	2																
Bill Sortet	OE-DE	22	6'1"	188	6																	1																
Ray Tesser	OE-DE	24	6'2"	207																																		

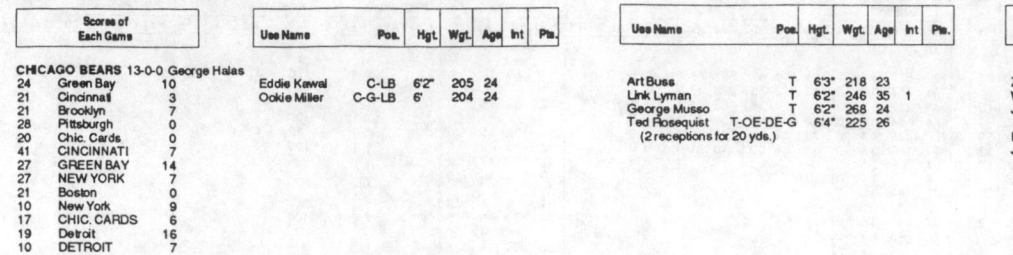

CHICAGO BEARS 13-0-0 George Halas

Scores of Each Game		
24	Green Bay	10
21	Cincinnati	3
21	Brooklyn	7
28	Pittsburgh	0
20	Chic. Cards	0
41	CINCINNATI	7
27	GREEN BAY	14
27	NEW YORK	7
21	Boston	0
10	New York	9
17	CHIC. CARDS	6
19	Detroit	16
10	DETROIT	7

Use Name	Pos.	Hgt.	Wgt.	Age	Int	Pts.
Eddie Kawal	C-LB	6'2"	205	24		
Ookie Miller	C-G-LB	6'	204	24		
Art Buss	T	6'3"	218	23		
Link Lyman	T	6'2"	246	35	1	
George Musso	T	6'2"	268	24		
Ted Rosequist	T-OE-DE-G	6'4"	225	26		
(2 receptions for 20 yds.)						
Zuck Carlson	G	6'	210	29		
Walt Kiesling	G-T	6'2"	252	31		
Joe Kopcha	G	6'	226	28		
(2 receptions for 24 yards)						
Bert Pearson	G-C-LB	6'	210	29		
Joe Zeller	G	6'1"	198	26	4	

The talent-laden Bears swept to the first perfect record in NFL history. George Halas had the ultimate fullback in Bronko Nagurski and a rookie sensation in halfback Beattie Feathers, who ran for over 1,000 yards behind Nagurski's blocking. Quarterback Carl Brumbaugh orchestrated the versatile offense with intelligence and the first-string line of Bill Hewitt, Link Lyman, Zuck Carlson, Eddie Kawal, Joe Kopcha, George Musso and Bill Karr was the best in the league. The talented reserves included fullback Jack Manders, who booted 10 field goals and finished second in the league in scoring. The Bears showed their depth by beating the string Detroit Lions in the final two games of the regular season despite having lost both Feathers and Kopcha with injuries.

DETROIT LIONS 10-3-0 Potsy Clark

9	NEW YORK	0
6	CHIC. CARDS	0
3	Green Bay	0
10	Philadelphia	0
24	BOSTON	0
28	BROOKLYN	0
38	Cincinnati at Portsmouth	0
40	PITTSBURGH	7
17	Chic. Cards	13
40	ST. LOUIS	7
0	GREEN BAY	3
16	CHIC. BEARS	19
7	Chic. Bears	10

Use Name	Pos.	Hgt.	Wgt.	Age	Int	Pts.
Chuck Bernard	C-LB	6'3"	225	22		
Clare Randolph	C-LB	6'2"	210	27	1	
George Christensen	T	6'2"	240	24		
Bob Emerick	T-G	6'2"	220	22		
Jack Johnson	T	6'4"	220	24		
Sam Knox	T-G	6'	200	24		
Maury Bodenger	G	5'10"	210	25		
Ox Emerson	G	5'11"	220	26		
Tom Hupke	G-T	5'10"	194	23		
Ray Richards	G-T	6'1"	240	28		

Pro football returned to Detroit when Dick Richards purchased the Portsmouth Spartans and transformed them into the Lions. Tailback Dutch Clark, back from last year's retirement, lured the paying customers with his exciting multiple talents and led the league in scoring. Other jewels in the lineup were Spartan veterans Glenn Presnell, Ace Gutowsky, Ernie Caddel, George Christensen, Ox Emerson, Bill McKalip and Harry Ebding. The Lions roared out of the gate, shutting out their first seven opponents and winning their first 10 games. The Packers broke the string with a 3-0 upset on November 25, but the Lion still had a shot at first place when they hosted the unbeaten Bears on Thanksgiving. Led by Gutowsky's running, the Lions led 16-7 at halftime, but the Bears came back to win 19-16 and end Detroit's first title bid.

GREEN BAY PACKERS 7-6-0 Curly Lambeau

19	PHILADELPHIA	6
10	CHIC. BEARS	24
20	NEW YORK	6
0	DETROIT	3
41	CINCINNATI	0
15	CHIC. CARDS	0
14	Chic. Bears	27
10	Boston	0
3	New York	17
0	CHIC. CARDS	9
3	Detroit	0
0	Chic. Cards	6
21	St. Louis	14

Use Name	Pos.	Hgt.	Wgt.	Age	Int	Pts.
Nate Barrager	C-G-LB	6'1"	190	24	1	
Red Bultman	C-LB	6'2"	200	27	3	
Frank Butler	C-LB	6'3"	226	25		
Lon Evans	T-G	6'2"	220	22		
Carl Jorgensen	T	6'	200	23		
Joe Kurth	T	6'1"	202	23		
Claude Perry	T	6'1"	210	32		
Ade Schwammel	T	6'2"	220	25		3
(1 field goal in 3 attempts)						
Bon Jones	G	6'2"	215	22		
Mike Michalske	G	6'	210	31		
Champ Seibold	G	6'4"	232	22		
Harry Wunsch	G	5'11"	212	22		

After the Packers' poor 1933 showing, Curly Lambeau continued dismantling the 1931 squad. Johnny Blood was sold to Pittsburgh, Cal Hubbard and Rudy Comstock retired and Lavie Dilweg was eased onto the second team. The new-look Packers fielded a young backfield featuring fullback Clarke Hinkle, passer Arnie Herber and versatile Bob Monnett. Th e line also showcased young talents, but the best work still came from championship veterans Mike Michalske and Nate Barrager. The offense relied on a strong passing attack, but it went through a four-game stretch in November without scoring a touchdown. The inconsistency of youth showed in two losses to the young Chicago Cardinals in November, sandwiched around a stirring 3-0 upset over unbeaten Detroit.

CHICAGO CARDINALS 5-6-0 Paul Schissler

9	Cincinnati at Dayton	0
0	Detroit	6
16	Cincinnati	0
0	CHIC. BEARS	20
0	Green Bay	15
0	Boston	9
21	Brooklyn	0
13	DETROIT	17
9	Green Bay	0
6	Chic. Bears	17
6	GREEN BAY	0

Use Name	Pos.	Hgt.	Wgt.	Age	Int	Pts.
Bernie Hughes	C-LB	6'1"	190	24		
Frank McNally	C-LB	6'1"	200	27		
Harry Field	T	6'1"	230	23		
Lou Gordon	T	6'5"	230	26		
Ted Isaacson	T	6'4"	272	22		
Pete Mehringer	T-G	6'2"	200	24		
Paul Shenefelt	T-G	6'	195	23	1	
Bree Cuppoletti	G	5'10"	198	24		
Phil Handler	G	6'	215	26		
Howie Tipton	G-OE-DE	5'11"	180	23	1	
Bill Volok	G	6'2"	215	24		

Coach Paul Schissler brought in a horde of rookies and swept out most of last year's cast. Schissler molded the young talent into a tough defensive squad which won five games, all by shutout. The fledging Cardinals fared poorer on offense, but they did convert kick returns into three victories. On opening day, Doug Russell took the opening kickoff and scooted 102 yards, paving the way for a 9-0 victory over Cincinnati. On November 18, Homer Griffith broke loose for a 65-yard punt return touchdown in a 9-0 triumph over the Packers. Less than two weeks later, Griffith ran 97 yards with the opening kickoff in a 6-0 whitewash of the Packers on Thanksgiving Day. The young defense profited from tough work by rookie Harry Field at tackle and Mike Mikulak at linebacker.

CINCINNATI REDS 0-8-0 Algy Clark — **ST. LOUIS GUNNERS** 1-2-0 Chile Walsh

	CINCINNATI	
0	Pittsburgh	13
0	CHIC. CARDS at Dayton	9
3	CHIC. BEARS	21
0	CHIC. CARDS	16
0	Green Bay	41
7	Chic. Bears	41
0	DETROIT at Portsmouth	38
0	Philadelphia	64
	St. LOUIS	
6	PITTSBURGH	0
7	Detroit	40
14	GREEN BAY	21

Use Name	Pos.	Hgt.	Wgt.	Age	Int	Pts.
Ted Maples	C-LB	6'	195	23		
Russ McLeod	C-LB	6'	190	27		
Lee Mulleneaux	C-LB FB-WB-DB	6'2"	216	27		
John Rogers	C-LB	5'8"	210	24		
Hal Weldin	C-LB	6'	198	23	1	
Ed Aspatore	T-G	6'1"	220	25		
Charlie Diehl	T	6'	215	27		
Earl Elser	T	6'1"	227	22		
Foster Howell	T	6'3"	215	23		
Babe Lyon	T	6'2"	235	27		
George Munday	T-G	6'2"	215	26		
Sandy Sandberg	T	6'2"	225	24		
Charlie Zunker	T	6'4"	227	26		
Les Caywood	G	6'	230	29		
Rosie Grant	G	5'10"	198	25		
Homer Hanson	G	6'	210	23		
Russ Lay (from DET)	G	5'11"	198	23		
Biff Lee	G	6'	235	26		1
(1 PAT in 1 attempt)						
Len McGirl	G	6'	206	25		
Bill Montgomery	G-T	5'9"	200	25		
Homer Reynolds	G	5'10"	190	24		
Harvey Sark	G	5'10"	210	27		

The Cincinnati defense hung tough for the first few games, but the offense was practically impotent. By mid-October, the dispirited Reds were regularly being crushed by clubs using their substitutes. With local interest nil, the management sold the franchise on November 5 to a St. Louis group which ran a strong independent pro team there. The Reds had one final game on November 6, and they faded into history with a 64-0 humiliation at the hands of the Eagles. On the next Sunday, the St. Louis Gunners took the Reds' place in the schedule and the standings. Without using any of the Cincinnati players, the Gunners broke into the NFL with a 6-0 victory over the Pirates. Although five former Reds joined the squad, the Gunners lost the remaining games against the Lions and Packers.

TEAM TOTALS	YARDS GAINED	OPP. YARDS	PASS ATT.	PASS COMP.	COMP. PCT.	TOTAL POINTS	RUSH TD	PASS TD	OTHER TD	PAT	FG	SAF	OPP. PTS.
CHICAGO BEARS	3783	2119	179	63	35.2	286	20	17	0	34	10	0	86
DETROIT	3510	1960	143	46	32.2	238	27	3	2	22	8	0	59
GREEN BAY	3372	2523	188	73	38.8	156	8	10	1	16	8	1	112
CHICAGO CARDS	1598	1578	140	34	24.3	80	7	1	3	5	3	0	84
CIN—ST. LOUIS	1608	3488	173	49	28.3	37	3	1	0	4	3	2	304

							RUSHING				PASSING								RECEIVING				PUNTING		KICKING						PUNT RETURNS				KICKOFF RETURNS			
Use Name - Backs & Ends	Pos.	Age	Hgt	Wgt	Pts	Int	No.	Yds.	Avg	TD	Att	Comp	%	Yds	Yd/Att	TD	Int-%	RK	No.	Yds.	Avg	TD	No.	Avg	Pat	Att	%	FG	Att	%	No.	Yds.	Avg	TD	No.	Yds.	Avg	TD
CHICAGO BEARS																																						
Carl Brumbaugh	QB-DB	26	5'10"	180	15	2	7	9	1.3	0	33	8	24	232	7.0	3	2- 6		5	84	17	2			3	3	100											
Bernie Masterson	QB-DB	23	6'3"	195	7	1	4	11	2.8	0	4	2	50	57	14.3	0	0- 0		5	89	18	1			1	2	50											
Beattie Feathers	HB-DB	26	5'10"	185	54		101	**1004**	**9.9**	8	12	4	33	41	3.4	1	1- 8		5	153	31	1																
Bronko Nagurski	FB-LB	25	6'2"	230	43	2	123	586	4.8	7	8	5	63	48	6.0	2	1- 12		3	32	11	0			1	2	50											
Gene Ronzani	HB-LB	25	5'9"	208	18	1	84	485	5.8	0	32	15	47	150	4.7	3	0- 0		8	114	14	3																
Jack Manders	FB-HB-LB	25	6'	210	71	2	57	184	3.2	2	3	2	67	35	11.7	0	0- 0		1	12	12	0			**29**	**30**	**97**	**10**										
Johnny Sisk	HB-LB	27	6'2"	200	6		41	156	3.8	1	9	2	22	22	2.4	0	1- 11		2	22	11	0																
Red Grange	HB-DB	31	6'	190	18		32	136	4.3	1	25	6	24	81	3.2	1	7- 28		3	61	20	2																
Keith Molesworth	HB-QB-DB	28	5'9"	168	12	1	60	136	2.3	1	36	13	36	225	6.3	5	4- 11		3	17	6	0																
George Corbett	HB-DB	26	5'9"	184			30	119	4.0	0	4	2	50	46	11.5	1	0- 0		2	7	4	0																
John Doehring	HB-LB	24	6'	215		1	7	16	2.3	0	11	3	27	48	4.4	1	0- 0		1	14	14	0																
Bill Hewitt	OE-DE	24	5'9"	195	30		1	14	14.0	0	2	1	50	4	2.0	0	0- 0		10	151	15	5																
Luke Johnsos	OE-DE	28	6'2"	198	12														6	94	16	2																
Bill Karr	OE-DE	23	6'1"	194	6														4	76	19	1																
DETROIT LIONS																																						
Dutch Clark	TB-DB	27	6'	190	74	1	122	763	6.3	**8**	49	23	**47**	383	**7.8**	0	3- 6	2	7	72	10	0			14	19	74	4											
Glenn Presnell	TB-WB-DB	29	5'10"	200	62	9	116	425	3.8	7	57	13	23	236	4.1	2	9-16	7							8	11	73	4											
Ace Gutowsky	FB-LB	25	5'11"	205	30	3	140	523	3.7	5																												
Frank Christensen	FB-BB-LB-DB	25	6'1"	205	12	3				2																												
Ernie Caddel	WB-DB	23	6'2"	205	36	1	101	428	4.2	4						1			9	125	14	1																
Bill McWilliams	WB-BB-DB	23	6'	200																																		
Father Lumpkin	BB-DB	26	6'2"	210	12	3				1																												
Bob Rowe	BB-WB-DB-FB-LB	23	6'	200		2																																
Harry Ebding	OE-DE	27	5'11"	205	12														9	**257**	**29**	2																
John Schneller	OE-DE	22	6'2"	205																																		
Buster Mitchell	OE-DE	28	6'	210		1																																
Bill McKalip	OE-DE	26	6'1"	195																																		
GREEN BAY PACKERS																																						
Arnie Herber	TB-HB-DB	24	5'11"	203		1	25	64	2.6	0	**115**	**42**	37	**799**	6.9	**8**	12- 10	1					20	36.2														
Bob Monnett	TB-DB	24	5'9"	180	30	1	66	158	2.4	2	47	16	34	223	5.0	2	4- 9	5	2	18	9	0			6	7	86	4	7	57								
Clarke Hinkle	FB-LB	24	5'11"	200	26	2	142	384	2.7	1	16	7	44	54	3.4	0	1- 6		10	123	12	1	64	35.5	5	5	100	3	12	25								
Roger Grove	HB-BB-TB-FB-DB	26	6'	184	25	3	50	226	4.5	1	5	4	80	25	5.0	0	0- 0		8	116	20	3			1	2	50											
Joe Laws	HB-BB-DB	23	5'9"	185	12	4	46	139	3.0	1	5	1	20	10	2.0	0	0- 0		6	137	23	1																
Hank Bruder	BB-FB-HB-TB-DB-LB	26	6'	197	22	4	41	115	2.8	1	6	2	33	23	3.8	0	1- 17		6	100	17	1	18	37.0	4	5	80											
Buckets Goldenberg	BB-FB-DB-LB	23	5'10"	215	12	3	29	68	2.3	2									3	17	6	0																
Earl Witte	BB-DB	26	6'	188			4	12	3.0	0																												
Milt Gantenbein	OE-DE	24	6'	193															14	250	18	0																
Lavie Dilweg	OE-DE	31	6'3"	202	12														7	134	19	2																
Al Rose	OE-DE	27	6'3"	200	12														5	73	15	2																
Les Peterson	OE-DE	24	6'3"	207															9	158	18	0																
Al Norgard	OE-DE	24	6'1"	194															2	8	4	0																
CHICAGO CARDINALS																																						
Doug Russell	TB-DB	22	6'	180	12					1																													1
Homer Griffith	TB-DB	22	5'11"	165	12	1																												1				1
Mike Mikulak	FB-WB-LB-DB	21	6'1"	210	24					4																												
Roy Horstmann	FB-LB	23	6'	190																																		
Dave Cook	WB-DB	22	6'2"	200	4	1																			1	3	33	1										
Curly Hinchman (to DET, BB-DB)	WB-TB-DB	27	5'10"	190		1																																
Phil Sarboe (from BOS)	BB-DB	22	5'10"	165		1																																
Frank Greene	BB-DB	23	5'11"	190																																		
Paul Pardonner	BB-DB	24	5'8"	170	3																							1										
Tom Murphy	BB-DB-FB-LB	27	5'11"	170																																		
Bill Smith	OE-DE	22	6'1"	198	25		5	74	14.8	2												1			4	6	67	1										
George Duggins	OE-DE	22	6'3"	200																																		
Milan Creighton	OE-DE	26	6'	190																																		
Bob Neuman	OE-DE	22	6'	200		1																																
Joe Krejci	OE-DE	28	6'	190																																		
CINCINNATI REDS — ST. LOUIS GUNNERS																																						
Lew Pope	TB-BB-DB	26	6'	196														1																				
Norris Steverson	TB-DB	24	5'10"	185																																		
Manny Rapp	TB-DB-FB-LB	24	6'	215																																		
Syl Saumer (from & to PIT, FB-BB)	TB-DB	22	6'1"	195	6					1																												
Gil LeFebvre	TB-DB	24	5'6"	156																																		
Charlie McLaughlin	TB-DB	24	6'	183																																		
Jabby Andrews	TB-DB			200																																		
Bill Senn	TB-BB-DB	29	6'	175	3																							1	1	100								
Red Corzine	FB-LB-BB-DB	25	6'	210	6	2				1																												
Swede Johnston (from GB)	FB-LB-WB-DB	24	5'10"	200	6					1																												
Otto Vokaty	FB-LB-WB-DB	25	6'1"	190																																		
Bill Parriott	FB-LB	23	5'10"	165																																		
Tom Bushby	WB-DB	22	5'10"	200																																		
Tiny Feather	WB-BB-DB	31	6'	205		1																																
Gene Alford	WB-DB	28	5'9"	180	6																				3	3	100	1	2	50								
Cy Casper (from GB, TB-DB)	WB-TB-DB	22	6'	188																																		
Benny Sohn	WB-DB-FB-LB	22	5'8"	170																																		
Cliff Moore	WB-DB		6'1"	202																																		
Algy Clark (to PHI)	BB-DB	30	6'	190	3																				0	1	0	1										
Blake Workman	BB-DB	24	5'11"	185																																		
Bill Lewis	BB-DB		5'11"	186																																		
Benny LaPresta	BB-DB	25	5'9"	185																																		
Jim Mooney	OE-DE	26	5'11"	197		1																																
Cookie Tackwell	OE-DE-WB-DB	27	6'2"	218																																		
Paul Moss	OE-DE	25	6'2"	200																		1																
Mack Gladden	OE-DE	25	6'2"	195																																		
Cole Wilging	OE-DE	22	6'3"	205																																		
George Rogge	OE-DE	26	6'	185																																		

NEW YORK GIANTS 9-3-0 Steve Owen

Scores of Each Game		
42	Pittsburgh	7
7	Green Bay	16
20	Boston	12
10	BROOKLYN	7
17	BOSTON	6
13	CHIC. CARDS	14
3	CHIC. BEARS	20
3	Chic. Bears	0
10	PHILADELPHIA	0
21	Brooklyn	0
21	Philadelphia	14
13	PITTSBURGH	0

Use Name	Pos.	Hgt	Wgt	Age	Int	Pts
Johnny Dell Isola	C-G-LB	5'11"	198	23		
Mel Hein	C-LB	6'2"	225	26		

Use Name – Tackles	Pos.	Hgt	Wgt	Age	Int	Pts
Len Grant	T	6'3"	235	29		
Tex Irvin	T	6'	230	28		
Bill Morgan	T	6'2"	235	25		
Jess Quatse	T	5'11"	230	28		

Use Name – Guards	Pos.	Hgt	Wgt	Age	Int	Pts
Bob Bellinger	G	5'11"	220	22		
Potsy Jones	G	5'11"	224	25		
Bernie Kaplan	G	6'	210	22		
Bill Owen	G-T	6'	225	31		

The Giants stood so far above the competition in the East, they practically rebuilt the club in midstream and still won the division title. With a rock-hard defense leading the way, the New Yorkers never lost a game to an Eastern opponent, suffering their only defeats at the hands of the Packers, Bears, and Cardinals.

Coach Steve Owen mostly achieved the season's success by inserting new players in key spots. Second-year tailback Ed Danowski pushed Harry Newman to the bench on the strength of his passing and running, and Kink Richards took over Ken Strong's rushing job. Owen also eased ends Red Badgro and Ray Flaherty to the sidelines in favor of rookie Tod Goodwin, the league's leading receiver, and Ike Frankian. Others who had to be replaced were Butch Gibson, who retired, and Dale Burnett, who was injured. Nevertheless, whomever Owen plugged into the gap invariably worked, and the Giants, as always, triumphed in the East.

BROOKLYN DODGERS 5-6-1 Paul Schissler

Scores of Each Game		
3	Boston	7
12	DETROIT	10
7	New York	10
14	Chic. Bears	24
17	PHILADELPHIA	6
13	Pittsburgh	7
3	Philadelphia	0
7	PITTSBURGH	16
14	CHIC. CARDS	12
0	NEW YORK	21
0	DETROIT	28
0	BOSTON	0

Use Name	Pos.	Hgt	Wgt	Age	Int	Pts
Walt McDonald	C-LB	5'10"	210	23		
Cap Oehler	C-LB	6'	205	24		

Use Name – Tackles	Pos.	Hgt	Wgt	Age	Int	Pts
Alex Eagle	T	6'2"	220	22		
Carl Heldt	T	6'2"	205	22		
Bill Lee	T	6'2"	240	23		
Lou Lubratovich	T	6'2"	230	28		
Jack Robinson	T	6'3"	220	23		

Use Name – Guards	Pos.	Hgt	Wgt	Age	Int	Pts
Gil Bergerson	G-T	6'6"	245	25		
Win Croft	G	5'11"	235	25		
Bo Kirkland	G	6'	215	22		
Frank Stojack	G	5'10"	190	23		

After seeing how the Chicago Cardinals had bettered themselves with an almost total rookie squad, the Dodgers hired Paul Schissler from the Cards to run the same sort of rebuilding program in Brooklyn—and fifteen rookies were infused into the team. Old pros Chris Cagle, Shipwreck Kelly, and Herman Hickman retired before the season started to give the youngsters a chance. But the newcomers could not lift the team, and they finished with the same mediocre record as 1934. The tragic fault in the Dodgers still was the lack of a major-league passer, a fact which came home to roost when Kercheval's punts—one which covered 86 yards—proved more effective than the team's forward passing.

PITTSBURGH PIRATES 4-8-0 Joe Bach

Scores of Each Game		
17	Philadelphia	7
7	NEW YORK	42
7	CHIC. BEARS	23
0	Green Bay	27
6	PHILADELPHIA	17
17	CHIC. CARDS	13
6	BOSTON	0
7	BROOKLYN	13
16	Brooklyn	7
14	GREEN BAY	34
3	Boston	13
0	New York	13

Use Name	Pos.	Hgt	Wgt	Age	Int	Pts
Ben Ciccone	C-LB	5'10"	208	**24**		
Joe Malkovich	C-LB	6'3"	205	23		
Lee Mulleneaux	C-LB	6'2"	225	28		
Swede Pittman	C-LB	6'	215	27		
Ed Skoronski	C-LB	6'2"	208	23		

Use Name – Tackles	Pos.	Hgt	Wgt	Age	Int	Pts
Mule Bray	T	6'2"	220	26		
Stan Oleniczak	T	6'	220	23		6
Sandy Sandberg	T	6'2"	225	25		
Joe Wiehl	T	5'11"	254	25		

Use Name – Guards	Pos.	Hgt	Wgt	Age	Int	Pts
Al Arndt	G	5'11"	205	24		
Norm Greeney	G	5'11"	210	25		
Henry Hayduk	G	6'	200	21		
Bob Hoel	G	6'	212	22		
George Rado	G	5'9"	197	22		
Dave Ribble	G	6'1"	212	28		
Bull Snyder	G	6'2"	230	23		

With their third new head coach in as many years, the Pirates rushed into the season with a 17-7 triumph at Philadelphia. Coach Joe Bach got a look at the real Pirates, though, when his club opened its home schedule by letting the New York Giants roll to a 42-7 romp and then encountering three more straight losses to shrivel the attendance and spell another year of hardship for owner Art Rooney.

Yet before the season ended, the Pirates won four games, the highest total in their short history, with back-to-back victories over the then unbeaten Cardinals and Redskins. Although the Pirates' forward wall had good success against teams that relied heavily on running attacks, they were most vulnerable when it came to stopping the passing game. The Pittsburgh offense itself threatened no outbursts of points and relied instead on Armand Niccolai's field goals to win close games.

BOSTON REDSKINS 2-8-1 Eddie Casey

Scores of Each Game		
7	BROOKLYN	3
12	NEW YORK	20
7	DETROIT	17
6	New York	17
0	Pittsburgh	6
0	Detroit	14
6	PHILADELPHIA	7
14	CHIC. BEARS	30
0	CHIC. CARDS	6
13	PITTSBURGH	3
0	Brooklyn	0

Use Name	Pos.	Hgt	Wgt	Age	Int	Pts
Frank Bausch	C-LB	6'3"	210	27		
Chief Johnson	LB	6'3"	225	26		
Larry Siemering	C-LB	6'3"	202	21		

Use Name – Tackles	Pos.	Hgt	Wgt	Age	Int	Pts
Jim Barber	T	6'3"	205	23		
Turk Edwards	T	6'2"	260	27		
Gail O'Brien	T	6'1"	216	23		
Steve Sinko	T	6'3"	230	24		

Use Name – Guards	Pos.	Hgt	Wgt	Age	Int	Pts
Rick Concannon	G	6'	215	26		
Herman Gundlach	G	6'	205	22		
Eddie Kahn	G	5'9"	190	23		
Jim Moran	G	6'1"	205	22		
Les Olsson	G	6'	225	27		

George Marshall had a perfect plan to draw more fans to the Redskin games. He hired Eddie Casey, an all-time great Harvard halfback, as his new head coach; with his previous college record and good looks, Casey would be a sure boost for the attendance. But the Marshall Plan did not work, and the Redskins bit the dust regularly from the start of the season.

Halfback Cliff Battles as usual made up almost the entire Boston offense with his end runs behind whatever blocking he could find. Without any passing game, a porous defense, and with owner Marshall sitting on the bench giving players instructions contradicting those of the coach, the Redskins were fortunate to win two games.

PHILADELPHIA EAGLES 2-9-0 Lud Wray

Scores of Each Game		
7	PITTSBURGH	17
0	Detroit	35
17	Pittsburgh	6
0	CHIC. BEARS	39
6	Brooklyn	17
7	Boston	6
0	BROOKLYN	3
3	Chic. Cards	12
0	New York	10
14	NEW YORK	21
6	GREEN BAY	13

Use Name	Pos.	Hgt	Wgt	Age	Int	Pts
Amy McPherson (from CHIB, G)	C-G-LB	5'11"	215	23		

Use Name – Tackles	Pos.	Hgt	Wgt	Age	Int	Pts
Howard Bailey	T	6'	205	22		
Bill Brian	T-C-LB	6'2"	200	22		
Paul Cuba	T	6'	212	27		
Carl Jorgensen (1 PAT in 1 attempt, 1 field goal)	T	6'	210	24		4
Joe Kresky (to and from PIT, G)	T-G	6'	220	27		
Jim MacMurdo	T	6'1"	210	**24**		
Leo Raskowski	T	6'3"	218	29		
Clyde Williams	T	6'2"	210	24		

Use Name – Guards	Pos.	Hgt	Wgt	Age	Int	Pts
Harry Benson	G	5'10"	218	25		
Tom Graham	G	6'3"	210	26		
Diddie Wilson	G	5'10"	195	24		
Vince Zizak	G	5'8"	208	26		
Jim Zyntell	G	6'1"	200	25		

The Eagles slipped back from the gains they had made in 1934 by falling to a new low of two wins. A fine crowd of 20,000 turned out on opening day, but the Eagles promptly turned them off by losing 17-7 to the lowly Pittsburgh Pirates.

Although coach Lud Wray had essentially the same players back from last year, an injury to back Swede Hanson slowed the attack and could not be overcome by the collection of mediocre football talent. Of the newcomers, only Eggs Manske added much to the Eagles, teaming with Joe Carter to give the club a fine set of ends.

Wray at least showed an open mind about trying new talent. He gave Alabama Pitts, a graduate not of any college but of the Sing Sing big house, a crack at a backfield post. But the legendary prison athlete had left his best days behind the bars.

							RUSHING				PASSING								RECEIVING				PUNTING		KICKING						PUNT RETURNS				KICKOFF RETURNS			
Use Name – Backs & Ends	Pos.	Age	Hgt	Wgt	Pts	Int	No.	Yds	Avg	TD	Att	Comp	%	Yds	Yd/Att	TD	Int–%	RK	No.	Yds	Avg	TD	No.	Avg	Pat	Att	%	FG	Att	%	No.	Yds	Avg	TD	No.	Yds	Avg	TD
NEW YORK GIANTS																																						
Ed Danowski	TB-DB	23	6'1"	198	12		130	335	2.6	2	113	57	50	795	7.0	11	9– 8	1																				
Harry Newman	TB-DB	25	5'8"	182	9		65	166	2.6	0	29	9	31	132	4.6	0									3	3	100	2										
Tony Sarausky	TB-FB-DB	23	5'11"	198	7					1	9	3	33	53	5.9	0									1	1	100											
John Mackorell	TB-DB	23	5'10"	178																																		
Kink Richards	FB-DB	24	5'11"	196	28		149	449	3.0	4									8	41	5	0			1	1	100	1										
Ken Strong	FB-DB	29	6'	205	29		46	151	3.3	1	3	0	0	0	0.0	0									11	12	92	4										
Stu Clancy	FB-WB-DB	29	5'10"	190	6					1																												
Max Krause	FB-DB	26	5'10"	200			32	121	3.8	0																												
Dale Burnett	WB-DB	26	6'1"	188	36														12	199	17	6																
Leland Shaffer	WB-DB	23	6'2"	200															7	123	18	0																
Red Corzine	BB-LB	26	6'	210	6		32	105	3.3	0																												
Bo Molenda	BB-LB	30	5'10"	215	11																				5	6	83											
Tod Goodwin	OE-DE	23	6'	184	24														26	432	17	4																
Ike Frankian	OE-DE	28	5'11"	207	6														7	39	6	0																
Walt Singer	OE-DE	22	6'	198	6																	1																
Red Badgro	OE-DE	32	6'	195																																		
Ray Flaherty	OE-DE	31	6'	195																																		
Les Borden	OE-DE	25	6'	185																																		
BROOKLYN DODGERS																																						
Red Franklin	TB-DB	23	5'10"	160	18		100	284	2.8	3	67	18	27	270	4.0	0		12																				
Jack Grossman	TB-DB	25	6'1"	190	13		67	208	3.1	2	35	9	26	149	4.3	1									1	1	100											
Wilbur White	TB-DB	23	6'	168							32	10	31	73	2.3	2																						
Bull Karcis	FB-LB	26	5'9"	220	6		68	188	2.8	1	5	2	40	23	4.6	0			5	58	12	0																
Stan Kostka	FB-LB	22	5'11"	215			63	249	4.0	0	6	0	0	0	0.0	0																						
Ralph Kercheval	HB-DB	24	6'1"	193	35		34	89	2.6	0	33	13	39	203	6.2	1			7	130	19	1			8	9	89	5	16	31								
Ollie Sansen	HB-DB	27	6'1"	198																																		
Father Lumpkin	BB-DB	27	6'2"	205																																		
John Norby	BB-DB	24	6'	195																																		
Jay Hornbeak	BB-DB	23	5'11"	185																																		
Wayland Becker	OE-DE	24	6'	185	6														10	131	13	1			0	1	0	0	3	0								
Ray Fuqua	OE-DE	23	6'	190	6														8	82	10	1																
Paul Riblett	OE-DE	27	5'10"	182															6	86	14	0																
Bud Hubbard	OE-DE	22	6'	190	6																	1																
PITTSBURGH PIRATES																																						
Johnny Gildea	TB-DB	25	6'2"	195			49	1	0.0	0	95	28	29	529	5.6	2		9																				
Warren Heller	TB-HB-DB	25	5'11"	195			37	112	3.0	0	41	9	22	88	2.1	0		14																				
Cy Casper	TB-BB-DB	23	6'	193	18		56	102	1.8	2	39	13	33	123	3.2	0			5	94	19	1																
John Doehring	TB-DB	25	6'	215			3	–6	–2.0	0	8	4	50	83	10.4	2																						
Silvio Zaninelli	FB-LB	21	5'10	210																																		
Buzz Wetzel (from CHIB)	FB-LB	24	5'10	190	6		22	41	1.9	1	8	2	25	21	2.6	0																						
Swede Ellstrom	FB-LB	27	6'1"	205			10	14	1.4	0	7	6	86	68	9.7	0																						
Art Strutt	HB-DB	22	6'	205	6		92	323	3.5	0	2	0	0	0	0.0	0			7	112	16	0																
Jim Levey	HB-DB	28	5'10"	170	24		42	69	1.6	2	5	1	20	12	2.4	0			11	112	10	2																
Heinie Weisenbaugh(to BOS,BB-LB)	HB-DB	21	5'11"	190	12		36	50	1.4	0	11	1	9	14	1.3	0			7	73	10	2																
Mike Nixon	HB-DB	23	5'11"	175																																		
John Turley	BB-DB	22	5'10"	180			4	7	1.8	0	27	6	22	92	3.4	1																						
Gene Augusterfer	BB-DB	23	5'9"	180																																		
Vic Vidoni	OE-DE	22	6'1"	210															11	111	10	0																
Ben Smith	OE-DE	24	6'3"	210															9	166	18	0																
Bill Sortet	OE-DE	23	6'1"	188															6	136	23	0																
Cliff Dolaway	OE-DE	22	6'	215																																		
Glenn Campbell	OE-DE	31	5'11"	210																																		
Armand Niccolai	T-OE-DE	28	6'2"	220	28																				10	12	83	6										
BOSTON REDSKINS																																						
Bill Shepherd (to DET, FB-LB)	TB BB FB DB LB	23	6'0"	190	26		143	425	3.0	4	64	20	44	417	6.5	2		6							1	2	50											
Cliff Battles	TB-DB	25	6'1"	195	12		84	310	3.7	1	22	5	23	92	4.2	0			2	22	11	0			0	2	0											1
Pug Rentner	TB-BB-WB-DB	24	6'1"	182	13		81	243	3.0	1	50	9	18	148	3.0	1		12							1	1	100											
Doug Nott (from DET)	TB-DB	24	6'	195			48	98	2.0	0	34	9	26	169	5.0	1																						
Hal McPhail	FB-DB	23	6'1"	230			45	105	2.3	0	2	0	0	0	0.0	0																						
Jim Musick	FB-DB	25	5'11"	205	14		60	174	2.9	2	1	0	0	0	0.0	0									2	3	67											
Steve Hokuf	FB-BB-LB-OE-DE	24	6'	202																																		
Ernie Pinckert	WB-DB	27	6'	200															5	60	12	0																
Vic Baltzell	WB-DB	23	5'11"	205																																		
Ted Wright (to BKN, BB-DB)	BB-LB	21	6'	185	1		65	45	0.7	0	18	4	22	51	2.8	0									1	2	50											
Charley Malone	OE-DE	25	6'4"	210	12														22	433	20	2																
Flavio Tosi	OE-DE	23	6'1"	187	6														10	169	17	1																
Paul Collins	OE-DE	27	6'1"	200																																		
PHILADELPHIA EAGLES																																						
Ed Matesic	TB-DB	24	6'1"	195	6		50	138	2.8	1	64	15	23	284	4.4	2		10																				
Ed Storm	TB-DB	27	6'1"	195			84	164	2.0	0	44	15	34	372	8.5	3		5																				
Jim Leonard	FB-LB	25	6'	204	6		74	171	2.3	1	32	11	34	119	3.7	0																						
Izzy Weinstock	FB-BB-LB	22	6'	205			58	176	3.1	0	5	1	20	12	2.4	0			8	107	13	0																
Bob Rowe	FB-LB	24	6'	195																																		
Swede Hanson	HB-DB	26	6'1"	197			77	209	2.7	0	1	1	100	23	23.0	0	0– 0																					
Rick Lackman	HB-DB	23	5'11"	186	1		22	56	2.6	0	1	1	100	8	8.0	0	0– 0		5	49	10	0			1	1	100											
Mike Sebastian (to PIT)	HB-DB	25	5'11"	185			18	76	4.2	0	1	0	0	0	0.0	0																						
Alabama Pitts	HB-DB	25	5'10"	185																																		
Dick Frahm (to BOS, WB-DB)	HB-DB	29	5'10"	190																																		
Stumpy Thomason (from BKN)	BB-DB	29	5'7"	190																																		
Steve Banas (from DET)	BB-DB	25	6'	190																																		
Irv Kupcinet	BB-DB	23	6'1"	190																																		
Red Kirkman	BB-DB	29	6'1"	195							10	3	30	30	3.0	1																						
Joe Carter	OE-DE	25	6'1"	203	12														11	260	24	2																
Eggs Manske	OE-DE	22	6'	185	24														9	205	23	4																
George Kenneally	OE-DE	33	6'	192																																		
Buke Robison	OE-DE-C-LB	25	6'4"	197																																		
Max Padlow	OE-DE	23	6'1"	198																																		
Hank Reese	C-LB	24	5'11"	210	7																				4	6	67	1										

TEAM TOTALS

	OFFENSE																	DEFENSE							
		RUSHING:		PASSING:							PENALTY:	FUMBLES:	POINTS:												
	FIRST DOWNS	Yards	TD	Att.	Comp	Comp Pct.	Yards	Yds/Att.	Yds/Comp	TD	Yards	Number	Total	TD	PAT	FG	Saf	Total Yards	Pass Att.	Pass Comp	Comp Pct.	No. Pass Int.	Oppos Fumb. Rec.	Points	TEAM TOTALS
NEW YORK	112	1451	9	154	69	44.8	980	6.4	14.2	11	175	20	180	23	21	7	0	2019	205	68	33.2	27	18	96	NEW YORK
BROOKLYN	90	1108	6	178	52	29.2	718	4.0	13.8	4	179	31	90	11	9	5	0	2960	163	55	33.7	26	38	141	BROOKLYN
PITTSBURGH	64	808	5	233	67	28.8	996	4.3	14.9	5	201	30	100	12	10	6	0	3204	189	66	34.9	21	27	209	PITTSBURGH
BOSTON	95	1263	5	175	47	26.9	752	4.3	16.0	3	166	30	65	10	5	0	0	1982	166	68	41.0	27	19	123	BOSTON
PHILADELPHIA	82	1054	2	158	47	29.7	848	5.4	18.0	6	330	28	60	8	6	2	0	2669	168	59	35.1	22	30	179	PHILADELPHIA

DETROIT LIONS 7-3-2 Potsy Clark

Scores of Each Game		
35	PHILADELPHIA	0
10	CHIC. CARDS	10
10	Brooklyn	12
17	Boston	7
9	Green Bay	13
14	BOSTON	0
7	Chic. Cards	6
7	Green Bay	31
20	GREEN BAY	10
20	Chic. Bears	20
14	CHIC. BEARS	2
28	Brooklyn	0

Use Name	Pos.	Hgt	Wgt	Age	Int	Pts
Clare Randolph	C-LB	6'2"	205	28		
Elmer Ward	C-LB	6'2"	215	22		

Use Name – Tackles	Pos.	Hgt	Wgt	Age	Int	Pts
George Christensen	T	6'2"	238	25		
Jack Johnson	T	6'4"	210	25		
Red Stacy	T-G	6'2"	207	23		
Jim Steen	T	6'2"	205	22		

Use Name – Guards	Pos.	Hgt	Wgt	Age	Int	Pts
Ox Emerson	G	5'11"	200	27		
Roy Gagnon	G	5'11"	210	22		
Tom Hupke	G	5'10"	192	24		
Sam Knox	G	6'	220	25		
Regis Monahan	G	5'10"	215	26		

With a squad as deep as it was talented, the Lions were unbeaten in their last four games to edge the Packers and bring home the NFL crown in only their second year in the league.

The Lions stalked their opponents on the ground. Of the NFL's top ten rushers, Ernie Caddel, Dutch Clark, Bill Shepherd, and Ace Gutowsky all wore Detroit blue jerseys; Caddel and Shepherd relied on speed, Clark on shifty moves, and Gutowsky on straight-ahead power. Frank Christensen and Buddy Parker filled the blocking back position, and Glenn Presnell completed the platoon of backs with his running and place kicking. Clearing the way for the backs was a line featuring George Christensen, Ox Emerson, and Clare Randolph.

GREEN BAY PACKERS 8-4-0 Curly Lambeau

Scores of Each Game		
6	CHIC. CARDS	7
7	CHIC. BEARS	0
16	NEW YORK	7
27	PITTSBURGH	0
0	Chic. Cards	3
13	DETROIT	9
17	Chic. Bears	14
31	DETROIT	7
10	Detroit	20
34	Pittsburgh	14
7	Chic. Cards	9
13	Philadelphia	6

Use Name	Pos.	Hgt	Wgt	Age	Int	Pts
Nate Barrager	C-LB	6'	210	28		
Frank Butler	C-LB	6'3"	230	26		
George Svendsen	C-LB	6'4"	214	22		

Use Name – Tackles	Pos.	Hgt	Wgt	Age	Int	Pts
Cal Hubbard	T-DE	6'4"	265	34		6
Buster Maddox	T	6'3"	240	23		
Claude Perry	T	6'1"	215	33		
Ade Schwammel	T	6'2"	230	26		15
(3 PAT's in 4 attempts, 4 field goals)						
Champ Seibold	T	6'4"	240	22		

Use Name – Guards	Pos.	Hgt	Wgt	Age	Int	Pts
Tiny Engebretsen	G	6'1"	235	25		1
(1 PAT in 1 attempt)						
Lon Evans	G	6'2"	220	23		
Walt Kiesling	G	6'2"	260	32		
Mike Michalske	G	6'	210	32		
Bob O'Connor	G-T-BB-DE	6'1"	220	25		

Don Hutson's first play for the Green Bay Packers served notice that a new era had arrived. After the Bear's opening exhibition game kickoff, the frail end from Alabama split out to the left while Johnny Blood, back again in Green Bay, lined up as a flanker to the right. Since Blood had burned many a secondary, the Bears concentrated on him, while Hutson went down, faked the halfback to the outside, and outran the Bear safetyman down the middle. Arnie Herber cut loose with a perfect pass which Hutson carried for an 83-yard touchdown. Hutson brought a full bag of pass patterns and moves to go with his sprinter's speed to send defensive backs around the league back to the drawing board in the advent of pro football's first modern wide receiver.

Although the new pass combination shot the Packers back into contention in the Western Division, their three losses to the Chicago Cardinals torpedoed their title hopes in this discovery year of the bomb.

CHICAGO BEARS 6-4-2 George Halas

Scores of Each Game		
0	Green Bay	7
23	Pittsburgh	7
39	Philadelphia	0
24	BROOKLYN	14
14	GREEN BAY	17
20	New York	3
30	Boston	14
0	NEW YORK	3
20	DETROIT	20
2	Detroit	14
7	CHIC. CARDS	7
13	Chic. Cards	0

Use Name	Pos.	Hgt	Wgt	Age	Int	Pts
Eddie Kawal	C-LB-G-T	6'2"	198	25		6
Ookie Miller	C-LB	6'	204	25		
Frank Sullivan	C-LB	6'3"	203	23		

Use Name – Tackles	Pos.	Hgt	Wgt	Age	Int	Pts
Art Buss	T	6'3"	218	24		
Dub Miller	T-G	6'	210	23		
George Musso	T	6'2"	258	25		
Ted Rosequist	T-OE-DE	6'4"	213	27		
Milt Trost	T-OE-DE	6'1"	203	22		

Use Name – Guards	Pos.	Hgt	Wgt	Age	Int	Pts
Zuck Carlson	G-T	6	210	30		
Joe Kopcha	G	6	226	29		3
(1 field goal missed 1 PAT attempt)						
Ray Richards	G	6'1"	235	29		
Joe Zeller	G	6'1"	203	27		

The Bears struggled to a third-place tie with the Cardinals due to injuries and a costly retirement. A bad hip laid Bronko Nagurski up for most of the campaign, while halfback Beattie Feathers missed a few games with injuries and quarterback Carl Brumbaugh called it quits—all of which contributed to forcing the Bears to using practically a second-string backfield. Place-kicker Jack Manders and Gene Ronzani filled in well as runners but could not replace the great Nagurski. Bernie Masterson handled the quarterbacking but lacked the savvy of the departed Brumbaugh.

If the Bears had any continuity at all, it came from the forward line, as end Bill Karr, giant tackle George Musso, and guard Joe Kopcha all won All-Pro honors, and end Bill Hewitt barely missed the team.

CHICAGO CARDINALS 6-4-2 Milan Creighton

Scores of Each Game		
7	Green Bay	6
10	Detroit	10
3	GREEN BAY	0
13	Pittsburgh	17
14	New York	13
6	DETROIT	7
12	PHILADELPHIA	3
12	Brooklyn	14
6	Boston	0
9	GREEN BAY	7
7	Chic. Bears	7
0	CHIC. BEARS	13

Use Name	Pos.	Hgt	Wgt	Age	Int	Pts
Bernie Hughes	C-LB	6'1"	195	25		
Bert Pearson	C-LB	6'	205	30		

Use Name – Tackles	Pos.	Hgt	Wgt	Age	Int	Pts
Tony Blazine	T	6'	237	23		
Harry Field	T	6'1"	230	24		
Lou Gordon	T-G	6'5"	230	27		
Ted Isaacson	T-C	6'4"	272	23		

Use Name – Guards	Pos.	Hgt	Wgt	Age	Int	Pts
Bree Cuppoletti	G	5'10"	198	25		
Phil Handler	G	6	215	27		
Homer Hanson	G-C-LB	6	220	24		
(to and from PHI. G)						
Pete Mehringer	G-T	6'2"	200	25		
Howie Tipton	G	5'11"	185	24		
Bill Volok	G-T	6'2"	215	25		6
(Missed 2 PAT attempts)						

Although the Cardinals' 1934 bumper crop of rookies matured to give the team the toughest defense in the NFL, the offense still had the anemic look of recent years and relied heavily on Doug Russell's fine ball carrying, Phil Sarboe's passing, and Bill Smith's field-goal kicking. Mike Mikulak led the defense with his inspired linebacking, and rookie tackle Tony Blazine lent his weight to the brick-wall unit. The league honored fullback Mikulak and end Smith with All-Pro status and Sarboe and Blazine with second-team spots.

The young Cardinals rushed out to three straight victories before the Pirates handed them their first loss. After the fine start, their lack of offensive power brought them back into the pack. The Cardinals brought the Green Bay Packers down with them, though, dealing a fatal blow to the Pack's title hopes by beating them three times, capped by a late-season 9-7 decision.

Use Name – Backs & Ends	Pos.	Age	Hgt	Wgt	Pts	Int	Rushing No.	Rushing Yds	Rushing Avg	Rushing TD	Passing Att	Passing Comp	Passing %	Passing Yds	Passing Yd/Att	Passing TD	Passing Int–%	Passing RK	Receiving No.	Receiving Yds	Receiving Avg	Receiving TD	Punting No.	Punting Avg	Kicking Pat	Kicking Att	Kicking %	Kicking FG	Kicking Att	Kicking %	Punt Returns No.	Punt Returns Yds	Punt Returns Avg	Punt Returns TD	Kickoff Returns No.	Kickoff Returns Yds	Kickoff Returns Avg	Kickoff Returns TD
DETROIT LIONS																																						
Dutch Clark	TB-DB	28	6'	180	55		120	412	3.4	4	26	11	42	133	5.1	2			9	124	14	2			16	19	84	1										
Glenn Presnell	TB-WB-DB	30	5'10"	190	28		72	206	2.9	0	45	15	33	193	4.3	0		11				1			4	4	100	4						1				
Pug Vaughan	TB-DB	24	5'11"	180			13	51	3.9	0	15	7	47	104	6.9	2																						
Ace Gutowsky	FB-LB	25	5'11'	200	12		102	295	2.9	2	9	5	56	95	10.6	2																						
Buddy Parker	FB-BB-LB-DB	21	6'	190			59	156	2.6	0	1	0	0	0	0.0	0																						
Tony Kaska	FB-LB	24	5'11"	185																																		
Ernie Caddel	WB-DB	24	6'2"	198	36		87	450	5.2	6	6	4	67	169	28.2	2			10	171	17	0																
Al Richins	WB-DB	24	5'9"	188																																		
Gil LeFebvre	WB-DB	25	5'6"	152																																		
Bill O'Neill	WB-DB	25	6'	185																																		
Frank Christensen	BB-DB	25	6'1"	195	8		11	6	0.5	0	21	6	29	92	4.4	0			5	57	11	1			2	2	100											
Harry Ebding	OE-DE	26	5'11"	195	6														8	128	16	1																
John Schneller	OE-DE	23	6'2"	205	12														7	149	21	2																
Butch Morse	OE-DE	23	6'2"	195															6	63	11	0																
Ed Klewicki	OE-DE	24	5'10"	210	12																	2																
Buster Mitchell (to NY)	OE-DE	29	6'	205																																		
GREEN BAY PACKERS																																						
Arnie Herber	TB-DB	25	5'11"	203	1		19	0	0.0	0	106	40	38	729	6.9	8	6– 6	4							1	1	100											
Bob Monnett	TB-DB	25	5'9"	180	11		68	336	4.9	1	65	31	47	454	7.0	2	6 – 9	3							2	3	67	1										
Clarke Hinkle	FB-LB	25	5'11"	200	18		76	258	3.4	2									1	4	4	0						2										
Swede Johnston	FB-LB	25	5'10"	200	6		52	176	3.4	1									6	59	10	0																
George Sauer	HB-TB-DB	24	6'2"	204	24		89	334	3.8	3	21	9	43	177	8.4	1																						
Johnny Blood	HB-DB	31	6'1"	190	24		42	115	2.7	0	33	11	33	164	5.0	0			25	404	16	3																
Joe Laws	HB-DB	24	5'9"	185	6		24	63	2.6	1	4	1	25	4	1.0	0																						
Roger Grove	HB-DB	27	6'	185																																		
Buckets Goldenberg	BB-DB	24	5'10"	215			15	52	3.5	0																												
Hank Bruder	BB-FB-DB-LB	27	6'	197	6		44	158	3.6	0	1	1	100	17	17.0	0																						
Herm Schneidman	BB-DB	21	5'11"	205																																		
Don Hutson	OE-DE	22	6'1"	185	43														18	420	23	7			1	1	100											
Milt Gantenbein	OE-DE	25	6'	193	6														12	165	14	1																
Al Rose	OE-DE	20	6'3"	200															0	01	11	0																
Bob Tenner	OE-DE	22	6'	212																																		
Dom Vairo	OE-DE	21	6'2"	203																																		
Ernie Smith	T	25	6'2"	234	14																				11	12	92	1										
CHICAGO BEARS																																						
Bernie Masterson	QB-DB	24	6'3"	195	6		21	2	0.1	0	44	18	41	456	10.4	7	4– 9	2	7	99	14	1																
Bob Dunlap	QB-DB	22	6'1"	187			7	–16	–2.3	0	37	11	30	111	3.0	1			1	10	10	0																
George Corbett	QB-DB	27	5'9"	177	3														2	5	3	0						1										
Gene Ronzani	FB-HB-LB	26	5'9"	190	15		79	356	4.5	1	41	16	39	230	5.6	3		6	8	122	15	1			3	4	75											
Beattie Feathers	HB-DB	27	5'10"	177	18		56	280	5.0	3	14	5	36	53	3.8	0			3	18	6	0																
Keith Molesworth	HB-DB	28	5'9"	168	24		59	286	4.8	4	36	13	36	266	7.4	2			7	154	22	0																
Jack Manders	FB-LB	26	6'	198	19		69	245	3.6	0									2	16	8	0			16	17	94	1	8	13								
Red Pollock	HB-LB	23	6'2"	187	24		45	254	5.6	3	12	1	8	18	1.5	0			7	135	18	1																
George Grosvenor	HB-DB	24	6'	172			55	234	4.3	0	15	6	40	69	4.6	0																						
Bronko Nagurski	FB-LB	26	6'2"	228	6		37	137	3.7	1	3	0	0	0	0.0	0																						
Johnny Sisk	HB-LB	28	6'2"	195	6		38	222	5.8	1	1	1	100	1	1.0	0	0– 0		1	44	44	0																
Luke Johnsos	OE-DE	28	6'2"	197	24		1	4	4.0	0									19	298	16	4																
Bill Karr	OE-DE	24	6'1"	187	36														9	220	24	6																
Bill Hewitt	OE-DE	25	5'9"	190															5	80	16	0																
Fred Crawford	OE-DE-T	25	6'2"	200															1	10	10	0																
CHICAGO CARDINALS																																						
Doug Russell	TB-DB	23	6'	180			140	499	3.6	0	28	7	25	108	3.9	0																						
Ike Peterson	TB-DB	23	5'9"	185			85	225	2.6	0	25	6	24	121	4.8	1																						
Gil Berry	TB-DB	23	5'10"	178			44	77	1.8	0	4	0	0	0	0.0	0																						
Mike Mikulak	FB-LB	22	6'1"	210	6		68	82	1.2	1									8	93	12	0																
Mule Dowell	FB-LB	22	6'2"	210																																		
Al Nichelini	WB-DB	25	6'2"	203	24		94	234	2.5	4	1	1	100	16	16.0	0	0– 0																					
Dave Cook	WB-DB	23	6'2"	200	6		31	121	3.9	1	1	1	100	7	7.0	0	0– 0																					
Phil Sarboe	BB-DB	23	5'10"	165	12		38	129	3.4	0	67	31	46	368	5.5	1		8																2				
Paul Pardonner	BB-DB	25	5'8"	170	4																				1	2	50	1										
Hal Pangle	BB-FB-DB-LB	23	5'10"	205			18	48	2.7	0	4	1	25	15	3.8	0																						
Bill Smith	OE-DE	23	6'1"	198	35														24	318	13	2			5	8	63	6										
Billy Wilson	OE-DE	23	5'10"	185																																		
Bob Neuman	OE-DE	23	6'	200	6																																	
Milan Creighton	OE-DE	27	6'	195																																		
Jim Mooney	OE-DE	27	5'11"	200																																		
Versil Deskin	OE-DE	22	6'	205																																		

TEAM TOTALS

Team	Offense: First Downs	Rushing: Yards	Rushing: TD	Passing: Att.	Passing: Comp	Passing: Comp Pct.	Passing: Yards	Passing: Yds/ Att.	Passing: Yds/ Comp	Passing: TD	Penalty: Yards	Fumbles: Number	Points: Total	Points: TD	Points: PAT	Points: FG	Points: Saf	Defense: Total Yards	Pass Att.	Pass Comp	Comp Pct.	No. Pass Int.	Oppos Fumb. Rec.	Points	Team Totals
DETROIT	121	1773	15	141	57	40.4	920	6.5	16.1	9	195	21	191	25	22	5	2	2023	181	58	32.0	9	27	111	DETROIT
GREEN BAY	125	1525	8	230	93	40.4	1545	6.7	16.6	11	295	29	181	23	19	8	0	2161	191	61	31.9	27	21	96	GREEN BAY
CHICAGO BEARS	140	2096	13	211	73	34.6	1229	5.8	16.8	13	354	36	192	27	19	3	1	2337	194	59	30.4	37	30	106	CHICAGO BEARS
CHICAGO CARDS	107	1521	6	130	47	36.2	635	4.9	13.5	2	255	27	99	12	6	7	0	2068	153	58	37.9	24	23	97	CHICAGO CARDS

BOSTON REDSKINS 7-5-0 Ray Flaherty

Scores of Each Game		
0	Pittsburgh	10
26	Philadelphia	3
14	Brooklyn	3
0	NEW YORK	7
2	Green Bay	31
17	PHILADELPHIA	7
13	CHIC. CARDS	10
3	GREEN BAY	7
0	CHIC. BEARS	26
30	BROOKLYN	6
30	PITTSBURGH	0
14	New York	0

Use Name	Pos.	Hgt	Wgt	Age	Int	Pts
Frank Bausch	C-LB	6'3"	215	28		
Larry Siemering	C-LB	6'3"	210	22		6

Use Name – Tackles	Pos.	Hgt	Wgt	Age	Int	Pts
Jim Barber	T	6'3"	215	24		
Vic Carroll	T-G	6'4"	212	23		6
Turk Edwards	T	6'2"	260	28		
Gail O'Brien	T	6'1"	220	24		
Steve Sinko	T	6'3"	235	25		

Use Name – Guards	Pos.	Hgt	Wgt	Age	Int	Pts
Rick Concannon	G	6'	217	27		
Eddie Kahn	G	5'9"	195	24		
Jim Karcher	G	6'	205	22		
Jim Moran	G	6'1"	210	23		
Les Olsson	G	6'	220	27		

New coach Ray Flaherty made it known that he was in charge when he insisted that owner George Marshall stay off the field and in the stands. Flaherty's positive attitude, developed by years of winning in New York, soon spread to his players. Going without a real passer on the squad but still fortunate enough to have Cliff Battles and Turk Edwards as All-Pros, the Redskins won the Eastern title by defeating the Giants 14-0 in the final game of the season.

Although the Skins had won the crown, they had no place to hang their hat. With the team winning, owner Marshall had raised ticket prices on the day of a game without any advance notice, and both the public and the press blew a hurricane of protest over this shabby treatment of long-suffering fans. With angry winds beating about his head, Marshall simply folded up his tent and moved the championship game to New York.

PITTSBURGH PIRATES 6-6-0 Joe Bach

Scores of Each Game		
10	BOSTON	0
10	BROOKLYN	6
10	NEW YORK	7
9	CHIC. BEARS	27
17	PHILADELPHIA	0
7	Chic. Bears	26
10	Green Bay	42
10'	BROOKLYN	7
6	Philadelphia	0
3	Detroit	28
6	Chic. Cards	14
0	Boston	30

Use Name	Pos.	Hgt	Wgt	Age	Int	Pts
Lee Mulleneaux	C-LB	6'2"	225	29		
Buster Raborn	C-LB	6'	195	23		
John Turley	BB-DB	5'10"	185	23		

Use Name – Tackles	Pos.	Hgt	Wgt	Age	Int	Pts
Mule Bray	T	6'2"	220	27		
Ed Karpowich	T	6'4"	220	23		
(1 reception for −6 yds.)						
Sandy Sandberg	T	6'2"	225	26		

Ben Ciccone – American Football League
Dave Ribble – American Football League
Ben Smith – American Football League

Use Name – Guards	Pos.	Hgt	Wgt	Age	Int	Pts
Win Croft	G	5'11"	235	26		
George Kakasic	G	5'10"	190	24		13
(1 PAT in 1 att., 2 FG, 1 rush for −8 yds.)						
Bill Lajousky	G	5'11"	200	23		
(1 rush for 1 yd.)						
Lindy Mayhew	G-T	6'1"	220	24		
George Rado	G	5'9"	198	23		

With a new unbalanced line offense, the Pirates roared out of the starting gate with victories over the Redskins, Dodgers, and Giants to grab the Eastern Division lead. If the Pirates had played only Eastern teams all year, they might have given owner Art Rooney his first championship. But such was not the case as they struck out in all five meetings against the Western clubs. The Pirates came into Boston on November 29 with a chance to ice away the crown by defeating the Redskins. Returning by train from an exhibition match in California the week before, the Bucs took the field tired and out of practice, and the sky-high Redskins blew them out of the stadium in a 30-0 rout. Rooney took the blame for scheduling the West Coast trip, for not even he had expected the Pirates to be in the title race as long as they were.

NEW YORK GIANTS 5-6-1 Steve Owen

Scores of Each Game		
7	Philadelphia	10
7	Pittsburgh	10
7	Boston	0
10	BROOKLYN	10
14	CHIC. CARDS	6
21	PHILADELPHIA	17
14	DETROIT	7
7	CHIC. BEARS	25
0	Detroit	38
14	GREEN BAY	26
14	Brooklyn	0
0	BOSTON	14

Use Name	Pos.	Hgt	Wgt	Age	Int	Pts
Len Dugan	C-LB	6'	210	24		
Mel Hein	C-LB	6'2"	225	27		
Chief Johnson	C-LB	6'3"	223	27		
Bob Tarrant	OE-DE	6'	180	22		
Bob Dunlap	DB	6'1"	195	23		

Use Name – Tackles	Pos.	Hgt	Wgt	Age	Int	Pts
Len Grant	T	6'3"	235	30		
Jack Haden	T	6'4"	230	21		
Cal Hubbard (from PIT G-T)	T	6'4"	255	35		
Art Lewis	T-G	6'3"	225	23		6
Bill Morgan	T	6'2"	235	26		
Bill Owen	T-G	6'	225	32		

Ken Strong – American Football League

Use Name – Guards	Pos.	Hgt	Wgt	Age	Int	Pts
Gaines Davis	G	5'11"	230	23		
Johnny Dell Isola	G-C-LB	5'11"	202	24		
Potsy Jones	G	5'11"	224	26		
Bernie Kaplan	G	6'	210	23		
Ewell Phillips	G	5'11"	210	26		
(1 reception for 5 yds.)						

When the Giants lost their first two contests to the Eagles and Pirates, the absence of some recently departed veterans stood out glaringly. Runner Ken Strong, second-string passer Harry Newman, end Red Badgro, and aging tackle Jess Quatse had all jumped to the outlaw American Football League, and end Ray Flaherty headed north to coach the Redskins. The young but talented Giants fought back into the Eastern title race behind the passing of Ed Danowski, the running of rookie Tuffy Leemans, and the line play of annual All-Pro Mel Hein. The division championship rode on the line in the season-ending confrontation between the Giants and Redskins in the Polo Grounds on December 6. Totally confident of victory, the Giants could not move the ball at all against the Skins and not only lost the game but also the first Eastern title since the divisions were formed in 1933.

BROOKLYN DODGERS 3-8-1 Paul Schissler

Scores of Each Game		
6	Pittsburgh	10
3	BOSTON	14
18	PHILADELPHIA	0
10	New York	10
7	DETROIT	14
9	CHIC. CARDS	0
7	Pittsburgh	10
7	GREEN BAY	38
6	Boston	30
0	NEW YORK	14
13	Philadelphia	7
6	Detroit	14

Use Name	Pos.	Hgt	Wgt	Age	Int	Pts
Wagner Jorgensen	C-LB	6'2"	205	23		
Red Krause	C-LB	6'1"	205	22		
Cap Oehler	C-LB	6'	205	25		
Jim Hartman	OE-DE	6'2"	205	23		
Jack Grossman	DB	6'1"	195	26		

Use Name – Tackles	Pos.	Hgt	Wgt	Age	Int	Pts
Carl Heldt	T	6'2"	206	23		
(2 receptions for 39 yds.)						
Bill Lee	T	6'2"	225	24		
Jim Whatley	T-OE-DE	6'5"	220	23		
John Yezerski	T	6'4"	240	22		

Use Name – Guards	Pos.	Hgt	Wgt	Age	Int	Pts
Gil Bergerson	G-T	6'6"	245	26		
Verdi Boyer	G	5'10"	195	24		
Bo Kirkland	G	6'	215	23		
Justin Rukas	G	6'	205	26		
Frank Stojack	G	5'10"	198	24		

As usual, the Dodgers got along without any passing attack to mention. Obtained from the Cardinals in mid-season, passer Phil Sarboe failed to give the offense a needed second dimension. Although rookie Bobby Wilson helped the running game, punter Ralph Kercheval still was the chief offensive threat with his booming kicks. Tackle Bill Lee headed a fair line, but the Dodgers, in general, were on a downslide which only new blood gave any hope of stopping. Unfortunately for coach Paul Schissler, new blood was also brought in at the top as the team's three victories and fourth-place Eastern Division finish was just not enough to give him employment the following year.

PHILADELPHIA EAGLES 1-11-0 Bert Bell

Scores of Each Game		
10	NEW YORK	7
3	BOSTON	26
0	CHIC. BEARS	17
0	Brooklyn	18
0	DETROIT	23
0	Pittsburgh	17
7	Boston	17
17	New York	21
0	PITTSBURGH	6
0	Chic. Cards	13
7	CHIC. BEARS	28
7	BROOKLYN	13

Use Name	Pos.	Hgt	Wgt	Age	Int	Pts
Pete Stevens	C-LB	6'	215	24		
Max Padlow	OE-DE	6'1"	200	24		
Carl Kane	HB-DB	5'11"	195	23		

Use Name – Tackles	Pos.	Hgt	Wgt	Age	Int	Pts
Bill Brian	T	6'2"	220	23		
Art Buss	T	6'3"	220	25		
Jim MacMurdo	T	6'1"	210	25		6

Jim Zyntell – American Football League

Use Name – Guards	Pos.	Hgt	Wgt	Age	Int	Pts
Rudy Gollomb	G	5'11"	205	24		
Amy McPherson	G	5'11"	214	24		
Joe Pivarnick	G	5'9"	217	24		
Jim Russell	G-T	5'11"	210	25		
Vince Zizak	G	5'8"	208	27		

President of the Eagles since their birth, Bert Bell expanded his duties this year by taking over Lud Wray's job as head coach. On the side, Bell also made travel arrangements, sold tickets, promoted the club, and handled almost every job connected with the team.

In his first game on the sidelines, Bell watched his club upset the New York Giants 10-7 at home to get the season off to a flying start. But as where **Bell could perform a solo show on the sidelines, he could do nothing in the** game itself, and the Eagles skidded into an eleven-game losing streak. Before the season, in the first college draft, Bell had chosen Jay Berwanger, Heisman Trophy halfback from the University of Chicago, and promptly traded the negotiating rights to the Bears for veteran tackle Art Buss. When Berwanger decided against a pro-football career, Bell looked like a genius—at least until the Eagles took to the field.

							RUSHING				PASSING								RECEIVING				PUNTING		KICKING						PUNT RETURNS				KICKOFF RETURNS			
Use Name – Backs & Ends	Pos.	Age	Hgt	Wgt	Pts	Int	No.	Yds	Avg	TD	Att	Comp	%	Yds	Yd/Att	TD	Int–%	RK	No.	Yds	Avg	TD	No.	Avg	Pat	Att	%	FG	Att	%	No.	Yds	Avg	TD	No.	Yds	Avg	TD
BOSTON REDSKINS																																						
Cliff Battles	TB-DB	26	6'1"	195	42		176	614	3.5	5	52	18	35	242	4.7	1	6–12	9	6	103	17	1												1				
Pug Rentner	FB-DB	25	6'1"	186	18		95	404	4.3	1	39	15	38	198	5.1	0	6–15		4	33	8	0																
Eddie Britt	FB-TB-DB	23	6'2"	205			72	180	2.5	0	44	18	41	294	6.7	3	5–11		6	106	18	0																
Don Irwin	FB-DB	23	6'1"	197	12		17	78	4.6	2	5	0	0	0	0.0	0	1–20		2	31	16	0																
Ed Smith	FB-TB-DB	23	6'2"	210	3		7	39	5.6	0	40	11	28	120	3.0	1	2–5											1										
Jim Musick	FB-DB	26	5'11"	205			6	14	2.3	0	1	1	100	9	9.0	0	0–0																					
Ernie Pinckert	WB-DB	28	6'	196			18	80	4.4	0									1	17	17	0																
Ed Justice	WB-DB	23	6'1"	205															8	132	17	0																
Riley Smith	BB-LB	25	6'2"	200	38		30	26	0.9	0	33	14	42	239	7.2	0	3–9		3	76	25	2			14	17	82	4										
Heinie Weisenbaugh	BB-LB	22	5'11"	190			3	9	3.0	0									3	37	12	0																
Wayne Millner	OE-DE	25	6'1"	190															18	211	12	0																
Charley Malone	OE-DE	26	6'4"	200	6														11	167	15	1																
Sam Busich	OE-DE	23	6'3"	190	10														6	57	10	1			1	2	50	1										
Bob McChesney	OE-DE	24	6'2"	195															5	62	12	0																
Flavio Tosi	OE-DE	24	6'1"	195	6														4	70	18	0																
PITTSBURGH PIRATES																																						
Ed Matesic	TB-DB	25	6'1"	205			46	58	1.3	0	138	64	46	850	6.2	5	16–12	3	1	13	13	0																
Max Fiske	TB-HB-DB	22	6'	195			58	92	1.6	0	15	6	40	64	4.3	0	3–20		7	96	14	0																
Jim Levey	TB-DB	29	5'10"	156			4	3	0.8	0																												
Bull Karcis	FB-LB	27	5'9"	220	13		89	272	3.1	2	4	0	0	0	0.0	0	2–50		8	71	9	0			1	1	100											
Dick Sandefur	FB-LB	24	5'10"	195			7	13	1.9	0																												
Warren Heller	HB-DB	26	5'11"	195	18		106	332	3.1	0	5	0	0	0	0.0	0	1–20		12	160	13	3																
Art Strutt	HB-DB	23	6'	200	6		84	180	2.1	1	1	1	100	15	15.0	0	0–0		11	166	15	0																
Jim McDonald	HB-DB		6'	195			9	18	2.0	0									1	8	8	0																
Johnny Gildea	BB-HB-DB	26	6'2"	205			35	31	0.9	0	29	9	31	147	5.1	1	5–17		5	70	14	0																
Silvio Zaninelli	BB-FB-DB-LB	22	5'10"	200			31	61	2.0	0	6	1	17	2	0.3	0	1–17		2	12	6	0																
Bill Sortet	OE-DE	24	6'1"	188	6		1	47	47.0	0									14	197	14	1																
Ed Skoronski	OE-DE	24	6'2"	210	6														8	95	12	1																
Jeep Brett (from CHIC)	OE-DE	22	6'2"	205															7	139	20	0																
Vic Vidoni	OE-DE	23	6'1"	210															2	35	18	0																
Vinnie Sites	OE-DE	24	6'2"	215	6														2	22	11	1																
Armand Niccolai	T	24	6'2"	220	28																				7	8	88	7										
NEW YORK GIANTS																																						
Ed Danowski	TB-DB	24	6'1"	198			91	259	2.8	0	104	47	45	515	5.0	6	10–10	5																				
Tony Sarausky	TB-DB	24	5'11"	198	10		32	150	4.7	1	27	6	22	87	3.2	1	1–4								1	1	100	1										
Tuffy Leemans	FB-DB	23	6'	188	12		206	830	4.0	2	42	13	31	258	6.1	3	6–14		4	22	6	0																
Kink Richards	FB-DB	25	5'11"	196	12		114	421	3.7	1									7	146	21	1																
Dale Burnett	WB-DB	27	6'1"	188	18		10	0	0.0	0									16	246	15	3																
Max Krause	WB-DB	27	5'10"	210	6		11	37	3.4	0									5	47	9	1																
Tilly Manton	BB-LB	24	5'11"	187	21		30	86	2.9	0	5	3	60	27	5.4	0	0–0		5	81	16	1			15	15	100											
Red Corzine	BB-LB	27	6'	210	6		7	12	1.7	0									1	36	36	1																
Leland Shaffer	BB-LB-DE-DE	24	6'2"	200	6		3	10	3.3	0									2	30	15	1																
Tod Goodwin	OE-DE	24	6'	184	12		3	−1	−0.3	0									7	79	11	2																
Winnie Anderson	OE-DE	24	6'	185															7	74	11	0																
Gene Rose	OE-DE	25	6'1"	185			2	13	6.5	0									6	73	12	0																
Walt Singer	OE-DE	23	6'	198	6														6	38	6	0																
Buster Mitchell	OE-DE	30	6'	205															2	10	5	0																
BROOKLYN DODGERS																																						
Bobby Wilson	TB-DB	23	5'9"	147	24		104	505	4.9	3	40	11	28	148	3.7	0	9–22		1	12	12	1																
Red Franklin	TB-DB	24	5'10"	165	6		15	70	4.7	1	7	1	14	17	2.4	0	0–0																					
Joe Maniaci	TB-HB-DB	22	6'1"	204			35	70	2.0	0	4	1	25	1	0.3	0	0–0		1	30	30	0																
Mark Temple (to BOS)	TB-DB	24	5'10"	175	6		5	4	0.8	1	7	0	0	0	0.0	0	5–71		1	10	10	0																
John Biancone	TB-DB	24	5'6"	165			8	34	4.3	0	3	1	33	29	9.7	0	0–0																					
Dick Crayne	FB-DB	23	6'	210	7		64	203	3.2	1	2	1	50	52	26.0	0	0–0		1	32	32	0			1	2	50											
Tony Kaska	FB-DB	25	5'11"	200	6		9	29	3.2	1	1	0		0	0.0	0	1–100		1	5	5	0																
Dave Cook (from CHIC)	FB-DB	24	6'2"	208			10	24	2.4	0									1	2	2	0																
Ralph Kercheval	HB-DB	25	6'1"	193	37		66	261	4.0	2	25	6	24	92	3.7	0	3–12		7	63	9	0			4	8	50	5										
Father Lumpkin	BB-LB	28	6'2"	205			11	29	2.6	0									6	34	6	0																
Jeff Barrett	OE-DE	23	6'1"	185	6														14	268	19	1																
Paul Riblett	OE-DE	28	5'10"	186			2	4	2.0	0									4	49	12	0																
Red Badgro	OE-DE	33	6'	190															3	59	20	0																
Ray Fuqua	OE-DE	24	6'	190															1	2	2	0			0	1	0											
PHILADELPHIA EAGLES																																						
Swede Hanson	TB-DB	27	6'1"	197	6		119	359	3.0	1	15	0	0	0	0.0	0	3–20		3	33	11	0																
Don Jackson	TB-DB	22	5'11"	184			46	76	1.7	0	35	7	20	80	2.3	0	11–31																					
Walt Masters	TB-DB	29	5'10"	180			7	18	2.6	0	6	1	17	11	1.8	0	1–17																					
Reds Bassman	TB-HB-DB	23	5'11"	180			4	19	4.8	0	3	1	33	3	1.0	0	1–33		2	38	19	0																
Dave Smukler	FB-LB	22	6'1"	228	5		99	321	3.2	0	68	21	31	345	5.1	3	6–9	8							2	2	100	1										
John Kusko	FB-LB	22	5'11"	203	6		49	209	4.3	1	27	6	22	108	4.0	0	9–33																					
Stumpy Thomason	HB-FB-DB-LB	30	5'7"	190	1		109	333	3.1	0	10	1	10	11	1.1	0	2–20								1	1	100											
Jim Leonard	BB-TB-HB-DB	26	6'	200	6		33	72	2.2	0	6	2	33	45	7.5	0	2–33		5	46	9	1																
Glenn Frey	BB-DB	24	5'10"	195			7	8	1.1	0									3	65	22	0																
Eggs Manske	OE-DE	23	6'	185															17	325	19	0																
Joe Pilconis	OE-DE	24	6'1"	190	6														4	51	13	1																
Joe Carter	OE-DE	26	6'1"	202	6														4	42	11	1																
George Mulligan	OE-DE-LB	22	6'1"	198															1	3	3	0																
Hank Reese	C-LB	25	5'11"	215	9																				3	3	100	2										

TEAM TOTALS — OFFENSE

		RUSHING:				PASSING:							PENALTY:	FUMBLES:	POINTS:				
TEAM TOTALS	FIRST DOWNS	No.	Yards	Avg. Yds.	TD	Att.	Comp.	Comp. Pct.	Yards	Yds/ Att.	Yds/ Comp.	TD	Yards	Number	Total	TD	PAT	FG	Saf
BOSTON	113	425	1444	3.4	8	214	77	36.0	1102	5.1	14.3	5	275	31	149	19	15	6	1
PITTSBURGH	117	472	1100	2.3	3	198	81	40.9	1078	5.4	13.3	6	336	34	98	10	9	9	1
NEW YORK	146	509	1817	3.6	4	178	69	38.8	887	5.0	12.9	10	205	37	115	16	16	1	0
BROOKLYN	90	340	1300	3.8	9	141	43	30.5	621	4.4	14.4	2	210	25	92	12	5	5	0
PHILADELPHIA	99	463	1415	3.1	2	170	39	22.9	603	3.5	15.5	3	159	33	51	6	6	3	0

DEFENSE

TEAM TOTALS	Total Yards	Pass Att.	Pass Comp.	Comp. Pct.	No. Pass Int.	Oppos. Fumb. Rec.	Points
BOSTON	2181	198	62	31.5	22	32	110
PITTSBURGH	3032	163	52	31.9	25	26	187
NEW YORK	2841	149	60	40.3	19	24	163
BROOKLYN	2798	174	65	37.4	24	27	161
PHILADELPHIA	2857	147	61	41.4	15	29	206

GREEN BAY PACKERS 10-1-1 Curly Lambeau

Scores of Each Game		
10	CHIC. CARDS	7
3	CHIC. BEARS	30
24	CHIC. CARDS	0
31	BOSTON	2
20	DETROIT	18
42	PITTSBURGH	10
21	Chic. Bears	10
7	Boston	3
38	Brooklyn	7
26	New York	14
26	Detroit	17
0	Chic. Cards	0

Use Name	Pos.	Hgt	Wgt	Age	Int	Pts
Frank Butler	C-LB	6'3"	246	27		
George Svendsen	C-LB	6'4"	224	23		
Al Rose	OE-DE	6'3"	205	29		

Use Name – Tackles	Pos.	Hgt	Wgt	Age	Int	Pts
Lou Gordon	T	6'5"	230	28		
Ade Schwammel	T	6'2"	230	27		8
(5 PAT's in 5 attempts, 1 field goal)						
Champ Seibold	T	6'4"	237	23		

Use Name – Guards	Pos.	Hgt	Wgt	Age	Int	Pts
Tiny Engebretsen	G	6'1"	238	26		17
(2 PAT's in 2 attempts. 5 field goals)						
Lon Evans	G-T	6'2"	220	24		
Buckets Goldenberg	G-BB-DB-LB	5'11"	210	25		
(6 rushing attempts for 9 yds.)						
Walt Kiesling	G	6'2"	257	33		
Russ Letlow	G	6'	203	22		
Tony Paulekas	G-C-LB	5'10"	210	24		

The first great NFL passing combination put the Packers back on top in the West, as tailback Arnie Herber filled the air with footballs aimed at fleet end Don Hutson. Due to extremely stubby fingers, Herber gripped the ball with his thumb across the seams, but this unorthodox hold did not stop him from being the best long passer in the league. While introducing hard-cutting fakes to defensive backs, Hutson hauled in a record thirty-four passes for eight touchdowns. But, as a defensive end, the slight Hutson took a beating.

On the ground, rugged Clarke Hinkle handled the heavy-duty power running. Despite the retirement of Mike Michalske, the line was the class of the circuit, with tackle Ernie Smith and guard Lon Evans winning All-Pro honors.

CHICAGO BEARS 9-3-0 George Halas

Scores of Each Game		
30	Green Bay	3
17	Philadelphia	0
27	Pittsburgh	9
7	CHIC. CARDS	3
26	PITTSBURGH	7
12	DETROIT	10
10	GREEN BAY	21
25	New York	7
26	Boston	0
28	Philadelphia	7
7	Detroit	13
7	Chic. Cards	14

Use Name	Pos.	Hgt	Wgt	Age	Int	Pts
Eddie Kawal	C-LB	6'2"	198	26		
Ookie Miller	C-LB	6'	204	26		6
Frank Sullivan	C-LB	6'3"	203	24		
Bob Allman	OE-DE	6'	198	22		

Use Name – Tackles	Pos.	Hgt	Wgt	Age	Int	Pts
George Musso	T	6'2"	258	26		
Joe Stydahar	T	6'4"	230	24		3
(3 PAT's in 4 attempts)						
Russ Thompson	T	6'5"	248	24		
Milt Trost	T	6'1"	203	23		

Use Name – Guards	Pos.	Hgt	Wgt	Age	Int	Pts
Zuck Carlson	G	6'	210	31		
Danny Fortmann	G	6'	210	20		
Eddie Michaels	G	5'11"	200	22		
Vern Oech	G	6'1"	207	23		
Joe Zeller	G	6'1"	206	28		

Three rookies led the Bears' charge back from the mediocrity of 1935. Halfback Ray Nolting exploded through small holes with his quick acceleration, while tough tackle Joe Stydahar provided running room for him and his fellow backs. When the Bears lost veteran guard Joe Kopcha when his medical studies forced a move to Detroit, rookie Danny Fortmann, also an aspiring doctor, more than made up for the loss with a hard-hitting internship in the line.

Veterans also contributed to the Chicago renaissance. Bronko Nagurski returned from his injury-filled 1935 season again to throw his weight around with considerable force and yards gained. Jack Manders booted seven field goals to lead the league for the third time, and bare-headed end Bill Hewitt won his third nod for All-Pro. With attendance up and both young and old players contributing, George Halas' heart was doubly warmed.

DETROIT LIONS 8-4-0 Potsy Clark

Scores of Each Game		
39	CHIC. CARDS	0
23	Philadelphia	0
14	Brooklyn	7
18	Green Bay	20
10	Chic. Bears	12
7	New York	14
28	PITTSBURGH	3
38	NEW YORK	0
14	Chic. Cards	7
13	CHIC. BEARS	7
17	GREEN BAY	26
14	BROOKLYN	6

Use Name	Pos.	Hgt	Wgt	Age	Int	Pts
Clare Randolph	C-LB	6'2"	207	29		
Del Ritchhart	C-LB	6'	195	25		6

Use Name – Tackles	Pos.	Hgt	Wgt	Age	Int	Pts
George Christensen	T	6'2"	238	26		
Jack Johnson	T	6'4"	210	26		
Red Stacy	T-G	6'2"	208	24		
Jim Steen	T	6'2"	205	23		

Use Name – Guards	Pos.	Hgt	Wgt	Age	Int	Pts
Ox Emerson	G	5'11"	200	28		
Tom Hupke	G	5'10"	192	25		
Sam Knox	G	6'	220	26		
Joe Kopcha	G	6'	226	30		
Regis Monahan	G-T	5'10"	215	27		6
Sid Wagner	G	5'11"	190	23		

Detroit went into key late-season contests without the services of fullback Ace Gutowsky, halfback Ernie Caddel, and center Clare Randolph, to lose all chances of repeating as Western Division winners.

The Detroit offense remained highly potent due largely to Dutch Clark's off-tackle slants and drop-kicking; from all his talents, Clark collected a league-leading 73 points. The loss of Randolph hurt the forward wall, but beefy George Christensen and small guard Ox Emerson opened more than a few holes for Clark to race through. No one could cover for Randolph at linebacker, though, and his absence hurt the defense the same way that Gutowsky's robbed the offense of its only solid power runner.

CHICAGO CARDINALS 3-8-1 Milan Creighton

Scores of Each Game		
7	Green Bay	10
0	Detroit	39
0	Green Bay	24
3	Chic. Bears	7
6	New York	14
0	Brooklyn	9
10	Boston	13
13	PHILADELPHIA	0
14	PITTSBURGH	6
7	DETROIT	14
14	CHIC. BEARS	7
0	GREEN BAY	0

Use Name	Pos.	Hgt	Wgt	Age	Int	Pts
Bernie Hughes	C-LB	6'1"	190	26		
Al Lind	C-LB	5'10"	185	23		
Bert Pearson	C-LB	6'	210	31		
Milan Creighton	OE-DE	6'	190	28		

Use Name – Tackles	Pos.	Hgt	Wgt	Age	Int	Pts
Conway Baker	T	5'11"	225	24		
Tony Blazine	T	6'	225	24		
Harry Field	T	6'1"	225	25		
Pete Mehringer	T	6'2"	218	26		
Jack Robinson (from BKN)	T	6'3"	220	24		

Use Name – Guards	Pos.	Hgt	Wgt	Age	Int	Pts
Ross Carter	G	6'	200	22		
Bree Cuppoletti	G	5'10"	200	26		
Phil Handler	G	6'	210	28		
Homer Hanson	G	6'	220	25		
Dub Miller	G	6'	225	24		
Howie Tipton	G-OE-DE	5'11"	185	25		
(1 reception for 15 yds.)						
Bill Volok	G	6'2"	215	26		

Despite slipping back into their losing ways, the Cardinals did experience one very satisfying moment. For the first time since Thanksgiving of 1929, when Ernie Nevers scored 40 points, the Cardinals defeated the Bears.

Aside from the Bear game, though, sparkling moments were few and far between for the Redbirds. With Doug Russell, the leading runner, knocked out for most of the year with an injury, the Cardinal offense went nowhere in a hurry. To pick up some of the backfield slack, the Cardinals obtained George Grosvenor from the Bears—who, predictably enough, turned in a key performance in the victory over his former teammates. Also helping Grosvenor in the backfield, especially on defense, was Mike Mikulak.

Use Name – Backs and Ends	Pos.	Age	Hgt	Wgt	Pts	Int	Rushing No.	Rushing Yds	Rushing Avg	Rushing TD	Passing Att	Passing Comp	Passing %	Passing Yds	Passing Yd/Att	Passing TD	Passing Int–%	Passing RK	Receiving No.	Receiving Yds	Receiving Avg	Receiving TD	Punting No.	Punting Avg	Kicking Pat	Kicking Att	Kicking %	Kicking FG	Kicking Att	Kicking %	Punt Returns No.	Punt Returns Yds	Punt Returns Avg	Punt Returns TD	Kickoff Returns No.	Kickoff Returns Yds	Kickoff Returns Avg	Kickoff Returns TD
GREEN BAY PACKERS																																						
Arnie Herber	TB-DB	26	5'11"	200			20	–32	–1.6	0	173	77	45	1239	7.2	11	13–8	1																				
Bob Monnett	TB-HB-DB	26	5'9"	185	3		104	224	2.2	0	52	20	38	280	5.4	4	2–4	4	13	169	13	0			3	3	100											
Harry Mattos	TB-DB	25	6'	200			1	2	2.0	0	12	4	33	32	2.7	0	2–17																					
Clarke Hinkle	FB-LB	26	5'11"	205	31		100	476	4.8	5	2	1	50	10	5.0	0	0–0								1	1	100											
George Sauer	FB-HB-LB-DB	25	6'2"	208	18		94	305	3.2	3	4	2	50	26	6.5	0	1–25		6	110	18	0																
Swede Johnston	FB-LB	26	5'10"	192	6		42	110	2.6	1									2	11	6	0																
Joe Laws	HB-DB	25	5'9"	185	18		50	296	5.9	1	4	1	25	22	5.5	1	0–0		10	132	13	2																
Paul Miller	HB-DB	23	5'11"	175	18		52	227	4.4	1	1	0	0	0	0.0	0	1–100		8	113	14	2																
Johnny Blood	HB-BB	32	6'1"	185	19		13	65	5.0	0	6	3	50	20	3.3	1	0–0		7	147	21	2			1	1	100 (Run)											
Hank Bruder	BB-DB	26	6'	197			4	–7	–1.7	0									2	25	13	0																
Cal Clemens	BB-DB-OE-DE	24	6'1"	195	1		3	–8	–2.7	0	1	0	0	0	0.0	0	0–0		1	18	18	0			1	1	100											
Herm Schneidman	OE-DE	22	5'11"	200	6														3	68	23	1																
Don Hutson	OE-DE	23	6'1"	185	54		1	–3	–3.0	0									34	526	15	8																
Milt Gantenbein	OE-DE	26	6'	208	6														15	231	15	1																
Wayland Becker	OE-DE	25	6'	190	6														5	66	13	1																
Bernie Scherer	OE-DE	23	6'1"	183	6														2	13	7	0																
Ernie Smith	T	26	6'2"	220	29																				17	18	94	4										
CHICAGO BEARS																																						
Bernie Masterson	QB-DB	25	6'3"	195	12		9	–7	–0.8	2	42	10	24	292	7.0	3	6–14		1	28	28	0																
Carl Brumbaugh	QB-DB	28	5'10"	178	12		9	–1	–0.1	0	28	8	29	140	5.0	5	3–11		5	39	8	2			0	1	0											
George Corbett	QB-HB-DB	28	5'9"	180	6		13	45	3.5	0	13	5	38	64	4.9	0	1–8		3	69	23	1																
Bronko Nagurski	FB-LB	27	6'2"	228	19		122	529	4.3	3	5	1	20	8	1.6	1	2–40		1	12	12	0			1	1	100											
Ray Nolting	HB-DB	22	5'11"	185	6		76	352	4.6	0	13	3	23	30	2.3	2	1–8		2	50	25	1																
Beattie Feathers	HB-DB	28	5'10"	185	12		97	350	3.6	2	11	1	9	10	0.9	0	2–18		2	5	3	0																
Keith Molesworth	HB-QB-DB	29	5'9"	170			60	276	4.6	0	31	15	48	188	6.1	4	4–13		9	146	16	0																
Jack Manders	FB-LB	27	6'	210	62		63	207	3.3	3	3	2	67	52	17.3	0	0–0		1	4	4	1			17	21	81	7	8	88								
Gene Ronzani	HB-QB-LB-DB	27	5'9"	200	12		37	186	5.0	0	12	8	67	170	14.2	1	2–17		4	58	15	2																
Johnny Sisk	HB-LB	29	6'2"	195			41	163	4.0	0									1	39	39	0																
John Doehring	HB-QB-LB	26	6'	215			18	101	5.6	0	12	5	42	145	12.1	1	0–0		1	19	19	0																
Bill Hewitt	OE-DE	26	5'9"	190	42		2	–9	–4.5	0									15	358	24	6																
Bill Karr	OE-DE	25	6'1"	190	18		4	11	2.8	1									6	121	20	2																
Luke Johnsos	OE-DE	29	6'2"	198	12														5	121	24	2																
Ted Rosequist	OE-DE-T	28	6'4"	225															1	15	15	0																
Red Pollock	OE-DE-HB-LB	24	6'2"	200															1	15	15	0																
DETROIT LIONS																																						
Dutch Clark	TB-DB	29	6'	180	73		123	628	5.1	7	71	38	54	467	6.6	4	6–8	2	1	5	5	0			19	23	83	4										
Glenn Presnell	TB-DB	31	5'10"	190	15		48	201	4.2	1	36	15	42	221	6.1	2	7–19								6	8	75	1										
Ace Gutowsky	FB-LB	26	5'11"	200	36		191	827	4.3	6	13	2	15	21	1.6	0	4–31		1	30	30	0																
Bill Shepherd	FB-LB	24	5'9"	200	13		74	292	3.9	1	9	3	33	57	6.3	0	1–11								1	1	100											
Ernie Caddel	WB-DB	25	6'2"	198	30		91	580	6.4	4	4	1	25	30	7.5	0	2–50		19	150	8	1																
Ike Peterson	WB-TB-DB	24	5'9"	185			60	276	4.6	3	6	0	0	0	0.0	0	1–17		8	38	5	0																
Wilbur White	WB-DB	24	6'	165			8	21	2.6	0	1	0	0	0	0.0	0	0–0		2	21	11	0																
Frank Christensen	BB-DB	26	6'1"	197	6		2	–2	–1.0	0	6	2	33	22	3.7	0	1–17		2	58	29	1																
Buddy Parker	BB-DB	22	6'	190			6	21	3.5	0									1	15	15	0																
Harry Ebding	OE-DE	27	5'11"	195	24														10	194	19	3																
John Schneller	OE-DE	24	6'2"	205	6														7	124	18	1																
Butch Morse	OE-DE	24	6'2"	195															5	83	17	0																
Ed Klewicki	OE-DE	25	5'10"	210															4	90	23	0																
Bill McKalip	OE-WB-DE-DB	28	6'1"	195			7	39	5.6	0									1	10	10	0																
CHICAGO CARDINALS																																						
Phil Sarboe (to BKN)	TB-DB	24	5'10"	170			83	103	1.2	0	114	47	41	680	6.0	3	13–11	6	1	18	18	0																
Pug Vaughan	TB-DB	25	5'11"	182			67	79	1.2	0	79	30	38	546	6.9	3	10–13	7																				
George Grosvenor (from CHIB, HB-DB)	TB-DB	25	6'	175	30		170	612	3.6	4	34	12	35	173	5.1	0	6–18		1	6	6	0												1				
Doug Russell	TB-DB	24	6'	190			3	11	3.7	0	1	0	0	0	0.0	0	0–0								6	7	86	1										
Clarence Kellogg	FB-DB	24	5'10"	205	9		66	164	2.5	0									4	11	3	0																
Mule Dowell	FB-DB	23	6'2"	202			54	151	2.8	0	2	1	50	6	3.0	0	0–0								2	3	67	1										
Hal Pangle	FB-BB-DB-LB	24	5'10"	196	6		38	101	2.7	1	2	0	0	0	0.0	0	0–0		9	195	22	0																
Swede Ellstrom	FB-DB	28	6'1"	205			4	12	3.0	0																												
Al Nichelini	WB-DB	26	6'2"	210	6		55	189	3.4	0									9	133	15	1																
Jimmy Lawrence	WB-DB	22	5'11"	195			26	84	3.2	0	2	0	0	0	0.0	0	1–50		8	98	12	0																
Mike Mikulak	BB-LB	23	6'1"	210			24	56	2.3	0									6	62	10	0																
Charlie McBride	BB-LB	22	5'10"	185	6		2	1	0.5	0									1	38	38	1																
Bill Smith	OE-DE	24	6'1"	198	11		2	13	6.5	0	1	0	0	0	0.0	0	1–100		20	414	21	1																
Versil Deskin	OE-DE	23	6'	190	6														3	60	20	1																
Bob Neuman	OE-DE	24	6'	195			1	3	3.0	0									3	41	14	0																
Ray Davis	OE-DE	29	6'1"	198															1	36	36	0																
Billy Wilson	OE-DE	24	5'10"	182															1	12	12	0																

TEAM TOTALS — OFFENSE

Team	First Downs	Rushing: No.	Rushing: Yards	Rushing: Avg. Yds.	Rushing: TD	Passing: Att.	Passing: Comp.	Passing: Comp Pct.	Passing: Yards	Passing: Yds/ Att.	Passing: Yds/ Comp.	Passing: TD	Penalty: Yards	Fumbles: Number	Points: Total	Points: TD	Points: PAT	Points: FG	Points: Saf
GREEN BAY	148	490	1664	3.4	11	255	108	42.4	1629	6.4	15.1	17	478	23	248	31	30	10	1
CHICAGO BEARS	145	552	2206	4.0	11	170	58	34.1	1099	6.5	18.9	17	435	24	222	30	21	7	0
DETROIT	170	610	2883	4.7	22	146	61	41.8	818	5.6	13.4	6	290	20	235	32	26	5	1
CHICAGO CARDS	138	552	1509	2.7	5	183	68	37.2	1123	6.1	16.5	4	415	34	74	10	8	2	0

DEFENSE — TEAM TOTALS

Total Yards	Pass Att.	Pass Comp.	Comp. Pct.	No. Pass Int.	Oppos Fumb. Rec.	Points	Team
2664	227	81	35.7	31	19	118	GREEN BAY
3000	227	86	37.9	35	24	94	CHICAGO BEARS
2489	194	70	36.1	21	13	102	DETROIT
2725	176	67	38.1	24	35	143	CHICAGO CARDS

WASHINGTON REDSKINS 8-3-0 Ray Flaherty

Scores of Each Game		
13	NEW YORK	3
14	CHIC. CARDS	21
11	BROOKLYN	7
0	PHILADELPHIA	14
34	PITTSBURGH	20
10	Philadelphia	7
21	Brooklyn	0
13	Pittsburgh	21
16	Cleveland	7
14	GREEN BAY	6
49	New York	14

Use Name	Pos.	Hgt	Wgt	Age	Int	Pts
Eddie Kawal	C-LB	6'2"	198	27		
George Smith	C-LB	6'2"	205	23		
Nels Peterson	WB-DB	5'8"	182	22		

Use Name – Tackles	Pos.	Hgt	Wgt	Age	Int	Pts
Jim Barber	T	6'3"	215	25		
Chuck Bond	T	6'2"	240	23		
Turk Edwards	T	6'2"	255	29		
Bill Young	T	6'1"	240	23		

Use Name – Guards	Pos.	Hgt	Wgt	Age	Int	Pts
Dick Bassi	G	5'11"	210	22		
Vic Carroll	G-T-C-LB	6'4"	225	24		
Eddie Kahn	G	5'9"	198	25		6
Jim Karcher	G	6'	207	23		
Eddie Michaels	G	5'11"	195	23		
Les Olsson	G	6'	250	28		

Long, lean rookie Sammy Baugh gave the transplanted Redskins the passing arm needed to round out their attack. In a pre-season practice, coach Ray Flaherty told Baugh to hit a downfield receiver in the eye with the ball, and Sammy calmly replied, "Which eye, Coach?"

In the Redskins' Washington debut, Baugh completed eleven of his sixteen passes and played the full sixty minutes in a 13-3 triumph over the Giants. By mid-season, his bullet aerials had meshed with Cliff Battle's running to give Washington the NFL's most explosive attack.

The New York Giants kept pace with the Redskins, though, and it took the season's finale—where 8,000 Washington fans traveled to New York—before the Skins could put a claim to the title in an upset victory.

NEW YORK GIANTS 6-3-2 Steve Owen

Scores of Each Game		
3	Washington	13
10	Pittsburgh	7
16	Philadelphia	7
21	PHILADELPHIA	0
21	BROOKLYN	0
3	CHIC. BEARS	3
17	PITTSBURGH	0
0	DETROIT	17
10	GREEN BAY	0
13	Brooklyn	13
14	WASHINGTON	49

Use Name	Pos.	Hgt	Wgt	Age	Int	Pts
Stan Galazin	C-LB	6'3"	215	22		
Mel Hein (1 reception for 7 yds.)	C-LB	6'2"	225	28		
Chief Johnson	C-LB	6'3"	225	28		

Use Name – Tackles	Pos.	Hgt	Wgt	Age	Int	Pts
Jerry Dennerlein	T	6'2"	235	24		
Len Grant	T	6'3"	235	31		
Jack Haden	T	6'4"	233	22		
Ox Parry	T	6'4"	230	22		
Ed Widseth	T	6'1"	225	27		

Ken Strong – American Football League

Use Name – Guards	Pos.	Hgt	Wgt	Age	Int	Pts
Pete Cole	G	5'11"	200	21		
Johnny Dell Isola	G-LB	5'11"	206	25		
Kayo Lunday	G-C-LB	6'3"	215	24		
Orville Tuttle	G	5'9"	210	24		
Tarzan White	G	5'9"	210	21		

With seventeen rookies on the twenty-five-man roster, the Giants surprised most observers by going into their final game as favorites for the Eastern title before falling to Washington in a 49-14 offensive blitz.

Starring on the revamped club was rookie Ward Cuff, who made the starting lineup as a wingback, while young veteran Ed Danowski did the passing and second-year-man Tuffy Leemans added his ball-carrying to the pot. Center Mel Hein, guard John Dell Isola, and rookie tackle Ed Widseth starred in a line which helped shut out four opponents during the season. The rebirth on the field sent the turnstiles clicking, with 50,000 fans turning out at the Polo Grounds to witness a 3-3 tie with the Chicago Bears.

PITTSBURGH PIRATES 4-7-0 Johnny Blood

Scores of Each Game		
27	PHILADELPHIA	14
21	Brooklyn	0
7	NEW YORK	10
0	CHIC. BEARS	7
3	Detroit	7
20	Washington	34
7	CHIC. CARDS	13
16	PHILADELPHIA	7
0	New York	17
21	WASHINGTON	13
0	BROOKLYN	23

Use Name	Pos.	Hgt	Wgt	Age	Int	Pts
Mike Basrak	C-LB	6'2"	220	24		
Buster Raborn	C-LB	6'	200	24		
Bill Harris	OE-DE	6'2"	196	23		
Dick Sandefur	DB	5'10"	195	25		

Use Name – Tackles	Pos.	Hgt	Wgt	Age	Int	Pts
Frank Billock	T	6'	230	24		
Joe Cardwell	T-DE	6'3"	240	23		
Tex Holcomb (to PHI)	T	6'2"	235	24		
Ed Karpowich (1 rush for 15 yds.)	T	6'4"	223	24		
Sandy Sandberg (to BKN)	T	6'2"	235	27		

Ben Ciccone – American Football League
Ed Matesic – American Football League
Lee Mulleneaux – American Football League
Dave Ribble – American Football League

Use Name – Guards	Pos.	Hgt	Wgt	Age	Int	Pts
Byron Gentry	G	5'11"	230	23		
George Kakasic (2 PAT's in 2 attempts)	G	5'10"	203	25		2
Walt Kiesling	G	6'2"	250	34		
Lindy Mayhew	G	6'1"	225	25		
John Perko (1 rush for 5 yds.)	G	6'1"	210	21		

Looking to push the Pirates to the top in the East, owner Art Rooney brought in the unpredictable Johnny Blood as head coach and big Walt Kiesling as his assistant. Both men—who played with Ernie Nevers on the 1926 Duluth Eskimos—played part time while directing their younger mates through a mediocre season.

The Pirates as usual lost all their games with Western teams but this time managed to split eight contests within their own division and upset the title-bound Redskins with a 21-13 triumph, but the defection of passer Ed Matesic to the rival American Football League left the burden of the attack on short-yardage runners like Bull Karcis and did not help the Pirates' cause.

BROOKLYN DODGERS 3-7-1 Potsy Clark

Scores of Each Game		
13	Philadelphia	7
0	PITTSBURGH	21
9	CLEVELAND	7
7	Washington	11
0	Detroit	30
0	New York	21
0	WASHINGTON	21
10	PHILADELPHIA	14
7	Chic. Bears	29
23	Pittsburgh	0
13	NEW YORK	13

Use Name	Pos.	Hgt	Wgt	Age	Int	Pts
Norm Cooper (1 reception for 14 yds.)	C-LB	6'4"	210	24		
Wagner Jorgensen	C-LB	6'2"	225	24		
Fred King	BB-LB	6'2"	205	24		
Father Lumpkin	BB-LB	6'2"	220	29		

Use Name – Tackles	Pos.	Hgt	Wgt	Age	Int	Pts
John Golemgeske	T-G	6'2"	225	22		
Pat Harrison	T	6'2"	215	23		
Roy Ilowit	T	6'2"	220	20		
Bill Lee (to GB)	T	6'2"	225	25		
Jim Whatley	T-DE	6'5"	223	24		

Use Name – Guards	Pos.	Hgt	Wgt	Age	Int	Pts
Sig Andrusking	G	5'8"	187	23		
Red Krause (to WAS C-LB)	G	6'1"	215	23		
Rube Leisk	G	6'	195	23		
Don Nelson	G	5'9"	205	23		
Ed Skoronski (from CLE T-C-LB)	G-T	6'2"	220	25		

The Dodgers finally found an offensive leader when former Duke tailback Ace Parker joined the club in November. Parker had been playing professional baseball and only late in the fall received permission from the Philadelphia Athletics to play football. Excelling both as a passer and runner, Parker immediately added a new punch to the Brooklyn offense, and he gave the Dodgers what Dutch Clark had long given the Detroit Lions, a general on the field.

With Ace, and a new coach in Potsy Clark, the Dodgers improved vastly, capping their season with a 23-0 victory at Pittsburgh and a 13-13 tie with the heavily favored Giants. Joe Maniaci and Ralph Kercheval scored all the Brooklyn points in the Giant game, finding their jobs easier with a real passer in the lineup.

PHILADELPHIA EAGLES 2-8-1 Bert Bell

Scores of Each Game		
14	Pittsburgh	27
7	BROOKLYN	13
3	CLEVELAND	21
6	CHIC. CARDS	6
7	NEW YORK	16
14	Washington	0
0	New York	21
7	WASHINGTON	10
7	Pittsburgh	16
14	Brooklyn	10
7	Green Bay	37

Use Name	Pos.	Hgt	Wgt	Age	Int	Pts
Moose Harper	C-LB	6'4"	218	23		6
Hank Reese (3 PAT's in 3 attempts)	C-LB	5'11"	215	26		3
Herb Roton	OE-DE	6'2"	210	24		
Jim Leonard	BB-DB	6'	200	27		

Use Name – Tackles	Pos.	Hgt	Wgt	Age	Int	Pts
Art Buss	T	6'3"	220	26		
John Dempsey	T	6'2"	225	26		
Fritz Ferko	T	6'1"	238	24		
Charlie Knox	T	5'11"	185			
Jim MacMurdo	T	6'1"	206	26		
Ray Spillers	T	6'3"	218	22		

Jim Zyntell – American Football League

Use Name – Guards	Pos.	Hgt	Wgt	Age	Int	Pts
Bill Hughes	G	6'1"	220	22		
Amy McPherson	G	5'11"	240	25		
George Rado (from PIT)	G	5'9"	197	24		
Jim Russell	G-T	5'11"	210	26		
Mule Stockton	G-T	6'1"	218	23		
Vince Zizak	G	5'8"	208	28		

Coach Bert Bell had the satisfaction of seeing his Eagles improve 100 percent over their 1936 season; they won two games this year instead of one. Bell had no worries about losing his job, though, since he owned the team.

For the second straight year, Bell traded off the first-draft choice, sending back Sam Francis of Nebraska to the Bears for veteran end Bill Hewitt. The bare-headed Hewitt turned in another All-Pro performance, while rookie back Emmett Mortell came through as a ball-carrier, and second-year man Dave Smukler grew into an effective runner and passer to complement Mortell. The youth-laden line was anchored by center Hank Reese.

Use Name — Backs & Ends	Pos.	Age	Hgt	Wgt	Pts	Int	Rushing No.	Rushing Yds	Rushing Avg	Rushing TD	Passing Att	Passing Comp	Passing %	Passing Yds	Passing Yd/Att	Passing TD	Passing Int–%	Passing RK
WASHINGTON REDSKINS																		
Sammy Baugh	TB-DB	23	6'2"	185	6		86	240	2.8	1	171	81	47	1127	6.6	8	14– 8	2
Dixie Howell	TB-DB	23	5'11"	175			5	9	1.8	0	6	1	17	14	2.3	0	3–50	
Cliff Battles	FB-TB-DB	27	6'1"	195	42		216	874	4.0	5	33	13	39	142	4.3	0	3– 9	
Don Irwin	FB-DB	24	6'1"	196	12		89	315	3.5	2	3	0	0	0	0.0	0	0– 0	
Max Krause	FB-BB-DB-LB	28	5'10"	198	6		21	47	2.2	1								
Eddie Britt	FB-DB	24	6'2"	205			7	21	3.0	0								
Ed Justice	WB-DB	24	6'1"	205	18		8	35	4.4	0								
Ernie Pinckert	WB-DB	29	6'	195	6		2	10	5.0	0								
Riley Smith	BB-LB	26	6'2"	200	55		12	39	3.3	2	9	4	44	33	3.7	3	0– 0	
Charley Malone	OE-DE	27	6'4"	200	24													
Wayne Millner	OE-DE	26	6'1"	190	18		2	6	3.0	0								
Bob McChesney	OE-DE	25	6'2"	195														
Ben Smith	OE-DE	26	6'3"	208														
NEW YORK GIANTS																		
Ed Danowski	QB-DB	25	6'1"	195	6		66	95	1.4	1	134	66	49	814	6.1	8	5– 4	3
Mickey Kobrosky	QB-DB	22	6'	187			13	41	3.2	0	13	2	15	18	1.4	0	2–15	
Tony Sarausky	QB-DB	25	5'11'	205			4	18	4.5	0	10	3	30	31	3.1	0	0– 0	
Hank Soar	FB-DB	23	6'2"	207	17		120	442	3.7	0	21	5	24	83	4.0	1	2–10	
Tuffy Leemans	FB-DB	24	6'	192	6		144	429	3.0	0	20	5	25	64	3.2	1	1– 5	
Kink Richards	FB-DB	26	5'11"	196	18		89	327	3.7	1								
Jim Neill	FB-DB	22	6'1"	190			7	55	7.9	0	3	1	33	0	0.0	0	1–33	
Ward Cuff	WB-DB	24	6'1"	198	30		4	32	8.0	2								
Dale Burnett	WB-DB	28	6'1"	188	6		7	4	0.6	0								
Red Corzine	BB-LB	28	6'	218	6		8	23	2.9	0	1	0	0	0	0.0	0	0– 0	
Leland Shaffer	BB-DB	25	6'2"	200			8	35	4.4	0								
Tilly Manton	BB-LB	25	5'11"	187	27		8	16	2.0	0	1	1	100	14	14.0	0	0– 0	
Will Walls	OE-DE	22	6'4"	205														
Jim Poole	OE-DE	21	6'3"	215	12													
Ray Hanken	OE-DE	24	5'11"	190														
Jim Lee Howell	OE-DE	22	6'6"	200														
Chuck Gelatka	OE-DE	24	6'1"	195														
PITTSBURGH PIRATES																		
Johnny Gildea	TB-BB-DB	27	6'2"	215	6		49	65	1.3	1	47	14	30	288	6.1	2	9–19	
Max Fiske	TB-DB	23	6'	205			28	44	1.6	0	43	17	40	318	7.4	4	4– 9	
Tuffy Thompson	TB-HB-DB	22	5'11"	175	6		43	80	1.9	0	14	6	43	100	7.1	1	4–29	
Bull Karcis	FB-LB	28	5'9"	225	18		128	511	4.0	3	3	1	33	2	0.7	1	1–33	
Stu Smith	FB-TB-LB-DB	21	6'	195			65	211	3.2	0	2	0	0	0	0.0	0	1–50	
Izzy Weinstock	FB-BB-LB	24	6'	212	4		33	88	2.7	0								
Bill Davidson	HB-TB-DB	22	6'	182	24		101	293	2.9	1	24	8	33	81	3.4	0	5–21	
Johnny Blood	HB-BB-TB-DB	33	6'1"	185	30		9	37	4.1	0	25	10	40	115	4.6	1	2– 8	
By Haines	HB-DB	23	5'11"	185			24	29	1.2	0	6	1	17	14	2.3	0	1–17	
Bill Breeden	HB-OE-DB	23	6'1"	210	1		10	25	2.5	0								
Silvio Zaninelli	BB-DB	23	5'10"	215			4	14	3.5	0								
Bill Sortet	OE-DE	25	6'1"	188	6													
Jeep Brett	OE-DE	23	6'2"	200	6													
Mac Cara	OE-DE	23	5'10"	185														
Vinnie Sites	OE-DE	25	6'2"	215														
Armand Niccolai	T	25	6'2"	225	17													
BROOKLYN DODGERS																		
Ace Parker	TB-DB	25	6'	184	13		34	26	0.8	1	61	28	46	514	8.4	1	7–11	7
Reino Nori	TB-DB	24	5'8"	168			26	81	3.1	0	23	11	48	168	7.3	1	3–13	
Carl Brumhaugh	TD-DB	29	5'10"	180			13	–3	–0.2	0	18	5	28	87	4.8	0	3–17	
(from CLE, BB-DB, to CHI B, QB-DB)																		
Shipwreck Kelly	TB-DB	27	6'2"	195			16	29	1.8	0	12	2	17	21	1.8	0	3–25	
Red Franklin	TB-DB	25	5'10"	165			4	12	3.0	0	4	0	0	0	0.0	0	0– 0	
Joe Maniaci	FB-HB-DB	23	6'1"	220	23		92	433	4.7	2	4	1	25	0	0.0	0	2–50	
Dick Crayne	FB-DB	24	6'	200	3		47	135	2.9	0	4	2	50	20	5.0	0	0– 0	
Vannic Albanese	FB-BB-DB-LB	24	6	184			21	53	2.5	0	2	1	50	5	2.5	0	0– 0	
Ralph Kercheval	HB-TB-DB	26	6 1	193	13		48	84	1.8	1	19	11	58	154	8.1	1	1– 5	
Bert Johnson	HB-TB-DB	25	6	205			41	59	1.4	0	11	0	0	0	0.0	0	1– 9	
Tony Kaska	BB-LB	26	5 11	196			1	4	4.0	0								
Jeff Barrett	OE-DE	24	6 1"	180	18		1	8	8.0	0								
Jim Austin	OE-DE	24	6'2"	200														
Buster Mitchell	OE-DE	31	6'	205	6													
Frank Cumiskey	OE-DE	22	6'2"	205														
PHILADELPHIA EAGLES																		
Emmett Mortell	TB-DB	23	6'1"	182			100	312	3.1	0	71	18	25	320	4.5	1	8–11	11
Dave Smukler	FB-LB	23	6'1"	229	17		92	247	2.6	1	118	42	36	432	3.7	6	14–12	10
Swede Hanson	FB-LB	28	6'1"	193	6		18	59	3.3	1	2	0	0	0	0.0	0	0– 0	
Rabbit Keen	WB-TB-DB	22	5'9"	174			34	154	4.5	0	6	1	17	86	14.3	1	0– 0	
Bob Masters	WB-DB	26	5'11"	200			9	32	3.6	0								
Winnie Baze	WB-TB-DB	23	5'11"	190			3	14	4.7	0	3	0	0	0	0.0	0	0– 0	
Jay Arnold	WB-BB-DB	23	6'1"	206			5	7	1.4	0								
John Kusko	BB-TB-DB	23	5'11"	190			17	27	1.6	0	7	2	29	11	1.6	0	2–29	
Glenn Frey	BB-DB	25	5'10"	190			5	11	2.2	0								
Bill Hewitt	OE-DE	27	5'9"	190	30													
Joe Carter	OE-DE	27	6'1"	208	18													
Joe Pilconis	OE-DE	25	6'1"	184	6		2	21	10.5	0								

Use Name — Backs & Ends	Receiving No.	Receiving Yds	Receiving Avg	Receiving TD	Punting No.	Punting Avg	Kicking Pat	Kicking Att	Kicking %	Kicking FG	Kicking Att	Kicking %	Punt Returns No.	Punt Returns Yds	Punt Returns Avg	Punt Returns TD	Kickoff Returns No.	Kickoff Returns Yds	Kickoff Returns Avg	Kickoff Returns TD
WASHINGTON REDSKINS																				
Sammy Baugh																				
Dixie Howell																				
Cliff Battles	9	81	9	1																
Don Irwin	8	112	14	0																
Max Krause	2	13	7	0																
Eddie Britt																				
Ed Justice	9	150	17	3																
Ernie Pinckert	10	145	15	1																
Riley Smith	11	93	8	0			22	26	85	5										
Charley Malone	28	419	15	4																
Wayne Millner	14	216	15	2																
Bob McChesney	6	50	8	0																
Ben Smith	2	37	19	0																
NEW YORK GIANTS																				
Ed Danowski																				
Mickey Kobrosky																				
Tony Sarausky																				
Hank Soar	6	77	13	1			2	3	67	1										
Tuffy Leemans	11	157	14	1																
Kink Richards	10	149	15	2																
Jim Neill																				
Ward Cuff	5	117	23	2						2										
Dale Burnett	10	121	12	1																
Red Corzine	9	75	8	1																
Leland Shaffer	7	72	10	0																
Tilly Manton	3	15	5	0			12	12	100	5										
Will Walls	7	55	8	0																
Jim Poole	5	79	16	2																
Ray Hanken	4	51	13	0																
Jim Lee Howell	4	32	8	0																
Chuck Gelatka	1	17	17	0																
PITTSBURGH PIRATES																				
Johnny Gildea	3	47	16	0																
Max Fiske	1	0	0	0																
Tuffy Thompson	6	126	21	1																
Bull Karcis	2	18	9	0																
Stu Smith							4	6	67											
Izzy Weinstock																				
Bill Davidson	4	169	42	2																
Johnny Blood	10	168	17	4																1
By Haines	2	17	9	0																
Bill Breeden	6	59	10	0			1	1	100											
Silvio Zaninelli	2	12	6	0																
Bill Sortet	9	121	13	1																
Jeep Brett	8	135	17	1																
Mac Cara	2	36	18	0																
Vinnie Sites	2	10	5	0																
Armand Niccolai							5	7	71	4										
BROOKLYN DODGERS																				
Ace Parker							1	2	50							1				
Reino Nori																				
Carl Brumhaugh																				
Shipwreck Kelly	1	7	7	0																
Red Franklin																				
Joe Maniaci	3	11	4	0			5	5	100	2										
Dick Crayne	1	4	4	0						1										
Vannic Albanese																				
Ralph Kercheval	5	57	11	0			1	3	33	2										
Bert Johnson	1	3	3	0																
Tony Kaska	4	84	21	0																
Jeff Barrett	20	461	23	3																
Jim Austin	13	185	14	0																
Buster Mitchell	8	115	14	1																
Frank Cumiskey	5	50	10	0																
PHILADELPHIA EAGLES																				
Emmett Mortell	1	0	0	0																
Dave Smukler	1	–4	–4	0			8	9	89	1										
Swede Hanson																				
Rabbit Keen	5	45	9	0																
Bob Masters	4	60	15	0																
Winnie Baze	1	2	2	0																
Jay Arnold	8	142	18	0																
John Kusko	2	47	24	0																
Glenn Frey	4	19	5	0																
Bill Hewitt	16	197	12	5																
Joe Carter	15	282	19	3																
Joe Pilconis	6	59	10	0																

TEAM TOTALS — OFFENSE

TEAM TOTALS	FIRST DOWNS	Rushing No.	Rushing Yards	Rushing Avg. Yds.	Rushing TD	Passing Att.	Passing Comp.	Passing Comp. Pct.	Passing Yards	Passing Yds/Att.	Passing Yds/Comp.	Passing TD	Passing Int.	Passing Pct. Int.	Fumbles: Number	Penalty: Yards	Points: Total	Points: TD	Points: PAT	Points: FG	Points: Saf
WASHINGTON	149	448	1596	3.6	11	222	99	44.6	1316	5.9	13.3	11	20	9.0	38	338	195	26	22	5	1
NEW YORK	127	478	1517	3.2	4	203	83	40.9	1024	5.0	12.3	10	11	5.4	25	275	128	15	14	8	0
PITTSBURGH	105	496	1417	2.9	5	164	57	34.8	918	5.6	16.1	9	27	16.5	31	358	122	16	12	4	1
BROOKLYN	88	375	978	2.6	5	179	64	35.8	995	5.6	15.5	4	23	12.8	28	190	82	10	7	5	0
PHILADELPHIA	68	285	884	3.1	2	207	63	30.4	849	4.1	13.5	8	24	11.6	17	146	86	12	11	1	0

DEFENSE

Total Yards	Pass Att.	Pass Comp.	Comp. Pct.	No. Pass Int.	Oppos. Fumb. Rec.	Points	TEAM TOTALS
2123	171	66	38.6	17	24	120	WASHINGTON
2158	182	71	39.0	30	14	109	NEW YORK
2232	185	60	32.4	17	23	145	PITTSBURGH
2821	165	74	44.8	21	16	174	BROOKLYN
3150	196	79	40.3	19	17	177	PHILADELPHIA

CHICAGO BEARS 9-1-1 George Halas

Scores of Each Game		
14	Green Bay	2
7	Pittsburgh	0
20	Cleveland	2
16	CHIC. CARDS	7
28	DETROIT	20
3	New York	3
14	GREEN BAY	24
29	BROOKLYN	7
13	Detroit	0
15	CLEVELAND	7
42	Chic. Cards	28

Use Name	Pos.	Hgt	Wgt	Age	Int	Pts
Frank Bausch	C-LB	6'2"	224	29		
Bill Conkright	C-LB	6'1"	200	23		
Frank Sullivan	C-LB	6'3"	203	25		
Henry Hammond	OE-DE	5'11"	190	23		
George Corbett	DB	5'9"	178	29		
Del Bjork	T	6'1"	218	23		
Joe Stydahar	T	6'4"	230	25		
Russ Thompson	T	6'5"	248	25		
Milt Trost	T	6'1"	203	24		
Zuck Carlson — knee injury						
Kay Bell	G-T	6'2"	210	22		
Danny Fortmann	G	6'	210	21		
George Musso	G	6'2"	258	27		
Joe Zeller	G	6'1"	203	29		

As the only NFL club still using the T formation, the Bears passed the word that they were back by winning their first five contests before the New York Giants held them to a 3-3 tie. A loss to the Green Bay Packers caused some people to doubt the Bears, but the Halas men ran off four straight victories to ice away the Western championship.

On the road to the top, quarterback Bernie Masterson had his pick of three hard-charging runners on ground plays. Halfback Ray Nolting relied on quickness to break clear, while both Bronko Nagurski and Jack Manders were straight-ahead power runners and blockers.

Up in the line, Joe Stydahar, George Musso, Danny Fortmann, and Frank Bausch all made either first-or second-team All-Pro with their trench play, and rookie George Wilson capably filled the traded Bill Hewitt's end slot.

GREEN BAY PACKERS 7-4-0 Curly Lambeau

Scores of Each Game		
7	CHIC. CARDS	14
2	CHIC. BEARS	14
26	DETROIT	6
34	CHIC. CARDS	13
35	Cleveland	10
35	CLEVELAND	7
14	Detroit	13
24	Chic. Bears	14
37	PHILADELPHIA	7
0	New York	10
6	Washington	14

Use Name	Pos.	Hgt	Wgt	Age	Int	Pts
Darrell Lester	C-LB	6'3"	220	27		
Bud Svendsen	C-LB	6'1"	195	22		
George Svendsen	C-LB	6'4"	230	24		
(1 reception for 11 yds.)						
Swede Johnston	FB-LB	5'10"	195	27		
Averell Daniell (to BKN)	T	6'3"	215	23		
Lou Gordon	T	6'5"	230	29		
Champ Seibold	T	6'4"	235	24		
Ernie Smith	T	6'2"	222	27		15
(12 PAT's in 14 attempts, 1 FG)						
Lyle Sturgeon	T	6'3"	250	23		
Tiny Engebretsen	G	6'1"	240	27		8
(5 PAT's in 6 attempts, 1 FG)						
Lon Evans	G	6'2"	230	25		
Russ Letlow	G	6'	210	23		
Mike Michalske	G	6'	230	34		
Zud Schammel	G-DE	6'2"	235	26		6

A bad hip and some added pounds around the middle cut down on Arnie Herber's never great mobility—enough to make him vulnerable to a strong pass rush—and the Cardinals and Bears applied enough pressure to hand the Packers two quick losses at the start of the season that even a seven-game winning streak could not make up for.

Herber's arm still sent many a long pass onto Don Hutson's outstretched fingertips for huge chunks of yardage. To balance this airmail service, fullback Clarke Hinkle carried the mail on the ground with enough power to merit All-Pro honors. Guards Russ Letlow and Lon Evans and center George Svendsen opened up holes for Hinkle and shielded Herber from too much hostile interference. But even with so much running talent, the Packers again stumbled at the end of the year by dropping games to the Giants and Redskins.

DETROIT LIONS 7-4-0 Dutch Clark

Scores of Each Game		
28	Cleveland	0
16	CHIC. CARDS	7
6	Green Bay	26
7	PITTSBURGH	3
30	BROOKLYN	0
20	Chic. Bears	28
13	GREEN BAY	14
27	CLEVELAND	7
17	New York	0
16	Chic. Cards	7
0	CHIC. BEARS	13

Use Name	Pos.	Hgt	Wgt	Age	Int	Pts
Hal Cooper	C-LB-G	5'10"	207	23		
Del Ritchhart	C-LB	6'	195	26		
Dixie Stokes	C-LB	6'	205	24		
Frank Christensen	BB-DB	6'1"	198	27		
Ray Reckmack (from BKN)	BB-DB	6'	200	23		
Charley Payne	WB-DB	5'11"	186	22		
George Christensen	T-G	6'2"	238	27		
Jack Johnson	T	6'4"	212	27		6
Bob Reynolds	T	6'4"	218	23		
Red Stacy	T	6'2"	215	25		
Ox Emerson	G	5'11"	200	29		
Bill Feldhaus	G-T	6'	230	25		
Tom Fena	G	5'11"	200	23		
Tom Hupke	G	5'10"	188	26		6
Sid Wagner	G	5'11"	190	24		

Dutch Clark had been running the Lions on the field since the team began, so it was only natural that he be chosen head coach when Potsy Clark decided to pack it in during the spring. Under Dutch's direction, the Lions lost only to the Packers and Bears. Clark's best player was an aging but still dangerous tailback named Dutch Clark.

Others who stood out in the Detroit lineup were Ace Gutowsky, who still crashed into the center of the line, Ernie Caddel, who still carried the ball to the outside, and George Christensen and Ox Emerson, both of whom helped stiffen the line. Although the Lions essentially had the same club that won the championship in 1935, they lacked the spark of that previous season and were beginning to get the label of a good team mired in a mediocre rut.

CHICAGO CARDINALS 5-5-1 Milan Creighton

Scores of Each Game		
14	Green Bay	7
7	Detroit	16
21	Washington	14
6	Philadelphia	6
6	Cleveland	0
13	Green Bay	34
7	Chic. Bears	16
13	Pittsburgh	7
13	CLEVELAND	7
7	DETROIT	16
28	CHIC. BEARS	42

Use Name	Pos.	Hgt	Wgt	Age	Int	Pts
Len Dugan	C-LB	6'	220	25		
Ham Harmon	C-LB	6'	220	23		
John Reynolds	C-LB	5'10"	185	23		
Milan Creighton	OE-DE	6'	190	29		
Bill Muellner	OE-DE	5'11"	175	22		
Conway Baker	T	5'11"	225	25		6
(6 PAT's in 6 attempts)						
Tony Blazine	T	6'	230	25		
(1 reception for 2 yds.)						
Dub Miller	T-G	6'	220	25		
Earl Nolan	T	6'1"	205	23		
(Missed 1 PAT attempt)						
Jack Robinson	T	6'3"	220	25		
Bert Pearson — American Football League						
Hal Carlson	G	6'3"	220	22		
Ross Carter	G	6'	200	23		
Bree Cuppoletti	G	5'10"	200	27		
Bob Hoel	G	6'	212	24		
John Morrow	G	5'11"	230			
Bill Volok	G	6'2"	215	27		
(1 reception for 9 yds.)						

The Cardinals flew back up to the .500 mark on the wings of a new passing combination to rival Herber & Hutson in Green Bay. Coming from LSU as a unit, passer Pat Coffee and receiver Gaynell Tinsley found NFL defenses not much more difficult than what they had faced in college. Tinsley gained 675 yards to set a receiving record, part of which came on a 97-yard pass play from Coffee in a game against the Bears.

While the two rookies ate up yardage, Doug Russell and Bill Smith again were hampered with injuries and played below their par. Both men had been promising young players two years before but found themselves aging prematurely because of the injury hex. Although George Grosvenor helped the running game, the Cardinals relied mostly on their new air express.

CLEVELAND RAMS 1-10-0 Hugo Bezdek

Scores of Each Game		
0	DETROIT	28
21	Philadelphia	3
7	Brooklyn	9
0	CHIC. CARDS	6
2	CHIC. BEARS	20
10	GREEN BAY	35
7	Green Bay	35
7	Chic. Cards	13
7	Detroit	27
7	WASHINGTON	16
7	Chic. Bears	15

Use Name	Pos.	Hgt	Wgt	Age	Int	Pts
Chuck Cerundolo	C-LB	6'1"	210	21		
Jim Turner	C-LB	6'2"	210	27		
Ollie Savatsky	OE-DE	6'2"	215	25		
Joe Williams	DB	5'9"	178	23		
Bob Emerick	T-G	6'2"	230	25		
Ted Livingston	T-G	6'3"	215	23		
Primo Miller	T	6'2"	220	21		6
Dale Prather	T-DE	6'2"	190	25		
Ted Rosequist	T	6'4"	225	29		
Wayne Underwood	T	6'1"	190	24		
Forrest Burmeister	G-T	6'3"	215	24		
Ralph Isselhardt (from DET)	G	6'1"	205	27		
Ookie Miller	G-C-LB	6'	215	27		
Dick Zoll	G	5'11"	220	23		

The first new club in the league since 1933, the Rams played like an expansion team by winning one out of eleven games. The offense scored the least points in the NFL, while the defense sprang for the most.

Coach Hugo Bezdek, the only man who managed a major-league baseball team and coached in the NFL, built his squad from a slew of rookies, a few defectors from the outlaw American Football League, and a handful of NFL veterans. Most of the rookies came from Midwest schools like Purdue and Ohio State, and the gems of the bunch were back Johnny Drake, the club's leading rusher, and center Chuck Cherundolo, a lineman who would have a long NFL career. The team's top passer, Bob Snyder, left the AFL along with five others to join the new NFL franchise. Two veterans of the Chicago Bears, center Ookie Miller and tackle Ted Rosequist, helped bring the club some respectability.

Use Name — Backs & Ends	Pos.	Age	Hgt	Wgt	Pts	Int	RUSHING				PASSING								RECEIVING				PUNTING		KICKING						PUNT RETURNS				KICKOFF RETURNS			
							No.	Yds	Avg	TD	Att	Comp	%	Yds	Yd/Att	TD	Int–%	RK	No.	Yds	Avg	TD	No.	Avg	Pat	Att	%	FG	Att	%	No.	Yds	Avg	TD	No.	Yds	Avg	TD
CHICAGO BEARS																																						
Bernie Masterson	QB-DB	26	6'3"	195	6		30	21	0.7	1	72	26	36	615	8.5	8	7–10	4																				
Ray Buivid	QB-HB-DB	22	6'1"	195	6		19	24	1.3	0	35	17	49	215	6.1	6	2– 6		1	4	4	1																
Gene Ronzani	QB-HB-DB	28	5'9"	190	6		12	17	1.4	0	13	4	31	84	6.5	0	1– 8		2	40	20	1																
Ray Nolting	HB-DB	23	5'11"	185	12		106	424	4.0	2	4	0	0	0	0.0	0	1–25		4	64	16	0																
Bronko Nagurski	FB-LB	28	6'2"	238	6		73	343	4.7	1	2	1	50	35	17.5	1	0– 0																					
Jack Manders	HB-DB	28	6'	200	69		73	319	4.4	0									7	155	22	3			15	20	75	8										
Beattie Feathers	HB-DB	29	5'10"	185	6		66	211	3.2	1	6	2	33	12	2.0	0	0– 0																					
Sam Francis	FB-LB	22	6'	205	7		48	129	2.7	0	6	3	50	34	5.7	1	2–33		1	9	9	0			1	1	100											
Pug Rentner	HB-DB	26	6'1"	185	6		21	70	3.3	0									6	101	17	1																
Keith Molesworth	HB-QB-DB	30	5'9"	168	1		20	53	2.7	0	6	1	17	4	0.7	0	0– 0		4	21	5	0			1	1	100											
John Doehring	HB-DB	27	6'	225			9	33	3.7	0	3	2	67	25	8.3	0	0– 0																					
Les McDonald	OE-DE	22	6'4"	200	24														11	179	16	4																
Eggs Manske	OE-DE	24	6'	185	24														9	225	25	3																
Bill Karr	OE-DE	26	6'1"	187	12		1	10	10.0	0									7	188	27	2																
Dick Plasman	OE-DE	23	6'3"	210	8														3	18	6	1			2	4	50											
George Wilson	OE-DE	23	6'1"	190	6														1	20	20	0																
GREEN BAY PACKERS																																						
Arnie Herber	TB-DB	27	5'11"	200			5	9	1.8	0	104	47	45	676	6.5	7	10–10	6																				
Bob Monnett	TB-HB-DB	27	5'9"	180	6		87	161	1.9	1	73	37	51	580	7.9	9	8–11	1	4	32	8	0																
Herb Banet	TB-HB-DB	23	6'2"	200			9	29	3.2	0	7	1	14	2	0.3	0	2–29		1	6	6	0																
Ray Peterson	TB-DB	21	6'	190							6	3	50	47	7.8	0	0– 0																					
Ed Smith	TB-DB	24	6'2"	204							2	0	0	0	0.0	0	1–50																					
Clarke Hinkle	FB-LB	27	5'11"	205	56		129	552	4.3	5	3	2	67	43	14.3	0	0– 0		8	116	15	2			8	9	89	2										
Ed Jankowski	FB-LB	24	5'9"	205	25		61	325	5.3	2									1	60	60	1			1	1	100											
George Sauer	FB-LB	26	6'2"	212			7	17	2.4	0																												
Joe Laws	HB-DB	26	5'9"	185	12		74	310	4.2	2	11	5	45	49	4.5	0	2–18		10	121	12	0																
Paul Miller	HB-DB	24	5'11"	180	6		71	265	3.7	0									6	66	11	1																
Hank Bruder	BB-TB-DB	29	6'	200	6		15	56	3.7	1	6	0	0	0	0.0	0	2–33																					
Herm Schneidman	BB-DB	23	5'11"	200	6		5	17	3.4	0									2	35	18	1																
Buckets Goldenberg	BB-G-DB-LB	26	5'10"	220	6		4	18	4.5	0																												
Don Hutson	OE-DE	24	6'1"	180	42		14	26	1.9	0	4	0	0	0	0.0	0	1–25		41	552	13	7																
Milt Gantenbein	OE-DE	27	6'	200	12														12	237	20	2																
Bernie Scherer	OE-DE	24	6'1"	190	12														7	148	21	2																
Wayland Becker	OE-DE	26	6'	205			2	4	2.0	0									2	13	7	0																
DETROIT LIONS																																						
Dutch Clark	TB-DB	30	6'	180	45		96	468	4.9	5	39	19	49	202	5.2	1	3– 8		2	33	17	1			6	10	60	1										
Bill Shepherd	TB-FB-DB-LB	25	5'9"	190	31		93	325	3.5	2	46	19	41	297	6.5	1	7–15								7	8	88	2										
Ace Gutowsky	FB-LB	27	5'11"	202	6		126	361	2.9	1	8	1	13	30	3.8	0	2–25																					
Lee Kizzire	FB-LB	23	6'	200			7	20	2.9	0																												
Ernie Caddel	WB-DB	26	6'2"	195	18		76	429	5.6	3	4	0	0	0	0.0	0	0– 0		9	80	9	0																
Lloyd Cardwell	WB-DB	24	6'2"	195	6		36	181	5.0	0									3	51	17	1																
Vern Huffman	BB-TB-WB-DB	22	6'2"	210	6		35	187	5.3	0	23	5	22	102	4.4	2	6–26		8	104	13	0																
Ed Klewicki	OE-WB-DE	26	5'10"	210	6		10	53	5.3	0									8	134	17	0																
Butch Morse	OE-DE	25	6'2"	202	6		1	–3	–3.0	0									8	131	16	1																
Harry Ebding	OE-DE	28	5'11"	195	18														5	89	18	1																
Chuck Hanneman	OE-DE	22	6'	195	6		2	53	26.5	1									1	9	9	0																
Regis Monahan	G	28	5'10"	215	20																				5	5	100	5										
CHICAGO CARDINALS																																						
Pat Coffee	TB-DB	23	5'11"	185	6		55	157	2.9	1	119	52	44	804	6.8	5	11– 9	5																				
George Grosvenor	TB-DB	26	6'	175	12		137	461	3.4	2	50	21	42	325	6.5	3	7–14	9																				
Hal Pangle	FB-DB	25	5'10"	200	12		61	203	3.3	2	2	0	0	0	0.0	0	1–50		5	58	12	0			0	1	0											
Buddy Parker	FB-DB	23	6'	195	7		50	115	2.3	1	1	0	0	0	0.0	0	0– 0		2	14	7	0			1	2	50											
Bill Crass	FB-DB	23	6'	205			5	8	1.6	0	1	0	0	0	0.0	0	0– 0																					
Doug Russell	WB-DB	25	6'	190	12		23	76	3.3	0	11	4	36	94	8.5	1	2–18		12	263	22	1												1				
Jimmy Lawrence	WB-DB	23	5'11"	185	6		19	60	3.2	1	3	0	0	0	0.0	0	0– 0		3	32	11	0																
Rock Reed	WB-DB	22	5'8"	170	6		10	33	3.3	0	1	0	0	0	0.0	0	0– 0		2	26	13	1																
Howie Tipton	BB-LB	26	5'11"	185			9	23	2.6	0									1	2	2	0																
Pete Tyler	BB-LB	23	5'11"	190	6		5	–5	–1.0	0	1	0	0	0	0.0	0	0– 0		7	60	9	1																
Bill May	BB-LB	23	5'11"	185	10		4	16	4.0	0															4	5	80	2										
Gus Tinsley	OE-DE	22	6'1"	195	36		1	2	2.0	0									36	675	19	5																
Bill Smith	OE-DE	25	6'1"	198	9														3	52	17	0			3	3	100											
Versil Deskin	OE-DE	24	6'	200	6														3	48	16	1																
Billy Wilson	OE-DE	25	5'10"	185															1	2	2	0																
CLEVELAND RAMS																																						
Bob Snyder	TB-DB	24	6'	190	16		82	232	2.8	1	66	25	38	378	5.7	2	6– 9	8	3	20	7	0			7	7	100	1										
Ed Goddard (from BKN)	TB-WB-DB	22	5'10"	180	13		57	162	2.8	1	41	13	32	180	4.4	2	8–20		6	61	10	0			1	1	100											
Harry Mattos	TB-DB	26	6'	195	8		26	16	0.6	1	22	5	23	94	4.3	1	4–18								2	2	100											
Joe Keeble	TB-WB-DB	28	6'	190	6		12	40	3.3	0	9	2	22	25	2.8	0	3–33		1	42	42	1																
Bud Cooper	TB-FB-DB	23	6'1"	204			19	45	2.4	0	5	2	40	21	4.2	0	1–20																					
Bill O'Neill	TB-DB	27	6'	185			4	12	3.0	0	2	1	50	20	10.0	0	1–50																					
Ray Johnson	TB-FB-DB	23	6'1"	200			7	28	4.0	0																												
Johnny Drake	FB-WB-LB-DB	21	6'1"	205	30		98	333	3.4	3	1	0	0	0	0.0	0	0– 0		10	172	17	2																
Mark Barber	FB-LB	23	5'11"	192			14	35	2.5	0	3	1	33	7	2.3	0	0– 0																					
John Bettridge (from CHIB)	FB-LB	27	5'10"	188			22	35	1.6	0									1	17	17	0																
Julie Alfonse	WB-TB-DB	23	5'8"	180			33	60	1.8	0	10	4	40	48	4.8	0	0– 0		5	113	23	0																
Mike Sebastian	WB-DB	27	5'11"	185			6	4	0.7	0																												
Stan Pincura	BB-DB	23	5'11"	175			5	–22	–4.4	0	27	9	33	92	3.4	0	3–11		12	139	12	0																
Wayne Gift	BB-DB	21	5'8"	175			3	7	2.3	0	3	0	0	0	0.0	0	0– 0		3	20	7	0																
Sam Busich	OE-DE	24	6'3"	190															13	136	10	0																
Paul Halleck	OE-DE	24	6'	195															3	57	19	0																
Phil Bucklew	OE-DE	22	6'1"	205															3	51	17	0																
Walt Uzdavinis	OE-DE	27	6'2"	210															1	15	15	0																

TEAM TOTALS	OFFENSE	RUSHING:				PASSING:									FUMBLES:	PENALTY:	POINTS:					DEFENSE							TEAM TOTALS
	FIRST DOWNS	No.	Yards	Avg. Yds.	TD	Att.	Comp.	Comp Pct.	Yards	Yds/ Att.	Yds/ Comp.	TD	Int.	Pct. Int.	Number	Yards	Total	TD	PAT	FG	Saf	Total Yards	Pass Att.	Pass Comp.	Comp. Pct.	No. Pass Int.	Oppos. Fumb. Rec.	Points	
CHICAGO BEARS	114	479	1654	3.5	5	147	56	38.1	1024	7.0	18.3	16	13	8.8	26	505	201	26	19	8	1	2255	195	78	40.0	17	21	100	CHICAGO BEARS
GREEN BAY	140	483	1789	3.7	11	216	95	44.0	1397	6.5	14.7	16	26	12.0	18	291	220	30	26	4	1	2297	197	70	35.5	22	11	122	GREEN BAY
DETROIT	120	482	2074	4.3	12	120	44	36.7	631	5.3	14.3	4	18	15.0	17	139	180	23	18	8	0	2102	165	59	35.8	25	17	105	DETROIT
CHICAGO CARDS	99	379	1149	3.0	7	189	77	40.7	1243	6.6	16.1	9	21	11.1	30	305	135	19	15	2	0	2526	204	73	35.8	24	21	165	CHICAGO CARDS
CLEVELAND	88	368	930	2.5	6	168	59	35.1	836	5.0	14.2	4	23	13.7	28	228	75	10	10	1	1	2702	166	67	43.2	15	15	207	CLEVELAND

NEW YORK GIANTS 8-2-1 Steve Owen

Scores of Each Game		
27	Pittsburgh	14
10	Philadelphia	14
10	PITTSBURGH	13
10	Washington	7
17	PHIALDELPHIA	7
28	BROOKLYN	14
6	CHIC. CARDS	0
28	CLEVELAND	0
15	GREEN BAY	3
7	Brooklyn	7
36	WASHINGTON	0

Use Name	Pos.	Hgt	Wgt	Age	Int	Pts
Stan Galazin	C-LB	6'3"	215	23		
Mel Hein	C-LB	6'2"	225	29		6
Cliff Johnson	C-LB	6'3"	225	29		

Use Name – Tackles	Pos.	Hgt	Wgt	Age	Int	Pts
Frank Cope	T	6'2"	213	22		
Jack Haden	T	6'4"	233	23		
John Mellus	T	6'	210	21		
Ox Parry	T	6'4"	230	23		
Ed Widseth	T	6'1"	225	28		

Ken Strong — suspended by N.F.L. for playing in A.F.L.

Use Name – Guards	Pos.	Hgt	Wgt	Age	Int	Pts
Pete Cole	G	5'11"	220	22		
Johnny Dell Isola	G-LB	5'11"	198	26		
Kayo Lunday	G-C-LB	6'3"	215	25		
Orville Tuttle (1 reception for −2 yds.)	G	5'9"	210	25		
Tarzan White	G	5'9"	205	22		

When the league awarded its first Most Valuable Player Award to Mel Hein, it was not a surprising choice, as the New York center had just made the All-Pro team for the sixth straight year. Hein's season performance was highlighted in a game against Green Bay when he picked off a pass at mid-field and rambled 50 yards for the only touchdown of his NFL career. Ed Danowski and Ed Widseth joined teammate Hein on the All-Pro team, and Tuffy Leemans barely missed a spot. Coach Owen had stockpiled so much talent, he formed two separate squads which alternated in the game by quarters, and after two early losses to the Eagles and Pirates, the deep Giants marched undefeated through the bulk of their schedule. With the Eastern crown again on the line, the Giants crushed the Redskins 36-0 in the final game of the year in New York.

WASHINGTON REDSKINS 6-3-2 Ray Flaherty

Scores of Each Game		
26	Philadelphia	23
16	BROOKLYN	16
37	CLEVELAND	13
7	NEW YORK	10
7	Detroit	5
20	PHILADELPHIA	14
6	Brooklyn	6
7	Pittsburgh	0
7	Chic. Bears	31
15	PITTSBURGH	0
0	New York	36

Use Name	Pos.	Hgt	Wgt	Age	Int	Pts
Vic Carroll	C-LB	6'4"	230	25		
Bud Erickson	C-LB	6'1"	195	22		
Red Krause	C-LB	6'1"	216	24		
Mickey Parks	C-LB	6'	220	21		
Rink Bond	BB-LB	5'10"	200	24		

Use Name – Tackles	Pos.	Hgt	Wgt	Age	Int	Pts
Jim Barber	T	6'3"	228	26		
Chuck Bond	T	6'2"	232	24		
Turk Edwards	T	6'2"	256	30		6
Willie Wilkin	T	6'4"	247	22		
Bill Young (1 reception for 62 yd. touchdown)	T	6'1"	242	24		6
Roy Young	T	6'2"	215	21		

Use Name – Guards	Pos.	Hgt	Wgt	Age	Int	Pts
Hank Bartos	G	6'1"	216	24		
Jim Karcher	G	6'	207	24		
Les Olsson	G	6'	243	29		
Clem Stralka	G	5'10"	202	24		

When Cliff Battles retired and the Eagles separated Sammy Baugh's shoulder early in the season's first game, visions of a long year passed before the Redskins' eyes. Two rookies, passer Bill Hartman and runner Andy Farkas, rushed to the rescue, though, pulled out a victory over the Eagles, and kept the Skins in contention in the East.

Although Baugh returned to action in mid-season below peak efficiency, and Washington kept pace with New York—thanks to an outstanding line led by tackles Turk Edwards and Jim Barber—the Skins could not duplicate last year's efforts and lost in the finale to the Giants with the Eastern crown at stake.

BROOKLYN DODGERS 4-4-3 Potsy Clark

Scores of Each Game		
16	Washington	16
3	PITTSBURGH	17
13	CHIC. CARDS	0
17	Pittsburgh	7
7	Green Bay	35
14	New York	28
6	WASHINGTON	6
10	Philadelphia	7
32	PHILADELPHIA	14
6	CHIC. BEARS	24
7	NEW YORK	7

Use Name	Pos.	Hgt	Wgt	Age	Int	Pts
Norm Cooper	C-LB	6'4"	205	25		
Lou Mark	C-LB	6'	195	23		
Gene Moore	C-LB	6'3"	205	25		
Eddie Britt	DB	6'2"	205	25		

Use Name – Tackles	Pos.	Hgt	Wgt	Age	Int	Pts
Leo Disend	T	6'2"	224	22		
John Golemgeske	T	6'2"	225	23		
Bruiser Kinard	T	6'1"	210	23		
Jim Whatley	T	6'5"	227	25		

Use Name – Guards	Pos.	Hgt	Wgt	Age	Int	Pts
Ox Emerson	G	5'11"	200	30		
Ed Merlin	G	5'10"	200	22		
Len Noyes	G	6'	214	24		
Jim Sivell	G	5'9"	200	24		

Though the Dodgers never threatened to take the lead in the Eastern Division, coach Potsy Clark had to consider the year a success. The team broke even in wins and losses for the first time in five years, and more young talent was gathering in Brooklyn.

Ace Parker developed into an All-Pro tailback in his first full pro season, excelling in all aspects of play and shining brightest as a passer. Each game, though, Parker had to wonder who his backfield mates would be. Veteran Beattie Feathers and rookie Boyd Brumbaugh were racked up with injuries, and Joe Maniaci was traded to the Bears in mid-year. Only fullback Scrapper Farrell kept Parker from being a one-man show, along with rookie tackle Bruiser Kinard, who, living up to his nickname, hit enough people to win second-team All-Pro honors.

PHILADELPHIA EAGLES 5-6-0 Bert Bell

Scores of Each Game		
23	WASHINGTON	26
27	Pittsburgh at Buffalo	7
14	NEW YORK	10
6	CHIC. BEARS	28
7	New York	17
14	Washington	20
7	CHIC. CARDS	0 at Erie
7	BROOKLYN	10
14	Brooklyn	32
14	PITTSBURGH	7 at Charleston W.Va.
21	Detroit	7

Use Name	Pos.	Hgt	Wgt	Age	Int	Pts
Moose Harper	C-LB	6'4"	223	24		
John Kusko	HB-DB	5'11"	190	24		
Bob Masters	BB-DB	5'11"	200	27		

Use Name – Tackles	Pos.	Hgt	Wgt	Age	Int	Pts
Drew Ellis	T	6'1"	215	23		
Fritz Ferko	T	6'1"	245	25		
Wimpy Giddens	T	6'2"	220	23		
Ray Keeling	T	6'3"	263	22		
Bob Pylman (1 reception for 1 yd.)	T	6'4"	215	24		6
Clem Woltman	T	6'1"	218	22		

Use Name – Guards	Pos.	Hgt	Wgt	Age	Int	Pts
Bill Fiedler	G	5'9"	200	22		
Bill Hughes	G	6'1"	227	23		
George Rado	G-DE	5'9"	185	25		
Ted Schmitt	G	5'11"	214	21		
Mule Stockton	G	6'1"	210	24		

The Eagles rewarded Bert Bell's hard work by winning five games, their best showing ever. The young players he had brought together jelled enough to finish the year with two strong victories and hope for the future.

Central to this rebirth was the development of Dave Smukler and Emmett Mortell into good ball carriers. The Eagle line progressed as the youngsters holding down trench slots were force-fed a diet of experience by more established opponents. Both starting tackles were rookies, and the two guards were just two-year pros. To steady the kids, Bell fielded veterans Bill Hewitt and Joe Carter at the ends and Hank Reese at center.

PITTSBURGH PIRATES 2-9-0 Johnny Blood

Scores of Each Game		
7	Detroit	16
14	NEW YORK	27
7	PHILADELPHIA at Buffalo	27
17	Brooklyn	3
13	New York	10
7	BROOKLYN	17
0	Green Bay	20
0	WASHINGTON	7
7	Philadelphia at Charleston,W.Va.	14
0	Washington	15
7	CLEVELAND at New Orleans	13

Use Name	Pos.	Hgt	Wgt	Age	Int	Pts
Mike Basrak	C-LB	6'2"	220	25		
Joe Maras	C-T-LB	6'1"	205	22		
Karl McDade	C-LB	6'3"	195	24		
Lou Tsoutsouvas	C-LB	5'11"	210	22		
Billy Wilson (to PHI)	OE-DE	5'10"	185	26		
Bernie Lee (from PHI)	BB-LB	5'11"	190	24		
Clarence Tommerson	DB	6'2"	197	23		

Use Name – Tackles	Pos.	Hgt	Wgt	Age	Int	Pts
Joe Cardwell	T	6'3"	230	24		
Ted Doyle	T	6'2"	220	24		
Ed Karpowich	T	6'4"	225	25		
Lou Lassahn	T-DE	6'	205	25		
John Nosich	T	6'3"	230	22		
Red Rorison	T	6'3"	250	24		

Use Name – Guards	Pos.	Hgt	Wgt	Age	Int	Pts
Shipley Farroh	G	5'11"	225	22		
Byron Gentry	G	5'11"	220	24		
George Kakasic	G	5'10"	202	26		
Walt Kiesling	G	6'2"	248	35		
Lindy Mayhew	G	6'1"	223	26		
John Perko	G	6'1"	210	22		

When Colorado halfback Whizzer White learned that he could delay his acceptance of a Rhodes scholarship, he signed a $15,800 contract with the Pirates. With the largest salary in the league, White received a lot of publicity before his debut against the Detroit Lions—so much so that as he lined up to take the opening kickoff, the jitters descended and the ball hit him squarely in the eye. White recovered from his embarrassment and black eye, though, to lead the NFL in yards gained rushing. While White got better as the season progressed, the Pirates, in general, got worse. But following three quick losses, Johnny Blood's merry men rose up and ambushed the Dodgers and Giants. Then, unknown to Blood, owner Art Rooney sold rookie Frankie Filchock, the team's main passer, to Washington. After that, the team never again won, as injuries and more sales chopped the Pirates down to mere bathtub sailors.

Use Name – Backs & Ends	Pos.	Age	Hgt	Wgt	Pts	Int	Rushing No.	Yds	Avg	TD	Passing Att	Comp	%	Yds	Yd/Att	TD	Int–%	RK	Receiving No.	Yds	Avg	TD	Punting No.	Avg	Kicking Pat	Att	%	FG	Att	%	Punt Returns No.	Yds	Avg	TD	Kickoff Returns No.	Yds	Avg	TD
NEW YORK GIANTS																																						
Ed Danowski	QB-DB	26	6'1"	198	6		48	215	4.5	1	129	70	54	848	6.6	7	8–6	2																				
Len Barnum	QB-WB-DB	25	6'	200	6		35	97	2.8	1	6	1	17	45	7.5	0	1–17		3	37	12	0																
Tuffy Leemans	FB-QB-DB	25	6'	192	24		121	463	3.8	4	42	19	45	249	5.9	3	6–14		4	68	17	0																
Hank Soar	FB-DB	24	6'2"	207	13		122	401	3.3	2	7	1	14	0	0.0	0	3–43		13	164	13	0			1	1	100											
Bull Karcis (from PIT)	FB-LB	38	5'9"	225	30		89	212	2.4	4																												
Kink Richards	FB-DB	27	5'11"	195	2		25	111	4.4	0	1	0	0	0	0.0	0	1–100		1	8	8	0			2	2	100											
Red Wolfe	FB-DB	25	6'	205			15	19	1.3	0	1	0	0	0	0.0	0	0–0		2	23	12	0			0	1	0											
Ward Cuff	WB-DB	25	6'1"	198	45		18	38	2.1	0									8	114	14	1			18	20	90	5	9	56								
Dale Burnett	WB-DB	29	6'1"	188	6		6	13	2.2	0									13	145	11	1																
Leland Shaffer	BB-DB	26	6'2"	200	12		1	4	4.0	0									12	86	7	2																
Nello Falaschi	BB-LB	24	6'	195			1	6	6.0	0																												
Johnny Gildea	BB-LB	28	6'2"	205			1	2	2.0	0									1	3	3	0																
Jim Lee Howell	OE-DE	23	6'6"	200	12														12	163	14	2																
Chuck Gelatka	OE-DB	25	6'1"	185	12														7	106	15	1			0	1	0											
Jim Poole	OE-DE	22	6'3"	215	6														7	98	14	1																
Ray Hanken	OE-DE	25	5'11"	190	12														5	73	15	2																
Hap Barnard	OE-DE	23	6'2"	190															1	33	33	0																
Will Walls	OE-DE	23	6'4"	205															1	23	23	0																
WASHINGTON REDSKINS																																						
Sammy Baugh	TB-DB	24	6'2"	185			15	35	2.3	0	128	63	49	853	6.7	5	11–9	4																				
Bill Hartman	TB-DB	23	6'	190			71	195	2.7	0	77	38	49	558	7.4	3	10–13	9	1	6	6	0																
Andy Farkas	FB-DB	22	5'10"	190	37		75	315	4.2	6									9	66	7	0			1	1	100											
Max Krause	FB-DB	29	5'10"	195	18		25	214	8.6	2									2	62	31	1																
George Karamatic	FB-DB	21	5'8"	187	11		50	185	3.7	0									4	99	25	1			2	3	67	1	2	50								
Don Irwin	FB-WB-TB-DB	25	6'1"	196	6		66	130	2.0	1	6	0	0	0	0.0	0	2–33		16	138	9	0			0	1	0											
Ed Justice	WB-DB	25	6'1"	200	6		10	11	1.1	0									14	173	12	1																
Ernie Pinckert	WB-DB	30	6'	198			3	7	2.3	0									3	20	7	0																
Riley Smith	BB-LB	27	6'2"	200	15		3	−7	−2.3	0	4	1	25	18	4.5	0	0–0		4	131	33	1			3	6	50	2	5	40								
Jay Turner	BB-LB	24	5'10"	198			5	25	5.0	0									2	10	5	0																
Tilly Manton (from NY)	BB-LB	26	5'11"	187	5		2	3	1.5	0															2	3	67	1	4	25								
Charley Malone	OE-DE	28	6'4"	210	6														24	257	11	1																
Wayne Millner	OE-DE	27	6'1"	190	6		3	5	1.7	0									18	232	13	1																
Bob Masterson	OE-DE	23	6'1"	186	14		3	89	29.7	0									10	213	21	1			5	6	83	1	1	100								
Bob McChesney	OE-DE	26	6'2"	193	6														3	49	16	1																
Hal Bradley (from CHIC)	OE-DE	24	6'4"	205															1	14	14	0																
BROOKLYN DODGERS																																						
Ace Parker	TB-DB	26	6'	180	29		93	253	2.7	2	148	63	43	865	5.8	5	7–5	5	1	19	19	1			5	7	71											
Tony Sarausky	TB-DB	26	5'11"	203			8	42	5.3	0	8	2	25	10	1.3	0	0–0																					
Scrapper Farrell (from PIT)	FB-DB	23	5'9"	202	18		108	425	3.9	3																												
Boyd Brumbaugh	FB-DB	23	5'11"	193	6		45	191	4.2	0									1	5	5	1																
Vannie Albanese	FB-DB	25	6'	183			27	97	3.6	0	1	0	0	0	0.0	0	0–0																					
Stan Kosel	FB-DB	21	5'11"	190			13	43	3.3	0	1	0	0	0	0.0	0	0–0																					
Beattie Feathers	HB-DB	30	5'10"	185	12		28	94	3.4	2									3	34	11	0																
Ralph Kercheval	HB-TB-DB	27	6'1"	193	28		51	86	1.7	1	9	3	33	98	10.9	0	1–11		11	136	12	0			7	9	78	5	13	38								
Wendell Butcher	BB-FB-LB-DB	24	6'1"	200	6		30	99	3.3	1									3	44	15	0																
Tony Kaska	BB-LB	27	5'11"	192			2	1	0.5	0									2	77	39	0																
Bill Reissig	BB-LB-DE	23	6'	195	6																							2	2	100								
Jim Austin	OE-DE	25	6'2"	196	6														14	180	13	1																
Jeff Barrett	OE-DE	25	6'1"	182	12		2	3	1.5	0									13	205	16	2																
Perry Schwartz	OE-DE	23	6'2"	204	6		2	−3	−1.5	0									8	132	17	1																
John Druze	OE-DE	24	6'	195															4	29	7	0																
Harold Hill	OE-DE	22	6'1"	200															3	61	20	0																
Bill Waller	OE-DE	23	6'1"	190															3	15	5	0																
PHILADELPHIA EAGLES																																						
Emmett Mortell	TB-DB	24	6'1"	183			110	296	2.7	0	57	12	21	201	3.5	7	7–12	14																				
Dick Riffle	TB-FB-DB	23	6'1"	194	6		65	227	3.5	1	31	9	29	178	5.7	1	4–13																					
Dave Smukler	FB-LB	24	6'1"	226	18		96	313	3.3	1	102	42	41	524	5.1	7	8–8	6							6	6	100	0	1	0								
Joe Bukant	FB-LB	22	6'	214			48	119	2.5	0	1	1	100	14	14.0	0	0–0																					
Jay Arnold	HB-DB	24	6'1"	209	27		19	22	1.2	0									6	74	12	2			3	3	100											
Rabbit Keen	HB-DB	23	5'8"	165			3	10	3.3	0																												
Woody Dow	BB-DB	21	6'	195	6		4	20	5.0	0									5	88	18	1																
John Cole	BB-FB-LB	23	5'9"	197			1	4	4.0	0									2	9	5	0																
Joe Carter	OE-DE	28	6'1"	195	48														27	386	14	7																
Bill Hewitt	OE-DE	28	5'9"	190	24														18	237	13	4																
Red Ramsey	OE-DE	23	6'	190	6														5	122	24	1																
Hank Reese	C-LB	27	5'11"	220	13																				10	13	77	1	6	17								
PITTSBURGH PIRATES																																						
Whizzer White	TB-HB-DB	21	6'1"	185	24		152	567	3.7	4	73	29	40	393	5.4	2	18–25	16	7	88	13	0																
Frankie Filchock (to WAS)	TB-DB	21	5'11"	188	6		69	198	2.9	1	101	41	41	469	4.6	3	11–11	13	2	4	2	0																
Max Fiske	TB-DB	24	6'	190			29	83	2.9	0	37	11	30	121	3.3	0	4–11																					
Stu Smith	FB-BB-LB	22	6'	195			80	241	3.0	0									3	30	10	0																
Swede Hanson	FB-DB	29	6'1"	195			15	50	3.3	0									1	2	2	0																
Bob Douglas	FB-DB	23	6'	195			4	10	2.5	0																												
Tuffy Thompson	HB-DB	23	5'11"	172	6		39	139	3.6	1	7	0	0	0	0.0	0	3–43		9	55	6	0																
Bill Davidson	HB-OE-DB	23	6'	183			33	52	1.6	0	2	2	100	10	5.0	0	0–0		12	229	19	0																
John Oelerich (to CHIB)	HB-DB	21	6'	192			14	23	1.6	0	1	1	100	10	10.0	0	0–0		3	23	8	0																
Johnny Blood	BB-DB	34	6'1"	184			21	−5	−0.2	0									2	5	3	0																
Tom Burnette (to PHI)	BB-LB	22	6'1"	194			1	0	0.0	0	1	0	0	0	0.0	0	0–0		1	3	3	0						0	1	0								
Izzy Weinstock	BB-LB	25	6'	215			1	0	0.0	0																												
Eggs Manske (to CHIB)	OE-HB-DE-DB	25	6'	185	18		5	29	5.8	0									19	310	16	2																
Bill Sortet	OE-DE	26	6'1"	188	24		1	−5	−5.0	0									11	166	15	4																
Paul McDonough	OE-DE	21	6'4"	215															6	86	14	0																
George Platukas	OE-DE	23	6'	188			3	6	2.0	0									4	82	21	0																
Mac Cara	OE-DE	24	5'10"	200			1	−1	−1.0	0									4	18	5	0																
Jess Tatum	OE-DE	23	6'1"	215															1	16	16	0																
Armand Niccolai	T	26	6'2"	230	13																				10	10	100	1	5	20								

TEAM TOTALS	OFFENSE First Downs	Rushing: No.	Yards	Avg. Yds.	TD	Passing Att.	Comp	Comp Pct.	Yards	Yds/ Att.	Yds/ Comp	TD	Int.	Pct. Int.	Fumbles: Number	Penalty: Yards	Points: Total	TD	PAT	FG Att.	FG	Saf	DEFENSE Total Yards	Pass Att.	Pass Comp.	Comp. Pct.	No. Pass Int.	Oppos. Fumb. Rec.	Points	TEAM TOTALS
NEW YORK	132	467	1550	3.3	12	186	91	48.9	1142	6.1	12.5	10	19	10.2	23	233	194	26	21	11	5	1	2029	226	77	34.1	34	14	79	NEW YORK
WASHINGTON	147	399	1424	3.6	10	248	114	46.0	1536	6.2	13.5	8	27	10.9	45	410	148	20	13	12	5	0	2174	195	69	35.4	19	9	154	WASHINGTON
BROOKLYN	96	379	1212	3.2	9	169	69	40.8	992	5.9	14.4	6	8	4.7	24	332	131	16	12	15	7	1	2958	246	105	42.7	28	9	161	BROOKLYN
PHILADELPHIA	86	346	1011	2.9	2	191	64	33.5	917	4.8	14.3	15	19	9.1	13	220	154	22	19	9	1	0	3270	197	97	49.2	16	17	164	PHILADELPHIA
PITTSBURGH	103	474	1414	3.0	5	194	72	37.1	916	4.7	12.7	5	33	17.0	14	225	79	11	10	6	1	0	2626	185	74	40.0	14	8	169	PITTSBURGH

GREEN BAY PACKERS 8-3-0 Curly Lambeau

Scores of Each Game		
26	CLEVELAND	17
0	CHIC. BEARS	2
28	CHIC. CARDS	7
24	Chic. Cards at Buffalo	22
7	DETROIT	17
35	BROOKLYN	7
20	PITTSBURGH	0
28	Cleveland	7
24	Chic. Bears	17
28	Detroit	7
3	New York	15

Use Name	Pos.	Hgt	Wgt	Age	Int	Pts
Darrell Lester	C-LB	6'3"	220	28		
Ookie Miller	C-LB	6'	215	28		
Lee Mulleneaux (from CHIC)	C-LB	6'2"	225	31		
Roy Schoemann	C-LB	6'1"	192	24		
Tony Borak	OE-DE	6'1"	190	25		
Voluntarily retired — Bud Svendsen						

Use Name – Tackles	Pos.	Hgt	Wgt	Age	Int	Pts
Frank Butler	T	6'3"	246	29		
Leo Katalinas	T	6'2"	240	22		
Bill Lee	T	6'2"	225	26		
Baby Ray	T	6'6"	250	23		
Champ Seibold	T	6'4"	240	25		

Use Name – Guards	Pos.	Hgt	Wgt	Age	Int	Pts
Tiny Engelbretsen	G	6'1"	240	28		15
(9 PAT's in 9 attempts, 2 FG in 4 attempts)						
Buckets Goldenberg	G-LB	5'10"	225	27		
Swede Johnston	G-LB	5'10"	195	28		
Potsy Jones	G	5'11"	230	28		
Russ Letlow	G	6'	212	24		
Pete Tinsley	G	5'8"	205	25		

With Arnie Herber slowing up, coach Curly Lambeau brought in a new rookie tailback with a strong passing arm. Cecil Isbell not only could throw the ball but could also carry it around the end for good yardage. Lambeau broke the rookie in gradually, alternating him with Herber at tailback and sometimes playing them both in the same backfield. Isbell hauled in a few Herber aerials, and the rookie sometimes caught defenses napping by throwing to the lead-footed Herber. Of course, both men often found their main targets in Don Hutson, who was heading for his usual receiving championship when he hurt his knee in Detroit on November 13. After the injury, the Packers grimly hung onto the lead in the West and won the title despite a 15-3 loss to the Giants in the finale.

DETROIT LIONS 7-4-0 Dutch Clark

Scores of Each Game		
16	PITTSBURGH	7
17	Cleveland	21
17	Green Bay	7
5	WASHINGTON	7
10	CHIC. CARDS	0
13	Chic. Bears	7
6	CLEVELAND	0
7	GREEN BAY	28
7	Chic. Cards	3
14	CHIC. BEARS	7
7	PHILADELPHIA	21

Use Name	Pos.	Hgt	Wgt	Age	Int	Pts
Jack Mackenroth	C-LB	6'2"	215	22		
Dixie Stokes	C-LB	6'	208	25		
Alex Wojciechowicz	C-LB	5'11"	204	23		
Lou Barle	BB-DB	6'1"	210	22		

Use Name – Tackles	Pos.	Hgt	Wgt	Age	Int	Pts
George Christensen	T	6'2"	250	28		
Jack Johnson	T	6'4"	220	28		
Tony Matisi	T	6'2"	230	24		
Bob Reynolds	T	6'4"	223	24		
Bill Rogers	T	5'11"	240	25		

Use Name – Guards	Pos.	Hgt	Wgt	Age	Int	Pts
Bill Feldhaus	G	6'	225	26		
Les Graham	G	6'	215	22		
Bill Radovich	G	5'10"	235	23		
Sid Wagner	G	5'11"	197	25		

The Lions' first game in spacious Briggs Stadium drew 55,000 spectators to see a close loss to the Washington Redskins. The irony of the season was that popular support should now be growing when the team was beginning to slip.

With Dutch Clark shelved by a bad ankle, Bill Shepherd handled most of the outside running until injuries sidelined him near the end of the season. Ace Gutowsky kept spinning into the line with elbows and knees flashing, and Lloyd Cardwell caught passes and defended well enough to make All-Pro. The forward wall also blended veterans with newcomers. George Christensen still excelled at tackle, while rookie Alex Wojciechowicz made a bigger name for himself with his hitting on both lines. With all the lineup changes, the Lions still had a chance to tie for the top with a final win, but the Eagles upset them 21-7.

CHICAGO BEARS 6-5-0 George Halas

Scores of Each Game		
16	CHIC. CARDS	13
2	Green Bay	0
28	Philadelphia	6
7	Cleveland	14
34	Chic. Cards	28
21	CLEVELAND	23
7	DETROIT	13
17	GREEN BAY	24
31	WASHINGTON	7
24	Brooklyn	6
7	Detroit	14

Use Name	Pos.	Hgt	Wgt	Age	Int	Pts
Frank Bausch	C-LB	6'2"	224	30		
Bill Conkright	C-OE-LB-DE	6'1"	200	24		6
(1 reception for 2 yd. touchdown)						
Frank Sullivan	C-LB	6'3"	203	26		
Red Corzine	LB	6'	218	29		

Use Name – Tackles	Pos.	Hgt	Wgt	Age	Int	Pts
Del Bjork	T	6'1"	218	24		
Lou Gordon	T	6'5"	230	30		
Joe Stydahar	T	6'4"	230	26		
Russ Thompson	T	6'5"	248	26		
Milt Trost	T	6'1"	208	25		

Use Name – Guards	Pos.	Hgt	Wgt	Age	Int	Pts
Dick Bassi	G	5'11"	210	23		6
Danny Fortmann	G	6'	210	22		
George Musso	G	6'2"	270	28		
Gust Zarnas	G	5'10"	212	23		
Joe Zeller	G	6'1"	203	30		6

With the veterans of the 1930s aging and the stars of the 1940s not yet arrived, the Bears—who sometimes displayed a powerful football machine—sputtered enough times to end with five losses, a calamity which had not occurred since the season of 1929.

Although Joe Maniaci ran well after his mid-season purchase from Brooklyn, he could not fill the gaping hole Bronko Nagurski's retirement left at the fullback spot. Quarterback Bernie Masterson passed infrequently but for good mileage, and Ray Nolting, Sam Francis, and Jack Manders picked up moderate yardage on the ground, but fumbles continually plagued the offense in an off-again, on-again year. The inconsistency of the Bear squad became evident by their victories over Green Bay and Washington and their double losses to Cleveland and Detroit.

CLEVELAND RAMS 4-7-0 Hugo Bezdek, Art Lewis

Scores of Each Game		
17	Green Bay	26
6	CHIC. CARDS	7
13	Washington	37
21	DETROIT	17
14	CHIC. BEARS	7
23	Chic. Bears	21
7	GREEN BAY	28
0	Detroit	6
0	New York	28
17	Chic. Cards	31
13	Pittsburgh at New Orleans	7

Use Name	Pos.	Hgt	Wgt	Age	Int	Pts
Chuck Cherundolo	C-LB	6'1"	220	22		
Gerry Conlee	C-LB	5'11"	190	22		
Jack May	C-LB	5'10"	210	23		
Jack Giannoni	OE-DE	6'1"	210	22		
Dale Prather	OE-DE	6'2"	190	26		

Use Name – Tackles	Pos.	Hgt	Wgt	Age	Int	Pts
Bill Krause	T	6'	210	23		
Art Lewis	T	6'3"	223	25		
Ted Livingston	T	6'3"	218	24		
Primo Miller	T	6'2"	220	22		
Chuck Ream	T	6'2"	225	23		
Jack Robinson (from PIT, T)	T-G	6'3"	218	26		

Use Name – Guards	Pos.	Hgt	Wgt	Age	Int	Pts
Red Chesbro	G	5'11"	190	23		
Tom Hupke	G	5'10"	195	27		
Vic Markov	G-T	6'	215	22		
Phil Ragazzo	G	6'	190	23		
Dick Zoll	G-T	5'11"	215	24		
(1 PAT in 1 attempt)						

Coach Hugo Bezdek handed in his resignation when the first four games resulted in only one victory, and assistant Art Lewis was given the thankless job of interim head coach for the rest of the year. Little did Lewis know what lay directly ahead. Two matches with the Chicago Bears approached, and the Rams surprised everyone by winning both. Although four losses followed, a final victory over Pittsburgh ended the season on a high note. On a team filled with rookies, only three Rams were older than twenty-five. Of these, first-draft choice Corby Davis bulled his way to enough hard yardage to lead the team in rushing, while tall end Jim Benton provided a big target for veteran Bob Snyder.

CHICAGO CARDINALS 2-9-0 Milan Creighton

Scores of Each Game		
13	Chic. Bears	16
7	Cleveland	6
7	Green Bay	28
22	GREEN BAY at Buffalo	24
0	Brooklyn	13
28	CHIC. BEARS	34
0	Detroit	10
0	Philadelphia at Erie	7
0	New York	6
3	DETROIT	7
31	CLEVELAND	17

Use Name	Pos.	Hgt	Wgt	Age	Int	Pts
Phil Dougherty	C-LB	5'11"	185	23		6
Len Dugan	C-LB	6'	220	26		

Use Name – Tackles	Pos.	Hgt	Wgt	Age	Int	Pts
Al Babartsky	T	6'	220	23		
Conway Baker	T	5'11"	225	26		
(missed 1 field goal attempt)						
Jon Bilbo	T-G	6'	195	23		
Tony Blazine	T	6'	230	26		6
Elwyn Dunstan	T	6'3"	235	23		
Bob McGee	T	6'	210	25		
Earl Nolan	T	6'1"	205	24		

Use Name – Guards	Pos.	Hgt	Wgt	Age	Int	Pts
Ross Carter	G	6'	200	24		
Bree Cuppoletti	G	5'10"	200	28		
Bob Hoel	G	6'	200	25		
John Morrow	G	5'11"	230			
Bill Volok	G	6'2"	215	28		

After breaking even last year, the Cardinals backslid, and coach Milan Creighton's efforts could only result in two wins over the Cleveland Rams. Of all his charges, end Gaynell Tinsley stood out for his All-Pro performance amidst the shambles. Making the honor roll a second time in two years, Tinsley grabbed forty-one passes to lead the NFL despite constant double coverage and the absence of a consistent passer for the Cardinals. In the only time he reached the end zone, Tinsley excited the crowd on a 98-yard pass play from Doug Russell in the second victory over Cleveland.

Use Name – Backs & Ends	Pos.	Age	Hgt	Wgt	Pts	Int	Rushing No.	Rushing Yds	Rushing Avg	Rushing TD	Passing Att	Passing Comp	Passing %	Passing Yds	Passing Yd/Att	Passing TD	Passing Int–%	Passing RK	Receiving No.	Receiving Yds	Receiving Avg	Receiving TD	Punting No.	Punting Avg	Kicking Pat	Kicking Att	Kicking %	Kicking FG	Kicking Att	Kicking %	Punt Returns No.	Punt Returns Yds	Punt Returns Avg	Punt Returns TD	Kickoff Returns No.	Kickoff Returns Yds	Kickoff Returns Avg	Kickoff Returns TD
GREEN BAY PACKERS																																						
Cecil Isbell	TB-HB-DB	23	6'1"	190	12		85	445	5.2	2	91	37	41	659	7.2	7	10–11	8	5	104	21	0																
Bob Monnett	TB-HB-DB	28	5'9"	180	7		75	225	3.0	0	57	31	54	465	8.2	9	4– 7	1	1	23	23	0			7	7	100											
Arnie Herber	TB-DB	28	5'11"	200	12		6	–1	–0.2	0	55	22	40	336	6.1	4	4– 7	11	5	84	17	2						0	1	0								
Clarke Hinkle	FB-LB	28	5'11"	203	58		114	299	2.6	3	2	1	50	6	3.0	0	0– 0		7	98	14	4			7	8	88	3	9	33								
Ed Jankowski	FB-LB	25	5'9"	195	14		24	124	5.1	2															2	3	67											
John Howell	FB-BB-LB	23	5'10"	185			7	7	1.0	0																												
Joe Laws	HB-DB	27	5'9"	185	12		60	253	4.2	0	5	0	0	0	0.0	0	2–40		6	55	9	1																
Andy Uram	HB-DB	23	5'10"	187	12		28	145	5.2	2									4	46	12	0																
Paul Miller	HB-DB	25	5'11"	185			20	48	2.4	0									4	36	9	0																
Dick Weisgerber	BB-DB	23	5'10"	205			6	13	2.2	0																												
Herm Schneidman	BB-DB	24	5'11"	200			4	8	2.0	0																												
Hank Bruder	BB-DB	30	6'	200			2	6	3.0	0									2	14	7	0																
Don Hutson	OE-DE	25	6'1"	185	57		3	–1	–0.3	0									32	548	17	9			3	3	100											
Milt Gantenbein	OE-DE	28	6'	205	6														12	164	14	1																
Wayland Becker	OE-DE	27	6'	205															7	166	24	0																
Moose Mulleneaux	OE-DE	21	6'3"	210	12														4	97	24	2																
Bernie Scherer	OE-DE	25	6'1"	193	6														2	31	16	1																
DETROIT LIONS																																						
Vern Huffman	TB-DB	23	6'2"	220	6		69	181	2.6	1	85	27	32	382	4.5	2	8– 9	15	1	17	17	0																
Dutch Clark	TB-DB	31	6'	190	8		7	25	3.6	0	12	6	50	50	4.2	1	2–17								2	2	100	2	2	100								
Bill Shepherd	FB-TB-LB-DB	26	5'9"	205	23		100	455	4.6	3	32	8	25	167	5.2	0	6–19								2	2	100	1	2	50								
Ace Gutowsky	FB-LB	28	5'11"	205	12		131	444	3.4	2	7	3	43	41	5.9	0	0– 0		1	25	25	0																
Paul Szakash	FB-LB	25	6'	215			20	55	2.8	0									1	0	0	0																
Lloyd Cardwell	WB-DB	25	6'2"	195	30		73	294	4.0	4	1	1	100	35	35.0	0	0– 0		9	138	15	1																
Rip Ryan	WB-DB	23	6'2"	190			24	180	7.5	0	9	2	22	27	3.0	0	0– 0		7	78	11	0																
Dick Nardi	WB-FB-DB	22	5'10"	200			20	109	5.5	0																												
Ernie Caddel	WB-DB	27	6'2"	195	6		14	38	2.7	1	2	2	100	45	22.5	0	0– 0		1	6	6	0																
Fred Vanzo	BB-LB	22	6'2"	230															4	52	13	0																
Jim McDonald	BB-DB	22	6'1"	190															2	41	21	0																
Maury Patt	OE-DE	24	6'2"	207			3	30	10.0	0									7	80	11	0																
Monk Moscrip	OE DE	24	6'	195	12														6	118	20	1			8	8	100	0	1	0								
Chuck Hanneman	OE-DE	23	6'	212	6		1	6	6.0	0									4	80	20	1																
Ed Klewicki	OE-WB-DE	27	5'10"	198			10	76	7.6	0									3	57	19	0																
Butch Morse	OE-DE	26	6'2"	206															3	55	18	0																
Regis Monahan	G	29	5'10"	220	14																				2	4	50	4	5	80								
CHICAGO BEARS																																						
Bernie Masterson	QB-DB	27	6'3"	195			13	–16	–1.2	0	112	46	41	848	7.6	7	9– 8	3	1	4	4	0																
Ray Buivid	QB-HB-DB	23	6'1"	195			32	65	2.0	0	48	17	35	295	6.1	5	2– 4		1	8	8	0																
George Corbett	QB-DB	30	5'9"	177	6		7	29	4.1	0	9	3	33	32	3.6	0	3–33		1	10	10	0																
Carl Brumbaugh	QB-DB	30	5'10"	175			3	–15	–5.0	0	4	2	50	25	6.3	0	0– 0		1	23	23	0																
Gene Ronzani	QB-DB	29	5'9"	190			7	12	1.7	0	1	0	0	0	0.0	0	0– 0																					
Reino Nori	QB-DB	25	5'8"	165			1	1	1.0	0																												
Joe Maniaci (from BKN)	FB-HB-LB	24	6'1"	210	32		88	345	3.6	3	2	1	50	19	9.5	1	0– 0		9	127	14	0			11	11	100	1	3	33								
Ray Nolting	HB-DB	24	5'11"	185	12		63	297	4.7	1	11	0	0	0	0.0	0	3–27		4	90	23	1																
Sam Francis	FB-HB-DB	23	6'	205	18		85	297	3.5	3	3	1	33	0	0.0	0	0– 0		1	8	8	0			0	2	0											
Jack Manders	HB-DB	29	6'	200	37		67	263	3.9	2	1	0	0	0	0.0	0	0– 0		2	27	14	1			10	12	83	3	9	33								
Bert Johnson	FB-LB	26	6'	215	12		37	138	3.7	2	2	1	50	4	2.0	0	0– 0																					
Bob Swisher	HB-DB	24	5'11"	165			22	133	6.0	0	4	1	25	8	2.0	0	1–25		4	65	16	0																
Gary Famiglietti	FB-LB	23	6'	214			33	129	3.9	0																												
Dick Schweidler	HB-DB	23	6'	185			16	57	3.6	0	1	0	0	0	0.0	0	0– 0		1	21	21	0																
Bill Karr	OE-DE	27	6'1"	187	24		1	6	6.0	0									14	253	18	4																
Les McDonald	OE-DE	23	6'4"	200	7		1	0	0.0	0									9	175	19	1			1	1	100											
Dick Plasman	OE-DE	24	6'3"	210	6														8	117	15	1																
George Wilson	OE-DE	24	6'1"	190	6														4	81	20	1																
Ferd Dreher	OE-DE	25	6'3"	205	6														3	69	23	1																
CLEVELAND RAMS																																						
Bob Snyder	TB-DB	25	6'	205	10		44	78	1.8	0	87	36	41	631	7.3	6	9–10	7	1	16	16	0			7	10	70	1	2	50								
Ed Goddard	TB-WB-DB	23	5'10"	186	7		40	–16	–0.4	0	43	18	44	238	5.5	0	6–14		6	128	21	1			1	1	100											
Dick Tuckey (from WAS)	TB-DB	24	6'2"	205	2		43	76	1.8	0	32	8	25	140	4.4	1	3– 9		1	10	10	0			2	3	67											
Bob Davis	TB-DB	24	6'	175			22	100	4.5	0	26	6	23	49	1.9	0	2– 8		3	31	10	0			0	1	0											
Carl Littlefield	TB-DB	22	6'	200	6		19	69	3.6	0	15	1	7	23	1.5	0	5–33		1	9	9	0																
Ray Johnson	TB-DB	24	6'1"	190							5	3	60	45	9.0	0	1–20																					
Corby Davis	FB-LB	23	5'11"	215	19		71	202	2.8	3	1	0	0	0	0.0	0	0– 0		1	2	2	0			1	1	100											
Johnny Drake	FB-WB-LB-DB	22	6'1"	210	6		74	188	2.5	1	3	1	33	8	2.7	0	0– 0		2	13	7	0																
Nels Peterson	WB-TB-DB	23	5'8"	175	20		21	70	3.3	1	6	0	0	0	0.0	0	2–33		4	43	11	1			2	2	100	2	2	100								
Julie Alfonse	WB-DB	24	5'8"	180	12		16	16	1.0	1	2	2	100	19	9.5	0	0– 0		2	47	24	0																
Stan Pincura	BB-DB	24	5'11"	175	6		2	–6	–3.0	0	33	13	39	240	7.3	2	7–21		6	72	12	1																
Vic Spadaccini	BB-WB-DB	22	6'	215			9	46	5.1	0									8	101	13	0																
Carl Brazell	BB-DB	21	5'10"	195			4	14	3.5	0									7	100	14	0																
Jim Benton	OE-DE	21	6'3"	205	36														21	418	20	5																
Ray Hamilton	OE-DE	22	6'4"	210															10	187	19	0																
Johnny Kovatch	OE-DE	23	5'11"	172	6														8	97	12	1																
Johnny Stephens	OE-DE	22	6'1"	190															6	75	13	0																
Phil Bucklew	OE-DE	23	6'1"	205															1	14	14	0																
CHICAGO CARDINALS																																						
John Robbins	TB-DB	22	6'2"	185			63	213	3.4	0	97	52	54	577	5.9	2	9– 9	10																				
Dwight Sloan	TB-DB	23	5'10"	180			56	126	2.3	0	79	37	48	333	4.2	1	7– 9	12	1	10	10	0																
Pat Coffee	TB-DB	24	5'11"	180	12		40	169	4.2	2	39	16	41	200	5.1	0	4–10																					
Ray Burnett	TB-DB						1	–10	–10.0	0	2	1	50	19	9.5	0	0– 0																					
Sam Agee	FB-DB	24	6'1"	208	6		48	178	3.7	1	2	2	100	27	13.5	0	0– 0		2	5	3	0																
Buddy Parker	FB-DB	24	6'	195	12		45	144	3.2	2	2	2	100	21	10.5	0	0– 0		16	142	9	0																
Ed Cherry	FB-DB	23	6'	205			6	18	3.0	0																												
Milt Popovich	FB-WB-DB	21	5'11"	190			6	13	2.2	0									1	8	8	0																
Jimmy Lawrence	WB-DB	24	5'11"	190	18		78	207	2.7	3	11	3	27	65	5.9	0	4–36		14	105	8	0																
Doug Russell	WB-DB	26	6'	190	6		31	60	1.9	1	7	1	14	98	14.0	1	2–29		6	36	6	0																
Frank Patrick	BB-LB	22	5'11"	190	17		1	1	1.0	0	1	0	0	0	0.0	0	0– 0		1	21	21	1			8	8	100	1	4	25								
Pete Tyler	BB-LB	24	5'11"	190	6		1	1	1.0	0									2	24	12	1																
Hal Pangle	BB-LB	26	5'10"	200			2	3	1.5	0									2	14	7	0																
Bill May	BB-LB	25	5'11"	190															1	16	16	0			0	2	0	0	1	0								
Gus Tinsley	OE-DE	23	6'1"	195	6		4	26	6.5	0									41	516	13	1																
Bill Smith	OE-DE	26	6'1"	198	16														18	338	19	1			4	5	80	2	2	100								
Versil Deskin	OE-DE	25	6'	200															6	57	10	0																
Ev Fisher	OE-BB-DE-LB	23	5'11'	205															3	48	16	0																

TEAM TOTALS	OFFENSE: FIRST DOWNS	RUSHING: No.	RUSHING: Yards	RUSHING: Avg. Yds.	RUSHING: TD	PASSING: Att.	PASSING: Comp.	PASSING: Comp. Pct.	PASSING: Yards	PASSING: Yds/ Att.	PASSING: Yds/ Comp.	PASSING: TD	PASSING: Pct. Int.	PASSING: Pct. Int.	FUMBLES: Number	PENALTY: Yards	POINTS: Total	POINTS: TD	POINTS: PAT	POINTS: FG Att.	POINTS: FG	POINTS: Saf	DEFENSE: Total Yards	DEFENSE: Pass Att.	DEFENSE: Pass Comp.	DEFENSE: Comp. Pct.	DEFENSE: No. Pass Int.	DEFENSE: Oppos. Fumb. Rec.	DEFENSE: Points	TEAM TOTALS
GREEN BAY	134	434	1571	3.6	9	210	91	43.3	1466	7.0	16.1	20	20	9.5	18	250	223	30	28	14	5	0	2594	232	92	39.7	21	12	118	GREEN BAY
DETROIT	129	472	1893	4.0	11	148	49	33.1	747	5.0	15.2	3	16	10.8	18	345	119	14	12	10	7	1	2199	205	77	37.6	23	13	108	DETROIT
CHICAGO BEARS	141	462	1686	3.6	11	197	72	36.5	1222	6.2	17.0	12	18	9.1	56	350	194	26	22	12	4	2	2187	190	76	40.0	24	14	148	CHICAGO BEARS
CLEVELAND	101	351	798	2.3	6	247	88	35.6	1363	5.5	15.5	9	34	13.8	23	195	131	18	14	4	3	0	3020	172	77	44.8	23	16	215	CLEVELAND
CHICAGO CARDS	121	382	1149	3.0	9	240	114	47.5	1340	5.6	11.8	4	26	10.8	34	286	111	15	12	8	3	0	2558	182	80	44.0	18	10	168	CHICAGO CARDS

NEW YORK GIANTS 9-1-1 Steve Owen

Scores of Each Game		
13	Philadelphia	3
0	Washington	0
14	Pittsburgh	7
27	PHILADELPHIA	10
16	CHIC. BEARS	13
7	Brooklyn	6
14	Detroit	18
17	CHIC. CARDS	7
23	PITTSBURGH	7
28	BROOKLYN	7
9	WASHINGTON	7

Use Name	Pos.	Hgt	Wgt	Age	Int	Pts
Stan Galazin	C-LB	6'3"	204	24		
Mel Hein	C-LB	6'2"	225	30		
Chief Johnson	C-LB	6'3"	225	30		

Use Name – Tackles	Pos.	Hgt	Wgt	Age	Int	Pts
Pete Cole	T	5'11"	225	23		
Frank Cope	T	6'2"	215	23		
John Mellus	T	6'	220	22		
Ox Parry	T	6'4"	230	24		
Ed Widseth	T	6'1"	220	29		

Use Name – Guards	Pos.	Hgt	Wgt	Age	Int	Pts
Johnny Dell Isola	G-LB	5'11"	200	27		
Kayo Lunday	G-C-LB	6'3"	215	26		
Doug Oldershaw	G-LB	6'	195	24		
Orville Tuttle	G	5'9"	202	26		
Tarzan White	G	5'9"	216	23		

With Hitler's blitzkrieg rolling through Europe this fall, the New York Giant defense was a lot sturdier than the Maginot Line. The blue-jerseyed Giants rudely turned back attempts to trespass on their turf, allowing enemies only 85 points in eleven confrontations. Aerial attacks did not bother the New Yorkers, as they intercepted thirty-five passes, a league high. The steadfast front line was manned by Mel Hein, Johnny Dell Isola, Orville Tuttle, Frank Cope, Ed Widseth, Jim Poole, and Will Walls, and if the enemy did get through these troops, mobile units in the secondary usually rushed to the scene and grounded the invader.

The Giants also could launch a powerful counterattack, Ed Danowski pin-pointed his passes better than any artillery could, and Tuffy Leemans ground out tough yardage in the infantry. When the smoke cleared, the Giants stood triumphant on the Eastern front.

WASHINGTON REDSKINS 8-2-1 Ray Flaherty

Scores of Each Game		
7	Philadelphia	0
0	NEW YORK	0
41	BROOKLYN	13
44	PITTSBURGH	14
21	Pittsburgh	14
14	Green Bay	24
7	PHILADELPHIA	6
42	Brooklyn	0
28	CHIC. CARDS	7
31	DETROIT	7
7	New York	9

Use Name	Pos.	Hgt	Wgt	Age	Int	Pts
Bud Erickson	C-LB	6'1"	200	23		
Mickey Parks	C-LB	6'	228	22		
(Missed 1 PAT attempt)						

Use Name – Tackles	Pos.	Hgt	Wgt	Age	Int	Pts
Jim Barber	T	6'3"	230	27		
Vic Carroll	T-C-LB	6'4"	230	28		
Turk Edwards	T	6'2"	270	31		
(Missed 1 PAT attempt)						
Willie Wilkin	T	6'4"	260	23		
(Missed 1 PAT attempt)						
Bill Young	T	6'1"	240	25		

Use Name – Guards	Pos.	Hgt	Wgt	Age	Int	Pts
Dick Farman	G	6'	215	23		
Jim Karcher	G	6'	200	25		
(8 punts for 39 yd. average)						
Clyde Shugart	G	6'1"	212	22		
Steve Slivinski	G	5'10"	210	22		
Clem Stralka	G	5'10"	210	25		
Steve Uhrinyak	G	6'2"	218	24		

For the fourth straight year, a large group of Washington fans traveled up to New York to see the Eastern Division championship decided between the Giants and Redskins on the final Sunday of the season. This year, a punishing defensive battle came down to a field-goal attempt by Washington's Bo Russell with forty-five seconds left. Alas, Russell missed, and New York picked up all the chips with a 9-7 win. Along the way to this showdown, coach Ray Flaherty kept Sammy Baugh in one piece by playing him only thirty minutes a game. Frankie Filchock handled the tailback job for two quarters a game and kept the offense moving with his own accurate passing. Alternating by quarters, both passers stayed healthy, and the Redskins' offense glowed.

Top honors went to halfback Andy Farkas and tackle Jim Barber, who capped the season with All-Pro performances.

BROOKLYN DODGERS 4-6-1 Potsy Clark

Scores of Each Game		
12	PITTSBURGH	7
23	CLEVELAND	12
7	Detroit	27
0	Philadelphia	0
13	Washington	41
23	PHILADELPHIA	14
6	NEW YORK	7
17	PITTSBURGH	13
0	WASHINGTON	42
0	GREEN BAY	28
7	New York	28

Use Name	Pos.	Hgt	Wgt	Age	Int	Pts
Paul Humphrey	C-LB	6'	195	22		
Lou Mark	C-LB	6'	195	24		
Joe Ratica	C-LB	6'	205	22		
George Lenc	OE-DE	6'3"	204	21		
Scrapper Farrell	FB-DB	5'9"	205	24		
Dick Falk	FB-DB	6'	200	23		

Use Name – Tackles	Pos.	Hgt	Wgt	Age	Int	Pts
Leo Disend	T	6'2"	224	23		
Bob Haak	T-G	6'1"	245	23		
Carl Kaplanoff	T-G	6'	235	22		
Bruiser Kinard	T	6'1"	210	24		7
(7 PAT's in 7 attempts)						
Alec Shellogg (from CHI B)	T	6	215	23		

Use Name – Guards	Pos.	Hgt	Wgt	Age	Int	Pts
John Golemgeske	G-T	6'2"	225	24		
Ralph Heikkenen	G	5'10"	180	22		
Les Lane	G	6'3"	193	23		
Ed Merlin	G	5'10"	200	23		
Jim Sivell	G	5'9"	200	25		

The Dodgers were running harder and harder on a treadmill and going no place. Coach Potsy Clark brought in some veterans and signed some rookies, but the Dodgers still wallowed in mediocrity. After a decade in the league, they showed no signs of challenging the Giants and Redskins as powers in the NFL East. In the last few years, the Dodgers had added one top-notch rookie to their ranks, and this year's sparkler was runner Pug Manders, Jack's brother of the Chicago Bears, a straight-ahead plunger. Tailback Ace Parker and tackle Bruiser Kinard, prize finds the last two years, led their teammates and won reputations as first-rate players on a second-rate team. Fullback Ace Gutowsky came over to Brooklyn from the Detroit Lions, but he, Beattie Feathers, and Ralph Kercheval all had left their best running behind them. None of the other linemen came close to matching Kinard's ferocity.

PHILADELPHIA EAGLES 1-9-1 Bert Bell

Scores of Each Game		
0	WASHINGTON	7
3	NEW YORK	13
0	BROOKLYN	0
10	New York	27
14	Brooklyn	23
6	Washington	7
16	GREEN BAY	23
14	Chic. Bears	27
17	PITTSBURGH	14
12	Pittsburgh	24
13	Cleveland at Colorado Springs	35

Use Name	Pos.	Hgt	Wgt	Age	Int	Pts
Zed Coston	C-LB	6'2"	222	23		
Moose Harper	C-LB	6'4"	230	25		
Jake Schueble	LB	6'	196	22		
Rankin Britt	DE	6'2"	206	24		

Use Name – Tackles	Pos.	Hgt	Wgt	Age	Int	Pts
Drew Ellis	T-FB	6'1"	216	24		
(6 rushing attempts for 1 yd.)						
Ray Keeling	T	6'3"	255	23		
Bob Pylman	T	6'4"	215	25		
George Somers	T	6'2"	242	23		
Clem Woltman	T	6'1"	212	23		

Use Name – Guards	Pos.	Hgt	Wgt	Age	Int	Pts
Bree Cuppoletti	G	5'10"	205	29		
Bill Hughes	G	6'1"	232	24		
Emmett Kriel	G	6'2"	200	23		
Hank Reese	G-C-LB	5'11"	216	28		7
(1 PAT in 1 attempt, 2 FG in 4 attempts)						
Ted Schmitt	G	5'11"	214	22		6
Allie White	G-T	5'11"	212	24		

Weighing in at 150 pounds, little Davey O'Brien learned to throw the ball often while an All-American at Texas Christian University, and Eagle owner Bert Bell gambled that the 5'7" passer would find pro defenses no more difficult to crack than college units. After luring O'Brien into uniform with a $12,000 contract, Bell insured his slight rookie against injury with Lloyds of London. The insurance policy called for a payment of $1,500 to the Eagles for each game O'Brien missed with an injury. Davey never missed a single game, and he lived up to expectations as a passer. He set a league record for yards gained in a season, surpassing Arnie Herber's 1936 mark. His twenty-one completions in one game also set a new standard. But O'Brien's passes could not help the Eagles win more than one game. After a strong 1938 campaign, the Eagles lapsed back into their losing ways again.

PITTSBURGH PIRATES 1-9-1 Johnny Blood, Walt Kiesling

Scores of Each Game		
7	Brooklyn	12
0	CHIC. CARDS	10
0	CHIC. BEARS	32
7	NEW YORK	14
14	Washington	44
14	WASHINGTON	21
14	Cleveland	14
13	Brooklyn	17
7	New York	23
14	Philadelphia	17
24	PHILADELPHIA	12

Use Name	Pos.	Hgt	Wgt	Age	Int	Pts
Ted Grabinski	C-LB	6'2"	200	24		
Joe Maras	C-T-LB	6'1"	202	23		
John Tosi (to BKN)	C-T-G-LB	5'10"	225	24		
Wayland Becker	OE-DE	6'	205	28		
Max Fiske	OE-DB	6'	205	25		
Earl Bartlett	HB-DB	6'	200	27		
Clarence Tommerson	HB-DB	6'2"	195	24		
Joe Williams	HB-DB	5'9"	178	25		

Use Name – Tackles	Pos.	Hgt	Wgt	Age	Int	Pts
Don Campbell	T	6'	215	22		
Ted Doyle	T-G	6'2"	220	25		
Ed Karpowich	T	6'4"	222	26		

Use Name – Guards	Pos.	Hgt	Wgt	Age	Int	Pts
Vinnie Farrar	G-BB-LB	5'10"	200	26		
Byron Gentry	G	5'11"	230	25		
George Kakasic	G	5'10"	205	27		
Lou Midler	G-T	6'1"	225	24		
Stan Pavkov	G	6'1"	215	24		
John Perko	G	6'1"	205	23		

Voluntarily retired – Whizzer White

An opening-day loss to Brooklyn was bad enough, but when the lowly Cardinals shut the Pirates out 10-0 and the Bears then shellacked them 32-0, Pittsburgh coach Johnny Blood packed his bags and quit. Two and a half years of losing was all the old star could take.

The coaching reigns fell to big Walt Kiesling, Blood's assistant for two years. Kiesling worked the players hard, a complete turnaround from Blood's country-club atmosphere, but the discipline did not stop the club from losing. With two games remaining, the Pirates started a home-and-away series with the Eagles in search of their first win, as was Philadelphia. The first game went to the Eagles 17-14, but Kiesling's men came back to win the curtain-dropper in Pittsburgh to end the season on the only positive note of the year.

Use Name – Backs & Ends	Pos.	Age	Hgt	Wgt	Pts	Int	RUSHING				PASSING								RECEIVING				PUNTING		KICKING						PUNT RETURNS				KICKOFF RETURNS			
							No.	Yds	Avg	TD	Att	Comp	%	Yds	Yd/Att	TD	Int–%	RK	No.	Yds	Avg	TD	No.	Avg	Pat	Att	%	FG	Att	%	No.	Yds	Avg	TD	No.	Yds	Avg	TD
NEW YORK GIANTS																																						
Ed Danowski	QB-DB	27	6'1"	198			25	21	0.8	0	101	42	42	437	4.3	3	6– 6	10					29	38														
Len Barnum	QB-WB-DB	26	6'	200	24		91	237	2.6	2	27	8	30	141	5.2	3	1– 4		3	50	17	0	29	41	3	3	100	3	7	43								
Eddie Miller	QB-DB	22	5'10"	165	6		30	99	3.3	1	23	13	57	195	8.5	2	2– 9						5	37														
Tuffy Leemans	FB-DB	26	6'	195	30		128	429	3.4	3	26	12	46	198	7.6	0	2– 8		8	185	23	2																
Hank Soar	FB-DB	25	6'2"	210	20		66	158	2.4	2									12	134	11	0			2	2	100	0	1	0								
Kink Richards	FB-DB	28	5'11"	195	6		40	117	2.9	1									2	8	4	0	1	39														
Bull Karcis	FB-LB	30	5'9"	225			31	93	3.0	0																												
Al Owen	FB-BB-DB-LB	26	6'	188	6		8	11	1.4	0									2	45	23	1																
Ken Strong	FB	33	6'	200	19		1	1	1.0	0													5	55	7	7	100	4	8	50								
Ward Cuff	WB-DB	26	6'1"	185	39		23	102	4.4	0									10	83	8	2			6	6	100	7	16	44								
Dale Burnett	WB-DB	30	6'1"	186			1	3	3.0	0									8	86	11	0																
Leland Shaffer	BB-DB	27	6'2"	205			3	6	2.0	0									2	8	4	0																
Nello Falaschi	BB-LB	25	6'	195			1	4	4.0	0									4	27	7	0																
Jim Poole	OE-DE	23	6'3"	215															7	99	14	0																
Chuck Gelatka	OE-DB	26	6'1"	180															6	71	12	0																
Jim Lee Howell	OE-DE	24	6'6"	200	12														5	112	22	2																
Jiggs Kline	OE-DE	25	6'1"	196	6														4	44	11	1																
Will Walls	OE-DE	24	6'4"	212															2	19	10	0																
WASHINGTON REDSKINS																																						
Frankie Filchock	TB-DB	22	5'11"	190	6		103	413	4.0	1	89	55	62	1094	12.3	11	7– 8	1																				
Sammy Baugh	TB-DB	25	6'2"	182			14	46	3.3	0	96	53	55	518	5.4	6	9– 9	9					26	38.4														
Jimmy German	TB-DB	22	6'	180	12		20	58	2.9	2	12	6	50	97	8.1	1	2–17																					
Andy Farkas	FB-DB	23	5'10"	190	68		139	547	3.9	5									16	437	27	5			2	3	67	0	1	0								1
Wilbur Moore	FB-DB	23	5'11"	190			27	100	3.7	0									1	2	2	0																
Don Irwin	FB-WB-DB	26	6'1"	196	6		10	63	6.3	1									1	8	8	0																
Jim Meade	FB-DB	25	6'1"	195			13	34	2.6	0									1	1	1	0	8	37														
Dick Todd	WB-FB-DB	24	5'11"	170	38		57	266	4.7	2	4	3	75	86	21.5	0	0– 0		19	230	12	3	5	32	2	3	67							1				
Jimmy Johnston	WB-DB	22	6'1"	190	7		7	47	6.7	0									11	111	10	1	8	39	1	1	100											
Ed Justice	WB-DB	26	6'1"	200	18		5	56	11.2	1									7	124	18	1																
Boyd Morgan	WB-DB	24	6'	196			1	0	0.0	0									1	4	4	0																
Ernie Pinckert	BB-LB	31	6'	198			5	17	3.4	0																												
Max Krause	BB-LB	30	5'10"	202			3	23	7.7	0																												
John Spirida	BB-OE-DE	23	6'	195			2	5	2.5	0									2	95	48	0	10	39														
Jay Turner	BB-LB	25	5'10"	205			2	1	0.5	0									2	15	8	0	1	33														
Wayne Millner	OE-DE	28	6'1"	190	24		4	12	3.0	0									19	294	15	4																
Charley Malone	OE-DE	29	6'4"	210	18														18	274	15	3			0	1	0											
Bob Masterson	OE-DE	24	6'1"	200	15														10	114	11	1			6	8	75	1	6	17								
Bob McChesney	OE-DE	27	6'2"	190	6		1	5	5.0	1									9	86	10	0																
Bo Russell	T	23	6'1"	218	24																				15	16	94	1	6	17								
BROOKLYN DODGERS																																						
Ace Parker	TB-DB	27	6'	168	33		104	271	2.6	5	157	72	46	977	6.2	4	13– 8	8	1	5	5	0	40	42	0	1	0	1	5	20								
Ray Carnelly	TB-HB-DB	22	6'2"	187			15	64	4.3	0	14	3	21	35	2.5	0	3–21		1	5	5	0						0	1	0								
Bill Leckorby	TB-DB	21	6'1"	185			4	−1	−0.2	0	1	0	0	0	0.0	0	0– 0																					
Pug Manders	FB-BB-DB-LB	26	6'	210	12		114	482	4.2	2									3	22	7	0																
Sam Francis (from PIT)	FB-HB-DB	24	6'	210	6		76	230	3.0	1									2	5	3	0	13	38														
Ace Gutowsky	FB-DB	29	5'11"	205			58	202	3.5	0	1	1	100	5	5.0	0	0– 0																					
Len Janiak	FB-BB-DB	23	6'1"	195			18	56	3.1	0									2	6	3	0																
Ralph Kercheval	HB-DB	28	6'1"	193	21		34	99	2.9	0	1	1	100	7	7.0	0	0– 0		3	8	3	0	28	39	3	3	100	6	13	46								
Beattie Feathers	HB-DB	31	5'10"	185			8	21	2.6	0									1	12	12	0																
Wendell Butcher	BB-LB	25	6'1"	200			2	2	1.0	0									9	73	8	0																
Stan Kosel	BB-LB	22	5'11"	190	6		2	6	3.0	0									2	40	20	1																
Bill Reissig	BB-LB-DE	24	6'	195	3																				0	1	0	1	1	100								
Perry Schwartz	OE-DE	24	6'2"	200	18														33	550	17	3																
Waddy Young	OE-DE	22	6'3"	205															8	100	13	0																
Harold Hill	OE-DE	23	6'1"	200															7	150	21	0																
Herman Hodges	OE-DE	24	6'1"	195	6														4	45	11	0																
PHILADELPHIA EAGLES																																						
Davey O'Brien	TB-DB	22	5'7"	150	6		108	−14	−0.1	1	201	99	49	1324	6.6	6	17– 8	6					3	40	0	1	0 (Pass)											
Emmett Mortell	TB-DB	25	6'1"	178			37	88	2.4	0	41	12	29	134	3.3	1	0– 0						23	43														
Dave Smukler	FB-LB	25	6'1"	224			45	218	4.8	0	20	7	35	56	2.8	0	4–20						10	40														
Franny Murray	WB-DB	23	6'	200	26		47	137	2.9	1									13	144	11	1	33	37	8	12	67	2	4	50								
Joe Bukant	FB-LB	23	6'	223	18		59	136	2.3	3	1	0	0	0	0.0	0	0– 0						1	54														
Dick Riffle	WB-TB-DB	24	6'1"	197			18	61	3.4	0	4	1	25	2	0.5	0	1–25		6	57	10	0	17	40														
Jay Arnold	BB-DB	25	6'1"	207	12		8	1	0.1	1									13	207	16	1	1	42														
Chuck Newton	BB-FB-DB	22	6'	205	6		1	0	0.0	0									9	123	14	1																
Woody Dow	FB-LB	22	6'	195			1	−7	−7.0	0									5	58	12	0																
Red Ramsey	OE-DE	24	6'	192	6														31	359	12	1																
Joe Carter	OE-DE	29	6'1"	200	12		1	4	4.0	0									24	292	12	2																
Bill Hewitt	OE-DE	29	5'9"	190	6		1	1	1.0	0									15	243	16	1																
Elmer Kolberg	OE-DB	23	6'4"	200															3	33	11	0																
PITTSBURGH PIRATES																																						
Hugh McCullough	TB-DB	23	6'	185	6		60	96	1.6	1	100	32	32	443	4.4	2	12–12	12	4	57	14	0	31	33														
Coley McDonough (from CHIC)	TB-DB	24	6'1"	195	6		27	75	2.8	0	47	17	36	365	7.8	2	8–17		1	3	3	1	10	37														
Lou Tomasetti	TB-HB-DB	23	6'	188	6		49	86	1.8	1	47	13	28	140	3.0	1	7–15		4	22	6	0	3	37														
Ernie Wheeler (to CHIC)	TB-DB	24	6'1"	180			17	0	0.0	0	17	5	29	94	5.5	1	7–41						10	46														
Boyd Brumbaugh (from BKN)	FB-TB-DB	24	5'11"	195	18		111	343	3.1	2	10	3	30	121	12.1	2	1–10		5	95	19	1	1	34														
Swede Johnston	FB-DB	29	5'10"	195	12		59	220	3.7	2													10	47														
Carl Littlefield	FB-DB	23	6'	200			39	141	3.6	0									1	18	18	0																
Bob Masters	HB-TB-DB	28	5'11"	195			9	39	4.3	0	3	1	33	9	3.0	0	1–33		2	12	6	0																
Bill Davidson	HB-TB-DB	24	6'	180			21	27	1.3	0	7	1	14	8	1.1	0	0– 0		6	27	5	0																
Dick Nardi (to BKN)	HB-TB-DB	23	5'10"	200			10	15	1.5	0	5	2	40	12	2.4	0	1–20		1	3	3	0	1	19														
Karl Schuelke	FB-DB	23	5'10"	200			2	2	1.0	0																												
Rink Bond	BB-LB	25	5'10"	200			1	4	4.0	0																												
Jack Lee	BB-LB	22	5'10"	205			1	−11	−11.0	0	1	0	0	0	0.0	0	0– 0						1	44														
Sam Boyd	OE-DE	25	6'1"	190	12														21	423	20	2																
Bill Sortet	OE-DE	27	6'1"	185	6														16	196	12	1																
George Platukas	OE-DE	24	6'	186	18														7	170	24	3																
Bernie Scherer	OE-DE	26	6'1"	195															2	49	25	0																
Frank Souchak	OE-DE	24	6'	205															1	12	12	0																
Armand Niccolai	T-G	27	6'2"	230	24																				15	15	100	3	8	38								

TEAM TOTALS	OFFENSE																						DEFENSE						TEAM TOTALS
	FIRST DOWNS	RUSHING: No.	Yards	Avg.	TD	PASSING: Att.	Comp.	Comp. Pct.	Yards	Yds. Att.	Yds. Comp.	TD	Int.	Pct. Int.	FUMBLES: Number	PENALTY: Yards	POINTS: Total	TD	PAT	FG Att.	FG	Saf	Total Yards	Pass Att.	Pass Comp.	Comp. Pct.	Int.	Points	
NEW YORK	109	448	1281	2.9	9	177	75	42.4	971	5.5	13.0	8	11	6.2	21	267	168	18	18	32	14	0	2482	222	89	40.1	35	85	NEW YORK
WASHINGTON	125	413	1693	4.1	13	201	117	58.2	1795	8.9	15.3	18	18	9.0	33	332	242	35	26	13	2	0	2116	243	90	37.0	24	94	WASHINGTON
BROOKLYN	113	400	1332	3.3	7	176	77	43.8	1024	5.8	13.3	4	16	9.1	21	210	108	12	10	20	8	1	3113	195	92	47.2	22	219	BROOKLYN
PHILADELPHIA	97	332	626	1.9	6	267	119	44.6	1516	5.7	12.7	7	22	8.2	28	237	105	14	9	8	4	0	2954	210	97	46.2	17	200	PHILADELPHIA
PITTSBURGH	113	432	1137	2.6	7	221	70	31.7	1084	4.9	15.5	8	34	15.4	25	279	114	15	15	8	3	0	3100	193	88	45.6	11	216	PITTSBURGH

GREEN BAY PACKERS 9-2-0 Curly Lambeau

Scores of Each Game		
14	CHIC. CARDS	10
21	CHIC. BEARS	16
24	CLEVELAND	27
27	CHIC. CARDS	20
26	DETROIT	7
24	WASHINGTON	14
27	Chic. Bears	30
23	Philadelphia	16
28	Brooklyn	0
7	Cleveland	6
12	Detroit	7

Use Name	Pos.	Hgt	Wgt	Age	Int	Pts
Charley Brock	C-LB	6'2"	193	23		6
Tom Greenfield	C-LB	6'4"	200	21		6
Bud Svendsen	C-LB	6'1"	183	24		6
Al Moore	DE	6'2"	218	25		
Frank Steen	OE-DE	6'1"	190	23		
Dick Weisgerber	BB-DB	5'10"	202	24		

Voluntarily retired – Champ Seibold

Use Name – Tackles	Pos.	Hgt	Wgt	Age	Int	Pts
Paul Kell	T	6'2"	217	22		
Wally Kilbourne	T	6'3"	240	23		
Bill Lee	T	6'2"	224	27		
Baby Ray	T	6'6"	238	24		
Charlie Schultz	T	6'3"	228	22		
Ernie Smith	T	6'2"	220	29		3
(3 PAT's in 4 attempts)						

Use Name – Guards	Pos.	Hgt	Wgt	Age	Int	Pts
Jack Brennan	G	6'1"	204	22		
Buckets Goldenberg	G-LB	5'10"	222	28		
Russ Letlow	G	6'	213	25		
Pete Tinsley	G	5'8"	196	26		
Frank Twedell	G	5'11"	220	22		
Gust Zarnas (from BKN)	G	5'10"	222	24		

In the middle of a game against the Lions, Curly Lambeau made a switch which added a few years to Don Hutson's career. Lambeau assigned rookie Larry Craig, a 205-pound bruiser, to play blocking back on offense and end on defense, freeing Hutson to use his speed at safety. His new secondary post spared Hutson the pounding of defensive line play and left him more energy for his pass-catching on offense. Passes from Cecil Isbell and Arnie Herber kept Hutson busy, while the running corps gained enough yards to make the Packers the top offensive club in the league. The foundation for this attack was a solid line featuring guards Russ Letlow and Buckets Goldenberg, all of which combined to give Green Bay a return trip to the championship game.

CHICAGO BEARS 8-3-0 George Halas

Scores of Each Game		
30	CLEVELAND	21
16	Green Bay	21
32	Pittsburgh	0
35	Cleveland	21
44	CHIC. CARDS	7
13	New York	16
0	DETROIT	10
30	GREEN BAY	27
23	Detroit	13
27	PHILADELPHIA	14
48	Chic. Cards	7

Use Name	Pos.	Hgt	Wgt	Age	Int	Pts
Frank Bausch	C-LB	6'2"	225	31		
Chet Chesney	C-LB	6'2"	227	22		
Frank Sullivan	C-LB	6'3"	205	27		
Chuck Apolskis	OE-DE	6'2"	207	22		
Charlie Heileman	OE-DE	6'2"	197	23		
Anton Stofa	QB-DB	6'	195	21		

Use Name – Tackles	Pos.	Hgt	Wgt	Age	Int	Pts
Joe Stydahar	T	6'4"	230	27		4
(1 reception for 9 yds., 4 PAT's in 6 attempts)						
Russ Thompson	T	6'5"	250	27		
John Torrance	T	6'3"	285	26		
Milt Trost	T	6'1"	208	26		

Use Name – Guards	Pos.	Hgt	Wgt	Age	Int	Pts
Dick Bassi	G	5'11"	210	24		
Ray Bray	G	6'	224	22		
Aldo Forte	G-T	6'	212	21		
Danny Fortmann	G-LB	6'	210	23		
George Musso	G	6'2"	270	29		

A single-wing tailback at Columbia University, rookie Sid Luckman had to start from scratch in learning to be a T-quarterback, and at first he was tripping over his own feet before getting the hang of handing off and faking. George Halas believed in the intelligent young man, though, and broke him in gradually at halfback while turning him over to veterans Carl Brumbaugh and Bernie Masterson for quarterback training. By the season's end, Luckman was settled in his new job, and the Bears had a new leader at quarterback. The club also came up with a new fullback in Bill Osmanski, a quick-starting rookie who played with his spikes filed sharp. The leading rusher in the league, Osmanski, joined veteran linemen Joe Stydahar and Danny Fortmann on the All-Pro team.

DETROIT LIONS 6-5-0 Gus Henderson

Scores of Each Game		
21	CHIC. CARDS	13
27	BROOKLYN	7
17	Chic. Cards	3
15	CLEVELAND	7
7	Green Bay	26
10	Chic. Bears	0
18	NEW YORK	14
13	CHIC. BEARS	23
3	Cleveland	14
7	Washington	31
7	GREEN BAY	12

Use Name	Pos.	Hgt	Wgt	Age	Int	Pts
Tony Calvelli	C-G-LB	5'10"	190	23		
Dixie Stokes	C-LB	6'	205	26		
Tony Tonelli	C-G-LB	6'	210	22		
Johnny Wiatrak	C-LB	6'	220	26		
Alex Wojciechowicz	C-LB	5'11"	200	24		
Connie Mack Berry	OE-DE	6'3"	200	23		
Hal Brill	TB-DB	5'10"	175	25		
Elvin Hutchinson	WB-DB	5'11"	195	26		

Use Name – Tackles	Pos.	Hgt	Wgt	Age	Int	Pts
Ray George	T	6'	230	23		
Jack Johnson	T	6'4"	220	29		
Steve Maronic	T	6'	225	23		
Bill Rogers	T	5'11"	240	26		

Use Name – Guards	Pos.	Hgt	Wgt	Age	Int	Pts
Bill Feldhaus	G-LB	6'	225	27		
Phil Martinovich	G	5'10"	220	24		9
(3 field goals in 6 attempts)						
Bill Radovich	G	5'10"	225	24		
Cal Thomas	G	6'2"	210	24		
John Wiethe	G-LB	6'	195	26		
(2 receptions for 5 yds.)						

With a new broom sweeping away many of the stars of the past decade, the Lions took the field a vastly different outfit from last year. Tailback Dutch Clark left Detroit to be head coach at Cleveland, tackle George Christensen became assistant coach at Brooklyn, Ace Gutowsky was sold to the Dodgers, and Ernie Caddel retired. For better or worse, new coach Gus Henderson had to go with a patchwork squad in the midst of rebuilding. At first, Henderson looked like a genius, as the Lions won their first four games and six of their first seven. But then the bottom fell out and the league-leading Lions lost their final four games to sink back into the mire in the Western Division.

CLEVELAND RAMS 5-5-1 Dutch Clark

Scores of Each Game		
21	Chic. Bears	30
12	Brooklyn	23
27	Green Bay	24
21	CHIC. BEARS	35
7	Detroit	15
24	Chic. Cards	0
14	PITTSBURGH	14
14	CHIC. CARDS	0
14	DETROIT	3
6	GREEN BAY	7
35	PHILADELPHIA at Colorado Springs	13

Use Name	Pos.	Hgt	Wgt	Age	Int	Pts
Chuck Cherundolo	C-LB	6'1"	217	23		
Bill Conkright	C-LB	6'1"	204	25		
Gerry Dowd	C-LB	6'	210	23		6
Mike Perry	BB-LB	5'11"	197	22		

Use Name – Tackles	Pos.	Hgt	Wgt	Age	Int	Pts
Chet Adams	T	6'3"	227	23		5
(5 PAT's in 5 attempts)						
Ben Friend	T	6'5"	248	22		
Art Lewis	T-G	6'3"	230	26		
Ted Livingston	T-G	6'3"	222	25		
Ralph Neihaus	T	6'4"	220	23		
Nate Schenker	T	6'2"	220	21		

Use Name – Guards	Pos.	Hgt	Wgt	Age	Int	Pts
Alex Atty	G	5'8"	216	22		
Lew Bostick	G	6'	197	22		2
(1 punt for 55 yds., 2 PAT's in 2 attempts)						
Tom Hupke	G	5'10"	190	28		
Riley Matheson	G-LB	6'2"	203	24		
Barney McGarry	G-LB	6'1"	205	21		
Phil Ragazzo	G-T	6'	210	24		

With Dutch Clark taking over as non-playing head coach, the Rams started the year with a rookie coach and a very inexperienced squad. Despite an upset of Green Bay, the early games chiefly gave the young Rams a chance to get used to each other while losing. But then, suddenly, in mid-season, the team jelled. The Rams twice shut out the Cardinals and upset the fading Lions before a record 25,000 home-town fans. After a close loss to the Packers, the Rams evened their final record by beating the Eagles. Rookie Parker Hall, known as "Bullet", was at center stage during the resurgence, topping all passers in the league statistics and winning the league MVP Award, and Jim Benton, Vic Spadaccini, Johnny Drake, and Chet Adams all blossomed during the second half of the season as the team rolled up 107 points to their opponents' 37.

CHICAGO CARDINALS 1-10-0 Ernie Nevers

Scores of Each Game		
13	Detroit	21
10	Green Bay	14
10	Pittsburgh	0
3	DETROIT	17
20	Green Bay	27
7	Chic. Bears	44
0	CLEVELAND	24
0	Cleveland	14
7	New York	17
7	Washington	28
7	CHIC. BEARS	48

Use Name	Pos.	Hgt	Wgt	Age	Int	Pts
Henry Adams	C-LB	6'1"	190	23		
Ki Aldrich	C-LB	6'	195	23		
Len Dugan (to PIT)	C-LB	6'	220	27		
Charlie Gainor	DE	6'3"	190	23		
Don Cosner	WB-DB	6'2"	200	22		
Jim Neill	WB-DB	6'1"	180	24		

Holdout — Gus Tinsley

Use Name – Tackles	Pos.	Hgt	Wgt	Age	Int	Pts
Al Babartsky	T	6'	220	24		6
Conway Baker	T	5'11"	225	27		
Jon Bilbo	T	6'	195	24		
Tony Blazine	T	6'	230	27		
Elwyn Dunstan (to CLE)	T	6'3"	235	24		
(3 rushing attempts for 2 yds)						
Frank Zelencik	T	6'1"	220	24		

Use Name – Guards	Pos.	Hgt	Wgt	Age	Int	Pts
Ross Carter	G-C-LB	6'	195	25		
Frank Huffman	G-LB	6'2"	205	24		
Mike Kochel	G-LB	5'11"	195	23		
Regis Monahan	G	5'10"	215	30		4
(1 PAT in 1 attempt, 1 FG in 1 attempt)						
Glynn Rogers	G	5'10"	220	24		
Andy Sabados	G	5'11"	208	22		
Jim Thomas	G	5'11"	200	22		
Bill Volok	G	6'2"	215	29		

To try and get the Cardinals back into a winning habit, owner Charles Bidwill hired all-time great Ernie Nevers to coach the club. Nevers had played with a never-say-die fervor, but that attitude didn't rub off on his charges. Right from training camp, the Cards did not expect to do much better than the two wins they picked up in 1938. As it turned out, they won only a single contest. The disorganized Cardinals suffered a mortal loss when end Gaynell Tinsley, the best player on the team, held out for more money and then retired to coach a high-school team. His absence killed any passing attack the team had.

Never's one consolation for the year came in the appearance of two blue-chip rookies, 195-pound center Ki Aldrich and All-American back Marshall Goldberg. A fine defensive back as well as a dangerous runner, Goldberg would last with the Cardinals into their winning days in the late 1940s.

Use Name – Backs & Ends	Pos.	Age	Hgt	Wgt	Pts	Int	Rushing No.	Rushing Yds	Rushing Avg	Rushing TD	Passing Att	Passing Comp	Passing %	Passing Yds	Passing Yd/Att	Passing TD	Passing Int–%	RK
GREEN BAY PACKERS																		
Arnie Herber	TB-DB	29	5'11"	200	6		18	–11	–0.6	1	139	57	41	1107	8.0	8	9– 6	4
Cecil Isbell	TB-HB-DB	24	6'1"	190	15		132	407	3.1	2	103	43	42	749	7.3	6	5– 5	3
Jim Lawrence (from CHIC,WB-DB)	TB-DB	25	5'11"	190			7	6	0.9	0	4	1	25	15	3.8	0	1–25	
Clarke Hinkle	FB-LB	29	5'11"	200	35		135	381	2.8	5								
Ed Jankowski	FB-LB	26	5'9"	202	12		75	278	3.7	2								
Frank Balasz	FB-LB	21	6'2"	215			11	41	3.7	0								
Andy Uram	HB-DB	24	5'10"	187	18		52	272	5.2	1	1	0	0	0	0.0	0	0– 0	
Joe Laws	HB-DB	28	5'9"	184	24		55	162	2.9	2	1	0	0	0	0.0	0	0– 0	
Tuffy Thompson	HB-DB	24	5'11"	170			6	9	1.5	0								
Larry Buhler	HB-BB-DB	22	6'2"	204			5	3	0.6	0								
Larry Craig	BB-DB-DE	23	6'1"	205			2	6	3.0	0								
Hank Bruder	BB-DB	31	6'	202	6													
Don Hutson	OE-DE-DB	26	6'1"	185	38		5	26	5.2	0								
Moose Mulleneaux	OE-DE	22	6'3"	206	6													
Milt Gantenbein	OE-DE	29	6'	195	6													
Harry Jacunski	OE-DE	23	6'2"	195	12													
Tiny Engebretsen	G	29	6'1"	245	30													
CHICAGO BEARS																		
Bernie Masterson	QB-DB	28	6'3"	195	12		21	–31	–1.5	2	113	44	39	914	8.1	8	9– 8	5
Sid Luckman	QB-HB-DB	22	6'	193	6		24	42	1.8	0	51	23	45	636	12.5	5	4– 8	
Billy Patterson	QB-HB-DB	21	5'10"	167	1		14	34	2.4	0	38	14	37	227	6.0	3	4–11	
Bob Snyder	QB-DB	26	6'	205	4		15	56	3.7	0	12	5	42	135	11.3	0	1– 8	
Solly Sherman	QB-DB	21	6'1"	190	6		3	–5	–1.7	0	4	2	50	43	10.8	0	0– 0	
Bill Osmanski	FB-LB	22	5'11"	195	48		121	699	5.8	7								
Joe Maniaci	FB-LB	25	6'1"	210	37		77	544	7.1	4	2	1	50	10	5.0	0	0– 0	
Ray Nolting	HB-DB	25	5'11"	185	24		50	216	4.3	2								
Bob Swisher	HB-DB	25	5'11"	165	18		30	192	6.4	2								
Gary Famiglietti	FB-LB	24	6'	214	1		33	128	3.9	0								
Bob MacLeod	HB-DB	21	6'	190	30		17	88	5.2	1								
Jack Manders	HB-DB	30	6'	200	50		25	63	2.5	3								
Dick Schweidler	HB-DB	24	6'	185			5	15	3.0	0								
Dick Plasman	OE-DE	25	6'3"	210	21						1	0	0	0	0.0	0	0– 0	
Les McDonald	OE-DE	24	6'4"	200	18		1	–2	–2.0	0								
Eggs Manske	OE-DE	26	6'	185	12													
George Wilson	OE-DE	25	6'1"	190														
John Siegal	OE-DE	21	6'1"	196	6													
DETROIT LIONS																		
Dwight Sloan	TB-DB	24	5'10"	180	24		79	225	2.8	4	107	45	42	658	6.1	2	3– 3	7
Darrell Tully	TB-DB	22	6'1"	200	6		31	50	1.6	1	69	20	29	356	5.2	2	13–19	13
Johnny Pingel	TB-DB	23	6'	180	6		72	301	4.2	1	48	27	56	343	7.1	3	4– 8	
Bill Shepherd	FB-LB	27	5'9"	205	18		85	420	4.9	2	1	0	0	0	0.0	0	0– 0	
Howie Weiss	FB-LB	22	6'	210			37	150	4.1	0								
Lloyd Cardwell	WB-DB	26	6'2"	200	18		29	141	4.9	1								
Jim McDonald	WB-FB-DB	23	6'1"	195			25	80	3.2	0								
Rip Ryan	WB-DB	24	6'2"	195	12		8	41	5.1	1								
Gordon Gore	WB-DB	26	6'	216			8	7	0.9	0	1	0	0	0	0.0	0	0– 0	
Fred Vanzo	BB-LB	23	6'2"	230			5	46	9.2	0								
Paul Szakash	BB-DB	26	6'	215			3	11	3.7	0								
Monk Moscrip	OE-DE	25	6'	195	15		1	8	8.0	0								
Chuck Hanneman	OE-DE	24	6'	212	29													
Bill Moore	OE-DE	27	6'1"	195	6		1	7	7.0	0								
Jim Austin	OE-DE	26	6'2"	200														
Ray Hamilton	OE-DE	23	6'4"	215														
Dave Diehl	OE-DE	20	6'	190														
Ray Clemons	G	26	6'	215														
CLEVELAND RAMS																		
Parker Hall	TB-DB	22	6'	205	12		120	458	3.8	2	208	106	51	1227	5.9	9	13– 6	2
Marty Slovak	TB-DB	22	5'9"	176			42	135	3.2	0	27	13	48	97	3.6	2	5–19	
Kelly Moan	TB-DB	26	6'	193	1		2	–15	–7.5	0	9	3	33	77	8.6	1	2–22	
Bronko Smilanich	TB-DB	23	5'11"	180			1	–3	–3.0	0	2	1	50	11	5.5	0	0– 0	
Johnny Drake	FB-DB-LB	23	6'1"	214	54		118	453	3.8	9								
Gaylon Smith	FB-WB-DB	23	5'11"	205	12		58	98	1.7	2	5	4	80	3	0.6	0	0– 0	
Corby Davis	FB-LB	24	5'11"	214	13		13	15	1.2	1								
Bill Lazetich	WB-DB	22	6'	200	6		6	23	3.8	0								
Doug Russell (from CHIC)	WB-DB	27	6'	190	6		9	21	2.3	0	1	0	0	0	0.0	0	0– 0	
Bill McRaven	WB-DB	21	5'11"	170			7	29	4.1	0								
Vic Spadaccini	BB-DB	23	6'	225	18													
Mike Rodak	BB-LB-DE	22	5'10"	195			1	–1	–1.0	0	1	0	0	0	0.0	0	1–100	
Lou Barle	BB-LB	23	6'1"	200														
Jim Benton	OE-DE	22	6'3"	197	48		7	19	2.7	0								
Maury Patt	OE-DE	25	6'2"	202			6	20	3.3	0								
Johnny Wilson	OE-DE	23	6'3"	200	6													
Paul McDonough	OE-DE	22	6'4"	218	6													
Joel Hitt	OE-DE	21	6'1"	180			1	3	3.0	0								
CHICAGO CARDINALS																		
John Robbins	TB-DB	23	6'2"	180			38	97	2.6	0	85	36	42	499	5.9	4	10–12	11
Frank Patrick	TB-DB	23	5'11"	190	7		30	84	2.8	1	79	22	28	291	3.7	1	13–16	14
Bert Johnson (from CHIB,FB-LB)	TB-DB	27	6'	215			38	95	2.5	0	40	14	35	208	5.2	0	5–12	
Marshall Goldberg	FB-TB-DB	21	5'11"	184	18		56	152	2.7	2	7	1	14	4	0.6	0	1–14	
Sam Agee	FB-DB	25	6'1"	218	6		45	137	3.1	1	3	0	0	0	0.0	0	0– 0	
Ed Cherry (to PIT)	FB-DB	24	6'	210			10	30	3.0	0								
Milt Popovich	WB-FB-DB	22	5'11"	190	6		26	78	3.0	0	6	5	83	52	8.7	0	0– 0	
Rock Reed	WB-DB	24	5'8"	175			5	–6	–1.2	0	1	1	100	2	2.0	0	0– 0	
George Faust	BB-LB	22	6'1"	205	1		22	71	3.2	0	5	0	0	0	0.0	0	1–20	
Ev Fisher	BB-OE-LB-DE	24	5'11"	205			18	63	3.5	0								
Buddy Parker	BB-LB	25	6'	196			12	37	3.1	0								
Earl Crowder	BB-LB	23	6'	198			6	–5	–0.8	0	7	2	29	6	0.9	0	0– 0	
Bill Smith	OE-DB	27	6'1"	198	36		1	3	3.0	0								
Joel Mason	OE-DB	26	6'	190														
Versil Deskin	OE-DE	26	6'	200														
John Klump	OE-DE	22	6'3"	195														
Hal Bradley (from WAS)	OE-DE	25	6'4"	205														
Keith Birlem (to WAS,WB-DB)	OE-DB	25	5'11"	198														

Use Name – Backs & Ends	Receiving No.	Receiving Yds	Receiving Avg	Receiving TD	Punting No.	Punting Avg	Kicking Pat	Kicking Att	Kicking %	Kicking FG	Kicking Att	Kicking %	Punt Returns No.	Punt Returns Yds	Punt Returns Avg	Punt Returns TD	Kickoff Returns No.	Kickoff Returns Yds	Kickoff Returns Avg	Kickoff Returns TD
GREEN BAY PACKERS																				
Arnie Herber	1	18	18	0	24	40														
Cecil Isbell	9	71	18	0	4	31	3	3	100											
Jim Lawrence (from CHIC,WB-DB)	3	41	14	0	3	38														
Clarke Hinkle	4	70	18	0	43	41	2	3	67	1	10	10								
Ed Jankowski	1	5	5	0																
Frank Balasz	1	11	11	0	1	35														
Andy Uram	7	93	13	2																
Joe Laws	11	177	16	1												1				
Tuffy Thompson	1	1	1	0																
Larry Buhler																				
Larry Craig	3	44	15	0																
Hank Bruder	5	65	16	1																
Don Hutson	34	846	25	6			2	2	100											
Moose Mulleneaux	12	218	18	1																
Milt Gantenbein	7	127	18	1																
Harry Jacunski	5	104	21	2																
Tiny Engebretsen							18	19	95	4	8	50								
CHICAGO BEARS																				
Bernie Masterson	2	37	19	0			0	1	0(Pass)											
Sid Luckman					27	44														
Billy Patterson					8	38	1	1	100											
Bob Snyder					7	42	1	2	50	1	1	100								
Solly Sherman	1	42	42	0																
Bill Osmanski	3	65	22	1																
Joe Maniaci							4	8	50	1	2	50								
Ray Nolting	6	87	15	1	12	39														
Bob Swisher	7	228	33	1	3	31														
Gary Famiglietti	3	72	24	0			1	1	100											
Bob MacLeod	10	231	23	3																
Jack Manders	1	29	29	1			17	20	85	3	7	43								
Dick Schweidler	2	43	22	0																
Dick Plasman	19	403	21	3			3	3	100	0	1	0								
Les McDonald	16	261	16	3																
Eggs Manske	10	321	32	2																
George Wilson	5	66	13	0																
John Siegal	3	71	24	1																
DETROIT LIONS																				
Dwight Sloan					1	43														
Darrell Tully																				
Johnny Pingel					32	43														
Bill Shepherd	14	143	10	1	23	37														
Howie Weiss	4	25	6	0																
Lloyd Cardwell	13	250	19	2																
Jim McDonald	5	71	14	0																
Rip Ryan	7	46	7	1	3	37														
Gordon Gore	1	20	20	0																
Fred Vanzo	4	110	28	0																
Paul Szakash							0	1	0											
Monk Moscrip	14	176	13	0			9	12	75	0	1	0								
Chuck Hanneman	12	257	21	2	1	31	5	5	100	4	5	80								
Bill Moore	6	82	14	1																
Jim Austin	5	102	20	0																
Ray Hamilton	3	53	18	0																
Dave Diehl	1	12	12	0																
Ray Clemons	1	5	5	0	15	43														
CLEVELAND RAMS																				
Parker Hall	1	–16	–16	0	58	41														
Marty Slovak					1	15														
Kelly Moan					1	30	1	1	100											
Bronko Smilanich																				
Johnny Drake	5	53	11	0																
Gaylon Smith	3	57	19	0																
Corby Davis	3	49	16	0	10	39	4	4	100	1	2	50								
Bill Lazetich	8	44	6	1																
Doug Russell (from CHIC)	5	67	13	1	8	41														
Bill McRaven	2	14	7	0																
Vic Spadaccini	32	292	9	1			12	16	75											
Mike Rodak	4	54	14	0																
Lou Barle	2	16	8	0																
Jim Benton	27	388	14	7																
Maury Patt	15	165	11	0																
Johnny Wilson	8	108	14	1																
Paul McDonough	8	73	9	1																
Joel Hitt	4	51	13	0																
CHICAGO CARDINALS																				
John Robbins	2	12	6	0	2	41														
Frank Patrick					16	40	1	1	100											
Bert Johnson (from CHIB,FB-LB)					14	37														
Marshall Goldberg	5	90	18	1																
Sam Agee	1	6	6	0																
Ed Cherry (to PIT)																				
Milt Popovich	2	10	5	0	27	33														
Rock Reed	3	67	22	0																
George Faust	4	85	21	0	25	44	1	1	100	1	1	0								
Ev Fisher	6	62	10	0																
Buddy Parker	5	33	7	0																
Earl Crowder	2	59	30	0																
Bill Smith	21	387	18	4	1	36	6	8	75	2	8	25								
Joel Mason	18	188	10	0																
Versil Deskin	4	84	21	0																
John Klump	4	21	6	0																
Hal Bradley (from WAS)	3	29	10	0																
Keith Birlem (to WAS,WB-DB)	2	17	9	0																

TEAM TOTALS	OFFENSE: First Downs	Rushing: No.	Rushing: Yards	Rushing: Avg.	Rushing: TD	Passing: Att.	Passing: Comp.	Passing: Comp. Pct.	Passing: Yards	Passing: Yds. Att.	Passing: Yds. Comp.	Passing: TD	Passing: Int.	Passing: Pct. Int.	Fumbles: Number	Penalty: Yards	Points: Total	Points: TD	Points: PAT	Points: FG Att.	Points: FG	Points: Saf	DEFENSE: Total Yards	Pass Att.	Pass Comp.	Comp. Pct.	Int.	Points	TEAM TOTALS
GREEN BAY	149	515	1574	3.1	13	248	101	40.7	1871	7.5	18.5	14	15	6.0	16	259	233	31	28	18	5	2	2770	239	106	44.4	26	153	GREEN BAY
CHICAGO BEARS	148	438	2043	4.7	21	221	89	40.3	1965	8.9	22.1	16	18	8.1	33	416	298	42	31	11	5	0	2604	319	133	41.7	25	157	CHICAGO BEARS
DETROIT	133	384	1487	3.9	10	226	92	40.7	1357	6.0	14.8	7	20	8.8	27	304	145	18	14	12	7	1	2603	217	92	42.4	14	150	DETROIT
CLEVELAND	131	390	1260	3.2	14	253	127	50.2	1415	5.6	11.1	12	21	8.3	28	220	195	28	24	2	1	0	2785	199	78	39.2	23	164	CLEVELAND
CHICAGO CARDS	101	325	835	2.6	4	248	84	33.9	1170	4.7	13.9	5	33	13.9	36	238	84	11	9	10	3	0	2998	201	86	42.8	12	254	CHICAGO BEARS

WASHINGTON REDSKINS 9-2-0 Ray Flaherty

Scores of Each Game		
24	BROOKLYN	17
21	NEW YORK	7
40	Pittsburgh	10
28	CHIC. CARDS	21
34	Philadelphia	17
20	Detroit	14
37	PITTSBURGH	10
14	Brooklyn	16
7	CHIC. BEARS	3
7	New York	21
13	PHILADELPHIA	6

Use Name	Pos.	Hgt	Wgt	Age	Int	Pts
Steve Andrako	C-LB	6'	210	24		
Mickey Parks	C-LB	6'	230	23		
Bob Titchenal	C-LB	6'2"	197	22		
Boyd Morgan	BB-LB	6'	200	25		
Keith Birlem – military service						

Use Name – Tackles	Pos.	Hgt	Wgt	Age	Int	Pts
Jim Barber	T	6'3"	230	28		
Vic Carroll	T-C-LB	6'4"	228	27		
Turk Edwards	T	6'2"	275	32		
Bob Fisher	T	6'2"	220	23		
Bo Russell	T	6'1"	228	24		14
(11 PAT's in 13 attempts, 1 FG in 1 attempt)						
Willie Wilkin	T	6'4"	265	24		
Bill Young	T	6'1"	250	26		

Use Name – Guards	Pos.	Hgt	Wgt	Age	Int	Pts
Dick Farman	G	6'	220	24		
Clyde Shugart	G	6'	226	23		
Steve Slivinski	G	5'10"	215	23		
Clem Stralka	G	5'10"	210	26		

In a late-season meeting between Chicago and Washington, the Bears had the ball on the Redskins' 6-yard line and were trailing 7-3 with time left for one play. Sid Luckman drilled a pass that hit Bill Osmanski in the chest and bounced away, and the entire Bear team screamed that Redskin Frankie Filchock had interfered with Osmanski. The officials didn't see it that way, so the Redskins were winners. But when Washington owner George Marshall commented to the press, "The Bears are front runners, quitters. They're not a second-half team, just a bunch of cry-babies," it gave the Bears something to ponder when they returned in three weeks for the championship game.

Although the Redskins took the Eastern title on a high-octane offense centered around Sammy Baugh's rifle passes and the playing of Dick Todd, Wayne Millner, Jim Barber, Wee Willie Wilkin, and Steve Slivinski, they could not overcome Marshall's words nor the Bears' playing when it came time for the NFL title.

BROOKLYN DODGERS 8-3-0 Jock Sutherland

Scores of Each Game		
17	Washington	24
10	Pittsburgh	3
30	PHILADELPHIA	17
21	PITTSBURGH	0
7	Chic. Bears	16
21	Philadelphia	7
7	NEW YORK	10
16	WASHINGTON	14
29	CLEVELAND	14
14	CHIC. CARDS	9
14	New York	6

Use Name	Pos.	Hgt	Wgt	Age	Int	Pts
Lou Mark	C-LB	6'	195	25		
Bud Svendsen	C-G-LB	6'1"	190	25		
Si Titus	C-LB	6'	195	21		
Sherrill Busby	DE	6'2"	200	22		
Bob Winslow (from DET)	DE	6'2"	205	24		

Use Name – Tackles	Pos.	Hgt	Wgt	Age	Int	Pts
John Golemgeske	T	6'2"	225	25		
Red Heater	T	6'2"	220	21		
Bruiser Kinard	T	6'1"	210	25		
Frank Kristufek	T	6'	210	24		
Walt Merrill	T	6'2"	220	23		

Use Name – Guards	Pos.	Hgt	Wgt	Age	Int	Pts
Ty Coon	G	6'	215	25		
Mike Gussie	G-LB	6'	204	22		6
(1 reception for 9 yd. touchdown)						
Art Jacher	G	6'1"	202	24		6
(1 reception for 2 yd. touchdown)						
Matt Kober	G	5'10"	190	24		
Steve Petro	G-LB	5'10"	200	25		
Jim Sivell	G	5'9"	215	26		

The hiring of Dr. Jock Sutherland, famous coach at the University of Pittsburgh, started the most successful Dodger season off on the right foot. Sutherland emphasized hard work and team spirit, and the Dodgers responded by chasing the Washington Redskins to the wire in the Eastern Division. With losses only to the Redskins, Bears, and Giants, Brooklyn's final record equaled the Bears' season mark. Centered around league MVP Ace Parker, a lively offense highlighted the Brooklyn revival. Passing, running, and punting with flair, Parker sparked a squad of some highly gifted football talent. Rookie Banks McFadden helped Pug Manders with the ball-carrying, end Perry Schwartz caught passes, blocked, and tackled well enough to win All-Pro honors, and Bruiser Kinard starred in a line which Sutherland had welded together into an effective unit. In all, it was enough of a pleasant change of pace from the recent menu to give Brooklyn fans something to shout about.

NEW YORK GIANTS 6-4-1 Steve Owen

Scores of Each Game		
10	Pittsburgh	10
7	Washington	21
20	Philadelphia	14
17	PHILADELPHIA	7
12	PITTSBURGH	0
21	CHIC. BEARS	37
10	Brooklyn	7
0	CLEVELAND	13
7	GREEN BAY	3
21	WASHINGTON	7
6	BROOKLYN	14

Use Name	Pos.	Hgt	Wgt	Age	Int	Pts
Wen Goldsmith	C-LB	6'	202	22		
Mel Hein	C-LB	6'2"	223	31		
Kayo Lunday	C-G-LB	6'3"	215	27		
Jiggs Kline	DE	6'1"	195	26		
Carl Tomasello	DE	6'	210	23		

Use Name – Tackles	Pos.	Hgt	Wgt	Age	Int	Pts
Frank Cope	T	6'2"	218	24		
Jerry Dennerlein	T	6'2"	245	27		
Gil Duggan	T	6'3"	235	22		
Monk Edwards	T	6'3"	218	20		
Ed McGee	T	6'1"	210	24		
John Mellus	T	6'	223	23		
Ed Widseth	T	6'1"	220	30		

Use Name – Guards	Pos.	Hgt	Wgt	Age	Int	Pts
Pete Cole	G	5'11"	223	24		
Johnny Dell Isola	G-LB	5'11"	200	28		
Ken Moore	G	6'	212	23		
Doug Oldershaw	G-LB-OE-DE	6'	195	25		
Orville Tuttle	G	5'9"	205	27		

Complacency caught up with the Giants, and so did the Washington Redskins. After two years on top of the Eastern Division, the New Yorkers fell off into third place despite a wealth of championship players. Even without the retired Ed Danowski, the offense moved the ball, and the defense was no pushover, but the spark that turns good players into a great team simply wasn't there. The club looked sluggish in an opening-day tie with Pittsburgh, and a loss to Washington the next week threw the Giants into a hole they never climbed out of.

There was nothing wrong with the line; Mel Hein made All-Pro, while guard Doug Oldershaw and tackle John Mellus won second-team honors. Tuffy Leemans, Eddie Miller, Leland Shaffer, and Ward Cuff kept the backfield in good shape. Yet the Giants lost four games and closed the season by bowing to Brooklyn, 14-6, to cast some shadow on the day the team chose to honor Mel Hein.

PITTSBURGH STEELERS 2-7-2 Walt Kiesling

Scores of Each Game		
7	CHIC. CARDS	7
10	NEW YORK	10
10	Detroit	7
3	BROOKLYN	10
10	WASHINGTON	40
0	Brooklyn	21
0	New York	12
3	Green Bay	24
10	Washington	37
7	PHILADELPHIA	3
0	Philadelphia	7

Use Name	Pos.	Hgt	Wgt	Age	Int	Pts
Ted Grabinski	C-G-LB	6'2"	204	25		
Joe Maras	C-T-LB	6'1"	203	24		
John Schmidt	C-LB	6'3"	210	23		
Frank Sullivan	C-LB	6'3"	220	28		
Sam Boyd	OE-DE	6'1"	185	26		
Rocco Pirro	HB-DB	6'	205	23		
John Yurchey	HB-DB	5'11"	188	22		

Use Name – Tackles	Pos.	Hgt	Wgt	Age	Int	Pts
Don Campbell	T	6'	235	23		
Ted Doyle	T	6'2"	220	26		
Clark Goff	T	6'3"	235	22		
John Woudenberg	T	6'3"	225	22		
Ed Karpowich – American Football League						

Use Name – Guards	Pos.	Hgt	Wgt	Age	Int	Pts
Frank Bykowski	G	6'	205	22		
Carl Nery	G	6'	212	23		
Stan Pavkov	G	6'	208	25		
John Perko	G	6'1"	195	24		
Jack Sanders	G	6'	225	23		

By tying the Cardinals and Giants and beating the Lions, the Pirates stood undefeated after three games. This impossible dream proved to be just that, as the Bucs dropped their next six games to return to the depths of the East. Even with a large recruitment of new players, coach Walt Kiesling simply couldn't keep his battered craft afloat.

Tailback Bill Patterson came over from the Bears but brought no winning magic with him. Rookies Merl Condit and George Kiick carried the ball conscientiously but not spectacularly. Kiesling strung together a respectable defense, but the Pittsburgh offense could not put more than 10 points on the scoreboard in any one game, nor score a touchdown in five of their contests. After the season, owner Art Rooney finally despaired and sold the team. But Rooney's exodus was only temporary, as he would be back on the Pittsburgh pro-football scene before the next season rolled around.

PHILADELPHIA EAGLES 1-10-0 Bert Bell

Scores of Each Game		
20	Green Bay	27
13	Cleveland	21
14	NEW YORK	20
17	Brooklyn	30
7	New York	17
17	WASHINGTON	34
7	BROOKLYN	21
3	Pittsburgh	7
0	DETROIT	21
7	PITTSBURGH	0
6	Washington	13

Use Name	Pos.	Hgt	Wgt	Age	Int	Pts
Chuck Cherundolo	C-LB	6'1"	212	24		
Moose Harper	C-LB	6'4"	230	26		
Ted Schmitt	C-LB	5'11"	220	23		
(1 rush for 6 yds., 1 reception for 8 yds.)						
Woody Dow	DB	6'	195	23		

Use Name – Tackles	Pos.	Hgt	Wgt	Age	Int	Pts
Ray George	T	6'	228	24		
Phil Ragazzo	T	6'	223	25		
Russ Thompson	T	6'5"	250	28		
Milt Trost	T	6'1"	210	27		
Clem Woltman	T	6'1"	212	24		
Hank Reese – American Football League						

Use Name – Guards	Pos.	Hgt	Wgt	Age	Int	Pts
Dick Bassi	G	5'11"	215	25		
Jerry Ginney	G	5'11"	217	24		
Bill Hughes	G	6'1"	228	25		
Elbie Schultz	G	6'4"	242	22		

Whatever flying the Eagles did was on the right wing of little Davey O'Brien. Blessed with a fine rookie receiver in Don Looney and cursed with a weak running corps and a porous line, O'Brien kept passing as a means of self-preservation to keep his 150-pound frame from being unduly manhandled by onrushing linemen. While O'Brien set new records for pass attempts and completions for a season, Looney reeled in enough aerials to set a receiving record. With little else besides the passing combination, the Eagles dropped their first nine games before beating the Pirates in a sort of Futility Bowl. The final game of the year, against the Redskins, turned into an aerial circus, with O'Brien pitted against fellow TCU graduate Slingin' Sammy Baugh. In a battle of the arms, little Davey sent a record sixty passes sailing off into the autumn air for thirty-three completions. But as usual, the Eagles lost, and Davey quit football to join the FBI.

Use Name – Backs & Ends	Pos.	Age	Hgt	Wgt	Pts	Int	RUSHING No.	Yds	Avg	TD	PASSING Att	Comp	%	Yds	Yd/Att	TD	Int–%	RK	RECEIVING No.	Yds	Avg	TD	PUNTING No.	Avg	KICKING Pat	Att	%	FG	Att	%	PUNT RETURNS No.	Yds	Avg	TD	KICKOFF RETURNS No.	Yds	Avg	TD
WASHINGTON REDSKINS																																						
Sammy Baugh	TB-DB	26	6'2"	183			20	16	0.8	0	177	111	63	1367	7.7	12	10– 6	1					35	51.3														
Frankie Filchock	TB-DB	23	5'11"	195	12		50	126	2.5	2	54	28	52	460	8.5	6	9–17																					
Roy Zimmerman	TB-FB-DB	22	6'2"	197			31	127	4.1	0	12	4	33	53	4.4	0	3–25						7	37														
Jimmy Johnston	FB-DB	23	6'1"	195	42		84	256	3.0	3									29	350	12	3	3	40														
Bob Seymour	FB-DB	24	6'2"	195	24		57	170	3.0	4									2	3	2	0																
Wilbur Moore	FB-WB-DB	24	5'11"	190	18		15	89	5.9	2									2	26	13	1																
Andy Farkas	FB-DB	24	5'10"	190			1	0	0.0	0																												
Dick Todd	WB-FB-DB	25	5'11"	165	54		76	408	5.4	4	1	1	100	7	7.0	0	0– 0		20	402	20	4	12	36										1				
Jim Meade	WB-DB	26	6'1"	198			48	115	2.4	0									4	39	10	0	9	40														
Ed Justice	WB-DB	27	6'1"	200	12		3	34	11.3	0									15	170	11	2																
Max Krause	BB-LB	31	5'10"	206			4	21	5.3	0																												
Ernie Pinckert	BB-LB	32	6'	205															2	27	14	0																
Bob Hoffman	BB-LB	22	6'1"	200			3	7	2.3	0																												
Ray Hare	BB-WB-LB-DB	22	6'1"	205			1	2	2.0	0																												
Wayne Millner	OE-DE	29	6'1"	190	18		3	31	10.3	0									22	233	11	3																
Charley Malone	OE-DE	30	6'4"	215															20	222	11	0																
Bob Masterson	OE-DE	25	6'1"	210	42		1	0	0.0	0									18	283	16	4			15	17	88	1	2	50								
Bob McChesney	OE-DE	28	6'2"	198	6														8	110	13	1																
Sandy Sanford	OE-DE	24	6'1"	210	3														1	13	13	0			3	4	75	0	2	0								
BROOKLYN DODGERS																																						
Ace Parker	TB-DB	28	6'	168	49	6	89	306	3.4	3	111	49	44	817	7.4	10	7– 6	2	3	139	46	2	49	38	19	22	86											
Dick Cassiano	TB-HB-DB	22	5'11"	175	12		35	84	2.4	0	30	9	30	128	4.3	1	2– 7		2	67	34	2																
George Cafego	TB-HB-DB	25	5'10"	180			41	109	2.7	0	17	7	41	105	6.2	1	2–12		9	105	12	0	1	18														
Bill Leckonby	TB-DB	22	6'1"	185	12		19	53	2.8	0	13	7	54	74	5.7	0	0– 0		1	8	8	1	2	27														
Ralph Kercheval	TB-DB	29	6'1"	185	15		11	19	1.7	0	7	4	57	38	5.4	1	0– 0		1	17	17	0	8	46	3	3	100	4	11	36								
Banks McFadden	HB-DB	23	6'2"	180	18		65	411	6.3	1	8	3	38	103	12.9	1	1–12		9	97	11	2																
Pug Manders	FB-DB	27	6'	212	36		80	311	3.9	5	1	0	0	0	0.0	0	0– 0		1	38	38	1																
Sam Francis	FB-DB	25	6'	207	6		44	217	4.9	1													16	45				0	1	0								
Frank Zadworney	HB-DB	23	6'	202			2	5	2.5	0																												
Rhoten Shetley	BB-LB	22	5'11"	200	6		7	30	4.3	0	4	1	25	2	0.5	0	1–25		8	126	16	1																
Ben Kish	BB-LB	23	6'	200															9	124	14	0	3	44														
Wendell Butcher	BB-LB	26	6'1"	200															2	21	11	0																
Perry Schwartz	OE-DE	25	6'2"	200	18														21	370	16	3																
Waddy Young	OE-DE	23	6'3"	205			1	1	1.0	0									7	85	12	0																
Herman Hodges	OE-DE	25	6'1"	195															3	38	13	0																
Bill Bailey	OE-DE	24	6'3"	205															1	12	12	0																
Harold Hill	OE-DE	24	6'1"	200															1	9	9	0																
NEW YORK GIANTS																																						
Eddie Miller	QB-DB	22	5'10"	165	6		65	206	3.2	1	73	35	48	505	6.9	3	7–10	6					19	39														
Kay Eakin	QB-DB	23	6'	183			14	20	1.4	0	43	17	40	199	4.6	0	3– 7						11	41														
Len Barnum	QB-FB-DB	27	6'	198	9		48	128	2.7	0	23	9	39	150	6.5	3	2– 9		1	15	15	0	39	40	6	7	86	1	4	25								
Grenny Landsdell	QB-DB	22	6'	190			7	9	1.3	0	3	2	67	23	7.7	1	0– 0																					
Tuffy Leemans	FB-DB	27	6'	195	6		132	474	3.6	1	31	15	48	159	5.1	2	3–10																					
Walt Nielsen	FB-DB	23	6'3"	220	6		73	269	3.7	1	1	0	0	0	0.0	0	0– 0		2	17	9	0	1	42														
Hank Soar	FB-DB	26	6'2"	207	12		80	246	3.1	1									4	36	9	1						0	1	0								
Dom Principe	FB-DB	23	6'	195			11	8	0.7	0																												
Ward Cuff	WB-DB	27	6'1"	185	42		15	86	5.7	1									13	220	17	1			9	9	100	5	8	63								
Leland Shaffer	WB-BB-DB	28	6'2"	202	18		7	20	2.9	1									15	121	8	2																
Nello Falaschi	BB-LB	26	6'	195															2	9	5	0																
Al Owen	BB-LB	27	6'	188			2	10	5.0	0									1	5	5	0																
Jack Hinkle	BB-LB	22	6'	190															3	23	8	0																
John McLaughry	BB-LB	23	6'1"	205															1	–1	–1	0																
Jim Lee Howell	OE-DE	25	6'6"	205	12														14	255	18	2																
Jim Poole	OE-DE	24	6'3"	217	18														10	156	16	3																
Chuck Gelatka	OE-DE	27	6'1"	182															6	56	9	0																
Max Harrison	OE-DE	24	6'1"	208															4	96	24	0																
Bolo Perdue	OE-DE	23	5'10"	207															2	28	14	0																
PITTSBURGH PIRATES																																						
Billy Patterson	TB-DB	22	5'10"	167			87	171	2.0	0	117	34	29	529	4.5	3	15–13	13					43	39														
Tommy Thompson	TB-HB-DB	24	6'1"	190			40	39	1.0	0	28	9	32	145	5.2	1	3–11		4	55	14	0																
Coley McDonough	TB-DB	25	6'1"	190	6		15	33	2.2	1	14	8	57	92	6.6	0	3–21						4	40														
Lou Tomasetti	HB-DB	24	6'	202	12		68	246	3.6	1	6	3	50	30	5.0	0	2–33		6	129	22	1																
George Kiick	FB-DB	23	6'	200			66	212	3.2	0	2	0	0	0	0.0	0	1–50		3	22	7	0																
Merl Condit	HB-DB	23	5'11"	195	6		52	205	3.9	0	15	2	13	33	2.2	0	2–13		4	30	8	1	12	38														
Swede Johnston	FB-DB	30	5'10"	205			41	113	2.8	0													8	40														
Boyd Brumbaugh	FB-DB	25	5'11"	195			32	79	2.5	0	7	2	29	46	6.6	0	1–14		1	0	0	0	6	32														
John Noppenberg	FB-OE-DB	22	6'	202			2	4	2.0	0									4	74	19	0	4	34														
Hank Bruder	BB-LB	32	6'	205															5	49	10	0																
Ev Fisher	BB-LB	25	5'11"	205															2	12	6	0																
George Platukas	OE-DE	25	6'	200	12														15	290	19	2																
Bill Sortet	OE-DE	28	6'1"	184															7	112	16	0																
Walt Kichefski	OE-DE	24	6'1"	210															4	26	7	0																
John Klumb (from CHIC)	OE-DE	23	6'3"	205															3	76	25	0																
Armand Niccolai	T	28	6'2"	230	24																				6	6	100	6	14	43								
PHILADELPHIA EAGLES																																						
Davey O'Brien	QB-DB	23	5'7"	151	6		100	–180	–1.8	1	277	124	45	1290	4.7	5	17– 6	5					6	41														
Foster Watkins	QB-DB	22	5'9"	160	2		14	–76	–5.4	0	85	28	33	565	6.6	1	3– 4	10							2	2	100											
Dick Riffle	HB-FB-DB	25	6'1"	197	30		81	238	2.9	4									8	58	7	1	14	34														
Elmer Hackney	FB-LB	24	6'2"	210	6		32	101	3.2	1									2	4	2	0																
Frank Emmons	FB-HB-LB	22	6'1"	213	12		29	77	2.7	1									3	19	6	1																
John Cole	FB-LB	25	5'9"	197	6		26	75	2.9	0									2	11	6	0	10	34	3	5	60	1	1	100								
Joe Bukant	FB-HB-LB	24	6'	220	6		18	50	2.8	1									1	13	13	0																
Jay Arnold	HB-DB	26	6'1"	213			3	9	3.0	0									7	145	21	0																
Franny Murray	HB-DB	24	6'	200	6		8	7	0.9	0									12	125	10	0	30	37	6	7	86	0	1	0								
Chuck Newton	HB-DB	23	6'	204															1	22	22	0																
Don Looney	OE-DB	22	6'2"	190	30		2	–4	–2.0	1									58	707	12	4																
Red Ramsey	OE-DE	25	6'	192															17	143	8	0																
Les McDonald (to DET)	OE-DE	25	6'4"	206			2	–2	–1.0	0									15	309	21	0																
Joe Carter	OE-DE	30	6'1"	200			1	–3	–3.0	0									12	201	18	0																
Joe Wendlick	OE-DE	24	6'	208															8	67	8	0																
Elmer Kolberg	OE-HB-DB	24	6'4"	198															6	43	7	0																
George Somers	T	24	6'2"	260	7																				1	1	100	2	9	22								

TEAM TOTALS	OFFENSE: FIRST DOWNS	RUSHING No.	Yds.	Avg. Yds.	TD	PASSING: Att.	Comp.	Comp. Pct.	Yds.	Yds/ Att.	Yds/ Comp.	TD	Int.	Pct. Int.	PUNT RETURNS Yds.	TD	KICKOFF RETURNS Yds.	TD	INT. RETURNS: No.	Yds.	Avg. Yds.	TD	PEN. Yds.	FUM. No.	POINTS: Total	PAT	FG Att.	FG Mde.	Saf	DEFENSE: Total Yards	Pass Att.	Pass Comp.	Comp Pct.	Oppos. Fumb. Rec.	Points	TEAM TOTALS
WASHINGTON	147	397	1402	3.5	15	244	144	59.0	1887	7.7	13.1	18	22	9.0	591	1	741	0	18	212	11.8	1	427	40	245	29	5	2	0	2847	287	125	43.6	9	142	WASHINGTON
BROOKLYN	115	394	1546	3.9	10	191	80	41.9	1267	6.6	15.8	14	13	6.8	408	0	793	1	18	287	15.9	0	285	23	186	22	12	4	1	2836	259	113	43.6	14	120	BROOKLYN
NEW YORK	127	454	1476	3.3	6	174	78	44.8	1036	6.0	13.3	9	15	8.6	448	0	282	0	23	224	9.7	0	349	28	131	15	13	6	1	2219	234	91	38.9	11	133	NEW YORK
PITTSBURGH	97	362	1102	3.0	2	189	58	30.7	875	5.2	15.1	4	27	14.3	441	0	843	0	8	62	7.8	0	336	26	60	6	14	6	0	2742	192	83	43.2	15	178	PITTSBURGH
PHILA.	122	317	298	0.9	9	362	152	42.0	1855	5.1	12.2	6	20	5.5	393	0	667	0	12	148	12.3	0	215	14	111	12	11	3	0	2780	151	80	53.0	13	211	PHILA.

CHICAGO BEARS 8-3-0 George Halas

Scores of Each Game		
41	Green Bay	10
7	Chic. Cards	21
21	Cleveland	14
7	DETROIT	0
16	BROOKLYN	7
37	New York	21
14	GREEN BAY	7
14	Detroit	17
3	Washington	7
47	CLEVELAND	25
31	CHIC. CARDS	23

Use Name	Pos.	Hgt	Wgt	Age	Int	Pts
Frank Bausch	C-LB	6'2"	225	32		
Chet Chesney	C-LB	6'2"	227	23		
Bulldog Turner	C-LB	6'1"	235	21		
Young Bussey	DB	5'9"	183	22		

Use Name – Tackles	Pos.	Hgt	Wgt	Age	Int	Pts
Lee Artoe	T	6'3"	218	24		4
(1 PAT in 2 attempts, 1 FG in 1 attempt)						
Ed Kolman	T	6'2"	225	22		
Joe Mihal	T	6'3"	230	24		
Joe Stydahar	T	6'4"	230	28		
John Torrance	T	6'3"	285	27		

Use Name – Guards	Pos.	Hgt	Wgt	Age	Int	Pts
Al Baisi	G	6'	215	22		
Ray Bray	G	6'	224	23		
Aldo Forte	G	6'	210	22		
Danny Fortmann	G-LB	6'	210	24		
Phil Martinovich	G	5'10"	220	25		6
(2 field goals in 2 attempts)						
George Musso	G	6'2"	270	30		

When Bert Bell looked at the pre-season roster, he said, "Nobody's going to beat the Bears. They're the greatest team ever assembled." Bell's remarks were prompted by an exceptional class of rookies which had transformed the Bears into the class of the league. One freshman was George McAfee, an explosive open-field runner who broke a 93-yard kickoff return in his first pro game. The others included end Ken Kavanaugh, tackles Lee Artoe and Ed Kolman, and center Bulldog Turner—a ferocious blocker and tackler who was as quick as he was big. Add these newcomers to veterans Luckman, Stydahar, Fortmann, Osmanski, Nolting, Maniaci, Musso, and Wilson, and the West had a new champion.

The Bears did lose three games, though, the last one a 7-3 defeat at Washington. After the game, Redskin owner George Marshall called the Bears "quitters" and "crybabies"—remarks he would later regret.

GREEN BAY PACKERS 6-4-1 Curly Lambeau

Scores of Each Game		
27	PHILADELPHIA	20
10	CHIC. BEARS	41
31	CHIC. CARDS	6
31	CLEVELAND	14
14	DETROIT	23
24	PITTSBURGH	3
7	Chic. Bears	14
28	Chic. Cards	7
3	New York	7
50	Detroit	7
13	Cleveland	13

Use Name	Pos.	Hgt	Wgt	Age	Int	Pts
Charley Brock	C-LB	6'2"	205	24		
Tom Greenfield	C-LB	6'4"	218	22		
George Svendsen	C-LB	6'4"	240	25		
George Seeman	OE-DE	6'1"	195	22		
Dick Weisgerber	BB-DE	5'10"	194	25		
(1 reception for 37 yds.)						

Use Name – Tackles	Pos.	Hgt	Wgt	Age	Int	Pts
Leo Disend	T	6'2"	224	24		
Paul Kell	T	6'2"	217	23		
Bill Lee	T	6'2"	235	28		
Baby Ray	T	6'6"	248	25		
Charlie Schultz	T	6'3"	230	23		
Champ Seibold	T	6'4"	246	27		

Use Name – Guards	Pos.	Hgt	Wgt	Age	Int	Pts
Tiny Engebretsen	G	6'1"	245	30		11
(8 PAT's in 8 attempts, 1 FG in 5 attempts)						
Buckets Goldenberg	G-LB	5'10"	225	29		
Smiley Johnson	G-LB	5'9"	200	29		
Russ Letlow	G	6'	215	26		
Lou Midler	G	6'1"	220	25		
Pete Tinsley	G-LB	5'8"	214	27		
Gust Zarnas	G	5'10"	225	25		

When the Chicago Bears trounced the Packers 41-10 to open their season, Green Bay fans knew that when 1941 rolled around they would no longer be the West's defending champions. The Packers still were a rugged team but unfortunately not as rugged as George Halas' powerhouse. After losses to the Lions, Bears again, and Giants, owner-coach Curly Lambeau became convinced that his team needed a body-building course before they could overtake the Bears.

But nothing was wrong with Don Hutson's body, as he bounced back from last year's knee injury to lead the NFL in scoring. The quick end found most of his passes coming from Cecil Isbell, with Arnie Herber getting less playing time at tailback. The same solid supporting cast filled the Green Bay line and backfield, with Clarke Hinkle and Russ Letlow shining especially bright to give the Packers a respectable but frustrating role as runners-up.

DETROIT LIONS 5-5-1 Potsy Clark

Scores of Each Game		
0	Chic. Cards at Buffalo	0
7	PITTSBURGH	10
6	CLEVELAND	0
43	CHIC. CARDS	14
0	Chic. Bears	7
23	Green Bay	14
14	WASHINGTON	20
0	Cleveland	24
17	CHIC. BEARS	14
21	Philadelphia	0
7	GREEN BAY	50

Use Name	Pos.	Hgt	Wgt	Age	Int	Pts
Tony Calvelli	C-LB	5'10"	190	24		6
Sam Tsoutsouvas	C-LB	6'	205	22		
Alex Wojciechowicz	C-LB	5'11"	200	25		6
Glenn Morris	OE-DE	6'	200	28		
Voluntarily retired – Paul Szakash						

Use Name – Tackles	Pos.	Hgt	Wgt	Age	Int	Pts
Clem Crabtree	T-G	6'3"	220	21		
Tony Furst	T	6'1"	220	22		
Johnny Hackenbruck	T	6'2"	215	25		
Jack Johnson	T	6'4"	220	30		6
(1 reception for 48 yds. touchdown)						
Steve Maronic	T	6'	225	24		
(Missed 1 field goal attempt)						
Bill Rogers	T	5'11"	240	27		
Harry Smith	T	5'11"	215	22		

Use Name – Guards	Pos.	Hgt	Wgt	Age	Int	Pts
Bill Feldhaus	G-LB	6'	225	28		
Bill Radovich	G	5'10"	225	25		
Harry Speelman	G	5'11"	220	24		
Cal Thomas	G	6'2"	210	25		
John Wiethe	G-LB	6'	195	27		

After being tipped off about an unheralded college center, owner George Richards ordered coach Gus Henderson to pick Bulldog Turner of Hardin-Simmons as Detroit's first draft choice. Richards then slipped Turner some money and free dental treatment to tell all other teams that he wasn't interested in pro football. But on the day of the draft, Henderson inexplicably named Doyle Nave of USC as his first pick, and George Halas promptly claimed Turner. Richards fired Henderson, who then revealed Richards' secret wooing of Turner. The league fined Richards $5,000, and he promptly sold the team to Fred Mandel and got out of pro football.

Although Nave didn't make the team, Mandel got Whizzer White, back from a year at Oxford, to play for the Lions. Preparing to enter Yale Law School, White led the NFL in rushing on a Detroit club that had few other good players.

CLEVELAND RAMS 4-6-1 Dutch Clark

Scores of Each Game		
21	PHILADELPHIA	13
0	Detroit	6
14	CHIC. BEARS	21
14	Green Bay	31
26	CHIC. CARDS	14
7	Chic. Cards	17
24	DETROIT	0
13	New York	0
14	Brooklyn	29
25	Chic. Bears	47
13	GREEN BAY	13

Use Name	Pos.	Hgt	Wgt	Age	Int	Pts
Bill Conkright	C-LB	6'1"	204	26		
Shag Goolsby	C-LB	6'2"	195	23		
Jack Haman	C-LB	6'1"	210	22		6
(1 reception for 5 yds.)						
Hank Rockwell	C-G-LB	6'4"	225	23		6
(1 rush for 5 yds., 1 reception for 5 yd. TD)						
Connie Mack Berry	OE-DE	6'3"	210	24		
Mike Kinek	OE-DE	6'1"	200	23		
Ham Murphy	OE-DE	5'10"	194	23		
Jack Nix	WB-DB	6'	175	23		
Glenn Olson	BB-DB	6'	195	24		

Use Name – Tackles	Pos.	Hgt	Wgt	Age	Int	Pts
Stan Anderson	T	6'2"	220	22		
Boyd Clay	T	6'1"	215	27		
(Missed 1 field goal attempt)						
Elwyn Dunstan	T	6'3"	235	25		
(1 rush for 4 yds.)						
Ted Livingston	T	6'3"	222	26		
Fred Shirey (from GB)	T	6'2"	225	24		

Use Name – Guards	Pos.	Hgt	Wgt	Age	Int	Pts
Pete Gudauskas	G-LB	6'2"	210	23		1
(1 PAT in 3 attempts)						
Riley Matheson	G-LB	6'2"	208	25		
Barney McGarry	G-LB	6'1"	205	22		
Ralph Stevenson	G-LB	5'10"	196	22		

When the Rams opened the season with a 21-13 victory over the Eagles, Cleveland fans expected the good showing of late 1939 to continue. But the Lions ended the spell, 16-0. The Bears and Packers then took on the Rams and dispelled whatever title hopes existed. With the Rams exposed as bogus contenders, the river of paying customers dried up, and the red ink began flowing in the front office—as even with back-to-back shutouts of the Lions and Giants later in the season, it was too late to rekindle the high hopes and enthusiasm of the fans.

For the most part, Johnny Drake and Parker Hall entertained the small audiences that remained loyal. Drake made All-Pro with his determined running, and Hall, a tailback, gave the rooters a treat with his passing, running, and punting.

CHICAGO CARDINALS 2-7-2 Jimmy Conzelman

Scores of Each Game		
7	Pittsburgh	7
0	DETROIT at Buffalo	0
21	CHIC. BEARS	7
6	Green Bay	31
14	Detroit	43
21	Washington	28
14	Cleveland	26
17	CLEVELAND	7
7	GREEN BAY	28
9	Brooklyn	14
23	Chic. Bears	31

Use Name	Pos.	Hgt	Wgt	Age	Int	Pts
Ki Aldrich	C-LB	6'	195	24		
Andy Chisick	C-LB	6'1"	205	23		
Rex Williams	C-LB	6'2"	195	24		
Keith Ranspot	OE-DE	6'3"	205	25		
Ev Elkins	WB-DB	5'11"	190	22		
Jimmy German	TB-DB	6'	180	23		
Herm Schneidman	BB-LB	5'11"	200	26		

Use Name – Tackles	Pos.	Hgt	Wgt	Age	Int	Pts
Conway Baker	T	5'11"	225	28		
Ed Beinor	T-DE	6'2"	230	22		
Tony Blazine	T	6'	230	28		
Ray Busler	T	6'1"	220	24		
Bill Davis	T	6'1"	235	23		
Bobby Wood	T	6'2"	230	24		
Joel Mason – American Football League						

Use Name – Guards	Pos.	Hgt	Wgt	Age	Int	Pts
Frank Huffman	G-LB	6'2"	205	25		
Joe Kuharich	G-LB	5'11"	195	23		
(Missed 1 field goal attempt)						
Bill Murphy	G	6'	205	26		
Rupert Pate	G	6'1"	205	23		
Andy Sabados	G	5'11"	210	23		
Tarzan White	G	5'9"	220	24		

With witty Jimmy Conzelman taking over as head coach, the Cardinals went into the season a loose if not a powerful team. With end Gaynell Tinsley back in action and Hugh McCullough the new tailback, the relaxed Cardinals tied the Pirates and Lions in their first two games before moving on to Comiskey Park and the Bears.

Conzelman wanted nothing better than to beat his friendly rival George Halas, and the Cardinals took the lead by driving to a quick touchdown. A little later, rookie Lloyd Madden took a handoff on a reverse and broke into the clear. Forgetting that pro goal posts are planted on the goal line and not behind the end zone, Madden quit running around the 10-yard line and was quickly tackled. But despite the mental error, the Cardinals went on to a 21-7 victory over their powerful neighbors—a great and lasting triumph in the face of the fact that Conzelman and company would win only one more game all year.

Use Name – Backs & Ends	Pos.	Age	Hgt	Wgt	Pts	Int	Rushing No.	Rushing Yds	Rushing Avg	Rushing TD	Passing Att	Passing Comp	Passing %	Passing Yds	Passing Yd/Att	Passing TD	Passing Int–%	Passing RK	Receiving No.	Receiving Yds	Receiving Avg	Receiving TD	Punting No.	Punting Avg	Kicking Pat	Kicking Att	Kicking %	Kicking FG	Kicking Att	Kicking %	Punt Returns No.	Punt Returns Yds	Punt Returns Avg	Punt Returns TD	Kickoff Returns No.	Kickoff Returns Yds	Kickoff Returns Avg	Kickoff Returns TD
CHICAGO BEARS																																						
Sid Luckman	QB-DB	23	6'	197			23	−65	−2.8	0	105	48	46	941	9.0	4	9– 9	4					27	42														
Bernie Masterson	QB-DB	29	6'3"	195	7		10	−7	−0.7	1	23	9	39	212	9.2	2	3– 13								1	1	100											
Bob Snyder	QB-DB	27	6'	205	7		7	12	1.7	0	22	5	23	145	6.6	1	1– 5						5	35	4	6	67	1	4	25								
Solly Sherman	QB-DB	22	6'1"	190			8	10	1.3	0	4	1	25	15	3.8	1	0– 0																					
Ray Nolting	HB-DB	26	5'11"	185	12		78	373	4.8	1	2	1	50	38	19.0	0	0– 0		3	36	12	0	2	34														1
Joe Maniaci	FB-LB	26	6'1"	210	19		84	368	4.4	2									1	−5	−5	0			1	1	100											
Gary Famiglietti	FB-HB-LB	25	6'	214	24		93	320	3.4	4									1	11	11	0																
Harry Clark	HB-DB	22	6'	180	18		56	258	4.6	2	3	0	0	0	0.0	0	2– 67		3	80	27	0	1	30														
George McAfee	HB-DB	22	6'	182	18		47	253	5.4	2	11	4	36	50	4.5	2	0– 0		7	117	17	0	22	39														1
Bill Osmanski	FB-LB	23	5'11"	197	18		50	192	3.8	3									1	13	13	0																
Bob Swisher	HB-DB	26	5'11"	165			15	70	4.7	0	1	0	0	0	0.0	0	0– 0		2	106	53	0																
Jack Manders	HB-DB	31	6'	200	23		8	20	2.5	0															17	18	95	2	3	67								
Ray McLean	HB-DB	24	5'10"	168	25		14	10	0.7	1									6	138	23	2			1	1	100 (reception)							1				
Ken Kavanaugh	OE-DE	23	6'3"	205	18														12	276	23	3																
Dick Plasman	OE-DE	26	6'3"	210	15														11	245	22	2			3	3	100											
Eggs Manske	OE-DE	27	6'	185															6	81	14	0																
Bob Nowaskey	OE-DE	22	6'	205	12		1	4	4.0	0									5	105	21	2																
George Wilson	OE-DE	26	6'1"	190	6														4	90	23	1																
John Siegal	OE-DE	22	6'1"	205	6														4	53	13	0																
Hamp Pool	OE-DE	25	6'3"	215															2	55	28	0																
GREEN BAY PACKERS																																						
Cecil Isbell	TB-DB	25	6'1"	190	24		97	270	2.8	4	150	68	45	1037	6.9	9	12– 8	3					2	32														
Arnie Herber	TB-DB	30	5'11"	208			6	−23	−3.8	0	89	38	43	560	6.3	5	7– 8	7					13	39														
Hal Van Every	TB-HB-DB	22	6'	195			38	154	4.1	0	41	12	29	199	4.9	4	6– 15		4	41	10	0	17	36														
Clarke Hinkle	FB-LB	30	5'11"	200	48		109	383	3.5	2									4	28	7	1	22	37	3	3	100	9	14	64								
Andy Uram	HB-DB	25	5'10"	188	19		71	270	3.8	1									10	188	19	2			1	2	50											
Ed Jankowski	FB-LB	27	5'9"	205	12		48	211	4.4	2																												
Harry Buhler	FB-HB-LB-DB	23	6'2"	210			36	118	3.3	0									1	17	17	0																
Frank Balasz	FB-LB	22	6'2"	213	6		25	107	4.3	1	1	0	0	0	0.0	0	1–100		1	7	7	0																
Lou Brock	HB-DB	22	6'	205			18	60	3.3	0	2	0	0	0	0.0	0	0– 0		5	97	19	0	3	42														
Joe Laws	HB-DB	29	5'9"	186	6		7	21	3.0	0									5	60	12	1																
Beattie Feathers	HB-DB	32	5'10"	190			4	19	4.8	0																												
Larry Craig	BB-DE	24	6'1"	206			3	9	3.0	0									6	67	11	0																
Bob Adkins	BB-LB-DE	23	6'1"	210	13		1	5	5.0	0									4	73	18	1			1	1	100	0	1	0								
Don Hutson	OE-DB	27	6'1"	185	57	6													45	664	15	7			15	16	94											
Moose Mulleneaux	OE-DE	23	6'3"	205	42														16	288	18	6																
Ray Riddick	OE-DE	22	6'1"	210															11	148	13	0																
Dick Evans	OE-DB	23	6'3"	195															2	40	20	0																
Harry Jacunski	OE-DE	24	6'2"	198															2	29	15	0																
Milt Gantenbein	OE-DE	30	6'	195															1	12	12	0																
DETROIT LIONS																																						
Whizzer White	TB-FB-DB	23	6'1"	190	32		146	514	3.5	5	80	35	44	461	5.8	0	11– 14	11	4	55	14	0	52	41	2	3	67	0	1	0								
Cotton Price	TB-DB	21	6'1"	185	16		42	122	2.9	2	66	33	50	456	6.9	3	7– 11	8					9	41	4	6	67											
Dwight Sloan	TB-DB	25	5'10"	180			58	225	3.9	0	46	18	39	260	5.7	0	8– 17						2	27														
Howie Weiss	FB-LB	23	6'	210	24		79	298	3.8	3									4	56	14	0																
Bill Shepherd	FB-DB	28	5'9"	205			24	67	2.8	0									2	12	6	0	1	40														
Lloyd Cardwell	WB-DB	27	6'2"	200	18		48	186	3.9	2	1	0	0	0	0.0	0	0– 0		20	349	17	1																
Rip Ryan	WB-FB-DB	25	6'2"	195		6	22	42	1.9	0	2	0	0	0	0.0	0	0– 0		9	96	11	0	9	39														
Jack Morlock	WB-DB	23	5'10"	165			1	0	0.0	0																												
Fred Vanzo	BB-LB	24	6'2"	230			1	−1	−1.0	0									7	75	11	0																
Bill Callihan	BB-DB	24	6'3"	210															4	38	10	0																
Paul Moore	BB-LB	22	5'9"	210	6		2	4	2.0	0									4	29	7	1																
Chuck Hanneman	OE-DE	25	6'	212	16														14	228	16	0			10	10	100	2	4	50								
Dave Diehl	OE-DE	21	6'	190	6														12	131	11	0																
Stillman Rouse	OE-DE	23	6'2"	205			2	0	0.0	0									2	17	9	0																
Butch Morse	OE-DE	27	6'2"	195															1	13	13	0																
Bill Fisk	OE-DE	23	6'	190			2	0	0.0	0									1	10	10	0																
CLEVELAND RAMS																																						
Parker Hall	TB-DB	23	6'	205	6		94	365	3.9	1	183	77	42	1108	6.1	6	16– 9	9					57	43														
Marty Slovak	TB-DB	23	5'9"	182	6		53	129	2.4	1	28	17	61	234	8.4	1	4– 14																					
Ken Heineman	TB-DB	22	5'9"	170	1		6	−5	−0.8	0	8	3	38	74	9.3	1	1– 12						2	32	1	1	100											
Jim Gillette	TB-DB	22	6'1"	185			1	1	1.0	0	4	0	0	0	0.0	0	2– 50																					
Fred Gehrke	TB-DB	22	5'11"	180							1	0	0	0	0.0	0	0– 0		1	−2	−2	0																
Johnny Drake	FB-DB-LB	24	6'1"	214	56		134	480	3.6	9	4	2	50	16	4.0	2	0– 0		8	81	10	0			2	6	25	0	1	0								
Len Janiak	FB-DB	24	6'1"	210			19	44	2.3	0									1	3	3	0	1	30														
Ollie Cordill	WB-DB	24	6'2"	190	12		24	73	3.0	0									14	158	11	2	5	45														
Dante Magnani	WB-DB	23	5'10"	183	6		7	19	2.7	0									11	119	11	1																
Vic Spadaccini	BB-DB	24	6'	225	23						1	0	0	0	0.0	0	0– 0		22	276	13	2			5	5	100											
Gaylon Smith	BB-TB-LB	24	5'11"	205			19	18	0.9	0	18	10	56	150	8.3	2	2– 11		3	65	22	0	11	36														
Earl Crowder	BB-LB	24	6'	198															2	33	17	0																
Mike Rodak	BB-LB	23	5'10"	196			1	4	4.0	0																												
Jim Benton	OE-DE	23	6'3"	197	18		1	0	0.0	0									22	351	16	3																
Paul McDonough	WB-OE-DE	23	6'4"	223	6		2	5	2.5	0									12	315	26	1																
Johnny Wilson	OE-DE	24	6'3"	200	6														7	93	13	1																
Maury Patt	OE-DE	26	6'2"	202	6		1	0	0.0	0									2	52	26	1																
Chet Adams	T-OE-DE	24	6'3"	228	10														2	28	14	0			7	10	70	1	5	20								
CHICAGO CARDINALS																																						
Hugh McCullough	TB-DB	24	6'	185	19		52	278	5.3	3	116	43	37	529	4.6	4	21– 18	12					30	40	1	3	33	0	1	0								
Beryl Clark	TB-DB	22	6'	200	3		39	9	0.2	0	58	25	43	316	5.4	2	6– 10		1	20	20	0	28	33	3	3	100											
Bob Kellogg	TB-DB	23	5'10"	175			9	31	3.4	0	18	6	33	42	2.3	0	4– 22						2	27														
Marshall Goldberg	FB-TB-DB	22	5'11"	188	18		87	325	3.7	2	2	0	0	0	0.0	0	0– 0		2	29	15	1	1	47														
Mario Tonelli	FB-DB	23	5'11"	200	6		51	148	2.9	1									5	53	11	0	1	15														
Milt Popovich	FB-DB	23	5'11"	190			41	138	3.4	0									5	32	6	0	5	42														
Marty Christiansen	FB-DB	23	6'	200	6		32	71	2.2	1																												
John Hall	WB-DB	23	6'	195	30		39	88	2.3	1	3	0	0	0	0.0	0	2– 67		4	111	28	2																1
Lloyd Madden	WB-DB	21	6'1"	195	18		29	186	6.4	2									4	90	23	1																
Buddy Parker	BB-LB	26	6'	195	9		6	8	1.3	1									6	45	8	0			3	3	100	0	1	0								
Bert Johnson	BB-LB	28	6'	210			6	15	2.5	0	1	1	100	25	25.0	0	0– 0		2	52	26	0	1	19														
Lou Zontini	BB-LB	23	5'9"	180	16		1	1	1.0	0													2	46	10	10	100	2	5	40								
Gus Tinsley	OE-DE	24	6'2"	205	6		1	17	17.0	0									16	165	10	1																
Al Coppage	OE-DE	24	6'1"	195	6														15	163	11	1																
John Shirk	OE-DE	22	6'4"	200															11	91	8	0																
Pop Ivy (from PIT)	OE-DE	24	6'3"	200															2	32	16	0																
Bill Dewell	OE-DE	23	6'4"	205															2	29	15	0																

TEAM TOTALS	OFFENSE: First Downs	Rushing: No.	Rushing: Yds.	Rushing: Avg. Yds.	Rushing: TD	Passing: Att.	Passing: Comp.	Passing: Comp. Pct.	Passing: Yds.	Passing: Yds/Att.	Passing: Yds/Comp.	Passing: TD	Passing: Int.	Passing: Pct. Int.	Punt Returns Yds.	Punt Returns TD	Kickoff Returns Yds.	Kickoff Returns TD	Int. Returns: No.	Int. Returns: Yds.	Int. Returns: Avg. Yds.	Int. Returns: TD	Pen. Yds	Fum. No.	Points: Total	Points: PAT	Points: FG Att.	Points: FG Mde.	Points: Saf	DEFENSE: Total Yards	Pass Att.	Pass Comp.	Comp. Pct.	Oppos. Fumb. Rec.	Points	TEAM TOTALS
CHI. BEARS	141	494	1818	3.7	16	171	68	39.8	1401	8.2	20.6	10	15	8.8	500	1	798	2	27	271	10.0	2	605	35	238	28	10	6	0	2750	269	133	49.4	11	152	CHI. BEARS
GREEN BAY	154	463	1604	3.5	10	283	118	41.7	1796	6.3	15.2	18	26	9.2	494	0	381	0	40	414	10.4	1	295	21	238	28	20	10	0	2532	252	98	38.9	7	155	GREEN BAY
DETROIT	133	427	1457	3.4	12	195	86	44.1	1177	6.0	13.7	3	26	13.3	300	0	714	0	29	298	10.3	2	259	27	138	16	6	2	1	2357	177	77	43.5	20	153	DETROIT
CLEVELAND	113	364	1142	3.1	11	247	109	44.1	1582	6.4	14.5	12	25	10.1	349	0	655	0	25	306	12.2	2	260	26	171	16	7	1	1	3102	247	99	40.1	14	191	CLEVELAND
CHI. CARDS	112	393	1315	3.3	11	198	75	37.9	912	4.6	12.2	6	33	16.7	346	0	632	1	23	389	16.9	1	331	23	139	17	8	2	1	2783	186	69	37.1	19	222	CHI.CARDS

Scores of Each Game		

Use Name	Pos.	Hgt	Wgt	Age	Int	Pts

Use Name – Tackles	Pos.	Hgt	Wgt	Age	Int	Pts

Use Name – Guards	Pos.	Hgt	Wgt	Age	Int	Pts

NEW YORK GIANTS 8-3-0 Steve Owen

24	Philadelphia	0
17	Washington	10
37	Pittsburgh	10
16	PHILADELPHIA	0
28	PITTSBURGH	7
13	Brooklyn	16
7	CHIC. CARDS	10
20	DETROIT	13
49	CLEVELAND	14
20	WASHINGTON	13
7	BROOKLYN	21

Use Name	Pos.	Hgt	Wgt	Age	Int	Pts
Lou DeFilippo	C-LB	6'1"	225	25		
Chet Gladchuk	C-T-LB	6'4"	245	24	1	
Mel Hein	C-LB	6'2"	230	32	1	
Kayo Lunday	C-G-LB	6'3"	215	28	1	
Dick Horne	DE	6'2"	212	23		
Don Vosberg	OE-DE	6'2"	188	21		

injured – Ed Widseth (broken leg)

Use Name – Tackles	Pos.	Hgt	Wgt	Age	Int	Pts
Tony Blazine	T	6'	240	29		
Frank Cope	T	6'2"	226	25		6
John Mellus	T	6'	220	24		
Win Pederson	T	6'3"	220	26	1	3
(1 field goal in 1 attempt)						

Al Owen – American Football League

Use Name – Guards	Pos.	Hgt	Wgt	Age	Int	Pts
Monk Edwards	G-T-LB	6'3"	210	21		
Doug Oldershaw	G-DE-LB	6'	195	26	1	6
Ben Sohn	G	6'2"	220	22		
Orville Tuttle	G	5'9"	215	28		
Len Younce	G-LB	6'1"	205	24	2	

With the Eastern Division championship already won, the Giants closed out their regular season by facing the Brooklyn Dodgers in the Polo Grounds on December 7. During the first half the public-address announcer urgently called out, "All armed forces personnel are requested to report to their commands immediately. Repeat . . ." Finally, at half time, the Giants heard the news of Pearl Harbor over the radio. They finished the game by losing in what turned out to be an insignificant contest in the face of all that was to come.

Soon to be broken up by the military draft, this Giant team rebounded from an off year to reassert its claim on the Eastern crown. Rookie backs Len Eshmont and Andy Manefos took some of the rushing burden off veteran Tuffy Leemans' shoulders, and freshman Len Younce helped John Mellus, Monk Edwards, Mel Hein, and the other linemen.

BROOKLYN DODGERS 7-4-0 Jock Sutherland

14	DETROIT	7
24	Philadelphia	13
0	Washington	3
7	Green Bay	30
6	CHIC. CARDS	20
16	NEW YORK	13
15	PHILADELPHIA	6
13	WASHINGTON	7
7	Pittsburgh	14
35	PITTSBURGH	7
21	New York	7

Use Name	Pos.	Hgt	Wgt	Age	Int	Pts
Ray Frick	C-LB	6'1"	205	22		
Joe Koons	C-LB	6'2"	195	24		
Tom Robertson	C-LB	6'	215	24		
Bud Svendsen	C-LB	6'1"	195	26	1	
(1 punt return for 2 yds.)						
Si Titus	C-LB-DE	6'	195	22	2	
Russ Cotton	BB-LB	6'2"	197	26		

Use Name – Tackles	Pos.	Hgt	Wgt	Age	Int	Pts
Pete Dobrus	T	6'	215	24		
Andy Fronczek	T	6'	200	24		
Mike Jurich	T	6'1"	225	22		
Bruiser Kinard	T	6'1"	218	26		9
(3 PAT's in 5 attempts)						
Frank Kristufek	T	6'	208	25		
Walt Merrill	T	6'2"	215	24		

Use Name – Guards	Pos.	Hgt	Wgt	Age	Int	Pts
Warren Alfson	G-LB	6'	198	26	2	
George Kinard	G-LB	6'1"	195	24		
Steve Petro	G-LB	5'10"	190	26		
Jim Sivell	G	5'9"	210	27		

The Dodgers enjoyed beating the local rival Giants twice during the year, but the Giants laughed last by finishing in first place ahead of Brooklyn. While the Giants lost only one other game besides the Brooklyn matches, the Dodgers dropped decisions to the Packers, Cardinals, Pirates, and Redskins to leave coach Jock Sutherland's boys one game away from the Eastern crown. Four young veterans pumped the life blood into the team. Tackle Bruiser Kinard held the line together and made up for his unimposing 218-pound frame by hitting often and hitting hard. End Perry Schwartz caught passes on offense and rushed passers on defense. Fullback Pug Manders cracked into enough holes narrowly to edge out George McAfee for the NFL rushing title, and the glue uniting all the parts was supplied by Ace Parker, the premier passer, runner, punter, defensive back, and team leader.

WASHINGTON REDSKINS 6-5-0 Ray Flaherty

10	NEW YORK	17
3	BROOKLYN	0
24	Pittsburgh	20
21	Philadelphia	17
17	CLEVELAND	13
23	PITTSBURGH	3
7	Brooklyn	13
21	Chic. Bears	35
13	New York	20
17	GREEN BAY	22
20	PHILADELPHIA	14

Use Name	Pos.	Hgt	Wgt	Age	Int	Pts
Ki Aldrich	C-LB	6'	215	25	2	7
(4 PAT's in 5 attempts, 1 FG in 3 attempts)						
Vic Carroll	C-G-LB	6'4"	230	28	2	6
(1 reception for 31 yds.)						
George Smith	C-LB	6'2"	222	27		
Bob Titchenal	C-DE-LB	6'2"	195	23	2	
Ken Dow	FB-DB	5'10"	198	22		

Use Name – Tackles	Pos.	Hgt	Wgt	Age	Int	Pts
Jim Barber	T	6'3"	235	29		
Fred Davis	T	6'3"	240	23		
Jim Stuart	T	6'	212	22		
Willie Wilkin	T	6'4"	260	25		
Bill Young	T	6'1"	255	27		

Use Name – Guards	Pos.	Hgt	Wgt	Age	Int	Pts
Dick Farman	G	6'	225	27		
Clyde Shugart	G	6'1"	220	24		
Steve Slivinski	G	5'10"	215	24	1	
Clem Stralka	G	5'10"	215	27		

With fullback Andy Farkas back from a knee injury and center Ki Aldrich obtained in a trade with the Cardinals, the Redskins looked stronger than last year. But a 17-10 opening-game loss to New York raised some doubts and rekindled the rumor that the team had not overcome the beating suffered at the hands of the Bears in the 1940 championship game. Although the Skins laughed at such suggestions and came back to win five in a row, Brooklyn upset them 13-7, the Bears soundly beat them 35-21, and the Giants and Packers edged out close victories to leave only thoughts of next year.

Prime in the Skins' attack was Sammy Baugh, who had some hard luck passing but managed to lead the league in punting as a result of his unexpected quick kicks, a line-drive punt on third down which often caught the defense flat-footed.

PHILADELPHIA EAGLES 2-8-1 Greasy Neale

0	NEW YORK	24
10	Pittsburgh	7
13	BROOKLYN	24
0	New York	16
17	WASHINGTON	21
21	CHIC. CARDS	14
6	Brooklyn	15
7	PITTSBURGH	7
17	Detroit	21
14	CHIC. BEARS	49
14	Washington	20

Use Name	Pos.	Hgt	Wgt	Age	Int	Pts
Frank Bausch	C-LB	6'2"	225	33		
Bob Bjorklund	C-LB	6'2"	225	23		
Bernie Feibish	C-LB	6'2"	223	23	1	
Lyle Graham	C-LB	6'3"	210	25	2	
Gran Harrison	DE	6'3"	212	24		

Use Name – Tackles	Pos.	Hgt	Wgt	Age	Int	Pts
John Eibner	T	6'2"	220	25		
Joe Frank	T	6'1"	220	26		
Phil Regazzo	T	6'	223	26		
Vic Sears	T	6'3"	208	23		
Cecil Sturgeon	T	6'2"	254	22		
Burr West	T	6'1"	220	22		

Use Name – Guards	Pos.	Hgt	Wgt	Age	Int	Pts
Tony Cemore	G	6'	210	24	1	
Enio Conti	G	5'11"	200	28		
(1 rush for –1 yd.)						
Dave diFilippo	G	5'10"	210	24		
Ralph Fritz	G	5'9"	202	23		
Woody Gerber	G	6'	225	21		
Bob Suffridge	G	6'	190	26		

The Philadelphia and Pittsburgh franchises were passed around during the off season like hot potatoes. Art Rooney started the ball rolling by selling the Pirates to Alexis Thompson in December and then buying a half interest in the Eagles from his friend Bert Bell. In April, Thompson mentioned a preference for a Philadelphia franchise, and Rooney, eager to return to Pittsburgh, talked Bell into swapping franchises.

Thompson started his Philadelphia tenure by hiring Greasy Neale, a long-time college coach, and Neale installed Tommy Thompson as his T-formation quarterback. Blind in one eye, Thompson was an uncanny long passer and a strong leader on a team almost totally comprised of rookies.

PITTSBURGH STEELERS 1-9-1 Bert Bell, Buff Donelli, Walt Kiesling

14	Cleveland	17
7	PHILADELPHIA	10
10	NEW YORK	37
20	WASHINGTON	24
7	New York	28
7	Chic. Bears	34
3	Washington	23
7	Philadelphia	7
14	BROOKLYN	7
7	GREEN BAY	54
7	Brooklyn	35

Use Name	Pos.	Hgt	Wgt	Age	Int	Pts
Chuck Cherundolo	C-LB	6'1"	210	25	1	
Moose Harper	C-LB	6'4"	235	27		
John Schiechl	C-LB	6'2"	232	24	1	
Dick Dolly	OE-DE	6'3"	210	23		
(1 rush for 2 yds.)						

Use Name – Tackles	Pos.	Hgt	Wgt	Age	Int	Pts
Joe Coomer	T	6'6"	265	22		
Ted Doyle	T	6'2"	222	27		
Royal Kahler	T	6'2"	225	23		
George Somers	T	6'2"	250	25		
(Missed 2 field goal attempts)						
John Woudenberg	T	6'3"	235	23		

Use Name – Guards	Pos.	Hgt	Wgt	Age	Int	Pts
Dick Bassi	G	5'11"	225	26		
(1 reception for 6 yds.)						
Carl Nery	G	6'	215	24		
Jack Sanders	G	6'	227	24		5
(5 PAT's in 5 attempts)						
Elbie Schultz	G	6'4"	245	23		
Don Williams	G	5'8"	210	22		

When Art Rooney sold the Pirates to Alexis Thompson after the 1940 season, he soon felt an itch to get back to the Steel City, and a complicated franchise swap saw Thompson get the Eagles and Rooney and Bert Bell wind up as co-owners of the newly renamed Steelers. Never again would Rooney wash his hands of Pittsburgh pro football. With Bell handling the coaching reigns, Rooney watched a pre-season workout for a few minutes, turned to a bystander, and sneered, "Well, we've got a new team, a new coach, a new nickname, and new uniforms, but they look like the same old Pirates to me." The bystander turned out to be a reporter, and Rooney's remarks made big news in the papers. With team morale undercut, Bell handed the coaching duties over to Buff Donelli after two games, but Walt Kiesling was back in charge by mid-season. Winning one game for the three coaches, the Steelers were off to a flying start.

TEAM TOTALS

OFFENSE	FIRST DOWNS: Tot	by Rsh	by Pas	by Pen	RUSHING: No.	Yds.	Avg. Yds.	TD	PASSING: Att.	Com	Comp. Pct.	Yds.	Avg. Yds. Att.	Avg. Yds. Comp	TD	Int.	Pct. Int.
N.Y.	110	68	33	9	433	1318	3.0	16	156	68	43.6	1088	7.0	16.0	11	12	7.7
BKN.	132	82	44	6	444	1665	3.7	14	202	90	44.6	1134	5.6	12.6	5	18	8.9
WASH.	135	62	64	9	406	1097	2.7	7	262	134	51.1	1563	6.0	11.7	11	30	11.5
PHIL.	128	60	59	9	360	849	2.4	6	249	115	46.2	1367	5.5	11.9	10	27	10.8
PITT.	75	49	18	8	381	1223	3.2	9	168	42	25.0	654	3.9	15.6	5	34	20.2

OFFENSE	PUNTING: No.	Avg. Yds.	PUNT RETURNS: No.	Yds.	Avg. Yds.	TD	KICKOFF RETURNS: No.	Yds.	Avg. Yds.	TD	INTERCEPTION RETURNS: No.	Yds.	Avg. Yds.	TD	PENALTIES: No.	Yds.	FUMBLES: No.	Lost	POINTS: Tot	PAT	FG Att	FG	Saf.	OFFENSE
N.Y.	64	41.5	47	717	15.3	0	20	467	23.4	0	29	569	19.6	1	40	323	25	14	238	28	20	10	0	N.Y.
BKN.	60	41.6	41	343	8.4	0	28	616	22.0	0	20	228	11.4	1	38	371	27	10	158	18	14	4	1	BKN.
WASH.	55	45.9	45	675	15.0	3	28	580	20.7	0	23	291	12.7	1	50	402	23	11	176	20	14	6	0	WASH.
PHIL.	69	41.0	27	210	7.8	0	31	734	23.7	0	21	213	10.1	0	54	407	24	15	119	14	8	3	0	PHIL.
PITT.	87	37.4	28	372	13.3	0	44	930	21.1	0	19	186	9.8	0	44	363	32	15	103	13	6	2	0	PITT.

Use Name – Backs & Ends	Pos.	Age	Hgt	Wgt	Pts	Int	RUSHING				PASSING								RECEIVING				PUNTING		KICKING						PUNT RETURNS				KICKOFF RETURNS			
							No.	Yds	Avg	TD	Att	Comp	%	Yds	Yd/Att	TD	Int–%	RK	No.	Yds	Avg	TD	No.	Avg	Pat	Att	%	FG	Att	%	No.	Yds	Avg	TD	No.	Yds	Avg	TD
NEW YORK GIANTS																																						
Ed Danowski	QB	29	6'1"	198							24	12	50	179	7.5	2	2–8		1	12	12	0	2	36.5														
Marion Pugh	QB-DB	21	6'1"	187			24	50	2.1	0	24	12	50	161	6.7	1	0–0								0	1	0				1	5	5	0				
Kay Eakin	QB-WB-DB	24	6'	178	6	2	27	17	0.6	0	19	5	26	71	3.7	1	4–21		5	81	16	1	20	47.4				0	1	0								
Tuffy Leemans	FB-DB	28	6'	200	24	3	100	332	3.3	4	66	31	47	475	7.2	4	5–8	5													14	170	12	0				
Len Eshmont	FB-DB	24	5'11"	180			50	164	3.3	0	3	2	67	32	10.7	1	0–0		1	4	4	0	11	38.9							6	131	22	0				
Andy Marefos	FB-DB	24	6'	225	30	2	60	153	2.5	2	8	2	25	79	9.9	1	1–12		1	5	5	0			6	6	100	4	5	80								
Frank Reagan	FB-DB	22	5'11"	185	24	1	35	146	4.2	4	6	1	17	16	2.7	0	0–0						13	37.5							6	113	19	0				
Hank Soar	FB-DB	27	6'2"	207	3	2	29	90	3.1	0	5	3	60	75	15.0	1	0–0								3	3	100				4	54	14	0				
Red McClain	FB-DB	23	5'9"	182	12	1	9	36	4.0	2																												
Ward Cuff	WB-DB	28	6'1"	190	46	4	28	157	5.6	0									19	317	17	2			19	20	95	5	13	38	1	10	10	0				
George Franck	WB-FB-DB	22	6'	175	24	4	48	101	2.1	3	1	0	0	0	0.0	0	0–0		8	95	12	1	18	39.8							13	194	15	0				
Howie Yeager	WB-DB	26	5'11"	173	24		22	67	3.0	1									11	237	22	3									2	40	20	0				
Dom Principe	BB-LB	24	6'	205			1	5	5.0	0									4	54	14	0																
Leland Shaffer	BB-DB	29	6'2"	205		1													1	5	5	0																
Nello Falaschi	BB-LB	27	6'	195		1													1	3	3	0																
Jim Poole	OE-DE	25	6'3"	220	18	1													6	74	12	2																
Will Walls	OE-DE	26	6'4"	220															4	89	17	0																
Jim Lee Howell	OE-DE	26	6'6"	218	6														4	62	16	1																
Vince Dennery	OE-DE	24	5'11"	190	6														1	65	65	1																
Jack Lummus	OE-DE	24	6'3"	194															1	5	5	0																
BROOKLYN DODGERS																																						
Ace Parker	TB-DB	29	6'	180		1	85	301	3.5	0	102	51	50	642	6.3	2	8–8	8	3	66	22	0	27	39.5							16	153	10	0				
Bill Leckonby	TB-DB	23	6'1"	185	6	3	54	202	3.7	0	64	25	39	299	4.7	1	5–8	11	1	9	9	1	15	39.2							15	119	8	0				
Dean McAdams	TB-HB-DB	23	6'1"	195	9	1	38	99	2.6	0	27	12	44	176	6.5	2	3–11		7	94	13	0	16	47.6	3	3	100	2	3	67	2	11	6	0				
Leo Stasica	TB-DB	25	5'11"	185			3	17	5.7	0	2	1	50	14	7.0	0	0–0														2	14	7	0				
Pug Manders	FB-DB	28	6'	200	42	4	111	486	4.4	6									6	67	11	0																
Merl Condit	HB-DB	23	5'11"	185	41	3	91	357	3.9	4	6	1	17	3	0.5	0	1–17		5	32	6	0	1	38.0	11	12	92	2	11	18	5	44	9	0				
George Kracum	FB-DB	23	6'1"	212	18	1	52	169	3.3	3									2	17	9	0																
Thurman Jones	FB-DB	23	5'10"	195			1	3	3.0	0																												
Larry Peace	HB-DB	24	5'11"	185	1		4	2	0.5	0															1	1	100											
Rhoten Shetley	BB-LB	23	5'11"	210	6	1	1	7	7.0	1	1	0	0	0	0.0	0	0–0		5	63	13	0																
Ben Kish	BB-LB	24	6'	200		1													4	50	13	0	1	35.0														
Wendell Butcher	BB-LB	27	6'1"	190			1	2	2.0	0																												
Perry Schwartz	OE-DE	26	6'2"	195	12		1	7	7.0	0									24	343	14	2																
Eddie Rucinski	OE-DE	25	6'2"	196	6		2	13	6.5	0									17	204	12	1																
Herman Hodges	OE-DE	26	6'1"	200															12	128	11	0																
Don Wemple	OE-DE	23	6'2"	195	6														2	37	19	1																
Bill Bailey	OE-DE	25	6'3"	220															1	14	14	0																
Dave Parker	OE-DE	23	6'3"	200															1	10	10	0																
WASHINGTON REDSKINS																																						
Sammy Baugh	TB-DB	27	6'2"	185		4	27	12	0.4	0	193	106	55	1236	6.4	10	19–10	4					30	48.7														
Frankie Filchock	TB-DB	24	5'11"	198	12		115	383	3.3	0	68	28	41	327	4.8	1	11–16	12					1	35.0							7	157	22	1				
Andy Farkas	FB-DB	25	5'10"	195	18	4	85	224	2.6	2									12	77	6	0									14	152	11	1				
Dick Todd	FB-DB	26	5'11"	170	18		55	138	2.5	1									8	125	16	1	10	43.5							14	238	17	1				
Bob Seymour	FB-WB-DB	25	6'2"	205	24	2	62	137	2.2	2									6	85	14	2									10	128	13	0				
Lee Gentry	FB-DB	22	6'	198		1	5	13	2.6	0																												
Roy Zimmerman	WB-FB-DB	23	6'2"	198			20	54	2.7	0	1	0	0	0	0.0	0	0–0		5	36	7	0	14	42.4														
Wilbur Moore	WB-BB-DB	25	5'11"	188	6		10	48	4.8	1									2	6	3	0																
Ed Justice	WB-DB	28	6'1"	198	6	2	4	–8	–2.0	0									8	149	19	1																
Ray Hare	BB-LB	23	6'1"	200	6		11	48	4.4	1									12	87	7	0																
Cecil Hare	BB-LB	22	5'11"	190	1		6	22	3.7	0									1	25	25	0																
Bob Hoffman	BB-LB	23	6'1"	194			1	2	2.0	0																												
Wayne Millner	OE-DE	30	6'1"	190			2	8	4.0	0									20	262	13	0																
Bob Mc Chesney	OE-DE	29	6'2"	195	12														19	213	11	2																
Bob Masterson	OE-DE	26	6'1"	220	23	1	1	3	3.0	0									11	135	12	1			8	8	100	3	6	50								
Joe Aguirre	OE-DE	22	6'4"	220	26														10	103	10	2			8	9	89	2	5	40								
Ed Cifers	OE-DE	25	6'2"	218	6														10	94	9	1																
Al Krueger	OE-DB	22	6'1"	190	6	1													7	123	18	1																
Frank Clair	OE-DE	24	6'1"	204															2	12	6	0																
PHILADELPHIA EAGLES																																						
Tommy Thompson	QB-DB	25	6'1"	187	6	3	54	28	0.5	0	162	86	53	974	6.0	8	14–9	7	2	10	5	1	1	43.0							5	27	5	0				
Len Barnum	QB-HB-FB-DB	28	6'	200	8	2	35	64	1.8	0	55	19	35	260	4.7	0	10–18		1	11	11	0	41	43.6	2	2	100	2	6	33								
Foster Watkins	QB-HB-DB	23	5'9"	165			15	11	0.7	0	10	6	60	51	5.1	1	0–0		3	27	9	0									3	17	6	0				
Jim Castiglia	FB-LB	22	5'11"	205	24	1	60	183	3.1	4	7	0	0	0	0.0	0	1–14		4	24	6	0																
Dan DeSantis	HB-DB	22	6'	180	1	2	45	125	2.8	0	7	3	43	78	11.1	1	1–14		4	53	13	0	7	29.4	1	1	100				9	80	9	0				
Terry Fox	FB-LB	22	6'1"	208			21	97	4.6	0									6	71	12	0																
Jack Banta	HB-DB	23	5'11"	192	6		29	93	3.2	1									2	42	21	0	9	45.6														
Sam Bartholomew	FB-LB	23	5'11"	188		1	21	71	3.4	0									3	15	5	0									1	1	1	0				
Mort Landsberg	HB-DB	22	5'11"	180		2	23	69	3.0	0									5	51	10	0									2	16	8	0				
Fred Gloden	HB-DB	22	5'10"	187			22	55	2.5	0									2	13	7	0																
Mike Basca	HB-DB	24	5'8"	170	18	3	14	43	3.1	1	4	0	0	0	0.0	0	1–25		2	45	23	0	10	34.8	9	9	100	1	2	50	1	8	8	0				
Lou Tomasetti (to DET,WB-DB)	HB-DB	25	6'	195	6	1	16	41	2.6	0									2	40	20	1									3	48	16	0				
Wes McAfee	HB-DB	22	5'11"	175	8		9	6	0.7	0	4	1	25	4	1.0	0	0–0		3	30	10	1	1	32.0	2	2	100				3	21	7	0				
Lou Ghecas	HB-DB	23	5'9"	175			2	3	1.5	0																					1	11	11	0				
Dick Humbert	OE-DB	22	6'1"	175	18	1													29	332	11	3																
Bob Krieger	OE-DE	23	6'1"	190	12														19	232	12	2																
Hank Piro	OE-DB	23	6'	186	6	1													10	141	14	1																
Kirk Hershey (from CLE)	OE-DE	22	6'2"	215															9	81	9	0																
Larry Cabrelli	OE-DE	24	5'11"	195	6														4	90	23	1																
John Shonk	OE-DB	23	6'1"	190		1													4	43	11	0																
Jack Ferrante	OE-DE	25	6'1"	195															2	22	11	0																
PITTSBURGH STEELERS																																						
Boyd Brumbaugh	TB-FB-DB	26	5'11"	197	12		68	114	1.7	2	41	13	32	260	6.3	2	8–20		1	1	1	0									7	60	9	0				
Coley McDonough	TB-DB	26	6'1"	182			20	64	3.2	0	41	12	29	200	4.9	1	5–12						7	37.1							2	28	14	0				
Art Jones	TB-HB-DB	22	6'2"	190	30	7	52	239	4.6	4	23	6	26	86	3.7	0	3–13		4	121	30	1	47	37.7							14	232	17	0				
Al Donelli	TB-HB-DB	22	5'7"	165		1	15	32	2.1	0	8	2	25	13	1.6	1	3–37		2	25	13	0	1	41.0							1	11	11	0				
Les Dodson	TB-DB	25	6'1"	180			2	–4	–2.0	0	8	1	13	7	0.9	0	3–37						1	34.0														
Ben Starret	TB-BB-LB	23	5'10"	200			7	9	1.3	0	2	0	0	0	0.0	0	1–50																					
Frank Zopetti	TB-DB	26	5'11"	185							1	0	0	0	0.0	0	0–0																					
Dick Riffle	FB-TB-DB	26	6'1"	210	12	6	109	388	3.6	1	39	8	21	88	2.3	1	9–23		2	24	12	1	7	35.3							3	38	13	0				
Elmer Hackney	FB-DB	25	6'2"	204	6		63	253	4.0	1	1	0	0	0	0.0	0	0–0		1	10	10	0									1	3	3	0				
Joe Hoague	FB-DB	23	6'2"	200	12		33	112	3.4	1	1	0	0	0	0.0	0	0–0		2	21	11	1	17	37.1														
John Noppenberg (to DET)	HB-TB-DB	23	6'	190			11	16	1.5	0	3	0	0	0	0.0	0	0–0						7	38.6														
Jay Arnold	BB-HB-LB	27	6'1"	215		1	2	4	2.0	0									1	5	5	0																
Rocco Pirro	BB-LB	24	6'	215		1	1	1	1.0	0									2	31	16	0																
John Patrick	BB-LB	23	6'	200		1													1	12	12	0																
Don Looney	OE-DB	23	6'2"	177	6														10	186	19	1																
Joe Wendlick	OE-DE	25	6'	206															7	84	12	0																
Walt Kichefski	OE-DE	25	6'1"	214	6														5	111	22	1																
George Platukas	OE-DE	26	6'	194															2	15	8	0																
Elmer Kolberg	OE-DE	25	6'4"	200															1	2	2	0																
Armand Niccolai	T	29	6'2"	230	14																				8	9	89	2	4	50								

TEAM TOTALS	FIRST DOWNS:				RUSHING:				PASSING:									PUNTING:		PUNT RETURNS:				KICKOFF RETURNS:				INTERCEPTION RETURNS:				PENALTIES:		FUMBLES:		POINTS:					TEAM TOTALS
DEFENSE	Tot	by Rsh	by Pas	by Pen	No.	Yds.	Avg. Yds.	TD	Att.	Com	Comp. Pct.	Yds.	Avg. Yds. Att.	Avg. Yds. Comp	TD	Int.	Pct. Int.	No.	Avg. Yds.	No.	Yds.	Avg. Yds.	TD	No.	Yds.	Avg. Yds.	TD	No.	Yds.	Avg. Yds.	TD	No.	Yds.	No.	Lost	Tot	PAT	FG Att	FG	Saf.	DEFENSE
N.Y.	116	64	47	5	408	1166	2.9	9	218	103	47.2	1212	5.6	11.8	6	29	13.3	76	40.3	33	469	14.2	1	45	1007	22.4	0	12	106	8.8	1	47	371	34	13	114	12	11	4	0	N.Y.
BKN.	110	58	45	7	376	1210	3.2	6	189	86	45.5	1169	6.2	13.6	6	20	10.6	72	40.1	34	463	13.6	1	29	625	21.6	0	18	261	14.5	1	47	370	17	8	127	13	10	4	0	BKN.
WASH.	129	66	56	7	410	1110	2.7	9	229	103	45.0	1338	5.8	13.0	14	23	10.0	65	41.6	28	351	12.5	0	36	698	19.4	0	30	309	10.3	0	37	269	33	12	174	19	13	5	1	WASH.
PHIL.	126	72	47	7	432	1498	3.5	14	238	100	42.0	1369	5.8	13.7	13	21	8.8	66	38.4	37	519	14.0	0	22	443	20.1	0	27	492	18.2	2	50	455	21	10	218	26	14	8	0	PHIL.
PITT.	116	72	34	10	426	1550	3.6	17	189	84	44.4	1168	6.2	13.9	10	19	10.1	65	40.6	41	416	10.1	0	21	536	25.5	1	34	596	17.5	2	54	495	17	8	276	34	12	4	1	PITT.

CHICAGO BEARS 10-1-0 George Halas

Scores of Each Game		
25	Green Bay	17
48	Cleveland	21
53	CHIC. CARDS	7
49	DETROIT	0
34	PITTSBURGH	7
14	GREEN BAY	16
31	CLEVELAND	13
35	WASHINGTON	21
24	Detroit	7
49	Philadelphia	14
34	Chic. Cards	24
	WEST playoff	
33	GREEN BAY	14

Use Name	Pos.	Hgt	Wgt	Age	Int	Pts
Bill Hughes	C-LB	6'1"	222	26	1	
(1 punt return for 6 yds.)						
Al Matuza	C-LB	6'2"	200	22	2	
Bulldog Turner	C-LB	6'1"	230	22	1	

Use Name – Tackles	Pos.	Hgt	Wgt	Age	Int	Pts
Lee Artoe	T	6'3"	230	25		6
(3 PAT's in 4 attempts, 1 FG in 7 attempts)						
John Federovich	T	6'5"	260	24	1	
Ed Kolman	T	6'2"	230	23		
Joe Mihal	T	6'3"	225	25		
Joe Stydahar	T	6'4"	230	29	1	4
(4 PAT's in 4 attempts)						

Use Name – Guards	Pos.	Hgt	Wgt	Age	Int	Pts
Al Baisi	G	6'	215	23		
Ray Bray	G	6'	245	24		
Aldo Forte	G	6'	212	23		
Danny Fortmann	G-LB	6'	207	25	3	
Hal Lahar	G	6'	225	22		4
(1 PAT in 3 attempts, 1 FG in 1 attempt)						
George Musso	G	6'2"	255	31		

As strong as the Bears looked last year, they were in even better shape this year. Two new horses, Norm Standlee and Hugh Gallarneau, were yoked into the backfield, and George McAfee grew into the most feared runner in the NFL. Combining a deer's speed with a rabbit's moves, McAfee led the league in average yards per carry, threatened to break punt and kickoff returns into touchdowns, and intercepted six passes as a cornerback on defense. But even with McAfee's overall play, Standlee's power running, Sid Luckman's passing, and the Bears averaging 36 points a game—capped by routs of 53-7 over the Cardinals and 49-0 over the Lions—it took a playoff game with the Green Bay Packers before the Western Division championship could be decided, as both clubs took turns to mar each other's perfect records and force the post-season game.

GREEN BAY PACKERS 10-1-0 Curly Lambeau

Scores of Each Game		
23	DETROIT	0
24	CLEVELAND	7
17	CHIC. BEARS	25
14	CHIC. CARDS	13
30	BROOKLYN	7
17	Cleveland	14
24	Detroit	7
16	Chic. Bears	14
17	CHIC. CARDS	9
54	Pittsburgh	7
22	Washington	17
	WEST Playoff	
14	Chic. Bears	33

Use Name	Pos.	Hgt	Wgt	Age	Int	Pts
Charley Brock	C-LB	6'2"	205	25		
Tom Greenfield	C-LB	6'4"	220	23		
George Svendesn	C-LB	6'4"	240	26	1	
Bob Adkins	BB-DE	6'1"	210	24	2	3
(3 PAT's in 3 attempts)						
Larry Buhler	BB-DE	6'2"	215	24		
Bill Johnson	DE	6'1"	196	24		

Use Name – Tackles	Pos.	Hgt	Wgt	Age	Int	Pts
Bill Lee	T	6'2"	240	29		
Ernie Pannell	T	6'2"	220	24	1	6
Baby Ray	T	6'6"	250	26		
Charlie Schultz	T	6'3"	235	24		

Use Name – Guards	Pos.	Hgt	Wgt	Age	Int	Pts
Amadeo Bucchianeri	G	5'10"	210	24		
Tiny Engebretsen	G	6'1"	245	31		3
(1 field goal in 3 attempts)						
Buckets Goldenberg	G-LB	5'10"	230	30	1	
Smiley Johnson	G-LB	5'9"	195	30	1	
Bill Kuusisto	G	6'	230	23		
Russ Letlow	G	6'	215	27		
Lee McLaughlin	G	6'1"	226	24		
Pete Tinsley	G-LB	5'8"	205	28	1	

With the Chicago Bears destroying all their opponents in the early going, everyone but Curly Lambeau was calling the Bears a superteam. Lambeau reminded his Packers that the Bears were only human and due for a fall, and when the two clubs met in mid-season, the hard-nosed Green Bay defense shut off the Bears and led the Packers to a 16-14 upset victory. That triumph made up for an opening-day loss to the Bears and led to both clubs having identical records when the regular season closed.

The Packers went into the playoff game with the NFL's premier receiver and league MVP in Don Hutson, a superb passer and strategist in Cecil Isbell, a stable of hard-charging runners headed by Clarke Hinkle, and a tough forward wall featuring Baby Ray and Buckets Goldenberg. But with all their talent, the Packers came up empty and fell before the George Halas machine 33-14.

DETROIT LIONS 4-6-1 Bill Edwards

Scores of Each Game		
0	Green Bay	23
7	Brooklyn	14
14	Chic. Cards	14
17	CLEVELAND	7
0	Chic. Bears	49
7	GREEN BAY	24
14	Cleveland	0
13	New York	20
21	PHILADELPHIA	17
7	CHIC. BEARS	24
21	CHIC. CARDS	3

Use Name	Pos.	Hgt	Wgt	Age	Int	Pts
Bob Nelson	C-T-LB	6'1"	215	21	1	
Dunc Obee	C-LB	5'11"	200	23		
Alex Wojciechowicz	C-LB	5'11"	205	26		
Paul Moore	BB-LB	5'9"	205	23		
Injured – Mike Rodak (broken leg)						

Use Name – Tackles	Pos.	Hgt	Wgt	Age	Int	Pts
Clem Crabtree	T	6'3"	230	22		
Tony Furst	T	6'1"	215	23	1	
Andy Logan	T	6'	222	23		
Ted Pavelic	T	6'	213	22		
Alex Schibanoff	T	6'1"	220	21		
John Tripson	T	6'3"	210	21		
Emil Uremovich	T	6'2"	220	24		

Use Name – Guards	Pos.	Hgt	Wgt	Age	Int	Pts
Stan Batinski	G	5'10"	215	24		
John Mattiford	G	5'10"	216	25		
(1 reception for 21 yds.)						
Bill Radovich	G	5'10"	230	26		
John Wiethe	G-LB	6'	200	28	2	

The Lions were offensive pussy cats, with no passing attack and a line that pushed no one around. Although they picked up four wins by beating the Rams twice, the Cardinals, and the Eagles, the stronger clubs lost no sleep over them. Against the Packers, Detroit dropped games by scores of 23-0 and 24-7, and the Bears took a pair via counts of 49-0 and 24-7—as the only score the Lions managed in the two games was a 101-yard kickoff return by Billy Jefferson.

New coach Bill Edwards, who had inherited a deteriorating club which would sink lower before starting to climb, also lost his ace Whizzer White after the season. White, who stood out amidst the rubble for his 100 percent effort at all times, went into military service and then on to pursue a legal career, which would lead to an appointment as Associate Justice of the United States Supreme Court.

CHICAGO CARDINALS 3-7-1 Jimmy Conzelman

Scores of Each Game		
6	CLEVELAND	10
14	DETROIT	14
13	Green Bay	14
7	Chic. Bears	53
20	Brooklyn	6
14	Philadelphia	21
10	New York	7
9	Green Bay	17
7	Cleveland	0
3	Detroit	21
24	CHIC. BEARS	34

Use Name	Pos.	Hgt	Wgt	Age	Int	Pts
Ray Apolskis	C-LB	5'11"	200	22	1	
Andy Chisick	C-LB	6'1"	208	24	1	
Fred Shook	C-LB	6'	218	22		
Walt Rankin	FB-DB	5'11"	190	23		
holdout – Gil Duggan						

Use Name – Tackles	Pos.	Hgt	Wgt	Age	Int	Pts
Al Bahartsky	T	6'	220	25		
Conway Baker	T	5'11"	230	29		
Ed Beinor (to WAS)	T	6'2"	215	23		
Ray Busler	T	6'1"	220	25		
Bill Davis	T	6'1"	235	24		6
John Kuzman	T	6'1"	235	25		
Joel Mason – American Football League						

Use Name – Guards	Pos.	Hgt	Wgt	Age	Int	Pts
John Higgins	G-LB	6'1"	210	21		
Frank Huffman	G-LB	6'2"	210	26		
Joe Kuharich	G-LB	5'11"	195	24	1	
(1 punt for 45 yds.)						
Joe Lokanc	G-LB	5'11"	205	22		
(1 reception for 2 yds.)						
Bill Murphy	G	6'	200	27		
Tarzan White	G	5'9"	225	25		

When the Bears trounced the Cardinals 53-7 in their first meeting of the season, Jimmy Conzelman knew he wouldn't be beating George Halas this year. But the coach could take satisfaction from other achievements. The Cardinals climbed up into fourth place in the West, finishing out of the last-place dungeon for the first time in four years, and their three wins included impressive upsets over Brooklyn and New York. With a better final record than Cleveland, Philadelphia, and Pittsburgh, the Cardinals felt they were making progress. Personal achievements also brightened the season. Guard Joe Kuharich won All-Pro status in his second pro year, and fullback Marshall Goldberg took a second-team place on the honor roll with his all-around play. Goldberg, whose reputation on defense was undisputed around the circuit, also led the NFL at mid-season in rushing, punt and kickoff returning, and interceptions.

CLEVELAND RAMS 2-9-0 Dutch Clark

Scores of Each Game		
17	PITTSBURGH	14
10	Chic. Cards	6
7	Green Bay	24
21	CHIC. BEARS	48
7	Detroit	17
14	GREEN BAY	17
13	Washington	17
0	DETROIT	14
13	Chic. Bears	31
14	New York	49
0	CHIC. CARDS	7

Use Name	Pos.	Hgt	Wgt	Age	Int	Pts
Bill Conkright	C-LB	6'1"	200	27	1	
Jack Haman	C-LB	6'1"	214	23	1	
Bill Rieth	C-LB	5'11"	203	25		
Frank Maher (from PIT)	DB	6'1"	195	23		
Pete Godauskas – American Football League						
Vic Spadaccini – American Football League						

Use Name – Tackles	Pos.	Hgt	Wgt	Age	Int	Pts
Graham Armstrong	T	6'4"	225	23		
Boyd Clay	T	6'1"	213	28		4
(1 PAT in 1 attempt, 1 FG in 2 attempts)						
Elwyn Dunstan	T	6'3"	245	26		6
(1 punt return for 35 yd. TD)						
Mike Kostiuk	T	6'	215	22		
Del Lyman (from GB)	T	6'3"	225	23		
Fred Shirey	T	6'2"	220	25		

Use Name – Guards	Pos.	Hgt	Wgt	Age	Int	Pts
Jack Gregory	G	6'2"	240	25		
Riley Matheson	G-LB	6'2"	203	26	1	
Barney McGarry	G-LB	6'1"	200	23		
Hank Rockwell	G-C-LB	6'4"	225	24	1	
Milt Simington	G	6'2"	213	23		
Wilfred Thorpe	G-LB-DE	6'3"	200	24	1	
Gordon Wilson	G-T	6'	225	25		

Looking to buy an NFL franchise he could eventually move to Los Angeles, Dan Reeves bought a controlling interest in the Cleveland Rams. In the opening game against Pittsburgh, Reeves and part owner Fred Levy were brought to their feet by Dante Magnani's opening kickoff which he returned 95 yards for a touchdown. When the Rams beat the Steelers and the Cardinals in their first two games, Reeves and Levy thought they had gotten into an easy business. But the bubble burst as the Rams lost their last nine contests.

Although coach Dutch Clark kept his job under the new ownership, he could not shake the Rams out of their mediocre habits. Parker Hall and Johnny Drake, as usual, handled the bulk of the passing and running but could not make up for the new blood which was needed in the backfield. And despite Riley Matheson's fine defensive work, the line also needed a transfusion.

TEAM TOTALS

OFFENSE	FIRST DOWNS: Tot	by Rsh	by Pas	by Pen	RUSHING: No.	Yds.	Avg Yds.	TD	PASSING: Att	Com	Comp Pct.	Yds.	Avg. Yds. Att.	Avg. Yds. Comp	TD	Int	Pct. Int.	PUNTING: No.	Avg. Yds.
CHI. B.	181	112	56	13	495	2290	4.6	30	196	98	50.0	2002	10.2	20.4	19	11	5.6	32	38.7
G.B	166	82	69	15	467	1550	3.3	13	253	133	52.6	1731	6.8	13.0	17	13	5.1	53	42.1
DET.	86	51	29	6	361	1009	2.8	7	187	58	31.0	848	4.5	14.6	5	20	10.6	79	39.7
CHI. C.	138	66	64	8	386	1098	2.8	8	252	117	46.4	1658	6.6	14.2	6	20	7.9	79	39.3
CLEVE.	121	68	44	9	343	984	2.9	4	285	123	43.2	1352	4.7	11.0	10	35	12.3	79	40.4

OFFENSE	PUNT RETURNS: No.	Yds.	Avg. Yds.	TD	KICKOFF RETURNS: No.	Yds.	Avg. Yds.	TD	INTERCEPTION RETURNS: No.	Yds.	Avg. Yds.	TD	PENALTIES: No.	Yds.	FUMBLES: No.	Lost	POINTS: Tot	PAT	FG Att	FG	Saf.
CHI. B.	27	546	20.2	2	29	685	23.6	1	34	556	16.4	3	77	677	37	19	396	45	11	5	0
G.B.	41	487	11.9	1	28	567	20.3	0	25	455	18.2	1	47	509	20	11	258	28	20	10	1
DET.	35	502	14.3	1	37	980	26.5	1	18	327	18.2	2	52	455	24	11	121	16	9	1	0
CHI. C.	32	311	9.7	0	31	705	22.7	0	16	145	9.1	1	41	446	19	12	127	13	12	4	0
CLEVE.	32	343	10.7	1	41	820	20.0	1	15	141	9.4	0	29	265	25	8	116	14	4	2	0

Use Name – Backs & Ends	Pos.	Age	Hgt	Wgt	Pts	Int	Rushing No.	Rushing Yds	Rushing Avg	Rushing TD	Passing Att	Passing Comp	Passing %	Passing Yds	Passing Yd/Att	Passing TD	Passing Int–%	Passing RK	Receiving No.	Receiving Yds	Receiving Avg	Receiving TD	Punting No.	Punting Avg	Kicking Pat	Kicking Att	Kicking %	Kicking FG	Kicking Att	Kicking %	Punt Returns No.	Punt Returns Yds	Punt Returns Avg	Punt Returns TD	Kickoff Returns No.	Kickoff Returns Yds	Kickoff Returns Avg	Kickoff Returns TD
CHICAGO BEARS																																						
Sid Luckman	QB-DB	24	6'	198	6	3	18	18	1.0	1	119	68	57	1181	9.9	9	6– 5	1					13	41.0														
Young Bussey	QB-DB	23	5'9"	185		2	13	9	0.7	0	40	13	33	353	8.8	5	3– 7						2	37.0							1	40	40	0				
Bob Snyder	QB-DB	28	6'	190	26	1	7	–10	–1.4	0	28	13	46	353	12.6	3	2– 7						2	38.0	20	24	83	2	2	100								
George McAfee	HB-DB	23	6'	180	72	6	65	474	7.3	6	3	1	33	44	14.7	1	0– 0		7	144	21	3	12	35.8							5	158	32	1				1
Norm Standlee	FB-LB	22	6'2"	230	30	2	81	414	5.1	5									2	–3	–1	0	2	63.0														
Bill Osmanski	FB-LB	24	5'11"	198	24	3	76	361	4.8	4	1	0	0	0	0.0	0	0– 0		4	52	13	0																
Hugh Gallarneau	HB-DB	24	6'	190	66	1	49	304	6.2	8									11	204	19	2	1	0.0							2	36	18	0				
Ray Nolting	HB-DB	27	5'11"	185	6		40	169	4.2	1	5	3	60	71	14.2	1	0– 0		4	68	17	0									4	50	13	0				
Bob Swisher	HB-DB	27	5'11"	160	18	1	37	149	4.0	0									6	179	30	2									7	101	14	0				
Harry Clark	HB-DB	23	6'	185	1	2	28	122	4.4	0									2	61	30	0			1	1	100				4	56	14	0				
Gary Famiglietti	FB-HB-LB	26	6'	220	6		36	101	2.8	1																												
Joe Maniaci	FB-LB	27	6'1"	215	29		28	95	3.4	3									2	21	11	0			8	8	100	1	1	100								
Ray McLean	HB-DB	25	5'10"	168	18	3	13	78	6.0	1									5	84	17	1									3	99	33	1				
Dick Plasman	OE-DE	27	6'3"	215	6		1	1	1.0	0									14	283	20	0			6	9	67											
Bob Nowaskey	OE-DE	23	6'	205	13		3	5	1.7	0									12	199	17	1			1	2	50											
Ken Kavanaugh	OE-DE	24	6'3"	206	37	1													11	314	29	6			1	1	100											
John Siegal	OE-DE	23	6'1"	205	18														9	220	24	3																
Hamp Pool	OE-DE	26	6'3"	225	6														5	101	20	1																
George Wilson	OE-DE	27	6'1"	200															4	75	19	0																
GREEN BAY PACKERS																																						
Cecil Isbell	TB-DB	26	6'1"	190	6	1	72	317	4.4	1	206	117	57	1479	7.2	15	11– 5	2	1	–1	–1	0									3	19	6	0				
Hal Van Every	TB-DB	23	6'	195	18	3	25	127	5.1	2	30	11	37	195	6.5	0	2– 7		1	3	3	0	13	38.8							4	58	15	0				
Tony Canadeo	TB-DB	22	5'11"	190	18	2	43	137	3.2	3	16	4	25	54	3.4	2	0– 0						10	40.5							4	26	7	0				
Clarke Hinkle	FB-LB	31	5'11"	198	56	1	129	393	3.0	5									8	78	10	1	22	44.5	2	2	100	6	14	43	2	61	31	0				
Andy Uram	HB-DB	26	5'10"	188	6	2	49	258	5.3	0									6	124	21	0									7	121	17	1				
George Paskvan	FB-DB	23	6'	190		2	38	116	3.1	0																												
Ed Jankowski	FB-LB	28	5'9"	200	4	1	47	65	1.4	0															1	2	50	1	1	100								
Joe Laws	HB-DB	30	5'9"	190	6	2	21	58	2.8	0									4	48	12	1									2	3	2	0				
Lou Brock	HB-DB	23	6'	197	12	2	14	44	3.1	0									22	307	14	2	3	42.7							15	153	10	0				
Herm Rohrig	HB-DB	23	5'8"	190	4	1	21	2	0.1	0	1	1	100	3	3.0	0	0– 0		11	58	5	0	5	42.8	1	1	100	1	1	100	4	46	12	0				
Larry Craig	BB-DE	25	6'1"	208			1	1	1.0	0									2	13	7	0																
Don Hutson	OE-DB	28	6'1"	185	95	1	4	22	5.5	2									58	738	13	10			20	24	83	1	1	100								
Moose Mulleneaux	OE-DE	24	6'3"	210	12														9	216	24	2																
Harry Jacunski	OE-DE	25	6'2"	200															4	48	12	0																
Ray Riddick	OE-DE	23	6'1"	215															3	33	11	0																
Ed Frutig	OE-DB	21	6'1"	185			1	11	11.0	0									2	40	20	0																
Alex Urban	OE-DE	24	6'3"	200	6														2	26	13	1																
DETROIT LIONS																																						
Whizzer White	TB-WB-DB	24	6'1"	185	24	1	89	238	2.7	2	62	22	35	338	5.5	2	5– 8	9	5	158	32	1	48	41.6							19	262	14	0				
Billy Jefferson	TB-DB	23	6'2"	205	12	1	56	164	2.9	1	72	18	25	181	2.5	0	9–12	13	2	14	7	0	20	37.5							7	69	10	0				1
Cotton Price	TB-DB	22	6'1"	182			16	36	2.3	0	33	9	27	112	3.4	0	4–12		1	6	6	0	5	38.2							3	48	16	0				
Harry Hopp	FB-DB	22	6'	205	6	1	69	202	2.9	1	3	0	0	0	0.0	0	1–33		2	7	4	0	2	42.0														
Steve Belichick	FB-LB	22	5'8"	190	18	1	28	118	4.2	2									1	13	13	0									1	77	77	1				
Milt Piepul	FB-LB	22	6'1"	215			20	56	2.8	0	1	1	100	23	23.0	0	0– 0						1	35.0														
Lloyd Parsons	FB-LB	23	5'11"	197			5	9	1.8	0									1	3	3	0																
Dick Booth	WB-DB	23	6'1"	190	6	1	29	79	2.7	1	8	5	63	135	16.9	2	1–12		7	103	15	0	1	25.0														
Ned Mathews	WB-DB	23	5'10"	185	6	5	31	56	1.8	0	8	3	38	59	7.4	1	0– 0		6	56	9	0	1	26.0							1	3	3	0				
Lloyd Cardwell	WB-DB	28	6'2"	195			10	19	1.9	0																					3	25	8	0				
Bill Callihan	BB-DB	25	6'3"	217															4	34	9	0																
Fred Vanzo (to CHIC)	BB-LB	25	6'2"	228															2	20	10	0																
Bill Fisk	OE-DE	24	6'	198	12														9	140	16	2																
Stan Anderson (from CLE)	OE-DE-T	23	6'2"	215															7	79	11	0																
John Jett	OE-DE	23	6'7"	225															4	50	13	0																
Chuck Hanneman (to CLE)	OE-DE	26	6'	215	13														4	48	12	1			4	4	100	1	4	25								
Paul Szakash	OE-DE-DB	28	6'	210															3	77	26	0																
Maury Britt	OE-DE	22	6'4"	210	6														1	45	45	1																
Augie Lio	G-LB	23	6'	225	18	3																	1	28.0	12	13	92	0	5	0								
CHICAGO CARDINALS																																						
Johnny Clement	TB-DB	21	6'	190	6		61	94	1.5	1	100	48	48	690	6.9	3	7– 7	6					4	31.3							13	113	9	0				
Ray Mallouf	TB-DB	23	5'11"	180			43	104	2.4	0	96	48	50	725	7.6	2	4– 4	3					28	41.0							4	11	3	0				
Hugh McCullough	TB-DB	25	6'	185			15	34	2.3	0	32	12	38	133	4.2	0	5–16						3	40.7							3	35	12	0				
Marshall Goldberg	FB-TB-DB	23	5'11"	190	24	7	117	427	3.6	3	19	9	47	110	5.8	1	1– 5		16	313	20	1									12	152	13	0	12	290	24	0
Bob Morrow	FB-DB	23	6'	220	6	1	37	128	3.5	1																												
Frank Balasz (from GB)	FB-DB	23	6'2"	210	1		23	81	3.5	0	4	0	0	0	0.0	0	2–50		2	17	9	0	7	37.0	1	1	100											
Milt Popovich	FB-G-LB	24	5'11"	200			5	4	0.8	0																												
John Hall	WB-DB	24	6'	200	24		53	165	3.1	2	1	0	0	0	0.0	0	0– 0		16	302	19	2																
John Martin	WB-DB	23	6'1"	192	12	1	25	56	2.2	1									4	53	13	1	24	39.9														
Avery Monfort	WB-DB	22	5'10"	178			3	8	2.7	0																												
Buddy Parker	BB-LB	27	6'	192		2	1	–1	–1.0	0									8	122	15	0			0	1	0											
Bert Johnson	BB-WB-LB-DB	29	6'	210	6	1	3	7	2.3	0									4	90	23	1																
Lou Zontini	BB-LB	24	5'9"	190	5		1	–9	–9.0	0									1	22	22	0	12	37.1	5	5	100	0	4	0								
Bill Dewell	OE-DE	24	6'4"	200	6		1	–1	–1.0	0									28	352	13	1																
Pop Ivy	OE-DE	25	6'3"	205	12	1													20	183	9	0																
Al Coppage	OE-DE	25	6'1"	195															8	117	15	0																
Bill Daddio	OE-DE	25	5'11"	202	20														5	39	8	0			8	9	89	4	8	50								
Dick Evans	OE-DE	24	6'3"	203															3	34	11	0																
CLEVELAND RAMS																																						
Parker Hall	TB-DB	24	6'	195	12	2	57	232	4.1	2	190	84	44	883	4.6	7	19–10	9					49	40.1							13	125	10	0				
Marty Slovak	TB-DB	24	5'9"	180			46	132	2.9	0	54	27	50	287	5.3	2	9–17														4	30	8	0				
Owen Goodnight	TB-DB	23	6'	195		2	21	–8	–0.4	0	36	12	33	182	5.1	1	5–14						16	39.8							2	27	14	0				
Johnny Drake	FB-DB	25	6'1"	220	18	2	101	246	2.4	2	2	0	0	0	0.0	0	0– 0		16	211	13	1																
Corby Davis	FB-BB-LB	26	5'11"	212			31	110	3.5	0									13	64	5	0	2	37.5							1	6	6	0				
Gaylon Smith	FB-DB	25	5'11"	195		1	11	22	2.0	0	2	0	0	0	0.0	0	1–50						1	23.0							1	33	33	0				
Len Janiak	FB-BB-DB	25	6'1"	200		1	14	20	1.4	0									2	5	3	0																
Dante Magnani	WB-DB	24	5'10"	175	12	2	24	137	5.7	0									14	189	14	1									5	54	11	0				
George Morris	WB-DB	22	5'11"	188			24	69	2.9	0									9	17	2	0									5	33	7	0				
Tony Gallovich	WB-DB	22	5'9"	170			1	1	1.0	0																												
Charlie Seabright	BB-LB	23	6'2"	195							1	0	0	0	0.0	0	1–100		5	44	9	0																
Rudy Mucha	BB-G-LB	23	6'1"	228			1	0	0.0	0									1	3	3	0	11	44.4														
Red Hickey	OE-DE	24	6'2"	195	24		7	7	1.0	0									21	294	14	4																
Paul McDonough	OE-DE	24	6'4"	230	12														14	198	14	2																
Maury Patt	OE-DE	27	6'2"	206	6		5	16	3.2	0									17	163	10	1																
Johnny Wilson	OE-DE	25	6'3"	205	6														5	115	23	1																
Ray Prochaska	OE-DE	22	6'3"	205															4	29	7	0																
Chet Adams	T	25	6'3"	230	16																				13	14	93	1	2	50								

TEAM TOTALS

DEFENSE	First Downs: Tot	by Rsh	by Pas	by Pen	Rushing: No.	Yds.	Avg. Yds.	TD	Passing: Att.	Com	Comp. Pct.	Yds.	Avg. Yds. Att.	Avg. Yds. Comp	TD	Int.	Pct. Int.	Punting: No.	Avg. Yds.	Punt Returns: No.	Yds.	Avg. Yds.	TD	Kickoff Returns: No.	Yds.	Avg. Yds.	TD	Interception Returns: No.	Yds.	Avg. Yds.	TD	Penalties: No.	Yds.	Fumbles: No.	Lost	Points: Tot	PAT	FG Att	FG	Saf.	DEFENSE
CHI. B.	143	60	63	20	373	1076	2.9	6	265	106	40.0	1463	5.5	13.8	9	34	12.8	56	39.5	20	340	17.0	2	48	1187	24.7	1	11	214	19.5	0	42	448	26	14	147	18	7	3	0	CHI. B.
G.B.	124	76	41	7	356	1221	3.4	10	233	104	44.6	1343	5.8	12.9	8	25	10.7	58	40.5	31	432	13.9	1	39	880	22.6	0	13	170	13.1	0	63	639	41	23	120	12	12	4	0	G.B.
DET.	160	89	61	10	475	1404	3.0	8	247	112	45.3	1605	6.5	14.3	8	18	7.3	67	42.8	40	546	13.7	1	29	628	21.7	0	20	215	10.8	0	36	415	20	12	195	24	18	9	0	DET.
CHI. C.	110	61	42	7	384	1301	3.4	13	196	90	45.9	1305	6.7	14.5	12	16	8.2	62	43.3	40	552	13.8	1	30	596	19.9	0	20	340	17.0	1	47	437	27	15	197	23	6	2	0	CHI. C.
CLEVE.	138	82	44	12	436	1547	3.5	23	206	90	43.7	1425	6.9	15.8	14	15	7.3	68	40.1	51	418	8.2	1	18	484	26.9	1	35	409	11.7	3	49	419	20	11	244	28	15	4	0	CLEVE.

WASHINGTON REDSKINS 10-1-0 Ray Flaherty

Scores of Each Game		
28	PITTSBURG	14
7	NEW YORK	14
14	Philadelphia	10
33	CLEVELAND	14
21	Brooklyn	10
14	Pittsburgh	0
30	PHILADELPHIA	27
28	CHIC. CARDS	0
14	New York	7
23	BROOKLYN	3
15	Detroit	3

Use Name	Pos.	Hgt	Wgt	Age	Int	Pts
Ki Aldrich	C-LB	6'	210	26		6
(1 kickoff return for 8 yds.)						
George Smith	C-LB	6'2"	215	28		
(Missed 1 field goal attempt)						
Bob Titchenal	OE-LB	6'2"	200	24	1	
(1 reception for 7 yds.)						

Use Name – Tackles	Pos.	Hgt	Wgt	Age	Int	Pts
Ed Beinor	T	6'2"	220	24		
Vic Carroll	T-G-C	6'4"	235	29		
Fred Davis	T	6'3"	240	24		
George Watts	T	6'1"	225	24		
Willie Wilkin	T	6'4"	265	26		8
(1 kickoff return for 15 yds.)						
Bill Young	T	6'1"	250	28		

Use Name – Guards	Pos.	Hgt	Wgt	Age	Int	Pts
Dick Farman	G	6'	220	26		
Clyde Shugart	G	6'1"	220	25		
Steve Slivinski	G	5'10"	216	25		
Clem Stralka	G	5'10"	220	28		
Joe Zeno	G	5'10"	220	23		

In the only game the Redskins lost, they held the Giants to no first downs and still dropped a rain-soaked 14-7 heartbreaker. After this early setback, the Washington offense caught up with the defense and led the Skins to nine straight wins, including a rematch with the Giants. In the last four games, the defense brilliantly held up its end of the bargain by allowing only one touchdown.

Although the defense, led by tackle Willie Wilkin, was the heart of the team, the explosive attack won most of the newsprint. Sammy Baugh drilled his passes from the tailback slot, Andy Farkas bulled his way to hard rushing yardage, and Dick Todd and Bob Masterson corraled most of Baugh's slings. Despite the loss of Wayne Millner, Frankie Filchock, and Jim Barber in the military buildup, the Redskins were armed to the teeth and hungry for revenge over the Bears in the upcoming championship game.

PITTSBURGH STEELERS 7-4-0 Walt Kiesling

14	PHILADELPHIA	24
14	Washington	28
13	NEW YORK	10
7	Brooklyn	0
14	Philadelphia	0
0	WASHINGTON	14
17	New York	9
35	Detroit	7
19	CHIC. CARDS	3
13	BROOKLYN	0
21	Green Bay	24

Art Albrecht	C-T-LB	6'1"	200	20		
Chuck Cherundolo	C-LB	6'1"	212	26	1	
Clure Mosher	C-G-LB	6'1"	215	22		
Hal Hinte (from GB)	DE	6'1"	195	22		
Ralph Wenzel	DE	6'	205	24		
John Naioti	DB	5'10"	175	20		

Ted Doyle	T	6'2"	220	28		
Eberle Schultz	T	6'4"	250	24		
George Somers	T	6'2"	260	26		1
(1 PAT in 1 attempt, missed 1 FG attempt)						
John Woudenberg	T	6'3"	220	24		
(1 reception for – 1 yd.)						

Joe Lamas	G	5'10"	216	26		6
Hubbard Law	G-LB	6'1"	210	21	1	
(1 rush for 6 yds.)						
Frank Pastin	G-LB	5'10"	197	21		
Mike Rodak	G-DE	5'10"	195	25		
Jack Sanders	G-LB	6'	215	25	1	7
(7 PAT in 8 attempts)						
Milt Simington	G	6'2"	220	24		4
(1 FG in 1 attempt, 1 PAT in 2 attempts)						
George Sirochman	G	6'2"	220	24		

After two early losses, the Steelers shockingly came alive and won seven of their last nine contests. In this totally unexpected transformation of the chaotic Steelers into contenders, rookie tailback Bill Dudley made the big difference.

Although Dudley stood only 5'10", had problems outrunning some linemen, and passed the ball with an awkward side-arm motion, he was a born winner. He ran slowly but knew how to use his blockers, which hole to hit, and when to cut back across an open field. He looked funny passing, but he completed passes, and his running, passing, kick-returning, defensive work, punting, and place-kicking all testified to a competitor's heart burning in his small body. He introduced himself to the league by running 55 yards for a touchdown in the first minute of play on opening day. Like Eddie Stanky in baseball, Bill Dudley had limited talent but always found a way to win.

NEW YORK GIANTS 5-5-1 Steve Owen

14	Washington	7
10	Pittsburgh	13
35	PHILADELPHIA	17
7	Chic. Bears	26
7	Brooklyn	17
9	PITTSBURGH	17
14	Philadelphia	0
7	WASHINGTON	14
21	GREEN BAY	21
21	CHIC. CARDS	7
10	BROOKLYN	0

Emmett Barrett	C-LB	6'2"	192	23		
Harold Hall	C-LB	6'2"	210	28		
Mel Hein	C-LB	6'2"	232	33	1	
Ed Hiemstra	C-G-LB	6'	200	22	1	
Jiggs Kline	DE	6'1"	198	28		
Harry Buffington	BB-LB	6'	195	23	1	

Kay Bell	T	6'2"	230	27		
Al Blozis	T	6'6"	250	23		
Frank Cope	T	6'2"	220	26		
Paul Stenn	T	6'2"	236	24		

Chuck Avedisian	G-LB	5'9"	200	24		
Monk Edwards	G-T-LB	6'3"	210	22		
Ed Lechner	G-T	6'1"	200	22		
Red Seick	G-LB	6'	195	31		

Cold in mid-season, hot at the end, the Giants finished a lukewarm third in the Eastern Division. Starting out with a victory over the Redskins, the Giants hoped to repeat as Eastern champs, but a three-game losing skid in October laid that ambition to rest, and the club had to win its last two games just to break even for the year.

The New Yorkers lost a lot of blood to the military, with runner Len Eshmont, blocking back Nello Falaschi, end Jim Poole, and tackle John Mellus lining up in different formations to the music of different signals. To compensate, Tuffy Leemans concentrated more on passing than on running, leaving the bulk of the ball-carrying to rookie Merle Hapes. The line was bolstered by rookie tackle Al Blozis, a 6'6" broth of a man who was a world champion shot-putter at Georgetown University. But the incoming talent hardly balanced the men trading in their blue jerseys for olive drab.

BROOKLYN DODGERS 3-8-0 Mike Getto

35	Philadelphia	14
28	Detroit	7
0	PITTSBURGH	7
10	WASHINGTON	21
17	NEW YORK	7
0	CLEVELAND	17
0	CHIC. BEARS	35
7	PHILADELPHIA	14
3	Washington	23
0	Pittsburgh	13
0	New York	10

Art Deremer	C-LB	6'3"	208	24		
Don Pierce	C-LB	6'1"	186	23		
Tom Robertson	C-LB	6'	218	25	1	
(1 kickoff return for 9 yds.)						
Si Titus	C-LB-DE	6'	195	23		
Mike Nixon	WB-DB	5'11"	187	30		
Bob Gifford	BB-LB	6'	200	23		

Mike Jurich	T	6'1"	235	23		
Duce Keahey (from NY)	T-G	6'2"	215	25		
Bruiser Kinard	T	6'1"	220	27		
Walt Merrill	T	6'2"	215	25		
Bernie Weiner	T-G	5'11"	222	24		

Bob Jeffries	G	6'2"	206	23		
Art Jocher	G	6'1"	207	26		
Bernie Kapitansky	G	6'1"	212	21		
George Kinard	G	6'1"	205	25		
Jim Sivell	G	5'9"	205	28		
Bud Svendsen	G-C-LB	6'1"	195	27	1	

With owner Dan Topping, coach Jock Sutherland, and star tailback Ace Parker all in the military, the Dodgers made an about-face. Sutherland had been the organizational genius and Parker the inspirational leader. Without their presence the team wandered through the season with very little direction. Mike Getto coached the club but could not replace Sutherland. Losers before the Scot arrived in Brooklyn, the Dodgers turned back into losers as soon as he left.

Dean McAdams played indifferently at tailback and could not fill Parker's shoes as a leader. Bruiser Kinard and Perry Schwartz kept up their good work on the line, and runners Pug Manders and Merl Condit gained yardage consistently although their jobs were tougher now that Parker's passes were no longer a threat. The Dodgers won only three games all year, but a victory over the rival Giants salvaged some of their local pride.

PHILADELPHIA EAGLES 2-9-0 Greasy Neale

24	Pittsburgh	14
14	Cleveland	24
14	BROOKLYN	35
10	WASHINGTON	14
17	New York	35
0	PITTSBURGH	14
14	Chic. Bears	45
27	Washington	30
0	NEW YORK	14
14	Brooklyn	7
0	GREEN BAY	7

Ray Graves	C-LB	6'1"	205	23	1	1
(1 PAT in 1 attempt)						
Ken Hayden	C-LB	6'	205	22	1	
Basilio Marchi	C-LB	6'2"	225	33		
Bob Wear	C-LB	5'11"	205	23		
Tex Williams	C-LB	5'11"	190	23		
Jack Smith	OE-DE	6'1"	200	25		
(1 kickoff return for 13 yds.)						
Al Thacker	DB	5'10"	200	23		
Jim Lankas	FB-LB	6'2"	215	24		

Leo Brennan	T	6'	210	22		
Leon Cook	T	5'11"	220	22		
John Eibner	T	6'2"	235	26		
Joe Frank	T	6'1"	215	27		
Bill Halverson	T	6'3"	242	24		
Frank Hrabetin	T	6'4"	235	26		
(1 kickoff return for 7 yds.)						
Ed Kasky	T	6'1"	220	23		
(Missed 1 field goal attempt)						
Steve Levanitis	T	6'1"	220	23		
Vic Sears	T	6'3"	210	24		6

Enio Conti	G	5'11"	205	29		
Woody Gerber	G	6'	220	22	1	
Bernie Kaplan	G	6'	205	29		
Al Milling	G	5'9"	170	22		
Rupert Pate	G	6'1"	205	25		6

Good ball players were scattered as rarely as four-leaf clovers on the Eagles, but Uncle Sam picked a handful of these gems for his own team. Linemen Bob Suffridge and Phil Ragazzo, starting end Bob Kreiger, and backs Jim Castiglia, Dan DeSantis, and Terry Fox (last year's top three rushers) all marched off into the military. Coach Greasy Neale made up for the losses by inviting hordes of rookies to training camp and keeping the best.

Tommy Thompson beat the draft because he could see in only one eye, and he spent the year directing the Eagles' T-formation offense. He led the team to an opening-day 24-14 victory over the Steelers, but eight straight losses followed for the young Eagles, and that fact, coupled with the prospect of more players being drafted, prompted the Eagles to merge with the Steelers when the 1943 season rolled around.

TEAM TOTALS

OFFENSE	FIRST DOWNS: Tot	by Rsh	by Pas	by Pen	RUSHING: No.	Yds.	Avg. Yds.	TD	PASSING: Att	Com	Comp Pct.	Yds.	Avg. Yds. Att.	Avg. Yds. Comp	TD	Int	Pct. Int.	PUNTING: No.	Avg. Yds.
WASH.	149	71	66	12	413	1521	3.7	9	257	137	53.3	1600	6.2	11.7	16	17	6.6	63	44.3
PITT.	130	86	29	15	490	1851	3.8	15	161	51	31.7	686	4.3	13.5	2	11	6.8	75	36.6
N.Y.	105	65	36	4	401	1221	3.0	10	148	67	45.3	957	6.5	14.3	10	14	9.5	65	38.5
BKN.	109	76	23	10	431	1495	3.5	9	159	56	35.2	714	4.5	12.8	3	24	15.1	73	40.6
PHI.	124	66	50	8	407	1105	2.7	8	213	96	45.1	1416	6.6	14.8	8	17	8.0	72	37.2

OFFENSE	PUNT RETURNS: No.	Yds.	Avg. Yds.	TD	KICKOFF RETURNS: No.	Yds.	Avg. Yds.	TD	INTERCEPTION RETURNS: No.	Yds	Avg. Yds.	TD	PENALTIES: No.	Yds.	FUMBLES: No.	Lost	POINTS: Tot	PAT	FG Att	FG	Saf.	OFFENSE
WASH.	45	544	12.1	0	23	640	27.8	2	19	225	11.8	0	67	610	26	13	227	28	9	3	2	WASH.
PITT.	43	662	15.4	2	30	699	23.3	1	21	420	20.0	0	58	383	22	10	167	20	16	3	0	PITT.
N.Y.	31	393	12.7	0	24	564	23.5	0	15	269	17.9	1	48	437	15	7	155	20	16	3	0	N.Y.
BKN.	29	309	10.7	0	31	656	21.2	0	14	229	16.4	1	32	288	23	10	100	13	6	3	0	BKN.
PHI.	42	596	14.2	1	42	882	21.0	1	18	179	9.9	0	47	392	26	11	134	17	8	3	0	PHI.

Use Name – Backs & Ends	Pos.	Age	Hgt	Wgt	Pts	Int	Rushing No.	Rushing Yds	Rushing Avg	Rushing TD	Passing Att	Passing Comp	Passing %	Passing Yds	Passing Yd/Att	Passing TD	Passing Int–%	Passing RK	Receiving No.	Receiving Yds	Receiving Avg	Receiving TD	Punting No.	Punting Avg	Kicking Pat	Kicking Att	Kicking %	Kicking FG	Kicking Att	Kicking %	Punt Returns No.	Punt Returns Yds	Punt Returns Avg	Punt Returns TD	Kickoff Returns No.	Kickoff Returns Yds	Kickoff Returns Avg	Kickoff Returns TD
WASHINGTON REDSKINS																																						
Sammy Baugh	TB-DB	28	6'2"	185	6	5	20	61	3.1	1	225	132	59	1524	6.8	16	11– 5	1					37	46.6							5	63	13	0				
Dick Poillon	TB-DB	22	6'	185	5		55	148	2.7	0	15	2	13	52	3.5	0	3–20						11	38.5	2	2	100	1	2	50	1	0	0	0	3	65	22	0
Roy Zimmerman	TB-DB	24	6'2"	200	4		12	56	4.7	0	10	2	20	13	1.3	0	2–20						4	50.5	1	1	100	1	1	100					1	25	25	0
Andy Farkas	FB-DB	26	5'10"	192	39	3	125	468	3.7	3									11	143	13	2			3	3	100				16	219	14	0	4	206	52	1
Bob Seymour	FB-DB	26	6'2"	208	6	3	54	190	3.5	1									3	20	7	0									4	79	20	0				
Steve Juzwik	FB-DB	24	5'8"	190	15		15	75	5.0	2															3	3	100				3	33	11	0	1	22	22	0
Rufus Deal	FB-DB	24	6'	205			5	12	2.4	0																												
Dick Todd	WB-FB-DB	27	5'11"	170	26	2	65	195	3.0	0	6	1	17	11	1.8	0	1–17		23	328	14	4	11	40.2	2	3	67				13	143	11	0	2	92	46	0
Wilbur Moore	WB-BB-DB	26	5'11"	190	12	3	10	25	2.5	0									10	114	11	2									1	3	3	0	1	24	24	0
Ed Justice	WB-DB	29	6'1"	195	6	1	3	–1	–0.3	0									9	108	12	1																
John Goodyear	WB-DB	22	6'1"	190			2	1	0.5	0																												
Ray Hare	BB-LB	24	6'1"	205	12	1	27	197	7.3	1									5	57	11	0									1	0	0	0	1	95	95	1
Cecil Hare	BB-LB	23	5'11"	195	12		14	57	4.1	1									3	35	12	1									1	4	4	0	1	11	11	0
Marv Whited	BB-LB	24	5'10"	210			1	3	3.0	0																												
Bob Masterson	OE-DE	27	6'1"	220	32		3	12	4.0	0	1	0	0	0	0.0	0	0– 0		22	308	14	2			17	19	89	1	5	20					3	45	15	0
Ed Cifers	OE-DE	26	6'2"	225	18														18	196	11	1													2	0	0	0
John Kovatch	OE-DE	22	6'3"	190	6														12	90	8	1													1	13	13	0
Al Krueger	OE-DE	23	6'1"	185															9	65	7	0													1	19	19	0
Bob McChesney	OE-DE	30	6'2"	200	12		2	22	11.0	0									8	100	13	2																
Charley Malone	OE-DE	32	6'4"	200															3	29	10	0																
PITTSBURGH STEELERS																																						
Bill Dudley	TB-DB	21	5'10"	175	36	3	162	696	4.3	5	94	35	37	438	4.7	2	5– 5	9	1	24	24	0	18	32.0							20	271	14	0	11	298	27	1
Andy Tomasic	TB-DB	22	6'	175	6	2	60	214	3.6	0	54	11	20	174	3.2	0	5– 9		1	27	27	0	17	35.5	0	1	0				12	199	17	1	4	94	24	0
Dick Riffle	FB-DB	27	6'1"	204	25	4	118	467	4.0	4	8	3	38	64	8.0	0	1–12		3	50	17	0	1	40.0	1	1	100				1	8	8	0	7	137	20	0
Joe Hoague	FB-DB	24	6'2"	200	6	1	65	168	2.6	1	1	0	0	0	0.0	0	0– 0						2	44.0														
Curt Sandig	HB-DB	24	5'10"	170	24	5	50	116	2.3	3	4	2	50	10	2.5	0	0– 0		6	103	17	0	37	38.8							6	142	24	1	7	168	24	0
George Gonda	HB-DB	21	5'10"	175	12	1	17	147	8.6	2									1	7	7	0									2	17	9	0				
John Binotto (to PHI)	HB-DB	22	5'10"	185	1		17	47	2.8	0															1	1	100				2	25	13	0				
Al Donelli (to PHI)	HB-DB	23	5'7"	165			2	–4	–2.0	0																												
Vern Martin	BB-LB	22	5'10"	195	12														7	64	9	1																
Russ Cotton	BB-LB	27	6'2"	195		1													2	58	29	0																
Walt Kichefski	OE-DE	26	6'1"	210															15	189	13	0																
Don Looney	OE-DB	24	6'2"	180	6														7	59	8	1																
Tom Brown	OE-DE	21	6'2"	216	6														4	69	17	0																
Tony Bova	OE-DB	25	6'1"	190		1													3	37	12	0													1	2	2	0
Armand Niccolai	T	30	6'2"	230	15																				9	9	100	2	14	14								
NEW YORK GIANTS																																						
Tuffy Leemans	QB-DB	29	6'	200	18		51	116	2.3	3	69	35	51	555	8.0	7	4– 6	4	1	–10	–10	0									2	26	13	0				
Andy Marefos	QB-FB-DB	25	6'	220	6	1	48	138	2.9	1	29	11	38	176	6.1	1	5–17											0	2	0								
Bob Trocolor	QB-DB	23	6'2"	205			26	18	0.7	0	5	3	60	52	10.4	1	1–20						16	41.3							2	24	12	0	1	35	35	0
Bill Hutchinson	QB-DB	26	5'9"	180			7	27	3.9	0	4	1	25	–3	–0.7	0	2–50						2	32.5							1	1	1	0				
Merle Hapes	FB-DB	23	5'10"	185	30	3	95	363	3.8	3	2	2	100	–12	–6.0	0	0– 0		10	79	8	2	15	37.1							11	170	15	0	9	215	24	0
Hank Soar	FB-DB	28	6'2"	210	8	3	49	187	3.8	1	10	3	30	34	3.4	0	1–10						3	42.0	2	3	67	0	2	0	3	29	10	0	5	134	27	0
Leo Cantor	FB-DB	23	6'1"	195	12	2	67	124	1.9	2	29	12	41	155	5.3	1	1– 3						20	38.1							5	69	14	0	1	24	24	0
Ward Cuff	WB-DB	29	6'	195	39	1	38	189	5.0	0									16	267	17	2			18	18	100	3	11	27	4	54	14	0	3	78	26	0
Don Lieberum	WB-DB	24	6'	175			11	29	2.6	0									6	65	11	0									1	0	0	0	1	12	12	0
Al Owen	BB-LB	29	6'	205			8	27	3.4	0									1	20	20	0									2	20	10	0				
Leland Shaffer	BB-LB	30	6'2"	205			1	3	3.0	0									3	20	7	0													2	40	20	0
Dom Principe	BB-LB	25	6'	210															2	33	17	0	1	32.0														
John Chickerneo	BB-LB	26	6'1"	205		1																	8	37.8														
Jim Lee Howell	OE-DE	27	6'6"	218															10	115	12	0																
Will Walls	OE-DE	27	6'4"	220	12														7	190	27	2													2	26	13	0
Neal Adams	OE-DE	23	6'3"	195	24	1													6	87	15	3																
John Lascari	OE-DE	24	6'2"	210	6														3	38	13	1						0	1	0								
Frank Liebel	OE-DE	22	6'1"	203															2	53	27	0																
BROOKLYN DODGERS																																						
Dean McAdams	TB-DB	24	6'1"	190	2		110	314	2.9	0	89	35	39	441	5.0	2	15–17	11	3	11	4	0	52	41.3	2	2	100				6	95	16	0	7	165	24	0
Harold McCullough	TB-DB	24	5'11"	170			21	11	0.5	0	38	12	32	211	5.6	1	3– 8						12	35.2							1	0	0	0				
Gerry Courtney	TB-DB	24	6'	195	6	1	8	12	1.5	1	4	1	25	14	3.5	0	2–50		1	1	1	0																
Curt Mecham	TB-DB	22	6'	180			3	0	0.0	0	4	1	25	9	2.3	0	0 0																					
Meril Condit	HB-DB	25	5'11"	185	37	6	129	647	5.0	2	17	5	29	27	1.6	0	3–18		9	111	12	0	7	45.0	10	10	100	3	6	50	21	210	10	0	8	172	22	0
Pug Manders	FB-DB	29	6'	200	36	2	93	316	3.4	6	1	0	0	0	0.0	0	0– 0		4	53	13	0													9	210	23	0
Bob Robertson	HB-DB	25	5'11"	185		2	46	132	2.9	0	3	1	33	1	0.3	0	1–33		5	61	12	0	1	32.0							1	4	4	0				
Walt Fedora	FB-DB	23	5'11"	190			16	34	2.1	0																									4	75	19	0
Jack Vetter	HB-DB	21	6'2"	198			1	4	4.0	0																												
Thurman Jones	FB-DB	24	5'10"	200	1		1	2	2.0	0															1	1	100											
Rhoten Shetley	BB-LB	24	5'11"	210	6	1													3	19	6	1																
Wendell Butcher	BB-LB	28	6'1"	195															1	16	16	0																
Perry Schwartz	OE-DE	27	6'2"	195	6		2	20	10.0	0									13	200	15	1													2	25	13	0
Eddie Rucinski	OE-DE	26	6'2"	198	6														9	99	11	1																
Herman Hodges	OE-DE	27	6'1"	200															4	74	19	0																
Joe Tofil	OE-DB	24	6'1"	205															3	33	11	0																
Don Eliason	OE-DE	24	6'2"	205															1	36	36	0																
PHILADELPHIA EAGLES																																						
Tommy Thompson	QB-DB	26	6'1"	190	6	4	92	9	0.1	1	203	95	47	1410	6.9	8	16– 8	5													7	60	9	0	5	76	15	0
Len Barnum	QB-DB	29	6'	200	16	1	30	64	2.1	0	9	1	11	6	0.7	0	1–11		3	54	18	0	50	38.1	7	8	88	3	7	43	1	44	44	0	1	16	16	0
Bob Davis	HB-DB	28	6'	180	18	2	43	207	4.8	2									6	93	16	1									10	84	8	0	8	140	18	0
Ted Williams	FB-LB	25	5'11"	185	12		50	183	3.7	2									9	58	6	0													3	58	19	0
Bosh Pritchard (from CLE)	HB-DB	23	5'11"	165	6	3	38	166	4.4	0									2	4	2	0	19	34.7							11	107	10	0	4	158	40	1
Ernie Steele	HB-DB	24	6'	190	13	2	24	124	5.2	0									7	114	16	1	2	30.5	1	1	100				10	264	26	1	7	160	23	0
Lou Tomasetti	HB-DB	26	6'	195		1	45	102	2.3	0									4	22	6	0									3	37	12	0	4	90	23	0
Dick Erdlitz	HB-DB	22	5'10"	182	14	1	21	69	3.3	1									5	78	16	0			8	8	100								1	25	25	0
Billy Jefferson (to BKN)	HB-DB	24	6'2"	210			12	58	4.8	0	4	1	25	11	2.8	0	0– 0						2	49.5											3	74	25	0
Bert Johnson	HB-DB	30	6'	215	12		27	54	2.0	0									9	123	14	2													2	40	20	0
Jack Stackpool	FB-LB	24	6'1"	207			15	47	3.1	0									2	59	30	0													1	13	13	0
Irv Hall	FB-LB	28	6'	210			8	14	1.8	0									2	18	9	0	1	36.0											1	22	22	0
Bob Masters	HB-DB	31	5'11"	200			1	3	3.0	0																												
Fred Meyer	OE-DE	23	6'2"	190	6		2	13	6.5	0									16	304	19	1													1	14	14	0
Larry Cabrelli	OE-DE	25	5'11"	195	6														15	249	17	1																
Len Supulski	OE-DB	21	6'	175	6	1	1	1	1.0	0									8	149	19	1																
Bob Priestley	OE-DE	30	5'11"	192															4	47	12	0																
Bill Combs	OE-DB	22	5'11"	183	6														4	44	11	1																

TEAM TOTALS

DEFENSE	First Downs: Tot	by Rsh	by Pas	by Pen	Rushing: No.	Yds.	Avg Yds.	TD	Passing: Att.	Com	Comp Pct.	Yds.	Avg. Yds. Att.	Avg. Yds. Comp	TD	Int.	Pct. Int.	Punting: No.	Avg. Yds.	Punt Returns: No.	Yds.	Avg. Yds.	TD	Kickoff Returns: No.	Yds.	Avg. Yds.	TD	Interception Returns: No.	Yds.	Avg. Yds.	TD	Penalties: No.	Yds.	Fumbles: No.	Lost	Points: Tot	PAT	FG Att	FG	Saf.	DEFENSE
WASH.	111	52	46	13	367	848	2.3	5	216	81	37.5	1093	5.1	13.5	5	19	8.8	83	38.1	30	375	12.5	0	37	829	22.4	2	17	319	18.8	1	43	340	16	7	102	12	8	4	0	WASH.
PITT.	114	59	50	5	366	1205	3.3	6	211	100	47.4	1183	5.6	11.8	9	21	10.0	71	41.3	40	412	10.3	0	27	500	18.5	0	11	131	11.9	0	60	512	19	7	119	14	17	5	0	PITT.
N.Y.	159	86	62	11	466	1485	3.2	13	228	114	50.0	1401	6.1	12.3	4	15	6.6	64	37.6	40	500	12.5	1	35	826	23.6	1	14	215	15.4	0	41	290	36	19	139	16	8	3	0	N.Y.
BKN.	131	77	49	5	426	1630	3.8	13	199	89	44.7	1175	5.9	13.2	9	14	7.0	62	40.0	37	551	14.9	1	22	526	23.9	0	24	173	7.2	0	61	495	26	12	168	21	13	3	0	BKN.
PHI.	131	78	40	13	464	1727	3.7	20	178	79	44.4	1241	7.0	15.7	12	18	10.1	65	40.5	31	446	14.4	0	26	632	24.3	1	17	224	13.2	0	51	452	20	10	239	32	9	3	0	PHI.

CHICAGO BEARS 11-0-0 George Halas, Luke Johnsos, Hunk Anderson, Paddy Driscoll

Scores of Each Game		
44	Green Bay	28
21	Cleveland	7
41	CHIC. CARDS	14
26	NEW YORK	7
45	PHILADELPHIA	14
16	DETROIT	0
35	Brooklyn	0
38	GREEN BAY	7
42	Detroit	0
47	CLEVELAND	0
21	Chic. Cards	7

Use Name	Pos.	Hgt	Wgt	Age	Int	Pts
Stu Clarkson	C-LB	6'2"	198	23		
Al Matuza	C-LB	6'2"	205	23	2	
Bulldog Turner	C-LB	6'1"	240	23	8	12
(1 kickoff return for 6 yds.)						
Clint Wager	OE-DE	6'6"	215	21		
Voluntarily retired – Bob Snyder						

Use Name – Tackles	Pos.	Hgt	Wgt	Age	Int	Pts
Lee Artoe	T	6'3"	230	26		20
(20 PAT's in 22 attempts, missed 1 FG attempt)						
Bill Hempel	T	6'	235	22		
Al Hoptowit	T	6'1"	216	26		
Ed Kolman	T	6'2"	230	24		
Joe Stydahar	T	6'4"	240	30		5
(5 PAT's in 8 attempts)						

Use Name – Guards	Pos.	Hgt	Wgt	Age	Int	Pts
Len Akin	G-LB	5'11"	207	26	1	
Ray Bray	G	6'	245	25		
Chuck Drulis	G-LB	5'10"	215	24	1	
Danny Fortmann	G-LB	6'	210	26	4	6
Nick Kerasiotis	G-LB	5'11"	197	24		
George Musso	G	6'2"	255	32		

With the Bears' first three fullbacks in the service, George Halas stuck fourth-stringer Gary Famiglietti into the lineup, and he simply responded by leading the club in rushing and winning a berth on the All-Pro team. Another Bear hero was rookie Frank Maznicki, who filled in for Navy-departed George McAfee with his own brand of speedy running. End Dick Plasman was also gone, as was tackle Joe Stydahar, who was called late in the year. Even George Halas was summonded back into the Navy in mid-season. But nothing could stop the talent-heavy Bears. They won eleven straight, easy games, by 14 points or more.

Halas left the club in the hands of assistants Hunk Anderson, Luke Johnsos, and Paddy Driscoll, and this triumvirate had close to a pushbutton job. They got passing from Sid Luckman, long-yardage receiving from halfback Scooter McLean, and superb line play from Bulldog Turner, Danny Fortmann, Lee Artoe, and George Wilson.

GREEN BAY PACKERS 8-2-1 Curly Lambeau

Scores of Each Game		
28	CHIC. BEARS	44
17	Chic. Cards	13
38	DETROIT	7
45	CLEVELAND	28
28	Detroit	7
55	CHIC. CARDS	24
30	Cleveland	12
7	Chic. Bears	38
21	New York	21
7	Philadelphia	0
24	PITTSBURGH	21

Use Name	Pos.	Hgt	Wgt	Age	Int	Pts
Charley Brock	C-LB	6'2"	210	26	6	6
Bob Flowers	C-LB	6'1"	205	25		
Bob Ingalls	C-LB	6'3"	200	23	1	6
Earl Ohlgren	DE	6'2"	210	24		
John Stonebraker	OE-DE	6'3"	200	24		
Ben Starret	BB-LE	5'11"	210	24		
(1 punt for 43 yds.)						

Use Name – Tackles	Pos.	Hgt	Wgt	Age	Int	Pts
Paul Berezney	T	6'2"	220	25		
(1 kickoff return for 7 yds.)						
Tiny Croft	T	6'3"	300	21		
Royal Kahler	T	6'2"	226	24		
Bill Lee	T	6'2"	240	30		
Ernie Pannell	T	6'2"	220	25		
Baby Ray	T	6'6"	245	27		

Use Name – Guards	Pos.	Hgt	Wgt	Age	Int	Pts
Buckets Goldenberg	G-LB	5'10"	220	31	4	
Bill Kuusisto	G	6'	225	24		
Russ Letlow	G	6'	222	28		
Pete Tinsley	G-LB	5'8"	205	29	1	
Fred Vant Hull	G-LB	6'	214	22		

Don Hutson caught lightning in a bottle this year, in addition to a lot of passes. With the Packer offense stressing the air game, Hutson set new NFL season records for receptions, yards gained on receptions, touchdown passes caught, and points scored. Passer Cecil Isbell set a few records himself, in yards gained passing and in touchdown passes. No one in the league had yet learned how to cover the crafty Hutson, and Isbell rarely missed the receiver in the open. Hutson also kicked extra points for Green Bay, building up a record 138 points that went unmatched until Paul Hornung came along in 1960.

Even with this premier combination, however, the Packers were only the second-best team in the league. They lost twice all year, but unfortunately did so at the hands of the unbeaten Bears. No excuses could be offered, as even with Clarke Hinkle in the Coast Guard, youngsters Ted Fritsch, Charlie Sample, and Tony Canadeo picked up the slack.

CLEVELAND RAMS 5-6-0 Dutch Clark

Scores of Each Game		
0	Chic. Cards	7
24	PHILADELPHIA	14
14	Detroit	0
7	CHIC. BEARS	21
14	Washington	33
28	Green Bay	45
7	CHIC. CARDS	3
17	Brooklyn	0
12	GREEN BAY	30
27	DETROIT	7
0	Chic. Bears	47

Use Name	Pos.	Hgt	Wgt	Age	Int	Pts
Bill Conkright	C-LB	6'1"	205	28	2	
Don Johnson	C-LB	6'	205	21		
Bill Rieth	C-LB	5'11"	203	26		
Hank Rockwell	C-LB-DE	6'4"	230	25	1	
Herb Godfrey	OE-DE	6'1"	187	23		
Maury Patt	DE	6'2"	205	28		

Use Name – Tackles	Pos.	Hgt	Wgt	Age	Int	Pts
Boyd Clay	T	6'1"	225	29		4
(4 PAT's in 4 attempts)						
Jake Fawcett	T	5'11"	225	23		
Tex Mooney	T	6'5"	270	25		
Joe Pasqua	T	6'1"	228	24		1
(1 PAT in 1 attempt)						

Use Name – Guards	Pos.	Hgt	Wgt	Age	Int	Pts
Larry Brahm	G-LB	5'10"	204	26	1	
Riley Matheson	G-LB	6'2"	205	27	1	
Barney McGarry	G-LB	6'1"	200	24		
Roy Stuart	G-LB	5'8"	185	22	1	
Wilfred Thorpe	G-LB	6'3"	210	25	1	

The Cleveland rise to a 5-6-0 record looked more impressive than it really was, since the five wins came against the Cardinals, Dodgers, Eagles, and Lions, all weaker sisters on the circuit. On the other hand, the Bears beat the Rams 21-7 and 47-0, the Packers stopped them 45-28 and 30-12, and the Redskins took a 33-14 decision. The Cardinals even downed the Rams 7-0 in their first meeting. The improved record showed only that the Rams were the best of the bad.

Although fullback Johnny Drake hung up his spikes, Dante Magnani developed into a good overall runner and receiver. Two of the linemen, Chet Adams and Riley Matheson, won compliments for their play, but neither Dan Reeves nor Fred Levy were around to add their praise. Both co-owners had been called back into the military and received permission to suspend operation for 1943 with their players being spread around the league.

CHICAGO CARDINALS 3-8-0 Jimmy Conzelman

Scores of Each Game		
7	CLEVELAND	0
13	DETROIT	0
13	GREEN BAY	17
14	Chic. Bears	41
7	Detroit	0
3	Cleveland	7
24	Green Bay	55
0	Washington	28
3	Pittsburgh	19
7	New York	21
7	CHIC. BEARS	21

Use Name	Pos.	Hgt	Wgt	Age	Int	Pts
Ray Apolskis	C-LB	5'11"	200	23	2	
Vince Banonis	C-LB	6'1"	220	21	2	
Ben Ciccone	C-LB	5'10"	220	**31**		
Ernie Wheeler	DB	6'1"	200	27		
(1 punt for 40 yds.)						
Dick Evans	OE-DE	6'3"	210	25		

Use Name – Tackles	Pos.	Hgt	Wgt	Age	Int	Pts
Joe Allton	T	6'2"	235	21	1	
Al Babartsky	T	6'	225	26		
Chet Bulger	T	6'3"	235	24		
Gil Duggan	T	6'3"	225	24	1	
Ross Nagel	T	6'4"	225	19		
Carl Olson	T	6'2"	206	25		
Champ Siebold	T	6'4"	237	29	1	6

Use Name – Guards	Pos.	Hgt	Wgt	Age	Int	Pts
Conway Baker	G	5'11"	225	**30**		
Libero Bertagnolli	G-LB	5'9"	190	26		
Frank Bohlmann	G	5'11"	212	25		
Ralph Fife	G-LB	6'	202	22		
Bob Maddock	G-LB	6'	200	22		
Gordon Wilson	G	6'	230	26		

With last year's top passer, receiver, and lineman in military service, the Cardinals expected a rough time this year. But even without Johnny Clement, Bill Dewell, and Joe Kuharich, the Cardinals opened the season by shutting out the Rams and Lions. Whatever faint hopes this beginning raised, eight losses in the next nine matches dashed them like crockery on the rocks. Bud Schwenk, the new passer, was no Sammy Baugh, but at least he kept busy by throwing the most passes in the league, and veteran end Pop Ivy grabbed twenty-seven aerials, a very distant second to Don Hutson's seventy-four receptions. Marshall Goldberg continued to be the backfield ace on offense and defense, but no one made up for Kuharich's loss in the line. After his third mediocre team in a row, coach Jimmy Conzelman quit to work in the front office of the St. Louis Browns baseball team. He would be back, though, bringing better times with him.

DETROIT LIONS 0-11-0 Bill Edwards, Bull Karcis

Scores of Each Game		
0	Chic. Cards	13
0	CLEVELAND	14
7	BROOKLYN	28
7	Green Bay	38
0	CHIC. CARDS	7
7	GREEN BAY	28
0	Chic. Bears	16
7	PITTSBURGH	35
7	Cleveland	27
0	CHIC. BEARS	42
3	WASHINGTON	15

Use Name	Pos.	Hgt	Wgt	Age	Int	Pts
Tony Arena	C-LB	6'	200	24		
Sloko Gill	C-G-LB	5'10"	185	24	1	
John Schiechl (from PIT)	C-LB	6'2"	245	25		
Alex Wojciechowicz	C-LB	5'11"	210	27	2	
(4 receptions for 44 yds., 3 kickoff rets. for 30 yds.)						
Bill Kennedy	DE	5'11"	194	23		

Use Name – Tackles	Pos.	Hgt	Wgt	Age	Int	Pts
Henry Goodman	T	6'3"	220	23		
Ted Pavelic	T	6'	210	23		3
(1 field goal in 2 attempts)						
Alex Schibanoff	T	6'1"	215	22		
George Speth	T	6'2"	220	24		
Emil Uremovich	T	6'2"	230	25		

Use Name – Guards	Pos.	Hgt	Wgt	Age	Int	Pts
Larry Sartori	G	6'	208	25		
(1 punt for 42 yds.)						
John Wiethe	G-LB	6'	200	29		
Tony Zuzzio	G	5'11"	210	26		

These Lions had no bite, no scratch, no offense, and no defense. The attack scored only five touchdowns all year, never posting more than 7 points in any one game, while the defense sprang so many leaks that 263 enemy points rushed through in a torrent. The closest the feeble Lions came to victory was a 7-0 loss to the Cardinals.

After three games, coach Bill Edwards quit, and Bull Karcis picked up the coaching reigns. The nightmare kept on going, though, and Karcis may have been tempted to play fullback himself, as none of his young backs showed any magnetism for the end zone. The only thing worse than the feeble passing attack was the attendance, a sparse 100,508 for seven home games. But owner Fred Mandel showed no discouragement. He never made any move to sell the club nor to fold for the duration of the war, as some other clubs had. In fact, Mandel insisted that the NFL and his team go on.

TEAM TOTALS

OFFENSE	FIRST DOWNS: Tot	by Rsh	by Pas	by Pen	RUSHING: No.	Yds.	Avg. Yds.	TD	PASSING: Att	Com	Comp Pct.	Yds.	Avg. Yds. Att.	Avg. Yds. Comp	TD	Int	Pct. Int.	PUNTING: No.	Avg. Yds.
CHI.B.	155	98	48	9	470	1911	4.1	23	194	94	48.5	1974	10.2	21.0	21	29	14.9	49	38.9
G.B.	176	65	97	14	422	1274	3.0	10	330	172	52.1	2407	7.3	14.0	28	18	5.5	58	37.4
LEVE.	103	36	60	7	310	1035	3.3	5	249	109	43.8	1537	6.2	14.1	13	27	10.8	77	40.3
C.	132	58	59	15	366	1021	2.8	4	316	131	41.5	1432	4.5	10.9	6	29	9.2	74	39.5
[illegible]	115	67	40	8	342	1261	3.7	4	222	73	32.9	885	4.0	12.1	1	33	14.9	71	40.6

PUNT RETURNS: No.	Yds.	Avg. Yds.	TD	KICKOFF RETURNS: No.	Yds.	Avg. Yds.	TD	INTERCEPTION RETURNS: No.	Yds.	Avg. Yds.	TD	PENALTIES: No.	Yds.	FUMBLES: No.	Lost	POINTS: Tot	PAT	FG Att	FG	Saf	OFFENSE
39	459	11.8	1	21	537	25.6	0	33	402	12.2	3	99	905	27	15	376	46	6	4	0	CHI.B
32	327	10.2	0	36	769	21.4	1	33	349	10.6	1	38	312	13	8	300	39	10	5	0	G.B.
30	307	10.2	0	39	739	18.9	0	23	255	11.1	0	45	315	20	8	150	19	6	3	1	CLEVE.
32	364	11.4	0	36	855	23.8	1	25	263	10.5	1	46	400	25	11	98	11	10	5	0	CHI.C.
34	378	11.1	0	38	687	18.1	0	18	188	10.4	0	43	364	35	23	38	5	6	1	0	DET.

Use Name – Backs & Ends	Pos.	Age	Hgt	Wgt	Pts	Int	Rushing No.	Rushing Yds	Rushing Avg	Rushing TD	Passing Att	Passing Comp	Passing %	Passing Yds	Passing Yd/Att	Passing TD	Passing Int–%	Passing RK	Receiving No.	Receiving Yds	Receiving Avg	Receiving TD	Punting No.	Punting Avg	Kicking Pat	Kicking Att	Kicking %	Kicking FG	Kicking Att	Kicking %	Punt Returns No.	Punt Returns Yds	Punt Returns Avg	Punt Returns TD	Kickoff Returns No.	Kickoff Returns Yds	Kickoff Returns Avg	Kickoff Returns TD
CHICAGO BEARS																																						
Sid Luckman	QB-DB	25	6'	200	6	4	13	24	1.8	0	105	57	54	1023	9.7	10	13–12	3					24	40.6							6	55	9	0				
Charlie O'Rourke	QB-DB	25	5'11"	175	6	3	18	−17	−0.9	1	88	37	42	951	**10.8**	11	16–18	6					23	35.5							2	8	4	0				
Gary Famiglietti	FB-LB	27	6'	225	48	1	118	503	4.3	**8**									1	12	12	0			0	1	0								1	9	9	0
Frank Maznicki	HB-DB	22	5'9"	178	45	4	54	343	**6.4**	1	1	0	0	0	0.0	0	0–0		2	17	9	1			21	22	95	4	5	80	6	50	8	0	1	33	33	0
Hugh Gallarneau	HB-DB	25	6'	190	42		68	292	4.3	4									14	291	21	3									9	101	11	0	6	151	25	0
Harry Clark	HB-DB	24	6'	190	36		58	273	4.7	4									6	131	22	2									5	76	15	0	5	159	32	0
Ray Nolting	HB-DB	28	5'11"	185	18		57	245	4.3	3									2	23	12	0									3	23	8	0	1	10	10	0
John Petty	FB-LB	23	6'1"	225	12	1	41	149	3.6	2									4	53	13	0	2	57.0														
Ray McLean	HB-DB	26	5'10"	165	54	3	26	63	2.4	0									19	571	**30**	8									6	118	20	1	4	106	27	0
Bill Geyer	HB-DB	22	5'10"	170			9	18	2.0	0									1	22	22	0									2	28	14	0				
Bill Osmanski	FB-LB	25	5'11"	198			2	9	4.5	0																												
Frank Morris	FB-LB	24	6'2"	214			3	7	2.3	0									3	24	8	0																
Adolph Kissell	HB-DB	21	5'11"	190			2	−1	−0.5	0																									2	63	32	0
John Siegal	OE-DE	24	6'1"	202	12														13	263	20	2																
Hamp Pool	OE-DE	27	6'3"	225	30														10	321	32	5																
George Wilson	OE-DE	28	6'1"	205	12	1													9	89	10	0																
Bob Nowaskey	OE-DE	24	6'	200			1	3	3.0	0									6	128	21	0																
Connie Mack Berry	OE-DE	26	6'3"	212	12														4	29	7	0																
GREEN BAY PACKERS																																						
Cecil Isbell	TB-DB	27	6'1"	190	6	6	36	83	2.3	1	268	**146**	54	**2021**	7.5	**24**	14–5	2					4	35.3							1	14	14	0	3	44	15	0
Tony Canadeo	TB-HB-DB	23	5'11"	190	18	1	89	272	3.1	3	59	24	41	310	5.3	3	4–7		10	66	7	0	18	35.8							7	76	11	0	6	137	23	0
Chuck Sample	FB-LB	22	5'9"	200	30		57	255	4.5	4									6	35	6	1													3	91	30	0
Lou Brock	FB-HB-DB	24	6'	192	20	2	95	237	2.5	2									20	139	7	1	32	38.1	2	2	100	0	1	0	8	86	11	0	9	179	20	0
Ted Fritsch	FB-LB	21	5'10"	210	13		74	223	3.0	0									9	60	7	0	3	40.7	1	1	100	4	5	**80**	1	31	31	0	2	43	22	0
Joe Laws	HB-DB	31	5'9"	180	6	3	29	100	3.4	0	3	2	67	76	25.3	1	0–0		6	96	16	1									7	56	8	0	2	36	18	0
Andy Uram	HB-DB	27	5'10"	188	31	2	24	75	3.1	0									21	420	20	4			1	1	100				7	50	7	0	8	208	26	1
Bob Kahler	HB-DB	25	6'3"	200			8	4	0.5	0									2	21	11	0									1	14	14	0				
Dick Weisgerber	BB-DE	27	5'10"	198	2		5	21	4.2	0															2	2	100											
Larry Craig	BB-DE	26	6'1"	205			2	0	0.0	0																									2	24	12	0
Don Hutson	OE-DB	29	6'1"	185	**138**	7	3	4	1.3	0									**74**	**1211**	15	**17**			**33**	**34**	97	1	4	25								
Harry Jacunski	OE-DE	26	6'2"	204	6														8	125	16	1																
Joel Mason	OE-DE	29	6'	195															7	86	12	0																
Ray Riddick	OE-DE	24	6'1"	202	6														6	104	17	1																
Joe Carter	OE-DE	32	6'1"	200	6														2	19	10	1																
Keith Ranspot (from DET)	OE-DB	27	6'3"	205	6														1	25	25	1																
CLEVELAND RAMS																																						
Parker Hall	TB-DB	25	6'	195	6	3	41	−3	−0.1	1	140	62	44	815	5.8	7	19–14	8					36	38.8							12	148	12	0	10	155	16	0
Jack Jacobs	TB-DB	23	6'1"	180		4	32	91	2.8	0	93	43	46	640	6.9	6	6–6	7					33	42.3							8	63	8	0	4	83	21	0
Gaylon Smith	FB-DB	26	5'11"	205	12	4	83	332	4.0	2	12	2	17	49	4.1	0	1–8		3	66	22	0									6	62	10	0	6	109	18	0
George Morris	FB-DB	23	5'11"	188		2	22	65	3.0	0																					1	2	2	0	1	15	15	0
Corby Davis	FB-DB	27	5'11"	205		1	28	55	2.0	0	2	1	50	22	11.0	0	1–50		2	18	9	0	7	39.3														
Dante Magnani	WB-DB	25	5'10"	178	30		59	344	5.8	1	1	0	0	0	0.0	0	0–0		24	276	12	4									2	27	14	0	11	250	23	0
Len Janiak	WB-FB-DB	26	6'1"	205	6		34	108	3.2	0	1	1	100	11	11.0	0	0–0		6	51	9	1																
Bill Lazetich	WB-DB	25	6'	195	12		3	19	6.3	1									6	65	11	1													1	27	27	0
Jack Boone	WB-DB	24	5'11"	175	6	1	3	−1	−0.3	0									2	58	29	1									1	5	5	0				
Art Elston	BB-LB	23	5'11"	195			1	15	15.0	0									4	58	15	0													2	46	23	0
Warren Plunkett	BB-LB	22	6'	200															2	16	16	0													1	4	4	0
John Petchel	BB-LB	23	5'11"	185			1	−2	−2.0	0									1	16	16	0													2	26	13	0
Jim Benton	OE-DE	25	6'3"	195	6														23	345	15	1																
Ben Hightower	OE-DB	23	6'2"	183	18														19	312	16	3																
Johnny Wilson	OE-DE	26	6'3"	205	12														6	113	19	1																
Joe Gibson	OE-DE	23	6'3"	204															6	79	13	0																
George Platukas	OE-DE	27	6'	205	12	1													5	64	13	1																
Chet Adams	T	26	6'3"	235	23																				14	15	93	3	6	50								
CHICAGO CARDINALS																																						
Bud Schwenk	TB-DB	24	6'2"	205	12	1	111	313	2.8	2	**295**	126	43	1360	4.6	6	27–9	9					3	38.0											2	24	12	0
Joe Bukant	TB-DB	26	6'	210			17	34	2.0	0	15	4	27	56	3.7	0	2–13																					
John Knolla	TB-WB-DB	23	5'10"	180		1	15	43	2.9	0	6	1	17	16	2.7	0	0–0		8	48	6	0									6	64	11	0	1	24	24	0
Marshall Goldberg	FB-DB	24	5'11"	195	12	3	116	369	3.2	1									9	108	12	0									6	60	10	0	15	393	26	1
Bob Morrow	FB-DB	24	6'	225	6		45	145	3.2	1																												
John Martin	WB-DB	24	6'1"	195		6	30	10	0.3	0									22	312	14	0	36	39.3							4	50	13	0	8	202	25	0
Steve Lach	WB-DB	22	6'2"	205	25	4	30	97	3.2	0									18	261	15	4	31	40.1	1	1	100				13	158	12	0	7	164	23	0
Lloyd Cheatham	WB-DB	23	6'2"	198	6	1	1	1	1.0	0									6	29	5	1									3	32	11	0	2	37	19	0
Buddy Parker	BB-LB	28	6'	190			1	9	9.0	0									2	7	4	0																
Milt Popovich	BB-G-LB	25	5'11"	208		1													2	21	11	0	3	36.3														
Pop Ivy	OE-DE	26	6'3"	220	2														27	259	10	0			2	2	100											
Al Coppage	OE-DE	26	6'1"	197															20	196	10	0													1	11	11	0
Bill Daddio	OE-DE	26	5'11"	204	29	1													11	108	10	1			8	8	100	5	10	50								
Ray Ebli	OE-DE	22	6'2"	210															6	83	14	0																
DETROIT LIONS																																						
Harry Hopp	TB-DB	23	6'	210		1	66	230	3.5	0	68	20	29	258	3.8	0	13–19	12					27	40.7							9	98	11	0	5	108	22	0
Chet Wetterlund	TB-DB	24	6'2"	185		1	23	6	0.3	0	44	13	30	230	5.2	0	10–23						11	40.8							3	26	9	0	5	89	18	0
Tom Colella	TB-DB	24	6'	185		1	23	51	2.2	0	41	18	44	178	4.3	0	4–10						16	38.1							2	14	7	0	4	74	19	0
Ned Mathews	TB-WB-DB	24	5'10"	185			21	79	3.8	0	22	6	27	43	2.0	1	2–9		3	38	13	0									7	82	12	0	5	97	19	0
Joe Stringfellow	TB-OE-DB	22	6'	185			16	41	2.6	0	13	5	38	67	5.2	0	2–15		8	89	11	0	9	40.3											2	54	27	0
Elmer Hackney	FB-LB	26	6'2"	200	12		34	208	6.1	2									3	22	7	0													1	4	4	0
Frank Grigonis	FB-LB	23	5'10"	182	6	1	37	131	3.5	1									1	17	17	0													2	49	25	0
John Polanski	FB-LB	23	6'2"	212		1	17	67	3.9	0																												
Harry Seltzer	FB-LB	23	5'9"	195			14	44	3.1	0									2	23	12	0																
Mickey Sanzotta	WB-TB-DB	21	5'9"	185		2	71	268	3.8	0	15	4	27	45	3.0	0	0–0		5	16	3	0	1	42.0							5	46	9	0				
Lloyd Cardwell	WB-DB	29	6'2"	190	6	2	6	78	13.0	1									5	125	25	0									2	45	23	0	1	13	13	0
Emil Banjavic	WB-DB	23	6'1"	194	6	1	11	67	6.1	0									5	50	10	1	5	47.0							2	29	15	0	4	69	17	0
John Hall	WB-DB	25	6'	190		1	2	−8	−4.0	0	1	0	0	0	0.0	0	0–0		1	42	42	0									4	38	10	0	4	86	22	0
Paul Szakash	BB-DB	29	6'	210															5	53	11	0																
Bill Callihan	BB-DB	26	6'3"	215		3					1	0	0	0	0.0	0	1–100		4	48	12	0	1	44.0														
Murray Evans	BB-DB	23	6'1"	205			1	−1	−1.0	0	17	7	41	64	3.8	0	1–6		2	32	16	0																
Bill Fisk	OE-DE	25	6'	200															15	177	12	0													1	10	10	0
Charlie Behan	OE-DE	22	6'3"	195															4	63	16	0																
Gran Harrison	OE-DE	25	6'3"	210															3	21	7	0																
Larry Knorr	OE-DE	25	6'2"	192															2	18	9	0																
Perry Scott	OE-DE	25	6'2"	210															1	7	7	0																
Augie Lio	G-LB	24	6'	235	5	1																			5	5	100	0	4	0					1	4	4	0

TEAM TOTALS

DEFENSE	First Downs: Tot	by Rsh	by Pas	by Pen	Rushing: No.	Yds.	Avg. Yds.	TD	Passing: Att.	Com	Comp Pct.	Yds.	Avg. Yds. Att.	Avg. Yds. Comp	TD	Int.	Pct. Int.	Punting: No.	Avg. Yds.	Punt Returns: No.	Yds.	Avg. Yds.	TD	Kickoff Returns: No.	Yds.	Avg. Yds.	TD	Interception Returns: No.	Yds.	Avg. Yds.	TD	Penalties: No.	Yds.	Fumbles: No.	Lost	Points: Tot	PAT	FG Att	FG	Saf.	DEFENSE
CHI. B.	**98**	35	47	16	**294**	**519**	**1.8**	**3**	280	111	39.6	1179	**4.2**	10.6	7	**33**	11.8	76	38.2	**25**	298	11.9	1	60	1194	19.9	0	29	282	9.7	1	34	324	33	18	**84**	12	2	0	0	CHI. B.
G.B.	147	79	59	9	376	1559	4.1	17	242	100	41.3	1471	6.1	14.7	8	33	**13.6**	56	37.0	38	395	10.4	0	45	1058	23.5	1	18	282	15.7	2	63	539	22	15	215	27	9	6	1	G.B.
CLEVE.	165	92	60	13	463	1764	3.8	11	262	125	47.7	1740	6.6	13.9	17	23	8.8	56	40.6	40	504	12.6	0	27	545	20.2	0	27	310	11.5	0	46	387	21	10	207	25	9	4	1	CLEVE.
CHI. C.	114	61	44	9	390	1495	3.8	11	214	84	39.3	1502	7.0	17.9	15	25	11.7	75	40.2	44	532	12.1	1	26	530	20.4	0	29	390	13.4	2	71	**636**	19	8	209	26	9	3	0	CHI. C.
DET.	128	69	51	8	440	1463	3.3	13	219	103	47.0	1623	7.4	15.8	22	18	8.2	69	41.0	32	326	10.2	0	15	**388**	25.9	1	33	453	13.7	1	53	441	20	10	263	33	9	2	1	DET.

WASHINGTON REDSKINS 6-3-1 Dutch Bergman

Scores of Each Game		
27	BROOKLYN	0
33	Green Bay	7
13	CHIC. CARDS	7
48	Brooklyn	10
14	Phil-Pitt	14
42	DETROIT	20
21	CHIC. BEARS	7
14	PHIL-PITT	27
10	New York	14
7	NEW YORK	31
	EAST Playoff	
28	New York	0

Use Name	Pos.	Hgt	Wgt	Age	Int	Pts
Ken Hayden	C-LB	6'	205	23		
George Smith	C-LB	6'2"	214	29	2	
(1 punt return for 3 yds.)						
Jack Smith	OE-DE	6'1"	200	26		
Joe Gibson*	BB-LB-DE	6'3"	210	24		
Coye Dunn	WB-DB	6'	198	27		

Use Name – Tackles	Pos.	Hgt	Wgt	Age	Int	Pts
Joe Pasqua*	T	6'1"	225	25		1
(1 PAT in 1 attempt)						
Lou Rymkus	T	6'4"	223	24	1	12
Willie Wilkin	T	6'4"	270	27		
Joe Zeno	T	5'10"	235	24		

Use Name – Guards	Pos.	Hgt	Wgt	Age	Int	Pts
Dick Farman	G-LB	6'	216	27		
Al Fiorentino	G-LB	5'7"	200	26		
Tony Leon	G-LB	5'9"	195	26		
Angelo Paternoster	G-LB	5'11"	195	23		
Frank Ribar	G-LB	6'1"	190	26		
Clyde Shugart	G-T-LB	6'1"	220	26	1	
Steve Slivinski	G-LB	5'10"	215	26	1	

After seven games, the Redskins were undefeated and sitting pretty atop the Eastern Division. Dutch Bergman was directing the club as coach, with Ray Flaherty in the Navy, and he worried only a little when the Skins lost to the war-mergered Eagles-Steelers club. A home-and-away series with the New York Giants capped the season for the Skins, who needed only a win or a tie to clinch the Eastern crown. But they got neither, as the Giants won both games to deadlock the title race. Expected to fold completely in the playoff game, the fading Redskins shot back into focus as Sammy Baugh threw for three touchdowns in a 28-0 put-down of the New Yorkers.

Baugh starred all year in the passing game. He ranked with Sid Luckman as the top passer in pro ball—and he also intercepted the most aerials by picking off eleven wayward tosses. On offense or defense, passes were Baugh's trademark.

NEW YORK GIANTS 6-3-1 Steve Owen

Scores of Each Game		
14	Phil-Pitt	28
20	Brooklyn	0
42	PHIL-PITT	14
21	GREEN BAY	35
0	Detroit	0
7	CHIC. BEARS	56
24	CHIC. CARDS	13
24	BROOKLYN	7
14	WASHINGTON	10
31	Washington	7
	EAST Playoff	
0	WASHINGTON	28

Use Name	Pos.	Hgt	Wgt	Age	Int	Pts
Mel Hein	C-LB	6'2"	234	34	1	
(Attempted 1 pass – incomplete)						
Bill Piccolo	C-LB	5'11"	185	23		
Hub Barker	BB-LB	5'10"	195	24		

Use Name – Tackles	Pos.	Hgt	Wgt	Age	Int	Pts
Verlin Adams	T-DE	6'	205	25		
Al Blozis	T	6'6"	250	24		6
(1 reception for 15 yds.)						
Vic Carroll	T	6'4"	230	30		
Frank Cope	T	6'2"	232	27		
Frank Umont	T	5'11"	220	25		

Use Name – Guards	Pos.	Hgt	Wgt	Age	Int	Pts
Chuck Avedisian	G-LB	5'9"	200	25		6
Walt Dubzinski	G-C-LB	5'10"	205	23	1	
Sal Marone	G	5'10"	195	25		
Tom Roberts	G-T	6'1"	215	28		
Larry Visnic	G-LB	5'11"	195	24		

Against the Bears, the New York defense looked like a kitchen strainer trying to hold water. Chicago quarterback Sid Luckman riddled the Giants with pinpoint passes, throwing for 433 yards and a record seven touchdowns in a 56-7 romp. After this performance, few expected the Giants to contain Sammy Baugh's slings, but the New Yorkers stiffened their defense and upset the Redskins 14-10 and 31-7 in a home-and-away series which ended the season with a tie for the Eastern lead. But the pass defense turned back into a pumpkin in the playoff game by allowing 28 points, while the offense never got to the scoreboard.

During the year, the young and the old helped the club. Rookie Bill Paschal bulled his way to a league-leading 572 yards behind the tough blocking of second-year tackle Al Blozis. Balancing this youth was thirty-four-year-old center Mel Hein, an instructor at Union College during the week and the pivot of the New York line on Sunday.

PHILADELPHIA EAGLES – PITTSBURGH STEELERS 5-4-1 Greasy Neale, Walt Kiesling

Scores of Each Game			
17	BROOKLYN	H	0
28	NEW YORK	H	14
21	Chic. Bears		48
14	New York		42
34	CHIC. CARDS	P	13
14	WASHINGTON	H	14
7	Brooklyn		13
35	DETROIT	P	34
27	Washington		14
28	GREEN BAY	H	38

H = at Philadelphia
P = at Pittsburgh

Use Name	Pos.	Hgt	Wgt	Age	Int	Pts
Ray Graves	C-LB	6'1"	205	24	1	
Al Wukits	C-LB	6'3"	190	23	1	6
Ray Reutt	DE	6'	195	26		
Hugh McCullough	DB	6'	185	27		

Use Name – Tackles	Pos.	Hgt	Wgt	Age	Int	Pts
Ted Doyle	T	6'2"	220	29		
Joe Frank	T	6'1"	215	28		
Bucko Kilroy	T	6'2"	240	22		
Elbie Schultz	T	6'4"	250	25		
Vic Sears	T	6'3"	220	25		
(1 kickoff return for 15 yds.)						
Al Wistert	T	6'1"	205	22		

Use Name – Guards	Pos.	Hgt	Wgt	Age	Int	Pts
Rocco Canale	G	5'11"	225	26		
Enio Conti	G	5'11"	205	30	1	
Eddie Michaels	G	5'11"	210	29		
Gordon Paschka	G	6'	205	23		2
(2 PAT's in 2 attempts)						

Faced with draining financial and manpower resources, the Eagles and Steelers merged into one team for a season. Philadelphia and Pittsburgh split the home schedule, coaches Greasy Neale and Walt Kiesling shared the reigns, and both teams pooled their players.

But with stars Bill Dudley and Tommy Thompson off to military service, the team was a true potpourri on the field. The Redskins sold Roy Zimmerman, Sammy Baugh's understudy, to the Phi-Pitt squad to play quarterback. Free-agent halfback Jack Hinkle shone as a ball carrier, while second-year tackle Vic Sears won a spot on the UPI All-Pro team. Rookies Al Wistert and Bucko Kilroy helped in the line, and veteran end Bill Hewitt came out of retirement, even wearing a helmet for the first time in his career. There was even a left-handed passer, Allie Sherman, who played little but whom coach Neale called "the smartest football player I ever coached." With a varied cast, the merged team managed to win five games.

BROOKLYN DODGERS 2-8-0 Pete Cawthorn

Scores of Each Game		
0	Detroit	27
0	Phil-Pitt	17
0	Washington	27
0	NEW YORK	20
21	Chic. Bears	33
10	WASHINGTON	48
7	CHIC. CARDS	0
13	PHIL-PITT	7
7	GREEN BAY	31
7	New York	24

Use Name	Pos.	Hgt	Wgt	Age	Int	Pts
Bill Conkright (from WAS)*	C-LB	6'1"	205	29	1	
Vaughn Stewart (from CHIC)	C-LB	6'1"	200	23		
Bud Svendsen	C-LB	6'1"	180	28	1	
John Bandura	OE-DE	6'	206	24		
Herm Schmaar	DE	6'2"	210	28		

Use Name – Tackles	Pos.	Hgt	Wgt	Age	Int	Pts
Bill Davis	T	6'1"	235	25		
Jake Fawcett*	T	5'11"	225	24		
John Matisi	T	6'2"	215	22	1	
Tex Mooney*	T	6'5"	290	26		
George Sergienko	T	6'1"	240	25		

Use Name – Guards	Pos.	Hgt	Wgt	Age	Int	Pts
Bill Armstrong	G	6'1"	210	23		
George Grandinette	G	5'9"	215	26		
Al Gutknecht	G-LB	6'	210	26		
Lew Jones	G-LB	6'	215	31	1	
(1 kickoff return for 5 yds.)						
Pete Owens	G-C-LB	5'11"	205	26		
Phil Swiadon	G	6'	220	28		

* = Property of CLEVELAND RAMS wh- suspended operations for the 1943 season.

Brooklyn sports fans suffered through a long year, as both baseball and football Dodgers plodded through dismal seasons. Although the baseball team finished seventh, it had a colorful manager in Leo Durocher and a flashy star in Dixie Walker. The football Dodgers also lost regularly, finishing dead last in the East, but had none of the color of their baseball brethren. Pete Cawthorn handled the coaching reigns on the war-ravaged football team, fielding a lineup which had problems scoring points. Dean McAdams again played tailback, and the fans again talked wistfully of the absent Ace Parker. McAdams' task was not made any easier when end Perry Schwartz went into the service, but runners Pug Manders and Merlin Condit kept the running game respectable and Bruiser Kinard starred in a patchwork line. Only wins over Philadelphia-Pittsburgh and the Cardinals broke the sports gloom hanging over Brooklyn.

TEAM TOTALS

	FIRST DOWNS:				RUSHING:				PASSING:									PUNTING:	
OFFENSE	Tot	by Rsh	by Pas	by Pen	No.	Yds.	Avg. Yds.	TD	Att.	Com	Comp. Pct.	Yds.	Avg. Yds. Att.	Avg. Yds. Comp	TD	Int.	Pct. Int.	No.	Avg. Yds.
WASH.	112	55	49	8	320	1069	3.3	7	254	139	54.7	1837	7.2	13.2	24	20	7.9	65	43.1
N.Y.	102	72	24	6	386	1436	3.7	14	149	63	42.3	760	5.1	12.1	8	9	6.0	69	39.5
PHI-PIT	138	96	32	10	459	1730	3.8	18	175	65	37.1	1138	6.5	17.6	11	20	11.4	62	34.4
BKN.	80	39	35	6	333	610	1.8	4	205	90	43.9	969	4.7	10.8	5	21	10.2	89	36.2
DEFENSE																			
WASH.	110	68	34	8	406	1330	3.3	10	193	77	39.9	1026	5.3	13.3	9	26	13.5	76	37.0
N.Y.	118	63	51	4	366	1006	2.7	8	229	119	52.0	1724	7.5	14.5	16	18	7.9	76	37.2
PHI-PIT	96	42	41	13	312	793	2.5	18	221	102	46.2	1393	6.3	13.7	15	22	10.0	60	39.9
BKN.	128	75	44	9	404	1562	3.9	16	219	86	39.3	1552	7.1	18.0	15	15	6.9	60	37.3

	PUNT RETURNS:				KICKOFF RETURNS:				INTERCEPTION RETURNS:				PENALTIES:		FUMBLES:		POINTS:					TEAM TOTALS
OFFENSE	No.	Yds.	Avg. Yds.	TD	No.	Yds.	Avg. Yds.	TD	No.	Yds.	Avg. Yds.	TD	No.	Yds.	No.	Lost	Tot	PAT	FG Att	FG	Saf.	OFFENSE
WASH.	41	442	10.8	0	26	616	23.7	0	26	247	9.5	1	65	499	30	11	229	28	7	1	0	WASH.
N.Y.	35	466	13.3	0	20	436	21.8	0	18	205	11.4	1	42	293	21	5	197	26	10	3	0	N.Y.
PHI-PIT	32	335	10.5	0	40	802	20.1	0	22	304	13.8	2	54	484	37	15	225	30	6	1	0	PHI-PIT
BKN.	30	268	8.9	0	40	968	24.2	0	15	163	10.9	0	36	292	22	9	65	8	6	1	0	BKN.
DEFENSE																						DEFENSE
WASH.	28	267	9.5	0	31	726	23.4	0	20	231	11.6	2	44	349	16	8	137	17	6	2	0	WASH.
N.Y.	39	391	10.0	0	41	791	19.3	0	9	135	15.0	0	49	329	33	10	170	23	7	1	0	N.Y.
PHI-PIT	28	348	12.4	0	34	772	22.7	2	20	258	12.9	1	59	466	20	8	230	29	11	1	0	PHI-PIT
BKN.	34	430	12.6	1	10	225	22.5	0	21	193	9.2	1	56	435	26	9	234	27	14	7	0	BKN.

Use Name — Backs & Ends	Pos.	Age	Hgt	Wgt	Pts	Int	RUSHING				PASSING								RECEIVING				PUNTING		KICKING						PUNT RETURNS				KICKOFF RETURNS			
							No.	Yds	Avg	TD	Att	Comp	%	Yds	Yd/Att	TD	Int–%	RK	No.	Yds	Avg	TD	No.	Avg	Pat	Att	%	FG	Att	%	No.	Yds	Avg	TD	No.	Yds	Avg	TD
WASHINGTON REDSKINS																																						
Sammy Baugh	TB-DB	29	6'2"	180		11	19	−42	−2.2	0	239	133	56	1754	7.3	23	19– 8	2					50	45.9							2	13	7	0				
Leo Stasica	TB-DB	27	5'11"	195		1	9	−10	−1.1	0	6	1	17	34	5.7	0	1– 17						1	38.0							1	11	11	0				
Andy Farkas	FB-DB	27	5'10"	195	54		110	331	3.0	5									19	202	11	4									15	168	11	0	9	279	31	0
Bob Seymour	FB-DB	27	6'2"	205	12	2	65	232	3.6	0									17	167	10	2									13	173	13	0	2	34	17	0
Frank Akins	FB-LB	24	5'10"	200			10	25	2.5	0									1	51	51	0	3	18.0														
Jack Jenkins	FB-LB	23	6'1"	210	1		4	20	5.0	0															1	1	100											
Wilbur Moore	WB-DB	27	5'11"	180	54	2	40	231	5.8	2									30	537	18	7									2	2	1	0	1	18	18	0
Frank Seno	WB-DB	22	6'	185		1	26	152	5.8	0									12	195	16	0									2	27	14	0	3	61	20	0
Ray Hare	BB-LB	25	6'1"	205		3	21	96	4.6	0									2	9	5	0									1	5	5	0	2	36	18	0
Joe Aguirre	OE-DE	24	6'4"	220	48														37	420	11	7			6	9	67	0	2	0					3	21	7	0
Bob Masterson	OE-DE	28	6'1"	220	41														16	200	13	3			20	21	95	1	5	20					2	66	33	0
Alex Piasecky	OE-DE	26	6'2"	197	6	1													3	17	6	1													1	17	17	0
Ted Lapka	OE-DE	23	6'1"	190															2	39	20	0																
NEW YORK GIANTS																																						
Tuffy Leemans	QB-DB	30	6'	202			37	69	1.9	0	87	37	43	366	4.2	5	5– 6	7													3	66	22	0	2	29	15	0
Emery Nix	QB-DB	23	5'11"	180		2	19	26	1.4	0	53	24	45	390	7.4	3	3– 6	4													4	50	13	0	1	12	12	0
Bob Trocolor	QB-DB	24	6'2"	205			6	−4	−0.7	0	7	2	29	4	0.6	0	1– 14						5	31.0							1	17	17	0	2	64	32	0
Bill Paschal	FB-DB	22	6'	195	72		147	572	3.9	10									9	74	8	2	12	35.0							9	92	10	0	7	183	26	0
Carl Kinscherf	FB-DB	23	6'1"	185	6		49	77	1.6	1									2	4	2	0	32	40.7											2	57	29	0
Bull Karcis	FB-LB	34	5'9"	225			12	25	2.1	0									1	1	1	0													1	21	21	0
Ward Cuff	WB-FB-DB	30	6'1"	192	53	3	80	523	6.5	3	1	0	0	0	0.0	0	0– 0		7	52	7	0			26	27	96	3	9	33	9	120	13	0	3	59	20	0
Dave Brown	WB-DB	24	5'11"	190		6	32	131	4.1	0									5	29	6	0									7	106	15	0				
Hank Soar	WB-DB	29	6'2"	210		3	2	8	4.0	0																					2	15	8	0				
Leland Shaffer	BB-LB	31	6'2"	200		1	1	3	3.0	0									3	66	22	0																
Joe Sulatis	BB-DE	22	6'2"	210			1	6	6.0	0									1	12	12	0																
Will Walls	OE-DE	28	6'4"	220	12														14	231	17	2													1	3	3	0
Frank Liebel	OE-DE	23	6'1"	203	18														11	199	18	3																
Neal Adams	OE-DE	24	6'3"	195	12														8	65	8	1													1	8	8	0
Steve Pritko*	OE-DE	21	6'2"	205	6														1	12	12	0																
Len Younce	G-LB	26	6'1"	205	6	1																	20	42.5				0	1	0								
PHILADELPHIA EAGLES – PITTSBURGH STEELERS																																						
Roy Zimmerman	QB-DB	25	6'2"	200	35	5	33	−41	−1.2	1	124	43	35	846	6.8	9	17– 14	6					44	34.6	26	28	93	1	6	17					3	55	18	0
Allie Sherman	QB-DB	20	5'11"	160	6		17	−20	−1.2	1	37	16	43	208	5.6	2	1– 3																					
Jack Hinkle	HB-DB	25	6'	215	24	4	116	571	4.9	4									1	3	3	0	4	19.5							4	45	11	0	11	217	20	0
Ernie Steel	HB-DB	25	6'	190	36		85	409	4.8	4	1	0	0	0	0.0	0	1–100		9	168	19	2									12	152	13	0	11	236	21	0
Johnny Butler	HB-DB	24	5'10"	185	18		87	362	4.2	3	13	6	46	84	6.5	0	1– 8		3	63	21	0	11	37.0							13	108	8	0	6	92	15	0
Bob Thurbon	HB-DB	25	5'10"	172	36	1	71	291	4.1	5									6	100	17	1									2	19	10	0	6	150	25	0
Charlie Gauer	FB-LB-DE	22	6'2"	215		1	12	69	5.8	0									2	18	9	0																
Ben Kish	FB-DB	26	6'	200	12	5	22	50	2.3	0									8	67	8	1	1	42.0														
Ted Laux	HB-DB	25	5'10"	185	2	1	9	23	2.6	0									2	19	10	0			2	2	100				1	11	11	0				
Bob Masters (to CHI B)	FB-LB	32	5'11"	200			4	16	4.0	0																									2	37	19	0
Steve Sader	FB-LB	22	5'11"	180			3	5	1.7	0																												
Dean Steward	HB	20	6'	210			1	−6	−6.0	0													2	42.0														
Tony Bova	OE-DB	26	6'1"	190	30		1	11	11.0	0									17	419	25	5																
Larry Cabrelli	OE-DB	26	5'11"	195	12	1													12	199	17	1																
Tom Miller	OE-DE	25	6'2"	198	6	1													3	60	20	1																
Bill Hewitt	OE-DE	33	5'9"	190															2	22	11	0																
BROOKLYN DODGERS																																						
Dean McAdams	TB-DB	25	6'1"	195		3	41	−38	−0.9	0	75	37	49	315	4.2	0	7– 9	10	2	6	3	0	36	37.6							4	54	14	0	5	102	20	0
Ken Heineman	TB-DB	25	5'9"	165		2	49	126	2.6	0	57	19	33	285	5.0	3	8– 14	12					14	34.6							10	78	8	0	16	442	28	0
George Cafego (to WAS)	TB-DB	28	5'10"	180			34	−12	−0.4	0	45	22	49	258	5.7	1	3– 7						21	34.3							6	52	9	0	9	218	24	0
Cecil Johnson	TB-HB-DB	21	5'11"	204	12	1	26	38	1.5	0	8	4	50	16	2.0	0	1– 12		9	136	15	2	10	34.9											3	68	23	0
Frank Sachse	TB-HB-DB	26	6'	195			8	14	1.8	0	9	5	56	72	8.0	1	1– 11		3	26	9	0									2	37	19	0				
Pug Manders	FB-LB	30	6'	200	24		89	266	3.0	3	5	4	80	31	6.2	1	0– 0		5	68	14	1													1	19	19	0
Jody Marek	FB-LB	27	5'11"	182			6	9	1.5	0									1	0	0	0						0	1	0								
Marshall Edwards	FB-LB	27	6'1"	190			1	5	5.0	0									1	−4	−4	0																
Merl Condit	HB-DB	26	5'11"	185	12	1	67	190	2.8	1	6	0	0	0	0.0	0	1– 17		7	101	14	1	19	38.1				0	3	0	6	47	8	0	6	178	30	0
Frank Martin	HB-DB	24	5'10"	165		2	25	50	2.0	0	4	2	50	15	3.8	0	0– 0		13	152	12	0									5	38	8	0				
Tilly Manton	BB-DB	31	5'11"	190			2	−7	−3.5	0	4	2	50	26	6.5	0	0– 0		6	26	4	0						0	1	0								
Joe Setcavage	BB-DB	25	5'11"	190		1	1	3	3.0	0	1	0	0	0	0.0	0	0– 0		5	26	5	0									1	2	2	0	1	5	5	0
Bill Brown	BB-DB	26	6'	190															4	42	11	0																
Andy Kowalski	OE-DE	23	6'	197		1													11	145	13	0																
Keith Ranspot	OE-DE	28	6'3"	205															7	80	11	0																
George Webb	OE-DE	27	6'1"	180															7	60	9	0																
Ray Wehba	OE-DE	27	6'	215															4	43	11	0													1	15	15	0
Bruiser Kinard	T	28	6'1"	218	17														5	62	12	1			8	9	89	1	1	100								

CHICAGO BEARS 8-1-1 Luke Johnsos, Hunk Anderson, Paddy Driscoll

Scores of Each Game		
21	Green Bay	21
27	Detroit	21
20	CHIC. CARDS	0
48	PHIL–PITT	21
33	BROOKLYN	21
35	DETROIT	14
21	GREEN BAY	7
56	New York	7
7	Washington	21
35	Chic. Cards	24

Use Name	Pos.	Hgt	Wgt	Age	Int	Pts
Al Matuza	C-LB	6'2"	195	24		
Fred Mundee	C-LB	6'1"	220	30	1	
Bulldog Turner	C-LB	6'1"	235	24		
Joe Vodicka	HB-DB	5'10"	190	22		

Use Name – Tackles	Pos.	Hgt	Wgt	Age	Int	Pts
Al Babartsky	T	6'	225	27		
Bernie Digris	T-G	6'	212	24		
Al Hoptowit	T	6'1"	218	27		
Dom Sigillo	T	6'	230	30		
Bill Steinkemper	T	6'2"	220	29		

Use Name – Guards	Pos.	Hgt	Wgt	Age	Int	Pts
Danny Fortmann	G-LB	6'	210	27		
Pete Gudauskas	G-LB	6'2"	222	26		
Tony Ippolito	G-LB	5'10"	220	25	1	
Jim Logan	G	5'11"	190	26		
(1 kickoff return for 2 yds.)						
Monte Merkel	G	5'10"	215	25		
George Musso	G	6'2"	270	33		

Still strong from working his farm, thirty-four-year-old Bronko Nagurski ended his five-year retirement to rejoin the draft-depleted Bears as a tackle. Nagurski played in the line until the final game of the schedule against the Cardinals. Needing a victory to clinch the Western title, the Bears trailed the Cardinals 24-14 at the end of three quarters. Coach Hunk Anderson then told the old pro to take over at his old fullback spot, and seven plays later Bronko smashed over for a touchdown after a 62-yard drive. The Bears later had the ball on fourth down with 4 yards to go; Nagurski plowed off-tackle for 6 yards and a first down, and a Sid Luckman touchdown pass to Harry Clark soon put the Bears ahead for keeps. Picking up 84 yards in sixteen carries, Nagurski said, "That game gave me my greatest kick out of football."

GREEN BAY PACKERS 7-2-1 Curly Lambeau

Scores of Each Game		
21	CHIC. BEARS	21
28	Chic. Cards	7
35	DETROIT	14
7	WASHINGTON	33
27	Detroit	6
35	New York	21
7	Chic. Bears	21
35	CHIC. CARDS	14
31	Brooklyn	7
38	Phil–Pitt	28

Use Name	Pos.	Hgt	Wgt	Age	Int	Pts
Charley Brock	C-LB	6'2"	210	27	4	
Bob Flowers	C-LB	6'1"	215	26	1	
Amy McPherson	C-DT	5'11"	248	31		
Don Perkins	LB	6'	195	25		

Use Name – Tackles	Pos.	Hgt	Wgt	Age	Int	Pts
Chet Adams*	T	6'3"	240	27		3
(1 field goal in 6 attempts)						
Paul Berezney	T	6'2"	220	26		
Tiny Croft	T	6'3"	298	22		
Baby Ray	T	6'6"	250	28		
Ade Schwammel	T	6'2"	230	34		

Use Name – Guards	Pos.	Hgt	Wgt	Age	Int	Pts
Sherwood Fries	G-LB	6'1"	238	22		2
Buckets Goldenberg	G-LB	5'10"	220	32		2
Bill Kuusisto	G	6'	230	25		
Glen Sorenson	G	6'	225	22		
(Missed 2 field goal attempts)						
Pete Tinsley	G-LB	5'8"	205	30	1	

Don Hutson had hauled many a pass into the end zone, but he got a chance to get on the other end of the pipe on one play. Hutson took a handoff and headed off on what looked like an end run. With all the defense converging on him, the fast end pulled up short and tossed a 38-yard pass to Harry Jacunski all alone in the end zone. After the play, the poker-faced Hutson broke into a grin. Passing, it seemed, was not that difficult. Most of the Green Bay passes were thrown by Tony Canadeo and Irv Comp, since star tailback Cecil Isbell had quit to coach at Purdue University. Isbell explained why he quit when still young: "I hadn't been up in Green Bay long when I saw Lambeau go around the locker room and tell players like Herber and Gatenbein and Hank Bruder that they were all done with the Packers. I sat there and watched and then I vowed it would never happen to me. I'd quit before they came around to tell me."

DETROIT LIONS 3-6-1 Gus Dorais

Scores of Each Game		
35	CHIC. CARDS	17
27	BROOKLYN	0
21	CHIC. BEARS	27
14	Green Bay	35
7	Chic. Cards at Buffalo	0
6	GREEN BAY	27
14	Chic. Bears	35
0	NEW YORK	0
20	Washington	42
34	Phil–Pitt	35

Use Name	Pos.	Hgt	Wgt	Age	Int	Pts
Gerry Conlee	C-LB	5'11"	200	27	1	
(1 kickoff return for 15 yds.)						
Ernie Rosteck	C-LB	6'1"	210	21		
Alex Wojciechowicz	C-LB	5'11"	210	28	2	
(1 kickoff return for 17 yds.)						
Sam Busich	DE	6'3"	188	30		1
(1 PAT in 1 attempt)						
Bob Layden	DE	6'2"	215	23		

Use Name – Tackles	Pos.	Hgt	Wgt	Age	Int	Pts
Al Kaporch	T	5'10"	215	29	1	
Alex Ketzko	T	5'11"	215	25		
Ed Opalewski	T	6'3"	220	23		
Lloyd Wickett	T	6'1"	205	23		

Use Name – Guards	Pos.	Hgt	Wgt	Age	Int	Pts
Stan Batinski	G	5'10"	212	26		
Sonny Liles	G-LB	5'9"	185	24		
Riley Matheson*	G-LB	6'2"	205	28		
Ted Pavelic	G	6'	225	24		
Lyle Rockenbach	G	5'9"	192	27		
Tony Rubino	G	5'10"	205	22		
Roy Stuart*	G-LB	5'8"	185	23		

New coach Gus Dorais took over a team that had no offense, a porous defense, and lost every game in 1942. To soup up the attack, Dorais selected Georgia tailback Frankie Sinkwich as the Lions' first draft pick, and the rookie made the passing game respectable and led the club in rushing. With the Cleveland Rams in mothballs for the year, guard Riley Matheson spent the season in Detroit, joining Alex Wojciechowicz and Augie Lio in a line far from the worst in the league. Most importantly, Dorais never let the club slip back into the chaos of last year. The new coach got the Lions off to a roaring start with a 35-17 victory over the Cardinals and a 27-0 shellacking of Brooklyn, outscoring last year's entire point total in two games. The offense did cool off, though, and in the game with the Giants both teams moved up and down the field without scoring, the last 0-0 tie to date.

CHICAGO CARDINALS 0-10-0 Phil Handler

Scores of Each Game		
17	Detroit	35
7	GREEN BAY	28
0	Chic. Bears	20
0	DETROIT at Buffalo	7
7	Washington	13
13	Phil–Pitt	34
0	Brooklyn	7
14	Green Bay	35
13	New York	24
24	CHIC. BEARS	35

Use Name	Pos.	Hgt	Wgt	Age	Int	Pts
Don Pierce	C-LB	6'1"	186	24		
Buddy Parker	BB-LB	6'	190	29		
Andy Puplis	WB-DB	5'9"	180	28	1	
(1 kickoff return for 9 yds.)						

Use Name – Tackles	Pos.	Hgt	Wgt	Age	Int	Pts
Art Albrecht	T-C	6'1"	200	21		
Clarence Booth	T	6'	220	23		
Chet Bulger	T	6'3"	235	25		1
(1 PAT in 1 attempt)						
Gil Duggan	T	6'3"	225	25		

Use Name – Guards	Pos.	Hgt	Wgt	Age	Int	Pts
Vern Ghersanich	G-LB	5'11"	210		1	
Lou Marotti	G	5'10"	195	25		
Floyd Rhea	G-LB	6'	215	22		
(1 kickoff return for 10 yds.)						
Marshall Robnett	G-LB	6'	200	24		
(1 kickoff return for 12 yds.)						
Gordon Wilson	G	6'	230	27		
(1 kickoff return for 6 yds.)						

With Jimmy Conzelman working in baseball, long-time assistant coach Phil Handler took over as head man. Handler may have been looking for another sport to pursue after the Cardinals dropped all ten games on their schedule. The high note of the season was the final game against the Bears, in which Bronko Nagurski's heroics foiled a fine effort by the Cardinals to upset their big neighbors. Outside of that game, the Cardinals pressed their opponents very little. For the second straight year, the team's top passer and receiver marched off into the service. To replace absent passer Bud Schwenk and end Pop Ivy, coach Handler put rookie Ronnie Cahill in the lineup at tailback and veteran Eddie Rucinski at end. Shining through the darkness of the winless season, Rucinski snagged enough passes to win a spot on the wire-service All-Pro teams. Few of the other Cardinals heard praise, though.

TEAM TOTALS

OFFENSE	First Downs: Tot	by Rsh	by Pas	by Pen	Rushing: No.	Yds.	Avg. Yds.	TD	Passing: Att.	Com	Comp. Pct.	Yds.	Avg. Yds. Att.	Avg. Yds. Comp	TD	Int.	Pct. Int.	Punting: No.	Avg. Yds.
CHIC. B.	161	84	66	11	424	1651	3.9	14	229	117	51.1	2310	10.1	19.7	28	17	7.4	48	37.2
G.B.	134	60	66	8	397	1442	3.6	13	253	114	45.1	1909	7.5	16.7	21	19	7.5	52	36.0
DET.	106	49	46	11	294	817	2.8	10	248	93	37.5	1290	5.2	13.9	11	37	14.9	65	41.4
CHIC. C.	102	48	43	11	334	709	2.1	5	219	88	40.2	1095	5.0	12.4	6	39	17.8	56	38.7
DEFENSE																			
CHIC. B.	100	49	33	18	332	1282	3.9	14	203	64	31.5	980	4.8	15.3	8	24	11.8	62	38.9
G.B.	122	62	56	4	350	1112	3.2	9	242	111	45.9	1420	5.9	12.8	16	42	17.4	55	36.6
DET.	130	69	54	7	381	1213	3.2	14	227	109	48.0	1606	7.1	14.7	16	19	8.4	66	41.9
CHIC. C.	131	75	48	8	396	1166	2.9	13	198	101	51.0	1607	8.1	15.9	21	16	8.1	51	37.2

OFFENSE	Punt Returns: No.	Yds.	Avg. Yds.	TD	Kickoff Returns: No.	Yds.	Avg. Yds.	TD	Interception Returns: No.	Yds.	Avg. Yds.	TD	Penalties: No.	Yds.	Fumbles: No.	Lost	Points: Tot	PAT	FG Att	FG	Saf.	OFFENSE
CHIC. B.	28	359	12.8	0	29	722	24.9	1	24	219	9.1	0	86	748	27	18	303	39	7	2	0	CHIC. B.
G.B.	32	371	11.6	0	28	661	23.6	0	42	606	14.4	2	52	403	15	6	264	36	16	4	0	G.B.
DET.	32	436	13.6	1	36	815	22.6	1	19	304	16.0	2	59	472	12	5	178	22	12	2	0	DET.
CHIC. C.	16	163	10.2	0	31	569	18.4	0	16	243	15.2	0	45	389	17	5	95	11	5	2	0	CHIC. C.
DEFENSE																						DEFENSE
CHIC. B.	31	426	13.7	0	50	1145	22.9	0	17	314	18.5	1	57	475	22	6	157	22	10	1	0	CHIC. B.
G.B.	28	332	11.9	0	31	660	21.3	0	19	188	9.9	0	51	391	22	9	172	22	3	0	0	G.B.
DET.	29	291	10.0	0	29	615	21.2	0	37	436	11.8	1	58	501	23	12	218	29	10	3	0	DET.
CHIC. C.	29	355	12.2	0	24	655	27.3	0	39	536	13.7	2	65	634	19	12	238	31	7	1	0	CHIC. C.

							RUSHING				PASSING								RECEIVING				PUNTING		KICKING						PUNT RETURNS				KICKOFF RETURNS			
Use Name – Backs & Ends	Pos.	Age	Hgt	Wgt	Pts	Int	No.	Yds	Avg	TD	Att	Comp	%	Yds	Yd/Att	TD	Int–%	RK	No.	Yds	Avg	TD	No.	Avg	Pat	Att	%	FG	Att	%	No.	Yds	Avg	TD	No.	Yds	Avg	TD
CHICAGO BEARS																																						
Sid Luckman	QB-DB	26	6'	195	6	4	22	−40	−1.8	1	202	110	54	2194	10.9	28	12– 6	1					34	35.9							4	46	12	0	1	7	7	0
Bob Snyder	QB-DB	30	6'	205	45	1	6	−20	−3.3	0	26	7	27	116	4.5	0	4– 15						10	37.8	39	42	93	2	7	29								
Harry Clark	HB-DB	25	6'	180	60	5	120	556	4.6	3	1	0	0	0	0.0	0	1–100		23	535	23	7									10	158	16	0	13	326	25	0
Dante Magnani*	HB-DB	26	5'10"	178	24	2	51	310	6.1	2									6	88	15	1									4	40	10	0	6	171	29	1
Gary Famiglietti	FB-LB	28	6'	225	12		64	229	3.6	2									1	10	10	0																
Ray Nolting	HB-DB	29	5'11"	190	6	1	38	209	5.5	1									5	90	18	0									2	13	7	0	2	40	20	0
Ray McLean	HB-DB	27	5'10"	168	18	4	35	127	3.6	1									18	435	24	2									7	94	13	0	4	105	26	0
Bill Osmanski	FB-LB	26	5'11"	198	6		37	102	2.8	1																												
Bronko Nagurski	T-FB-LB	34	6'2"	235	6		16	84	5.3	1																												
Doug McEnulty	HB-DB	21	6'3"	215	6	1	16	45	2.8	0									1	10	10	1	4	46.8														
Bill Geyer	HB-DB	23	5'10"	170	24	2	16	36	2.3	2									5	123	25	2									1	8	8	0	2	71	36	0
Bob Steuber	HB-DB	21	6'2"	200			1	3	3.0	0																												
George Wilson	OE-DE	29	6'1"	205	30	2													21	293	14	5																
Hamp Pool	OE-DE	28	6'3"	215	30														18	363	20	5																
Jim Benton*	OE-DE	26	6'3"	195	18														13	235	18	3																
Connie Mack Berry	OE-DE	27	6'3"	218	12														4	99	25	2																
John Siegal	OE-DE	25	6'1"	205															2	29	15	0																
GREEN BAY PACKERS																																						
Tony Canadeo	TB-DB	24	5'11"	195	30	2	94	489	5.2	3	129	56	43	875	6.8	9	12– 9	5	3	31	10	2	3	34.0							8	93	12	0	10	242	24	0
Irv Comp	TB-DB	24	6'2"	192	24	10	77	182	2.4	3	92	46	50	662	7.2	7	4– 4	3					12	37.8							1	20	20	0	4	81	20	0
Lou Brock	TB-HB-DB	25	6'	195	18	1	45	67	1.5	2	22	9	41	274	12.5	3	1– 5		4	57	14	1	32	36.4							8	126	16	0	5	112	22	0
Joe Laws	HB-DB	32	5'9"	188		7	43	232	5.4	0									5	33	7	0									10	84	8	0	2	47	24	0
Tony Falkenstein	FB-LB	28	5'10	210	6		58	198	3.4	1									3	39	13	0													2	47	24	0
Ted Fritsch	FB-LB	22	5'10"	205	24		54	169	3.1	4									2	55	28	0	5	30.2				0	2	0					4	99	25	0
Andy Uram	HB-TB-DB	28	5'10"	190	12	2	15	53	3.5	0	6	2	33	60	10.0	1	1– 7		10	212	21	2									5	48	10	0				
Bob Kabler	HB-DB	26	6'3"	200			1	5	5.0	0																												
Jim Lankas	FB-LB	25	6'2"	225			2	2	1.0	0																												
Larry Craig	BB-DE	27	6'1"	208			1	3	3.0	0																												
Ben Starret	BB-DE	25	5'11"	215		1	1	1	1.0	0																												
Don Hutson	OE-DB	30	6'1"	178	117	8	6	41	6.8	0	4	1	25	38	9.5	1	1– 25		47	776	17	11			36	36	100	3	5	60								
Harry Jacunski	OE-DE	27	6'2"	198	18	1													24	528	22	3													1	33	33	0
Joel Mason	OE-DE	30	6'	200	12														8	107	13	2																
Dick Evans	OE-DB	26	6'3"	210															8	71	9	0																
DETROIT LIONS																																						
Frankie Sinkwich	TB-DB	22	5'11"	185	12	1	93	266	2.9	1	126	50	40	699	5.5	7	20– 16	8	1	8	8	0	12	45.9				0	1	0	11	228	21	0	5	128	26	0
Chuck Fenenbock	TB-WB-DB	25	5'9"	172	6	1	46	180	3.9	0	58	20	34	338	5.8	3	9– 16	11	5	45	9	1	4	46.0							6	54	9	0	11	224	20	0
Tom Colella	TB-DB	25	6'	185			15	25	1.7	0	31	11	35	103	3.3	0	4– 13		1	−1	−1	0	6	46.7							2	11	6	0				
Harry Hopp	FB-LB-DB	24	6'	200	54	2	56	99	1.8	5	8	5	63	60	7.5	0	0– 0		17	229	13	3	42	39.1							1	−7	−7	0	3	57	19	0
Elmer Hackney	FB-LB	27	6'2"	200	18	2	27	87	3.2	2	3	1	33	−1	−0.3	0	0– 0		5	51	10	0									1	40	40	1	2	36	18	0
Mike Corgan	FB-LB	24	5'10"	188			5	14	2.8	0									1	9	9	0																
Ned Mathews	WB-TB-DB	25	5'10"	184	18	4	38	124	3.3	1	12	4	33	76	6.3	1	0– 0		9	193	21	1	1	35.0							4	37	9	0	7	246	35	1
Art Van Tone	WB-DB	24	5'10"	185	6	2	2	1	0.5	0	3	1	33	7	2.3	0	1– 33		6	112	19	1									3	47	16	0				
Lloyd Cardwell	WB-DB	30	6'2"	190			3	6	2.0	0									1	9	9	0									2	21	11	0	3	56	19	0
Bob Keene	WB-DB	24	5'11"	190			1	1	1.0	0									1	27	27	0													1	12	12	0
Bill Callihan	BB-DB	27	6'3"	230	24	1	5	17	3.4	1	2	0	0	0	0.0	0	1– 50		8	108	14	3									2	5	3	0				
Murray Evans	BB-DB	24	6'1"	206			2	3	1.5	0	5	1	20	8	1.6	0	2– 40		3	31	10	0																
Jack Matheson	OE-DE	23	6'2"	204	6														13	156	12	1													1	19	19	0
Bill Fisk	OE-DE	26	6'	198															11	137	12	0													1	5	5	0
Ben Hightower*	OE-DB	24	6'2"	185	6	1	1	−6	−6.0	0									10	172	17	1																
Bert Kuczynski	OE-DE	23	6'	197															1	4	4	0																
Augie Lio	G-LB	25	6'	236	27	1																			21	23	91	2	11	18								
CHICAGO CARDINALS																																						
Ronnie Cahill	TB-DB	26	5'8"	170			62	−11	−0.2	0	109	50	46	608	5.6	3	21– 19	8					3	29.3							1	19	19	0	3	56	19	0
Joe Bukant	TB-DB	27	6'	208			42	87	2.1	0	40	14	35	109	2.7	1	5– 12		1	0	0	0	5	36.2														
Walt Masters	TB-DB	36	5'10"	200			14	−17	−1.2	0	45	17	38	249	5.5	2	7– 16						10	36.8							1	13	13	0	2	39	20	0
John Grigas	FB-DB	23	6'	205	18	5	105	333	3.2	3	19	4	21	98	5.2	0	4– 21		19	225	12	0									2	−2	−1	0	3	72	24	0
Bob Morrow	FB-DB	25	6'	225	12	2	38	129	3.4	2									3	20	7	0													3	66	22	0
George Smith	FB-DB	22	6'1"	200			4	12	3.0	0									1	18	18	0																
Walt Rankin	FB-DB	25	5'11"	200		3	2	1	0.5	0									10	44	4	0													4	57	14	0
John Martin	WB-DB	25	6'1"	195		1	30	98	3.3	0									7	138	20	0	30	39.6							9	95	11	0	7	130	19	0
John Hall	WB-DB	26	6'	200	6	2	22	51	2.3	0	4	2	50	24	6.0	0	2– 50		7	82	12	0									1	17	17	0	2	35	18	0
Marshall Goldberg	WB-DB	25	5'11"	190	6	1	6	6	1.0	0									4	31	8	1									1	15	15	0	2	53	27	0
Cal Purdin	WB-DB	21	6'2"	190			9	20	2.2	0	2	1	50	7	3.5	0	0– 0		3	35	12	0	8	42.6							1	6	6	0	1	24	24	0
Eddie Rucinski	OE-DE	27	6'2"	198	18														26	398	15	3																
Don Currivan	OE-DE	22	6'	195	12														5	79	16	1																
Freeman Rexer	OE-DE	25	6'1"	210															1	14	14	0																
Clint Wager	OE-DE	22	6'6"	220															1	11	11	0																
Conway Baker	G	31	5'11'	235	14																				5	6	83	1	2	50								
Dixie Stokes	C-LB	30	6'	200	8																				5	6	83	1	3	33								

NEW YORK GIANTS 8-1-1 Steve Owen

Scores of Each Game		
22	Boston	10
14	Brooklyn	7
23	CARD–PITT	0
17	PHILADELPHIA	24
31	BOSTON	0
21	Philadelphia	21
24	GREEN BAY	0
7	BROOKLYN	0
16	WASHINGTON	13
31	Washington	0

Use Name	Pos.	Hgt	Wgt	Age	Int	Pts
Mel Hein	C-LB	6'2"	230	35	3	
Bill Piccolo	C-LB	5'11"	185	24	2	
Larry Visnic	BB-LB	5'11"	195	25	2	
Roy Clay	WB-DB	6'	185	21		

Use Name – Tackles	Pos.	Hgt	Wgt	Age	Int	Pts
Al Blozis	T	6'6"	250	25		
(Killed in military service – Jan. 31, 1945)						
Roland Caranci	T	6'1"	227	23		
Vic Carroll	T	6'4"	235	31	1	8
(1 punt return for 28 yd. touchdown)						
Frank Cope	T	6'2"	220	28		
Frank Damiani	T	6'1"	225	22		
Herb Kane	T	6'1"	215	23		

Use Name – Guards	Pos.	Hgt	Wgt	Age	Int	Pts
Chuck Avedisian	G-LB	5'9"	210	26	1	6
Jim Sivell (from BKN)	G	5'9"	205	30		
Frank Umont	G-T	5'11"	220	26		

When passer Arnie Herber showed up at training camp, he was so overweight that one reporter called him "a tub of lard." The ex-Packer worked hard, though, shook off the cobwebs of his three-year retirement, and soon recaptured his fine touch at throwing the bomb. With Herber throwing and the tough defense hanging up five shutouts, the Giants edged out the Eagles for the Eastern Division title. Among the whitewashings were a satisfying 24-0 triumph over Herber's old mates in Green Bay and a 31-0 victory over Washington to clinch the divisional crown.

Coach Steve Owen built this year's squad with parts salvaged from many sources. Herber and kicker Ken Strong came out of retirement, Mel Hein commuted from his full-time job at Union College, Bill Paschal was a second-year pro, and Howie Livingston came out of the service. Fortunately, Ward Cuff, Frank Cope, Al Blozis, and Len Younce were no farther than the locker room.

PHILADELPHIA EAGLES 7-1-2 Greasy Neale

Scores of Each Game		
28	Boston	7
31	WASHINGTON	31
38	BOSTON	0
24	New York	17
21	Brooklyn	7
21	NEW YORK	21
37	Washington	7
7	CHIC. BEARS	28
34	BROOKLYN	0
26	CLEVELAND	13

Use Name	Pos.	Hgt	Wgt	Age	Int	Pts
Vic Lindskog	C-LB	6'1"	205	28	1	6
Bap Manzini	C-LB	5'11"	200	24	1	
Walt Nowak	OE-DB	5'11"	185	17		
John Yovicsin	DE	6'3"	195	25		
Vic Sears (broken ankle)						

Use Name – Tackles	Pos.	Hgt	Wgt	Age	Int	Pts
Rocco Canale	T	5'11"	235	27		
Bob Friedman	T	6'2"	215	22	1	
Bucko Kilroy	T	6'2"	240	23		
Al Wistert	T	6'1"	215	23		

Use Name – Guards	Pos.	Hgt	Wgt	Age	Int	Pts
Bruno Banducci	G	5'11"	205	22		
Enio Conti	G	5'11"	205	31		
Carl Fagiolo	G	6'	200			
Mike Mandarino	G-T-C	5'11"	240	23		
Duke Maronic	G	5'9"	205	23	1	
Eddie Michaels	G	5'11"	210	30		

Shucking off the Steelers to go it alone, the Eagles abruptly shot into the upper reaches of the NFL. Coach Greasy Neale was building a powerhouse which had not reached its peak, yet just missed winning the Eastern Division championship. The chief addition to the flock was Steve Van Buren, a hard-charging runner with a halfback's moves and a fullback's power. Running with head down and knees pumping furiously, Van Buren usually bowled over tacklers in his way, and he could cut and dance his way through an open field when he wanted to, so much so that in the late 1940s he was the league's dominant runner.

Coach Neale fielded other good players around Van Buren. Passer Roy Zimmerman, runner Jack Hinkle, and defensive ace Ernie Steele stocked the backfield with quality, and Al Wistert, Bucko Kilroy, and Bruno Banducci filled the line with able-bodied bruisers.

WASHINGTON REDSKINS 6-3-1 Dud DeGroot

Scores of Each Game		
31	Philadelphia	31
21	Boston	14
17	BROOKLYN	14
42	CARD–PITT	20
14	CLEVELAND	10
10	Brooklyn	0
7	PHILADELPHIA	37
14	BOSTON	7
13	New York	16
0	NEW YORK	31

Use Name	Pos.	Hgt	Wgt	Age	Int	Pts
Nick Campofreda	C-DT	6'1"	240	30		
Vern Foltz	C-LB	6'1"	205	26		
Chief Johnson	C-LB	6'3"	233	35		
Pete Marcus	DE	6'2"	200	25		

Use Name – Tackles	Pos.	Hgt	Wgt	Age	Int	Pts
Jack Keenan	T	5'10"	220	25		
Jim North	T	6'3"	235	25		
Ev Sharp	T	6'1"	220	25		
Mitch Ucovich	T	5'11"	208	28		
Joe Ungerer	T	6'	225	27		
Joe Zeno	T	5'10"	240	25		

Use Name – Guards	Pos.	Hgt	Wgt	Age	Int	Pts
Tom Bedore	G-LB	5'11"	193	18		
Al Fiorentino	G-LB	5'7"	204	27	1	
(1 kickoff return for 5 yds.)						
Ed Merkle	G-LB	5'10"	215	27		
Ray Monaco	G-LB	5'10"	208	26		
Clyde Shugart	G	6'1"	230	27		
Frank Walton	G	5'11"	240	32		

With long-time coach Ray Flaherty in the Navy, owner George Marshall again started going through field managers like water. This year's head man, Dud DeGroot, brought the T-formation with him to Washington, forcing Sammy Baugh to learn a completely new system of offense. Sammy missed the old single-wing and double-wing attack at first, but he slowly got the hang of taking a direct snap from the center. Fresh out of the Navy, Frankie Filchock split the quarterback duties with Baugh and celebrated his civilian status by leading the league in passing. With these two arms throwing to Joe Aguirre, Wilbur Moore, and Les Dye, the Redskins won five straight games after an opening-day tie to climb to the top in the East. Although three losses in their last four matches placed the Skins in a third-place finish, they were hopeful that Baugh and the new offensive system would soon produce a winner.

BOSTON YANKS 2-8-0 Herb Kopf

Scores of Each Game		
7	PHILADELPHIA	28
10	NEW YORK	22
14	WASHINGTON	21
0	Philadelphia	38
17	Brooklyn	14
0	New York	31
7	Chic. Bears	21
13	BROOKLYN	6
7	Washington	14
7	Detroit	38

Use Name	Pos.	Hgt	Wgt	Age	Int	Pts
Walt Dubzinski	C-LB	5'10"	205	24		
Ed Korisky	C-LB	6'1"	210	26	1	
Jim Magee	C-LB	6'1"	200	23		
Morgan Tiller	OE-DE	6'1"	195	24		
(1 kickoff return for 12 yds.)						
Bob McRoberts	HB-DB	5'11"	190	20		
Frank Santora	QB-DB	5'10"	166	18		
(1 kickoff return for 27 yds.)						

Use Name – Tackles	Pos.	Hgt	Wgt	Age	Int	Pts
Art Albrecht	T	6'1'	210	22		
Ed Franco	T	5'8"	205	28		
Wimpy Giddens	T	6'2"	220	29		
Ed McGee	T	6'1"	230	28	1	
Thron Riggs	T	6'1"	225	23		

Use Name – Guards	Pos.	Hgt	Wgt	Age	Int	Pts
Vince Commisa	G	5'9"	190			
Frank Gaziano	G	5'8"	218	28		
John Morelli	G-LB	5'10"	190	21		12
Bill Walker	G	6'	220	23		

While singer Kate Smith was selling lots of war bonds, her manager, Ted Collins, was buying a pro-football team. He purchased an NFL franchise for Boston and set up the Yanks, hiring Herb Kopf to run the club on the field. The first Yank roster listed both rookies and veteran pros cut loose by other teams. The top passer, George Cafego, had been the first player picked in the 1940 collegiate draft, but he had shown little since then for the Brooklyn Dodgers and Washington Redskins. Of the leading runners, Bob Davis had bounced around with three clubs since 1938, while Milt Crain was playing his first pro season. The Yanks were end Keith Ranspot's seventh team in four years, but he settled in Boston long enough to lead the club in receiving. Of the interior linemen, only ex-Lion Augie Lio would have started elsewhere. With the league's weakest attack, the Yanks could beat only the inept Brooklyn Tigers.

BROOKLYN TIGERS 0-10-0 Pete Cawthorn, Ed Kuhale, Frank Bridges

Scores of Each Game		
7	Green Bay	14
14	Detroit	19
7	NEW YORK	14
14	Washington	17
14	BOSTON	17
7	PHILADELPHIA	21
0	WASHINGTON	10
6	Boston	13
0	New York	7
0	Philadelphia	34

Use Name	Pos.	Hgt	Wgt	Age	Int	Pts
George Smith	C-LB	6'2"	215	30	1	
(6 punts for 37.2 yd. average)						
Vaughn Stewart	C-LB	6'1"	180	24		
(1 punt for 58 yds.)						
George Weeks	DE	6'2"	200	25		

Use Name – Tackles	Pos.	Hgt	Wgt	Age	Int	Pts
George Doherty	T	6'1"	215	23		
George Sergienko	T	6'1"	250	26		
Frank Strom	T	6'2"	252	28		
Charlie Ware	T	6'3"	245	26		

Use Name – Guards	Pos.	Hgt	Wgt	Age	Int	Pts
John Ellis	G	5'10"	212	24		
Tony Leon	G-LB	5'9"	197	27	1	
Floyd Rhea	G-LB	6'	215	23	1	
Gordon Wilson (from BOS)	G	6'	230	28		

The old Dodgers were rechristened the Tigers, but the only bite was on owner Dan Topping's wallet. Brooklyn fans never warmed up to the new name, and they didn't bother coming out to see the winless squad. After all, a ticket to a Tiger game gave the buyer the privilege of watching a parade of scatter-arm passers throw lots of incompleted passes. Or the paying customer could watch fullback Pug Manders, a good runner, fling himself at nonexistent holes that were never cleared out by the line. If he appreciated line play, the fan could watch Bruiser Kinard get double- and triple-teamed while some of his trench mates were ignored by the enemy. The Tigers unfortunately never played the Card-Pitt squad; one of them would have had to win, if only one could score some points. Although the Card-Pitt team hardly was an encouraging example, owner Topping arranged a merger for next year with the Boston Yanks—and Brooklyn would never return to the NFL.

TEAM TOTALS

OFFENSE	First Downs: Tot	by Rsh	by Pas	by Pen	Rushing: No.	Yds.	Avg. Yds.	TD	Passing: Att.	Com	Comp. Pct.	Yds.	Avg. Yds. Att.	Avg. Yds. Comp	TD	Int.	Pct. Int.	Punting: No.	Avg. Yds.
N.Y.	99	72	23	4	416	1532	3.7	11	125	47	37.6	857	6.9	18.2	9	17	13.6	60	38.6
PHIL.	110	73	27	10	424	1661	3.9	23	136	55	40.4	941	6.9	17.1	9	12	8.8	55	39.9
WASH.	133	59	70	4	342	904	2.6	6	299	170	56.9	2021	6.8	11.9	17	17	5.7	59	39.0
BOSTON	87	36	41	10	324	471	1.5	3	197	85	43.1	1030	5.2	12.1	6	22	11.2	72	35.0
BKN.	110	53	47	10	365	964	2.6	6	213	76	35.7	996	4.7	13.1	3	29	13.6	74	38.0
DEFENSE																			
N.Y.	137	66	64	7	374	1000	2.7	6	258	114	44.2	1290	5.0	11.3	3	34	13.1	60	37.2
PHIL.	86	43	35	8	321	558	1.7	7	231	105	45.5	1379	6.0	13.1	12	33	14.3	71	39.8
WASH.	123	71	47	5	409	1492	3.7	15	188	84	44.7	1166	6.2	13.9	9	19	10.1	55	36.6
BOSTON	126	81	44	1	446	1575	3.5	20	166	76	45.8	1131	6.8	14.9	11	16	9.6	62	35.8
BKN.	95	41	41	13	362	1181	3.3	14	181	78	43.1	1227	6.8	15.7	9	10	5.5	71	38.6

OFFENSE	Punt Returns: No.	Yds.	Avg. Yds.	TD	Kickoff Returns: No.	Yds.	Avg. Yds.	TD	Interception Returns: No.	Yds.	Avg. Yds.	TD	Penalties: No.	Yds.	Fumbles: No.	Lost	Points: Tot	PAT	FG Att	FG	Saf.
N.Y.	33	399	12.1	1	17	466	27.4	0	34	549	16.1	4	68	502	14	7	206	25	16	7	2
PHIL.	41	563	13.7	1	26	630	24.2	1	33	544	16.4	3	66	523	36	20	267	33	8	4	0
WASH.	26	269	10.3	0	37	682	18.4	0	19	177	9.3	0	68	545	28	12	169	19	8	4	0
BOSTON	37	457	12.4	0	39	797	20.4	0	16	236	14.8	0	34	228	29	8	82	10	9	2	0
BKN.	31	359	11.6	1	26	578	22.2	0	10	76	7.6	0	81	639	27	8	69	9	6	0	0
DEFENSE																					
N.Y.	32	323	10.1	1	40	957	23.9	0	17	197	11.5	0	54	412	30	11	75	9	10	4	0
PHIL.	26	265	10.2	0	46	830	18.0	1	12	160	13.3	0	79	570	29	4	131	14	5	1	0
WASH.	32	426	13.3	0	26	566	21.8	0	17	302	17.7	3	60	421	22	9	180	21	13	5	0
BOSTON	42	483	11.5	2	18	425	23.6	0	22	302	13.7	1	77	561	24	11	233	30	7	5	1
BKN.	35	465	13.3	0	15	293	19.5	0	29	268	9.2	1	63	539	21	9	166	19	13	3	0

Use Name – Backs & Ends	Pos.	Age	Hgt	Wgt	Pts	Int	RUSHING No.	Yds	Avg	TD	PASSING Att	Comp	%	Yds	Yd/Att	TD	Int–%	RK	RECEIVING No.	Yds	Avg	TD	PUNTING No.	Avg	KICKING Pat	Att	%	FG	Att	%	PUNT RETURNS No.	Yds	Avg	TD	KICKOFF RETURNS No.	Yds	Avg	TD
NEW YORK GIANTS																																						
Arnie Herber	QB	34	5'11"	210			7	-58	-8.3	0	86	36	42	651	7.6	6	8- 9	7					1	39.0														
Joe Sulatis	QB-DE	23	6'2"	210			9	38	4.2	0	17	4	24	53	3.1	1	4- 24																					
Hank Soar	QB-DB	30	6'2"	210		1	9	10	1.1	0	10	4	40	113	11.3	2	1- 10														6	52	9	0				
Bill Paschal	FB-DB	23	6'	200	54		196	737	3.8	9	8	2	25	31	3.9	0	2- 25						1	6.0							7	102	15	0	9	260	29	0
Howie Livingston	FB-DB	22	6'1"	190	18	9	84	313	3.7	1	1	0	0	0	0.0	0	1-100		1	12	12	1	2	39.5							4	44	11	0	4	114	29	0
Carl Kinscherf	FB-DB	24	6'1"	190		1	9	21	2.3	0									1	9	9	0																
Ken Strong	FB	38	6'	210	41		2	-2	-1.0	0													1	44.0	23	24	96	6	12	50								
Ward Cuff	WB-DB	31	6'1"	195	17	2	76	425	5.6	0									11	135	12	2			2	2	100	1	4	25	11	115	10	0	2	63	32	0
Bill Petrilas	WB-DB	26	6'1"	195	12	5	12	29	2.4	0																					4	58	15	0				
Keith Beebe	BB-DB	23	5'9"	180		3	8	12	1.5	0	3	1	33	9	3.0	0	1- 11						7	30.0														
Len Calligaro	BB-LB	23	5'11"	190	6		3	4	1.3	1									2	11	6	0																
Hub Barker	BB-LB	25	5'10"	190			1	3	3.0	0									3	34	11	0																
Neal Adams	OE-DE	25	6'3"	195	6														14	342	24	1													2	29	15	0
Frank Liebel	OE-DB	24	6'1"	205	36	1													13	292	22	5																
Verlin Adams	OE-DE	26	6'	205															1	12	12	0																
John Weiss	OE-DB	22	6'3"	195															1	10	10	0																
Len Younce	G-LB	27	6'1"	210		3																	48	40.4														
PHILADELPHIA EAGLES																																						
Roy Zimmerman	QB-DB	26	6'2"	200	62	4	26	-84	-3.2	3	105	39	37	785	7.5	8	10- 10	9					39	39.3	32	34	94	4	8	50								
Allie Sherman	QB-DB	21	5'11"	175	6	2	22	-42	-1.9	1	31	16	52	156	5.0	1	2- 6						1	27.0														
Steve Van Buren	HB-DB	23	6'	200	42	5	80	444	5.6	5													1	35.0							15	230	15	1	8	266	33	1
Jack Hinkle	HB-DB	26	6'	195	18	2	92	421	4.6	2									2	34	17	0									4	32	8	0	6	134	22	0
Mel Bleeker	HB-DB	24	5'11"	185	48	1	60	315	5.3	4									8	299	37	4									1	3	3	0				
Ernie Steele	HB-DB	26	6'	180	30	6	59	247	4.2	5									1	22	22	0									11	181	16	0	5	128	26	0
Jack Banta	HB-DB	26	5'11"	190	18	1	38	198	5.2	3									1	8	8	0	9	44.2							7	81	12	0	3	54	18	0
Ben Kish	FB-LB	27	6'	200	7	4	22	96	4.4	0									5	73	15	1	4	45.5	1	1	100								2	36	18	0
Art Macioszczyk	FB-LB	23	5'9"	210			16	55	3.4	0									3	28	9	0									1	14	14	0	1	4	4	0
Toimi Jarvi	HB-DB	24	6'	200		1	5	16	3.2	0									1	9	9	0									2	22	11	0				
Ted Laux	HB-DB	26	5'10"	185			2	-1	-0.5	0									1	6	6	0	1	18.0														
Larry Cabrelli	OE-DB	27	5'11"	190	6		1	-2	-2.0	0									14	169	12	1																
Tom Miller	OE-DE	26	6'2"	205	6	1	1	-2	-2.0	0									8	135	17	0													1	8	8	0
Flip McDonald (from BKN)	OE-DB	23	6'2"	195	6	1													4	26	7	1																
Jack Ferrante	OE-DE	28	6'1"	205	6														3	66	22	1																
Charlie Gauer	OE-DE	23	6'2"	215		1													2	35	18	0																
John Durko	OE-DE	25	6'4"	235	6														2	31	16	1																
WASHINGTON REDSKINS																																						
Frankie Filchock	QB-HB-DB	27	5'11"	198			33	-34	-1.0	0	147	84	57	1139	7.7	13	9- 6	1	3	51	17	0									3	5	2	0	3	42	14	0
Sammy Baugh	QB-DB	30	6'2"	180		4	19	-38	-2.0	0	146	82	56	849	5.8	4	8- 5	4	1	0	0	0	44	40.5							4	23	6	0				
Larry Weldon	QB-DB	27	6'	198	4		8	8	1.0	0	6	4	67	33	5.5	0	0- 0								4	4	100								3	28	9	0
Bob Seymour	FB-DB	28	6'2"	208	36	2	92	315	3.4	3									19	263	14	3	10	35.5							1	8	8	0				
Frank Akins	FB-LB	26	6'10"	205	0		48	154	3.3	1									5	27	5	0	1	39.0											1	14	14	0
Frank Seno	HB-DB	23	6'	195		2	43	140	3.3	0									17	146	9	0									10	129	13	0	8	193	24	0
Wilbur Moore	HB-DB	28	5'11"	185	42	5	37	140	3.8	2									33	424	13	5									1	12	12	0	8	143	18	0
Mike Micka	FB-DB	23	6'	190		1	25	94	3.8	0									2	16	8	0	2	21.0														
Andy Farkas	FB-HB-DB	28	5'10"	192		3	21	85	4.0	0									4	29	7	0									7	94	13	0	11	229	21	0
Bob Sneddon	HB-DB	23	5'10"	180		1	14	30	2.1	0									3	42	14	0																
Larry Fuller	HB-DB	21	5'10"	187	6		4	10	2.5	0									5	82	16	1																
Andy Natowich	HB-DB	24	5'10"	175																															1	16	16	0
Joe Aquirre	OE-DE	25	6'4"	234	51														34	410	12	4	2	43.5	15	18	83	4	8	50								
Les Dye	OE	26	6'1"	182	12														24	281	12	2																
Doug Turley	OE-DE	25	6'2"	212	6														8	112	14	1													1	12	12	0
Alex Piasecky	OE-DE	27	6'2"	197															8	77	10	0																
Ted Lapka	OE-DE	24	6'1"	196	6														4	61	15	1																
BOSTON YANKS																																						
George Cafego	QB-DB	29	5'10"	180	6	1	61	31	0.5	1	73	35	48	454	6.2	3	7- 10	10	2	8	4	0	16	36.4							4	49	12	0	3	48	16	0
Leo Stasica	QB-DB	28	5'11"	185		1	22	-16	-0.7	0	47	21	45	225	4.8	1	7- 15						1	38.0							3	30	10	0	3	75	25	0
Scott Gudmundson	QB-DB	23	5'10"	175			14	-21	-1.5	0	38	16	42	226	5.9	1	4- 11						12	33.5							1	27	27	0	3	55	18	0
Frank Turbert	QB-DB	26	5'11"	200			14	-16	-1.1	0	14	5	36	37	2.6	0	0- 0		1	16	16	0									1	7	7	0				
Bob Davis	HB-DB	32	6'	190	6	4	95	363	3.8	1	18	8	44	88	4.9	1	2- 11		19	97	5	0	3	20.0							22	271	12	0	7	152	22	0
Milt Crain	FB-LB	23	6'2"	225		1	26	78	3.0	0									1	16	16	0	1	40.0							2	10	5	0	2	33	17	0
Ken Steinmetz	FB-LB	20	6'	186			11	24	2.2	0	1	0	0	0	0.0	0	0- 0						1	17.0														
Ted Williams	HB-DB	27	5'11"	180	6	1	52	13	0.3	1	6	0	0	0	0.0	0	2- 33		6	28	5	0									1	13	13	0	6	82	14	0
John Martin (from C-P)	HB-DB	26	6'1"	195		3	19	7	0.4	0									6	56	9	0	41	36.4							3	50	17	0	8	265	33	0
Dave Smukler	FB-LB	27	6'1"	225			2	7	3.5	0													2	24.5														
Paul Sanders	HB-DB	25	5'11"	192			6	4	0.7	0									4	5	1	0																
Tony Falkenstein (from BKN,BB)	FB-LB	29	5'10"	200			4	2	0.5	0									1	21	21	0																
Keith Ranspot	OE-DE	29	6'3"	205	18														19	269	14	3						0	1	0					3	37	12	0
Joe Crowley	OE-DB	25	6'	190	18	1													13	279	21	3																
Harry Wynne	OE-DE	24	6'4"	205															10	205	21	0													1	11	11	0
Sam Goldman	OE-DE	27	6'3"	220															2	21	11	0													1	0	0	0
Dick Harrison	OE-DB	28	6'	195															1	9	9	0																
Augie Lio	G-LB	26	6'	235	16	2																			10	11	91	2	8	25								
BROOKLYN TIGERS																																						
Charlie McGibbony	TB-DB	26	5'10"	160		1	26	81	3.1	0	48	18	38	262	5.5	1	10- 21						8	36.8							5	66	13	0	2	40	20	0
Frankie Sachse	TB-DB	27	6'	197			9	13	1.4	0	45	18	40	226	5.0	0	5- 11														1	23	23	0	1	25	25	0
Cecil Johnson	TB-DB	22	5'11"	190			30	41	1.4	0	25	10	40	193	7.7	2	4- 16						23	42.6							7	102	15	0				
Kenny Fryer	TB-DB	25	6'	200			15	15	1.0	0	24	9	38	91	3.8	0	2- 8						7	39.0														
Johnny Butler (from C-P,HB-DB)	TB-DB	25	5'10"	185	12	3	60	94	1.6	0	23	8	35	107	4.7	0	1- 4		3	109	36	2	13	37.3							9	99	11	0	4	92	23	0
Steve Marko	TB-DB	20	6'	200			6	10	1.7	0	7	1	14	2	0.3	0	2- 29																		3	80	27	0
John McMichaels	TB-DB	26	5'11"	190			3	1	0.3	0	1	0	0	0	0.0	0	1-100						2	42.5							1	5	5	0				
Pug Manders	FB-LB	31	6'	200	30	1	127	430	3.4	5	34	9	26	96	2.8	0	4- 12		6	78	13	0						0	1	0					11	227	21	0
Ray Hare	HB-FB-DB	26	6'1"	202	6	1	72	196	2.7	0	1	0	0	0	0.0	0	0- 0		9	206	23	1									2	5	3	0	4	120	30	0
Bill Reynolds	HB-DB	25	5'8"	175	6		11	71	6.5	1																					1	12	12	0	1	18	18	0
Frank Martin	HB-DB	25	5'10"	180		1	11	18	1.6	0	1	1	100	7	7.0	0	0- 0		3	15	5	0	1	2.0							3	16	5	0				
Bob Trocolor	HB-DB	25	6'2"	210			3	8	2.7	0													1	10.0														
Charlie Taylor	BB-LB	24	5'10"	210			7	19	2.7	0									2	22	11	0									2	25	13	0	1	12	12	0
Bill Brown	BB-LB	27	6'	205		1	4	10	2.5	0	3	1	33	11	3.7	0	0- 0		2	10	5	0									2	16	8	0	1	12	12	0
Bob Masterson	OE-DE	29	6'1"	218	6						1	1	100	1	1.0	0	0- 0		24	258	11	1	4	34.0				0	5	0								
Joe Carter	OE-DE	34	6'1"	197															13	143	11	0	9	36.1														
Andy Kowalski	OE-DE	24	6'1"	200	6														9	155	17	1																
Rocky Uguccioni	OE-DE	26	6'	195	6														7	94	13	0									1	12	12	1				
Bill LaFitte	OE	18	6'1"	170															1	15	15	0																
Bruiser Kinard	T	29	6'1"	218	9	1																			9	9	100								1	22	22	0

GREEN BAY PACKERS 8-2-0 Curly Lambeau

Scores of Each Game		
14	BROOKLYN	7
42	CHIC. BEARS	28
27	DETROIT	6
34	CARD–PITT	7
30	CLEVELAND	21
14	Detroit	0
0	Chic. Bears	21
42	Cleveland	7
0	New York	24
35	Card–Pitt	20

Use Name	Pos.	Hgt	Wgt	Age	Int	Pts
Charley Brock	C-LB	6'2"	210	28	1	
Bob Flowers	C-LB	6'1"	210	27		
Amy McPherson	C-DT	5'11"	240	32		
Bob Kercher	DE	6'2"	196	26		
Bob Kahler	DB	6'3"	204	27		

Use Name – Tackles	Pos.	Hgt	Wgt	Age	Int	Pts
Paul Berezney	T	6'2"	220	27		
Tiny Croft	T	6'3"	285	23		
Baby Ray	T	6'6"	250	29		
Ade Schwammel	T	6'2"	215	35		

Use Name – Guards	Pos.	Hgt	Wgt	Age	Int	Pts
Amadeo Bucchianeri	G	5'10"	215	27		
Buckets Goldenberg	G-LB	5'10"	220	33		
Bill Kuusisto	G	6'	230	26		
Glen Sorenson	G-LB	6'	215	23		1
(Missed 2 FG attempts, 1 PAT in 1 attempt)						
Pete Tinsley	G-LB	5'8"	210	31		
Charlie Tollefson	G	6'	215	27		

Far from the greatest Green Bay team ever, this year's edition of the Packers was good enough to win the Western Division crown. The Packers ran off six straight victories at the start of the season and coasted home the rest of the way, leaving the Bears and Lions to snarl over the second-place spoils. Although Don Hutson, as usual, burned defensive backs for long gains, most of the faces in the Green Bay backfield were new. Rangy Irv Comp was Hutson's new passing partner, and popular Ted Fritsch picked up the tough yardage on the ground as Clarke Hinkle once did. Baby Ray, Buckets Goldenberg, and Charlie Brock gave the strong forward line a veteran flavor. Like most wartime clubs, the Packers mixed veterans and youngsters together with a salad-bowl effect that was sometimes interesting and sometimes boringly inept. But with Don Hutson on hand, Green Bay remained the best around.

CHICAGO BEARS 6-3-1 Luke Johnsos, Hunk Anderson, Paddy Driscoll

Scores of Each Game		
28	Green Bay	42
7	Cleveland	19
34	CARD–PITT	7
21	DETROIT	21
28	CLEVELAND	21
21	GREEN BAY	0
21	BOSTON	7
21	Detroit	41
28	Philadelphia	7
49	Card–Pitt	7

Use Name	Pos.	Hgt	Wgt	Age	Int	Pts
Fred Mundee	C-LB	6'1"	220	31	1	
Bulldog Turner	C-LB-HB	6'1"	255	25	2	6
(1 rush for 48 yd. TD, 1 punt return for 9 yds.)						
Elmo Kelly	DE	6'1"	210	27		
Max Burnell	HB-DB	5'11"	180	29		
Duke Greenrich	HB-DB	5'11"	185	20		

Use Name – Tackles	Pos.	Hgt	Wgt	Age	Int	Pts
Al Babartsky	T	6'	225	28		
Al Hoptowit	T	6'1"	222	28		
Tom Roberts	T	6'1"	215	28		
Dom Sigillo	T	6'	220	31		
Jake Sweeney	T	6'3"	240	22		

Use Name – Guards	Pos.	Hgt	Wgt	Age	Int	Pts
George Musso	G	6'2"	260	34		
Paul Podmajersky	G	5'11"	220	28		
Ed Sprinkle	G-LB	6'1"	200	20	1	
George Zorich	G-LB	6'2"	210	25	1	

The Bears dropped their first two games of the year to Green Bay and Cleveland, then spent the rest of the season trying to catch up with the Packers. Although they had to settle for a second-place tie, the Bears received several noteworthy performances. Quarterback Sid Luckman spent most of his week in the Merchant Marine but usually got away on Sunday to direct the attack. Sid's understudy was thirty-five-year-old Gene Ronzani, back in the NFL for the first time since 1938.

Bulldog Turner kept up his superior work at center, but also showed hidden talent as a ball carrier. When several Bears were ejected for fighting in a game against the Card-Pitt team, Bulldog volunteered for emergency duty at halfback. The only time he got the ball he plowed straight ahead for a 48-yard touchdown. Card-Pitt coach Walt Kiesling was so angry he kicked Turner in the rump the next time there was a pile-up in front of his bench.

DETROIT LIONS 6-3-1 Gus Dorais

Scores of Each Game		
6	Green Bay	27
19	BROOKLYN	14
17	CLEVELAND	20
21	Chic. Bears	21
0	GREEN BAY	14
27	Card–Pitt	6
21	CARD–PITT	7
41	CHIC. BEARS	21
26	Cleveland	14
38	BOSTON	7

Use Name	Pos.	Hgt	Wgt	Age	Int	Pts
Ed Eiden (from PHI)	C-LB	6'	205	22		
Ernie Rosteck	C-LB	6'1"	226	22		
Alex Wojciechowicz	C-LB	5'11"	220	29	7	
Paul Blessing	OE-DE	6'4"	215	25		
Dale Nansen	DE-T	6'3"	225	23		
Freeman Rexer (from BOS)	DE	6'1"	212	26		
John Greene	BB-DB	6'	215	24	2	

Use Name – Tackles	Pos.	Hgt	Wgt	Age	Int	Pts
Joe D'Orazio	T	5'11"	220	29		
Tony Furst	T	6'1"	215	26		
Tom Kennedy	T	6'	218	24		
Luke Lindon	T	5'10"	240	27		
Ed Opalewski	T	6'3"	240	24		
Bill Rogers	T	5'11"	250	31		

Use Name – Guards	Pos.	Hgt	Wgt	Age	Int	Pts
Stan Batinski	G	5'10"	218	27		
Al Kaporch	G-LB	5'10"	215	30	1	
(1 punt return for 14 yds.)						
Sonny Liles	G-LB	5'9"	185	25	1	
(1 punt return for 5 yds.)						
George Sirochman	G	6'2"	210	26		

The Lions began the season by posting a 1-3-1 record. But then, with the emergence of a powerful offense, Detroit won its last five games to climb up into a second-place perch along with the Bears. One of the victories in the closing streak was a 41-21 upset over the Chicagoans that fatally slashed their slim title hopes. Although the Lions never threatened to catch the Packers, Detroit fans relished the turn-around in form by a team which only two years ago had not won a single game all season.

Leading the resurgence was tailback Frankie Sinkwich, a strong passer, shifty runner, and a top-notch punter. Coach Gus Dorais constructed his offense around Sinkwich's passes to end Jack Matheson, and the tailback spurred the Lions on well enough to win the league MVP Award and put some teeth back in his team's attack.

CLEVELAND RAMS 4-6-0 Buff Donelli

Scores of Each Game		
30	Card–Pitt	28
19	CHIC. BEARS	7
20	Detroit	17
21	Green Bay	30
21	Chic. Bears	28
10	Washington	14
7	GREEN BAY	42
33	Card–Pitt	6
14	DETROIT	26
13	Philadelphia	26

Use Name	Pos.	Hgt	Wgt	Age	Int	Pts
Bill Conkright	C-LB	6'1"	205	30		
Joe Gibson	C-LB-DE	6'3"	220	25		
Bill Rieth	C-LB	5'11"	203	28	1	
Mo Scarry	C-T-LB	6'	220	24	1	
Floyd Konetsky	DE	6'	195	24		
Howie Carson	HB-DB	6'	190	29		

Use Name – Tackles	Pos.	Hgt	Wgt	Age	Int	Pts
Boyd Clay	T	6'1"	225	31		
Jake Fawcett	T	5'11"	220	25		
(1 reception for 9 yds., 2 kickoff rets. for 2 yds.)						
Del Lyman	T	6'3"	220	27		
Norm Olsen	T	6'2"	220	22		
(1 kickoff return for 19 yds.)						
Chet Pudloski	T	6'1"	210	29		

Use Name – Guards	Pos.	Hgt	Wgt	Age	Int	Pts
Tom Corbo	G-LB	5'11"	210	26	1	
Al Gutknecht	G-LB	6'	200	27		
Les Lear	G-LB	5'11"	223	26		
Riley Matheson	G-LB	6'2"	205	29	3	
Charley Riffle	G-LB	6'	210	26		

After a year in deep freeze, the Rams rushed back into the football wars, hiring Buff Donelli as head coach and recalling their players who had been spread around the league in 1943. Returning to Cleveland were Jim Benton, Bill Conkright, Jake Fawcett, Joe Gibson, Riley Matheson, John Petchel, and Bill Rieth, the only seven Rams still active. Donelli bolstered this nucleus with rookies and free agents. At the heart of the attack was passer Albie Reisz and runner Walt West, both rookies. With the team pasted together again, the Rams celebrated their rebirth with a 30-28 victory over Card-Pitt. The next week they upset the Bears 19-7 and then beat Detroit 20-17. Green Bay, as expected, burst the bubble by downing the Rams 30-21, throwing them into a tailspin which lasted the rest of the year.

CHICAGO CARDINALS – PITTSBURGH STEELERS 0-10-0 Phil Handler, Walt Kiesling

Scores of Each Game		
28	CLEVELAND	P 30
7	Green Bay	34
7	Chic. Bears	34
0	New York	23
20	Washington	42
6	DETROIT	P 27
7	Detroit	21
6	CLEVELAND	C 33
20	GREEN BAY	C 35
7	CHIC. BEARS	P 49

P=at Pittsburgh
C=at Chicago

Use Name	Pos.	Hgt	Wgt	Age	Int	Pts
Vince Banonis	C-LB	6'1"	220	23		
Al Wukits	C-LB	6'3"	215	24		

Use Name – Tackles	Pos.	Hgt	Wgt	Age	Int	Pts
Clarence Booth	T	6'	225	24		
Chet Bulger	T	6'3"	245	26		
(1 kickoff return for 5 yds.)						
Ted Doyle	T	6'2"	230	30		
Gil Duggan	T	6'3"	225	26		
Al Merkovsky	T	6'1"	238	27		
Elbie Schultz	T	6'4"	250	26		6
(touchdown on kickoff return lateral)						

Use Name – Guards	Pos.	Hgt	Wgt	Age	Int	Pts
Lou Marotti	G	5'10"	212	26		
(1 kickoff return for 2 yds.)						
John Perko	G	6'1"	210	28	1	
(1 kickoff return for 3 yds.)						

Known affectionately around the league as the Carpets, this joint effort of the Cardinals and Steelers lost every time it took the field. Pittsburgh, in 1943, had merged with the Eagles, and this year pooled resources with the hard-pressed Cards. The losing season was a true team effort, with both organizations liable for the blame. Co-coaches Phil Handler and Walt Kiesling fielded a line in which only Conway Baker and Vince Banonis were big-league players. John Grigas threw and ran more than any other back, grinding out enough yardage to rank second in the league rushing statistics, and veteran end Eddie Rucinski played well as a receiver.

The closest the Carpets came to getting off the floor was a close 30-28 opening-game loss to Cleveland. After that, they were rarely long in the game after the opening gun. After their disastrous combined showing, both clubs decided to go it alone in 1945.

TEAM TOTALS

OFFENSE	First Downs: Tot	by Rsh	by Pas	by Pen	Rushing: No.	Yds.	Avg. Yds.	TD	Passing: Att.	Com	Comp. Pct.	Yds.	Avg. Yds. Att.	Avg. Yds. Comp	TD	Int.	Pct. Int.
G.B.	147	70	63	14	395	1517	3.8	16	253	105	41.5	1471	5.8	14.0	15	24	9.5
CHIC. B.	140	73	57	10	412	1562	3.8	16	217	107	49.3	1616	7.4	15.1	21	18	8.3
DET.	106	52	47	7	326	1141	3.5	14	207	89	43.0	1475	7.1	16.6	16	28	13.5
CLEVE.	104	51	43	10	358	1141	3.2	11	209	85	40.7	1261	6.0	14.8	13	26	12.4
CARD-PITT	109	56	44	9	360	1019	2.8	7	258	87	33.7	1257	4.9	14.4	8	41	15.9
DEFENSE																	
G.B.	114	56	49	9	357	1130	3.2	10	227	89	39.4	1229	5.4	13.8	10	29	12.8
CHIC. B.	110	49	38	23	298	954	3.2	14	208	69	33.2	1052	5.1	15.2	10	24	11.5
DET.	129	63	57	9	403	1216	3.0	7	246	106	43.1	1442	5.9	13.6	15	26	10.5
CLEVE.	116	69	41	6	387	1412	3.7	16	206	87	42.3	1434	7.0	16.5	16	27	13.1
CARD-PITT	109	56	46	7	365	1394	3.8	25	204	98	48.0	1575	7.7	16.1	22	16	7.8

OFFENSE	Punting: No.	Avg. Yds.	Punt Returns: No.	Yds.	Avg. Yds.	TD	Kickoff Returns: No.	Yds.	Avg. Yds.	TD	Interception Returns: No.	Yds.	Avg. Yds.	TD	Penalties: No.	Yds.	Fumbles: No.	Lost	Points: Tot	PAT	FG Att	FG	Saf.	OFFENSE
G.B.	48	36.9	27	241	8.9	0	30	612	20.4	0	29	454	15.6	3	62	558	11	7	238	32	6	0	1	G.B.
CHIC. B.	57	36.6	29	263	9.1	0	31	670	21.6	0	24	387	16.1	0	121	1025	24	14	258	36	0	0	0	CHIC. B.
DET.	54	40.5	31	440	14.2	0	25	589	23.6	1	26	307	11.8	0	56	417	22	8	216	24	8	2	0	DET.
CLEVE.	57	38.4	28	326	11.6	0	41	923	22.5	0	27	310	11.5	0	64	441	28	15	188	20	7	4	0	CLEVE.
CARD-PITT	60	32.7	17	159	9.4	0	53	1119	21.1	1	16	146	9.1	0	65	479	30	12	108	12	2	0	0	CARD-PITT
DEFENSE																								DEFENSE
G.B.	57	36.8	18	193	10.7	0	34	804	23.6	0	24	344	14.3	1	88	700	25	12	141	18	2	1	0	G.B.
CHIC. B.	58	38.4	32	393	12.3	0	46	949	20.6	1	18	283	15.7	2	59	489	23	10	172	22	6	2	0	CHIC. B.
DET.	57	35.8	20	252	12.6	0	39	898	23.0	0	28	351	12.5	0	51	405	25	16	151	19	3	0	0	DET.
CLEVE.	55	38.5	24	290	12.1	0	36	872	24.2	1	26	289	11.1	0	77	627	27	17	224	27	3	1	1	CLEVE.
CARD-PITT	50	37.2	39	386	9.9	0	25	472	18.8	0	41	690	16.8	2	77	633	23	12	328	41	7	1	1	CARD-PITT

Use Name – Backs & Ends	Pos.	Age	Hgt	Wgt	Pts	Int	RUSHING				PASSING								RECEIVING				PUNTING		KICKING						PUNT RETURNS				KICKOFF RETURNS			
							No.	Yds	Avg	TD	Att	Comp	%	Yds	Yd/Att	TD	Int–%	RK	No.	Yds	Avg	TD	No.	Avg	Pat	Att	%	FG	Att	%	No.	Yds	Avg	TD	No.	Yds	Avg	TD
GREEN BAY PACKERS																																						
Irv Comp	TB-DB	25	6'2"	214	18	6	52	134	2.6	2	177	80	45	1159	6.5	12	21–12	7	2	16	8	1									2	32	16	0	2	37	19	0
Tony Canadeo	TB-DB	25	5'11"	190			31	149	4.8	0	20	9	45	89	4.5	0	0– 0		1	12	12	0	13	36.9							1	4	4	0	1	12	12	0
Tex McKay	TB-DB	24	6'	190			5	12	2.4	0	14	6	43	72	5.1	1	2–14						8	37.1							2	19	10	0				
Dick Bilda	TB-DB	25	6'	200		1					1	0	0	0	0.0	0	0– 0																					
Ted Fritsch	FB-LB	23	5'10"	210	30	6	94	322	3.4	4									3	5	2	0	10	40.8											11	288	26	0
Don Perkins	FB-LB	26	6'	197	12	2	58	207	3.6	0									1	1	1	0	1	31.0											2	34	17	0
Joe Laws	HB-DB	33	5'9"	190	24	3	45	200	4.4	3	4	1	25	15	3.8	0	1–25		7	61	9	1									15	118	8	0	8	132	17	0
Lou Brock	HB-DB	26	6'	190	30		36	200	5.6	3	21	5	24	94	4.5	2	0– 0		4	74	19	2	14	35.0							4	36	9	0	2	41	21	0
Paul Duhart	HB-DB	23	6'	180	24	4	51	183	3.6	2	13	3	31	42	3.2	0	0– 0		9	176	20	2									3	32	11	0	1	18	18	0
Larry Craig	BB-DE	28	6'1"	205		1													2	17	9	0													1	17	17	0
Ben Starret	BB-DE	26	5'11"	220	12		10	21	2.1	2									1	6	6	0	2	33.0											11	13	13	0
Don Hutson	OE-DB	31	6'1"	180	85	4	12	87	7.3	0	3	0	0	0	0.0	0	0– 0		58	866	15	9			31	33	94	0	3	0								
Harry Jacunski	OE-DE	28	6'2"	205															9	151	17	0																
Ray Wehba	OE-DE	28	6'	215		1													6	67	11	0																
Alex Urban	OE-DE	27	6'3"	210			1	2	2.0	0									1	10	10	0													1	20	20	0
Joel Mason	OE-DE	31	6'	210															1	9	9	0																
CHICAGO BEARS																																						
Sid Luckman	QB-DB	27	6'	200	6	2	20	–96	–4.8	1	143	71	50	1018	7.1	11	11– 8	2					20	34.2							1	6	6	0				
Gene Ronzani	QB-DB	35	5'9"	210		3	12	26	2.2	0	56	26	46	448	8.0	9	5– 9	2																				
John Long	QB-DB	29	6'	185			24	2	0.1	0	14	9	64	128	9.1	1	1– 7						7	35.4							2	14	7	0	1	14	14	0
Bill Glenn	QB-DB	26	6'	157			1	1	1.0	0	4	1	25	22	5.5	0	1–25																					
Bob Margarita	HB-DB	23	5'11"	175	24	3	88	463	5.3	4									15	130	9	0	1	34.0							5	9	2	0	12	279	23	0
Jim Fordham	FB-LB	27	5'11"	215	24		73	381	5.2	4									1	13	13	0													2	42	21	0
Al Grygo	HB-DB	26	5'10"	172	12	4	53	322	6.1	2									5	42	8	0	4	30.8							11	100	9	0	7	162	23	0
Gary Famiglietti	FB-LB	29	6'	238	18		63	282	4.5	2									1	23	23	1																
Tipp Mooney	HB-DB	25	6'	187	6	1	29	88	3.0	0									2	74	37	1									1	46	46	0	3	65	22	0
Ray McLean	HB-DB	28	5'10"	165	42	3	29	35	0.9	2									19	414	22	5									8	79	10	0	4	102	26	0
Doug McEnulty	HB-DB	22	6'3"	227	6	1	8	11	1.4	0									2	10	5	1	25	39.8														
Bob Masters	FB-LB	33	5'11"	204			11	9	0.8	0																												
George Wilson	OE-DE	30	6'1"	205	24														24	265	11	4																
Connie Mack Berry	OE-DE	28	6'3"	212	36														21	378	18	6																
Abe Craft	OE-DB	22	6'	180	12	1													9	140	16	2																
Rudy Smeja	OE-DE	23	6'2"	195	6														7	110	16	1													1	7	7	0
Dick Plasman	OE-DE	30	6'3"	220															1	17	17	0													1	–1	–1	0
Pete Gudauskas	G-LB	27	6'2"	220	36	1																			36	37	97											
DETROIT LIONS																																						
Frankie Sinkwich	TB-DB	23	5'11"	195	66	3	150	563	3.8	6	148	58	39	1060	7.2	12	20–14	6					45	41.0	24	30	80	2	8	25	11	148	13	0	6	144	24	0
Russ Lowther	TB-DB	21	5'8"	165		1	9	18	2.0	0	10	7	70	54	5.4	0	2–20						5	41.0							2	28	14	0				
Bob Westfall	FB-TB-LB	25	5'8"	195	30	1	65	277	4.3	3	47	23	49	342	7.3	4	6–13		16	218	14	2	1	11.0							3	38	13	0	3	78	26	0
Elmer Hackney	FB-LB	28	6'2"	198	30	3	58	184	3.2	4	1	1	100	19	19.0	0	0– 0		8	48	6	1																
Fred Dawley	FB-LB	23	5'9"	190			2	16	8.0	0																												
Art Van Tone	WB-DB	25	5'10"	185	36	4	25	30	1.2	1	1	0	0	0	0.0	0	0– 0		9	237	26	4	2	47.0							5	78	16	0	9	227	25	1
Bob Keene	WB-DB	25	5'11"	190	12	2	9	26	2.9	0									5	91	18	2	1	30.0							7	120	17	0	4	93	23	0
Tony Aiello (to BKN,HB-DB)	WB-DB	23	5'6"	165			6	22	3.7	0																					1	9	9	0				
Bill Callihan	BB-DB	28	6'3"	220			1	3	3.0	0									8	67	8	0													3	46	15	0
Buzz Trebotich	BB-DB	23	5'10"	210			1	2	2.0	0																												
Jack Matheson	OE-DE	24	6'2"	220	18	1													23	361	16	3																
Dave Diehl	OE-DE	25	6'	200	24														18	426	24	4																
Wayne Clark	OE-DE	26	6'3"	210															2	27	14	0																
CLEVELAND RAMS																																						
Albie Reisz	TB-DB	26	5'10"	170	12	3	69	134	1.9	2	113	49	43	777	6.9	8	10– 9	5					24	40.0							5	68	14	0	12	285	24	0
Tom Colella	TB-DB	26	6'	190	21	4	53	208	3.9	2	76	27	36	336	4.4	4	10–13	12	2	64	32	1	33	37.8				1	1	100	4	65	16	0	10	241	24	0
Walt West	FB-DB	25	6'	197	12	2	66	220	3.3	0									9	64	7	0			6	8	75				1	0	0	0	1	15	15	0
Mike Kabealo	HB-DB	28	5'8"	185	6	2	47	152	3.2	1	1	1	100	54	54.0	1	0– 0		2	20	10	0									7	64	9	0	4	126	32	0
Harvey Jones	FB-DB	23	6'	175	6	3	38	133	3.5	1									6	59	10	0									6	66	11	0	1	33	33	0
Jim Gillette	HB-DB	26	6'1"	185	12	3	26	131	5.0	2																					1	16	16	0	4	115	29	0
Lou Zontini	HB-DB	27	5'9"	190	47	2	33	105	3.2	3	2	2	100	18	9.0	0	0– 0		3	88	29	1			14	16	88	3	6	50	4	47	12	0	3	66	22	0
Roy Huggins	FB-LB	25	5'11"	195			12	41	3.4	0									1	0	0	0																
Stan Skoczen	HB-DB	23	5'11"	187			1	0	0.0	0																												
John Karrs	BB-LB	28	6'1"	210			7	0	0.0	0	10	4	40	49	4.9	0	4–40																					
John Petchel	BB-DB	25	5'11"	185	6	1	5	11	2.2	0	3	2	67	27	9.0	0	0– 0		1	43	43	1													1	17	17	0
Dave Bernard	BB-LB	31	5'10"	190			1	6	6.0	0	4	0	0	0	0.0	0	2–50																					
Jim Benton	OE-DE	27	6'3"	195	42														39	505	13	6													2	4	2	0
Steve Pritko	OE-DE	22	6'2"	210	18	1													18	296	16	3																
Ray Hamilton	OE-DE	28	6'4"	210	6														3	113	38	1																
CHICAGO CARDINALS – PITTSBURGH STEELERS																																						
John McCarthy	QB-DB	28	5'8"	160			6	–49	–8.2	0	67	20	30	250	3.6	0	13–19						24	33.4							1	9	9	0				
Tony Bova	QB-OE-DB	27	6'1"	192	12		14	–22	–1.6	0	30	6	20	96	3.2	0	1– 3		19	287	15	2																
Coley McDonough	QB-DB	29	6'1"	190			3	7	2.3	0	23	10	43	208	9.0	2	4–17																					
Walt Masters	QB	37	5'10"	197			1	–14	–14.0	0	7	1	14	13	1.9	0	2–29						2	45.5														
John Grigas	FB-LB	24	6'	203	18	1	185	610	3.3	3	131	50	38	690	5.3	6	21–16	11	2	33	17	0	12	35.1							5	40	8	0	23	471	20	0
Bob Thurbon	HB-DB	26	5'10"	176	30	2	69	185	2.7	4									7	134	19	1	15	30.0							1	2	2	0	12	291	24	0
George Magulick	HB-DB	25	5'9"	150		2	17	102	6.0	0									6	48	8	0									7	86	12	0	5	101	20	0
John Popovich	HB-DB	26	5'8"	160			8	29	3.6	0									3	1	0	0													3	75	25	0
Walt Rankin	FB-LB	26	5'11"	200		2	3	13	4.3	0									4	18	5	0																
Bernie Semes	HB-DB	25	5'7"	188		1	17	38	2.2	0									3	22	7	0																
Eddie Rucinski	OE-DB	28	6'2"	198	6	4	16	72	4.5	0									22	284	13	1													3	67	22	0
Don Currivan	OE-DB	23	6'	195	12														7	163	23	2													1	14	14	0
Walt Kichefski	OE-DE	28	6'1"	215															6	85	14	0																
Clint Wager	OE-DE	23	6'6"	222															5	73	15	0																
Marshall Robnett	C-G-LB	25	6'	208	1	1																	1	14.0	1	1	100	0	2	0								
Conway Baker	G	32	5'11"	230	11																				11	15	73											

WASHINGTON REDSKINS 8-2-0 Dud DeGroot

Scores of Each Game		
20	Boston	28
14	Pittsburgh	0
24	PHILADELPHIA	14
24	New York	14
24	CHIC. CARDS	21
34	BOSTON	7
28	CHIC. BEARS	21
0	Philadelphia	16
24	PITTSBURGH	0
17	NEW YORK	0

Use Name	Pos.	Hgt	Wgt	Age	Int	Pts
Ki Aldrich	C-LB	6'	215	29		
Ernie Barber	C-LB	6'1"	225	30		
Al DeMao	C-LB	6'2"	200	25	1	
Lee Pressley	C-FB-LB	6'2"	230	22		
(1 rush for 1 yd.)						
John Watson	C-LB	6'	205	24		
Larry Weldon	DE	6'	198	28		1
(1 PAT in 1 attempt)						

Use Name – Tackles	Pos.	Hgt	Wgt	Age	Int	Pts
John Adams	T	6'7"	245	25		
Earl Audet	T	6'2"	250	24		
Fred Davis	T	6'3"	240	27		
John Koniszewski	T	6'3"	228	26		
Ev Sharp	T	6'1"	225	26		
Joe Ungerer	T	6'	260	28		

Use Name – Guards	Pos.	Hgt	Wgt	Age	Int	Pts
Zip Hanna	G	5'10"	218	28		
Jack Keenan	G	5'10"	208	26		
Al Lolotai	G-T	6'	215	24	1	
(1 kickoff return for 15 yds.)						
Reid Lennan	G	6'	228	23		
Clem Stralka	G	5'10"	228	31		
Frank Walton	G	5'11"	235	33		
Marv Whited	G	5'10"	205	27	1	

An arm, a toe, and a pair of legs gave the Redskins sharp weapons in their drive to the top of the East. The arm, quarterback Sammy Baugh, completed a record 70.3 percent of his passes and kept the Washington attack moving in the air. The toe, Joe Aguirre, belted seven field goals, with one of them beating the Cardinals 24-21 in the last minute of play. To complete this tale of limbs, Steve Bagarus' quick legs often sprang the little halfback into the open on pass plays and end runs, one time leaving the Bears in the jet stream of a 55-yard weaving dash which made the difference in a 28-21 Redskin victory. An anatomy of the Washington offense would place these three players at the heart of the attack.

The framework for this talent was the T formation which had given Sammy Baugh trouble last year. But now that he was used to it, Sammy said he could play in top hat and tails—a remark fostered by his having no running duties in the T formation.

PHILADELPHIA EAGLES 7-3-0 Greasy Neale

Scores of Each Game		
21	CHIC. CARDS	6
24	Detroit	28
14	Washington	24
28	CLEVELAND	14
45	Pittsburgh	3
38	NEW YORK	17
30	PITTSBURGH	6
16	WASHINGTON	0
21	New York	28
35	BOSTON	7

Use Name	Pos.	Hgt	Wgt	Age	Int	Pts
Terry Fox	LB	6'1"	208	26		
Vic Lindskog	C-LB	6'1"	200	29	1	
Mike Mandarino	C	5'11"	240	24		
Bap Manzini	C-LB	5'11"	190	25		
Charlie Gauer	DE	6'2"	210	24		
Red Ramsey	DE	6'	210	30		
Milt Smith	DB-OE	6'3"	185	25		

Use Name – Tackles	Pos.	Hgt	Wgt	Age	Int	Pts
Rocco Canale	T	5'11"	235	28		
George Fritts	T	5'11"	205	25		
Bucko Kilroy	T	6'2"	240	24		
(1 kickoff return for 7 yds.)						
Vic Sears	T	6'3"	215	27		
Abe Shires	T	6'2"	220	26		
John Smith	T	6'2"	200	26		
Al Wistert	T	6'1"	215	24		

Use Name – Guards	Pos.	Hgt	Wgt	Age	Int	Pts
Bruno Banducci	G	5'11"	205	23		
Enio Conti	G	5'11"	207	32		
Duke Maronic	G	5'9"	205	24		
Eddie Michaels	G	5'11"	215	31		
Jack Sanders	G	6'	210	28		
Bob Suffridge	G	6'	220	30		

With his weak left arm useless for straight-arm tactics, Steve Van Buren had to get past tacklers by trampling them under his pistonlike legs. He did enough trampling, with some dodging thrown in, to win his first rushing title as well as the scoring championship. The Lions tasted Van Buren's wares when he stormed to a 69-yard touchdown run, and the Giants had to endure a 98-yard Van Buren kickoff return. With Van Buren snorting up yardage in storms, the Eagles stayed close to the Redskins until the Giants shot them down, 28-21, in their second meeting of the year.

Rock-hard tackles Al Wistert and Vic Sears also starred in this campaign. Passer Tommy Thompson was discharged from the Army and balanced the run-oriented attack as coach Greasy Neale was slowly but surely assembling a championship team.

NEW YORK GIANTS 3-6-1 Steve Owen

Scores of Each Game		
34	Pittsburgh	6
13	Boston	13
7	PITTSBURGH	21
14	WASHINGTON	24
17	CLEVELAND	21
17	Philadelphia	38
35	DETROIT	14
14	GREEN BAY	23
28	PHILADELPHIA	21
0	Washington	17

Use Name	Pos.	Hgt	Wgt	Age	Int	Pts
Lou DeFilippo	C-LB	6'1"	225	29		
Mel Hein	C-LB	6'2"	230	36	2	
Bill Piccolo	C-LB	5'11"	185	25		6
Elmer Barbour	BB-LB	6'1"	200	23		
Hub Barker	BB-LB	5'10"	195	26		
Bob Morrow	BB-LB	6'	220	27		
Leland Shaffer	BB-LB	6'2"	210	33		
(2 kickoff returns for 42 yds.)						
Bill Petrilas	DB	6'1"	195	27	2	

Use Name – Tackles	Pos.	Hgt	Wgt	Age	Int	Pts
Vic Carroll	T-C	6'4"	235	32		
Frank Cope	T	6'2"	235	29		
Lou Eaton	T	6'2"	215	30		
Herb Kane	T	6'1"	220	24		
Tom Kearns	T	6'4"	245	25		
Jim Little	T	6'1"	200	24		
Win Pederson	T	6'3"	225	30		
Phil Ragazzo	T	6'	223	30	1	
Army Tomaini	T	6'	235	27		

Use Name – Guards	Pos.	Hgt	Wgt	Age	Int	Pts
Verlin Adams	G-LB-DE	6'	205	27	1	
Bob Garner	G	6'	238	22		
Carl Grate	G-LB	6'	215	25		
Virgil Lindahl	G-OE-LB	6'1"	197	24		
(1 reception for 32 yds.)						
Jim Sivell	G	5'9"	205	31		
Frank Umont	G	5'11"	215	27		
Larry Visnic	G-LB	5'11"	180	26	1	
(1 kickoff return for 0 yds.)						
Tarzan White	G	5'9"	225	29		

The death of Al Blozis in France began the year on a tragic note which made the football games seem less important. Lieutenant Blozis met a hero's death when he went back for a missing member of his platoon and stopped a German bullet, cutting short a brilliant NFL career that lasted only three seasons.

Guard Len Younce also joined the military, and fullback Bill Paschal spent half the season in service, leaving the Giants a much weaker team. From its perch atop the Eastern Division, New York tumbled into third place with a squad made up of untried rookies and overaged veterans. One of the old-timers, passer Arnie Herber, had a last fling at glory in a late-season game against the Eagles. After Philadelphia had built up a big first-half lead, Herber came into the game in the second half and threw three touchdown passes to Frank Liebel in a five-minute span, bringing the Giants back to victory.

BOSTON YANKS 3-6-1 Herb Kopf

Scores of Each Game		
28	PITTSBURGH	7
28	WASHINGTON	20
13	NEW YORK	13
14	Green Bay	38
10	Pittsburgh	6
9	DETROIT	10
7	Washington	34
0	GREEN BAY	28
7	Cleveland	20
7	Philadelphia	35

Use Name	Pos.	Hgt	Wgt	Age	Int	Pts
Jim Magee	C-LB	6'1"	200	24	1	
Jack Sachse	C-LB	6'	210	24		
Bill Anderson	DE	6'2"	190	24		
Andy Kowalski	DE	6'1"	200	25		
Lou Mark	DE-LB	6'	200	30		

Use Name – Tackles	Pos.	Hgt	Wgt	Age	Int	Pts
Don Deeks	T	6'4"	240	22		
George Doherty	T	6'1"	220	24		
Ed McGee	T	6'1"	225	29		
George Sergienko	T	6'1"	250	27		

Use Name – Guards	Pos.	Hgt	Wgt	Age	Int	Pts
Al Fiorentino	G	5'7"	200	28		
Ellis Jones	G-LB	6'	190	24		
Tony Leon	G	5'9"	210	28		
John Morelli	G-LB	5'10"	192	22	1	
Floyd Rhea	G	6'	220	24		
Bill Walker	G	6'	220	24		
(1 kickoff return for 3 yds.)						

The Brooklyn Tigers joined forces with the Yanks for this year, but the marriage of two weak clubs only gave birth to an anemic offspring. Playing four home games in Boston and one in New York, the Yanks inherited the pop-gun offense characteristic of both parent squads. Even worse, the Yanks were duds at the box office in both cities, forcing owner Ted Collins to use the team as a tax write-off. The other NFL clubs also wrote off the Yanks as serious threats on the field. But the team did win three games, two from Pittsburgh plus an upset of Washington, and stayed very close in several losses. The lack of scoring punch was a ball and chain on the Yanks' movement. Passer Scott Gudmundson never showed a major-league arm, and leading runner Pug Manders ranked only fifteenth in the league statistics. The biggest asset on the Brooklyn roster, tackle Bruiser Kinard, was snatched away by Uncle Sam before he could make it to New England.

PITTSBURGH STEELERS 2-8-0 Jim Leonard

Scores of Each Game		
7	Boston	28
6	NEW YORK	34
0	WASHINGTON	14
21	New York	7
6	BOSTON	10
3	PHILADELPHIA	45
23	CHIC. CARDS	0
6	Philadelphia	30
7	Chic. Bears	28
0	Washington	24

Use Name	Pos.	Hgt	Wgt	Age	Int	Pts
Art Brandau	C-LB	6'2"	215	23		
Chuck Cherundolo	C-LB	6'1"	215	29	1	
Vern Foltz	C-LB	6'1"	205	27		
Si Titus	C-LB-DE	6'	195	26		
Al Wukits	C-LB	6'3"	230	25		
Carmine DePascal	OE-DB	6'	188	27		
John Pierre	OE-DE	6'	185	24		
(1 kickoff return for 10 yds.)						
Julie Koshlap	HB-DB	5'11"	180	27		

Use Name – Tackles	Pos.	Hgt	Wgt	Age	Int	Pts
Joe Cibulas	T	6'	220	22		
Joe Coomer (missed 1 FG attempt)	T	6'6"	290	26		
Ted Doyle	T	6'2"	240	31	1	6
Len Frketich	T	6'1"	290	27		
John Kondria	T	6'	185	25		
Ed McNamara	T	6'2"	225	25		
Ross Sorce	T	6'4"	255	25		
Glenn Stough	T	6'5"	240	24		
(1 kickoff return for 6 yds.)						

Use Name – Guards	Pos.	Hgt	Wgt	Age	Int	Pts
Carl Buda	G	5'11"	220	26		
Garth Chamberlain	G	6'	215	20		
Henry DePaul	G	5'11"	225	28		
Hubbard Law	G	6'1"	210	24		
Al Merkovsky	G-T	6'1"	210	28		
John Perko	G	6'1"	210	29		
Bill Brown	BB-DB	6'	205	28		
John Partick	BB-FB-LB	6'	200	27		
Mel O'Delli	HB-DB	5'8"	176	22		

After two years in merger situations, the Steelers decided that they could field a last-place team without help from any other club. Under coach Jim Leonard, the Steelers beat the Cardinals and Giants for their only wins, a pretty good showing for a team that didn't throw a single touchdown pass all year. The bright note of the season was the return of tailback Bill Dudley. In his first game back in uniform, Dudley ran for two touchdowns in leading his team to victory over the Cardinals. In the four games he played, Dudley scored more points than any other Pittsburgh back could score in the entire year.

TEAM TOTALS

OFFENSE	First Downs: Tot	by Rsh	by Pas	by Pen	Rushing: No.	Yds.	Avg Yds.	TD	Passing: Att	Com	Comp Pct.	Yds.	Avg. Yds. Att.	Avg. Yds. Comp	TD	Int	Pct. Int.	Punting: No.	Avg. Yds.
WASH.	154	77	71	6	394	1708	4.3	15	228	146	64.0	1838	8.1	12.6	12	11	4.8	33	43.3
PHIL.	131	74	47	10	391	1647	4.2	26	192	98	51.0	1321	6.9	13.5	11	14	7.3	47	37.8
N.Y.	98	50	38	10	317	791	2.5	6	201	92	45.8	1534	7.6	16.7	16	16	8.0	50	38.4
BOSTON	83	44	30	9	345	846	2.5	9	160	66	41.3	1000	6.3	15.2	6	21	13.1	66	36.4
PITT.	96	56	30	10	367	951	2.6	8	164	61	37.2	652	4.0	10.7	0	21	12.8	65	39.3
DEFENSE																			
WASH.	111	60	39	12	337	1003	3.0	8	209	95	45.5	1121	5.4	11.8	9	16	7.7	46	40.1
PHIL.	104	54	37	13	318	817	2.6	8	205	89	43.4	1243	6.1	14.0	10	19	9.3	63	37.5
N.Y.	140	77	55	8	395	1643	4.2	17	186	99	53.2	1410	7.6	14.2	6	13	7.0	44	40.0
BOSTON	133	62	61	10	387	1364	3.5	15	227	104	45.8	1427	6.3	13.7	10	30	13.2	43	38.9
PITT.	116	64	49	3	363	1371	3.8	16	191	102	53.4	1617	8.5	15.9	14	13	6.8	48	38.2

Punt Returns: No.	Yds.	Avg. Yds.	TD	Kickoff Returns: No.	Yds.	Avg. Yds.	TD	Interception Returns: No.	Yds.	Avg. Yds.	TD	Penalties: No.	Yds.	Fumbles: No.	Lost	Points: Tot	PAT	FG Att	FG	Saf.	OFFENSE
31	390	12.6	0	29	628	21.7	0	16	233	14.6	0	80	672	23	9	209	26	13	7	0	WASH.
37	452	12.2	0	30	734	24.5	1	19	257	13.5	0	61	529	27	10	272	32	8	4	0	PHIL.
26	277	10.7	0	30	649	21.6	0	13	116	8.9	0	56	492	27	9	179	23	13	6	0	N.Y.
27	233	8.6	0	41	845	20.6	0	30	264	8.8	0	61	533	31	15	123	15	6	4	0	BOSTON
32	361	11.3	0	30	652	21.7	0	13	212	16.3	1	53	436	26	8	79	7	5	4	0	PITT.
																					DEFENSE
23	254	11.1	0	37	692	18.7	0	11	140	12.7	0	49	411	23	6	121	16	5	1	0	WASH.
28	288	10.3	0	39	866	22.2	0	14	127	9.1	0	56	422	22	7	133	16	6	3	0	PHIL.
28	305	10.9	0	30	825	27.5	1	16	336	21.0	2	55	472	31	14	198	24	14	6	0	N.Y.
38	461	12.1	1	25	678	27.1	0	21	252	12.0	1	94	811	22	8	211	25	16	8	0	BOSTON
42	436	10.4	0	25	520	20.8	0	21	229	10.9	0	61	600	40	14	220	25	8	5	0	PITT.

Use Name – Backs & Ends	Pos.	Age	Hgt	Wgt	Pts	Int	RUSHING				PASSING								RECEIVING				PUNTING		KICKING						PUNT RETURNS				KICKOFF RETURNS			
							No.	Yds	Avg	TD	Att	Comp	%	Yds	Yd/Att	TD	Int–%	RK	No.	Yds	Avg	TD	No.	Avg	Pat	Att	%	FG	Att	%	No.	Yds	Avg	TD	No.	Yds	Avg	TD
WASHINGTON REDSKINS																																						
Sammy Baugh	QB-DB	31	6'2"	185	1	4	19	–71	–3.7	0	182	128	70	1669	9.2	11	4– 2	1					33	43.3	1	1	100											
Frankie Filchock	QB-HB-DB	28	5'11"	190		1	9	21	2.3	0	46	18	39	169	3.7	1	7–15		3	33	11	0									1	17	17	0				
Frank Akins	FB-LB	26	5'10"	210	36		147	797	5.4	6									8	57	7	0													1	21	21	0
Wilbur Moore	HB-DB	29	5'11"	180	12		29	206	7.1	1									13	115	9	1									1	10	10	0				
Merl Condit	HB-DB	28	5'11"	185	19		36	173	4.8	3									3	16	5	0			1	1	100											
Steve Bagarus	HB-DB	26	6'	170	36		39	154	3.9	1									35	517	15	5									21	251	12	0	12	325	27	0
Bob Seymour	FB-DB	29	6'2"	208	18	4	30	102	3.4	2									8	91	11	1																
Bill deCorrevont	HB-DB	26	6'	185			22	91	4.1	0									4	36	9	0									3	45	15	0	11	210	19	0
Sal Rosato	FB-LB	27	6'1"	220	12		23	85	3.7	2									1	7	7	0													1	17	17	0
Mike Micka (to BOS)	FB-LB	24	6'	190		1	19	62	3.3	0									2	74	37	0													2	31	16	0
Dick Todd	HB-DB	30	5'11"	182		4	7	54	7.7	0																					5	67	13	0				
Bob DeFruiter	HB-DB	28	6'	190			7	36	5.1	0									1	19	19	0																
Vito Ananis	HB-DB	29	5'10"	195			3	8	2.7	0																												
Ceril Hare	HB-DB	26	5'11"	200			3	0	0.0	0									3	83	28	0													2	30	15	0
Jim Gaffney	HB-DB	24	6'1"	208			1	–6	–6.0	0																												
Doug Turley	OE-DE	26	6'2"	210	6														17	185	11	1																
Joe Aguirre	OE-DE	26	6'4"	230	44														16	289	18	0			23	24	96	7	13	54								
Wayne Millner	OE-DE	34	6'1"	190	12														13	130	10	2																
Tom Miller	OE-DE	27	6'2"	198															11	84	8	0																
Les Dye	OE	27	6'1"	180	12														7	84	12	2																
Alex Piasecky	OE-DE	28	6'2"	198															1	18	18	0																
PHILADELPHIA EAGLES																																						
Roy Zimmerman	QB-DB	27	6'2"	205	47	7	29	–11	–0.4	1	132	67	51	991	7.5	9	8– 6	4					47	37.8	29	33	88	4	8	50	1	7	7	0				
Allie Sherman	QB-DB	22	5'11"	173	6		16	–7	–0.4	1	29	15	52	172	5.9	2	3–10																					
Tommy Thompson	QB-DB	29	6'1"	190		2	8	–13	–1.6	0	28	15	54	146	5.2	0	2– 7																					
Steve Van Buren	HB-DB	24	6'	205	110	1	143	832	5.8	15	1	0	0	0	0.0	0	0– 0		10	123	12	2			2	2	100				14	154	11	0	13	373	29	1
Ernie Steele	HB-DB	27	6'	190	12	1	20	212	10.6	2	2	1	50	12	6.0	0	1–50		3	42	14	0									2	22	11	0	3	72	24	0
Mel Bleeker	HB-DB	25	5'11"	195	12		50	167	3.3	2									3	32	11	0									4	37	9	0				
Sonny Karnofsky	HB-DB	22	5'10"	175	12	1	41	134	3.3	2									5	113	23	0									7	103	15	0	6	164	27	0
Ben Kish	FB-LB	28	6'	215		1	9	82	9.1	0									8	78	10	0																
Johnny Butler	HB-DB	26	5'10"	185	6	1	21	61	2.9	1									2	14	7	0													1	21	21	0
Jack Banta	HB-DB	27	5'11"	192	6		15	49	3.3	1									1	10	10	0									4	74	19	0	2	37	19	0
Gil Steinke	HB-DB	25	6'	180	6		7	46	6.6	1									2	12	6	0									2	27	14	0	1	18	18	0
Jack Hinkle	HB-DB	27	6'	193		1	11	40	3.6	0									1	8	8	0									3	28	9	0	1	17	17	0
Jim Castiglia	FB-LB	26	5'11"	210			13	29	2.2	0																												
Dick Erdlitz	HB-DB	25	5'10"	180		1	6	24	4.0	0																												
John Rogalla	FB-LB	27	6'	215	1		2	2	1.0	0									2	22	11	0			1	1	100											
Jack Ferrante	OE-DE	29	6'1"	195	42	1													21	474	23	7																
Larry Cabrelli	OE-DB	28	5'11"	190		1													15	140	9	0													2	25	13	0
Fred Meyer	OE-DE	26	6'2"	195	6														11	125	11	1																
Flip McDonald	OE-DB	24	6'2"	195	6														8	75	9	1																
Dick Humbert	OE-DB	26	6'1"	105															6	53	9	0																
NEW YORK GIANTS																																						
Arnie Herber	QB	35	5'11"	220			6	–27	–4.5	0	80	35	44	641	8.0	9	8–10	5					1	51.0														
Marion Pugh	QB	25	6'1"	187			24	–52	–2.2	0	58	27	47	390	6.7	3	3– 5																					
Junie Hovious	QB	26	5'8"	180			22	–7	–0.3	0	46	22	48	373	8.1	4	5–11																		1	20	20	0
Joe Sulatis	QB-WB	24	6'2"	205			10	37	3.7	0	13	7	54	126	9.7	0	0– 0		2	12	6	0													3	50	17	0
Bill Paschal	FB-DB	24	6'	196	12		59	247	4.2	2	1	0	0	0	0.0	0	0– 0		2	11	6	0													2	43	22	0
Steve Filipowicz	FB-LB	24	5'8"	200	12		53	142	2.7	1	2	0	0	0	0.0	0	0– 0		4	49	12	1									1	18	18	0	1	32	32	0
Howie Livingston	FB-DB	23	6'1"	190	30	3	40	109	2.7	3									14	250	18	2	13	37.0							13	106	8	0	4	104	26	0
Ward Cuff	WB-DB	32	6'1"	187		1	48	214	4.5	0									12	172	14	0									10	124	12	0	4	105	26	0
George Franck	WB-DB	26	6'	180			29	61	2.1	0	1	1	100	4	4.0	0	0– 0		3	39	13	0	22	37.8											3	58	19	0
Jack Doolan (from WAS)	WB-DB	26	6'1"	190			10	26	2.6	0									6	50	8	0													3	87	29	0
Mike Klotovich	WB-DB	28	5'10"	180			5	26	5.2	0									1	7	7	0	11	38.4														
Ed Shedlosky	WB-DB	25	6'	185			9	11	1.2	0									2	15	8	0									1	19	19	0	2	40	20	0
Frank Martin (from BOS)	WB-DB	26	5'10"	185	6	1	3	11	3.7	0									4	67	17	1									1	10	10	0	1	18	18	0
Frank Liebel	OE-DB	25	6'1"	205	60	1													22	593	27	10																
Sam Fox	OE-DE	25	6'2"	215	12														10	120	12	2													1	14	14	0
John Weiss	OE-DB	23	6'3"	195	6														4	82	21	1													2	36	18	0
Hal Springer	OE DE	23	6'4"	212															4	63	16	0																
Harry Wynne	OE-DE	25	6'4"	200															2	25	13	0																
Ken Strong	K	39	6'	210	41																		3	44.7	23	23	100	6	13	46								
BOSTON YANKS																																						
Scott Gudmundson	QB-DB	24	5'10"	180		2	23	4	0.2	0	43	17	40	200	7.0	1	5–12		1	–8	–8	0	17	36.0							4	36	9	0				
George Cafego	QB-DB	30	5'10"	178		1	19	–51	–2.7	0	26	13	50	149	5.8	0	3–12		2	20	10	0	6	35.5							1	0	0	0	2	47	24	0
Ace Parker	QB-DB	33	6'	187			18	–49	–2.7	0	24	10	42	123	5.1	0	5–21						7	32.0														
Frank Sachse	QB-DB	28	6'	198		2	5	9	1.8	0	21	9	43	203	9.7	2	1– 5																					
Hugh McCullough	QB-DB	29	6'	185			2	1	0.5	0	5	0	0	0	0.0	0	3–60		1	17	17	0	2	32.0														
Pug Manders	FB-LB	32	6'	200	36	3	76	238	3.1	6	9	5	56	42	4.7	0	1–11																		2	10	5	0
John Martin	HB-DB	27	6'1"	198	12	1	39	191	4.9	1									2	20	10	0	14	41.1							4	7	2	0	13	302	23	0
John Grigas	FB-LB	25	6'	203	12	1	64	160	2.5	2	14	5	36	85	6.1	0	1– 7		5	54	11	0													4	65	16	0
Ned Mathews	HB-DB	27	5'10"	185	6	3	27	146	5.4	0	1	0	0	0	0.0	0	0– 0		4	56	14	1													4	108	27	0
Bob Davis	HB-DB	31	6'	190		6	29	91	3.1	0	10	5	50	73	7.3	3	0– 0		9	56	6	0	3	41.0							10	91	9	0	6	131	22	0
Babe Dimancheff	HB-DB	23	5'11"	178		1	30	69	2.3	0									1	15	15	0									8	99	12	0	4	123	31	0
Paul Duhart (from PIT)	HB-QB-DB	24	6'	180	6		17	17	1.0	1	9	3	33	27	3.0	0	2–22																		4	81	20	0
Ken Steinmetz	FB-LB	21	6'	190		1	4	12	3.0	0													8	30.0														
Don Currivan	OE-DB	24	6'	190	24														16	397	25	4													1	3	3	0
Bob Masterson	OE-DE	30	6'1"	220															15	191	13	0						0	1	0								
Keith Ranspot	OE-DE	30	6'3"	205															8	117	15	0																
Joe Crowley	OE-DB	26	6'	198		1													1	12	12	0																
Augie Lio	G-LB	27	6'	230	27	3																			15	16	94	4	5	80								
George Smith	C-LB	31	6'2"	225		2																	9	39.4											1	0	0	0
PITTSBURGH STEELERS																																						
Busit Warren (from PHI, HB-DB)	TB-DB	28	5'11"	175	12	1	96	285	3.0	2	92	36	39	368	4.0	0	10–11	10	1	–1	–1	0									13	168	13	0	5	137	27	0
Bill Dudley	TB-DB	24	5'10"	176	20	2	57	204	3.6	3	32	10	31	58	1.8	0	2– 6						2	18.0	2	3	67				5	20	4	0	3	65	22	0
Ed Stofko	TB-DB	25	6'1"	192			13	–16	–1.2	0	17	7	41	94	5.5	0	4–24						3	36.3														
Toimi Jarvi	TB-DB	25	6'	200			9	24	2.7	0	10	4	40	50	5.0	0	3–30						2	34.5														
Russ Lowther	TB-DB	22	5'8"	165			15	54	3.6	0	4	0	0	0	0.0	0	1–25						1	35.0	0	1	0				2	35	18	0	1	20	20	0
Al Postus	TB-DB	23	5'10"	180			2	4	2.0	0	5	2	40	73	14.6	0	1–20																		1	14	14	0
John Lucente	FB-LB	23	5'9"	200	12		82	242	3.0	1									11	45	4	0													5	102	20	0
Art Jones	HB-DB	26	6'2"	193		1	15	64	4.3	0									5	8	2	0									6	62	12	0	1	26	26	0
George Kiick	HB-DB	28	6'	195	6		15	45	3.0	1									1	–2	–2	0													1	19	19	0
John Petrella	HB-DB	25	5'7"	160		1	15	33	2.2	0																					6	52	9	0	3	85	28	0
John Itzel	FB-LB	20	6'	190		1	4	11	2.8	0									1	4	4	0																
Al Nichols	FB-LB	28	5'10"	205			10	5	0.5	0																												
Sid Tinsley	HB-DB	24	5'9"	168		1	5	3	0.6	0													57	40.4														
John Popovich	HB-DB	27	5'8"	160			4	–8	–2.0	0																									1	39	39	0
John Naioti	HB-DB	23	5'10"	185	4		1	–17	–17.0	0									2	14	7	0			4	4	100											
Leon Pense	BB-DB	23	6'	170		3	6	1	0.2	0									1	32	32	0													1	21	21	0
John Petchel	BB-DB	26	5'11"	185		1	2	2	1.0	0	1	1	100	8	8.0	0	0– 0		2	25	13	0																
Tony Bova	OE-HB-DB	28	6'1"	185			0	11	1.8	0	1	0	0	0	0.0	0	0– 0		15	220	15	0									1	24	24	0				
Morgan Tiller	OE-DE	25	6'1"	195															10	141	14	0													3	47	16	0
Dick Dolly	OE-DE	27	6'3"	212															8	122	15	0																
Al Olszewski	OE-DB	24	6'2"	185															2	28	14	0																
Frank Kimble	OE-DE	27	6'5"	205															2	16	8	0																
Ben Agajanian (from PHI)	K	26	6'	195	13																				1	2	50	4	4	100								

CLEVELAND RAMS 9-1-0 Adam Walsh

Scores of Each Game		
21	CHIC. CARDS	0
17	CHIC. BEARS	0
27	Green Bay	14
41	Chic. Bears	21
14	Philadelphia	28
21	New York	17
20	GREEN BAY	7
35	Chic. Cards	21
28	Detroit	21
20	BOSTON	7

Use Name	Pos.	Hgt	Wgt	Age	Int	Pts
Dave Bernard	LB	5'10"	197	32		
Bob deLauer	C-LB	6'1"	218	25		
Roger Harding	C-LB	6'2"	195	22	1	
George Phillips	LB	6'3"	215	24		
Bill Rieth	C-G-LB	5'11"	203	29		
Mo Scarry	C-LB	6'	220	25	4	
Joe Winkler	C-LB	6'1"	200	23	1	
Floyd Konetsky	DE	6'	195	25		
Bob Shaw	OE-DE	6'4"	229	24		
(1 kickoff return for 1 yd.)						

Use Name – Tackles	Pos.	Hgt	Wgt	Age	Int	Pts
Graham Armstrong	T	6'4"	215	27		
Gil Bouley	T	6'2"	233	24		
Roger Eason	T	6'2"	220	27		
Len Levy	T	6'	260	24		
Elbie Schultz	T	6'4"	245	27		
Rudy Sikich	T	6'1"	220	24		

Use Name – Guards	Pos.	Hgt	Wgt	Age	Int	Pts
Mike Lazetich	G-LB	6'1"	195	24		
Les Lear	G-LB	5'11"	223	27		
Sonny Liles (from DET)	G-LB	5'9"	195	26	1	
Riley Matheson	G-LB	6'2"	210	30	2	
(1 punt return for 5 yds.)						
Art Mergenthal	G-LB	5'11"	215	25		
Ray Monaco	G-LB	5'10"	215	27		

The husband of movie star Jane Russell and a Rose Bowl star at UCLA rookie quarterback Bob Waterfield added to his credits by leading the Rams to the NFL championship. At the controls of Cleveland's new T offense, Waterfield loved to throw the long ball, ran the bootleg play with great poise, and had a knack for rallying his teammates when faced with defeat. He also found time to kick field goals, punt, and intercept six passes while on defense. Injuries could not stop him; taped like a mummy because of torn rib muscles, he hit end Jim Benton with ten passes for 303 yards in defeating Detroit and clinching the Western crown. Waterfield got lots of help from running backs, Fred Gehrke, Jim Gillette, and Don Greenwood, while ends Benton and Steve Pritko both were mentioned on All-Pro teams. But even with such a fine squad, owner Dan Reeves still lost $50,000 in this championship season.

DETROIT LIONS 7-3-0 Gus Dorais

Scores of Each Game		
10	Chic. Cards	0
21	Green Bay	57
28	PHILADELPHIA	24
26	CHIC. CARDS	0
16	CHIC. BEARS	10
10	Boston	9
35	Chic. Bears	28
14	New York	35
21	CLEVELAND	28
14	GREEN BAY	3

Use Name	Pos.	Hgt	Wgt	Age	Int	Pts
Frank Kring	LB	6'	190	26		
Bob Nelson	C-LB	6'1"	215	25	1	3
(1 field goal in 4 attempts)						
Frank Szymanski	C-LB	6'	225	22	1	
Rex Williams	C-LB	6'2"	210	29		
Alex Wojciechowicz	C-LB	5'11"	220	31		
Ted Grefe	OE-DE	6'	205	27		
Larry Knorr	OE-DB	6'2"	195	28		
Vince Mazza	DE	6'1"	210	24		
Arch Milano	OE-DE	6'	197	26		
Lake Robertson	DE	6'1"	210	26		

Use Name – Tackles	Pos.	Hgt	Wgt	Age	Int	Pts
Al Kaporch	T	5'10"	215	31	1	
Mike Kostiuk	T	6'	210	26		
Luke Lindon	T	5'10"	245	28		
Joe Manzo	T	6'1"	220	28		
Dick Mesak	T	6'2"	225	25		
Garvin Mugg	T	6'1"	215	24		
Dom Sigillo	T	6'	230	32		
Emil Uremovich	T	6'2"	240	28		
Joe Krol	DB	6'1"	210	26		
(2 punts for 37.0 average)						
Bob Sneddon	WB-DB	5'10"	180	24		

Use Name – Guards	Pos.	Hgt	Wgt	Age	Int	Pts
Stan Batinski	G	5'10"	215	28		
Bill Radovich	G	5'10"	240	30		
Larry Sartori	G	6'	208	28		
Damon Tassos	G-LB	6'1"	220	21	3	

Star tailback Frankie Sinkwich spent the year in the service, but Uncle Sam made up for it by discharging two linemen who immediately beefed up the Detroit line. Emil Uremovich and Bill Radovich put their military training to use in the football trenches and opened up enough holes for Detroit runners to carry the club to a second-place finish. Bob Westfall, ex-GI Chuck Fenenbock, and newly acquired Andy Farkas blasted away for enough yards to compensate for the loss of Sinkwich's passing. On defense, the Lions saw lots of passes. On October 7, Green Bay's Don Hutson burned the secondary for four touchdown catches in just the second period of a 57-21 Packer romp. And in a late-season showdown with the Rams, the Lions watched sure-handed Jim Benton haul in ten passes for 303 yards in a 28-21 Cleveland win, to more than point up the Lions' inability to deal with the aerial attack.

GREEN BAY PACKERS 6-4-0 Curly Lambeau

Scores of Each Game		
31	CHIC. BEARS	21
57	DETROIT	21
14	CLEVELAND	27
38	BOSTON	14
33	CHIC. CARDS	14
24	Chic. Bears	28
7	Cleveland	20
28	Boston	0
23	New York	14
3	Detroit	14

Use Name	Pos.	Hgt	Wgt	Age	Int	Pts
Charley Brock	C-LB	6'2"	210	29	4	12
Bob Flowers	C-LB	6'1"	210	28	1	
Bob Adkins	BB-G-DE	6'1"	220	28		
Larry Craig	BB-DE	6'1"	215	29		6
(1 kickoff return for 11 yds.)						
Ken Keuper	BB-DE	6'	215	27		
(1 punt for 12 yds.)						

Use Name – Tackles	Pos.	Hgt	Wgt	Age	Int	Pts
Solon Barnett	T	6'1"	235	24		
Tiny Croft	T	6'3"	285	24		
Paul Lipscomb	T	6'4"	230	22		
Amy McPherson	T-C	5'11"	240	33		
Ed Neal	T	6'4"	287	27		
Ernie Pannell	T	6'2"	220	28		
(1 kickoff return for 10 yds.)						
Baby Ray	T	6'6"	256	30		

Use Name – Guards	Pos.	Hgt	Wgt	Age	Int	Pts
Amadeo Bucchianeri	G	5'10"	210	28		
Bernie Crimmins	G-LB	5'11"	195	26	1	6
Ray Frankowski	G	5'11"	220	26		
Buckets Goldenberg	G	5'10"	220	34		
Bill Kuusisto	G	6'	230	27		
Glen Sorenson	G	6'	210	24		
(missed 1 field goal attempt)						
Pete Tinsley	G-LB	5'8"	205	32	1	
Charlie Tollefson	G	6'	215	28		

After the 1944 season, Don Hutson announced his retirement by saying, "If I every play on this field again, I'll jump off the Empire State Building." Evidently, he changed his mind, since he was back in uniform at the start of the season with no sign of carrying out his threat. Even though the Packers fell off to third place, Hutson still soared above all the receivers in the NFL. In the second quarter of the October 7 game against Detroit, Hutson caught four touchdown passes and kicked five extra points, chalking up a record 29 points in one period. The Packers also had a colorful twenty-seven-year-old rookie tackle named Ed Neal. Bulldog Turner best described him: "Ed Neal weighed two hundred and eighty-seven pounds stripped. His arms were as big as my leg and as hard as a table." Turner's remarks were not ill-founded, as Neal would break Turner's nose five times during the course of their many encounters.

CHICAGO BEARS 3-7-0 Luke Johnsos, Hunk Anderson, Paddy Driscoll, George Halas

Scores of Each Game		
21	Green Bay	31
0	Cleveland	17
7	CHIC. CARDS	16
21	CLEVELAND	41
10	Detroit	16
28	GREEN BAY	24
28	DETROIT	35
21	Washington	28
28	PITTSBURGH	7
28	Chic. Cards	20

Use Name	Pos.	Hgt	Wgt	Age	Int	Pts
Forest Masterson	C-G	6'3"	246	26		
Fred Mundee	C-LB	6'1"	220	32		
John Schiechl	C-LB	6'2"	245	28		
Bulldog Turner	C-LB	6'1"	230	26		
Milt Vucinich	C-LB	6'	215	25		
Charlie Mitchell	DB	6'	185	24		

Use Name – Tackles	Pos.	Hgt	Wgt	Age	Int	Pts
Lee Artoe	T	6'3"	237	29		
(Missed 1 field goal attempt)						
Al Barbartsky	T	6'	225	29		
Glen Burgeis	T	6'1"	220	23		
Jim Daniell	T	6'2"	230	27		
(1 kickoff return for 14 yds.)						
Al Hoptowit	T	6'1"	212	29		
Frank Ramsey	T	6'1"	240	29		
Tom Roberts	T	6'1"	215	29		
Joe Stydahar	T	6'4"	230	33		

Use Name – Guards	Pos.	Hgt	Wgt	Age	Int	Pts
Chuck Drulis	G-LB	5'10"	215	27		
Nick Kerasiotis	G-LB	5'11"	193	27		
Rudy Mucha (from CLE)	G	6'1"	246	27		
Pete Perez	G	5'9"	220	21		
Ed Sprinkle	G-DE	6'1"	200	21		
George Zorich	G	6'2"	210	26		

After eight games, the Bears had won only once. Too many players had gone off into the military for coaches Hunk Anderson, Luke Johnsos, and Paddy Driscoll to keep the Bears on top of the NFL heap. The club was practicing on Thanksgiving morning when Sid Luckman noticed a middle-aged man in a Navy uniform walking across the field, and when he waved he knew that George Halas was back. With two games left on the slate, Papa Bear again took over the coaching reigns of the once Monsters of the Midway.

Other prewar Bears also started trickling back as Ken Kavanaugh, Joe Stydahar, George McAfee, and Hugh Gallarneau all put the Chicago jersey back on after years of military uniforms. When McAfee reported in time for a game against Pittsburgh, Halas promised to use him sparingly. True to his word, Halas used him for only twelve minutes; in that time, McAfee ripped off three quick touchdowns.

CHICAGO CARDINALS 1-9-0 Phil Handler

Scores of Each Game		
0	DETROIT	10
0	Cleveland	21
6	Philadelphia	21
16	Chic. Bears	7
0	Detroit	26
14	Green Bay	33
21	Washington	24
0	Pittsburgh	23
21	CLEVELAND	35
20	CHIC. BEARS	28

Use Name	Pos.	Hgt	Wgt	Age	Int	Pts
Ray Apolskis	C-LB	5'11"	200	26		
Bill Campbell	C-LB-DB	6'	195	25		
Larry Fuller (from WAS)	LB	5'10"	196	22		
Bob Norman	C-LB	6'1"	185	25		
Hal Robl	LB	6'	227	27		
Marshall Robnett	C-LB	6'	208	26		
Cliff Speegle	C-LB	6'1"	195	27	2	
John Durko	DE	6'4"	235	26		
Pop Ivy	DE	6'3"	205	29	1	
Freeman Rexer	OE-DE	6'1"	210	27		
Les Bruckner	FB-LB	6'1"	195	26		
(1 kickoff return for 13 yds.)						
Hal Blackwell	HB-DB	6'1"	205	26		
(17 punts for 38.9 yd. overage)						

Use Name – Tackles	Pos.	Hgt	Wgt	Age	Int	Pts
Chet Bulger	T	6'3"	235	27		6
Ray Busler	T	6'1"	225	29		
Gil Duggan	T	6'3"	225	27		
Bob Eckl	T	6'1"	233	27		
Ralph Foster	T	6'1"	230	28		
Mitch Ucovich	T	5'11"	208	29		
Bob Zimny	T	6'1"	220	24		
(1 kickoff return for 12 yds.)						
Chet Maeda	HB-DB	5'10"	187	26		
(1 pass attempt – incomplete)						

Use Name – Guards	Pos.	Hgt	Wgt	Age	Int	Pts
Conway Baker	G	5'11"	230	33		
(Missed 1 FG and 1 PAT attempt)						
Libero Bertagnolli	G		188	29		
Dave Braden	G-LB	6'	210	26		
Steve Enich	G	5'10"	212	22		
Ralph Fife	G-LB	6'	210	25		
Lou Marotti	G	5'10"	223	27		
Vic Obeck	G	6'	225	27		
Gordon Wilson	G	6'	225	29		

Although the Cardinals still finished in last place, owner Charles Bidwill and coach Phil Handler were laying the groundwork for future success. Imitating the Bears, Handler remodeled the offense with the T-formation. To run this new offense, Bidwill signed quarterback Paul Christman of Missouri, a fine passer who suffered a rough rookie season but grew into a crafty field general with time. Further reinforcements came from military returnees Bill Dewell and Joe Kuharich and from ex-Redskin Frank Seno. Dewell especially helped Christman, giving him a target to aim at while enemy linemen poured through the thin Cardinal line at him. The new attack got off the ground slowly, scoring 98 points and only beating the Bears, the one team they most wanted to beat.

TEAM TOTALS

OFFENSE	First Downs: Tot	by Rsh	by Pas	by Pen	Rushing: No.	Yds.	Avg Yds.	TD	Passing: Att	Com	Comp Pct.	Yds.	Avg. Yds. Att.	Avg. Yds. Comp	TD	Int	Pct. Int.	Punting: No.	Avg. Yds.
CLEVE.	137	68	60	9	372	1714	4.6	19	199	100	50.3	1767	8.9	17.7	16	20	10.1	47	40.1
DET.	102	40	47	15	313	857	2.7	8	238	87	36.6	1544	6.5	17.7	15	36	15.1	53	38.0
G.B.	131	73	44	14	377	1325	3.5	15	218	81	37.2	1536	7.0	19.0	14	24	11.0	46	39.9
CHIC. B.	164	86	60	18	422	1497	3.5	13	244	128	52.5	1857	7.6	14.5	14	12	4.9	44	35.7
CHIC. C.	115	47	51	17	334	933	2.8	8	267	99	37.1	1328	5.0	13.4	5	18	6.7	62	36.7

OFFENSE	Punt Returns: No.	Yds.	Avg. Yds.	TD	Kickoff Returns: No.	Yds.	Avg. Yds.	TD	Interception Returns: No.	Yds.	Avg. Yds.	TD	Penalties: No.	Yds.	Fumbles: No.	Lost	Points: Tot	PAT	FG Att	FG	Saf.
CLEVE.	31	353	11.4	0	26	458	17.6	0	28	398	14.2	0	67	593	34	18	244	31	3	1	0
DET.	39	563	14.4	1	30	662	22.1	0	23	424	18.4	1	66	673	32	10	195	25	7	2	1
G.B.	34	310	9.1	0	33	670	20.3	0	24	464	19.3	5	69	723	21	7	258	31	13	5	1
CHIC. B.	17	165	9.7	0	39	677	17.4	0	15	101	6.7	0	67	666	21	10	192	27	3	1	0
CHIC. C.	27	276	10.2	0	46	924	20.1	0	12	133	11.1	0	50	389	35	13	98	12	4	0	1

Use Name – Backs & Ends	Pos.	Age	Hgt	Wgt	Pts	Int	RUSHING No.	Yds	Avg	TD	PASSING Att	Comp	%	Yds	Yd/Att	TD	Int–%	RK	RECEIVING No.	Yds	Avg	TD	PUNTING No.	Avg	KICKING Pat	Att	%	FG	Att	%	PUNT RETURNS No.	Yds	Avg	TD	KICKOFF RETURNS No.	Yds	Avg	TD
CLEVELAND RAMS																																						
Bob Waterfield	QB-DB	25	6'1"	190	64	6	18	18	1.0	5	171	88	52	1609	9.4	14	16–9	2					39	40.7	31	34	91	1	3	33	2	34	17	0				
Albie Reisz	QB-DB	27	5'10"	170		2	12	-2	-0.2	0	21	9	43	146	7.0	2	4–19		1	11	11	0	7	34.4							8	78	10	0				
Jack Jacobs	QB-DB	26	6'1"	180			2	0	0.0	0	5	3	60	12	2.4	0	0–0						1	43.0							1	6	6	0				
Steve Nemeth	QB-DB	23	5'10"	172							1	0	0	0	0.0	0	0–0																					
Fred Gehrke	HB-DB	27	5'11"	190	48	4	74	467	6.3	7									8	90	11	1									8	120	15	0	9	173	19	0
Jim Gillette	HB-DB	27	6'1"	185	6	4	63	390	6.1	1									6	48	8	0									7	53	8	0	4	66	17	0
Don Greenwood	FB-LB	24	6'	190	24		101	376	3.7	4									3	72	24	0													5	106	21	0
Tom Colella	HB-DB	27	6'	185	24		46	224	4.9	2	1	0	0	0	0.0	0	0–0		7	64	9	2									1	10	10	0	3	89	30	0
George Koch	HB-DB	26	6'	200			12	101	8.4	0																									1	7	7	0
Ralph Ruthstrom	FB-LB	24	6'5"	208		1	10	74	7.4	0																					3	47	16	0				
Pat West	FB-LB	22	6'	204			19	45	2.4	0									1	-2	-2	0																
Harvey Jones	HB-DB	24	6'	175	6	2	8	15	1.9	0									2	36	18	1																
Jim Worden	HB-DB	29	5'10"	180			4	3	0.8	0																												
Walt Zirinsky	HB-DB	24	5'11"	187			3	3	1.0	0																												
Jim Benton	OE-DE	28	6'3"	195	48														45	1067	24	8													3	16	5	0
Steve Pritko	OE-DE	23	6'2"	210	24														19	255	13	4																
Red Hickey	OE-DE	28	6'2"	195															4	76	19	0																
Ray Hamilton	OE-DE	29	6'4"	210															4	50	13	0																
DETROIT LIONS																																						
Chuck Fenenbock	TB-DB	27	5'9"	175	12	1	72	143	2.0	1	110	45	41	752	6.8	7	11–10	7	1	24	24	0	29	37.2							5	69	14	0	7	192	27	0
Charley Price	TB-DB	26	6'1"	185		1	24	71	3.0	0	52	16	31	256	4.9	3	8–15						4	37.0							3	32	11	0	4	79	20	0
Dave Ryan	TB-DB	22	5'10"	190	15	3	36	93	2.6	1	44	13	30	331	7.5	3	10–23		2	67	34	1	17	39.3				1	3	33	15	220	15	0	6	138	23	0
Dick Weber	TB-DB	26	5'11"	195			7	10	1.4	0	22	6	27	72	3.3	0	5–23						1	42.0											1	24	24	0
Bob Westfall	FB-LB	26	5'8"	190	54		82	234	2.9	6	4	3	75	91	22.8	1	0–0		12	209	17	3									1	16	16	0	2	26	13	0
Andy Farkas	FB-WB-LB	29	5'10"	195	12		31	137	4.4	0									9	132	15	2									7	101	14	0	8	165	21	0
Elmer Hackney	FB-LB	29	6'2"	203			6	13	2.2	0																												
Dick Booth	WB-DB	27	6'1"	190	6		4	20	5.0	0									3	90	30	1									2	8	4	0	1	26	26	0
Art Van Tone	WB-DB	26	5'10"	185			3	14	4.7	0									3	67	22	0																
Bob Brumley	WB-DB	23	6'	200			5	18	3.6	0									2	27	14	0																
Jim Thomason	WB-DB	25	6'	200			9	9	1.0	0									1	6	6	0																
Tippy Madarik	WB-DB	23	5'11"	197		1	2	5	2.5	0																												
Bob Keene	WB-DB	26	5'11"	193			2	2	1.0	0																												
Bill Callihan	BB-FB-LB	29	6'3"	230	31	2	27	85	3.1	0	5	3	60	34	6.8	1	2–40		4	88	22	1			25	27	93											
Chuck DeShane	BB-DB	26	6'1"	192	12	3													2	29	15	0									5	107	21	1				
Buzz Trebotich	BB-DB	24	5'10"	210		3	3	3	1.0	0	1	1	100	8	8.0	0	0–0																					
John Greene	OE-DB	25	6'	215	30	3													26	450	17	5																
Jack Matheson	OE-DE	25	6'2"	210	14														19	341	18	1									1	10	10	0				
Ed Frutig (from GB)	OE-DB	25	6'1"	185	6														2	5	3	1													1	12	12	0
Dave Diehl	OE-DE	26	6'	200															1	9	9	0																
GREEN BAY PACKERS																																						
Irv Comp	TB-DB	26	6'2"	205	18	2	57	75	1.3	1	106	44	43	865	8.2	7	11–10	6	1	50	50	1									4	36	9	0	5	110	22	0
Tex McKay	TB-DB	25	6'	195	12	3	71	231	3.3	2	89	32	36	520	5.8	5	9–10	9					44	41.2							7	66	9	0	4	67	17	0
Lou Brock	TB-HB-DB	27	6'	195	18	3	46	196	4.3	3	22	5	23	151	6.9	2	4–18		4	87	22	0									4	37	9	0	1	12	12	0
Ted Fritsch	FB-LB	24	5'10"	210	57	1	88	282	3.2	7									3	13	4	0						3	8	38					8	279	35	0
Don Perkins (to CHIB)	FB-LB	27	6'	198	12		46	273	5.9	2									2	11	6	0	1	13.0														
Bruce Smith	HB-DB	25	6'	197			21	94	4.5	0																					6	67	11	0	2	46	23	0
Joe Laws	HB-DB	34	5'9"	185		3	16	82	5.1	0									2	11	6	0									11	71	6	0	4	72	18	0
Russ Mosley	HB-DB	27	5'10"	170			16	49	3.1	0	1	0	0	0	0.0	0	0–0		1	10	10	0									1	13	13	0				
Ken Snelling	FB-LB	26	6'	210			3	10	3.3	0																												
Chuck Sample	FB-LB	25	5'9"	210			2	2	1.0	0																												
Ben Starret	BB-DE	27	5'11"	220		1	5	26	5.2	0																									1	3	3	0
Don Hutson	OE-DB	32	6'1"	180	97	4	8	60	7.5	1									47	834	18	9			31	35	89	2	4	50					4	37	9	0
Nolan Luhn	OE-DE	24	6'3"	200	6														10	151	15	1																
Clyde Goodnight	OE-DB	21	6'1"	195	18		8	26	3.3	0									7	283	40	3													1	8	8	0
Moose Mulleneaux	OE-DE	28	6'3"	210															3	31	10	0																
Alex Urban	OE-DE	28	6'3"	210															1	55	55	0																
Joel Mason	DE	32	6'	200																											1	20	20	0	1	15	15	0
CHICAGO BEARS																																						
Sid Luckman	QB-DB	28	6'	205			36	-118	-3.3	0	217	117	54	1726	7.9	14	10–5	2					36	36.0											2	31	16	0
Gene Ronzani	QB-DB	36	5'9"	210			3	-20	-6.7	0	24	10	42	119	5.0	0	2–8														1	6	6	0	1	0	0	0
John Long	QB-DB	30	6'	185			2	3	1.5	0													1	42.0							1	12	12	0				
Bob Margarita	HB-DB	24	5'11"	175	30	6	112	497	4.4	3									23	394	17	2	1	29.0							7	66	9	0	10	155	16	0
Hugh Gallarneau	HB-DB	28	6'	190	18	2	75	260	3.5	2									7	58	8	1									3	30	10	0	6	90	15	0
Gary Famiglietti	FB-LB	30	6'	235	18		65	235	3.6	3									4	42	11	0						0	1	0					1	19	19	0
Jim Fordham	FB-LB	28	5'11"	215	6		45	153	3.4	1									4	34	9	0																
George McAfee	HB-DB	27	6'	185	24	1	16	139	8.7	3	1	0	0	0	0.0	0	0–0		3	85	28	1	2	31.0							1	8	8	0	5	98	20	0
Tipp Mooney	HB-DB	26	6'	187			17	105	6.2	0									2	10	5	0													3	51	17	0
Al Grygo	HB-DB	27	5'10"	173	6	3	23	98	4.3	0	1	1	100	13	13.0	0	0–0		5	82	16	1	2	43.0											4	80	20	0
Special Delivery Jones	HB-DB	26	5'10"	175			8	41	5.1	0	1	0	0	0	0.0	0	0–0		1	0	0	0													2	72	36	0
Ray McLean	HB-DB	29	5'10"	168		1	9	22	2.4	0									8	107	13	0									3	41	14	0	3	60	20	0
Jackie Hunt	HB-DB	26	6'	192			1	1	1.0	0													2	27.0														
Bob Swisher	HB-DB	31	5'11"	160		1													2	4	2	0																
George Wilson	OE-DE	31	6'1"	200	18														28	259	9	3									1	2	2	0				
Ken Kavanaugh	OE-DE	28	6'3"	205	36														25	539	22	6													1	7	7	0
Connie Mack Berry	OE-DE	29	6'3"	218															12	202	17	0																
Abe Croft	OE-DB	23	6'	185															2	12	6	0																
John Morton	OE-DB	23	6'	190															1	18	18	0																
Rudy Smeja	OE-DE	24	6'2"	195															1	11	11	0																
Pete Gudauskas	G-LB	28	6'2"	222	30	1																			27	27	100	1	2	50								
CHICAGO CARDINALS																																						
Paul Christman	QB	27	6'	218	6		30	-34	-1.1	1	219	89	41	1147	5.3	5	12–5	8																	1	44	44	0
Paul Collins	QB	22	5'11"	178			10	13	1.3	0	17	3	18	43	2.5	0	2–12																					
Vince Oliver	QB	26	5'11"	180			11	-3	-0.3	0	10	4	40	22	2.2	0	0–0																					
Frank Seno	HB-DB	24	6'	185	12	1	93	355	3.8	2	1	0	0	0	0.0	0	0–0		7	129	18	0									10	103	10	0	19	408	21	0
Leo Cantor	HB-DB	26	6'	195	30	5	83	291	3.5	5	18	3	17	116	6.4	0	4–22		15	159	11	0	5	33.2							5	59	12	0	6	123	21	0
Buzz Mertes	HB-DB	24	6'	195			24	107	4.5	0									2	1	1	0									1	7	7	0	1	12	12	0
Ernie Bonelli	FB-LB	25	5'11"	197		1	32	93	2.9	0									3	9	3	0									3	37	12	0	2	45	23	0
Al Drulis	FB-LB	24	5'10"	195			12	49	4.1	0									6	49	8	0													4	44	11	0
John Knolla	HB-DB	26	5'10"	180			15	36	2.4	0	1	0	0	0	0.0	0	0–0		1	15	15	0	2	33.0							3	43	14	0	6	114	19	0
Walt Rankin	FB-LB	27	5'11"	190		1	7	11	1.6	0									3	25	8	0													1	14	14	0
Bill Reynolds	HB-DB	26	5'8"	190			7	10	1.4	0													38	36.4														
Walt Watt	HB-DB	23	6'	187			6	7	1.2	0									1	22	22	0													1	18	18	0
Al Lindow	HB-DB	26	6'	165																											1	18	18	0	1	13	13	0
Joe Vodicka (from CHIB)	HB-DB	24	5'10"	187			3	-1	-0.3	0									1	3	3	0									4	9	2	0	1	20	20	0
Frank Balasz	FB-LB	27	6'2"	210			1	-1	-1.0	0									1	15	15	0																
Bill Dewell	OE-DE	28	6'4"	200	6														26	370	14	1																
Eddie Rucinski	OE-DE	29	6'2"	195	12														23	400	17	2																
Jim Poole (to NY)	OE-DE	29	6'3"	220	12	1													6	82	14	2																
Joe Carter	OE-DE	35	6'1"	200															3	17	6	0													1	44	44	0
Clint Wager	OE-DE	24	6'6"	215															1	32	32	0																
Joe Kuharich	G-LB	28	5'11"	195	12																				12	13	92	0	3	0								

TEAM TOTALS

DEFENSE	FIRST DOWNS: Tot	by Rsh	by Pas	by Pen	RUSHING: No.	Yds.	Avg. Yds.	TD	PASSING: Att.	Com	Comp. Pct.	Yds.	Avg. Yds. Att.	Avg. Yds. Comp	TD	Int.	Pct. Int.	PUNTING: No.	Avg. Yds.	PUNT RETURNS: No.	Yds.	Avg. Yds.	TD
CLEVE.	129	67	51	11	349	1026	2.9	10	253	99	39.1	1463	5.8	14.8	9	28	11.1	52	36.4	28	333	11.9	0
DET.	105	46	42	17	356	912	2.6	7	227	89	39.2	1615	7.1	18.1	17	23	10.1	64	35.5	32	314	9.8	0
G.B.	137	65	57	15	388	1349	3.5	16	231	111	48.1	1708	7.4	15.4	9	24	10.4	59	37.2	25	283	11.3	0
CHIC. B.	126	63	44	19	357	1464	4.1	20	195	83	42.6	1283	6.6	15.5	10	15	7.7	42	39.7	24	353	14.7	0
CHIC. C.	110	57	43	10	382	1320	3.5	17	187	87	46.5	1490	8.0	17.1	15	12	6.4	52	41.6	33	353	10.7	0

DEFENSE	KICKOFF RETURNS: No.	Yds.	Avg. Yds.	TD	INTERCEPTION RETURNS: No.	Yds.	Avg. Yds.	TD	PENALTIES: No.	Yds.	FUMBLES: No.	Lost	POINTS: Tot	PAT	FG Att	FG	Saf.
CLEVE.	45	923	20.5	0	20	353	17.7	0	43	391	31	16	136	19	4	1	0
DET.	37	614	16.6	0	36	334	9.3	2	64	568	27	10	194	24	5	4	2
G.B.	39	725	18.6	0	24	376	15.6	0	68	701	31	17	173	23	2	0	0
CHIC. B.	37	688	18.6	0	12	236	19.6	2	63	581	24	6	235	30	7	3	1
CHIC. C.	20	368	18.4	0	18	220	12.2	0	77	749	26	11	228	27	8	3	0

WORLD WAR II - MILITARY SERVICE

Full seasons missed by active players
(Only men who played in an official N.F.L. game before entering military service are listed.)

BROOKLYN DODGERS and TIGERS, BOSTON YANKS (1941=11 1942=25 1943=46 1944=51 1945=57)

41	42	43	44	45	Player
				45	Art Albrecht
	42	43	44	45	Warren Alfson
	42	43	44	45	Bill Bailey
41	42	43	44	45	Sherrill Busby
41	42				George Cafego
41	42	43	44	45	Dick Cassiano
			44		Merl Condit
41	42	43	44	45	Ty Coon
		43	44	45	Gerry Courtney
		43	44	45	Art Deremer
				45	Walt Dubzinski
		43	44	45	Don Eliason
				45	Tony Falkenstein
		43	44	45	Walt Fedora
41	42	43	44	45	Sam Francis
	42	43	44	45	Ray Frick
	42	43	44	45	Andy Fronczek
		43	44	45	Bob Gifford
				45	Sam Goldman
41	42	43	44	45	Mike Gussie
				45	Dick Harrison
			44	45	Ken Heineman
		43	44	45	Herman Hodges
		43	44	45	Bob Jeffries
		43	44	45	Art Jocher
				45	Cecil Johnson
			44	45	Lew Jones
		43	44	45	Thurman Jones
		43	44	45	Mike Jurich
		43	44	45	Bernie Kapitansky
		43	44	45	Duce Keahey
41	42	43	44	45	Ralph Kercheval
				45	Bruiser Kinard
		43	44	45	George Kinard
	42				Ben Kish
	42	43	44	45	Joe Koons
	42	43	44	45	George Kracum
	42	43	44	45	Frank Kristufek
				45	Bill LaFitte
	42	43	44	45	Bill Leckonby
41	42	43	44		Lou Mark
			44	45	John Matisi
41	42	43	44	45	Banks McFadden
		43	44	45	Curt Mecham
		43	44	45	Walt Merrill
			44	45	Tex Mooney
	42	43	44		Ace Parker
	42	43	44	45	Dave Parker
	42	43	44	45	Larry Peace
	42	43	44	45	Steve Petro
				45	Thron Riggs
		43	44	45	Bob Robertson
		43	44	45	Tom Robertson
				45	Frank Santora
		43	44	45	Perry Schwartz
		43	44	45	Rhoten Shetley
		43			Jim Sivell
			44	45	Bud Svendsen
		43	44		Si Titus
		43	44	45	Joe Tofil
				45	Rocky Uguccioni
		43	44	45	Jack Vetter
		43	44	45	Bernie Weiner
	42				Don Wemple (killed in action June 23, 1943)
41	42	43	44		Waddy Young (shot down and killed during first B-29 raid over Tokyo, Jan. 9, 1945)
41	42	43	44	45	Frank Zadworney

NEW YORK GIANTS (1941=5 1942=27 1943=44 1944=47 1945=41)

41	42	43	44	45	Player
				45	Neal Adams
		43	44		Emmett Barrett
			44	45	Dave Brown
		43	44	45	Harry Buffington
		43	44		Leo Cantor
		43	44	45	John Chickerneo
41	42	43	44	45	Pete Cole
				45	Frank Damiani
	42	43	44	45	Ed Danowski
	42	43	44		Lou DeFilippo
	42	43	44	45	Vince Dennery
	42	43	44	45	Kay Eakin
		43	44	45	Mank Edwards
	42	43	44	45	Len Eshmont
	42	43	44	45	Nello Falaschi
	42	43	44		George Franck
41	42	43	44	45	Chuck Gelatka
	42	43	44	45	Chet Gladchuk
		43	44	45	Merle Hapes
		43	44	45	Ed Hiemstra
	42	43	44	45	Dick Horne
		43	44	45	Jim Lee Howell
		43	44		Jiggs Kline
41	42	43	44		Grenny Landsdell
		43	44	45	John Lascari
		43	44	45	Ed Lechner
		43	44	45	Don Lieberum
	42	43	44		Jack Lummus (killed in action on IwoJima, March 8, 1945)
	42	43	44	45	Kayo Lunday
		43	44	45	Andy Marefos
	42	43	44	45	Red McClain
	42	43	44	45	John Mellus
41	42	43	44	45	Eddie Miller
41	42	43	44	45	Walt Nielsen
			44	45	Emery Nix
	42	43	44	45	Doug Oldershaw
		43	44	45	Al Owen
	42	43	44		Win Pederson
	42	43	44		Jim Poole
		43	44	45	Dom Principe
	42	43	44		Marion Pugh
	42	43	44	45	Frank Reagan
		43	44	45	Red Seick
				45	Hank Soar
	42	43	44	45	Ben Sohn
		43	44	45	Paul Stenn
	42	43	44	45	Orville Tuttle
	42	43	44	45	Don Vosberg
			44	45	Will Walls
	42	43	44	45	Howie Yeager
				45	Len Younce

Al Blozis—played in 1944—killed in action Jan. 31, 1945

PHILADELPHIA EAGLES (1941=1 1942=28 1943=47 1944=48 1945=40)

41	42	43	44	45	Player
	42	43			Jack Banta
		43	44	45	Len Barnum
	42	43	44	45	Sam Bartholomew
	42	43	44		Mike Basca (killed in action in France Nov. 11, 1944)
		43	44	45	John Binotti
	42	43	44	45	Bob Biorklund
		43	44	45	Leo Brenner
	42	43	44	45	Tony Cemore
	42	43	44		Jim Castiglia
		43	44	45	Bill Combs
	42	43	44	45	Dan DeSantis
	42	43	44	45	Dave diFilippo
		43	44	45	Al Donelli
		43	44	45	John Eibner
41	42	43	44	45	Frank Emmons
		43	44		Dick Erdlitz
	42	43	44	45	Bernie Feibish
	42	43	44		Terry Fox
			44	45	Joe Frank
	42	43	44	45	Ralph Fritz
		43	44	45	Woody Gerber
	42	43	44	45	Lou Ghecas
	42	43	44	45	Fred Gloden
	42	43	44	45	Lyle Graham
			44	45	Ray Graves
		43	44	45	Irv Hall
		43	44	45	Bill Halverson
	42				Jack Hinkle
		43	44	45	Frank Hrabetin
	42	43	44		Dick Humbert
		43	44	45	Ed Kasky
	42	43	44	45	Bob Krieger
	42	43	44	45	Mort Landsberg
		43	44	45	Steve Levanitis
				45	Art Macioszczyk (also 1946)
		43	44	45	Basilio Marchi
	42	43	44	45	Wes McAfee
	42				Hugh McCullough
		43	44		Fred Meyer
		43	44	45	Rupert Pate
	42	43	44	45	Hank Piro
		43	44	45	Bosh Pritchard
	42	43	44		Phil Ragazzo
	42	43	44	45	John Shonk
	42	43	44	45	Jack Stackpool
	42				Leo Stasica
			44	45	Dean Steward
	42	43	44		Bob Suffridge
		43			Len Supulski (killed in airplane crash in France in 1944)
		43	44		Tommy Thompson
		43	44	45	Lou Tomasetti
	42	43	44	45	Foster Watkins
	42	43	44	45	Burr West
		43	44	45	Tex Williams

PITTSBURGH STEELERS (1941=3 1942=14 1943=33 1944=30 1945=21)

41	42	43	44	45	Player
	42	43	44	45	Dick Bassi
		43	44	45	Tom Brown
		43	44		Chuck Cherundolo
	42	43	44		Joe Coomer
		43	44	45	Russ Cotton
		43			Milt Crain
	42	43	44		Dick Dolly
		43	44		Bill Dudley
41	42	43	44	45	Clark Goff
		43	44	45	Goerge Gonda
	42	43	44	45	Moose Harper
		43	44	45	Joe Hoague
	42	43	44		Art Jones
		43			Walt Kichefski
41	42	43	44		George Kiick
		43	44	45	Joe Lamas
		43	44		Hubbard Law
		43	44	45	Don Looney
		43	44	45	Vern Martin
	42	43			Coley McDonough
		43	44	45	Clure Mosher
	42	43	44	45	Carl Nery
	42	43	44		John Patrick
41	42	43	44	45	Stan Pavkov
	42	43	44	45	Rocco Pirro
	42	43	44	45	Mike Rodak
		43	44		Jack Sanders
		43	44	45	Curt Sandig
		43	44	45	Andy Tomasic
		43	44	45	Ralph Wenzel
	42	43	44	45	Don Williams
		43	44	45	John Woudenberg
	42	43	44	45	Frank Zopetti

WASHINGTON REDSKINS (1941=7 1942=14 1943=33 1944=37 1945=34)

41	42	43	44	45	Player
		43	44		Ki Aldrich
41	42	43	44	45	Steve Andrako
	42	43	44	45	Jim Barber
		43	44	45	Ed Beinor
41	42				Keith Birlem (killed in action, May 7, 1943)
		43	44	45	Ed Cifers
	42	43	44	45	Frank Clair
		43	44		Fred Davis
		43	44	45	Rufus Deal
	42	43	44	45	Ken Dow
	42	43			Frankie Filchock
	42	43	44	45	Lee Gentry
		43	44	45	John Goodyear
		43	44		Cecil Hare
			44	45	Ken Hayden
	42	43	44	45	Bob Hoffman
			44	45	Jack Jenkins
		43	44	45	Ed Justice
		43	44	45	Steve Juzwik
		43	44	45	John Kovatch
		43	44	45	Al Krueger
				45	Ted Lapka
		43			Charley Malone
		43	44	45	Bob McChesney
41	42	43	44	45	Jim Meade
			44	45	Ed Merkle
	42	43	44		Wayne Millner
41	42	43	44	45	Boyd Morgan
				45	Andy Natowich
41	42	43	44	45	Mickey Parks
		43	44	45	Dick Poillon
			44	45	Frank Ribar
41	42	43	44	45	Bo Russell
			44	45	Lou Rymkus
41	42	43	44	45	Sandy Sanford
			44	45	Jack Smith
		43	44		Clem Stralka
		43	44	45	Bob Titchenal
		43	44		Dick Todd
		43	44	45	George Watts
		43	44		Marv Whited
			44	45	Willie Wilkin
		43	44	45	Bill Young
				45	Joe Zeno

WORLD WAR II - MILITARY SERVICE

Full seasons missed by active players
(Only men who played in an official N.F.L. game before entering military service are listed.)

CHICAGO BEARS (1941=1 1942=15 1943=31 1944=43 1945=32)

41	42	43	44	45	Player
		43	44	45	Len Akin
		43	44		Lee Artoe
	42	43	44	45	Al Baisi
		43	44	45	Ray Bray
	42	43	44		Young Bussey (missing in action Jan. 7, 1945)
41	42	43	44	45	Chet Chesney
			44	45	Harry Clark
		43	44	45	Stu Clarkson
		43	44		Chuck Drulis
	42	43	44	45	John Federovich
	42	43	44	45	Aldo Forte
			44	45	Danny Fortmann
		43	44		Hugh Gallarneau
			44	45	Bill Geyer
		43	44	45	Bill Hempel
	42	43	44	45	Bill Hughes
			44	45	Tony Ippolito
	42	43	44		Ken Kavanaugh
		43	44		Nick Keriasotis
		43	44	45	Adolph Kissell
		43	44	45	Ed Kolman
	42	43	44	45	Hal Lahar
			44	45	Jim Logan
	42	43	44	45	Joe Maniaci
	42	43	44	45	Phil Martinovich
			44	45	Al Matuza
		43	44	45	Frank Maznicki
	42	43	44	45	George McAfee
			44	45	Monte Merkel
	42	43	44	45	Joe Mihal
		43	44	45	Frank Morris
		43	44	45	Bob Nowaskey
		43	44	45	Charlie O'Rourke
			44	45	Bill Osmanski
		43	44	45	John Petty
	42	43			Dick Plasman
			44	45	Hamp Pool
			44	45	John Siegal
	42	43	44	45	Norm Standlee
			44		Bill Steinkemper
			44	45	Bob Steuber
		43	44		Joe Stydahar
	42	43	44		Bob Swisher
			44		Joe Vodicka

CHICAGO CARDINALS (1941=5 1942=22 1943=36 1944=42 1945=30)

41	42	43	44	45	Player
		43	44	45	Joe Allton
		43	44		Ray Apolskis
	42	43	44		Frank Balasz
		43			Vince Banonis
		43	44		Libero Bertagnolli
			44	45	Joe Bukant
	42	43	44		Ray Rusler
			44	45	Ronnie Cahill
		43	44	45	Lloyd Cheatham
	42	43	44	45	Andy Chisick
	42	43	44	45	Johnny Clement
		43	44	45	Al Coppage
		43	44	45	Bill Daddio
	42				Bill Davis
	42	43	44		Bill Dewell
		43	44	45	Ray Elli
41	42	43	44	45	Ev Elkins
		43	44		Ralph Fife
			44	45	Marshall Goldberg
	42	43	44	45	John Higgins
	42	43	44	45	Frank Huffman
		43	44		Pop Ivy
41	42	43	44	45	Jimmy Johnston
		43	44		John Knolla
	42	43	44		Joe Kuharich
	42	43	44	45	John Kuzman
		43	44	45	Steve Lach
	42	43	44	45	Joe Lokenc
		43	44	45	Bob Maddock
	42	43	44	45	Ray Mallouf
	42	43	44	45	Avery Monfort
			44		Bob Morrow
	42	43	44	45	Bill Murphy
			44	45	Andy Puplis
			44	45	Cal Purdin
		43	44	45	Bud Schwenk
41	42	43	44	45	John Shirk
	42	43	44	45	Fred Shook
			44	45	George Smith
41	42	43	44		Marin Tonelli
	42	43	44	45	Fred Vanzo
		43	44	45	Ernie Wheeler
	42	43	44		Tarzan White
41	42	43	44	45	Bobby Wood

CLEVELAND RAMS (1941=4 1942=18 1943=36 1944=39 1945=38)

41	42	43	44	45	Player
			44	45	Chet Adams
	42	43	44		Graham Armstrong
		43	44	45	Jack Boone
				45	Boyd Clay
41	42	43	44	45	Ollie Cordill
		43	44	45	Corby Davis
		43	44	45	Art Elston
				45	Jake Fawcett
41	42	43	44		Fred Gehrke
				45	Joe Gibson
41	42	43			Jim Gillette
	42	43	44	45	Owen Goodnight
		43	44	45	Parker Hall
	42	43	44	45	Jack Haman
	42	43	44	45	Kirk Hershey
	42	43	44		Red Hickey
			44	45	Ben Hightower
		43	44		Jack Jacobs
		43	44	45	Ben Janiak
		43	44	45	Don Johnson
	42	43	44		Mike Kostiuk
		43	44	45	Bill Lazetich
	42	43	44	45	Ted Livingston
			44	45	Dante Magnani
	42	43	44	45	Frank Maher
	42	43	44	45	Paul McDonough
		43	44	45	Barney McGarry
		43	44	45	George Morris
	42	43	44		Rudy Mucha
			44	45	Joe Pasqua
		43	44		Maury Parr
		43	44	45	George Platukis
		43	44	45	Warren Plunkett
	42	43	44	45	Ray Prochaska
				45	Chet Pudloski
		43			Bill Rieth
				45	Charley Riffle
		43	44	45	Hank Rockwell
	42	43	44	45	Charlie Seabright
	42	43	44	45	Marty Slovak
		43	44	45	Gaylon Smith
	42	43	44	45	Vic Spadaccini
41	42	43	44	45	Ralph Stevenson
			44	45	Roy Stuart
		43	44	45	Wilfred Thorpe
		43	44	45	Johnny Wilson
				45	Lou Zontini

DETROIT LIONS (1941=6 1942=23 1943=45 1944=54 1945=42)

41	42	43	44	45	Player
	42	43	44	45	Stan Anderson
		43	44	45	Tony Arena
		43	44	45	Emil Baniavcic
	42				Stan Batinski
		43	44		Charlie Behan (killed in action May 18, 1945—Okinawa)
	42	43	44	45	Steve Belichick
	42	43	44		Dick Booth
	42	43	44	45	Maury Britt (right arm amputated after being wounded in combat)
41	42	43	44	45	Tony Calvelli
			44	45	Gerry Conlee
			44	45	Mike Corgan
	42	43	44	45	Clem Crabtree
			44	45	Murray Evans
			44		Chuck Fenenbock
			44	45	Bill Fisk
	42	43			Tony Furst
		43	44		Sloko Gill
		43	44	45	Henry Goodman
		43	44	45	Frank Grigonis
41	42	43	44	45	John Hackenbruck
		43	44	45	Gran Harrison
			44	45	Harry Hopp
		43	44	45	Bill Kennedy (also 1946)
			44		Alex Ketzko (killed in action Dec. 23, 1944)
		43	44		Larry Knorr
			44	45	Bert Kuczynski
	42	43	44	45	Andy Logan
	42	43	44	45	John Mattiford
	42	43	44		Paul Moore
41	42	43	44	45	Butch Morse
	42	43	44		Bob Nelson
	42	43	44	45	Dunc Obee
	42	43	44	45	Lloyd Parsons
			44	45	Ted Pavelic
		43	44	45	John Polanski
	42	43	44		Cotton Price
	42	43	44		Bill Radovich
			44	45	Lyle Rockenbach
41	42	43	44	45	Stillman Rouse
			44	45	Tony Rubino
41	42	43	44	45	Rip Ryan
		43	44	45	Mickey Sanzotta
		43	44		Larry Sartori
		43	44	45	Alex Schibanoff
		43	44		John Schiechl
		43	44	45	Perry Scott
		43	44	45	Harry Seltzer
				45	Frankie Sinkwich
41	42	43	44	45	Dwight Sloan
		43			Dave Smukler
		43	44	45	George Speth
		43	44	45	Joe Stringfellow
		43	44	45	Paul Szakash
	42	43	44	45	John Tripson
		43	44		Emil Uremovich
		43			Chet Wetterlund (killed in action Sept. 5, 1944)
			44	45	Lloyd Wickett
	42	43	44	45	Whizzer White
		43	44	45	Tony Zuzzio

GREEN BAY PACKERS (1941=1 1942=16 1943=25 1944=27 1945=23)

41	42	43	44	45	Player
	42	43	44		Bob Adkins
				45	Tony Canadeo
		43			Joe Carter
			44	45	Dick Evans
			44	45	Sherwood Fries
	42	43	44		Ed Frutig
	42	43	44		Tom Greenfield
	42	43	44	45	Clarke Hinkle
		43	44	45	Bob Ingalls
	42	43	44	45	Ed Jankowski
	42	43	44	45	Bill Johnson
	42	43	44		Smiley Johnson (killed in action at Iwo Jima)
				45	Bob Kahler
			44	45	Jim Lankas
		43	44	45	Bill Lee
		43	44	45	Russ Letlow
	42	43	44	45	Lee McLaughlin
	42	43	44		Moose Mulleneaux
		43	44		Ernie Pannell
	42	43	44	45	George Paskvan
		43	44	45	Ray Riddick
	42	43	44	45	Herm Rohrig
		43	44		Chuck Sample
	42	43	44	45	Charlie Schultz
	42	43	44	45	George Svendsen
			44	45	Andy Uram
	42	43			Alex Urban
	42	43	44	45	Hal Van Every
		43	44	45	Fred Vant Hull
				45	Ray Wehba
		43	44	45	Dick Weisgerber
41	42	43	44	45	Gust Zarnas

Total N.F.L. 1941=44 1942=202 1943=376 1944=418 1945=358

Championship Games 1933–1936

1933
December 17 at Chicago
(Attendance: Approximately 26,000)

Beginning History on a Seesaw

Two strong divisional champions and clear, crisp weather set a perfect table for the NFL's first championship game between the Bears and Giants. Both clubs moved the ball in the first half, the Bears mostly by running and the Giants by passing, but the defenses had limited the scoring to a pair of Jack Manders field goals for Chicago and a 29-yard touchdown pass from Harry Newman to Red Badgro plus the conversion for New York. In the third quarter, Manders' third field goal put the Bears on top 9-7, and the Giants came right back with a 61-yard drive, capped by Max Krause's 1-yard plunge into the end zone. Six plays later, the Bears recaptured the lead on an 8-yard pass from Bronko Nagurski to Bill Karr after a fake run. With Chicago leading 16-14, the Giants scored on the first play of the final quarter. With the ball on the Chicago 8-yard line, Newman pitched out to Ken Strong, who lateraled back to Newman when trapped behind the line; after scrambling around for a few seconds, Newman then threw a pass to Strong in the end zone. But with their backs to the wall, and under three minutes left, Nagurski passed to Bill Hewitt, who took a few steps and lateraled to Bill Karr, who went all the way to give the Bears a 23-21 win.

SCORING

NEW YORK	0	7	7	7–21
CHICAGO	3	3	10	7–23

1st Qtr: CHI.	Manders, FG 16 yards	
2nd Qtr: CHI.	Manders, FG 40 yards	
N.Y.	Badgro, 29 yard pass from Newman	PAT–Strong (kick)
3rd Qtr: CHI.	Manders, FG 28 yards	
N.Y.	Krause, 1 yard rush	PAT–Strong (kick)
CHI.	Karr, 8 yard pass from Nagurski	PAT–Manders (kick)
4th Qtr: N.Y.	Strong, 8 yard pass from Newman	PAT–Strong (kick)
CHI.	Karr, 36 yards on lateral from Hewitt on pass from Nagurski	PAT–Manders (kick)

TEAM STATS

CHI.		N.Y.
12	First Downs	13
161	Rushing Yardage	99
16	Pass Attempts	20
7	Pass Completions	14
.438	Completion Percentage	.700
147	Passing Yardage	200
1	Interceptions	1
10	Punts	13
39.8	Punting Average	28.6
58	Punt Return Yards	59
0	Fumbles Lost	0
7	Penalties	3
40	Penalty Yards	15

1934
December 9 at New York
(Attendance: 35,059)

Sneaking to the Throne

Although the Bears had gone undefeated through the season and the Giants had lost three of their last six games to barely hold onto first place in the East, injuries and the weather leveled the differences between the clubs. Bears guard Joe Kopcha and rookie sensation Beattie Feathers were left at home with injuries, while the Giants had to play without passer Harry Newman and end Red Badgro. Overnight rain and freezing temperatures turned the field into a sheet of ice that favored neither team. Both clubs slipped and skidded on the ice through the first half, with the Bears leading 10-3 at halftime. When the Giants came out for the second half, the Bears and spectators were surprised to see most of them wearing sneakers instead of football cleats. The only score of the third quarter was a Jack Manders field goal which put the Bears ahead 13-3, but the Giants exploded for 27 points in the fourth quarter. With the sneakers providing better footing on the icy turf, the Giants closed the gap to 13-10 on a 28-yard pass from Ed Danowski to Ike Frankian. Then, in short order, Ken Strong ran 42 yards past the sliding Bears for a touchdown, and the Giants added two more touchdowns by Strong and Danowski to ice away the victory 30-13.

SCORING

CHICAGO	0	10	3	0–13
NEW YORK	3	0	0	27–30

1st Qtr: N.Y.	Strong, FG 38 yards	
2nd Qtr: CHI.	Nagurski, 1 yard rush	PAT–Manders (kick)
CHI.	Manders, FG 17 yards	
3rd Qtr: CHI.	Manders, FG 24 yards	
4th Qtr: N.Y.	Frankian, 28 yard pass from Danowski	PAT–Strong (kick)
N.Y.	Strong, 42 yard rush	PAT–Strong (kick)
N.Y.	Strong, 11 yard rush	PAT–Strong–(No Good)
N.Y.	Danowski, 6 yard rush	PAT–Strong (kick)

TEAM STATS

N.Y.		CHI.
7	First Downs	7
170	Rushing Yardage	93
13	Pass Attempts	13
7	Pass Completions	6
.538	Completion Percentage	.462
115	Passing Yardage	74
2	Interceptions	3
6	Punts	9
38	Punting Average	35
2	Fumbles Lost	0
0	Penalty Yards	30

1935
December 15 at Detroit
(Attendance: 15,000)

Finding Glory in the Mud

A muddy field, freezing rain, and biting wind gave an advantage to the Lions, who were a running club, and hurt the Giants, who relied on the pass. On the first series after the opening kickoff, however, the Lions completed two long passes in a 61-yard drive climaxed by Ace Gutowsky's 5-yard smash into the end zone. The Giants drove back to the Detroit 13-yard line, but Ken Strong's field-goal attempt was unsuccessful; even more costly for New York on this drive were two broken ribs receiver Tod Goodwin suffered in making a catch. Detroit added a second touchdown late in first quarter when Dutch Clark broke loose for a 40-yard run to make the score 13-0. In the second the Giants closed the gap to 13-7 with a 42-yard pass from Ed Danowski to Ken Strong. New York struggled to get the tying touchdown in the fourth quarter, but fell short with a streak of bad luck. With three minutes left to play, the Lions blocked Danowski's punt and recovered it on the New York 26-yard line. Six plays later, Ernie Caddel skirted around end from the one-foot line for the clinching points. With Danowski then heaving desperation passes, Buddy Parker picked one off and returned it to the Giant 10. Three plays later, Parker carried the ball in but missed the extra point in a final 26-7 outcome.

SCORING

NEW YORK	0	7	0	0– 7
DETROIT	13	0	0	13–26

1st Qtr: Det.	Gutowsky, 2 yard rush	PAT–Presnell (kick)
Det.	Clark, 40 yard rush	PAT–Clark (No Good)
2nd Qtr: N.Y.	Strong, 42 yard pass from Danowski	PAT–Strong (kick)
3rd Qtr:	None	
4th Qtr: Det.	Caddel, 4 yard rush	PAT–Clark (kick)
Det.	Parker, 9 yard rush	PAT–Parker (No Good)

TEAM STATS

N.Y.		DET.
8	First Downs	13
106	Rushing Yardage	235
13	Pass Attempts	5
4	Pass Completions	2
.308	Completion Percentage	.400
88	Passing Yardage	68
2	Interceptions	0
5	Punts	4
43	Punting Average	39
3	Fumbles Lost	4
15	Penalty Yards	25

1936
December 13 at New York
(Attendance: 29,543)

Getting Neutralized on Neutral Ground

With the game scheduled for the home park of the Eastern champion, Redskin owner George Marshall showed his contempt for what he considered Boston's poor support of his team by moving the title match to the neutral Polo Grounds in New York. The orphaned Redskins were given little chance of upending the favored Green Bay Packers, and when star runner Cliff Battles was injured on the first Boston series of downs, they faced a bleak afternoon. Moments after Battles left the field, Green Bay's Arnie Herber launched a 43-yard pass play to Don Hutson that swung momentum completely over to the Packers. The Redskins fought gamely back and drove seventy-eight yards, capped by Pug Rentner's plunge from the one-yard line. Riley Smith's conversion attempt sailed wide, however, and the Skins still trailed 7-6. The Packers upped the count to 14-6 by driving 74 yards in six plays after the second-half kickoff. The key play in the drive was a 52-yard pass play from Herber to veteran Johnny Blood, and the touchdown itself came on an 8-yard pass from Herber to Milt Gantenbein. The Redskins meanwhile suffered a further blow when Frank Bausch, their only healthy center, was ejected from the game for fighting. In the final period, the Packers again scored after blocking a Boston punt to run the score to 21-6.

SCORING

GREEN BAY	7	0	7	7–21
BOSTON	0	6	0	0– 6

1st Qtr: G.B.	Hutson, 43 yard pass from Herber	PAT–E. Smith (kick)
2nd Qtr: Bos.	Rentner, 1 yard rush	PAT–R. Smith (No Good)
3rd Qtr: G.B.	Gantenbein, 8 yard pass from Herber	PAT–E. Smith (kick)
4th Qtr: G.B.	Monnett, 2 yard rush	PAT–E. Smith (kick)

TEAM STATS

G.B.		BOS.
7	First Downs	8
67	Rushing Yardage	39
23	Pass Attempts	26
9	Pass Completions	7
.391	Completion Percentage	.269
153	Passing Yardage	77
2	Interceptions	1
10	Punts	7
34	Punting Average	35
4	Punt Returns	5
27	Punt Return Yards	58
2	Fumbles	5
1	Fumbles Lost	2
3	Penalties	4
15	Penalty Yards	25

1937

December 12, at Chicago
(Attendance 15,878)

SCORING

WASHINGTON	7	0	21	0–28
CHIC. BEARS	14	0	7	0–21

First Quarter

Was.	Battles, 7 yard rush PAT–R. Smith (kick)	8:04
Chi.	Manders, 10 yard rush PAT–Manders (kick)	11:12
Chi.	Manders, 39 yard pass from Masterson PAT–Manders (kick)	14:25

Third Quarter

Was.	Milner, 55 yard pass from Baugh PAT–R. Smith (kick)	1:13
Chi.	Manske, 4 yard pass from Masterson PAT–Manders (kick)	5:56
Was.	Milner, 78 yard pass from Baugh PAT–R. Smith (kick)	6:26
Was.	Justice, 35 yard pass from Baugh PAT–R. Smith (kick)	14:06

TEAM STATISTICS

CHI.			WASH.
14	First Downs	– Total*	22
8		– by Rushing	9
6		– by Passing	13
0		– by Penalty	0
2	Punt Returns	– Number	1
3	Fumbles	– Number	4
1		– Times Lost Ball	3
1	Penalties	– Number	1
15		– Yards Penalized	5

*includes Touchdowns

Washington and the Golden Arm

Sammy Baugh, Washington's marvelous rookie passer, showed the Bears his skill and daring by passing from his own end zone to Cliff Battles for a 43-yard gain on the Redskins' first play from scrimmage. The Redskins were forced to punt, but they did drive 53 yards the next time they got the ball, with Battles going over from the seven-yard line for the score. The Bears fought back and, with Jack Manders, Bronko Nagurski, and Eggs Manske leading the way, scored two touchdowns to make the halftime score 14-7 in favor of Chicago. Baugh hit Wayne Millner with a 55-yard bomb to tie the score in the third quarter, but the Bears used the power of Nagurski and Manders to smash away at the Redskins for another touchdown, making the count 21-14, Chicago. But Baugh then unleashed the full power of his arm. On the first play after the kickoff, he hit Millner for a 78-yard touchdown, and minutes later he threw 35 yards to Ed Justice to take the lead, 28-21. Although the fourth quarter was enlivened by a free-for-all, the 28-21 Washington lead stayed untouched, as the Bears simply could not mount a passing attack any thing like what Slingin' Sam had done.

INDIVIDUAL STATISTICS

RUSHING

CHICAGO	No.	Yds.	Avg.	WASHINGTON	No.	Yds.	Avg.
Manders	10	64	6.4	Battles	17	51	3.0
Nagurski	7	47	6.7	Irwin	10	33	3.3
Nolting	10	38	3.8	Baugh	3	32	10.7
Buivid	1	6	6.0	Justice	1	4	4.0
Rentner	1	0	0.0	Krause	1	4	4.0
Masterson	1	–2	–2.0	Millner	1	–2	–2.0
Ronzani	1	–3	–3.0		33	122	3.7
	31	150	4.8				

RECEIVING

CHICAGO	No.	Yds.	Avg.	WASHINGTON	No.	Yds.	Avg.
Manske	2	55	27.5	Millner	8	181	22.6
Plasman	2	44	22.0	Battles	3	82	27.3
McDonald	2	39	19.5	Justice	3	63	21.0
Manders	1	37	37.0	Malone	3	27	9.0
Rentner	1	32	32.0	R. Smith	2	20	10.0
	8	207	25.9	Pinckert	1	18	18.0
				Irwin	1	7	7.0
					21	398	19.0

PUNTING

CHICAGO	No.	Avg.	WASHINGTON	No.	Avg.
Nolting	4	45.0	Baugh	5	23.2
Francis	1	62.0	R. Smith	1	12.0
Feathers	1	44.0	Battles	1	27.0
	6	49.5		7	24.8

PASSING

CHICAGO	Att.	Comp.	Comp. Pct.	Yds.	Int.	Yds/ Att.	Yds/ Comp.	Yards Lost Tackled
Masterson	17	4	23.5	131	2	7.7	32.8	1– 7
Buivid	11	3	27.3	41	1	3.7	13.7	2–18
Molesworth	1	1	100.0	35	0	35.0	35.0	
Nagurski	1	0	0.0	0	0	0.0	0.0	
	30	8	26.7	207	3	6.9	25.9	3–25
WASHINGTON								
Baugh	34	17	50.0	358	1	10.5	21.1	1–26
Battles	5	3	60.0	23	1	4.6	7.7	2– 6
R. Smith	2	1	50.0	17	1	8.5	17.0	1–13
	41	21	51.2	398	3	9.7	19.0	4–45

1938

December 12, at New York
(Attendance 48,120)

SCORING

GREEN BAY	0	14	3	0–17
NEW YORK	9	7	7	0–23

First Quarter

N.Y.	Cuff, 13 yard Field Goal
N.Y.	Leemans, 6 yard rush PAT–Gildea (No Good)

Second Quarter

G.B.	C. Mulleneaux, 40 yard pass from Herber PAT – Engebretsen (kick)
N.Y.	Barnard, 20 yard pass from Danowski PAT – Cuff (kick)
G.B.	Hinkle, 1 yard rush PAT – Engebretsen (kick)

Third Quarter

G.B.	Engebretsen, 15 yard Field Goal
N.Y.	Soar, 23 yard pass from Danowski PAT – Cuff (kick)

TEAM STATISTICS

N.Y.			G.B.
13	First Downs	– Total*	16
7		– by Rushing	10
4		– by Passing	6
2		– by Penalty	0
2	Fumbles	– Number	4
0		– Times Lost Ball	2
2	Penalties	– Number	3
10		– Yards Penalized	20

*includes Touchdowns

Start with Defense, End with Victory

Two blocked punts gave the Giants an early first-quarter lead before the largest crowd yet to see an NFL championship game. The first blocked kick led to Ward Cuff's 13-yard field goal; the second led to Tuffy Leemans' six-yard run for a touchdown. Trailing 9-0 although holding the New York offense, the Packers came back in the second quarter on a 40-yard pass from Arnie Herber to Moose Mulleneaux, who was the Packers' primary receiver because Don Hutson was injured. The teams traded touchdowns before the half ended to bring the score up to 16-14 in favor of the Giants at halftime. Within the first three minutes of the second half, the Packers had taken the lead on a Tiny Engebretsen field goal, but the Giants promptly drove 61 yards behind Hank Soar's running and Ed Danowski's passing for the winning touchdown in the 23-17 contest.

INDIVIDUAL STATISTICS

PUNT RETURNS

NEW YORK	No.	Yds.	Avg.	GREEN BAY	No.	Yds.	Avg.
Leemans	2	34	17.0	Monnett	1	10	10.0
				Herber	1	0	0.0
				Uram	1	0	0.0
					3	10	3.3

KICKOFF RETURNS

NEW YORK	No.	Yds.	Avg.	GREEN BAY	No.	Yds.	Avg.
Cuff	1	20	20.0	Laws	1	29	29.0
Soar	1	16	16.0	Hinkle	1	22	22.0
Howell	1	12	12.0	Herber	1	15	15.0
Shaffer	1	8	8.0		3	66	22.0
	4	56	14.0				

INTERCEPTION RETURNS

NEW YORK	No.	Yds.	Avg.	GREEN BAY	No.	Yds.	Avg.
Danowski	1	0	0.0	Engebretsen	1	0	0.0

INDIVIDUAL STATISTICS

RUSHING

NEW YORK	No.	Yds.	Avg.	GREEN BAY	No.	Yds.	Avg.
Soar	21	65	3.1	Hinkle	18	63	3.5
Leemans	13	42	3.2	Monnett	4	29	7.3
Barnum	3	8	2.7	Herber	3	22	7.3
Danowski	1	4	4.0	Isbell	11	20	1.8
Karcis	3	3	1.0	Laws	4	20	5.0
Cuff	2	–7	–3.5	Jankowski	3	14	4.7
	43	115	2.7	Uram	2	–1	–0.5
				Miller	1	–3	–3.0
					46	164	4.6

RECEIVING

NEW YORK	No.	Yds.	Avg.	GREEN BAY	No.	Yds.	Avg.
Soar	3	41	13.7	Becker	2	79	39.5
Howell	2	3	1.5	C. Mulleneaux	2	54	27.0
Barnard	1	20	20.0	Uram	1	24	24.0
Barnum	1	20	20.0	Isbell	1	22	22.0
Leemans	1	5	5.0	Scherer	1	19	19.0
Perry	0	8	–	Gantenbein	1	6	6.0
	8	97	12.1	Hutson	0	10	–
					8	214	26.8

PUNTING

NEW YORK	No.	Avg.	GREEN BAY	No.	Avg.
Danowski	6	39.5	Herber	3	41.3
Gildea	1	55.0	Hinkle	2	18.5
Barnum	1	33.0	Isbell	1	0.0
	8	40.6		6	26.8

PASSING

NEW YORK	Att.	Comp.	Comp. Pct.	Yds.	Int.	Yds/ Att.	Yds/ Comp.
Danowski	11	7	63.6	77	0	7.0	11.0
Leemans	2	1	50.0	20	1	10.0	20.0
Barnum	1	0	0.0	0	0	0.0	0.0
Soar	1	0	0.0	0	0	0.0	0.0
	15	8	53.3	97	1	6.5	12.1
GREEN BAY							
Herber	14	5	35.7	123	0	8.8	24.6
Isbell	5	3	60.0	91	1	18.2	30.3
	19	8	42.1	214	1	11.3	26.8

1939

December 10, at Milwaukee
(Attendance 32,279)

SCORING

NEW YORK	0	0	0	0– 0
GREEN BAY	7	0	10	10–27

First Quarter

G.B.	Gantenbein, 7 yard pass from Herber PAT – Engebretsen (kick)

Third Quarter

G.B.	Engebretsen, 29 yard Field Goal
G.B.	Laws, 27 yard pass from Isbell PAT – Engebretsen (kick)

Fourth Quarter

G.B.	Smith, 42 yard Field Goal
G.B.	Jankowski, 1 yard rush PAT – Smith (kick)

TEAM STATISTICS

G.B.			N.Y.
13	First Downs	– Total*	9
7		– by Rushing	5
4		– by Passing	3
2		– by Penalty	1
2	Fumbles	– Number	1
0		– Times Lost Ball	0
4	Penalties	– Number	5
50		– Yards Penalized	21

*includes Touchdowns

Shackles and Humiliation

The Packers avenged last year's championship-game loss by completely shackling the Giants and running off to a 27-0 victory. The Green Bay defense kept the Giants bottled up in their own territory most of the game, with the Packer line constantly smashing through into the New York backfield. The only score of the first half was a seven-yard pass from Arnie Herber to Milt Gantenbein, plus the conversion, but the Packers put the game away in the second half on touchdowns by Joe Laws and Ed Jankowski and field goals by Tiny Engebretsen and Ernie Smith. Unable to launch an attack all day, the Giants suffered the worst championship beating yet.

INDIVIDUAL STATISTICS

PUNT RETURNS

GREEN BAY	No.	Yds.	Avg.	NEW YORK	No.	Yds.	Avg.
Laws	1	15	15.0	Leemans	2	25	12.5
Uram	1	10	10.0				
	2	25	12.5				

KICKOFF RETURNS

GREEN BAY	No.	Yds.	Avg.	NEW YORK	No.	Yds.	Avg.
				Leemans	3	41	13.7
None				Cuff	1	13	13.0
					4	54	13.5

INTERCEPTION RETURNS

GREEN BAY	No.	Yds.	Avg.	NEW YORK	No.	Yds.	Avg.
Brock	2	14	7.0	Miller	1	5	5.0
Svendson	1	15	15.0	Barnum	1	0	0.0
Uram	1	10	10.0	Cuff	1	0	0.0
Gantenbein	1	5	5.0		3	5	1.7
Lawrence	1	0	0.0				
	6	44	7.3				

INDIVIDUAL STATISTICS

RUSHING

GREEN BAY	No.	Yds.	Avg.	NEW YORK	No.	Yds.	Avg.
Uram	10	38	3.8	Leemans	12	24	2.0
Isbell	14	28	2.0	Miller	2	19	9.5
Hinkle	13	23	1.8	Soar	4	14	3.5
Laws	3	20	6.7	Richards	7	12	1.7
Jankowski	7	14	2.0	Cuff	3	7	2.3
Jacunski	1	11	11.0	Barnum	4	4	1.0
Herber	2	3	1.5	Kline	1	1	1.0
Hutson	1	3	3.0	Owen	1	–2	–2.0
	51	140	2.7		34	79	2.3

RECEIVING

GREEN BAY	No.	Yds.	Avg.	NEW YORK	No.	Yds.	Avg.
Hutson	2	21	10.5	Shaffer	2	16	8.0
Craig	2	6	3.0	Falaschi	2	6	3.0
Jacunski	1	31	31.0	Leemans	1	37	37.0
Laws	1	31	31.0	Gelatka	1	24	24.0
Gantenbein	1	7	7.0	Barnum	1	6	6.0
	7	96	13.7	Cuff	1	5	5.0
					8	94	11.8

PUNTING

GREEN BAY	No.	Avg.	NEW YORK	No.	Avg.
Hinkle	5	22.6	Danowski	4	42.5
Herber	2	34.5	Barnum	2	36.0
	7	26.0		6	40.3

PASSING

GREEN BAY	Att.	Comp.	Comp. Pct.	Yds.	Int.	Yds/ Att.	Yds/ Comp.	Yards Lost Tackled
Herber	8	5	62.5	59	3	7.4	11.8	1–6
Isbell	2	2	100.0	37	0	18.5	18.5	
	10	7	70.0	96	3	9.6	13.7	1–6
NEW YORK								
Danowski	12	4	33.3	48	3	4.0	12.0	
Miller	6	3	50.0	40	1	6.7	13.3	1–9
Leemans	4	1	25.0	6	1	1.5	6.0	
Barnum	3	0	0.0	0	1	0.0	0.0	
	25	8	32.0	94	6	3.8	11.8	1–9

1940
December 8, at Washington
(Attendance 36,034)

SCORING

CHIC. BEARS	21	7	26	19	–73
WASHINGTON	0	0	0	0	– 0

First Quarter		
Chi.	Osmanski, 68 yard rush PAT – Manders (kick)	00:55
Chi.	Luckman, 1 yard rush PAT – Snyder (kick)	10:50
Chi.	Maniaci, 42 yard rush PAT – Martinovick (kick)	12:25
Second Quarter		
Chi.	Kavanaugh, 30 yard pass from Luckman PAT – Snyder (kick)	11:45
Third Quarter		
Chi.	Pool, 15 yard interception return PAT – Plasman (kick)	00:45
Chi.	Nolting, 23 yard rush PAT – Plasman (No Good)	4:25
Chi.	McAfee, 35 yard interception return PAT – Stydahar (kick)	5:12
Chi.	Turner, 20 yard interception return PAT – Maniaci (No Good)	12:56
Fourth Quarter		
Chi.	Clark, 44 yard rush PAT – Famiglietti (no Good)	4:47
Chi.	Famiglietti, 2 yard rush PAT – Maniaci, pass from Sherman	6:15
Chi.	Clark, 1 yard rush PAT – Snyder, pass (No Good)	12:36

TEAM STATISTICS

WASH.		CHI.
15	First Downs – Total*	26
3	– by Rushing	20
10	– by Passing	5
2	– by Penalty	1
0	Fumbles – Number	1
0	– Times Lost Ball	0
6	Penalties – Number	7
71	– Yards Penalized	36

* – includes touchdowns

The Worst Vengence Ever

Still bristling from a 7-3 loss to the Redskins three weeks earlier, the Bears administered the worst beating ever in an NFL game by crushing Washington 73-0 in a perfect display of football. Using their T-formation instead of the single wing generally used around the league, the Bears served notice right at the start that this afternoon was theirs. On the second play from scrimmage, Bill Osmanski went around end for 68 yards for a touchdown, sprung loose by George Wilson's flying block which erased the two last Redskin defenders in one shot. Washington's Max Krause then returned the kickoff back to the Chicago 39-yard line, and five plays later Sammy Baugh threw a perfect pass to Charlie Malone all alone on the five. Malone dropped it, and the Redskins never came close again. By the end of the first quarter the score was 21-0 and the game was turning into a rout. With the Chicago defense shutting off the Redskin runners and intercepting passes freely, the score mounted to 28-0 at halftime. Rather than slack off in the second half, the Bears poured it on, running the final score to 73-0 with three fourth-quarter touchdowns.

INDIVIDUAL STATISTICS

WASHINGTON	No	Yds	Avg.	CHICAGO	No	Yds	Avg.
PUNT RETURNS							
Moore	1	6	6.0	McAfee	1	17	17.0
				Clark	1	9	9.0
				Luckman	1	3	3.0
					3	29	9.7
INTERCEPTION RETURNS							
				Maniaci	2	26	13.0
				McAfee	1	35	35.0
				Turner	1	20	20.0
				Pool	1	15	15.0
				Nolting	1	10	10.0
				McLean	1	0	0.0
				Osmanski	1	0	0.0
					8	106	13.3

INDIVIDUAL STATISTICS

WASHINGTON	No	Yds	Avg.	CHICAGO	No	Yds	Avg.
RUSHING							
Filchock	2	20	10.0	Osmanski	10	107	10.7
Seymour	4	17	4.3	Clark	7	75	10.7
Johnson	4	14	3.5	Nolting	11	67	6.1
Justice	1	2	2.0	Maniaci	5	62	12.4
Zimmerman	1	2	2.0	McAfee	7	32	4.6
	12	55	4.6	Famiglietti	4	19	4.8
				McLean	3	18	6.0
				Nowaskey	1	7	7.0
				Snyder	1	2	2.0
				Manders	2	1	0.5
				Luckman	1	1	1.0
					52	391	7.5
RECEIVING							
Millner	6	94	15.7	Maniaci	2	44	22.0
Masterson	3	34	11.3	Kavanaugh	2	32	16.0
Johnson	3	9	3.0	Swisher	1	36	36.0
Malone	2	51	25.5	Mihal	1	14	14.0
Hoffman	2	8	4.0	Nolting	1	12	12.0
Farkas	1	19	19.0		7	138	19.7
Seymour	1	7	7.0				
Justice	1	4	4.0				
McChesney	1	0	0.0				
	20	226	11.3				
PUNTING							
Zimmerman	1		61.0	Luckman	1		58.0
Todd	1		35.0	McAfee	1		38.0
Baugh	1		31.0		2		48.0
	3		42.3				
KICKOFF RETURNS							
Filchock	3	65	21.7	Nolting	1	22	22.0
Krause	1	51	51.0				
Farkas	1	35	35.0				
Zimmerman	1	33	33.0				
Pinckert	1	10	10.0				
Malone	1	9	9.0				
	8	203	25.4				

PASSING

WASHINGTON	Att	Comp	Comp Pct.	Yds	Int	Yds/ Att.	Yds/ Comp	Yards Lost Tackled
Filchock	23	8	34.8	101	4	4.4	12.6	1–17
Baugh	16	9	56.3	91	2	5.7	10.1	1–16
Zimmerman	12	3	25.0	34	2	2.8	11.3	1–17
	51	20	39.2	226	8	4.4	11.3	3–50
CHICAGO								
Luckman	6	4	66.7	102	0	17.0	25.5	
Snyder	3	3	100.0	36	0	12.0	12.0	1–10
McAfee	1	0	0.0	0	0	–	–	
	10	7	70.0	138	0	13.8	19.7	1–10

1941
December 21, at Chicago
(Attendance 13,341)

SCORING

NEW YORK	6	0	3	0	– 9
CHIC. BEARS	3	6	14	14	–37

First Quarter		
Chi.	Snyder, 14 yard Field Goal	10:34
N.Y.	Franck, 31 yard pass from Leemans PAT – Cuff (No Good)	12:40
Second Quarter		
Chi.	Snyder, 39 yard Field Goal	0:44
Chi.	Snyder, 37 yard Field Goal	9:58
Third Quarter		
N.Y.	Cuff, 17 yard Field Goal	4:25
Chi.	Standlee, 2 yard rush PAT – Snyder (kick)	7:48
Chi.	Standlee, 7 yard rush PAT – Maniaci (kick)	13:05
Fourth Quarter		
Chi.	McAfee, 5 yard rush PAT – Artoe (kick)	10:55
Chi.	Kavanaugh, 42 yard fumble return PAT – McLean (kick)	14:51

The Anticlimactic Affair

With attendance held down by concern over the recent attack on Pearl Harbor, the Bears wore the Giants down in the first half and broke the game open in the final half for a 37-9 victory. After the first thirty minutes the score read 9-6, with the Bears tallying three Bob Snyder field goals and the Giants a 31-yard touchdown pass from Tuffy Leemans to George Franck. A Ward Cuff field goal tied the score at 9-9 early in the third quarter, but the Bears took charge from that point on. With Sid Luckman's passes on target and Norm Standlee almost unstoppable on short yardage plays, the Bears drove 71 yards for six points, with Standlee taking it over from the two. Minutes later, Standlee climaxed another Bear drive with a seven-yard dash into the end zone, with the extra point making the score 23-9 at the end of three quarters. The deep Bears completely routed the Giants in the final period, notching two touchdowns and adding the final extra point on a drop kick, already a forgotten play in football.

TEAM STATISTICS

CHI.		N.Y.
20	First Downs	8
192	Rushing Yardage	84
19	Passing – Attempts	15
11	– Completions	3
57.9	– Completion Pct.	20.0
182	– Yards	73
9.6	– Yards per Attempt	4.9
16.5	– Yards per Completion	24.3
0	– Intercepted	3
2	Punting – Number	5
53.5	– Average Yards	38.6
3	Fumbles – Number	2
1	– Times Lost Ball	2
9	Penalties – Number	3
80	– Yards Penalized	31

1942
December 13, at Washington
(Attendance 36,006)

SCORING

CHIC. BEARS	0	6	0	0	– 6
WASHINGTON	0	7	7	0	–14

Second Quarter		
CHI.	Artoe, 52 yard fumble return PAT – Artoe (No Good)	1:22
WAS.	Moore, 39 yard pass from Baugh PAT – Masterson (kick)	8:56
Third Quarter		
Was.	Farkas, 1 yard rush PAT – Masterson (kick)	7:25

TEAM STATISTICS

WASH.		CHI.
10	First Downs – Total	10
6	– by Rushing	6
2	– by Passing	3
2	– by Penalty	1
1	Fumbles – Number	1
1	– Times Lost Ball	1
4	Penalties – Number	7
26	– Yards Penalized	47

Somewhat Healing the Wounds

The Redskins won a measure of revenge for their 1940 humiliation by beating the undefeated Chicago Bears 14-6 for the NFL championship. The Washington line played inspired football, completely shredding the Chicago running game and rushing the Bear passers so that the Bears spent most of the game mired in their own territory. Chicago did score first, with no thanks to their offense, as tackle Lee Artoe returned a fumble 52 yards for a touchdown. Baugh hit Wilbur Moore for a 39-yard touchdown pass, and the extra point made it 7-6 Washington at the halftime break. With the Bear attack unable to get untracked, the Redskins added an Andy Farkas touchdown in the second half for the 14-6 win.

INDIVIDUAL STATISTICS

WASHINGTON	No	Yds	Avg.	CHICAGO	No	Yds	Avg.
KICKOFF RETURNS							
Hare	1	29	29.0	McLean	1	25	25.0
Moore	1	23	23.0	Nolting	1	23	23.0
	2	52	26.0	Clark	1	21	21.0
					3	69	23.0
INTERCEPTION RETURNS							
Moore	1	14	14.0	Nolting	1	0	0.0
Baugh	1	0	0.0	O'Rourke	1	0	0.0
Hare	1	0	0.0		2	0	0.0
	3	14	4.7				

INDIVIDUAL STATISTICS

WASHINGTON	No	Yds	Avg.	CHICAGO	No	Yds	Avg.
RUSHING							
Farkas	13	46	3.5	Osmanski	13	38	2.9
Seymour	14	34	2.4	Nolting	8	26	3.3
Todd	2	12	6.0	Famiglietti	7	22	3.1
Hare	4	7	1.8	Maznicki	5	14	2.8
Baugh	2	6	3.0	McLean	1	3	3.0
Masterson	1	–1	–1.0	Gallarneau	1	0	0.0
	36	104	2.9	Petty	3	–1	–0.3
					38	102	2.7
RECEIVING							
Moore	2	41	20.5	McLean	3	26	8.7
Todd	1	9	9.0	Siegel	2	11	5.5
Cifers	1	8	8.0	Maznicki	1	39	39.0
Masterson	1	8	8.0	Nowaskey	1	32	32.0
	5	66	13.2	Nolting	1	11	11.0
					8	119	14.9
PUNTING							
Baugh	1		52.5	Luckman	6		42.0
PUNT RETURNS							
Todd	2	5	2.5	Gallarneau	1	13	13.0
Farkas	2	0	0.0				
Seymour	2	0	0.0				
	6	5	0.8				

PASSING

WASHINGTON	Att	Comp	Comp Pct.	Yds	Int	Yds/ Att.	Yds/ Comp	Yards Lost Tackled
Baugh	13	5	38.5	66	2	5.1	13.2	
CHICAGO								
Luckman	11	4	36.4	9	2	0.8	2.3	3–33
O'Rourke	6	4	66.7	110	0	18.3	27.5	
Maznicki	1	0	0.0	0	1	–	–	
	18	8	44.4	119	3	6.6	14.9	3–33

1943

December 26, at Chicago
(Attendance 34,320)

SCORING

WASHINGTON	0	7	7	7–21
CHIC. BEARS	0	14	13	14–41

Second Quarter		
Was.	Farkas, 1 yard rush PAT – Masterson (kick)	0:02
Chi.	Clark, 31 yard pass from Luckman PAT – Snyder (kick)	2:23
Chi.	Nagurski, 3 yard rush PAT – Snyder (kick)	12:57
Third Quarter		
Chi.	Magnani, 36 yard pass from Luckman PAT – Snyder (kick)	2:59
Chi.	Magnani, 66 yard pass from Luckman PAT – Snyder (No Good)	11:33
Was.	Farkas, 17 yard pass from Baugh PAT – Masterson kick	13:44
Fourth Quarter		
Chi.	Benton, 29 yard pass from Luckman PAT – Snyder (kick)	3:30
Chi.	Clark, 16 yard pass from Luckman PAT – Snyder (kick)	11:50
Was.	Aguirre, 26 yard pass from Baugh PAT – Aguirre (kick)	12:02

Five Strikes for Luckman, One Kick for Baugh

Sid Luckman turned in a marvelous all-around performance in leading the Bears to a 41-21 triumph over the Washington Redskins. Luckman threw five touchdown passes, ran for 64 yards, deftly picked the Redskin defense apart with his play-calling, and intercepted two passes on defense. Sammy Baugh, Luckman's opposite number on the Redskins, missed most of the first half when kicked in the head while making a tackle. With George Cafego filling in at tailback, the Redskins drew first blood when Andy Farkas bucked over from the one-yard line. Luckman went to work after that and soon put the game out of reach. A 31-yard pass play to Harry Clark tied the score, and a 3-yard plunge by Bronko Nagurski, back from five years of retirement, gave the Bears a 14-7 halftime edge. In the first few minutes of the second half, halfback Dante Magnani twice went all the way with short passes, running 36 and 66 yards to break the game wide open. Sammy Baugh, still dizzy from a mild concussion, returned to action in the third quarter and rallied his mates to a touchdown before the end of the period. The Bears, leading 27-14 after three quarters, completely dominated the final quarter. They held onto the ball for the first eleven minutes and fifty seconds of the period by launching an extended drive that resulted in a Jim Benton touchdown, then recovered an onside kick and again marched steadily downfield for another score.

TEAM STATISTICS

CHI.		WASH.
14	First Downs	11
169	Rushing Yardage	50
27	Passing – Attempts	24
15	– Completions	11
55.6	– Completion Pct.	45.8
276	– Yards	199
10.2	– Yards per Attempt	8.3
18.4	– Yards per Completion	18.1
0	– Had Intercepted	4
5	Punting – Number	5
32.0	– Average Yards	40.8
3	Punt Returns – Number	2
60	– Yards	37
20.0	– Average Yards	18.5
2	Kickoff Returns – Number	7
21	– Yards	107
10.5	– Average Yards	15.3
0	Fumbles – Number	1
0	– Times Lost Ball	0
9	Penalties – Number	3
81	– Yards Penalized	35

1944

December 17, at New York
(Attendance 46,016)

SCORING

GREEN BAY	0	14	0	0–14
NEW YORK	0	0	0	7– 7

Second Quarter		
G.B.	Fritsch, 1 yard rush PAT – Hutson (kick)	2:26
G.B.	Fritsch, 28 yard pass from Comp PAT – Hutson (kick)	13:43
Fourth Quarter		
N.Y.	Cuff, 1 yard rush PAT – Strong (kick)	0:03

TEAM STATISTICS

N.Y.		G.B.
9	First Downs – Total	13
6	– by Rushing	10
2	– by Passing	3
1	– by Penalty	0
2	Fumbles – Number	2
0	– Times Lost Ball	0
11	Penalties – Number	4
90	– Yards Penalized	48

One Decoy and a Lot of Defense

Although the Giants had beaten them 24-0 only four weeks earlier, the Packers won the NFL championship by downing New York 14-7 in a strong defensive battle. The Giants got next to nothing out of runner Bill Paschal, who hurt his ankle in the final game of the regular season, so they relied on their defense to keep them in the game. The Packers knew that the Giants would have to double-team end Don Hutson, so they wisely used him as a decoy most of the afternoon and hit at the weakened sectors of the New York defense. After a scoreless first quarter, the Packers returned a New York punt to the Giant 48-yard line to start a drive at the beginning of the second period. On the first play, Joe Laws broke through the line for 20 yards, and Ted Fritsch ran 27 yards down to the one on the next play. The Giants held firm for three plays, but Fritsch plunged over on fourth down for the touchdown. Later in the quarter they started another drive from their own 38-yard line. On third and three, Irv Comp hit Hutson with a pass good for 24 yards down to the New York 30, and three plays later, with the Giants concentrating on Hutson, Comp hit Fritsch with a pass which he ran untouched all the way to the end zone. Hutson added the extra point after both touchdowns to give Green Bay a 14-0 bulge at the half. The teams traded punts and interceptions through the third quarter until a long pass from ex-Packer Arnie Herber to Frank Liebel gave the Giants a first down on the Green Bay one-yard line when the period ended. On the first play of the final quarter, Ward Cuff drove in for New York's only touchdown of the day, with the extra point making the count 14-7. The Giants launched a final drive to tie the game late in the period, only to have a long pass by Herber intercepted by Paul Duhart on the 20-yard line.

INDIVIDUAL STATISTICS

NEW YORK	No	Yds	Avg.	GREEN BAY	No	Yds	Avg.
RUSHING							
Cuff	12	76	6.3	Fritsch	18	59	3.3
Livingston	12	22	1.8	Laws	13	72	5.5
Paschal	2	4	2.0	Comp	7	42	6.0
Sulaitis	1	–1	–1.0	Duhart	7	15	2.1
	27	101	3.7	Perkins	2	–4	–2.0
					47	184	3.9
RECEIVING							
Liebel	3	70	23.3	Hutson	2	46	23.0
Cuff	2	23	11.5	Fritsch	1	28	28.0
Livingston	2	21	10.5		3	74	24.7
Barker	1	0	0.0				
	8	114	14.3				
PUNTING							
Younce	10		41.0	L. Brock	6		36.8
				Fritsch	4		41.0
					10		38.5
PUNT RETURNS							
Cuff	3	29	9.7	Comp	4	46	11.5
Livingston	1	2	2.0	Laws	3	37	12.3
	4	31	7.8	Duhart	1	5	5.0
					8	88	11.0
KICKOFF RETURNS							
Cuff	1	24	24.0	Laws	1	9	9.0
Livingston	1	22	22.0				
Herber	1	17	17.0				
Sulaitis	1	16	16.0				
	4	79	19.8				
INTERCEPTION RETURNS							
Younce	1	5	5.0	Laws	3	28	9.3
Livingston	1	0	0.0	Duhart	1	0	0.0
Hein	1	–3	–3.0		4	28	7.0
	3	2	0.7				

PASSING

	Att	Comp	Comp Pct.	Yds	Int	Yds/ Att.	Yds/ Comp	Yards Lost Tackled
NEW YORK								
Herber	22	8	36.4	114	4	5.2	14.3	3–16
GREEN BAY								
Comp	10	3	30.0	74	3	7.4	24.7	2–21
L. Brock	1	0	0.0	0	0	–	–	
	11	3	27.3	74	3	6.7	24.7	2–21

1945

December 16, at Cleveland
(Attendance 32,178)

SCORING

WASHINGTON	0	7	7	0–14
CLEVELAND	2	7	6	0–15

First Quarter	
Cle.	Safety – Automatic; Baugh's pass from inside of end zone hit goal post.
Second Quarter	
Was.	Bagarus, 38 yard pass from Filchock PAT – Aguirre (kick)
Cle.	Benton, 37 yard pass from Waterfield PAT – Waterfield (kick)
Third Quarter	
Cle.	Gillette, 53 yard pass from Waterfield PAT – Waterfield (No Good)
Was.	Seymour, 8 yard pass from Filchock PAT – Aguirre (kick)

Goal Posts and Crossbars

As young Bob Waterfield led his Cleveland Rams against the Washington Redskins and veteran passing star Sammy Baugh, a strong wind whipping across the field directly figured in the first score of the game and eventual outcome. Early in the first quarter the Skins stopped a Cleveland drive on the five-yard line. Baugh then faded back into his end zone to throw a long pass, but when he let it fly a gust of wind blew it into the goal post. The ball bounced back into the end zone, which was a safety under the rules then in effect. The 2-0 lead held up through the first quarter, but Baugh didn't; bruised ribs knocked him out of action in the opening period, and he played only a few minutes in the second half. Frankie Filchock took over at tailback and hit Steve Bagarus with a 38-yard touchdown pass, but Cleveland took a 9-7 lead before the half on a Waterfield to Jim Benton pass covering 37 yards. Waterfield's extra-point try hit the crossbar, bounced up in the air and dropped over, giving the Rams a point which proved to be the winning margin, as both teams scored a touchdown in the third period although Cleveland missed the conversion to give them a final 15-14 victory.

TEAM STATISTICS

CLE.		WASH.
14	First Downs	8
180	Rushing Yardage	35
27	Passing – Attempts	20
14	– Completions	9
51.9	– Completion Pct.	45.0
192	– Yards	179
7.1	– Yards per Attempt	9.0
13.7	– Yards per Completion	19.9
2	– Had Intercepted	2
8	Punting – Number	7
38	– Average Yards	36
1	Fumbles Lost	1
60	Yards Penalized	34

INDIVIDUAL STATISTICS

CLEVELAND	No	Yds	Avg.	WASHINGTON	No	Yds	Avg.
KICKOFF RETURNS							
Greenwood	2	33	16.5	Condit	1	34	34.0
Nemeth	1	5	5.0	Bagarus	1	24	24.0
	3	38	12.7		2	58	29.0
INTERCEPTION RETURNS							
West	1	23	23.0	Aldrich	2	11	5.5
Reisz	1	15	15.0				
	2	38	19.0				

UseName(Nicknames)-Positions	Team by Year	See Section	Hgt	Wgt	College	Int	Pts
Abbruzzino, Frank LB-BB-C-G-OE-DE-WB-DB	31Bkn 33Cin		6'	193	Colgate	2	
Adams (born Adamczyk), Chet DT-OT-OE-DE	39-42Cle 43GB 44-45MS 46-48CleAA 49BufAA 50NYY	5	6'3"	233	Ohio U.	1	173
Adams, Henry C-LB	39ChiC		6'1"	190	Pittsburgh		
Adams, Neal OE-DE	42-44NYG 45MS 46-47BknAA 42-43 played in N.B.L.	2	6'3"	195	Arkansas	1	54
Adams, Verlin (Sparky) DE-T-G-OE-LB	43-45NYG		6'	205	Charleston	1	
Adkins, Bob BB-DE-G-LB	40-41GB 42-44MS 45GB		6'1"	213	Marshall	2	16
Agee, Sam FB-DB	38-39ChiC	2	6'1"	218	Vanderbilt		12
Aquirre, Joe OE-DE	41,43-45Was 46-49LA-AA 50CFL	2 5	6'4"	225	St. Mary's		310
Aiello, Tony WB-DB	44Det 44Bkn		5'6"	165	Youngstown State		
Akin, Len (Tex) G-LB	40-41AFL 42ChiB 43-45MS		5'11"	207	Baylor	1	
Akins, Frank FB-LB	43-46Was	2	5'10"	208	Washington State		42
Albanese, Vannie FB-DB-BB-LB	37-38Bkn 40-41AFL	2	6'	184	Syracuse		
Albrecht, Art T-C-LB	42Pit 43ChiC 44Bos 45MS		6'1"	203	Wisconsin		
Aldrich, Ki C-LB-G	39-40ChiC 41-42Was 43-44MS 45-47Was		6'	207	Texas Christian	7	19
Alfonse, Julie WB-DB-TB	37-38Cle 40-41AFL	2	5'8"	180	Minnesota		12
Alford, Gene WB-DB-BB-FB-LB	31-33Port 34C-S	0	5'9"	180	Texas Tech	1	24
Alfson, Warren G-LB	41Bkn 42-45MS		6'	198	Nebraska	2	
Allman, Bob OE-DE	36ChiB		6'	198	Michigan State		
Allton, Joe T	42ChiC 43-45MS		6'2"	235	Oklahoma	1	
Ananis, Vito HB-DB	40AFL 45Was		5'10"	195	Boston College		
Anderson, Bill DE	45Bos		6'2"	190	West Virginia		
Anderson, Stan T-OE-DE	40-41Cle 41Det 42-45MS		6'2"	218	Stanford		
Anderson, Winnie OE-DE	36NYG		6'	185	Colgate		
Andrako, Steve C-LB	40Was 41-45MS		6'	210	Ohio State		
Andrews, Jabby TB-DB	34C-S			200	none		
Andrusking, Sig G	36-37AFL 37Bkn		5'8"	187	Detroit		
Apolskis, Chuck OE-DE	39ChiB 41AFL		6'2"	207	DePaul		
Apsit, Megs BB-LB-DB-WB-HB	31Fra 31Bkn 32GB 33Bos		5'11"	200	Southern Calif.		
Arena, Tony C-LB	42Det 43-45MS		6'	200	Michigan State		
Arenz, Arnie BB-LB	34Bos		6'1"	215	St. Louis		
Ariail, Gump OE-DE	34Bkn 34C-S		5'11"	205	Auburn		
Armstrong, Bill G	43Bkn		6'1"	210	U.C.L.A.		
Arndt, Al G	35Pit		5'11"	205	S. Dakota State		
Arnold, Jay HB-DB-BB-WB-LB	37-40Phi 40AFL 41Pit	2	6'1"	210	Texas	2	39
Artman, Corrie (Whitey, Chang) T-G	31NYG 32Bos 33Pit		6'2"	240	Stanford		
Artoe, Lee T	40-42ChiB 43-44MS 45ChiB 46-47LA-AA 48BalAA	5	6'3"	234	Santa Clara, California		31
Aspatore, Ed T-G	34C-S		6'1"	220	Marquette		
Atty, Alex G	39Cle		5'8"	216	West Virginia		
Auer, Howie T	33Phi		6'1"	205	Michigan		
Augusterfer, Gene BB-DB	35Pit		5'9"	180	Catholic		
Austin, Jim OE-DE	37AFL 37-38Bkn 39Det	2	6'2"	199	St. Mary's		6
Avedisian, Chuck G-LB	42-44NYG		5'9"	203	Providence	1	12
Babartsky, Al T	38-39,41-42ChiC 43-45ChiB		6'	223	Fordham		6
Bach, Joe	HC35-36,52-53Pit				Notre Dame		
Badgro, Red OE-DE	27-28NYY 29RB 30-35NYG 36Bkn 29-30 played major league baseball PC36AFL	0 2	6'	191	Southern Calif.	3	42
Bailey, Bill OE-DE	40-41Bkn 42-45MS		6'3"	213	Duke		
Bailey, Howard (Screeno) T	35Phi		6'	205	Tennessee		
Baisi, Al G	40-41ChiB 42-45MS 46ChiB 47Phi		6'	217	West Virginia		
Baker, Conway T-G	36-43ChiC 44C-P 45ChiC	5	5'11"	228	Centenary		31
Balasz, Frank FB-LB-DB	39-41GB 41ChiC 42-44MS 45ChiC	2	6'2"	212	Iowa		7
Baltzell, Vic WB-DB	35Bos 36AFL		5'11"	205	Southwestern (Kan.)		
Banas, Steve BB-DB	35Det 35Phi 40-41AFL		6'	190	Notre Dame		
Bandura, John OE-DE	43Bkn		6'	206	Southwestern La.		
Banet, Herb TB-HB-DB	37GB		6'2"	200	Manchester		
Banjavic, Emil (Banji) WB-DB	42Det 43-45MS		6'1"	194	Arizona	1	6
Barber, Ernie C-LB	45Was		6'1"	225	San Francisco		
Barber, Jim T	35-36Bos 37-41Was 42-45MS		6'3"	223	San Francisco		
Barber, Mark FB-LB	37Cle		5'11"	192	S. Dakota State		
Barbour, Elmer BB-LB	45NYG		6'1"	200	Wake Forest		
Barker, Hubert BB-LB	43-45NYG		5'10"	193	Arkansas		
Barle, Lou (Fats) BB-DB-LB	38Det 39Cle 39-43 played in the N.B.L.		6'1"	205	Minnesota-Duluth		
Barnard, Hap OE-DE	38NYG		6'2"	190	Central St. - Okla.		
Barnett, Solon T-G	45-46GB		6'1"	235	Southwestern (Tex.), Baylor		
Barnhart, Dan (Chief) TB-DB	34Phi 37AFL		6'	200	St. Mary's, Centenary		
Barnum, Len (Feets, Bear Tracks) QB-DB-FB-WB-HB	38-40NYG 41-42Phi 43-45MS	12 45	6'	200	West Va. Wesleyan	3	63
Barrager, Nate C-LB-G	30Min and 30Fra 31Fra 31-32,34-35GB		6'	212	Southern Calif.	2	
Barrett, Emmett C-LB	42NYG 43-44MS		6'2"	192	Portland		
Barrett, Jeff OE-DE	36-38Bkn	2	6'1"	182	Louisiana State		36
Bartholomew, Sam FB-LB	41Phi 42-45MS		5'11"	188	Tennessee	1	
Bartlett, Earl (Cowboy) HB-DB	36-37AFL 39Pit		6'	200	Centre		
Bartos, Hank G	38Was		6'1"	216	North Carolina		
Basca, Mike HB-DB	41Phi 42-44MS - killed in action		5'8"	170	Villanova	3	18
Basrak, Mike C-LB	37-38Pit		6'2"	220	Duquesne		
Bassi, Dick G-LB	37Was 38-39ChiB 40Phi 41Pit 42-45MS 46-47SF-AA		5'11"	214	Santa Clara	1	6
Bassman, Reds TB-HB-DB	36Phi		5'11"	180	Ursinus		
Batinski, Stan G	41Det 42MS 43-47Det 48Bos 49NYB		5'10"	215	Temple		
Battles, Cliff (Gyp) TB-DB-WB-FB	32-36Bos 37Was HC46-47BknAA	012	6'1"	195	West Va. Wesleyan	8	190
Baugh, Sammy (Slingin' Sammy) QB-TB-DB	37-52Was HC60-61NYA HC64HouA	12 4	6'2"	182	Texas Christian	28	55
Bausch, Frank (Pete) C-LB	34-36Bos 37-40ChiB 41Phi		6'3"	220	Kansas	2	
Bausch, Jim TB-FB-DB-LB	33ChiC 33Cin		6'1"	200	Wichita State, Kansas		
Baze, Winnie WB-TB-DB	37Phi		5'11"	190	Texas Tech		
Becker, Wayland OE-DE	34ChiB 34-35Bkn 36-38GB 39Pit 40-41AFL	2	6'	198	Marquette		12
Bedore, Tom G-LB	44Was		5'11"	193	Pepperdine		
Beebe, Keith BB-DB	44NYG		5'9"	180	Occidental	3	
Behan, Charlie OE-DE	42Det 43-44MS - killed in action		6'3"	195	Northern Illinois		
Beinor, Ed T-DE	40-41ChiC 41-42Was 43-45MS		6'2"	222	Notre Dame		
Belichick, Steve FB-LB	41Det 42-45MS	2	5'8"	190	Case Reserve	1	18
Bell, Bert	HC38-40Phi HC41Pit				Pennsylvania		
Bell, Kay T-G	37ChiB 40-41AFL 42NYG		6'2"	220	Washington State		
Bellinger, Bob G	34-35NYG		5'11"	216	Gonzaga		
Bennett, Chuck WB-DB-BB	30-31Port 33ChiC	0	5'9"	193	Indiana	1	42
Benson, Harry G	35Phi		5'10"	218	Western Maryland		
Benton, Jim (Big Jim) OE-DE	38-40,42Cle 43ChiB 44-45Cle 46-47LA	2	6'3"	200	Arkansas		288
Berezney, Paul T	41AFL 42-44GB 46MiaAA		6'2"	221	Fordham		
Bergerson, Gil G-T	32-33ChiB 33ChiC 35-36Bkn		6'6"	245	Oregon State	1	
Bergman, Dutch	HC43Was 16 played major league baseball				Notre Dame, Detroit		

UseName(Nicknames)-Positions	Team by Year	See Section	Hgt	Wgt	College	Int	Pts
Bernard, Chuck C-LB	34Det		6'3"	225	Michigan		
Bernard, Dave (King) LB-BB	40-41AFL 44-45Cle		5'10"	194	Mississippi		
Berner, Mil C-LB	33Cin		6'2"	204	Syracuse		
Berry, Connie Mack DE-OE	39Det 40Cle 40-41AFL 42-26ChiB 47ChiAA 39-46 played in N.B.L.	2	6'3"	215	N. Carolina State		60
Berry, Gil TB-DB	35ChiC		5'10"	178	Illinois		
Bertagnolli, Libero G-LB	42ChiC 43-44MS 45ChiC		5'9"	189	Washington-St.L.		
Bettencourt, Larry C-LB	33GB 28,31-32 played major league baseball		5'11"	205	St. Mary's		
Bettridge, John FB-LB	37ChiB 37Cle		5'10"	188	Ohio State		
Bezdek, Hugo	HC37-38Cle 17-19 manager — major league baseball				Chicago		
Biancone, John TB-DB	36Bkn		5'6"	165	Oregon State		
Bilbo, Jon T-G	38-39ChiC		6'	195	Mississippi		
Bilda, Dick TB-DB	44GB		6'	200	Marquette	1	
Billock, Frank T	37Pit		6'	230	St. Mary's (Minn.)		
Binotto, John HB-DB	42Pit 42Phi 43-45MS		5'10"	185	Duquesne		1
Birlem, Keith DB-OE-WB	39ChiC 39Was 40-42MS — killed in action		5'11"	198	San Jose State		
Bjork, Del T	37-38ChiB		6'1"	218	Oregon		
Bjorklund, Bob C-LB	41Phi 42-45MS		6'2"	225	Minnesota		
Blackwell, Hal HB=DB	45ChiC		6'1"	205	South Carolina		
Blazine, Tony T	35-40ChiC 41NYG		6'	232	Illinois Wesleyan		6
Bleeker, Mel HB-DB	44-46Phi 47LA	2	5'11"	189	Southern Calif.	2	66
Blessing, Paul OE-DE	44Det		6'4"	215	Kearney State		
Blondin, Tom G	33Cin		6'	195	West Va. Wesleyan		
Blood (born McNally), Johnny (The Vagabond Halfback) HB-WB-DB-TB-BB-FB	25Mil 26-27Dul 28Pott 29-33GB, 34Pit 35-36GB PC37-38Pit HC39Pit 41AFL	012	6'1"	188	Wis.-River Falls, St. John's (Minn.), Notre Dame	33	297
Blozis, Al (The Human Howitzer) T	42-44NYG MS — killed in action		6'6"	250	Georgetown		6
Blumer, Herb OE-DE-G-T-C	25-30,33ChiC		6'1"	200	Missouri		12
Bodenger, Maury G	31-33Port 34Det 36AFL		5'10"	214	Tulane	2	
Bohlmann, Frank G	40-41AFL 42ChiC		5'11"	212	Marquette		
Bond, Chuck T	37-38Was		6'2"	234	Washington		
Bond, Rink BB-LB	38Was 39Pit		5'10"	200	Washington		
Bonelli, Ernie FB-LB-HB-DB	45ChiC 46Pit	2	5'11"	194	Pittsburgh	1	
Boone, Jack WB-DB	42Cle 43-45MS		5'11"	175	Elon	1	6
Booth, Clarence T	43ChiC 44C-P		6'	223	S.M.U.		
Booth, Dick WB-DB	41Det 42-44MS 45Det	2	6'1"	190	Case Reserve	1	12
Borak, Tony DE	38GB		6'1"	190	Creighton		
Borden, Les OE-DE	35NYG 36AFL		6'	185	Fordham		
Bostick, Lew G	39Cle		6'	197	Alabama		2
Boswell, Ben T	33Port 34Bos		6'	245	Texas Christian		
Bova, Tony OE-DB-DE-QB-HB	42Pit 43P-P 44C-P 45-47Pit	12	6'1"	190	St. Francis (Pa.)	1	44
Bowdoin, Jim (Goofy) G	28-31GB 32Bkn 32NYG 33Port 34Bkn		6'1"	227	Alabama		
Boyd, Sam OE-DE	39-40Pit	2	6'1"	188	Baylor		12
Boyer, Verdi T	36Bkn 37AFL		5'10"	195	U.C.L.A.		
Boyle, Knuckles T	34NYG		5'11"	232	none		
Braden, Dave G-LB	45ChiC		6'	210	Marquette		
Bradley, Hal OE-DE	38ChiC 38-39Was 39ChiC		6'4"	205	Elon		
Brahm, Larry G-LB	42Cle		5'10"	204	Temple		
Braidwood, Chuck OE-DE	30Port 31Cle 32ChiC 33Cin		6'	199	Loyola (Chic.), Tenn-Chattanooga	1	
Bray, Mule T	35-36Pit		6'2"	220	S.M.U.		
Brazell, Carl BB-DB	38Cle		5'10"	195	Baylor		
Breeden, Bill HB-OE-DB	37Pit		6'1"	210	Oklahoma		
Brennan, Jack G	39GB		6'1"	204	Michigan		
Brennan, Leo T	42Phi 43-45MS		6'	210	Holy Cross		
Brett, Jeep OE-DE	36ChiC 36-37 Pit	2	6'2"	203	Washington State		6
Brian, Bill T-C-LB	35-36Phi		6'2"	210	Gonzaga		
Bridges, Frank	HC44Bkn				Baylor		
Brill, Hal TB-DB	39Det		5'10"	175	Wichita State		
Britt, Eddie DB-FB-TB	36Bos 37Was 38Bkn 40AFL	12	6'2"	205	Holy Cross		
Britt, Maury OE-DE	41Det 42-45MS — arm amputated		6'4"	210	Arkansas		6
Britt, Rankin DE	39Phi		6'2"	206	Texas A&M		
Brock, Charley (Ears) C-LB	39-47GB		6'2"	207	Nebraska	17	24
Brock, Lou HB-DB-FB-TB	40-45GB	1234	6'	195	Purdue	8	98
Brodnicki, Chuck G	34Bkn		6'2"	225	Villanova		
Brovelli, Angie DB-TB-FB-HB-BB-LB	33-34Pit		6'	193	St. Mary's		20
Brown, Bill BB-DB-LB	43-44Bkn 45Pit		6'	202	Texas Tech	1	
Brown, Tom OE-DE	42Pit 43-45MS		6'2"	216	William & Mary		6
Bruckner, Les FB-LB	45ChiC		6'1"	195	Michigan State		
Bruder, Hank BB-DB-LB-TB-HB-FB	31-39GB 40Pit	0	6'	199	Northwestern	7	100
Brumbaugh, Boyd FB-TB-DB-HB	38-39Bkn 39-41Pit	12	5'11'	195	Duquesne		36
Brumbaugh, Carl QB-TB-DB-BB	30-34,36ChiB 37Cle 37Bkn	012	5'10"	170	Florida	7	40
Brumley, Bob WB-DB	45Det		6'	200	Rice		
Bucchianeri, Mike G	41,44-45GB		5'10"	212	Indiana		
Buckler, Bill G-T-OE-DE-C	26-28,31-33ChiB		6'	224	Alabama		2
Bucklew, Phil OE-DE	37-38Cle 40-41AFL		6'1"	205	Xavier-Ohio		
Buda, Carl G	45Pit		5'11"	220	Creighton, Tulsa		
Buhler, Larry FB-HB-BB-DB-LB-DE	39-41GB	2	6'2"	210	Minnesota		
Buivid, Ray (Buzz) QB-HB-DB	37AFL 37-38ChiB	12	6'1"	195	Marquette		6
Bukant, Joe (Buckin' Joe) FB-TB-HB-LB-DB	38-40Phi 42-43ChiC 44-45MS	12	6'	216	Washington-St. L.		24
Bultman, Red C-LB-T	31Bkn 32-34GB		6'2"	201	Indiana, Marquette	5	
Burdick, Lloyd (Tiny, Shorty) T	31-32ChiB 33Cin		6'4"	248	Illinois	1	
Burgeis, Glen T	45ChiB		6'1"	220	Tulsa		
Burleson, John (Tex) T-G	33Port 33Pit 33Cin		6'2"	237	S.M.U.		
Burmeister, Forrest G-T	37Cle		6'3"	215	Purdue		
Burnell, Max HB-DB	44ChiB		5'11"	180	Notre Dame		
Burnett, Dale WB-DB-FB-BB	30-39NYG	0 2	6'1"	187	Emporia State	18	172
Burnett, Ray (Rabbit) TB-DB	38ChiC				Arkansas Tech, Central Arkansas		
Burnette, Tom BB-LB	38Pit 38Phi		6'1"	194	North Carolina		
Busby, Sherrill DE	40Bkn 41-45MS		6'2"	200	Troy State		
Bushby, Tom WB-DB	34C-S		5'10"	200	Kansas State		
Busich, Sam OE-DE	36Bos 37Cle 43Det	2	6'3"	189	Ohio State		10
Busler, Ray T	40-41ChiC 42-44MS 45ChiC		6'1"	222	Marquette		
Buss, Art T	34-35ChiB 36-37Phi		6'3"	219	Michigan State		
Bussey, Young DB-QB	40-41ChiB 42-44MS — killed in action	1	5'9"	184	Louisiana State	2	
Butcher, Wendell BB-LB-FB-DB	38-42Bkn	2	6'1"	197	Gustavus Adolphus		6
Butler, Frank C-LB-T	34-36,38GB		6'3"	237	Michigan State		
Butler, Johnny HB-DB-TB	43P-P 44C-P 44Bkn 45Phi	12	5'10"	185	Tennessee	4	36
Bykowski, Frank G	40Pit 40-41AFL		6'	205	Purdue		
Cabrelli, Larry OE-DE-DB	41-42Phi 43P-P 44-47Phi	2	5'11"	194	Colgate	2	36

UseName(Nicknames)-Positions	Team by Year	See Section	Hgt	Wgt	College	Int	Pts
Caddel, Ernie WB-DB	33Port 34-38Det	2	6'2"	199	Stanford	1	150
Cafego, George (Bad News) QB-TB-DB-HB	40Bkn 41-42MS 43Bkn 43Was 44-45Bos	12 4	5'10"	183	Tennessee	2	6
Cagle, Chris (Red) DB-FB-TB-WB	30-32NYG 33-34Bkn	01	5'10"	174	Southwestern La., Army	4	30
Cahill, Ronnie TB-DB	43ChiC 44-45MS	12	5'8"	170	Holy Cross		
Calligaro, Len BB-LB	44NYG		5'11"	190	Wisconsin		6
Callihan, Bill BB-DB-LB-FB	40-45Det	2 5	6'3"	217	Nebraska	6	55
Calvelli, Tony C-LB-G	39-40Det 41-45MS 47SF-AA		5'10"	189	Stanford	1	6
Campbell, Don (Pop) T	39-40Pit		6'	225	Carnegie-Mellon		
Campbell, Glenn (Turtle,Flash) OE-DE	29-33NYG 34IL 35Pit	0	5'11"	190	Emporia State	1	48
Campiglio, Bob DB-TB-WB-BB	32SI 33Bos	0	6'1"	183	W. Liberty State	1	
Campofreda, Nick C-DT	44Was		6'1"	240	Western Maryland		
Canale, Rocco T-G	43P-P 44-45Phi 46-47Bos		5'11"	240	Boston College		
Cannella, John G-C-LB-T	33-34NYG 34Bkn		6'1"	199	Fordham		
Cantor, Leo DB-HB-FB	42NYG 43-44MS 45ChiC	12 4	6'	195	U.C.L.A.	7	42
Cara, Mac OE-DE	37-38Pit		5'10"	193	N. Carolina State		
Caranci, Roland T	44NYG		6'1"	227	Colorado		
Cardwell, Joe T-DE	37-38Pit		6'3"	235	Duke		
Cardwell, Lloyd WB-DB-FB	37-43Det	2	6'2"	195	Nebraska	2	78
Carlson, Hal G	37AFL 37ChiC		6'3"	220	Northwestern, DePaul	1	
Carlson, Zuck G-T-C-LB	29-36ChiB 37KJ		6'	208	Oregon State		
Carnelly, Ray TB-HB-DB	39Bkn		6'2"	187	Carnegie-Mellon		
Carpe, Joe T-DE-OE-LB-C-WB	26Fra 28Pott 29Bos 33Phi		6'	203	Millikin		
Carroll, Vic T-C-G-LB-OE	36Bos 37-42Was 43-47NYG		6'4"	231	Nevada-Reno	4	32
Carson, Howie HB-DB	40-41AFL 44Cle		6'	190	Illinois		
Carter, Joe OE-DE	33-40Phi 42GB 43MS 44Bkn 45ChiC	2	6'1"	201	S.M.U., Austin		139
Carter, Ross (Timber Beast) G-C-LB	36-39ChiC		6'	238	Oregon		
Casey, Eddie	HC35Bos				Harvard		
Casper, Cy TB-DB-BB-WB	34GB 34C-S 35Pit	1	6'	190	Texas Christian		18
Cassiano, Dick TB-HB-DB	40Bkn 41-45MS	12	5'11"	175	Pittsburgh		12
Cavosie, John FB-LB-BB-DB-WB-OE-DE-T	31-33Port	0	6'	207	Butler	6	28
Cawthon, Pete	HC43-44Bkn				Southwestern (Tex.)		
Caywood, Les (Wimpy) G-T	26KC 26Buf 27Pott 27NYG 27Cle 28Det 29-30NYG 31ChiC 31-32NYG 32Bkn 33Cin 34C-S		6'	231	St. John's (N.Y.)	3	6
Cemore, Tony G	41Phi 42-45MS		6'	210	Creighton	1	
Chalmers, George C-LB	33Bkn		6'	196	N.Y.U.		
Chamberlain, Garth G	45Pit		6'	215	Brigham Young		
Cherne, Hal T-G	33Bos		6'	230	DePaul		
Cherry, Ed FB-DB	38-39ChiC 39Pit		6'	208	Hardin-Simmons		
Cherundolo, Chuck C-LB	37-39Cle 40Phi 41-42Pit 43-44MS 45-48Pit		6'1"	215	Penn State	4	
Chesbro, Red G	38Cle		5'11"	190	Colgate		
Chesney, Chet C-LB	39-40ChiB 41-45MS		6'2"	227	DePaul		
Chickerneo, John (Chick) BB-LB	42NYG 43-45MS		6'1"	205	Pittsburgh	1	
Chisick, Andy C-LB	40-41ChiC 42-45MS		6'1"	207	Villanova	1	
Christiansen, Marty FB-DB	40ChiC	2	6'	200	Minnesota		6
Christensen, Frank BB-DB-FB-LB	34-37Det	1	6'1"	199	Utah	3	26
Christensen, George (Chris) T-G	31-33Port 34-38Det		6'2"	238	Oregon	1	
Cibulas, Joe T	45Pit		6'	220	Duquesne		
Ciccone, Ben (Scaggie) C-LB	34-35Pit 36-37AFL 42ChiC		5'10"	207	Duquesne		
Clair, Frank OE-DE	41Was 42-45MS		6'1"	204	Ohio State		
Clancy, Stu DB-FB-TB-WB-LB-HB	30Nwk 31-32SI 32-35NYG 36AFL	0	5'10"	189	Holy Cross	6	36
Clark, Algy DB-BB-HB-WB-TB-LB-FB-OE-DE	30Bkn 31Cle 32Bos 33Cin PC34C-S 34Phi	0	6'	188	Ohio State	6	36
Clark, Beryl TB-DB	40ChiC	12 4	6'	200	Oklahoma		3
Clark, Dutch TB-DB	31-32Port 33VR 34-36,PC37-38Det HC39-42Cle	012 5	6'	182	Colorado College	10	370
Clark, Harry HB-DB	40-43ChiB 44-45MS 46-48LA-AA 48ChiAA	23	6'	186	West Virginia	9	139
Clark, Jimmy FB-HB-DB	33-34Pit 36AFL		5'9"	174	Pittsburgh	2	6
Clark, Potsy (The Little Colonel)	HC30-33Port HC34-36Det HC37-39Bkn HC40Det				Illinois		
Clark, Wayne OE-DE	44Det		6'3"	210	Utah		
Clay, Boyd T	40-42,44Cle 45MS		6'1"	220	Tennessee		8
Clay, Roy WB-DB	44NYG		6'	185	Colorado State		
Clemens, Cal BB-DB	36GB 37AFL		6'1"	195	Southern Calif.		1
Clemons, Ray G	37AFL 39Det		6'	215	Central St.-Okla.		
Coffee, Pat TB-DB	37-38ChiC	12	5'11"	183	Louisiana State		18
Cole, John (King) FB-LB-BB	38,40Phi	2	5'9"	197	St. Joseph's-Pa.		6
Cole, Pete G-T	37-40NYG 41-45MS		5'11"	222	Trinity (Texas)		
Colella, Tom DB-HB-TB	42-43Det 44-45Cle 46-48CleAA 49BufAA	1234	6'	187	Canisius	26	93
Colins, Paul (Rip) OE-DE	32-35Bos		6'1"	198	Pittsburgh		
Collins, Paul QB	45ChiC		5'11"	178	Missouri		
Combs, Bill OE-DB	42Phi 43-45MS		5'11"	183	Purdue		6
Commisa, Vince G	44Bos		5'9"	190	Notre Dame		
Comstock, Rudy G-T	23Can 24Cle 25Can 26-29Fra 30NYG 31-33GB PC36AFL		5'10"	209	Georgetown		
Concannon, Rick G-T	32SI 34-36Bos 36-37AFL		6'	217	N.Y.U.		
Condit, Merl (Merlyn the Magician) HB-DB	40Pit 41-43Bkn 44MS 45Was 46Pit	12345	5'11"	187	Carnegie-Mellon	10	125
Conkright, Bill (Red) C-LB-OE-DE	37-38ChiB 39-42Cle 43Was 43Det 44Cle HC62OakA		6'1"	203	Oklahoma	4	6
Conlee, Gerry C-LB	38Cle 43Det 44-45MS 46-47SF-AA		5'11"	203	St. Mary's	1	
Conti, Enio G	41-42Phi 43P-P 44-45Phi		5'11"	204	Bucknell	1	
Cook, Dave DB-WB-FB	34-36ChiC 36Bkn		6'2"	203	Illinois	1	10
Cook, Leon T	42Phi		5'11"	220	Northwestern		
Coon, Ty G	40Bkn 41-45MS		6'	215	N. Carolina State		
Cooper, Bud TB-FB-DB	36AFL 37Cle		6'1"	204	Penn State		
Cooper, Hal C-LB-G	37Det		5'10"	207	Detroit		
Cooper, Norm C-LB	37-38Bkn		6'4"	210	Samford		
Cooper, Sam T	33Pit		6'	200	Geneva		
Cope, Frank T	38-47NYG		6'2"	225	Santa Clara		6
Coppage, Al OE-DE-DB	40-42ChiC 43-45MS 46CleAA 47BufAA	2	6'1"	195	Oklahoma		18
Corbett, George QB-HB-DB	32-38ChiB	0 2	5'9"	179	Millikin	3	22
Corbo, Tom G-LB	44Cle		5'11"	210	Duquesne	1	
Cordill, Ollie WB-DB	40Cle 41-45MS	2	6'2"	190	Rice		12
Corgan, Mike FB-LB	43Det 44-45MS		5'10"	188	Notre Dame		
Corzine, Red (Lefty) LB-BB-FB	33Cin 34C-S 35-37NYG 38ChiB	2	6'	213	Davis & Elkins	3	30
Cosner, Don WB-DB	39ChiC		6'2"	200	Montana State		
Coston, Zed C-LB	39Phi		6'2"	222	Texas A&M		
Cotton, Russ BB-LB	41Bkn 42Pit 43-45MS		6'2"	196	Texas-El Paso	1	
Courtney, Gerry TB-DB	42Bkn 43-45MS		6'	195	Syracuse	1	6
Crabtree, Clem T-G	40-41Det 42-45MS		6'3"	225	Wake Forest		

UseName(Nicknames)-Positions	Team by Year	See Section	Hgt	Wgt	College	Int	Pts
Craig, Larry (Superman) BB-DE-LB-OE-DB	39-49GB	2	6'1"	211	South Carolina	1	6
Crain, Milt FB-LB	44Bos	2	6'2"	225	Baylor	1	
Crakes, Joe (Buster) OE-DE	32ChiC 33Cin		6'1"	205	South Dakota		
Crass, Bill FB-DB	37ChiC		6'	205	Louisiana State		
Crawford, Fred OE-DE-T	35ChiB		6'2"	200	Duke		
Crayne, Dick (Baldy) FB-DB	36-37Bkn	2	6'	205	Iowa		10
Creighton, Milan DE-OE	31-34,PC35-37 HC38ChiC	0	6'	190	Arkansas		12
Crimmins, Bernie G-LB	45GB		5'11"	195	Notre Dame	1	6
Critchfield, Larry G	33Pit		5'11"	195	Grove City		
Croft, Abe OE-DB	44-45ChiB	2	6'	183	S.M.U.	1	12
Croft, Tiny T	42-47GB		6'3"	287	Alabama, Ripon		
Croft, Win G	35Bkn 36Pit		5'11"	235	Utah		
Cronkhite, Doc OE-DE	34Bkn		6'5"	210	Kansas State	1	
Crow, Orien C-LB	33-34Bos		6'	220	Haskell Indian		
Crowder, Earl BB-LB	39ChiC 40Cle		6'	198	Oklahoma		
Crowley, Joe OE-DB	44-45Bos	2	6'	194	Dartmouth	2	18
Cuba, Paul T	33-35Phi		6'	212	Pittsburgh		
Cuff, Ward WB-DB-HB-FB	37-45NYG 46ChiC 47GB	23 5	6'1"	192	Marquette	11	417
Cumiskey, Frank OE-DE	37Bkn		6'2"	205	Ohio State		
Cuppoletti, Bree G	34-38ChiC 39Phi		5'10"	200	Oregon		
Daddio, Bill DE-OE	41-42ChiC 43-45MS 46BufAA	2 5	5'11"	207	Pittsburgh	1	52
Dailey, Ted OE-DE	33Pit		5'9"	170	Pittsburgh		
Damiani, Frank T	44NYG 45MS		6'1"	225	Manhatten		
Daniell, Averell T	37GB 37Bkn		6'3"	215	Pittsburgh		
Daniell, Jim T	45ChiB 46CleAA		6'2"	230	Ohio State		
Danowski, Ed QB-TB-DB-WB	34-39,41NYG 42-45MS	12 4	6'1"	198	Fordham		24
Davidson, Bill HB-DB-TB-OE	37-39Pit	12	6'	182	Temple		24
Davis, Bill T	40-41ChiC 42MS 43Bkn 46MiaAA		6'1"	234	Texas Tech		6
Davis, Bob (Twenty Grand) HB-DB-TB	38Cle 40-41AFL 42Phi 44-46Bos	123	6'	185	Kentucky	19	30
Davis, Corby FB-LB-DB-BB	38-39,41-42Cle 43-45MS	2	5'11"	212	Indiana	1	32
Davis, Gaines G	36NYG		5'11"	230	Texas Tech		
Davis, Ray G-C-T-OE-DE-LB	32-33Port 36AFL 36ChiC		6'1"	198	Samford		
Davis, Red TB-DB	33Phi		5'11'	195	Geneva		9
Dawley, Fred FB-LB	44Det		5'9"	190	Michigan		
Deal, Rufus FB-DB	42Was 43-45MS		6'	205	Auburn		
DeCarbo, Nick G	33Pit		5'9"	185	Duquesne		
DeFilippo, Lou C-LB-DT	41NYG 42-44MS 45-47NYG		6'1"	230	Purdue, Fordham		
Dell Isola, Johnny G-LB-C	34-40NYG		5'11"	201	Fordham	1	
Demas, George G	32SI 34Bkn		6'	194	Washington & Jeff.		
Dempsey, John T	34Phi 34Pit 37Phi		6'2"	225	Bucknell		
Dennerlein, Jerry T	37,40NYG		6'2"	240	St. Mary's		
Dennery, Vince OE-DE	41NYG 42-45MS		5'11"	190	Fordham		
DePascal, Carmine DB-OE	45Pit		6'1"	200	Wichita State		
DePaul, Henry G	45Pit		5'11"	225	Duquesne		
Deremer, Art C-LB	42Bkn 43-45MS		6'3"	208	Niagara		
DeSantis, Dan HB-DB	41Phi 42-45MS	2	6'	180	Niagara	2	1
Deskin, Versil OE-DE	35-39ChiC	2	6'	199	Drake		12
Diehl, Charlie G-T	30-31ChiC 34C-S		6'	208	Idaho		
Diehl, Dave OE-DE	39-40,44-45Det	2	6'	195	Michigan State		30
Dietz, Lone Star	HC33-34Bos				Carlisle		
diFilippo, Dave G	41Phi 42-45MS		5'10"	210	Villanova		
Digris, Bernie T-G	43ChiB		6'	212	Holy Cross		
Dilweg, Lavie OE-DE	26Mil 27-34GB	0 2	6'3"	200	Marquette	27	92
DiMelio, Luby	HC34Pit				Pittsburgh		
Disend, Leo (Moose) T	38-39Bkn 40GB		6'2"	224	Albright		
Dobrus, Pete T	41Bkn		6'	215	Carnegie-Mellon		
Dodson, Les TB-DB	41Pit		6'1"	180	Mississippi		
Doehring, John (Bull) HB-LB-TB-DB-QB	32-34ChiB 35Pit 36-37ChiB 40AFL	0 2	6'	216	none		6
Doell, Sonny (Tex) T	33Cin		6'	200	Texas		
Dolaway, Cliff OE-DE	35Pit		6'	215	Carnegie-Mellon		
Dolly, Dick OE-DE	41Pit 42-44MS 45Pit		6'3"	211	West Virginia		
Donelli, Al HB-DB	41-42Pit 42Phi 43-45MS		5'7"	165	Duquesne	1	
Donelli, Buff	HC41Pit HC44Cle				Duquesne		
Dorais, Gus	HC43 47Det				Notre Dame		
D'Orazio, Joe T	44Det		5'11"	220	Ithaca		
Douds, Jap T-G-C-LB-BB	30Prov 30-31Port 32ChiC PC33-34Pit		5'10"	216	Washington & Jeff.	1	
Dougherty, Phil C-LB	38ChiC		5'11"	185	Santa Clara		6
Douglas, Ben WB-DB	33Bkn		6'	185	Grinnell	2	6
Douglas, Bob FB-DB	37AFL 38Pit		6'	195	Kansas State		
Dow, Ken FB-DB	41Was 42-45MS		5'10"	198	Oregon State		
Dow, Woody (Rowdy, Cub) BB-FB-DB-LB	38-40Phi	2	6'	195	West Texas State		6
Dowd, Gerry C-LB	39Cle		6'	210	St. Mary's		6
Dowell, Mule FB-DB-LB	35-36ChiC	2	6'2"	206	Texas Tech		
Doyle, Ted T-G	38-42Pit 43P-P 44C-P 45Pit		6'2"	224	Nebraska	1	6
Drake, Johnny FB-DB-LB-WB	37-41Cle	2	6'1"	213	Purdue	2	164
Draveling, Leo (Firpo) T	33Cin		6'2"	210	Michigan		
Dreher, Fred OE-DE	38ChiB		6'3"	205	Denver		6
Druze, John OE-DE	38Bkn		6'	195	Fordham		
Dubzinski, Walt LB-C-G	43NYG 44Bos 45MS		5'10"	205	Boston College	1	
Dugan, Len C-LB	36NYG 37-39ChiC 39Pit		6'	218	Wichita State		
Duggan, Gil (Cactus Face) T	40NYG 41HO 42-43ChiC 44C-P 45ChiC 46LA-AA 47Buf-AA		6'3"	229	Oklahoma	1	
Duggins, George OE-DE	34ChiC		6'3"	200	Purdue		
Duhart, Paul HB-DB-QB	44GB 45Pit 45Bos	2	6'	180	Florida	4	30
Dunlap, Bob DB-QB	35ChiB 36NYG	1	6'1"	191	Oklahoma		
Dunn, Coye WB-DB	43Was		6'	198	Southern Calif.		
Dunstan, Elwyn T	38-39ChiC 39-41Cle		6'3"	238	Portland		6
Durko, John DE-OE	44Phi 45ChiC		6'4"	235	Albright		6
Dye, Les OE	44-45Was	2	6'1"	181	Syracuse		24
Eagle, Alex T	35Bkn		6'2"	220	Oregon		
Eakin, Kay QB-DB-WB-HB	40-41NYG 42-45MS 46MiaAA	12 4	6'	180	Arkansas	4	6
Eaton, Lou T	45NYG		6'2"	215	California		
Ebding, Harry (Irish) OE-DE	31-33Port 34-37Det	0 2	5'11"	199	St. Mary's	2	66
Eckl, Bob T	40-41AFL 45ChiC		6'1"	233	Wisconsin		
Edwards, Bill (Big Bill)	HC41-42Det				Wittenberg		
Edwards, Marshall FB-LB	43Bkn		6'1"	190	Wake Forest		
Edwards, Monk G-T-LB	40-42NYG 43-45MS 46NYG		6'3"	213	Baylor		
Edwards, Turk T	32-36Bos 37-40,HC46-48Was		6'2"	255	Washington State	2	12
Eibner, John T	41-42Phi 43-45MS 46Phi		6'2"	228	Kentucky		
Eiden, Ed C-LB	44Phi 44Det		6'	205	Scranton		

UseName(Nicknames)-Positions	TeambyYear	See Section	Hgt	Wgt	College	Int	Pts
Eliason, Don OE-DE	42Bkn 43-45MS 46Bos		6'2"	215	Hamline		
	46-47 played in B.A.A.						
Elkins, Chief (Pete) DB-WB-FB-LB-TB-BB-OE-DE	28Fra	0	5'11"	190	Haskell Indian,	5	16
	29ChiC 29Fra 33Cin				Southeastern Okla.,		
					Nebraska		
Elkins, Ev (Boot) WB-DB	40AFL 40ChiC 41-45MS		5'11"	190	Marshall		
Ellis, Drew T-FB	38-39Phi		6'1"	215	Texas Christian		
Ellis, John G	44Bkn		5'10"	212	Vanderbilt		
Ellstrom, Swede FB-DB-HB-LB	34Bos 34Phi 35Pit		6'1"	203	Oklahoma		6
	36ChiC 36-37AFL						
Elser, Earl T	33Port 34C-S 36AFL		6'1"	229	Butler		
Ely, Harold T-G	32ChiB 32-34Bkn		6'2"	268	Iowa		
Emerick, Bob T-G	34Det 36AFL 37Cle		6'2"	225	Miami-Ohio		
Emerson, Ox G-LB-C	31-33Port 34-37Det 38Bkn		5'11"	203	Texas	2	
Emmons, Frank FB-HB-LB	40Phi 41-45MS	2	6'1"	213	Oregon		12
Engebretsen, Tiny G-T	32ChiB 33Pit 33ChiC 34Bkn	0 5	6'1"	238	Northwestern		101
	34-41GB						
Engelmann, Wuert DB-HB-TB-BB-FB-LB	30-33GB	0	6'3"	191	S. Dakota State	9	60
Enich, Steve G	45ChiC		5'10"	212	Marquette		
Erdlitz, Dick HB-DB	42Phi 43-44MS 45Phi 46MiaAA	2 5	5'10"	181	Northwestern	3	48
Erickson, Bud C-LB	38-39Was		6'1"	198	Washington		
Evans, Dick OE-DB-DE	40GB 41-42ChiC 43GB	2	6'3"	205	Iowa		
40-43,44-45 played in N.B.L.	44-45MS						
Evans, Lon G-T	33-37GB		6'2"	223	Texas Christian		
Evans Murray BB-DB	42-43Det 44-45MS		6'1"	205	Hardin-Simmons		
Fagiolo, Carl G	44Phi		6'	200	none		
Falaschi, Nello (Flash) BB-LB	38-41NYG 42-45MS		6'	195	Santa Clara	1	
Falkenstein, Tony (Hawk) FB-LB-BB	43GB 44Bkn 44Bos	2	5'10"	205	St. Mary's		6
	45MS						
Famiglietti, Gary FB-LB-HB	38-45ChiB 46Bos	2	6'	225	Boston U.	1	151
Farkas, Andy FB-DB-HB-WB-LB	38-44Was 45Det	23	5'10"	192	Detroit	10	228
Farman, Dick G-LB	39-43Was		6'	219	Washington State		
Farrar, Vinnie G-BB-LB	36-37AFL 39Pit		5'10"	200	N. Carolina State		
Farrell, Scrapper FB-DB	38Pit 38-39Bkn	2	5'9"	204	Muhlenberg		18
Farroh, Shipley (King Kong) G	38Pit		5'11"	225	Iowa		
Faust, George BB-LB	39ChiC		6'1"	205	Minnesota		1
Fawcett, Jake T	42Cle 43Bkn 44Cle 45MS 46LA		5'11"	223	S.M.U.	1	
Feather, Tiny DB-FB-BB-WB-OE-DE-LB-HB-TB	27Cle	0	6'	197	Kansas State	16	86
	28Det 29-30NYG 31SI 31-33NYG 34C-S						
Feathers, Beattie HB-DB	34-37ChiB 38-39Bkn 40GB	12	5'10"	185	Tennessee		102
Federovich, John (Ace) T	41ChiB 42-45MS 46ChiB		6'5"	261	Davis & Elkins	1	
Fedora, Walt FB-DB	42Bkn 43-45MS		5'1"	190	George Washington		
Feibish, Bernie C-LB	41Phi 42-45MS		6'2"	223	N.Y.U.	1	
Felber, Nip OE-DE	32Bos 33Phi		6'2"	190	North Dakota		
Feldhaus, Bill G-LB-T	37-40Det		6'	226	Cincinnati		
Fena, Tom G	37Det		5'11"	200	Denver		
Fencl, Dick OE-DE	33Phi		5'11"	160	Northwestern		
Ferko, Fritz T	37-38Phi		6'1"	242	West Chester		
Fiedler, Bill G	38Phi		5'9"	200	Pennsylvania		
Field, Harry T	34-36ChiC 37AFL		6'1"	228	Oregon State		
Fife, Ralph G-LB	42ChiC 43-44MS 45ChiC 46Pit		6'	207	Pittsburgh		
Filchock, Frankie TB-QB-DB-HB	38Pit 38-41Was	12	5'11"	193	Indiana	1	48
	42-43MS 44-45Was 46NYG 47-49DE 50Bal						
	HC60-61DenA						
Filipowicz, Steve LB-FB-BB	45-46NYG	2	5'8"	200	Fordham	4	30
	44-45,48 played major league baseball						
Fiorentino, Al G-LB	43-44Was 45Bos		5'7"	201	Boston College	1	
Fishel, Dick BB-LB-DB-WB-TB	33-34Bkn		5'9"	190	Syracuse		6
Fisher, Bob T	40Was		6'2"	220	Southern Calif.		
Fisher, Ev (King) BB-LB-OE-DE	38-39ChiC 40Pit	2	5'11"	205	Santa Clara		
Fisk, Bill OE-DE	40-43Det 44-45MS 46-47SF-AA	2	6'	199	Southern Calif.		18
	48LA-AA						
Fiske, Max (Baxie) TB-DB-OE-HB	36-39Pit	12	6'	199	DePaul		
Flaherty, Ray OE-DE	26AFL 27NYY 28NYG 28NYY	0 2	6'	190	Washington State,	7	127
	28,29,31-35NYG 30RC HC36Bos HC37-42Was				Gonzaga		
	43-45MS HC46-48NY-AA HC49ChiAA						
Folk, Dick FB-DB	39Bkn		6'	200	Arkansas State,		
					Illinois Wesleyan		
Foltz, Vern C-LB	44Was 45Pit 46MS		6'1"	205	St. Vincent		
Fordham, Jim FB-LB	44-45ChiB	2	5'11"	215	Georgia		30
Forte, Aldo G-T 39-41ChiB 42-45MS 46Det 46ChiB 47GB			6'	213	Montana		
Fortmann, Danny G-LB	36-43ChiB 44-45MS		6'	210	Colgate	7	6
Foster, Ralph (Burley) T	45-46ChiC		6'1"	230	Idaho,		
					Oklahoma State		
Fox, Sam OE-DE	45NYG	2	6'2"	215	Ohio State		12
Fox, Terry FB-LB	41Phi 42-44MS 45Phi 46MiaAA	2	6'1"	208	Miami (Fla.)		
Frahm, Dick DB-WB-HB	32SI 35Phi 35Bos 36AFL		5'10"	195	Nebraska	3	2
Francis, Sam FB-DB-HB-LB	37-38ChiB 39Pit 39-40Bkn	2 4	6'	207	Nebraska		37
	41-45MS						
Franck, George WB-DB-FB	41NYG 42-44MS 45-47NYG	2 4	6'	176	Minnesota	5	48
Franco, Ed T	44Bos		5'8"	205	Fordham		
Frank, Joe T	41-42Phi 43P-P 44-45MS		6'1"	217	Georgetown		
Frankian, Ike OE-DE	33Bos 34-35NYG 37AFL		5'11"	208	St. Mary's	1	12
Franklin, Paul (Ben) FB-LB-OE-DE-HB-DB	31-33ChiB		6'2"	198	Franklin (Ind.)	2	6
Franklin, Red TB-DB	35-37Bkn	1	5'10"	163	Oregon State		24
Frey, Glenn (Wackie) BB-DB	36-37Phi		5'10"	193	Temple		
Frick, Ray C-LB	41Bkn 42-45MS		6'1"	205	Pennsylvania		
Friedman, Benny TB-DB	27Cle 28Det 29,PC30,31NYG	01	5'10"	183	Michigan	17	185
	PC32,33-34Bkn						
Friedman, Bob T	44Phi		6'2"	215	Washington	1	
Friend, Ben T	39Cle		6'5"	248	Louisiana State		
Fries, Sherwood, G-LB	43GB 44-45MS		6'1"	235	Colorado State	2	
Fritts, George T	45Phi		5'11"	205	Clemson		
Fritz, Ralph G	41Phi 42-45MS		5'9"	202	Michigan		
Frketich, Len T	45Pit		6'1"	290	Penn State		
Fronczek, Andy T	41Bkn 42-45MS		6'	200	Richmond		
Frutig, Ed OE-DB-DE	41GB 42-44MS 45GB 45-46Det	2	6'1"	190	Michigan		18
Fryer, Kenny TB-DB	44Bkn		6'	200	West Virginia		
Fuller, Larry HB-DB-LB	44-45Was 45ChiC		5'10"	192	none		6
Fuqua, Ray OE-DE	35-36Bkn		6'	190	S.M.U.		6
Furst, Tony T	40-41Det 42-43MS 44Det		6'1"	217	Dayton	1	
Gagnon, Roy (Rosy) G	35Det		5'11"	210	Oregon		
Gainor, Charlie DE	39ChiC		6'3"	190	North Dakota		
Galazin, Stan C-LB	37-39NYG		6'3"	211	Villanova		
Gallarneau, Hugh HB-DB	41-42ChiB 43-44MS 45-47ChiB	2	6'	190	Stanford	4	210
Gallovich, Tony WB-DB	41Cle		5'9"	170	Wake Forest		
Gantenbein, Milt OE-DE	31-40GB	0 2	6'	199	Wisconsin	3	48
Garner, Bob G	45NYG		6'	238	none		
Gauer, Charlie DE-FB-OE-LB	43P-P 44-45Phi		6'2"	213	Colgate	2	
Gaziano, Frank G	44Bos		5'8"	218	Holy Cross		
Gelatka, Chuck OE-DB-DE	37-40NYG 41-45MS	2	6'1"	185	Mississippi State		12
Gentry, Byron (Pills) G	37AFL 37-39Pit		5'11"	227	Southern Calif.		
Gentry, Lee FB-DB	41Was 42-45MS		6'	198	Tulsa	1	
George, Ray T	39Det 40Phi		6'	229	Southern Calif.		
Gerber, Woody G	41-42Phi 43-45MS		6'	223	Alabama	1	

UseName(Nicknames)-Positions	TeambyYear	See Section	Hgt	Wgt	College	Int	Pts
German, Jimmy TB-DB	39Was 40ChiC		6'	180	Centre		12
Getto, Mike	HC42Bkn				Pittsburgh		
Geyer, Bill HB-DB	42-43ChiB 44-45MS 46ChiB	2	5'10"	173	Colgate	2	24
Ghecas, Lou HB-DB	41Phi 42-45MS		5'9"	175	Georgetown		
Ghersanich, Vern G-LB	43ChiC		5'11"	210	Auburn	1	
Giannoni, Jack OE-DE	38Cle		6'1"	210	St. Mary's		
Gibson, Butch G-T	30NYG 30Nwk 31-34NYG		5'9"	204	Grove City	1	
Gibson, Joe LB-DE-C-OE-BB	42Cle 43Was 44Cle 45MS		6'3"	213	Tulsa		
	46-47BknAA						
Giddens, Wimpy T	38Phi 44Bos		6'2"	220	Louisiana Tech		
Gifford, Bob BB-LB	42Bkn 43-45MS		6'	200	Denver		
Gift, Wayne BB-DB	37Cle		5'8"	175	Purdue		
Gildea, Johnny TB-BB-DB-LB-HB	35-37Pit 38NYG	12	6'2"	205	St. Boneventure		6
Gill, Sloko C-LB-G	42Det 43-44MS		5'10"	185	Youngstown State	1	
Ginney, Jerry G	40Phi		5'11"	217	Santa Clara		
Gladden, Mack OE-DE	34C-S 36AFL		6'2"	195	Missouri		
Glenn, Bill QB-DB	44ChiB		6'	157	Eastern Illinois		
Gloden, Fred HB-DB	41Phi 42-45MS 46MiaAA	2	5'10"	187	Tulane		6
Goddard, Ed (Rip) TB-DB-WB	37Bkn 37-38Cle	12	5'10"	183	Washington State		20
Godfrey, Herb OE-DE	42Cle		6'1"	187	Washington State		
Goff, Clark T	40Pit 41-45MS		6'3"	235	Florida		
Goldberg, Marshall (Biggie) DB-FB-HB-TB-WB	39-43ChiC	123	5'11"	190	Pittsburgh	17	102
	44-45MS 46-48ChiC						
Goldenberg, Buckets G-LB-BB-DB-FB	33-45GB		5'10"	220	Wisconsin	13	60
Goldsmith, Wen C-LB	40NYG		6'	202	Emporia State		
Golemgeske, John T-G	37-40Bkn		6'2"	225	Wisconsin		
Gollomb, Rudy G	36Phi		5'11"	205	Wisconsin,		
					Carroll (Wis.)		
Gonda, George HB-DB	42Pit 43-45MS		5'10"	175	Duquesne	1	12
Gonya, Bob T-OE-DE	33-34Phi		6'2"	208	Northwestern		6
Goodman, Henry T	42Det 43-45MS		6'3"	220	West Virginia		
Goodnight, Owen TB-DB	41Cle 42-45MS	1	6'	195	Hardin-Simmons	2	
Goodwin, Tod OE-DE	35-36NYG	2	6'	184	West Virginia		36
Goodyear, John WB-DB	42Was 43-45MS		6'	190	Marquette		
Goolsby, Shag C-LB	40Cle		6'2"	195	Mississippi State		
Gordon, Lou T-G-OE-DE	30-31ChiC 31Bkn 32-35ChiC		6'5"	224	Illinois	1	
	36-37GB 38ChiB						
Gore, Gordon WB-DB	37AFL 39Det		6'	215	Southwestern Okla.		
Grabinski, Ted LB-C-G	39-40Pit		6'2"	207	Duquesne		
Graham, Al (Pup) G	25-29Day 30Prov 30Port 31Prov		6'	211	none	1	12
	32-33ChiC						
Graham, Les G	38Det		6'	215	Tulsa		
Graham, Lyle C-LB	41Phi 42-45MS		6'3"	210	Richmond	2	
Graham, Tom G	35Phi		6'3"	210	Temple		
Grandinette, George G	43Bkn		5'9"	215	Fordham		
Grange, Red (The Wheaton Iceman) HB-DB-TB-BB	25ChiB	0 2	5'11"	183	Illinois	10	194
(The Galloping Ghost)	26AFL 27NYY 28KJ 29-34ChiB						
Grant, Len (Fish) T	30-37NYG		6'3"	235	N.Y.U.	1	
	killed by lightning Aug. 6, 1938						
Grant, Rosie G-C-LB	32SI 33Cin 34C-S		5'10"	198	N.Y.U.		
Grate, Carl G-LB	45NYG		6'	215	Georgia		
Graves, Ray C-LB	42Phi 43P-P 44-45MS 46Phi		6'1"	205	Tennessee	2	1
Greene, Frank (Toadie) BB-DB	34ChiC		5'11"	190	Tulsa		
Greeney, Norm G-T	34-35Pit		5'11"	212	Notre Dame		
Greenfield, Tom C-LB	39-41GB 42-44MS		6'4"	213	Arizona		6
Greenich, Duke HB-DB	44ChiB		5'11"	185	Mississippi		
Greenshields, Don T	32-33Bkn		6'1"	190	Penn State		
Grefe, Ted OE-DE	45Det		6'	205	Northwestern		
Gregory, Jack G	40AFL 41Cle		6'2"	210	Tenn.-Chattanooga		
Griffith, Homer TB-DB	34ChiC		5'11'	165	Southern Calif.	1	12
Grigas, John FB-LB-DB	43ChiC 44C-P 45-47Bos	123	6'	204	Holy Cross	8	66
Grigonis, Frank FB-LB	42Det 43-45MS	2	5'10"	182	Tenn.-Chattanooga	1	6
Grossman, Jack DB-TB-FB-WB	32,34-36Bkn	012	6'1"	193	Rutgers	1	55
Grosvenor, George TB-DB-HB	35-36ChiB 36-37ChiC	12	6'	174	Colorado		42
Grove, Roger (Roy) DB-BB-HB	31-35GB	0 2 5	6'	182	Michigan State	14	58
Grygo, Al HB-DB	44-45ChiB	2	5'10"	173	South Carolina	7	18
Gudauskas, Pete G-LB	40Cle 40-41AFL 43-45ChiB	5	6'2"	219	Murray State	2	67
Gudd, Len OE-DE	34Phi		6'3"	220	Temple		
Gudmundson, Scott QB-DB	44-45Bos	12 4	5'10"	178	George Washington	2	
Gundlach, Herman G	35Bos		6'	205	Harvard		
Gussie, Mike G-LB	40Bkn 41-45MS		6'	204	West Virginia		6
Gutknecht, Al G-LB	43Bkn 44Cle		6'	205	Niagara		
Gutowsky, Ace FB-LB-DB-TB	32-33Port 34-38Det 39Bkn	012	5'11"	201	Oklahoma City	5	121
Haak, Bob (Spanky) T-G	39Bkn		6'1"	245	Indiana		
Hackenbruck, Johnny T	40Det 41-45MS		6'2"	215	Oregon State		
Hackney, Elmer FB-LB-DB	40Phi 41Pit 42-46Det	2	6'2"	202	Kansas State	5	72
Haden, Jack T	36-38NYG		6'4"	232	Arkansas		
Haines, By HB-DB	37Pit		5'11"	185	Washington		
Hajek, Chuck C-LB	34Phi		6'1"	210	South Carolina,	1	1
					Northwestern		
Hall, Harold C-LB	42NYG		6'2"	210	Springfield		
Hall, Irv (Shine) FB-LB	42Phi 43-45MS		6'	210	Brown		
Hall, John WB-DB	40-41ChiC 42Det 43ChiC	2	6'	196	Texas Christian	3	60
Hall, Parker (Bullet)TB-DB-QB	39-42Cle 43-45MS 46SF-AA	1234	6'	198	Mississippi	5	36
Halleck, Paul OE-DE	37Cle		6'	195	Ohio U.		
Halverson, Bill T	42Phi 43-45MS		6'3"	242	Oregon State		
Haman, Jack C-LB	40-41Cle 42-45MS		6'1"	212	Northwestern	1	6
Hamilton, Ray OE-DE	38Cle 39Det 44-45Cle 46-47LA	2	6'4"	212	Arkansas		12
Hammond, Henry OE-DE	37ChiB		5'11"	190	Rhodes		
Handler, Phil (Motsy) G	30-36,HC43,45,49ChiC HC44C-P		6'	212	Texas Christian	1	
Hanken, Ray OE-DE	37-38NYG		5'11"	190	George Washington		12
Hanna, Zip G	45Was		5'10"	218	South Carolina		
Hanneman, Chuck OE-DE	37-41Det 41Cle	2 5	6'	209	Eastern Michigan		70
Hansen, Cliff TB-DB-FB-LB	33ChiC		6'1"	190	Luther	1	
Hanson, Homer G-C-LB	34C-S 35ChiC 35Phi 35-36ChiC		6'	217	Kansas State		
Hanson, Swede FB-DB-LB-TB-HB-WB	31Bkn 32SI	0 2	6'1"	192	Temple	6	90
	33-37Phi 38Pit						
Hapes, Merle FB-DB	42NYG 43-45MS 46NYG 47-49DE	2 4	5'10"	190	Mississippi	4	60
Hare, Cecil BB-LB-DB-HB	41-42Was 43-44MS 45Was		5'11"	195	Gonzaga	1	12
	46NYG						
Hare, Ray BB-LB-DB-WB-HB-FB	40-43Was 44Bkn	2	6'1"	204	Gonzaga	5	24
	46NY-AA						
Harmon, Ham C-LB	37ChiC		6'	220	Tulsa		
Harper, Moose C-LB	37-40Phi 41Pit 42-45MS		6'4"	227	Austin		6
Harris, Bill OE-DE	37Pit 37AFL		6'2"	196	Hardin-Simmons		
Harrison, Dick OE-DB	44Bos 45MS		6'	195	Boston College		
Harrison, Gran DE-OE	41Phi 42Det 43-45MS		6'3"	211	Mississippi State		
Harrison, Max OE-DE	40NYG		6'1"	208	Auburn		
Harrison, Pat T	36AFL 37Bkn 37,41AFL		6'2"	215	Samford		

UseName(Nicknames)-Positions	Team by Year	See Section	Hgt	Wgt	College	Int	Pts
Hartman, Bill TB-DB	38Was	12	6'	190	Georgia		
Hartman, Jim OE-DE	36Bkn		6'2"	205	Colorado State		
Hayden, Ken C-LB	42Phi 43Was 44-45MS		6'	205	Arkansas	1	
Hayduk, Henry G	35Pit		6'	200	Washington State		
Heater, Rod T	40Bkn		6'2"	220	Syracuse		
Heikkinen, Ralph G	39Bkn		5'10"	180	Michigan		
Heileman, Charlie OE-DE	39ChiB		6'2"	197	Iowa State		
Hein, Mel C-LB	31-45NYG HC47LA-AA		6'2"	225	Washington State	17	6
Heineman, Ken TB-DB	40Cle 43Bkn 44-45MS	12	5'9"	168	Texas-El Paso	2	1
Heldt, Carl T	35-36Bkn		6'2"	206	Purdue		
Heller, Warren (Fats) TB-DB-HB	34-36Pit	12	5'11"	195	Pittsburgh	3	24
Hempel, Bill T	42ChiB 43-45MS		6'	235	Carroll (Wis.)		
Henderson, Gus	HC39Det				Oberlin		
Herber, Arnie (Flash) TB-DB-QB-BB-HB	30-40GB 44-45NYG	012 4	5'11"	203	Wisconsin, Regis	13	44
Hershey, Kirk OE-DE	41Cle 41Phi 42-45MS		6'2"	215	Carroll (Wis.)		
Hewitt, Bill OE-DE	32-36ChiB 37-39Phi 43P-P	0 2	5'9"	190	Michigan	2	156
Hickman, Herman G	32-34Bkn		5'10"	246	Tennessee		8
Hiemstra, Ed LB-C-G	42NYG 43-45MS		6'	200	Sterling	1	
Higgins, John G-LB	41ChiC 42-45MS		6'1"	200	Trinity (Texas)		
Hightower, Ben OE-DB	42Cle 43Det 44-45MS	2	6'2"	184	Sam Houston St.	1	24
Hill, Harold OE-DE	38-40Bkn	2	6'	200	Samford		
Hill, Irv FB-LB-BB-DB-OE-DE	31-32ChiC 33Bos	0	6'1"	207	Trinity (Texas)		22
Hilpert, Hal OE-DE-WB-DB	30NYG 33Cin		5'9"	188	Oklahoma City		
Hinchman, Curly FB-TB-LB-BB-WB	33-34ChiC 34Det		5'10"	190	Butler	1	
Hinkle, Clarke FB-LB-HB-DB	32-41GB 42-45MS	0 2 45	5'11"	202	Bucknell	10	371
Hinkle, Jack HB-DB-BB-LB	40NYG 41AFL 42MS 43P-P 44-47Phi	2	6'	195	Syracuse	9	42
Hinte, Hal DE	42GB 42Pit		6'1"	195	Pittsburgh		
Hitt, Joel OE-DE	39Cle		6'1"	180	Mississippi Coll.		
Hoague, Joe FB-DB-LB	41-42Pit 43-45MS 46Bos	2	6'2"	203	Colgate	2	18
Hodges, Herman (Country) OE-DE	39-42Bkn 43-45MS	2	6'1"	198	Samford		6
Hoel, Bob G	35Pit 37-38ChiC		6'	208	Pittsburgh		
Hokuf, Steve BB-LB-OE-DE-FB-DB	33-35Bos	1	6'	199	Nebraska	3	4
Holcomb, Tex T	37Pit 37Phi		6'2"	235	Texas Tech		
Holm, Tony FB-LB-TB-DB-BB	30Prov 31Port 32ChiC 33Pit	01	6'1"	214	Alabama	1	12
Holmer, Walt TB-DB-FB-HB-WB-BB	29-30ChiB 31-32ChiC 33Bos 33Pit	0	6'	185	Northwestern	1	38
Hood, Frank HB-DB-BB	33Pit		6'	235	Pittsburgh		
Hopp, Harry FB-DB-TB-LB-QB	41-43Det 44-45MS 46BufAA 46MiaAA 47LA-AA	12 4	6'	209	Nebraska	5	70
Hoptowit, Al T	42-45ChiB		6'1"	217	Washington State		
Hornbeak, Jay BB-DB	35Bkn		5'11"	185	Washington		
Horstmann, Roy FB-LB-DB-WB	33Bos 34ChiC		6'	188	Purdue	1	
Hovious, Junie QB	45NYG	1	5'8"	180	Mississippi		
Howell, Dixie TB-DB	37Was		5'11"	175	Alabama		
Howell, Foster T	34C-S		6'3"	215	Texas Christian		
Howell, Jim Lee OE-DE	37-42NYG 43-45MS 46-48NYG HC54-60NYG	2	6'6"	210	Arkansas		42
Howell, John FB-LB-BB	38GB		5'10"	185	Nebraska		
Hrabetin, Frank T	42Phi 43-45MS 46BknAA 46MiaAA		6'4"	233	Loyola Marymount		
Hubbard, Bud OE-DE	35Bkn		6'	190	San Jose State		6
Hubbard, Cal T-DE-OE-G-LB-C	27-28NYG 29-33,35GB 36Pit 36NYG		6'4"	253	Centenary, Geneva	7	12
Huffman, Frank G-LB	39-41ChiC 42-45MS		6'2"	207	Marshall		
Huffman, Vern TB-DB-BB-WB	37-38Det 38-39 played in N.B.L.	12	6'2"	215	Indiana		12
Huggins, Roy FB-LB	44Cle		5'11"	195	Vanderbilt		
Hughes, Bernie C-LB	34-36ChiC 37AFL		6'1"	192	Oregon		
Hughes, Bill (Hoss) G-C-LB	37-40Phi 41ChiB 42-45MS		6'1"	226	Texas	1	
Hugret, Joe (Sugar) OE-DE	34Bkn		6'2"	195	N.Y.U.		
Humphrey, Paul C-LB	39Bkn 40-41AFL		6'	195	Purdue		
Hunt, Jackie HB-DB	45ChiB		6'	192	Marshall		
Hunter, Ramey OE-DE	33Port		6'	178	Marshall		
Hupke, Tom G-T	34-37Det 38-39Cle		5'10"	192	Alabama		6
Hurley, George G	32-33Bos		6'	200	Washington State		
Hutchinson, Bill QB-DB	40-41AFL 42NYG		5'9"	180	Dartmouth		
Huchinson, Elvin (The Red Oak Express) WB-DB	39Det		5'11"	195	Whittier		
Hutson, Don OE-DB-DE	35-45GB	2 5	6'1"	183	Alabama	30	823
Illowit, Roy T	37Bkn		6'2"	220	C.C.N.Y.		
Ingalls, Bob C-LB	42GB 43-45MS		6'3"	200	Michigan	1	6
Intrieri, Marne G-T-C-LB-DE-OE	32SI 33-34Bos		5'8"	250	Loyola (Balt.)		
Ippolito, Tony G-LB	43ChiB 44-45MS		5'10"	220	Purdue	1	
Irvin, Tex T-FB-LB-G	31Prov 32-35NYG		6'	225	Davis & Elkins		6
Irwin, Don (Bull) FB-DB-WB-TB	PC36AFL 36Bos37-39Was	2	6'1"	196	Colgate		36
Isaacson, Ted T-C	34-35ChiC		6'4"	272	Washington		
Isbell, Cecil TB-DB-HB	38-42GB HC47-49BalAA	12	6'1"	190	Purdue	7	63
Isselhardt, Ralph G	37Det 37Cle		6'1"	205	Franklin (Ohio)		
Itzel, John FB-LB	45Pit		6'	190	Pittsburgh, Georgetown	1	
Ivy, Pop DE-OE	40Pit 40-42ChiC 43-44MS 45-47ChiC HC58-59ChiC HC60-61StL HC62-63HouA	2	6'3"	208	Oklahoma	3	20
Jackson, Don TB-DB	36Phi	12	5'11"	184	North Carolina		
Jacunski, Harry OE-DE	39-44GB	2	6'2"	200	Fordham	1	36
Janecek, Clarence (Janny) G	33Pit		6'	200	Purdue		
Janiak, Len DB-FB-BB-WB	39Bkn 40-42Cle 43-45MS	2	6'1"	203	Ohio U.	1	6
Jankowski, Ed FB-LB	37-41GB 42-45MS	2	5'9"	201	Wisconsin	1	67
Jarvi, Toimi DB-TB-HB	44Phi 45Pit		6'	200	Northern Illinois	1	
Jefferson, Billy TB-DB-HB	41Det 42Phi 42Bkn	12	6'2"	208	Mississippi State	1	12
Jeffries, Bob G	42Bkn 43-45MS		6'2"	206	Missouri		
Jett, John OE-DE	41Det		6'7"	225	Wake Forest		
Jocher, Art G	40,42Bkn 43-45MS		6'1"	205	Manhatten		6
Johnson, Bert (Man O' War) DB-LB-FB-BB-TB-HB-WB	37Bkn 38-39ChiB 39-41ChiC 42Phi	12	6'	212	Kentucky	1	30
Johnson, Bill DE	41GB 42-45MS		6'1"	196	Minnesota		
Johnson, Cecil TB-DB-HB	43-44Bkn 45MS	12 4	5'11"	197	East Texas State	1	12
Johnson, Chief LB-C-OE-DE	33-35Bos 36AFL 36-39NYG 44Was		6'3"	223	Haskell Indian		
Johnson, Don C-LB	42Cle 43-45MS		6'	205	Northwestern		
Johnson, Jack T	34-40Det		6'4"	216	Utah		12
Johnson, Lorne FB-LB	34Phi		6'2"	195	Temple		
Johnson, Ray DB-TB-FB	37-38Cle 40AFL		6'1"	195	Denver		
Johnson, Smiley G-LB	40-41GB 42-44MS — Killed in action		5'9"	198	Georgia	1	
Johnsos, Luke OE-DE	29-36,HC42-45ChiB	0 2	6'2"	195	Northwestern	2	163
Johnston, Jimmy DB-FB-WB-HB	39-40Was 41-45MS 46ChiC	2	6'1"	193	Washington	1	49
Johnston, Swede FB-LB-DB-G-WB	34GB 34C-S 35-38GB 39-40Pit	2	5'10"	197	Elmhurst, Marquette		30

UseName(Nicknames)-Positions	Team by Year	See Section	Hgt	Wgt	College	Int	Pts
Jones, Art DB-HB-TB	41Pit 42-44MS 45Pit	2 4	6'2"	192	Richmond	8	30
Jones, Bob G	34GB		6'2"	215	Indiana		
Jones, Bruce G-T-DE-OE	27-28GB 30Nwk 32-34Bkn		6'1"	219	Alabama	1	
Jones, Ellis G-LB	45Bos		6'	190	Tulsa		
Jones, Harvey DB-FB-HB	44-45Cle 47Was	2	6'	175	Baylor	5	12
Jones, Lew G-LB	43Bkn 44-45MS		6'	215	Weatherford J.C.	1	
Jones, Potsy G	30Fra and 30Min 31Fra 32-36NYG 37AFL 38GB		5'11"	216	Bucknell		
Jones, Thurman FB-DB	41-42Bkn 43-45MS		5'10"	198	Abilene Christian		1
Jorgensen, Carl T	34GB 35Phi		6'	205	St. Mary's		4
Jorgensen, Wagner C-LB	36-37Bkn		6'2"	215	St. Mary's		
Jurich, Mike T	41-42Bkn 43-45MS		6'1"	230	Denver		
Justice, Ed WB-DB-OE	36Bos 37-42Was 43-45MS	2	6'1"	200	Gonzaga	3	66
Kabealo, Mike HB-DB	44Cle	2	5'8"	185	Ohio State	2	6
Kahler, Bob DB-HB	42-44GB 45MS		6'3"	201	Nebraska		
Kahler, Royal T	41Pit 42GB		6'2"	226	Nebraska		
Kahn, Eddie (King Kong) G	35-36Bos 37Was		5'9"	194	North Carolina		6
Kakasic, George (Bunko) G 39 played as George Kase	36-39Pit		5'10"	200	Duquesne		15
Kamp, Jim T-G	32SI 33Bos		6'	210	Oklahoma City		
Kane, Carl HB-DB	36Phi		5'11"	195	St. Louis		
Kane, Herb T	44-45NYG		6'1"	218	EC Oklahoma		
Kapitnansky, Bernie G	42Bkn 43-45MS		6'1"	212	Long Island U.		
Kaplan, Bernie G	35-36NYG 42Phi		6'	208	Western Maryland		
Kaplanoff, Carl T-G	39Bkn 40AFL		6'	235	Ohio State		
Kaporch, Al T-G-LB	43-45Det		5'10"	215	St. Boneventure	3	
Karamatic, George (Automatic) FB-DB	38Was 40AFL	2	5'8"	187	Gonzaga		11
Karcher, Jim G	36Bos 37-39Was 40AFL		6'	205	Ohio State		
Karcis, Bull (Five Yards) FB-LB-BB	32-35Bkn 36-38Pit 38-39NYG HC42Det 43NYG	0 2	5'9"	223	Carnegie-Mellon	2	73
Karpowich, Ed T 38-39 played as Ed Karp	36-39Pit 40AFL		6'4"	223	Catholic		
Karr, Bill OE-DE	33-38ChiB	2	6'1"	190	West Virginia	1	120
Karrs, John BB-LB	44Cle		6'1"	210	Duquesne		
Kaska, Tony FB-LB-BB-DB	35Det 36-38Bkn		5'11"	193	Illinois Wesleyan		6
Kasky, Ed T	42Phi 43-45MS		6'1"	220	Villanova		
Kassel, Chuck OE-DE	27ChiB 27-28Fra 29-33ChiC	0	6'1"	191	Illinois	4	48
Katalinas, Leo T	38GB		6'2"	240	Catholic		
Kavel, George HB-DB	34Pit 34Phi		5'11"	170	Cenegie-Mellon		
Kawal, Eddie C-LB-G-T	31,34-36ChiB 37Was		6'2"	200	Illinois, Widener		6
Keahey, Duce T-G	41AFL 42NYG 42Bkn 43-45MS		6'2"	215	George Washington		
Keeble, Joe TB-WB-DB	36-37AFL 37Cle		6'	190	U.C.L.A.		6
Keeling, Ray (King Kong) T	38-39Phi		6'3"	259	Texas		
Keen, Rabbit WB-DB-HB-TB	37-38Phi	2	5'9"	170	Arkansas		
Keenan, Jack T-G	44-45Was		5'10"	214	South Carolina		
Keene, Bob WB-DB	43-45Det		5'11"	191	Detroit	2	12
Kell, Paul T	39-40GB		6'2"	217	Notre Dame		
Kellogg, Bob TB-DB	40ChiC		5'10"	175	Tulane		
Kellogg, Clarence FB-DB	36ChiC	2	5'10"	205	St. Mary's		9
Kelly, Elmo DE	44ChiB		6'1"	210	Wichita State		
Kelly, Shipwreck DB-TB-WB-FB	32NYG 33-34,37Bkn	0 2	6'2"	190	Kentucky	2	49
Kelsch, Mose HB-FB-DB-LB	33-34Pit killed in auto accident July, 1935		5'10"	223	none		16
Kemp, Ray T	33Pit		6'1"	215	Duquesne		
Kenneally, George (Gus) OE-DE-G	26-28Pott 29Bos 30ChiC 32Bos 33-35Phi HC36-37AFL	0	6'	190	St. Boneventure		
Kennedy, Tom T	44Det		6'	218	Wayne State		
Kerasiotis, Nick G-LB	41AFL 42ChiB 43-44MS 45ChiB		5'11"	195	St. Ambrose		
Kercher, Bob DE	44GB		6'2"	196	Georgetown		
Kercheval, Ralph DB-HB-TB-WB	34-40Bkn 41-45MS	12 45	6'1"	190	Kentucky	1	185
Ketzko, Alex T	43Det 44MS-killed in action		5'11"	215	Michigan State		
Kichefski, Walt OE-DE	40-42Pit 43MS 44C-P	2	6'1"	212	Miami (Fla.)		6
Kiesling, Walt (Babe) G-T	26-27Dul 28Pott 29-33ChiC 34ChiB 35-36GB 37-38,HC39-42Pit HC43P-P HC44C-P HC54-56Pit		6'2"	249	St. Thomas	1	
Kiick, George DB-FB-HB	40Pit 41-44MS 45Pit	2	6'	198	Bucknell		6
Kilbourne, Wally (Cleats) T	39GB 40-41AFL		6'3"	240	Minnesota		
Kimble, Frank OE-DE	45Pit		6'5"	205	West Virginia		
Kinard, Bruiser T	38-44Bkn 45MS 46-47NY-AA	5	6'1"	216	Mississippi	1	42
Kinard, George G-LB	41-42Bkn 43 45MS 46NY-AA		6'1"	202	Mississippi		
Kinek, Mike DE-OE	40Cle		6'1"	200	Michigan State		
King, Fred BB-LB	37Bkn		6'2"	205	Hobart		
Kinscherf, Carl FB-DB	43-44NYG	2 4	6'1"	188	Colgate	1	6
Kirkland, Bo G	35-36Bkn		6'	215	Alabama		
Kirkman, Red BB-DB-TB	33-35Phi	1	6'1"	195	Case Reserve, Washington & Jeff.		19
Kish, Ben LB-FB-BB-DB	40-41Bkn 42MS 43P-P 44-49Phi	2	6'	207	Pittsburgh	16	25
Kissell, Adolph HB-DB	42ChiB 43-45MS		5'11"	190	Boston College		
Kizzire, Lee FB-LB	37Det		6'	200	Wyoming		
Klewicki, Ed OE-DE-WB	35-38Det	2	5'10"	209	Michigan State		18
Kline, Jiggs DE-OE	39-40,42NYG 43-44MS		6'1"	196	Emporia State		6
Kloppenburg, Harry OE-DE-G	30SI 31,33-34Bkn		6'1"	210	Fordham	2	
Klotovich, Mike WB-DB	45NYG		5'10"	180	St. Mary's		
Klumb, John OE-DE	39-40ChiC 40Pit		6'3"	200	Washington State		
Knapper, Jack HB-DB	34Phi		6'3"	190	Ottawa (Kan.)	1	
Knolla, John DB-HB-TB-WB	42ChiC 43-44MS 45ChiC	2	5'10"	180	Creighton	1	
Knorr, Larry OE-DE-DB	42Det 43-44MS 45Det		6'2"	194	Dayton		
Knox, Charlie T	37Phi		5'11"	185	St. Edmonds		
Knox, Sam (Dutch) G-T	34-36Det		6'	213	Illinois, New Hampshire		
Kober, Matt G	40Bkn		5'10"	190	Villanova		
Kobrosky, Mickey QB-DB	37NYG		6'	187	Trinity (Conn.)		
Kochel, Mike G-LB	39ChiC		5'11"	195	Fordham		
Koeninger, Art C-LB-T	31Fra 32SI 33Phi		6'1"	202	Tenn.-Chattanooga	1	
Koken, Mike TB-DB-BB	33ChiC		5'11"	180	Notre Dame		1
Kolberg, Elmer OE-DB-DE-HB	39-40Phi 41Pit	2	6'4"	199	Oregon State		
Kolman, Ed T	40-42ChiB 43-45MS 46-47ChiB 49NYG		6'2"	232	Temple		
Kondria, John T	45Pit		6'	185	St. Vincent		
Konetsky, Floyd DE	44-45Cle 47BalAA		6'	197	Florida	1	
Koons, Joe C-LB	41Bkn 42-45MS		6'2"	195	Scranton		
Kopcha, Joe (Doc) G-T	29ChiB 30-31VR 32-35ChiB 36Det		6	221	Tenn.-Chattanooga		3
Kopf, Herb	HC44-46Bos				Washington & Jeff.		
Korisky, Ed C-LB	44Bos		6'1"	210	Villanova	1	
Kosel, Stan FB-DB-BB-LB	38-39Bkn		5'11"	190	Albright		6
Koshlap, Julie HB-DB	45Pit		5'11"	180	Georgetown		
Kostiuk, Mike T	40AFL 41Cle 42-44MS 45Det		6'	212	Detroit Tech		
Kostka, Stan FB-LB	35Bkn		5'11"	215	Oregon, Minnesota		
Kottler, Marty (Butch) FB-LB	33Pit		5'9"	180	Centre	1	6

UseName(Nicknames)-Positions	Team by Year	See Section	Hgt	Wgt	College	Int	Pts
Kovatch, Johnny OE-DE	38Cle		5'11"	172	Northwestern		6
Kowalski, Andy DE-OE	43-44Bkn 45Bos	2	6'1"	199	Mississippi State	1	6
Kracum, George FB-DB	41Bkn 42-45MS	2	6'1"	212	Pittsburgh	1	18
Krause, Bill T	38Cle		6'	210	Baldwin-Wallace		
Krause, Max (Bananas) BB-DB-LB-FB-WB	33-36NYG	2	5'10"	202	Gonzaga		37
	37-40Was						
Krause, Red C-LB-G	36-37Bkn 37-38Was		6'1"	212	St. Louis		
Krejci, Joe OE-DE	34ChiC		6'	190	Peru State		
Kresky, Joe (Mink) G-T	32Bos 33-35Phi 35Pit 35Phi		6'	215	Wisconsin		
Krieger, Bob OE-DE	41Phi 42-45MS 46Phi	2	6'1"	190	Dartmouth		12
Kriel, Emmett (Sally) G	39Phi		6'2"	200	Baylor		
Kring, Frank LB	45Det		6'	190	Texas Christian		
Kristufek, Frank T	40-41Bkn 42-45MS		6'	209	Pittsburgh		
Krol, Joe DB	45Det		6'1"	210	Western Ontario		
Krueger, Al OE-DE-DB	41-42Was 43-45MS 46LA-AA	2	6'1"	188	Southern Calif.	1	12
Kubale, Ed	HC44Bkn				Centre		
Kuczynski, Bert OE-DE	43Det 44-45MS 46Phi		6'	196	Pennsylvania		6
	43played major league baseball						
Kuharich, Joe G-LB	40-41ChiC 42-44MS 45,HC52ChiC	5	5'11"	195	Notre Dame	1	12
	HC54-58Was HC64-68Phi						
Kupcinet, Irv BB-DB	35Phi		6'1"	190	Northwestern, North Dakota		
Kurth, Joe T	33-34GB		6'1"	202	Notre Dame		
Kusko, John FB-LB-DB-BB-TB-HB	36-38Phi	12	5'11'	194	Temple		6
Kuusisto, Bill G	41-46GB		6'	228	Minnesota		
Kvaternick, Zvonimir G	34Pit		5'11"	210	Kansas		
Lackman, Rick HB-DB-TB	33-35Phi		5'11"	186	none	1	1
LaFitte, Bill OE	44Bkn 45MS		6'1"	170	Ouachita Baptist		
Lainhart, Porter BB-DB	33Phi		6'	180	Washington State		
Lajousky, Bill G	36Pit		5'11"	200	Catholic		
Lamas, Joe G	42Pit 43-45MS		5'10"	216	Mt. St. Mary's		6
Lamb, Roddy TB-DB-BB-WB	25RI 26-27,33ChiC	0	5'6"	160	Lombard	5	40
Landsberg, Mort HB-DB	41Phi 42-45MS 47LA-AA	2	5'11"	180	Cornell	2	
Landsdell, Grenny QB-DB	40NYG 41-44MS		6'	190	Southern Calif.		
Lane, Les G	39Bkn 40AFL		6'3"	193	South Dakota		
Lankas, Jim FB-LB	42Phi 43GB 44-45MS		6'2"	220	St. Mary's		
Lantz, Mose C-LB	33Pit		5'11"	185	Grove City		
Lapka, Ted OE-DE	43-44Was 45MS 46Was		6'1"	193	St. Ambrose		12
LaPresta, Benny BB-LB-DB	33Bos 34C-S		5'9"	185	St. Louis		1
Lascari, John OE-DE	42NYG 43-45MS		6'2"	210	Georgetown		6
Lassahn, Lou T-DE	38Pit		6'	205	Western Maryland		
Laux, Ted HB-DB	43P-P 44Phi		5'10"	185	St. Joseph's-Pa.	1	2
Law, Hubbard G-LB	42Pit 43-44MS 45Pit		6'1"	210	Sam Houston St.	1	
Lawrence, Jimmy WB-DB-TB	36-39ChiC 39GB	2	5'11"	190	Texas Christian		24
Laws, Joe HB-DB-BB	34-45GB	123	5'9"	186	Iowa	22	126
Lay, Russ G	34Det 34C-S		5'11"	198	Michigan State		
Layden, Bob DE	43Det		6'2"	215	Southwestern (Kan.)		
Lazetich, Bill WB-DB	39,42Cle 43-45MS	2	6'	198	Montana		18
Leathers, Red G	33Phi		5'11"	198	Georgia		
Lechner, Ed G-T	42NYG 43-45MS		6'1"	200	Minnesota		
Lechthaler, Roy G	33Phi		5'10"	198	Lebanon Valley		
Leckonby, Bill (Wild Bill) TB-DB	39-41Bkn 42-45MS	12	6'1"	185	St. Lawrence	3	18
Ledbetter, Doc FB-LB-WB-DB	32SI 32-33ChiC	0	5'10"	190	Arkansas		12
Lee, Bernie BB-LB	38Phi 38Pit		5'11"	190	Villanova		
Lee, Biff G	31Port 31Cle 33Cin 34C-S		6'	226	Missouri, Oklahoma		4
Lee, Bill T	35-37Bkn 37-42GB 43-45MS 46GB		6'2"	231	Alabama		
Lee, Jack (Whitey) BB-LB	39Pit		5'10"	205	Carnegie-Mellon		
Leemans, Tuffy FB-DB-QB	36-43NYG	12	6'	195	Oregon, George Washington	3	120
LeFebvre, Gil (Frenchy) TB-WB-DB	33Cin 34C-S 35Det		5'6"	155	none		6
	37AFL						
Leisk, Rube G	37Bkn		6'	195	Louisiana State		
Lenc, George (Chilly) OE-DE	39Bkn 40AFL		6'3"	204	Augustana (Ill.)		
Leon, Tony G-LB	43Was 44Bkn 45-46Bos		5'9"	203	Alabama	1	
Leonard, Jim BB-FB-DB-LB-TB-HB	34-37Phi HC45Pit	12	6'	202	Notre Dame		18
Lester, Darrell C-LB	37-38GB		6'3"	220	Texas Christian		
Letlow, Russ G	36-42GB 43-45MS 46GB		6'	214	San Francisco		
Letsinger, Jim G	33Pit		5'10"	190	Purdue		
Levanitis, Steve T	42Phi 43-45MS		6'1"	220	Boston College		
Levey, Jim HB-DB-TB	34-36Pit	2	5'10"	163	none		24
	30-33 played major league baseball						
Lewis, Art (Pappy) T-G	36NYG PC38,39Cle		6'3"	226	Ohio U.		6
Lewis, Bill BB-DB	34C-S		5'11"	186	none		
Leyendecker, Tex T-C-LB	33Phi		6'1"	235	Vanderbilt		
Liebel, Frank OE-DE-DB	42-47NYG 48ChiC	2	6'1"	211	Norwich	7	144
Lieberum, Don WB-DB	42NYG 43-45MS		6'	175	Manchester		
Liles, Sonny G-LB	43-45Det 45Cle		5'9"	188	Oklahoma State	2	
Lillard, Joe TB-DB	32-33ChiC	0	6'	185	Oregon	3	21
Lindahl, Virgil G-LB-OE	45NYG		6'1"	197	Wayne St.-Neb., Kentucky		
Lind, Al C-LB	36ChiC		5'10"	185	Northwestern		
Lindon, Luke T	40AFL 44-45Det		5'10"	243	Kentucky		
Lindow, Al HB-DB	45ChiC		6'	165	Washington-St.L.		
Lio, Augie G-LB	41-43Det 44-45Bos 46Phi 47BalAA	5	6'	234	Georgetown	10	172
Lipski, Bull C-LB	33-34Phi		5'11"	200	Temple	3	
Little, Jim T	45NYG		6'1"	200	Kentucky		
Littlefield, Carl (Moon Eyes) DB-FB-TB	38Cle 39Pit 40AFL	2	6'	200	Washington State		6
Livingston, Ted T-G	37-40Cle 41AFL		6'3"	219	Indiana		
Logan (born Wyhowanec), Andy T	41Det 42-45MS		6'	222	Case Reserve		
Logan, Jim G	43ChiB 44-45MS		5'11"	190	Indiana		
Lokanc, Joe G-LB	41ChiC 42-45MS		5'11'	205	Northwestern		
Long, John QB-DB	44-45ChiB	2	6'	185	Colgate		
Looney, Don OE-DB	40Phi 41-42Pit 43-45MS	2	6'2"	182	Texas Christian		42
Lowther, Russ TB-DB	44Det 45Pit		5'8"	165	Detroit	1	
Lubratovich, Lou T	31-35Bkn		6'2"	230	Wisconsin	3	
Lucente, John FB-LB	45Pit	2	5'9"	200	West Virginia		12
Luckman, Sid QB-DB-HB	39-50ChiB	12 4	6'	197	Columbia	14	37
Lummus, Jack OE-DE	41NYG 42-44MS-killed in action		6'3"	194	Baylor		
Lumpkin, Father BB-DB-LB-FB-TB	30-33Port 34Det	0	6'2"	211	Georgia Tech	13	54
	35-37Bkn						
Lunday, Kayo LB-G-C	37-41NYG 42-45MS 46-47NYG		6'3"	217	Arkansas	1	
Lyman, Del T	41GB 41,44Cle		6'3"	223	U.C.L.A.		
Lyman, Link T	22-23Can 24Cle 25Can 25Fra		6'2"	233	Nebraska	3	37
	27-28,30-31,33-34ChiB						
Lyon, Babe T-G	29NYG 30Port 31ChiB 31Cle		6'2"	235	Kansas State		
	32Bkn 34C-S 36AFL						

UseName(Nicknames)-Positions	Team by Year	See Section	Hgt	Wgt	College	Int	Pts
Lyons, John OE-DE	33Bkn		6'1"	185	Tulsa		
Mackenroth, Jack C-LB	38Det		6'2"	215	North Dakota		
Mackorell, John TB-DB	35NYG		5'10"	178	Davidson		
MacLeod, Bob HB-DB 39-40 played in N.B.L.	39ChiB	2	6'	190	Dartmouth		30
MacMurdo, Jim (Big Jim) T-G	32-33Bos 34-37Phi		6'1"	209	Pittsburgh	1	6
Madden, Lloyd WB-DB	40ChiC	2	6'1"	195	Colorado Mines		18
Maddock, Bob G-LB	42ChiC 43-45MS 46ChiC		6'	200	Notre Dame		
Maddox, Buster T	35GB		6'3"	240	Kansas State		
Maeda, Chet HB-DB	45ChiC		5'10"	187	Colorado State		
Magee, Jim C-LB	44-46Bos		6'1"	202	Villanova	1	
Magulick, George HB-DB	44C-P		5'9"	150	St. Francis (Pa.)	2	
Maher, Frank DB	41Pit 41Cle 42-45MS		6'1"	195	Toledo		
Malkovich, Joe (Hunk) C-LB	35Pit		6'3"	205	Duquesne		
Malloy, Les BB-DB-WB-TB	31-33ChiC		6'	200	Loyola (Chic.)	1	6
Malone, Charley (Chuck) OE-DE	34-36Bos	2	6'4"	206	Texas A&M		78
	37-40,42Was 43MS						
Mandarino, Mike C-G-T	44-45Phi		5'11"	240	LaSalle		
Manders, Jack FB-LB-HB-DB	33-40ChiB	2 5	6'	203	Minnesota	4	363
Manders, Pug FB-LB-DB-BB	39-44Bkn 45Bos	12	6'	202	Drake	10	234
	46NY-AA 47BufAA						
Maniaci, Joe FB-LB-HB-DB-TB	36-38Bkn 38-41ChiB	2 5	6'1"	212	Fordham		140
	42-45MS						
Manske, Eggs OE-DE-HB-DB	35-36Phi 37ChiB 38Pit	2	6'	185	Northwestern		84
	38-40ChiB						
Manton, Tilly BB-LB-DB	36-38NYG 38Was 43Bkn	2 5	5'11"	188	Texas Christian		53
Manzini, Bap C-LB	44-45,48Phi		5'11"	195	St. Vincent	1	
Manzo, Joe T	45Det		6'1"	220	Boston College		
Maples, Tal (Sheriff) C-LB	34C-S		6'	195	Tennessee		
Maras, Joe C-LB-T	38-40Pit		6'1"	203	Duquesne		
Marchi, Basilio G-C-LB	34Pit 42Phi 43-45MS		6'2"	220	N.Y.U.		
Marcus, Pete DE	44Was		6'2"	200	Kentucky		
Marefos, Andy (Anvil Andy) FB-DB-QB-LB	41-42NYG	12	6'	223	St. Mary's	3	62
	43-45MS 46LA-AA						
Marek, Jodey FB-LB	43Bkn		5'11"	182	Texas Tech		
Margarita, Hank HB-DB	44-46ChiB	2	5'11"	178	Brown	9	54
Mark, Lou LB-D-DE	38-40Bkn 41-44MS 45Bos		6'	196	N. Carolina State		
Marker, Harry BB-DB	34Pit		5'6"	155	West Virginia		
Marko, Steve TB-DB	44Bkn		6'	200	none		
Markov, Vic G-T	38Cle		6'	215	Washington		
Marone, Sal G	43NYG		5'10"	195	Manhatten		
Maronic, Steve T	39-40Det		6'	225	North Carolina		
Marotti, Lou G	40AFL 43ChiC 44C-P 45ChiC		5'10"	210	Toledo		
Marsh, Dick G	33NYG		6'2"	200	Phillips, Oklahoma		
Martin, Frank DB-HB-WB	43-44Bkn 45Bos 45NYG	2	5'10"	177	Alabama	4	6
Martin, John DB-WB-HB	41-43ChiC 44C-P 44-45Bos	234	6'1"	195	Oklahoma	12	24
Martin, Vern BB-LB	42Pit 43-45MS		5'10"	195	Texas		12
Mason, Joel OE-DE-DB	39ChiC 40-41AFL 42-45GB	2	6'	201	Western Michigan		12
	42-43 played, 46-47 coached in N.B.L.						
Masters, Bob (Chief) DB-HB-LB-FB-WB-BB-TB	37-38Phi	2	5'11"	200	Baylor		
	39Pit 42Phi 43P-P 43-44ChiB						
Masters, Walt TB-DB-QB	36Phi 43ChiC 44C-P	1	5'10"	192	Pennsylvania		
	31,37,39 played major league baseball						
Masterson, Bernie QB-DB	34-40ChiB	12	6'3"	195	Nebraska	1	50
Masterson, Bob OE-DE	38-43Was 44Bkn 45Bos 46BY-AA	2 5	6'1"	213	Miami (Fla.)	2	173
Masterson, Forest C-G	45ChiB		6'3"	246	Iowa		
Matesic, Ed (Dick) TB-DB	34-35Phi 36Pit 37AFL	12	6'1"	198	Pittsburgh	1	13
Matheson, Jack OE-DE	43-46Det 47ChiB	2	6'2"	221	Western Michigan	2	38
Matheson, Riley G-LB	39-42Cle 43Det 44-45Cle		6'2"	207	Texas-El Paso	14	
	46-47LA 48SF-AA						
Mathews, Ned DB-HB-WB-TB	41-43Det 45Bos	12	5'10"	187	U.C.L.A.	18	78
	PC46ChiAA 46-47SF-AA						
Matisi, John T	43Bkn 44-45MS 46BufAA		6'2"	218	Duquesne	1	
Matisi, Tony T	38Det		6'2"	230	Pittsburgh		
Mattiford, John G	41Det 42-45MS		5'10"	216	Marshall		
Mattos, Harry (The Toe, Horse) TB-DB	36GB 36-37AFL	12	6'	198	St. Mary's		8
	37Cle						
Matuza, Al C-LB	41-43ChiB 44-45MS 46JJ		6'2"	200	Georgetown	4	
May, Bill BB-LB	37-38ChiC		5'11"	188	Louisiana State		10
May, Jack C-LB	38Cle		5'10"	210	Centenary		
Mayhew, Lindy G-T	36-38Pit		6'1"	223	Texas-El Paso		
McAdams, Dean TB-DB-HB	41-43Bkn	12 4	6'1"	193	Washington	4	11
McAfee, Wes HB-DB	41Phi 42-45MS		5'11"	175	Duke		8
McBride, Charlie BB-LB	36AFL 36ChiC		5'10"	185	Washington State		6
McBride, Jack DB-FB-TB-BB	25-28NYG 29Prov	0	5'11"	186	Syracuse	17	287
	30-32Bkn 32-34NYG HC36AFL						
McCarthy, John QB-DB	44C-P	1	5'8"	160	St. Francis (Pa.)		
McChesney, Bob OE-DE	36Bos 37-42Was 43-45MS	2	6'2"	195	U.C.L.A.		42
McCalin, Red FB-DB	41NYG 42-45MS		5'9"	182	S.M.U.	1	12
McCrary, Hurdis FB-LB-HB-DB-TB	29-33GB	0	6'	207	Georgia	7	66
McCullough, Harold TB-DB	42Bkn	1	5'11"	170	Cornell		
McCullough, Hugh DB-TB-QB	39Pit 40-41ChiC	12 4	6'	185	Oklahoma		25
	42MS 43P-P 45Bos						
McDade, Karl C-LB	38Pit		6'3"	195	Portland		
McDonald, Flip OE-DB-DE	44Bkn 44-46Phi 48NY-AA	2	6'2"	200	Oklahoma	1	6
McDonald, Jim HB-DB	36Pit		6'	195	Duquesne		
McDonald, Jim DB-WB-BB-FB	38-39Det	2	6'1"	193	Ohio State		
McDonald, Les OE-DE	37-39ChiB 40Phi 40Det	2	6'4"	202	Nebraska		49
McDonald, Walt C-LB	35Bkn		5'10"	210	Utah		
McDonough, Coley TB-DB-QB	39ChiC 39-41Pit	12	6'1"	189	Dayton		12
	42-43MS 44C-P						
McDonough, Paul OE-DE-WB	38Pit 39-41Cle 42-45MS	2	6'4"	222	Utah		24
McEnulty, Doug HB-DB	43-44ChiB	4	6'3"	221	Wichita State	2	12
McEwen, Cap	HC33-34Bkn				Minnesota, Army		
McFadden, Banks HB-DB	40Bkn 41-45MS	2	6'2"	180	Clemson		18
McGarry, Barney G-LB	39-42Cle 43-45MS		6'1"	203	Utah		
McGee, Bob T	38ChiC		6'	210	Santa Clara		
McGee, Ed T	40AFL 40NYG 44-46Bos		6'1"	224	Temple	1	
McGibbony, Charlie TB-DB	44Bkn	12	5'10"	160	Central Arkansas		
McGirl, Len G	34C-S		6'	206	Missouri		
McKalip, Bill OE-DE-WB-DB	31-32Port 34,36Det	0	6'1"	195	Oregon State		24
McKay, Tex DB-TB-FB-HB	44-47GB	12 4	6'	193	Texas	4	21
McLaughlin, Charlie TB-DB	34C-S		6'	183	Wichita State		
McLaughlin, Lee G	41GB 42-45MS		6'1"	226	Virginia		
McLaughry, John BB-LB	40NYG		6'1"	205	Brown		
McLean, Ray (Scooter) HB-DB	40-47ChiB HC53,58GB	23 5	5'10"	167	St. Anselm's	17	225
McLeod, Russ C-LB	34C-S		6'	190	St. Louis		
McMichaels, John TB-DB	44Bkn		5'11"	180	Birmingham-South.		
McNally, Frank C-LB-T-G	31-34ChiC		6'1"	203	St. Mary's	1	8
McNamara, Ed T	45Pit		6'2"	225	Holy Cross		
McPhail, Hal (Bumper) FB-DB	34-35Bos 37AFL		6'1"	230	Army, Xavier-Ohio	4	22

UseName(Nicknames)-Positions	Team by Year	See Section	Hgt	Wgt	College	Int	Pts
McPherson, Amy C-G-T-LB	35ChiB 35-37Phi 43-45GB		5'11"	233	Nebraska		
McRaven, Bill (Bullet Bill) WB-DB	39Cle 40AFL		5'11"	170	Murray State		
McRoberts, Bob HB-DB	44Bos		5'11"	190	Wisconsin-Stout		
McWilliams, Bill WB-DB	34Det		6'	200	Iowa		
	31 played major league baseball						
Meade, Jim DB-WB-FB	39-40Was 41-45MS	2	6'1"	197	Maryland		
Mecham, Curt TB-DB	42Bkn 43-45MS		6'	180	Oregon		
Mehringer, Pete (Champ) T-G	34-36ChiC 37AFL		6'2"	206	Kansas		
Mellus, John T	38-41NYG 42-45MS 46SF-AA		6'	214	Villanova		7
	47-49BalAA						
Mergenthal, Art G-LB	40AFL 45Cle 46LA		5'11"	215	Notre Dame		
Merkel, Monte G	43ChiB 44-45MS		5'10"	215	Kansas		
Merkle, Ed G-LB	44Was 45MS		5'10"	215	Oklahoma State		
Merkovsky, Al T-G	44C-P 45-46Pit		6'1"	223	Pittsburgh		
Merlin, Ed G	38-39Bkn 40AFL		5'10"	210	Vanderbilt		
Merril, Walt T	40-42Bkn 43-45MS		6'2"	217	Alabama		
Mesak, Dick T	45Det		6'2"	225	St. Mary's		
Meyer, Fred OE-DE	42Phi 43-44MS 45Phi	2	6'2"	193	Stanford		12
Michaels (born Mikolajewski), Eddie (Whitey) G	36ChiB		5'11"	205	Villanova		
	37Was 43P-P 44-46Phi 47CFL						
Michalske, Mike G-T-LB-BB	27-28NYY 29-35,37GB		6'	210	Penn State	4	14
Midler, Lou G-T	39Pit 40GB		6'1"	223	Minnesota		
Mielziner, Saul C-T-G-LB	29-30NYG 31-34Bkn		6'1"	245	Carnegie-Mellon		
Mihal, Joe T	40-41ChiB 42-45MS 46LA-AA 47ChiAA		6'3"	234	Purdue		
Mikulak, Mike (Iron Mike) FB-LB-BB-WB-DB	34-36ChiC	2	6'1"	210	Oregon		30
Milam, Barnes G-T	34Phi				Austin		
Milano, Arch OE-DE	45Det		6'	197	St. Francis (Pa.)		
Miller, Dub G-T	35ChiB 36-37ChiC		6'	218	Chadron State		
Miller, Eddie QB-DB	39-40NYG 41-45MS	12	5'10"	165	New Mexico State		12
Miller, Ookie C-LB-G	32-36ChiB 37Cle 38GB		6'	209	Purdue	1	6
Miller, Paul HB-DB	36-38GB	2	5'11"	180	S. Dakota State		24
Miller, Primo T	37-38Cle		6'2"	220	Rice		6
Miller, Tom DE-OE	43P-P 44Phi 45Was 46GB	2	6'2"	202	Hampden-Sydney	2	12
Milling, Al G	42Phi		5'9"	170	Richmond		
Millner, Wayne OE-DE	36Bos 37-41Was 42-44MS	2	6'1"	190	Notre Dame		78
	45Was HC51Phi						
Mitchell, Buster (Tex) OE-DE-T	31-33Port 34-35Det	0 2	6'	205	Davis & Elkins	1	6
	35-36NYG 37Bkn						
Moan, Kelly TB-DB	39Cle		6'	193	West Virginia		1
Moe, Hal WB-DB	33ChiC		5'10"	182	Oregon State	1	12
Molenda, Bo FB-LB-BB	27-28NYY 28-32GB 32-35NYG	0	5'10'	210	Michigan	24	108
Molesworth, Keith (Rabbit) DB-HB-QB	31-37ChiB HC53Bal	012	5'9"	167	Monmouth	5	67
Monaco, Ray G-LB	44Was 45Cle		5'10"	212	Holy Cross		
Monahan, Regis (Monty) G-T	35-38Det 39ChiC	5	5'10"	216	Ohio State		44
Monfort, Avery WB-DB	41ChiC 42-45MS		5'10"	178	New Mexico		
Monnett, Bob TB-DB-HB	33-38GB	12 5	5'9"	182	Michigan State	2	91
Montgomery, Bill G-T	34C-S		5'9"	200	St. Louis		
Montgomery, Cliff TB-DB	34Bkn		5'9"	165	Columbia		
Mooney, Jim OE-DE-T-G-BB-LB	30Nwk 30-31Bkn	0	5'11"	200	Georgetown	1	3
	33Cin 34C-S 35ChiC 36,PC37AFL						
Mooney (born Schupbach), Tex T	42Cle 43Bkn 44-45MS		6'5"	280	West Texas State		
Mooney, Tipp HB-DB	44-45ChiB	2	6'	187	Abilene Christian	1	6
Moore, Al DE	39GB		6'2"	218	Texas A&M		
Moore, Bill OE-DE	37AFL 39Det		6'1"	195	North Carolina		6
Moore, Bucky (The Dixie Flyer) DB-HB-WB	32ChiC 33Pit		5'11"	185	Loyola (N. Orl.)	1	
Moore, Cliff WB-DB	34C-S		6'1"	202	Penn State		
Moore, Gene C-LB	38Bkn		6'3"	205	Colorado		
Moore, Ken G	40NYG		6'	212	West Va. Wesleyan		
Moore, Paul (June) BB-LB	40-41Det 42-44MS		5'9"	208	Presbyterian		6
Moore, Wilbur (Little Indian) DB-WB-HB-FB BB	39-46Was	2	5'11"	187	Minnesota	12	144
Moran, Hap DB-TB-WB-LB-BB-FB-OE-DE	26-27Fra	0	6'1"	190	Grinnell,	15	167
	27ChiC 28Pott 28-33NYG				Carnegie-Mellon		
Moran, Jim G	35-36Bos		6'1"	208	Holy Cross		
Morelli, John G-LB	44-45Bos		5'10"	191	Georgetown		
Morgan, Bill T	33-36NYG		6'2"	232	Oregon		
Morgan, Boyd (Red) DB-LB-WB-DB	39-40Was 41-45MS		6'	198	Southern Calif.		
Morlock, Jack WB-DB	40Det		5'10"	165	Marshall		
Morris, Frank FB-LB	42ChiB 43-45MS		6'2"	214	Boston U.		
Morris, George DB-WB-FB	41-42Cle 43-45MS	2	5'11"	188	Baldwin-Wallace	2	
Morris, Glenn OE-DE	40Det 40AFL		6'	200	Colorado State		
Morrison, Doc C-LB	33-34Bkn		5'11"	210	Michigan	2	
Morrow, Bob FB-DB-BB-LB	41-43ChiC 44MS 45NYG	2	6'	222	Illinois Wesleyan	3	24
	46NY-AA						
Morrow, John G	37-38ChiC		5'11"	230	Kearney State		
Morse, Butch OE-DE	35-38,40Det 41-45MS	2	6'2"	199	Oregon		6
Mortell, Emmett TB-DB-QB	37-39Phi	12	6'1"	181	Wisconsin		
Moscrip, Monk OE-DE	38-39Det	2 5	6'	195	Stanford		27
Moses, Don BB-DB	33Cin		5'11"	185	Southern Calif.		
Mosher, Clure C-G-LB	42Pit 43-45MS		6'1"	215	Louisville		
Mosley, Russ DB-HB	45-46GB		5'10"	170	Alabama	2	
Moss, Paul OE-DE	33Pit 34C-S	2	6'2"	200	Purdue		18
Mott, Buster DB-BB-HB-FB-LB	33GB 34C-S 34Pit		5'8"	193	Georgia		
Moynihan, Tim C-LB-G	32-33ChiC		6'1"	204	Notre Dame	1	12
Mucha, Rudy G-LB-BB	41Cle 42-44MS 45Cle 45-46ChiB	4	6'1"	236	Washington		
Muellner, Bill OE-DE	37ChiC 37AFL		5'11"	175	DePaul		
Mugg, Garvin T	45Det		6'1"	215	North Texas		
Mulleneaux, Lee (Brute) LB-C-DB-WB-BB-FB	32NYG		6'2"	221	Northern Arizona		
	33Cin 34C-S 35-36Pit 37AFL 38ChiC 38GB 40AFL						
Mulleneaux, Moose DE-OE	38-41GB 42-44MS 45-46GB	2	6'3"	209	Utah State		72
Mulligan, George OE-DE-LB	36Phi 36AFL		6'1"	198	Catholic		
Munday, George (Sunny) T-G	31Cle 31-32NYG 33Cin		6'2"	213	Emporia State		
	34C-S 36AFL						
Mundee, Fred C-LB	43-45ChiB		6'1"	220	Notre Dame	2	
Murphy, Bill G	40-41ChiC 42-45MS		6'	203	Washington-St.L.		
Murphy, Ham OE-DE	40Cle		5'10"	194	Mississippi		
Murphy, Tom (Smiling Tom) BB-DB-FB-LB	34ChiC		5'11"	170	Arkansas		
(The Red Knight of Arkansas)							
Murray, Franny DB-WB-HB	39-40Phi	2 45	6'	200	Pennsylvania		32
Musick, Jim (Sweet) FB-DB	32-33Bos 34HO 35-36Bos	0 2 5	5'11"	205	Southern Calif.	3	64
Musso, George (Moose) G-T	33-44ChiB		6'2"	262	Millikin		
Nagurski, Bronko FB-LB-T	30-37,43ChiB	0 2	6'2"	226	Minnesota	7	153
Maiotl, John DB-HB	42,45Pit		5'10"	180	St. Francis (Pa.)		4
Nardi, Dick DB-WB-HB-TB-FB	38Det 39Pit 39Bkn	2	5'10"	200	Ohio State		
Nash, Tom OE-DE	28-32GB 33-34Bkn	0	6'3"	208	Georgia	6	32
Natowich, Andy HB-DB	44Was 45MS		5'10"	175	Holy Cross		
Neihaus, Ralph T	39Cle 40-41AFL		6'4"	220	Dayton		
Neill, Jim DB-FB-WB	37NYG 39ChiB		6'1"	185	Texas Tech		
Nelson, Don G	37Bkn		5'9"	205	Iowa		

UseName(Nicknames)-Positions	Team by Year	See Section	Hgt	Wgt	College	Int	Pts
Nery, Carl G	40-41Pit 42-45MS		6'	214	Duquesne		
Nesbitt, Dick HB-DB-FB-LB-BB-WB	30-33ChiB	0	6'	204	Drake	5	36
	33ChiC 34Bkn						
Neuman, Bob OE-DE	34-36ChiC		6'	198	Illinois Wesleyan	1	6
Newman, Harry TB-DB	33-35NYG 36-37AFL	12 5	5'8"	179	Michigan	6	78
Newton, Chuck DB-BB-HB-FB	39-40Phi	2	6'	205	Washington		6
Niccolai, Armand (Nick) T-G-DE-OE	34-42Pit	5	6'2"	226	Duquesne		173
Nichelini, Al WB-DB	35-36ChiC 37AFL	2	6'2"	207	St. Mary's		30
Nichols, Al FB-LB	45Pit		5'10"	205	Temple		
Nielsen, Walt FB-DB	40NYG 41-45MS	2	6'3"	220	Arizona		6
Nisbet, Dave OE-DE	33ChiC		6'1"	180	Washington		
Nix, Emery QB-DB	43NYG 44-45MS 46NYG	12	5'11"	180	Texas Christian	2	
Nix, Jack WB-DB	40Cle		6'	175	Mississippi State		
Nixon (born Nicksick), Mike DB-HB-WB	35Pit		5'11"	181	Pittsburgh		
	42Bkn HC59-61Was HC65Pit						
Nolan, Earl T	37-38ChiC		6'1"	205	Arizona		
Nolting, Ray HB-DB	36-43ChiB	12	5'11"	186	Cincinnati	1	96
Noppenberg, John DB-HB-FB-TB-OE	40-41Pit 41Det		6'	196	Miami (Fla.)		
Norby, John DB-WB-BB-HB	34NYG 34Phi 34C-S 35Bkn		6'	195	Idaho		
Norgard, Al OE-DE	34GB		6'1"	194	Stanford		
Norl, Reino TB-DB-QB	37Bkn 38ChiB	2	5'8"	167	Norhtern Illinois		
Norman, Bob C-LB	45ChiC		6'1"	185	none		
North, Jim T	44Was		6'3"	235	Central Washington		
Nosich, John T	38Pit		6'3"	230	Duquesne		
Nott, Doug TB-DB	35Det 35Bos	1	6'	195	Detroit		
Nowak, Walt OE-DB	44Phi		5'11"	185	Villanova		
Noyes, Len G	38Bkn		6'	214	Montana		
Obee, Dunc C-LB	41Det 42-45MS		5'11"	200	Dayton		
O'Boyle, Harry BB-DB-FB-LB	28GB 29-31RC 32GB 33Phi	0	5'9"	178	Notre Dame	4	30
O'Brien, Davey (Slingshot) QB-DB-TB	39-40Phi	12	5'7"	151	Texas Christian		12
O'Brien, Gail T	34-36Bos 37AFL		6'1"	219	Nebraska		
Obst, Henry G	31SI 33Phi 36AFL		5'11"	192	Syracuse		
O'Connor, Bob G-T-DE-BB	35GB		6'1"	220	Stanford		
O'Delli, Mel HB-DB	45Pit		5'8"	176	Duquesne		
Oech, Vern G	36ChiB		6'1"	207	Minnesota		
Oehler, Cap C-LB	33-34Pit 35-36Bkn		6'	204	Purdue	8	
Oelerich, John HB-DB	38Pit 38ChiB		6'	192	St. Ambrose		
Ohlgren, Earl DE	40-41AFL 42GB		6'2"	210	Minnesota		
Oldershaw, Doug G-LB-DE-OE	39-41NYG 42-45MS		6'	195	Cal.-Santa Barbara	1	6
Oleniczak, Stan (Oleo) T	35Pit		6'	220	Pittsburgh		6
Oliver, Vince QB	45ChiC		5'11"	180	Indiana		
Olsen, Norm T	44Cle		6'2"	220	Alabama		
Olson, Carl T	42ChiC		6'2"	206	U.C.L.A.		
Olson, Glenn BB-DB	40Cle 41AFL		6'	195	Iowa		
Olsson, Les (Swede) G	34-36Bos 37-38Was		6'	232	Mercer		
Olszewski, Al OE-DB	45Pit		6'2"	185	Penn State,		
					Pittsburgh		
O'Neill, Bill (Speedy, Sidecar) TB-DB-WB	35Det		6'	185	Detroit		
	36-37AFL 37Cle						
Opalewski, Ed T	43-44Det		6'3"	230	Eastern Michigan		
Osmanski, Bill FB-LB	39-43ChiB 44-45MS 46-47ChiB	2	5'11"	197	Holy Cross	4	126
Owen, Al BB-LB-FB-DB	39-40NYG 41AFL 42NYG		6'	194	Mercer		6
	43-45MS						
Owen, Bill (Red) T-G	26KC 27Cle 28Det 29-36NYG		6'	211	Oklahoma State		
Owen, Steve T-G	24-25KC 25Cle		5'10"	235	Phillips		
	26-29,PC30-31,33,HC32,34-53NYG						
Owens, Pete G-C-LB	43Bkn		5'11"	205	Texas Tech		
Padlow, Max OE-DE	35-36Phi 36-37,41AFL		6'1"	199	Ohio State		
Palm, Mike DB-BB-WB	25-26NYG,PC33Cin HC36-37AFL		5'10"	170	Penn State	1	6
Pangle, Hal FB-DB-LB-BB	35-38ChiC	2	5'10"	200	Oregon State		18
Pannell, Ernie T	41-42GB 43-44MS 45GB		6'2"	220	Texas A&M	1	6
Pardonner, Paul (Pudge) BB-DB	34-35ChiC		5'8"	170	Purdue		7
Parker, Ace TB-DB-QB	37-41Bkn 42-44MS	12 45	6'	178	Duke	7	148
37-38 played major league baseball	45Bos 46NY-AA						
Parker, Buddy BB-LB-FB-DB	35-36Det 37-43,HC49ChiC	2	6'	193	Centenary	2	28
	HC51-56Det HC57-64Pit						
Parker, Dave OE-DE	41Bkn 42-45MS		6'3"	200	Hardin-Simmons		
Parks, Mickey C-LB	38-40Was 41-45MS 46ChiAA		6'	225	Oklahoma		
Parriott, Bill FB-LB	34C-S		5'10"	165	West Virginia		
Parry, Ox T	37-39NYG		6'4"	230	Baylor		
Parsons, Lloyd FB-LB	41Det 42-45MS		5'11"	197	Gustavus Adolphus		
Paschal, Bill FB-DB-LB	43-47NYG 47-48Bos	23	6'	201	Georgia Tech		210
Paskvan, George FB-DB	41GB 42-45MS	2	6'	190	Wisconsin	2	
Pasqua, Joe T	42Cle 43Was 44-45MS 46LA		6'1"	226	S.M.U.		2
Pastin, Frank G-LB	42Pit		5'10"	197	Waynesburg		
Pate, Rupert G	40ChiC 41AFL 42Phi 43-45MS		6'1"	205	Wake Forest		6
Paternoster, Angelo G-LB	43Was		5'11"	195	Georgetown		
Patt, Maury (Babe) OE-DE	38Det 39-42Cle 43-44MS	2	6'2"	205	Carnegie-Mellon		12
Patterson, Billy TB-DB-QB-HB	39ChiB 40Pit	12 4	5'10"	167	Baylor		1
Patrick, Frank TB-DB-BB-LB	38-39ChiC 40-41AFL	12	5'11"	190	Pittsburgh		24
Patrick, John BB-LB-FB	41Pit 42-44MS 45-46Pit		6'	202	Penn State	1	
Paulekas, Tony G-C-LB	36GB		5'10"	210	Washington & Jeff.		
Pavelic, Ted T-G	41-43Det 44-45MS		6'	218	Detroit		3
Pavkov, Stan G	39-40Pit 41-45MS		6'	212	Idaho		
Payne, Charlie WB-DB	37Det		5'11"	186	Detroit		
Peace, Larry HB-DB	40AFL 41Bkn 42-45MS		5'11"	185	Pittsburgh		1
Pearson, Bert C-LB-G-T	29-34ChiB 35-36ChiC 37AFL		6'	206	Kansas State	1	
Pederson, Win T	40AFL 41NYG 42-44MS 45NYG 46Bos		6'3"	223	Minnesota	1	3
Pense, Leon BB-DB	45Pit		6'	170	Arkansas	3	
Perdue, Bolo DE-OE	40NYG 46BknAA		5'10"	206	Duke		
Perez, Pete G	45ChiB		5'9"	220	Illinois		
Perkins, Don FB-LB	41AFL 43-45GB 45-46ChiB	2	6'	198	Wis.-Platteville	2	24
Perko, John G-LB	37-40Pit 44C-P 45-47Pit		6'1"	207	Duquesne	1	
Perry, Claude T-G-DE-OE	27-31GB 31Bkn 32-35GB		6'1"	210	Alabama		
	36-37AFL						
Perrie, Mike (Iron Mike) BB-LB	39Cle		5'11"	197	St. Mary's		
Petchel, John BB-DB-LB	43-44Cle 45Pit		5'11"	185	Duquesne	2	6
Peterson, Ike TB-DB-WB	35ChiC 36Det	12	5'9"	185	Gonzaga		18
Peterson, Les (Tex) OE-DE-T	31Port 32GB 32SI	0 2	6'3"	206	Texas		
	32GB 33Bkn 34GB						
Peterson, Nels (Banty) WB-DB-TB	37Was 38Cle 40-41AFL		5'8"	179	West Va. Wesleyan		20
Peterson, Phil OE-DE	34Bkn		5'11"	195	Wisconsin		
Peterson, Ray TB-DB	37GB		6'	190	San Francisco		
Petrella, John HB-DB	45Pit		5'7"	160	Penn State	1	
Petrilas, Bill DB-WB	44-45NYG		6'1"	195	none	7	12
Petro, Steve G-LB	40-41Bkn 42-45MS		5'10"	195	Pittsburgh		

UseName(Nicknames)-Positions	Team by Year	See Section	Hgt	Wgt	College	Int	Pts
Petty, John FB-LB	42ChiB 43-45MS	2	6'1"	225	Purdue	1	12
Phillips, Ewell G	36NYG 37AFL		5'11"	210	Oklahoma Baptist		
Phillips, George LB	45Cle		6'3"	215	U.C.L.A.		
Piasecky, Alex OE-DE	43-45Was	2	6'2"	197	Duke	1	6
Piccolo, Bill C-LB	43-45NYG		5'11"	185	Canisius	2	6
Piepul, Milt FB-LB	41Det		6'1"	215	Notre Dame		
Pierce, Don C-LB	42Bkn 43ChiC		6'1"	186	Kansas		
Pierre, John OE-DE	45Pit		6'	185	Pittsburgh		
Pilconis, Joe OE-DE	34,36-37Pit	2	6'1"	189	Temple	1	12
Pinckert, Ernie WB-DB-BB-LB	32-36Bos 37-40Was	0 2	6'	197	Southern Calif.	12	18
Pincura, Stan BB-DB	36AFL 37-38Cle	12	5'11"	175	Ohio State		6
Pingel, Johnny TB-DB	39Det	12 4	6'	180	Michigan State		6
Piro, Hank OE-DB	41Phi 42-45MS	2	6'	186	Syracuse	1	6
Pittman, Swede C-LB	35Pit		6'	215	Hardin-Simmons		
Pitts, Alabama HB-DB	35Phi		5'10"	185	none		
Pivarnick, Joe (Butch) G	36Phi		5'9"	217	Notre Dame		
Plasman, Dick DE-OE-T	37-41ChiB 42-43MS 44ChiB 46-47ChiC	2 5	6'3"	218	Vanderbilt		56
Platukas, George OE-DE	38-41Pit 42Cle 43-45MS	2	6'	196	Duquesne	1	42
Plunkett, Warren BB-LB	42Cle 43-45MS		6'	200	Minnesota		
Podmajersky, Paul G	44ChiB		5'11"	220	Illinois		
Pollock, Red HB-LB-OE-DE	35-36ChiB		6'2"	194	Widener		24
Pool, Hamp OE-DE	40-42ChiB 44-45MS PC46MiaAA HC47ChiAA HC52-54LA	2	6'3"	221	Stanford		66
Poole, Jim OE-DE	37-41NYG 42-44MS 45ChiC 45-46NYG	2	6'3"	218	Mississippi	2	84
Pope, Lew (Chicken) DB-TB-WB-BB-FB-LB	31Prov 33Cin 34C-S	0	6'	196	Purdue	1	6
Popovich, John HB-DB	44C-P 45Pit		5'8"	160	St. Vincent		
Popovich, Milt FB-DB-WB-LB-G-BB	38-42ChiC	2 4	5'11"	196	Montana	1	6
Postus, Al TB-DB	45Pit		5'10"	180	Villanova		
Poth, Phil G	34Phi		5'11"	195	Gonzaga		
Powell, Dick (Tiny) OE-DE	32NYG 33Cin		6'2"	215	Davis & Elkins		
Prather, Dale OE-DE-T	37AFL 37-38Cle		6'2"	190	George Washington		
Presnell, Glenn TB-DB-WB-FB-LB	31-33Port 34-36Det	0 12 5	5'10"	195	Nebraska	23	216
Pressley, Lee C-LB-FB	45Was		6'2"	230	Oklahoma		
Price, Cotton TB-DB-QB	40-41Det 42-44MS 45Det 46MiaAA	12	6'1"	183	Texas A&M	1	16
Priestley, Bob OE-DE	42Phi		5'11"	192	Brown		
Principe, Dom LB-BB-FB-DB	40-42NYG 43-45MS 46BknAA	2	6'	205	Fordham		12
Prisco, Nick TB-DB	33Phi		5'8"	193	Rutgers		
Prochaska, Ray OE-DE	41Cle 42-45MS HC61StL		6'3"	205	Nebraska		
Pudloski, Chet T	44Cle 45MS		6'1"	210	Villanova		
Pugh, Marion QB-DB	41NYG 42-44MS 45NYG 46MiaAA	12	6'1"	187	Texas A&M		12
Puplis, Andy WB-DB	43ChiC 44-45MS		5'9"	180	Notre Dame	1	
Pylman, Bob T	38-39Phi		6'4"	214	S. Dakota State		6
Quatse, Jess T	33GB 33-34Pit 35NYG 36,PC37AFL		5'11"	226	Pittsburgh		
Raborn, Buster C-LB	36-37Pit		6'	198	S.M.U.		
Rado, Alex (Pug, Moose) HB-DB	34Pit		6'1"	200	West Virginia Tech		
Rado, George (Mousie) G-DE	35-37Pit 37-38Phi		5'9"	194	Duquesne		
Radovich, Bill G	38-41Det 42-44MS 45Det 46-47LA-AA		5'10"	238	Southern Calif.		
Ragazzo, Phil T-G	38-40Cle 40-41Phi 42-44MS 45-47NYG		6'	216	Case Reserve		
Rajkovich, Pete FB-LB	34Pit		5'10"	190	Detroit		
Ramsey, Frank T	45ChiB		6'1"	240	Oregon State		
Ramsey, Red OE-DE	38-40Phi	2	6'	196	Texas Tech		12
Randolph, Clare C-LB-G-OE-DE	30ChiC 31-33Port 34-36Det		6'2"	204	Indiana	5	
Rankin, Walt (Bull) LB-FB-DB	41,43ChiC 44C-P 45-47ChiC	2	5'11"	197	Texas Tech	8	
Ranspot, Keith OE-DE-DB	40ChiC 40-41AFL 42Det 43Bkn 44-45Bos	2	6'3"	205	S.M.U.		24
Rapp, Manny TB-DB-FB-LB	34C-S		6'	215	St. Louis		
Raskowski, Leo (Fat) T	32SI 33Bkn 33Pit 35Phi		6'3"	219	Ohio State	1	
Ratica, Joe C-LB	39Bkn 40-41AFL		6'	205	St. Vincent		
Ray, Baby T	38-48GB		6'6"	249	Vanderbilt	1	
Rayburn, Van OE-DE	33Bkn		6'1"	180	Tennessee		
Ream, Chuck T	38Cle		6'2"	225	Ohio State		
Reckmack, Ray BB-DB	37Bkn 37Det		6'	200	Syracuse		
Reed, Rock WB-DB	37,39ChiC		5'8"	173	Louisiana State		6
Reese, Hank C-LB-G	33-34NYG 35-39Phi 40AFL	5	5'11"	214	Temple	1	39
Reissig, Bill BB-LB-DE	37AFL 38-39Bkn		6'	195	Ft. Hays State		9
Reisz, Albie TB-DB-QB	44-45Cle 46LA 47BufAA	12 4	5'10"	174	Southwestern La.	5	12
Rentner, Pug DB-WB-FB-HB-TB-BB	34-36Bos 37ChiB	12	6'1"	187	Northwestern	3	43
Reutt, Ray DE	43P-P		6'	195	V.M.I.		
Rexner, Freeman DE-OE	43ChiC 44Bos 44Det 45ChiC		6'1"	211	Tulane		
Reynolds, Bill HB-DB	44Bkn 45ChiC	4	5'8"	183	Mississippi		6
Reynolds, Bob T	37-38Det		6'4"	221	Stanford		
Reynolds, Homer G	34C-S 37AFL		5'10"	190	Tulsa		
Reynolds, John (Tex) C-LB	37ChiC		5'10"	185	Baylor		
Rhea, Floyd G-LB	43ChiC 44Bkn 45Bos 47Det		6'	218	Oregon	1	
Rhea, Hughie G	33Bkn 36AFL		6'3"	225	Nebraska		
Rhodes, Don T	33Pit 36AFL		6'2"	225	Washington & Jeff.		
Ribar, Frank G-LB	43Was 44-45MS		6'1"	190	Duke		
Ribble, Dave (Tex, Babe) G-T	32Port 33ChiC 34-35Pit 36-37AFL		6'1"	216	Hardin-Simmons		
Riblett, Paul OE-DE	32-36Bkn	0 2	5'10"	184	Pennsylvania	1	13
Richards, Dick WB-DB	33Bkn		6'	194	Kentucky		
Richards, Kink FB-DB-TB	33-39NYG	2	5'11"	195	Simpson	1	122
Richards, Ray G-T-OE-DE	30Fra 33ChiB 34Det 35ChiB 37AFL HC55-57ChiC		6'1"	230	Nebraska		
Richins, Al WB-DB	35Det		5'9"	188	Utah		
Riddick, Ray DE-OE	40-42GB 43-45MS 46GB	2	6'1"	211	Fordham		6
Rieth, Bill C-LB-G	41-42Cle 43MS 44-45Cle		5'11"	203	Carnegie-Mellon	1	
Riffle, Dick DB-FB-TB-HB-WB	38-40Phi 41-42Pit	12 4	6'1"	200	Albright	10	73
Riggs, Thron T	44Bos 45MS		6'1"	225	Washington		
Riley, Jack T	33Bos		6'2"	230	Northwestern		
Ritchhart, Del C-LB	36-37Det		6'	195	Colorado		
Robbins, Jack TB-DB	38-39ChiC	12	6'2"	183	Arkansas		
Roberts, Jack (Ripper) HB-DB-FB-LB-TB-BB	32Bos 32SI 33-34Phi 34Pit	0	6'	210	Georgia	2	6
Roberts, Tom T-G	43NYG 44-45ChiB		6'1"	215	DePaul		
Robertson, Bob HB-DB	42Bkn 43-45MS	2	5'11"	185	Southern Calif.	2	
Robertson, Lake DE	45Det		6'1"	210	Mississippi		
Robertson, Tom C-LB	41-42Bkn 43-45MS 46NY-AA		6'	199	Tulsa	1	
Robinson, Gil OE-DE	33Pit		6'	180	Catawba		
Robinson, Jack T-G	35-36Bkn 36-37ChiC 38Pit 38Cle		6'3"	220	NE Missouri St.		
Robison, Buke OE-DE-C-LB	35Phi		6'4"	197	Brigham Young		
Robl, Hal LB	45ChiC		6'	227	Wis.-Oshkosh		

UseName(Nicknames)-Positions	Team by Year	See Section	Hgt	Wgt	College	Int	Pts
Robnett, Marshall LB-C-G	43ChiC 44C-P 45ChiC		6'	205	Texas A&M	1	1
Rockenbach, Lyle G	43Det 44-45MS		5'9"	192	Michigan State		
Rockwell, Hank C-G-LB-DE	40-42Cle 43-45MS 46,48LA-AA		6'4"	231	Arizona State	2	6
Rodak, Mike BB-LB-DE-G	39-40Cle 41BL 42Pit 43-45MS		5'10"	196	Case Reserve		
Rogalla, John FB-LB	45Phi		6'	215	Scranton		1
Rogers, Bill T	38-40,44Det		5'11"	243	Villanova		
Rogers, Glynn G	39ChiC		5'10"	220	Texas Christian		
Rogers, John (Bee) C-LB	33Cin 34C-S 36AFL		5'8"	208	Notre Dame	1	
Rogge, George OE-DE	31-33ChiC 34C-S		6'	186	Iowa	1	6
Ronzani, Gene QB-HB-DB-LB-FB	33-38,44-45ChiB HC50-53GB	12	5'9"	200	Marquette	4	57
Rorison, Red T	38Pit		6'3"	250	Southern Calif.		
Rose, Al (Big Un) OE-DE	30-31Prov 32-36GB 36AFL	0	6'3"	201	Texas	2	48
Rose, Gene OE-DE	36NYG		6'1"	185	Tennessee		
Rosequist, Ted T-DE-OE-G	34-36ChiB 37Cle		6'4"	222	John Carroll, Ohio State		
Rosteck, Ernie C-LB	43-44Det		6'1"	218	none		
Roton, Herb (Bummy) OE-DE	37Phi		6'2"	210	Auburn		
Rouse, Stillman OE-DE	40Det 41-45MS		6'2"	205	Missouri		
Rovinski, Tony OE-DE	33NYG		5'9"	195	Holy Cross		
Rowan, Ev (Deb) OE-DE-DB-FB-HB	30,32Bkn 33Phi		6'1"	197	Ohio State		
Rowe, Bob DB-BB-WB-FB-LB	34Det 35Phi		6'	198	Colgate	2	
Rubino, Tony G	43Det 44-45MS 46Det		5'10"	208	Wake Forest		
Rucinski, Eddie OE-DE-DB	41-42Bkn 43ChiC 44C-P 45-46ChiC	2	6'2"	197	Indiana	4	48
Rukas, Justin (Ruke) G	36Bkn		6'	205	Louisiana State		
Russell, Bo T	39-40Was 41-45MS	5	6'1"	223	Auburn		38
Russell, Doug TB-WB-DB	34-39ChiC 39Cle	12	6'	187	Kansas State		36
Russell, Jim G-T	36-37Phi		5'11"	210	Temple		
Russell, Reb DB-HB-LB-FB-BB	33NYG 33Phi		6'1"	195	Northwestern	1	
Ryan, Rip WB-DB-FB	38-40Det 41-45MS	2	6'2"	193	Utah State	6	12
Sabados, Andy G	39-40ChiC		5'11"	209	The Citadel		
Sachse, Frank DB-TB-QB-HB	43-44Bkn 45Bos 43-45 played in N.B.L.	1	6'	197	Texas Tech	2	
Sachse, Jack C-LB	45Bos		6'	210	Southwestern (Tex.), Texas		
Sader, Steve FB-LB	43P-P		5'11"	180	none		
Sample, Chuck FB-LB	42GB 43-44MS 45GB	2	5'9"	205	Toledo		30
Sandberg, Sandy T	34C-S 35-37Pit 37Bkn		6'2"	228	Iowa Wesleyan		
Sandefur, Dick FB-LB-DB	36-37Pit 37AFL		5'10"	195	Purdue		
Sanders, Jack G-LB	40-42Pit 43-44MS 45Phi	5	6'	219	S.M.U.	1	12
Sanders, Paul HB-DB	44Bos		5'11"	192	Utah State		
Sandig, Curt HB-DB	42Pit 43-45MS 46BufAA	2 4	5'10"	173	St. Mary's (Tex.)	5	30
Sanford, Sandy OE-DE	40Was 41-45MS		6'1"	210	Alabama		3
Sansen, Ollie DB-WB-HB-FB-OE-DE	32-35Bkn		6'1"	193	Iowa		12
Santora, Frank DB-QB	44Bos 45MS		5'10"	166	none		
Sanzotta, Mickey WB-DB-TB	42Det 45MS 46Det	2	5'9"	188	Case Reserve	2	
Sarafiny, Al C-LB	33GB		5'11"	235	St. Edward's	1	
Sarausky, Tony TB-DB-QB-FB	35-37NYG 38Bkn	12	5'11"	201	Fordham		17
Sarboe, Phil DB-BB-TB	34Bos 34-36ChiC 36Bkn	12	5'10"	167	Washington State	1	12
Sark, Harvey G	31NYG 34C-S		5'10"	210	Phillips		
Sartori, Larry G	42Det 43-44MS 45Det		6'	208	Fordham		
Satenstein, Ollie G-OE-DE-T-LB-C	29-32SI 33NYG		6'	213	N.Y.U.		
Sauer, George HB-FB-DB-LB-TB	35-37GB	2	6'2"	208	Nebraska		42
Saumer, Syl TB-DB-FB-LB-BB	34Pit 34C-S 34Pit		6'1"	195	St. Olaf		6
Savatsky, Ollie OE-DE	37Cle 37AFL		6'2"	215	Miami-Ohio		
Scafide, John T	33Bos		6'	210	Tulane		
Scarry, Mo C-LB-T	44-45Cle 46-47CleAA		6'	214	Waynesburg	7	
Schaake, Elmer (Dutch) FB-LB-WB-TB-DB	33Port	2	5'11"	207	Kansas	2	6
Schammel, Zud G-DE	37GB		6'2"	235	Iowa		6
Schenker, Nate T	39Cle		6'2"	220	Samford		
Scherer, Bernie OE-DE	36-38GB 39Pit	2	6'1"	190	Nebraska		24
Scheuer, Babe T	34NYG		6'3"	240	N.Y.U.		
Schibanoff, Alex T	41-42Det 43-45MS		6'1"	218	Franklin & Marshall		
Schiechl, John C-LB	41-42Pit 42Det 43-44MS 45-46ChiB 47SF-AA		6'2"	244	Santa Clara	6	
Schissler, Paul	HC33-34ChiC HC35-36Bkn				Doane, Hastings, St. Viator		
Schmaar, Herm DE	43Bkn		6'2"	210	Catholic		
Schmidt, John C-LB	40Pit		6'3"	210	Carnegie-Mellon		
Schmidt, Kermit (Dutch) OE-DE-WB-DB	32Bos 33Cin		6'	200	Cal. Poly-Pomona		
Schmitt, Ted G-C-LB	38-40Phi		5'11"	216	Pittsburgh		6
Schneidman, Herm (Biff) BB-DB-LB-OE-DE	35-38GB 40ChiC		5'11"	201	Iowa		12
Schneller, John OE-DE	33Port 34-36Det	2	6'2"	204	Wisconsin		18
Schoemann, Roy C-LB	38GB		6'1"	192	Marquette		
Schuehle, Jake LB	39Phi		6'	196	Rice		
Schuelke, Karl FB-DB	39Pit		5'10"	200	Wisconsin		
Schultz, Charlie T	39-41GB 42-45MS		6'3"	231	Minnesota		
Schultz, Elbie T-G	40Phi 41-42Pit 43P-P 44C-P 45Cle 46-47LA		6'4"	252	Oregon State		6
Schwammel, Ade (Tar) T	34-36,43-44GB		6'2"	225	Oregon State		26
Schwartz, Elmer FB-LB-HB-DB-WB	31Port 32ChiC 33Pit	0	6'	212	Washington State	2	18
Schwartz, Perry OE-DE	38-42Bkn 43-45MS 46NY-AA	2	6'2"	199	California		60
Schweidler, Dick HB-DB	38-39,46ChiB	2	6'	182	none	1	18
Scott, Perry OE-DE	42Det 43-45MS		6'2"	210	Muhlenberg		
Sebastian, Mike DB-HB-WB	35Phi 35Pit 36AFL 37Cle 37AFL		5'11"	185	Pittsburgh		
Seeman, George OE-DE	40GB		6'1"	195	Nebraska		
Seibold, Champ T-G	34-38GB 39VR 40GB 42ChiC		6'4"	238	Wisconsin	1	6
Seick, Red G-LB	41AFL 42NYG 43-45MS		6'	195	Manhatten		
Seltzer, Harry FB-LB	42Det 43-45MS		5'9"	195	Charleston		
Semes, Bernie HB-DB	44C-P		5'7"	188	Duquesne	1	
Senn, Bill HB-DB-TB-WB-FB-LB-BB	26-31ChiB 31Bkn 33Cin 34C-S	0	6'	177	Knox	4	158
Sergienko, George T	43-44Bkn 45Bos 46BknAA		6'1"	248	American Inter.		
Setcavage, Joe BB-DB	43Bkn		5'11"	190	Duquesne	1	
Seymour, Bob DB-FB-HB-WB	40-45Was 46LA-AA	23	6'2"	205	Oklahoma	17	138
Shaffer, George BB-DB	33Pit		6'	190	Washington & Jeff.		
Shaffer, Leland BB-DB-LB-WB-OE-DE	35-43,45NYG	2	6'2"	203	Kansas State	2	36
Sharp, Ev T	44-45Was		6'1"	223	Cal. Poly-Pomona		
Shedlosky, Ed WB-DB	45NYG		6'	185	Tulsa, Fordham		
Shellogg, Alec T	39ChiB 39Bkn 40-41AFL		6'	215	Notre Dame		
Shenefelt, Paul T	34ChiC		6'	195	Manchester	1	
Shepherd, Bill FB-LB-TB-DB-BB	35Bos 35-40Det	12 5	5'9"	199	Western Maryland		110
Sherman, Allie QB-DB	43P-P 44-47Phi HC61-68NYG	12	5'11"	170	Brooklyn	2	24
Sherman, Solly QB-DB	39-40ChiB		6'1"	190	Chicago		6
Shetley, Rhoten BB-LB-FB	40-42Bkn 43-45MS 46BknAA	2	5'11"	208	Furman	2	18
Shires, Abe T	45Phi		6'2"	220	Tennessee		

UseName(Nicknames)-Positions	Team by Year	See Section	Hgt	Wgt	College	Int	Pts
Shirley, Fred T	40GB 40-41Cle		6'2"	223	Nebraska		
Shirk, John OE-DE	40ChiC 41-45MS	2	6'4"	200	Oklahoma		
Shonk, John OE-DB	41Phi 42-45MS		6'1"	190	West Virginia	1	
Shook, Fred C-LB	41ChiC 42-45MS		6'	218	Texas Christian		
Shugart, Clyde G-LB-T	39-44Was		6'1"	221	Iowa State	1	
Siano, Tony C-LB	32Bos 34Bkn		5'8"	172	Fordham	1	
Siegal, John OE-DE	39-43ChiB 44-45MS	2	6'1"	203	Columbia		42
Siemering, Larry C-LB	35-36Bos		6'3"	206	San Francisco		6
Sigillo, Dom T	37,40-41AFL 45Det		6'	230	Xavier-Ohio		
Sikich, Rudy T	45Cle		6'1"	220	Minnesota		
Simas, Butch BB-DB	32-33ChiC		5'10"	185	St. Mary's	1	
Simington, Milt G	41Cle 42Pit		6'2"	217	Arkansas		4
died Jan. 18, 1943 — heart attack							
Singer, Walt OE-DE	35-36NYG		6'	198	Syracuse		12
Sinko, Steve T-G	34-36Bos 37AFL		6'3"	232	Duquesne		
Sinkwich, Frankie TB-DB-HB	43-44Det 45MS 46-47NY-AA	12 45	5'11"	190	Georgia	4	78
	47BalAA						
Sirochman, George G	42Pit 44Det		6'2"	215	Duquesne		
Sisk, Johnny (Big Train) HB-LB	32-36ChiB	0 2	6'2"	197	St. Viator, Marquette	3	18
Sites, Vinnie OE-DE	36-37Pit 37AFL		6'2"	215	Pittsburgh		6
Sivell, Jim (Happy) G	38-42Bkn 43MS 44Bkn		5'9"	205	Auburn		
	44-45NYG 46MiaAA						
Skladany, Joe (Muggsy) OE-DE	34Pit	2	5'10"	210	Pittsburgh		12
Skoczen, Stan HB-DB	44Cle		5'11"	187	Case Reserve		
Skoronski, Ed OE-DE-C-LB-G-T	35-36Pit 37Bkn 37Cle		6'2"	213	Pudue		6
Slivinski, Steve G-LB	39-43Was		5'10"	214	Washington	2	
Sloan, Dwight (Paddlefoot) TB-DB	38ChiC	12	5'10"	180	Arkansas		24
	39-40Det 41-45MS						
Slovak, Marty (The Elliston Eel) TB-DB	39-41Cle	12	5'9"	179	Toledo		6
	42-45MS						
Smeja, Rudy OE-DE	44-45ChiB 46Phi	2	6'2"	195	Michigan		6
Smilanich, Bronko TB-DB	39Cle		5'11"	180	Arizona		
Smith, Ben (Big Ben) OE-DE	33GB34-35Pit 36AFL 37Was	2	6'3"	208	Alabama		
Smith, Bill OE-DE	34-39ChiC	2 5	6'1"	198	Washington		132
Smith, Dick C-LB	33Bos 33ChiB		6'2"	225	Ohio State		
Smith, Ed FB-TB-DB	36Bos 37GB	1	6'2"	207	N.Y.U.		3
Smith, Ernie T	35-37,39GB	5	6'2"	224	Southern Calif.		61
Smith, Gaylon FB-DB-LB-WB-BB-TB	39-42Was	12	5'11"	202	Rhodes	6	54
	43-45MS 46CleAA						
Smith, George C-LB	37,41-43Was 44Bkn 45Bos 47SF-AA		6'2"	220	California	6	
Smith, George FB-DB	43ChiC 44-45MS		6'1"	200	Villanova		
Smith, Harry (Blackjack) T	40Det		5'11"	215	Southern Calif.		
Smith, Jack DE-OE	42Phi 43Was 44-45MS		6'1"	200	Stanford		
Smith, John T	45Phi		6'2"	200	Florida		
Smith, Milt DB-OE	45Phi		6'3"	185	U.C.L.A.		
Smith, Ray C-LB	30-31Prov 33Phi		5'10'	195	Missouri	5	
Smith, Riley (General) BB-LB	36Bos 37-38Was	12 5	6'2"	200	Alabama		108
Smith, Stu FB-LB-TB-DB-BB	37-38Pit	2	6'	195	Bucknell		
Smith, Wee Willie DB-TB-FB	34NYG	2	5'6"	148	Idaho		12
Smukler, Dave (Dynamite) FB-LB	36-39Phi 43MS 44Bos	12 5	6'1"	226	Temple		40
Sneddon, Bob DB-HB-WB	44Was 45Det 46LA-AA		5'10"	180	St. Mary's	2	
Snelling, Ken FB-LB	45GB		6'	210	U.C.L.A.		
Snyder, Bob QB-DB-TB	36AFL 37-38Cle 39-41ChiB	12 5	6'	200	Ohio U.	2	108
	42VR 43ChiB HC47LA						
Snyder, Bull G-T	34-35Pit		6'2"	230	Ohio U.		
Soar, Hank DB-FB-WB-QB	36AFL 37-44NYG 45MS	12 5	6'2"	209	Providence	12	73
47-48 coached in B.A.A.	46NYG						
Sohn, Ben G	41NYG 42-45MS		6'2"	220	Southern Calif.		
Sohn, Benny WB-DB-FB-LB	34C-S		5'8"	170	Washington		
Somers, George T	39-40Phi 41-42Pit	5	6'2"	253	LaSalle		8
Sorce, Ross T	45Pit		6'4"	255	Georgetown		
Sorenson, Glen (Goof) G-LB	43-45GB		6'	217	Utah State		1
Sortet, Bill OE-DE	33-40Pit	2	6'1"	187	West Virginia		48
Souchak, Frank OE-DE	39Pit		6'	205	Pittsburgh		
Spadaccini, Vic BB-DB-WB	38-40Cle 41AFL 42-45MS	2 5	6'	222	Minnesota		41
Speegle, Cliff C-LB	45ChiC		6'1"	195	Oklahoma	2	
Speelman, Harry G	40Det		5'11"	220	Michigan State		
Speth, George T	42Det 43-45MS		6'2"	220	Murray State		
Spillers, Ray (Brush) T	37Phi		6'3"	218	Arkansas		
Spirida, John BB-DE-OE	39Was		6'	195	St. Anselm's		
Springer, Hal OE-DE	45NYG		6'4"	212	Central St.-Okla.		
Squyres, Seaman (Cob) TB-DB	33Cin		6'3"	200	Rice		
Stackpool, Jack FB-LB	42Phi 43-45MS		6'1"	207	Washington		
Stacy, Red T-G	35-37Det		6'2"	210	Oklahoma		
Stafford, Harry WB-DB	34NYG		5'11"	205	Texas		
Stahlman, Dick T-G-OE-DE	24Ken 24KC 24Ken 24-25Akr		6'2"	219	DePaul, Northwestern		
	26AFL 27,30NYG 31-32GB 33ChiB						
Starret, Ben BB-DE-LB-TB	41Pit 42-45GB		5'11"	213	St. Mary's	2	12
Stasica, Leo DB-QB-TB	41Bkn 42MS 43Was 44Bos	12	5'11"	185	Colorado	2	
Steele, Ernie HB-DB	42Phi 43P-P 44-48Phi	23	6'	187	Washington	24	115
Steen, Frank OE-DE	39GB		6'1"	190	Rice		
Steen, Jim T	35-36Det		6'2"	205	Syracuse		
Steinbach, Larry T-G	30-31ChiB 31-33ChiC 33Phi		6'	214	St. Thomas		
Steinkemper, Bill T	37AFL 43ChiB 44MS		6'2"	220	Notre Dame		
Steinmetz, Ken FB-LB	44-45Bos		6'	188	none	1	
Stephens, Johnny OE-DE	38Cle		6'1"	190	Marshall		
Steponovich, Mike G	33Bos		5'9"	205	St. Mary's		
Stevens, Pete C-LB	36Phi		6'	215	Temple		
Stevenson, Ralph G-LB	40Cle 41-45MS		5'10"	196	Oklahoma		
Steverson, Norris TB-DB	34C-S		5'10"	185	Arizona State		
Steward, Dean HB	43P-P 44-45MS		6'	210	Ursinus		
Stewart, Vaughn C-LB	43ChiC 43-44Bkn		6'1"	190	Alabama		
Stockton, Mule G-T	37-38Phi		6'1"	214	McMurry		
Stofko, Ed TB-DB	45Pit		6'1"	192	St. Francis (Pa.)		
Stojack, Frank (Toughie) G	35-36Bkn		5'10"	194	Washington State		
Stokes, Dixie C-LB	37-39Det 43ChiC		6'	205	Centenary		8
Stolfa, Anton (Butch) QB-DB	39ChiB		6'	195	Luther		
Stonebraker, John OE-DE	42GB		6'3"	200	Southern Calif.		
Storm, Ed TB-DB-FB-LB-HB-BB	34-35Phi	1	6'1"	195	Santa Clara		12
Stough, Glenn T	45Pit		6'5"	240	Duke		
Stralka, Clem (Little Bull) G	38-42Was 43 44MS 45-46Was		5'10"	215	Georgetown		
Stramiello, Mike OE-DE	30-32Bkn 32SI 34Bkn		6'1"	198	Colgate	1	18
Stringfellow, Joe TB-DB-OE	42Det 43-45MS		6'	185	Southern Miss.		
Strom, Frank T	44Bkn		6'2"	252	Claremore J.C.		
Strong, Ken FB-DB-TB-K	29-32SI 33-35NYG	0 2 5	6'	206	N.Y.U.	18	479
	36-37AFL 38SL 39,44-47NYG						
Strutt, Art HB-DB	35-36Pit	2	6'	202	Duquesne		12
Stuart, Jim T	41Was		6'	212	Oregon		

UseName(Nicknames)-Positions	Team by Year	See Section	Hgt	Wgt	College	Int	Pts
Stuart, Roy G-LB	42Cle 43Det 44-45MS 46BufAA		5'8"	188	Tulsa		
Sturgeon, Cecil T	41Phi		6'2"	254	N. Dakota State		
Sturgeon, Lyle T	37GB		6'3"	250	N. Dakota State		
Stydahar, Joe T	36-42ChiB 43-44MS 45-46ChiB	5	6'4"	233	Pittsburgh, West Virginia	1	28
	HC50-51LA HC53-54ChiC						
Suffridge, Bob G	41Phi 42-44MS 45Phi		6'	205	Tennessee		
Sullivan, Frank C-LB	35-39ChiB 40Pit		6'3"	206	Loyola (N. Orl.)		
Supulski, Len OE-DB	42Phi 43-44MS-killed in action		6'	175	Dickinson	1	6
Sutherland, Jock	HC40-41Bkn 42-45MS HC46-47Pit				Pittsburgh		
died April 11, 1948 — brain tumor							
Svendsen, Bud C-LB-G	37,39GB 38VR 40-43Bkn		6'1"	190	Minnesota	3	6
	44-45MS						
Svendsen, George C-LB	35-37,40-41GB 42-45MS		6'4"	230	Oregon, Minnesota	1	
37-38 played in N.B.L.							
Sweeney, Jake T	44ChiB		6'3"	240	Cincinnati		
Swiadon, Phil G	43Bkn		6'	220	N.Y.U.		
Swisher, Bob HB-DB	38-41GB 42-44MS 45ChiB	2	5'11"	163	Northwestern	2	36
Szakash, Paul (Socko) BB-DB-FB-LB-OE-DE	38-39Det		6'	213	Montana		
	40VR 41-42Det 43-45MS						
Tackwell, Cookie OE-DE-T-G	30Fra 30Min 31Fra	0	6'2"	215	Kansas State	1	12
	31-33ChiB 33Cin 34C-S						
Tanguay, Bill TB-DB	33Pit		6'	190	N.Y.U.		
Tarrant, Bob OE-DE	36NYG 36AFL		6'	180	Pittsburg State		
Tatum, Jess OE-DE	38Pit		6'1"	215	N. Carolina State		
Taylor, Charlie BB-LB	44Bkn		5'10"	210	Ouachita Baptist		
Temple, Mark TB-DB	36Bkn 36Bos 36AFL		5'10"	175	Oregon		6
Tenner, Bob OE-DE	35GB		6'	212	Minnesota		
Tesser, Ray OE-DE	33-34Pit	2	6'2"	204	Carnegie-Mellon		
Thacker, Al DB	42Phi		5'10"	200	Charleston		
Thayer, Harry (Hobo) T-G	33Port		6'1"	215	Tennessee		
Thomas, Cal G	39-40Det		6'2"	210	Tulsa		
Thomas, Jim G	39ChiC		5'11"	200	Oklahoma		
Thomason, Jim WD-DB	45Det		6'	200	Texas A&M		
Thomason, Stumpy DB-FB-LB-BB-HB-TB-WB	30-35Bkn	0 2	5'7"	189	Georgia Tech	2	37
	35-36Phi						
Thompson, Russ T	36-39ChiB 40Phi		6'5"	249	Nebraska		
Thompson, Tuffy HB-DB-TB	37-39Phi 39GB	2	5'11"	172	Minnesota		12
Thornton, Dick BB-DB	33Phi		5'8"	165	Missouri-Rolla		
Thorpe, Wilfred G-LB-DE	41-42Cle 43-45MS		6'3"	205	Arkansas	2	
Thurbon, Bob HB-DB	43P-P 44C-P 46BufAA	2	5'10"	176	Pittsburgh	3	66
Tiller, Morgan OE-DE	44Bos 45Pit	2	6'1"	195	Denver		
Tinsley, Gus OE-DE	37-38ChiC 39HO 40ChiC	2	6'1"	198	Louisiana State	1	48
Tinsley, Jess T-OE-DE	29-33ChiC		6'	201	Louisiana State	1	
Tinsley, Pete G-LB	38-45GB		5'8"	205	Georgia	4	
Tinsley, Sid HB-DB	45Pit	4	5'9"	168	Clemson	1	
Tipton, Howie G-OE-DE-LB-DB-BB-WB-TB	33-37ChiC		5'11"	186	Southern Calif.	1	6
Titchenal, Bob LB-OE-C-DE	40-42Was 43-45MS	2	6'2"	194	San Jose State	3	12
	46SF-AA 47LA-AA						
Titus, Si C-LB-DE	40-42Bkn 43-44MS 45Pit		6'	195	Holy Cross	2	
Todd, Dick DB-HB-WB-FB	39-42Was 43-44MS	234	5'11"	172	Texas A&M	14	208
	45-48Was HC51Was						
Tofil, Joe OE-DB	42Bkn 43-45MS		6'1"	205	Indiana		
Tollefson, Charlie G	44-46GB		6'	215	Iowa		
Tomaini, Army T	45NYG		6'	235	Catawba		
Tomasello, Carl DE	40NYG		6'	210	Scranton		
Tomasic, Andy TB-DB	42Pit 43-45MS 46Pit	12	6'	175	Temple	2	6
played major league baseball							
Tommerson, Clarence DB-HB	38-39Pit		6'2"	196	Wisconsin		
Tonelli, Mario FB-DB	40ChiC 41-44MS	2	5'11"	200	Notre Dame		6
Tonelli, Tony C-LB-G	39Det		6'	210	Southern Calif.		
Torrance, Jack (Baby Jack) T	39-40ChiB		6'3"	285	Louisiana State		
Tosi, Flavio (Bull) OE-DE	34-36Bos	2	6'1"	101	Boston College		12
Tosi, John C-LB-T-G	39Pit 39Bkn		5'10"	225	Niagara		
Trebotich, Buzz BB-DB-LB-FB	44-45Det 47BalAA		5'10"	208	St. Mary's	3	
Tripson, John T	41Det 42-45MS		6'3"	210	Mississippi State		
Trocolor, Bob QB-DB-HB	42-43NYG 44Bkn	2	6'2"	207	Long Island U.		
Trost, Milt (Bud) T-DE-OE	35 30ChiD 40Phi 41AFL		6'1"	206	Marquette		
Tsoutouvas, Lou C-LB	38Pit		5'11"	210	Stanford		
Tsoutouvas, Sam C-LB	40Det		6'	205	Oregon State		
Tuckey, Dick TB-DB	38Was 38Cle	12	6'2"	205	Manhattan		2
Tully, Darrell TB-DB	39Det	12	6'1"	200	East Texas State		6
Turbert, Frank QB-DB	44Bos		5'11'	200	Charleston		
Turley, John BB-DB	35-36Pit	1	5'10"	183	Ohio Wesleyan		
Turnbow, Guy T-OE-DB	33-34Phi		6'2"	217	Mississippi		3
Turner, Jay BB-LB	38-39Was		5'10"	202	George Washington		
Turner, Jim C-LB	36AFL 37Cle		6'2"	210	Oklahoma State		
Tuttle, Orville G	37-41NYG 42-45MS 46NYG		5'9"	210	Oklahoma City		
Twedell, Frank G	39GB		5'11"	220	Minnesota		
Tyler, Pete BB-LB	37-38ChiC		5'11"	190	Hardin-Simmons		12
Ucovich, Mitch T	44Was 45ChiC		5'11"	208	San Jose State		
Ugoccioni, Rocky OE-DE	44Bkn 45MS		6'	195	Murray State		6
Uhrinyak, Steve G	39Was		6'2"	218	Franklin & Marshall		
Umont, Frank G-T	43-45NYG		5'11"	218	none		
Underwood, Wayne (Forest) T	37Cle 37AFL		6'1"	190	Davis & Elkins		
Ungerer, Joe T	44-45Was		6'	243	Fordham		
Uram, Andy HB-DB-TB	38-43GB 44-45MS	2	5'10"	188	Minnesota	6	98
Urban, Alex DE-OE	41GB 42-43MS 44-45GB		6'3"	207	South Carolina		6
Uremovich, Emil T	41-42Det 43-44MS 45-46Det 48ChiAA		6'2"	233	Indiana	1	
Uzdavinis, Walt DE-OE-T	36AFL 37Cle		6'2"	210	Fordham		
Vairo, Dom OE-DE	35GB		6'2"	203	Notre Dame		
Van Every, Hal TB-DB-HB	40-41GB 42-45MS	12 4	6'	195	Minnesota	3	18
Van Sickle, Clyde G	32-33GB		6'1"	220	Arkansas		
Vant Hull, Fred G-LB	42GB 43-45MS		6'	214	Minnesota		
Van Tone, Art WB-DB	43-45Det 46BknAA	2	5'10"	185	Southern Miss.	7	60
Vanzo, Fred (Chopper) BB-LB	38-41Det 41ChiC 42-45MS	2	6'2"	230	Northwestern		
Vaughn, Harp DB-TB-BB-HB	33-34Pit	1	5'7"	150	none		6
Vaughan, Pug TB-DB	35Det 36ChiC	12	5'11"	181	Tennessee	3	
Vetter, Jack HB-DB	42Bkn 43-45MS		6'2"	198	McPherson		
Vidoni, Vic (Putt) OE-DE	35-36Pit	2	6'1"	210	Duquesne		
Visnic, Larry LB-G-BB	43-45NYG		5'11"	190	St. Benedict's	3	
Vodicka, Joe HB-DB	43ChiB 44MS 45ChiB 45ChiC		5'10"	189	none		
Vokaty, Otto (Lefty) FB-LB-BB-TB-DB	31Cle 32NYG	0	6'1"	191	Heidelberg	1	24
	33ChiC 34C-S						
Volok, Bill G-T	34-39ChiC		6'2"	215	Tulsa		6
Vosberg, Don OE-DE	41NYG 42-45MS		6'2"	188	Marquette		
Vucinich, Milt C-LB	45ChiB		6'	215	Stanford		
Wager, Clint OE-DE	42ChiB 43ChiC 44C-P 45ChiC		6'6"	218	St. Mary's (Minn.)		
43-46,47-49 played in N.B.L., 49-50 played in N.B.A.							
Wager, John (Popeye, Red) C-LB-G-T	31-33Port		5'11"	203	Carthage	5	
Wagner, Sid G	36-38Det		5'11"	192	Michigan State		

UseName(Nicknames)-Positions	Team by Year	See Section	Hgt	Wgt	College	Int	Pts
Walker, Bill G	44-45Bos		6'	220	V.M.I.		
Waller, Bill (Blondy) OE-DE	37AFL 38Bkn		6'1"	190	Illinois		
Walls, Will OE-DE	37-39,41-43NYG 44-45MS	2	6'4"	214	Texas Christian		24
Walsh, Adam	HC45Cle HC46LA				Notre Dame		
Walsh, Chile	HC34C-S				Notre Dame		
Walton, Frank (Tiger) G	34Bos 44-45Was		5'11"	230	Pittsburgh		
Ward, David (Nubbin) OE-DE	33Bos		5'10"	195	Haskell Indian, New Mexico		
Ward, Elmer (Bear) C-LB	35Det		6'2"	215	Utah State		
Ware, Charlie T	44Bkn		6'3"	245	Birmingham-South.		
Warren, Busit TB-DB-HB	45Phi 45Pit	12	5'11"	175	Tennessee	1	12
Waters, Dale (Muddy) T-OE-DE-G-WB-DB	31Port 31Cle 32-33Bos		6'2"	212	Florida		
Watkins, Foster (Flippin') QB-DB-HB	40-41Phi 42-45MS	12	5'9"	163	West Texas State		2
Watson, Jim C-LB	45Was		6'	205	U. of Pacific		
Watt, Walt HB-DB	45ChiC		6'	187	Miami (Fla.)		
Watts, George T	42Was 43-45MS		6'1"	225	Appalachian State		
Wear, Bob C-LB	42Phi		5'11"	205	Penn State		
Webb, George OE-DE	43Bkn		6'1"	180	Texas Tech		
Weber, Dick TB-DB	45Det		5'11"	195	St. Louis		
Weeks, George DE	44Bkn		6'2"	200	Alabama		
Wehba, Ray OE-DE	43Bkn 44GB 45MS	2	6'	215	Southern Calif.	1	
Weinberg, Henry G-T	34Pit		5'7"	190	Duquesne		
Weiner, Bernie T-G	42Bkn 43-45MS		5'11"	222	Kansas State		
Weiner, Reds FB-LB-BB-DB	34Phi		5'9"	180	Muhlenberg	1	6
Weinstock, Izzy LB-FB-BB	35Phi 37-38Pit	2	6'	211	Pittsburgh		4
Weisenbaugh, Heinie BB-LB-HB-DB	35Pit 35-36Bos	2	5'11"	190	Pittsburgh		12
Weisgerber, Dick BB-DE-DB	38-40,42GB 43-45MS		5'10"	200	Willamette		2
Weiss, Howie FB-LB	39-40Det 41AFL	2	6'	210	Wisconsin		24
Weiss, John OE-DB	44-46NYG		6'3"	198	none		12
Weldin, Hal C-LB	34C-S		6'	198	Northwestern	1	
Weldon, Larry QB-DB-DE	44-45Was		6'	198	Presbyterian		5
Weller, Rabbit (Bub) WB-DB	33Bos		5'6"	150	Haskell Indian		13
Wemple, Don OE-DE	41Bkn 42-44MS-killed in action		6'2"	195	Colgate		6
Wendlick, Joe OE-DE	40Phi 41Pit	2	6'	207	Oregon State		
Wenzel, Ralph DE	42Pit 43-45MS		6'	205	Tulane		
West, Burr T	41Phi 42-45MS		6'1"	220	Tennessee		
West, Walt FB-DB	44Cle	2	6'	197	Pittsburgh	2	12
Westfall, Bob FB-LB-TB	45-47Det	12	5'8"	190	Michigan	1	96
Westfall, Ed TB-DB-BB	32-33Bos 33Pit		5'9"	170	Ohio Wesleyan	1	13
Wetterlund, Chet TB-DB	42Det 43-44MS-killed in action	1	6'2"	185	Illinois Wesleyan	1	
Wetzel, Buzz FB-LB	35ChiB 35Pit PC36AFL		5'10"	190	Ohio State		6
Whalen, Tammy (Moose) TB-DB	33Pit		5'8"	165	Catholic		
Whatley, Jim T-DE-OE	36-38Bkn		6'5"	223	Alabama		
Wheeler, Ernie DB-TB	39Pit 39ChiC 40-41AFL 42ChiC 43-45MS		6'1"	190	N. Dakota State		
Whire, Jodie FB-LB	33Phi		6'1"	185	Georgia		
White, Allie G-T	39Phi		5'11"	212	Texas Christian		
White, Tarzan G	37-39NYG 40-41ChiC 42-44MS 45NYG		5'9"	217	Alabama		
White, Whizzer TB-DB-HB-FB-WB	38Pit 39VR 40-41Det 42-45MS	12 4	6'1"	187	Colorado	1	80
White, Wilbur (Red) TB-DB-WB	35Bkn 36AFL 36Det	1	6'	167	Colorado State		
Whited, Marv LB-BB-G	42Was 43-44MS 45Was		5'10"	208	Oklahoma	1	
Wiatrak, Johnny C-LB	39Det		6'	220	Washington		
Wiberg, Ossie (Swede) BB-LB-DB-FB-HB-WB-G-OE-DE	27Cle 28Det 30NYG 32Bkn 33Cin	0	5'11"	207	Neb. Wesleyan	3	75
Wickett, Lloyd T	43Det 44-45MS 46Det		6'1"	208	Oregon State		
Widseth, Ed T	37-40NYG 41BL		6'1"	223	Minnesota		
Wiehl, Joe (Tiny) T	35Pit		5'11"	254	Duquesne		
Wiethe, John (Sock) G-LB 37-38 player-coach in N.B.L.	39-42Det		6'	198	Xavier-Ohio	2	
Wilging, Cole OE-DE	34C-S		6'3"	205	Xavier-Ohio		
Wilkerson, Basil OE-DE-T	32Bos 32SI 34C-S		6'	215	Oklahoma City		
Wilkin, Willie (Wee Willie) T	38-43Was 44-45MS PC46AA		6'4"	261	St. Mary's		8
Williams, Clyde T	35Phi 36AFL		6'2"	210	Georgia Tech		
Williams, Don G	41Pit 42-45MS		5'8"	210	Texas		
Williams, Jake OE-DE-G	29-33ChiC		6'	205	Texas Christian	1	
Williams, Joe (Jumpin' Joe) DB-HB	37Cle 39Pit 40AFL		5'9"	178	Ohio State		
Williams, Rex (Pinky) C-LB	40ChiC 40AFL 45Det		6'2"	203	Texas Tech		
Williams, Ted FB-LB-HB-DB	42Phi 44Bos	2	5'11"	183	Boston College	1	18
Williams, Tex C-LB	42Phi 43-45MS 46MiaAA		5'11"	193	Auburn	1	
Willson, Diddie G-0OE-DE	33-35Phi		5'10"	196	Pennsylvania	2	
Wilson, Billy OE-DE	35-37ChiC 38Pit 38Phi		5'10"	184	Gonzaga		
Wilson, Bobby TB-DB	36Bkn	12	5'9"	147	S.M.U.		24
Wilson, George OE-DE 39-40 played in N.B.L.	37-46ChiB HC57-64Det HC66-69MiaA	2	6'1"	199	Northwestern	3	108
Wilson, Gordon G-T	41AFL 41Cle 42-43ChiC 44Bos 44Bkn 45ChiC		6'	228	Texas-El Paso		
Wilson, Johnny (Long John) OE-DE	39-42Cle 43-45MS	2	6'3"	203	Case Reserve		30
Wilson, Mule WB-DB-FB-TB-HB-BB-LB	26Buf 27-30NYG 30SI 30-31GB 32-33Port	0	5'11"	192	Texas A&M	16	85
Winkler, Joe C-LB	45Cle		6'1"	200	Purdue	1	
Winslow, Bob DE	40Det 40Bkn		6'2"	205	Southern Calif.		
Witte, Earl BB-DB	34GB		6'	188	Gustavus Adolphus		
Wojciechowicz, Alex C-LB	38-46Det 46-50Phi		5'11"	217	Fordham	14	6
Wolfe, Red FB-DB	38NYG		6'	205	Texas		
Woltman, Clem T	38-40Phi		6'1"	214	Purdue		
Wood, Bobby T	40ChiC 41-45MS		6'2"	230	Alabama		
Woodruff, Lee (Cowboy) FB-LB-DB-TB-WB-HB	31Prov 32Bos 33Phi	0	6'	202	Mississippi	2	37
Worden, Jim HB-DB	45Cle		5'10"	180	Waynesburg		
Worden, Stu G-T-C-LB	30,32-34Bkn		6'	210	Hampden-Sydney		
Workman, Blake (Sheriff) DB-TB-BB	33Cin 34C-S		5'11"	185	Tulsa		
Wright, Ralph T	33Bkn		6'	230	Kentucky		
Wright, Ted WB-DB-BB-LB	34-35Bos 35Bkn		6'	185	North Texas		9
Wukits, Al LB-C-G	43P-P 44C-P 45Pit 46BufAA 46MiaAA		6'3"	213	Duquesne	3	6
Wunsch, Harry G	34GB		5'11"	212	Notre Dame		
Wycoff, Doug FB-DB-TB-BB-LB	26AFL 27NYG 29PC,30SI 31NYG 32SI 34Bos 36AFL	0	6'	206	Georgia Tech	13	73
Wynne, Harry OE-DE	44Bos 45NYG	2	6'4"	203	Arkansas		
Yarr, Tommy C-LB	33ChiC		5'10"	205	Notre Dame	1	
Yeager, Howie WB-DB	41NYG 42-45MS	2	5'11"	173	Cal.-Santa Barbara		24
Yezerski, John T	36Bkn		6'4"	240	St. Mary's		
Younce, Len G-LB	41,43-44NYG 45MS 46-48NYG	45	6'1"	208	Oregon State	10	49
Young, Bill (Bubbles) T	37-42Was 43-45MS 46Was		6'1"	247	Alabama		6
Young, Paul C-LB	33GB		6'4"	195	Oklahoma	1	
Young, Ray T	38Was		6'2"	215	Texas A&M		
Young, Waddy OE-DE	39-40Bkn 41-44MS-killed in action	2	6'3"	205	Oklahoma		
Yovicsin, John DE	44Phi		6'3"	195	Gettysburg		
Yurchey, John HB-DB	40Pit		5'11"	188	Duquesne		
Zadworney, Frank HB-DB	40Bkn 41-45MS		6'	202	Ohio State		
Zaninelli, Silvio BB-DB-LB-FB	34-37Pit	2	5'10"	207	Duquesne	2	6
Zapustas, Joe OE-DE	33NYG 36-37AFL		6'	198	Fordham		
Zarnas, Gust G	38ChiB 39Bkn 39-40GB 41-45MS		5'10"	220	Ohio State		
Zelencik, Frank T	39ChiC		6'1"	220	Ogelthorpe		
Zeller, Joe G-OE-DE	32GB 33-38ChiB		6'1"	203	Indiana	8	12
Zeno, Goe G-T	42-44Was 45MS 46-47Bos		5'10"	234	Holy Cross	1	
Zimmerman, Roy QB-DB-TB-FB-WB	40-42Was 43P-P 44-46Phi 47Det 48Bos	12 45	6'2"	201	San Jose State	19	229
Zirinsky, Walt HB-DB	45Cle		5'11"	187	Lafayette		
Zizak, Vince G-T	34-37Phi 37AFL		5'8"	208	Villanova		
Zoll, Dick G-T	37-38Cle		5'11"	218	Indiana		1
Zontini, Lou HB-LB-DB-BB-FB	40-41ChiC 44Cle 45MS 46BufAA	2 45	5'9"	189	Notre Dame	3	110
Zopetti, Frank TB-DB	41Pit 42-45MS		5'11"	185	Duquesne		
Zorich, George G-LB	44-45ChiB 46MiaAA 47BalAA		6'2"	213	Northwestern	1	
Zunker, Charlie T	34C-S		6'4"	227	SW Texas State		
Zuzzio, Tony G	42Det 43-45MS		5'11"	210	Muhlenberg		
Zyntell, Jim G	33NYG 33-35Phi 36-37AFL		6'1"	200	Holy Cross		

The number "0" in "See Section" means that the player's statistics are also shown in the statistical register sections for 1920-1932.

Lifetime Statistics — 1933-1945 Players Section 1 — PASSING
(All men with 25 or more passing attempts)

Name	Years*	Att.	Comp.	Comp. Pct.	Yards	Yds./ Att.	TD	Int.	Pct. Int.
Len Barnum	38-42	120	38	31.7	602	5.0	6	15	12.5
Cliff Battles	35-37	107	36	33.6	476	4.4	1		
Sammy Baugh	37-52	2995	1693	56.5	21886	7.3	187	203	6.8
Johnny Blood	33, 35-39	68	25	36.8	312	4.6	2		
Tony Bova	42-47	31	6	19.4	96	3.1	0	1	3.2
Eddie Britt	36-38	44	18	40.9	294	6.7	3	5	11.4
Lou Brock	40-45	67	19	28.4	519	7.7	77	5	7.5
Boyd Brumbaugh	38-41	58	18	31.0	427	7.4	4	10	17.2
Carl Brumbaugh	34, 36-38	83	23	27.7	484	5.8	9	8	9.6
Ray Buivid	37-38	83	34	41.0	510	6.1	11	4	4.8
Joe Bukant	38-40, 42-43	57	19	33.3	179	3.1	1	7	12.3
Young Bussey	40-41	40	13	32.5	353	8.8	5	3	7.5
Johnny Butler	43-45	36	14	38.9	191	5.3	0	2	5.6
George Cafego	40, 43-45	161	77	47.8	966	6.0	5	15	9.3
Chris Cagle	33	74	31	41.9	385	5.2	2	9	12.2
Ronnie Cahill	43	109	50	45.9	608	5.6	3	21	19.3
Leo Cantor	42, 45	47	15	31.9	271	5.8	1	5	10.6
Cy Casper	35	39	13	33.3	123	3.2	0		
Dick Cassiano	40	30	9	30.0	128	4.3	1	2	6.7
Frank Christensen	35-36	27	8	29.6	114	4.2	0		
Beryl Clark	40	58	25	43.1	316	5.4	2	6	10.3
Dutch Clark	34-38	197	97	49.2	1235	6.3	8		
Pat Coffee	37-38	158	68	43.0	1004	6.4	4	15	9.5
Tom Colella	42-49	149	56	37.6	617	4.1	4	18	12.1
Merl Condit	40-43, 45-46	48	10	20.8	152	3.2	1	7	14.6
George Corbett	34-38	26	10	38.5	142	5.5	1	4	15.4
Ed Danowski	34-39, 41	645	311	48.2	3867	6.0	39	44	6.8
Bill Davidson	37-39	33	11	33.3	99	3.0	0	5	15.2
Bob Davis	38, 42, 44-46	55	20	36.4	177	3.2	4	4	7.3
John Doehring	34-37	34	14	41.2	297	8.7	5	0	0.0
Bob Dunlap	35-36	37	11	29.7	111	3.0	1		
Kay Eakin	40-41, 46	107	41	38.3	601	5.6	3	12	11.2
Beattie Feathers	34-40	43	12	27.9	116	2.7	1		
Frankie Filchock	38-41, 44-46, 50	677	342	50.5	4921	7.3	47	79	11.7
Max Fiske	36-38	95	34	35.8	503	5.3	4	11	11.6
Red Franklin	35-37	78	19	24.4	287	3.7	1		
Benny Friedman	33	80	42	52.5	597	7.5	5	7	8.7
Johnny Gildea	35-38	171	51	29.8	964	5.6	5		
Ed Goddard	37-38	84	32	38.1	418	5.0	2	14	10.7
Marshall Goldberg	39-43, 46-48	28	10	35.7	114	4.1	1	2	7.1
Owen Goodnight	41	36	12	33.3	182	5.1	1	5	13.9
Red Grange	34	25	6	24.0	81	3.2	1	7	28.0
John Grigas	43-47	166	60	36.1	889	5.4	6	27	16.3
Jack Grossman	35-36	35	9	25.7	149	4.3	2		
George Grosvenor	35-37	99	39	39.4	567	5.7	3		
Scott Gudmundson	44-45	81	33	40.7	525	6.5	2	9	11.1
Ace Gutowsky	35-39	38	12	31.6	192	5.1	3		
Parker Hall	39-42, 46	729	331	45.4	4048	5.6	29	67	9.2
Bill Hartman	38	77	38	49.4	558	7.4	3	10	13.0
Ken Heineman	40, 43	65	22	33.8	359	5.5	4	9	13.8
Warren Heller	34-36	158	40	25.3	599	3.8	2		
Arnie Herber	33-40, 44-45	1072	445	41.5	7556	7.0	70	88	8.2
Clarke Hinkle	33-34, 36-41	52	21	40.4	265	5.1	0	6	11.5
Steve Hokuf	34	51	13	25.5	203	4.0	3	10	19.6
Tony Holm	33	52	16	30.8	406	7.8	2	13	25.0
Harry Hopp	41-43, 46-47	101	36	35.6	508	5.0	0	14	13.9
John Hovious	45	46	22	47.8	373	8.1	4	5	10.9
Vern Huffman	37-38	108	32	29.6	484	4.5	4	14	13.0
Cecil Isbell	38-42	818	411	50.2	5945	7.3	61	52	6.4
Don Jackson	36	35	7	20.0	80	2.3	0	11	31.4
Billy Jefferson	41-42	76	19	25.0	192	2.5	0	9	11.8
Bert Johnson	37-42	54	16	29.6	237	4.4	0	6	11.1
Cecil Johnson	43-44	33	14	42.4	209	6.3	2	5	15.2
Ralph Kercheval	35-40	94	38	40.4	592	6.3	3		
Red Kirkman	33,35	83	25	30.1	384	4.6	4		
John Kusko	36-38	34	8	23.5	119	3.5	0	11	32.3
Joe Laws	34-45	37	11	29.7	176	4.8	3		
Bill Leckonby	39-41	78	32	41.0	373	4.8	1	5	6.4
Tuffy Leemans	36-43	383	167	43.6	2324	6.1	25	32	8.4
Jim Leonard	35-36	38	13	34.2	164	4.3	0		
Sid Luckman	39-50	1744	904	51.8	14683	8.4	137	131	7.5
Pug Manders	39-47	53	20	37.7	183	3.5	1	5	9.4
Andy Marefos	41-42, 46	37	13	35.1	255	6.9	2	6	16.2
Walt Masters	36, 43-44	58	19	32.8	273	4.7	2	10	17.2
Bernie Masterson	34-40	410	155	37.8	3394	8.3	35	38	9.3
Ed Matesic	34-36	262	99	37.8	1406	5.4	9		
Ned Mathews	41-43, 45-47	46	14	30.4	204	4.4	3	2	4.3
Harry Mattos	36-37	34	9	26.5	126	3.7	1	6	17.6
Dean McAdams	41-43	191	84	44.0	932	4.9	4	25	13.1
John McCarthy	44	67	20	29.9	250	3.6	0	13	19.4
Harold McCullough	42	38	12	31.6	211	5.6	1	3	7.9
Hugh McCullough	39-43, 45	253	87	34.4	1105	4.4	6	41	16.2
Coley McDonough	39-41, 44	125	47	37.6	865	6.9	5	20	16.0
Charlie McGibbony	44	48	18	37.5	262	5.5	1	10	20.8
Tex McKay	44-47	103	38	36.9	592	5.7	6	11	10.7
Eddie Miller	39-40	96	48	50.0	700	7.3	5	9	9.4
Keith Molesworth	33-37	159	61	38.4	1104	6.9	15		
Bob Monnett	33-38	338	154	45.6	2281	6.7	23	26	7.7
Emmett Mortell	37-39	169	42	24.9	655	3.9	9	15	8.9
Harry Newman	33-35	269	105	39.0	1696	6.3	12	25	9.3
Emery Nix	43,46	72	34	47.2	546	7.6	5	3	4.2
Ray Nolting	36-43	35	7	20.0	139	4.0	3	5	14.3
Doug Nott	35	34	9	26.5	169	5.0	1		
Davey O'Brien	39-40	478	223	46.7	2614	5.5	11	34	7.1
Ace Parker	37-41, 45-46	718	335	46.7	4701	6.5	30	50	7.0
Billy Patterson	39-40	155	48	31.0	756	4.9	6	19	12.3
Frank Patrick	38-39	80	22	27.5	291	3.6	1	13	16.2
Ike Peterson	35-36	31	6	19.4	121	3.9	1		
Stan Pincura	37-38	60	22	36.7	332	5.5	2	10	16.7
Johnny Pingel	39	48	27	56.3	343	7.1	3	4	8.3
Glenn Presnell	33-36	263	90	34.2	1424	5.4	9		
Cotton Price	40-41, 45-46	225	94	41.8	1308	5.8	8	24	10.7
Marion Pugh	41, 45-46	200	94	47.0	1159	5.8	9	15	7.5
Albie Reisz	44-47	134	58	43.3	923	6.9	10	14	10.4
Pug Rentner	35-37	89	24	27.0	346	3.9	1	6	15.4
Dick Riffle	38-42	82	21	25.6	332	4.0	2	15	18.3
John Robbins	38-39	182	88	48.4	1076	5.9	6	19	10.4
Gene Ronzani	34-38, 44-45	179	79	44.1	1201	6.7	16		
Doug Russell	35-39	48	12	25.0	300	6.3	2		
Frank Sachse	43-45	75	32	42.7	501	6.7	3	7	9.3
Tony Sarausky	35-38	54	14	25.9	181	3.4	1		
Phil Sarboe	35-36	181	78	43.1	1048	5.8	5		
Bill Shepherd	36-40	88	30	34.1	521	5.9	3	14	15.9
Allie Sherman	43-47	135	66	48.9	823	6.1	9	9	6.7
Frankie Sinkwich	43-44, 46-47	301	121	40.2	1913	6.4	19	42	14.0
Dwight Sloan	38-40	232	100	43.1	1251	5.4	3	18	7.8
Marty Slovak	39-41	109	57	52.3	618	5.7	5	18	16.5
Ed Smith	36-37	42	11	26.2	120	2.9	1	3	7.1
Gaylon Smith	39-42, 46	37	16	43.2	202	5.5	2	4	10.8
Riley Smith	36-38	46	19	41.3	290	6.3	3	3	6.5
Dave Smukler	36-39, 44	308	112	36.4	1357	4.4	16	32	10.4
Bob Snyder	37-41, 43	241	91	37.8	1758	7.3	12	23	9.5
Hank Soar	37-46	53	16	30.2	305	5.8	4	7	13.2
Leo Stasica	41, 43-44	55	23	41.8	273	5.0	1	8	14.5
Ed Storm	35	44	15	34.1	372	8.5	3		
Ken Strong	34-35, 39, 44-47	26	12	46.2	159	6.1	1	2	7.7
Andy Tomasic	42, 46	66	15	22.7	227	3.4	0	6	9.1
Dick Tuckey	38	32	8	25.0	140	4.4	1	3	9.4
Darrell Tully	39	69	20	29.0	356	5.2	2	13	18.8
John Turley	35	27	6	22.2	92	3.4	1		
Hal Van Every	40-41	71	23	32.4	394	5.5	4	8	11.3
Harp Vaughan	34	39	14	35.9	272	7.0	2	5	12.8
Pug Vaughan	35-36	94	37	39.4	650	6.9	5		
Busit Warren	45	92	36	39.1	368	4.0	0	10	10.9
Foster Watkins	40-41	95	34	35.8	616	6.5	2	3	3.2
Bob Westfall	44-47	53	27	50.9	428	8.1	5	7	13.2
Chet Wetterlund	42	44	13	29.5	230	5.2	0	10	22.7
Whizzer White	38, 40-41	215	86	40.0	1192	5.5	4	34	15.8
Wilbur White	35-36	33	10	30.3	73	2.2	2		
Bobby Wilson	36	40	11	27.5	148	3.7	0	9	22.5
Roy Zimmerman	40-48	708	291	41.1	4801	6.8	44	70	9.9

* — Years for which statistics are avialable

Lifetime Statistics Section 2 — **RUSHING and RECEIVING**
(All men with 25 or more rushing attempts or 10 or more receptions)

Name	Years*	RUSHING Att.	Yards	Avg.	TD	RECEIVING Rec.	Yards	Avg.	TD
Neal Adams	42-47					43	719	16.7	7
Sam Agee	38-39	93	315	3.4	2	3	11	3.7	0
Joe Aguirre	41-49	3	16	5.3	0	160	2262	14.1	29
Frank Atkins	43-46	244	1142	4.7	7	16	150	9.4	0
Vannie Albanese	37-38	48	150	3.1	0				
Julie Alfonse	37-38	49	76	1.6	1	7	160	22.9	0
Jay Arnold	37-41	37	43	1.2	1	35	573	16.4	3
Jim Badgro	37-39					32	467	14.6	1
Red Badgro	33-34,36					32	521	16.3	2
Frank Balasz	39-41,45	60	228	3.8	1	5	50	10.0	0
Len Barnum	38-42	239	590	2.5	3	11	167	15.2	0
Jeff Barrett	36-38	3	11	3.7	0	47	944	20.1	5
Cliff Battles	33-37	725	3037	4.2	21	33	486	14.7	3
Sammy Baugh	37-52	318	324	1.0	9	1	0	0.0	0
Wayland Becker	34-39	2	4	2.0	0	25	394	15.8	2
Steve Belichick	41	28	118	4.2	2	1	13	13.0	0
Jim Benton	38-40,42-47	8	19	2.4	0	288	4801	16.7	45
Connie Mack Berry	39-40,42-47					45	766	17.0	8
Gil Berry	35	44	77	1.8	0				
Mel Bleeker	44-47	139	586	4.2	6	14	360	25.7	4
Johnny Blood	33,35-39	98	243	2.5	0	54	930	17.2	12
Ernie Bonelli	45-46	38	100	2.6	0	4	35	8.8	0
Dick Booth	41,45	33	99	3.0	1	10	193	19.3	1
Tony Bova	42-47	21	0	0.0	0	60	1134	18.9	7
Sam Boyd	39-40					21	423	20.1	2
Jeep Brett	36-37					15	274	18.3	1
Eddie Britt	36-38	79	201	2.5	0	6	106	17.7	0
Lou Brock	40-45	254	804	3.2	10	59	761	12.9	6
Hank Bruder	33-40 + 33-34,36-40	180	602	3.3	5	23	347	15.1	2
Boyd Brumbaugh	38-41	256	727	2.8	4	8	101	12.6	2
Carl Brumbaugh	33-34,36-38, +34,36-38	51	31	0.6	1	11	146	13.3	4
Larry Buhler	39-41	41	121	3.0	0	1	17	17.0	0
Ray Buivid	37-38	51	89	1.7	1	2	12	6.0	1
Joe Bukant	38-40,42-43	184	426	2.3	4	2	13	6.5	0
Dale Burnett	33-39	45	62	1.4	0	82	1190	14.5	17
Sam Busich	36-37,43					19	193	10.2	1
Wendell Butcher	38-42	33	103	3.1	1	15	154	10.3	0
Johnny Butler	43-45	168	517	3.1	4	8	186	23.3	2
Larry Cabrelli	41-47	1	-2	-2.0	0	68	945	13.9	5
Ernie Caddel	33-38 + 34-38	443	2211	5.0	20	48	532	11.1	4
George Cafego	40,43-45	155	77	0.5	1	13	133	10.2	0
Ronnie Cahill	43	62	-11	-0.2	0				
Bill Calihan	40-45	33	105	3.2	1	32	383	12.0	4
Leo Cantor	42,45	150	415	2.8	7	15	159	10.6	0
Lloyd Cardwell	37-43	205	905	4.4	8	51	922	18.1	5
Joe Carter	34-45	2	1	0.5	0	127	1880	14.8	21
Cy Casper	35	56	102	1.8	2	5	94	18.8	1
Dick Cassiano	40	35	84	2.4	0	2	67	33.5	2
Marty Christiansen	40	32	71	2.2	1				
Stu Clancy	33-34+	58	226	3.9	3				
Beryl Clark	40	39	9	0.2	0	1	20	20.0	0
Dutch Clark	34-38	468	2296	4.9	24	19	234	12.3	0
Harry Clark	40-43,46-48	390	1711	4.4	11	51	1022	20.0	11
Pat Coffee	37-38	95	326	3.4	3				
John Cole	38,40	27	79	2.9	0	4	20	5.0	0
Tom Colella	42-49	199	754	3.8	8	18	215	11.9	5
Merl Condit	40-43,45-46	421	1713	4.1	11	32	323	10.1	2
Dave Cook	35-36 + 36	41	145	3.5	0	1	2	2.0	0
Al Coppage	40-42,46-47					65	736	11.3	3
George Corbett	33-34,36-38 + 34-38	75	247	3.3	0	8	91	11.4	1
Ollie Cordill	40	24	73	3.0	0	14	158	11.3	2
Red Corzine	35-38 + 36-38	47	140	3.0	2	10	111	11.1	2
Larry Craig	39-49	10	16	1.6	0	14	155	11.1	0
Milt Crain	44	26	78	3.0	0	1	16	16.0	0
Dick Crayne	36-37	111	338	3.0	1	2	36	18.0	0
Abe Croft	44-45					11	152	13.8	2
Joe Crowley	44-45					14	291	20.8	3
Ward Cuff	37-47	344	1851	5.4	7	106	1559	14.7	13
Bill Daddio	41-42,46					16	147	9.2	1
Ed Danowski	34-39,41	455	1232	2.7	4	1	12	12.0	0
Bill Davidson	37-39	155	370	2.4	1	22	425	19.3	2
Bob Davis	38,42,44-46	230	904	3.9	3	47	427	9.1	2
Corby Davis	38-39, 41-42	143	382	2.7	4	19	133	7.0	0
Dan DeSantis	41	45	125	2.8	0	4	53	13.3	0
Versil Deskin	36-39					16	249	15.6	2
Dave Diehl	39-40,44-45					32	578	18.1	4
Lavie Dilweg	33-34					25	334	13.4	2
John Doehring	33-37 + 34-37	49	212	4.3	0	2	33	16.5	0
Woody Dow	38-40	5	13	2.6	0	10	146	14.6	1
Mule Dowell	36	54	151	2.8	0				
Johnny Drake	37-41	525	1700	3.2	24	41	530	12.9	3
Paul Duhart	44-45	68	200	3.9	3	9	176	19.6	2
Les Dye	44-45					31	365	11.8	4
Kay Eakin	40-41,46	56	-4	-0.1	0	11	148	13.5	1
Harry Ebding	34-37					32	668	20.9	7
Frank Emmons	40	29	77	2.7	1	3	19	6.3	1
Dick Erdlitz	42,45-46	53	131	2.5	2	12	109	9.1	0
Dick Evans	40-43					13	145	11.2	0
Tony Falkenstein	43-44	62	200	3.2	1	3	60	15.0	0
Gary Famiglietti	38-46	528	1981	3.8	24	12	187	15.6	1
Andy Farkas	38-45	587	2103	3.6	21	80	1086	13.6	13
Scrapper Farrell	38-39	109	425	3.9	3				
Beattie Feathers	34-40	360	1979	5.5	16	14	222	15.9	1
Frankie Filchock	38-41,44-46,50	477	1478	3.1	6	8	88	11.0	0
Steve Filipowicz	45-46	55	145	2.6	2	11	133	12.1	2
Ev Fisher	38-40	18	63	3.5	0	11	122	11.1	0
Bill Fisk	40-43,46-48	2	0	0.0	0	69	791	11.5	3
Max Fiske	36-38	115	219	1.9	0	8	96	12.0	0
Ray Flaherty	33-34					25	396	15.8	1
Jim Fordham	44-45	118	534	4.5	5	5	47	9.4	0

Name	Years*	RUSHING Att.	Yards	Avg.	TD	RECEIVING Rec.	Yards	Avg.	TD
Sam Fox	45					10	120	12.0	2
Terry Fox	41,45-46	33	123	3.7	0	9	98	10.9	0
Sam Francis	37-40	253	873	3.5	5	4	22	5.5	0
George Franck	41,45-47	144	525	3.6	3	27	536	19.9	5
Red Franklin	35-37 + 36-37	119	366	3.1	4				
Ed Frutig	41,45-46	1	11	11.0	0	12	117	9.8	3
Hugh Gallerneau	41-42,45-47	343	1421	4.1	26	51	794	15.6	7
Milt Gantenbein	33-40					80	1329	16.6	7
Chuck Gelatka	37-40					20	250	12.5	1
Bill Geyer	42-43,46	25	54	2.2	2	6	145	24.2	2
Johnny Gildea	35-38 + 36-38	134	99	0.7	1	9	120	13.3	0
Fred Gloden	41,46	35	79	2.3	1	2	13	6.5	0
Ed Goddard	37-38	97	146	1.5	2	12	189	15.8	1
Marshall Goldberg	39-43,46-48	476	1644	3.5	11	60	775	12.9	5
Buckets Goldenberg	33-45 + 33-34, 36-45	110	356	3.2	6	10	64	6.4	1
Ted Goodwin	35-36	3	-1	-0.3	0	33	511	15.5	6
Red Grange	33-34	111	433	3.9	2	6	135	22.5	2
John Grigas	43-47	465	1581	3.4	10	30	374	12.5	1
Frank Grigonis	42	37	131	3.5	1	1	17	17.0	0
Jack Grossman	35-36 + 34,36	67	208	3.1	2	10	158	15.8	1
George Grosvenor	35-37 + 36-37	362	1307	3.6	6	1	6	6.0	0
Roger Grove	33-34	53	227	4.3	1	26	351	13.5	3
Al Grygo	44-45	76	420	5.5	2	10	124	12.4	1
Scott Gudmundson	44-45	37	-17	-0.5	0	1	-8	-8.0	0
Ace Gutowsky	33-39+36-39	851	3037	3.6	17	2	55	27.5	0
Elmer Hackney	40-46	220	846	3.8	10	19	135	7.1	1
John Hall	40-43	116	296	2.6	3	28	537	19.2	5
Parker Hall	39-42, 46	329	1083	3.3	6	3	9	3.0	0
Ray Hamilton	38-39,44-47					40	688	17.2	2
Chuck Hanneman	37-41	3	59	19.7	1	35	622	17.8	4
Swede Hanson	33-38 + 36-38	507	2001	3.9	12	4	35	8.8	2
Merle Hapes	42,46	146	524	3.6	8	13	119	9.2	2
Ray Hare	40-44,46	132	539	4.1	2	28	359	12.8	1
Bill Hartman	38	71	195	2.7	0	1	6	6.0	0
Ken Heineman	40,43	55	121	2.2	0				
Warren Heller	34-36 + 36	274	987	3.5	1	12	160	13.3	3
Arnie Herber	33-40,44-45	161	46	0.3	1	8	124	15.5	2
Bill Hewitt	33-39,43	4	6	1.5	0	97	1562	16.1	23
Ben Hightower	42-43	1	-6	-6.0	0	29	484	16.7	4
Harold Hill	38-40					11	220	20.0	0
Clarke Hinkle	33-41	1079	3545	3.3	31	47	561	11.9	9
Jack Hinkle	40,43-47	238	1067	4.5	6	7	68	9.7	0
Joe Hoague	41-42, 46	99	282	2.8	2	3	25	8.3	1
Herman Hodges	39-42					23	285	12.4	0
Harry Hopp	41-43,46-47	262	801	3.1	9	24	294	12.3	3
Jim Lee Howell	37-42,46-47					61	921	15.1	7
Vern Huffman	37-38	104	368	3.5	1	9	121	13.4	0
Don Hutson	35-45	56	262	4.7	3	488	7981	16.4	100
Don Irwin	36-39	182	586	3.2	6	27	289	10.4	0
Cecil Isbell	38-42	422	1522	3.6	10	15	174	11.6	0
Pop Ivy	40-42,45-47					53	513	9.7	1
Don Jackson	36	46	76	1.7	0				
Harry Jacunski	39-44					52	985	18.9	6
Len Janiak	39-42	85	228	2.7	0	11	65	5.9	1
Ed Jankowski	37-41	255	1003	3.9	8	2	65	32.5	1
Billy Jefferson	41-42	68	222	3.3	1	2	14	7.0	0
Bert Johnson	37-42	152	368	2.4	2	16	268	16.8	3
Cecil Johnson	43-44	56	79	1.4	0	9	136	15.1	2
Luke Johnsos	33-36	1	4	4.0	0	40	688	17.2	11
Jimmy Johnston	39-40,46	97	321	3.3	3	40	461	11.5	4
Swede Johnston	35-40	194	619	3.2	5	8	70	8.8	0
Art Jones	41,45	67	303	4.5	4	9	129	14.3	1
Harvey Jones	44-45,47	46	148	3.2	1	8	95	11.9	1
Ed Justice	36-42	33	127	3.8	1	70	1006	14.4	9
Mike Kabealo	44	47	152	3.2	1	2	20	10.0	0
George Karamatic	38	50	185	3.7	0	4	99	24.8	1
Bull Karcis	35-39,43	417	1301	3.1	10	16	148	9.3	0
Bill Karr	36-38 + 33-38	6	27	4.5	1	48	1042	21.7	18
Ribbit Keen	37-38	37	164	4.4	0	5	45	9.0	0
Clarence Kellogg	36	66	164	2.5	0	4	11	2.8	0
Shipwreck Kelly	37 + 33,37	16	29	1.8	3	23	253	11.0	3
Ralph Kercheval	35-40	244	638	2.6	4	34	411	12.1	4
Walt Kichefski	40-42,44					30	411	13.7	1
George Klick	40,45	81	257	3.2	1	4	20	5.0	0
Carl Kinscherf	43-44	58	98	1.7	1	3	13	4.3	0
Ben Kish	40-41,43-49	74	344	4.6	1	38	420	11.1	2
Ed Klewicki	36-38	20	129	6.5	0	15	281	18.7	2
John Knolla	42,45	30	79	2.6	0	9	63	7.0	0
Elmer Kolberg	39-41					10	78	7.8	0
Stan Kostka	35+	63	249	4.0	0				
Andy Kowalski	43-45					20	300	15.0	1
George Kracum	41	52	169	3.3	3	2	17	8.5	0
Max Krause	33-40 + 34,36-40	155	593	3.8	3	10	126	12.6	3
Bob Krieger	41,46					21	279	13.3	2
Al Krueger	41-42,46					35	401	11.5	2
John Kusko	36-38	66	236	3.6	1	2	47	23.5	0
Mort Landsberg	41,47	25	58	2.3	0	6	51	8.5	0
Jimmy Lawrence	36-39	130	357	2.7	4	28	276	9.9	0
Joe Laws	34-35 + 34,36-45	470	1916	4.1	10	72	931	12.9	9
Bill Lazetich	39,42	9	42	4.7	1	14	109	7.8	2
Bill Leckonby	39-41	77	254	3.3	0	2	17	8.5	2
Tuffy Leemans	36-43	919	3142	3.4	17	28	422	15.1	3
Joe Leonard	35-37 + 36-37	107	243	2.3	2	5	46	9.2	1
Jim Levey	35-36+35	46	72	1.6	2	11	112	10.2	2
Frank Liebel	42-48					82	1755	21.4	23
Carl Littlefield	38-39	58	210	3.6	0	2	27	13.5	0
John Long	44-45	26	5	0.2	0				
Don Looney	40-42	2	-4	-2.0	1	75	952	12.7	6
John Lucente	45	82	242	3.0	1	11	45	4.1	0
Sid Luckman	39-50	204	-209	-1.0	4	1	15	15.0	0

* — Years for which the player's statistics are available

+ — Indicates that Rushing statistics and Receiving statistics are available for different years. Rushing years are before the +, and Receiving years are after the +.

Lifetime Statistics — 1933-1945 Players Section 2 — RUSHING and RECEIVING (continued)
(All men with 25 or more rushing attempts or 10 or more receptions)

		RUSHING				RECEIVING			
Name	Years*	Att.	Yards	Avg.	TD	Rec.	Yards	Avg.	TD
Bob MacLeod	39	17	88	5.2	1	10	231	23.1	3
Lloyd Madden	40	29	186	6.4	2	4	90	22.5	1
Charley Malone	34-40,42					137	1922	14.0	13
Jack Manders	33-40+34-40	427	1545	3.6	10	14	243	17.4	6
Pug Manders	39-47	742	2712	3.7	36	28	375	13.4	2
Joe Maniaci	36-41	404	1855	4.6	14	16	184	11.5	0
Eggs Manske	35-40	5	29	5.8	0	70	1467	21.0	11
Tilly Manton	36-38,43	42	98	2.3	0	14	122	8.7	1
Andy Marefos	41-42,46	138	384	2.8	7	2	18	9.0	0
Hank Margarita	44-46	204	960	4.7	7	38	524	13.8	2
Frank Martin	43-45	39	79	2.0	0	20	234	11.7	0
John Martin	41-45	143	362	2.5	2	41	579	14.1	1
Joel Mason	39,42-45					34	390	11.5	2
Bob Masters	37-39,42-44	34	99	2.9	0	6	72	12.0	0
Bernie Masterson	34-40	108	-27	-0.2	6	16	257	16.1	2
Bob Masterson	38-46	8	104	13.0	0	136	1821	13.4	13
Ed Matesic	35+36	96	196	2.0	1	1	13	13.0	0
Jack Matheson	43-47					73	1044	14.3	5
Ned Mathews	41-43,45-47	186	752	4.0	4	34	494	14.5	6
Harry Mattos	36-37	27	18	0.7	1				
Dean McAdams	41-43	189	375	2.0	0	12	111	9.3	0
Jack McBride	33-34+	37	101	2.7	0				
Bob McChesney	36-42	3	27	9.0	1	59	679	11.5	6
Hugh McCullough	39-43,45	129	409	3.2	4	5	74	14.8	0
Flip McDonald	44-46,48					15	131	8.7	2
Jim McDonald	38-39	25	80	3.2	0	7	112	16.0	0
Les McDonald	37-40	4	-4	-1.0	0	51	924	18.1	8
Coley McDonough	39-41,44	65	179	2.8	1	1	3	3.0	1
Paul McDonough	38-41	2	5	2.5	0	40	672	16.8	4
Banks McFadden	40	65	411	6.3	1	9	97	10.8	2
Charlie McGibbony	44	26	81	3.1	0				
Tex McKay	44-47	100	288	2.9	3				
Ray McLean	40-47	152	412	2.7	6	103	2222	21.6	21
Hal McPhail	35+	45	105	2.3	1				
Jim Meade	39-40	61	149	2.4	0	5	40	8.0	0
Fred Meyer	42,45	2	13	6.5	0	27	429	15.9	2
Mike Mikulak	35-36	92	138	1.5	5	14	155	11.1	0
Eddie Miller	39-40	95	305	3.2	2				
Paul Miller	36-38	143	540	3.8	1	18	215	11.9	3
Tom Miller	43-46	1	-2	-2.0	3	22	279	12.7	1
Wayne Millner	36-41,45	14	62	4.4	0	124	1578	12.7	12
Buster Mitchell	36-37	2	4	2.0	0	10	125	12.5	1
Bo Molenda	33-34+34	105	302	2.9	3	4	70	17.5	0
Keith Molesworth	33-37+34-37	259	895	3.5	6	213	338	14.7	1
Bob Monnett	33-38+33-34,36-38	508	1516	3.0	7	24	320	13.3	0
Tipp Mooney	44-45	46	193	4.2	0	4	84	21.0	1
Wilbur Moore	39-46	183	901	4.9	8	91	1224	13.5	16
George Morris	41-42	46	134	2.9	0	9	17	1.9	0
Bob Morrow	41-43,45-46	128	456	3.6	4	4	26	6.5	0
Butch Morse	35-38,40	1	-3	-3.0	0	23	345	15.0	1
Emmett Mortell	37-39	247	696	2.8	0	1	0	0.0	0
Moose Moscrip	38-39	1	8	8.0	0	20	294	14.7	1
Paul Moss	33					18	383	21.3	3
Moose Mulleneaux	38-41,45-46					44	850	19.3	11
Franny Murray	39-40	55	144	2.6	1	25	269	10.8	1
Jim Musick	33,35-36+33,36	239	997	4.2	7				
Bronko Nagurski	33-37,43	499	2212	4.4	14	5	67	13.4	0
Dick Narki	38-39	30	124	4.1	0	1	3	3.0	0
Harry Newman	33-35+34	333	1145	3.4	6	4	55	13.8	1
Chuck Newton	39-40	1	0	0.0	0	10	145	14.5	1
Al Nichelini	35-36+36	149	423	2.8	4	9	133	14.8	1
Walt Nielsen	40	73	269	3.7	1	2	17	8.5	0
Emery Nix	43,46	27	1	0.0	0				
Ray Nolting	36-43	508	2285	4.5	11	30	508	16.9	3
Reino Nori	37-38	27	82	3.0	0				
Doug Nott	35+	48	98	2.0	0				
Davey O'Brien	39-40	209	-194	-0.9	2				
Bill Osmanski	39-43,46-47	374	1743	4.7	20	12	170	14.2	1
Hal Pangle	35-38+36-38	119	355	3.0	3	16	267	16.7	0
Ace Parker	37-41,45-46	498	1292	2.6	14	8	229	28.6	3
Buddy Parker	35-43+36-43	180	489	2.7	4	40	378	9.5	0
Bill Paschal	43-48	677	2430	3.6	27	32	326	10.2	8
George Paskvan	41	38	116	3.1	0				
Maury Patt	38-42	15	66	4.4	0	41	460	11.2	2
Billy Patterson	39-40	101	205	2.0	0				
Frank Patrick	38-39	31	85	2.7	1	1	21	21.0	1
Don Perkins	43-46	138	585	4.2	2	5	53	10.6	0
Ike Peterson	35-36+36	145	501	3.5	3	8	38	4.8	0
Les Peterson	33-34					22	328	14.9	0
John Petty	42	41	149	3.6	2	4	53	13.3	0
Alex Piasecky	43-45					12	112	9.3	1
Joe Pilconis	36-37	2	21	10.5	0	10	110	11.0	1
Ernie Pinckert	36-40+35-40	28	114	4.1	1	21	269	12.8	1
Stan Pincura	37-38	7	-28	-4.0	0	18	211	11.7	1
Johnny Pingel	39	72	301	4.2	1				
Hank Piro	41					10	141	14.1	1
Dick Plasman	37-41,44,46-47	1	1	1.0	0	56	1083	19.3	7
George Platukas	38-42	3	6	2.0	0	33	621	28.8	6
Red Pollack	35+35-36	45	254	5.6	3	8	150	18.8	1
Hamp Pool	40-43,46					38	903	23.8	11
Jim Poole	37-41,45-46					65	895	13.8	13
Milt Popovich	38-42	78	233	3.0	0	10	71	7.1	0
Glenn Presnell	33-36+36	354	1354	3.8	14				1
Cotton Price	40-41,45-46	97	174	1.8	2	3	23	7.7	0
Dom Principe	40-42,46	51	152	3.0	2	9	112	12.4	0
Marion Pugh	41,45,46	77	-127	-1.6	2	4	43	10.8	0
Red Ramsey	38-40,45					53	624	11.8	2
Walt Rankin	41,43-47	20	30	1.5	0	17	87	5.1	0
Keith Ranspot	40,42-45					35	491	14.0	4
Albie Reisz	44-47	83	164	2.0	2	1	11	11.0	0
Pug Rentner	35-37+36-37	197	717	3.6	2	10	134	13.4	2
Paul Riblett	36+33,35-36	2	4	2.0	0	22	307	14.0	2
Kink Richards	33-39+34-39	568	1884	3.3	11	36	337	9.4	8
Ray Riddick	40-42,46					20	285	14.3	1
Dick Riffle	38-42	391	1381	3.5	10	19	189	9.9	2
John Robbins	38-39	101	310	3.1	0	2	12	6.0	0
Bob Robertson	42	46	132	2.9	0	5	61	12.2	0
Gene Ronzani	33-38,44-45 +34-38,44-45	260	1153	4.4	1	22	334	15.2	8
Al Rose	33-36					19	256	13.5	3
Eddie Rucinski	41-46	18	85	4.7	0	99	1408	14.2	8
Doug Russell	35-39+36-39	206	667	3.2	2	23	366	15.9	2
Rip Ryan	38-40	54	263	4.9	1	23	220	9.6	1
Charlie Sample	41,45	59	257	4.4	4	6	35	5.8	1
Curt Sandig	42,46	72	168	2.3	4	8	118	14.8	0
Mickey Sanzotta	42,46	77	340	4.4	0	7	35	5.0	0
Tony Sarausky	36-38	44	210	4.8	2				
Phil Sarboe	35-36+36	121	232	1.9	0	1	18	18.0	0
George Sauer	35-37+36-37	190	656	3.5	6	6	110	18.3	0
Elmer Schaake	33+	125	412	3.3	0				
Bernie Scherer	36-39					13	241	18.5	3
John Schneller	35-36					14	273	19.5	3
Perry Schwartz	38-42,46	5	24	4.8	0	104	1677	16.1	10
Dick Schweidler	38-39,46	41	166	4.0	3	4	75	18.8	0
Bob Seymour	40-46	397	1311	3.3	12	72	817	11.3	11
Leland Shaffer	36-43,45+35-43,45	24	81	3.4	1	52	531	10.2	5
Bill Shepherd	35-40+36-40	519	1984	3.8	12	16	155	9.7	1
Allie Sherman	43-47	92	-44	-0.5	4				
Rhoten Shetley	40-42,46	17	58	3.4	1	17	218	12.8	2
John Shirk	40					11	91	8.3	0
John Siegal	39-43					31	636	20.5	6
Frankie Sinkwich	43-44,46-47	321	1090	3.4	7	2	11	5.5	0
Johnny Sisk	33-36+34-36	172	760	4.4	4	4	105	26.3	0
Joe Skladany	34					10	246	24.6	2
Dwight Sloan	38-40	193	576	3.0	4	1	10	10.0	0
Marty Slovak	39-41	141	396	2.8	1				
Rudy Smeja	44-46					,11	166	15.1	1
Ben Smith	33-35,37					25	434	17.4	0
Bill Smith	34,36-39+35-39	8	90	11.3	2	86	1509	17.5	9
Gaylon Smith	39-42,46	233	710	3.0	9	16	261	16.3	0
Riley Smith	36-38	45	58	1.3	2	18	300	16.7	3
Stu Smith	37-38	145	452	3.1	0	3	30	10.0	0
Wee Willie Smith	34	45	232	5.2	2	2	32	16.0	0
Dave Smukler	36-39,44	334	1106	3.3	2	1	-4	-4.0	0
Bob Snyder	37-41,43	161	348	2.2	1	4	36	9.0	0
Hank Soar	37-46	478	1545	3.2	6	35	411	11.7	2
Bill Sortet	35-40	2	42	21.0	0	63	928	14.7	8
Vic Spadaccini	38-40	9	46	5.1	0	62	669	10.8	3
Leo Stasica	41,43-44	34	-9	-0.3	0				
Ernie Steele	42-48	258	1337	5.2	14	31	520	16.8	4
Ed Storm	35+	84	164	2.0	2				
Ken Strong	33-35,39,44-47	265	974	3.7	9	16	278	17.4	2
Art Strutt	35-36	176	503	2.9	1	18	278	15.4	0
Bob Swisher	38-41,45	104	544	5.2	2	21	582	27.7	3
Ray Tesser	33					14	274	19.6	0
Stumpy Thomason	36+	109	333	3.1	0				
Tuffy Thompson	37-39	88	228	2.6	1	16	182	11.4	1
Bob Thurbon	43-44,46	143	478	3.3	9	14	231	16.5	2
Morgan Tiller	44-45					10	141	14.1	0
Gaynell Tinsley	37-38,40	6	45	7.5	0	93	1356	14.6	7
Bob Titchenal	40-42,46-47	2	2	1.0	0	15	264	17.6	0
Dick Todd	39-42,45-48	368	1573	4.3	11	119	1826	15.3	20
Andy Tomasic	42,46	60	214	3.6	0	1	27	27.0	0
Mario Tonelli	40	51	148	2.9	1	5	53	10.6	0
Flavio Tosi	35-36					14	239	17.1	1
Bob Trocolor	42-44	35	22	0.6	0				
Dick Tuckey	38	43	76	1.8	0	1	10	10.0	0
Darrell Tully	39	31	50	1.6	1				
Andy Uram	38-43	239	1073	4.5	4	58	1083	18.7	10
Hal Van Every	40-41	63	281	4.5	2	5	44	8.8	0
Art Van Tone	43-46	34	55	1.6	1	25	568	22.7	8
Fred Vanzo	38-41	6	45	7.5	0	17	257	15.1	0
Pug Vaughan	35+36	80	130	1.6	0				
Vic Vidoni	35-36					13	146	11.2	0
Will Walls	37-39,41-43					35	587	16.8	4
Busit Warren	45	96	285	3.0	2	1	-1	-1.0	0
Foster Watkins	40-41	29	-65	-2.2	0	3	27	9.0	0
Ray Wehba	43-44					10	110	11.0	0
Izzy Weinstock	35,37-38	92	264	2.9	0	8	107	13.4	0
Heinie Weisenbaugh	35-36	39	59	1.5	0	10	110	11.0	2
Howie Weiss	39-40	116	448	3.9	3	8	81	10.1	0
Joe Wendlick	40-41					15	151	10.1	0
Walt West	44	66	220	3.3	0	9	64	7.1	0
Bob Westfall	44-47	209	697	3.3	11	47	588	12.5	5
Whizzer White	38,40-41	387	1319	3.4	11	16	301	18.8	1
Ted Williams	42,44	102	196	1.9	3	15	86	5.7	0
Bobby Wilson	36	104	505	4.9	3	1	12	12.0	1
George Wilson	37-46					111	1342	12.1	15
Johnny Wilson	39-42					26	429	16.5	4
Ted Wright	35+	65	45	0.7	1				
Harry Wynne	44-45					12	230	19.2	0
Howie Yeager	41	22	67	3.0	1	11	239	21.7	3
Waddy Young	39-40	1	1	1.0	0	15	185	12.3	0
Silvio Zaninelli	36-37	35	75	2.1	0	4	24	6.0	0
Roy Zimmerman	40-48	200	244	1.2	7	5	36	7,2	0
Lou Zontini	40-41,44,46	48	133	2.8	3	4	110	27.5	1

Section 3 — **PUNT RETURNS and KICKOFF RETURNS**
(All men with 25 or more Punt Returns or 25 or more Kickoff Returns)

Name	Years	PUNT RETURNS No.	Yards	Avg.	TD	KICKOFF RETURNS No.	Yards	Avg.	TD
Lou Brock	P 42-45	39	438	11.2	0	17	344	20.2	0
Harry Clark	P 42-43,46-48	26	379	14.6	0	32	854	26.7	0
Tom Colella	42-49	32	487	15.2	1	26	553	21.3	0
Merl Condit	P 42-43,45-46	35	332	9.5	0	17	369	21.7	0
Ward Cuff	P 42-47	37	447	12.1	0	12	305	25.4	0
Bob Davis	42,44-46	55	576	10.5	0	26	515	19.8	0
Andy Farkas	P 42-45	59	734	12.4	1	32	879	27.5	2
(includes 1 kickoff return touchdown in 1939)									
Marshall Goldberg	41-43,46-48	21	259	12.3	0	34	844	24.8	1
John Grigas	43-47	7	38	5.4	0	32	635	19.8	0
Parker Hall	P 42,46	25	273	10.9	0	11	177	16.1	0
Joe Laws	P 42-45	45	332	7.4	1	16	287	17.9	0
(includes 1 punt return touchdown in 1939)									
John Martin	P 42-45	20	202	10.1	0	36	899	25.0	0
Ray McLean	P 42-47	39	575	14.7	3	20	461	23.1	0
(includes 1 punt return touchdown in 1940)									
Bill Paschal	43-48	29	395	13.6	0	53	1245	23.5	0
Bob Seymour	P 42-46	46	597	13.0	0	6	121	20.2	0
Ernie Steele	42-48	56	889	15.9	1	38	763	20.1	0
Dick Todd	P 42, 45-48	44	581	13.2	3	17	378	22.2	0
(includes 1 punt return touchdown in 1939 and 1 punt return touchdown in 1940)									

Kickoff Return statistics start in 1942.
Punt Return statistics start in 1941.

P — includes Punt Return statistics for 1941

Section 4 — **PUNTING**
(All men with 25 or more punts)

Name	Years	No.	Avg.
Len Barnum	39-42	159	40.5
Sammy Baugh	39-52	338	44.9
Lou Brock	40-45	84	37.2
George Cafego	40,43-45	44	34.9
Leo Cantor	42,45	25	37.1
Beryl Clark	40	28	33.0
Tom Colella	42-49	196	37.4
Merl Condit	40-43,45-46	39	39.4
Ed Danowski	39,41	31	37.9
Kay Eakin	40-41,46	68	43.1
Sam Francis	39-40	29	41.7
George Franck	41,45-47	63	39.2
Scott Gudmundson	44-45	29	35.0
Parker Hall	39-42	200	41.0
Merle Hapes	42,46	27	38.3
Arnie Herber	33-34,39-40, 44-45	109	37.4
Clarke Hinkle	33-34,39-41	234	37.6
Harry Hopp	41-43,46-47	86	38.2
Cecil Johnson	43-44	33	40.2
Art Jones	41,45	47	37.7
Ralph Kercheval	39-40	36	40.6
Carl Kinschert	43-44	32	40.7
Sid Luckman	39-50	230	38.4
John Martin	41-45	145	38.8
Dean McAdams	41-43	104	41.0
Hugh McCullough	39-43,45	66	36.5
Doug McEnuty	43-44	29	40.8
Tex McKay	44-47	124	41.9
Rudy Mucha	41,45-46	34	40.7
Franny Murray	39-40	63	37.0
Ace Parker	39-41,45-46	150	38.3
Billy Patterson	39-40	51	39.1
Johnny Pingel	39	32	42.7
Milt Popovich	39-42	35	34.6
Albie Reisz	44-47	88	37.6
Bill Reynolds	44-45	38	36.4
Dick Riffle	39-42	39	37.0
Curt Sandig	42,46	41	38.8
Frankie Sinkwich	43-44,46-47	64	41.5
Sid Tinsley	45	57	40.4
Dick Todd	39-42,45-48	38	38.7
Hal Van Every	40-41	30	37.3
Whizzer White	40-41	100	41.4
Len Younce	41,43-44,46-48	70	40.6
Roy Zimmerman	40-48	278	39.8
Lou Zontini	40-41,44,46	58	36.8

Punting statistics start in 1939

Section 5 — **KICKING**
(All men with 10 or more PAT or Field Goal Attempts)

Name	Years	PAT	PAT Att.	PAT Pct.	FG	FG Att.	FG Pct.
Chet Adams	39-43,46-50	122	131	93	13	40	33
Joe Aguirre	41-49	85	95	89	17	39	44
Lee Artoe	40-42,45-48	25	30	83	2	10	20
Conway Baker	36-45	22	28	79	1	3	33
Len Barnum	38-42	18	20	90	9	24	38
Bill Callihan	40-45	25	27	93			
Dutch Clark	34-38	57	73	78	12		
Merl Condit	40-43,45-46	26	27	96	5	22	23
Ward Cuff	37-47	156	162	96	43		
Bill Daddio	41-42,46	19	20	95	9	18	50
Tiny Engebretsen	33-41	43	45	96	15		
Dick Erdlitz	42,45-46	30	30	100	2	7	29
Roger Grove	33-35	9	11	82	0	1	0
Pete Gudauskas	40,43-45	64	67	96	1	2	50
Chuck Hanneman	37-41	19	19	200	7	13	54
Clarke Hinkle	33-41	28	31	90	28		
Don Hutson	35-45	172	184	93	7	17	41
Ralph Kercheval	34-40	32	41	78	31		
Bruiser Kinard	38-47	27	30	90	1	1	100
Joe Kuharich	40-41,45	12	13	92	0	4	0
Augie Lio	41-47	109	115	95	17	52	33
Jack Manders	33-40	137	154	89	40		
Joe Maniaci	36-41	29	33	88	5		
Tilly Manton	36-38,43	29	30	97	6		
Bob Masterson	38-46	71	79	90	8	32	25
Ray McLean	40-47	44	52	85	0	1	0
Regis Monahan	35-39	8	10	80	10		
Bob Monnett	33-38	28	31	90	5		
Monk Moscrip	38-39	15	18	83	0	2	0
Franny Murray	39-40	14	19	74	2	5	40
Jim Musick	33,35-36	13	15	87	1		
Harry Newman	33-35	12	15	80	6		
Armand Niccolai	34-42	71	78	91	34		
Ace Parker	37-41,45-46	25	32	78	1	5	20
Dick Plasman	37-41,44,46-47	14	19	74	0	1	0
Glenn Presnell	33-36	30	37	81	14		
Hank Reese	33-39	21	26	81	6		
Bo Russell	39-40	26	29	90	2	7	29
Jack Sanders	40-42,45	12	13	92			
Bill Shepherd	35-40	11	13	85	3		
Frankie Sinkwich	43-44,46-47	24	30	80	2	9	22
Bill Smith	34-39	24	33	73	12		
Ernie Smith	35-37,39	43	48	90	6		
Riley Smith	36-38	39	49	80	11		
Dave Smukler	36-39,43-44	16	17	94	2		
Bob Snyder	37-43,47	78	91	86	8		
Hank Soar	37-46	10	12	83	1		
George Somers	39-42	2	2	100	2	12	17
Vic Spadaccini	38-40	17	21	81			
Ken Strong	33-35,39,44-47	142	147	97	35		
Joe Stydahar	36-42,45-46	28	35	80	0	2	0
Len Younce	41,43-44,46-48	37	38	97	2	9	22
Roy Zimmerman	40-48	133	144	92	18	42	43
Lou Zontini	40-41,44-46	59	62	95	9	23	39

Field Goal Attempts statistics start in 1938.

1946—1959

1946—1959
Beginning and Ending with Confrontation

The postwar boom in the American economy put money in the pockets of football fans, and a new professional league took the field in 1946 to win a share of that money. The All-American Football Conference, organized by Arch Ward, sports editor of the Chicago Tribune, had wealthy owners backing almost every franchise, and the new league lured over 100 players away from the NFL and drove player salaries up to new heights. With ex-Notre Dame star Jim Crowley as commissioner, the AAFC brought good-quality football to New York, Brooklyn, Buffalo, Miami, Cleveland, Chicago, San Francisco, and Los Angeles in 1946.

To face this challenge, the NFL named Bert Bell, part owner of the Pittsburgh Steelers, as its commissioner. A tough, likable man with an immense love of football, Bert would guide the NFL through fourteen crucial years in which pro football reached a dazzling level of prosperity.

The 1946 season was prosperous for few pro-football clubs, as the high price of financial warfare put most of the clubs in the red for the season. The most notable exception was the Cleveland Browns of the AAFC. Captivating a city which the NFL champion Rams had abandoned, the Browns drew an average of 57,000 fans to each of their home games as they swept to the league championship.

But although the financial picture suffered in 1946, pro football advanced on several fronts. Both leagues placed clubs in California, with the NFL Rams moving from Cleveland to Los Angeles and the AAFC fielding teams in San Francisco and Los Angeles. Pro football became the first major-league sport to invade the West Coast.

Both leagues also employed black players, who had been unofficially barred from pro football since the early 1930s. The AAFC Browns signed fullback Marion Motley and guard Bill Willis, while the NFL Rams hired halfback Kenny Washington and end Woody Strode. These players had to walk the same unpleasant path of abuse that baseball player Jackie Robinson walked in 1947, but the football pioneers have never received anything close to the publicity that Robinson attracted.

The 1946 season also gave NFL Commissioner Bell his first test of leadership. On the morning of the championship game between the Giants and Bears, Bell learned that New York players Frank Filchock and Merle Hapes had been offered bribes to throw the game. Although neither had accepted the bribes, neither had reported the offer to the authorities. Bell released the news to the press, keeping everything out in the open so as to preserve confidence in the game, and he suspended Hapes while allowing Filchock to play. Although Filchock played an outstanding game in a 24-14 Bear win, Bell later suspended him indefinitely from NFL competition. The cumulative effect of the incident was to underline Bell's determination to lead the NFL firmly and openly.

Most pro teams continued to lose money in the late 1940's as the war between the leagues raged. Attendance was high in both leagues in 1946 and 1947, but the bidding war over players washed away most of the ticket revenues. When the postwar economic boom died out in 1948 and attendance dropped, the clubs felt a tight financial pinch—a major factor in the new league beginning to prod the NFL for peace terms. AAFC Commissioner Jonas Ingram, who succeeded Crowley in 1947, tried in vain to arrange a merger after the 1948 season. With Scrappy Kessing as its new commissioner, the league hobbled through 1949 before finally reaching a merger agreement with the NFL. The merger was dictated along NFL terms. The Cleveland Browns, San Francisco '49ers, and Baltimore Colts were admitted from the AAFC into the NFL, but the other four clubs in the young league were disbanded. The players on these four clubs went into a special pool and were distributed among the NFL teams, with the Giants profiting most by obtaining several stars from the AAFC Yankees.

The NFL entered the 1950s with the field to itself and with wise leadership in Commissioner Bell. One of the most important innovations of Bell's administration was the free-substitution rule. This rule, temporarily adopted during World War II and given a one-year trial in 1949, allowed coaches to develop separate platoons for offense and defense. Permanently adopted in 1950, the rule gave full bloom to the era of specialists who would charge the game with their highly polished skills. Another innovation after the merger was face masks, which became standard equipment on helmets and spared modern players the battle scars old-time players carried around on their faces.

But Bell's master stroke was a wise and firm policy toward the young medium of television. Bell insisted on permitting only road games to be televised into a team's home city. Television thus brought in added revenues without hurting paid attendance, and a national contract signed with the Columbia Broadcasting System in 1956 spread the game's following throughout the country.

Pro football soared in popularity in the 1950s and rivaled baseball as the national pastime. The total NFL attendance of 1,977,556 in 1950 set a new record for the sport, and the record continued to mount year by year in a steady climb through the end of the decade. Attendance broke two million in 1952 and went over three million in 1958. The team owners who had stuck out the frugal days of the Depression and the war with the AAFC suddenly found themselves raking in money hand over fist.

The NFL entered the 1950s with a lineup of thirteen clubs, but not all the teams shared in the prosperity. The Baltimore Colts franchise folded after the 1950 season, and the New York Yanks became the Dallas Texans in 1952. When pro football flopped in Texas, the team was transferred to Baltimore for the 1953 campaign, and the Colts took root in this second chance to give the NFL twelve solid franchises.

As the decade drew to a close, a new group of businessmen were looking to get into the game. But when Lamar Hunt and Bud Adams were turned down in applications for NFL clubs, they held organizational meetings and formed a new American Football League in the summer of 1959, with plans to start play in 1960. Once again, the NFL prepared itself to go to war. A new general would have to be found for the struggle, however, for as Commissioner Bell was watching the Eagles and Steelers play in Philadelphia on October 11, 1959, a massive heart attack ended his life in the very setting where he had spent most of his energies.

NEW YORK GIANTS 7-3-1 Steve Owen

Scores of Each Game		
17	Boston	0
17	Pittsburgh	14
14	Washington	24
28	CHIC. CARDS	24
14	CHIC. BEARS	0
14	Philadelphia	24
45	PHILADELPHIA	17
28	BOSTON	28
7	PITTSBURGH	0
21	LOS ANGELES	31
31	WASHINGTON	0

Use Name	Pos.	Hgt	Wgt	Age	Int	Pts
Lou DeFilippo	C-DT	6'1"	240	30		
Chet Gladchuk	C-DT	6'4"	245	29		
Lou Palazzi	C-LB	6'	195	25		
Pete Gorgone	BB-LB	6'	220	25		

Use Name – Tackles	Pos.	Hgt	Wgt	Age	Int	Pts
Joe Byler	T	6'5"	240	23		
Vic Carroll	T	6'4"	240	33		
(1 kickoff return for 11 yds.)						
Frank Cope	T	6'2"	230	30		
Tex Coulter	T	6'4"	225	21		
Phil Ragazzo	T	6'	220	31		
Jim White	T	6'2"	225	25		6

Use Name – Guards	Pos.	Hgt	Wgt	Age	Int	Pts
Bob Dobelstein	G-LB	5'11"	210	24		
Monk Edwards	G-LB	6'3"	215	26		
Kayo Lunday	G	6'3"	220	33		
Orville Tuttle	G	5'9"	215	33		
Len Younce	G-LB	6'1"	210	29	1	
(1 punt for 10 yds.)						

The Giants bounced back from an off year to grab the Eastern Division championship with a tough defense and recharged offense. The new battery in the attack was tailback Frankie Filchock, a flashy performer obtained from the Washington Redskins. Unchained from Sammy Baugh's shadow after six seasons Filchock came into his own with elusive running and a strong passing arm, winning an All-Pro berth for his efforts. The defense was built on the shoulders of a strong line stocked with healthy young men like Jim White, Frank Cope, Tex Coulter, Len Younce, Monk Edwards, and Chet Gladchuk. Even with the departure of veterans Mel Hein, Arnie Herber, and Ward Cuff, the Giants flexed too much muscle for their Eastern opponents. And at the box office, the Giant fans showed their own power, turning out for an average crowd of 50,000 at each home game, making the season profitable both in the standings and in the financial accounts.

PHILADELPHIA EAGLES 6-5-0 Greasy Neale

Scores of Each Game		
25	Los Angeles	14
49	BOSTON	25
7	GREEN BAY	19
14	Chic. Bears	21
28	Washington	24
24	NEW YORK	14
17	New York	45
7	Pittsburgh	10
10	WASHINGTON	27
10	PITTSBURGH	7
40	Boston	14

Use Name	Pos.	Hgt	Wgt	Age	Int	Pts
Ray Graves	C-LB	6'1"	205	27		
Henry Gude	C-G	6'1"	225	24		
(1 kickoff return for 0 yds.)						
Vic Lindskog	C-LB	6'1"	200	30	1	
Alex Wojciechowicz	C-LB	5'11"	225	31		
(from DET)						
Bob Friedlund	OE-DE	6'3"	210	26		
Bert Kuczynski	OE-DE	6'	195	26		6
(1 reception for 9 yd. touchdown)						
Flip McDonald	OE-DE	6'2"	200	25		
Art Macioszczyk – military service						

Use Name – Tackles	Pos.	Hgt	Wgt	Age	Int	Pts
Otis Douglas	T	6'1"	220	34		
John Eibner	T	6'2"	230	30		
Bucko Kilroy	T	6'2"	240	25	1	
Jay MacDowell	T-OE	6'2"	210	27		2
(1 reception for 28 yds.)						
Vic Sears	T	6'3"	225	28		
Al Wistert	T	6'1"	215	25	1	

Use Name – Guards	Pos.	Hgt	Wgt	Age	Int	Pts
Duke Maronic	G	5'9"	205	25	1	
Bob McDonough	G	5'11"	205	29		
Eddie Michaels	G	5'11"	210	32		
Cliff Patton	G	6'2"	240	22		
John Wyhonic	G	6'	210	26		

The lackluster Eagle record hid the fact that coach Greasy Neale was still adding talent to his developing club. This year's new arrivals were Alex Wojciechowicz, a tough veteran center and linebacker picked up from Detroit, ex-Boston guard Augie Lio, rookie fullback and linebacker Joe Muha, and wiry halfback Bosh Pritchard. Already settled in at quarterback was Tommy Thompson. Steve Van Buren had made a habit of storming through the enemy like a one-man stampede, while linemen Vic Sears, Al Wistert, and Bucko Kilroy made opponents pay a price for facing the Eagles.

But this season the array of talent did not quite jell into a first-class team. Although the defense still needed some patchwork and the offense sputtered when injuries shelved Steve Van Buren, the Eagles still looked like a team on the verge of breaking through.

WASHINGTON REDSKINS 5-5-1 Turk Edwards

Scores of Each Game		
14	PITTSBURGH	14
17	DETROIT	16
24	NEW YORK	14
14	Boston	6
24	PHILADELPHIA	28
7	Pittsburgh	14
7	BOSTON	14
20	Chic. Bears	24
27	Philadelphia	10
7	GREEN BAY	20
0	New York	31

Use Name	Pos.	Hgt	Wgt	Age	Int	Pts
Ki Aldrich	C-LB	6'	206	30	3	6
Al DeMao	C-LB	6'2"	205	26	2	
Clyde Ehrhardt	C-LB	6'1"	240	25	1	
Ralph Schilling	DE-OE	6'3"	218	25		
(to BUF AA) (1 reception for 14 yds.)						

Use Name – Tackles	Pos.	Hgt	Wgt	Age	Int	Pts
John Adams	T	6'7"	245	24		
Don Avery	T	6'4"	245	25		
John Koniszewski	T	6'3"	250	27		
Paul Stenn	T	6'2"	245	28		
Bill Young	T	6'1"	254	32		

Use Name – Guards	Pos.	Hgt	Wgt	Age	Int	Pts
Oscar Britt	G	5'11"	193	28		
Al Couppee	G-FB	6'	225	27		
(3 rushing attempts for 22 yds.)						
John Jaffurs	G	5'10"	200	24		
John Steber	G	6'	200	23		
Clem Stralka	G	5'10"	228	32		
Bill Ward	G	6'	230	25		
(1 kickoff return for 2 yds.)						

George Marshall did New York owner Tim Mara a favor and ended up suffering because of it. Sending passer Frankie Filchock to the punchless Giants, Marshall figured that Sammy Baugh was all the quarterback any team needed. As things turned out, injuries to Baugh left the Skins without a passer for several games, while Filchock sparked the Giants to the Eastern title. But more than Baugh's hurts caused the drop to third place. Owner Marshall refused to compete with the AAFC in offering high salaries to his players, and with offers too good to resist, the new league lured away ace tackle Willie Wilkin, star end and kicker Joe Aguirre, and even head coach Dud DeGroot.

Despite these losses, coach Turk Edwards kept the team in the race through the autumn, with wins needed in the last two games to clinch the crown. The Packers killed the title hopes with a 20-7 win, and then the Giants added insult to injury with a 31-0 triumph.

PITTSBURGH STEELERS 5-5-1 Jock Sutherland

Scores of Each Game		
14	CHIC. CARDS	7
14	Washington	14
14	NEW YORK	17
16	BOSTON	7
7	Green Bay	17
33	Boston	7
14	WASHINGTON	7
7	Detroit	17
10	PHILADELPHIA	7
0	New York	7
7	Philadelphia	10

Use Name	Pos.	Hgt	Wgt	Age	Int	Pts
Art Brandau	C-LB	6'2"	204	24		
Chuck Cherundolo	C-LB	6'1"	222	30	1	
George Titus	C-LB	5'10"	185	24		
Jim Reynolds	DB	6'	193	25		
John Patrick	BB-LB	6'	205	28		
Vern Foltz – military service						

Use Name – Tackles	Pos.	Hgt	Wgt	Age	Int	Pts
Joe Coomer	T	6'6"	280	27		
Earl Klapstein	T	6'	220	24		
Art McCaffray	T	5'11"	190	25		
Al Merkovsky	T	6'1"	220	29		
Joe Repko	T	6'	235	25		
Jack Wiley	T	5'11"	203	25		

Use Name – Guards	Pos.	Hgt	Wgt	Age	Int	Pts
Ray Bucek	G-LB	6'	186	26		
Ralph Fife	G-LB	6'	208	26		
(2 kickoff returns for 31 yds.)						
Frank Mattioli	G-LB	6'	210	23		
John Perko	G-LB	6'1"	210	30		
Nick Skorich	G-LB	5'9"	200	25		

With stern coach Jock Sutherland running a tight ship, and with Bill Dudley in uniform for the whole year, owner Art Rooney felt that the Steelers were on the road to the top in the East. Rooney could not have expected, however, that the coach and star player would immediately grow to dislike each other. Dudley always chewed out teammates who put out less than a full effort, and Sutherland saw this as overstepping his bounds. Deciding that Dudley had become a prima donna in the Army, Sutherland chose to reassert his authority over the Steelers by constantly needling the back about his running style and side-arm passing. Dudley accepted his coach's distain and sarcasm in silence, answering him with his performance on the field. He led the NFL in rushing and in interceptions, and he spurred the mediocre team into a third-place finish. At the end of the season, Dudley finally answered his hostile coach: He quit professional football.

BOSTON YANKS 2-8-1 Herb Kopf

Scores of Each Game		
0	NEW YORK	17
25	Philadelphia	49
7	Pittsburgh	16
6	WASHINGTON	14
7	PITTSBURGH	33
14	CHIC. CARDS	28
14	Washington	17
28	New York	28
40	LOS ANGELES	21
34	Detroit	10
14	PHILADELPHIA	40

Use Name	Pos.	Hgt	Wgt	Age	Int	Pts
Joe Domnanovich	C-LB	6'1"	205	27		
Gene Lee	C-LB	6'3"	226	24	1	
(1 kickoff return for 0 yds.)						
Jim Magee	C-LB	6'1"	205	25		
Joe Sulatis	LB	6'2"	210	25		
Sam Bailey	OE-DE	6'2"	195	22		

Use Name – Tackles	Pos.	Hgt	Wgt	Age	Int	Pts
Ralph Calacagni	T	6'3"	225	24		
Tom Dean	T	6'2"	248	22		
Don Deeks	T	6'4"	235	23		
Rube Juster	T	6'2"	230	22		
Ed McGee	T	6'1"	230	30		
Win Pederson	T	6'3"	225	31		
Steve Sierocinski	T	6'3"	245	24		

Use Name – Guards	Pos.	Hgt	Wgt	Age	Int	Pts
John Badaczewski	G	6'1"	235	24		
Rocco Canale	G	5'11"	253	29		
Tony Leon	G	5'9"	210	29		
(1 kickoff return for 6 yds.)						
Joe Zeno	G	5'10"	238	27	1	

With New York regularly drawing 50,000 fans to home games, with the Los Angeles Rams averaging 38,700 despite AAFC competition, the Boston Yanks still drew very few paying customers to their games. Owner Ted Collins still used the team mainly as a tax write-off, with the operation showing no signs of turning a profit after three years in existence. On the field, the team set no records either, although rookie Paul Governali did give the Yanks a solid passing threat, beating out first draft choice Boley Dancewicz for the signal-calling job. Veteran runners Gary Famiglietti and Jim Gillette joined the club through trades, but both had too much mileage to help the attack. The line folded under pressure like an accordion, and the Yanks could only shake their heads when guard Augie Lio was traded to the Eagles and immediately made All-Pro.

TEAM TOTALS

OFFENSE	FIRST DOWNS: Tot	by Rsh	by Pas	by Pen	RUSHING: No.	Yds.	Avg. Yds.	TD	PASSING: Att.	Com	Comp. Pct.	Yds.	Avg. Yds. Att.	Avg. Yds. Comp	TD	Int.	Pct. Int.
N.Y.	163	81	63	19	413	1467	3.6	15	194	100	51.5	1450	7.5	14.5	14	25	12.9
PHIL.	156	75	69	12	422	1263	3.0	12	217	116	53.5	1641	7.6	14.1	14	19	8.8
WASH.	161	84	67	10	435	1492	3.4	10	221	112	50.7	1613	7.3	14.4	10	22	10.0
PITT.	120	75	35	10	414	1307	3.2	13	161	58	36.0	970	6.0	16.6	4	13	8.1
BOSTON	147	67	59	21	365	1109	3.0	10	239	103	43.1	1566	6.6	15.1	15	18	7.5

OFFENSE	PUNTING: No.	Avg. Yds.	PUNT RETURNS: No.	Yds.	Avg. Yds.	TD	KICKOFF RETURNS: No.	Yds.	Avg. Yds.	TD	INTERCEPTION RETURNS: No.	Yds.	Avg. Yds.	TD	PENALTIES: No.	Yds.	FUMBLES: No.	Lost	POINTS: Tot	PAT	FG Att	FG	Saf.	OFFENSE
N.Y.	50	43.4	33	378	11.5	0	24	625	26.0	0	19	295	15.5	1	76	785	36	16	236	32	8	4	0	N.Y.
PHIL.	57	38.2	39	504	12.9	1	41	881	21.5	0	26	413	15.9	1	86	769	54	27	231	29	15	8	2	PHIL.
WASH.	45	44.1	43	470	10.9	0	36	784	21.8	0	24	337	14.0	1	85	843	36	22	171	21	18	8	0	WASH.
PITT.	70	39.7	37	498	13.5	0	26	474	18.2	0	14	295	21.1	1	69	534	38	15	136	16	9	2	0	PITT.
BOSTON	72	40.2	29	363	12.5	0	52	1063	20.4	1	17	236	13.9	1	83	691	33	18	189	21	2	0	0	BOSTON

Use Name – Backs & Ends	Pos.	Age	Hgt	Wgt	Pts	Int	Rushing No.	Rushing Yds	Rushing Avg	Rushing TD	Passing Att	Passing Comp	Passing %	Passing Yds	Passing Yd/Att	Passing TD	Passing Int–%	Passing RK	Receiving No.	Receiving Yds	Receiving Avg	Receiving TD	Punting No.	Punting Avg	Kicking Pat	Kicking Att	Kicking %	Kicking FG	Kicking Att	Kicking %	Punt Returns No.	Punt Returns Yds	Punt Returns Avg	Punt Returns TD	Kickoff Returns No.	Kickoff Returns Yds	Kickoff Returns Avg	Kickoff Returns TD
NEW YORK GIANTS																																						
Frankie Filchock	QB	29	5'11"	190	12		98	371	3.8	2	169	87	51	1262	7.5	12	25–15	8													6	50	8	0	4	109	27	0
Emery Nix	QB	26	5'11"	180			8	–25	–3.1	0	19	10	53	156	8.2	2	0– 0																					
Bill Paschal	FB-DB	25	6'	200	36		117	362	3.1	4									9	78	9	2	1	47.0							9	111	12	0	6	158	26	0
Frank Reagan	FB-DB	27	5'11"	185	12		62	246	4.0	2	6	3	50	32	5.3	0	0– 0		4	71	18	0	20	42.8							5	48	10	0	2	77	39	0
Merle Hapes	FB-DB	27	5'10"	195	30	1	51	161	3.2	5									3	40	13	0	12	39.9							2	5	3	0	2	43	22	0
Hank Soar	FB-DB	32	6'2"	215		3	1	3	3.0	0																					3	57	19	0				
George Franck	WB-DB	27	6'	180	6		43	270	6.3	0									6	137	23	1	16	39.0											6	162	27	0
Howie Livingston	WB-DB	24	6'1"	195	18	4	10	38	3.8	1									2	36	18	1													1	30	30	0
Jack Doolan	WB-DB	27	6'1"	195			12	33	2.8	0									3	28	9	0									3	49	16	0				
Dave Brown	WB-DB	27	5'11"	190			9	5	0.6	0																					1	0	0	0				
Steve Filipowicz	BB-LB	25	5'8"	200	18	4	2	3	1.5	1									7	84	12	1									4	58	15	0	1	16	16	0
Cecil Hare	BB-LB	27	5'11"	195															2	30	15	0													1	19	19	0
Jim Poole	OE-DE	30	6'3"	225	18														24	307	13	3																
Frank Liebel	OE-DB	26	6'1"	220	24	5													18	360	20	4																
Jim Lee Howell	OE-DE	31	6'6"	215															9	141	16	0																
John Weiss	OE-DB	24	6'3"	205	6														4	70	18	1																
Don McCafferty	OE-DE	25	6'4"	220	6														3	38	13	1																
Jack Mead	OE-DB	24	6'3"	215		1													3	26	12	0																
Ken Strong	K	40	6'	210	44																				32	32	100	4	9	44								
PHILADELPHIA EAGLES																																						
Tommy Thompson	QB	30	6'1"	190			34	–116	–3.4	0	103	57	55	745	7.4	6	9– 9	3																				
Roy Zimmerman	QB-DB	28	6'2"	200	14	3	23	43	1.9	1	79	41	50	597	7.6	4	8–10	6					23	38.7	2	2	100	2	4	50								
Allie Sherman	QB	23	5'11"	170			20	8	0.4	0	33	17	52	264	8.0	4	2– 6																					
Steve Van Buren	HB-DB	25	6'	205	36		116	529	4.6	5	1	1	100	35	35.0	0	0– 0		6	55	9	0	1	41.0							5	89	18	1	11	319	29	0
Bosh Pritchard	HB-DB	27	5'11"	170	36	3	42	218	5.2	3	1	0	0	0	0.0	0	0– 0		14	309	22	3	7	34.6							12	166	14	0	8	164	21	0
Gil Steinke	HB-DB	26	6'	175	24	6	38	154	4.1	1									5	107	21	2									8	116	15	0	3	92	31	0
Ernie Steele	HB-DB	28	6'	190	6	3	31	108	3.5	1									5	69	14	0									9	82	9	0	8	120	15	0
Russ Craft	HB-DB	26	5'9"	175		3	27	108	4.0	0									4	48	12	0									4	47	12	0	4	86	22	0
Jim Castiglia	FB-LB	27	5'11"	210	6		39	87	2.2	1									11	51	5	0													1	17	17	0
Joe Muha	FB-LB	25	6'1"	205		1	12	41	3.4	0													22	38.3											1	23	23	0
Jack Hinkle	HB-DB	28	6'	195		2	18	33	1.8	0																					1	4	4	0	1	25	25	0
Pete Kmetovic	HB-DB	26	5'9"	173			5	30	6.0	0									4	68	17	0																
Ben Kish	FB-LB	29	6'	215		1	6	13	2.2	0									3	16	5	0	4	40.8														
Elliott Ormsbee	HB-DB	24	5'11"	185			4	12	3.0	0																									1	5	5	0
Mel Bleeker	HB-DB	26	5'11"	190			6	–7	–1.2	0									3	29	10	0																
Jack Ferrante	OE-DE	30	6'1"	195	24														28	451	16	4																
Dick Humbert	OE-DB	27	6'1"	175	18		1	2	2.0	0									18	191	11	3													1	18	18	0
Larry Cabrelli	OE-DE	29	5'11"	195	6														8	98	12	1																
Rudy Smeja	OE-DE	25	6'2"	196															3	45	15	0													1	12	12	0
Bob Krieger	OE-DE	28	6'1"	190															2	47	24	0																
Augie Lio	G	28	6'	235	51																				27	27	100	6	11	55								
WASHINGTON REDSKINS																																						
Sammy Baugh	QB	32	6'2"	180	6		18	–76	–4.2	1	161	87	54	1163	7.2	8	17–11	7					33	45.1														
Jim Youel	QB-DB	24	6'	175	6	2	13	60	4.6	1	48	20	42	352	7.3	2	3– 6						2	34.0							13	150	12	0	2	29	15	0
Jack Jacobs	QB-HB-DB	27	6'1"	185		2	18	34	1.9	0	12	5	42	98	8.2	0	2–17		4	53	13	0	10	42.8							2	23	12	0				
Dick Todd	HB-DB	31	5'11"	173	30	4	41	266	6.5	3									8	107	13	2									5	64	13	0	3	47	16	0
Sal Rosato	FB-LB	28	6'1"	228	12		62	238	3.8	2									1	17	17	0									1	12	12	0				
Eddie Saenz	HB-DB	23	5'11"	170	24	1	55	213	3.9	1									12	242	20	3													11	264	24	0
Jack Jenkins	FB-LB	26	6'1"	205	6	3	64	200	3.1	1									2	27	14	0									2	14	7	0				
Steve Bagarus	HB-DB	27	6'	170	18	4	53	168	3.0	0									31	438	14	3									18	192	11	0	13	332	26	0
Frank Akins	FB-LB	27	5'10"	215			41	166	4.0	0									2	15	8	0																
Jim Gaffney	HB-DB	25	6'1"	200	6		25	96	3.8	0									7	85	12	1													1	24	24	0
Wilbur Moore	HB-DB	30	5'11"	190		2	15	62	4.1	0																					1	2	2	0				
Dick Poillon	HB-DB	26	6'	186	45		25	45	1.8	1									7	114	16	0			21	21	100	6	16	38	1	13	13	0	5	86	17	0
Bob DeFruiter	HB-DB	29	6'	190			2	–2	–1.0	0									1	9	9	0																
Jim Peebles	OE-DE	26	6'4"	218	6														9	164	18	1						0	2	0								
Doug Turley	OE-DE	27	6'2"	210															6	105	18	0																
John Kovatch	OE-DE	26	6'3"	200															6	67	11	0																
Don Lookabaugh	OE-DE	26	6'4"	212															6	67	11	0																
Ed Cifers	OE-DE	30	6'2"	234															6	61	10	0																
Ted Lapka	OE-DE	26	6'1"	192	6														3	28	9	0																
PITTSBURGH STEELERS																																						
Bill Dudley	TB-DB	25	5'10"	172	48	10	146	604	4.1	3	90	32	36	452	5.0	2	9–10	10	4	109	27	1	60	40.0	12	14	86	2	7	29	27	385	14	0	14	280	20	0
Johnny Clement	TB-DB	28	6'	190	6		43	60	1.4	1	47	16	34	345	7.2	1	3– 6		1	22	22	0	9	35.0							3	26	9	0	3	66	22	0
Andy Tomasic	TB-DB	26	6'	175							12	4	33	53	4.4	0	1– 8						1	56.0							1	20	20	0				
Tony Campagno	FB-DB	25	5'11"	200	6	1	67	217	3.2	1									7	77	11	0													1	27	27	0
Bill Dutton	HB-DB	25	5'10"	180	12		53	169	3.2	2	6	4	67	31	5.2	0	0– 0		2	68	34	0									3	36	12	0	1	22	22	0
Merl Condit	HB-DB	29	5'11"	186	10		46	141	3.1	1	4	2	50	89	22.3	1	0– 0		4	33	8	0			4	4	100	0	2	0	3	31	10	0	3	19	6	0
Steve Lach	FB-DB	26	6'2"	200	30	1	42	111	2.6	5	1	0	0	0	0.0	0	0– 0		2	11	6	0																
Ernie Bonelli	HB-DB	26	5'11"	190			6	7	1.2	0									1	26	26	0																
Walt Gorinski	FB-DB	26	6'1"	207			1	3	3.0	0																												
Max Kielbasa	HB-DB	25	6'1"	185			2	–2	–1.0	0																												
Cullen Rogers	HB-DB	25	5'10"	178			6	–8	–1.3	0	1	0	0	0	0.0	0	0– 0																					
Charlie Seabright	BB-LB	28	6'2"	210	6	1													4	77	19	1																
Bill Garnaas	BB-LB	25	5'11"	195	6														3	56	19	1													2	29	15	0
Val Jansante	OE-DE	25	6'1"	188	6		2	5	2.5	0									10	136	14	1																
Charlie Mehelich	OE-DE	24	6'1"	205															10	116	12	0																
Tony Bova	OE-DE	29	6'1"	190															6	171	29	0																
Sam Gray	OE-DE	26	6'	195															1	20	20	0																
Bob Davis	OE-DE	25	5'11"	195	6														1	13	13	0																
BOSTON YANKS																																						
Paul Governali	QB	25	5'11"	195	12		33	–187	–5.7	2	192	83	43	1293	6.7	13	10– 5	5					11	43.7														
Boley Dancewicz	QB-DB	21	5'10"	185		1	14	81	5.8	0	34	13	38	162	4.8	1	5–15																					
Howie Maley	QB-HB-DB	24	5'11"	188			13	67	5.2	0	8	3	38	71	8.9	1	2–25		2	35	18	0	60	39.4							3	12	4	0	1	3	3	0
John Grigas	FB-LB	26	6'	205	18	1	84	426	5.1	2	2	1	50	16	8.0	0	1–50		3	61	20	1	1	45.0											1	8	8	0
Babe Dimancheff	HB-DB	24	5'11"	178	6	1	57	238	4.2	0									5	121	24	1									7	98	14	0	5	96	19	0
Bob Davis	HB-DB	31	6'	190	6	7	41	143	3.5	0	1	1	100	7	7.0	0	0– 0		10	150	15	1									13	130	10	0	5	92	18	0
Jim Gillette	HB-DB	28	6'1"	185	12	1	30	99	3.3	1									5	96	19	1									2	62	31	0	3	43	14	0
Sonny Karnofsky	HB-DB	23	5'10"	175	18		36	84	2.3	1									8	139	17	1									2	38	19	0	21	599	29	1
Mike Micka	HB-DB	25	6'	184	6	2	20	76	3.8	0																												
Gary Famiglietti	FB	31	6'	238	24		23	54	2.3	4	1	1	100	6	6.0	0	0– 0		1	17	17	0						0	1	0								
Lou Abbruzzi	HB-DB	27	5'10"	175			6	26	4.3	0	1	1	100	11	11.0	0	0– 0		2	55	28	0									1	1	1	0	8	127	16	0
Joe Hoague	FB-LB	28	6'2"	210		1	1	2	2.0	0									1	4	4	0																
Rudy Romboli	FB-LB	23	5'10"	215		1	1	–3	–3.0	0																												
Hal Crisler	OE-DE	22	6'4"	215	30		4	6	1.5	0									32	385	12	5													2	22	11	0
Sam Goldman	OE-DE	29	6'3"	228			2	–3	–1.5	0									15	154	10	0													2	41	21	0
Don Currivan	OE-DB	25	6'	195	24														11	262	24	4									1	22	22	0	1	14	14	0
Nick Scollard	OE-DE	26	6'4"	218	33														7	78	11	1			21	24	88	0	1	0					1	12	12	0
Don Eliason	OE-DE	28	6'2"	225															1	9	9	0			0	1												

TEAM TOTALS

DEFENSE	First Downs Tot	First Downs by Rsh	First Downs by Pas	First Downs by Pen	Rushing No.	Rushing Yds.	Rushing Avg Yds.	Rushing TD	Passing Att	Passing Com	Passing Comp Pct.	Passing Yds.	Passing Avg. Yds. Att.	Passing Avg. Yds. Comp	Passing TD	Passing Int	Passing Pct. Int.	Punting No.	Punting Avg. Yds.	Punt Returns No.	Punt Returns Yds.	Punt Returns Avg. Yds.	Punt Returns TD	Kickoff Returns No.	Kickoff Returns Yds.	Kickoff Returns Avg. Yds.	Kickoff Returns TD	Interception Returns No.	Interception Returns Yds.	Interception Returns Avg. Yds.	Interception Returns TD	Penalties No.	Penalties Yds.	Fumbles No.	Fumbles Lost	Points Tot	Points PAT	Points FG Att	Points FG	Points Saf.	DEFENSE
N.Y.	161	77	72	12	394	1289	3.3	12	258	128	49.6	1823	7.7	14.3	9	19	7.4	58	38.9	28	250	8.9	0	52	1279	24.6	2	25	246	9.8	1	94	837	42	26	162	21	9	5	0	N.Y
PHIL.	146	72	56	18	418	1123	2.7	19	220	95	43.2	1360	6.2	14.3	11	26	11.8	64	40.2	30	356	11.9	0	40	822	20.5	0	19	380	20.0	1	91	817	36	18	220	26	10	4	1	PHIL.
WASH.	147	71	56	20	407	1103	2.7	16	216	101	46.8	1342	6.2	13.3	10	24	11.1	58	41.0	28	404	14.4	0	32	652	20.4	0	22	459	20.9	4	66	552	29	10	191	24	13	3	1	WASH.
PITT.	147	94	44	9	466	1754	3.8	9	162	64	39.5	939	5.8	14.7	6	14	8.6	68	42.2	32	247	7.7	0	28	684	24.4	0	13	131	10.1	0	75	707	28	17	117	15	10	4	0	PITT.
BOSTON	182	104	69	9	452	1852	4.1	22	227	106	46.7	1642	7.3	15.5	15	17	7.5	52	38.7	49	705	14.4	1	36	670	18.6	0	18	346	19.2	0	84	871	34	14	273	34	14	5	1	BOSTON

CHICAGO BEARS 8-2-1 George Halas

Scores of Each Game		
30	Green Bay	7
34	Chic. Cards	17
28	LOS ANGELES	28
21	PHILADELPHIA	14
0	New York	14
10	GREEN BAY	7
27	Los Angeles	21
24	WASHINGTON	20
42	DETROIT	6
28	CHIC. CARDS	35
45	Detroit	24

Use Name	Pos.	Hgt	Wgt	Age	Int	Pts
Stu Clarkson	C-LB	6'2"	215	27	3	6
John Schiechl	C-LB	6'2"	250	29	3	
Bulldog Turner	C-LB	6'1"	240	27	1	
(1 kickoff return for 2 yds.)						
Walt Lamb	DE-OE	6'1"	195	25		
(1 reception for 10 yds.)						
Bill Geyer	HB-DB	5'10"	180	26		
(1 kickoff return for 14 yds.)						
Bob Margarita	HB-DB	5'11"	185	25		
(4 rushing attempts for 0 yds.)						
injured – Al Matuza						

Use Name – Tackles	Pos.	Hgt	Wgt	Age	Int	Pts
Fred Davis	T	6'3"	245	28		
John Federovich	T	6'5"	262	29		
Mike Jarmoluk	T	6'5"	260	23		
Ed Kolman	T	6'2"	235	28		
Walt Stickel	T	6'3"	245	24		
Joe Stydahar	T	6'4"	250	34		12
(12 PAT 's in 13 attempts, 2 missed FG attempts)						

Use Name – Guards	Pos.	Hgt	Wgt	Age	Int	Pts
Al Baisi	G	6'	215	28		
Ray Bray	G	6'	240	29		
Chuck Drulis	G-LB	5'10"	215	28	1	
Aldo Forte (from DET)	G	6'	215	28		
Pat Preston	G-LB	6'2"	215	23		

With World War II over, Americans wanted to return to a normal life without war bonds, ration stamps, and blackouts. The Chicago Bears did their part to recreate the prewar scene by recapturing the NFL flag with a platoon of old Bears back from the war. George McAfee, Bill Osmanski, and Hugh Gallarneau ran with the ball just as in the good old days, while Ken Kavanaugh and Ray Bray again filled the line. Sid Luckman, Bulldog Turner, and George Wilson had been around right through the war and kept up their good work now that the big boys were back. To round out the squad, newcomers like tough Ed Sprinkle, Fred Davis, and Dante Magnani gave George Halas new troops to deploy. Many key players were aging, but the Bears looked more experienced than old in easily taking the Western Division crown.

LOS ANGELES RAMS 6-4-1 Adam Walsh

Scores of Each Game		
14	PHILADELPHIA	25
21	Green Bay	17
28	Chic. Bears	28
35	DETROIT	14
10	Chic. Cards	34
41	Detroit	20
21	CHIC. BEARS	27
17	CHIC. CARDS	14
21	Boston	40
31	New York	21
38	GREEN BAY	17

Use Name	Pos.	Hgt	Wgt	Age	Int	Pts
Bod deLauer	C-LB	6'1"	218	26		
(Missed 2 FG attempts)						
Roger Harding	C-LB	6'2"	215	23	1	
Fred Naumetz	C-LB	6'1"	220	24	1	
Albie Reisz	DB	5'10"	175	28		

Use Name – Tackles	Pos.	Hgt	Wgt	Age	Int	Pts
Gil Bouley	T	6'2"	235	25		
Jake Fawcett	T	5'11"	220	27	1	
Clyde Johnson	T	6'6"	265	29		
Joe Pasqua	T	6'1"	225	28		
Elbie Schultz	T	6'4"	260	28		

Use Name – Guards	Pos.	Hgt	Wgt	Age	Int	Pts
Roger Eason	G	6'2"	225	28		
Mike Lazetich	G-LB	6'1"	215	25		
Les Lear	G-LB	5'11"	227	28	1	
Len Levy	G	6'	260	25		6
Riley Matheson	G-LB	6'2"	210	31	4	
Art Mergenthal	G-LB	5'11"	215	26		

Less than a month after the Cleveland Rams had won the 1945 championship, owner Dan Reeves picked them up and replanted them in the promised land of Southern California. The other NFL owners had been reluctant to approve the switch, but an average attendance of 38,700 in the face of AAFC competition convinced the doubters that Los Angeles indeed was ready for big-league sports. The team, though, by never winning more than two games in a row, could not capture another title for its new home. Bob Waterfield kept shooting passes to Jim Benton, but the rest of the squad never reached the edge of last year. Three newcomers kept the team interesting if not victorious. Tommy Harmon, the 1940 Heisman Trophy winner, came out of the Army to make a solid debut in the NFL, and two UCLA graduates, Kenny Washington and Woody Strode, won attention as the first blacks in the league since 1933.

GREEN BAY PACKERS 6-5-0 Curly Lambeau

Scores of Each Game		
7	CHIC. BEARS	30
17	LOS ANGELES	21
19	Philadelphia	7
17	PITTSBURGH	7
10	DETROIT	7
7	Chic. Bears	10
19	Chic. Cards	7
9	Detroit	0
6	CHIC. CARDS	24
20	Washington	7
17	Los Angeles	38

Use Name	Pos.	Hgt	Wgt	Age	Int	Pts
Charley Brock	C-LB	6'2"	210	30		
Bob Flowers	C-LB	6'1"	210	29		
Les Gatewood	C-LB	6'2"	195	25		
Tom Miller	DE-OE	6'2"	208	28		
Moose Mulleneaux	DE	6'3"	210	29		
Ray Riddick	DE	6'1"	220	28		
Ken Keuper	BB-DB	6'	205	28	3	
(1 kickoff return for 6 yds.)						
Al Zupek	BB-DE	6'1"	205	23		
Charlie Mitchell	DB	6'	190	25	1	
Russ Mosley	DB	5'10"	170	28	1	

Use Name – Tackles	Pos.	Hgt	Wgt	Age	Int	Pts
Tiny Croft	T	6'3"	275	25		
Bill Lee	T	6'2"	225	34		
Paul Lipscomb	T	6'4"	240	23		
Urban Odson	T	6'3"	255	27		2
Baby Ray	T	6'6'	250	31	1	

Use Name – Guards	Pos.	Hgt	Wgt	Age	Int	Pts
Solon Barnett	G	6'1"	235	25		
Earl Bennett	G-LB	5'8"	188	26		
Bill Kuusisto	G	6'	225	28		
Russ Letlow	G	6'	218	32		
Ed Neal	G-T	6'4"	290	28		
Merv Pregulman	G-LB	6'3"	215	24		
Al Sparlis	G-LB	5'11"	185	26		
Charlie Tollefson	'G	6'	215	29		
Dick Wildung	G	6'	220	24		

Green Bay lost a hero and Curly Lambeau an ace when Don Hutson finally made his retirement stick. The Packers long had counted on the wiry end to put points on the scoreboard, and not until the coming of Vince Lombardi would the team adjust to his loss. To make matters worse, the new AAFC was driving player salaries up to the sky, making it hard for the non-profit Packers to sign new talent.

Coach Lambeau relied on a strong running game to make up for the diminished air attack. Ex-GI Tony Canadeo, veteran Ted Fritsch, and rookie Walt Schlinkman handled the bulk of the ball-carrying with little help from passer Irv Comp and his undistinguished receivers. Quick losses to the Bears and Rams uncovered chinks in the Packer defense, and a strong mid-season spurt petered out into two losses in the last three games.

CHICAGO CARDINALS 6-5-0 Jimmy Conzelman

Scores of Each Game		
7	Pittsburgh	14
34	DETROIT	14
17	CHIC. BEARS	34
36	Detroit	14
24	New York	28
34	LOS ANGELES	10
28	Boston	14
7	GREEN BAY	19
14	Los Angeles	17
24	Green Bay	6
35	Chic. Bears	28

Use Name	Pos.	Hgt	Wgt	Age	Int	Pts
Vince Banonis	C-LB	6'1"	230	24	2	
Bill Campbell	C-LB	6'	195	26		
(1 kickoff return for 17 yds.)						
Dick Plasman	DE	6'3"	230	32		
Al Drulis	FB-LB	5'10"	195	25		
(1 rush for 0 yds.)						

Use Name – Tackles	Pos.	Hgt	Wgt	Age	Int	Pts
Chet Bulger	T	6'3"	238	28		
Ralph Foster	T	6'1"	230	29		
Tom Kearns	T	6'4"	248	26		
Stan Mauldin	T	6'2"	224	25		
(1 kickoff return for 16 yds.)						
Walt Szot	T	6'1"	215	27		
Bob Zimny	T	6'1"	230	25		

Use Name – Guards	Pos.	Hgt	Wgt	Age	Int	Pts
Ray Apolskis	G-LB	5'11"	215	27	1	
Lloyd Arms	G	6'1"	215	27		
Jake Colhouer	G	6'1"	210	24		
Bill Conoly	G	6'	227	26		
Bob Maddock	G-LB	6'	200	26		
Buster Ramsey	G-LB	6'1"	210	26	1	
(1 rush for 5 yds.)						

Owner Charles Bidwill opened his wallet wide, shelling out enough money to buy a championship nucleus for the Cardinals. He started the renovation by luring Jimmy Conzelman back as coach and giving him a marvelous rookie crop to work with. Bruising fullback Pat Harder lived up to expectations as a first draft choice, while Elmer Angsman starred at halfback despite a lack of press clippings. Speedster Mal Kutner gave the team a deep pass threat, and linemen Buster Ramsey and Stan Mauldin plugged holes in the line with hard-hitting bulk. Veterans Paul Christman, Marshall Goldberg, and Bill Dewell blended in with the newcomers to turn the Cardinals into a winning team with a bright future. The final game of the year with the Bears ended the season on an up note. With the score tied 28-28 and time for one more play, Paul Christman ignored Conzelman's signals for a field goal and threw a 5-yard touchdown pass to Mal Kutner for the victory.

DETROIT LIONS 1-10-0 Gus Dorais

Scores of Each Game		
14	Chic. Cards	34
16	Washington	17
14	CHIC. CARDS	36
14	Los Angeles	35
7	Green Bay	10
20	LOS ANGELES	41
17	PITTSBURGH	7
0	GREEN BAY	9
6	Chic. Bears	42
10	BOSTON	34
24	CHIC. BEARS	45

Use Name	Pos.	Hgt	Wgt	Age	Int	Pts
Elmer Hackney	LB	6'2"	200	30		
Walt Jurkiewicz	C-LB	6'1"	220	27		
Frank Szymanski	C-LB	6'	215	23		
Vince Mazza	OE-DE	6'1"	210	25		
Bill Kennedy – military service						

Use Name – Tackles	Pos.	Hgt	Wgt	Age	Int	Pts
Leon Fichman	T	6'1"	215	25		
Jim Montgomery	T	6'4"	235	24		
Russ Thomas	T	6'3"	230	22	1	
Emil Uremovich	T	6'2"	240	29		
Lloyd Wickett	T	6'1"	210	26		

Use Name – Guards	Pos.	Hgt	Wgt	Age	Int	Pts
Stan Batinski	G	5'10"	215	29		
Tony Rubino	G	5'10"	210	25		
Damon Tassos	G	6'1"	225	22	1	3
(3 PAT's in 3 attempts, missed 1 FG attempt)						
Walt Vezmar	G	5'11"	235	21		

The Lions lost tailback Frankie Sinkwich to the military after the 1944 season, and when he got his discharge from the service he signed with the New York Yankees of the new AAFC instead of with Detroit. That defection killed the Lions' passing game, and a rash of pre-season injuries to backs and linemen wiped out the running game. With the offense thus crippled, coach Gus Dorais watched his team drop six games before it beat the Steelers 17-7. Any hopes the victory may have raised were dashed to bits when the Lions ran out the season with four more losses.

This year's collapse underlined the deterioration of last year's team. Tailback Chuck Fenenbock jumped to the AAFC, runner Andy Farkas retired, and center Alex Wojciechowicz was traded to Philadelphia early in the campaign, and those players who stayed behind in Detroit never reached the heights of last year's second-place finish.

TEAM TOTALS

OFFENSE	FIRST DOWNS: Tot	by Rsh	by Pas	by Pen	RUSHING: No.	Yds.	Avg Yds.	TD	PASSING: Att	Com	Comp Pct.	Yds.	Avg. Yds. Att.	Avg. Yds. Comp	TD	Int	Pct. Int.	PUNTING: No.	Avg. Yds.	PUNT RETURNS: No.	Yds.	Avg. Yds.	TD	KICKOFF RETURNS: No.	Yds.	Avg. Yds.	TD	INTERCEPTION RETURNS: No.	Yds.	Avg. Yds.	TD	PENALTIES: No.	Yds.	FUMBLES: No.	Lost	POINTS: Tot	PAT	FG Att	FG	Saf.	OFFENSE
CHIC. B.	211	112	82	17	506	1762	3.5	19	253	120	47.4	1950	7.7	16.2	18	19	7.5	58	38.1	29	336	11.6	0	37	800	21.6	0	27	465	17.2	1	104	940	35	16	289	37	11	4	0	CHIC. B.
L.A.	214	102	91	21	404	1683	4.2	15	326	153	46.9	2080	6.4	13.6	19	24	7.4	45	44.4	26	295	11.3	0	43	934	21.7	1	23	376	16.3	1	80	764	31	20	277	37	11	6	0	L.A.
G.B.	160	112	34	14	561	1765	3.1	12	178	54	30.3	841	4.7	15.5	4	18	10.1	65	42.8	28	284	10.2	0	34	739	21.7	0	24	399	16.6	0	82	693	24	11	148	15	17	9	2	G.B.
CHIC. C.	175	77	84	14	371	1529	4.1	16	266	115	43.2	1951	7.3	16.9	17	20	7.5	50	39.6	23	255	11.1	0	40	825	20.6	1	24	262	10.9	0	84	761	44	29	260	33	12	5	1	CHIC. C.
DET.	120	49	59	12	274	470	1.7	7	287	119	41.5	1674	5.8	14.6	11	33	11.5	67	43.4	28	332	11.9	0	59	1127	19.1	0	13	230	17.7	0	82	635	26	12	142	17	6	3	1	DET.

Use Name — Backs & Ends	Pos.	Age	Hgt	Wgt	Pts	Int	RUSHING No.	Yds	Avg	TD	PASSING Att	Comp	%	Yds	Yd/Att	TD	Int–%	RK	RECEIVING No.	Yds	Avg	TD	PUNTING No.	Avg	KICKING Pat	Att	%	FG	Att	%	PUNT RETURNS No.	Yds	Avg	TD	KICKOFF RETURNS No.	Yds	Avg	TD
CHICAGO BEARS																																						
Sid Luckman	QB-DB	29	6'	195		1	25	−76	−3.0	0	229	110	48	1826	8.0	17	16– 7	1					33	37.4														
Tom Farris	QB-DB	25	6'1"	185		4	22	17	0.8	0	21	8	38	108	5.1	1	3–14		1	16	16	0									2	4	2	0	1	27	27	0
Hugh Gallarneau	HB-DB	29	6'	190	48		112	476	4.3	6									12	185	15	1									10	99	10	0	5	115	23	0
Bill Osmanski	FB-LB	29	5'11"	200	30	1	78	343	4.4	5									4	40	10	0									1	10	10	0	8	203	25	0
Dante Magnani	HB-DB	29	5'10"	180	6	1	68	277	4.1	0									14	156	11	1													3	50	17	0
Joe Osmanski	FB-LB	27	6'2"	220	12		55	201	3.7	2									2	14	7	0													3	54	18	0
Noah Mullins	HB-DB	27	5'11"	185		3	20	117	5.9	0	1	1	100	16	16.0	0	0– 0														4	50	13	0	1	22	22	0
Don Perkins	FB-LB	28	6'	200			34	105	3.1	0									2	41	21	0									1	14	14	0	1	25	25	0
Dick Schweidler	HB-DB	31	6'	175	18	1	20	94	4.7	3									1	11	11	0									1	13	13	0	3	63	21	0
Lloyd Reese	FB-LB	24	6'2"	240	12		18	84	4.7	2																												
George McAfee	HB-DB	28	6'	180	18	3	14	53	3.8	0	2	1	50	0	0.0	0	0– 0		10	137	14	3									1	24	24	0	3	96	32	0
Frank Maznicki	HB-DB	26	5'9"	185	37	2	19	43	2.3	0									2	38	19	0			25	26	96	4	9	44	1	12	12	0	2	65	33	0
Ray McLean	HB-DB	30	5'10"	170	18	2	16	29	1.8	1									17	348	20	2									7	86	12	0	3	53	18	0
Ken Kavanaugh	OE-DE	29	6'3"	210	30														18	337	19	5																
Jim Keane	OE-DE	22	6'4"	220	18														14	331	24	3	2	39.5							1	23	23	0				
George Wilson	OE-DE	32	6'1"	210	6														11	104	9	1																
Ed Sprinkle	OE-DE	22	6'1"	205	18	1													7	124	18	2													2	11	6	0
Connie Mack Berry	OE-DE	30	6'3"	220															4	58	15	0																
Rudy Mucha	G	28	6'1"	235			1	−1	−1.0	0													23	39.0														
LOS ANGELES RAMS																																						
Bob Waterfield	QB-DB	26	6'1"	190	61	5	16	−60	−3.7	1	251	127	51	1747	7.0	18	17– 7	2					39	44.6	37	37	100	6	9	67	1	12	12	0				
Jim Hardy	QB-DB	24	6'	185		1	10	−10	−1.0	0	64	24	38	285	4.5	1	7–11	13					5	41.8														
Fred Gehrke	HB-DB	28	5'11"	190	30	3	71	371	5.2	3	1	1	100	29	29.0	0	0– 0		11	83	8	2									8	59	7	0	8	186	23	0
Tommy Harmon	HB-DB	26	6'1"	197	30	3	47	236	5.0	2									10	199	20	2									5	57	11	0	6	134	22	0
Pat West	FB-LB	23	6'	200	6		40	226	5.7	1																									4	49	12	0
Mike Holovak	FB-LB	26	6'1"	220	18		55	211	3.8	3									2	6	3	0													1	18	18	0
Jack Banta	HB-DB	28	5'11"	192	6	2	44	209	4.7	0									8	81	10	1	1	44.0							2	26	13	0	8	142	18	0
Bob Hoffman	FB-LB	28	6'1"	210	18		42	162	3.9	3																												
Jack Wilson	HB-DB	28	6'	200	6	1	19	120	6.3	0									3	30	10	1									5	99	20	0	6	145	24	0
Kenny Washington	HB-DB	28	6'1"	200	6		23	114	5.0	1	8	1	13	19	2.4	0	0– 0		6	83	14	0													2	39	20	0
Tom Farmer	HB-DB	25	5'11"	195	6		28	90	3.2	1	2	0	0	0	0.0	0	0– 0		6	17	3	0									4	40	10	0	4	129	32	0
Steve Sucic	FB-LB	25	6'	200			7	18	2.6	0									1	1	1	0													1	20	20	0
Ralph Ruthstrom	FB-LB	25	6'5"	208			2	−4	−2.0	0									1	9	9	0									1	2	2	0				
Jim Benton	OE-DE	29	6'3"	206	36														63	981	16	6																
Steve Pritko	OE-DE	24	6'2"	210	12														18	185	10	2																
Red Hickey	OE-DE	29	6'2"	203	18														8	213	27	3													1	14	14	0
Ray Hamilton	OE-DE	30	6'4"	210															8	92	11	0																
Bob Shaw	OE-DE	25	6'4"	225	18														4	63	16	2													1	52	52	1
Woody Strode	OE-DE	31	6'3"	205															4	37	9	0													1	6	6	0
GREEN BAY PACKERS																																						
Irv Comp	TB-DB	27	6'2"	205	6	2	61	62	1.0	1	94	27	29	333	3.5	1	8– 8	12																	1	29	29	0
Cliff Aberson	TB-DB	24	6'	195		3	48	161	3.4	0	41	14	34	184	4.5	0	5–12																		3	69	23	0
Tony Canadeo	TB-HB-DB	27	5'11"	190		1	122	476	3.9	0	27	7	26	189	7.0	1	3–11		2	25	13	0									6	76	13	0	6	163	27	0
Bruce Smith	TB-DB	26	6'	197			22	119	5.4	0																					2	12	6	0	1	20	20	0
Ted Fritsch	FB-LB	25	5'10"	210	100	1	128	444	3.4	9									2	13	7	1	1	62.0	13	15	87	9	17	53					3	68	23	0
Walt Schlinkman	FB	24	5'8"	190	12		97	379	3.9	2									1	5	5	0													2	43	22	0
Tex McKay	FB-DB	26	6'	193	8	1	21	34	1.6	1													64	42.7	2	2	100								2	41	21	0
Bob Nussbaumer	HB-DB	22	5'11"	175		3	29	43	1.5	0	1	1	100	10	10.0	0	0– 0		10	143	14	0									12	98	8	0	6	148	25	0
Bob Forte	HB-DB	24	6'	195		2	17	73	4.3	0	7	3	43	28	4.0	1	1–14		2	5	3	0																
Herm Rohrig	HB-TB-DB	28	5'8"	190		5	15	−23	−1.6	0	8	2	25	97	12.1	1	1–12		2	30	15	0									8	98	12	0	5	106	21	0
Larry Craig	BB-DE	30	6'1"	218			1	−3	−3.0	0																									2	18	9	0
Clyde Goodnight	OE-DB	22	6'1"	195	6														16	308	19	1																
Nolan Luhn	OE-DE	25	6'3"	200	14														16	224	14	2													2	28	14	0
Don Wells	OE-DE	24	6'2"	200															2	74	37	0																
Hal Prescott	OE-DB	25	6'2"	210															1	8	8	0																
CHICAGO CARDINALS																																						
Paul Christman	QB	28	6'	210	18		28	−61	−2.2	3	229	100	44	1656	7.2	13	18– 8	4																				
Ray Mallouf	QB-DB	28	5'11"	180		1	4	6	1.5	0	34	14	41	260	7.6	4	2– 6						15	34.5														
Pat Harder	FB-LB	24	5'11"	205	36		106	545	5.1	4									11	128	12	1			5	5	100				1	10	10	0	5	92	18	0
Elmer Angsman	HB	20	5'11"	190	12		48	328	6.8	2	1	0	0	0	0.0	0	0– 0		2	44	22	0													1	13	13	0
Marshall Goldberg	HB-DB	28	5'11"	192	24	4	43	210	4.9	3									17	152	9	1									1	11	11	0	5	108	22	0
Frank Seno	HB-DB	25	6'	185	12	4	62	191	3.1	0	1	0	0	0	0.0	0	0– 0		12	124	10	1									17	176	10	0	13	408	31	1
Jimmy Strausbaugh	HB-DB	28	5'9"	190	18		37	183	4.9	3	1	1	100	35	35.0	0	0– 0		5	56	11	0									2	34	17	0	6	104	17	0
Ward Cuff	HB-DB	33	6'1"	192	55		13	78	6.0	1									5	82	16	1			28	30	93	5	12	42	2	24	12	0				
Jimmy Johnston	HB-DB	29	6'1"	195		1	6	18	3.0	0																									2	22	11	0
Bill Montgomery	FB-LB	23	6'	205			8	11	1.4	0																												
George Sutch	HB-DB	25	6'1"	205			5	4	0.8	0																									1	4	4	0
Walt Rankin	FB-LB	28	5'11"	197		2	5	1	0.2	0																									1	11	11	0
Paul Sarringhaus	HB-DB	25	6'	185			2	1	0.5	0																												
Bill Dewell	OE-DE	29	6'4"	210	42														27	643	24	7																
Mal Kutner	OE-DB	25	6'2"	197	30	4	1	−1	−1.0	0									27	634	23	5													3	30	10	0
Pop Ivy	OE-DE	30	6'3"	210	6	1													4	39	10	1																
Eddie Rucinski	OE-DB	30	6'2"	195															2	23	12	0																
Joe Parker	OE-DE	23	6'1"	220															2	17	9	0													1	0	0	0
Al Hust	OE-DE	25	6'1"	220															1	9	9	0																
Bill Blackburn	C-LB	24	6'6"	225	8	3	1	10	10.0	0													35	41.9														
DETROIT LIONS																																						
Dave Ryan	TB-DB	23	5'10"	190	12	4	71	65	0.9	1	154	73	47	965	6.3	6	17–11	9	1	−5	−5	0									7	57	8	0	15	308	21	0
Jim Callahan	TB-DB	25	5'11"	185	12	2	52	86	1.7	2	68	22	32	359	5.3	2	7–10	11					4	45.5							6	71	12	0	6	133	22	0
Bill deCorrevont	TB-WB-DB	27	6'	185	12		8	−32	−4.0	0	19	8	42	155	8.2	2	2–11		10	278	28	2	5	58.6							6	81	14	0	10	183	18	0
Joel McCoy	TB-DB	26	5'10"	170			19	−29	−1.5	0	18	6	33	72	4.0	0	4–22														1	8	8	0	1	7	7	0
Tippy Madarik	TB-WB-DB	24	5'11"	200		3	8	7	0.9	0	14	7	50	104	7.4	1	0– 0		6	38	6	0									5	71	14	0	5	131	26	0
Jim Jones	TB	26	6'	180			3	3	1.0	0	4	0	0	0	0.0	0	1–25						1	−9.0														
Camp Wilson	FB-LB	24	6'2"	200	18		64	207	3.2	3									7	62	9	0	22	34.9											7	127	18	0
Bob Westfall	FB-LB	27	5'8"	190	6		28	54	1.9	1	2	1	50	−5	−5.0	0	1–50		17	142	8	0													4	58	15	0
Mickey Sanzotta	WB-DB	25	5'9"	190			6	72	12.0	0	1	0	0	0	0.0	0	0– 0		2	19	10	0									2	41	21	0	2	40	20	0
Gene Spangler	WB-DB	23	5'10"	195			1	1	1.0	0									2	1	1	0													2	30	15	0
Bob Cifers	BB-DB	25	5'11"	200	24		8	18	2.3	0	6	2	33	24	4.0	0	1–17		4	178	45	5	30	45.6							1	3	3	0				
Ivan Schottel	BB-DB	25	6'2"	200	6		4	12	3.0	0									4	146	36	1	5	41.6											1	20	20	0
Chuck DeShane	BB-LB	27	6'1"	218	10	1	2	3	1.5	0	1	0	0	0	0.0	0	0– 0		2	13	7	0			10	10	100	0	1	0								
John Greene	OE-DE	26	6'	210	14														20	289	14	2													2	29	15	0
Jack Matheson	OE-DE	26	6'2"	235		1													17	178	10	0													1	17	17	0
Ted Cremer	OE-DE	27	6'2"	205															15	179	12	0																
Ed Frutig	OE-DE	26	6'1"	200	12														8	72	9	2																
Ralph Jones	OE-DE	25	6'3"	200															4	84	21	0													3	44	15	0
Jack Helms	DE	25	6'4"	215	13																				4	6	67	3	4	75								

TEAM TOTALS

DEFENSE	FIRST DOWNS: Tot	by Rsh	by Pas	by Pen	RUSHING: No.	Yds.	Avg. Yds.	TD	PASSING: Att.	Com	Comp. Pct.	Yds.	Avg. Yds. Att.	Avg. Yds. Comp	TD	Int.	Pct. Int.	PUNTING: No.	Avg. Yds.	PUNT RETURNS: No.	Yds.	Avg. Yds.	TD	KICKOFF RETURNS: No.	Yds.	Avg. Yds.	TD	INTERCEPTION RETURNS: No.	Yds.	Avg. Yds.	TD	PENALTIES: No.	Yds.	FUMBLES: No.	Lost	POINTS: Tot	PAT	FG Att	FG	Saf.	DEFENSE
CHIC. B.	138	57	68	12	334	1044	3.1	12	257	108	42.0	1610	6.3	14.9	14	27	10.5	59	44.6	24	256	10.6	0	50	798	16.0	0	19	300	15.8	0	76	716	38	22	193	25	11	4	0	CHIC. B.
L.A.	170	76	75	19	402	1325	3.3	14	265	112	42.3	2154	8.1	19.2	21	23	8.7	51	40.2	27	350	13.0	0	52	1301	25.0	1	24	386	16.1	0	89	702	35	15	257	30	11	5	1	L.A.
G.B.	158	84	59	15	367	1372	3.7	15	214	94	43.9	1288	6.0	13.7	8	24	11.2	60	41.8	35	414	11.8	0	28	683	24.4	0	18	275	15.3	1	76	628	45	28	158	20	7	4	0	G.B.
CHIC. C.	176	95	66	15	438	1249	2.9	12	273	118	43.2	1603	5.9	14.9	14	25	9.2	57	41.3	29	399	13.8	0	46	748	16.3	0	20	355	17.8	0	80	673	39	20	198	25	10	5	1	CHIC. C.
DET.	203	104	78	21	481	1698	3.5	21	249	123	49.4	1975	7.9	16.0	20	13	5.2	52	40.3	33	334	10.1	0	28	601	21.5	0	33	430	13.0	0	100	912	31	16	310	38	15	8	1	DET.

NEW YORK YANKEES 10-3-1 Ray Flaherty

Scores of Each Game		
21	San Francisco	7
21	BUFFALO	10
17	Chicago	17
7	Cleveland	24
21	Buffalo	13
0	CLEVELAND	7
21	BROOKLYN	10
31	Los Angeles	17
24	MIAMI	21
17	LOS ANGELES	12
10	SAN FRANCISCO	9
28	CHICAGO	38
21	Brooklyn	7
31	Miami	0

Use Name	Pos.	Hgt	Wgt	Age	Int	Pts
Jack Baldwin	C-LB	6'3"	225	25		
Tom Robertson	C-LB	6'	225	29		
Lou Sossamon	C-LB	6'1"	207	25		
Ray Hare	BB-LB	6'1"	205	28		

Use Name – Tackles	Pos.	Hgt	Wgt	Age	Int	Pts
George Bentz	T	6'2"	230	27		
Nate Johnson	T	6'3"	240	26		
Bruiser Kinard	T	6'1"	218	31		
Harley McCollum	T	6'4"	245	28		
Darrell Palmer	T	6'2"	245	24		
Roman Piskor	T	6'	245	28		

Use Name – Guards	Pos.	Hgt	Wgt	Age	Int	Pts
Mike Karmazin	G	5'11"	210	27		
George Kinard	G	6'1"	205	29		
Charley Riffle	G	6'	212	28		
Joe Yackanich	G	5'10"	205	24		

His Brooklyn team had not done well in the NFL, so owner Dan Topping jumped the club into the AAFC as the Yankees. After a year in mothballs, the team took back its players from the Boston franchise and set up shop in Yankee Stadium. With ex-Redskin coach Ray Flaherty at the helm, the Yankees won the Eastern title with a mixed squad of NFL veterans and freshmen pros. Frankie Sinkwich slated to be the star tailback, was hobbled by an old knee injury, so Ace Parker, a step slower than in his prewar days, directed the single-win attack. Old Dodgers Bruiser Kinard, Pug Manders, Perry Schwartz, and Bob Masterson rejoined Parker in the lineup. The brightest star, however, was rookie Spec Sanders, a standout runner, passer, receiver, and defensive back. Of the three games the Yankees lost, two came at the hands of the powerful Cleveland Browns.

BROOKLYN DODGERS 3-10-1 Mal Stevens, Cliff Battles

Scores of Each Game		
27	Buffalo	14
14	Los Angeles	20
13	San Francisco	32
7	Cleveland	26
21	CHICAGO	21
10	New York	21
30	MIAMI	7
21	Chicago	14
14	BUFFALO	17
14	LOS ANGELES	19
14	SAN FRANCISCO	30
7	NEW YORK	21
14	CLEVELAND	66
20	Miami	31

Use Name	Pos.	Hgt	Wgt	Age	Int	Pts
Joe Gibson	C-LB-DE	6'3"	215	27		
Russ Morrow (1 reception for 8 yds. and TD, 22 yds. on rushing lateral)	C-LB-OE	6'7"	200	22		12
Caleb Warrington	C-LB	6'2"	210	25		
Bolo Perdue	DE	5'10"	205	29		

Use Name – Tackles	Pos.	Hgt	Wgt	Age	Int	Pts
Nick Daukas (2 receptions for 19 yds.)	T	6'4"	225	23	1	
Frank Hrabetin (to MIA) (1 reception for 17 yds.)	T	6'4"	230	30		
Herb Maack	T	6'2"	210	29		
Ed Mieszkowski	T	6'2"	220	21		
George Perpich (1 punt return for 16 yds.)	T	6'2"	230	26		
Martin Ruby (1 reception for 3 yds.)	T	6'3"	250	26		
George Sergienko	T	6'1"	250	28		

Use Name – Guards	Pos.	Hgt	Wgt	Age	Int	Pts
George Bernhardt (1 kickoff return for 13 yds.)	G	5'10"	210	27		
John Billman	G	6'1"	202	26		
Harry Buffington	G	6'	210	27		
Jack Freeman	G	6'	198	24		
Vic Obeck (1 punt return for 3 yds.)	G	6'	225	28		

Brooklyn fans supported the baseball Dodgers in royal style but treated the football team like an unwanted stepchild as the attendance averaged under 20,000 per game. This edition of the Dodgers gave fans little reason to turn out, winning only three games all year and ending the season with a six-game losing streak. The entire offense rested on the shoulders of rookie tailback Glen Dobbs, a great passer who won the league MVP Award. Receivers Saxon Judd and Joe Davis kept the offense alive with their catches, but the runners made no headway at all. Even with All-Pro tackle Martin Ruby, the line sprang many leaks. The losing, both of games and money, cost coach Mal Stevens his job after seven games, but replacements Cliff Battles and Tom Scott offered no magic potions for victory.

BUFFALO BISONS 3-10-1 Red Dawson

Scores of Each Game		
14	BROOKLYN	27
10	New York	21
0	CLEVELAND	28
35	Chicago	38
21	LOS ANGELES	21
13	NEW YORK	21
14	MIAMI	17
17	SAN FRANCISCO	14
49	CHICAGO	17
14	San Francisco	27
17	Brooklyn	14
14	Miami	21
17	Cleveland	42
14	Los Angeles	62

Use Name	Pos.	Hgt	Wgt	Age	Int	Pts
Sam Brazinsky	C-LB	6'1"	215	24	2	
Jim Martinelli	C-LB	6'	227	26	1	
Felto Prewitt	C-LB	5'11"	210	22	4	
Bill Daddio (3 PAT's in 3 attempts)	DE	5'11"	215	30		3
Ralph Schilling (from WAS-NFL)	DE-OE	6'3"	218	25		
John Fekete (1 rush for −1 yd.)	HB-DB	5'11"	200	25		

Use Name – Tackles	Pos.	Hgt	Wgt	Age	Int	Pts
Jack Dugger (1 reception for 15 yds.)	T-DE-OE	6'3"	225	23		6
Chubby Grigg	T	6'2"	330	20		
Jack Kramer	T	6'	220	23		
John Matisi	T	6'2"	220	25		
Ben Pucci	T	6'4"	260	21		
C.B. Stanley	T	6'4"	225	27		

Use Name – Guards	Pos.	Hgt	Wgt	Age	Int	Pts
George Doherty (from NY) (1 kickoff return for 0 yds.)	G	6'1"	218	25		
Elmer Jones	G-LB	6'	233	26	2	
Al Klug	G	6'1"	220	25		
Hal Lahar	G	6'	225	27		
Jim Lecture	G	5'10"	220	22		
John Perko	G	5'11"	225	27		
Rocco Pirro	G	6'	235	29		
Roy Stuart	G-LB	5'8"	195	26		
Gene White	G	6'	205	27		

Buffalo had tried pro football several times before and now took another shot at it in the AAFC. In the early 1920s the Buffalo All-Americans had been a powerful contender for the championship of professional football. As late as 1929 Buffalo had held a franchise in the NFL, and in 1940-41 she had been part of the outlaw American Football League. Undaunted by the litter of these past failures, Sam Cordovano purchased a franchise.

Under the direction of coach Red Dawson, the Bisons had a lot of problems keeping other teams out of the end zone. They lost games 38-35 to Chicago, 42-17 to Cleveland, and 62-14 to Los Angeles. Yet, with a pair of tough runners in Vic Kulbitski and Steve Juzwik, the Bisons also broke out with a flurry of points, as the Chicago Rockets learned in a 49-17 Buffalo blitzkrieg.

MIAMI SEAHAWKS 3-11-0 Jack Meagher, Hamp Pool (retired as player when named head coach)

Scores of Each Game		
0	Cleveland	44
14	San Francisco	21
14	Los Angeles	30
7	SAN FRANCISCO	34
17	Buffalo	14
7	Chicago	28
7	Brooklyn	30
21	New York	24
7	CHICAGO	20
21	BUFFALO	14
21	LOS ANGELES	34
0	CLEVELAND	34
0	NEW YORK	31
31	BROOKLYN	20

Use Name	Pos.	Hgt	Wgt	Age	Int	Pts
Daryl Cato (3 yds. rushing on lateral)	C-LB	6'2"	195	26	1	
John Tavener	C-LB	6'	225	25		
Ken Whitlow	C-LB	6'1"	190	28	2	
Tex Williams	C-LB	6'	195	27	1	
Al Wukits (from BUF)	C-LB-G	6'3"	218	26	2	
Stan Stasica	HB-DB	5'10"	175	25		

Use Name – Tackles	Pos.	Hgt	Wgt	Age	Int	Pts
Paul Berezney	T	6'2"	225	29		
Bill Davis	T	6'1"	230	29		
Gene Ellenson	T	6'1"	210	25		
George Hekkers	T	6'4"	225	23		
Mitch Olenski (1 kickoff return for 2 yds.)	T	6'3"	218	26		

Use Name – Guards	Pos.	Hgt	Wgt	Age	Int	Pts
Ed Bell	G	6'1"	210	24		
Hal Jungmichel	G	5'9"	200	26	1	
Joe Krivonak	G	6'2"	230	28		
Jim Sivell	G	5'9"	200	32		
Charlie Taylor	G	5'11"	205	26		
George Zorich (1 punt return for 18 yds.)	G	6'2"	215	27		

Miami may have been a booming city, but it hardly was ready to support a pro-football team. Playing before tiny home crowds, the Seahawks gave their fans little reason to come back a second time, as they lost eleven games, most of them by lopsided scores. A collection of marginal NFL veterans and undistinguished rookies filled the Miami roster but left the victory column of the standings close to empty. The year began with a 44-0 trouncing in Cleveland, and only wins over Brooklyn and Buffalo (twice) broke the monotony.

As unimpressive as they were on the field, the Seahawks were the financial albatross around the AAFC's neck. The Miami owners quickly sank into a sea of red ink, and only contributions from other clubs kept the Seahawks from drowning in mid-season. But the scant attendance finally sent the Seahawks to Davey Jones's locker after one season.

TEAM TOTALS

OFFENSE	First Downs: Tot	by Rsh	by Pas	by Pen	Rushing: No.	Yds.	Avg Yds.	TD	Passing: Att	Com	Comp Pct.	Yds.	Avg. Yds. Att.	Avg. Yds. Comp	TD	Int	Pct. Int.	Punting: No.	Avg. Yds.
N.Y.	158	98	54	6	512	1880	3.7	17	274	129	47.1	1645	6.0	12.8	13	21	7.7	79	36.0
BKN.	135	54	70	11	374	1017	2.7	9	327	162	49.5	2258	6.9	13.9	17	23	7.0	90	46.5
BUFF.	147	85	45	17	501	2046	4.1	13	238	96	40.3	1367	5.7	14.2	16	23	9.7	88	35.6
MIAMI	121	50	59	12	408	848	2.1	13	295	131	44.4	1725	5.9	13.2	10	33	11.2	80	40.6
DEFENSE																			
N.Y.	119	61	47	11	449	1055	2.3	9	252	123	48.4	1564	6.2	12.7	13	16	6.3	88	42.3
BKN.	192	114	69	9	575	2458	4.3	24	255	132	51.9	2077	8.2	15.7	19	12	4.7	73	40.6
BUFF.	170	94	68	8	497	2075	4.2	21	295	146	49.5	2370	8.0	16.2	23	22	7.5	67	41.5
MIAMI	155	93	53	9	528	2248	4.3	24	252	123	48.4	1876	7.4	15.3	19	24	9.5	51	42.0

OFFENSE	Punt Returns: No.	Yds.	Avg. Yds.	TD	Kickoff Returns: No.	Yds.	Avg. Yds.	TD	Interception Returns: No.	Yds.	Avg. Yds.	TD	Penalties: No.	Yds.	Fumbles: No.	Lost	Points: Tot	PAT	FG Att	FG	Saf.
N.Y.	61	778	15.3	3	44	1050	23.9	1	16	266	16.6	1	65	558	63	24	270	36	9	6	0
BKN.	30	389	13.0	1	55	1005	18.3	0	12	209	17.4	0	56	453	43	17	226	27	11	5	2
BUFF.	37	534	14.4	0	59	1265	21.4	0	22	297	13.5	1	46	296	55	36	249	33	8	4	0
MIAMI	27	301	11.1	0	61	1344	22.0	0	24	279	11.6	0	56	402	47	23	167	23	7	2	0
DEFENSE																					
N.Y.	40	432	10.8	0	47	968	20.6	0	21	392	18.7	1	51	449	39	18	192	22	16	8	1
BKN.	44	619	14.1	1	46	1182	25.7	1	23	354	15.4	1	53	395	56	26	339	42	16	5	3
BUFF.	47	810	17.2	2	42	1046	24.9	1	23	208	9.0	0	73	588	42	29	370	49	9	3	0
MIAMI	44	595	13.5	1	37	685	18.5	0	33	569	16.9	3	68	625	47	20	378	45	16	13	0

Use Name – Backs & Ends	Pos.	Age	Hgt	Wgt	Pts	Int	RUSHING				PASSING								RECEIVING				PUNTING		KICKING						PUNT RETURNS				KICKOFF RETURNS			
							No.	Yds	Avg	TD	Att	Comp	%	Yds	Yd/Att	TD	Int–%	RK	No.	Yds	Avg	TD	No.	Avg	Pat	Att	%	FG	Att	%	No.	Yds	Avg	TD	No.	Yds	Avg	TD
NEW YORK YANKEES																																						
Ace Parker	TB-DB	34	6'	180	24		75	184	2.5	3	115	62	54	763	6.6	8	3– 3	3					27	33.7							8	85	11	0	2	27	14	0
Spec Sanders	TB-WB-DB	27	6'1"	196	72	2	140	709	5.1	6	79	33	42	411	5.2	4	9–11		17	259	15	3	33	36.6							17	257	15	1	13	395	30	1
Bob Perina	TB-DB	25	6'1"	205	6	2	45	135	3.0	1	48	21	44	279	5.8	1	4– 8						11	37.5							15	205	14	0	4	81	20	0
Frankie Sinkwich	TB-DB	25	5'11"	190			7	20	2.9	0	12	5	42	61	5.1	0	2–17																					
Eddie Prokop	FB-DB	24	5'11"	200	18	1	65	236	3.6	1	11	4	36	72	6.5	0	0– 0		5	52	10	1									4	116	29	1	2	47	24	0
Bob Kennedy	FB-DB	25	5'11"	195	12	3	58	179	3.1	2	6	2	33	45	7.5	0	3–50		11	59	5	0	7	37.0							3	20	7	0	4	105	26	0
Pug Manders	FB-LB	33	6'	200	18		49	168	3.4	3	3	2	67	14	4.7	0	0– 0		3	49	16	0													1	26	26	0
Dewey Proctor	FB-LB	25	5'11"	215	12		23	76	3.3	1									3	32	11	1																
Harvey Johnson	FB-LB	27	5'11"	210	54		16	63	3.9	0									2	19	10	0			36	36	100	6	8	75								
Lowell Wagner	WB-DB	22	6'	193	12		15	29	1.9	0									9	126	14	1									2	55	28	1	4	119	30	0
Bob Sweiger	WB-DB	27	6'	209	6	4	7	22	3.1	0									8	55	7	1	1	52.0							1	14	14	0	5	103	21	0
Lloyd Cheatham	BB-LB	27	6'2"	215	6	1	3	2	0.7	0									4	54	14	1									1	26	26	0	1	7	7	0
Bob Morrow	BB-LB	28	6'	220			8	54	6.8	0									1	6	6	0																
Jack Russell	OE-DE	26	6'1"	215	24														23	223	10	4																
Bruce Alford	OE-DB	25	6'	190															13	173	13	0													1	62	62	0
Harry Burrus	OE-WB-DB	25	6'1"	195	6	2	1	3	3.0	0									10	251	25	1																
Bob Masterson	OE-DE	31	6'1"	225		1													10	119	12	0						0	1	0					5	55	11	0
Perry Schwartz	OE-DE	31	6'2"	200															5	82	16	0													2	23	12	0
Mel Conger	OE-DE	27	6'2"	225															3	61	20	0																
Hank Stanton	OE-DE	26	6'2"	200															2	25	13	0																
BROOKLYN DODGERS																																						
Glenn Dobbs	TB-DB	26	6'4"	210	36	2	95	208	2.2	4	269	135	50	1886	7.0	13	15– 6	5	1	–5	–5	0	80	47.8							7	146	21	1	12	214	18	0
Lew Mayne	TB-DB	26	6'1"	190	12		70	191	2.7	1	25	14	56	219	8.8	3	4–16		5	9	2	0	3	26.3							6	47	8	0	4	90	23	0
Charlie Armstrong	TB-DB	27	5'10"	180		2	22	78	3.6	0	21	9	43	126	6.0	1	2–10						6	38.5							6	97	16	0	3	93	31	0
Harry Connolly	TB-DB	26	5'11"	190			8	18	2.3	0	8	2	25	29	3.6	0	1–12														1	6	6	0	2	41	21	0
Dom Principe	FB-LB	29	6'	210	12		39	139	3.6	2									3	25	8	0													6	117	20	0
Charlie Timmons	FB-LB	28	5'10"	210			23	65	2.8	0									1	4	4	0																
Bill Daley (to MIA)	FB-LB	26	6'2"	210			14	63	4.5	0									2	–5	–2	0													1	10	10	0
Rhoten Shetley	FB-LB	28	5'11"	210			9	21	2.3	0									1	10	10	0																
Cal Purdin (to MIA, HB-DB)	WB-DB	24	6'2"	185			10	12	1.2	0	1	1	100	–2	–2.0	0	0– 0		12	108	9	0									4	52	13	0	4	77	19	0
Doyle Tackett	WB-BB-DB	22	6'	201	12	1	11	–6	–0.5	0									10	191	19	2									1	3	3	0	5	76	15	0
Art Van Tone	WB-DB	27	5'10"	185	18	1	4	10	2.5	0									7	152	22	3									1	5	5	0	2	25	13	0
Dub Jones (from MIA, HB-DB)	WB-DB	21	6'4"	200			43	163	3.8	0	2	1	50	0	0.0	0	1–50														1	6	6	0	6	91	15	0
Mickey Colmer	BB-LB	27	6'2"	218	6	1	46	155	3.4	0									22	327	15	1									1	9	9	0	1	9	9	0
Walt McDonald (from MIA, QB)	BB-DB	25	6'1"	210		2	4	–11	–2.7	0	3	1	33	24	8.0	0	1–33		12	126	11	0													3	32	11	0
Saxon Judd	OE	25	6'1"	190	30														34	443	13	4													3	54	18	0
Joe Davis	OE-DE	25	6'2"	195	7														22	337	15	1			1	1	100								2	32	16	0
Neal Adams	OE-DE	27	6'3"	195	12														12	225	15	2																
Jim McCarthy	OE-DE	24	6'1"	205	23	1													11	296	27	3			6	7	71	0	1	0					1	8	8	0
Bob McCain	OE-DE	24	5'11"	105															3	27	9	0																
Phil Martinovich	G	31	5'10"	220	36																				21	22	95	5	10	50								
BUFFALO BISONS																																						
George Terlep	QB-DB	24	5'10"	180	6		36	29	0.8	1	123	48	39	574	4.7	7	14–11	9					1	31.0											1	23	23	0
Al Dekdebrun	QB-DB	25	5'11"	180		3	25	–55	–2.2	0	66	28	42	517	7.8	8	8–12																		6	116	19	0
Ken Stofer	QB-DB	27	5'9"	188			16	36	2.3	0	26	9	35	86	3.3	1	1– 4		1	14	14	0	3	36.0							5	53	11	0	2	81	41	0
Harry Hopp (to MIA)	QB-FB-LB	27	6'1"	215	18		61	218	3.6	3	22	11	50	190	8.6	0	0– 0		2	–1	0	0	15	30.7											6	113	19	0
Vic Kulbitski	FB-LB	25	5'11"	205	12	1	97	605	6.2	2									1	0	0	0													5	81	16	0
Steve Juzwik	HB-DB	28	5'8"	184	42	5	71	455	6.4	3									23	357	16	3									11	135	12	0	21	452	22	0
Chet Mutryn	HB-DB	25	5'9"	180	30		57	289	5.1	1									7	168	24	3									5	57	11	0	4	79	20	0
Pres Johnston (from MIA)	FB-LB	25	6'	205	19	1	45	218	4.8	2	1	1	100	9	9.0	0	0– 0		6	54	9	1	28	39.7	1	1	100								2	21	11	0
Lou Tomasetti	HB-DB	30	6'	198	12	1	43	139	3.2	1									6	81	14	1									7	138	20	0	2	85	43	0
Andy Dudish	HB-DB	25	5'11"	180			30	106	3.5	0									2	33	17	0									5	73	15	0	7	196	28	0
Curt Sandig	HB-DB	28	5'10"	175	6		22	52	2.4	1									2	15	8	0	4	38.8							2	20	10	0	2	43	22	0
Jim Thibaut	FB-LB	27	5'11"	205	6		10	48	4.8	1																												
Lou Zontini	FB-LB	29	5'8"	195	42	1	13	36	2.8	0	1	0	0	0	0.0	0	0– 0						44	36.3	30	31	97	4	8	50					1	19	19	0
Blondy Black	FB-DB	26	5'11"	195		1	1	10	10.0	0									1	21	21	0									2	58	29	0				
Bob Thurbon	HB-DB	28	5'10"	180			3	2	0.7	0									1	–3	–3	0													1	15	15	0
Fay King	OE	24	6'3"	195	36														30	466	16	6																
Al Vandeweghe	OE-DE	25	5'11"	200	12														6	67	11	1													1	16	16	0
Herb Nelson	OE-DE	25	6'4"	218			1	1	1.0	0									4	47	12	0																
John Batorski	OE-DE	25	6'2"	238															2	27	14	0																
Marty Comer	OE-DE	28	6'	202	6														2	17	9	0																
Ray Ebli	OE-DE	26	6'2"	210	6														2	15	8	1																
Nick Klutka	OE-DE	25	5'11"	200															1	9	9	0																
MIAMI SEAHAWKS																																						
Marion Pugh	QB	26	6'1"	187	12		29	–125	–4.3	2	118	55	47	608	5.2	5	12–10	8	4	43	11	0													1	24	24	0
Cotton Price	QB	27	6'1"	180			15	–55	–3.7	0	74	36	49	484	6.5	2	5– 7		2	17	9	0	4	26.3											2	32	16	0
Kay Eakin	QB-HB-DB	29	6'	180		2	15	–41	–2.7	0	45	19	42	331	7.4	2	5–11		6	67	11	0	37	41.4							3	30	10	0	4	51	13	0
Jimmy Nelson	HB-QB-DB	27	5'11"	180	12	2	39	163	4.2	2	24	8	33	135	5.6	0	4–17		4	20	5	0	16	39.7							7	71	10	0	10	192	19	0
Jim Tarrant	QB	25	5'9"	160			5	–46	–9.2	0	12	5	42	95	7.9	1	0– 0																					
Ken Holley	QB	26	5'10"	185			2	–22	–11.0	0	11	3	27	36	3.3	0	4–36																					
Frank Trigilio (from LA)	FB-LB	27	5'11"	200	6		41	126	3.1	1																												
Don Reece	FB-LB-T	26	6'1"	230	12	1	30	109	3.6	2									1	5	5	0																
Bob Paffrath (from BKN, BB-DB)	HB-DB	28	5'8"	190	12		31	100	3.2	2	1	0	0	0	0.0	0	0– 0		4	–6	–1	0	1	50.0							1	1	1	0	4	76	19	0
Jim Reynolds	FB-LB	26	6'1"	190		2	32	96	3.0	0									1	32	32	0	1	39.0											1	13	13	0
Monk Gafford (from BKN, WB-DB)	HB-DB	25	5'11"	195	30	4	24	66	2.8	1	5	1	20	–3	–0.6	0	2–40		14	270	19	4	13	40.3							9	117	13	0	11	345	31	0
Stan Koslowski	FB-LB	21	6'1"	200			18	61	3.4	0									2	27	14	0									1	4	4	0	3	72	24	0
Dick Erdlitz	HB-DB	26	5'10"	180	34	1	26	38	1.5	1	1	1	100	10	10.0	0	0– 0		7	31	4	0			22	22	100	2	7	29					6	104	17	0
Terry Fox	FB-LB	27	6'1"	208			12	26	2.2	0									3	27	9	0	2	44.0											1	24	24	0
Fred Gloden	HB-DB	27	5'10"	187	6		13	24	1.9	1																									1	20	20	0
Fondren Mitchell	HB-DB	25	6'	185		1	5	17	3.4	0									8	131	16	0													4	52	13	0
John Vardian	HB-DB	21	5'8"	165			5	–8	–1.6	0	1	1	100	–4	–4.0	0	0– 0		7	108	15	0													1	23	23	0
Lamar Davis	OE-DB	25	6'1"	185	12	4	14	64	4.6	0									22	275	13	2									4	54	14	0	5	235	47	0
Lamar Blount	OE-DB	26	6'1"	190	6														13	218	17	1																
Prince Scott	OE-DB	27	6'1"	190	12	1													13	180	14	2									1	6	6	0	2	28	14	0
Dick Horne	OE-DE	28	6'2"	215															5	48	10	0																
Hub Ulrich	OE-DE	25	6'	205	6														4	75	19	1																
Hamp Pool	OE-DE	31	6'3"	225															3	63	21	0																

CLEVELAND BROWNS 12-2-0 Paul Brown

Scores of Each Game		
44	MIAMI	0
20	Chicago	6
28	Buffalo	0
24	NEW YORK	7
26	BROOKLYN	7
7	New York	0
31	LOS ANGELES	14
20	SAN FRANCISCO	34
16	Los Angeles	17
14	San Francisco	7
51	CHICAGO	14
42	BUFFALO	17
34	Miami	0
66	Brooklyn	14

Use Name	Pos.	Hgt	Wgt	Age	Int	Pts
Frank Gatski	C-LB	6'3"	210	24	1	6
Mel Maceau	C-LB	6'	203	24		
Mo Scarry	C-LB	6'	208	26	2	

Use Name – Tackles	Pos.	Hgt	Wgt	Age	Int	Pts
Chet Adams	T	6'3"	228	30	1	17
(5 PAT's in 5 attempts)						
Ernie Blandin	T	6'4"	245	27		
Jim Daniell	T	6'2"	230	28		
Lou Rymkus	T	6'4"	230	27		

Use Name – Guards	Pos.	Hgt	Wgt	Age	Int	Pts
George Cheroke	G	5'9"	195	25		
Lin Houston	G	6'	205	25		
Alex Kapter	G	6'	205	24		
Bob Kolesar	G	5'10"	200	25		
Ed Ulinski	G	5'11"	200	25		
(1 rush for 2 yds.)						
Bill Willis	G	6'2"	206	25		

Cleveland lost a champion when the Rams left but gained a dynasty with the birth of the Browns. Coached by Paul Brown and manned by a platoon of war-hardened ex-GIs, the Browns overwhelmed their opponents and went on to take the newly created All American Football Conference championship. Cleveland fans were captivated as they never were by the Rams, turning out for a record average attendance of 57,000 per game.

With Paul Brown welding the parts together with a rigorous discipline, the Browns boasted of a full squad of first-rate players. Leading the pack was quarterback Otto Graham, a fine passer, safetyman, and field leader. Ends Mac Speedie and Dante Lavelli gave Graham a superb pair of targets, tackle Lou Groza led the league in scoring on the strength of his toe, Tom Colella picked off the most enemy passes, and Marion Motley and Bill Willis, two black players signed by Brown, gave Cleveland the league's best fullback and guard. Motley led the team in rushing even though he and Willis did not play in the game at Miami after receiving death threats.

SAN FRANCISCO 49ers 9-5-0 Buck Shaw

Scores of Each Game		
7	NEW YORK	21
21	MIAMI	14
32	BROOKLYN	13
7	Chicago	21
34	Miami	7
23	Los Angeles	14
14	Buffalo	17
34	Cleveland	20
27	BUFFALO	14
7	CLEVELAND	14
9	New York	10
30	Brooklyn	14
14	CHICAGO	0
48	LOS ANGELES	7

Use Name	Pos.	Hgt	Wgt	Age	Int	Pts
Gerry Conlee	C-LB	5'11"	210	30		
Art Elston	C-LB	5'11"	190	27	1	
Ed Forrest	C-LB	5'11"	210	25		
Bill Remington	C-LB	6'1"	185	25		

Use Name – Tackles	Pos.	Hgt	Wgt	Age	Int	Pts
Bob Bryant	T	6'3"	225	27		
John Kuzman	T	6'1"	230	30		6
John Mellus	T	6'	210	29		1
(1 PAT in 2 attempts and missed 1 FG attempt)						
John Woudenberg	T	6'3"	225	28		

Use Name – Guards	Pos.	Hgt	Wgt	Age	Int	Pts
Bruno Banducci	G	5'11"	215	24		
Dick Bassi	G-LB	5'11"	215	31	1	
Garland Gregory	G-LB	5'11"	185	27		
(1 kickoff return for 0 yds.)						
Visco Grgich	G	5'11"	210	23		
Charlie Pavlich	G	6'2"	210	25		
Bob Thornton	G	5'10"	205	27		

When the NFL brushed off his application for a franchise, Tony Morabito organized the '49ers for the AAFC. In this debut season, the '49ers established that they were the second-best franchise in the league, trailing the Browns not only this year but for the whole span of the AAFC. Both in attendance and in the standings, San Francisco would grow accustomed to being listed right below Cleveland.

Coach Buck Shaw built the team around quarterback Frankie Albert, a little left-handed passer who scrambled before it was fashionable. Albert's favorite receiver was Alyn Beals, a quick end from Santa Clara who loved to run deep patterns. Ex-Bear Norm Standlee was the top runner and ex-Eagle Bruno Banducci the leading lineman.

LOS ANGELES DONS 7-5-2 Dud DeGroot

Scores of Each Game		
20	BROOKLYN	14
30	MIAMI	14
21	Buffalo	21
21	Chicago	9
14	SAN FRANCISCO	23
14	Cleveland	31
17	NEW YORK	31
17	CLEVELAND	16
12	New York	17
19	Brooklyn	14
34	Miami	21
62	BUFFALO	14
7	San Francisco	48
17	CHICAGO	17

Use Name	Pos.	Hgt	Wgt	Age	Int	Pts
Don Nolander	C-LB	6'1"	210	25	1	
Hank Rockwell	C-G	6'4"	230	29		
John McQuary	HB-DB	6'1"	208	26		

Use Name – Tackles	Pos.	Hgt	Wgt	Age	Int	Pts
Lee Artoe	T	6'3"	240	30		1
((1 kickoff return for 13 yds., 1 PAT in 2 attempts)						
Earl Audet	T	6'2"	252	25		
Gil Duggan	T	6'3"	235	28		
Joe Mihal	T	6'3"	240	30		
Paul Mitchell	T	6'3"	225	26		

Use Name – Guards	Pos.	Hgt	Wgt	Age	Int	Pts
Ray Frankowski	G	5'11"	220	27		6
Al Lolotai	G	6'	220	25		
Bill Radovich	G	5'10"	255	31		
Frank Yokas	G	5'11"	210	22		

After having no pro teams last year, Los Angeles suddenly had two, the Rams and Dons, and both of them lost money in the battle for paying customers—a financial bleeding which would go on until the Dons gave up the ghost in 1949.

The Dons raked in points like leaves on an October Saturday, but their opponents in return marched all over the Los Angeles defense. Even with 1943 Heisman Trophy winner Angelo Bertelli injured, veteran pro backs Charlie O'Rourke, John Kimbrough, Chuck Fenenbock, and Harry Clark kept the ball moving steadily. Dale Gentry was the team's top receiver, and Bob Nelson, Lee Artoe, Bill Radovich, and Bob Reinhard gave the Dons four of the AAFC's best linemen. The defense did turn in a standout game in a 17-16 upset of the Browns, but a 48-7 trouncing by San Francisco pointed out the leaks in the dam.

CHICAGO ROCKETS 5-6-3 Dick Hanley, Bob Dove, Ned Mathews, Willie Wilkin, Pat Boland

Scores of Each Game		
6	CLEVELAND	20
17	NEW YORK	17
38	BUFFALO	35
21	SAN FRANCISCO	7
9	LOS ANGELES	21
21	Brooklyn	21
28	MIAMI	7
17	Buffalo	49
14	BROOKLYN	21
20	Miami	7
14	Cleveland	51
38	New York	28
0	San Francisco	14
17	Los Angeles	17

Use Name	Pos.	Hgt	Wgt	Age	Int	Pts
Herb Coleman	C-LB	6'	200	23	1	
(1 kickoff return for 20 yds.)						
Mickey Parks	C-LB	6'	220	29		

Use Name – Tackles	Pos.	Hgt	Wgt	Age	Int	Pts
Jim Brutz	T	6'	230	27		
Charlie Huneke	T	6'3"	225	25		
Quentin Klenk (from BUF)	T	6'2"	225	27		
Norm Verr	T	6'1"	240	23		
Lloyd Wasserbach	T	5'11"	205	25	1	
(1 kickoff return for 13 yds.)						
Willie Wilkin	T	6'4"	260	30		
(3 yds. receiving on lateral)						

Use Name – Guards	Pos.	Hgt	Wgt	Age	Int	Pts
Jim O'Neal	G	6'1"	230	22		
Jim Pearcy	G	5'11"	210	27		
Joe Ruetz	G-LB	6'	200	29	2	
Tony Sumpter	G	6'1"	215	24		
Red Vogds	G	5'10"	204	23		

The Rockets faced the hardest road in the AAFC, sharing the Chicago football dollar with the NFL Bears and Cardinals. With the Bears perennial champions and the Cardinals on the rise, the Rockets had problems enough without the chaos in their higher command. Dick Hanley began the year as coach but quit after three games. Then three players, Bob Dove, Ned Mathews, and Willie Wilkin, took over as a committee of coaches for five games, with Pat Boland finally coming in as full-time coach for the last six contests.

Through all these changes, the Rockets managed to stay around the break-even point in wins and losses. Bob "Hunchy" Hoernschemeyer sparked the offense with his passing and running, and Elroy "Crazy Legs" Hirsch added his speed to the team.

TEAM TOTALS

	FIRST DOWNS:				RUSHING:				PASSING:									PUNTING:	
OFFENSE	Tot	by Rsh	by Pas	by Pen	No.	Yds.	Avg Yds.	TD	Att	Com	Comp Pct.	Yds.	Avg. Yds. Att.	Avg. Yds. Comp	TD	Int	Pct. Int.	No.	Avg. Yds.
CLEVE.	146	79	60	7	494	2007	4.1	27	237	123	51.9	2266	9.6	18.4	22	7	3.0	58	39.2
S.F.	170	113	52	5	582	2175	3.7	22	252	130	51.6	1721	6.8	13.2	18	21	8.3	67	40.6
L.A.	183	92	84	7	549	1949	3.6	17	322	176	54.7	2193	6.8	12.5	19	30	9.3	57	44.2
CHI.	149	76	63	10	511	1559	3.1	10	310	144	46.5	1898	6.1	13.1	18	29	9.4	91	41.9
DEFENSE																			
CLEVE.	160	89	56	15	546	1616	3.0	8	299	125	41.8	1317	4.4	10.5	8	41	13.7	71	41.6
S.F.	140	56	79	5	425	873	2.1	7	359	185	51.5	2150	5.9	11.6	15	21	5.8	87	38.8
L.A.	144	71	65	8	451	1356	3.0	19	284	138	48.6	2101	7.4	15.2	17	20	7.0	84	38.7
CHI.	129	69	50	10	475	1718	3.6	16	259	119	46.0	1618	6.3	13.6	19	31	12.0	89	40.0

	PUNT RETURNS:				KICKOFF RETURNS:				INTERCEPTION RETURNS:				PENALTIES:		FUMBLES:		POINTS:					TEAM TOTALS
OFFENSE	No.	Yds.	Avg. Yds.	TD	No.	Yds.	Avg. Yds.	TD	No.	Yds.	Avg. Yds.	TD	No.	Yds.	No.	Lost	Tot	PAT	FG Att	FG	Saf.	OFFENSE
CLEVE.	39	537	13.8	0	36	841	23.4	1	41	589	14.4	4	71	600	54	30	423	52	29	13	1	CLEVE.
S.F.	51	640	12.5	0	37	777	21.0	0	21	391	18.6	1	56	440	35	21	307	35	8	4	1	S.F
L.A.	49	724	14.8	0	57	1307	22.9	1	20	293	14.7	1	50	379	31	13	305	37	17	6	2	L.A.
CHI.	48	652	13.6	3	54	1323	24.5	2	31	516	16.6	1	63	514	40	18	263	32	12	9	0	CHI.
DEFENSE																						DEFENSE
CLEVE.	39	510	13.1	1	61	1397	22.9	0	7	116	16.6	0	48	326	58	23	137	17	9	4	0	CLEVE.
S.F.	34	433	12.7	1	61	1360	22.3	1	21	292	13.9	1	47	377	46	26	189	24	9	3	0	S.F.
L.A.	36	530	14.7	1	54	1161	21.5	2	30	387	12.9	0	50	329	32	17	290	35	12	7	0	L.A.
CHI.	48	626	13.0	0	55	1117	20.3	0	29	532	18.3	3	73	553	48	22	315	41	14	6	2	CHI.

							RUSHING				PASSING								RECEIVING				PUNTING		KICKING						PUNT RETURNS				KICKOFF RETURNS			
Use Name – Backs & Ends	Pos.	Age	Hgt	Wgt	Pts	Int	No.	Yds	Avg	TD	Att	Comp	%	Yds	Yd/Att	TD	Int–%	RK	No.	Yds	Avg	TD	No.	Avg	Pat	Att	%	FG	Att	%	No.	Yds	Avg	TD	No.	Yds	Avg	TD
CLEVELAND BROWNS																																						
Otto Graham	QB-DB	24	6'1"	190	12	5	30	–125	–4.2	1	174	95	55	1834	10.5	17	5–3	1													12	129	11	0				
Cliff Lewis	QB-DB	23	5'11"	165		5	24	–34	–1.4	0	30	11	37	125	4.2	1	1–3														8	133	17	0	3	70	23	0
Bud Schwenk	QB	28	6'2"	200	6		6	–1	–0.2	1	23	15	65	276	12.0	4	0–0																					
Marion Motley	FB-LB	26	6'1"	218	36	1	73	601	8.2	5									10	188	19	1									1	0	0	0	3	53	18	0
Special Delivery Jones	HB-DB	27	5'10"	195	36	2	77	539	7.0	4	4	1	25	4	1.0	0	0–0		4	120	30	1									7	73	10	0	12	307	26	1
Don Greenwood	HB-DB	25	6'	198	36	2	77	274	3.6	6	1	1	100	27	27.0	0	0–0		4	0	0	0													5	105	21	0
Gaylon Smith	FB-LB	30	5'11"	200	30	1	62	240	3.9	5									7	73	10	0																
Tom Colella	HB-DB	28	6'	187	18	10	30	118	3.9	2									1	12	12	1	47	40.3							8	172	22	0	1	29	29	0
Ray Terrell	HB-DB	27	6'	185	6	3	39	117	3.0	0	2	0	0	0	0.0	0	0–0		4	21	5	0													3	80	27	0
Gene Fekete	FB-LB	24	6'	195	6		26	106	4.1	1									1	2	2	0													1	21	21	0
Bill Lund	HB-DB	22	5'10"	180	18	1	23	72	3.1	1									4	64	16	2									2	30	15	0	1	32	32	0
Al Akins	HB-DB	25	6'1"	195	6	1	5	42	8.4	1																									2	74	37	0
Fred Evans	HB-DB	25	5'11"	185		1	8	27	3.4	0									1	7	7	0	8	37.0							1	0	0	0				
Bob Steuber	HB-DB	24	6'2"	200		1	8	19	2.4	0									1	9	9	0													2	53	27	0
Lou Saban	FB-LB	24	6'	198		4	4	–4	–1.0	0	3	0	0	0	0.0	0	1–33		1	45	45	0																
Dante Lavelli	OE	23	6'	190	48		1	14	14.0	0									40	843	21	8																
Mac Speedie	OE-DE	26	6'3"	200	43														24	564	24	7	3	28.0	1	1	100								1	1	1	0
John Harrington	OE-DE	24	6'3"	198															8	136	17	0													2	16	8	0
John Yonakor	OE-DE	25	6'5"	218	12														7	98	14	2																
George Young	OE-DE	22	6'3"	210															3	37	12	0																
Al Coppage	OE-DE	30	6'1"	195															2	34	17	0																
John Rokisky	OE-DE	26	6'2"	200	1														1	13	13	0			1	1	100											
Lou Groza	T	22	6'3"	215	84																				45	47	96	13	29	45								
SAN FRANCISCO 49ers																																						
Frankie Albert	QB-DB	26	5'10"	160	24		69	–10	–0.1	4	197	104	53	1404	7.1	14	14–7	2					54	41.0							1	6	6	0	4	74	19	0
Jess Freitas	QB-DB	25	5'10"	170		2	6	–21	–3.5	0	44	22	50	234	5.3	3	7–16														1	10	10	0				
Parker Hall	QB-DB	29	6'	192			17	31	1.8	0	8	2	25	15	1.9	0	0–0		2	25	13	0													1	22	22	0
Norm Standlee	FB-LB	27	6'2"	245	12		134	651	4.9	2									2	–5	–2	0	1	34.0											1	33	33	0
Earle Parsons	HB-DB	26	6'	180	12		74	362	4.9	2									8	52	7	0									15	198	13	0	4	94	24	0
Johnny Strzykalski	HB-DB	23	5'9"	190	12	3	79	346	4.4	2									9	80	9	0									3	26	9	0	7	142	20	0
Len Eshmont	HB-DB	29	5'11"	178	54		73	340	4.7	6	2	1	50	42	21.0	1	0–0		17	287	17	2									2	26	13	0	10	264	26	0
Don Durdan	HB-DB	26	5'9"	175	6	2	32	132	4.1	0									2	27	14	1	6	39.8							3	37	12	0				
Ken Casanega	HB-DB	25	5'11"	175	12	8	29	90	3.1	1									5	102	20	1									18	248	14	0	3	61	20	0
Dick Renfro	FB-LB	27	5'10"	200	18		18	85	4.7	3																									1	20	20	0
Joe Vetrano	HB-DB	24	5'9"	170	49	3	23	69	3.0	1									4	37	9	0	6	39.3	31	38	82	4	7	57	7	84	12	0	3	49	16	0
Ken Roskie	FB-LB	26	6'1"	230			9	16	1.8	0									0	7	–	0																
Pete Franceschi	HB-DB	26	5'9"	170	12		8	–5	–0.6	1									3	35	12	1									1	6	6	0				
Alyn Beals	OE-DB	25	6'	185	61		2	–7	–3.5	0									40	586	15	10			1	1	100											
Bill Fisk	OE-DE	29	6'	200	6														19	186	10	1																
Bob Titchenal	OE-DE	28	6'2"	190	12		1	2	2.0	0									7	160	23	2																
Nick Susoeff	OE-DE	25	6'1"	210															5	98	20	0													1	10	10	0
Ed Balatti	OE-DB	22	6'1"	190	8														4	15	4	0			2	2	100											
Hank Norberg	OE-DE	27	6'2"	225		1													3	29	10	0																
LOS ANGELES DONS																																						
Charlie O'Rourke	QB-DB	29	5'11"	175	6		47	50	1.1	1	182	105	58	1250	6.9	12	14–8	4					8	39.0											1	28	28	0
Angelo Bertelli	QB	25	6'1"	190	6		11	–16	–1.5	1	127	67	53	917	7.2	7	14–11	7					2	38.0														
Bob Mitchell	QB-DB	25	5'11"	195		1	8	–12	–1.5	0	10	3	30	19	1.9	0	2–20		1	1	1	0	1	44.0														
John Kimbrough	FB-LB	28	6'2"	210	42		122	473	3.9	6									9	162	18	1													5	111	22	0
Chuck Fenenbock	HB-DB	28	5'9"	175	24		50	420	8.4	3	1	0	0	0	0.0	0	0–0		11	67	6	0									16	299	19	0	17	479	28	1
Harry Clark	HB-DB	28	6'	195	12	2	62	250	4.0	0									10	123	12	2									2	24	12	0	2	48	24	0
Earl Elsey	HB-DB	27	5'8"	175		2	47	165	3.5	0									14	179	13	0									9	147	16	0	15	335	22	0
Bob Seymour	HB-DB	30	6'2"	208	18	4	37	165	4.5	0									17	188	11	3									18	211	12	0	4	87	22	0
Buzz Mertes	HB-DB	25	6'	195	6	1	40	111	2.8	0									5	61	12	1													2	35	18	0
Bernie Nygren	HB-DB	26	5'9"	193	6	2	26	111	4.3	0									13	170	13	1													4	88	22	0
Andy Marefos	FB-LB	29	6'	225	26		30	93	3.1	4									1	13	13	0			2	2	100											
John Polanski	FB-LB	27	6'2"	210	12	1	28	77	2.7	1									2	15	8	1																
Paul Vinnola	HB-DB	24	5'10"	180		1	23	36	1.6	0									4	39	10	0									2	24	12	0	5	83	17	0
Bob Sneddon	HB-DB	25	5'10"	180		1	3	6	2.0	0									2	11	6	0																
Dale Gentry	OE-DE	29	6'3"	223	30		5	29	5.8	1									24	341	14	3									1	14	14	0				
Al Krueger	OE-DE	27	6'1"	190	6														19	213	11	1																
Bob Nowaskey	OE-DE	28	6'	200	24	1	3	14	4.7	0									19	198	10	3									1	5	5	0				
Joe Aguirre	OE-DE	27	6'4"	225	55		2	–5	–2.5	0	1	0	0	0	0.0	0	0–0		14	246	18	2	2	46.5	31	32	97	4	11	36								
Bill Kerr	OE-DE	30	6'	220		1	1	10	10.0	0									7	122	17	0																
John Morton	OE-DE	24	6'	200	6	1													4	44	11	1																
Bob Reinhard	T	25	6'4"	225	6		1	–30	–30.0	0	1	1	100	7	7.0	0	0–0						44	45.4														
Bob Nelson	C-LB	26	6'1"	215	9	1																			3	5	60	2	6	33					1	0	0	0
CHICAGO ROCKETS																																						
Bob Hoernschemeyer	TB-DB	20	5'11"	192		1	111	375	3.4	0	193	95	49	1266	6.6	14	14–7	6	1	11	11	0	11	44.0							6	91	15	0	9	275	31	0
Walt Williams	TB-DB	27	6'1"	195	12	2	21	19	0.9	1	30	13	48	226	7.5	1	5–17		1	3	3	0	24	41.6							1	6	6	0	1	18	18	0
Steve Nemeth	TB-DB	24	5'10"	175	59		4	10	2.5	0	23	5	22	68	3.0	0	0–0						2	46.0	32	33	97	9	12	75	1	14	14	0				
Bill Schroeder	TB-DB	23	6'	190		1	12	42	3.5	0	2	1	50	10	5.0	0	0–0		1	9	9	0									0	7	–	0	1	19	19	0
Norm Cox	TB	20	6'2"	210			1	12	12.0	0																												
Walt Clay	HB-TB-DB	22	5'11"	195	6	6	65	283	4.4	1	27	12	44	140	5.2	2	3–11		4	48	12	0	1	45.0							8	70	9	0	2	43	22	0
Crazy Legs Hirsch	HB-DB	22	6'2"	190	36	6	87	226	2.6	1	20	12	60	156	7.8	1	2–10		27	347	13	3			0	1	0				17	235	14	1	14	384	27	1
Bill Kellagher	FB-LB	26	5'11"	205	18		49	178	3.6	3	3	2	67	15	5.0	0	1–33		2	36	18	0	1	56.0											3	48	16	0
Billy Hillenbrand	HB-DB	24	6'	188	48	3	50	175	3.5	2	3	0	0	0	0.0	0	2–67		21	315	15	4									13	180	14	1	8	220	28	1
Ernie Lewis	FB-LB	22	6'1"	215	6	1	57	164	2.9	1	8	4	50	17	2.1	0	1–12		2	26	13	0	50	41.7											2	22	11	0
Ned Mathews (to SF)	HB-DB	28	5'10"	192	18	2	30	109	3.6	1	1	1	100	26	26.0	0	0–0		6	100	17	2													6	118	20	0
Pete Lamana	FB-LB	25	5'11"	210	6	1	6	21	3.5	0																					0	20	–	1	1	18	18	0
Don Griffin	HB-DB	23	5'11"	195		1	28	13	0.5	0	1	0	0	0	0.0	0	1–100		5	28	6	0													2	31	16	0
Bill Boedecker	HB-DB	22	5'11"	190	6	1	6	8	1.3	0									5	82	16	1									2	29	15	0	2	84	42	0
Ralph Heywood	OE-DE	24	6'2"	195	24														20	287	14	4	2	28.5														
Tom Lahey	OE-DE	28	6'2"	218		1	1	–2	–2.0	0									17	203	12	0													1	5	5	0
Frank Quillen	OE-DE	24	6'5"	225	12	1													13	143	11	2													1	13	13	0
Bob Motl	OE-DE	26	6'3"	195	6														9	124	14	1																
Bob Dove	OE-DE	25	6'2"	220	6														7	67	10	1																
Max Morris	OE-DE	21	6'2'	200			1	20	20.0	0									3	66	22	0																

N.F.L. — December 15, at New York (Attendance 58, 436)

Hapes and Filchock, and Luckman's Run

On the morning of the game, news broke that Merle Hapes and Frankie Filchock, two New York backs, were under investigation in a bribe attempt. Hapes, who had declined a bribe to throw the game but had not reported the attempt, was suspended by Commissioner Bert Bell, but Filchock, who knew of the bribe offer only through Hapes, was allowed to play. With suspicion hanging over his head, Filchock played a hard fifty minutes, despite a broken nose, in the Giants' losing effort against the Bears. Chicago, with a host of stars back from military service, scored two touchdowns in the first quarter, the first after recovering a fumble and the second on an interception return. Filchock cut the Bear lead down with a 38-yard touchdown pass to Frank Liebel late in the quarter. At the start of the second half, the Giants recovered a Chicago fumble deep in Bear territory, and a short pass from Filchock to Steve Filipowicz plus the extra point knotted the score at 14 all. The tie held until early in the fourth quarter, when, aided by a 16-yard punt by Howie Livingston of New York, the Bears drove to a first down on the Giant 19. Sid Luckman, who never ran with the ball, then shocked the Giants by running for the touchdown to put the game out of reach. For Filchock, it was all bad news, as he was also suspended soon after the game for his failure to report what Hapes had told him.

SCORING

NEW YORK	7	0	7	0	–14
CHIC. BEARS	14	0	0	10	–24

First Quarter

Chi.	Kavanaugh, 21 yard pass from Luckman PAT – Maznicki (kick)	4:36
Chi.	Magnani, 19 yard interception return PAT – Maznicki (kick)	8:52
N.Y.	Liebel, 38 yard pass from Filchock PAT – Strong (kick)	13:26

Third Quarter

N.Y.	Filipowicz, 5 yard pass from Filchock PAT – Strong (kick)	3:44

Fourth Quarter

Chi.	Luckman, 19 yard rush PAT – Maznicki (kick)	2:45
Chi.	Maznicki, 26 yard Field Goal	9:44

TEAM STATISTICS

N.Y.		CHI.
13	First Downs	10
120	Rushing Yardage	101
26	Pass Attempts	23
9	Pass Completions	9
34.6	Completion Percentage	39.1
128	Passing Yardage	144
4.9	Average Yards per Attempt	6.3
14.2	Average Yards per Comp.	16.0
6	Passes had Intercepted	2
4	Punts	7
31.7	Average Punt Distance	42.3
9	Punt Return Yards	13
3	Fumbles	2
2	Lost Ball	1
6	Penalties	9
70	Yards Penalized	112

A.A.F.C. — December 22, at Cleveland (Attendance 41,181)

Nearly Avoiding a Futile Finish

The Cleveland Browns had beaten the New York Yankees twice during the season, by scores of 24-7 and 7-0, and were clear favorites to sweep the first AAFC championship game. New York did not roll over dead for the Browns, however, and fought them closely all afternoon. The Yankees got up on the scoreboard in the first period after Eddie Prokop picked off an Otto Graham pass and returned it to the Cleveland 34-yard line. After an Ace Parker—Jack Russell pass and a Spec Sanders run netted two first downs, the New York drive stalled on the Cleveland four, and Harvey Johnson booted a 12-yard field goal to make the score 3-0. The Browns knew they were in for a rough afternoon when they had a first down on the Yankee six-yard line, and the New York defense held for four downs. The Browns again reached New York territory early in the second quarter, only to have Lou Groza's field-goal attempt fail. Late in the period, the Browns took possession after a punt on their own 30, and Graham passes to Dub Jones, Mac Speedie, and Dante Lavelli moved the ball quickly to the New York 12. Marion Motley carried the ball in from there on two running plays; Groza's conversion made the score 7-3. The Yankees took a 9-7 lead in the third period on Spec Sanders' two-yard run after an 80-yard drive, but the extra-point attempt was blocked. With defeat staring them in the face, the Browns drove 22 yards on eleven plays, most of them passes, with the score coming on a 16-yard Graham-to-Lavelli pass with under five minutes left in the game. New York's final drive ended when Graham picked off Parker's pass on the Cleveland 30-yard line, and the game ended 14-9 in favor of Cleveland.

SCORING

CLEVELAND	0	7	0	7	–14
NEW YORK	3	0	6	0	– 9

First Quarter

N.Y.	H. Johnson, 12 yard F.G.	5:31

Second Quarter

Cle.	Motley, 1 yard rush PAT – Groza (kick)	13:58

Third Quarter

N.Y.	Sanders, 2 yard rush PAT – H. Johnson (No Good)	9:28

Fourth Quarter

Cle.	Lavelli, 16 yard pass from Graham PAT – Groza (kick)	10:47

TEAM STATISTICS

CLE.		N.Y.
18	First Downs – Total	10
8	by Rushing	6
10	by Passing	4
0	by Penalty	0
3	Fumbles – Number	2
0	Lost Ball	1
5	Penalties – Number	4
25	Yards Penalized	20

INDIVIDUAL STATISTICS

CLEVELAND	No	Yds	Avg.	NEW YORK	No	Yds	Avg.
			RUSHING				
Motley	13	98	7.5	Sanders	14	55	3.9
Jones	10	16	1.6	Parker	9	5	0.6
Greenwood	5	14	2.8	Prokop	5	5	1.0
Colella	4	14	3.5	Wagner	1	0	0.0
Terrell	1	–4	–4.0		29	65	2.2
Lavelli	1	–7	–7.0				
Graham	3	–19	–6.3				
	37	112	3.0				
			RECEIVING				
Lavelli	6	87	14.5	Russell	5	58	11.6
Speedie	6	71	11.8	Schwartz	1	12	12.0
Jones	3	45	15.0	Masterson	1	7	7.0
Yonakor	1	8	8.0	Prokop	1	4	4.0
Greenwood	(Lat)	2	–		8	81	10.1
	16	213	13.3				
			PUNTING				
Colella	2		38.5	Parker	4		29.0
				Sanders	1		45.0
					5		32.2
			PUNT RETURNS				
Graham	5	20	4.0	Perina	1	5	5.0
			KICKOFF RETURNS				
Greenwood	2	25	12.5	Sanders	2	52	26.0
Jones	1	12	12.0	Morrow	1	25	25.0
	3	37	12.3		3	77	25.7
			INTERCEPTION RETURNS				
Graham	1	4	4.0	Prokop	1	16	16.0

PASSING

Cleveland	Att	Comp	Comp Pct.	Yds	Int	Yds/ Att.	Yds/ Comp
Graham	27	16	59.3	213	1	7.9	13.3
New York							
Parker	18	8	44.4	81	1	4.5	10.1
Sanders	2	0	0.0	0	0	–	–
	20	8	40.0	81	1	4.1	10.1

N.F.L. —December 28, at Chicago (Attendance 30,759)

Icing the Eagles

The Cardinals had beaten the Eagles 45-21 during the season and had a strategy designed to exploit Philadelphia's 4-4-3 defensive. Midway through the first quarter, on an icy field, the Cards double-teamed the Eagle defensive guard and sent Charlie Trippi roaring up the middle. Since there was no middle linebacker in the Philadelphia defense, Trippi went 44 yards for a touchdown. The Cards scored again in the second quarter on another quick opener through the Eagle defense, but just before the half Tommy Thompson's long pass to Pat McHugh made the score 14-7. With the Cardinal offense stalled, the Eagles hoped to climb back into the game, only to have Trippi return a punt 75 yards to make the score 21-7. Another Eagle touchdown brought them within seven points, but Elmer Angsman's second 70-yard touchdown dash nailed down the championship.

SCORING

CHIC. Cards	7	7	7	7	–28
PHILADELPHIA	0	7	7	7	–21

First Quarter
- Chi. Trippi, 44 yard rush 6:22
  - PAT — Harder (kick)

Second Quarter
- Chi. Angsman, 70 yard rush 6:54
  - PAT — Harder (kick)
- Phi. McHugh, 70 yard pass from Thompson 14:00
  - PAT — Patton (kick)

Third Quarter
- Chi. Trippi, 75 yard punt return 8:44
  - PAT — Harder (kick)
- Phi. Van Buren, 1 yard rush 13:10
  - PAT — Patton (kick)

Fourth Quarter
- Chi. Angsman, 70 yard rush 7:30
  - PAT — Harder (kick)
- Phi. Craft, 1 yard rush 10:30
  - PAT — Patton (kick)

TEAM STATISTICS

CHI.		PHIL.
11	First Downs—Total	22
7	First Downs—Rushing	10
2	First Downs—Passing	11
1	First Downs—Penalty	1
282	Rushing Yardage	60
14	Pass Attempts	44
3	Pass Completions	27
21.4	Completion Percentage	61.4
54	Passing Yardage	297
3.9	Average Yards per Attempt	6.8
18.0	Average Yards per Comp.	11.0
8	Punts	8
32	Average Distance	34.5
3	Interception Returns	2
45	Yards	11
15.0	Average Yards	5.5
4	Punt Returns	4
150	Yards	10
37.5	Average Yards	2.5
3	Kickoff Returns	5
70	Yards	63
23.3	Average Yards	12.6
2	Fumbles	2
1	Fumbles Lost	0
10	Penalties	7
97	Yards Penalized	55

A.A.F.C.— December 14, at New York (Attendance 60,103)

A Fumble, Roughness, and Cleveland Makes it Two

The rematch between the Browns and Yankees again was a defensive battle, although they had played two high-scoring games during the season. The Browns launched the first extended drive of the game late in the first quarter. Starting from their own 32-yard line, the Browns drove down to the New York one-yard line, with the key play in the drive a 51-yard end run by Marion Motley. Otto Graham snuck over for the touchdown, and Lou Groza added the extra point. The Yankees came right back with a drive of their own, as little Buddy Young and Spec Sanders led the New Yorkers down to the Cleveland five-yard line, where the attack petered out. Harvey Johnson salvaged three points with a 12-yard field goal, bringing the score to 7-3. Groza missed two three-point tries before halftime broke the action. Neither club could mount a consistent attack in the third quarter, but the Browns got a break when Tom Colella picked off a Sanders pass and returned it to the New York 41. Martion Motley then ran for 16 yards, Graham threw to Dub Jones for eleven more, and Lew Mayne hauled in another Graham pass for eight more yards. Two power plays with Jones carrying the ball gave Cleveland a first down on the 4-yard line. On the next play, Graham faked handoffs to Motley and Mayne and gave the ball to Jones, who made it to the end zone unmolested. The Yanks had two scoring threats left, marching to Cleveland's 19-yard line before losing the ball on a fumble and reaching the 29 late in the game, only to have an unnecessary-roughness penalty push them back out of scoring range.

SCORING

NEW YORK	0	3	0	0	– 3
CLEVELAND	7	0	7	0	–14

First Quarter
- Cle. Graham, 1 yard rush 13:00
  - PAT – Groza (kick)

Second Quarter
- N.Y. H.Johnson, 12 field goal 4:14

Third Quarter
- Cle. Jones, 4 yard rush 10:04
  - PAT – Saban (kick)

TEAM STATISTICS

N.Y.		CLE.
13	First Downs—Total*	17
8	by Rushing	12
5	by Passing	4
0	by Penalty	1
3	Fumbles—Number	2
2	Lost Ball	1
3	Penalties—Number	7
21	Yards Penalized	45
0	Field Goals Missed	2

*—Includes Touchdowns

INDIVIDUAL STATISTICS

RUSHING

NEW YORK	No	Yds	Avg.	CLEVELAND	No	Yds	Avg.
Young	16	69	4.3	Motley	13	109	8.4
Sanders	12	40	3.3	Jones	10	27	2.7
Prokop	5	14	2.8	Graham	4	21	5.3
	33	123	3.7	Lewis	1	9	9.0
				Colella	1	6	6.0
				Mayne	4	0	0.0
					33	172	5.2

RECEIVING

NEW YORK	No	Yds	Avg.	CLEVELAND	No	Yds	Avg.
Young	2	25	12.5	Speedie	4	25	6.3
Sweiger	2	12	6.0	Lavelli	3	37	12.3
Kurrasch	1	20	20.0	Jones	3	31	10.3
Davis	1	18	18.0	Colella	2	7	3.5
Russell	1	14	14.0	Mayne	1	8	8.0
	7	89	12.7	Lewis	1	4	4.0
					14	112	8.0

PUNTING

NEW YORK	No		Avg.	CLEVELAND	No		Avg.
Kennedy	6		36.0	Gillom	5		45.0

PUNT RETURNS

NEW YORK	No	Yds	Avg.	CLEVELAND	No	Yds	Avg.
Young	2	4	2.0	Lewis	3	25	8.3
Prokop	1	10	10.0	Motley	1	2	2.0
	3	14	4.7		4	27	6.8

KICKOFF RETURNS

NEW YORK	No	Yds	Avg.	CLEVELAND	No	Yds	Avg.
Young	2	51	25.5	Colella	1	16	16.0
Sanders	1	32	32.0	Allen	1	10	10.0
	3	83	27.7		2	26	13.0

INTERCEPTION RETURNS

NEW YORK	No	Yds	Avg.	CLEVELAND	No	Yds	Avg.
None				Colella	1	13	13.0

PASSING

NEW YORK	Att	Comp	Comp Pct.	Yds	Int	Yds/ Att.	Yds/ Comp.
Sanders	17	7	41.2	89	1	5.2	12.7
Prokop	1	0	0.0	0	0	–	–
	18	7	38.9	89	1	4.9	12.7
CLEVELAND							
Graham	21	14	66.7	112	0	5.3	8.0

PHILADELPHIA EAGLES 8-4-0 Greasy Neale

Scores of Each Game		
45	WASHINGTON	42
23	NEW YORK	0
7	Chic. Bears	40
24	Pittsburgh	35
14	LOS ANGELES	7
38	Washington	14
41	New York	24
32	BOSTON	0
14	Boston	21
21	PITTSBURGH	0
21	CHIC. CARDS	45
28	GREEN BAY	14
	EAST playoff	
21	Pittsburgh	0

Use Name	Pos.	Hgt	Wgt	Age	Int	Pts
Roger Harding	C-LB	6'2"	215	24		
Vic Lindskog	C-LB	6'1"	205	31	1	
Boyd Williams	C-LB	6'3"	218	25		
Alex Wojciechowicz	C-LB	5'11"	225	32	1	
Larry Cabrelli	DE	5'11"	195	30		
John Green	DE	6'1"	190	25		
Eddie Michaels – Canadian Football League						

Use Name – Tackles	Pos.	Hgt	Wgt	Age	Int	Pts
Alf Bauman (from CHI-AAFC)	T	6'2"	218	27		
T.G. Campion	T	6'2"	235	26		
Otis Douglas	T	6'1"	224	35		
Jim Kekeris	T	6'1"	275	23		2
(Missed 1 Field Goal Attempt, 2 PAT in 3 attempts)						
Jay MacDowell	T	6'2"	220	28		
Vic Sears	T	6'3"	230	29		
(1 punt return for 6 yds.)						
Don Talcott	T	6'2"	235	25		
Al Wistert	T	6'1"	215	26		

Use Name – Guards	Pos.	Hgt	Wgt	Age	Int	Pts
Al Baisi	G	6'	225	29		
Bucko Kilroy	G	6'2"	245	26		
Duke Maronic	G	5'9"	205	26		
Don Weedon	G	5'11"	220	26		
John Wyhonic	G	6'	210	27		

With Steve Van Buren running over defenders for a record 1,008 yards rushing and Tommy Thompson making his infrequent passes count for good yardage, the Philadelphia offense kept the Eagles flying high in the Eastern Division. Greasy Neale's T-formation attack jelled in fine fashion, with the addition of end Pete Pihos adding the finishing touch. A fullback in college, Pihos blocked like an avalanche, hugged every pass like a falling baby, and joined Jack Ferrante in the toughest end combination in the league. Enemy runners found it hard to move against a line of Pihos, Ferrante, Vic Sears, annual All-Pro Al Wistert, Vic Lindskog, and Bucko Kilroy, with linebackers Alex Wojciechowicz and Joe Muha around to erase any mistakes.

PITTSBURGH STEELERS 8-4-0 Jock Sutherland

Scores of Each Game		
17	DETROIT	10
7	LOS ANGELES	48
26	Washington	27
30	Boston	14
35	PHILADELPHIA	24
38	New York	21
18	Green Bay	17
21	WASHINGTON	14
24	NEW YORK	7
7	Chic. Bears	49
0	Philadelphia	21
17	BOSTON	7
	EAST playoff	
0	PHILADELPHIA	21

Use Name	Pos.	Hgt	Wgt	Age	Int	Pts
Chuck Cherundolo	C-LB	6'1"	215	31		
Bryant Meeks	C-LB	6'2"	190	21		
Frank Sinkovitz	C-LB	6'1"	217	24	3	6
Tony Bova	OE-DE	6'1"	190	30		2
(1 kickoff return for 16 yds.)						
Sam Gray	DE	6'	194	27		
Al Drulis	BB-LB	5'10"	188	26		

Use Name – Tackles	Pos.	Hgt	Wgt	Age	Int	Pts
Ralph Calacagri	T	6'3"	235	25		2
Bill Hornick	T	6'1"	207	28		
Joe Repko	T	6'	230	26		6
Paul Stenn	T	6'2"	240	29		
Jack Wiley	T	5'11"	206	26		
Frank Wydo	T	6'4"	208	23		

Use Name – Guards	Pos.	Hgt	Wgt	Age	Int	Pts
Bill Cregar	G-LB	5'11"	190	22		
John Mastrangelo	G	6'1"	215	21		6
Bill Moore	G	5'11"	215	24		
John Perko	G-LB	6'1"	207	31		
Nick Skorich	G-LB	5'9"	192	26		

When Bill Dudley made it definite that he was not returning, owner Art Rooney reluctantly traded him to Detroit. Although he considered Dudley "the best all-around ballplayer I've ever seen," Rooney still was confident that coach Jock Sutherland could mold the remaining players into a winning team. Stressing teamwork on a club with no superstars, Sutherland spurred the anonymous Steelers, led by tailback Johnny Clement and fullback Steve Lach into a first-place tie with the Eagles. The two clubs had split their meetings during the season, but the Steelers headed into the Eastern playoff with Clement shelved with injuries, and the Eagles held the nameless Steelers pointless via a 21-0 score.

BOSTON YANKS 4-7-1 Clipper Smith

Scores of Each Game		
7	NEW YORK	7
7	DETROIT	21
14	PITTSBURGH	30
14	New York	0
7	Chic. Cards	27
24	CHIC. BEARS	28
27	Los Angeles	16
0	Philadelphia	32
21	PHILADELPHIA	14
27	WASHINGTON	24
7	Pittsburgh	17
13	Washington	40

Use Name	Pos.	Hgt	Wgt	Age	Int	Pts
Joe Domnanovich	C-LB	6'1"	210	28	1	
Bill Godwin	C-LB	6'3"	236	28	2	
Joe Sabasteanski	C-LB	6'	205	26	1	
Sam Goldman	DE-OE	6'3"	224	30		
(1 reception for 9 yds.)						
Ed Fiorentino	DE	6'1"	210	25		
Bob Long	HB-DB	5'10"	190	25		

Use Name – Tackles	Pos.	Hgt	Wgt	Age	Int	Pts
Rocco Canale	T	5'11"	253	30		
Tom Dean	T	6'2"	247	23		
Tom Rodgers	T	6'	248	24		
Alex Sidorik	T	6'	255	25		
Carroll Vogelaar	T	6'3"	238	27		

Use Name – Guards	Pos.	Hgt	Wgt	Age	Int	Pts
John Badaczewski	G	6'1"	235	25		
Fritz Barzilauskas	G	6'1..	228	26		
Bill Collins	G	5'8"	195	25		
Bill Kennedy	G	5'11"	205	28		
Bob McClure	G	6'1"	224	23		
(1 kickoff return for 12 yds.)						
Jim Wright	G	6'1"	222	26		
Joe Zeno	G	5'10"	238	28		

The Yanks welcomed new coach Clipper Smith to Boston by winning a new high of four games, but few fans paid their way in to see the resurgence. Of the victories, a 14-0 shutout over New York and a 21-14 upset of the Philadelphia Eagles especially would have caused the fans to buzz if there had been any fans. The Yanks even boasted of a statistical leader, as Frank Seno tied for top honors in interceptions. The new coach revamped his offense, trading quarterback Paul Governali to the Giants for fullback Bill Paschal and installing second-year man Boley Dancewicz as signal-caller—all to no avail, either on the field or at the box office.

WASHINGTON REDSKINS 4-8-0 Turk Edwards

Scores of Each Game		
42	Philadelphia	45
27	PITTSBURGH	26
28	NEW YORK	20
10	Green Bay	27
20	CHIC. BEARS	56
14	PHILADELPHIA	38
14	Pittsburgh	21
21	Detroit	38
45	CHIC. CARDS	21
24	Boston	27
10	New York	35
40	BOSTON	13

Use Name	Pos.	Hgt	Wgt	Age	Int	Pts
Ki Aldrich	C-G-LB	6'	215	31	2	
Al DeMao	C-LB	6'2"	211	27	2	
Jack Sommers	C-LB	6'3"	232	28		
(Missed 1 field goal attempt)						
Harvey Jones	HB-DB	6'	175	26		
(1 kickoff return for 30 yds.)						

Use Name – Tackles	Pos.	Hgt	Wgt	Age	Int	Pts
John Adams	T	6'7"	254	25		
Don Avery	T	6'4"	258	26		
(2 kickoff returns for 24 yds.)						
Don Deeks (from BOS)	T	6'4"	232	24		
John Sanchez (from CHI-AAFC and DET)	T	6'3"	234	26	1	
Ernie Williamson	T	6'4"	235	24		
(1 kickoff return for 28 yds.)						

Use Name – Guards	Pos.	Hgt	Wgt	Age	Int	Pts
Fred Boensch	G-LB	6'4"	225	27	1	
Mike Garzoni	G	5'11"	213	23		
Bill Gray	G	5'11"	210	24		
Hank Harris	G	6'	260	24		
Leo Nobile	G-LB	5'10"	210	25		
John Steber	G	6'	220	24		

The tone of the season was set on opening day when the Skins lost a 45-42 shootout with the Eagles. Scoring points came easy for the Skins; it was stopping the other team that presented problems. At the helm of the attack was passer Sammy Baugh, improving with age in his eleventh pro season. Slingin' Sam was honored with a special day before a game against the strong Chicago Cardinals, and the Washington linemen pledged as their gift to keep the passer off the ground and safe from Cardinal pass-rushers. With the blockers coming through as promised, Baugh riddled the Cardinals for twenty-five completions in thirty-three attempts, good for 355 yards, six touchdown passes, and a 45-21 victory.

But even with top performances from Baugh, runner Jim Castiglia, and halfback Bob Nussbaumer, the Redskins could win only four games. They exploded for 40 or more points against the Eagles, Cardinals, and Boston Yanks, but tasted their own medicine against the Eagles and Bears. Sammy Baugh had hit his peak, but the Redskins in general were on a steady downhill slide.

NEW YORK GIANTS 2-8-2 Steve Owen

Scores of Each Game		
7	Boston	7
0	Philadelphia	33
20	Washington	28
0	BOSTON	14
21	PITTSBURGH	38
7	Detroit	35
21	PHILADELPHIA	41
7	Pittsburgh	24
24	GREEN BAY	24
35	CHIC. CARDS	31
35	WASHINGTON	10
10	Los Angeles	35

Use Name	Pos.	Hgt	Wgt	Age	Int	Pts
Lou DeFilippo	C-LB	6'1"	235	31		
Chet Gladchuk	C-DT	6'4"	255	30		
Lou Palazzi	C-LB	6'	200	26		
Bill Miklich	BB-LB	6'	208	26		
(1 reception for –5 yds.)						
Declared ineligible – Frankie Filchock, Merle Hapes						

Use Name – Tackles	Pos.	Hgt	Wgt	Age	Int	Pts
Frank Cope	T	6'2"	240	31		
Phil Ragazzo	T	6'	225	32		
Bill Schuler	T	6'	215	25		
Jim White	T	6'2"	228	26	1	6

Use Name – Guards	Pos.	Hgt	Wgt	Age	Int	Pts
Bob Dobelstein	G-LB	5'11"	212	25	1	6
Bill Hachten	G-LB	6'	210	22		
Kayo Lunday	G	6'3"	225	34		
George Tobin	G-LB	5'10"	205	26		
Leo Younce	G-LB	6'1"	210	30	3	4
(1 PAT in 1 att., 1 FG in 1 att., 1 punt for 43 yds.)						

With Frankie Filchock and Merle Hapes suspended by the league for not reporting a bribe offer to throw the 1946 championship game, the Giants headed into the season without a quarterback to run the attack. Not until Paul Governali was obtained from Boston in mid-season did the Giants come up with a major-league passer, but by then it was too late to salvage the season. New York lost seven games before it won a contest, dropping to the bottom of the East for keeps. Coach Steve Owen had expected the season to be a rebuilding year, with a slew of rookies on the roster, but he could not anticipate what fate had in store. The only bright notes were a 35-31 upset of the Cardinals and top-notch seasons by Len Younce and Frank Reagen.

TEAM TOTALS

OFFENSE	First Downs: Tot	by Rsh	by Pas	by Pen	Rushing: No.	Yds.	Avg Yds.	TD	Passing: Att	Com	Comp Pct.	Yds.	Avg. Yds. Att.	Avg. Yds. Comp	TD	Int	Pct. Int.
PHILA.	203	109	68	26	474	1971	4.2	21	223	116	52.0	1761	7.9	15.2	18	19	8.5
PITT.	176	108	57	11	496	1948	3.9	15	209	86	41.1	1410	6.8	16.4	10	19	9.1
BOSTON	117	49	52	16	343	973	2.8	5	238	95	39.9	1661	6.9	17.5	15	27	11.3
WASH.	242	76	140	26	384	1343	3.5	11	416	231	55.5	3336	8.0	14.4	28	18	4.3
N.Y.	149	56	71	22	366	1195	3.3	7	293	123	42.0	1999	6.8	16.4	17	26	8.9

OFFENSE	Punting: No.	Avg. Yds.	Punt Returns: No.	Yds.	Avg. Yds.	TD	Kickoff Returns: No.	Yds.	Avg. Yds.	TD	Interception Returns: No.	Yds.	Avg. Yds.	TD	Penalties: No.	Yds.	Fumbles: No.	Lost	Points: Tot	PAT	FG Att	FG	Saf.
PHILA.	63	42.4	54	716	13.3	2	44	854	19.4	1	23	287	12.5	0	92	848	37	14	308	38	20	4	0
PITT.	68	41.1	40	583	14.6	0	50	975	19.5	0	18	397	22.1	4	60	527	28	16	240	30	14	6	3
BOSTON	93	40.6	25	378	15.1	1	52	1130	21.7	0	28	336	12.0	0	93	855	21	8	168	21	4	3	0
WASH.	52	40.3	36	445	12.4	0	66	1456	22.1	2	21	172	8.2	0	102	860	34	21	295	37	7	4	0
N.Y.	77	42.3	44	371	8.4	0	48	905	18.9	0	27	435	16.1	0	98	945	30	16	190	25	6	3	0

Use Name – Backs & Ends	Pos.	Age	Hgt	Wgt	Pts	Int	Rushing No.	Rushing Yds	Rushing Avg	Rushing TD	Passing Att	Passing Comp	Passing %	Passing Yds	Passing Yd/Att	Passing TD	Passing Int–%	Passing RK	Receiving No.	Receiving Yds	Receiving Avg	Receiving TD	Punting No.	Punting Avg	Kicking Pat	Kicking Att	Kicking %	Kicking FG	Kicking Att	Kicking %	Punt Returns No.	Punt Returns Yds	Punt Returns Avg	Punt Returns TD	Kickoff Returns No.	Kickoff Returns Yds	Kickoff Returns Avg	Kickoff Returns TD
PHILADELPHIA EAGLES																																						
Tommy Thompson	QB	31	6'1"	195	12		23	52	2.4	2	201	106	53	1680	8.4	16	15–7	3																				
Bill Mackrides	QB	22	5'11"	187	6		7	–15	–2.1	0	17	8	47	58	3.4	2	3–8																					
Allie Sherman	QB	24	5'11"	173	6		17	17	1.0	1	5	2	40	23	4.6	0	1–20																					
Steve Van Buren	HB-DB	26	6'	205	84	1	217	1008	4.5	13									9	79	9	0													13	282	29	1
Bosh Pritchard	HB-DB	28	5'11"	160	24	1	69	294	4.3	1									16	315	20	3	2	32.0							24	271	11	0	8	148	19	0
Pat McHugh	HB-DB	27	5'11"	165	12	3	22	171	7.8	1									2	16	8	0									10	156	16	1	3	50	17	0
Ernie Steele	HB-DB	29	6'	182	6	6	26	138	5.3	1									4	62	16	0									11	183	17	0	2	17	9	0
Joe Muha	FB-LB	26	6'1"	205	15		27	107	4.0	2									1	10	10	0	53	43.5				1	5	20					3	55	18	0
Art Macioszczyk	FB-LB	26	5'9"	215			30	104	3.5	0									3	20	7	0													2	36	18	0
Gil Steinke	HB-DB	27	6'	172	6	1	16	50	3.1	0									4	90	23	1									6	69	12	0				
Noble Doss	HB-DB	27	6'	180		2	11	45	4.1	0									2	17	9	0																
Jack Hinkle	HB-DB	29	6'	185			1	2	2.0	0																												
Russ Craft	HB-DB	27	5'9"	175	6	1	5	–1	–0.2	0									2	66	33	1									1	5	5	0				
Ben Kish	FB-LB	30	6'	212		1	3	–1	–0.3	0									1	12	12	0	8	37.6											1	10	10	0
Pete Pihos	OE-DE	23	6'1"	210	48														23	382	17	7									1	26	26	1	1	17	17	0
Jack Ferrante	OE-DE	31	6'1"	200	24														18	341	19	4													7	99	14	0
Neill Armstrong	OE-DB	21	6'2"	188	12														17	197	12	2													3	38	13	0
Dick Humbert	OE-DB	28	6'1"	175		2													13	139	11	0																
Hal Prescott	OE-DB	26	6'2"	200		3													1	15	15	0																
Cliff Patton	G	23	6'2"	255	45																				36	40	90	3	14	21								
PITTSBURGH STEELERS																																						
Johnny Clement	TB	27	6'	188	24		129	670	5.2	4	123	52	42	1004	8.2	7	9–7	8	1	6	6	0													1	24	24	0
Walt Slater	TB-DB	27	5'11"	187		4	46	167	3.6	0	39	18	46	215	5.5	1	5–13														28	435	16	0	22	480	22	0
Gonzales Morales	TB-DB	24	6'	190		1	29	96	3.3	0	27	8	30	78	2.9	1	4–15														6	88	15	0	5	113	23	0
Gene Hubka	TB-DB	23	5'10"	175			2	4	2.0	0																												
Steve Lach	FB	27	6'2"	215	54		120	372	3.1	8	5	2	40	12	2.4	1	0–0		11	77	7	1													3	59	20	0
Bob Cifers	HB-DB	26	5'11"	198		1	87	356	4.1	0	3	2	67	28	9.3	0	0–0		3	58	19	0	68	41.1											2	30	15	0
Tony Compagno	FB-DB	26	5'11"	197	30	4	34	126	3.7	2									9	190	21	1													2	32	16	0
Paul White	HB-DB	25	6'1"	183		2	22	85	3.9	0	3	1	33	21	7.0	0	0–0		2	55	28	0									5	50	10	0	3	50	17	0
Bob Sullivan	HB-TB-DB	22	5'9"	187	12		21	61	2.9	1	9	3	33	52	5.8	0	1–11		4	72	18	1									1	10	10	0	4	86	22	0
Paul Davis	FB-DB	22	6'1"	185			4	5	1.3	0																												
Joe Glamp	HB-DB	24	5'11"	185	48		1	2	2.0	0															30	31	97	6	14	43								
Bill Garnaas	WB	26	5'11"	183	12														5	144	29	2													1	17	17	0
Charlie Seabright	BB-LB	29	6'2"	201	6	3	1	4	4.0	0									7	16	2	0													3	23	8	0
Val Jansante	OE-DE	26	6'1"	190	32														35	599	17	5													2	42	21	0
Bob Davis	OE-DE	26	5'11"	190															5	145	29	0													1	3	3	0
Charlie Mehelich	OE-DE	25	6'1"	195															3	38	13	0																
Elbie Nickel	OE-DE	24	6'1"	188															1	10	10	0																
BOSTON YANKS																																						
Boley Dancewicz	QB	22	5'10"	190	6		47	145	3.1	1	169	66	39	1203	7.1	11	18–11	11					1	40.0														
Howie Maley	QB-HB	25	5'11"	185			32	132	4.1	0	12	6	50	144	12.0	1	1–8						92	40.6											1	23	23	0
Bill Paschal (from NY)	FB-LB	26	6'	205	6		78	263	3.4	1	1	0	0	0	0.0	0	0–0		4	70	18	0									1	11	11	0	5	103	21	0
Frank Seno	HB-DB	26	6'	195	12	10	69	212	3.1	0									12	118	10	1									12	213	18	1	27	636	24	0
Frank Maznicki	HB-DB	27	5'9"	180	37	4	34	77	2.3	0	1	0	0	0	0.0	0	1–100		6	76	13	0			19	21	90	2	2	100	2	48	24	0				
Joe Golding	HB-DB	26	6'	180	18	5	26	71	2.7	1									6	52	9	2									7	63	9	0	9	173	19	0
Jim Mello	FB-LB	26	5'10"	190		1	33	62	1.9	0									2	26	13	0																
John Griggs	FB-LB	27	6'	205			27	52	1.9	0									1	1	1	0													1	19	19	0
Rudy Romboli	FB-LB	24	5'10"	215		1	23	50	2.2	0									4	30	8	0													3	64	21	0
John Poto	HB-DB	21	5'10"	197	6		6	27	4.5	1																					1	12	12	0	4	99	25	0
Mike Micka	HB-DB	26	6'	193		2	1	–4	–4.0	0									2	11	6	0																
Walt Williams	HB-DB	28	6'1"	192							1	0	0	0	0.0	0	1–100		1	2	2	0									1	14	14	0				
Hal Crisler	OE-DE	23	6'4"	215	12														25	363	15	2																
Don Currivan	OE-DB	26	6'	192	60	1													24	782	33	9																
Bill Chipley	OE-DB	27	6'3"	200	6		1	3	3.0	0									5	105	21	1																
Nick Scollard	OE-DE	27	6'4"	218	5														2	18	9	0			2	2	100	1	4	25								
WASHINGTON REDSKINS																																						
Sammy Baugh	QB	33	6'2"	182	12		25	47	1.9	2	354	210	59	2938	8.3	25	15–4	1					35	43.7														
Jim Youel	QB	25	6'	174	6		10	44	4.4	1	62	21	34	398	6.4	3	3–5						2	17.5														
Jim Castiglia (from BAL-AAFC)	FB	28	5'11"	210	30		104	426	4.2	5									11	88	8	0													1	10	10	0
Sal Rosato	FB-LB	29	6'1"	236	6		74	297	4.0	0									7	107	15	1													2	36	18	0
Eddie Saenz	HB-DB	24	5'11"	168	36		51	143	2.8	0									34	598	18	4									24	308	13	0	29	797	27	2
Bob Nussbaumer	HB-DB	23	5'11"	170	24	1	43	136	3.2	0									47	597	13	4									2	15	8	0	8	154	19	0
Dick Poillon	HB-DB	27	6'	197	85	2	28	104	3.7	2									20	250	13	4	15	35.5	37	41	90	4	6	67	3	37	12	0	4	23	6	0
Jack Jenkins	FB-LB	27	6'1"	202		1	16	54	3.4	0									5	96	19	0																
Dick Todd	HB-DB	32	5'11"	173		4	10	45	4.5	0									4	84	21	0									4	48	12	0	19	189	21	0
Tom Farmer	HB-DB	26	5'11"	183	6	6	15	29	1.9	1									8	137	17	0													4	118	30	0
Tommy Mont	HB-DB	25	6'	192		1	1	7	7.0	0									2	14	7	0									3	37	12	0				
Ralph Ruthstrom	FB-LB	26	6'5"	215			2	5	2.5	0																									1	5	5	0
George Wilde	HB-DB	24	6'1"	193	6		4	–1	–0.2	0									6	45	8	1													1	19	19	0
Vince Pacewic	HB-DB	25	6'1"	205															5	42	8	0																
Hugh Taylor	OE	24	6'4"	197	36		1	7	7.0	0									26	511	20	6																
Paul McKee	OE-DE	24	6'3"	214	12														16	242	15	2																
Joe Duckworth	OE-DE	26	6'2"	220	18														14	250	18	3																
Joe Tereshinski	OE-DE	23	6'2"	205	6														10	76	8	1																
Doug Turley	OE-DE	28	6'2"	215	6														6	95	16	1													1	10	10	0
John Lookabaugh	OE-DE	27	6'4"	220	6														6	78	13	1																
Jim Peebles	OE-DE	27	6'4"	232															4	26	7	0						0	1	0					1	13	13	0
NEW YORK GIANTS																																						
Paul Governali (from BOS)	QB	26	5'11"	194	12		40	151	3.8	2	252	108	43	1775	7.0	17	22–9	7					4	35.5														
Jerry Niles	QB	27	6'1"	195			8	24	3.0	0	57	19	33	269	4.7	1	7–12																		1	12	12	0
Frank Reagan	QB-DB	28	5'11"	180		10	14	22	1.6	0	25	12	48	191	7.6	1	2–8						61	42.8							27	182	17	0	2	35	18	0
Art Faircloth	QB-DB	27	6'	190			10	9	0.9	0	5	3	60	30	6.0	1	0–0						4	39.7											2	62	31	0
Choo-Choo Roberts	FB	23	5'11"	188	6		86	296	3.5	1									4	58	15	0													8	141	18	0
Jim Blumenstock	FB-DB	28	5'11"	190	12		54	168	3.1	2	8	4	50	48	6.0	0	1–13		4	15	4	0									1	8	8	0	2	77	39	0
Gordon Paschka	FB-LB	27	6'	220	12		48	143	3.0	2									1	–6	–6	0													1	20	20	0
George Cheverko	WB-DB	26	6'1"	195	18	3	19	63	3.3	0									17	300	18	3									5	88	18	0	7	135	19	0
Howie Livingston	WB-DB	25	6'1"	190	18	4	19	87	4.6	0									12	273	23	3													9	203	23	0
George Franck	WB-DB	28	6'	180	18	1	24	93	3.9	0									10	265	27	3	7	42.4							6	60	10	0	7	121	17	0
Dave Brown	WB-DB	28	5'11"	190			6	5	0.8	0									1	5	5	0									4	22	6	0	1	30	30	0
Joe Sulaitis	BB-LB-DE	26	6'2"	210		1													7	53	8	0													2	23	12	0
John Cannady	BB-LB	23	6'2"	220		1	1	14	14.0	0									1	3	3	0																
Duke Iverson	BB-LB	27	6'2"	200															1	11	11	0													1	16	16	0
Ray Poole	OE-DE	25	6'2"	215	24	1													24	395	17	4																
Frank Liebel	OE-DE	27	6'1"	220	6														16	258	16	1													1	12	12	0
Tex Coulter	OE-T	22	6'4"	262	6														8	107	13	1													2	16	8	0
Vic Carroll	OE-T	34	6'4"	240	12	1													7	123	18	2																
Jack Mead	OE-DE	25	6'3"	210															6	91	15	0																
Jim Lee Howell	OE-DE	32	6'6"	220															3	41	14	0																
Greg Browning	OE	25	6'	190															1	12	12	0																
Ken Strong	K	41	6'	210	30																				24	25	96	2	5	40								

TEAM TOTALS

DEFENSE	First Downs: Tot	by Rsh	by Pas	by Pen	Rushing: No.	Yds.	Avg. Yds.	TD	Passing: Att.	Com	Comp. Pct.	Yds.	Avg. Yds. Att.	Avg. Yds. Comp	TD	Int.	Pct. Int.	Punting: No.	Avg. Yds.	Punt Returns: No.	Yds.	Avg. Yds.	TD	Kickoff Returns: No.	Yds.	Avg. Yds.	TD	Interception Returns: No.	Yds.	Avg. Yds.	TD	Penalties: No.	Yds.	Fumbles: No.	Lost	Points: Tot	PAT	FG Att	FG	Saf.	DEFENSE
PHILA.	188	76	86	27	380	1329	3.5	13	334	152	45.5	2410	7.2	16.0	19	23	6.9	70	38.4	32	350	10.9	0	49	889	20.2	1	19	236	12.4	2	110	1017	28	13	242	32	10	2	0	PHILA.
PITT.	170	88	68	14	403	1622	4.0	11	244	98	40.2	1847	7.6	18.8	20	18	7.4	70	42.5	30	330	11.0	0	43	892	20.7	0	19	287	15.1	0	78	622	34	14	259	34	7	5	0	PITT.
BOSTON	219	112	94	13	493	2020	4.1	18	303	158	52.1	2042	6.7	12.9	17	28	9.2	61	41.8	63	913	14.5	1	32	562	17.6	0	27	236	8.7	1	99	1030	34	17	256	29	11	3	1	BOSTON
WASH.	196	80	88	28	409	1564	3.8	18	282	146	51.8	2422	8.6	16.6	26	21	7.5	60	40.8	38	512	13.5	1	51	1130	22.2	1	18	428	23.8	3	87	745	24	8	367	47	17	8	1	WASH.
N.Y.	190	101	75	14	457	1836	4.0	18	276	121	43.8	2015	7.3	16.6	19	27	9.8	70	41.8	50	719	14.4	1	47	859	18.3	1	26	350	13.5	2	95	861	33	12	309	39	17	8	0	N.Y.

CHICAGO CARDINALS 9-3-0 Jimmy Conzelman

Scores of Each Game		
45	DETROIT	21
31	CHIC. BEARS	7
14	Green Bay	10
7	Los Angeles	27
27	BOSTON	7
17	LOS ANGELES	10
17	Detroit	7
21	GREEN BAY	20
21	Washington	45
31	New York	35
45	Philadelphia	21
30	Chic. Bears	21

Use Name	Pos.	Hgt	Wgt	Age	Int	Pts
Vince Banonis	C-LB	6'1"	230	25	3	6
Bill Blackburn	C-LB	6'6"	225	25	3	
(1 punt for 19 yds.)						
Bill Campbell	LB	6'	195	27		
Clarence Esser	DE-T	6'	190	23		
Pop Ivy	DE	6'3"	210	31		
(Missed 1 field goal attempt)						
Joe Parker	DE	6'	220	24		

Use Name – Tackles	Pos.	Hgt	Wgt	Age	Int	Pts
Chet Bulger	T	6'3"	238	29		
Joe Coomer	T	6'6"	287	28		
Caleb Martin	T	6'4"	245	24		
Stan Mauldin	T	6'2"	225	26	1	
Dick Plasman	T-DE	6'3"	238	33		
Walt Szot	T	6'1"	225	28		
Bob Zimny	T	6'1"	235	26		

Use Name – Guards	Pos.	Hgt	Wgt	Age	Int	Pts
Plato Andros	G	6'	235	26		
Ray Apolskis	G-LB	5'11"	210	28		
Lloyd Arms	G	6'1"	215	28		
Jake Colhover	G	6'1"	210	25		
(2 kickoff returns for 16 yds.)						
Ham Nichols	G-LB	5'11"	200	23	1	
Buster Ramsey	G-LB	6'1"	220	27	4	

Owner Charles Bidwill had slowly built up a championship team, but he never lived to see it. He died on April 19, just as the Cardinals were on the verge of climbing to the top of the NFL mountain. Another tragedy was the death of rookie Jeff Burkett in a plane crash on October 24. Just before his death, Bidwill signed rookie halfback Charley Trippi, the final member of the Dream Backfield with Paul Christman, Pat Harder, and Elmer Angsman. But even with a solid line, the Cardinals could not shake the Bears until beating them 30-21 in the season's finale.

CHICAGO BEARS 8-4-0 George Halas

Scores of Each Game		
20	Green Bay	29
7	Chic. Cards	31
40	PHILADELPHIA	7
33	DETROIT	24
56	Washington	20
28	Boston	24
20	GREEN BAY	17
41	Los Angeles	31
49	PITTSBURGH	7
34	Detroit	14
14	LOS ANGELES	17
21	CHIC. CARDS	30

Use Name	Pos.	Hgt	Wgt	Age	Int	Pts
Stu Clarkson	C-LB	6'2"	215	28	2	
Thurman Garrett	C-G	6'3"	275	23	1	
(Missed 1 field goal attempt)						
Bulldog Turner	C-LB	6'1"	235	28	2	6
Allen Smith	DE	6'2"	215	24		
(2 kickoff returns for 18 yds.)						
Russ Reader	DB	6'	185	28		

Use Name – Tackles	Pos.	Hgt	Wgt	Age	Int	Pts
Fred Davis	T	6'3"	245	29		
Ed Ecker	T	6'7"	290	24		
Fred Hartman	T	6'1"	235	27	1	6
Ed Kolman	T	6'2"	235	29		
Walt Stickel	T	6'3"	250	25		

Use Name – Guards	Pos.	Hgt	Wgt	Age	Int	Pts
Ray Bray	G	6'	240	30		
Chuck Drulis	G-LB	5'10"	215	29	1	
Bill Johnson	G-LB	6'	210	26		
Bill Milner	G-LB	6'1"	212	23	1	
Pat Preston	G-LB	6'2"	215	24		

The Bears got off to a sluggish start with a 29-20 loss to Green Bay, then hit rock bottom with a 31-7 humiliation at the hands of the rising Cardinals. Staring prospects for a dismal season straight in the face, George Halas rallied his defending champs and drove them back into the Western Division race. Going into the final game with the Cardinals, both Chicago clubs were tied for the division lead. On the first play after the opening kickoff, Cardinal quarterback Paul Christman launched an 80-yard touchdown pass to speedy halfback Babe Dimancheff, and the Bears spent the rest of the afternoon trying to catch up. They never did.

Even with the final disappointment, the Bears boasted of several outstanding individual performances. Sid Luckman, Ken Kavanaugh, and Fred Davis all won All-Pro honors, while second-year end Jim Keane led the league in receiving. Center Bulldog Turner won applause for his 96-yard return of an interception in which he dodged and weaved more like a 180-pound halfback than a 235-pound center.

GREEN BAY PACKERS 6-5-1 Curly Lambeau

Scores of Each Game		
29	CHIC. BEARS	20
17	LOS ANGELES	14
10	CHIC. CARDS	14
27	WASHINGTON	10
34	DETROIT	17
17	PITTSBURGH	18
17	Chic. Bears	20
20	Chic. Cards	21
24	New York	24
30	Los Angeles	10
35	Detroit	14
14	Philadelphia	28

Use Name	Pos.	Hgt	Wgt	Age	Int	Pts
Charley Brock	C-LB	6'2"	210	31	2	
Bob Flowers	C-LB	6'1"	210	30	1	
Les Gatewood	C-LB	6'2"	200	26		
John Kovatch	DE	6'3"	200	27		
Bob Skoglund	DE	6'1"	198	22		
Don Wells	DE	6'2"	200	25		
Bob McDougal	FB-LB	6'2"	205	26		

Use Name – Tackles	Pos.	Hgt	Wgt	Age	Int	Pts
Tiny Croft	T	6'3"	280	26		
Paul Lipscomb	T	6'5"	245	24		
Urban Odson	T	6'3"	250	28		
Baby Ray	T	6'6"	250	32		

Use Name – Guards	Pos.	Hgt	Wgt	Age	Int	Pts
Ed Bell	G	6'1"	233	25		
Ray Clemons	G	5'10"	220	26		
Ralph Davis	G	5'11"	205	25		
Aldo Forte	G	6'	215	29		
Ed Neal	G-T	6'4"	290	29		6
Damon Tassos	G	6'1"	225	23		
Dick Wildung	G	6'	220	25		2

Curly Lambeau installed the T formation at Green Bay and developed a respectable passing attack; but quarterback Jack Jacobs was no Cecil Isbell, and ends Nolan Luhn and Clyde Goodnight were no Don Hutsons. What Lambeau did have was a short-passing offense which moved the ball sporadically but couldn't break games open like the old Packer air combinations. Tony Canadeo and Walt Schlinkman kept the running game healthy, moving behind a line which stayed strong despite the retirement of Bill Lee and Russ Letlow. The Packers were a solid if unspectacular team, with only a cruel streak of bad luck killing their title hopes, as they lost 18-17 to Pittsburgh, 20-17 to the Bears, and 21-20 to the Cardinals.

LOS ANGELES RAMS Bob Snyder 6-6-0

Scores of Each Game		
48	Pittsburgh	7
14	Green Bay	17
27	Detroit	13
27	CHIC. CARDS	7
7	Philadelphia	14
10	Chic. Cards	17
16	BOSTON	27
21	CHIC. BEARS	41
28	DETROIT	17
10	GREEN BAY	30
17	Chic. Bears	14
34	NEW YORK	10

Use Name	Pos.	Hgt	Wgt	Age	Int	Pts
Jack Martin	C-LB	6'3"	235	25	1	
Fred Naumetz	C-LB	6'1"	223	25	1	
Woody Strode – Canadian Football League						

Use Name – Tackles	Pos.	Hgt	Wgt	Age	Int	Pts
Gil Bouley	T	6'2"	238	26		6
(1 reception for 15 yds., 1 punt return for 24 yds.)						
Ed Champagne	T	6'3"	225	25		
Dick Huffman	T	6'2"	250	24		6
Clyde Johnson	T	6'6"	273	30		
Elbie Schultz	T	6'4"	274	29		
Bill Smyth	T-OE	6'3"	245	25		
(3 receptions for 26 yds.)						

Use Name – Guards	Pos.	Hgt	Wgt	Age	Int	Pts
Bob David	G-LB	6'	222	25		
Hal Dean	G-LB	6'	205	24		
Roger Eason	G	6'2"	230	29		
Jack Finlay	G-LB	6'1"	216	26		
Mike Lazetich	G-LB	6'1"	212	26		
Riley Matheson	G-LB	6'2"	210	32	1	

After the season ended, Rams fans could talk about Kenny Washington's 92-yard run against the Cardinals on November 2. Or else they could remember Bob Waterfield's 86-yard punt in the October 5 game with Green Bay. Unfortunately, the Rams lost both games, and the fans preferred not to discuss the team's mediocre season record.

The Rams fluctuated from one extreme to another like an excited Geiger counter. They impressed all observers with a 48-7 victory over Pittsburgh, a 27-7 upset of the title-bound Cardinals, and a 17-14 late-season triumph over the Bears. But mixed in with these gems were a 27-16 loss to the anemic Boston Yanks, a 41-21 trouncing at the hands of the Bears, and a 30-10 defeat by the Packers.

New head coach Bob Snyder directed an explosive squad which just as often laid a dud as detonated. Bob Waterfield kept winging the ball to steady Jim Benton, Kenny Washington developed into a dangerous runner, Tommy Harmon starred as a defensive back, 250-pound tackle Dick Huffman ate enemy ball carriers alive, and the rest of the squad listed lots of top-drawer players. Still, the Rams stumbled, bumbled, and butted no one in the end.

DETROIT LIONS Gus Dorais 3-9-0

Scores of Each Game		
10	Pittsburgh	17
21	Chic. Cards	45
21	Boston	7
13	LOS ANGELES	27
24	Chic. Bears	33
17	Green Bay	34
35	NEW YORK	7
7	CHIC. CARDS	17
38	WASHINGTON	21
17	Los Angeles	28
14	CHIC. BEARS	34
14	GREEN BAY	35

Use Name	Pos.	Hgt	Wgt	Age	Int	Pts
Reed Nilson	C-LB	6'	230	26		
Merv Pregulman	C-LB	6'3"	215	25	2	
(1 punt return for 9 yds.)						
Dick Stovall	C-LB	6'	208	23	1	
Frank Szymanski	C-LB	6'	225	24		

Use Name – Tackles	Pos.	Hgt	Wgt	Age	Int	Pts
Jack Dugger	T	6'3"	240	24	1	
Leon Fichman	T	6'1"	215	26		
George Hekkers (from BAL-AAFC)	T	6'4"	225	24		
Mitch Olenski	T	6'3"	225	27		
Ed Stacco	T	6'2"	250	22		
Russ Thomas	T	6'3"	235	23		

Use Name – Guards	Pos.	Hgt	Wgt	Age	Int	Pts
Stan Batinski	G	5'10"	215	30		
Ben Chase	G	6'3"	235	24		
Chuck DeShane	G	6'1"	218	28		
Bob Ivory	G	6'2"	212	23		
Elmer Jones	G	6'	225	27		
Les Lear	G	5'11"	227	29		
Floyd Rhea	G	6'	220	26		
Walt Vezmer	G	5'11"	235	22		
Bill Ward (from WAS)	G	6'	230	26		

When Steeler tailback Bill Dudley announced his retirement, the Lions traded two players and a first draft choice to Pittsburgh for rights to talk to the star player. During the spring, Lion coach Gus Dorais visited Dudley at the University of Virginia, where he was coaching, and offered him a three-year contract at $20,000 per year. Dudley could not turn down a pact which made him the highest paid pro player. The other Lion players at first were apprehensive, hearing rumors that the back was arrogant and pushy. But from the first day of training, Dudley kept his mouth shut and put out 100 percent effort, and the Lion players elected him team captain as a sign of their respect. Unfortunately, this did not help the defense. In six games against the Cardinals, Bears, and Packers, the Lions allowed an average of 33 points per game.

TEAM TOTALS

OFFENSE	FIRST DOWNS: Tot	by Rsh	by Pas	by Pen	RUSHING: No.	Yds.	Avg Yds.	TD	PASSING: Att	Com	Comp Pct.	Yds.	Avg. Yds. Att.	Avg. Yds. Comp	TD	Int	Pct. Int.
CHIC. C.	241	101	110	30	468	1735	3.7	20	340	160	47.1	2580	7.6	16.1	18	25	7.4
CHIC. B.	283	122	123	18	448	1959	4.4	21	378	194	51.3	3093	8.2	15.9	29	35	9.3
G.B.	206	105	82	19	510	2149	4.2	14	253	112	44.3	1724	6.8	15.4	17	19	7.5
L.A.	206	112	82	12	459	2171	4.7	15	283	123	42.0	1660	5.7	13.5	13	28	9.6
DET.	189	77	93	19	333	1234	3.7	6	348	167	48.0	2446	7.1	14.7	23	34	9.8

OFFENSE	PUNTING: No.	Avg. Yds.	PUNT RETURNS: No.	Yds.	Avg. Yds.	TD	KICKOFF RETURNS: No.	Yds.	Avg. Yds.	TD	INTERCEPTION RETURNS: No.	Yds.	Avg. Yds.	TD	PENALTIES: No.	Yds.	FUMBLES: No.	Lost	POINTS: Tot	PAT	FG Att	FG	Saf.	OFFENSE
CHIC. C.	56	40.8	27	370	13.7	0	43	716	16.7	0	27	438	16.2	2	89	688	32	16	306	39	10	7	0	CHIC. C.
CHIC. B.	38	41.5	39	495	12.7	0	41	871	21.2	0	27	481	18.2	3	107	1020	34	23	363	45	1	0	0	CHIC. B
G.B.	65	43.6	45	563	12.5	0	42	874	20.8	0	30	428	14.3	1	104	1019	24	13	274	33	29	13	2	G.B.
L.A.	72	40.1	44	640	14.5	2	36	727	20.2	0	24	288	12.0	1	87	800	33	20	259	31	17	8	0	L.A.
DET.	65	43.0	34	452	13.3	1	50	926	18.5	0	25	226	9.0	1	78	704	30	18	231	30	11	5	0	DET.

Use Name – Backs & Ends	Pos.	Age	Hgt	Wgt	Pts	Int	Rushing No.	Rushing Yds	Rushing Avg	Rushing TD	Passing Att	Passing Comp	Passing %	Passing Yds	Passing Yd/Att	Passing TD	Passing Int–%	Passing RK	Receiving No.	Receiving Yds	Receiving Avg	Receiving TD	Punting No.	Punting Avg	Kicking Pat	Kicking Att	Kicking %	Kicking FG	Kicking Att	Kicking %	Punt Returns No.	Punt Returns Yds	Punt Returns Avg	Punt Returns TD	Kickoff Returns No.	Kickoff Returns Yds	Kickoff Returns Avg	Kickoff Returns TD
CHICAGO CARDINALS																																						
Paul Christman	QB	29	6'	208	12		8	11	1.4	2	301	138	46	2191	7.3	17	22– 7	4																				
Ray Mallouf	QB	29	5'11"	180			5	13	2.6	0	36	21	58	340	9.4	1	2– 6						43	39.9														
Elmer Angsman	HB	21	5'11"	205	48		110	412	3.7	7									5	138	28	1													2	17	9	0
Charlie Trippi	HB-DB	24	6'	190	18	1	83	401	4.8	2	2	1	50	49	24.5	0	1– 50		23	240	10	0									8	141	18	0	15	321	21	0
Pat Harder	FB-LB	25	5'11"	205	102		113	371	3.3	7									9	78	9	0			39	40	98	7	10	70								
Marshall Goldberg	HB-FB-DB	29	5'11"	190			51	155	3.0	0									7	52	7	0									1	21	21	0				
Bill deCorrevont	HB-DB	28	6'	190	6	1	29	149	5.1	1									4	52	13	0									8	61	8	0	7	102	15	0
Babe Dimancheff	HB	25	5'11"	175	24		30	116	3.9	0									22	438	20	4													10	180	18	0
Red Cochran	FB-DB	25	6'	200	12	8	14	36	2.6	1	1	0	0	0	0.0	0	0– 0		1	7	7	1	1	25.0							10	147	15	0	4	46	12	0
Vic Schwall	HB	23	5'8"	190			12	33	2.8	0																									1	20	20	0
Charlie Smith	HB-DB	24	5'11"	170		1	9	23	2.6	0									1	–6	–6	0													1	14	14	0
Walt Rankin	FB-LB	29	5'11"	202			3	4	1.3	0																												
Mal Kutner	OE-DB	26	6'2"	195	48	3													43	944	22	7																
Bill Dewell	OE-DE	30	6'4"	210	24														42	576	14	4																
Jeff Burkett – died Oct. 24	OE-DB	26	6'1"	190	6	1	1	11	11.0	0									2	44	22	1	11	47.4														
Jack Doolan	OE-DE	28	6'1"	190															1	17	17	0																
CHICAGO BEARS																																						
Sid Luckman	QB	30	6'	197	7		10	86	8.6	1	323	176	54	2712	8.4	24	31– 10	2	1	15	15	0	5	35.4	1	1	100											
Nick Sacrinty	QB-DB	23	5'11"	185		1	4	4	1.0	0	48	15	31	299	6.2	5	3– 6																					
Tom Farris	QB-DB	26	6'1"	185		1	1	–3	–3.0	0	2	0	0	0	0.0	0	0– 0																					
Joe Osmanski	FB-LB	28	6'2"	220	6		64	328	5.4	1									7	134	19	0																
Mike Holovak	FB-LB	27	6'1"	215	6		51	281	5.5	1									7	119	17	0													2	47	24	0
Don Kindt	HB-DB	21	6'1"	200	12	3	61	266	4.4	2									2	24	12	0													10	220	22	0
George Gulyanics	HB-DB	26	6'	195	24	2	35	212	6.1	4	2	1	50	55	27.5	0	1– 50		3	22	7	0	23	44.8							1	7	7	0	5	124	25	0
George McAfee	HB-DB	29	6'	175	24	1	63	209	3.3	3									32	490	15	1	2	35.5							18	261	15	0	1	23	23	0
Bob Fenimore	HB-DB	21	6'1"	195	18	2	53	189	3.8	1	3	2	67	27	9.0	0	0– 0		15	219	15	2									2	16	8	0				
Frank Minini	HB-DB	23	6'1"	215	12	1	26	132	5.1	2									2	23	12	0													11	261	24	0
Hugh Gallarneau	HB-DB	30	6'	190	36	1	39	89	2.3	6									7	56	8	0													2	43	22	0
Ray McLean	HB-DB	31	5'10"	165	50	1	10	58	5.8	0									11	125	11	1			44	52	85	0	1	0	5	58	12	0	2	35	18	0
Noah Mullins	HB-DB	28	5'11"	185		6	9	55	6.1	0									1	4	4	0									13	153	12	0				
Bill Osmanski	FB	30	5'11"	195			10	37	3.7	0																									3	67	22	0
Eddie Allen	FB-LB	29	6'1"	200			12	16	1.3	0													8	37.4														
Jim Keane	OE-DE	23	6'4"	220	60														64	910	14	10																
Ken Kavanaugh	OE-DE	30	6'3"	210	78														32	818	26	13																
Ed Sprinkle	OE-DE	23	6'1"	207															4	43	11	0																
Ed Cifers	OE-DE	31	6'2"	228	12	1													3	48	16	1													2	33	17	0
Mike Jarmoluk	OE-T	24	6'5"	250	6														2	33	17	1																
Jack Matheson	OE-DE	27	6'2"	235															1	8	8	0																
GREEN BAY PACKERS																																						
Jack Jacobs	QB-DB	28	6'1"	190	6	4	18	64	3.6	1	242	108	45	1615	6.7	16	17– 7	5					57	43.5							1	4	4	0				
Irv Comp	QB-DB	28	6'2"	205		5	5	46	9.2	0	1	0	0	0	0.0	0	1–100														1	0	0	0				
Tony Canadeo	HB-DB	28	5'11"	190	12		103	464	4.5	2	8	3	38	101	12.6	1	1– 13														10	111	11	0	15	312	21	0
Walt Schlinkman	FB	25	5'8"	190	12		115	439	3.8	2									2	–6	–3	0																
Bruce Smith	HB-DB	27	6'	197	14	2	47	288	6.1	1									4	50	13	1									1	22	22	0	3	61	20	0
Ted Fritsch	FB-LB	26	5'10"	210	56	1	68	247	3.6	6															2	2	100	6	13	46					5	100	20	0
Jim Gillette	HB-DB	29	6'1"	185	6		50	207	4.1	0									12	224	19	1									11	168	15	0	3	66	22	0
Ed Cody	FB-DB	24	5'10"	190	12		56	263	4.7	2									1	2	2	0									2	30	15	0	10	269	27	0
Bob Forte	HB-DB	25	6'	195	18	8	29	80	2.4	0	2	1	50	8	4.0	0	0– 0		7	80	11	2									1	15	15	0	2	28	14	0
Herm Rohrig	HB-DB	29	5'8"	190		5	7	22	3.1	0																					18	213	12	0	1	15	15	0
Ken Keuper	HB-DB	29	6'	209		2	6	14	2.3	0									2	37	19	0																
Tex McKay	HB	27	6'	195	1		3	11	3.7	0													8	43.8	1	1	100											
Ward Cuff	HB-DB	34	6'1"	192	51		1	7	7.0	0															30	30	100	7	16	44								
Nolan Luhn	OE-DE	26	6'3"	200	42														42	696	17	7													2	30	15	0
Clyde Goodnight	OE-DB	23	6'1"	195	36		1	–1	–1.0	0									38	593	16	6													1	7	7	0
Gene Wilson	OE-DB	21	5'10"	175			1	–2	–2.0	0									3	34	11	0																
Larry Craig	OE-DE	31	6'1"	218															1	14	14	0																
LOS ANGELES RAMS																																						
Bob Waterfield	QB-DB	27	6'1"	193	54	5	3	6	2.0	1	221	96	43	1210	5.5	8	18– 8	10	2	14	7	0	59	42.4	27	30	90	7	16	44	1	2	2	0				
Jim Hardy	QB	25	6'	175			3	–6	–2.0	0	57	23	40	388	6.8	5	7– 12						10	26.3														
John Ksionzyk	QB	26	5'10"	190							7	1	14	17	2.4	0	2– 29																					
Kenny Washington	HB-DB	29	6'1"	215	30		60	444	7.4	5	5	2	40	14	2.8	0	1– 20		3	40	13	0									3	44	15	0	2	52	26	0
Tommy Harmon	HB-DB	27	6'1"	200	24	8	60	306	5.1	1	3	1	33	31	10.3	0	0– 0		5	89	18	1									27	392	15	1	9	208	23	0
Fred Gehrke	HB-DB	29	5'11"	190	13	1	59	304	5.2	0									6	19	3	0			4	4	100	1	1	100	4	112	28	1	2	29	15	0
Jack Banta	HB-DB	29	5'11"	190	6	2	40	193	4.8	1									14	198	14	0	3	41.7							2	19	10	0	2	50	25	0
Dante Magnani	HB	30	5'10"	184	6		48	178	3.7	0									4	57	14	1													6	186	31	0
Pat West	FB-LB	24	6'	200	12	1	42	162	3.9	2																									1	21	21	0
Bob Hoffman	FB-LB	29	6'1"	210	18	1	42	159	3.8	3									2	22	11	0													1	12	12	0
Dick Hoerner	FB-LB	25	6'4"	217	12	1	30	124	4.1	2									1	20	20	0																
Mel Bleeker	HB-DB	27	5'11"	187	6	1	23	111	4.8	0																									3	50	17	0
Gerry Cowhig	FB-LB	26	6'2"	217		1	25	104	4.2	0																									2	29	15	0
Les Horvath	HB-DB	26	5'10"	168			18	68	3.8	0									3	29	10	0									4	29	7	0	3	58	19	0
Steve Bagarus	HB-DB	28	6'	178		1	3	15	5.0	0																					2	18	9	0	1	11	11	0
Jack Wilson	HB-DB	29	6'	200			3	3	1.0	0									1	–5	–5	0																
Jim Benton	OE-DE	30	6'3"	216	36														35	511	15	6																
Red Hickey	OE-DE	30	6'2"	212	12														12	196	16	2																
Ray Hamilton	OE-DE	31	6'4"	214	6														12	193	16	1													1	10	10	0
Steve Pritko	OE-DE	25	6'2"	200															10	101	10	0																
Jack Zilly	OE-DE	25	6'2"	206															7	75	11	0													1	10	10	0
Frank Hubbell	OE-DE	25	6'2"	222	12														2	60	30	2																
DETROIT LIONS																																						
Clyde LeForce	QB-DB	24	5'11"	178		3	18	143	7.9	0	175	94	54	1384	7.9	13	20– 11	6													6	78	13	0	4	98	25	0
Roy Zimmerman	QB	29	6'2"	205	51		13	28	2.2	1	138	57	41	867	6.3	7	9– 7	9					49	42.4	30	31	97	5	11	45								
Joe Margucci	QB-HB-DB	24	5'10"	180	12		26	97	3.7	1	31	13	42	171	5.5	1	5– 16		10	125	13	1									2	23	12	0	5	94	19	0
Camp Wilson	FB-LB	25	6'2"	205			89	412	4.6	0									5	96	19	0													3	46	15	0
Bill Dudley	HB-DB	26	5'10"	178	66	5	80	302	3.8	2	4	3	75	24	6.0	2	0– 0		27	375	14	7	15	43.8							11	182	17	1	15	359	24	0
Bob Westfall	FB-LB	28	5'8"	185	6		34	132	3.9	1									2	19	10	0													2	27	14	0
Bob Wiese	HB-DB	24	6'3"	200		5	20	61	3.1	0									5	53	11	0	1	61.0														
Tippy Madarik	HB-DB	25	5'11"	200	6		19	29	1.5	1									4	75	19	0									1	7	7	0	3	49	16	0
Pete Kmetovic	HB-DB	27	5'9"	177	12		14	23	1.6	0									6	143	24	0									3	26	9	0	4	62	16	0
Joe Watt (from BOS)	HB-DB	26	5'11"	183	12	2	11	7	0.6	0									4	104	26	2									10	143	14	0	4	68	17	0
Steve Sucic (from BOS)	FB-LB	26	6'	210			3	3	1.0	0									1	20	20	0													1	18	18	0
Bill O'Brien	HB-DB	23	6'	180			1	2	2.0	0																												
Ken Reese	HB-DB	25	5'11"	175			3	1	0.3	0																									2	40	20	0
Bill Hillman	FB-LB	27	5'11"	200			2	0	0.0	0									1	25	25	0													1	15	15	0
Tommy James	HB-DB	23	5'10"	180			2	–1	–0.5	0																					1	2	2	0				
Bob DeFruiter (from WAS)	HB-DB	30	6'	190		3	1	–2	–2.0	0																												
John Greene	OE-DE	27	6'	200	30														38	621	16	5													2	19	10	0
Kelley Mote	OE-DB	24	6'2"	193	6	1													16	180	11	1													1	17	17	0
Cecil Souders	OE-DE	25	6'1"	210	6														15	184	12	1																
Ralph Heywood	OE-DE	25	6'2"	205	12														13	198	15	2																
Ted Cremer	OE-DE	28	6'2"	212	6														13	117	9	1																
Ted Cook	OE-DB	26	6'2"	195	6	2													7	111	16	1									1	10	10	0	2	14	7	0

TEAM TOTALS

OFFENSE	First Downs: Tot	by Rsh	by Pas	by Pen	Rushing: No.	Yds.	Avg Yds.	TD	Passing: Att	Com	Comp Pct.	Yds.	Avg. Yds. Att.	Avg. Yds. Comp	TD	Int	Pct. Int.	Punting: No.	Avg. Yds.	Punt Returns: No.	Yds.	Avg. Yds.	TD	Kickoff Returns: No.	Yds.	Avg. Yds.	TD	Interception Returns: No.	Yds.	Avg. Yds.	TD	Penalties: No.	Yds.	Fumbles: No.	Lost	Points: Tot	PAT	FG Att	FG	Saf.	DEFENSE
CHIC. C.	201	90	101	10	400	1759	4.4	10	314	148	47.1	2206	7.3	14.9	18	27	8.6	58	41.2	36	337	9.4	0	53	1037	19.6	0	25	331	13.2	0	90	852	25	18	231	30	14	5	0	CHIC. C.
CHIC. B.	206	78	96	32	392	1423	3.6	6	345	161	46.7	2449	7.1	15.2	20	27	7.8	64	42.4	27	433	16.0	2	57	1000	17.5	0	35	408	11.7	0	75	580	27	20	241	29	15	8	1	CHIC. B.
G.B.	193	96	71	26	433	1606	3.7	13	277	122	44.0	1790	6.5	14.7	14	30	10.8	65	43.5	44	483	11.0	0	48	1034	21.5	0	19	293	15.4	1	88	759	41	21	210	25	11	5	1	G.B
L.A.	209	99	93	17	453	1544	3.4	12	306	145	47.4	2059	6.7	14.2	14	24	7.8	76	41.1	29	352	12.1	0	47	1002	21.3	0	28	487	17.4	1	76	761	34	24	214	26	6	4	1	L.A.
DET.	220	96	106	18	461	1975	4.3	18	310	156	50.3	2430	7.8	15.6	21	25	8.1	55	42.2	39	584	15.0	1	45	929	20.6	0	34	442	13.0	2	112	1039	23	18	305	38	15	5	0	DET.

NEW YORK YANKEES 11-2-1 Ray Flaherty

Scores of Each Game		
24	Buffalo	28
48	CHICAGO	26
30	Los Angeles	14
21	San Francisco	16
21	Baltimore	7
17	Cleveland	26
31	BROOKLYN	7
28	Chicago	7
35	BALTIMORE	21
24	SAN FRANCISCO	16
16	LOS ANGELES	13
28	CLEVELAND	28
35	BUFFALO	13
20	Brooklyn	17

Use Name	Pos.	Hgt	Wgt	Age	Int	Pts
Fred Cardinal	LB	5'11"	220	22		
Paul Duke	C-LB	6'1"	210	21		
Lou Sossamon	C-LB	6'1"	207	26		6
Ralph Stewart	C-LB	6'	205	21		
Ray Ruskusky	DE	6'3"	200	26	1	
Hank Stanton	OE-DE	6'2"	200	27		

Use Name – Tackles	Pos.	Hgt	Wgt	Age	Int	Pts
Jack Durishan (1 kickoff return for 3 yds.)	T-G	6'2"	230	25		
Charlie Elliott	T	6'2"	240	25		
Nate Johnson	T	6'3"	240	27		
Bruiser Kinard	T	6'1"	218	32		
Ted Ossowski	T	6'	218	25		
Darrell Palmer	T	6'2"	245	25		
Vic Schleich	T	6'3"	240	26		

Use Name – Guards	Pos.	Hgt	Wgt	Age	Int	Pts
Dick Barwegan	G	6'1"	215	25		
Roman Bentz	G	6'2"	230	28		
Charley Riffle	G	6'	212	29		
Ed Sharkey	G	6'3"	215	21		
Joe Yackanich	G	5'10"	205	25		

Yankee coach Ray Flaherty had no stars like Joe DiMaggio on his squad, but he did have a versatile tailback in Spec Sanders, a quick scatback in 5'5" rookie Buddy Young, a tough two-way end in John Russell, and solid linemen in Nate Johnson, Bruiser Kinard, Dick Barwegan, and Lou Sossamon. Sanders slithered and sprinted to a pro record of 1,432 yards rushing, passed well, and played defensive back, replacing the retired Ace Parker as backfield leader on the team. Building around Sanders, Flaherty programmed a hard-hitting attack that averaged 27 points a game. But the New Yorkers could not escape the Browns' shadow. In their first meeting, the Browns won a 26-17 decision. In the rematch, the Yankees had the Browns down 28-0, but let them get off the hook for a 28-28 tie—a tipoff how the championship game would go.

BUFFALO BILLS 8-4-2 Red Dawson

28	NEW YORK	24
14	Cleveland	30
28	CHICAGO	20
31	Chicago	14
24	SAN FRANCISCO	41
27	Los Angeles	25
20	BALTIMORE	15
14	Brooklyn	14
35	BROOKLYN	7
7	CLEVELAND	28
25	LOS ANGELES	0
33	Baltimore	14
13	New York	35
21	San Francisco	21

Use Name	Pos.	Hgt	Wgt	Age	Int	Pts
Bert Corley	C-LB	6'2"	210	27	1	
Joe Haynes	C-G	6'3"	225	26		
Felto Prewitt	C-LB	5'11"	210	23	2	
John Morton	OE-DE	6'	200	25		

Use Name – Tackles	Pos.	Hgt	Wgt	Age	Int	Pts
Jack Carpenter	T	6'	235	24		
Gil Duggan	T	6'3"	235	29		
John Kerns	T	6'3"	245	24		
Chet Kozel (1 kickoff return for 11 yds.)	T	6'2"	207	27		

Use Name – Guards	Pos.	Hgt	Wgt	Age	Int	Pts
George Doherty	G	6'1"	218	26		
George Groves	G	5'11"	195	26		
Hal Lahar	G	6'	225	28		
John Maskas	G	5'11"	212	27		
Rosco Pirro	G	6'	235	30		
Vin Scott	G	5'8"	215	25		

The Bills came up with a new name, a new quarterback, and a new lease on life. While the change of name from the Bisons to the Bills didn't help the team on the field, the arrival of passer George Ratterman certainly did. The rookie quarterback from Notre Dame stepped right in as a starter, zipping passes to ends Fay King and Al Baldwin from the first game on. With the new passer spreading out the defenses, halfback Chet Mutryn blossomed into a fine runner, and the Bills suddenly were scoring points in a steady flow. Up until the final two weeks of the season, the Bills were in the running for the Eastern Division crown, but a 35-13 defeat by the Yankees ended any hopes of a mini-miracle. The fans reacted to the new winning image by almost doubling the 1946 attendance, a favor much appreciated by the owners.

BROOKLYN DODGERS 3-10-1 Cliff Battles

7	San Francisco	23
7	Baltimore	16
7	CLEVELAND	55
21	Los Angeles	48
35	Chicago	31
7	New York	31
14	BUFFALO	14
7	Buffalo	35
7	CHICAGO	3
12	Cleveland	13
21	BALTIMORE	13
12	LOS ANGELES	16
7	SAN FRANCISCO	21
17	NEW YORK	20

Use Name	Pos.	Hgt	Wgt	Age	Int	Pts
Lou Daukas (1 kickoff return for 1 yd.)	C-LB	6'	203	26	1	
Joe Gibson	LB-DE	6'3"	215	28	1	
Ed Gustafson	C-LB	6'3"	205	25		
Frank Laurinaitis	LB	5'10"	200	25		
Russ Morrow	LB-DE	6'7"	210	23		
Caleb Warrington (2 yds. on pass reception lateral)	C-G	6'2"	210	26		
Neal Adams	OE-DE	6'3"	195	28		
Mel Conger	DE	6'2"	225	28		
Mike Patanelli	DE	6'2"	215	22		
Bernie Nygren	HB-DB	5'9"	193	27		
Adolph Kowalski	BB-DB	6'3"	205	26		
Doyle Tackett (25 yds. on pass reception lateral)	BB-DB	6'	205	23	1	

Use Name – Tackles	Pos.	Hgt	Wgt	Age	Int	Pts
Nick Daukas	T	6'4"	225	24		
Charlie Huneke (from CHI)	T	6'3"	225	26		
Ed Mieszkowski	T	6'2"	220	22		
Martin Ruby	T	6'3"	250	27		
Leroy Schneider	T	5'11"	237	24		
Harlan Wetz	T	6'5"	265	22		
Garland Williams	T	6'3"	220	26		

Use Name – Guards	Pos.	Hgt	Wgt	Age	Int	Pts
George Bernhardt	G	5'10"	215	28		
Harry Buffington	G	6'	210	28		
Amos Harris	G	6'	210	26		
Ed Jeffers	G	6'3"	215	24		
Billy Jones	G	6'	220	27		

Tailback Glen Dobbs learned how quickly football fame can evaporate. Last year, he led the AAFC in passing, made the All-League team, won the first league MVP Award, and established himself as a rising star in the pro-football sky. This year, he got off to a slow start and found out how short coach Cliff Battles' memory was when the Dodgers traded with Chicago for tailback Bob Hoernschemeyer. Before the season was over, Hoernschemeyer had won the starter's position, and Dobbs was playing for the Los Angeles Dons.

Since Hoernschemeyer ran with the ball better than he passed, the Brooklyn offense shifted focus by concentrating on a ground attack. Fullback Mickey Colmer helped Hoernschemeyer with the running and also led the league in punting. Up front, only Martin Ruby was above average. With good players scattered thinly across the roster, the Dodgers lost all but three games, and with fans scattered thinly throughout the stands, the front office lost quite a few dollars.

BALTIMORE COLTS 2-11-1 Cecil Isbell

16	BROOKLYN	7
7	San Francisco	14
0	Cleveland	28
7	NEW YORK	21
28	SAN FRANCISCO	28
15	Buffalo	20
10	LOS ANGELES	38
0	Los Angeles	56
21	New York	35
21	Chicago	27
14	Brooklyn	21
14	BUFFALO	33
14	CHICAGO	7
0	CLEVELAND	42

Use Name	Pos.	Hgt	Wgt	Age	Int	Pts
Dick Handley	C-LB	6'1"	215	25		
Joe Kodba	C-LB	5'11"	190	26		
Mike Phillips	C-LB	6'	208	25		
Bill Baumgartner	OE-DE	6'3"	202	26		
Floyd Konetsky	DE	6'	200	27	1	
Armand Cure (2 rushing attempts for –1 yd.)	HB-DB	6'	198	28		

Use Name – Tackles	Pos.	Hgt	Wgt	Age	Int	Pts
George Hekkers (to DET-NFL)	T	6'4"	225	24		
Mike Kasap	T	6'2"	255	26		
Al Klug	T	6'1"	212	26		
Jim Landrigan	T	6'4"	235	24		
John Mellus (5 yds. on pass reception lateral)	T	6'	210	30		
George Perpich	T	6'2"	235	27		

Use Name – Guards	Pos.	Hgt	Wgt	Age	Int	Pts
Barry French (1 kickoff return for 11 yds.)	G	6'	225	26		
Ed Grain (from NY)	G	6'	230	25		
Luke Higgins	G	6'	210	26		
Vic Marino	G	5'8"	206	28		
Frank Yokas	G	5'11"	210	23		
George Zorich	G	6'2"	215	28		

When the Miami Seahawks ran aground on financial reefs, the franchise was set afloat in the virgin football waters of Baltimore. The new owners started building their team by hiring Cecil Isbell as head coach. The ex-Packer star emphasized the passing game, and he came up with a representative quarterback in Bud Schwenk, Otto Graham's backup in 1946 and an NFL veteran. Schwenk kept the fans alert by throwing spades of passes to end Lamar Davis and halfback Billy Hillenbrand; he had to keep throwing, since the running attack had all the force of a feather. The Colts picked up former Detroit Lion star Frankie Sinkwich in mid-season, but he was past his prime and less effective in the T formation. Isbell did acquire two good linemen in tackle John Mellus and guard Augie Lio, but the rest of the line badly needed shoring up. Even though the Colts won only two games, they won enough of a following to come back for a second year.

TEAM TOTALS

OFFENSE	First Downs: Tot	by Rsh	by Pas	by Pen	Rushing: No.	Yds.	Avg. Yds.	TD	Passing: Att.	Com	Comp. Pct.	Yds.	Avg. Yds. Att.	Avg. Yds. Comp.	TD	Int	Pct. Int.	Punting: No.	Avg.	Punt Returns: No.	Yds.	Avg. Yds.	TD	Kickoff Returns: No.	Yds.	Avg. Yds.	TD	Interception Returns: No.	Yds.	Avg. Yds.	TD	Penalties: No.	Yds.	Fumbles: No.	Lost	Points: Tot	PAT	FG Att	FG	Saf.	OFFENSE
N.Y.	187	120	54	13	534	2930	5.5	27	216	111	51.4	1795	8.3	16.2	16	18	8.3	55	40.0	32	489	15.3	2	53	1351	25.5	3	17	342	20.1	1	67	522	45	17	378	49	8	7	1	N.Y.
BUFFALO	175	109	59	7	496	2217	4.5	18	267	129	48.3	1891	7.1	14.7	24	23	8.6	57	37.0	42	545	13.0	0	50	1282	25.6	2	18	404	22.4	2	48	390	36	17	320	38	4	2	0	BUFFALO
BKN.	138	92	39	7	495	1936	3.9	21	232	92	39.7	1060	4.6	11.5	4	17	7.3	84	42.8	32	425	13.3	0	56	1296	23.1	0	16	157	9.8	0	46	374	37	13	181	22	20	3	0	BKN.
BALT.	161	65	85	11	417	1161	2.8	7	352	177	50.3	2337	6.6	13.2	13	24	6.8	78	36.2	33	546	16.5	0	59	1356	23.0	1	14	213	15.2	0	47	360	36	23	167	21	10	4	1	BALT.
DEFENSE																																									DEFENSE
N.Y.	140	67	60	13	371	1237	3.3	13	304	144	47.4	1910	6.3	13.3	17	17	5.6	78	41.4	39	473	12.1	0	68	1401	20.6	0	18	237	13.2	1	54	382	33	12	239	26	15	7	0	N.Y.
BUFFALO	182	109	64	9	507	2218	4.4	22	260	133	51.2	1929	7.4	14.5	14	18	6.9	64	42.8	29	312	10.8	0	58	1357	23.4	0	23	327	14.2	2	52	456	34	14	288	36	10	4	3	BUFFALO
BKN.	178	112	57	9	514	2516	4.9	16	265	124	46.8	2130	8.0	17.2	21	16	6.0	55	40.0	50	744	14.9	1	37	1032	27.9	2	17	218	12.8	3	43	261	40	20	340	40	18	12	0	BKN.
BALT.	183	118	59	6	571	2665	4.7	29	239	124	51.9	1791	7.5	14.4	17	14	5.9	56	40.0	46	627	13.6	1	38	646	17.0	1	24	417	17.4	4	59	488	60	25	377	50	12	3	0	BALT.

							RUSHING				PASSING								RECEIVING				PUNTING		KICKING						PUNT RETURNS				KICKOFF RETURNS			
Use Name – Backs & Ends	Pos.	Age	Hgt	Wgt	Pts	Int	No.	Yds	Avg	TD	Att	Comp	%	Yds	Yd/Att	TD	Int–%	RK	No.	Yds	Avg	TD	No.	Avg	Pat	Att	%	FG	Att	%	No.	Yds	Avg	TD	No.	Yds	Avg	TD
NEW YORK YANKEES																																						
Spec Sanders	TB-DB	28	6'1"	196	114	3	231	1432	6.2	18	171	93	54	1442	8.4	14	17– 10	3	1	13	13	0	46	42.1							6	164	27	0	22	593	27	1
Ben Raimondi	TB	22	5'10"	175			6	11	1.8	0	15	3	20	54	3.6	0	0– 0																					
Buddy Young	FB-HB-DB	21	5'5"	170	42		116	712	6.1	3	2	1	50	13	6.5	0	0– 0		27	303	11	2									8	127	16	1	12	332	28	1
Eddie Prokop	FB-DB	25	5'11"	200	30	3	76	324	4.3	4	8	4	50	137	17.1	2	1– 13		3	79	26	1									7	78	11	0	7	188	27	0
Bob Kennedy	FB-DB	26	5'11"	195	6	2	44	258	5.9	1	3	2	67	56	18.7	0	0– 0						5	25.2							6	44	7	0				
Dewey Proctor	FB-LB	26	5'11"	215	6	1	15	15	1.0	1	1	0	0	0	0.0	0	0– 0		1	4	4	0													1	15	15	0
John Sylvester	HB-DB	25	6'	183			17	101	5.9	0	1	0	0	0	0.0	0	0– 0		1	5	5	0	1	42.0							3	37	12	0	1	25	25	0
Harry Burrus	WB-DB	26	6'1"	195	12	1	1	5	5.0	0									8	192	24	2																
Harmon Rowe	HB-DB	25	6'	182		2	2	–3	–1.5	0																									1	18	18	0
Lowell Wagner	WB-DB	23	6'	193	6														4	50	13	1																
Bob Sweiger	BB-LB	28	6'	209	12	2	9	44	4.9	0									11	108	10	1													1	12	12	0
Lloyd Cheatham	BB	28	6'2"	215	12		1	–2	–2.0	0									4	124	31	2																
Harvey Johnson	BB-LB	28	5'11"	210	70																				49	51	98	7	8	88								
Jack Russell	OE-DE	27	6'1"	215	18	1													20	368	18	2													4	66	17	0
Bruce Alford	OE-DB	26	6'	190	42	1													20	298	15	5									1	34	34	1	2	90	45	1
Van Davis	OE-DE	25	6'2"	215															8	179	22	0													1	9	9	0
Roy Kurrasch	OE-DE	25	6'2"	195															2	53	27	0																
Ollie Poole	OE-DE	25	6'3"	220															1	19	19	0									1	5	5	0				
BUFFALO BILLS																																						
George Ratterman	QB	20	6'1"	175	6		17	–49	–2.9	1	244	124	51	1840	7.5	22	20– 8	3							0	1	0											
George Terlep	QB-DB	25	5'10"	180		1	4	11	2.8	0	23	5	22	51	2.2	2	3– 13														1	17	17	0				
Albie Reisz	QB	29	5'10"	180			2	32	16.0	0													57	37.0														
Chet Mutryn	HB-DB	26	5'9"	180	73	1	140	868	6.2	9									10	176	18	2			1	2	50				13	187	14	0	21	691	33	1
Julie Rykovich	HB-DB	23	6'2"	200	24	2	92	414	4.5	4									4	44	11	0									7	93	13	0	12	257	21	0
Lou Tomasetti	HB-DB	31	6'	198	18	1	92	326	3.5	2									13	125	10	0													4	74	19	0
Vic Kulbitski	FB-LB	26	5'11"	205	31	1	56	249	4.4	1									9	117	13	4			1	1	100				1	13	13	0	1	19	19	0
George Koch	HB-DB	28	6'	200	6	3	37	149	4.0	1									1	10	10	0									4	84	21	0	1	12	12	0
Steve Juzwik	HB-DB	29	5'8"	184	40		26	130	5.0	0									5	35	7	1			28	32	88	2	3	67	4	36	9	0	1	20	20	0
Alex Wizbicki	HB-DB	25	5'11"	188	6		9	44	4.9	0																					9	105	12	0	5	164	33	1
Pug Manders	FB-LB	34	6'	200			3	15	5.0	0																												
Buckets Hirsch	FB-LB	26	5'10"	205	6	3	4	7	1.8	0																												
Fay King	OE	25	6'3"	195	36														26	382	15	6																
Al Baldwin	OE-DB	24	6'2"	187	42	2													25	468	19	7													1	6	6	0
Al Coppage	OE-DB	31	6'1"	195	12														20	226	11	2													2	28	14	0
Paul Gibson	OE-DB	22	6'2"	190															8	154	19	0																
Ray Kuffel	OE-DE	25	6'3"	210															3	37	12	0																
Marty Comer	OE-DE	29	6'	202	6														2	75	38	1																
Vince Mazza	OE-DE	26	6'1"	210		1													2	11	6	0																
Graham Armstrong	T	28	6'4"	240	8																				8	10	80	0	1	0								
BROOKLYN DODGERS																																						
Bob Hoernschemeyer (from CHI)	TB-DB	21	5'11"	192	36	1	152	704	4.6	5	173	73	42	926	5.4	4	11– 6	9	1	4	4	1	2	28.0							1	19	19	0	1	11	11	0
Bob Perina	TB-HB-DB	26	6'1"	205	24	4	67	116	1.7	3	24	11	46	91	3.8	0	2– 8		9	67	7	1	7	29.9							4	27	7	0	3	67	22	0
Dub Jones	TB-DB	22	6'4"	200	6	2	43	136	3.2	1	15	3	20	37	2.5	0	2– 13														14	157	11	0	7	121	17	0
Mickey Colmer	FB-LB	28	6'2"	224	60		152	578	3.8	9	3	1	33	20	6.7	0	0– 0		18	190	11	1	56	44.7											3	77	26	0
Monk Gafford	HB-DB	26	5'11"	195	6	3	46	232	5.0	1									8	113	14	0									11	186	17	0	21	565	27	0
Al Akins	HB-DB	26	6'1"	195	12	1	15	79	5.3	1									6	101	17	1									1	17	17	0	5	131	26	0
Lee Tevis	FB-LB	25	5'11"	190		2	4	44	11.0	0	3	0	0	0	0.0	0	0– 0						5	49.2														
George Benson	HB-DB	28	6'1"	205			2	5	2.5	0																												
Elmore Harris	HB	25	5'11"	175			3	–2	–0.7	0																									14	329	24	0
Walt McDonald	BB	26	6'1"	210			1	1	1.0	0									3	30	10	0									1	19	19	0				
Saxon Judd	OE	26	6'1"	190	6														18	204	11	1													2	5	3	0
Hal Thompson	OE-DE	25	6'1"	205			1	4	4.0	0									15	148	10	0																
Jim McCarthy	OE-DE	25	6'1"	205							2	1	50	17	8.5	0	1– 50		10	147	15	0																
Herb Nelson	OE-DE	26	6'4"	218															2	17	9	0																
Ed Scruggs	OE-DE	24	6'1"	195															2	9	5	0																
Bob Hein	OE-DE	26	6'3"	220															1	7	7	0																
Phil Martinovich	G	32	5'10"	220	31																				22	25	88	3	20	15								
BALTIMORE COLTS																																						
Bud Schwenk	QB	29	6'2"	200	6		25	58	2.3	1	327	168	51	2236	6.8	13	20– 6	5																				
Ernie Case	QB-DB	27	5'10"	170	4	2	1	0	0.0	0	11	4	36	49	4.5	0	1– 9						5	30.4	1	1	100	1	1	100	2	18	9	0	4	104	26	0
John Galvin	QB	27	5'10"	170			1	–4	–4.0	0	6	3	50	34	5.7	0	0– 0						66	36.0											2	38	19	0
Steve Nemeth	QB	25	5'10"	175	1		1	1	1.0	0	6	2	33	18	3.0	0	2– 33						3	42.0	1	1	100	0	1	0								
Buzz Mertes	FB	26	6'	205	12		95	321	3.4	2									2	28	14	0																
Frankie Sinkwich (from NY, TB)	HB-DB	26	5'11"	190			71	241	3.4	0	15	8	53	93	6.2	0	0– 0		1	3	3	0	7	37.1							1	15	15	0	5	118	24	0
Billy Hillenbrand	HB-DB	25	6'	188	60	1	66	204	3.1	2	1	0	0	0	0.0	0	1–100		39	702	18	7									13	201	15	0	18	466	26	1
John Wright	FB-LB	26	5'11"	225		1	38	113	3.0	0																												
Rudy Mobley	HB-DB	25	5'7"	155	12	2	26	90	3.5	1									11	121	11	1									5	74	15	0	1	18	18	0
John Vardian	HB-DB	22	5'8"	168	6	3	35	57	1.6	0									16	280	18	1									5	66	13	0	6	128	21	0
Ray Terrell (to CLE)	HB-DB	28	6'	185		1	26	48	1.8	0									6	21	4	0									1	18	18	0	9	204	23	0
Blondy Black	HB-DB	27	5'11"	195			5	39	7.8	0									1	7	7	0																
Andy Dudish	HB-DB	26	5'11"	180	12		28	30	1.1	1									7	130	19	1									5	121	24	0	8	184	23	0
Jim Castiglia (to WAS–NFL)	FB	28	5'11"	210	6		9	18	2.0	0									1	10	10	0																
Buzz Trebotich	FB-LB	26	5'10"	205			3	–4	–1.3	0																									1	17	17	0
Lamar Davis	OE-DB	26	6'1"	185	12	1	3	14	4.7	0	1	0	0	0	0.0	0	0– 0		46	515	11	2									1	33	33	0	2	44	22	0
Hub Bechtol	OE-DE	21	6'3"	200	6	1	2	–1	–0.5	0									17	167	10	1													1	13	13	0
Lamar Blount (from BUF)	OE-HB-DB	27	6'1"	190			4	5	1.3	0									8	148	19	0																
Sig Sigurdson	OE-DE	28	6'2"	206															8	104	13	0																
Elmer Madar	OE-DB	26	5'11"	185															8	53	7	0													1	14	14	0
Ralph Jones	OE-DE	26	6'3"	200															3	23	8	0																
Gorham Getchell	OE-DE	27	6'4"	225															2	17	9	0																
Gil Meyer	OE-DE	26	6'2"	200															1	3	3	0																
Augie Lio	G	29	6'	230	28																				19	20	95	3	8	38								

CLEVELAND BROWNS 12-1-1 Paul Brown

Scores of Each Game		
30	BUFFALO	14
55	Brooklyn	7
28	BALTIMORE	0
41	Chicago	21
26	NEW YORK	17
10	LOS ANGELES	13
31	CHICAGO	28
14	San Francisco	7
28	Buffalo	7
13	BROOKLYN	12
37	SAN FRANCISCO	14
28	New York	28
27	Los Angeles	17
42	Baltimore	0

Use Name	Pos.	Hgt	Wgt	Age	Int	Pts
Frank Gatski	C-LB	6'3"	210	25	2	
(1 kickoff return for 17 yds.)						
Mel Maceau	C-LB	6'	203	25		
Lou Saban	LB	6'	198	25	2	10
(10 PAT in 11 attempts)						
Mo Scarry	C-LB	6'	208	27		
George Young	DE	6'3"	210	23		

Use Name – Tackles	Pos.	Hgt	Wgt	Age	Int	Pts
Ernie Blandin	T	6'4"	245	28		
(1 rush for –6 yds.)						
Roman Piskor	T	6'	245	29		
Lou Rymkus	T	6'4"	230	28		
Len Simonetti	T	5'11"	225	28	1	

Use Name – Guards	Pos.	Hgt	Wgt	Age	Int	Pts
Bob Gaudio	G-LB	5'10"	215	22		
Lin Houston	G	6'	205	26		
Weldon Humble	G-LB	6'1"	215	26	2	
(1 rush for 0 yds.)						
Ed Ulinski	G	5'11"	200	26		
Bill Willis	G	6'2"	206	26		

Since the Browns obviously outclassed the rest of the AAFC, people already were discussing how they would fare in the established NFL. The Browns lost only one game this year, and the Cleveland fans kept turning out in the highest numbers in pro football. The team's riches began with coach Paul Brown, a demanding leader who combined Spartan discipline with endless blackboard analyses. The attack dazzled opponents with passes as quarterback Otto Graham calmly shot unstoppable sideline passes to Dante Lavelli and Mac Speedie, then crossed up the defense with an occasional long bomb. The linemen made sure Graham had plenty of time to sight his receivers, and fullback Marion Motley kept defenses honest with his pile-driving running. The Browns also had a lot of heart, showing their mettle when they fell behind 28-0 to the New York Yankees and came back to salvage a 28-28 tie.

SAN FRANCISCO 49ers 8-4-2 Buck Shaw

Scores of Each Game		
23	BROOKLYN	7
17	LOS ANGELES	14
14	BALTIMORE	7
16	NEW YORK	21
41	Buffalo	24
28	Baltimore	28
42	CHICAGO	28
7	CLEVELAND	14
26	Los Angeles	16
16	New York	24
14	Cleveland	37
41	Chicago	16
21	Brooklyn	7
21	BUFFALO	21

Use Name	Pos.	Hgt	Wgt	Age	Int	Pts
Jack Baldwin (from NY)	C-LB	6'3"	225	26		
Tony Calvelli	C-LB	5'10"	187	31	1	
Gerry Conlee	C-LB	5'11"	210	31		
(1 punt return for 1 yd.)						
John Schiechl	C-LB	6'2"	250	30	2	
George Smith	C-LB	6'2"	245	33	1	

Use Name – Tackles	Pos.	Hgt	Wgt	Age	Int	Pts
Bob Bryant	T	6'3"	225	28		
Odis Crowell	T	6'2"	220	23		
Visco Grgich	T	5'11"	210	24		
(1 kickoff return for 21 yds.)						
Al Satterfield	T	6'3"	225	25		
Bob Thornton	T	5'10"	205	28		
(1 punt return for 32 yds.)						
John Woudenberg	T	6'3"	225	29		
(1 kickoff return for 2 yds.)						

Use Name – Guards	Pos.	Hgt	Wgt	Age	Int	Pts
Bruno Banducci	G	5'11"	215	25		
(1 punt ret. for 19 yds., 1 kickoff ret. for 27 yds.)						
Dick Bassi	G-LB	5'11"	215	32		
Art Elston	G-C-LB	5'11"	190	28	2	
Ed Forrest	G-LB	5'11"	210	26		
Garland Gregory	G-LB	5'11"	185	28		
(1 punt return for 31 yds.)						

Althought the '49ers could not challenge the Browns for first place, quarterback Frankie Albert kept fans and players buzzing with his magical ball-handling and unpredictable play-calling. Little Frankie dealt out fakes in the backfield like the girl next door by sending defenders in hot pursuit of runners who didn't even have the ball. Close to the end zone, he often would fake to all three backs, hide the ball behind his hip, and roll unmolested around end for a touchdown. Although his long passes wobbled like a crippled pigeon, Albert never hesitated to throw the ball to ends Alyn Beals and Nick Susoeff on quick short patterns or on deep bombs. With Albert deftly shuffling pass plays, handoffs to his running backs, and bootleg keepers, enemy defenders never knew what was coming next.

LOS ANGELES DONS 7-7-0 Dud DeGroot, Mel Hein, Ted Shipkey

Scores of Each Game		
24	Chicago	21
14	San Francisco	17
14	NEW YORK	30
48	BROOKLYN	21
25	BUFFALO	27
13	Cleveland	10
38	Baltimore	10
56	BALTIMORE	0
16	SAN FRANCISCO	26
0	Buffalo	25
13	New York	16
16	Brooklyn	12
17	CLEVELAND	27
34	CHICAGO	14

Use Name	Pos.	Hgt	Wgt	Age	Int	Pts
John Brown	C-LB	6'4"	230	25	1	
Dick Danahe	C-T	6'2"	235	22		
(8 yds. on pass reception lateral)						
Bob Steuber	FB-LB	6'2"	200	25		
(1 rush for 2 yds.)						

Use Name – Tackles	Pos.	Hgt	Wgt	Age	Int	Pts
Lee Artoe	T	6'3"	240	31		
(1 kickoff return for 16 yds.)						
Earl Audet	T	6'2"	252	26		
Pete Berezney	T	6'2"	240	23		
Paul Mitchell	T	6'3"	225	27		
Jim Smith	T	6'4"	270	23		

Use Name – Guards	Pos.	Hgt	Wgt	Age	Int	Pts
Ray Frankowski	G	5'11"	220	28		
Bernie Gallagher	G	6'	235	24		
Reid Lennan	G	6'	235	25		
Len Levy	G	6'	252	26		
Al Lolotai	G	6'	220	26		
Bill Radovich	G	5'10"	255	32		

Los Angeles football fans warmed up to the Dons by more than doubling the total attendance to a figure of 304,177. The Browns alone outdrew the Dons in the AAFC, and only a handful of NFL clubs could match their total. Even with the healthy ticket sales, the club still lost money because of high costs in this time of football war.

But the Dons did field an interesting team which could rise to dazzling heights. They hung the only loss of the season on the Cleveland Browns in a 13-10 upset. They trounced the Baltimore Colts 56-0 and 38-10 and downed Brooklyn 48-21. Yet the Dons also lost three close games by a total of 8 points to bring their final record down to the break-even point. The fans could single out any number of players for fine play, with John Kimbrough, Dale Gentry, Len Levy, and Bob Nelson especially worthy of attention from the newly found customers. Coach Dud DeGroot also drew attention; he was fired in mid-season.

CHICAGO ROCKETS 1-13-0 Jim Crowley, Hamp Pool

Scores of Each Game		
21	LOS ANGELES	24
26	New York	48
20	Buffalo	28
14	BUFFALO	31
21	CLEVELAND	41
31	BROOKLYN	35
28	San Francisco	42
28	Cleveland	31
7	NEW YORK	28
3	Brooklyn	7
27	BALTIMORE	21
16	SAN FRANCISCO	41
7	Baltimore	14
14	Los Angeles	34

Use Name	Pos.	Hgt	Wgt	Age	Int	Pts
Herb Coleman	C-LB	6'	200	24		
Pete Lamana	C-LB	5'11"	210	26		
Fred Negus	C-LB	6'1"	205	25		
Cliff Rothrock	C-LB	5'10"	198	25		
Connie Mack Berry	DE	6'3"	230	31		

Use Name – Tackles	Pos.	Hgt	Wgt	Age	Int	Pts
Alf Bauman (to PHI-NFL)	T	6'2"	218	27		
Chubby Grigg	T	6'2"	330	21		
John Kuzman	T	6'1"	230	31		
(1 kickoff return for 7 yds.)						
Harley McCollum	T	6'4"	245	29		
(1 kickoff return for 9 yds.)						
Joe Mihal	T	6'3"	240	31		
Bruno Niedziela	T	6'2"	225	24		
Ben Pucci	T	6'4"	260	22		
John Sanchez (to DET-NFL & WAS-NFL)	T	6'3"	234	26		
Norm Verry	T	6'1"	240	24		
Lloyd Wasserbach	T	5'11"	205	26		

Use Name – Guards	Pos.	Hgt	Wgt	Age	Int	Pts
Alex Agase (from LA)	G-LB	5'10"	210	25	1	
John Billman	G-LB	6'1"	202	27		
Al Hecht	G	6'	235	25		
Fran Mattingly	G-LB	5'11"	215	27	1	
Jim O'Neal	G	6'1"	230	23		
Jim Pearcy	G	5'11"	210	28		
Tony Sumpter	G	6'1"	215	25		
Red Vogds	G	5'10"	204	24		

Jim Crowley resigned as AAFC commissioner to take over as general manager and head coach of the Rockets, leading some people to doubt his sanity. As general manager, Crowley had to worry about a 33 percent drop in attendance and the renewed gate pull of the NFL Bears and Cardinals. As coach, he watched his team lose its first ten games and end the season with only one victory. In an effort to get the Rockets moving, general manager Crowley fired head coach Crowley, replacing him with Hamp Pool, and when new ownership took over the club after the season, general manager Crowley joined his alter ego on the unemployment line.

On the field, the Rockets hardly fielded a team equal to the Cardinals and Bears. Injuries robbed the club of backs Angelo Bertelli, Crazy Legs Hirsch, and Ray Ramsey for stretches of action, and none of the remaining players could stop the skid to the bottom.

TEAM TOTALS

	FIRST DOWNS:				RUSHING:				PASSING:									PUNTING:	
OFFENSE	Tot	by Rsh	by Pas	by Pen	No.	Yds.	Avg. Yds.	TD	Att.	Com	Comp. Pct.	Yds.	Avg. Yds. Att.	Avg. Yds. Comp	TD	Int.	Pct. Int.	No.	Avg. Yds.
CLEVE.	214	108	91	15	479	2557	5.3	24	296	174	58.8	2990	10.1	17.2	26	12	4.1	52	43.6
S.F.	218	138	72	8	587	2767	4.7	22	297	147	49.5	1993	6.7	13.6	22	19	6.4	50	43.5
L.A.	161	86	62	13	487	1780	3.7	17	300	141	47.0	2127	7.1	15.1	19	25	8.3	58	45.0
CHICAGO	155	69	75	11	401	1520	3.8	9	341	157	46.0	2358	6.9	15.0	23	26	7.6	67	39.1
DEFENSE																			
CLEVE.	188	102	75	11	503	2181	4.3	12	303	129	42.6	1707	5.8	13.2	11	32	10.6	58	43.0
S.F.	178	87	78	13	405	1631	4.0	10	332	177	53.3	2502	7.5	14.1	23	24	7.2	62	37.1
L.A.	160	76	68	16	461	1668	3.6	9	310	157	50.6	2376	7.7	15.1	24	24	7.7	75	40.9
CHICAGO	200	116	76	8	564	2752	4.9	34	288	140	48.6	2206	7.7	15.8	20	19	6.6	53	39.7

PUNT RETURNS:				KICKOFF RETURNS:				INTERCEPTION RETURNS:				PENALTIES:		FUMBLES:		POINTS:					TEAM TOTALS
No.	Yds.	Avg. Yds.	TD	No.	Yds.	Avg. Yds.	TD	No.	Yds.	Avg. Yds.	TD	No.	Yds.	No.	Lost	Tot	PAT	FG Att	FG	Saf.	OFFENSE
32	503	15.7	1	42	889	21.2	0	32	474	14.8	3	80	660	29	16	410	50	20	8	0	CLEVE.
44	500	11.4	1	43	845	19.7	0	24	406	16.9	1	58	472	47	18	327	39	12	4	0	S.F.
47	583	12.4	0	55	1287	23.4	0	24	345	14.4	2	58	478	29	14	328	39	24	15	2	L.A.
28	289	10.3	0	69	1483	21.5	0	19	400	21.1	3	38	264	50	26	263	33	9	4	1	CHICAGO
																					DEFENSE
31	506	16.3	0	63	1449	23.0	0	12	208	17.3	1	47	385	40	19	185	23	11	4	0	CLEVE.
24	324	13.5	1	58	1346	23.2	1	19	356	18.7	1	56	416	37	21	264	34	10	4	1	S.F.
30	324	10.8	0	60	1494	24.9	1	25	465	18.6	0	59	507	43	13	256	26	13	6	1	L.A.
41	570	13.9	1	45	1067	23.7	1	26	512	19.7	0	72	610	32	20	425	56	18	7	0	CHICAGO

Use Name – Backs & Ends	Pos.	Age	Hgt	Wgt	Pts	Int	RUSHING				PASSING								RECEIVING				PUNTING		KICKING						PUNT RETURNS				KICKOFF RETURNS			
							No.	Yds	Avg	TD	Att	Comp	%	Yds	Yd/Att	TD	Int–%	RK	No.	Yds	Avg	TD	No.	Avg	Pat	Att	%	FG	Att	%	No.	Yds	Avg	TD	No.	Yds	Avg	TD
CLEVELAND BROWNS																																						
Otto Graham	QB-DB	25	6'1"	190	6	1	19	72	3.8	1	269	163	61	2753	10.2	25	11–4	1													10	121	12	0				
Ermal Allen	QB-DB	28	5'11"	165		4	7	11	1.6	0	13	4	31	88	6.8	0	0–0						4	33.8							4	28	7	0				
Cliff Lewis	QB-DB	24	5'11"	165		4	11	66	6.0	0	11	5	45	70	6.4	1	1–9														7	84	12	0	4	71	18	0
Marion Motley	FB-LB	27	6'1"	218	60	1	146	889	6.1	8									7	73	10	1													13	322	25	0
Special Delivery Jones	HB-DB	28	5'10"	195	36		69	443	6.4	5	3	2	67	79	26.3	0	0–0		5	92	18	1									2	37	19	0	2	48	24	0
Bill Boedecker	HB-DB	23	5'11"	190	30		31	194	6.3	4									8	175	22	1									3	82	27	0	6	133	22	0
Bob Cowan	HB-DB	24	5'11"	185	18		38	181	4.8	2									5	60	12	1													3	55	18	0
Spiro Dellerba	FB-LB	24	5'11"	200	6		29	176	6.1	0									1	14	14	0													1	34	34	0
Bill Lund	HB-DB	23	5'10"	180	18	2	14	105	7.5	1									6	110	18	1													2	37	19	0
Tony Adamle	FB-LB	23	6'	210	6	1	23	95	4.1	1									1	22	22	0									0	36	–	0	1	22	22	0
Don Greenwood	HB-DB	26	6'	198		4	18	94	5.2	0									5	49	10	0																
Tom Colella	HB-DB	29	6'	187	24	6	11	77	7.0	1									4	63	16	1	1	36.0							5	113	23	1	1	13	13	0
Lew Mayne	HB-DB	27	6'1"	190	18		41	75	1.8	0									6	238	40	3													5	102	20	0
Jim Dewar	HB-DB	25	6'1"	190	6	1	14	64	4.6	1																					1	2	2	0	1	25	25	0
Mac Speedie	OE	27	6'3"	200	42		1	−7	−7.0	0									67	1146	17	6																
Dante Lavelli	OE	24	6'	190	54														49	799	16	9													1	10	10	0
John Yonakor	OE-DE	26	6'5"	218	12														6	95	16	2													1	0	0	0
Marshall Shurnas	OE-DE	25	6'1"	205															2	30	15	0																
Horace Gillom	OE-DE	26	6'1"	208		1													2	24	12	0	47	44.6														
Lou Groza	T	23	6'3"	214	60																				39	42	93	7	19	37								
Chet Adams	T	31	6'3"	228	4																				1	2	50	1	1	100								
SAN FRANCISCO 49ers																																						
Frankie Albert	QB	27	5'10"	160	30		46	179	3.9	5	242	128	53	1692	7.0	18	15–6	2					40	44.0	0	2	0								1	23	23	0
Jess Freitas	QB	26	5'10"	170		1	6	−9	−1.5	0	33	13	39	215	6.5	4	2–6						8	42.0														
Bev Wallace	QB	24	6'2"	180							16	5	31	48	3.0	0	2–13						2	39.0														
Johnny Strzykalski	HB-DB	24	5'9"	190	48	2	143	906	6.3	5	4	1	25	38	9.5	0	0–0		15	258	17	3									8	70	9	0	6	124	21	0
Norm Standlee	FB-LB	28	6'2"	245	48		145	585	4.0	8									2	22	11	0													3	24	8	0
Len Eshmont	HB-DB	30	5'11"	178	12	6	84	381	4.5	0									19	303	16	2									1	3	3	0	9	177	20	0
Ned Mathews	HB-DB	29	5'10"	182	30	4	39	238	6.1	2	2	0	0	0	0.0	0	0–0		6	51	9	2									4	44	11	0	2	46	23	0
Len Masini	FB-LB	26	6'	225	12	1	38	167	4.4	2																												
Earle Parsons	HB-DB	27	6'	180	12		33	125	3.8	0									9	163	18	2									10	106	11	0	4	99	25	0
Wally Yonamine	HB-DB	23	5'9"	180		1	19	74	3.9	0									3	40	13	0									2	29	15	0	7	127	18	0
Ed Carr	HB-DB	20	6'	185		2	11	42	3.8	0									4	41	10	0									1	20	20	0	2	42	21	0
Ed Robnett	FB-LB	27	5'8"	205			7	18	2.6	0																												
Joe Vetrano	HB-DB	25	5'9"	170	50		10	11	1.1	0															38	43	88	4	12	33	12	137	11	0	5	117	23	0
Don Durdan	HB-DB	27	5'9"	175			1	2	2.0	0																												
Alyn Beals	OE-DB	26	6'	185	60	1	5	48	9.6	0									47	655	14	10																
Nick Susoeff	OE-DE	26	6'1"	210	12														24	223	9	2																
Ed Balatti	OE-DB	23	6'1"	190	13														8	98	12	1			1	1	100				2	8	4	1	1	16	16	0
Bill Fisk	OE-DE	30	6'	200															5	39	8	0																
Dick Horne	OE-DE	29	6'2"	215															3	69	23	0																
Hank Norberg	OE-DE	28	6'2"	225															2	31	16	0																
LOS ANGELES DONS																																						
Charlie O'Rourke	QB	30	5'11"	175	6		24	55	2.3	1	178	89	50	1449	8.2	13	16–9	7																	1	24	24	0
Glenn Dobbs (from BKN)	QB-DB	27	6'4"	210	12	5	42	131	3.1	1	143	61	43	762	5.3	7	8–6	8	2	21	11	0	44	43.4							19	215	11	0	5	119	24	0
Bill Reinhard	QB-DB	25	5'10"	165	6	1	1	2	2.0	1	2	0	0	0	0.0	0	0–0														2	22	11	0				
John Kimbrough	FB	29	6'2"	210	66		131	562	4.3	8									16	281	18	3													4	96	24	0
Bob Kelly	HB-DB	22	5'10"	190	18	2	51	205	4.0	2									9	68	8	1									4	69	17	0	3	61	20	0
Chuck Fenenbock	HB-DB	29	5'9"	175	36		58	185	3.2	3	7	1	14	7	1.0	0	2–29		20	276	14	2									17	210	12	0	18	452	25	0
Harry Clark	HB-DB	29	6'	195	12		44	173	3.9	2									3	54	18	0									3	38	13	0	8	225	28	0
Bert Pigott	HB-DB	26	6'2"	195	6	1	46	161	3.5	0									7	63	9	1									1	7	7	0	5	120	24	0
Bob Reinhard	FB-DT	26	6'4"	230	6	1	41	150	3.7	0	4	2	50	21	5.3	0	0–0		3	34	11	1	28	45.7											3	42	14	0
Bob Mitchell	HB-DB	26	5'11"	195	6	2	32	85	2.7	0									3	36	12	1													6	119	20	0
Walt Clay (from CHI)	HB-DB	23	5'11"	195		1	9	42	4.7	0									1	52	52	0																
Mort Landsberg	HB-DB	28	5'11"	180			2	−11	−5.5	0									1	0	0	0																
Harry Hopp	FB-LB	28	6'	215		1	10	52	5.2	0									3	59	20	0													1	13	13	0
Walt Heap	HB-DB	25	6'1"	210	12	5	5	3	0.6	0									2	0	0	1																
Dale Gentry	OE-DE	30	6'3"	223	12														22	352	16	2																
Burr Baldwin	OE-DE	25	6'1"	200	6														12	275	23	1																
Ezz Anderson	OE-DE	27	6'4"	215	6		3	24	8.0	0									11	126	11	1																
Joe Aguirre	OE-DE	28	6'4"	225	24														8	158	20	4																
Bob Nowaskey	OE-DE	29	6'	200		2													8	106	13	0									1	22	22	0				
Bob Titchenal	OE-LB	29	6'2"	190			1	0	0.0	0									7	97	14	0																
Bob Nelson	C-LB-OE	27	6'1"	215	12	2													3	61	20	1																
Ben Agajanian	K	28	6'1"	210	84																				39	40	98	15	24	63								
CHICAGO ROCKETS																																						
Sam Vacanti	QB	25	5'11"	200	6		11	−9	−0.8	1	225	96	43	1571	7.0	16	16–7	6																				
Al Dekdebrun	QB-TB-DB	26	5'11"	180			20	71	3.6	0	75	45	60	556	7.4	5	7–9																					
Angelo Bertelli	QB	26	6'1"	190			1	2	2.0	0	7	2	29	−5	−0.7	0	2–29											0	1	0								
Norm Cox	QB	21	6'2"	210			1	−3	−3.0	0	2	1	50	9	4.5	0	0–0																					
Bill Daley	FB-DB	27	6'2"	210	24		121	447	3.7	4	6	3	50	70	11.7	1	1–17		12	116	10	0									1	3	3	0	7	145	21	0
Ray Ramsey	HB-DB	26	6'2"	170	60	5	70	433	6.2	2									35	768	22	8									11	131	12	0	16	406	25	0
Bill Kellagher	FB-DB	27	5'11"	205		6	42	243	5.8	0									3	22	7	0																
Fred Evans (from BUF)	HB-DB	26	5'11"	185	12		31	124	4.0	1	2	0	0	0	0.0	0	0–0		5	84	17	1	2	36.5							5	30	6	0	9	159	18	0
Crazy Legs Hirsch	HB-DB	23	6'2"	190	24		23	51	2.2	1	1	0	0	0	0.0	0	0–0		10	282	28	3									2	24	12	0	6	172	29	0
Ernie Lewis	FB-LB	23	6'1"	215			13	47	3.6	0													65	39.2														
Bill Schroeder	HB-DB	24	6'	190	18	4	11	45	4.1	0									2	19	10	1													5	92	18	0
Bill Bass	HB-DB	25	5'10"	180	12	2	28	44	1.6	0	1	1	100	14	14.0	0	0–0		8	79	10	1									10	85	9	0	12	264	22	0
Ted Scalissi	HB-DB	25	5'8"	173	12		35	37	1.1	0									5	67	13	2									2	26	13	0	8	171	21	0
Max Morris	OE	22	6'2"	200	12														22	239	11	1													1	13	13	0
John Harrington	OE	25	6'3"	198	18														17	233	14	3																
Tom Lahey	OE-DE	29	6'2"	218															13	148	11	0													2	18	9	0
Frank Quillen	OE-DE	25	6'5"	225	6														7	113	16	1																
Jerry Mulready	OE-DE	25	6'1"	205															7	108	15	0																
Bob Dove	OE-DE	26	6'2"	220	6														6	61	10	1													1	16	16	0
Ray Elbi	OE-DE	27	6'2"	210	6														4	38	10	1																
John Rokisky	OE-DE	27	6'2"	200	45														1	8	8	0			33	35	94	4	8	50								

PHILADELPHIA EAGLES 9-2-1 Greasy Neale

Scores of Each Game		
14	Chic. Cards.	21
28	Los Angeles	28
45	NEW YORK	0
45	Washington	0
12	CHIC. BEARS	7
34	Pittsburgh	7
35	New York	14
45	BOSTON	0
42	WASHINGTON	21
17	PITTSBURGH	0
14	Boston	37
45	DETROIT	21

Use Name	Pos.	Hgt	Wgt	Age	Int	Pts
Vic Lindskog	C-LB	6'1"	205	32		
Bap Manzini	C-LB	5'11"	195	28		
Frank Szymanski	C	6'	230	25		
Alex Wojciechowicz	C-LB	5'11"	232	33	1	
John Green	OE-DE	6'1"	192	26		
(2 kickoff returns for 24 yds.)						
Hal Prescott	OE-DB	6'2"	193	27		
Al Johnson	DB	6'	175	23		
(1 punt for 5 yards)						

Use Name – Tackles	Pos.	Hgt	Wgt	Age	Int	Pts
Otis Douglas	T	6'1"	225	36		
Fred Hartman	T	6'1"	222	28		
Jay MacDowell	T	6'2"	215	29		
George Savitsky	T	6'2"	245	24		
Vic Sears	T	6'3"	225	30		
Al Wistert	T	6'1"	214	27		

Use Name – Guards	Pos.	Hgt	Wgt	Age	Int	Pts
Walt Barnes	G	6'1"	233	30		2
Mario Giannelli	G	6'	270	27		
Bucko Kilroy	G	6'2"	244	27		
John Magee	G	5'10"	220	25		
Duke Maronic	G	5'9"	210	27		

An opening-day loss to the defending champion Cardinals didn't discourage the Eagles from riding roughshod over the Eastern Division for another trip to the championship game. Coach Greasy Neale had the best of everything at his command—the league's best runner in Steve Van Buren, a passer in Tommy Thompson, second only to Sammy Baugh in the NFL, an outstanding two-way end in Pete Pihos, fine tackles in Al Wistert and Vic Sears, a league-leading kicker in Cliff Patton, and a league-leading punter in Joe Muha. Aided by a supporting cast of strong players, the Eagles confidently entered into the title rematch with the Cardinals.

WASHINGTON REDSKINS 7-5-0 Turk Edwards

Scores of Each Game		
17	PITTSBURGH	14
41	NEW YORK	10
7	Pittsburgh	10
0	PHILADELPHIA	45
23	Green Bay	7
59	BOSTON	21
23	Boston	7
46	DETROIT	21
21	Philadelphia	42
13	Chic. Bears	48
13	LOS ANGELES	41
28	New York	21

Use Name	Pos.	Hgt	Wgt	Age	Int	Pts
Don Corbitt	C-LB	6'4"	224	24		
Al DeMao	C-LB	6'2"	223	28	1	
Clyde Ehrhardt	C-LB	6'1"	232	27	2	
Jim Peebles	DE	6'4"	234	28		1
(1 PAT in 2 attempts)						
Hal Shoener	DE	6'3"	207	25		
Art Macioszczyk	FB-LB	5'9"	200	27		
Howie Livingston	DB	6'1"	197	26		

Use Name – Tackles	Pos.	Hgt	Wgt	Age	Int	Pts
John Adams	T	6'7"	237	26		
Carl Butkus (to NY-AAFC)	T	6'1"	245	26		
Weldon Edwards	T	6'	225	24		
John Koniszewski	T	6'3"	252	29		2
Mike Roussos	T	6'3"	235	22		
John Sanchez	T	6'3"	240	27		
Ed Stacco	T	6'2"	272	23		

Use Name – Guards	Pos.	Hgt	Wgt	Age	Int	Pts
Fred Boensch	G	6'4"	230	28		
Bill Gray	G	5'11"	210	25		
Hank Harris	G-T	6'	270	25		
Mike Katrishen	G	6'1"	215	25		
John Steber	G	6'	233	25		

The time had come to groom a successor for Sammy Baugh, so the Redskins drafted Alabama quarterback Harry Gilmer. Owner George Marshall had been so impressed by Gilmer's college career that he sold the draft rights to rookie passer Charlie Conerly to the New York Giants. It was a decision that Marshall would regret, as Gilmer's career became plagued with injuries while Conerly played fourteen years as the Giant quarterback.

Baugh, meantime, wasn't so old that he couldn't hold down the fort. Against the Boston Yanks, he threw for 446 yards in driving the Skins to a 59-21 laugher, and the Skins' offense pumped out points at a steady clip. But the defense had a talent for making mediocre passers look like Baugh himself. Opponents passed so often against the Skins that rookie safetyman Dan Sandifer wound up with a record thirteen interceptions.

NEW YORK GIANTS 4-8-0 Steve Owen

Scores of Each Game		
27	Boston	7
10	Washington	41
0	Philadelphia	45
35	CHIC. CARDS	63
34	PITTSBURGH	27
14	Chic. Bears	35
14	PHILADELPHIA	35
37	LOS ANGELES	52
49	Green Bay	3
28	BOSTON	14
28	Pittsburgh	38
21	WASHINGTON	28

Use Name	Pos.	Hgt	Wgt	Age	Int	Pts
John Cannady	C-LB	6'2"	225	24	2	
Carl Fennema	C-LB	6'2"	210	22		6
Art Faircloth	DB-HB	6'	190	28	3	
(1 rush for –1 yd.)						
Ken Keuper	DB	6'	200	30	1	
Declared ineligible – Frankie Filchock, Merle Hapes						

Use Name – Tackles	Pos.	Hgt	Wgt	Age	Int	Pts
Larry Beil	T	6'2"	235	24		
Tex Coulter	T	6'4"	245	23		
Bill Schuler	T	6'	215	26		
John Treadaway	T	6'5"	250	28		
Jim White	T	6'2"	228	27		6
(1 kickoff return for 6 yds.)						
Ernie Williamson	T	6'4"	250	25		

Use Name – Guards	Pos.	Hgt	Wgt	Age	Int	Pts
Bob Dobelstein	G-LB	5'11"	212	26	1	6
Bill Erickson	G-LB	6'2"	210	26		
Don Ettinger	G-LB	6'2"	210	25	2	
Mike Garzoni (to NY-AAFC)	G	5'11"	220	24		
Ed Royston	G	6'1"	220	25		
(1 kickoff return for 5 yds.)						

The Redskins did the Giants more favors than anyone in the last few years. The Skins had sent Frankie Filchock to New York in 1946, and Filchock promptly led the Giants to an Eastern title. This year, the Redskins sold the draft rights to passer Chuck Conerly to the Giants. Although he demonstrated his passing ability by completing a record thirty-six passes in fifty-three attempts against the Steelers, Pittsburgh won the game 38-28—a game that seemed to summarize the Giants' season. The New Yorkers could score but could not stop their opponents from doing the same. Seven times they gave up 35 or more points in a game, grounding the offense with a handicap too heavy to overcome. Since Conerly was not a gifted runner, and the Giants did not have an outstanding center like Mel Hein (a necessity for a successful A-formation team), Steve Owen installed the T formation as the Giants basic offense in mid-season. So 1948 was truly a "rebuilding" season for New York.

PITTSBURGH STEELERS 4-8-0 John Michelosen

Scores of Each Game		
14	Washington	17
24	BOSTON	14
10	WASHINGTON	7
7	Boston	13
27	New York	34
7	PHILADELPHIA	34
38	GREEN BAY	7
7	CHIC. CARDS	24
14	Detroit	17
0	Philadelphia	17
38	NEW YORK	28
14	Los Angeles	31

Use Name	Pos.	Hgt	Wgt	Age	Int	Pts
Chuck Cherundolo	C-LB	6'1"	220	32		
Bryant Meeks	C-LB	6'2"	195	22		
Frank Sinkovitz	C-LB	6'1"	215	25	1	
Roy Kurrasch	DE	6'2"	195	26		
Ed Ryan	DE	6'2"	200	22		
Bill Garnaas	WB	5'11"	183	27		
(1 kickoff return for 18 yds.)						

Use Name – Tackles	Pos.	Hgt	Wgt	Age	Int	Pts
John Mastrangelo	T	6'1"	225	22		
Carl Samuelson	T	6'4"	245	25	1	
Hubert Shurtz	T	6'3"	235	25		
Jack Wiley	T	5'11"	210	27		
Frank Wydo	T	6'4"	215	24		

Use Name – Guards	Pos.	Hgt	Wgt	Age	Int	Pts
Bill Cregar	G-LB	5'11"	200	23		
Bill Moore	G	5'11"	220	25		
Leo Nobile	G-LB	5'10"	215	26		
Nick Skorich	G	5'9"	200	27		
Steve Suhey	G	5'11"	215	26		
(1 kickoff return for 11 yds.)						

Coach Jock Sutherland was scouring the South for talent in April when his recurrent headaches forced him into the hospital. Within six days he was dead of a brain tumor. Assistant John Michelosen took over as head coach but could not inspire the team to perform as Sutherland had done. The single-wing offense rolled like a steamroller some days and rolled over dead on others. The defense also fluctuated between generous and miserly, and the team's fortunes, consistently tough under Sutherland, went from Jekyll to Hyde from week to week.

BOSTON YANKS 3-9-0 Clipper Smith

Scores of Each Game		
0	GREEN BAY	31
7	NEW YORK	28
14	Pittsburgh	24
17	Detroit	14
13	PITTSBURGH	7
27	Chic. Cards	49
21	Washington	59
7	WASHINGTON	23
0	Philadelphia	45
17	CHIC. BEARS	51
14	New York	28
37	PHILADELPHIA	14

Use Name	Pos.	Hgt	Wgt	Age	Int	Pts
Joe Domnanovich	C-LB	6'1"	215	29	1	
(1 punt return for 29 yds.)						
Bill Godwin	C-LB	6'3"	245	29		
Vaughn Mancha	C-LB	6'1"	230	27		
George Sullivan	OE-DE	6'2"	205	22		
Mike Micka	DB-HB	6'	185	27	3	
(4 rushing attempts for 3 yds.)						
Dave Ryan	DB-HB	5'10"	190	25		
(3 rushing attempts for 1 yd.)						

Use Name – Tackles	Pos.	Hgt	Wgt	Age	Int	Pts
Bob Davis	T	6'4"	235	21		
Mike Jarmoluk	T	6'5"	252	25	2	
John Nolan	T	6'2"	230	22		
George Roman	T	6'4"	232	22		
Carroll Vogelaar	T	6'3"	260	28		

Use Name – Guards	Pos.	Hgt	Wgt	Age	Int	Pts
John Badaczewski (to CHIC)	G	6'1"	235	26		
Fritz Barzilauskas	G	6'1"	230	27		
Stan Batinski	G	5'10"	215	31		
Bob McClure	G	6'1"	224	24		
(2 kickoff returns for 14 yds.)						
Joe Sebasteanski	G-LB	6'	208	27	2	

The fact that a low number of fans showed up to see the Yanks did not stop them from having some shining moments in yet another losing season. In one mid-season stretch, the defense got tough enough to post back-to-back victories over the Lions and Steelers. Aided by Philadelphia's overconfidence, the Yanks reached their highest peak when they upset the title-bound Eagles 37-14 in a late-season encounter. They lost their other nine games, though—most of them not even close—and wound up with a financial statement far short of the break-even point. The fact was enough to prompt owner Ted Collins to move the club to New York for the 1949 season.

TEAM TOTALS

	FIRST DOWNS:				RUSHING:				PASSING:									PUNTING:		PUNT RETURNS:				KICKOFF RETURNS:				INTERCEPTION RETURNS:				PENALTIES:		FUMBLES:		POINTS:					
OFFENSE	Tot	by Rsh	by Pas	by Pen	No.	Yds.	Avg. Yds.	TD	Att.	Com	Comp. Pct.	Yds.	Avg. Yds. Att.	Avg. Yds. Comp	TD	Int.	Pct. Int.	No.	Avg. Yds.	No.	Yds.	Avg. Yds.	TD	No.	Yds.	Avg. Yds.	TD	No.	Yds.	Avg. Yds.	TD	No.	Yds.	No.	Lost	Tot	PAT	FG Att	FG	Saf.	OFFENSE
PHIL.	241	119	99	23	528	2378	4.5	21	301	159	52.8	2241	7.5	14.1	27	16	5.3	62	45.9	51	554	10.9	1	32	681	21.3	0	23	228	9.9	0	86	773	35	18	376	50	17	8	1	PHIL.
WASH.	236	93	120	23	434	1603	3.7	11	360	202	56.1	2861	7.9	14.2	24	26	7.2	51	42.2	34	370	10.9	0	54	1164	21.6	1	24	482	20.1	2	122	1100	30	17	291	34	7	5	1	WASH.
N.Y.	212	81	114	17	362	1219	3.4	12	363	191	52.6	2504	6.9	13.1	24	16	4.4	78	38.6	24	212	8.8	0	57	1238	21.7	1	39	561	14.4	2	95	815	36	20	297	40	8	1	1	N.Y.
PITT.	210	122	68	20	510	1934	3.8	17	266	108	40.6	1529	5.8	14.2	8	29	10.9	63	39.0	36	353	9.8	0	42	846	20.1	0	13	320	24.6	1	63	616	43	17	200	26	10	4	0	PITT.
BOSTON	121	55	55	11	365	1170	3.2	4	261	101	38.7	1308	5.0	13.0	13	34	13.0	93	42.0	40	507	12.7	0	54	1090	20.2	0	18	374	20.8	3	81	813	40	20	174	21	7	3	0	BOSTON

Use Name – Backs & Ends	Pos.	Age	Hgt	Wgt	Pts	Int	RUSHING				PASSING								RECEIVING				PUNTING		KICKING						PUNT RETURNS				KICKOFF RETURNS			
							No.	Yds	Avg	TD	Att	Comp	%	Yds	Yd/Att	TD	Int–%	RK	No.	Yds	Avg	TD	No.	Avg	Pat	Att	%	FG	Att	%	No.	Yds	Avg	TD	No.	Yds	Avg	TD
PHILADELPHIA EAGLES																																						
Tommy Thompson	QB	32	6'1"	195	6		12	46	3.8	1	246	141	57	1965	8.0	25	11–4	2																				
Bill Mackrides	QB	23	5'11"	180			7	4	0.6	0	53	18	34	276	5.2	2	4–8																					
Steve Van Buren	HB-DB	27	6'	205	60	2	201	945	4.7	10	1	0	0	0	0.0	0	0–0		10	96	10	0													14	292	21	0
Bosh Pritchard	HB-DB	29	5'11"	163	48		117	517	4.4	4									27	252	9	2									24	282	12	1	9	249	28	0
Noble Doss	HB-DB	28	6'	189			62	193	3.1	0									8	96	12	0									1	0	0	0	1	26	26	0
Jim Parmer	HB-DB	21	6'	190	18	1	30	167	5.6	3																									1	14	14	0
Jack Myers	FB-LB	23	6'2"	200	6	2	21	118	5.6	1									7	57	8	0																
Ben Kish	FB-LB	31	6'	210	6	3	10	106	10.6	1																					1	0	0	0				
Ernie Steele	HB-DB	30	6'	186	12	6	13	99	7.6	1	1	0	0	0	0.0	0	1–100		2	43	22	1									1	5	5	0	2	30	15	0
Joe Muha	FB-LB	27	6'1"	205	6		25	90	3.6	0									2	22	11	1	57	47.2				0	5	0								
Russ Craft	HB-DB	28	5'9"	170	12		13	67	5.2	0									4	138	35	2									3	32	11	0				
Gil Steinke	HB-DB	28	6'	172			5	17	3.4	0																									1	17	17	0
Pat McHugh	HB-DB	28	5'11"	165		2	4	12	3.0	0																					18	220	12	0				
Les Palmer	HB-DB	24	6'	180																			4	37.0							1	8	8	0	1	20	20	0
Pete Phios	OE-DE	24	6'1"	215	66		8	−3	−0.4	0									46	766	17	11													1	9	9	0
Jack Ferrante	OE-DE	32	6'1"	205	42														28	444	16	7																
Neill Armstrong	OE-DB	22	6'2"	188	18	2													24	325	14	3																
Dick Humbert	OE-DB	29	6'1"	180		4													1	2	2	0									2	7	4	0				
Cliff Patton	G	24	6'2"	240	74																				50	50	100	8	12	67								
WASHINGTON REDSKINS																																						
Sammy Baugh	QB	34	6'2"	180	6		4	4	1.0	1	315	185	59	2599	8.3	22	23–7	1																				
Tommy Mont	QB-DB	26	6'	197	6	2	11	103	9.4	1	28	12	43	157	5.6	2	2–7																					
Harry Gilmer	QB	22	6'	160							5	2	40	69	13.8	0	0–0																					
Jim Castiglia	FB	29	5'11"	205	12		97	330	3.4	0									7	73	10	2													1	18	18	0
Ed Quirk	FB-LB	23	6'1"	230	24		77	328	4.3	4									9	40	4	0																
Dick Poillon	HB	28	6'	198	66		71	233	3.3	1									9	105	12	1	51	42.2	33	38	87	5	7	71								
Dick Todd	HB-DB	33	5'11"	174	42		57	201	3.5	1									37	550	15	6									3	21	7	0	3	50	17	0
Tom Farmer	HB-DB	27	5'11"	193	18		52	188	3.6	1									12	148	12	2									4	34	9	0	8	192	24	0
Dan Sandifer	HB-DB	21	6'1"	190	24	13	18	67	3.7	0									9	181	20	1									20	236	12	0	26	594	23	1
Bob Nussbaumer	HB-DB	24	5'11"	176	6		23	59	2.6	0									19	252	13	1									1	−8	−8	0	2	38	19	0
Howard Hartley	HB-DB	24	6'	185	6	3	5	40	8.0	1									1	10	10	0									2	41	21	0	4	64	16	0
Eddie Saenz	HB-DB	25	5'11"	168			8	21	2.6	0									4	62	16	0									2	26	13	0	8	173	22	0
John Holler	FB-LB	26	6'	220			4	7	1.8	0																												
Tippy Madarik	HB-DB	26	5'11"	205			2	7	3.5	0																									1	20	20	0
Steve Bagarus	HB-DB	29	6'	173	6		3	6	2.0	0									15	100	7	1													1	15	15	0
Hal Crisler	OE-DB	24	6'4"	215	36	2													33	599	18	6									2	20	10	0				
Hugh Taylor	OE	25	6'4"	192	18						1	0	0	0	0.0	0	0–0		20	341	17	3																
Paul McKee	OE-DE	25	6'3"	220															14	171	12	0																
Doug Turley	OE-DE	29	6'2"	230	6														8	111	14	0																
Joe Tereshinski	OE-DE	24	6'2"	214	6														4	98	25	1																
NEW YORK GIANTS																																						
Charlie Conerly	QB	24	6'1"	183	30		40	180	4.0	5	299	162	54	2175	7.3	22	13–4	6					17	39.9											4	72	18	0
Paul Governali	QB	27	5'11"	190			6	−48	−8.0	0	56	27	48	280	5.0	1	1–2																					
Choo-Choo Roberts	FB	24	5'11"	188	18		145	491	3.4	0									14	222	16	3									1	10	10	0	7	160	23	0
Joe Scott	HB-DB	22	6'1"	200	30	5	48	198	4.1	2									17	235	14	2									3	25	8	0	20	568	28	1
Ray Coates	HB-DB	24	6'1"	190	18		50	176	3.6	3	2	1	50	28	13.0	1	0–0																		6	107	18	0
Skippy Minisi	HB-DB	21	5'11"	190	12	2	36	160	4.4	1	3	0	0	0	0.0	0	2–67		13	123	9	1									3	25	8	0	4	82	21	0
Em Tunnell	HB-DB	26	6'1"	187	6	7	17	43	2.5	0	2	1	50	23	11.5	0	0–0		4	32	8	0									12	115	10	0	1	21	21	0
George Cheverko (from WAS)	HB-WB-DB	27	6'1"	195		6	3	10	3.3	0									1	41	41	0									1	5	5	0	3	80	27	0
John Atwood	HB-WB-DB	23	5'11"	185	6	1	9	6	0.7	0									10	141	14	1									4	32	8	0	3	58	19	0
Frank Williams	FB-LB	26	6'	212	4														1	5	5	0			4	5	80	0	1	0								
Jules Siegle	FB-LB	25	6'	210			2	6	3.0	0																									1	12	12	0
Joe Sulaitis	BB-DE	27	6'2"	210	12		5	18	3.6	1	1	0	0	0	0.0	0	0–0		26	298	11	1													4	66	17	0
Joe Johnson	WB-DB	23	6'2"	195	12														19	217	11	2																
Frank Reagan	DB	29	5'11"	180		9																	61	38.2														
Bill Swiacki	OE	23	6'2"	195	60														39	550	14	10													1	0	0	0
Ray Poole	OE-DE	26	6'2"	215	26														35	492	14	3																
Bruce Gehrke	OE-DB	23	6'2"	190	6														9	109	12	1																
Joyce Pipkin	OE-DE	24	6'1"	203															2	28	14	0																
Paul Walker	OE-DB	23	6'3"	210		1													1	11	11	0																
Len Younce	G-LB	31	6'1"	210	39																				39	37	97	1	7	14								
PITTSBURGH STEELERS																																						
Ray Evans	TB-DB	25	6'1"	195	12		99	343	3.5	2	137	64	47	924	6.7	5	17–12	11	7	93	13	0	1	0.0							10	133	13	0	7	122	17	0
Johnny Clement	TB	28	6'	190	12		67	261	3.9	2	58	18	32	281	4.8	3	7–12																					
Gonzales Morales	TB-DB	25	6'	185	6	1	13	29	2.2	0	4	3	75	30	7.5	0	0–0														8	83	10	0	3	62	21	0
Norm Mosley	TB-DB	26	5'9"	185	6		13	39	3.0	1	2	0	0	0	0.0	0	0–0														7	52	7	0	1	31	31	0
Bob Cifers	HB-DB	27	5'11"	195	6		112	361	3.2	1	4	0	0	0	0.0	0	1–25		4	55	14	0	62	39.6							1	8	8	0	9	245	27	0
George Papach	FB-DB	23	6'2"	205	18		60	324	5.4	2									4	72	18	1													1	16	16	0
Jerry Shipkey	FB-DB	23	6'1"	210	48		64	199	3.1	8									10	106	11	0													2	34	17	0
Joe Glamp	HB-DB	25	5'11"	185	56		28	167	5.9	1	1	0	0	0	0.0	0	0–0		9	138	15	2			26	27	96	4	10	40	1	15	15	0	7	158	23	0
Jerry Nuzum	HB-DB	25	6'1"	195		1	26	109	4.2	0									2	37	19	0									1	7	7	0	6	122	20	0
Tony Compagno	FB-DB	27	5'11"	200	6	7	24	101	4.2	0									1	4	4	0									4	21	5	0				
Paul Davis	FB-DB	23	6'1"	190		1	2	−1	−0.5	0																					4	34	9	0	1	13	13	0
Joe Gasparella	BB-LB	21	6'4"	225			1	5	5.0	0	57	23	40	294	5.2	0	4–7																					
Charlie Seabright	BB-LB	30	6'2"	205	6	1					1	0	0	0	0.0	0	0–0		8	63	8	1													1	4	4	0
Val Jansante	OE	27	6'1"	190	18		1	−3	−3.0	0									39	623	16	3																
Elbie Nickel	OE-DE	25	6'1"	190	6														22	324	15	1																
Bob Davis	OE-DE	27	5'11"	190															2	14	7	0													1	8	8	0
Charlie Mehelich	OE-DE	26	6'1"	195							2	0	0	0	0.0	0	0–0																		1	2	2	0
BOSTON YANKS																																						
Roy Zimmerman	QB	30	6'2"	205	16		13	72	5.5	0	107	46	43	649	6.1	7	13–12	12					51	43.4	13	15	87	1	4	25								
Jim Youel (to WAS)	QB	26	6'	175	6		19	79	4.1	1	36	9	25	99	2.8	2	4–11		1	20	20	0	2	32.5														
Boley Dancewicz	QB	23	5'10"	188	6		4	3	0.8	1	35	17	49	186	5.3	0	5–14																					
Gene Malinowski	TB-DB	23	6'1"	210		1	11	21	1.9	0	54	15	28	218	4.0	3	7–13		3	−10	−3	0																
Phil Slosburg	TB-HB-DB	21	5'10"	170			32	89	2.8	0	20	8	40	119	6.0	1	3–15		2	29	15	0									10	141	14	0	1	37	37	0
Frank Nelson	TB-HB-DB	25	5'9"	167		1	18	60	3.3	0	17	8	47	71	4.2	0	2–12		1	10	10	0									2	27	14	0	3	34	11	0
Al Dekdebrun (from NY-AAFC)	TB-DB	27	5'11"	185			2	14	7.0	0	3	1	33	2	0.7	1	1–33																					
Bill Paschal	FB-LB	27	6'	212	30		80	249	3.1	1									8	93	12	4	2	40.0							3	79	26	0	24	498	21	0
Frank Seno	HB-DB	27	6'	204	18	1	71	242	3.4	0									13	322	25	3									13	99	8	0	8	171	21	0
Frank Muehlheuser	FB-LB	22	6'2"	215	6		38	169	4.4	1									3	19	6	0	1	46.0											1	27	27	0
Rudy Romboli	FB-LB	25	5'10"	210	6		25	90	3.6	1									8	77	10	0													1	22	22	0
Joe Golding	HB-DB	27	6'	184	36	4	24	36	1.5	0									9	159	18	4									10	129	13	0	7	192	27	0
John Poto	HB-DB	22	5'10"	190			13	32	2.5	0									10	101	10	0									1	3	3	0	1	16	16	0
Bob Hazelhurst	HB-DB	24	6'	188			11	15	1.4	0													2	50.0											2	31	16	0
Ralph Heywood (from DET)	OE-DE	26	6'2"	205	18		1	11	11.0	0									14	208	15	1	46	38.4											1	8	8	0
Bill Chipley	OE-DB	28	6'3"	192	12	3													13	131	10	1																
Jim Tyree	OE-DE	26	6'3"	204	6														13	106	8	0													1	17	17	0
Steve Pritko	OE-DE	26	6'2"	210	6														3	42	14	0													2	23	12	0
Nick Scollard	OE-DE	28	6'4"	215	14														2	23	12	0			8	8	100	2	3	67								

TEAM TOTALS

DEFENSE	FIRST DOWNS: Tot	by Rsh	by Pas	by Pen	RUSHING: No.	Yds.	Avg Yds.	TD	PASSING: Att	Com	Comp Pct.	Yds.	Avg. Yds. Att.	Avg. Yds. Comp	TD	Int	Pct. Int.	PUNTING: No.	Avg. Yds.	PUNT RETURNS: No.	Yds.	Avg. Yds.	TD	KICKOFF RETURNS: No.	Yds.	Avg. Yds.	TD	INTERCEPTION RETURNS: No.	Yds.	Avg. Yds.	TD	PENALTIES: No.	Yds.	FUMBLES: No.	Lost	POINTS: Tot	PAT	FG Att	FG	Saf.	DEFENSE
PHIL.	158	62	83	13	376	1208	3.2	5	338	139	41.1	1951	5.8	14.0	14	23	6.8	88	38.8	38	411	10.8	0	48	990	20.6	0	16	257	16.1	2	87	860	33	16	156	21	5	1	0	PHIL.
WASH,	233	114	93	26	482	1958	4.1	17	289	135	46.7	1953	6.8	14.5	20	24	8.3	52	43.8	30	383	12.8	0	44	1079	24.5	1	26	389	15.0	0	81	771	40	18	287	38	10	3	0	WASH.
N.Y.	227	109	106	12	481	2168	4.5	26	311	157	50.5	2406	7.7	15.3	25	30	12.6	57	39.5	55	812	14.8	2	56	1242	22.2	0	16	216	13.5	1	104	880	34	11	388	52	8	4	0	N.Y.
PITT.	188	90	83	15	434	1648	3.8	7	279	149	53.4	1987	7.1	13.3	18	13	4.7	67	42.8	33	374	11.3	1	35	622	17.8	0	29	378	13.0	0	106	927	29	18	243	30	16	7	0	PITT.
BOSTON	244	124	100	20	511	2320	4.5	19	356	161	45.2	2483	6.9	15.3	27	18	5.1	69	40.2	51	469	9.2	0	36	702	19.5	0	34	507	14.9	0	104	929	46	24	372	48	11	6	0	BOSTON

CHICAGO CARDINALS 11-1-0 Jimmy Conzelman

Scores of Each Game		
21	PHILADELPHIA	14
17	CHIC. BEARS	28
17	Green Bay	7
63	New York	35
49	BOSTON	27
27	Los Angeles	22
56	DETROIT	20
24	Pittsburgh	7
27	LOS ANGELES	24
28	Detroit	14
42	GREEN BAY	7
24	Chic. Bears	21

Use Name	Pos.	Hgt	Wgt	Age	Int	Pts
Vince Banonis	C-LB	6'1"	232	26	2	
Bill Blackburn	C-LB	6'6"	230	26	2	12
Bill Campbell	LB	6'	195	28		
Bob Dove	DE	6'2"	220	27		
(1 rush for –2 yds.)						
Sam Goldman	DE	6'3"	235	31		
Frank Liebel	OE-DE	6'1"	220	28		
Jack Doolan	DE	6'1"	190	29		
Marshall Goldberg	DB	5'11"	195	30	2	
Bob Ravensburg	DB	6'	190	23	1	

Use Name – Tackles	Pos.	Hgt	Wgt	Age	Int	Pts
Chet Bulger	T	6'3"	238	30		
Joe Coomer	DG-T	6'6"	283	29		
Marv Jacobs	T	6'2"	235	23		
Dick Loepfe	T	6'2"	230	27		
Stan Mauldin	T	6'2"	226	27		
died of heart attack – September 24.						
Walt Szot	T	6'1"	218	29		
Bob Zimny	T	6'1"	235	27		

Use Name – Guards	Pos.	Hgt	Wgt	Age	Int	Pts
Plato Andros	G	6'	242	27		
Ray Apolskis	G-LB	5'11"	210	29		
Lloyd Arms	G	6'1"	215	29		
Jake Colhauer	G	6'1"	215	26		
Ham Nichols	G-LB	5'11"	210	24		
Buster Ramsey	G-LB	6'1"	215	28	1	
Dick Wedel	G	5'11"	205	25		

After the opening-day victory over the Eagles, the Cardinal clubhouse should have been a scene of jubilation. Instead, tragedy and grief filled the room. Star tackle Stan Mauldin had keeled over after the game and died of a heart attack. The Cardinals rekindled their spirits, though, and came down to the final game of the season tied with the Bears for the Western Division lead. Earlier in the year, the Bears had beaten the Cardinals 28-17, but this time the Cardinals came through with a 24-21 victory and the Western crown.

CHICAGO BEARS 10-2-0 George Halas

Scores of Each Game		
45	Green Bay	7
28	Chic. Cards	17
42	LOS ANGELES	21
28	DETROIT	0
7	Philadelphia	12
35	NEW YORK	14
21	Los Angeles	6
7	GREEN BAY	6
51	Boston	17
48	WASHINGTON	13
42	Detroit	14
21	CHIC. CARDS	24

Use Name	Pos.	Hgt	Wgt	Age	Int	Pts
Stu Clarkson	C-LB	6'2"	220	29	2	
Thurman Garrett	C	6'3"	260	24		
Bulldog Turner	C-LB	6'1"	235	29	2	
Ed Cifers	OE-DE	6'2"	230	32		
(1 rush for 5 yds.)						
Hank Norberg	OE-DE	6'2"	225	29		
(1 reception for 4 yds.)						

Use Name – Tackles	Pos.	Hgt	Wgt	Age	Int	Pts
Alf Bauman	T	6'2"	235	28		
George Connor	T	6'3"	240	23		
(1 kickoff return for 5 yds.)						
Fred Davis	T	6'3"	248	30		
Paul Stenn	T	6'2"	240	30		
Walt Stickel	T	6'3"	245	26		

Use Name – Guards	Pos.	Hgt	Wgt	Age	Int	Pts
Ray Bray	G	6'	240	31		
(1 kickoff return for 8 yds.)						
Chuck Drulis	G-LB	5'10"	215	30	1	
Bill Milner	G-LB	6'1"	215	24		
Pat Preston	G-LB	6'2"	220	25		
Wash Serini	G	6'2"	235	24		

George Halas opened his wallet wide to outbid the AAFC for three blue-chip rookies, quarterbacks Johnny Lujack and Bobby Layne and tackle George Connor. Lujack signed an $18,000 contract, Layne got a $10,000 bonus to ink a $22,500 pact, and Connor signed a no-cut contract, all exceptional deals for freshman pro-football players. With veteran Sid Luckman still running the offense, Lujack played mostly on defense, while Layne mostly sat and watched and Connor saw action both on offense and defense.

Yet even with these fine rookies, it was the veteran ball players who kept the Bears in the running for the Western Division crown right to the end. Going into the season's finale with the Cardinals, the two Chicago teams were tied for the lead, but the Cardinals won a return trip to the championship game with a 24-21 victory. Once again, the Bears had been beaten at the wire.

LOS ANGELES RAMS 6-5-1 Clark Shaughnessy

Scores of Each Game		
44	DETROIT	7
28	PHILADELPHIA	28
21	Chic. Bears	42
0	Green Bay	16
34	Detroit	27
22	CHIC. CARDS	27
6	CHIC. BEARS	21
52	New York	37
24	Chic. Cards	27
24	GREEN BAY	10
41	Washington	13
31	PITTSBURGH	14

Use Name	Pos.	Hgt	Wgt	Age	Int	Pts
Jack Martin	C-LB	6'3"	240	26		
Fred Naumetz	C-LB	6'1"	222	26	4	
Don Paul	C-LB	6'1"	230	23		
Bob DeFruiter	DB-HB	6'	190	31		
(3 rushing attempts for 4 yds.)						

Use Name – Tackles	Pos.	Hgt	Wgt	Age	Int	Pts
Gil Bouley	T	6'2"	235	27		
(1 reception for 15 yds., 1 kickoff return for 8 yds.)						
Ed Champagne	T	6'3"	240	26		
Dick Huffman	T	6'2"	256	25		
Joe Repko	T	6'	240	27		
Al Sparkman	T	6'6"	253	23		

Use Name – Guards	Pos.	Hgt	Wgt	Age	Int	Pts
Bob David (to CHI-AAFC)	G-LB	6'	215	26		
Hal Dean	G-LB	6'	205	25	1	
Roger Eason	G	6'2"	230	30		
Jack Finlay	G-LB	6'1"	215	27		
Mike Lazetich	G-LB	6'1"	214	27		
Ray Yagiello	G-LB	6'	220	25		

When the Rams made Clark Shaughnessy their new head coach, they brought in one of football's greatest strategic minds. George Halas had hired the ex-Stanford coach as a consultant in the early 1940s, and Shaughnessy added subtle changes to the T formation which made the Bears the scourge of the league. Rams owner Dan Reeves had hoped that the little tactician could give the Los Angeles attack some of the same medicine he had provided the Bears. But even with some of the players resenting Shaughnessy's strict method of dealing with them, all were amazed by the scope of his football theories.

And score the Rams did, despite the loss of last year's top passing combination. Big Jim Benton called it a career, leaving quarterback Bob Waterfield without his favorite receiver, and Waterfield himself soon was on the sidelines with an injury. Shaughnessy gave the quarterback job to second-stringer Jim Hardy and turned the vacant end position over to rookie Tom Fears. Freezing defensive backs with a variety of moves, Fears caught the most passes of any end in the league. Hardy also came through in fine fashion, shining most brightly by passing for 406 yards in a game against the Cardinals. But a soft defense held the Rams down in third place as enemy quarterbacks simply ran their plays away from big tackle Dick Huffman.

GREEN BAY PACKERS 3-9-0 Curly Lambeau

Scores of Each Game		
31	Boston	0
7	CHIC. BEARS	45
33	DETROIT	21
7	CHIC. CARDS	17
16	LOS ANGELES	0
7	WASHINGTON	23
20	Detroit	24
7	Pittsburgh	38
6	Chic. Bears	7
3	NEW YORK	49
10	Los Angeles	24
7	Chic. Cards	42

Use Name	Pos.	Hgt	Wgt	Age	Int	Pts
Lloyd Baxter	C	6'2"	210	25		
Bob Flowers	C-LB	6'1"	210	31	4	
Jay Rhodemyre	C-LB	6'1"	210	26	1	
Larry Craig	DE-LB	6'1"	218	32		
Ted Cremer	DE	6'2"	210	29		
Don Wells	DE	6'2"	200	26		

Use Name – Tackles	Pos.	Hgt	Wgt	Age	Int	Pts
Ed Bell	T	6'1"	233	26		
Jim Kekeris	T	6'1"	257	24		
Paul Lipscomb	T	6'5"	245	25		
Urban Odson	T	6'3"	250	29		
Baby Ray	T	6'6"	250	33		
Dick Wildung	T	6'	220	26		

Use Name – Guards	Pos.	Hgt	Wgt	Age	Int	Pts
Ralph Davis	G	5'11"	205	26		
Don Deeks	G	6'4"	245	25		
Ed Neal	G	6'4"	290	30		
Larry Olsonoski	G	6'2"	214	23		
Damon Tassos	G	6'1"	225	24		
Red Vogds	G	5'10"	215	25		

After an early-season 17-7 loss to the Cardinals, coach Curly Lambeau fined the entire squad half of one week's salary for "indifferent play." The players did not feel they had been indifferent, but they believed that a good game against the Rams would get their money back. The Packers easily downed the Rams 16-0, bringing their season's record up to 3-2-0. Expecting an extra-large paycheck, the players blew their stacks when they did not get back the fine money. Morale dropped to zero, and the Packers lost every other game this year. Finally, in January, when it was too late, Lambeau returned the players' money.

DETROIT LIONS 2-10-0 Bo McMillin

Scores of Each Game		
7	Los Angeles	44
21	Green Bay	33
14	BOSTON	17
0	Chic. Bears	28
27	LOS ANGELES	24
24	GREEN BAY	20
20	Chic. Cards	56
21	Washington	46
17	PITTSBURGH	14
14	CHIC. CARDS	28
14	CHIC. BEARS	42
21	Philadelphia	45

Use Name	Pos.	Hgt	Wgt	Age	Int	Pts
Larry Ellis	LB	6'1"	204	26		
Roger Harding	C-LB	6'2"	215	25		
Bob Wiese	LB	6'3"	195	25		
Max Bumgardner	DE	6'2"	190	24		
Ivan Schottel	DE	6'2"	208	27		
Earl Maves	DB-WB	5'9"	180	25		

Use Name – Tackles	Pos.	Hgt	Wgt	Age	Int	Pts
Paul Briggs	T	6'4"	248	28		
Jack Dugger	T	6'3"	227	25		
Dale Hansen	T	6'3"	220	27		
George Hekkers	T	6'4"	230	25		
Russ Thomas	T	6'3"	240	24		

Les Lear – Canadian Football League

Use Name – Guards	Pos.	Hgt	Wgt	Age	Int	Pts
Les Bingaman	G	6'3"	240	23		
Howie Brown	G	5'11"	215	25		
Chuck DeShane	G-LB	6'1"	217	29		
Elmer Jones	G-LB	6'	215	28		
Bill Miklich (from NY)	G-LB	6'	208	27		
Dick Stovall	G-LB	6'	200	24		
Bill Ward	G	6'	230	27		

New owner D. Lyle Fyfe dipped into the college ranks for a new head coach and came up with ex-Indiana mentor Bo McMillin, whom he wooed with a lucrative five-year contract. Many of the players thought that the aging McMillin was behind the times in his thinking, and Bo's opinion of his players wasn't too high when they won only two games all year. Rookie quarterback Fred Enke kept the offense moving fairly steadily, but the defense gave up twice as many points as the attack could score—which prompted McMillin to have lots of new faces in next year's lineup.

TEAM TOTALS

OFFENSE	First Downs: Tot	by Rsh	by Pas	by Pen	Rushing: No.	Yds.	Avg. Yds.	TD	Passing: Att.	Com	Comp. Pct.	Yds.	Avg. Yds. Att.	Avg. Yds. Comp	TD	Int.	Pct. Int.	Punting: No.	Avg. Yds.
CHIC. C.	233	136	81	17	531	2560	4.8	26	285	134	47.0	2134	7.5	15.9	22	12	4.2	68	39.7
CHIC. B.	242	134	93	15	567	2452	4.4	24	287	142	49.5	1894	6.6	13.3	22	19	6.6	69	42.8
L.A.	239	100	123	16	427	1743	4.1	13	395	201	50.9	2748	7.0	13.7	28	25	6.3	63	41.8
G.B.	172	89	58	25	446	1758	3.9	11	274	109	39.8	1364	5.0	12.5	8	29	10.6	78	40.3
DET.	187	84	92	11	389	1360	3.5	6	324	151	46.6	2288	7.1	15.2	20	26	8.0	67	35.4

OFFENSE	Punt Returns: No.	Yds.	Avg. Yds.	TD	Kickoff Returns: No.	Yds.	Avg. Yds.	TD	Interception Returns: No.	Yds.	Avg. Yds.	TD	Penalties: No.	Yds.	Fumbles: No.	Lost	Points: Tot	PAT	FG Att	FG	Saf.
CHIC. C.	35	669	19.1	4	38	915	24.1	0	23	350	15.2	2	83	749	21	16	395	53	21	8	0
CHIC. B.	55	781	14.2	1	29	751	25.9	1	30	388	12.9	1	122	1066	33	21	375	51	7	2	0
L.A.	41	514	12.5	0	42	894	21.3	1	19	223	11.7	1	98	859	32	17	327	39	11	6	0
G.B.	47	527	11.2	0	47	926	19.7	0	29	405	14.0	0	104	941	30	19	154	16	16	6	0
DET.	33	289	8.8	0	61	1114	18.3	0	14	91	6.5	0	49	395	35	20	200	26	6	2	0

Use Name – Backs & Ends	Pos.	Age	Hgt	Wgt	Pts	Int	RUSHING				PASSING								RECEIVING				PUNTING		KICKING						PUNT RETURNS				KICKOFF RETURNS			
							No.	Yds	Avg	TD	Att	Comp	%	Yds	Yd/Att	TD	Int–%	RK	No.	Yds	Avg	TD	No.	Avg	Pat	Att	%	FG	Att	%	No.	Yds	Avg	TD	No.	Yds	Avg	TD
CHICAGO CARDINALS																																						
Ray Mallouf	QB	30	5'11"	180	6		13	17	1.3	1	143	73	51	1160	8.1	13	6–4	4					45	39.0														
Paul Christman	QB	30	6'	212	6		8	6	0.8	1	114	51	45	740	6.5	5	4–4	9																				
Charley Eikenberg	QB	25	6'2"	205			2	9	4.5	0	19	6	32	116	6.1	3	2–11						2	36.0														
Charlie Trippi	HB	25	6'	185	60		128	690	5.4	6	8	4	50	118	14.8	1	0–0		22	228	10	2	13	43.4							11	213	19	2	16	354	22	0
Elmer Angsman	HB	22	5'11"	205	54		131	638	4.9	8									9	142	16	1																
Pat Harder	FB-LB	26	5'11"	205	110		126	554	4.4	6									13	93	7	0			53	53	100	7	17	41								
Vinnie Yablonski	FB-LB	26	5'8"	195	3		48	233	4.9	0									1	13	13	0						1	4	25								
Babe Dimancheff	HB	26	5'11"	180	24		27	117	4.3	1									13	260	20	3													6	118	20	0
Vic Schwall	HB	24	5'8"	185	6		15	107	7.1	1	1	0	0	0	0.0	0	0–0		2	13	7	0																
Jerry Davis	HB-DB	26	5'10"	175	12	4	12	77	6.4	0																					16	334	21	2	15	437	29	0
Corwin Clatt	FB-LB	25	6'	210		1	6	38	6.3	0																												
Red Cochran	HB-DB	26	6'	190		7	3	15	5.0	0													6	38.2							8	122	15	0	1	6	6	0
Bob Hanlon	HB-DB	23	6'1"	195		1	6	11	1.8	0																												
Mal Kutner	OE-DB	27	6'2"	197	90	2	5	50	10.0	1									41	943	23	14																
Bill Dewell	OE-DE	31	6'4"	215	12														33	442	13	2																
CHICAGO BEARS																																						
Sid Luckman	QB	31	6'	195			8	11	1.4	0	163	89	55	1047	6.4	13	14–9	8					10	38.4														
Johnny Lujack	QB-DB	23	6'	185	50	8	15	110	7.3	1	66	36	55	611	9.3	6	3–5								44	46	96	0	3	0								
Bobby Layne	QB	21	6'1"	198	6		13	80	6.1	1	52	16	31	232	6.4	3	2–4						1	24.0				0	1	0								
George Gulyanics	HB	27	6'	198	30		119	439	3.7	4									8	130	16	1	55	44.2														
George McAfee	HB-DB	30	6'	175	48	2	92	392	4.3	5	4	0	0	0	0.0	0	0–0		17	227	13	2	1	18.0							30	417	14	1	1	25	25	0
Joe Osmanski	FB	29	6'2"	215	6		74	341	4.6	1									9	43	5	0													2	26	13	0
J. R. Boone	HB-DB	22	5'8"	158	42	1	48	266	5.5	5	1	1	100	4	4.0	0	0–0		10	143	14	2									11	137	12	0	2	31	16	0
Mike Holovak	FB-LB	28	6'1"	205	12	1	30	228	7.6	2									4	30	8	0																
Noah Mullins	HB-DB	29	5'11"	180	36	7	36	208	5.8	1	1	0	0	0	0.0	0	0–0		9	127	14	4									3	33	11	0	1	41	41	0
Don Kindt	FB-LB	22	6'1"	210	12	1	54	189	3.5	2									11	137	12	0																
Frank Minini	HB	24	6'1"	212	30		24	79	3.3	2									1	14	14	1													12	370	31	1
Al Lawler	HB-DB	24	5'10"	175	6		9	44	4.9	0									3	40	13	0			3	3	100	1	1	100	5	81	16	0	3	85	28	0
Bill deCorrevont	HB-DB	29	6'	185		5	16	25	1.5	0									2	7	4	0									4	61	15	0	6	160	27	0
Fred Evans (frim CHI-AAFC)	HB-DB	27	5'11"	186	12		10	15	1.5	0									1	−2	−2	0									1	15	15	0				
Dick Flanagan	HB-DB	21	6'	205			5	14	2.8	0																												
Jim Canady	HB-DB	22	5'10"	178			2	8	4.0	0																					1	37	37	0				
Jim Keane	OE-DE	24	6'4"	218	18														30	414	14	3																
Ken Kavanaugh	OE-DE	31	6'3"	207	42														18	352	20	6																
Ed Sprinkle	OE-DE	24	6'1"	207	18		1	−2	−2.0	0									10	132	13	3																
Joe Abbey	OE-DE	22	6'1"	198															5	67	13	0																
Allen Smith	OE-DE	25	6'2"	220															3	29	10	0																
Fred Venturelli	K	30	5'11"	235	7																				4	4	100	1	2	50								
LOS ANGELES RAMS																																						
Jim Hardy	QB	26	6'	180			5	14	2.8	0	211	112	53	1390	6.6	14	7–3	4					3	50.3														
Bob Waterfield	QB-DB	28	6'1"	193	56	4	7	12	1.7	0	180	87	48	1354	7.5	14	18–10	7					43	42.6	38	44	86	6	11	55								
Paul Rickards	QB	22	6'1"	190			2	21	10.5	0	2	2	100	4	2.0	0	0–0																					
Dick Hoerner	FB-DB	26	6'4"	214	36	1	76	354	4.7	4									18	227	13	2									1	6	6	0	2	35	18	0
Kenny Washington	HB-DB	30	6'1"	220	18	2	57	301	5.3	2	1	0	0	0	0.0	0	0–0		6	104	17	1									1	12	12	0	2	54	27	0
Fred Gehrke	HB-DB	30	5'11"	190	19	2	56	246	4.4	1	1	0	0	0	0.0	0	0–0		16	173	11	1			1	1	100				19	217	11	0	17	464	27	1
Gerry Cowhig	FB-DB	27	6'2"	214	12	1	46	206	4.5	2									3	18	6	0									1	3	3	0	1	3	3	0
Dante Magnani	HB	31	5'10"	193	6		38	144	3.8	0									3	28	9	1													3	49	16	0
Les Horvath	HB-DB	27	5'10"	176	6	2	30	118	3.9	0									4	42	11	0									13	203	16	0	2	31	16	0
Jack Banta	HB-DB	30	5'11"	188			32	105	3.3	0									4	34	9	0	17	37.6							1	14	14	0	6	119	20	0
Bob Hoffman	FB-LB	30	6'1"	212	30		22	68	3.1	4									3	28	9	1													2	19	10	0
Bruce Smith (from GB)	HB-DB	28	6'	197			18	59	3.3	0	1	0	0	0	0.0	0	0–0		4	29	7	0									1	10	10	0				
Bob Alger	HB-DB	25	6'1"	205			8	41	5.1	0																												
Joe Corn	HB-DB	26	5'6"	168			11	27	2.5	0																					4	49	12	0	5	112	22	0
Tom Keane	HB-DB	21	6'1"	196	12		7	16	2.3	0									11	195	18	2																
Jim Mello (to CHI-AAFC)	FB-DB	27	5'10"	190			7	3	0.4	0									1	17	17	0																
Tom Fears	OE-DB	24	6'2"	216	30	2	2	8	4.0	0									51	698	14	4																
Red Hickey	OE-DE	31	6'2"	215	42														30	509	17	7																
Jack Zilly	OE-DE	26	6'2"	210	24														13	169	13	4																
Don Currivan (from BOS)	OE-DB	27	6'	192	24		1	−4	−4.0	0									12	218	18	3																
Frank Hubbell	OE-DE	26	6'2"	222	6														10	134	13	1																
Bill Smyth	OE-DE	26	6'3"	235	6														6	66	11	1																
Larry Brink	OE-DE	25	6'5"	217			1	−3	−3.0	0									4	36	9	0																
GREEN BAY PACKERS																																						
Jack Jacobs	QB-DB	29	6'1"	190	6		24	73	3.0	1	184	82	45	848	4.6	5	21–11	13					69	40.3							1	3	3	0				
Irv Comp	QB-DB	29	6'2"	205		5	3	3	1.0	0	49	16	33	335	6.8	1	7–14														3	35	12	0				
Perry Moss	QB	24	5'10"	170			5	2	0.4	0	17	4	24	20	1.2	0	0–0																					
Tony Canadeo	HB-DB	29	5'11"	190	24	3	123	598	4.8	4	8	2	25	24	3.0	0	0–0		9	81	9	0	1	38.0							4	55	14	0	9	166	18	0
Walt Schlinkman	FB	26	5'8"	193	24		106	441	4.2	4																									4	89	22	0
Ted Fritsch	FB-LB	27	5'10"	210	29	1	37	173	4.7	0															5	6	83	6	16	38					1	17	17	0
Ralph Earhart	HB-DB	25	5'10"	165	18		30	140	4.7	1									17	194	11	2									11	137	12	0	2	51	26	0
Fred Provo	HB-DB	26	5'9"	185			29	90	3.1	0	1	1	100	20	20.0	1	0–0		4	−9	−2	0									18	208	12	0	10	205	21	0
Oscar Smith	HB-DB	25	6'	185			27	85	3.1	0									12	121	10	0									8	71	9	0	12	287	24	0
Ed Cody	FB-DB	25	5'10"	190	11		26	58	2.2	0															11	13	85								2	31	16	0
Bob Forte	HB-DB	26	6'	195	6	5	12	30	2.5	0									6	63	11	1													2	30	15	0
Jug Girard	HB-DB	21	5'11"	175		1	13	26	2.0	0	14	4	29	117	8.4	1	1–7		1	2	2	0	8	40.0											1	20	20	0
Pat West (from LA)	FB	25	6'	200			4	24	6.0	0									3	37	12	0																
Clyde Goodnight	OE-DB	24	6'1"	195	18														28	448	16	3													1	12	12	0
Nolan Luhn	OE-DE	27	6'3"	200	12														17	285	17	2													3	18	6	0
Ted Cook	OE-DB	27	6'2"	195		6													13	156	12	0									2	18	9	0				
Gene Wilson	OE-DB	22	5'10"	180		2													2	23	12	0																
DETROIT LIONS																																						
Fred Enke	QB	23	6'1"	200			74	365	4.9	0	221	100	45	1328	6.0	11	17–8	10	1	6	6	0													5	76	15	0
Clyde LeForce	QB-WB-DB	25	5'11"	175	30	1	28	86	3.1	1	101	50	50	912	9.0	9	8–8	6	8	122	15	3									1	9	9	0	1	10	10	0
Charley Sarratt	QB-DB	24	6'1"	185			3	3	1.0	0	1	1	100	48	48.0	0	0–0		1	3	3	0	5	33.2							1	2	2	0				
Camp Wilson	FB	26	6'2"	200	12		157	612	3.9	2									2	9	5	0													10	228	23	0
Bill Dudley	HB-WB-DB	27	5'10"	176	42	1	33	97	2.9	0	1	0	0	0	0.0	0	1–100		20	210	11	6	23	35.9							8	67	8	0	10	204	20	0
Joe Watt	HB-DB	27	5'11"	183		4	20	54	2.7	0									2	29	15	0									8	87	11	0	12	180	15	0
Paul Serringhaus	HB	27	6'	185			19	38	2.0	0									1	−1	−1	0													5	96	19	0
Ken Roskie (from GB)	FB-LB	28	6'1"	220	6	1	6	29	4.8	1																									1	30	30	0
Steve Sucic	FB-LB	27	6'	210			6	20	3.3	0																												
Andy Dudish	HB-DB	27	5'11"	185			1	5	5.0	0																					2	10	5	0	2	38	19	0
Jim Gillette	HB-DB	30	6'1"	185		6	2	3	1.5	0									1	8	8	0									2	10	5	0				
Joe Margucci	WB-DB	25	5'10"	184	30		34	14	0.4	3									36	450	13	2									10	100	10	0	10	199	20	0
George Grimes	WB-DB	26	5'11"	190	6	1	1	8	8.0	0									1	17	17	1	28	35.9							1	4	4	0				
Mel Groomes	WB-DB	21	6'	175			2	1	0.5	0									2	18	9	0																
Bob Mann	OE	24	5'11"	170	18		6	46	7.6	0									33	560	17	3													1	16	16	0
John Greene	OE-DE	28	6'	210	30														25	595	24	5													1	11	11	0
Kelley Mote	OE	25	6'2"	182															13	212	16	0													3	27	9	0
Cecil Souders	OE-DE	26	6'1"	210															2	19	10	0																
Merv Pregulman	C-LB	26	6'3"	214	32	1																			26	27	96	2	6	33								

TEAM TOTALS

DEFENSE	FIRST DOWNS: Tot	by Rsh	by Pas	by Pen	RUSHING: No.	Yds.	Avg. Yds.	TD	PASSING: Att.	Com	Comp. Pct.	Yds.	Avg. Yds. Att.	Avg. Yds. Comp	TD	Int.	Pct. Int.	PUNTING: No.	Avg. Yds.	PUNT RETURNS: No.	Yds.	Avg. Yds.	TD	KICKOFF RETURNS: No.	Yds.	Avg. Yds.	TD	INTERCEPTION RETURNS: No.	Yds.	Avg. Yds.	TD	PENALTIES: No.	Yds.	FUMBLES: No.	Lost	POINTS: Tot	PAT	FG Att	FG	Saf.	DEFENSE
CHIC. C.	190	85	94	11	408	1516	3.7	8	336	159	47.3	2520	7.5	15.8	22	23	6.8	72	39.2	42	504	12.0	0	64	1207	18.9	1	12	143	11.9	0	87	743	30	24	226	28	11	2	0	CHIC. C.
CHIC. B.	174	71	78	33	384	1254	3.3	8	336	139	41.4	1646	4.9	11.8	12	30	8.9	82	39.5	45	413	9.2	0	59	1101	18.7	0	19	225	11.8	0	72	633	29	16	151	17	8	4	1	CHIC. B.
L.A.	204	90	97	17	441	1570	3.6	13	309	164	53.1	2143	6.9	13.1	20	19	6.1	77	41.0	32	445	13.9	1	53	1157	21.8	1	25	311	12.4	3	77	719	42	24	269	33	11	6	1	L.A.
G.B.	222	132	74	16	537	2153	4.0	21	298	134	51.5	1626	6.3	12.1	13	29	11.2	70	43.3	38	473	12.4	1	22	611	27.8	1	29	457	15.8	2	91	771	23	15	290	38	14	6	0	G.B.
DET.	253	135	103	15	495	2382	4.8	27	302	161	53.3	2176	7.2	13.5	25	14	4.6	56	40.5	32	492	15.4	1	39	908	23.3	0	26	539	20.7	4	94	894	29	19	407	51	16	6	1	DET.

BUFFALO BILLS 7-7-0 Red Dawson

Scores of Each Game		
14	San Francisco	35
42	CHICAGO	7
13	CLEVELAND	42
28	SAN FRANCISCO	38
31	BROOKLYN	21
13	NEW YORK	14
14	Cleveland	31
35	Los Angeles	21
35	BALTIMORE	17
26	Brooklyn	21
20	LOS ANGELES	27
39	Chicago	35
35	New York	14
15	Baltimore	35
	EAST Playoff	
28	Baltimore	17

Use Name	Pos.	Hgt	Wgt	Age	Int	Pts
Jack Baldwin	C-LB	6'3"	220	27		
Bob Callahan	C-LB	6'	205	24		
Buckets Hirsch	LB	5'10"	205	27		
Felto Prewitt	C-LB	5'11"	204	24		
Art Statuto	C	6'2"	220	23		
(2 yds. on pass reception lateral)						
Jerry Whalen	C-G	6'1"	235	20		
Bob Stefik	DE	5'11"	180	24		
(missed 1 PAT attempt)						
Ed Balatti (from SF and NY)	DE	6'1	205	24		
Vince Mazza	DE	6'1"	224	27		6
Carl Schuette	DB	6'1"	200	26	4	6
Alex Wizbicki	DB	5'11"	188	26	3	
(3 punt returns for 33 yds.)						

Use Name – Tackles	Pos.	Hgt	Wgt	Age	Int	Pts
Jack Carpenter	T	6'	242	25		
John Kerns	T	6'3"	240	25		
(1 kickoff return for 3 yds.)						
(2 yds. on punt return lateral)						
John Kissell	T	6'3"	234	25		

Use Name – Guards	Pos.	Hgt	Wgt	Age	Int	Pts
Ed King	G-DE	6'	218	23		
Hal Lahar	G	6'	207	29		
Rocco Pirro	G	6'	230	31		
Vin Scott	G	5'8"	215	26		
John Wyhonic	G	6'	214	28		

In the Eastern Division, a mere 7-7 record earned the Bills a share of the division lead and forced a playoff game with the Colts in Baltimore for the Eastern title. After three quarters, the Colts were sitting on a 17-7 lead before a dancing crowd of 27,327. But early in the final period George Ratterman hit Bill Gompers for a 66-yard touchdown pass to bring the count up to 17-14. A few minutes later, the Bills started on another drive deep in their own territory. Buffalo picked up two first downs before star halfback Chet Mutryn took a short pass, ran a few steps, and dropped the ball. The Colts recovered the ball, but the officials ruled it an incomplete pass. Six plays later, Al Baldwin scored on a 35-yard pass, and Buffalo wound up with a final 28-17 victory and a trip to Cleveland.

BALTIMORE COLTS 7-7-0 Cecil Isbell

Scores of Each Game		
45	NEW YORK	28
14	Chicago	21
27	New York	14
35	BROOKLYN	20
10	CLEVELAND	14
14	SAN FRANCISCO	56
29	Los Angeles	14
10	San Francisco	21
17	Buffalo	35
7	Cleveland	28
38	CHICAGO	24
14	LOS ANGELES	17
38	Brooklyn	20
35	BUFFALO	15
	EAST Playoff	
17	BUFFALO	28

Use Name	Pos.	Hgt	Wgt	Age	Int	Pts
Herb Coleman (from CHI)	C-LB	6'	200	25		
Bert Corley	C-LB	6'2"	210	28		
Len McCormick	C-LB	6'3"	232	25	1	
Ralph Stewart (from NY)	C-LB	6'	205	22		
John Sylvester	DB	6'	183	26	1	
(2 punt returns for 16 yds.)						
injured – Barry French						

Use Name – Tackles	Pos.	Hgt	Wgt	Age	Int	Pts
Lee Artoe	T	6'3"	240	32		
Pete Berezney	T	6'2"	240	24		
Ernie Blandin	T	6'4"	245	29		
John Mellus	T	6'	210	31		
Alex Sidorik	T	6'	245	26		
Jim Spruill	T	6'3"	225	25		

Use Name – Guards	Pos.	Hgt	Wgt	Age	Int	Pts
Dick Barwegan	G-LB	6'1"	215	26	1	
Bill Garrett	G	6'1"	235	24		
(1 kickoff return for 6 yds.)						
Ed Grain	G	6'	230	26		
George Groves	G-LB	5'11"	195	27		
Al Klug	G	6'1"	212	27		
Jack Simmons	G	6'4"	235	22		

The Cleveland Browns were set at quarterback with Otto Graham, so they dealt Baltimore the draft rights to a rookie passer from LSU. Y.A. Tittle, his hair already thinning, proved just the medicine to make the Colts well. In his pro debut, Tittle threw four touchdown passes to lead the Colts to a 45-28 upset of the New York Yankees. With Y.A. throwing the ball to halfback Billy Hillenbrand and end Lamar Davis, and with Buzz Mertes carrying the ball on the ground, the offense heated up enough to carry the club to a tie for first place in the Eastern Division. Two newcomers, tackle Lee Artoe and guard Dick Barwegan, beefed up the line, and rookie back Rex Grossman led the league in field goals.

NEW YORK YANKEES 6-8-0 Ray Flaherty, Red Strader

Scores of Each Game		
21	Brooklyn	3
28	Baltimore	45
0	San Francisco	41
14	BALTIMORE	27
10	Los Angeles	20
14	Buffalo	13
7	SAN FRANCISCO	21
7	Cleveland	35
42	CHICAGO	7
38	LOS ANGELES	6
21	BROOKLYN	7
21	CLEVELAND	34
14	BUFFALO	35
28	Chicago	7

Use Name	Pos.	Hgt	Wgt	Age	Int	Pts
Joe Magliolo	LB	6'	210	26	1	
Roland Nabors	C-LB	6'2"	200	24	1	
Frank Perantoni	C	6'	220	24		
Lou Sossamon	C-LB	6'1"	207	27		
John Rokisky	DE	6'2"	205	28		
Harmon Rowe	DB	6'	182	25		
(1 punt return for 12 yds.)						
Steve Sieradzki	DB	6'	194	23		

Use Name – Tackles	Pos.	Hgt	Wgt	Age	Int	Pts
Carl Butkus (from WAS-NFL)	T	6'1"	245	26		
Bill Chambers	T	6'2"	230	25		
Denver Crawford	T	6'	210	27		
Nelson Greene	T	6'2"	235	25		
Glenn Johnson	T	6'4"	260	26		
Clayton Lane	T	6'	215	26		
Paul Mitchell (from LA)	T	6'3"	240	28		
Darrell Palmer	T	6'2"	245	26		
Marion Shirley	T	6'4"	260	26		
Arnie Weinmeister	T	6'4"	235	25		

Use Name – Guards	Pos.	Hgt	Wgt	Age	Int	Pts
Mike Garzoni (from NYG-NFL)	G	5'11"	220	24		
Charley Riffle	G-LB	6'	212	30	1	
Ed Sharkey	G-LB	6'3"	215	22		
Joe Signiago	G	6'1"	215	25		
Dick Werder	G	5'9"	210	26		
Joe Yackanich	G	5'10"	205	26		

Even with a trio of blue-chip rookies, the Yankees could not repeat as Eastern champions. Tackle Arnie Weinmeister took over for the retired Bruiser Kinard with little drop in efficiency. Pete Layden, after finishing the baseball season as an outfielder with the St. Louis Browns, joined the football Yankees and backed up Spec Sanders at tailback. Defensive back Otto "The Claw" Schnellbacher earned his nickname by leading the league with eleven interceptions and then spent the winter playing professional basketball. But when the Yankees offense sputtered and faltered, they dropped six of their first eight contests. Coach Ray Flaherty paid with his job despite his two divisional crowns, and a late-season spurt under new coach Red Strader left the Yankees one game out of first place at the end of the disappointing campaign.

One mark of the team's decline is found in their two games with the Cleveland Browns. In 1947, the New Yorkers lost a close decision and then held the Browns to a tie. This year, however, the Browns took easy 35-7 and 34-21 victories.

BROOKLYN DODGERS 2-12-0 Carl Voyles

Scores of Each Game		
3	NEW YORK	21
20	San Francisco	36
7	Los Angeles	17
20	Baltimore	35
21	Buffalo	31
17	Cleveland	30
21	CHICAGO	7
35	Chicago	14
0	LOS ANGELES	17
21	BUFFALO	26
7	New York	21
40	SAN FRANCISCO	63
20	BALTIMORE	38
21	CLEVELAND	31

Use Name	Pos.	Hgt	Wgt	Age	Int	Pts
Jim Cooper	C-LB	6'	205	24		
Ed Gustafson	C-LB	6'3"	205	26		
(1 rush for 7 yds.)						
George Strohmeyer	C-LB	5'10"	200	24	4	
(1 punt return for 5 yds.)						
Caleb Warrington	C-G	6'2"	210	27		
Tom Mikula	FB-LB	5'10"	200	21		
Jim Dewar	WB-DB	6'1"	190	26		
John Klasnic	WB-DB	6'	185	21		
Doyle Tackett	BB-DB	6'	205	24		
(1 punt return for 10 yds.)						

Use Name – Tackles	Pos.	Hgt	Wgt	Age	Int	Pts
John Clowes	T	6'1"	235	26		
Charlie Huneke	T	6'3"	225	27		
Herb Nelson	T-DE	6'4"	220	27		
Martin Ruby	T	6'3"	250	28		6
Ralph Sazio	T	6'1"	220	26		
(5 yds. on rushing lateral)						
Joe Spencer	T	6'3"	235	25		
Garland Williams	T	6'3"	220	27		

Use Name – Guards	Pos.	Hgt	Wgt	Age	Int	Pts
Harry Buffington	G	6'	210	29		
Amos Harris	G	6'	210	27		
(1 kickoff return for 10 yds.)						
Bob Leonetti (from BUF)	G	6'	230	25		
Herb St. John	G	5'10"	215	22		
John Wozniak	G-LB	6'	210	27	1	
(13 yds. on rushing lateral)						

Branch Rickey had built the baseball Dodgers into a successful franchise, and now he wanted to take a crack at football. At Rickey's suggestion, the baseball club purchased the football Brooklyn Dodgers. The success of the baseball team didn't wear off on their football counterparts, as they won only two of their fourteen games. Had the Chicago Rockets not been around for the Dodgers to beat twice, Brooklyn may never have won on the gridiron. The team's only bright spots included fullback Mickey Colmer, tailbacks Bob Hoernschemeyer and Bob Chappuis, and tackle Martin Ruby—a quartet that earned the highest marks on the club.

The fans who filled Ebbets Field in the summer stayed away from the ballpark on fall Sundays. By the end of the year, Rickey and the owners of the baseball team had had enough of pro football, and they turned the club back to the league—a move which necessitated the Dodgers' merger with the New York Yankees for the 1949 season.

TEAM TOTALS

	FIRST DOWNS:				RUSHING:				PASSING:									
OFFENSE	Tot	by Rsh	by Pas	by Pen	No.	Yds.	Avg Yds.	TD	Att	Com	Comp Pct.	Yds.	Avg. Yds. Att.	Avg. Yds. Comp	TD	Int	Pct. Int.
BUFFALO	223	120	89	14	539	2738	5.1	29	360	177	49.2	2683	7.5	15.2	17	26	7.2
BALT.	218	120	84	14	532	2166	4.1	22	340	185	54.4	2899	8.5	15.7	19	13	3.8
N.Y.	178	93	70	15	464	1977	4.3	20	316	139	44.0	1966	6.2	14.1	15	24	7.6
BKN.	194	101	79	14	409	1787	4.4	12	410	188	45.9	2524	6.2	13.4	20	32	7.8
DEFENSE																	
BUFFALO	207	98	95	14	463	1983	4.3	25	414	211	51.0	2829	6.8	13.4	23	14	3.4
BALT.	224	125	84	15	504	2522	5.0	21	364	177	48.6	2438	6.7	13.8	18	22	6.0
N.Y.	192	94	85	13	467	2015	4.3	18	341	160	46.9	2767	8.1	17.3	19	27	7.9
BKN.	226	146	72	8	585	3146	5.4	30	296	160	54.1	1986	6.7	12.4	23	25	8.4

	PUNTING:		PUNT RETURNS:				KICKOFF RETURNS:				INTERCEPTION RETURNS:				PENALTIES:		FUMBLES:		POINTS:					TEAM TOTALS
OFFENSE	No.	Avg. Yds.	No.	Yds.	Avg. Yds.	TD	No.	Yds.	Avg. Yds.	TD	No.	Yds.	Avg. Yds.	TD	No.	Yds.	No.	Lost	Tot	PAT	FG Att	FG	Saf.	OFFENSE
BUFFALO	63	38.7	33	557	16.9	3	53	1033	19.5	0	14	294	21.0	2	88	644	34	13	360	43	3	1	1	BUFFALO
BALT.	66	38.6	40	597	14.9	1	52	1062	20.4	0	22	262	11.9	0	84	743	33	21	333	43	18	10	1	BALT.
N.Y.	77	40.4	39	515	13.2	1	49	1128	23.0	0	27	481	17.1	1	84	690	35	15	265	37	7	2	0	N.Y.
BKN.	63	42.8	30	314	10.5	1	60	1336	22.3	0	25	438	17.5	1	56	410	41	15	253	31	8	2	0	BKN.
																								DEFENSE
BUFFALO	67	43.5	40	620	15.5	1	57	1333	23.4	0	26	447	17.2	0	76	616	44	26	358	49	11	5	0	BUFFALO
BALT.	58	43.4	31	318	10.3	0	61	1176	19.3	0	13	208	16.0	2	73	556	30	14	327	43	11	2	1	BALT.
N.Y.	64	41.3	48	566	11.8	1	47	944	20.1	0	24	341	14.2	1	89	733	35	16	301	37	12	6	0	N.Y.
BKN.	51	39.8	38	689	18.4	2	48	1007	21.0	1	32	321	10.3	1	82	775	37	17	387	48	12	7	0	BKN.

							RUSHING				PASSING								RECEIVING				PUNTING		KICKING						PUNT RETURNS				KICKOFF RETURNS			
Use Name – Backs & Ends	Pos.	Age	Hgt	Wgt	Pts	Int	No.	Yds	Avg	TD	Att	Comp	%	Yds	Yd/Att	TD	Int–%	RK	No.	Yds	Avg	TD	No.	Avg	Pat	Att	%	FG	Att	%	No.	Yds	Avg	TD	No.	Yds	Avg	TD
BUFFALO BILLS																																						
George Ratterman	QB	21	6'1"	182	18		12	-18	-1.5	3	335	168	50	2577	7.7	16	22- 7	4																				
Jim Still	QB-DB	24	6'3"	190		1	5	-26	-5.2	0	14	5	36	89	6.4	1	3-21						47	38.8														
Chet Mutryn	HB-DB	27	5'9"	173	96		147	823	5.6	10	6	2	33	21	3.5	0	0- 0		39	794	20	5									10	171	17	1	19	500	26	0
Lou Tomasetti	HB	32	6'	205	48		134	716	5.3	7									22	213	10	1													2	14	7	0
Bob Steuber	FB-LB	26	6'2"	200	41		69	437	6.3	3	2	1	50	-4	-2.0	0	0- 0		2	14	7	0	1	40.0	20	23	87	1	2	50					6	123	21	0
Bill Gompers	HB-DB	20	6'1'	185	6	2	48	219	4.6	1																					1	10	10	0	4	62	16	0
Vic Kulbitski	FB-LB	27	5'10"	206	14		40	152	3.8	0									3	37	12	0			8	10	80								1	18	18	0
Rex Bumgardner	HB-DB	24	5'11"	193	12	2	14	82	5.9	0									1	63	63	0									16	336	21	2	9	141	16	0
Don Schneider	HB	24	5'9"	170			15	70	4.7	0									1	14	14	0									1	4	4	0	4	77	19	0
Chick Maggioli	HB-DB	26	5'11"	180		1	11	27	2.5	0	1	1	100	0	0.0	0	0- 0		3	23	8	0	2	47.5							1	0	0	0	2	38	19	0
Al Akins (from BKN)	HB-DB	27	6'1"	208			4	-9	-2.2	0									3	12	4	0																
Al Baldwin	OE	25	6'2"	198	48														54	916	17	8			0	1	0											
Bill O'Connor	OE-DE	22	6'4"	220	12														31	301	10	2													1	0	0	0
Paul Gibson	OE-DB	23	6'2"	190															11	216	20	0																
Marty Comer	OE-DE	30	6'	205	6														5	66	13	1																
George Kisiday	OE-DE	25	6'1"	220															1	20	20	0																
Graham Armstrong	T	29	6'4"	240	15														1	0	0	0			15	17	88	0	1	0					1	9	9	0
BALTIMORE COLTS																																						
Y. A. Tittle	QB	21	6'	190	24		52	157	3.0	4	289	161	56	2522	8.7	16	9- 3	1																				
Charlie O'Rourke	QB	31	5'11"	175	6		7	15	2.1	1	51	24	47	377	7.4	3	4- 8						66	38.6														
Buzz Mertes	FB	27	6'	205	24		155	680	4.4	4									6	56	9	0													1	15	15	0
Billy Hillenbrand	HB-DB	26	6'	188	78		100	510	5.1	7									50	970	19	6									18	231	13	0	16	356	22	0
Bob Pfohl	HB-DB	22	6'	200	36		107	455	4.3	4									13	134	10	1									2	102	51	1	17	366	22	0
Lu Gambino	FB-LB	24	6'1"	205	6		54	194	3.6	1									6	28	5	0													3	57	19	0
Jake Leicht	HB-DB	27	5'9"	170	12	5	20	88	4.4	1									12	134	11	1									8	139	17	0	4	83	21	0
Aubrey Fowler	HB-DB	28	5'10"	160		3	6	30	5.0	0																					4	41	10	0	2	16	8	0
Lew Mayne	HB-DB	28	6'1"	190			14	26	1.9	0									2	33	17	0									2	24	12	0	3	61	20	0
John Vardian	HB-DB	23	5'8"	168			6	13	2.2	0									3	26	9	0									3	34	11	0	3	66	22	0
Spiro Dellerba	FB-LB	25	5'11"	200		2	2	0	0.0	0																									1	12	12	0
Rex Grossman	FB-LB	24	6'1"	215	73	2	8	-3	-0.4	0															43	43	100	10	18	56								
Lamar Davis	OE-DB	27	6'1"	185	42	5													41	765	19	7									1	10	10	0				
Win Williams	OE	25	6'2"	185	12														32	360	11	2													1	20	20	0
John North	OE-DB	27	6'2"	198	12	1													8	204	26	1																
Joe Smith	OE-DB	26	6'1"	183	6	1	1	1	1.0	0									8	131	16	1																
Hub Bechtol	OE-DE	22	6'3"	200															2	25	13	0													0	4	–	0
Bob Nowaskey (from LA)	OE-DE	30	6'	200															1	31	31	0																
Ollie Poole	OE-DE	26	6'3"	220															1	2	2	0																
NEW YORK YANKEES																																						
Spec Sanders	TB-DB	29	6'1"	196	54	1	169	759	4.5	9	168	78	46	918	5.5	5	11- 7	9					42	40.6							13	128	10	0	9	217	24	0
Pete Layden	TB-DB	28	5'11"	195	18	3	95	576	6.1	3	105	43	41	816	7.8	9	8- 8	7					21	42.1							7	64	9	0	8	211	26	0
Al Dekdebrun (to BOS-NFL)	TB-DB	27	5'11"	185		1	7	24	3.4	0	20	10	50	149	7.5	0	2-10														1	12	12	0	1	15	15	0
Bud Schwenk	TB	30	6'2"	200			3	6	2.0	0	17	6	35	52	3.1	0	3-18																					
Tom Casey	TB-DB	24	5'11"	175	6		18	75	4.2	0	5	2	40	31	6.2	1	0- 0						6	40.3							9	229	25	1	7	170	24	0
Buddy Young	FB-DB	22	5'5"	170	30		70	245	3.5	1									21	259	12	4									2	11	6	0	12	303	25	0
Bill Daley	FB-DB	28	6'2"	210	6		40	102	2.6	1									4	31	8	0	1	41.0											4	88	22	0
Lowell Tew	FB	21	5'11"	195	30		24	95	4.0	5									7	97	14	0													3	75	25	0
Bob Kennedy	FB-DB	27	5'11"	195	6	4	33	90	2.7	1	1	0	0	0	0.0	0	0- 0		5	23	5	0	7	33.9							1	14	14	0	2	20	10	0
Lowell Wagner	WB-DB	24	6'	193	6	1													6	99	17	1																
Duke Iverson	WB-DB	28	6'2"	188		1													4	30	8	0																
Lloyd Cheatham	BB	29	6'2"	215			2	1	0.5	0									7	76	11	0													1	18	18	0
Bob Sweiger	BB-LB	29	6'	209			3	4	1.3	0									12	129	11	0													1	3	3	0
Howie Parker	BB-LB	22	6'2"	220															1	17	17	0																
Harvey Johnson	BB-LB	29	5'11"	210	43														1	6	6	0			37	37	100	2	7	29								
Bruce Alford	OE	27	6'	190	18														32	578	18	3																
Jack Russell	OE-DE	28	6'1"	215	36	1													23	433	19	6																
Otto Schnellbacher	OE-DB	25	6'2"	185	6	11													5	72	14	0									5	45	9	0				
Van Davis	OE-DE	26	6'2"	215	6	1													4	49	12	1																
Paul Cleary	OE-DE	26	6'1"	196															4	37	9	0													1	8	8	0
Flip McDonald	OE-DE	27	6'2"	210															3	30	10	0																
BROOKLYN DODGERS																																						
Bob Chappuis	TB-DB	25	6'	190	6		52	310	6.0	1	213	100	47	1402	6.6	8	15- 7	8													1	8	8	0	3	55	18	0
Bob Hoernschemeyer	TB-WB-DB	22	5'11"	192	42		110	574	5.2	3	155	71	46	854	5.5	8	15-10	10	11	173	16	3	1	40.0							1	3	3	0	6	138	23	0
Monk Gafford	TB-WB-DB	27	5'11"	195	30		30	51	1.7	1	39	17	44	268	6.9	4	2- 5		15	274	18	4									14	130	9	0	23	559	24	0
Mickey Colmer	FB-LB	29	6'2"	218	60		164	704	4.3	6	1	0	0	0	0.0	0	0- 0		21	372	18	4	56	42.5											8	163	20	0
Morrie Warren	FB-LB	24	5'11"	208			1	1	1.0	0																									1	36	36	0
Bob Sullivan	FB-LB	23	5'9"	195			2	-1	-0.5	0																									1	22	22	0
Lee Tevis	FB-LB	26	5'11"	190	10						1	0	0	0	0.0	0	0- 0		1	-8	-8	0	5	42.8	4	4	100	2	7	29	6	59	10	0	2	40	20	0
Nick Forkovitch	FB-LB	28	5'11"	195			1	4	4.0	0																												
Ray Ramsey	WB-DB	27	6'2"	170	18	7	22	48	2.2	0	1	0	0	0	0.0	0	0- 0		13	315	24	2									5	82	16	1	10	233	23	0
Jim Camp	WB-DB	24	6'	170		1	8	43	5.4	0									1	43	43	0													1	12	12	0
Hardy Brown	WB-DB	24	6'	185	37	1	6	23	3.8	1									3	36	12	1			25	29	86	0	1	0								
Hugo Marcolini	WB-DB	25	6'	203			5	11	2.2	0									2	38	19	0													2	33	17	0
Carl Allen	WB-DB	27	6'	175	6	2	1	9	9.0	0																					1	17	17	0				
Jim Smith (from BUF)	WB-DB	23	6'1"	188		4	1	7	7.0	0													14	38.4							1	1	1	0				
Walt McDonald	BB-DB	27	6'1"	210	6	3	6	15	2.5	0									7	41	6	1																
Saxon Judd	OE	27	6'1"	190	12														32	350	11	2													1	14	14	0
Max Morris	OE	23	6'2"	200	6														28	372	13	1													1	21	21	0
Dan Edwards	OE-DE	22	6'1"	200															23	176	8	0																
Hank Foldberg	OE-DE	25	6'1"	200	6														16	129	8	0																
Harry Burrus (from CHI)	OE-DB	27	6'1"	195	8	3	1	-3	-3.0	0									10	227	23	1			2	3	67											
Hal Thompson	OE-DE	26	6'1"	205	6														4	37	9	1																
Ed Scruggs	OE-DE	25	6'1"	195															1	8	8	0																

CLEVELAND BROWNS 14-0-0 Paul Brown

Scores of Each Game			
19	LOS ANGELES	14	
42	Buffalo	13	
28	Chicago	7	
21	CHICAGO	10	
14	Baltimore	10	
30	BROOKLYN	17	
31	BUFFALO	14	
35	NEW YORK	7	
28	BALTIMORE	7	
14	SAN FRANCISCO	7	
34	New York	21	
31	Los Angeles	14	
31	San Francisco	28	
31	Brooklyn	21	

Use Name	Pos.	Hgt	Wgt	Age	Int	Pts
Frank Gatski	C	6'3"	220	26		
Mel Maceau	C-LB	6'	203	26		
Lou Saban	LB	6'	198	26	5	
Frank Kosikowski	DE	6'1"	200	22		
injured – Warren Lahr						

Use Name – Tackles	Pos.	Hgt	Wgt	Age	Int	Pts
Chet Adams	T	6'3"	230	32		
Chubby Grigg	T	6'2"	280	22		
Ben Pucci	T	6'4"	245	23		
Lou Rymkus	T	6'4"	230	29		
Len Simonetti	T	5'11"	225	29		

Use Name – Guards	Pos.	Hgt	Wgt	Age	Int	Pts
Alex Agase	G-LB	5'10"	212	26		
Bob Gaudio (1 rush for 2 yds.)	G-LB	5'10"	215	23		
Lin Houston	G	6'	205	27		
Weldon Humble	G-LB	6'1"	215	27	1	
Ed Ulinski	G	5'11"	200	27		
Bill Willis	G	6'2"	210	27		

They hardly needed any strengthening, but the Browns went into the season with new help in halfback Dub Jones, guard Alex Agase, and tackle Chubby Grigg. With last year's powerhouse intact, the Browns ripped through the league undefeated, untied, and unthreatened by any other team. Only San Francisco had hopes of knocking off the Browns, and their two meetings became the high points of the AAFC season. A pulsating crowd of 82,769 in Cleveland watched the Browns tumble the '49ers from the undefeated ranks with a hard-fought 14-7 decision. Their rematch in San Francisco drew an audience of 59,785 and wound up in a 31-28 Brown victory.

A look at the Cleveland roster explained their dominance of the league. Eight Browns won spots on the first or second All-League teams, with Otto Graham, Marion Motley, Mac Speedie, Dante Lavelli, Lou Rymkus, Bill Willis, Ed Ulinski, and Lou Saban thus honored. With San Francisco disposed of, the title game against the Eastern champion Buffalo Bills had to be anticlimactic.

SAN FRANCISCO 49ers 12-2-0 Buck Shaw

Scores of Each Game			
35	BUFFALO	14	
36	BROOKLYN	20	
41	NEW YORK	0	
36	LOS ANGELES	14	
38	Buffalo	28	
31	Chicago	14	
56	Baltimore	14	
21	New York	7	
21	BALTIMORE	10	
44	CHICAGO	21	
7	Cleveland	14	
63	Brooklyn	40	
28	CLEVELAND	31	
38	Los Angeles	21	

Use Name	Pos.	Hgt	Wgt	Age	Int	Pts
Art Elston	C-G-LB	5'11"	190	29	1	
Bill Johnson	C-LB	6'3"	210	22	1	
Walt McCormick	C-LB	6'1"	215	21		
Joel Williams	C-LB	6'1"	215	20		
Ken Casanega	HB-DB	5'11"	175	27		

Use Name – Tackles	Pos.	Hgt	Wgt	Age	Int	Pts
Bob Bryant (1 punt return for 14 yds.)	T	6'3"	225	29		
Floyd Collier	T	6'1"	215	24		
Charlie Elliott (from CHI)	T	6'2"	240	26		
Visco Grgich	T	5'11"	210	25		
Fred Land	T-G	6'1"	220	23		
Bob Mike	T	6'1"	220	24		
Hal Puddy	T	6'3"	220	23		
John Woudenberg	T	6'3"	225	30		

Use Name – Guards	Pos.	Hgt	Wgt	Age	Int	Pts
Bruno Banducci	G	5'11"	215	26		
Roman Bentz (from NY)	G	6'2"	230	29		
Don Clark	G-LB	5'11"	197	24	1	
Jim Cox	G-LB	6'1"	208	27		
Paul Evansen	G	6'3"	240	26		
Riley Matheson	G-LB	6'2"	210	33	2	

Joe "the Jet" Perry got his pro career off the ground with a flash of light when, on his first play, he jetted 58 yards to the end zone. Perry would face insults and violence because of his black skin, but his talents and determination kept him in the league long after the black man had made his mark in pro football. But Perry was just one back on the team with the greatest running in the history of pro football. The '49ers gained 3,663 yards rushing, averaged 6.1 yards per carry, 262 yards per game, scored thirty-five rushing TDs, and a total of 495 points, all records which still stand. The starting backfield of Albert, Strzykalski, Eshmont and Perry rushed for 2,122 yards on 337 carries, and the second-string unit of Wallace, Lillywhite, Hall, and Standlee racked up 1,016 yards on only 174 attempts! The stand-out linemen leading the way for these ball carriers were tackles Visco Grgich and John Woudenberg and guards Bruno Banducci and Riley Matheson. Despite this, the '49ers still were bridesmaids for the Browns and their superior defense.

LOS ANGELES DONS 7-7-0 Jim Phelan

Scores of Each Game			
7	Chicago	0	
14	Cleveland	19	
17	BROOKLYN	7	
14	San Francisco	36	
20	NEW YORK	10	
49	CHICAGO	28	
14	BALTIMORE	29	
21	BUFFALO	35	
17	Brooklyn	0	
6	New York	38	
27	Buffalo	20	
17	Baltimore	14	
14	CLEVELAND	31	
21	SAN FRANCISCO	38	

Use Name	Pos.	Hgt	Wgt	Age	Int	Pts
John Brown	C-LB	6'4"	230	26	1	
Jack Flagerman (6 yds. on pass reception lateral)	C-LB	6'	218	26		
Bob Nelson (1 rush for –7 yds.)	C-LB	6'1"	215	28	1	
Ezz Anderson – Canadian Football League						

Use Name – Tackles	Pos.	Hgt	Wgt	Age	Int	Pts
Earl Audet	T	6'2"	252	27		
Don Avery	T	6'4"	260	27		
Dick Danabe	T	6'2"	235	23		
Clyde Johnson	T	6'6"	270	31		
Mike Perrotti (7 yds. on pass reception lateral)	T	6'3"	240	25		
Bill Smith (from CHI)	T	6'2"	250	21		
Bernie Winkler	T	6'1"	232	22		

Use Name – Guards	Pos.	Hgt	Wgt	Age	Int	Pts
Ray Frankowski	G	5'11"	230	29		
Len Levy	G	6'	252	27		
Al Lolotai	G	6'	233	27		
Knox Ramsey	G	6'1"	210	22		
Hank Rockwell (6 yds. on pass reception lateral)	G-C	6'4"	245	31		

Attendance at Dons' games dropped off this year, but wealthy owner Ben Lindheimer kept shelling out money to sign new talent. He brought halfback Herm Wedemeyer into the fold with a $12,000 contract, which was big money for a rookie. He signed Len Ford, a 230-pound end who would later become a great defensive end for the Browns. But all of Lindheimer's money couldn't get the Dons past Cleveland or San Francisco.

But the Dons did showcase some excellent football players. Phelan put in a spread formation specially for Glenn Dobbs and the great tailback regained his 1946 form. Veteran Joe Aguirre and rookies Wedemeyer and Ford gave Dobbs easy targets to throw to, linemen Bob Nelson and Bob Reinhard gave the passer plenty of time to set up, and place-kicker Ben Agajanian put his toeless right foot to good use in belting field goals — enough of an array of talent to claim show money in a difficult field.

CHICAGO ROCKETS 1-13-0 Ed McKeever

Scores of Each Game			
0	LOS ANGELES	7	
7	Buffalo	42	
21	BALTIMORE	14	
7	CLEVELAND	28	
10	Cleveland	21	
14	SAN FRANCISCO	31	
28	Los Angeles	49	
7	Brooklyn	21	
14	BROOKLYN	35	
7	New York	42	
21	San Francisco	44	
24	Baltimore	38	
35	BUFFALO	39	
7	NEW YORK	28	

Use Name	Pos.	Hgt	Wgt	Age	Int	Pts
Pete Lamana	C-LB	5'11"	210	27	1	
Fred Negus	C-LB	6'1"	205	26	5	6
John Rapacz	C	6'4"	230	23		
Farnham Johnson (2 PAT in 2 attemnts)	DE	6'	210	24		2
Ike Owens	DE	6'1"	190	27		
Fred Evans (to CHIB-NFL)	HB-DB	5'11"	186	27		
Joe Prokop	HB-DB	6'2"	170	27		

Use Name – Tackles	Pos.	Hgt	Wgt	Age	Int	Pts
Jim Brutz	T	6'	230	29		
Ziggy Czarobski	T	6'	225	25		
Ed Ecker	T	6'7"	285	25		
Nate Johnson	T	6'3"	240	28		
Roman Piskor	T	6'	245	30		
Emil Uremovich	T	6'2"	235	31	1	
Bill Bass – Canadian Football League						

Use Name – Guards	Pos.	Hgt	Wgt	Age	Int	Pts
George Bernhardt (from BKN)	G	5'10"	215	29		
Bob David (from LA-NFL)	G	6'	215	26		
Chet Kozel (from BUF)	G	6'2"	215	28		
Jim Pearcy	G	5'11"	220	29		
Joe Ruetz	G	6'	200	31		
Gasper Urban	G-LB	6'1"	215	25	1	

For the third straight year, the Rockets had new owners and a new coach. This year's head coach was Ed McKeever, privileged with a sideline seat for the Rockets' miserable season. The Rockets had the worst situation of any pro-football franchise; in addition to battling both the Bears and Cardinals for the Chicago sports dollar, the Rockets had to contend with constant turnover in their own leadership. Their pitiful performance on the field drove whatever fans they had away and forced this year's owners to look for a new buyer.

The Rockets fielded a collection of rookies, NFL rejects, and marginal veterans in their march to nowhere. The only player on the roster destined to go far in pro football spent most of the season in a hospital bed. Elroy "Crazy Legs" Hirsch got hit in an early game and didn't get up; when he awoke, he was in the hospital with a fractured skull and a loss of body coordination. Doctors told him to forget football; he instead forgot the doctors' advice and worked his way back to become a star pass receiver in the 1950s.

TEAM TOTALS

OFFENSE	First Downs: Tot	by Rsh	by Pas	by Pen	Rushing: No.	Yds.	Avg. Yds.	TD	Passing: Att.	Com	Comp. Pct.	Yds.	Avg. Yds. Att.	Avg. Yds. Comp	TD	Int.	Pct. Int.	Punting: No.	Avg. Yds.	Punt Returns: No.	Yds.	Avg. Yds.	TD	Kickoff Returns: No.	Yds.	Avg. Yds.	TD	Interception Returns: No.	Yds.	Avg. Yds.	TD	Penalties: No.	Yds.	Fumbles: No.	Lost	Points: Tot	PAT	FG Att	FG	Saf.	OFFENSE
CLEVE.	243	123	104	16	544	2557	4.7	25	344	178	51.7	2809	8.2	15.8	26	16	4.7	56	35.0	39	385	9.9	0	40	752	18.8	0	24	283	11.8	0	77	761	25	11	389	51	19	8	1	CLEVE.
S.F.	227	152	67	8	603	3663	6.1	35	288	162	56.3	2104	7.3	13.0	30	14	4.9	44	42.6	44	676	15.4	0	45	1098	24.4	1	32	357	11.2	2	89	794	38	21	495	64	8	5	1	S.F.
L.A.	186	78	93	15	400	1554	3.9	11	406	195	48.0	2497	6.2	12.8	21	24	5.9	76	47.2	44	730	16.6	1	56	1093	19.5	0	24	295	12.3	2	77	715	36	16	258	33	15	5	0	L.A.
CHICAGO	180	102	65	13	484	1719	3.6	8	341	146	42.8	2290	6.7	15.7	19	38	11.1	60	44.7	32	348	10.9	0	60	1265	21.1	0	19	247	13.0	0	78	659	51	27	202	28	4	2	0	CHICAGO
DEFENSE																																									DEFENSE
CLEVE.	171	84	74	13	436	1519	3.5	10	354	159	44.9	2097	5.9	13.2	14	24	6.8	73	39.7	32	356	11.1	0	48	1151	24.0	0	16	359	22.4	1	76	657	44	16	190	25	8	3	0	CLEVE.
S.F.	203	100	90	13	468	1906	4.1	11	374	184	49.2	2615	7.0	13.2	23	32	8.6	68	40.5	24	314	13.1	0	70	1511	21.6	0	14	119	8.5	0	72	567	35	20	248	32	5	2	0	S.F.
L.A.	209	125	70	14	514	2456	4.8	14	344	164	47.7	2473	7.5	15.7	24	24	7.0	67	40.7	52	644	12.4	1	45	962	21.4	0	24	206	8.6	0	76	806	38	16	305	38	12	7	3	L.A.
CHICAGO	217	117	81	19	538	2614	4.9	33	318	155	48.7	2568	7.8	16.0	23	19	6.0	57	42.3	36	605	16.8	2	38	683	17.5	0	38	636	16.7	3	89	707	30	14	439	58	11	3	0	CHICAGO

							RUSHING				PASSING								RECEIVING				PUNTING		KICKING						PUNT RETURNS				KICKOFF RETURNS			
Use Name – Backs & Ends	Pos.	Age	Hgt	Wgt	Pts	Int	No.	Yds	Avg	TD	Att	Comp	%	Yds	Yd/Att	TD	Int–%	RK	No.	Yds	Avg	TD	No.	Avg	Pat	Att	%	FG	Att	%	No.	Yds	Avg	TD	No.	Yds	Avg	TD
CLEVELAND BROWNS																																						
Otto Graham	QB-DB	26	6'1"	190	36	1	23	146	6.3	6	333	173	52	2713	8.1	25	15– 5	3													1	12	12	0				
Cliff Lewis	QB-DB	25	5'11"	165		9	5	44	8.8	0	8	4	50	69	8.6	1	0– 0						1	18.0							26	258	10	0	7	147	21	0
George Terlep (from BUF)	QB	26	5'10"	180			1	4	4.0	0	4	1	25	27	6.8	0	2– 50																					
Marion Motley	FB-LB	28	6'1"	220	42		157	964	6.1	5	1	0	0	0	0.0	0	0– 0		13	192	15	2													14	337	24	0
Special Delivery Jones	HB	29	5'10"	195	60		100	400	4.0	5									14	293	21	5																
Bill Boedecker	HB-DB	24	5'11"	190	30		78	254	3.3	3									13	237	18	2									2	8	4	0	4	61	15	0
Dub Jones	HB-DB	23	6'4"	200	18		33	149	4.5	1									9	119	13	2													2	35	18	0
Ara Parseghian	HB-DB	25	5'10"	192	12	1	32	135	4.2	1									2	31	16	1													2	41	21	0
Ollie Cline	FB-LB	22	6'	200			29	129	4.4	0																									3	55	18	0
Bob Cowan	HB-DB	25	5'11"	185	30		33	99	3.0	1									15	265	18	4													3	53	18	0
Tony Adamle	FB-LB	24	6'	210	6		17	88	5.2	1																												
Tom Colella	HB-DB	30	6'	187	6	2	14	60	4.3	1									1	7	7	0	49	35.0							5	60	12	0				
Dean Sensenbaugher	HB-DB	23	5'9"	190	6		18	59	3.3	1																												
Tommy James	HB-DB	24	5'10"	180		4	1	8	8.0	0									1	44	44	0									5	47	9	0				
Mac Speedie	OE	28	6'3"	200	24		1	7	7.0	0									68	816	14	4													1	13	13	0
Dante Lavelli	OE	25	6'	190	30		1	9	9.0	0									25	463	19	5													1	0	0	0
Horace Gillom	OE-DE	27	6'1"	208	6														20	295	15	1	6	37.8											3	10	3	0
John Yonakor	OE-DE	27	6'5"	218		1													5	27	5	0																
George Young	OE DE	24	6'3"	210	6														2	20	10	0																
Lou Groza	T	24	6'3"	215	75																				51	52	98	8	19	42								
SAN FRANCISCO 49ers																																						
Frankie Albert	QB	28	5'10"	160	49		69	349	5.1	8	264	154	58	1990	7.6	29	10– 4	2	1	1	1	0	35	44.8	1	2	50											
Bev Wallace	QB	25	6'2"	180			3	2	0.7	0	22	8	36	114	5.2	1	3– 14						4	38.4														
Johnny Strzykalski	HB-DB	25	5'9"	190	66	3	141	915	6.5	4	1	0	0	0	0.0	0	0– 0		26	485	19	7									13	201	15	0	9	185	21	0
Joe Perry	FB-DB	21	6'	195	72	1	77	562	7.3	10									8	79	10	1													4	145	36	1
Forrest Hall	HB	25	5'8"	155	12		66	413	6.3	2									4	87	22	0									3	97	32	0	13	369	28	0
Verl Lillywhite	HB-DB	21	5'10"	185	18	3	53	340	6.4	3	1	0	0	0	0.0	0	1–100		1	–1	–1	0	3	25.3							3	41	14	0				
Len Eshmont	HB-DB	31	5'11"	178	12	1	50	296	5.9	1									14	214	15	0													1	32	32	0
Norm Standlee	FB-LB	29	6'2"	245	18		52	261	5.0	3									1	1	1	0													1	31	31	0
Jim Cason	HB-DB	21	6'	168	18	5	20	146	7.3	2									4	99	25	1									22	309	14	0	10	212	21	0
Bob Sullivan	HB-DB	25	5'10"	190	6	1	33	121	3.7	0									4	58	15	1													2	40	20	0
Ed Carr	HB-DB	21	6'	185	12	7	14	121	8.6	1									3	40	13	0													1	16	16	0
Joe Vetrano	HB	26	5'9"	170	83		12	71	5.9	1									1	34	34	0	1	38.0	62	66	94	5	8	63					1	38	38	0
Paul Crowe	HB-DB	24	6'1"	195	12	5	12	65	5.4	0									0	16	–	1									2	14	7	0	2	18	9	0
Alyn Beals	OE	27	6'	185	84														46	591	13	14																
Nick Susoeff	OE-DE	27	6'1"	210	6														27	237	9	1													1	12	12	0
Hal Shoener	OE-DE	25	6'3"	200	18														15	76	5	3																
Gail Bruce	OE-DE	24	6'1"	205			1	1	1.0	0									5	49	10	0																
Norm Maloney	OE-DE	25	6'1"	190	7														1	29	29	1			1	1	100											
Clarence Howell	OE-DE	21	6'1"	188		1													1	9	9	0																
LOS ANGELES DONS																																						
Glenn Dobbs	TB-DB	28	6'4"	210	24	1	91	539	5.9	4	369	185	50	2403	6.5	21	20– 5	5	2	11	6	0	68	49.1											2	38	19	0
Herm Wedemeyer	TB-HB	24	5'10"	178	12		79	249	3.2	0	30	9	30	79	2.6	0	3– 10		36	330	9	2	1	10.0							23	368	16	0	11	240	22	0
Bill Reinhard	TB-HB-DB	26	5'10"	170	12	4	6	31	5.2	0	5	0	0	0	0.0	0	0– 0		5	48	10	0									16	276	17	1	2	41	21	0
Walt Clay	HB-DB	24	5'11"	195	24	2	86	293	3.4	3									10	118	12	1													4	48	12	0
John Kimbrough	FB	30	6'2"	210	30		76	189	2.5	3									10	131	13	0													4	54	14	0
Mike Graham	FB-LB	23	6'	200	6	1	19	69	3.6	1									0	2	–	0													6	145	24	0
Jeff Durkota	FB-LB	24	6'	205		1	14	66	4.7	0									2	12	6	0													9	198	22	0
Lin Sexton	HB-DB	22	6'	180		1	7	39	5.6	0																					3	47	16	0	3	49	16	0
Bob Reinhard	FB-DT	27	6'4"	238			1	21	21.0	0									4	54	14	0	6	34.0							1	23	23	0	3	51	17	0
Len Masini (from SF)	FB-LB	27	6'	225			3	12	4.0	0									1	–1	–1	0																
Bob Kelly	HB-DB	23	5'10"	183		3	3	10	3.3	0																												
John Naumu	HB	27	5'8"	175			1	0	0.0	0													1	34.0											6	131	22	0
Walt Heap	BB-DB	26	6'1"	210	6	5	3	12	4.0	0									2	9	5	0																
Dick Ottele	BB-DB	21	6'3"	210			2	11	5.5	0																									3	47	16	0
Bob Mitchell	BB-DB	27	5'11"	195		3	2	–2	–1.0	0	2	1	50	15	7.5	0	1– 50																					
Joe Aguirre	OE-DE	29	6'4"	225	56														38	599	16	9			2	3	67								1	10	10	0
Len Ford	OE-DE	22	6'4"	230	42	1													31	598	19	7													1	24	24	0
Dale Gentry	OE-DE	31	6'3"	223															28	308	11	0																
Burr Baldwin	OE-DE	26	6'1"	195															10	96	10	0																
Bill Fisk	OE-DE	31	6'	205															9	102	11	0																
Lou Mihajlovich	OE	23	5'11"	175															4	42	11	0																
Ben Agajanian	K	29	6'	215	46																				31	32	97	5	15	33								
CHICAGO ROCKETS																																						
Jess Freitas	QB	27	5'10"	170			24	25	1.0	0	167	84	50	1425	8.5	14	16– 10	5																				
Sam Vacanti (to BAL)	QB	26	5'11"	200	12		7	7	1.0	2	116	47	41	633	5.5	2	15– 13	11																				
Angelo Bertelli	QB	27	6'1"	190			2	–1	–0.5	0	32	7	22	60	1.9	1	3– 9																					
Tom Farris	QB	27	6'1"	185			4	5	1.3	0	9	3	33	24	2.7	0	3– 33																					
Julie Rykovich (from BUF)	HB-DB	24	6'2"	200	36	3	96	425	4.4	6	1	1	100	12	12.0	0	0– 0		5	71	14	0									1	23	23	0	7	129	18	0
Eddie Prokop	HB-DB	26	5'11"	200	24		54	266	4.9	1	1	0	0	0	0.0	0	0– 0		7	223	32	3									6	80	13	0	15	323	22	0
Jim Mello (from LA-NFL)	FB-DB	27	5'10"	190	6		50	243	4.9	1									3	38	13	0													2	30	15	0
Dewey Proctor	FB-LB	27	5'11"	215	6		47	190	4.0	1									2	18	9	0																
Bob Livingstone	HB-DB	26	6'	175	12		55	174	3.2	0									15	240	16	2									3	24	8	0	9	211	23	0
Chuck Fenenbock (from LA)	HB-DB	30	5'9"	175	6		43	174	4.0	0	15	4	27	136	9.1	2	1– 7		8	111	14	1									17	169	10	0	14	311	22	0
Floyd Simmons	HB-DB	23	6'1"	200	12		36	121	3.4	1									2	60	31	1													3	77	26	0
Bill Kellagher	FB-LB	28	5'11"	205	6		33	97	2.9	1																									3	54	18	0
Crazy Legs Hirsch	HB-DB	24	6'2"	190	6	2	23	93	4.0	0									7	101	14	1									2	27	14	0	1	10	10	0
Harry Clark (from LA)	HB-DB	30	6'	195			22	79	3.6	0									4	38	10	0									2	27	14	0	4	96	24	0
Ernie Lewis	FB-LB	24	6'1"	215			13	54	4.2	0									1	6	6	0	60	44.7														
Steve Juzwik	HB	30	5'8"	184	5		13	19	1.5	0									1	5	5	0			5	5	100											
Bob Perina	HB-DB	27	6'1"	205		6	6	1	0.2	0									2	13	7	0									2	14	7	0	3	52	17	0
Fay King	OE	26	6'3"	195	42														50	647	13	7													1	11	11	0
Bob Jensen	OE-DE	22	6'4"	207	6														20	276	14	1													1	10	10	0
Ray Kuffel	OE-DE	26	6'3"	215	18														19	365	19	3													1	16	16	0
Jim McCarthy	OE-DE	26	6'1"	205	27														3	30	10	0			21	21	100	2	3	67								

N. F. L. – December 19, at Philadelphia (Attendance 36,309)

Fit for Neither Man Nor Beast

A heavy snowstorm that fell throughout the game made football a makeshift operation in this championship game. The tarpaulin was taken off the field only thirty minutes before the opening kickoff, obliterating all the yard markers as it was rolled up; all first down and out-of-bounds decisions were pure judgment decisions by the officials. Before the game was very old, several inches of snow coated the field and made secure footing a pipe dream. A consistent passing attack was out of the question, but both clubs had a full stable of strong runners. On their first play from scrimmage, the Eagles went for broke, with Tommy Thompson heaving a long bomb which Jack Ferrante hauled 65 yards to the end zone; an offside penalty nullified the score, however, and the game settled into a contest of power running. The Cardinals used smashes by Elmer Angsman, Pat Harder, and Charlie Trippi to move the ball down to the Philadelphia 29-yard line, where the attack stalled. Several Cardinal players cleared a spot with their hands for the ball to be spotted for a field-goal attempt, but Harder's boot sailed wide. The Eagles had a scoring opportunity in the second quarter when they recovered Angsman's fumble on the Chicago 21. The Cards then intercepted one of Thompson's passes but put the ball into play on the 7-yard line, within the shadow of their own goal post. After three plays, Ray Mallouf punted out to the 45, but Philadelphia's Pat McHugh returned the ball to the 21. Sticking strictly to running plays and one screen pass, Thompson drove his team down to the 8-yard line before the Cards stiffened, but Cliff Patton's field-goal attempt from the 12 missed the mark. The half ended with the score 0-0, with visibility cut to a minimum and with snowbanks piling up on the field and along the sidelines. The hardy fans stayed with the game, waiting to see which club would get a break to enable them to score. On the first series of downs in the second half, the Cards recovered Steve Van Buren's fumble at mid-field and drove down to the 30-yard line before losing the ball when a fourth-and-one power play failed. The big break finally came near the end of the third quarter, when the Eagles recovered a fumble from a poor exchange between Mallouf and Angsman on the Chicago 17. Bosh Pritchard then ran through the left side for six yards as the quarter ended. After the teams went to the other end of the field and the officials lined the ball up as closely as they could, Joe Muha plowed through the middle down to the eight. Thompson then snuck down to the 5, and Van Buren blasted through a big hole on the right side for the remaining yardage. Cliff Patton added the extra point to make the score 7-0, a truly imposing lead in these weather conditions. The Eagles later in the period were pinned deep in their own territory, with a third down and 16 to go on their own 8-yard line. Thompson got the Eagles out of the hole by faking a pitch-out to Van Buren and running up the middle for 17 yards and the first down. The Eagles ate up most of the remaining time and were camped on the Chicago five-yard line when the clock ran out and mercifully sent the players and fans to the warmth of their homes.

INDIVIDUAL STATISTICS

PHILADELPHIA	No	Yds	Avg.	CHICAGO	No	Yds	Avg.
RUSHING							
Van Buren	26	98	3.8	Angsman	10	33	3.3
Pritchard	16	67	4.2	Harder	11	30	2.7
Thompson	11	50	4.5	Trippi	9	26	2.9
Myers	2	7	3.5	Mallouf	2	5	2.5
Muha	2	3	1.5	Clatt	1	2	1.2
	57	225	3.9	Schwall	1	0	0.0
					34	96	2.8
RECEIVING							
Ferrante	1	7	7.0	Kutner	2	19	9.5
Pihos	1	0	0.0	Dewell	1	16	16.0
	2	7	3.5		3	35	11.7
PUNTING							
Muha	5		38.6	Mallouf	8		37.4
PUNT RETURNS							
McHugh	2	22	11.0	Trippi	2	11	5.5
KICKOFF RETURNS							
McHugh	1	18	18.0	Schwall	1	20	20.0
				Trippi	1	15	15.0
					2	35	17.5
INTERCEPTION RETURNS							
Steele	1	0	0.0	Cochran	2	20	10.0

PASSING

PHILADELPHIA	Att	Comp	Comp Pct.	Yds	Int	Yds/ Att.	Yds/ Comp
Thompson	12	2	16.7	7	2	0.6	3.5
CHICAGO							
Mallouf	7	3	42.9	35	0	5.0	11.7
Trippi	2	0	0.0	0	0	–	–
Eikenburg	2	0	0.0	0	1	–	–
	11	3	27.3	35	1	3.2	11.7

SCORING

PHILADELPHIA	0	0	0	7–7
CHICAGO CARDS	0	0	0	0–0

Fourth Quarter
Phi. Van Buren, 5 yard rush
PAT – Patton (kick) 1:04

TEAM STATISTICS

PHIL.		CHIC.
16	First Downs – Total	6
15	by Rushing	3
0	by Passing	3
1	by Penalty	0
1	Fumbles – Number	3
1	Lost Ball	2
3	Penalties – Number	4
17	Yards	33
3	Field Goals Missed	1

A. A. F. C – December 19, at Cleveland (Attendance 22,981)

Handily Capping a Perfect Season

The game was considered no contest before it even started, and that was exactly how it turned out. The Cleveland Browns, champions of the Western Division, had swept undefeated through their fourteen-game schedule with a blistering offense and stubborn defense. The Eastern champion Buffalo Bills had a potent offense but allowed almost as many points as they scored. They evenly split their fourteen games and had to beat Baltimore in a divisional playoff to take the title in the weak Eastern sector. The Browns began by converting an interception into a first-quarter touchdown. After Tommy James returned the ball 30 yards to the Buffalo 20-yard line, the Browns took seven plays to cover the distance, with Special Delivery Jones's three-yard run scoring the points. Completely stymying George Ratterman's passes, the Browns got their second first-half score when George Young returned Rex Bumgardner's fumble 18 yards for a touchdown. The score was 14-0 at halftime, but the Browns really poured it on in the second half. Within three minutes they had intercepted a Ratterman pass and driven 21 yards for the score, with an Otto Graham to Special Delivery Jones pass covering the final nine yards. Later in the quarter, Marion Motley ran 29 yards to score, with Lou Groza's conversion running the score to 28-0. With the game now out of hand, the Bills replaced Ratterman at quarterback with Jim Still and promptly went on to score their only touchdown of the afternoon. After making one first down on the drive, Still punted the ball to Cleveland, but the Bills retained possession on a roughing-the-kicker penalty. On the next play, Still passed to Bumgardner for 25 yards, bringing the ball down to the Cleveland 28. After one running play, Still passed to Bill O'Connor for another first down on the 10-yard line. A pass to Al Baldwin then put the Bills on the scoreboard, and Graham Armstrong's kick made it 28-7. The Browns added on three fourth-period touchdowns to make the final count an embarrassing 49-7. Dub Jones returned the kickoff after the Buffalo score 46 yards down to the Bills' 34-yard line, and after Jones ran the ball for three yards Marion Motley blasted through the Bills for the final 31 yards. The final two touchdowns came after interceptions, the first on a drive of 60 yards and the second on Lou Saban's 39-yard return of the pilfered pass, and by the time the clock ended the match, both clubs had their second-stringers on the field.

SCORING

CLEVELAND	7	7	14	21–49
BUFFALO	0	0	7	0– 7

First Quarter
Cle. E. Jones, 3 yard rush 14:50
PAT – Groza (kick)

Second Quarter
Cle. Young, 18 yard fumble return PAT – Groza (kick) 3:25

Third Quarter
Cle. E. Jones, 9 yard pass from Graham 2:02
PAT – Groza (kick)
Cle. Motley, 29 yard rush 10:35
PAT – Groza (kick)
Buf. A. Baldwin, 10 yard pass from Still 14:56
PAT – Armstrong (kick)

Fourth Quarter
Cle. Motley, 31 yard rush 0:44
PAT – Groza (kick)
Cle. Motley, 5 yard rush 9:44
PAT – Groza (kick)
Cle. Saban, 39 yard pass interception (by Still) 11:49
PAT – Groza (kick)

TEAM STATISTICS

CLE.		BUF.
20	First Downs – Total*	13
10	by Rushing	4
8	by Passing	7
2	by Penalty	2
6	Fumbles – Number	3
3	Lost Ball	3
9	Penalties – Number	7
90	Yards	27
1	Field Goals Missed	0

* – Includes Touchdowns

INDIVIDUAL STATISTICS

CLEVELAND	No	Yds	Avg.	BUFFALO	No	Yds	Avg.
RUSHING							
Motley	14	133	9.5	Bumgardner	11	34	3.1
E. Jones	8	29	3.6	Tomasetti	11	20	1.8
D. Jones	5	22	4.4	Mutryn	8	8	1.0
Cline	1	20	20.0	Kulbitski	2	1	0.5
Parseghian	4	14	3.5	Still	1	0	0.0
Sensenb'her	2	2	1.0		33	63	1.9
Colella	1	1	1.0				
Graham	1	0	0.0				
Adamle	2	–1	–0.5				
Terlep	2	–5	–2.5				
	40	215	5.4				
RECEIVING							
E. Jones	3	39	13.0	O'Connor	3	41	13.7
Speedie	2	22	11.0	Mutryn	2	5	2.5
Lavelli	2	16	8.0	Bumgardner	1	25	25.0
D. Jones	2	13	6.5	Kulbitski	1	14	14.0
Gillom	1	15	15.0	A. Baldwin	1	10	10.0
Motley	1	13	13.0	Gibson	1	7	7.0
	11	118	10.7	Snyder	1	4	4.0
				Tomasetti	1	–2	–2.0
					11	104	9.5
PUNTING							
Colella	2		31.0	Still	6		42.5
Gillom	1		36.0				
	3		32.7				
PUNT RETURNS							
Lewis	2	10	5.0	None			
Colella	1	18	18.0				
Terlep	1	13	13.0				
	4	41	10.3				
KICKOFF RETURNS							
D. Jones	1	46	46.0	Schneider	2	33	16.5
Motley	1	20	20.0	Mutyrn	1	18	18.0
	2	66	33.0		3	51	17.0
INTERCEPTION RETURNS							
James	2	36	18.0	Maggioli	1	2	2.0
Saban	1	39	39.0				
Adamle	1	4	4.0				
Colella	1	1	1.0				
	5	80	16.0				

PASSING

CLEVELAND	Att	Comp	Comp Pct.	Yds	Int	Yds/ Att.	Yds/ Comp
Graham	24	11	45.8	118	1	4.9	10.7
E. Jones	2	0	0.0	0	0	–	–
	26	11	42.3	118	1	4.5	10.7
BUFFALO							
Still	18	6	33.3	80	2	4.4	13.3
Ratterman	18	5	27.8	24	3	1.3	4.8
	36	11	30.6	104	5	2.9	9.5

N.F.L. – December 18, at Los Angeles (Attendance 27,980)

Flying High in the Mud

A steady downpour of rain turned the playing field into a quagmire. It was a terrain which helped the Eagles, who relied on their big backs to move the ball on the ground, and hurt the Rams, who were primarily a passing team. Both teams slid around in the mud all afternoon, with only Steve Van Buren of the Eagles showing any ability to run in the mud; he picked up 196 yards rushing to set a new championship-game record. The Eagles' first-half touchdown came on a 63-yard drive during which Tommy Thompson completed three key passes, a weapon that the Rams could not ignite today. Thompson hit Jack Ferrante for 11 yards on one toss, hit him again for 15 yards, and fired a deep pass over the middle to Pete Pihos that covered 31 yards and scored six points. The Rams meanwhile could get no attack rolling in the mud, and a blocked punt in the third quarter made the final margin 14-0, Philadelphia.

SCORING

LOS ANGELES	0	0	0	0	– 0
PHILADELPHIA	0	7	7	0	–14

Second Quarter
Phi. Pihos, 31 yard pass from Thompson
PAT – Patton (kick)

Third Quarter
Phi. Skladany, 2 yard blocked punt return
PAT – Patton (kick)

TEAM STATISTICS

L.A.		PHIL.
7	First Downs – Total	17
0	First Downs – Rushing	12
6	First Downs – Passing	4
1	First Downs – Penalty	1
9	Punts	6
38.1	Average Punt Distance	36.3
17	Punt Return Yards	14
1	Fumbles	4
0	Fumbles Lost	1
4	Penalties	6
25	Yards Penalized	40

INDIVIDUAL STATISTICS

RUSHING

LOS ANGELES	No	Yds	Avg.	PHILADELPHIA	No	Yds	Avg.
Gehrke	3	13	4.3	Van Buren	31	196	6.3
V. T. Smith	6	11	1.8	Parmer	15	41	2.7
Hoerner	7	10	1.4	Scott	6	23	3.8
Waterfield	2	3	1.5	Thompson	4	7	1.8
Hirsch	2	0	0.0	Ziegler	3	4	1.3
Kalmanir	2	0	0.0	Pritchard	1	2	2.0
Van Brocklin	2	–16	–8.0	Myers	1	1	1.0
	24	21	0.9		61	274	4.5

PASSING

LOS ANGELES	Att	Comp	Comp Pct.	Yds	Int	Yds/ Att.	Yds/ Comp
Waterfield	13	5	38.5	43	1	3.3	8.6
Van Brocklin	14	5	35.7	55	0	3.9	11.0
	27	10	37.0	98	1	3.6	9.8
PHILADELPHIA							
Thompson	9	5	55.6	68	2	7.6	13.6

A.A.F.C. – December 11, at Cleveland (Attendance 22,550)

The Final Championship

With the league not arranged into divisions this year, a playoff system was installed in which the first- and fourth-place and the second- and third-place teams played each other. In these first-round matches the Browns beat Buffalo 31-21 and the '49ers beat New York 17-7, putting Cleveland and San Francisco into the championship game. Several days before the contest news broke that the NFL and the AAFC would merge, so that it was fitting for the two most successful AAFC clubs to play in the final league game. Attendance at the game was unusually low, but the Browns and '49ers fought a spirited battle in the snow and slush for the final AAFC crown. The Browns had won each previous championship but had never before faced the '49ers in the title game. This year's playoff system gave the '49ers, always finishing second behind Cleveland in the Western Division, their first shot at all the marbles. The Browns' defense turned out to be the key of the game, foiling the running of Norm Standlee and Joe Perry and rushing Frankie Albert whenever he attempted to pass. The only score of the first half came when Cleveland's Special Delivery Jones blasted into the end zone from two yards out, with Lou Groza adding the extra point. When Marion Motley broke loose on a trap play for a 63-yard touchdown in the third quarter, San Francisco's prospects appeared bleak. A Frankie Albert to Paul Salata touchdown pass brought the '49ers back to within seven points of the Browns in the final period, but a final Cleveland touchdown ended the game 21-7 and gave the Browns a complete set of AAFC championship trophies.

SCORING

CLEVELAND	7	0	7	7	–21
SAN FRANCISCO	0	0	0	7	– 7

First Quarter
Cle. E. Jones, 2 yard rush
PAT – Groza (kick) 7:20

Third Quarter
Cle. Motley, 63 yard rush
PAT – Groza (kick) 9:30

Fourth Quarter
S.F. Salata, 23 yard pass from Albert 0:14
PAT – Yetrano (kick)
Cle. D. Jones, 4 yard rush
PAT – Groza (kick) 6:13

TEAM STATISTICS

CLE.		S. F.
16	First Downs – Total	14
11	by Rushing	7
5	by Passing	7
0	by Penalty	0
0	Fumbles – Number	2
0	Lost Ball	0
1	Penalties – Number	0
5	Yards Penalized	0
0	Field Goals Missed	1

INDIVIDUAL STATISTICS

RUSHING

CLEVELAND	No	Yds	Avg.	SAN FRANCISCO	No	Yds	Avg.
Motley	8	75	9.4	Albert	5	41	8.2
E. Jones	16	63	3.9	Perry	6	36	6.0
Graham	9	62	6.9	Standlee	10	21	2.1
Lahr	1	7	7.0	Garlin	3	13	4.3
James	2	7	3.5	Cathcart	9	11	1.2
D. Jones	4	2	0.5		33	122	3.7
Lewis	1	1	1.0				
	41	217	5.3				

RECEIVING

CLEVELAND	No	Yds	Avg.	SAN FRANCISCO	No	Yds	Avg.
Lavelli	4	56	14.0	Salata	3	47	15.7
Speedie	1	37	37.0	Beals	3	26	8.7
D. Jones	1	25	25.0	Shoener	2	25	12.5
E. Jones	1	10	10.0	Garlin	1	10	10.0
	7	128	18.3		9	108	12.0

PUNTING

CLEVELAND	No	Yds	Avg.	SAN FRANCISCO	No	Yds	Avg.
Gillom	4		43.0	Albert	6		44.0

PUNT RETURNS

CLEVELAND	No	Yds	Avg.	SAN FRANCISCO	No	Yds	Avg.
Lewis	3	38	12.7	Cathcart	1	13	13.0
Lahr	2	23	11.5	Cason	1	10	10.0
	5	61	12.2		2	23	11.5

KICKOFF RETURNS

CLEVELAND	No	Yds	Avg.	SAN FRANCISCO	No	Yds	Avg.
Lahr	2	41	20.5	Cathcart	1	22	22.0

PASSING

CLEVELAND	Att	Comp	Comp Pct.	Yds	Int	Yds/ Att.	Yds/ Comp
Graham	17	7	41.2	128	0	7.5	18.3
SAN FRANCISCO							
Albert	24	9	37.5	108	0	4.5	12.0
Lillywhite	1	0	0.0	0	0	–	–
	25	9	36.0	108	0	4.3	12.0

PHILADELPHIA EAGLES 11-1-0 Greasy Neale

Scores of Each Game		
7	N.Y. Bulldogs	0
22	Detroit	14
28	CHIC. CARDS	3
21	Chic. Bears	38
49	WASHINGTON	14
38	Pittsburgh	7
38	LOS ANGELES	14
44	Washington	21
42	N.Y. BULLDOGS	0
34	PITTSBURGH	17
24	N.Y. Giants	3
17	N.Y. GIANTS	3

Use Name	Pos.	Hgt	Wgt	Age	Int	Pts
Chuck Bednarik	C-LB	6'3"	230	24		
Vic Lindskog	C	6'1"	200	33		
Alex Wojciechowicz	C-LB	5'11"	235	34	2	
Leo Skladany	DE	6'1"	205	22		
Jay MacDowell	DE-T	6'2"	222	30		
Dick Humbert	DB-OE	6'1"	186	30	7	
(1 reception for 14 yds.)						

Use Name – Tackles	Pos.	Hgt	Wgt	Age	Int	Pts
Otis Douglas	T	6'1"	226	37		
Mike Jarmoluk (from NYB)	T	6'5"	265	26	1	
George Savitsky	T	6'2"	242	25		
Vic Sears	T	6'3"	225	31		
Al Wistert	T	6'1"	217	28		

Use Name – Guards	Pos.	Hgt	Wgt	Age	Int	Pts
Walt Barnes	G	6'1"	240	31		
Mario Giannelli	G	6'	265	28		2
Bucko Kilroy	G	6'2"	248	28		
John Magee	G	5'10"	222	26		
Duke Maronic	G	5'9"	215	28		

The Eagles may have been champions, but the high expenses of running the team were making a pauper of owner Alexis Thompson. Thus, before the season opened, a group of 100 Philadelphians, each paying $3,000, bought themselves the NFL champions.

The Eagles welcomed their new benefactors by rolling through their schedule to an easy Eastern Division title. The Philadelphia attack moved mostly on the ground, with Steve Van Buren and Bosh Pritchard punching out yardage play after play. Especially devastating was the Eagles' end run, with both guards and fullback Joe Muha leading Van Buren around the flank. To complement his powerful offense, coach Greasy Neale devised a 5-2-4 defense which stopped enemy passers cold in the new era of aerial warfare.

PITTSBURGH STEELERS 6-5-1 John Michelosen

Scores of Each Game		
28	N.Y. GIANTS	7
14	WASHINGTON	27
14	DETROIT	7
21	N.Y. Giants	17
24	N.Y. BULLDOGS	13
7	PHILADELPHIA	38
14	Washington	27
7	LOS ANGELES	7
30	Green Bay	7
17	Philadelphia	34
21	Chic. Bears	30
27	N.Y. Bulldogs	0

Use Name	Pos.	Hgt	Wgt	Age	Int	Pts
Bob Balog	C-LB	6'2"	225	25		
Vince Ragunas	LB	5'11"	200	25		
Frank Sinkovitz	C-LB	6'1"	215	26	1	
Bill Walsh	C	6'2"	230	22		
Bob Davis	DE	5'11"	190	28		
Bill McPeak	DE	6'1"	200	24		
Charlie Mehelich	DE	6'1"	200	27		

Use Name – Tackles	Pos.	Hgt	Wgt	Age	Int	Pts
Pete Barbolak	T	6'3"	235	23		
Carl Samuelson	T	6'4"	245	26		8
Walt Szot	T	6'1"	225	30		
Jack Wiley	T	5'11"	210	28		
(1 reception for 10 yds.)						
Frank Wydo	T	6'4"	215	25		
(2 receptions for 21 yds.)						

Use Name – Guards	Pos.	Hgt	Wgt	Age	Int	Pts
Darrell Hogan	G-LB	5'10"	210	23	1	
Bill Moore	G	5'11"	220	26		
Leo Nobile	G-LB	5'10"	215	27	1	
Steve Suhey	G	5'11"	215	27		

With every other team in the league lining up in the explosive T formation, the Steelers stuck with the hard-hitting, conservative single-wing attack. While other clubs were throwing the ball in what old-timers considered reckless fashion, Pittsburgh still ground out its yardage with off-tackle power plays and wingback reverses. Rookie Joe Geri was the last of the triple-threat tailbacks, but his passing was much less threatening than his running and kicking. With the attack relying almost completely on the running of Jerry Nuzum and Geri, the Steelers needed a rock-rib defense to win six games. The free-substitution rule, in on a trial basis this year, enabled coach John Michelosen to devote certain players like rookie end Bill McPeak exclusively to defense and to save his entire starting offensive backfield of Seabright, Geri, Nuzum and Papich from the rigors of playing defense.

NEW YORK GIANTS 6-6-0 Steve Owen

Scores of Each Game		
7	Pittsburgh	28
38	N.Y. Bulldogs	14
45	Washington	35
17	PITTSBURGH	21
35	CHIC. BEARS	28
41	Chic. Cards	38
24	N.Y. BULLDOGS	31
30	Green Bay	10
21	DETROIT	45
23	WASHINGTON	7
3	PHILADELPHIA	24
3	Philadelphia	17

Use Name	Pos.	Hgt	Wgt	Age	Int	Pts
John Cannady	LB	6'2"	225	25	1	
Tex Coulter	C	6'4"	245	24		
Carl Fennema	C-LB	6'2"	210	23		
George Kershaw	DE	6'4"	210	22		
Declared ineligible – Frankie Filchock, Merle Hapes						

Use Name – Tackles	Pos.	Hgt	Wgt	Age	Int	Pts
Bill Austin	OT	6'1"	218	20	1	
Carl Butkus	T	6'1"	245	27		
Al DeRogatis	DT	6'4"	235	22		6
Ralph Hutchinson	T	6'2"	230	24		
Ed Kolman	DT	6'2"	235	30		
(2 kickoff returns for 24 yds.)						
John Sanchez (from WAS)	T	6'3"	240	28		
Jim White	OT	6'2"	225	28		

Use Name – Guards	Pos.	Hgt	Wgt	Age	Int	Pts
Jon Baker	G-LB	6'2"	210	26		
Jake Colhouer	G	6'1"	210	27		
Don Ettinger	G-LB	6'2"	215	26	2	
Ed Royston	G	6'1"	220	26		

Gaping holes were still evident in the Giants' lineup as coach Steve Owen slowly filled his squad with young quality players. Second-year pro Chuck Conerly had staked out the quarterback job for his own with his pinpoint passing. Halfback Choo-Choo Roberts had a real taste for the end zone, scoring seventeen touchdowns to lead the league in TDs and scoring, and, with free substitution now in effect, coach Owen began developing specialists in the modern tradition. Sophomore safetyman Em Tunnell was a ball hawk for interceptions and a one-man offense when returning a punt or interception. Two rookie linemen were assigned to the different platoons, Bill Austin to the offense and Al DeRogatis to the defense, while Ben Agajanian—a fourth-year man—provided Owen with a kicking specialist.

WASHINGTON REDSKINS 4-7-1 John Whelchel, Herman Ball

Scores of Each Game		
7	Chic. Cards.	38
27	Pittsburgh	14
35	N.Y. GIANTS	45
38	N.Y. BULLDOGS	14
14	Philadelphia	49
14	N.Y. Bulldogs	14
27	PITTSBURGH	14
21	PHILADELPHIA	44
21	CHIC. BEARS	31
7	N.Y. Giants	23
30	GREEN BAY	0
27	Los Angeles	53

Use Name	Pos.	Hgt	Wgt	Age	Int	Pts
Al DeMao	C-LB	6'2"	210	29	1	
Clyde Ehrhardt	C	6'1"	223	28		
Jim Peebles	DE	6'4"	232	29		
(1 rushing attempt for –3 yds.)						
Herb Shoener	DE	6'3"	202	26		6
Frank Seno	DB	6'	190	28		
(2 kickoff returns for 39 yds.)						

Use Name – Tackles	Pos.	Hgt	Wgt	Age	Int	Pts
John Adams	T	6'7"	230	27		
Bob Hendren	T	6'8"	240	26		
Laurie Niemi	T	6'1"	236	24		
Len Szafaryn	T	6'2"	212	21		

Use Name – Guards	Pos.	Hgt	Wgt	Age	Int	Pts
John Badaczewski	G	6'1"	237	27		
Mike Katrishen	G	6'1"	212	26		
Herb Siegert	G-LB	6'3"	210	25	2	
Joe Soboleski (from CHI-AAFC)	G	6'	215	23		
John Steber	G	6'	230	26		
Dick Stovall	G-LB	6'	198	25		

Owner George Marshall decided that his team needed discipline, so he hired John Whelchel, a retired admiral and ex-coach at Navy, as his new head coach. As things turned out, Whelchel got along fine with the players but couldn't stomach interference from the owner. Marshall figured that Whelchel was using his players all wrong, so he came to a practice and told the coach where to play his men. Whelchel looked Marshall in the eye, pulled an about-face, and marched off the field. Marshall turned a dark shade of purple, gathered a few of the players together, and yelled, "How could you let that man ruin the ball club?" When the players answered that Whelchel, after all, was the coach, the owner replied, "Hell, I hired him for a disciplinarian, not for a goddamn coach." This behavior, plus Marshall's unwillingness to sign any black players on the Redskins, assured Washington fans of another losing season.

NEW YORK BULLDOGS 1-10-1 Charley Ewart

Scores of Each Game		
0	PHILADELPHIA	7
14	N.Y. GIANTS	38
0	GREEN BAY	19
14	Washington	38
13	Pittsburgh	24
14	WASHINGTON	14
31	N.Y. Giants	24
20	CHIC. CARDS	65
0	Philadelphia	42
20	Los Angeles	42
27	Detroit	28
0	PITTSBURGH	27

Use Name	Pos.	Hgt	Wgt	Age	Int	Pts
Bill Campbell (from CHIC)	LB	6'	195	29		
Joe Domnanovich	C-LB	6'1"	215	30	1	
Herb Ellis	C-LB	6'2"	205	23		
Merv Pregulman	C	6'3"	214	27		
Sam Tamburo	DE	6'2"	200	23		
Joe Watt	DB	5'11"	185	28	1	
Al Dekdebrun – Canadian Football League						

Use Name – Tackles	Pos.	Hgt	Wgt	Age	Int	Pts
Tom Blake	T	6'2"	220	23		
(1 punt return for 6 yds.)						
Frank Gaul	T	6'	200	23		
John Nolan	T	6'2"	240	23		
George Roman	T	6'4"	245	23		
Carroll Vogelaar	T	6'3"	260	29		

Use Name – Guards	Pos.	Hgt	Wgt	Age	Int	Pts
Fritz Barzilauskas	G	6'1"	230	28		
Stan Batinski	G	5'10"	215	32		
Larry Olsonoski (from GB)	G	6'2"	214	24		
Joe Sebasteanski	G	6'	208	28		
John Weaver	G	6'2"	215	23		

Owner Ted Collins moved his Boston Yanks to New York in hopes for a colorful season as the Bulldogs. Using the Polo Grounds when the Giants were away, the Bulldogs played before echoing, empty stands; not even half-time circus acts brought customers in. The show on the field resembled a circus, too. Collins bought quarterback Bobby Layne from the Bears, and Layne learned how to eat the ball without flinching behind his pitiful offensive line. Coach Charley Ewart wanted to run a ball-control offense like the Eagles, but, according to Layne, "We didn't have any Steve Van Burens." Layne was even forced to make up plays in the huddle by drawing pass patterns in the dirt with his finger. With no one paying money to see this show, Collins cut expenses by releasing many of the squad, and by season's end only nineteen players were suiting up.

TEAM TOTALS

OFFENSE	FIRST DOWNS: Tot	by Rsh	by Pas	by Pen	RUSHING: No.	Yds.	Avg Yds.	TD	PASSING: Att	Com	Comp Pct.	Yds.	Avg. Yds. Att.	Avg. Yds. Comp	TD	Int	Pct. Int.	PUNTING: No.	Avg. Yds.
PHIL.	243	143	87	13	632	2607	4.1	26	251	130	51.8	1909	7.6	14.7	18	14	5.6	53	40.8
PITT.	189	126	50	13	535	2209	4.1	19	209	81	38.8	1310	6.3	16.2	10	18	8.6	77	40.9
N.Y.G.	177	75	87	15	419	1404	3.4	15	322	155	48.1	2157	6.7	13.9	17	23	7.1	73	36.9
WASH.	217	78	121	18	407	1579	3.9	14	394	197	50.0	2816	7.1	14.3	22	29	7.4	68	40.4
N.Y.B	183	76	88	19	353	1184	3.4	9	343	172	50.1	2025	5.9	11.8	10	23	6.7	77	41.2

PUNT RETURNS: No.	Yds.	Avg. Yds.	TD	KICKOFF RETURNS: No.	Yds.	Avg. Yds.	TD	INTERCEPTION RETURNS: No.	Yds.	Avg. Yds.	TD	PENALTIES: No.	Yds.	FUMBLES: No.	Lost	POINTS: Tot	PAT	FG Att	FG	Saf.	OFFENSE
48	577	12.0	2	25	542	21.7	0	29	409	14.1	2	81	729	29	12	384	47	19	9	1	PHIL.
34	449	13.2	0	37	792	21.4	0	22	310	14.1	0	52	460	31	9	224	30	7	2	1	PITT.
39	457	11.7	1	37	961	26.0	1	22	336	15.3	2	88	800	23	10	287	35	13	8	0	N.Y.G.
35	377	10.8	0	55	1113	20.2	0	18	223	12.4	0	85	675	24	13	268	34	7	4	0	WASH.
37	211	5.7	0	58	1191	20.5	0	14	211	15.1	1	51	420	41	22	153	18	10	3	0	N.Y.B.

Use Name – Backs & Ends	Pos.	Age	Hgt	Wgt	Pts	Int	Rushing No.	Rushing Yds	Rushing Avg	Rushing TD	Passing Att	Passing Comp	Passing %	Passing Yds	Passing Yd/Att	Passing TD	Passing Int–%	Passing RK	Receiving No.	Receiving Yds	Receiving Avg	Receiving TD	Punting No.	Punting Avg	Kicking Pat	Kicking Att	Kicking %	Kicking FG	Kicking Att	Kicking %	Punt Returns No.	Punt Returns Yds	Punt Returns Avg	Punt Returns TD	Kickoff Returns No.	Kickoff Returns Yds	Kickoff Returns Avg	Kickoff Returns TD
PHILADELPHIA EAGLES																																						
Tommy Thompson	QB	33	6'1"	195	12		15	17	1.1	2	214	116	54	1727	8.1	16	11– 5	2																				
Bill Mackrides	QB	24	5'11"	182	6		14	17	1.2	1	36	14	39	182	5.1	2	2– 6																					
Steve VanBuren	HB	28	6'	200	72		263	1146	4.4	11									4	88	22	1													12	288	24	0
Bosh Pritchard	HB	30	5'11"	163	30		84	506	6.0	3	1	0	0	0	0.0	0	1–100		8	185	23	2									13	99	8	0	5	99	20	0
Frank Ziegler	HB-DB	25	5'11"	175	6	1	84	283	3.4	1									3	33	11	0									2	20	10	0	1	21	21	0
Jim Parmer	HB-DB	22	6'	190	30	2	66	234	3.5	5									5	33	7	0																
Clyde Scott	HB	25	6'	175	18		40	195	4.9	1									8	148	19	1									5	114	23	1	1	54	54	0
Jack Myers	FB	24	6'2"	200	6		48	182	3.8	1									7	98	14	0													2	27	14	0
Joe Muha	FB-LB	28	6'1"	205	11	2	3	19	6.3	0									1	10	10	0	45	40.0	5	5	100	0	1	0	1	2	2	0	1	20	20	0
Russ Craft	HB-DB	29	5'9"	172	6	1	11	5	0.5	0									1	37	37	0									3	50	17	0				
Pat McHugh	HB-DB	29	5'11"	165	6	6	2	5	2.5	0																					3	26	9	0				
Ben Kish	FB-LB	32	6'	207			2	–2	–1.0	0																												
Frank Reagan	DB	30	5'11"	180	6	7																	8	45.3							21	266	13	1				
John Green	DE	27	6'1"	194																															2	33	17	0
Jack Ferrante	OE	33	6'1"	205	30														34	508	15	5																
Pete Pihos	OE-DE	25	6'1"	210	24														34	484	14	4													1	0	0	0
Neill Armstrong	OE-DB	23	6'2"	188	30														24	271	11	5																
Cliff Patton	G	25	6'2"	240	69																				42	43	98	9	18	50								
PITTSBURGH STEELERS																																						
Joe Geri	TB	25	5'10"	180	45		133	543	4.1	5	77	31	40	554	7.2	5	5– 6						43	43.2	12	13	92	1	1	100	2	28	14	0				
Jim Finks	TB-DB	22	6'	175	12	1	35	135	3.9	1	71	24	34	322	4.5	2	8– 11		1	17	17	1																
Bob Gage	TB-DB	22	5'11"	175	18	5	46	228	5.0	3	36	17	47	329	9.1	2	4– 11		1	8	8	0	4	40.8							16	254	16	0	1	25	25	0
Jerry Nuzum	HB	26	6'1"	200	42		139	611	4.4	5	1	1	100	21	21.0	0	0– 0		4	81	20	2													1	17	17	0
George Papach	FB	24	6'2"	210			99	407	4.1	0	1	0	0	0	0.0	0	0– 0		6	18	3	0													3	57	19	0
Don Samuel	HB-TB-DB	25	5'11"	190	6	1	39	163	4.2	1	21	7	33	67	3.2	0	1– 5		1	2	2	0									7	80	11	0				
Jerry Shipkey	FB-DB	24	6'1"	210	30	3	26	93	3.6	5									2	32	16	0																
Bob Hanlon	HB-DB	24	6'1"	195		3	6	13	2.2	0									1	4	4	0													11	213	19	0
Joe Hollingsworth	FB	24	6'	200			6	13	2.2	0	1	0	0	0	0.0	0	0– 0																					
Joe Glamp	HB	26	5'11"	185	21		3	–8	–2.7	0									1	14	14	0			18	18	100	1	7	14								
Charlie Seabright	BB	31	6'2"	208							1	1	100	17	17.0	1	0– 0		4	4	1	0													1	24	24	0
Frank Minini	BB	25	6'1"	200			1	5	5.0	0																									16	390	24	0
Howard Hartley	DB	25	6'	185		6																									9	87	10	0				
Elbie Nickel	OE	26	6'1"	190	18														26	633	24	3													1	20	20	0
Val Jansante	OE	28	6'1"	190	24														29	445	15	4													3	46	15	0
Bill Long	OE	23	6'1"	200			2	6	3.0	0									2	21	11	0	30	37.6														
NEW YORK GIANTS																																						
Chuck Conerly	QB	25	6'1"	185			23	42	1.8	0	305	152	50	2138	7.0	17	20– 7	4					2	35.0														
Ray Mallouf	QB-DB	31	5'11"	180		1	1	–1	–1.0	0	16	3	19	19	1.2	0	2– 13						57	37.4														
Choo-Choo Roberts	HB	25	5'11"	188	102		152	634	4.2	9	1	0	0	0	0.0	0	1–100		35	711	20	8													1	16	16	0
Joe Scott	HB-DB	23	6'1"	200	42	1	70	224	3.2	6									15	111	7	1													7	203	29	0
Bob Greenhalgh	FB	25	6'1"	200			62	188	3.0	0									3	23	8	0																
Jack Salscheider	HB	24	5'10"	185	6		26	105	4.0	0									4	9	2	0	14	35.4											15	474	32	1
Clete Fischer	HB-DB	24	5'9"	170	6	2	26	72	2.8	0									3	45	15	1									7	64	9	0	8	188	24	0
Ray Coates	HB-DB	25	6'1"	200	6	1	27	55	2.0	0									8	152	19	1									6	78	13	0				
Buzz Mertes (from BAL-AAFC)	FB	28	6'	205			16	46	2.9	0									2	14	7	0																
Joe Sulaitis	FB-DE	28	6'2"	215			14	42	3.0	0									3	35	12	0													1	27	27	0
Noah Mullins	HB-DB	30	5'11"	177	6	3	2	–3	–1.5	0									2	45	23	1																
Em Tunnell	HB-DB	27	6'1"	187	18	10													1	7	7	0									26	315	12	1	2	26	13	0
Bill Swiacki	OE	24	6'2"	195	24														47	652	14	4																
Ray Poole	OE-DE	27	6'2"	215	6														25	277	11	1													1	3	3	0
Dick Hensley	OE-DE	23	6'4"	210															3	24	8	0																
Frank LoVuolo	OE-DE	25	6'2"	210	6														2	37	19	0																
Dick Duden	OE-DE	22	6'3"	212															2	15	8	0																
Ben Agajanian	K	30	6'	210	59																				35	36	97	8	13	62								
WASHINGTON REDSKINS																																						
Sammy Baugh	QB	35	6'2"	182	12		13	67	5.2	2	255	145	57	1903	7.5	18	14– 5	1					1	53.0														
Harry Gilmer	QB-HB	23	6'	164			31	167	5.4	0	132	49	37	869	6.6	4	15– 11	12	5	77	15	0																
Tommy Mont	QB-HB	27	6'	192	12		14	75	5.4	0	7	3	43	44	6.3	0	0– 0		8	105	13	2													1	22	22	0
Rob Goode	HB-DB	22	6'4"	210	12	2	61	261	4.3	2									16	279	17	0													3	50	17	0
Pete Stout	FB-LB	26	6'	200	36	1	62	245	4.0	4									8	102	13	2																
Harry Dowda	HB-DB	25	6'2"	194	18	3	65	239	3.7	2									11	187	17	1																
Eddie Saenz	HB	26	5'11"	168			53	170	3.2	0									23	251	11	0									17	178	10	0	24	465	19	0
Ed Quirk	FB	24	6'1"	226	6		40	139	3.5	1									5	33	7	0																
Tom Cochran	FB	25	6'	209	6		34	135	4.0	1									7	82	12	0													1	19	19	0
Dan Sandifer	HB-DB	22	6'1"	190	18	5	20	64	3.2	0									19	293	15	3									18	199	11	0	24	518	22	0
John Hollar (from DET)	FB	27	6'2"	225	12		13	35	2.7	1									4	38	10	1																
Dick Poillon	HB	29	6'	198	46		7	5	0.7	0									1	8	8	0	66	40.9	34	37	97	4	7	57								
Howie Livingston	HB-DB	27	6'1"	190	6	4	1	1	1.0	1									3	41	14	0																
Hugh Taylor	OE	26	6'4"	192	54														45	781	17	9																
Hal Crisler	OE	25	6'4"	207	24														26	388	15	4																
Clyde Goodnight	OE-DE	25	6'1"	200															11	150	14	0																
Joe Tereshinski	OE-DE	25	6'2"	214															4	36	9	0																
Ed Berrang	OE-DE	24	6'2"	203															1	5	5	0																
NEW YORK BULLDOGS																																						
Bobby Layne	QB	22	6'1"	198	18		54	196	3.6	3	299	155	52	1796	6.0	9	18– 6	6																				
Johnny Rauch	QB-DB	22	6'	200	6	2	3	46	15.3	1	25	11	44	169	6.8	1	3– 12																					
Bob DeMoss	QB	22	6'2"	185			5	1	0.2	0	18	6	33	60	3.3	0	2– 11																					
Joe Osmanski (from CHIB)	FB	30	6'2"	215	12		81	312	3.8	2									18	138	8	0													4	46	12	0
Joe Golding	HB-DB	28	6'	184	18	1	63	240	3.8	0									12	78	7	2									5	27	5	0	13	289	22	0
Paul Shoults	HB	23	5'11"	178			46	124	2.7	0									10	124	12	0									8	27	3	0	14	271	19	0
Phil Slosburg	HB-DB	22	5'10"	170	6	1	37	121	3.3	1									4	11	3	0									4	32	8	0	4	98	25	0
Jim Canady (from CHIB)	HB-DB	23	5'10"	178		5	23	91	4.0	0									5	80	16	0									4	36	9	0	10	233	23	0
Dean Sensenbaugher	HB	24	5'9"	190	6		20	36	1.8	1																					1	9	9	0	3	81	27	0
Frank Nelson	HB-DB	26	5'9"	167		1	8	26	3.3	0																					3	14	5	0	3	52	17	0
Oscar Smith (from GB)	HB-DB	26	6'	185		2	16	24	1.5	0																					5	31	6	0	2	36	18	0
Jim Wade	HB-DB	23	5'11"	175		1	9	23	2.6	0									4	58	15	0									7	32	5	0	3	58	19	0
Frank Muehlheuser	FB-LB	23	6'2"	220	6		9	10	1.1	1									2	26	13	0	1	0.0											1	40	40	0
Mike Boyda	FB-LB	27	6'1"	205		1					1	0	0	0	0.0	0	0– 0						56	44.2														
Bill Chipley	OE	29	6'3"	205	12														57	631	11	2													1	7	7	0
Ralph Heywood	OE	27	6'2"	205	24		3	–6	–2.0	1									37	499	13	3	20	34.9														
Hal Prescott (from PHI)	OE	28	6'2"	193	6														10	162	16	1																
Joe Abbey (from CHIB)	OE-DE	23	6'1"	205															8	110	14	0																
Nick Scollard	OE-DE	29	6'4"	225	39	1													3	81	27	2			18	21	86	3	10	30	1	6	6	0	2	16	8	0
Bob Sponaugle	OE-DE	21	6'1"	203															2	26	13	0																

TEAM TOTALS

DEFENSE	First Downs: Tot	by Rsh	by Pas	by Pen	Rushing: No.	Yds.	Avg Yds.	TD	Passing: Att	Com	Comp Pct.	Yds.	Avg. Yds. Att.	Avg. Yds. Comp	TD	Int	Pct. Int.	Punting: No.	Avg. Yds.	Punt Returns: No.	Yds.	Avg. Yds.	TD	Kickoff Returns: No.	Yds.	Avg. Yds.	TD	Interception Returns: No.	Yds.	Avg. Yds.	TD	Penalties: No.	Yds.	Fumbles: No.	Lost	Points: Tot	PAT	FG Att	FG	Saf.	DEFENSE
PHIL.	148	60	68	20	353	1217	3.4	5	303	121	39.9	1607	5.3	13.3	11	29	9.6	81	38.6	36	384	10.7	0	53	1087	20.5	0	14	241	17.2	1	62	533	30	14	134	17	8	5	0	PHIL.
PITT.	210	100	98	12	463	1862	4.0	17	337	161	47.8	2043	6.1	12.7	9	22	6.5	66	40.7	27	373	13.8	1	35	687	19.6	0	18	334	18.6	1	97	862	26	9	214	25	14	7	0	PITT.
N.Y.G.	232	104	110	18	465	1664	3.6	20	374	193	51.6	2460	6.7	12.7	16	22	5.9	65	38.6	52	598	11.5	2	48	1092	22.8	0	23	226	9.8	1	64	559	32	18	298	40	12	6	0	N.Y.G.
WASH.	233	120	95	18	487	2316	4.8	23	316	148	46.8	2409	7.6	16.3	24	18	5.7	59	40.7	38	442	11.6	0	42	917	21.8	0	29	377	13.0	0	74	676	30	13	339	42	15	5	0	WASH.
N.Y.B.	238	131	92	15	535	2360	4.4	20	303	147	48.5	2132	7.0	14.5	25	14	4.6	63	39.7	52	660	12.7	2	31	618	19.9	0	23	356	15.5	1	90	766	33	14	368	47	12	7	0	N.Y.B.

LOS ANGELES RAMS 8-2-2 Clark Shaughnessy

Scores of Each Game		
27	DETROIT	24
48	Green Bay	7
31	Chic. Bears	16
21	Detroit	10
35	GREEN BAY	7
27	CHIC. BEARS	24
14	Philadelphia	38
7	Pittsburgh	7
28	Chic. Cards	28
42	N. Y. BULLDOGS	20
27	CHIC. CARDS	31
53	WASHINGTON	27

Use Name	Pos.	Hgt	Wgt	Age	Int	Pts
Jack Martin	C-LB	6'3"	240	27		
Fred Naumetz	C-LB	6'1"	223	27		
Don Paul	LB	6'1"	230	24	2	
(2 kickoff returns for 32 yds.)						
Larry Brink	DE	6'5"	230	26		
George Sims	DB	5'11"	170	21	9	6

Use Name – Tackles	Pos.	Hgt	Wgt	Age	Int	Pts
Gil Bouley	T	6'2"	235	28		
Ed Champagne	T	6'3"	240	27		
Dick Huffman	T	6'2"	256	26		
(2 receptions for 36 yds.)						
Joe Repko	T	6'	240	28		
Al Sparkman	T	6'6"	253	24		

Use Name – Guards	Pos.	Hgt	Wgt	Age	Int	Pts
Hal Dean	G	6'	205	26		
(1 kickoff return for 0 yds.)						
Jack Finlay	G-LB	6'1"	216	28		
Mike Lazetich	G-LB	6'1"	214	28	2	
Ray Yagiello	G	6'	220	26		

Clark Shaughnessy, one of the creators of the modern T offense, came up with another far-reaching innovation this year. Already blessed with two fine ends in Tom Fears and Bob Shaw, Shaughnessy wanted to use newly acquired halfback Crazy Legs Hirsch as a wide receiver, and he did so by cleverly splitting Hirsch wide as a flanker. With three fine targets to aim at, quarterbacks Bob Waterfield and rookie Norm Van Brocklin directed pro football's most dynamic air show.

But after winning their first six games on the strength of their offense, the Rams took on the defensive-minded Philadelphia Eagles and lost. The match proved to be the Rams' Waterloo, and they struggled through the rest of their games with great difficulty. Yet the Rams did beat the Bears twice during that season to finish ahead of Halas' squad by percentage points and to win the first divisional crown for the West Coast.

CHICAGO BEARS 9-3-0 George Halas

17	Green Bay	0
17	Chic. Cards	7
16	LOS ANGELES	21
38	PHILADELPHIA	21
28	N. Y. Giants	35
24	Los Angeles	27
24	GREEN BAY	3
27	DETROIT	24
31	Washington	21
28	Detroit	7
30	PITTSBURGH	21
52	CHIC. CARDS	21

Use Name	Pos.	Hgt	Wgt	Age	Int	Pts
Stu Clarkson	LB	6'2"	220	30	2	
Frank Szymanski	C	6'	215	26		
Bulldog Turner	C-LB	6'1"	235	30		
Bill Milner	DE	6'1"	215	25		
Bill deCorrevont	DB-HB	6'	185	30	4	
(1 reception for 44 yds.)						

Use Name – Tackles	Pos.	Hgt	Wgt	Age	Int	Pts
Alf Bauman	T	6'2"	235	29		
George Connor	T	6'3"	240	24		
(3 receptions for 51 yds.)						
Fred Davis	T	6'3"	245	31		
Paul Stenn	T	6'2"	245	31		
(2 receptions for 11 yds.)						
Walt Stickel	T	6'3"	245	27		

Use Name – Guards	Pos.	Hgt	Wgt	Age	Int	Pts
Ray Bray	G	6'	235	32		
Chuck Drulis	G-LB	5'10"	215	31	1	
Dick Flanagan	G-FB	6'	210	22		
(5 kickoff returns for 88 yds.)						
Pat Preston	G-LB	6'2"	215	26		
Wash Serini	G	6'2"	235	25		

George Halas started the season by selling quarterback Bobby Layne to the New York Bulldogs. Although the move would later haunt him, it was not a foolish decision at the time. When veteran Sid Luckman was sidetracked for most of the season with a thyroid condition, Halas considered himself fortunate to have Johnny Lujack, the former Heisman Trophy winner from Notre Dame. Showing a strong arm and unexpected poise, Lujack came through in flying colors, leading the Bears to a season-ending six-game winning streak which fell just short of the title. With Lujack capping his successful season by passing for a record 468 yards, and six touchdowns against the Cardina's in the season finale, and the presence of a third quarterback in promising rookie George Blanda, there was no evidence of the passing misfortunes which would haunt the Bears within a few short years.

CHICAGO CARDINALS 6-5-1 Buddy Parker, Phil Handler

38	WASHINGTON	7
7	CHIC. BEARS	17
3	Philadelphia	28
39	Green Bay	17
7	DETROIT	24
38	N. Y. GIANTS	41
42	Detroit	19
65	N. Y. Bulldogs	20
28	LOS ANGELES	28
41	GREEN BAY	21
31	Los Angeles	27
21	Chic. Bears	52

Use Name	Pos.	Hgt	Wgt	Age	Int	Pts
Vince Banonis	C-LB	6'1"	232	27	4	6
Bill Blackburn	C-LB	6'6"	230	27	3	6
(1 kickoff return for 4 yds.)						
Jim Cain	DE	6'1"	210	22		
Bob Dove	DE	6'2"	220	28		
Corwin Clatt	DB	6'	210	26	2	
(1 punt return for 22 yds.)						
Jerry Davis	DB	5'10"	175	27	6	6
(1 punt return for 14 yds.)						
Bob Nussbaumer	DB	5'11"	170	25	12	
(1 punt return for 16 yds.)						

Use Name – Tackles	Pos.	Hgt	Wgt	Age	Int	Pts
Chet Bulger	T	6'3"	238	31		
Joe Coomer	T	6'6"	283	30		
Bill Fischer	T	6'2"	250	22	1	
John Goldsberry	T	6'2"	245	23	1	
Dick Loepfe	T	6'2"	230	28		
George Petrovich	T	6'2"	225	24		
Bob Zimny	T	6'1"	235	28		

Use Name – Guards	Pos.	Hgt	Wgt	Age	Int	Pts
Plato Andros	G	6'	242	28		
Ray Apolskis	G-LB	5'11"	210	30	1	
Ham Nichols	G-LB	5'11"	210	25		
Buster Ramsey	G-LB	6'1"	220	29	1	2
(1 kickoff return for 0 yds.)						

The championship squads of 1947-48 slowly were breaking up on the reefs of time. The death of Stan Mauldin robbed the Cardinals of a great lineman, defensive back Marshall Goldberg retired, and injuries were turning Paul Christman into an ordinary passer. To further worsen the team's plight, head coach Jimmy Conzelman decided to quit after the 1948 season—a move which left the widow of late owner Charles Bidwill in a dither. She couldn't decide between assistants Phil Handler and Buddy Parker for the vacated spot—and unwisely made them co-coaches, a chaotic arrangement which lasted half a year and four losses in six games before Handler moved into the front office. But it was too late for Parker to do more than bring the club up above the break-even point, or prevent the 52-21 trouncing by the Bears in the season's finale, which returned the Cardinals to the roll of bridesmaid in Chicago.

DETROIT LIONS 4-8-0 Bo McMillin

24	Los Angeles	27
14	PHILADELPHIA	22
7	Pittsburgh	14
10	LOS ANGELES	21
24	Chic. Cards	7
14	Green Bay	16
19	CHIC. CARDS	42
24	Chic. Bears	27
45	N. Y. Giants	21
7	CHIC. BEARS	28
28	N. Y. BULLDOGS	27
21	GREEN BAY	7

Use Name	Pos.	Hgt	Wgt	Age	Int	Pts
George Karstens	C	6'4"	205	25		
Bob Pifferini	C-LB	6'	210	24	3	
Jack Simmons	C-T	6'4"	240	23		
Abe Addams	DE	6'2"	220	23		
Sam Goldman	DE	6'3"	235	32		
Ollie Poole	DE	6'3"	220	27		
Chick Maggioli	DB-HB	5'11"	174	27	3	6
(1 reception for 9 yds.)						
Jim Mello	DB	5'10"	190	28	3	
(3 kickoff returns for 37 yds.)						

Use Name – Tackles	Pos.	Hgt	Wgt	Age	Int	Pts
George Hekke	T	6'4"	240	26		
John Prchlik	T	6'4"	230	24		
Mike Roussos (from WAS)	T	6'3"	240	23		
Al Russas	T-DE	6'2"	210	25		
Cecil Souders	T-DE	6'1"	210	27		
(1 kickoff return for 7 yds.)						
Russ Thomas	T	6'3"	242	25		
John Treadway	T	6'5"	266	29		

Use Name – Guards	Pos.	Hgt	Wgt	Age	Int	Pts
Les Bingaman	DG	6'3"	250	24		
Howie Brown	G-T	5'11"	215	26		
Mario DeMarco	G-LB	5'11"	200	22		
Chuck DeShane	G-LB	6'1"	217	30	1	
Bill Ward	G	6'	230	28		

Even while mired in mediocrity, the Lions were sowing the seeds for a defensive unit which would win as much press space as many offensive units. Coach Bo McMillin uncovered some of these specialists this year who would man the great Detroit defense of the early 1950s.

A pair of backs, Don Doll and Jim Smith, each showed a flair for picking off interceptions and running them back a long way. Smith ran one of his nine thefts back 102 yards for a score against the Bears, and Doll averaged over 25 yards a return for his eleven interceptions. At middle guard, Les Bingaman plugged up holes with his considerable bulk; one writer said that Bingaman stops runners the same way Pepper Martin stopped ground balls, with his stomach. Once Bingaman was taking a rest in practice, and a teammate yelled, "Move around Bing,you're killing the grass." Thus, it seemed, the Lions were on their way.

GREEN BAY PACKERS 2-10-0 Curly Lambeau

0	CHIC. BEARS	17
7	LOS ANGELES	48
19	N. Y. Bulldogs	0
17	CHIC. CARDS	39
7	Los Angeles	35
16	DETROIT	14
3	Chic. Bears	24
10	N. Y. GIANTS	30
7	PITTSBURGH	30
21	Chic. Cards	41
0	Washington	30
7	Detroit	21

Use Name	Pos.	Hgt	Wgt	Age	Int	Pts
Ben Flowers	C-LB	6'1"	210	32		
Roger Harding (from NYB)	C-LB	6'2"	215	26	1	
Ed Neal	C-T	6'4"	290	31		
Jay Rhodemyre	C-LB	6'1"	210	27	4	
Larry Craig	DE-LB	6'1"	218	33		
Ralph Olsen	DE	6'4"	220	25		
Don Wells	DE	6'2"	200	27		
Irv Comp	DB	6'2"	205	30	3	
Ken Kranz	DB	5'10"	190	25		

Use Name – Tackles	Pos.	Hgt	Wgt	Age	Int	Pts
Ed Bell	T	6'1"	233	27		
Lou Ferry	T	6'2"	233	22		
Glenn Johnson	T	6'4"	265	27		6
Paul Lipscomb	T	6'5"	245	26		
Urban Odson	T	6'3"	250	30		
Dick Wildung	T	6'	220	27		

Use Name – Guards	Pos.	Hgt	Wgt	Age	Int	Pts
Buddy Burris	G-LB	5'11"	215	26	1	
Roger Eason	G	6'2"	230	31		
Damon Tassos	G-LB	6'1"	225	25	1	
Red Vogds	G	5'10"	215	26		
(1 kickoff return for 0 yds.)						

With the wolves howling for Curly Lambeau's head, the Packers ran the gauntlet of their worst season in history. Outside of gutsy runner Tony Canadeo, the Packers fielded a pitiful team which won only twice all year. In addition, the Packer organization tottered on the brink of bankruptcy, relying on a new sale of shares to restock the team treasury. The governing board wanted a larger voice in running the club, while Lambeau still insisted on concentrating power in his own hands. When the coach and governing board reached an impasse over the issue, Lambeau read the handwriting on the wall and resigned on February 1, 1950. Some of the executives heaved a sigh of relief, but former player Buckets Goldenberg summed up popular opinion: "I don't see how the Packers can last without him. He was the Packers."

TEAM TOTALS

OFFENSE	First Downs: Tot	by Rsh	by Pas	by Pen	Rushing: No.	Yds.	Avg Yds.	TD	Passing: Att	Com	Comp Pct.	Yds.	Avg. Yds. Att.	Avg. Yds. Comp	TD	Int	Pct. Int.
L.A.	245	103	125	17	445	1732	3.9	17	366	192	52.5	2819	7.7	14.7	23	27	7.4
CHIC. B.	248	111	119	18	483	1785	3.7	18	385	193	50.1	3055	7.9	15.8	24	30	7.8
CHIC. C.	207	106	82	19	467	2130	4.6	21	307	138	45.0	1763	5.8	12.8	21	26	8.5
DET.	206	81	104	21	397	1381	3.5	10	399	178	44.6	2291	5.8	12.9	18	28	7.0
G.B	182	99	68	15	503	2061	4.1	7	299	91	30.4	1291	4.3	14.2	5	29	9.7

OFFENSE	Punting: No.	Avg. Yds.	Punt Returns: No.	Yds.	Avg. Yds.	TD	Kickoff Returns: No.	Yds.	Avg. Yds.	TD	Interception Returns: No.	Yds.	Avg. Yds.	TD	Penalties: No.	Yds.	Fumbles: No.	Lost	Points: Tot	PAT	FG Att	FG	Saf.
L.A.	52	44.4	43	624	14.5	2	37	690	18.6	0	30	359	12.0	4	83	795	29	18	360	45	17	5	0
CHIC. B.	52	43.3	52	583	11.2	0	38	874	23.0	0	27	257	9.5	2	92	901	25	18	332	42	16	8	1
CHIC. C.	65	40.9	30	546	18.2	2	51	1013	19.9	0	33	486	14.7	3	67	590	20	16	360	46	11	8	1
DET.	62	37.9	39	557	14.3	2	49	1064	21.7	0	32	656	20.5	2	71	682	34	21	237	30	14	5	0
G.B.	87	40.2	37	310	8.4	1	42	815	19.4	0	20	187	9.4	0	76	722	32	16	114	12	22	6	0

Use Name — Backs & Ends	Pos.	Age	Hgt	Wgt	Pts	Int	Rushing				Passing								Receiving				Punting		Kicking						Punt Returns				Kickoff Returns			
							No.	Yds	Avg	TD	Att	Comp	%	Yds	Yd/Att	TD	Int–%	RK	No.	Yds	Avg	TD	No.	Avg	Pat	Att	%	FG	Att	%	No.	Yds	Avg	TD	No.	Yds	Avg	TD
LOS ANGELES RAMS																																						
Bob Waterfield	QB	29	6'1"	200	76		5	–4	–0.8	1	296	154	52	2168	7.3	17	24– 8	4					49	44.4	43	45	98	9	16	56								
Norm Van Brocklin	QB	23	6'1"	190			4	–1	–0.3	0	58	32	55	601	10.3	6	2– 3						2	45.5														
Bobby Thomason	QB	21	6'1"	198							12	6	50	50	4.2	0	1– 8																					
Dick Hoerner	FB	27	6'4"	220	36		155	582	3.8	6									17	213	13	0	1	43.0														
Crazy Legs Hirsch	HB-DB	25	6'2"	192	36	2	68	287	4.2	2									22	326	15	4																
Tommy Kalmanir	HB	23	5'8"	170	12		29	218	7.5	1									2	36	18	0									14	164	12	1	18	403	22	0
Fred Gehrke	HB-DB	31	5'11"	190	32		58	203	3.5	3									9	140	16	2			2	3	67	0	1	0								
Tank Younger	HB-FB	21	6'3"	217			52	191	3.7	0									7	119	17	0																
Vitamin Smith	HB	25	5'8"	180	24		40	117	2.9	2									5	63	13	1									27	427	16	1	13	235	18	0
Jerry Williams	HB-DB	25	5'10"	165	24	5	19	103	5.4	3									7	102	15	0									2	33	17	0				
Gerry Cowhig	FB-DB	28	6'2"	214	12	4	10	32	3.2	1																												
Bob Agler	FB-LB	26	6'1"	210			4	7	1.8	0																									2	20	10	0
Tom Fears	OE	25	6'2"	216	54		1	–3	–3.0	0									77	1013	13	9																
Bob Shaw	OE-DE	28	6'4"	225	36														29	535	18	6																
Tom Keane	OE-DB	22	6'1"	196															4	70	18	0																
Don Currivan	OE-DB	28	6'	190	6	5													3	78	26	1																
Jack Zilly	OE-DE	27	6'2"	210															3	35	12	0													1	0	0	0
Frank Hubbell	OE-DE	27	6'2"	222	6	1													3	32	11	0																
Bill Smyth	OE-DE	27	6'3"	245															2	21	11	0																
CHICAGO BEARS																																						
Johnny Lujack	QB	24	6'	185	57		8	64	8.0	2	312	162	52	2658	8.2	23	22– 7	3					3	41.0	42	44	98	1	1	100								
Sid Luckman	QB	32	6'	195			3	4	1.3	0	50	22	44	200	4.0	1	3– 6						1	16.0														
George Blanda	QB-LB	21	6'1"	195	27		2	9	4.5	1	21	9	43	197	9.4	0	5–24						19	39.3				7	15	47								
George Gulyanics	HB	28	6'	195	36		102	452	4.4	5	1	0	0	0	0.0	0	0– 0		16	165	10	1	29	47.2														
Julie Rykovich	HB	25	6'2"	208	48		88	340	3.9	6									16	210	13	2																
John Hoffman	FB	23	6'2"	215	18		53	216	4.1	1									25	373	15	2													10	249	25	0
Wally Dreyer	HB	24	5'10"	170			45	172	3.8	0									7	94	13	0									13	130	10	0	13	338	26	0
George McAfee	HB-DB	31	6'	175	30	6	42	161	3.8	3									9	157	17	1									24	279	12	0				
Don Kindt	FB-DB	23	6'1"	207		2	41	118	2.9	0									12	118	10	0																
J.R. Boone	HB-DB	23	5'8"	160	18	1	35	111	3.2	0									14	336	24	3									14	170	12	0				
Dante Magnani	HB	32	5'10"	178			33	59	1.8	0									3	29	10	0																
Ed Cody	FB-DB	26	5'10"	195	6	2	11	25	2.3	0																					1	4	4	0	8	181	23	0
Bob Perina	HB-DB	28	6'1"	205		6	4	4	1.0	0									3	33	11	0													1	10	10	0
Jim Keane	OE	25	6'4"	215	36														47	696	15	6																
Ken Kavanaugh	OE-DE	32	6'3"	207	54														29	655	23	9																
Ed Sprinkle	OE-DE	25	6'1"	207	2		1	5	5.0	0	1	0	0	0	0.0	0	0– 0		4	69	17	0																
Jack Dugger	OE-DE	26	6'3"	230															1	11	11	0													1	8	8	0
CHICAGO CARDINALS																																						
Paul Christman	QB	31	6'	212			4	34	8.5	0	151	75	50	1015	6.7	11	13– 9	7																				
Jim Hardy	QB	27	6'	180	6		7	6	0.9	1	150	63	42	748	5.0	10	13– 9	11					5	36.0														
Elmer Angsman	HB	23	5'11"	205	36		125	674	5.4	6	1	0	0	0	0.0	0	0– 0		5	57	11	0													5	66	13	0
Charlie Trippi	HB-DB	26	6'	185	54		112	553	4.9	3	2	0	0	0	0.0	0	0– 0		34	412	12	6	8	36.5							10	160	16	0	18	427	24	0
Pat Harder	FB-LB	27	5'11"	205	102		106	447	4.2	7									12	100	8	1			45	47	98	3	5	60								
Babe Dimancheff	HB	27	5'11"	180	24		38	151	4.0	3									10	130	13	1													2	43	22	0
Vinnie Yablonski	FB-LB	27	5'8"	195	16		32	97	3.0	0									6	35	6	0			1	1	100	5	6	83								
Red Cochran	HB	27	6'	190	24		20	87	4.4	1	1	0	0	0	0.0	0	0– 0		7	107	15	1	52	42.0							15	314	21	2	20	410	21	0
Vic Schwall	HB	25	5'8"	185	12		12	47	3.9	0	2	0	0	0	0.0	0	0– 0		3	8	3	2													4	63	16	0
Clarence Self	HB-DB	24	5'8"	170		1	4	16	4.0	0																					2	20	10	0				
Mal Kutner	OE-DB	28	6'2"	197	30		5	10	2.0	0									30	465	16	5																
Bill Dewell	OE-DE	32	6'4"	215	12														20	235	12	2																
Bob Ravensburg	OE	24	6'1"	190	18		2	8	4.0	0									10	203	20	3																
Tom Wham	OE-DE	25	6'2"	215	6	1													1	11	11	0																
DETROIT LIONS																																						
Frank Tripucka	QB	21	6'2"	180	6		12	36	3.0	1	145	62	43	833	5.7	9	14–10	10					28	38.4														
Fred Enke	QB	24	6'1"	200	6		36	134	3.7	1	142	63	44	793	5.6	6	5– 4	8	1	14	14	0																
Clyde LeForce	QB	26	5'11"	175	6		13	58	4.5	1	112	53	47	665	5.9	3	9– 8	9																				
Bill Dudley	HB	28	5'10"	176	81		125	402	3.2	3									27	190	7	2	32	39.9	30	32	97	5	14	36	11	199	18	1	13	246	19	0
Camp Wilson	FB	27	6'2"	200	6		68	222	3.3	1									6	31	5	0																
Wally Triplett	HB	22	5'10"	175	12		53	221	4.2	1									8	90	11	0									21	281	13	1				
Jim Smith (from CHI-AAFC)	HB-DB	24	6'1"	190	6	9	33	162	4.9	0									2	16	8	0									2	25	13	0	7	172	25	0
Cloyce Box	HB	25	6'4"	220	24		30	62	2.1	0									15	276	18	4													3	50	17	0
John Panelli	FB-LB	23	5'11"	200		1	10	37	3.7	0									1	13	13	0													1	16	16	0
Don Doll	HB-DB	22	5'10"	185	12	11	8	25	3.1	1									1	–5	–5	0									5	52	10	0	21	536	26	0
Mel Groomes	HB-DB	22	6'	180	6	1	1	1	1.0	0									3	33	11	1																
Bob Mann	OE	25	5'11"	167	24														66	1014	15	4																
John Greene	OE	29	6'	210	42														42	542	13	7																
Kelley Mote	OE	26	6'2"	190															4	58	15	0																
Bernie Hafen	OE	26	6'2"	195															1	10	10	0																
GREEN BAY PACKERS																																						
Jug Girard	QB-HB-DB	22	5'11"	175	6	1	45	198	4.4	1	175	62	35	881	5.0	4	12– 7	12	1	13	13	0	69	39.0							11	70	6	0	2	45	23	0
Stan Heath	QB	22	6'1"	190	6		10	25	2.5	1	106	26	25	355	3.3	1	14–13	14																				
Jack Jacobs	QB-DB	30	6'1"	190		2					16	3	19	55	3.4	0	3–19						17	44.5							1	9	9	0				
Tony Canadeo	HB	30	5'11"	190	24		208	1052	5.1	4									3	–2	–1	0													2	20	10	0
Ted Fritsch	FB	28	5'10"	210	32		69	227	3.3	1	1	0	0	0	0.0	0	0– 0		6	81	14	0			11	13	85	5	20	25					1	23	23	0
Walt Schlinkman	FB	27	5'8"	190			47	196	4.2	0																									1	23	23	0
Bob Forte	HB-DB	27	6'	195		2	40	135	3.4	0	1	0	0	0	0.0	0	0– 0		7	85	12	0									1	13	13	0	7	159	23	0
Bob Summerhays	FB	22	6'1"	207			29	101	3.5	0									1	34	34	0																
Ralph Earhart	HB	26	5'10"	165	6		20	54	2.7	0									5	109	22	0									14	161	12	1	11	187	17	0
Bob Cifers	HB	28	5'11"	210			23	52	2.3	0									1	5	5	0	1	49.0														
Jack Kirby	HB-DB	26	5'11"	185			3	6	2.0	0																					8	48	6	0	14	315	23	0
Ted Cook	OE-DB	28	6'2"	195	6	5													25	442	18	1													1	7	7	0
Bill Kelley	OE	23	6'2"	195	6														17	222	13	1																
Nolan Luhn	OE-DE	28	6'3"	200	6														15	169	11	1																
Steve Pritko (from NYB)	OE-DE	27	6'2"	215	12														7	98	14	2																
Dan Orlich	OE-DE	24	6'5"	215															4	39	10	0																
Joe Ethridge	T	21	6'	230	4																				1	1	100	1	2	50								

TEAM TOTALS

DEFENSE	First Downs: Tot	by Rsh	by Pas	by Pen	Rushing: No.	Yds.	Avg Yds.	TD	Passing: Att	Com	Comp Pct.	Yds.	Avg. Yds. Att.	Avg. Yds. Comp	TD	Int	Pct. Int.	Punting: No.	Avg. Yds.	Punt Returns: No.	Yds.	Avg. Yds.	TD	Kickoff Returns: No.	Yds.	Avg. Yds.	TD	Interception Returns: No.	Yds.	Avg. Yds.	TD	Penalties: No.	Yds.	Fumbles: No.	Lost	Points: Tot	PAT	FG Att	FG	Saf.	DEFENSE
L.A.	213	101	92	20	472	1679	3.6	14	335	144	43.0	2084	6.2	14.5	16	30	9.0	68	44.2	26	215	8.3	0	55	1144	20.8	0	27	229	8.5	1	72	676	30	18	239	30	13	5	1	L.A.
CHIC. B.	170	56	95	19	428	1196	2.8	6	320	152	47.5	2147	6.7	14.1	20	27	8.4	78	41.4	32	359	11.2	0	44	963	21.9	0	30	499	16.6	2	56	521	27	16	218	29	7	5	0	CHIC. B.
CHIC. C.	231	113	107	11	446	1874	4.2	19	383	174	45.4	2617	6.8	15.0	18	33	8.6	59	38.4	43	361	8.4	1	54	1262	23.2	1	26	401	15.4	1	67	625	26	21	301	37	14	6	0	CHIC. C.
DET.	204	103	85	16	491	1827	3.7	15	312	149	47.8	1814	5.8	12.2	14	32	10.3	59	43.5	38	367	9.7	1	38	712	18.7	0	28	365	13.0	4	73	700	31	17	259	32	15	5	1	DET.
G.B.	218	110	89	19	501	2077	4.1	20	292	138	47.3	2123	7.3	15.4	15	20	6.8	68	39.8	50	932	18.6	3	29	583	20.1	0	29	406	14.0	4	91	836	23	15	329	40	26	11	2	G.B.

CLEVELAND BROWNS 9-1-2 Paul Brown

Scores of Each Game		
28	Buffalo	28
21	BALTIMORE	0
14	NEW YORK	3
28	Baltimore	20
42	LOS ANGELES	7
28	San Francisco	56
61	Los Angeles	14
30	SAN FRANCISCO	28
35	CHICAGO	2
7	BUFFALO	7
31	New York	0
14	Chicago	6

Use Name	Pos.	Hgt	Wgt	Age	Int	Pts
Frank Gatski	C	6'3"	240	27		
Lou Saban	LB	6'	215	27	2	17
(11 for 11 PAT – 0 for 2 Field Goal Attempts)						
Tommy Thompson	C-LB	6'1"	220	22	1	
Bill O'Connor	DE	6'4"	220	23		
John Yonakor	DE	6'5"	227	28		
(1 punt return for 1 yd.)						
George Young	DE	6'3"	215	25		

Use Name – Tackles	Pos.	Hgt	Wgt	Age	Int	Pts
Chubby Grigg	T	6'2"	280	23		
(2 yds. on reception lateral)						
Darrell Palmer	T	6'2"	235	27		
Lou Rymkus	T	6'4"	235	30		
(1 kickoff return for 16 yds.)						
Joe Spencer	T	6'3"	240	26		

Use Name – Guards	Pos.	Hgt	Wgt	Age	Int	Pts
Alex Agase	G-LB	5'10"	210	27	3	
Bob Gaudio (1 rush for –2 yds.)	G-LB	5'10"	225	24		
Lin Houston	G	6'	215	28		
(19 yds. on reception lateral)						
Weldon Humble	G-LB	6'1"	225	28	2	
Ed Ulinski	G	5'11"	210	28		
Bill Willis	G	6'2"	215	28	1	

The Browns looked so good on paper that many experts predicted a second straight perfect season. Otto Graham and Co. began the campaign with a tie and then four straight victories before running their unbeaten streak to twenty-seven games over three seasons. But then, out on the Coast, the '49ers knocked the complacent Browns from their pedestal with a whopping 56-28 upset. On the flight back to Cleveland, coach Paul Brown entertained his players with a blistering tirade and the team went on to five wins and one tie.

Although the Browns proved the class of their breed, the AAFC was not considered the class of pro football, and when the two leagues merged to begin the 1950 season, Cleveland heroes like Otto Graham, Marion Motley, Mac Speedie, Dante Lavelli, Bill Willis, Lou Groza, and Lou Rymkus welcomed the chance to show they could win in any league.

SAN FRANCISCO 49ers 9-3-0 Buck Shaw

Scores of Each Game		
31	BALTIMORE	17
42	CHICAGO	7
42	LOS ANGELES	14
17	Buffalo	28
42	Chicago	24
56	CLEVELAND	28
51	BUFFALO	7
3	New York	24
28	Cleveland	30
28	Baltimore	10
41	Los Angeles	24
35	NEW YORK	14

Use Name	Pos.	Hgt	Wgt	Age	Int	Pts
Bill Johnson	C-LB	6'3"	210	23	1	6
Tino Sabuco	C	6'1"	206	22		
Pete Wissman	C-LB	6'	215	25	1	

Use Name – Tackles	Pos.	Hgt	Wgt	Age	Int	Pts
Bob Bryant	T	6'3"	230	30		
Jack Carpenter	T	6'	242	26		
(from BUF, 2 receptions for 20 yds.)						
Ray Evans	T	6'1"	225	25		
Bob Mike	T	6'1"	220	25		
Joe Morgan	T	6'1"	245	20		
(–1 yd. on rushing lateral)						
Charley Quilter	T	6'1"	240	23		
John Woudenberg	T	6'3"	225	31		

Use Name – Guards	Pos.	Hgt	Wgt	Age	Int	Pts
Bruno Banducci	G	5'11"	220	27		
Don Clark	G-LB	5'11"	197	25	1	
Visco Grgich	G	5'11"	220	26		
Homer Hobbs	G	5'11"	210	26		

The '49ers enjoyed their finest moment in the AAFC when the Cleveland Browns came into Kezar Stadium for a mid-season clash. The Browns had last been beaten early in the 1947 season, but behind Frankie Albert's passing and the running of Joe Perry and Johnny Strzykalski, the '49ers destroyed the Browns' cloak of invincibility with a convincing romp. As the Browns left town, the '49ers moved into first place—a position which their fans had almost forgotten existed.

But injuries to halfbacks Strzykalski and Ed Carr the next week crippled the San Francisco running game, and the '49ers lost two in a row, 24-3 to the Yankees and 30-28 to the Browns, once again to lock the team into the familiar surroundings of second place.

NEW YORK YANKEES 8-4-0 Red Strader

Scores of Each Game		
17	Buffalo	14
3	Cleveland	14
10	LOS ANGELES	7
38	Chicago	24
24	Baltimore	21
24	SAN FRANCISCO	3
21	BALTIMORE	14
14	BUFFALO	17
14	CHICAGO	10
0	CLEVELAND	31
17	Los Angeles	16
14	San Francisco	35

Use Name	Pos.	Hgt	Wgt	Age	Int	Pts
Brad Ecklund	C-LB	6'3"	215	27		
Frank Perantoni	C	6'	220	25		

Use Name – Tackles	Pos.	Hgt	Wgt	Age	Int	Pts
Paul Mitchell	T	6'3"	240	29		
(1 punt return for 15 yds.)						
Martin Ruby	T	6'3"	250	29	1	6
Marion Shirley	T	6'4"	260	27		
Arnie Weinmeister	T	6'4"	235	26		
Ralph Sazio – Canadian Football League						
Spec Sanders (knee injury)						

Use Name – Guards	Pos.	Hgt	Wgt	Age	Int	Pts
George Brown	G	6'2"	223	26		
Bill Chambers	G	6'2"	230	26		
Bill Erickson	G-LB	6'2"	210	27		
John Mastrangelo	G	6'1"	235	23		
Ed Sharkey	G-LB	6'3"	215	23	1	
Joe Signiago	G	6'1"	225	26		
John Wozniak	G-LB	6'	218	28		

Although the New York Yankees and Brooklyn Dodgers were the most hated of rivals in baseball, their football namesakes could not afford such luxury and ended their feuding and pooled their players under the banner of the New York Yankees when economics forced the Brooklyn management out of business. Yet while the cluster of talent produced a solid team, it did not contain a passer.

With Spec Sanders sidelined all year with a knee injury, the Yankees switched to the T formation. They got running help from tiny Buddy Young, a halfback, who bounced up sprightly after each tackle and threatened to break away for big yardage every time he got the ball, and Arnie Weinmeister, Martin Ruby, and Joe Signaigo, who ranked among the best linemen in the league. The Yankees even had two outstanding young defensive backs in Otto Schnellbacher and rookie Tom Landry. But the lack of a passer put a ceiling on the team's progress.

BUFFALO BILLS 5-5-2 Red Dawson, Clem Crowe

Scores of Each Game		
14	Chicago	17
28	CLEVELAND	28
14	NEW YORK	17
28	SAN FRANCISCO	17
28	BALTIMORE	35
28	Los Angeles	42
7	San Francisco	51
17	LOS ANGELES	14
17	New York	14
7	Cleveland	7
10	CHICAGO	0
38	Baltimore	14

Use Name	Pos.	Hgt	Wgt	Age	Int	Pts
Hal Herring	C-LB	6'1"	215	25	1	
Buckets Hirsch	LB	5'10"	210	28		
Bill Schroll	LB	6'	210	23	1	
Carl Schuette	C-LB	6'1"	205	27		
Art Statuto	C	6'2"	223	24		
Bob Logel	DE	6'3"	210	21		
Vince Mazza	DE	6'1"	224	28		
Bill Stanton	DE	6'2"	210	24		

Use Name – Tackles	Pos.	Hgt	Wgt	Age	Int	Pts
John Kerns	T	6'3"	245	26		
John Kissell	T	6'2"	247	26		
John Maskas	T	5'11"	212	29		
Vin Scott – Canadian Football League						

Use Name – Guards	Pos.	Hgt	Wgt	Age	Int	Pts
Abe Gibron	G	5'10"	231	23		
(3 yds. on reception lateral)						
Ed King	G	6'	218	24		
Rocco Pirro	G	6'	235	32		
Odell Stautzenberger	G	6'	218	24		
Vic Vasicek	G	5'11"	220	23		
(5 yds. on reception lateral)						
John Wyhonic	G	6'	218	29		

The Bills became the only team in AAFC history to go through a season without losing to the Cleveland Browns. In both their meetings, the Bills and Browns battled to a draw, by scores of 28-28 and 7-7. The rest of the schedule saw the Bills on a treadmill, as they lost four of their first six games, then won four of their final six. Their final resting place was in the middle of the pack.

But off-the-field developments angered Buffalo fans more than did the stumbling Bills. The merger of the NFL and the AAFC was announced at the end of the season, with the Cleveland Browns, San Francisco '49ers, and Baltimore Colts all admitted into the established league. Buffalo, whose fans had supported the team, was consigned to pro football's junk pile along with the other AAFC teams.

							RUSHING				PASSING								RECEIVING				PUNTING		KICKING						PUNT RETURNS				KICKOFF RETURNS			
Use Name – Backs & Ends	Pos.	Age	Hgt	Wgt	Pts	Int	No.	Yds	Avg	TD	Att	Comp	%	Yds	Yd/Att	TD	Int–%	RK	No.	Yds	Avg	TD	No.	Avg	Pat	Att	%	FG	Att	%	No.	Yds	Avg	TD	No.	Yds	Avg	TD
CLEVELAND BROWNS																																						
Otto Graham	QB	27	6'1"	195	18		27	107	4.0	3	285	161	56	2785	9.8	19	10– 4	1																				
Cliff Lewis	QB-DB	26	5'11"	168	6	6	9	−17	−1.9	1	10	5	50	144	14.4	2	2–20														20	174	9	0				
Marion Motley	FB-LB	29	6'1"	238	48		113	570	5.0	8									15	191	13	0													12	262	22	0
Dub Jones	HB	24	6'4"	204	30		77	312	4.1	4									12	241	20	1													8	204	26	0
Bill Boedecker	HB	25	5'11"	195	18		50	269	5.4	1									11	371	34	2													9	189	21	0
Special Delivery Jones	HB	30	5'10"	205	42		43	127	3.0	4	1	0	0	0	0.0	0	0– 0		9	130	14	3													1	15	15	0
Ed Susteric	FB-LB	25	6'	205	6		23	114	5.0	1									1	7	7	0													2	39	20	0
Tony Adamle	FB-LB	25	6'	215		4	17	64	3.8	0									1	13	13	0																
Warren Lehr	HB-DB	25	5'11"	185	6	4	9	36	4.0	1									1	20	20	0	4	31.3							6	83	14	0				
Les Horvath	HB-DB	28	5'10"	175	18	2	10	35	3.5	1									2	71	36	1									3	19	6	0				
Ara Parseghian	HB	26	5'10"	195			12	31	2.6	0									1	2	2	0																
Tommy James	HB-DB	25	5'10"	185	6	4	10	28	2.8	0																												
Mac Speedie	OE	29	6'3"	205	42														62	1028	17	7																
Dante Lavelli	OE	26	6'	192	42														28	475	17	7																
Horace Gillom	OE-DE	28	6'1"	220			2	8	4.0	0									23	359	16	0	54	37.2														
Lou Groza	T	25	6'3"	235	40																				34	35	97	2	9	22					1	2	2	0
SAN FRANCISCO 49ers																																						
Frankie Albert	QB	29	5'10"	170	18		35	249	7.1	3	260	129	50	1862	7.2	27	16– 6	3					31	48.2	0	1	0											
Bev Wallace	QB	26	6'2"	180	6		2	2	1.0	1	23	9	39	95	4.1	0	4–17						1	30.0														
Joe Perry	FB	22	6'	195	66		115	783	6.8	8	2	0	0	0	0.0	0	0– 0		11	146	13	3													14	337	24	0
Sam Cathcart	HB-DB	24	6'	175	6	1	69	412	6.0	1									12	182	15	0									18	306	17	0	7	138	20	0
Johnny Strzykalski	HB	26	5'9"	190	24		66	287	4.3	3									6	99	17	1									2	19	10	0	2	57	29	0
Verl Lillywhite	HB-DB	22	5'10"	185	24	1	69	263	3.8	2									8	82	10	2	4	50.5											1	16	16	0
Norm Standlee	FB	30	6'2"	230	24		44	237	5.4	4													8	34.5														
Len Eshmont	HB-DB	32	5'11"	180	12	3	25	164	6.6	0									3	107	36	2													1	13	13	0
Ed Carr	HB-DB	22	6'	185	42	7	19	120	6.3	2									7	165	24	3									1	6	6	0				
Don Garlin	HB-DB	22	5'11"	188	6	1	21	113	5.4	1									6	64	11	0													1	21	21	0
Jim Cason	HB-DB	22	6'	168	6	9	21	70	3.3	1	2	1	50	38	19.0	1	0-- 0		5	38	38	0									21	351	17	0	11	247	22	0
Joe Vetrano	HB	27	5'9"	170	65		11	50	4.5	0															56	56	100	3	7	43	1	16	16	0				
Lowell Wagner	HB-DB	25	6'	193	6	6	3	17	5.7	0																					1	2	2	0				
Alyn Beals	OE	28	6'	190	73		4	32	8.0	0									44	678	15	12			1	1	100											
Paul Salata	OE	22	6'2"	190	24														24	289	12	4																
Hal Shoener	OE	26	6'3"	200															7	84	12	0									1	8	8	0	1	17	17	0
Nick Susoeff	OE-DE	28	6'1"	215	6														5	52	10	1																
Gail Bruce	OE-DE	25	6'1"	205		1													1	9	9	0													1	8	8	0
Norm Maloney	OE-DE	26	6'1"	190																											1	5	5	0				
NEW YORK YANKEES																																						
Don Panciera	QB	26	6'1"	195			10	−4	−0.4	0	150	51	34	801	5.3	5	16–11	9																				
Gil Johnson	QB	28	5'11"	195			3	21	7.0	0	36	12	33	179	5.0	0	5–14																					
Buddy Young	HB	23	5'5"	170	48		76	495	6.5	5									12	171	14	2									9	171	19	0	11	316	29	1
Bob Kennedy	FB-HB-LB	28	5'11"	195	36	2	118	490	4.2	5	1	1	100	27	27.0	0	0– 0		7	55	8	1													1	15	15	0
Sherman Howard	HB-DB	25	5'11"	192	18	1	117	459	3.9	3									1	24	24	0													4	95	24	0
Lou Kusserow	FB	25	6'1"	200			39	136	3.5	0	1	0	0	0	0.0	0	0– 0																		6	136	23	0
Eddie Prokop	FB-LB	27	5'11"	200	12		31	109	3.5	2									1	7	7	0													3	62	21	0
Mickey Colmer	FB	30	6'2"	215			36	100	2.8	0	1	0	0	0	0.0	0	0– 0		2	10	5	0	5	46.4											1	16	16	0
Pete Layden	HB-DB	29	5'11"	195	6	7	19	96	5.1	0	10	2	20	25	2.5	0	1–10		1	0	0	0	15	41.7							29	287	10	0	1	28	28	0
Tom Landry	HB-DB	24	6'1"	195		1	29	91	3.1	0									6	109	18	0	51	44.1							3	52	17	0	2	39	20	0
Lowell Tew	HB	22	5'11"	195	6		14	65	4.6	1																									1	17	17	0
Duke Iverson	HB-DB	29	6'2"	198		1	6	50	8.3	0																									2	18	9	0
Harmon Rowe	DB-HB	26	6'	182	3		6	21	3.5	0																												
Noble Doss	HB	29	6'	189			5	15	3.0	0																									1	22	22	0
Dewey Proctor	FB-LB	28	5'11"	215			1	−1	−1.0	0																												
Bruce Alford	OE	28	6'	190	6														11	213	19	1													2	31	16	0
Dan Garza	OE	25	6'3"	200															9	193	21	0													1	21	21	0
Jack Russell	OE-DE	29	6'1"	215	12	1													7	130	19	1																
Barney Poole	OE-DE	26	6'2"	220		1													6	83	14	0									1	6	6	0				
Van Davis	OE-DE	27	6'2"	215															2	26	13	0																
Otto Schnellbacher	DB-OE	26	6'2"	185		4													1	11	11	0									4	31	8	0				
Harvey Johnson	G-LB	30	5'11"	210	46	1																			25	25	100	7	15	47								
BUFFALO BILLS																																						
George Ratterman	QB	22	6'1"	190	24		36	85	2.4	4	252	146	58	1777	7.1	14	13 15	2																				
Jim Still	QB	25	6'3"	195			2	6	3.0	0	12	6	50	86	7.2	1	1– 8						16	38.4														
Jess Freitas	QB	28	5'10"	170			3	13	4.3	0	9	4	44	10	1.1	0	2–22																					
Chet Mutryn	HB	28	5'9"	183	30		131	696	5.3	5									29	333	11	0									7	77	11	0	10	224	22	0
Ollie Cline	FB	23	6'	200	18		125	518	4.1	3									15	110	7	0													1	21	21	0
Rex Bumgardner	HB	25	5'11"	193	30		101	391	3.9	1									7	168	24	4									4	35	9	0	9	163	18	0
Lou Tomasetti	HB	33	6'	205	18		54	249	4.6	2									9	56	6	1									2	13	7	0	1	19	19	0
Joe Sutton	HB-DB	25	5'11"	180	6		9	63	7.0	0									5	63	13	1									6	62	10	0	4	82	21	0
Vito Kissell	FB-LB	22	5'10"	205		1	10	19	1.9	0									3	37	12	0													1	1	1	0
Larry Joe	HB	26	5'9"	190			2	18	9.0	0									2	52	26	0													1	12	12	0
Wilbur Volz	HB-DB	25	6'	192	6		4	7	1.8	1									1	6	6	0													3	43	14	0
Tom Colella	HB-DB	31	6'	187		3	7	−9	−1.3	0									2	6	3	0	44	35.3							5	42	8	0	7	107	15	0
Alex Wizbicki	HB-DB	27	5'11"	188		1	5	−10	−2.0	0																									1	22	22	0
Bob Livingstone (from CHI)	HB-DB	27	6'	175	6	1	1	0	0.0	0									3	80	27	0									17	292	17	1	6	85	14	0
Al Baldwin	OE	26	6'2"	210	42		2	1	0.5	0									53	719	14	7																
Jim Lukens	OE	25	6'4"	205	12														24	249	10	2																
Paul Gibson	OE-DE	24	6'2"	205		1													3	32	11	0																
Bob Oristaglio	OE-DE	25	6'2"	210															1	14	14	0																
Chet Adams	T	33	6'3"	240	44																				32	32	100	4	11	36								

CHICAGO HORNETS 4-8-0 Ray Flaherty

Scores of Each Game		
17	BUFFALO	14
7	San Francisco	42
23	Los Angeles	21
35	BALTIMORE	7
24	SAN FRANCISCO	42
24	NEW YORK	38
17	Baltimore	7
14	LOS ANGELES	24
2	Cleveland	35
10	New York	14
0	Buffalo	10
6	CLEVELAND	14

Use Name	Pos.	Hgt	Wgt	Age	Int	Pts
Fred Negus	C-LB	6'1"	210	27	2	6
John Rapacz	C	6'4"	235	24		
George Strohmeyer	C-LB	5'10"	210	25	3	
Paul Cleary	DE	6'1"	196	27		
Bob Heck	DE	6'3"	207	24		
Ray Kuffel	DE	6'3"	215	27		

Use Name – Tackles	Pos.	Hgt	Wgt	Age	Int	Pts
John Clowes	T	6'1"	239	27		
Ziggy Czarobski	T	6'	235	26		
Ted Hazelwood	T	6'1"	235	25		
Nate Johnson	T	6'3"	245	29		
Homer Paine	T	6'	235	26		
Joe Soboleski (to WAS-NFL)	T	6'	215	23		

Use Name – Guards	Pos.	Hgt	Wgt	Age	Int	Pts
Jim Bailey	G	6'2"	215	22		
Jim Pearcy	G	5'11"	210	30		
Ray Richeson	G	6'	235	26		
(1 kickoff return for 0 yds.)						
Herb St. John	G	5'10"	215	23		
Marty Wendell	G	5'10"	215	22		

The AAFC Chicago franchise began the season with its fourth set of new owners, a new nickname in the Hornets, a new coach in Ray Flaherty, and paper-thin chances for survival. Chicago simply would not support three pro-football franchises, and the Hornets offered no competition for the Bears and Cardinals, who already were set with established followings and colorful teams. The Rockets had starved for customers for three years, and as the Hornets, the dollar famine got worse. An unappetizing production on the field killed any hopes the franchise had of beating the squeeze play in the oncoming merger. Those fans who did show up this year saw a club greatly improved over last year's punching bag, as the Hornets used a much tighter defense to chalk up four victories, their highest total since 1946.

LOS ANGELES DONS 4-8-0 Jim Phelan

Scores of Each Game		
49	BALTIMORE	17
21	CHICAGO	23
14	San Francisco	42
7	New York	10
7	Cleveland	42
42	BUFFALO	28
14	CLEVELAND	61
14	Buffalo	17
24	Chicago	14
24	SAN FRANCISCO	41
21	Baltimore	10
16	NEW YORK	17

Use Name	Pos.	Hgt	Wgt	Age	Int	Pts
John Brown	C-LB	6'4"	230	27	3	12
Dick Woodward	C-LB	6'2"	220	23	2	6
Dan Dworsky	BB-LB	6'	211	21	1	
(1 kickoff return for 14 yds.)						
Joyce Pipkin	BB	6'1"	205	25		

Use Name – Tackles	Pos.	Hgt	Wgt	Age	Int	Pts
Ed Henke	T-G	6'3"	217	21		
(1 reception for 15 yds.)						
Ed Kelley (1 rush for --2 yds.)	T	6'4"	230	25		
Mike Perrotti	T	6'3"	245	26		
Bob Reinhard						
(1 reception for 2 yds.)	T	6'4"	236	28		
Bob Tinsley	T	6'4"	245	25		
Ernie Williamson	T	6'4"	250	26		

Use Name – Guards	Pos.	Hgt	Wgt	Age	Int	Pts
Bob Dobelstein	G	5'11"	220	27		
Ollie Fletcher	G	6'3"	210	26		
Al Lolotai	G	6'	230	28		
Knox Ramsey	G	6'1"	216	23		
Ben Whaley	G	5'11"	210	22		

The Dons gave one the impression of a man going the wrong way on an escalator. The attendance never improved, the team's record kept slipping, and more of the press coverage was captured by the Rams. Owner Ben Lindheimer couldn't be faulted though, as he unstintingly shelled out good money after bad to keep the Dons going. Several other AAFC franchises also owed their lives to Lindheimer. The Los Angeles owner contributed some of his own funds to help the tottering Chicago Hornets, and the Baltimore Colts tasted Lindheimer's hospitality in a unique player deal. When the Colts traded for Los Angeles halfback Herm Wedemeyer, they found out that they couldn't afford his $12,000 contract. Lindheimer told the Colts that if they could pay $8,000, he would take care of the rest.

BALTIMORE COLTS 1-11-0 Cecil Isbell, Walt Driskill

Scores of Each Game		
17	San Francisco	31
17	Los Angeles	49
0	Cleveland	21
7	Chicago	35
20	CLEVELAND	28
35	Buffalo	28
21	NEW YORK	24
7	CHICAGO	17
14	New York	21
10	SAN FRANCISCO	28
10	LOS ANGELES	21
14	BUFFALO	38

Use Name	Pos.	Hgt	Wgt	Age	Int	Pts
Warren Beson	C	6'	205	22		
Spiro Dellerba	LB	5'11"	200	26		
Felto Prewitt	C-LB	5'11"	204	25		
Ralph Ruthstrom	LB	6'5"	215	28	1	
Al Tillman	C-LB	6'	210	26		
Hub Bechtol	DE	6'3"	205	23	1	
Bill Leonard	DE	6'2"	200	22	1	
(1 kickoff return for 25 yds.)						
Bob Nowaskey	DE	6'	220	31	1	

Use Name – Tackles	Pos.	Hgt	Wgt	Age	Int	Pts
Ernie Blandin	T	6'4"	245	30		
Jon Jenkins	T	6'2"	225	23		
John Mellus	T	6'	210	32		
Alex Sidorik	T	6'	245	27		
Jim Spruill	T	6'3"	225	26		

Use Name – Guards	Pos.	Hgt	Wgt	Age	Int	Pts
Dick Barwegan	G	6'1"	230	27		
Ken Cooper	G	6'1"	205	26		
Barry French	G	6'	225	28		
Bill Garrett	G	6'1"	235	25		

It was the theory of some onlookers that Y.A. Tittle developed his strong passing arm while throwing the ball with tacklers constantly on his back. While the pass protection leaked like a strainer, the running attack was so anemic that Y.A. had little choice but to retreat a few steps and try to hit a receiver while defensive linemen clawed and pummeled him. Tittle came out of the year healthy, but the Colts wound up with a sickly 1-11-0 record. Outside of the quarterback, few of the Colts showed any long-range potential. Only guard Dick Barwegan would make his weight felt in the NFL in coming years. Although coach Cecil Isbell paid in mid-season for the lack of talent with his job, his replacement, Walt Driskill, had no Midas touch when it came to turning losers into winners. Consequently, the Colts, doormats of the AAFC, would also play the same role when joining the NFL in 1950.

Use Name – Backs & Ends	Pos.	Age	Hgt	Wgt	Pts	Int	RUSHING				PASSING								RECEIVING				PUNTING		KICKING						PUNT RETURNS				KICKOFF RETURNS			
							No.	Yds	Avg	TD	Att	Comp	%	Yds	Yd/Att	TD	Int–%	RK	No.	Yds	Avg	TD	No.	Avg	Pat	Att	%	FG	Att	%	No.	Yds	Avg	TD	No.	Yds	Avg	TD
CHICAGO HORNETS																																						
Bob Hoernschemeyer	TB	23	5'11"	195	12		133	456	3.4	2	167	69	41	1063	6.4	6	11– 7	6					4	48.8							1	4	2	0	14	373	27	0
Johnny Clement	TB	29	6'	185	30		106	388	3.7	5	114	58	51	906	7.9	6	13–11	5																				
Bob Chappuis	TB	26	6'	190			4	13	3.3	0	14	2	14	40	2.9	0	4–29																					
John Donaldson (from LA)	TB-DB	24	5'10"	180			1	–2	–2.0	0	1	0	0	0	0.0	0	0– 0														1	18	18	0	1	27	27	0
Rip Collins	FB-DB	22	6'	190		1	28	88	3.1	0	1	0	0	0	0.0	0	0– 0		6	161	27	0	41	42.1											2	23	12	0
Ernie Lewis	FB	25	6'1"	210	6		11	43	3.9	1													16	42.5														
George Buksar	FB-LB	23	6'	200	6		13	16	1.2	1	1	0	0	0	0.0	0	0– 0																					
Frank Aschenbrenner	FB	24	5'10"	188			8	14	1.8	0									2	–4	–2	0													2	35	18	0
Hardy Brown	FB-DB	25	6'	185		3	1	2	2.0	0									1	10	10	0	10	39.7														
Ray Ramsey	WB-DB	28	6'2"	165	24	2	32	43	1.3	0									17	366	22	4									8	64	8	0	14	407	29	0
Paul Patterson	WB-DB	23	5'9"	185	24	3	2	0	0.0	0									16	304	19	4									4	33	8	0				
Jim Smith (to DET-NFL)	WB	24	6'1"	190															1	31	31	0																
Bob Sweiger	BB-LB	30	6'	209		1	3	17	5.7	0									11	126	11	0													3	59	20	0
Walt McDonald	BB	28	6'1"	210			1	0	0.0	0																												
Dan Edwards	OE	23	6'1"	203	24														42	573	14	3													2	29	15	1
Hank Foldberg	OE-DE	26	6'1"	205															15	202	13	0																
Fay King	OE	27	6'3"	195	6														9	88	10	1													1	13	13	0
Jim McCarthy	OE-DE	27	6'1"	205	39														4	58	15	0			21	23	91	6	13	46								
Bob Jensen	OE-DE	23	6'4"	222															2	14	7	0																
LOS ANGELES DONS																																						
Glenn Dobbs	TB	29	6'4"	214	18		34	161	4.7	3	153	65	42	825	5.4	4	9– 6	6					39	42.3														
George Taliaferro	TB	22	5'11"	195	42		95	472	5.0	5	124	45	36	790	6.4	4	14–11	8	0	42	–	1	27	36.4							2	53	27	1	13	313	24	0
Walt Clay	TB	25	5'11"	198			9	34	3.8	0	1	1	100	8	8.0	0	0– 0																					
Hosea Rodgers	FB	27	6'1"	192	30		131	494	3.8	5	1	0	0	0	0.0	0	0– 0		7	97	14	0																
Billy Grimes	HB	22	6'1"	192	36		83	429	5.2	4	3	3	100	105	35.0	1	0– 0		13	189	15	2									5	67	13	0	16	411	26	0
Earl Howell	HB	24	5'10"	189	12		31	116	3.7	1									5	11	2	1									1	7	7	0	4	74	19	0
Jimmie Spavital	FB-LB	23	6'1"	215		4	15	44	2.9	0									1	–1	–1	0									6	58	10	0	1	32	32	0
Harper Davis	DB-HB	23	5'11"	175	6	2	13	33	2.5	1									2	13	7	0									7	37	19	0	4	87	22	0
Tom McWilliams	DB-HB	23	5'11"	185		2	3	15	5.0	0	2	0	0	0	0.0	0	0– 0														8	112	14	0				
Bob Kennedy	DB-HB	21	6'	178		1	2	14	7.0	0																												
Paul Crowe (from SF)	DB-FB	25	6'1"	195	6	1	3	2	0.7	0																					6	96	16	0				
Bob Hoffman	BB-LB	31	6'1"	220		1													2	21	11	0													1	14	14	0
George Murphy	BB	22	6'	200			1	0	0.0	0									1	17	17	0																
Len Ford	OE-DE	23	6'4"	235	6	1													36	577	16	1																
Dick Wilkins	OE	23	6'2"	192	18		8	28	3.5	0	1	0	0	0	0.0	0	0– 0		32	589	18	3																
Lew Holder	OE	25	6'1"	191			1	–1	–1.0	0									5	71	14	0																
Joe Aguirre	OE-DE	30	6'4"	225	6														3	37	12	1																
Ab Wimberly	OE-DE	23	6'2"	212	12	1													3	22	7	0																
Burr Baldwin	OE-DB	27	6'1"	195		2	1	1	1.0	0									2	26	13	0																
Bob Nelson	C-LB	29	6'1"	210	43																				34	35	97	3	6	50								
BALTIMORE COLTS																																						
Y. A. Tittle	QB	22	6'	190	12		29	89	3.1	2	289	148	51	2209	7.6	14	18– 6	4																				
Sam Vacanti	QB	27	5'11"	210	3		7	10	1.4	0	27	11	41	134	5.0	0	1– 4								3	3	100	0	2	0					1	10	10	0
Charlie O'Rourke	QB	32	5'11"	175							7	1	14	12	1.7	0	1–14						28	39.2														
Herm Wedemeyer	HB	25	5'10"	178			64	291	4.5	0	1	0	0	0	0	0	1–100		10	112	11	0	3	18.0							16	221	14	0	30	602	20	0
Lu Gambino	FB	25	6'1"	205	6		56	208	3.7	0									10	67	7	1																
Billy Stone	HB	23	6'	190	48		51	205	4.0	2									31	621	20	6													1	25	25	0
Bob Pfohl	HB	23	6'	200	12		67	205	3.1	2									7	62	9	0													4	98	25	0
Chick Jagade	FB	22	6'	200	12		33	174	5.3	2									8	44	6	0													6	75	13	0
Paul Page	HB-DB	22	6'	180			25	81	3.2	0									4	62	16	0									1	16	16	0	4	108	27	0
Bob Kelly	HB-DB	24	5'10"	193		3	9	17	1.9	0									2	25	13	0													2	31	16	0
Buzz Mertes (to NYG-NFL)	FB	28	6'	205	6		11	8	0.7	0									2	22	11	1																
Wayne Kingery	HB-DB	22	5'11"	175		1	3	3	1.0	0									1	–2	–2	0	3	36.3							2	19	10	0				
Bob Cowan	HB-DB	26	5'11"	185		3	1	0	0.0	0									1	26	26	0																
Jake Leicht	HB-DB	28	5'9"	170		1	6	–7	–1.2	0									1	12	12	0									9	109	12	0	8	171	21	0
Lamar Davis	OE-DB	28	6'1"	185	6	1													38	548	14	1													1	13	13	0
John North	OE	28	6'2"	200	24														25	490	20	4																
Win Williams	OE	26	6'2"	185	6														20	266	13	1																
Rex Grossman	K	25	6'1"	215	37						1	0	0	0	0.0	0	1–100						28	38.8	19	19	100	6	11	55								

TEAM TOTALS	FIRST DOWNS:				RUSHING:				PASSING:									PUNTING:		PUNT RETURNS:				KICKOFF RETURNS:				INTERCEPTION RETURNS:				PENALTIES:		FUMBLES:		POINTS:					TEAM TOTALS
OFFENSE	Tot	by Rsh	by Pas	by Pen	No.	Yds.	Avg. Yds.	TD	Att	Com	Comp. Pct.	Yds.	Avg. Yds. Att.	Avg. Yds. Comp	TD	Int.	Pct. Int.	No.	Avg. Yds.	No.	Yds.	Avg. Yds.	TD	No.	Yds.	Avg. Yds.	TD	No.	Yds.	Avg. Yds.	TD	No.	Yds.	No.	Lost	Tot	PAT	FG Att	FG	Saf.	OFFENSE
CLEVE.	176	62	100	14	403	1682	4.2	24	296	166	56.1	2929	9.9	17.6	21	12	4.1	58	36.8	30	277	9.2	0	34	727	21.4	0	29	331	11.4	2	72	617	33	21	339	45	11	2	0	CLEVE.
S.F.	175	117	53	5	506	2798	5.5	26	287	139	48.4	1995	7.0	14.4	28	20	7.0	44	45.5	46	713	15.5	0	39	854	21.9	0	32	474	14.8	3	65	595	47	22	416	57	7	3	1	S.F.
N.Y.	135	91	37	7	510	2143	4.2	16	199	66	33.2	1032	5.2	15.6	5	22	11.1	71	43.8	47	562	12.0	0	36	816	22.7	1	24	321	13.4	2	52	358	35	20	196	25	15	7	0	N.Y.
BUFFALO	184	111	61	12	492	2047	4.2	16	273	156	57.1	1873	6.9	12.0	15	16	5.9	60	36.1	34	400	11.8	1	40	729	18.2	0	9	84	9.3	0	59	454	34	18	236	32	11	4	0	BUFFALO
CHICAGO	122	46	63	13	342	1080	3.2	9	297	129	43.4	2009	6.8	15.6	12	28	9.4	71	42.2	21	240	11.4	0	43	989	23.0	1	15	323	21.5	0	63	426	29	19	179	21	13	6	1	CHICAGO
L.A.	157	82	63	12	430	1838	4.3	19	286	114	39.9	1728	6.0	15.2	9	23	8.0	66	39.9	30	430	14.3	1	41	972	23.7	0	21	316	16.0	2	59	530	31	17	253	34	6	3	0	L.A.
BALT.	151	66	78	7	362	1284	3.5	8	326	160	40.2	2355	7.3	14.7	14	22	6.8	62	37.9	28	365	13.0	0	58	1158	20.0	0	13	113	8.7	0	49	369	32	21	172	22	13	6	0	BALT.
DEFENSE																																									DEFENSE
CLEVE.	156	75	67	14	437	1905	4.4	13	304	120	39.5	1677	5.5	14.0	9	29	9.5	63	39.6	27	314	11.6	0	32	694	21.7	0	12	153	12.8	0	45	359	32	13	171	22	10	3	1	CLEVE.
S.F.	150	74	68	8	401	1364	3.4	12	318	137	43.1	1949	6.1	14.2	15	32	10.1	75	39.3	27	317	11.7	0	61	1216	19.9	0	20	229	11.5	1	51	374	27	15	227	29	10	6	0	S.F.
N.Y.	129	55	68	6	360	1134	3.2	8	316	159	50.3	2189	6.9	13.8	13	24	7.6	78	41.8	44	485	11.0	1	44	994	22.6	1	22	349	15.9	3	56	414	33	17	206	26	9	6	0	N.Y.
BUFFALO	139	69	62	8	385	1616	4.2	13	282	132	46.8	2109	7.5	16.0	18	9	3.2	58	42.4	29	343	11.8	0	41	959	23.4	0	16	250	15.6	1	54	419	34	22	256	35	16	3	1	BUFFALO
CHICAGO	163	92	61	10	467	2309	4.9	24	197	107	54.3	1732	8.8	16.2	9	15	7.6	54	37.6	44	583	13.3	1	36	868	24.1	1	28	335	12.0	2	73	521	52	37	268	37	10	3	0	CHICAGO
L.A.	174	89	69	16	484	2148	4.4	20	290	148	51.0	2414	8.3	16.3	22	21	7.2	52	40.0	30	398	13.3	0	43	824	19.2	0	23	268	11.7	1	68	678	35	17	322	40	12	6	0	L.A.
BALT.	189	121	60	8	511	2396	4.7	28	256	127	49.6	1851	7.2	14.6	18	13	5.1	52	40.7	35	547	15.6	0	34	690	20.3	0	22	378	17.2	1	72	590	28	17	341	47	9	4	0	BALT.

1950 Gathering in the Best of the Flock

The death of the AAFC gathered all the strong clubs into the NFL under a strong commissioner in Bert Bell and exiled the weaker franchises into the history books. The Cleveland Browns, San Francisco '49ers, and Baltimore Colts moved into the established league, swelling its membership up to 13 clubs, while the players from the defunct teams went into a pool and were spread around the league.

The new era also brought with it the permanent adoption of the "free substitution" rule which relieved coaches of the necessity of playing most men both ways and that gave the opportunity to develop offensive and defensive specialists who would excel in one aspect of the game. This division of labor made pro football a faster, more exciting game to watch, and while sold-out stadiums were still the exception rather than the rule, attendance soared to a record total of 1,977,556.

Only the new medium of television did not fit smoothly into the picture. The Los Angeles Rams televised all their games, both home and away, and watched their attendance shrink to almost half of the 1949 total despite a very attractive football team. It was an example that Bell would later use to support the TV blackout of all home games throughout the league.

AMERICAN CONFERENCE

Cleveland Browns—The NFL schedule-maker indulged his sense of drama by pitting the 1949 NFL champion Philadelphia Eagles against the 1949 AAFC champion Cleveland Browns on the Saturday night before the other teams opened their seasons. The oddsmakers favored the Eagles, but coach Paul Brown had his team ready to break into the established league with a bang. A crowd of 71,000 jammed Philadelphia's Municipal Stadium but found little cause for cheering. With Otto Graham slinging sideline passes to Mac Speedie, Dub Jones, and Dante Lavelli, the Browns ran away from the Eagles in the second half for a stunningly easy 35-10 upset. The Browns then marched briskly through their NFL opponents, winning ten games and losing twice to the New York Giants. But in the conference playoff, the Browns rebounded to down New York 8-3.

New York Giants—The death of the AAFC Yankees brought back to the Giants defensive tackle Arnie Weinmeister and defensive backs Otto Schnellbacher, Tom Landry, and Harmon Rowe, while the college draft brought scrappy fullback Eddie Price into the fold. Coach Steve Owen built his offense around runners Price and Choo-Choo Roberts, and he constructed the famous "umbrella defense" to defuse free-passing clubs like the Browns. In this defense, the two defensive ends dropped off the line to cover receivers, while backs Em Tunnell, Landry, Schnellbacher, and Rowe formed the "umbrella" in the zone pass defense.

Philadelphia Eagles—A tight budget and an injured foot killed the Eagles' chances of repeating as NFL champs. The tight budget of the front office did not allow for any pay raises, and several holdouts riddled the club with dissension. Coach Greasy Neale had no use for owner Jim Clark when he rewarded the holdouts with raises after most of the players agreed to play for the same salary as last year, and their deteriorating relations came to a head when the players had to pull Neale off Clark in the Polo Grounds dressing room. The injured foot belonged to Steve Van Buren. An off-season operation failed to heal properly and left the punishing halfback a shadow of his former self. But with Tommy Thompson throwing the ball, Frank Ziegler running it, and young Chuck Bednarik bolstering the defense at linebacker, the Eagles stayed close behind the Browns and Giants until dropping their last four games.

Pittsburgh Steelers—The Steeler offense still looked like something out of the 1930s. While every other pro team now used the T formation, coach John Michelosen still stuck with the conservative single wing. Although tailback Joe Geri picked up yardage in bits and pieces with off-tackle smashes, his pass completions came few and far between. The earthbound Steelers scored only 180 points, less than half of what the pass-oriented Rams tallied, but a hard-nosed defense, led by lineman Bill McPeak and Ernie Stautner, kept them in most of their games. Of their six victories, the most impressive was a 17-6 triumph over the New York Giants. The most characteristic win, though, was a bruising 9-7 fray with the Eagles in which all the Steeler points came on three Geri field goals. Coach Michelosen liked this kind of hard-hitting football so much that he let Jim Finks, a promising passer, waste away unused.

Chicago Cardinals—After thirty-one years in Green Bay, Curly Lambeau began anew as coach of the Cards, but he brought with him none of the magic of his six NFL championships with the Packers. Still emphasizing the pass, he elevated strong-armed Jim Hardy from second string to starting quarterback. Hardy enjoyed some good days, such as the game in which he threw five touchdown passes to end Bob Shaw, but he also had his bad days—one of which made the record books when the Eagles intercepted him eight times. Despite Hardy's inconsistency, Lambeau had to stick with him, since he had unloaded incumbent quarterback Paul Christman before the season.

Washington Redskins—Quarterback Harry Gilmer still showed no signs of growing into the starting lineup, and heralded rookie Choo-Choo Justice impressed no one with his running. Only fullback Rob Goode and end Hugh Taylor helped aging Sammy Baugh and Bill Dudley shoot some life into the attack, and despite rookie Chuck Drazenovich's fine play at linebacker, the defense had as much trouble stopping the enemy as the offense had moving the ball. The result was predictable, as the Skins went on an eight-game losing streak in mid-season to turn the year into a shambles. But coach Herman Ball somehow survived and would be back for more next year.

NATIONAL CONFERENCE

Los Angeles Rams—The modern passing attack hit a new peak as the Rams threw their way to the top of the National Conference by chalking up 466 points, sixty-four touchdowns, and 70 points in one game—all records. New head coach Joe Stydahar, replacing the fired Clark Shaughnessy, managed a superb pair of quarterbacks in young Norm Van Brocklin and veteran Bob Waterfield. Ends Tom Fears and Crazy Legs Hirsch and halfback ex-Army star Glenn Davis were all among the league's top receivers. The defense fell far short of immovable, but the offense carried the team into a tie with the Bears for the conference crown. In the playoff game, Fears, who had set a new season's receiving record, hauled in three touchdown passes as the Rams won 24-14.

Chicago Bears—Johnny Lujack was completing his passes, but he wasn't getting his usual zing into the ball. After the season, the word leaked out that Lujack had hurt his shoulder and, with veteran Sid Luckman unable to play for any extended stretch, had to keep playing with the injury. The young passer boosted the Bears into a tie for the conference title, but his arm was never again the same. In engineering a strong offense, Lujack ran well, hit end Jim Keane with short passes, and often handed off to George Gulyanics. George Connor and Dick Barwegan excelled in the offensive line with Connor doubling as a big linebacker on defense.

New York Yanks—Ted Collins still owned the team, but the Yanks were a far different outfit from last year's Bulldogs. The club had a new name, moved to Yankee Stadium, had a respected coach in Red Strader, and a practically whole new cast of players. Only three men returned from the Bulldog roster, with most of the squad recruited from AAFC veterans. Quarterback George Ratterman, runners Sherman Howard, George Taliaferro, and Buddy Young, receiver Dan Edwards, linemen Joe Signiago and Martin Ruby, and defensive back Spec Sanders all came from the AAFC to bring the franchise alive. Add solid rookie seasons from runner Zollie Toth and end Art Weiner, and the Yanks had a pretty fair team. Only two things remained the same: New Yorkers still kept away from the ballpark, and Collins kept losing money.

Detroit Lions—The Lions hadn't won a championship since 1935, but they gathered together a nucleus of players who would soon bring the NFL title to Detroit. Quarterback Bobby Layne was puchased from the New York Bulldogs, giving the squad a leader both on the field and off it. Layne sparkled on long, time-consuming downfield marches, as well as on late-night extra curricular activities. Like Babe Ruth, however, Layne could ignore all training rules and still turn in an outstanding performance on the gridiron. The rookie crop yielded a fine runner, receiver, and kicker in Doak Walker, a bruising two-way end in Leon Hart, and a tough tackle in Thurman McGraw. Further additions included halfback Bob Hoernschemeyer and offensive lineman Lou Creekmur, both from AAFC rosters.

Green Bay Packers—New coach Gene Ronzani inherited a deteriorating squad, and constant front-office interference didn't make his task any easier. Some new talent, however, kept the season from being a total loss. Rookie quarterback Tobin Rote showed flair both in passing and running, end Al Baldwin and halfback Billy Grimes both fit into the attack after coming over from the AAFC, and rookie Clayton Tonnemaker graded out as the best Packer lineman. But the defense leaked horrendously, five times allowing 40 or more points, while the offense was inconsistent.

San Francisco '49Ers—Fullback Joe Perry and halfback Johnny Strzykalski both carried the ball above and beyond the call of duty, but they could not make up for a weakened passing attack. Saddled with his first losing season in San Francisco, coach Buck Shaw did uncover two fine rookies, pass receiver and place kicker Gordy Soltau and tackle Leo Nomellini, a brute of a tackle equally effective in the offensive or defensive line.

Baltimore Colts—The Colts started out their NFL career by dropping all seven of their pre-season games and six of their regular season's games. Only at quarterback were the Colts well fortified, with Y. A. Tittle and rookie Adrian Burk both worthy of better supporting casts. But even these two were not enough to keep attendance from dwindling, the club from continually losing, and owner Abraham Watner from selling the franchise back to the league.

FINAL TEAM STATISTICS

OFFENSE

	BALT.	CHI.B.	CHI.C.	CLEVE.	DET.	G.BAY	L.A.	N.Y.G.	N.Y.Y.	PHIL.	PITT.	S.F.	WASH.
FIRST DOWNS:													
Total	188	234	194	199	209	174	278	173	210	231	177	201	187
by Rushing	56	141	84	104	92	82	112	114	94	142	97	107	92
by Passing	109	85	87	86	98	70	142	53	102	79	68	83	84
by Penalty	23	10	23	9	19	22	24	6	14	10	12	11	11
RUSHING:													
Number	345	574	386	457	389	398	404	515	397	581	477	460	410
Yards	1148	2308	1604	2089	1626	1706	1711	2336	1832	2328	1659	1955	1773
Average Yards	3.3	4.0	4.2	4.6	4.2	4.3	4.2	4.5	4.6	4.0	3.5	4.3	4.3
Touchdowns	12	25	8	20	14	15	28	21	16	13	12	14	10
PASSING:													
Attempts	438	296	368	260	403	367	453	187	355	285	255	326	314
Completions	206	135	165	139	176	140	253	81	174	121	100	164	154
Completion Percent	47.0	45.6	44.8	53.5	43.7	38.1	55.8	43.3	49.0	42.5	39.2	50.3	49.0
Yards	2687	1927	2375	1984	2772	1831	3709	1338	2894	1836	1729	1875	2093
Avg. Yards per Att.	6.1	6.5	6.5	7.6	6.9	5.0	8.2	7.2	8.2	6.4	6.8	5.8	6.7
Avg. Yards per Comp.	13.0	14.3	14.4	14.3	15.8	13.1	14.7	16.5	16.6	15.2	17.3	11.4	13.6
Touchdowns	14	5	21	15	22	14	31	12	29	15	10	14	18
Interceptions	31	24	31	21	29	37	27	10	26	28	29	25	25
Percent Intercepted	7.1	8.1	8.4	8.1	7.2	10.1	6.0	5.3	7.3	9.8	11.4	7.7	8.0
PUNTING:													
Number	83	66	76	66	68	74	63	78	72	56	61	63	64
Average Distance	40.2	41.7	40.6	43.2	40.2	38.1	40.5	37.1	42.2	41.4	41.3	38.7	40.6
PUNT RETURNS:													
Number	26	60	33	30	36	44	45	42	27	52	33	33	43
Yards	378	601	338	469	389	729	393	410	305	401	387	406	407
Average Yards	15.5	10.0	10.2	15.6	10.8	16.6	8.7	9.8	11.3	7.7	11.7	12.3	9.5
Touchdowns	1	0	1	1	0	2	0	0	0	0	0	0	1
KICKOFF RETURNS:													
Number	66	35	51	32	40	56	56	25	58	38	32	40	51
Yards	1286	818	1064	670	1067	1233	1424	592	1280	867	748	800	1242
Average Yards	19.5	23.4	20.9	20.9	26.7	22.0	25.4	23.7	22.1	22.8	23.4	20.0	24.4
Touchdowns	0	0	0	0	1	0	3	0	1	1	0	0	0
INTERCEPTION RETURNS:													
Number	34	16	22	31	31	27	31	27	30	31	22	22	19
Yards	571	283	190	262	480	337	512	408	438	401	295	304	221
Average Yards	16.8	17.7	8.6	8.5	15.5	12.5	16.5	15.1	14.6	12.9	13.4	13.8	11.6
Touchdowns	4	4	0	2	3	2	1	0	2	3	0	1	2
PENALTIES:													
Number	63	85	76	104	86	85	110	68	85	63	57	93	80
Yards	579	738	609	968	804	757	1038	562	762	612	477	851	829
FUMBLES:													
Number	32	23	25	26	35	35	30	36	32	32	41	35	42
Number Lost	21	17	14	12	18	20	17	20	13	15	29	21	22
POINTS:													
Total	213	279	233	310	321	244	466	268	366	254	180	213	232
PAT Attempts	31	35	31	38	43	34	63	35	51	33	22	29	31
PAT Made	27	34	29	38	39	31	59	30	48	32	22	27	31
FG Attempts	4	20	12	21	18	17	14	12	9	22	14	8	10
FG Made	0	9	6	14	8	3	7	6	2	8	8	4	5
Percent FG Made	0.0	45.0	50.0	66.7	44.5	17.6	50.0	50.0	22.2	36.4	57.1	50.0	50.0
Safeties	0	1	0	1	0	0	1	2	3	0	1	0	0

DEFENSE

	BALT.	CHI.B.	CHI.C.	CLEVE.	DET.	G.BAY	L.A.	N.Y.G.	N.Y.Y.	PHIL.	PITT.	S.F.	WASH.
FIRST DOWNS:													
Total	257	178	216	184	200	220	217	176	249	141	198	204	217
by Rushing	150	67	126	96	70	91	113	87	119	66	111	111	110
by Passing	96	88	79	71	113	110	88	76	112	65	77	81	90
by Penalty	11	23	11	17	17	19	16	13	18	10	10	12	17
RUSHING:													
Number	514	388	525	451	399	422	431	473	434	391	460	443	462
Yards	2857	1449	2132	1573	1367	1885	1882	1387	2445	1603	1889	1662	1944
Average Yards	5.6	3.7	4.1	3.5	3.4	4.5	4.4	2.9	5.6	4.1	4.1	3.8	4.2
Touchdowns	28	14	21	10	13	23	12	8	28	5	12	17	17
PASSING:													
Attempts	304	354	269	292	381	379	385	295	396	277	300	347	328
Completions	156	169	130	121	191	185	165	145	189	102	146	164	145
Completion Percent	51.3	47.7	48.3	41.4	50.1	48.8	42.9	49.2	47.7	36.8	48.7	47.3	44.2
Yards	2545	2265	2075	1581	2580	2818	2576	1848	2775	1621	1801	2289	2276
Avg. Yards per Att.	8.4	6.4	7.7	5.4	6.8	7.4	6.7	6.3	7.0	5.9	6.0	6.6	6.9
Avg. Yards per Comp.	16.3	13.4	16.0	13.1	13.5	15.2	15.6	12.7	14.7	15.9	12.3	14.0	15.7
Touchdowns	31	11	14	8	23	24	26	11	17	10	10	16	19
Interceptions	34	16	22	31	31	27	31	27	30	31	22	22	19
Percent Intercepted	11.2	4.5	8.2	10.6	8.1	7.1	8.1	9.1	7.6	11.2	7.3	6.3	5.8
PUNTING:													
Number	56	87	57	69	73	72	72	77	58	77	70	62	60
Average Distance	39.1	39.7	43.3	41.5	42.7	40.2	39.3	41.2	38.8	38.9	40.8	39.4	40.3
PUNT RETURNS:													
Number	44	24	46	32	45	49	28	43	53	32	35	37	36
Yards	531	303	400	210	529	372	394	420	699	392	504	413	446
Average Yards	12.1	12.6	8.7	6.6	11.8	7.6	14.1	9.8	13.2	12.3	14.4	11.2	12.4
Touchdowns	0	1	1	0	0	0	0	0	0	1	1	0	2
KICKOFF RETURNS:													
Number	36	44	46	43	54	41	48	55	53	38	37	41	44
Yards	900	848	1063	988	1218	845	1411	1166	1148	834	710	1014	946
Average Yards	25.0	19.3	23.1	23.0	22.6	20.6	29.4	21.2	21.7	21.9	19.2	24.7	21.5
Touchdowns	1	0	0	0	2	0	2	0	0	0	0	1	0
INTERCEPTION RETURNS:													
Number	31	24	31	21	29	37	27	10	26	28	29	25	25
Yards	622	396	410	262	372	575	294	120	343	289	244	429	346
Average Yards	20.1	16.5	13.2	12.5	12.8	15.5	10.9	12.0	13.2	10.3	8.4	17.2	13.8
Touchdowns	2	2	1	1	0	5	3	0	2	1	1	3	3
PENALTIES:													
Number	96	77	93	62	86	95	93	70	88	73	77	71	74
Yards	967	671	876	554	803	919	859	553	824	590	733	599	638
FUMBLES:													
Number	29	24	37	37	35	34	31	43	28	32	30	39	25
Number Lost	14	16	24	24	24	15	15	27	14	17	16	21	12
POINTS:													
Total	462	207	287	144	285	406	309	150	367	141	195	300	326
PAT Attempts	63	27	38	19	39	55	43	19	49	17	25	39	43
PAT Made	61	24	35	18	37	50	42	18	46	15	24	35	42
FG Attempts	13	12	18	11	11	13	13	11	17	18	12	14	18
FG Made	7	5	8	4	4	6	3	6	9	8	5	7	8
Percent FG Made	53.8	41.7	44.4	36.4	36.4	46.1	23.1	54.5	53.0	44.4	41.7	50.0	44.4
Safeties	1	0	0	0	1	1	0	0	0	0	3	2	1

SCORING

CLEVELAND	7	6	7	10—30
LOS ANGELES	14	0	14	0—28

First Quarter
- L.A. Davis, 82 yard pass from Waterfield
  PAT—Waterfield (Kick)
- Cle. Jones, 27 yard pass from Graham
  PAT—Groza (Kick)
- L.A. Hoerner, 3 yard rush
  PAT—Waterfield (Kick)

Second Quarter
- Cle. Lavelli, 37 yard pass from Graham
  PAT—Bad Center Snap

Third Quarter
- Cle. Lavelli, 39 yard pass from Graham
  PAT—Groza (Kick)
- L.A. Hoerner, 1 yard rush
  PAT—Waterfield (Kick)
- L.A. Brink, 6 yard Fumble return
  PAT—Waterfield (Kick)

Fourth Quarter
- Cle. Bumgardner, 14 yard pass from Graham
  PAT—Groza, (Kick)
- Cle. Groza, 16 yard field goal

TEAM STATISTICS

CLEVE.		L.A.
22	First Downs	22
116	Rushing Yardage	106
33	Pass Attempts	32
22	Pass Completions	18
66.7	Completion Percentage	56.3
298	Passing Yardage	312
9.0	Avg. Yards per Attempt	9.8
13.5	Avg. Yards per Completion	17.3
1	Had Intercepted	5
5	Number of Punts	4
38.4	Average Punt Distance	50.8
22	Punt Return Yardage	14
3	Fumbles	0
3	Fumbles Lost	0
3	Penalties	4
26	Yards Penalized	48

1950
CHAMPIONSHIP GAME
December 24, at Cleveland
(Attendance 29,751)

Different League, Same Title

In their first season in the NFL the Browns beat the Giants in a playoff for the Eastern title, and now only the Rams stood in the way of the league championship. Both clubs depended on strong passing attacks, and footballs filled the air right from the start of the game. On the first play from scrimmage, Bob Waterfield hit Glenn Davis on a fly pattern good for 82 yards and a touchdown. Within three minutes Cleveland tied the score on an Otto Graham to Dub Jones pass, but Los Angeles again went ahead by driving 81 yards in eight plays after the kickoff. Both teams slowed up for the rest of the quarter, but the Browns struck again midway through the second period. With the ball on the Los Angeles 37-yard line, Dante Lavelli grabbed a Graham pass between two Ram defenders on the 8-yard line and ran it in for six points. On the extra point, holder Tommy James fumbled the snap, so the Browns trailed 14-13 at the half. Graham hit Lavelli with another touchdown pass four minutes into the third quarter to put Cleveland into the lead 20-14, but the Rams came right back with a score of their own. Waterfield hit on three straight passes to bring the ball down to the Cleveland 17, and then he turned to fullback Dick Hoerner. The powerful Hoerner carried the ball seven straight times, scoring from the 1-yard line on fourth down. On the first play after the kickoff, Marion Motley fumbled deep in his own territory, and Ram end Larry Brink scooped the ball up and carried it in for the second Los Angeles touchdown in twenty-one seconds. Waterfield's conversion made it 28-20, with the Browns' missed extra point looking very large. The Cleveland defense, however, tightened up and gave the offense a chance to get back in the game. Late in the third period, Warren Lahr intercepted a Waterfield pass on his own 35-yard line, and Graham then drove his team 65 yards with nine completed passes, including five in a row to Lavelli, with the touchdown coming on a diving catch by Rex Bumgardner. Now Cleveland trailed by only one point, but the Ram defense followed Cleveland's in stiffening up. Neither team could launch an extended drive, trading punts for most of the fourth quarter. With two minutes left in the game, Cliff Lewis returned Waterfield's punt to the Brown 32-yard line, giving Cleveland one last shot at winning it. Graham kept the ball and ran 19 yards on the first play, then passed to Bumgardner for 10 more yards. His next pass was incomplete, but completions to Jones and Bumgardner then brought the ball down to the Ram 11. After a quarterback sneak to get the ball in the center of the field, Graham turned the ball over to kicker Lou Groza. The kick from the 16 split the goal posts with only twenty-eight seconds left, and the Browns took the NFL crown with a 30-28 win.

CLEVELAND BROWNS 10-2-0 Paul Brown

Scores of Each Game		
35	Philadelphia	10
31	Baltimore	0
0	N.Y. GIANTS	6
30	Pittsburgh	17
34	CHIC. CARDS	24
13	N.Y. Giants	17
45	PITTSBURGH	7
10	Chic. Cards	7
34	SAN FRANCISCO	14
20	WASHINGTON	14
13	PHILADELPHIA	7
45	Washington	21
	Playoff	
8	N.Y. GIANTS	3

Use Name	Pos.	Hgt	Wgt	Age	Int	Pts
Lou Groza	OT	6'3"	235	26		74
Lou Rymkus	OT	6'4"	235	31		
Abe Gibron	OG	5'11"	236	24		
Lin Houston	OG	6'	215	29		
Weldon Humble	OG	6'1"	225	29		
Frank Gatski	C	6'3"	240	28		
Bill Willis	DG	6'2"	215	29		
Len Ford	DE	6'4"	238	24		
George Young	DE	6'3"	215	26		
Jim Martin	OT-DE	6'2"	215	26	2	
Chubby Grigg	DT	6'2"	280	24		12
John Kissell	DT	6'3"	247	27		2
Darrell Palmer	DT	6'2"	235	28		
John Sandusky	DT	6'1"	250	24		
Alex Agase	LB	5'10"	212	28	1	
Tommy Thompson	LB	6'1"	220	23		
Hal Herring	C-LB	6'1"	210	26	2	
Tony Adamle	FB-LB	6'1"	220	26	1	
Ken Gorgal	DB	6'2"	200	21	6	
Warren Lahr	DB	5'11"	185	26	8	12
Cliff Lewis	QB-DB	5'11"	168	27	1	
Tommy James	HB-DB	5'10"	185	26	9	
Otto Graham	QB	6'1"	195	28		36
Rex Baumgardner	HB	5'11"	193	26		18
Ken Carpenter	HB	6'1"	192	24		6
Dub Jones	HB	6'4"	205	25		66
Dom Moselle	HB	6'	192	24		
Don Phelps	DB-HB	5'11"	185	25	1	18
Emerson Cole	FB	6'2"	215	22		
Marion Motley	LB-FB	6'1"	238	30		24
Dante Lavelli	OE	6'	192	27		30
Mac Speedie	OE	6'3"	205	30		6
Horace Gillom	DE-OE	6'1"	225	29		6

Chick Jagade – Broken Foot
Special Delivery Jones – Canadian Football League

NEW YORK GIANTS 10-2-0 Steve Owen

Scores of Each Game		
18	Pittsburgh	7
6	Cleveland	0
21	Washington	17
6	PITTSBURGH	17
17	CLEVELAND	13
3	Chic. Cards	17
24	WASHINGTON	21
51	CHIC. CARDS	21
55	Baltimore	20
7	PHILADELPHIA	3
51	N.Y. YANKS	7
9	Philadelphia	7
	Playoff	
3	Cleveland	8

Use Name	Pos.	Hgt	Wgt	Age	Int	Pts
John Sanchez	OT	6'3"	240	29		
Jim White	OT	6'2"	230	29		
George Roman	DT-OT	6'4"	250	24		
Bill Austin	OG	6'1"	220	21		
Jon Baker	DG-LB	6'2"	215	27		
Don Ettinger	OG	6'2"	215	27		
John Mastrangelo	DG-LB-OG	6'1"	235	24		
Bill Milner	DG-LB	6'1"	225	26		
Joe Sulaitis	BB-OG	6'2"	215	29		
John Rapacz	LB-C	6'4"	260	25		
Jim Duncan	DE	6'2"	205	24		
Ray Poole	DE	6'2"	215	28	1	45
Leo Skladany	DE	6'1"	210	23		
Al DeRogatis	DT	6'4"	240	23		6
Arnie Weinmeister	DT	6'4"	235	27		
John Cannady	LB	6'2"	225	26	2	
Dick Woodward	C-LB	6'2"	225	24	1	6
Tom Landry	DB	6'1"	195	25	2	6
Harmon Rowe	DB	6'	182	27	3	
Otto Schnellbacner	DB	6'2"	190	27	8	
Em Tunnell	DB	6'1"	187	28	7	
Chuck Conerly	QB	6'1"	185	26		6
Travis Tidwell	QB	5'10"	185	25		12
Forrest Griffith	HB	5'11"	190	21		12
Jim Ostendarp	HB	5'8"	178	25		12
Joe Scott	HB	6'1"	200	24		18
Randy Clay	DB-HB	6'	185	22	2	15
Choo-Choo Roberts	DB-HB	5'11"	188	26		32
Bob Jackson	FB	5'11"	210	25		12
Eddie Price	FB	5'11"	190	24		24
Bob McChesney	OE	6'2"	190	23		36
Bill Swiacki	OE	6'2"	195	25		18
Ellery Williams	OE	6'	185	24		
Kelley Mote	DE-OE	6'2"	190	27	1	6

Dick Hensley — Military Service

PHILADELPHIA EAGLES 6-6-0 Greasy Neale

Scores of Each Game		
10	CLEVELAND	35
45	Chic. Cards	7
56	LOS ANGELES	20
24	Baltimore	14
17	Pittsburgh	10
35	WASHINGTON	3
7	PITTSBURGH	9
33	Washington	0
10	CHIC. CARDS	14
3	N.Y. Giants	7
7	Cleveland	13
7	N.Y. GIANTS	9

Use Name	Pos.	Hgt	Wgt	Age	Int	Pts
Al Wistert	OT	6'1"	217	29		
Vic Sears	DT-OT	6'3"	237	32		
John Magee	OG	5'10"	220	27		
Duke Maronic	OG	5'9"	209	29		
Cliff Patton	OG	6'2"	240	26		56
Bucko Kilroy	OT-DT-OG	6'2"	240	29		
Vic Lindskog	C	6'1"	205	34		
Walt Barnes	OG-DG	6'1"	248	32		
Mario Gianelli	OG-DG	6'	265	29		
John Green	DE	6'1"	192	28		6
Norm Willey	DE	6'2"	210	23	1	6
Walt Stickel	OT	6'3"	245	28		
Mike Jarmoluk	DE-DT	6'5"	250	27		
Jay MacDowell	DE-DT	6'2"	215	31		
Joe Muha	LB	6'1"	206	29	2	6
Chuck Bednarik	C-LB	6'3"	233	25	1	
Alex Wojciechowicz	C-LB	5'11"	232	35	1	
Russ Craft	HB-DB	5'9"	172	30	7	6
Pat McHugh	HB-DB	5'11"	166	30	4	
Frank Reagan	HB-DB	5'11"	180	31	4	6
Dan Sandifer (from SF)	HB-DB	6'2"	190	23	2	
Joe Sutton	HB-DB	5'11"	180	26	8	
Tommy Thompson	QB	6'1"	196	33		
Bill MacKrides	QB	5'11"	179	25		
Clyde Scott	HB	6'	175	26		
Steve Van Buren	HB	6'	205	29		24
Frank Ziegler	HB	5'11"	172	26		18
Toy Ledbetter	DB-HB	5'10"	190	23		18
Jack Myers	LB-FB	6'2"	200	25		
Jim Parmer	DB-FB	6'	189	23		48
Jack Ferrante	OE	6'1"	188	34		18
Billy Hix	OE	6'2"	215	22		
Pete Pihos	DE-OE	6'1"	215	26		36
Neill Armstrong	DB-OE	6'2"	188	24	3	6

Bosh Pritchard – Injury

PITTSBURGH STEELERS 6-6-0 John Michelosen

Scores of Each Game		
7	N.Y. GIANTS	18
7	Detroit	10
26	Washington	7
17	CLEVELAND	30
17	N.Y. Giants	6
10	PHILADELPHIA	17
7	Cleveland	45
5	Philadelphia	7
17	BALTIMORE	7
28	Chic. Cards	17
7	WASHINGTON	24
28	CHIC. CARDS	7

Use Name	Pos.	Hgt	Wgt	Age	Int	Pts
Lou Allen	OT	6'3"	215	27		
Frank Wydo	OT	6'4"	220	26		
Jack Wiley	DT-OT	5'11"	210	29		
George Hughes	OG	6'1"	225	25		
Dick Tomlinson	OG	6'1"	205	22		
Bob Balog	C	6'2"	225	26		
Bill Walsh	C	6'2"	230	23		
Bob Davis	DE	5'11"	195	29		
George Hays	DE	6'2"	210	25		
Bill McPeak	DE	6'1"	200	25		
Carl Samuelson	DT	6'4"	250	27		
Ernie Stautner	DT	6'1"	218	25		2
Walt Szot	DT	6'1"	225	31		
Darrell Hogan	LB	5'10"	210	24	1	
George Nicksich	OG-LB	6'	225	22	3	
Frank Sinkovitz	C-LB	6'1"	220	27	2	
Joe Hollingsworth	FB-LB	6'	200	25		
Jerry Shipkey	FB-LB	6'1"	210	25	2	18
Don Samuel	DB	5'11"	190	26		
Jim Finks	TB-DB	6'	175	23		
Tom McWilliams	TB-DB	5'11"	180	24	2	
Howard Hartley	WB-DB	6'	185	26	5	
Joe Geri	TB	5'10"	190	26		64
Bob Gage	DB-TB	5'11"	175	23	4	30
Lynn Chandnois	WB	6'2"	195	26		
Jerry Nuzum	HB	6'1"	200	27		12
Fran Rogel	FB	5'11"	200	23		24
Joe Gasparella	BB	6'4"	220	23		
Charlie Seabright	BB	6'2"	210	32		6
Truett Smith	BB	6'2"	210	26		
Val Jansante	OE	6'1"	190	29		
Elbie Nickel	OE	6'1"	195	27		24
Bill Long	DE-OE	6'1"	200	24		
Charlie Mehelich	DE-OE	6'1"	200	28		

CHICAGO CARDINALS 5-7-0 Curly Lambeau

Scores of Each Game		
7	PHILADELPHIA	45
55	BALTIMORE	13
6	Chic. Bears	27
24	Cleveland	34
38	Washington	28
17	N.Y. GIANTS	3
7	CLEVELAND	10
21	N.Y. Giants	51
14	Philadelphia	10
17	PITTSBURGH	28
20	CHIC. BEARS	10
7	Pittsburgh	28

Use Name	Pos.	Hgt	Wgt	Age	Int	Pts
Plato Andros	OT	6'	240	29		
Bill Fischer	OT	6'2"	250	23		
John Hock	OT	6'2"	217	22		
George Petrovich	OG	6'2"	225	25		
Buster Ramsey	OG	6'1"	225	30		
Knox Ramsey	OG	6'1"	210	24		
Ed Bagdon	LB-OG	5'10"	200	24		
Bill Blackburn	C	6'6"	230	28		
Bob Dove	DE	6'2"	220	29	1	
Jerry Hennessey	DE	6'2"	211	24		
Tom Wham	DE	6'2"	215	26		6
John Goldsberry	DT	6'2"	245	24		
Lloyd McDermott (from DET)	DT	6'2"	240	24		
Jack Jennings	OT-DT	6'4"	245	23		
Jim Lipinski	OT-DT	6'4"	238	23		
Gerry Cowhig	LB	6'2"	214	29		
Bill Svoboda	LB	6'	210	23		
Ray Apolskis	OG-LB	5'11"	210	31	1	
Vince Banonis	C-LB	6'1"	235	28		
Red Cochran	DB	6'	190	28		
Jerry Davis	DB	5'10"	180	28	9	
Bob Nussbaumer	DB	5'11"	170	26		
Mike Swistowicz	DB	5'10"	185	25		
Don Paul	HB-DB	6'	185	24	4	12
Ray Ramsey	OE-DB	6'2"	165	29	1	
Jim Hardy	QB	6'	180	28		6
Frank Tripucka	QB	6'2"	175	22		6
Elmer Angsman	HB	5'11"	197	24		12
Babe Dimancheff	HB	5'11"	180	28		
Vic Schwall	HB	5'8"	190	26		
Charlie Trippi	HB	6'	185	27		24
Fred Gehrke (from SF)	DB-HB	5'11"	190	32	3	12
Pat Harder	FB	5'11"	200	28		40
Vinnie Yablonski	FB	5'8"	195	28		19
Fran Polsfoot	OE	6'3"	200	23		36
Bob Shaw	OE	6'4"	225	29		72
Mal Kutner	DB-OE	6'2"	197	29	3	

WASHINGTON REDSKINS 3-9-0 Herman Ball

Scores of Each Game		
38	Baltimore	14
21	Green Bay	35
7	PITTSBURGH	26
17	N.Y. GIANTS	21
28	CHIC. CARDS	38
3	Philadelphia	35
21	N.Y. Giants	24
0	PHILADELPHIA	33
14	Cleveland	20
38	BALTIMORE	28
24	Pittsburgh	7
21	CLEVELAND	45

Use Name	Pos.	Hgt	Wgt	Age	Int	Pts
Laurie Niemi	OT	6'1"	247	25		
Bob Hendren	DT-OT	6'8"	246	27		
Jerry Houghton	DT-OT	6'2"	226	24		
John Badaczewski	OG	6'1"	238	28		
Herb Siegert	OG	6'3"	213	26		
John Steber	OG	6'	240	27		
Slug Witucki	OG	5'11"	240	22		
Gene Pepper	OT-DT-LB-OG	6'2"	230	23		
Harry Ulinski	C	6'4"	226	25		
Dan Brown	DE	6'1"	200	25		
Roland Dale	DE	6'3"	210	23		
Ed Berrang	OE-DE	6'2"	203	25		
Lou Karras	DT	6'4"	240	23		
Paul Lipscomb	DT	6'5"	248	27		
Al DeMao	C-LB	6'2"	215	30		
Ed Quirk	C-LB	6'1"	228	25	2	
Chuck Drazenovich	FB-LB	6'1"	225	23	2	6
Pete Stout	FB-LB	6'	202	27	1	
Hardy Brown (from BAL)	DB-LB	6'	195	26	1	
Joe Bartos	HB-DB	6'2"	194	24		
Harry Dowda	HB-DB	6'2"	197	26	4	6
Hall Haynes	HB-DB	6'	190	21	4	6
Eddie Saenz	HB-DB	5'11"	166	27	1	12
Sammy Baugh	QB	6'2"	184	36		6
Nick Sebek	QB	6'	194	23		
Harry Gilmer	HB-QB	6'	170	24		6
Choo-Choo Justice	HB	5'10"	172	26		12
Frank Spaniel (from BAL)	HB	5'10"	185	22	1	12
George Thomas	HB	6'1"	184	22		
Bill Dudley	DB-HB	5'10"	175	29	2	64
Rob Goode	LB-FB	6'4"	220	23	2	36
Clyde Goodnight	OE	6'1"	195	26		12
Hugh Taylor	OE	6'4"	191	27		54
Joe Tereshinski	DE-OE	6'2"	209	26		

CLEVELAND BROWNS

RUSHING

Last Name	No.	Yds	Avg	TD
Motley	140	810	5.8	3
Jones	83	384	4.6	6
Bumgardner	67	231	3.4	2
Phelps	39	198	5.1	2
Carpenter	35	181	5.2	1
Graham	55	145	2.6	6
Cole	26	105	4.0	0
Moselle	5	39	7.8	0
Adamle	3	8	2.7	0
James	1	-1	-1.0	0
Lewis	2	-1	-0.5	0
Humble	1	-10	-10.0	0

RECEIVING

Last Name	No.	Yds	Avg	TD
Speedie	42	548	13	1
Lavelli	37	565	15	5
Jones	31	458	15	5
Motley	11	151	14	1
Bumgardner	9	112	12	1
Carpenter	5	45	16	0
Gillom	2	54	27	1
Phelps	1	28	28	0
Groza	1	23	23	1

PUNT RETURNS

Last Name	No.	Yds	Avg	TD
Phelps	13	174	13	1
Moselle	7	126	18	0
Gorgal	4	83	21	0
Carpenter	4	58	15	0
Lewis	2	13	7	0
James	0	15	0	0

KICKOFF RETURNS

Last Name	No.	Yds	Avg	TD
Phelps	12	325	27	0
Moselle	5	107	21	0
Carpenter	5	98	20	0
Adamle	4	53	13	0
Gillom	3	51	17	0
Cole	1	22	22	0
Martin	1	14	14	0
Rymkus	1	0	0	0

PASSING

Last Name	Att	Comp	%	Yds	Yd/Att	TD	Int–%	RK
Graham	253	137	54	1943	7.7	14	20– 8	2
Lewis	4	1	25	38	9.5	1	0– 0	
Gillom	1	1	100	3	3.0	0	0– 0	
Carpenter	1	0	0	0	0	0	1–100	
Groza	1	0	0	0	0	0	0– 0	

PUNTING

Last Name	No	Avg
Gillom	66	43.2

KICKING

Last Name	XP	Att	%	FG	Att	%
Groza	29	29	100	13	19	68
Grigg	9	9	100	1	2	50

NEW YORK GIANTS

RUSHING

Last Name	No.	Yds	Avg	TD
Price	126	703	5.6	4
Roberts	116	483	4.2	4
Scott	72	322	4.5	2
Clay	74	254	3.4	2
Griffith	45	162	3.6	2
Ostendarp	18	144	8.0	2
Tidwell	29	133	4.6	2
Jackson	12	113	9.4	2
Conerly	23	22	0.9	1

RECEIVING

Last Name	No.	Yds	Avg	TD
Swiacki	20	280	14	3
McChesney	19	380	20	6
Roberts	11	144	13	1
Scott	9	240	27	1
Clay	7	69	10	0
Williams	4	78	20	0
Mote	4	72	18	1
Price	4	30	8	0
Griffith	1	26	26	0
Weinmeister	1	16	16	0
Sulaitis	1	3	3	0

PUNT RETURNS

Last Name	No.	Yds	Avg	TD
Tunnell	31	305	10	0
Ostendarp	7	60	9	0
Schnellbacher	3	22	7	0
Scott	1	23	23	0

KICKOFF RETURNS

Last Name	No.	Yds	Avg	TD
Scott	14	351	25	0
Sulaitis	4	112	28	0
Ostendarp	3	68	23	0
Clay	1	25	25	0
Roberts	1	13	13	0
Poole	1	12	12	0
Swiacki	1	11	11	0

PASSING

Last Name	Att	Comp	%	Yds	Yd/Att	TD	Int–%	RK
Conerly	132	56	42	1000	7.6	8	7– 5	6
Tidwell	55	25	45	338	6.2	4	3– 5	

PUNTING

Last Name	No	Avg
Landry	58	36.8
Conerly	20	38.0

KICKING

Last Name	XP	Att	%	FG	Att	%
Poole	30	34	88	5	11	45
Clay	0	1	0	1	1	100

PHILADELPHIA EAGLES

RUSHING

Last Name	No.	Yds	Avg	TD
Ziegler	172	733	4.3	1
Van Buren	188	629	3.3	4
Ledbetter	67	320	4.8	1
Parmer	60	203	3.4	7
Myers	29	159	5.5	0
MacKrides	21	82	3.9	0
Reagan	3	55	18.3	0
Craft	8	52	6.5	0
Scott	13	46	3.5	0
Thompson	15	34	2.3	0
McHugh	4	14	3.5	0
Sandifer	1	3	3.0	0
Sutton	1	1	1.0	0

RECEIVING

Last Name	No.	Yds	Avg	TD
Pihos	38	447	12	6
Ferrante	35	588	17	3
Ziegler	13	216	17	2
Myers	12	204	17	0
Armstrong	8	124	16	1
Parmer	6	103	17	1
Ledbetter	4	81	20	2
Van Buren	2	34	17	0
Hix	2	25	13	0
Craft	1	14	14	0

PUNT RETURNS

Last Name	No.	Yds	Avg	TD
Sandifer	15	155	10	0
Craft	19	113	6	0
Sutton	9	75	8	0
Reagan	6	38	6	0
Ziegler	3	20	7	0

KICKOFF RETURNS

Last Name	No.	Yds	Avg	TD
Craft	10	327	33	1
Ziegler	10	204	20	0
Van Buren	5	110	22	0
Sandifer	5	108	22	0
McHugh	2	45	23	0
Muha	2	28	14	0
Myers	2	25	13	0
Sutton	1	21	21	0
Green	1	14	14	0
Maronic	1	4	4	0

PASSING

Last Name	Att	Comp	%	Yds	Yd/Att	TD	Int–%	RK
Thompson	239	107	45	1608	6.7	11	22– 9	11
MacKrides	46	14	30	228	5.0	4	6–13	

PUNTING

Last Name	No	Avg
Reagan	54	42.0
Muha	2	24.0

KICKING

Last Name	XP	Att	%	FG	Att	%
Patton	32	33	97	8	17	47
Muha	0	0	0	0	5	0

PITTSBURGH STEELERS

RUSHING

Last Name	No.	Yds	Avg	TD
Geri	188	705	3.8	2
Rogel	92	418	4.5	3
Chandnois	71	216	3.0	0
Nuzum	57	154	2.7	1
Gage	39	106	2.7	3
McWilliams	10	39	3.9	0
Shipkey	18	17	0.9	3
Finks	1	2	2.0	0
Hollingsworth	1	2	2.0	0

RECEIVING

Last Name	No.	Yds	Avg	TD
Jansante	26	353	14	0
Rogel	24	304	13	1
Nickel	22	527	24	4
Chandnois	7	158	23	0
Nuzum	6	142	24	1
Gage	6	127	21	2
Seabright	3	37	12	1
Hartley	2	27	14	0
Mehelich	2	18	9	0
Geri	1	33	33	1
Gasparella	1	3	3	0

PUNT RETURNS

Last Name	No.	Yds	Avg	TD
Gage	14	192	14	0
McWilliams	11	139	13	0
Hartley	5	23	5	0
Chandnois	3	33	11	0

KICKOFF RETURNS

Last Name	No.	Yds	Avg	TD
Chandnois	12	351	29	0
Gage	9	196	22	0
Nuzum	2	47	24	0
McWilliams	3	45	15	0
Hartley	1	44	44	0
Hollingsworth	1	22	22	0
Rogel	1	20	20	0
Mehelich	2	16	8	0
Wydo	1	7	7	0

PASSING

Last Name	Att	Comp	%	Yds	Yd/Att	TD	Int–%	RK
Geri	113	41	36	866	7.7	6	15–13	16
Gage	58	21	36	294	5.1	1	5– 9	
Gasparella	54	23	43	383	7.1	3	5– 9	
Finks	9	5	56	35	3.9	0	1–11	
McWilliams	8	5	63	113	14.1	0	1–13	
Chandnois	6	1	17	5	0.8	0	2–33	
Rogel	4	3	75	30	7.5	0	0– 0	
Seabright	3	1	33	3	1.0	0	0– 0	

PUNTING

Last Name	No	Avg
Geri	55	40.7
Gage	3	48.7
McWilliams	3	45.0

KICKING

Last Name	XP	Att	%	FG	Att	%
Geri	22	22	100	8	14	57

CHICAGO CARDINALS

RUSHING

Last Name	No.	Yds	Avg	TD
Harder	99	454	4.6	1
Trippi	99	426	4.3	3
Angsman	102	362	3.5	1
Schwall	17	114	6.7	0
Yablonski	30	110	3.7	1
Gehrke	25	73	2.9	1
Paul	14	80	5.7	0
Tripucka	4	35	8.8	1
Hardy	10	14	1.4	1
Dimancheff	8	5	0.6	0

RECEIVING

Last Name	No.	Yds	Avg	TD
Shaw	48	971	20	12
Polsfoot	38	653	17	6
Trippi	32	270	8	1
Harder	15	111	7	0
Yablonski	7	71	10	0
Angsman	7	56	8	1
Paul	5	93	19	1
Dimancheff	5	53	11	0
Gehrke	5	26	5	1
Kutner	4	74	19	0
Bagdon	1	19	19	0
Schwall	1	7	7	0

PUNT RETURNS

Last Name	No.	Yds	Avg	TD
Paul	18	194	11	1
Swistowicz	4	59	15	0
Trippi	7	54	8	0
Gehrke	5	44	9	0
Davis	3	29	10	0
Blackburn	1	2	2	0

KICKOFF RETURNS

Last Name	No.	Yds	Avg	TD
Paul	28	693	25	0
Trippi	8	139	17	0
Harder	6	112	19	0
Gehrke	2	57	29	0
Wham	2	53	27	0
Davis	3	25	8	0
Schwall	1	21	21	0
Bagdon	1	11	11	0
Hennessey	1	5	5	0
Hock	1	5	5	0

PASSING

Last Name	Att	Comp	%	Yds	Yd/Att	TD	Int–%	RK
Hardy	257	117	46	1636	6.4	17	24– 9	10
Tripucka	108	47	44	720	6.8	4	7– 6	13
Trippi	3	1	33	19	6.3	0	0– 0	

PUNTING

Last Name	No	Avg
Hardy	56	39.4
Tripucka	18	43.7
Trippi	2	47.0

KICKING

Last Name	XP	Att	%	FG	Att	%
Harder	22	24	92	4	9	44
Yablonski	7	7	100	2	3	67

WASHINGTON REDSKINS

RUSHING

Last Name	No.	Yds	Avg	TD
Goode	136	560	3.4	5
Dudley	66	339	5.1	1
Justice	59	285	4.8	0
Drazenovich	35	155	4.1	1
Gilmer	22	145	6.6	1
Saenz	20	64	3.2	1
Stout	9	53	5.9	0
Dowda	23	47	2.0	0
Thomas	20	41	2.1	0
Bartos	9	36	4.0	0
Baugh	7	27	3.9	1
Spaniel	15	22	1.5	1
Haynes	2	20	10.0	0

RECEIVING

Last Name	No.	Yds	Avg	TD
Taylor	39	833	21	9
Dudley	22	172	8	1
Justice	19	180	9	2
Goode	19	160	8	1
Tereshinski	17	148	9	0
Goodnight	12	185	15	2
Saenz	10	165	17	1
Spaniel	5	84	17	0
Drazenovich	3	38	13	0
Dowda	2	16	8	0
Stout	2	15	8	0
Thomas	2	7	4	0
Berrang	1	14	14	0
DeMao	1	4	4	0

PUNT RETURNS

Last Name	No.	Yds	Avg	TD
Dudley	12	185	15	1
Saenz	14	125	9	0
Justice	7	46	7	0
Haynes	3	22	7	0
Thomas	3	15	5	0
Spaniel	2	11	6	0

KICKOFF RETURNS

Last Name	No.	Yds	Avg	TD
Saenz	12	347	29	0
Spaniel	14	316	23	0
Justice	9	223	25	0
Haynes	5	214	43	0
Thomas	8	169	21	0
Dudley	1	43	43	0
Drazenovich	3	38	13	0
Goodnight	1	12	12	0
H. Brown	3	21	7	0
Siegert	1	0	0	0

PASSING

Last Name	Att	Comp	%	Yds	Yd/Att	TD	Int–%	RK
Baugh	166	90	54	1130	6.8	10	11– 7	6
Gilmer	141	63	45	948	6.7	8	12– 9	13
Justice	4	1	25	15	3.8	0	0– 0	
Sebek	3	0	0	0	0.0	0	2–67	

PUNTING

Last Name	No	Avg
Justice	22	41.3
Haynes	19	39.8
Dudley	14	41.8
Baugh	9	39.1

KICKING

Last Name	XP	Att	%	FG	Att	%
Dudley	31	31	100	5	10	50
H. Brown	0	1	0	0	0	0

LOS ANGELES RAMS 9-3-0 Joe Stydahar

Scores of Each Game		
20	CHIC. BEARS	24
45	N.Y. YANKS	28
35	San Francisco	14
20	Philadelphia	56
30	Detroit	28
70	BALTIMORE	27
65	DETROIT	24
28	SAN FRANCISCO	21
45	Green Bay	14
43	N.Y. Yanks	35
14	Chic. Bears	24
51	GREEN BAY	14
	Playoff	
24	CHIC. BEARS	14

Use Name	Pos.	Hgt	Wgt	Age	Int	Pts
Gil Bouley	DT-OT	6'2"	235	29		
Ed Champagne	DT-OT	6'3"	240	28		6
Harry Thompson	OG	6'2"	225	23		
Jack Finlay	LB-OG	6'1"	215	29		
Dave Stephenson	DG-OG	6'2"	235	24		
Art Statuto	C	6'2"	220	25		
Fred Naumetz	LB-C	6'1"	223	28	1	
Stan West	DG	6'2"	245	23		
Larry Brink	DE	6'5"	235	27		2
Jack Zilly	DE	6'2"	215	28		
Bill Smyth	OE-DE	6'3"	245	28		
Dick Huffman	OT-DT	6'2"	256	27		
Bob Reinhard	DT	6'4"	240	29		6
Mike Lazetich	OG-LB	6'1"	195	24		
Vic Vasicek	OG-LB	5'11"	225	24	1	
Don Paul	C-LB	6'1"	230	25	3	
Tank Younger	HB-FB-LB	6'3"	220	22		12
Woodley Lewis	DB	6'1"	185	25	12	6
George Sims	DB	5'11"	170	22	1	
Jerry Williams	HB-DB	5'10"	175	26	3	12
Tom Keane	OE-DB	6'1"	195	23	6	6
Norm Van Brocklin	QB	6'1"	190	24		6
Bob Waterfield	QB	6'1"	200	30		81
Paul Barry	HB	6'	210	24		12
Glenn Davis	HB	5'11"	170	25		42
Tommy Kalmanir	HB	5'8"	175	24		6
Vitamin Smith	HB	5'8"	175	26		48
Ralph Pasquariello	FB	6'2"	240	23		6
Dan Towler	FB	6'2"	225	22		36
Dick Hoerner	LB-FB	6'4"	220	28		66
Bob Boyd	OE	6'2"	205	22		24
Tom Fears	OE	6'2"	215	26		42
Crazy Legs Hirsch	DB-OE	6'2"	190	26	4	47

CHICAGO BEARS 9-3-0 George Halas

Scores of Each Game		
24	Los Angeles	20
32	San Francisco	20
21	Green Bay	31
27	CHIC. CARDS	6
28	GREEN BAY	14
27	N.Y. Yanks	38
35	Detroit	21
28	N.Y. YANKS	20
17	SAN FRANCISCO	0
24	LOS ANGELES	14
10	Chic. Cards	20
6	DETROIT	3
	Playoff	
14	Los Angeles	24

Use Name	Pos.	Hgt	Wgt	Age	Int	Pts
Paul Stenn	OT	6'2"	245	32		
George Connor	LB-OT	6'3"	240	25	1	
Dick Barwegan	OG	6'1"	230	28		
Frank Dempsey	OT-OG	6'3"	235	25		
Wash Serini	DG-OG	6'2"	235	26		2
Wayne Hansen	LB-OG	6'2"	228	22		
Bulldog Turner	LB-C	6'1"	235	31		
Ed Bradley	DE	6'	208	24		
Ed Sprinkle	OE-DE	6'1"	207	26		
Bill Wightkin	OE-DE	6'3"	235	23		
Alf Bauman	DT	6'2"	235	30		
Bill Garrett	DT	6'1"	240	26		6
Fred Davis	OT-DT	6'3"	245	32		
Ray Bray	OG-DG	6'	240	33		
Fred Negus	LB	6'1"	212	28		
Jerry Weatherley	LB	6'5"	215	21	2	12
Stu Clarkson	C-LB	6'2"	225	31		
Ed Cody	DB	5'10"	190	27		
Red O'Quinn	DB	6'2"	195	25	3	6
J.R. Boone	HB-DB	5'8"	163	24		
Al Campana	HB-DB	5'11"	185	24	1	6
Harper Davis	HB-DB	5'11"	172	24	5	6
George McAfee	HB-DB	6'	175	32	2	
Don Kindt	FB-DB	6'1"	205	24		6
George Blanda	DB-LB-QB	6'1"	198	22		18
Sid Luckman	QB	6'	195	33		
Steve Romanik	QB	6'1"	190	26		
Johnny Lujack	DB-QB	6'	185	25	1	109
George Gulyanics	HB	6'	195	29		12
Chuck Hunsinger	HB	6'	188	25		12
Julie Rykovich	HB	6'2"	205	26		42
Curley Morrison	FB	6'2"	215	24		6
John Hoffman	LB-FB	6'2"	218	24	1	18
Jim Keane	OE	6'4"	215	26		
Ken Kavanaugh	OE	6'3"	207	33		18

NEW YORK YANKS 7-5-0 Red Strader

Scores of Each Game		
21	San Francisco	17
28	Los Angeles	45
44	DETROIT	21
44	Green Bay	31
29	SAN FRANCISCO	24
35	GREEN BAY	17
38	CHIC. BEARS	27
20	Chic. Bears	28
35	LOS ANGELES	43
14	Detroit	49
7	N.Y. Giants	51
51	BALTIMORE	14

Use Name	Pos.	Hgt	Wgt	Age	Int	Pts
John Nolan	OT	6'2"	226	24		
Jon Jenkins (from BAL)	DT-OT	6'2"	225	24		
Carroll Vogelaar	DT-OT	6'1"	255	30		
John Clowes	OG-DT-OT	6'1"	240	28		
George Brown	OG	6'2"	220	27		
Joe Signiago	OG	6'1"	220	27		
John Wozniak	OG	6'	220	29		
Brad Ecklund	LB-C	6'3"	215	28		
John Yonakor	DE	6'5"	227	29	1	
Barney Poole	OE-DE	6'2"	220	27		6
Chet Adams	DT	6'3"	240	34		51
Nate Johnson	DT	6'3"	255	30		
Paul Mitchell	DT	6'3"	240	30		
Martin Ruby	DT	6'4"	245	30		2
Bob Kennedy	LB	5'11"	195	29	1	
Jim Champion	OT-LB	6'	230	23		2
Ed Sharkey	OG-LB	6'3"	240	24	1	
Joe Domnanovich	C-LB	6'1"	215	31		
Lou Kusserow	FB-LB	6'1"	200	26		
Duke Iverson	DB	6'2"	208	30	3	8
Pete Layden	DB	5'11"	185	30	3	3
Joe Golding	HB-DB	6'	187	29	7	12
Spec Sanders	HB-DB	6'1"	197	31	13	
George Ratterman	QB	6'1"	180	23		18
Johnny Rauch	QB	6'	195	23		
Sherman Howard	HB	5'11"	192	26		54
George Taliaferro	HB	5'11"	195	23		54
Buddy Young	HB	5'5"	170	24		12
Ben Aldridge	DB-HB	6'	195	23	1	
Zollie Toth	FB	6'2"	215	26		48
Bruce Alford	OE	6'	190	29		6
Dan Edwards	OE	6'1"	195	24		36
Art Weiner	DE-OE	6'3"	212	26		36
Jack Russell	DE-OE	6'1"	215	30		18

DETROIT LIONS 6-6-0 Buddy Parker

Scores of Each Game		
45	Green Bay	7
10	PITTSBURGH	7
21	N.Y. Yanks	44
24	SAN FRANCISCO	7
28	LOS ANGELES	30
27	San Francisco	28
24	Los Angeles	65
21	CHIC. BEARS	35
24	GREEN BAY	21
49	N.Y. YANKS	14
45	Baltimore	21
3	Chic. Bears	6

Use Name	Pos.	Hgt	Wgt	Age	Int	Pts
Gus Cifelli	OT	6'4"	240	24		
Floyd Jaszewski	OT	6'4"	230	23		
Howie Brown	OG	5'11"	215	27		
Joe Sobeleski	OG	6'	210	24		
Lou Creekmur	DT-OG	6'4"	240	23		
Dick Flanagan	LB-OG	6'	220	23		
Jack Simmons	C	6'4"	240	24		
Les Bingaman	DG	6'3"	250	25		
Jim Cain	OE-DE	6'1"	200	23		6
Bernie Hafen	OE-DE	6'2"	195	27		
Thurman McGraw	DT	6'5"	235	23	1	
John Prchlik	DT	6'4"	235	25		
Chet Bulger	OT-DT	6'3"	250	32		
Ray Lininger	C-LB	5'11"	217	23	3	
Joe Watson	C-LB	6'3"	235	24	1	
Rex Grossman (From BAL)	FB-LB	6'1"	215	26		16
John Panelli	FB-LB	5'11"	200	24		
Bill Schroll	FB-LB	6'1"	215	24	2	
Don Doll	DB	5'10"	185	23	12	6
Jim Smith	DB	6'1"	185	25	5	6
Don Panciera	QB-DB	6'1"	195	27	1	
Gerry Krall	HB-DB	5'10"	185	23		
Clarence Self	HB-DB	5'8"	185	25	3	6
Bobby Layne	QB	6'1"	195	23		25
Fred Enke	HB-QB	6'1"	200	25		
Bob Hoernschemeyer	HB	5'11"	195	24		12
Dante Magnani	HB	5'10"	185	33		
Lindy Pearson	HB	6'	195	21		12
Wally Triplett	HB	5'10"	173	23		12
Doak Walker	DB-HB	5'11"	173	23	1	128
Ollie Cline	FB	6'	200	24		12
Cloyce Box	OE	6'4"	220	26		66
John Greene	OE	6'	210	30		18
Leon Hart	OE	6'5"	262	21		6
Dick Rifenburg	OE	6'3"	195	23		6

GREEN BAY PACKERS 3-9-0 Gene Ronzani

Scores of Each Game		
7	DETROIT	45
35	WASHINGTON	21
31	CHIC. BEARS	21
31	N.Y. YANKS	44
14	Chic. Bears	28
17	N.Y. Yanks	35
21	Baltimore	41
14	LOS ANGELES	45
21	Detroit	24
25	SAN FRANCISCO	21
14	Los Angeles	51
14	San Francisco	30

Use Name	Pos.	Hgt	Wgt	Age	Int	Pts
Ed Ecker	OT	6'7"	270	27		
Dick Wildung	DT-OT	6'	220	28		
Ray DiPierro	OG	5'11"	210	23		
Willie Manley	OT-OG	6'2"	210	24		
Len Szafaryn	LB-OG	6'2"	230	22		
Ed Neal	DG-C	6'4"	275	32		
Dan Orlich	DE	6'5"	215	26	1	6
Steve Pritko	OE-DE	6'2"	210	28		12
Ab Wimberly	OE-DE	6'1"	210	24	1	
Clarence McGeary	DT	6'5"	250	24		
Don Stansauk	DT	6'1"	255	25		
Joe Spencer	OT-DT	6'3"	240	27	1	
Buddy Burris	LB	5'11"	215	27		
Chuck Drulis	LB	5'10"	220	32		
Carl Schuette	LB	6'1"	210	28	1	
Bob Summerhays	LB	6'1"	207	23	1	
Clayton Tonnemaker	C-LB	6'2"	235	22	1	1
Rebel Steiner	DB	6'1"	185	24	7	6
Alex Wizbicki	DB	5'11"	188	28	2	
Tony Cannava	HB-DB	5'10"	180	26		
Wally Dreyer	HB-DB	5'10"	170	25	5	6
Bob Forte	HB-DB	6'	205	28	1	
Jug Girard	HB-DB	5'11"	175	23	1	
Paul Christman	QB	6'	200	32		6
Tom O'Malley	QB	5'11"	185	26		
Tobin Rote	QB	6'3"	200	22		
Bill Boedecker (to PHI)	HB	5'11"	195	26		
Larry Coutre	HB	5'10"	175	21		18
Billy Grimes	HB	6'1"	197	23		48
Breezy Reid (From ChiB)	HB	5'10"	187	23		18
Tony Canadeo	FB	5'11"	190	31		24
Jack Cloud	FB	5'10"	220	25		18
Ted Fritsch	FB	5'10"	215	29		39
Ted Cook	OE	6'2"	195	29		18
Bob Mann	OE	5'11"	175	26		6
Al Baldwin	DB-OE	6'2"	210	27	5	18

Stan Heath – Canadian Football League
Jack Jacobs – Canadian Football League

SAN FRANCISCO FORTY NINERS 3-9-0 Buck Shaw

Scores of Each Game		
17	N.Y. YANKS	21
20	CHIC. BEARS	32
14	LOS ANGELES	35
7	Detroit	24
24	N.Y. Yanks	29
28	DETROIT	27
17	BALTIMORE	14
21	Los Angeles	28
14	Cleveland	34
0	Chic. Bears	17
21	Green Bay	25
30	GREEN BAY	14

Use Name	Pos.	Hgt	Wgt	Age	Int	Pts
Charley Quilter	OT	6'1"	240	24		
Harley Dow	OG-OT	6'2"	220	25		
Leo Nomellini	DT-OT	6'3"	270	25		
Bruno Banducci	OG	5'11"	220	28		6
Ray Evans	OG	6'1"	225	26		
Homer Hobbs	OG	5'11"	210	26		
Charlie Shaw	OG	6'2"	220	23		
Bill Johnson	LB-C	6'3"	210	24		
Hal Shoener	DE	6'3"	200	27	1	
Gail Bruce	OE-DE	6'1"	205	26	1	
Don Campora	DT	6'3"	270	23		
Ray Collins	DT	5'11"	230	22		
Clay Matthews	DT	6'3"	215	22		
Don Burke	LB	6'	230	24		
Visco Grgich	LB	5'11"	220	27	1	
Pete Wissman	C-LB	6'	215	26	1	
Norm Standlee	FB-LB	6'2"	230	31		6
Jim Powers	QB-LB	6'	185	22	5	
Verl Lillywhite	HB-DB	5'10"	185	23	1	
Howie Livingston (From WAS)	HB-DB	6'1"	190	28	5	18
Lowell Wagner	HB-DB	6'	195	26	4	
Frankie Albert	QB	5'10"	170	30		18
Royal Cathcart	HB	6'	185	24		
Don Garlin	HB	5'11"	188	23		
Emil Sitko	HB	5'8"	180	26		12
Johnny Strzykalski	HB	5'9"	190	27		18
Jim Cason	DB-HB	6'	168	23	1	24
Sam Cathcart	DB-HB	6'	175	25	3	
Joe Perry	FB	6'	195	23		36
Alyn Beals	OE	6'	190	29		18
Alex Loyd	OE	6'4"	198	23		
Jack Nix	OE	6'2"	200	22		1
Gordie Soltau	OE	6'2"	195	25		44

BALTIMORE COLTS 1-11-0 Clem Crowe

Scores of Each Game		
14	WASHINGTON	38
0	CLEVELAND	31
13	Chic. Cards	55
14	PHILADELPHIA	24
27	Los Angeles	70
14	San Francisco	17
41	GREEN BAY	21
7	Pittsburgh	17
20	N.Y. GIANTS	55
28	Washington	38
21	DETROIT	45
14	N.Y. Yanks	51

Use Name	Pos.	Hgt	Wgt	Age	Int	Pts
Barry French	OT	6'	225	29		
Ernie Blandin	DT-OT	6'4"	245	31		
Ken Cooper	OG	6'1"	205	27		
Ed King	OG	6'	215	25		
Earl Murray	OG	6'2"	240	24		
John Schweder	OG	6'1"	220	23		
Bob Nelson	LB-C	6'1"	210	30		
Bob Jensen	DE	6'4"	224	24		
Bob Nowaskey	DE	6'	210	32		
Art Spinney	OE-DE	6'	215	23		
Don Colo	DT	6'3"	245	25		
Art Donovan	OT-DT	6'2"	245	25		
Sisto Averno	LB	5'11"	230	24		
Ollie Fletcher	OG-LB	6'3"	210	26		
Joel Williams	C-LB	6'1"	225	22		6
George Buksar	FB-LB	6'	202	24	6	
Vito Kissell	FB-LB	5'10"	205	23	2	11
Chick Maggioli	DB	5'11"	180	28	8	
Bob Livingstone	HB-DB	6'	170	28	3	
Bob Perina	HB-DB	6'1"	205	29		
Herb Rich	HB-DB	5'11"	180	21	3	12
Billy Stone	HB-DB	6'	190	24	6	30
Adrian Burk	QB	6'2"	185	22		6
Frankie Filchock	QB	5'11"	200	33		
Y.A. Tittle	QB	6'	190	23		12
Gino Mazzanti	HB	5'11"	190	21		6
Chet Mutryn	HB	5'9"	180	29		24
Rip Collins	DB-HB	6'	190	23	1	
Ernie Zaleiski	DB-HB	6'	185	23	2	12
Leon Campbell	FB	6'	207	23		
Jimmie Spavital	FB	6'1"	205	24		18
Hal Crisler	OE	6'4"	215	26		30
John North	OE	6'2"	200	29		
Paul Salata (From SF)	OE	6'2"	192	23		24
Bob Oristaglio	DE-OE	6'2"	215	26		
Jim Owens	DE-OE	6'3"	205	23	1	6

LOS ANGELES RAMS

RUSHING

Last Name	No.	Yds	Avg	TD
Davis	88	416	4.7	3
Hoerner	95	381	4.0	10
Smith	51	250	4.9	1
Barry	50	231	4.6	2
Towler	46	130	2.8	6
Williams	13	108	8.3	1
Kalmanir	20	83	4.2	0
Pasquariello	7	31	4.4	1
Younger	8	28	3.5	2
Van Brocklin	15	22	1.5	1
Hirsch	2	19	9.5	0
Waterfield	8	14	1.8	1
Boyd	1	–2	–2.0	0

RECEIVING

Last Name	No.	Yds	Avg	TD
Fears	84	1116	13	7
Hirsch	42	687	16	7
Davis	42	592	14	4
Hoerner	26	446	17	1
Smith	16	279	17	4
Boyd	9	220	24	4
Towler	8	63	8	0
Barry	7	122	17	0
Kalmanir	5	58	12	1
Champagne	4	52	13	1
Williams	4	21	5	1
Smyth	2	10	5	0
Keane	1	19	19	0
Bouley	1	11	11	0
Reinhard	1	11	11	1
Pasquariello	1	2	2	0

PUNT RETURNS

Last Name	No.	Yds	Avg	TD
Smith	22	218	10	0
Kalminir	13	116	9	0
Williams	6	35	6	0
Davis	3	24	8	0
Lewis	1	0	0	0

KICKOFF RETURNS

Last Name	No.	Yds	Avg	TD
Smith	22	742	34	3
Kalmanir	13	358	28	0
Davis	8	167	21	0
Towler	5	47	9	0
Lewis	2	47	24	0
Vasicek	2	30	15	0
Finlay	2	14	7	0
Pasquariello	1	14	14	0
Stephenson	1	5	5	0

PASSING – PUNTING – KICKING

PASSING	Att	Comp	%	Yds	Yd/Att	TD	Int–%	RK
Van Brocklin	233	127	55	2061	8.8	18	14– 6	1
Waterfield	213	122	57	1540	7.2	11	13– 6	2
Davis	5	3	60	97	19.4	2	0– 0	
Smith	1	1	100	11	11.0	0	0– 0	
Hirsch	1	0	0	0	0.0	0	0– 0	

PUNTING	No.	Avg
Waterfield	52	40.1
Van Brocklin	11	42.4

KICKING	XP	Att	%	FG	Att	%
Waterfield	54	58	93	7	14	50
Hirsch	5	5	100	0	0	0

CHICAGO BEARS

RUSHING

Last Name	No.	Yds	Avg	TD
Gulyanics	146	571	3.9	2
Lujack	63	397	6.3	11
Rykovich	122	394	3.2	7
Hunsinger	61	326	5.3	2
Morrison	66	252	3.8	1
Hoffman	42	154	3.7	0
Campana	45	134	3.0	1
H. Davis	10	57	5.7	1
Boone	13	15	1.2	0
Kindt	1	4	4.0	0
McAfee	2	4	2.0	0
Luckman	2	1	.5	0
Sprinkle	1	–1	–1.0	0

RECEIVING

Last Name	No.	Yds	Avg	TD
Keane	36	433	12	0
Rykovich	21	344	16	0
Kavanaugh	17	331	19	2
Morrison	13	86	7	0
Gulyanics	12	137	11	0
Hoffman	8	161	20	2
Boone	8	139	17	0
Campana	5	58	12	0
Sprinkle	4	70	18	0
Kindt	3	72	24	1
Wightkin	3	24	8	0
H. Davis	2	15	8	0
Connor	1	21	21	0
Hunsinger	1	20	20	0
Lujack	1	16	16	0

PUNT RETURNS

Last Name	No.	Yds	Avg	TD
McAfee	33	284	9	0
Boone	17	215	13	0
Hoffman	7	75	11	0
H. Davis	1	19	19	0
Kindt	1	4	4	0
Hunsinger	1	4	4	0

KICKOFF RETURNS

Last Name	No.	Yds	Avg	TD
Hunsinger	12	343	29	0
Morrison	10	261	26	0
Campana	4	54	14	0
Hoffman	2	52	26	0
Kindt	2	33	17	0
McAfee	1	23	23	0
Stenn	1	16	16	0
H. Davis	1	13	13	0
Bauman	1	9	9	0
Sprinkle	1	5	5	0
Connor	0	9	0	0

PASSING – PUNTING – KICKING

PASSING	Att	Comp	%	Yds	Yd/Att	TD	Int–%	RK
Lujack	264	121	48	1731	6.8	4	21– 8	12
Luckman	37	13	35	180	4.9	1	2– 5	
Romanik	2	0	0	0	0.0	0	0– 0	
Gulyanics	1	1	100	16	16.0	0	0– 0	
Blanda	1	0	0	0	0.0	0	0– 0	
McAfee	1	0	0	0	0.0	0	1–100	

PUNTING	No.	Avg
Morrison	57	43.3
Gulyanics	6	33.5
Blanda	2	15.0
Rykovich	1	48.0

KICKING	XP	Att	%	FG	Att	%
Blanda	0	0	0	6	15	40
Lujack	34	35	97	3	5	60

NEW YORK YANKS

RUSHING

Last Name	No.	Yds	Avg	TD
Toth	131	636	4.9	5
Taliaferro	88	411	4.7	4
Howard	71	362	5.0	3
Young	76	334	4.6	1
Aldridge	16	69	4.3	0
Rauch	2	12	6.0	0
Kusserow	1	6	6.0	0
Golding	1	2	2.0	0
Ratterman	11	0	0.0	3

RECEIVING

Last Name	No.	Yds	Avg	TD
Edwards	52	775	15	6
Weiner	35	722	21	6
Taliaferro	21	299	14	5
Young	20	302	15	1
Toth	15	189	13	3
Howard	12	278	23	5
Russell	10	177	18	2
Poole	4	82	21	1
Aldridge	4	56	14	0
Alford	1	14	14	0

PUNT RETURNS

Last Name	No.	Yds	Avg	TD
Taliaferro	9	129	14	0
Sanders	6	93	16	0
Young	9	54	6	0
Aldridge	2	17	9	0
Howard	1	12	12	0

KICKOFF RETURNS

Last Name	No.	Yds	Avg	TD
Young	20	536	27	0
Taliaferro	25	473	19	0
Howard	8	240	30	1
Poole	2	8	4	0
Russell	2	8	4	0
Kennedy	1	15	15	0

PASSING – PUNTING – KICKING

PASSING	Att	Comp	%	Yds	Yd/Att	TD	Int–%	RK
Ratterman	294	140	48	2251	7.7	22	24– 8	4
Rauch	51	29	57	502	9.8	6	2– 4	
Taliaferro	7	3	43	83	11.9	1	0– 0	
Sanders	3	2	67	58	19.3	0	0– 0	

PUNTING	No.	Avg
Sanders	71	42.3
Taliaferro	1	39.0

KICKING	XP	Att	%	FG	Att	%
Adams	45	48	94	2	9	22
Layden	3	3	100	0	0	0

DETROIT LIONS

RUSHING

Last Name	No.	Yds	Avg	TD
Hoernschemeyer	84	471	5.6	1
Walker	83	386	4.7	5
Layne	56	250	4.5	4
Cline	69	227	3.3	2
Triplett	14	92	6.6	0
Pearson	31	82	2.6	2
Panelli	32	82	2.6	0
Enke	9	16	1.8	0
Self	3	9	3.0	0
Magnani	3	7	2.3	0
Schroll	1	1	1.0	0
Krall	3	0	0.0	0

RECEIVING

Last Name	No.	Yds	Avg	TD
Box	50	1009	20	11
Walker	35	534	15	6
Hart	31	505	16	1
Greene	22	368	17	2
Rifenburg	10	96	10	1
Hoernschemeyer	8	78	10	1
Cline	7	18	3	0
Triplett	6	70	12	0
Krall	2	61	31	0
Panelli	2	9	5	0
Self	1	12	12	0
Cain	1	8	8	0
Grossman	1	4	4	0
Pearson	1	4	4	0

PUNT RETURNS

Last Name	No.	Yds	Avg	TD
Self	12	129	11	0
Triplett	11	94	9	0
Walker	5	77	15	0
Doll	5	71	14	0
Krall	1	9	9	0
Pearson	1	6	6	0
Enke	1	3	3	0

KICKOFF RETURNS

Last Name	No.	Yds	Avg	TD
Triplett	8	411	51	1
Walker	10	225	23	0
Self	6	155	25	0
Pearson	7	120	17	0
Doll	2	52	26	0
Panelli	2	48	24	0
Cline	1	20	20	0
Grossman	1	15	15	0
Enke	1	11	11	0
Cain	1	10	10	0
Brown	1	0	0	0

PASSING – PUNTING – KICKING

PASSING	Att	Comp	%	Yds	Yd/Att	TD	Int–%	RK
Layne	336	152	45	2323	6.9	16	18– 5	4
Enke	53	22	42	424	8.0	5	7– 13	
Walker	7	1	14	6	.9	0	0– 0	
Hoernschemeyer	4	1	25	19	4.8	1	1– 25	
Pearson	3	0	0	0	0.0	0	3–100	

PUNTING	No	Avg
Smith	32	40.9
Walker	32	39.9
Hoernschemeyer	4	36.8

KICKING	XP	Att	%	FG	Att	%
Walker	38	41	93	8	18	44
Layne	1	2	50	0	0	0
Grossman	16	19	84	0	3	0

GREEN BAY PACKERS

RUSHING

Last Name	No.	Yds	Avg	TD
Grimes	84	480	5.7	5
Reid	87	394	4.5	1
Coutre	41	283	6.9	1
Canadeo	93	247	2.6	4
Rote	27	158	5.9	0
Cloud	18	52	2.9	3
Girard	14	39	2.8	0
Christman	7	18	2.6	1
Boedecker	8	16	2.0	0
Fritsch	7	13	1.9	0
Forte	9	13	1.4	0
Cannava	1	2	2.0	0
Dreyer	1	0	0.0	0
O'Malley	1	–9	–9.0	0

RECEIVING

Last Name	No.	Yds	Avg	TD
Baldwin	28	555	20	3
Grimes	17	261	15	1
Coutre	17	206	12	2
Pritko	17	125	7	2
Cook	16	182	11	3
Reid	11	120	11	2
Canadeo	10	54	5	0
Mann	6	89	15	1
Manley	5	66	13	0
Girard	4	89	22	0
Cloud	3	19	6	0
Wimberly	2	18	9	0
Forte	2	9	5	0
Cannava	1	28	28	0
Boedecker	1	10	10	0

PUNT RETURNS

Last Name	No.	Yds	Avg	TD
Grimes	29	555	19	2
Canadeo	5	68	14	0
Boedecker	5	49	10	0
Dreyer	3	48	16	0
Cannava	2	9	5	0

KICKOFF RETURNS

Last Name	No.	Yds	Avg	TD
Grimes	26	600	23	0
Canadeo	16	411	26	0
Forte	3	73	24	0
DiPierro	3	42	14	0
Fritsch	2	34	17	0
Girard	1	25	25	0
Boedecker	1	20	20	0
Burris	3	18	6	0
Canava	1	10	10	0

PASSING – PUNTING – KICKING

PASSING	Att	Comp	%	Yds	Yd/Att	TD	Int–%	RK
Rote	224	83	37	1231	5.5	7	24– 11	17
Christman	126	51	40	545	4.3	7	7– 6	15
O'Malley	15	4	27	31	2.1	0	6– 40	
Forte	2	2	100	24	12.0	0	0– 0	

PUNTING	No	Avg
Girard	71	38.2
Forte	3	35.7

KICKING	XP	Att	%	FG	Att	%
Fritsch	30	33	91	3	17	18
Tonnemaker	1	1	100	0	0	0

SAN FRANCISCO FORTY NINERS

RUSHING

Last Name	No.	Yds	Avg	TD
Perry	124	647	5.2	5
Strzykalski	136	612	4.5	2
Albert	53	272	5.1	3
Cason	38	129	3.4	1
Sitko	23	105	4.6	1
S. Cathcart	33	76	2.3	0
Standlee	12	23	1.9	1
Wagner	2	5	2.5	0
R. Cathcart	3	5	1.7	0
Powers	3	4	1.3	0
Lillywhite	7	4	.6	0
Garlin	3	3	1.0	0
Shoener	1	1	1.0	0
Livingston	1	0	0.0	0

RECEIVING

Last Name	No.	Yds	Avg	TD
Loyd	32	402	13	0
Cason	30	374	12	3
Strzykalski	24	187	8	1
Beals	22	315	14	3
Soltau	14	170	12	1
Perry	13	69	5	1
Nix	9	114	13	0
S. Cathcart	7	99	14	0
Livingston	5	156	31	2
Sitko	3	43	14	1
Bruce	1	10	10	0
Lillywhite	1	6	6	0
Banducci	0	11	0	1

PUNT RETURNS

Last Name	No.	Yds	Avg	TD
S. Cathcart	16	185	12	0
Cason	11	173	16	0
Wagner	1	4	4	0
Livingston	2	3	2	0

KICKOFF RETURNS

Last Name	No.	Yds	Avg	TD
S. Cathcart	13	311	24	0
Perry	12	223	19	0
Shoener	4	53	13	0
Cason	2	48	24	0
Lillywhite	2	36	18	0
Garlin	1	24	24	0
Standlee	1	17	17	0
Matthews	1	10	10	0
Evans	1	2	2	0

PASSING – PUNTING – KICKING

PASSING	Att	Comp	%	Yds	Yd/Att	TD	Int–%	RK
Albert	306	155	51	1767	5.8	14	23– 8	8
Powers	20	9	45	108	5.4	0	2– 10	

PUNTING	No.	Avg
Albert	37	38.5
Lillywhite	26	39.1

KICKING	XP	Att	%	FG	Att	%
Soltau	26	28	93	4	7	57
Nix	1	1	100	0	0	0

BALTIMORE COLTS

RUSHING

Last Name	No.	Yds	Avg	TD
Mutryn	108	355	3.3	2
Spavital	58	246	4.2	2
Stone	14	113	8.1	1
Cullins	69	101	1.5	0
Campbell	20	93	4.7	0
Tittle	20	77	3.9	2
Williams	0	50	0.0	1
Buksar	12	44	3.7	0
Mazzanti	7	22	3.1	1
Burk	11	19	1.7	1
Kissell	2	6	3.0	0
Rich	2	6	3.0	0
Zalejski	7	–2	–0.3	1
Livingston	1	–3	–3.0	0

RECEIVING

Last Name	No.	Yds	Avg	TD
Salata	50	618	12	4
Mutryn	36	379	13	2
Spavital	21	238	11	1
Crisler	19	307	16	5
Collins	19	295	16	0
Owens	19	188	10	0
Oristaglio	14	134	10	0
Stone	12	324	27	4
North	5	90	18	0
Spinney	2	19	10	0
Fletcher	2	18	9	0
Buksar	2	2	1	0
Blandin	1	16	16	0
Mazzanti	1	11	11	0
Campbell	1	5	5	0
Zalejski	1	1	1	0

PUNT RETURNS

Last Name	No.	Yds	Avg	TD
Rich	12	276	23	1
Mutryn	6	45	8	0
Livingstone	3	33	11	0
Zalejski	3	17	6	0
Stone	2	7	4	0

KICKOFF RETURNS

Last Name	No.	Yds	Avg	TD
Rich	17	434	26	0
Mutryn	19	408	21	0
Zalejski	7	101	14	0
Stone	2	35	18	0
Collins	2	33	17	0
Oristaglio	2	32	16	0
Blandin	3	31	10	0
Owens	2	29	15	0
Kissell	2	19	10	0
Salata	3	12	4	0
Livingston	1	11	11	0

PASSING – PUNTING – KICKING

PASSING	Att	Comp	%	Yds	Yd/Att	TD	Int–%	RK
Tittle	315	161	51	1884	6.0	8	19– 6	8
Burk	119	43	36	798	6.7	6	12– 10	17
Filchock	3	1	33	1	.3	0	0– 0	
Mutryn	1	1	100	4	4.0	0	0– 0	

PUNTING	No.	Avg
Burk	81	40.0
Collins	2	45.5

KICKING	XP	Att	%	FG	Att	%
Kissell	11	11	100	0	1	0

1951 Blackout: Rams, Fadeout: Colts

One franchise saw the error of its ways, while another never saw the light of the season. The Los Angeles Rams this year telecast only their road games, reversing last year's policy of showing all their games on TV. With the home giveaway stopped, fans poured back into the Coliseum to see the explosive Rams, shooting attendance up to the highest in pro football. Commissioner Bert Bell, the leading proponent of the television blackout of home games, grew even firmer in his position because of this Los Angeles episode.

Bell had a less pleasant experience dealing with the Baltimore Colts franchise. After losing money on the team for several seasons, team owner Abraham Watner turned the franchise back to the league at the NFL meeting in February. Although Baltimore fans protested loudly, their team was dismantled and the players spread around the league as part of the collegiate draft. By-products of the death of the Colts were the strengthening of the remaining teams and the reduction of league membership to a more manageable twelve clubs.

The wire services recognized the modern shape of the game by naming for the first time separate All-Pro teams for the offense and defense. Although the two-platoon system now was common, many players still played both ways, due partly to the low roster limit of thirty-three men.

AMERICAN CONFERENCE

Cleveland Browns—When the '49ers beat the Browns 24-10 on opening day, the other clubs in the conference took hope that Cleveland was ready to fall from the top. By the end of the season, however, the Browns, as usual, had captured the conference flag. After that opening loss, Paul Brown's men had won all their games, with only two of the victories by less than 10 points. Sportswriters began comparing the Browns to the great Chicago Bears of 1940-41. Both had inspirational coaches in George Halas and Paul Brown, and both had marvelous quarterbacks in Sid Luckman and Otto Graham. With Marion Motley slowing up, the Cleveland running game could not match the old Bears' ground attack, but ends Dante Lavelli and Mac Speedie caught more passes than any of the early Chicago receivers. The comparisons could never be resolved, but one thing was definite: With nine men named to All-Pro teams, the Browns had to be called the best of the present—until someone could prove otherwise.

New York Giants—The Giants were a strong team, but their tragic flaw was an inability to beat Cleveland. In their first meeting, the Browns squeezed by with a 14-13 victory, and their November rematch wound up with the Browns ahead 10-0. The Giants won all their other games, but the two losses were enough to shut them into a second-place finish. The losses to Cleveland, however, could not dull several stellar individual performances. Fullback Eddie Price, a small man for his position, hustled his way to the rushing championship and set a record for rushing attempts in one season. Defensive lineman Arnie Weinmeister, Al Derogatis, and linebacker Jon Baker all won All-Pro honors, as did offensive tackle Tex Coulter.

Washington Redskins—When the Redskins dropped their first three games, owner George Marshall predictably fired head coach Herman Ball. Marshall then offered the pilot's position to Hunk Anderson, an assistant coach for the Bears. Anderson was willing, but George Halas refused to let him out of his contract with the Bears unless Washington sent star tackle Paul Lipscomb to Chicago. Marshall called Halas a few uncomplimentary names, and named former Redskin star Dick Todd as his new coach. The Skins came alive under Todd, winning their first two games and climbing up to third place by the season's end.

Philadelphia Eagles—With the firing of Greasy Neale and the retirement of Tommy Thompson, the Eagles needed a new head coach and quarterback for 1951. They came up with an adequate quarterback in Adrian Burk, a survivor of the Baltimore Colts, but the appointment of Bo McMillin as coach ended in tragedy. A highly successful college coach at Indiana, McMillin came to Philadelphia after three unspectacular seasons with the Detroit Lions. The Eagles won their first two games for the new coach, but then McMillin resigned, revealing that stomach cancer made it impossible for him to continue. With assistant Wayne Millner at the helm, the Eagles lost their next three games and finished a weak fifth. Steve Van Buren's continued foot ailments figured greatly in the collapse, with both the Eagles and Van Buren looking as if they would never be the same.

Pittsburgh Steelers—Jock Sutherland had been in his grave for over three years, but the Steelers still looked like a Sutherland team. Coach John Michelosen, an assistant under the stern Scot, still deployed the Steelers in the single-wing formation on offense. The defense still was a hard-nosed unit which only grudgingly allowed points. And the Steelers still were a faceless outfit, one without a dynamic star who would make good copy for the reporters. One thing had changed, though: The rest of the NFL teams had developed high-power passing attacks which could leave the Steelers hopelessly behind with one good outburst. Only when the defense held the enemy to 14 points or less did the Steelers win, and although Bill McPeak, Ernie Stautner, Dale Dodrill, Howard Hartley, Jack Butler, Jerry Shipkey, and the other defenders six times limited the opponent to two touchdowns or less, the Steelers still could win only four games.

Chicago Cardinals—In dire need of a quarterback, the Cards moved Charlie Trippi to the signal caller's position after four years at halfback. Although he had starred as a single-wing tailback in college, Trippi was not the sort of quarterback who could lift this talent-thin club above mediocrity. As if below-average personnel were not problem enough, club president Walter Wolfner and coach Curly Lambeau quarreled all year, Wolfner claiming that the coach was lax on discipline, Lambeau saying that the front office was meddling in coaching matters. With two games left on the schedule, Lambeau bitterly resigned, leaving the club in the hands of his assistants, but a moment of glory still remained for the Cards. Losing 14-0 at halftime, the Cards came back to defeat the Bears on the final Sunday and end the Bears' hopes for a conference crown.

NATIONAL CONFERENCE

Los Angeles Rams—Large crowds consistently turned out to see the Rams, the most dynamic club in pro football. The explosive offense had two superb quarterbacks in Norm Van Brocklin and Bob Waterfield, one of whom was bound to be hot on the day of a game, and two superb receivers in Tom Fears and Crazy Legs Hirsch. Tying Don Hutson's season record of seventeen touchdown catches, Hirsch also set a new standard of 1,495 yards gained receiving in one year. Coach Joe Stydahar came up with an innovation in his "bull elephant" backfield, with three big fullbacks in Dan Towler, Dick Hoerner, and Tank Younger giving the Rams unmatched pass blocking and power running. The offense kept the club at the head of the conference most of the season, but the Lions knocked the Rams out of first place with a 24-22 upset one week from the end. Los Angeles snuck back into first, however, by beating the Packers while San Francisco beat Detroit on the final Sunday.

Detroit Lions—New coach Buddy Parker had much less of the schoolmaster in him than deposed coach Bo McMillin, and the Lions reacted to the relaxed atmosphere by going all out for victory. Attendance at Briggs Stadium doubled as the Lions ran neck and neck with the Rams all season. Quarterback Bobby Layne, runner Bob Hoernschemeyer, two-way end Leon Hart, offensive guard Lou Creekmur, and defensive guard Les Bingaman all starred as the Lions just missed the title by losing to the '49ers 21-17 on the last Sunday of the season. However, the Lions were finally on their way.

San Francisco '49ers—It took them a year to get used to NFL competition, but the '49ers finished with three straight wins to recapture their usual second-place spot. The quarterback for these final three games was Y. A. Tittle, the refugee from Baltimore who had been taken aboard when the Colts sank. For most of the campaign Tittle sat on the bench, watched Frankie Albert run the team, and learned the San Francisco system. Coach Buck Shaw started "the Bald Eagle" down the stretch, and the results established Tittle as Albert's successor. Fullback Joe Perry, receivers Gordy Soltau and Billy Wilson, and tackle Leo Nomellini also contributed to the strong finish and gave the club a youthful look. The '49ers played the spoiler role to the hilt, handing the Browns their only loss, knocking off the Rams in mid-season, and twice beating the Lions late in the year.

Chicago Bears—An era ended for the Bears when Sid Luckman, George McAfee, and Ken Kavanaugh, all stars of the 1940s, retired. Coach George Halas especially could have used a young Luckman, as quarterback Johnny Lujack was plagued with a sore shoulder that turned his bullet passes into easy floaters. With the air game crippled, the Bears relied on runners Kayo Dottley, George Gulyanics, and Julie Rykovich to bang out the yardage on the ground. The offensive line did its part to make the running game work, as George Connor, Dick Barwegan, and veteran Bulldog Turner all cleared the way for the backs. Connor also starred on the adequate defensive unit which three times broke down and gave up 40 or more points. With all their problems, the Bears still could have tied the Rams for the conference lead by winning their final game, but the Cards upset them.

Green Bay Packers—The Packers lost their last seven games to finish a limp fifth in the National Conference. Even the hapless New York Yanks downed the Packers 31-28 for their only win of the season. Coach Gene Ronzani looked high and low for running backs, and the best he could find were Fred Cone, whose kicking far surpassed his ball-carrying, and Tony Canadeo, a veteran of the Lambeau era who had long ago left his best days behind. That left the burden of the running as well as the throwing to quarterback Tobin Rote. Ends Bob Mann and Ray Pelfrey caught many of Rote's passes, but so, unfortunately, did enemy defensive backs.

New York Yanks—The year got off to a flying start when quarterback George Ratterman, fullback Lou Kusserow, tackle Martin Ruby, and end Jack Russell decided to do their football playing in the Canadian League. But Ratterman did not find Canada to his liking and rejoined the Yanks, still winless, in mid-season. With Ratterman and Bob Celeri sharing the passer's job, the Yanks showed some life down the stretch, tying the '49ers and beating the Packers on successive weekends. They ended their season by bowing to the Giants.

FINAL TEAM STATISTICS

OFFENSE

	CHI.B.	CHI.C.	CLEVE.	DET.	G.BAY	L.A.	N.Y.G.	N.Y.Y.	PHIL.	PITT.	S.F.	WASH.
FIRST DOWNS:												
Total	256	224	203	231	218	272	151	211	200	172	237	199
by Rushing	141	108	92	109	75	114	81	89	111	76	134	128
by Passing	80	101	99	105	115	130	54	99	73	79	92	62
by Penalty	25	15	12	17	28	28	16	23	16	17	11	9
RUSHING:												
Number	539	440	415	410	313	426	491	364	509	425	523	547
Yards	2408	1963	1708	1841	1196	2210	1713	1337	1562	1428	2366	2151
Average Yards	4.5	4.5	4.1	4.5	3.8	5.2	3.5	3.7	3.1	3.4	4.5	3.9
Touchdowns	24	14	20	11	8	22	10	12	13	9	18	14
PASSING:												
Attempts	315	334	271	351	478	373	210	428	284	330	281	226
Completions	143	161	151	158	231	189	101	172	120	130	154	99
Completion Percentage	45.4	48.2	55.7	45.0	48.3	50.2	48.1	40.2	42.3	39.4	54.8	43.8
Yards	2239	2244	2273	2500	2846	3296	1432	2634	1713	1842	1955	1508
Avg. Yards per Attempt	7.1	6.7	8.4	7.1	6.0	8.8	6.8	6.2	6.0	5.6	7.0	6.8
Avg. Yards per Completion	15.7	13.9	15.1	15.8	12.3	17.4	14.2	15.3	14.3	14.2	12.7	15.2
Touchdowns	12	13	18	29	26	26	11	16	17	10	14	8
Interceptions	20	24	17	24	29	22	26	27	29	26	19	25
Percent Intercepted	6.3	7.2	6.3	6.8	6.1	5.9	12.4	6.3	10.2	7.9	6.8	11.1
PUNTING:												
Number	62	70	73	58	61	52	87	81	77	80	54	59
Average Distance	38.5	39.8	45.5	41.3	41.0	41.5	40.2	38.3	39.1	38.6	43.6	38.7
PUNT RETURNS:												
Number	44	30	30	32	29	37	48	29	43	47	35	40
Yards	374	192	230	483	213	344	675	379	382	464	407	333
Average Yards	8.5	6.4	7.7	15.1	7.3	9.3	14.1	13.1	8.9	9.9	11.6	8.3
Touchdowns	1	0	0	4	0	1	4	1	0	1	1	0
KICKOFF RETURNS:												
Number	46	43	27	45	60	44	28	55	48	34	38	47
Yards	974	1051	496	1053	1449	826	724	1256	920	858	820	896
Average Yards	21.2	24.4	18.4	23.4	24.2	18.8	25.9	22.8	19.2	25.2	21.6	19.1
Touchdowns	0	0	0	0	0	0	1	1	0	0	0	0
INTERCEPTION RETURNS:												
Number	21	27	22	15	22	19	41	22	18	30	33	18
Yards	216	390	235	235	292	193	542	235	256	461	498	166
Average Yards	10.3	14.4	10.7	15.7	13.3	10.2	13.2	10.7	14.2	16.4	15.1	9.2
Touchdowns	0	0	2	0	1	1	4	0	0	3	1	0
PENALTIES:												
Number	118	82	117	80	90	94	64	63	51	50	75	67
Yards	1107	729	1017	746	790	813	569	605	428	430	694	560
FUMBLES:												
Number	23	26	26	19	23	22	27	22	36	31	26	34
Number Lost	15	20	19	9	15	15	13	9	18	17	20	18
POINTS:												
Total	286	210	331	336	254	392	254	241	234	183	255	183
PAT Attempts	38	27	43	44	35	51	31	31	31	23	33	22
PAT Made	37	27	43	43	29	47	30	31	28	22	31	21
FG Attempts	19	13	23	17	8	24	16	14	11	14	18	13
FG Made	7	7	10	9	5	13	12	6	6	7	6	10
Percent FG Made	36.8	53.8	43.5	52.9	62.5	54.2	75.0	42.9	54.5	50.0	33.3	76.9
Safeties	0	0	0	1	0	0	1	0	1	1	1	0

DEFENSE

	CHI.B.	CHI.C.	CLEVE.	DET.	G.BAY	L.A.	N.Y.G.	N.Y.Y.	PHIL.	PITT.	S.F.	WASH.
FIRST DOWNS:												
Total	228	212	201	235	236	231	174	257	183	188	188	241
by Rushing	100	116	88	102	127	125	60	125	92	97	91	135
by Passing	101	83	81	107	95	84	103	118	77	74	84	92
by Penalty	27	13	32	26	14	22	11	14	14	17	13	14
RUSHING:												
Number	372	476	428	454	496	478	392	464	462	499	417	464
Yards	1958	1977	1454	1509	2152	2206	913	2397	1816	1859	1549	2093
Average Yards	5.3	4.2	3.4	3.3	4.3	4.6	2.3	5.1	3.9	3.7	3.7	4.5
Touchdowns	15	15	8	13	22	17	8	23	12	13	9	20
PASSING:												
Attempts	337	265	330	374	313	329	377	355	287	266	353	295
Completions	160	123	151	181	157	140	162	182	119	136	158	140
Completion Percentage	47.5	46.4	45.8	48.4	50.2	42.6	43.0	51.3	41.5	51.1	44.7	47.4
Yards	2431	1973	1978	2608	2535	1992	2337	2776	1748	1687	2313	2104
Avg. Yards per Attempt	7.2	7.4	6.0	7.0	8.1	6.1	6.2	7.8	6.1	6.3	6.5	7.1
Avg. Yards per Completion	15.2	16.0	13.1	14.4	16.1	14.2	14.4	15.2	14.7	12.4	14.6	15.0
Touchdowns	21	18	10	18	25	13	11	24	17	12	15	16
Interceptions	21	27	22	15	22	19	41	22	18	30	33	18
Percent Intercepted	6.2	10.2	6.7	4.0	7.0	5.8	10.9	6.2	6.3	10.3	9.4	6.1
PUNTING:												
Number	66	62	69	56	62	75	86	66	70	77	70	55
Average Distance	37.7	40.9	39.8	41.7	37.6	40.9	40.2	39.9	44.4	40.7	40.4	40.8
PUNT RETURNS:												
Number	25	47	49	33	38	33	54	33	34	40	21	37
Yards	251	677	340	386	365	375	399	333	261	411	140	349
Average Yards	10.0	14.4	6.9	11.7	11.2	11.4	7.4	10.1	7.7	10.3	6.7	9.5
Touchdowns	0	4	0	1	2	3	0	1	1	0	0	1
KICKOFF RETURNS:												
Number	38	42	34	58	40	54	49	48	41	32	44	35
Yards	977	801	763	1328	741	1478	1002	1077	923	597	957	679
Average Yards	25.7	19.1	22.4	22.9	18.5	27.4	20.4	22.4	22.5	18.7	21.8	19.4
Touchdowns	0	0	0	0	0	0	1	1	0	0	0	0
INTERCEPTION RETURNS:												
Number	20	24	17	24	29	22	26	27	29	26	19	25
Yards	321	342	95	277	387	313	280	299	475	446	223	261
Average Yards	16.1	14.3	5.6	11.5	13.3	14.2	10.8	11.1	16.4	17.2	11.7	10.4
Touchdowns	0	1	1	0	1	1	0	1	2	3	0	2
PENALTIES:												
Number	102	80	59	81	99	107	60	87	53	84	68	71
Yards	1022	711	505	656	924	1028	506	797	458	725	526	630
FUMBLES:												
Number	25	21	35	22	23	26	37	18	28	30	22	28
Number Lost	21	16	29	16	13	10	12	12	19	16	9	15
POINTS:												
Total	282	287	152	259	375	261	161	382	264	235	205	296
PAT Attempts	39	38	20	32	50	35	20	49	32	30	24	40
PAT Made	37	38	18	31	49	33	20	44	31	28	22	38
FG Attempts	5	17	14	22	17	12	15	18	21	12	24	13
FG Made	3	7	4	12	8	6	7	12	13	7	13	6
Percent FG Made	60.0	41.2	28.6	54.5	47.0	50.0	46.7	66.7	61.9	58.3	54.2	46.2
Safeties	1	0	1	0	1	0	0	1	1	0	0	0

1951 CHAMPIONSHIP GAME

December 23, at Los Angeles
(Attendance 59,475)

SCORING

LOS ANGELES	0	7	7	10–24
CLEVELAND	0	10	0	7–17

Second Quarter

L.A.	Hoerner, 1 yard rush PAT–Waterfield (Kick)	5:44
Cle.	Groza, 52 yard field goal	11:08
Cle.	Jones, 17 yard pass from Graham PAT–Groza (Kick)	12:54

Third Quarter

L.A.	Towler, 1 yard rush PAT–Waterfield (Kick)	6:16

Fourth Quarter

L.A.	Waterfield, 17 yard field goal	3:10
Cle.	Carpenter, 5 yard rush PAT–Groza (Kick)	7:10
L.A.	Fears, 73 yard pass from Van Brocklin PAT–Waterfield (Kick)	7:35

TEAM STATISTICS

L.A.		CLEVE.
20	First Downs–Total	22
9	First Downs–Rushing	6
9	First Downs–Passing	16
2	First Downs–Penalty	0
2	Fumbles	4
1	Fumbles Lost	1
5	Penalties	6
25	Yards Penalized	41
1	Field Goals Missed	1

Van Brocklin to Fears to the Championship

In the rematch with the Rams, the Browns were not as precise as in last year's game, as Lou Groza missed a 23-yard field goal on the first drive. The first quarter ended with the match still scoreless, but Bob Waterfield led the Rams 55 yards in twelve plays, mixing passes and runs, with Dick Hoerner plowing into the end zone from the 1-yard line. Leading 7-0, the Rams bothered Otto Graham with blitzing linebackers, but the Browns put three points on the scoreboard with a 52-yard field goal by Groza. After three plays, the Rams kicked the ball back to the Browns, and then Otto Graham began picking the Los Angeles defense apart. First he hit Mac Speedie for 14 yards, then passed to Marion Motley over the middle for 23 yards, and finally threw to Dub Jones for 17 yards and a touchdown. The Browns took a 10-7 lead into the locker room at halftime, but the Rams went ahead six minutes into the third period. Otto Graham was back to pass on his own 24-yard line when Los Angeles end Larry Brink blindsided him and knocked the ball loose. Andy Robustelli picked it up and ran it all the way down to the 2. From there, Dan Towler needed three attempts to make it into the end zone, and Waterfield's conversion made it 14-10. The Rams upped the lead to 17-10 with a fourth-quarter Waterfield field goal, but the Browns drove 70 yards in ten plays to tie the score at 17-17. Less than a minute later, however, Norm Van Brocklin, who had relieved Waterfield at quarterback for the Rams, hit Tom Fears with a perfect pass that resulted in a 73-yard touchdown and the championship.

INDIVIDUAL STATISTICS

LOS ANGELES	No.	Yds	Avg.	CLEVELAND	No.	Yds	Avg.
RUSHING							
Towler	16	36	2.3	Graham	5	43	8.6
Younger	4	20	5.0	Motley	5	23	4.6
Smith	9	15	1.7	Carpenter	4	14	3.5
Waterfield	2	8	4.0	Jones	9	12	1.3
Hoerner	5	5	1.0		23	92	4.0
Van Brocklin	1	3	3.0				
Davis	6	–6	–1.0				
	43	81	1.9				
RECEIVING							
Fears	4	146	36.5	Speedie	7	81	11.6
Hirsch	4	66	16.5	Lavelli	4	66	16.5
Davis	3	10	3.3	Jones	4	62	15.5
Smith	1	18	18.0	Carpenter	3	48	16.0
Hoerner	1	13	13.0	Motley	1	23	23.0
	13	253	19.5		19	280	14.7
PUNTING							
Waterfield	5		43.4	Gillom	4		37.0
PUNT RETURNS							
				Lewis	1	13	13.0
None				Carpenter	1	1	1.0
					2	14	7.0
KICKOFF RETURNS							
Williams	1	21	21.0	Carpenter	5	132	26.4
INTERCEPTION RETURNS							
Johnson	1	35	35.0	James	1	0	0.0
Paul	1	26	26.0	Lahr	1	0	0.0
Williams	1	15	15.0		2	0	0.0
	3	76	25.3				

PASSING

LOS ANGELES	Att	Comp	Comp Pct.	Yds	Int	Yds/ Att.	Yds/ Comp	Yards Lost Tackled
Waterfield	24	9	37.5	125	2	5.2	13.9	0
Van Brocklin	6	4	66.7	128	0	21.3	32.0	0
	30	13	43.3	253	2	8.4	19.5	0
CLEVELAND								
Graham	40	19	47.5	280	3	7.0	14.7	5–47
Carpenter	1	0	0	0	0	–	–	0
	41	19	46.3	280	3	6.8	14.7	5–47

CLEVELAND BROWNS 11-1-0 Paul Brown

Scores of Each Game			Use Name	Pos.	Hgt	Wgt	Age	Int	Pts
10	San Francisco	24	Lou Groza	OT	6'3"	235	27		73
38	Los Angeles	23	Lou Rymkus	OT	6'4"	235	32		
45	WASHINGTON	0	John Sandusky	OT	6'1"	250	25		
17	PITTSBURGH	0	Bob Gaudio	OG	5'10"	220	26		
14	N.Y. GIANTS	13	Abe Gibron	OG	5'11"	230	25		
34	Chic. Cards	17	Lin Houston	OG	6'	215	30		
20	PHILADELPHIA	17	Frank Gatski	C	6'3"	240	29		
10	N.Y. Giants	0	Bill Willis	DG	6'2"	215	30		
42	CHIC. BEARS	21	Len Ford	DE	6'4"	230	25		
49	CHIC. CARDS	28	George Young	DE	6'3"	215	27		6
28	Pittsburgh	0	Bob Oristaglio	OE-DE	6'2"	215	27		6
24	Philadelphia	9	Chubby Grigg	DT	6'2"	280	25		
			John Kissell	DT	6'3"	247	28		
			Darrell Palmer	DT	6'2"	235	29		
			Tony Adamle	LB	6'	215	27	1	
			Alex Agase	LB	5'10"	210	29	2	
			Tommy Thompson	LB	6'1"	220	24	2	
			Hal Herring	C-LB	6'1"	210	27	1	
			Chick Jagade	FB-LB	6'	210	24		
			Tommy James	DB	5'10"	185	27	2	
			Warren Lahr	DB	5'11"	185	27	5	12
			Don Shula	DB	5'11"	190	21	4	
			Cliff Lewis	QB-DB	5'11"	168	28	5	
			Carl Taseff	HB-DB	5'11"	192	22		12
			Otto Graham	QB	6'1"	195	29		24
			Rex Baumgardner	HB	5'11"	193	27		12
			Ken Carpenter	HB	6'	187	25		36
			Dub Jones	HB	6'4"	205	26		72
			Don Phelps	HB	5'11"	185	26		6
			Emerson Cole	FB	6'2"	215	23		6
			Marion Motley	LB-FB	6'1"	238	31		6
			Dante Lavelli	OE	6'	192	28		36
			Mac Speedie	OE	6'3"	205	31		18
			Horace Gillom	DE-OE	6'1"	220	30		6

Ken Gorgal – Military Service
Weldon Humble — Military Service
Art Spinney – Military Service

NEW YORK GIANTS 9-2-1 Steve Owen

Scores of Each Game			Use Name	Pos.	Hgt	Wgt	Age	Int	Pts
13	Pittsburgh	13	Tex Coulter	OT	6'4"	260	26		
35	Washington	14	Herb Hannah	OT	6'3"	220	29		
28	CHIC. CARDS	17	Ray Krouse	DT-OT	6'3"	250	24		
26	PHILADELPHIA	24	Earl Murray	OG	6'2"	240	25		
13	Cleveland	14	Bill Albright	OT-DT-OG	6'1"	232	22		
37	N.Y. YANKS	31	Jon Baker	DG-LB	6'2"	215	28		
28	WASHINGTON	14	Fritz Barzilaukas	DG-LB-OG	6'1"	230	30		
0	CLEVELAND	10	Duke Maronic	DG-LB-OG	5'9"	218	30		
10	Chic. Cards	0	Joe Sulaitis	BB-OG	6'2"	215	30		
14	PITTSBURGH	0	John Rapacz	C	6'4"	260	26		
23	Philadelphia	7	Jim Duncan	DE	6'2"	205	25	2	
27	N.Y. Yanks	17	Ray Poole	DE	6'2"	215	29		66
			Al DeRogatis	DT	6'4"	240	24		
			Arnie Weinmeister	DT	6'4"	235	28		
			John Cannady	LB	6'2"	225	27	3	
			Dick Woodward	C-LB	6'2"	225	25	2	
			Tom Landry	DB	6'1"	195	26	8	18
			Harmon Rowe	DB	6'	182	28	2	2
			Otto Schnellbacher	DB	6'2"	190	28	11	12
			Em Tunnell	DB	6'1"	183	29	9	24
			John Amberg	HB-DB	5'11"	195	23	3	
			Bob Wilkinson	OE-DB	6'3"	215	24	1	6
			Chuck Conerly	QB	6'1"	185	27		6
			Travis Tidwell	QB	5'10"	185	26		
			Forrest Griffith	HB	5'11"	190	22		
			Jim Ostendarp	HB	5'8"	178	26		
			Kyle Rote	HB	6'	195	22		6
			Joe Scott	HB	6'1"	195	25		18
			Bob Jackson	FB	5'11"	210	26		
			Eddie Price	FB	5'11"	190	25		42
			Bob Hudson	OE	6'4"	215	21		
			Bob McChesney	OE	6'2"	190	24		12
			Bill Stribling	OE	6'1"	205	24		12
			Kelley Mote	DE-OE	6'2"	190	28		24

Bill Austin — Military Service
Randy Clay — Military Service
Dick Hensley — Military Service
Choo-Choo Roberts — Canadian Football League
George Roman — Canadian Football League
Bill Milner — Military Service

WASHINGTON REDSKINS 5-7-0 Herman Ball Dick Todd

Scores of Each Game			Use Name	Pos.	Hgt	Wgt	Age	Int	Pts
17	Detroit	35	Laurie Niemi	OT	6'1"	256	26		
14	N.Y. GIANTS	35	Gene Pepper	OG-OT	6'2"	244	24		
0	Cleveland	45	Jim Peebles	DE-OT	6'4"	237	31		
7	CHIC. CARDS	3	Buddy Brown	OG	6'1"	211	24		
27	Philadelphia	23	Herb Siegert	OG	6'3"	225	27		
0	CHIC. BEARS	27	Slug Witucki	OG	5'11"	239	23		
14	N.Y. Giants	28	Harry Ulinski	C	6'4"	230	26		
22	Pittsburgh	7	John Badaczewski	OG	6'1"	255	29		
31	LOS ANGELES	21	Jim Ricca	DG	6'4"	268	24		
21	PHILADELPHIA	35	Walt Yowarsky	DE	6'2"	230	23		
20	Chic. Cards	17	Bob Hendren	OT-DE	6'8"	245	28		
10	PITTSBURGH	20	Lou Karras	DT	6'4"	248	24		
			Paul Lipscomb	DT	6'5"	252	28	1	
			Jim Staton	DT	6'4"	246	24		
			George Buksar	LB	6'	202	25	1	
			Ed Quirk	LB	6'1"	240	26		
			Al DeMao	C-LB	6'2"	220	31	1	
			Chuck Drazenovich	FB-LB	6'1"	222	24	2	18
			Jack Dwyer	DB	5'11"	175	24	1	
			Neil Ferris	DB	5'11"	178	23		
			Ed Salem	QB-DB	5'11"	193	23	5	
			Billy Cox	HB-DB	6'3"	194	22	2	
			Harry Dowda	HB-DB	6'2"	200	27		
			Sammy Baugh	QB	6'2"	175	37		
			Harry Gilmer	DB-QB	6'	162	25	5	
			Johnny Papit	HB	6'	190	23		
			Eddie Saenz	HB	5'10"	170	28		
			Bill Dudley	DB-HB	5'10"	175	30		69
			George Thomas	DB-HB	6'1"	180	23		12
			Rob Goode	FB	6'4"	224	24		54
			Leon Heath	FB	6'1"	202	23		
			Gene Brito	OE	6'1"	216	25		
			Hugh Taylor	OE	6'4"	190	28		18
			Joe Tereshinski	DE-LB-OE	6'2"	217	27		12

Hall Haynes – Military Service
Choo-Choo Justice – Voluntarily Retired
Joe Bartos — Military Service
John Steber — Military Service

PITTSBURGH STEELERS 4-7-1 John Michelosen

Scores of Each Game			Use Name	Pos.	Hgt	Wgt	Age	Int	Pts
13	N.Y. GIANTS	13	Lou Allen	OT	6'3"	215	28		
33	Green Bay	35	Frank Wydo	OT	6'4"	220	27		
24	SAN FRANCISCO	28	Paul Lea	DT-OT	6'2"	240	21		
0	Cleveland	17	George Hughes	OG	6'1"	225	26		
28	Chic. Cards	14	Dick Tomlinson	OG	6'1"	205	23		
13	PHILADELPHIA	34	Lou Levanti	C-OG	6'1"	215	25		
28	GREEN BAY	7	Tony Momsen	C	6'1"	215	24		
7	WASHINGTON	22	Bill Walsh	C	6'2"	230	24		
17	Philadelphia	13	Bill McPeak	DE	6'1"	200	26		
0	N.Y. Giants	14	Charlie Mehelich	DE	6'1"	200	29	2	
0	CLEVELAND	28	George Hays	DT-DE	6'2"	210	26		
20	Washington	10	Carl Samuelson	DT	6'4"	260	28		
			Ernie Stautner	DT	6'1"	230	26		
			Dale Dodrill	LB	6'1"	205	26		
			Darrell Hogan	LB	5'10"	210	25	1	
			Frank Sinkovitz	LB	6'1"	220	28	2	
			John Schweder	OG-LB	6'1"	225	24	1	
			Jack Butler	DB	6'	195	23	5	6
			Howard Hartley	DB	6'	185	27	10	
			Jerry Shipkey	DB	6'1"	215	26	6	6
			Jim Finks	TB-DB	6'	175	24	3	6
			Joe Geri	TB	5'10"	185	27		61
			Chuck Ortmann	DB-TB	6'1"	190	22	1	
			Jerry Nuzum	HB	6'1"	200	28		6
			Ray Mathews	DB-HB	6'	185	22	1	6
			Lynn Chandnois	TB-HB	6'2"	195	27		42
			Joe Hollingsworth	FB	6'	200	26		
			Fran Rogel	FB	5'11"	200	24		18
			Joe Gasparella (to Chic C)	BB	6'4"	220	24		
			Dick Hendley	BB	6'	198	25		
			Truett Smith	BB	6'2"	205	27		
			Val Jansante (to GB)	OE	6'1"	190	30		6
			Tom Jelley	OE	6'5"	225	24		
			Henry Minarik	OE	6'2"	200	24		6
			Elbie Nickel	OE	6'1"	195	28		18

Tom McWilliams — Military Service
Walt Szot — Military Service

PHILADELPHIA EAGLES 4-8-0 Bo McMillin Wayne Millner

Scores of Each Game			Use Name	Pos.	Hgt	Wgt	Age	Int	Pts
17	Chic. Cards	14	Bucko Kilroy	OT	6'2"	235	30		
21	SAN FRANCISCO	14	Vic Sears	DT-OT	6'3"	225	33		
24	Green Bay	37	Walt Barnes	OG	6'1"	230	33		
24	N.Y. Giants	26	Ray Romero	OG	5'11"	213	24		
23	WASHINGTON	27	Dick Steere	OG	6'4"	240	24		
34	Pittsburgh	13	Al Wistert	OG	6'1"	214	30		
17	Cleveland	20	John Magee	LB-OG	5'10"	220	28		
10	DETROIT	28	Vic Lindskog	C	6'1"	203	35		
13	PITTSBURGH	17	Mario Gianelli	DG	6'	260	30		
35	Washington	21	John Green	DE	6'1"	190	29		
7	N.Y. GIANTS	23	Jay MacDowell	DE	6'2"	220	32		
9	CLEVELAND	24	Norm Willey	DE	6'2"	215	24		
			Bud Grant	OE-DE	6'3"	200	24		
			Walt Stickel	DT	6'3"	250	29	2	
			Roscoe Hansen	OT-DT	6'3"	215	22		
			Mike Jarmoluk	DE-DT	6'5"	250	28	1	
			Gerry Cowhig	LB	6'2"	218	30		6
			Chuck Bednarik	C-LB	6'3"	230	26		
			Ken Farragut	C-LB	6'4"	230	23		
			Ebert Van Buren	FB-LB	6'2"	210	26	1	
			Russ Craft	DB	5'9"	175	31	2	
			Pat McHugh	DB	5'11"	166	31	1	
			Frank Reagan	DB	5'11"	185	32	4	
			Joe Sutton	DB	5'11"	180	27	2	
			Neill Armstrong	OE-DB	6'2"	195	25	4	
			Adrian Burk	QB	6'2"	190	23		6
			Bill MacKrides	QB	5'11"	179	26		
			Al Pollard (from NYY)	HB	6'	196	23		
			Bosh Pritchard (to NYG)	HB	5'11"	163	32		6
			Clyde Scott	HB	6'	170	27		24
			Steve Van Buren	HB	6'	202	30		36
			Frank Ziegler	HB	5'11"	175	27		12
			Dan Sandifer	DB-HB	6'2"	190	24	1	12
			Jim Parmer	DB-FB	6'	195	24		12
			Bobby Walston	OE	6'	190	22		94
			Red O'Quinn (from ChiB)	OE	6'2"	195	26		
			Pete Pihos	DE-OE	6'1"	205	27	2	30

Toy Ledbetter – Military Service

CHICAGO CARDINALS 3-9-0 Curley Lambeau

Scores of Each Game			Use Name	Pos.	Hgt	Wgt	Age	Int	Pts
14	PHILADELPHIA	17	Bill Fischer	OT	6'2"	250	24		
28	CHIC. BEARS	14	Jack Jennings	OT	6'4"	245	24		
17	N.Y. Giants	28	Ed Bagdon	OG	5'10"	200	25		
3	Washington	7	Lynn Lynch	OG	6'2"	225	23		
14	PITTSBURGH	28	Buster Ramsey	LB-OG	6'1"	225	31		
17	CLEVELAND	34	Knox Ramsey	LB-OG	6'1"	210	25		
21	Los Angeles	45	Jack Simmons	C	6'4"	240	25		
27	San Francisco	21	Bob Dove	DE	6'2"	225	30		
0	N.Y. GIANTS	10	Jerry Hennessey	DE	6'2"	215	25		
28	Cleveland	49	Tony Klimak	DE	5'11"	200	25		
17	WASHINGTON	20	Tom Wham	DE	5'11"	200	25	3	
24	Chic. Bears	14	Lou Ferry	DT	6'2"	220	27		
			Don Joyce	DT	6'3"	250	21		
			Lloyd McDermott	DT	6'2"	240	25	1	
			Jerry Groom	LB	6'3"	235	22		
			Jerry Houghton	LB	6'2"	226	25		
			Fred Wallner	LB	6'2"	230	22	1	
			Cliff Patton	OT-LB	6'2"	240	27	3	34
			Leo Sanford	C-LB	6'1"	220	22	1	
			John Panelli	FB-LB	5'11"	200	25		
			Bill Svoboda	FB-LB	6'	210	24		
			Billy Gay	DB	5'11"	180	23		
			Lindy Lauro	DB	5'10"	195	27		
			S.J. Whitman	DB	5'11"	185	25	7	
			Jerry Davis	HB-DB	5'10"	180	29	2	
			Tom Bienemann	OE-DB	6'3"	220	23	1	
			Ray Ramsey	OE-DB	6'2"	165	30	5	
			Jim Hardy	QB	6'	180	29		
			Charlie Trippi	QB	6'	185	28		24
			Frank Tripucka	QB	6'2"	175	23		
			Elmer Angsman	HB	5'11"	197	25		24
			Billy Cross	HB	5'6"	155	22		36
			Emil Sitko	HB	5'8"	185	27		
			Don Paul	DB-HB	6'	180	25	3	36
			Ralph Pasquariello	FB	6'2"	235	24		6
			Vinnie Yablonski	FB	5'8"	195	29		14
			Fran Polsfoot	OE	6'3"	200	24		24
			Don Stonesifer	OE	6'	200	24		12

Bob Shaw – Canadian Football League
John Hock – Military Service
Bill Blackburn – Canadian Football League
Jim Lipinski – Canadian Football League

CLEVELAND BROWNS

RUSHING

Last Name	No.	Yds	Avg	TD
Jones	104	492	4.7	7
Carpenter	85	402	4.7	4
Motley	61	273	4.5	1
Cole	46	252	5.5	1
Bumgardner	45	126	2.8	1
Phelps	16	65	4.1	1
Taseff	13	49	3.8	2
Jagade	7	30	4.3	0
Graham	35	29	.8	3
Lewis	3	−10	−3.3	0

RECEIVING

Last Name	No.	Yds	Avg	TD
Lavelli	43	586	14	6
Speedie	34	589	17	3
Jones	30	570	19	5
Carpenter	12	183	15	2
Gillom	11	164	15	0
Motley	10	52	5	0
Bumgardner	5	61	12	1
Cole	4	30	8	0
Oristaglio	1	20	20	1
Taseff	1	18	18	0

PUNT RETURNS

Last Name	No.	Yds	Avg	TD
Carpenter	14	173	12	0
Lewis	14	48	3	0
Taseff	1	6	6	0
Phelps	1	3	3	0

KICKOFF RETURNS

Last Name	No.	Yds	Avg	TD
Carpenter	9	196	22	0
Bumgardner	3	75	25	0
Phelps	3	66	22	0
Taseff	3	56	19	0
Jagade	2	36	18	0
Cole	2	28	14	0
Gillom	2	25	13	0
Gaudio	1	8	8	0
Shula	1	6	6	0
Gibron	1	0	0	0

PASSING – PUNTING – KICKING

PASSING	Att	Comp	%	Yds	Yd/Att	TD	Int–%	RK
Graham	265	147	55	2205	8.3	17	16– 6	1
Lewis	6	4	67	68	11.3	1	1–17	

PUNTING	No	Avg
Gillom	73	45.5

KICKING	XP	Att	%	FG	Att	%
Groza	43	43	100	10	23	43

NEW YORK GIANTS

RUSHING

Last Name	No.	Yds	Avg	TD
Price	271	971	3.6	7
Scott	94	367	3.9	1
Griffith	54	115	2.1	0
Rote	21	114	5.4	1
Conerly	17	65	3.8	1
Amberg	7	35	5.0	0
Tidwell	11	14	1.3	0
Jackson	5	9	1.8	0

RECEIVING

Last Name	No.	Yds	Avg	TD
Scott	23	356	15	2
Stribling	18	226	13	2
McChesney	14	230	16	2
Mote	11	187	17	4
Wilkinson	11	182	17	1
Rote	8	62	8	0
Price	5	19	4	0
Hudson	4	122	31	0
Sulaitis	4	25	6	0
Griffith	2	19	10	0
Murray	1	−4	−4	0
Hannah	0	8	0	0

PUNT RETURNS

Last Name	No.	Yds	Avg	TD
Tunnell	34	489	14	3
Ostendarp	2	57	29	0
Schnellbacher	7	32	5	0
Landry	1	0	0	0

KICKOFF RETURNS

Last Name	No.	Yds	Avg	TD
Tunnell	6	227	38	1
Rote	6	185	31	0
Scott	6	154	26	0
Sulaitis	1	37	37	0
Griffith	2	28	14	0
Jackson	1	27	27	0
Ostendarp	1	15	15	0
Coulter	1	12	12	0
Landry	1	0	0	0
Murray	1	0	0	0

PASSING – PUNTING – KICKING

	Att	Comp	%	Yds	Yds/Att	TD	Int–%	RK
Conerly	189	93	49	1277	6.8	10	22–12	11
Tidwell	21	8	38	155	7.4	1	4–19	

PUNTING	No	Avg
Conerly	72	39.7
Landry	15	42.5

KICKING	XP	Att	%	FG	Att	%
Poole	30	31	97	12	16	75

WASHINGTON REDSKINS

RUSHING

Last Name	No.	Yds	Avg	TD
Goode	208	951	4.6	9
Dudley	91	398	4.4	2
Papit	44	175	4.0	0
Heath	64	159	2.5	0
Gilmer	19	141	7.4	0
Thomas	42	130	3.1	0
Dowda	29	111	3.8	0
Drazenovich	34	76	2.2	3
Saenz	3	8	2.7	0
Cox	2	7	3.5	0
Baugh	11	−5	−0.5	0

RECEIVING

Last Name	No.	Yds	Avg	TD
Taylor	29	444	15	3
Brito	24	313	13	0
Dudley	22	303	14	1
Thomas	7	193	28	2
Tereshinksi	6	74	12	2
Goode	3	45	15	0
Papit	3	43	14	0
Dowda	2	54	27	0
Drazenovich	1	27	27	0
Saenz	1	9	9	0
Heath	1	3	3	0

PUNT RETURNS

Last Name	No.	Yds	Avg	TD
Dudley	22	172	8	0
Gilmer	6	132	22	0
Dwyer	7	22	3	0
Saenz	2	6	3	0
Ferris	2	1	1	0
Buksar	1	0	0	0

KICKOFF RETURNS

Last Name	No.	Yds	Avg	TD
Dowda	13	341	26	0
Dudley	11	248	23	0
Saenz	9	145	16	0
Buksar	4	56	14	0
Brito	4	39	10	0
Lipscomb	2	27	14	0
Hendren	2	21	11	0
Dwyer	1	10	10	0
Siegert	1	0	0	0

PASSING – PUNTING – KICKING

PASSING	Att	Comp	%	Yds	Yd/Att	TD	Int–%	RK
Baugh	154	67	44	1104	7.2	7	17–11	16
Gilmer	68	31	46	391	5.8	1	6– 9	
Salem	3	0	0	0	0.0	0	2–67	
Dudley	1	1	100	13	13.0	0	0– 0	

PUNTING	No	Avg
Cox	28	40.0
Dudley	27	34.9
Baugh	4	55.3

KICKING	XP	Att	%	FG	Att	%
Dudley	21	22	95	10	13	77

PITTSBURGH STEELERS

RUSHING

Last Name	No.	Yds	Avg	TD
Rogel	109	385	3.5	3
Chandnois	108	332	3.1	2
Ortmann	59	327	5.5	0
Geri	90	252	2.8	3
Nuzum	27	56	2.1	1
Mathews	21	37	1.8	0
Finks	3	27	9.0	0
Hollingsworth	7	11	1.6	0
Smith	1	1	1.0	0

RECEIVING

Last Name	No.	Yds	Avg	TD
Minarik	35	459	13	1
Chandnois	29	490	17	5
Nickel	28	447	16	3
Jansante	16	200	13	1
Rogel	10	59	6	0
Smith	4	71	18	0
Ortmann	4	62	16	0
Nuzum	2	43	22	0
Geri	2	9	5	0
Jelley	1	8	8	0

PUNT RETURNS

Last Name	No.	Yds	Avg	TD
Mathews	15	231	15	1
Hartley	18	156	9	0
Chandnois	12	55	5	0
Finks	1	20	20	0
Butler	1	2	2	0

KICKOFF RETURNS

Last Name	No.	Yds	Avg	TD
Chandnois	12	390	33	0
Mathews	13	327	25	0
Geri	2	108	54	0
Hartley	1	14	14	0
McPeak	3	10	3	0
Rogel	2	9	5	0
Wydo	1	0	0	0

PASSING – PUNTING – KICKING

PASSING	Att	Comp	%	Yds	Yd/Att	TD	Int–%	RK
Ortmann	139	56	40	671	4.8	3	13– 9	17
Geri	90	29	32	506	5.6	2	7– 8	
Chandnois	43	16	37	256	6.0	2	4– 9	
Mathews	31	15	48	208	6.7	2	0– 0	
Finks	24	14	58	201	8.4	1	1– 4	
Gasparella	2	0	0	0	0.0	0	1–50	
Rogel	1	0	0	0	0	0	0– 0	

PUNTING	No	Avg
Geri	73	38.2
Ortmann	7	43.1

KICKING	XP	Att	%	FG	Att	%
Geri	22	23	96	7	14	50

PHILADELPHIA EAGLES

RUSHING

Last Name	No.	Yds	Avg	TD
Ziegler	113	418	3.7	2
S. Van Buren	112	327	2.9	6
Parmer	92	316	3.4	2
Scott	45	161	3.6	1
Pollard	26	121	4.7	0
Sandifer	35	113	3.2	1
E. Van Buren	16	60	3.8	0
Pritchard	42	29	.7	0
Burk	28	12	.4	1
MacKrides	7	9	1.3	0

RECEIVING

Last Name	No.	Yds	Avg	TD
Pihos	35	536	15	5
Walston	31	512	17	8
Parmer	13	80	6	0
Scott	10	212	21	3
Pritchard	8	103	13	0
Ziegler	8	59	7	0
S. Van Buren	4	28	7	0
O'Quinn	3	58	19	0
Armstrong	3	44	15	0
Pollard	3	35	12	0
Sandifer	2	36	18	1
Lindskog	0	21	0	0
Magee	0	7	0	0

PUNT RETURNS

Last Name	No.	Yds	Avg	TD
Pollard	18	148	8	0
Pritchard	11	147	13	1
Sandifer	14	137	10	0
Scott	4	72	18	0
Grant	1	9	9	0
Craft	2	0	0	0

KICKOFF RETURNS

Last Name	No.	Yds	Avg	TD
Pollard	19	464	22	0
Scott	8	171	21	0
Sandifer	8	147	18	0
Pritchard	7	120	17	0
Walston	5	57	11	0
Craft	2	53	27	0
Pihos	3	40	13	0
Kilroy	1	18	18	0
Barnes	1	15	15	0
Cowhig	1	12	12	0

PASSING – PUNTING – KICKING

PASSING	Att	Comp	%	Yds	Yd/Att	TD	Int–%	RK
Burk	218	92	42	1329	6.1	14	23–11	15
MacKrides	54	23	43	333	6.2	3	5– 9	

PUNTING	No	Avg
Burk	67	39.5
Reagan	10	36.7

KICKING	XP	Att	%	FG	Att	%
Walston	28	31	90	6	11	55

CHICAGO CARDINALS

RUSHING

Last Name	No.	Yds	Avg	TD
Trippi	78	501	6.4	4
Angsman	121	380	3.1	3
Cross	53	283	5.3	3
Pasquareillo	53	251	4.7	1
Paut	37	247	6.7	3
Sitko	52	183	3.5	0
Hardy	12	38	3.2	0
Panelli	13	38	2.9	0
Yablonski	14	20	1.4	0
Svoboda	5	15	3.0	0
Tripucka	1	14	14.0	0
Davis	1	−7	−7.0	0

RECEIVING

Last Name	No.	Yds	Avg	TD
Polsfoot	57	796	14	4
Stonesifer	27	343	13	2
Paul	23	398	17	3
Cross	18	322	18	3
Angsman	9	195	22	1
R. Ramsey	8	135	17	0
Svoboda	6	−9	−1	0
Sitko	4	28	7	0
Davis	4	24	6	0
Pasquariello	2	−9	−5	0
Bieneman	1	8	8	0
Yablonski	1	8	8	0
Panelli	1	5	5	0

PUNT RETURNS

Last Name	No.	Yds	Avg	TD
Paul	19	143	8	0
Cross	7	39	6	0
Davis	4	10	3	0

KICKOFF RETURNS

Last Name	No.	Yds	Avg	TD
Sitko	17	429	25	0
Paul	15	424	28	0
Panelli	2	57	29	0
Angsman	2	51	26	0
Bieneman	2	34	17	0
Svoboda	1	29	29	0
Jennings	1	16	16	0
Hennessy	1	11	11	0
Fischer	1	0	0	0
R. Ramsey	1	0	0	0

PASSING – PUNTING – KICKING

PASSING	Att	Comp	%	Yds	Yd/Att	TD	Int–%	RK
Trippi	191	88	46	1191	6.2	8	13– 7	10
Hardy	114	56	49	809	7.1	3	10– 9	14
Tripucka	29	17	59	244	8.4	2	1– 3	

PUNTING	No	Avg
Polsfoot	47	40.7
Trippi	12	37.2
Tripucka	11	39.0

KICKING	XP	Att	%	FG	Att	%
Patton	19	19	100	5	8	63
Yablonski	8	8	100	2	5	40

LOS ANGELES RAMS 8-4-0 Joe Stydahar

Scores of Each Game		
54	N.Y. YANKS	14
23	CLEVELAND	38
27	Detroit	21
28	Green Bay	0
17	San Francisco	44
23	SAN FRANCISCO	16
45	CHIC. CARDS	21
48	N.Y. YANKS	21
21	Washington	31
42	Chic. Bears	17
22	DETROIT	24
42	GREEN BAY	14

Use Name	Pos.	Hgt	Wgt	Age	Int	Pts
Tom Dahms	OT	6'5"	240	23		
Don Simensen	OT	6'2"	220	24		
Dick Daugherty	OG	6'1"	214	22		
Bill Lange	OG	6'1"	245	24		
Harry Thompson	DE-DG-OG	6'2"	225	24		
Leon McLaughlin	C	6'2"	228	25		
Stan West	DG	6'2"	258	24		
Larry Brink	DE	6'5"	240	28		
Andy Robustelli	DE	6'1"	220	25		
Jack Zilly	DE	6'2"	215	29		
Charlie Toogood	DT	6'	233	23	1	
Jim Winkler	DT	6'2"	248	24		
Bobby Collier	OT-DT	6'3"	230	21		
Jack Halliday	OT-DT	6'3"	238	23		
Don Paul	LB	6'1"	230	26	1	
Jack Finlay	OG-LB	6'1"	222	30		
Joe Reid	C-LB	6'3"	225	21		
Tank Younger	HB-FB-LB	6'3"	226	23	1	6
Woodley Lewis	DB	6'	195	26	3	
Herb Rich	DB	5'11"	180	22	3	
Marvin Johnson	HB-DB	5'11"	180	23		
Jerry Williams	HB-DB	5'10"	176	27	3	24
Bob Boyd	OE-DB	6'2"	198	23	2	6
Norb Hecker	OE-DB	6'2"	190	24	3	6
Norm Van Brocklin	QB	6'1"	200	25		12
Bob Waterfield	QB	6'1"	200	31		98
Glen Davis	HB	5'11"	170	26		12
Tommy Kalmanir	HB	5'8"	170	25		12
Vitamin Smith	HB	5'8"	180	27		12
Dick Hoerner	FB	6'4"	220	29		42
Dan Towler	FB	6'2"	220	23		36
Tom Fears	OE	6'2"	215	27		24
Tom Keane	DB-OE	6'1"	190	24	2	
Crazy Legs Hirsch	HB-OE	6'2"	190	27		102

Paul Barry – Military Service
Dick Huffman – Canadian Football League
Ed Champagne-Canadian Football League
George Sims — Military Service

DETROIT LIONS 7-4-1 Buddy Parker

Scores of Each Game		
35	WASHINGTON	17
37	N. Y. Yanks	10
21	LOS ANGELES	27
24	N.Y. YANKS	24
23	CHIC. BEARS	28
24	Green Bay	17
41	Chic. Bears	28
28	Philadelphia	10
52	GREEN BAY	35
10	SAN FRANCISCO	20
24	Los Angeles	22
17	San Francisco	21

Use Name	Pos.	Hgt	Wgt	Age	Int	Pts
Gus Cifelli	OT	6'4"	240	25		
Floyd Jaszewski	OT	6'4"	230	24		
Dan Rogas	DT-OT	6'1"	225	24		
Barry French	OG	6'	225	30		
Bob Momsen	OG	6'3"	225	21		
Bruce Womack	OG	6'3"	210	22		
Lou Creekmur	DT-OG	6'4"	230	24		
Vince Banonis	LB-C	6'1"	235	29	1	
Les Bingaman	DG	6'3"	260	26		
Ed Berrang (From WAS)	DE	6'2"	203	26	1	
Jim Martin	OT-DE	6'2"	220	27		
Jim Doran	OE-DE	6'2"	195	23	1	12
Thurman McGraw	DT	6'5"	235	24		
John Prchlik	DT	6'4"	235	26		2
Dick Flanagan	OG-LB	6'	215	24	2	
Roy Lininger	C-LB	5'11"	217	24		
Lavern Torgeson	C-LB	6'	210	22	1	
Art Murakowski	FB-LB	6'	195	25		
Jack Christiansen	DB	6'1"	180	22	2	24
Don Doll	DB	5'10"	185	24	1	
Jim Hill	DB	6'	185	22		
Clarence Self	DB	5'8"	185	26		
Jim Smith	DB	6'1"	195	26	3	
Fred Enke	QB	6'1"	200	26		
Bobby Layne	QB	6'1"	190	24		6
Bob Hoernschemeyer	HB	5'11"	195	25		30
Lindy Pearson	HB	6'	200	22		
Doak Walker	HB	5'11"	173	24		97
Ollie Cline	FB	6'	200	25		
Pete D'Alonzo	FB	5'10"	210	21		
Pat Harder	FB	5'11"	202	29		57
Leon Hart	OE	6'5"	262	22	2	72
Bill Swiacki	OE	6'2"	195	26		
Dorne Dibble	DB-OE	6'2"	195	22	1	36

Cloyce Box – Military Service
Jim Cain – Military Service
Wally Triplett – Military Service

SAN FRANCISCO FORTY NINERS 7-4-1 Buck Shaw

Scores of Each Game		
24	CLEVELAND	10
14	Philadelphia	21
28	Pittsburgh	24
7	Chic. Bears	13
44	LOS ANGELES	17
16	Los Angeles	23
19	N. Y. YANKS	14
21	CHIC. CARDS	27
10	N. Y. Yanks	10
20	Detroit	10
31	GREEN BAY	19
21	DETROIT	17

Use Name	Pos.	Hgt	Wgt	Age	Int	Pts
Ray Collins	OT	5'11"	230	23		
Leo Nomellini	DT-OT	6'3"	270	26		6
Bruno Banducci	OG	5'11"	220	29		
Bob Downs	OG	5'10"	210	24		
Nick Feher	OG	6'	220	24		
Dave Sparks	OG	6'1"	222	22		
Bill Johnson	C	6'3"	225	25		
Gail Bruce	DE	6'1"	210	27		1
Ed Henke	DT-DE	6'3"	225	23		
Al Carapella	DT	6'	235	24	1	
Hamp Tanner	OT-DT	6'2"	280	24		2
Hardy Brown	LB	6'	196	27	1	
Don Burke	OG-LB	6'	235	25		
Visco Grgich	OG-LB	5'11"	225	28		
Pete Wissman	C-LB	6'	220	27	2	
Norm Standlee	FB-LB	6'2"	240	32		
Lowell Wagner	DB	6'	195	27	9	
Jim Powers	QB-DB	6'	185	23	4	
Rex Berry	HB-DB	5'11"	180	25	4	
Jim Cason	HB-DB	6'	168	24	8	6
Bob White	HB-DB	5'11"	174	22	1	
Frankie Albert	QB	5'10"	170	31		18
Y. A. Tittle	QB	6'	190	24		6
Joe Arenas	HB	5'11"	180	25		24
Jim Monachino	HB	5'10"	190	22		12
Pete Schabarum	HB	5'11"	185	22		12
Johnny Strzykalski	HB	5'9"	190	28		18
Verl Lillywhite	DB-HB	5'10"	185	24	3	12
Joe Perry	FB	6'	210	24		24
Bishop Strickland	FB	5'10"	195	22		
Alyn Beals	OE	6'	190	30		
Bill Jessup	OE	6'1"	190	22		6
Gordie Soltau	OE	6'2"	195	26		90
Billy Wilson	OE	6'3"	195	24		18

Clay Mathews – Military Service
Jack Nix-Canadian Football League
Sam Cathcart — Military Service

CHICAGO BEARS 7-5-0 George Halas

Scores of Each Game		
31	Green Bay	20
14	Chic. Cards	28
24	N. Y. YANKS	21
13	SAN FRANCISCO	7
28	Detroit	23
27	Washington	0
28	DETROIT	41
24	GREEN BAY	13
21	Cleveland	42
17	LOS ANGELES	42
45	N. Y. Yanks	21
14	CHIC. CARDS	24

Use Name	Pos.	Hgt	Wgt	Age	Int	Pts
Paul Stenn	DT-OT	6'2"	245	33		
George Conner	LB-OT	6'3"	240	26	2	
Dick Barwegan	OG	6'1"	228	29		
Frank Dempsey	OG	6'3"	235	26		
Wayne Hansen	OG	6'2"	230	23		
Wash Serini	OG	6'2"	235	27		
Bob Moser	C	6'3"	240	22		
Bulldog Turner	OG-C	6'1"	235	32		
Ed Neal (From GB)	DG-C	6'4"	275	33		
Les Cowan	DT-DE	6'5"	235	24		
Ed Sprinkle	OE-DE	6'1"	207	27	1	12
Fred Davis	OT-DT	6'3"	248	33		
Ray Bray	DG	6'	235	34		
Jerry Stoutberg	OG-LB	6'2"	228	23		
Stu Clarkson	LB	6'2"	225	32	1	
J. R. Boone	HB	5'8"	163	25		
Al Campana	HB-DB	5'11"	180	25		
Billy Stone	HB-DB	6'	188	25	4	12
Don Kindt	FB-DB	6'1"	208	25	4	6
Gene Schroeder	OE-DB	6'3"	190	22	5	18
Steve Romanik	QB	6'1"	190	27		6
Bob Williams	QB	6'1"	198	22		
George Blanda	LB-DB-QB	6'1"	204	23	1	44
Johnny Lujack	DB-QB	6'	188	26	3	52
George Gulyanics	HB	6'	204	30		24
Chuck Hunsinger	HB	6'	188	26		24
Brad Rowland	HB	6'1"	190	23		
Julie Rykovich	HB	6'2"	205	27		24
Wilford White	HB	5'9"	172	23		16
Kayo Dottley	FB	6'1"	200	23		24
Curley Morrison	FB	6'2"	215	25		
Jim Keane	OE	6'4"	215	27		6
Bill Wightkin	OE	6'3"	238	24		6
John Hoffman	LB-OE	6'2"	218	25		12

JerryWeatherley – Military Service

GREEN BAY PACKERS 3-9-0 Gene Ronzani

Scores of Each Game		
20	CHIC. BEARS	31
35	PITTSBURGH	33
37	PHILADELPHIA	24
0	LOS ANGELES	28
29	N. Y. Yanks	27
17	DETROIT	24
7	Pittsburgh	28
13	Chic. Bears	24
35	Detroit	52
28	N. Y. YANKS	31
19	San Francisco	31
14	Los Angeles	42

Use Name	Pos.	Hgt	Wgt	Age	Int	Pts
Willie Manley	OG-OT	6'2"	225	25		
Joe Spencer	DT-OT	6'3"	240	28		
Dick Wildung	DT-OT	6'	220	29		
Ray DiPierro	OG	5'11"	210	24		
Dave Stephenson	OG	6'2"	235	25		
Buddy Burris	LB-OG	5'11"	215	28		
Jay Rhodemyre	C	6'1"	210	29		
Dick Afflis	DG	6'	252	22		
Art Felker	DE	6'3"	205	23		
John Martinkovic	DE	6'3"	235	24		
Dan Orlich	OE-DE	6'5"	215	26		
Ab Wimberly	OE-DE	6'1"	215	25		
Howie Ruetz	DT	6'3"	265	23	1	
Don Stansauk	DT	6'1"	255	26		
Ed Ecker	OT-DT	6'7"	270	28		
Walt Michaels	LB	6'	225	22		
Bill Schroll	LB	6'	218	25		
Bob Summerhays	LB	6'1"	215	24	2	6
Ham Nichols	OG-LB	5'11"	215	27		
Carl Schuette	C-LB	6'1"	210	29		
Bob Nussbaumer	DB	5'11"	170	27		
Rebel Steiner	DB	6'	185	25	3	
Rip Collins	HB-DB	6'	190	24	2	
Harper Davis	HB-DB	5'11"	172	25	4	
Jug Girard	HB-DB	5'11"	175	24	5	12
Ace Loomis	HB-DB	6'1"	190	23	4	
Tobin Rote	QB	6'3"	200	23		18
Bobby Thomason	QB	6'1"	197	22		
Tony Canadeo	HB	5'11"	190	32		18
Billy Grimes	HB	6'1"	197	24		12
Breezy Reid	HB	5'10"	180	24		
Dom Moselle	DB-HB	6'	192	25	1	18
Jack Cloud	FB	5'10"	220	26		12
Fred Cone	FB	5'11"	197	25		50
Carl Elliott	OE	6'4"	215	24		30
Bob Mann	OE	5'11"	172	27		48
Dick Moje	OE	6'2"	210	24		
Ray Pelfrey	HB-OE	6'	190	23		30

Larry Coutre – Military Service
Bob Forte – Military Service
Len Szafaryn – Military Service
Clayton Tonnemaker – Military Service

NEW YORK YANKS 1-9-2 Red Strader

Scores of Each Game		
14	Los Angeles	54
10	DETROIT	37
21	Chic. Bears	24
24	Detroit	24
27	GREEN BAY	29
31	N. Y. Giants	37
14	San Francisco	19
21	Los Angeles	48
10	SAN FRANCISCO	10
31	Green Bay	28
21	CHIC. BEARS	45
17	N. Y. GIANTS	27

Use Name	Pos.	Hgt	Wgt	Age	Int	Pts
Jim Champion	DT-OT	6'	245	24		
John Clowes (To DET)	DT-OT	6'1"	245	29		
Ross Nagel	DT-OT	6'4"	243	28	1	
Jim Cullom	OG	5'11"	235	25		
Sisto Averno	LB-OG	5'11"	228	25		
Wayne Siegert	OT-LB-OG	6'3"	225	21		
Joe Domnanovich	C	6'1"	215	32		
Brad Ecklund	C	6'3"	215	29		
Barney Poole	DE	6'2"	228	28		
Breck Stroschein	DE	6'1"	205	22		
Art Tait	DE	5'11"	205	22		12
Don Colo	DT	6'3"	252	26		
Art Donovan	DT	6'2"	240	26		
Mike McCormack	DT	6'4"	230	24		
Paul Mitchell	DT	6'3"	240	31		
Harvey Johnson	LB	5'11"	220	32		49
Vito Kissell	LB	5'10"	205	24		
John Wozniak	OG-LB	6'	220	30		
Ben Aldridge	DB	6'	195	24	5	
Joe Golding	DB	6'	187	30	2	
Bobby Griffin	DB	6'	180	23	4	
Duke Iverson	DB	6'2"	208	31		
Darrell Meisenheimer	DB	5'10"	195	25	3	
Paul Crowe	HB-DB	6'1"	195	27	3	
Bob Celeri	QB	5'10"	180	24		6
George Ratterman	QB	6'1"	180	24		
Johnny Rauch (To PHI)	QB	6'	195	24		
Bev Wallace	QB	6'2"	180	28		
Sherman Howard	HB	5'11"	192	27		42
Buddy Young	HB	5'5"	170	25		36
George Taliaferro	DB-QB-HB	5'11"	195	24	4	30
Zollie Toth	FB	6'2"	215	27		24
Bruce Alford	OE	6'	190	30		
Dan Edwards	OE	6'1"	195	25		18
Dan Graza	OE	6'3"	205	27		24
Bill O'Connor	DE-OE	6'4"	220	25		

Lou Kusserow – Canadian Football League
Martin Ruby – Canadian Football League
Jack Russell – Canadian Football League
John Yonakor — Canadian Football League
Ed Sharkey — Military Service

LOS ANGELES RAMS

RUSHING

Last Name	No.	Yds	Avg	TD
Towler	126	854	6.8	6
Hoerner	94	569	6.1	6
Younger	36	223	6.2	1
Davis	64	200	3.1	1
Smith	52	143	2.8	1
Williams	21	106	5.0	2
Kalmanir	16	61	3.8	0
Waterfield	9	49	5.4	3
Hirsch	1	3	3.0	0
Van Brocklin	7	2	.3	2

RECEIVING

Last Name	No.	Yds	Avg	TD
Hirsch	66	1495	23	17
Fears	32	528	17	3
Smith	16	278	17	1
Towler	16	257	16	0
Keane	12	133	11	0
Boyd	9	128	14	1
Hoerner	8	102	13	1
Davis	8	90	11	1
Kalmanir	6	91	15	1
Younger	5	72	14	0
Williams	5	49	10	0
Hecker	4	35	9	1
Johnson	2	38	19	0

PUNT RETURNS

Last Name	No.	Yds	Avg	TD
Smith	12	139	12	0
Kalmanir	5	86	17	1
Davis	15	85	6	0
Williams	4	22	6	0
Lewis	1	12	12	0

KICKOFF RETURNS

Last Name	No.	Yds	Avg	TD
Smith	15	274	18	0
Davis	9	179	20	0
Williams	6	133	22	0
Kalmanir	6	120	20	0
Lewis	4	67	17	0
Hoerner	1	22	22	0
Simensen	1	13	13	0
Towler	1	10	10	0
Collier	1	8	8	0

PASSING – PUNTING – KICKING

PASSING	Att	Comp	%	Yds	Yd/Att	TD	Int–%	RK
Van Brocklin	194	100	52	1725	8.9	13	11– 6	2
Waterfield	176	88	50	1566	8.9	13	10– 6	2
Davis	2	1	50	5	2.5	0	0– 0	
Keane	1	0	0	0	0	0	1–100	

PUNTING	No	Avg
Van Brocklin	48	41.5
Waterfield	4	41.5

KICKING	XP	Att	%	FG	Att	%
Waterfield	41	43	95	13	23	57
Fears	6	7	86	0	0	0
Hirsch	0	1	0	0	0	0
Hecker	0	0	0	0	1	0

DETROIT LIONS

RUSHING

Last Name	No.	Yds	Avg	TD
Hoernschemeyer	132	678	5.1	2
Harder	101	380	3.8	6
Walker	79	356	4.5	2
Layne	61	290	4.8	1
Pearson	22	88	4.0	0
Doran	2	23	11.5	0
Cline	3	15	5.0	0
D'Alonzo	2	11	5.5	0
Enke	4	6	1.5	0
Hart	4	–6	–1.5	0

RECEIVING

Last Name	No.	Yds	Avg	TD
Hart	35	544	16	12
Dibble	30	613	20	6
Hoernschemeyer	23	263	11	3
Walker	22	421	19	4
Harder	17	193	11	2
Swiacki	16	188	12	0
Doran	10	225	23	2
Pearson	5	43	9	0
Martin	0	10	0	0

PUNT RETURNS

Last Name	No.	Yds	Avg	TD
Christiansen	18	343	19	4
Walker	7	85	12	0
Doll	5	39	8	0
Hoernschemeyer	2	16	8	0

KICKOFF RETURNS

Last Name	No.	Yds	Avg	TD
Walker	15	408	27	0
Christiansen	11	270	25	0
Doll	9	220	24	0
Hoernschemeyer	3	78	26	0
Cline	3	48	16	0
Harder	1	14	14	0
Prchlik	1	12	12	0
French	1	3	3	0
Murakowski	1	0	0	0

PASSING – PUNTING – KICKING

PASSING	Att	Comp	%	Yds	Yd/Att	TD	Int–%	RK
Layne	332	152	46	2403	7.2	26	23– 7	6
Enke	9	2	22	22	2.4	0	1–11	
Walker	5	2	40	29	5.8	1	0– 0	
Hoernschemeyer	4	2	50	46	12.0	2	0– 0	
Harder	1	0	0	0	0.0	0	0– 0	

PUNTING	No	Avg
Smith	49	42.5
Walker	9	35.1

KICKING	XP	Att	%	FG	Att	%
Walker	43	44	98	6	12	50
Harder	0	0	0	3	5	60

SAN FRANCISCO FORTY NINERS

RUSHING

Last Name	No.	Yds	Avg	TD
Perry	136	677	5.0	3
Lillywhite	67	397	5.9	1
Schabarum	76	311	4.1	2
Strzykalski	81	296	3.7	3
Arenas	34	183	5.4	3
Strickland	34	165	4.9	0
Albert	35	146	4.2	3
Monachino	21	74	3.5	2
Standlee	16	65	4.1	0
White	8	33	4.1	0
Tittle	13	18	1.4	1
Cason	1	5	5.0	0
Soltau	1	–4	–4.0	0

RECEIVING

Last Name	No.	Yds	Avg	TD
Soltau	59	826	14	7
Wilson	18	268	15	3
Perry	18	167	9	1
Beals	12	126	11	0
Strzykalski	12	105	9	0
Lillywhite	11	125	11	1
Schabarum	10	162	16	0
Jessup	7	99	14	1
White	3	36	12	0
Arenas	1	12	12	1
Berry	1	12	12	0
Cason	1	8	8	0
Monachino	1	6	6	0
Johnson	0	3	0	0

PUNT RETURNS

Last Name	No.	Yds	Avg	TD
Arenas	21	272	13	0
Cason	13	115	9	0
Nomellini	1	20	20	1

KICKOFF RETURNS

Last Name	No.	Yds	Avg	TD
Arenas	21	542	26	0
Cason	10	196	20	0
Perry	1	32	32	0
Nomellini	2	27	14	0
Strickland	1	14	14	0
Collins	1	6	6	0
Banducci	1	3	3	0
Wilson	1	0	0	0

PASSING – PUNTING – KICKING

PASSING	Att	Comp	%	Yds	Yd/Att	TD	Int–%	RK
Albert	166	90	54	1116	6.7	5	10– 6	9
Tittle	114	63	55	808	7.1	8	9– 8	8
Perry	1	1	100	31	31.0	1	0– 0	

PUNTING	No	Avg
Albert	34	44.3
Lillywhite	20	42.4

KICKING	XP	Att	%	FG	Att	%
Soltau	30	32	94	6	18	33
Bruce	1	1	100	0	0	0

CHICAGO BEARS

RUSHING

Last Name	No.	Yds	Avg	TD
Dottley	127	670	5.3	3
Gulyanics	105	403	3.8	4
Rykovich	83	399	4.8	4
Hunsinger	73	369	5.1	3
Lujack	47	171	3.6	7
Stone	30	123	4.1	1
Morrison	29	96	3.3	0
White	9	86	9.6	1
Rowland	10	50	5.0	0
Romanik	12	23	1.9	1
Boone	3	9	3.0	0
Kindt	2	5	2.5	0
Schroeder	1	4	4.0	0
Campana	2	3	1.5	0
Williams	5	0	0.0	0
Hoffman	1	–3	–3.0	0

RECEIVING

Last Name	No.	Yds	Avg	TD
Hoffman	28	394	14	2
Schroeder	24	461	19	3
Stone	18	320	18	1
Keane	15	247	16	1
Dottley	14	225	16	1
Gulyanics	13	146	11	0
Rykovich	6	133	22	0
Boone	6	117	20	0
Hunsinger	6	59	10	1
White	4	45	11	1
Kindt	4	39	10	1
Sprinkle	2	11	6	1
Wightkin	1	47	47	0
Rowland	1	–2	–2	0
Morrison	1	–3	–3	0

PUNT RETURNS

Last Name	No.	Yds	Avg	TD
White	14	131	9	0
Stone	14	120	9	0
Boone	14	113	8	0
Hunsinger	1	7	7	0
Wightkin	1	3	3	1

KICKOFF RETURNS

Last Name	No.	Yds	Avg	TD
Morrison	13	353	27	0
Rowland	15	350	23	0
Stone	5	108	22	0
Hunsinger	4	66	17	0
Davis	3	26	9	0
Hansen	1	23	23	0
Blanda	2	19	10	0
Schroeder	1	18	18	0
Connor	1	9	9	0
Sereni	1	2	2	0

PASSING – PUNTING – KICKING

PASSING	Att	Comp	%	Yds	Yd/Att	TD	Int–%	RK
Lujack	176	85	48	1295	7.4	8	8– 5	5
Romanik	101	43	43	791	7.8	3	9– 8	11
Williams	33	14	42	146	4.4	1	2– 6	
Rykovich	3	0	0	0	0.0	0	1–33	
Morrison	1	1	100	7	7.0	0	0– 0	
White	1	0	0	0	0.0	0	0– 0	

PUNTING	No	Avg
Morrison	57	39.1
Williams	4	36.3
Rowland	1	18.0

KICKING	XP	Att	%	FG	Att	%
Blanda	26	26	100	6	17	35
Lujack	10	11	91	0	0	0
White	1	1	100	1	2	50

GREEN BAY PACKERS

RUSHING

Last Name	No.	Yds	Avg	TD
Rote	76	523	6.9	3
Cone	56	190	3.4	1
Canadeo	54	131	2.4	1
Grimes	44	123	2.8	1
Reid	23	73	3.2	0
Cloud	29	61	2.1	1
Pelfrey	3	44	14.7	0
Moselle	12	23	2.0	1
Girard	4	20	5.0	0
Mann	2	9	4.5	0
Collins	5	4	.8	0
Thomason	5	–5	–1.0	0

RECEIVING

Last Name	No.	Yds	Avg	TD
Mann	50	696	14	8
Pelfrey	38	462	12	5
Elliott	35	317	9	5
Cone	28	315	11	0
Canadeo	22	226	10	2
Grimes	15	170	11	1
Moselle	14	233	17	2
Girard	10	220	22	2
Reid	9	115	13	0
Cloud	3	16	5	1
Davis	1	15	15	0
Moje	1	11	11	0
Wimberly	1	10	10	0
Loomis	1	9	9	0
Orlich	1	9	9	0
Collins	1	5	5	0
Rote	0	11	0	0

PUNT RETURNS

Last Name	No.	Yds	Avg	TD
Grimes	16	100	6	0
Moselle	9	80	9	0
Davis	2	21	11	0
Girard	1	9	9	0
Wussbaumer	1	3	3	0

KICKOFF RETURNS

Last Name	No.	Yds	Avg	TD
Grimes	23	582	25	0
Moselle	20	547	27	0
Canadeo	4	101	25	0
Michaels	5	86	17	0
Collins	1	40	40	0
Martinkovic	2	34	17	0
Summerhays	1	21	21	0
Cone	1	20	20	0
Elliott	1	14	14	0
Wimberly	2	4	2	0

PASSING – PUNTING – KICKING

PASSING	Att	Comp	%	Yds	Yd/Att	TD	Int–%	RK
Rote	256	106	41	1540	6.0	15	20– 8	11
Thomason	221	125	57	1306	5.9	11	9– 4	4
Reid	1	0	0	0	0.0	0	0– 0	

PUNTING	No	Avg
Girard	52	40.4
Pelfrey	5	44.0
Collins	2	40.5
Rote	1	55.0
Cone	1	47.0

KICKING	XP	Att	%	FG	Att	%
Cone	29	35	83	5	7	71
Michaels	0	0	0	0	1	0

NEW YORK YANKS

RUSHING

Last Name	No.	Yds	Avg	TD
Toth	119	384	3.2	4
Howard	94	343	3.6	4
Taliaferro	62	330	5.3	3
Young	46	165	3.6	1
Celeri	36	107	3.0	0
Rauch	7	26	3.7	0
Ratterman	3	9	3.0	0
Wallace	1	–8	–8.0	0

RECEIVING

Last Name	No.	Yds	Avg	TD
Edwards	39	509	13	3
Young	31	508	16	3
Garza	31	470	15	4
Howard	21	447	21	3
Taliaferro	16	230	14	2
O'Connor	14	192	14	0
Toth	10	100	10	0
Alford	4	65	16	0
Crowe	3	20	7	0
Celeri	2	71	36	1
Wozniak	1	4	4	0

PUNT RETURNS

Last Name	No.	Yds	Avg	TD
Young	12	231	19	1
Taliaferro	9	68	8	0
Griffin	4	46	12	0
Aldridge	1	0	0	0

KICKOFF RETURNS

Last Name	No.	Yds	Avg	TD
Taliaferro	27	622	23	0
Young	14	427	31	1
Averno	3	28	9	0
Iverson	1	14	14	0
Mitchell	1	11	11	0
O'Connor	1	10	10	0
Johnson	1	4	4	0
Siegert	1	2	2	0
McCormack	1	0	0	0

PASSING – PUNTING – KICKING

PASSING	Att	Comp	%	Yds	Yd/Att	TD	Int–%	RK
Celeri	238	102	43	1797	7.6	12	15– 6	7
Rauch	94	30	32	288	3.1	1	4– 4	
Ratterman	67	31	46	340	5.1	2	6– 9	
Taliaferro	33	13	39	251	7.6	1	3– 9	
Wallace	8	1	13	9	1.1	0	0– 0	

PUNTING	No	Avg
Taliaferro	76	37.9
Celeri	5	44.8

KICKING	XP	Att	%	FG	Att	%
Johnson	31	31	100	6	14	43

1952 Texas: Everything but the Pros

Two rookies joined the league who perfectly illustrated the modern pro game. Both Hugh McElhenny of San Francisco and Ollie Matson of the Cardinals had blazing speed and the ability to bring a crowd to its feet with a breakaway run or pass reception. Pro football in general was fast, offense-oriented, and spiced with exciting stars on most of the teams and the fans showed their approval by turning out in a record number of 2,052,126 for seventy-two league games.

Eleven of the clubs prospered in these booming times, but the twelfth franchise was a pain in the neck for the league. Tired of losing money, New York Yank owner Ted Collins sold his franchise back to the league. Bert Bell and the league then sold the team to a group from Dallas, Texas. Long a hotbed for college and high-school football, Texas looked like an untapped source of riches just waiting for an NFL team. Instead, the Dallas Texans went through their first few games waiting for customers, while the fans ignored the team. After four home games, the Texans were averaging under 15,000 attendance per game, convincing the owners to get out immediately. They turned the club over to the league in mid-season, and the commissioner's office operated the Texans as a road team for the remainder of the year.

AMERICAN CONFERENCE

Cleveland Browns—Even in an off year, the Browns marched off with a conference title. They lost four games, the most in the history of the team, yet still came home a game ahead of the Giants and Eagles. The Giants beat the Browns twice but had problems with the rest of the league. The Eagles downed the Browns in their second meeting but lost two of their last three contests to fall out of contention. The other Cleveland loss was administered by the Detroit Lions, the Browns' opponent in the upcoming championship game. The Browns nevertheless headed into the title match with a lot of guns at their side. Lou Groza and Horace Gillom fueled the potent kicking game. Otto Graham and Mac Speedie hooked up in a dangerous passing combination, Marion Motley came back from knee injuries to have a good year, and Len Ford and Bill Willis kept the defensive backbone stiff.

New York Giants—Safetyman Em Tunnell gave the New York defense a lot of offensive power. Very fast and shifty, Tunnell returned interceptions, punts, and kickoffs with such electric flair that he actually outgained the league rushing leader in yards gained. Dan Towler of Los Angeles won the running title with 894 yards, while Tunnell, never lining up on offense, ran for 924 yards on his various returns. But even with Tunnell, Tom Landry, and Arnie Weinmeister starring on defense, and with Eddie Price sparking the offense, the Giants still finished short of the title in second place.

Philadelphia Eagles—The Eagles broke in a new coach and lost their greatest star during the pre-season. Jim Trimble took over the coaching reigns but never had the pleasure of using Steve Van Buren in action. In a training-camp scrimmage, a hard tackle ripped up Van Buren's knee, ending the powerful halfback's glowing career. Trimble rallied his forces, however, and drove the Eagles through the season fast on the heels of the Cleveland Browns. The new coach installed Bobby Thomason, a pick-up from Green Bay, as quarterback, and youngsters Bud Grant and Bobby Walston as the offensive ends, shifted tough Pete Pihos to the defensive unit, and was smart enough to leave Chuck Bednarik alone at linebacker.

Pittsburgh Steelers—The Steelers came out of the dark ages this year, led by a coach from the 1930s. Joe Bach had coached the team back in 1935-36 and had been canned by owner Art Rooney, at whose wedding he had been best man. Now Rooney rehired him, saying, "I never should have let him get away in the first place. That bull-headed Dutchman was the best organizer I ever had." An all-out passing attack from the T-formation is what Bach organized for this year. The single wing went out, and passer Jim Finks came off the bench to take over as quarterback. The Steelers still lost more than they won, but their new system generated more offense and more excitement.

Chicago Cardinals—The Cards won three of their first four games but hardly had the personnel to keep that pace up. Under freshman coach Joe Kuharich, the Cards dropped seven of their last eight contests, as the offense had problems scoring more than two touchdowns. Quarterback Charlie Trippi ran the ball well but could not give the team a real passing threat; essentially, he was a halfback playing quarterback out of necessity. Filling one halfback spot was rookie Ollie Matson, a marvelous overall athlete who combined power and speed in his 6' 2", 205-pound frame. The bronze medal winner in the 400-meter sprint at the 1952 Olympics, Matson returned kicks explosively, gave the Cards a breakaway threat in the backfield, and played defense often enough and well enough to win All-Pro honors as a cornerback.

Washington Redskins—Owner George Marshall canned another coach, replacing Dick Todd with Curly Lambeau before the regular season even began, but the fans were concerned more with the imminent departure of Sammy Baugh. Breaking his hand in a pre-season contest, Slingin' Sam spent most of the year holding the ball on place kicks and coaching little Eddie LeBaron in the tricks of quarterbacking. Like most recent seasons, this campaign was a dismal one, with the Redskins riding a six-game losing streak heading into their final two games. At this point Baugh returned to the starting lineup for his pro finale and rallied the team to beat the Giants 27-17 and knock them out of the conference race, and then Sammy wrapped up his career as the Redskins topped the Eagles 27-21.

NATIONAL CONFERENCE

Detroit Lions—The Lions dropped two of their first three contests, but then Bobby Layne and his merry men roared back to deadlock the Rams for the National Conference title. Even with Doak Walker hurt most of the year, the Lion attack moved on Bob Hoernschemeyer's legs, Layne's arm, receiver Cloyce Box's hands, and blocker Lou Creekmur's shoulders. The Lions also developed a defensive unit which fans would recognize and applaud as much as the offense. Big Les Bingaman, quick and clever as a fox, held down the middle of the line, mean Thurman McGraw piled up runners and passers from his tackle spot, and Jack Christiansen, Yale Lary, Jim David, and Jim Smith gave the Lion secondary strength matched only by the Giants—all of which was enough to give the Lions their first conference crown when, on a foggy Sunday in Los Angeles, they ended the Rams' reign with a 31-21 playoff triumph.

Los Angeles Rams—All of a sudden the high-riding Rams were rolling in the dirt. The defense wasn't holding anybody, head coach Joe Stydahar was feuding with chief assistant Hamp Pool, and the club lost its last three pre-season games. When the Browns murdered the Rams 37-7 on opening day, the internal feud came to a head. Stydahar quit, leaving the club in Pool's control, and the Rams quickly dropped to a 1-3 mark. Then, in mid-October, the defending champs regrouped. The defense shaped up, thanks largely to defensive backs Herb Rich and Night Train Lane, a free-agent rookie who picked off a record fourteen passes, while the offense regained its top stride.

San Francisco '49ers—With five straight wins to begin the year, the '49ers were on the way to a conference crown until one play turned it all around. With the '49ers ahead of the Bears 17-10 in the second half, Frankie Albert dropped back deep to punt. When he got the ball, he instead decided to run for the first down, only to be dropped short of the needed yardage. The Bears quickly drove to a tying touchdown and won the game on a last-minute 48-yard field goal by George Blanda. After that, relations between Albert and coach Buck Shaw were strained, contributing to a second-half collapse by the team. Thus, a season highlighted by the arrival of Hugh McElhenny, a long-legged halfback who was the best open-field runner since Red Grange and George McAfee, ended in bitterness.

Green Bay Packers—The Packers got away from their limp-rag image of recent years, showing enough life to break even in wins and losses for the first time since 1947. The team for once signed a strong crop of rookies. Tackle Dave Hanner, a jolly bald-headed man who used his tremendous strength on the field, and smart back Bobby Dillon, who was blind in one eye, shored up a defense which sorely needed reinforcements, while Babe Parilli and Billy Howton broke into the offensive lineup. Parilli shared the quarterback job with Tobin Rote, and both men found the sure-handed Howton open for many key passes. The veterans on the squad may have had a funny feeling when the Packers, for the first time ever in a regular season game, lined up against a Curly Lambeau team. Sentiment went out the window, though, as the Packers defeated Lambeau's Redskins 35-20.

Chicago Bears—Four years ago George Halas had a marvelous stable of quarterbacks in Sid Luckman, Johnny Lujack, and Bobby Layne; now Luckman was gracefully retired, Lujack had quit with a bad shoulder, and Layne was leading the Detroit Lions to a league championship. Stuck with a pair of unproven quarterbacks in George Blanda and Steve Romanik, the Bears dropped below the .500 mark for the first time since 1945 and only the second time since 1929.

Dallas Texans—It was a promising venture that ended as a joke. The league transferred the New York Yanks franchise to Dallas, but after four echo-filled games in the Cotton Bowl, the club owners threw in the sponge and turned the operation over to the league. For the second half of the season the Texans traveled the country as a road team, using Hershey, Pennsylvania, as their home base for loosely organized practices. With morale lower than the floor, the Texans shocked the world by beating the Bears 27-23 on Thanksgiving Day in Akron, Ohio, before a rousing throng of 3,000 paid customers for the only win of their existence.

FINAL TEAM STATISTICS

OFFENSE

	CHI.B.	CHI.C.	CLEVE.	DALLAS	DET.	G.BAY	L.A.	N.Y.	PHIL.	PITT.	S.F.	WASH.
FIRST DOWNS:												
Total	194	176	228	172	219	197	205	155	181	187	213	206
by Rushing	90	91	106	79	92	84	92	78	72	67	97	95
by Passing	87	74	119	78	115	95	102	66	98	110	104	90
by Penalty	17	11	4	15	12	18	11	11	11	10	12	21
RUSHING:												
Number	411	477	394	381	442	405	411	442	434	384	421	467
Yards	1543	1748	1786	1397	1780	1485	1811	1636	1370	1204	1905	1655
Average Yards	3.8	3.7	4.5	3.7	4.0	3.7	4.4	3.7	3.2	3.1	4.5	3.5
Touchdowns	11	10	12	13	14	11	17	11	10	12	16	10
PASSING:												
Attempts	347	289	374	352	362	337	329	280	361	365	342	286
Completions	141	124	184	149	171	161	167	121	154	167	177	147
Completion Percentage	40.6	42.9	49.2	42.3	47.2	47.8	50.8	43.2	42.7	45.8	51.8	51.4
Gross Yards	2015	1512	2839	1807	2495	2688	2438	1713	2272	2504	2371	2127
Yards Lost Tackled	280	301	273	423	287	314	146	321	307	313	396	387
Net Yards	1735	1211	2566	1384	2208	2374	2292	1392	1965	2191	1975	1740
Avg. Yards per Attempt (Gross)	5.8	5.2	7.6	5.1	6.9	8.0	7.4	6.1	6.3	6.9	6.9	7.4
Avg. Yards per Comp. (Gross)	14.3	12.2	15.4	12.1	14.6	16.7	14.6	14.2	14.8	15.0	13.4	14.5
Touchdowns	18	10	22	12	24	26	17	16	13	21	19	20
Interceptions	27	22	26	30	28	25	31	22	19	23	23	21
Percent Intercepted	7.8	7.6	7.0	8.5	7.7	7.4	9.4	7.9	5.3	6.3	6.7	7.3
PUNTS:												
Number	66	76	61	84	66	65	59	82	83	81	68	68
Average Yards	42.4	37.3	45.7	36.7	44.1	40.7	42.8	41.0	40.2	43.0	42.6	41.3
PUNT RETURNS:												
Number	41	49	55	21	35	38	38	41	53	47	40	41
Yards	223	450	410	160	520	370	527	502	446	557	436	452
Average Yards	5.4	9.2	7.5	7.6	14.9	9.7	13.9	12.2	8.4	11.9	10.9	11.0
Touchdowns	0	0	1	0	3	0	2	0	2	3	2	2
KICKOFF RETURNS:												
Number	50	45	47	67	39	52	40	45	47	39	36	51
Yards	1168	1008	823	1586	882	1085	967	999	1173	1128	798	1052
Average Yards	23.4	22.4	17.5	23.7	22.6	20.9	24.2	22.2	25.0	28.9	22.2	20.6
Touchdowns	2	2	0	0	0	0	0	0	0	2	0	0
INTERCEPTION RETURNS:												
Number	20	25	22	28	32	22	38	28	20	27	17	18
Yards	281	232	250	397	477	254	712	371	290	409	252	301
Average Yards	14.1	9.3	11.4	14.2	14.9	11.5	18.7	13.3	14.5	15.1	14.8	16.7
Touchdowns	0	0	0	1	2	1	4	1	3	1	1	1
PENALTIES												
Number	73	87	85	67	77	83	100	64	80	57	79	69
Yards	583	743	744	621	799	739	891	626	747	520	628	669
FUMBLES:												
Number	39	33	21	35	17	40	32	27	43	27	26	32
Number Lost	24	23	11	25	10	31	17	14	22	14	13	17
POINTS:												
Total	245	172	310	182	344	295	349	234	252	300	285	240
PAT Attempts	31	24	35	27	43	39	45	29	31	42	37	32
PAT Made	31	22	35	20	42	37	44	28	31	36	35	26
FG Attempts	28	18	33	4	28	21	19	17	20	11	12	10
FG Made	8	2	19	0	14	6	11	10	11	4	6	4
Percent FG Made	28.6	11.1	57.6	0.0	50.0	28.6	57.9	58.8	55.0	36.4	50.0	40.0
Safeties	2	0	1	0	1	0	1	1	1	0	2	2

DEFENSE

	CHI.B.	CHI.C.	CLEVE.	DALLAS	DET.	G.BAY	L.A.	N.Y.	PHIL.	PITT.	S.F.	WASH.
FIRST DOWNS:												
Total	209	176	186	197	195	202	212	189	187	224	167	189
by Rushing	98	85	78	97	74	87	93	72	81	100	81	96
by Passing	98	82	95	90	105	97	97	110	93	115	76	80
by Penalty	13	9	13	10	16	18	22	7	13	9	10	13
RUSHING:												
Number	463	455	411	421	353	415	441	404	408	460	412	426
Yards	1921	1588	1386	2334	1145	1507	1613	1303	1396	1744	1566	1817
Average Yards	4.1	3.5	3.4	5.5	3.2	3.6	3.7	3.2	3.4	3.8	3.8	4.3
Touchdowns	20	8	11	17	8	16	10	8	12	8	10	19
PASSING:												
Attempts	311	307	348	310	382	340	360	337	343	369	342	275
Completions	160	149	141	150	182	162	161	162	157	167	151	121
Completion Percentage	51.4	48.5	40.5	48.4	47.6	47.6	44.7	48.1	45.8	45.3	44.2	44.0
Gross Yards	2350	1942	2028	2394	2421	2205	2252	2514	2164	2765	1929	1817
Yards Lost Tackled	259	177	339	346	321	443	369	336	410	220	291	237
Net Yards	2091	1765	1689	2048	2100	1762	1883	2178	1754	2545	1638	1580
Avg. Yards per Attempt (Gross)	7.6	6.3	5.8	7.7	6.3	6.5	6.3	7.5	6.3	7.5	5.6	6.6
Avg. Yards per Comp. (Gross)	14.7	13.0	14.4	16.0	13.3	13.6	14.0	15.5	13.8	16.6	12.8	15.0
Touchdowns	16	16	17	31	15	17	18	18	19	24	15	12
Interceptions	20	25	22	28	32	22	38	28	20	27	17	18
Percent Intercepted	6.4	8.1	6.3	9.0	8.4	6.5	10.6	8.3	5.8	7.3	5.0	6.5
PUNTS:												
Number	67	69	84	50	73	72	66	84	88	73	78	55
Average Yards	41.5	42.1	40.6	43.3	40.6	39.0	42.8	40.5	41.3	42.4	41.3	41.2
PUNT RETURNS:												
Number	38	54	39	36	41	36	22	52	55	50	29	47
Yards	612	600	307	399	305	281	178	348	571	483	359	610
Average Yards	16.1	11.1	7.9	11.1	7.4	7.8	8.1	6.7	10.4	9.7	12.4	13.0
Touchdowns	2	1	0	3	0	1	0	2	1	1	1	3
KICKOFF RETURNS:												
Number	36	35	47	35	63	51	48	49	44	56	52	42
Yards	906	774	1107	732	1338	1312	1149	957	1111	1024	1242	1017
Average Yards	25.2	22.1	23.6	20.9	21.2	25.7	23.9	19.5	25.3	18.3	23.9	24.2
Touchdowns	2	2	0	0	0	0	0	0	0	2	0	0
INTERCEPTION RETURNS:												
Number	27	22	26	30	28	25	31	22	19	23	23	21
Yards	323	240	389	632	364	339	518	306	187	426	299	203
Average Yards	12.0	10.9	15.0	21.1	13.0	13.6	16.7	13.9	9.8	18.5	13.0	9.7
Touchdowns	0	0	1	4	1	3	3	0	1	0	0	2
PENALTIES												
Number	91	91	46	91	62	96	77	66	74	71	65	91
Yards	795	883	425	926	596	752	746	518	699	623	530	817
FUMBLES:												
Number	44	30	23	27	34	28	26	35	36	26	31	32
Number Lost	26	18	14	18	25	19	18	17	19	13	18	16
POINTS:												
Total	326	221	213	427	192	312	234	231	271	273	221	287
PAT Attempts	43	28	27	56	25	40	30	30	37	35	27	37
PAT Made	40	25	25	54	21	39	28	27	31	35	27	35
FG Attempts	20	20	11	24	15	20	16	19	14	18	21	23
FG Made	8	8	4	11	7	11	6	8	4	8	10	10
Percent FG Made	40.0	40.0	36.3	45.8	46.7	55.0	37.5	42.1	28.6	44.4	47.6	43.5
Safeties	2	2	1	2	0	1	0	0	0	2	1	0

1952
CHAMPIONSHIP GAME
December 28 at Cleveland
(Attendance 50,934)

Roaring Back After Seventeen Years

The Browns came into the game with a long injury list but hurt themselves more with mistakes during the contest. Dub Jones, Mac Speedie, and John Kissell all missed the game, and Lou Groza played with cracked ribs, which made him miss all three of his field-goal attempts. The Browns made their first mistake in the opening quarter when Horace Gillom got off a poor 22-yard punt which gave Detroit the ball at mid-field. Bobby Layne then took the Lions into the end zone after eight plays, with the touchdown scored by Layne himself on a quarterback sneak. The Detroit defense meanwhile kept the Browns scoreless, and the halftime score was 7-0 in favor of the Lions. Doak Walker, the versatile halfback out most of the season with injuries, lengthened the lead to 14-0 in the third quarter with a 67-yard dash through a massive hole opened on the right side. After the kickoff, the Browns went on their only extended drive of the game, driving 67 yards to make the score 14-7. Then the mistakes started flowing. The Browns had a first down on the Detroit 5-yard line, only to lose the ball on downs. In the fourth quarter, Ken Carpenter fumbled a punt, which the Lions converted into a Pat Harder field goal and their first NFL title in seventeen years.

SCORING

DETROIT	0	7	7	3	–17
CLEVELAND	0	0	7	0	– 7

First Quarter
None

Second Quarter
Det.
Layne, 2 yard rush; PAT – Harder (kick)

Third Quarter
Det.
Walker, 67 yard rush; PAT – Harder (kick)
Cle.
Jagade, 7 yard rush; PAT – Groza (kick)

Fourth Quarter
Det.
Harder, 36 yard Field Goal

TEAM STATISTICS

DET.		CLE.
10	First Downs – Total	22
8	– by Rushing	15
2	– by Passing	7
0	– by Penalty	0
34	Rushing – Attempts	34
199	– Yards	227
5.9	– Average Yards	6.7
10	Passing – Attempts	36
7	– Completions	20
68	– Yards	191
0	– Had Intercepted	1
6	Punts – Number	3
40.8	– Average Distance	43.3
18	Punt Return Yards	18
0	Fumbles – Number	1
0	– Times Lost Ball	1
3	Penalties – Number	7
25	– Yards Penalized	65
0	Giveaways	2
2	Takeaways	0
+2	Difference	–2

INDIVIDUAL STATISTICS

RUSHING	No.	Yds.	Avg.	RECEIVING	No.	Yds.	Avg.
Cleveland							
Jagade	15	104	6.9	Bumg'ner	4	43	10.8
Motley	6	74	12.3	Lavelli	4	23	5.8
Graham	7	23	3.3	Renfro	4	26	6.5
Carpenter	3	13	4.3	Motley	3	21	7.0
Renfro	3	13	4.3	Brewster	2	53	26.5
				Carpenter	2	7	3.5
				Gillom	1	8	8.0
Detroit							
Walker	10	97	9.7	Harder	2	18	9.0
Layne	9	47	5.2	Walker	2	11	5.5
Harder	8	28	3.5	Hart	1	15	15.0
Horn'meyer	7	27	3.9	Swiacki	1	14	14.0
				Box	1	10	10.0

PASSING

	Att.	Comp	Comp Pct.	Yds	Yds/ Att	Yds/ Comp
Cleveland						
Graham	35	20	57.1	191	5.5	9.6
Motley	1	0	00.0	0	–	–
Detroit						
Layne	9	7	77.8	68	7.6	9.7
Walker	1	0	00.0	0	–	–

CLEVELAND BROWNS 8-4-0 Paul Brown

Scores of Each Game		
37	LOS ANGELES	7
21	Pittsburgh	20
9	NEW YORK	17
49	Philadelphia	7
19	WASHINGTON	15
6	Detroit	17
28	CHIC. CARDS	13
29	PITTSBURGH	28
20	PHILADELPHIA	28
48	Washington	24
10	Chic. Cards	0
34	New York	37

Use Name	Pos.	Hgt	Wgt	Age	Int	Pts
Lou Groza	OT	6'3"	235	28		89
John Sandusky	OT	6'1"	250	26		
Bob Gain	DT-OT	6'3"	245	24		3
Abe Gibron	OG	5'11"	240	26		
Lin Houston	OG	6'	215	31		
Joe Skibinski	OG	5'11"	220	24		
Frank Gatski	C	6'3"	240	30		
Bill Willis	DG	6'2"	215	31		
Len Ford	DE	6'4"	240	26		6
George Young	DE	6'3"	215	28		2
Jerry Helluin	DT	6'2"	280	22		
John Kissell	DT	6'3"	247	29		
Darrell Palmer	DT	6'2"	235	30		

Use Name	Pos.	Hgt	Wgt	Age	Int	Pts
Walt Michaels	LB	6'	215	23	4	
Tommy Thompson	LB	6'1"	220	25	1	
Ed Sharkey	OG-LB	6'3"	240	25		
Hal Herring	C-LB	6'1"	210	28		
Emerson Cole (to Chi B)	DB-LB	6'2"	215	24		
Tommy James	DB	5'10"	185	28	4	
Warren Lahr	DB	5'11"	185	28	5	
Don Phelps	DB	5'11"	185	27		
Bert Rechichar	DB	6'1"	200	22	6	
Don Shula	DB	5'11"	190	22		

Tony Adamle – Voluntarily retired
Ken Gorgal – Military Service
Carl Taseff – Military Service
Art Spinney – Military Service

Use Name	Pos.	Hgt	Wgt	Age	Int	Pts
Otto Graham	QB	6'1"	195	30		24
George Ratterman	QB	6'1"	185	25		
Ken Carpenter	HB	6'	190	26		30
Sherman Howard	HB	5'11"	195	28		18
Dub Jones	HB	6'4"	205	27		36
Ray Renfro	HB	6'1"	185	21		
Rex Bumgardner	DB-HB	5'11"	193	28	2	
Chick Jagade	FB	6'	210	25		18
Marion Motley	LB-FB	6'1"	238	32		18
Darrell Brewster	OE	6'3"	210	22		6
Dante Lavelli	OE	6'	192	29		24
Mac Speedie	OE	6'3"	205	32		30
Horace Gillom	DE-OE	6'1"	225	31		6

NEW YORK GIANTS 7-5-0 Steve Owen

Scores of Each Game		
24	Dallas	6
31	Philadelphia	7
17	Cleveland	9
23	CHIC. CARDS	24
10	PHILADELPHIA	14
28	Chic. Cards	6
23	SAN FRANCISCO	14
3	GREEN BAY	17
14	Washington	10
7	Pittsburgh	63
17	WASHINGTON	27
37	CLEVELAND	34

Use Name	Pos.	Hgt	Wgt	Age	Int	Pts
Dick Yelvington	OT	6'2"	230	25		
Hal Mitchell	OG-OT	6'1"	225	20		
Ray Krouse	DT-OT	6'3"	250	25		
Bill Albright	OG	6'1"	232	23		
Ray Beck	OG	6'2"	220	20		
George Kennard	OG	6'	205	23		
Bob Patton	OG	6'	226	24		
John Rapacz	C	6'4"	260	27		
Tex Coulter	OT-C	6'4"	260	27		
Jim Duncan	DE	6'2"	205	26	2	
Ray Poole	DE	6'2"	215	30	1	56
Horrace Sherrod	OE-DE	6'	190	25		6
Al DeRogatis	DT	6'4"	240	25		
Arnie Weinmeister	DT	6'4"	235	29		2

Use Name	Pos.	Hgt	Wgt	Age	Int	Pts
Jon Baker	LB	6'2"	215	29		
John Cannady	LB	6'2"	225	28	2	
Joe Sulaitis	OG-BB-LB	6'2"	215	31		
Pat Knight	DE-BB-LB	6'2"	200	23		
Don Menasco	DB	6'	185	22	4	
Harmon Rowe	DB	6'	182	29	1	
Em Tunnell	DB	6'1"	183	30	7	
Tom Landry	QB-DB	6'1"	195	27	8	12
John Amberg	HB-DB	5'11"	195	24	2	

Bill Austin – Military Service
Randy Clay – Military Service
Bill Milner — Military Service

Use Name	Pos.	Hgt	Wgt	Age	Int	Pts
Fred Benners	QB	6'3"	195	22		
Chuck Conerly	QB	6'1"	185	28		2
Kyle Rote	HB	6'	195	23		24
Joe Scott	HB	6'1"	195	26		24
George Thomas	HB	6'1"	185	24		
Frank Gifford	DB-HB	6'1"	190	22	1	
Eddie Price	FB	5'11"	190	26		30
Bob Hudson	OE	6'4"	215	22		
Bob McChesney	OE	6'2"	190	25		36
Bill Stribling	OE	6'1"	205	25		30
Kelley Mote	DE-OE	6'2"	190	29		
Bob Wilkinson	HB-DB-OE	6'3"	215	25		12

PHILADELPHIA EAGLES 7-5-0 Jim Trimble

Scores of Each Game		
31	Pittsburgh	25
7	NEW YORK	31
26	PITTSBURGH	21
7	CLEVELAND	49
14	New York	10
10	Green Bay	12
38	WASHINGTON	20
10	CHIC. CARDS	7
28	Cleveland	20
22	Chic. Cards	28
38	DALLAS	21
21	Washington	27

Use Name	Pos.	Hgt	Wgt	Age	Int	Pts
Lum Snyder	OT	6'5"	225	22		
Frank Wydo	OT	6'4"	235	28		
Bill Horrell	OG	5'11"	222	22		
Maury Nipp	OG	6'	218	22		
John Magee	OG	5'10"	220	29		
Dan Rogas	OG	6'1"	230	25		
Joe Tyrrell	OG	5'11"	216	23		
Ken Farragut	LB-C	6'4"	240	24		
Bucko Kilroy	OT-DG	6'2"	240	31		
Bob Oristaglio	DE	6'2"	215	28		
Jack Zilly	DE	6'2"	215	30		
Norm Willey	OG-DE	6'2"	225	25	1	
Mike Jarmoluk	DT	6'5"	240	29	2	12
Vic Sears	DT	6'3"	230	34	1	6

Use Name	Pos.	Hgt	Wgt	Age	Int	Pts
Chuck Bednarik	C-LB	6'3"	230	27	2	
Wayne Robinson	C-LB	6'2"	220	22		
Ebert Van Buren	HB-LB	6'2"	210	27		8
Bob Stringer	FB-LB	6'1"	200	22	1	
Russ Craft	DB	5'9"	175	32	1	6
Joe Restic	DB	6'2"	180	25		
Joe Sutton	DB	5'11"	180	28	3	
Neil Ferris (from WAS)	HB-DB	5'11"	185	24		6
Bibbles Bawel	OE-DB	6'1"	186	22	8	6

Neill Armstrong – Canadian Football League
Roscoe Hansen – Military Service
Toy Ledbetter – Military Service
Red O'Quinn – Canadian Football League
Ray Romero – Military Service
Steve Van Buren – Knee Injury

Use Name	Pos.	Hgt	Wgt	Age	Int	Pts
Adrian Burk	QB	6'2"	190	24		
Fred Enke	QB	6'1"	200	27		
Bobby Thomason	QB	6'1"	195	23		
Ralph Goldston	HB	5'11"	195	24		18
Al Pollard	HB	6'	197	24		6
Don Stevens	HB	5'9"	176	25		6
Frank Ziegler	HB	5'11"	175	28		24
John Brewer	FB	6'4"	230	24		12
John Huzvar	FB	6'4"	240	23		12
Jim Parmer	FB	6'	190	25		
Bud Grant	OE	6'3"	198	25		42
Bobby Walston	OE	6'	185	23		82
Pete Pihos	DE-OE	6'1"	215	28		12

PITTSBURGH STEELERS 5-7-0 Joe Bach

Scores of Each Game		
25	PHILADELPHIA	31
20	CLEVELAND	21
21	Philadelphia	26
24	WASHINGTON	28
34	Chic. Cards	28
24	Washington	23
6	DETROIT	31
28	Cleveland	29
17	CHIC. CARDS	14
63	NEW YORK	7
24	San Francisco	7
14	Los Angeles	28

Use Name	Pos.	Hgt	Wgt	Age	Int	Pts
Dick Fugler	OT	6'2"	235	22		
George Hughes	OG-OT	6'1"	225	27		
Rudy Andabaker	OG	6'	205	23		
Earl Murray	OG	6'2"	240	26		
Pete Ladygo	LB-OG	6'2"	215	24		
Bill Walsh	C	6'2"	230	25		
George Hays	DE	6'2"	210	27	1	12
Bill McPeak	DE	6'1"	200	27		
George Tarasovic	C	6'4"	235	23		
Lou Ferry	DT	6'2"	245	25		6
Ernie Stautner	DT	6'1"	230	27		

Use Name	Pos.	Hgt	Wgt	Age	Int	Pts
Dale Dodrill	LB	6'1"	210	27		6
Darrell Hogan	LB	5'10"	210	26	4	6
John Schweder	OG-LB	6'1"	225	25		
Lou Levanti	C-LB	6'1"	215	26		
Frank Sinkovitz	C-LB	6'1"	220	29	1	
Jerry Shipkey	FB-LB	6'1"	215	27	2	
Jim Brandt	DB	6'1"	200	24		
Howard Hartley	DB	6'	185	28	4	
Claude Hipps	DB	6'1"	188	26	3	
Ed Kissell	DB	6'1"	190	24	5	
Jack Butler	OE-DB	6'	195	24	7	12

Tom McWilliams — Military Service
Walt Szot — Military Service

Use Name	Pos.	Hgt	Wgt	Age	Int	Pts
Pat Brady	QB	6'1"	195	24		
Jim Finks	QB	6'	175	25		30
Gary Kerkorian	QB	5'11"	185	23		47
Tom Calvin	HB	6'	200	26		
Lynn Chandnois	HB	6'2"	195	28		30
Ray Mathews	HB	6'	185	23		43
Ed Modzelewski	FB	6'	210	23		18
Fran Rogel	FB	5'11"	200	25		18
Jack Spinks	FB	6'	238	22		
Dick Hensley	OE	6'4"	210	26		12
Elbie Nickel	OE	6'1"	195	29		54
George Sulima	OE	6'2"	200	25		6

CHICAGO CARDINALS 4-8-0 Joe Kuharich

Scores of Each Game		
7	WASHINGTON	23
21	CHIC. BEARS	10
17	Washington	6
24	New York	23
28	PITTSBURGH	34
6	NEW YORK	28
13	Cleveland	28
7	Philadelphia	10
14	Pittsburgh	17
28	PHILADELPHIA	22
0	CLEVELAND	10
7	Chic. Bears	10

Use Name	Pos.	Hgt	Wgt	Age	Int	Pts
Volney Peters	DT-OT	6'4"	225	24		6
Jack Jennings	OT	6'4"	245	25		
Bill Fischer	OG	6'2"	245	25		
Ed Listopad	OG	6'2"	230	22		
Mike Sikora	OG	6'2"	230	24		
Jack Simmons	C	6'4"	230	26		
Tom Bienemann	DE	6'3"	220	24		
Bob Dove	DE	6'2"	225	31		
Tony Klimek	DE	5'11"	200	26	2	
Don Joyce	DT	6'3"	250	22		
Mike Mergen	DT	6'5"	245	23		
Jerry Groom	C-DT	6'3"	235	23		

Use Name	Pos.	Hgt	Wgt	Age	Int	Pts
Eli Popa	LB	5'10"	202	21		
Bill Svoboda	LB	6'	210	25	2	
Fred Wallner	LB	6'2"	230	23		
Gordon Polofsky	OG-LB	6'1"	218	21		
Leo Sanford	OG-LB	6'1"	220	23	2	
John Panelli	FB-LB	5'11"	200	26	3	
Roy Barni	DB	5'11"	185	25	6	
Billy Gay	DB	5'11"	180	24		
S. J. Whitman	DB	5'11"	185	26	3	
Don Paul	HB-DB	6'	180	26		6
Ray Ramsey	OE-DB	6'2"	165	31	5	

John Hock – Military Service

Use Name	Pos.	Hgt	Wgt	Age	Int	Pts
Don Panciera	QB	6'1"	185	29		
Charlie Trippi	HB-QB	6'	185	29		24
Elmer Angsman	HB	5'11"	200	26		6
Billy Cross	HB	5'6"	150	23		24
Joe Geri	HB	5'10"	185	28		28
Johnny Karras	HB	5'11"	187	24		6
Emil Sitko	HB	5'8"	185	28		6
Wally Triplett	HB	5'10"	175	25		
Ralph Pasquariello	FB	6'2"	235	25		
Ollie Matson	DB-FB	6'2"	205	22	2	54
Cliff Anderson	OE	6'2"	215	22		12
Fran Polsfoot	OE	6'3"	200	25		
Don Stonesifer	OE	6'	200	25		
Ralph Thomas	DE-OE	5'11"	195	22		

WASHINGTON REDSKINS 4-8-0 Curly Lambeau

Scores of Each Game		
23	Chic. Cards	7
20	Green Bay	35
6	CHIC. CARDS	17
28	Pittsburgh	24
15	Cleveland	19
23	PITTSBURGH	24
20	Philadelphia	38
17	SAN FRANCISCO	23
10	NEW YORK	14
24	CLEVELAND	48
27	New York	17
27	PHILADELPHIA	21

Use Name	Pos.	Hgt	Wgt	Age	Int	Pts
Joe Moss	OT	6'1"	221	22		
Laurie Niemi	DT-OT	6'1"	257	27		
Ed Bagdon	OG	5'10"	213	26		7
Buddy Brown	OG	6'1"	212	25		
Jim Clark	OG	6'1"	230	23		
Knox Ramsey (from PHI)	LB-OG	6'1"	225	26		
Gene Pepper	OT-DT-DG-OG	6'2"	237	25		
Tony Momsen	C	6'1"	235	25		
Dick Woodward	C	6'2"	225	26		
Jim Ricca	OT-DG	6'4"	267	25		
Ed Berrang	DE	6'2"	211	27	2	
Jerry Hennessey	DE	6'2"	224	26		2
John Yonakor	DT-DE	6'5"	225	31		
Lou Karras	DT	6'4"	234	25		
Paul Lipscomb	DT	6'5"	255	29	1	
Ed Ecker	OT-DT	6'7"	265	29		

Use Name	Pos.	Hgt	Wgt	Age	Int	Pts
Al DeMao	C-LB	6'2"	220	32		
George Buksar	FB-LB	6'	220	26		24
Chuck Drazenovich	FB-LB	6'1"	226	25	3	18
Joe Tereshinski	OE-LB	6'2"	217	28	1	
Dick Alban	DB	6'	185	23	1	
Andy Davis	DB	6'	188	25		
Billy Cox	HB-DB	6'3"	184	23	3	
Harry Dowda	HB-DB	6'2"	200	28	2	6
Johnny Williams	HB-DB	5'11"	170	25	5	18

Bill Dudley – Voluntarily Retired
Rob Goode – Military Service
Hall Haynes – Military Service
Harry Ulinski – Military Service
Slug Witucki – Military Service
Walt Yowarsky – Military Service
Joe Bartos — Military Service
John Steber — Military Service

Use Name	Pos.	Hgt	Wgt	Age	Int	Pts
Sammy Baugh	QB	6'2"	175	38		
Eddie LeBaron	QB	5'9"	173	22		18
Harry Gilmer	HB-QB	6'	172	26		6
Choo-Choo Justice	HB	5'10"	178	28		6
Johnny Papit	HB	6'	188	24		6
Julie Rykovich	HB	6'2"	200	28		13
Sam Venuto	HB	6'1"	195	24		6
Jack Cloud	FB	5'10"	220	27		
Leon Heath	FB	6'1"	198	24		18
Bob Sykes	FB	6'1"	218	24		
Gene Brito	OE	6'1"	215	26		12
Hugh Taylor	OE	6'4"	188	29		72

CLEVELAND BROWNS

RUSHING

Last Name	No.	Yds	Avg	TD
Motley	104	444	4.3	1
Carpenter	72	408	5.7	3
Jagade	57	373	6.5	2
Jones	65	270	4.2	2
Graham	42	130	3.1	4
Howard	34	95	2.8	0
Bumgardner	9	38	4.2	0
Renfro	10	26	2.6	0
Ratterman	1	2	2.0	0

RECEIVING

Last Name	No.	Yds	Avg	TD
Speedie	62	911	15	5
Jones	43	651	15	4
Lavelli	21	336	16	4
Carpenter	16	136	9	1
Motley	13	213	16	2
Howard	11	219	20	3
Jagade	9	203	23	1
Brewster	4	117	29	1
Gillom	4	45	11	1
Renfro	1	8	8	0

PUNT RETURNS

Last Name	No.	Yds	Avg	TD
Renfro	22	169	7	0
Carpenter	10	139	14	1
Rechichar	14	58	4	0
Bumgardner	4	24	6	0
Phelps	5	15	3	0
Skibinski	0	5	0	0

KICKOFF RETURNS

Last Name	No.	Yds	Avg	TD
Carpenter	11	234	21	0
Renfro	8	130	16	0
Cole	5	99	20	0
Bumgardner	5	89	18	0
Motley	3	88	29	0
Rechichar	4	70	18	0
Jagade	3	58	19	0
Sharkey	2	24	12	0
Howard	1	22	22	0
Michaels	1	16	16	0
Brewster	1	11	11	0
Skibinski	1	8	8	0
Gillom	1	2	2	0
Gain	1	0	0	0
Gibron	1	0	0	0

PASSING – PUNTING – KICKING

PASSING	Att	Comp	%	Yds	Yd/Att	TD	Int–%	RK
Graham	364	181	50	2816	7.7	20	24– 7	2
Ratterman	6	2	33	20	3.3	1	2–33	
Jones	2	1	50	3	1.5	1	0– 0	
Motley	2	0	0	0	0.0	0	0– 0	

PUNTING	No	Avg
Gillom	61	45.7

KICKING	XP	Att	%	FG	Att	%
Groza	32	32	100	19	33	58
Gain	3	3	100	0	0	0

NEW YORK GIANTS

RUSHING

Last Name	No.	Yds	Avg	TD
Price	183	748	4.1	5
Rote	103	421	4.1	2
Gifford	38	116	3.1	0
Conerly	27	115	4.3	0
Scott	38	107	2.8	3
Landry	7	40	5.7	1
Amberg	7	27	3.9	0
Wilkinson	26	26	1.0	0
Thomas	6	18	3.0	0
Benners	5	16	3.2	0
McChesney	2	2	1.0	0

RECEIVING

Last Name	No.	Yds	Avg	TD
Stribling	26	399	15	5
McChesney	21	430	20	6
Rote	21	240	11	2
Scott	14	251	18	1
Price	11	36	3	0
Wilkinson	6	148	24	2
Gifford	5	36	7	0
Mote	4	45	11	0
Hudson	4	40	10	0
Sulaitis	4	31	8	0
Amberg	3	40	13	0
Coulter	1	9	9	0
Thomas	1	8	8	0

PUNT RETURNS

Last Name	No.	Yds	Avg	TD
Tunnell	30	411	14	0
Landry	10	88	9	0
Gifford	1	3	3	0

KICKOFF RETURNS

Last Name	No.	Yds	Avg	TD
Tunnell	15	364	24	0
Scott	7	190	27	0
Gifford	4	124	31	0
Rote	6	110	18	0
Sulaitis	4	91	23	0
Sherrod	2	33	17	0
McChesney	3	28	9	0
Price	1	21	21	0
Landry	1	20	20	0
Stribling	1	11	11	0
Kennard	1	0	0	0
Beck	0	7	0	0

PASSING – PUNTING – KICKING

PASSING	Att	Comp	%	Yds	Yd/Att	TD	Int–%	RK
Conerly	169	82	49	1090	6.5	13	10– 6	9
Benners	58	25	43	320	5.5	0	5– 9	
Landry	47	11	23	172	3.7	1	7–15	
Rote	4	2	50	113	28.3	1	0– 0	
Gifford	2	1	50	18	9.0	1	0– 0	

PUNTING	No	Avg
Landry	82	41.0

KICKING	XP	Att	%	FG	Att	%
Poole	26	27	96	10	17	59
Conerly	2	2	100	0	0	0

PHILADELPHIA EAGLES

RUSHING

Last Name	No.	Yds	Avg	TD
Huzvar	105	349	3.3	2
Goldston	65	210	3.2	3
Brewer	50	188	3.8	2
Pollard	55	186	3.4	1
Ziegler	67	172	2.6	2
Stevens	33	95	2.9	0
Thomason	17	88	5.2	0
Burk	7	28	4.0	0
Enke	14	25	1.8	0
Parmer	12	23	1.9	0
Ferris	11	22	2.0	1
Stringer	2	5	2.5	0
E. Van Buren	7	1	0.1	0

RECEIVING

Last Name	No.	Yds	Avg	TD
Grant	56	997	18	7
Walston	26	469	18	3
Stevens	13	174	13	0
Huzvar	13	37	2	0
Pihos	12	219	18	1
Ziegler	8	120	15	2
Pollard	8	59	7	0
Brewer	5	19	4	0
E. Van Buren	4	73	18	0
Bawel	2	60	30	0
Enke	2	19	10	0
Goldston	2	12	6	0
Parmer	2	10	5	0
Ferris	1	8	8	0
Stringer	1	4	4	0

PUNT RETURNS

Last Name	No.	Yds	Avg	TD
Bawel	34	261	8	1
Stevens	16	172	11	1
Walston	2	13	7	0
Ferris	2	11	6	0
E. Van Buren	1	0	0	0

KICKOFF RETURNS

Last Name	No.	Yds	Avg	TD
Pollard	21	528	25	0
Stevens	16	433	27	0
Ziegler	4	82	21	0
Ferris	3	76	25	0
Sears	1	45	45	0
Parmer	2	33	17	0
Stringer	1	22	22	0
Craft	1	18	18	0
E. Van Buren	1	12	12	0

PASSING – PUNTING – KICKING

PASSING	Att	Comp	%	Yds	Yd/Att	TD	Int–%	RK
Thomason	212	95	45	1334	6.3	8	9– 4	10
Burk	82	37	45	561	6.8	4	5– 6	
Enke	67	22	33	377	5.6	1	5– 7	

PUNTING	No	Avg
Burk	83	40.2

KICKING	XP	Att	%	FG	Att	%
Walston	31	31	100	11	20	55

PITTSBURGH STEELERS

RUSHING

Last Name	No.	Yds	Avg	TD
Mathews	66	315	4.8	0
Chandnois	97	298	3.1	1
Rogel	84	230	2.7	3
Modzelewski	82	195	2.4	3
Spinks	22	94	4.3	0
Finks	23	37	1.6	5
Kerkorian	2	20	10.0	0
Calvin	7	14	2.0	0
Shipley	1	1	1.0	0

RECEIVING

Last Name	No.	Yds	Avg	TD
Nickel	55	884	16	9
Mathews	33	543	16	5
Chandnois	28	370	13	2
Hensley	12	217	18	2
Rogel	12	140	12	0
Modzelewski	11	109	10	0
Sulima	9	176	20	1
Butler	3	37	12	2
Spinks	2	22	11	0
Calvin	2	4	2	0
Hughes	0	2	0	0

PUNT RETURNS

Last Name	No.	Yds	Avg	TD
Mathews	26	397	15	2
Chandnois	17	111	7	0
Hartley	1	34	34	0
Calvin	2	12	6	0
Hays	1	3	3	1

KICKOFF RETURNS

Last Name	No.	Yds	Avg	TD
Chandnois	17	599	35	2
Mathews	14	367	26	0
Calvin	5	120	24	0
Brandt	1	24	24	0
Murray	1	14	14	0
Ladygo	1	4	4	0

PASSING – PUNTING – KICKING

PASSING	Att	Comp	%	Yds	Yd/Att	TD	Int–%	RK
Finks	336	158	47	2307	6.9	20	19– 6	4
Mathews	13	3	23	104	8.0	0	1– 8	
Kerkorian	11	5	45	79	7.2	1	3–27	
Brady	3	1	33	14	4.7	0	0– 0	
Chandnois	2	0	0	0	0.0	0	0– 0	

PUNTING	No	Avg
Brady	17	43.2
Finks	4	39.0

KICKING	XP	Att	%	FG	Att	%
Kerkorian	35	41	85	4	9	44
Kissell	0	0	0	0	2	0
Mathews	1	1	100	0	0	0

CHICAGO CARDINALS

RUSHING

Last Name	No.	Yds	Avg	TD
Trippi	72	350	4.9	4
Sitko	88	348	4.0	1
Cross	71	347	4.9	2
Matson	96	344	3.6	3
Pasquariello	48	129	2.7	0
Angsman	46	114	2.5	0
Geri	20	50	2.5	0
Karras	24	42	1.8	0
Paul	6	28	4.7	0
Panciera	4	6	1.5	0
Peters	1	−7	−7.0	0

RECEIVING

Last Name	No.	Yds	Avg	TD
Stonesifer	54	617	11	0
Cross	17	234	14	2
Anderson	11	191	17	2
Matson	11	187	17	3
Pasquariello	7	46	7	0
Trippi	5	66	13	0
Karras	5	63	13	1
Paul	4	32	8	1
Angsman	4	22	6	1
Ramsey	3	27	9	0
Sitko	2	16	8	0

PUNT RETURNS

Last Name	No.	Yds	Avg	TD
Cross	21	177	8	0
Paul	10	97	10	0
Matson	9	86	10	0
Karras	4	47	12	0
Triplett	2	26	13	0
Barni	2	17	9	0
Peters	1	0	0	0

KICKOFF RETURNS

Last Name	No.	Yds	Avg	TD
Matson	20	624	31	2
Cross	9	169	19	0
Karras	4	69	17	0
Paul	3	54	18	0
Stonesifer	2	27	14	0
Sitko	1	19	19	0
Mergen	1	13	13	0
Pasquariello	1	13	13	0
Anderson	1	8	8	0
Peters	1	4	4	0
Fischer	1	0	0	0

PASSING – PUNTING – KICKING

PASSING	Att	Comp	%	Yds	Yd/Att	TD	Int–%	RK
Trippi	181	84	46	890	4.9	5	13– 7	12
Panciera	96	35	36	582	6.1	5	9– 9	

PUNTING	No	Att
Geri	29	37.7
Trippi	16	36.8

KICKING	XP	Att	%	FG	Att	%
Geri	22	24	92	2	18	11

WASHINGTON REDSKINS

RUSHING

Last Name	No.	Yds	Avg	TD
Heath	90	388	4.3	2
Gilmer	100	365	3.7	0
Rykovich	94	361	3.8	1
LeBaron	43	164	4.0	2
Justice	36	129	3.6	0
Papit	34	102	3.0	0
Drazenovich	29	66	2.3	3
Cloud	7	21	3.0	0
Venuto	4	16	4.0	1
Sykes	4	10	2.5	0
Dowda	6	5	.8	0
Williams	2	3	1.5	0
Buksar	3	3	1.0	0
Baugh	1	1	1.0	0
Cox	3	−1	−0.3	0

RECEIVING

Last Name	No.	Yds	Avg	TD
Taylor	41	961	23	12
Heath	12	146	6	1
Brito	21	270	13	2
Rykovich	16	283	18	1
Gilmer	15	143	10	1
Justice	11	106	10	1
Drazenovich	4	62	16	0
Papit	3	71	24	1
Dowda	3	20	7	1
Cox	2	19	10	0
Tereshinski	2	19	10	0
Buksar	2	3	2	0
Williams	1	13	13	0
Sykes	1	5	5	0
Karras	1	−2	−2	0

PUNT RETURNS

Last Name	No.	Yds	Avg	TD
Williams	24	366	15	2
Justice	12	47	4	0
Gilmer	3	28	9	0

KICKOFF RETURNS

Last Name	No.	Yds	Avg	TD
Williams	20	486	24	0
Justice	10	209	21	0
Gilmer	7	157	22	0
Buksar	4	43	11	0
Venuto	2	28	14	0
Papit	1	25	25	0
Cloud	1	18	18	0
Brito	2	5	3	0
Lipscomb	1	5	5	0

PASSING – PUNTING – KICKING

PASSING	Att	Comp	%	Yds	Yd/Att	TD	Int–%	RK
LeBaron	194	95	49	1420	7.3	14	15– 8	5
Gilmer	58	31	53	555	9.6	4	4– 7	
Baugh	33	20	61	152	4.6	2	1– 3	
Justice	1	0	0	0	0.0	0	1–100	

PUNTING	No	Att
LeBaron	51	42.2
Justice	11	39.2
Cox	5	35.4
Baugh	1	48.0

KICKING	XP	Att	%	FG	Att	%
Buksar	15	18	83	3	7	43
Bagdon	4	6	67	1	3	33
LeBaron	6	7	86	0	0	0
Rykovich	1	1	100	0	0	0

DETROIT LIONS 9-3-0 Buddy Parker

Scores of Each Game		
3	San Francisco	17
17	Los Angeles	14
0	SAN FRANCISCO	28
24	LOS ANGELES	16
52	Green Bay	17
17	CLEVELAND	6
31	Pittsburgh	6
43	DALLAS	13
23	Chic. Bears	24
48	GREEN BAY	24
45	CHIC. BEARS	21
41	DALLAS	6
	Playoff	
31	Los Angeles	21

Use Name	Pos.	Hgt	Wgt	Age	Int	Pts
Gus Cifelli	OT	6'4"	240	26		
Bob Miller	DT-OT	6'3"	235	22		
Stan Campbell	OG	6'	215	22		
Dick Stanfel	OG	6'3"	240	25		
Lou Creekmur	OT-OG	6'4"	230	25		
Vince Banonis	C	6'1"	235	30		
Les Bingaman	DG	6'3"	285	27	1	
Blaine Earon	DE	6'1"	195	23		
Sonny Gandee (from DAL)	DE	6'1"	210	23		2
Jim Doran	OE-DE	6'2"	195	24		6
Pat Summerall	OE-DE	6'4"	220	22		
Thurman McGraw	DT	6'5"	235	25		
John Prchlik	DT	6'4"	235	27		
Dick Flanagan	OG-LB	6'	215	25	1	
Jim Martin	OG-LB	6'2"	220	28		
Lavern Torgeson	C-LB	6'	210	23	5	6
Jim David	DB	5'11"	172	25	7	
Don Doll	DB	5'10"	185	25	2	
Jim Hill	DB	6'	185	23	1	
Yale Lary	DB	6'	180	21	4	6
Jack Christiansen	HB-DB	6'1"	180	23	2	24
Clyde Scott (from PHI)	HB-DB	6'	175	28	1	
Jim Smith	HB-DB	6'1"	195	27	9	6
Jim Cain — Military Service						
Dorne Dibble — Military Service						
Tom Dublinski	QB	6'2"	190	22		
Jim Hardy	QB	6'	180	30		1
Bobby Layne	QB	6'1"	190	25		8
Byron Bailey	HB	5'10"	185	22		12
Jug Girard	HB	5'11"	175	25		24
Bob Hoernschemeyer	HB	5'11"	195	26		24
Doak Walker	HB	5'11"	173	25		14
Ollie Cline	FB	6'	200	26		6
Pete D'Alonzo	FB	5'10"	210	22		
Pat Harder	FB	5'11"	202	30		85
Cloyce Box	OE	6'4"	220	28		90
Leon Hart	OE	6'5"	262	23		24
Bill Swiacki	OE	6'2"	195	27		6

LOS ANGELES RAMS 9-3-0 Hamp Pool

Scores of Each Game		
7	Cleveland	37
14	DETROIT	17
30	Green Bay	28
16	Detroit	24
31	CHIC. BEARS	7
42	DALLAS	20
27	Dallas	6
40	Chic. Bears	24
35	SAN FRANCISCO	9
34	San Francisco	21
45	GREEN BAY	27
28	PITTSBURGH	14
	Playoff	
21	DETROIT	31

Use Name	Pos.	Hgt	Wgt	Age	Int	Pts
Tom Dahms	OT	6'5"	240	24		
Don Simensen	OT	6'2"	220	25		
Len Teeuws	OT	6'4"	235	25		
Dick Daugherty	OG	6'1"	214	23		
Bill Lange	OG	6'1"	245	25		
Bud McFadin	OG	6'3"	245	24		
Harry Thompson	DE-OG	8'2"	225	25		
Leon McLaughlin	C	6'2"	228	26		
Stan West	DG	6'2"	240	25	1	
Larry Brink	DE	6'5"	240	29		
Andy Robustelli	DE	6'1"	220	26	1	12
Ken Casner	DT	6'2"	245	22		6
Charlie Toogood	DT	6'	233	24		
Jim Winkler	DT	6'2"	248	25		
Duane Putnam	OG-LB	6'	215	24		
Don Paul	C-LB	6'1"	230	27	2	
Tank Younger	HB-FB-LB	6'3"	226	24	2	6
Jack Dwyer	DB	5'11"	176	25	4	12
Night Train Lane	DB	6'1"	190	24	14	14
Herb Rich	DB	5'11"	180	23	8	6
Woodley Lewis	HB-DB	6'	195	27	1	12
Jerry Williams	HB-DB	5'10"	176	28	4	
Norb Hecker	OE-DB	6'2"	190	25	1	
Bob Boyd — Military Service						
George Sims — Military Service						
Don Klosterman	QB	5'10"	180	22		
Norm Van Brocklin	QB	6'1"	200	26		
Bob Waterfield	QB	6'1"	200	32		83
Paul Barry	HB	6'	200	26		6
Carl Mayes	HB	6'	190	22		
Skeets Quinlan	HB	5'11"	175	24		18
Vitamin Smith	HB	5'8"	180	28		36
Jack Myers	FB	6'2"	202	27		6
Dan Towler	FB	6'2"	226	24		60
Bob Carey	OE	6'5"	215	24		12
Tom Fears	OE	6'2"	215	28		36
Crazy Legs Hirsch	OE	6'2"	190	28		24

SAN FRANCISCO FORTY NINERS 7-5-0 Buck Shaw

Scores of Each Game		
17	DETROIT	3
37	Dallas	14
28	Detroit	0
40	Chic. Bears	16
48	DALLAS	21
17	CHIC. BEARS	20
14	New York	23
23	Washington	17
9	Los Angeles	35
21	LOS ANGELES	34
7	PITTSBURGH	24
24	GREEN BAY	14

Use Name	Pos.	Hgt	Wgt	Age	Int	Pts
Rry Collins	DT-OT	5'11"	230	24		
Leo Nomellini	DT-OT	6'3"	265	27		
Bruno Banducci	OG	5'11"	220	30		
Nick Feher	OG	6'	225	25		
Jerry Smith	LB-OG	6'1"	230	22		
Bill Johnson	C	6'3"	240	26		
Ed Henke	DE	6'3"	225	24		
Pat O'Donahue	DE	6'1"	200	22		7
Charley Powell	DE	6'2"	215	20		2
Al Endriss	OE-DE	6'2"	200	23		
Don Campora	DT	6'3"	265	25		
Al Carapella	OT-DT	6'	235	25		
Bob Toneff	OT-DT	6'2"	252	22		
Hardy Brown	LB	6'	196	28	1	
Don Burke	OG-LB	6'	235	26	1	6
Visco Grgich	OG-LB	5'11"	225	29		
Bob Momsen	OG-LB	6'3"	225	22		2
Pete Wismann	C-LB	6'	220	28		
Jim Cason	DB	6'	168	25	2	
Rex Berry	HB-DB	5'11"	180	26	2	
Sam Cathcart	HB-DB	6'	175	27	3	
Lowell Wagner	HB-DB	6'	195	28	6	
Jim Powers	LB-QB-DB	6'	185	24	2	
Verl Lillywhite — Military Service						
Clay Mathews — Military Service						
Pete Schabarum — Military Service						
Dave Sparks — Military Service						
Jim Monachino — Military Service						
Frankie Albert	QB	5'10"	170	32		6
Y. A. Tittle	QB	6'	190	25		
Ben Aldridge	HB	6'	195	25		6
Joe Arenas	HB	5'11"	180	26		6
Hugh McElhenny	HB	6'1"	198	23		60
Johnny Strzykalski	HB	5'9"	190	29		
Bob White	HB	5'11"	174	23		18
J. R. Boone	DB-HB	5'8"	163	26		6
Bob Meyers	FB	6'2"	284	22		
Joe Perry	FB	6'	210	25		48
Norm Standlee	FB	6'2"	240	33		
Bill Jessup	OE	6'1"	200	23		6
Gordie Soltau	OE	6'2"	195	27		94
Billy Wilson	OE	6'3"	195	25		18

GREEN BAY PACKERS 6-6-0 Gene Ronzani

Scores of Each Game		
14	CHIC. BEARS	24
35	WASHINGTON	20
28	LOS ANGELES	30
24	Dallas	14
17	DETROIT	52
12	PHILADELPHIA	10
41	Chic. Bears	28
17	New York	3
42	DALLAS	14
24	Detroit	48
27	Los Angeles	45
14	San Francisco	24

Use Name	Pos.	Hgt	Wgt	Age	Int	Pts
Dick Afflis	OT	6'	250	23		
Steve Dowden	OT	6'2"	235	23		
Bob Dees	DT-OT	6'4"	245	22		
Ray Bray	OG	6'	240	35		
Steve Ruzich	OG	6'2"	225	24		
Dave Stephenson	OG	6'2"	235	26		
Dick Logan	DT-OG	6'2"	225	22		
Jay Rhodemyre	C	6'1"	210	30		
John Martinkovic	DE	6'3"	235	25		12
Ab Wimberly	DE	6'1"	215	26	1	
Dave Hanner	DT	6'2"	245	23		
Tom Johnson	DT	6'2"	230	22		
Howie Ruetz	DT	6'3"	265	24		
Wash Serini	OG-DT-DG	6'2"	240	28		
Deral Teteak	OG-LB	5'10"	210	23	1	
George Schmidt	C-LB	6'2"	230	25		
Bob Forte	HB-LB	6'	205	30	4	
Hal Faverty	C-DE-LB	6'2"	220	25		
Bobby Dillon	DB	6'1"	185	22	4	
Marvin Johnson (from LA)	DB	5'11"	185	24	2	
Ace Loomis	DB	6'1"	190	24	4	6
Dom Moselle	DB	6'	192	26	3	
Dan Sandifer	DB	6'2"	190	25	2	
Clarence Self	DB	5'8"	180	27	1	
Larry Coutre — Military Service						
Len Szafaryn — Military Service						
Clayton Tonnemaker — Military Service						
Babe Parilli	QB	6'1"	190	22		6
Tobin Rote	QB	6'3"	200	24		18
Tony Canadeo	HB	5'11"	190	33		18
Billy Grimes	HB	6'1"	195	25		
Lindy Pearson (from DET)	HB	6'	200	23		
Breezy Reid	HB	5'10"	185	25		24
Bill Robinson	HB	6'	195	23		
Fred Cone	FB	5'11"	198	26		53
Bobby Jack Floyd	FB	6'	210	23		6
Bill Reichardt	FB	5'11"	210	22		26
Billy Howton	OE	6'2"	185	22		78
Jim Keane	OE	6'4"	215	28		6
Bob Mann	OE	5'11"	170	28		36
Carl Elliott	DE-OE	6'4"	215	25		6

CHICAGO BEARS 5-7-0 George Halas

Scores of Each Game		
24	Green Bay	14
10	Chic. Cards	21
38	DALLAS	20
16	SAN FRANCISCO	40
7	Los Angeles	31
20	San Francisco	17
28	GREEN BAY	41
24	LOS ANGELES	40
24	DETROIT	23
23	Dallas at Akron	27
21	Detroit	45
10	CHIC. CARDS	7

Use Name	Pos.	Hgt	Wgt	Age	Int	Pts
Bulldog Turner	OG-OT	6'1"	235	33		
George Connor	LB-OT	6'3"	240	27	2	
Dick Barwegan	OG	6'1"	230	30		
Ed Bradley	OG	6'	215	26		
Bob Moser	C	6'3"	240	23		
Wayne Hansen	OG-C	6'2"	233	24		
Jack Hoffman	DE	6'5"	230	23	1	
Ed Sprinkle	OE-DE	6'1"	207	28		6
Bill Bishop	DT	6'4"	248	21		
Fred Williams	DT	6'4"	250	22	1	
Bob Cross	OT-DT	6'4"	240	21		
Jerry Weatherley	LB	6'5"	220	23	3	
Herman Clark	OG-LB	6'3"	260	21	1	
Frank Dempsey	OG-LB	6'3"	234	27	1	
John Hoffman	OE-LB	6'2"	212	26	2	
Bill George	OG-DT-LB	6'2"	235	21		
Al Campana	HB-DB	5'11"	180	26		
Jim Dooley	HB-DB	6'4"	200	22	5	
Jimmy Lesane	HB-DB	5'10"	172	21		
Billy Stone	HB-DB	6'	194	26	1	24
Don Kindt	FB-DB	6'1"	208	26	3	2
Stu Clarkson — Canadian Football League						
Johnny Lujack — Shoulder Injury						
Steve Romanik	QB	6'1"	190	28		
Bob Williams	QB	6'1"	195	23		
George Blanda	DB-QB	6'1"	200	24		54
Babe Dimancheff	HB	5'11"	175	30		12
George Gulyanics	HB	6'	200	31		
Chuck Hunsinger	HB	6'	188	27		12
Eddie Macon	HB	6'	175	24		12
Wilford White	HB	5'9"	172	24		7
Leon Campbell	FB	6'	197	25		6
Kayo Dottley	FB	6'1"	200	24		24
Curley Morrison	FB	6'2"	215	26		24
Bill McColl	OE	6'4"	230	22		12
Bill Wightkin	DE-OE	6'3"	238	25		12
Gene Schroeder	DB-OE	6'3"	190	23		36

DALLAS TEXANS 1-11-0 Jimmy Phelan

Scores of Each Game		
6	NEW YORK	24
14	SAN FRANCISCO	37
20	Chic. Bears	38
14	GREEN BAY	24
21	San Francisco	48
20	Los Angeles	42
6	LOS ANGELES	27
13	Detroit	43
14	Green Bay	42
27	CHIC. BEARS at Akron	23
21	Philadelphia	38
6	Detroit	41

Use Name	Pos.	Hgt	Wgt	Age	Int	Pts
Ken Jackson	OT	6'2"	225	23		
Jim Lansford	OT	6'3"	235	22		
Hamp Tanner	OT	6'2"	280	25		
Sisto Averno	OG	5'11"	235	26		
Weldon Humble	OG	6'1"	225	31		
George Robison	OG	6'2"	215	21		
John Wozniak	OG	6'	220	31		
Brad Ecklund	C	6'3"	215	30		
Art Tait	DE	5'11"	205	23		
Gino Marchetti	OT-DE	6'4"	235	26		6
Barney Poole	OE-DE	6'2"	225	29		
Joe Campanella	DT	6'2"	235	21		
Don Colo	DT	6'3"	252	27	1	
Art Donovan	DT	6'2"	260	27		
Chubby Grigg	DT	6'2"	280	26		9
Joe Soboleski	DT	8'	210	26		
Pat Cannamela	LB	6'	195	23		8
Keever Jankovich	LB	6'	215	23		
Joe Reid	DG-LB	6'3"	225	22	1	
Keith Flowers	C-LB	6'	211	21	1	3
Jerry Davis	DB	5'10"	180	30	3	6
Dick McKissack	DB	6'2"	208	26		
Will Sherman	DB	6'2"	197	23	1	
Billy Baggett	HB-DB	5'11"	175	23	1	6
Johnny Petitbon	HB-DB	5'11"	185	21	5	
Tom Keane	OE-DB	6'1"	190	25	10	
Stan Williams	OE-DB	6'2"	195	23	5	6
Mike McCormack — Military Service						
Bob Celeri	QB	5'10"	180	25		6
Chuck Ortmann	QB	6'1"	190	23		
Frank Tripucka (from CHI C)	QB	6'2"	180	24		18
Hank Lauricella	HB	5'11"	175	22		
Buddy Young	HB	5'5"	180	26		30
George Taliaferro	QB-HB	5'11"	200	25		12
Dick Hoerner	FB	6'4"	220	30		12
Zollie Toth	FB	6'2"	215	28		24
Dan Edwards	OE	6'1"	195	26		
Gene Felker	OE	6'1"	198	23		6
Ray Pelfrey (to CHI C)	OE	6'	190	24		12
Dick Wilkins	OE	6'2"	195	26		18

DETROIT LIONS

RUSHING

Last Name	No.	Yds	Avg	TD
Hoernschemeyer	106	457	4.3	4
Layne	94	411	4.4	1
Harder	81	244	3.0	2
Girard	61	222	3.6	2
Christiansen	19	148	7.8	2
Walker	26	106	4.1	0
Bailey	19	74	3.9	2
Doran	1	36	36.0	0
Cline	13	36	2.8	1
Hardy	5	16	3.2	0
Smith	3	12	4.0	0
Hart	3	10	3.3	0
D'Alonzo	5	7	1.4	0
Dublinski	1	3	3.0	0
Scott	2	−2	−1.0	0

RECEIVING

Last Name	No.	Yds	Avg	TD
Box	42	924	22	15
Hart	32	376	12	4
Girard	17	316	19	2
Swiacki	17	213	13	1
Hoernschemeyer	17	139	8	0
Harder	14	142	10	1
Walker	11	90	8	0
Doran	10	147	15	1
Christiansen	3	32	11	0
Cline	2	45	23	0
Bailey	2	28	14	0
D'Alonzo	2	4	2	0
Scott	1	21	21	0
Smith	1	18	18	0

PUNT RETURNS

Last Name	No.	Yds	Avg	TD
Christiansen	15	322	21	2
Lary	16	182	11	1
Scott	3	14	5	0
Hill	1	2	2	0

KICKOFF RETURNS

Last Name	No.	Yds	Avg	TD
Christiansen	16	409	26	0
Lary	12	303	25	0
Scott	3	68	23	0
Girard	2	31	16	0
Earon	3	25	8	0
Bailey	1	23	23	0
Hoernschemeyer	1	23	23	0
Miller	1	0	0	0

PASSING – PUNTING – KICKING

PASSING	Att	Comp	%	Yds	Yd/Att	TD	Int–%	RK
Layne	287	139	48	1999	7.0	19	20– 7	6
Hardy	59	28	48	434	7.4	3	5– 8	
Dublinski	6	1	17	39	6.5	0	1–17	
Hoernschemeyer	4	2	50	14	3.5	2	1–25	
Girard	4	0	0	0	0.0	0	0– 0	
Walker	2	1	50	9	4.5	0	1–50	

PUNTING	No	Avg
Smith	61	44.7
Lary	5	36.2

KICKING	XP	Att	%	FG	Att	%
Harder	34	35	97	11	23	48
Walker	5	5	100	3	5	60
Layne	2	2	100	0	0	0
Hardy	1	1	100	0	0	0

LOS ANGELES RAMS

RUSHING

Last Name	No.	Yds	Avg	TD
Towler	156	894	5.7	10
Younger	63	331	5.3	1
Quinlan	52	224	4.3	1
Smith	57	133	2.3	3
Lewis	19	114	6.0	0
Myers	27	82	3.0	1
Williams	11	65	5.9	0
Mayes	5	2	0.4	0
Fears	1	0	0.0	0
Barry	2	−1	−0.5	0
Klosterman	1	−9	−9.0	0
Van Brocklin	7	−10	−1.4	0
Waterfield	9	−14	−1.6	1

RECEIVING

Last Name	No.	Yds	Avg	TD
Fears	48	600	13	6
Carey	36	539	15	1
Hirsch	25	590	24	4
Smith	16	254	16	3
Quinlan	14	265	19	2
Younger	12	73	6	0
Towler	11	68	6	0
Barry	2	43	22	1
Myers	2	1	1	0
Waterfield	1	5	5	0

PUNT RETURNS

Last Name	No.	Yds	Avg	TD
Lewis	19	351	18	2
Quinlan	14	167	12	0
Williams	1	9	9	0
Smith	2	0	0	0
Rich	1	0	0	0
Towler	1	0	0	0

KICKOFF RETURNS

Last Name	No.	Yds	Avg	TD
Quinlan	17	440	26	0
Lewis	16	345	22	0
Smith	5	158	32	0
Towler	1	9	9	0
West	1	0	0	0

PASSING – PUNTING – KICKING

PASSING	Att	Comp	%	Yds	Yd/Att	TD	Int–%	RK
Van Brocklin	205	113	55	1736	8.5	14	17– 8	3
Waterfield	109	51	47	655	6.0	3	11–10	15
Klosterman	10	3	30	47	4.7	0	3– 3	
Quinlan	4	0	0	0	0.0	0	0– 0	
Smith	1	0	0	0	0.0	0	0– 0	

PUNTING	No	Avg
Waterfield	30	42.5
Van Brocklin	29	43.1

KICKING	XP	Att	%	FG	Att	%
Waterfield	44	46	96	11	18	61
Carey	0	0	0	0	1	0

SAN FRANCISCO FORTY-NINERS

RUSHING

Last Name	No.	Yds	Avg	TD
Perry	158	725	4.6	8
McElhenny	98	684	7.0	6
Arenas	44	183	4.2	0
Albert	22	87	4.0	1
Boone	24	72	3.0	0
Strzykalski	16	53	3.3	0
Aldridge	13	36	2.8	0
White	24	33	1.4	1
Cathcart	6	21	3.5	0
Standlee	2	8	4.0	0
Berry	1	7	7.0	0
Nomellini	1	5	5.0	0
Meyers	1	2	2.0	0
Tittle	11	−11	−1.0	0

RECEIVING

Last Name	No.	Yds	Avg	TD
Soltau	55	774	14	7
McElhenny	26	367	14	3
Boone	25	461	18	1
Wilson	23	304	13	3
Perry	15	81	5	0
White	12	173	14	2
Jessup	6	108	18	1
Arenas	5	47	9	1
Aldridge	4	22	6	1
Cathcart	2	15	8	0
Henke	1	13	13	0
Wagner	1	6	6	0
Strzykalski	1	4	4	0
Banducci	1	−4	−4	0

PUNT RETURNS

Last Name	No.	Yds	Avg	TD
McElhenny	20	284	14	1
Boone	11	66	6	0
Arenas	7	40	6	0
Cathcart	1	23	23	0
O'Donahue	1	23	23	1

KICKOFF RETURNS

Last Name	No.	Yds	Avg	TD
McElhenny	18	396	22	0
Arenas	11	291	26	0
Brown	2	31	16	0
Burke	1	25	25	0
Cathcart	1	20	20	0
Nomellini	1	18	18	0
O'Donahue	2	17	9	0

PASSING – PUNTING – KICKING

PASSING	Att	Comp	%	Yds	Yd/Att	TD	Int–%	RK
Tittle	208	106	51	1407	6.8	11	12– 6	6
Albert	129	71	55	964	7.5	8	10– 8	8
Perry	2	0	0	0	0.0	0	0– 0	
Arenas	1	0	0	0	0.0	0	0– 0	
Cathcart	1	0	0	0	0.0	0	1 100	
Powers	1	0	0	0	0.0	0	0– 0	

PUNTING	No	Avg
Albert	68	42.6

KICKING	XP	Att	%	FG	Att	%
Soltau	34	36	94	6	12	50
O'Donahue	1	1	100	0	0	0

GREEN BAY PACKERS

RUSHING

Last Name	No.	Yds	Avg	TD
Rote	58	313	5.4	2
Cone	70	276	3.9	2
Floyd	61	236	3.9	1
Canadeo	65	191	2.9	2
Reid	58	156	2.7	2
Reichardt	39	121	3.1	1
Parilli	32	106	3.3	1
Grimes	17	59	3.5	0
Robinson	3	4	1.3	0
Pearson	5	2	0.4	0
Self	0	21	21.0	0

RECEIVING

Last Name	No.	Yds	Avg	TD
Howton	53	1231	23	13
Mann	30	517	17	6
Keane	18	191	11	1
Reid	12	250	21	2
Elliott	12	114	10	1
Floyd	11	129	12	0
Canadeo	9	86	10	1
Cone	8	98	12	1
Reichardt	5	18	4	0
Rote	1	28	28	1
Pearson	1	16	16	0

PUNT RETURNS

Last Name	No.	Yds	Avg	TD
Grimes	18	179	10	0
Loomis	8	83	10	0
Moselle	7	77	11	0
Dillon	2	22	11	0
Sandifer	2	5	3	0
Canadeo	1	4	4	0

KICKOFF RETURNS

Last Name	No.	Yds	Avg	TD
Grimes	18	422	23	0
Loomis	10	207	21	0
Self	3	85	28	0
Moselle	5	83	17	0
Floyd	5	75	15	0
Canadeo	2	62	31	0
Robinson	2	49	25	0
Cone	2	23	12	0
Dees	1	20	20	0
Reichardt	1	19	19	0
Schmidt	1	14	14	0
Martinkovic	1	0	0	0

PASSING – PUNTING – KICKING

PASSING	Att	Comp	%	Yds	Yd/Att	TD	Int–%	RK
Parilli	177	77	44	1416	8.0	13	17–10	11
Rote	157	82	52	1268	8.1	13	8– 5	1
Forte	2	2	100	4	2.0	0	0– 0	
Canadeo	1	0	0	0	0.0	0	0– 0	

PUNTING	No	Avg
Parilli	65	40.7

KICKING	XP	Att	%	FG	Att	%
Cone	32	34	94	1	1	100
Reichardt	5	5	100	5	20	25

CHICAGO BEARS

RUSHING

Last Name	No.	Yds	Avg	TD
Morrison	95	367	3.9	3
Dottley	65	302	4.6	3
Stone	50	196	3.9	2
Macon	30	194	6.5	1
Hunsinger	58	139	2.4	0
Dimancheff	17	106	6.2	1
Blanda	20	104	5.2	1
Campbell	24	76	3.2	0
B. Williams	11	33	3.0	0
Campana	9	14	1.6	0
Kindt	3	13	4.3	0
Romanik	6	9	1.5	0
Lesane	1	5	5.0	0
Gulyanics	2	4	2.0	0
Dooley	1	0	0.0	0
White	19	−19	−1.0	0

RECEIVING

Last Name	No.	Yds	Avg	TD
Schroeder	39	660	17	6
McColl	20	277	14	2
Hunsinger	16	170	11	2
Stone	13	283	22	2
Morrison	10	129	13	1
Dottley	9	113	13	1
White	8	152	19	0
Macon	8	25	3	0
Wightkin	7	120	17	2
Dimancheff	5	69	1	1
Campbell	2	1	1	0
Jo. Hoffman	1	9	9	0
Campana	1	3	3	0
Sprinkle	1	2	2	1
Turner	1	2	2	0

PUNT RETURNS

Last Name	No.	Yds	Avg	TD
White	23	117	5	0
Macon	7	74	11	0
Lesane	9	25	3	0
Kindt	1	7	7	0
Dimancheff	1	0	0	0

KICKOFF RETURNS

Last Name	No.	Yds	Avg	TD
Hunsinger	15	308	21	0
Macon	9	299	33	1
White	5	134	27	0
Dimancheff	4	110	28	0
Campbell	2	106	53	1
Morrison	4	41	10	0
Stone	2	40	20	0
Sprinkle	4	39	10	0
Jo. Hoffman	2	34	17	0
Turner	1	29	29	0
McColl	1	0	0	0

PASSING – PUNTING – KICKING

PASSING	Att	Comp	%	Yds	Yd/Att	TD	Int–%	RK
Blanda	131	47	36	664	5.1	8	11– 8	14
Romanik	126	49	39	772	6.1	4	11– 9	15
B. Williams	87	45	52	579	6.7	6	5– 6	
White	2	0	0	0	0.0	0	0– 0	
Lesane	1	0	0	0	0.0	0	0– 0	

PUNTING	No	Avg
Morrison	64	42.3
Williams	2	45.0

KICKING	XP	Att	%	FG	Att	%
Blanda	30	30	100	6	25	24
White	1	1	100	2	3	67

DALLAS TEXANS

RUSHING

Last Name	No.	Yds	Avg	TD
Taliaferro	100	419	4.2	1
Toth	82	266	3.2	4
Young	71	243	3.4	3
Hoerner	56	162	2.9	2
Celeri	17	135	7.9	0
Baggett	19	65	3.4	0
Lauricella	19	55	2.9	0
Tripucka	10	25	2.5	3
Ortmann	8	24	3.0	0

RECEIVING

Last Name	No.	Yds	Avg	TD
Wilkins	32	416	13	3
Young	22	269	12	2
Taliaferro	21	244	12	1
Pelfrey	20	264	13	2
Toth	13	54	4	0
Hoerner	10	172	17	0
Williams	9	123	14	0
Felker	6	63	11	1
Celeri	4	37	9	1
Keane	3	73	24	0
Baggett	3	41	14	1
Edwards	3	22	7	0
Poole	2	23	12	0
Marchetti	1	17	17	1
Petitbon	1	11	11	0
Wozniak	1	−1	−1	0

PUNT RETURNS

Last Name	No.	Yds	Avg	TD
Baggett	13	102	9	0
Young	6	35	6	0
Davis	1	11	11	0
Keane	1	8	8	0
Taliaferro	1	4	4	0

KICKOFF RETURNS

Last Name	No.	Yds	Avg	TD
Young	23	643	28	0
Baggett	23	567	25	0
Taliaferro	6	146	24	0
Jankovich	3	45	15	0
Campanella	3	40	13	0
Pelfrey	2	34	17	0
Hoerner	1	33	33	0
Lauricella	1	26	26	0
Tanner	1	19	19	0
Toth	1	18	18	0
Humble	1	17	17	0
Reid	1	17	17	0
Petitbon	1	11	11	0
Wozniak	1	4	4	0
Tait	1	0	0	0

PASSING – PUNTING – KICKING

PASSING	Att	Comp	%	Yds	Yd/Att	TD	Int–%	RK
Tripucka	186	91	49	809	4.3	3	17– 9	13
Celeri	75	31	40	490	6.5	3	3– 4	
Taliaferro	63	16	25	298	4.7	2	6–10	
Lauricella	22	11	50	177	8.1	4	2– 9	
Ortmann	15	5	33	73	4.9	0	1– 7	
Young	3	0	0	0	0.0	0	1–33	

PUNTING	No	Avg
Lauricella	58	35.1
Tripucka	36	36.7
Celeri	21	41.7

KICKING	XP	Att	%	FG	Att	%
Grigg	9	12	75	0	3	0
Cannamela	8	10	80	0	1	0
Flowers	3	5	60	0	0	0

1953 Bring on the Defense

This season's rookie class sprouted no spectacular runners or passers, but blockers and defenders who would star in the league for years made a mass debut. Offensive linemen like Rosey Brown, Jack Stroud, Ray Wietecha, Bob St. Clair, Jim Ringo, Harley Sewell, and Charlie Ane and defensive behemoths like Joe Schmidt, Doug Atkins, Big Daddy Lipscomb, Dick Modzelewski, and Bill Pellington excited crowds with the violence of their crunching blocks and punishing tackles. The offense had dominated the game in recent years, but now the defense was getting some brawny reinforcements to help it catch up.

The league itself got some help from the courts and from the citizens of Baltimore. Federal Judge Allan K. Grim ruled that the TV blackout of home games did not violate the anti-trust laws, thus giving legal approval to Commissioner Bert Bell's television policy. The citizens of Baltimore did their share to help the NFL by buying 15,000 season's tickets for the new Baltimore Colts, who took the place of the wandering Dallas Texans. With Carroll Rosenbloom at the head of the organization, the Colts drew an average attendance of 28,000 and gave the league twelve solid franchises. The Baltimore renaissance helped boost the total NFL attendance 5 percent more to another new record of 2,164,585. The one tragic footnote to the year came in March when Jim Thorpe, pro football's first superstar and its first league president, passed away.

EASTERN CONFERENCE

Cleveland Browns—Owner and founder Mickey McBride sold the team to Dave R. Jones, but the Browns kept right on winning under the new regime. Now at the peak of his powers, quarterback Otto Graham picked defenses apart like a safecracker and shot his arrow passes like another William Tell picking off apples. Mac Speedie jumped to the Canadian League, but Dante Lavelli still hauled in Graham's passes regularly. In addition, young halfback Ray Renfro showed talent both as a receiver and a runner. With Marion Motley's bad knees bothering him, Chick Jagade answered the call to duty at fullback, and the Cleveland defense as always was tough. The Browns rolled through their first eleven games in blitzkreig fashion, but let up and dropped their finale 42-27 to the Eagles.

Philadelphia Eagles—When offensive end Bud Grant skipped up to Canada to play and eventually to begin a coaching career, Eagle pilot Jim Trimble replaced him by using Pete Pihos mostly on offense. A tough character who had played a lot at defensive end, Pihos nonetheless had sure hands which sucked in any passes thrown his way. With Pihos and Bobby Walston at the ends, quarterback Bobby Thomason kept the Eagles moving with a flood of passes. The defense, featuring pass-rushing Norm Willey and hard-tackling Chuck Bednarik, improved on last year's performance, and only an outstanding year by the Browns kept the surprising Eagles off the Eastern throne.

Washington Redskins—The world saw one last glimpse of Curly Lambeau's genius as he molded the Redskins into a very tough outfit down the stretch. Of the final six games, Washington won four and lost the other two by a grand total of four points. Lambeau used Eddie LeBaron at quarterback but kept the little man alive by spelling him often with rookie Jack Scarbath. Halfback Choo-Choo Justice pleasantly surprised the team by looking like the runner he was in college instead of like the lackluster pro he had been. Sparked by end Gene Brito, rookie tackle Dick Modzelewski, linebacker Chuck Drazenovich, and cornerback Don Doll, the defense shone in the second half of the season, with a 10-0 shutout of the Eagles. That triumph was Lambeau's 231st NFL victory and his last.

Pittsburgh Steelers—Owner Art Rooney still was waiting for his first NFL title after twenty-one years in the league. After World War II, Jock Sutherland had almost made it to the top with a hard-running single-wing attack, and now coach Joe Bach had the Steelers throwing the ball around the clock from the T-formation. Bach, unfortunately, did not even get as close as did Sutherland, with this club reaching the break-even point only by winning its last two games. After a good start, the offense had bogged down, so the defense had to carry the team to those final two victories.

New York Giants—Despite a fine catch of raw material for the offensive line in rookies Rosey Brown, Jack Stroud, and Ray Wietecha, the Giants were far from a finished masterpiece. With workhorse fullback Eddie Price hurt, the New York offense ground to a halt, with Sonny Grandelius, Kyle Rote, and Frank Gifford hardly able to take up the slack. The Giants put only 30 points on the scoreboard in their opening three losses, which shot all their hopes to pieces. Injuries and Ray Poole's jumping to Canada plagued the defense, and young Gifford often found himself going both ways as a running back and cornerback, wearing himself ragged in the process. One week from the end came the crowning humiliation, a 62-14 shellacking by the Cleveland Browns. The Mara family, owners and operators of the club, took action after the season by firing Steve Owen as coach after over thirty-one years at the helm, closing the book on a large chapter in Giant history.

Chicago Cardinals—Joe Stydahar's only previous port of call as a head coach had been at Los Angeles, where his Rams always finished on top. He was thus hardly prepared for the situation of the Chicago Cardinals, who won only a single game all year. Stydahar tried to install the same free-wheeling passing attack he had used in Los Angeles, but his passer here was neither Norm Van Brocklin nor Bob Waterfield but instead a very average quarterback named Jim Root. The only speed on the team marched off into the Army in the person of Ollie Matson, leaving Stydahar with no game-breaker to spark the attack. Through eleven games the Cards were winless, although they did manage a very satisfying tie against the coach's old charges, the Rams. But the Cards did save the best for last, whipping the Bears 24-17 in the finale to avoid a shutout for the year.

WESTERN CONFERENCE

Detroit Lions—Even though they were the defending champions, the Lions signed an immensely talented bunch of rookies. Offensive linemen Harley Sewell, Charlie Ane, and Ollie Spencer, tough linebacker Joe Schmidt, and halfback Gene Gedman all fit right in with this winning club. In addition, all the key veterans returned to drive for another title. Bobby Layne still ran the offense and inspired his teammates with his infectious enthusiasm, Bob Hoernschemeyer and Doak Walker again gave the club a pair of versatile halfbacks, and Lou Creekmur and Dick Stanfel kept up their good work in the offensive line. On defense, Les Bingaman guided his 300-pound body with an uncanny knack for smelling out plays, while Jack Christiansen had a nose for picking off enemy passes.

San Francisco '49ers—The '49ers jumped off to early wins over the Eagles and Rams but ran into disaster in their next game against the Lions. On a quarterback keeper play near the goal line, passer Y.A. Tittle was knocked out of action with a triple fracture of his cheekbone. Defensive back Jim Powers doubled as the back-up quarterback, and while he could not avoid a 24-21 loss to the Lions, he did drive his team to a 35-28 victory the next week against the Bears. In the rematch with the Lions, however, Detroit triumphed 14-10, practically ending San Francisco's title hopes

Los Angeles Rams—Even with Bob Waterfield retired, the Rams felt strong enough to grab the Western Conference title back from the Lions, and they proved their point by beating Detroit in both their meetings. The only problem was that the Rams couldn't reach the same peak effort in all their games. They lost twice to San Francisco, once to the Bears, and settled for a tie with the lowly Cardinals. At their best, though, the Rams were a spectacularly exciting football team, with Norm Van Brocklin, Dan Towler, Skeets Quinlan, and Crazy Legs Hirsch the stars on offense and Andy Robustelli, Big Daddy Lipscomb, Don Paul, and Night Train Lane the defensive standouts.

Chicago Bears—No doubt about it, this was the worst Bear team ever. Bulldog Turner had retired, leaving none of the 1940-41 champions in action for this dismal 3-8-1 season, while the George Halas well of talent had dried up. Although there were a few good players, such as George Connor, Jim Dooley, Bill George, and Ed Sprinkle, they were scattered like diamonds in a pigsty. The once powerful backfield had no runners of note and an erratic quarterback in George Blanda, whose kicks hit the mark more often than his passes. On defense, the secondary especially needed patching up. But even with all these holes, the Bears still could recapture their old glory on occasion, as when they dealt a fatal blow to Los Angeles' title hopes by knocking the Rams off 24-21 late in the year.

Baltimore Colts—Only thirteen Dallas players caught on with the Colts, but among them were All-Pro cornerback Tom Keane and defensive linemen Gino Marchetti and Art Donovan, both of whom would be around when the team started winning championships. The Colts began the season in fine fashion, beating the Bears 13-9 as cornerback Bert Rechichar ran a George Blanda interception back 39 yards for a touchdown and also kicked a record 56-yard field goal in his first NFL attempt. The Colts slipped back into the pack by losing their last seven games, but this time the Colts were here to stay.

Green Bay Packers—The Packers fell back into last place, and the executive committee openly second-guessed coach Gene Ronzani at every opportunity. Certain members of the committee even asked players what they thought the coach was doing wrong. The players backed up their coach, but the turmoil did not help a team that was weak to start with. Finally, with two games left on the schedule, the committee fired Ronzani, issuing a statement that he had resigned. Assistants Chuck Drulis, Hugh Devore, and Ray McLean were appointed to take over, but after three days the committee dropped Drulis from the triumvirate.

FINAL TEAM STATISTICS

OFFENSE

	BALT.	CHI.B.	CHI.C.	CLEVE.	DET.	G.BAY	L.A.	N.Y.	PHIL.	PITT.	S.F.	WASH.
FIRST DOWNS:												
Total	157	214	184	213	206	189	214	166	256	206	243	181
by Rushing	75	79	75	79	105	93	105	66	97	98	128	90
by Passing	66	119	95	122	96	79	104	87	144	97	99	82
by Penalty	16	16	14	12	5	17	5	13	15	11	16	9
RUSHING:												
Number	376	367	322	379	427	424	426	398	410	432	443	413
Yards	1459	1129	1179	1577	1812	1665	2148	1049	1722	1549	2230	1726
Average Yards	3.9	3.1	3.7	4.2	4.2	3.9	5.0	2.6	4.2	3.6	5.0	4.2
Touchdowns	7	9	7	20	12	14	23	6	22	13	26	10
PASSING:												
Attempts	319	446	408	303	316	352	324	345	438	416	322	278
Completions	126	206	181	191	144	147	173	158	224	189	174	107
Completion Percentage	39.5	46.2	44.4	63.0	45.6	41.8	53.4	45.8	51.1	45.4	54.0	38.5
Gross Yards	1625	2637	2191	3059	2309	1833	2672	1985	3357	2014	2407	1736
Yards Lost Tackled	368	138	328	245	163	278	107	274	268	164	239	228
Net Yards	1257	2499	1863	2814	2146	1555	2565	1711	3089	1850	2168	1508
Avg. Yards per Attempt (Gross)	5.1	5.9	5.4	10.1	7.3	5.2	8.2	5.8	7.7	4.8	7.5	6.2
Avg. Yards per Comp. (Gross)	12.9	12.8	12.1	16.0	16.0	12.5	15.4	12.6	15.0	10.7	13.8	16.2
Touchdowns	13	15	14	16	18	9	19	16	25	10	22	12
Interceptions	27	30	27	9	27	34	18	34	31	21	19	29
Percent Intercepted	8.5	6.7	6.6	3.0	8.5	9.7	5.6	9.9	7.1	5.0	5.9	10.4
PUNTS:												
Number	83	66	76	63	68	80	60	86	53	80	42	68
Average Yards	38.4	42.6	41.6	43.8	40.6	37.6	42.2	39.2	42.4	46.9	40.6	38.5
PUNT RETURNS:												
Number	29	38	50	43	35	39	55	55	46	50	33	36
Yards	184	143	349	175	233	348	326	334	166	269	250	306
Average Yards	6.3	4.0	7.0	4.1	6.7	8.9	5.9	6.1	3.6	5.4	7.6	8.5
Touchdowns	1	0	0	0	1	1	1	0	0	0	0	0
KICKOFF RETURNS:												
Number	53	48	50	30	43	56	48	41	37	44	43	41
Yards	1258	1089	1120	579	926	1197	1136	1077	787	1101	1105	797
Average Yards	23.7	22.7	22.4	19.3	21.5	21.4	23.7	26.3	21.3	25.0	25.7	19.4
Touchdowns	1	0	0	0	0	0	0	0	0	1	0	0
INTERCEPTION RETURNS:												
Number	29	14	24	25	38	28	30	23	24	21	23	27
Yards	308	292	439	246	663	351	417	412	299	273	388	247
Average Yards	10.6	20.9	18.3	9.8	17.4	12.5	13.9	17.9	12.5	13.0	16.9	9.1
Touchdowns	1	1	2	1	2	2	3	1	1	1	1	2
PENALTIES:												
Number	69	61	73	86	52	67	73	44	84	54	90	49
Yards	623	530	611	680	427	624	597	411	779	546	772	408
FUMBLES:												
Number	34	32	39	27	24	29	32	19	37	28	28	31
Number Lost	21	21	21	15	15	14	22	9	15	14	19	18
POINTS:												
Total	182	218	190	348	271	200	366	179	352	211	372	208
PAT Attempts	23	27	23	40	33	25	48	24	49	28	49	25
PAT Made	21	27	23	39	31	23	45	22	46	27	48	25
FG Attempts	18	21	24	26	23	16	25	12	15	12	18	22
FG Made	7	7	9	23	14	5	11	3	4	4	10	11
Percent FG Made	38.9	33.3	37.5	88.5	60.9	31.3	44.0	25.0	26.7	33.3	55.6	50.0
Safeties	1	1	1	0	0	0	0	2	0	2	0	0

DEFENSE

	BALT.	CHI.B.	CHI.C.	CLEVE.	DET.	G.BAY	L.A.	N.Y.	PHIL.	PITT.	S.F.	WASH.
FIRST DOWNS:												
Total	232	213	216	206	194	199	194	189	186	184	206	210
by Rushing	121	94	95	89	91	95	91	81	69	63	99	102
by Passing	95	109	111	101	96	91	92	99	98	110	95	93
by Penalty	16	10	10	16	7	13	11	9	19	11	12	15
RUSHING:												
Number	445	437	440	374	404	407	375	385	331	366	398	455
Yards	2315	1776	1662	1560	1580	1746	1570	1360	1117	1125	1548	1886
Average Yards	5.2	4.1	3.8	4.2	3.9	4.3	4.2	3.5	3.4	3.1	3.9	4.1
Touchdowns	21	15	24	11	10	24	10	12	6	9	12	15
PASSING:												
Attempts	321	364	341	389	354	312	366	368	374	372	356	350
Completions	165	174	176	164	159	144	161	173	167	193	173	171
Completion Percentage	51.4	47.8	51.6	42.2	44.9	46.2	44.0	47.0	44.7	51.9	48.6	48.9
Gross Yards	2411	2530	2619	2271	2162	2341	2181	2558	2289	2413	2100	1950
Yards Lost Tackled	240	154	255	256	197	236	299	177	408	157	223	198
Net Yards	2171	2376	2364	2015	1965	2105	1882	2381	1881	2256	1877	1752
Avg. Yards per Attempt (Gross)	7.5	7.0	7.7	5.8	6.1	7.5	6.0	6.5	6.1	6.5	5.9	5.6
Avg. Yards per Comp. (Gross)	14.6	14.5	14.9	13.8	13.6	16.3	13.5	14.8	13.7	12.5	12.1	11.4
Touchdowns	21	14	17	10	13	15	15	20	17	22	17	8
Interceptions	29	14	24	25	38	28	30	23	24	21	23	27
Percent Intercepted	9.0	3.8	7.0	6.4	10.7	9.0	8.2	6.3	6.4	5.6	6.5	7.7
PUNTS:												
Number	55	73	74	72	62	66	75	72	79	83	60	54
Average Yards	40.3	36.5	42.0	40.8	40.4	41.7	40.5	43.0	42.5	42.5	41.0	41.7
PUNT RETURNS:												
Number	40	34	44	35	41	41	45	69	45	50	27	38
Yards	307	234	68	156	275	232	356	521	257	403	109	165
Average Yards	7.7	6.9	1.5	4.5	6.7	5.7	7.9	7.6	5.7	8.1	4.0	4.3
Touchdowns	1	1	0	0	1	1	0	0	0	0	0	0
KICKOFF RETURNS:												
Number	40	36	35	46	54	40	59	36	49	37	59	43
Yards	724	844	852	1114	1193	851	1600	705	1208	604	1264	1213
Average Yards	18.1	23.4	24.3	24.2	22.1	21.3	27.1	19.6	24.7	16.3	21.4	28.2
Touchdowns	0	0	0	0	0	0	0	1	1	0	0	0
INTERCEPTION RETURNS:												
Number	27	30	27	9	27	34	18	34	31	21	19	29
Yards	469	449	202	94	426	407	373	526	351	373	204	461
Average Yards	17.4	15.0	7.5	10.4	15.8	12.0	20.7	15.5	11.3	17.8	10.7	15.9
Touchdowns	3	3	0	1	2	2	2	1	1	1	0	2
PENALTIES:												
Number	87	79	72	40	53	84	51	68	63	66	71	68
Yards	757	711	615	335	463	617	465	625	606	603	615	596
FUMBLES:												
Number	42	34	23	25	31	28	22	32	27	29	33	34
Number Lost	27	23	12	16	15	19	13	14	17	14	17	17
POINTS:												
Total	350	262	337	162	205	338	236	277	215	263	237	215
PAT Attempts	46	33	45	22	26	43	29	35	27	33	30	25
PAT Made	45	31	43	20	23	41	27	34	26	32	30	25
FG Attempts	16	30	13	13	19	22	23	20	18	19	16	23
FG Made	9	11	8	2	6	11	11	9	9	11	9	12
Percent FG Made	56.3	36.7	61.5	15.4	31.6	50.0	47.8	45.0	50.0	57.9	56.3	52.2
Safeties	1	0	0	2	1	0	1	0	0	0	0	2

1953 CHAMPIONSHIP GAME

December 27 at Detroit
(Attendance 54,577)

Throwing It Up and Away

Even with Otto Graham suffering through his worst day as a professional, the Browns battled the Lions evenly through most of the game. Graham's long afternoon of frustration began when Lavern Torgeson made him fumble deep in his own territory on the first series of downs in the game. Les Bingaman recovered the ball on the 13-yard line, and the Lions took six plays to cover that distance, with Doak Walker crashing over from the 1-yard line. The Browns returned the favor by recovering a Detroit fumble on the Lion 6-yard line, but they had to settle for three points on a Lou Groza field goal. Late in the second quarter, Jim David picked off a Graham pass, and Doak Walker converted this turnover into three points with a 23-yard field goal. Trailing 10-3 at halftime, the Browns quickly tied the game up in the third period. Ken Gorgal intercepted a Bobby Layne pass and returned it to the Cleveland 49; the Browns then covered 51 yards in eight plays, with only one pass in the drive. Neither team could break the 10-10 deadlock in the third quarter, but Lou Groza booted a 15-yard field goal forty-four seconds into the final period to put the Browns ahead 13-10. Detroit's bid to tie the game failed when Walker's 33-yard field-goal attempt sailed wide, and Groza added another three-pointer with less than five minutes left in the game to make the score 16-10. After Groza kicked the ball into the end zone for a touchback, Bobby Layne marched his club downfield on a winning drive. He hit Jim Doran with a pass good for 17 yards, and after two incompleted passes he again threw to Doran, this time for 18 yards. Cloyce Box then hauled in a pass for 9 yards, and after Bob Hoernschemeyer failed to get the first down, Layne picked up 3 yards on a keeper play. With a first down on the Cleveland 33, Layne then hit Doran with a deep pass that carried all the way to the end zone. Doak Walker's extra point gave the Lions a 17-16 lead with two minutes left, and Otto Graham's first pass was intercepted to insure defeat for the Browns in the championship game for the third consecutive year.

SCORING

DETROIT	7	3	0	7	–17
CLEVELAND	0	3	7	6	–16

First Quarter
Det. Walker, 1 yard rush; PAT – Walker (kick) 4:05

Second Quarter
Cle. Groza, 13 yard FG 0:09
Det. Walker, 23 yard FG 13:45

Third Quarter
Cle. Jagade, 9 yard rush; PAT – Groza (kick) 6:48

Fourth Quarter
Cle. Groza, 15 yard FG 0:44
Cle. Groza, 43 yard FG 10:50
Det. Doran, 33 yard pass from Layne; PAT – Walker (kick) 12:52

TEAM STATISTICS

DET.		CLE.
18	First Downs – Total	11
10	by Rushing	9
7	by Passing	1
1	by Penalty	1
3	Fumbles – Number	2
2	Times Lost Ball	2
4	Penalties – Number	4
50	Yards Penalized	30
4	Giveaways	4
4	Takeaways	4
0	Difference	0

INDIVIDUAL STATISTICS

RUSHING

DETROIT	No.	Yds	Avg.	CLEVELAND	No.	Yds	Avg.
Horn'meyer	17	47	2.8	Jagade	15	104	6.9
Layne	11	46	4.2	Jones	3	28	9.3
Gedman	8	29	3.6	Reynolds	6	16	2.7
Walker	3	7	2.3	Carpenter	3	14	4.7
	39	129	3.3	Renfro	4	11	2.8
				Graham	5	9	1.8
					36	182	5.1

RECEIVING

DETROIT	No.	Yds	Avg.	CLEVELAND	No.	Yds	Avg.
Doran	4	95	23.8	Jagade	1	18	18.0
Box	4	54	13.5	Lavelli	1	13	13.0
Horn'meyer	2	–2	–1.0	Reynolds	1	7	7.0
Dibble	1	22	22.0		3	38	12.7
Walker	1	10	10.0				
	12	179	14.9				

PUNTING

DETROIT	No	Avg	CLEVELAND	No.	Avg.
Lary	4	49.3	Gillom	5	42.6

PUNT RETURNS

DETROIT	No.	Yds	Avg.	CLEVELAND	No.	Yds	Avg.
None				Reynolds	2	32	16.0
				Carpenter	1	3	3.0
					3	35	11.7

KICKOFF RETURNS

DETROIT	No.	Yds	Avg.	CLEVELAND	No.	Yds	Avg.
Girard	2	39	19.5	Jagade	1	29	29.0
Walker	1	7	7.0	Reynolds	1	21	21.0
	3	46	15.3	Carpenter	1	18	18.0
				Young	1	2	2.0
					4	70	17.5

INTERCEPTION RETURNS

DETROIT	No.	Yds	Avg.	CLEVELAND	No.	Yds	Avg.
David	1	36	36.0	Gorgal	2	9	4.5
Karilivacz	1	12	12.0				
	2	48	24.0				

PASSING

	Att	Comp	Comp Pct.	Yds	Yds/ Att.	Yds/ Comp	Yds Lost Tackled
Detroit							
Layne	25	12	48.0	179	7.2	14.9	
Walker	1	0	0.0	0	–	–	
	26	12	46.2	179	6.9	14.9	2–15
Cleveland							
Graham	15	2	13.3	20	1.3	10.0	
Ratterman	1	1	100.0	18	18.0	18.0	
	16	3	18.8	38	2.4	12.7	3–28

CLEVELAND BROWNS 11-1-0 Paul Brown

Scores of Each Game		
27	Green Bay	0
27	Chic. Cards	7
37	PHILADELPHIA	13
30	Washington	14
7	New York	0
27	WASHINGTON	3
34	PITTSBURGH	16
23	SAN FRANCISCO	21
20	Pittsburgh	16
27	Chic. Cards	16
62	NEW YORK	14
27	Philadelphia	42

Use Name	Pos.	Hgt	Wgt	Age	Int	Pts
Lou Groza	OT	6'3"	240	29		108
John Sandusky	OT	6'1"	258	27		
Don Steinbrunner	OT	6'3"	220	21		
Gene Donaldson	OG	5'9"	215	23		
Abe Gibron	OG	5'11"	245	27		
Lin Houston	OG	6'	225	32		
Chuck Noll	OG	6'1"	218	21		
Frank Gatski	C	6'3"	240	31		
Bill Willis	DG	6'2"	218	32		
Doug Atkins	DE	6'8"	250	23		
Len Ford	DE	6'4"	254	27	1	
George Young	DE	6'3"	220	29		
Don Colo	DT	6'3"	258	28		
Jerry Helluin	DT	6'2"	292	23		6
Darrell Palmer	DT	6'2"	242	31		
Walt Michaels	LB	6'	232	24	1	6
Tommy Thompson	LB	6'1"	227	26	2	
Tom Catlin	C-LB	6'1"	210	22	1	
Ken Gorgal	DB	6'2"	200	24	4	
Tommy James	DB	5'10"	185	29	5	6
Kenny Konz	DB	5'10"	182	25	5	
Warren Lahr	DB	5'11"	192	29	5	
Sherman Howard	HB-DB	5'11"	196	29	1	
Otto Graham	QB	6'1"	200	31		36
George Ratterman	QB	6'1"	182	26		
Ken Carpenter	HB	6'	195	27		30
Dub Jones	HB	6'4"	200	28		
Ray Renfro	HB	6'1"	185	22		54
Billy Reynolds	HB	5'10"	188	21		18
Chick Jagade	FB	6'	220	26		24
Marion Motley	LB-FB	6'1"	238	33		
Darrell Brewster	OE	6'3"	205	23		24
Dante Lavelli	OE	6'	192	30		36
Horace Gillom	DE-OE	6'1"	225	32		

Tony Adamle – Voluntarily Retired
Bob Gain – Military Service
John Kissell – Canadian Football League
Joe Skibinski – Military Service
Mac Speedie – Canadian Football League

PHILADELPHIA EAGLES 7-4-1 Jim Trimble

Scores of Each Game		
21	San Francisco	31
21	WASHINGTON	21
13	Cleveland	37
23	PITTSBURGH	7
56	Chic. Cards	17
35	Pittsburgh	7
30	NEW YORK	7
45	BALTIMORE	14
38	CHIC. CARDS	0
28	New York	37
0	Washington	10
42	CLEVELAND	27

Use Name	Pos.	Hgt	Wgt	Age	Int	Pts
Lum Snyder	OT	6'5"	230	23		
Frank Wydo	OT	6'4"	235	29		
George Mrkonic	DT-OT	6'2"	225	24		
John Magee	OG	5'10"	220	30		
John Michels	OG	5'11"	200	22		
Maury Nipp	OG	6'	218	23		
Ken Farragut	LB-C	6'4"	245	25		
Bucko Kilroy	DG	6'2"	245	32		
Tom Scott	DE	6'2"	210	23		6
Norm Willey	DE	6'2"	225	26		
Willie Irvin	OE-DE	6'3"	203	23		
Mike Jarmoluk	DT	6'5"	250	30	1	
Jess Richardson	DT	6'2"	235	23		
Vic Sears	DT	6'3"	220	35		
Wayne Robinson	LB	6'2"	220	23		
Ebert Van Buren	LB	6'2"	210	28	1	
Chuck Bednarik	C-LB	6'3"	230	28	6	6
Bob Stringer	FB-LB	6'1"	193	23	1	
Tom Brookshier	DB	6'	185	21	8	
Russ Craft	DB	5'9"	175	33	4	
Bob Hudson	DB	6'4"	220	23	3	
Al Pollard	FB-DB	6'	195	25		1
Adrian Burk	QB	6'2"	190	25		18
Bob Gambold	QB	6'4"	215	23		
Bobby Thomason	QB	6'1"	193	24		6
Skippy Giancanelli	HB	5'10"	173	24		36
Don Johnson	HB	6'	187	22		42
Toy Ledbetter	HB	5'10"	200	26		18
Jerry Williams	HB	5'10"	176	29		24
Frank Ziegler	HB	5'11"	176	29		30
John Brewer	FB	6'4"	230	25		6
Jim Parmer	DB-FB	6'	195	26		12
Bob Schnelker	OE	6'3"	208	23		
Bobby Walston	OE	6'	188	24		87
Pete Pihos	DE-OE	6'1"	212	29		60

Bibbles Bawel – Military Service
Ralph Goldston – Broken Leg
Bud Grant – Canadian Football League
Roscoe Hansen – Military Service
Bill Horrell – Military Service
Ray Romero – Military Service

WASHINGTON REDSKINS 6-5-1 Curly Lambeau

Scores of Each Game		
24	Chic. Cards	13
21	Philadelphia	21
13	NEW YORK	9
14	CLEVELAND	30
17	Baltimore	27
3	Cleveland	27
28	CHIC. CARDS	17
24	CHIC. BEARS	27
24	New York	21
17	Pittsburgh	9
10	PHILADELPHIA	0
13	PITTSBURGH	14

Use Name	Pos.	Hgt	Wgt	Age	Int	Pts
Don Boll	OT	6'2"	265	26		
Ted Hazelwood	OT	6'1"	235	29		
Laurie Niemi	DT-OT	6'1"	257	28		6
Slug Witucki	OG	5'11"	245	25		
Gene Pepper	OG	6'2"	242	26		
Jim Clark	OT-DT-LB-OG	6'1"	230	24		
Harry Ulinski	C	6'4"	225	28		
Jim Ricca	OT-DT-DG	6'4"	268	26		
Jerry Hennessey	DE	6'2"	224	27		
Bill Hegarty (from PIT)	DT-DE	6'4"	240	23		
Joe Tereshinski	LB-DE	6'2"	220	29		
Gene Brito	OE-DE	6'1"	223	27		
Don Campora	DT	6'3"	270	26		
Paul Lipscomb	DT	6'5"	250	30		
Dick Modzelewski	DT	6'	248	22		
Knox Ramsey	OG-LB	6'1"	222	27		
Al DeMao	C-LB	6'2"	220	33		
Jack Cloud	FB-LB	5'10"	222	28	2	6
Chuck Drazenovich	FB-LB	6'1"	222	26		6
Dick Alban	DB	6'1"	190	24	4	
Don Doll	DB	5'10"	185	26	10	
Johnny Williams	DB	5'11"	180	26	6	
Harry Dowda	HB-DB	6'2"	200	29	5	6
Hall Haynes	HB-DB	6'	190	24		
Eddie LeBaron	QB	5'9"	168	23		12
Jack Scarbath	QB	6'2"	205	23		
Paul Barry	HB	6'	210	27		
Bill Dudley	HB	5'10"	175	32		58
Choo-Choo Justice	HB	5'10"	175	29		24
Johnny Papit (to GB)	HB	6'	190	25		6
Julie Rykovich	HB	6'2"	210	29		6
Sam Baker	FB	6'2"	210	21		6
Leon Heath	FB	6'1"	208	25		24
Paul Dekker	OE	6'5"	220	22		6
Fran Polsfoot	OE	6'3"	210	26		
Hugh Taylor	OE	6'4"	190	30		48

Billy Cox – Military Service
Rob Goode – Military Service
Walt Yowarsky – Military Service
Harry Gilmer – Injury

PITTSBURGH STEELERS 6-6-0 Joe Bach

Scores of Each Game		
21	Detroit	38
24	NEW YORK	14
31	CHIC. CARDS	28
7	Philadelphia	23
31	GREEN BAY	14
7	PHILADELPHIA	35
16	Cleveland	34
14	New York	10
16	CLEVELAND	20
9	WASHINGTON	17
21	Chic. Cards	17
14	Washington	13

Use Name	Pos.	Hgt	Wgt	Age	Int	Pts
George Hughes	OT	6'1"	225	28		
Bob Gaona	DT-OT	6'3"	235	23		
Marv McFadden	OG	6'	215	23		
John Schweder	LB-OG	6'1"	225	26		
Lou Tepe	C	6'2"	205	23		
Bill Walsh	C	6'2"	225	26		
John Alderton	DE	6'1"	200	22		
Bill McPeak	DE	6'1"	200	28		
George Tarasovic	DE	6'4"	240	24		
Lou Ferry	DT	6'2"	245	26		2
Tom Palmer	DT	6'2"	240	25		
Ernie Stautner	DT	6'1"	235	28		
Nick Bolkovac	OT-DT	6'1"	230	26		45
Dale Dodrill	LB	6'1"	210	28	1	6
Dick Flanagan	LB	6'	220	26	2	
Darrell Hogan	LB	5'10"	210	27		
Marv Matuszak	OG-LB	6'3"	230	22	1	
Art DeCarlo	DB	6'2"	195	23	5	
Ed Fullerton	DB	5'10"	190	23		
Claude Hipps	DB	6'1"	190	27	2	
Jack Butler	OE-DB	6'	195	25	9	12
Pat Brady	QB	6'1"	195	25		
Jim Finks	QB	6'	175	26		12
Bill Mackrides (from NY)	QB	5'11"	185	27		6
Ted Marchibroda	QB	5'10"	170	22		
Tom Calvin	HB	6'	200	27		
Lynn Chandnois	HB	6'2"	195	29		24
Jim Brandt	DB-HB	6'1"	200	25		18
Ray Mathews	DB-HB	6'	185	24	1	44
Leo Elter	FB-HB	5'10"	200	24		
Fran Rogel	FB	5'11"	205	26		12
Ed Barker	OE	6'3"	198	22		6
Elbie Nickel	OE	6'1"	195	30		24
George Sulima	OE	6'2"	200	26		

Pete Ladygo – Injury
Rudy Andabaker – Military Service
Ed Kissell – Military Service
Ed Modzelewski – Military Service

NEW YORK GIANTS 3-9-0 Steve Owen

Scores of Each Game		
7	Los Angeles	21
14	Pittsburgh	24
9	Washington	13
21	CHIC. CARDS	7
0	CLEVELAND	7
23	Chic. Cards	20
7	Philadelphia	30
10	PITTSBURGH	14
21	WASHINGTON	24
37	PHILADELPHIA	28
14	Cleveland	62
16	DETROIT	27

Use Name	Pos.	Hgt	Wgt	Age	Int	Pts
Rosey Brown	OT	6'3"	245	20		
Everett Douglas	OT	6'3"	240	21		
Dick Yelvington	OT	6'2"	230	26		
Bill Austin	OG	6'1"	225	24		
George Kennard	OG	6'	205	24		
Chester Lagod	OG	6'2"	220	25		
Jack Stroud	OG	6'1"	215	24		
Bill Albright	DT-OG	6'2"	232	24		6
John Rapacz	C	6'4"	260	28		
Jim Duncan	DE	6'2"	205	27	3	
Joe Sulaitis	LB-DE	6'2"	215	32	1	
Ray Krouse	DT	6'3"	250	26		
Arnie Weinmeister	DT	6'4"	235	30		
John Cannady	LB	6'2"	225	29	1	
Bob Peviani	LB	6'1"	210	21		
Joe Remona	OG-LB	6'1"	210	22		
Ray Wietecha	C-LB	6'1"	215	24	1	
Dick Woodward	C-LB	6'2"	225	27	1	
Tom Landry	DB	6'1"	195	28	3	
Don Menasco	DB	6'	185	23	1	
Leo Miles	DB	6'	200	21		
Em Tunnell	DB	6'1"	183	31	6	
Randy Clay	HB-DB	6'	190	25	2	32
Chuck Conerly	QB	6'1"	185	29		
Arnie Galiffa	QB	6'2"	195	26		
Sonny Grandelius	HB	6'	195	23		6
Kyle Rote	HB	6'	195	24		36
Frank Gifford	DB-HB	6'1"	190	23	1	47
Cutter Long	DB-HB	6'1"	190	21	3	14
Clarence Avinger	FB	6'1"	215	24		
Merwin Hodel	FB	6'2"	205	22		
Eddie Price	FB	5'11"	190	27		18
Cliff Anderson (from CHI C)	OE	6'2"	215	23		
Ray Pelfrey	OE	6'	190	25		18
Joe Scott	OE	6'1"	195	27		
Bill Stribling	OE	6'1"	205	26		

Ray Beck – Military Service
Tex Coulter – Canadian Football League
Pat Knight – Military Service
Ray Poole – Canadian Football League

CHICAGO CARDINALS 1-10-1 Joe Stydahar

Scores of Each Game		
13	WASHINGTON	24
7	CLEVELAND	27
28	Pittsburgh	31
7	New York	21
17	PHILADELPHIA	56
20	NEW YORK	23
17	Washington	28
24	LOS ANGELES	24
0	Philadelphia	38
16	Cleveland	27
17	PITTSBURGH	21
24	Chic. Bears	17

Use Name	Pos.	Hgt	Wgt	Age	Int	Pts
Jack Jennings	OT	6'4"	245	26		
Tom Higgins	DT-OT	6'2"	230	24		
Volney Peters	DT-OT	6'4"	225	25		
Bill Fischer	OG	6'2"	245	26		
Dave Suminski (from WAS)	OG	5'11"	230	22		
Jerry Watford	DE-OG	6'3"	205	23		
Ed Husmann	LB-OG	6'	218	22		
Jack Simmons	C	6'4"	230	27		
Tom Bienemann	DE	6'3"	220	25		
Keever Jankovich	DE	6'	215	24		
George Schmidt	DE	6'2"	230	26	2	
Pat Summerall	DE	6'4"	220	23		50
Jerry Groom	DT	6'3"	235	24		
Don Joyce	DT	6'3"	250	23		
George Gilchrist	DG-DT	6'	260	25		
John Panelli	LB	5'11"	200	27	1	
Bill Svoboda	LB	6'	210	26	1	
Nick Chickillo	OG-LB	5'11"	220	22		
Gordon Polofsky	OG-LB	6'1"	218	22		
Leo Sanford	C-LB	6'1"	220	24	2	6
Roy Barni	DB	5'11"	185	26		
Jim Psaltis	DB	6'1"	190	26	2	
Dan Sandifer (from GB)	DB	6'2"	190	26		
Tony Curcillo	HB-DB	6'1"	200	22	2	
Don Paul	HB-DB	6'	180	27	5	12
Ray Ramsey	OE-DB	6'2"	165	32	10	6
Ray Nagel	QB	5'11"	177	26		
Steve Romanik (from Chi B)	QB	6'1"	190	29		6
Jim Root	QB	6'1"	185	22		6
Billy Cross	HB	5'6"	147	24		12
Wally Triplett	HB	5'10"	175	26		
Charlie Trippi	HB	6'	185	30		12
Al Campana	DB-HB	5'11"	180	27		
Willie Carter	DB-HB	5'11"	198	22		
Johnny Olszewski	FB	5'11"	195	22		30
Jack Spinks	FB	6'	235	23		
Gern Nagler	OE	6'2"	190	20		36
Don Stonesifer	OE	6'	200	26		12

Ralph Pasquariello – Injury
Dick Fugler – Military Service
Ollie Matson – Military Service
Ralph Thomas – Military Service
Fred Wallner – Military Service

CLEVELAND BROWNS

RUSHING

Last Name	No.	Yds	Avg	TD
Renfro	60	352	5.9	4
Jagade	86	344	4.0	4
Reynolds	72	313	4.3	3
Carpenter	46	195	4.2	3
Motley	32	161	5.0	0
Graham	43	143	3.3	6
Howard	7	42	6.0	0
Jones	31	28	0.9	0
Ratterman	2	6	3.0	0
Gibron	0	−7	–	0

RECEIVING

Last Name	No.	Yds	Avg	TD
Lavelli	45	783	17	6
Renfro	39	722	19	4
Brewster	32	632	20	4
Jones	24	373	16	0
Jagade	20	193	10	0
Reynolds	9	120	13	0
Carpenter	9	109	12	2
Gillom	7	80	11	0
Motley	6	47	8	0

PUNT RETURNS

Last Name	No.	Yds	Avg	TD
Reynolds	18	111	6	0
Renfro	17	53	3	0
Jones	1	7	7	0
Konz	1	4	4	0
Carpenter	6	0	0	0

KICKOFF RETURNS

Last Name	No.	Yds	Avg	TD
Carpenter	16	367	23	0
Reynolds	4	74	19	0
Motley	3	60	20	0
Michaels	2	40	20	0
Steinbrunner	1	23	23	0
Donaldson	1	7	7	0
Howard	1	6	6	0
Noll	1	2	2	0
Young	1	0	0	0

PASSING – PUNTING – KICKING

PASSING	Att	Comp	%	Yds	Yd/Att	TD	Int–%	RK
Graham	258	167	65	2722	10.6	11	9– 3	1
Ratterman	41	23	56	301	7.3	4	0– 0	
Renfro	3	1	33	36	12.0	1	0– 0	
Jones	1	0	0	0	0.0	0	0– 0	

PUNTING	No	Avg
Gillom	63	43.8

KICKING	XP	Att	%	FG	Att	%
Groza	39	40	98	23	26	88

PHILADELPHIA EAGLES

RUSHING

Last Name	No.	Yds	Avg	TD
Johnson	83	439	5.3	5
Williams	61	345	5.7	3
Ziegler	83	320	3.9	5
Parmer	38	158	4.2	2
Giancanelli	44	131	3.0	1
Ledbetter	41	120	2.9	1
Brewer	17	85	5.0	1
Burk	8	54	6.8	3
Pollard	23	44	1.9	0
Thomason	9	23	2.6	1
Stringer	1	5	5.0	0
Gambold	2	−2	−1.0	0

RECEIVING

Last Name	No.	Yds	Avg	TD
Pihos	63	1049	17	10
Walston	41	750	18	5
Williams	31	438	14	1
Giancanelli	20	346	17	5
Ziegler	15	211	14	0
Parmer	14	89	6	0
Ledbetter	13	137	11	2
Johnson	12	227	19	2
Pollard	7	33	5	0
Brewer	4	43	11	0
Schnelker	4	34	9	0

PUNT RETURNS

Last Name	No.	Yds	Avg	TD
Pollard	20	106	5	0
Williams	15	25	2	0
Johnson	5	14	3	0
Giancanelli	4	11	3	0
Hudson	2	10	5	0

KICKOFF RETURNS

Last Name	No.	Yds	Avg	TD
Williams	14	343	25	0
Pollard	13	301	23	0
Johnson	4	69	17	0
Giancanelli	2	45	23	0
Parmer	1	18	18	0
Stringer	1	11	11	0
Hudson	1	0	0	0
Scott	1	0	0	0

PASSING – PUNTING – KICKING

PASSING	Att	Comp	%	Yds	Yd/Att	TD	Int–%	RK
Thomason	304	162	53	2462	8.1	21	20– 7	4
Burk	119	56	47	788	6.6	4	9– 8	8
Gambold	14	6	43	107	7.6	0	2–14	
Ziegler	1	0	0	0	0.0	0	0– 0	

PUNTING	No	Avg
Burk	41	43.0
Bednarik	12	40.3

KICKING	XP	Att	%	FG	Att	%
Walston	45	48	94	4	13	31
Pollard	1	1	100	0	2	0

WASHINGTON REDSKINS

RUSHING

Last Name	No.	Yds	Avg	TD
Justice	115	616	5.4	2
Heath	70	200	3.5	4
Rykovich	73	251	3.4	0
Barry	56	218	3.9	0
Papit	17	102	6.0	1
Scarbath	22	98	4.5	0
LeBaron	21	95	4.5	2
Baker	17	72	4.2	1
Drazenovich	11	27	2.5	1
Dudley	5	15	3.0	0
Cloud	3	7	2.3	0
Dowda	1	3	3.0	0
Haynes	2	0	0.0	0

RECEIVING

Last Name	No.	Yds	Avg	TD
Taylor	35	703	20	8
Justice	22	434	20	2
Dekker	14	182	13	1
Polsfoot	11	164	15	0
Barry	8	70	9	0
Rykovich	7	73	10	1
Heath	5	45	9	0
Brito	2	35	18	0
Baker	2	21	11	0
Papit	1	9	9	0

PUNT RETURNS

Last Name	No.	Yds	Avg	TD
Williams	18	172	10	0
Haynes	5	92	18	0
Dudley	8	34	4	0
Justice	4	6	2	0
Doll	1	2	2	0

KICKOFF RETURNS

Last Name	No.	Yds	Avg	TD
Williams	9	224	25	0
Baker	9	186	21	0
Haynes	7	123	18	0
Barry	6	112	19	0
Cloud	4	68	17	0
Rykovich	2	39	20	0
Papit	2	38	19	0
Justice	1	20	20	0
Boll	1	11	11	0
Lipscomb	1	8	8	0
Brito	1	6	6	0

PASSING – PUNTING – KICKING

PASSING	Att	Comp	%	Yds	Yd/Att	TD	Int–%	RK
LeBaron	149	62	42	874	5.0	3	17–11	17
Scarbath	129	45	35	862	6.7	9	12– 9	13

PUNTING	No	Avg
LeBaron	51	39.3
Baker	17	36.1

KICKING	XP	Att	%	FG	Att	%
Dudley	25	25	100	11	22	50

PITTSBURGH STEELERS

RUSHING

Last Name	No.	Yds	Avg	TD
Rogel	137	527	3.8	2
Chandnois	123	470	3.8	3
Mathews	65	260	4.0	2
Brandt	42	106	2.5	3
Elter	26	81	3.1	0
Calvin	13	65	5.0	0
Mackrides	14	27	1.9	1
Marchibroda	1	15	15.0	0
Finks	12	0	0.0	2

RECEIVING

Last Name	No.	Yds	Avg	TD
Nickel	62	743	12	4
Chandnois	43	412	10	0
Mathews	27	346	13	4
Rogel	19	95	5	0
Barker	17	172	10	1
Sulima	10	131	13	0
Calvin	4	28	7	0
Elter	3	29	10	0
Butler	2	43	22	1
Brandt	2	15	8	0

PUNT RETURNS

Last Name	No.	Yds	Avg	TD
Mathews	16	128	8	0
Chandnois	26	101	4	0
Brandt	6	34	6	0
Butler	1	5	5	0
DeCarlo	1	1	1	0

KICKOFF RETURNS

Last Name	No.	Yds	Avg	TD
Chandnois	21	610	29	1
Mathews	10	261	26	0
Brandt	6	135	23	0
Tepe	3	47	16	0
Marchibroda	1	25	25	0
Elter	1	23	23	0
Gaona	1	0	0	0
Hughes	1	0	0	0

PASSING – PUNTING – KICKING

PASSING	Att	Comp	%	Yds	Yd/Att	TD	Int–%	RK
Finks	292	131	45	1484	5.1	8	14– 5	8
Mackrides	109	54	50	506	4.6	2	8– 7	12
Marchibroda	22	9	41	66	3.0	1	2– 9	
Chandnois	3	1	33	11	3.7	0	0– 0	
Mathews	2	0	0	0	0.0	0	0– 0	
Brady	1	0	0	0	0.0	0	0– 0	
Brandt	1	0	0	0	0.0	0	0– 0	
Rogel	1	0	0	0	0.0	0	0– 0	

PUNTING	No	Avg
Brady	**80**	**46.9**

KICKING	XP	Att	%	FG	Att	%
Bolkovac	27	28	96	4	12	33

NEW YORK GIANTS

RUSHING

Last Name	No.	Yds	Avg	TD
Grandelius	108	278	2.6	1
Rote	63	213	3.4	1
Price	101	206	2.0	2
Gifford	50	157	3.1	2
Conerly	24	91	3.8	0
Long	20	58	2.9	0
Clay	16	26	1.6	0
Hodel	5	11	2.2	0
Avinger	5	6	1.2	0
Galiffa	5	1	0.2	0

RECEIVING

Last Name	No.	Yds	Avg	TD
Rote	26	440	17	5
Price	26	233	9	1
Gifford	18	292	16	4
Anderson	17	266	16	0
Pelfrey	17	233	14	3
Stribling	16	175	11	0
Grandelius	15	80	5	0
Long	14	220	16	2
Clay	5	51	10	1
Avinger	2	8	4	0
Hodel	2	−15	−7	0
Scott	1	10	10	0

PUNT RETURNS

Last Name	No.	Yds	Avg	TD
Tunnell	**38**	223	6	0
Gifford	16	106	7	0
Landry	1	5	5	0

KICKOFF RETURNS

Last Name	No.	Yds	Avg	TD
Tunnell	17	479	28	0
Gifford	13	327	25	0
Long	7	198	28	0
Landry	2	38	19	0
Clay	1	20	20	0
Sulaitis	1	15	15	0

PASSING – PUNTING – KICKING

PASSING	Att	Comp	%	Yds	Yd/Att	TD	Int–%	RK
Conerly	303	143	47	1711	5.7	13	25– 8	8
Galiffa	13	4	31	129	9.9	1	5–38	
Rote	8	2	25	45	5.6	0	1–13	
Gifford	6	3	50	47	7.8	1	0– 0	

PUNTING	No	Avg
Landry	44	40.3
Avinger	42	38.1

KICKING	XP	Att	%	FG	Att	%
Clay	20	22	91	2	7	29
Gifford	2	2	100	1	5	20

CHICAGO CARDINALS

RUSHING

Last Name	No.	Yds	Avg	TD
Trippi	97	433	4.5	0
Olszewski	106	386	3.6	4
Cross	51	196	3.8	1
Paul	16	114	7.1	0
Curcillo	8	29	3.6	0
Root	26	12	0.5	1
Nagel	4	8	2.0	0
Triplett	3	1	2.7	1
Romanik	2	1	0.5	1
Spinks	6	0	0.0	0
Carter	2	−3	−1.5	0
Campana	2	−5	−2.5	0

RECEIVING

Last Name	No.	Yds	Avg	TD
Stonesifer	56	684	12	2
Nagler	43	610	14	6
Olszewski	21	210	10	1
Cross	17	285	17	1
Paul	16	167	10	2
Ramsey	12	118	10	0
Trippi	11	87	8	2
Triplett	3	15	5	0
Spinks	1	6	6	0

PUNT RETURNS

Last Name	No.	Yds	Avg	TD
Trippi	21	239	11	0
Paul	18	85	5	0
Sandifer	3	35	12	0
Carter	4	20	5	0
Cross	6	5	1	0
Olszewski	1	0	0	0

KICKOFF RETURNS

Last Name	No.	Yds	Avg	TD
Cross	12	257	21	0
Triplett	10	253	25	0
Trippi	8	199	25	0
Carter	8	178	22	0
Paul	4	106	27	0
Campana	3	56	19	0
Curcillo	1	17	17	0
Olszewski	1	17	17	0
Jennings	1	15	15	0
Svoboda	1	15	15	0
Joyce	1	7	7	0

PASSING – PUNTING – KICKING

PASSING	Att	Comp	%	Yds	Yd/Att	TD	Int–%	RK
Root	192	80	42	1149	6.0	8	11– 6	7
Romanik	125	51	41	650	5.2	4	11– 9	15
Nagel	62	30	48	192	3.1	0	5– 8	
Trippi	34	20	59	195	5.7	2	1– 3	
Paul	2	1	50	13	6.5	0	0– 0	
Olszewski	1	0	0	0	0.0	0	1–100	

PUNTING	No	Avg
Trippi	54	42.9
Simmons	22	38.4

KICKING	XP	Att	%	FG	Att	%
Summerall	23	23	100	9	24	38

DETROIT LIONS 10-2-0 Buddy Parker

Scores of Each Game		
38	PITTSBURGH	21
27	Baltimore	17
24	SAN FRANCISCO	21
19	LOS ANGELES	31
14	San Francisco	10
24	Los Angeles	37
17	BALTIMORE	7
14	Green Bay	7
20	Chic. Bears	16
34	GREEN BAY	15
13	CHIC. BEARS	7
27	New York	16

Use Name	Pos.	Hgt	Wgt	Age	Int	Pts
Charlie Ane	OT	6'2"	265	22		
Ollie Spencer	OT	6'2"	230	22		
Lou Creekmur	OG-OT	6'4"	250	26		
Dick Stanfel	OG	6'3"	235	26		
Harley Sewell	LB-OG	6'1"	220	22	1	
Vince Banonis	C	6'1"	235	31		
Les Bingaman	OG	6'3"	300	28	1	
Jim Cain	DE	6'1"	200	26		
Bob Dove (from Chi C)	DE	6'2"	225	32		
Blaine Earon	DE	6'1"	195	24		
Sonny Gandee	DE	6'1"	210	24	1	
Jim Doran	OE-DE	6'2"	195	25		
Thurman McGraw	DT	6'5"	235	26	1	
John Prchlik	DT	6'4"	235	28		
Bob Miller	OT-DT	6'3"	235	23	1	
Joe Schmidt	LB	6'1"	218	21	2	
Jim Martin	OG-LB	6'2"	225	29	1	10
Lavern Torgeson	C-LB	6'	215	24	5	
Jack Christiansen	DB	6'1"	185	24	12	6
Jim David	DB	5'11"	175	26	4	
Carl Karilivacz	DB	6'	185	22		
Yale Lary	DB	6'	185	22	5	6
Jim Smith	HB-DB	6'1"	195	28	3	
Tom Dublinski	QB	6'2"	190	23		
Bobby Layne	QB	6'1"	195	26		
Gene Gedman	HB	5'11"	195	21		18
Jug Girard	HB	5'11"	175	26		
Bob Hoernschemeyer	HB	5'11"	195	27		54
Doak Walker	HB	5'11"	172	26		93
Lew Carpenter	DB-HB	6'1"	200	21	1	6
Ollie Cline	FB	6'	200	27		6
Pat Harder	FB	5'11"	202	31		
Bob Smith	FB	6'	204	24		
Cloyce Box	OE	6'4"	220	29		12
Dorne Dibble	OE	6'2"	195	24		18
Leon Hart	OE	6'5"	265	24		42

Stan Campbell – Military Service
Jim Hill – Military Service

SAN FRANCISCO FORTY NINERS 9-3-0 Buck Shaw

Scores of Each Game		
31	PHILADELPHIA	21
31	LOS ANGELES	30
21	Detroit	24
35	Chic. Bears	28
10	DETROIT	14
24	CHIC. BEARS	14
31	Los Angeles	27
21	Cleveland	23
37	Green Bay	7
38	Baltimore	21
48	GREEN BAY	14
45	BALTIMORE	14

Use Name	Pos.	Hgt	Wgt	Age	Int	Pts
Hal Miller	OT	6'4"	230	23		
Bob St. Clair	OT	6'9"	245	22		
Doug Hogland	OG-OT	6'3"	225	22		
Bruno Banducci	OG	5'11"	220	31		
Nick Feher	OG	6'	225	26		
Jerry Smith	LB-OG	6'1"	230	23		
Bill Johnson	C	6'3"	240	27		
Clay Mathews	DE	6'3"	220	25		
Charley Powell	DE	6'2"	220	21		
Bob Van Doren	DE	6'3"	215	24		
Al Carapella	DT	6'	235	26		
Leo Nomellini	OT-DT	6'3"	252	28		
Hardy Brown	LB	6'	196	29	1	
John Morton	LB	6'2"	220	24	2	
Don Burke	OG-LB	6'	235	27		
Art Michalik	OG-LB	6'2"	225	23		
Pete Brown	C-LB	6'2"	210	22		
Jack Manley	C-LB	6'3"	215	24		
Rex Berry	DB	5'11"	180	27	7	6
Fred Bruney	DB	5'10"	177	22	5	
Lowell Wagner	HB-DB	6'	195	29	6	
Jim Monachino	FB-DB	5'10"	187	24		
Hal Ledyard	QB	6'	185	22		
Y. A. Tittle	QB	6'	190	26		36
Jim Powers	DB-QB	6'	185	25		
Hugh McElhenny	HB	6'1"	198	24		30
Joe Arenas	DB-HB	5'11"	180	27	2	42
Billy Mixon	DB-HB	5'11"	185	23		6
Pete Schabarum	DB-HB	5'11"	185	24		
Ken Bahnsen	FB	5'10"	200	23		
Joe Perry	FB	6'	210	26		78
Harry Babcock	OE	6'2"	195	22		
Gordie Soltau	OE	6'2"	195	28		114
Billy Wilson	OE	6'3"	190	26		60

Jim Cason – Canadian Football League
Ed Henke – Military Service

Bill Jessup – Military Service
Pat O'Donahue – Military Service
Dave Sparks – Military Service
Bob Toneff – Military Service

Bob White – Military Service
Verl Lillywhite – Military Service

LOS ANGELES RAMS 8-3-1 Hamp Pool

Scores of Each Game		
21	NEW YORK	7
30	San Francisco	31
38	Green Bay	20
31	Detroit	19
38	CHIC. BEARS	24
37	DETROIT	24
27	SAN FRANCISCO	31
24	Chic. Cards	24
21	Baltimore	13
21	Chic. Bears	24
45	BALTIMORE	2
33	GREEN BAY	17

Use Name	Pos.	Hgt	Wgt	Age	Int	Pts
Tom Dahms	OT	6'5"	240	25		
Bob Fry	OT	6'4"	220	22		
Len Teeuws	DT-OT	6'4"	235	26		
Dick Daugherty	OG	6'1"	214	24		
John Hock	OG	6'2"	235	25		
Duane Putnam	OG	6'	215	25		
Harry Thompson	DE-OG	6'2"	225	26		
Leon McLaughlin	C	6'2"	228	27		
Stan West	OG	6'2"	230	26	1	
Larry Brink	DE	6'5"	240	30		
Big Daddy Lipscomb	DE	6'5"	272	22		
Andy Robustelli	DE	6'1"	220	27		
Charlie Toogood	DT	6'	233	25	1	
Frank Fuller	C-DT	6'4"	235	24		
Bud McFadin	LB	6'3"	245	25	1	
Don Paul	LB	6'1"	225	28	3	
Harland Svare	LB	6'	210	22	1	
Bob Griffin	C-LB	6'3"	215	24		
Jack Dwyer	DB	5'11"	175	26	2	6
Neil Ferris	DB	5'11"	180	25		
Night Train Lane	DB	6'1"	190	25	3	12
Herb Rich	DB	5'11"	180	24	3	6
Woodley Lewis	HB-DB	6'	195	28	7	12
Norb Hecker	OE-DB	6'2"	190	26	7	
Rudy Bukich	QB	6'1"	193	22		6
Norm Van Brocklin	QB	6'1"	200	27		
Tom McCormick	HB	5'11"	190	23		
Brad Myers	HB	6'1"	200	23		18
Skeets Quinlan	HB	5'11"	175	25		36
Vitamin Smith	HB	5'8"	180	29		18
Dan Towler	FB	6'2"	226	25		48
Tank Younger	LB-HB-FB	6'3"	226	25		54
Tom Fears	OE	6'2"	215	29		32
Crazy Legs Hirsch	OE	6'2"	190	29		28
Bob Boyd	DB-OE	6'2"	200	25	1	24
Ben Agajanian	K	6'	215	34		66

Bob Carey – Military Service
Don Klosterman – Military Service

CHICAGO BEARS 3-8-1 George Halas

Scores of Each Game		
9	Baltimore	13
17	Green Bay	13
14	BALTIMORE	16
28	SAN FRANCISCO	35
24	Los Angeles	38
14	San Francisco	24
21	GREEN BAY	21
27	Washington	24
16	DETROIT	20
24	LOS ANGELES	21
7	Detroit	13
17	CHIC. CARDS	24

Use Name	Pos.	Hgt	Wgt	Age	Int	Pts
Kline Gilbert	OT	6'2"	224	22		
Art Davis	DT-OT	6'2"	235	23		
George Connor	OG-LB-OT	6'3"	240	28		
John Badaczewski	OG	6'1"	235	31		
John Hatley	OG	6'3"	245	22		
Billy Autrey	C	6'3"	220	20		
Bob Moser	C	6'3"	235	24		
Wayne Hansen	OT-OG-LB-C	6'2"	235	25		
Ed Sprinkle	DE	6'1"	210	29		6
Bill Wightkin	OE-DE	6'3"	233	26		6
Bill Bishop	DT	6'4"	250	22	1	
John Kreamcheck	DT	6'5"	255	25		
Fred Williams	DT	6'4"	250	23		
John Helwig	LB	6'2"	208	25		
Jerry Shipkey	LB	6'1"	215	28		
Jerry Weatherley	LB	6'5"	218	24	1	
Frank Dempsey	OG-LB	6'3"	235	28		
Bill George	OG-LB	6'2"	240	22		
George Figner	DB	6'	185	24	1	
Don Kindt	DB	6'1"	208	27	6	6
Howie Livingston	DB	6'1"	198	31		
Rex Proctor	DB	5'10"	180	24	1	
S. J. Whitman (from Chi C)	DB	5'11"	185	27	3	
Billy Anderson	HB-DB	6'	198	24		
Lloyd Lowe	HB-DB	5'10"	155	24	1	
George Blanda	QB	6'1"	197	25		48
Tom O'Connell	QB	5'11"	182	21		
Willie Thrower	QB	5'11"	182	23		
Eddie Macon	HB	6'	175	25		18
Billy Stone	HB	6'	195	27		36
John Hoffman	DE-LB-OE-FB-HB	6'2"	215	27	1	24
Leon Campbell	FB	6'	197	26		
Kayo Dottley	FB	6'1"	200	25		6
Bobby Jack Floyd	FB	6'	210	24		
Curley Morrison	HB-FB	6'2"	215	27		12
Jim Dooley	OE	6'4"	198	23		24
Dick Hensley	OE	6'4"	218	27		2
Bill McColl	OE	6'4"	230	23		30

Ed Bradley – Canadian Football League
Herman Clark – Military Service

Bob Cross – Military Service
Jack Hoffman – Military Service
Chuck Hunsinger – Canadian Football League
Jimmy Lesane – Military Service

Gene Schroeder – Military Service
Bob Williams – Military Service

BALTIMORE COLTS 3-9-0 Keith Molesworth

Scores of Each Game		
13	CHIC. BEARS	9
17	DETROIT	27
16	Chic. Bears	14
14	Green Bay	37
27	WASHINGTON	17
24	GREEN BAY	35
7	Detroit	17
14	Philadelphia	45
13	LOS ANGELES	21
21	SAN FRANCISCO	38
2	Los Angeles	45
14	San Francisco	45

Use Name	Pos.	Hgt	Wgt	Age	Int	Pts
Ernie Blandin	OT	6'4"	260	34		
Ken Jackson	OT	6'2"	235	24		
Jack Little	OT	6'4"	235	22		
Dick Barwegan	OG	6'1"	230	31		
Bill Lange	OG	6'1"	230	26		
Sisto Averno	LB-OG	5'11"	245	27		
Brad Ecklund	C	6'3"	215	31		
Barney Poole	DE	6'2"	250	30		
Art Spinney	DE	6'	235	26		
Elmer Wingate	DE	6'3"	230	25		
Joe Campanella	DT	6'2"	245	22		
Art Donovan	DT	6'2"	270	28		2
Tom Finnin	DT	6'2"	255	25		
Gino Marchetti	DT	6'4"	245	27		
Jim Winkler	OG-DT	6'2"	255	26		
Alex Agase	LB	5'10"	220	31	1	
Bill Pellington	LB	6'2"	235	24	2	
Ed Sharkey	OG-LB	6'3"	240	26		
Ed Mioduszewski	QB-DB	5'10"	185	23	1	
Bert Rechichar	HB-DB	6'1"	210	23	7	33
Don Shula	HB-DB	5'11"	190	23	3	
Carl Taseff	HB-DB	5'11"	195	24	2	12
Tom Keane	OE-DB	6'1"	185	26	11	
Jack Del Bello	QB	6'1"	190	25		
Fred Enke	QB	6'1"	205	28		
Dick Flowers	QB	6'	190	25		
Larry Coutre (from GB)	HB	5'10"	175	24		
Tommy Kalmanir	HB	5'8"	170	27		6
Buddy Young	HB	5'5"	180	27		24
George Taliaferro	QB-HB	5'11"	200	26		24
John Huzvar	FB	6'4"	250	24		30
Buck McPhail	FB	6'1"	195	23		27
Dan Edwards	OE	6'1"	190	27		18
Mel Embree	OE	6'3"	190	26		6
Monte Brethauer	DB-OE	6'1"	175	22	1	

Johnny Petitbon – Military Service
Mike McCormack – Military Service
Stan Williams – Canadian Football League
John Wozniak – Canadian Football League
Zollie Toth – Knee Injury

GREEN BAY PACKERS 2-9-1 Gene Ronzani Hugh Devore Ray McLean

Scores of Each Game		
0	CLEVELAND	27
13	CHIC. BEARS	17
20	LOS ANGELES	38
37	BALTIMORE	14
14	Pittsburgh	31
35	Baltimore	24
21	Chic. Bears	21
7	DETROIT	14
7	SAN FRANCISCO	37
15	Detroit	34
14	San Francisco	48
17	Los Angeles	33

Use Name	Pos.	Hgt	Wgt	Age	Int	Pts
Gus Cifelli	OT	6'4"	250	27		
Len Szafaryn	OG-OT	6'2"	230	25		
Dick Afflis	OG-OT	6'	250	24		
Buddy Brown	OG	6'1"	220	26		
Steve Ruzich	OG	6'2"	230	25		
Dick Logan	DT-OG	6'2"	230	23		
Jim Ringo	C	6'1"	225	22		
Dave Stephenson	OG-C	6'2"	225	27		
John Martinkovic	DE	6'3"	240	26		
George Hays	DE	6'2"	215	28		
Carl Elliott	OE-DE	6'4"	220	26		6
Dave Hanner	DT	6'2"	250	24	1	
Howie Ruetz	DT	6'3"	265	25		
Dick Wildung	DT	6'	230	31		
Bob Forte	LB	6'	205	31		
Clayton Tonnemaker	LB	6'2"	235	25		
Deral Teteak	OG-LB	5'10"	210	24		
Roger Zatkoff	DE-LB	6'2"	215	22		
Bill Forester	DT-LB	6'3"	230	22	1	
Ben Aldridge	DB	6'	195	26	5	
Bobby Dillon	DB	6'1"	180	23	9	6
Marvin Johnson	DB	5'11"	185	25	4	
Ace Loomis	DB	6'1"	190	25	4	
Val Joe Walker	DB	6'1"	180	22	4	6
Babe Parilli	QB	6'1"	190	23		24
Tobin Rote	QB	6'3"	200	25		
Byron Bailey (from DET)	HB	5'10"	198	23		
Al Carmichael	HB	6'1"	190	23		6
Gib Dawson	HB	5'11"	180	23		6
Breezy Reid	HB	5'10"	188	26		18
Don Barton	DB-HB	5'11"	175	23		6
J. R. Boone	DB-HB	5'8"	167	27		6
Fred Cone	FB	5'11"	197	27		74
Howie Ferguson	FB	6'2"	210	23		
Billy Howton	OE	6'2"	188	23		24
Bob Mann	OE	5'11"	175	29		12
Clive Rush	OE	6'2"	197	22		

Clarence Self – Military Service

DETROIT LIONS

RUSHING

Last Name	No.	Yds	Avg	TD
Hoernschemeyer	101	482	4.8	7
Layne	87	343	3.9	0
Walker	66	337	5.1	2
Gedman	83	255	3.1	3
Cline	42	169	4.0	0
Girard	19	73	3.8	0
B. Smith	6	51	8.5	0
Dublinski	6	39	6.5	0
Carpenter	7	24	3.4	0
Harder	8	21	2.6	0
Lary	1	21	21.0	0
Hart	1	2	2.0	0
Christiansen	0	–5	–	0

RECEIVING

Last Name	No.	Yds	Avg	TD
Walker	30	502	17	3
Hart	25	472	19	7
Hoernschemeyer	23	282	12	2
Box	16	403	25	2
Dibble	16	274	17	3
Gedman	14	121	9	0
Cline	10	126	13	1
Doran	6	75	13	0
Girard	2	24	12	0
Harder	1	19	19	0
J. Smith	1	11	11	0

PUNT RETURNS

Last Name	No.	Yds	Avg	TD
Lary	13	115	9	1
Girard	9	86	10	0
Christiansen	8	22	3	0
Gedman	4	10	3	0
Schmidt	1	0	0	0

KICKOFF RETURNS

Last Name	No.	Yds	Avg	TD
Girard	9	252	28	0
Christiansen	10	183	18	0
Carpenter	8	172	22	0
Walker	4	139	35	0
Lary	6	116	19	0
Gedman	2	47	24	0
Hoernschemeyer	1	10	10	0
Stanfel	1	4	4	0
Bingaman	1	3	3	0
Cline	1	0	0	0

PASSING – PUNTING – KICKING

PASSING	Att	Comp	%	Yds	Yd/Att	TD	Int–%	RK
Layne	273	125	46	2088	7.7	16	21– 8	5
Dublinski	30	14	47	174	5.8	0	5–17	
Walker	7	3	43	31	4.4	1	0– 0	
Hoernschemeyer	5	2	40	16	3.2	1	1–20	
Girard	1	0	0	0	0.0	0	0– 0	

PUNTING	No	Avg
J. Smith	40	41.2
Lary	28	39.7

KICKING	XP	Att	%	FG	Att	%
Walker	27	29	93	12	19	63
Martin	4	4	100	2	4	50

SAN FRANCISCO FORTY NINERS

RUSHING

Last Name	No.	Yds	Avg	TD
Perry	192	1018	5.3	10
McElhenny	112	503	4.5	3
Arenas	72	380	5.3	6
Mixon	25	176	7.0	1
Schabarum	18	104	5.8	0
Tittle	14	41	2.9	6
Monachino	4	10	2.5	0
Wagner	1	4	4.0	0
Ledyard	1	3	3.0	0
Bahnsen	1	1	1.0	0
Powers	3	–10	–3.3	0

RECEIVING

Last Name	No.	Yds	Avg	TD
Wilson	51	840	16	10
Soltau	43	620	14	6
McElhenny	30	474	16	2
Perry	19	191	10	3
Arenas	10	113	11	1
Schabarum	10	96	10	0
Babcock	7	59	8	0
Monachino	2	9	5	0
Mixon	1	7	7	0
Hogland	1	–2	–2	0

PUNT RETURNS

Last Name	No.	Yds	Avg	TD
McElhenny	15	104	7	0
Arenas	8	93	12	0
Berry	7	42	6	0
Bruney	1	11	11	0
Schabarum	2	0	0	0

KICKOFF RETURNS

Last Name	No.	Yds	Avg	TD
Arenas	16	551	34	0
McElhenny	15	368	25	0
Schabarum	2	50	25	0
Bruney	2	46	23	0
Berry	1	37	37	0
Perry	2	21	11	0
Bahnsen	1	21	21	0
Nomellini	1	5	5	0
Babcock	2	3	2	0
H. Brown	1	3	3	0

PASSING – PUNTING – KICKING

PASSING	Att	Comp	%	Yds	Yd/Att	TD	Int–%	RK
Tittle	259	149	58	2121	8.2	20	16– 6	3
Powers	49	22	45	259	5.3	1	2– 4	
Ledyard	9	0	0	0	0.0	0	1–11	
McElhenny	3	2	67	13	4.3	1	0– 0	
Perry	1	1	100	14	14.0	0	0– 0	
Arenas	1	0	0	0	0.0	0	0– 0	

PUNTING	No	Avg
Powers	42	40.6

KICKING	XP	Att	%	FG	Att	%
Soltau	48	49	98	10	15	67
Perry	0	0	0	0	3	0

LOS ANGELES RAMS

RUSHING

Last Name	No.	Yds	Avg	TD
Towler	152	879	5.8	7
Quinlan	97	705	7.3	4
Younger	84	350	4.2	8
Myers	40	124	3.1	3
McCormick	20	29	1.5	0
Bukich	14	28	2.0	1
Smith	8	26	3.3	0
Van Brocklin	8	11	1.4	0
Lewis	2	2	1.0	0
Hirsch	1	–6	–6.0	0

RECEIVING

Last Name	No.	Yds	Avg	TD
Hirsch	61	941	15	4
Boyd	24	548	23	4
Fears	23	278	12	4
Younger	20	259	13	1
Quinlan	17	260	15	2
Towler	11	125	11	1
Smith	6	151	25	3
McCormick	5	72	14	0
Myers	4	13	3	0
Hecker	2	25	13	0

PUNT RETURNS

Last Name	No.	Yds	Avg	TD
Lewis	35	267	8	1
Smith	12	30	3	0
Boyd	5	26	5	0
McCormick	2	2	1	0
Myers	1	1	1	0

KICKOFF RETURNS

Last Name	No.	Yds	Avg	TD
Lewis	32	830	26	0
McCormick	5	134	27	0
Smith	2	44	22	0
Myers	3	42	14	0
Quinlan	2	38	19	0
Younger	1	24	24	0
Toogood	1	19	19	0
McFadin	1	5	5	0
Thompson	1	0	0	0

PASSING – PUNTING – KICKING

PASSING	Att	Comp	%	Yds	Yd/Att	TD	Int–%	RK
Van Brocklin	286	156	55	2393	8.4	19	14– 5	2
Bukich	32	14	44	169	5.3	0	3– 9	
Quinlan	4	2	50	60	15.0	0	1–25	
Smith	2	1	50	50	25.0	0	0– 0	

PUNTING	No	Avg
Van Brocklin	60	42.2

KICKING	XP	Att	%	FG	Att	%
Agajanian	36	37	97	10	24	42
Fears	5	6	83	1	1	100
Hirsch	4	5	80	0	0	0

CHICAGO BEARS

RUSHING

Last Name	No.	Yds	Avg	TD
Morrison	95	307	3.2	2
Stone	72	169	2.3	2
Dottley	58	150	2.6	0
Macon	40	130	3.3	1
Campbell	22	130	5.9	0
Hoffman	32	95	3.0	3
Floyd	16	70	4.4	0
Blanda	24	62	2.6	0
O'Connell	7	16	2.3	0

RECEIVING

Last Name	No.	Yds	Avg	TD
Dooley	53	841	16	4
McColl	36	453	13	4
Stone	34	376	11	4
Hoffman	28	341	12	1
Morrison	16	214	13	0
Floyd	9	63	7	0
Macon	6	24	4	2
Campbell	5	74	15	0
Dottley	5	21	4	0
Hensley	4	117	29	0
Lowe	4	34	9	0
Anderson	3	33	11	0
Wightkin	2	22	11	0
Connor	1	17	17	0
Blanda	0	7	0	0

PUNT RETURNS

Last Name	No.	Yds	Avg	TD
Macon	17	68	4	0
Lowe	15	51	3	0
Stone	4	12	3	0
Anderson	1	7	7	0
Dempsey	1	5	5	0

KICKOFF RETURNS

Last Name	No.	Yds	Avg	TD
Campbell	19	455	24	0
Macon	13	373	29	0
Anderson	5	127	25	0
Morrison	4	43	11	0
Hoffman	2	32	16	0
Lowe	1	26	26	0
Connor	1	21	21	0
Helwig	1	12	12	0
Sprinkle	1	1	1	0
Wightkin	1	0	0	0

PASSING – PUNTING – KICKING

PASSING	Att	Comp	%	Yds	Yd/Att	TD	Int–%	RK
Blanda	362	169	47	2164	6.0	14	23– 7	6
O'Connell	67	33	49	437	6.5	1	4– 6	
Thrower	8	3	38	27	3.4	0	1–13	
Macon	1	0	0	0	0.0	0	0– 0	

PUNTING	No	Avg
Morrison	65	42.6
Anderson	1	46.0

KICKING	XP	Att	%	FG	Att	%
Blanda	27	27	100	7	20	35
George	0	0	0	0	1	0

BALTIMORE COLTS

RUSHING

Last Name	No.	Yds	Avg	TD
Huzvar	119	515	4.3	4
Taliaferro	102	479	4.7	2
McPhail	53	138	2.6	0
Young	40	135	3.4	0
Enke	28	91	3.3	0
Kalmanir	16	53	3.3	0
Coutre	22	39	1.8	0
Mioduszewski	3	33	11.0	0
Del Bello	14	14	1.0	0
Taseff	1	1	1.0	1

RECEIVING

Last Name	No.	Yds	Avg	TD
Edwards	35	312	9	3
Embree	23	272	12	1
Taliaferro	20	346	17	2
Young	12	201	17	3
Brethauer	10	133	13	0
McPhail	10	38	4	0
Huzvar	6	55	9	1
Rechichar	3	151	50	2
Keane	3	61	20	0
Kalmanir	3	31	10	1
Shula	1	6	6	0
Coutre	1	–4	–4	0
Marchetti	0	19	0	0

PUNT RETURNS

Last Name	No.	Yds	Avg	TD
Taseff	1	71	71	1
Coutre	5	43	9	0
Taliaferro	10	31	3	0
Kalmanir	2	19	10	0
Mioduszewski	4	13	3	0
Young	6	9	2	0
Keane	1	3	3	0
Rechichar	1	0	0	0

KICKOFF RETURNS

Last Name	No.	Yds	Avg	TD
Young	11	378	34	1
Taliaferro	16	331	21	0
Coutre	12	318	27	0
Taseff	4	87	22	0
Kalmanir	3	51	17	0
Jackson	3	37	12	0
Rechichar	1	28	28	0
Mioduszewski	1	25	25	0
Poole	2	24	12	0
Finnin	1	18	18	0
Campanella	2	13	7	0

PASSING – PUNTING – KICKING

PASSING	Att	Comp	%	Yds	Yd/Att	TD	Int–%	RK
Enke	169	71	42	1054	6.2	8	15– 9	11
Del Bello	61	27	44	229	3.8	1	5– 8	
Taliaferro	55	15	27	211	3.8	2	5– 9	
Mioduszewski	30	11	37	113	3.8	2	2– 7	
Flowers	4	2	50	18	4.5	0	0– 0	

PUNTING	No	Avg
Taliaferro	65	37.5
Keane	18	41.8

KICKING	XP	Att	%	FG	Att	%
McPhail	21	23	91	2	5	40
Rechichar	0	0	0	5	13	38

GREEN BAY PACKERS

RUSHING

Last Name	No.	Yds	Avg	TD
Reid	95	492	5.2	3
Cone	92	301	3.3	5
Carmichael	49	199	4.1	1
Rote	33	180	5.5	0
Parilli	42	171	4.1	4
Ferguson	52	134	2.6	0
Barton	7	40	5.7	0
Bailey	13	29	2.2	0
Boone	7	24	3.4	0
Dawson	5	18	3.6	0
Rush	1	–6	–6.0	0

RECEIVING

Last Name	No.	Yds	Avg	TD
Howton	25	463	19	4
Mann	23	327	14	2
Cone	18	165	9	1
Ferguson	15	86	6	0
Rush	14	190	14	0
Elliott	13	150	12	0
Carmichael	12	131	11	0
Reid	10	100	10	0
Bailey	8	119	15	0
Boone	6	55	9	1
Barton	2	51	26	1

PUNT RETURNS

Last Name	No.	Yds	Avg	TD
Carmichael	20	198	10	0
Dawson	7	72	10	1
Boone	5	24	5	0
Barton	2	13	7	0
Aldridge	1	0	0	0

KICKOFF RETURNS

Last Name	No.	Yds	Avg	TD
Carmichael	26	641	25	0
Ferguson	7	123	18	0
Dawson	4	102	26	0
Reid	4	82	21	0
Teteak	2	62	31	0
Bailey	2	34	17	0
Loomis	1	19	19	0
Barton	1	14	14	0
Martinkovic	2	12	6	0
Forester	1	12	12	0
Wildung	1	6	6	0

PASSING – PUNTING – KICKING

PASSING	Att	Comp	%	Yds	Yd/Att	TD	Int–%	RK
Rote	185	72	39	1005	5.4	5	15– 8	14
Parilli	166	74	45	830	5.0	4	19–11	16
Boone	1	1	100	–1	–1.0	0	0– 0	

PUNTING	No	Avg
Rush	60	37.7
Parilli	19	36.1
Rote	1	57.0

KICKING	XP	Att	%	FG	Att	%
Cone	23	25	92	5	16	31

1954 Putting Some Tarnish on the Golden Glow

The sun was shining brightly on the NFL, giving the team owners a radiant financial glow. Attendance climbed to another new record total of 2,190,571, and most of the clubs had lucrative local TV contracts to line the owners' pockets doubly with green. The veteran owners like Tim Mara, George Marshall, Art Rooney, and George Halas now raked in the dollars faster than they had lost them in the rugged 1930s and 1940s. Another old-time owner, Bert Bell, was also making out well. With his contract as commissioner renewed for twelve years, the frog-voiced Bell combined universal popularity with complete authority and an unblemished record of making the right move at the right time.

But one mosquito from the north buzzed annoyingly around the NFL's head. The Canadian Football League had also been growing fat off the postwar boom and now felt strong enough to make some inroads south of the border. American fans could watch a Canadian game every Saturday on television, often recognizing famous American players who had been lured north with healthy contracts. Nineteen fifty-two Heisman Trophy winner Billy Vessels had scorned the Baltimore Colts to cross the border, and NFL veterans Arnie Weinmeister, Eddie LeBaron, and Gene Brito this year signed with Canadian teams. But the American teams responded with their own raids, and NFL clubs soon were drawing Canadian stars south.

EASTERN CONFERENCE

Cleveland Browns—When the Browns dropped two of their first three games, the second a 55-27 loss to the Steelers, the other Eastern clubs smelled the blood of a dying champion. The obituaries were premature, however, as the Browns then won every game until the final Sunday of the season again to take their conference crown. The slow settling in of Mo Bassett, Mike McCormack, and Walt Michaels as replacements for the retired Marion Motley, Bill Willis, and Tommy Thompson partly accounted for the slow start, but renewed concentration by the long-time champs got the club back on the winning path. Led by charging end Len Ford, the defense allowed only nine touchdowns in the last nine games, while quarterback Otto Graham kept the attack moving through the air.

Philadelphia Eagles—The Eagles opened the season perfectly by beating Cleveland 28-10 and then won their next three contests to take the Eastern lead. The Philadelphia passing game drove the club, as when quarterback Adrian Burk threw seven touchdown passes in a 49-21 romp over the Redskins. But, suddenly, the attack dried up, as the Steelers, Packers, Giants, and Browns beat the Eagles in a mid-season stretch of five games. A rematch with the Redskins helped retune the offense, but with the Browns by then in high gear, the Eagles could not make up the lost ground.

New York Giants—With long-time coach Steve Owen gone, the Giants began a new era with a fantastic influx of coaching talent. Jim Lee Howell, a popular Giant end in the 1930s and 1940s, took over as head coach with the philosophy of keeping his troops loose as well as disciplined. Coming in from West Point to take control of the offense was Vince Lombardi, a forty-one-year-old inspirational leader and master tactician. Lombardi installed the power sweep, in which both guards escorted the runner around end, and the halfback option, in which the back may either pass or run as the play develops. Promoted to playing coach in charge of the defense was Tom Landry, another football genius who kept his All-Pro status as a cornerback as well as technically refining the modern 4-3-4 defense as a coach.

Pittsburgh Steelers—Promoted to head coach for the third time, Walt Kiesling got the Steelers off to a rousing 4-1 start highlighted by a 55-27 trouncing of the mighty Cleveland Browns. Most pre-season predictions had expected little of the Steelers, and the club finally lived up to those small expectations by losing six of their last seven starts. The defense, led by Ernie Stautner, Dale Dodrill, and Jack Butler, stayed tough all season, but the offense faded away after a great start.

Washington Redskins—New head coach Joe Kuharich never had much of a chance to build a winning team this year. Even before the season started, quarterback Eddie LeBaron and defensive end Gene Brito, both key performers, jumped the team to play in the Canadian League. To make matters worse, the trade of Don Doll to the Rams and the retirement of Bill Dudley left the defensive secondary quite threadbare. A 41-7 thrashing by the '49ers started the Skins on their way to five quick losses and a trip to the basement in the East, as passing teams found the Washington defense easy to throw against. Seven times the Redskins gave up over 35 points, with a 62-3 loss to Cleveland the height of the club's ineptitude. Finally, to crown an ineffective year with tragedy, guard Dave Sparks died of a heart attack after the 34-14 loss to Cleveland on December 5.

Chicago Cardinals—Even with Ollie Matson back from military service, the Cards plunged to the depths of the standings right from the first Sunday of the season. Five quick losses established the Cardinals as doormats, and the team was fortunate to beat Pittsburgh and Washington for its only victories. The offense never found the proper groove, as rookie quarterback Lamar McHan floundered about in his inexperience. Matson starred as an explosive runner and receiver, using his powerful legs to break tackles when he couldn't outrun a defender. He also found time to fill in on defense, often joining ex-runner Charlie Trippi and ex-Ram Night Train Lane in the secondary. A bargain pick-up, Lane led the league with ten interceptions.

WESTERN CONFERENCE

Detroit Lions—For the third time running, the Lions convincingly won the Western Conference title with the same cast of starring characters. Bobby Layne engineered long drives with his wobbly passes, imaginative play-calling, and driving enthusiasm, while reporters wrote stories of equal length about his late-night carousing. Doak Walker, so slight that he looked fragile, ran well behind his blockers and kicked long field goals regularly. Big Les Bingaman, a bulky 320-pounder whose tiny feet seemed out of place with his giant frame, moved like a cat both in diagnosing enemy plays and in pursuing enemy runners. The defensive secondary, dubbed Chris's Crew after safetyman Jack Christiansen, won cheers from even offense-minded fans, while Layne did his best to publicize the unsung offensive linemen.

Chicago Bears—George Halas hadn't lost the Midas touch after all, as his refurbished Bears won their last four games to capture second place in the West and re-establish themselves as NFL powers. Halas regenerated the offense with talented newcomers in key spots. Rookie Harlon Hill, a tall, lanky end from tiny Florence State College in Alabama, set the league on its ear with his spectacular grabs of long bombs and short sideline passes. At quarterback, Halas alternated rookie Zeke Bratkowski with veteran George Blanda, while ex-Brown Chick Jagade juiced up the running game at the fullback spot. Two more rookies, Stan Jones and Larry Strickland, won jobs in the offensive line, partially offsetting the loss of George Connor to injuries. The Bears grew stronger as the year progressed, and while they began the season with a 48-23 loss to Detroit, they ended it by beating those same Lions 28-24.

San Francisco '49ers—Undefeated after five games, the '49ers then fell apart, dropping three straight games to fall back into the Western Conference pack. The slide began when halfback Hugh McElhenny, heading for the league rushing title, was sidelined with a shoulder separation. Joe Perry and rookie John Henry Johnson, recruited from the Canadian Football League, both ate up yardage with their power running but could not make up for the breakaway threat lost in McElhenny. The defense also collapsed during the three-game skid, giving up 121 points to the Bears, Rams, and Lions in that span. But even with the fatal slump, the '49ers still showcased many top stars, as Perry and Johnson finished 1-2 in the NFL rushing statistics. After this season, Coach Buck Shaw was fired, taking with him a nine-year winning record but no championship trophies to grace his den.

Los Angeles Rams—Despite a 48-0 opening-day victory over Baltimore, the Rams could win only two of their first six games. The offense was still explosive, with Norm Van Brocklin passing, Tank Younger and Dan Towler running, and speedy Bob Boyd joining Tom Fears and Crazy Legs Hirsch as dangerous receivers, but the explosions now came in spurts instead of with machine-gun rapidity. Even as the attack scored 35 or more points four times, it chalked up fewer than 20 points four times. Les Richter, for whom the Rams had traded eleven players to the Dallas Texans in 1952, came out of the Army to make his pro debut as a linebacker, but the defense still coughed up 49 points more than in 1953.

Green Bay Packers—New coach Lisle Blackbourn hardly endeared himself to the populace as the Packers lost their first three games, but the club suddenly came alive, beating the Rams, Eagles, and Colts twice for four wins in their next five tilts. Blackbourn hardly had time to enjoy the renaissance, though, as the Lions twice, the '49ers, and the Rams handed the Packers four straight losses to end the year.

Baltimore Colts—In looking for a new head coach to direct the team's rebuilding, owner Carroll Rosenbloom narrowed the field down to two of Paul Brown's assistants at Cleveland. He first offered the job to Blanton Collier, only to be turned down when Collier instead chose the head job at the University of Kentucky. Then Weeb Ewbank was offered the post, and the stubby Cleveland lieutenant accepted the challenge of building the Colts into champions. Ewbank set a timetable of five years to reach the top and immediately began bringing together the players who would win the title.

FINAL TEAM STATISTICS

OFFENSE

	BALT.	CHI.B.	CHI.C.	CLEVE.	DET.	G.BAY	L.A.	N.Y.	PHIL.	PITT.	S.F.	WASH.
FIRST DOWNS:												
Total	169	219	184	238	236	207	**255**	197	221	205	252	188
by Rushing	66	63	83	113	91	79	115	85	66	71	**125**	94
by Passing	90	**144**	86	112	134	112	125	99	139	115	109	76
by Penalty	13	12	15	13	11	16	15	13	16	**19**	18	18
RUSHING:												
Number	364	353	418	**476**	393	321	432	380	401	368	442	427
Yards	1275	1142	1612	1793	1608	1328	2140	1482	1196	1282	**2498**	1626
Average Yards	3.5	3.2	3.9	3.8	4.1	4.1	5.0	3.9	3.0	3.5	**5.7**	3.8
Touchdowns	4	8	10	23	11	13	24	8	4	10	**28**	9
PASSING:												
Attempts	313	**429**	349	295	395	412	321	334	401	386	340	257
Completions	163	208	148	174	**215**	195	171	163	206	189	187	116
Completion Percentage	52.1	48.5	42.4	**59.0**	54.4	47.3	53.3	48.8	51.4	49.0	55.0	45.1
Gross Yards	1995	**3299**	1903	2557	2972	2454	3180	2467	2982	2321	2444	1813
Yards Lost Tackled	336	195	241	226	147	295	**133**	141	375	148	238	319
Net Yards	1659	**3104**	1662	2331	2825	2159	3047	2326	2607	2173	2206	1494
Avg. Yards per Attempt (Gross)	6.4	7.7	5.5	8.7	7.5	6.0	**9.9**	7.4	7.4	6.0	7.2	7.1
Avg. Yards per Comp. (Gross)	12.3	15.9	12.9	14.7	13.8	12.6	**18.6**	15.1	14.5	12.3	13.1	15.6
Touchdowns	9	26	8	14	25	14	15	27	**33**	15	10	15
Interceptions	22	35	30	22	21	19	23	22	30	26	**12**	32
Percent Intercepted	7.0	8.2	8.6	7.5	5.3	4.6	7.2	6.6	7.5	6.7	**3.5**	12.5
PUNTS:												
Number	72	57	63	52	63	72	44	64	**73**	66	60	62
Average Yards	37.2	40.1	39.2	42.9	41.0	41.7	42.6	42.5	40.0	**43.2**	37.0	40.2
PUNT RETURNS:												
Number	33	42	39	**61**	37	40	**44**	52	49	32	36	26
Yards	168	186	208	324	364	**394**	201	305	273	110	205	121
Average Yards	5.1	4.4	5.3	5.3	9.8	**9.9**	4.6	5.9	5.6	3.4	5.7	4.7
Touchdowns	0	0	1	0	**2**	1	0	1	0	0	0	0
KICKOFF RETURNS:												
Number	48	50	58	31	39	49	56	29	45	45	39	**69**
Yards	899	942	**1420**	783	822	1193	1202	662	946	987	930	1380
Average Yards	18.7	18.8	24.5	**25.3**	21.1	24.3	21.5	22.8	21.0	21.9	23.8	20.0
Touchdowns	0	0	**3**	0	1	0	1	0	0	0	0	1
INTERCEPTION RETURNS:												
Number	20	27	24	23	30	19	23	**33**	28	30	19	18
Yards	166	458	294	369	372	285	274	370	326	**569**	282	133
Average Yards	8.3	17.0	12.3	16.0	12.4	15.0	11.9	11.2	11.6	**19.0**	14.8	7.4
Touchdowns	0	1	0	**4**	2	1	1	0	1	3	2	0
PENALTIES:												
Number	71	71	**91**	83	75	57	77	61	85	54	73	54
Yards	662	592	819	796	689	522	757	502	**874**	471	614	455
FUMBLES:												
Number	**20**	30	32	25	22	21	27	25	38	28	30	41
Number Lost	12	15	23	17	**11**	12	18	15	22	17	13	23
POINTS:												
Total	131	301	183	336	**337**	234	314	293	284	219	313	207
PAT Attempts	13	38	23	41	**43**	29	41	36	39	28	40	27
PAT Made	12	37	21	40	**43**	27	41	36	36	25	37	26
FG Attempts	23	22	19	24	23	16	16	**25**	10	13	21	10
FG Made	11	12	8	**16**	12	9	9	13	4	8	12	5
Percent FG Made	47.8	54.5	42.1	**66.7**	52.2	56.3	56.3	52.0	40.0	61.5	57.1	50.0
Safeties	1	0	0	1	0	0	0	1	1	1	0	2

DEFENSE

	BALT.	CHI.B.	CHI.C.	CLEVE.	DET.	G.BAY	L.A.	N.Y.	PHIL.	PITT.	S.F.	WASH.
FIRST DOWNS:												
Total	234	221	226	**147**	199	228	240	195	171	221	207	282
by Rushing	95	94	85	**56**	85	101	92	77	64	120	74	108
by Passing	120	106	123	**73**	99	119	129	110	84	93	122	163
by Penalty	19	21	18	18	15	**8**	19	**8**	23	**8**	11	11
RUSHING:												
Number	425	427	400	372	397	403	368	415	354	466	**348**	400
Yards	1630	1917	1532	**1050**	1520	1871	1615	1332	1063	2193	1371	1888
Average Yards	3.8	4.5	3.8	**2.8**	3.8	4.6	4.4	3.2	3.0	4.7	3.9	4.7
Touchdowns	21	15	13	**4**	13	13	14	9	8	14	8	20
PASSING:												
Attempts	330	369	356	300	357	374	393	352	345	**295**	374	387
Completions	178	177	193	**126**	150	208	219	164	143	167	193	217
Completion Percentage	53.9	48.0	54.2	42.0	42.0	55.6	55.7	46.6	**41.4**	56.6	51.6	56.1
Gross Yards	2503	2432	3006	**1784**	2390	2690	2697	2322	2030	2458	3015	3060
Yards Lost Tackled	203	244	212	176	164	211	130	306	346	281	**366**	155
Net Yards	2300	2188	2794	**1608**	2226	2479	2567	2016	1684	2177	2649	2905
Avg. Yards per Attempt (Gross)	7.6	6.6	8.4	5.9	6.7	7.2	6.9	6.6	**5.9**	8.3	8.1	7.9
Avg. Yards per Comp. (Gross)	14.1	13.7	15.6	14.2	15.9	12.9	**12.3**	14.2	14.2	14.7	15.6	14.1
Touchdowns	12	13	29	15	**10**	17	16	11	13	18	24	33
Interceptions	20	27	24	23	30	19	23	**33**	28	30	19	18
Percent Intercepted	6.1	7.3	6.7	6.4	10.0	5.1	5.9	9.4	8.1	**10.2**	5.1	4.7
PUNTS:												
Number	57	65	55	**84**	65	64	58	71	71	54	59	45
Average Yards	39.8	39.4	41.7	40.1	**39.3**	40.1	43.0	40.2	42.3	39.9	41.0	39.6
PUNT RETURNS:												
Number	45	40	46	38	**29**	43	32	45	49	44	40	40
Yards	150	430	**55**	128	67	290	373	152	304	302	269	411
Average Yards	3.3	10.8	**1.2**	3.4	2.3	6.7	11.7	3.4	6.2	6.9	6.7	10.3
Touchdowns	**0**	2	**0**	1	**0**	1	**0**	**0**	1	**0**	**0**	**0**
KICKOFF RETURNS:												
Number	**29**	47	36	51	61	45	46	53	52	42	57	39
Yards	**587**	1018	832	1060	1257	832	1058	1274	1235	1003	1145	865
Average Yards	20.2	21.7	23.1	20.8	20.6	**18.5**	23.0	24.0	23.8	23.9	20.1	22.2
Touchdowns	**0**	1	1	**0**	**0**	**0**	**0**	1	2	1	**0**	**0**
INTERCEPTION RETURNS:												
Number	22	35	30	22	21	19	23	22	30	26	**12**	32
Yards	232	397	397	368	187	380	293	352	476	332	**167**	317
Average Yards	10.5	11.3	13.2	16.7	**8.9**	20.0	12.7	16.0	15.9	12.8	13.9	9.9
Touchdowns	1	2	1	2	**0**	1	1	1	2	1	**0**	3
PENALTIES:												
Number	92	87	74	58	53	72	63	65	58	**97**	51	82
Yards	**834**	696	716	608	489	666	605	562	589	823	426	739
FUMBLES:												
Number	28	31	30	26	22	22	18	**38**	32	31	29	32
Number Lost	10	18	19	19	12	14	6	**22**	**22**	20	18	18
POINTS:												
Total	279	279	347	**162**	189	251	285	184	230	263	251	432
PAT Attempts	36	34	44	**22**	23	33	34	23	27	34	32	56
PAT Made	36	32	42	21	21	32	33	**20**	25	33	32	54
FG Attempts	19	25	16	**9**	18	14	26	15	28	17	19	16
FG Made	9	13	11	**3**	10	7	16	8	13	8	9	12
Percent FG Made	47.4	52.0	68.8	**33.3**	55.6	50.0	61.5	53.3	46.4	47.1	47.4	75.0
Safeties	**0**	2	1	**0**	**0**	**0**	**0**	1	2	1	**0**	**0**

1954 CHAMPIONSHIP GAME

December 26 at Cleveland
(Attendance 43,827)

1954 Nearly Leaving on a Laugher

This was to be Otto Graham's last game, and he wanted to go out a winner. His first pass of the day was intercepted, leading to a Detroit field goal, but every move after that helped the Browns to a crushing 56-10 victory over the Lions. Before the first quarter had ended, the Browns led 14-3 on touchdown passes from Graham to Ray Renfro and Darrell Brewster. A 52-yard run by Lew Carpenter set up Detroit's only touchdown of the game in the second quarter, but the Browns scored three times before the half to run the score to 35-10; Graham made two touchdowns himself and passed to Renfro for another. The Cleveland defense shut the Lions out in the second half, while Graham and Co. poured it on. Graham and Fred Morrison scored in the third period, and Chet Hanulak added a final touchdown in the fourth quarter. It was a perfect farewell for Graham, but he would be back for a curtain call.

SCORING

CLEVELAND	14	21	14	7	–56
DETROIT	3	7	0	0	–10

First Quarter
- Det. Walker, 36 yard Field Goal
- Cle. Renfro, 35 yard pass from Graham; PAT – Groza (kick)
- Cle. Brewster, 8 yard pass from Graham; PAT – Groza (kick)

Second Quarter
- Cle. Graham, 1 yard rush; PAT – Groza (kick)
- Det. Bowman, 5 yard rush; PAT – Walker (kick)
- Cle. Graham, 5 yard rush; PAT – Groza (kick)
- Cle. Renfro, 31 yard pass from Graham; PAT – Groza (kick)

Third Quarter
- Cle. Graham, 1 yard rush; PAT – Groza (kick)
- Cle. Morrison, 12 yard rush; PAT – Groza (kick)

Fourth Quarter
- Cle. Hanulak, 10 yard rush; PAT – Groza (kick)

TEAM STATISTICS

DET.		CLE.
16	First Down – Total	17
5	by Rushing	8
9	by Passing	6
2	by Penalty	3
3	Fumbles – Number	2
3	Times Lost Ball	2
4	Penalties – Number	5
49	Yards Penalized	50
9	Giveaways	4
4	Takeaways	9
–5	Difference	+5

INDIVIDUAL STATISTICS

DETROIT	No	Yds	Avg.	CLEVELAND	No	Yds	Avg.
RUSHING							
Carpenter	8	34	8.0	Hanulak	5	44	8.8
Bowman	7	61	8.7	Graham	9	27	3.0
Walker	3	13	4.3	Bassett	8	27	3.4
Layne	7	7	1.0	Morrison	10	19	1.9
Horn'meyer	2	2	1.0	Reynolds	6	16	2.7
Dublinski	2	–11	–5.5	Jones	3	3	1.0
	29	136	4.7	Renfro	3	2	1.5
				Ratterman	1	2	2.0
					45	140	3.1
RECEIVING							
Carpenter	6	17	2.8	Renfro	5	94	18.8
Girard	5	57	11.4	Brewster	2	53	26.5
Dibble	4	63	15.8	Bassett	1	10	10.0
Walker	2	39	19.5	Lavelli	1	6	6.0
Hart	1	19	19.0		9	163	18.1
Bowman	1	0	0.0				
	19	195	10.3				
PUNT RETURNS							
Girard	1	0	0.0	Reynolds	1	42	42.0
				Konz	1	0	0.0
					2	42	21.0
KICKOFF RETURNS							
Girard	3	52	17.3	Reynolds	3	85	28.3
Christianson	2	36	18.0				
Walker	1	20	20.0				
	6	108	18.0				
INTERCEPTION RETURNS							
Schmidt	1	14	14.0	Ford	2	46	23.0
Christianson	1	0	0.0	Konz	2	28	14.0
	2	14	7.0	Paul	1	31	31.0
				Michaels	1	17	17.0
					6	122	20.3
PUNTING							
Girard	6		41.3	Gillom	4		43.0

PASSING

	Att	Comp	Comp Pct.	Yds	Yds/ Att.	Yds/ Comp	Yds Lost Tackled	Int
DETROIT								
Layne	42	18	42.9	177	4.2	9.8	0–0	6
Dublinski	2	1	50.0	18	9.0	18.0	0–0	0
	44	19	43.2	195	4.4	10.3	0–0	6
CLEVELAND								
Graham	12	9	75.0	163	13.6	18.1	0–0	2

CLEVELAND BROWNS 9-3-0 Paul Brown

Scores of Each Game		
10	Philadelphia	28
31	CHIC. CARDS	7
27	Pittsburgh	55
35	Chic. Cards	3
24	NEW YORK	14
62	WASHINGTON	3
39	Chic. Bears	10
6	PHILADELPHIA	0
16	New York	7
34	Washington	14
42	PITTSBURGH	7
10	DETROIT	14

Use Name	Pos.	Hgt	Wgt	Age	Int	Pts
Lou Groza	OT	6'3"	235	30		85
John Sandusky	OT	6'1"	250	28		
Don King	DT-OT	6'3"	260	24		
Harold Bradley	OG	6'2"	230	25		
Herschel Forester	OG	6'	230	24		
Abe Gibron	OG	5'11"	240	28		
Frank Gatski	C	6'3"	240	32		
Mike McCormack	DG	6'4"	248	27	1	
Doug Atkins	DE	6'8"	250	24		
Len Ford	DE	6'4"	250	28		2
Carlton Massey	DE	6'2"	215	25		
Don Colo	DT	6'3"	260	29		
John Kissell	DT	6'3"	238	31		
Bob Gain	OT-DG-DT	6'3"	250	26		
Tony Adamle	LB	6'	218	30		
Walt Michaels	LB	6'	225	25	1	
Chuck Noll	OG-LB	6'1"	210	22		
Tom Catlin	C-LB	6'1"	210	23	1	
Ken Gorgal	DB	6'2"	200	25	1	6
Kenny Konz	DB	5'10"	180	26	7	15
Don Paul	DB	6'	190	28	3	
Tommy James	HB-DB	5'10"	185	30	4	
Warren Lahr	HB-DB	5'11"	190	30	5	6
Otto Graham	QB	6'1"	205	32		48
George Ratterman	QB	6'1"	185	27		6
Chet Hanulak	HB	5'10"	180	21		24
Dub Jones	HB	6'4"	200	29		12
Ray Renfro	HB	6'1"	190	23		6
Billy Reynolds	HB	5'10"	190	22		12
Mo Bassett	FB	6'1"	230	24		36
Curley Morrison	FB	6'2"	215	28		12
Darrell Brewster	OE	6'3"	210	24		24
Dante Lavelli	OE	6'	190	31		42
Horace Gillom	DE-OE	6'1"	225	33		

Joe Skibinski – Military Service
Marion Motley-Leg Injury

PHILADELPHIA EAGLES 7-4-1 Jim Trimble

Scores of Each Game		
28	CLEVELAND	10
35	Chic. Cards	16
24	PITTSBURGH	22
49	Washington	21
7	Pittsburgh	17
14	GREEN BAY	37
30	CHIC. CARDS	14
14	New York	27
0	Cleveland	6
41	WASHINGTON	33
13	Detroit	13
29	NEW YORK	14

Use Name	Pos.	Hgt	Wgt	Age	Int	Pts
Gus Cifelli (to PIT)	OT	6'4"	250	28		
Lum Snyder	OT	6'5"	225	24		
Frank Wydo	OT	6'4"	235	30		
Ken Huxhold	OG	6'1"	215	25		
John Magee	OG	5'10"	220	31		
Menil Mavraides	OG	6'1"	235	20		
Tom Higgins	OT-OG	6'2"	230	25		
Ken Farragut	LB-C	6'4"	245	26		
Bucko Kilroy	DG	6'2"	250	33	4	
Tom Scott	DE	6'2"	218	24		
Don Luft	OE-DE	6'5"	220	25		
Norm Willey	OE-DE	6'2"	225	27		6
Mike Jarmoluk	DT	6'5"	250	31		
Jess Richardson	DT	6'2"	240	24	1	
Wayne Robinson	LB	6'2"	230	24	4	
Chuck Bednarik	C-LB	6'3"	230	29	1	
Ed Sharkey	OT-OG-LB	6'3"	230	27	1	
Roy Barni	DB	5'11"	185	27	2	
Harry Dowda	DB	6'2"	200	30	2	
Ralph Goldston	DB	5'11"	195	26		
Bob Hudson	DB	6'4"	220	24	8	
Don Miller (from GB)	DB	6'2"	195	23		
Bud Roffler	DB	6'1"	200	25		
Don Stevens	DB	5'9"	176	27		
Jerry Norton	HB-DB	5'11"	183	24	5	6
Adrian Burk	QB	6'2"	190	26		
Bobby Thomason	QB	6'1"	200	25		
Skippy Giancanelli	HB	5'10"	173	25		24
Don Johnson	HB	6'	187	23		
Toy Ledbetter	HB	5'10"	200	27		24
Jerry Williams	HB	5'10"	185	30		24
Dom Moselle	DB-HB	6'	193	28		18
Jim Parmer	FB	6'	195	27		
Neil Worden	FB	5'10"	190	24		6
Bobby Walston	OE	6'	190	25		114
Pete Pihos	DE-OE	6'1"	210	30		60

Bibbles Bawel – Military Service
Tom Brookshier – Military Service
Bill Horrell – Military Service
Maury Nipp – Military Service

NEW YORK GIANTS 7-5-0 Jim Lee Howell

Scores of Each Game		
41	Chic. Cards	10
14	Baltimore	20
51	Washington	21
31	CHIC. CARDS	17
24	WASHINGTON	7
14	Cleveland	24
30	Pittsburgh	6
27	PHILADELPHIA	14
16	LOS ANGELES	17
7	CLEVELAND	16
24	PITTSBURGH	3
14	Philadelphia	29

Use Name	Pos.	Hgt	Wgt	Age	Int	Pts
Rosey Brown	OT	6'3"	245	21		
Dick Yelvington	OT	6'2"	230	27		
Bill Austin	OG	6'1"	225	25		
John Bauer	OG	6'3"	235	22		
Russ Carroccio	OG	6'1"	235	23		
George Kennard	OG	6'	215	25		
Jack Stroud	OG	6'1"	215	25		
Bill Albright	OT-DT-OG	6'1"	235	25		
John Rapacz	C	6'4"	260	29		
Barney Poole	DE	6'2"	250	31		
Pat Knight	LB-DE	6'2"	210	25	3	
Ray Collins	DT	5'11"	235	26		
Ray Krouse	DT	6'3"	260	27		
Billy Shipp	DT	6'5"	275	23		
John Cannady	LB	6'2"	245	30	2	
Pete Mangum	LB	6'	218	22		
Bill Svoboda	LB	6'	210	27	1	
Ray Wietecha	C-LB	6'1"	225	25		
Cliff Livingston	DE-LB	6'3"	205	24		
Tom Landry	DB	6'1"	195	29	8	
Dick Nolan	DB	6'1"	185	22	6	2
Herb Rich	DB	5'11"	180	25	5	
Em Tunnell	DB	6'1"	185	32	8	
Wayne Berry	HB-DB	6'	175	21		
Bobby Clatterbuck	QB	6'3"	195	22		6
Chuck Conerly	QB	6'1"	185	30		7
Don Heinrich	QB	6'	185	22		
Frank Gifford	HB	6'1"	195	24		18
Herb Johnson	HB	5'10"	172	25		12
Cutter Long	HB	6'1"	195	22		12
Kyle Rote	HB	6'	195	25		12
Bobby Epps	FB	5'9"	195	23		
Eddie Price	FB	5'11"	190	28		30
Ken MacAfee	OE	6'2"	205	24		48
Bob Schnelker	OE	6'3"	215	24		48
Bob Topp	OE	6'2"	190	22		18
Dick Wilkins	OE	6'2"	195	28		6
Ben Agajanian	K	6'	215	35		74

Ray Beck – Military Service
Arnie Weinmeister – Canadian Football League

PITTSBURGH STEELERS 5-7-0 Joe Bach Walt Kiesling

Scores of Each Game		
21	Green Bay	20
37	WASHINGTON	7
22	Philadelphia	24
55	CLEVELAND	27
17	PHILADELPHIA	7
14	Chic. Cards	17
6	NEW YORK	30
14	Washington	17
3	SAN FRANCISCO	31
20	CHIC. CARDS	17
3	New York	24
7	Cleveland	42

Use Name	Pos.	Hgt	Wgt	Age	Int	Pts
Bob Gaona	OT	6'3"	245	24		
George Hughes	OT	6'1"	225	29		
Nick Bolkovac	DT-OT	6'1"	230	27		12
Joe Matesic	DT-OT	6'4"	250	26		
Rudy Andabaker	OG	6'	210	25		
Pete Ladygo	OG	6'2"	220	26		
John Schweder	LB-OG	6'1"	225	27		
Bill Walsh	C	6'2"	238	27		
Dewey Brundage	DE	6'3"	210	23		
Bill McPeak	DE	6'1"	200	29		2
Joe Zombek	DE	6'1"	195	22		
Ernie Cheatham (to BAL)	DT	6'4"	245	26		
Lou Ferry	DT	6'2"	245	27		
Tom Palmer	DT	6'2"	240	26		
Ernie Stautner	DT	6'1"	235	29	1	
Dale Dodrill	LB	6'1"	210	29	3	
Dick Flanagan	LB	6'	220	27	3	
Stan Sheriff	C-LB	6'1"	230	23	1	
Lou Tepe	C-LB	6'2"	205	24	3	
Paul Cameron	DB	6'	185	23	7	
Russ Craft	DB	5'9"	180	34	3	6
Ed Kissell	DB	6'1"	195	26	1	14
Jack Butler	OE-DB	6'	195	26	4	12
Dewey McConnell	OE-DB	6'	190	25	3	
Jim Finks	QB	6'	175	27		
Paul Held	QB	6'2"	195	26		23
Tom Calvin	HB	6'	200	28		
Lynn Chandnois	HB	6'2"	195	30		6
Johnny Lattner	HB	6'1"	195	22		42
Ray Mathews	HB	6'	185	25		48
Jim Brandt	DB-HB	6'1"	200	26		6
Burrell Shields	DB-HB	6'2"	205	22	1	
Leo Elter	FB	5'10"	200	25		
Fran Rogel	FB	5'11"	205	27		12
Elbie Nickel	OE	6'1"	195	31		30
George Sulima	OE	6'2"	200	27		6
Jack O'Brien	DE-OE	6'2"	215	23		
Pat Brady	K	6'1"	195	26		

Marv Matuszak – Military Service
Marv McFadden – Military Service
Ed Modzelewski – Military Service
George Tarasovic – Military Service

WASHINGTON REDSKINS 3-9-0 Joe Kuharich

Scores of Each Game		
7	San Francisco	41
7	Pittsburgh	37
21	NEW YORK	51
21	PHILADELPHIA	49
7	New York	24
24	BALTIMORE	21
3	Cleveland	62
17	PITTSBURGH	14
16	Chic. Cards	38
33	Philadelphia	41
14	CLEVELAND	34
37	CHIC. CARDS	20

Use Name	Pos.	Hgt	Wgt	Age	Int	Pts
Don Boll	OT	6'2"	274	27		
Dave Sparks – died Dec. 5	OT	6'1"	238	25		
Ken Barfield	DT-OT	6'2"	238	25		
Slug Witucki	OG	5'11"	253	26		
Marv Berschet	DE-OG	6'2"	220	25		
Ron Hansen	LB-OG	6'	220	22		
Harry Ulinski	C	6'4"	228	29		
Jim Schrader	OT-C	6'2"	233	22		
Jim Ricca	OT-DT-DG	6'4"	274	27		8
Chet Ostrowski	DE	6'1"	225	24	1	
Walt Yowarsky	DE	6'2"	235	26		
Dick Modzelewski	DT	6'	260	23		2
Volney Peters	DT	6'4"	230	26		
Bob Morgan (from Chi C)	OT-DT	6'	235	21		
Nick Adducci	LB	5'10"	210	25		
Walt Cudzik	C-LB	6'2"	215	21		
Joe Tereshinski	DE-LB	6'2"	220	30		
Chuck Drazenovich	FB-LB	6'1"	224	27	1	
Ralph Felton	FB-LB	5'11"	210	22	2	19
Dick Alban	DB	6'	192	25	9	
Jim Kincaid	DB	5'11"	180	23		1
Don Menasco	DB	6'	185	24		
George Rosso	DB	5'11"	177	24	4	
Scooter Scudero	HB-DB	5'10"	175	24	1	6
Al Dorow	QB	6'	194	24		18
Jack Scarbath	QB	6'2"	208	24		
Vic Janowicz	HB	5'9"	184	24		21
Choo-Choo Justice	HB	5'10"	178	30		18
Billy Wells	HB	5'9"	178	22		24
Harry Gilmer	DB-HB	6'	173	28		
Dale Atkeson	FB	6'2"	210	24		18
Rob Goode	FB	6'4"	226	27		6
Ed Barker	OE	6'3"	193	31		18
Johnny Carson	OE	6'3"	200	24		
Hugh Taylor	OE	6'4"	208	31		48
Sam Morley	OE	6'2"	182	22		

Sam Baker – Military Service
Gene Brito – Canadian Football League
Billy Cox – Military Service
Art DeCarlo – Military Service
Paul Dekker – Canadian Football League
Norb Hecker – Canadian Football League
Eddie LeBaron – Canadian Football League

CHICAGO CARDINALS 2-10-0 Joe Stydahar

Scores of Each Game		
10	NEW YORK	41
16	PHILADELPHIA	35
7	Cleveland	31
17	New York	31
3	CLEVELAND	35
17	PITTSBURGH	14
14	Philadelphia	30
17	Los Angeles	28
38	WASHINGTON	16
17	Pittsburgh	20
7	CHIC. BEARS	29
20	Washington	37

Use Name	Pos.	Hgt	Wgt	Age	Int	Pts
Jack Jennings	OT	6'4"	248	27		
Len Teeuws	OT	6'4"	245	27		
Ledio Fanucchi	DT-OT	6'2"	225	23		
Dick Fugler	DT-OT	6'2"	240	24		
John Hatley	OG	6'3"	245	23		
Jerry Watford	DE-OG	6'3"	205	24		
Bill Lange	LB-OG	6'1"	230	27		
Jack Simmons	C	6'4"	230	28		
Tom Bienemann	DE	6'3"	215	26		
Leo Sugar	DE	6'1"	200	25		6
Pat Summerall	DE	6'4"	220	24		45
Jerry Groom	DT	6'3"	235	25		
Chuck Ulrich	DT	6'4"	225	23		
Gordon Polofsky	OG-LB	6'1"	220	23		
Fred Wallner	OG-LB	6'2"	230	25		
Leo Sanford	C-LB	6'1"	220	25	2	
Elmer Arterburn	DB	5'10"	175	25		
Al Brosky	DB	5'11"	175	24	2	
Ellsworth Kingery	DB	5'11"	180	25	1	
Charley Oakley	DB	5'10"	170	23		
Bill Bredde	HB-DB	6'1"	195	21	2	6
George Kinek	OE-DB	6'2"	190	25	2	
Night Train Lane	OE-DB	6'1"	190	26	10	
Lamar McHan	QB	6'1"	190	22		6
Steve Romanik	QB	6'1"	190	30		6
Paul Barry	HB	6'	210	28		
Emmett King	HB	5'9"	195	21		6
George Brancato	DB-HB	5'9"	177	23		
Les Goble	DB-HB	5'11"	160	22	1	18
Ollie Matson	DB-HB	6'2"	210	24	1	54
Jimmy Sears	DB-HB	5'11"	178	23		
Charlie Trippi	DB-HB	6'	185	31	3	6
Johnny Olszewski	FB	5'11"	195	23		12
Jack Crittendon	OE	6'1"	190	23		
Mel Embree	OE	6'3"	190	27		
Jim Ladd	OE	6'4"	205	21		
Don Stonesifer	OE	6'	200	27		18

Ed Husmann – Military Service
Gern Nagler – Military Service
Jim Root – Military Service
Dave Suminski – Canadian Football League
Ralph Thomas – Military Service

CLEVELAND BROWNS

RUSHING

Last Name	No.	Yds	Avg	TD
Bassett	144	588	4.1	6
Hanulak	59	296	5.0	4
Morrison	54	234	4.3	2
Jones	51	231	4.5	0
Reynolds	64	180	2.8	2
Renfro	29	151	5.2	0
Graham	63	114	1.8	8
Lahr	3	18	6.0	0
James	1	–6	–6.0	0
Ratterman	8	–13	–1.6	1

RECEIVING

Last Name	No.	Yds	Avg	TD
Lavelli	47	802	17	7
Brewster	42	676	16	4
Bassett	20	205	10	0
Jones	19	347	18	2
Renfro	13	228	18	1
Morrison	12	81	7	0
Reynolds	10	76	8	0
Hanulak	6	80	13	0
Gillom	5	62	12	0

PUNT RETURNS

Last Name	No.	Yds	Avg	TD
Reynolds	25	138	6	0
Hanulak	27	92	3	0
Paul	1	57	57	0
Konz	7	37	5	0
Gorgal	1	0	0	0

KICKOFF RETURNS

Last Name	No.	Yds	Avg	TD
Reynolds	14	413	30	0
Hanulak	9	213	24	0
Konz	2	53	27	0
Paul	1	31	31	0
Renfro	1	24	24	0
Bassett	1	20	20	0
Gorgal	1	11	11	0
Massey	1	10	10	0
Morrison	1	8	8	0

PASSING – PUNTING – KICKING

PASSING	Att	Comp	%	Yds	Yd/Att	TD	Int–%	RK
Graham	240	142	59	2092	8.7	11	17– 7	3
Ratterman	53	32	60	465	8.8	3	3– 5	
Lahr	1	0	0	0	0.0	0	1–100	
Renfro	1	0	0	0	0.0	0	1–100	

PUNTING	No	Avg
Gillom	52	42.9

KICKING	XP	Att	%	FG	Att	%
Groza	37	38	97	16	24	67
Konz	3	3	100	0	0	0

PHILADELPHIA EAGLES

RUSHING

Last Name	No.	Yds	Avg	TD
Parmer	119	408	3.4	0
Ledbetter	81	241	3.0	1
Williams	47	183	3.9	1
Worden	58	128	2.2	1
Moselle	29	114	3.9	1
Giancanelli	33	47	1.4	0
Thomason	10	45	4.5	0
Burk	15	18	1.2	0
Johnson	7	16	2.3	0
Pihos	1	–1	–1.0	0
Norton	1	–3	–3.0	0

RECEIVING

Last Name	No.	Yds	Avg	TD
Pihos	60	872	15	10
Williams	44	668	15	15
Walston	31	581	19	11
Moselle	17	242	14	2
Ledbetter	15	192	13	3
Giancanelli	14	195	14	4
Parmer	12	40	3	0
Worden	7	63	9	0
Luft	3	59	20	0
Willey	2	50	25	0
Johnson	1	20	20	0

PUNT RETURNS

Last Name	No.	Yds	Avg	TD
Williams	23	153	7	0
Norton	21	89	4	0
Bednarik	2	26	13	0
Sharkey	1	5	5	0
Barni	1	0	0	0
Cifelli	1	0	0	0

KICKOFF RETURNS

Last Name	No.	Yds	Avg	TD
Giancanelli	17	387	23	0
Ledbetter	8	175	22	0
Johnson	6	152	25	0
Moselle	7	149	21	0
Bednarik	3	40	13	0
Roffler	1	19	19	0
Snyder	2	17	9	0
Stevens	1	6	6	0

PASSING – PUNTING – KICKING

PASSING	Att	Comp	%	Yds	Yd/Att	TD	Int–%	RK
Burk	231	123	53	1740	7.5	23	17– 7	5
Thomason	170	83	49	1242	7.3	10	13– 8	14

PUNTING	No	Avg
Burk	73	40.0

KICKING	XP	Att	%	FG	Att	%
Walston	36	39	92	4	10	40

NEW YORK GIANTS

RUSHING

Last Name	No.	Yds	Avg	TD
Price	135	555	4.1	2
Gifford	66	368	5.6	2
Johnson	42	168	4.0	1
Epps	30	110	3.7	0
Conerly	24	107	4.5	1
Long	32	106	3.3	1
Rote	30	60	2.0	0
Berry	1	30	30.0	0
Heinrich	1	0	0.0	0
Clatterbuck	19	–21	–1.1	1

RECEIVING

Last Name	No.	Yds	Avg	TD
Schnelker	30	550	18	8
Rote	29	551	19	2
Price	28	352	13	3
MacAfee	24	438	18	8
Gifford	14	154	11	1
Long	13	178	14	1
Johnson	10	89	9	0
Topp	6	90	15	3
Epps	5	20	4	0
Wilkins	4	45	11	1

PUNT RETURNS

Last Name	No.	Yds	Avg	TD
Johnson	16	164	10	1
Tunnell	21	70	3	0
Long	6	54	9	0
Gifford	8	12	2	0
Rich	1	5	5	0

KICKOFF RETURNS

Last Name	No.	Yds	Avg	TD
Johnson	10	251	25	u
Long	10	237	24	0
Tunnell	5	98	20	0
Gifford	1	29	29	0
Svoboda	1	21	21	0
Kennard	1	16	16	0
Topp	1	10	10	0

PASSING – PUNTING – KICKING

PASSING	Att	Comp	%	Yds	Yd/Att	TD	Int–%	RK
Conerly	210	103	49	1439	6.9	17	11– 5	7
Clatterbuck	101	50	50	781	7.7	6	7– 7	12
Heinrich	9	4	44	56	6.2	0	2– 22	
Gifford	8	4	50	155	19.4	3	1– 13	
Rote	6	2	33	36	6.0	1	1– 17	

PUNTING	No	Avg
Landry	64	42.5

KICKING	XP	Att	%	FG	Att	%
Agajanian	35	35	100	13	25	52
Conerly	1	1	100	0	0	0

PITTSBURGH STEELERS

RUSHING

Last Name	No.	Yds	Avg	TD
Rogel	111	415	3.7	1
Mathews	80	242	3.0	2
Lattner	69	237	3.4	5
Chandnois	45	147	3.3	1
Brandt	19	82	4.3	1
Calvin	12	57	4.8	0
Elter	13	54	4.2	0
Shields	7	28	4.0	0
Finks	9	17	1.9	0
Held	3	3	1.0	0

RECEIVING

Last Name	No.	Yds	Avg	TD
Mathews	44	652	15	6
Nickel	40	584	15	5
Sulima	30	439	15	1
Lattner	25	305	12	2
Chandnois	22	176	8	0
Rogel	18	51	3	1
Elter	4	16	4	0
Shields	1	22	22	0
Calvin	1	19	19	0
Butler	1	12	12	0
Brandt	1	9	9	0
O'Brien	1	9	9	0
McConnell	1	2	2	0
Gaona	0	25	0	0

PUNT RETURNS

Last Name	No.	Yds	Avg	TD
Lattner	17	73	4	0
Cameron	2	19	10	0
Chandnois	8	12	2	0
Mathews	2	6	3	0
Shields	3	0	0	0

KICKOFF RETURNS

Last Name	No.	Yds	Avg	TD
Lattner	16	413	26	0
Chandnois	13	256	20	0
Shields	9	183	20	0
Mathews	4	88	22	0
Elter	2	32	16	0
Calvin	1	15	15	0

PASSING – PUNTING – KICKING

PASSING	Att	Comp	%	Yds	Yd/Att	TD	Int–%	RK
Finks	306	164	54	2003	6.6	14	19– 6	7
Held	73	24	33	305	4.2	1	6– 8	
Mathews	4	0	0	0	0.0	0	1– 25	
Chandnois	3	1	33	13	4.3	0	0– 0	

PUNTING	No	Avg
Brady	66	43.2

KICKING	XP	Att	%	FG	Att	%
Held	14	16	88	3	5	60
Kissell	8	9	89	2	4	50
Bolkovac	3	3	100	3	4	75

WASHINGTON REDSKINS

RUSHING

Last Name	No.	Yds	Avg	TD
Wells	100	516	5.2	3
Goode	108	462	4.3	0
Justice	56	254	4.5	1
Atkeson	68	176	2.6	2
Dorow	34	117	3.4	3
Scarbath	17	36	2.1	0
Gilmer	6	19	3.2	0
Scudero	21	19	0.9	0
Janowicz	6	13	2.2	0
Felton	3	8	2.7	0
Drazenovich	8	6	0.8	0

RECEIVING

Last Name	No.	Yds	Avg	TD
Taylor	37	659	18	8
Barker	23	353	15	3
Wells	19	295	16	1
Carson	12	139	12	0
Justice	11	242	22	2
Atkeson	4	75	19	0
Scudero	4	32	8	1
Goode	4	4	1	0
Drazenovich	1	15	15	0
Janowicz	1	–1	–1	0

PUNT RETURNS

Last Name	No.	Yds	Avg	TD
Scudero	14	53	4	0
Atkeson	4	29	7	0
Wells	3	24	8	0
Rosso	4	15	4	0
Felton	1	0	0	0

KICKOFF RETURNS

Last Name	No.	Yds	Avg	TD
Atkeson	24	623	26	1
Wells	17	319	19	0
Goode	16	284	18	0
Scudero	3	70	23	0
Felton	2	18	9	0
Janowicz	1	18	18	0
Drazenovich	1	17	17	0
Yowarsky	1	13	13	0
Ostrowski	3	9	3	0
Ricca	1	9	9	0

PASSING – PUNTING – KICKING

PASSING	Att	Comp	%	Yds	Yd/Att	TD	Int–%	RK
Dorow	138	70	51	997	7.2	8	17– 12	15
Scarbath	109	44	40	798	7.3	7	13– 12	16
Gilmer	7	2	29	18	2.6	0	1– 14	
Justice	2	0	0	0	0.0	0	1– 50	
Janowicz	1	0	0	0	0.0	0	0– 0	

PUNTING	No	Avg
Justice	61	40.3
Janowicz	1	32.0

KICKING	XP	Att	%	FG	Att	%
Felton	16	17	94	1	2	50
Janowicz	9	9	100	4	8	50
Kincaid	1	1	100	0	0	0

CHICAGO CARDINALS

RUSHING

Last Name	No.	Yds	Avg	TD
Matson	101	506	5.0	4
Olszewski	106	352	3.3	1
King	57	167	2.9	0
Barry	50	156	3.1	0
Trippi	18	152	8.4	1
McHan	34	152	4.5	1
Bredde	13	57	4.4	1
Goble	30	42	1.4	1
Brancato	2	26	13.0	0
Romanik	7	2	0.3	1

RECEIVING

Last Name	No.	Yds	Avg	TD
Stonesifer	44	607	14	3
Matson	34	611	18	3
Ladd	22	254	12	0
Olszewski	12	133	11	1
Barry	7	29	4	0
King	6	43	7	1
Crittendon	5	48	10	0
Lane	4	58	15	0
Bredde	3	44	15	0
Brancato	3	28	9	0
Trippi	3	18	6	0
Embree	2	20	10	0
Goble	1	–1	–1	0

PUNT RETURNS

Last Name	No.	Yds	Avg	TD
Matson	11	100	9	1
Trippi	6	57	10	0
Goble	22	51	2	0

KICKOFF RETURNS

Last Name	No.	Yds	Avg	TD
Goble	27	749	28	2
Matson	17	449	26	1
Barry	5	80	16	0
Sears	2	38	19	0
Olszewski	1	21	21	0
Bredde	1	19	19	0
King	1	19	19	0
Trippi	1	17	17	0
Hatley	1	11	11	0
Jennings	1	10	10	0
Sugar	1	7	7	0

PASSING – PUNTING – KICKING

PASSING	Att	Comp	%	Yds	Yd/Att	TD	Int–%	RK
McHan	255	105	41	1475	5.8	6	22– 9	17
Romanik	79	36	46	343	4.3	2	5– 6	
Trippi	13	7	54	85	6.5	0	3– 23	
Matson	2	0	0	0	0.0	0	0– 0	

PUNTING	No	Avg
Trippi	59	39.1
McHan	4	39.8

KICKING	XP	Att	%	FG	Att	%
Summerall	21	23	91	8	18	44
Crittendon	0	0	0	0	1	0

DETROIT LIONS 9-2-1 Buddy Parker

Scores of Each Game		
48	CHIC. BEARS	23
21	LOS ANGELES	3
35	BALTIMORE	0
31	San Francisco	37
27	Los Angeles	24
27	Baltimore	3
48	SAN FRANCISCO	7
21	Green Bay	17
28	GREEN BAY	24
13	PHILADELPHIA	13
24	Chic. Bears	28
14	Cleveland	10

Use Name	Pos.	Hgt	Wgt	Age	Int	Pts
Charlie Ane	OT	6'2"	250	23		
Lou Creekmur	DT-OT	6'4"	255	27		
Dick Stanfel	OG	6'3"	240	27		
Harley Sewell	LB-OG	6'1"	225	23		6
Andy Miketa	C	6'2"	210	23		
Les Bingaman	DG	6'3"	320	29		
Jim Cain	DE	6'1"	200	27		
Bob Dove	DE	6'2"	220	33		
Sonny Gandee	DE	6'1"	220	25	3	
Hal Turner	DE	6'2"	235	24		
Jim Doran	OE-DE	6'2"	200	26		24
Gil Mains	DT	6'2"	235	24		
Jerry Perry	DT	6'4"	235	23		
Thurman McGraw	OT-DT	6'5"	235	27		
Bob Miller	OT-DT	6'3"	235	24		
Joe Schmidt	LB	6'1"	220	22	2	
Jim Martin	OG-LB	6'2"	230	30		3
Lavern Torgeson	C-LB	6'	215	25	2	
Jack Christiansen	DB	6'1"	190	25	8	12
Jim David	DB	5'11"	175	27	7	
Carl Karilivacz	DB	6'	185	23	2	6
Bill Stits	DB	6'	190	23	6	
Tom Dublinski	QB	6'2"	190	24		6
Bobby Layne	QB	6'1"	200	27		12
Bob Hoernschemeyer	HB	5'11"	195	28		18
Doak Walker	HB	5'11"	172	27		106
Dick Kercher	DB-HB	6'2"	205	22		
Lew Carpenter	FB-HB	6'1"	200	22		30
Jug Girard	OE-HB	5'11"	175	27		42
Bill Bowman	FB	6'2"	210	23		30
Bob Smith	FB	6'	205	25		
Cloyce Box	OE	6'4"	220	30		
Dorne Dibble	OE	6'2"	195	25		36
Leon Hart	OE	6'5"	250	25		6

Stan Campbell – Military Service
Gene Gedman – Military Service
Jim Hill – Military Service
Yale Lary – Military Service
Ollie Spencer – Military Service

CHICAGO BEARS 8-4-0 George Halas

Scores of Each Game		
23	Detroit	48
10	Green Bay	3
28	BALTIMORE	9
24	SAN FRANCISCO	31
38	Los Angeles	42
31	San Francisco	27
28	GREEN BAY	23
10	CLEVELAND	39
28	Baltimore	13
24	LOS ANGELES	13
29	Chic. Cards	7
28	DETROIT	24

Use Name	Pos.	Hgt	Wgt	Age	Int	Pts
Stan Jones	OT	6'1"	255	23		
Bill Wightkin	OT	6'3"	233	27		
George Connor	LB-OT	6'3"	240	29	1	
Kline Gilbert	OG	6'2"	235	23		
Fred Williams	OG	6'4"	250	24		
Larry Strickland	C	6'4"	255	23		
Larry Brink	DE	6'5"	240	31		6
Ted Daffer	DE	6'	198	24		
Ed Meadows	DE	6'2"	220	22		
Ed Sprinkle	DE	6'1"	210	30	1	
Bill Bishop	DT	6'4"	245	23		
John Kreamcheck	DT	6'5"	255	26		
Paul Lipscomb (from WAS)	DT	6'5"	250	31		
Herman Clark	LB	6'3"	255	23		
John Helwig	LB	6'2"	208	26	3	
Jerry Weatherley	C-LB	6'5"	218	25	2	6
Bill George	OG-LB	6'2"	240	23	2	25
Pete Perini	FB-LB	6'	225	26		1
Wayne Hansen	OT-OG-C-LB	6'2"	235	26	1	6
Lloyd Lowe	DB	5'10"	155	25		
McNeil Moore	DB	6'	185	21	3	
Stan Wallace	DB	6'3"	208	22	4	
S. J. Whitman	DB	5'11"	185	28	5	6
Don Kindt	HB-DB	6'1"	208	28	2	
Ray Gene Smith	HB-DB	5'10"	188	24	2	
George Blanda	QB	6'1"	207	26		47
Zeke Bratkowski	QB	6'2"	202	22		6
Ed Brown	DB-QB	6'2"	205	25	1	
Bucky McElroy	HB	5'11"	195	25		
Billy Stone	HB	6'	190	28		36
Billy Anderson	DB-HB	6'	198	25		
John Hoffman	OE-HB	6'2"	215	28		12
Leon Campbell	FB	6'	197	27		
Chick Jagade	FB	6'	220	27		18
Jim Dooley	OE	6'4"	198	24		42
Harlon Hill	OE	6'3"	198	22		72
Bill McColl	OE	6'4"	230	24		12
Gene Schroeder	OE	6'3"	190	25		6

Frank Dempsey – Canadian Football League
Jack Hoffman – Military Service
Eddie Macon – Canadian Football League
Tom O'Connell – Military Service
Bob Williams – Military Service

SAN FRANCISCO FORTY NINERS 7-4-1 Buck Shaw

Scores of Each Game		
41	WASHINGTON	7
24	Los Angeles	24
23	Green Bay	17
31	Chic. Bears	24
37	DETROIT	31
27	CHIC. BEARS	31
34	LOS ANGELES	42
7	Detroit	48
31	Pittsburgh	3
13	Baltimore	17
35	GREEN BAY	0
10	BALTIMORE	7

Use Name	Pos.	Hgt	Wgt	Age	Int	Pts
Bob St. Clair	OT	6'9"	262	23		
Doug Hogland	OG-OT	6'3"	235	23		
Bruno Banducci	OG	5'11"	220	32		
Ted Connolly	OG	6'3"	225	22		
Nick Feher	OG	6'	225	27		
Bob Hantla	LB-OG	6'1"	220	22		
Bill Johnson	C	6'3"	240	28		
Jack Brumfield	DE	6'2"	215	22		
Clay Matthews	DE	6'3"	220	26		
Al Carapella	DT	6'	235	27	2	
Leo Nomellini	OT-DT	6'3"	252	29		
Bob Toneff	OT-DG	6'2"	252	24	1	
Marion Campbell	OT-DE-DT	6'3"	245	25		
Hardy Brown	LB	6'	196	30	3	6
Don Burke	OG-LB	6'	240	28		
Art Michalik	OG-LB	6'2"	230	24		
Pete Brown	C-LB	6'2"	210	23	1	
Pete Wissman	C-LB	6'	220	30		
Frank Cassara	FB-LB	6'	215	27		
Rex Berry	DB	5'11"	180	28	3	6
Johnny Williams	DB	5'11"	180	27	3	
Jim Cason	HB-DB	6'	175	27		
Billy Mixon	HB-DB	5'11"	197	24	2	
Billy Tidwell	HB-DB	5'9"	178	23		
Floyd Sagely	OE-DB	6'1"	187	22		
Maury Duncan	QB	6'1"	185	23		
Arnie Galiffa	QB	6'2"	190	27		
Y. A. Tittle	QB	6'	190	27		24
John Henry Johnson	HB	6'2"	205	24		54
Hugh McElhenny	HB	6'1"	198	25		36
Joe Arenas	DB-HB	5'11"	180	28	3	
Pete Schabarum	DB-HB	5'11"	185	25	1	6
Joe Perry	FB	6'	210	27		57
Bill Jessup	OE	6'1"	195	25		18
Gordie Soltau	OE	6'2"	195	29		76
Billy Wilson	OE	6'3"	190	27		30
Harry Babcock	DE-OE	6'2"	195	23		

Fred Bruney – Military Service
Ed Henke – Military Service
Pat O'Donahue – Military Service
Charley Powell – Military Service
Verl Lillywhite – Military Service
Jerry Smith – Military Service
Bob White – Military Service

LOS ANGELES RAMS 6-5-1 Hamp Pool

Scores of Each Game		
48	Baltimore	0
24	SAN FRANCISCO	24
3	Detroit	21
17	Green Bay	35
42	CHIC. BEARS	38
24	DETROIT	27
42	San Francisco	34
28	CHIC. CARDS	17
17	New York	16
13	Chic. Bears	24
21	BALTIMORE	22
35	GREEN BAY	27

Use Name	Pos.	Hgt	Wgt	Age	Int	Pts
Bob Cross	OT	6'4"	250	23		
Tom Dahms	OT	6'5"	240	26		
Duane Putnam	OG	6'	230	26		
Harry Thompson	OG	6'2"	225	27		
Art Hauser	DT-OG	6'	230	23		
Leon McLaughlin	C	6'2"	228	28		
Stan West	DG	6'2"	235	27	1	
Duane Wardlow	DE	6'4"	215	22		
Paul Miller	C-DE	6'2"	215	22	1	
Andy Robustelli	DE	6'1"	220	28		6
Big Daddy Lipscomb	DT	6'6"	280	23		
Charlie Toogood	OT-DT	6'	235	26	1	
Bob Griffin	LB	6'3"	220	25		
Les Richter	LB	6'3"	240	23	1	62
Harland Svare	LB	6'	210	23		
Don Paul	C-LB	6'1"	230	29		
Bud McFadin	OG-DT-LB	6'3"	245	26		
Bill Bowers	DB	6'	198	23		
Don Doll	DB	5'10"	185	27	5	
Jack Dwyer	DB	5'11"	175	27	4	6
Hall Haynes	DB	6'	185	25	1	
Ed Haynes	DB	6'1"	185	26	2	
Will Sherman	DB	6'2"	200	25	6	
Norm Van Brocklin	QB	6'1"	200	28		
Billy Wade	QB	6'2"	215	23		6
Tom McCormick	HB	5'11"	190	24		
Skeets Quinlan	HB	5'11"	175	26		36
Woodley Lewis	DB-OE-HB	6'	195	29		6
Tank Younger	LB-FB-HB	6'3"	226	26		48
Dan Towler	FB	6'2"	226	26		66
Bob Boyd	OE	6'2"	200	26		36
Bob Carey	OE	6'5"	215	26		5
Tom Fears	OE	6'2"	215	30		19
Crazy Legs Hirsch	DB-OE	6'2"	190	30	1	18

Rudy Bukich – Military Service
Dick Daugherty – Military Service
Bob Fry – Military Service
Don Klosterman – Military Service
Brad Myers – Military Service

GREEN BAY PACKERS 4-8-0 Lisle Blackbourn

Scores of Each Game		
20	PITTSBURGH	21
3	CHIC. BEARS	10
17	SAN FRANCISCO	23
35	LOS ANGELES	17
7	Baltimore	6
37	Philadelphia	14
23	Chic. Bears	28
24	BALTIMORE	13
17	DETROIT	21
24	Detroit	28
0	San Francisco	35
27	Los Angeles	35

Use Name	Pos.	Hgt	Wgt	Age	Int	Pts
Art Hunter	OT	6'4"	240	21		
Len Szafaryn	OT	6'2"	225	26		
Al Barry	OG	6'2"	225	23		
Buddy Brown	OG	6'1"	225	27		
Dave Stephenson	C-OG	6'2"	230	28		
Jim Ringo	C	6'1"	230	23		
Dick Afflis	OT-OG-DG	6'1"	250	25	1	
Carl Elliott	DE	6'4"	230	27		
Gene Knutson	DE	6'2"	205	22		
John Martinkovic	DE	6'3"	245	27		
Gene White	DE	6'2"	205	22	1	
Dave Hanner	DT	6'2"	260	25		
Jerry Helluin	DT	6'2"	280	24		
Bill Forester	LB	6'3"	235	23	1	
Deral Teteak	LB	5'10"	210	25	1	
Clayton Tonnemaker	LB	6'2"	240	26	1	
Roger Zatkoff	LB	6'2"	215	23	1	
Steve Ruzich	OT-OG-DT-LB	6'2"	230	26		
Bobby Dillon	DB	6'1"	180	24	7	6
Jim Psaltis	DB	6'1"	190	27		
Clarence Self	DB	5'8"	185	29	2	
Val Joe Walker	DB	6'1"	178	23	4	
Bob Garrett	QB	6'1"	198	22		
Tobin Rote	QB	6'3"	205	26		48
Al Carmichael	HB	6'1"	190	24		
Joe Johnson	HB	6'	185	24		6
Breezy Reid	HB	5'10"	190	27		30
Verl Switzer	DB-HB	5'11"	190	22		24
Fred Cone	FB	5'11"	200	28		54
Howie Ferguson	FB	6'2"	210	24		
Billy Howton	OE	6'2"	190	24		12
Gary Knafelc (from Chi C)	OE	6'4"	205	22		
Max McGee	OE	6'2"	203	22		54

Babe Parilli – Military Service

BALTIMORE COLTS 3-9-0 Weeb Ewbank

Scores of Each Game		
0	LOS ANGELES	48
20	NEW YORK	14
9	Chic. Bears	28
0	Detroit	35
6	GREEN BAY	7
21	Washington	24
3	DETROIT	27
13	Green Bay	24
13	CHIC. BEARS	28
17	SAN FRANCISCO	13
22	Los Angeles	21
7	San Francisco	10

Use Name	Pos.	Hgt	Wgt	Age	Int	Pts
Jack Little	OT	6'4"	235	23		
Ken Jackson	OG-OT	6'2"	240	25		
Dick Barwegan	OG	6'1"	235	32		
Gene Pepper	OG	6'2"	242	27		
Alex Sandusky	OG	6'1"	220	22		
Art Spinney	OG	6'	235	27		
Sisto Averno	LB-OG	5'11"	245	28		
George Radosevich	C	6'2"	230	27		
Buzz Nutter	LB-C	6'4"	225	23		
Don Joyce	DE	6'3"	255	24		
Bob Langas	DE	6'4"	230	24		
Gino Marchetti	DE	6'4"	245	28		
Jim Mutscheller	OE-DE	6'1"	210	24		
Art Donovan	DT	6'2"	270	29		
Tom Finnin	DT	6'2"	275	26		2
Doug Eggers	LB	6'	210	24	3	
Bill Pellington	LB	6'2"	230	25		
Charley Robinson	OG-LB	6'	240	26		6
Joe Campanella	OT-DT-LB	6'2"	245	23	1	
Bob Leberman	DB	6'1"	180	22	2	
Jimmy Lesane (from Chi B)	DB	5'10"	180	23		
Chuck McMillan	DB	6'3"	175	23		
Bert Rechichar	DB	6'1"	210	24	2	19
Tom Keane	HB-DB	6'1"	190	27	5	
Don Shula	HB-DB	5'11"	190	24	5	
Cotton Davidson	QB	6'1"	180	23		
Fred Enke	QB	6'1"	205	29		
Gary Kerkorian	QB	5'11"	185	25		32
George Taliaferro	HB	5'11"	195	27		6
Royce Womble	HB	6'	185	22		18
Buddy Young	HB	5'5"	170	28		30
Carl Taseff	DB-HB	5'11"	195	25	2	6
John Huzvar	FB	6'4"	250	25		
Zollie Toth	FB	6'2"	230	30		6
Lloyd Colteryahn	OE	6'2"	220	24		
Dan Edwards	OE	6'1"	200	28		6
Jack Bighead	DE-OE	6'3"	215	24		

Monte Brethauer – Military Service
Johnny Petitbon – Military Service

DETROIT LIONS

RUSHING

Last Name	No.	Yds	Avg	TD
Carpenter	104	476	4.6	3
Bowman	96	397	4.1	2
Hoernschemeyer	94	242	2.6	2
Walker	32	240	7.5	1
Layne	30	119	4.0	2
Dublinski	21	76	3.6	1
Girard	9	36	4.0	0
Box	1	20	20.0	0
Kercher	3	1	0.3	0
Smith	3	1	0.3	0

RECEIVING

Last Name	No.	Yds	Avg	TD
Dibble	46	768	17	6
Bowman	34	288	8	2
Walker	32	564	18	3
Girard	27	421	16	7
Hart	24	377	16	0
Hoernschemeyer	20	153	8	1
Carpenter	16	145	9	2
Doran	10	203	20	4
Box	6	53	9	0

PUNT RETURNS

Last Name	No.	Yds	Avg	TD
Christiansen	23	225	10	1
Walker	3	117	29	1
Girard	9	22	2	0
Schmidt	1	0	0	0

KICKOFF RETURNS

Last Name	No.	Yds	Avg	TD
Girard	12	248	21	0
Bowman	6	178	30	1
Walker	8	172	22	0
Christiansen	5	102	20	0
Hoernschemeyer	4	73	18	0
Carpenter	2	46	23	0
Mains	1	3	3	0
Sewell	1	0	0	0

PASSING – PUNTING – KICKING

PASSING	Att	Comp	%	Yds	Yd/Att	TD	Int–%	RK
Layne	246	135	55	1818	7.4	14	12– 5	1
Dublinski	138	77	56	1073	7.8	8	7– 5	4
Hoernschemeyer	7	3	43	81	11.6	3	1–14	
Walker	4	0	0	0	0.0	0	1–25	

PUNTING	No	Avg
Girard	63	41.0

KICKING	XP	Att	%	FG	Att	%
Walker	43	43	100	11	17	65
Martin	0	0	0	1	6	17

CHICAGO BEARS

RUSHING

Last Name	No.	Yds	Avg	TD
Jagade	157	498	3.2	3
Stone	79	306	3.9	3
Hoffman	39	178	4.6	1
Blanda	19	41	2.2	0
Campbell	18	38	2.1	0
Brown	9	36	4.0	0
Bratkowski	15	35	2.3	1
Perini	4	11	2.8	0
Anderson	3	8	2.7	0
Kindt	10	–9	–0.9	0

RECEIVING

Last Name	No.	Yds	Avg	TD
Hill	45	1124	25	12
Stone	35	395	11	3
Dooley	34	658	19	7
Hoffman	28	354	13	1
McColl	24	368	15	2
Jagade	24	172	7	0
Kindt	9	101	11	0
Perini	5	56	11	0
Campbell	3	0	0	0
Schroeder	1	71	71	1

PUNT RETURNS

Last Name	No.	Yds	Avg	TD
Moore	11	80	7	0
Smith	7	43	6	0
Stone	14	40	3	0
Hoffman	1	5	5	0
Lowe	2	4	2	0
Kindt	1	1	1	0

KICKOFF RETURNS

Last Name	No.	Yds	Avg	TD
Stone	8	215	27	0
Jagade	11	195	18	0
Moore	8	156	20	0
Campbell	3	77	26	0
Perini	3	44	15	0
Smith	2	38	19	0
Connor	2	32	16	0
Hoffman	1	23	23	0
McElroy	1	21	21	0
Meadows	1	17	17	0
Anderson	1	15	15	0
Kindt	1	10	10	0
Sprinkle	3	8	3	0
Lowe	1	0	0	0

PASSING – PUNTING – KICKING

PASSING	Att	Comp	%	Yds	Yd/Att	TD	Int–%	RK
Blanda	281	131	47	1929	6.9	15	17– 6	11
Bratkowski	130	67	52	1087	8.4	8	17–13	12
Brown	17	10	59	283	16.7	3	1– 6	

PUNTING	No	Avg
Bratkowski	39	41.0
Brown	18	38.0

KICKING	XP	Att	%	FG	Att	%
Blanda	23	23	100	8	16	50
George	13	14	93	4	6	67
Perini	1	1	100	0	0	0

SAN FRANCISCO FORTY NINERS

RUSHING

Last Name	No.	Yds	Avg	TD
Perry	173	1049	6.1	8
J.H. Johnson	129	681	5.3	9
McElhenny	64	515	8.0	6
Schabarum	21	79	3.8	1
Arenas	11	77	7.0	0
Tittle	28	68	2.4	4
Mixon	7	19	2.7	0
Cassara	3	17	5.7	0
Galiffa	1	2	2.0	0
Tidwell	1	1	1.0	0
Cason	2	1	0.5	0
Jessup	1	–5	–5.0	0
P. Brown	1	–6	–6.0	0

RECEIVING

Last Name	No.	Yds	Avg	TD
Wilson	60	830	14	5
Jessup	30	565	19	3
J.H. Johnson	28	183	7	0
Perry	26	203	8	0
Soltau	22	316	14	2
McElhenny	8	162	20	0
Babcock	6	91	15	0
Schabarum	4	70	18	0
Arenas	2	12	6	0
Cassara	1	12	12	0

PUNT RETURNS

Last Name	No.	Yds	Avg	TD
Arenas	23	117	5	0
McElhenny	8	78	10	0
Schabarum	2	10	5	0
Tidwell	3	0	0	0

KICKOFF RETURNS

Last Name	No.	Yds	Avg	TD
Arenas	16	362	23	0
Tidwell	10	287	29	0
McElhenny	8	210	26	0
Schabarum	1	34	34	0
J.H. Johnson	2	25	13	0
Toneff	1	10	10	0
Hogland	1	2	2	0

PASSING – PUNTING – KICKING

PASSING	Att	Comp	%	Yds	Yd/Att	TD	Int–%	RK
Tittle	295	170	58	2205	7.5	9	9– 3	2
Duncan	14	4	29	82	5.9	0	2–14	
Cason	13	7	54	40	3.1	0	1– 8	
Galiffa	12	3	25	54	4.5	0	0– 0	
J.H. Johnson	2	1	50	10	5.0	1	0– 0	
P. Brown	1	1	100	19	19.0	0	0– 0	
Perry	1	1	100	34	34.0	0	0– 0	
Schabarum	1	0	0	0	0.0	0	0– 0	
Tidwell	1	0	0	0	0.0	0	0– 0	

PUNTING	No	Avg
P. Brown	49	37.5
H. Brown	10	38.4
Berry	1	0.0

KICKING	XP	Att	%	FG	Att	%
Soltau	31	33	94	11	18	61
Perry	6	7	86	1	3	33

LOS ANGELES RAMS

RUSHING

Last Name	No.	Yds	Avg	TD
Younger	91	610	6.7	8
Towler	149	599	4.0	11
Quinlan	82	490	6.0	4
Wade	28	190	6.8	1
McCormick	48	173	3.6	0
Lewis	26	72	2.8	0
Fears	1	10	10.0	0
Hirsch	1	6	6.0	0
Van Brocklin	6	–10	–1.7	0

RECEIVING

Last Name	No.	Yds	Avg	TD
Boyd	53	1212	23	6
Fears	36	546	15	3
Hirsch	35	720	21	3
Quinlan	18	324	18	2
Towler	10	127	13	0
Younger	8	76	10	0
Carey	5	49	10	0
McCormick	3	58	19	0
Lewis	2	19	10	0
Robustelli	1	49	49	1

PUNT RETURNS

Last Name	No.	Yds	Avg	TD
Sherman	6	89	15	0
Lewis	22	82	4	0
Dwyer	6	18	3	0
McCormick	7	8	1	0
Quinlan	1	4	4	0
Doll	1	0	0	0
Hughes	1	0	0	0

KICKOFF RETURNS

Last Name	No.	Yds	Avg	TD
Lewis	34	836	25	1
Sherman	6	130	22	0
Quinlan	4	69	17	0
Dwyer	3	65	22	0
McCormick	3	49	16	0
Dahms	2	23	12	0
Putnam	1	13	13	0
Toogood	1	11	11	0
Lipscomb	1	6	6	0
Robustelli	1	0	0	0

PASSING – PUNTING – KICKING

PASSING	Att	Comp	%	Yds	Yd/Att	TD	Int–%	RK
Van Brocklin	260	139	53	2637	10.1	13	21– 8	6
Wade	59	31	53	509	8.6	2	1– 2	
Quinlan	2	1	50	34	17.0	0	1–50	

PUNTING	No	Avg
Van Brocklin	44	42.6

KICKING	XP	Att	%	FG	Att	%
Richter	38	38	100	8	15	53
Carey	2	2	100	1	1	100
Fears	1	1	100	0	0	0

GREEN BAY PACKERS

RUSHING

Last Name	No.	Yds	Avg	TD
Reid	99	507	5.1	5
Rote	67	301	4.5	8
Ferguson	83	276	3.3	0
Carmichael	33	130	3.9	0
Switzer	15	59	3.9	0
Johnson	7	31	4.4	0
Cone	15	18	1.2	0
McGee	1	9	9.0	0
Garrett	1	–3	–3.0	0

RECEIVING

Last Name	No.	Yds	Avg	TD
Howton	52	768	15	2
Ferguson	41	398	10	0
McGee	36	614	17	9
Carmichael	18	251	14	0
Switzer	17	166	10	2
Reid	14	129	9	0
Johnson	10	72	7	1
Knafelc	5	48	10	0
Cone	4	19	5	0

PUNT RETURNS

Last Name	No.	Yds	Avg	TD
Switzer	24	306	13	1
Carmichael	9	43	5	0
Johnson	5	38	8	0
Dillon	1	7	7	0
Psaltis	1	0	0	0

KICKOFF RETURNS

Last Name	No.	Yds	Avg	TD
Carmichael	20	531	27	0
Switzer	20	500	25	0
Johnson	4	91	23	0
Ferguson	2	31	16	0
Cone	1	22	22	0
Forester	1	18	18	0
Brown	1	0	0	0

PASSING – PUNTING – KICKING

PASSING	Att	Comp	%	Yds	Yd/Att	TD	Int–%	RK
Rote	382	180	47	2311	6.1	14	18– 5	10
Garrett	30	15	50	143	4.8	0	1– 3	

PUNTING	No	Avg
McGee	72	41.7

KICKING	XP	Att	%	FG	Att	%
Cone	27	29	93	9	16	56

BALTIMORE COLTS

RUSHING

Last Name	No.	Yds	Avg	TD
Young	70	311	4.4	2
Toth	86	303	3.5	1
Taseff	41	228	5.6	0
Womble	60	174	2.9	0
Taliaferro	48	157	3.3	0
Kerkorian	22	36	1.6	1
Davidson	11	31	2.8	0
Huzvar	19	29	1.5	0
Shula	2	3	1.5	0
Enke	5	3	0.6	0

RECEIVING

Last Name	No.	Yds	Avg	TD
Edwards	40	531	13	1
Colteryahn	30	384	13	0
Womble	30	338	11	3
Taseff	16	159	10	1
Young	15	272	18	3
Taliaferro	14	122	9	1
Toth	11	51	5	0
Bighead	6	89	15	0
Mutscheller	1	49	49	0

PUNT RETURNS

Last Name	No.	Yds	Avg	TD
Young	14	60	4	0
Taseff	8	52	7	0
Taliaferro	5	34	7	0
Rechichar	6	22	4	0
Lesane	6	13	2	0

KICKOFF RETURNS

Last Name	No.	Yds	Avg	TD
Young	13	308	24	0
Womble	9	170	19	0
Taseff	7	167	24	0
Taliaferro	7	134	19	0
Lesane	4	91	23	0
Hechichar	3	26	9	0
Pellington	2	26	13	0
Robinson	1	19	19	0
Langas	1	18	18	0
Joyce	1	13	13	0
Toth	1	13	13	0
McMillan	1	5	5	0
Huzvar	1	0	0	0
Radosevich	1	0	0	0

PASSING – PUNTING – KICKING

PASSING	Att	Comp	%	Yds	Yd/Att	TD	Int–%	RK
Kerkorian	217	117	54	1515	7.0	9	12– 6	7
Davidson	64	28	44	309	4.8	0	5– 8	
Enke	28	17	61	171	6.1	0	3– 7	
Taliaferro	2	0	0	0	0.0	0	1– 50	
Keane	1	1	100	0	0.0	0	0– 0	
Lesane	1	0	0	0	0.0	0	0– 0	
Toth	1	0	0	0	0.0	0	1–100	

PUNTING	No	Avg
Davidson	72	37.2

KICKING	XP	Att	%	FG	Att	%
Kerkorian	11	12	91	5	10	50
Rechichar	1	1	100	6	13	46

1955 Continuing the Bloodless War

Disarmament talks between the United States and Canada fell through in February, but no ambassadors spoke at these meetings, and nuclear weapons never were mentioned. Representatives of the Canadian Football League and NFL commissioner Bert Bell were trying to thrash out a "no raiding" treaty for each other's players. No agreement was signed, leaving some clubs free to pirate players across national borders. The NFL captured Eddie LeBaron, Gene Brito, and Norb Hecker, all of whom had fled north a year ago, and also Alex Webster, a talented Canadian League runner. The Toronto Argonauts of the CFL signed quarterback Tom Dublinski of the Detroit Lions, but the Lions went to court and forced Dublinski to sit out this year before joining the Canadian club. But this was more a war of threats than of deeds, as most players simply stayed right where they were.

On the field itself, the players in the NFL were witnessing a gradual change in defensive tactics. The six-man line, standard at the start of the decade, had gradually turned into a 5-2-4 defense geared to deal with strong passing attacks. Now the five-man line was slowly evolving into a four-man line, as more and more teams replaced the middle guard with a mobile middle linebacker who could cover both the pass and the run. By the end of the decade, the 4-3-4 defense was used throughout the league, and middle linebackers like Joe Schmidt, Bill George, and Sam Huff were winning as many cheers as any of the offensive stars.

EASTERN CONFERENCE

Cleveland Browns—Coach Paul Brown was ready to defend the NFL championship without retired quarterback Otto Graham, but when the Browns looked pitiful in their pre-season games, Brown sent out an S.O.S, for his veteran passer. Answering the call in time for the final exhibition game, Graham still could not prevent an opening-day loss to the improved Washington Redskins. But after this warm-up, Graham and his mates hit their stride, winning their next six contests and driving to a conference crown for the tenth straight year.

Washington Redskins—The Redskins shed their recent mediocrity to make a surprisingly strong run at the Browns for the Eastern crown. Returning to the NFL after a year in Canada were quarterback Eddie LeBaron, defensive end Gene Brito, and defensive back Norb Hecker. Along with Brito's strong defensive work and little LeBaron's slick ball-handling, Vic Janowicz's all-around talent highlighted the club's dramatic rise. Abandoning his baseball career with the Pittsburgh Pirates, Janowicz combined his dogged running with accurate placekicking to finish eight points behind scoring leader Doak Walker.

New York Giants—The Giants had too much talent to keep losing, as they did in their first three games, and all the parts finally did fit together over the second half of the schedule. In the last seven games, the Giants won five, lost one, and tied one to finish in a rush behind Cleveland and Washington in the East. Head coach Jim Lee Howell needed time to blend rookies Mel Triplett, Rosie Grier, Jimmy Patton, and ex-Canadian star Alex Webster into the lineup, but the late-season results upheld the coach's faith in the newcomers. Of the holdovers, halfback Frank Gifford, guard Bill Austin, and safetyman Em Tunnell made All-Pro teams. Gifford blossomed into stardom with his ability to run the pass-option play, run behind his blockers, and catch passes. Relieved of any duties on defense, the handsome Gifford concentrated on honing his offensive skills to a fine point.

Chicago Cardinals—New head coach Ray Richards tasted sweet victory when his Cards met the Bears late in the year for their annual intercity battle. The Bears were riding a six-game winning streak to the Western Division crown, but the Cards derailed them with a stunning 53-14 upset. Aside from the Bear game, however, highlights for the Cardinals fell widely over the landscape. Ollie Matson continued to quicken pulses with his dramatic kick returns and runs from scrimmage, while Night Train Lane kept up his good work in the defensive backfield. Lane did take a few turns as an offensive end, though, and on one shift he grabbed a 97-yard TD pass from Ogden Compton.

Philadelphia Eagles—Coming from 10 points behind to beat the New York Giants on opening day, the Eagles nevertheless began the year on a bad note as middle guard Bucko Kilroy, playing in his 101st consecutive game, tore ligaments in his knee. Outstanding seasons by Norm Willey, Tom Scott, Chuck Bednarik, and Bibbles Bawel kept the defense on an even keel, but the offense dragged it's feet with a sluggish performance for the year. Quarterbacks Adrian Burk and Bobby Thomason found ends Pete Pihos and Bill Stribling open for frequent passes, but no Eagle runner consistently moved the ball on the ground.

Pittsburgh Steelers—Coach Walt Kiesling needed a back-up quarterback to spell Jim Finks, so he brought three young passers to training camp—Ted Marchibroda, Vic Eaton, and John Unitas. A ninth-round draft pick from the University of Louisville, Unitas never caught Kiesling's eye and was cut without ever getting into even a pre-season game. So, while Unitas spent the season quarterbacking the semi-pro Bloomington Rams, the Steeler offense struggled along under Finks, Marchibroda, and Eaton, scoring 20 points only three times all season.

WESTERN CONFERENCE

Los Angeles Rams—The Rams looked high and low for a new head coach, and they came up with unheralded Sid Gillman of the University of Cincinnati. A master organizer and offensive genius, Gillman took the Rams right to the top of the Western Conference for the first time since 1951. Rookies Ron Waller and Don Burroughs were the only key newcomers, as veterans Norm Van Brocklin, Tank Younger, Tom Fears, and Crazy Legs Hirsch spearheaded the attack, while Andy Robustelli and Will Sherman led the defense. Two mid-season losses to the Bears pushed the Rams back into second place, but three straight wins at the end of the year enabled them to sneak into first when the Cardinals upset the Bears two weeks from the end of the season. With a tougher defense and a breakaway runner in Waller to complement Van Brocklin's passing, the Rams were looking forward again to fighting the Browns for the NFL crown.

Chicago Bears—Told that George Halas was retiring as coach after the season, the Bears went all out to win the championship for their departing leader. Three losses to open the year doubled the players' determination to win, and the Bears then took off on a six-game winning streak, twice beating the Rams to take the lead in the West. Second-year man Ed Brown, a superb short passer, took charge at quarterback, rookies Rick Casares and Bobby Watkins beefed up the running attack, and Harlon Hill again starred as a pass receiver. Of the linemen, Bill Wightkin and Stan Jones stood out on offense, Bill George and George Connor on defense. The tough Bears were riding high until the Cards shot the horse out from under them with a 53-14 upset.

Green Bay Packers—Armed with a rejuvenated offense, the Packers moved up into third place by evenly splitting their season with wins and losses. Howie Ferguson, a hustling fullback, developed into a top-flight runner and gave the club a strong ground game to balance the attack. Tobin Rote's passes to Billy Howton and Gary Knafelc ate up yardage in large bites, keeping enemy defenses spread for Ferguson's runs. Spearheaded by linebacker Roger Zatkoff and safety Bobby Dillon, the defense kept the Packers in most of their games, while field-goal kicker Fred Cone helped win some close contests with his toe.

Baltimore Colts—Rookie fullback Alan Ameche broke into the professional ranks with a thunderbolt of a run. On his first play from scrimmage, he took a handoff, banged through the middle of the line, and rumbled 79 yards for a touchdown. The Colts went on to win that game, and Ameche went on to take the NFL rushing crown. Besides Ameche, the strong rookie crop turned up quarterback George Shaw, halfback L.G. Dupre, sure-handed end Ray Berry, and linemen George Preas and Dick Szymanski. After a fine beginning of three straight wins, the Colts fell off into mediocrity, but winning was less important right now to coach Weeb Ewbank than the building process.

San Francisco '49ers—For a second straight year, injuries bothered Hugh McElhenny, and for a second straight year the '49ers offense had problems scoring points. The bad foot which hobbled McElhenny robbed the attack of football's premier breakaway runner and left it without punch. The Redskins beat the '49ers 7-0, the first shutout hung on them since 1950, and the Browns and Packers just missed blanking them in other games. A five-game mid-season losing streak did nothing to improve new head coach Red Strader's disposition, and owner Tony Morabito sent Strader packing after just one season on the job.

Detroit Lions—Two off-season events sent the Lions reeling down into the Western Conference basement after three years in the penthouse. Middle guard Les Bingaman, literally the center of the defense, decided to quit, and a horse on which Bobby Layne's young son was riding bolted and separated Papa Layne's shoulder. Layne didn't miss any time from the lineup, but he left the zip in his arm back on a horse trail in Texas. With the offense thus crippled, the defense had problems of its own, trying to replace Bingaman's bulk and brains in the defensive line. Coach Buddy Parker eventually shifted offensive lineman Lou Creekmur to the middle guard spot, but by that time the Lions had lost their first six games.

FINAL TEAM STATISTICS

OFFENSE

	BALT.	CHI.B.	CHI.C.	CLEVE.	DET.	G.BAY	L.A.	N.Y.	PHIL.	PITT.	S.F.	WASH.
FIRST DOWNS:												
Total	206	**235**	150	224	224	213	233	189	219	211	204	193
by Rushing	93	**118**	84	111	88	106	**118**	92	71	74	102	101
by Passing	92	101	53	98	119	95	103	86	**128**	119	89	71
by Penalty	**21**	16	13	15	17	12	12	11	20	18	13	**21**
RUSHING:												
Number	456	487	438	**536**	392	433	451	414	392	420	408	478
Yards	1833	**2388**	1626	2020	1477	1883	1943	1693	1317	1284	1713	2000
Average Yards	4.0	**4.9**	3.7	3.8	3.8	4.3	4.3	4.1	3.4	3.1	4.2	4.2
Touchdowns	15	19	10	**20**	11	11	17	13	9	13	12	17
PASSING:												
Attempts	266	306	280	234	**400**	348	344	292	**400**	390	303	257
Completions	134	145	106	130	**204**	159	175	137	198	189	151	101
Completion Percentage	50.4	47.4	37.9	**55.6**	51.0	45.7	50.9	46.9	49.5	48.5	49.8	39.3
Gross Yards	1795	2108	1520	2225	2542	2004	2206	1865	**2696**	2550	2225	1549
Yards Lost Tackled	164	180	175	275	132	225	145	**105**	224	163	287	201
Net Yards	1631	1928	1345	1950	2410	1779	2061	1760	**2472**	2387	1938	1348
Avg. Yards per Attempt (Gross)	6.7	6.9	5.4	**9.5**	6.4	5.8	6.4	6.4	6.7	6.5	7.3	6.0
Avg. Yards per Comp. (Gross)	13.4	14.5	14.3	**17.1**	12.5	12.6	12.6	13.6	13.6	13.5	14.7	15.3
Touchdowns	11	17	14	**21**	15	17	9	17	19	12	17	11
Interceptions	22	23	25	**11**	22	19	18	15	24	30	28	21
Percent Intercepted	8.3	7.5	8.9	**4.7**	5.5	5.5	5.2	5.1	6.0	7.7	9.2	8.2
PUNTS:												
Number	55	57	**75**	58	67	56	60	**75**	61	71	63	62
Average Yards	39.3	39.9	40.3	41.2	41.0	43.2	**44.6**	40.3	42.9	38.4	40.6	41.6
PUNT RETURNS:												
Number	**48**	35	34	44	41	36	44	36	41	46	39	43
Yards	178	147	**408**	337	224	280	229	230	95	88	118	407
Average Yards	3.7	4.2	**12.0**	7.7	5.5	7.8	5.2	6.4	2.3	1.9	3.0	9.5
Touchdowns	0	0	**2**	1	0	1	1	**2**	0	0	0	**2**
KICKOFF RETURNS:												
Number	40	44	44	41	45	39	44	39	39	44	**51**	43
Yards	941	1085	835	949	839	1002	1013	848	922	**1157**	1147	1097
Average Yards	23.5	24.7	19.0	23.1	18.6	25.7	23.0	21.7	23.6	**26.3**	22.5	25.5
Touchdowns	0	0	0	0	0	**1**	0	**1**	**1**	0	0	**1**
INTERCEPTION RETURNS:												
Number	19	19	29	25	15	**31**	**31**	23	16	10	21	19
Yards	260	299	360	287	224	**400**	353	250	302	85	242	215
Average Yards	13.7	15.7	12.7	11.5	14.9	12.9	11.4	10.9	**18.9**	8.5	11.5	11.3
Touchdowns	0	0	**3**	**3**	1	0	**3**	0	2	0	1	0
PENALTIES:												
Number	59	57	**82**	64	51	41	64	50	61	67	64	60
Yards	565	498	**695**	603	526	401	612	458	542	604	541	648
FUMBLES:												
Number	**18**	23	35	27	28	37	23	25	35	26	25	25
Number Lost	**8**	18	20	18	19	25	10	16	21	17	18	21
POINTS:												
Total	214	294	224	**349**	230	258	260	267	248	195	216	246
PAT Attempts	26	37	29	**45**	29	30	31	34	31	27	30	33
PAT Made	25	37	23	**44**	27	30	30	33	29	21	27	30
FG Attempts	26	16	21	22	17	24	**32**	15	26	18	12	21
FG Made	11	11	9	11	9	**16**	14	10	11	4	3	6
Percent FG Made	42.3	**68.8**	42.9	50.0	52.9	66.7	43.8	66.7	42.3	22.2	25.0	28.6
Safeties	0	**1**	0	**1**	**1**	0	**1**	0	0	0	0	0

DEFENSE

	BALT.	CHI.B.	CHI.C.	CLEVE.	DET.	G.BAY	L.A.	N.Y.	PHIL.	PITT.	S.F.	WASH.
FIRST DOWNS:												
Total	234	216	224	**171**	217	196	245	209	174	176	250	189
by Rushing	120	96	100	**65**	95	118	95	77	89	98	132	73
by Passing	98	106	102	83	110	71	122	119	69	**67**	103	104
by Penalty	16	14	22	23	12	**7**	28	13	16	11	15	12
RUSHING:												
Number	448	398	465	**351**	449	475	423	418	455	494	538	391
Yards	2035	2100	1902	**1189**	1851	2174	1624	1441	1637	1814	2135	1275
Average Yards	4.5	5.3	4.1	3.4	4.1	4.6	3.8	3.4	3.6	3.7	4.0	**3.3**
Touchdowns	18	17	11	12	16	18	10	10	12	11	24	**8**
PASSING:												
Attempts	320	354	371	323	304	259	351	373	272	**242**	311	340
Completions	158	177	154	126	163	**118**	**193**	181	124	123	147	165
Completion Percentage	49.4	50.0	41.5	**39.0**	53.6	45.6	55.0	48.5	45.6	50.8	47.3	48.5
Gross Yards	2288	2369	2146	1775	2304	1768	2518	2543	1810	**1530**	2045	2189
Yards Lost Tackled	201	**312**	138	123	140	80	209	176	216	235	172	274
Net Yards	2087	2057	2008	1652	2164	1688	2309	2367	1594	**1295**	1873	1915
Avg. Yards per Attempt (Gross)	7.2	6.7	5.8	**5.5**	7.6	6.8	7.2	6.8	6.7	6.3	6.6	6.4
Avg. Yards per Comp. (Gross)	14.5	13.4	13.9	14.1	14.1	15.0	13.0	14.0	14.6	**12.4**	13.9	13.3
Touchdowns	12	14	16	15	18	13	18	16	12	19	**10**	17
Interceptions	19	19	29	25	15	**31**	**31**	23	16	10	21	19
Percent Intercepted	5.9	5.4	7.8	7.7	4.9	**12.0**	8.8	6.2	5.9	4.1	6.8	5.6
PUNTS:												
Number	56	65	61	70	60	52	56	64	74	**80**	57	65
Average Yards	39.9	42.0	40.6	39.1	40.6	41.8	42.4	41.6	**39.1**	42.1	42.6	41.2
PUNT RETURNS:												
Number	37	40	42	37	42	**36**	41	52	**36**	42	40	42
Yards	**71**	201	288	186	152	223	264	181	206	304	369	296
Average Yards	**1.9**	5.0	6.9	5.0	3.6	6.2	6.4	3.5	5.7	7.2	9.2	7.0
Touchdowns	**0**	1	2	1	**0**	1	**0**	**0**	1	1	1	1
KICKOFF RETURNS:												
Number	36	43	46	50	44	48	**35**	54	40	38	37	42
Yards	724	943	1133	1220	942	1157	**690**	1370	987	779	867	1023
Average Yards	20.1	21.9	24.6	24.4	21.4	24.1	**19.7**	25.4	24.7	20.5	23.4	24.4
Touchdowns	**0**	**0**	**0**	1	**0**	**0**	**0**	2	**0**	**0**	**0**	1
INTERCEPTION RETURNS:												
Number	22	23	25	**11**	22	19	18	15	24	30	28	21
Yards	269	247	261	**181**	306	268	338	194	228	494	299	200
Average Yards	12.2	10.7	10.4	16.5	13.9	14.1	18.8	12.9	**9.5**	16.5	10.7	9.5
Touchdowns	**0**	**0**	**0**	1	1	1	**0**	2	**0**	5	2	1
PENALTIES:												
Number	69	54	65	58	62	56	50	46	57	66	58	**79**
Yards	681	530	677	560	544	490	430	439	463	657	528	**694**
FUMBLES:												
Number	24	28	23	21	33	27	20	34	27	35	19	**36**
Number Lost	14	15	18	15	**24**	18	15	16	20	19	13	**24**
POINTS:												
Total	239	251	252	**218**	275	276	231	223	231	285	298	222
PAT Attempts	30	32	31	29	36	36	29	30	28	36	37	28
PAT Made	29	26	31	**23**	35	36	27	26	27	33	36	27
FG Attempts	**14**	24	29	15	23	17	17	20	23	25	24	19
FG Made	10	11	11	7	8	8	10	**5**	12	12	12	9
Percent FG Made	71.4	45.8	37.9	46.7	34.8	47.1	58.8	**25.0**	52.2	48.0	50.0	47.4
Safeties	**0**	**0**	1	**0**	**0**	**0**	**0**	1	**0**	**0**	2	**0**

Winning on a Final Bow

Paul Brown had talked Otto Graham out of retirement last fall, so Graham was back for his second farewell performance in the championship game. This year's opponent was the Los Angeles Rams, whom rookie coach Sid Gillman had led to the Western title for the first time since 1951. The Rams intercepted a Graham pass early in the game, but the Browns promptly picked off a Norm Van Brocklin pass and turned it into a 26-yard Lou Groza field goal. Cleveland's Don Paul intercepted another Van Brocklin pass early in the second quarter and returned it 65 yards for a touchdown, making the score 10-0. The Rams quickly scored on a Van Brocklin to Skeets Quinlan pass, but a 50-yard pass from Graham to Dante Lavelli ran the halftime count to 17-7. The second half was all Cleveland, as the Browns' pass rush kept Van Brocklin off balance, and Graham ran for a pair of touchdowns and threw to Ray Renfro for a third. The Rams added a touchdown late in the game, and the final score was 38-14 in favor of Cleveland, a championship for Paul Brown and a final bow for Otto Graham.

1955 CHAMPIONSHIP GAME

December 26 at Los Angeles
(Attendance 87,695)

SCORING

LOS ANGELES	0	7	0	7	–14
CLEVELAND	3	14	14	7	–38

First Quarter
- Cle. Groza, 26 yard Field Goal – 12:21

Second Quarter
- Cle. Paul, 65 yard Interception Return – 4:12
  PAT – Groza (kick)
- L.A. Quinlan, 67 yard pass from Van Brocklin – 6:04
  PAT – Richter (kick)
- Cle. Lavelli, 50 yard pass from Graham – 14:21
  PAT – Groza (kick)

Third Quarter
- Cle. Graham, 15 yard rush – 8.06
  PAT – Groza (kick)
- Cle. Graham, 1 yard rush – 12:44
  PAT – Groza (kick)

Fourth Quarter
- Cle. Renfro, 35 yard pass from Graham – 0:11
  PAT – Groza (kick)
- L.A. Waller, 4 yard rush – 12:42
  PAT – Richter (kick)

TEAM STATISTICS

CLE.		L.A.
17	First Downs – Total	17
7	by Rushing	8
10	by Passing	8
0	by Penalty	1
0	Fumbles – Number	1
0	Times Lost Ball	1
5	Penalties – Number	2
74	Yards Penalized	10
3	Giveaways	8
8	Takeaways	3
+5	Difference	–5

INDIVIDUAL STATISTICS

RUSHING

CLEVELAND	No.	Yds.	Avg.	LOS ANGELES	No.	Yds.	Avg.
Modzelewski	13	61	4.7	Towler	14	64	4.6
Bassett	11	49	4.5	Walker	11	48	4.4
Morrison	11	33	3.0	Wade	1	4	4.0
Graham	9	21	2.3		26	116	4.5
Jones	1	3	3.0				
Smith	3	2	0.7				
	48	169	3.5				

RECEIVING

CLEVELAND	No.	Yds.	Avg.	LOS ANGELES	No.	Yds.	Avg.
Modzelewski	5	34	6.8	Quinlan	5	116	23.2
Lavelli	3	95	31.7	Waller	3	18	6.0
Renfro	2	49	24.5	Fears	1	16	16.0
Jones	1	11	11.0	Hirsch	1	9	9.0
Brewster	1	9	9.0	Towler	1	7	7.0
Morrison	1	7	7.0		11	166	15.1
Bassett	1	4	4.0				
	14	209	14.9				

PUNT RETURNS

CLEVELAND	No.	Yds.	Avg.	LOS ANGELES	No.	Yds.	Avg.
Konz	2	27	13.5	Lewis	1	9	9.0
Paul	1	0	0.0				
	3	27	9.0				

KICKOFF RETURNS

CLEVELAND	No.	Yds.	Avg.	LOS ANGELES	No.	Yds.	Avg.
Smith	2	41	20.5	Lewis	4	127	31.8
Paul	1	0	0	Waller	3	88	29.3
	3	41	13.7		7	215	30.7

INTERCEPTION RETURNS

CLEVELAND	No.	Yds.	Avg.	LOS ANGELES	No.	Yds.	Avg.
Konz	2	12	6.0	Burroughs	1	24	24.0
Paul	1	65	65.0	Morris	1	22	22.0
James	1	11	11.0	Hughes	1	0	0.0
Palumbo	1	10	10.0		3	46	15.3
Michaels	1	5	5.0				
Ford	1	0	0.0				
	7	103	14.7				

PUNTING

CLEVELAND	No.		Avg.	LOS ANGELES	No.		Avg.
Gillom	3		42.7	Van Brocklin	4		45.0

PASSING

	Att	Comp	Comp Pct.	Yds	Yds/ Att.	Yds/ Comp	Yds Lost Tackled	Int
Cleveland								
Graham	25	14	56.0	209	8.4	14.9	1– 7	3
Los Angeles								
Van Brocklin	25	11	44.0	166	6.6	15.1	0– 0	6
Wade	3	0	0.0	0	–	–	2–23	1
	28	11	39.3	166	5.9	15.1	2–23	7

CLEVELAND BROWNS 9-2-1 Paul Brown

Scores of Each Game		
17	WASHINGTON	27
38	San Francisco	3
21	PHILADELPHIA	17
24	Washington	14
41	GREEN BAY	10
26	Chic. Cards	20
24	NEW YORK	14
17	Philadelphia	33
41	PITTSBURGH	14
35	New York	35
30	Pittsburgh	7
35	CHIC. CARDS	24

Use Name	Pos.	Hgt	Wgt	Age	Int	Pts
Lou Groza	OT	6'3"	242	31		77
Mike McCormack	OT	6'4"	248	28		
John Sandusky	DT-OT	6'1"	252	29		
Harold Bradley	OG	6'2"	230	26		
Herschel Forester	OG	6'	230	25		
Abe Gibron	OG	5'11"	250	29		
Frank Gatski	C	6'3"	240	33		
Bob Gain	DG	6'3"	250	27		
Len Ford	DE	6'4"	258	29		
Carlton Massey	DE	6'2"	218	26	1	
Don Colo	DT	6'3"	250	30		
John Kissell	DT	6'3"	248	32		
Tom Jones	OT-DT	6'6"	300	24		
Walt Michaels	LB	6'	230	26	1	6
Chuck Noll	LB	6'1"	220	23	5	8
Sam Palumbo	C-LB	6'2"	225	24		
Pete Perini (from Chi B)	FB-LB	6'	225	27		
Chuck Weber	OG-DE-LB	6'1"	225	26		
Kenny Konz	DB	5'10"	182	27	5	6
Warren Lahr	DB	5'11"	194	31	5	
Don Paul	DB	6'	195	29	4	6
Bob White (to BAL)	DB	5'11"	180	26		
Tommy James	HB-DB	5'10"	185	31	2	
Johnny Petitbon	HB-DB	5'11"	195	24	2	
Otto Graham	QB	6'1"	205	33		36
George Ratterman	QB	6'1"	180	28		6
Henry Ford	HB	6'	175	24		
Dub Jones	HB	6'4"	200	30		6
Curley Morrison	HB	6'2"	218	29		18
Ray Renfro	HB	6'1"	190	24		48
Bob Smith	HB	5'10"	195	23		6
Mo Bassett	FB	6'1"	232	25		18
Ed Modzelewski	FB	6'	215	26		48
Darrell Brewster	OE	6'3"	210	25		36
Dante Lavelli	OE	6'	192	32		24
Horace Gillom	DE-OE	6'1"	225	34		

Tom Catlin – Military Service
Chet Hanulak – Military Service
Don King-Canadian Football League
Billy Reynolds – Military Service

WASHINGTON REDSKINS 8-4-0 Joe Kuharich

Scores of Each Game		
27	Cleveland	17
31	Philadelphia	30
10	CHIC. CARDS	24
14	CLEVELAND	24
14	Baltimore	13
7	New York	35
34	PHILADELPHIA	21
7	SAN FRANCISCO	0
31	Chic. Cards	0
23	Pittsburgh	14
20	NEW YORK	27
28	PITTSBURGH	17

Use Name	Pos.	Hgt	Wgt	Age	Int	Pts
Don Boll	OT	6'2"	263	28		
Mike Davlin	OT	6'1"	230	27		
Fred Miller	OT	6'3"	225	24		
Walt Houston	OG	6'	217	22		
Ron Marciniak	OG	6'1"	218	23		
Red Stephens	OG	6'	230	25		
Slug Witucki	OG	5'11"	257	27		
Johnny Allen	C	6'2"	217	23		
Harry Ulinski	C	6'4"	235	30		
Gene Brito	DE	6'1"	230	30		
Chet Ostrowski	DE	6'1"	228	25		
Marv Berschet	OG-DE	6'2"	220	26		
J. D. Kimmel	DT	6'4"	245	26		
Volney Peters	DT	6'4"	242	27		
Jim Norman	OT-DT	6'2"	248	21		
Nick Adducci	LB	5'10"	204	26		
Ralph Felton	LB	5'11"	210	23		
Lavern Torgeson	C-LB	6'	222	26	3	
Chuck Drazenovich	FB-LB	6'2"	227	28	2	
Dick Alban	DB	6'	197	26	2	
Roy Barni (from PHI)	DB	5'11"	187	28	1	6
Hal Norris	LB-DB	5'11"	194	23		
Scooter Scudero	HB-DB	5'10"	176	25	5	12
Norb Hecker	OE-DB	6'2"	190	28	6	8
Al Dorow	QB	6'	190	25		
Ralph Guglielmi	QB	6'1"	200	22		6
Eddie LeBaron	QB	5'9"	168	25		24
Vic Janowicz	HB	5'9"	190	25		88
Jim Monachino	HB	5'10"	185	26		12
Bert Zagers	HB	5'10"	186	22		18
Dale Atkeson	FB	6'2"	210	25		12
Leo Elter	HB-FB	5'10"	197	26		24
Johnny Carson	OE	6'3"	203	25		18
Billy Cox	OE	6'3"	190	26		
Charlie Jones	OE	6'1"	202	26		
Ralph Thomas	OE	5'11"	190	25		18

Sam Baker – Military Service
Art DeCarlo – Military Service
Jim Schrader – Military Service
Billy Wells – Military Service
Bob Morgan-Canadian Football League

NEW YORK GIANTS 6-5-1 Jim Lee Howell

Scores of Each Game		
17	Philadelphia	27
17	Chic. Cards	28
23	Pittsburgh	30
10	CHIC. CARDS	0
17	PITTSBURGH	19
35	WASHINGTON	7
14	Cleveland	24
17	BALTIMORE	7
31	PHILADELPHIA	7
35	CLEVELAND	35
27	Washington	20
24	Detroit	19

Use Name	Pos.	Hgt	Wgt	Age	Int	Pts
Rosey Brown	OT	6'3"	245	22		
Dick Yelvington	OT	6'2"	230	28		
Bill Austin	OG	6'1"	225	26		
George Kennard	OG	6'	215	26		
Jack Stroud	OG	6'1"	215	26		
Ray Beck	DG-OG	6'2"	225	23		
Ray Wietecha	C	6'1"	225	26		
Stan West	OG-DG	6'2"	235	28		
John Hall	DE	6'1"	220	22		
Cliff Livingston	DE	6'3"	205	25		6
Walt Yowarsky (from DET)	DE	6'2"	235	27		
Rex Boggan	DT	6'3"	245	25		
Rosey Grier	DE-DT	6'5"	260	22		
Ray Krouse	DT	6'3"	260	28		
Pat Knight	LB	6'2"	210	26	2	
Harland Svare	LB	6'	215	24	2	
Bill Svoboda	LB	6'	210	28	1	
Tom Landry	DB	6'1"	195	30	2	
Dick Nolan	DB	6'1"	185	23	1	
Jimmy Patton	DB	6'	180	23	1	12
Herb Rich	DB	5'11"	180	26	6	
Em Tunnell	DB	6'1"	185	33	7	6
Larry Weaver	HB-DB	5'11"	190	22		
Bobby Clatterbuck	QB	6'3"	195	23		
Chuck Conerly	QB	6'1"	185	31		1
Don Heinrich	QB	6'	185	23		12
Frank Gifford	HB	6'1"	195	25		42
Joe Heap	HB	5'11"	185	23		
Kyle Rote	HB	6'	195	26		48
Alex Webster	HB	6'3"	210	24		36
Bobby Epps	FB	5'9"	195	23		12
Eddie Price	FB	5'11"	190	29		
Mel Triplett	FB	6'1"	215	23		
Ken MacAfee	OE	6'2"	205	25		6
Bob Schnelker	OE	6'3"	215	25		18
Cutter Long	HB-OE	6'1"	195	23		6
Ben Agajanian	K	6'	215	36		62

Bill Albright – Canadian Football League
Ray Collins – Canadian Football League
Billy Shipp – Canadian Football League
Arnie Galiffa-Canadian Football League

CHICAGO CARDINALS 4-7-1 Ray Richards

Scores of Each Game		
7	Pittsburgh	14
28	NEW YORK	17
24	Washington	10
0	New York	10
24	PHILADELPHIA	24
20	CLEVELAND	26
27	PITTSBURGH	13
14	Green Bay	31
0	WASHINGTON	31
53	CHIC. BEARS	14
3	Philadelphia	27
24	Cleveland	35

Use Name	Pos.	Hgt	Wgt	Age	Int	Pts
Burt Delevan	OT	6'2"	235	25		
Jack Jennings	OT	6'4"	245	28		
Len Teeuws	DT-OT	6'4"	245	28		
Larry Hartshorn	OG	6'	225	22		
John Hatley	OG	6'3"	245	24		
Bill Lange	LB-OG	6'1"	245	28		
Jack Simmons	C	6'4"	240	29		
Tom Bienemann	DE	6'3"	225	27	2	
Leo Sugar	DE	6'1"	210	26	1	
Pat Summerall	DE	6'4"	225	25	1	53
Jerry Groom	DT	6'3"	240	26		
Tony Pasquesi	DT	6'4"	235	21		
Chuck Ulrich	DT	6'4"	240	24		
Fred Wallner	LB	6'2"	230	26	2	
Harry Thompson	OG-LB	6'2"	230	28		
Leo Sanford	C-LB	6'1"	225	26	3	6
Lindon Crow	DB	6'1"	187	22	3	
Jimmy Hill	DB	6'2"	190	26		
Tom Keane	DB	6'1"	190	28	6	
Jim Psaltis	DB	6'1"	190	28	4	6
Charlie Trippi	DB	6'	185	32		
Night Train Lane	OE-DB	6'1"	190	27	6	6
Ogden Compton	QB	6'1"	180	22		
Lamar McHan	QB	6'1"	197	23		12
Dave Leggett	DB-QB	6'2"	198	21		
Dave Mann	HB	6'1"	190	22		33
Ollie Matson	HB	6'2"	210	25		30
Frank Bernardi	DB-HB	5'9"	180	22	1	6
Jimmy Carr	DB-HB	6'1"	195	22		
Les Goble	DB-HB	5'11"	155	23		
Mal Hammack	FB	6'2"	200	22		12
Johnny Olszewski	FB	5'11"	200	24		6
Max Boydston	OE	6'2"	207	22		6
Gern Nagler	OE	6'2"	190	22		18
Don Stonesifer	OE	6'	200	28		30
Dick Brubaker	DE-OE	6'	205	23		
Frank McPhee	DB-OE	6'3"	195	24		

Ed Husmann – Military Service
Jim Root – Military Service
Jimmy Sears – Military Service

PHILADELPHIA EAGLES 4-7-1 Jim Trimble

Scores of Each Game		
27	NEW YORK	17
30	WASHINGTON	31
17	Cleveland	21
7	Pittsburgh	13
24	Chic. Cards	24
24	PITTSBURGH	0
21	Washington	34
33	CLEVELAND	17
7	New York	31
21	LOS ANGELES	23
27	CHIC. CARDS	3
10	Chic. Bears	17

Use Name	Pos.	Hgt	Wgt	Age	Int	Pts
Lum Snyder	OT	6'5"	230	25		
Jim Weatherall	OT	6'4"	235	25		
Frank Wydo	OT	6'4"	235	31		
Tom Higgins	OG-OT	6'2"	230	26		
Ken Huxhold	OG	6'1"	215	26		
Buck Lansford	OG	6'2"	230	22		
John Magee	OG	5'10"	220	32		
Ed Sharkey (to SF)	OG	6'3"	235	28		
*Russ Carroccio	OT-DG-DT-OG	6'1"	235	24	1	
Bob Kelley	C	6'2"	225	26		
Bucko Kilroy	DG	6'2"	250	34		
Jim Ricca (from DET)	OT-DT-DG	6'4"	270	28	1	
Tom Scott	DE	6'2"	220	25		
Norm Willey	OE-DE	6'2"	225	28		
Jess Richardson	DT	6'2"	235	25		
Mike Jarmoluk	DG-DT	6'5"	250	32		
Wayne Robinson	LB	6'2"	220	25	1	
Chuck Bednarik	C-LB	6'3"	230	30	1	
Eddie Bell	DB	6'1"	205	24	1	
Harry Dowda	DB	6'2"	200	31		
Bob Hudson	LB-DB	6'4"	220	25	3	
Ralph Goldston	HB-DB	5'11"	195	27		
Bibbles Bawel	OE-DB	6'1"	185	25	9	12
Adrian Burk	QB	6'2"	190	27		12
Bobby Thomason	QB	6'1"	200	26		
Skippy Giancanelli	HB	5'10"	180	26		18
Don Johnson	HB	6'	187	24		
Toy Ledbetter	HB	5'10"	200	28		6
Jim Parmer	HB	6'	195	28		6
George Taliaferro	HB	5'11"	195	28		
Ted Wegert	HB	5'11"	195	23		12
Jerry Norton	DB-HB	5'11"	200	25	1	18
Dick Bielski	FB	6'1"	215	23		56
Rob Goode (from WAS)	FB	6'4"	230	28		
Pete Pihos	OE	6'1"	210	31		42
Bill Stribling	OE	6'1"	205	28		36
Bobby Walston	HB-OE	6'	190	26		30

Tom Brookshier – Military Service
Menil Mavraides – Military Service
Maury Nipp – Military Service
Neil Worden – Military Service

*(from NY)

PITTSBURGH STEELERS 4-8-0 Walt Kiesling

Scores of Each Game		
14	CHIC. CARDS	7
26	Los Angeles	27
30	NEW YORK	23
13	PHILADELPHIA	7
19	New York	17
0	Philadelphia	24
13	Chic. Cards	27
28	DETROIT	31
14	Cleveland	41
14	WASHINGTON	23
7	CLEVELAND	30
17	Washington	28

Use Name	Pos.	Hgt	Wgt	Age	Int	Pts
Bob Gaona	OT	6'3"	250	25		
Frank Varrichione	OT	6'1"	235	23		
Nick Feher	OG	6'	225	28		
Dick Oniskey	OG	6'2"	225			
John Schweder	LB-OG	6'1"	225	28		
Fred Broussard (to NY)	C	6'3"	235	22		
Dick Flanagan	C	6'	220	28		
Bill McPeak	DE	6'1"	215	30		
Ed Meadows	DE	6'2"	218	23		
Joe O'Malley	DE	6'2"	220	22		6
Lou Ferry	DT	6'2"	250	28		
Willie McClung	DT	6'2"	215	26		
Dick Modzelewski	DT	6'	250	24		
Ernie Stautner	OG-DT	6'1"	235	30		
Dale Dodrill	LB	6'1"	210	30	2	
Marv Matuszak	LB	6'3"	235	24	1	
Art Michalik	LB	6'2"	230	25		12
John Reger	OG-LB	6'	220	24	2	
Lou Tepe	C-LB	6'2"	215	25		
Marion Motley	FB-LB	6'1"	240	35		
Jack Butler	DB	6'	195	27		
Dick Doyle	DB	6'	195	24	1	
Jim Hill	DB	6'	195	26	1	
Richie McCabe	DB	6'1"	185	21	3	6
Vic Eaton	QB-DB	6'2"	200	22		
Jim Finks	QB	6'	175	28		24
Ted Marchibroda	QB	5'10"	180	24		6
Lynn Chandnois	HB	6'2"	205	31		30
Ray Mathews	HB	6'	185	26		42
Sid Watson	HB	5'11"	185	22		6
Leon Campbell	FB	6'	197	28		
Fran Rogel	FB	5'11"	205	28		12
Ed Bernet	OE	6'3"	200	22		6
Jack McClairen	OE	6'4"	215	24		
Elbie Nickel	OE	6'1"	195	32		12
Jack O'Brien	DE-OE	6'2"	215	24		12
Tad Weed	K	5'5"	140	22		21

Paul Cameron – Military Service
Johnny Lattner – Military Service
Marv McFadden – Military Service
Pat Brady-Foot Injury
Stan Sheriff – Military Service
George Tarasovic – Military Service

CLEVELAND BROWNS

RUSHING

Last Name	No.	Yds	Avg	TD
Morrison	156	824	5.3	3
Modzelewski	185	619	3.3	6
Bassett	38	174	4.6	3
Smith	37	142	3.8	1
Graham	68	121	1.8	6
Renfro	29	90	3.1	0
Jones	10	44	4.4	0
Petitbon	3	10	3.3	0
Ratterman	6	8	1.3	1
James	1	2	2.0	0
H. Ford	2	1	0.5	0
Perini	2	0	0.0	0
Gillom	1	−15	−15.0	0

RECEIVING

Last Name	No.	Yds	Avg	TD
Brewster	34	622	18	6
Lavelli	31	492	16	4
Renfro	29	603	21	8
Modzelewski	13	113	9	2
Morrison	9	185	21	0
Bassett	9	83	9	0
Jones	3	115	38	1
Smith	2	12	6	0
Perini	1	3	3	0

PUNT RETURNS

Last Name	No.	Yds	Avg	TD
Paul	19	148	8	1
Konz	17	138	8	0
White	2	28	14	0
H. Ford	4	15	4	0
Smith	1	5	5	0
Renfro	1	3	3	0

KICKOFF RETURNS

Last Name	No.	Yds	Avg	TD
White	14	400	29	0
Smith	13	320	25	0
Bassett	7	151	22	0
Paul	5	109	23	0
Konz	3	66	22	0
Michaels	3	45	15	0

PASSING – PUNTING – KICKING

PASSING	Att	Comp	%	Yds	Yd/Att	TD	Int–%	RK
Graham	185	98	53	1721	9.3	15	8– 4	1
Ratterman	47	32	68	504	10.7	6	3– 6	
Renfro	2	0	0	0	0.0	0	0– 0	

PUNTING	No	Avg
Gillom	58	41.2

KICKING	XP	Att	%	FG	Att	%
Groza	44	45	98	11	22	50

WASHINGTON REDSKINS

RUSHING

Last Name	No.	Yds	Avg	TD
Janowicz	93	397	4.3	4
Zagers	89	395	4.4	2
Elter	97	361	3.7	3
Atkeson	77	300	3.9	1
Monachino	46	207	4.5	2
LeBaron	37	190	5.1	4
Guglielmi	18	51	2.8	1
Dorow	8	49	6.1	0
Scudero	6	27	4.5	0

RECEIVING

Last Name	No.	Yds	Avg	TD
Carson	23	443	19	3
Zagers	14	306	22	0
Elter	13	219	17	1
Janowicz	11	149	14	3
Thomas	9	105	12	2
Atkeson	9	81	9	1
Monachino	8	74	9	0
Cox	5	71	14	0
Jones	4	58	15	0
Hecker	3	31	10	1
Drazenovich	1	−3	−3	0

PUNT RETURNS

Last Name	No.	Yds	Avg	TD
Scudero	25	241	10	1
Zagers	7	125	18	1
Monachino	6	26	4	0
Adduci	1	10	10	0
Felton	1	5	5	0
Alban	3	0	0	0

KICKOFF RETURNS

Last Name	No.	Yds	Avg	TD
Scudero	25	699	28	1
Zagers	11	280	25	0
Atkeson	4	106	27	0
Felton	1	12	12	0
Barni	1	0	0	0
Marciniak	1	0	0	0

PASSING – PUNTING – KICKING

PASSING	Att	Comp	%	Yds	Yd/Att	TD	Int–%	RK
LeBaron	178	79	44	1270	7.1	9	15– 8	12
Guglielmi	62	20	32	242	3.9	2	4– 7	
Dorow	12	2	17	37	3.1	0	1– 8	
Janowicz	5	0	0	0	0.0	0	1–20	

PUNTING	No	Avg
LeBaron	62	41.6

KICKING	XP	Att	%	FG	Att	%
Janowicz	28	31	90	6	20	30
Hecker	2	2	100	0	1	0

NEW YORK GIANTS

RUSHING

Last Name	No.	Yds	Avg	TD
Webster	128	634	5.0	5
Epps	95	375	3.9	2
Gifford	86	351	4.1	3
Triplett	34	138	4.1	0
Price	30	109	3.6	0
Rote	10	46	4.6	0
Heap	8	29	3.6	0
Conerly	12	10	0.8	0
Heinrich	7	4	0.6	2
Weaver	3	0	0.0	0
Clatterbuck	1	−3	−3.0	0

RECEIVING

Last Name	No.	Yds	Avg	TD
Gifford	33	437	13	4
Rote	31	580	19	8
Schnelker	25	326	13	2
Webster	22	269	12	1
MacAfee	11	170	15	1
Long	6	64	11	1
Epps	5	8	2	0
Triplett	3	9	3	0
Price	1	2	2	0

PUNT RETURNS

Last Name	No.	Yds	Avg	TD
Tunnell	25	98	4	1
Patton	3	69	23	1
Heap	8	63	8	0

KICKOFF RETURNS

Last Name	No.	Yds	Avg	TD
Heap	12	230	19	0
Patton	5	229	46	1
Long	6	172	29	0
Gifford	5	114	23	0
Triplett	3	47	16	0
Kennard	3	36	12	0
Brown	1	14	14	0
West	1	0	0	0
Yowarsky	3	0	0	0

PASSING – PUNTING – KICKING

PASSING	Att	Comp	%	Yds	Yd/Att	TD	Int–%	RK
Conerly	202	98	49	1310	6.5	13	13– 6	7
Heinrich	67	31	46	413	6.2	2	2– 3	
Clatterbuck	16	6	38	46	2.9	0	0– 0	
Gifford	6	2	33	96	16.0	2	0– 0	
Rote	1	0	0	0	0.0	0	0– 0	

PUNTING	No	Avg
Landry	75	40.3

KICKING	XP	Att	%	FG	Att	%
Agajanian	32	33	97	10	15	67
Conerly	1	1	100	0	0	0

CHICAGO CARDINALS

RUSHING

Last Name	No.	Yds	Avg	TD
Matson	109	475	4.4	1
Mann	87	336	3.9	4
Olszewski	84	326	3.9	1
McHan	56	194	3.5	2
Hammack	51	160	3.1	2
Carr	30	115	3.8	0
Bernardi	8	17	2.1	0
Goble	7	11	1.6	0
Compton	6	−8	−1.3	0

RECEIVING

Last Name	No.	Yds	Avg	TD
Stonesifer	28	330	12	5
Matson	17	237	14	2
Mann	16	137	9	1
Carr	9	157	17	0
Olszewski	9	37	4	0
Nagler	7	218	31	3
Brubaker	6	125	21	0
Hammack	5	13	3	0
Bernardi	4	77	19	1
Boydston	3	79	26	1
Lane	2	110	55	1

PUNT RETURNS

Last Name	No.	Yds	Avg	TD
Matson	13	245	19	2
Bernardi	19	163	9	0
Carr	1	0	0	0
Hill	1	0	0	0

KICKOFF RETURNS

Last Name	No.	Yds	Avg	TD
Matson	15	368	25	0
Goble	8	160	20	0
Mann	6	136	23	0
Carr	4	93	23	0
Hammack	2	32	16	0
Olszewski	2	26	13	0
Hatley	2	13	7	0
Simmons	1	7	7	0
Delevan	2	0	0	0
Lange	2	0	0	0

PASSING – PUNTING – KICKING

PASSING	Att	Comp	%	Yds	Yd/Att	TD	Int–%	RK
McHan	207	78	38	1085	5.2	11	19– 9	14
Compton	61	22	36	339	5.6	1	6–10	
Mann	10	5	50	53	5.3	2	0– 0	
Leggett	1	0	0	0	0.0	0	0– 0	
Matson	1	1	100	43	43.0	0	0– 0	

PUNTING	No	Avg
Mann	43	40.1
Trippi	32	40.7

KICKING	XP	Att	%	FG	Att	%
Summerall	23	25	92	8	19	42
Mann	0	2	0	1	1	100
Keane	0	0	0	0	1	0
McHan	0	2	0	0	0	0

PHILADELPHIA EAGLES

RUSHING

Last Name	No.	Yds	Avg	TD
Giancanelli	97	385	4.0	2
Goode	83	297	3.6	0
Norton	36	144	4.0	1
Burk	36	132	3.7	2
Parmer	34	129	3.8	1
Wegert	26	120	4.6	2
Bielski	28	67	2.4	1
Ledbetter	21	48	2.3	0
Thomason	17	29	1.7	0
Johnson	3	1	0.3	0
Taliaferro	3	−2	−0.7	0
Walston	1	−3	−3.0	0
Goldston	14	−7	−0.5	0

RECEIVING

Last Name	No.	Yds	Avg	TD
Pihos	62	864	14	7
Stribling	38	568	15	6
Walston	27	443	16	3
Giancanelli	25	379	15	1
Goode	11	152	14	0
Norton	11	125	11	1
Bielski	8	48	6	0
Ledbetter	7	88	13	1
Taliaferro	3	17	6	0
Wegert	3	17	6	0
Goldston	2	8	4	0
Bawel	1	6	6	0
Parmer	1	−4	−4	0

PUNT RETURNS

Last Name	No.	Yds	Avg	TD
Norton	20	33	2	0
Bawel	15	32	2	0
Giancanelli	5	30	6	0
Hudson	1	0	0	0

KICKOFF RETURNS

Last Name	No.	Yds	Avg	TD
Norton	8	281	35	1
Giancanelli	11	267	24	0
Bawel	8	169	21	0
Wegert	4	87	22	0
Goode	2	36	18	0
Snyder	3	34	11	0
Ledbetter	1	21	21	0
Taliaferro	1	16	16	0
Sharkey	1	11	11	0

PASSING – PUNTING – KICKING

PASSING	Att	Comp	%	Yds	Yd/Att	TD	Int–%	RK
Burk	228	110	48	1359	6.0	9	17– 8	11
Thomason	171	88	51	1337	7.8	10	7– 4	2
Norton	1	0	0	0	0.0	0	0– 0	

PUNTING	No	Avg
Burk	61	42.9

KICKING	XP	Att	%	FG	Att	%
Bielski	23	24	96	9	23	39
Walston	6	7	86	2	3	67

PITTSBURGH STEELERS

RUSHING

Last Name	No.	Yds	Avg	TD
Rogel	168	588	3.5	2
Chandnois	105	353	3.4	5
Mathews	57	187	3.3	1
Finks	35	76	2.2	4
Campbell	18	42	2.3	0
Watson	29	31	1.1	0
Motley	2	8	4.0	0
Marchibroda	6	−1	−0.2	1

RECEIVING

Last Name	No.	Yds	Avg	TD
Mathews	42	762	18	6
Nickel	36	488	14	2
Chandnois	27	385	14	0
Rogel	24	222	9	0
Bernet	22	276	13	1
Watson	19	223	12	1
O'Brien	9	105	12	2
Campbell	9	76	8	0
McClairen	1	13	13	0

PUNT RETURNS

Last Name	No.	Yds	Avg	TD
Eaton	23	73	3	0
Watson	23	15	1	0

KICKOFF RETURNS

Last Name	No.	Yds	Avg	TD
Watson	27	716	27	0
Chandnois	9	223	25	0
Campbell	4	133	33	0
Rogel	1	81	81	0
Gaona	2	4	2	0
Matuszak	1	0	0	0

PASSING – PUNTING – KICKING

PASSING	Att	Comp	%	Yds	Yd/Att	TD	Int–%	RK
Finks	344	165	48	2270	6.6	10	26– 8	10
Marchibroda	43	24	56	280	6.5	2	3– 7	
Eaton	2	0	0	0	0.0	0	0– 0	
Chandnois	1	0	0	0	0.0	0	1–100	

PUNTING	No	Avg
Eaton	66	38.2
Zombek	5	40.2

KICKING	XP	Att	%	FG	Att	%
Weed	12	12	100	3	6	50
Michalik	9	15	60	1	12	8

LOS ANGELES RAMS 8-3-1 Sid Gillman

Scores of Each Game		
23	San Francisco	14
27	PITTSBURGH	26
17	Detroit	10
28	Green Bay	30
24	DETROIT	13
20	CHIC. BEARS	31
27	SAN FRANCISCO	14
3	Chic. Bears	24
17	Baltimore	17
23	Philadelphia	21
20	BALTIMORE	14
31	GREEN BAY	17

Use Name	Pos.	Hgt	Wgt	Age	Int	Pts
Bob Cross	OT	6'4"	250	24		
Glenn Holtzman	OT	6'3"	240	25		
Charlie Toogood	OT	6'	228	27		
Jack Ellena	OG	6'1"	226	23		
Sid Fournet	OG	6'	238	22		
John Hock	OG	6'2"	230	27		
Duane Putnam	OG	6'	230	27		
Leon McLaughlin	C	6'2"	228	29		
Paul Miller	DE	6'2"	220	23		
Andy Robustelli	DE	6'1"	230	29	1	12
Art Hauser	DT	6'	236	24		
Big Daddy Lipscomb	DT	6'6"	286	24		
Bud McFadin	DT	6'3"	250	27		3
Frank Fuller	OG-DE-DT	6'4"	245	26		
Don Paul	LB	6'1"	222	30		
Les Richter	LB	6'3"	230	24	2	69
Bob Griffin	C-LB	6'3"	230	26	1	2
Larry Morris	HB-LB	6'2"	210	21		6
Don Burroughs	DB	6'4"	176	24	9	
Jim Cason	DB	6'	175	28	5	6
Hall Haynes	DB	6'	182	26		
Ed Hughes	DB	6'1"	180	27		
Will Sherman	DB	6'2"	194	26	11	
Norm Van Brocklin	QB	6'1"	200	29		
Billy Wade	QB	6'2"	195	24		
Tom McCormick	HB	5'11"	180	25		6
Skeets Quinlan	HB	5'11"	170	27		6
Ron Waller	HB	5'11"	174	22		48
Corky Taylor	DB-HB	5'10"	192	21	2	12
Dan Towler	FB	6'2"	226	27		18
Tank Younger	FB	6'3"	228	27		30
Jack Bighead	OE	6'3"	215	25		
Bob Boyd	OE	6'2"	200	27		18
Tom Fears	OE	6'2"	203	31		12
Crazy Legs Hirsch	OE	6'2"	190	31		12
Woodley Lewis	OE	6'	188	30		

Rudy Bukich – Military Service
Dick Daugherty – Military Service
Bob Fry – Military Service
Brad Myers – Military Service
Duane Wardlow – Military Service

CHICAGO BEARS 8-4-0 George Halas

Scores of Each Game		
17	Baltimore	23
3	Green Bay	24
19	SAN FRANCISCO	20
38	BALTIMORE	10
34	San Francisco	23
31	Los Angeles	20
52	GREEN BAY	31
24	LOS ANGELES	3
24	Detroit	14
14	Chic. Cards	53
21	DETROIT	20
17	PHILADELPHIA	10

Use Name	Pos.	Hgt	Wgt	Age	Int	Pts
Kline Gilbert	OT	6'2"	235	24		
Bill Wightkin	OT	6'3"	235	28		
Stan Jones	OG	6'1"	255	24		
Herman Clark	LB-OG	6'3"	255	24		
Larry Strickland	C	6'4"	250	24		
Doug Atkins	DE	6'8"	255	25		
John Helwig	DE	6'2"	208	27		
Ed Sprinkle	DE	6'1"	207	31		
Jack Hoffman	OE-DE	6'5"	235	26		
Bill Bishop	DT	6'4"	250	24	1	
John Kreamcheck	DT	6'5"	255	27		
Fred Williams	DT	6'4"	250	25		
Joe Fortuanto	LB	6'	225	25		
Bill George	LB	6'2"	240	24	2	
George Connor	OT-LB	6'3"	240	30	1	6
Ralph Jecha	OG-LB	6'2"	235	24		
Wayne Hansen	C-DT-LB	6'2"	235	27		
Ken Gorgal	DB	6'2"	200	26	6	
Charlie Sumner	DB	6'1"	190	25	7	
Don Kindt	HB-DB	6'1"	208	29		
Ray Gene Smith	HB-DB	5'10"	188	25	2	
George Blanda	QB	6'1"	207	27		82
Ed Brown	QB	6'2"	205	26		12
Bob Williams	QB	6'1"	197	26		
Henry Mosley	HB	6'2"	210	25		
Bobby Watkins	HB	5'10"	195	23		48
Ron Drzewiecki	DB-HB	5'11"	185	23		6
Harry Hugasian (from BAL)	DB-HB	6'1"	192	24		
John Hoffman	FB-OE-HB	6'2"	215	29		8
Rick Casares	FB	6'2"	225	24		30
Chick Jagade	FB	6'	220	28		12
Harlon Hill	OE	6'3"	200	23		54
Bill McColl	OE	6'4"	230	25		24
Gene Schroeder	OE	6'3"	190	26		12

Zeke Bratkowski – Military Service

Jim Dooley – Military Service
McNeil Moore – Military Service
Tom O'Connell – Military Service
Stan Wallace – Military Service

GREEN BAY PACKERS 6-6-0 Lisle Blackbourn

Scores of Each Game		
20	DETROIT	17
24	CHIC. BEARS	3
20	BALTIMORE	24
30	LOS ANGELES	28
10	Cleveland	41
10	Baltimore	14
31	Chic. Bears	52
31	CHIC. CARDS	14
27	SAN FRANCISCO	21
10	Detroit	24
28	San Francisco	7
17	Los Angeles	31

Use Name	Pos.	Hgt	Wgt	Age	Int	Pts
Tom Dahms	OT	6'5"	240	27		
Len Szafaryn	OT	6'2"	230	27		6
Buddy Brown	OG	6'1"	225	28		
Joe Skibinski	OG	5'11"	228	27		
Jack Spinks	OG	6'	240	25		
Jim Ringo	C	6'1"	230	24		
Dave Stephenson	C	6'2"	230	29		
Nate Borden	DE	6'	205	23		
John Martinkovic	DE	6'3"	245	28		
Pat O'Donahue	DE	6'1"	215	25		
Dave Hanner	DT	6'2"	250	26		
Jerry Helluin	DT	6'2"	260	25		
Bill Lucky	DT	6'3"	250	24		
Tom Bettis	LB	6'2"	225	22		
Bill Forester	LB	6'3"	235	24	4	
Deral Teteak	LB	5'10"	210	26	2	
Roger Zatkoff	LB	6'2"	215	24	3	
Hank Bullough	OG-LB	6'	220	21		
George Timberlake	OG-LB	6'1"	220	23		
Billy Bookout	DB	5'11"	180	23	2	
Bobby Dillon	DB	6'1"	180	25	9	
Doyle Nix	DB	6'1"	188	22	5	
Clarence Self	DB	5'8"	180	30		
Val Joe Walker	DB	6'1"	178	24	6	
Jim Capuzzi	QB-DB	6'	190	23		
Charlie Brackins	QB	6'2"	202	23		
Paul Held	QB	6'2"	194	27		
Tobin Rote	QB	6'3"	215	27		30
Al Carmichael	HB	6'1"	190	25		12
Joe Johnson	HB	6'	180	25		6
Breezy Reid	HB	5'10"	190	28		18
Al Romine	DB-HB	6'2"	190	22		
Veryl Switzer	DB-HB	5'11"	190	23		6
Bob Clemens	FB	6'2"	200	23		
Fred Cone	FB	5'11"	200	29		78
Howie Ferguson	FB	6'2"	212	25		24
Billy Howton	OE	6'2"	190	25		30
Jim Jennings	OE	6'3"	195	22		
Gary Knafelc	OE	6'4"	215	23		48
Dick Deschaine	K	6'	190	25		

Al Barry – Military Service
Max McGee – Military Service

Art Hunter – Military Service
Gene Knutson – Military Service
Babe Parilli – Military Service

BALTIMORE COLTS 5-6-1 Weeb Ewbank

Scores of Each Game		
23	CHIC. BEARS	17
28	DETROIT	13
24	Green Bay	20
10	Chic. Bears	38
13	WASHINGTON	14
14	GREEN BAY	10
14	Detroit	24
7	New York	17
17	LOS ANGELES	17
26	SAN FRANCISCO	14
14	Los Angeles	20
24	San Francisco	35

Use Name	Pos.	Hgt	Wgt	Age	Int	Pts
Dick Chorovich	OT	6'4"	260	22		
Ken Jackson	OT	6'2"	235	26		
George Radosevich	OT	6'2"	225	28		
George Preas	OG-OT	6'2"	228	23		
Alex Sandusky	OG	6'1"	215	23		
Art Spinney	OG	6'	230	28		
Buzz Nutter	LB-C	6'4"	220	24		
Don Joyce	DE	6'3"	255	25		
Gino Marchetti	DE	6'4"	245	29		
Art Donovan	DT	6'2"	265	30		
Tom Finnin	DT	6'2"	255	27		
Bob Myers	DT	6'	260	24		
Doug Eggers	LB	6'	210	25		
Bill Pellington	LB	6'2"	230	26	2	
Jack Patera	OG-LB	6'1"	230	23	1	
Dick Szymanski	C-LB	6'3"	230	23		
Joe Campanella	OT-DT-LB	6'2"	245	24	2	
Bert Rechichar	DB	6'1"	210	25	6	55
Don Shula	DB	5'11"	190	25	5	
Jesse Thomas	DB	5'10"	180	26	1	
Walter Bryant	HB-DB	6'1"	185	22	1	
Carl Taseff	HB-DB	5'11"	190	26	1	
Monte Brethauer	OE-DB	6'1"	180	24		
Gary Kerkorian	QB	5'11"	185	26		9
George Shaw	QB	6'1"	180	22		18
L. G. Dupre	HB	5'11"	190	23		6
Dean Renfro	HB	5'11"	180	22		
Burrell Shields	HB	6'2"	200	23		
Royce Womble	HB	6'	185	23		
Buddy Young	HB	5'5"	176	29		12
Alan Ameche	FB	6'	217	22		54
Dick Young	HB-FB	5'11"	210	24		
Ray Berry	OE	6'2"	190	22		
Lloyd Colteryahn	OE	6'2"	220	25		18
Jim Mutscheller	OE	6'1"	218	25		42

Cotton Davidson – Military Service

SAN FRANCISCO FORTY NINERS 4-8-0 Red Strader

Scores of Each Game		
14	LOS ANGELES	23
3	CLEVELAND	38
20	Chic. Bears	19
27	Detroit	24
23	CHIC. BEARS	34
38	DETROIT	21
14	Los Angeles	27
0	Washington	7
21	Green Bay	27
14	Baltimore	26
7	GREEN BAY	28
35	BALTIMORE	24

Use Name	Pos.	Hgt	Wgt	Age	Int	Pts
Bob St. Clair	OT	6'9"	263	24		
Leo Nomellini	DT-OT	6'3"	252	30		
Doug Hogland	OG	6'3"	240	24		
Eldred Kraemer	OG	6'2"	225	25		
Lou Palatella	LB-OG	6'2"	230	22		
Bob Hantla	DE-LB-OG	6'1"	220	23		
Ed Beatty	C	6'3"	230	23		
Bill Johnson	C	6'3"	240	29		
Clay Matthews	DE	6'3"	220	27	1	
Charley Powell	DE	6'2"	230	23		
Marion Campbell	DT	6'3"	245	26	1	
Al Carapella	DT	6'	235	28		
Sid Youngelman	DT	6'3"	240	23		
Hardy Brown	LB	6'	196	31	2	
Paul Carr	LB	6'	205	23	1	
Matt Hazeltine	LB	6'1"	205	22		
Tom Stolhandske	DE-LB	6'2"	210	23	1	
Bob Toneff	DT-LB	6'2"	252	25		
Rex Berry	DB	5'11"	180	29	3	6
Bobby Luna	DB	5'11"	183	22	2	
George Maderos	DB	6'1"	187	22	2	
Lowell Wagner	DB	6'	195	31		
Dick Moegle	HB-DB	6'	180	21	6	30
Ernie Smith	HB-DB	6'3"	190	22		
Maury Duncan	QB	6'1"	185	24		
Y. A. Tittle	QB	6'	190	28		
Carroll Hardy	HB	6'	185	22		24
Hugh McElhenny	HB	6'1"	198	26		36
Joe Arenas	DB-HB	5'11"	180	29	1	12
John Henry Johnson	DB-HB	6'2"	205	25	1	6
Lem Harkey (from PIT)	FB	6'1"	205	21		
Bud Laughlin	FB	6'1"	200	24		
Joe Perry	FB	6'	210	28		18
Harry Babcock	OE	6'2"	190	24		
Gordie Soltau	OE	6'2"	194	30		42
Billy Wilson	OE	6'3"	190	28		42
Ted Vaught	DE-OE	6'	208	23		

Bill Jessup – Injury

Fred Bruney – Military Service
Ted Connolly – Military Service
Ed Henke – Canadian Football League
Verl Lillywhite – Military Service

Jerry Smith – Military Service

DETROIT LIONS 3-9-0 Buddy Parker

Scores of Each Game		
17	Green Bay	20
13	Baltimore	28
10	LOS ANGELES	17
24	SAN FRANCISCO	27
13	Los Angeles	24
21	San Francisco	38
24	BALTIMORE	14
31	Pittsburgh	28
14	CHIC. BEARS	24
24	GREEN BAY	10
20	Chic. Bears	21
19	NEW YORK	24

Use Name	Pos.	Hgt	Wgt	Age	Int	Pts
Charlie Ane	OT	6'2"	260	24		
Jim Salsbury	OG-OT	6'1"	220	23		
George Atkins	OG	6'1"	210	23		
Stan Campbell	OG	6'	220	25		
Harley Sewell	OG	6'1"	235	24		
Dick Stanfel	OG	6'3"	245	28		
Andy Miketa	C	6'2"	210	24		
Lou Creekmur	OT-DG	6'4"	250	28		
Jim Cain	DE	6'1"	200	28		
Sonny Gandee	LB-DE	6'1"	220	26		6
Walt Jenkins	DT-DE	6'1"	223	24		
Gil Mains	DT	6'2"	235	25		6
Darris McCord	DT	6'4"	248	22		
Bob Miller	DT	6'3"	235	25		
Jim Martin	LB	6'2"	230	31		
Joe Schmidt	LB	6'1"	220	23		
Ted Topor	LB	6'1"	210	25		
Leon Cunningham	C-LB	6'2"	215	24		
Bob Long	DE-LB	6'3"	223	21		2
Jack Christiansen	DB	6'1"	195	26	3	
Jim David	DB	5'11"	175	28	3	
Dom Fucci	DB	5'11"	190	27		
Carl Karilivacz	DB	6'	185	24	2	
Lee Riley	DB	6'1"	190	23	2	
Dick Woit	DB	5'8"	175	24		
Harry Gilmer	QB	6'	180	29		
Bobby Layne	QB	6'1"	200	28		
Bob Hoernschemeyer	HB	5'11"	195	29		6
Bill Stits	DB-HB	6'	190	24	3	6
Doak Walker	DB-HB	5'11"	172	28	1	96
Lew Carpenter	FB-HB	6'1"	200	23		48
Jug Girard	OE-HB	5'11"	175	28		
Dave Middleton	OE-HB	6'1"	190	22		30
Leon Hart	OE-FB	6'5"	255	26		6
Dorne Dibble	OE	6'2"	195	26		12
Jim Doran	OE	6'2"	200	27		12

Bill Bowman – Military Service
Tom Dublinski – Canadian Football League
Gene Gedman – Military Service
Dick Kercher-Military Service

Yale Lary – Military Service
Jerry Perry – Military Service
Ollie Spencer – Military Service

LOS ANGELES RAMS

RUSHING

Last Name	No.	Yds	Avg	TD
Waller	151	716	4.7	7
Younger	138	644	4.7	5
Morris	40	148	3.7	1
Towler	43	137	3.2	3
Taylor	26	95	3.7	0
Quinlan	15	70	4.7	0
McCormick	16	66	4.1	1
Wade	11	43	3.9	0
Van Brocklin	11	24	2.2	0

RECEIVING

Last Name	No.	Yds	Avg	TD
Fears	44	569	13	2
Hirsch	25	460	18	2
Waller	24	228	10	1
Boyd	22	383	17	3
Quinlan	19	245	13	0
Lewis	19	199	10	0
Taylor	7	47	7	1
Younger	6	51	9	0
Towler	6	25	4	0
McCormick	3	−1	−0	0

PUNT RETURNS

Last Name	No.	Yds	Avg	TD
Lewis	29	105	4	0
Waller	14	60	4	0
Quinlan	1	55	55	1
Ellena	0	9	0	0

KICKOFF RETURNS

Last Name	No.	Yds	Avg	TD
Waller	17	461	27	0
Lewis	20	450	23	0
McCormick	2	42	21	0
Lipscomb	2	32	16	0
Hauser	2	17	9	0
Toogood	1	11	11	0

PASSING – PUNTING – KICKING

PASSING	Att	Comp	%	Yds	Yd/Att	TD	Int–%	RK
Van Brocklin	272	144	53	1890	7.0	8	15– 6	6
Wade	71	31	44	316	4.5	1	3– 4	
Waller	1	0	0	0	0.0	0	0– 0	

PUNTING	No	Avg
Van Brocklin	60	44.6

KICKING	XP	Att	%	FG	Att	%
Richter	30	31	97	13	24	54
McFadin	0	0	0	1	5	20
Fears	0	0	0	0	3	0

CHICAGO BEARS

RUSHING

Last Name	No.	Yds	Avg	TD
Casares	125	672	5.4	4
Watkins	110	553	5.0	8
Jo. Hoffman	94	454	4.8	0
Jagade	72	309	4.3	2
Brown	43	203	4.7	2
Williams	13	79	6.1	0
Drzewiecki	10	54	5.4	1
Blanda	15	54	3.6	2
Hugasian	12	34	2.8	0
Mosley	3	10	3.3	0

RECEIVING

Last Name	No.	Yds	Avg	TD
Hill	42	789	19	9
McColl	35	502	14	4
Schroeder	17	315	19	2
Casares	16	136	9	1
Jo. Hoffman	11	153	14	1
Jagade	7	16	2	0
Ja. Hoffman	6	86	14	0
Watkins	6	79	13	0
Hugasian	3	32	11	0
Kindt	2	15	8	0
Smith	1	13	13	0
Drzewiecki	1	1	1	0

PUNT RETURNS

Last Name	No.	Yds	Avg	TD
Drzewiecki	20	100	5	0
Smith	12	47	4	0
Kindt	1	0	0	0
Sumner	1	0	0	0

KICKOFF RETURNS

Last Name	No.	Yds	Avg	TD
Drzewiecki	25	591	24	0
Sumner	10	288	29	0
Watkins	5	145	29	0
Smith	1	24	24	0
Jagade	1	23	23	0
Mosley	1	14	14	0
Hugasian	1	0	0	0

PASSING – PUNTING – KICKING

PASSING	Att	Comp	%	Yds	Yd/Att	TD	Int–%	RK
Brown	164	85	52	1307	8.0	9	10– 6	4
Blanda	97	42	43	459	4.7	4	7– 7	
Williams	40	15	38	256	6.4	3	5–13	
Casares	3	2	67	27	9.0	1	1–33	
McColl	2	1	50	59	30.0	0	0– 0	

PUNTING	No	Avg
Brown	44	40.1
Williams	13	39.1

KICKING	XP	Att	%	FG	Att	%
Blanda	37	37	100	11	16	69

GREEN BAY PACKERS

RUSHING

Last Name	No.	Yds	Avg	TD
Ferguson	192	859	4.5	4
Rote	74	332	4.5	5
Reid	83	303	3.7	2
Johnson	49	210	4.3	0
Switzer	16	101	6.3	0
Carmichael	6	45	7.5	0
Cone	12	25	2.1	0
Held	1	8	8.0	0

RECEIVING

Last Name	No.	Yds	Avg	TD
Howton	44	697	16	5
Knafelc	40	613	15	8
Ferguson	22	153	7	0
Carmichael	16	222	14	1
Switzer	14	104	7	1
Reid	13	138	11	1
Johnson	9	71	8	1
Cone	1	7	7	0

PUNT RETURNS

Last Name	No.	Yds	Avg	TD
Switzer	24	158	7	0
Carmichael	10	89	9	0
Szafaryn	1	28	28	1
Johnson	1	5	5	0
Romine	1	0	0	0

KICKOFF RETURNS

Last Name	No.	Yds	Avg	TD
Switzer	17	445	26	0
Carmichael	14	418	30	1
Forester	3	52	17	0
Johnson	2	46	23	0
Reid	2	21	11	0
Ferguson	1	20	20	0

PASSING – PUNTING – KICKING

PASSING	Att	Comp	%	Yds	Yd/Att	TD	Int–%	RK
Rote	342	157	46	1977	5.8	17	19– 6	7
Held	4	2	50	27	6.8	0	0– 0	
Brackins	2	0	0	0	0.0	0	0– 0	

PUNTING	No	Avg
Deschaine	56	43.2

KICKING	XP	Att	%	FG	Att	%
Cone	30	30	100	16	24	67

BALTIMORE COLTS

RUSHING

Last Name	No.	Yds	Avg	TD
Ameche	213	961	4.5	9
Dupre	88	338	3.8	1
Shaw	68	301	4.4	3
B. Young	32	87	2.7	1
D. Young	17	39	2.3	0
Shields	10	34	3.4	0
Kerkorian	6	20	3.3	1
Renfro	4	13	3.3	0
Bryant	2	4	2.0	0
Womble	4	2	0.5	0

RECEIVING

Last Name	No.	Yds	Avg	TD
Mutscheller	33	518	16	7
Ameche	27	141	5	0
Colteryahn	21	261	12	3
B. Young	19	426	22	1
Berry	13	205	16	0
Dupre	10	153	15	0
Shields	3	27	9	0
D. Young	2	15	8	0
Womble	1	14	14	0
Pellington	1	10	10	0
Taseff	1	3	3	0

PUNT RETURNS

Last Name	No.	Yds	Avg	TD
Rechichar	30	121	4	0
Taseff	14	46	3	0
Pellington	1	6	6	0
D. Young	1	3	3	0
Peters	1	2	2	0
B. Young	1	0	0	0

KICKOFF RETURNS

Last Name	No.	Yds	Avg	TD
Rechichar	9	235	26	0
B. Young	9	222	25	0
Taseff	7	162	23	0
Ameche	4	60	15	0
D. Young	2	37	19	0
Pellington	2	36	18	0
Berry	2	27	14	0
Renfro	1	20	20	0

PASSING – PUNTING – KICKING

PASSING	Att	Comp	%	Yds	Yd/Att	TD	Int–%	RK
Shaw	237	119	50	1586	6.7	10	19– 8	9
Kerkorian	29	15	52	209	7.2	1	3–10	

PUNTING	No	Avg
Brethauer	55	39.3

KICKING	XP	Att	%	FG	Att	%
Rechichar	25	26	96	10	24	42
Kerkorian	0	0	0	1	2	50

SAN FRANCISCO FORTY NINERS

RUSHING

Last Name	No.	Yds	Avg	TD
Perry	156	701	4.5	2
McElhenny	90	327	3.6	4
Moegle	41	235	5.7	5
Arenas	37	150	4.1	0
Tittle	23	114	5.0	0
J. Johnson	19	69	3.6	1
Laughlin	20	58	2.9	0
Hardy	15	37	2.5	0
Harkey	6	27	4.5	0
Duncan	1	−5	−5.0	0

RECEIVING

Last Name	No.	Yds	Avg	TD
Wilson	53	831	16	7
Soltau	26	358	14	1
Perry	19	55	3	1
Arenas	13	255	20	2
Hardy	12	338	28	4
McElhenny	11	203	18	2
Laughlin	8	54	7	0
Moegle	4	94	24	0
Babcock	3	31	10	0
J. Johnson	2	6	3	0

PUNT RETURNS

Last Name	No.	Yds	Avg	TD
Arenas	21	55	3	0
Moegle	8	36	5	0
Berry	1	11	11	0
McElhenny	7	10	1	0
J. Johnson	1	6	6	0
Carapella	1	0	0	0

KICKOFF RETURNS

Last Name	No.	Yds	Avg	TD
Arenas	24	594	25	0
Moegle	10	249	25	0
McElhenny	9	189	21	0
Hardy	3	65	22	0
Laughlin	1	25	25	0
Toneff	1	13	13	0
Hazeltine	1	9	9	0
Powell	1	2	2	0
Palatella	1	1	1	0

PASSING – PUNTING – KICKING

PASSING	Att	Comp	%	Yds	Int–%	TD	Int–%	RK
Tittle	287	147	51	2185	7.6	17	28–10	5
Duncan	12	4	33	40	3.3	0	0– 0	
Perry	2	0	0	0	0.0	0	0– 0	
Arenas	1	0	0	0	0.0	0	0– 0	
Moegle	1	0	0	0	0.0	0	0– 0	

PUNTING	No	Avg
Luna	63	40.6

KICKING	XP	Att	%	FG	Att	%
Soltau	27	30	90	3	12	25

DETROIT LIONS

RUSHING

Last Name	No.	Yds	Avg	TD
Carpenter	137	543	4.0	6
Middleton	59	201	3.4	2
Stits	46	165	3.6	0
Hart	35	159	4.5	0
Layne	31	111	3.6	0
Hoernschemeyer	36	109	3.0	1
Walker	23	95	4.1	2
Gilmer	15	67	4.5	0
Girard	10	27	2.7	0

RECEIVING

Last Name	No.	Yds	Avg	TD
Middleton	44	663	15	3
Carpenter	44	312	7	2
Doran	38	552	15	2
Girard	23	301	13	0
Walker	22	428	19	5
Dibble	14	179	13	2
Hart	9	54	6	1
Hoernschemeyer	5	36	7	0
Stits	5	17	3	0

PUNT RETURNS

Last Name	No.	Yds	Avg	TD
Riley	14	107	8	0
Christiansen	12	87	7	0
Girard	9	25	3	0
Walker	2	5	3	0
David	1	0	0	0
Karilivacz	1	0	0	0
Schmidt	1	0	0	0
Stits	1	0	0	0

KICKOFF RETURNS

Last Name	No.	Yds	Avg	TD
Middleton	11	188	17	0
Christiansen	7	169	24	0
Girard	7	117	17	0
Riley	5	111	22	0
Hart	4	86	22	0
Carpenter	4	78	20	0
Walker	1	24	24	0
Martin	1	14	14	0
Cunningham	1	13	13	0
Toper	1	13	13	0
Woit	1	13	13	0
Gandee	1	7	7	0
Schmidt	1	6	6	0

PASSING – PUNTING – KICKING

PASSING	Att	Comp	%	Yds	Yd/Att	TD	Int–%	RK
Layne	270	143	53	1830	6.8	11	17– 6	3
Gilmer	122	58	48	633	5.2	2	4– 3	
Walker	3	0	0	0	0.0	0	0– 0	
Hornschemeyer	2	1	50	17	8.5	1	1–50	
Stits	2	2	100	62	31.0	1	0– 0	
Girard	1	0	0	0	0.0	0	0 0	

PUNTING	No	Avg
Girard	56	41.3
Walker	9	40.2
Fucci	2	36.0

KICKING	XP	Att	%	FG	Att	%
Walker	27	29	93	9	16	56
Martin	0	0	0	0	1	0

1956 Wiring the Quarterback

The television tube now was creating pro-football fans in every corner of the country, as the NFL signed a lucrative contract with the Columbia Broadcasting System for TV coverage of all league games. With home contests blacked out for a fifty-mile radius, CBS captured huge audiences every Sunday afternoon with regional telecasts of most games and coast-to-coast coverage of all post-season action. Besides handsomely rewarding the teams financially, the TV contract further fueled the league's already skyrocketing attendance and started some people to thinking of pro football as the new national pastime.

The world of electronics did create some problems for Commissioner Bert Bell, as walkie-talkie radios came into vogue on the field. Instead of sending plays into the quarterback via alternating guards, as had been his custom, Cleveland coach Paul Brown installed radio receivers in his quarterbacks' helmets and called the plays by radio. Very quickly, several teams were broadcasting their signals from the bench, leading other clubs to tune in on the enemy's wave length to try to decode their messages. The Pittsburgh Steelers even installed special wiring in the turf at Forbes Field to aid radio reception, but Bell quickly ended this sideshow by banning, on October 19, all such electronic gadgetry.

Bell this year faced no threats from Canada, as the Canadian teams had tired of waging a raiding war, but he did face a new adversary in the new NFL players' association. This union was seeking benefits such as the establishment of a pension and a minimum salary of $5,000, but the owners felt strong enough to ignore this group for now.

EASTERN CONFERENCE

New York Giants—The Giants moved into Yankee Stadium this year, and once the New Yorkers beat the quick-starting Chicago Cards in a mid-season showdown, they easily charged down the home stretch. While the offense jelled after several seasons of playing together, the defense was bolstered by four fine newcomers. Defensive coach Tom Landry, no longer a player, replaced himself in the secondary with ex-Ram Ed Hughes, installed rookie Sam Huff, whose crunching tackles won him a hero's status with Giant fans, as a full-time middle linebacker, and traded for two excellent linemen in ex-Ram Andy Robustelli and ex-Steeler Dick Modzelewski. Em Tunnell and Rosie Grier shone among the returning defenders, and although the Chuck Conerly-led offense consistently ground out points, it was the defensive unit that gave this team its image and won the fans' imagination.

Chicago Cardinals—For a team with an unsure quarterback, the Cards got off to an amazing start by beating the Browns, Giants, Redskins, and Eagles in their first four games. Directing the attack through these victories was young Lamar McHan, a talented passer whose lack of confidence required constant pep talks from his teammates, even in the huddle. After the opening spurt, however, the entire Card team faded into inconsistency. Although Night Train Lane and Lindon Crow starred in the secondary, the improved defense fell into a mid-season skid when injuries shelved tackles Chuck Ulrich and Tony Pasquesi.

Washington Redskins—One evening during training camp, halfback Vic Janowicz was riding in a friend's car when the vehicle left the road in an accident. Janowicz was thrown from the car against a tree, suffering brain damage, which ended his football career. The Redskins as a team were shocked by the loss of their star back, but the players as individuals were repelled by owner George Marshall's policy toward the crippled Janowicz. Stating that the accident happened on off-duty hours, Marshall put the injured player off the Redskin payroll. Fully aware of the staggering medical costs facing him, each Redskin player contributed $10 each week to help Janowicz through the crisis. Morale on the squad sank to an ugly level, and although injuries to quarterbacks Eddie LeBaron and Al Dorow hurt the team, the Redskin season was unalterably ruined before it began.

Cleveland Browns—All monarchies eventually fall, and the Browns this year ran into a revolt by their former abject subjects in the Eastern Conference. The retirement of Otto Graham left the dynasty on shaky ground, with four losses in the first five games signaling the death of the king. George Ratterman began the year at quarterback but ripped up his knee in the season's fourth game. Babe Parilli was next on the firing line, lasting three games before a shoulder separation shelved him and left the Browns without a quarterback. In desperation, the team signed free-agent Tom O'Connell, who did surprisingly well in the remaining games. A loss to the Cards in the final game of the year saddled the Browns with their first losing season ever, but this cloudy season had a silver lining. With an early pick in the collegiate draft, the Browns would wind up with Jimmy Brown.

Pittsburgh Steelers—The Steelers' rebuilding program fielded several promising first- and second-year men. Youngsters Joe Krupa, John Reger, and Gary Glick worked their way onto the defensive platoon, while Frank Varrichione, Willie McClung, and Lowell Perry got their feet wet on offense. Of all these young gems, Perry shone the brightest, with his darting speed put to good use as a pass receiver and a punt returner until a mid-season tackle fractured his pelvis and ended his career before it really began. But even with Perry's loss, the Steelers played respectable football while breaking in the new men.

Philadelphia Eagles—Pete Pihos was gone, Bucko Kilroy was gone, and any resemblance to the championship teams of the Greasy Neale era was gone. The Eagles still had not signed any reliable, heavy-duty runner, relying instead on Bobby Thomason and Adrian Burk to pass the club to victory in the face of expectant enemy defenses. With the sticky-finger Pihos retired, even the air attack bogged down, with the offense dropping 105 points off from its 1955 production.

WESTERN CONFERENCE

Chicago Bears—This season both started a new era in Bear history and recaptured the glory of the pre-World War II Bear teams. Although George Halas still called the shots from the front office, he kept his promise to install a younger coach by turning over the reigns to long-time assistant Paddy Driscoll, who was a full two years younger. But even without Halas prowling the sidelines, this Bear club looked a lot like the team which won four straight divisional crowns from 1940 to 1943. The defense, led by Bill George, stood like a granite wall for enemy offenses to beat their heads against, while the Bear attack combined hard running with accurate passing.

Detroit Lions—With Bobby Layne's shoulder healed and Joe Schmidt's coming into his own as a middle linebacker, the Lions had an inspirational leader at the head of both the offensive and defensive platoons. With last year's collapse to motivate them further, the Lions roared out of the pack with six straight wins and ran head and head with the Bears for the Western crown. Two weeks from the end of the year, Detroit took a half-game lead by destroying the Bears 42-10, and that same slim margin was on the line when the clubs again met on the last day of the season. With Detroit favored to win, disaster struck when Chicago's Ed Meadows blindsided Layne, knocking him out of action with a concussion. Bitterness and anger filled the field, and when the final gun sounded, Chicago had won 38-21.

San Francisco '49ers—Popular ex-quarterback Frankie Albert returned to the '49ers as head coach but couldn't make up his mind on which quarterback to use. At the start of the year, he benched veteran Y. A. Tittle and gave the starting job to rookie Earl Morrall. Pro football, however, had reached the stage where no rookie could step right into the lineup and turn a club into a winner, so Albert put Tittle back into the signal caller's spot and the '49ers rallied to four wins and a tie in their last five games.

Baltimore Colts—When a hard tackle by the Bears' Fred Williams broke quarterback George Shaw's kneecap in the Colts' fourth game, into the lineup trotted rookie Johnny Unitas, signed as an unheralded free agent during training camp. With Unitas' timing rusty from inactivity, the Colts kept fumbling the ball, and the Bears coasted to a 58-27 triumph. With little expected from him, Unitas then led the Colts to successive upsets over the Packers and Browns and later engineered a 56-21 thrashing of the Rams. Two other key newcomers figured in the mid-season surge—rookie speedster Lenny Moore and ex-Ram defensive tackle Big Daddy Lipscomb.

Green Bay Packers—On successive weekends the Packers knocked the Lions temporarily out of first place with a 24-20 triumph, then killed the Cardinals' Eastern Division hopes with a 24-21 upset. But outside of these two spoiler victories, the season bogged down in a swamp of internal turmoil. The team executive committee began growling at head coach Lisle Blackbourn when the Packers won only two of their first eight games. One executive member blasted Blackbourn for not playing first draft choice Jack Losch more often, another wanted Blackbourn's head for trading off defensive end John Martinkovic.

Los Angeles Rams—The Rams' decisive loss in last year's championship game led coach Sid Gillman to replace some of the parts in his football machine, only to have the entire unit break down in the process. Gillman unloaded Andy Robustelli, Big Daddy Lipscomb, and Ed Hughes from the defensive unit and started young Billy Wade at quarterback over Norm Van Brocklin. With ten rookies on the thirty-five-man roster, the Rams opened the season by beating the Eagles 27-7 and then dropped three straight to reveal the flaws in the new lineup.

FINAL TEAM STATISTICS

OFFENSE

	BALT.	CHI.B.	CHI.C.	CLEVE.	DET.	G.BAY	L.A.	N.Y.	PHIL.	PITT.	S.F.	WASH.
FIRST DOWNS:												
Total	216	244	191	173	247	212	227	223	160	184	221	176
by Rushing	106	140	116	94	122	86	103	124	73	83	101	91
by Passing	99	92	63	63	111	112	111	82	74	83	107	71
by Penalty	11	12	12	16	14	14	13	17	13	18	13	14
RUSHING:												
Number	432	536	527	480	507	337	384	499	418	413	419	501
Yards	2202	2468	2053	1845	2011	1421	1978	2129	1377	1350	1836	1743
Average Yards	5.1	4.6	3.9	3.8	4.0	4.2	5.2	4.3	3.3	3.3	4.4	3.5
Touchdowns	21	22	14	8	21	13	15	18	11	14	17	5
PASSING:												
Attempts	279	250	214	202	301	353	329	275	249	318	297	215
Completions	158	135	100	105	160	171	170	133	122	136	162	104
Completion Percentage	56.6	54.0	46.7	52.0	53.2	48.4	51.7	48.4	49.0	42.8	54.5	48.4
Gross Yards	2210	2193	1492	1358	2250	2591	2601	1601	1556	1793	2262	1335
Yards Lost Tackled	289	124	123	183	55	193	182	34	279	127	285	117
Net Yards	1921	2069	1369	1175	2195	2398	2419	1567	1277	1666	1977	1218
Avg. Yards per Attempt (Gross)	7.9	8.8	7.0	6.7	7.5	7.3	7.9	5.8	6.2	5.6	7.6	6.2
Avg. Yards per Comp. (Gross)	14.0	16.2	14.9	12.9	14.1	15.2	15.3	12.0	12.8	13.2	14.0	12.8
Touchdowns	14	19	13	8	13	21	18	17	6	14	8	11
Interceptions	18	19	14	18	23	18	28	14	27	24	19	18
Percent Intercepted	6.5	7.6	6.5	8.9	7.6	5.1	8.5	5.1	10.8	7.5	6.4	8.4
PUNTS:												
Number	58	44	55	50	52	62	48	60	68	77	59	63
Average Yards	38.4	39.3	37.8	41.9	41.3	42.7	43.1	41.8	41.8	38.2	38.4	42.4
PUNT RETURNS:												
Number	42	30	32	41	43	30	43	36	36	45	35	29
Yards	297	195	305	317	233	239	253	162	241	299	160	273
Average Yards	7.1	6.5	9.5	7.7	5.4	8.0	5.9	4.5	6.7	6.6	4.6	9.4
Touchdowns	1	1	1	1	1	0	1	0	0	0	1	0
KICKOFF RETURNS:												
Number	54	37	33	34	33	59	44	35	45	40	51	44
Yards	1043	830	700	830	687	1442	1011	719	1073	1042	1257	864
Average Yards	19.3	22.4	21.2	24.4	20.8	24.4	23.0	20.5	23.8	26.1	24.6	19.6
Touchdowns	0	1	1	0	0	1	1	0	0	0	1	0
INTERCEPTION RETURNS:												
Number	13	23	33	18	28	19	20	17	16	18	17	18
Yards	134	420	451	274	360	406	328	198	246	312	126	148
Average Yards	10.3	18.3	13.7	15.2	12.9	21.4	16.4	11.6	15.4	17.3	7.4	8.2
Touchdowns	0	3	1	1	1	1	2	0	1	0	1	0
PENALTIES:												
Number	53	67	78	52	66	42	57	52	59	74	57	44
Yards	507	553	626	457	668	393	583	474	542	614	562	383
FUMBLES:												
Number	18	18	29	18	14	24	32	27	25	16	17	29
Number Lost	14	10	21	12	11	11	18	13	11	10	12	17
POINTS:												
Total	270	363	240	167	300	264	291	264	143	217	233	183
PAT Attempts	38	47	30	19	36	35	38	35	18	29	28	19
PAT Made	33	45	30	18	36	33	36	34	17	26	26	16
FG Attempts	16	28	22	20	25	8	19	15	14	9	20	25
FG Made	3	12	10	11	16	5	9	6	6	5	13	17
Percent FG Made	18.8	42.9	45.5	55.0	64.0	62.5	47.4	40.0	42.9	55.6	65.0	68.0
Safeties	0	0	0	1	0	0	0	1	0	1	0	1

DEFENSE

	BALT.	CHI.B	CHI.C.	CLEVE.	DET.	G.BAY	L.A.	N.Y.	PHIL.	PITT.	S.F.	WASH.
FIRST DOWNS:												
Total	238	207	211	188	181	246	224	188	200	167	236	188
by Rushing	109	80	117	108	81	129	109	82	110	93	124	97
by Passing	115	113	79	62	84	104	100	90	69	66	103	83
by Penalty	14	14	15	18	16	13	15	16	21	8	9	8
RUSHING:												
Number	447	384	478	463	373	512	473	415	513	468	481	446
Yards	1916	1483	2075	2032	1503	2619	1944	1443	1893	1743	2192	1570
Average Yards	4.3	3.9	4.3	4.4	4.0	5.1	4.1	3.5	3.7	3.7	4.6	3.5
Touchdowns	16	14	14	13	9	20	21	10	10	14	23	15
PASSING:												
Attempts	297	332	287	226	297	260	290	297	243	234	279	240
Completions	165	159	129	107	138	144	156	149	114	128	147	120
Completion Percentage	55.6	47.9	44.9	47.3	46.5	55.4	53.8	50.2	46.9	54.7	52.7	50.0
Gross Yards	2463	2413	1670	1215	2045	2166	2374	1890	1506	1646	2115	1739
Yards Lost Tackled	203	220	146	112	140	75	212	252	173	203	145	110
Net Yards	2260	2193	1524	1103	1905	2091	2162	1638	1333	1443	1970	1629
Avg. Yards per Attempt (Gross)	8.3	7.3	5.8	5.4	6.9	8.3	8.2	6.4	6.2	6.8	7.6	7.2
Avg. Yards per Comp. (Gross)	14.9	15.2	12.9	11.4	14.8	15.0	15.2	12.7	13.2	12.9	14.4	14.5
Touchdowns	22	16	8	7	11	17	17	12	15	14	12	11
Interceptions	13	23	33	18	28	19	20	17	16	18	17	18
Percent Intercepted	4.4	6.9	11.5	8.0	9.4	7.3	6.9	5.7	6.6	7.7	6.1	7.5
PUNTS:												
Number	56	64	52	59	59	50	58	62	68	65	42	61
Average Yards	44.4	40.0	39.2	40.7	39.4	40.8	42.0	36.5	41.0	41.6	40.7	40.7
PUNT RETURNS:												
Number	39	29	28	26	32	49	31	34	50	45	35	44
Yards	153	243	132	137	197	280	342	337	283	451	123	296
Average Yards	3.9	8.4	4.7	5.3	6.2	5.7	11.0	9.9	5.7	10.0	3.5	6.7
Touchdowns	2	1	0	0	0	1	0	0	0	1	0	2
KICKOFF RETURNS:												
Number	43	47	40	33	48	48	52	46	27	43	42	40
Yards	1015	1249	889	819	1041	924	1068	1033	666	817	988	989
Average Yards	23.6	26.6	22.2	24.8	21.7	19.3	20.5	22.5	24.7	19.0	23.5	24.7
Touchdowns	1	1	0	0	1	0	1	0	0	0	0	1
INTERCEPTION RETURNS:												
Number	18	19	14	18	23	18	28	14	27	24	19	18
Yards	275	343	173	279	243	312	331	235	365	364	330	153
Average Yards	15.3	18.1	12.4	15.5	10.6	17.3	11.8	16.8	13.5	15.2	17.4	8.5
Touchdowns	2	1	0	0	1	3	0	1	0	3	0	0
PENALTIES:												
Number	62	60	60	61	48	52	62	56	76	69	37	58
Yards	486	624	543	529	519	493	512	495	686	606	321	548
FUMBLES:												
Number	23	24	23	11	16	17	13	32	17	39	27	25
Number Lost	15	15	12	8	12	8	8	16	11	22	17	16
POINTS:												
Total	322	246	182	177	188	342	307	197	215	250	284	225
PAT Attempts	43	34	23	21	22	44	39	25	25	33	34	29
PAT Made	40	33	21	21	21	42	37	24	23	31	32	25
FG Attempts	19	18	16	17	20	18	20	16	21	16	25	15
FG Made	8	3	7	10	11	12	12	7	14	7	14	8
Percent FG Made	42.1	16.7	43.8	58.8	55.0	66.7	60.0	43.8	66.7	43.8	56.0	53.3
Safeties	0	0	1	0	1	0	0	1	0	0	0	1

1956
CHAMPIONSHIP GAME
December 30, at New York
(Attendance 56,836)

Icing the Bears on Giant Footing

Just as in 1934, the Giants and Bears met for the NFL title on an icy field in New York, with the Giants again getting superior footing from sneakers. New York established itself right at the outset as Gene Filipski ran the opening kickoff 53 yards back to the Chicago 38-yard line. Four plays later, Mel Triplett barged 17 yards over left tackle for the first touchdown of the game. Two plays after the kickoff, the Giants recovered Rick Casares' fumble deep in his own territory and converted it into three points on Ben Agajanian's toe. After Jimmy Patton picked off an Ed Brown pass, Agajanian kicked another field goal to make the score 13-0 at the end of the first quarter. Three minutes into the second period, Alex Webster's three-yard run plus the extra point ran the lead to 20-0. With a rout staring them in the face, the Bears got a break when Em Tunnell fumbled a punt on the New York 25-yard line and John Mellekas recovered for Chicago. Five plays later, Rick Casares ran nine yards for the Bears' only touchdown of the day. The Giants put the game in their hip pocket with a pair of touchdowns late in the second period. The Giants drove 72 yards in five plays, with a 50-yard pass from Chuck Conerly to Alex Webster the key play. Within two minutes, New York's Ray Beck blocked Ed Brown's punt, and Henry Moore fell on it in the end zone for another Giant touchdown. The halftime score of 34-7 convinced quite a few fans to leave the frigid stadium for the warmth at home. The Bears, however, had to endure a second half in which the Giant linemen constantly pressured Ed Brown and George Blanda, the linebackers hounded fullback Rick Casares, and the secondary blanketed ace receiver Harlon Hill. The Chicago attack was throttled so completely that the Bears abandoned the T formation and switched to the double wing in the third quarter. The Giants, however, scored the only points of the period by driving 80 yards in four plays, with the final nine yards coming on a Conerly-to-Kyle Rote pass as Conerly continued to pick on rookie defensive back J.C. Caroline. Conerly's 14-yard touchdown pass to Frank Gifford midway through the final period ran the score to 47-7, and that total stood up through the final eight minutes of the game. By the end of the game, third-string quarterback Bobby Clatterbuck was directing the New York offense, but the Bears were able to keep him from lengthening the lead.

SCORING

NEW YORK	13	21	6	7–47
CHIC. BEARS	0	7	0	0– 7

First Quarter			
	N. Y.	Triplett, 17 yard rush PAT – Agajanian (kick)	2:40
	N. Y.	Agajanian, 17 yard Field Goal	4:59
	N. Y.	Agajanian, 43 yard Field Goal	12:21
Second Quarter			
	N. Y.	Webster, 3 yard rush PAT – Agajanian (kick)	2:34
	Chi.	Casares, 9 yard rush PAT – Blanda (kick)	6:52
	N. Y.	Webster, 1 yard rush PAT – Agajanian (kick)	9:54
	N.Y.	Moore, recovered blocked punt in end zone PAT – Agajanian (kick)	11:32
Third Quarter			
	N.Y.	Rote, 9 yard pass from Conerly PAT – Agajanian (No Good)	10:10
Fourth Quarter			
	N.Y.	Gifford, 14 yard pass from Conerly PAT – Agajanian (kick)	6:23

TEAM STATISTICS

N.Y.		CHI.
16	First Downs – Total	19
8	First Downs – Rushing	8
8	First Downs – Passing	10
0	First Downs – Penalty	1
126	Rushing Yardage	67
20	Pass Attempts	47
11	Pass Completions	20
55.0	Completion Percentage	42.5
228	Yards Gained Passing	247
6	Yards Lost Attempting to Pass	34
222	Net Passing Yards	213
11.4	Average Yards per Attempt	5.3
20.7	Average Yards per Completion	12.4
3	Punts	8
37	Average Punting Distance	34
46	Punt Return Yardage	1
2	Interceptions	0
48	Interception Return Yardage	0
6	Penalties	4
40	Yards Penalized	50
3	Fumbles	2
2	Fumbles Lost	1

NEW YORK GIANTS 8-3-1 Jim Lee Howell

Scores of Each Game		
38	San Francisco	21
27	Chic. Cards	35
21	Cleveland	9
38	PITTSBURGH	10
20	PHILADELPHIA	3
17	Pittsburgh	14
23	CHIC. CARDS	10
7	Washington	33
17	CHIC. BEARS	17
28	WASHINGTON	14
7	CLEVELAND	24
21	Philadelphia	7

Use Name	Pos.	Hgt	Wgt	Age	Int	Pts
Rosey Brown	OT	6'3"	245	23		
Dick Yelvington	OT	6'2"	235	29		
Bill Austin	OG	6'1"	225	27		
Jerry Huth	OG	6'	215	23		
Jack Spinks (from GB)	OG	6'	235	26		
Jack Stroud	OG	6'1"	235	27		
Ray Wietecha	C	6'1"	225	27		
Ray Beck	OG-DG	6'2"	225	24	1	
Jim Katcavage	DE	6'3"	235	21		
Andy Robustelli	DE	6'1"	235	30		2
Walt Yowarsky	DE	6'2"	235	28		
Rosey Grier	DT	6'5"	275	23		
Dick Modzelewski	DT	6'	260	25		
Sam Huff	LB	6'1"	230	21	3	
Cliff Livingston	LB	6'3"	210	26		
Harland Svare	LB	6'	215	25		
Bill Svoboda	LB	6'	210	29	2	
Ed Hughes	DB	6'1"	185	28	1	
Dick Nolan	DB	6'1"	185	24	2	
Jimmy Patton	DB	6'	180	24	1	
Herb Rich	DB	5'11"	185	27	1	
Em Tunnell	DB	6'1"	200	34	6	
Henry Moore	HB-DB	6'1"	195	22		
Bobby Clatterbuck	QB	6'3"	195	24		
Chuck Conerly	QB	6'1"	185	32		
Don Heinrich	QB	6'	180	24		
Don Chandler	HB	6'2"	205	21		3
Gene Filipski	HB	5'11"	185	25		6
Frank Gifford	HB	6'1"	205	26		65
Alex Webster	HB	6'3"	210	25		60
Mel Triplett	FB	6'1"	215	24		36
Ken MacAfee	OE	6'2"	215	26		24
Kyle Rote	OE	6'	205	27		24
Bob Schnelker	OE	6'3"	215	26		6
Ben Agajanian	K	6'	215	37		38

CHICAGO CARDINALS 7-5-0 Ray Richards

Scores of Each Game		
9	CLEVELAND	7
35	NEW YORK	27
31	Washington	3
20	Philadelphia	6
14	WASHINGTON	17
28	PHILADELPHIA	17
10	New York	23
7	Pittsburgh	14
38	PITTSBURGH	27
21	GREEN BAY	24
3	Chic. Bears	10
24	Cleveland	7

Use Name	Pos.	Hgt	Wgt	Age	Int	Pts
Tom Dahms	OT	6'5"	247	28		
Burt Delevan	OT	6'2"	236	26		
Jack Jennings	OT	6'4"	245	29		
John Dittrich	OG	6'1"	230	23		
Doug Hogland	OG	6'3"	240	25		
Bob Konovsky	OT-OG	6'2"	245	22		
Jack Simmons	C	6'4"	240	30		
Stan West	OG	6'2"	235	29		
Tom Bienemann	DE	6'3"	225	28	1	
Leo Sugar	DE	6'1"	210	27		
Pat Summerall	DE	6'4"	225	26		60
Chuck Ulrich	DT	6'4"	250	25		
Len Teeuws	DT	6'4"	245	29		
Tony Pasquesi	LB-DT	6'4"	250	22		
Carl Brettschneider	LB	6'1"	220	24		
Hardy Brown (from SF)	LB	6'	196	32		
Ed Husmann	OG-LB	6'	225	25		
Leo Sanford	C-LB	6'1"	230	27	5	
Chuck Weber (from CLE)	DE-LB	6'1"	225	27	1	
Lindon Crow	DB	6'1"	187	23	11	
Jimmy Hill	DB	6'2"	190	27	5	
Woodley Lewis	DB	6'	195	31	1	
Julian Spence	DB	5'11"	175	27	1	
John Roach	QB-DB	6'4"	190	23		
Night Train Lane	OE-DB	6'1"	190	28	7	6
Lamar McHan	QB	6'1"	197	24		30
Jim Root	QB	6'1"	185	25		12
Alex Burl	HB	5'10"	165	24		6
Ollie Matson	HB	6'2"	210	26		48
Frank Bernardi	DB-HB	5'9"	180	23	1	6
Dave Mann	OE-HB	6'1"	190	23		6
Joe Childress	FB	6'	195	22		6
Johnny Olszewski	FB	5'11"	200	25		12
Max Boydston	OE	6'2"	207	23		12
Gern Nagler	OE	6'2"	190	23		24
Don Stonesifer	OE	6'	200	29		12
Charlie Anderson	DE-OE	6'	230	22		

Mal Hammack – Military Service
Jimmy Sears – Military Service

WASHINGTON REDSKINS 6-6-0 Joe Kuharich

Scores of Each Game		
13	Pittsburgh	30
9	Philadelphia	13
3	CHIC. CARDS	31
20	CLEVELAND	9
17	Chic. Cards	14
18	DETROIT	17
33	NEW YORK	7
20	Cleveland	17
14	New York	28
19	PHILADELPHIA	17
0	PITTSBURGH	23
17	Baltimore	19

Use Name	Pos.	Hgt	Wgt	Age	Int	Pts
Don Boll	OT	6'2"	270	29		
Johnny Miller	DT-OT	6'5"	242	22		2
H. Jagielski (from Chi C)	DT-OT	6'	250	24		
Dick Stanfel	OG	6'3"	230	29		
Red Stephens	OG	6'	227	26		
Slug Witucki	OG	5'11"	234	28		
Bill Fulcher	LB-OG	6'	190	22	1	
Johnny Allen	C	6'2"	224	24		
Jim Schrader	C	6'2"	235	24		
Harry Ulinski	C	6'4"	232	31		
Gene Brito	DE	6'1"	230	30	1	
Erik Christensen	DE	6'3"	235	25		
Chet Ostrowski	DE	6'1"	232	26	1	
Ralph Thomas	OE-DE	5'11"	184	26		
J. D. Kimmel	DT	6'4"	250	27		
Volney Peters	DT	6'4"	237	28		
John Paluck	DE-DT	6'2"	235	23		6
Chuck Drazenovich	LB	6'1"	224	29		
Ralph Felton	LB	5'11"	210	24		
Tony Sardisco (to SF)	LB	6'2"	215	23		
Lavern Torgeson	LB	6'	220	27	1	
Roy Barni	DB	5'11"	184	29	2	
Art DeCarlo	DB	6'2"	193	26	1	
Norb Hecker	DB	6'2"	196	29	8	6
Gary Lowe	DB	5'11"	198	22	1	
Hal Norris	LB-DB	5'11"	194	24		
Scooter Scudero	HB-DB	5'10"	170	26	2	
Al Dorow	QB	6'	190	26		
Eddie LeBaron	QB	5'9"	165	26		
Fred Wyant	QB	6'	200	22		
Jerry Planutis	HB	5'9"	175	26		
Tom Runnels	HB	5'10"	184	22		6
Billy Wells	HB	5'9"	178	24		12
Dick James	DB-HB	5'9"	174	22		18
Dale Atkeson	FB	6'2"	212	26		6
Sam Baker	FB	6'2"	210	24		67
Leo Elter	FB	5'10"	202	27		12
Johnny Carson	OE	6'3"	198	26		18
Steve Meilinger	OE	6'2"	220	26		30

Vic Janowicz – Brain injury in automobile accident
Ralph Guglielmi – Military Service
Bert Zagers – Military Service

CLEVELAND BROWNS 5-7-0 Paul Brown

Scores of Each Game		
7	Chic. Cards	9
14	Pittsburgh	10
9	NEW YORK	21
9	Washington	20
16	PITTSBURGH	24
24	Green Bay	7
7	BALTIMORE	21
16	Philadelphia	0
17	WASHINGTON	20
17	PHILADELPHIA	14
24	New York	7
7	CHIC. CARDS	24

Use Name	Pos.	Hgt	Wgt	Age	Int	Pts
Lou Groza	OT	6'3"	240	32		51
Mike McCormack	OT	6'4"	248	29		
John Macerelli	OG-OT	6'2"	230	26		
Harold Bradley	OG	6'2"	230	27		
Herschel Forester	OG	6'	230	26		
Abe Gibron (to PHI)	OG	5'11"	240	30		
Frank Gatski	C	6'3"	240	34		
Art Hunter	DE-DT-C	6'4"	225	23		
Len Ford	DE	6'4"	250	30		
Carlton Massey	DE	6'2"	220	27		
Jim Ray Smith	DE	6'3"	220	25		
Horace Gillom	OE-DE	6'1"	225	35		
Don Colo	DT	6'3"	245	31	1	
John Kissell	DT	6'3"	248	33		
Don Goss	OT-DT	6'5"	260	24		
Bob Gain	DE-LB-DT	6'3"	250	28		
Galen Fiss	LB	6'	215	26	1	
Walt Michaels	LB	6'	230	27		
Chuck Noll	LB	6'1"	220	24	1	6
Sam Palumbo	C-LB	6'2"	220	25		
Kenny Konz	DB	5'10"	180	28	4	6
Warren Lahr	DB	5'11"	190	32	3	
Don Paul	DB	6'	190	30	7	6
Johnny Petitbon	DB	5'11"	185	25		
Junior Wren	DB	6'	185	26	1	2
Billy Kinard	HB-DB	6'	185	22		6
Tom O'Connell	QB	5'11"	190	24		12
Babe Parilli	QB	6'1"	190	26		
George Ratterman	QB	6'1"	185	29		6
Preston Carpenter	HB	6'2"	190	22		
Curley Morrison	HB	6'2"	215	30		12
Skeets Quinlan (from LA)	HB	5'11"	170	28		
Mo Bassett	FB	6'1"	230	26		12
Ed Modzelewski	FB	6'	215	27		12
Darrell Brewster	OE	6'3"	210	26		6
Dante Lavelli	OE	6'	192	33		6
Ray Renfro	HB-FL	6'1"	192	25		24

Tom Catlin – Military Service
Chet Hanulak – Military Service
Billy Reynolds – Military Service

PITTSBURGH STEELERS 5-7-0 Walt Kiesling

Scores of Each Game		
30	WASHINGTON	13
10	CLEVELAND	14
21	PHILADELPHIA	35
10	New York	38
24	Cleveland	16
14	NEW YORK	17
7	Philadelphia	14
14	CHIC. CARDS	7
27	Chic. Cards	38
30	LOS ANGELES	13
7	Detroit	45
23	Washington	0

Use Name	Pos.	Hgt	Wgt	Age	Int	Pts
Bob Gaona	OT	6'3"	245	26		
Frank Varrichione	OT	6'1"	240	24		
Ralph Jecha	OG	6'2"	235	25		
Marv McFadden	OG	6'	230	26		
Bob O'Neil	DE-OG	6'1"	220	23		
John Cenci	C	6'	215	22		
Jim Taylor	C	6'2"	230	22		
Bill McPeak	DE	6'1"	220	31		2
Joe O'Malley	DE	6'2"	215	23		
George Tarasovic	C-LB-DE	6'4"	245	27	3	
Joe Krupa	DT	6'2"	240	23		
Ernie Stautner	DT	6'1"	230	31		
Willie McClung	OT-DT	6'2"	245	27		
Dale Dodrill	LB	6'1"	210	31	1	
Marv Matuszak	LB	6'3"	230	25	2	
Art Michalik	LB	6'2"	230	26		
John Reger	LB	6'	220	25	2	
Dick Alban	DB	6'	195	27	2	
Fred Bruney (from SF)	DB	5'10"	180	25	1	
Gary Glick	DB	6'2"	195	25		28
Art Davis	HB-DB	6'1"	195	22		
Jack Butler	OE-DB	6'	195	28	6	12
Ted Marchibroda	QB	5'10"	180	25		12
Jack Scarbath	QB	6'2"	205	26		
Lou Baldacci	HB	6'2"	200	22		
Lynn Chandnois	HB	6'2"	205	32		30
Sid Watson	HB	5'11"	185	23		37
Henry Ford	DB-HB	6'	184	25	1	12
Fran Rogel	FB	5'11"	205	29		12
Charlie Shepard	HB-FB	6'2"	215	23		
Fred Glatz	OE	6'1"	200	22		
Ray Mathews	OE	6'	190	27		30
Jack McClairen	OE	6'4"	210	25		
Elbie Nickel	OE	6'1"	210	33		30
Jack O'Brien	OE	6'2"	210	25		
John Stock	OE	6'2"	210	22		
Lowell Perry	HB-OE	6'	195	24		12

Paul Cameron – Military Service
Johnny Lattner – Military Service
Richie McCabe – Military Service

PHILADELPHIA EAGLES 3-8-1 Hugh Devore

Scores of Each Game		
7	Los Angeles	27
13	WASHINGTON	9
35	Pittsburgh	21
6	CHIC. CARDS	20
3	New York	20
17	Chic. Cards	28
14	PITTSBURGH	7
0	CLEVELAND	16
10	SAN FRANCISCO	10
14	Cleveland	17
17	Washington	19
7	NEW YORK	21

Use Name	Pos.	Hgt	Wgt	Age	Int	Pts
Dick Murley (from PIT)	OT	6'	247	22		
Frank Wydo	OT	6'4"	228	32		
Tom Dimmick	C-LB-OT	6'6"	250	25		
Ken Huxhold	OG	6'1"	230	27		
Maury Nipp	OG	6'	220	26		
Frank D'Agostino	OT-OG	6'1"	244	22		
Buck Lansford	OT-OG	6'2"	235	23		
Bob Kelley	C	6'2"	238	27		
Tom Scott	DE	6'2"	225	26	1	
Norm Willey	DE	6'2"	230	29		
Marion Campbell	DT	6'3"	250	27	1	
Jess Richardson	DT	6'2"	275	26		
Jim Weatherall	DT	6'4"	245	26		
Sid Youngelman	DT	6'3"	255	24		
Chuck Bednarik	LB	6'3"	235	31	2	
Wayne Robinson	LB	6'2"	236	26		
Bob Pellegrini	OG-LB	6'2"	237	21		
Jim Ricca	OT-DT-LB	6'4"	270	29		
Bibbles Bawel	DB	6'1"	185	26	1	
Eddie Bell	DB	6'1"	212	25	4	6
Tom Brookshier	DB	6'	195	24	1	
Jerry Norton	DB	5'11"	200	26	2	
Lee Riley	DB	6'1"	200	24	3	
Rocky Ryan	HB-DB	6'1"	202	24	1	
Adrian Burk	QB	6'2"	194	28		
Bobby Thomason	QB	6'1"	190	27		12
Will Berzinski	HB	6'2"	195	22		
Skippy Giancanelli	HB	5'10"	180	27		6
Ken Keller	HB	5'11"	185	22		24
Bob Smith (from CLE)	HB	5'10"	195	24		
Ted Wegert	HB	5'11"	210	24		6
Jim Parmer	FB-HB	6'	195	29		
Dick Bielski	FB	6'1"	225	24		6
Don Schaefer	FB	6'	210	22		12
John Bredice	OE	6'1"	213	22		6
Hank Burnine (from NY)	OE	6'2"	185	24		12
Pete Retzlaff	OE	6'1"	208	26		
Bill Stribling	OE	6'1"	205	29		
Bobby Walston	OE	6'	190	27		53

Bob Hudson – Voluntarily Retired
Menil Mavraides – Military Service
Lum Snyder – Military Service
Neil Worden – Military Service

NEW YORK GIANTS

RUSHING

Last Name	No.	Yds	Avg	TD
Gifford	159	819	5.2	5
Webster	178	694	3.9	7
Triplett	125	515	4.1	5
Filipski	13	85	6.5	1
Conerly	11	11	1.0	0
Chandler	1	7	7.0	0
Rote	3	5	1.7	0
Patton	2	–1	–0.5	0
Moore	2	–2	–1.0	0
Heinrich	5	–4	–0.8	0

RECEIVING

Last Name	No.	Yds	Avg	TD
Gifford	51	603	12	4
Rote	28	405	14	4
Webster	21	197	9	3
MacAfee	14	184	13	4
Schnelker	9	122	14	1
Triplett	6	48	8	1
Filipski	3	37	12	0
Chandler	1	5	5	0

PUNT RETURNS

Last Name	No.	Yds	Avg	TD
Tunnell	22	120	5	0
Filipski	1	25	25	0
Patton	12	17	1	0

KICKOFF RETURNS

Last Name	No.	Yds	Avg	TD
Filipski	19	390	21	0
Patton	13	283	22	0
Hughes	1	27	27	0
Triplett	1	2	2	0

PASSING – PUNTING – KICKING

PASSING	Att	Comp	%	Yds	Yd/Att	TD	Int–%	RK
Conerly	174	90	52	1143	6.6	10	7– 4	3
Heinrich	88	37	42	369	4.2	5	5– 6	
Clatterbuck	7	4	57	54	7.7	0	1– 14	
Gifford	5	2	40	35	7.0	2	1– 20	
Rote	1	0	0	0	0.0	0	0– 0	

PUNTING	No	Avg
Chandler	59	41.9
Conerly	1	33.0

KICKING	XP	Att	%	FG	Att	%
Agajanian	23	23	100	5	13	38
Gifford	8	9	89	1	2	50
Chandler	3	3	100	0	0	0

CHICAGO CARDINALS

RUSHING

Last Name	No.	Yds	Avg	TD
Matson	192	924	4.8	5
Olszewski	157	598	3.8	2
Childress	43	203	4.7	0
McHan	58	161	2.8	5
Mann	45	116	2.6	0
Root	17	45	2.6	2
Bernardi	14	4	0.3	0
Burl	1	2	2.0	0

RECEIVING

Last Name	No.	Yds	Avg	TD
Stonesifer	22	320	15	2
Olszewski	17	182	11	0
Matson	15	199	13	2
Nagler	14	268	19	4
Mann	13	170	13	1
Boydston	6	116	19	2
Childress	6	82	14	1
Bernardi	4	56	14	0
Burl	2	24	12	1
Lane	1	75	75	0

PUNT RETURNS

Last Name	No.	Yds	Avg	TD
Bernardi	18	217	12	1
Matson	5	39	8	0
Lewis	5	22	4	0
Crow	1	21	21	0
Sanford	1	6	6	0
Lane	2	0	0	0

KICKOFF RETURNS

Last Name	No.	Yds	Avg	TD
Matson	13	362	28	1
Mann	7	131	19	0
Bernardi	4	101	25	0
Burl	3	59	20	0
Olszewski	3	25	8	0
Lewis	1	22	22	0
Weber	2	3	2	0
Childress	1	0	0	0

PASSING – PUNTING – KICKING

PASSING	Att	Comp	%	Yds	Yd/Att	TD	Int–%	RK
McHan	152	72	47	1159	7.6	10	8– 5	6
Root	57	28	49	333	5.8	3	5– 9	
Matson	3	0	0	0	0.0	0	0– 0	
Mann	2	0	0	0	0.0	0	1– 50	

PUNTING	No	Avg
Mann	36	37.4
Roach	11	40.8
McHan	8	35.6

KICKING	XP	Att	%	FG	Att	%
Summerall	30	30	100	10	22	46

WASHINGTON REDSKINS

RUSHING

Last Name	No.	Yds	Avg	TD
Elter	145	544	3.8	2
Runnels	96	334	3.5	0
James	58	280	4.8	1
Wells	69	185	2.7	1
Atkeson	63	163	2.6	1
Baker	25	117	4.7	0
Dorow	30	105	3.5	0
LeBaron	11	6	0.5	0
Planutis	2	6	3.0	0
Scudero	2	3	1.5	0

RECEIVING

Last Name	No.	Yds	Avg	TD
Carson	39	504	13	3
Meilinger	24	395	16	5
Elter	11	99	9	0
James	7	127	18	2
Wells	6	86	14	0
Runnels	6	56	9	1
Atkeson	6	28	5	0
Baker	4	35	9	0
Planutis	1	5	5	0

PUNT RETURNS

Last Name	No.	Yds	Avg	TD
Runnels	8	91	11	0
James	6	84	14	0
Scudero	10	50	5	0
Wells	2	36	18	0
Atkeson	1	12	12	0
Baker	1	0	0	0
Lowe	1	0	0	0

KICKOFF RETURNS

Last Name	No.	Yds	Avg	TD
Runnels	17	375	22	0
James	9	181	20	0
Scudero	9	157	17	0
Elter	4	87	22	0
Atkeson	1	25	25	0
Sardisco	1	15	15	0
Kimmel	1	12	12	0
Wells	1	12	12	0
Thomas	1	0	0	0

PASSING – PUNTING – KICKING

PASSING	Att	Comp	%	Yds	Yd/Att	TD	Int–%	RK
Dorow	112	55	49	730	6.5	8	8– 7	11
LeBaron	98	47	48	554	5.7	3	10– 10	
Runnels	3	1	33	34	11.3	0	0– 0	
Wyant	2	1	50	17	8.5	0	0– 0	

PUNTING	No	Avg
Baker	59	42.5
LeBaron	4	40.3

KICKING	XP	Att	%	FG	Att	%
Baker	16	19	84	17	25	68

CLEVELAND BROWNS

RUSHING

Last Name	No.	Yds	Avg	TD
Carpenter	188	756	4.0	0
Modzelewski	107	431	4.0	2
Morrison	83	340	4.1	1
Bassett	41	129	3.1	1
Parilli	18	65	3.6	0
O'Connell	24	40	1.7	2
Kinard	1	27	27.0	1
Quinlan	12	25	2.1	0
Renfro	4	24	6.0	0
Ratterman	10	19	1.9	1

RECEIVING

Last Name	No.	Yds	Avg	TD
Brewster	28	417	15	1
Lavelli	20	344	17	1
Renfro	17	325	19	4
Carpenter	16	124	8	0
Modzelewski	10	27	3	0
Quinlan	7	87	12	0
Morrison	6	29	5	1
Bassett	4	29	7	1

PUNT RETURNS

Last Name	No.	Yds	Avg	TD
Konz	13	187	14	1
Paul	17	103	6	0
Quinlan	14	50	4	0
Carpenter	1	18	18	0

KICKOFF RETURNS

Last Name	No.	Yds	Avg	TD
Carpenter	15	381	25	0
Quinlan	12	256	21	0
Kinard	7	196	28	0
Morrison	1	17	17	0

PASSING – PUNTING – KICKING

PASSING	Att	Comp	%	Yds	Yd/Att	TD	Int–%	RK
O'Connell	96	42	44	551	5.7	4	8– 8	
Ratterman	57	39	68	398	7.0	1	3– 5	
Parilli	49	24	49	409	8.4	3	7– 14	

PUNTING	No	Avg
Morrison	38	41.1
Gillom	12	44.7

KICKING	XP	Att	%	FG	Att	%
Groza	18	18	100	11	20	55

PITTSBURGH STEELERS

RUSHING

Last Name	No.	Yds	Avg	TD
Rogel	131	476	3.6	2
Watson	112	298	2.7	4
Marchibroda	39	152	3.9	2
Baldacci	31	140	4.5	0
Chandnois	44	118	2.7	4
Shepard	30	91	3.0	0
Perry	2	37	18.5	0
Ford	12	26	2.2	2
Scarbath	4	19	4.8	0
Davis	5	6	1.2	0
Varrichione	0	–2	–	0
Mathews	3	–11	–3.7	0

RECEIVING

Last Name	No.	Yds	Avg	TD
Mathews	31	540	17	5
Nickel	27	376	14	5
Rogel	23	88	4	0
Perry	14	334	24	2
Watson	12	138	12	0
Chandnois	7	71	10	1
O'Brien	6	71	12	0
Baldacci	5	62	12	0
McClairen	5	56	11	0
Ford	3	7	2	0
Shepard	1	31	31	0
Butler	1	10	10	1
Davis	1	9	9	0

PUNT RETURNS

Last Name	No.	Yds	Avg	TD
Ford	25	145	6	0
Perry	11	127	12	0
Bruney	5	20	4	0
Davis	3	5	2	0
Watson	1	2	2	0

KICKOFF RETURNS

Last Name	No.	Yds	Avg	TD
Chandnois	8	291	36	0
Bruney	9	235	26	0
Perry	9	219	24	0
Ford	6	135	23	0
Watson	4	110	28	0
Mathews	1	26	26	0
Reger	1	13	13	0
Varrichione	1	8	8	0
Matuszak	1	5	5	0

PASSING – PUNTING – KICKING

PASSING	Att	Comp	%	Yds	Yd/Att	TD	Int–%	RK
Marchibroda	275	124	45	1585	5.8	12	19– 7	10
Scarbath	41	12	29	208	5.1	2	5– 12	
Baldacci	1	0	0	0	0.0	0	0– 0	
Chandnois	1	0	0	0	0.0	0	0– 0	

PUNTING	No	Avg
Baldacci	26	38.8
Shepard	26	36.6
Glatz	25	39.4

KICKING	XP	Att	%	FG	Att	%
Glick	16	17	94	4	7	57
Watson	10	12	83	1	1	100
Michalik	0	0	0	0	1	0

PHILADELPHIA EAGLES

RUSHING

Last Name	No.	Yds	Avg	TD
Keller	112	433	3.9	4
Schaefer	102	320	3.1	2
Bielski	52	162	3.1	1
Giancanelli	42	148	3.5	1
Wegert	47	127	2.7	1
Berzinski	15	72	4.8	0
Burk	17	61	3.6	0
Thomason	21	48	2.3	2
Smith	11	18	1.6	0
Parmer	1	–2	–2.0	0

RECEIVING

Last Name	No.	Yds	Avg	TD
Walston	39	590	15	3
Schaefer	13	117	9	0
Retzlaff	12	159	13	0
Burnine	10	208	21	2
Bredice	10	146	15	1
Giancanelli	10	104	10	0
Bielski	8	63	8	0
Keller	7	36	5	0
Wegert	6	46	8	0
Berzinski	3	35	12	0
Stribling	2	11	6	0
Ryan	1	31	31	0
Riley	1	10	10	0

PUNT RETURNS

Last Name	No.	Yds	Avg	TD
Keller	15	146	10	0
Riley	17	73	4	0
Giancanelli	4	22	6	0

KICKOFF RETURNS

Last Name	No.	Yds	Avg	TD
Riley	15	381	25	0
Keller	15	353	24	0
Giancanelli	8	187	23	0
Pellegrini	2	47	24	0
Willey	2	32	16	0
Norton	1	31	31	0
Bawel	1	25	25	0
Bednarik	1	17	17	0
Smith	1	14	14	0

PASSING – PUNTING – KICKING

PASSING	Att	Comp	%	Yds	Yd/Att	TD	Int–%	RK
Thomason	164	82	50	1119	6.8	4	21– 12	12
Burk	82	39	48	426	5.2	1	6– 7	
Schaefer	3	1	33	11	3.7	1	0– 0	

PUNTING	No	Avg
Burk	68	41.8

KICKING	XP	Att	%	FG	Att	%
Walston	17	18	94	6	13	46
Bielski	0	0	0	0	1	0

CHICAGO BEARS 9-2-1 Paddy Driscoll

Scores of Each Game		
21	Baltimore	28
37	Green Bay	21
31	SAN FRANCISCO	7
58	BALTIMORE	27
38	San Francisco	21
35	Los Angeles	24
38	GREEN BAY	14
30	LOS ANGELES	21
17	New York	17
10	Detroit	42
10	CHIC CARDS	3
38	DETROIT	21

Use Name	Pos.	Hgt	Wgt	Age	Int	Pts
Kline Gilbert	OT	6'2"	235	25		
John Mellekas	OT	6'3"	255	23		
Bill Wightkin	OT	6'3"	235	29		
Herman Clark	OG	6'3"	255	25		
Stan Jones	OG	6'1"	255	25		
Tom Roggeman	OG	6'	235	25		
Dick Klawitter	C	6'7"	270	26		
Larry Strickland	C	6'4"	245	25		
Doug Atkins	DE	6'8"	255	26		
John Helwig	DE	6'2"	208	28		
Jack Hoffman	DE	6'5"	235	27		
Ed Meadows	DE	6'2"	220	24		
Bill Bishop	DT	6'4"	250	25		
Fred Williams	DT	6'4"	245	26	1	
M. L. Brackett	DE-LB-DT	6'5"	248	23	1	
Joe Fortunato	LB	6'	225	26	2	6
Bill George	LB	6'2"	240	25	2	
Wayne Hansen	LB	6'2"	230	28	1	
Ken Gorgal (to GB)	DB	6'2"	200	27	2	
McNeil Moore	DB	6'	185	23	3	
Ray Gene Smith	DB	5'10"	185	26	4	
Stan Wallace	DB	6'3"	207	24	1	
J. C. Caroline	HB-DB	6'1"	190	23	6	24
George Blanda	QB	6'1"	207	28		81
Ed Brown	QB	6'2"	205	27		12
Jim Haluska	QB	6'	190	23		
Don Bingham	HB	6'	185	26		6
Harland Carl	HB	6'	195	25		6
Perry Jeter	HB	5'7"	178	22		18
Bobby Watkins	HB	5'10"	195	24		18
John Hoffman	FB-HB	6'2"	215	30		12
Rick Casares	FB	6'2"	225	25		84
Jim Dooley	OE	6'4"	198	26		
Harlon Hill	OE	6'3"	198	24		66
Bill McColl	OE	6'4"	230	26		24
Gene Schroeder	OE	6'3"	195	27		6

Zeke Bratkowski – Military Service
Ron Drzewiecki – Military Service
Charlie Sumner – Military Service

DETROIT LIONS 9-3-0 Buddy Parker

Scores of Each Game		
20	Green Bay	16
31	Baltimore	14
24	LOS ANGELES	21
20	SAN FRANCISCO	17
16	Los Angeles	7
17	San Francisco	13
17	Washington	18
27	BALTIMORE	3
20	GREEN BAY	24
42	CHIC. BEARS	10
45	PITTSBURGH	7
21	Chic. Bears	38

Use Name	Pos.	Hgt	Wgt	Age	Int	Pts
Lou Creekmur	OT	6'4"	250	29		
Ollie Spencer	OT	6'2"	245	25		
Jim Salsbury	OG-OT	6'1"	235	24		
Stan Campbell	OG	6'	225	26		
Harley Sewell	OG	6'1"	235	25		
Charlie Ane	C	6'2"	260	25		
Bob Lusk	C	6'1"	222	23		
Gene Cronin	OG-DE	6'2"	230	23		
Gil Mains	DT-DE	6'2"	235	26		
Ray Krouse	DT	6'3"	265	29		
Darris McCord	DT	6'4"	240	23		
Bob Miller	DT	6'3"	245	26		
Jerry Perry	DT	6'4"	235	25		
Sonny Gandee	LB	6'1"	220	27		
Jim Martin	LB	6'2"	225	32		15
Joe Schmidt	LB	6'1"	220	24	1	
Bob Long	DE-LB	6'3"	230	22	2	
Jack Christiansen	DB	6'1"	195	27	8	6
Jim David	DB	5'11"	175	29	7	
Carl Karilivacz	DB	6'	185	25	1	
Yale Lary	DB	6'	185	25	8	6
Bill Stits	HB-DB	6'	200	25	1	
Harry Gilmer	QB	6'	180	30		
Bobby Layne	QB	6'1"	200	29		99
Jerry Reichow	OE-QB	6'2"	210	21		6
Hopalong Cassady	HB	5'10"	178	22		
Gene Gedman	HB	5'11"	195	24		48
Don McIlhenny	HB	6'	195	21		30
Jug Girard	OE-HB	5'11"	175	29		
Bill Bowman	FB	6'2"	215	25		12
Leon Hart	FB	6'5"	248	27		36
Tom Tracy	FB	5'9"	200	24		
Dorne Dibble	OE	6'2"	195	27		12
Jim Doran	OE	6'2"	200	28		
Dave Middleton	OE	6'1"	195	23		30

Lew Carpenter – Military Service
Dick Kercher-Military Service

SAN FRANCISCO FORTY NINERS 5-6-1 Frankie Albert

Scores of Each Game		
21	NEW YORK	38
33	LOS ANGELES	30
7	Chic. Bears	31
17	Detroit	20
21	CHIC. BEARS	38
13	DETROIT	17
6	Los Angeles	30
17	Green Bay	16
10	Philadelphia	10
20	Baltimore	17
38	GREEN BAY	20
30	BALTIMORE	17

Use Name	Pos.	Hgt	Wgt	Age	Int	Pts
Bob Cross	OT	6'4"	250	25		
Bob St. Clair	OT	6'9"	265	25		
John Gonzaga	DE-OT	6'3"	240	23		
Ted Connolly	OG	6'3"	240	24		
Lou Palatella	OG	6'2"	230	23		
Ed Beatty	C	6'3"	230	24		
Bill Johnson	C	6'3"	240	30		
Bruce Bosley	DE	6'2"	240	22		
Ed Henke	DE	6'3"	227	28		
Charley Powell	DE	6'2"	220	24		
Charlie Smith	DE	6'2"	205	23	1	
Bill Herchman	DT	6'2"	240	23		
Leo Nomellini	DT	6'3"	255	31		
Bob Toneff	OG-DG-DT	6'3"	263	26		
Matt Hazeltine	LB	6'1"	205	23	1	
Leo Rucka	LB	6'3"	212	24		
Stan Sheriff	LB	6'1"	218	25		
Ed Sharkey	OG-LB	6'3"	235	30	1	
George Morris	C-LB	6'2"	220	25		
Paul Carr	DB-LB	6'	205	24	2	
Rex Berry	DB	5'11"	185	30	3	
Bob Holladay (from LA)	DB	5'11"	175	23	1	
George Maderos	DB	6'1"	187	23	2	
Ernie Smith	DB	6'3"	190	23		
J. D. Smith (from Chi B)	DB	6'1"	200	23		
Earl Morrall	QB	6'1"	190	22		
Y. A. Tittle	QB	6'	190	29		24
Joe Arenas	HB	5'11"	180	30		18
Tom McCormick	HB	5'11"	180	26		
Hugh McElhenny	HB	6'1"	198	27		48
Dick Moegle	HB-DB	6'	185	22	6	6
John Henry Johnson	FB-HB	6'2"	205	26		12
Paul Goad	FB	6'	195	21		
Joe Perry	FB	6'	210	29		18
Clyde Conner	OE	6'2"	195	23		6
Floyd Sagely	OE	6'1"	195	24		
Gordie Soltau	OE	6'2"	195	31		71
Billy Wilson	OE	6'3"	190	29		30
Bill Jessup	FL-OE	6'1"	195	27		

BALTIMORE COLTS 5-7-0 Weeb Ewbank

Scores of Each Game		
28	CHIC. BEARS	21
14	DETROIT	31
33	Green Bay	38
27	Chic. Bears	58
20	GREEN BAY	21
21	Cleveland	7
3	Detroit	27
56	LOS ANGELES	21
17	SAN FRANCISCO	20
7	Los Angeles	31
17	San Francisco	30
19	WASHINGTON	17

Use Name	Pos.	Hgt	Wgt	Age	Int	Pts
Dick Chorovich	OT	6'4"	260	23		
Tom Feamster	DE-OT	6'7"	260	25		24
Ken Jackson	OG-OT	6'2"	235	27		
Alex Sandusky	OG	6'1"	230	24		
Art Spinney	OG	6'	230	29		
George Preas	OT-LB-OG	6'2"	230	24		
Buzz Nutter	C	6'4"	225	25		
George Radosevich	OT-C	6'2"	230	29		
Don Joyce	DE	6'3"	255	26		
Gino Marchetti	DE	6'4"	245	30		
Art Donovan	DT	6'2"	265	31		
Tom Finnin	DT	6'2"	255	28		
Big Daddy Lipscomb	DT	6'6"	282	25		
Jerry Peterson	DT	6'3"	290	22		
Joe Campanella	LB	6'2"	245	25		
Doug Eggers	LB	6'	215	26	1	
Bill Koman	LB	6'2"	220	22		
Jack Patera	LB	6'1"	240	24	2	
Bill Pellington	LB	6'2"	230	27	1	
Jim Harness	DB	5'11"	180	22		
John Hermann (from NY)	DB	6'1"	180	22		
Tommy James	DB	5'10"	185	32		
Don Shula	DB	5'11"	190	26	1	
Jesse Thomas	DB	5'10"	180	27	2	6
Bert Rechichar	HB-DB	6'1"	210	26	4	17
Carl Taseff	HB-DB	5'11"	190	27	2	12
Gary Kerkorian	QB	5'11"	185	27		1
George Shaw	QB	6'1"	180	23		
Johnny Unitas	QB	6'1"	190	23		6
L. G. Dupre	HB	5'11"	190	24		24
Lenny Moore	HB	6'1"	190	23		54
Billy Vessels	HB	6'	190	25		18
Royce Womble	HB	6'	185	24		12
Dick Nyers	DB-HB	5'11"	178	22		
Alan Ameche	FB	6'	217	23		48
Dick Young	FB	5'11"	210	25		
Ray Berry	OE	6'2"	190	23		12
Lloyd Colteryahn	OE	6'2"	220	26		
Bernie Flowers	OE	6'2"	190	26		
Jim Mutscheller	OE	6'1"	210	26		36

Cotton Davidson – Military Service
Dick Szymanski – Military Service

GREEN BAY PACKERS 4-8-0 Lisle Blackbourn

Scores of Each Game		
16	DETROIT	20
21	CHIC. BEARS	37
38	BALTIMORE	33
42	LOS ANGELES	17
21	Baltimore	28
7	CLEVELAND	24
14	Chic. Bears	38
16	SAN FRANCISCO	17
24	Detroit	20
24	Chic. Cards	21
20	San Francisco	38
21	Los Angeles	49

Use Name	Pos.	Hgt	Wgt	Age	Int	Pts
Bob Skoronski	OT	6'3"	250	23		
Don King (from PHI)	DT-OT	6'3"	265	26		
John Sandusky	DT-OT	6'1"	250	30		
Buddy Brown	OG	6'1"	225	29		
Joe Skibinski	OG	5'11"	230	28		
Jerry Smith (from SF)	OG	6'1"	230	26		
Len Szafaryn	OG	6'2"	225	28		
Forrest Gregg	OT-DT-OG	6'4"	240	23		
Larry Lauer	C	6'3"	235	27		
Jim Ringo	C	6'1"	235	25		
Emery Barnes	DE	6'6"	235	27		
Nate Borden	DE	6'	225	24		
Gene Knutson	DE	6'2"	230	24		
John Martinkovic	DE	6'3"	245	29		
Dave Hanner	DT	6'2"	255	27		
Jerry Helluin	DT	6'2"	265	26		
Tom Bettis	LB	6'2"	230	23		
Bill Forester	LB	6'3"	235	25	4	
Deral Teteak	LB	5'10"	210	27	2	
Roger Zatkoff	LB	6'2"	215	25		
Billy Bookout	DB	5'11"	180	24	1	
Jim Capuzzi	DB	6'	190	24	2	
Bobby Dillon	DB	6'1"	180	26	7	6
Hank Gremminger	DB	6'1"	195	23	2	
Val Joe Walker	DB	6'1"	180	25	1	
Glenn Young	DB	6'2"	205	26		
Tobin Rote	QB	6'3"	215	28		66
Bart Starr	QB	6'1"	200	23		
Al Carmichael	HB	6'1"	190	26		12
Joe Johnson	HB	6'	180	26		
Jack Losch	HB	6'1"	205	23		
Breezy Reid	HB	5'10"	190	29		
Bill Roberts	HB	6'	200	27		
Fred Cone	FB	5'11"	200	30		72
Howie Ferguson	FB	6'2"	215	26		
Billy Howton	OE	6'2"	190	26		72
Gary Knafelc	OE	6'4"	215	24		36
Dick Deschaine	K	6'	210	26		

Al Barry – Military Service
Hank Bullough – Military Service
Max McGee – Military Service
Doyle Nix – Military Service

LOS ANGELES RAMS 4-8-0 Sid Gillman

Scores of Each Game		
27	PHILADELPHIA	7
30	San Francisco	33
21	Detroit	24
17	Green Bay	42
7	DETROIT	16
24	CHIC. BEARS	35
30	SAN FRANCISCO	6
21	Chic. Bears	30
21	Baltimore	56
13	Pittsburgh	30
31	BALTIMORE	7
49	GREEN BAY	21

Use Name	Pos.	Hgt	Wgt	Age	Int	Pts
Bob Fry	OT	6'4"	225	25		
Glenn Holtzman	OT	6'3"	250	26		
Charlie Toogood	OT	6'	230	28		
John Hock	OG	6'2"	234	28		
Duane Putnam	OG	6'	230	28		
John Morrow	OG-DE-C	6'3"	237	23		
Dick Daugherty	OG-LB-C	6'1"	223	27		
Paul Miller	DE	6'2"	215	24		
Duane Wardlow	DE	6'4"	215	24		
Sid Fournet	LB-DE	6'	238	23	1	
Art Hauser	DT	6'	230	25		
Bud McFadin	DT	6'3"	250	28		9
Ken Panfil	OT-DT	6'6"	255	25		
Jack Ellena	LB	6'1"	223	24		
Bob Griffin	LB	6'3"	243	27		
Larry Morris	LB	6'2"	212	22		
Hugh Pitts	LB	6'2"	220	22	3	
Les Richter	LB	6'3"	243	25		60
Don Burroughs	DB	6'4"	173	25	2	
Jim Cason	DB	6'	175	29	4	
Jesse Castete (from Chi B)	DB	5'11"	175	21	2	
Will Sherman	DB	6'2"	197	27	4	12
Ray Shiver	DB	6'	190	24	1	
Jesse Whittenton	DB	6'	182	22	3	6
Rudy Bukich	QB	6'1"	190	25		
Norm Van Brocklin	QB	6'1"	200	30		6
Billy Wade	QB	6'2"	190	25		18
Ron Waller	HB	5'11"	180	23		6
Tom Wilson	HB	6'	197	23		6
Joe Marconi	FB	6'2"	220	22		42
Brad Myers	FB	6'1"	196	26		
Tank Younger	FB	6'3"	226	28		18
Bob Boyd	OE	6'2"	203	28		42
Bob Carey	OE	6'5"	220	28		6
Leon Clarke	OE	6'4"	220	23		24
Tom Fears	OE	6'2"	207	32		
Crazy Legs Hirsch	OE	6'2"	190	32		36
Ron Miller	OE	6'4"	200	23		

CHICAGO BEARS

RUSHING

Last Name	No.	Yds	Avg	TD
Casares	234	1126	4.8	12
Jeter	60	316	5.3	2
Watkins	68	276	4.1	2
Jo. Hoffman	56	272	4.9	2
Brown	40	164	4.1	1
Caroline	34	141	4.1	2
Carl	29	66	2.3	1
Blanda	6	47	7.8	0
Bingham	7	36	5.1	0
Hill	2	24	12.0	0

RECEIVING

Last Name	No.	Yds	Avg	TD
Hill	47	1128	24	11
McColl	24	322	13	4
Casares	23	203	9	2
Schroeder	20	315	16	1
Jo. Hoffman	7	85	12	0
Jeter	5	52	10	0
Dooley	4	47	12	0
Carl	2	31	16	0
Watkins	2	3	2	1
Bingham	1	7	7	0

PUNT RETURNS

Last Name	No.	Yds	Avg	TD
Jeter	6	66	11	1
Smith	6	65	11	0
Moore	3	28	9	0
Caroline	2	29	15	0
Bingham	13	7	1	0

KICKOFF RETURNS

Last Name	No.	Yds	Avg	TD
Bingham	17	444	26	1
Jeter	5	105	21	0
Carl	4	102	26	0
Casares	3	95	32	0
Caroline	2	32	16	0
Moore	1	19	19	0
Smith	1	16	16	0
Wallace	1	13	13	0
McColl	2	4	2	0
Atkins	1	0	0	0

PASSING – PUNTING – KICKING

PASSING	Att	Comp	%	Yds	Yd/Att	TD	Int–%	RK
Brown	168	96	57	1667	9.9	11	12– 7	1
Blanda	69	37	54	439	6.4	7	4– 6	
Haluska	4	1	25	8	2.0	0	0– 0	
McColl	4	1	25	79	19.8	1	2– 50	
Casares	3	0	0	0	0.0	0	1– 33	
Hill	1	0	0	0	0.0	0	0– 0	
Jeter	1	0	0	0	0.0	0	0– 0	

PUNTING	No	Avg
Brown	42	39.1
Blanda	1	33.0
Casares	1	51.0

KICKING	XP	Att	%	FG	Att	%
Blanda	45	47	96	12	28	43

DETROIT LIONS

RUSHING

Last Name	No.	Yds	Avg	TD
Gedman	135	479	3.5	7
Cassady	97	413	4.3	0
McIlhenny	87	372	4.3	3
Hart	76	348	4.6	5
Layne	46	169	3.7	5
Bowman	20	84	4.2	1
Girard	17	67	3.9	0
Tracy	12	32	2.7	0
Gilmer	8	19	2.4	0
Lary	1	10	10.0	0
Middleton	3	9	3.0	0
Dibble	1	8	8.0	0
Reichow	1	1	1.0	0
Stits	3	0	0.0	0

RECEIVING

Last Name	No.	Yds	Avg	TD
Middleton	39	606	16	5
Dibble	32	597	19	2
Doran	25	448	18	0
Gedman	15	142	9	1
Hart	14	116	8	1
Cassady	9	83	9	0
McIlhenny	8	70	9	2
Bowman	5	34	7	1
Reichow	4	63	16	1
Stits	3	52	17	0
Girard	3	33	11	0
Tracy	3	6	2	0

PUNT RETURNS

Last Name	No.	Yds	Avg	TD
Cassady	13	83	6	0
Christiansen	6	73	12	1
Lary	22	70	3	0
Girard	2	7	4	0

KICKOFF RETURNS

Last Name	No.	Yds	Avg	TD
Cassady	16	382	24	0
Christiansen	6	116	19	0
Lary	4	76	19	0
Stits	3	48	16	0
Bowman	1	24	24	0
Ane	1	19	19	0
Salsbury	1	13	13	0
Reichow	1	9	9	0

PASSING – PUNTING – KICKING

PASSING	Att	Comp	%	Yds	Yd/Att	TD	Int–%	RK
Layne	244	129	53	1909	7.8	9	17– 7	5
Gilmer	46	27	59	303	6.6	4	3– 7	
Reichow	6	3	50	19	3.2	0	1– 17	
Cassady	2	0	0	0	0.0	0	1– 50	
Girard	1	1	100	19	19.0	0	0– 0	
McIlhenny	1	0	0	0	0.0	0	0– 0	
Stits	1	0	0	0	0.0	0	1–100	

PUNTING	No	Avg
Lary	42	40.4
Girard	10	44.8

KICKING	XP	Att	%	FG	Att	%
Layne	33	33	100	12	15	80
Martin	3	3	100	4	10	40

SAN FRANCISCO FORTY NINERS

RUSHING

Last Name	No.	Yds	Avg	TD
McElhenny	185	916	5.0	8
Perry	115	520	4.5	3
J.H. Johnson	80	301	3.8	2
Tittle	24	67	2.8	4
Moegle	7	18	2.6	0
Morrall	6	10	1.7	0
McCormick	2	4	2.0	0

RECEIVING

Last Name	No.	Yds	Avg	TD
Wilson	60	889	15	5
Conner	22	362	16	1
Soltau	18	299	17	1
Perry	18	104	6	0
McElhenny	16	193	12	0
Arenas	14	226	16	1
J.H. Johnson	8	90	11	0
Moegle	3	79	26	0
Jessup	2	7	4	0

PUNT RETURNS

Last Name	No.	Yds	Avg	TD
Arenas	19	117	6	1
McElhenny	15	38	3	0
Moegle	1	5	5	0

KICKOFF RETURNS

Last Name	No.	Yds	Avg	TD
Arenas	27	801	30	1
McElhenny	13	300	23	0
Moegle	2	39	20	0
J.H. Johnson	1	23	23	0
Maderos	2	21	11	0
Goad	1	18	18	0
McCormick	1	18	18	0
Carr	1	11	11	0
Gonzaga	1	6	6	0
Herschman	1	6	6	0

PASSING – PUNTING – KICKING

PASSING	Att	Comp	%	Yds	Yd/Att	TD	Int–%	RK
Tittle	218	124	57	1641	7.5	7	12– 6	8
Morrall	78	38	49	621	8.0	1	6– 8	
McElhenny	1	0	0	0	0.0	0	1–100	

PUNTING	No	Avg
Morrall	45	37.9
Jessup	14	40.2

KICKING	XP	Att	%	FG	Att	%
Soltau	26	28	93	13	20	65

BALTIMORE COLTS

RUSHING

Last Name	No.	Yds	Avg	TD
Ameche	178	858	4.8	8
Moore	86	649	7.5	8
Vessels	44	215	4.9	2
Dupre	49	182	3.7	2
Unitas	28	155	5.5	1
Womble	20	72	3.6	0
Shaw	20	63	3.2	0
Young	5	7	1.4	0
Taseff	1	2	2.0	0
Rechichar	1	0	0.0	0

RECEIVING

Last Name	No.	Yds	Avg	TD
Mutscheller	44	715	16	6
Berry	37	601	16	2
Ameche	26	189	7	0
Dupre	16	216	14	2
Vessels	11	177	16	1
Moore	11	102	9	1
Womble	9	180	20	2
Colteryahn	3	29	10	0
Unitas	1	1	1	0

PUNT RETURNS

Last Name	No.	Yds	Avg	TD
Taseff	27	233	9	1
Moore	8	38	5	0
Nyers	2	16	8	0
Rechichar	5	10	2	0
Hermann	1	0	0	0

KICKOFF RETURNS

Last Name	No.	Yds	Avg	TD
Vessels	16	379	24	0
Taseff	9	206	23	0
Dupre	7	148	21	0
Moore	10	129	13	0
Nyers	3	69	23	0
Young	3	40	13	0
Ameche	2	38	19	0
Sandusky	1	24	24	0
Hermann	1	17	17	0
Spinney	1	10	10	0
Pellington	1	0	0	0
Shula	1	0	0	0

PASSING – PUNTING – KICKING

PASSING	Att	Comp	%	Yds	Yd/Att	TD	Int–%	RK
Unitas	198	110	56	1498	7.6	9	10– 5	2
Shaw	75	45	60	645	8.6	3	7– 9	
Moore	4	1	25	8	2.0	1	1– 25	
Kerkorian	2	2	100	59	29.5	1	0– 0	

PUNTING	No	Avg
Rechichar	33	38.7
Dupre	25	38.1

KICKING	XP	Att	%	FG	Att	%
Feamster	24	26	92	0	3	0
Rechichar	8	10	80	3	13	23
Kerkorian	1	2	50	0	0	0

GREEN BAY PACKERS

RUSHING

Last Name	No.	Yds	Avg	TD
Rote	84	398	4.7	11
Ferguson	99	367	3.7	0
Cone	49	211	4.3	2
Carmichael	32	199	6.2	0
Johnson	35	129	3.7	0
Losch	19	43	2.3	0
Reid	14	39	2.8	0
Starr	5	35	7.0	0

RECEIVING

Last Name	No.	Yds	Avg	TD
Howton	55	1188	22	12
Knafelc	30	418	14	6
Johnson	28	258	9	0
Ferguson	22	214	10	0
Carmichael	13	180	14	1
Cone	12	218	18	2
Losch	7	85	12	0
Reid	3	16	5	0
Roberts	1	14	14	0
Smith	1	13	13	0

PUNT RETURNS

Last Name	No.	Yds	Avg	TD
Carmichael	21	165	8	0
Losch	8	74	9	0
Reid	1	0	0	0

KICKOFF RETURNS

Last Name	No.	Yds	Avg	TD
Carmichael	33	927	28	1
Losch	15	390	26	0
Ferguson	5	83	17	0
Forester	4	36	9	0
Smith	1	14	14	0
Gremminger	1	6	6	0
Borden	1	0	0	0

PASSING – PUNTING – KICKING

PASSING	Att	Comp	%	Yds	Yd/Att	TD	Int–%	RK
Rote	308	146	47	2203	7.1	18	15– 5	3
Starr	44	24	55	325	7.4	2	3– 7	
Losch	1	1	100	63	63.0	1	0– 0	

PUNTING	No	Avg
Deschaine	62	42.7

KICKING	XP	Att	%	FG	Att	%
Cone	33	35	94	5	8	63

LOS ANGELES RAMS

RUSHING

Last Name	No.	Yds	Avg	TD
Waller	83	543	6.5	1
Younger	114	518	4.5	3
Wilson	64	470	7.3	0
Marconi	75	298	4.0	7
Wade	26	93	3.6	3
Myers	6	33	5.5	0
Bukich	1	8	8.0	0
Van Brocklin	4	1	0.3	1
Boyd	1	−7	−7.0	0

RECEIVING

Last Name	No.	Yds	Avg	TD
Clarke	36	650	18	4
Hirsch	35	603	17	6
Boyd	30	586	20	7
Younger	18	268	15	0
Marconi	12	70	6	0
R. Miller	11	129	12	0
Waller	9	76	8	0
Wilson	6	86	14	0
Carey	5	60	12	1
Fears	5	49	10	0

PUNT RETURNS

Last Name	No.	Yds	Avg	TD
Sherman	12	100	8	1
Waller	14	65	5	0
Myers	1	26	26	0
Whittenton	10	21	2	0
Wilson	2	0	0	0

KICKOFF RETURNS

Last Name	No.	Yds	Avg	TD
Wilson	15	477	32	1
Waller	11	276	25	0
Whittenton	4	85	21	0
Boyd	4	62	16	0
Myers	3	57	19	0
Toogood	1	13	13	0
Richter	1	4	4	0
Panfil	1	0	0	0
Putnam	1	0	0	0

PASSING – PUNTING – KICKING

PASSING	Att	Comp	%	Yds	Yd/Att	TD	Int–%	RK
Wade	178	91	51	1461	8.2	10	13– 7	6
Van Brocklin	124	68	55	966	7.8	7	12– 10	9
Bukich	23	10	43	130	5.7	1	3– 13	
Waller	3	1	33	44	14.7	0	0– 0	
Wilson	1	0	0	0	0.0	0	0– 0	

PUNTING	No	Avg
Van Brocklin	48	43.1

KICKING	XP	Att	%	FG	Att	%
Richter	36	38	95	8	15	53
McFadin	0	0	0	1	4	25

1957 No Ticket, No Television

When the NFL championship game at Detroit was sold out weeks in advance, Commissioner Bert Bell resisted popular pressure for him to relax the home-game blackout rule and allow local television coverage in the Motor City. "It's not honest," he said, "to sell tickets to thousands of people on the basis of no television and then, afterward, when all the tickets are gone to give the game away on television." The game stayed blacked out in Detroit, and Lion fans in the city had to follow the game on radio.

But regardless of the merits of this one case, attendance figures backed up the blackout rule. Attendance had been growing each year, but with CBS broadcasts of road games whetting the fans' interest in their home team, total league attendance bounced a robust 11 percent up to 2,836,318, setting a new record for the eighth year in a row. With sell-out crowds happening more often, such as the record 102,368 who watched the '49ers and Rams play in Los Angeles on November 10, Bell and the team owners had to wonder where the boom would level off.

The individual fan who followed the teams on TV and in the ballpark (when he could get a ticket) was learning a new football term—the flanker back. More and more of the NFL coaches began stationing one halfback out beyond an end and close to the line of scrimmage, thus creating in effect a third pass receiving end. Offenses now took on the look of the modern pro set, with two running backs behind the quarterback, a tight end lined up next to a tackle, and a split end and flanker set wide toward the sidelines as primary pass receivers.

EASTERN CONFERENCE

Cleveland Browns—Paul Brown had hoped to pick quarterback Len Dawson in the college draft, but when Pittsburgh chose him first, Brown instead selected fullback Jimmy Brown from Syracuse. From the start of training camp, coach Brown knew he had something special. Here was the consummate ball-carrier, so heavily muscled as to be impossible for one tackler to bring down, yet fast enough to outrun defensive backs and shifty enough to slip tackles with straight-arms and sidesteps. Young Brown could not block like Marion Motley, Cleveland's great fullback of the Otto Graham era, but he made up for it by running inside, running outside, and catching passes. Coach Brown immediately centered the offense around his young star, with occasional passes from Tom O'Connell and Milt Plum to divert the enemy—as Jimmy Brown captured his first rushing title and the Browns recaptured the Eastern crown.

New York Giants—From the first time the Giants played Cleveland with its star rookie runner, Jimmy Brown, the New Yorkers assigned middle linebacker Sam Huff to tail him wherever he went. The results of their meetings would be the same for years. Brown often would gain his yardage but would have a tougher time against the Giants than any other team. Opening day pitted the Giants against the Browns, and while the New York defense bottled up young Brown in his pro debut, Cleveland still won 6-3. After that, both clubs battled through the autumn for the Eastern lead until the Giants folded in their final three games.

Pittsburgh Steelers—Coach Walt Kiesling passed over Jimmy Brown to choose quarterback Len Dawson in the collegiate draft and counted on the rookie to take charge of the offense. However, by the end of the exhibition season, Kiesling was out as coach, with Buddy Parker coming over from Detroit to take command of the Steelers. Parker decided against going into the season with only rookies Dawson and Jack Kemp at quarterback, so he engineered a trade with San Francisco for second-year man Earl Morrall. The price was hard for some to swallow, as Parker handed over two first draft picks plus linebacker Marv Matuszak to the '49ers for Morrall and rookie lineman Mike Sandusky. But even with Morrall at quarterback and the blooming of Jack McClairen into a fine receiver, the Steelers still had problems scoring points.

Washington Redskins—For a second straight year, tragedy touched the Washington training camp when defensive back Roy Barni was shot to death in a barroom brawl. The Redskins trudged listlessly through most of the season, losing some close games and some runaways, until a surprising late-season turn-about. The defense jelled into a solid unit in the last three games as it allowed the Bears, Eagles, and Steelers a total of only 13 points.

Philadelphia Eagles—Rookies Clarence Peaks and Billy Barnes, a pair of strong runners, broke into the starting lineup immediately, while passer Sonny Jurgensen and receiver Tommy McDonald sat and learned for future seasons. But no newcomers helped out up front, where only Buck Lansford earned high grades, or at end, where Bill Stribling and Bobby Walston showed good hands but no speed. Quarterback Adrian Burk had retired, leaving long-time partner Bobby Thomason in charge of an offense without a breakaway threat among the runners or receivers. The defense held its own, even with the transfer of Chuck Bednarik to offense, but it could not save head coach Hugh Devore from getting the ax.

Chicago Cardinals—The Cards' plunge to last place was swift and complete, as an offensive collapse saddled the team with seven losses in its last eight games. Shining through the gloom was Ollie Matson, still one of the NFL's blue-chip halfbacks, but none of his mates could draw the defense's attention away from him. The plodding Cards gave fans very little to cheer about, and the deteriorating neighborhood around Comiskey Park discouraged paying customers from coming to the games. It was a bad situation that called for a new deal, but the only change made was to fire head coach Ray Richards.

WESTERN CONFERENCE

Detroit Lions—Two days before the first pre-season game, coach Buddy Parker stood to address the Detroit Boosters' banquet. "This team of ours has been the worst I've ever seen in training," he said, leaving his audience openmouthed in shock. "I don't want to get involved in another losing season, so I'm leaving Detroit. As a matter of fact, I'm leaving tonight." With those words, Parker had quit as coach, leaving assistant George Wilson in charge of the talented but listless squad. Shaken into action by Parker's resignation, the Lions battled the Colts and Bears all through the season for the Western crown. One innovation in the offense was a two-quarterback system, with Bobby Layne sharing the job with ex-Packer Tobin Rote. Neither man was pleased with the arrangement, but the depth at the spot came in handy when Layne broke his leg in a late-season game and Rote led the Lions to victories in the last two games to tie the '49ers for the conference crown.

San Francisco '49ers—After a three-game losing streak in mid-season slowed them up, the '49ers finished in a hurry, winning their last three games by close scores and deadlocking the Lions for first place as the season ended. Starring on the road to this finish were passer Y. A. Tittle, runner Hugh McElhenny, receivers Billy Wilson and R. C. Owens, and defenders Leo Nomellini and Marv Matuszak, a pre-season pick-up from Pittsburgh. In the playoff game for the Western title, Tittle had a hot first half and carved out a 27-7 San Francisco lead at halftime, only to have the Lions storm back in the second half for a 31-27 Detroit victory.

Baltimore Colts—Undefeated after three games, the Colts blew a 10-point lead with three minutes left to bow 31-27 in a rematch with the Lions. After two more losses the Colts regained their touch and regained the conference lead down the stretch. With a one-game lead over the '49ers and Lions with two games left, the Colts headed for California. In San Francisco, a Unitas-to-Lenny Moore touchdown pass put the Colts in front 13-10 with two minutes left in the game, only to have the '49ers come back to win on a Hugh McElhenny touchdown. Then, needing a win to tie for the crown, the Colts played the Rams and came away 37-21 losers.

Los Angeles Rams—The passing attack, the Rams' long suit since heading West, suddenly looked a little threadbare. The great receivers weren't around any longer, as Tom Fears had retired and Crazy Legs Hirsch had lost his game-breaking speed, and quarterbacks Norm Van Brocklin and Billy Wade weren't frightening defenses as the old Ram teams did. Coach Sid Gillman did find some strong runners to lug the ball, as second-year men Tom Wilson and Joe Marconi and veteran Tank Younger punched out hard yardage regularly. But even with impressive wins over the Packers and Colts to end the season, the Rams were still in the midst of a rebuilding program.

Chicago Bears—With rookie Willie Galimore, billed as the league's next great breakaway runner, and promising quarterback Zeke Bratkowski to bolster the offense, the Bears expected to improve on last year's title winning record. Instead, the Packers, Colts, and '49ers all beat them in the first three weeks of the season, and the Bears never did put more than two wins together in a row. The defense took no blame for the slump, as it actually allowed fewer points than last year, but all accusing fingers tabbed the offense as the culprit.

Green Bay Packers—It looked as though the Packers had signed a Heisman Trophy winner without a position when Paul Hornung, the golden-haired All-American from Notre Dame, bounced around the Green Bay backfield like a pinball. Coach Lisle Blackbourn first tried him at quarterback, but the rookie didn't have the arm for the position. Then came a trial at fullback, but Hornung had neither the bulk nor the inclination to be a work-horse power runner. The Packers had evidently chosen another lemon as their first draft choice, bringing a new round of calls for coach Blackbourn's firing. Another rookie, end Ron Kramer, made a good showing, while Bart Starr showed promise in replacing the traded Tobin Rote. But the season as a whole was a dismal way in which to open Green Bay's new football stadium and to end Blackbourn's three-year reign.

FINAL TEAM STATISTICS

OFFENSE

	BALT.	CHI.B.	CHI.C.	CLEVE.	DET.	G.BAY	L.A.	N.Y.	PHIL.	PITT.	S.F.	WASH.
FIRST DOWNS:												
Total	222	188	174	180	221	179	235	216	149	159	223	197
by Rushing	91	82	77	93	103	72	112	95	80	59	92	107
by Passing	117	92	75	76	105	90	104	103	51	92	115	78
by Penalty	14	14	22	11	13	17	19	18	18	8	16	12
RUSHING:												
Number	434	457	365	501	409	380	474	441	424	390	377	500
Yards	1735	1686	1442	1958	1811	1441	2142	1649	1582	1174	1622	1873
Average Yards	4.0	3.7	4.0	3.9	4.4	3.8	4.5	3.7	3.7	3.0	4.3	3.7
Touchdowns	12	15	12	19	12	13	15	13	9	7	15	17
PASSING:												
Attempts	314	286	271	195	381	325	296	269	204	312	305	201
Completions	177	130	111	108	163	157	144	147	99	149	191	109
Completion Percentage	56.4	45.5	41.0	55.4	45.2	48.3	48.6	54.6	48.5	47.8	62.6	54.2
Gross Yards	2608	1945	1969	1873	2239	2157	2256	2158	1379	2013	2407	1741
Yards Lost Passing	220	177	194	161	210	366	255	58	224	297	371	120
Net Yards	2388	1768	1775	1712	2029	1791	2001	2100	1155	1716	2036	1621
Avg. Yards per Attempt (Gross)	8.3	6.8	7.3	9.6	6.2	6.6	7.6	8.0	6.8	6.5	7.9	8.7
Avg. Yards per Comp. (Gross)	14.7	15.0	17.7	17.3	13.7	13.7	15.7	14.7	13.9	13.5	12.6	16.0
Touchdowns	25	7	12	12	17	12	21	15	10	11	17	11
Interceptions	19	28	22	14	22	23	23	12	23	14	18	13
Percent Intercepted	6.1	9.8	8.1	7.2	6.1	7.1	7.8	4.5	11.3	4.5	5.9	6.5
PUNTS:												
Number	55	63	59	61	54	63	56	60	68	70	57	50
Average Distance	34.5	38.8	42.5	39.3	39.9	42.0	44.4	44.6	41.1	40.1	44.7	42.8
PUNT RETURNS:												
Number	33	43	40	48	41	36	36	43	37	51	37	44
Yards	133	146	258	231	200	256	198	180	199	276	122	460
Average Yards	4.0	3.4	6.5	4.8	4.9	7.1	5.5	4.2	5.4	5.4	3.3	10.5
Touchdowns	0	0	0	0	0	0	0	0	0	0	0	2
KICKOFF RETURNS:												
Number	42	39	47	33	37	58	49	42	41	25	42	38
Yards	948	836	1167	686	747	1261	1150	976	838	581	1096	874
Average Yards	22.6	21.4	24.8	20.8	20.2	21.7	23.5	23.2	20.4	23.2	26.1	23.0
Touchdowns	1	0	0	0	0	0	1	0	0	1	0	0
INTERCEPTION RETURNS:												
Number	28	15	12	19	25	30	14	18	17	19	18	16
Yards	349	185	183	223	311	561	236	276	442	195	264	203
Average Yards	12.5	12.3	15.3	11.7	12.4	18.7	16.9	15.3	26.0	10.3	14.7	12.7
Touchdowns	2	0	0	0	1	1	1	3	2	0	1	0
PENALTIES:												
Number	67	63	51	66	65	43	60	66	75	48	66	31
Yards	712	614	468	597	673	516	580	597	654	405	629	321
FUMBLES:												
Number	22	25	22	19	29	28	24	36	25	39	22	30
Number Lost	12	15	15	10	13	18	14	20	16	18	14	17
POINTS:												
Total	303	203	200	269	251	218	307	254	173	161	260	251
PAT Attempts	41	23	26	32	30	26	39	32	21	20	33	30
PAT Made	36	23	24	32	30	26	38	32	20	15	33	29
FG Attempts	19	26	17	22	25	21	19	18	14	26	15	23
FG Made	7	14	6	15	13	12	11	10	9	8	9	14
Percent FG Made	36.8	53.8	35.3	68.2	52.0	57.1	57.9	55.6	64.3	30.8	60.0	60.9
Safeties	0	0	1	0	1	0	1	0	0	1	1	0

DEFENSE

	BALT.	CHI.B.	CHI.C.	CLEVE.	DET.	G.BAY	L.A.	N.Y.	PHIL.	PITT.	S.F.	WASH.
FIRST DOWNS:												
Total	204	185	208	164	198	226	216	174	199	156	239	174
by Rushing	69	68	120	79	81	117	96	92	83	69	107	82
by Passing	118	96	79	66	100	97	101	64	94	77	117	89
by Penalty	17	21	9	19	17	12	19	18	22	10	15	3
RUSHING:												
Number	375	419	521	396	406	462	440	442	451	412	434	394
Yards	1174	1383	2201	1502	1521	2159	1845	1777	1714	1425	1847	1567
Average Yards	3.1	3.3	4.2	3.8	3.7	4.7	4.2	4.0	3.8	3.5	4.3	4.0
Touchdowns	10	10	19	11	13	18	15	12	15	7	18	11
PASSING:												
Attempts	342	306	233	242	290	314	301	226	257	234	332	262
Completions	175	153	117	105	163	153	153	104	133	112	182	135
Completion Percentage	51.2	50.0	50.2	43.4	56.2	48.7	50.8	46.0	51.8	47.9	54.8	51.5
Gross Yards	2548	2212	2027	1511	2099	2185	2186	1596	2083	1523	2582	2193
Yards Lost Passing	316	479	120	211	255	147	306	202	114	157	181	165
Net Yards	2232	1733	1907	1300	1844	2038	1880	1394	1969	1366	2401	2028
Avg. Yards per Attempt (Gross)	7.5	7.2	8.7	6.2	7.2	7.0	7.3	7.1	8.1	6.5	7.8	8.4
Avg. Yards per Comp. (Gross)	14.6	14.4	17.3	14.4	12.9	14.3	14.3	15.3	15.7	13.6	14.2	16.2
Touchdowns	19	15	17	8	15	18	15	10	10	12	13	18
Interceptions	28	15	12	19	25	30	14	18	17	19	18	16
Percent Intercepted	8.2	4.9	5.2	7.9	8.6	9.6	4.7	8.0	6.6	8.1	5.4	6.1
PUNTS:												
Number	56	76	60	72	55	50	61	60	58	62	47	59
Average Distance	42.5	42.0	39.7	41.8	40.9	43.0	40.2	38.8	42.8	42.7	40.3	39.6
PUNT RETURNS:												
Number	34	47	46	47	33	40	37	45	45	45	35	35
Yards	109	244	266	315	54	149	229	325	351	324	205	88
Average Yards	3.2	5.2	5.8	6.7	1.6	3.7	6.2	7.2	7.8	7.2	5.9	2.5
Touchdowns	0	0	0	1	0	0	0	1	0	0	0	0
KICKOFF RETURNS:												
Number	49	33	31	42	47	42	53	42	31	35	45	43
Yards	1120	860	783	917	1044	897	1268	964	737	704	928	938
Average Yards	22.9	26.1	25.3	21.8	22.2	21.4	23.9	23.0	23.8	20.1	20.6	21.8
Touchdowns	0	1	1	0	0	0	1	0	0	0	0	0
INTERCEPTION RETURNS:												
Number	19	28	22	14	22	23	23	12	23	14	18	13
Yards	180	574	340	141	292	252	381	190	340	230	336	172
Average Yards	9.5	20.5	15.5	10.1	13.3	11.0	16.6	15.8	14.8	16.4	18.7	13.2
Touchdowns	0	2	0	1	1	2	1	1	1	1	1	0
PENALTIES:												
Number	60	65	68	42	65	75	49	49	65	43	55	65
Yards	546	744	726	412	577	709	516	423	642	370	502	599
FUMBLES:												
Number	29	22	27	20	28	26	24	34	26	39	25	21
Number Lost	12	15	13	12	18	17	11	14	19	23	16	12
POINTS:												
Total	235	211	299	172	231	311	278	211	230	178	264	230
PAT Attempts	29	29	37	22	29	39	33	25	27	21	32	30
PAT Made	29	25	35	19	27	39	33	25	26	20	31	29
FG Attempts	21	19	23	14	17	22	26	17	29	19	24	14
FG Made	10	4	14	7	10	12	15	12	14	10	13	7
Percent FG Made	47.6	21.1	60.9	50.0	58.8	54.5	57.7	70.6	48.3	52.6	54.2	50.0
Safeties	1	0	0	0	0	1	1	0	0	1	1	0

1957 CHAMPIONSHIP GAME

December 29, at Detroit
(Attendance 55,263)

SCORING

DETROIT	17	14	14	14–59
CLEVELAND	0	7	7	0–14

First Quarter			
	Det.	Martin, 31 yard Field goal	7:36
	Det.	Rote, 1 yard rush PAT – Martin (kick)	11:04
	Det.	Gedman, 1 yard rush PAT – Martin (kick)	13:52
Second Quarter			
	Cle.	Brown, 29 yard rush PAT – Groza (kick)	0:10
	Det.	Junker, 26 yard pass from Rote PAT – Martin (kick)	7:41
	Det.	Barr, 19 yard interception return (by O'Connell) PAT – Martin (kick)	11:36
Third Quarter			
	Cle.	L. Carpenter, 5 yard rush PAT – Groza (kick)	7:59
	Det.	Doran, 78 yard pass from Rote PAT – Martin (kick)	8:43
	Det.	Junker, 23 yard pass from Rote PAT – Martin (kick)	13:21
Fourth Quarter			
	Det.	Middleton, 32 yard pass from Rote PAT – Martin (kick)	0:07
	Det.	Cassady, 16 yard pass from Richlow PAT – Martin (kick)	12:40

TEAM STATISTICS

DET.		CLE.
22	First Downs – Totals	17
9	First Downs – Rushing	11
10	First Downs – Passing	5
3	First Downs – Penalty	1
4	Fumbles – Number	2
1	Fumbles – Lost Ball	2
6	Penalties – Number	5
52	Yards – Penalized	64
1	Field Goals Missed	0

Parker and the Unsleeping Lions

The Detroit Lions entered the championship game against the Cleveland Browns with at least three strikes against them. Their star field general, Bobby Layne, was out with a broken ankle; Charlie Ane, one of the league's best tackles, was hampered by a bad ankle; and head coach George Wilson found himself in a peculiar position. He had replaced Buddy Parker in training camp after Parker publicly denounced the team and walked out before the first exhibition game. To say the least, it seemed as if the Lions were in for a long afternoon. But Tobin Rote, who had filled in admirably after Layne's injury, and the Detroit team in general were prepared to cap the season successfully, to prove to Parker and their fans that they were not deadbeats nor an uncoachable football team. By the time the first half ended, the throng in Briggs Stadium were in near hysteria with the scoreboard reading Lions 31, Browns 7. In the third quarter, Cleveland put a little fear in the crown as they marched 80 yards in ten plays to make the score 31-14. But then, after the Lions had returned the kickoff to their own 22-yard line, Rote uncorked a 78-yard bomb to Jim Doran to give Detroit, after the conversion, a 38-14 lead. Before the quarter ended, Rote struck again to put the game out of reach. On the first play of the final quarter, Jerry Perry recovered a fumble on the Cleveland 32, and Rote and Co. returned to the field. A Rote-to-Dave Middleton pass pushed the score to 52-14 after Jim Martin's conversion. The final Cleveland embarrassment and Detroit vindication came when Jerry Reichow, in relief of Rote, capped a 56-yard drive by drilling a 16-yard pass to Hopalong Cassady, which, following Martin's eighth extra-point conversion, ran the score to 59-14—the second biggest championship-game drubbing ever.

INDIVIDUAL STATISTICS

DETROIT	No.	Yds.	Avg.	CLEVELAND	No.	Yds.	Avg.
RUSHING							
Cassady	8	48	6.0	L. Carpenter	14	82	5.9
Johnson	8	40	5.0	Brown	20	69	3.5
Rote	7	27	3.9	Plum	3	46	15.3
Redman	12	27	2.3	Renfro	1	21	21.0
Reichow	1	0	0.0		38	218	5.7
	36	142	3.9				
RECEIVING							
Junker	5	109	21.8	P. Carpenter	4	43	10.8
Doran	3	101	33.7	Brewster	3	52	17.3
Cassady	2	22	11.0	Renfro	1	9	9.0
Middleton	1	32	32.0	L. Carpenter	1	8	8.0
Johnson	1	16	16.0		9	112	12.4
Tracy	1	16	16.0				
	13	296	22.8				
PUNTING							
Lary	4		36.3	Konz	4		35.5
PUNT RETURNS							
Lary	1	12	12.0	Reynolds	2	1	0.5
Barr	1	1	1.0				
	2	13	6.5				
KICKOFF RETURNS							
Lary	3	85	28.3	Brown	4	106	26.5
				Reynolds	3	58	19.3
				Campbell	1	19	19.0
					8	183	22.9
INTERCEPTION RETURNS							
Barr	1	19	19.0				
Long	1	17	17.0	None			
Schmidt	1	2	2.0				
David	1	0	0.0				
Perry	1	0	0.0				
	5	38	7.6				

PASSING

	Att.	Comp.	Comp Pct.	Yds.	Int.	Yds/ Att.	Yds/ Comp.	Yards Lost Tackled
DETROIT								
Rote	19	12	63.2	280	0	14.7	23.3	0
Reichow	3	1	33.3	16	0	5.3	16.0	0
	22	13	59.1	296	0	13.5	22.8	0– 0
CLEVELAND								
Plum	13	5	38.5	51	2	3.9	10.2	1–10
O'Connell	8	4	50.0	61	2	7.6	15.3	0
Hanulak	1	0	0.0	0	1	–	–	1– 7
	22	9	40.9	112	5	5.1	12.4	2–17

CLEVELAND BROWNS 9-2-1 Paul Brown

Scores of Each Game		
6	NEW YORK	3
23	Pittsburgh	12
24	PHILADELPHIA	7
7	Philadelphia	17
17	Chic. Cards	7
21	WASHINGTON	17
24	PITTSBURGH	0
30	Washington	30
45	LOS ANGELES	31
31	CHIC. CARDS	0
7	Detroit	20
34	New York	28

Use Name	Pos.	Hgt	Wgt	Age	Int	Pts
Lou Groza	OT	6'3"	248	33		77
Mike McCormack	OT	6'4"	247	30		
Herschel Forester	OG	6'	230	27		
Fred Robinson	OG	6'1"	242	27		
Stan Sheriff (from SF)	OG	6'1"	225	26		
Jim Ray Smith	OG	6'3"	240	26		
Joe Amstutz	C	6'5"	264	23		
Art Hunter	C	6'4"	242	24		
Len Ford	DE	6'4"	258	31		
Bill Quinlan	DE	6'3"	245	25		
Paul Wiggin	DE	6'3"	237	23		
Don Colo	DT	6'3"	250	32		
Bob Gain	DT	6'3"	260	29		
Henry Jordan	DT	6'3"	242	23		
Tom Catlin	LB	6'1"	210	26		
Vince Costello	LB	6'	224	25	2	
Galen Fiss	LB	6'	227	27	1	
Walt Michaels	LB	6'	237	28	1	
Chuck Noll	LB	6'1"	210	25		
Bobby Freeman	DB	6'1"	200	24	3	
Kenny Konz	DB	5'10"	187	29	4	
Warren Lahr	DB	5'11"	192	33	2	
Don Paul	DB	6'	192	31	4	6
Junior Wren	DB	6'	188	27	2	
John Borton	QB	6'	208	25		
Tom O'Connell	QB	5'11"	195	25		6
Milt Plum	QB	6'1"	205	23		
Milt Campbell	HB	6'3"	217	24		6
Lew Carpenter	HB	6'1"	205	25		24
Chet Hanulak	HB	5'10"	190	24		18
Billy Reynolds	HB	5'10"	195	25		6
Jimmy Brown	FB	6'2"	228	21		60
Ed Modzelewski	FB	6'	222	28		
Darrell Brewster	OE	6'3"	210	27		12
Preston Carpenter	OE	6'2"	192	23		18
Frank Clarke	OE	6'	207	24		
Ray Renfro	FL	6'1"	190	26		36

NEW YORK GIANTS 7-5-0 Jim Lee Howell

Scores of Each Game		
3	Cleveland	6
24	Philadelphia	20
24	Washington	20
35	PITTSBURGH	0
14	WASHINGTON	31
31	Green Bay	17
27	CHIC. CARDS	14
13	PHILADELPHIA	0
28	Chic. Cards	21
17	SAN FRANCISCO	27
10	Pittsburgh	21
28	CLEVELAND	34

Use Name	Pos.	Hgt	Wgt	Age	Int	Pts
Rosey Brown	OT	6'3"	245	24		
Dick Yelvington	OT	6'2"	235	30		
Bill Austin	OG	6'1"	225	28		
Ray Beck	OG	6'2"	225	25		
Jack Spinks	OT-OG	6'	235	27		
Jack Stroud	OT-OG	6'1"	235	28		
Ray Wietecha	C	6'1"	225	28		
Andy Robustelli	DE	6'1"	235	31		
Walt Yowarsky	OT-DE	6'3"	235	29		
John Martinkovic	DT-DE	6'3"	245	30		
Jim Katkavage	DT	6'3"	235	22		
Dick Modzelewski	DT	6'	260	26		
Sam Huff	LB	6'1"	230	22	1	6
Cliff Livingston	LB	6'3"	210	27		
Bill Svoboda	LB	6'	210	30	2	
Harland Svare	LB-DT	6'	215	26	1	
Johnny Bookman	DB	5'11"	175	22	3	6
Ed Crawford	OE-DB	6'3"	185	23	1	
Ed Hughes	DB	6'1"	185	29		
Dick Nolan	DB	6'1"	185	25	1	
Jimmy Patton	DB	6'	180	25	3	6
Em Tunnell	DB	6'1"	200	35	6	6
Bobby Clatterbuck	QB	6'3"	195	25		
Chuck Conerly	QB	6'1"	185	33		6
Don Heinrich	QB	6'	180	25		12
Don Chandler	HB	6'2"	205	22		
Gene Filipski	HB	5'11"	185	26		
Frank Gifford	HB	6'1"	205	27		54
Alex Webster	HB	6'3"	210	26		36
Bobby Epps	FB	5'9"	205	25		
Mel Triplett	FB	6'1"	215	25		
Ken MacAfee	OE	6'2"	215	27		12
Kyle Rote	OE	6'	205	28		18
Bob Schnelker	OE	6'3"	215	27		30
Ben Agajanian	K	6'	215	38		62

Jerry Huth – Military Service
Rosey Grier – Military Service

PITTSBURGH STEELERS 6-6-0 Buddy Parker

Scores of Each Game		
28	WASHINGTON	7
12	CLEVELAND	23
29	CHIC. CARDS	20
0	New York	35
6	PHILADELPHIA	0
19	Baltimore	13
0	Cleveland	24
10	GREEN BAY	27
6	Philadelphia	7
21	NEW YORK	10
3	Washington	10
27	Chic. Cards	2

Use Name	Pos.	Hgt	Wgt	Age	Int	Pts
Jerry Leahy	OT	6'2"	220	23		
Frank Varrichione	OT	6'1"	230	25		
Willie McClung	DT-OT	6'2"	250	28		
Sid Fournet	OG	6'	215	24		
Herm Lee	OG	6'4"	220	26		
Bill Michael	OG	6'2"	240	23		
John Nisby	OG	6'1"	230	24		
Bob O'Neil	OG	6'1"	230	24		
Mike Sandusky	OG	6'	235	24		
Ed Beatty	C	6'3"	230	25		
Bill McPeak	DE	6'1"	220	32		2
George Tarasovic	LB-DE	6'4"	250	28	2	
Joe Krupa	DT	6'2"	240	24		
Dave Liddick	DT	6'2"	240	23		
Ernie Stautner	DE-DT	6'1"	230	32		
Dale Dodrill	LB	6'1"	215	32	2	
Bill Priatko	LB	6'2"	220	26		
John Reger	LB	6'	220	26		6
Aubrey Rozelle	LB	6'2"	215	24	1	
Dick Alban	DB	6'	195	28	1	
Fred Bruney	DB	5'10"	180	26	1	
Jack Butler	DB	6'	195	29	10	
Gene Cichowski	DB	6'	195	23		
Gary Glick	DB	6'2"	190	26	2	25
Richie McCabe	DB	6'1"	185	23		
Len Dawson	QB	6'	195	23		
Jack Kemp	QB	6'1"	200	23		
Earl Morrall	QB	6'1"	205	23		12
Dick Hughes	HB	5'9"	185	25		
Sid Watson	HB	5'11"	185	24		
Billy Wells (from WAS)	HB	5'9"	170	25		6
Dean Derby	DB-HB	6'	185	23		21
Ray Mathews	OE-HB	6'	195	28		24
Bill Bowman	FB	6'2"	220	26		
Fran Rogel	FB	5'11"	205	30		6
Dick Young	FB	5'11"	210	26		12
Bob Gunderman	OE	6'2"	195	23		
Jug Girard	OE	5'11"	185	30		29
Jack McClairen	OE	6'4"	215	26		12
Elbie Nickel	OE	6'1"	205	34		6
Perry Richards	OE	6'2"	205	23		

Lynn Chandnois – Injury
Lowell Perry – Injury

WASHINGTON REDSKINS 5-6-1 Joe Kuharich

Scores of Each Game		
7	Pittsburgh	28
37	Chic. Cards	14
20	NEW YORK	24
14	CHIC. CARDS	44
31	New York	14
17	Cleveland	21
17	BALTIMORE	21
30	CLEVELAND	30
12	Philadelphia	21
14	Chic. Bears	3
42	PHILADELPHIA	7
10	PITTSBURGH	3

Use Name	Pos.	Hgt	Wgt	Age	Int	Pts
Don Boll	OT	6'7"	266	30		
Ray Lemek	OT	6'	232	23		
Ed Khayat	DT-OT	6'3"	220	22		
Dick Stanfel	OG	6'3"	230	30		
Red Stephens	OG	6'	230	27		
Ed Voytek	OG	6'2"	230	22		
Bill Fulcher	LB-OG	6'	190	23		
Johnny Allen	C	6'2"	228	25		
Jim Schrader	C	6'2"	232	25		
Gene Brito	DE	6'1"	230	31		
Chet Ostrowski	DE	6'1"	235	27		
Bob Dee	DT-DE	6'3"	225	24		
Don Owens	DT	6'5"	258	25		
Volney Peters	DT	6'4"	240	29		
Will Renfro	DT	6'5"	230	25		
Chuck Drazenovich	LB	6'1"	222	30	2	
Ralph Felton	LB	5'11"	200	25	1	
Lavern Torgeson	LB	6'	217	28	1	
Norb Hecker	DB	6'2"	200	30	3	
Don Shula	DB	5'11"	190	27	3	
Bert Zagers	DB	5'10"	185	24	2	12
Dick James	HB-DB	5'9"	180	23	2	
Scooter Scudero	HB-DB	5'10"	170	27		
Rudy Bukich	QB	6'1"	200	26		
Eddie LeBaron	QB	5'9"	165	27		
Jim Podoley	HB	6'2"	190	24		36
Tom Runnels	HB	5'10"	190	23		
Ed Sutton	DB-HB	6'1"	202	22	1	36
Sam Baker	FB	6'2"	217	25		77
Don Bosseler	FB	6'1"	212	21		42
Leo Elter	FB	5'10"	200	28		18
Tom Braatz	OE	6'1"	213	24		
Johnny Carson	OE	6'3"	202	27		18
Steve Meilinger	OE	6'2"	223	27		12
Joe Walton	DE-OE	5'11"	205	22	1	

J. D. Kimmel – Injury
Ralph Guglielmi – Military Service
Johnny Miller – Military Service
John Paluck – Military Service
Roy Barni – Shot to death Aug. 1957

PHILADELPHIA EAGLES 4-8-0 Hugh Devore

Scores of Each Game		
13	Los Angeles	17
20	NEW YORK	24
7	Cleveland	24
17	CLEVELAND	7
0	Pittsburgh	6
38	Chic. Cards	21
16	DETROIT	27
0	New York	13
21	WASHINGTON	12
7	PITTSBURGH	6
7	Washington	42
27	CHIC. CARDS	31

Use Name	Pos.	Hgt	Wgt	Age	Int	Pts
Bob Gaona	OT	6'3"	240	27		
Buck Lansford	OT	6'2"	232	24		
Len Szafaryn	OT	6'2"	225	29		
Abe Gibron	OG	5'11"	260	31		
Ken Huxhold	OG	6'1"	235	28		
Menil Mavraides	OG	6'1"	235	28		
John Simerson	C	6'3"	258	22		
Tom Scott	DE	6'2"	220	27		
Norm Willey	DE	6'2"	235	30		
Marion Campbell	DT	6'3"	255	28		
Tom Saidock	DT	6'5"	263	25		
Jim Weatherall	DT	6'4"	252	27		
Frank Wydo	DT	6'4"	232	33	1	
Sid Youngelman	DT	6'3"	255	25		
Chuck Bednarik	C-LB	6'3"	235	32	3	
Bill Koman	LB	6'2"	223	23		
Bob Hudson	DB-LB	6'4"	230	27		
Eddie Bell	DB	6'1"	215	26	2	
Tom Brookshier	DB	6'	198	25	4	
Jimmy Harris	DB	6'1"	180	22	3	6
Jerry Norton	DB	5'11"	195	27	4	6
Al Dorow	QB	6'	190	27		12
Sonny Jurgensen	QB	5'11"	200	23		12
Bobby Thomason	QB	6'1"	197	28		18
Billy Barnes	HB	5'11"	202	22		12
Ken Keller	HB	5'11"	185	23		
Rocky Ryan	OE-HB	6'1"	202	25		12
Tommy McDonald	FL-HB	5'10"	182	23		18
Clarence Peaks	FB	6'1"	218	21		6
Neil Worden	FB	5'10"	205	27		
Dick Bielski	OE	6'1"	236	25		12
Hank Burnine	OE	6'2"	190	25		
Bill Stribling	OE	6'1"	210	30		6
Bobby Walston	OE	6'	190	28		53
Pete Retzlaff	FL	6'1"	209	27		

Jess Richardson – Injury
Lum Snyder – Military Service

CHICAGO CARDINALS 3-9-0 Ray Richards

Scores of Each Game		
20	San Francisco	10
14	WASHINGTON	37
20	Pittsburgh	29
44	Washington	14
7	CLEVELAND	17
21	PHILADELPHIA	38
14	New York	27
21	NEW YORK	28
0	Cleveland	31
6	CHIC. BEARS	14
31	Philadelphia	27
2	PITTSBURGH	27

Use Name	Pos.	Hgt	Wgt	Age	Int	Pts
Jack Jennings	OT	6'4"	245	30		
Dave Lunceford	OT	6'4"	240	23		
Charlie Toogood	OG-OT	6'	230	29		
Doug Hogland	OG	6'3"	245	26		
Bob Konovsky	OG	6'2"	245	23		
Earl Putnam	C	6'6"	308	25		
Jim Taylor	LB-C	6'2"	235	23		
Stan West	C-DG	6'2"	235	30		
Leo Sugar	DE	6'1"	210	28		12
Pat Summerall	DE	6'4"	230	27		42
Chuck Weber	LB-DE	6'1"	225	28		
Wayne Bock	DT	6'4"	250	23		
Tom Finnin	DT	6'2"	270	29		
Len Teeuws	DT	6'4"	245	30		
Chuck Ulrich	DT	6'4"	250	26		
Carl Brettschneider	LB	6'1"	200	25		
Ed Husmann	OG-LB	6'	225	26		
Leo Sanford	C-LB	6'1"	230	28	1	
Jerry Tubbs	C-LB	6'2"	216	22		
Tony Pasquesi	DT-LB	6'4"	255	23		
Jimmy Carr	DB	6'1"	200	24		
Lindon Crow	DB	6'1"	187	24	1	
Jimmy Hill	DB	6'2"	190	28	3	
Night Train Lane	DB	6'1"	190	29	2	
Floyd Sagely	DB	6'1"	190	25	1	
Frank Bernardi	HB-DB	5'9"	180	24	2	
Paul Larson	QB	5'11"	185	25		
Ted Marchibroda	QB	5'10"	180	26		
Lamar McHan	QB	6'1"	197	25		12
Joe Childress	HB	6'	200	23		6
Ollie Matson	HB	6'2"	210	27		54
Jimmy Sears	HB	5'11"	180	26		6
Dave Mann	OE-HB	6'1"	190	24		
Mal Hammack	FB	6'2"	200	24		
Johnny Olszewski	FB	5'11"	196	26		12
Max Boydston	OE	6'2"	207	24		
Dick Brubaker	OE	6'	205	25		
Gern Nagler	OE	6'2"	190	24		24
Woodley Lewis	DB-OE	6'	195	32	2	30

John Dittrich – Military Service
John Roach – Military Service

CLEVELAND BROWNS

RUSHING

Last Name	No.	Yds	Avg	TD
Brown	202	942	4.7	9
Hanulak	125	375	3.0	3
L. Carpenter	83	315	3.8	4
Plum	26	118	4.5	0
P. Carpenter	3	86	28.7	1
Reynolds	29	57	2.0	1
Campbell	7	23	3.3	0
Renfro	2	22	11.0	0
Modzelewski	10	21	2.1	0
McCormack	0	4	0.0	0
O'Connell	14	–5	–0.4	1

RECEIVING

Last Name	No.	Yds	Avg	TD
Brewster	30	614	21	2
P. Carpenter	27	398	15	2
Renfro	21	589	28	6
Brown	16	55	3	1
L. Carpenter	5	65	13	0
Clarke	4	77	19	0
Hanulak	3	38	13	0
Campbell	1	25	25	1
Reynolds	1	12	12	0

PUNT RETURNS

Last Name	No.	Yds	Avg	TD
Reynolds	24	114	5	0
Paul	9	75	8	0
Hanulak	11	29	3	0
Konz	3	13	4	0
Robinson	1	0	0	0

KICKOFF RETURNS

Last Name	No.	Yds	Avg	TD
Campbell	11	263	24	0
Reynolds	7	152	22	0
Brown	6	136	23	0
Modzelewski	5	74	15	0
L. Carpenter	1	24	24	0
Clarke	2	22	11	0
Freeman	1	15	15	0

PASSING – PUNTING – KICKING

PASSING	Att	Comp	%	Yds	Yd/Att	TD	Int–%	RK
O'Connell	110	63	57	1229	11.2	9	8– 7	5
Plum	76	41	54	590	7.8	2	5– 7	
Borton	6	3	50	22	3.7	0	1– 17	
Hanulak	2	1	50	32	16.0	1	0– 0	
Campbell	1	0	0	0	0.0	0	0– 0	

PUNTING	No	Avg
Konz	61	39.3

KICKING	XP	Att	%	FG	Att	%
Groza	32	32	100	15	22	68

NEW YORK GIANTS

RUSHING

Last Name	No.	Yds	Avg	TD
Gifford	136	528	3.9	5
Webster	135	478	3.5	5
Epps	63	286	4.5	0
Triplett	61	216	3.5	0
Filipski	22	89	4.0	0
Conerly	15	24	1.6	1
Rote	1	13	13.0	0
Heinrich	4	10	2.5	2
Clatterbuck	3	3	1.0	0
Chandler	1	2	2.0	0

RECEIVING

Last Name	No.	Yds	Avg	TD
Gifford	41	588	14	4
Webster	30	330	11	1
Rote	25	358	14	3
Schnelker	20	450	23	5
MacAfee	16	229	14	2
Epps	8	81	10	0
Triplett	4	75	19	0
Crawford	2	40	20	0
Filipski	1	7	7	0

PUNT RETURNS

Last Name	No.	Yds	Avg	TD
Filipski	20	91	5	0
Tunnell	12	60	5	0
Patton	11	29	3	0

KICKOFF RETURNS

Last Name	No.	Yds	Avg	TD
Filipski	26	613	24	0
Patton	10	223	22	0
Bookman	4	102	26	0
Crawford	2	38	19	0

PASSING – PUNTING – KICKING

PASSING	Att	Comp	%	Yds	Yd/Att	TD	Int–%	RK
Conerly	232	128	55	1712	7.4	11	11– 5	4
Heinrich	26	11	42	224	8.6	1	1– 4	
Gifford	6	4	67	143	23.8	2	0– 0	
Chandler	2	2	100	40	20.0	0	0– 0	
Clatterbuck	2	2	100	39	19.5	1	0– 0	
Epps	1	0	0	0	0.0	0	0– 0	

PUNTING	No	Avg
Chandler	60	44.6

KICKING	XP	Att	%	FG	Att	%
Agajanian	32	32	100	10	18	56

PITTSBURGH STEELERS

RUSHING

Last Name	No.	Yds	Avg	TD
Wells	154	532	3.5	0
Rogel	68	232	3.4	1
Young	56	153	2.7	2
Murrall	41	81	2.0	2
Bowman	28	76	2.7	0
Derby	18	49	2.7	2
Dawson	3	31	10.3	0
Watson	12	21	1.8	0
Hughes	2	6	3.0	0
Kemp	3	–1	–0.3	0
Mathews	3	–1	–0.3	0
Girard	1	–5	–2.5	0

RECEIVING

Last Name	No.	Yds	Avg	TD
McClairen	46	630	14	2
Girard	21	419	20	4
Rogel	20	128	6	0
Mathews	15	369	25	4
Wells	14	89	6	0
Bowman	11	107	10	0
Nickel	10	115	12	1
Derby	4	79	20	0
Young	4	38	10	0
Watson	3	24	8	0
Richards	1	15	15	0

PUNT RETURNS

Last Name	No.	Yds	Avg	TD
Wells	21	143	7	0
Bruney	17	86	5	0
Derby	9	32	4	0
Butler	1	10	10	0
Hughes	1	5	5	0
Glick	1	0	0	0
Rozelle	1	0	0	0

KICKOFF RETURNS

Last Name	No.	Yds	Avg	TD
Wells	12	325	27	1
Derby	6	137	23	0
Bruney	5	101	20	0
Alban	2	33	17	0
Rogel	1	4	4	0

PASSING – PUNTING – KICKING

PASSING	Att	Comp	%	Yds	Yd/Att	TD	Int–%	RK
Morrall	289	139	48	1900	6.6	11	12– 4	6
Kemp	18	8	44	88	4.9	0	2– 11	
Dawson	4	2	60	26	6.3	0	0– 0	
Girard	1	0	0	0	0.0	0	0– 0	

PUNTING	No	Avg
Girard	68	40.5
Kemp	2	27.5

KICKING	XP	Att	%	FG	Att	%
Glick	10	12	83	5	18	28
Derby	3	3	100	2	4	50
Girard	2	3	67	1	3	33
Dawson	0	2	0	0	1	0

WASHINGTON REDSKINS

RUSHING

Last Name	No.	Yds	Avg	TD
Bosseler	167	673	4.0	7
Podoley	114	442	3.9	2
Sutton	108	407	3.8	5
Elter	45	211	3.8	2
Scudero	9	60	6.7	0
Runnels	20	52	2.6	0
Baker	2	23	11.5	1
James	7	19	2.7	0
Bukich	8	–2	–0.2	0
LeBaron	20	–12	–0.6	0

RECEIVING

Last Name	No.	Yds	Avg	TD
Carson	34	583	17	3
Podoley	27	554	21	4
Bosseler	19	152	8	0
Meilinger	13	183	14	2
Elter	6	94	16	1
Walton	3	57	19	0
Braatz	2	52	26	0
Sutton	2	32	16	1
Scudero	2	30	15	0
Runnels	1	4	4	0

PUNT RETURNS

Last Name	No.	Yds	Avg	TD
Zagers	14	217	16	2
Scudero	9	84	9	0
James	11	83	8	0
Runnels	10	76	8	0

KICKOFF RETURNS

Last Name	No.	Yds	Avg	TD
Zagers	15	348	23	0
James	12	259	22	0
Scudero	3	95	32	0
Runnels	2	66	33	0
Podoley	3	56	19	0
Sutton	1	19	19	0
Khayat	1	12	12	0

PASSING – PUNTING – KICKING

PASSING	Att	Comp	%	Yds	Yd/Att	TD	Int–%	RK
LeBaron	167	99	59	1508	9.0	11	10– 6	3
Bukich	28	6	21	103	3.7	0	3– 11	
Sutton	5	3	60	95	19.0	0	0– 0	
Runnels	1	1	100	35	35.0	0	0– 0	

PUNTING	No	Avg
Baker	50	42.8

KICKING	XP	Att	%	FG	Att	%
Baker	29	30	97	14	23	61

PHILADELPHIA EAGLES

RUSHING

Last Name	No.	Yds	Avg	TD
Barnes	143	529	3.7	1
Peaks	125	495	4.0	1
Keller	57	195	3.4	0
Worden	42	133	3.2	0
Norton	2	73	36.5	0
Thomason	15	62	4.1	3
Dorow	17	52	3.1	2
McDonald	12	36	3.0	0
Walston	1	7	7.0	0
Youngelman	0	3	0.0	0
Jurgensen	10	–3	–0.3	2

RECEIVING

Last Name	No.	Yds	Avg	TD
Barnes	19	212	11	1
Stribling	14	194	14	1
Walston	11	266	24	1
Peaks	11	99	9	0
Retzlaff	10	120	12	0
McDonald	9	228	25	3
Bielski	8	81	10	2
Burnine	7	63	9	0
Ryan	4	91	23	2
Keller	4	31	8	0
Worden	1	3	3	0
Gaona	1	–9	0	0

PUNT RETURNS

Last Name	No.	Yds	Avg	TD
McDonald	26	127	5	0
Keller	9	59	7	0
Norton	1	13	13	0
Harris	1	0	0	0

KICKOFF RETURNS

Last Name	No.	Yds	Avg	TD
Keller	15	320	21	0
McDonald	11	304	28	0
Peaks	5	98	20	0
Worden	4	63	16	0
Norton	2	33	17	0
Bielski	2	11	6	0
Bell	1	7	7	0
Wydo	1	2	2	0

PASSING – PUNTING – KICKING

PASSING	Att	Comp	%	Yds	Yd/Att	TD	Int–%	RK
Thomason	92	46	50	630	6.9	4	10– 11	
Jurgensen	70	33	47	470	6.7	5	8– 11	
Dorow	36	17	47	212	5.9	1	4– 11	
Peaks	3	2	67	56	18.7	0	1– 33	
Barnes	1	0	0	0	0.0	0	0– 0	
McDonald	1	1	100	11	11.0	0	0– 0	
Norton	1	0	0	0	0.0	0	0– 0	

PUNTING	No	Avg
Norton	68	41.4

KICKING	XP	Att	%	FG	Att	%
Walston	20	21	95	9	12	75
Bielski	0	0	0	0	2	0

CHICAGO CARDINALS

RUSHING

Last Name	No.	Yds	Avg	TD
Matson	134	577	4.3	6
Olszewski	83	271	3.3	2
Childress	41	168	4.1	1
Hammack	30	158	5.3	0
Mann	22	92	4.2	0
McHan	25	82	3.3	2
Sears	17	68	4.0	1
Larson	8	12	1.5	0
Marchibroda	4	10	2.5	0
Bernardi	1	4	4.0	0

RECEIVING

Last Name	No.	Yds	Avg	TD
Nagler	27	475	18	4
Lewis	21	424	20	5
Matson	20	451	23	3
Boydston	14	193	14	0
Childress	10	146	15	0
Mann	8	137	17	0
Sears	5	66	13	0
Olszewski	3	36	12	0
Hammack	1	14	14	0
Sugar	1	14	14	0
Bernardi	1	13	13	0

PUNT RETURNS

Last Name	No.	Yds	Avg	TD
Lewis	24	175	7	0
Matson	10	54	5	0
Bernardi	2	12	6	0
Hill	1	9	9	0
Lane	1	8	8	0
Mann	1	0	0	0
Sears	1	0	0	0

KICKOFF RETURNS

Last Name	No.	Yds	Avg	TD
Lewis	26	682	26	0
Sears	8	220	28	0
Matson	7	154	22	0
Carr	2	39	20	0
Hammack	2	33	17	0
Mann	1	23	23	0
Summerall	1	3	3	0
Olszewski	0	13	0	0

PASSING – PUNTING – KICKING

PASSING	Att	Comp	%	Yds	Yd/Att	TD	Int–%	RK
McHan	200	87	44	1568	7.8	10	15– 8	9
Marchibroda	45	15	33	238	5.3	1	5– 11	
Larson	14	6	43	61	4.4	0	1– 7	
Matson	5	2	40	59	11.8	0	0– 0	
Sears	3	0	0	0	0.0	0	0– 0	
Childress	2	1	50	43	21.5	0	1– 50	
Bernardi	1	0	0	0	0.0	0	0– 0	
Mann	1	0	0	0	0.0	0	0– 0	

PUNTING	No	Avg
Mann	59	42.5

KICKING	XP	Att	%	FG	Att	%
Summerall	24	26	92	6	17	35

DETROIT LIONS 8-4-0 George Wilson

Scores of Each Game		
14	Baltimore	34
24	Green Bay	14
10	LOS ANGELES	7
31	BALTIMORE	27
17	Los Angeles	35
31	San Francisco	35
27	Philadelphia	16
31	SAN FRANCISCO	10
7	CHIC. BEARS	27
18	GREEN BAY	6
20	CLEVELAND	7
21	Chic. Bears	13
	Playoff	
31	San Francisco	27

Use Name	Pos.	Hgt	Wgt	Age	Int	Pts
Charlie Ane	OT	6'2"	265	26		
Ken Russell	OT	6'3"	255	21		
Lou Creekmur	OG-OT	6'4"	254	30		
Stan Campbell	OG	6'	228	27		
Harley Sewell	OG	6'1"	226	26		
John Gordy	OT-OG	6'3"	238	21		
Frank Gatski	C	6'3"	240	35		
Gene Cronin	OG-DE	6'2"	228	24		
Gil Mains	DT-DE	6'2"	255	27		
Darris McCord	DT-DE	6'4"	245	24		
Ray Krouse	DT	6'3"	275	30		
Bob Miller	DT	6'3"	255	27		
Jerry Perry	DT	6'4"	237	26		2
Bob Long	LB	6'3"	230	23	1	
Jim Martin	LB	6'2"	223	33	1	26
Joe Schmidt	LB	6'1"	222	25	1	
Roger Zatkoff	LB	6'2"	220	26		
Terry Barr	DB	6'	185	22	1	
Jack Christiansen	DB	6'1"	196	28	10	6
Jim David	DB	5'11"	185	30	3	
Carl Karilivacz	DB	6'	190	26	5	
Gary Lowe (from WAS)	DB	5'11"	195	23	1	
Yale Lary	DB	6'	186	26	2	
Sonny Gandee – Injury						
Bobby Layne	QB	6'1"	208	30		43
Tobin Rote	QB	6'3"	215	29		6
Marv Brown	HB	5'8"	150	25		
Hopalong Cassady	HB	5'10"	180	23		36
Gene Gedman	HB	5'11"	196	25		18
John Henry Johnson	FB	6'2"	207	27		30
Tom Tracy	FB	5'9"	205	25		
Leon Hart	OE-FB	6'5"	250	28		
Dorne Dibble	OE	6'2"	197	28		
Jim Doran	OE	6'2"	202	29		30
Steve Junker	OE	6'3"	218	22		24
Dave Middleton	OE	6'1"	195	24		12
Jerry Reichow	QB-OE	6'2"	210	22		18

SAN FRANCISCO FORTY NINERS 8-4-0 Frankie Albert

Scores of Each Game		
10	CHIC. CARDS	20
23	LOS ANGELES	20
21	Chic. Bears	17
24	Green Bay	14
21	CHIC. BEARS	17
35	DETROIT	31
24	Los Angeles	37
10	Detroit	31
21	Baltimore	27
27	New York	17
17	BALTIMORE	13
27	GREEN BAY	20
	Playoff	
27	DETROIT	31

Use Name	Pos.	Hgt	Wgt	Age	Int	Pts
Bob Cross	OT	6'4"	250	26		
Tom Dahms	OT	6'5"	250	29		
John Gonzaga	OT	6'3"	240	24		
Bob St. Clair	OT	6'9"	263	26		
Bruce Bosley	OG	6'2"	240	23		
Ted Connolly	OG	6'3"	240	25		
Lou Palatella	OG	6'2"	230	24		
Frank Morze	C	6'4"	280	23		
Ed Henke	LB-DE	6'3"	227	29		
Charley Powell	OE-LB-DE	6'2"	225	25		
Bill Herchman	DT	6'2"	240	24	1	6
Leo Nomellini	DT	6'3"	255	32		2
Bob Toneff	DT	6'3"	255	27		
Matt Hazeltine	LB	6'1"	205	24	2	
Marv Matuszak	LB	6'3"	235	26		
Karl Rubke	C-LB	6'4"	235	21	1	
Paul Carr	DB-LB	6'	205	25		
Bob Holladay	DB	5'11"	175	24		
Jimmy Ridlon	DB	6'1"	195	22		
J. D. Smith	DB	6'1"	200	24	2	
Julian Spence	DB	5'11"	175	28		
Bill Stits	DB	6'	195	26	2	
Val Joe Walker	DB	6'1"	178	26	2	
Dick Moegle	HB-DB	6'	195	23	8	6
John Brodie	QB	6'1"	195	22		
Y. A. Tittle	QB	6'	195	30		36
Joe Arenas	HB	5'11"	180	31		6
Hugh McElhenny	HB	6'1"	198	28		18
Gene Babb	FB	6'3"	207	22		18
Larry Barnes	FB	6'1"	225	24		
Joe Perry	FB	6'	210	30		18
Clyde Conner	OE	6'2"	195	24		24
Gordie Soltau	OE	6'2"	195	32		60
Billy Wilson	OE	6'3"	190	30		36
Bill Jessup	OE-FL	6'1"	195	28		
R. C. Owens	OE-FL	6'3"	205	22		30

BALTIMORE COLTS 7-5-0 Weeb Ewbank

Scores of Each Game		
34	DETROIT	14
21	CHIC. BEARS	10
45	Green Bay	17
27	Detroit	31
21	GREEN BAY	24
13	PITTSBURGH	19
21	Washington	17
29	Chic. Bears	14
27	SAN FRANCISCO	21
31	LOS ANGELES	14
13	San Francisco	17
21	Los Angeles	37

Use Name	Pos.	Hgt	Wgt	Age	Int	Pts
Luke Owens	OT	6'2"	242	24		
Jim Parker	OT	6'3"	262	23		
Ken Jackson	OG-OT	6'2"	235	28		
Alex Sandusky	OG	6'1"	235	25		
Art Spinney	OG	6'	228	30		
George Preas	OT-LB-OG	6'2"	230	25		
Buzz Nutter	C	6'4"	225	26		
Dick Szymanski	LB-C	6'3"	228	25		
Ordell Braase	DE	6'4"	215	25		
Don Joyce	DE	6'3"	250	27	1	
Gino Marchetti	DE	6'4"	240	31		6
Art Donovan	DT	6'2"	265	32		
Big Daddy Lipscomb	DT	6'6"	282	26		
Joe Campanella	LB	6'2"	235	26		
Doug Eggers	LB	6'	214	27		
Jack Patera	LB	6'1"	225	25	1	
Bill Pellington	LB	6'2"	228	28		
Don Shinnick	LB	6'	230	22	2	
Steve Myhra	OG-LB	6'1"	235	23		26
Milt Davis	DB	6'1"	190	28	10	12
Art DeCarlo (from WAS)	DB	6'2"	195	27	1	
Henry Moore	DB	6'1"	195	23	1	
Andy Nelson	DB	6'1"	180	24	5	
Dick Nyers	DB	5'11"	175	23		
Bert Rechichar	DB	6'1"	210	27	5	31
Carl Taseff	DB	5'11"	190	28	1	
Jesse Thomas	DB	5'10"	180	28	1	
Cotton Davidson	QB	6'1"	185	25		
George Shaw	QB	6'1"	190	24		6
Johnny Unitas	QB	6'1"	190	24		6
Jack Call	HB	6'1"	200	22		
L. G. Dupre	HB	5'11"	190	25		24
Lenny Moore	HB	6'1"	190	24		66
Royce Womble	HB	6'	185	25		
Alan Ameche	FB	6'	217	24		42
Billy Pricer	FB	5'10"	195	22		
Ray Berry	OE	6'2"	190	24		36
Jim Mutscheller	OE	6'1"	215	27		48

LOS ANGELES RAMS 6-6-0 Sid Gillman

Scores of Each Game		
17	PHILADELPHIA	13
20	San Francisco	23
7	Detroit	10
26	Chic. Bears	34
35	DETROIT	17
10	CHIC. BEARS	16
37	SAN FRANCISCO	24
31	Green Bay	27
31	Cleveland	45
14	Baltimore	31
42	GREEN BAY	17
37	BALTIMORE	21

Use Name	Pos.	Hgt	Wgt	Age	Int	Pts
Bob Fry	OT	6'4"	238	26		
Glenn Holtzman	DE-OT	6'3"	254	27		
Ken Panfil	DT-OT	6'6"	268	26		
John Hock	OG	6'2"	234	29		
Duane Putnam	OG	6'	230	29		
John Houser	OG-C	6'3"	237	21		
Bob Griffin	LB-C	6'3"	250	28		
Paul Miller	DE	6'2"	220	25		
Billy Ray Smith	DE	6'4"	227	22		
Lamar Lundy	OE-DE	6'7"	235	22		18
Frank Fuller	DT	6'4"	243	28		
Art Hauser	DT	6'	246	26		6
George Strugar	DT	6'5"	258	22		
Dick Daugherty	LB	6'1"	223	28	1	8
Bob Dougherty	LB	6'	234	23	1	
Larry Morris	LB	6'2"	220	23	1	
Jack Pardee	LB	6'2"	215	21		
Les Richter	LB	6'3"	248	26	4	
Alex Bravo	DB	6'1"	190	25		
Don Burroughs	DB	6'4"	186	26	3	
Jesse Castete	DB	5'11"	180	22		
Will Sherman	DB	6'2"	197	28	1	
Del Shofner	DB	6'3"	185	21	2	
Corky Taylor	DB	5'10"	185	23		
Jesse Whittenton	DB	6'	190	23	1	
John Morrow – Military Service						
Norm Van Brocklin	QB	6'1"	202	31		24
Billy Wade	QB	6'2"	203	26		
Jon Arnett	HB	5'11"	194	22		36
Ron Waller	HB	5'11"	180	24		
Tom Wilson	HB	6'	204	24		24
Joe Marconi	FB	6'2"	230	23		24
Tank Younger	FB	6'3"	226	29		18
Bob Boyd	OE	6'2"	203	29		18
Leon Clarke	OE	6'4"	230	24		24
Crazy Legs Hirsch	OE	6'2"	190	33		36
Paige Cothren	K	5'11"	212	22		71

CHICAGO BEARS 5-7-0 Paddy Driscoll

Scores of Each Game		
17	Green Bay	21
10	Baltimore	21
17	SAN FRANCISCO	21
34	LOS ANGELES	26
17	San Francisco	21
16	Los Angeles	10
21	GREEN BAY	14
14	BALTIMORE	29
27	Detroit	7
3	WASHINGTON	14
14	Chic. Cards	6
13	DETROIT	21

Use Name	Pos.	Hgt	Wgt	Age	Int	Pts
Kline Gilbert	OT	6'2"	235	26		
Bob Kilcullen	OT	6'3"	245	21		
Bill Wightkin	OT	6'3"	235	30		
Herman Clark	OG	6'3"	255	26		
Stan Jones	OG	6'1"	255	26		
Tom Roggeman	OG	6'	235	26		
Larry Strickland	C	6'4"	245	26		
John Damore	OG-C	6'2"	228	24		
Doug Atkins	DE	6'8"	255	27		
Jack Hoffman	DE	6'5"	235	28		
Ed Meadows	DE	6'2"	220	25		
Bill Bishop	DT	6'4"	246	26		
Earl Leggett	DT	6'3"	250	23		
Fred Williams	DT	6'4"	245	27		
M. L. Brackett	DE-DT	6'5"	248	24		
Bill George	LB	6'2"	235	26		
Wayne Hansen	LB	6'2"	228	29	1	
Joe Fortunato	FB-LB	6'	225	27		6
Jack Johnson	DB	6'3"	198	23	4	
McNeil Moore	DB	6'	185	24	2	
Stan Wallace	DB	6'3"	210	25	2	
Vic Zucco	DB	6'	187	22	3	6
J. C. Caroline	HB-DB	6'1"	190	24	2	
Ray Gene Smith	HB-DB	5'10"	185	27	1	
John Mellekas – Military Service						
Charlie Sumner – Military Service						
George Blanda	QB	6'1"	207	29		71
Zeke Bratkowski	QB	6'2"	203	25		
Ed Brown	QB	6'2"	205	28		6
Ronnie Knox	QB	6'1"	198	23		
Ron Drzewiecki	HB	5'11"	185	25		
Willie Galimore	HB	6'1"	188	22		42
Perry Jeter	HB	5'7"	178	23		
Bobby Watkins	HB	5'10"	197	25		12
Rick Casares	FB	6'2"	224	26		36
Jim Dooley	OE	6'4"	198	27		6
Harlon Hill	OE	6'3"	198	25		12
Bill McColl	OE	6'4"	230	27		6
Gene Schroeder	OE	6'3"	195	28		

GREEN BAY PACKERS 3-9-0 Lisle Blackbourn

Scores of Each Game		
21	CHIC. BEARS	17
14	DETROIT	24
17	BALTIMORE	45
14	SAN FRANCISCO	24
24	Baltimore	21
17	NEW YORK	31
14	Chic. Bears	21
27	LOS ANGELES	31
27	Pittsburgh	10
6	Detroit	18
17	Los Angeles	42
20	San Francisco	27

Use Name	Pos.	Hgt	Wgt	Age	Int	Pts
Norm Masters	OT	6'2"	240	24		
Ollie Spencer	OT	6'2"	250	26		
Carl Vereen	OT	6'2"	247	21		
Norm Amundsen	OG	5'11"	245	24		
Al Barry	OG	6'2"	230	26		
Jim Salsbury	OG	6'1"	235	26		
Larry Lauer	C	6'2"	235	28		
Jim Ringo	C	6'1"	230	26		
Nate Borden	DE	6'	235	25		
Carlton Massey	DE	6'2"	225	28		
Jim Temp	DE	6'4"	230	24		
Dave Hanner	DT	6'2"	250	28		
Jerry Helluin	DT	6'2"	265	27	1	
Tom Bettis	LB	6'2"	235	24		
Ernie Danjean	LB	6'	230	23		
Bill Forester	LB	6'3"	235	26	4	
Sam Palumbo	LB	6'2"	230	26	1	
Bobby Dillon	DB	6'1"	180	27	9	6
Hank Gremminger	DB	6'1"	195	24	5	
Billy Kinard	DB	6'	185	23		
Johnny Petitbon	DB	5'11"	190	26	1	
Johnny Symank	DB	5'11"	180	22	9	
Hank Bullough – Military Service						
Forrest Gregg – Military Service						
Doyle Nix – Military Service						
Bob Skoronski – Military Service						
Babe Parilli	QB	6'1"	190	27		12
Bart Starr	QB	6'1"	200	24		18
Al Carmichael	HB	6'1"	190	27		6
Joe Johnson	HB	6'	180	27		6
Don McIlhenny	HB	6'	200	22		18
Paul Hornung	FB-HB	6'2"	215	21		18
Fred Cone	FB	5'11"	205	31		74
Howie Ferguson	FB	6'2"	220	27		12
Frank Purnell	FB	5'11"	230	24		
Billy Howton	OE	6'2"	190	27		30
Gary Knafelc	OE	6'4"	215	25		12
Ron Kramer	OE	6'3"	220	22		
Max McGee	OE	6'3"	205	25		6
Dick Deschaine	K	6'	215	27		

DETROIT LIONS

RUSHING

Last Name	No.	Yds	Avg	TD
Johnson	129	621	4.8	5
Rote	70	366	5.2	1
Gedman	67	278	4.1	3
Cassady	73	250	3.4	3
Hart	24	99	4.1	0
Layne	24	99	4.1	0
Tracy	16	46	2.9	0
Lary	1	32	32.0	0
Reichow	2	9	4.5	0
Brown	2	6	3.0	0
Dibble	1	5	5.0	0

RECEIVING

Last Name	No.	Yds	Avg	TD
Doran	33	624	19	5
Cassady	25	325	13	3
Junker	22	305	14	4
Johnson	20	141	7	0
Middleton	18	294	16	2
Reichow	17	215	13	3
Gedman	10	135	14	0
Dibble	8	121	15	0
Tracy	6	24	4	0
Hart	4	55	14	0

PUNT RETURNS

Last Name	No.	Yds	Avg	TD
Lary	25	139	6	0
Barr	9	33	4	0
Brown	3	16	5	0
Christiansen	3	12	4	0
Karilivacz	1	0	0	0

KICKOFF RETURNS

Last Name	No.	Yds	Avg	TD
Cassady	10	232	23	0
Gedman	6	158	26	0
Barr	9	153	17	0
Brown	6	106	18	0
Christiansen	4	80	20	0
Perry	1	18	18	0
Cronin	1	0	0	0

PASSING – PUNTING – KICKING

PASSING	Att	Comp	%	Yds	Yd/Att	TD	Int–%	RK
Layne	179	87	49	1169	6.5	6	12– 7	11
Rote	177	76	42	1070	6.1	11	10– 6	9
Gedman	2	0	0	0	0.0	0	0– 0	
Reichow	2	0	0	0	0.0	0	0– 0	
Lary	1	0	0	0	0.0	0	0– 0	

PUNTING	No	Avg
Lary	54	39.9

KICKING	XP	Att	%	FG	Att	%
Layne	25	25	100	6	11	55
Martin	5	5	100	7	14	50

SAN FRANCISCO FORTY NINERS

RUSHING

Last Name	No.	Yds	Avg	TD
McElhenny	102	478	4.7	1
Perry	97	454	4.7	3
Babb	102	330	3.2	3
Tittle	40	220	5.5	6
Barnes	20	78	3.9	0
Moegle	9	48	5.3	1
Arenas	5	14	2.8	1
Brodie	2	0	0.0	0

RECEIVING

Last Name	No.	Yds	Avg	TD
Wilson	**52**	757	15	6
McElhenny	37	458	12	2
Conner	30	412	14	4
Owens	27	395	15	5
Babb	20	141	7	0
Perry	15	130	9	0
Soltau	5	47	9	0
Jessup	2	29	15	0
Powell	1	27	27	0
Arenas	1	10	10	0
Barnes	1	1	1	0

PUNT RETURNS

Last Name	No.	Yds	Avg	TD
Arenas	25	80	3	0
McElhenny	10	41	4	0
Hazeltine	1	1	1	0
Moegle	1	0	0	0

KICKOFF RETURNS

Last Name	No.	Yds	Avg	TD
Arenas	24	657	27	0
Smith	14	368	26	0
Hazeltine	1	23	23	0
Carr	1	10	10	0
Jessup	1	8	8	0
Babb	1	0	0	0
Palatella	0	30	0	0

PASSING – PUNTING – KICKING

PASSING	Att	Comp	%	Yds	Yd/Att	TD	Int–%	RK
Tittle	279	**176**	**63**	2157	7.7	13	15– 5	2
Brodie	21	11	52	160	7.6	2	3– 14	
Arenas	3	3	100	92	30.7	2	0– 0	
Barnes	1	1	100	–2	–2.0	0	0– 0	
Perry	1	0	0	0	0.0	0	0– 0	

PUNTING	No	Avg
Jessup	38	43.6
Barnes	19	47.1

KICKING	XP	Att	%	FG	Att	%
Soltau	33	33	100	9	15	60

BALTIMORE COLTS

RUSHING

Last Name	No.	Yds	Avg	TD
Ameche	144	493	3.4	5
L. Moore	98	488	**5.0**	3
Dupre	101	375	3.7	2
Unitas	42	171	4.1	1
Call	33	145	4.4	0
Shaw	5	30	6.0	1
Pricer	2	18	9.0	0
Womble	7	18	2.6	0
Myhra	1	1	1.0	0
Nyers	1	–4	–4.0	0

RECEIVING

Last Name	No.	Yds	Avg	TD
Berry	47	**800**	17	6
L. Moore	40	687	17	7
Mutscheller	32	558	17	**8**
Dupre	32	339	11	2
Ameche	15	137	9	2
Womble	7	69	10	0
Call	4	18	5	0

PUNT RETURNS

Last Name	No.	Yds	Avg	TD
Rechichar	22	71	3	0
Taseff	7	60	9	0
Shinnick	1	2	2	0
L. Moore	2	0	0	0
Davis	1	0	0	0

KICKOFF RETURNS

Last Name	No.	Yds	Avg	TD
Nyers	17	350	21	0
Call	14	329	24	0
Moore*	1	108	–	1
Davidson	5	79	16	0
Pricer	2	40	20	0
Owens	1	23	23	0
Myhra	1	19	19	0
Rechichar	1	0	0	0

*TD on 92 yard lateral, also has a 16 yd return.

PASSING – PUNTING – KICKING

PASSING	Att	Comp	%	Yds	Yd/Att	TD	Int–%	RK
Unitas	**301**	172	57	**2550**	8.5	**24**	17– 6	**1**
Shaw	9	5	56	58	6.4	1	1– 11	
Davidson	2	0	0	0	0.0	0	1– 50	
L. Moore	2	0	0	0	0.0	0	0– 0	

PUNTING	No	Avg
Davidson	47	35.4
Rechichar	5	31.4
Dupre	3	25.0

KICKING	XP	Att	%	FG	Att	%
Rechichar	22	25	88	3	13	23
Myhra	14	16	88	4	6	67

LOS ANGELES RAMS

RUSHING

Last Name	No.	Yds	Avg	TD
Wilson	127	616	4.9	3
Marconi	104	481	4.6	3
Younger	96	401	4.2	3
Arnett	86	347	4.0	2
Waller	48	292	6.1	0
Hirsch	1	8	8.0	0
Wade	1	5	5.0	0
Clarke	1	–4	–4.0	0
Van Brocklin	10	–4	–0.4	4

RECEIVING

Last Name	No.	Yds	Avg	TD
Hirsch	32	477	15	6
Boyd	29	534	18	3
Clarke	23	442	19	4
Arnett	18	322	18	3
Marconi	16	171	11	1
Younger	8	61	8	0
Wilson	7	95	14	1
Lundy	6	114	19	3
Waller	5	40	8	0

PUNT RETURNS

Last Name	No.	Yds	Avg	TD
Arnett	14	85	6	0
Taylor	3	41	14	0
Waller	16	33	2	0
Wilson	1	28	28	0
Burroughs	1	11	11	0
Sherman	1	0	0	0

KICKOFF RETURNS

Last Name	No.	Yds	Avg	TD
Arnett	18	504	**28**	1
Wilson	11	290	26	0
Waller	13	289	22	0
Taylor	1	35	35	0
Pardee	3	21	7	0
Putnam	2	11	6	0
Lundy	1	0	0	0

PASSING – PUNTING – KICKING

PASSING	Att	Comp	%	Yds	Yd/Att	TD	Int–%	RK
Van Brocklin	265	132	50	2105	7.9	20	21– 8	6
Wade	24	10	42	116	4.8	1	1– 4	
Waller	6	2	33	35	5.8	0	0– 0	
Younger	1	0	0	0	0.0	0	1–100	

PUNTING	No	Avg
Van Brocklin	54	44.3
Shofner	2	48.5

KICKING	XP	Att	%	FG	Att	%
Cothren	**38**	**38**	**100**	11	19	58

CHICAGO BEARS

RUSHING

Last Name	No.	Yds	Avg	TD
Casares	**204**	700	3.4	6
Galimore	127	538	4.2	5
Watkins	57	212	3.7	1
Brown	31	129	4.2	1
Bratkowski	12	83	6.9	0
Drzewiecki	5	11	2.2	0
Jeter	10	11	1.1	0
Smith	1	8	8.0	0
Hill	2	7	3.5	0
Caroline	1	1	1.0	0
Blanda	5	5	–1.0	1
Fortunato	2	–9	–4.5	1

RECEIVING

Last Name	No.	Yds	Avg	TD
Dooley	37	530	14	1
Casares	25	225	9	0
Hill	21	483	23	2
McColl	19	282	15	1
Galimore	15	201	13	2
Watkins	3	90	30	1
Schroeder	3	48	16	0
Smith	3	37	12	0
Jeter	2	9	5	0
Caroline	1	33	33	0
Drzewiecki	1	7	7	0

PUNT RETURNS

Last Name	No.	Yds	Avg	TD
Drzewiecki	22	64	3	0
Zucco	11	58	5	0
Caroline	6	20	3	0
Jeter	2	3	2	0
Smith	2	1	1	0

KICKOFF RETURNS

Last Name	No.	Yds	Avg	TD
Drzewiecki	13	315	24	0
Zucco	8	224	28	0
Galimore	5	140	28	0
Caroline	4	77	19	0
Jeter	3	62	21	0
Damore	1	7	7	0
Williams	1	6	6	0
Brackett	3	5	2	0
Casares	1	0	0	0

PASSING – PUNTING – KICKING

PASSING	Att	Comp	%	Yds	Yd/Att	TD	Int–%	RK
Brown	185	84	45	1321	7.1	6	16– 9	12
Bratkowski	80	37	46	527	6.6	1	9– 11	
Blanda	19	8	42	65	3.4	0	3– 16	
Casares	2	1	50	32	16.0	0	0– 0	

PUNTING	No	Avg
Brown	34	40.1
Bratkowski	16	38.6
Johnson	11	36.2
Casares	2	33.5

KICKING	XP	Att	%	FG	Att	%
Blanda	23	23	100	14	**26**	53

GREEN BAY PACKERS

RUSHING

Last Name	No.	Yds	Avg	TD
McIlhenny	100	384	3.8	1
Hornung	60	319	5.3	3
Ferguson	59	216	3.7	1
Cone	53	135	2.5	2
Carmichael	37	118	3.2	1
Starr	31	98	3.2	3
Parilli	24	83	3.5	2
McGee	5	40	8.0	0
Purnell	5	22	4.4	0
Howton	4	20	5.0	0
Johnson	2	6	3.0	0

RECEIVING

Last Name	No.	Yds	Avg	TD
Howton	38	727	19	5
Kramer	28	337	12	0
McIlhenny	18	210	12	2
McGee	17	273	16	1
Ferguson	15	107	7	1
Carmichael	13	184	14	0
Knafelc	9	164	18	2
Johnson	7	75	11	1
Hornung	6	34	6	0
Cone	4	30	8	0
Purnell	2	16	8	0

PUNT RETURNS

Last Name	No.	Yds	Avg	TD
Carmichael	25	190	8	0
Johnson	4	39	10	0
Kinard	3	19	6	0
Dillon	1	8	8	0
Symank	3	0	0	0

KICKOFF RETURNS

Last Name	No.	Yds	Avg	TD
Carmichael	**31**	**690**	22	0
McIlhenny	14	362	26	0
Cone	5	83	17	0
McGee	4	69	17	0
Forester	4	57	14	0

PASSING – PUNTING – KICKING

PASSING	Att	Comp	%	Yds	Yd/Att	TD	Int–%	RK
Starr	215	117	54	1489	6.9	8	10– 5	8
Parilli	102	39	38	669	6.6	4	12– 12	13
Hornung	6	1	17	–1	–0.2	0	0– 0	
Ferguson	1	0	0	0	0.0	0	0– 0	
Kramer	1	0	0	0	0.0	0	1–100	

PUNTING	No	Avg
Deschaine	63	42.0

KICKING	XP	Att	%	FG	Att	%
Cone	26	26	100	12	17	71
Hornung	0	0	0	0	4	0

1958 Recognition in Overtime

By putting in a few minutes of overtime, the NFL reaped a multitude of favorable comment from fans, reporters, and television executives. The championship game between the Baltimore Colts and the New York Giants in Yankee Stadium on December 28 was a hard-fought, entertaining contest all afternoon, but when the final gun sounded with the score tied, this match transcended any previous football game. Sudden-death overtime, on the books since 1955 for post-season action, was being played for the first time, with 64,185 paid customers and many millions of television viewers riding the fine edge of tantalizing suspense. With the rule declaring the first team to score the winner, Baltimore's touchdown after eight minutes and fifteen seconds of overtime play gave them the NFL championship, but the league itself won the most, in publicity, in fan approval, and in the television industry's realization of the gem that pro football could be on the tube.

EASTERN CONFERENCE

New York Giants—Needing to win their two final games to tie the Cleveland Browns for the Eastern crown, the Giants trailed Detroit 17-12 at the start of the fourth quarter. With the ball at mid-field, Lions punter Yale Lary faked the kick and tried to run for the first down, only to be collared short of the needed yards. Chuck Conerly then drove his offense to the end zone in five plays, and the defense protected the 19-17 lead to the end. Then came the do-or-die battle with the Browns in New York. With Jimmy Brown running 65 yards for a touchdown on the first play of the game, Cleveland led 10-3 in the fourth quarter until a Conerly TD pass tied the score late in the game. Then, with snow falling and less than a minute left in the game, Pat Summerall drove a 49-yard field goal to win the game 13-10 and force a playoff.

Cleveland Browns—While people last year said that Jimmy Brown could be the greatest runner in football history, Brown this year proved that he already was. Brown shattered Steve Van Buren's old season's rushing mark, establishing a new standard of 1,527 yards. With defenses around the league looking for a way to stop him, only the gang-tackling Giants had any success in stopping Brown and in stopping the Browns. With Milt Plum clicking on short passes and Bobby Mitchell loosening defenses with his outside running, the Browns lost only to the Giants and Lions before meeting the Giants again on the last Sunday of the season. Needing only a tie to clinch the Eastern crown, the Browns lost. In the playoff game the next week in New York, Brown could gain only 8 yards in a 10-0 defeat.

Pittsburgh Steelers—Coach Buddy Parker had won three divisional titles at Detroit with Bobby Layne as his quarterback, so Parker jumped at the chance to get Layne from the Lions two weeks into the regular season. Traded for Earl Morrall and two draft choices, Layne immedicately took over at quarterback and took the winless Steelers to a 24-3 victory over the Philadelphia Eagles. Losses to Cleveland and New York followed, but then the Steelers hit their stride. Over the last seven weeks the Steelers won six and tied one to rush into third place in the East. Tom Tracy, a powerful halfback who also came to Pittsburgh from the Lions, handled the heavy-duty running chores, while Layne quickly hooked up with rookie end Jimmy Orr to form a productive passing combination.

Washington Redskins—With his four-year record at Washington under .500, coach Joe Kuharich needed a winning season to stay on owner George Marshall's payroll. But the club he was running had added no major new talent in years and was sliding from mediocrity into the ranks of the cellar dwellers. Of their last five first draft choices, only fullback Don Bosseler was playing regularly; Steve Meilinger, Ralph Guglielmi, Ed Vereb, and Mike Sommer were either riding the bench or playing elsewhere. Marshall's policy of not signing black players also was hampering the team from getting needed new blood. Another losing season just underlined the need for new players. Marshall responded by firing Kuharich.

Chicago Cardinals—With Pop Ivy the new head coach, the Cards scored more points but kept on losing. Ivy emphasized the offense, often using a double-wing T formation which fostered a pass-oriented attack. Ollie Matson still led the club in ground gaining, but a rookie halfback, John David Crow, showed promise. At quarterback, Ivy alternated Lamar McHan and M. C. Reynolds, while first draft choice King Hill did more watching than playing. The most surprising offensive star was thirty-two-year-old Woodley Lewis, who had become the team's leading receiver after spending most of his career as a defensive back with the Rams.

Philadelphia Eagles—When Buck Shaw, the genial ex-coach of the San Francisco '49ers, took over as the Eagles' new head coach, he immediately went into the market for an experienced quarterback. He came up with a fine passer and strong leader in Norm Van Brocklin, for whom he had to send tackle Buck Lansford, defensive back Jimmy Harris, and a first draft choice to the Los Angeles Rams. Van Brocklin gave the offense a boost with his passing, finding a pair of congenial young receivers in Pete Retzlaff and swift Tommy McDonald, but he needed better blocking from his linemen before he could consistently put points on the scoreboard. The defense also needed redoing, with Jess Richardson, Bob Pellegrini, and Tom Brookshier the only regulars destined to last through 1960 with the club.

WESTERN CONFERENCE

Baltimore Colts—With Baltimore fans packing Municipal Stadium for every game and fanatically cheering their team on, the Colts stormed out to a large lead in the West by winning their first six decisions handily. But in the sixth game, a 56-0 rout of the Packers, a hard tackle by Green Bay's Johnny Symank put quarterback Johnny Unitas in the hospital with three broken ribs and a punctured lung. With Unitas out indefinitely, George Shaw took over at quarterback and threw three touchdown passes in New York, although the Giants won the game 24-21. Then the Colts shut out the Bears 17-0 and swamped the Rams 34-7, a game in which Unitas returned to action briefly. The next week, with Unitas at the helm, the Colts fought back from a 27-7 halftime deficit to beat the '49ers 35-27 and clinch the crown.

Chicago Bears—After last year's 5-7-0 record, owner George Halas threw aside his past promises to hire a younger coach and again took up the coaching reigns, saying, "There's some new stuff I have in mind that I would like to try." The Bears didn't show much new stuff, but they did carry out their assignments with the hard-hitting precision of earlier Halas teams. The defense, staffed with the likes of Bill George, Doug Atkins, and Joe Fortunato, turned in ten good performances, falling down only in early-season losses to Baltimore and Los Angeles. And even without a full recovery by injured receiver Harlon Hill, the attack showed new life and muscle in moving the ball. The Bears had a chance to pull within one game of the top by beating the Colts late in the season, but the Baltimore defense knocked the Bears out of contention by shutting them out.

Los Angeles Rams—Sid Gillman made three moves which jazzed up the Ram offense and made the team interesting to watch: He junked the two-quarterback system, he put Jon Arnett into the starting backfield, and he shifted Del Shofner from defense to offense. Gillman installed young Billy Wade as his full-time quarterback, dealing veteran Norm Van Brocklin off to the Eagles, and Wade responded with a fine season. Given a starting halfback job in addition to his kick-return duties, Arnett rocketed to stardom with his jackrabbit quickness, using his speed and moves best on end runs and on screen passes. And Shofner turned out to be a worthy successor to the retired Crazy Legs Hirsch, shifting from the defensive backfield to become one of the league's top deep receiving threats.

San Francisco '49ers—The '49ers had entertained fans for years with their wide-open offensive style, but as the decade began to reach the end of the string, so were many of the '49er players. A lifeless break-even season underlined the advancing age of Y. A. Tittle, Joe Perry, Hugh McElhenny, Billy Wilson and Leo Nomellini. Coach Frankie Albert started easing some young talent into the lineup, as John Brodie often spelled Tittle at quarterback, J.D. Smith saw action at halfback, Clyde Connor and R.C. Owens were starting receivers, and rookie Abe Woodson filled a defensive secondary spot in addition to running back kicks.

Detroit Lions—After two games of this year, the Lions closed out an era in their history by trading quarterback Bobby Layne, ring leader of the champions of the early 1950s, to the Pittsburgh Steelers. Coach George Wilson was protected at quarterback with Tobin Rote, but injuries decimated the ranks at other positions to turn the season into a dragging catastrophe. A slow start of three losses and a tie in the first four contests wiped out any dreams of another championship, and a mid-season drive for a .500 season was stymied by close losses on the last two Sundays of the season.

Green Bay Packers—Bart Starr, Jim Taylor, and Paul Hornung were in the backfield, Jim Ringo, Jerry Kramer, and Forrest Gregg held jobs in the offensive line, and Ray Nitschke, Jess Whittenton, Dan Currie, and Bill Forester played on defense. But these were not the championship Packers of Vince Lombardi that would take the league by storm in the early 1960s; these were the pitiful Packers of Ray McLean, a team that would win only one game in a brutally demoralizing season. Although Taylor, Kramer, Nitschke, and Currie were rookies, the Packer fans saw no hope at all in this abject squad, and the executive committee went hunting for a new head coach after the season.

FINAL TEAM STATISTICS

OFFENSE

	BALT.	CHI.B.	CHI.C.	CLEVE.	DET.	G.BAY	L.A.	N.Y.	PHIL.	PITT.	S.F.	WASH.
FIRST DOWNS:												
Total	253	202	219	206	195	177	209	191	222	202	237	213
by Rushing	117	95	80	127	89	76	93	93	72	77	93	111
by Passing	120	94	124	71	95	87	104	83	125	107	126	90
by Penalty	16	13	15	8	11	14	12	15	25	18	18	12
RUSHING:												
Number	456	437	366	475	364	345	345	450	334	394	359	480
Yards	2127	1770	1456	2526	1360	1421	1734	1725	1093	1521	1628	1977
Average Yards	4.7	4.1	4.0	5.3	3.7	4.1	5.0	3.8	3.3	3.9	4.5	4.1
Touchdowns	24	15	9	24	9	7	18	14	13	14	18	11
PASSING:												
Attempts	354	321	407	206	319	348	358	266	402	336	383	251
Completions	178	146	198	110	141	161	186	119	214	156	223	121
Completion Percentage	50.3	45.5	48.6	53.4	44.2	46.3	52.0	44.7	53.2	46.4	58.2	48.2
Gross Yards	2537	2021	2735	1758	2148	2118	2909	1718	2772	2895	2691	1989
Yards Lost Passing	125	210	161	177	279	298	237	113	75	143	208	293
Net Yards	2412	1811	2574	1581	1869	1820	2672	1605	2697	2752	2483	1696
Avg. Yards per Attempt (Grs)	7.2	6.3	6.7	8.5	6.7	6.1	8.1	6.5	6.9	8.6	7.0	7.9
Avg. Yards per Comp. (Gross)	14.3	13.8	13.8	16.0	15.2	11.4	15.6	14.4	13.0	18.6	12.1	16.4
Touchdowns	26	18	23	12	20	15	19	15	18	16	15	14
Interceptions	11	24	27	14	14	27	26	12	21	21	29	17
Percent Intercepted	3.1	7.5	6.6	6.8	4.4	7.8	7.3	4.5	5.2	6.3	7.6	6.8
PUNTS:												
Number	62	59	57	51	60	62	51	65	54	51	48	48
Average Distance	36.7	39.4	37.8	41.2	42.5	42.3	40.9	44.0	41.2	39.7	38.3	45.4
PUNT RETURNS:												
Number	39	38	39	39	41	33	41	42	47	45	35	32
Yards	237	156	259	318	223	179	239	168	333	301	146	143
Average Yards	6.1	4.1	6.6	8.2	5.4	5.4	5.8	4.0	7.1	6.7	4.2	4.5
Touchdowns	0	0	0	1	1	0	0	0	0	0	0	0
KICKOFF RETURNS:												
Number	34	37	61	38	39	60	43	34	45	36	39	40
Yards	864	954	1532	908	839	1309	835	700	900	774	790	891
Average Yards	25.4	25.8	25.1	23.9	21.5	21.8	19.4	20.6	20.0	21.5	20.3	22.3
Touchdowns	2	1	2	2	1	0	0	0	0	0	0	0
INTERCEPTION RETURNS:												
Number	35	22	15	18	22	13	28	21	15	24	16	16
Yards	514	221	121	285	328	174	490	294	206	248	114	191
Average Yards	14.7	10.0	8.1	17.8	14.9	13.4	17.5	14.0	13.7	10.3	7.1	11.9
Touchdowns	1	1	0	1	1	1	5	0	0	0	1	0
PENALTIES:												
Number	55	76	71	59	52	52	67	44	55	78	58	40
Yards	518	742	615	554	513	545	636	379	570	875	619	365
FUMBLES:												
Number	26	29	37	14	36	26	34	29	41	32	31	18
Number Lost	11	19	22	8	19	17	23	14	22	21	11	16
POINTS:												
Total	381	298	261	302	261	193	344	246	235	261	257	214
PAT Attempts	52	38	35	40	32	23	42	30	31	31	33	25
PAT Made	48	37	33	38	30	22	42	28	31	31	29	25
FG Attempts	14	23	17	19	23	21	25	23	14	28	21	26
FG Made	5	11	6	8	11	11	14	12	6	14	8	13
Percent FG Made	35.7	47.8	35.3	42.1	47.8	52.4	56.0	52.2	42.9	50.0	38.1	50.0
Safeties	0	0	0	0	0	0	1	1	0	1	0	0

DEFENSE

	BALT.	CHI.B.	CHI.C.	CLEVE.	DET.	G.BAY	L.A.	N.Y.	PHIL.	PITT.	S.F.	WASH.
FIRST DOWNS:												
Total	188	168	253	201	199	236	235	170	225	209	227	215
by Rushing	70	67	121	82	94	109	109	83	101	81	106	100
by Passing	106	84	114	104	95	111	110	80	100	114	106	102
by Penalty	12	17	18	15	10	16	16	7	24	14	15	13
RUSHING:												
Number	331	351	449	369	407	427	405	399	488	403	380	396
Yards	1291	1297	2133	1448	1720	2040	1777	1440	1929	1491	2038	1734
Average Yards	3.9	3.7	4.8	3.9	4.2	4.8	4.4	3.6	4.0	3.7	5.4	4.4
Touchdowns	13	12	26	6	19	24	12	7	15	14	15	13
PASSING:												
Attempts	363	327	337	312	320	336	381	311	289	334	341	300
Completions	168	153	171	162	167	175	188	142	138	173	163	153
Completion Percentage	46.3	46.8	50.7	51.9	52.2	52.1	49.3	45.7	47.8	51.8	47.8	51.0
Gross Yards	2248	2142	2793	2387	2255	2653	2303	2130	2244	2136	2218	2782
Yards Lost Passing	255	373	166	175	138	78	252	152	126	244	246	114
Net Yards	1993	1769	2627	2212	2117	2575	2051	1978	2118	1892	1972	2668
Avg. Yards per Attempt (Grs)	6.2	6.6	8.3	7.7	7.0	7.9	6.0	6.8	7.8	6.4	6.5	9.3
Avg. Yards per Comp. (Gross)	13.4	14.0	16.3	14.7	13.5	15.2	12.3	15.0	16.3	12.3	13.6	18.2
Touchdowns	9	14	18	20	15	24	21	11	22	11	25	21
Interceptions	35	22	15	16	22	13	28	21	15	24	16	16
Percent Intercepted	9.6	6.7	4.5	5.1	6.9	3.9	7.3	6.8	5.2	7.2	4.7	5.3
PUNTS:												
Number	62	73	54	55	55	42	65	56	53	62	49	42
Average Distance	44.1	37.5	41.2	42.7	40.2	41.6	37.9	41.7	43.1	42.0	40.7	36.8
PUNT RETURNS:												
Number	40	36	35	38	44	46	33	51	41	38	38	33
Yards	176	376	154	95	151	268	143	376	363	233	132	235
Average Yards	4.4	10.4	4.4	2.5	3.4	5.8	4.3	7.4	8.9	6.1	3.7	7.1
Touchdowns	1	0	0	0	0	0	0	0	1	0	0	0
KICKOFF RETURNS:												
Number	43	48	41	48	33	32	53	40	40	50	42	36
Yards	1241	1072	933	1045	683	710	1116	889	961	1115	739	792
Average Yards	28.9	22.3	22.8	21.8	20.7	22.2	21.1	22.2	24.0	22.3	17.6	22.0
Touchdowns	1	1	1	0	0	0	1	0	1	2	0	1
INTERCEPTION RETURNS:												
Number	11	24	27	14	14	27	26	12	21	21	29	17
Yards	169	380	210	134	193	371	316	123	242	330	448	270
Average Yards	15.4	15.8	7.8	9.6	13.8	13.7	12.2	10.3	11.5	15.7	15.4	15.9
Touchdowns	3	1	0	0	1	1	2	1	0	0	2	0
PENALTIES:												
Number	60	77	68	37	52	72	47	45	74	62	52	61
Yards	555	832	696	347	458	657	476	451	722	585	510	642
FUMBLES:												
Number	31	34	29	27	27	31	22	35	18	34	32	33
Number Lost	17	18	16	18	16	19	13	19	12	18	15	22
POINTS:												
Total	203	230	356	217	276	382	278	183	306	230	324	268
PAT Attempts	26	28	46	26	35	49	37	22	39	28	41	35
PAT Made	23	26	44	26	34	46	35	21	39	26	40	34
FG Attempts	17	24	25	23	19	25	21	19	23	20	17	21
FG Made	6	12	12	11	8	12	7	10	11	12	10	8
Percent FG Made	35.3	50.0	48.0	47.8	42.1	48.0	30.0	52.6	47.8	60.0	58.8	38.1
Safeties	0	0	0	1	1	0	0	0	0	0	1	0

1958 CHAMPIONSHIP GAME

December 28, at New York
(Attendance 64,185)

SCORING

NEW YORK	3	0	7	7	0–17
BALTIMORE	0	14	0	3	6–23

First Quarter

N. Y.	Summerall, 36 yard field goal	12:58

Second Quarter

Balt.	Ameche, 2 yard rush	2:26
	PAT – Myhra (kick)	
Balt.	Berry, 15 yard pass from Unitas	13:40
	PAT – Myhra (kick)	

Third Quarter

N. Y.	Triplett, 1 yard rush	11:14
	PAT – Summerall (kick)	

Fourth Quarter

N.Y.	Gifford, 15 yard pass from Conerly	0:53
	PAT – Summerall (kick)	
Balt.	Myhra, 20 yard field goal	14:53

Sudden Death

Balt.	Ameche, 1 yard rush	8:15
	No PAT Attempt made	

TEAM STATISTICS

N. Y.		BALT.
10	First Downs – Total	27
3	First Downs – Rushing	10
7	First Downs – Passing	17
0	First Downs – Penalty	0
6	Fumbles – Number	2
4	Fumbles – Lost Ball	2
2	Penalties – Number	3
22	Yards Penalized	15
0	Field Goals Missed	2
4	Giveaways	3
3	Takeaways	4
–1	Difference	+1

One for the Books

When the game began it was simply a showdown for the championship of professional football between the Baltimore Colts and New York Giants. When the game ended it became the kind of contest which inspires folklore as well as finding a special place in the history books. The action began on a Johnny Unitas to Lenny Moore 60-yard pass play. That quick drive soon ended in a Steve Myhra 27-yard field-goal attempt that was blocked by Sam Huff. Before the first quarter was over, Frank Gifford took the ball 38 yards on an end sweep to put the Giants on the Colts' 27-yard line. Pat Summerall then sent the ball 36 yards for a 3-0 Giant lead. In the second quarter Gifford fumbled on the Giants' 20, and five plays later Alan Ameche went over for the score. Several plays later, on another Gifford fumble, the Colts marched downfield, Unitas passed 15 yards to Ray Berry, and Myhra converted to make it 14-3. In the third period the Giants tallied to make the score 14-10. In the beginning of the fourth quarter Chuck Conerly fired to Gifford to put the Giants in front, after the extra point, 17-14. Then, with less than two minutes to go, Unitas moved the ball to the New York 13, and with seven seconds remaining Myhra booted the tying field goal. It was now sudden death and the Giants got the ball, but they were unable to reach the scoreboard. The Colts then moved from their own 20 and, 12 plays later, including a 33-yard pass from Unitas to Berry, reached the Giants' one-yard line, where Ameche went over at 8:15 to give the Colts the historic 23-17 victory.

INDIVIDUAL STATISTICS

NEW YORK	No.	Yds	Avg.	BALTIMORE	No.	Yds	Avg.
RUSHING							
Gifford	12	60	5.0	Ameche	14	59	4.2
Webster	9	24	2.7	Dupre	11	30	2.7
Triplett	5	12	2.4	Unitas	4	26	6.5
Conerly	2	5	2.5	Moore	9	24	2.7
King	3	–13	–4.3		38	139	3.7
	31	88	2.8				
RECEIVING							
Gifford	3	14	4.7	Berry	12	178	14.8
Rote	2	76	38.0	Moore	5	99	19.8
Schnelker	2	63	31.5	Mutscheller	4	63	15.8
Webster	2	17	8.5	Ameche	3	14	4.7
Triplett	2	15	7.5	Dupre	2	7	3.5
McAfee	1	15	15.0		26	361	13.9
	12	200	16.7				
PUNTING							
Chandler	6		45.6	Brown	4		50.8
PUNT RETURNS							
Maynard	2	13	6.5	Taseff	2	8	4.0
Patton	1	14	14.0	Simpson	1	0	0.0
Crow	1	0	0.0		3	8	2.7
	4	27	6.8				
KICKOFF RETURNS							
Maynard	2	28	14.0	Lyle	2	38	19.0
Brown	1	0	0.0	Simpson	1	23	23.0
Triplett	Lat	18	–		3	61	20.3
	3	46	15.3				
INTERCEPTION RETURNS							
Crow	1	5	5.0	None			

PASSING

	Att	Comp	Comp Pct.	Yds	Int	Yds/ Att.	Yds/ Comp	Yards Lost Tackled
NEW YORK								
Conerly	14	10	71.4	187	0	13.4	18.7	3–30
Heinrich	4	2	50.0	13	0	3.3	6.5	0
	18	12	66.7	200	0	11.1	16.7	3–30
BALTIMORE								
Unitas	40	26	65.0	361	1	9.0	13.9	5–38

NEW YORK GIANTS 9-3-0 Jim Lee Howell

Scores of Each Game		
37	Chic. Cards	7
24	Philadelphia	27
21	Washington	14
6	CHIC. CARDS	23
17	PITTSBURGH	6
21	Cleveland	17
24	BALTIMORE	21
10	Pittsburgh	31
30	WASHINGTON	0
24	PHILADELPHIA	10
19	Detroit	17
13	CLEVELAND	10
	Playoff	
10	CLEVELAND	0

Use Name	Pos.	Hgt	Wgt	Age	Int	Pts
Rosey Brown	OT	6'3"	245	25		
Frank Youso	OT	6'4"	260	22		
Al Barry	OG	6'2"	230	27		
Buzz Guy	OG	6'3"	248	23		
Jon Jelacic	OG	6'3"	230	21		
Bob Mischak	OG	6'	240	25		
Jack Stroud	OG	6'1"	235	29		
Ray Wietecha	C	6'1"	225	29		
Jim Katkavage	DE	6'3"	235	23		2
Andy Robustelli	DE	6'1"	235	32		
Pat Summerall	DE	6'4"	230	28		64
Rosey Grier	DT	6'5"	275	25		
Dick Modzelewski	DT	6'	260	27		
M. L. Brackett	DE-DT	6'5"	248	25		

Use Name	Pos.	Hgt	Wgt	Age	Int	Pts
Sam Huff	LB	6'1"	230	23	2	
Cliff Livingston	LB	6'3"	210	28		
Harland Svare	LB	6'	215	27	1	
Bill Svoboda	LB	6'	210	31		
Lindon Crow	DB	6'1"	187	25	3	
Ed Hughes	DB	6'1"	185	30		
Carl Karilivacz	DB	6'	190	27	3	6
Jimmy Patton	DB	6	180	26	11	
Em Tunnell	DB	6'1"	200	36	1	
Billy Lott	HB-DB	6'	195	23		

Jerry Huth — Military Service

Use Name	Pos.	Hgt	Wgt	Age	Int	Pts
Chuck Conerly	QB	6'1"	185	34		
Tom Dublinski	QB	6'2"	208	28		
Don Heinrich	QB	6'	180	26		6
Don Chandler	HB	6'2"	205	23		
Frank Gifford	HB	6'1"	205	28		60
Don Maynard	HB	6'	178	22		
Alex Webster	HB	6'3"	210	27		36
Phil King	FB-HB	6'4"	225	22		6
Mel Triplett	FB	6'1"	215	26		6
Ken MacAfee	OE	6'2"	215	28		12
Kyle Rote	OE	6'	205	29		18
Bob Schnelker	OE	6'3"	215	28		30

CLEVELAND BROWNS 9-3-0 Paul Brown

Scores of Each Game		
30	Los Angeles	27
45	Pittsburgh	12
35	CHIC. CARDS	28
27	PITTSBURGH	10
38	Chic. Cards	24
17	NEW YORK	21
10	DETROIT	30
20	Washington	10
28	PHILADELPHIA	14
21	WASHINGTON	14
21	Philadelphia	14
10	New York	13
	Playoff	
0	New York	10

Use Name	Pos.	Hgt	Wgt	Age	Int	Pts
Lou Groza	OT	6'3"	248	34		60
Mike McCormack	OT	6'4"	247	31		
Willie McClung	DT-OT	6'2"	260	29		
Gene Hickerson	OG	6'3"	242	23		
Jim Ray Smith	OG	6'3"	242	27		
Chuck Noll	C-OG	6'1"	224	26		
Art Hunter	C	6'4"	242	25		
Bill Quinlan	DE	6'3"	250	26		
Paul Wiggin	DE	6'3"	237	24		
Willie Davis	OT-DE	6'3"	240	25		
Don Colo	DT	6'3"	254	33		
Bob Gain	DT	6'3"	260	30		
Henry Jordan	DT	6'3"	247	23		

Use Name	Pos.	Hgt	Wgt	Age	Int	Pts
Tom Catlin	LB	6'1"	213	27		
Vince Costello	LB	6'	224	26		
Galen Fiss	LB	6'	227	28		
Walt Michaels	LB	6'	230	29		
Kenny Konz	DB	5'10"	187	30	4	6
Warren Lahr	DB	5'11"	192	34	1	
Don Paul	DB	6'	192	32	4	
Jim Shofner	DB	6'2"	196	22	1	
Junior Wren	DB	6'	192	28	3	
Bobby Freeman	HB-DB	6'1"	205	25	3	

Use Name	Pos.	Hgt	Wgt	Age	Int	Pts
Jim Ninowski	QB	6'1"	210	22		
Milt Plum	QB	6'1"	205	24		26
Leroy Bolden	HB	5'8"	170	25		6
Lew Carpenter	HB	6'1"	210	26		12
Bobby Mitchell	HB	6'	188	23		36
Jimmy Brown	FB	6'2"	228	22		108
Ed Modzelewski	FB	6'	222	29		
Ray Renfro	HB-FL	6'1"	190	27		36
Darrell Brewster	OE	6'3"	210	28		6
Preston Carpenter	OE	6'2"	192	24		6
Frank Clarke	OE	6'	207	25		
Dick Deschaine	K	6'	210	28		

PITTSBURGH STEELERS 7-4-1 Buddy Parker

Scores of Each Game		
20	San Francisco	23
12	CLEVELAND	45
24	PHILADELPHIA	3
10	Cleveland	27
6	New York	17
24	WASHINGTON	16
31	Philadelphia	24
31	NEW YORK	10
27	Chic. Cards	20
24	CHIC. BEARS	10
14	Washington	14
38	CHIC. CARDS	21

Use Name	Pos.	Hgt	Wgt	Age	Int	Pts
Darrell Dess	OT	6'	235	22		
Frank Varrichione	OT	6'1"	230	26		
Ted Karras	LB-OT	6'1"	235	25		
Billy Krisher	OG	6'1"	230	22		
John Nisby	OG	6'1"	230	25		
Mike Sandusky	OG	6'	230	25		
Ed Beatty	C	6'3"	225	26		
Billy Ray Smith	DE	6'4"	230	23		
George Tarasovic	DE	6'4"	245	29		
Joe Krupa	DT	6'2"	225	25		
Joe Lewis	DT	6'2"	260	23	1	
Ernie Stautner	DE-DT	6'1"	230	33		2

Use Name	Pos.	Hgt	Wgt	Age	Int	Pts
Dick Campbell	LB	6'1"	225	22	1	
Dale Dodrill	LB	6'1"	215	33	1	
Bob Dougherty	LB	6'	235	24		
Dick Lasse	LB	6'2"	220	22		
John Reger	LB	6'	230	27	1	
Dick Alban	DB	6'	195	29	5	
Jack Butler	DB	6'	195	30	9	
Dean Derby	DB	6'	185	24	4	
Gary Glick	DB	6'2"	190	27	2	6
Richie McCabe	DB	6'1"	185	24		

Use Name	Pos.	Hgt	Wgt	Age	Int	Pts
Len Dawson	QB	6'	180	24		
Bobby Layne (from DET)	QB	6'1"	208	31		19
Dick Christy	HB	5'10"	180	22		
Billy Reynolds	HB	5'10"	200	26		6
Tom Tracy	HB	5'9"	205	26		54
Leo Elter	FB	5'10"	205	29		12
Larry Krutko	FB	6'	220	23		
Tank Younger	FB	6'3"	230	30		18
Don Bishop	HB-FL	6'2"	210	23		
Joe Evans	OE	6'4"	205	22		
Dick Lucas	OE	6'2"	210	24		
Jack McClairen	OE	6'4"	210	27		6
Jimmy Orr	OE	5'11"	195	22		42
Ray Mathews	HB-OE	6'	195	29		24
Tom Miner	K	6'4"	235	28		73

WASHINGTON REDSKINS 4-7-1 Joe Kuharich

Scores of Each Game		
24	Philadelphia	14
10	Chic. Cards	37
14	NEW YORK	21
37	GREEN BAY	21
10	Baltimore	35
16	Pittsburgh	24
45	CHIC. CARDS	31
10	CLEVELAND	20
0	New York	30
14	Cleveland	21
14	PITTSBURGH	14
20	PHILADELPHIA	0

Use Name	Pos.	Hgt	Wgt	Age	Int	Pts
Don Boll	OT	6'2"	272	31		
Ray Lemek	OT	6'	237	24		
Will Renfro	DT-OT	6'5"	240	26		
Dick Stanfel	OG	6'3"	230	31		
Red Stephens	OG	6'	232	28		
Ed Voytek	OG	6'2"	240	23		
Jim Schrader	C	6'2"	236	26		
Johnny Allen	LB-C	6'2"	227	26		
Gene Brito	DE	6'1"	230	31		
Bob Dee	DE	6'3"	230	25		
Chet Ostrowski	DT-DE	6'1"	235	28		
Jim Weatherall	DT	6'4"	245	28		
Johnny Miller	OT-DT	6'5"	250	24		

Use Name	Pos.	Hgt	Wgt	Age	Int	Pts
Charlie Brueckman	LB	6'2"	220	22		
Chuck Drazenovich	LB	6'1"	230	31	2	
Ralph Felton	LB	5'11"	210	26		
Bill Fulcher	LB	6'	200	24		
Frank Kuchta	LB	6'2"	220	22		
Gene Cichowski	DB	6'	195	24		
Dick Lynch	DB	6'1"	200	22	2	
Doyle Nix	DB	6'1"	188	25	3	
Mike Sommer	DB	5'11"	187	23		
Les Walters	DB	6'	185	21	1	
Dick James	HB-DB	5'9"	180	24	4	6
Scooter Scudero	HB-DB	5'10"	174	28	2	

John Paluck — Military Service

Use Name	Pos.	Hgt	Wgt	Age	Int	Pts
Rudy Bukich (to Chi B)	QB	6'1"	200	27		
Ralph Guglielmi	QB	6'1"	195	25		
Eddie LeBaron	QB	5'9"	165	28		
Jim Podoley	HB	6'2"	200	25		24
Ed Sutton	HB	6'1"	207	23		18
Sid Watson	HB	5'11"	194	25		6
Bert Zagers	DB-HB	5'10"	185	25	2	6
Don Bosseler	FB	6'1"	207	22		24
Johnny Olszewski	FB	5'11"	202	27		12
Bill Anderson	OE	6'3"	195	22		12
Tom Braatz (from LA)	OE	6'1"	215	25		
Johnny Carson	OE	6'3"	200	28		12
Joe Walton	OE	5'11"	205	23		30
Sam Baker	K	6'2"	217	26		64

CHICAGO CARDINALS 2-9-1 Pop Ivy

Scores of Each Game		
7	NEW YORK	37
37	WASHINGTON	10
28	Cleveland	35
23	New York	6
24	CLEVELAND	38
21	PHILADELPHIA	21
31	Washington	45
21	Philadelphia	49
20	PITTSBURGH	27
14	LOS ANGELES	20
14	Chic. Bears	30
21	Pittsburgh	38

Use Name	Pos.	Hgt	Wgt	Age	Int	Pts
Ed Cook	OT	6'2"	250	26		
Bob Cross	OT	6'4"	250	27		
Jim McCusker	OT	6'2"	245	22		
Bob Konovsky	OG	6'2"	245	24		
Dale Meinert	OT-OG	6'4"	218	25		
Ed Husmann	DE-LB-OG	6'	230	27		
Don Gillis	C	6'3"	240	24		
Jim Taylor	LB-C	6'2"	230	24	1	
Leo Sugar	DE	6'1"	210	29		
Luke Owens	DT-DE	6'2"	255	25		
Ed Culpepper	DT	6'1"	255	24		
Chuck Ulrich	DT	6'4"	250	27		

Jimmy Hill — Arm Injury

Use Name	Pos.	Hgt	Wgt	Age	Int	Pts
Carl Brettschneider	LB	6'1"	220	26		
Doug Eggers	LB	6'	215	28		
Ken Gray	LB	6'2"	235	22		
Jack Patera	LB	6'1"	225	26		
Jerry Tubbs (to SF)	LB	6'2"	216	23		
Chuck Weber	LB	6'1"	225	29		
Bobby Joe Conrad	DB	6'	180	23	4	51
Bobby Gordon	DB	6'	195	22	2	
Charlie Jackson	DB	5'11"	180	22	1	
Lowell Lander	DB	6'	195	25		
Night Train Lane	DB	6'1"	190	30	2	
Dick Nolan	DB	6'1"	185	26	5	

John Roach — Military Service
John Dittrich — Military Service

Use Name	Pos.	Hgt	Wgt	Age	Int	Pts
King Hill	QB	6'3"	207	22		
Lamar McHan	QB	6'1"	200	26		6
M. C. Reynolds	QB	6'	190	23		
Joe Childress	HB	6'	200	24		24
Ollie Matson	HB	6'2"	210	28		60
Jimmy Sears	HB	5'11"	185	27		12
Bobby Watkins	HB	5'10"	195	26		6
Mal Hammack	FB	6'2"	205	25		6
Dean Philpott	FB	6'	200	23		
John David Crow	HB-FB	6'2"	215	23		38
Max Boydston	OE	6'2"	207	25		6
Woodley Lewis	OE	6'	195	33		24
Gern Nagler	OE	6'2"	190	25		30

PHILADELPHIA EAGLES 2-9-1 Buck Shaw

Scores of Each Game		
14	WASHINGTON	24
27	NEW YORK	24
3	Pittsburgh	24
24	SAN FRANCISCO	30
35	Green Bay	38
21	Chic. Cards	21
24	PITTSBURGH	31
49	CHIC. CARDS	21
14	Cleveland	28
10	New York	24
14	CLEVELAND	21
0	Washington	20

Use Name	Pos.	Hgt	Wgt	Age	Int	Pts
Proverb Jacobs	OT	6'4"	255	23		
Lum Snyder	OT	6'5"	230	28		
Len Szafaryn	OT	6'2"	230	30		
Harold Bradley	OG	6'2"	230	29		
Ken Huxhold	OG	6'1"	235	29		
Galen Laack*	OG	6'	230	26		
Chuck Bednarik	C	6'3"	235	33		
John Simerson (to PIT)	C	6'3"	258	23		
Marion Campbell	DE	6'3"	255	29		
Ed Cooke (from Chi B)	DE	6'4"	238	23		
Ed Meadows	DE	6'2"	225	26		
Ed Khayat	DT	6'3"	225	23		
Don Owens	DT	6'5"	250	26		
Jess Richardson	DT	6'2"	272	28		
Sid Youngelman	DT	6'3"	255	26		
Volney Peters	DE-DT	6'4"	245	30		

Use Name	Pos.	Hgt	Wgt	Age	Int	Pts
Bill Koman	LB	6'2"	235	24	1	
Bob Pellegrini	LB	6'2"	225	23	4	
Tom Scott	LB	6'2"	220	28	2	
Tom Louderback	OG-C-LB	6'2"	234	24		
Eddie Bell	DB	6'1"	212	27	2	
Tom Brookshier	DB	6'	198	26	1	
Jerry Norton	DB	5'11"	195	28	1	
Lee Riley	DB	6'1"	190	26	1	
Bob Hudson	LB-DB	6'4"	230	28	1	

Ken Keller — Military Service
Tom Saidock — Military Service

*Laack — died 1/1/59 — Auto Accident

Use Name	Pos.	Hgt	Wgt	Age	Int	Pts
Sonny Jurgensen	QB	5'11"	200	24		
Norm Van Brocklin	QB	6'1"	202	32		6
Billy Barnes	HB	5'11"	202	23		42
Billy Wells	HB	5'9"	178	26		6
Brad Myers	DB-OE-HB	6'1"	195	28		
Clarence Peaks	FB	6'1"	218	22		30
Walt Kowalczyk	DB-FB	6'	205	23	1	6
Tommy McDonald	FL	5'10"	182	24		54
Pete Retzlaff	FL-OE	6'1"	210	27		12
Dick Bielski	OE	6'1"	218	26		6
Gene Mitcham	OE	6'2"	206	26		6
Andy Nacrelli	OE	6'1"	190	25		
Bobby Walston	OE	6'	190	29		67

NEW YORK GIANTS

RUSHING

Last Name	No.	Yds	Avg	TD
Gifford	115	468	4.1	8
Triplett	118	466	3.9	1
Webster	100	398	4.0	3
King	83	316	3.8	1
Maynard	12	45	3.8	0
Lott	4	30	7.5	0
Chandler	1	15	15.0	0
Heinrich	5	4	0.8	1
Conerly	12	−17	−1.4	0

RECEIVING

Last Name	No.	Yds	Avg	TD
Gifford	29	330	11	2
Webster	25	279	11	3
Schnelker	24	460	19	5
Rote	12	244	20	3
King	11	132	12	0
Triplett	7	110	16	0
Maynard	5	84	17	0
MacAfee	5	52	10	2
Mischak	1	27	27	0

PUNT RETURNS

Last Name	No.	Yds	Avg	TD
Maynard	24	117	5	0
Crow	11	46	4	0
Patton	1	5	5	0
Tunnell	6	0	0	0

KICKOFF RETURNS

Last Name	No.	Yds	Avg	TD
Maynard	11	284	26	0
King	13	279	21	0
Lott	5	78	16	0
Triplett	4	59	15	0
Brown	1	0	0	0

PASSING – PUNTING – KICKING

PASSING	Att	Comp	%	Yds	Yd/Att	TD	Int–%	RK
Conerly	184	88	48	1199	6.0	10	9– 5	11
Heinrich	68	26	38	369	5.4	4	2– 3	
Gifford	10	3	30	109	10.9	1	1– 10	
Dublinski	3	1	33	14	4.7	0	0– 0	
Chandler	1	1	100	27	27.0	0	0– 0	

PUNTING	No	Avg
Chandler	65	44.0

KICKING	XP	Att	%	FG	Att	%
Summerall	28	30	93	12	23	52

CLEVELAND BROWNS

RUSHING

Last Name	No.	Yds	Avg	TD
Brown	257	1527	5.9	17
Mitchell	80	500	6.3	1
L. Carpenter	73	308	4.2	2
Plum	37	107	2.8	4
Bolden	15	55	3.7	0
Renfro	3	17	5.7	0
Modzelewski	3	8	2.7	0
P. Carpenter	3	2	0.7	0
Freeman	2	1	0.5	0
Ninowski	1	1	0.5	0

RECEIVING

Last Name	No.	Yds	Avg	TD
P. Carpenter	29	474	16	1
Renfro	24	573	24	6
Brewster	16	294	18	1
Brown	16	138	9	1
Mitchell	16	131	8	3
L. Carpenter	5	47	9	0
Clarke	3	91	30	0
Modzelewski	1	10	10	0

PUNT RETURNS

Last Name	No.	Yds	Avg	TD
Mitchell	14	165	9	1
Konz	18	143	8	0
Shofner	4	10	3	0
Paul	2	0	0	0
Wren	1	0	0	0

KICKOFF RETURNS

Last Name	No.	Yds	Avg	TD
Mitchell	18	454	25	1
Bolden	14	362	26	1
Brown	3	74	25	0
L. Carpenter	1	18	18	0
McClung	1	0	0	0
Paul	1	0	0	0

PASSING – PUNTING – KICKING

PASSING	Att	Comp	%	Yds	Yd/Att	TD	Int–%	RK
Plum	189	102	54	1619	8.6	11	11– 6	2
Ninowski	17	8	47	139	8.2	1	3– 18	

PUNTING	No	Avg
Deschaine	50	41.3
Wren	1	38.0

KICKING	XP	Att	%	FG	Att	%
Groza	36	38	94	8	19	42
Plum	2	2	100	0	0	0

PITTSBURGH STEELERS

RUSHING

Last Name	No.	Yds	Avg	TD
Tracy	169	714	4.2	5
Younger	88	344	3.9	3
Layne	40	154	3.9	3
Elter	37	104	2.8	2
Christy	38	101	2.7	0
Reynolds	10	29	2.9	1
Mathews	4	24	6.0	0
Orr	1	8	8.0	0
Krutko	4	6	1.5	0
Dawson	2	−1	−0.5	0

RECEIVING

Last Name	No.	Yds	Avg	TD
Orr	33	910	28	7
Tracy	32	535	17	4
McClairen	29	491	17	1
Mathews	25	525	21	4
Younger	16	188	12	0
Christy	7	73	10	0
Elter	6	68	11	0
Lucas	4	47	12	0
Bishop	3	57	19	0
Reynolds	1	1	1	0

PUNT RETURNS

Last Name	No.	Yds	Avg	TD
Christy	17	153	9	0
Reynolds	25	143	6	0
Dodrill	1	5	5	0
Glick	2	0	0	0

KICKOFF RETURNS

Last Name	No.	Yds	Avg	TD
Christy	16	384	24	0
Reynolds	15	346	23	0
Varrichione	3	38	13	0
Karras	1	6	6	0
McClairen	1	0	0	0

PASSING – PUNTING – KICKING

PASSING	Att	Comp	%	Yds	Yd/Att	TD	Int–%	RK
Layne	294	145	49	2510	8.5	14	12– 4	2
Tracy	16	6	38	270	16.9	2	2– 12	
Dawson	6	1	17	11	1.8	0	2– 33	

PUNTING	No	Avg
Orr	61	39.7

KICKING	XP	Att	%	FG	Att	%
Miner	31	31	100	14	28	50
Layne	1	3	33	0	0	0

WASHINGTON REDSKINS

RUSHING

Last Name	No.	Yds	Avg	TD
Olszewski	98	505	5.2	2
Bosseler	109	475	4.4	4
Sutton	93	335	3.6	3
Podoley	48	169	3.5	0
Watson	46	166	3.6	0
James	24	88	3.7	1
Zagers	27	82	3.0	1
Guglielmi	17	74	4.4	0
Scudero	5	30	6.0	0
LeBaron	12	30	2.5	0
Bukich	2	16	8.0	0

RECEIVING

Last Name	No.	Yds	Avg	TD
Walton	32	532	17	5
Anderson	18	396	22	2
Podoley	16	381	24	4
Carson	14	244	17	2
Bosseler	14	101	7	0
Olszewski	11	102	9	0
Sutton	6	112	19	0
Watson	5	38	8	1
Zagers	3	50	17	0
James	2	33	17	0

PUNT RETURNS

Last Name	No.	Yds	Avg	TD
Zagers	7	41	6	0
James	6	37	6	0
Scudero	8	27	3	0
Watson	4	21	5	0
Nix	1	12	12	0
Sommer	3	3	1	0
Bosseler	1	2	2	0
Olszewski	2	0	0	0

KICKOFF RETURNS

Last Name	No.	Yds	Avg	TD
Watson	19	443	23	0
James	9	212	24	0
Scudero	4	122	31	0
Sommer	4	77	19	0
Miller	1	15	15	0
Renfro	1	12	12	0
Braatz	1	8	8	0
Olszewski	1	2	2	0

PASSING – PUNTING – KICKING

PASSING	Att	Comp	%	Yds	Yd/Att	TD	Int–%	RK
LeBaron	145	79	54	1365	9.4	11	10– 7	5
Guglielmi	81	34	42	458	5.7	2	6– 7	
Bukich	23	8	35	166	7.2	1	1– 4	
Sutton	3	0	0	0	0.0	0	0– 0	

PUNTING	No	Avg
Baker	48	45.4

KICKING	XP	Att	%	FG	Att	%
Baker	25	25	100	13	26	50

CHICAGO CARDINALS

RUSHING

Last Name	No.	Yds	Avg	TD
Matson	129	505	3.9	5
Reynolds	48	252	5.3	0
Crow	52	221	4.3	2
Childress	50	170	3.4	0
Hammack	35	121	3.5	1
McHan	17	65	3.8	1
Sears	17	51	3.0	0
Philpott	12	44	3.7	0
Watkins	3	17	5.7	0
Gordon	2	10	5.0	0
Hill	1	0	0.0	0

RECEIVING

Last Name	No.	Yds	Avg	TD
Lewis	46	690	15	4
Nagler	36	469	13	5
Childress	35	406	12	4
Matson	33	465	14	3
Crow	20	362	18	3
Sears	13	187	14	2
Watkins	4	62	16	1
Philpott	4	30	8	0
Boydston	3	42	14	1
Hammack	3	11	4	0
Lane	1	10	10	0
McHan	0	1	0	0

PUNT RETURNS

Last Name	No.	Yds	Avg	TD
Conrad	19	129	7	0
Sears	14	94	7	0
Lewis	2	12	6	0
Gordon	1	12	12	0
Jackson	2	10	5	0
Nolan	1	2	2	0

KICKOFF RETURNS

Last Name	No.	Yds	Avg	TD
Sears	32	756	24	0
Matson	14	497	36	2
Crow	6	145	24	0
Lewis	2	46	23	0
Conrad	1	33	33	0
Watkins	1	24	24	0
Philpott	3	18	6	0
Tubbs	1	11	11	0
Weber	1	2	2	0

PASSING – PUNTING – KICKING

PASSING	Att	Comp	%	Yds	Yd/Att	TD	Int–%	RK
McHan	198	91	46	1291	6.5	12	13– 7	11
Reynolds	195	105	54	1422	7.3	11	11– 6	
Hill	9	1	11	18	2.0	0	2– 22	
Matson	2	1	50	4	2.0	0	0– 0	
Childress	1	0	0	0	0.0	0	0– 0	
Crow	1	0	0	0	0.0	0	1–100	
Sears	1	0	0	0	0.0	0	0– 0	

PUNTING	No	Avg
Gordon	55	38.0
McHan	2	32.5

KICKING	XP	Att	%	FG	Att	%
Conrad	33	35	94	6	17	35

PHILADELPHIA EAGLES

RUSHING

Last Name	No.	Yds	Avg	TD
Barnes	156	551	3.5	7
Peaks	115	386	3.4	3
Wells	24	92	3.8	1
Kowalczyk	17	43	2.5	1
Myers	9	23	2.6	0
Van Brocklin	8	5	0.6	1
Jurgensen	1	1	1.0	0
Retzlaff	1	−4	−4.0	0
McDonald	3	−4	−1.3	0

RECEIVING

Last Name	No.	Yds	Avg	TD
Retzlaff	56	766	14	2
Barnes	35	423	12	0
McDonald	29	603	21	9
Peaks	29	248	9	2
Bielski	23	234	10	1
Walston	21	298	14	3
Kowalczyk	8	72	9	0
Wells	4	49	12	0
Myers	4	25	6	0
Mitcham	3	39	13	1
Nacrelli	2	15	8	0

PUNT RETURNS

Last Name	No.	Yds	Avg	TD
Wells	19	158	8	0
McDonald	18	135	8	0
Riley	7	27	4	0
Norton	1	8	8	0
Koman	1	5	5	0

KICKOFF RETURNS

Last Name	No.	Yds	Avg	TD
Wells	14	336	24	0
McDonald	14	262	19	0
Riley	9	205	23	0
Bielski	5	66	13	0
Jacobs	2	24	12	0
Koman	1	7	7	0

PASSING – PUNTING – KICKING

PASSING	Att	Comp	%	Yds	Yd/Att	TD	Int–%	RK
Van Brocklin	374	198	53	2409	6.4	15	20– 5	7
Jurgensen	22	12	55	259	11.8	0	1– 5	
Barnes	6	4	67	104	17.3	3	0– 0	

PUNTING	No	Avg
Van Brocklin	54	41.2

KICKING	XP	Att	%	FG	Att	%
Walston	31	31	100	6	14	43

BALTIMORE COLTS 9-3-0 Weeb Ewbank

Scores of Each Game		
28	DETROIT	15
51	CHIC. BEARS	38
24	Green Bay	17
40	Detroit	14
35	WASHINGTON	10
56	GREEN BAY	0
21	New York	24
17	Chic. Bears	0
34	LOS ANGELES	7
35	SAN FRANCISCO	27
28	Los Angeles	30
12	San Francisco	21

Use Name	Pos.	Hgt	Wgt	Age	Int	Pts
Jim Parker	OT	6'3"	270	24		
Sherman Plunkett	OT	6'4"	265	24		
George Preas	OT	6'2"	245	26		
Alex Sandusky	OG	6'1"	235	26		
Art Spinney	OG	6'	230	31		
Fuzzy Thurston	OG	6'1"	245	25		
Buzz Nutter	C	6'4"	235	27		
Ordell Braase	DE	6'4"	235	26		
Don Joyce	DE	6'3"	255	28		
Gino Marchetti	DE	6'4"	240	32		
Art Donovan	DT	6'2"	270	33		
Big Daddy Lipscomb	DT	6'6"	288	27		
Ray Krouse	DE-DT	6'3"	275	31		
Bill Pellington	LB	6'2"	230	29	4	
Leo Sanford	LB	6'1"	230	29	1	
Don Shinnick	LB	6'	230	23	3	
Steve Myhra	OG-LB	6'1"	235	24		60
Dick Szymanski	C-LB	6'3"	230	26		
Bert Rechichar	OE-LB	6'1"	210	28		9
Milt Davis	DB	6'1"	190	29	4	
Andy Nelson	DB	6'1"	180	25	8	6
Johnny Sample	DB	6'1"	203	21		
Jackie Simpson	DB	5'10"	180	24		
Carl Taseff	DB	5'11"	190	29	7	
Ray Brown	QB-DB	6'2"	195	22	8	
Art DeCarlo	OE-DB	6'2"	196	28		
Dick Horn	QB	6'1"	195	28		
George Shaw	QB	6'1"	190	25		6
Johnny Unitas	QB	6'1"	190	25		18
Jack Call	HB	6'1"	200	23		
L. G. Dupre	HB	5'11"	190	26		18
Lenny Moore	HB	6'1"	190	25		84
Avatus Stone	HB	6'1"	195	27		
Lenny Lyles	DB-HB	6'2"	198	22		24
Alan Ameche	FB	6'	220	25		54
Billy Pricer	FB	5'10"	210	23		6
Ray Berry	OE	6'2"	190	25		54
Jim Mutscheller	OE	6'1"	215	28		42

CHICAGO BEARS 8-4-0 George Halas

Scores of Each Game		
34	Green Bay	20
38	Baltimore	51
28	SAN FRANCISCO	6
31	LOS ANGELES	10
27	San Francisco	14
35	Los Angeles	41
24	GREEN BAY	10
0	BALTIMORE	17
20	Detroit	7
10	Pittsburgh	24
30	CHIC. CARDS	14
21	DETROIT	16

Use Name	Pos.	Hgt	Wgt	Age	Int	Pts
Bob Kilcullen	OT	6'3"	245	22		
Dick Klein	OT	6'4"	255	24		
Herm Lee	OT	6'4"	248	27		
Abe Gibron	OG	5'11"	250	32		
Don Healy	OG	6'3"	250	22		
Stan Jones	OG	6'1"	250	27		
John Mellekas	C	8'3"	255	25		
Larry Strickland	C	6'4"	245	27		
Doug Atkins	DE	6'8"	255	28		
Jack Hoffman	DE	6'5"	235	29	1	
Bill Bishop	DT	6'4"	248	27		6
Earl Leggett	DT	6'3"	250	24		
Fred Williams	DT	6'4"	248	28		
Joe Fortunato	LB	6'	225	28	1	
Bill George	LB	6'2"	235	27	1	1
Wayne Hansen	LB	6'2"	228	30	1	
Chuck Howley	LB	6'3"	228	22	1	
Bill Raehnelt	LB	6'1"	225	22		
Erich Barnes	DB	6'2"	198	23	4	12
Jack Johnson	DB	6'3"	198	24	1	
Charlie Sumner	DB	6'1"	195	28	6	6
Stan Wallace	DB	6'3"	205	26	3	
Vic Zucco	DB	6'	187	23	3	
Rocky Ryan (from PHI)	OE-DB	6'1"	202	26	1	
George Blanda	QB	6'1"	208	30		69
Zeke Bratkowski	QB	6'2"	203	26		
Ed Brown	QB	6'2"	208	29		18
Willie Galimore	HB	6'1"	187	23		72
Johnny Morris	HB	5'10"	180	23		12
J. C. Caroline	DB-HB	6'1"	190	25		6
Rick Casares	FB	6'2"	225	27		18
Merrill Douglas	HB-FB	6'	204	22		
Ralph Anderson	OE	6'4"	220	21		8
Bob Carey	OE	6'5"	224	30		
Harlon Hill	OE	6'3"	200	26		18
Bob Jewett	OE	6'2"	198	24		6
Bill McColl	OE	6'4"	230	28		48

Jim Dooley – Broken Ankle

LOS ANGELES RAMS 8-4-0 Sid Gillman

Scores of Each Game		
27	CLEVELAND	30
33	San Francisco	3
42	Detroit	28
10	Chic. Bears	31
24	DETROIT	41
41	CHIC. BEARS	35
56	SAN FRANCISCO	7
20	Green Bay	7
7	Baltimore	34
20	Chic. Cards	14
30	BALTIMORE	28
34	GREEN BAY	20

Use Name	Pos.	Hgt	Wgt	Age	Int	Pts
John Baker	OT	6'6"	290	23		
Charlie Bradshaw	OT	6'6"	240	22		
Bob Fry	OT	6'4"	238	27		
Buck Lansford	OG	6'2"	235	25		
Duane Putnam	OG	6'	230	30		
John Houser	C-OG	6'3"	237	22		
John Morrow	C	6'3"	235	25		
Glenn Holtzman	DE	6'3"	254	28		2
Lou Michaels	DE	6'2"	238	22	2	6
Roy Wilkins	LB-DE	6'3"	220	24		
Frank Fuller	DT	6'4"	243	29		
George Strugar	DT	6'5"	258	23		
Ken Panfil	OT-DT	6'6"	268	27		
Dick Daugherty	LB	6'1"	223	29	1	6
Bill Jobko	LB	6'2"	220	22		
Jack Pardee	LB	6'2"	215	22		
Les Richter	LB	6'3"	248	27	3	
Alex Bravo	DB	6'	190	26		
Fred Bruney	DB	5'10"	180	27		
Don Burroughs	DB	6'4"	186	27	7	
Jimmy Harris	DB	6'1"	176	23	4	
Floyd Iglehart	DB	6'4"	197	23		
Jim Jones	DB	6'1"	196	22		
Jack Morris	DB	6'	188	26	6	6
Will Sherman	DB	6'2"	197	29	5	12
Clendon Thomas	DB	6'2"	190	21		
Frank Ryan	QB	6'3"	190	22		
Billy Wade	QB	6'2"	203	27		12
Jon Arnett	HB	5'11"	194	23		42
Ron Waller	HB	5'11"	180	25		
Tom Wilson	HB	6'	204	25		60
Joe Marconi	FB	6'2"	230	24		6
Leon Clarke	OE	6'4"	230	25		30
Jim Phillips	OE	6'1"	200	21		12
Del Shofner	OE	6'3"	185	22		48
Lamar Lundy	DE-OE	6'7"	235	23		18
Paige Cothren	K	5'11"	195	23		84

SAN FRANCISCO FORTY NINERS 6-6-0 Frankie Albert

Scores of Each Game		
23	PITTSBURGH	20
3	LOS ANGELES	33
6	Chic. Bears	28
30	Philadelphia	24
14	CHIC. BEARS	27
24	DETROIT	21
7	Los Angeles	56
21	Detroit	35
33	Green Bay	12
27	Baltimore	35
48	GREEN BAY	21
21	BALTIMORE	12

Use Name	Pos.	Hgt	Wgt	Age	Int	Pts
John Gonzaga	OT	6'3"	245	25		
Bob St. Clair	OT	6'9"	265	27		
John Thomas	OT	6'4"	237	23		
Bruce Bosley	OG	6'2"	244	24		
Ted Connolly	OG	6'3"	245	26		
Lou Palatella	OG	6'2"	230	25		
John Wittenborn	OG	6'2"	233	22		
Frank Morze	C	6'4"	270	24		
Ed Henke	DE	6'3"	230	30		
Bob Toneff	DE	6'3"	260	28	1	
Walt Yowarsky	DE	6'2"	235	30		
Bill Herchman	DT	6'2"	245	25		
Leo Nomellini	DT	6'3"	255	33		
Matt Hazeltine	LB	6'1"	215	25	3	6
Marv Matuszak (to GB)	LB	6'3"	235	27	1	
Dennit Morris	LB	6'1"	230	22		
Karl Rubke	C-LB	6'4"	240	22		
Billy Atkins	DB	6'1"	200	23	1	
Jerry Mertens	DB	6'	185	22	2	
Dick Moegle	DB	6'	190	24		
Jimmy Ridlon	DB	6'1"	180	23	4	
Bill Stits	DB	6'	195	27	3	
Abe Woodson	HB-DB	5'11"	188	23	1	
John Brodie	QB	6'1"	195	23		6
Y. A. Tittle	QB	6'	195	31		12
Hugh McElhenny	HB	6'1"	198	29		48
Jim Pace	HB	6'	195	22		12
Tony Teresa	HB	5'9"	190	23		
J. D. Smith	FB-HB	6'1"	210	25		18
Gene Babb	FB	6'3"	215	23		
Joe Perry	FB	6'	197	31		30
R. C. Owens	OE-FL	6'3"	207	23		6
Bill Jessup	OE-FL	6'1"	195	29		6
Clyde Conner	OE	6'2"	202	25		30
Fred Dugan	OE	6'3"	195	24		
Gordie Soltau	OE	6'2"	195	33		53
Billy Wilson	OE	6'3"	190	31		30

DETROIT LIONS 4-7-1 George Wilson

Scores of Each Game		
15	Baltimore	28
13	Green Bay	13
28	LOS ANGELES	42
14	BALTIMORE	40
41	Los Angeles	24
21	San Francisco	24
30	Cleveland	10
35	SAN FRANCISCO	21
7	CHIC. BEARS	20
24	GREEN BAY	14
17	NEW YORK	19
16	Chic. Bears	21

Use Name	Pos.	Hgt	Wgt	Age	Int	Pts
Ken Russell	OT	6'3"	250	22		
Lou Creekmur	OG-OT	6'4"	254	31		
Stan Campbell	OG	6'	228	28		
Doug Hogland (from Chi C)	OG	6'3"	240	27		
Karl Koepfer	OG	6'2"	230	22		
Harley Sewell	OG	6'1"	233	27		
Charlie Ane	OT-C	6'2"	260	27		
Bill Glass	OT-C	6'5"	236	22		
Gene Cronin	DE	6'2"	230	25		
Darris McCord	DE	6'4"	240	25		
Jerry Perry	DT-DE	6'4"	235	27		13
Alex Karras	DT	6'2"	254	22		
Gil Mains	DT	6'2"	250	28		
Bob Miller	DT	6'3"	257	28		
Bob Long	LB	6'3"	234	24	2	
Jim Martin	LB	6'2"	230	34		49
Joe Schmidt	LB	6'1"	217	26	6	
Wayne Walker	LB	6'2"	220	21	1	12
Roger Zatkoff	LB	6'2"	217	27		
Terry Barr	DB	6'	190	23	3	6
Jack Christiansen	DB	6'1"	196	29	1	
Jim David	DB	5'11"	185	31	3	
Gary Lowe	DB	5'11"	195	24	2	
Dave Whitsell	DB	6'	184	22	1	
Yale Lary	DB	6'	190	27	3	6
Earl Morrall (from PIT)	QB	6'1"	200	24		
Tobin Rote	QB	6'3"	212	30		18
Hopalong Cassady	HB	5'10"	180	24		42
Gene Gedman	HB	5'11"	195	26		42
Dan Lewis	HB	6'1"	197	22		
Ken Webb	FB-HB	5'11"	208	23		18
John Henry Johnson	FB	6'2"	213	28		
Jim Doran	OE	6'2"	200	30		24
Jim Gibbons	OE	6'2"	215	22		12
Dave Middleton	OE	6'1"	195	25		18
Perry Richards	OE	6'2"	205	24		
Tom Rychlec	OE	6'3"	215	24		

John Gordy – Voluntarily Retired
Steve Junker – Knee Injury
Jerry Reichow – Knee Injury

GREEN BAY PACKERS 1-10-1 Ray McLean

Scores of Each Game		
20	CHIC. BEARS	34
13	DETROIT	13
17	BALTIMORE	24
21	Washington	37
38	PHILADELPHIA	35
0	Baltimore	56
10	Chic. Bears	24
7	LOS ANGELES	20
12	SAN FRANCISCO	33
14	Detroit	24
21	San Francisco	48
20	Los Angeles	34

Use Name	Pos.	Hgt	Wgt	Age	Int	Pts
Norm Masters	OT	6'2"	250	25		
Ollie Spencer	OT	6'2"	245	27		
Forrest Gregg	OG-DT-OT	6'4"	245	25		
Hank Bullough	OG	6'	240	24		
Jerry Kramer	OG	6'3"	235	23		
Jim Salsbury	OG	6'1"	240	26		
Jim Ringo	C	6'1"	236	27		
Nate Borden	DE	6'	240	26		
Len Ford	DE	6'4"	250	32		
Carlton Massey	DE	6'2"	226	29		
Jim Temp	DE	6'4"	250	25		
Dave Hanner	DT	6'2"	266	29		
J. D. Kimmel	DT	6'4"	250	29		
Tom Bettis	LB	6'2"	225	25		
Dan Currie	LB	6'3"	235	24		
Bill Forester	LB	6'3"	240	27		
Ray Nitschke	LB	6'3"	220	22	1	
Bobby Dillon	DB	6'1"	190	28	6	6
Hank Gremminger	DB	6'1"	200	25	3	
Johnny Symank	DB	5'11"	180	23	1	
Jesse Whittenton	DB	6'	195	24	1	
Billy Kinard	HB-DB	6'	202	24		
Al Romine	HB-DB	6'2"	184	25	1	
Babe Parilli	QB	6'1"	196	28		
Bart Starr	QB	6'1"	200	25		6
Joe Francis	HB-QB	6'1"	194	23		6
Al Carmichael	HB	6'1"	195	28		6
Paul Hornung	HB	6'2"	211	22		67
Joe Johnson	FL	6'	188	28		6
Don McIlhenny	HB	6'	200	23		12
Jim Shanley	HB	5'9"	174	22		
Howie Ferguson	FB	6'2"	213	28		6
Jim Taylor	FB	6'	205	23		12
Billy Howton	OE	6'2"	195	28		12
Gary Knafelc	OE	6'4"	217	26		6
Max McGee	OE	6'3"	196	26		42
Steve Meilinger	OE	6'2"	230	28		6

Ron Kramer – Military Service
Bob Skoronski – Military Service

BALTIMORE COLTS

RUSHING

Last Name	No.	Yds	Avg	TD
Ameche	171	791	4.6	8
Moore	82	598	7.3	7
Dupre	95	390	4.1	3
Call	37	154	4.2	0
Unitas	33	139	4.2	3
Lyles	22	41	1.9	1
Pricer	10	26	2.6	1
Shaw	5	−3	−0.6	1
Brown	1	−9	−9.0	0

RECEIVING

Last Name	No.	Yds	Avg	TD
Berry	56	794	14	9
Moore	50	938	19	7
Mutscheller	28	504	18	7
Dupre	13	111	9	0
Ameche	13	81	6	1
Lyles	5	24	5	1
Rechichar	4	34	9	1
Call	4	28	7	0
Pricer	3	14	5	0
DeCarlo	1	10	10	0
Pellington	1	−1	−1	0

PUNT RETURNS

Last Name	No.	Yds	Avg	TD
Taseff	29	196	7	0
Rechichar	7	29	4	0
Moore	2	11	6	0
Simpson	1	1	1	0

KICKOFF RETURNS

Last Name	No.	Yds	Avg	TD
Lyles	11	398	36	2
Pricer	9	168	19	0
Moore	4	91	23	0
Simpson	3	59	20	0
Rechichar	3	50	17	0
Taseff	1	50	50	0
Call	2	48	24	0
DeCarlo	1	0	0	0

PASSING – PUNTING – KICKING

PASSING	Att	Comp	%	Yds	Yd/Att	TD	Int–%	RK
Unitas	263	136	52	2007	7.6	19	7– 3	1
Shaw	89	41	46	531	6.0	7	4– 4	
Brown	2	1	50	−1	−0.5	0	0– 0	

PUNTING	No	Avg
Brown	41	39.9
Horn	19	34.1
Stone	1	28.0
Dupre	1	0.0

KICKING	XP	Att	%	FG	Att	%
Myhra	48	51	94	4	10	40
Rechichar	0	0	0	1	4	25
Shaw	0	1	0	0	0	0

CHICAGO BEARS

RUSHING

Last Name	No.	Yds	Avg	TD
Casares	176	651	3.7	2
Galimore	130	619	4.8	8
Morris	52	239	4.6	2
Caroline	33	121	3.7	0
Brown	32	94	2.9	3
Douglas	10	53	5.3	0
Bratkowski	3	0	0.0	0

RECEIVING

Last Name	No.	Yds	Avg	TD
McColl	35	517	15	8
Casares	32	290	9	1
Hill	27	365	14	3
Jewett	15	192	13	1
Anderson	11	177	16	1
Morris	11	170	15	0
Galimore	8	151	19	3
Caroline	5	78	16	1
Ryan	1	66	66	0
Carey	1	15	15	0

PUNT RETURNS

Last Name	No.	Yds	Avg	TD
Morris	14	96	7	0
Zucco	15	35	2	0
Sumner	9	25	3	0
Ryan	1	0	0	0

KICKOFF RETURNS

Last Name	No.	Yds	Avg	TD
Morris	16	399	25	0
Galimore	9	338	38	1
Caroline	6	123	21	0
Zucco	3	63	21	0
Sumner	1	19	19	0
Gibron	1	12	12	0
Barnes	1	0	0	0

PASSING – PUNTING – KICKING

PASSING	Att	Comp	%	Yds	Yd/Att	TD	Int–%	RK
Brown	218	102	47	1418	6.5	10	17– 8	13
Bratkowski	90	41	46	571	6.3	7	6– 7	
Blanda	7	2	29	19	2.7	0	0– 0	
Casares	4	1	25	13	3.3	1	0– 0	
Galimore	1	0	0	0	0.0	0	1–100	

PUNTING	No	Avg
Brown	27	42.2
Johnson	18	34.8
Bratkowski	14	39.6

KICKING	XP	Att	%	FG	Att	%
Blanda	36	37	97	11	23	48
George	1	1	100	0	0	0

LOS ANGELES RAMS

RUSHING

Last Name	No.	Yds	Avg	TD
Arnett	133	683	5.1	6
Wilson	73	475	6.5	9
Marconi	89	428	4.8	1
Wade	42	90	2.1	2
Ryan	5	45	9.0	0
Waller	3	13	4.3	0

RECEIVING

Last Name	No.	Yds	Avg	TD
Shofner	51	1097	22	8
Phillips	35	524	15	2
Arnett	35	494	14	1
Lundy	25	396	16	3
Clarke	18	135	8	4
Marconi	10	87	9	0
Wilson	9	101	11	1
Waller	3	75	25	0

PUNT RETURNS

Last Name	No.	Yds	Avg	TD
Arnett	18	223	12	0
Morris	8	9	1	0
Waller	13	7	1	0
Sherman	1	0	0	0
Wilkins	1	0	0	0

KICKOFF RETURNS

Last Name	No.	Yds	Avg	TD
Arnett	16	331	21	0
Wilson	16	324	20	0
Waller	7	120	17	0
Morris	2	37	19	0
Fry	2	23	12	0

PASSING – PUNTING – KICKING

PASSING	Att	Comp	%	Yds	Yd/Att	TD	Int–%	RK
Wade	341	181	53	2875	8.4	18	22– 6	2
Ryan	14	5	36	34	2.4	1	3– 2	
Arnett	1	0	0	0	0.0	0	0– 0	
Shofner	1	0	0	0	0.0	0	0– 0	
Wilson	1	0	0	0	0.0	0	1–100	

PUNTING	No	Avg
Shofner	49	41.2
Thomas	2	33.0

KICKING	XP	Att	%	FG	Att	%
Cothren	42	42	100	14	25	56

SAN FRANCISCO FORTY NINERS

RUSHING

Last Name	No.	Yds	Avg	TD
Perry	125	758	6.1	4
McElhenny	113	451	4.0	6
Smith	26	209	8.0	3
Pace	52	161	3.1	2
Tittle	22	35	1.6	2
Woodson	2	12	6.0	0
Babb	7	9	1.3	0
Atkins	1	5	5.0	0
Brodie	11	−12	−1.1	1

RECEIVING

Last Name	No.	Yds	Avg	TD
Conner	49	512	10	5
Wilson	43	592	14	5
Owens	40	620	16	1
McElhenny	31	366	12	2
Perry	23	218	9	1
Pace	10	59	6	0
Dugan	9	122	14	0
Soltau	7	77	11	0
Smith	6	59	10	0
Jessup	5	66	13	1

PUNT RETURNS

Last Name	No.	Yds	Avg	TD
McElhenny	24	93	4	0
Woodson	7	53	8	0
Jessup	2	0	0	0
Pace	2	0	0	0

KICKOFF RETURNS

Last Name	No.	Yds	Avg	TD
Smith	15	356	24	0
Woodson	11	239	22	0
Pace	8	134	17	0
McElhenny	2	31	16	0
Babb	2	30	15	0
Connolly	1	0	0	0

PASSING – PUNTING – KICKING

PASSING	Att	Comp	%	Yds	Yd/Att	TD	Int–%	RK
Tittle	208	120	58	1467	7.1	9	15– 7	9
Brodie	172	103	60	1224	7.1	6	13– 8	8
McElhenny	2	0	0	0	0.0	0	0– 0	
Jessup	1	0	0	0	0.0	0	1–100	

PUNTING	No	Avg
Atkins	25	39.3
Jessup	23	37.2

KICKING	XP	Att	%	FG	Att	%
Soltau	29	33	88	8	21	38

DETROIT LIONS

RUSHING

Last Name	No.	Yds	Avg	TD
Rote	77	351	4.6	3
Johnson	56	254	4.5	0
Gedman	92	209	2.3	4
Cassady	45	198	4.4	0
Webb	56	172	3.1	2
Lewis	25	131	5.2	0
Morrall	11	80	7.3	0
Lary	1	2	2.0	0
Middleton	2	1	0.5	0

RECEIVING

Last Name	No.	Yds	Avg	TD
Middleton	29	506	17	3
Gibbons	25	367	15	2
Cassady	23	406	18	7
Doran	22	495	23	4
Gedman	14	106	8	3
Webb	11	85	8	1
Richards	7	90	13	0
Johnson	7	60	9	0
Rychlec	2	21	11	0
Lewis	1	12	12	0

PUNT RETURNS

Last Name	No.	Yds	Avg	TD
Lary	27	196	7	1
Barr	11	23	2	0
Cassady	3	4	1	0

KICKOFF RETURNS

Last Name	No.	Yds	Avg	TD
Barr	4	197	49	1
Webb	7	154	22	0
Gedman	7	131	19	0
Cassady	6	126	21	0
Lewis	6	110	18	0
Whitsell	3	63	21	0
Creekmur	2	23	12	0
Karras	1	16	16	0
Middleton	1	15	15	0
Gibbons	1	4	4	0
Rychlec	1	0	0	0

PASSING – PUNTING – KICKING

PASSING	Att	Comp	%	Yds	Yd/Att	TD	Int–%	RK
Rote	257	118	46	1678	6.5	14	10– 4	8
Morrall	78	25	32	463	5.9	5	9– 12	
Gedman	3	2	67	111	37.0	1	0– 0	
Lary	1	0	0	0	0.0	0	0– 0	

PUNTING	No	Avg
Lary	59	42.8
Morrall	1	25.0

KICKING	XP	Att	%	FG	Att	%
Martin	28	28	100	7	19	37
Perry	1	1	100	4	4	100

GREEN BAY PACKERS

RUSHING

Last Name	No.	Yds	Avg	TD
Hornung	69	310	4.5	2
Ferguson	59	268	4.5	1
Taylor	52	247	4.8	1
McIlhenny	74	239	3.2	1
Francis	24	153	6.4	1
Starr	25	113	4.5	1
Shanley	23	30	1.3	0
Carmichael	9	21	2.3	0
Parilli	8	15	1.9	0
Ringo	0	13	0.0	0
McGee	1	9	9.0	0
Salsbury	0	3	0.0	0
Romine	1	0	0.0	0

RECEIVING

Last Name	No.	Yds	Avg	TD
McGee	37	655	18	7
Howton	36	507	14	2
McIlhenny	20	154	8	1
Hornung	15	137	9	0
Meilinger	13	139	11	1
Ferguson	12	121	10	0
Johnson	10	176	18	1
Knafelc	8	118	15	1
Taylor	4	72	18	1
Carmichael	3	26	9	1
Shanley	3	13	4	0

PUNT RETURNS

Last Name	No.	Yds	Avg	TD
Shanley	14	105	8	0
Carmichael	15	67	4	0
Romine	2	7	4	0
McIlhenny	1	0	0	0
Symank	1	0	0	0

KICKOFF RETURNS

Last Name	No.	Yds	Avg	TD
Carmichael	29	700	24	0
Hornung	10	248	25	0
Taylor	7	185	26	0
McIlhenny	7	146	21	0
Currie	2	14	7	0
Massey	1	10	10	0
Forester	1	6	6	0
Kramer	1	0	0	0
Nitschke	1	0	0	0
Temp	1	0	0	0

PASSING – PUNTING – KICKING

PASSING	Att	Comp	%	Yds	Yd/Att	TD	Int–%	RK
Parilli	157	68	43	1068	6.8	10	13– 8	14
Starr	157	78	50	875	5.6	3	12– 8	15
Francis	31	15	48	175	5.7	2	2– 6	
Ferguson	1	0	0	0	0.0	0	0– 0	
Hornung	1	0	0	0	0.0	0	0– 0	
McGee	1	0	0	0	0.0	0	0– 0	

PUNTING	No	Avg
McGee	62	42.3

KICKING	XP	Att	%	FG	Att	%
Hornung	22	23	96	11	21	52

1959 The Passing of Greatness

While the Philadelphia Eagles and Pittsburgh Steelers were battling on the turf at Franklin Field on October 11, Commissioner Bert Bell collapsed and died of a heart attack in the grandstand while watching the two clubs he had once owned and coached. The league mourned him both as a kind friend and a wise leader, a man who had led the NFL from the backwoods to center stage in the sporting world. Since becoming commissioner in 1946, Bell had successfully ended the war with the All-American Football Conference, had firmly upheld the game's honesty in the 1946 championship-game gambling affair, had used television to promote the game rather than give it away, and had administered the league office in truly big-league fashion. Bell was the second NFL pioneer to die this year, as New York Giant founder Tim Mara had passed on in February after a long illness.

League treasurer Austin Gunsel assumed Bell's duties until a new commissioner could be named by the owners. The new man would have to be a strong leader, since a new threat to the NFL was gathering in the wilderness. Organized by rich Texans Lamar Hunt and Bud Adams, the American Football League announced plans to operate an eight-team circuit starting next fall. With Houston, Dallas, New York, Los Angeles, Boston, Buffalo, Denver, and Minneapolis–St. Paul lined up as AFL franchises, the now established NFL was not quaking in its boots but could not afford to snear at this newcomer on the block.

EASTERN CONFERENCE

New York Giants—Heroics by the defense and by quarterback Chuck Conerly flavored the Giants' drive to the top of the East. After getting burned by the Eagles 49-21 the week before, the Giant defense vindicated itself on October 12 by shutting down Jimmy Brown and the Browns for a 10-6 victory. Two weeks later, this defense passed the supreme test in Pittsburgh. With New York leading 21-16, the Steelers recovered Joe Morrison's fumble on the Giant 16-yard line with 1:30 left in the game. Two plays took the Steelers to the 6½-yard line, but the Giant front wall held firm, twice stopping Tom Tracy from plunging for the first down. Then came Conerly's turn to shine. After missing two mid-season games with a bad leg, old Chuck limped into the lineup and passed the Giants to a 30-20 victory over the Cards. The next Sunday was officially celebrated as Chuck Conerly Day, with the guest of honor celebrating by leading his club to a 45-14 triumph over Washington.

Cleveland Browns—The Browns ran even with the Giants at the head of the East for eight weeks until bad luck and a bad day did them in. On the last two weeks of November, they lost a pair of 21-20 heartbreakers to Pittsburgh and San Francisco: On the first Sunday of December, they got the worst beating in the club's history. After being stopped in the first period, Jimmy Brown had to sit out the second quarter after being kicked in the head, and Chuck Conerly led the Giants to a 48-0 lead through three quarters, settling for a final 48-7 score. With Cleveland's sound defense and Jimmy Brown at fullback, fans now wondered out loud why Paul Brown couldn't win the Eastern title with this team. The Giants, though, had discovered how to shut the door on the Browns: Intimidate quarterback Milt Plum with a stiff pass rush and assign a watchdog named Sam Huff to stick with Brown like flypaper.

Philadelphia Eagles—With the interior line made up of Chuck Bednarik and four newcomers, giving him good protection, Norm Van Brocklin passed the Eagles to a 49-21 upset of the Giants in an early-October contest. After that, the young Eagles believed in themselves, driving to a second-place finish in the East and their first winning season in five years. Old pro Van Brocklin led by example, zipping passes to Tommy McDonald, Pete Retzlaff, and Bobby Walston and inspiring his mates with his own determination to win. Three pro-football greats blessed the Philadelphia offensive huddles, with Van Brocklin, center Bednarik, and split end Bobby Watson all veterans at the top of their game. Another old pro, Tom Brookshier, helped glue the young defense together.

Pittsburgh Steelers—When the Steelers beat the Browns 17-7 to open the season, they ran their unbeaten streak to eight regular-season games. The Redskins ended the string a week later, and the Steelers would not come close to running off another long streak this year. But even with the Steelers' mediocre final record of 6-5-1, quarterback Bobby Layne showed Pittsburgh fans their first great T-formation quarterback. He wisely deployed a strong but slow corps of runners, using Tom Tracy to pick up vital short yardage, while his passes moved the ball in large bites. Jimmy Orr kept up his good work on short and medium passes, but rookie Buddy Dial, a pre-season cut by the Giants, won the headlines with his speed on long downfield passes.

Washington Redskins—After a 49-21 trouncing at the hands of the Cardinals on opening day, the Redskins seemed to hit their stride by beating the Steelers and the Cards on the next two weekends. But the victories were a false alarm, as the Skins dropped eight of their last nine contests to sink to fifth place in the East. Mike Nixon, an assistant under Joe Kuharich, was promoted to head coach to head up a new rebuilding program, but he had hoped to win more than three games this season.

Chicago Cardinals—With John David Crow developing into a top runner, the Cards decided to trade star Ollie Matson to get help at the other positions. Eight players and a draft choice came over from the Rams, with offensive tackle Ken Panfil and defensive tackle Frank Fuller the gems in the bunch. The Cards could hardly do worse than their recent seasons with Matson, but they actually did lose one more game than last year. By and large, the Cards were a dismal outfit on the field, and general manager Walter Wolfner was looking to get a fresh start for the team away from Chicago. So the Cardinals, one of the NFL's charter members, fled to St. Louis for the start of the new decade.

WESTERN CONFERENCE

Baltimore Colts—With their defense showing signs of creeping old age, the Colts trailed the San Francisco '49ers by two games in the West with only five weeks left to play. Even during this slow start, Johnny Unitas had kept the attack moving at a high clip, and now he shifted the offense into top speed for the final five games. Scoring an average of 37 points per game during this final stretch, the Colts swept all five games, twice beating the fading '49ers by scores of 45-14 and 34-14 to clear a path to the top of the conference. The Colts moved best through the air, with all the parts needed for a top-flight passing attack. Unitas set a league record of thirty-two touchdown passes, aided by superb pass blocking from linemen like Jim Parker and Art Spinney, and by a collection of receivers featuring swift Lenny Moore, sure-handed Ray Berry, and hard-working Jim Mutscheller.

Chicago Bears—With four losses in their first five games, the Bears found themselves mired in fifth place in the Western Conference. But George Halas' team was just a little slow out of the starting gate, as both the offensive and defensive platoons came alive for the last seven games. As the Bears began winning, they quickly passed the Rams and Packers on the way to the top and closed in on the '49ers and Colts. On the morning of the final Sunday of the season, the Colts held a one-game lead over the '49ers and Bears for the Western title. San Francisco, fading since early November, dropped out of contention by losing to Green Bay, while the Bears kept their chances alive by beating Detroit. But the late drive fell short, as the Colts beat Los Angeles to make that one-game margin permanent.

Green Bay Packers—Vince Lombardi's first statements in Green Bay made his position perfectly clear. To the executive committee he said, "Let's get one thing straight right now: I'm in complete command here." To his players he said, "Gentlemen, I've never been associated with a losing team. I do not intend to start now." The Packers took him at his word and gave their coach a winning season, a complete turn-around from last year's fiasco. Three quick wins began the Lombardi era with a flourish as halfback Paul Hornung responded to the coach's confidence in him by developing into a marvelous all-purpose halfback. When a five-game losing streak in mid-season threatened to drag this new coach under into losing waters, Lombardi came up with a master stroke: He replaced quarterback Lamar McHan with Bart Starr and won the last four games of this year.

San Francisco '49ers—A revitalized offense and rebuilt defense got the '49ers off winging to six wins in their first seven starts. New coach Red Hickey had promoted J. D. Smith to starting halfback, and Smith rewarded the coach with strong running week after week. Another Hickey project was the defensive secondary, where second-year men Abe Woodson and Jerry Mertens and rookies Eddie Dove and Dave Baker effectively shut off enemy passing attacks over the first half of the season. Over the final month of the season, however, the high-flying '49ers fell into a nose dive and the club blew a two-game lead with five games left by winning only once.

Detroit Lions—Even with a fine rookie fullback in Nick Pietrosante, the Detroit offense looked very tired most of the time. Age had caught up with the front line, as Lou Creekmur, Harley Sewell, and Charlie Ane could no longer play up to their earlier standards, and quarterback Tobin Rote now had as many bad days as good days. While ends Jim Gibbons and Dave Middleton weren't old, their speed was nothing to write home about. With the defense being rebuilt around Alex Karras, Joe Schmidt, and Yale Lary, the Lions dropped thier first four games before upsetting the Rams.

Los Angeles Rams—General manager Pete Rozelle had built a surefire championship club by trading for runner Ollie Matson and defensive end Gene Brito over the summer. Matson had cost the Rams eight players and a draft choice but was expected to join Billy Wade, Jon Arnett, and Del Shofner in an unstoppable offense, while Brito was to fit into the Les Richter-led defense. The Rams were favored to beat the New York Giants on opening day, but 71,000 fans in the Coliseum saw them bow 23-21. After the '49ers shellacked them 34-0 the next week, the dreams of glory began to fade.

FINAL TEAM STATISTICS

OFFENSE

	BALT.	CHI.B	CHI.C	CLEVE.	DET.	G.BAY	L.A.	N.Y.	PHIL.	PITT.	S.F.	WASH.
FIRST DOWNS:												
Total	**267**	190	179	234	198	212	232	198	211	207	182	193
by Rushing	95	69	85	**118**	90	109	101	82	78	82	93	94
by Passing	**148**	110	80	109	87	87	116	106	120	103	76	80
by Penalty	**24**	11	14	7	21	16	15	10	13	22	13	19
RUSHING:												
Number	435	392	367	**457**	399	421	371	433	391	406	407	422
Yards	1705	1438	1613	**2149**	1792	1907	1778	1646	1315	1543	1839	1964
Average Yards	3.9	3.7	4.4	4.7	4.5	4.5	**4.8**	3.8	3.4	3.8	4.5	4.7
Touchdowns	13	14	10	**20**	13	15	15	11	13	10	16	9
PASSING:												
Attempts	**375**	310	280	276	328	268	356	302	352	319	264	284
Completions	**196**	156	125	159	136	128	**196**	165	194	150	132	121
Completion Percentage	52.3	50.3	44.6	**57.6**	41.5	47.8	55.1	54.6	55.1	47.0	50.0	42.6
Gross Yards	**2938**	2284	1766	2033	2131	1963	2723	2633	2644	2298	1685	1824
Yards Lost Passing	185	211	207	167	467	131	241	106	**72**	246	136	301
Net Yards	**2753**	2073	1559	1866	1664	1832	2482	2527	2572	2052	1549	1523
Avg. Yards per Attempt (Gross)	7.8	7.4	6.3	7.4	6.5	7.3	7.6	**8.7**	7.5	7.2	6.4	6.4
Avg. Yards per Comp. (Gross)	15.0	14.6	14.1	12.8	15.7	15.3	13.9	**16.0**	13.6	15.3	12.8	15.1
Touchdowns	**33**	15	14	14	10	16	14	18	17	21	12	13
Interceptions	14	16	19	**9**	27	17	22	13	16	23	22	23
Percent Intercepted	3.7	5.2	6.8	**3.3**	8.2	6.3	6.2	4.3	4.5	7.2	8.3	8.1
PUNTS:												
Number	53	68	62	50	56	64	50	55	54	**71**	59	49
Average Distance	42.1	41.3	44.6	37.1	46.5	42.4	41.7	**46.6**	42.7	40.4	45.7	45.5
PUNT RETURNS:												
Number	38	26	**56**	26	50	33	36	50	36	38	37	30
Yards	233	243	**548**	211	197	316	251	164	239	152	269	119
Average Yards	6.1	9.3	**9.8**	8.1	3.9	9.6	7.0	3.3	6.6	4.0	7.3	4.0
Touchdowns	0	1	**5**	1	0	1	1	0	2	0	0	0
KICKOFF RETURNS:												
Number	38	33	**52**	29	42	43	43	31	42	30	41	50
Yards	792	735	**1080**	551	846	949	1054	703	842	613	980	1006
Average Yards	20.8	22.3	20.8	19.0	20.1	22.1	**24.5**	22.7	20.0	20.4	23.9	20.1
Touchdowns	0	0	0	0	0	0	0	0	0	0	**1**	0
INTERCEPTION RETURNS:												
Number	**40**	22	15	18	14	14	7	22	20	22	14	13
Yards	**677**	100	301	242	216	231	5	288	167	363	189	147
Average Yards	14.4	9.0	**20.1**	13.4	15.4	16.5	0.7	13.1	8.4	16.5	13.5	11.3
Touchdowns	**4**	1	1	1	0	0	0	2	0	0	1	0
PENALTIES:												
Number	56	**66**	44	36	65	49	51	54	52	60	57	51
Yards	**634**	597	431	329	496	435	465	480	501	532	489	453
FUMBLES:												
Number	22	26	48	**8**	36	24	34	30	26	22	24	25
Number Lost	9	15	36	**5**	19	16	19	20	9	10	10	17
POINTS:												
Total	**374**	252	234	270	203	248	242	284	268	257	255	185
PAT Attempts	**51**	32	31	37	25	32	29	32	35	32	31	22
PAT Made	**50**	28	30	33	23	31	27	32	34	32	31	21
FG Attempts	18	19	9	16	23	17	26	**30**	24	18	26	22
FG Made	6	10	6	5	10	7	11	**20**	8	11	12	10
Percent FG Made	33.3	52.6	**66.7**	31.3	43.5	41.2	42.3	**66.7**	33.3	61.1	46.2	45.5
Safeties	0	1	0	0	0	**2**	1	0	0	0	1	1

DEFENSE

	BALT.	CHI.B.	CHI.C.	CLEVE.	DET.	G.BAY	L.A.	N.Y.	PHIL.	PITT.	S.F.	WASH.
FIRST DOWNS:												
Total	195	208	212	205	196	215	216	**167**	220	179	238	252
by Rushing	**65**	95	99	75	79	101	96	66	103	85	123	109
by Passing	118	91	100	115	103	102	100	85	101	**80**	102	125
by Penalty	**12**	22	13	15	14	**12**	20	16	16	14	13	18
RUSHING:												
Number	**325**	429	477	360	403	430	427	379	429	405	433	404
Yards	1557	1783	1874	1422	1562	1770	1704	**1261**	2068	1500	1974	2214
Average Yards	4.8	4.2	3.9	4.0	3.9	4.1	4.0	**3.3**	4.8	3.7	4.6	5.5
Touchdowns	16	11	15	9	13	14	15	**6**	15	10	16	19
PASSING:												
Attempts	351	333	**266**	319	288	329	287	304	292	285	341	319
Completions	171	144	138	168	147	169	151	137	144	**128**	176	185
Completion Percentage	48.7	43.2	51.9	52.7	51.0	51.4	52.6	45.1	49.3	**44.9**	51.6	58.0
Gross Yards	2497	2147	2359	2457	2340	2030	2315	**1811**	2074	2014	2272	2606
Yards Lost Passing	155	**254**	218	115	246	248	225	229	204	172	228	176
Net Yards	2342	1893	2141	2342	2094	1782	2090	**1582**	1870	1842	2044	2430
Avg. Yards per Attempt (Gross)	7.1	6.4	8.9	7.7	8.1	6.2	8.1	**6.0**	7.1	7.1	6.7	8.2
Avg. Yards per Comp. (Gross)	14.6	14.9	17.1	14.6	15.9	**12.0**	13.7	13.2	14.4	15.7	12.9	14.1
Touchdowns	13	14	22	17	19	14	17	**11**	17	12	15	26
Interceptions	**40**	22	15	18	14	14	7	22	20	22	14	13
Percent Intercepted	**11.4**	6.6	5.6	5.6	4.9	4.3	2.4	7.2	6.8	7.7	4.1	4.1
PUNTS:												
Number	50	61	67	50	69	56	60	**72**	48	59	57	42
Average Distance	44.7	42.3	41.3	42.4	43.7	44.3	44.1	42.7	41.1	46.5	41.6	**40.8**
PUNT RETURNS:												
Number	33	**46**	39	32	36	40	**30**	38	40	49	35	38
Yards	120	360	181	**39**	230	291	205	527	312	418	186	73
Average Yards	3.6	7.8	4.6	**1.2**	6.4	7.3	6.8	13.9	7.8	8.5	5.3	1.9
Touchdowns	**0**	1	**0**	**0**	**0**	1	1	4	1	3	**0**	**0**
KICKOFF RETURNS:												
Number	46	38	33	38	37	40	42	52	37	43	40	**28**
Yards	950	754	692	734	774	917	980	1229	819	753	924	**625**
Average Yards	20.7	19.8	21.0	19.3	20.9	22.9	23.3	23.6	22.1	**17.5**	23.1	22.3
Touchdowns	**0**	**0**	**0**	**0**	**0**	**0**	1	**0**	**0**	**0**	**0**	**0**
INTERCEPTION RETURNS:												
Number	14	18	19	**9**	27	17	22	13	16	23	22	23
Yards	199	**96**	158	139	370	227	305	173	360	287	272	339
Average Yards	14.2	**6.0**	8.3	15.4	13.7	13.4	13.9	13.3	22.5	12.5	12.4	14.7
Touchdowns	2	**0**	1	1	1	1	1	**0**	2	**0**	1	**0**
PENALTIES:												
Number	**65**	62	61	32	64	51	60	40	47	55	45	59
Yards	**610**	553	528	285	603	450	562	324	457	483	417	570
FUMBLES:												
Number	18	**38**	25	20	31	28	25	29	28	22	34	27
Number Lost	9	17	15	12	19	15	14	16	20	12	**22**	14
POINTS:												
Total	251	196	324	214	275	246	315	**170**	278	216	237	350
PAT Attempts	31	26	41	28	34	30	38	**22**	36	26	31	46
PAT Made	29	26	40	28	34	28	36	**20**	35	24	28	44
FG Attempts	22	17	22	**13**	21	22	31	16	20	32	**13**	19
FG Made	12	**4**	12	6	11	12	17	6	9	12	5	10
Percent FG Made	54.5	**23.5**	54.5	46.2	52.4	54.5	54.8	37.5	45.0	37.5	38.5	52.6
Safeties	**0**	1	1	**0**	2	1	**0**	**0**	**0**	**0**	1	**0**

1959 CHAMPIONSHIP GAME

December 27, at Baltimore
(Attendance 57,545)

SCORING

BALTIMORE	7	0	0	24–31
NEW YORK	3	3	3	7–16

First Quarter

Bal.	Moore, 60 yard pass from Unitas PAT – Myhra (kick)	4:55
N. Y.	Summerall, 23 yard field goal	13:16

Second Quarter

N. Y.	Summerall, 37 yard field goal	14:49

Third Quarter

N. Y.	Summerall, 23 yard field goal	5:45

Fourth Quarter

Bal.	Unitas, 4 yard rush PAT – Myhra (kick)	2:42
Bal.	Richardson, 12 yard pass from Unitas PAT – Myhra (kick)	7:21
Bal.	Sample, 42 yard interception return PAT – Myhra (kick)	9:31
Bal.	Myhra, 25 yard field goal	12:40
N. Y.	Schnelker, 32 yard pass from Conerly PAT – Summerall (kick)	14:28

TEAM STATISTICS

BAL.		N.Y.
12	First Downs – Total	17
3	First Downs – Rushing	4
9	First Downs – Passing	12
0	First Downs – Penalty	1
1	Fumbles – Number	1
0	Fumbles – Lost Ball	0
4	Penalties – Number	3
20	Yards Penalized	23
1	Field Goals Missed	0

Convincingly If Not Easily

Meeting in a rematch of the famous 1958 sudden-death overtime confrontation, the Baltimore Colts and New York Giants gave fans an exciting but anticlimactic finish to one of the most thrilling championship matchups in NFL history. Although Baltimore drew first blood by driving 80 yards in six plays, capped by a 60-yard pass from Johnny Unitas to Lenny Moore, the Giants responded three times on Pat Summerall's toe to move in front 9-7 by the time the third quarter drew to a close. Unfortunately for the Giants, they entered the second half without the services of their star end Kyle Rote, the victim of a concussion, and safety Jimmy Patton, who injured his foot late in the second period and had to leave the game. Yet beyond the injuries, which surely hurt the Giants in the final and all-important fourth quarter, the turning point of the game came in the third quarter, when, with New York in front 9-7, the ball was on the Colts' 28-yard line with fourth down and inches to go. The Giants decided to go for the first down behind Alex Webster only to meet a stone-wall defense led by Gino Marchetti. The backfired strategy changed the momentum of the game, as the Colts scored four times in the fourth period, three on touchdowns, with one coming off an interception and the last on a field goal by Steve Myhra to bring the score to 31-9 before New York finally struck pay dirt with thirty-two seconds remaining to make the final count a little more respectable. The game was best summed up by Colt general manager Don Kellert, who said, "We didn't win easily, but we won convincingly."

INDIVIDUAL STATISTICS

BALTIMORE	No.	Yds.	Avg.	NEW YORK	No.	Yds.	Avg.
RUSHING							
Ameche	9	30	3.3	Gifford	9	50	5.6
Sommer	6	15	2.5	Triplett	6	39	6.5
Pricer	4	14	3.5	Webster	8	25	3.1
Moore	4	8	2.0	King	2	4	2.0
Unitas	2	6	3.0		25	118	4.7
	25	73	2.9				
RECEIVING							
Berry	5	68	13.6	Schnelker	9	178	19.8
Mutsch'ler	5	40	8.0	King	4	17	4.3
Moore	3	127	42.3	Rote	2	41	20.5
Price	2	6	3.0	Gifford	1	19	19.0
Ameche	1	13	13.0	Triplett	1	–2	–2.0
Richardson	1	12	12.0		17	253	14.9
Sommer	1	–1	–1.0				
	18	265	14.7				
PUNTING							
Sherer	6		37.9	Chandler	6		47.9
PUNT RETURNS							
Sample	2	23	11.5	Morrison	1	5	5.0
Taseff	1	10	10.0	King	1	2	2.0
	3	33	11.0		2	7	3.5
KICKOFF RETURNS							
Hawkins	2	63	31.5	King	2	52	26.0
Myhra	1	31	31.0	Morrison	2	43	21.5
Sample	1	8	8.0	Triplett	1	21	21.0
	4	102	25.5		5	116	23.2
INTERCEPTION RETURNS							
Sample	2	76	38.0	None			
Nelson	1	17	17.0				
	3	93	31.0				

PASSING

BALTIMORE	Att	Comp	Comp Pct.	Yds	Int	Yds/ Att.	Yds/ Comp	Yards Lost Tackled
Unitas	29	18	62.1	265	0	9.1	14.7	7-58
NEW YORK								
Conerly	35	16	45.7	234	2	6.7	14.6	5–47
Gifford	2	1	50.0	19	1	9.5	19.0	0– 0
King	1	0	0.0	0	0	–	–	0– 0
	38	17	44.7	253	3	6.7	14.9	5–47

NEW YORK GIANTS 10-2-0 Jim Lee Howell

Scores of Each Game		
23	Los Angeles	21
21	Philadelphia	49
10	Cleveland	6
24	PHILADELPHIA	7
21	Pittsburgh	16
20	GREEN BAY	3
9	CHIC. CARDS	3
9	PITTSBURGH	14
30	Chic. Cards (at Minneapolis)	20
45	WASHINGTON	14
48	CLEVELAND	7
24	Washington	10

Use Name	Pos.	Hgt	Wgt	Age	Int	Pts
Rosey Brown	OT	6'3"	245	26		
Frank Youso	OT	6'4"	260	23		
Bob Schmidt	C-OT	6'4"	245	23		
Al Barry	OG	6'2"	230	28		
Darrell Dess	OG	6'	235	23		
Ellison Kelly	OG	6'1"	235	23		
Jack Stroud	OG	6'1"	235	30		
Buzz Guy	OT-DT-OG	6'3"	248	24		
Ray Wietecha	C	6'1"	225	30		
Jim Katcavage	DE	6'3"	230	24		
Andy Robustelli	DE	6'1"	230	33		
Rosey Grier	DT	6'5"	285	26		
Art Hauser (from Chi C)	DT	6'	235	28		
Dick Modzelewski	DT	6'	260	28		
Sam Huff	LB	6'1"	230	24	1	6
Cliff Livingston	LB	6'3"	215	29	2	
Harland Svare	LB	6'	215	28	3	6
Tom Scott	DE-LB	6'2"	220	29		
Lindon Crow	DB	6'1"	200	26	5	6
Dick Lynch	DB	6'1"	200	23	1	
Dick Nolan	DB	6'1"	185	27	5	
Jimmy Patton	DB	6'	180	27	5	
Bill Stits (from WAS)	DB	6'	195	28		
Chuck Conerly	QB	6'1"	185	35		6
Don Heinrich	QB	6'	180	27		
George Shaw	QB	6'1"	180	26		
Don Chandler	HB	6'2"	205	24		2
Frank Gifford	HB	6'1"	205	29		42
George Scott	HB	6'1"	180	21		
Alex Webster	HB	6'3"	225	28		42
Joe Morrison	DB-HB	6'1"	195	21		12
Mel Triplett	FB	6'1"	215	27		6
Phil King	HB-FB	6'4"	225	23		6
Joe Biscaha	OE	6'1"	190	22		
Bill Kimber	OE	6'2"	195	23		
Kyle Rote	OE	6'	200	30		24
Bob Schnelker	OE	6'3"	215	29		36
Pat Summerall	OE	6'4"	235	29		90

CLEVELAND BROWNS 7-5-0 Paul Brown

Scores of Each Game		
7	Pittsburgh	17
34	Chic. Cards	7
6	NEW YORK	10
17	CHIC. CARDS	7
34	WASHINGTON	7
38	Baltimore	31
28	PHILADELPHIA	7
31	Washington	17
20	PITTSBURGH	21
20	SAN FRANCISCO	21
7	New York	48
28	Philadelphia	21

Use Name	Pos.	Hgt	Wgt	Age	Int	Pts
Lou Groza	OT	6'3"	248	35		48
Mike McCormack	OT	6'4"	247	32		
Fran O'Brien	DE-OT	6'1"	235	24		
Gene Hickerson	OG	6'3"	242	24		
Jim Ray Smith	OG	6'3"	242	28		
John Wooten	OG	6'2"	235	24		
Dick Schafrath	DE-OG	6'3"	230	23		
Art Hunter	C	6'4"	242	26		
Bob Gain	DE	6'3"	260	31		
Paul Wiggin	DE	6'3"	237	25		
Willie Davis	OT-DE	6'3"	240	26		
Willie McClung	DT	6'2"	260	30		
Floyd Peters	DT	6'4"	250	24		
Sid Youngelman	DT	6'3"	262	27		
Vince Costello	LB	6'	225	27		
Galen Fiss	LB	6'	227	29	1	
Walt Michaels	LB	6'	237	30	1	
Chuck Noll	OG-LB	6'1"	224	27	2	
Dave Lloyd	C-LB	6'3"	240	23		
Kenny Konz	DB	5'10"	187	31	1	
Warren Lahr	DB	5'11"	192	35	1	
Bernie Parrish	DB	5'11"	190	24	5	6
Jim Shofner	DB	6'2"	187	23	2	
Junior Wren	DB	6'	192	29	5	6
Jim Ninowski	QB	6'1"	210	23		
Milt Plum	QB	6'1"	205	25		6
Bob Ptacek	QB	6'1"	205	23		
Leroy Bolden	HB	5'8"	170	26		
Bobby Mitchell	HB	6'	180	24		60
Jimmy Brown	FB	6'2"	228	23		84
Ed Modzelewski	FB	6'	222	30		6
Ray Renfro	FL	6'1"	190	28		36
Preston Carpenter	OE	6'2"	195	25		12
Frank Clarke	OE	6'	207	26		
Billy Howton	OE	6'2"	195	29		6
Rich Kreitling	OE	6'2"	205	24		

PHILADELPHIA EAGLES 7-5-0 Buck Shaw

Scores of Each Game		
14	San Francisco	24
49	NEW YORK	21
28	PITTSBURGH	24
7	New York	24
28	Chic. Cards	24
30	WASHINGTON	23
7	Cleveland	28
27	CHIC. CARDS	17
23	LOS ANGELES	20
0	Pittsburgh	31
34	Washington	14
21	CLEVELAND	28

Use Name	Pos.	Hgt	Wgt	Age	Int	Pts
Jerry DeLucca	OT	6'3"	245	23		
Jim McCusker	OT	6'2"	245	23		
J. D. Smith	OT	6'5"	250	23		
Darrell Aschbacher	OG	6'1"	220	24		
Stan Campbell	OG	6'	230	29		
Jerry Huth	OG	6'	228	26		6
Bill Striegel	OG	6'2"	230	23		
Chuck Bednarik	C	6'3"	235	34		
Ed Khayat	DE	6'3"	225	24	1	
Joe Robb	DE	6'3"	225	22		
Jerry Wilson	DE	6'3"	240	22		
Jess Richardson	DT	6'2"	262	29		
Don Owens	OT-DT	6'5"	255	27		6
Marion Campbell	DE-DT	6'3"	250	30	1	
Tom Catlin	LB	6'1"	220	28		
John Nocera	LB	6'1"	215	25		
Bob Pellegrini	LB	6'2"	235	24	3	
Chuck Weber	LB	6'1"	235	30	2	6
Tom Louderback	C-LB	6'2"	234	25		
Tom Brookshier	DB	6'	198	27	3	
Jimmy Carr	DB	6'1"	198	26	5	
Gene Johnson	DB	6'	190	24	1	
Art Powell	DB	6'3"	200	22	3	6
Lee Riley	DB	6'1"	190	27	1	
Sonny Jurgensen	QB	5'11"	200	25		
Norm Van Brocklin	QB	6'1"	202	33		12
Billy Barnes	HB	5'11"	202	24		54
Theron Sapp	HB	6'1"	200	24		6
Walt Kowalczyk	FB	6'	205	24		
Joe Pagliei	FB	6'	220	25		
Clarence Peaks	FB	6'1"	220	23		18
Tommy McDonald	FL	5'10"	182	25		66
Dick Bielski	OE	6'1"	218	27		6
Pete Retzlaff	OE	6'1"	210	28		6
Bobby Walston	OE	6'	190	30		51
Paige Cothren	K	5'11"	195	24		25

PITTSBURGH STEELERS 6-5-1 Buddy Parker

Scores of Each Game		
17	CLEVELAND	7
17	WASHINGTON	23
24	Philadelphia	28
27	Washington	6
16	NEW YORK	21
24	Chic. Cards	45
10	DETROIT	10
14	New York	9
21	Cleveland	20
31	PHILADELPHIA	0
21	Chic. Bears	27
35	CHIC. CARDS	20

Use Name	Pos.	Hgt	Wgt	Age	Int	Pts
Frank Varrichione	OT	6'1"	230	27		
Ray Fisher	OG-DT-OT	6'	230	25		
John Nisby	OG	6'1"	230	26		
Mike Sandusky	OG	6'	230	26		
Ted Karras	OT-OG	6'1"	235	26		
Ed Beatty	C	6'3"	225	27		
Billy Ray Smith	DE	6'4"	230	24		
George Tarasovic	C-DE	6'4"	245	30		6
Joe Krupa	DT	6'2"	240	26		
Joe Lewis	DT	6'2"	260	24		
Byron Beams	OT-DT	6'6"	250	25		
Ernie Stautner	DE-DT	6'1"	230	34		
Dick Campbell	LB	6'1"	230	23	1	
Dale Dodrill	LB	6'1"	215	34		
Rudy Hayes	LB	6'	220	24		
Mike Henry	LB	6'2"	230	23	2	
Dick Lasse	LB	6'2"	215	23		
John Reger	LB	6'	230	28		
Dick Alban	DB	6'	195	30	6	
Don Bishop (to Chi B)	DB	6'2"	210	24		
Jack Butler	DB	6'	195	31	2	
Dean Derby	DB	6'	185	25	7	
Ron Hall	DB	6'	190	22	1	
Bobby Luna	DB	5'11"	190	26	3	
Don Sutherin (from NY)	DB	5'10"	195	23		
Len Dawson	QB	6'	180	25		
Bobby Layne	QB	6'1"	208	32		77
Jack Call	HB	6'1"	200	24		
Tom Tracy	HB	5'9"	210	27		48
Tom Barnett	DB-HB	5'11"	190	22		12
Leo Elter	FB	5'10"	205	30		
Larry Krutko	FB	6'	215	24		24
Ray Mathews	FL	6'	190	30		
Buddy Dial	OE-FL	6'1"	185	22		36
Darrell Brewster	OE	6'3"	215	29		12
Jack McClairen	OE	6'4"	210	28		
Gern Nagler	OE	6'2"	190	26		12
Jimmy Orr	OE	5'11"	195	23		30

WASHINGTON REDSKINS 3-9-0 Mike Nixon

Scores of Each Game		
21	Chic. Cards	49
23	Pittsburgh	17
23	CHIC. CARDS	14
6	PITTSBURGH	27
7	Cleveland	34
23	Philadelphia	30
27	BALTIMORE	24
17	CLEVELAND	31
0	Green Bay	21
14	New York	45
14	PHILADELPHIA	34
10	NEW YORK	24

Use Name	Pos.	Hgt	Wgt	Age	Int	Pts
Ray Lemek	OT	6'	237	25		
Don Boll	OG-OT	6'2"	282	32		
Johnny Miller	DT-OT	6'5"	260	25		
Don Lawrence	OG	6'1"	245	22		
Red Stephens	OG	6'	232	29		
Frank Kuchta	C	6'2"	220	23		
Jim Schrader	C	6'2"	250	27		
Art Gob	DE	6'4"	230	22		2
Ed Meadows	DE	6'2"	225	27		
John Paluck	DE	6'2"	235	26		
Chet Ostrowski	DT-DE	6'1"	235	29		
Don Churchwell	DT	6'1"	250	22		
Will Renfro	DT	6'5"	240	27		
Bob Toneff	DT	6'3"	250	29		
Tom Braatz	LB	6'1"	215	26	1	
Chuck Drazenovich	LB	6'1"	224	32	1	
Ralph Felton	LB	5'11"	210	27	2	
Emil Karas	DE-LB	6'3"	227	25	1	
Bob Hudson	DB-LB	6'4"	230	29		
Gene Cichowski	DB	6'	195	25		
Gary Glick (from PIT)	DB	6'2"	190	28	2	
Richie McCabe	DB	6'1"	182	25	1	
Doyle Nix	DB	6'1"	188	26	1	
Ben Scotti	DB	6'1"	185	22		
Eagle Day	QB	6'	180	27		
Ralph Guglielmi	QB	6'1"	200	26		
Eddie LeBaron	QB	5'9"	167	29		
Jim Podoley	HB	6'2"	205	26		12
Ed Sutton	HB	6'1"	205	24		6
Dick James	DB-HB	5'9"	175	25	3	24
Dick Haley	DB-OE-HB	5'10"	190	22	1	6
Sam Baker	FB	6'2"	217	27		51
Don Bosseler	FB	6'1"	215	23		18
Johnny Olszewski	HB-FB	5'11"	202	28		6
Bill Anderson	OE	6'3"	211	23		36
Johnny Carson	OE	6'3"	205	29		
Ken MacAfee (from PHI)	OE	6'2"	215	29		6
Joe Walton	OE	5'11"	200	24		18

CHICAGO CARDINALS 2-10-0 Pop Ivy

Scores of Each Game		
49	WASHINGTON	21
7	CLEVELAND	34
14	Washington	23
7	Cleveland	17
24	PHILADELPHIA	28
45	PITTSBURGH	24
3	New York	9
17	Philadelphia	27
20	NEW YORK (at Minneapolis)	30
7	CHIC. BEARS	31
21	Detroit	45
20	Pittsburgh	35

Use Name	Pos.	Hgt	Wgt	Age	Int	Pts
Bob Cross	OT	6'4"	250	28		
Ken Panfil	OT	6'6"	265	28		
Ed Cook	OG-OT	6'2"	237	27		
Ken Gray	OG	6'2"	235	23		
Dale Meinert	OG	6'2"	218	26		
Dale Memmelaar	OT-OG	6'2"	230	22		
Don Gillis	C	6'3"	240	24		
Mac Lewis	OT-C	6'6"	290	22		
Leo Sugar	DE	6'1"	210	30		
Luke Owens	DT-DE	6'2"	255	26		
Maury Schleicher	LB-DE	6'3"	232	22		
Ed Culpepper	DT	6'1"	255	25		
Frank Fuller	DT	6'4"	245	30		
Ed Husmann	DT	6'	230	28		
Ted Bates	LB	6'3"	215	22		
Carl Brettschneider	LB	6'1"	220	27	1	
Bill Koman	LB	6'2"	230	25		
Jack Patera	LB	6'1"	235	27	1	
Marion Rushing	LB	6'2"	210	22		
Freddy Glick	DB	6'1"	185	22		
Jimmy Hill	DB	6'2"	190	30	2	6
Night Train Lane	DB	6'1"	190	31	3	6
Jerry Norton	DB	5'11"	195	29	3	
Billy Stacy	DB	6'1"	190	23	5	12
Jim Wagstaff	DB	6'2"	195	23		
King Hill	QB	6'3"	207	23		30
M. C. Reynolds	QB	6'	190	24		
John Roach	DB-QB	6'4"	195	26		
Joe Childress	HB	6'	200	25		6
Bobby Joe Conrad	HB	6'	195	24		84
Ken Hall	HB	6'1"	205	23		12
Mal Hammack	FB	6'2"	205	26		6
Larry Hickman	FB	6'2"	223	23		
John David Crow	HB-FB	6'2"	215	24		42
Woodley Lewis	OE	6'	195	34		18
Sonny Randle	OE	6'2"	187	23		6
Perry Richards	OE	6'2"	205	25		6
John Tracey	OE	6'3"	218	25		

NEW YORK GIANTS

RUSHING

Last Name	No.	Yds	Avg	TD
Gifford	106	540	5.1	3
Triplett	91	381	4.2	1
Webster	79	250	3.2	5
King	72	232	3.2	0
Morrison	62	165	2.7	1
Conerly	15	38	2.5	1
Chandler	1	24	24.0	0
Scott	2	10	5.0	0
Heinrich	2	3	1.5	0
Shaw	3	3	1.0	0

RECEIVING

Last Name	No.	Yds	Avg	TD
Gifford	42	768	18	4
Schnelker	37	714	19	6
Webster	27	381	14	2
Rote	25	362	14	4
Morrison	17	183	11	1
King	7	98	14	1
Triplett	6	78	13	0
Summerall	2	32	16	0
Scott	1	12	12	0
Biscaha	1	5	5	0

PUNT RETURNS

Last Name	No.	Yds	Avg	TD
Crow	11	66	6	0
Morrison	15	51	3	0
Patton	8	23	3	0
Scott	12	17	1	0
Stits	4	7	2	0

KICKOFF RETURNS

Last Name	No.	Yds	Avg	TD
Morrison	15	345	23	0
Scott	10	253	25	0
King	4	84	21	0
Brown	1	18	18	0
Summerall	1	3	3	0

PASSING – PUNTING – KICKING

PASSING	Att	Comp	%	Yds	Yd/Att	TD	Int–%	RK
Conerly	194	113	58	1706	8.8	14	4– 2	1
Heinrich	58	22	38	329	5.7	1	6– 10	
Shaw	36	24	67	433	12.0	1	1– 3	
Gifford	11	5	45	151	13.7	2	2– 18	
Morrison	2	1	50	14	7.0	0	0– 0	
Webster	1	0	0	0	0.0	0	0– 0	

PUNTING	No	Avg
Chandler	55	46.6

KICKING	XP	Att	%	FG	Att	%
Summerall	30	30	100	20	29	69
Chandler	2	2	100	0	1	0

CLEVELAND BROWNS

RUSHING

Last Name	No.	Yds	Avg	TD
Brown	290	1329	4.6	14
Mitchell	131	743	5.7	5
Plum	21	20	1.0	1
Modzelewski	6	18	3.0	0
Ptacek	3	13	4.3	0
Bolden	4	11	2.8	0
Ninowski	1	11	11.0	0
Carpenter	1	4	4.0	0

RECEIVING

Last Name	No.	Yds	Avg	TD
Howton	39	510	13	1
Mitchell	35	351	10	4
Renfro	30	528	18	6
Carpenter	24	372	16	2
Brown	24	190	8	0
Clarke	3	44	15	0
Modzelewski	3	18	6	1
Plum	1	20	20	0

PUNT RETURNS

Last Name	No.	Yds	Avg	TD
Mitchell	17	177	10	1
Konz	9	34	4	0

KICKOFF RETURNS

Last Name	No.	Yds	Avg	TD
Mitchell	11	236	21	0
Bolden	9	170	19	0
Brown	4	88	22	0
Modzelewski	4	37	9	0
Noll	1	20	20	0

PASSING – PUNTING – KICKING

PASSING	Att	Comp	%	Yds	Yd/Att	TD	Int–%	RK
Plum	266	156	59	1992	7.5	14	8– 3	3
Ninowski	10	3	33	41	4.1	0	1– 10	

PUNTING	No	Avg
Wren	27	36.9
Shofner	23	37.4

KICKING	XP	Att	%	FG	Att	%
Groza	33	37	89	5	16	31

PHILADELPHIA EAGLES

RUSHING

Last Name	No.	Yds	Avg	TD
Barnes	181	687	3.8	7
Peaks	124	451	3.6	3
Sapp	41	145	3.5	1
Kowalczyk	26	37	1.4	0
Van Brocklin	11	13	1.2	2
Walston	2	8	4.0	0
Pagliei	2	–5	–2.5	0
McDonald	2	–10	–5.0	0
Retzlaff	2	–11	–5.5	0

RECEIVING

Last Name	No.	Yds	Avg	TD
McDonald	47	846	18	10
Retzlaff	34	595	18	1
Barnes	32	314	10	2
Peaks	28	209	7	0
Walston	16	279	17	3
Bielski	15	264	18	1
Kowalczyk	9	33	4	0
Sapp	6	47	8	0
Pagliei	2	9	5	0

PUNT RETURNS

Last Name	No.	Yds	Avg	TD
Powell	15	124	8	1
Mcdonald	21	115	5	1

KICKOFF RETURNS

Last Name	No.	Yds	Avg	TD
McDonald	24	444	19	0
Powell	14	379	27	0
Nocera	1	15	15	0
Wilson	2	4	2	0
DeLucca	1	0	0	0

PASSING – PUNTING – KICKING

PASSING	Att	Comp	%	Yds	Yd/Att	TD	Int–%	RK
Van Brocklin	340	191	56	2617	7.7	16	14– 4	4
Barnes	7	0	0	0	0.0	0	2– 29	
Jurgensen	5	3	60	27	5.4	1	0– 0	

PUNTING	No	Avg
Van Brocklin	53	42.7
Pagllei	1	45.0

KICKING	XP	Att	%	FG	Att	%
Walston	33	34	97	0	1	0
Cothren	1	1	100	8	18	44
Bielski	0	0	0	0	5	0

PITTSBURGH STEELERS

RUSHING

Last Name	No.	Yds	Avg	TD
Tracy	199	794	4.0	3
Barnett	75	238	3.2	1
Krutko	75	226	3.0	4
Layne	33	181	5.5	2
Orr	5	43	8.6	0
Elter	8	25	3.1	0
Dawson	4	20	5.0	0
Call	3	9	3.0	0
Mathews	1	4	4.0	0
Luna	3	3	1.0	0

RECEIVING

Last Name	No.	Yds	Avg	TD
Orr	35	604	17	5
Tracy	23	273	12	5
Brewster	22	360	16	2
Dial	16	428	27	6
Nagler	14	222	16	2
Mathews	13	182	14	0
Krutko	13	100	8	0
Barnett	7	52	7	1
McClairen	3	46	15	0
Elter	3	31	10	0
Call	1	0	0	0

PUNT RETURNS

Last Name	No.	Yds	Avg	TD
Sutherin	12	68	6	0
Hall	5	23	5	0
Mathews	2	17	9	0
Derby	9	16	2	0
Luna	2	13	7	0
Bishop	4	10	3	0
Tracy	4	5	1	0

KICKOFF RETURNS

Last Name	No.	Yds	Avg	TD
Sutherin	11	225	20	0
Call	6	146	24	0
Tracy	7	145	21	0
Derby	2	32	16	0
Barnett	2	24	12	0
Hall	1	22	22	0
Hayes	1	19	19	0

PASSING – PUNTING – KICKING

PASSING	Att	Comp	%	Yds	Yd/Att	TD	Int–%	RK
Layne	297	142	48	1986	6.7	20	21 7	8
Tracy	12	3	25	159	13.3	0	2– 17	
Dawson	7	3	43	60	8.6	1	0– 0	
Luna	1	1	100	55	55.0	0	0– 0	
Mathews	1	1	100	38	38.0	0	0– 0	
Orr	1	0	0	0	0.0	0	0– 0	

PUNTING	No	Avg
Luna	63	40.7
Orr	8	37.8

KICKING	XP	Att	%	FG	Att	%
Layne	32	32	100	11	17	65
Sutherin	0	0	0	0	1	0

WASHINGTON REDSKINS

RUSHING

Last Name	No.	Yds	Avg	TD
Bosseler	119	644	5.4	3
Olszewski	65	432	6.6	1
James	100	384	3.8	3
Sutton	61	232	3.8	1
Guglielmi	26	97	3.7	0
Podoley	18	83	4.6	0
Haley	14	51	3.6	1
Day	3	27	9.0	0
LeBaron	13	7	0.5	0
Baker	2	3	1.5	0

RECEIVING

Last Name	No.	Yds	Avg	TD
Anderson	35	734	21	6
Walton	21	317	15	3
Podoley	18	282	16	2
James	13	192	15	1
Bosseler	11	47	4	0
MacAfee	9	87	10	1
Olszewski	7	62	9	0
Carson	6	74	12	0
Sutton	4	63	16	0
Haley	2	14	7	0

PUNT RETURNS

Last Name	No.	Yds	Avg	TD
James	21	95	5	0
Haley	7	15	2	0
Glick	1	9	9	0
Olszewski	1	0	0	0

KICKOFF RETURNS

Last Name	No.	Yds	Avg	TD
James	23	503	22	0
Haley	17	346	20	0
Podoley	5	126	25	0
MacAfee	1	12	12	0
Gob	1	0	0	0
Renfro	1	0	0	0
Scotti	1	0	0	0

PASSING – PUNTING – KICKING

PASSING	Att	Comp	%	Yds	Yd/Att	TD	Int–%	RK
LeBaron	173	77	45	1077	6.2	8	11– 6	11
Guglielmi	89	36	40	617	6.9	4	11– 12	
Day	13	6	46	79	6.1	0	1– 8	
Sutton	7	2	29	51	7.3	1	0– 0	
Bosseler	1	0	0	0	0.0	0	0– 0	
Podoley	1	0	0	0	0.0	0	0– 0	

PUNTING	No	Avg
Baker	49	45.5

KICKING	XP	Att	%	FG	Att	%
Baker	21	22	95	10	22	45

CHICAGO CARDINALS

RUSHING

Last Name	No.	Yds	Avg	TD
Crow	140	666	4.8	3
Conrad	74	328	4.4	2
Hammack	49	237	4.8	0
K. Hill	39	167	4.3	5
Hall	14	81	5.8	0
Childress	30	59	2.0	0
Norton	2	41	20.5	0
Roach	9	20	2.2	0
Hickman	5	18	3.6	0
Reynolds	5	–4	–0.8	0

RECEIVING

Last Name	No.	Yds	Avg	TD
Lewis	34	534	16	3
Crow	27	328	12	4
Tracey	17	258	15	0
Randle	15	202	13	1
Conrad	14	142	10	3
Richards	5	89	18	1
Childress	4	73	18	1
Hammack	4	69	17	0
Hall	4	60	15	1
Hickman	1	11	11	0

PUNT RETURNS

Last Name	No.	Yds	Avg	TD
Stacy	29	281	10	2
Conrad	16	133	8	1
Hall	3	91	30	1
Richards	3	22	7	0
Norton	3	4	1	0
J. Hill	1	0	0	0
Sugar	1	0	0	0
Hammack	0	17	0	1

KICKOFF RETURNS

Last Name	No.	Yds	Avg	TD
Conrad	18	388	22	0
Stacy	12	280	23	0
Crow	5	185	37	0
Hall	6	99	17	0
Norton	3	70	23	0
Randle	2	33	17	0
Tracey	1	14	14	0
Gray	1	11	11	0
Cross	1	0	0	0
Hammack	1	0	0	0
Panfil	1	0	0	0
Patera	1	0	0	0

PASSING – PUNTING – KICKING

PASSING	Att	Comp	%	Yds	Yd/Att	TD	Int–%	RK
K. Hill	181	82	45	1015	5.6	7	13– 7	14
Roach	57	22	39	340	6.0	2	4– 7	
Reynolds	39	19	49	329	8.4	4	1– 3	
Conrad	3	2	67	82	27.3	1	1– 33	

PUNTING	No	Avg
Norton	59	44.9
K. Hill	3	39.3

KICKING	XP	Att	%	FG	Att	%
Conrad	30	31	97	6	9	67

BALTIMORE COLTS 9-3-0 Weeb Ewbank

Scores of Each Game			Use Name	Pos.	Hgt	Wgt	Age	Int	Pts	Use Name	Pos.	Hgt	Wgt	Age	Int	Pts	Use Name	Pos.	Hgt	Wgt	Age	Int	Pts
21	DETROIT	9	Jim Parker	OT	6'3"	270	25			Marv Matuszak	LB	6'3"	232	28	1		Johnny Unitas	QB	6'1"	190	26		12
21	CHIC. BEARS	26	Sherman Plunkett	OT	6'4"	265	25			Bill Pellington	LB	6'2"	230	30	4	6	L. G. Dupre	HB	5'11"	190	27		6
31	Detroit	24	George Preas	OT	6'2"	245	27			Bert Rechichar	LB	6'1"	210	29			Alex Hawkins	HB	6'1"	190	22		
21	Chic. Bears	7	Steve Myhra	OG	6'1"	235	25		68	Don Shinnick	LB	6'	230	24	7		Lenny Moore	HB	6'1"	190	26		48
38	GREEN BAY	21	Alex Sandusky	OG	6'1"	235	27			Dick Szymanski	LB	6'3"	230	27	5	6	Mike Sommer (from WAS)	HB	5'11"	190	24		12
31	CLEVELAND	38	Art Spinney	OG	6'	230	32			Milt Davis	DB	6'1"	190	30	7	6	Harold Lewis	DB-HB	6'	195	23		
24	Washington	27	Buzz Nutter	C	6'4"	235	28			Andy Nelson	DB	6'1"	180	26	6	6	Alan Ameche	FB	6'	217	26		48
28	Green Bay	24	Ordell Braase	DE	6'4"	242	27			Johnny Sample	DB	6'1"	203	22	1		Billy Pricer	FB	5'10"	210	24		
45	SAN FRANCISCO	14	Gino Marchetti	DE	6'4"	240	33	1		Jackie Simpson	DB	5'10"	180	25			Jerry Richardson	FL	6'3"	185	23		18
35	LOS ANGELES	21	Don Joyce	DT-DE	6'3"	255	29			Carl Taseff	DB	5'11"	190	30	2	6	Ray Berry	OE	6'2"	190	26		84
34	San Francisco	14	Art Donovan	DT	6'2"	270	34			Ray Brown	QB-DB	6'2"	195	23	5		Jim Mutscheller	OE	6'1"	215	29		48
45	Los Angeles	26	Big Daddy Lipscomb	DT	6'6"	288	28	1		Art DeCarlo	OE-DB	6'2"	196	29			Dave Sherer	OE	6'3"	210	22		
			Ray Krouse	DE-DT	6'3"	275	32																

CHICAGO BEARS 8-4-0 George Halas

Scores of Each Game			Use Name	Pos.	Hgt	Wgt	Age	Int	Pts	Use Name	Pos.	Hgt	Wgt	Age	Int	Pts	Use Name	Pos.	Hgt	Wgt	Age	Int	Pts
6	Green Bay	9	Dick Klein	OT	6'4"	255	25			Joe Fortunato	LB	6'	225	29	2		Zeke Bratkowski	QB	6'2"	203	27		
26	Baltimore	21	Herm Lee	OT	6'4"	247	28			Bill George	LB	6'2"	235	28	2		Ed Brown	QB	6'2"	208	30		6
21	LOS ANGELES	28	Ed Nickla	OT	6'3"	240	26			Chuck Howley	LB	6'3"	228	23			Rudy Bukich	QB	6'1"	200	28		
7	BALTIMORE	21	Abe Gibron	OG	5'11"	248	33			Larry Morris	LB	6'2"	230	24	1	6	Willie Galimore	HB	6'1"	187	24		18
17	San Francisco	20	Don Healy	OG	6'3"	255	23			Bill Roehnelt	LB	6'1"	225	23			Johnny Morris	HB	5'10"	180	24		18
26	Los Angeles	21	Stan Jones	OG	6'1"	250	28			Erich Barnes	DB	6'2"	198	24	5		John Adams	FB	6'3"	235	22		
28	GREEN BAY	17	John Damore	C-OG	6'	228	26			J. C. Caroline	DB	6'1"	190	26	5		Rick Casares	FB	6'2"	225	28		72
14	SAN FRANCISCO	3	John Mellekas	C	6'3"	255	26			Jack Johnson	DB	6'3"	198	25	1		Merrill Douglas	FB	6'	204	23		12
24	Detroit	14	Larry Strickland	C	6'4"	245	28			Pete Johnson	DB	6'2"	200	22			Jim Dooley	FL	6'4"	198	29		18
31	Chic. Cards	7	Doug Atkins	DE	6'8"	255	29			Richie Petitbon	DB	6'3"	205	21	3	6	Lionel Taylor	FL	6'2"	215	23		
27	PITTSBURGH	21	Earl Leggett	DT-DE	6'3"	250	25		2	Charlie Sumner	DB	6'1"	195	29	3		Willard Dewveall	OE	6'4"	218	22		18
25	DETROIT	14	Bill Bishop	DT	6'4"	248	28			Vic Zucco	DB	6'	187	24			Harlon Hill	OE	6'3"	200	27		18
			Fred Williams	DT	6'4"	248	29										Bill McColl	OE	6'4"	230	29		
										Bob Kilcullen – Military Service							John Aveni	K	6'3"	210	24		58

GREEN BAY PACKERS 7-5-0 Vince Lombardi

Scores of Each Game			Use Name	Pos.	Hgt	Wgt	Age	Int	Pts	Use Name	Pos.	Hgt	Wgt	Age	Int	Pts	Use Name	Pos.	Hgt	Wgt	Age	Int	Pts
9	CHIC. BEARS	6	Forrest Gregg	OT	6'4"	245	26			Tom Bettis	LB	6'2"	225	26	1		Joe Francis	QB	6'1"	195	24		
28	DETROIT	10	Norm Masters	OT	6'2"	250	26			Dan Currie	LB	6'3"	235	25	1		Lamar McHan	QB	6'1"	205	27		
21	SAN FRANCISCO	20	Bob Skoronski	OT	6'3"	250	26			Bill Forester	LB	6'3"	240	28	2	2	Bart Starr	QB	6'1"	200	26		
6	LOS ANGELES	45	John Dittrich	OG	6'1"	235	26			Ray Nitschke	LB	6'3"	230	23			Timmy Brown	HB	5'10"	195	22		
21	Baltimore	38	Jerry Kramer	OG	6'3"	245	24			Bobby Dillon	DB	6'1"	180	29	1		Bill Butler	HB	5'10"	180	22		6
3	New York	20	Fuzzy Thurston	OG	6'1"	245	26			Bobby Freeman	DB	6'1"	205	26	2		Paul Hornung	HB	6'2"	215	23		94
17	Chic. Bears	28	Jim Ringo	C	6'1"	230	28			Hank Gremminger	DB	6'1"	205	26	1		Don McIlhenny	HB	6'	200	24		12
24	BALTIMORE	28	Nate Borden	DE	6'	240	27			Johnny Symank	DB	5'11"	180	24	2		Lew Carpenter	FB-HB	6'1"	210	27		6
21	WASHINGTON	0	Bill Quinlan	DE	6'3"	250	27	1		Em Tunnell	DB	6'1"	215	37	2		Jim Taylor	FB	6'	212	24		48
24	Detroit	17	Jim Temp	DE	6'4"	250	26	1		Jesse Whittenton	DB	6'	195	25			Boyd Dowler	OE	6'5"	225	22		24
38	Los Angeles	20	Ken Beck	DT	6'2"	240	24										Gary Knafelc	OE	6'4"	220	27		24
36	San Francisco	14	Dave Hanner	DT	6'2"	260	30		2	Steve Meilinger – Broken Arm							Ron Kramer	OE	6'3"	230	24		
			Henry Jordan	DT	6'3"	250	24										Max McGee	OE	6'3"	205	27		30
																	A. D. Williams	OE	6'2"	210	26		

SAN FRANCISCO FORTY NINERS 7-5-0 Red Hickey

Scores of Each Game			Use Name	Pos.	Hgt	Wgt	Age	Int	Pts	Use Name	Pos.	Hgt	Wgt	Age	Int	Pts	Use Name	Pos.	Hgt	Wgt	Age	Int	Pts
24	PHILADELPHIA	14	John Gonzaga	OT	6'3"	245	26			Bob Harrison	LB	6'2"	227	22			John Brodie	QB	6'1"	192	24		
34	LOS ANGELES	0	Bob St. Clair	OT	6'9"	265	28			Matt Hazeltine	LB	6'1"	220	26		6	Y. A. Tittle	QB	6'	195	32		
20	Green Bay	21	John Thomas	OT	6'4"	243	24			Clancy Osborne	LB	6'3"	220	24			Lenny Lyles	HB	6'2"	198	23		6
34	Detroit	13	Bruce Bosley	OG	6'2"	237	25			Jerry Tubbs	LB	6'2"	220	24	2		Hugh McElhenny	HB	6'1"	198	30		24
20	CHIC. BEARS	17	Ted Connolly	OG	6'3"	240	27			Karl Rubke	C-LB	6'4"	248	23			Dick Moegle	HB	6'	190	25		
33	DETROIT	7	John Wittenborn	OG	6'2"	233	23			Billy Atkins	DB	6'1"	192	24			J. D. Smith	FB-HB	6'1"	210	26		66
24	Los Angeles	16	Frank Morze	DT-C	6'4"	275	25			Dave Baker	DB	6'	190	22	5		Joe Perry	FB	6'	197	32		18
3	Chic. Bears	14	Charlie Krueger	DE	6'4"	245	23		2	Eddie Dove	DB	6'2"	183	22	1		C. R. Roberts	FB	6'3"	215	23		6
14	Baltimore	45	Monte Clark	DT-DE	6'6"	255	22			Jerry Mertens	DB	6'	187	23	2	6	R. C. Owens	OE-FL	6'3"	196	24		18
21	Cleveland	20	Ed Henke	LB-DE	6'3"	227	31			Jimmy Ridlon	DB	6'1"	186	24			Clyde Conner	OE	6'2"	193	26		6
14	BALTIMORE	34	Bill Herchman	DT	6'2"	245	26			Abe Woodson	DB	5'11"	188	24	4	6	Fred Dugan	OE	6'3"	197	25		
14	GREEN BAY	36	Leo Nomellini	DT	6'3"	255	34										Billy Wilson	FL-OE	6'3"	190	32		24
			Henry Schmidt	DT	6'4"	245	22			Jim Pace – Injury							Tommy Davis	K	6'	212	24		67

DETROIT LIONS 3-8-1 George Wilson

Scores of Each Game			Use Name	Pos.	Hgt	Wgt	Age	Int	Pts	Use Name	Pos.	Hgt	Wgt	Age	Int	Pts	Use Name	Pos.	Hgt	Wgt	Age	Int	Pts
9	Baltimore	21	Lou Creekmur	OT	6'4"	250	32			Bob Long	LB	6'3"	234	25			Earl Morrall	QB	6'1"	200	25		
10	Green Bay	28	Ken Russell	OT	6'3"	250	23			Jim Martin	LB	6'3"	230	35	2	21	Tobin Rote	QB	6'3"	220	31		12
24	BALTIMORE	31	Ollie Spencer	OT	6'2"	250	28			Joe Schmidt	LB	6'1"	217	27	1		Jerry Reichow	OE-QB	6'2"	215	24		6
13	SAN FRANCISCO	34	Bob Grottkau	OG	6'4"	220	22			Wayne Walker	LB	6'2"	220	22		5	Hopalong Cassady	HB	5'10"	182	25		30
17	Los Angeles	7	Mike Rabold	OG	6'2"	235	22			Jim David	DB	5'10"	178	32	2		Dan Lewis	HB	6'1"	197	23		12
7	San Francisco	33	Harley Sewell	OG	6'1"	233	28			Dick LeBeau	DB	6'1"	187	22			Ken Webb	FB-HB	5'11"	208	24		12
10	Pittsburgh	10	John Gordy	OT-OG	6'3"	240	23			Gary Lowe	DB	5'11"	197	25	5		John Henry Johnson	FB	6'2"	213	29		18
23	LOS ANGELES	17	Charlie Ane	OT-C	6'2"	260	28			Jim Steffen	DB	6'	195	22			Nick Pietrosante	FB	6'2"	225	22		18
14	CHIC. BEARS	24	Gene Cronin	DE	6'2"	227	26			Dave Whitsell	DB	6'	185	23			Gene Cook	OE	6'3"	215	25		
17	GREEN BAY	24	Bill Glass	DE	6'5"	236	23			Terry Barr	HB-DB	6'	190	24	1	6	Jim Doran	OE	6'2"	200	31		12
45	CHIC. CARDS	21	Darris McCord	DE	6'4"	240	26			Yale Lary	DB	6'	185	28	3	6	Jim Gibbons	OE	6'2"	212	23		6
14	Chic. Bears	25	Alex Karras	DT	6'2"	254	23										Steve Junker	OE	6'3"	215	24		
			Gil Mains	DT	6'2"	242	29			Gene Gedman – Knee Injury							Dave Middleton	OE	6'1"	196	26		12
			Ben Paolucci	DT	6'2"	240	22																
			Jerry Perry	DT	6'4"	234	28		27														
			Jim Weatherall	DT	6'4"	245	29																

LOS ANGELES RAMS 2-10-0 Sid Gillman

Scores of Each Game			Use Name	Pos.	Hgt	Wgt	Age	Int	Pts	Use Name	Pos.	Hgt	Wgt	Age	Int	Pts	Use Name	Pos.	Hgt	Wgt	Age	Int	Pts
21	NEW YORK	23	Charlie Bradshaw	OT	6'6"	255	23			John Guzik	LB	6'3"	230	22			Buddy Humphrey	QB	6'1"	190	23		
0	San Francisco	34	Paul Dickson	OT	6'5"	245	22			Bill Jobko	LB	6'2"	218	23	1		Frank Ryan	QB	6'3"	190	23		6
28	Chic. Bears	21	Gene Selawski	OT	6'4"	252	23			Jack Pardee	LB	6'2"	215	23			Billy Wade	QB	6'2"	203	28		12
45	Green Bay	6	Bob Fry	OG	6'4"	238	28			Les Richter	LB	6'3"	232	28			Tom Wilson	HB	6'	204	26		6
7	DETROIT	17	Buck Lansford	OG	6'2"	232	26			Roy Wilkins	LB	6'3"	223	25			Joe Marconi	FB-HB	6'2"	225	25		30
21	CHIC. BEARS	26	Duane Putnam	OG	6'	230	31			Don Burroughs	DB	6'4"	186	28			Jon Arnett	FL-OE-HB	5'11"	193	24		24
16	SAN FRANCISCO	24	John Morrow	C	6'3"	236	26			Tom Franckhauser	DB	6'	192	22	3		Ollie Matson	FB	6'2"	210	29		36
17	Detroit	23	John Houser	OG-C	6'3"	240	23			Carl Karilivacz	DB	6'	190	28			Clendon Thomas	DB-OE-FL	6'2"	190	22		
20	Philadelphia	23	Gene Brito	DE	6'1"	230	34			Ed Meador	DB	5'11"	185	22	3		Leon Clarke	OE	6'4"	230	26		
21	Baltimore	35	Lou Michaels	DE	6'2"	238	23		36	Jack Morris	DB	6'	188	27		24	Jim Phillips	OE	6'1"	200	22		24
20	GREEN BAY	38	Lamar Lundy	OE-DE	6'7"	240	24			Will Sherman	DB	6'2"	197	30			Del Shofner	OE	6'3"	185	23		42
26	BALTIMORE	45	Sam Williams	OE-DE	6'5"	225	28		2														
			John Baker	DT	6'6"	290	24			Ron Waller – Knee Injury													
			John Lovetere	DT	6'4"	266	23																
			George Strugar	DT	6'5"	258	24																

BALTIMORE COLTS

RUSHING

Last Name	No.	Yds	Avg	TD
Ameche	178	679	3.8	7
Moore	92	422	4.6	2
Sommer	62	231	3.7	2
Unitas	29	145	5.0	2
Pricer	34	128	3.8	0
Dupre	23	54	2.3	0
Hawkins	12	44	3.7	0
Brown	2	4	2.0	0
Lewis	4	2	0.5	0

RECEIVING

Last Name	No.	Yds	Avg	TD
Berry	66	959	15	14
Moore	47	846	18	6
Mutscheller	44	699	16	8
Ameche	13	129	10	1
Sommer	7	111	16	0
Richardson	7	81	12	3
Dupre	6	47	8	1
Lewis	3	54	18	0
Pricer	2	3	2	0
Sherer	1	9	9	0

PUNT RETURNS

Last Name	No.	Yds	Avg	TD
Sample	22	129	6	0
Taseff	15	104	7	0
Shinnick	1	0	0	0

KICKOFF RETURNS

Last Name	No.	Yds	Avg	TD
Sample	17	457	27	0
Sommer	9	185	21	0
Pricer	6	66	11	0
Rechichar	2	39	20	0
Lewis	2	31	16	0
Hawkins	1	21	21	0
Plunkett	1	12	12	0
Davis	1	0	0	0

PASSING – PUNTING – KICKING

PASSING	Att	Comp	%	Yds	Yd/Att	TD	Int–%	RK
Unitas	367	193	53	2899	7.9	32	14– 4	2
Brown	4	1	25	14	3.5	0	0– 0	
Moore	3	2	67	25	8.3	0	0– 0	
Dupre	1	0	0	0	0.0	0	0– 0	

PUNTING	No	Avg
Sherer	51	41.8
Brown	2	44.5

KICKING	XP	Att	%	FG	Att	%
Myhra	50	51	98	6	17	35
Rechichar	0	0	0	0	1	0

CHICAGO BEARS

RUSHING

Last Name	No.	Yds	Avg	TD
Casares	177	699	3.9	10
J. Morris	87	312	3.6	0
Galimore	58	199	3.4	1
Brown	33	108	3.3	1
Bratkowski	7	86	12.3	0
Douglas	24	47	2.0	2
Bukich	1	0	0.0	0
Hill	1	0	0.0	0
Adams	4	−13	−3.2	0

RECEIVING

Last Name	No.	Yds	Avg	TD
Dooley	41	580	14	3
Hill	36	578	16	3
Casares	27	273	10	2
Dewveall	20	420	21	3
J. Morris	13	197	15	2
Galimore	10	125	13	2
McColl	8	94	12	0
Douglas	1	17	17	0

PUNT RETURNS

Last Name	No.	Yds	Avg	TD
J. Morris	14	171	12	1
Petitbon	11	72	7	0
Zucco	1	0	0	0

KICKOFF RETURNS

Last Name	No.	Yds	Avg	TD
J. Morris	17	438	26	0
Galimore	11	229	21	0
Petitbon	4	68	17	0
Roehnelt	1	0	0	0

PASSING – PUNTING – KICKING

PASSING	Att	Comp	%	Yds	Yd/Att	TD	Int–%	RK
Brown	247	125	51	1881	7.6	13	10– 4	6
Bratkowski	62	31	50	403	6.5	2	5– 8	
Casares	1	0	0	0	0.0	0	1–100	

PUNTING	No	Avg
Brown	64	41.2
Casares	3	46.3
J. Johnson	1	32.0

KICKING	XP	Att	%	FG	Att	%
Aveni	28	32	88	10	19	53

GREEN BAY PACKERS

RUSHING

Last Name	No.	Yds	Avg	TD
Hornung	152	681	4.5	7
Taylor	120	452	3.8	6
Carpenter	60	322	5.4	1
McIlhenny	47	231	4.9	1
Starr	16	83	5.2	0
McHan	16	64	4.0	0
Butler	7	49	7.0	0
Dowler	1	20	20.0	0
Francis	2	5	2.5	0

RECEIVING

Last Name	No.	Yds	Avg	TD
Dowler	32	549	17	4
McGee	30	695	23	5
Knafelc	27	384	14	4
Hornung	15	113	8	0
Taylor	9	71	8	2
McIlhenny	8	95	12	1
Carpenter	5	47	9	0
Williams	1	11	11	0
Butler	1	−2	−2	0

PUNT RETURNS

Last Name	No.	Yds	Avg	TD
Butler	18	163	9	1
Carpenter	13	150	12	0
Tunnell	1	3	3	0
Symank	1	0	0	0

KICKOFF RETURNS

Last Name	No.	Yds	Avg	TD
Butler	21	472	22	0
Symank	14	338	24	0
Francis	2	52	26	0
McIlhenny	3	50	17	0
Carpenter	1	24	24	0
Nitschke	2	13	7	0

PASSING – PUNTING – KICKING

PASSING	Att	Comp	%	Yds	Yd/Att	TD	Int–%	RK
Starr	134	70	52	972	7.3	6	7– 5	9
McHan	108	48	44	805	7.5	8	9– 8	13
Francis	18	5	28	91	5.1	0	1– 6	
Hornung	8	5	63	95	11.9	2	0– 0	

PUNTING	No	Avg
McGee	64	42.4

KICKING	XP	Att	%	FG	Att	%
Hornung	31	32	97	7	17	41

SAN FRANCISCO FORTY NINERS

RUSHING

Last Name	No.	Yds	Avg	TD
Smith	207	1036	5.0	10
Perry	139	602	4.4	3
McElhenny	18	67	3.7	1
Roberts	10	67	6.7	1
Lyles	13	28	2.2	1
Tittle	11	24	2.2	0
Moegle	3	9	3.0	0
Brodie	5	6	1.2	0
Owens	1	0	0.0	0

RECEIVING

Last Name	No.	Yds	Avg	TD
Wilson	44	540	12	4
McElhenny	22	329	15	3
Owens	17	347	20	3
Conner	13	162	12	1
Smith	13	133	10	1
Perry	12	53	4	0
Dugan	6	72	12	0
Lyles	3	33	11	0
Moegle	1	12	12	0
Tittle	1	4	4	0

PUNT RETURNS

Last Name	No.	Yds	Avg	TD
Woodson	15	143	10	0
Dove	22	126	6	0

KICKOFF RETURNS

Last Name	No.	Yds	Avg	TD
Lyles	25	565	23	0
Woodson	13	382	29	1
Hazeltine	2	26	13	0
Herchman	1	7	7	0

PASSING – PUNTING – KICKING

PASSING	Att	Comp	%	Yds	Yd/Att	TD	Int–%	RK
Tittle	199	102	51	1331	6.7	10	15– 8	10
Brodie	64	30	47	354	5.5	2	7– 11	
Moegle	1	0	0	0	0.0	0	0– 0	

PUNTING	No	Avg
Davis	59	45.7

KICKING	XP	Att	%	FG	Att	%
Davis	31	31	100	12	26	46

DETROIT LIONS

RUSHING

Last Name	No.	Yds	Avg	TD
Pietrosante	76	447	5.9	3
Johnson	82	270	3.3	2
Webb	60	222	3.7	2
Cassady	52	203	3.9	1
Lewis	49	199	4.1	2
Rote	35	156	4.5	2
Morrall	26	112	4.3	0
Reichow	13	98	7.5	0
Barr	5	57	11.4	1
Lary	1	18	18.0	0
Ane	0	10	–	0

RECEIVING

Last Name	No.	Yds	Avg	TD
Gibbons	31	431	14	1
Middleton	18	402	22	2
Pietrosante	16	140	9	0
Cassady	15	316	21	4
Doran	14	191	14	1
Webb	12	201	17	0
Barr	10	180	18	0
Reichow	7	118	17	1
Johnson	7	34	5	1
Lewis	5	75	15	0
Cook	1	43	43	0

PUNT RETURNS

Last Name	No.	Yds	Avg	TD
Barr	16	102	6	0
Lary	21	43	2	0
Middleton	3	30	10	0
Cassady	1	14	14	0
Lowe	6	8	1	0
Steffens	3	0	0	0

KICKOFF RETURNS

Last Name	No.	Yds	Avg	TD
Webb	16	352	22	0
Barr	9	224	25	0
Cassady	8	163	20	0
Pietrosante	5	98	20	0
Lewis	1	9	9	0
Martin	1	0	0	0
Rabold	1	0	0	0
Russell	1	0	0	0

PASSING – PUNTING – KICKING

PASSING	Att	Comp	%	Yds	Yd/Att	TD	Int–%	RK
Rote	162	62	38	861	5.3	5	19– 11	12
Morrall	137	65	47	1102	8.0	5	6– 4	7
Reichow	27	9	33	168	6.2	0	2– 11	
Barr	1	0	0	0	0.0	0	0– 0	
Lary	1	0	0	0	0.0	0	0– 0	

PUNTING	No	Avg
Lary	45	47.1
Morrall	11	43.7

KICKING	XP	Att	%	FG	Att	%
Perry	18	18	100	3	6	50
Martin	0	1	0	7	17	41
Walker	5	6	83	0	0	0

LOS ANGELES RAMS

RUSHING

Last Name	No.	Yds	Avg	TD
Matson	161	863	5.4	6
Arnett	73	371	5.1	2
Wilson	40	210	5.3	0
Marconi	52	176	3.4	4
Wade	25	95	3.8	2
Ryan	19	57	3.0	1
Shofner	1	6	6.0	0

RECEIVING

Last Name	No.	Yds	Avg	TD
Shofner	47	936	20	7
Arnett	38	419	11	1
Phillips	37	541	15	4
Clarke	20	453	16	0
Matson	18	130	7	0
Wilson	12	83	7	1
Marconi	10	81	8	1
Lundy	4	74	19	0
Thomas	1	6	6	0

PUNT RETURNS

Last Name	No.	Yds	Avg	TD
Arnett	17	184	11	1
Matson	14	61	4	0
Thomas	3	6	2	0
Burroughs	1	0	0	0
Meador	1	0	0	0

KICKOFF RETURNS

Last Name	No.	Yds	Avg	TD
Matson	16	367	23	0
Arnett	14	320	23	0
Wilson	7	243	35	0
Thomas	3	95	32	0
Wilkins	2	29	15	0
Dickson	1	0	0	0

PASSING – PUNTING – KICKING

PASSING	Att	Comp	%	Yds	Yd/Att	TD	Int–%	RK
Wade	261	153	59	2001	7.7	12	17– 7	5
Ryan	89	42	47	709	8.0	2	4– 4	
Arnett	5	1	20	13	2.6	0	0– 0	
Matson	1	0	0	0	0.0	0	1–100	

PUNTING	No	Avg
Shofner	48	41.8
Marconi	2	40.5

KICKING	XP	Att	%	FG	Att	%
Michaels	12	14	86	8	17	47
Morris	15	15	100	3	8	38
Richter	0	0	0	0	1	0

Use Name (Nicknames) – Positions	Team by Year	See Section	Hgt	Wgt	College	Int	Pts
Abbey, Joe OE-DE	48-49ChiB 49NYB	2	6'1"	202	North Texas		
Abbruzzi, Lou HB-DB	46Bos		5'10"	175	Rhode Island		
Aberson, Cliff TB-DB	46GB	12	6'	195	none	3	
47-49 played major league baseball							
Adamle, Tony LB-FB	47-49CleAA 50-51Cle 52-53VR 54Cle	2	6'	215	Ohio State	7	12
Adams, John (Tree) T	45-49Was		6'7"	242	Notre Dame		
Addams, Abe DE	49Det		6'2"	220	Indiana		
Adducci, Nick LB	54-55Was		5'10"	207	Nebraska		
Afflis, Dick OT-DG-OG	51-54GB		6'	251	Nevada-Reno	1	
Agajanian, Ben (The Toeless Wonder) K	45Phi 45Pit 47-48LA-AA 49NYG 53LA 54-57NYG 60LA-A 61DalA 61GB 62OakA 64SDA	5	6'	215	New Mexico		655
Agase, Alex LB-G	47LA-AA 47ChiAA 48-49CleAA 50-51Cle 53Bal		5'10"	212	Illinois, Purdue	8	
Agler, Bob HB-DB-FB-LB	48-49LA		6'1"	208	Otterbein		
Akins, Al DB-HB	46CleAA 47-48BknAA 48BufAA		6'1"	199	Washington, Washington State	2	18
Alban, Dick DB	52-55Was 56-59Pit		6'	193	Northwestern	14	
Albert, Frankie QB-DB	46-49SF-AA 50-52,HC56-58SF	12 4	5'10"	166	Stanford		169
Albright, Bill OG-OT-DT	51-54NYG 55CFL		6'1"	233	Wisconsin		6
Alderton, John DE	53Pit		6'1"	200	Maryland		
Aldridge, Ben DB-HB	50-51NYY 52SF 53GB	2	6'	195	Oklahoma State	11	6
Alford, Bruce OE-DB	46-49NY-AA 50-51NYY	2	6'	190	Texas Christian	1	72
Allen, Carl DB-WB	48BknAA		6'	175	Ouachita Baptist	2	6
Allen, Eddie FB-LB	47ChiB		6'1"	200	Pennsylvania		
Allen, Ermal DB-QB	47CleAA		5'11"	165	Kentucky	4	
Allen, Johnny C-LB	55-58Was		6'2"	224	Purdue		
Allen, Lou OT	50-51Pit		6'3"	215	Duke		
Amberg, John DB-HB	51-52NYG		5'11"	195	Kansas	5	
Ameche, Alan (The Horse) FB	55-60Bal	2	6'	218	Wisconsin		264
Amstutz, Joe C	57Cle		6'5"	264	Indiana		
Amundsen, Norm OG	57GB		5'11"	245	Wisconsin		
Andabaker, Rudy OG	52Pit 53MS 54Pit		6'	208	Pittsburgh		
Anderson, Billy HB-DB	53-54ChiB		6'	198	Compton J.C.		
Anderson, Charlie DE-OE	56ChiC		6'	230	Louisiana Tech		
Anderson, Cliff OE	52-53ChiC 53NYG	2	6'2"	215	Indiana		12
Anderson, Ezz (Sugarfoot) OE-DE	47LA-AA 48CFL	2	6'4"	215	Kentucky State		6
Andros, Plato G-OT	47-50ChiC		6'	240	Oklahoma		
Ane, Charlie OT-C	53-59Det		6'2"	260	Southern Calif.		
Angsman, Elmer HB	46-52ChiC	2	5'11"	200	Notre Dame		192
Apolskis, Ray LB-OG-C	41-42ChiC 43-44MS 45-50ChiC		5'11"	206	Marquette	6	
Arenas, Joe HB-DB	51-57SF	23	5'11"	180	Nebraska-Omaha	6	108
Arms, Lloyd G	46-48ChiC		6'1"	215	Oklahoma State		
Armstrong, Charlie DB-TB	41AFL 42-45MS 46BknAA		5'10"	180	Mississippi Coll.	2	
Armstrong, Graham T	41Cle 42-44MS 45Cle 47-48BufAA	5	6'4"	230	John Carroll		23
Armstrong, Neill OE-DB	47-51Phi 52CFL HC78-81ChiB	2	6'2"	189	Oklahoma State	9	66
Arterburn, Elmer DB	54ChiC		5'10"	175	Texas Tech		
Aschbacher, Darrell OG	59Phi		6'1"	220	Oregon		
Aschenbrenner, Frank FB	49ChiAA		5'10"	188	Northwestern		
Atkeson, Dale FB	54-56Was	23	6'2"	211	none		36
Atkins, George OG	55Det		6'1"	210	Auburn		
Atwood, John HB-WB-DB	48NYG	2	5'11"	185	Wisconsin	1	6
Audet, Earl T	45Was 46-48LA-AA		6'2"	252	Southern Calif.		
Austin, Bill OG-T	49-50NYG 51-52MS 53-57NYG HC66-68Pit HC70Was		6'1"	223	Oregon State	1	
Autrey, Billy C	53ChiB		6'3"	220	Austin		
Averno, Sisto OG-LB	50Bal 51NYY 52Dal 53-54Bal		5'11"	237	Muhlenberg		
Avery, Don T	46-47Was 48LA-AA		6'4"	254	Southern Calif.		
Avinger, Clarence FB	53NYG	4	6'1"	215	Alabama		
Babcock, Harry OE-DE	53-55SF	2	6'2"	193	Georgia		
Badaczewski, John OG-DG	46-48Bos 48ChiC 49-51 Was 53ChiB		6'1"	239	Case Reserve		
Bagarus, Steve HB-DB	45-46Was 47LA 48Was	23	6'	173	Notre Dame	5	60
Bagdon, Ed OG-LB	50-51ChiC 52Was		5'10"	204	Michigan State		7
Baggett, Billy HB-DB	52Dal		5'11"	175	Louisiana State	1	6
Bahnsen, Ken FB	53SF		5'10"	200	North Texas		
Bailey, Byron HB	52-53Det 53GB	2	5'10"	192	Washington State		12
Bailey, Jim G	49ChiAA		6'2"	215	West Virginia St.		
Bailey, Sam DE-OE	46Bos		6'2"	195	Georgia		
Baker, Jon LB-DG-OG	49-52NYG		6'2"	214	California		
Balatti, Ed OE-DB-DE	46-48SF-AA 48NY-AA 48BufAA	2	6'1"	195	none		21
Baldacci, Lou HB	56Pit	2 4	6'2"	200	Michigan		
Baldwin, Al OE-DB	47-49BufAA 50GB	2	6'2"	201	Arkansas	7	150
Baldwin, Burr OE-DE	47-49LA-AA	2	6'1"	197	U.C.L.A.	2	6
Baldwin, Jack C-LB	46-47NY-AA 47SF-AA 48BufAA		6'3"	223	Centenary		
Ball, Herman	HC49-51Was				Davis & Elkins		
Balog, Bob C-LB	49-50Pit		6'2"	225	Denver		
Banducci, Bruno OG-DG	44-45Phi 46-49SF-AA 50-54SF		5'11"	216	Stanford		6
Banonis, Vince C-LB	42ChiC 43MS 44C-P 46-50ChiC 51-53Det		6'1"	230	Detroit	14	12
Banta, Jack HB-DB	41Phi 42-43MS 44-45Phi 46-48LA	2 4	5'11"	191	Southern Calif.	5	42
Barbolak, Pete T	49Pit		6'3"	235	Purdue		
Barfield, Ken OT-DT	54Was		6'2"	238	Mississippi		
Barker, Ed OE	53Pit 54Was	2	6'3"	196	Washington State		24
Barnes, Emery DE	56GB		6'6"	235	Oregon		
Barnes, Larry FB-DE	57SF 60OakA	5	6'1"	228	Colorado State		55
Barnes, Walt (Piggy) OG-DG	48-51Phi		6'1"	238	Louisiana State		2
Barnett, Tom HB-DB	59-60Pit	2	5'11"	190	Purdue		12
Barni, Roy DB	52-53ChiC 54-55Phi 55-56Was		5'11"	185	San Francisco	11	6
Shot and killed – August 57							
Barry, Al OG	54GB 55-56MS 57GB 58-59NYG 60LA-A		6'2"	230	Southern Calif.		
Barry, Paul HB	50LA 51MS 52LA 53Was 54ChiC	2	6'	208	Tulsa		18
Barton, Don HB-DB	53GB		5'11"	175	Texas		6
Bartos, Joe HB	50Was 51-52MS		6'2"	194	Navy		
Barwegan, Dick OG-DG-LB	47NY-AA 48-49BalAA 50-52ChiB 53-54Bal		6'1"	227	Purdue	1	
Barzilauskas, Fritz OG-DG-LB	47-48Bos 49NYB 51NYG		6'1"	230	Holy Cross, Yale		
Bass, Bill HB-DB	47ChiAA 48CFL	2	5'10"	180	Nevada-Reno	2	12
Bassett, Mo FB	54-56Cle	2	6'1"	231	Langston		66
Batorski, John OE-DE	46BufAA		6'2"	238	Colgate		
Bauer, John OG	54NYG		6'3"	235	Illinois		
Bauman, Alf DT-OT	47ChiAA 47Phi 48-50ChiB		6'2"	228	Northwestern		
Baumgartner, Bill OE-DE	47BalAA		6'3"	202	Minnesota		
Bawel, Bibbles DB-OE	52Phi 53-54MS 55-56Phi 56-57CFL	3	6'1"	185	Evansville	18	18
Baxter, Lloyd C	48GB		6'2"	210	S.M.U.		
Beals, Alyn OE-DB	46-49SF-AA 50-51SF	2	6'	188	Santa Clara	1	296
Beatty, Ed C	55-56SF 57-61Pit 61Was		6'3"	229	Mississippi		
Bechtol, Hub DE-OE	47-49BalAA	2	6'3"	202	Texas	2	6
Beck, Ken DT-DE	59-60GB		6'2"	245	Texas A&M		
Beck, Ray OG-DG	52NYG 53-54MS 55-57NYG		6'2"	224	Georgia Tech	1	
Bednarik, Chuck LB-C	49-62Phi		6'3"	233	Pennsylvania	20	6
Beil, Larry T	48NYG		6'2"	235	Portland		
Bell, Ed G-T	46MiaAA 47-49GB		6'1"	227	Indiana		
Bell, Eddie DB	55-58Phi 59CFL 60NY-A		6'1"	212	Pennsylvania	11	6
Benners, Fred QB	52NYG	1	6'3"	195	S.M.U.		
Bennett, Earl G-LB	46GB		5'8"	188	Hardin-Simmons		
Benson, George HB-DB	47BknAA		6'1"	205	Northwestern		
Bentz,Roman G-T	46-48NY-AA 48SF-AA		6'2"	230	Tulane		
Berezney, Pete T	47LA-AA 48BalAA		6'2"	240	Notre Dame		
Bernardi, Frank DB-HB	55-57ChiC 60DenA	3	5'9"	181	Colorado	4	12
Bernet, Ed OE	55Pit 60DalA	2	6'3"	203	S.M.U.		6
Bernhardt, George G	46-48BknAA 48ChiAA		5'10"	213	Illinois		
Berrang, Ed DE-OE	49-51Was 51Det 52Was		6'2"	205	Villanova	3	
Berry, Rex DB-HB	51-56SF		5'11"	181	Brigham Young	22	18
Berry, Wayne HB-DB	54NYG		6'	175	Washington State		
Berschet, Marv OG-DE	54-55Was		6'2"	220	Illinois		
Bertelli, Angelo (The Springfield Rifle) QB	46LA-AA 47-48ChiAA	1	6'1"	190	Notre Dame		6
Berzinski, Will HB	56Phi		6'2"	195	Wis.-La Crosse		
Boson, Warren C	49BalAA		6'	205	Minnesota		
Bettis, Tom LB	55-61GB 62Pit 63ChiB HC77KC		6'2"	228	Purdue	1	
Bielski, Dick OE-FB	55-59Phi 60-61Dal 62-63Bal	2 5	6'1"	224	Maryland		208
Bienemann, Tom DE-OE	51-56ChiC		6'3"	221	Drake	4	
Bighead, Jack DE-OE	54Bal 55LA		6'3"	215	Pepperdine		
Billman, John G-LB	46BknAA 47ChiAA		6'1"	202	Minnesota		
Bingaman, Les DG-OG	48-54Det		6'3"	272	Illinois	2	
Bingham, Don HB	56ChiB		6'	185	Sul Ross State		6
Biscaha, Joe OE	59NYG 60BosA		6'1"	190	Richmond		
Bishop, Bill DT-OT	52-60ChiB 61Min		6'4"	248	North Texas	2	6
Black, Blondy DB-HB-FB	46BufAA 47BalAA		5'11"	195	Mississippi State	1	
Blackbourn, Lisle (Liz)	HC54-57GB				Lawrence		
Blackburn, Bill LB-C	46-50ChiC 51CFL	4	6'6"	228	Rice	11	26
Blake, Tom T	49NYB		6'2"	220	Cincinnati		
Blandin, Ernie DT-OT	46-47CleAA 48-49BalAA 50,53Bal		6'4"	248	Tulane		
Blount, Lamar OE-DB-HB	46MiaAA 47BufAA 47BalAA	2	6'1"	190	Mississippi State		6
Blumenstock, Jim FB-DB	47NYG	2	5'11"	190	Fordham		12
Bock, Wayne DT	57ChiC		6'4"	250	Illinois		
Boedecker, Bill HB-DB	46ChiAA 47-49CleAA 50GB 50Phi	2	5'11"	192	DePaul	1	84
Boensch, Fred G-LB	47-48Was		6'4"	228	Stanford	1	
Boggan, Rex DT	55NYG		6'3"	245	Mississippi		
Boland, Pat	HC46ChiAA				Minnesota		
Bolden, Leroy HB	58-59Cle		5'8"	170	Michigan State		6
Bolkovac, Nick DT-OT	53-54Pit	5	6'1'	230	Pittsburgh		57
Boll, Don OT-OG	53-59Was 60NYG		6'2"	270	Nebraska		
Bookout, Billy DB	55-56GB		5'11"	180	Austin	3	
Boone, J. R. HB-DB	48-51ChiB 52SF 53GB	23	5'8"	162	Tulsa	2	72
Borden, Nate DE	55-59GB 60-61Dal 62BufA		6'	234	Indiana		
Borton, John QB	57Cle		6'	208	Ohio State		
Bouley, Gil DT-OT	45Cle 46-50LA		6'2"	235	Boston College		6
Bowers, Bill DB	54LA		6'	198	Southern Calif.		
Bowman, Bill FB	54Det 55MS 56Det 57Pit	2	6'2"	215	William & Mary		42
Box, Cloyce OE-HB	49-50Det 51MS 52-54Det	2	6'4"	220	West Texas State		192
Boyd, Bob OE-DB	50-51LA 52MS 53-57LA	2	6'2"	201	Loyola Marymount	3	168
Boyda, Mike LB-FB	49NYB	4	6'1"	205	Washington & Lee	1	
Boydston, Max OE	55-58ChiC 60-61DalA 62OakA	2	6'2"	210	Oklahoma		48
Braatz, Tom LB-OE	57Was 58LA 58-59Was 60Dal		6'1"	216	Marquette	2	
Brackett, M. L. DE-DT-LB	56-57ChiB 58NYG		6'5"	248	Auburn	1	
Brackins, Charlie QB	55GB		6'2"	202	Prairie View		
Bradley, Ed OG-DE	50,52ChiB 53CFL		6'	212	Wake Forest		
Bradley, Harold OG	54-56Cle 58Phi		6'2"	230	Iowa		
Brady, Pat QB-K	52-54Pit 55FJ	4	6'1"	195	Bradley, Nevada-Reno		
Brancato, George HB-DB	54ChiC		5'9"	177	Louisiana State		
Brandau, Art C-LB	45-46Pit		6'2"	210	Tennessee		
Brandt, Jim HB-DB	52-54Pit	2	6'1"	200	St. Thomas		24
Bray, Ray DG-OG	39-42ChiB 43-45MS 46-51ChiB 52GB		6'	237	Western Michigan		
Brazinsky, Sam C-LB	46BufAA		6'1"	215	Villanova	2	
Bredde, Bill HB-DB	54ChiC		6'1"	195	Oklahoma State	2	6
Bredice, John OE	56Phi	2	6'1"	213	Boston U.		6
Brethauer, Monte DB-OE	53Bal 54MS 55Bal	2 4	6'1"	178	Oregon	1	
Brettschneider, Carl LB	56-59ChiC 60-63Det		6'1"	223	Iowa State	3	
Brewer, John FB	52-53Phi	2	6'4"	230	Louisville		18
Brewster, Darrell (Pete) OE	52-58Cle 59-60Pit	2	6'3"	210	Purdue		126
Briggs, Paul T	48Det		6'4"	248	Colorado		
Brink, Larry DE-OE	48-53LA 54ChiB		6'5"	235	Northern Illinois		8
Brito, Gene DE-OE	51-53Was 54CFL 55-58Was 59-60LA 61IL	2	6'1"	226	Loyola Marymount	1	12
Britt, Oscar G	46Was		5'11"	193	Mississippi		
Brookshier, Tom DB	53Phi 54-55MS 56-61Phi		6'	196	Colorado	20	
Brosky, Al DB	54ChiC		5'11"	175	Illinois	2	
Broussard, Fred C	55Pit 55NYG		6'3"	235	Texas A & M, Northwestern La.		
Brown, Buddy OG	51-52Was 53-56GB		6'1"	220	Arkansas		
Brown, Dan DE	50Was		6'1"	200	Villanova		
Brown, Dave DB-WB	43NYG 44-45MS 46-47NYG	2	5'11"	190	Alabama	6	
Brown, Ed QB-DB	54-61ChiB 62-65Pit 65Bal	12 4	6'2"	209	San Francisco		84
Brown, George OG-DG	49NY-AA 50NYY		6'2"	222	Texas Christian		
Brown, Hardy LB-DB-FB	48BknAA 49ChiAA 50Bal 50Was 51-56SF 56ChiC 60DenA	5	6'	193	Tulsa	13	43
Brown, Howie OG-DG-OT-DT	48-50Det		5'11"	215	Indiana		
Brown, John LB-C	47-49LA-AA		6'4"	230	N.Car. Central	5	12
Brown, Marv HB	57Det		5'8"	150	East Texas State		
Brown, Paul	HC46-49CleAA HC50-62Cle HC68-69CinA HC70-75Cin				Miami–Ohio		
Brown, Pete C-LB	53-54SF	4	6'2"	210	Georgia Tech	1	
Brown, Ray DB-QB	58-60Bal	4	6'2"	195	Mississippi	13	
Brown, Rosey OT	53-65NYG		6'3"	249	Morgan State		
Browning, Greg OE	47NYG		6'	190	Denver		
Brubaker, Dick OE-DE	55,57ChiC 60BufA	2	6'	202	Ohio State		6

Use Name (Nicknames) – Positions	Team by Year	See Section	Hgt	Wgt	College	Int	Pts
Bruce Gail, DE-OE	48-49SF-AA 50-51SF		6'1"	206	Washington	2	1
Brueckman, Charlie LB	58Was 60LA-A		6'2"	223	Pittsburgh		
Brumfield, Jack DE	54SF		6'2"	215	Southern Miss.		
Brundage, Dewey DE	54Pit		6'3"	210	Brigham Young		
Bruney, Fred DB	53SF 54-55MS 56SF 56-57Pit 58LA 60-62BosA	3	5'10"	184	Ohio State	15	6
Brutz, Jim T	46,48ChiAA		6'	230	Notre Dame		
Bryant, Bob T	46-49SF-AA		6'3"	220	Texas Tech		
Bryant, Walter DB-HB	55Bal		6'1"	185	Texas Tech	1	
Bucek, Ray G-LB	46Pit		6'	186	Texas A & M		
Buffington, Harry G-LB-BB	42NYG 43-45MS 46-48BknAA		6'	206	Oklahoma State	1	
Buksar, George LB-FB	49ChiAA 50Bal 51-52Was	2 5	6'	206	Purdue	7	30
Bulger, Chet OT-DT	42-43ChiC 44C-P 45-49ChiC 50Det		6'3"	239	Auburn		7
Bullough, Hank OG-LB	55GB 56-57MS 58GB		6'	230	Michigan State		
Bumgardner, Max DE	48Det		6'2"	190	Texas		
Bumgardner, Rex HB-DB	48-49BufAA 50-52Cle	23	5'11"	193	West Virginia	4	72
Burk, Adrian QB	50Bal 51-56Phi	12 4	6'2"	190	Baylor		42
Burke, Don LB-OG	50-54SF		6'	235	Southern Calif.	1	6
Burkett, Jeff OE-DB	47ChiC		6'1"	190	Louisiana State	1	6
killed in plane crash October 24, 1947							
Burl, Alex HB	56ChiC		5'10"	165	Colorado State		6
Burnine, Hank OE	56NYG 56-57Phi	2	6'2"	188	Missouri		12
Burris, Buddy LB-OG	49-51GB		5'11"	215	Oklahoma	1	
Burrus, Harry DB-OE-WB	46-47NY-AA 48ChiAA 48BknAA	2	6'1"	195	Hardin-Simmons	6	26
Butkus, Carl T	48Was 48NY-AA 49NYG		6'1"	245	George Washington		
Butler, Jack DB-OE	51-59Pit		6'	195	St. Bonaventure	52	54
Byler, Joe T	46NYG		6'5"	240	Nebraska		
Cain, Jim DE-OE	49ChiC 50Det 51-52MS 53-55Det		6'1"	202	Alabama		6
Calacagni, Ralph T	46Bos 47Pit		6'3"	230	Pennsylvania		2
Call, Jack HB	57-58Bal 59Pit	2	6'1"	200	Colgate		
Callahan, Bob C-LB	48BufAA		6'	205	Michigan		
Callahan, Jim TB-DB	46Det	12	5'11"	185	Texas	2	12
Calvin, Tom HB	52-54Pit	2	6'	200	Alabama		
Cameron, Paul DB	54Pit 55-56MS		6'	185	U. C. L. A.	7	
Camp, Jim WB-DB	48BknAA		6'	170	North Carolina	1	
Campana, Al HB-DB	50-52ChiB 53ChiC	2	5'11"	181	Youngstown State	1	6
Campanella, Joe LB-DT-OT	52Dal 53-57Bal		6'2"	242	Ohio State	3	
Campbell, Bill LB-C-DB	45-49ChiC 49NYB		6'	195	Oklahoma		
Campbell, Dick LB	58-60Pit		6'1"	227	Marquette	3	
Campbell, Leon FB	50Bal 52-54ChiB 55Pit	23	6'	199	Arkansas		6
Campbell, Marion DT-DE-OT	54-55SF 56-61Phi HC74-76Atl HC83-84Phi		6'3"	250	Georgia	3	
Campbell, Milt HB	57Cle		6'3"	217	Indiana		6
Campbell, Stan OG	52Det 53-54MS 55-58Det 59-61Phi 62OakA		6'	226	Iowa State		
Campion, T.G. T	47Phi		6'2"	235	Southeastern La.		
Campora, Don DT	50,52SF 53Was		6'3"	268	U. of Pacific		
Canadeo, Tony (The Gray Ghost of Gonzaga) HB-DB-TB-FB	41-44GB 45MS 46-52GB	1234	5'11"	190	Gonzaga	9	186
Canady, Jim DB-HB	48-49ChiB 49NYB	2	5'10"	178	Texas	5	
Cannady, John LB-C-BB	47-54NYG		6'2"	227	Indiana	14	
Cannamela, Pat LB	52Dal	5	6'	195	Southern Calif.		8
Cannava, Tony HB-DB	50GB		5'10"	180	Boston College		6
Capuzzi, Jim DBD-QB	55-56GB		6'	190	Cincinnati	2	
Carapella, Al DT-OT	51-55SF		6'	235	Miami (Fla.)	3	
Cardinal, Fred LB	47NY-AA		5'11"	220	Baldwin-Wallace		
Carey, Bob OE	52LA 53MS 54,56LA 58ChiB	2	6'5"	219	Michigan State		23
Carl, Harland HB	56ChiB	2	6'	195	Wisconsin		6
Carmichael, Al HB	53-58GB 60-61DenA	23	6'1"	192	Southern Calif.		84
Carpenter, Jack T	47-49BufAA 49SF-AA 50CFL		6'	240	Missouri, Michigan		
Carpenter, Ken HB-OE	50-53Cle 60DenA	23	6'	195	Oregon State		108
Carpenter, Lew HB-FB-FL-OE-DB	53-55Det 56MS 57-58Cle 59-63GB	23	6'1"	209	Arkansas	1	126
Carr, Ed DB-HB	47-49SF-AA	2	6'	185	none	16	54
Carr, Paul DB-LB	55-57SF		6'	205	Houston	3	
Carroccio, Russ OG-OT-DG-DT	54-55NYG 55Phi		6'1"	235	Virginia	1	
Carson, Johnny OE	54-59Was 60HouA	2	6'3"	202	Georgia		90
Carter, Willie HB-DB	53ChiC		5'11"	198	Tennessee State		
Casanega, Ken DB-HB	46,48SF-AA	2	5'11"	175	Santa Clara	8	12
Case, Ernie DB-QB	47BalAA		5'10"	170	U. C. L. A.	2	4
Casey, Tom TB-DB	48NY-AA		5'11"	175	Hampton U		6
Casner, Ken DT	52LA		6'2"	245	Baylor		6
Cason, Jim DB-HB	48-49SF-AA 50-52SF 53CFL 54SF 55-56LA	23	6'	171	Louisiana State	34	60
Cassady, Hopalong HB-FL	56-61Det 62Cle 62Phi 63Det	23	5'10"	183	Ohio State		144
Cassara, Frank FB-LB	54SF		6'	215	St. Mary's		
Castete, Jesse DB	56ChiB 56-57LA		5'11"	178	McNeese State	2	
Castiglia, Jim FB-LB	41Phi 42-44MS 45-46Phi 47BalAA 47-48Was	2	5'11"	208	Georgetown	1	78
42 played major league baseball							
Cathcart, Royal HB	50SF		6'	185	Cal.-Santa Barbara		
Cathcart, Sam DB-HB	49SFAA 50SF 51MS 52SF	23	6'	175	Cal.-Santa Barbara	7	6
Catlin, Tom LB-C	53-54Cle 55-56MS 57-58Cle 59Phi		6'1"	213	Oklahoma	2	
Cato, Daryl C-LB	46MiaAA		6'2"	195	Arkansas	1	
Celeri, Bob QB	51NYY 52Dal	12 4	5'10"	180	California		12
Cenci, John C	56Pit		6'	215	Pittsburgh		
Chambers, Bill T-G	48-49NY-AA		6'2"	230	Alabama, Georgia Tech, U. C. L. A.		
Champagne, Ed DT-OT	47-50LA 51CFL		6'3"	236	Louisiana State		6
Champion, Jim OT-DT-LB	50-51NYY		6'	238	Mississippi State		2
Chandnois, Lynn HB-TB	50-56Pit	123	6'2"	198	Michigan State		162
Chappuis, Bob TB-DB	48BknAA 49ChiAA	12	6'	190	Michigan		6
Chase, Ben G	47Det		6'3"	235	Navy		
Cheatham, Ernie DT	54Pit 54Bal		6'4"	245	Loyola Marymount		
Cheatham, Lloyd BB-LB-DB-WB	42ChiC 43-45MS 46-48NY-AA	2	6'2"	211	Auburn	2	24
Cheroke, George G	46CleAA		5'9"	195	Ohio State		
Cheverko, George DB-WB-HB	47NYG 48Was 48NYG	2	6'1"	195	Fordham	9	18
Chickillo, Nick LB-OG	53ChiC		5'11"	220	Miami (Fla.)		
Chipley, Bill OE-DB	47-48Bos 49NYB	2	6'3"	199	Washington & Lee	3	30
Chorovich, Dick OT	55-56Bal 60LA-A		6'4"	260	Miami-Ohio		
Christensen, Erik DE	56Was		6'3"	235	Richmond		
Christiansen, Jack DB-HB	51-58Det HC63-67SF	3	6'1"	190	Colorado State	46	78
Christman, Paul (Pitchin' Paul) QB	45-49ChiC 50GB	12	6'	210	Missouri		48
Churchwell, Don OT-DT	59Was 60OakA		6'1"	253	Mississippi		
Cichowski, Gene DB	57Pit 58-59Was		6'	195	Indiana		
Cifelli, Gus OT	50-52Det 53GB 54Phi 54Pit		6'4"	244	Notre Dame		
Cifers, Bob HB-DB-BB	46Det 47-48Pit 49GB	2 4	5'11"	201	Tennessee	1	30

Use Name (Nicknames) – Positions	Team by Year	See Section	Hgt	Wgt	College	Int	Pts
Cifers, Ed OE-DE	41-42Was 43-45MS 46 Was 47-48ChiB	2	6'2"	227	Tennessee	1	36
Clark, Don LB-G	48-49SF-AA		5'11"	197	Southern Calif.	2	
Clark, Herman OG-LB	52ChiB 53MS 54-57ChiB		6'3"	256	Oregon State	1	
Clark, Jim OG-OT-DT-LB	52-53Was		6'1"	230	Oregon State		
Clarke, Leon OE-FL	56-59LA 60-62Cle 63Min	2	6'4"	232	Southern Calif.		114
Clarkson, Stu LB-C	42ChiB 43-MS 46-51ChiB 52CFL		6'2"	217	Texas A & I	10	6
Clatt, Corwin DB-FB-LB	48-49ChiC		6'	210	Notre Dame	3	
Clatterbuck, Bobby QB	54-57NYG 60LA-A	12	6'3"	195	Houston		6
Clay, Randy HB-DB	50NYG 51-52MS 53NYG	2 5	6'	188	Texas	4	47
Clay, Walt DB-HB-TB	46-47ChiAA 47-49LA-AA	12	5'11"	196	Colorado	9	30
Cleary, Paul DE-OE	48NY-AA 49ChiAA		6'1"	196	Southern Calif.		
Clemens, Bob FB	55GB		6'2"	200	Georgia		
Clement, Johnny (Mr Zero) TB-DB	41ChiC 42-45MS 46-48Pit 49ChiAA	12	6'	189	S. M. U.		78
Clemons, Ray G	47GB		5'10"	220	St. Mary's		
Cline, Ollie FB-LB	48CleAA 49BufAA 50-53Det	2	6'	200	Ohio State		42
Cloud, Jack (Flying) FB-LB	50-51GB 52-53Was	2	5'10"	220	William & Mary	2	36
Clowes, John DT-OT-OG	48BknAA 49ChiAA 50-51NYY 51Det		6'1"	240	William & Mary		
Coates, Ray HB-DB	48-49NYG	2	6'1"	195	Louisiana State	1	24
Cochran, Red DB-HB-FB	47-50ChiC	234	6'	193	Wake Forest	15	36
Cochran, Tom FB	49Was	2	6'	209	Auburn		6
Cody, Ed DB-FB	47-48GB 49-50ChiB	2 5	5'10"	191	Purdue	2	29
Cole, Emerson FB-DB-LB	50-52Cle 52ChiB	2	6'2"	215	Toledo		6
Coleman, Herb C-LB	46-48ChiAA 48BalAA		6'	200	Notre Dame	1	
Colhouer, Jake G	46-48ChiC 49NYG		6'1"	211	Oklahoma State		
Collier, Bobby OT-DT	51LA		6'3"	230	S. M. U.		
Collier, Floyd T	48SF-AA		6'1"	215	San Jose State		
Collins, Bill G	47Bos		5'8"	195	Texas		
Collins, Ray DT-OT	50-52SF 54NYG 55-59CFL 60 61DalA		5'11"	230	Louisiana State		
Collins, Rip HB-FB	49ChiAA 50Bal 51GB	2 4	6'	190	Louisiana State	4	
Colmer, Mickey FB-LB-BB	46-48BknAA 49NY-AA	2 4	6'2"	219	Miramonte J.C.	1	126
Colo, Don DT	50Bal 51NYY 52Dal 53-58Cle		6'3"	252	Brown	2	
Colteryahn, Lloyd OE	54-56Bal	2	6'2"	220	Maryland		18
Comer, Marty DE-OE	46-48BufAA		6'	203	Tulane		18
Comp, Irv DB-TB-QB	43-49GB	12	6'2"	204	St. Benedict's	33	66
Compagno, Tony FB-DB	46-48Pit	2	5'11"	199	St. Mary's	12	42
Compton, Ogden QB	55ChiC	1	6'1"	180	Hardin-Simmons		
Cone, Fred FB-K	51-57GB 60 Dal	2 5	5'11"	199	Clemson		491
Conerly, Chuck QB	48-61NYG	12 4	6'1"	185	Mississippi		64
Conger, Mel DE-OE	46NY-AA 47BknAA		6'2"	225	Georgia		
Conner, Clyde OE	56-63SF	2	6'2"	193	U. of Pacific		108
Connolly, Harry TB-DB	46BknAA		5'11"	190	Boston College		
Connolly, Ted OG	54SF 55MS 56-62SF 63Cle		6'3"	240	Tulsa, Santa Clara		
Connor, George OT-LB-DT-OG	48-55ChiB		6'3"	240	Notre Dame	7	6
Conoly, Bill G	46ChiC		6'	227	Texas		
Cook, Gene OE	59Det		6'3"	215	Toledo		
Cook, Ted OE-DB	47Det 48-50GB	2	6'2"	195	Alabama	13	30
Coomer, Joe T-DG	41Pit 42-44MS 45-46Pit 47-49ChiC		6'6"	281	Austin		
Cooper, Jim C-LB	48BknAA		6'	205	North Texas		
Cooper, Ken OG-DG	49BalAA 50Bal		6'1"	205	Vanderbilt		
Corbitt, Don C-LB	48Was		6'4"	224	Arizona		
Corley, Bert C-LB	47BufAA 48BalAA		6'2"	210	Mississippi State	1	
Corn, Joe HB-DB	48LA		5'6"	168	none		
Cothren, Paige K	57-58LA 59Phi	5	5'11"	201	Mississippi		180
Coulter, Tex OT-DT-C-OE	46-49,51-52NYG 53 CFL		6'4"	250	Army		6
Couppee, Al G-FB	46Was		6'	225	Iowa		
Coutre, Larry HB	50GB 51-52MS 53GB 53Bal	2	5'10"	175	Notre Dame		18
Cowan, Bob HB-DB	47-48CleAA 49BalAA	2	5'11"	185	Michigan	3	48
Cowan, Les OT-DE	51ChiB		6'5"	235	McMurry		
Cowhig, Gerry LB-FB-DB	47-49LA 50ChiC 51Phi	2	6'2"	215	Notre Dame	6	30
Cox, Billy DB-HB-OE	51-52Was 53-54MS 55Was	4	6'3"	189	Duke	5	
Cox, Jim G-LB	48SF-AA		6'1"	208	Stanford		
Cox, Norm QB-TB	46-47ChiAA		6'2"	210	Texas Christian		
Craft, Russ DB-HB	46-53Phi 54Pit	23	5'9"	174	Alabama	22	42
Crawford, Denver T	48NY-AA		6'	210	Tennessee		
Crawford, Ed DB-OE	57NYG		6'3"	185	Mississippi	1	
Creekmur, Lou OT-OG-DT-DG	50-59Det		6'4"	246	William & Mary		
Cregar, Bill G-LB	47-48Pit		5'11"	195	Holy Cross		
Cremer, Ted DE-OE	46-47Det 48GB	2	6'2"	209	Auburn		6
Crisler, Hal OE-DE-DB 46-47 played in B.A.A.	46-47Bos 48-49Was 50Bal	2	6'4"	213	San Jose State	2	132
Crittendon, Jack OE	54ChiC		6'1"	190	Wayne State		
Cronin, Gene DE-OG-LB	56-59Det 60Dal 61-62Was		6'2"	229	U. of Pacific	1	
Cross, Billy HB	51-53ChiC	23	5'6"	151	West Texas State		72
Cross, Bob OT-DT	52ChiB 53MS 54-55LA 56-57SF 58-59ChiC 60BosA		6'4"	248	Kilgore J. C.		
Crow, Lindon DB	55-57ChiC 58-60NYG 61-64LA	3	6'1"	195	Southern Calif	38	20
Crowe, Clem	HC49 BufAA HC50Bal				Notre Dame		
Crowe, Paul DB-HB-FB	48-49SF-AA 49LA-AA 51NYY		6'1"	195	St. Mary's	9	18
Crowell, Odis T	47SF-AA		6'2"	220	Hardin-Simmons		
Cullom, Jim OG	51NYY		5'11"	235	California		
Cunningham, Leon LB-C	55Det		6'2"	215	South Carolina		
Curcillo, Tony DB-HB	53ChiC		6'1"	200	Ohio State	2	
Cure, Armand HB 46-47 played in B.A.A.	47BalAA		6'	198	Rhode Island		
Currivan, Don OE-DB-DE	43ChiC 44C-P 45-48Bos 48-49LA	2	6'	193	Boston College	6	162
Czarobski, Ziggy T	48-49ChiAA		6'	230	Notre Dame		
Daffer, Ted DE	54ChiB		6'	198	Tennessee		
D'Agostino, Frank OG-OT	56Phi 60NY-A		6'1"	245	Auburn		
Dahms, Tom OT	51-54LA 55GB 56ChiC 57SF		6'5"	242	San Diego State		
Dale, Roland DE	50Was		6'3"	210	Mississippi		
Daley, Bill FB-DB-LB	46BknAA 46MiaAA 47ChiAA 48NY-AA	2	6'2"	210	Minnesota, Michigan		30
D'Alonzo, Pete FB	51-52Det		5'10"	210	Villanova		
Damore, John C-OG	57,59ChiB		6'	228	Northwestern		
Danahe, Dick T-C	47-48LA-AA		6'2"	235	Southern Calif.		
Dancewicz, Boley QB-DB	46-48Bos	12	5'10"	187	Notre Dame	1	12
Danjean, Ernie LB	57GB		6'	230	Auburn		
Daugherty, Dick OG-LB-C	51-53LA 54-55MS 56-58LA		6'1"	219	Oregon	2	14
Daukas, Lou LB-C	47BknAA		6'	203	Cornell	1	
Daukas, Nick T	46-47BknAA		6'4"	225	Dartmouth	1	
David, Bob G-LB	47-48LA-AA 48ChiAA		6'	219	Villanova		

Use Name (Nicknames) – Positions	Team by Year	See Section	Hgt	Wgt	College	Int	Pts
David, Jim DB	52-59Det		5'11"	178	Colorado State	36	
Davis, Andy DB	52Was		6'	188	George Washington		
Davis, Art OT-DT	53ChiB		6'2"	235	Alabama State		
Davis, Art HB-DB	56Pit		6'1"	195	Mississippi State		
Davis, Bob T	48Bos		6'4"	235	Georgia Tech		
Davis, Bob DE-OE	46-50Pit		5'11"	192	Penn State		6
Davis, Fred OT-DT	41-42Was 43-44MS 45Was 46-51ChiB		6'3"	244	Alabama		
Davis, Glenn HB	50-51LA	2	5'11"	170	Army		54
Davis, Harper DB-HB	49LA-AA 50ChiB 51GB		5'11"	173	Mississippi State	11	12
Davis, Jerry DB-HB	48-51ChiC 52Dal	3	5'10"	178	Southeastern La.	24	24
Davis, Joe OE-DE	46BknAA	2	6'2"	195	Southern Calif.		7
Davis, Lamar (Racehorse) OE-DB	46MiaAA 47-49BalAA	2	6'1"	185	Georgia	11	72
Davis, Milt DB	57-60Bal		6'1"	188	U. C. L. A.	27	18
Davis, Paul FB-DB	47-48Pit		6'1"	188	Otterbein	1	
Davis, Ralph G	47-48GB		5'11"	205	Wisconsin		
Davis, Van DE-OE	47-49NY-AA	2	6'2"	215	Georgia	1	6
Davlin, Mike OT	55Was		6'1"	230	Notre Dame, San Francisco		
Dawson, Gib HB	53GB		5'11"	180	Texas		6
Dawson, Red	HC46-49 BufAA				Tulane		
Dean, Hal G-LB	47-49LA		6'	205	Ohio State	1	
Dean, Tom T	46-47Bos		6'2"	248	S. M. U.		
DeCarlo, Art DB-OE	53Pit 54-55MS 56-57Was 57-60Bal		6'2"	196	Georgia	7	
deCorrevont, Bill DB-HB-TB-WB	45Was 46Det 47ChiC 48-49ChiB	23	6'	186	Northwestern	10	18
Deeks, Don T-G	45-47Bos 47Was 48GB		6'4"	238	Washington		
Dees, Bob OT-DT	52GB		6'4"	245	SW Missouri St.		
DeFruiter, Bob DB-HB	45-47Was 47Det 48LA		6'	190	Nebraska	3	
DeGroot, Dud	HC44-45Was HC46-47LA-AA				Stanford		
Dekdebrun, Al TB-QB-DB	46BufAA 47ChiAA 48NY-AA 48Bos 49CFL	12	5'11"	182	Cornell	4	
Dekker, Paul OE	53Was 54CFL	2	6'5"	220	Michigan State		6
deLauer, Bob C-LB	45Cle 46LA		6'1"	218	Southern Calif.		
Del Bello, Jack QB	53Bal	1	6'1"	190	Miami (Fla.)		
Delevan, Burt OT	55-56ChiC		6'2"	236	U. of Pacific		
Dellerba, Spiro LB-FB	47CleAA 48-49BalAA	2	5'11"	200	Ohio State	2	6
DeMao, Al C-LB	45-53Was		6'2"	214	Duquesne	8	
DeMarco, Mario G-LB	49Det		5'11"	200	Miami (Fla.)		
DeMoss, Bob QB	49NYB		6'2"	185	Purdue		
Dempsey, Frank OG-LB-OT	50-53ChiB 54CFL		6'3"	235	Florida	1	
Derby, Dean DB-HB	57-61Pit 61-62Min		6'	187	Washington	21	21
DeRogatis, Al DT	49-52NYG		6'4"	239	Duke		12
Deschaine, Dick K	55-57GB 58Cle	4	6'	206	none		
DeShane, Chuck G-LB-BB-DB	45-49Det	5	6'1"	212	Alabama	5	22
Devore, Hugh	HC53GB HC56-57Phi				Notre Dame		
Dewar, Jim DB-HB-WB	47CleAA 48BknAA		6'1"	190	Indiana	1	6
Dewell, Bill OE-DE	40-41ChiC 42-44MS 45-49ChiC	2	6'4"	208	S. M. U.		102
Dibble, Dorne OE-DB	51Det 52MS 53-57Det	2	6'2"	195	Michigan State	1	114
Dillon, Bobby DB	52-59GB		6'1"	182	Texas	52	30
Dimancheff, Babe HB-DB	45-46Bos 47-50ChiC 52ChiB	23	5'11"	178	Purdue, Butler	2	90
Dimmick, Tom C-OT-LB	56Phi 60DalA		6'6"	253	Houston		
DiPierro, Ray OG	50-51GB		5'11"	210	Ohio State		
Dittrich, John OG	56ChiC 57-58MS 59GB 60OakA 61BufA		6'1"	236	Wisconsin		
Dobbs, Glenn TB-DB-QB	46-47BknAA 47-49LA-AA 50CFL	1234	6'4"	211	Tulsa	8	90
Dobelstein, Bob G-LB	46-48NYG 49LA-AA		5'11"	214	Tennessee	1	6
Dodrill, Dale LB	51-59Pit		6'1"	211	Colorado State	10	12
Doherty, George G-T	44Bkn 45Bos 46NY-AA 46-47BufAA		6'1"	218	Louisiana Tech		
Doll, Don DB-HB	49-52Det 53Was 54LA	3	5'10"	185	Southern Calif.	41	18
Domnanovich, Joe C-LB	46-48Bos 49NYB 50-51NYY		6'1"	213	Alabama	3	
Donaldson, Gene OG	53Cle		5'9"	215	Kentucky		
Donaldson, John DB-TB	49LA-AA 49ChiAA		5'10"	180	Georgia		
Donovan, Art DT-OT	50Bal 51NYY 52Dal 53-61Bal		6'2"	263	Boston College		2
Doolan, Jack DB-WB-OE-DE	45Was 45-46NYG 47-48ChiC	2	6'1"	191	Georgetown		
Dooley, Jim OE-FL-HB-DB	52-54ChiB 55MS 56-57ChiB 58BN 59-62,HC68-71ChiB	2	6'4"	198	Miami (Fla.)	5	96
Doran, Jim OE-DE	51-59Det 60-61Dal	2	6'2"	201	Iowa State	1	150
Dorow, Al QB	54-56Was 57Phi 58-59CFL 60-61NY-A 62BufA	12	6'	193	Michigan State		96
Doss, Noble HB-DB	47-48Phi 49NY-AA	2	6'	186	Texas	2	
Dottley, Kayo FB	51-53ChiB	2	6'1"	200	Mississippi		54
Douglas, Everett OT	53NYG		6'3"	240	Florida		
Douglas, Otis T	46-49Phi		6'1"	224	William & Mary		
Dove, Bob DE-OE	PC46,47ChiAA 48-53ChiC 53-54Det	2	6'2"	222	Notre Dame	1	12
Dow, Harley OG-OT	50SF		6'2"	220	San Jose State		
Dowda, Harry DB-HB	49-53Was 54-55Phi	2	6'2"	199	Wake Forest	16	36
Dowden, Steve OT	52GB		6'2"	235	Baylor		
Downs, Bob OG	51SF		5'10"	210	Southern Calif.		
Doyle, Dick DB	55Pit 60DenA		6'	193	Ohio State	2	
Drazenovich, Chuck LB-FB	50-59Was	2	6'1"	225	Penn State	15	48
Dreyer, Wally HB-DB	49ChiB 50GB	2	5'10"	170	Wisconsin	5	6
			5'8"	165	Northwestern		421
Driskill, Walt	HC49BalAA				Maryland		
Drulis, Al LB-FB-BB	45-46ChiC 47Pit		5'10"	193	Temple		
Drulis, Chuck LB-G	42ChiB 43-44MS 45-49ChiB 50GB HC61StL		5'10"	216	Temple	4	
Drzewiecki, Ron HB-DB	55ChiB 56MS 57ChiB	3	5'11"	185	Marquette		6
Dublinski, Tom QB	52-54Det 55-57CFL 58NYG 60DenA	12	6'2"	197	Utah		6
Duckworth, Joe OE-DE	47Was	2	6'2"	220	Colgate		18
Duden, Dick DE-OE	49NYG		6'3"	212	Navy		
Dudish, Andy HB-DB	46BufAA 47BalAA 48Det	2	5'11"	182	Georgia		12
Dudley, Bill (Bullet Bill) HB-TB-DB-WB	42Pit 43-44MS 45-46Pit 47-49Det 50-51Was 52VR 53Was	12345	5'10"	175	Virginia	23	484
Dugger, Jack T-DE-OE 46-47 played in N.B.L.	46BufAA 47-48Det 49ChiB		6'3"	230	Ohio State	1	6
Duke, Paul C-LB	47NY-AA		6'1"	210	Georgia Tech		
Duncan, Jim DE	50-53NYG		6'2"	205	Duke, Wake Forest	7	
Duncan, Maury QB	54-55SF	1	6'1"	185	San Fran. State		
Dupre, L. G. (Long Gone) HB	55-59Bal 60-61Dal	2 4	5'11"	190	Baylor		108
Durdan, Don HB-DB	46-47SF-AA	2	5'9"	175	Oregon State	2	6
Durishan, Jack T-G	47NY-AA		6'2"	230	Pittsburgh		
Durkota, Jeff FB-LB	48LA-AA		6'	205	Penn State	1	
Dutton, Bill HB-DB	46Pit	2	5'10"	180	Pittsburgh		12
Dworsky, Dan LB-BB	49LA-AA		6'	211	Michigan	1	
Dwyer, Jack DB	51Was 52-54LA		5'11"	175	Loyola Marymount	11	24

Use Name (Nicknames) – Positions	Team by Year	See Section	Hgt	Wgt	College	Int	Pts
Earhart, Ralph HB-DB	48-49GB	23	5'10"	165	Texas Tech		24
Earon, Blaine DE	52-53Det		6'1"	195	Duke		
Eason, Roger G-T	45Cle 46-48LA 49GB		6'2"	227	Oklahoma		
Eaton, Vic QB-DB	55Pit	4	6'2"	200	Missouri		
Ebli, Ray DE-OE	42ChiC 43-45MS 46BufAA 47ChiAA	2	6'2"	210	Notre Dame		12
Ecker, Ed OT-DT	47ChiB 48ChiAA 50-51GB 52Was		6'7"	276	John Carroll		
Ecklund, Brad C-LB	49NY-AA 50-51NYY 52Dal 53Bal		6'3"	215	Oregon		
Edwards, Dan OE-DE	48BknAA 49ChiAA 50-51NYY 52Dal 53-54Bal	2	6'1"	197	Georgia		102
Edwards, Weldon (Scratch) T	48Was		6'	225	Texas Christian		
Ehrhardt, Clyde C-LB	46,48-49Was		6'1"	232	Georgia	3	
Eikenberg, Charley QB	48ChiC		6'2"	205	Rice		
Eggers, Doug LB	54-57Bal 58ChiC		6'	213	S. Dakota State	4	
Ellena, Jack OG-LB	55-56LA		6'1"	225	U. C. L. A.		
Ellenson, Gene T	46MiaAA		6'1"	210	Georgia		
Elliott, Carl (Stretch) OE-DE	51-54GB	2	6'4"	220	Virginia		42
Elliott, Charlie T	47NY-AA 48ChiAA 48SF-AA		6'2"	240	Oregon		
Ellis, Herb C-LB	49NYB		6'2"	205	Texas A & M		
Ellis, Larry LB	48Det		6'1"	204	Syracuse		
Elsey, Earl HB-DB	46LA-AA	2	5'8	175	Loyola Marymount	2	
Elston, Art (Dutch) LB-C-G-BB	42Cle 43-45MS 46-48SF-AA		5'11"	191	South Carolina	4	
Elter, Leo FB-HB	53-54Pit 55-57Was 58-59Pit	2	5'10"	201	Villanova Duquesne		66
Embree, Mel OE	53Bal 54ChiC	2	6'3"	190	Pepperdine		6
Endriss, Al DE-OE	52SF		6'2"	200	San Fran. State		
Enke, Fred QB-HB	48-51Det 52Phi 53-54Bal	12	6'1"	201	Arizona		6
Epps, Bobby FB	54-55,57NYG	2	5'9"	198	Pittsburgh		12
Erickson, Bill G-LB	48NYG 49NY-AA		6'2"	210	Mississippi		
Eshmont, Len HB-DB-FB	41NYG 42-45MS 46-49SF-AA	2	5'11"	179	Fordham	10	90
Esser, Clarence DE-T	47ChiC		6'	190	Wisconsin		
Ethridge, Joe T	49GB		6'	230	S. M. U.		4
Ettinger, Don LB-OG	48-50NYG		6'2"	213	Kansas	4	
Evans, Fred HB-DB	46CleAA 47BufAA 47-48ChiAA 48ChiB	2	5'11"	185	Notre Dame	1	24
Evans, Jon OE	58Pit		6'4"	205	Oklahoma State		
Evans, Ray TB-DB	48Pit	12	6'1"	195	Kansas		12
Evans, Ray OG-OT-DT	48SF-AA 50SF		6'1"	225	Texas-El Paso		
Evansen, Paul G	48SF-AA		6'3"	240	Oregon State		
Ewart, Charley	HC49NYB				Yale		
Faircloth, Art DB-QB-HB	47-48 NYG		6'	190	N. Carolina State	3	
Fanucchi, Ledio OT-DT	54ChiC		6'2"	225	Fresno State		
Farmer, Tom HB-DB	46LA 47-48Was	2	5'11"	190	Iowa	6	30
Farragut, Ken C-LB	51-54Phi		6'4"	240	Mississippi		
Farris, Tom QB-DB	46-47ChiB 48ChiAA	12	6'1"	185	Wisconsin	5	
Faverty, Hal LB-DE-C	52GB		6'2"	220	Wisconsin		
Feamster, Tom OT-DE	56Bal	5	6'7"	260	Florida State		24
Fears, Tom OE-DB	48-56LA HC67-70NO	2 5	6'2"	213	U. C. L. A.	2	249
Feher, Nick OG	51-54SF 55Pit		6'	224	Georgia		
Fekete, Gene FB-LB	46CleAA	2	6'	195	Ohio State		6
Fekete, John HB-DB	46BufAA		5'11"	200	Ohio U.		
Felker, Art DE	51GB		6'3"	205	Marquette		
Felker, Gene OE	52Dal		6'1"	198	Wisconsin		6
Felton, Ralph LB-FB	54-60Was 61-62BufA	5	5'11"	210	Maryland	7	19
Fenenbock, Chuck TB-HB-DB-WB	43Det 44MS 45Det 46-48LA-AA 48ChiAA	1234	5'9"	174	U. C. L. A.	2	84
Fenimore, Bob HB-DB	47ChiB	2	6'1"	195	Oklahoma State	2	18
Fennema, Carl C-LB	48-49NYG		6'2"	210	Washington		6
Ferguson, Howie FB	53-58GB 60LA-A	2	6'2"	214	none		78
Ferrante, Jack OE-DE	41,44-50Phi	2	6'1"	197	none	1	186
Ferris, Neil DB-HB	51-52Was 52Phi 53LA		5'11"	181	Loyola Marymount		6
Ferry, Lou DT-OT	49GB 51ChiC 52-55Pit		6'2"	244	Villanova		8
Fichman, Leon T	46-47Det		6'1"	215	Alabama		
Figner, George DB	53ChiB		6'	185	Colorado	1	
Filipski, Gene HB	56-57NYG	23	5'11"	185	Army, Villanova		6
Finks, Jim QB-TB-DB	49-55Pit	12	6'	175	Tulsa	4	84
Finlay, Jack OG-LB	47-51LA		6'1"	217	U. C. L. A.		
Finnin, Tom DT	53-56Bal 57ChiC		6'2"	262	Detroit		2
Fiorentino, Ed DE	47Bos		6'1"	210	Boston College		
Fischer, Bill OT-OG-DT	49-53ChiC		6'2"	248	Notre Dame	1	
Fischer, Clete HB-DB	49NYG	2	5'9"	170	Nebraska	2	6
Fisher, Ray DT-OT-OG	59Pit 60JJ		6'	230	Eastern Illinois		
Flagerman, Jack C-LB	48LA-AA		6'	218	St. Mary's		
Flanagan, Dick LB-OG-C-HB-DB-DG-FB	48-49ChiB 50-52Det 53-55Pit		6'	216	Ohio State	8	
Fletcher, Ollie OG-LB-DG	49LA-AA 50Bal		6'3"	210	Southern Calif.		
Flowers, Bernie OE	56Bal		6'2"	190	Purdue		
Flowers, Bob C-LB	42-49GB		6'1"	210	Texas Tech	6	
Flowers, Dick QB	53Bal		6'	190	Northwestern		
Flowers, Keith C-LB	52Dal		6'	211	Texas Christian	1	3
Floyd, Bobby Jack FB	52GB 53ChiB	2	6'	210	Texas Christian		6
Foldberg, Hank OE-DE	48BknAA 49ChiAA	2	6'1"	203	Army		6
Ford, Henry HB-DB	55Cle 56Pit	3	6'	180	Pittsburgh	1	12
Ford, Len DE-OE 48-49 played in N.B.L.	48-49LA-AA 50-57Cle 58GB	2	6'4	245	Michigan	3	56
Forester, Bill LB-DT	53-63GB		6'3"	237	S. M. U.	21	2
Forester, Herschel OG	54-57Cle		6'	230	S. M. U.		
Forkovitch, Nick FB-LB	48BknAA		5'11"	195	William & Mary		
Forrest, Ed G-LB	46-47SF-AA		5'11"	210	Santa Clara		
Forte, Bob HB-DB-LB	46-50GB 51MS 52-53GB	2	6'	199	Arkansas	22	24
Fowler, Aubrey DB-HB	48BalAA		5'10"	160	Arkansas	3	
Franceschi, Pete HB-DB	46SF-AA		5'9"	170	San Francisco		12
Francis, Joe QB-HB	58-59GB	12	6'1"	195	Oregon State		6
Frankowski, Ray G	45GB 46-48LA-AA		5'11"	223	Washington		6
Freeman, Jack G	46BknAA		6'	198	Texas		
Freitas, Jess QB-DB	46-47SF-AA 48ChiAA 49BufAA	12	5'10"	170	Santa Clara	3	
French, Barry OG-DG-OT	47,49BalAA 48JJ 50Bal 51Det		6'	225	Purdue		
Friedlund, Bob DE-OE	46Phi		6'3"	210	Michigan State		
Fritsch, Ted FB-LB 44-45,46-47 played in N.B.L.	42-50GB	23 5	5'10"	210	Wis.-Stevens Point	10	380
Fry, Bob OT-OG	53LA 54-55MS 56-59LA 60-64Dal		6'4"	235	Kentucky		
Fucci, Dom DB	55Det		5'11"	190	Kentucky		
Fugler, Dick OT-DT	52Pit 53MS 54ChiC		6'2"	238	Tulane		
Fulcher, Bill LB-OG	56-58Was		6'	193	Georgia Tech	1	
Fuller, Frank DT-OG-C-DE	53,55,57-58LA 59ChiC 60-62StL 63Phi		6'4"	244	Kentucky		2
Fullerton, Ed DB	53Pit		5'10"	190	Maryland		

Use Name (Nickname)-Positions	Team by Year	See Section	Hgt	Wgt	College	Int	Pts
Gaffney, Jim HB-DB	45-46Was	2	6'1"	204	Tennessee		6
Gafford, Monk DB-HB-TB-WB	46MiaAA 46-48BknAA	123	5'11"	195	Auburn	7	66
Gage, Bob TB-DB	49-50Pit	123	5'11"	175	Clemson	9	48
Gain, Bob DT-DE-DG-OT-LB	52Cle 53MS 54-64Cle	123	6'3"	256	Kentucky	1	9
Galiffa, Arnie QB	53NYG 54SF 55CFL	1	6'2"	193	Army		
Gallagher, Bernie G	47LA-AA		6'	234	Pennsylvania		
Galvin, John QB	47BalAA	4	5'10"	170	Purdue		
Gambino, Lu FB-LB	48-49BalAA	2	6'1"	205	Maryland		12
Gambold, Bob QB	53Phi		6'4"	215	Washington State		
Gandee, Sonny DE-LB	52Dal 52-56Det 57JJ		6'1"	216	Ohio State	4	8
Gaona, Bob OT-DT	53-56Pit 57Phi		6'3"	243	Wake Forest		
Garlin, Don HB-DB	49SF-AA 50SF		5'11"	188	Southern Calif.	1	6
Garnaas, Bill WB-BB-LB	46-48Pit		5'11"	187	Minnesota		18
Garrett, Bill DG-OG-DT	48-49BalAA 50 ChiB		6'1"	237	Mississippi State		6
Garrett, Bob QB	54GB	1	6'1"	198	Stanford		
Garrett, Thurman C-G	47-48ChiB		6'3"	268	Oklahoma State	1	
Garza, Dan OE	49NY-AA 51NYY	2	6'3"	203	Oregon		24
Garzoni, Mike G	47Was 48NYG 48NY-AA		5'11"	218	Southern Calif.		
Gasparella, Joe BB-LB	48,50-51Pit 51ChiC	1	6'4"	222	Notre Dame		
Gatewood, Les C-LB	46-47GB		6'2"	198	Baylor		
Gatski, Frank (Gunner) C-LB	46-49CleAA 50-56Cle 57Det		6'3"	233	Marshall, Auburn	3	6
Guadio, Bob OG-LB-DG	47-49CleAA 51Cle		5'10"	219	Ohio State		
Gaul, Frank T	49NYB		6'	200	Notre Dame		
Gay, Billy DB	51-52ChiC		5'11"	180	Notre Dame		
Gedman, Gene (The Baron) HB	53Det 54-55MS 56-58Det 59KJ	2	5'11"	195	Indiana		126
Gehrke, Bruce OE-DB	48NYG		6'2"	190	Columbia		6
Gehrke, Fred HB-DB-TB	40Cle 41-44MS 45Cle 46-49LA 50SF 50ChiC	23	5'11"	189	Utah	13	154
Gentry, Dale OE-DE	46-48LA-AA	2	6'3"	223	Washington State		42
George, Bill LB-OG-DT	52-65ChiB 66LA	5	6'2"	237	Wake Forest	18	26
Geri, Joe TB-HB	49-51Pit 52ChiC	12 45	5'10"	185	Georgia		198
Getchell, Gorham OE-DE	47BalAA		6'4"	225	Temple		
Giancanelli, Skippy HB	53-56Phi	23	5'10"	177	Loyola Marymount		84
Giannelli, Mario OG-DG	48-51Phi		6'	265	Boston College		2
Gibron, Abe OG-DG	49BufAA 50-56Cle 56-57Phi 58-59,HC72-74ChiB		5'11"	243	Valparaiso, Purdue		
Gibson, Paul OE-DB-DE	47-49BufAA	2	6'2"	195	N. Carolina State	1	
Gifford, Frank HB-FL-DB	52-60NYG 61VR 62-64NYG	123 5	6'1"	197	Southern Calif.	2	484
Gilbert, Kline OT-OG	53-57ChiB		6'2"	233	Mississippi		
Gilchrist, George DT-DG	53ChiC		6'	260	Tennessee State		
Gillom, Horace DE-OE	47-49CleAA 50-56Cle	2 4	6'1"	221	Nevada-Reno	1	24
Gillette, Jim HB-DB-TB	40Cle 41-43MS 44-45Cle 46Bos 47GB 48Det	2	6'1"	185	Virginia	14	36
Gilmer, Harry QB-HB-DB	48-52Was 53JJ 54Was 55-56,HC65-66Det	12	6'	169	Alabama	5	12
Girard, Jug HB-OE-DB-QB	48-51GB 52-56Det 57Pit	1234	5'11"	176	Wisconsin	8	113
Gladchuck, Chet C-DT-LB	41NYG 42-45MS 46-47NYG		6'4"	248	Boston College	1	
Glamp, Joe HR-DB	47-49Pit	2 5	5'11'.	185	Louisiana State		125
Glatz, Fred OE	56Pit	4	6'1"	200	Pittsburgh		
Glick, Gary DB-HB	56-59Pit 59-61Was 61Bal 63SD-A	5	6'2"	195	Colorado State	14	65
Goad, Paul FB	56SF		6'	195	Abilene Christian		
Gob, Art DE	59-60Was 60LA-A		6'4"	230	Pittsburgh		2
Goble, Les HB-DB	54-55ChiC	23	5'11"	158	Alfred	1	18
Godwin, Bill C-LB	47-48Bos		6'3"	241	Georgia	2	
Golding, Joe DB-HB	47-48Bos 49NYB 50-51NYY	23	6'	184	Oklahoma	19	84
Goldman, Sam DE-OE	44Bos 45MS 46-47Bos 48ChiC 49Det	2	6'3"	228	Samford		
Goldsberry, John DT-OT	49-50ChiC		6'2"	245	Indiana	1	
Goldston, Ralph HB-DB	52Phi 53BL 54-55Phi 56CFL	2	5'11"	195	Youngstown State		18
Gompers, Bill HB-DB	48BufAA	2	6'1"	185	Notre Dame	2	6
Goode, Rob FB-HB-LB-DB	49-51,54-55Was 52-53MS 55Phi	2	6'4"	222	Texas A&M	4	108
Goodnight, Clyde OE-DB	45-48GB 49-50Was	2	6'1"	196	Tulsa		90
Gordon, Bobby DB	58ChiC 60HouA	4	6'	195	Tennessee	5	
Gorgal, Ken DB	50Cle 51-52MS 53-54Cle 55-56ChiB 56GB		6'2"	200	Purdue	19	6
Gorgone, Pete BB-LB	46NYG		6'	220	Muhlenberg		
Gorinski, Walt FB-DB	48Pit		6'1"	207	Louisiana State		
Goss, Don OT-DT	56Cle		6'5"	260	S. M. U.		
Governali, Paul (Pitching Paul) QB	46-47Bos 47-48NYG	12	5'11"	193	Columbia		24
Graham, Mike FB-LB	48LA-AA		6'	200	Cincinnati		6
Graham Otto QB-DB	46-49CleAA 50-55Cle HC66-68Was	12	6'1"	196	Northwestern	7	276
45-46 played in N.B.L.							
Grain, Ed G	47NY-AA 47-48BalAA		6'	230	Pennsylvania		
Grandelius, Sonny HB	53NYG	2	6'	195	Michigan State		6
Grant, Bud OE-DE	51-52Phi 53CFL HC67-83,85Min	2	6'3"	199	Minnesota		42
49-51 played in N.B.A.							
Gray, Bill G	47-48Was		5'11"	210	Oregon State		
Gray, Sam DE-OE	46-47Pit		6'	195	Tulsa		
Green, John DE-OE	47-51Phi		6'1"	192	Tulsa		6
Greene, John OE-DE-DB-BB	44-50Det	2	6'	210	Michigan	5	164
Greene, Nelson T	48NY-AA		6'2"	235	Tulsa		
Greenhalgh, Bob FB	49NYG	2	6'1"	200	San Francisco		
Greenwood, Don DB-HB-FB-LB	45Cle 46-47CleAA	2	6'	195	Missouri, Illinois	6	60
Gregory Garland G-LB	46-47SF-AA		5'11"	185	Louisiana Tech		
Grgich, Visco OG-LB-DG-OT-DT	46-49SF-AA 50-52SF		5'11"	217	Santa Clara	1	
Griffin, Bob LB-C	53-57LA 61DenA 61StL		6'3"	225	Arkansas	1	2
Griffin, Bobby DB	51NYY		6'	180	Baylor	4	
Griffin, Don HB-DB	46ChiAA	2	5'11"	195	Illinois	1	
Griffith, Forrest HB	50-51NYG	2	5'11"	190	Kansas		12
Grigg, Chubby DT-OT	46BufAA 47ChiAA 48-49CleAA 50-51Cle 52Dal	5	6'2"	294	Tulsa		21
Grimes, Billy HB	49LA-AA 50-52GB	23	6'1"	195	Oklahoma State		96
Grimes, George DB-WB	48Det	4	5'11"	190	Virginia	1	6
Groom Jerry DT-C-LB	51-55ChiC		6'3"	236	Notre Dame	1	
Groomes, Mel DB-WB-HB	48-49Det		6'	178	Indiana	1	6
Grossman, Rex LB-FB-K	48-49BalAA 50Bal 50Det	45	6'1"	215	Indiana	2	126
Groves, George G-LB	47BufAA 48BalAA		5'11"	195	Marquette		
Groza, Lou (The Toe) OT-DT-K	46-49ClaAA 50-59Cle 60VR 61-67Cle	5	6'3"	240	Ohio State		1608
Gude, Henry C-G	46Phi		6'1"	225	Vanderbilt		
Gulyanics, George HB-DB	47-52ChiB	2 4	6'	198	Ellisville J.C.	2	126
Gunderman, Bob OE	57Pit		6'2"	195	Virginia		
Gustafson, Ed C-LB	47-48BknAA		6'3"	205	George Washington		
Guy, Buzz OG-DT-OT	58-59NYG 60Dal 61HouA 61DenA		6'3"	248	Duke		
Hachten, Bill G-LB	47NYG		6'	210	Stanford		
Hafen Bernie OE-DE	49-50Det		6'2"	195	Utah		

Use Name (Nicknames)-Positions	Team by Year	See Section	Hgt	Wgt	College	Int	Pts
Hall, Forrest HB	48SF-AA	2	5'8"	155	Duquesne, San Francisco		12
Hall, John DE	55NYG		6'1"	220	Iowa		
Halliday, Jack OT-DT	51LA		6'3"	238	S. M. U.		
Haluska, Jim QB	56ChiB		6'	190	Wisconsin		
Handley, Dick C-LB	47BalAA		6'1"	215	Fresno State		
Hanlon, Bob DB-HB	48ChiC 49Pit		6'1"	195	Notre Dame, Loras	4	
Hannah, Herb OT	51NYG		6'3"	220	Alabama		
Hanner, Dave DT	52-64GB		6'2"	257	Arkansas	4	2
Hansen, Dale T-DE	44,48Det		6'3"	223	Michigan State		
Hansen, Ron G-LB	54Was		6'	220	Minnesota		
Hansen, Roscoe OT-DT	51Phi 52-53MS		6'3"	215	North Carolina		
Hansen, Wayne LB-C-OG-OT-DT	50-58ChiB 60Dal		6'2"	231	Texas-El Paso	6	6
Hantla, Bob OG-LB-DE	54-55SF		6'1"	220	Kansas		
Hanulak, Chet HB	54Cle 55-56MS 57Cle	23	5'10"	185	Maryland		42
Harder, Pat FB-LB	46-50ChiC 51-53Det	2 5	5'11"	203	Wisconsin		531
Harding, Roger C-LB	45Cle 46LA 47Phi 48Det 49NYB 49GB		6'2"	211	California	3	
Hardy, Carroll HB	55SF	2	6'	185	Colorado		24
58-64,67 played major league baseball							
Hardy, Jim QB-DB	46-48LA 49-51ChiC 52Det	12 4	6'	180	Southern Calif.		13
Harkey, Lem FB	55Pit 55SF		6'1"	205	Coll. of Emporia		
Harmon, Tommy HB-DB	41AFL 42-45MS 46-47LA	23	6'1"	199	Michigan	11	54
Harness, Jim DB	56Bal		5'11"	180	Mississippi State		
Harrington, John OE-DE	46CleAA 47ChiAA	2	6'3"	198	Marquette		18
Harris, Amos G	47-48BknAA		6'	210	Mississippi State		
Harris, Elmore HB	47BknAA		5'11"	175	Morgan State		
Harris, Hank G-T	47-48Was		6'	265	Texas		
Harris, Jimmy DB	57Phi 58LA 60DalA 61Dal		6'1"	178	Oklahoma	11	6
Hart, Leon OE-FB	50-57Det	2	6'5"	257	Notre Dame	2	192
Hartley, Howard DB-HB-WB	48Was 49-52Pit	3	6'	185	Duke	28	6
Hartman, Fred T	47ChiB 48Phi		6'1"	229	Rice	1	6
Hartshorn, Larry OG	55ChiC		6'	225	Kansas State		
Hatley, John OG-DT	53ChiB 54-55ChiC 60DenA		6'3"	249	Sul Ross State		
Hauser, Art DT-OG	54-57LA 59ChiC 59NYG 60BosA 61DenA		6'	237	Xavier-Ohio		6
Haynes, Hall DB-HB	50Was 51-52MS 53Was 54-55LA		6'	187	Santa Clara	5	6
Haynes, Joe C-G	47BufAA		6'3"	225	Tulsa		
Hays, George DE-DT	50-52Pit 53GB		6'2"	211	St. Bonaventure	1	12
Hazelhurst, Bob HB-DB	48Bos		6'	188	Denver		
Hazelwood, Ted OT-DT	49ChiAA 53Was		6'1"	235	North Carolina		
Heap, Joe HB	55NYG		5'11"	185	Notre Dame		
Heap, Walt DB-BB-HB	47-48LA-AA		6'1"	210	Texas	10	18
Heath, Leon FB	51-53Was	2	6'1"	203	Oklahoma		42
Heath, Stan QB	49GB 50CFL	1	6'1"	190	Nevada-Reno		6
Hecht, Al G	47ChiAA		6'	235	Alabama		
Heck, Bob DE	49ChiAA		6'3"	207	Purdue		
Hecker, Norb DB-OE	51-53LA 54CFL 55-57Was HC66-68Atl		6'2"	193	Baldwin-Wallace	28	20
Hein, Bob DE-OE	47BknAA		6'3"	220	Kent State		
Hegarty, Bill DE-OT	53Pit 53Was		6'4"	240	Georgia, Villanova		
Heinrich, Don QB	54-59NYG 60Dal 62OakA	2	6'	182	Washington		30
Hekkers, George T	46MiaAA 47BalAA 47-49Det		6'4"	229	Wisconsin		
Held, Paul QB	54Pit 55GB	1 5	6'2"	195	San Jose State		23
Helluin, Jerry DT	52-53Cle 54-57GB 60HouA		6'2"	272	Tulane	1	6
Helms, Jack DE	46Det		6'4"	215	Georgia Tech		13
Helwig, John LB-DE	53-56ChiB		6'2"	208	Notre Dame	3	
Hendley, Dick BB	51Pit		6'	198	Clemson		
Hendren, Bob OT-DT-DE	49-51Was		6'0"	244	Southern Calif.		
Henke, Ed DE-LB-OG-DG-OT-DT	49LA-AA 51-52SF 53-54MS 55CFL 56-60SF 61-63StL		6'3"	227	Southern Calif.		
Hennessey, Jerry DE	50-51ChiC 52-53Was		6'2"	219	Sant Clara		2
Hensley, Dick OE-DE	49NYG 50-51MS 52Pit 53ChiB	2	6'4"	213	Kentucky		14
Herchman, Bill DT	56-59SF 60-61Dal 62HouA		6'2"	246	Texas Tech	1	6
Hermann, John DB	* 56NYG 56Bal		6'1"	180	U. C. L. A.		
Herring, Hal LB-C	49BufAA 50-52Cle		6'1"	211	Auburn	4	
Heywood, Ralph OE-DE	46ChiAA 47-48Det 48Bos 49NYB	2 4	6'2"	203	Southern Calif.		78
Hickey, Red OE-DE	41Cle 42-44MS 45Cle 46-48LA HC59-63SF	2	6'2"	204	Arkansas		96
Higgins, Luke G	47BalAA		6'	210	Notre Dame		
Higgins, Tom OT-OG-DT	53ChiC 54-55Phi		6'2"	230	North Carolina		
Hill, Harlon OE-DB	54-61ChiB 62Pit 62Det	2	6'3"	199	North Alabama	3	240
Hill, Jim DB	51-52Det 53-54MS 55Pit		6'	188	Tennessee	2	
Hillenbrand, Billy HB-DB	46ChiAA 47-48BalAA	23	6'	188	Indiana	4	186
Hillman, Bill FB-LB	47Det		5'11"	200	Tennessee		
Hipps, Claude DB	52-53Pit		6'1"	189	Georgia	5	
Hirsch, Buckets LB-FB	47-49BufAA 50CFL		5'10"	207	Northwestern	3	6
Hirsch, Crazy Legs OE-HB-DB	46-48ChiAA 49-57LA	2 5	6'2"	190	Wisconsin, Michigan	15	405
Hix, Billy OE	50Phi		6'2"	215	Arkansas		
Hobbs, Homer OG-DG	49SF-AA 50SF		5'11"	210	Georgia		
Hock, John OG-OT	50ChiC 51-52MS 53,55-57LA		6'2"	230	Santa Clara		
Hodell, Merwin FB	53NYG		6'2"	205	Colorado		
Hoerner, Dick FB-LB-DB	47-51LA 52Dal		6'4"	219	Iowa	1	204
Hoernschemeyer, Bob (Hunchy) HB-TB-DB-WB	46-47ChiAA 47-48BknAA 49ChiAA 50-55Det	123	5'11"	194	Indiana	2	234
Hoffman, Bob LB-FB-BB	40-41Was 42-45MS 46-49LA	2	6'1"	208	Southern Calif.	2	66
Hoffman, Jack DE-OE	52ChiB 53-54MS 55-58ChiB		6'5"	234	Xavier-Ohio	2	6
Hoffman, John FB-OE-LB-HB-DE	49-56ChiB	2	6'2"	215	Arkansas	4	104
Hogan, Darrell LB-OG	49-53Pit		5'10"	210	Trinity(Texas)	7	6
Hogland, Doug OG-OT	53-55SF 56-58ChiC 58Det		6'3"	239	Oregon State		
Holder, Lew OE	49LA-AA		6'	191	Texas		
Holladay, Bob DB	56LA 56-57SF		5'11"	175	Tulsa	1	
Hollar, John FB-LB	48Was 49Det 49Was		6'	223	Appalachian State		12
Holley, Ken QB	46MiaAA		5'10"	185	Holy Cross		
Hollingsworth, Joe FB	49-51Pit		6'	200	Eastern Kentucky		
Holovak, Mike FB-LB	46LA 47-48ChiB HC61-68BosA	2	6'1"	213	Boston College	1	36
Holtzman, Glenn OT-DE	55-58LA		6'3"	250	North Texas		2
Horn, Dick QB	58Bal		6'1"	195	Stanford		
Horne, Dick DE-OE	41NYG 42-45MS 46MiaAA 47SF-AA		6'2"	214	Oregon		
Hornick, Bill T	47Pit		6'1"	207	Tulane		
Horrell, Bill OG	52Phi 53-54MS		5'11"	222	Michigan State		
Horvath, Les HB-DB	47-48LA 49CleAA	2	5'10"	173	Ohio State	4	24
Houghton, Jerry LB-DT-OT	50Was 51ChiC		6'2"	226	Washington State		
Houston, Lin OG-DG	46-49CleAA 50-53Cle		6'	213	Ohio State		

Use Name (Nicknames)-Positions	Team by Year	See Section	Hgt	Wgt	College	Int	Pts
Houston, Walt OG	55Was		6'	217	Purdue		
Howard, Sherman HB-DB	49NY-AA 50-51NYY 52-53Cle	2	5'11"	193	Iowa, Nevada-Reno	2	132
Howell, Clarence OE-DE	48SF-AA		6'1"	188	Texas A&M	1	
Howell, Earl HB	49LA-AA	2	5'10"	189	Mississippi		12
Howton, Billy OE	52-58GB 59Cle 60-63Dal	2	6'2"	191	Rice		366
Hubbell, Frank DE-OE	47-49LA	2	6'2"	222	Tennessee	1	24
Hubka, Gene TB-DB	47Pit		5'10"	175	Bucknell		
Hudson, Bob LB-DB-OE	51-52NYG 53-55Phi 56VR 57-58Phi 59Was 60DalA 60-61DenA		6'4"	225	Clemson	19	
Huffman, Dick OT-DT	47-50LA 51CFL		6'2"	255	Tennessee		6
Hugasian, Harry HB-DB	55Bal 55ChiB		6'1"	192	Stanford		
Hughes, Dick HB	57Pit		5'9"	185	Tulsa		
Hughes, Ed DB	54-55LA 56-58NYG HC71Hou		6'1"	184	N. Carolina State, Tulsa	3	
Hughes, George OT-OG	50-54Pit		6'1"	225	William & Mary		
Humbert, Dick OE-DB	41Phi 42-44MS 45-49Phi	2	6'1"	179	Richmond	14	36
Humble, Weldon OG-LB	47-49CleAA 50 Cle 51 MS 52Dal		6'1"	221	Rice	5	
Huneke, Charlie T	46-47ChiAA 47-48BknAA		6'3"	225	St. Benedict's		
Hunsinger, Chuck HB	50-52ChiB 53CFL	23	6'	188	Florida		48
Hust, Al DE-OE	46ChiC		6'1"	220	Tennessee		
Hutchinson, Ralph T	49NYG		6'2"	230	Tenn.-Chattanooga		
Huxhold, Ken OG	54-58Phi		6'1"	226	Wisconsin		
Huzvar, John FB	52Phi 53-54Bal	2	6'4"	247	N. Carolina State, Pittsburgh		42
Iglehart, Floyd DB	58LA		6'4"	197	Wiley		
Irvin, Willie DE-OE	53Phi		6'3"	203	Florida A&M		
Iverson, Duke DB-WB-HB-BB-LB	47NYG 48-49NY-AA 50-51NYY		6'2"	200	Oregon	5	8
Ivory, Bob G	47Det		6'2"	212	Detroit		
Jackson, Bob FB	50-51NYG		5'11"	210	N. Carolina A&T		12
Jackson, Charlie DB	58ChiC 60DalA		5'11"	180	S. M. U.	1	
Jackson, Ken OT-OG	52Dal 53-57Bal		6'2"	236	Texas		
Jacobs, Jack (Indian Jack) QB-DB-TB-HB	42Cle 43-44MS 45Cle 46Was 47-49GB 50CFL	12 4	6'1"	186	Oklahoma	12	18
Jacobs, Marv T	48ChiC		6'2"	235	none		
Jaffurs, John G	46Was		5'10"	200	Penn State		
Jagade, Chick FB-LB	49BalAA 50BF 51-53Cle 54-55ChiB	2	6'	213	Indiana		84
James, Tommy DB-HB	47Det 48-49CleAA 50-55Cle 56Bal		5'10"	184	Ohio State	34	12
Jankovich, Keever LB-DE	52Dal 53ChiC		6'	215	U. of Pacific		
Janowicz, Vic HB	54-55Was	2 5	5'9"	187	Ohio State		109
	56 brain injury in auto accident						
53-54 played major league baseball							
Jansante, Val OE-DE	46-50Pit 51GB	2	6'1"	190	Duquesne		86
Jarmoluk, Mike DT-OT-DE-DG-OE	46-47ChiB 48Bos 49NYB 49-55Phi		6'5"	252	Temple	7	18
Jaszewski, Floyd OT	50-51Det		6'4"	230	Minnesota		
Jecha, Ralph OG-LB	55ChiB 56Pit		6'2"	235	Northwestern		
Jeffers, Ed G	47BknAA		6'3"	215	Oklahoma State		
Jelley, Tom OE	51Pit		6'5"	225	Miami (Fla)		
Jenkins, Jack FB-LB	43Was 44-45MS 46-47Was	2	6'1"	206	Vanderbilt	4	7
Jenkins, Jon DT-OT	49BalAA 50Bal 50NYY		6'2"	225	Dartmouth		
Jenkins, Walt DE-DT	55Det		6'1"	223	Wayne State		
Jennings, Jack OT-DT	50-57ChiC		6'4"	245	Ohio State		
Jennings, Jim DE-OE	55GB		6'3"	195	Missouri		
Jensen, Bob DE-OE	48-49ChiAA 50Bal	2	6'2"	218	Iowa State		6
Jessup, Bill OE-FL	51-52SF 53MS 54SF 55HJ 56-58SF 60DenA	2 4	6'1"	195	Southern Calif.		42
Jeter, Perry HB	56-57ChiB	2	5'7"	178	Cal. Poly-Pomona		18
Jewett, Bob OE	58ChiB	2	6'2"	198	Michigan State		6
Joe, Larry HB	49BufAA		5'9"	190	Penn State		
Johnson, Al DB	48Phi		6'	175	Hardin-Simmons		
Johnson, Bill G-LB	47ChiB		6'	210	S. M. U.		
Johnson, Bill C-LB	48-49SF-AA 50-56SF HC76-78Cin		6'3"	228	Tyler J. C.	2	6
Johnson, Clyde T	46-47LA 48LA-AA		6'6"	269	Kentucky		
Johnson, Don HB	53-55Phi	2	6'	187	California		42
Johnson, Farnham DE	48ChiAA		6'	210	Wisconsin, Michigan		2
Johnson, Gil QB	49NY-AA	1 •	5'11"	195	S. M. U.		
Johnson, Glenn T	48NY-AA 49GB		6'4"	263	Arizona State		6
Johnson, Harvey LB-BB-FB-G	46-49NY-AA 51NYY HC68BufA HC71Buf	5	5'11"	212	William & Mary	1	262
Johnson, Herb HB	54NYG	2	5'10"	172	Washington		12
Johnson, Jack DB	57-59ChiB 60-61BufA 61DalA	4	6'3"	198	Miami (Fla.)	8	
Johnson, Joe WB-DB	48NYG	2	6'2"	195	Mississippi		12
Johnson, Joe HB-OE-FL	54-58GB 60-61BosA	2	6'	185	Boston College		48
Johnson, Marvin DB-HB	51-52LA 52-53GB		5'11"	183	San Jose State	6	
Johnson, Nate DT-OT	46-47NY-AA 48-49ChiAA 50NYY		6'3"	244	Illinois		
Johnson, Pete DB	59ChiB		6'2"	200	V.M.I.		
Johnson, Tom DT	52GB		6'2"	230	Michigan		
Johnston, Pres FB-LB	46MiaAA 46BufAA	2 4	6'	205	S. M. U.	1	19
Jones, Billy G	47BknAA		6'	220	West Va. Wesleyan		
Jones, Charlie OE	55Was		6'1"	202	George Washington		
Jones, Dub HB-DB-WB-TB	46MiaAA 46-47BknAA 48-49CleAA 50-55Cle	2	6'4"	202	Tulane, Louisiana State	2	246
Jones, Elmer G-LB	46BufAA 47-48Det		6'	224	Wake Forest		2
Jones, Jim DB-FB	58LA 61OakA		6'1"	204	Washington		
Jones, Jim (Casey) TB-DB	46Det		6'	180	Union (Tenn.)		
Jones, Ralph OE-DE	46Det 47BalAA		6'3"	200	Alabama		
Jones, Special Delivery HB-DB	45ChiB 46-49CleAA 50CFL	2	5'10"	193	Pittsburgh	2	174
Jones, Tom (Emperor) DT-OT	55Cle		6'6"	300	Miami–Ohio		
Joyce, Don DE-DT	51-53ChiC 54-60Bal 61Min 62DenA		6'3"	253	Tulane	1	
Judd, Saxon, OE	46-48BknAA	2	6'1"	190	Tulsa		48
Jungmichel, Hal G	46MiaAA		5'9"	200	Texas	1	
Jurkiewicz, Walt C-LB	46Det		6'1"	220	Indiana		
Juster, Rube T	46Bos		6'2"	230	Minnesotta		
Justice, Choo-Choo HB	50Was 51VR 52-54Was	2 4	5'10	176	North Carolina		60
Juzwik, Steve HB-DB-FB	42Was 43-45MS 46-47BufAA 48ChiAA	2 5	5'8"	186	Notre Dame	5	102
Kalmanir, Tommy HB	49-51LA 53Bal	23	5'8"	171	Nevada-Reno		36
Kapter, Alex G	46CleAA		6'	205	Northwestern		
Karilivacz, Carl DB	53-57Det 58NYG 59-60LA		6'	188	Syracuse	13	12
Karmazin, Mike G	46NY-AA		5'11"	210	Duke		
Karnofsky, Sonny HB-DB	45Phi 46Bos	23	5'10"	175	Arizona	1	30
Karras, Johnny HB	52ChiC		5'11"	187	Illinois		6
Karras, Lou DT	50-52Was		6'4"	241	Purdue		
Karstens, George C	49Det		6'4"	205	Indiana		
Kasap, Mike T	47BalAA		6'2"	255	Illinois, Purdue		
Katrishen, Mike G	48-49Was		6'1"	214	Southern Miss.		

Use Name (Nicknames)-Positions	Team by Year	See Section	Hgt	Wgt	College	Int	Pts
Kavanaugh, Ken OE-DE	40-41ChiB 42-44MS 45-50ChiB	2	6'3"	207	Louisiana State	1	313
Keane, Jim OE-DE	46-51ChiB 52GB	2	6'4"	217	Iowa		144
Keane, Tom DB-OE-HB	48-51LA 52Dal 53-54Bal 55ChiC	2	6'1"	192	Ohio State, West Virginia	40	18
Kearns, Tom T	45NYG 48ChiC		6'4"	247	Miami (Fla.)		
Kekeris, Jim T	47Phi 48GB		6'1"	266	Missouri		2
Kellagher, Bill FB-LB-DB	46-48ChiAA	2	5'11"	205	Fordham	6	24
Keller, Ken HB	56-57Phi 58JJ	23	5'11"	185	North Carolina		24
Kelley, Bill OE	49GB	2	6'2"	195	Texas Tech		6
Kelley, Bob C	55-56Phi		6'2"	232	West Texas State		
Kelley, Ed T	49LA-AA		6'4"	230	Texas		
Kelly, Bob DB-HB	47-48LA-AA 49BalAA	2	5'10"	192	Notre Dame	8	18
Kelly, Ellison OG	59NYG		6'1"	235	Michigan State		
Kennard, George OG	52-55NYG		6'	210	Kansas		
Kennedy, Bill DE-G	42Det 43-46MS 47Bos		5'11"	200	Michigan State		
Kennedy, Bob FB-DB-LB-HB	46-49NY-AA 50NYY	2	5'11"	195	Washington State	12	60
Kennedy, Bob DB-HB	49LA-AA		6'	178	North Carolina	1	
Kercher, Dick HB-DB	54Det 55-56MS		6'2"	205	Tulsa		
Kerkorian, Gary QB	52Pit 54-56Bal	12 5	5'11"	185	Stanford		89
Kerns, John T	47-49BufAA 50CFL		6'3"	243	Ohio U.		
Kerr, Bill OE-DE	46LA-AA		6'	220	Notre Dame	1	
Kershaw, George DE	49NYG		6'4"	210	Colgate		
Keuper, Ken DB-BB-HB-DE45	45-47GB 48NYG		6'	207	Georgia	6	
Kielbasa, Max HB-DB	46Pit		6'1"	185	Duquesne		
Kilroy, Bucko DG-OT-DG-OG	43P-P 44-55Phi		6'2"	243	Temple	5	
Kimbrough, John (Jarrin' John) FB-LB	41AFL 46-48LA-AA	2	6'2"	210	Texas A&M		138
Kimmel, J. D. DT	55-56Was 57BL 58GB		6'4"	248	Army, Houston		
Kinard, Billy DB-HB	56Cle 57-58GB 60BufA		6'	189	Mississippi	4	6
Kincaid, Jim DB	54Was		5'11"	180	South Carolina		1
Kindt, Don DB-FB-HB-LB	47-55ChiB	2	6'1"	207	Wisconsin	21	50
Kinek, George DB-OE	54ChiC		6'2"	190	Tulane	2	
King, Don OT-DT	54Cle 55CFL 56Phi 56GB 60DenA		6'3"	260	Kentucky	2	
King, Ed OG-DE-DG	48-49BufAA 50Bal		6'	217	Boston College		
King, Emmett HB	54ChiC	2	5'9"	195	none		6
King, Fay (Dolly) OE	46-47BufAA 48-49ChiAA	2	6'3"	195	Georgia		120
Kingery, Ellsworth DB	54ChiC		5'11"	180	Tulane	1	
Kingery, Wayne HB-DB	49BalAA		5'11"	175	Louisiana State	1	
Kirby, Jack HB-DB	49GB		5'11"	185	Southern Calif.		
Kisiday, George OE-DE	48BufAA		6'1"	220	Duquesne, Columbia		
Kissell, Ed DB	52Pit 53MS 54Pit		6'1"	193	Wake Forest	6	14
Kissell, John DT-OT	48-49BufAA 50-52,54-56Cle 53CFL		6'3"	245	Boston College		2
Kissell, Vito LB-FB	49BufAA 50Bal 51NYY	5	5'10"	205	Holy Cross	3	11
Klapstein, Earl T	46Pit		6'	220	U. of Pacific		
Klasnic, John WB-DB	48BknAA		6'	185	none		
Klawitter, Dick C	56ChiB		6'7"	270	S. Dakota State		
Klenk, Quentin T	46BufAA 46ChiAA		6'2"	225	Southern Calif.		
Klimek, Tony DE	51-52ChiC		5'11"	200	Illinois	5	
Klosterman, Don QB	52LA 53-54MS		5'10"	180	Loyola Marymount		
Klug, Al G-T	46BufAA 47-48BalAA		6'1"	215	Marquette		
Klutka, Nick OE-DE	46BufAA		5'11"	200	Florida		
Kmetovic, Pete HB-DB	46Phi 47Det	2	5'9"	175	Stanford		12
Knafelc, Gary OE	54ChiC 54-62GB 63SF	2	6'4"	217	Colorado		138
Knight, Pat LB-DE-BB	52NYG 53MS 54-55NYG		6'2"	207	S.M.U.	5	
Knox, Ronnie QB	57ChiB		6'1"	198	U. C. L. A.		
Knutson, Gene DE	54GB 55MS 56GB		6'2"	218	Michigan		
Koch, George HB-DB	45Cle 47BufAA	2	6'	200	Baylor, St. Mary's (Tex.)	3	6
Kodba, Joe C-LB	47BalAA		5'11"	190	Purdue	1	
Koepfer, Karl OG	58Det		6'2"	230	Bowling Green		
Kolesar, Bob G	46CleAA		5'10"	200	Michigan		
Koniszewski, John T	45-46, 48Was		6'3"	243	George Washington		2
Konovsky, Bob OG-DE-OT	56-58ChiC 60ChiB 61DenA		6'2"	246	Wisconsin		
Konz, Kenny DB	53-59Cle	34	5'10"	184	Louisiana State	30	33
Kosikowski, Frank DE	48CleAA		6'1"	200	Marquette, Notre Dame		
Koslowski, Stan FB-LB	46MiaAA		6'1"	200	Holy Cross		
Kovatch, John DE-OE	42Was 43-45MS 46Was 47GB	2	6'3"	197	Notre Dame		6
Kowalski, Adolph BB-DB	47BknAA		6'3"	205	Tulsa		
Kozel, Chet G-T	47-48BufAA 48ChiAA		6'2"	211	Mississippi		
Kraemer, Eldred OG	55SF		6'2"	225	Pittsburgh		
Krall, Gerry HB-DB	50Det		5'10"	185	Ohio State		
Kramer, Jack T	46BufAA		6'	220	Marquette		
Kranz, Ken DB	49GB		5'10"	190	Wis.–Milwaukee		
Kreamcheck, John DT	53-55ChiB		6'5"	255	William & Mary		
Krivonak, Joe G	46MiaAA		6'2"	230	South Carolina		
Krouse, Ray DT-DE-OT	51-55NYG 56-57Det 58-59Bal 60Was		6'3"	263	Maryland		
Krutko, Larry FB	58-60Pit	2	6'	220	West Virginia		24
Ksionzyk, John QB	47LA		5'10"	190	St. Bonaventure		
Kuchta, Frank C-LB	58-59Was 60DenA		6'2"	225	Notre Dame		
Kuffel, Ray DE-OE	47BufAA 48-49ChiAA	2	6'3"	213	Marquette, Notre Dame		18
Kulbitski, Vic FB-LB	46-48BufAA	2 5	5'11	205	Minnesota, Notre Dame	2	57
Kurrasch, Roy DE-OE	47NY-AA 48Pit		6'2"	195	U.C.L.A.		
Kusserow, Lou FB-LB	49NY-AA 50NYY 51CFL	2	6'1"	200	Columbia		
Kutner, Mal OE-DB	46-50ChiC	2	6'2"	197	Texas	12	198
Kuzman, John T	41ChiC 42-45MS 46SF-AA 47ChiAA		6'1"	232	Fordham		6
Laack, Galen OG	58Phi		6'	230	U. of Pacific		
Killed in auto accident – Jan. 1, 1959							
Lach, Steve FB-DB-WB	42ChiC 43-45MS 46-47Pit	2 4	6'2"	207	Duke	5	109
Ladd, Jim OE	54ChiC	2	6'4"	205	Bowling Green		
Ladygo, Pete OG-LB	52Pit 53JJ 54Pit		6'2"	218	Maryland		
Lagod, Chet OG	53NYG		6'2"	220	Tenn-Chattanooga		
Lahar, Hal G	41ChiB 42-45MS 46-48BufAA		6'	221	Oklahoma		4
Lahey, Tom OE-DE	46-47ChiAA	2	6'2"	218	John Carroll	1	
Lahr, Warren DB-HB	49CleAA 50-59Cle		5'11"	189	Case Reserve	44	36
Lamana, Pete LB-C-FB	46-48ChiAA		5'11"	210	Boston U.	2	6
Lamb, Walt DE-OE	46ChiB		6'1"	195	Oklahoma		
Land, Fred T-G	48SF-AA		6'1"	220	Louisiana State		
Lander, Lowell DB	58ChiC		6'	195	Westminster (Pa.)		
Landrigan, Jim T	47BalAA		6'4"	235	Holy Cross, Dartmouth		
Landry, Tom DB-HB-QB	49NY-AA 50-55NYG HC60-87Dal	12 4	6'1	195	Texas	32	36
Lane, Clayton T	48NY-AA		6'	215	New Hampshire		

Use Name (Nicknames) – Positions	Team by Year	See Section	Hgt	Wgt	College	Int	Pts
Lane, Night Train DB-OE	52-53LA 54-59ChiC 60-65Det		6'1"	194	Western Neb. C.C.	68	50
Langas, Bob DE	54Bal		6'4"	230	Wayne State		
Lange, Bill OG-LB	51-52LA 53Bal 54-55ChiC		6'1"	239	Dayton		
Lansford, Buck OG-OT	55-57Phi 58-60LA		6'2"	232	Texas		
Lansford, Jim OT	52Dal		6'3"	235	Texas		
Larson, Paul QB	57ChiC 60OakA		5'11"	183	California		
Lary, Yale DB	52-53Det 54-55MS 56-64Det	34	6'	187	Texas A&M	50	36
Lattner, Johnny HB	54Pit 55-56MS	2	6'1"	195	Notre Dame		42
Lauer, Larry C	56-57GB		6'3"	235	Alabama		
Laughlin, Bud FB	55SF		6'1"	200	Kansas		
Lauricella, Hank HB	52Dal	4	5'11"	175	Tennessee		
Laurinaitis, Frank LB	47BknAA		5'10"	200	Richmond		
Lauro, Lindy DB	51ChiC		5'10"	195	Pittsburgh		
Lavelli, Dante OE	46-49CleAA 50-56Cle	2	6'	191	Ohio State		372
Lawler, Al HB-DB	48ChiB		5'10"	175	Texas		6
Layden, Pete DB-TB-HB	48-49NY-AA 50NYY	1234	5'11"	192	Texas	13	27
48 played major league baseball							
Layne, Bobby QB	48ChiB 49NYB 50-58Det 58-62Pit	12 5	6'1"	201	Texas		372
Lazetich, Mike OG-LB	45Cle 46-50LA		6'1"	211	Montana, Michigan	2	
Lee, Paul DT-OT	51Pit		6'2"	240	Tulane		
Leahy, Jerry OT	57Pit		6'2"	220	Colorado		
Lear, Les G-LB	44-45Cle 46LA 47Det 48CFL		5'11"	225	Manitoba	1	
LeBaron, Eddie QB	52-53Was 54CFL 55-59Was 60-63Dal	12 4	5'9"	166	U. of Pacific		60
Leberman, Bob DB	54Bal		6'1"	180	Syracuse	2	
Lecture, Jim G	46BufAA		5'10"	220	Northwestern		
Ledbetter, Toy HB-DB	50Phi 51-52MS 53-55Phi	2	5'10"	198	Oklahoma State		66
Ledyard, Hal QB	53SF		6'	185	Tenn.–Chattanooga		
Lee, Gene C-LB	46Bos		6'3"	226	Florida	1	
LeForce, Clyde QB-DB-WB	47-49Det	12	5'11"	176	Tulsa	4	36
Leggett, Dave QB-DB	55ChiC		6'2"	198	Ohio State		
Leicht, Jake DB-HB	48-49BalAA	2	5'9"	170	Oregon	6	12
Lennan, Reid G	47LA-AA		6'	232	none		
Leonard, Bill DE	49BalAA		6'2"	200	Notre Dame	1	
Leonetti, Bob G	48BufAA 48BknAA		6'	230	Wake Forest		
Lesane, Jimmy DB-HB	52ChiB 53MS 54ChiB 54Bal		5'10"	176	Virginia		
Levanti, Lou C-OG-LB	51-52Pit		6'1"	215	Illinois		
Levy, Len G-T	45Cle 46LA 47-48LA-AA		6'	256	Minnesota		6
Lewis, Cliff DB-QB	46-49CleAA 50-51Cle	123	5'11"	167	Duke	30	6
Lewis, Ernie FB-LB	48-49ChiAA	2 4	6'1"	211	Colorado	1	12
Lewis, Mac OT-C	59ChiC		6'6"	290	Iowa		
Lewis, Woodley DB-OE-HB	50-55LA 56-59ChiC 60Dal	23	6'	193	Oregon	26	108
Liddick, Dave DT	57Pit		6'2"	240	George Washington		
Lillywhite, Verl HB-DB	48-49SF-AA 50-51SF 52-55MS	2 4	5'10"	185	Southern Calif.	8	54
Lindskog, Vic C-LB	44-51Phi		6'1"	203	Stanford	4	6
Lininger, Ray LB-C	50-51Det		5'11"	217	Ohio State	3	
Lipinski, Jim OT-DT	50ChiC 51CFL		6'4"	238	Fairmont State		
Lipscomb, Big Daddy DT-DE	53-55LA 56-60Bal 61-62Pit		6'6"	284	none	1	2
died May 10, 1963							
Lipscomb, Paul DT-OT	45-49GB 50-54Was 54ChiB		6'5"	246	Tennessee	2	
Listopad, Ed OG	52ChiC		6'2"	230	Wake Forest		
Little, Jack OT	53-54Bal		6'4"	235	Texas A&M		
Livingston, Howie DB-FB-WB-HB	44-47NYG 48-50Was 50SF 53ChiB	2	6'1"	193	Fullerton J.C.	29	108
Livingstone, Bob DB-HB	48-49ChiAA 49BufAA 50Bal	2	6'	173	Notre Dame	4	18
Loepfe, Dick T	48-49ChiC		6'2"	230	Wisconsin		
Logan, Dick OG-OT	52-53GB		6'2"	228	Ohio State		
Logel, Bob DE	49BufAA		6'3"	210	none		
Lolotai, Al G-T	45Was 46-49LA-AA		6'	224	Weber State	1	
Long, Bill OE-DE	49-50Pit	4	6'1"	200	Oklahoma State		
Long, Bob HB-DB	47Bos		5'10"	190	Tennessee		
Long, Bob LB-DE	55-59Det 60-61LA 62Dal		6'3"	232	U.C.L.A.	7	2
Long, Cutter HB-DB-DE	53-55NYG	2	6'1"	193	Florida	3	32
Lookabaugh, John OE-DE	46-47Was	2	6'4"	216	Maryland		6
Loomis, Ace DB-HB	51-53GB		6'1"	190	Wis.-La Crosse	12	6
Losch, Jack HB	56GB		6'1"	205	Miami (Fla.)		
LoVuolo, Frank OE-DE	49NYG		6'2"	210	St. Bonaventure		6
Lowe, Lloyd DB-HB	53-54ChiB		5'10"	155	North Texas	1	
Loyd, Alex OE	50SF	2	6'4"	198	Oklahoma State		
Lucky, Bill DT	55GB		6'3"	250	Baylor		
Luft, Don DE-OE	54Phi		6'5"	220	Indiana		
Luhn, Nolan OE-DE	45-49GB	2	6'3"	200	Tulsa		80
Lujack, Johnny QB-DB	48-51ChiB 52SJ	12 5	6'	186	Notre Dame	12	268
Lukens, Jim OE	49BufAA	2	6'4"	205	Washington & Lee		12
Luna, Bobby DB	55SF 59Pit	4	5'11"	187	Alabama	5	
Lunceford, Dave OT	57ChiC		6'4"	240	Baylor		
Lund, Bill HB-DB	46-47CleAA	2	5'10"	180	Case Reserve	3	36
Lusk, Bob C	56Det		6'1"	222	William & Mary		
Lynch, Lynn OG	51ChiC		6'2"	225	Illinois		
Maack, Herb T	46BknAA		6'2"	210	Columbia		
MacAfee, Ken OE	54-58NYG 59Phi 59Was	2	6'2"	212	Alabama		108
MacDowell, Jay DT-OT-DE-OE	46-51Phi		6'2"	217	Washington		2
Maceau, Mel C-LB	46-48CleAA		6'	203	Marquette		
Macerelli, John OG-OT	56Cle		6'2"	230	St. Vincent		
Macioszczyk, Art FB-LB	44Phi 45-46MS 47Phi 48Was	2	5'9"	208	Western Michigan		
Mackrides, Bill QB	47-51Phi 53NYG 53Pit	12	5'11"	182	Nevada-Reno		18
Macon, Eddie HB-DB	52-53ChiB 54-59CFL 60OakA	2	6'	177	U. of Pacific	9	36
Mader, Elmer OE-DB	47BalAA		5'11"	185	Michigan		
Madarik, Tippy DB-HB-WB-TB	45-47Det 48Was	2	5'11"	200	Detroit	4	6
Maderos, George DB	55-56SF		6'1"	187	Chico State	4	
Magee, John (Maggie) OG-DG-LB	48-55Phi		5'10"	220	Rice		
Maggioli, Chick DB-HB	48BufAA 49Det 50Bal		5'11"	178	Illinois, Notre Dame	12	6
Magliolo, Joe LB	48NY-AA		6'	210	Texas	1	
Magnani, Dante HB-DB-WB	40-42Cle 43ChiB 44-45MS 46ChiB 47-48LA 49ChiB 50Det	23	5'10"	182	St. Mary's	5	90
Mains, Gil DT-DE	54-61Det		6'2"	243	Murray State		6
Maley, Howie QB-HB-DB	46-47Bos	2 4	5'11"	187	S.M.U.		6
Malinowski, Gene TB-DB	48Bos	1	5'11"	210	Detroit	1	
Mallouf, Ray QB-DB-TB	41ChiC 42-45MS 46-48ChiC 49NYG	12 4	5'11"	180	S.M.U.	2	6
Maloney, Norm OE-DE	48-49SF-AA		6'1"	190	Purdue		7
Mancha, Vaughn C-LB	48Bos		6'1"	230	Alabama		
Mangum, Pete LB	54NYG 60DenA		6'	219	Mississippi		
Manley, Jack C-LB	53SF		6'3"	215	Mississippi State		

Use Name (Nicknames) – Positions	Team by Year	See Section	Hgt	Wgt	College	Int	Pts
Manley, Willie OG-OT	50-51GB		6'2"	218	Oklahoma		
Mann, Bob OE	48-49Det 50-53GB	2	5'11"	172	Michigan		144
Mann, Dave HB-OE	55-57ChiC 58CFL	2 4	6'1"	190	Oregon State		39
Marchetti, Gino DE-DT-OT	52Dal 53-64Bal 65VR 66Bal		6'4"	244	San Francisco	1	20
Marchibroda, Ted QB	54-56Pit 57ChiC HC75-79Bal	12	5'10"	178	St. Bonaventure, Detroit		18
Marciniak, Ron OG	55Was		6'1"	218	Kansas State		
Marcolini, Hugo WB-DB	58BknAA		6'	203	St. Bonaventure		
Marcucci, Joe WB-QB-HB-DB	47-48Det	12	5'10"	182	Southern Calif.		42
Marino, Vic G	40AFL 42-45MS 47BalAA		5'8"	205	Ohio State		
Maronic, Duke OG-DG-LB	44-50Phi 51NYG		5'9"	209	none	2	
Martin, Caleb T	47ChiC		6'4"	245	Louisiana Tech		
Martin, Jack C-LB	47-49LA		6'3"	238	Navy	1	
Martin, Jim LB-OG-DE-OT-K	50Cle 51-61Det 62VR 63Bal 64Was	5	6'2"	227	Notre Dame	6	434
Martinelli, John C-LB	46BufAA		6	227	Scranton	1	
Martinkovic, John DE-DT	51-56GB 57NYG		6 3	241	Xavier-Ohio		12
Martinovich, Phil (Iron Mike) G	39Det 40ChiB 41AFL 42-45MS 46-47BknAA	5	5 10	220	U. of Pacific		82
Masini, Len FB-LB	47-48SF-AA 48LA-AA	2	6'	225	Fresno State	1	12
Maskas, John G-T	47,49BufAA		5'11"	212	Virginia Tech		
Massey, Carlton DE	54-56Cle 57-58GB		6'2"	221	Texas	1	
Mastrangelo, John OG-DG-LB-OT-DT	47-48Pit 49NY-AA 50NYG		6'1"	228	Notre Dame		6
Matesic, Joe OT-DT	54Pit		6'4"	250	Arizona State		
Mathews, Ray HB-OE-FL-DB	51-59Pit 60Dal	123	6'	190	Clemson	2	261
Matson, Ollie HB-FB-DB-FL	52ChiC 53MS 54-58ChiC 59-62LA 63Det 64-66Phi	23	6'2"	210	San Francisco	3	438
Matthews, Clay DE-DT	50SF 51-52MS 53-55SF		6'3"	219	Georgia Tech	1	
Mattingly, Fran G-LB	47ChiAA		5'11"	215	Texas A&I	1	
Mattioli, Frank G-LB	46Pit		6'	210	Pittsburgh		
Matuszak, Marv LB-OG	53Pit 54MS 55-56Pit 57-58SF 58GB 59-61Bal 62-63BufA 64DenA		6'3"	232	Tulsa	14	
Mauldin, Stan T	46-48ChiC		6'2"	225	Texas	1	
died Sept. 24, 1948 – heart attack							
Maves, Earl WB-DB	48Det		5'9"	180	Wisconsin		
Mavraides, Menil OG	54Phi 55-56MS 57Phi		6'1"	235	Notre Dame		
Mayes, Carl HB	52LA		6'	190	Texas		
Mayne, Lew HB-TB-DB	46BknAA 47CleAA 48BalAA	12	6'1"	190	Texas		30
Maznicki, Frank HB-DB	42ChiB 43-45MS 46ChiB 47Bos	2 5	5'9"	181	Boston College	10	119
Mazzo, Vince DE OE	45-46Det 47-49BufAA 50CFL		6'1"	210	none	1	6
Mazzanti, Gino HB	50Bal		5'11"	190	Arkansas		6
McAfee, George HB-DB	40-41ChiB 42-44MS 45-50ChiB	234	6'	178	Duke	21	234
McCabe, Richie DB	55Pit 56MS 57-58Pit 59Was 60-61BufA		6'1"	185	Pittsburgh	9	6
McCafferty, Don OE-DE	46NYG HC70-72Bal HC73Det		6'4"	220	Ohio State		6
McCaffray, Art T	46Pit		5'11"	190	U. of Pacific		
McCain, Bob OE-DE	46BknAA		5'11"	195	Mississippi		
McCarthy, Jim OE-DE	46-47BknAA 48-49ChiAA	2 5	6'1"	205	Illinois	1	89
McChesney, Bob OE	50-52NYG	2	6'2"	190	Hardin-Simmons		84
McClairen, Jack OE	55-60Pit	2	6'4"	213	Bethune-Cookman		18
McClung, Willie OT-DT	55-57Pit 58-59Cle 60-61Det		6'2"	250	Florida A&M		
McClure, Bob G	47-48Bos		6'1"	224	Drake, Nevada-Reno		
McColl, Bill OE	52-59ChiB	2	6'4"	230	Stanford		156
McCollum, Harley T	46NY-AA 47ChiAA		6'4"	245	Tulane		
McConnell, Dewey DB-OE	54Pit		6'	190	Wyoming	3	
McCormack, Mike OT-DG-DT	51NYY 52-53MS 54-62Cle HC73 75Phi HC80-81Bal HC82Sea		6'4"	246	Kansas	1	
McCormick, Len C-LB	48BalAA		6'3"	232	Baylor	1	
McCormick, Tom HB	53-55LA 56SF	2	5'11"	185	U. of Pacific		6
McCormick, Walt C-LB	48SF-AA		6'1"	215	Southern Calif.		
McCoy, Joel TB-DB	46Det		5'10"	170	Alabama		
McDermott, Lloyd DT	50Det 50-51ChiC		6'2"	240	Kentucky	1	
McDonald, Walt BB-DB-QB	46MiaAA 46-48BknAA 49ChiAA	2	6'1"	210	Tulane	5	6
McDonough, Bob G	46Phi		5'11"	205	Duke		
McDougal, Bob LB-FB	47GB		6'2"	205	Miami (Fla.)		
McElhenny, Hugh (Hurryin' Hugh, The King) HB	52-60SF 61-62Min 63NYG 64Det	23	6'1"	197	Washington		360
McElroy, Bucky HB	54ChiB		5'11"	195	Southern Miss.		
McFadden, Marv OG	53Pit 54-55MS 56Pit		6'	223	Michigan State		
McGeary, Clarence DT	50GB		6'5"	250	N. Dakota State		
McGraw, Thurman DT-OT	50-54Det		6'5"	235	Colorado State	2	
McHan, Lamar QB	54-58ChiC 59-60GB 61-63Bal 63SF 64CFL	12	6'1"	201	Arkansas		72
McHugh, Pat DB-HB	47-51Phi	23	5'11"	165	Georgia Tech	16	18
McIlhenny, Don HB	56Det 57-59GB 60-61Dal 61SF	23	6'	197	S.M.U.		84
McKee, Paul OE-DE	47-48Was	2	6'3"	217	Syracuse		12
McKeever, Ed	HC48ChiAA				Texas Tech		
McKissack, Dick DB	52Dal		6'2"	208	S.M.U.		
McLaughlin, Leon C	51-55LA		6 2	228	U.C.L.A.		
McMillan, Chuck DB	54Bal		6 3	175	John Carroll		
McPeak, Bill DE	49-57Pit HC61-65Was		6 1	206	Pittsburgh		6
McPhail, Buck FB	53Bal	2 5	6 1	195	Oklahoma		27
McPhee, Frank DB-OE	55ChiC		6'3"	195	Princeton		
McQuary, John HB-DB	46LA-AA		6'1"	208	California		
McWilliams, Tom DB-TB-HB	49LA-AA 50Pit 51-52MS		5'11"	183	Mississippi State	4	
Mead, Jack OE-DB-DE	46-47NYG		6'3"	213	Wisconsin	1	
Meadows, Ed DE	54ChiB 55Pit 56-57ChiB 58Phi 59Was		6'2"	221	Duke		
Meeks, Bryant C-LB	47-48Pit		6'2"	193	South Carolina		
Mehelich, Charlie DE-OE	46-51Pit	2	6'1"	199	Duquesne		2
Meilinger, Steve OE	56-57Was 58GB 59BA 60GB 61Pit 61StL	2	6'2"	277	Kentucky		48
Meisenheimer, Darrell DB	51NYY		5'10"	195	Oklahoma State	3	
Mello, Jim DB-FB-LB	47Bos 48LA 48ChiAA 49Det	2	5'10"	190	Notre Dame	4	6
Menasco, Don DB	52-53NYG 54Was		6'	186	Texas	6	
Mergen, Mike DT	52ChiC		6'5"	245	San Francisco		
Mertes, Buzz FB-HB-DB	46ChiC 46LA-AA 47-49BalAA 49NYG	2	6'	201	Iowa	1	48
Meyer, Gil DE-OE	47BalAA		6'2"	200	Wake Forest		
Meyers, Bob FB	52SF		6'2"	184	Stanford		
Michael, Bill OG	57Pit		6'2"	240	Ohio State		
Michaels, Walt LB	51GB 52-61Cle 63NY-A HC77-82NYJ		6'	231	Washington & Lee	11	12
Michalik, Art LB-OG	53-54SF 55-56Pit	5	6'2"	229	St. Ambrose		12
Michelosen, John	HC48-51Pit				Pittsburgh		
Michels, John OG	53Phi		5'11"	200	Tennessee		
Micka, Mike DB-HB-FB-LB	44-45Was 45-48Bos	2	6'	188	Colgate	9	6

Use Name (Nicknames) – Positions	Team by Year	See Section	Hgt	Wgt	College	Int	Pts
Middleton, Dave OE-HB-FL	55-60Det 61Min	2	6'1"	194	Auburn		
Mieszkowski, Ed T	46-47BknAA		6'2"	220	Notre Dame		
Mihajlovich, Lou OE	48LA-AA		5'11"	175	Indiana		
Mike, Bob T	48-49SF-AA		6'1"	220	U. C. L. A.		
Miketa, Andy C	54-55Det		6'2"	210	North Carolina		
Miklich, Bill LB-BB-G	47-48NYG 48Det		6'	208	Idaho		
Mikula, Tom FB-LB	48BknAA		5'10"	200	William & Mary		
Miles, Leo DB	53NYG		6'	200	Virginia State		
Miller, Bob DT-OT	52-58Det		6'3"	242	Virginia	1	
Miller, Don DB	54GB 54Phi		6'2"	195	S. M. U.		
Miller, Fred OT	55Was		6'3"	225	U. of Pacific		
Miller, Hal OT	53SF		6'4"	230	Georgia Tech		
Miller, Johnny OT-DT-DE	56Was 57MS 58-59Was 60GB		6'5"	253	Boston College		2
Miller, Paul DE-C	54-57LA 60-61DalA 62SD-A		6'2"	226	Louisiana State	1	
Miller, Ron OE	56LA	2	6'4"	200	Southern Calif.		
Milner, Bill LB-OG-DG-DE	47-49ChiB 50NYG 51-52MS		6'1"	217	Duke	1	
Minarik, Henry OE	51Pit	2	6'2"	200	Michigan State		6
Miner, Tom K	58Pit	5	6'4"	235	Tulsa		73
Minini, Frank HB-BB-DB	47-48ChiB 49Pit	23	6'1"	209	San Jose State	1	42
Minisi, Skippy HB-DB	48NYG	2	5'11"	190	Pennsylvania	2	12
Mioduszewski, Ed QB-DB	53Bal	1	5'10"	185	William & Mary	1	
Mitcham, Gene OE	58Phi		6'2"	206	Arizona State		6
Mitchell, Bob DB-HB-BB-QB	46-48LA-AA	2	5'11"	195	Stanford	6	6
Mitchell, Charlie DB	45ChiB 46GB		6'	188	Tulsa	1	
Mitchell, Fondren HB-DB	46MiaAA		6'	185	Florida	1	
Mitchell, Hal OT-OG	52NYG		6'1"	225	U. C. L. A.		
Mitchell, Paul DT-OT	46-48LA-AA 48-49NY-AA 50-51NYY		6'3"	235	Minnesota		
Mixon, Billy HB-DB	53-54SF	2	5'11"	191	Georgia	2	6
Mobley, Rudy (Little Doc) HB-DB	47BalAA	2	5'7"	155	Hardin-Simmons	2	12
Modzelewski, Dick (Little Mo) DT	53-54Was 55Pit		6'	258	Maryland		4
	56-63NYG 64-66, HC77Cle						
Modzelewski, Ed (Big Mo) FB	52Cle 53-54MS 55-59Cle	2	6'	217	Maryland		84
Moegle, Dick DB-HB	55-59SF 60Pit 61Dal	2	6'	190	Rice	28	42
Moje, Dick OE	51GB		6'2"	210	Loyola Marymount		
Momsen, Bob OG-LB	51Det 52SF		6'3"	225	Ohio State		2
Momsen, Tony C	51Pit 52Was		6'1"	215	Michigan		
Monachino, Jim HB-FB-DB	51SF 52MS 53SF 55Was	2	5'10"	187	California		24
Mont, Tommy QB-DB-HB	47-49Was	12	6'	194	Maryland	3	18
Montgomery, Bill FB-LB	46ChiC		6'	205	Louisiana State		
Montgomery, Jim T	46Det		6'4"	235	Texas A & M		
Moore, Bill G	47-49Pit		5'11"	218	Penn State		
Moore, Henry DB-HB	56NYG 57Bal		6'1"	195	Arkansas	1	
Moore, McNeil DB	54ChiB 55MS 56-57ChiB		6'	185	Sam Houston St.	8	
Morales, Gonzales TB-DB	47-48Pit	12	6'	188	St. Mary's	2	6
Morgan, Bob DT-OT	54ChiC 54Was 55CFL		6'	235	Maryland		
Morgan, Joe T	49SF-AA		6'1"	245	Southern Miss.		
Morley, Sam OE	54Was		6'2"	182	Stanford		
Morris, George C-LB	56SF		6'2"	220	Georgia Tech		
Morris, Jack DB	58-60LA 60Pit 61Min	5	6'	189	Oregon	8	30
Morris, Max OE-DE	46-47ChiAA 48BknAA	2	6'2"	200	Illinois,		18
46-49 played in N. B. L., 49-50 played in N. B. A.					Northwestern		
Morrison, Curley FB-HB	50-53ChiB 54-56Cle	2345	6'2"	215	Ohio State		84
Morrow, Russ LB-C-DE-OE	46-47BknAA		6'7"	205	Tennessee		12
Morton, John OE-DE-DB	45ChiB 46LA-AA 47BufAA		6'	197	Missouri, Purdue	1	6
Morton, John LB	53SF		6'2"	220	Texas Christian	2	
Moselle, Dom DB-HB	50Cle 51-52GB 54Phi	23	6'	192	Wis.-Superior	4	36
Moser, Bob C	51-53ChiB		6'3"	238	U. of Pacific		
Mosley, Henry HB	55ChiB		6'2"	210	Morris Brown		
Mosley, Norm TB-DB	48Pit		5'9"	185	Alabama		6
Moss, Joe OT	52Was		6'1"	221	Maryland		
Moss, Perry QB	48GB		5'10"	170	Illinois		
Mote, Kelley OE-DE-DB	47-49Det 50-52NYG	2	6'2"	189	Duke	2	36
Motl, Bob OE-DE	46ChiAA		6'3"	195	Northwestern		6
Motley, Marion FB-LB	46-49CleAA 50-53Cle 54LJ 55Pit	23	6'1"	232	S. Carolina State,	2	234
					Nevada-Reno		
Mrkonic, George OT-DT	53Phi		6'2"	225	Kansas		
Muehlheuser, Frank (Moose) FB-LB	48Bos 49NYB	2	6'2"	218	Colgate		12
Muha, Joe LB-FB	46-50Phi	2 4	6'1"	205	V. M. I.	5	38
Mullins, Noah DB-HB	46-48ChiB 49NYG	2	5'11"	182	Kentucky	19	42
Mulready, Jerry OE-DE	47ChiAA		6'1"	205	N. Dakota State		
Murakowski, Art FB-LB	51Det		6'	195	Northwestern		
Murley, Dick OT	56Pit 56Phi		6'	247	Purdue		
Murphy, George BB	49LA-AA		6'	200	Southern Calif.		
Murray, Earl OG	50Bal 51NYG 52Pit		6'2"	240	Purdue		
Mutryn, Chet HB-DB	46-49BufAA 50Bal	23	5'9"	179	Xavier-Ohio	1	253
Mutscheller, Jim OE-DE	54-61Bal	2	6'1"	213	Notre Dame		240
Myers, Bob DT	55Bal		6'	260	Ohio State		
Myers, Brad HB-FB-OE-DB	53LA 54-55MS 56LA 58Phi	2	6'1"	197	Bucknell		18
Myers, Jack FB-LB	48-50Phi 52LA	2	6'2"	200	U. C. L. A.	2	18
Myhra, Steve OG-LB	57-61Bal	5	6'1"	237	North Dakota		312
Nabors, Roland LB-C	48NY-AA		6'2"	200	Texas Tech	1	
Nacrelli, Andy OE	58Phi		6'1"	190	Fordham		
Nagel, Ray QB	53ChiC	1	5'11"	177	U. C. L. A.		
Nagel, Ross DT-OT	42ChiC 51NYY		6'4"	234	St. Louis	1	
Nagler, Gern OE	53ChiC 54MS 55-58ChiC 59Pit 60-61Cle	2	6'2"	190	Santa Clara		168
Naumetz, Fred C-LB	46-50LA		6'1"	222	Boston College	7	
Naumu, John HB	48LA-AA		5'8"	175	Southern Calif.		
Neal, Ed DG-DT-OT-OG-C	45-51GB 51ChiB		6'4"	285	Tulane,		6
					Louisiana State		
Neale, Greasy	HC41-42Phi HC43P-P HC44-50Phi				West Va. Wesleyan		
16-22, 24 played major league baseball							
Negus, Fred LB-C	47-49ChiAA 50ChiB		6'1"	208	Wisconsin,	7	12
					Michigan		
Nelson, Bob C-LB-OT-DT-OE	41Det 42-44MS 45Det	5	6'1"	214	Baylor	6	67
	46-49LA-AA 50Bal						
Nelson, Frank DB-HB-TB	48Bos 49NYB	2	5'9"	167	Utah	2	
Nelson, Herb DE-OE-T	46BufAA 47-48BknAA		6'4"	219	Pennsylvania		
Nelson, Jimmy HB-QB-DB	46MiaAA	2	5'11"	180	Alabama	2	12
Nemeth, Steve QB-TB-DB	45Cle 46ChiAA 47BalAA	1 5	5'10"	174	Notre Dame		60
Nichols, Ham OG-LB	47-49ChiC 51GB		5'11"	209	Rice	1	
Nickel, Elbie OE-DE	47-57Pit	2	6'1"	196	Cincinnati		222
Nickla, Ed OT	59ChiB		6'3"	240	Maryland,		
					Tennessee		
Nicksich, George LB-OG	50Pit		6'	225	St. Bonaventure	3	

Use Name (Nicknames) – Positions	Team by Year	See Section	Hgt	Wgt	College	Int	Pts
Niedziela, Bruno T	47ChiAA		6'2"	225	Iowa		
Niemi, Laurie (Finn) OT-DT	49-53Was		6'1"	251	Washington State		6
Niles, Jerry QB	47NYG	1	6'1"	195	Iowa		
Nilson, Reed C-LB	47Det		6'	230	Brigham Young		
Nipp, Maury OG	52-53Phi 54-55MS 56Phi		6'	219	Loyola Marymount		
Nix, Doyle DB	55GB 56-57MS 58-59Was 60LA-A 61DalA		6'1"	191	S. M. U.	16	6
Nix, Jack OE	50SF 51CFL		6'2"	200	Southern Calif.		
Nobile, Leo G-LB	48-49Pit		5'10"	213	Penn State	1	
Nolan, Dick DB	54-57NYG 58ChiC 59-61NYG 62Dal		6'1"	185	Maryland	23	2
	HC68-75SF HC78-80NO						
Nolan, John OT-DT	48Bos 49NYB 50NYY		6'2"	232	Penn State		
Nolander, Don C-LB	46LA-AA		6'1"	210	Minnesota	1	
Noll, Chuck LB-OG-C	53-59Cle HC69-87Pit		6'1"	218	Dayton	8	14
Nomellini, Leo (The Lion) DT-OT	50-63SF		6'3"	259	Minnesota		10
Norberg, Hank DE-OE	46-47SF-AA 48ChiB		6'2"	225	Stanford	1	
Norman, Jim DT-OT	55Was		6'2"	248	none		
Norris, Hal LB-DB	55-56Was		5'11"	194	California		
North, John OE-DB	48-49BalAA 50Bal HC73-75NO	2	6'2"	199	Vanderbilt	1	36
Norton, Jerry DB-HB	54-58Phi 59ChiC 60-61StL 62Dal	234	5'11"	195	S. M. U.	35	42
	63-64GB						
Nowaskey, Bob DE-OE	40-42ChiB 43-45MS 46-48LA-AA	2	6'	205	George Washington	4	49
	48-49BalAA 50Bal						
Nussbaumer, Bob DB-HB	46GB 47-48Was 49-50ChiC 51GB	2	5'11"	172	Michigan	16	30
Nutter, Buzz C-LB	54-60Bal 61-64Pit 65Bal		6'4"	230	Virginia Tech		
Nuzum, Jerry HB-DB	48-51Pit	2	6'1"	199	New Mexico State	1	60
Nyers, Dick DB-HB	56-57Bal		5'11"	177	Indiana Central		
Nygren, Bernie HB-DB	46LA-AA 47BknAA	2	5'9"	193	San Jose State	2	6
Oakley, Charley DB	54ChiC		5'10"	170	Louisiana State		
Obeck, Vic G	40AFL 42-44MS 45ChiC 46BknAA		6'	225	Springfield		
O'Brien, Bill HB-DB	47Det		6'	180	none		
O'Brien, Jack OE-DE	54-56Pit	2	6'2"	213	Florida		12
O'Connell, Tom QB	53ChiB 54-55MS 56-57Cle 60-61BufA	12	5'11"	187	Illinois		26
O'Connor, Bill OE-DE	48BufAA 49CleAA 51NYY	2	6'4"	220	Notre Dame		12
O'Donahue, Pat DE	52SF 53-54MS 55GB		6'1"	208	Wisconsin		7
Odson, Urban T	46-49GB		6'3"	251	Minnesota		2
Olenski, Mitch T	46MiaAA 47Det		6'3"	222	Alabama		
Olsen, Ralph DE	49GB		6'4"	220	Utah		
Olsonoski, Larry G	48-49GB 49NYB		6'2"	214	Minnesota		
Olszewski, Johnny (Johnny O) FB-HB	53-57ChiC 58-60Was	2	5'11"	200	California		114
	61Det 62DenA						
O'Malley, Joe DE	55-56Pit		6'2"	218	Georgia		6
O'Malley, Tom QB	50GB		5'11"	185	Cincinnati		
O'Neal, Jim G	46-47ChiAA		6'1"	230	Texas Christian		
O'Neil, Bob OG-DE	56-57Pit 61NY-A		6'1"	229	Notre Dame		
Oniskey, Dick OG	55Pit		6'2"	225	Tenn. Chattanooga		
O'Quinn, Red DB-OE-DE	50-51ChiB 51Phi 52CFL		6'2"	195	Wake Forest	3	6
Oristaglio, Bob DE-OE	49BufAA 50Bal 51Cle 52Phi	2	6'2"	214	Pennsylvania		6
Orlich, Dan DE-OE	49-51GB		6'5"	215	Nevada-Reno	1	6
Ormsbee, Elliott HB-DB	46Phi		5'11"	185	Bradley		
O'Rourke, Charlie QB-DB	42ChiB 43-45MS 46-47LA-AA	12 4	5'11"	175	Boston College	3	24
	48-49BalAA						
Ortmann, Chuck TB-DB-QB	51Pit 52Dal	12	6'1"	190	Michigan	1	
Osmanski, Joe FB-LB	46-49ChiB 49NYB	2	6'2"	218	Holy Cross		36
Ossowski, Ted T	47NY-AA		6'	218	Oregon State		
Ostendarp, Jim HB	50-51NYG		5'8"	178	Bucknell		12
Ostrowski, Chet DE-DT	54-59Was		6'1"	232	Notre Dame	2	
Ottele, Dick BB-DB	48LA-AA		6'3"	210	Washington		
Owens, Ike DE	48ChiAA		6'1"	190	Illinois		
Owens, Jim OE-DE	50Bal	2	6'3"	205	Oklahoma	1	6
Pace, Jim HB	58SF 59JJ 60CFL	2	6'	195	Michigan		12
Pacewic, Vince HB-DB	47Was		6'1"	205	San Francisco		
Paffrath, Bob HB-DB-BB	46BknAA 46MiaAA 47CFL	2	5'8"	190	Minnesota		12
Page, Paul HB-DB	49BalAA	2	6'	180	S. M. U.		
Paine, Homer T	49ChiAA		6'	235	Oklahoma		
Palatella, Lou OG-LB	55-58SF		6'2"	230	Pittsburgh		
Palazzi, Lou C-LB	46-47NYG		6'	198	Penn State		
Palmer, Darrell DT-OT	46-48NY-AA 49CleAA 50-53Cle		6'2"	240	Texas Christian		
Palmer, Les DB-HB	48Phi		6'	180	N. Carolina State		
Palmer, Tom DT	53-54Pit		6'2"	240	Wake Forest		
Palumbo, Sam LB-C	55-56Cle 57GB 60BufA		6'2"	226	Notre Dame	1	
Panciera, Don QB-DB	49NY-AA 50Det 52ChiC	1	6'1"	192	San Francisco	1	
Panelli, John LB-FB	49-50Det 51-53ChiC	2	5'11"	200	Notre Dame	5	
Panfil, Ken OT-DT	56-58LA 59ChiC 60-62StL		6'6"	262	Purdue		
Paolucci, Ben DT	59Det		6'2"	240	Wayne State		
Papach, George FB-DB	48-49Pit	2	6'2"	208	Purdue		18
Papit, Johnny HB	51-53Was 53GB	2	6'	190	Virginia		12
Parker, Howie BB-LB	48NY-AA		6'2"	220	S. M. U.		
Parker, Joe DE-OE	46-47ChiC		6'1"	220	Texas		
Parmer, Jim HB-FB-DB	48-56Phi	2	6'	193	Oklahoma State	3	126
Parseghian, Ara HB-DB	48-49CleAA	2	5'10"	194	Miami-Ohio	1	12
Parsons, Earle HB-DB	46-47SF-AA	23	6'	180	Southern Calif.		24
Paschka, Gordon FB-LB-G	43P-P 47NYG	2	6'	213	Minnesota		14
Pasquariello, Ralph FB	50LA 51-52ChiC 53JJ	2	6'2"	237	Villanova		12
Pasquesi, Tony DT-LB	55-57ChiC		6'4"	245	Notre Dame		
Patanelli, Mike DE	47BknAA		6'2"	215	Ball State		
Patera, Jack LB-OG	55-57Bal 58-59ChiC 60-61Dal		6'1"	234	Oregon	6	
	HC76-82Sea						
Patterson, Paul WB-DB	49ChiAA	2	5'9"	185	Illinois	3	24
Patton, Bob OG	52NYG		6'	226	Clemson		
Patton, Cliff OG-DG-LB	46-50Phi 51ChiC	5	6'2"	243	Texas Christian	3	278
Paul, Don LB-C	48-55LA		6'1"	228	U. C. L. A.	11	
Paul, Don DB-HB	50-53ChiC 54-58Cle	23	6'	187	Washington State	34	84
Pavlich, Charlie G	46SF-AA		6'2"	210	none		
Pearcy, Jim G	46-49ChiAA		5'11"	210	Marshall		
Pearson, Lindy HB	50-52Det 52GB	2	6'	198	Oklahoma		12
Peebles, Jim DE-OE-OT	46-49, 51Was	2	6'4"	231	Vanderbilt		7
Pelfrey, Ray OE-HB	51GB 52Dal 52ChiC 53NYG	2	6'	190	Eastern Kentucky		
Pellington, Bill LB-OG	53-64Bal		6'2"	234	Rutgers	21	6
Pepper, Gene OG-OT-DT-LB-DG	50-53Was 54Bal		6'2"	239	Missouri		
Perantoni, Frank C	48-49NY-AA		6'	220	Princeton		
Perina, Bob DB-TB-HB	46NY-AA 47BknAA 48ChiAA 49ChiB	12	6'1"	205	Princeton	18	30
	50Bal						
Perini, Pete FB-LB	54-55ChiB 55Cle		6'	225	Ohio State		1
Perko, John G	46BufAA		5'11"	225	Minnesota,		
					Notre Dame		
Perpich, George T	46BknAA 47BalAA		6'2"	233	Georgetown		
Perotti, Mike T	48-49LA-AA		6'3"	243	Cincinnati		

Use Name (Nicknames) – Positions	Team by Year	See Section	Hgt	Wgt	College	Int	Pts
Perry, Jerry DT-DE-OT-OG	54Det 55MS 56-59Det 60-62StL	5	6'4"	237	California		190
Perry, Joe FB-DB	48-49SF-AA 50-60SF 61-62Bal 63SF	23	6'	203	Compton J.C.	1	513
Perry, Lowell OE-HB	56Pit	2	6'	195	Michigan		12
Peters, Volney DT-OT-DE	52-53ChiC 54-57Was 58Phi 60LA-A 61OakA		6'4"	237	Southern Calif.		6
Peterson, Jerry (The Heap) DT	56Bal		6'3"	290	Texas		
Petitbon, Johnny DB-HB	52Dal 53-54MS 55-56Cle 57GB		5'11"	186	Notre Dame	8	
Petrovich, George OG-OT-DT	49-50ChiC		6'2"	225	Texas		
Peviani, Bob LB	53NYG		6'1"	210	Southern Calif.		
Pfohl, Bob HB-DB	48-49BalAA	2	6'	200	Purdue		48
Phelan, Jimmy	HC48-49LA-AA HC52Dal				Notre Dame		
Phelps, Don (Dopey) HB-DB	50-52Cle	2	5'11"	185	Kentucky	1	24
Phillips, Mike C-LB	47BalAA		6'	208	Western Maryland		
Philpott, Dean FB	58ChiC		6'	200	Fresno State		
Pifferini, Bob LB-C	49Det		6'	210	San Jose State	3	
Piggott, Bert HB-DB	47LA-AA	2	6'2"	195	Illinois	1	6
Pihos, Pete OE-DE	47-55Phi	2	6'1"	211	Indiana	2	378
Pipkin, Joyce OE-DE-BB	48NYG 49LA-AA		6'1"	204	Arkansas		
Pirro, Rocco G-BB-LB-DB-HB	40-41Pit 42-45MS 46-49BufAA		6'	226	Catholic	1	
Piskor, Roman T	46NY-AA 47CleAA 48ChiAA		6'	245	Niagara		
Pitts, Hugh LB	56LA 60HouA		6'2"	223	Texas Christian	3	
Planutis, Jerry HB	56Was		5'9"	175	Michigan State		
Podoley, Jim HB-OE	57-60Was 61JJ	2	6'2"	200	Central Michigan		78
Poillon, Dick HB-DB-TB	42Was 43-45MS 46-49Was	2 45	6'	193	Canisius	2	247
Polanski, John FB-LB	42Det 43-45MS 46LA-AA	2	6'2"	211	Wake Forest	2	12
Pollard, Al HB-FB-DB	51NYY 51-53Phi	23	6'	196	Army, Loyola Marymount		7
Polofsky, Gordon OG-LB	52-54ChiC		6'1"	219	Tennessee		
Polsfoot, Fran OE	50-52ChiC 53Was	2 4	6'3"	203	Washington State		60
Poole, Barney DE-OE	49NY-AA 50-51NYY 52Dal 53Bal 54NYG	2	6'2"	231	North Carolina, Army, Mississippi	1	6
Poole, Ollie DE-OE	47NY-AA 48BalAA 49Det		6'3"	220	Mississippi		
Poole, Ray DE-OE	47-52NYG 53CFL	2 5	6'2"	215	Mississippi	3	223
Pope, Eli LB	52ChiC		5'10"	202	Illinois		
Poto, John HB-DB	47-48Bos	2	5'10"	194	none		6
Powell, Charley DE-LB-OE	52-53SF 54MS 55-57SF 58-59 retired for pro boxing career 60-61OakA		6'2"	226	none		2
Powers, Jim DB-QB LB	50-53SF	1 4	6'	185	Southern Calif.	11	
Prchlik, John DT-OT	49-53Det		6'4"	234	Yale		2
Pregulman, Merv C-LB	46GB 47-48Det 49NYB	5	6'3"	215	Michigan	3	32
Prescott, Hal OE-DB	46GB 47-49Phi 49NYB	2	6'2"	199	Hardin-Simmons	3	6
Preston, Pat G-LB	46-49ChiB		6'2"	216	Wake Forest		
Prewitt, Felto LB-C	46-48BufAA 49BalAA		5'11"	207	Tulsa	6	
Priatko, Bill LB	57Pit		6'2"	220	Pittsburgh		
Price, Eddie FB	50-55NYG	2	5'11	190	Tulane		144
Pricer, Billy FB	57-60Bal 61DalA	2	5'10"	208	Oklahoma		18
Pritchard, Bosh HB-DB	42Cle 42Phi 43-45MS 46-49Phi 50JJ 51Phi 51NYG	234	5'11"	164	V.M.I.	7	150
Pritko, Steve OE-DE	43NYG 44-45Cle 46-47LA 48Bos 49NYB 49-50GB	2	6'2"	209	Villanova	1	90
Proctor, Dewey FB-LB	46-47NY-AA 48ChiAA 49NY-AA	2	5'11"	215	Furman	1	24
Proctor, Rex DB	53ChiB		5'10"	180	Rice	1	
Prokop, Eddie FB-DB-HB-LB	46-47NY-AA 48ChiAA 49NY-AA	23	5'11"	200	Georgia Tech	4	84
Prokop, Joe HB-DB	48ChiAA		6'2"	170	Bradley		
Provo, Fred HB-DB	48GB	2	5'9"	185	Washington		18
Psaltis, Jim DB	53ChiC 54GB 55ChiC		6'1"	190	Southern Calif.	6	6
Ptacek, Bob QB	59Cle		6'1"	205	Michigan		
Pucci, Ben T	46BufAA 47ChiAA 48CleAA		6'4"	255	none		
Puddy, Hal T	48SF-AA		6'3"	220	Oregon State		
Purdin, Cal WB-DB-HB	43ChiC 44-45MS 46BknAA 46MiaAA	2	6'2"	188	Tulsa		
Purnell, Frank FB	57GB		5'11"	230	Alcorn State		
Putman, Earl C	57ChiC		6'6"	308	Arizona State		
Putnam, Duane OG-LB	52-59LA 60Dal 61Cle 62LA		6'	228	U. of Pacific		
Quillen, Frank OE-DE	46-47ChiAA	2	6'5"	225	Pennsylvania	1	18
Quilter, Charley OT-DT	49SF-AA 50SF		6'1"	240	Tyler J.C.		
Quinlan, Skeets HB	52-56LA 56Cle	23	5'11"	173	San Diego State		96
Quirk, Ed FB-LB-C	48-51Was	2	6'1"	231	Missouri	2	30
Radosevich, George C-OT	54-56Bal		6'2"	228	Pittsburgh		
Ragunas, Vince LB	49Pit		5'11"	200	V.M.I.		
Raimondi, Ben TB	47NY-AA		5'10"	175	Indiana		
Ramona, Joe LB-OG	53NYG		6'1"	210	Santa Clara		
Ramsey, Buster OG-LB	46-51ChiC HC60-61BufA		6'1"	219	William & Mary	7	2
Ramsey, Knox OG-LB-DG	48-49LA-AA 50-51ChiC 52Phi 52-53Was		6'1"	216	William & Mary		
Ramsey, Ray DB-OE-WB-HB	47ChiAA 48BknAA 49ChiAA 47-49 played in B. A. A. 50-53ChiC	23	6'2"	166	Bradley	35	108
Rapacz, John C-LB	48-49ChiAA 50-54NYG		6'4"	252	Oklahoma		
Ratterman, George QB	47-49BufAA 50-51NYY 52-56Cle	12	6'1"	182	Notre Dame		84
Rauch, Johnny QB-DB	49NYB 50-51NYY 51Phi HC66-68OakA HC69BufA HC70Buf	1	6'	197	Georgia	2	6
Ravensburg, Bob OE-DB	48-49ChiC	2	6'	190	Indiana	1	18
Reader, Russ DR	47ChiB		6'	185	Michigan State		
Reagan, Frank DB-FB-QB-HB	41NYG 42-45MS 46-48NYG 49-51Phi	1234	5'11"	182	Pennsylvania	35	48
Rechichar, Bert DB-LB-HB-OE	52Cle 53-59Bal 60Pit 61NY-A	345	6'1"	209	Tennessee	31	179
Reece, Don FB-LB-T	46MiaAA	2	6'1"	230	Missouri	1	12
Reese, Ken HB-DB	47Det		5'11"	175	Alabama		
Reese, Lloyd FB-LB	46ChiB	2	6'2"	240	Tennessee		6
Reichardt, Bill FB	52GB	2 5	5'11"	210	Iowa		26
Reid, Breezy HB	50ChiB 50-56GB	2	5'10"	187	Georgia		108
Reid, Joe LB-C-DG	51LA 52Dal		6'3"	225	Louisiana State	1	
Reinhard, Bill DB-TB-HB-QB	47-48LA-AA		5'10"	168	California	5	18
Reinhard, Bob DT-FB-OT	46-49LA-AA 50LA	2 4	6'4"	234	California	1	18
Remington, Bill C-LB	46SF-AA		6'1"	185	Washington State		
Renfro, Dean HB	55Bal		5'11"	180	North Texas		
Renfro, Dick FB-LB	46SF-AA		5'10"	200	Washington State		18
Renfro, Ray FL-HB	52-63Cle	23	6'1"	190	North Texas		330
Renfro, Will DT-DE-OT	57-59Was 60Pit 61Phi		6'5"	233	Memphis State		18
Repko, Joe T	46-47Pit 48-49LA		6'	236	Boston College		6
Restic, Joe DB	52Phi		6'2"	180	Villanova		
Reynolds, Billy HB	53-54Cle 55-56MS 57Cle 58Pit 60OakA	23	5'10"	195	Pittsburgh		42
Reynolds, Jim FB-LB	46MiaAA	2	6'1"	190	Auburn	2	
Reynolds, Jim DB	46Pit		6'	193	Oklahoma State	1	
Rhodemyre, Jay C-LB	48-49, 51-52GB		6'1"	210	Kentucky	5	
Ricca, Jim OT-DG-DT	51-54Was 55Det 55-56Phi		6'4"	270	Georgetown	1	8
Rich, Herb DB-HB	50Bal 51-53LA 54-56NYG		5'11"	181	Vanderbilt	29	24

Use Name (Nicknames) – Positions	Team by Year	See Section	Hgt	Wgt	College	Int	Pts
Richardson, Jess DT	53-56Phi 57JJ 58-61Phi 62-64BosA		6'2"	261	Alabama	1	
Richeson, Roy G	49ChiAA		6'	235	Alabama		
Richter, Les LB	54-62LA	5	6'3"	238	California	16	193
Rickards, Paul QB	48LA		6'1"	190	Pittsburgh		
Rifenburg, Dick OE	50Det	2	6'3"	195	Michigan		6
Riffle, Charley G-LB	44Cle 45MS 46-48NY-AA		6'	212	Notre Dame	1	
Riley, Lee DB	55Det 56,58-59Phi 60NYG 61-62NY-A	3	6'1"	192	Detroit	23	
Roberts, Bill HB	56GB		6'	200	Dartmouth		
Roberts, Choo-Choo HB-FB-DB	47-50NYG 51CFL	2	5'11"	188	Tenn.-Chattanooga		158
Robinson, Bill HB	52GB		6"	195	Lincoln (Pa.)		
Robinson, Charley OG-LB	54Bal		6'	240	Morgan State		6
Robinson, Fred OG	57Cle		6'1"	242	Washington		
Robinson, Wayne LB-C	52-56Phi		6'2"	225	Minnesota	5	
Robison, George OG	52Dal		6'2"	215	V.M.I.		
Robnett, Ed FB-LB	47SF-AA		5'8"	205	Texas Tech		
Robustelli, Andy DE	51-55LA 56-64NYG		6'1"	230	Arnold	2	32
Rodgers, Hosea FB	49LA-AA	2	6'1"	192	North Carolina		30
Rodgers, Tom T	47Bos		6'	248	Bucknell		
Roffler, Bud DB	54Phi		6'1"	200	Washington State		
Rogas, Dan OG-DT-OT	51Det 52Phi		6'1"	228	Tulane		
Rogel, Fran FB	50-57Pit	2	5'11"	203	Penn State		114
Rogers, Cullen HB-DB	46Pit		5'10"	178	Texas A&M		
Roggeman, Tom OG	56-57ChiB		6'	235	Purdue		
Rohrig, Herm (Stumpy) DB-HB-TB	41GB 42-45MS 46-47GB	23	5'8"	190	Nebraska	11	4
Rokisky, John DE-OE	46CleAA 47ChiAA 48NY-AA	5	6'2"	202	Duquesne		46
Roman, George DT-OT	48Bos 49NYB 50NYG 51CFL		6'4"	242	Case Reserve		
Romanik, Steve QB	50-53ChiB 53-54ChiC	12	6'1"	190	Villanova		18
Romboli, Rudy FB-LB	46-48Bos	2	5'10"	213	none	2	6
Romero, Ray OG	51Phi 52-53MS		5'11"	213	Kansas State		
Romine, Al DB-HB	55,58GB 60DenA 61BosA		6'2"	191	North Alabama	4	
Root, Jim QB	53ChiC 54-55MS 56ChiC	12	6'1"	185	Miami-Ohio		18
Rosato, Sal FB-LB	45-47Was	2	6'1"	228	Villanova		30
Roskie, Ken FB-LB	46SF-AA 48GB 48Det		6'1"	225	South Carolina	1	6
Rosso, George DB	54Was		5'11"	177	Ohio State	4	
Rote, Kyle OE-HB	51-61NYG	2	6'	199	S.M.U.		312
Rote, Tobin QB	50-56GB 57-59Det 60-62CFL 63-64SD-A 66DenA	12	6'3"	211	Rice		228
Rothrock, Cliff C-LB	47ChiAA		5'10"	108	N. Dakota State		
Roussos, Mike T	48-49Was 49Det		6'3"	238	Pittsburgh		
Rowe, Harmon DB-HB-WB	47-49NY-AA 50-52NYG		6'	182	San Francisco	11	2
Rowland, Brad HB	51ChiB		6'1"	190	McMurry		
Royston, Ed G	48-49NYG		6'1"	220	Wake Forest		
Rozelle, Aubrey LB	57Pit		6'2"	215	Delta State	1	
Ruby, Martin DT-OT	46-48BknAA 49NY-AA 50NYY 51CFL		6'4"	249	Texas A & M	1	8
Rucka, Leo LB	56SF		6'3"	212	Rice		
Ruetz, Howie DT	51-53GB		6'3"	265	Loras	1	
Ruetz, Joe G-LB	46,48ChiAA		6'	200	Notre Dame	2	
Runnels, Tom HB	56-57Was	2	5'10"	187	North Texas		6
Rush, Clive OE	53GB HC69BosA HC70Bos	2 4	6'2"	197	Miami-Ohio		
Ruskusky, Ray DE	47NY-AA		6'3"	200	St. Mary's	1	
Russas, Al T-DE	49Det		6'2"	210	Tennessee		
Russell, Jack OE-DE-DB	46-49NY-AA 50NYY 51CFL	2	6'1"	215	Baylor	3	108
Russell, Ken OT	57-59Det		6'3"	252	Bowling Green		
Ruthstrom, Ralph LB-FB	45Cle 46LA 47Was 49BalAA		6'5"	212	S. Houston St.,SMU	2	
Ruzich, Steve OG-LB-OT-DT	52-54GB		6'2"	228	Ohio State		
Ryan, Dave TB-DB-HB	45-46Det 48Bos	12	5'10"	190	Hardin-Simmons	7	27
Ryan, Ed DE	48Pit		6'2"	200	St. Mary's		
Ryan, Rocky OE-DB-HB	56-58Phi 58ChiB		6'1"	202	Illinois	2	12
Rykovich, Julie HB-DB	47-48BufAA 48ChiAA 49-51ChiB 52-53Was	2	6'2"	204	Illinois, Notre Dame	5	193
Rymkus, Lou OT-DT	43Was 44-45MS 46-49CleAA 50-51Cle HC60HouA		6'4"	231	Notre Dame	1	12
Saban, Lou LB-FB	46-49CleAA HC60-61BosA HC62-65BufA HC67-69DenA HC70-71Den HC72-76Buf	5	6'	202	Indiana	13	27
Sabasteanski, Joe G-LB-C	47-48Bos 49NYB		6'	207	Fordham	3	
Sabuco, Tino C	49SF-AA		6'1"	206	San Francisco		
Sacrinty, Nick QB-DB	47ChiB	1	5'11"	185	Wake Forest	1	
Saenz, Eddie HB-DB	46-51Was	23	5'11"	169	Southern Calif.	3	72
Sagely, Floyd DB-OE	54,56SF 57ChiC		6'1"	191	Arkansas	1	
St. Clair, Bob OT	53-63SF 64FJ		6'9"	263	Tulsa, San Francisco		
St. John, Herb G	48BknAA 49ChiAA		5'10"	215	Georgia		
Salata, Paul OE	49SFAA 50SF 50 Bal	2	6'2"	191	Southern Calif.		48
Salem, Ed QB-DB	51Was		5'11"	193	Alabama	5	
Salsbury, Jim OG-OT	55-56Det 57-58GB		6'1"	233	U. C. L. A.		
Salscheider, Jack HB	49NYG	2	5'10"	185	St. Thomas		6
Samuel, Don DB-HB	49-50Pit	2	5'11"	190	Oregon State	1	6
Samuelson, Carl DT-OT	48-51Pit		6'4"	250	Nebraska	1	8
Sanchez, John OT-DT	47ChiAA 47Det 47-49Was 49-50NYG		6'3"	239	San Francisco	1	
Sanders, Spec TB-DB-WB-HB	46-48NY-AA 49KJ 50NYY	1234	6'1"	196	Texas	19	240
Sandifer, Dan DB-HB	48-49Was 50SF 50-51Phi 52-53GB 53ChiC	23	6'1"	190	Louisiana State	23	54
Sandusky, John OT-DT	50-55Cle 56GB		6'1"	251	Villanova		
Sanford, Leo LB-C-OG	51-57ChiC 58Bal		6'1"	224	Louisiana Tech	17	12
Sarratt, Charley QB-DB	48Det		6'1"	185	Oklahoma		
Sarringhaus, Paul HB-DB	46ChiC 48Det		6'	185	Ohio State		
Satterfield, Al T	47SF-AA		6'3"	225	Vanderbilt		
Savitsky, George T	48-49Phi		6'2"	244	Pennsylvania		
Sazio, Ralph T	48BknAA 49CFL		6'1"	220	William & Mary		
Scalissi, Ted HB-DB	47ChiAA		5'8"	173	Ripon		12
Scarbath, Jack QB	53-54Was 56Pit	12	6'2"	206	Maryland		12
Schabarum, Pete HB-DB	51SF 52MS 53-54SF	2	5'11"	185	California	1	18
Schaefer, Don FB	56Phi	2	6'	210	Notre Dame		12
Schilling, Ralph DE-OE	46Was 46BufAA		6'3"	218	Oklahoma City		
Schleich, Vic T	47NY-AA		6'3"	240	Nebraska		
Schlinkman, Walt FB	46-49GB	2	5'8"	191	Texas Tech		48
Schmidt, George DE-C-LB	52GB 53ChiC		6'2"	230	Illinois Tech		2
Schmidt, Joe LB	53-65, HC67-72Det		6'1"	220	Pittsburgh	24	18
Schneider, Don HB	48BufAA		5'9"	170	Pennsylvania		
Schneider, Leroy T	47BknAA		5'11"	237	Tulane		
Schnelker, Bob OE	53Phi 54-60NYG 61Min 61Pit	2	6'3"	214	Bowling Green		204
Schnellbacher, Otto (The Claw) DB-OE	48-49NY-AA 48-49 played in B. A. A. 50-51NYG		6'2"	188	Kansas	34	18

Use Name (Nicknames) – Positions	Team by Year	See Section	Hgt	Wgt	College	Int	Pts
Schottel, Ivan BB-DB-DE 47 played in P.B.A.	46,48Det		6'2"	204	NW Missouri St.		
Schrader, Jim C-OT	54Was 55MS 56-61Was 62-64Phi		6'2"	244	Notre Dame		
Schroeder, Bill DB HB-TB	46-47ChiAA		6'	190	Wisconsin	5	18
46-47 played in N.B.L.							
Schroeder, Gene OE-DB	51-52ChiB 53MS 54-57ChiB	2	6'3"	192	Virginia	5	78
Schroll, Bill LB-FB	49BufAA 50Det 51GB		6'	214	Louisiana State	3	
Schuette, Carl LB-C-DB	48-49BufAA 50-51GB		6'1"	206	Marquette	5	6
Schuler, Bill T	47-48NYG		6'	215	Yale		
Schwall, Vic HB	47-50ChiC	2	5'8"	188	Northwestern		18
Schweder, John OG-LB	50Bal 51-55Pit		6'1"	224	Pennsylvania	1	
Schwenk, Bud QB-TB-DB	42ChiC 43-45MS 46CleAA 47BalAA	12	6'2"	201	Washington-St. L.	1	24
	48NY-AA						
Scollard, Nick DE-OE	46-48Bos 49NYB	2 5	6'4"	217	St. Joseph's-Ind.	1	91
Scott, Clyde (Smackover) HB-DB	49-52Phi 52Det	2	6'	174	Navy, Arkansas	1	42
Scott, George HB	59NYG		6'1"	180	Miami-Ohio		
Scott, Joe HB-DB-OE	48-53NYG	23	6'1"	198	San Francisco	6	132
Scott, Prince OE-DB	46MiaAA	2	6'1"	190	Texas Tech	1	12
Scott, Tom LB-DE	53-58Phi 59-64NYG		6'2"	219	Virginia	8	18
Scott, Vin G	47-48BufAA 49CFL		5'8"	215	Notre Dame		
Scruggs, Ed OE-DE	47-48BknAA		6'1"	195	Rice		
Scudero, Scooter DB-HB	54-58Was 60Pit	23	5'10"	173	San Francisco	10	18
Seabright, Charlie (Lefty) BB-LB	41Cle 42-45MS 46-50Pit	2	6'2"	204	West Virginia	5	24
Sears, Jimmy HB-DB	54ChiC 55-56MS 57-58ChiC 60LA-A 61DenA	23	5'11"	183	Southern Calif.	2	18
Sears, Vic DT-OT	41-42Phi 43P-P 44BN 45-53Phi		6'3"	223	Oregon State	1	12
Sebek, Nick QB	50Was		6'1"	194	Indiana		
Self, Clarence DB-HB	49ChiC 50-51Det 52GB 53MS		5'8"	181	Wisconsin	7	6
	54-55GB						
Seno, Frank DB-HB-WB	43-44Was 45-46ChiC 47-48Bos	23	6'	191	George Washington	19	54
	49Was						
Sensenbaugher, Dean HB-DB	48CleAA 49NYB	2	5'9"	190	Army, Ohio State		12
Serini, Wash OG-DG-DT	48-51ChiB 52GB		6'2"	236	Kentucky		2
Sewell, Harley OG-LB	53-62Det 63LA		6'1"	230	Texas	1	6
Sexton, Lin HB-DB	48LA-AA		6'	180	Wichita State	1	
Shanley, Jim HB	58GB		5'9"	174	Oregon		
Sharkey, Ed OG-LB-OT-DG	47-49NY-AA 50NYY 51MS		6'3"	229	Nevada-Reno,	4	
	52Cle 53Bal 54-55 Phi 55-56SF				Duke		
Shaughnessy, Clark	HC48-49LA				Minnesota		
Shaw, Bob OE-DE	45Cle 46,49LA 50ChiC 51CFL	2	6'4"	226	Ohio State		126
45-47 played in N.B.L.							
Shaw, Buck	HC46-49SF-AA HC50-54SF HC58-60Phi				Notre Dame		
Shaw, Charlie OG	50SF		6'2"	220	Oklahoma State		
Shaw, George QB	55-58Bal 59-60NYG 61Min 62DenA	12	6'1"	183	Oregon		30
Shepard, Charlie HB-DB	56Pit 57CFL	2 4	6'2"	215	North Texas		
Sheriff, Stan LB-OG-C	54Pit 55MS 56-57SF 57Cle		6'1"	224	Cal. Poly-Pomona	1	
Sherman, Will DB-HB	52Dal 54-60LA 61Min		6'2"	197	St. Mary's	29	24
Sherrod, Horace OE-DE	52NYG		6'	190	Tennessee		6
Shields, Burrell HB-DB	54Pit 55Bal		6'2"	203	John Carroll	1	
Shipkey, Jerry FB-DB-LB	48-52Pit 53ChiB	2	6'1"	213	U. C. L. A.	13	102
Shipkey, Ted	HC47LA-AA				Stanford		
Shipp, Billy DT	54NYG 55CFL		6'5"	275	Alabama		
Shirley, Marion T	48-49NY-AA		6'4"	260	Oklahoma City		
Shiver, Ray DB	56LA		6'	190	Miami (Fla.)	1	
Shoener, Hal OE-DE	48-49SF-AA 50SF	2	6'3"	200	Iowa	1	18
Shoener, Herb DE	48-49Was		6'3"	205	Iowa		6
Shoults, Paul HB	49NYB	2	5'11"	178	Miami-Ohio		
Shula, Don DB-HB	51-52Cle 53-56Bal 57Was HC63-69Bal		5'11"	190	John Carroll	21	
	HC70-87Mia						
Shurnas, Marshall OE-DE	47CleAA		6'1"	205	Missouri		
Shurtz, Hubert T	48Pit		6'3"	235	Louisiana State		
Sidorik, Alex T	47Bos 48-49BalAA		6'	248	Mississippi State		
Siegert, Herb OG-LB	49-51Was		6'3"	216	Illinois	2	
Siegert, Wayne OT-LB-OG	51NYY		6'3"	225	Illinois		
Siegle, Jules FB-LB	48NYG		6'	210	Northwestern		
Sieradzki, Steve DB	48NY-AA		6'	194	Michigan State		
Sierocinski, Steve T	46Bos		6'3"	245	none		
Signiago, Joe OG-DG	48-49NY-AA 50NYY		6'1"	220	Notre Dame		
Sigurdson, Sig OE-DE	47Bal AA		6'2"	206	Pacific Lutheran		
Sikora, Mike OG	52ChiC		6'2"	230	Oregon		
Simensen, Don OT	51-52LA		6'2"	220	St. Thomas		
Simerson, John C-OT	57-58Phi 58Pit 60HouA 61BosA		6'3"	257	Purdue		
Simmons, Floyd HB-DB	48ChiAA	2	6'1"	200	Notre Dame		12
Simmons, Jack C-G-T	48BalAA 49-50Det 51-56 ChiC		6'4"	236	Detroit		
Simonetti, Len (Meatball) T	47-48CleAA		5'11"	225	Tennessee	1	
Sims, George DB	49-50LA 51-52MS		5'11"	170	Baylor	10	6
Sinkovitz, Frank LB-C	47-52Pit		6'1"	218	Duke	10	6
Sitko, Emil (Red, 6-Yard) HB	50SF 51-52ChiC	2	5'8"	183	Notre Dame		18
Skibinski, Joe OG	52Cle 53-54MS 55-56GB		5'11"	226	Purdue		
Skladany, Leo DE	49Phi 50NYG		6'1"	208	Pittsburgh		
Skoglund, Bob DE	47GB		6'1"	198	Notre Dame		
Skorich, Nick G-LB	46-48Pit HC61-63Phi HC71-74Cle		5'9"	197	Cincinnati		
Slater, Walt TB-DB	47Pit	123	5'11"	187	Tennessee	4	
Slosburg, Phil DB-HB-TB	48Bos 49NYB	2	5'10"	170	Temple	1	6
Smith, Allen DE-OE	47-48ChiB		6'2"	218	Mississippi		
Smith, Bill T	48ChiAA 48LA-AA		6'2"	250	North Carolina		
Smith, Bob FB	53-54Det		6'	205	Texas A&M		
Smith, Bob HB	55-56Cle 56Phi	2	5'10"	195	Nebraska		6
Smith, Bruce HB-DB-TB	45-48GB 48LA	2	6'	197	Minnesota	2	14
Smith, Charlie HB-DB	47ChiC		5'11"	170	Georgia	1	
Smith, Charlie DE	56SF		6'2"	205	Abilene Christian	1	
Smith, Clipper	HC47-48Bos				Notre Dame		
Smith, Ernie DB-HB	55-56SF		6'3"	190	Compton J.C.		
Smith, Jerry OG-LB	52-53SF 54-55MS 56SF 56GB HC71Den		6'1"	230	Wisconsin		
Smith, Jim T	47LA-AA		6'4"	270	Colorado		
Smith, Jim DB-HB-WB	48BufAA 48BknAA 49ChiAA 49-53Det	2 4	6'1"	191	Iowa	33	18
Smith, Joe OE-DB	48BalAA		6'1"	183	Texas Tech	1	6
Smith, Oscar HB-DB	48-49GB 49NYB	2	6'	185	Texas-El Paso	2	
Smith, Ray Gene DB-HB	54-57ChiB	3	5'10"	187	Midwestern State	9	
Smith, Truett BB	50-51Pit		6'2"	208	Wyoming,		
					Mississippi State		
Smith, Vitamin HB	49-53LA	23	5'8"	179	Abilene Christian		138
Smyth, Bill DE-OE-T	47-50LA	2	6'3"	243	Cincinnati		6
Snyder, Lum OT	52-55Phi 56-57MS 58Phi		6'5"	228	Georgia Tech		
Soboleski, Joe OG-OT-DT-DG	49ChiAA 49Was 50Det 52Dal		6'	213	Michigan		
Soltau, Gordie OE	50-58SF	2 5	6'2"	195	Minnesota		644
Sommers, Jack C-LB	47Was		6'3"	232	U. C. L. A.		

Use Name (Nicknames) – Positions	Team by Year	See Section	Hgt	Wgt	College	Int	Pts
Sossamon, Lou C-LB	46-48NY-AA		6'1"	207	South Carolina		6
Souders, Cecil DE-OE-T	47-49Det	2	6'1"	210	Ohio State		6
Spangler, Gene WB-DB	46Det		5'10"	195	Tulsa		
Spaniel, Frank HB	50Bal 50Was		5'10"	185	Notre Dame		12
Sparkman, Al T	48-49LA		6'6"	253	Texas A & M		
Sparks, Dave OG-OT	51SF 52-53MS 54Was		6'1"	229	South Carolina		
died of heart attack Dec. 5, 1954							
Sparlis, Al G-LB	46GB		5'11"	185	U. C. L. A.		
Spavital, Jimmie FB-LB	49LA-AA 50Bal	2	6'1"	210	Oklahoma State	4	18
Speedie, Mac OE-DE	46-49CleAA 50-52Cle 53CFL	2	6'3"	203	Utah		205
Spencer, Joe DT-OT	48BknAA 49CleAA 50-51GB		6'3"	239	Oklahoma State	1	
Spencer, Ollie OT-OG-C	53Det 54-55MS 56Det 57-58GB		6'2"	245	Kansas		
	59-61Det 63OakA						
Spinks, Jack OG-FB-OT	52Pit 53ChiC 55-56GB 56-57NYG	2	6'	236	Alcorn State		
Spinney, Art OG-DE-OE	50Bal 51-52MS 53-60Bal		6'	230	Boston College		
Sponaugle, Bob OE-DE	49NYB		6'1"	203	Pennsylvania		
Sprinkle, Ed DE-OE-OG-LB	44-55ChiB	2	6'1"	206	Hardin-Simmons	4	62
Spruill, Jim T	48-49BalAA		6'3"	225	Rice		
Stacco, Ed T	47Det 48Was		6'2"	261	Colgate		
Standlee, Norm FB-LB	41ChiB 42-45MS 46-49SF-AA	2	6'2"	238	Stanford	2	138
	50-52SF						
Stanfel, Dick OG	52-55Det 56-58Was HC80NO		6'3"	236	San Francisco		
Stanley, C. B. T	46BufAA		6'4"	225	Tulsa		
Stansauk,Don DT	50-51GB		6'1"	255	Denver		
Stanton, Bill DE	49BufAA		6'2"	210	N. Carolina State		
Stanton, Henry DE-OE	46-47NY-AA		6'2"	200	Arizona		
Stasica, Stan HB-DB	46MiaAA		5'10"	175	South Carolina		
Staton, Jim DT	51Was		6'4"	246	Wake Forest		
Statuto, Art C	48-49BufAA 50LA		6'2"	221	Notre Dame		
Stautner, Ernie DT-DE-OG	50-63Pit		6'1"	230	Boston College	2	6
Stautzenberger, Odell G	49BufAA		6'	218	Texas A & M		
Steber, John OG-DG	46-50Was 51-52MS		6'	225	Georgia Tech		
Steere, Dick OG	51Phi		6'4"	240	Drake		
Stefik, Bob OE	48BufAA		5'11"	180	Niagara		
Steinbrunner, Don OT	53Cle		6'3"	220	Washington State		
Steiner, Rebel DB	50-51GB		6'	185	Alabama	10	6
Steinke, Gil HB-DB	45-48Phi	2	6'	175	Texas A & I	7	36
Stenn (born Stenko), Paul OT-DT	42NYG 43-45MS 46Was 47Pit		6'2"	242	Villanova		
	48-51ChiB						
Stephens, Red OG	55-60Was		6'	230	San Francisco		
Stephenson, Dave OG-C-DG	51-55GB		6'2"	232	West Virginia		
Steuber, Bob FB-HB-LB-DB	43ChiB 44-45MS 46CleAA	2 5	6'2"	200	Missouri, DePauw	1	41
	47LA-AA 48BufAA						
Stevens, Don HB-DB	52,54Phi	2	5'9"	176	Illinois		6
Stevens, Mal	HC46BknAA				Yale		
Stewart, Ralph C-LB	47-48NY-AA 48BalAA		6'	205	Missouri,		
					Notre Dame		
Stickel, Walt DT-OT	46-49ChiB 50-51Phi		6'3"	247	Pennsylvania		2
Still, Jim QB-DB	48-49BufAA	1 4	6'3"	193	Georgia Tech	1	
Stits, Bill DB-HB	54-56Det 57-58SF 59Was 59-61NYG	23	6'	194	U. C. L. A.	15	6
Stock, John OE	56Pit		6'2"	210	Pittsburgh		
Stofer, Ken QB-DB	46BufAA	1	5'9"	188	Cornell		
Stolhandske, Tom LB-DE	55SF		6'2"	210	Texas	1	
Stone, Avatus HB	58Bal		6'1"	195	Syracuse		
Stone, Billy HB-DB	49-50BalAA 51-54ChiB	23	6'	191	Bradley	11	186
Stonesifer, Don OE	51-56ChiC	2	6'	200	Northwestern		84
Stout, Pete FB-LB	49-50Was	2	6'	201	Texas Christian	2	36
Stoutberg, Jerry OG-LB	51ChiB		6'2"	228	Cincinnati		
Stovall, Dick LB-G-C	47-48Det 49Was		6'	202	Abilene Christian	1	
Strausbaugh, Jimmy HB-DB	46ChiC	2	5'9"	190	Ohio State		18
Stribling, Bill OE	51-53NYG 55-57Phi 58CFL	2	6'1"	206	Mississippi		84
Strickland, Bishop FB	51SF		5'10"	195	South Carolina		
Strickland, Larry C	54-59ChiB		6'4"	248	North Texas		
Striegel, Bill OG-OT-LB	59Phi 60BosA 60OakA		6'2"	235	U. of Pacific		
Stringer, Bob LB-FB	52-53Phi		6'1"	197	Tulsa	2	
Strode, Woody OE-DE	46LA 47CFL		6'3"	205	U. C. L. A.		
Strohmeyer, George LB-C	48BknAA 49ChiAA		5'10"	205	Notre Dame	7	
Stroschein, Breck DE	51NYY		6'1"	205	U. C. L. A.		
Stroud, Jack OG-OT	53-64NYG		6'1"	235	Tennessee		
Strzykalski, Johnny (Strike) HB-DB	46-49SF-AA 50-52SF	23	5'9"	190	Marquette	8	186
Sucic, Steve FB-LB	46LA 47Bos 47-48Det		6'	207	Illinois		
Sugar, Leo DE	54-59ChiC 60StL 61Phi 62Det		6'1"	214	Purdue	1	18
Suhey, Steve G	48-49Pit		5'11"	215	Penn State		
Sulatis, Joe BB-DE-LB-OG-QB-FB-WB	43-45NYG 46Bos	12	6'2"	212	none	2	12
	47-53NYG						
Sulima, George OE	52-54Pit	2	6'2"	200	Boston U.		12
Sullivan, Bob HB-TB-DB-LB-FB	47Pit 48BknAA		5'9"	191	Iowa		12
Sullivan, Bob HB-DB	48SF-AA	2	5'10"	190	Holy Cross	1	6
Sullivan, George DE-OE	48Bos		6'2"	205	Notre Dame		
Suminski, Dave OG	53Was 53ChiC 54CFL		5'11"	230	Wisconsin		
Summerall, Pat DE-OE-K	52Det 53-57ChiC 58-61NYG	5	6'4"	228	Arkansas		563
Summerhays, Bob LB-FB	49-51GB	2	6'1"	210	Utah	3	6
Sumner, Charlie DB	55ChiB 56-57MS 58-60ChiB 61-62Min		6'1"	194	William & Mary	21	6
Sumpter, Tony G	46-47ChiAA		6'1"	215	Cameron		
Susoeff, Nick OE-DE	46-49SF-AA	2	6'1"	211	Washington State		24
Susteric, Ed FB-LB	49CleAA		6'	205	Findlay		6
Sutch, George HB-DB	46ChiC		6'1"	205	Temple		
Sutherin, Don DB	59NYG 59-60Pit		5'10"	193	Ohio State	1	
Sutton, Ed HB-DB	57-59Was 60NYG	2	6'1"	205	North Carolina	1	60
Sutton, Joe DB-HB	49BufAA 50-52Phi		5'11"	180	Temple	13	6
Svare, Harland (Swede) LB-DT	53-54LA 55-60NYG		6'	214	Washington State	9	6
	HC62-65LA HC71-73SD						
Svoboda, Bill LB-FB	50-53ChiC 54-58NYG		6'	210	Tulane	9	
Sweiger, Bob BB-LB-DB-WB	46-48NY-AA 49ChiAA	2	6'	209	Minnesota	7	18
Swiacki, Bill OE	48-50NYG 51-52Det	2	6'2"	195	Columbia		108
Swistowicz, Mike DB	50NYY 50ChiC		5'10"	185	Notre Dame		
Switzer, Veryl HB-DB	54-55GB	23	5'11"	190	Kansas State		30
Sykes, Bob FB	52Was		6'1"	218	San Jose State		
Sylvester, John DB-HB	47NY-AA 48BalAA		6'	183	Temple	1	
Szafaryn, Len OT-OG-LB-DT	49Was 50GB 51-52MS		6'2"	226	North Carolina		6
	53-56GB 57-58Phi						
Szot, Walt DT-OT	46-48ChiC 49-50Pit 51-52MS		6'1"	222	Bucknell		
Szymanski, Frank C-LB	45-47Det 48Phi 49ChiB		6'	220	Notre Dame	1	

Use Name (Nicknames) – Positions	Team By Year	See Section	Hgt	Wgt	College	Int	Pts
Tackett, Doyle BB-DB-WB	46-48BknAA	2	6'	205	none	2	12
Tait, Art DE	51NYY 52Dal		5'11"	205	Mississippi State		12
Talcott, Dan T	47Phi		6'2"	235	Nevada-Reno		
Taliaferro, George HB-QB-TB-DB	49LA-AA 50-51NYY 52Dal 53-54Bal 55Phi	1234	5'11"	196	Indiana	4	168
Tamburo, Sam DE	49NYB		6'2"	200	Penn State		
Tanner, Hamp OT-DT	51SF 52Dal		6'2"	280	Georgia		2
Tarrant, Jim QB	46MiaAA		5'9"	160	Samford, Tennessee		
Taseff, Carl DB-HB	51Cle 52MS 53-61Bal 61Phi 62BufA	23	5'11"	192	John Carroll	20	48
Tassos, Damon G-LB	45-46Det 47-49GB		6'1"	224	Texas A&M	5	3
Tavener, John C-LB	46MiaAA		6'	225	Indiana		
Taylor, Charlie G	46MiaAA		5'11"	205	Stanford		
Taylor, Corky DB-HB	55,57LA	2	5'10"	189	Kansas State	2	12
Taylor, Hugh (Bones) OE	47-54Was HC65HouA	2	6'4"	194	Oklahoma City		348
Taylor, Jim C-LB	56Pit 57-58ChiC		6'2"	232	Baylor	1	
Teeuws, Len DT-OT	52-53LA 54-57ChiC		6'4"	242	Tulane		
Temp, Jim DE	57-60GB		6'4"	245	Wisconsin	1	
Tepe, Lou C-LB	53-55Pit		6'2"	208	Duke	3	
Tepo, George OE-DE	46Bos		6'2"	210	Fordham		
Tereshinski, Joe DE-OE-LB	47-54Was	2	6'2"	215	Georgia	1	24
Terlep, George QB-DB	46-48BufAA 48CleAA	12	5'10"	180	Notre Dame	1	6
Terrell, Ray HB-DB	46CleAA 47BalAA 47CleAA	2	6'	185	Mississippi	4	6
Teteak, Deral LB-OG	52-56GB		5'10"	210	Wisconsin	6	
Tevis, Lee FB-LB	47-48BknAA		5'11"	190	Miami-Ohio, Washington-St.L.		
Tew, Lowell FB	48-49NY-AA	2	5'11"	195	Alabama		36
Thibaut, Jim FB-LB	46BufAA		5'11"	205	Tulane		6
Thomas, George HB-DB	50-51Was 52NYG	2	6'1"	183	Oklahoma		12
Thomas, Jesse DB	55-57Bal 60LA-A		5'10"	180	Michigan State	4	6
Thomas, Ralph OE-DE	52ChiC 53-54MS 55-56Was		5'11"	190	San Francisco		18
Thomas, Russ T	46-49Det		6'3"	237	Ohio State	1	
Thomason, Bobby QB	49LA 51GB 52-57Phi	12	6'1"	196	V. M. I.		36
Thompson, Hal OE-DE	47-48BknAA	2	6'1"	205	Delaware		6
Thompson, Harry OG-DE-LB-DG	50-54LA 55ChiC		6'2"	226	U. C. L. A.		
Thompson, Tommy QB-DB-TB-HB	40Pit 41-42Phi 43-44MS 45-50Phi	12	6'1"	192	Tulsa	9	42
Thompson, Tommy LB-C	49CleAA 50-53Cle		6'1"	221	William & Mary	6	
Thornton, Bob G-T	46-47SF-AA		5'10"	205	Santa Clara		
Thrower, Willie QB	53ChiB		5'11"	182	Michigan State		
Tidwell, Billy HB-DB	54SF		5'9"	178	Texas A&M		
Tidwell, Travis QB	50-51NYG	12	5'10"	185	Auburn		12
Tillman, Al C-LB	49BalAA		6'	210	Oklahoma		
Timberlake, George LB-OG	55GB		6'1"	220	Southern Calif.		
Timmons, Charlie FB-LB	46BknAA		5'10"	210	Clemson		
Tinsley, Buddy T	49LA-AA 50CFL		6'4"	245	Baylor		
Tittle, Y. A. (Ya-Ya, The Bald Eagle) QB	48-49BalAA 50Bal 51-60SF 61-64NYG	12	6'	192	Louisiana State		234
Titus, George C-LB	46Pit		5'10"	185	Holy Cross		
Tobin, George G-LB	47NYG		5'10"	205	Notre Dame		
Tomasetti, Lou HB-DB-TB-WB	39-40Pit 41Phi 41Det 42Phi 43-45MS 46-49BufAA	12	6'	198	Bucknell	4	120
Tomlinson, Dick OG	50-51Pit		6'1"	205	Kansas		
Toneff, Bob DT-DG-DE-OT-OG	52SF 53MS 54-58SF 59-64Was		6'2"	260	Notre Dame	2	
Tonnemaker, Clayton (Clayt) LB-C	50GB 51-52MS 53-54GB		6'2"	237	Minnesota	2	1
Toogood, Charlie DT-OT-OG	51-56LA 57ChiC		6'	232	Nebraska	3	
Topor, Ted LB	55Det		6'1"	210	Michigan		
Topp, Bob OE	54NYG		6'2"	190	Michigan		18
Torgeson, Lavern (Torgy) LB-C	51-54Det 55-57Was		6'	215	Washington State	18	6
Toth, Zollie FB	50-51NYY 52Dal 53KJ 54Bal	2	6'2"	219	Louisiana State		102
Towler, Dan (Deacon Dan) FB	50-55LA	2	6'2"	225	Washington & Jeff.		264
Treadway, John T	48NYG 49Det		6'5"	258	Hardin-Simmons		
Trigillo, Frank FB-LB	46LA-AA 46MiaAA	2	5'11"	200	Alfred, Vermont, Indiana		6
Trimble, Jim	HC52-55Phi						
Triplett, Mel FB	55-60NYG 61-62Min	2	6'1"	215	Toledo		108
Triplett, Wally HB	49-50Det 51MS 52-53ChiC	23	5'10"	175	Penn State		24
Trippi, Charlie HB-DB-QB	47-55ChiC	1234	6'	186	Georgia	4	222
Tunnell, Em (Emlen the Gremlin) DB-HB	48-58NYG 59-61GB	3	6'1"	193	Toledo, Iowa	79	60
Turley, Doug DE-OE	44-48Was	2	6'2"	215	Scranton		24
Turner, Bulldog C-LB-OG-OT-HB	40-52ChiB HC62NY-A		6'1"	237	Hardin-Simmons	16	24
Turner, Hal DE	54Det		6'2"	235	Tennessee State		
Tyree, Jim OE-DE	48Bos	2	6'3"	204	Oklahoma		6
Tyrrell, Joe OG	52 Phi		5'11"	216	Temple		
Ulinski, Ed G	46-49CleAA		5'11"	203	Marshall		
Ulinski, Harry C	50-51Was 52MS 53-56Was		6'4"	229	Kentucky		
Ulrich, Chuck DT	54-58ChiC		6'4"	243	Illinois		
Ulrich, Hub OE-DE	46MiaAA		6'	205	Kansas		6
Urban, Gasper G-LB	48ChiAA		6'1"	215	Notre Dame	1	
Vacanti, Sam QB	47-48ChiAA 48-49BalAA	12	5'11"	203	Nebraska, Iowa		21
Van Brocklin, Norm (The Dutchman) QB	49-57LA 58-60Phi HC61-66Min HC68-74Atl	12 4	6'1"	199	Oregon		66
Van Buren, Ebert LB-FB-HB	51-53Phi		6'2"	210	Louisiana State	2	8
Van Buren, Steve HB-DB	44-51Phi 52KJ	23	6'	203	Louisiana State	9	464
Vandeweghe, Al OE-DE	46BufAA		5'11"	200	William & Mary		12
Van Doren, Bob DE	53SF		6'3"	215	Southern Calif.		
Vardian, John HB-DB	46MiaAA 47-48BalAA	2	5'8"	167	none	3	6
Vasicek, Vic OG-LB-DG	49BufAA 50LA		5'11"	223	Southern Calif., Texas	1	
Vaught, Ted DE-OE	55SF		6'	208	Texas Christian		
Venturelli, Fred K	48ChiB		5'11"	235	none		7
Venuto, Sam HB	52Was		6'1"	195	Guilford		6
Vereen, Carl OT	57GB		6'2"	247	Georgia Tech		
Verry, Norm T	46-47ChiAA		6'1"	240	Southern Calif.		
Vessels, Billy HB	56Bal	2	6'	190	Oklahoma		18
Vetrano, Joe HB-DB	46-49SF-AA	2 5	5'9"	170	Southern Miss.	3	247
Vezmar, Walt G	46-47Det		5'11"	235	Michigan State		
Vinnola, Paul HB DB	46LA-AA		5'10"	180	Santa Clara	1	
Vogds, Red G	46-47ChiAA 48-49GB		5'10"	210	Wisconsin		
Vogelaar, Carroll DT-OT	47-48Bos 49NYB 50NYY		6'3"	253	Loyola Marymount, San Francisco		
Volz, Wilbur HB-DB	49BufAA 50MS		6'	192	Missouri		6
Voyles, Carl	HC48BknAA				Oklahoma State		
Voytek, Ed OG	57-58Was		6'2"	235	Purdue		
Wade, Jim HB-DB	49NYB		5'11"	175	Oklahoma City	1	
Wagner, Lowell DB-WB-HB	46-48NY-AA 49SF-AA 50-53SF 54CFL 55SF	2	6'	194	Southern Calif.	32	30
Walker, Doak HB-DB	50-55Det	2345	5'11"	173	S. M. U.	2	534

Use Name (Nicknames) – Positions	Team by Year	See Section	Hgt	Wgt	College	Int	Pts
Walker, Paul DB-OE	48NYG		6'3"	210	Yale	1	
Walker, Val Joe DB	53-56GB 57SF		6'1"	179	S. M. U.	17	6
Wallace, Bev QB	47-49SF-AA 51NYY	1	6'2"	180	Compton J.C.		6
Wallace, Stan DB	54ChiB 55MS 56-58ChiB		6'3"	208	Illinois	10	
Waller, Ron HB	55-58LA 59KJ 60LA-A HC73SD	23	5'11"	180	Maryland		54
Wallner, Fred LB-OG	51-52ChiC 53MS 54-55ChiC 60 HouA		6'2"	231	Notre Dame	3	
Walsh, Bill C	49-54Pit		6'2"	230	Notre Dame		
Walston, Bobby OE-FL-HB	51-62Phi	2 5	6'	190	Georgia		881
Walters, Les DB	58Was		6'	185	Penn State	1	
Ward, Bill G	46-47Was 47-49Det		6'	230	Washington State		
Wardlow, Duane DE	54LA 55MS 56LA		6'4"	215	Washington		
Warren, Morrie FB-LB	48BknAA		5'11"	208	Arizona State		
Warrington, Caleb C-G-LB	46-48BknAA		6'2"	210	William & Mary, Auburn		
Washington, Kenny HB-DB	46-48LA	2	6'1"	212	U. C. L. A.	2	54
Wasserbach, Lloyd T	46-47ChiAA		5'11"	205	Wisconsin	1	
Waterfield, Bob QB-DB	45Cle 46-52,HC60-62LA	12 45	6'1"	196	U. C. L. A.	20	573
Watford, Jerry OG-DE	53-54ChiC		6'3"	205	Alabama		
Watkins, Bobby HB	55-57ChiB 58ChiC	2	5'10"	196	Ohio State		84
Watson, Joe C-LB	50Det		6'3"	235	Rice	1	
Watson, Sid HB	55-57Pit 58Was	23 5	5'11"	187	Northeastern		49
Watt, Joe DB-HB	47Bos 47-48Det 49NYB	2	5'11"	184	Syracuse	7	12
Weatherall, Jim DT-OT	55-57Phi 58Was 59-60Det		6'4"	245	Oklahoma		
Weatherley, Jerry LB	50ChiB 51MS 52-54ChiB		6'5"	218	Rice	8	18
Weaver, John G	49NYB		6'2"	215	Miami-Ohio		
Weaver, Larry HB-DB	55NYG		5'11"	190	Fullerton J.C.		
Weber, Chuck LB-DE-OG	55-56Cle 56-58ChiC 59-61Phi		6'1"	229	West Chester	10	6
Webster, Alex (Big Red) HB-FB	55-64, HC69-73NYG	2	6'3"	218	N. Carolina State		336
Wedel, Dick G	48ChiC		5'11"	205	Wake Forest		
Wedemeyer, Horm (Squirmin' Herman, The Hawaiian Hurricane) HB-TB	48LA-AA 49BalAA	123	5'10"	178	St. Mary's		12
Weed, Tad K	55Pit	5	5'5"	140	Ohio State		21
Weedon, Don G	47Phi		5'11"	220	Texas		
Wegert, Ted HB	55-56Phi 60NY-A 60DenA 60BufA	2	5'11"	202	none		30
Weiner, Art OE-DE	50NYY	2	6'3"	212	North Carolina		36
Weinmeister, Arnie DT-OT	48-49NY-AA 50-53NYG 54CFL		6'4"	235	Washington		2
Wells, Billy HB	54Was 55MS 56-57Was 57Pit 58Phi 60BosA	23	5'9"	176	Michigan State		54
Wells, Don DE-OE	46-49GB		6'2"	200	Georgia		
Wendell, Marty G	49ChiAA		5'10"	215	Notre Dame		
Werder, Dick G	48NY-AA		5'9"	210	Georgetown		
West, Pat FB-LB	45Cle 46-48LA 48GB	2	6'	201	Southern Calif.	1	18
West, Stan DG-OG-C	50-54LA 55NYG 56-57ChiC		6'2"	239	Oklahoma	3	
Wetz, Harlan T	47BknAA		6'5"	265	Texas		
Whalen, Jerry C-G	48BufAA		6'1"	235	Canisius		
Whaley, Ben G	49LA-AA		5'11"	210	Virginia State		
Wham, Tom DE-OE	49-51ChiC		6'2"	217	Furman	1	12
Whelchel, John	HC49Was				Navy		
White, Bob DB-HB	51-52SF 53-54MS 55Cle 55Bal	2	5'11"	176	Stanford	1	18
White, Gene G	46BufAA		6'	205	Indiana		
White, Gene DE	54GB		6'2"	205	Georgia	1	
White, Jim OT-DT	46-50NYG		6'2"	227	Notre Dame	1	18
White, Paul HB-DB	47Pit		6'1"	183	Michigan	2	
White, Wilford HB	51-52ChiB	23	5'9"	172	Arizona State		23
Whitlow, Ken LB-C	46MiaAA		6'1"	190	Rice	2	
Whitman, S. J. DB	51-53ChiC 53-54ChiB		5'11"	185	Tulsa	18	6
Wiese, Bob DB-HB-LB	47-48Det		6'3"	198	Michigan	5	
Wietecha, Ray C-LB	53-62NYG		6'1"	225	Northwestern	1	
Wightkin, Bill OT-OE-DE	50-57ChiB	2	6'3"	235	Notre Dame		24
Wilde, George HB-DB	47Was		6'1"	193	Texas A&M		6
Wildung, Dick DT-OT-OG-DG	46-51,53GB		6'	221	Minnesota		2
Wiley, Jack OT-DT	46-50Pit		5'11"	208	Waynesburg		
Wilkins, Dick OE	49LA-AA 52Dal 54NYG	2	6'2"	194	Oregon		42
Wilkins, Roy LB-DE	58-59LA 60-61Was		6'3"	224	Georgia		
Wilkinson, Bob OE-DB-HB	51-52NYG	2	6'3"	215	U. C. L. A.	1	18
Willey, Norm (Wild Man) DE-OG-OE	50-57Phi		6'2"	224	Marshall	2	12
Williams, Bob QB	51-52ChiB 53-54MS 55ChiB	12	6'1"	197	Notre Dame		
Williams, Boyd C-LB	47Phi		6'3"	218	Syracuse		
Williams, Ellery OE	50NYG		6'	185	Santa Clara		
Williams, Frank FB-LB	48NYG		6'	212	Utah State		4
Williams, Fred DT-OG	52-63ChiB 64-65Was		6'4"	249	Arkansas	2	
Williams, Garland T	47-48BknAA		6'3"	220	Georgia		
Williams, Jerry HB-DB	49-52LA 53-54,HC69-71Phi	23	5'10"	175	Washington State	15	108
Williams, Joel C-LB	48SF-AA 50Bal		6'1"	220	Texas		6
Williams, Johnny DB-HB	52-53Was 54SF	3	5'11"	177	Southern Calif.	14	18
Williams, Stan DB-OE	52Dal 53CFL		6'2"	195	Baylor	5	6
Williams, Walt DB-TB-HB	46ChiAA 47Bos	1	6'1"	194	Boston U.	2	12
Williams, Win OE	48-49BalAA	2	6'2"	185	Rice		18
Williamson, Ernie T	47Was 48NYG 49LA-AA		6'4"	245	North Carolina		
Willis, Bill DG-OG	46-49CleAA 50-53Cle		6'2"	213	Ohio State	1	
Wilson, Billy OE-FL	51-60SF	2	6'3"	191	San Jose State		294
Wilson, Camp FB-LB	46-49Det	2	6'2"	201	Tulsa		36
Wilson, Gene DB-OE	47-48GB		5'10"	178	S. M. U.	2	
Wilson, Jack HB-DB	46-47LA		6'	200	Baylor	1	6
Wilson, Jerry LB-DE	59-60Phi 60SF		6'3"	238	Auburn		
Wilson, Tom (Touchdown Tommy) HB-FB	56-61LA 62Cle 63Min	23	6'	203	none		144
Wimberly, Ab DE-OE	49LA-AA 50-52GB		6'1"	213	Louisiana State	3	12
Wingate, Elmer DE	53Bal		6'3"	230	Maryland		
Winkler, Bernie T	48LA-AA		6'1"	232	Texas Tech		
Winkler, Jim DT-OG	51-52LA 53Bal		6'2"	250	Texas A&M		
Wissman, Pete C-LB	49SF-AA 50-52,54SF		6'	218	St. Louis	4	
Wistert, Al OT-DT-OG	43P-P 44-51Phi		6'1"	214	Michigan	1	
Witucki, Slug OG	50-51Was 52MS 53-56Was		5'11"	245	Indiana		
Wizbicki, Alex DB-HB	47-49BufAA 50GB		5'11"	188	Holy Cross	6	6
Woit, Dick DB	55Det		5'8"	175	Arkansas State		
Womack, Bruce OG	51Det		6'3"	210	West Texas State		
Womble, Royce HB-FL	54-57Bal 60LA-A	2	6'	185	North Texas		54
Woodward, Dick C-LB	49LA-AA 50-51NYG 52Was 53NYG		6'2"	224	Iowa	6	12
Worden, Neil FB	54Phi 55-56MS 57Phi	2	5'10"	198	Notre Dame		6
Woudenberg, John T	40-42Pit 43-45MS 46-49SF-AA		6'3"	226	Denver		
Wozniak, John OG-LB	48BknAA 49NY-AA 50-51NYY 52Dal 53CFL		6'	218	Alabama	1	

Use Name (Nicknames) – Positions	Team by Year	See Section	Hgt	Wgt	College	Int	Pts
Wren, Junior DB	56-59Cle 60Pit 61NY-A	4	6'	192	Missouri	14	8
Wright, Jim G	47Bos		6'1"	222	S. M. U.		
Wright, John FB-LB	47BalAA	2	5'11"	225	Maryland	1	
Wyant, Fred QB	56Was		6'	200	West Virginia		
Wydo, Frank OT-DT	47-51Pit 52-57Phi		6'4"	225	Cornell	1	
Wyhonic, John G	46-47Phi 48-49BufAA		6'	213	Alabama		
Yablonski, Vinnie FB-LB	48-51ChiC	2 5	5'8"	195	Columbia		52
Yackanich, Joe G	46-48NY-AA		5'10"	205	Fordham		
Yagiello, Ray G-LB	48-49LA		6'	220	Catawba		
Yelvington, Dick OT	52-57NYG		6'2"	232	Georgia		
Yokas, Frank G	46LA-AA 47BalAA		5'11"	210	none		
Yonakor, John DE-OE-DT	46-49CleAA 50NYY 51CFL 52Was	2	6'5"	222	Notre Dame	2	24
Yonamine, Wally HB-DB	47SF-AA		5'9"	180	none	1	
Youel, Jim QB-DB	46-47Was 48Bos 48Was	12	6'	175	Iowa	2	18
Young, Buddy HB-DB-FB	47-49NY-AA 50-51NYY 52Dal 53-55Bal	23	5'5"	173	Illinois		264
Young, Dick FB-HB	55-56Bal 57Pit	2	5'11"	210	Tenn.-Chattanooga		12
Young, George DE-OE	46-49CleAA 50-53Cle		6'3"	214	Georgia		14
Young, Glenn DB	56GB		6'2"	205	Purdue		
Youngelman, Sid DT-DE	55SF 56-58Phi 59Cle 60-61NY-A 62-63BufA		6'3"	257	Alabama		
Younger, Tank FB-HB-LB	49-57LA 58Pit	2	6'3"	225	Grambling	3	210
Yowarsky, Walt DE-OT	51Was 52-53MS 54Was 55Det 55-57NYG 58SF		6'2"	234	Kentucky		
Zagers, Bert HB-DB	55Was 56MS 57-58Was	23	5'10"	185	Michigan State	4	36
Zalejski, Ernie DB-HB	50Bal		6'	185	Notre Dame	2	12
Zatkoff, Roger LB-DE	53-56GB 57-58Det		6'2"	216	Michigan	4	
Ziegler, Frank HB-DB	49-53Phi	2	5'11"	175	Georgia Tech	1	90
Zilly, Jack DE-OE	47-51LA 52Phi	2	6'2"	212	Notre Dame		24
Zimny, Bob T	45-49ChiC		6'1"	233	Indiana		
Zombek, Joe OE	54Pit		6'1"	195	Pittsburgh		
Zucco, Vic DB	57-60ChiB	3	6'	187	Michigan State	8	6
Zupek, Al BB-DE	46GB		6'1"	205	Lawrence		

Lifetime Statistcis - 1946-1959 Players   Section 1 - PASSING
(All men with 25 or more passing attempts)

Name	Years	Att.	Comp.	Comp Pct.	Yards	Yds./ Att.	TD	Int.	Pct. Int.
Cliff Aberson	46	41	14	34.1	184	4.5	0	5	12.2
Frankie Albert	46-52	1564	831	53.1	10795	6.9	115	98	6.3
Fred Benners	52	58	25	43.1	320	5.5	0	5	8.6
Angelo Bertelli	46-48	166	76	45.8	972	5.9	8	19	11.4
Ed Brown	54-65	1987	949	47.8	15600	7.9	102	138	6.9
Adrien Burk	50-56	1079	500	46.3	7001	6.5	61	89	8.2
Jim Callahan	46	68	22	32.4	359	5.3	2	7	10.3
Tony Canadeo	41-44,46-52	268	105	39.2	1642	6.1	15	20	7.5
Bob Celeri	51-52	313	133	42.5	2287	7.3	15	18	5.8
Lynn Chandnois	50-56	59	19	32.2	285	4.8	2	7	11.9
Bob Chappuis	48-49	227	102	44.9	1442	6.4	8	23	10.1
Paul Christman	45-50	1140	504	44.2	7294	6.4	58	76	6.7
Bobby Clatterbuck	54-57,60	149	77	51.7	1032	6.9	8	9	6.0
Walt Clay	46-49	28	13	46.4	148	5.3	2	3	10.7
Johnny Clement	41,46-49	442	192	43.4	3226	7.3	20	39	8.8
Irv Comp	43-49	519	213	41.0	3364	6.5	28	52	10.0
Ogden Compton	55	61	22	36.1	339	5.6	1	6	9.8
Chuck Conerly	48-61	2833	1418	50.1	19488	6.9	173	167	5.9
Boley Dancewicz	46-48	238	96	40.3	1651	6.9	12	28	11.8
Al Dekdebrun	46-48	164	84	51.2	1224	7.5	13	18	11.0
Jack Del Bello	53	61	27	44.3	229	3.8	1	5	8.2
Glenn Dobbs	46-49	934	446	47.8	5876	6.3	45	52	5.6
Al Dorow	54-57,60-62	1207	572	47.4	7708	6.4	64	93	7.7
Tom Dublinski	52-54,58,60	177	93	52.5	1300	7.3	8	13	7.3
Bill Dudley	42,45-51,53	222	81	36.5	985	4.4	6	17	7.7
Maury Duncan	54-55	26	8	30.8	122	4.7	0	2	7.7
Fred Enke	48-54	689	297	43.1	4169	6.1	31	53	7.7
Ray Evans	48	137	64	46.7	924	6.7	5	17	12.4
Tom Farris	46-48	32	11	34.4	132	4.1	1	6	18.8
Chuck Fenenbock	43,45-48	191	70	36.6	1233	6.5	12	23	12.0
Jim Finks	49-55	1382	661	47.8	8622	6.2	55	88	6.4
Joe Francis	58-59	49	20	40.8	266	5.4	2	3	6.1
Jess Freitas	46-49	253	123	48.6	1884	7.4	21	27	10.7
Monk Gafford	46-48	44	18	40.9	265	6.0	4	4	9.1
Bob Gage	49-50	94	38	40.4	623	6.6	3	9	9.6
Arnie Galiffa	53-54	25	7	28.0	183	7.3	1	5	20.0
Bob Garrett	54	30	15	50.0	143	4.8	0	1	3.3
Joe Gasparella	48,50-51	113	46	40.7	677	6.0	3	10	8.8
Joe Geri	49-52	280	101	36.1	1926	6.9	13	27	9.6
Frank Gifford	52-60,62-64	63	29	46.0	823	13.1	14	6	9.5
Harry Gilmer	48-52,54-56	579	263	45.4	3786	6.5	23	45	7.8
Jug Girard	48-57	197	67	34.0	1017	5.2	5	13	6.6
Paul Governali	46-48	500	218	43.6	3348	6.7	31	33	6.6
Otto Graham	46-55	2626	1464	55.8	23584	9.0	174	135	5.1
Jim Hardy	46-52	912	423	46.4	5690	6.2	53	73	8.0
Stan Heath	49	106	26	24.5	355	3.3	1	14	13.2
Don Heinrich	54-60,62	406	164	40.4	2287	5.6	17	23	5.7
Paul Held	54-55	77	26	33.8	332	4.3	1	6	7.8
Bob Hoernschemeyer	46-55	714	319	44.7	4302	6.0	42	56	7.8
Jack Jacobs	42,45-49	552	244	44.2	3268	5.9	27	49	8.9
Gil Johnson	49	36	12	33.3	179	5.0	0	5	13.9
Gary Kerkorian	52,54-56	259	139	53.7	1862	7.2	12	18	6.9
Tom Landry	49-55	47	11	23.4	172	3.7	1	7	14.9
Pete Layden	48-50	115	45	39.1	841	7.3	9	9	7.8
Bobby Layne	48-62	3700	1814	49.0	26768	7.2	196	243	6.6
Eddie LeBaron	52-53,55-63	1796	897	49.9	13399	7.5	104	141	7.9
Clyde LeForce	47-49	388	197	50.8	2961	7.6	25	37	9.5
Cliff Lewis	46-51	69	30	43.5	514	7.4	7	5	7.2
Johnny Lujack	48-51	808	404	50.0	6295	7.8	41	54	6.7
Bill Mackrides	47-51,53	315	131	41.6	1583	5.0	15	28	8.9
Gene Malinowski	48	54	15	27.8	218	4.0	3	7	13.0
Ray Mallouf	41,46-49	325	159	48.9	2504	7.7	20	16	4.9
Ted Marchibroda	53,55-57	385	172	44.7	2169	5.6	16	29	7.5
Joe Margucci	47-48	31	13	41.9	171	5.5	1	5	16.1
Ray Mathews	51-60	51	19	37.3	350	6.9	2	2	3.9
Lew Mayne	46-48	25	14	56.0	219	8.8	3	4	16.0
Lamar McHan	54-63	1351	610	45.2	9449	7.0	72	108	8.0
Ed Mioduszewski	53	30	11	36.7	113	3.8	2	2	6.7
Tommy Mont	47-49	35	15	42.9	201	5.7	2	2	5.7
Gonzales Morales	47-48	31	11	35.5	108	3.5	1	4	12.9
Ray Nagel	53	62	30	48.4	192	3.1	0	5	8.1
Steve Nemeth	45-47	30	7	23.3	86	2.9	0	2	6.7
Jerry Niles	47	57	19	33.3	269	4.7	1	7	12.3
Tom O'Connell	53,56-57,60-61	423	204	48.2	3261	7.7	21	34	8.0
Charlie O'Rourke	42,46-49	506	256	50.6	4039	8.0	39	51	10.1
Chuck Ortmann	51-52	154	61	39.6	744	4.8	3	14	9.1
Don Panciera	49-50,52	246	86	35.0	1383	5.6	10	25	10.2
Bob Perina	46-50	72	32	44.4	370	5.1	1	6	8.3
Jim Powers	50-53	70	31	44.3	367	5.2	1	4	5.7
George Ratterman	47-56	1396	737	52.8	10473	7.5	91	96	6.9
Johnny Rauch	49-51	170	70	41.2	959	5.6	8	9	5.3
Frank Reagan	41,46-51	37	16	43.2	239	6.5	1	2	5.4
Steve Romanik	50-54	433	179	41.3	2556	5.9	13	36	8.3
Jim Root	53,56	249	108	43.4	1482	6.0	11	16	6.4
Tobin Rote	50-59,63-64,66	2907	1329	45.7	18850	6.5	148	191	6.6
Dave Ryan	45-46,48	198	86	43.4	1296	6.5	9	27	13.6
Nick Sacrinty	47	48	15	31.3	299	6.2	5	3	6.2
Spec Sanders	46-48,50	421	206	48.9	2829	6.7	23	37	8.8
Jack Scarbath	53-54,56	279	101	36.2	1868	6.7	18	30	10.8
Bud Schwenk	42,46-48	662	316	47.6	3024	5.0	23	50	7.6
George Shaw	55-62	802	405	50.5	5829	7.3	41	63	7.9
Walt Slater	47	39	18	46.2	215	5.5	1	5	12.8
Jim Still	48-49	26	11	42.3	175	6.7	2	4	15.4
Ken Stofer	46	26	9	34.6	86	3.3	1	1	3.8
Joe Sulatis	43-53	31	11	35.5	179	5.8	1	4	12.9
George Taliaferro	49-55	284	92	32.4	1633	5.8	10	29	10.2
George Terlep	46-48	150	54	36.0	652	4.3	9	19	12.7
Bobby Thomason	49,51-57	1346	687	51.0	9480	7.0	68	90	6.7
Tommy Thompson	40-42,45-50	1424	732	51.4	10400	7.3	91	103	7.2
Travis Tidwell	50-51	76	33	43.4	493	6.5	5	7	9.2
Y. A. Tittle	48-64	4395	2427	55.2	33070	7.5	242	248	5.6
Lou Tomasetti	39-42,46-49	53	16	30.2	170	3.2	1	9	17.0
Charlie Trippi	47-55	434	205	47.2	2547	5.9	16	31	7.1
Sam Vacanti	47-49	368	154	41.8	2338	6.4	18	32	8.7
Norm Van Brocklin	49-60	2895	1553	53.6	23611	8.2	173	178	6.1
Bev Wallace	47-49,51	69	23	33.3	266	3.9	1	9	13.0
Bob Waterfield	45-52	1617	813	50.3	11849	7.3	98	127	7.9
Herm Wedemeyer	48-49	31	9	29.0	79	2.5	0	4	12.9
Bob Williams	51-52,55	160	74	46.3	981	6.1	10	12	7.5
Walt Williams	46-47	31	13	41.9	226	7.3	1	6	19.4
Jim Youel	46-48	146	50	34.2	849	5.8	7	10	6.8

Lifetime Statistics · 1946-1959 Players Section 2 · RUSHING and RECEIVING
(All men with 25 or more rushing attempts or 10 or more receptions)

Name	Years	RUSHING Att.	Yards	Avg.	TD	RECEIVING Rec.	Yards	Avg.	TD
Joe Abbey	48-49					13	177	13.6	0
Cliff Aberson	46	48	161	3.4	0				
Tony Adamle	47-51,54	60	255	4.3	2	2	35	17.5	0
Frankie Albert	46-52	329	1272	3.9	27	1	1	1.0	0
Ben Aldridge	50-53	29	105	3.6	0	8	78	9.8	1
Bruce Alford	46-51					81	1341	16.6	9
Alan Ameche	55-60	964	4045	4.2	40	101	733	7.3	4
Cliff Anderson	52-53					28	457	16.3	2
Ezz Anderson	47	3	24	8.0	0	11	126	11.5	1
Elmer Angsman	46-52	683	2908	4.3	27	41	654	16.0	5
Joe Arenas	51-57	203	987	4.9	10	46	675	14.7	6
Neill Armstrong	47-51					76	961	12.6	11
Dale Atkeson	54-56	208	639	3.1	4	19	184	9.7	1
John Atwood	48	9	6	0.7	0	10	141	14.1	1
Harry Babcock	53-55					16	181	11.3	0
Steve Bagarus	45-48	98	343	3.5	1	81	1055	13.0	9
Byron Bailey	52-53	32	103	3.2	2	10	147	14.7	0
Ed Balatti	46-48					12	113	9.4	1
Lou Baldacci	56	31	140	4.5	0	5	62	12.4	0
Al Baldwin	47-50	2	1	0.5	0	160	2658	16.6	25
Burr Baldwin	47-49	1	1	1.0	0	24	397	16.5	1
Jack Banta	41,44-48	198	847	4.3	6	30	373	12.4	1
Ed Barker	53-54					40	525	13.1	4
Tom Barnett	59-60	81	263	3.2	1	7	52	7.4	1
Paul Barry	50,52-54	158	604	3.8	2	24	264	11.0	1
Bill Bass	47	28	44	1.6	0	8	79	9.9	1
Mo Bassett	54-56	223	891	4.0	10	33	317	9.6	1
Alyn Beals	46-51	11	73	6.6	0	211	2951	14.0	49
Hub Bechtol	47-49	2	−1	−0.5	0	19	192	10.1	1
Ed Bernet	55-60					26	325	12.5	1
Dick Bielski	55-63	80	229	2.9	2	107	1305	12.2	10
Lamar Blount	46-47	4	5	1.3	0	21	366	17.4	1
Jim Blumenstock	47	54	168	3.1	2	4	15	3.8	0
Bill Boedecker	46-50	173	741	4.3	8	38	875	23.0	6
J. R. Boone	48-53	130	497	3.8	5	69	1251	18.1	7
Bill Bowman	54,56-57	144	557	3.9	3	50	429	8.6	3
Cloyce Box	49-50,52-54	31	82	2.6	0	129	2665	20.7	32
Bob Boyd	51-51,53-57	2	−9	−4.5	0	176	3611	20.5	28
Max Boydston	55-58,60-62					97	1328	13.7	8
Jim Brandt	52-54	61	188	3.1	4	3	24	8.0	0
John Bredice	56					10	146	14.6	1
Monte Brethauer	53,55					10	133	13.3	0
John Brewer	52-53	67	273	4.1	3	9	62	6.9	0
Darrell Brewster	52-60					210	3758	17.9	21
Gene Brito	51-53,55-60					47	618	13.1	2
Dave Brown	43,46-47	47	141	3.0	0	6	34	5.7	0
Ed Brown	54-65	265	920	3.6	14				
Dick Brubaker	55,57,60					13	200	15.4	1
George Buksar	49-52	28	63	2.3	1	4	5	1.3	0
Rex Bumgardner	48-52	236	868	3.7	4	22	404	18.4	6
Adrian Burk	50-56	122	324	2.7	7				
Hank Burnine	56-57					17	271	15.9	2
Harry Burrus	46-48	3	5	1.7	0	28	670	23.9	4
Jack Call	57-59	73	308	4.2	0	9	46	5.1	0
Jim Callahan	46	52	86	1.7	2				
Tom Calvin	52-54	32	136	4.3	0	7	51	7.3	0
Al Campana	50-53	58	146	2.5	1	6	61	10.2	0
Leon Campbell	50,52-55	102	379	3.7	0	20	156	7.8	0
Tony Canadeo	41-44,46-52	1025	4197	4.1	26	69	579	8.4	5
Jim Canady	48-49	25	99	4.0	0	5	80	16.0	0
Bob Carey	52-54,56,58					47	663	14.1	2
Harland Carl	56	29	66	2.3	1	2	31	15.5	0
Al Carmichael	53-58,60-61	222	947	4.3	4	112	1633	14.6	8
Ken Carpenter	50-53,60	242	1199	5.0	11	71	823	11.6	6
Lew Carpenter	53-55,57-63	468	2025	4.3	16	87	782	9.0	4
Ed Carr	47-49	44	283	6.4	3	14	246	17.6	3
Johnny Carson	54-60					173	2591	15.0	15
Ken Casanega	46,48	29	90	3.1	1	5	102	20.4	1
Jim Cason	48-56	82	351	4.3	4	40	519	13.0	4
Hopalong Cassady	56-63	316	1229	3.9	6	111	1601	14.4	18
Jim Castiglia	41,45-48	322	1073	3.3	10	34	246	7.2	2
Sam Cathcart	49-50,52	108	509	4.7	1	21	296	14.1	0
Bob Celeri	51-52	53	242	4.6	0	6	108	18.0	2
Lynn Chandnois	50-56	593	1934	3.3	16	163	2062	12.7	8
Bob Chappuis	48-49	56	323	5.8	1				
Lloyd Cheatham	42,46-48	7	2	0.3	0	21	283	13.5	4
George Cheverko	47-48	22	73	3.3	0	18	341	18.9	3
Bill Chipley	47-49	1	3	3.0	0	75	867	11.6	4
Paul Christman	45-50	85	−26	−0.3	8				
Bob Cifers	46-49	230	787	3.4	1	12	296	24.7	4
Ed Cifers	41-42,46-48	1	5	5.0	0	37	399	10.8	3
Leon Clarke	56-63	1	−4	−4.0	0	141	2215	15.7	18
Bobby Clatterbuck	54-57,60	29	−27	−0.9	1				
Randy Clay	50,53	90	280	3.1	2	12	120	10.0	1
Walt Clay	46-49	169	652	3.9	4	15	218	14.5	1
Johnny Clement	41,46-49	406	1473	3.6	13	2	28	14.0	0
Ollie Cline	48-53	281	1094	3.9	6	34	299	8.8	1
Jack Cloud	50-53	57	141	2.5	4	6	35	5.8	1
Ray Coates	48-49	77	231	3.0	3	8	152	19.0	1
Red Cochran	47-50	37	138	3.7	2	8	114	14.3	2
Tom Cochran	49	34	135	4.0	1	7	82	11.7	0
Ed Cody	47-50	93	346	3.7	2	1	2	2.0	0
Emerson Cole	50-52	72	357	5.0	1	4	30	7.5	0
Rip Collins	49-51	102	193	1.9	0	26	461	17.7	0
Mickey Colmer	46-49	398	1537	3.9	15	63	899	14.3	6

Name	Years	RUSHING Att.	Yards	Avg.	TD	RECEIVING Rec.	Yards	Avg.	TD
Lloyd Colteryahn	54-56					54	664	12.3	3
Irv Comp	43-49	255	502	2.0	7	3	66	22.0	2
Tony Campagno	46-48	125	444	3.6	3	17	271	15.9	1
Fred Cone	51-57,60	347	1156	3.3	12	75	852	11.4	4
Chuck Conerly	48-61	270	685	2.5	10				
Clyde Conner	56-63					203	2643	13.0	18
Ted Cook	47-50					61	891	14.6	5
Larry Coutre	50,53	63	322	5.1	1	18	202	11.2	2
Bob Cowan	47-49	72	280	3.9	3	21	351	16.7	5
Gerry Cowhig	47-51	81	342	4.2	3	3	18	6.0	0
Rus Craft	46-54	64	231	3.6	0	12	303	25.3	3
Ted Cremer	46-48					28	296	10.6	1
Hal Crisler	46-50	4	6	1.5	0	135	2042	15.1	22
Billy Cross	51-53	175	826	4.7	6	52	841	16.2	6
Don Currivan	43-49	1	−4	−4.0	0	78	1979	25.4	24
Bill Daley	46-48	175	612	3.5	5	18	142	7.9	0
Boley Dancewicz	46-48	65	229	3.5	2				
Glenn Davis	50-51	152	616	4.1	4	50	682	13.6	5
Joe Davis	46					22	337	15.3	1
Lamar Davis	46-49	17	78	4.6	0	147	2103	14.3	12
Van Davis	47-49					14	254	18.1	1
Bill deCorrevont	45-49	75	233	3.1	1	21	417	19.9	2
Al Dekdebrun	46-48	54	54	1.0	0				
Paul Dekker	53					14	182	13.0	1
Spiro Dellerba	47-49	31	176	5.7	0	1	14	14.0	0
Bill Dewell	40-41,45-49	1	−1	−1.0	0	178	2647	14.9	17
Dorne Dibble	51,53-57	2	13	6.5	0	146	2552	17.5	19
Babe Dimancheff	45-50,52	207	802	3.9	5	61	1086	17.8	10
Glen Dobbs	46-49	262	1039	4.0	12	5	27	5.4	0
Jack Doolan	45-48	22	59	2.7	0	10	95	9.5	0
Jim Dooley	52-54,56-57,59-62	1	0	0.0	0	211	3172	15.0	16
Jim Doran	51-61	3	59	19.7	0	212	3667	17.3	24
Al Dorow	54-57,60-62	282	864	3.1	16				
Noble Doss	47-49	78	253	3.2	0	10	113	11.3	0
Kayo Dottley	51-53	250	1122	4.5	7	28	359	12.8	2
Bob Dove	46-54	1	−2	−2.0	0	13	128	9.8	2
Harry Dowda	49-55	124	405	3.3	2	18	277	15.4	2
Chuck Drazenovich	50-59	117	330	2.8	8	10	139	13.9	0
Wally Dreyer	49-50	46	172	3.7	0	7	94	13.4	0
Tom Dublinski	52-54,58,60	28	118	4.2	1				
Joe Duckworth	47					14	250	17.9	3
Andy Dudish	46-48	59	141	2.4	1	9	163	18.1	1
Bill Dudley	42,45-51,53	765	3057	4.0	19	123	1383	11.2	18
L. G. Dupre	55-61	476	1761	3.7	11	104	1131	10.9	7
Don Durdan	46-47	33	134	4.1	0	2	27	13.5	1
Bill Dutton	46	53	169	3.2	2	2	68	34.0	0
Ralph Earhart	48-49	50	194	3.9	1	22	303	13.8	2
Ray Ebli	42,46-47					12	138	11.5	2
Dan Edwards	48-54					234	2898	12.4	16
Carl Elliott	51-54					60	581	9.7	6
Earl Elsey	46	47	165	3.5	0	14	179	12.8	0
Leo Elter	53-59	371	1380	3.7	9	46	556	12.1	2
Mel Embree	53-54					25	292	11.7	1
Fred Enke	48-54	170	640	3.8	1	4	39	9.8	0
Bobby Epps	54-55,57	188	771	4.1	2	18	109	6.1	0
Len Eshmont	41,46-49	282	1345	4.8	7	54	915	16.9	6
Fred Evans	46-48	49	166	3.4	1	7	89	12.7	1
Ray Evans	48	99	343	3.5	2	7	93	13.3	0
Tom Farmer	46-48	95	307	3.2	3	26	302	11.6	2
Tom Farris	46-48	27	19	0.7	0	1	16	16.0	0
Tom Fears	48-56	5	15	3.0	0	400	5397	13.5	38
Gene Fekete	46	26	106	4.1	1	1	2	2.0	0
Chuck Fenenbock	43,45-48	269	1102	4.1	7	45	523	11.6	4
Bob Fenimore	47	53	189	3.8	1	15	219	14.6	2
Howie Ferguson	53-58,60	670	2558	3.8	10	148	1247	8.4	3
Jack Ferrante	41,44-50					169	2894	17.1	31
Gene Filipski	56-57	35	174	5.0	1	4	44	11.0	0
Jim Finks	49-55	118	294	2.5	12	1	17	17.0	1
Clete Fischer	49	26	72	2.8	0	3	45	15.0	1
Bobby Jack Floyd	52-53	77	306	4.0	1	20	192	9.6	0
Hank Foldberg	48-49					31	331	10.7	0
Len Ford	48-58					67	1175	17.5	8
Bob Forte	46-50,52-53	101	331	3.3	0	24	242	10.1	3
Joe Francis	58-59	26	158	6.1	1				
Jess Freitas	46-49	39	8	0.2	0				
Ted Fritsch	42-50	619	2100	3.4	31	25	227	9.1	1
Jim Gaffney	45-46	26	90	3.5	0	7	85	12.1	1
Monk Gafford	46-48	100	349	3.5	3	37	657	17.8	8
Bob Gage	49-50	85	334	3.9	6	7	135	19.3	2
Lu Gambino	48-49	110	402	3.7	1	16	95	5.9	1
Dan Garza	49,51					40	663	16.6	4
Gene Gedman	53,56-58	377	1221	3.2	17	53	504	9.5	4
Fred Gehrke	40,45-50	343	1664	4.9	15	56	529	9.4	7
Dale Gentry	46-48	5	29	5.8	1	74	1001	13.5	5
Joe Geri	49-52	431	1550	3.6	10	3	42	14.0	1
Skippy Giancanelli	53-56	216	711	3.3	4	69	1024	14.8	10
Paul Gibson	47-49					22	402	18.3	0
Frank Gifford	52-60,62-64	840	3609	4.3	34	367	5434	14.8	43
Horace Gillom	47-56	3	−7	−2.3	0	74	1083	14.6	3
Jim Gillette	40,44-48	172	831	4.8	4	24	376	15.7	2
Harry Gilmer	48-52,54-56	201	923	4.6	1	20	220	11.0	1
Jug Girard	48-57	194	703	3.6	3	109	1838	16.9	15
Joe Glamp	47-49	32	161	5.0	1	10	152	15.2	2
Les Goble	54-55	37	53	1.4	1	1	−1	−1.0	0
Joe Golding	47-51	114	349	3.0	1	27	289	10.7	8

Lifetime Statistics · 1946-1959 Players — Section 2 · **RUSHING and RECEIVING** (continued)
(All men with 25 or more rushing attempts or 10 or more receptions)

Name	Years	Rushing Att.	Rushing Yards	Rushing Avg.	Rushing TD	Receiving Rec.	Receiving Yards	Receiving Avg.	Receiving TD
Sam Goldman	44,46-49	2	−3	−1.5	0	18	184	10.2	0
Ralph Goldston	52,54-55	79	203	2.6	3	4	20	5.0	0
Bill Gompers	48	48	219	4.6	1				
Rob Goode	49-51,54-55	596	2531	4.2	16	53	640	12.1	1
Clyde Goodnight	45-50	9	25	2.8	0	112	1967	17.6	15
Paul Governali	46-48	79	−84	−1.1	4				
Otto Graham	46-55	405	882	2.2	44				
Sonny Grandelius	53	108	278	2.6	1	15	80	5.3	0
Bud Grant	51-52					56	997	17.8	7
John Greene	44-50					173	2865	16.6	26
Bob Greenhalgh	49	62	188	3.0	0	3	23	7.7	0
Don Greenwood	45-47	196	744	3.8	10	12	121	10.1	0
Don Griffin	46	28	13	0.5	0	5	28	5.6	0
Forrest Griffith	50-51	99	277	2.8	2	3	45	15.0	0
Billy Grimes	49-52	228	1091	4.8	10	45	620	13.8	4
George Gulyanics	47-52	509	2081	4.1	19	52	600	11.5	2
Forrest Hall	48	66	413	6.3	2	4	87	21.8	0
Chet Hanulak	54,57	184	671	3.6	7	9	118	13.1	0
Pat Harder	46-53	740	3016	4.1	33	92	864	9.4	5
Carroll Hardy	55	15	37	2.5	0	12	338	28.2	4
Jim Hardy	46-52	52	72	1.4	2				
Tommy Harmon	46-47	107	542	5.1	3	15	288	19.2	3
John Harrington	46-47					25	369	14.8	3
Leon Hart	50-57	143	612	4.3	5	174	2499	14.4	26
Leon Heath	51-53	230	813	3.5	6	29	194	6.7	1
Don Heinrich	54-60,62	27	24	0.9	5				
Dick Hensley	49,52-53					19	358	18.8	2
Ralph Heywood	46-49	4	5	1.3	1	84	1192	14.2	10
Red Hickey	41,45-48	7	7	1.0	0	75	1288	17.2	16
Harlon Hill	54-62	12	103	8.6	0	233	4717	20.2	40
Billy Hillenbrand	46-48	216	889	4.1	11	110	1987	18.1	17
Crazy Legs Hirsch	46-57	207	687	3.3	4	387	7029	18.2	60
Dick Hoerner	47-52	506	2172	4.3	30	80	1180	14.8	4
Bob Hoernschemeyer	46-55	1059	4548	4.3	27	109	1139	10.4	11
Bob Hoffman	40-41,46-49	110	398	3.6	10	7	71	10.1	1
John Hoffman	49-56	317	1366	4.3	7	136	1870	13.8	9
Mike Holovak	46-48	136	720	5.3	6	13	155	11.9	0
Les Horvath	47-49	58	221	3.8	1	9	142	15.8	1
Sherman Howard	49-53	323	1301	4.0	10	45	968	21.5	11
Earl Howell	49	31	116	3.7	1	5	11	2.2	1
Billy Howton	52-63	5	29	5.8	0	503	8459	16.8	61
Frank Hubbell	47-49					15	226	15.1	3
Dick Humbert	41,45-49	1	2	2.0	0	68	731	10.8	6
Chuck Hunsinger	50-52	192	834	4.3	5	23	249	10.8	3
John Huzvar	52-54	243	893	3.7	6	19	92	4.8	1
Jack Jacobs	42,45-49	94	262	2.8	2	4	53	13.3	0
Chick Jagade	49,51-55	412	1728	4.2	13	68	628	9.2	1
Vic Janowicz	54-55	99	410	4.1	4	12	148	12.3	3
Val Jansante	46-51	3	2	0.7	0	155	2356	15.2	14
Jack Jenkins	43,46-47	84	274	3.3	1	7	123	17.6	0
Bob Jensen	48-50					22	290	13.2	1
Bill Jessup	51-52,54,56-58,60	1	−5	−5.0	0	61	994	16.3	7
Perry Jeter	56-57	70	327	4.7	2	7	61	8.7	0
Bob Jewett	58					15	192	12.8	1
Don Johnson	53-55	93	456	4.9	5	13	247	19.0	2
Herb Johnson	54	42	168	4.0	1	10	89	8.9	0
Joe Johnson	48					19	217	11.4	2
Joe Johnson	54-58,60-61	93	376	4.0	0	84	920	11.0	8
Pres Johnston	46	45	218	4.8	2	6	54	9.0	1
Dub Jones	46-55	540	2209	4.1	21	171	2874	16.8	20
Special Delivery Jones	45-49	297	1550	5.2	18	33	635	19.2	10
Saxon Judd	46-48					84	997	11.9	7
Choo-Choo Justice	50,52-54	266	1284	4.8	3	63	962	15.3	7
Steve Juzwik	42,46-48	125	679	5.4	5	29	397	13.7	4
Tommy Kalmanir	49-51,53	81	415	5.1	1	16	216	13.5	3
Sonny Karnofsky	45-46	77	218	2.8	3	13	252	19.4	1
Ken Kavanaugh	40-41,45-50					162	3622	22.4	50
Jim Keane	46-52					224	3222	14.4	24
Tom Keane	48-55	7	16	2.3	0	34	551	16.2	2
Bill Kellagher	46-48	124	518	4.2	4	5	58	11.6	0
Ken Keller	56-57	169	628	3.7	4	11	67	6.1	0
Bill Kelley	49					17	222	13.1	1
Bob Kelly	47-49	63	232	3.7	2	11	93	8.5	1
Bob Kennedy	46-50	253	1017	4.0	9	23	137	6.0	1
Gary Kerkorian	52,54-56	30	76	2.5	2				
John Kimbrough	46-48	329	1224	3.7	17	35	574	16.4	6
Don Kindt	47-55	172	586	3.4	4	43	506	11.8	2
Emmett King	54	57	167	2.9	0	6	43	7.2	1
Fay King	46-49					115	1583	13.8	20
Pete Kmetovic	46-47	19	53	2.8	0	10	211	21.1	2
Gary Knafelc	54-63					154	2162	14.0	23
George Koch	45,47	49	250	5.1	1	1	10	10.0	0
John Kovatch	42,46-47					18	157	8.7	1
Larry Krutko	58-60	96	331	3.4	4	14	108	7.7	0
Ray Kuffel	47-49					22	402	18.3	3
Vic Kulbitski	46-48	193	1006	5.2	3	13	154	11.8	4
Lou Kusserow	49-50	40	142	3.6	0				
Mal Kutner	46-50	11	59	5.4	1	145	3060	21.1	31
Steve Lach	42,46-47	192	580	3.0	13	31	349	11.3	5
Jim Ladd	54					22	254	11.5	0
Tom Lahey	46-47	1	−2	−2.0	0	30	351	11.7	0
Tom Landry	49-55	36	131	3.6	1	6	109	18.2	0
Johnny Lattner	54	69	237	3.4	5	25	305	12.2	2
Dante Lavelli	46-56	2	23	11.5	0	386	6488	16.8	62
Pete Layden	48-50	114	672	5.9	3	1	0	0.0	0

Name	Years	Rushing Att.	Rushing Yards	Rushing Avg.	Rushing TD	Receiving Rec.	Receiving Yards	Receiving Avg.	Receiving TD
Bobby Layne	48-62	611	2451	4.0	25				
Eddie LeBaron	52-53,55-63	202	650	3.2	9				
Toy Ledbetter	50,53-55	210	729	3.5	3	39	498	12.8	8
Clyde LeForce	47-49	59	287	4.9	2	8	122	15.3	3
Jake Leicht	48-49	26	81	3.1	1	13	146	11.2	1
Cliff Lewis	46-51	54	48	0.9	1				
Ernie Lewis	46-49	94	308	3.3	2	3	32	10.7	0
Woodley Lewis	50-60	47	188	4.0	0	123	1885	15.3	12
Verl Lillywhite	48-51	196	1004	5.1	6	21	212	10.1	3
Howie Livingston	44-50,53	155	548	3.5	6	37	768	20.8	9
Bob Livingstone	48-50	57	171	3.0	0	18	320	17.8	2
Cutter Long	53-55	52	164	3.2	1	33	462	14.0	4
John Lookabaugh	46-47					12	145	12.1	1
Alex Loyd	50					32	402	12.6	0
Nolan Luhn	45-49					100	1525	15.3	13
Johnny Lujack	48-51	133	742	5.6	21	1	16	16.0	0
Jim Lukens	49					24	249	10.4	2
Bill Lund	46-47	37	177	4.8	2	10	174	17.4	3
Ken MacAfee	54-59					79	1160	14.7	18
Art Macioszczyk	44,47-48	46	159	3.5	0	6	48	8.0	0
Bill Mackrides	47-51,53	70	124	1.8	2				
Eddie Macon	52-53,60	70	324	4.6	2	14	49	3.5	2
Elmer Madarik	45-48	31	48	1.5	1	10	113	11.3	0
Dante Magnani	40-43,46-50	331	1475	4.5	3	79	942	11.9	10
Howie Maley	46-47	45	199	4.4	0	2	35	17.5	0
Ray Mallouf	41,46-49	66	139	2.1	1				
Bob Mann	48-53	8	55	6.9	0	208	3203	15.4	24
Dave Mann	55-57	154	544	3.5	4	37	444	12.0	2
Ted Marchibroda	53,55-57	50	176	3.5	3				
Joe Margucci	47-48	60	111	1.9	4	46	575	12.5	3
Len Masini	47-48	41	179	4.4	2	1	−1	−1.0	0
Ray Mathews	51-60	300	1057	3.5	5	233	3963	17.0	34
Ollie Matson	52,54-66	1170	5173	4.4	40	222	3285	14.8	23
Lew Mayne	46-48	125	292	2.3	1	13	280	21.5	3
Frank Maznicki	42,46-47	107	463	4.3	1	10	131	13.1	1
George McAfee	40-41,45-50	341	1685	4.9	22	85	1357	16.0	11
Jim McCarthy	46-49					28	531	19.0	3
Bob McChesney	50-52	2	2	1.0	0	54	1040	19.3	14
Jack McClairen	55-60					85	1253	14.7	3
Bill McColl	52-59					201	2815	14.0	25
Tom McCormick	53-56	86	272	3.2	1	11	129	11.7	0
Walt McDonald	46-49	12	5	0.4	0	22	197	9.0	1
Hugh McElhenny	52-64	1124	5281	4.7	38	264	3247	12.3	20
Lamar McHan	54-63	239	849	3.6	12	0	1	—	0
Pat McHugh	47-51	32	202	6.3	1	2	16	8.0	0
Don McIlhenny	56-61	414	1581	3.8	7	70	655	9.4	7
Paul McKee	47-48					30	413	13.8	2
Buck McPhail	53	53	138	2.6	0	10	38	3.8	0
Charlie Mehelich	46-51					15	172	11.5	0
Steve Meilinger	56-58,60-61	1	6	6.0	0	60	863	14.4	8
Jim Mello	47-49	90	308	3.4	1	6	81	13.5	0
Buzz Mertes	45-49	341	1273	3.7	6	19	182	9.6	2
Mike Micka	44-48	69	231	3.3	0	6	101	16.8	0
Dave Middleton	55-61	67	210	3.1	2	183	2966	16.2	17
Ron Miller	56					11	129	11.7	0
Henry Minarik	51					35	459	13.1	1
Frank Minini	47-49	51	216	4.2	4	3	37	12.3	1
Skippy Minisi	48	36	160	4.4	1	13	123	9.5	1
Bob Mitchell	46-48	42	71	1.7	0	4	37	9.3	1
Billy Mixon	53-54	32	195	6.1	1	1	7	7.0	0
Rudy Mobley	47	26	90	3.5	1	11	121	11.0	1
Ed Modzelewski	52,55-59	393	1292	3.3	11	38	277	7.3	3
Dick Moegle	55-61	60	310	5.2	6	8	185	23.1	0
Jim Monachino	51,53,55	71	291	4.1	4	11	89	8.1	0
Tommy Mont	47-49	26	185	7.1	1	10	119	11.9	2
Gonzales Morales	47-48	42	125	3.0	0				
Max Morris	46-48	1	20	20.0	0	53	677	12.8	2
Curley Morrison	50-56	578	2420	4.2	12	67	721	10.8	2
Dom Moselle	50-52,54	46	176	3.8	2	31	475	15.3	4
Kelley Mote	47-52					52	754	14.5	6
Marion Motley	46-53,55	828	4720	5.7	31	85	1107	13.0	7
Frank Muehlheuser	48-49	47	179	3.8	2	5	45	9.0	0
Joe Muha	46-50	67	257	3.8	2	4	42	10.5	0
Noah Mullins	46-49	67	377	5.6	1	12	176	14.7	5
Chet Mutryn	46-50	583	3031	5.2	27	121	1850	15.3	12
Jim Mutscheller	54-61					220	3684	16.7	40
Brad Myers	53,56,58	55	180	3.3	3	8	38	4.8	0
Jack Myers	48-50,52	125	541	4.3	3	28	360	12.9	0
Gern Nagler	53,55-61					196	3119	15.9	28
Frank Nelson	48-49	26	86	3.3	0	1	10	10.0	0
Jimmy Nelson	46	39	163	4.2	2	4	20	5.0	0
Elbie Nickel	47-57					329	5131	15.6	37
John North	48-50					38	784	20.6	5
Jerry Norton	54-64	47	341	7.3	1	11	125	11.4	1
Bob Nowaskey	40-42,46-50	8	26	3.3	0	51	767	15.0	6
Bob Nussbaumer	46-51	95	238	2.5	0	76	992	13.1	5
Jerry Nuzum	48-51	249	930	3.7	7	14	303	21.6	3
Bernie Nygren	46-47	26	111	4.3	0	13	170	13.1	1
Jack O'Brien	54-56					16	185	11.6	2
Tom O'Connell	53,56-57,60-61	67	27	0.4	4				
Bill O'Connor	48-49,51					45	493	11.0	2
Johnny Olszewski	53-62	837	3320	4.0	16	104	988	9.5	3
Bob Oristaglio	49-52	1	20	20.0	1	15	148	9.9	0
Charlie O'Rourke	43,46-49	96	103	1.1	4				
Chuck Ortmann	51-52	67	351	5.2	0	4	62	15.5	0

Lifetime Statistics · 1946-1959 Players   Section 2 · **RUSHING and RECEIVING** (continued)
(All men with 25 or more rushing attempts or 10 or more receptions)

Name	Years	RUSHING				RECEIVING			
		Att.	Yards	Avg.	TD	Rec.	Yards	Avg.	TD
Joe Osmanski	46-49	274	1182	4.3	6	36	329	9.1	0
Jim Owens	50					19	188	9.9	0
Jim Pace	58	52	161	3.1	2	10	59	5.9	0
Bob Paffrath	46	31	100	3.2	2	4	−6	−1.5	0
Paul Page	49	25	81	3.2	0	4	62	15.5	0
John Panelli	49-53	55	157	2.9	0	4	27	6.8	0
George Papach	48-49	159	731	4.6	2	10	90	9.0	1
Johnny Papit	51-53	95	379	4.0	1	7	123	17.6	1
Jim Parmer	48-56	452	1636	3.6	20	53	351	6.6	1
Ara Parseghian	48-49	44	166	3.8	1	3	33	11.0	1
Earle Parsons	46-47	107	487	4.6	2	17	215	12.6	2
Gordon Paschka	43-47	48	143	3.0	2	1	−6	−6.0	0
Ralph Pasquariello	50-52	108	411	3.8	2	10	39	3.9	0
Paul Patterson	49	2	0	0.0	0	16	304	19.0	4
Don Paul	50-58	73	469	6.4	3	48	690	14.4	7
Lindy Pearson	50-52	58	172	3.0	2	7	63	9.0	0
Jim Peebles	46-49,51	1	−3	−3.0	0	13	190	14.6	1
Ray Pelfrey	51-53	3	44	14.7	0	75	959	12.8	10
Bob Perina	46-50	122	256	2.1	4	14	113	8.1	1
Joe Perry	48-63	1929	9723	5.0	71	260	2021	7.8	12
Lowell Perry	56	2	37	18.5	0	14	334	23.9	2
Bob Pfohl	48-49	174	660	3.8	6	20	196	9.8	1
Don Phelps	50-52	55	263	4.8	3	1	28	28.0	0
Bert Piggott	47	46	161	3.5	0	7	63	9.0	1
Pete Pihos	47-55	9	−4	−0.4	0	373	5619	15.1	61
Jim Podoley	57-60	209	746	3.6	2	78	1461	18.7	11
Dick Poillon	42,46-49	186	535	2.9	4	37	477	12.9	5
John Polanski	42,46	45	144	3.2	1	2	15	7.5	1
Al Pollard	51-53	104	351	3.4	1	18	127	7.1	0
Fran Polsfoot	50-53					106	1613	15.2	10
Barney Poole	49-54					12	188	15.5	1
Ray Poole	47-52					83	1164	14.0	8
John Poto	47-48	19	59	3.1	1	10	101	10.1	0
Hal Prescott	46-49					12	185	15.4	1
Eddie Price	50-55	846	3292	3.9	20	75	672	9.0	4
Billy Pricer	57-61	97	316	3.3	2	15	115	7.7	1
Bosh Pritchard	42,46-49,51	392	1730	4.4	11	75	1166	15.6	10
Steve Pritko	43-50					93	1114	12.0	13
Dewey Proctor	46-49	86	280	3.3	3	6	54	9.0	0
Eddie Prokop	46-49	226	935	4.1	8	16	361	22.6	5
Fred Provo	48	29	90	3.1	0	4	−9	−2.2	0
Cal Purdin	43,46	19	32	1.7	0	15	143	9.5	0
Frank Quillen	46-47					20	256	12.8	3
Skeets Quinlan	52-56	258	1514	5.9	9	75	1181	15.7	6
Ed Quirk	48-51	117	467	4.0	5	14	73	5.2	0
Ray Ramsey	47-53	124	524	4.2	2	88	1729	19.6	14
George Ratterman	47-56	106	49	0.5	14				
Bob Ravensburg	48-49	2	8	4.0	0	10	203	20.3	3
Frank Reagan	41,46-51	114	469	4.1	6	4	71	17.8	0
Don Reece	46	30	109	3.6	2	1	5	5.0	0
Bill Reichardt	52	39	121	3.1	1	5	18	3.6	0
Breezy Reid	50-56	459	1964	4.3	13	72	868	12.1	5
Bob Reinhard	46-50	43	141	3.3	0	9	101	11.2	2
Ray Renfro	52-63	137	682	5.0	4	281	5508	19.6	50
Billy Reynolds	53-54,57-58,60	176	585	3.3	7	24	252	10.5	0
Jim Reynolds	46	32	96	3.0	0	1	32	32.0	0
Dick Rifenburg	50					10	96	9.6	1
Choo-Choo Roberts	47-50	499	1904	3.8	14	64	1135	17.7	12
Hosea Rodgers	49	131	494	3.8	5	7	97	13.9	0
Fran Rogel	50-57	900	3271	3.6	17	150	1087	7.2	2
Herm Rohrig	41,46-47	43	1	0.0	0	13	88	6.8	0
Steve Romanik	50-54	27	35	1.3	3				
Rudy Romboli	46-48	49	137	2.8	1	12	107	8.9	0
Jim Root	53,56	43	57	1.3	3				
Sal Rosato	45-47	159	620	3.9	4	9	131	14.6	1
Kyle Rote	51-61	231	871	3.8	4	300	4797	16.0	48
Tobin Rote	50-59,63-64,66	635	3128	4.9	37	2	28	14.0	1
Tom Runnels	56-57	116	386	3.3	0	7	60	8.6	1
Clive Rush	53	1	−6	−6.0	0	14	190	13.6	0
Jack Russell	46-50					83	1331	16.0	15
Dave Ryan	45-46,48	110	159	1.4	2	3	62	20.7	1
Julie Rykovich	47-53	648	2584	4.0	28	75	1158	15.4	4
Eddie Saenz	46-51	190	619	3.3	2	84	1327	15.8	8
Paul Salata	49-50					74	907	12.3	8
Jack Salschneider	49	26	105	4.0	0	4	9	2.3	0
Don Samuel	49-50	39	163	4.2	1	1	2	2.0	0
Spec Sanders	46-48,50	540	2900	5.4	33	18	272	15.1	3
Don Sandifer	48-53	74	247	3.3	1	30	510	17.0	5
Ted Scalissi	47	35	37	1.1	0	5	67	13.4	2
Jack Scarbath	53-54,56	43	153	3.6	0				
Pete Schabarum	51,53-54	115	494	4.3	3	24	328	13.7	0
Don Schaefer	56	102	320	3.1	2	13	117	9.0	0
Walt Schlinkman	46-49	365	1455	4.0	8	3	−1	−0.3	0
Bob Schnelker	53-61					211	3667	17.4	33
Gene Schroeder	51-52,54-57	1	4	4.0	0	104	1870	18.0	13
Vic Schwall	47-50	56	301	5.4	1	6	28	4.7	2
Bud Schwenk	42,46-48	145	376	2.6	4				
Nick Scollard	46-49					14	200	14.3	3
Clyde Scott	49-52	100	400	4.0	2	19	381	20.1	4
Joe Scott	48-53	322	1218	3.8	14	79	1203	15.2	7
Prince Scott	46					13	180	13.8	2
Scooter Scudero	54-58,60	43	139	3.2	0	6	62	10.3	1
Charlie Seabright	41,46-50	1	4	4.0	0	31	241	7.8	3
Jimmy Sears	54,57-58,60-61	34	119	3.5	1	18	253	14.1	2
Frank Seno	43-49	364	1292	3.5	2	73	1034	14.2	5

Name	Years	RUSHING				RECEIVING			
		Att.	Yards	Avg.	TD	Rec.	Yards	Avg.	TD
Dean Sensenbaugher	48-49	38	95	2.5	2				
Bob Shaw	45-46,49-50					81	1569	19.4	20
George Shaw	55-62	130	431	3.3	5				
Charlie Shepard	6	30	91	3.0	0	1	31	31.0	0
Jerry Shipkey	48-53	109	310	2.8	16	12	138	11.5	0
Hal Shoener	48-50	1	1	1.0	0	22	160	7.3	3
Paul Shoults	49	46	124	2.7	0	10	124	12.4	0
Floyd Simmons	48	36	121	3.4	1	2	60	30.0	1
Emil Sitko	50-52	163	636	3.9	2	9	87	9.7	1
Walt Slater	47	46	167	3.6	0				
Phil Slosburg	48-49	69	210	3.0	1	6	40	6.7	0
Bob Smith	55-56	48	160	3.3	1	2	12	6.0	0
Bruce Smith	45-48	108	560	6.2	1	8	79	9.9	1
Jim Smith	48-53	37	181	4.9	0	5	76	15.2	0
Oscar Smith	48-49	43	109	2.5	0	12	121	10.1	0
Vitamin Smith	49-53	208	669	3.2	7	59	1025	17.4	12
Bill Smyth	47-50					13	123	9.5	1
Gordie Soltav	50-58	1	−4	−4.0	0	249	3487	14.0	25
Cecil Souders	47-49					17	203	11.9	1
Jimmie Spavital	49-50	73	290	4.0	2	22	237	10.8	1
Mac Speedie	46-52	2	0	0.0	0	349	5602	16.1	33
Jack Spinks	52-53,55-57	28	94	3.4	0	3	28	9.3	0
Ed Sprinkle	44-55	3	2	0.7	0	32	451	14.1	7
Norm Standlee	41,46-52	486	2244	4.6	23	7	15	2.1	0
Gil Steinke	45-48	66	267	4.0	2	11	209	19.0	3
Bob Steuber	46-48	79	461	5.8	3	3	23	7.7	0
Don Stevens	52,54	33	95	2.9	0	13	174	13.4	0
Bill Stits	54-61	49	165	3.4	0	8	69	8.6	0
Billy Stone	49-54	296	1112	3.8	11	143	2319	16.2	20
Don Stonesifer	51-56					231	2901	12.6	14
Pete Stout	49-50	71	298	4.2	4	10	117	11.7	2
Jim Strausbaugh	46	37	183	4.9	3	5	56	11.2	0
Bill Stribling	51-53,55-57					114	1573	13.8	14
Bishop Strickland	51	34	165	4.9	0				
Johnny Strzykalski	46-52	662	3415	5.2	19	93	1218	13.1	12
Joe Sulatis	43-53	39	141	3.6	1	48	469	9.8	1
George Sulima	52-54					49	746	15.2	2
Bob Sullivan	48	33	121	3.7	0	4	58	14.5	1
Bob Summerhays	49-51	29	101	3.5	0	1	34	34.0	0
Nick Susoeff	46-49					61	610	10.0	4
Ed Sutton	57-60	282	1109	3.9	9	14	237	16.9	1
Bob Sweiger	46-49	22	87	4.0	0	42	418	10.0	2
Bill Swiacki	48-52					139	1883	13.5	18
Veryl Switzer	54-55	31	160	5.2	0	31	269	8.7	3
Doyle Tackett	46-48	11	−6	−0.5	0	10	216	21.6	2
George Taliaferro	49-55	498	2266	4.6	15	95	1300	13.7	12
Carl Taseff	51,53-62	60	283	4.7	3	19	193	10.2	1
Corky Taylor	55,57	26	95	3.7	0	7	47	6.7	1
Hugh Taylor	47-54	1	7	7.0	0	272	5233	19.2	58
Joe Tereshinski	47-54					43	451	10.5	4
George Terlep	46-48	41	44	1.1	1				
Ray Terrell	46-47	65	165	2.5	0	10	42	4.2	0
Lowell Tew	48-49	38	160	4.2	6	7	97	13.9	0
George Thomas	50-52	68	189	2.8	0	10	208	20.8	2
Bobby Thomason	49,51-57	98	290	3.0	6				
Hal Thompson	47-48	1	4	4.0	0	19	187	9.8	1
Tommy Thompson	40-42,45-50	293	96	0.3	6	6	65	10.8	1
Travis Tidwell	50-51	40	147	3.7	2				
Y. A. Tittle	48-64	372	1245	3.3	39	1	4	4.0	0
Lou Tomasetti	39-42,46-49	501	1905	3.8	14	66	688	10.4	5
Zollie Toth	50-52,54	418	1589	3.8	14	49	394	8.0	3
Dan Towler	50-55	672	3493	5.2	43	62	665	10.7	1
Frank Trigillo	46	41	126	3.1	1				
Mel Triplett	55-62	685	2856	4.2	14	43	439	10.2	4
Wally Triplett	49-50,52-53	70	321	4.6	1	17	175	10.3	0
Charlie Trippi	47-55	687	3506	5.1	23	130	1321	10.2	11
Doug Turley	44-48					45	608	13.5	3
Jim Tyree	48					13	106	8.2	0
Sam Vacanti	47-49	25	8	0.3	3				
Norm Van Brocklin	49-60	102	40	0.4	11				
Steve Van Buren	44-51	1320	5860	4.4	69	45	503	11.2	3
John Vardian	46-48	46	62	1.3	0	26	414	15.9	1
Billy Vessels	56	44	215	4.9	2	11	177	16.1	1
Joe Vetrano	46-49	56	201	3.6	2	5	71	14.2	0
Lowell Wagner	46-53,55	21	55	2.6	0	20	281	14.1	3
Doak Walker	50-55	309	1520	4.9	12	152	2539	16.7	21
Ron Waller	55-58,60	294	1569	5.3	8	44	443	10.1	1
Bobby Walston	51-62	4	12	3.0	0	311	5363	17.2	46
Kenny Washington	46-48	140	859	6.1	8	15	227	15.1	1
Bob Waterfield	45-52	75	21	0.3	13	3	19	6.3	0
Bobby Watkins	55-58	238	1058	4.4	11	15	234	15.6	3
Sid Watson	55-58	199	516	2.6	4	39	423	10.8	2
Joe Watt	47-49	31	61	2.0	0	6	133	22.2	2
Alex Webster	55-64	1196	4638	3.9	39	240	2679	11.2	17
Herm Wedemeyer	48-49	143	540	3.8	0	46	442	9.6	2
Ted Wegert	55-56,60	109	408	3.7	4	14	131	9.4	1
Art Weiner	50					35	722	20.6	6
Billy Wells	54,56-58,60	361	1384	3.8	5	57	725	12.7	2
Pat West	45-48	105	457	4.4	3	4	35	8.8	0
Bob White	51-52,55	32	66	2.1	1	15	209	13.9	2
Wilford White	51-52	28	67	2.4	1	12	197	16.4	1
Bill Wightkin	50-57					13	213	16.4	2
Dick Wilkins	49,52,54	8	28	3.5	0	68	1050	15.4	7
Bob Wilkinson	51-52	26	26	1.0	0	17	330	19.4	3
Bob Williams	51-52,55	29	112	3.9	0				

Lifetime Statistics - 1946-1959 Players Section 2 - RUSHING and RECEIVING (continued)
(All men with 25 or more rushing attempts or 10 or more receptions)

		RUSHING				RECEIVING			
Name	Years	Att.	Yards	Avg.	TD	Rec.	Yards	Avg.	TD
Jerry Williams	49-54	172	910	5.3	10	91	1278	14.0	5
Win Williams	48-49					52	626	12.0	3
Billy Wilson	51-60					407	5902	14.5	49
Camp Wilson	46-49	378	1453	3.8	6	20	198	9.9	0
Tom Wilson	56-63	508	2553	5.0	18	61	617	10.1	5
Royce Womble	54-57,60	91	266	2.9	0	79	917	11.6	9
Neil Worden	54,57	100	261	2.6	1	8	66	8.3	0
John Wright	47	38	113	3.0	0				
Vinnie Yablonski	48-51	124	460	3.7	1	15	127	8.5	0
John Yonakor	46-50,52					18	220	12.2	4
Jim Youel	46-48	42	183	4.4	3	1	20	20.0	0
Buddy Young	47-55	597	2727	4.6	17	179	2711	15.1	21
Dick Young	55-57	78	199	2.6	2	6	53	8.8	0
Tank Younger	49-58	770	3640	4.7	34	100	1167	11.7	1
Bert Zagers	55,57-58	116	477	4.1	3	17	356	20.9	0
Frank Ziegler	49-53	519	1926	3.7	11	47	639	13.6	4
Jack Zilly	47-52					23	279	12.1	4

Section 3 - PUNT RETURNS and KICKOFF RETURNS
(All men with 25 or more Punt Returns or 25 or more Kickoff Returns)

		PUNT RETURNS				KICKOFF RETURNS			
Name	Years	No.	Yards	Avg.	TD	No.	Yards	Avg.	TD
Joe Arenas	51-57	124	774	6.2	1	139	3798	27.3	1
Dale Atkeson	54-56	5	41	8.2	0	29	754	26.0	1
Steve Bagarus	45-48	41	461	11.2	0	27	683	25.3	0
Bibbles Bawel	52,55-56	49	293	6.2	1	9	194	21.6	0
Frank Bernardi	55-57,60	39	392	10.1	1	4	101	25.3	0
J. R. Boone	48-53	72	725	10.1	0	2	31	15.5	0
Fred Bruney	53,56-58,60-62	53	265	5.0	0	18	421	23.4	0
Rex Bumgardner	48-52	24	395	16.5	2	26	468	18.0	0
Leon Campbell	50,52-55					28	771	27.5	1
Tony Canadeo	41-44,46-52	46	513	11.2	0	71	1626	22.9	0
Al Carmichael	53-58,60-61	122	912	7.5	0	191	4798	25.1	2
Ken Carpenter	50-53,60	34	370	10.9	1	41	895	21.8	0
Lew Carpenter	53-55,57-63	28	339	12.1	0	34	686	20.2	0
Jim Cason	48-52,54-56	67	948	14.1	0	33	703	21.3	0
Hopalong Cassady	56-63	43	341	7.9	0	77	1594	20.7	0
Sam Cathcart	49-50,52	35	514	14.7	0	21	469	22.3	0
Lynn Chandnois	50-56	66	312	4.7	0	92	2720	29.6	3
Jack Christiansen	51-58	85	1084	12.8	8	59	1329	22.5	0
Red Cochran	47-50	33	583	17.7	2	25	462	18.5	0
Russ Craft	46-54	32	247	7.7	0	17	484	28.5	1
Billy Cross	51.53	34	221	6.5	0	21	426	20.3	0
Lindon Crow	55-64	25	134	5.4	0				
Jerry Davis	48-52	25	398	15.9	2	18	462	25.7	0
Bill deCorrevont	45-49	21	248	11.8	0	34	655	19.3	0
Babe Dimancheff	45-50,52	16	197	12.3	0	31	670	21.6	0
Glenn Dobbs	46-49	26	361	13.9	1	19	371	19.5	0
Don Doll	49-54	17	164	9.6	0	32	808	25.3	0
Ron Drzewiecki	55,57	42	164	3.9	0	38	906	23.8	0
Bill Dudley	42,45-51,53	124	1515	12.2	3	78	1743	22.3	1
Ralph Earhart	48-49	25	298	11.9	1	13	238	18.3	0
Chuck Fenenbock	43.46-48	61	801	13.1	0	67	1658	24.7	1
Gene Filipski	56-57	21	116	5.5	0	45	1003	22.3	0
Henry Ford	55-56	29	160	5.5	0	6	135	22.5	0
Ted Fritsch	42-50	1	31	31.0	0	37	951	25.7	0
Monk Gafford	46-48	34	433	12.7	0	55	1469	26.7	0
Bob Gage	49-50	30	446	14.9	0	10	221	22.1	0
Fred Gehrke	40,45-50	44	552	12.5	1	38	909	23.9	1
Skippy Giancanelli	53-56	13	63	4.8	0	38	986	25.9	0
Frank Gifford	52-60,62-64	25	121	4.8	0	23	594	25.8	0
Jug Girard	48-57	41	219	5.3	0	34	738	21.7	0
Les Goble	54-55	22	51	2.3	0	35	909	26.0	2
Joe Golding	47-51	22	219	10.0	0	29	654	22.6	0
Billy Grimes	49-52	68	901	13.3	2	83	2015	24.3	0
Chet Hanulak	54,57	38	121	3.2	0	9	213	23.7	0
Tommy Harmon	46-47	32	449	14.0	1	15	342	22.8	0
Howard Hartley	48-52	35	341	9.7	0	6	122	20.3	0
Billy Hillenbrand	46-48	44	612	13.9	1	42	1042	24.8	2
Bob Hoernschemeyer	46-55	11	133	12.1	0	39	981	25.2	0
Chuck Hunsinger	50-52	2	11	5.5	0	31	717	23.1	0
Tommy Kalmanir	49-51,53	34	385	11.3	2	40	932	23.3	0
Sonny Karnofsky	45-46	9	141	15.7	0	27	763	28.3	1
Ken Keller	56-57	24	205	8.5	0	30	673	22.4	0
Kenny Konz	53-59	68	556	8.2	1	5	119	23.8	0
Yale Lary	52-53,56-64	126	758	6.0	3	22	495	22.5	0
Pete Layden	48-50	36	351	9.8	0	9	239	26.6	0
Cliff Lewis	46-51	77	710	9.2	0	14	288	20.6	0
Woodley Lewis	50-60	138	1026	7.4	3	137	3325	24.3	1
Dante Magnani	40-43,46-50	11	121	11.0	0	29	706	24.3	2
Ray Mathews	51-60	61	779	12.8	3	42	1069	25.5	0
Ollie Matson	52,54-66	65	595	9.2	3	143	3746	26.2	6
George McAfee	40-41,45-50	112	1431	12.8	2	11	265	24.1	2
Hugh McElhenny	52-64	126	920	7.3	2	83	1921	23.1	0
Pat McHugh	47-51	31	402	13.0	1	5	95	19.0	0
Don McIlhenny	56-61	1	0	0.0	0	30	747	24.9	0
Frank Minini	47-49					39	1021	26.2	1
Curley Morrison	50-56					33	723	21.9	0
Dom Moselle	50-52,54	23	283	12.3	0	37	886	23.9	0
Marion Motley	46-53,55	1	0	0.0	0	48	1122	23.3	0
Chet Mutryn	46-50	41	537	13.1	1	73	1902	26.1	1
Jerry Norton	54-64	46	147	3.2	0	14	415	29.6	1
Earle Parsons	46-47	25	304	12.2	0	8	193	24.1	0
Don Paul	50-58	113	902	8.0	2	57	1417	24.9	0
Joe Perry	48-63					33	758	23.0	1
Al Pollard	51-53	38	254	6.7	0	53	1293	24.4	0
Bosh Pritchard	42,46-49,51	95	1072	11.3	2	41	938	22.9	1
Eddie Prokop	46-49	17	274	16.1	1	27	620	23.0	0
Skeets Quinlan	52-56	30	276	9.2	1	35	803	22.9	0
Ray Ramsey	47-53	24	277	11.5	1	41	846	20.6	0
Frank Reagan	41,46-51	65	647	10.0	1	4	112	28.0	0
Bert Rechichar	52-61	85	311	3.7	0	23	448	19.5	0
Ray Renfro	52-63	40	225	5.6	0	9	154	17.1	0
Billy Reynolds	53-54,57-58,60	99	530	5.4	0	40	985	24.6	0
Lee Riley	55-56,58-61	48	249	5.2	0	32	764	23.9	0
Herm Rohrig	41,46-47	30	357	11.9	0	6	121	20.2	0
Eddie Saenz	46-51	59	643	10.9	0	93	2191	23.6	2
Spec Sanders	46-48,50	42	642	15.3	1	44	1205	27.4	2
Dan Sandifer	48-53	72	767	10.7	0	63	1367	21.7	1
Joe Scott	48-53	4	48	12.0	0	54	1467	27.2	1
Scooter Scudero	54-58,60	68	458	6.7	1	44	1143	26.0	1
Jimmy Sears	54,57-58,60-61	24	195	8.1	0	50	1169	23.4	0
Frank Seno	43-49	64	747	11.7	1	80	1916	24.0	1
Walt Slater	47	28	435	15.5	0	22	480	21.8	0
Ray Gene Smith	54-57	27	156	5.8	0	4	78	19.5	0
Vitamin Smith	49-53	75	814	10.9	1	57	1453	25.5	3
Bill Stits	54-61	40	305	7.6	0	27	621	23.0	0
Billy Stone	49-54	34	179	5.3	0	18	423	23.5	0
Johnny Strzykalski	46-52	26	316	12.2	0	24	508	21.2	0
Veryl Switzer	54-55	48	464	9.7	1	37	945	25.5	0
George Taliaferro	49-55	36	319	8.9	1	95	2035	21.4	0
Carl Taseff	51,53-62	117	850	7.3	2	45	1019	22.6	0
Wally Triplett	49-50,52-53	44	401	9.1	1	18	664	36.9	1
Charlie Trippi	47-55	63	864	13.7	2	66	1457	22.1	0
Em Tunnell	48-61	258	2209	8.6	5	46	1215	26.4	1
Steve Van Buren	44-51	34	473	13.9	2	76	2030	26.7	3
Doak Walker	50-55	18	284	15.8	1	38	968	25.5	0
Ron Waller	55-58,60	57	165	2.9	0	48	1146	23.9	0
Sid Watson	55-58	28	38	1.4	0	50	1269	25.4	0
Herm Wedemeyer	48-49	39	589	15.1	0	41	842	20.5	0
Billy Wells	54,56-58,60	57	427	7.5	0	55	1267	23.0	
Wilford White	51-52	37	248	6.7	0	5	134	26.8	0
Jerry Williams	49-54	51	277	5.4	0	20	476	23.8	0
Johnny Williams	52-54	42	538	12.8	2	29	710	24.5	0
Tom Wilson	56-63	3	28	9.3	0	62	1689	27.2	1
Buddy Young	47-55	67	698	10.4	2	125	3465	27.7	4
Bert Zagers	55,57-58	28	383	13.7	3	26	628	24.2	0
Vic Zucco	57-60	37	176	4.8	0	12	304	25.3	0

Section 4 · PUNTING
(All men with 25 or more punts)

Name	Years	No.	Avg.
Frankie Albert	46-52	299	43.0
Clarence Avinger	53	42	38.1
Lou Baldacci	56	26	38.8
Jack Banta	41,44-48	39	41.4
Bill Blackburn	46-50	36	41.3
Mike Boyda	49	56	44.2
Pat Brady	52-54	223	44.5
Monte Brethauer	53,55	55	39.3
Ed Brown	54-65	493	40.5
Pete Brown	53-54	49	37.5
Ray Brown	58-60	95	39.2
Adrian Burk	50-56	474	40.9
Tony Canadeo	41-44,46-52	45	37.1
Bob Celeri	51-52	26	42.3
Bob Cifers	46-49	161	41.4
Red Cochran	47-50	59	41.3
Rip Collins	49-51	45	42.2
Mickey Colmer	46-49	117	43.7
Chuck Conerly	48-61	130	38.9
Billy Cox	51-52,55	33	39.3
Dick Deschaine	55-58	231	42.3
Glenn Dobbs	46-49	231	46.4
Bill Dudley	42,45-51,53	191	38.2
L. G. Dupre	55-61	29	35.4
Vic Eaton	55	66	38.2
Chuck Fenenbock	43,45-48	33	38.3
John Galvin	47	66	36.0
Joe Geri	49-52	200	39.9
Horace Gillom	47-56	492	43.1
Jug Girard	48-57	397	40.1
Fred Glatz	56	25	39.4
Bobby Gordon	58,60	55	38.0
George Grimes	48	28	35.9
Rex Grossman	48-50	28	38.8
George Gulyanics	47-52	113	44.6
Jim Hardy	46-52	79	38.1
Ralph Heywood	46-49	68	37.1
Jack Jacobs	42,45-49	187	42.2
Bill Jessup	51-52,54,56-58,60	75	41.0
Jack Johnson	57-61	30	35.2
Pres Johnston	46	28	39.7
Choo-Choo Justice	50,52-54	94	40.4
Kenny Konz	53-59	61	39.3
Steve Lach	42,46-47	31	40.1
Tom Landry	49-55	389	40.9
Yale Lary	52-53,56-64	503	44.3
Hank Lauricella	52	58	35.1
Pete Layden	48-50	36	41.9
Eddie LeBaron	52-53,55-63	171	40.9
Ernie Lewis	46-49	191	41.9
Verl Lillywhite	48-51	53	40.4
Bill Long	49-50	30	37.6
Bobby Luna	55,59	126	40.7
Howie Maley	46-47	152	40.1
Ray Mallouf	41,46-49	188	38.7
Dave Mann	55-57	138	40.4
George McAfee	40-41,45-50	39	36.9
Curley Morrison	50-56	281	41.8
Joe Muha	46-50	179	42.9
Jerry Norton	54-64	358	43.8
Charlie O'Rourke	42,46-49	125	38.2
Dick Poillon	42,46-49	143	40.6
Fran Polsfoot	50-53	47	40.7
Jim Powers	50-53	42	40.6
Bosh Pritchard	42,46-51	28	34.5
Frank Reagan	41,46-51	227	40.9
Bert Rechichar	52-61	38	37.7
Bob Reinhard	46-50	78	44.6
Clive Rush	53	60	37.7
Spec Sanders	46-48,50	192	40.9
Charlie Shepard	56	26	36.6
Jim Smith	48-53	196	42.4
Jim Still	48-49	63	38.7
George Taliaferro	49-55	169	37.5
Charlie Trippi	47-55	196	40.4
Norm Van Brocklin	49-60	523	42.9
Doak Walker	50-55	50	39.1
Bob Waterfield	45-52	315	42.4
Junior Wren	56-61	36	36.3

Section 5 · KICKING
(All men with 10 or more PAT or Field Goal attempts)

Name	Years	PAT	PAT Att.	PAT Pct.	FG	FG Att.	FG Pct.
Ben Agajanian	45,47-49,53-57,60-62,64	343	351	98	104	204	51
Graham Armstrong	41,45,47-48	23	27	85	0	2	0
Larry Barnes	57,60	37	39	95	6	25	24
Dick Bielski	55-63	58	62	94	26	65	40
Nick Bolkovac	53-54	30	31	97	7	16	44
Hardy Brown	48-56,60	25	30	83	0	1	0
George Buksar	49-52	15	18	83	3	7	43
Pat Cannamela	52	8	10	80	0	1	0
Randy Clay	50,53	20	23	87	3	8	38
Ed Cody	47-50	11	13	85			
Fred Cone	51-57,60	221	237	93	59	102	58
Paige Cothren	57-59	81	81	100	33	62	53
Chuck DeShane	45-49	10	10	100	0	1	0
Bill Dudley	42,45-51,53	121	127	95	33	66	50
Tom Feamster	56	24	26	92	0	3	0
Tom Fears	48-56	12	14	86	1	4	25
Ralph Felton	54-62	16	17	94	1	2	50
Ted Fritsch	42-50	62	70	89	36	98	37
Bill George	52-66	14	15	93	4	8	50
Joe Geri	49-52	78	82	95	18	47	38
Frank Gifford	52-60,62-64	10	11	91	2	7	29
Joe Glamp	47-49	74	76	97	11	31	35
Gary Glick	56-61,63	26	29	90	9	25	36
Chubby Grigg	46-52	18	21	86	1	5	20
Rex Grossman	48-50	78	81	96	16	32	50
Lou Groza	46-59,61-67	810	834	97	264	481	55
Pat Harder	46-53	198	204	97	35	69	51
Paul Held	54-55	14	16	88	3	5	60
Crazy Legs Hirsch	46-57	9	12	75			
Vic Janowicz	54-55	37	40	93	10	28	36
Harvey Johnson	46-49,51	178	180	99	28	52	54
Steve Juzwik	42,46-48	36	40	90	2	3	67
Gary Kerkorian	52,54-56	47	55	85	10	21	48
Vito Kissell	49-51	11	11	100	0	1	0
Vic Kulbitski	46-48	9	11	82			
Bobby Layne	48-62	120	124	97	34	50	68
Johnny Lujack	48-51	130	136	96	4	9	44
Jim Martin	50-61,63-64	158	169	93	92	192	48
Phil Martinovich	39-40,46-47	43	47	91	13	38	34
Frank Maznicki	42,46-47	65	69	94	10	16	63
Jim McCarthy	46-49	47	51	92	8	17	47
Buck McPhail	53	21	23	91	2	5	40
Art Michalik	53-56	9	15	60	1	13	8
Tom Miner	58	31	31	100	14	28	50
Jack Morris	58-61	15	15	100	3	8	38
Steve Myhra	57-61	180	189	95	44	91	48
Bob Nelson	41,45-50	37	40	93	6	16	38
Steve Nemeth	45-47	33	34	97	9	13	69
Cliff Patton	46-51	179	185	97	33	69	48
Jerry Perry	54,56-62	92	96	96	32	58	55
Dick Poillon	42,46-49	127	139	91	20	38	53
Ray Poole	47-52	86	92	93	27	44	61
Merv Pregulman	46-49	26	27	96	2	6	33
Bert Rechichar	52-61	62	68	91	31	78	40
Bill Reichardt	52	5	5	100	5	20	25
Les Richter	54-62	106	109	97	29	55	53
John Rokisky	46-48	34	36	94	4	8	50
Lou Saban	46-49	21	22	95	0	2	0
Nick Scollard	46-49	49	55	89	6	18	33
Gordie Soltau	50-58	284	302	94	70	138	51
Bob Steuber	43,46-48	20	23	87	1	2	50
Pat Summerall	52-61	257	265	97	100	212	47
Joe Vetrano	46-49	187	203	92	16	34	47
Doak Walker	50-55	183	191	96	49	87	56
Bobby Walston	51-62	365	384	95	80	157	51
Bob Waterfield	45-52	315	336	94	60	110	55
Sid Watson	55-58	10	12	83	1	1	100
Tad Weed	55	12	12	100	3	6	50
Vinnie Yablonski	48-51	16	16	100	10	18	56

Leaders and Features

The mention of any sport brings certain images to mind.When it comes to pro football the pictures are vivid and swift. Mostly though it is an extreme of functions. For those in love with risk and the dramatics of suddenness, there is nothing more serene than the aerial ballet of a 50-yard pass play. And for those who like to chew their fantasy in small, but certain chunks of yardage, there is nothing more pleasurable than the fullback who eludes a mammoth of flesh in search of four yards of daylight. Yet these two simplified illustrations have not always held true for pro football. If nothing else, football is a game of constant change. From year to year records are constantly changing with the times of football as the newer types of strategies, equipment and fields of play are introduced.

It is for this reason that many of the records which appear on the following pages have no continuity with the players of one period to the next.

Yet beyond the comparison of any era, more important are the achievements of the men who made up their time, and the fact that whatever the criteria, each contributed the fullest and best of his talents. It is on this basis that each must be measured and appreciated in the light of pro football's changing game.

The rules of the game have changed drastically in the periods covered in this book. Suffice to say that there are to many rule changes to explain here but to say that these changes do have an effect on the records as seen on these pages. It seems that a glance at the yearly leaders will show how evolutions occur, but as stated in the first paragraphs above there is no continuity and here we are listing those who the authors feel have made their contributions....through single season leader lists—and as lifetime leaders— and as category leaders.

YEARLY CHAMPIONSHIP GAMES

Year	Team	Winner (Share)	Loser (Share)	Score
1933	NFL	CHICAGO BEARS ($210.34)	New York Giants ($140.22)	23–21
1934	NFL	NEW YORK GIANTS ($621)	Chicago Bears ($414.02)	30–13
1935	NFL	DETROIT LIONS ($313.35	New York Giants ($200.20)	26–7
1936	NFL	Green Bay Packers ($250)	Boston Redskins ($180)	21–6
		(At New York)		
1937	NFL	Washington Redskins ($225.90)	CHICAGO BEARS ($127.78)	28–21
1938	NFL	NEW YORK GIANTS ($504.45)	Green Bay Packers ($368.81)	23–17
1939	NFL	GREEN BAY PACKERS ($703.97)	New York Giants ($455.57)	27–0
		(At Milwaukee)		
1940	NFL	Chicago Bears ($873)	WASHINGTON REDSKINS ($606)	73–0
1941	NFL	CHICAGO BEARS ($430)	New York Giants ($288)	37–9
1942	NFL	WASHINGTON REDSKINS ($965)	Chicago Bears ($637)	14–6
1943	NFL	CHICAGO BEARS ($1,146)	Washington Redskins ($765)	41–21
1944	NFL	Green Bay Packers ($1,449)	NEW YORK GIANTS ($814)	14–7
1945	NFL	CLEVELAND RAMS ($1,469)	Washington Redskins ($902)	15–14
1946	NFL	Chicago Bears (1,975)	NEW YORK GIANTS ($1,295)	24–14
1946	AAFC	CLEVELAND BROWNS ($931.57)	New York Yankees ($645.88)	14–9
1947	NFL	CHICAGO CARDINALS ($1,132)	Philadelphia Eagles ($754)	28–21
1947	AAFC	Cleveland Browns ($1,191.99)	NEW YORK YANKEES ($794.66)	14–3
1948	NFL	PHILADELPHIA EAGLES ($1,540)	Chicago Cardinals ($874)	7–0
1948	AAFC	CLEVELAND BROWNS ($594.18)	Buffalo Bills ($386.22)	49–7
1949	NFL	Philadelphia Eagles ($1,094)	LOS ANGELES RAMS ($739)	14–0
1949	AAFC	CLEVELAND BROWNS ($266.11)	San Francisco 49ers ($172.61)	21–7
1950		CLEVELAND BROWNS ($1,113)	Los Angeles Rams ($686)	30–28
1951		LOS ANGELES RAMS ($2,108)	Cleveland Browns ($1,483)	24–17
1952		Detroit Lions (2,274)	CLEVELAND BROWNS ($1,712)	17–7
1953		DETROIT LIONS ($2,424)	Cleveland Browns ($1,654)	17–16
1954		CLEVELAND BROWNS ($2,478)	Detroit Lions ($1,585)	56–10
1955		Cleveland Browns ($3,508)	LOS ANGELES RAMS ($2,316)	38–14
1956		NEW YORK GIANTS ($3,779)	Chicago Bears ($2,485)	47–7
1957		DETROIT LIONS ($4,295)	Cleveland Browns ($2,750)	59–14
1958		Baltimore Colts ($4,718)	NEW YORK GIANTS ($3,111)	*23–17
1959		BALTIMORE COLTS ($4,674)	New York Giants ($3,083)	31–16

Note: Home Team in Upper Case.

* – Sudden Death Game

Team	Games	Wins	Losses	Pct.	Total Share
Colts	2	2	0	1.000	9,392
Lions	5	4	1	.800	13,691.35
Packers	4	3	1	.750	2,771.78
Eagles	3	2	1	.667	3,388
Browns	10	6	4	.600	17,681.85
Bears	9	5	4	.556	8,298.14
Cardinals	2	1	1	.500	2,006.
Rams	5	2	3	.400	7,318
Redskins	6	2	4	.333	3,643.90
Giants	11	3	8	.273	14,291.44
Yankees	2	0	2	.000	1,440.54
Bills	1	0	1	.000	386.22
Forty Niners	1	0	1	.000	172.61

YEARLY TEAM LEADERS

OFFENSE

YEAR	LGUE	POINTS	PTS/G	FIRST DOWNS	RUSH YARDS	YDS/GAME	RUSH AVERAGE	RUSH TD	PASS COMPLETION PERCENTAGE	PASS YARDS	YDS/GAME	PASS YARDS/ATTEMPT	PASS TD	FEWEST INT.	LEAST INT.%	PUNTING AVERAGE	YEAR	LGUE
1920	NFL	Day. 127	15.9					R.I.,Buf. 8 Day 8					Day. 8				1920	NFL
1921	NFL	Buf. 211	17.6					Akr. 15					Buf. 11 ChiB 5				1921	NFL
1922	NFL	Can. 184	R.I. 22.0					Can, RI 19					Akr. 4				1922	NFL
1923	NFL	Can. 246	20.5					Can. 25					Can.,Col. 7				1923	NFL
1924	NFL	Fra. 326	Cle. 25.4					Fra. 38					Cle. 11				1924	NFL
1925	NFL	Pott. 270	22.5					Pott. 23					G.B. 11				1925	NFL
1926	NFL	Fra. 236	13.9					Fra. 20					ChiB 8 G.B. 8				1926	NFL
1927	NFL	Cle. 209	16.1					NY G,Cle. 16					Cle. 12				1927	NFL
1928	NFL	Det. 189	18.9					Det. 15					Det. 12				1928	NFL
1929	NFL	NY G 312	20.8					NY G 19					NY G 25				1929	NFL
1930	NFL	NY G 308	18.1					NY G 27					NY G 16				1930	NFL
1931	NFL	G.B. 291	20.8					G.B. 18					G.B. 17 G.B. 21				1931	NFL
1932	NFL	ChiB 160	11.4					ChiB 13					G.B. 9				1932	NFL
1933	NFL	NY G 244	17.4						Bkn. 46.7								1933	NFL
1934	NFL	ChiB 286	22.0						NY G 40.9								1934	NFL
1935	NFL	ChiB 192	16.0	ChiB 140	ChiB 2096	175		Det. 15	NY G 44.8	G.B. 1645	129	G.B. 6.72	ChiB 13				1935	NFL
1936	NFL	G.B. 248	20.7	Det. 170	Det. 2883	240	Det. 4.73	Det. 22	G.B. 42.4	G.B. 1629	136	ChiB 6.46	ChiB,G.B. 17				1936	NFL
1937	NFL	G.B. 220	20.0	Was. 149	Det. 2074	189	Det. 4.30	Det. 12	Was. 44.6	G.B. 1397	127	ChiB 6.97	ChiB,G.B. 16	NY G 11	NY G 5.42		1937	NFL
1938	NFL	G.B. 223	20.7	Was. 147	Det. 1893	172	Det. 4.01	NY G 12	NY G 48.9	Was. 1536	140	G.B. 6.98	G.B. 20	Bkn. 8	Bkn. 4.73		1938	NFL
1939	NFL	ChiB 298	27.1	G.B. 149	ChiB 2043	186	ChiB 4.66	ChiB 21	Was. 58.2	ChiB 1965	179	Was. 8.93	Was. 18	NY G 11	NY G 6.21		1939	NFL
1940	NFL	Was. 245	22.2	G.B. 154	ChiB 1818	165	Bkn. 3.92	ChiB 16	Was. 59.0	Was. 1887	172	ChiB 8.19	G.B.,Was. 18	Bkn. 13	Phi. 5.52		1940	NFL
1941	NFL	ChiB 396	36.0	ChiB 181	ChiB 2290	208	ChiB 4.63	ChiB 30	G.B. 52.6	ChiB 2002	182	ChiB 10.21	ChiB 19	ChiB 11	G.B. 5.14	Was. 45.9	1941	NFL
1942	NFL	ChiB 376	34.2	G.B. 176	ChiB 1911	174	ChiB 4.07	ChiB 23	Was. 53.3	G.B. 2407	219	ChiB 10.18	G.B. 28	Pit. 11	G.B. 5.45	Was. 44.3	1942	NFL
1943	NFL	ChiB 303	30.3	ChiB 161	P-P 1730	173	ChiB 3.89	P-P 18	Was. 54.7	ChiB 2310	231	ChiB 10.09	ChiB 28	NY G 9	NY G 6.04	Was. 43.1	1943	NFL
1944	NFL	Phi. 267	26.7	G.B. 147	Phi. 1661	166	Phi. 3.92	Phi. 23	Was. 56.9	Was. 2021	202	ChiB 7.45	ChiB 21	Phi. 12	Was. 5.69	Det. 40.5	1944	NFL
1945	NFL	Phi. 272	27.2	ChiB 164	Cle. 1714	171	Cle. 4.61	Phi. 26	Was. 64.0	ChiB 1857	186	Cle. 8.88	Cle. 16	Was. 11	Was. 4.82	Was. 43.3	1945	NFL
1946	NFL	ChiB 289	26.3	L.A. 214	G.B. 1765	160	L.A. 4.17	ChiB 19	Phi. 53.5	L.A. 2080	189	ChiB 7.71	L.A. 19	Pit. 13	L.A. 7.36	L.A. 44.4	1946	NFL
1946	AAFC	Cle. 423	30.2	L.A. 183	S.F. 2175	155	Buf. 4.08	Cle. 27	L.A. 54.7	Cle. 2266	162	Cle. 9.56	Cle. 22	Cle. 7	Cle. 2.95	Bkn. 46.5	1946	AAFC
1947	NFL	ChiB 363	30.3	ChiB 263	L.A. 2171	181	L.A. 4.73	ChiB 21 Phi. 21	Was. 55.5	Was. 3336	278	ChiB 8.18	ChiB 29	Was. 18	Was. 4.33	G.B. 43.6	1947	NFL
1947	AAFC	Cle. 410	29.8	S.F. 218	N.Y. 2930	209	N.Y. 5.49	N.Y. 27	Cle. 58.8	Cle. 2990	214	Cle. 10.10	Cle. 26	Cle. 12	Cle. 4.05	L.A. 45.0	1947	AAFC
1948	NFL	ChiC 395	32.9	ChiB 242	ChiC 2560	213	ChiC 4.82	ChiC 25	Was. 56.1	Was. 2861	238	Was. 7.95	L.A. 28	ChiC 12	ChiC 4.21	Phi. 45.9	1948	NFL
1948	AAFC	S.F. 495	35.4	Cle. 243	S.F. 3663	262	S.F. 6.07	S.F. 35	S.F. 56.3	Bal. 2899	207	Bal. 8.53	S.F. 30	Bal. 13	Bal. 3.82	L.A. 47.2	1948	AAFC
1949	NFL	Phi. 364	30.3	ChiB 248	Phi. 2607	217	ChiC 4.56	Phi. 25	L.A. 52.5	ChiB 3055	255	ChiB 7.94	ChiB 24	Phi. 14	Phi. 5.56	L.A. 44.4	1949	NFL
1949	AAFC	S.F. 416	34.7	Buf. 184	S.F. 2798	233	S.F. 5.53	S.F. 26	Buf. 57.1	Cle. 2929	244	Cle. 9.90	S.F. 28	Cle. 12	Cle. 4.05	S.F. 45.5	1949	AAFC
1950	NFL	L.A. 466	38.8	L.A. 278	NY G 2336	195	NYY 4.56	L.A. 28	L.A. 55.8	L.A. 3709	309	L.A. 8.19	L.A. 31	NY G 10	NY G 5.35	Cle. 43.2	1950	NFL
1951	NFL	L.A. 392	32.7	L.A. 272	ChiB 2408	201	L.A. 5.19	ChiB 24	Cle. 55.7	L.A. 3296	275	L.A. 8.84	Det. 29	Cle 7	L.A. 5.90	Cle. 45.5	1951	NFL
1952	NFL	L.A. 349	29.1	Cle. 228	S.F. 1905	159	Cle. 4.53	L.A. 17	S.F. 51.8	Cle. 2839	237	G.B. 7.98	G.B. 26	Phi. 19	Phi. 5.26	Cle. 45.7	1952	NFL
1953	NFL	S.F. 372	31.0	Phi. 256	S.F. 2230	186	L.A. 5.04	S.F. 26	Cle. 63.0	Phi. 3357	280	Cle. 10.10	Phi. 25	Cle. 9	Cle. 2.97	Pit. 46.9	1953	NFL
1954	NFL	Det. 337	28.1	L.A. 255	S.F. 2498	208	S.F. 5.65	S.F. 28	Cle. 59.0	ChiB 3299	275	L.A. 9.91	Phi. 33	S.F. 12	S.F. 3.53	Pit. 43.2	1954	NFL
1955	NFL	Cle. 349	29.1	ChiB 235	ChiB 2388	199	ChiB 4.90	Cle. 20	Cle. 55.6	Phi. 2696	225	Cle. 9.51	Cle. 21	Cle. 11	Cle. 4.70	L.A. 44.6	1955	NFL
1956	NFL	ChiB 363	30.3	Det. 247	ChiB 2468	206	L.A. 5.15	ChiB 22	Bal. 56.6	L.A. 2601	217	ChiB 8.77	G.B. 21	ChiC 14	NY G 5.09	L.A. 43.1	1956	NFL
1957	NFL	L.A. 307	25.6	L.A. 235	L.A. 2142	179	L.A. 4.52	Cle. 19	S.F. 62.6	Bal. 2608	217	Cle. 9.61	Bal. 25	NY G 12	NY G 4.46	S.F. 44.7	1957	NFL
1958	NFL	Bal. 381	31.8	Bal. 253	Cle. 2526	211	Cle. 5.32	Bal. 24 Cle. 24	S.F. 58.2	L.A. 2909	242	Pit. 8.62	Bal. 26	Bal. 11	Bal. 3.11	Was. 45.4	1958	NFL
1959	NFL	Bal. 374	31.2	Bal. 267	Cle. 2149	179	L.A. 4.79	Cle. 20	Cle. 57.6	Bal. 2938	245	NY G 8.72	Bal. 22	Cle. 9	Cle. 3.26	NY G 46.6	1959	NFL

DEFENSE

YEAR	LGUE	POINTS	PTS/G	FIRST DOWNS	RUSH YARDS	YARDS/GAME	RUSH AVERAGE	RUSH TD	PASS COMPLETION PERCENTAGE	PASS YARDS	YARDS/GAME	PASS YARDS/ATTEMPT	TD PASS	MOST INT.	HIGHEST INT. %	YEAR	LGUE
1933	NFL	Bkn. 54	5.4													1933	NFL
1934	NFL	Det. 59	4.5													1934	NFL
1935	NFL	G.B. 96 NY G 96	8.0 8.0						ChiB 30.4					ChiB 37	ChiB 19.1	1935	NFL
1936	NFL	ChiB 94	7.8						Bos. 31.5					ChiB 35	ChiB 15.4	1936	NFL
1937	NFL	ChiB 100	9.1						Pit. 32.4					NY G 30	NY G 16.5	1937	NFL
1938	NFL	NY G 79	7.2						NY G 35.1					NY G 44	NY G 15.0	1938	NFL
1939	NFL	NY G 85	7.7						Was. 37.0					NY G 35	NY G 15.8	1939	NFL
1940	NFL	Bkn. 120	10.9						ChiC 37.1					G.B. 40	Det. 16.4	1940	NFL
1941	NFL	NY G 114	10.3	Bkn. 110 ChiC 110	ChiB 1076	98	Was. 2.71	Bkn. 6 ChiB 6	ChiB 40.0	Pit. 1168	106	ChiB 5.5	Bkn. 6 NY G 6	ChiB 34	NY G 13.3	1941	NFL
1942	NFL	ChiB 84	7.6	ChiB 98	ChiB 519	47	ChiB 1.77	ChiB 3	Was. 37.5	Was. 1083	99	ChiB 4.2	NY G 4	ChiB 33 G.B. 33	G.B. 13.6	1942	NFL
1943	NFL	Was. 137	13.7	P-P 96	P-P 793	79	P-P 2.54	NY G 8	ChiB 31.5	ChiB 980	98	ChiB 4.8	ChiB 8	G.B. 42	G.B. 17.4	1943	NFL
1944	NFL	NY G 75	7.5	Phi. 86	Phi. 558	56	Phi. 1.74	NY G 6	ChiB 33.2	ChiB 1052	105	NY G 5.0	NY G 3	NY G 34	Phi. 14.3	1944	NFL
1945	NFL	Was. 121	12.1	Phi. 104	Pbi. 817	82	Det. 2.56	Det. 7	Cle. 39.1	Was. 1121	112	Was. 5.4	NY G 6	Bos. 30	Bos. 13.2	1945	NFL
1946	NFL	Pit. 117	10.6	ChiB 138	ChiB 1044	95	Phi. 2.69	Pit. 9	Pit. 39.5	Pit. 939	85	Pit. 5.8	G.B. 6 Pit. 6	ChiB 27	Phi. 11.8	1946	NFL
1946	AAFC	Cle. 137	9.8	N.Y. 119	S.F. 873	62	S.F. 2.05	S.F. 7	Cle. 41.8	Cle. 1317	94	Cle. 4.4	Cle. 8	Cle. 41	Cle. 13.7	1946	AAFC
1947	NFL	G.B. 210	17.5	Pit. 170	Phi. 1329	111	L.A. 3.41	ChiB 6	Pit. 40.2	G.B. 1790	149	G.B. 6.5	G.B. 14 L.A. 14	G.B. 30	G.B. 10.8	1947	NFL
1947	AAFC	Cle. 185	13.2	N.Y. 140	N.Y. 1237	88	N.Y. 3.33	L.A. 9	Cle. 42.6	Cle. 1707	122	Cle. 5.6	Cle. 11	Cle. 32	Cle. 10.6	1947	AAFC
1948	NFL	ChiB 151	12.6	Phi. 158	Phi. 1209	101	Phi. 3.22	Phi. 5	Phi. 41.1	G.B. 1626	135	ChiB 4.9	ChiB 12	NY G 39	NY G 12.5	1948	NFL
1948	AAFC	Cle. 190	13.6	Cle. 171	Cle. 1519	108	Cle. 3.48	Cle. 10	Cle. 44.9	Bkn. 1985	142	Cle. 5.9	Cle. 14	S.F. 32	S.F. 8.6	1948	AAFC
1949	NFL	Phi. 134	11.2	Phi. 148	ChiB 1196	100	ChiB 2.79	Phi. 5	Phi. 39.9	Phi. 1607	134	Phi. 5.3	Pit. 9	ChiC 33	Det. 10.3	1949	NFL
1949	AAFC	Cle. 171	14.2	N.Y. 129	N.Y. 1134	94	N.Y. 3.15	N.Y. 8	Cle. 39.5	Cle. 1677	140	Cle. 5.5	Cle. 9	S.F. 32	S.F. 10.1	1949	AAFC
1950	NFL	Phi. 141	11.7	Phi. 141	Det. 1367	114	NY G 2.93	Phi. 5	Phi. 36.8	Cle. 1581	132	Cle. 5.4	Cle. 8	Bal. 34	Phi. 11.2	1950	NFL
1951	NFL	Cle. 152	12.7	NY G 174	NY G 913	76	NY G 2.33	Cle. 8	Phi. 41.5	Pit. 1687	141	Cle. 6.0	Cle. 10	NY G 41	NY G 10.9	1951	NFL
1952	NFL	Det. 192	16.0	S.F. 167	Det. 1145	95	NY G 3.23	NY G 8 ChiC 8 Det. 8 NY G 8 Pit. 8	Cle. 40.5	Was. 1817	151	S.F. 5.6	Was. 12	L.A. 38	L.A. 10.6	1952	NFL
1953	NFL	Cle. 162	13.5	Pit. 184	Phi. 1117	93	Pit. 3.07	Phi. 6	Cle. 42.2	Was. 1950	162	Was. 5.6	Was. 8	Det. 38	Det. 10.7	1953	NFL
1954	NFL	Cle. 162	13.5	Cle. 147	Cle. 1050	88	Cle. 2.82	Cle. 4	Phi. 41.4	Cle. 1784	149	Phi. 5.9	Det. 10	NY G 33	Pit. 10.2	1954	NFL
1955	NFL	Cle. 218	18.2	Cle. 171	Cle. 1189	99	Was. 3.26	Was. 8	Cle. 39.0	Pit. 1530	127	Cle. 5.5	S.F. 10	G.B. 31 L.A. 31	G.B. 12.0	1955	NFL
1956	NFL	Cle. 177	14.7	Pit. 167	NY G 1443	120	NY G 3.48	Det. 9	ChiC 44.9	Cle. 1215	101	Cle. 5.4	Cle. 7	ChiC 33	ChiC 11.5	1956	NFL
1957	NFL	Cle. 172	14.3	Pit. 156	Bal. 1174	98	Bal. 3.13	Pit. 7	Cle. 43.4	Cle. 1511	126	Cle. 6.2	Cle. 8	G.B. 30	G.B. 9.6	1957	NFL
1958	NFL	NY G 183	15.2	ChiB 168	Bal. 1291	108	NY G 3.61	Cle. 6	NY G 45.7	NY G 2130	177	L.A. 6.0	Bal. 9	Bal. 35	Bal. 9.6	1958	NFL
1959	NFL	NY G 170	14.2	NY G 167	NY G 1261	105	NY G 3.33	NY G 6	Pit. 44.9	NY G 1811	151	NY G 6.0	NY G 11	Bal. 40	Bal. 11.4	1959	NFL

YEARLY LEADERS

PASSING

YEAR	LGUE	YARDS			COMPLETIONS			COMP. PCT.			TOUCHDOWNS			YARDS/ATT.			FEWEST PCT. INT.			YEAR	LGUE
1920	NFL										Mahrt	Day.	7							1920	NFL
1921	NFL										Oliphant	Buf.	7							1921	NFL
1922	NFL										Conzelman	RI-Mil.	3							1922	NFL
1923	NFL										Smythe	Can.	6							1923	NFL
1924	NFL										Workman	Cle.	9							1924	NFL
1925	NFL										Dunn	ChiC.	9							1925	NFL
1926	NFL										Driscoll	ChiB.	6							1926	NFL
1927	NFL										Friedman	Cle.	12							1927	NFL
1928	NFL										Friedman	Det.	10							1928	NFL
1929	NFL										Friedman	NY G	20							1929	NFL
1930	NFL										Friedman	NY G	13							1930	NFL
1931	NFL										Dunn	G.B.	8							1931	NFL
1932	NFL	Herber	G.B.	774	Herber	G.B.	44				Herber	G.B.	9							1932	NFL
1933	NFL	Newman	NY G	973	Newman	NY G	53	Friedman	Bkn.	52.5	Newman	NY G	11	Molesworth	ChiB.	8.4	Monnett	G.B.	6.5	1933	NFL
1934	NFL	Herber	G.B.	799	Herber	G.B.	42	Clark	Det.	46.9	Herber	G.B.	8	Clark	Det	7.8	Newman	NY G	5.5	1934	NFL
1935	NFL	Danowski	NY G	795	Danowski	NY G	57	Danowski	NY G	50.4	Danowski	NY G	11	Masterson	ChiB.	10.4	Not Available			1935	NFL
1936	NFL	Herber	G.B.	1239	Herber	G.B.	77	Clark	Det.	53.5	Herber	G.B.	11	Herber	G.B.	7.2	Monnett	G.B.	3.8	1936	NFL
1937	NFL	Baugh	Was.	1127	Baugh	Was.	81	Monnett	G.B.	50.7	Monnett	G.B.	9	Masterson	ChiB.	8.5	Danowski	NY G	3.7	1937	NFL
1938	NFL	Parker	Bkn.	865	Danowski	NY G	70	Monnett	G.B.	54.4	Monnett	G.B.	9	Monnett	G.B.	8.2	Parker	Bkn.	4.7	1938	NFL
1939	NFL	O'Brien	Phi.	1324	Hall	Cle.	106	Filchock	Was.	61.8	Filchock	Was.	11	Filchock	Was.	12.3	Sooan	Det.	2.8	1939	NFL
1940	NFL	Baugh	Was.	1367	O'Brien	Phi.	124	Baugh	Was.	62.7	Baugh	Was.	12	Luckman	ChiB.	9.0	Watkins	Phi.	3.5	1940	NFL
1941	NFL	Isbell	G.B.	1479	Isbell	G.B.	117	Luckman	ChiB.	57.1	Isbell	G.B.	15	Luckman	ChiB.	9.9	Mallouf	ChiC.	4.2	1941	NFL
1942	NFL	Isbell	G.B.	2021	Isbell	G.B.	146	Baugh	Was.	58.7	Isbell	G.B.	24	O'Rourke	ChiB.	10.8	Baugh	Was.	4.9	1942	NFL
1943	NFL	Luckman	ChiB.	2194	Baugh	Was.	133	Baugh	Was.	56.2	Luckman	ChiB.	28	Luckman	ChiB.	10.9	Comp	G.B.	4.3	1943	NFL
1944	NFL	Comp	G.B.	1159	Filchock	Was.	84	Filchock	Was.	57.1	Filchock	Was.	13	Ronzani	ChiB.	8.0	Baugh	Was.	5.5	1944	NFL
1945	NFL	Luckman	ChiB.	1725	Baugh	Was.	128	Baugh	Was.	70.3	Luckman	ChiB.	14	Waterfield	Cle.	9.4	Baugh	Was.	2.2	1945	NFL
											Waterfield	Cle.	14								
1946	NFL	Luckman	ChiB.	1826	Waterfield	L.A.	127	Thompson	Phi.	55.3	Waterfield	L.A.	18	Luckman	ChiB.	8.0	Governali	Bos.	5.2	1946	NFL
1946	AAFC	Dobbs	Bkn.	1886	Dobbs	Bkn.	135	O'Rourke	L.A.	57.7	Graham	Cle.	17	Graham	Cle.	10.5	Parker	N.Y.	2.6	1946	AAFC
1947	NFL	Baugh	Was.	2938	Baugh	Was.	210	Baugh	Was.	59.3	Baugh	Was.	25	Luckman	ChiB.	8.4	Baugh	Was.	4.2	1947	NFL
1947	AAFC	Graham	Cle.	2753	Schwenk	Bal.	168	Graham	Cle.	60.6	Graham	Cle.	25	Graham	Cle.	10.2	Graham	Cle.	4.1	1947	AAFC
1948	NFL	Baugh	Was.	2599	Baugh	Was.	185	Baugh	Was.	58.7	Thompson	Phi.	25	LeForce	Det.	9.0	Hardy	L.A.	3.3	1948	NFL
1948	AAFC	Graham	Cle.	2713	Dobbs	L.A.	185	Albert	S.F.	58.3	Albert	S.F.	29	Tittle	Bal.	8.7	Tittle	Bal.	3.1	1948	AAFC
1949	NFL	Lujack	ChiB.	2658	Lujack	ChiB.	162	Baugh	Was.	56.9	Lujack	ChiB.	23	Lujack	ChiB.	8.2	Enke	Det.	3.5	1949	NFL
1949	AAFC	Graham	Cle.	2785	Graham	Cle.	161	Ratterman	Buf.	57.9	Albert	S.F.	27	Graham	Cle.	9.8	Graham	Cle.	3.5	1949	AAFC
1950	NFL	Layne	Det.	2323	Tittle	Bal.	161	Waterfield	L.A.	57.3	Ratterman	NY Y	22	Van Brocklin	L.A.	8.8	Conerly	NY G	5.3	1950	NFL
1951	NFL	Layne	Det.	2403	Layne	Det.	152	Thomason	G.B.	56.6	Layne	Det.	26	Waterfield	L.A.	8.9	Thomason	G.B.	4.1	1951	NFL
1952	NFL	Graham	Cle.	2816	Graham	Cle.	181	Van Brocklin	L.A.	55.1	Finks	Pit.	20	Van Brokclin	L.A.	8.5	Thomason	Phi.	4.2	1952	NFL
											Graham	Cle.	20								
1953	NFL	Graham	Cle.	2722	Blanda	ChiB.	169	Graham	Cle.	64.7	Thomason	Phi.	21	Graham	Cle.	10.6	Graham	Cle.	3.5	1953	NFL
1954	NFL	Van Brocklin	L.A.	2637	Rote	G.B.	180	Graham	Cle.	59.2	Burk	Phi.	23	Van Brocklin	L.A.	10.1	Tittle	S.F.	3.1	1954	NFL
1955	NFL	Finks	Pit.	2270	Finks	Pit.	165	Graham	Cle.	53.0	Rote	G.B.	17	Graham	Cle.	9.3	Gilmer	Det.	3.3	1955	NFL
											Tittle	S.F.	17								
1956	NFL	Rote	G.B.	2203	Rote	G.B.	146	Brown	ChiB.	57.1	Rote	G.B.	18	Brown	ChiB.	9.9	Conerly	NY G	4.0	1956	NFL
1957	NFL	Unitas	Bal.	2550	Tittle	S.F.	176	Tittle	S.F.	63.1	Unitas	Bal.	24	O'Connell	Cle.	11.2	Morrall	Pit.	4.2	1957	NFL
1958	NFL	Wade	L.A.	2875	Van Brocklin	Phi.	198	Brodie	S.F.	59.9	Unitas	Bal.	19	Le Baron	Was.	9.4	Unitas	Bal.	2.7	1958	NFL
1959	NFL	Unitas	Bal.	2899	Unitas	Bal.	193	Wade	L.A.	58.6	Unitas	Bal.	32	Conerly	NY G	8.8	Conerly	NY G	2.1	1959	NFL

PUNT RETURNS / KICKOFF RETURNS

		PUNT RETURNS NUMBER			PUNT RETURNS YARDS			PUNT RETURNS AVERAGE			KICKOFF RETURNS NUMBER			KICKOFF RETURNS YARDS			KICKOFF RETURNS AVERAGE				
YEAR	LGUE	NAME	TEAM		NAME	TEAM		NAME	TEAM		NAME	TEAM		NAME	TEAM		NAME	TEAM		YEAR	LGUE
1941	NFL	Whizzer White	Det.	19	Whizzer White	Det.	262													1941	NFL
1942	NFL	Merl Condit	Bkn.	21	Bill Dudley	Pit.	271	Ernie Steele	Phi.	26.4	Marshall Goldberg	ChiC	15	Marshall Golberg	ChiC	393	Bill Dudley	Pit.	27.1	1942	NFL
1943	NFL	Andy Farkas	Was.	15	Frankie Sinkwich	Det.	228	Frankie Sinkwich	Det.	20.7	Ken Heineman	Bkn.	16	Ken Heineman	Bkn.	442	Ned Matthews	Det.	35.1	1943	NFL
1944	NFL	Bob Davis	Bos.	22	Bob Davis	Bos.	271	Ernie Steele	Phi.	16.5	John Grigas	C–P	23	John Grigas	C–P	471	Steve Van Buren	Phi.	33.3	1944	NFL
1945	NFL	Steve Bagarus	Was.	21	Steve Bagarus	Was.	251	Fred Gehrke	Cle.	15.0	Frank Seno	ChiC	19	Frank Seno	ChiC	408	Ted Fritsch	G.B.	34.9	1945	NFL
1946	NFL	Bill Dudley	Pit.	27	Bill Dudley	Pit.	385	Gil Steinke	Phi.	14.5	Sonny Karnofsky	Bos.	21	Sonny Karnofsky	Bos.	599	Frank Seno	ChiC	31.4	1946	NFL
1946	AAFC	Ken Casanega	S.F.	18	Chuck Fenenbock	L.A.	299	Chuck Fenenbock	L.A.	18.7	Steve Juzwik	Buf.	21	Chuck Fenenbock	L.A.	479	Monk Gafford	Bkn–Mia	31.4	1946	AAFC
		Bob Seymour	L.A.	18																	
1947	NFL	Walt Slater	Pit.	28	Walt Slater	Pit.	435	Frank Seno	Bos.	17.8	Eddie Saenz	Was.	29	Eddie Saenz	Was.	797	Steve Van Buren	Phi.	29.4	1947	NFL
1947	AAFC	Glenn Dobbs	Bkn–L.A.	19	Glenn Dobbs	Bkn–L.A.	215	Spec Sanders	N.Y.	27.3	Spec Sanders	N.Y.	22	Chet Mutryn	Buf.	691	Chet Mutryn	Buf.	32.9	1947	AAFC
1948	NFL	George McAfee	ChiB	30	George McAfee	ChiB	417	Jerry Davis	ChiC	20.9	Dan Sandifer	Was.	26	Dan Sandifer	Was.	594	Frank Minini	G.B.	30.8	1948	NFL
1948	AAFC	Cliff Lewis	Cle.	26	Herm Wedemeyer	L.A.	368	Tom Casey	N.Y.	25.4	Monk Gafford	Bkn.	23	Monk Gafford	Bkn.	559	Forrest Hall	S.F.	28.4	1948	AAFC
1949	NFL	Vitamin Smith	L.A.	27	Vitamin Smith	L.A.	427	Red Cochran	ChiC	20.9	Eddie Saenz	Was.	24	Don Doll	Det.	536	J. Salschneider	NY G	31.6	1949	NFL
											Dan Sandifer	Was.	24								
1949	AAFC	Pete Layden	N.Y.	29	Jim Cason	S.F.	351	Buddy Young	N.Y.	19.0	Herm Wedemeyer	Bal.	30	Herm Wedemeyer	Bal.	602	Ray Ramsey	Chi.	29.2	1949	AAFC
1950	NFL	George McAfee	ChiB	33	Billy Grimes	G.B.	555	Herb Rich	Bal.	23.0	Don Paul	ChiC	28	Vitamin Smith	L.A.	742	Vitamin Smith	L.A.	33.7	1950	NFL
1951	NFL	Em Tunnell	NY G	34	Em Tunnell	NY G	489	Buddy Young	NY Y	19.3	George Taliaferro	NY Y	27	George Taliaferro	NY Y	622	Lynn Chadnois	Pit.	32.5	1951	NFL
1952	NFL	Bibbles Bawel	Phi.	34	Em Tunnell	NY G	411	J. Christiansen	Det.	21.5	Billy Baggett	Dal.	23	Buddy Young	Dal.	643	Lynn Chadnois	Pit.	35.2	1952	NFL
											Buddy Young	Dal.	23								
1953	NFL	Em Tunnell	NY G	38	Woodley Lewis	L.A.	267	Charlie Trippi	ChiC	11.4	Woodley Lewis	L.A.	32	Woodley Lewis	L.A.	830	Joe Arenas	S.F.	34.4	1953	NFL
1954	NFL	Chet Hanulak	Cle.	27	Veryl Switzer	G.B.	306	Veryl Switzer	G.B.	12.8	Woodley Lewis	L.A.	34	Woodley Lewis	L.A.	836	Billy Reynolds	Cle.	29.5	1954	NFL
1955	NFL	Bert Rechichar	Bal.	30	Ollie Matson	ChiC	245	Ollie Matson	ChiC	18.8	Sid Watson	Pit.	27	Sid Watson	Pit.	716	Al Carmichael	G.B.	29.9	1955	NFL
1956	NFL	Carl Taseff	Bal.	27	Carl Taseff	Bal.	233	Kenny Konz	Cle.	14.4	Al Carmichael	G.B.	33	Al Carmichael	G.B.	927	Tom Wilson	L.A.	31.8	1956	NFL
1957	NFL	Tommy McDonald	Phi.	26	Bert Zagers	Was.	217	Bert Zagers	Was.	15.5	Al Carmichael	G.B.	31	Al Carmichael	G.B.	690	Jon Arnett	L.A.	28.0	1957	NFL
1958	NFL	Carl Taseff	Bal.	29	Jon Arnett	L.A.	223	Jon Arnett	L.A.	12.4	Jimmy Sears	ChiC	32	Jimmy Sears	ChiC	756	Ollie Matson	ChiC	35.5	1958	NFL
1959	NFL	Bill Stacy	ChiC	29	Bill Stacy	ChiC	281	Johnny Morris	ChiB	12.2	Lenny Lyles	S.F.	25	Lenny Lyles	S.F.	565	Abe Woodson	S.F.	29.4	1959	NFL

YEARLY LEADERS

RUSHING | POINTS | PUNTING AVERAGE | INTERCEPTIONS

YEAR	LGUE	ATTEMPTS			YARDS			AVERAGE YARDS			TOUCHDOWNS			POINTS			PUNTING AVERAGE			INTERCEPTIONS			YEAR	LGUE
1920	NFL.										Smith	Buf.	4	Bacon	Day.	32							1920	NFL
1921	NFL.										Pollard	Akr.	7	Oliphant	Buf.	47							1921	NFL
1922	NFL.										Conzelman	RI-Mil.	7	Gillo	Rac.	52							1922	NFL
1923	NFL.										Smythe	Can.	7	Driscoll	ChiC.	78							1923	NFL
1924	NFL.										Hamer	Fra.	12	J. Sternaman	ChiB.	75							1924	NFL
1925	NFL.										Latone	Pott.	7	Berry	Pott.	74							1925	NFL
1926	NFL.										Wentz	Pott.	10	Driscoll	ChiB.	86							1926	NFL
1927	NFL.										McBride	NY G	6	McBride	NY G	57							1927	NFL
1928	NFL										Lewellen	G.B.	6	Friedman	Det.	55							1928	NFL
											Friedman	Det.	6											
1929	NFL										Nevers	ChiC.	12	Nevers	ChiC.	85							1929	NFL
1930	NFL										Lewellen	G.B.	8	McBride	Bkn.	56							1930	NFL
1931	NFL										Clark	Port.	9	Blood	G.B.	84							1931	NFL
1932	NFL	Clark	Port.	149	Battles	Bos.	576	Nagurski	ChiB.	4.5	Nagurski	ChiB.	4	Clark	Port.	55							1932	NFL
1933	NFL	Musick	Bos.	173	Musick	Bos.	809	Richards	NYG	6.2	Presnell	Det.	6	Presnell	Det.	63							1933	NFL
1934	NFL	Hanson	Phi.	147	Feathers	ChiB.	1004	Feathers	ChiB.	9.9	Clark	Det.	8	Clark	Det.	74							1934	NFL
											Feathers	ChiB.	8											
1935	NFL	Richards	NY G.	149	Russell	ChiC.	499	Caddel	Det.	5.2	Caddel	Det.	6	Clark	Det.	55							1935	NFL
1936	NFL	Leemans	NY G.	206	Leemans	NY G.	830	Caddel	Det.	6.4	Clark	Det.	7	Clark	Det.	73							1936	NFL
1937	NFL	Battles	Was.	216	Battles	Was.	874	Caddel	Det.	5.6	Battles	Was.	5	Manders	Chi B	69							1937	NFL
											Clark	Det.	5											
											Hinkle	G.B.	5											
1938	NFL	White	Pit.	152	White	Pit.	567	Isbell	G.B.	5.2	Farkas	Was.	6	Hinkle	G.B.	58							1938	NFL
1939	NFL	Farkas	Was.	139	Osmanski	ChiB.	699	Maniaci	ChiB.	7.1	Drake	Cle.	9	Farkas	Was.	68	Faust	Chi C	44				1939	NFL
																	Sid Luckman	Chi B	44					
1940	NFL	White	Det.	146	White	Det.	514	McFadden	Bkn.	6.3	Drake	Cle.	9	Hutson	G.B.	57	Baugh	Was.	51.3	Hutson	G.B.	6	1940	NFL
																				Parker	Bkn.	6		
																				Ryan	Det.	6		
1941	NFL	Hinkle	G.B.	129	Manders	Bkn.	486	McAfee	ChiB.	7.3	Gallarneau	ChiB.	8	Hutson	G.B.	95	Baugh	Was.	48.7	Goldberg	ChiC	7	1941	NFL
																				Jones	Pit.	7		
1942	NFL	Dudley	Pit.	162	Dudley	Pit.	696	Maznicki	ChiB.	6.4	Famiglietti	ChiB.	8	Hutson	G.B.	138	Baugh	Was.	46.6	Turner	Chi B	8	1942	NFL
1943	NFL	Paschal	NY G.	147	Paschal	NY G.	572	Cuff	NY G.	6.5	Paschal	NY G.	10	Hutson	G.B.	117	Baugh	Was.	45.9	Baugh	Was.	11	1943	NFL
1944	NFL	Paschal	NY G.	196	Paschal	NY G.	737	Grygo	ChiB.	6.1	Paschal	NY G.	9	Hutson	G.B.	85	Johnson	Bkn.	42.6	Livingston	NY G	9	1944	NFL
1945	NFL	Akins	Was.	147	Van Buren	Phi.	832	Gehrke	Cle.	6.3	Van Buren	Phi.	15	Van Buren	Phi.	110	Baugh	Was.	43.3	Zimmerman	Phi.	7	1945	NFL
1946	NFL	Dudley	Pit.	146	Dudley	Pit.	604	Angsman	ChiC.	6.8	Fritsch	G.B.	9	Fritsch	G.B.	100	Cifers	Det.	45.6	Dudley	Pit.	10	1946	NFL
1946	AAFC	Sanders	N.Y.	140	Sanders	N.Y.	709	Fenenbock	L.A.	8.4	Eshmont	S.F.	6	Groza	Cle.	84	Dobbs	Bkn.	47.8	Colella	Cle.	10	1946	AAFC
											Greenwood	Cle.	6											
											Kimbrough	L.A.	6											
											Sanders	N.Y.	6											
1947	NFL	Van Buren	Phi.	217	Van Buren	Phi.	1008	Washington	L.A.	7.4	Van Buren	Phi.	13	Harder	Chi C	102	Gulyanics	Chi B	44.8	Reegan	NY G	10	1947	NFL
																				Seno	Bos.	10		
1947	AAFC	Sanders	N.Y.	231	Sanders	N.Y.	1432	Jones	Cle.	7.0	Sanders	N.Y.	18	Sanders	N.Y.	114	Reinhard	L.A.	45.7	Collella	Cle.	6	1947	AAFC
																				Eshmont	S.F.	6		
																				Killagher	Chi.	6		
1948	NFL	Van Buren	Phi.	201	Van Buren	Phi.	945	Trippi	ChiC.	5.4	Van Buren	Phi.	10	Harder	Chi C	110	Muha	Phi.	47.2	Sandifer	Was.	13	1948	NFL
1948	AAFC	Sanders	N.Y.	169	Motley	Cle.	964	Perry	S.F.	7.3	Mutryn	Buf.	10	Mutryn	Buf.	96	Dobbs	L.A.	49.1	Schnellbacher	N.Y.	11	1948	AAFC
											Perry	S.F.	10											
1949	NFL	Van Buren	Phi.	263	Van Buren	Phi.	1146	Pritchard	Phi.	6.0	Van Buren	Phi.	11	Harder	Chi C	102	Gulyanics	Chi B	47.2	Nussbaumer	Chi C	12	1949	NFL
														Roberts	NY G	102								
1949	AAFC	Hoernschemeyer	Chi.	133	Perry	S.F.	783	Albert	S.F.	7.1	Motley	Cle.	8	Beals	S.F.	73	Albert	S.F.	48.2	Cason	S.F.	9	1949	AAFC
											Perry	S.F.	8											
1950	NFL	Geri	Pit.	188	Motley	Cle.	810	Lujack	ChiB.	6.3	Lujack	ChiB.	11	Walker	Det.	128	Morrison	Chi B	43.3	Sanders	NY Y	13	1950	NFL
		Van Buren	Phi.	188																				
1951	NFL	Price	NY G.	271	Price	NY G.	971	Rote	G.B.	6.9	Goode	Was.	9	Hirsch	L.A.	102	Gillom	Cle.	45.5	Schnellbacher	NY G	11	1951	NFL
1952	NFL	Price	NY G.	183	Towler	L.A.	894	McElhenny	S.F.	7.0	Towler	L.A.	10	Soltau	S.F.	94	Gillom	Cle.	45.7	Lane	L.A.	14	1952	NFL
1953	NFL	Perry	S.F.	192	Perry	S.F.	1018	Quinlan	L.A.	7.3	Perry	S.F.	10	Soltau	S.F.	114	Brady	Pit.	46.9	Christiansen	Det.	12	1953	NFL
1954	NFL	Perry	S.F.	173	Perry	S.F.	1049	McElhenny	S.F.	8.0	Towler	L.A.	11	Walston	Phi.	114	Brady	Pit.	43.2	Lane	Chi C	10	1954	NFL
1955	NFL	Ameche	Bal.	213	Ameche	Bal.	961	Casares	ChiB.	5.4	Ameche	Bal.	9	Walker	Det.	96	Van Brocklin	L.A.	44.6	Sherman	L.A.	11	1955	NFL
1956	NFL	Casares	ChiB.	234	Casares	ChiB.	1126	Moore	Bal.	7.5	Casares	ChiB.	12	Layne	Det.	99	Van Brocklin	L.A.	43.1	Crow	Chi C	11	1956	NFL
1957	NFL	Casares	ChiB.	204	Brown	Cle.	942	Moore	Bal.	5.0	Brown	Cle.	9	Baker	Was.	77	Chandler	NY G	44.6	Butler	Pit.	10	1957	NFL
																				Christiansen	Det.	10		
																				Davis	Bal.	10		
1958	NFL	Brown	Cle.	257	Brown	Cle.	1527	Moore	Bal.	7.3	Brown	Cle.	17	Brown	Cle.	108	Baker	Was.	45.4	Patton	NY G	11	1958	NFL
1959	NFL	Brown	Cle.	290	Brown	Cle.	1329	Olszewski	Was.	6.6	Brown	Cle.	14	Hornung	G.B.	94	Lary	Det.	47.1	Davis	Bal.	7	1959	NFL
																				Derby	Pit.	7		
																				Shinnick	Bal.	7		

YEARLY LEADERS

Year	Lgue	Receiving: Receptions	Receiving: Yards	Receiving: Average Yards	Receiving: Touchdowns	Field Goals: Made	Field Goals: Percentage	PATs: Made	Year	Lgue
1920	NFL				Sacksteder Day. 3	D. Sternaman Dec. 3		Copley Akr. 12	1920	NFL
						Thorpe Can. 3		Kinderdine Day. 12		
1921	NFL				Halas Chi B 3	D. Sternaman Chi B 5		Oliphant Buf. 26	1921	NFL
						Oliphant Buf. 5				
1922	NFL				Annan Tol. 2	Driscoll Chi C 8		Hathaway Day.&Can. 9	1922	NFL
					Bierce Akr. 2					
					Mathys G.B. 2					
					Driscoll Chi C 2					
1923	NFL				Rapp Col. 3	Driscoll Chi C 10		Henry Can. 25	1923	NFL
1924	NFL				Rapp Col. 5	J. Sternaman Chi B 9		Welsh Fra. 17	1924	NFL
					Voss G.B. 5					
1925	NFL				Berry Pott. 4	Driscoll Chi C 11		Berry Pott. 29	1925	NFL
					Norton G.B. 4					
1926	NFL				Hanny Chi B 4	Driscoll Chi B 12		McBride NY G 15	1926	NFL
								Welsh Pott. 15		
1927	NFL				Flaherty NY Y 4	Mercer Fra. 5		McBride NY G 15	1927	NFL
					Haines NY G 4					
1928	NFL				Welch NY Y 6	O'Boyle G.B. 3		Friedman Det. 19	1928	NFL
1929	NFL				Flaherty NY G 8	Weimer Buf. 3		Friedman NY G 20	1929	NFL
1930	NFL				Blood G.B. 5	Peters Prov.-Port. 2		Dunn G.B. 14	1930	NFL
					Thomas Bkn. 5					
1931	NFL				Blood G.B. 9	Strong S.I. 2		Nevers Chi C 15	1931	NFL
								Dunn G.B. 15		
1932	NFL	Johnson Chi B 24			Flaherty NY G 5	Clark Port. 3		Clark Port. 10	1932	NFL
								Engerbretsen Chi B 10		
1933	NFL	Kelly Bkn. 22	Moss Pit. 383	Karr Chi B 23.0	Burnett NY G 4	Manders Chi B 5		Manders Chi B 14	1933	NFL
						Pressnell Det. 5		Strong NY G 14		
						Strong NY G 5				
1934	NFL	Badgro NY G 16	Ebding Det. 257	Ebding Det. 28.6	Hewitt Chi B 5	Manders Chi B 10		Manders Chi B 29	1934	NFL
		Carter Phi. 16								
1935	NFL	Goodwin NY G 26	Malone Bos. 433	Carter Phi. 23.6	Hutson G.B. 7	Niccolai Pit. 6		Clark Det. 16	1935	NFL
						Smith Chi C 6		Manders Chi B 16		
1936	NFL	Hutson G.B. 34	Hutson G.B. 526	Hewitt Chi B 23.9	Hutson G.B. 8	Manders Chi B 7		Clark Det. 19	1936	NFL
						Niccolai Pit. 7				
1937	NFL	Hutson G.B. 41	Tinsley Chi C 675	Barrett Bkn. 23.1	Hutson G.B. 7	Manders Chi B 8		Smith Was. 22	1937	NFL
1938	NFL	Tinsley Chi C 41	Hutson G.B. 548	Benton Cle. 19.9	Hutson G.B. 9	Cuff NY G 5	Monahan Det. 80	Cuff NY G 18	1938	NFL
						Kercheval Bkn. 5				
1939	NFL	Hutson G.B. 34	Hutson G.B. 846	Farkas Was. 27.3	Benton Cle. 7	Cuff NY G 7	Hanneman Det. 80	Engrebretsen G.B. 18	1939	NFL
1940	NFL	Looney Phi. 58	Looney Phi. 707	McDounough Cle. 26.3	Hutson G.B. 7	Hinkle G.B. 9	Hinkle G.B. 64	Parker Bkn. 19	1940	NFL
1941	NFL	Hutson G.B. 58	Hutson G.B. 738	Kavenaugh Chi B 28.5	Hutson G.B. 10	Hinkle G.B. 6	Marefos NY G 80	Hutson G.B. 20	1941	NFL
								Snyder Chi B 20		
1942	NFL	Hutson G.B. 74	Hutson G.B. 1211	McLean Chi B 30.1	Hutson G.B. 17	Daddio Chi C 5	Fritsch G.B. 80	Hutson G.B. 33	1942	NFL
							Maznicki Chi B 80			
1943	NFL	Hutson G.B. 47	Hutson G.B. 776	Bova P–P 24.6	Hutson G.B. 11	Cuff NY G 3	Hutson G.B. 60	Snyder Chi B 39	1943	NFL
						Hutson G.B. 3				
1944	NFL	Hutson G.B. 58	Hutson G.B. 866	Bleeker Phi. 37.4	Hutson G.B. 9	Strong NY G 6	Strong NY G 50	Gudauskas Chi B 36	1944	NFL
1945	NFL	Hutson G.B. 47	Benton Cle. 1067	Liebel NY G 27.0	Liebel NY G 10	Aguirre Was. 7	Agajanian Phi. + Pit. 100	Hutson G.B. 31	1945	NFL
								Waterfield Cle. 31		
1946	NFL	Benton L.A. 63	Benton L.A. 981	Dewell Chi C 23.8	Dewell Chi C 7	Fritsch G.B. 9	Waterfield L.A. 67	Waterfield L.A. 37	1946	NFL
1946	AAFC	Beals S.F. 40	Lavelli Cle. 843	McCarthy Bkn. 26.9	Beals S.F. 10	Groza Cle. 13	Nemeth Chi. 75	Groza Cle. 45	1946	AAFC
		Lavelli Cle. 40								
1947	NFL	Keane Chi B 64	Kutner Chi C 944	Currivan Bos. 32.6	Kavanaugh Chi B 13	Cuff G.B. 7	Harder Chi C 70	McLean Chi B 44	1947	NFL
						Harder Chi C 7				
						Waterfield L.A. 7				
1947	AAFC	Speedie Cle. 67	Speedie Cle. 1146	Hirsch Chi. 28.2	Beals S.F. 10	Agajanian L.A. 15	Johnson N.Y. 88	Johnson N.Y. 49	1947	AAFC
1948	NFL	Fears L.A. 51	Kutner Chi.C 943	Seno Bos. 24.8	Kutner Chi C 14	Patton Phi. 8	Poillon Was. 71	Harder Chi C 53	1948	NFL
1948	AAFC	Speedie Cle. 58	Hillenbrand Bal. 970	North Bal. 26.0	Beals S.F. 14	Grossman Bal. 10	Vetrano S.F. 63	Vetrano S.F. 62	1948	AAFC
1949	NFL	Fears L.A. 77	Mann Det. 1014	Nickel Pit. 24.3	Fears L.A. 9	Patton Phi. 9	Yablonski Chi C 83	Harder Chi C 45	1949	NFL
					Kavanaugh Chi B 9	Waterfield L.A. 9				
					Taylor Was. 9					
1949	AAFC	Speedie Cle. 62	Speedie Cle. 1028	Boedecker Cle. 33.7	Beals S.F. 12	Johnson N.Y. 7	Grossman Bal. 55	Vetrano S.F. 56	1949	AAFC
1950	NFL	Fears L.A. 84	Fears L.A. 1116	Taylor Was. 21.4	Shaw Chi C 12	Groza Cle. 13	Groza Cle. 68	Waterfield L.A. 54	1950	NFL
1951	NFL	Hirsch L.A. 66	Hirsch L.A. 1495	Hirsch L.A. 22.7	Hirsch L.A. 17	Waterfield L.A. 13	Dudley Was. 77	Groza Cle. 43	1951	NFL
								Walker Det. 43		
1952	NFL	Speedie Cle. 62	Howton G.B. 1231	Taylor Was. 23.4	Box Det. 15	Groza Cle. 19	Waterfield L.A. 61	Waterfield L.A. 44	1952	NFL
1953	NFL	Pihos Phi. 63	Pihos Phi. 1049	Boyd L.A. 22.8	Pihos Phi. 10	Groza Cle. 23	Groza Cle. 88	Soltau S.F. 48	1953	NFL
					Wilson S.F. 10					
1954	NFL	Pihos Phi. 60	Boyd L.A. 1212	Hill Chi B 25.0	Hill Chi B 12	Groza Cle. 16	Groza Cle. 67	Walker Det. 43	1954	NFL
		Wilson S.F. 60								
1955	NFL	Pihos Phi. 62	Pihos Phi. 864	Renfro Cle. 20.8	Hill Chi B 9	Cone G.B. 16	Cone G.B. 67	Groza Cle. 44	1955	NFL
1956	NFL	Wilson S.F. 60	Howton G.B. 1188	Hill Chi B 24.0	Howton G.B. 12	Baker Was. 17	Layne Det. 80	Blanda Chi B 45	1956	NFL
1957	NFL	Wilson S.F. 52	Berry Bal. 800	Renfro Cle. 28.0	Mutscheller Bal. 8	Groza Cle. 15	Walston Phi. 75	Cothren L.A. 38	1957	NFL
1958	NFL	Berry Bal. 56	Shofner L.A. 1097	Orr Pit. 27.6	Berry Bal. 9	Cothren L.A. 14	Cothren L.A. 56	Myhra Bal. 48	1958	NFL
		Retzlaff Phi. 56			McDonald Phi. 9	Miner Pit. 14				
1959	NFL	Berry Bal. 66	Berry Bal. 959	McGee G.B. 23.2	Berry Bal. 14	Summerall NY G 20	Summerall NY G 69	Myhra Bal. 50	1959	NFL

SINGLE SEASON LEADERS

PASSING

COMPLETIONS
(150)

1	Sammy Baugh	1947	210
2	Norm Van Brocklin	1958	198
3	Johnny Unitas	1959	193
4	Norm Van Brocklin	1959	191
5	Sammy Baugh	1948	185
	Glenn Dobbs	1948	185
7	Otto Graham	1952	181
	Billy Sade	1958	181
9	Tobin Rote	1954	180
10	Sid Luckman	1947	176
	Y. A. Tittle	1957	176
12	Otto Graham	1948	173
13	Johnny Unitas	1957	172
14	Y. A. Tittle	1954	170
15	George Blanda	1953	169
16	Bud Schwenk	1947	168
	George Ratterman	1948	168
18	Otto Graham	1953	167
19	Jim Finks	1955	165
20	Jim Finks	1954	164
21	Otto Graham	1947	163
22	Chuck Conerly	1948	162
	Johnny Lujack	1949	162
	Bobby Thomason	1953	162
25	Y. A. Tittle	1948	161
	Otto Graham	1949	161
	Y. A. Tittle	1950	161
28	Jim Finks	1952	158
29	Tobin Rote	1955	157
30	Norm Van Brocklin	1953	156
	Milt Plum	1959	156
32	Bobby Layne	1949	155
	Frankie Albert	1950	155
34	Frankie Albert	1948	154
	Bob Waterfield	1949	154
36	Billy Wade	1959	153
37	Chuck Conerly	1959	152
	Bobby Layne	1950	152
	Bobby Layne	1951	152

COMPLETION PERCENTAGE
(55%) (Minimum 100 attempts)

			Att.	Comp.	Pct.
1	Sammy Baugh	1945	182	128	70.3
2	Otto Graham	1953	258	167	64.7
3	Y. A. Tittle	1957	279	176	63.1
4	Sammy Baugh	1940	177	111	62.7
5	Otto Graham	1947	269	163	60.6
6	John Brodie	1958	172	103	59.9
7	Sammy Baugh	1947	354	210	59.3
8	Eddie LeBaron	1957	167	99	59.3
9	Otto Graham	1954	240	142	59.2
10	Sammy Baugh	1948	315	185	58.7
11	Sammy Baugh	1942	225	132	58.7
12	Milt Plum	1959	266	156	58.6
13	Billy Wade	1959	261	153	58.6
14	Frankie Albert	1948	264	154	58.3
15	Chuck Conerly	1959	194	113	58.2
16	George Ratterman	1949	252	146	57.9
17	Y. A. Tittle	1958	208	120	57.7
18	Y. A. Tittle	1954	295	170	57.6
19	Y. A. Tittle	1953	259	149	57.5
20	Charlie O'Rourke	1946	182	105	57.7
21	Tommy Thompson	1948	246	141	57.3
22	Bob Waterfield	1957	213	122	57.3
23	Tom O'Connell	1958	110	63	57.3
24	Sid Luckman	1941	119	68	57.1
25	Frankie Filchock	1944	147	84	57.1
26	Ed Brown	1956	168	96	57.1
27	Johnny Unitas	1957	301	172	57.1
28	Sammy Baugh	1949	255	145	56.9
29	Cecil Isbell	1941	206	117	56.8
30	Bobby Thomason	1951	221	125	56.6
31	Otto Graham	1949	285	161	56.5
32	Norm Van Brocklin	1959	340	191	56.2
33	Sammy Baugh	1944	144	82	56.2
34	Tom Dublinski	1954	138	77	55.8
35	Y. A. Tittle	1948	289	161	55.7
36	Sammy Baugh	1943	239	133	55.6
37	Johnny Unitas	1956	198	110	55.6
38	Otto Graham	1951	265	147	55.5
39	Tommy Thompson	1946	103	57	55.3
40	Y. A. Tittle	1951	114	63	55.3
41	Chuck Conerly	1957	232	128	55.2
42	Norm Van Brocklin	1952	205	113	55.1
43	Frankie Albert	1952	129	71	55.0

YARDS
(2000)

1	Sammy Baugh	1947	2938
2	Johnny Unitas	1959	2899
3	Billy Wade	1958	2875
4	Otto Graham	1952	2816
5	Otto Graham	1949	2785
6	Otto Graham	1947	2753
7	Otto Graham	1953	2722
8	Otto Graham	1948	2713
9	Sid Luckman	1947	2712
10	Johnny Lujack	1949	2658
11	Norm Van Brocklin	1954	2637
12	Norm Van Brocklin	1959	2617
13	Sammy Baugh	1948	2599
14	George Ratterman	1948	2577
15	Johnny Unitas	1957	2550
16	Y. A. Tittle	1948	2522
17	Bobby Layne	1958	2510
18	Bobby Thomason	1953	2462
19	Norm Van Brocklin	1958	2409
20	Glenn Dobbs	1948	2403
	Bobby Layne	1951	2403
22	Norm Van Brocklin	1953	2393
23	Bobby Layne	1950	2323
24	Tobin Rote	1954	2311
25	Jim Finks	1953	2307
26	Jim Finks	1955	2270
27	George Ratterman	1950	2251
28	Bud Schwenk	1947	2236
29	Y. A. Tittle	1949	2209
30	Otto Graham	1951	2205
	Y. A. Tittle	1954	2205
32	Tobin Rote	1956	2203
33	Sid Luckman	1943	2194
34	Paul Christman	1947	2191
35	Y. A. Tittle	1955	2185
36	Chuck Conerly	1948	2175
37	Bob Waterfield	1949	2168
38	George Blanda	1953	2164
39	Y. A. Tittle	1957	2157
40	Chuck Conerly	1949	2138
41	Y. A. Tittle	1953	2121
42	Norm Van Brocklin	1957	2105
43	Otto Graham	1954	2092
44	Bobby Layne	1953	2088
45	Norm Van Brocklin	1950	2061
46	Cecil Isbell	1942	2021
47	Johnny Unitas	1958	2007
48	Jim Finks	1954	2003
49	Billy Wade	1959	2001

YARDS PER ATTEMPT (8.5)
(Minimum 100 Attempts)

			Att.	Yards	Y/A
1	Tom O'Connell	1957	110	1229	11.2
2	Sid Luckman	1943	202	2194	10.9
3	Otto Graham	1953	258	2722	10.6
4	Otto Graham	1946	174	1834	10.5
5	Otto Graham	1947	269	2753	10.2
6	Norm Van Brocklin	1954	260	2637	10.1
7	Sid Luckman	1941	119	1181	9.9
8	Ed Brown	1956	168	1667	9.9
9	Otto Graham	1949	285	2785	9.8
10	Sid Luckman	1942	105	1023	9.7
11	Eddie LeBaron	1958	145	1365	9.4
12	Bob Waterfield	1945	171	1609	9.4
13	Otto Graham	1955	185	1721	9.3
14	Sammy Baugh	1945	182	1669	9.2
15	Eddie LeBaron	1957	167	1508	9.0
16	Clyde LeForce	1948	101	912	9.0
17	Sid Luckman	1940	105	941	9.0
18	Bob Waterfield	1951	176	1566	8.9
19	Norm Van Brocklin	1951	194	1725	8.9
20	Norm Van Brocklin	1950	233	2061	8.9
21	Chuck Conerly	1959	194	1706	8.8
22	Benny Friedman	1930*	105	922	8.8
23	Y. A. Tittle	1948	289	2522	8.7
24	Otto Graham	1954	240	2092	8.7
25	Milt Plum	1958	189	1619	8.6
26	Bobby Layne	1958	294	2510	8.5
27	Jess Freitas	1948	167	1425	8.5

TOUCHDOWN PASSES
(20)

1	Johnny Unitas	1959	32
2	Frankie Albert	1948	29
3	Sid Luckman	1943	28
4	Frankie Albert	1949	27
5	Bobby Layne	1951	26
6	Sammy Baugh	1947	25
	Otto Graham	1947	25
	Otto Graham	1948	25
	Tommy Thompson	1948	25
10	Cecil Isbell	1942	24
	Sid Luckman	1947	24
	Johnny Unitas	1957	24
13	Sammy Baugh	1943	23
	Johnny Lujack	1949	23
	Adrian Burk	1954	23
16	George Ratterman	1947	22
	Sammy Baugh	1948	22
	Chuck Conerly	1948	22
	George Ratterman	1950	22
20	Glenn Dobbs	1948	21
	Bobby Thomason	1953	21
22	Benny Friedman	1929	20
	Jim Finks	1952	20
	Otto Graham	1952	20
	Y. A. Tittle	1953	20
	Norm Van Brocklin	1957	20
	Bobby Layne	1959	20

LOWEST PASS INTERCEPTION PERCENTAGE
(3.85) (Minimum 100 Attempts)

			Att.	Int.	Pct.
1	Chuck Conerly	1959	194	4	2.06
2	Sammy Baugh	1945	182	4	2.20
3	Ace Parker	1946	115	3	2.61
4	Johnny Unitas	1958	263	7	2.66
5	Dwight Sloan	1939	107	3	2.80
6	Otto Graham	1946	174	5	2.87
7	Milt Plum	1959	266	8	3.01
8	Y. A. Tittle	1954	295	9	3.05
9	Y. A. Tittle	1948	289	9	3.11
10	Harry Gilmer	1955	122	4	3.28
11	Jim Hardy	1948	211	7	3.32
12	Otto Graham	1953	258	9	3.49
13	Paul Christman	1948	114	4	3.51
14	Otto Graham	1949	285	10	3;51
15	Fred Enke	1949	142	5	3.52
16	Ed Danowski	1937	134	5	3.73
17	Frankie Albert	1948	260	16	3.79
18	Johnny Unitas	1959	367	14	3.81

* Incomplete

SINGLE SEASON LEADERS
RUSHING

ATTEMPTS
(175)

1	Jimmy Brown	1959	290
2	Eddie Price	1951	271
3	Steve Van Buren	1949	263
4	Jimmy Brown	1958	257
5	Rick Casares	1956	234
6	Spec Sanders	1947	231
7	Barney Wentz	1926	220
8	Steve Van Buren	1947	217
9	Cliff Battles	1937	216
10	Alan Ameche	1955	213
11	Tony Canadeo	1949	208
	Rob Goode	1951	208
13	J.D. Smith	1959	207
14	Tuffy Leemans	1936	206
15	Rick Casares	1957	204
16	Jimmy Brown	1957	202
17	Tom Tracy	1959	199
18	Bill Paschal	1944	196
19	Joe Perry	1953	192
	Howie Ferguson	1955	192
	Ollie Matson	1956	192
22	Ace Gutowsky	1936	191
23	Joe Geri	1950	188
	Steve Van Buren	1950	188
	Preston Carpenter	1956	188
26	John Griggs	1944	185
	Ed Modzelewski	1955	185
	Hugh McElhenny	1956	185
29	Eddie Price	1952	183
30	Billy Barnes	1959	181
31	Alex Webster	1956	178
	Alan Ameche	1956	178
33	Cliff Battles	1936	176
	Rick Casares	1958	176

YARDS
(800)

1	Jimmy Brown	1958	1527
2	Spec Sanders	1947	1432
3	Jimmy Brown	1959	1329
4	Steve Van Buren	1949	1146
5	Rick Casares	1956	1126
6	Tony Canadeo	1949	1052
7	Joe Perry	1954	1049
8	J.D. Smith	1959	1036
9	Joe Perry	1953	1018
10	Steve Van Buren	1947	1008
11	Beattie Feathers	1934	1004
12	Eddie Price	1951	971
13	Marion Motley	1948	964
14	Alan Ameche	1955	961
15	Rob Goode	1951	951
16	Jimmy Brown	1957	942
17	Ollie Matson	1956	924
18	Hugh McElhenny	1956	916
19	Johnny Stryzkalski	1948	915
20	Johnny Stryzkalski	1947	906
21	Dan Towler	1952	894
22	Marion Motley	1947	889
23	Dan Towler	1953	879
24	Cliff Battles	1937	874
25	Chet Mutryn	1947	868
26	Ollie Matson	1949	863
27	Howie Ferguson	1955	859
28	Alan Ameche	1956	858
29	Dan Towler	1951	854
30	Steve Van Buren	1945	832
31	Tuffy Leemans	1936	830
32	Ace Gutowsky	1936	827
33	Chet Mutryn	1948	823
34	Frank Gifford	1956	819
35	Marion Motley	1950	810
36	Jim Musick	1933	809
37	Swede Hanson	1934	805

AVERAGE YARDS (5.5)
(Minimum 75 Attempts)

			Att.	Yards	Avg.
1	Beattie Feathers	1934	101	1004	9.94
2	Lenny Moore	1956	86	649	7.55
3	Joe Perry	1948	77	562	7.30
4	Lenny Moore	1958	82	598	7.29
5	Skeets Quinlan	1953	97	705	7.27
6	Joe Maniaci	1939	77	544	7.07
7	Hugh McElhenny	1952	98	684	6.98
8	Tobin Rote	1951	76	523	6.88
9	Joe Perry	1949	115	783	6.81
10	Dan Towler	1951	126	854	6.78
11	Tank Younger	1954	91	610	6.70
12	Ron Waller	1956	83	543	6.54
13	Ward Cuff	1943	80	523	6.54
14	Buddy Young	1949	76	495	6.51
15	Johnny Stryzkalski	1948	141	915	6.49
16	Charlie Trippi	1951	78	501	6.42
17	Ernie Caddel	1936	91	580	6.37
18	Johnny Stryzkalski	1947	143	906	6.34
19	Dutch Clark	1934	122	763	6.25
20	Bobby Mitchell	1958	80	500	6.25
21	Vic Kulbitski	1946	97	605	6.24
22	Chet Mutryn	1947	140	868	6.20
23	Spec Sanders	1947	231	1432	6.20
24	Marion Motley	1948	157	964	6.14
25	Buddy Young	1947	116	712	6.14
26	Pete Layden	1948	95	576	6.09
27	Marion Motley	1947	146	889	6.09
28	Joe Perry	1958	125	758	6.06
29	Joe Perry	1954	173	1049	6.06
30	Dick Hoerner	1951	94	569	6.05
31	Bosh Pritchard	1949	84	506	6.02
32	Skeets Quinlan	1954	82	490	5.98
33	Jimmy Brown	1958	257	1527	5.94
34	Nick Pietrosante	1959	78	477	5.88
35	Steve Van Buren	1945	143	832	5.82
36	Marion Motley	1950	140	810	5.79
37	Dan Towler	1953	152	879	5.78
38	Bill Osmanski	1939	121	699	5.78
39	Gene Ronzani	1934	84	485	5.77
40	Dan Towler	1952	156	894	5.73
41	Billy Grimes	1950	84	480	5.71
42	Bobby Mitchell	1959	131	743	5.67
43	Ernie Caddel	1937	76	429	5.64
44	Bob Hoernschemeyer	1950	84	471	5.61
45	Chet Mutryn	1948	147	823	5.60
46	Glenn Dobbs	1948	91	539	5.59
47	Eddie Price	1950	126	703	5.58
48	Steve Van Buren	1944	80	444	5.55

TOUCHDOWNS (8)

1	Spec Sanders	1947	18
2	Jimmy Brown	1958	17
3	Steve Van Buren	1945	15
4	Jimmy Brown	1959	14
5	Steve Van Buren	1947	13
6	Tex Hamer	1924	12
	Ernie Nevers	1929	12
	Rick Casares	1956	12
9	Steve Van Buren	1949	11
	Johnny Lujack	1950	11
	Dan Towler	1954	11
	Tobin Rote	1956	11
13	Barney Wentz	1926	10
	Bill Paschal	1943	10
	Chet Mutryn	1948	10
	Joe Perry	1948	10
	Steve Van Buren	1948	10
	Dick Hoerner	1950	10
	Dan Towler	1952	10
	Joe Perry	1953	10
	Rick Casares	1959	10
	J.D. Smith	1959	10
23	Tony Latone	1929	9
	Dutch Clark	1931	9
	Johnny Drake	1939	9
	Johnny Drake	1940	9
	Bill Paschal	1944	9
	Ted Fritsch	1946	9
	Chet Mutryn	1947	9
	Mickey Colmer	1947	9
	Spec Sanders	1948	9
	Choo-Choo Roberts	1949	9
	Rob Goode	1951	9
	John Henry Johnson	1954	9
	Alan Ameche	1955	9
	Jimmy Brown	1957	9
	Tom Wilson	1959	9
38	Ernie Nevers	1926	8
	Tony Plansky	1929	8
	Vern Lewellen	1930	8
	Ernie Nevers	1931	8
	Dutch Clark	1934	8
	Beattie Feathers	1934	8
	Hugh Gallarneau	1941	8
	Gary Famiglietti	1942	8
	John Kimbrough	1947	8
	Steve Lach	1947	8
	Marion Motley	1947	8
	Norm Standlee	1947	8
	Elmer Angsman	1948	8
	Jerry Shipkey	1948	8
	Marion Motley	1949	8
	Joe Perry	1949	8
	Joe Perry	1952	8
	Tank Younger	1953	8
	Joe Perry	1954	8
	Tobin Rote	1954	8
	Tank Younger	1954	8
	Bobby Watkins	1955	8
	Alan Ameche	1956	8
	Hugh McElhenny	1956	8
	Lenny Moore	1956	8
	Alan Ameche	1958	8
	Willie Galimore	1958	8
	Frank Gifford	1958	8

SINGLE SEASON LEADERS

RECEIVING

RECEPTIONS (50)

1	Tom Fears	1950	84
2	Tom Fears	1949	77
3	Don Hutson	1942	74
4	Mac Speedie	1947	67
5	Bob Mann	1949	66
	Crazy Legs Hirsch	1951	66
	Ray Berry	1959	66
8	Jim Keane	1947	64
9	Jim Benton	1946	63
	Pete Pihos	1953	63
11	Mac Speedie	1949	62
	Mac Speedie	1952	62
	Elbie Nickel	1953	62
	Pete Pihos	1955	62
15	Crazy Legs Hirsch	1953	61
16	Pete Pihos	1954	60
	Billy Wilson	1954	60
	Billy Wilson	1956	60
19	Gordie Soltau	1951	59
20	Don Looney	1940	58
	Don Hutson	1941	58
	Don Hutson	1944	58
	Mac Speedie	1948	58
24	Bill Chipley	1949	57
	Fran Polsfoot	1951	57
26	Bud Grant	1952	56
	Don Stonesifer	1958	56
	Ray Berry	1958	56
	Pete Retzlaff	1958	56
30	Elbie Nickel	1952	55
	Gordie Soltau	1952	55
	Billy Howton	1956	55
33	Al Baldwin	1948	54
	Don Stonesifer	1952	54
35	Al Baldwin	1949	53
	Billy Howton	1952	53
	Jim Dooley	1953	53
	Bob Boyd	1954	53
	Billy Wilson	1955	53
40	Dan Edwards	1950	52
	Billy Howton	1954	52
	Billy Wilson	1957	52
43	Tom Fears	1948	51
	Billy Wilson	1953	51
	Frank Gifford	1956	51
	Del Shofner	1958	51
47	Billy Hillenbrand	1948	50
	Fay King	1948	50
	Cloyce Box	1950	50
	Paul Salata	1950	50
	Bob Mann	1951	50
	Lenny Moore	1958	50

YARDS (800)

1	Crazy Legs Hirsch	1951	1495
2	Billy Howton	1952	1231
3	Bob Boyd	1954	1212
4	Don Hutson	1942	1211
5	Billy Howton	1956	1188
6	Mac Speedie	1947	1146
7	Harlon Hill	1956	1128
8	Harlon Hill	1954	1124
9	Tom Fears	1950	1116
10	Del Shofner	1958	1097
11	Jim Benton	1945	1067
12	Pete Pihos	1953	1049
13	Mac Speedie	1949	1028
14	Bob Mann	1949	1014
15	Tom Fears	1949	1013
16	Cloyce Box	1950	1009
17	Bud Grant	1952	997
18	Jim Benton	1946	981
19	Bob Shaw	1950	971
20	Billy Hillenbrand	1948	970
21	Hugh Taylor	1952	961
22	Ray Berry	1959	959
23	Mal Kutner	1947	944
24	Mal Kutner	1948	943
25	Crazy Legs Hirsch	1953	941
26	Del Shofner	1959	936
27	Cloyce Box	1952	924
28	Al Baldwin	1948	916
29	Mac Speedie	1951	911
30	Jim Keane	1947	910
	Jimmy Orr	1958	910
32	Billy Wilson	1956	889
33	Elbie Nickel	1952	884
34	Pete Pihos	1954	872
35	Don Hutson	1944	866
36	Pete Pihos	1955	864
37	Don Hutson	1939	846
	Tommy McDonald	1959	846
	Lenny Moore	1959	846
40	Dante Lavelli	1946	843
41	Jim Dooley	1953	841
42	Billy Wilson	1953	840
43	Don Hutson	1945	834
44	Hugh Taylor	1950	833
45	Billy Wilson	1955	831
46	Billy Wilson	1954	830
47	Gordie Soltau	1951	826
48	Mac Speedie	1948	816
49	Dante Lavelli	1954	802
50	Ray Berry	1957	800

AVERAGE YARDS (20.0)
(Minimum 30 Receptions)

			Rec.	Yards	Avg.
1	Jimmy Orr	1958	33	910	27.6
2	Ken Kavanaugh	1947	32	818	25.6
3	Harlon Hill	1954	45	1124	25.0
4	Don Hutson	1939	34	846	24.9
5	Harlon Hill	1956	47	1128	24.0
6	Jim Benton	1945	45	1067	23.7
7	Hugh Taylor	1952	41	961	23.4
8	Billy Howton	1952	53	1231	23.2
9	Max McGee	1959	30	695	23.2
10	Mal Kutner	1948	41	943	23.0
11	Bob Boyd	1953	53	1212	22.9
12	Crazy Legs Hirsch	1951	66	1495	22.7
13	Cloyce Box	1952	42	924	22.0
14	Mal Kutner	1947	42	944	22.0
15	Ray Ramsey	1947	35	768	21.9
16	Billy Howton	1956	55	1188	21.6
17	Del Shofner	1958	51	1097	21.5
18	Hugh Taylor	1950	39	833	21.4
19	Dante Lavelli	1946	40	843	21.1
20	Bill Anderson	1959	35	734	21.0
21	Crazy Legs Hirsch	1954	35	720	20.6
22	Dorne Dibble	1951	30	613	20.4
23	Chet Mutryn	1948	39	794	20.4
24	Choo-Choo Roberts	1949	35	711	20.3
25	Bob Shaw	1950	48	971	20.2
26	Cloyce Box	1950	50	1009	20.2
27	Hugh Taylor	1953	35	703	20.1
28	Billy Stone	1949	31	621	20.0

TOUCHDOWNS (9)

1	Don Hutson	1942	17
	Crazy Legs Hirsch	1951	17
3	Cloyce Box	1952	15
4	Alyn Beals	1948	14
	Mal Kutner	1948	14
	Ray Berry	1959	14
7	Ken Kavanaugh	1947	13
	Billy Howton	1952	13
9	Alyn Beals	1949	12
	Bob Shaw	1950	12
	Leon Hart	1951	12
	Hugh Taylor	1952	12
	Harlon Hill	1954	12
	Billy Howton	1956	12
15	Johnny Blood	1931	11
	Pete Pihos	1948	11
	Cloyce Box	1950	11
	Bobby Walston	1954	11
	Harlon Hill	1956	11
20	Frank Liebel	1945	10
	Alyn Beals	1946	10
	Alyn Beals	1947	10
	Jim Keane	1947	10
	Pete Pihos	1953	10
	Billy Wilson	1953	10
	Pete Pihos	1954	10
	Tommy McDonald	1959	10
28	Don Hutson	1938	9
	Don Hutson	1944	9
	Don Hutson	1945	9
	Don Currivan	1947	9
	Joe Aguirre	1948	9
	Hugh Taylor	1949	9
	Tom Fears	1949	9
	Ken Kavanaugh	1949	9
	Hugh Taylor	1950	9
	Elbie Nickel	1952	9
	Max McGee	1954	9
	Harlon Hill	1955	9
	Ray Berry	1958	9
	Tommy McDonald	1958	9

POINTS

POINTS (70)

1	Don Hutson	1942	138
2	Doak Walker	1950	128
3	Don Hutson	1943	117
4	Spec Sanders	1947	114
	Gordie Soltau	1953	114
	Bobby Walston	1954	114
7	Steve Van Buren	1945	110
	Pat Harder	1948	110
9	Johnny Lujack	1950	109
10	Lou Groza	1953	108
	Jimmy Brown	1958	108
12	Doak Walker	1954	106
13	Pat Harder	1947	102
	Pat Harder	1949	102
	Choo-Choo Roberts	1949	102
	Crazy Legs Hirsch	1951	102
17	Ted Fritsch	1946	100
18	Bobby Layne	1956	99
19	Bob Waterfield	1951	98
20	Don Hutson	1945	97
	Doak Walker	1951	97
22	Chet Mutryn	1948	96
	Doak Walker	1955	96
24	Don Hutson	1941	95
25	Gordie Soltau	1952	94
	Paul Hornung	1959	94
27	Doak Walker	1953	93
28	Mal Kutner	1948	90
	Gordie Soltau	1951	90
	Cloyce Box	1952	90
	Pat Summerall	1959	90
32	Lou Groza	1952	89
33	Vic Janowicz	1955	88
34	Bobby Walston	1953	87
35	Paddy Driscoll	1926	86
36	Ernie Nevers	1929	85
	Don Hutson	1944	85
	Dick Poillon	1947	85
	Pat Harder	1952	85
	Lou Groza	1954	85
41	Johnny Blood	1931	84
	Lou Groza	1946	84
	Ben Agajanian	1947	84
	Steve Van Buren	1947	84
	Alyn Beals	1948	84
	Paige Cothren	1958	84
	Lenny Moore	1958	84
	Ray Berry	1959	84
	Jimmy Brown	1959	84
	Bobby Joe Conrad	1959	84
51	Joe Vetrano	1948	83
	Bob Waterfield	1952	83
53	Bobby Walston	1952	82
54	Bill Dudley	1949	81
	Bob Waterfield	1950	81
	George Blanda	1956	81
57	Jack Manders	1934	79
58	Paddy Driscoll	1923	78
	Ken Kavanaugh	1947	78
	Billy Hillenbrand	1948	78
	Fred Cone	1955	78
	Billy Howton	1952	78
63	Sam Baker	1957	77
	Lou Groza	1957	77
	Bobby Layne	1959	77
66	Bob Waterfield	1949	76
67	Joey Sternaman	1924	75
	Lou Groza	1948	75
69	Charlie Berry	1925	74
	Cliff Patton	1948	74
	Lou Groza	1950	74
	Fred Cone	1953	74
	Ben Agajanian	1954	74
	Fred Cone	1957	74
75	Dutch Clark	1934	73
	Dutch Clark	1936	73
	Chet Mutryn	1947	73
	Rex Grossman	1948	73
	Alyn Beals	1949	73
	Lou Groza	1951	73
81	Tex Hamer	1924	72
	George McAfee	1941	72
	Bill Paschal	1943	72
	Spec Sanders	1946	72
	Joe Perry	1948	72
	Steve Van Buren	1949	72
	Bob Shaw	1950	72
	Dub Jones	1951	72
	Leon Hart	1951	72
	Harlon Hill	1954	72
	Fred Cone	1956	72
	Willie Galimore	1958	72
	Rick Casares	1959	72
94	Paddy Driscoll	1923	71
	Ernie Nevers	1926	71
	Gordie Soltau	1956	71
	Paige Cothren	1957	71
	George Blanda	1957	71
99	Harvey Johnson	1947	70

SINGLE SEASON LEADERS
PUNT RETURNS

(30)

1	Charley Rogers	1927*	44
2	Charley Rogers	1928*	43
3	Jack Ernst*	1926	41
	Red Dunn	1929	41
5	Em Tunnell	1953	38
6	Red Dunn	1928	36
	Ken Strong	1931	36
8	Woodley Lewis	1953	35
9	Em Tunnell	1951	34
10	Bibbles Bawel	1952	34
11	Ken Strong	1930*	33
	George McAfee	1950	33
13	Em Tunnell	1950	31
	Two Bits Homan	1929*	31
15	Dutch Clark	1932	30
	George McAfee	1948	30
	Em Tunnell	1951	30
	Em Tunnell	1952	30
	Bert Rechichar	1955	30

YARDS
300

1	Charley Rogers	1927*	620
2	Billy Grimes	1950	555
3	Charley Rogers	1928*	528
4	Em Tunnell	1951	489
5	Jack Ernst	1926	453
6	Two Bits Homan	1929*	439
7	Walt Slater	1947	435
8	Ken Strong	1931	428
9	Vitamin Smith	1949	427
10	George McAfee	1948	417
11	Em Tunnell	1952	411
12	Glenn Presnell	1931	407
13	Red Dunn	1929	406
14	Ray Mathews	1952	397
15	Tom Harmon	1947	392
16	Ken Strong	1930*	389
17	Curly Oden	1926*	387
18	Bill Dudley	1946	385
19	Jack Ernst	1925*	370
20	Herm Wedemeyer	1948	368
21	Johnny Williams	1952	366
22	Curly Oden	1928*	365
23	Jim Cason	1949	351
	Woodley Lewis	1952	351

AVERAGE RETURN (15.0)
(Minimum 1 return per game)

			Ret	Yards	Avg.
1	Ernie Steele	1942	10	264	26.4
2	Herb Rich	1950	12	276	23.0
3	Jack Christiansen	1952	15	322	21.5
4	Rex Baumbardner	1948	16	336	21.0
5	Red Cochran	1949	15	314	20.9
6	Jerry Davis	1948	16	334	20.9
7	Frankie Sinkwich	1943	11	228	20.7
8	Buddy Young	1951	12	231	19.3
9	Paddy Driscoll	1921	8	154	19.3
10	Billy Grimes	1950	29	555	19.1
11	Jack Christiansen	1951	18	343	19.1
12	Ollie Matson	1955	13	245	18.9
13	Chuck Fenenbock	1946	16	269	18.7
14	Woodley Lewis	1952	19	351	18.5
15	Frank Seno	1947	12	213	17.8
16	Bill Reinhard	1948	16	276	17.3
17	Bob Livingstone	1949	17	292	17.2
18	Bob Seymour	1941	14	238	17.0
19	Sam Cathcart	1949	18	306	17.0
20	Curly Oden	1928*	17	288	16.9
21	Jim Cason	1949	21	351	16.7
22	Andy Tomasic	1942	12	199	16.6
23	Art Jones	1941	14	232	16.6
24	Ernie Steele	1944	11	181	16.5
25	Glen Presnell	1931	25	407	16.3
26	Herm Wedemeyer	1948	23	368	16.0
27	Roddy Lamb	1925*	18	286	15.9
28	Bob Gage	1949	16	254	15.9
29	Vitamin Smith	1949	27	427	15.8
30	Henry Clark	1943	10	158	15.8
31	Les Horvath	1948	13	203	15.6
32	Walt Slater	1947	28	435	15.5
33	Bert Zagers	1957	14	217	15.5
34	Merle Hapes	1942	11	170	15.5
35	Bill Dudley	1950	12	185	15.4
36	Ray Mathews	1951	15	231	15.4
37	Steve Van Buren	1944	15	230	15.3
38	Ray Mathews	1952	26	397	15.3
39	Johnny Williams	1952	24	366	15.3
40	Spec Sanders	1946	17	257	15.1

TOUCHDOWNS (2)

1	Jack Christiansen	1951	4
2	Em Tunnell	1951	3
3	Curly Oden	1926	2
	Shipwreck Kelly	1933	2
	Phil Sarboe	1935	2
	Charlie Trippi	1948	2
	Rex Baumgardner	1948	2
	Billy Grimes	1950	2
	Jack Christiansen	1952	2
	Woodley Lewis	1952	2
	Ray Mathews	1952	2
	Johnny Williams	1952	2
	Ollie Matson	1955	2
	Bert Zagers	1957	2

PUNTING

PUNTS (70)

1	Verne Lewellen	1928	136
2	Verne Lewellen	1926	116
3	Tex Hamer	1925*	100
4	Verne Lewellen	1927	99
5	Frank Kirkleski	1927*	97
6	Jesse Brown	1926	94
7	Wally Diehl	1928*	92
	Howie Maley	1947	92
9	Verne Lewellen	1925	91
10	Wally Diehl	1929*	89
	Verne Lewellen	1930*	89
12	Cub Buck	1923	88
13	Verne Lewellen	1929	85
14	Adrian Burk	1952	83
15	Cub Buck	1924	82
	Tom Landry	1952	82
17	Adrian Burk	1950	81
18	Glenn Dobbs	1946	80
	Pat Brady	1953	80
20	Wooky Roberts	1922*	77
21	Ken Strong	1931	76
	George Taliaferro	1951	76
23	Ken Strong	1929	75
	Tom Landry	1955	75
25	Joe Geri	1951	73
	Horace Gillom	1951	73
	Adrian Burk	1954	73
28	Arnie Herber	1932	72
	Charlie Conerly	1951	72
	Cotton Davidson	1954	72
	Max McGee	1954	72
32	Jug Girard	1950	71

PUNTING AVERAGE (43.0)
(Minimum 30 Punts)

1	Sammy Baugh	1940	51.3
2	Glenn Dobbs	1948	49.1
3	Sammy Baugh	1941	48.7
4	Frankie Albert	1949	48.2
5	Glenn Dobbs	1946	47.8
6	Joe Muha	1948	47.2
7	Yale Lary	1959	47.1
8	Pat Brady	1953	46.9
9	Sammy Baugh	1942	46.8
	Don Chandler	1959	46.6
11	Sammy Baugh	1943	45.9
12	Horace Gillom	1952	45.7
	Tommy Davis	1959	45.7
14	Bob Cifers	1946	45.6
15	Sam Baker	1959	45.5
16	Bob Reinhard	1946	45.4
	Horace Gillom	1951	45.4
	Sam Baker	1958	45.4
19	Sammy Baugh	1946	45.1
20	Jerry Norton	1959	44.9
21	Mickey Colmer	1947	44.7
	Ernie Lewis	1948	44.7
	Jim Smith	1952	44.7
24	Bob Waterfield	1946	44.6
	Horace Gillom	1947	44.6
	Norm Van Brocklin	1955	44.6
	Don Chandler	1957	44.6
28	Bob Waterfield	1949	44.4
29	Frankie Albert	1951	44.3
	Norm Van Brocklin	1957	44.3
31	George Gulyanics	1948	44.2
	Mike Boyda	1949	44.2
33	Tom Landry	1949	44.1
34	Frankie Albert	1947	44.0
	Don Chandler	1958	44.0
36	Horace Gillom	1953	43.8
37	Sammy Baugh	1947	43.7
38	Len Barnham	1941	43.6
	Bill Jessup	1957	43.6
40	Jack Jacobs	1947	43.5
	Joe Muha	1947	43.5

SINGLE SEASON LEADERS
KICKOFF RETURNS

(22)

1	Woodley Lewis	1954	34
2	Al Carmichael	1956	33
3	Woodley Lewis	1953	32
	Jimmy Sears	1958	32
5	Al Carmichael	1957	31
6	Herm Wedemeyer	1949	30
7	Eddie Saenz	1947	29
	Al Carmichael	1958	29
9	Don Paul	1950	28
10	Frank Seno	1947	27
	George Taliaferro	1951	27
	Les Goble	1954	27
	Sid Watson	1955	27
	Joe Arenas	1956	27
15	Don Sandifer	1948	26
	Billy Grimes	1950	26
	Al Carmichael	1953	26
	Gene Filipski	1957	26
	Woodley Lewis	1957	26
20	George Taliaferro	1950	25
	Scooter Scudero	1955	25
	Ron Drzewiecki	1955	25
	Lenny Lyles	1959	25
24	Bill Paschal	1948	24
	Eddie Saenz	1949	24
	Don Sandifer	1949	24
	Dale Atkeson	1954	24
	Joe Arenas	1955	24
	Joe Arenas	1957	24
	Tommy McDonald	1959	24
31	Bob Thurbon	1944	23
	Billy Grimes	1951	23
	Billy Baggett	1952	23
	Buddy Young	1952	23
	Dick James	1959	23
36	Spec Sanders	1947	22
	Walt Slater	1947	22
	Vitamin Smith	1950	22

YARDS (550)

1	Al Carmichael	1956	927
2	Woodley Lewis	1954	836
3	Woodley Lewis	1953	830
4	Joe Arenas	1956	801
5	Eddie Saenz	1947	797
6	Jimmy Sears	1958	756
7	Les Goble	1954	749
8	Vitamin Smith	1950	742
9	Sid Watson	1955	716
10	Al Carmichael	1958	700
11	Scooter Scudero	1955	699
12	Don Paul	1950	693
13	Chet Mutryn	1947	691
14	Al Carmichael	1957	690
15	Woodley Lewis	1957	682
16	Joe Arenas	1957	657
17	Buddy Young	1952	643
18	Al Carmichael	1953	641
19	Frank Seno	1947	636
20	Ollie Matson	1952	624
21	Dale Atkeson	1954	623
22	George Taliaferro	1951	622
23	Gene Filipski	1957	613
24	Lynn Chadnois	1953	610
25	Herm Wedemeyer	1949	602
26	Billy Grimes	1950	600
27	Sonny Karnofsky	1946	599
	Lynn Chadnois	1952	599
29	Don Sandifer	1948	594
	Joe Arenas	1955	594
31	Spec Sanders	1947	593
32	Ron Drzewiecki	1955	591
33	Billy Grimes	1951	582
34	Joe Scott	1948	569
35	Billy Baggett	1952	567
36	Monk Gafford	1947	565
	Lenny Lyles	1959	565
38	Monk Gafford	1948	559

AVERAGE RETURN (28.0)
(Minimum 1 return per game)

			Ret.	Yards	Avg.
1	Ollie Matson	1958	14	497	35.50
2	Lynn Chadnois	1952	17	599	35.24
3	Joe Arenas	1953	16	551	34.44
4	Vitamin Smith	1950	22	742	33.73
5	Chet Mutryn	1947	21	691	32.90
6	Lynn Chadnois	1951	12	390	32.70
7	Tom Wilson	1956	15	477	31.80
8	Jack Salschneider	1949	15	474	31.60
9	Frank Seno	1946	13	408	31.38
10	Ollie Matson	1952	20	624	31.20
11	Frank Minini	1948	12	370	30.83
12	Buddy Young	1951	14	427	30.50
13	Al Carmichael	1955	14	418	29.86
14	Joe Arenas	1956	27	801	29.67
15	Billy Reynolds	1954	14	413	29.50
16	Steve Van Buren	1947	13	382	29.38
	Abe Woodson	1959	13	382	29.38
18	Lynn Chadnois	1950	12	351	29.25
19	Jerry Davis	1948	15	437	29.13
20	Ray Ramsey	1949	14	407	29.07
21	Lynn Chadnois	1953	21	610	29.05
22	Steve Van Buren	1946	11	319	29.00
23	Eddie Saenz	1950	12	347	28.92
24	Steve Van Buren	1945	13	373	28.69
	Eddie Macon	1953	13	373	28.69
26	Chuck Hunsinger	1950	12	343	28.58
27	Bob White	1955	14	400	28.57
28	Sonny Karnofsky	1946	21	599	28.52
29	Don Paul	1951	15	424	28.27
30	Chuck Fenenbock	1946	17	479	28.18
	Em Tunnell	1953	17	479	28.18
32	Al Carmichael	1956	33	927	28.09
33	Jon Arnett	1957	18	504	28.00

TOUCHDOWNS (2)

1	Vitamin Smith	1950	3
2	Eddie Saenz	1947	2
	Les Goble	1954	2

INTERCEPTIONS

(8)

1	Night Train Lane	1952	14
2	Don Sandifer	1948	13
	Spec Sanders	1950	13
4	Bob Nussbaumer	1949	12
	Don Doll	1950	12
	Woodley Lewis	1950	12
	Jack Christiansen	1953	12
8	Sammy Baugh	1943	11
	Otto Schnellbacher	1948	11
	Don Doll	1949	11
	Otto Schnellbacher	1951	11
	Tom Keane	1953	11
	Will Sherman	1955	11
	Lindon Crow	1956	11
	Jimmy Patton	1956	11
16	Eddie Kotal	1928	10
	Irv Comp	1943	10
	Tom Colella	1946	10
	Bill Dudley	1946	10
	Frank Seno	1947	10
	Frank Reagan	1947	10
	Em Tunnell	1949	10
	Howard Hartley	1951	10
	Tom Keane	1952	10
	Don Doll	1953	10
	Ray Ramsey	1953	10
	Night Train Lane	1954	10
	Jack Butler	1957	10
	Jack Christiansen	1957	10
	Milt Davis	1957	10
31	Verne Lewellen	1926	9
	Howie Livingston	1944	9
	Cliff Lewis	1948	9
	Frank Reagan	1948	9
	Jim Cason	1949	9
	Jim Smith	1949	9
	Tommy James	1950	9
	Jerry Davis	1950	9
	Em Tunnell	1951	9
	Jim Smith	1952	9
	Jack Butler	1953	9
	Bobby Dillon	1953	9
	Dick Alban	1954	9
	Bibbles Bawel	1955	9
	Bobby Dillon	1955	9
	Bobby Dillon	1957	9
	Johnny Symank	1957	9
	Jack Butler	1958	9
49	Tillie Voss	1924	8
	Wes Fry	1927*	8
	Dale Burnett	1930*	8
	Bulldog Turner	1942	8
	Don Hutson	1943	8
	Red Cochran	1947	8
	Bob Forte	1947	8
	Tommy Harmon	1947	8
	Warren Lahr	1950	8
	Chick Maggioli	1950	8
	Otto Schnellbacher	1950	8
	Joe Sutton	1950	8
	Bibbles Bawel	1952	8
	Tom Landry	1952	8
	Herb Rich	1952	8
	Tom Brookshier	1953	8
	Jack Christiansen	1954	8
	Bob Hudson	1954	8
	Tom Landry	1954	8
	Em Tunnell	1954	8
	Jack Christiansen	1956	8
	Norb Hecker	1956	8
	Yale Lary	1956	8
	Dick Moegle	1957	8
	Andy Nelson	1958	8
	Ray Brown	1958	8

* Incomplete

SINGLE SEASON LEADERS

FIELD GOALS

ATTEMPTS (24)

1	Lou Groza	1952	33
2	Paddy Driscoll	1926	29
	Lou Groza	1946	29
	Pat Summerall	1959	29
5	George Blanda	1956	28
	Tom Miner	1958	28
7	Jim Welsh	1926	27
8	Lou Groza	1953	26
	George Blanda	1957	26
	Sam Baker	1958	26
	Tommy Davis	1959	26
12	Pete Henry	1923	25
	Ben Agajanian	1954	25
	George Blanda	1952	25
	Sam Baker	1956	25
	Paige Cothren	1958	25
17	Ben Agajanian	1947	24
	Ben Agajanian	1953	24
	Pat Summerall	1953	24
	Lou Groza	1954	24
	Fred Cone	1955	24
	Bert Rechichar	1955	24
	Les Richter	1955	24

MADE (11)

1	Lou Groza	1953	23
2	Pat Summerall	1959	20
3	Lou Groza	1952	19
4	Sam Baker	1956	17
5	Lou Groza	1954	16
	Fred Cone	1955	16
7	Ben Agajanian	1947	15
	Lou Groza	1957	15
9	Sam Baker	1957	14
	George Blanda	1957	14
	Paige Cothren	1958	14
	Tom Miner	1958	14
13	Lou Groza	1946	13
	Lou Groza	1950	13
	Bob Waterfield	1951	13
	Ben Agajanian	1954	13
	Les Richter	1955	13
	Gordie Soltau	1956	13
	Sam Baker	1958	13
	Lou Groza	1958	13
21	Paddy Driscoll	1925	12
	Ray Poole	1951	12
	Doak Walker	1953	12
	George Blanda	1956	12
	Bobby Layne	1956	12
	Fred Cone	1957	12
	Pat Summerall	1958	12
	Tommy Davis	1959	12
29	Paddy Driscoll	1924	11
	Pat Harder	1952	11
	Bobby Walston	1952	11
	Bob Waterfield	1952	11
	Bill Dudley	1953	11
	Gordie Soltau	1954	11
	Doak Walker	1954	11
	George Blanda	1955	11
	Lou Groza	1955	11
	Lou Groza	1956	11
	Paige Cothren	1957	11
	George Blanda	1958	11
	Paul Hornung	1958	11
	Bobby Layne	1959	11

PERCENTAGE FIELD GOALS MADE (55)

(Minimum 10 Attempts)

			Good	Att.	Pct.
1	Lou Groza	1953	23	26	88.46
2	Bobby Layne	1956	12	15	80.00
3	Bill Dudley	1951	10	13	76.92
4	Steve Nemeth	1946	9	12	75.00
	Ray Poole	1951	9	12	75.00
	Bobby Walston	1957	12	16	75.00
7	Paddy Driscoll	1923	10	14	71.43
8	Fred Cone	1957	12	17	70.58
9	Pat Harder	1947	7	10	70.00
10	Pat Summerall	1959	20	29	68.96
11	George Blanda	1955	11	16	68.75
12	Lou Groza	1950	13	19	68.42
13	Lou Groza	1957	15	22	68.18
14	Sam Baker	1956	17	25	68.00
15	Cliff Patton	1948	8	12	66.67
	Gordie Soltau	1953	10	15	66.67
	Lou Groza	1954	16	24	66.67
	Ben Agajanian	1955	10	15	66.67
	Fred Cone	1955	16	24	66.67
20	Gordie Soltau	1956	13	20	65.00
21	Doak Walker	1954	11	17	64.70
	Bobby Layne	1959	11	17	64.70
23	Clarke Hinkle	1940	9	14	64.29
24	Red Dunn	1924	7	11	63.64
25	Doak Walker	1953	12	19	63.15
26	Ben Agajanian	1947	15	24	62.50
27	Paddy Driscoll	1922	8	13	61.54
	Ben Agajanian	1949	8	13	61.54
29	Bob Waterfield	1952	11	18	61.11
30	Sam Baker	1957	14	23	60.86
31	Joey Sternaman	1923	6	10	60.00
	Gordie Soltau	1957	9	15	60.00
33	Ray Poole	1952	10	17	58.82
34	Paddy Driscoll	1925	11	19	57.89
	Paige Cothren	1957	11	19	57.89
36	Lou Groza	1952	19	33	57.58
37	Joe Geri	1950	8	14	57.14
38	Bob Waterfield	1951	13	23	56.52
39	Bob Waterfield	1949	9	16	56.25
	Fred Cone	1954	9	16	56.25
	Doak Walker	1955	9	16	56.25
42	Paige Cothren	1958	14	25	56.00
43	Rex Grossman	1948	10	18	55.56
	Ben Agajanian	1957	10	18	55.56
45	Bobby Walston	1952	11	20	55.00
	Lou Groza	1956	11	20	55.00

POINTS AFTER TOUCHDOWNS

GOOD (35)

1	Joe Vetrano	1948	62
2	Joe Vetrano	1949	56
3	Bob Waterfield	1950	54
4	Pat Harder	1948	53
5	Lou Groza	1948	51
6	Cliff Patton	1948	50
	Steve Myhra	1959	50
8	Harvey Johnson	1947	49
9	Gordie Soltau	1953	48
	Steve Myhra	1958	48
11	Lou Groza	1946	45
	Pat Harder	1949	45
	Chet Adams	1950	45
	Bobby Walston	1953	45
	George Blanda	1956	45
16	Ray McLean	1947	44
	Johnny Lujack	1948	44
	Bob Waterfield	1952	44
	Lou Groza	1955	44
20	Rex Grossman	1948	43
	Bob Waterfield	1949	43
	Lou Groza	1951	43
	Doak Walker	1951	43
	Doak Walker	1954	43
25	Johnny Lujack	1949	42
	Cliff Patton	1949	42
	Paige Cothren	1958	42
28	Bob Waterfield	1951	41
29	Bob Snyder	1943	39
	Pat Harder	1947	39
	Ben Agajanian	1947	39
	Lou Groza	1947	39
	Len Younce	1948	39
	Lou Groza	1953	39
35	Joe Vetrano	1947	38
	Bob Waterfield	1948	38
	Doak Walker	1950	38
	Les Richter	1954	38
	Paige Cothren	1957	38
40	Bob Waterfield	1946	37
	Dick Poillon	1947	37
	Harvey Johnson	1948	37
	Lou Groza	1954	37
	George Blanda	1955	37
45	Don Hutson	1943	36
	Pete Gudauskas	1944	36
	Harvey Johnson	1947	36
	Cliff Patton	1947	36
	Ben Agajanian	1953	36
	Bobby Walston	1954	36
	Les Richter	1956	36
	George Blanda	1958	36
	Lou Groza	1958	36
54	Ben Agajanian	1949	35
	Gary Kerkorian	1952	35
	Ben Agajanian	1954	35

MOST PAT's – NO MISSES (30)

1	Joe Vetrano	1949	56
2	Pat Harder	1948	53
3	Cliff Patton	1948	50
4	Rex Grossman	1948	43
	Lou Groza	1951	43
	Doak Walker	1954	43
7	Paige Cothren	1958	42
8	Les Richter	1954	38
	Paige Cothren	1957	38
10	Bob Waterfield	1946	37
	Harvey Johnson	1948	37
	George Blanda	1955	37
13	Don Hutson	1943	36
	Harvey Johnson	1947	36
15	Ben Agajanian	1954	35
16	Bobby Layne	1956	33
	Gordie Soltau	1957	33
18	Ken Strong	1946	32
	Chet Adams	1949	32
	Lou Groza	1952	32
	Ben Agajanian	1957	32
	Lou Groza	1957	32
	Bobby Layne	1959	32
24	Harvey Johnson	1951	31
	Bobby Walston	1952	31
	Tom Miner	1958	31
	Bobby Walston	1958	31
	Tommy Davis	1959	31
29	Ward Cuff	1947	30
	George Blanda	1952	30
	Fred Cone	1955	30
	Pat Summerall	1956	30
	Pat Summerall	1959	30

LIFETIME LEADERS
PASSING

ATTEMPTS (800)

1	Boby Layne	1948-59	3109
2	Sammy Baugh	1937-52	2995
3	Y.A. Tittle	1948-59	2960
4	Otto Graham	1946-55	2626
5	Norm Van Brocklin	1949-59	2611
6	Chuck Conerly	1948-59	2593
7	Tobin Rote	1950-59	2450
8	Sid Luckman	1939-50	1744
9	Bob Waterfield	1945-52	1617
10	Frankie Albert	1946-52	1564
11	Tommy Thompson	1940-42, 45-50	1424
12	George Ratterman	1947-56	1396
13	Jim Finks	1949-55	1382
14	Bobby Thomason	1949, 51-57	1346
15	Arnie Herber*	1932-40, 44-45	1223
16	Paul Christman	1945-50	1140
17	Johnny Unitas	1956-59	1129
18	Lamar McHan	1954-59	1120
19	Eddie LeBaron	1952-53, 55-59	1104
20	Adrian Burk	1950-56	1079
21	Ed Brown	1954-59	999
22	George Blanda	1949-58	988
23	Glenn Dobbs	1946-49	934
	Billy Wade	1954-59	934
25	Jim Hardy	1946-52	912
26	Cecil Isbell	1938-42	818
27	Benny Friedman*	1927-34	815
28	Johnny Lujack	1948-51	808

COMPLETIONS (600)

1	Sammy Baugh	1937-52	1693
2	Y.A. Tittle	1948-59	1627
3	Bobby Layne	1948-59	1520
4	Otto Graham	1946-55	1464
5	Norm Van Brocklin	1949-59	1400
6	Chuck Conerly	1948-59	1308
7	Tobin Rote	1950-59	1082
8	Sid Luckman	1939-50	904
9	Frankie Albert	1946-52	831
10	Bob Waterfield	1945-52	813
11	George Ratterman	1947-56	737
12	Tommy Thompson	1940-42, 45-50	732
13	Bobby Thomason	1949, 51-57	687
14	Jim Finks	1949-55	661
15	Johnny Unitas	1956-59	611

COMPLETION PERCENTAGE
(All with over 800 Attempts)

			Att.	Comp.	Pct.
1	Sammy Baugh	1937-52	2995	1693	56.53
2	Otto Graham	1946-55	2626	1464	55.75
3	Y.A. Tittle	1948-59	2960	1627	54.97
4	Johnny Unitas	1956-59	1129	611	54.11
5	Norm Van Brocklin	1949-59	2611	1400	53.63
6	Billy Wade	1954-59	934	497	53.21
7	Frankie Albert	1946-52	1564	831	53.13
8	George Ratterman	1947-56	1396	737	52.79
9	Sid Luckman	1939-50	1657	904	51.83
10	Tommy Thompson	1940-42, 45-50	1424	732	51.40
11	Bobby Thomason	1949, 51-57	1346	687	51.04
12	Chuck Conerly	1948-59	2593	1308	50.44
13	Bob Waterfield	1945-52	1617	813	50.28
14	Ed Brown	1954-59	999	502	50.25
15	Cecil Isbell	1938-42	818	411	50.24
16	Johnny Lujack	1948-51	808	404	50.00
17	Bobby Layne	1948-59	3109	1520	48.89
18	Eddie LeBaron	1952-53, 55-59	1104	538	48.73
19	Jim Finks	1949-55	1382	661	47.83
20	Glenn Dobbs	1946-49	934	446	47.75
21	Jim Hardy	1946-52	912	423	46.38
22	Adrian Burk	1950-56	1079	500	46.34
23	Benny Friedman*	1927-34	702	324	46.15
24	George Blanda	1949-58	988	445	45.04
25	Paul Christman	1945-50	1140	504	44.21
26	Tobin Rote	1950-59	2450	1082	44.16
27	Lamar McHan	1954-59	1120	481	42.95
28	Arnie Herber*	1932-40, 44-45	1221	502	41.11

YARDS (6,000)

1	Otto Graham	1946-55	23594
2	Bobby Layne	1948-59	22063
3	Y.A. Tittle	1948-59	21937
4	Sammy Baugh	1937-52	21886
5	Norm Van Brocklin	1949-59	21140
6	Chuck Conerly	1948-59	17900
7	Tobin Rote	1950-59	15144
8	Sid Luckman	1939-50	14683
9	Bob Waterfield	1945-52	11849
10	Frankie Albert	1946-52	10795
11	George Ratterman	1947-56	10473
12	Tommy Thompson	1940-52, 45-50	10400
13	Bobby Thomason	1949, 51-57	9480
14	Johnny Unitas	1956-59	8954
15	Jim Finks	1949-55	8622
16	Arnie Herber*	1932-40, 44-45	8613
17	Billy Wade	1954-59	8278
18	Eddie LeBaron	1952-53, 55-59	8068
19	Ed Brown	1954-59	7877
20	Lamar McHan	1954-59	7383
21	Paul Christman	1945-50	7294
22	Benny Friedman*	1927-34	7292
23	Adrian Burk	1950-56	7001
24	Johnny Lujack	1948-51	6295

YARDS PER ATTEMPT
(All with over 800 Attempts)

			Yards	Att.	Yd/A
1	Otto Graham	1946-55	23594	2626	8.98
2	Billy Wade	1954-59	8278	934	8.86
3	Sid Luckman	1939-50	14683	1657	8.42
4	Norm Van Brocklin	1949-59	21140	2611	8.10
5	Johnny Unitas	1956-59	8954	1129	7.93
6	Ed Brown	1954-59	7877	999	7.88
7	Johnny Lujack	1948-51	6295	808	7.79
8	Benny Friedman*	1927-34	5326	702	7.59
9	George Ratterman	1947-56	10473	1396	7.50
10	Y.A. Tittle	1948-59	21937	2960	7.41
11	Bob Waterfield	1945-52	11849	1617	7.33
12	Eddie LeBaron	1952-53, 55-59	8068	1104	7.31
13	Sammy Baugh	1937-52	21886	2995	7.31
14	Tommy Thompson	1940-42, 45-50	10400	1424	7.30
15	Cecil Isbell	1938-42	5945	818	7.27
16	Bobby Layne	1948-59	22063	3109	7.10
17	Bobby Thomason	1949, 51-57	9480	1346	7.04
18	Arnie Herber*	1932-40, 44-45	8573	1221	7.02
19	Chuck Conerly	1948-59	17900	2593	6.90
20	Frankie Albert	1946-52	10795	1564	6.90
21	Lamar McHan	1954-59	7383	1120	6.59
22	Adrian Burk	1950-56	7001	1079	6.49
23	Paul Christman	1945-50	7294	1140	6.40
24	Glenn Dobbs	1946-49	5876	934	6.29
25	Jim Hardy	1946-52	5690	912	6.24
26	Jim Finks	1949-55	8622	1382	6.24
27	Tobin Rote	1950-59	15144	2450	6.18
28	George Blanda	1949-58	5436	988	6.01

TOUCHDOWN PASSES (55)

1	Sammy Baugh	1937-52	187
2	Otto Graham	1946-55	174
3	Bobby Layne	1948-59	163
4	Chuck Conerly	1948-59	158
5	Norm Van Brocklin	1949-59	149
6	Y.A. Tittle	1948-59	142
7	Sid Luckman	1939-50	137
8	Tobin Rote	1950-59	119
9	Frankie Albert	1946-52	115
10	Bob Waterfield	1945-52	98
11	George Ratterman	1947-56	91
	Tommy Thompson	1940-42, 45-50	91
13	Johnny Unitas	1956-59	84
14	Arnie Herber	1932-40, 44-45	82
15	Benny Friedman	1927-34	68
	Bobby Thomason	1949, 51-57	68
17	Cecil Isbell	1938-42	61
	Adrian Burk	1950-56	61
19	Eddie LeBaron	1952-53, 55-59	59
20	Paul Christman	1945-50	58
21	Lamar McHan	1954-59	57
22	Jim Finks	1949-55	55

INTERCEPTIONS (70)

1	Sammy Baugh	1937-52	203
2	Bobby Layne	1948-59	193
3	Y.A. Tittle	1948-59	177
4	Norm Van Brocklin	1949-59	161
5	Tobin Rote	1950-59	158
6	Chuck Conerly	1948-59	152
7	Otto Graham	1946-55	135
8	Sid Luckman	1939-50	131
9	Bob Waterfield	1945-52	127
10	Tommy Thompson	1940-42, 45-50	103
11	Frankie Albert	1946-52	98
12	Arnie Herber*	1932-40, 44-45	97
13	George Ratterman	1947-56	96
14	Bobby Thomason	1949, 51-57	90
15	Adrian Burk	1950-56	89
16	Jim Finks	1949-55	88
	Eddie LeBaron	1952-53, 55-59	88
18	Lamar McHan	1954-59	86
19	Curly Lambeau*	1921-29	78
20	Paul Christman	1945-50	76
21	Jim Hardy	1946-52	73
22	George Blanda	1949-58	70

PERCENT INTERCEPTED
(All with over 800 Attempts)

			Att.	Int.	Pct.
1	Johnny Unitas	1956-59	1129	48	4.25
2	Otto Graham	1946-55	2626	135	5.14
3	Glenn Dobbs	1946-49	934	52	5.57
4	Chuck Conerly	1948-59	2593	152	5.86
5	Y.A. Tittle	1948-59	2960	177	5.98
6	Billy Wade	1954-59	934	57	6.10
7	Norm Van Brocklin	1949-59	2611	161	6.17
8	Bobby Layne	1948-59	3109	193	6.21
9	Frankie Albert	1946-52	1564	98	6.26
10	Cecil Isbell	1938-42	818	52	6.36
11	Jim Finks	1949-55	1382	88	6.37
12	Tobin Rote	1950-59	2450	158	6.45
13	Ed Brown	1954-59	999	66	6.61
14	Paul Christman	1945-50	1140	76	6.67
15	Johnny Lujack	1948-51	808	54	6.68
16	Bobby Thomason	1949, 51-57	1346	90	6.69
17	Sammy Baugh	1937-52	1693	203	6.78
18	George Ratterman	1947-56	1396	96	6.88
19	George Blanda	1949-58	988	70	7.09
20	Tommy Thompson	1940-42, 45-50	1424	103	7.23
21	Benny Friedman*	1927-34	702	51	7.26
22	Sid Luckman	1939-50	1744	131	7.51
23	Lamar McHan	1954-59	1120	86	7.68
24	Bob Waterfield	1946-52	1617	127	7.85
25	Arnie Herber*	1932-40, 44-45	1221	97	7.94
26	Eddie LeBaron	1952-53, 55-59	1104	88	7.98
27	Jim Hardy	1946-52	912	73	8.00
28	Adrian Burk	1950-56	1079	89	8.25

* Incomplete

LIFETIME LEADERS

RUSHING

ATTEMPTS (600)

1	Joe Perry	1948-59	1607
2	Steve Van Buren	1944-51	1320
3	Clarke Hinkle	1932-41	1192
4	Bob Hoernschemeyer	1946-55	1099
5	Tony Canadeo	1941-44,46-52	1025
6	Ace Gutkowsky*	1932-39	946
7	Ollie Matson	1952,54-59	922
8	Tuffy Leemans	1936-43	919
8	Hugh McElhenny	1952-59	3941
9	Rick Casares	1955-59	3838
10	Jimmy Brown	1957-59	3798
11	Alan Ameche	1955-59	3782
12	Tank Younger	1949-58	3640
13	Cliff Battles	1932-37	3613
14	Charlie Trippi	1947-55	3506
18	Frank Gifford	1952-59	756
19	Bronko Nagurski*	1930-37,43	750
20	Jimmy Brown	1957-59	749
21	Tony Latone*	1925-30	744
22	Pug Manders	1939-47	742
23	Pat Harder	1946-53	740
24	Dutch Clark	1931-32,34-38	706
25	Verne Lewellen*	1924-32	705
26	Johnny Olszewski	1953-59	699
27	Charlie Trippi	1947-55	687
28	Elmer Angsman	1946-52	683
29	Bill Paschal	1943-48	677
30	Dan Towler	1950-55	672
31	Johnny Strzykalski	1946-52	662
32	Julie Rykovich	1947-53	648
33	Alex Webster	1955-59	620
34	Ted Fritsch	1942-50	619
35	Tobin Rote	1950-59	601

YARDS (3,000)

1	Joe Perry	1948-59	8496
2	Steve Van Buren	1944-51	5860
3	Marion Motley	1946-53,55	4720
4	Bob Hoernschmeyer	1946-55	4548
5	Tony Canadeo	1941-44,46-52	4197
6	Ollie Matson	1952,54-59	4194
7	Clarke Hinkle	1932-41	3996
8	Hugh McElhenny	1952-59	3941
9	Rick Casares	1955-59	3838
10	Jimmy Brown	1957-59	3798
11	Alan Ameche	1955-59	3782
12	Tank Younger	1949-58	3640
13	Cliff Battles	1932-37	3613
14	Charlie Trippi	1947-55	3506
15	Dan Towler	1950-55	3493
16	Bronko Nagurski*	1930-37,43	3430
17	Johnny Strzykalski	1946-52	3415
18	Ace Gutowsky*	1932-39	3381
19	Frank Gifford	1952-59	3347
20	Eddie Price	1950-55	3292
21	Dutch Clark	1931-32,34-38	3272
22	Fran Rogel	1950-57	3271
23	Tuffy Leemans	1936-43	3142
24	Tobin Rote	1950-59	3078
25	Bill Dudley	1942,45-51,53	3057
26	Chet Mutryn	1946-50	3031
27	Pat Harder	1946-53	3016

AVERAGE YARDS (4.0)
(Minimum 500 Rushes)

			Att.	Yards	Avg.
1	Marion Motley	1946-53,55	828	4720	5.70
2	Spec Sanders	1946-48,50	540	2900	5.37
3	Joe Perry	1948-59	1607	8496	5.29
4	Dan Towler	1950-55	672	3493	5.20
5	Chet Mutryn	1946-50	583	3031	5.20
6	Johnny Strzykalski	1946-52	662	3415	5.16
7	Tobin Rote	1950-59	601	3078	5.12
8	Charlie Trippi	1947-55	687	3506	5.10
9	Jimmy Brown	1957-59	749	3782	5.05
10	Hugh McElhenny	1952-59	782	3941	5.04
11	Tank Younger	1949-58	770	3640	4.73
12	Dutch Clark	1932-32,34-38	706	3272	4.63
13	Buddy Young	1947-55	597	2727	4.57
14	Ollie Matson	1952,54-59	922	4194	4.55
15	Bronko Nagurski*	1930-37,43	738	3430	4.54
16	Ray Nolting	1936-43	508	2285	4.50
17	Steve Van Buren	1944-51	1320	5860	4.44
18	Frank Gifford	1952-59	756	3347	4.43
19	Dick Hoerner	1947-52	500	2172	4.29
20	Alan Ameche	1955-59	884	3782	4.28
21	Elmer Angsman	1946-52	683	2908	4.26
22	Rob Goode	1949-51,54-55	596	2531	4.25
23	Curley Morrison	1950-56	578	2420	4.19
24	Red Grange*	1925,27,29-34	548	2286	4.17
25	Cliff Battles	1932-37	873	3613	4.14
26	Bob Hoernschemeyer	1946-55	1099	4548	4.14
27	Rick Casares	1955-59	916	3782	4.13
28	Johnny Olszewski	1953-59	699	2872	4.11
29	Tony Canadeo	1941-44,46-52	1025	4197	4.09
30	Dub Jones	1946-55	540	2209	4.09
31	George Gulyanics	1947-52	509	2081	4.09
32	Pat Harder	1946-53	740	3016	4.08

TOUCHDOWNS (26)

1	Steve Van Buren	1944-51	69
2	Joe Perry	1948-59	67
3	Otto Graham	1946-55	44
4	Dan Towler	1950-55	43
5	Jimmy Brown	1957-59	40
6	Ernie Nevers	1926-27,29-31	38
7	Alan Ameche	1955-59	37
	Verne Lewellen	1924-32	37
9	Dutch Clark	1931-32,34-38	36
	Pug Manders	1939-47	36
11	Tobin Rote	1950-59	35
	Hugh McElhenny	1952-59	35
13	Clarke Hinkle	1932-41	34
	Tank Younger	1949-58	34
	Rick Casares	1955-59	34
16	Spec Sanders	1946-48,50	33
	Pat Harder	1946-53	33
18	Ted Fritsch	1942-50	31
	Marion Motley	1946-53,55	31
	Y.A. Tittle	1948-59	31
21	Dick Hoerner	1947-52	30
	Ollie Matson	1952,54-59	30
23	Julie Rykovich	1947-53	28
24	Bill Paschal	1943-48	27
	Chet Mutryn	1946-50	27
	Elmer Angsman	1946-52	27
	Bob Hoernschemeyer	1946-55	27
	Paddy Driscoll	1920-29	27
29	Tony Latone	1925-30	26
	Tony Canadeo	1941-44,46-52	26
	Frank Gifford	1952-59	26
	Jack McBride	1925-34	26
33	Bronko Nagurski	1930-37,43	25
	Lenny Moore	1956-59	25

INTERCEPTIONS

(25)

1	Em Tunnell	1948-59	76
2	Night Train Lane	1952-59	57
3	Jack Butler	1951-59	56
	Bobby Dillon	1952-59	56
5	Jack Christiansen	1951-58	46
6	Warren Lehr	1949-59	44
7	Don Doll	1949-54	41
8	Tom Keane	1948-55	40
9	Jim David	1952-59	36
10	Frank Reagan	1941,46-51	35
	Ray Ramsey	1947-53	35
12	Tommy James	1947-56	34
	Jim Cason	1948-52,54-56	34
	Otto Schnellbacher	1948-51	34
	Don Paul	1950-58	34
16	Irv Comp	1943-49	33
	Jim Smith	1948-53	33
18	Lowell Wagner	1946-53,55	32
	Tom Landry	1949-55	32
20	Johnny Blood*	1925-39	31
21	Don Hutson	1935-45	30
	Cliff Lewis	1946-51	30
	Kenny Kunz	1953-59	30
	Bert Rechichar	1952-59	30
25	Howie Livingston	1944-50,53	29
	Herb Rich	1950-56	29
27	Howard Hartley	1948-52	28
	Norb Hecker	1951-53,55-57	28
	Will Sherman	1952-59	28
30	Lavie Dilweg*	1926-34	27
31	George Trafton*	1920-21,23-32	26
	Woodley Lewis	1950-59	26

* Incomplete

LIFETIME LEADERS
RECEIVING

RECEPTIONS (200)

1	Don Hutson	1935-45	488
2	Billy Wilson	1951-59	404
3	Tom Fears	1948-56	400
4	Crazy Legs Hirsch	1946-57	387
5	Dante Lavelli	1946-56	376
6	Pete Pihos	1947-55	373
7	Mac Speedie	1946-52	349
8	Billy Howton	1952-59	342
9	Elbie Nickel	1947-57	329
10	Jim Benton	1938-40,42-47	288
11	Hugh Taylor	1947-54	272
12	Gordie Soltau	1950-58	249
13	Bobby Walston	1951-59	243
14	Dan Edwards	1948-54	234
15	Frank Gifford	1952-59	233
16	Don Stonesifer	1951-56	231
17	Ray Mathews	1951-59	230
18	Jim Keane	1946-52	224
19	Ray Berry	1955-59	219
20	Harlon Hill	1954-59	218
21	Alyn Beals	1946-51	211
22	Bob Mann	1948-53	208
	Darrel Brewster	1952-59	208
24	Kyle Rote	1951-59	205
25	Bill McColl	1952-59	201

YARDS (3000)

1	Don Hutson	1935-45	7981
2	Crazy Legs Hirsch	1946-57	7029
3	Dante Lavelli	1946-56	6488
4	Billy Howton	1952-59	6091
5	Billy Wilson	1951-59	5851
6	Pete Pihos	1947-55	5619
7	Mac Speedie	1946-52	5602
8	Tom Fears	1948-56	5397
9	Hugh Taylor	1947-54	5233
10	Elbie Nickel	1947-57	5131
11	Jim Benton	1938-40,42-47	4801
12	Harlon Hill	1954-59	4467
13	Bobby Walston	1951-59	4285
14	Ray Mathews	1951-59	3919
15	Darrel Brewster	1952-59	3732
16	Ken Kavanaugh	1940-41,45-50	3622
17	Bob Boyd	1950-51,53-57	3611
18	Ray Renfro	1952-59	3576
19	Gordie Soltau	1950-58	3487
20	Ray Berry	1955-59	3359
21	Kyle Rote	1951-59	3242
22	Jim Keane	1946-52	3222
23	Frank Gifford	1952-59	3208
24	Bob Mann	1948-53	3203
25	Johnny Blood*	1925-39	3164
26	Mal Kutner	1946-50	3060
27	Jim Mutscheller	1954-59	3043

AVERAGE YARDS (16.0)
(Minimum 150 Receptions)

			Rec.	Yards	Avg.
1	Ken Kavanaugh	1940-41,45-50	162	3622	22.36
2	Ray Renfro	1952-59	174	3576	20.55
3	Bob Boyd	1950-51,53-57	176	3611	20.52
4	Harlon Hill	1954-59	218	4467	20.49
5	Hugh Taylor	1947-54	272	5233	19.24
6	Crazy Legs Hirsch	1946-57	387	7029	18.16
7	Darrel Brewster	1952-59	208	3732	17.94
8	Johnny Blood*	1925-39	178	3173	17.83
9	Billy Howton	1952-59	342	6091	17.81
10	Bobby Walston	1951-59	243	4285	17.63
11	Jim Doran	1951-59	168	2960	17.62
12	Jack Ferrante	1941,44-50	169	2894	17.12
13	Ray Mathews	1951-59	230	3919	17.04
14	Dante Lavelli	1946-56	376	6488	16.81
15	Dub Jones	1946-55	171	2874	16.81
16	Jim Mutscheller	1954-49	182	3043	16.72
17	Jim Benton	1938-40,42-47	288	4801	16.67
18	Al Baldwin	1947-50	160	2658	16.61
19	John Greene	1944-50	173	2865	16.56
20	Don Hutson	1935-45	488	7981	16.36
21	Mac Speedie	1946-52	349	5602	16.05

TOUCHDOWNS (30)

1	Don Hutson	1935-45	100
2	Dante Lavelli	1946-56	62
3	Pete Pihos	1947-55	61
4	Crazy Legs Hirsch	1946-57	60
5	Hugh Taylor	1947-54	58
6	Ken Kavanaugh	1940-41,45-50	50
7	Alyn Beals	1946-51	49
8	Billy Wilson	1951-59	48
9	Jim Benton	1938-40,42-47	45
10	Billy Howton	1952-59	44
11	Bobby Walston	1951-59	42
12	Harlon Hill	1954-59	40
13	Tom Fears	1948-56	38
14	Johnny Blood	1925-39	37
	Elbie Nickel	1947-57	37
16	Jim Mutscheller	1954-59	36
17	Ray Renfro	1952-59	35
18	Ray Mathews	1951-59	34
19	Mac Speedie	1946-52	33
20	Cloyce Box	1949-50,52-54	32
21	Jack Ferrante	1941,44-50	31
	Kyle Rote	1951-59	31
	Ray Berry	1955-59	31

POINTS

(250)

1	Lou Groza	1946-59	1001
2	Don Hutson	1935-45	823
3	Gordie Soltau	1950-58	644
4	Bobby Walston	1951-59	631
5	Bob Waterfield	1945-52	573
6	George Blanda	1949-58	541
7	Doak Walker	1950-55	534
8	Pat Harder	1946-53	531
9	Ben Agajanian	1945,47-49,53-57	491
10	Bill Dudley	1942,45-51,53	484
11	Joe Perry	1948-59	483
12	Ken Strong	1929-35,39,44-47	479
13	Steve Van Buren	1944-51	464
14	Fred Cone	1951-57	455
15	Paddy Driscoll	1920-29	418
16	Ward Cuff	1937-47	417
17	Crazy Legs Hirsch	1946-57	405
18	Pat Summerall	1952-59	404
19	Ted Fritsch	1942-50	380
20	Pete Pihos	1947-55	378
21	Clarke Hinkle	1932-41	377
22	Dante Lavelli	1946-56	372
23	Dutch Clark	1931-32,34-38	370
24	Jack Manders	1933-40	363
25	Hugh Taylor	1947-54	348
26	Ollie Matson	1952,54-59	336
27	Ken Kavanaugh	1940-41,45-50	313
	Bobby Layne	1948-59	313
29	Joe Aguirre	1941,48-49	310
30	Verne Lewellen	1924-32	307
31	Ernie Nevers	1926-27,29-31	301
32	Hugh McElhenny	1952-59	300
33	Alyn Beals	1946-51	296
34	Jim Benton	1938-40,42-47	288
	Billy Wilson	1951-59	288
36	Johnny Blood	1925-39	279
37	Johnny Lujack	1948-51	268
38	Sam Baker	1953,56-59	265
39	Dan Towler	1950-55	264
	Buddy Young	1947-55	264
	Billy Howton	1952-59	264
42	Harvey Johnson	1946-49,51	262
43	Ray Mathews	1951-59	261
44	Chet Mutryn	1946-50	253

* Incomplete

LIFETIME LEADERS
PUNT RETURNS

(90)

1	Em Tunnell	1948-59	258
2	Woodley Lewis	1950-59	138
3	Red Dunn*	1924-31	136
4	Bill Dudley	1942,45-51,53	124
	Joe Arenas	1951-57	124
	Yale Lary	1952-53,56-59	124
7	Don Paul	1950-58	113
8	George McAfee	1940,41,45-50	112
9	Carl Taseff	1951,53-59	102
10	Two Bits Homan*	1925-30	100
	Al Carmichael	1953-58	100
12	Hugh McElhenny	1952-59	99
13	Bosh Pritchard	1942,46-49,51	95
14	Charley Rogers*	1927-29	94
15	Billy Reynolds	1953-54,57-58	92

YARDS (750)

1	Em Tunnell	1948-59	2209
2	Bill Dudley	1942,45-51,53	1515
3	Two Bits Homan*	1925-30	1439
4	George McAfee	1940-41,45-50	1431
5	Curly Oden*	1925-28,30-32	1336
6	Charley Rogers*	1927-29	1255
7	Red Dunn*	1924-31	1248
8	Ken Strong*	1929-35,39,44-47	1112
9	Jack Christiansen	1951-58	1084
10	Bosh Pritchard	1942,46-49,51	1072
11	Jack Ernst*	1925-30	1060
12	Woodley Lewis	1950-59	1026
13	Jim Cason	1948-52,54-56	948
14	Don Paul	1950-58	902
15	Billy Grimes	1949-52	901

AVERAGE RETURN (10.0)
(Minimum 75 Returns)

			Ret.	Yards	Avg.
1	Two Bits Homan*	1925-30	82	1114	13.59
2	Charley Rogers*	1927-29	91	1199	13.18
3	George McAfee	1940-41,45-50	112	1431	12.78
4	Jack Christianson	1951-58	85	1084	12.75
5	Ken Strong*	1929-35,39,44-47	88	1112	12.64
6	Bill Dudley	1942,46-49,51	124	1515	12.22
7	Jack Ernst*	1925-30	89	1060	11.91
8	Bosh Pritchard	1942,46-49,51	95	1072	11.28
9	Vitamin Smith	1949-53	75	814	10.85

TOUCHDOWNS (2)

1	Jack Christiansen	1951-58	8
2	Em Tunnell	1948-59	5
3	Curly Oden	1925-28,30-32	4
4	Dick Todd	1939-40,42,45-58	3
	Ray McLean	1940,42-47	3
	Bill Dudley	1942,45-51,53	3
	Woodley Lewis	1950-59	3
	Ray Mathews	1951-59	3
	Bert Zagers	1955,57-58	3
	Ollie Matson	1952,54-59	3
11	Don Paul	1950-58	2
	Bosh Pritchard	1942,46-49,51	2
	Charlie Trippi	1947-55	2
	Billy Grimes	1949-52	2
	Tommy Kalmanir	1949-51,53	2
	Rex Bumgardner	1948-52	2
	Red Cochran	1947-50	2
	Johnny Williams	1952-54	2
	Buddy Young	1947-55	2
	Yale Lary	1952-53,56-59	2
	Ken Strong	1929-35,39,44-47	2

KICKOFF RETURNS

(70)

1	Al Carmichael	1953-58	153
2	Joe Arenas	1951-57	139
3	Woodley Lewis	1950-59	137
4	Buddy Young	1947-55	125
5	Ollie Matson	1952,54-59	103
6	George Taliaferro	1949-55	95
7	Eddie Saenz	1946-51	93
8	Lynn Chadnois	1950-56	92
9	Billy Grimes	1949-52	83
10	Frank Seno	1943-49	80
11	Bill Dudley	1942,45-51,53	78
12	Steve Van Buren	1944-51	76
13	Chet Mutryn	1946-50	73
14	Tony Canadeo	1941-44,46-52	71

YARDS (1700)

1	Al Carmichael	1953-58	3907
2	Joe Arenas	1951-57	3798
3	Buddy Young	1947-55	3465
4	Woodley Lewis	1950-59	3325
5	Ollie Matson	1952,54-59	2821
6	Lynn Chadnois	1950-56	2720
7	Eddie Saenz	1946-51	2191
8	George Taliaferro	1949-55	2035
9	Steve Van Buren	1944-51	2030
10	Billy Grimes	1949-52	2015
11	Frank Seno	1943-49	1916
12	Chet Mutryn	1946-50	1902
13	Bill Dudley	1942,45-51,53	1743

AVERAGE RETURN (20.0)
(Minimum 70 Returns)

			Ret.	Yards	Avg.
1	Lynn Chadnois	1950-56	92	2720	29.57
2	Buddy Young	1947-55	125	3465	27.72
3	Ollie Matson	1952,54-59	103	2821	27.39
4	Joe Arenas	1951-57	139	3798	27.32
5	Steve Van Buren	1944-51	76	2030	26.71
6	Chet Mutryn	1946-50	73	1902	26.05
7	Al Carmichael	1953-58	153	3907	25.54
8	Billy Grimes	1949-52	83	2015	24.28
9	Woodley Lewis	1950-59	137	3325	24.27
10	Frank Seno	1943-49	80	1916	23.95
11	Eddie Saenz	1946-51	93	2191	23.56
12	Tony Canadeo	1941-44,46-52	71	1626	22.90
13	Bill Dudley	1942,45-51,53	78	1743	22.35
14	George Taliaferro	1949-55	95	2035	21.42

TOUCHDOWNS (2)

1	Ollie Matson	1952,54-59	6
2	Buddy Young	1947-55	4
3	Vitamin Smith	1949-53	3
	Steve Van Buren	1944-51	3
	Lynn Chadnois	1950-56	3
6	Andy Farkas	1938-45	2
	Dante Magnani	1940-43,46-50	2
	Billy Hillebrand	1946-48	2
	Eddie Saenz	1946-51	2
	Spec Sanders	1946-48,50	2
	Al Carmichael	1953-58	2
	Les Goble	1954-55	2

* Incomplete

LIFETIME LEADERS

POINTS AFTER TOUCHDOWN

ATTEMPTS (200)

1	Lou Groza	1946-59	528
2	Bob Waterfield	1945-52	336
3	Gordie Soltau	1945-52	302
4	Ben Agajanian	1945,47-49,53-57	268
5	Bobby Walston	1951-59	260
6	George Blanda	1949-58	250
7	Fred Cone	1951-57	214
8	Pat Harder	1946-53	204
9	Joe Vetrano	1946-49	203

GOOD (150)

1	Lou Groza	1946-59	512
2	Bob Waterfield	1945-52	315
3	Gordie Soltau	1945-52	284
4	Ben Agajanian	1945,47-49,53-57	263
5	George Blanda	1949-58	247
	Bobby Walston	1951-59	247
7	Fred Cone	1951-57	200
8	Pat Harder	1946-53	198
9	Joe Vetrano	1946-49	187
10	Doak Walker	1950-55	183
11	Cliff Patton	1946-51	179
	Pat Summerall	1952-59	179
13	Harvey Johnson	1946-49,51	178
14	Don Hutson	1935-45	172
15	Ken Strong	1929-35,39,44-47	167
16	Ward Cuff	1937-47	156

PERCENT MADE (90.0)
(Mimimum 175 Attempts)

			Good	Att.	Pct.
1	Harvey Johnson	1946-49,51	178	180	98.89
2	George Blanda	1949-58	247	250	98.80
3	Ben Agajanian	1945,47-49,53-57	263	268	98.13
4	Pat Harder	1946-53	198	204	97.05
5	Lou Groza	1946-59	512	528	96.96
6	Cliff Patton	1946-51	179	185	96.75
7	Doak Walker	1950-55	183	191	95.81
8	Pat Summerall	1952-59	179	187	95.72
9	Bobby Walston	1951-59	247	260	95.00
10	Gordie Soltau	1945-52	284	302	94.03
11	Bob Waterfield	1945-52	315	336	93.75
12	Don Hutson	1935-45	172	184	93.47
13	Fred Cone	1951-57	200	214	93.45
14	Joe Vetrano	1946-49	187	203	92.11

FIELD GOALS

ATTEMPTS (125)

1	Lou Groza	1946-59	300
2	George Blanda	1949-58	201
3	Pat Summerall	1952-59	152
4	Ben Agajanian	1945,47-49,53-57	147
5	Gordie Soltau	1945-52	138
6	Bob Waterfield	1945-52	110
7	Ted Fritsch	1942-50	98
8	Bobby Walston	1951-59	97
9	Sam Baker	1953,56-59	96
10	Fred Cone	1951-57	89
11	Doak Walker	1950-55	87

GOOD (50)

1	Lou Groza	1946-59	161
2	George Blanda	1949-58	88
3	Ben Agajanian	1945,47-49,53-57	76
4	Pat Summerall	1952-59	73
5	Gordie Soltau	1945-52	70
6	Bob Waterfield	1945-52	60
7	Sam Baker	1953,56-59	54
8	Fred Cone	1951-57	53
9	Paddy Driscoll	1920-29	51

PERCENT MADE (50.0)
(Minimum 70 Attempts)

			Good	Att.	Pct.
1	Fred Cone	1951-57	53	89	59.55
	Doak Walker	1950-55	49	87	56.32
	Sam Baker	1953,56-59	54	96	56.25
4	Bob Waterfield	1945-52	60	110	54.54
5	Lou Groza	1946-59	161	300	53.67
6	Ben Agajanian	1945,47-49,53-57	76	147	51.70
7	Gordie Soltau	1945-52	70	138	50.72

PUNTING

PUNTS (200)

1	Verne Lewellen*	1924-32	681
2	Horace Gillom	1947-56	492
3	Adrian Burk	1950-56	474
4	Norm Van Brocklin	1949-59	463
5	Jug Girard	1948-57	397
6	Tom Landry	1949-55	389
7	Sammy Baugh	1937-52	338
8	Bob Waterfield	1945-52	315
9	Frankie Albert	1946-52	299
10	Paddy Driscoll*	1920-29	291
11	Curley Morrison	1950-56	281
12	Clarke Hinkle*	1932-41	279
13	Roy Zimmerman	1940-48	278
14	Cub Buck*	1920-25	257
15	Yale Lary	1952-53,56-59	253
16	Ed Brown	1954-59	243
17	Don Chandler	1956-59	239
18	Glenn Dobbs	1946-49	231
	Dick Deschaine	1955-58	231
20	Sid Luckman	1939-50	230
21	Ken Strong*	1929-35,39-44-47	227
	Frank Reagan	1941,46-51	227
23	Pat Brady	1952-54	223
24	Sam Baker	1953,56-59	221
25	Arnie Herber*	1930-40,44-45	205
26	Parker Hall	1939-42	200
	Joe Geri	1949-52	200

PUNTING AVERAGE (40.0)
(Minimum 175 Punts)

1	Glenn Dobbs	1946-49	46.4
2	Sammy Baugh	1937-52	44.9
3	Pat Brady	1952-54	44.5
4	Don Chandler	1956-59	44.2
5	Sam Baker	1953,56-59	43.8
6	Horace Gillom	1947-56	43.1
7	Frankie Albert	1946-52	43.0
8	Joe Muha	1946-50	42.9
9	Norm Van Brocklin	1949-59	42.8
10	Bob Waterfield	1945-52	42.4
11	Jim Smith	1948-53	42.4
12	Dick Deschaine	1955-58	42.3
13	Jack Jacobs	1942,45-49	42.2
14	Ernie Lewis	1946-49	41.9
15	Curley Morrison	1950-56	41.8
16	Parker Hall	1939-42	41.0
17	Frank Reagan	1941,46-51	40.9
	Spec Sanders	1946-48,50	40.9
	Tom Landry	1949-55	40.9
	Adrian Burke	1950-56	40.9
21	Charlie Trippi	1947-53	40.4
22	Jug Girard	1948-57	40.1

* Incomplete

1960—1969

1960-1969
From 12 to 26

The established National Football League faced yet another challenge from a rival league in the 1960's, but unlike the previous tests, this one produced far-reaching changes in the NFL. It eventually resulted in a two-fold increase in the number of teams, the adoption of many innovations to attract new fans, much-improved salaries and retirement benefits for the players, a big expansion of television coverage and the establishment of a Super Bowl championship game which attracted as much attention as baseball's World Series. Inevitably, these changes turned professional football into a big business for owners and players alike.

Having survived the challenge from the All-American Football Conference in the late 1940's, the NFL prepared to do battle with the new American Football League. The first step was to find a new commissioner to replace Bert Bell, under whose leadership the NFL had prospered for 13 years. When the owners reached a stalemate between the two primary candidates, 33-year-old Alvin (Peter) Rozelle was accepted by both factions as a compromise. In 1957 Rozelle had been named general manager of the Los Angeles Rams and one of his more noteworthy trades during the three-year stint was the acquisition of four-time All-Pro halfback Ollie Matson from the Chicago Cardinals in exchange for the rights to nine Ram players.

In an effort to head off the AFL's colonization of virgin football territory, the NFL decided to test two of the more promising areas by placing a club in Dallas beginning in 1960 and another in Minnesota to begin play in 1961. In addition, the desperate financial condition of the Cardinals and the desirability of St. Louis as an NFL city persuaded chairman of the board Violet Bidwill Wolfner and her husband, managing director Walter Wolfner, to move the team after 62 years in Chicago.

Meanwhile, the AFL laid plans for starting play in 1960, trying to avoid the pitfalls which caused the demise of three separate leagues using the same name earlier in the century. The AFL representatives and their cities were chief organizer Lamar Hunt, Dallas; William H. Sullivan, Boston; Ralph C. Wilson, Buffalo; Bob Howsam, Denver; K.S. (Bud) Adams, Houston; Barron Hilton, Los Angeles; Max Winter and William Boyer, Minneapolis-St. Paul; and Harry Wismer, New York City. Several of these men had been frustrated in attempts to buy NFL franchises previously.

When Minnesota was granted an NFL franchise, Winter and Boyer decided they had a better future in the more established league and thus withdrew from the AFL. The vacancy opened the door for an Oakland group headed by Y.C. (Chet) Soda and it included Ed McGah, Robert Osborne and Wayne Valley. The Raiders became the last of the original eight AFL teams to begin play in 1960 and eventually one of the more successful ones. Despite competition from NFL teams in Dallas, Los Angeles and New York, the AFL owners decided to stay in those cities, although the former two were later abandoned in favor of untested cities.

The AFL set out to differentiate its games from the NFL contests by adding several innovations. The new league adopted a rule for conversions whereby a team could elect to run or pass the ball across the goal line for two points as an alternative to the traditional one-point placekick used in the NFL. This added a new dimension of excitement and strategy to a play which had become nearly automatic. The AFL owners also decided to put the players' names on the backs of the jerseys and to make the scoreboard clock official, instead of having an official on the field keep the correct time as was done in the NFL. Both of these rules made the game more accessible to the average fan.

Joe Foss, a former pilot and South Dakota governor, was appointed as the first commissioner of the AFL, and a draft of college players similar to the one held annually by the NFL was scheduled. The competition for players was expected to cause sharp increases in player salaries, just as it had done during the previous challenge from the AAFC. Because of the tempting offers made to college seniors, several players signed contracts with both leagues and soon found themselves as subjects of court battles.

The AFL won its first court cast over a player when a Los Angeles court declared Billy Cannon's contract with the Rams invalid, freeing him to sign with Houston. The Louisiana State University halfback had been the first player selected in the 1960 NFL draft, and his defection to the upstart AFL signalled the beginning of a long and costly bidding war between the two leagues. In the same year, however, Southern Methodist quarterback Don Meredith signed with the NFL's new entry in Dallas, the Cowboys, instead of with Hunt's Dallas Texans. In 1961 end Willard Dewveall became the first player to voluntarily switch leagues when he joined Houston of the AFL after playing out his option with the Chicago Bears.

The AFL received its biggest shot in the arm in 1965 when Sonny Werblin, who had taken over a shaky New York franchise from the league after Wismer had gone bankrupt in 1963, signed quarterbacks Joe Namath and John Huarte to sizeable contracts. Namath received a $225,000 bonus, an annual salary of $25,000 for three years, and no-cut and no-trade clauses in his contract, as the bidding war reached new heights. Although the cost seemed high at the time, Werblin proved himself to be a shrewd businessman, because Namath provided the charisma which made the important New York franchise a financial success and gave the league a degree of legitimacy previously unattained in th eyes of the New York media and many of the football fans across the country. As a measure of Namath's appeal, his first regular-season appearance in a Jet uniform attracted a crowd of 52,680 to Rice Stadium, where the Oilers were playing their first regular-season game after attracting an average of only 20,000 the previous year at Jeppeson Stadium. Three years later, Namath struck another blow for AFL pride when he predicted an AFL victory in Super Bowl III and then proceeded to direct the Jets to a win over the heavily favored Colts, giving the AFL its first Super Bowl triumph.

Although the New York franchise had floundered in its early years under the leadership of Wismer, Werblin wasted little time in upgrading the team. He hired Weeb Ewbank, a former Baltimore head coach, as his field boss in 1963 and the following year moved the team from the rundown Polo Grounds to new Shea Stadium, where it immediately set AFL attendance records. Werblin had a show-business background and he proved adept at utilizing that experience to attract new fans. Commissioner Foss also played a key role in preserving the franchise when he decided to have the league run the operation until the syndicate headed by Werblin came on the scene.

Another major reason behind the AFL's success was its ability to sell itself to a major television network at its inception. Under a contract signed with the American Broadcasting company, each AFL team received $150,000, and this needed revenue kept the league afloat when it otherwise might have folded. During the early years of its existence, the AFL suffered from a lack of superstars, poor attendance, the high cost of signing top draft choices and, in some cases, inadequate stadia. Attendance in the first year averaged only 16,500 but by 1962 began to climb steadily.

While the AFL may have had a shortage of quality players in its initial years, the games didn't lack for excitement or unpredictability. Most AFL teams used a wide-open, passing style which produced a lot of scoring. Although the defenses sometime seemed invisible, the style of play appealed immensely to the average fan. In the very first year Denver's Lionel Taylor caught 92 passes, and in 1964 George Blanda attempted 505 passes and Houston Teammate Charley Hennigan caught 101 of them for a total of 1,546 yards. Although Johnny Morris of the NFL's Chicago Bears caught 93 passes that same year, the older league with its stronger defenses couldn't quite match its young challenger when it came to high-scoring football.

When the Dallas Texans found their future growth limited by the presence of the NFL Cowboys and attendance figures below expectations, Hunt moved them to Kansas City after winning the 1962 AFL championship. As an inducement, Kansas City mayor H. Roe Bartle offered to enlarge Municipal Stadium and rent it to the team at $1 per year for the first two seasons, in addition to promising three times as many season tickets as the Texans sold in Dallas. With St. Louis the nearest competitor 250 miles away, Hunt saw a much brighter future in Kansas City, which became the AFL's first team in the Midwest.

The Los Angeles Chargers were actually the first AFL franchise to move to a new city, heading south for San Diego after their first year of play, in which they won the AFL's Western Division. Only 9,928 fans witnessed their title-clinching victory over Denver in 1960, and the club lost a total of $900,000 that first year. Those figures, combined with an enthusiastic appeal by San Diego officials, convinced Hilton to move the team without delay to the 34,000-seat Balboa Stadium.

Unknown to Commissioner Foss, AFL owners held a secret draft in 1961, hoping to sign the premium college players before the NFL teams held their draft. But when Foss learned of the plan, he declared the secret draft void and insisted another one be held. This infuriated Wismer, who had drafted Syracuse fullback Ernie Davis at the secret draft but saw Buffalo pick him at the official draft. Wismer tried to effect Foss' ouster but a majority of the owners backed the commissioner. While the competition for college seniors was fierce, the AFL refrained from signing established players currently under contract to NFL teams.

Rozelle convinced NFL owners that their interests would be better served if they united and sold the television rights to their games to one network in a single package. Such a plan brought added stability to the league, because the weaker clubs were able to share equally in the television revenue. Rozelle went before Congress in 1961 and convinced that body to pass a bill legalizing single-network contracts by professional sports leagues. He was rewarded the next year by being given a new five-year contract.

In 1962 a U.S. District judge ruled against the AFL's charges of monopoly by the NFL in the areas of expansion, player signings and television contracts, and the U.S. Fourth Circuit Court of Appeals refused to overturn that decision a year later. Meanwhile, both leagues competed for the spectators' dollars, the AFL instituting in 1961 a post-season All-Star game which got television exposure and the NFL experimenting in 1962 with a pre-season doubleheader involving four teams that drew a capacity house at Cleveland. The AFL had an all-Texas championship game in 1962 that went into a second overtime period before the Texans finally beat the Oilers in front of a full house of 37,981.

In 1963 the NFL was rocked by a gambling scandal which threatened the credibility of the entire league. Acting decisively, Rozelle suspended Green Bay's "Golden Boy" Paul Hornung and Detroit's defensive star Alex Karras for betting on football games in which they were not involved. In addition, five Detroit players — Joe Schmidt, Wayne Walker, John Gordy, Gary Lowe and Sam Williams — were fined $2,000 each for betting and the Lions' management was fined $4,000. Both players were reinstated 11 months later, but Rozelle's action served to maintain the public's faith in the integrity of the sport.

While Werblin was taking control of the AFL's New York franchise (changing its name from Titans to Jets) and Hunt was moving his team to Kansas City (changing its name from Texans to Chiefs), Al Davis left his job as an assistant coach at San Diego at age 33 to become the general manager and head coach at Oakland. With the Raiders finishing 2-12 and 1-13 in the previous two seasons, Davis' task seemed formidable, but he somehow blended several free agents and rookies with the holdovers and produced a team which went 10-4 and fell only one game short of the Western Division title. That season was only the beginning of what would prove to be a very successful career for Davis.

The survival of the AFL took a giant step in 1964 when Foss signed a five-year television contract with NBC for $36 million, guaranteeing each team $900,000 per year from television rights alone. The NFL also signed a new television contract, getting $14.1 million from CBS for the next two years of regular-season games. The new contract also permitted for the first time the telecasts of several games during prime time and also the telecasts of other games in the area of a team playing at home on a given Sunday.

With both leagues now having a measure of security because of the television revenue, they looked toward opening up new markets. They expanded into the Deep South for the first time in 1965, the NFL awarding a franchise to Atlanta and the AFL adding Miami, with both teams scheduled to begin league play in 1966. Following the same trend, New Orleans was slated to join the NFL in 1967.

While Kansas City's Hunt and Dallas' Tex Schramm were secretly discussing a merger, the war between the two leagues over signing players escalated in 1966 when placekicker Pete Gogolak played out his option with the Buffalo Bills and then signed with the NFL's New York Giants. The AFL interpreted this move as a deliberate attempt to lure away its top players, and Davis, who had replaced Foss as AFL commissioner in April 1966 after three impressive years at Oakland, set out to retaliate. The agressive 36-year-old league boss began efforts to sign top NFL players, forcing the NFL owners to seriously consider a truce in the war. The two leagues spent an estimated $7 million on draft choices alone in 1966, including $1 million by Green Bay for running backs Donny Anderson and Jim Grabowski.

To the surprise of nearly everyone, Rozelle announced on June 8, 1966 a merger agreement between the two leagues, with the AFL paying $26 million for the added financial security of joining the stable NFL. The two sides agreed to a championship game between the two leagues beginning with the 1966 season. Starting in 1967, a common draft and inter-league pre-season games were scheduled. Expansion to 26 teams by 1968 and a total merger of the two leagues into one unit by 1970 was planned. Rozelle was chosen as commissioner of the two leagues and, with the goal of a merger agreement behind him, Davis resigned his post with the AFL and returned to Oakland as managing general partner. Milt Woodward was appointed AFL president until the two leagues realigned under one banner.

At the first common draft in 1967, the AFL demonstrated its uncanny ability to assess young talent — an ability that would later prove to be a major factor in its quick rise to equality with the NFL teams. The AFL drafted such future stars as Bob Griese, Gene Upshaw, George Webster and Floyd Little, while the best the NFL could do was Mel Farr and Charles (Bubba) Smith, the No. 1 choice in the entire draft. Rozelle announced at that draft that "futures" (players whose college class had graduated but who still had a year of eligibility left) no longer could be drafted.

The AFL also had some success in inter-league games during the 1967 pre-season, Denver beating Detroit 13-7 for the first AFL triumph and defending AFL champion Kansas City embarrassing Chicago 66-27. The regular season started on an explosive note, as four kickoffs were returned for touchdowns on the opening weekend. For the season, 14 touchdowns were scored on kickoff returns, including a record four by Green Bay rookie Travis Williams and three by Chicago's Gale Sayers. Both players had record-breaking kickoff return averages — Williams 41.1 and Sayers 37.7. There also was a single-season record of nine ties during that exciting 1967 season.

Cincinnati was granted a franchise to join the AFL in 1968, and the team chose the same nickname (Bengals) that was used by the Cincinnati team in the old AFL of 1941. Former Cleveland coach Paul Brown was the leader of a group which bought the franchise, and he became its first head coach. Although his fellow owners weren't overly generous in the veteran allocation draft which supplied 40 players to the Bengals, Brown and player personnel director Al LoCasale used the draft wisely, building the Bengals into the first expansion team ever to win a division title in its third year of existence.

Two of the greatest names in NFL coaching annals retired in early 1968 — George Halas and Vince Lombardi. For Halas, 73, it was the fourth and final retirement after 40 years of professional coaching in Chicago, where he had owned a team since 1921. His coaching record was an impressive 320-147-30, giving him the most victories of any coach in NFL history. Lombardi resigned at the pinnacle of his career, having won five NFL championships during his nine-year reign at Green Bay and the frist two Super Bowls during his last two years. After one year in the sole capacity of general manager of the Packers, Lombardi took up a new challenge as part-owner, general manager and head coach of Washington in 1969 — a challenge that would be cut short by cancer after one season.

While AFL owners and players had agreed upon a pension increase in early 1968, the NFL was less sucessful. The resulting dispute prompted the NFL Players Association to declare a strike in July, and a compromise was reached only a few days before training camps were scheduled to open. The television networks learned just how powerful the influence of the football viewers had become when NBC switched at the appointed hour from its coverage of a close game between the Jets and the Raiders to begin a dramatic special of "Heidi." Enraged football fans jammed the network's switchboard, becoming even more upset when they learned that Oakland had scored two touchdowns in 17 seconds during the final minute of the game. Television had indeed created a "monster" that would have to be accommodated even further in the near future.

The AFL gained in respectability by leaps and bounds after the 1968 regular season had ended. PRO FOOTBALL WEEKLY announced the first-ever All-Pro team combining AFL and NFL players, and the AFL captured 10 of 22 positions. While Earl Morrall led the Baltimore Colts to an NFL title as a replacement for the injured Johnny Unitas, a young Joe Namath was making headlines with three touchdown passes in a 27-23 win over Oakland for the AFL championship. Because the AFL hadn't come close in either of the first two Super Bowl games, nobody gave the brash, young Jets much of a chance against the once-beaten Colts. When Namath was quoted a few days before the game as saying that the Jets would beat Baltimore, the statement was interpreted as a typical example of Super bowl "hype." Namath fulfilled his promise on Super Bowl Sunday, however, completing 17 of 28 passes for 206 yards as the Jets defeated the Colts 16-7. It was a momentous day for the AFL, and four underdogs everywhere.

When the excitement surrounding Super Bowl III began to subside, the NFL and AFL owners began deliberations on the realignment of the two leagues under one roof. The procedure wasn't as simple as some owners had expected. Many NFL owners were determined to maintain the separate identities of the two leagues within one organization. Some AFL owners also were willing to accept this plan, until Paul Brown and several other owners (New York's Phil Iselin, Denver's Gerald Phipps and Miami's Joe Robbie insisted that the AFL could never achieve parity with the NFL as long as the teams in the NFL outnumbered their AFL counterparts 16 to 10.

Once the NFL owners realized that a 16-10 split of the teams would not be approved, they had to decide which three teams would move to the AFL. At first, none of the owners wanted to move, fearing that their reputation and attendance would suffer and that they would lose important rivalries. The New York Giants and the San Francisco 49ers were exempted from switching to the AFL by the terms of the original merger agreement, because it was deemed essential that they be in a different conference from their next-door neighbors, the New York Jets and the Oakland Raiders. Reasons for not joining the AFL seemed to be numerous, while reasons for switching were hard to find.

In a non-stop meeting that lasted nearly 36 hours, the owners finally agreed on a new alignment, with Baltimore, Cleveland and Pittsburgh moving to the AFL. Baltimore owner Carroll Rosenbloom had taken the initiative, agreeing to move his Colts to the AFL, and Cleveland's Art Modell followed Rosenbloom's lead. Modell wanted Pittsburgh to join him in a new division of the realigned American Conference and, after some hesitation, Steeler bosses Art and Dan Rooney agreed. The move by Baltimore and Cleveland came as a surprise to many fans because the clubs were two of the NFL's better teams at that time. While Pittsburgh had been a member of the NFL since 1933, its switch was less surprising in light of its five consecutive losing seasons.

Al Davis, who had been a thorn in the sides of NFL owners during his two-month tenure as AFL commissioner prior to the merger agreement, didn't win any new friends when he prolonged the marathon realignment session an additional 12 hours by insisting upon knowing the exact alignment of the 13 remaining NFL teams before giving his ratification vote. Nevertheless, the meeting adjourned without an agreement on the new setup of the 13 NFL teams, forcing the approval of the overall realignment plan to be postponed.

Two divisional arrangements came within one vote of the unanimous approval needed at that May 9-10 meeting in 1969. The first had the Vikings, Redskins, Cardinals, Giants and Eagles in the Eastern Division; the Cowboys, Packers, Bears and Lions in the Central; the Rams, 49ers, Saints and Falcons in the Western. The second plan had the Cowboys, Redskins, Cardinals and Giants in the East; the Packers, Bears, Lions and Saints in the Central; the Vikings, Rams, 49ers, Falcons And Eagles in the West. The First proposal was closer to the alignment eventually adopted, needing only a reversal of the Vikings' and Cowboys' positions.

Because the NFL owners never were able to agree on an equitable divisional setup for their 13 teams, Rozelle eventually submitted five plans and had one drawn in a lottery.

The financial aspects of the merger agreement included an $18 million indemnity payment by the AFL, which also gave the NFL an $8 million franchise fee paid by the Cincinnati owners to join the league. On the other hand, the AFL was getting assets estimated at a value of $55 million in the form of the three NFL teams which joined the AFL teams. In addition, the 13 NFL clubs agreed to pay each of the three teams who switched to the AFL approximately $2.5 million as compensation for the move.

The persistence of the AFL owners in demanding an equal share of the pie virtually guaranteed the equality of the two factions within a relatively short period of time. While the existence of the AFL vanished along with the decade, just as it had arisen from nowhere at the beginning of the 1960's, the memory of the league lingered on. The rivalry between the NFL and AFL was continued as an NFC-AFC rivalry, although the divisions had been blurred by the realignment. More than a decade after the initial merger agreement, the controversy between NFC and AFC factions continued to rage. The spirit and innovations of the American Football League pervaded professional football long after its disappearance, making the sport a more popular attraction than ever.

The end of the decade also provided some touchy decisions for Rozelle. The commissioner signed a three-year contract with the ABC television network for weekly telecasts of Monday night football games, while some observers feared that overexposure might result. Whereas the armchair quarterback had previously been limited to weekends for most of his football viewing, he now would have the opportunity to witness a football game as a prime-time "production." More importantly, the move of pro football to prime-time television meant large-scale advertising revenue and, as a result, more money in the coffers of the individual teams. Inevitably, this increase in revenue would be reflected in the salary demands of the players. Taken to its conclusion, the rapid spread in television exposure meant that the networks would have more control and the average fan less influence over the development of the sport.

Having dealt decisively with the gambling scandal in 1963, Rozelle faced a lesser but still noteworthy decision in 1969 when Namath was reportedly linked to several underworld figures through his part-ownership of a New York City nightclub. When Rozelle gave Namath the ultimatum of either selling his interest in the business or being suspended, Namath "retired" from football in a fit of pique. Although Namath was charged with "guilt by association" rather than any illegal activities, Rozelle was clearly within his broad authority as outlined in the league's constitution and by-laws and the standard player contract. Faced with the prospect of losing a substantial sum of money through a forfeited football contract and the possible loss of endorsements, Namath reconsidered his "retirement," choosing instead to sell his interest in Bachelors III and return to football.

Progress in the area of racial equality was achieved more quickly in professional football circles than in the surrounding environment, but some vestiges of foot-dragging were evident during the 1960's. Washington became the last NFL team to end the color barrier when it drafted Heisman Trophy winner Ernie Davis of Syracuse in 1962. Before the season started, the Redskins traded Davis to Cleveland for Bobby Mitchell, a black who became one of the league's leading receivers. Other blacks signed by the Redskins that year where Ron Hatcher, Leroy Jackson and John Nisby. After the 1965 season, several players in New Orleans for the AFL All-Star game charged that they were discriminated against, so the game was moved to Houston. In 1968 Merlin Briscoe of the Denver Broncos became the first black in pro football history to play regularly at quarterback, when an injury to the regular quarterback forced the rookie from Omaha to take over. Briscoe was traded to Buffalo the following year and he became a wide receiver.

A number of rule changes were adopted during the 1960's many of which made the game easier for the average fan to follow. The color of the officials' penalty flags was changed from white to gold, the uprights of the goal post were lengthened to a minimum of 20 feet above the crossbar and were painted gold, and the playing field was rimmed with a white border six feet wide. The major rule changes affecting the conduct of the game made it illegal for a player to grab the facemask of an opponent and required kicking shoes to be of standard production and not modified in any manner.

As the 1960's drew to a close, the emphasis on wide-open offensive football was beginning to change to a more conservative style of ball-control offense and short passes, as zone defenses became increasingly effective. While the influx of soccer-style kickers had accompanied a surge in the number of field goals, the number of touchdowns per game dropped significantly near the end of the decade. With 26 teams united under one organization and attendance booming, pro football was ready to begin a new era.

ALL-NFL TEAM OF THE 1960's

OFFENSE

Name	Position
Del Shofner	Split End
Charley Taylor	Split End
Gary Collins	Flanker
Boyd Dowler	Flanker
John Mackey	Tight End
Bob Brown	Tackle
Forrest Gregg	Tackle
Ralph Neely	Tackle
Gene Hickerson	Guard
Jerry Kramer	Guard
Howard Mudd	Guard
Jim Ringo	Center
Sonny Jurgensen	Quarterback
Bart Starr	Quarterback
Johnny Unitas	Quarterback
John David Crow	Halfback
Paul Hornung	Halfback
Leroy Kelly	Halfback
Gale Sayers	Halfback
Jim Brown	Fullback
Jim Taylor	Fullback
Jim Bakken	Kicker
Don Chandler	Punter

DEFENSE

Name	Position
Doug Atkins	End
Willie Davis	End
David (Deacon) Jones	End
Alex Karras	Tackle
Bob Lilly	Tackle
Merlin Olsen	Tackle
Dick Butkus	Linebacker
Larry Morris	Linebacker
Ray Nitschke	Linebacker
Tommy Nobis	Linebacker
Dave Robinson	Linebacker
Herb Adderley	Cornerback
Lem Barney	Cornerback
Bobby Boyd	Cornerback
Eddie Meador	Safety
Larry Wilson	Safety
Willy Wood	Safety

ALL-AFL TEAM OF THE 1960's

OFFENSE

Name	Position
Lance Alworth	Flanker
Don Maynard	End
Fred Arbanas	Tight End
Ron Mix	Tackle
Jim Tyrer	Tackle
Ed Budde	Guard
Billy Shaw	Guard
Jim Otto	Center
Joe Namath	Quarterback
Clem Daniels	Running Back
Paul Lowe	Running Back
George Blanda	Kicker
Jarrel Wilson	Punter

DEFENSE

Name	Position
Jerry Mays	End
Gerry Philbin	End
Houston Antwine	Tackle
Tom Sestak	Tackle
Bobby Bell	Linebacker
George Webster	Linebacker
Nick Buoniconti	Linebacker
Willie Brown	Cornerback
Dave Grayson	Cornerback
Johnny Robinson	Safety
George Saimes	Safety

(Both teams were chosen by the Pro Football Hall of Fame Selection Committee).

1960 N.F.L. Mara's Compromise

After four days of meetings and twenty-one deadlocked ballots, the league owners had still not elected a new commissioner to succeed the late Bert Bell. With the older owners supporting acting commissioner Austin Gunsel and the young owners supporting San Francisco attorney Marshall Leahy, New York Giant vice-president Wellington Mara presented an acceptable compromise candidate. He nominated Pete Rozelle, thirty-three-year-old general manager of the Los Angeles Rams, and the other owners quickly confirmed the young man as commissioner. Like Bell, Rozelle faced the challenge of a new league, the American Football League, at the start of his administration, but the NFL was strong enough at this time also to expand, shifting the Cardinals to St. Louis, putting a new team in Dallas this year, and granting Minneapolis-St. Paul a franchise for 1961. The new league would drive player salaries up, but the NFL owners had no worries about their league surviving.

EASTERN CONFERENCE

Philadelphia Eagles—The Eagles hardly looked like champions when they lost to Cleveland on opening day and barely beat the new Dallas team 27-25 the next week. But the club slowly gained momentum and by mid-season was battling the Giants and Browns for the Eastern lead. They eliminated the Giants by beating them 17-10 and 31-23 in back-to-back games, while the Browns eliminated themselves with three mid-season losses. Quarterback Norm Van Brocklin moved the team with his passes, but reserve depth was the key to the title drive. When fullback Clarence Peaks was sidelined, rookie Ted Dean filled in splendidly, and when injuries depleted the linebacking corps, center Chuck Bednarik moved over to defense. The thirty-five-year-old Bednarik was the story of the year, playing most of the game while starring at center and middle linebacker.

Cleveland Browns—The Browns opened their year with an impressive 41-24 rout of the Eagles, but the Philadelphia club evened the score three weeks later with a 31-29 squeaker. Then, while the Eagles went on a hot streak, the Browns ran into trouble in mid-season. The Giants came to Cleveland in early November and held Jimmy Brown and Bobby Mitchell to a total of six yards rushing. The 17-13 New York victory was their sixth in a row over the Browns. After the Browns edged the Cards 28-27, a 14-10 loss to Pittsburgh and a 17-17 tie with the Cards put them too far behind the Eagles to catch up. But one element of satisfaction did come from the strong finale, a 48-34 victory over the Giants at Yankee Stadium.

New York Giants—A good early-season showing kept the Giants in the Eastern race into November, but the aging New York squad was barely holding together with paste and string. A bad knee sidelined Alex Webster for most of the year, elbow and leg troubles made Chuck Conerly's availability a week-to-week affair, and an injured shoulder put Jim Katcavage out of action for the last half of the season. The Eagles, holding a slim half-game lead, came to Yankee Stadium in mid-November and beat the New Yorkers 17-10. The biggest loss of the day, however, was halfback Frank Gifford, knocked unconscious with a concussion by Chuck Bednarik's vicious tackle. Another loss in Philadelphia made the Giants' chances slim, and a tie with the fledgling Cowboys ended their hopes completely.

St. Louis Cardinals—The team's move to St. Louis had an immediate effect, as the Cards beat the Rams 43-21 to open their new history. Long-time losers in Chicago, these new Cardinals moved up to fourth place in the East behind an improved defense and versatile offense. The defensive line, led by Frank Fuller, put strong pressure on enemy passers, while the mobile linebacking crew of Bill Koman, Dale Meinert, and Ted Bates improved with experience. In the secondary, Jerry Norton starred at safety, while rookie Larry Wilson broke into the lineup as a cornerback. John Roach was the third new starting quarterback in three years, but the main forces in the offensive resurgence were end Sonny Randle and halfback John David Crow.

Pittsburgh Steelers—After beating the new Dallas Cowboys to start the season, the Steelers won only once in their next seven games, with only a matching effort by the Redskins keeping them from dropping to the bottom of the East. Injuries plagued the Steelers along the way. Bobby Layne hurt his throwing hand, a bad leg slowed John Henry Johnson, and various physical ills bothered Jimmy Orr, Mike Sandusky, and Mike Henry. Flanker Buddy Dial stayed healthy and was the main offensive threat with his speed on long passes. The defense slacked off a bit, due partly to the retirement of All-Pro cornerback Jack Butler, but still was no pushover. Starting in late November, the Steelers drove back to respectabiltiy with a three-game win streak, crippling the Browns' title hopes 14-10, locking Washington into the basement 22-10, and ending the Eagles' nine-game win streak 27-21.

Washington Redskins—The Redskin defense sprang some major leaks in the secondary, but they were nothing compared to the leaks in the offensive line. Quarterback Ralph Guglielmi watched a flood of defensive linemen pour in on him every Sunday, forcing him either to hurry his pass or hang onto the ball and get smashed to the ground. The ends he was throwing to, Bill Anderson and Joe Walton, did not have good speed, and fullback Don Bosseler, the leading rusher, was no sprinter, so the Redskins scored 16 points or less in eight of their nine losses.

WESTERN CONFERENCE

Green Bay Packers—After a close five-team race, the Packers emerged from the fray with their first Western title since 1944. They did not back into the crown but won it by taking their last three contests, two of which included head-to-head victories over the Bears and the '49ers. The Packers again were national news, and their biggest star was halfback Paul Hornung, who grabbed headlines with his unprecedented point production. As a runner, he had a nose for the end zone; as a kicker, his toe churned out points with field goals and extra points. After twelve games Hornung had set a new season's scoring record of 176 points.

Detroit Lions—With their defense jelling into a top unit, the Lions won their last four games to capture second place in the West. Rookie tackle Roger Brown joined Alex Karras, Darris McCord, and Bill Glass in a powerful front line, while Carl Brettschneider came from the Cardinals to complete the linebacking trio with Joe Schmidt and Wayne Walker. Another ex-Card, Night Train Lane, tightened up a secondary that already featured Yale Lary, Dick LeBeau, and Gary Lowe. Newcomers also helped the offense, as ex-Cleveland quarterback Jim Ninowski and freshman end Gail Cogdill made the pass a vital weapon in the Detroit attack again.

San Francisco '49ers—In a turn-about in the club's image, the defense carried the '49ers through the season. The young secondary of Abe Woodson, Jerry Mertens, Eddie Dove, and Dave Baker had meshed into a fine unit, while veterans Matt Hazeltine and Leo Nomellini anchored the linebacking front line units. The offense, however, bucked and sputtered, relying more than usual on Tommy Davis' field goals to bail it out. Head coach Red Hickey did experiment with the shotgun formation, with both ends split, a flanker and two wingbacks up near the line of scrimmage, and a quarterback all alone in the backfield, five yards back from the center. With the mobile John Brodie beating out Y. A. Tittle for the quarterback slot, the new formation often caught enemy defenses by surprise.

Baltimore Colts—Playing with a fractured vertebra in his back, Johnny Unitas still had his Colts at the head of the West. In mid-November, Baltimore held a one-game lead over Green Bay and had just won three straight games, apparently on the way to a third straight Western title. But when a torn Achilles tendon ended fullback Alan Ameche's career in mid-season, the Colt running game withered away and died. With only Unitas' passing to Ray Berry and Lenny Moore to worry about, enemy defenses concentrated solely on rushing the fragile Unitas and blanketing his receivers.

Chicago Bears—Neither Zeke Bratkowski nor Ed Brown had impressed at quarterback, fullback Rick Casares was slowing up, and the ends had no speed, but the Bears had scrapped their way to a 5-3-1 record, a half game behind the first-place Colts, by late November. The defense, led by Bill George and Doug Atkins, had kept the Bears in the race with several strong efforts through the fall. But the visions of championships dancing in George Halas' head were just so many sugar plums. The Packers just about killed any Bear hopes with a 41-13 drubbing two weeks from the end of the year, and the last two games turned into a nightmare, with a 42-0 beating by Cleveland and a 36-0 loss to Detroit.

Los Angeles Rams—It would have made great newspaper copy for new head coach Bob Waterfield and new general manager Elroy "Crazy Legs" Hirsch, great players in the salad days of the early 1950s, to lead the Rams back to glory, but it wasn't to be. Four losses right at the start established the Rams as also-rans in the West and prompted Waterfield to shake his club up. Young Frank Ryan began sharing the quarterback job with Billy Wade, Ollie Matson was shifted to a flanker position where his main duties were blocking and receiving, and Del Shofner became a defensive back after losing his offensive end job to rookie Carroll Dale. Although the Rams did beat the Packers and Colts down the stretch, the season was a troubled one all around.

Dallas Cowboys—Former New York assistant Tom Landry came in as head coach and tried to combine young talent with a coating of experienced players. For quarterbacks, Landry traded for little Eddie LeBaron and got rookie Don Meredith in the expansion draft, but the offense they commanded was practically invisible. Of the other players, end Jim Doran and linebacker Jerry Tubbs showed the most, with the roster in general an arid stretch of mediocrity. A perfect record of losses seemed inevitable for the Cowboys until they visited New York in December and gained a 31-31 tie with the Giants.

FINAL TEAM STATISTICS

OFFENSE

	BALT.	CHI.	CLEVE.	DALL.	DET.	G.BAY	L.A.	N.Y.	PHIL.	PITT.	ST.L.	S.F.	WASH.
FIRST DOWNS:													
Total	227	183	219	180	192	237	194	202	190	198	229	201	166
by Rushing	64	83	107	57	89	135	76	81	54	81	127	90	83
by Passing	143	90	96	105	88	86	101	107	121	104	89	96	71
by Penalty	20	10	16	18	15	16	17	14	15	13	13	15	12
RUSHING:													
Number	345	373	383	312	392	463	343	406	351	411	484	413	415
Yards	1289	1639	1930	1049	1714	2150	1449	1440	1134	1623	2356	1681	1313
Average Yards	3.7	4.4	5.0	3.4	4.4	4.6	4.2	3.5	3.2	3.9	4.9	4.1	3.2
Touchdowns	10	11	18	6	19	29	9	10	9	9	13	9	9
PASSING:													
Attempts	392	324	264	354	333	279	335	322	331	285	285	336	274
Completions	196	146	160	163	166	137	177	156	177	139	126	174	147
Completion Pct.	50.0	45.1	60.6	46.0	49.8	49.1	52.8	48.4	53.5	48.8	44.2	51.8	53.6
Gross Yards	3164	2130	2343	2388	2022	1993	2188	2385	2957	2511	1990	1866	1816
Yards Lost Tackled	208	304	299	284	344	118	366	131	141	89	179	287	385
Net Yards	2956	1826	2044	2104	1678	1875	1822	2254	2816	2422	1811	1579	1431
Avg. Yds per Att (Gs)	8.1	6.6	8.9	6.7	6.1	7.1	6.5	7.4	8.9	8.8	7.0	5.6	6.6
Avg. Yds per Com (Gs)	16.1	14.6	14.6	14.7	12.2	14.5	12.4	15.3	16.7	18.1	15.8	10.7	12.4
Touchdowns	26	13	22	17	6	9	19	20	29	20	20	11	9
Interceptions	24	32	5	33	21	13	22	23	20	21	25	12	23
Percent Intercepted	6.1	9.9	1.9	9.3	6.3	4.7	6.6	7.1	6.0	7.4	8.8	3.6	8.4
PUNTING:													
Number	52	64	55	60	64	49	64	49	60	64	44	65	60
Average Distance	38.5	39.7	42.0	42.0	43.8	41.2	42.3	39.2	43.1	44.2	44.9	44.3	42.1
PUNT RETURNS:													
Number	23	27	21	23	31	26	25	31	28	30	30	24	15
Yards	127	182	208	175	227	172	129	209	119	183	232	217	65
Average Yards	5.5	6.7	9.9	7.6	7.3	6.6	5.2	6.7	4.3	6.1	7.7	9.0	4.3
Touchdowns	0	0	0	0	0	0	1	0	0	0	0	0	0
KICKOFF RETURNS:													
Number	47	47	45	69	43	35	40	41	52	44	45	43	62
Yards	1030	1055	900	1264	916	852	941	894	973	964	1045	1167	1363
Average Yards	21.9	22.4	20.0	18.3	21.3	24.3	23.5	21.8	18.7	21.9	23.2	27.1	22.0
Touchdowns	1	0	1	0	0	0	0	0	0	0	0	1	0
INTERCEPTION RETURNS:													
Number	30	10	31	15	19	22	23	22	30	16	21	20	15
Yards	297	111	624	97	365	358	362	294	341	130	178	141	189
Average Yards	9.9	11.1	20.1	6.5	19.2	16.3	15.7	13.4	11.4	8.1	8.5	7.1	12.6
Touchdowns	0	0	6	0	2	1	3	2	0	0	0	0	0
PENALTIES:													
Number	51	83	49	62	68	64	64	48	57	61	46	63	69
Yards	504	707	534	600	726	578	625	460	544	606	456	604	713
FUMBLES:													
Number	24	18	20	22	13	18	17	49	24	27	42	14	29
Number Lost	12	10	12	17	9	12	9	26	10	14	22	4	15
POINTS:													
Total	288	194	362	177	239	332	265	271	321	240	288	208	178
PAT Attempts	37	25	46	23	28	41	31	32	40	28	34	21	19
PAT Made	35	23	44	21	26	41	31	32	39	27	33	21	19
FG Attempts	19	16	20	13	24	28	22	26	20	19	25	35	23
FG Made	9	7	12	6	13	15	14	13	14	11	15	19	15
Percent FG Made	47.4	43.8	60.0	46.2	54.2	53.6	63.6	50.0	70.0	57.9	60.0	54.3	65.2
Safeties	2	0	0	0	3	0	0	1	0	0	3	2	0

DEFENSE

	BALT.	CHI.	CLEVE.	DALL.	DET.	G.BAY	L.A.	N.Y.	PHIL.	PITT.	ST.L.	S.F.	WASH.
FIRST DOWNS:													
Total	195	202	208	216	204	199	221	183	205	224	158	180	223
by Rushing	86	94	92	106	87	74	87	79	117	90	56	82	77
by Passing	98	84	102	97	94	110	114	89	81	120	93	89	126
by Penalty	11	24	14	13	23	15	20	15	7	14	9	9	20
RUSHING:													
Number	379	403	405	447	360	350	419	396	449	414	344	363	362
Yards	1591	1679	1643	2242	1348	1285	1718	1267	2200	1493	1212	1587	1502
Average Yards	4.2	4.2	4.1	5.0	3.7	3.7	4.1	3.2	4.9	3.6	3.5	4.4	4.1
Touchdowns	17	17	10	20	9	7	16	8	14	13	8	13	9
PASSING:													
Attempts	298	291	319	293	354	365	339	297	283	361	300	293	321
Completions	144	246	163	146	175	192	168	142	139	184	156	140	169
Completion Pct.	48.3	50.2	51.1	49.8	49.4	52.6	49.6	47.8	49.1	51.0	52.0	47.8	52.6
Gross Yards	2068	1808	2370	2305	2275	2432	2510	2010	1984	3075	2147	2001	2768
Yards Lost Tackled	342	420	207	175	226	275	155	177	157	284	330	183	204
Net Yards	1726	1388	2163	2130	2049	2157	2355	1833	1827	2791	1817	1818	2564
Avg. Yds per Att (Gs)	6.9	6.2	7.4	7.9	6.4	6.7	7.4	6.8	7.0	8.5	7.2	6.8	8.6
Avg. Yds per Com (Gs)	14.4	12.4	14.5	15.8	13.0	12.7	14.9	14.2	14.3	16.7	13.8	14.3	16.4
Touchdowns	8	14	15	22	17	19	18	19	14	20	20	11	24
Interceptions	30	10	31	15	19	22	23	22	30	16	21	20	15
Percent Intercepted	10.1	3.4	9.7	5.1	5.4	6.0	6.8	7.4	10.6	4.4	7.0	6.8	4.7
PUNTING:													
Number	54	72	46	50	69	66	50	66	48	54	63	62	50
Average Distance	46.4	41.3	45.5	42.1	39.0	39.4	43.8	40.8	43.6	43.4	44.3	41.2	39.5
PUNT RETURNS:													
Number	15	35	24	20	34	22	27	17	34	21	26	28	31
Yards	48	249	168	91	296	144	199	100	166	198	162	182	242
Average Yards	3.2	7.1	7.0	4.6	8.7	6.5	7.4	5.9	4.9	9.4	6.2	6.5	7.8
Touchdowns	0	1	0	0	0	0	0	0	0	0	0	0	0
KICKOFF RETURNS:													
Number	44	37	62	31	45	57	52	47	53	48	57	38	42
Yards	1253	1029	1177	803	979	1158	1083	995	1076	1078	1245	769	719
Average Yards	28.5	27.8	19.0	25.9	21.8	20.3	20.8	21.2	20.3	22.5	21.8	20.2	17.1
Touchdowns	1	1	0	1	0	0	0	0	0	0	0	0	0
INTERCEPTION RETURNS:													
Number	24	32	5	33	21	13	22	23	20	21	25	12	23
Yards	272	627	58	366	314	185	182	253	277	165	419	159	210
Average Yards	11.3	19.6	11.6	11.1	15.0	14.2	8.3	11.0	13.9	7.9	16.8	13.3	9.1
Touchdowns	1	4	1	2	2	0	0	2	1	0	0	0	1
PENALTIES:													
Number	59	75	48	72	60	61	59	55	54	58	52	64	68
Yards	538	704	526	671	637	636	517	532	597	565	500	580	654
FUMBLES:													
Number	20	13	27	21	19	23	29	28	31	25	35	15	31
Number Lost	9	9	14	11	11	15	13	12	15	13	23	8	19
POINTS:													
Total	234	299	217	369	212	209	297	261	246	275	230	205	309
PAT Attempts	27	38	26	45	28	25	35	32	27	33	30	25	34
PAT Made	27	37	25	44	27	24	34	31	24	33	29	23	34
FG Attempts	30	20	21	25	12	13	29	23	28	21	16	20	32
FG Made	15	8	12	17	5	9	17	12	16	14	7	10	21
Percent FG Made	50.0	40.0	57.1	68.0	41.7	69.2	58.6	52.2	57.1	66.7	43.8	50.0	65.6
Safeties	0	2	0	2	1	1	1	1	0	1	0	1	1

1960 NFL CHAMPIONSHIP GAME
December 26, at Philadelphia
(Attendance 67,325)

Start with Hornung, End with Dean

The Green Bay Packers, a tough, young team built by coach Vince Lombardi, came to Franklin Field to face the Eagles, a veteran team centering around Norm Van Brocklin and Chuck Bednarik, for the NFL title. The Packers got the first break of the game by recovering an Eagle fumble on the Philadelphia 14-yard line on the first play from scrimmage, but four Green Bay running plays gained only nine yards. The Eagles took the ball on downs but fumbled it away three plays later on the 22-yard line. Again the Packers couldn't move the ball, and they had to settle for a Paul Hornung field goal. The quarter ended with the score 3-0, as both defenses played well against the enemy's strength. The Eagles shut off the Green Bay running game; the Packers stopped Van Brocklin's passes. The halftime score was Philadelphia 10, Green Bay 6, and neither team scored in the third quarter. Within two minutes of the fourth period, however, Green Bay capped an 80-yard drive with a Bart Starr-to-Max McGee touchdown pass to give the Packers a 13-10 lead. On the kickoff following the touchdown, Ted Dean brought the Eagles back into the game by returning the ball to the Green Bay 39. Seven plays later, Dean carried the ball over from the 5-yard line. The Packers drove downfield in the waning minutes, but time ran out with the ball on the Philadelphia 9-yard line and the score 17-13 in favor of the Eagles.

SCORING

PHILADELPHIA	0	10	0	7	–17
GREEN BAY	3	3	0	7	–13

First Quarter
G. B. Hornung, 20 yard field goal 6:20

Second Quarter
G. B. Hornung, 23 yard field goal 1:44
PHI. McDonald, 35 yard pass from Van Brocklin 8:08
PAT – Walston (kick)
PHI. Walston, 15 yard field goal 11:48

Fourth Quarter
G. B. McGee, 7 yard pass from Starr 1:53
PAT – Hornung (kick)
PHI. Dean, 5 yard rush 5:21
PAT – Walston (kick)

TEAM STATISTICS

PHI.		G.B.
13	First Downs – Total	22
5	First Downs – Rushing	14
6	First Downs – Passing	8
2	First Downs – Penalty	0
99	Rushing Yardage	223
20	Pass Attempts	35
9	Pass Completions	21
45.0	Completion Percentage	60.0
204	Passing Yardage	178
10.2	Avg. Yards per Attempt	5.1
22.7	Avg. Yards per Completion	8.5
7	Yards Lost Tackled	0
107	Net Passing Yardage	178
0	Interceptions By	1
0	Interception Return Yardage	0
3	Fumbles – Number	1
2	Fumbles – Lost Ball	1
0	Penalties – Number	4
0	Yards Penalized	27
0	Missed Field Goals	1

INDIVIDUAL STATISTICS

PHILADELPHIA	No.	Yds.	Avg.	GREEN BAY	No.	Yds.	Avg.
PUNTING							
Van Brocklin	6		39.5	McGee	5		45.2
PUNT RETURNS							
Dean	1	10	10.0	Wood	2	11	5.5
				Carpenter	2	7	3.5
					4	18	4.5
KICKOFF RETURNS							
Dean	1	58	58.0	Symank	2	49	24.5
Brown	1	20	20.0				
Lucas	1	9	9.0				
Robb	1	4	4.0				
	4	91	22.8				

PHILADELPHIA EAGLES 10-2-0 Buck Shaw

Scores of Each Game		
24	CLEVELAND	41
27	Dallas	25
31	ST. LOUIS	27
28	DETROIT	10
31	Cleveland	29
34	PITTSBURGH	7
19	WASHINGTON	13
17	New York	10
31	NEW YORK	23
20	St. Louis	6
21	Pittsburgh	27
38	Washington	28

Use Name	Pos.	Hgt	Wgt	Age	Int	Pts
Jim McCusker	OT	6'2"	245	24		
J. D. Smith	OT	6'5"	250	24		6
Howard Keys	C-OT	6'3"	235	25		
John Wilcox	DE-OT	6'5"	230	22		
Stan Campbell	OG	6'	230	30		
Jerry Huth	OG	6'	228	27		
John Wittenborn (from SF)	OG	6'2"	230	24		
Bill Lapham	C	6'3"	250	26		
Marion Campbell	DE	6'3"	250	31		
Joe Robb	LB-DE	6'3"	225	23		
Gene Gossage	DT-DE	6'3"	236	25		
Riley Gunnels	DT	6'3"	240	23		
Jess Richardson	DT	6'2"	262	30		
Ed Khayat	DE-DT	6'3"	240	25		

Use Name	Pos.	Hgt	Wgt	Age	Int	Pts
Maxie Baughan	LB	6'1"	220	22	3	
John Nocera	LB	6'1"	215	26		
Chuck Weber	LB	6'1"	235	31	6	
Bob Pellegrini	OG-LB	6'2"	235	25		
Chuck Bednarik	C-LB	6'3"	235	35	2	
Tom Brookshier	DB	6'	198	28	1	
Don Burroughs	DB	6'4"	186	29	9	
Jimmy Carr	DB	6'1"	198	27	2	6
Bobby Freeman	DB	6'1"	200	27	4	
Bobby Jackson	DB	6'1"	190	24		
Gene Johnson	DB	6'	190	25	3	

Use Name	Pos.	Hgt	Wgt	Age	Int	Pts
Sonny Jurgensen	QB	5'11"	200	26		
Norm Van Brocklin	QB	6'1"	202	34		
Jerry Reichow	OE-QB	6'2"	220	25		
Billy Barnes	HB	5'11"	198	25		36
Timmy Brown	HB	5'10"	195	23		24
Theron Sapp	HB	6'1"	200	25		
Ted Dean	FB-HB	6'2"	210	22		18
Clarence Peaks	FB	6'1"	220	24		18
Tommy McDonald	FL	5'10"	182	26		78
Dick Lucas	OE	6'2"	210	26		
Pete Retzlaff	OE	6'1"	210	29		30
Bobby Walston	FL-OE	6'	190	31		105

CLEVELAND BROWNS 8-3-1 Paul Brown

Scores of Each Game		
41	Philadelphia	24
28	PITTSBURGH	20
48	Dallas	7
29	PHILADELPHIA	31
31	Washington	10
13	NEW YORK	17
28	ST. LOUIS	27
10	Pittsburgh	14
17	St. Louis	17
27	WASHINGTON	16
42	CHICAGO	0
48	New York	34

Use Name	Pos.	Hgt	Wgt	Age	Int	Pts
Bob Denton	OT	6'4"	240	26		
Mike McCormack	OT	6'4"	247	33		
Dick Schafrath	OT	6'3"	245	24		
Gene Selawski	OT	6'4"	252	24		
Gene Hickerson	OG	6'3"	248	25		
Jim Ray Smith	OG	6'3"	245	29		
John Wooten	OG	6'2"	248	25		
John Morrow	C	6'3"	240	27		
Jim Houston	DE	6'2"	230	23		
Jim Marshall	DE	6'3"	220	23		
Paul Wiggin	DE	6'3"	240	26	1	6
Bob Gain	DT	6'3"	260	32	1	6
Floyd Peters	DT	6'4"	250	25		
Jim Prestel	DT	6'5"	250	23		
Larry Stephens	DT	6'4"	248	22	1	6

Use Name	Pos.	Hgt	Wgt	Age	Int	Pts
Vince Costello	LB	6'	225	28		
Galen Fiss	LB	6'	227	30	1	
Walt Michaels	LB	6'	237	31		
Dave Lloyd	C-LB	6'3"	248	24		
Ross Fichtner	DB	6'	185	22		
Don Fleming	DB	6'	185	23	5	
Bobby Franklin	DB	5'11"	180	24	8	12
Rich Mostardi	DB	5'11"	188	22		
Bernie Parrish	DB	5'11"	195	25	6	6
Jim Shofner	DB	6'2"	190	24	8	

Lou Groza – Voluntarily Retired

Use Name	Pos.	Hgt	Wgt	Age	Int	Pts
Len Dawson	QB	6'	195	26		
Milt Plum	QB	6'1"	205	26		12
Prentice Gautt	HB	6'	195	22		6
Bobby Mitchell	HB	6'	188	25		72
Jamie Caleb	FB-HB	6'1"	210	23		6
Jimmy Brown	FB	6'2"	228	24		66
Ray Renfro	FL	6'1"	192	29		24
A. D. Williams	OE-FL	6'2"	210	27		
Leon Clarke	OE	6'4"	234	27		24
Rich Kreitling	OE	6'2"	208	25		18
Fred Murphy	OE	6'3"	205	22		
Gern Nagler	OE	6'2"	190	27		18
Sam Baker	K	6'2"	217	28		80

NEW YORK GIANTS 6-4-2 Jim Lee Howell

Scores of Each Game		
21	San Francisco	19
35	St. Louis	14
19	Pittsburgh	17
24	WASHINGTON	24
13	ST. LOUIS	20
17	Cleveland	13
27	PITTSBURGH	24
10	PHILADELPHIA	17
23	Philadelphia	31
31	DALLAS	31
17	Washington	3
34	CLEVELAND	48

Use Name	Pos.	Hgt	Wgt	Age	Int	Pts
Don Boll	OT	6'2"	270	33		
Rosey Brown	OT	6'3"	245	27		
Frank Youso	OT	6'4"	260	24		
Lou Cordileone	OG	6'	240	23		
Bill Crawford	OG	6'1"	235	23		
Darrell Dess	OG	6'	235	24		
Jack Stroud	OG	6'1"	235	31		
Ray Wietecha	C	6'1"	225	31		
Bob Schmidt	OT-OG-C	6'4"	245	24		
Jim Katcavage	DE	6'3"	230	25		
Andy Robustelli	DE	6'1"	230	34		
Tom Scott	LB-DE	6'2"	220	30	1	6
Rosey Grier	DT	6'5"	285	27		2
Proverb Jacobs	DT	6'4"	255	25		
Dick Modzelewski	DT	6'	260	29		

Use Name	Pos.	Hgt	Wgt	Age	Int	Pts
Sam Huff	LB	6'1"	230	25	3	
Jim Leo	LB	6'1"	215	22		
Cliff Livingston	LB	6'3"	215	30	1	
Harland Svare	LB	6'	215	29	1	
Lindon Crow	DB	6'1"	205	27	3	6
Dick Lynch	DB	6'1"	200	24	3	6
Dick Nolan	DB	6'1"	185	28	3	
Jimmy Patton	DB	6'	180	28	6	
Lee Riley	DB	6'1"	190	28	1	
Bill Stits	DB	6'	195	29		

Use Name	Pos.	Hgt	Wgt	Age	Int	Pts
Chuck Conerly	QB	6'1"	185	36		
Lee Grosscup	QB	6'1"	185	23		
George Shaw	QB	6'1"	180	27		
Don Chandler	HB	6'2"	205	25		
Frank Gifford	HB	6'1"	200	30		42
Joe Morrison	HB	6'1"	195	22		30
Ed Sutton	HB	6'1"	207	25		
Alex Webster	HB	6'3"	220	29		
Mel Triplett	FB	6'1"	215	28		36
Phil King	HB-FB	6'4"	225	24		
Bill Kimber	OE	6'2"	190	24		
Kyle Rote	OE	6'	200	31		60
Bob Schnelker	OE	6'3"	215	30		12
Pat Summerall	OE	6'4"	235	30		71
Bob Simms	DE-LB-OE	6'1"	210	22		

ST. LOUIS CARDINALS 6-5-1 Pop Ivy

Scores of Each Game		
43	Los Angeles	21
14	NEW YORK	35
27	Philadelphia	31
14	Pittsburgh	27
12	DALLAS	10
20	New York	13
44	WASHINGTON	7
27	Cleveland	28
26	Washington	14
17	CLEVELAND	17
6	PHILADELPHIA	20
38	PITTSBURGH	7

Use Name	Pos.	Hgt	Wgt	Age	Int	Pts
Ed Cook	OT	6'2"	245	28		
Dale Memmelaar	OT	6'2"	265	23		
Ken Panfil	OT	6'6"	265	29		
Tom Day	OG-OT	6'2"	240	25		
Ken Gray	OG	6'2"	245	24		
Mike McGee	OG	6'1"	230	22		
Mike Rabold	OG	6'2"	235	23		
Don Gillis	C	6'3"	250	25		
Ernie Fritsch	LB-C	6'	230	23		
Luke Owens	DE	6'2"	255	27		2
Jerry Perry	DE	6'4"	240	29		44
Leo Sugar	DE	6'1"	220	31		
Ed Culpepper	DT	6'1"	255	26		
Frank Fuller	DT	6'4"	245	31		2
Don Owens (from PHI)	DT	6'5"	255	28		
Tom Redmond	DT	6'5"	250	23		

Use Name	Pos.	Hgt	Wgt	Age	Int	Pts
Ted Bates	LB	6'3"	220	23		
Bill Koman	LB	6'2"	230	26	1	
Dale Meinert	LB	6'2"	218	27	3	
John Tracey	LB	6'3"	228	26	1	2
Charley Ellzey	C-LB	6'3"	245	22		
Joe Driskill	DB	6'1"	195	23		
Freddy Glick	DB	6'1"	185	23		
Jimmy Hill	DB	6'2"	190	31		
Billy Stacy	DB	6'1"	195	24	4	6
Larry Wilson	DB	6'	187	22	2	
Jerry Norton	DB	5'11"	195	30	10	
Bobby Towns	HB-OE-DB	6'1"	180	22		

Use Name	Pos.	Hgt	Wgt	Age	Int	Pts
King Hill	QB	6'3"	207	24		6
George Izo	QB	6'3"	230	23		
John Roach	QB	6'4"	195	27		6
Joe Childress	HB	6'	200	26		12
Bobby Joe Conrad	HB	6'	195	25		34
John David Crow	HB	6'2"	215	25		54
Willie West	HB	5'10"	185	22		
Mal Hammack	FB	6'2"	205	27		12
Frank Mestnik	FB	6'2"	200	22		18
Hugh McInnis	OE	6'3"	215	22		
Sonny Randle	OE	6'2"	187	24		90
Perry Richards	OE	6'2"	205	26		

PITTSBURGH STEELERS 5-6-1 Buddy Parker

Scores of Each Game		
35	Dallas	28
20	Cleveland	28
17	NEW YORK	19
27	ST. LOUIS	14
27	Washington	27
13	GREEN BAY	19
7	Philadelphia	34
24	New York	27
14	CLEVELAND	10
22	WASHINGTON	10
27	PHILADELPHIA	21
7	St. Louis	38

Use Name	Pos.	Hgt	Wgt	Age	Int	Pts
Byron Beams	OT	6'6"	248	26		
John Kapele	OT	6'	240	23		
Frank Varrichione	OT	6'1"	230	28		
Dan James	C-OT	6'4"	275	23		
John Nisby	OG	6'1"	230	27		
Mike Sandusky	OG	6'	230	27		
Ron Stehouwer	OT-OG	6'2"	240	23		
Ed Beatty	C	6'3"	225	28		
Billy Ray Smith	DE	6'4"	230	25		
George Tarasovic	DE	6'4"	245	31	1	
Ernie Stautner	DT-DE	6'1"	230	35		
Joe Krupa	DT	6'2"	225	27		
Joe Lewis	DT	6'2"	260	25		6
Ken Longenecker	DT	6'4"	285	22		
Will Renfro	DE-DT	6'5"	220	28		

Use Name	Pos.	Hgt	Wgt	Age	Int	Pts
Dick Campbell	LB	6'1"	225	24	1	
Rudy Hayes	LB	6'	215	25		
Mike Henry	LB	6'2"	215	24		
John Reger	LB	6'	230	29	1	
Dean Derby	DB	6'	185	26	3	
Dick Moegle	DB	6'	195	26	6	
Jack Morris (from LA)	DB	6'	190	28		
Bert Rechichar	DB	6'1"	210	30	1	15
Scooter Scudero	DB	5'10"	174	30		
Don Sutherin	DB	5'10"	190	24	1	
Fred Williamson	DB	6'2"	205	22		
Junior Wren	DB	6'	205	30	2	

Ron Hall – Military Service

Use Name	Pos.	Hgt	Wgt	Age	Int	Pts
Rudy Bukich	QB	6'1"	200	29		
Bobby Layne	QB	6'1"	210	33		48
Rex Johnston	HB	6'1"	195	22		
Tom Tracy	FB-HB	5'9"	205	28		63
Tom Barnett	DB-HB	5'11"	190	23		
John Henry Johnson	FB	6'2"	215	30		18
Larry Krutko	FB	6'	225	25		
Charlie Scales	FB	5'11"	210	21		
Buddy Dial	FL	6'1"	195	23		54
Darrell Brewster	OE	6'3"	210	30		
Jack McClairen	OE	6'4"	215	29		
Preston Carpenter	HB-OE	6'2"	205	26		12
Jimmy Orr	FL-OE	5'11"	200	24		24
Bobby Joe Green	K	5'11"	175	22		

WASHINGTON REDSKINS 1-9-2 Mike Nixon

Scores of Each Game		
0	Baltimore	20
26	DALLAS	14
24	New York	24
27	PITTSBURGH	27
10	CLEVELAND	31
7	St. Louis	44
13	Philadelphia	19
14	ST. LOUIS	26
10	Pittsburgh	22
16	Cleveland	27
3	NEW YORK	17
28	PHILADELPHIA	38

Use Name	Pos.	Hgt	Wgt	Age	Int	Pts
Ray Lemek	OT	6'	240	26		
Don Lawrence	DT-OT	6'1"	245	23		
Don Stallings	DE-DT-OT	6'4"	250	21		
Fran O'Brien	OG	6'1"	240	25		
Vince Promuto	OG	6'1"	240	22		
Red Stephens	OG	6'	232	30		
Bob Whitlow	OG	6'1"	232	24		
Jim Schrader	C	6'2"	252	28		
Bob Khayat	OG-C	6'2"	230	22		64
John Paluck	DE	6'2"	235	27		
Art Gob (to LA-A)	DE	6'4"	230	23		
Andy Stynchula	C-DE	6'3"	255	21		
Ray Krouse	DT	6'3"	270	33		
Bob Toneff	DT	6'3"	265	30		

Use Name	Pos.	Hgt	Wgt	Age	Int	Pts
Rod Breedlove	LB	6'2"	220	22	3	
Ralph Felton	LB	5'11"	210	28		
Dick Lasse	LB	6'2"	225	24	3	
Bill Roehnelt	LB	6'1"	230	24		
Roy Wilkins	LB	6'3"	223	26		
Billy Brewer	DB	6'	190	25		
Jim Crotty	DB	5'11"	195	22	1	
Ben Scotti	DB	6'1"	185	23	4	
Jim Wulff	DB	5'11"	185	24		
Gary Glick	HB-DB	6'2"	200	29	3	6
Pat Heenan	OE-DB	6'1"	190	22	1	

Use Name	Pos.	Hgt	Wgt	Age	Int	Pts
Eagle Day	QB	6'	185	28		
Ralph Guglielmi	QB	6'1"	195	27		
M. C. Reynolds	QB	6'	195	25		
Dick Haley	HB	5'10"	195	23		
Ed Vereb	HB	6'	190	26		
Sam Horner	DB-HB	6'	195	22		
Dick James	DB-HB	5'9"	180	26		36
Jim Podoley	OE-HB	6'2"	205	27		6
Don Bosseler	FB	6'1"	212	24		12
Johnny Olszewski	FB	5'11"	202	29		18
Bill Anderson	OE	6'3"	210	24		18
Tom Osborne	OE	6'3"	190	23		
Joe Walton	OE	5'11"	205	25		18

PHILADELPHIA EAGLES

RUSHING

Last Name	No.	Yds	Avg	TD
Peaks	86	465	5.4	3
Barnes	117	315	2.7	4
Dean	113	304	2.7	0
Brown	9	35	3.2	2
Sapp	9	20	2.2	0
Jurgensen	4	5	1.3	0
Retzlaff	2	3	1.5	0
Van Brocklin	11	−13	−1.2	0

RECEIVING

Last Name	No.	Yds	Avg	TD
Retzlaff	46	826	18	5
McDonald	39	801	21	13
Walston	30	563	19	4
Barnes	19	132	7	2
Dean	15	218	15	3
Peaks	14	116	8	0
Brown	9	247	27	2
Lucas	3	34	11	0
Sapp	2	20	10	0

PUNT RETURNS

Last Name	No.	Yds	Avg	TD
Dean	16	65	4	0
Brown	10	47	5	0
Jackson	1	5	5	0
McDonald	1	2	2	0

KICKOFF RETURNS

Last Name	No.	Yds	Avg	TD
Dean	26	533	21	0
Brown	11	295	27	0
McDonald	2	45	23	0
Robb	4	44	11	0
Reichow	4	28	7	0
Baughan	2	18	9	0
Carr	1	5	5	0
Lucas	1	5	5	0

PASSING – PUNTING – KICKING

PASSING	Att	Comp	%	Yds	Yd/Att	TD	Int–%	RK
Van Brocklin	284	153	54	2471	8.7	24	17– 6	2
Jurgensen	44	24	55	486	11.0	5	1– 2	
Barnes	3	0	0	0	0.0	0	2– 67	

PUNTING	No	Avg
Van Brocklin	60	43.1

KICKING	XP	Att	%	FG	Att	%
Walston	39	40	98	14	20	70
Wittenborn	0	0	0	0	3	0

CLEVELAND BROWNS

RUSHING

Last Name	No.	Yds	Avg	TD
Brown	215	1257	5.8	9
Mitchell	111	506	4.6	5
Gautt	28	159	5.7	1
Caleb	8	60	7.5	1
Dawson	1	0	0.0	0
Baker	1	−11	−11.0	0
Kreitling	2	−17	−8.5	0
Plum	17	−24	−1.4	2

RECEIVING

Last Name	No.	Yds	Avg	TD
Mitchell	45	612	14	6
Nagler	36	616	17	3
Renfro	24	378	16	4
Brown	19	204	11	2
Kreitling	16	316	20	3
Clarke	11	184	17	4
Caleb	5	−18	−4	0
Murphy	2	36	18	0
Gautt	1	10	10	0
Williams	1	5	5	0

PUNT RETURNS

Last Name	No.	Yds	Avg	TD
Shofner	11	105	10	0
Mitchell	9	101	11	0
Franklin	1	2	2	0

KICKOFF RETURNS

Last Name	No.	Yds	Avg	TD
Mitchell	17	432	25	1
Brown	14	300	21	0
Caleb	5	90	18	0
Gautt	3	47	16	0
Franklin	1	23	23	0
Fleming	1	8	8	0
Parrish	2	0	0	0
Fichtner	1	0	0	0
Stephens	1	0	0	0

PASSING – PUNTING – KICKING

PASSING	Att	Comp	%	Yds	Yd/Att	TD	Int–%	RK
Plum	250	151	60	2297	9.2	21	5– 2	1
Dawson	13	8	62	23	1.8	0	0– 0	
Mitchell	1	1	100	23	23.0	1	0– 0	

PUNTING	No	Avg
Baker	55	42.0

KICKING	XP	Att	%	FG	Att	%
Baker	44	46	96	12	20	60

NEW YORK GIANTS

RUSHING

Last Name	No.	Yds	Avg	TD
Triplett	124	573	4.6	4
Morrison	103	346	3.4	2
Gifford	77	232	3.0	4
Sutton	20	135	6.8	0
King	26	97	3.7	0
Webster	22	48	2.2	0
Chandler	2	19	9.5	0
Conerly	14	1	0.1	0
Grosscup	3	1	0.3	0
Shaw	15	−12	−0.8	0

RECEIVING

Last Name	No.	Yds	Avg	TD
Rote	42	750	18	10
Schnelker	38	610	16	2
Morrison	29	367	13	3
Gifford	24	344	14	3
Webster	8	106	13	0
Triplett	5	40	10	2
King	3	6	2	0
Kimber	2	48	24	0
Sutton	2	30	15	0
Simms	1	58	58	0
Summerall	1	15	15	0
Dess	1	3	3	0

PUNT RETURNS

Last Name	No.	Yds	Avg	TD
Stits	18	166	9	0
Riley	10	42	4	0
Crow	2	1	1	0
Patton	1	0	0	0

KICKOFF RETURNS

Last Name	No.	Yds	Avg	TD
Stits	20	486	24	0
Sutton	2	223	19	0
King	2	73	37	0
Riley	3	67	22	0
Triplett	2	38	19	0
Youso	1	7	7	0
Brown	1	0	0	0

PASSING – PUNTING – KICKING

PASSING	Att	Comp	%	Yds	Yd/Att	TD	Int–%	RK
Shaw	155	76	49	1263	8.1	11	13– 8	9
Conerly	134	66	49	954	7.1	8	7– 5	7
Grosscup	25	11	44	144	5.8	1	1– 4	
Gifford	6	3	50	24	4.0	0	1– 17	
Morrison	1	0	0	0	0.0	0	1–100	
Summerall	1	0	0	0	0.0	0	0– 0	

PUNTING	No	Avg
Chandler	31	40.5
Conerly	18	36.9

KICKING	XP	Att	%	FG	Att	%
Summerall	32	32	100	13	26	50

ST. LOUIS CARDINALS

RUSHING

Last Name	No.	Yds	Avg	TD
Crow	183	1071	5.9	6
Mestnick	104	429	4.1	3
Hammack	96	347	3.6	2
Childress	34	240	7.5	0
Conrad	23	91	4.0	0
Hill	16	47	2.9	1
Norton	2	47	23.5	0
West	7	45	6.4	0
Roach	19	39	2.1	1

RECEIVING

Last Name	No.	Yds	Avg	TD
Randle	62	893	14	15
Crow	25	462	18	3
McInnis	13	260	20	0
Childress	11	202	18	2
Conrad	7	103	15	0
Hammack	4	36	9	0
Mestrick	3	24	8	0
Richards	1	10	10	0

PUNT RETURNS

Last Name	No.	Yds	Avg	TD
Conrad	8	86	11	0
Stacy	14	62	4	0
West	5	58	12	0
Wilson	3	26	9	0

KICKOFF RETURNS

Last Name	No.	Yds	Avg	TD
West	13	370	28	0
Conrad	12	338	28	0
Stacy	6	146	24	0
Wilson	6	115	19	0
Mestnick	3	39	13	0
Hammack	2	23	12	0
Memmelaar	1	8	8	0
Bates	1	6	6	0
Driskill	1	0	0	0

PASSING – PUNTING – KICKING

PASSING	Att	Comp	%	Yds	Yd/Att	TD	Int–%	RK
Roach	188	87	46	1423	7.6	17	19– 10	13
K. Hill	55	20	36	205	3.7	1	5– 9	
Izo	24	10	42	115	4.8	0	0– 0	
Crow	18	9	50	247	13.7	2	1– 6	

PUNTING	No	Avg
Norton	39	45.6
Hill	5	39.6

KICKING	XP	Att	%	FG	Att	%
Conrad	28	29	97	2	5	40
Perry	5	5	100	13	20	65

PITTSBURGH STEELERS

RUSHING

Last Name	No.	Yds	Avg	TD
Tracy	192	680	3.5	5
Johnson	118	621	5.3	2
Krutko	17	99	5.8	0
Scales	26	81	3.1	0
Orr	8	57	7.1	0
Carpenter	17	36	2.1	0
Barnett	6	25	4.2	0
Layne	19	12	0.6	2
Johnston	4	12	3.0	0
Dial	1	8	8.0	0
Bukich	3	−8	−2.7	0

RECEIVING

Last Name	No.	Yds	Avg	TD
Dial	40	972	24	9
Orr	29	541	19	4
Carpenter	29	495	17	2
Tracy	24	349	15	4
Johnson	12	112	9	1
Brewster	2	26	13	0
McClairen	1	17	17	0
Krutko	1	8	8	0
Scales	1	−2	−2	0
Varrichione	0	−7	0	0

PUNT RETURNS

Last Name	No.	Yds	Avg	TD
Carpenter	13	120	9	0
Johnston	12	45	4	0
Moegle	3	15	5	0
Scudero	2	3	2	0

KICKOFF RETURNS

Last Name	No.	Yds	Avg	TD
Johnston	18	393	22	0
Carpenter	10	255	26	0
Moegle	7	174	25	0
Scales	5	100	20	0
Tracy	1	30	30	0
Hayes	1	11	11	0
McClairen	1	1	1	0
Varrichione	1	0	0	0

PASSING – PUNTING – KICKING

PASSING	Att	Comp	%	Yds	Yd/Att	TD	Int–%	RK
Layne	209	103	49	1814	8.7	13	17– 8	6
Bukich	51	25	49	358	7.0	2	3– 6	
Tracy	22	9	41	322	14.6	4	1– 5	
Carpenter	2	1	50	2	1.0	0	0– 0	
Johnson	1	1	100	15	15.0	1	0– 0	

PUNTING	No	Avg
Green	64	44.2

KICKING	XP	Att	%	FG	Att	%
Layne	21	22	95	5	6	83
Rechichar	6	6	100	3	7	43
Tracy	0	0	0	3	6	50

WASHINGTON REDSKINS

RUSHING

Last Name	No.	Yds	Avg	TD
Bosseler	109	428	3.9	2
Guglielmi	79	247	3.1	0
Olszewski	75	227	3.0	3
James	73	199	2.7	4
Horner	22	80	3.6	0
Podoley	29	52	1.8	0
Vereb	19	38	2.0	0
Reynolds	4	20	5.0	0
Glick	1	15	15.0	0
Anderson	1	6	6.0	0
Day	3	1	0.3	0

RECEIVING

Last Name	No.	Yds	Avg	TD
Anderson	38	488	13	3
Walton	27	401	15	3
Podoley	17	244	14	1
James	16	243	15	2
Bosseler	13	86	7	0
Olszewski	10	62	6	0
Vereb	9	119	13	0
Horner	7	106	15	0
Osborne	7	46	7	0
Haley	3	21	7	0

PUNT RETURNS

Last Name	No.	Yds	Avg	TD
James	7	46	7	0
Horner	3	16	5	0
Podoley	3	3	1	0
Olszewski	1	0	0	0
Vereb	1	0	0	0

KICKOFF RETURNS

Last Name	No.	Yds	Avg	TD
Horner	24	511	21	0
James	19	458	24	0
Olszewski	5	119	24	0
Vereb	5	119	24	0
Podoley	4	87	22	0
Wilkins	2	24	12	0
Stallings	1	19	19	0
O'Brien	1	16	16	0
Lawrence	1	10	10	0

PASSING – PUNTING – KICKING

PASSING	Att	Comp	%	Yds	Yd/Att	TD	Int–%	RK
Guglielmi	223	125	56	1547	6.9	9	19– 9	9
Reynolds	30	13	44	154	5.1	0	3– 10	
Day	19	9	47	115	6.1	0	1– 5	
James	1	0	0	0	0.0	0	0– 0	
Vereb	1	0	0	0	0.0	0	0– 0	

PUNTING	No	Avg
Day	59	42.0
Horner	1	48.0

KICKING	XP	Att	%	FG	Att	%
Khayat	19	19	100	15	23	65

GREEN BAY PACKERS 8-4-0 Vince Lombardi

Scores of Each Game		
14	CHICAGO	17
28	DETROIT	9
35	BALTIMORE	21
41	SAN FRANCISCO	14
19	Pittsburgh	13
24	Baltimore	38
41	DALLAS	7
31	LOS ANGELES	33
10	Detroit	23
41	Chicago	13
13	San Francisco	0
35	Los Angeles	21

Use Name	Pos.	Hgt	Wgt	Age	Int	Pts
Forrest Gregg	OT	6'4"	250	27		
Norm Masters	OT	6'2"	250	27		
Bob Skoronski	OT	6'3"	250	27		
Andy Cvercko	OG	6'	240	23		
Jerry Kramer	OG	6'3"	250	25		
Fuzzy Thurston	OG	6'1"	250	27		
Ken Iman	C	6'1"	230	21		
Jim Ringo	C	6'1"	235	29		
Willie Davis	DE	6'3"	240	27		6
Bill Quinlan	DE	6'3"	250	28		
Jim Temp	DE	6'4"	250	27		
Dave Hanner	DT	6'2"	260	31		
Henry Jordan	DT	6'3"	250	25		
Ken Beck	DE-DT	6'2"	250	25		
Johnny Miller	DE-DT	6'5"	260	26		
Tom Bettis	LB	6'2"	225	27		
Dan Currie	LB	6'3"	240	26	4	
Bill Forester	LB	6'3"	240	29	2	
Ray Nitschke	LB	6'3"	235	24	3	6
Hank Gremminger	DB	6'1"	205	27	3	
Dale Hackbart	DB	6'3"	200	24		
Dick Pesonen	DB	6'	190	22		
Johnny Symank	DB	5'11"	180	25	1	
Em Tunnell	DB	6'1"	210	38	3	
Jesse Whittenton	DB	6'	195	26	6	
Willie Wood	DB	5'10"	185	24		
Lamar McHan	QB	6'1"	210	28		6
Bart Starr	QB	6'1"	200	27		
Paul Hornung	HB	6'2"	215	24		176
Tom Moore	HB	6'2"	215	22		30
Paul Winslow	HB	5'11"	200	22		6
Larry Hickman	FB	6'2"	230	24		
Jim Taylor	FB	6'	215	25		66
Boyd Dowler	FL	6'5"	220	23		12
Lew Carpenter	OE-FL	6'1"	215	28		
Gary Knafelc	OE	6'4"	220	28		
Ron Kramer	OE	6'3"	230	25		
Max McGee	OE	6'3"	205	28		24
Steve Meilinger	OE	6'2"	230	30		

DETROIT LIONS 7-5-0 George Wilson

Scores of Each Game		
9	Green Bay	28
10	SAN FRANCISCO	14
10	Philadelphia	28
30	BALTIMORE	17
35	Los Angeles	48
24	San Francisco	0
12	LOS ANGELES	10
7	Chicago	28
23	GREEN BAY	10
20	Baltimore	15
23	DALLAS	14
36	CHICAGO	0

Use Name	Pos.	Hgt	Wgt	Age	Int	Pts
Ollie Spencer	C-OT	6'2"	250	29		
John Gordy	OG-OT	6'3"	250	24		
Willie McClung	DT-OT	6'2"	260	31		
Grady Alderman	OG	6'2"	230	21		
Bob Grottkau	OG	6'4"	235	23		
Harley Sewell	OG	6'1"	230	29		
Bob Scholtz	C	6'4"	250	22		
Bill Glass	DE	6'5"	255	24		
Gil Mains	DE	6'2"	250	30		
Darris McCord	OT-DE	6'4"	250	27		
Sam Williams	LB-DE	6'5"	235	29		
Roger Brown	DT	6'5"	290	23		
Alex Karras	DT	6'2"	245	24		
Jim Weatherall	DT	6'4"	250	30		
Carl Brettschneider	LB	6'1"	225	28		
Jim Martin	LB	6'2"	230	36		65
Max Messner	LB	6'3"	225	22	1	
Joe Schmidt	LB	6'1"	220	28	2	12
Wayne Walker	LB	6'2"	225	23	1	2
Night Train Lane	DB	6'1"	195	32	5	6
Dick LeBeau	DB	6'1"	185	23	4	
Gary Lowe	DB	5'11"	195	26	2	
Bruce Maher	DB	5'11"	190	23	1	2
Jim Steffen	DB	6'	195	23		
Dave Whitsell	DB	6'	190	24		
Yale Lary	DB	6'	190	29	3	
Earl Morrall	QB	6'1"	206	26		6
Jim Ninowski	QB	6'1"	200	24		30
Warren Rabb	QB	6'1"	196	23		
Terry Barr	HB	6'	190	25		12
Dan Lewis	HB	6'1"	200	24		12
Ken Webb	FB-HB	5'11"	210	25		12
Nick Pietrosante	FB	6'2"	225	23		48
Hopalong Cassady	HB-FL	5'10"	185	26		12
Dave Middleton	OE-FL	6'1"	195	27		
Gail Cogdill	OE	6'2"	195	23		6
Glenn Davis	OE	6'	180	26		
Jim Gibbons	OE	6'2"	220	24		12
Steve Junker	OE	6'3"	220	25		

SAN FRANCISCO FORTY NINERS 7-5-0 Red Hickey

Scores of Each Game		
19	NEW YORK	21
13	LOS ANGELES	9
14	Detroit	10
10	Chicago	27
14	Green Bay	41
25	CHICAGO	7
0	DETROIT	24
26	Dallas	14
30	Baltimore	22
23	Los Angeles	7
0	GREEN BAY	13
34	BALTIMORE	10

Use Name	Pos.	Hgt	Wgt	Age	Int	Pts
Len Rohde	OT	6'4"	240	22		
Bob St. Clair	OT	6'9"	265	29		
John Thomas	OT	6'4"	246	25		
Bruce Bosley	OG	6'2"	240	26		
Ted Connolly	OG	6'3"	242	28		
Mike Magac	OG	6'3"	240	22		
Karl Rubke	C	6'4"	240	24		
Frank Morze	DT-C	6'4"	264	26		
Dan Colchico	DE	6'4"	236	23		
Ed Henke	DE	6'3"	227	32		
Charlie Krueger	DE	6'4"	245	24		2
Monte Clark	DT	6'6"	260	23		
Leo Nomellini	DT	6'3"	262	35		2
Henry Schmidt	DT	6'4"	260	23		
Bob Harrison	LB	6'2"	220	23	1	
Matt Hazeltine	LB	6'1"	220	27		
Gorden Kelley	LB	6'3"	230	22	2	
Clancy Osborne	LB	6'3"	218	25		
Jerry Wilson (from PHI)	LB	6'2"	235	23		
Dave Baker	DB	6'	193	23	10	
Eddie Dove	DB	6'2"	180	23	3	
Lenny Lyles	DB	6'2"	202	24		6
Jerry Mertens	DB	6'	183	24	2	
Jimmy Ridlon	DB	6'1"	177	25		
Abe Woodson	HB-DB	5'11"	188	25	2	
John Brodie	QB	6'1"	186	25		6
Y. A. Tittle	QB	6'	195	33		
Bob Waters	QB	6'2"	184	22		
Hugh McElhenny	HB	6'1"	198	31		6
Ray Norton	HB	6'2"	184	23		
J. D. Smith	FB-HB	6'1"	200	27		36
Joe Perry	FB	6'	206	33		6
C. R. Roberts	FB	6'3"	197	24		12
R. C. Owens	OE-FL	6'3"	190	25		36
Clyde Conner	OE	6'2"	190	27		12
Dee Mackey	OE	6'5"	236	24		
Monte Stickles	OE	6'4"	230	22		
Billy Wilson	FL-OE	6'3"	190	33		6
Tommy Davis	K	6'	212	25		78

BALTIMORE COLTS 6-6-0 Weeb Ewbank

Scores of Each Game		
20	WASHINGTON	0
42	CHICAGO	7
21	Green Bay	35
31	LOS ANGELES	17
17	DETROIT	30
45	Dallas	7
38	GREEN BAY	24
24	Chicago	20
22	SAN FRANCISCO	30
15	DETROIT	20
3	Los Angeles	10
10	San Francisco	34

Use Name	Pos.	Hgt	Wgt	Age	Int	Pts
Jim Parker	OT	6'3"	275	26		
Sherman Plunkett	OT	6'4"	270	26		
George Preas	OT	6'2"	255	28		
Lebron Shields	DE-OT	6'4"	240	23		2
Steve Myhra	OG	6'1"	240	26		62
Palmer Pyle	OG	6'2"	240	23		
Alex Sandusky	OG	6'1"	238	28		
Art Spinney	OG	6'	236	33		
Buzz Nutter	C	6'4"	240	29		
Ordell Braase	DE	6'4"	242	28		
Gino Marchetti	DE	6'4"	245	34		
Jim Colvin	OG-DE	6'2"	240	23		
Don Joyce	DT-DE	6'3"	250	30		
Art Donovan	DT	6'2"	270	35		
Big Daddy Lipscomb	DT	6'6"	288	29		2
Marv Matuszak	LB	6'3"	228	29		
Bill Pellington	LB	6'2"	238	31	1	
Don Shinnick	LB	6'	235	25	5	
Dick Szymanski	LB	6'3"	235	28	1	
Zeke Smith	DE-LB	6'2"	230	24		
Bobby Boyd	DB	5'10"	190	22	7	
Milt Davis	DB	6'1"	180	31	6	
Andy Nelson	DB	6'1"	180	27	6	
Jackie Simpson	DB	5'10"	185	26		
Johnny Sample	HB-DB	6'1"	203	23	4	6
Carl Taseff	HB-DB	5'11"	194	31		
Ray Brown	QB	6'2"	195	24		
Johnny Unitas	QB	6'1"	194	27		
Alex Hawkins	HB	6'1"	190	23		30
Ed Kovac	HB	6'	197	22		
Lenny Moore	HB	6'1"	190	27		78
Mike Sommer	HB	5'11"	190	25		
Jim Welch	HB	6'	190	22		
Alan Ameche	FB	6'	220	27		18
Billy Pricer	FB	5'10"	210	25		12
Ray Berry	OE	6'2"	190	27		60
Jim Mutscheller	OE	6'1"	204	30		12
Art DeCarlo	DB-OE	6'2"	202	30		
Jerry Richardson	HB-OE	6'3"	185	24		6

CHICAGO BEARS 5-6-1 George Halas

Scores of Each Game		
17	Green Bay	14
7	Baltimore	42
34	LOS ANGELES	27
27	SAN FRANCISCO	10
24	Los Angeles	24
7	San Francisco	25
20	BALTIMORE	24
28	DETROIT	7
17	DALLAS	7
13	GREEN BAY	41
0	Cleveland	42
0	Detroit	36

Use Name	Pos.	Hgt	Wgt	Age	Int	Pts
Stan Fanning	OT	6'6"	252	22		
Bob Kilcullen	OT	6'3"	245	24		
Herm Lee	OT	6'4"	247	29		
Bob Wetoska	OT	6'3"	250	22		
Roger Davis	OG	6'3"	235	22		
Stan Jones	OG	6'1"	250	29		
Ted Karras	OG	6'1"	235	27		
Bob Konovsky	OG	6'2"	245	26		
John Mellekas	C	6'3"	255	27		
Doug Atkins	DE	6'8"	255	30		
Maury Youmans	OT-DE	6'6"	230	23		
Fred Williams	DT	6'4"	248	30		
Bill Bishop	OT-DT	6'4"	248	29		
Earl Leggett	DE-DT	6'3"	250	26	1	
Joe Fortunato	LB	6'	225	30		
Bill George	LB	6'2"	235	29	1	
Ken Kirk	LB	6'2"	230	22		
Larry Morris	LB	6'2"	230	25	1	
Roger LeClerc	C-DT-LB	6'3"	235	22		
Erich Barnes	DB	6'2"	198	25		
J. C. Caroline	DB	6'1"	190	27	3	6
Pete Manning	DB	6'3"	208	24		
Richie Petitbon	DB	6'3"	205	22	2	
Justin Rowland	DB	6'2"	188	22		
Charlie Sumner	DB	6'1"	195	30		
Vic Zucco	DB	6'	187	25	2	
Zeke Bratkowski	QB	6'2"	203	28		
Ed Brown	QB	6'2"	208	31		12
Charlie Bivins	HB	6'2"	212	21		
Willie Galimore	HB	6'1"	187	25		6
Johnny Morris	HB	5'10"	180	25		36
Glen Shaw	HB	6'1"	217	21		
John Adams	FB	6'3"	235	23		
Rick Casares	FB	6'2"	225	29		30
Merrill Douglas	FB	6'	204	24		
Angie Coia	OE	6'2"	211	22		24
Willard Dewveall	OE	6'4"	218	23		30
Jim Dooley	OE	6'4"	198	30		6
Bo Farrington	OE	6'3"	217	24		
Harlon Hill	OE	6'3"	200	28		
John Aveni	K	6'3"	210	25		44

LOS ANGELES RAMS 4-7-1 Bob Waterfield

Scores of Each Game		
21	ST. LOUIS	43
9	San Francisco	13
27	Chicago	34
17	Baltimore	31
24	CHICAGO	24
48	DETROIT	35
38	Dallas	13
10	Detroit	12
33	Green Bay	31
7	SAN FRANCISCO	23
10	BALTIMORE	3
21	GREEN BAY	35

Use Name	Pos.	Hgt	Wgt	Age	Int	Pts
Jim Boeke	OT	6'5"	230	21		
Charlie Bradshaw	OT	6'6"	255	24		
John Guzik	OG	6'3"	236	23		
Roy Hord	OG	6'4"	232	25		
Chuck Janerette	OG	6'3"	240	21		
Buck Lansford	OG	6'2"	232	27		
Art Hunter	C	6'4"	248	27		
Gene Brito	DE	6'1"	230	34		
Lamar Lundy	DE	6'7"	235	25	1	6
Lou Michaels	DE	6'2"	248	24		7
John Baker	DT-DE	6'6"	290	25	1	
John Lovetere	DT	6'4"	280	24		6
George Strugar	DT	6'5"	260	25		
John Kennerson	DE-DT	6'3"	255	21		
Bill Jobko	LB	6'2"	218	24	1	
Bob Long	LB	6'3"	234	26	1	
Jack Pardee	LB	6'2"	220	24	1	
Les Richter	LB	6'3"	232	29	2	2
Jerry Stalcup	OG-LB	6'	220	22	1	
Charley Britt	DB	6'2"	180	22	5	6
Don Ellersick	DB	6'1"	193	22	2	
Carl Karilivacz	DB	6'	190	29		
Ed Meador	DB	5'11"	185	23	4	6
Will Sherman	DB	6'2"	197	31	1	
Vern Valdez	DB	5'11"	190	24	1	
Buddy Humphrey	QB	6'1"	200	24		
Frank Ryan	QB	6'3"	195	4		12
Billy Wade	QB	6'2"	203	29		12
Jon Arnett	HB	5'11"	193	25		24
Dick Bass	HB	5'10"	190	23		
Tom Wilson	HB	6'	204	27		12
Clendon Thomas	DB-FL-HB	6'2"	190	23	1	12
Joe Marconi	FB	6'2"	220	26		18
Ollie Matson	FL-FB	6'2"	210	30		6
Carroll Dale	OE	6'1"	194	22		18
Jim Phillips	OE	6'1"	200	23		48
Del Shofner	DB-OE	6'3"	192	24	1	6
Danny Villanueva	K	5'11"	200	22		64

DALLAS COWBOYS 0-11-1 Tom Landry

Scores of Each Game		
28	PITTSBURGH	35
25	PHILADELPHIA	27
14	Washington	26
7	CLEVELAND	48
10	St. Louis	12
7	BALTIMORE	45
13	LOS ANGELES	38
7	Green Bay	41
14	SAN FRANCISCO	26
7	Chicago	17
31	New York	31
14	Detroit	23

Use Name	Pos.	Hgt	Wgt	Age	Int	Pts
Byron Bradfute	OT	6'3"	243	22		
Paul Dickson	OT	6'5"	250	23		
Bob Fry	OT	6'4"	240	29		
Dick Klein	OT	6'4"	255	26		
Mike Falls	OG	6'1"	240	26		
Buzz Guy	OG	6'3"	247	25		
Duane Putnam	OG	6'	233	32		
Mike Connelly	C	6'3"	235	24		
John Houser	C	6'3"	238	24		
Nate Borden	DE	6'	240	28		
Gene Cronin	DE	6'2"	232	27	1	
John Gonzaga	DE	6'3"	244	27		
Don Healy	DT	6'3"	264	24		
Bill Herchman	DT	6'2"	245	27		
Ed Husmann	DT	6'	238	29		
Tom Braatz	LB	6'1"	220	27	1	
Wayne Hansen	LB	6'2"	228	32	2	
Jack Patera	LB	6'1"	240	28	1	
Jerry Tubbs	LB	6'2"	220	25	1	
Bob Bercich	DB	6'1"	198	23	2	
Don Bishop	DB	6'2"	204	25	3	
Bill Butler	DB	5'10"	182	23	1	
Fred Doelling	DB	5'10"	190	21		
Tom Franckhauser	DB	6'	196	23	3	
Jim Mooty	DB	5'11"	177	22		
Gary Wisener	OE-DB	6'1"	206	22		
Ray Fisher – Injury						
Chuck Howley – Injury						
Don Heinrich	QB	6'	182	28		
Eddie LeBaron	QB	5'9"	166	30		6
Don Meredith	QB	6'2"	198	22		
L. G. Dupre	HB	5'11"	190	28		30
Don McIlhenny	HB	6'	204	25		12
Gene Babb	FB	6'3"	218	25		6
Mike Dowdle	FB	6'3"	210	22		
Walt Kowalczyk	FB	6'	205	25		12
Ray Mathews	FL	6'	200	31		
Dick Bielski	OE	6'1"	227	28		6
Frank Clarke	OE	6'	215	27		18
Jim Doran	OE	6'2"	211	32		18
Fred Dugan	OE	6'3"	200	26		6
Billy Howton	OE	6'2"	195	30		24
Woodley Lewis	OE	6'	195	35		
Dave Sherer	OE	6'3"	225	23		
Fred Cone	K	5'11"	198	34		39

GREEN BAY PACKERS

RUSHING

Last Name	No.	Yds	Avg	TD
Taylor	230	1101	4.8	11
Hornung	160	671	4.2	13
Moore	45	237	5.3	4
McHan	8	67	8.4	1
Carpenter	1	24	24.0	0
Hickman	7	22	3.1	0
Starr	7	12	1.7	0
McGee	2	11	5.5	0
Dowler	1	8	8.0	0
Winslow	2	−3	−1.5	0

RECEIVING

Last Name	No.	Yds	Avg	TD
McGee	38	787	21	4
Dowler	30	505	17	2
Hornung	28	257	9	2
Taylor	15	121	8	0
Knafelc	14	164	12	0
Moore	5	40	8	1
R. Kramer	4	55	14	0
Meilinger	2	43	22	0
Carpenter	1	21	21	0

PUNT RETURNS

Last Name	No.	Yds	Avg	TD
Wood	16	106	7	0
Carpenter	9	59	7	0
Forester	1	7	7	0

KICKOFF RETURNS

Last Name	No.	Yds	Avg	TD
Moore	12	397	33	0
Carpenter	12	249	21	0
Symank	4	103	26	0
Hickman	3	54	18	0
Nitschke	2	33	17	0
Temp	1	16	16	0
Meilinger	1	0	0	0

PASSING – PUNTING – KICKING

PASSING	Att	Comp	%	Yds	Yd/Att	TD	Int–%	RK
Starr	172	98	57	1358	7.9	4	8– 5	5
McHan	91	33	36	517	5.7	3	5– 5	
Hornung	16	6	38	118	7.4	2	0– 0	

PUNTING	No	Avg
McGee	31	41.6
Dowler	18	40.5

KICKING	XP	Att	%	FG	Att	%
Hornung	41	41	100	15	28	54

DETROIT LIONS

RUSHING

Last Name	No.	Yds	Avg	TD
Pietrosante	161	872	5.4	8
Lewis	92	438	4.8	1
Webb	59	166	2.8	2
Ninowski	32	81	2.5	5
Barr	17	74	4.4	1
Morrall	10	37	3.7	1
Cassady	17	28	1.6	1
Lary	1	19	19.0	0
Middleton	3	−1	−0.3	0

RECEIVING

Last Name	No.	Yds	Avg	TD
Gibbons	51	604	12	2
Cogdill	43	642	15	1
Cassady	20	238	12	1
Pietrosante	13	129	10	0
Lewis	12	192	16	1
Webb	10	68	7	0
Junker	6	55	9	0
Middleton	5	51	10	0
Barr	5	26	5	1
Davis	1	17	17	0

PUNT RETURNS

Last Name	No.	Yds	Avg	TD
Barr	14	104	7	0
Steffen	14	83	6	0
Cassady	1	25	25	0
Maher	1	10	10	0
Lary	1	5	5	0

KICKOFF RETURNS

Last Name	No.	Yds	Avg	TD
Steffen	8	225	28	0
Maher	10	214	21	0
Lewis	10	202	20	0
Cassady	4	82	21	0
Barr	4	81	20	0
Pietrosante	2	58	29	0
Webb	3	38	13	0
LeBeau	2	16	8	0

PASSING – PUNTING – KICKING

PASSING	Att	Comp	%	Yds	Yd/Att	TD	Int–%	RK
Ninowski	283	134	47	1599	5.7	2	18– 6	17
Morrall	49	32	65	423	8.6	4	3– 6	
Barr	1	0	0	0	0.0	0	0– 0	

PUNTING	No	Avg
Lary	64	43.8

KICKING	XP	Att	%	FG	Att	%
Martin	26	28	93	13	24	54

SAN FRANCISCO FORTY NINERS

RUSHING

Last Name	No.	Yds	Avg	TD
Smith	174	780	4.5	5
McElhenny	95	347	3.7	0
Roberts	73	213	2.9	2
Brodie	18	171	9.5	1
Perry	36	95	2.6	1
Tittle	10	61	6.1	0
Waters	1	8	8.0	0
Woodson	4	4	1.0	0
Norton	2	2	1.0	0

RECEIVING

Last Name	No.	Yds	Avg	TD
Connor	38	531	14	2
Owens	37	532	14	6
Smith	36	181	5	1
Stickles	22	252	11	0
McElhenny	14	114	8	1
Mackey	12	159	13	0
Roberts	9	49	5	0
Wilson	3	51	17	1
Perry	3	−3	−1	0

PUNT RETURNS

Last Name	No.	Yds	Avg	TD
Woodson	13	174	13	0
Dove	11	43	4	0

KICKOFF RETURNS

Last Name	No.	Yds	Avg	TD
Lyles	17	526	31	1
Woodson	17	498	29	0
Colchico	5	68	14	0
Roberts	3	60	20	0
Clark	1	15	15	0
J. Wilson	1	0	0	0

PASSING – PUNTING – KICKING

PASSING	Att	Comp	%	Yds	Yd/Att	TD	Int–%	RK
Brodie	207	103	50	1111	5.4	6	9– 4	12
Tittle	127	69	54	694	5.5	4	3– 2	8
Waters	2	2	100	61	30.5	1	0– 0	

PUNTING	No	Avg
Davis	62	44.1
Baker	3	47.7

KICKING	XP	Att	%	FG	Att	%
Davis	21	21	100	19	32	59

BALTIMORE COLTS

RUSHING

Last Name	No.	Yds	Avg	TD
Moore	91	374	4.1	4
Hawkins	76	267	3.5	2
Ameche	80	263	3.3	3
Unitas	36	195	5.4	0
Pricer	46	131	2.8	1
Brown	2	25	12.5	0
Welch	5	23	4.6	0
Sample	1	7	7.0	0
Taseff	4	3	0.8	0
Kovac	4	1	0.3	0

RECEIVING

Last Name	No.	Yds	Avg	TD
Berry	74	1298	18	10
Moore	45	936	21	9
Hawkins	25	280	11	3
Mutscheller	18	271	15	2
DeCarlo	8	116	15	0
Richardson	8	90	11	1
Pricer	8	77	10	1
Ameche	7	56	8	0
Kovac	2	27	14	0
Taseff	1	13	13	0

PUNT RETURNS

Last Name	No.	Yds	Avg	TD
Sample	14	101	7	0
Taseff	6	25	4	0
Nelson	3	1	0	0

KICKOFF RETURNS

Last Name	No.	Yds	Avg	TD
Sample	18	519	29	1
Taseff	14	291	21	0
Pricer	6	88	15	0
Welch	4	80	20	0
Moore	1	23	23	0
Pellington	2	11	6	0
Sommer	1	10	10	0
Kovac	1	8	8	0

PASSING – PUNTING – KICKING

PASSING	Att	Comp	%	Yds	Yd/Att	TD	Int–%	RK
Unitas	378	190	50	3099	8.2	25	24– 6	3
Brown	13	6	46	65	5.0	1	0– 0	
Moore	1	0	0	0	0.0	0	0– 0	

PUNTING	No	Avg
Brown	52	38.5

KICKING	XP	Att	%	FG	Att	%
Myhra	35	37	95	9	19	47

CHICAGO BEARS

RUSHING

Last Name	No.	Yds	Avg	TD
Casares	160	566	3.5	5
J. Morris	73	417	5.7	3
Galimore	74	368	5.0	1
Adams	23	114	5.0	0
Brown	19	89	4.7	2
Douglas	11	82	7.5	0
Bratkowski	8	20	2.5	0
Farrington	1	2	−2.0	0
Coia	3	−4	−1.3	0
Bivens	1	−11	−11.0	0

RECEIVING

Last Name	No.	Yds	Avg	TD
Dewveall	43	804	19	5
Dooley	36	426	12	1
Coia	25	478	19	4
J. Morris	20	224	11	3
Casares	8	64	8	0
Hill	5	98	20	0
Galimore	3	35	12	0
Douglas	2	11	6	0
Adams	2	−20	−10	0
Lee	1	16	16	0
Brown	1	−6	0	0

PUNT RETURNS

Last Name	No.	Yds	Avg	TD
Zucco	10	83	8	0
J. Morris	13	75	6	0
Petitbon	2	22	11	0
Coia	2	2	1	0

KICKOFF RETURNS

Last Name	No.	Yds	Avg	TD
J. Morris	19	384	20	0
Bivens	15	362	24	0
Galimore	12	292	24	0
Zucco	1	17	17	0

PASSING – PUNTING – KICKING

PASSING	Att	Comp	%	Yds	Yd/Att	TD	Int–%	RK
Bratkowski	175	87	50	1051	6.0	6	21– 12	16
Brown	149	59	40	1079	7.2	7	11– 7	14

PUNTING	No	Avg
Brown	56	39.8
Bratkowski	7	36.0
Casares	1	60.0

KICKING	XP	Att	%	FG	Att	%
Aveni	23	25	92	7	16	44

LOS ANGELES RAMS

RUSHING

Last Name	No.	Yds	Avg	TD
Arnett	104	436	4.2	2
Marconi	42	240	5.7	3
Wade	26	171	6.6	2
Matson	61	170	2.9	1
Bass	31	153	4.9	0
Wilson	41	139	3.4	0
Ryan	19	85	4.5	1
Thomas	16	63	3.9	0
Humphrey	2	7	3.5	0
Shofner	1	−15	−15.0	0

RECEIVING

Last Name	No.	Yds	Avg	TD
Phillips	52	883	17	8
Arnett	29	226	8	2
Dale	19	336	18	3
Thomas	17	275	16	2
Matson	15	98	7	0
Bass	13	92	7	0
Shofner	12	122	10	1
Wilson	11	82	7	2
Marconi	9	32	4	0
Ryan	0	32	0	1
Wade	0	10	0	0

PUNT RETURNS

Last Name	No.	Yds	Avg	TD
Bass	11	62	6	0
Arnett	10	60	6	0
Lovetere	1	6	6	1
Sherman	1	1	1	0
Matson	1	0	0	0
Meador	1	0	0	0

KICKOFF RETURNS

Last Name	No.	Yds	Avg	TD
Arnett	17	416	24	0
Bass	11	246	22	0
Matson	9	216	24	0
Wilson	2	48	24	0
Michaels	1	15	15	0

PASSING – PUNTING – KICKING

PASSING	Att	Comp	%	Yds	Yd/Att	TD	Int–%	RK
Wade	182	106	58	1294	7.1	12	11– 6	4
Ryan	128	62	48	816	6.4	7	9– 7	14
Humphrey	24	9	38	78	3.3	0	2– 8	
Arnett	1	0	0	0	0.0	0	0– 0	

PUNTING	No	Avg
Shofner	54	42.6
Marconi	10	40.8

KICKING	XP	Att	%	FG	Att	%
Villaneuva	28	28	100	12	19	63
Richter	2	2	100	0	0	0
Michaels	1	1	100	2	3	67

DALLAS COWBOYS

RUSHING

Last Name	No.	Yds	Avg	TD
Dupre	104	362	3.5	3
McIlhenny	96	321	3.3	1
Kowalczyk	50	156	3.1	1
Babb	39	115	2.9	0
LeBaron	17	94	5.5	1
Meredith	3	4	1.3	0
Heinrich	2	3	1.5	0
Clarke	1	−6	−6.0	0

RECEIVING

Last Name	No.	Yds	Avg	TD
Doran	31	554	18	3
Dugan	29	461	16	1
Howton	23	363	16	4
Dupre	21	216	10	2
McIlhenny	15	120	8	1
Kowalczyk	14	143	10	1
Babb	13	140	11	1
Clarke	9	290	32	3
Bielski	4	38	10	1
Mathews	3	44	15	0
Lewis	1	19	19	0

PUNT RETURNS

Last Name	No.	Yds	Avg	TD
Butler	13	131	10	0
Mooty	8	37	5	0
Franckhauser	2	7	4	0

KICKOFF RETURNS

Last Name	No.	Yds	Avg	TD
Franckhauser	26	526	20	0
Butler	20	399	20	0
Mooty	12	210	18	0
Babb	3	46	15	0
Dupre	2	44	22	0
Dowdle	2	22	11	0
Putnam	1	13	13	0
Bielski	1	4	4	0
Kowalczyk	1	0	0	0
Sherer	1	0	0	0

PASSING – PUNTING – KICKING

PASSING	Att	Comp	%	Yds	Yd/Att	TD	Int–%	RK
LeBaron	225	111	49	1736	7.7	12	25– 11	9
Meredith	68	29	43	281	4.1	2	5– 7	
Heinrich	61	23	38	371	6.1	3	3– 5	

PUNTING	No	Avg
Sherer	67	42.5
LeBaron	3	33.0

KICKING	XP	Att	%	FG	Att	%
Cone	21	23	91	6	13	46

1960 A.F.L. A New Competitor

Even before the first game was played the new American Football League was a flurry of activity. Commissioner Joe Foss, the former South Dakota governor chosen by the team owners to run the league, faced a major problem when the Minneapolis owners quit the circuit in January to accept an NFL team in 1961. This strategic move by the NFL shut the new circuit out of the Midwest and almost killed it in the cradle, but the upstarts did not give up. After several days of discussion the league owners turned down a bid from an Atlanta group and instead granted the eighth franchise to a syndicate from Oakland, California. The AFL finally had its full contingent of cities—Boston, New York, Buffalo, Houston, Dallas, Denver, Los Angeles, and Oakland. In New York, Dallas, and Los Angeles, the new league would be bucking NFL teams. Oakland in reality would have to compete with the NFL San Francisco '49ers. Buffalo and Boston were both graveyards for previous pro-football failures, while Denver and Houston were virgin territory.

Work went on during the summer, when players had to be signed. The AFL honored existing NFL contracts with players and lured away no players from the established league. The new teams picked up experience by signing NFL rejects and oldsters. Most of the AFL quarterbacks had NFL credits, such as George Blanda, Jack Kemp, Babe Parilli, Tom O'Connell, Al Dorow, and Cotton Davidson. Some players from the Canadian League seized upon the AFL as a chance to play again in the United States. Frank Tripuka, Dave Kocourek, Goose Gonsoulin, Butch Songin, Al Jamison, and Sherrill Headrick all had been playing north of the border before signing with the AFL. And a flock of unknown rookies and free agents were signing, hard-working if unspectacular football players with a desire to play football for a living. Such unheralded names as Charley Hennigan, Abner Haynes, Jim Otto, and Larry Grantham went unnoticed by pro scouts until turning up in AFL training camps.

But the most spectacular aspect of the player recruiting was the bidding war with NFL teams over well-known college players. The new league wanted to build its image by signing the cream of the graduating college class, and some clubs engaged in financial combat with an NFL team to woo an All-American collegian. Some young men found this courtship so intoxicating that they signed contracts with both contestants. A series of court battles ensued that gave the AFL such dual signers as Heisman Trophy winner Billy Cannon, Johnny Robinson, and Charlie Flowers.

Another item on the agenda was finding a place to play. New York and Oakland fared the worst in the stadium hunt, with New York having to settle for the grimy old Polo Grounds, while Oakland had to play its home games in San Francisco because there was no stadium in Oakland. Houston played its games in a high-school facility and Denver used a minor-league baseball field.

A fourteen-game schedule was adopted for the league, and the two-point conversion rule, where the team may run or pass for two points after a touchdown, was put into effect for all games. But the most important move by Commissioner Foss was the signing of a national television contract with the American Broadcasting System which provided a needed $150,000 to each team.

After all this, play was ready to begin. Although average attendance per game was only 16,000, the AFL would survive 1960 and be back for more.

EASTERN DIVISION

Houston Oilers—The players came from all over. Billy Cannon, the Heisman Trophy halfback from Louisiana State, had signed a three-year contract for $100,000, one of the richest pacts in pro history. George Blanda had come out off a year's retirement after a ten-year career with the Chicago Bears. Charley Hennigan had been teaching high-school biology, and he taped his final paycheck from the school inside his helmet for inspiration in dull moments. Bill Groman was an unknown rookie from Heidelberg. Al Jamison came down from the Canadian League. Coach Lou Rymkus blended all the parts together into a high-scoring machine which took command in the Eastern Division right from the start. The Oilers at first relied on Blanda's long bombs to Groman and Hennigan, but Cannon recovered from a slow start to give the ground game some punch and the Oilers won the first AFL Eastern crown.

New York Titans—The drab old Polo Grounds, abandoned since 1957, was dusted off to serve as home for the Titans. While Titan games were played in virtual anonymity (with highly inflated announced attendance figures), the NFL Giants were playing to a packed house week after week within walking distance at Yankee Stadium. The Titans admittedly were no match for the Giants yet, but they did play interesting, wide-open football. Although fullback Bill Mathis showed promise as a runner after winning a job in mid-season, the attack lived on quarterback Al Dorow's scrambling runs and long passes to speedsters Art Powell and Don Maynard. The Titan defense was virtually nonexistent, although young Larry Grantham showed well at linebacker. The Titans won interesting games, as when they beat Denver 28-24 by blocking a punt with twenty seconds left in the game, and they lost interesting games, like a 50-43 shootout with the Chargers. But the death of guard Howard Glenn with a broken neck after the October 9 game with Houston and the dearth of paying fans cast a deep shadow over this debut season.

Buffalo Bills—The Bills were an early-AFL rarity, a team trying to live on its defense. They had two tough linemen in Lavern Torczon and Chuck McMurtry, a mobile, hard-hitting middle linebacker in Archie Matsos, and one of the league's better secondaries, headed by NFL veterans Richie McCabe and Jim Wagstaff. But the offense couldn't launch an effective passing attack, the staple of most AFL clubs this year. Tom O'Connell, the old Cleveland quarterback, could not hold the starting passer's job given to him at the outset of the season, and Penn State All-American Rickie Lucas flopped both at quarterback and halfback. Johnny Green, an unheralded rookie, eventually took charge of the offense, whose main weapons were runner Wray Carlton and flanker Elbert Dubenion. The high point of the year was a 32-3 upset of the Los Angeles Chargers, but the Buffalo attack stalled too often to do any better than third place in the East.

Boston Patriots—The AFL broke into the box scores in Boston on Friday night, September 9. A crowd of 21,597 fans turned out at Boston University Field to watch the first regular-season AFL game ever, between the Patriots and the Denver Broncos. The Patriots displayed their weak attack right from the start by losing 13-10 to the Broncos. Coach Lou Saban had little speed in an offense led by quarterback Butch Songin, a thirty-six-year-old veteran of the Canadian League who doubled as a local high-school coach, but the defense held together well around a nucleus of Bob Dee, Tom Addison, Fred Bruney, and Ross O'Hanley. With a 35-0 trouncing of the Chargers and a 42-14 beating of the Texans to their credit, the Patriots stayed at the break-even point until losing all four of their final games. In the season's finale, before a sell-out Boston crowd of 27,123, the Pats lost 37-21 to Houston. More importantly, coach Saban shifted Gino Cappelletti from defensive back to split end for this game and discovered Boston's top receiver for the next few years.

WESTERN DIVISION

Los Angeles Chargers—The eeriest sight in pro football was the Los Angeles Chargers playing to vast stretches of empty seats in the huge Memorial Coliseum. But despite the sparse fan support, coach Sid Gillman, who had coached the Rams last season, built a high-scoring outfit which took the Western Division crown in this first AFL season. The Chargers dropped three of their first five contests before hitting their stride, losing only once in their last nine games. The offense led this second-half charge, scoring 41 or more points in each of the last four games. Although the Chargers had shelled out a lot of money for Mississippi fullback Charlie Flowers, the offensive stars were quarterback Jack Kemp, rejected by the Steelers, Giants, and '49ers in the NFL; halfback Paul Lowe, an unknown rookie from Oregon State; and tackle Ron Mix, a first-draft choice of the NFL Colts. Tragedy hit the club when end Ralph Anderson, the team's leading receiver, died of a diabetes attack in November. But in general the Chargers were an artistic if not a financial success.

Dallas Texans—The Texans had the league's best runner, best defense, and worst luck. Halfback Abner Haynes, a speedster from North Texas State, was the AFL's first running star, carrying the ball for 875 yards, catching passes out of the backfield, and running back kicks with an exciting flair. The defense posted three shutouts and allowed a grand total of seven points in its last three games, the stingiest unit in this offense-oriented season. End Mel Branch, tackle Paul Rochester, middle linebacker Sherrill Headrick, and backs Dave Webster and Johnny Bookman were the main pillars of coach Hank Stram's defense. Only a couple of heartbreaking losses kept the Texans from challenging for the Western crown, as they lost 21-20 to the Chargers, 37-35 to the Titans, and 20-19 to the Raiders. But after the season the Texans could look back on a 17-0 victory over the Chargers and a 24-0 victory over the Oilers, shutouts over both divisional champions.

Oakland Raiders—Because of the problem of getting a late start, due to Oakland replacing Minneapolis as the eighth club in the new circuit, businessman Chet Soda, who headed the group granted the Oakland franchise, did not have an easy time when it came to signing players. But coach Ernie Erdelatz weeded through the available talent and built a surprisingly respectable team. He found two quarterbacks in rookie Tom Flores and NFL veteran Babe Parilli and three hard-working runners in Tony Teresa, Billy Lott, and Jack Larscheid. From this quickly organized squad, two players would stick with the Raiders through the entire ten-year life of the AFL—center Jim Otto and guard Wayne Hawkins.

Denver Broncos—With Gene Mingo returning a punt 76 yards for a touchdown, the Broncos beat the Boston Patriots 13-10 in the first regular-season AFL game. But Denver's main offensive weapon didn't join the team until the third week of the season. End Lionel Taylor, a slow-footed but sure-handed receiver, practiced with the Broncos for four days before catching eleven passes against the Titans on September 25, and he went on to catch enough passes in twelve games to lead the league in receiving. The Broncos lived on the pass, with thirty-two-year-old Frank Tripuka throwing 478 passes all year, including fifty-two against the Oilers on November 6. The airborne Denver attack boasted the league's top point producer in halfback and kicker Gene Mingo, but the defense leaked profusely despite fine seasons by tackle Bud McFadin and safety Goose Gonsoulin. With opposing teams scoring freely, the Broncos went winless in their last eight games, salvaging only a 38-38 tie with Boston by coming back from a 38-7 deficit in the third quarter.

FINAL TEAM STATISTICS

	OFFENSE								DEFENSE							
	BOSTON	BUFFALO	DALLAS	DENVER	HOUSTON	L.A.	NEW YORK	OAKLAND	BOSTON	BUFFALO	DALLAS	DENVER	HOUSTON	L.A.	NEW YORK	OAKLAND
FIRST DOWNS:																
Total	234	211	272	248	262	263	286	254	237	225	253	254	282	259	252	268
by Rushing	86	77	119	84	83	96	111	98	78	103	76	112	90	97	99	99
by Passing	126	109	136	141	153	141	152	138	135	109	148	123	164	138	133	146
by Penalty	22	25	17	23	26	26	23	18	24	13	29	19	28	24	20	23
RUSHING:																
Number	401	462	483	440	474	437	485	475	477	474	422	541	438	414	449	442
Yards	1218	1211	1814	1195	1565	1536	1460	1785	1513	1393	980	2145	1027	1750	1378	1598
Average Yards	3.0	2.6	3.8	2.7	3.3	3.5	3.0	3.7	3.2	2.9	2.3	4.0	2.3	4.2	3.1	3.6
Touchdowns	11	15	24	10	15	24	14	23	21	15	14	19	6	24	20	17
PASSING:																
Attempts	475	447	435	508	456	441	474	463	429	429	503	387	557	467	450	477
Completions	223	184	209	259	218	229	236	235	210	185	261	189	271	227	216	234
Completion Percentage	46.9	41.2	48.0	51.0	47.8	51.9	49.8	50.8	49.0	43.1	51.2	48.8	48.7	48.6	48.0	49.1
Yards	2865	2689	2831	3247	3371	3177	3334	2923	2958	2461	3002	2987	3874	2851	2919	3385
Average Yards per Attempt	6.0	6.0	6.5	6.4	7.4	7.2	7.0	6.3	6.9	5.7	6.0	7.7	7.0	6.1	6.5	7.1
Average Yards per Completion	12.8	14.6	13.5	12.5	15.5	13.9	14.1	12.4	14.1	13.3	11.5	15.8	14.3	12.6	13.5	14.5
Touchdowns	25	19	16	24	31	21	32	18	19	19	19	25	28	21	27	28
Interceptions	23	29	19	35	28	29	28	28	25	33	32	27	25	28	24	25
Percent Intercepted	4.8	6.5	4.4	6.9	6.1	6.6	5.9	6.0	5.8	7.7	6.4	7.0	4.5	6.0	5.3	5.2
PUNTING:																
Number	78	89	61	70	72	58	62	76	74	77	78	67	68	62	65	75
Average Distance	35.8	39.0	39.3	37.3	35.8	39.7	37.1	38.9	37.2	37.6	37.5	39.0	37.1	40.2	37.0	37.5
PUNT RETURNS:																
Number	28	27	33	29	15	32	17	26	21	33	27	20	28	17	31	30
Yards	203	185	496	261	208	301	120	151	361	232	157	149	258	197	342	229
Average Yards	7.3	6.9	15.0	9.0	13.9	9.4	7.1	5.8	17.2	7.0	5.8	7.5	9.2	11.6	11.0	7.6
Touchdowns	0	0	1	1	0	1	1	0	3	0	0	1	0	0	0	0
KICKOFF RETURNS:																
Number	60	47	40	67	48	58	62	63	50	55	57	54	46	70	70	43
Yards	1421	945	845	1547	1225	1213	1580	1504	1123	1402	1347	1087	1096	1481	1785	959
Average Yards	23.7	20.1	21.1	23.1	25.5	20.9	25.5	23.9	22.5	25.5	23.6	20.1	23.8	21.2	25.5	22.3
Touchdowns	0	0	0	0	2	0	2	1	1	0	1	1	0	0	1	1
INTERCEPTION RETURNS:																
Number	25	33	32	27	25	28	24	25	23	29	19	35	28	29	28	28
Yards	312	356	410	417	190	317	201	278	336	422	171	343	316	284	228	381
Average Yards	12.6	10.8	12.8	15.4	7.6	11.3	8.4	11.1	14.6	14.6	9.0	9.8	11.3	9.8	8.1	13.6
Touchdowns	0	4	4	2	0	2	1	1	3	2	0	3	2	1	0	3
PENALTIES:																
Number	69	57	80	54	75	70	63	71	77	62	59	62	74	59	77	59
Yards	730.5	615	753	501	750	648	672	718	825	608.5	579	633	664	569	911	598
FUMBLES:																
Number	36	30	30	32	36	31	36	41	41	27	34	26	42	39	27	36
Number Lost	22	15	18	17	17	16	20	18	20	16	16	17	26	17	16	15
POINTS:																
Total	286	296	362	309	379	373	382	319	349	303	253	393	285	336	399	388
PAT (Kick) Attempts	32	34	44	36	47	47	50	39								
PAT (Kick) Made	30	28	42	33	46	46	47	37	43	37	31	48	33	40	51	46
PAT (Rush or Pass) Attempts	5	3	2	1	0	0	1	4								
PAT (Rush or Pass) Made	4	2	1	0	0	0	1	2								
FG Attempts	23	26	34	28	34	24	21	25	27	27	23	28	27	28	25	30
FG Made	8	12	14	18	15	13	9	6	10	14	4	17	12	14	10	14
Percent FG Made	34.8	46.2	41.2	64.3	44.1	54.2	42.9	24.0	37.0	51.9	17.4	60.7	44.4	50.0	40.0	46.7
Safeties	1	0	0	0	0	0	0	1	0	1	0	0	0	1	0	0

1960 AFL CHAMPIONSHIP GAME

January 1, at Houston
(Attendance 32,183)

SCORING

HOUSTON	0	10	7	7–24
LOS ANGELES	6	3	7	0–16

First Quarter

L.A.	Agajanian, 38 yard field goal	4:02
L.A.	Agajanian, 22 yard field goal	8:16

Second Quarter

Hous.	Smith, 17 yard pass from Blanda PAT–Blanda (kick)	3:51
Hous.	Blanda, 18 yard field goal	8:45
L.A.	Agajanian, 27 yard field goal	14:55

Third Quarter

Hous.	Groman, 7 yard pass from Blanda PAT–Blanda (kick)	
L.A.	Lowe, 2 yard rush PAT–Agajanian (kick)	

Fourth Quarter

Hous.	Cannon, 88 yard pass from Blanda PAT–Blanda (kick)	

TEAM STATISTICS

HOUS.		L.A.
17	First Downs–Total	21
4	First Downs–Rushing	11
13	First Downs–Passing	9
0	First Downs–Penalty	1
0	Fumbles–Number	2
0	Fumbles–Lost Ball	0
4	Penalties–Number	3
54	Yards Penalized	15
0	Giveaways	2
2	Takeaways	0
+2	Difference	–2

Age and Blanda and a Crown

The Oilers and Chargers met on New Year's Day to decide the first AFL championship. Both clubs had high scoring offenses, but the defensive units turned in surprisingly strong performances. The only scoring of the first quarter came on a pair of field goals by Ben Agajanian, Los Angeles' forty-one-year-old kicking specialist. George Blanda, the old man in the Houston lineup, put the Oilers ahead early in the second period with a 17-yard touchdown pass to fullback Dave Smith and the successful conversion. Blanda and Agajanian both added three-pointers late in the quarter to make the score 10-9 Houston at the half. The offenses moved better in the second half, with the Oilers relying on Blanda's passing and the Chargers on Paul Lowe's running. Houston upped its lead to eight points with a seven-yard Blanda-to-Bill Groman touchdown pass, but the Chargers came right back on a long drive culminating in Lowe's two-yard dash into the end zone. Leading 17-16 after three quarters, the Oilers broke open a long pass play, a very common occurrence in the early AFL. Billy Cannon came out of the backfield and took a George Blanda pass 88 yards to a touchdown, with the extra point running the score to 24-16. The Oilers led by eight points, but the Chargers could tie the game in one swoop with a touchdown and a two-point conversion. Twice the Chargers drove deep into Houston territory only to lose the ball on downs on the 35-yard line and on the 22-yard line. The final Los Angeles drive died with one minute left, turning the ball and the league championship over to the Oilers.

INDIVIDUAL STATISTICS

HOUSTON	No.	Yds.	Avg.	LOS ANGELES	No.	Yds.	Avg.
RUSHING							
Cannon	18	50	2.8	Lowe	21	165	7.9
Smith	19	45	2.4	Ferguson	4	11	2.8
Hall	3	5	1.6	Ford	2	–5	–2.5
	40	100	2.5	Kemp	6	–9	–1.5
					33	162	4.9
RECEIVING							
Smith	5	52	10.4	Norton	6	55	9.2
Hennigan	4	71	17.8	Womble	6	29	4.8
Cannon	3	128	42.7	Kocourek	3	57	19.0
Groman	3	37	12.3	Lowe	3	5	1.7
Carson	1	13	13.0	Ferguson	2	19	9.5
	16	301	18.8	Flowers	1	6	6.0
					21	171	8.1
PUNTING							
Milstead	5		34.0	Laraba	4		41.0
PUNT RETURNS							
None				Harris	1	27	27.0
				Sears	1	15	15.0
					2	42	21.0
KICKOFF RETURNS							
Cannon	3	81	27.0	Lowe	4	101	25.3
Hall	2	47	23.5	Ford	1	22	22.0
	5	128	25.6		5	123	24.6
INTERCEPTION RETURNS							
Gordon	1	27	27.0	None			
Dukes	1	8	8.0				
	2	35	17.5				

PASSING

	Att.	Comp.	Comp. Pct.	Yds.	Int.	Yds/ Att.	Yds/ Comp.
HOUSTON							
Blanda	31	16	51.6	301	0	9.7	18.8
Cannon	1	0	0.0	0	0	–	–
	32	16	50.0	301	0	9.4	18.8
LOS ANGELES							
Kemp	41	21	51.2	171	2	4.2	8.1

HOUSTON OILERS 10-4-0 Lou Rymkus

Scores of Each Game		
37	Oakland	22
38	LOS ANGELES	28
13	OAKLAND	14
27	NEW YORK	21
20	DALLAS	10
42	New York	28
24	Buffalo	25
45	Denver	25
21	Los Angeles	24
20	DENVER	10
24	Boston	10
0	Dallas	24
31	BUFFALO	23
37	BOSTON	21

Use Name	Pos.	Hgt	Wgt	Age	Int	Pts
Gary Greaves	OT	6'3"	235	24		
Al Jamison	OT	6'5"	240	23		
Rich Michael	OT	6'3"	230	21		
Fred Wallner	OG	6'2"	235	31		
Hogan Wharton	OG	6'2"	245	24		
Wahoo McDaniel	OG	6'	230	23		
Bob Talamini	OG	6'1"	230	21		
George Belotti	C	6'4"	255	25		
John Simerson	C	6'3"	255	25		
Dalva Allen	DE	6'5"	245	24	1	
Don Floyd	DE	6'4"	230	21		
Dan Lanphear	DE	6'2"	220	22		
Pete Davidson	DT	6'5"	255	26		
Jerry Helluin	DT	6'2"	260	30		
George Shirkey	DT	6'4"	260	23		
Orville Trask	DT	6'4"	260	25		
Mike Dukes	LB	6'3"	225	24	2	
Dennit Morris	LB	6'1"	225	24	4	
Phil Perlo	LB	6'	220	24		
Hugh Pitts	LB	6'2"	225	26		
Tony Banfield	DB	6'1"	185	21	3	
Bobby Gordon	DB	6'	195	24	3	
Mark Johnston	DB	6'	203	22	4	
Charlie Kendall	DB	6'2"	185	25	2	
Jim Norton	DB	6'3"	182	21	1	
Julian Spence	DB	5'11"	170	31	4	
George Blanda	QB	6'1"	210	32		115
Jacky Lee	QB	6'1"	185	21		
Charley Milstead	QB	6'2"	190	22		
Don Brown	HB	6'1"	205	23		
Billy Cannon	HB	6'1"	210	23		42
Ken Hall	HB	6'1"	200	24		6
Charley Tolar	HB	5'7"	195	22		18
Doug Cline	FB	6'2"	210	21		12
Dave Smith	FB	6'1"	205	23		42
Bob White	FB	6'2"	220	22		
Jack Atchason (from BOS)	OE	6'4"	215	23		6
Johnny Carson	OE	6'3"	205	30		24
Bill Groman	OE	6'	194	24		72
Charley Hennigan	OE	6'	190	24		36
John White	OE	6'4"	230	22		
Al Witcher	DE-OE	6'1"	200	23	1	6

NEW YORK TITANS 7-7-0 Sammy Baugh

Scores of Each Game		
27	BUFFALO	3
24	BOSTON	28
28	DENVER	24
37	Dallas	35
21	Houston	27
17	Buffalo	13
28	HOUSTON	42
27	OAKLAND	28
7	LOS ANGELES	21
21	Boston	38
41	DALLAS	35
30	Denver	27
31	Oakland	28
43	Los Angeles	50

Use Name	Pos.	Hgt	Wgt	Age	Int	Pts
Larry Baker	OT	6'2"	240	23		
Ernie Barnes	OT	6'3"	257	21		
Gene Cockrell	OT	6'3"	247	27		
Jack Klotz	OT	6'5"	260	26		
Dan Callahan	OG	6'	230	22		
Frank D'Agostino	OG	6'1"	245	26		
Howard Glenn (died Oct. 9)	OG	6'	235	25		
John McMullan	OG	6'	244	25		
Bob Mischak	OG	6'	238	27		
Mike Hudock	C	6'2"	245	25		
Ed Cooke	DE	6'4"	245	25		
Bob Reifsnyder	DE	6'2"	250	23		
Joe Ryan	DE	6'2"	235	26		
Nick Mumley	OT-DE	6'6"	245	24	1	6
Dick Guesman	DT	6'4"	255	24		
Joe Katchik	DT	6'9"	290	26		
Tom Saidock	DT	6'5"	260	28		
Sid Youngelman	DT	6'3"	265	28		
Leon Dumbrowski	LB	6'	215	22		
Roger Ellis	LB	6'3"	233	22	1	
Larry Grantham	LB	6'	195	21	5	
Bob Marques	LB	6'	220	23		
Hall Whitley	LB	6'2"	225	25		
Eddie Bell	DB	6'1"	215	29	2	
Roger Donnahoo	DB	6'	185	22	5	12
Charlie Dupre	DB	6'1"	195	24		
Dick Felt	DB	6'	180	27	2	
Fred Julian	DB	5'9"	185	22	6	
Corky Tharp	DB	5'10"	180	27	2	
Rick Sapienza	HB-DB	5'11"	185	24		
Al Dorow	QB	6'	195	30		42
Dick Jamieson	QB	6'1"	190	24		
Bob Scrabis	QB	6'3"	220	24		
Dewey Bohling	HB	5'11"	190	21		36
Leon Burton	HB	5'9"	172	25		18
Don Herndon	HB	6'	195	26		6
Bill Shockley	HB	6'	185	22		86
Pete Hart	FB	5'9"	190	22		
Bill Mathis	FB	6'1"	205	21		12
Joe Pagliei	FB	6'	220	26		6
Ken Campbell	OE	6'1"	213	21		
Don Maynard	OE	6'	185	24		36
Art Powell	OE	6'3"	210	23		84
Dave Ross	OE	6'3"	210	22		6
Thurlow Cooper	DE-OE	6'4"	228	27		20

BUFFALO BILLS 5-8-1 Buster Ramsey

Scores of Each Game		
3	New York	27
21	DENVER	27
13	Boston	0
10	LOS ANGELES	24
13	NEW YORK	17
38	OAKLAND	9
25	HOUSTON	24
28	DALLAS	45
7	Oakland	20
32	Los Angeles	3
38	Denver	38
38	BOSTON	14
23	Houston	31
7	Dallas	24

Use Name	Pos.	Hgt	Wgt	Age	Int	Pts
Tony Discenzo (from BOS)	OT	6'5"	240	24		
Ed Meyer	OT	6'2"	240	23		
Harold Olson	OT	6'3"	266	21		
Bob Sedlock	OT	6'4"	295	23		
Phil Blazer	OG	6'1"	235	24		
Don Chelf	OG	6'3"	235	25		
Ed Muelhaupt	OG	6'3"	230	24		
Dan McGrew	C	6'2"	250	22		
Leroy Moore	DE	6'	230	24		
Charlie Rutkowski	DE	6'3"	248	22		
Lavern Torczon	DE	6'2"	240	24		
Mack Yoho	DE	6'2"	240	24	1	12
Gene Grabosky	DT	6'5"	275	23		
Chuck McMurtry	DT	6'	310	22		
John Scott	DT	6'4"	260	24		
Jim Sorey	DT	6'4"	270	23		
Bernie Buzynski	LB	6'3"	228	22	1	
Joe Hergert	LB	6'1"	217	24	1	12
Jack Laraway	LB	6'1"	220	24		
Archie Matsos	LB	6'	220	25	8	6
Sam Palumbo	LB	6'2"	230	29		
Dennis Remmert	LB	6'3"	215	21		
Joe Schaffer	LB	6'	210	22	1	
Jack Johnson	DB	6'3"	195	26	2	
Billy Kinard	DB	6'	185	26	4	
Richie McCabe	DB	6'1"	185	26	4	
Jim Wagstaff	DB	6'2"	190	24	6	6
Billy Atkins	HB-DB	6'1"	195	25	5	45
Bob Brodhead	QB	6'2"	207	23		2
Johnny Green	QB	6'3"	198	23		12
Tom O'Connell	QB	5'11"	190	28		8
Richie Lucas	HB-QB	6'	190	21		18
Elbert Dubenion	HB	6'	190	25		48
Willmer Fowler	HB	5'11"	185	23		6
Darrell Harper	HB	6'1"	195	21		7
Joe Kulbacki	HB	6'	185	22		6
Harold Lewis	HB	6'	200	24		
Wray Carlton	FB	6'2"	210	22		66
Carl Smith	FB	6'	200	25		6
Bob Barrett	OE	6'3"	200	24		
Dick Brubaker	OE	6'	195	28		6
Dan Chamberlain	OE	6'4"	200	23		24
Monte Crockett	OE	6'3"	210	21		6
Al Hoisington (from OAK)	OE	6'3"	200	25		12
Tom Rychlec	OE	6'3"	220	26		

BOSTON PATRIOTS 5-9-0 Lou Saban

Scores of Each Game		
10	DENVER	13
28	New York	24
0	BUFFALO	13
35	Los Angeles	0
14	Oakland	27
24	Denver	31
16	LOS ANGELES	45
34	OAKLAND	28
38	NEW YORK	21
42	DALLAS	14
10	HOUSTON	24
14	Buffalo	38
0	Dallas	34
21	Houston	37

Use Name	Pos.	Hgt	Wgt	Age	Int	Pts
Bob Cross	OT	6'4"	245	29		
Jerry DeLucca	OT	6'3"	250	24		
George McGee	OT	6'2"	255	24		
Abe Cohen	OG	5'11"	230	26		
Jack Davis	OG	6'	226	27		
Bob Lee	OG	6'1"	245	24		
Charlie Leo	OG	6'	233	25		
Walt Cudzik	C	6'2"	226	27		
Bill Danenhauer (from DEN)	DE	6'4"	245	25		
Bob Dee	DE	6'3"	234	27	1	
Harry Jacobs	DE	6'2"	235	23	4	
Don McComb	DE	6'4"	240	26		
Al Richardson	DE	6'3"	250	25		
Al Crow	DT	6'6"	260	27		
Art Hauser	DT	6'	243	29		
Jim Hunt	DT	5'11"	245	21		
Harry Jagielski	DT	6'	260	28		
Bob Yates	DT	6'3"	250	21		
Tom Addison	LB	6'3"	230	24		
Phil Bennett	LB	6'3"	225	24		
Bill Brown	LB	6'1"	230	23	1	
Jack Rudolph	LB	6'3"	225	22	2	
Tony Sardisco	LB	6'2"	225	27		
Fred Bruney	DB	5'10"	188	29	3	
Ross O'Hanley	DB	6'	185	21	3	
Chuck Shonta	DB	6'	190	22	2	6
Bob Soltis	DB	6'2"	205	23	2	
Clyde Washington	DB	6'	195	22	3	
Gino Cappelletti	OE-DB	6'	190	26	4	60
Tom Dimitroff	QB	5'11"	200	25		
Tom Greene	QB	6'1"	190	22		
Butch Songin	QB	6'2"	190	36		12
Harvey White	QB	6'1"	190	22		
Walter Beach	HB	6'	180	25		6
Ron Burton	HB	5'10"	190	23		6
Dick Christy	HB	5'10"	192	24		36
Jake Crouthamel	HB	5'11"	195	22		
Larry Garron	HB	6'	185	23		
Jerry Green	HB	6'	190	23		
Walt Livingston	HB	6'	185	25		6
Ger Schwedes	HB	6'1"	205	21		
Billy Wells	HB	5'9"	175	28		6
Jim Crawford	FB	6'1"	205	24		14
Bill Larson	FB	5'10"	190	21		
Alan Miller	FB	6'	195	22		18
Joe Biscaha	OE	6'1"	190	23		
Jim Colclough	OE	6'	185	24		54
Joe Johnson	OE	6'	185	30		18
Oscar Lofton	OE	6'6"	218	22		24
Mike Long	OE	6'	188	21		
Tom Stephens	OE	6'1"	190	24		18

HOUSTON OILERS

RUSHING

Last Name	No.	Yds	Avg	TD
Cannon	152	644	4.2	1
Smith	154	643	4.2	5
Tolar	54	179	3.3	3
Hall	30	118	3.9	0
Cline	37	105	2.8	2
Talamini	0	14	0.0	0
Milstead	6	–21	–3.5	0
Lee	16	–57	–3.6	0
Blanda	25	–60	–2.4	4

RECEIVING

Last Name	No.	Yds	Avg	TD
Groman	72	**1473**	**20**	12
Carson	45	604	13	4
Hennigan	44	722	16	6
Smith	22	216	10	2
Cannon	15	187	12	5
Tolar	7	71	10	0
Atchason	5	48	10	1
Witcher	4	34	9	1
Cline	4	15	4	0
J. White	1	18	18	0
Norton	1	5	5	0

PUNT RETURNS

Last Name	No.	Yds	Avg	TD
Cannon	4	96	24	0
Hall	6	72	12	0
Tolar	5	40	8	0

KICKOFF RETURNS

Last Name	No.	Yds	Avg	TD
Hall	19	594	**31**	1
Cannon	8	266	33	1
Tolar	13	249	19	0
Dukes	4	58	15	0
Cline	3	42	14	0
Jamison	1	5	5	0
J. White	0	11	11	0

PASSING – PUNTING – KICKING

PASSING	Att	Comp	%	Yds	Yd/Att	TD	Int–%	RK
Blanda	363	169	47	2413	6.6	24	22– 6	5
Lee	77	41	53	842	10.9	5	6– 8	
Milstead	7	4	57	43	6.1	0	0– 0	
Smith	5	3	60	70	14.0	1	0– 0	
Cannon	3	0	0	0	0.0	0	0– 0	
Groman	1	1	100	3	3.0	1	0– 0	

PUNTING	No	Avg
Milstead	66	35.8
Hall	6	35.0

KICKING	XP	Att	%	FG	Att	%
Blanda	46	47	**98**	15	**34**	44

NEW YORK TITANS

RUSHING

Last Name	No.	Yds	Avg	TD
Bohling	123	431	3.5	2
Mathis	92	307	3.3	2
Dorow	124	167	1.3	7
Shockley	37	156	4.2	0
Burton	16	119	7.4	1
Hart	25	113	4.5	0
Pagliei	17	69	4.1	1
Jamieson	8	–61	–7.6	0

RECEIVING

Last Name	No.	Yds	Avg	TD
Maynard	72	1265	18	6
Powell	69	1167	17	**14**
Bohling	30	268	9	4
Mathis	18	103	6	0
Ross	10	122	12	1
Cooper	9	161	18	3
Shockley	8	69	9	2
Herndon	5	57	11	1
Hart	3	19	6	0
Burton	3	8	3	0
Pagliei	1	13	13	0
Sapienza	1	4	4	0
Klotz	0	5	0	0

PUNT RETURNS

Last Name	No.	Yds	Avg	TD
Burton	12	93	8	0
Donnahoo	1	15	15	1
Shockley	3	12	4	0
Tharp	1	0	0	0

KICKOFF RETURNS

Last Name	No.	Yds	Avg	TD
Burton	**31**	**897**	29	2
Shockley	17	411	24	0
Herndon	6	114	23	0
Powell	2	63	32	0
Maynard	3	59	20	0
Baker	1	18	18	0
Reifsnyder	1	16	16	0
Klotz	1	8	8	0
Cooper	1	0	0	0

PASSING – PUNTING – KICKING

PASSING	Att	Comp	%	Yds	Yd/Att	TD	Int–%	RK
Dorow	396	201	51	2748	6.9	**26**	26– 7	2
Jamieson	70	35	50	586	8.4	6	2– 3	
Bohling	5	0	0	0	0.0	0	0– 0	
Scrabis	3	0	0	0	0.0	0	0– 0	

PUNTING	No	Avg
Pagliei	48	37.1
Sapienza	8	32.4
Dorow	6	44.0

KICKING	XP	Att	%	FG	Att	%
Shockley	**47**	**50**	94	9	21	43

2 POINT XP
Cooper (1)

BUFFALO BILLS

RUSHING

Last Name	No.	Yds	Avg	TD
Carlton	137	533	3.9	7
Fowler	93	370	4.0	1
Kulbacki	41	108	2.6	1
Dubenion	16	94	5.9	1
Lucas	46	90	1.9	2
Smith	19	61	3.2	0
Atkins	2	47	23.5	0
Brodhead	21	45	2.1	0
Harper	1	3	3.0	0
O'Connell	22	–24	–1.0	1
Green	46	–156	–3.4	2

RECEIVING

Last Name	No.	Yds	Avg	TD
Rychlec	45	590	13	0
Dubenion	42	752	18	7
Carlton	29	477	16	4
Chamberlain	17	279	16	4
Crockett	14	173	12	1
Fowler	10	99	10	0
Hoisington	8	141	18	2
Smith	7	127	18	1
Brubaker	7	75	11	1
Lucas	5	58	12	1
Kulbacki	2	9	5	0
Green	1	0	0	0

PUNT RETURNS

Last Name	No.	Yds	Avg	TD
Kulbacki	12	100	8	0
Kinard	2	24	12	0
Matsos	1	20	20	0
Dubenion	2	6	3	0
Crockett	1	5	5	0
Lucas	4	3	1	0
Lewis	1	2	2	0

KICKOFF RETURNS

Last Name	No.	Yds	Avg	TD
Kulbacki	13	226	17	0
Fowler	12	201	17	0
Lewis	4	97	24	0
Smith	2	72	36	0
Dubenion	4	68	17	0
Kinard	1	39	39	0
Hoisington	2	25	13	0
Chamberlain	1	24	24	0
Rychlec	1	3	3	0

PASSING – PUNTING – KICKING

PASSING	Att	Comp	%	Yds	Yd/Att	TD	Int–%	RK
Green	228	89	39	1267	5.6	10	10– 4	8
O'Connell	145	65	45	1033	7.1	7	13– 9	8
Lucas	49	23	47	314	6.4	2	3– 6	
Brodhead	26	7	28	76	3.0	0	3– 12	

PUNTING	No	Avg
Atkins	**89**	39.0

KICKING	XP	Att	%	FG	Att	%
Atkins	27	32	84	6	13	46
Harper	1	2	50	2	3	67
Hergert	0	0	0	2	4	50
Yoho	0	0	0	2	5	40
O'Connell	0	0	0	0	1	0

2 POINT XP
Brodhead (1)
O'Connell (1)

BOSTON PATRIOTS

RUSHING

Last Name	No.	Yds	Avg	TD
Miller	101	416	4.2	1
Christy	78	363	4.7	4
Burton	66	280	4.3	1
Crawford	51	238	4.7	2
Wells	14	59	4.2	0
Garron	8	27	3.4	0
Crouthamel	4	16	4.0	0
Livingston	10	16	1.6	1
Washington	2	10	5.0	0
White	5	7	1.4	0
Beach	6	–4	–0.7	0
Dimitroff	2	–10	–5.0	0
Greene	16	–27	–1.7	0
Songin	36	–140	–3.9	2

RECEIVING

Last Name	No.	Yds	Avg	TD
Colclough	49	666	14	9
Miller	29	284	10	2
Christy	26	268	10	2
Stephens	22	320	15	3
Burton	21	196	9	0
Lofton	19	360	19	4
Wells	14	206	15	1
Johnson	11	186	17	3
Crawford	10	92	9	0
Beach	9	132	15	1
Green	3	52	17	0
White	2	24	12	0
Long	2	10	5	0
Cappelletti	1	28	28	0
Cudzik	1	11	11	0
Garron	1	8	8	0
Livingston	1	0	0	0

PUNT RETURNS

Last Name	No.	Yds	Avg	TD
Christy	8	73	9	0
Wells	12	66	6	0
Bruney	4	31	8	0
Beach	1	21	21	0
Cohen	1	9	9	0
Cappelletti	1	3	3	0
Burton	1	0	0	0

KICKOFF RETURNS

Last Name	No.	Yds	Avg	TD
Christy	24	617	26	0
Wells	11	275	25	0
Burton	4	161	40	0
Beach	7	146	21	0
Cappelletti	4	100	25	0
Bruney	2	39	20	0
Crouthamel	2	27	14	0
Garron	1	21	21	0
Hunt	1	8	8	0
Team	1	8	8	0
Greene	1	3	3	0
Livingston	1	3	3	0

PASSING – PUNTING – KICKING

PASSING	Att	Comp	%	Yds	Yd/Att	TD	Int–%	RK
Songin	392	187	48	2476	6.3	22	15– 4	4
Greene	63	27	43	251	4.0	1	6– 10	
Christy	11	6	55	94	8.5	2	2– 18	
White	7	3	43	44	6.3	0	0– 0	
Dimitroff	2	0	0	0	0.0	0	0– 0	

PUNTING	No	Avg
Greene	59	37.9
Washington	17	31.7

KICKING	XP	Att	%	FG	Att	%
Cappelletti	30	32	94	8	21	38
Crawford	0	0	0	0	1	0
Cudzik	0	0	0	0	1	0

2 POINT XP
Cappelletti (3)
Crawford (1)

LOS ANGELES 10-4-0 Sid Gillman

Scores of Each Game		
21	DALLAS	20
28	Houston	38
0	Dallas	17
24	Buffalo	10
0	BOSTON	35
23	Denver	19
45	Boston	16
21	New York	7
24	HOUSTON	21
3	BUFFALO	32
52	OAKLAND	28
41	Oakland	17
41	DENVER	33
50	NEW YORK	43

Use Name	Pos.	Hgt	Wgt	Age	Int	Pts
Dick Chorovich	OT	6'4"	260	27		
Sam DeLuca	OT	6'2"	245	24		
Ron Mix	OT	6'4"	245	22		
Ernie Wright	OT	6'4"	270	21		
Al Barry	OG	6'2"	235	29		
Fred Cole	OG	5'11"	226	23		
Orlando Ferrante	OG	6'	230	27		
Charlie Kempinski	OG	6'	235	21		
Don Rogers	C	6'2"	235	23		
Ben Donnell	DE	6'5"	248	23		
Art Gob (from WAS-N)	DE	6'4"	230	23		
Ron Nery	DE	6'6"	226	25		
Maury Schleicher	DE	6'3"	240	23	1	
Paul Maguire	OE-DE	6'	210	22	3	6
Gary Finneran	DT	6'3"	240	26		
John Kompara	DT	6'2"	245	23		
Volney Peters	DT	6'4"	240	31		

Use Name	Pos.	Hgt	Wgt	Age	Int	Pts
Al Bansavage	LB	6'2"	230	22		
Hubert Bobo	LB	6'1"	214	25		
Ron Botcham	LB	6'1"	238	25	2	
Charlie Brueckman	LB	6'2"	225	24		
Emil Karas	LB	6'3"	225	26		
Rommie Loudd	LB	6'3"	226	26	3	
Bob Garner	DB	5'10"	190	25	2	
Dick Harris	DB	5'11"	174	23	5	6
Charley McNeil	DB	5'11"	178	24	3	
Doyle Nix	DB	6'1"	195	27	4	6
Jesse Thomas	DB	5'10"	180	31		
Henry Wallace	DB	6'	195	22		
Bob Zeman	DB	6'1"	203	23	2	
Jimmy Sears	HB-DB	5'11"	187	29	2	

Use Name	Pos.	Hgt	Wgt	Age	Int	Pts
Bobby Clatterbuck	QB	6'3"	196	28		
Jack Kemp	QB	6'1"	200	26		48
Bob Laraba	LB-QB	6'3"	194	27	1	
Fred Ford (from BUF)	HB	5'8"	180	22		12
Paul Lowe	HB	6'	180	23		66
Ron Waller	HB	5'11"	184	27		
Howie Ferguson	FB	6'2"	217	30		36
Charlie Flowers	FB	6'1"	207	23		12
Blanche Martin (from NY)	FB	6'	195	23		6
Royce Womble	FL	6'	184	28		24
Ralph Anderson*	OE	6'4"	225	23		30
Howard Clark	OE	6'2"	204	25		
Dave Kocourek	OE	6'5"	225	23		6
Trusse Norris	OE	6'1"	190	23		
Don Norton	OE	6'1"	180	22		30
Ben Agajanian	K	6'	220	41		85

* died Nov. 26 of diabetes

DALLAS TEXANS 8-6-0 Hank Stram

Scores of Each Game		
20	Los Angeles	21
34	Oakland	16
17	LOS ANGELES	0
35	NEW YORK	37
19	OAKLAND	20
10	Houston	20
17	Denver	14
45	Buffalo	28
34	DENVER	7
14	Boston	42
35	New York	41
24	HOUSTON	0
34	BOSTON	0
24	BUFFALO	7

Use Name	Pos.	Hgt	Wgt	Age	Int	Pts
Jerry Cornelison	OT	6'3"	250	23		
Charley Diamond	OT	6'2"	235	24		
R. B. Nunnery	OT	6'4"	275	26		
Jack Stone	OT	6'2"	245	23		
Sid Fournet	OG	6'	235	27		
Billy Krisher	OG	6'1"	235	24		
Al Reynolds	OG	6'3"	225	22		
Marvin Terrell	OG	6'1"	235	22		
Jim Barton	C	6'5"	250	25		
Tom Dimmick	C	6'6"	255	29		
Mel Branch	DE	6'2"	220	23		
Dick Frey	DE	6'2"	230	29		
Paul Miller	DE	6'2"	235	28		
Ray Collins	DT	5'11"	250	32		
Rufus Granderson	DT	6'5"	277	23		
Walter Napier	DT	6'4"	280	24		
Paul Rochester	DT	6'2"	250	23		

Use Name	Pos.	Hgt	Wgt	Age	Int	Pts
Walt Corey	LB	6'	215	22	3	
Ted Greene	LB	6'1"	230	26	3	
Sherrill Headrick	LB	6'2"	215	23	2	
Bob Hudson (to DEN)	LB	6'4"	230	30	1	
Smokey Stover	LB	6'	215	21	1	
Johnny Bookman	DB	5'11"	185	25	4	
Don Flynn	DB	6'	205	25	3	6
Jimmy Harris	DB	6'1"	175	25	2	
Charlie Jackson	DB	5'11"	180	24		
Dave Webster	DB	6'4"	215	22	6	18
Duane Wood	DB	6'1"	190	24	4	6
Carroll Zaruba	DB	5'9"	210	26		
Clem Daniels	HB-DB	6'1"	220	23	3	

Use Name	Pos.	Hgt	Wgt	Age	Int	Pts
Cotton Davidson	QB	6'1"	180	28		17
Hunter Enis	QB	6'2"	190	23		18
Abner Haynes	HB	6'	185	22		72
Curley Johnson	HB	6'	215	25		14
Johnny Robinson	HB	6'	195	21		54
Jim Swink	HB	6'1"	185	24		
Bo Dickinson	FB	6'2"	220	25		6
Jack Spikes	FB	6'2"	220	22		103
Ed Bernet	OE	6'3"	205	27		
Max Boydston	OE	6'2"	215	27		18
Bob Bryant	OE	6'5"	230	23		
Chris Burford	OE	6'3"	210	22		30

OAKLAND RAIDERS 6-8-0 Eddie Erdalatz

Scores of Each Game		
22	HOUSTON	37
16	DALLAS	34
14	Houston	13
14	Denver	31
20	Dallas	19
27	BOSTON	14
9	Buffalo	38
28	New York	27
28	Boston	34
20	BUFFALO	7
28	Los Angeles	52
17	LOS ANGELES	41
28	NEW YORK	31
48	DENVER	10

Use Name	Pos.	Hgt	Wgt	Age	Int	Pts
Don Churchwell	OT	6'1"	255	23		
Bill Striegel (from BOS)	OT	6'2"	240	24		
Dalton Truax	OT	6'2"	235	25		
Don Deskins	OG	6'3"	240	27		
John Dittrich	OG	6'1"	240	27		
Wayne Hawkins	OG	6'	235	22		
Don Manoukian	OG	5'9"	242	25		
Ron Sabal	OG	6'2"	230	23		
Jim Otto	C	6'2"	227	22		
Larry Barnes	DE	6'1"	230	27		55
Carmen Cavalli	DE	6'4"	245	22		
George Fields	DE	6'3"	245	24	2	
Charley Powell	DE	6'2"	227	28		
Ray Armstrong	DT	6'1"	235	22		
Joe Barbee	DT	6'3"	250	25		
Paul Oglesby	DT	6'4"	235	20		
Ron Warzeka	DT	6'4"	250	29		

Use Name	Pos.	Hgt	Wgt	Age	Int	Pts
Bob Dougherty	LB	6'1"	240	26		
Billy Locklin	LB	6'2"	225	22		
Tom Louderback	LB	6'2"	235	26	2	
Riley Morris	LB	6'2"	230	23		
Alex Bravo	DB	6'	190	28	4	
Joe Cannavino	DB	5'11"	185	24	4	
Wayne Crow	DB	6'	205	22	4	
L. C. Joyner	DB	6'1"	187	25		
Eddie Macon	DB	6'	180	32	9	6
John Harris	HB-DB	6'1"	195	27		

Use Name	Pos.	Hgt	Wgt	Age	Int	Pts
Tom Flores	QB	6'1"	190	23		18
Paul Larson	QB	5'11"	180	28		
Babe Parilli	QB	6'1"	190	30		6
Bob Keyes	HB	5'10"	183	24		
Jack Larscheid	HB	5'6"	162	26		12
Nyle McFarlane	HB	6'2"	205	24		12
Billy Reynolds	HB	5'10"	200	28		
Tony Teresa	HB	5'9"	185	25		60
Billy Lott	FB	6'	205	25		38
J. D. Smith	FB	6'	220	25		50
Doug Asad	OE	6'3"	200	22		6
Al Goldstein	OE	6'	204	24		12
Charley Hardy	OE	6'	183	26		18
Gene Prebola	OE	6'3"	215	22		12

DENVER BRONCOS 4-9-1 Frankie Filchock

Scores of Each Game		
13	Boston	10
27	Buffalo	21
24	New York	28
31	OAKLAND	14
19	LOS ANGELES	23
31	BOSTON	24
14	DALLAS	17
25	HOUSTON	45
7	Dallas	34
10	Houston	20
38	BUFFALO	38
27	NEW YORK	30
33	Los Angeles	41
10	Oakland	48

Use Name	Pos.	Hgt	Wgt	Age	Int	Pts
Eldon Danenhauer	OT	6'4"	235	24		
Gordy Holz	OT	6'4"	270	26		
Willie Smith	OT	6'2"	255	22		
Ken Adamson	OG	6'2"	215	21		
Jack Davis	OG	6'2"	235	25		
Carl Larpenter	OG	6'4"	235	23		
Dave Strickland	OG	6'	220	28		
Frank Kuchta	C	6'2"	235	24		
Mike Nichols	C	6'3"	225	21		
Chuck Gavin	DE	6'1"	235	26		
Bill Yelverton	DE	6'4"	220	26	1	6
Joe Young	DE	6'3"	245	25		
John Hatley	DT	6'3"	260	29		
Bud McFadin	DT	6'3"	260	32		
Hal Smith (from BOS)	DT	6'5"	250	25		
Don King	OT-DT	6'3"	255	30	2	

Use Name	Pos.	Hgt	Wgt	Age	Int	Pts
Vaughan Alliston	LB	6'	218	26	1	
Hardy Brown	LB	6'	190	36		
Al Day	LB	6'2"	216	22		
Pete Mangum	LB	6'	220	28		
Frank Bernardi	DB	5'9"	185	27		
Dick Doyle	DB	6'	190	29	1	
Goose Gonsoulin	DB	6'3"	205	22	11	
John Pyeatt	DB	6'3"	204	26	4	6
Al Romine	DB	6'2"	195	27	3	
Bob McNamara	HB-DB	6'	188	26	4	12

Use Name	Pos.	Hgt	Wgt	Age	Int	Pts
Tom Dublinski	QB	6'2"	205	30		
George Herring	QB	6'2"	200	25		
Frank Tripucka	QB	6'2"	205	32		
Henry Bell	HB	5'10"	210	23		
Al Carmichael	HB	6'1"	195	30		42
Gene Mingo	HB	6'1"	200	21		123
Bob Stransky	HB	6'1"	180	24		
Ted Wegert (from NY-to BUF)	HB	5'11"	200	28		12
Don Allen	FB	6'	200	23		6
J. W. Brodnax	FB	6'	208	23		6
Dave Rolle	FB	6'	215	22		18
Don Carothers	OE	6'5"	225	24		
Pat Epperson	OE	6'3"	225	24		
Jim Greer	OE	6'3"	215	26		6
Bill Jessup	OE	6'1"	195	31		6
Lionel Taylor	OE	6'2"	214	24		72
Ken Carpenter	HB-OE	6'	212	34		6

LOS ANGELES CHARGERS

RUSHING

Last Name	No.	Yds	Avg	TD
Lowe	136	855	6.3	9
Ferguson	126	438	3.5	4
Ford	38	194	5.1	2
Flowers	39	161	4.1	1
Martin	18	58	3.2	0
Laraba	4	7	1.8	0
Waller	9	5	0.6	0
Norton	1	2	2.0	0
Clatterbuck	6	−6	−1.0	0
Kemp	90	−103	−1.1	8

RECEIVING

Last Name	No.	Yds	Avg	TD
Anderson	44	614	14	5
Kocourek	40	662	17	1
Womble	32	316	10	4
Clark	27	431	16	0
Norton	25	414	17	5
Lowe	23	377	16	2
Ferguson	21	168	8	2
Flowers	12	153	13	1
Martin	4	23	6	1
Waller	3	24	8	0
Ford	1	5	5	0

PUNT RETURNS

Last Name	No.	Yds	Avg	TD
Harris	13	105	8	0
Sears	9	101	11	0
Garner	6	85	14	0
Ford	2	6	3	0
Maguire	1	4	4	1
Lowe	1	0	0	0

KICKOFF RETURNS

Last Name	No.	Yds	Avg	TD
Lowe	28	611	22	0
Ford	18	400	22	0
Sears	8	155	19	0
Norton	8	153	19	0
DeLuca	1	0	0	0

PASSING – PUNTING – KICKING

PASSING	Att	Comp	%	Yds	Yd/Att	TD	Int–%	RK
Kemp	406	211	52	3018	7.4	20	25– 6	1
Clatterbuck	23	15	65	112	4.9	1	1– 4	
Laraba	7	2	29	23	3.3	0	2– 29	
Lowe	3	1	33	24	8.0	0	0– 0	
Ford	1	0	0	0	0.0	0	0– 0	
Waller	1	0	0	0	0.0	0	1–100	

PUNTING	No	Avg
Maguire	43	40.5
Laraba	15	37.2

KICKING	XP	Att	%	FG	Att	%
Agajanian	46	47	98	13	24	54

DALLAS TEXANS

RUSHING

Last Name	No.	Yds	Avg	TD
Haynes	156	875	5.6	9
Robinson	98	458	4.8	4
Spikes	115	457	4.0	5
Dickinson	35	143	4.1	1
Johnson	23	43	1.9	1
Swink	10	15	1.5	0
Daniels	1	−2	−2.0	0
Enis	12	−12	−1.0	3
Davidson	31	−122	−3.9	1

RECEIVING

Last Name	No.	Yds	Avg	TD
Haynes	55	576	10	3
Burford	46	789	17	5
Robinson	41	611	15	4
Boydston	29	357	12	3
Spikes	11	158	14	0
Johnson	10	174	17	1
Bryant	5	43	9	0
Bernet	4	49	12	0
Swink	4	37	9	0
Dickinson	3	38	13	0
Davidson	1	−1	−1	0

PUNT RETURNS

Last Name	No.	Yds	Avg	TD
Haynes	14	215	15	0
Robinson	14	207	15	1
Daniels	3	69	23	0
Harris	1	5	5	0
Rochester	1	0	0	0

KICKOFF RETURNS

Last Name	No.	Yds	Avg	TD
Haynes	19	434	23	0
Daniels	9	162	18	0
Harris	5	117	23	0
Robinson	3	54	18	0
Swink	1	36	36	0
Dickinson	2	29	15	0
Johnson	1	13	13	0

PASSING – PUNTING – KICKING

PASSING	Att	Comp	%	Yds	Yd/Att	TD	Int–%	RK
Davidson	379	179	47	2474	6.5	15	16– 4	5
Enis	54	30	56	357	6.6	1	2– 4	
Haynes	1	0	0	0	0.0	0	0– 0	
Robinson	1	0	0	0	0.0	0	1–100	

PUNTING	No	Avg
Davidson	58	39.4
Johnson	3	36.7

KICKING	XP	Att	%	FG	Att	%
Spikes	34	36	94	13	31	42
Davidson	8	8	100	1	1	100
Flynn	0	0	0	0	1	0
Johnson	0	0	0	0	1	0

2 POINT XP
Johnson (1)

OAKLAND RAIDERS

RUSHING

Last Name	No.	Yds	Avg	TD
Teresa	139	608	4.4	6
Lott	99	520	5.3	5
Larscheid	94	397	4.2	1
Smith	63	214	3.4	6
McFarlane	4	52	13.0	0
Parilli	32	25	0.8	1
Keyes	1	7	7.0	0
Reynolds	1	6	6.0	0
Goldstein	3	−2	−0.7	1
Flores	38	42	1.1	3

RECEIVING

Last Name	No.	Yds	Avg	TD
Lott	49	524	11	1
Teresa	35	393	11	4
Prebola	33	404	12	2
Goldstein	27	354	13	1
Hardy	24	423	18	3
Larscheid	22	187	9	1
Smith	17	194	11	1
Asad	14	197	14	1
McFarlane	5	89	18	2
Reynolds	3	43	14	0
Keyes	1	19	19	0
Parilli	1	0	0	0

PUNT RETURNS

Last Name	No.	Yds	Avg	TD
Larscheid	12	106	9	0
Reynolds	7	24	3	0
Teresa	5	12	2	0
Keyes	1	5	5	0
Cannavino	1	4	4	0

KICKOFF RETURNS

Last Name	No.	Yds	Avg	TD
Larscheid	30	852	28	0
Smith	14	373	27	1
McFarlane	5	71	14	0
Asad	3	66	22	0
Teresa	4	61	15	0
Harris	3	38	13	0
Deskins	1	15	15	0
Morris	1	3	3	0

PASSING – PUNTING – KICKING

PASSING	Att	Comp	%	Yds	Yd/Att	TD	Int–%	RK
Flores	252	136	54	1738	6.9	12	12– 5	2
Parilli	187	87	47	1003	5.4	5	11– 6	10
Teresa	18	9	50	111	6.2	1	3– 17	
Larscheid	6	3	50	71	11.8	0	2– 33	

PUNTING	No	Avg
Crow	76	38.9

KICKING	XP	Att	%	FG	Att	%
Barnes	37	39	95	6	25	24

2 POINT XP
Lott (1)
Smith(1)

DENVER BRONCOS

RUSHING

Last Name	No.	Yds	Avg	TD
Rolle	130	501	3.9	2
Mingo	83	323	3.9	4
Bell	43	238	5.5	0
Carmichael	41	211	5.1	2
Wegert	36	161	4.5	1
Stransky	28	78	2.8	0
McNamara	17	33	1.9	1
Brodnax	15	18	1.2	0
Allen	30	18	0.6	1
Carpenter	4	13	3.3	0
Nichols	0	3	0.0	0
Taylor	2	−6	−3.0	0
Herring	5	−46	−9.2	0
Tripucka	37	−226	−6.1	0

RECEIVING

Last Name	No.	Yds	Avg	TD
Taylor	92	1235	13	12
Carmichael	32	616	19	5
Carpenter	29	350	12	1
Greer	22	284	13	1
Rolle	21	122	6	1
Mingo	19	156	8	1
Epperson	11	99	9	0
Jessup	9	120	13	1
McNamara	7	143	20	1
Wegert	5	68	14	1
Brodnax	5	39	8	1
Allen	5	34	7	0
Stransky	3	11	4	0
Carothers	2	25	13	0
Bell	2	13	7	0

PUNT RETURNS

Last Name	No.	Yds	Avg	TD
Carmichael	15	101	7	0
Mingo	3	92	31	1
McNamara	11	68	6	0
Wegert	4	25	6	0

KICKOFF RETURNS

Last Name	No.	Yds	Avg	TD
Carmichael	22	581	26	0
Wegert	10	252	25	0
Mingo	9	209	23	0
McNamara	9	192	21	0
Stransky	7	153	22	0
Brodnax	5	117	23	0
Allen	5	72	14	0
Bell	2	60	30	0
W. Smith	1	13	13	0
Greer	1	11	11	0
Strickland	1	9	9	0

PASSING – PUNTING – KICKING

PASSING	Att	Comp	%	Yds	Yd/Att	TD	Int–%	RK
Tripucka	478	248	52	3038	6.4	24	34– 7	7
Herring	22	9	41	137	6.2	0	1– 5	
Mingo	7	1	14	46	6.6	0	0– 0	
Carmichael	1	1	100	26	26.0	0	0– 0	

PUNTING	No	Avg
Herring	70	37.3

KICKING	XP	Att	%	FG	Att	%
Mingo	33	36	92	18	28	64

1961 N.F.L. Bypassing the Crisis

For some teams, the forward pass became less important than the weekend pass. President Kennedy's activation of reserve units because of the Berlin crisis drafted many players into active military duty, among them Paul Hornung, Bobby Mitchell, Ray Nitschke, Boyd Dowler, Dick Schafrath, Bob DeMarco, John Gordy, and John Paluck. Since all of the reservists were stationed within the continental United States, most of the affected players could get back to their teams on a weekend pass, then return to their military base on Monday morning. Commissioner Pete Rozelle also had contact with the federal government, but not as a soldier. He successfully persuaded Congress to pass a bill officially exempting the NFL's package TV deal with CBS from anti-trust legislation.

EASTERN CONFERENCE

New York Giants—After the Giants lost to the Cards on opening day and looked sluggish in the first half against the Steelers, Giant coach Allie Sherman yanked quarterback Chuck Conerly and replaced him with newly acquired Y. A. Tittle. The bald-headed Tittle won the first-string job by pulling out a victory over the Steelers and flawlessly directed the New York attack through the season. With Del Shofner, Joe Walton, and Erich Barnes—all, like Tittle, acquired in off-season trades—blending in with the holdover Giant stars, New York climbed into a first-place tie with Philadelphia by beating the Eagles 38-21 in Yankee Stadium on November 12 and took sole possession of the top spot by knocking off the Eagles 28-24 in Philadelphia on December 10. Needing at least a tie to clinch the title, the Giants played Cleveland to a 7-7 deadlock to end the season.

Philadelphia Eagles—Starting with Timmy Brown's 105-yard kickoff return on the first play of the season, the Eagles displayed the league's most explosive offense. Sonny Jurgensen replaced the retired Norm Van Brocklin at quarterback and surpassed all expectations by throwing thirty-two touchdown passes in a superior air attack featuring receivers Tommy McDonald and Pete Retzlaff. But two flaws sabotaged the Eagles' title chances—a weak running game and a thin defensive secondary. Cornerback Tom Brookshier broke a leg in a 16-14 victory over the Bears, and the Giants exploited substitute Glen Amerson's inexperience the next week in a 38-21 New York win.

Cleveland Browns—Paul Brown may have been the coach of the 1950s, but a storm was gathering against him in the 1960s. Several Cleveland players, including Jimmy Brown, found the coach's stern way of dealing with his men increasingly hard to take, and quarterback Milt Plum was openly critical of Brown's system of sending every play in via alternating messenger guards. But despite the growing dissension and a disappointing defensive secondary, the Browns again were in the thick of the Eastern title chase. They trailed New York by only one game until a 37-21 Giant win on November 26 ended their hopes.

St. Louis Cardinals—Injuries crippled the Cardinal offense even before the season started. Halfback John David Crow broke an ankle, and quarterback Sam Etcheverry, debuting in the NFL after a great nine-year career in Canada, came up with a sore arm to put a dent in the running and passing attacks. Coach Pop Ivy kept his team together, throwing Prentice Gautt into Crow's spot and spelling Etcheverry with Ralph Guglielmi, and the Cards came up with upset wins over New York and Philadelphia. But more injuries, such as Ken Panfil's bad knee, dropped the club into the lower ranks in the East and prompted coach Ivy to resign with two games left.

Pittsburgh Steelers—Old age was catching up with the Steelers. Bobby Layne spent several weeks in drydock with a bad shoulder, ends Preston Carpenter and Bob Schnelker had lost their speed, and defensive linemen Ernie Stautner, Big Daddy Lipscomb, and Joe Krupa all were on the decline. With Layne out, Rudy Bukich, who had done more sitting than playing in his past six seasons, took over at quarterback and showed a good arm and no consistency. Only fullback John Henry Johnson, flanker Buddy Dial, defensive back Johnny Sample, and linebackers John Reger and Myron Pottios had top-notch seasons.

Dallas Cowboys—After going winless through their inaugural 1960 season, the Cowboys quickly picked up their first victory by beating Pittsburgh 27-24 on opening day. After four weeks, the Cowboys had also beaten Minnesota twice to climb to a 3-1 record before the league caught up with them. Two blue-chip rookies made the Cowboys a much improved team. Halfback Don Perkins, who missed the 1960 season with a broken foot, raced to 815 yards rushing with a fine showing late in the season. The defensive addition was Bob Lilly, a quick and strong defensive end who put heavy pressure on enemy passers. Veterans Eddie LeBaron and Billy Howton combined for many short pass completions, while Frank Clarke suddenly developed into a dangerous deep receiver.

Washington Redskins—Rookie head coach Bill McPeak and rookie quarterback Norm Snead both suffered through a frightening debut. McPeak found himself in charge of a club with no runners, no blockers, and a porous defensive secondary. Snead learned quickly how to throw under pressure, with his line giving him no protection from swarms of defenders clawing and thrashing him. After thirteen losses and heavy underdogs against the Dallas Cowboys, the Redskins won 34-24 to avert the stigma of a victoryless season.

WESTERN CONFERENCE

Green Bay Packers—Coach Vince Lombardi had built his team around good blocking and good tackling. His offense had the league's best running attack, with two superb guards in Jerry Kramer and Fuzzy Thurston escorting runners Jim Taylor, Paul Hornung, and Tommy Moore around end in the famous Green Bay power sweep. Against the run the Packers defense was murder, with a quick forward wall of Bill Quinlan, Henry Jordan, Dave Hanner, and Willie Davis perfectly complemented by smart linebackers Bill Forester, Ray Nitschke, and Dan Currie. The Packers were a brutally physical team, with quarterback Bart Starr directing the violence with pinpoint passing and a knack for picking apart enemy defenses. After losing to the Lions on opening day, Green Bay won its next six games and had the Western title sewed up with two weeks left in the season.

Detroit Lions—Detroit fans found it hard to believe that the Lions were NFL powers. Five times the Lions lost at home, with a 49-0 pasting by the '49ers the ultimate humiliation. But the Lions saved their best for the road by going undefeated. Coach George Wilson had built a defense to match Green Bay's, a unit with size, speed, and experience in all sectors. No other team could match tackles Alex Karras and Roger Brown, Joe Schmidt had no peer as a middle linebacker, and Yale Lary and Night Train Lane had a world of savvy in the secondary.

Baltimore Colts—Johnny Unitas' passes still packed the Baltimore attack with explosives, but the Colt defense no longer could defuse enemy offenses. With Big Daddy Lipscomb and Johnny Sample traded to Pittsburgh and Art Donovan at the end of his career, opponents found it easier to move the ball against the Colts than it had been in the late 1950s. A slow start of two wins in the first five games made any title hopes seem very slim, and even a 45-21 mid-season ambush of the Packers couldn't halt the Colts' decline into mediocrity. But the colts still showcased several fine individual performances, such as the explosive running and receiving of Lenny Moore, the continued superb pass-catching of Ray Berry, and All-Pro seasons from Jim Parker and Gino Marchetti.

Chicago Bears—First place in the West rode on the November 12 meeting of the Bears and Packers in Wrigley Field. Green Bay's record was 6-2, coming off a 45-21 pasting by the Colts; the Bears' record was 5-3, fresh from a close 16-14 loss to the Eagles. Although the Packers had shut the Bears out 24-0 in an earlier meeting, Chicago fans whipped themselves into a fury over the game. They saw a good game, as the Packers ran out to a 28-7 lead and then barely held on for a 31-28 triumph. The Bears did not recapture first place, but they did refurbish their passing attack this year. The main addition was rookie Mike Ditka, the first tight end to win a national following for his devastating blocking and effective receiving.

San Francisco '49ers—The shotgun formation burned the league up for five weeks. Using this pass-oriented formation, the '49ers won four of their first five games, including triumphs of 35-3 over Washington, 49-0 over Detroit, and 35-0 over Los Angeles. Coach Red Hickey was alternating John Brodie, rookie Bill Kilmer, and Bobby Waters at the quarterback slot on alternate plays, loading the shotgun with quarterback plunges, halfback reverses, and a spate of passes. But the dream ended on October 22 in Chicago. Knowing that a center could not block well while looking between his legs to hike a ball back to a tailback, Bear defensive coach Clark Shaughnessy put middle linebacker Bill George right over the center and had him charge straight through to the quarterback on every play. By halftime, the Bears had demoralized the '49ers; by the final gun, the Bears had won 31-0. Thus exposed, the shotgun never again exploded.

Los Angeles Rams—The Rams had a lot of offensive talent for a sixth-place team. Jon Arnett and Dick Bass were top-notch runners, Ollie Matson a multitalented back, and both Jim Phillips and Carroll Dale fine receivers. There was no fuse at quarterback, however, to start the machine rolling, as neither Zeke Bratkowski nor Frank Ryan showed any consistency in running the attack. The porous offensive line helped neither passers nor runners, and outside of rookie end Deacon Jones, bright spots were scarce for the defensive unit.

Minnesota Vikings—The Vikings, this year's expansion team, quickly surpassed Dallas' 1960 record as a new team by beating the Chicago Bears 37-13 in their first league game. The three wins the Vikes captured for the season surprised most experts and made Norm Van Brocklin's coaching debut a success. Van Brocklin stepped right from the playing ranks as quarterback with the Eagles into the head coach's job at Minnesota, and his quarterback was one with a style most unlike his own. While Van Brocklin was a pocket passer whom only a tidal wave could force to run, rookie Fran Tarkenton became the talk of the league with his scrambling.

FINAL STATISTICS

OFFENSE

	BALT.	CHI.	CLEVE.	DALLAS	DET.	G.BAY	L.A.	MINN.	N.Y.	PHIL.	PITT.	ST.L.	S.F.	WASH.
FIRST DOWNS:														
Total	274	239	246	239	233	274	236	236	**275**	252	239	202	258	193
by Rushing	124	103	116	100	96	**142**	109	104	99	78	102	83	116	55
by Passing	135	113	120	130	122	115	111	123	**160**	158	123	110	132	124
by Penalty	15	**23**	10	9	15	17	16	9	16	16	14	9	10	14
RUSHING:														
Number	456	436	476	416	439	474	415	419	464	373	**543**	386	448	361
Yards	2119	1890	2163	1819	1868	**2350**	1958	1897	1857	1507	1761	1405	2100	1072
Average Yards	4.6	4.3	4.5	4.4	4.3	**5.0**	4.7	4.5	4.0	4.0	3.2	3.6	4.7	3.0
Touchdowns	17	16	15	6	16	**27**	17	14	13	10	10	8	**27**	9
PASSING:														
Attempts	**438**	349	320	422	398	306	386	377	416	429	334	351	346	420
Completions	232	186	185	215	186	177	199	203	215	**241**	176	168	187	189
Completion Pct.	53.0	53.3	57.8	50.9	46.7	**57.8**	51.6	53.8	51.7	56.2	52.7	47.9	54.0	45.0
Passing Yards (Gross)	3018	3011	2538	2918	2830	2502	2709	2527	3035	**3824**	2622	2434	3057	2566
Yards Lost Tackled	215	339	164	257	286	**138**	372	538	295	219	290	461	253	391
Net Yards	2803	2672	2374	2661	2544	2364	2337	1989	2740	**3605**	2332	1973	2804	2175
Yds. per Att (Gross)	6.9	8.6	7.9	6.9	7.1	8.2	7.0	6.7	7.3	**8.9**	7.9	6.9	8.8	6.1
Yds. per Comp (Gross)	13.0	16.2	13.7	13.6	15.2	14.1	13.6	12.4	14.1	15.9	14.9	14.5	**16.3**	13.6
Touchdowns	17	26	20	23	14	18	13	22	27	**34**	23	21	15	12
Interceptions	29	24	**13**	27	27	16	21	22	23	26	34	23	19	28
Pct. Intercepted	6.6	6.9	**4.1**	6.4	6.8	5.2	5.4	5.8	5.5	6.1	10.2	6.6	5.5	6.7
PUNTING:														
Number	42	60	53	61	56	51	64	63	68	55	73	**85**	59	70
Average Distance	43.0	41.7	43.3	36.7	**47.6**	43.0	40.1	39.0	43.9	43.7	47.0	44.7	44.6	38.1
PUNT RETURNS:														
Number	33	27	28	23	38	20	14	23	**42**	34	40	26	24	28
Yards	269	170	283	103	357	355	184	309	289	353	**447**	236	232	197
Average Yards	8.2	6.3	10.1	4.5	9.4	**17.8**	13.1	13.4	6.9	10.4	11.2	9.1	9.7	7.0
Touchdowns	0	0	1	0	0	**2**	1	1	0	1	1	1	1	0
KICKOFF RETURNS:														
Number	53	51	50	64	50	41	56	**72**	38	53	49	47	49	64
Yards	1182	1247	1115	1345	1097	1077	1463	**1568**	850	1313	1020	992	1302	1661
Average Yards	22.3	24.5	22.3	21.0	21.9	26.3	26.1	21.8	22.4	24.8	20.8	21.1	**26.6**	26.0
Touchdowns	0	0	**1**	0	**1**	0	**1**	0	0	**1**	0	0	**1**	0
INTERCEPTION RETURNS:														
Number	16	24	20	25	29	29	23	22	**33**	17	25	24	19	26
Yards	123	371	160	374	312	446	277	356	**526**	239	498	459	322	325
Average Yards	7.7	15.5	8.0	15.0	10.8	15.4	12.0	16.2	15.9	14.1	**19.9**	19.1	16.9	12.5
Touchdowns	0	0	0	0	1	2	0	0	4	0	2	**5**	0	2
PENALTIES:														
Number	69	**81**	47	47	69	66	63	36	59	47	57	57	66	70
Yards	680	710.5	455	427	678	647	599	375	629	500	486	535	635	651
FUMBLES:														
Number	21	23	28	46	25	**18**	21	36	40	25	34	39	25	18
Number Lost	13	14	20	21	15	**10**	11	22	20	14	22	18	17	12
POINTS:														
Total	302	326	319	236	270	**391**	263	285	368	361	295	279	346	174
PAT Attempts	34	42	39	29	32	**49**	32	37	46	46	36	37	44	23
PAT Made	33	41	37	29	31	**49**	32	36	46	43	34	34	44	21
FG Attempts	**39**	27	23	24	33	24	27	21	34	25	28	17	22	28
FG Made	**21**	11	16	11	15	16	13	9	14	14	15	7	12	5
Percent FG Made	53.8	40.7	**69.6**	45.8	45.5	66.7	48.1	42.9	41.2	56.0	53.6	41.2	54.5	17.9
Safeties	1	0	0	0	1	0	0	0	**2**	0	0	1	1	0

DEFENSE

	BALT.	CHI.	CLEVE.	DALLAS	DET.	G.BAY	L.A.	MINN.	N.Y.	PHIL.	PITT.	ST.L.	S.F.	WASH.
FIRST DOWNS:														
Total	232	223	243	254	222	245	279	291	**212**	267	218	215	234	261
by Rushing	108	80	87	122	89	110	136	147	86	116	**71**	91	90	94
by Passing	**110**	124	146	120	121	117	121	132	**110**	145	132	112	132	154
by Penalty	14	19	10	12	12	18	22	12	16	**6**	15	12	12	13
RUSHING:														
Number	418	401	411	454	412	412	508	493	419	474	**396**	477	419	412
Yards	1869	1652	1605	2161	1520	1694	2440	2667	1761	2007	**1463**	1676	1701	1550
Average Yards	4.5	4.1	3.9	4.8	3.7	4.1	4.8	5.4	4.2	4.2	3.7	**3.5**	4.1	3.8
Touchdowns	17	10	16	20	14	12	26	29	**6**	12	11	9	13	10
PASSING:														
Attempts	351	398	358	**326**	385	414	328	365	386	383	420	389	380	409
Completions	**161**	209	200	168	203	218	184	194	176	224	201	187	196	238
Completion Pct.	45.9	52.5	55.9	51.5	52.7	52.7	56.1	53.2	**45.6**	58.5	47.9	48.1	51.6	58.2
Passing Yards (Gross)	**2320**	3164	2831	2635	2744	2630	2642	3051	2600	3183	2780	2644	2874	3493
Yards Lost Tackled	**407**	367	305	204	326	273	269	125	399	263	334	334	394	218
Net Yards	**1913**	2797	2526	2431	2418	2357	2373	2926	2201	2920	2446	2310	2480	3275
Yds. per Att (Gross)	6.6	7.9	7.9	8.1	7.1	**6.4**	8.1	8.4	6.7	8.3	6.6	6.8	7.6	8.5
Yds. per Comp (Gross)	14.4	15.1	14.2	15.7	13.5	**12.1**	14.4	15.7	14.8	14.2	13.8	14.1	14.7	14.7
Touchdowns	18	27	16	21	**11**	13	19	21	21	23	22	18	18	37
Interceptions	16	24	20	25	29	29	23	22	**33**	17	25	24	19	26
Pct. Intercepted	4.6	6.0	5.6	7.7	7.5	7.0	7.0	6.0	**8.5**	4.4	6.0	6.2	5.0	6.4
PUNTING:														
Number	64	66	54	43	67	49	51	46	83	64	**86**	67	62	58
Average Distance	41.4	42.7	42.9	45.5	43.0	**37.8**	43.3	41.4	42.4	41.8	43.8	42.0	44.0	44.2
PUNT RETURNS:														
Number	18	24	27	**17**	21	25	36	23	32	30	32	53	32	30
Yards	248	302	213	193	273	313	384	**138**	247	235	251	438	269	280
Average Yards	13.8	12.6	7.9	11.4	13.0	12.5	10.7	**6.0**	7.7	7.8	7.8	8.3	8.4	9.3
Touchdowns	1	1	**0**	**0**	1	1	**0**	**0**	**0**	1	1	1	1	1
KICKOFF RETURNS:														
Number	57	55	56	43	49	69	53	51	59	58	50	50	58	**29**
Yards	1552	1219	1465	978	1184	1597	1380	1148	1288	1224	1156	1007	1368	**666**
Average Yards	27.2	22.2	26.2	22.7	24.2	23.1	26.0	22.5	21.8	21.1	23.1	**20.1**	23.6	23.0
Touchdowns	**0**	1	1	**0**	2	**0**	**0**	**0**	**0**	1	**0**	**0**	**0**	**0**
INTERCEPTION RETURNS:														
Number	29	24	**13**	27	27	16	21	22	23	26	34	23	19	28
Yards	406	346	302	589	314	**238**	280	219	246	294	510	318	249	477
Average Yards	14.0	14.4	23.2	21.8	11.6	14.9	13.3	**10.0**	10.7	11.3	15.0	13.8	13.1	17.0
Touchdowns	1	**0**	1	6	**0**	**0**	**0**	2	1	1	2	**0**	**0**	2
PENALTIES:														
Number	66	**86**	38	38	39	52	75	66	67	62	57	59	56	63
Yards	547.5	**860**	367	362	381	609	662	638	677	684	533	546	456	603
FUMBLES:														
Number	19	22	23	30	21	30	27	31	**43**	27	36	38	21	33
Number Lost	8	13	18	18	12	17	16	**23**	21	16	20	20	12	15
POINTS:														
Total	307	302	270	380	258	223	333	407	**220**	297	287	267	272	392
PAT Attempts	37	39	34	49	28	**26**	45	52	29	38	37	30	32	50
PAT Made	37	36	33	44	28	**26**	45	50	29	36	35	30	32	49
FG Attempts	26	27	28	28	34	21	21	26	**20**	24	26	38	29	24
FG Made	16	10	11	14	20	13	6	15	**5**	11	10	19	16	13
Percent FG Made	61.5	37.0	39.3	50.0	58.8	61.9	28.6	57.7	**25.0**	45.8	38.5	50.0	55.2	54.2
Safeties	**0**	1	**0**	**0**	1	1	**0**	**0**	1	**0**	**0**	**0**	**0**	2

SCORING

GREEN BAY	0	24	10	3–37
NEW YORK	0	0	0	0– 0

Second Quarter

G.B.	Hornung, 6 yard rush PAT – Hornung (kick)	0:04
G.B.	Dowler, 13 yard pass from Starr PAT – Hornung (kick)	4:19
G.B.	R. Kramer, 14 yard pass from Starr PAT – Hornung (kick)	10:04
G.B.	Hornung, 17 yard field goal	15:00

Third Quarter

G.B.	Hornung, 22 yard field goal	9:55
G.B.	R. Kramer, 13 yard pass from Starr PAT – Hornung (kick)	12:12

Fourth Quarter

G.B.	Hornung, 19 yard field goal	6:48

TEAM STATISTICS

G.B.		N.Y.
19	First Downs – Total	6
10	First Downs – Rushing	1
8	First Downs – Passing	4
1	First Downs – Penalty	1
1	Fumbles – Number	5
0	Fumbles – Number Lost	1
4	Penalties – Number	4
16	Yards Penalized	38
0	Giveaways	5
5	Takeaways	0
+5	Difference	–5

1961 NFL CHAMPIONSHIP GAME
December 31, at Green Bay
(Attendance 39,029)

New York's Cold Reception

Although the Packers had won five Western titles before this year, this was the first NFL championship game ever staged in Green Bay. The sub-freezing Wisconsin weather suited the Packers fine as they easily rolled over the Giants. The first quarter was scoreless, but New York's Kyle Rote dropped a sure touchdown pass deep in Green Bay territory. The Giants blew another touchdown in the second quarter when halfback Bob Gaiters overthrew Rote in the end zone. The Packers, meanwhile, took a comfortable lead by scoring three touchdowns in the quarter. Paul Hornung, on leave from the Army, scored from the 6-yard line after an 80-yard Packer drive, Boyd Dowler scored on a Bart Starr pass after a Ray Nitschke interception, and a Starr-to-Ron Kramer touchdown pass followed another Packer interception. Hornung added all the extra points and a 17-yard field goal to run the halftime score to 24-0. With their running game ineffective, the Giants turned to the pass, but Green Bay's Jess Whittenton blanketed top receiver Del Shofner like a shadow. While their defense continued to thwart the Giants, the Packers added ten more points in the third quarter to put the game on ice. The Packers turned a fumbled punt by Joe Morrison into a Hornung field goal, and another sustained drive resulted in Ron Kramer's second touchdown catch. A fourth-quarter Hornung field goal made the final score 37-0 and gave Hornung a record 19 points for the championship game.

INDIVIDUAL STATISTICS

GREEN BAY	No	Yds	Avg	NEW YORK	No	Yds	Avg.
RUSHING							
Hornung	20	89	4.5	Webster	7	19	2.7
Taylor	14	69	4.9	Wells	3	9	3.0
Moore	6	25	4.2	King	2	5	2.5
Roach	1	0	0.0	Gaiters	1	2	2.0
Pitts	3	–2	–0.7	Tittle	1	–4	–4.0
	44	181	4.1		14	31	2.2
RECEIVING							
R. Kramer	4	80	20.0	Rote	3	54	18.0
Hornung	3	47	15.7	Shofner	3	41	13.7
Dowler	3	37	12.3	Webster	3	5	1.7
	10	164	16.4	Walton	1	19	19.0
					10	119	11.9
PUNTING							
Dowler	5		42.0	Chandler	5		39.2
PUNT RETURNS							
Wood	1	4	4.0	Morrison	2	10	5.0
KICKOFF RETURNS							
Nitschke	1	18	18.0	Wells	5	98	19.6
				Gaiters	1	21	21.0
					6	119	19.8
INTERCEPTION RETURNS							
Adderley	1	14	14.0				
Gremminger	1	13	13.0	None			
Nitschke	1	9	9.0				
Whittenton	1	0	0.0				
	4	36	9.0				

PASSING

GREEN BAY	Att	Comp	Comp Pct.	Yds	Int	Yds/ Att.	Yds/ Comp	Yards Lost Tackled
Starr	17	10	58.8	164	0	9.6	16.4	0
Hornung	2	0	0.0	0	0	–	–	0
	19	10	52.6	164	0	8.6	16.4	0
NEW YORK								
Tittle	20	6	30.0	65	4	3.3	10.8	2–15
Conerly	8	4	50.0	54	0	6.8	13.5	1– 5
Gaiters	1	0	0.0	0	0	–	–	0
	29	10	34.5	119	4	4.1	11.9	3–20

Scores of Each Game			Use Name	Pos.	Hgt	Wgt	Age	Int	Pts	Use Name	Pos.	Hgt	Wgt	Age	Int	Pts	Use Name	Pos.	Hgt	Wgt	Age	Int	Pts
NEW YORK GIANTS 10-3-1 Allie Sherman																							
10	ST. LOUIS	21	Rosey Brown	OT	6'3"	255	28			Larry Hayes	LB	6'3"	230	26		6	Chuck Conerly	QB	6'1"	185	37		
17	Pittsburgh	14	Chuck Janerette	OT	6'3"	250	22			Sam Huff	LB	6'1"	230	26	3	6	Lee Grosscup	QB	6'1"	185	24		
24	Washington	21	Darrell Dess	OG	6'	245	25			Cliff Livingston	LB	6'3"	215	31	3		Y. A. Tittle	QB	6'	195	34		18
24	St. Louis	9	Zeke Smith	OG	6'2"	235	25			Tom Scott	LB	6'2"	220	31	1	6	Don Chandler	HB	6'2"	210	26		
31	Dallas	10	Jack Stroud	OG	6'1"	250	32			Bob Simms	LB	6'1"	230	23			Bob Gaiters	HB	5'11"	210	23		42
24	LOS ANGELES	14	Mickey Walker	OG	6'	230	21			Gene Johnson (from MIN)	DB	6'	180	26			Phil King	HB	6'4"	225	25		
16	DALLAS	17	Ray Wietecha	C	6'1"	230	32			Dick Lynch	DB	6'1"	205	25	9		Joel Wells	HB	6'1"	198	20		12
53	WASHINGTON	0	Greg Larson	OT-C	6'2"	245	22			Dick Nolan	DB	6'1"	185	29			Joe Morrison	DB-HB	6'1"	212	23	2	12
38	PHILADELPHIA	21	Jim Katcavage	DE	6'3"	240	26		2	Jimmy Patton	DB	6'	185	29	8	6	Alex Webster	FB	6'3"	225	30		30
42	PITTSBURGH	21	Andy Robustelli	DE	6'1"	235	35			Bill Stits	DB	6'	195	30			Pete Hall	OE	6'2"	200	23		
37	Cleveland	21	Rosey Grier	DT	6'5"	290	28			Erich Barnes	HB-DB	6'2"	198	26	7	18	Kyle Rote	OE	6'	200	32		42
17	GREEN BAY	20	Dick Modzelewski	DT	6'	260	30		2	Allan Webb	HB-DB	5'11"	180	26			Del Shofner	OE	6'3"	185	25		66
28	Philadephia	24															Joe Walton	OE	5'11"	200	26		12
7	CLEVELAND	7	Frank Gifford – Voluntarily Retired							Jim Podoley – Injury							Pat Summerall	K	6'4"	235	31		88
PHILADELPHIA EAGLES 10-4-0 Nick Skorich																							
27	CLEVELAND	20	Jim McCusker	OT	6'2"	245	25			Maxie Baughan	LB	6'1"	226	23	1		King Hill	QB	6'3"	213	25		
14	WASHINGTON	7	Don Oakes	OT	6'3"	245	23			Chuck Bednarik	LB	6'3"	235	36	2		Sonny Jurgensen	QB	5'11"	200	27		
27	ST. LOUIS	30	J. D. Smith	OT	6'5"	250	25			John Nocera	LB	6'1"	220	27			Billy Barnes	HB	5'11"	202	26		24
21	PITTSBURGH	16	Stan Campbell	OG	6'	230	31			Bob Pellegrini	LB	6'2"	225	26			Timmy Brown	HB	5'10"	190	24		30
20	St. Louis	7	John Wittenborn	OG	6'2"	240	25			Chuck Weber	LB	6'1"	235	32	1		Ted Dean	HB	6'2"	210	23		18
43	Dallas	7	Howard Keys	C	6'3"	240	26			Glen Amerson	DB	6'1"	186	22			Clarence Peaks	FB	6'1"	220	25		30
27	Washington	24	Gene Gossage	DE	6'3"	240	26			Tom Brookshier	DB	6'	198	29	2		Theron Sapp	FB	6'1"	205	26		6
16	CHICAGO	14	Will Renfro	DE	6'5"	235	29			Don Burroughs	DB	6'4"	190	30	7		Tommy McDonald	FL	5'10"	172	27		78
21	New York	38	Leo Sugar	DE	6'1"	230	32			Jimmy Carr	DB	6'1"	210	28	2		Dick Lucas	OE	6'2"	216	27		30
24	Cleveland	45	Marion Campbell	DT	6'3"	250	32			Irv Cross	DB	6'1"	190	22	2		Pete Retzlaff	OE	6'1"	212	30		48
35	DALLAS	13	Riley Gunnels	DT	6'3"	250	24			Bobby Freeman	DB	6'1"	200	28			John Tracey	OE	6'3"	225	28		
35	Pittsburgh	24	Ed Khayat	DT	6'3"	248	26										Bobby Walston	OE	6'	195	32		97
24	NEW YORK	28	Jess Richardson	DT	6'2"	265	31																
27	Detroit	24																					
CLEVELAND BROWNS 8-5-1 Paul Brown																							
20	Philadelphia	27	Lou Groza	OT	6'3"	248	37		85	Vince Costello	LB	6'	232	29		6	Len Dawson	QB	6'	195	27		
20	ST. LOUIS	17	Errol Linden	OT	6'5"	260	24			Galen Fiss	LB	6'	227	31	1		Milt Plum	QB	6'1"	205	27		6
25	DALLAS	7	Mike McCormack	OT	6'4"	250	34			Walt Michaels	LB	6'	237	32	2		Bobby Mitchell	HB	6'	192	26		60
31	WASHINGTON	7	Ed Nutting	OT	6'4"	246	22			Dave Lloyd	C-LB	6'3"	248	25			Tom Watkins	HB	6'1"	195	24		6
17	GREEN BAY	49	Dick Schafrath	OT	6'3"	255	25			Ross Fichtner	DB	6'	185	23			Jimmy Brown	FB	6'2"	228	25		60
30	Pittsburgh	28	Duane Putnam	OG	6'	233	33			Don Fleming	DB	6'	188	24	3		Preston Powell	FB	6'2"	225	24		
21	St. Louis	10	Jim Ray Smith	OG	6'3"	245	30			Bernie Parrish	DB	5'11"	195	26	7	6	Ray Renfro	FL	6'1"	192	30		36
13	PITTSBURGH	17	John Wooten	OG	6'2"	250	26			Jim Shofner	DB	6'2"	190	25	5		Leon Clarke	OE	6'4"	235	28		12
17	Washington	6	John Morrow	C	6'3"	248	28			Bobby Franklin	DB	5'11"	182	25	2	6	Bob Crespino	OE	6'4"	217	23		6
45	PHILADELPHIA	24	Jim Houston	DE	6'2"	235	24										Charley Ferguson	OE	6'5"	217	21		6
21	NEW YORK	37	Paul Wiggin	DE	6'3"	245	27			Gene Hickerson – Broken Leg							Rich Kreitling	OE	6'2"	208	26		18
38	Dallas	17	Johnny Brewer	DE	6'4"	225	24										Gern Nagler	OE	6'2"	190	28		6
14	Chicago	17	Bob Gain	DT	6'3"	260	33										Sam Baker	K	6'2"	217	29		
7	New York	7	Floyd Peters	DT	6'4"	255	26																
			Larry Stephens	DT	6'4"	260	23																
ST. LOUIS CARDINALS 7-7-0 Pop Ivy Chuck Drulis Ray Prochaska Ray Willsey																							
21	New York	10	Ed Cook	OT	6'2"	240	29			Ted Bates	LB	6'3"	220	24			Sam Etcheverry	QB	5'11"	190	31		
17	Cleveland	20	Charley Granger (from DAL)	OT	6'2"	240	23			Bill Koman	LB	6'2"	230	27	1		Ralph Guglielmi	QB	6'1"	195	28		6
30	Philadelphia	27	Ernie McMillan	OT	6'6"	255	23			Monte Lee	LB	6'4"	225	23	1		Charley Johnson	QB	6'	190	24		
9	NEW YORK	24	Dale Memmelaar	OT	6'2"	245	24			Dale Meinert	LB	6'2"	220	28	2		Bobby Joe Conrad	HB	6'	195	26		22
7	PHILADELPHIA	20	Ken Panfil	OT	6'6"	255	30			Joe Driskill	DB	6'1"	195	24			John David Crow	HB	6'2"	215	26		24
24	Washington	0	Jerry Perry	OT	6'4"	240	30		51	Jimmy Hill	DB	6'2"	190	32	4	6	Prentice Gautt	HB	6'	200	23		36
10	CLEVELAND	21	Bob DeMarco	OG	6'3"	240	23			Jerry Norton	DB	5'11"	195	31	7	12	Ken Hall (from HOU-A)	HB	6'1"	210	25		
31	Dallas	17	Ken Gray	OG	6'2"	240	25			Willie West	DB	5'10"	185	23	1	6	Mal Hammack	FB	6'2"	205	28		6
14	DETROIT	45	Mike McGee	OG	6'1"	230	23			Larry Wilson	DB	6'	187	23	3	2	Frank Mestnik	FB	6'2"	200	23		12
0	Baltimore	16	Tom Redmond	OG	6'5"	240	24			Pat Fischer	HB-DB	5'10"	165	21			Taz Anderson	OE	6'2"	200	22		18
27	Pittsburgh	30	Charley Ellzey	C	6'3"	240	23			Billy Stacy	HB-DB	6'1"	190	25	4	24	Dick Lage	OE	6'4"	228	21		
38	WASHINGTON	24	Don Gillis	C	6'3"	250	26										Hugh McInnis	OE	6'3"	220	23		
31	DALLAS	13	Bob Griffin (from DEN-A)	LB-C	6'3"	250	32			Joe Childress – Injury							Sonny Randle	OE	6'2"	187	25		54
20	PITTSBURGH	0	Ed Henke	DE	6'3"	230	33																
			Luke Owens	DE	6'2"	255	28																
			Joe Robb	DE	6'3"	230	24	1															
			Frank Fuller	DT	6'4"	245	32																
			Ron McDole	DT	6'3"	250	21																
			Don Owens	DT	6'5"	255	29																
PITTSBURGH STEELERS 6-8-0 Buddy Parker																							
24	Dallas	27	Charlie Bradshaw	OT	6'6"	255	25			Mike Henry	LB	6'2"	215	25	1		Rudy Bukich	QB	6'1"	205	30		12
14	NEW YORK	17	Dan James	OT	6'4"	280	24			Myron Pottios	LB	6'2"	240	22	2		Bobby Layne	QB	6'1"	210	34		5
14	Los Angeles	24	Dick Klein (to BOS-A)	OT	6'4"	255	27			John Reger	LB	6'	230	30	1		Terry Nofsinger	QB	6'4"	205	23		
16	Philadelphia	21	John Nisby	OG	6'1"	230	28			Bob Schmitz	LB	6'1"	235	23			Dick Hoak	HB	5'11"	190	22		
20	WASHINGTON	0	Mike Sandusky	OG	6'	230	28			Wilbert Scott	LB	6'	215	22			Jack Stanton	HB	6'1"	190	23		
28	CLEVELAND	30	Ron Stehouwer	OG	6'2"	230	24			George Tarasovic	LB	6'4"	245	32	1		Tom Tracy	HB	5'9"	205	29		20
20	SAN FRANCISCO	10	Buzz Nutter	C	6'4"	230	30			Len Burnett	DB	6'1"	195	22			John Henry Johnson	FB	6'2"	215	31		42
17	Cleveland	13	George Demko	DE	6'3"	240	26			Bill Butler	DB	5'10"	185	24	3	6	Charlie Scales	FB	5'11"	215	22		
37	DALLAS	7	John Kapele	DE	6'	240	24			Willie Daniel	DB	5'11"	185	23	3		Buddy Dial	FL	6'1"	195	24		72
21	New York	42	Lou Michaels	DE	6'2"	235	25	1	72	Johnny Sample	DB	6'1"	200	24	8	12	Red Mack	HB-FL	5'10"	185	24		12
30	ST. LOUIS	27	Ernie Stautner	DT-DE	6'1"	230	36			Jackie Simpson	DB	5'10"	185	27	2		Preston Carpenter	OE	6'2"	190	27		24
24	PHILADELPHIA	35	Joe Krupa	DT	6'2"	225	28			Brady Keys	HB-DB	6'	185	25	2		Henry Clement	OE	6'2"	200	21		
30	Washington	14	Big Daddy Lipscomb	DT	6'6"	288	30			Dick Haley (from MIN)	FL-DB	5'10"	195	24	1		Bob Coronado	OE	6'1"	195	25		
0	St. Louis	20															Steve Meilinger (to STL)	OE	6'2"	230	31		
																	Bob Schnelker (from MIN)	OE	6'3"	215	31		24
																	Bobby Joe Green	K	5'11"	175	23		

NEW YORK GIANTS

RUSHING

Last Name	No.	Yds	Avg	TD
Webster	196	928	4.7	2
Gaiters	116	460	4.0	6
Wells	65	216	3.3	1
Tittle	25	85	3.4	3
Webb	6	51	8.5	0
Morrison	33	48	1.5	1
Chandler	3	30	10.0	0
Conerly	13	16	1.2	0
Grosscup	2	10	5.0	0
King	4	7	1.8	0
Shofner	1	6	6.0	0

RECEIVING

Last Name	No.	Yds	Avg	TD
Shofner	68	1125	17	11
Rote	53	805	15	7
Walton	36	544	15	2
Webster	26	313	12	3
Morrison	11	67	6	1
Gaiters	11	54	5	1
Wells	6	31	5	1
Barnes	2	74	37	1
Hall	2	22	11	0

PUNT RETURNS

Last Name	No.	Yds	Avg	TD
Stits	17	132	8	0
Wells	17	90	5	0
Webb	5	61	12	0
Morrison	3	6	2	0

KICKOFF RETURNS

Last Name	No.	Yds	Avg	TD
Gaiters	11	288	26	0
Wells	12	273	23	0
Webb	8	156	20	0
Stits	4	87	22	0
Morrison	2	32	16	0
Simms	1	14	14	0

PASSING – PUNTING – KICKING

PASSING	Att	Comp	%	Yds	Yd/Att	TD	Int–	%	RK
Tittle	285	163	57	2272	8.0	17	12–	4	3
Conerly	106	44	42	634	6.0	7	8–	8	
Grosscup	22	5	23	87	4.0	1	3–	14	
Gaiters	3	3	100	42	14.0	2	0–	0	

PUNTING	No	Avg
Chandler	68	43.9

KICKING	XP	Att	%	FG	Att	%
Summerall	46	46	100	14	34	41

PHILADELPHIA EAGLES

RUSHING

Last Name	No.	Yds	Avg	TD
Peaks	135	471	3.5	5
Brown	50	338	6.8	1
Dean	66	321	4.9	2
Barnes	92	309	3.4	1
Jurgensen	20	27	1.4	0
Sapp	7	24	3.4	1
Hill	2	9	4.5	0
Retzlaff	1	8	8.0	0

RECEIVING

Last Name	No.	Yds	Avg	TD
McDonald	64	1144	18	13
Retzlaff	50	769	15	8
Walston	34	569	17	2
Peaks	32	472	15	0
Dean	21	335	16	1
Barnes	15	194	13	3
Brown	14	264	19	2
Lucas	8	67	8	5
Sapp	3	10	3	0

PUNT RETURNS

Last Name	No.	Yds	Avg	TD
Dean	18	140	8	0
Brown	8	125	16	1
Cross	7	77	11	0
Baughan	1	11	11	0

KICKOFF RETURNS

Last Name	No.	Yds	Avg	TD
Brown	29	811	28	1
Dean	21	462	22	0
Peaks	2	29	15	0
Cross	1	11	11	0

PASSING – PUNTING – KICKING

PASSING	Att	Comp	%	Yds	Yd/Att	TD	Int–	%	RK
Jurgensen	416	235	56	3723	8.9	32	24–	6	5
Hill	12	6	50	101	8.4	2	2–	17	
Peaks	1	0	0	0	0.0	0	0–	0	

PUNTING	No	Avg
Hill	55	43.7

KICKING	XP	Att	%	FG	Att	%
Walston	43	46	93	14	25	56

CLEVELAND BROWNS

RUSHING

Last Name	No.	Yds	Avg	TD
Brown	305	1408	4.6	8
Mitchell	101	548	5.4	5
Watkins	43	209	4.9	0
Franklin	1	12	12.0	1
Powell	1	5	5.0	0
Kreitling	0	4	0.0	0
McCormack	0	4	0.0	0
Dawson	1	–10	–10.0	0
Plum	24	–17	–0.7	1

RECEIVING

Last Name	No.	Yds	Avg	TD
Renfro	48	834	17	6
Brown	46	459	10	2
Mitchell	32	368	12	3
Kreitling	21	229	11	3
Nagler	19	241	13	1
Clarke	11	211	19	2
Watkins	4	66	17	1
Ferguson	2	68	34	0
Crespino	2	62	31	1

PUNT RETURNS

Last Name	No.	Yds	Avg	TD
Mitchell	14	164	12	1
Shofner	14	119	9	0

KICKOFF RETURNS

Last Name	No.	Yds	Avg	TD
Mitchell	16	428	27	1
Powell	16	321	20	0
Watkins	9	226	25	0
Baker	3	57	19	0
Brown	2	50	25	0
Stephens	1	15	15	0
Fichtner	1	11	11	0
Linden	1	5	5	0
Brewer	1	2	2	0

PASSING – PUNTING – KICKING

PASSING	Att	Comp	%	Yds	Yd/Att	TD	Int–	%	RK
Plum	302	177	59	2416	8.0	18	10–	3	1
Dawson	15	7	47	85	5.7	1	3–	20	
Brown	3	1	33	37	12.3	1	0–	0	

PUNTING	No	Avg
Baker	53	43.3

KICKING	XP	Att	%	FG	Att	%
Groza	37	38	97	16	23	70

ST. LOUIS CARDINALS

RUSHING

Last Name	No.	Yds	Avg	TD
Gautt	129	523	4.1	3
Mestnik	95	334	3.5	1
Crow	48	192	4.0	1
Guglielmi	22	101	4.6	1
Hammack	18	79	4.4	1
Etcheverry	33	73	2.2	0
Anderson	15	39	2.6	1
McInnis	4	30	7.5	0
Conrad	20	22	1.1	0
Norton	1	15	15.0	0
Johnson	1	–3	–3.0	0

RECEIVING

Last Name	No.	Yds	Avg	TD
Randle	44	591	13	9
Conrad	30	499	17	2
Anderson	22	359	16	2
Crow	20	306	15	3
Stacy	12	241	20	1
Gautt	12	132	11	3
Mestnik	12	29	2	1
McInnis	7	107	15	0
Hammack	5	70	14	0
Hall	3	38	13	0
Fischer	1	22	22	0

PUNT RETURNS

Last Name	No.	Yds	Avg	TD
Conrad	5	103	21	1
West	11	98	9	0
Fischer	4	18	5	0
Stacy	5	9	2	0
Driskill	1	8	8	0

KICKOFF RETURNS

Last Name	No.	Yds	Avg	TD
Fischer	17	426	25	0
West	16	340	21	0
Wilson	4	83	21	0
Stacy	3	60	20	0
Conrad	1	28	28	0
Mestnik	2	27	14	0
Lee	1	12	12	0
Driskill	2	8	4	0
Hammack	1	8	8	0

PASSING – PUNTING – KICKING

PASSING	Att	Comp	%	Yds	Yd/Att	TD	Int–	%	RK
Etcheverry	196	96	49	1275	6.5	14	11–	6	11
Guglielmi	116	56	48	927	8.0	5	8–	7	
Crow	14	4	29	76	5.4	1	1–	7	
Johnson	13	5	38	51	4.0	0	2	15	
Gautt	11	6	55	100	9.1	1	1–	9	
Conrad	1	1	100	5	5.0	0	0–	0	

PUNTING	No	Avg
Norton	35	44.7

KICKING	XP	Att	%	FG	Att	%
Perry	30	33	91	7	16	44
Conrad	4	4	100	0	1	0

PITTSBURGH STEELERS

RUSHING

Last Name	No.	Yds	Avg	TD
Johnson	213	787	3.7	6
Tracy	147	402	2.7	2
Hoak	85	302	3.6	0
Scales	50	184	3.7	0
Green	2	37	18.5	0
Keys	6	14	2.3	0
Layne	8	11	1.4	0
Carpenter	7	9	1.3	0
Meilinger	1	6	6.0	0
Dial	3	6	2.0	0
Nofsinger	6	6	1.0	0
Bukich	14	4	0.3	2
Coronado	1	–7	–7.0	0

RECEIVING

Last Name	No.	Yds	Avg	TD
Dial	53	1047	20	12
Carpenter	33	460	14	4
Schnelker	24	401	17	4
Johnson	24	262	11	1
Tracy	14	133	10	1
Mack	8	128	16	2
Meilinger	8	103	13	0
Scales	7	43	6	0
Clement	5	65	13	0
Haley	3	43	14	0
Coronado	3	32	11	0
Hoak	3	18	6	0

PUNT RETURNS

Last Name	No.	Yds	Avg	TD
Sample	26	283	11	1
Keys	9	135	15	0
Carpenter	3	18	6	0
Butler	2	11	6	0

KICKOFF RETURNS

Last Name	No.	Yds	Avg	TD
Sample	23	532	23	0
Haley	13	278	21	0
Butler	6	117	20	0
Scales	3	41	14	0
Keys	2	41	21	0
Johnson	1	11	11	0
Schmitz	1	0	0	0

PASSING – PUNTING – KICKING

PASSING	Att	Comp	%	Yds	Yd/Att	TD	Int–	%	RK
Bukich	156	89	57	1253	8.0	11	16–	10	9
Layne	149	75	50	1205	8.1	11	16–	11	14
Tracy	12	4	33	73	6.1	0	0–	0	
Nofsinger	11	7	64	78	7.1	0	0–	0	
Hoak	3	1	33	13	4.3	1	1–	33	
Johnson	2	0	0	0	0.0	0	1–	50	
Green	1	0	0	0	0.0	0	0–	0	

PUNTING	No	Avg
Green	73	47.0

KICKING	XP	Att	%	FG	Att	%
Michaels	27	29	93	15	26	58
Layne	5	5	100	0	0	0
Tracy	2	2	100	0	1	0
Green	0	0	0	0	1	0

EASTERN CONFERENCE – Continued

DALLAS COWBOYS 4-9-1 Tom Landry

Scores of Each Game		
27	PITTSBURGH	24
21	MINNESOTA	7
7	Cleveland	25
28	Minnesota	0
10	NEW YORK	31
7	PHILADELPHIA	43
17	New York	16
17	ST. LOUIS	31
7	Pittsburgh	37
28	WASHINGTON	28
13	Philadelphia	35
17	CLEVELAND	38
13	St. Louis	31
24	Washington	34

Use Name	Pos.	Hgt	Wgt	Age	Int	Pts
Byron Bradfute	OT	6'3"	243	23		
Bob Fry	OT	6'4"	240	30		
Bob McCreary	OT	6'5"	256	22		
Andy Cvercko	OG	6'	240	24		
Mike Falls	OG	6'1"	240	27		
Bob Grottkau	OG	6'4"	230	24		
John Houser	OG	6'3"	242	25		
Mike Connelly	C	6'3"	235	25		
Nate Borden	DE	6'	240	29		
Bob Lilly	DE	6'4"	248	22		
Ken Frost	DT	6'4"	245	22	1	
Don Healy	DT	6'3"	264	25	1	
Bill Herchman	DT	6'2"	250	28		
Sonny Davis	LB	6'2"	220	22		
Mike Dowdle	LB	6'3"	210	23	1	
Chuck Howley	LB	6'3"	230	25	1	
Jack Patera	LB	6'1"	240	29		
Jerry Tubbs	LB	6'2"	220	26	3	
Gene Babb	FB-LB	6'3"	218	26		
Bob Bercich	DB	6'1"	198	24	3	
Don Bishop	DB	6'2"	204	26	8	
Tom Franckhauser	DB	6'	196	24	1	
Jimmy Harris	DB	6'1"	180	26	2	
Warren Livingston	DB	5'10"	180	23	1	
Dick Moegle	DB	6'	195	27	2	
Buddy Humphrey	QB	6'1"	200	25		
Eddie LeBaron	QB	5'9"	160	31		
Don Meredith	QB	6'2"	198	23		6
L. G. Dupre	HB	5'11"	190	29		
Don Perkins	HB	5'10"	198	23		30
J. W. Lockett (from SF)	FB	6'2"	230	24		18
Amos Marsh	FB	6'1"	208	22		18
Merrill Douglas	HB-FB	6'	204	25		
Dick Bielski	OE	6'1"	227	29		46
Frank Clarke	OE	6'	215	28		54
Jim Doran	OE	6'2"	211	33		12
Billy Howton	OE	6'2"	185	31		24
Lee Murchison	OE	6'3"	205	23		
Glynn Gregory	DB-OE	6'2"	200	22	1	
Allen Green	K	6'2"	215	23		34

WASHINGTON REDSKINS 1-12-1 Bill McPeak

Scores of Each Game		
3	San Francisco	35
7	Philadelphia	14
21	NEW YORK	24
7	Cleveland	31
0	Pittsburgh	20
0	ST. LOUIS	24
24	PHILADELPHIA	27
0	New York	53
6	CLEVELAND	17
28	Dallas	28
6	BALTIMORE	27
24	St. Louis	38
14	PITTSBURGH	30
34	DALLAS	24

Use Name	Pos.	Hgt	Wgt	Age	Int	Pts
Ray Lemek	OT	6'	240	27		
Riley Mattson	OT	6'4"	248	22		
Fran O'Brien	OT	6'1"	250	26		
Bernie Darre	OG	6'2"	230	21		
Vince Promuto	OG	6'1"	243	23		
Ed Beatty (from PIT)	C	6'3"	237	29		
Fred Hageman	C	6'4"	244	23		
Jim Schrader	C	6'2"	252	29		
John Paluck	DE	6'2"	240	28	1	
Andy Stynchula	DE	6'3"	250	22		
Gene Cronin	LB-DE	6'2"	228	28		
Don Lawrence	DT	6'1"	245	24		
Joe Rutgens	DT	6'2"	265	22		
Bob Toneff	DT	6'3"	270	31		
Rod Breedlove	LB	6'2"	225	23	2	
Dick Lasse	LB	6'2"	225	25		
Doyle Schick	LB	6'1"	210	22		
Roy Wilkins	LB	6'3"	228	27		
Jim Crotty (to BUF-A)	DB	5'11"	190	23		
Dale Hackbart	DB	6'3"	210	25	6	12
Jim Kerr	DB	6'	195	22	7	
Joe Krakoski	DB	6'2"	200	24	4	
Ben Scotti	DB	6'1"	186	24	1	
Jim Steffen (from DET)	DB	6'	195	24	1	
Jim Wulff	HB-DB	5'11"	184	25	3	
George Izo	QB	6'3"	214	24		
Norm Snead	QB	6'4"	215	21		18
Lew Luce	HB	6'	187	23		
Mike Sommer (from BAL)	HB	5'11"	190	26		
Sam Horner	DB-HB	6'	198	23		6
Dick James	DB-HB	5'9"	175	27	1	30
Don Bosseler	FB	6'1"	212	25		18
Jim Cunningham	FB	5'11"	220	22		12
Bill Anderson	OE	6'3"	214	25		
John Aveni	OE	6'3"	215	26		42
Fred Dugan	OE	6'3"	198	27		24
Steve Junker	OE	6'3"	217	26		
Tom Osborne	OE	6'3"	190	24		12

WESTERN CONFERENCE

GREEN BAY PACKERS 11-3-0 Vince Lombardi

Scores of Each Game		
13	DETROIT	17
30	SAN FRANCISCO	10
24	CHICAGO	0
45	BALTIMORE	7
49	Cleveland	17
33	Minnesota	7
28	MINNESOTA	10
21	Baltimore	45
31	Chicago	28
35	LOS ANGELES	17
17	Detroit	9
20	NEW YORK	17
21	San Francisco	22
24	Los Angeles	17

Use Name	Pos.	Hgt	Wgt	Age	Int	Pts
Forrest Gregg	OT	6'4"	250	28		
Norm Masters	OT	6'2"	250	28		
Bob Skoronski	OT	6'3"	250	28		
Jerry Kramer	OG	6'3"	250	26		
Fuzzy Thurston	OG	6'1"	250	28		
Ken Iman	C	6'1"	230	22		
Jim Ringo	C	6'1"	235	30		
Ben Davidson	DE	6'8"	275	21		
Willie Davis	DE	6'3"	240	28		
Bill Quinlan	DE	6'3"	250	29		
Dave Hanner	DT	6'2"	260	32	1	
Henry Jordan	DT	6'3"	250	26		
Ron Kostelnik	DT	6'4"	260	21		
Tom Bettis	LB	6'2"	225	28		
Dan Currie	LB	6'3"	240	27	3	6
Bill Forester	LB	6'3"	240	30	2	
Ray Nitschke	LB	6'3"	235	25	2	
Nelson Toburen	LB	6'3"	235	22		
Herb Adderley	DB	6'1"	205	22	1	
Hank Gremminger	DB	6'1"	205	28	5	
Johnny Symank	DB	5'11"	180	26	5	
Em Tunnell	DB	6'1"	210	39		
Jesse Whittenton	DB	6'	195	27	5	6
Willie Wood	DB	5'10"	185	25	5	12
John Roach	QB	6'4"	200	28		6
Bart Starr	QB	6'1"	200	28		6
Lew Carpenter	HB	6'1"	215	29		
Paul Hornung	HB	6'2"	215	25		146
Tom Moore	HB	6'2"	215	23		12
Elijah Pitts	HB	6'1"	200	22		6
Jim Taylor	FB	6'	215	26		96
Boyd Dowler	FL	6'5"	220	24		18
Lee Folkins	OE	6'5"	220	22		
Gary Knafelc	OE	6'4"	220	29		24
Ron Kramer	OE	6'3"	230	26		24
Max McGee	OE	6'3"	205	29		42
Ben Agajanian (from DAL-A)	K	6'	220	42		11

DETROIT LIONS 8-5-1 George Wilson

Scores of Each Game		
17	Green Bay	13
16	Baltimore	15
0	SAN FRANCISCO	49
17	CHICAGO	31
14	LOS ANGELES	13
14	BALTIMORE	17
28	Los Angeles	10
20	San Francisco	20
45	St. Louis	14
37	Minnesota	10
9	GREEN BAY	17
16	Chicago	15
13	MINNESOTA	7
24	PHILADELPHIA	27

Use Name	Pos.	Hgt	Wgt	Age	Int	Pts
Dan LaRose	OT	6'5"	250	21		
Willie McClung	OT	6'2"	260	32		
Ollie Spencer	OG-OT	6'2"	250	30		
Harley Sewell	OG	6'1"	230	30		
Dick Mills	OG	6'3"	240	21		
John Gordy	OT-OG	6'3"	250	25		
Bob Scholtz	C	6'4"	250	23		
Bob Whitlow (from WAS)	OG-C	6'1"	236	25		
Bill Glass	DE	6'5"	255	25		
Darris McCord	DE	6'4"	250	28	1	
Sam Williams	OE-DE	6'5"	235	30		
Roger Brown	DT	6'5"	300	24	1	
John Gonzaga	DT	6'3"	250	28		
Alex Karras	DT	6'2"	245	25		
Gil Mains	DT	6'2"	250	31		
Paul Ward	DT	6'3"	247	24		
Carl Brettschneider	LB	6'1"	225	29		
Jim Martin	LB	6'2"	230	37		70
Max Messner	LB	6'3"	225	23		
Joe Schmidt	LB	6'1"	220	29	4	6
Wayne Walker	LB	6'2"	225	24	2	6
Night Train Lane	DB	6'1"	200	33	6	
Dick LeBeau	DB	6'1"	185	24	3	
Gary Lowe	DB	5'11"	195	27	5	2
Bruce Maher	DB	5'11"	190	24	1	
Yale Lary	DB	6'	190	30	6	
Earl Morrall	QB	6'1"	206	27		
Jim Ninowski	QB	6'1"	200	25		30
Hopalong Cassady	HB	5'10"	185	27		12
Dan Lewis	HB	6'1"	200	25		24
Johnny Olszewski	FB	5'11"	202	30		
Nick Pietrosante	FB	6'2"	225	24		30
Ken Webb	FB	5'11"	205	26		6
Terry Barr	FL	6'	190	26		36
Pat Studstill	FL	6'1"	180	23		6
Gail Cogdill	OE	6'2"	195	24		36
Glenn Davis	OE	6'	180	27		
Jim Gibbons	OE	6'2"	220	25		6

BALTIMORE COLTS 8-6-0 Weeb Ewbank

Scores of Each Game		
27	LOS ANGELES	24
15	DETROIT	16
34	MINNESOTA	33
7	Green Bay	45
10	Chicago	24
17	Detroit	14
20	CHICAGO	21
45	GREEN BAY	21
20	Minnesota	28
16	ST. LOUIS	0
27	Washington	6
20	SAN FRANCISCO	17
17	Los Angeles	34
27	San Francisco	24

Use Name	Pos.	Hgt	Wgt	Age	Int	Pts
Tom Gilburg	OT	6'5"	245	22		
Jim Parker	OT	6'3"	275	27		
George Preas	OT	6'2"	250	29		
Wiley Feagin	OG	6'2"	235	24		
Alex Sandusky	OG	6'1"	242	29		
Palmer Pyle	OG	6'2"	250	24		
Dick Szymanski	C	6'3"	235	28		
Ordell Braase	DE	6'4"	242	29		
Gino Marchetti	DE	6'4"	245	35		2
John Diehl	DT	6'7"	285	25		
Art Donovan	DT	6'2"	265	36		
Joe Lewis	DT	6'2"	250	26		
Jim Colvin	DE-DT	6'2"	250	24		
Billy Ray Smith	DE-DT	6'4"	235	26		
Marv Matuszak	LB	6'3"	230	32		
Bill Pellington	LB	6'2"	238	32	3	
Don Shinnick	LB	6'	235	26	2	
Steve Myhra	OG-LB	6'1"	240	27		96
Jackie Burkett	C-LB	6'4"	230	24	1	
Bobby Boyd	DB	5'10"	190	23	2	
Gary Glick (from WAS)	DB	6'2"	200	30	4	
Bob Harrison	DB	5'11"	187	22	3	
Lenny Lyles	DB	6'2"	202	25		
Andy Nelson	DB	6'1"	180	28		
Carl Taseff (to PHI)	DB	5'11"	194	32	1	
Jim Welch	HB-DB	6'	190	23		6
Lamar McHan	QB	6'1"	205	29		
Johnny Unitas	QB	6'1"	194	28		12
Alex Hawkins	HB	6'1"	190	24		30
Jerry Hill	HB	5'11"	210	21		
Tom Matte	HB	6'	192	22		
Lenny Moore	HB	6'1"	190	28		90
Joe Perry	FB	6'	195	34		24
Mark Smolinski	FB	6'	222	22		6
Ray Berry	OE	6'2"	190	28		
Ken Gregory	OE	6'	190	24		
Aubrey Linne	OE	6'7"	235	22		
Dee Mackey	OE	6'5"	236	25		
Jim Mutscheller	OE	6'1"	205	31		12
Jimmy Orr	OE	5'11"	180	25		24

EASTERN CONFERENCE—Continued

DALLAS COWBOYS

RUSHING

Last Name	No.	Yds	Avg	TD
Perkins	200	815	4.1	4
Marsh	84	379	4.5	1
Lockett	77	298	3.9	1
Meredith	22	176	8.0	1
LeBaron	20	72	3.6	0
Dupre	16	60	3.8	0
Douglas	5	24	4.8	0
Howton	1	9	9.0	0

RECEIVING

Last Name	No.	Yds	Avg	TD
Howton	56	785	14	4
Clarke	41	919	22	9
Perkins	32	298	9	1
Bielski	26	377	15	3
Marsh	21	189	9	2
Lockett	19	149	8	2
Doran	13	153	12	2
Dupre	6	49	8	0
Gregory	3	30	10	0
Douglas	1	−2	−2	0

PUNT RETURNS

Last Name	No.	Yds	Avg	TD
Marsh	14	71	5	0
Livingston	6	20	3	0
Perkins	1	8	8	0
Dupre	2	4	2	0

KICKOFF RETURNS

Last Name	No.	Yds	Avg	TD
Marsh	26	667	26	0
Perkins	22	443	20	0
Dupre	6	110	18	0
Lockett	5	61	12	0
Babb	2	34	17	0
Dowdle	2	33	17	0
Douglas	1	12	12	0
Doran	1	0	0	0

PASSING – PUNTING – KICKING

PASSING	Att	Comp	%	Yds	Yd/Att	TD	Int–	%	RK
LeBaron	236	120	51	1741	7.4	14	16–	7	12
Meredith	182	94	52	1161	6.4	9	11–	6	15
Humphrey	2	1	50	16	8.0	0	0–	0	
Lockett	2	0	0	0	0.0	0	0–	0	

PUNTING	No	Avg
Green	61	36.7

KICKING	XP	Att	%	FG	Att	%
Green	19	19	100	5	15	33
Bielski	10	10	100	6	9	67

WASHINGTON REDSKINS

RUSHING

Last Name	No.	Yds	Avg	TD
James	71	374	5.3	3
Horner	96	275	2.9	0
Bosseler	77	220	2.9	2
Cunningham	69	160	2.3	1
Snead	34	47	1.4	3
Anderson	3	5	1.7	0
Luce	3	1	0.3	0
Sommer	11	1	0.9	0
Izo	3	−1	−0.3	0

RECEIVING

Last Name	No.	Yds	Avg	TD
Dugan	53	817	15	4
Anderson	40	637	16	0
Osborne	22	297	14	2
James	20	298	15	2
Bosseler	16	94	6	1
Cunningham	12	90	8	1
Horner	10	113	11	1
Junker	9	130	14	0
Aveni	6	84	14	1
Sommer	1	31	31	0
Wulff	1	6	6	0

PUNT RETURNS

Last Name	No.	Yds	Avg	TD
Steffen	19	153	8	0
James	12	90	8	0
Sommer	2	26	13	0
Kerr	5	23	5	0
Luce	1	0	0	0

KICKOFF RETURNS

Last Name	No.	Yds	Avg	TD
Steffen	29	691	24	0
James	21	617	29	0
Kerr	14	385	28	0
Sommer	4	98	25	0
Cunningham	4	80	20	0
Luce	4	77	19	0
Horner	4	75	19	0
Stynchula	2	73	37	0
Junker	1	0	0	0

PASSING – PUNTING – KICKING

PASSING	Att	Comp	%	Yds	Yd/Att	TD	Int–	%	RK
Snead	375	172	46	2337	6.2	11	22–	6	16
Izo	40	16	40	214	5.4	1	6–	15	
James	4	1	25	15	3.8	0	0–	0	
Aveni	1	0	0	0	0.0	0	0–	0	

PUNTING	No	Avg
Horner	63	38.2
James	6	35.0
Cunningham	1	46.0

KICKING	XP	Att	%	FG	Att	%
Aveni	21	23	91	5	28	18

WESTERN CONFERENCE

GREEN BAY PACKERS

RUSHING

Last Name	No.	Yds	Avg	TD
Taylor	243	1307	5.4	15
Hornung	127	597	4.7	8
Moore	61	302	5.0	1
Pitts	23	75	3.3	1
Starr	12	56	4.7	1
R. Kramer	5	13	2.6	0
Carpenter	1	5	5.0	0
Roach	2	−5	−2.5	1

RECEIVING

Last Name	No.	Yds	Avg	TD
McGee	51	883	17	7
Dowler	36	633	18	3
R. Kramer	35	559	16	4
Taylor	25	175	7	1
Hornung	15	145	10	2
Moore	8	41	5	1
Knafelc	3	32	11	0
Carpenter	3	29	10	0
Pitts	1	5	5	0

PUNT RETURNS

Last Name	No.	Yds	Avg	TD
Wood	14	225	16	2
Carpenter	6	130	22	0

KICKOFF RETURNS

Last Name	No.	Yds	Avg	TD
Adderley	18	478	27	0
Moore	15	409	27	0
Symank	4	121	30	0
Forester	3	55	18	0
Pitts	1	14	14	0

PASSING – PUNTING – KICKING

PASSING	Att	Comp	%	Yds	Yd/Att	TD	Int–	%	RK
Starr	295	172	58	2418	8.2	16	16–	5	3
Hornung	5	3	60	42	8.4	1	0–	0	
Roach	4	0	0	0	0.0	0	0–	0	
Moore	2	2	100	42	21.0	1	0–	0	

PUNTING	No	Avg
Dowler	38	44.1
McGee	13	40.0

KICKING	XP	Att	%	FG	Att	%
Hornung	41	41	100	15	22	68
Agajanian	8	8	100	1	2	50

DETROIT LIONS

RUSHING

Last Name	No.	Yds	Avg	TD
Pietrosante	201	841	4.2	5
Lewis	110	451	4.1	4
Ninowski	33	238	7.2	5
Cassady	31	131	4.2	1
Olszewski	30	109	3.6	0
Morrall	20	86	4.3	0
Lary	1	14	14.0	0
Webb	7	6	0.9	1
Barr	6	−8	−1.3	0

RECEIVING

Last Name	No.	Yds	Avg	TD
Cogdill	45	956	21	6
Gibbons	45	566	13	1
Barr	40	630	16	6
Peitrosante	26	315	12	0
Davis	9	115	13	0
Lewis	8	118	15	0
Studstill	5	54	11	0
Cassady	5	45	9	1
Olszewski	1	14	14	0
Williams	1	10	10	0
Webb	1	7	7	0

PUNT RETURNS

Last Name	No.	Yds	Avg	TD
Cassady	16	159	10	0
Studstill	8	75	9	0
Gibbons	1	14	14	0
Lary	1	8	8	0
Lane	1	6	6	0

KICKOFF RETURNS

Last Name	No.	Yds	Avg	TD
Studstill	16	448	28	1
Cassady	9	127	14	0
Olszewski	4	59	15	0
Maher	1	19	19	0
Williams	1	4	4	0
Webb	0	5	0	0

PASSING – PUNTING – KICKING

PASSING	Att	Comp	%	Yds	Yd/Att	TD	Int–	%	RK
Ninowski	247	117	47	1921	7.8	7	18–	7	17
Morrall	150	69	46	909	6.1	7	9–	6	18
Cassady	1	0	0	0	0.0	0	0–	0	

PUNTING	No	Avg
Lary	52	48.4
Morrall	3	37.7
Studstill	1	32.0

KICKING	XP	Att	%	FG	Att	%
Martin	25	26	96	15	30	50
Walker	6	6	100	0	3	0

BALTIMORE COLTS

RUSHING

Last Name	No.	Yds	Avg	TD
Perry	168	675	4.0	3
Moore	92	648	7.0	7
Hawkins	86	379	4.4	4
Unitas	54	190	3.5	2
Smolinski	31	98	3.2	0
Welch	1	60	60.0	1
Matte	13	54	4.2	0
Hill	1	4	4.0	0
McHan	4	1	0.3	0

RECEIVING

Last Name	No.	Yds	Avg	TD
Berry	75	873	12	0
Moore	49	728	15	8
Perry	34	322	9	1
Mutscheller	20	370	19	2
Hawkins	20	158	8	1
Orr	18	357	20	4
Smolinski	9	100	11	1
Mackey	4	66	17	0
Matte	1	8	8	0
Szymanski	1	5	5	0

PUNT RETURNS

Last Name	No.	Yds	Avg	TD
Boyd	18	173	10	0
Taseff	5	39	8	0
Hawkins	4	20	5	0
Nelson	4	19	5	0
Harrison	1	16	16	0
Smolinski	1	2	2	0

KICKOFF RETURNS

Last Name	No.	Yds	Avg	TD
Lyles	28	672	24	0
Harrison	11	250	23	0
Welch	5	146	29	0
Matte	2	50	25	0
Smolinski	3	27	9	0
Lewis	1	14	14	0
Matuszak	1	14	14	0
Mackey	1	6	6	0
Gregory	1	3	3	0

PASSING – PUNTING – KICKING

PASSING	Att	Comp	%	Yds	Yd/Att	TD	Int–	%	RK
Unitas	420	229	55	2990	7.1	16	24–	6	8
McHan	15	3	20	28	1.9	1	4–	27	
Moore	2	0	0	0	0.0	0	1–	50	
Boyd	1	0	0	0	0.0	0	0–	0	

PUNTING	No	Avg
Gilburg	42	43.0

KICKING	XP	Att	%	FG	Att	%
Myhra	33	34	97	21	39	54

WESTERN CONFERENCE – Continued

CHICAGO BEARS 8-6-0 George Halas

Scores of Each Game			Use Name	Pos.	Hgt	Wgt	Age	Int	Pts
13	Minnesota	37	Art Anderson	OT	6'3"	244	24		
21	Los Angeles	17	Herm Lee	OT	6'4"	247	30		
0	Green Bay	24	Stan Fanning	OT	6'6"	270	23		
31	Detroit	17	Roger Davis	OG	6'3"	235	23		
24	BALTIMORE	10	Stan Jones	OG	6'1"	250	30		
31	SAN FRANCISCO	0	Ted Karras	OG	6'1"	243	28		
21	Baltimore	20	Bob Wetoska	OG	6'3"	240	23		
14	Philadelphia	16	Roger LeClerc	C	6'3"	235	23		70
28	GREEN BAY	31	Mike Pyle	C	6'3"	240	22		
31	San Francisco	41	Doug Atkins	DE	6'8"	255	31		
28	LOS ANGELES	24	Bob Kilcullen	DE	6'3"	245	25		
15	DETROIT	16	Maury Youmans	DE	6'6"	260	24		
17	CLEVELAND	14	John Mellekas	DT	6'3"	255	28		
52	MINNESOTA	35	Fred Williams	DT	6'4"	248	31		

Use Name	Pos.	Hgt	Wgt	Age	Int	Pts
Joe Fortunato	LB	6'	225	31	3	
Bill George	LB	6'2"	235	30	3	
Larry Morris	LB	6'2"	230	26	1	
Ken Kirk	C-LB	6'2"	230	23		
J.C. Caroline	DB	6'1"	190	28	3	
Bobby Jackson	DB	6'1"	190	25		
Pete Manning	DB	6'3"	208	25		
Don Mullins	DB	6'1"	195	22		
Richie Petitbon	DB	6'3"	205	23	5	
Rosey Taylor	DB	5'11"	186	22		
Dave Whitsell	DB	6'	190	25	6	

Earl Leggett – Knee Injury

Use Name	Pos.	Hgt	Wgt	Age	Int	Pts
Ed Brown	QB	6'2"	210	32		4
Dick Norman	QB	6'3"	210	23		
Billy Wade	QB	6'2"	210	30		12
Charlie Bivins	HB	6'2"	212	22		6
Willie Galimore	HB	6'1"	187	26		42
J. D. Smith	HB	6'	210	26		
John Adams	FB	6'3"	235	24		6
Bill Brown	FB	5'11"	218	23		
Rick Casares	FB	6'2"	225	30		48
Johnny Morris	FL	5'10"	180	26		24
Angie Coia	OE	6'2"	202	23		18
Mike Ditka	OE	6'3"	230	21		72
Jim Dooley	OE	6'4"	198	31		
Bo Farrington	OE	6'3"	217	25		24
Harlon Hill	DB-OE	6'3"	200	29	3	

SAN FRANCISCO FORTY NINERS 7-6-1 Red Hickey

Scores of Each Game			Use Name	Pos.	Hgt	Wgt	Age	Int	Pts
35	WASHINGTON	3	Len Rohde	OT	6'4"	240	23		
10	Green Bay	30	Bob St. Clair	OT	6'9"	265	30		
49	Detroit	0	John Thomas	LB-OT	6'4"	246	26		
35	LOS ANGELES	0	Bruce Bosley	OG	6'2"	240	27		
38	Minnesota	24	Ted Connolly	OG	6'3"	242	29		
0	Chicago	31	Bill Lopasky	OG	6'2"	235	24		
10	Pittsburgh	20	Mike Magac	OG	6'3"	240	23		
20	DETROIT	20	Frank Morze	C	6'4"	264	27		
7	Los Angeles	17	Dan Colchico	DE	6'4"	236	24		
41	CHICAGO	31	Lou Cordileone	DE	6'	245	24		
38	MINNESOTA	28	Charlie Krueger	DE	6'4"	245	25		2
17	Baltimore	20	Roland Lakes	OT-DE	6'4"	247	21		
22	GREEN BAY	21	Monte Clark	DT	6'6"	260	24		
24	BALTIMORE	27	Leo Nomellini	DT	6'3"	262	36		

Use Name	Pos.	Hgt	Wgt	Age	Int	Pts
Bob Harrison	LB	6'2"	220	24	2	
Matt Hazeltine	LB	6'1"	220	28	1	
Carl Kammerer	LB	6'3"	237	24		
Gorden Kelley	LB	6'3"	230	23	1	
Dave Baker	DB	6'	193	24	6	
Eddie Dove	DB	6'2"	180	24	3	
Jim Johnson	DB	6'2"	190	23	5	
Jerry Mertens	DB	6'	183	25		
Jimmy Ridlon	DB	6'1"	177	26		
Abe Woodson	HB-DB	5'11"	188	26	1	12

Use Name	Pos.	Hgt	Wgt	Age	Int	Pts
John Brodie	QB	6'1"	186	26		12
Billy Kilmer	QB	6'	190	21		60
Bob Waters	QB	6'2"	184	23		18
Don McIlhenny	HB	6'	185	26		
Dale Messer	HB	5'10"	175	24		
Ray Norton	HB	6'2"	184	24		
J. D. Smith	FB-HB	6'1"	200	28		54
Bill Cooper	FB	6'1"	215	22		6
C. R. Roberts	FB	6'3"	197	25		6
Bernie Casey	OE	6'4"	215	22		6
Clyde Conner	OE	6'2"	190	28		6
R. C. Owens	OE	6'3"	195	26		36
Monte Stickles	OE	6'4"	230	23		30
Aaron Thomas	OE	6'3"	208	23		12
Tommy Davis	K	6'	212	26		80

LOS ANGELES RAMS 4-10-0 Bob Waterfield

Scores of Each Game			Use Name	Pos.	Hgt	Wgt	Age	Int	Pts
24	Baltimore	27	Jim Boeke	OT	6'5"	245	22		
17	CHICAGO	21	Willie Hector	OT	6'2"	220	21		
24	PITTSBURGH	14	Frank Varrichione	OT	6'1"	235	29		
0	San Francisco	35	Charley Cowan	OG	6'4"	250	23		
13	Detroit	14	Roy Hord	OG	6'4"	250	26		
14	New York	24	Joe Scibelli	OG	6'1"	250	22		
10	DETROIT	28	Bruce Tarbox	OG	6'2"	230	22		
31	MINNESOTA	17	Art Hunter	C	6'4"	248	28		
17	SAN FRANCISCO	7	Deacon Jones	DE	6'5"	240	22		
17	Green Bay	35	Lamar Lundy	DE	6'7"	235	26		
24	Chicago	28	John Baker	DT-DE	6'6"	290	26		
21	Minnesota	42	Urban Henry	DT	6'4"	265	26		
34	BALTIMORE	17	John Lovetere	DT	6'4"	280	25		
17	GREEN BAY	24	George Strugar	DT	6'5"	258	26	1	

Use Name	Pos.	Hgt	Wgt	Age	Int	Pts
Bill Jobko	LB	6'2"	220	25	1	
Bob Long	LB	6'3"	235	27	1	
Marlin McKeever	LB	6'1"	230	21		
Jack Pardee	LB	6'2"	225	25	1	
Les Richter	LB	6'3"	235	30	4	
Charley Britt	DB	6'2"	185	23	5	
Ross Coyle	DB	6'2"	195	25		
Lindon Crow	DB	6'1"	200	28	6	
Alvin Hall	DB	6'	193	28		
Elbert Kimbrough	DB	5'11"	195	22		
Ed Meador	DB	5'11"	185	24	1	
Clendon Thomas	DB	6'2"	192	24	3	

Gene Brito – Illness

Use Name	Pos.	Hgt	Wgt	Age	Int	Pts
Zeke Bratkowski	QB	6'2"	203	29		18
Frank Ryan	QB	6'3"	200	25		
Jon Arnett	HB	5'11"	194	26		30
Pervis Atkins	HB	6'1"	195	25		
Ollie Matson	HB	6'2"	210	31		30
Tom Wilson	HB	6'	204	28		6
Dick Bass	FB	5'10"	200	24		30
Joe Marconi	FB	6'2"	225	27		24
Frank Williams	FB	6'2"	215	29		
Duane Allen	OE	6'4"	210	23		12
Carroll Dale	OE	6'1"	195	23		12
Jim Phillips	OE	6'1"	198	24		30
Danny Villanueva	K	5'11"	200	23		71

MINNESOTA VIKINGS 3-11-0 Norm Van Brocklin

Scores of Each Game			Use Name	Pos.	Hgt	Wgt	Age	Int	Pts
37	CHICAGO	13	Bob Denton	OT	6'4"	240	27		
7	Dallas	21	Frank Youso	OT	6'4"	260	25		
33	Baltimore	34	Paul Dickson	DT-OT	6'5"	250	24		
0	DALLAS	28	Grady Alderman	OG	6'2"	235	22		
24	SAN FRANCISCO	38	Jerry Huth	OG	6'	228	28		
7	GREEN BAY	33	Ken Petersen	OG	6'2"	235	22		
10	Green Bay	28	Mike Rabold	OG	6'2"	238	24		
17	Los Angeles	31	Bill Lapham	C	6'3"	250	27		
28	BALTIMORE	20	Don Joyce	DE	6'3"	250	31		
10	DETROIT	37	Jim Leo	DE	6'1"	225	23		
28	San Francisco	38	Jim Marshall	DE	6'3"	230	23		
42	LOS ANGELES	21	Lebron Shields	DE	6'4"	245	24		
7	Detroit	13	Bill Bishop	DT	6'4"	248	30		
35	Chicago	52	Ed Culpepper	DT	6'1"	255	27		
			Jim Prestel	DT	6'5"	250	24		

Use Name	Pos.	Hgt	Wgt	Age	Int	Pts
Dick Grechi	LB	6'1"	230	23	1	
Rip Hawkins	LB	6'3"	230	22	5	
Clancy Osborne	LB	6'3"	217	26	4	
Karl Rubke	C-LB	6'4"	240	25	1	
Dean Derby (from PIT)	DB	6'	190	27	3	
Jack Morris	DB	6'	190	29	2	
Rich Mostardi	DB	5'11"	188	23	2	
Dick Pesonen	DB	6'	190	23	1	
Justin Rowland	DB	6'2"	188	23	1	
Charlie Sumner	DB	6'1"	195	31	2	
Will Sherman	HB-DB	6'2"	197	32		

Use Name	Pos.	Hgt	Wgt	Age	Int	Pts
George Shaw	QB	6'1"	180	28		
Fran Tarkenton	QB	6'1"	190	21		30
Jamie Caleb	HB	6'1"	210	24		
Billy Gault	HB	6'1"	185	24		
Tommy Mason	HB	6'	195	22		18
Hugh McElhenny	HB	6'1"	198	32		42
Ray Hayes	FB	6'3"	235	26		12
Doug Mayberry	FB	6'1"	225	24		
Mel Triplett	FB	6'1"	215	29		6
Dave Middleton	OE	6'1"	190	28		12
Fred Murphy	OE	6'3"	205	23		
Jerry Reichow	OE	6'2"	220	26		66
Gordon Smith	OE	6'2"	200	22		24
A. D. Williams	OE	6'2"	210	28		6
Mike Mercer	K	6'	220	25		63

WESTERN CONFERENCE – Continued

CHICAGO BEARS

RUSHING

Last Name	No.	Yds	Avg	TD
Galimore	153	707	4.6	4
Casares	135	588	4.4	8
Wade	45	255	5.7	2
Bivins	43	188	4.4	1
B. Brown	22	81	3.7	0
J. Morris	8	49	6.1	0
E. Brown	13	18	1.4	0
Smith	3	6	2.0	0
Adams	14	−2	−0.1	1

RECEIVING

Last Name	No.	Yds	Avg	TD
Ditka	56	1076	19	12
J. Morris	36	548	15	4
Galimore	33	502	15	3
Farrington	21	349	17	4
Coia	12	249	21	3
Casares	8	69	9	0
Dooley	6	90	15	0
Adams	5	80	16	0
Bivins	4	−9	−2	0
Hill	3	51	17	0
B. Brown	2	6	3	0

PUNT RETURNS

Last Name	No.	Yds	Avg	TD
J. Morris	23	155	7	0
Petitbon	2	9	5	0
Taylor	1	4	4	0
L. Morris	1	2	2	0

KICKOFF RETURNS

Last Name	No.	Yds	Avg	TD
Bivins	25	668	27	0
Taylor	14	379	27	0
Galimore	5	82	16	0
B. Brown	4	54	14	0
J. Morris	2	46	23	0
Smith	1	18	18	0

PASSING – PUNTING – KICKING

PASSING	Att	Comp	%	Yds	Yd/Att	TD	Int–	%	RK
Wade	250	139	56	2258	9.0	22	13–	5	2
E. Brown	98	46	47	742	7.6	4	11–	11	
Adams	1	1	100	11	11.0	0	0–	0	

PUNTING	No	Avg
E. Brown	58	42.2
Adams	2	28.0

KICKING	XP	Att	%	FG	Att	%
LeClerc	40	41	98	10	24	42
E. Brown	1	1	100	1	2	50
George	0	0	0	0	1	0

SAN FRANCISCO FORTY NINERS

RUSHING

Last Name	No.	Yds	Avg	TD
Smith	167	823	4.9	8
Kilmer	96	509	5.3	10
Roberts	63	338	5.4	1
Waters	47	233	5.0	3
Brodie	28	90	3.2	2
McIlhenny	10	34	3.4	0
Woodson	14	23	1.6	0
Cooper	8	17	2.1	1
Messer	3	13	4.3	0
Norton	2	−2	−1.0	0
A. Thomas	1	−15	−15.0	0
Owens	0	23	0.0	1

RECEIVING

Last Name	No.	Yds	Avg	TD
Owens	55	1032	19	5
Stickles	43	794	18	5
Smith	28	343	12	1
A. Thomas	15	301	20	2
Conner	11	177	16	1
Casey	10	185	19	1
Roberts	10	83	8	0
Woodson	8	74	9	0
Messer	3	33	11	0
McIlhenny	1	6	6	0

PUNT RETURNS

Last Name	No.	Yds	Avg	TD
Woodson	16	172	11	1
Dove	6	49	8	0
Messer	2	11	6	0

KICKOFF RETURNS

Last Name	No.	Yds	Avg	TD
Woodson	27	782	29	1
McIlhenny	6	189	32	0
Smith	7	158	23	0
Norton	1	60	60	0
Cooper	3	44	15	0
Messer	3	36	12	0
Kammerer	1	18	18	0

PASSING – PUNTING – KICKING

PASSING	Att	Comp	%	Yds	Yd/Att	TD	Int–	%	RK
Brodie	283	155	55	2588	9.1	14	12–	4	5
Kilmer	34	19	56	286	8.4	0	4–	12	
Waters	28	13	46	183	6.5	1	2–	7	
Smith	1	0	0	0	0.0	0	1–	100	

PUNTING	No	Avg
Davis	50	45.4
Kilmer	9	40.4

KICKING	XP	Att	%	FG	Att	%
Davis	44	44	100	12	22	55

LOS ANGELES RAMS

RUSHING

Last Name	No.	Yds	Avg	TD
Arnett	158	609	3.9	4
Bass	98	608	6.2	4
Wilson	44	220	5.0	1
Matson	24	181	7.5	2
Marconi	36	146	4.1	3
Ryan	38	139	3.7	0
Bratkowski	12	36	3.0	3
Atkins	5	19	3.8	0

RECEIVING

Last Name	No.	Yds	Avg	TD
Phillips	78	1092	14	5
Dale	35	561	16	2
Matson	29	537	19	3
Arnett	28	194	7	0
Bass	16	145	9	0
Atkins	5	67	13	0
Marconi	4	20	5	1
Allen	2	80	40	2
Wilson	1	12	12	0
Scibelli	1	1	1	0

PUNT RETURNS

Last Name	No.	Yds	Avg	TD
Bass	4	109	27	1
Arnett	10	75	8	0

KICKOFF RETURNS

Last Name	No.	Yds	Avg	TD
Bass	23	698	30	0
Arnett	25	653	26	1
Atkins	4	77	19	0
Varrichione	3	23	8	0
Jones	1	12	12	0

PASSING – PUNTING – KICKING

PASSING	Att	Comp	%	Yds	Yd/Att	TD	Int–	%	RK
Bratkowski	230	124	54	1547	6.7	8	13–	6	13
Ryan	142	72	51	1115	7.9	5	7–	5	10
Arnett	13	3	23	47	3.6	0	1–	8	
Villanueva	1	0	0	0	0.0	0	0–	0	

PUNTING	No	Avg
Villanueva	46	40.1
Bratkowski	12	38.2
Marconi	6	44.2

KICKING	XP	Att	%	FG	Att	%
Villanueva	32	32	100	13	27	48

MINNESOTA VIKINGS

RUSHING

Last Name	No.	Yds	Avg	TD
McElhenny	120	570	4.8	3
Triplett	80	407	5.1	1
Hayes	73	319	4.4	2
Tarkenton	56	308	5.5	5
Mason	60	226	3.8	3
Mayberry	13	40	3.1	0
Shaw	10	39	3.9	0
Caleb	3	11	3.7	0
Reichow	3	9	3.0	0
Mercer	1	−32	−32.0	0

RECEIVING

Last Name	No.	Yds	Avg	TD
Reichow	50	859	17	11
McElhenny	37	283	8	3
Middleton	30	444	15	2
Mason	20	122	6	0
Hayes	16	121	8	0
Williams	13	174	13	1
Smith	12	320	27	4
Triplett	10	41	4	0
Sherman	2	40	20	0
Mayberry	2	18	9	0
Caleb	2	−8	−4	0

PUNT RETURNS

Last Name	No.	Yds	Avg	TD
McElhenny	8	155	19	1
Mason	14	146	10	0
Caleb	1	8	8	0

KICKOFF RETURNS

Last Name	No.	Yds	Avg	TD
Mason	25	603	24	0
Caleb	22	504	23	0
Rowland	8	175	22	0
Pesonen	6	136	23	0
McElhenny	2	59	30	0
Triplett	3	41	14	0
Gault	2	41	21	0
Leo	3	9	3	0
Hayes	1	0	0	0

PASSING – PUNTING – KICKING

PASSING	Att	Comp	%	Yds	Yd/Att	TD	Int–	%	RK
Tarkenton	280	157	56	1997	7.1	18	17–	6	7
Shaw	91	46	51	530	5.8	4	4–	4	
Reichow	3	0	0	0	0.0	0	1–	33	
Caleb	1	0	0	0	0.0	0	0–	0	
Mason	1	0	0	0	0.0	0	0–	0	
McElhenny	1	0	0	0	0.0	0	0–	0	

PUNTING	No	Avg
Mercer	63	39.0

KICKING	XP	Att	%	FG	Att	%
Mercer	36	37	97	9	21	43

1961 A.F.L. The Feuding Ends at the Altar

Commissioner Joe Foss had enough problems to keep him busy this year. His authority to govern the league was actually at stake in one incident. To get a jump on the NFL in signing rookies, the team owners conducted a secret draft of college seniors in November, with each club taking six name players. Foss, who set the date for the draft in December, was not informed of this draft, and when he found out about it he declared it invalid. A potential revolt of the owners narrowed down to a public feud between Foss and New York Titan owner Harry Wismer. The Titans had selected Syracuse runner Ernie Davis in the November draft that Foss nullified, and when Buffalo picked Davis in the official December draft Wismer let loose his full vocal fury on Foss. Despite Wismer's calls for Foss's ouster, the commissioner stayed in office, directed the official draft, and won a five-year renewal of his contract from the owners when the season ended. The most amazing development came in the spring of 1962 when Foss was Wismer's best man at his wedding.

Attendance around the league also troubled Foss. League attendance rose a slight amount, up to 17,000, and Houston, Buffalo, Boston, and San Diego showed increases in home attendance. In these cases, though, it was generally a case of going from horrible to merely bad. The AFL was providing exciting, wide-open games for television, but fans did not yet think it reasonable to pay to see these new teams play.

The anti-trust suit filed by the AFL against the NFL was still going through the judicial process, so the main confrontation between the two leagues was still taking place at the box office and in the signing of rookie players. The NFL was winning on all fronts in the attendance war, and the old league also grabbed off the lion's share of graduating seniors from the class of 1961. With the element of surprise gone, the AFL signed only a handful of name collegians, among them Ken Rice, Art Baker, E. J. Holub, and Earl Faison.

The league also signed a new player from a different route, one who had played out his option in the NFL. Willard Dewveall, an offensive end with the Chicago Bears, played through 1960 without signing a new contract and agreed to terms with the Houston Oilers for the 1961 season. Dewveall thus became the first player to jump to the AFL from the active ranks of the NFL.

While new players were coming into the league, some of the old ones were lost to the federal activation of Reserve units in response to the Berlin crisis. The activated players all were stationed in the continental United States, and most were able to make the league games on weekend passes. These weekday soldiers and weekend football warriors included Ron Mix, Larry Grantham, Ross O'Hanley, Proverb Jacobs, Richie Lucas, Bill Roehnelt, George McGee, Oscar Lofton, John Jelacik, and Herm Urenda.

A new city also joined the circuit as owner Barron Hilton picked up his Los Angeles Chargers and transplanted them in the virgin soil of San Diego. Attendance in San Diego topped that of Los Angeles, but the Chargers still lost money while winning on the field.

One innovation by the league this season was the scheduling of an All-Star Game after the season to showcase the league's talent. Although some NFL boosters snickered at the contest, it provided one more television date for the league to win new fans.

EASTERN DIVISION

Houston Oilers—The Oilers were mired in last place with a 1-3-1 record when owner Bud Adams canned head coach Lou Rymkus and replaced him with assistant Wally Lemm. The club's fortunes immediately turned around, as the Oilers won all their remaining nine games with a blistering offensive blitzkrieg. Lemm gave the quarterback job back to George Blanda, whom Rymkus had benched in favor of Jacky Lee, and Blanda responded with a pro record of thirty-six touchdown passes, a pair of 400 passing-yards games, and reliable long-range place-kicking, including boots of 55 and 53 yards. Charley Hennigan and Bill Groman were Blanda's deep targets, while Billy Cannon and Charley Tolar punched out yardage on the ground at a steady clip. The Oilers took over first place by beating Boston 27-15 on November 12, and they kept on wining right to the end. Coach Lemm summed up his perfect relief job by saying, "I feel like someone who inherited a million dollars in tarnished silverware. All I did was polish it."

Boston Patriots—Like the Oilers, the Patriots profited from a mid-season switch in coaches. After Mike Holovak succeeded Lou Saban as head coach, the Patriots won seven of nine games to streak into first place, only to have the Oilers win nine out of nine over the same span to win the title. The Boston attack featured no stars but still was second in the league in points scored. Butch Songin and Babe Parilli, a pair of senior citizens, shared the quarterback job and found converted defensive back Gino Cappelletti their favorite receiver. Cappelletti's kicking, however, was the spearhead of the Boston attack and won him the AFL scoring title. The Pats lost only to Houston over the last eight games, but that one loss was enough to foil the late-season drive.

New York Titans—Owner Harry Wismer made news this year. He made news with his feud with coach Sammy Baugh. He made news by publicly calling for Commissioner Joe Foss's ouster and more news when they finally made up. And he made news by announcing that his losses for 1960 and 1961 totaled $1.2 million. Wismer made more news than his football team, which played its games in virtual privacy. Three wins in the first four games got the Titans out to an early lead in the East, but a rash of injuries plus hot streaks by Houston and Boston pushed New York back into third place. Although fullback Billy Mathis developed into a bruising runner, the Titans still relied on Al Dorow's passes to Don Maynard and Art Powell for most of the offense. But while the Titans moved well through the air, enemy passers found the New York secondary easy pickings in return.

Buffalo Bills—In a league not known for great quarterbacks, the Bills had the worst quarterback situation. Ex-Redskin M. C. Reynolds, sophomore Johnny Green, and ex-Lion Warren Raab were uniformly unimpressive, and the offense sputtered despite some fine rookies in the lineup. Fullback Art Baker contributed power running, end Glenn Bass injected speed into the attack after being cut by San Diego, and Al Bemiller, Billy Shaw, Stew Barber, and Ken Rice all won jobs in the offensive line. But without a competent quarterback, the Bills had to rely on the defense to stay competitive. Lavern Torczon, Chuck McMurtry, Archie Matsos, and Billy Atkins stood out as defenders, but the unbalanced team effort cost head coach Buster Ramsey his job at the end of the season.

WESTERN DIVISION

San Diego Chargers—The Chargers celebrated their move to San Diego by winning their first eleven games to make a shambles out of the Western Division race. Head coach and general manager Sid Gillman built his defensive unit into the league's best with the addition of three excellent rookies. End Earl Faison put steady pressure on enemy passers, tackle Ernie Ladd contributed 315 pounds of muscle to the center of the line, and middle linebacker Chuck Allen, a lightly regarded twenty-eighth draft choice, was a sensation until breaking his ankle late in the year. With Dick Harris and Charley McNeil heading up a solid secondary, the San Diego defense had no weak spots. The offense held up its end of the bargain, with Jack Kemp, Paul Lowe, Dave Kocourek, and Ron Mix starring. But the team's real star was Gillman, one of the few AFL general managers who was successfully signing most of the rookies on his draft list.

Dallas Texans—The Texans matched the Chargers in signing blue-chip rookies but fell farther behind them in the standings. Professional debuts by Jim Tyrer, Jerry Mays, E. J. Holub, and Dave Grayson did not prevent a slump by the defense and the team's dropping below .500 for the season. After winning three of their first four games, the Texans went into a six-game losing streak that ended the Western Division race. The team's passing attack did not live up to expectations, as quarterback Cotton Davidson was very erratic, but the running corps of Abner Haynes, Jack Spikes, Frank Jackson, and Bo Dickinson led the league in rushing yardage. Both lines had weak links, though, and suffered periodic breakdowns, throwing a mid-season monkey wrench into high pre-season hopes.

Denver Broncos—Without a balanced offensive diet, the Broncos grew weaker as the season progressed. The Denver running attack was dead last in the league, with the offense totally dependent on the passing of Frank Tripuka and George Herring. The Broncos threw the ball so often that split end Lionel Taylor set a new professional record with 100 catches for the season, not bad for a man the Chicago Bears had cut two years ago. Taylor's strong suit was his glue-fingered hands, but his lack of speed was underlined by his scoring only four touchdowns on the 100 receptions. After seven games, the Broncos had a respectable 3-4 record, but by then enemy defenses had wised up to the Denver air show. The Broncos lost their last seven games, and coach Frankie Filchock lost his job in the process.

Oakland Raiders—When the Raiders lost their first game 55-0 to Houston and their second game 44-0 to San Diego, the tone for a disastrous season was set. Coach Ernie Erdelatz was fired after the two opening massacres, but replacement Marty Feldman couldn't do much better with this squad. The Raiders scored the fewest points in the league, allowed the most points, and attracted minuscule crowds to their home games on the foreign turf of San Francisco's Candlestick Park. Not all the Raider players were inept, only most of them. Center Jim Otto won praise as the league's best at his position, Fred Williamson played well at cornerback, and halfback Clem Daniels showed promise after being picked up as a free agent. But a pair of mid-season victories over Denver and Buffalo was the best the Raiders could do as they lost their last six games of the season.

FINAL TEAM STATISTICS

OFFENSE

	BOSTON	BUFFALO	DALLAS	DENVER	HOUSTON	NEW YORK	OAKLAND	SAN DIEGO
FIRST DOWNS:								
Total	238	243	**247**	219	**293**	247	200	208
by Rushing	93	92	**112**	66	97	100	65	81
by Passing	120	128	122	127	**182**	126	116	110
by Penalty	25	23	13	**26**	14	21	19	17
RUSHING:								
Number	389	438	439	333	**452**	426	350	391
Yards	1675	1606	**2183**	1091	1896	1678	1234	1466
Average Yards	4.3	3.7	**5.0**	3.3	4.2	3.9	3.5	3.7
Touchdowns	15	18	23	11	15	17	10	**24**
PASSING:								
Attempts	420	439	399	**568**	498	460	423	423
Completions	206	194	177	**265**	254	204	209	190
Completion Percentage	49.0	44.2	44.4	46.7	**51.0**	44.3	49.4	44.9
Passing Yards	2795	2786	2815	3004	**4568**	2733	2514	3121
Average Yards per Attempt	6.7	6.3	7.1	5.3	**9.2**	5.9	5.9	7.4
Average Yards per Completion	13.6	14.4	15.9	11.3	**18.0**	13.4	12.0	16.4
Times Tackled Attempting to Pass	33	63	24	33	**14**	41	45	28
Yards Lost Attempting to Pass	256	442	239	284	**176**	346	463	274
Net Yards	2539	2344	2576	2720	**4392**	2387	2051	2847
Touchdowns	29	15	18	18	**48**	20	17	17
Interceptions	**21**	25	27	45	29	32	28	25
Percent Intercepted	**5.0**	5.7	6.8	7.9	5.8	7.0	6.6	5.9
PUNTING:								
Number	62	**85**	62	80	56	74	75	63
Average Distance	38.8	**44.5**	39.9	39.4	39.1	41.8	39.0	41.5
PUNT RETURNS:								
Number	**35**	19	26	33	19	26	15	29
Yards	288	187	219	369	118	**463**	117	458
Average Yards	8.2	9.8	8.4	11.2	6.2	**17.8**	7.8	15.8
Touchdowns	2	0	0	**2**	0	**2**	0	**2**
KICKOFF RETURNS:								
Number	49	57	53	66	43	66	**68**	39
Yards	1136	1208	1465	**1501**	940	1213	1383	642
Average Yards	23.2	21.2	**27.6**	22.7	21.9	18.4	20.3	16.5
Touchdowns	**2**	1	1	1	0	0	0	0
INTERCEPTION RETURNS:								
Number	22	29	24	26	33	26	24	**49**
Yards	326	311	418	355	528	315	285	**929**
Average Yards	14.8	10.7	17.4	13.7	16.0	12.6	11.9	**19.0**
Touchdowns	2	1	3	0	0	1	2	**9**
PENALTIES:								
Number	64	65	**89**	60	83	60	53	88
Yards	659	549	874.5	560	**889**	585	456	682.5
FUMBLES:								
Number	24	32	32	40	**21**	32	28	32
Number Lost	**9**	17	18	23	10	20	16	19
POINTS:								
Total	413	294	334	251	**513**	301	237	396
PAT (kick) Attempts	50	31	40	27	**66**	39	25	50
PAT (kick) Made	48	29	37	27	**65**	37	24	43
PAT (Rush or Pass) Attempts	2	**7**	4	5	0	1	4	2
PAT (Rush or Pass) Made	1	**4**	3	3	0	0	2	1
FG Attempts	**32**	26	24	25	26	23	26	27
FG Made	**17**	9	7	8	16	8	11	13
Percent FG Made	53.1	34.6	29.2	32.0	**61.5**	34.8	42.3	48.1
Safeties	0	1	0	1	**2**	0	1	0

DEFENSE

	BOSTON	BUFFALO	DALLAS	DENVER	HOUSTON	NEW YORK	OAKLAND	SAN DIEGO
FIRST DOWNS:								
Total	243	**200**	238	233	235	242	280	224
by Rushing	72	**61**	89	83	87	100	135	79
by Passing	151	124	129	127	126	**121**	129	124
by Penalty	20	**15**	20	23	22	21	16	21
RUSHING:								
Number	350	**349**	410	435	365	414	494	401
Yards	**1041**	1377	1525	1633	1634	1880	2382	1357
Average Yards	**3.0**	3.9	3.7	3.8	4.5	4.5	4.8	3.4
Touchdowns	9	9	18	17	17	20	36	**7**
PASSING:								
Attempts	479	430	439	433	493	462	**409**	485
Completions	241	206	219	194	212	211	**192**	224
Completion Percentage	50.3	47.9	49.9	44.8	**43.0**	45.7	46.9	46.2
Passing Yards	3490	3237	3077	3060	2750	3044	2942	**2736**
Average Yards per Attempt	7.3	7.5	7.0	7.1	**5.6**	6.6	7.2	5.6
Average Yards per Completion	14.5	15.7	14.1	15.8	13.0	14.4	15.3	**12.2**
Times Tackled Attempting to Pass	**44**	36	34	33	41	31	20	42
Yards Lost Attempting to Pass	**408**	350	300	275	359	247	168	373
Net Yards	3082	2887	2777	2785	2391	2797	2774	**2363**
Touchdowns	27	28	20	30	**13**	26	22	16
Interceptions	22	29	24	26	33	25	24	**49**
Percent Intercepted	4.6	6.7	5.7	6.0	6.7	5.4	5.6	**10.1**
PUNTING:								
Number	71	75	63	77	**81**	70	50	70
Average Distance	40.7	**38.7**	41.7	40.8	40.7	42.4	40.4	40.1
PUNT RETURNS:								
Number	**15**	45	20	26	20	20	34	22
Yards	245	291	216	368	271	284	352	**192**
Average Yards	16.3	**6.5**	10.8	14.2	13.6	14.2	10.4	8.7
Touchdowns	2	1	1	2	**0**	**0**	1	1
KICKOFF RETURNS:								
Number	53	54	65	**42**	66	51	45	65
Yards	1255	1112	1249	**720**	1481	1084	1066	1521
Average Yards	23.7	20.6	19.2	**17.1**	22.4	21.3	23.7	23.4
Touchdowns	1	1	1	**0**	1	1	**0**	**0**
INTERCEPTION RETURNS:								
Number	**21**	25	27	45	29	32	28	25
Yards	**198**	398	424	818	407	670	280	272
Average Yards	**9.4**	15.9	15.7	18.2	14.0	20.9	10.0	10.9
Touchdowns	**1**	4	**1**	5	2	3	**1**	**1**
PENALTIES:								
Number	67	76	62	**98**	57	86	62	54
Yards	661.5	693	619	799	588	**869.5**	524	501
FUMBLES:								
Number	**36**	20	31	25	31	**36**	29	33
Number Lost	20	15	18	14	15	**21**	12	17
POINTS:								
Total	313	342	343	432	242	390	458	**219**
PAT (kick) Attempts	40	42	38	55	**26**	48	53	**26**
PAT (kick) Made	40	41	37	51	**22**	46	50	23
PAT (Rush or Pass) Attempts	1	1	6	1	7	**2**	6	**1**
PAT (Rush or Pass) Made	**0**	1	3	1	2	1	5	1
FG Attempts	**23**	28	31	26	24	27	27	**23**
FG Made	9	13	12	13	**6**	14	12	10
Percent FG Made	39.1	46.4	38.7	50.0	**25.0**	51.9	44.4	43.5
Safeties	**0**	1	**0**	2	**0**	**0**	1	1

1961 AFL CHAMPIONSHIP GAME

December 24, at San Diego
(Attendance 29,556)

Oiling the Defense

For a second straight year, the defensive units excelled in the AFL championship game. The Chargers and Oilers, repeat winners of their divisional races, both found interceptions easy to come by, the Chargers picking off six passes and the Oilers four. Played on a sunny, 59-degree Christmas Eve, the game was a showcase for turnovers, with seven fumbles plus all the interceptions thwarting most offensive drives. Neither club generated much offense in the first half, with the only score coming on a 46-yard field goal by George Blanda late in the second quarter. The Oilers, who hadn't lost a game since Wally Lemm took over as head coach three months back, stubbornly defended their 3-0 lead throughout the third quarter and added to it late in the period. The Oilers had the ball on the San Diego 35-yard line with a third-and-five situation when a strong Charger pass rush forced Blanda out of his protective pocket. Rolling to his right, Blanda saw halfback Billy Cannon open down the middle and hit him with a pass on the 17-yard line. Cannon made a leaping catch, sidestepped a defender, and raced into the end zone. Blanda's extra point made the score 10-0 and put a heavy load of pressure on the San Diego offense. With Jack Kemp throwing freely, the Chargers broke the ice with a 12-yard George Blair field goal in the first minute of the fourth quarter, but a final San Diego bid fell short when Houston's Julian Spence picked off a Kemp pass on the Oiler 30-yard line with under two minutes left in the game.

SCORING

SAN DIEGO	0	0	0	3	– 3
HOUSTON	0	3	7	0	–10

Second Quarter
Hous. Blanda, 46 yard field goal 8:06

Third Quarter
Hous. Cannon, 35 yard pass from Blanda
PAT–Blanda (kick) 11:39

Fourth Quarter
S.D. Blair, 12 yard field goal 0:39

TEAM STATISTICS

S.D.		HOUS.
15	First Downs–Total	18
6	First Downs–Rushing	6
8	First Downs–Passing	8
1	First Downs–Penalty	4
2	Fumbles–Number	5
2	Fumbles–Number Lost	1
10	Penalties–Number	5
106	Yards Penalized	68
6	Giveaways	7
7	Takeaways	6
+1	Difference	–1

INDIVIDUAL STATISTICS

SAN DIEGO	No.	Yds.	Avg.	HOUSTON	No.	Yds.	Avg.
RUSHING							
Roberson	8	37	4.6	Tolar	16	52	3.3
Lowe	5	30	6.0	Cannon	15	48	3.2
Lincoln	3	7	2.3	Blanda	2	–4	–2.0
Kemp	4	5	1.3		33	96	2.9
	20	79	4.0				
RECEIVING							
Kocourek	7	123	17.6	Cannon	5	53	10.6
D. Norton	3	48	16.0	Hennigan	5	43	8.6
Flowers	2	17	8.5	Groman	3	32	10.7
Roberson	1	11	11.0	Dewveall	2	10	5.0
Lowe	1	10	10.0	Tolar	2	2	1.0
Scarpitto	1	9	9.0	McLeod	1	20	20.0
Hayes	1	5	5.0		18	160	8.9
Lincoln	1	3	3.0				
	17	226	13.3				
PUNTING							
Maguire	6		33.3	J. Norton	4		41.5
PUNT RETURNS							
Lincoln	1	16	16.0	None			
KICKOFF RETURNS							
Lowe	1	27	27.0	None			
Roberson	1	23	23.0				
	2	50	25.0				
INTERCEPTION RETURNS							
Whitehead	2	45	15.0	Cline	1	7	7.0
McNeil	2	15	7.5	Glick	1	0	0.0
Zeman	2	0	0.0	Johnston	1	0	0.0
	6	60	10.0	Spence	1	0	0.0
					4	7	1.8

PASSING

	Att.	Comp.	Comp. Pct.	Yds.	Int.	Yds/ Att.	Yds/ Comp.	Yards Lost Tackled
SAN DIEGO								
Kemp	32	17	53.1	226	4	7.1	13.3	6–49
HOUSTON								
Blanda	40	18	45.0	160	5	4.0	8.9	0
Gorman	1	0	0.0	0	1	–	–	0
	41	18	43.9	160	6	3.9	8.9	0

HOUSTON OILERS 10-3-1 Lou Rymkus Wally Lemm

Scores of Each Game		
55	OAKLAND	0
24	San Diego	34
21	Dallas	26
12	BUFFALO	22
31	Boston	31
38	DALLAS	7
28	Buffalo	16
55	Denver	14
27	BOSTON	15
49	NEW YORK	13
45	DENVER	14
33	SAN DIEGO	13
48	New York	21
47	Oakland	16

Use Name	Pos.	Hgt	Wgt	Age	Int	Pts
Al Jamison	OT	6'5"	245	24		
Bob Kelly	OT	6'3"	250	21		
Rich Michael	OT	6'3"	230	22		
Leo Reed (to DEN)	OG	6'4"	240	21		
Bob Talamini	OG	6'1"	230	22		
Hogan Wharton	OG	6'2"	245	25		
Bob Schmidt	C	6'4"	245	25		
Dalva Allen	DE	6'5"	245	25		
Don Floyd	DE	6'4"	225	22		
Dick Frey	OG-DE	6'2"	235	30		
Byron Beams	DT	6'6"	250	27		
Ed Husmann	DT	6'	238	30		
George Shirkey	DT	6'4"	240	24		
Orville Trask	DT	6'4"	260	26	1	

Use Name	Pos.	Hgt	Wgt	Age	Int	Pts
Ron Botcham	LB	6'1"	230	26		
Doug Cline	LB	6'2"	220	22	1	12
Mike Dukes	LB	6'3"	230	25	2	
John Guzik	LB	6'3"	228	24		
Gene Jones	LB	6'	200	24		
Jack Laraway	LB	6'1"	215	25	1	
Dennit Morris	LB	6'1"	225	25	1	
Tony Banfield	DB	6'1"	185	22	8	
Freddy Glick	DB	6'1"	190	24	4	
Mark Johnston	DB	6'	200	23	3	6
Charley Milstead	DB	6'2"	190	23	2	1
Jim Norton	DB	6'3"	190	22	9	
Gary Wisener	DB	6'1"	205	23		
Julian Spence	FL-DB	5'11"	158	32	1	

Use Name	Pos.	Hgt	Wgt	Age	Int	Pts
George Blanda	QB	6'1"	210	33		112
Jacky Lee	QB	6'1"	185	22		
Billy Cannon	HB	6'1"	212	24		90
Ken Hall (to STL-N)	HB	6'1"	210	25		6
Claude King	HB	5'11"	185	22		18
Dave Smith	FB	6'1"	210	24		18
Charley Tolar	FB	5'7"	200	23		30
Charley Hennigan	FL	6'	185	25		72
Willard Dewveall	OE	6'4"	220	24		18
Bill Groman	OE	6'	195	25		108
Bob McLeod	OE	6'5"	225	22		12
John White	OE	6'4"	230	23		6

BOSTON PATRIOTS 9-4-1 Lou Saban Mike Holovak

Scores of Each Game		
20	NEW YORK	21
45	DENVER	17
23	Buffalo	21
30	New York	37
27	SAN DIEGO	38
31	HOUSTON	31
52	BUFFALO	21
18	Dallas	17
28	DALLAS	21
15	Houston	27
20	OAKLAND	17
28	Denver	24
35	Oakland	21
41	San Diego	0

Use Name	Pos.	Hgt	Wgt	Age	Int	Pts
Jerry DeLucca	OT	6'3"	250	25		
Milt Graham	OT	6'6"	235	27		
Dick Klein (from PIT-N)	OT	6'4"	255	27		
Charley Long	OT	6'3"	240	23		
John Simerson	OT	6'3"	255	26		
Charlie Leo	OG	6'	240	26		
Willis Perkins (from HOU)	OG	6'	240	24		
Tony Sardisco	OG	6'2"	235	28		
Walt Cudzik	C	6'2"	235	28		
Bob Yates	C	6'3"	230	22		
Bob Dee	DE	6'3"	240	28		
Larry Eisenhauer	DE	6'5"	235	21		
Leroy Moore	DE	6'	232	25		
Houston Antwine	DT	6'	250	22		
Jim Hunt	DT	5'11"	245	22		
Paul Lindquist	DT	6'3"	265	23		

Use Name	Pos.	Hgt	Wgt	Age	Int	Pts
Tom Addison	LB	6'3"	235	25	4	
Harry Jacobs	LB	6'2"	235	24		
Rommie Loudd	LB	6'3"	230	27	1	
Frank Robotti	LB	6'	220	22	2	
Walter Beach	DB	6'	185	26	1	
Fred Bruney	DB	5'10"	190	30	2	
Ron Hall	DB	6'	190	24	2	
Ross O'Hanley	DB	6'	175	22		
Al Romine	DB	6'2"	195	28		
Chuck Shonta	DB	6'	190	23	1	
Bob Soltis	DB	6'2"	205	24		
Bobby Towns	DB	6'1"	180	23		
Don Webb	DB	5'10"	180	22	5	24
Clyde Washington	HB-DB	6'	195	23	4	

Oscar Lofton – Military Service

Use Name	Pos.	Hgt	Wgt	Age	Int	Pts
Babe Parilli	QB	6'1"	190	31		32
Butch Songin	QB	6'2"	205	37		6
Tom Yewcic	HB-QB	5'11"	185	29		6
Ron Burton	HB	5'10"	190	24		18
Larry Garron	HB	6'	200	24		36
Ray Ratkowski	HB	6'	195	21		
Ger Schwedes	HB	6'1"	205	22		
Jim Crawford	FB	6'1"	205	25		
Billy Lott	FB	6'	205	26		66
Gino Cappelletti	FL	6'	190	27		147
Jim Colclough	OE	6'	185	25		54
Joe Johnson	OE	6'	195	31		6
Bill Kimber	OE	6'2"	190	25		
Tom Stephens	OE	6'1"	195	25		18

George McGee – Military Service

NEW YORK TITANS 7-7-0 Sammy Baugh

Scores of Each Game		
21	Boston	20
31	Buffalo	41
35	DENVER	28
37	BOSTON	30
10	SAN DIEGO	25
10	Denver	27
14	Oakland	6
13	San Diego	48
23	OAKLAND	12
13	Houston	49
21	BUFFALO	14
28	DALLAS	7
21	HOUSTON	48
24	Dallas	35

Use Name	Pos.	Hgt	Wgt	Age	Int	Pts
Gene Cockrell	OT	6'3"	247	28		
Moses Gray	OT	6'3"	260	23		
Jack Klotz	OT	6'5"	260	27		
Ed Walsh	OT	6'4"	243	25		
Tom Budrewicz	OG	6'2"	245	24		
John McMullan	OG	6'	244	26		
Bob Mischak	OG	6'	240	28		
Bob O'Neil	OG	6'1"	238	28		
Roger Ellis	C	6'3"	233	23		
Mike Hudock	C	6'2"	245	26		
Ed Cooke	DE	6'4"	250	26	3	
Nick Mumley	DE	6'6"	255	25		
Bob Reifsnyder	DE	6'2"	260	24		
Dick Guesman	DT	6'4"	255	25		39
Proverb Jacobs	DT	6'4"	255	26		
Tom Saidock	DT	6'5"	260	29		
Sid Youngelman	DE-DT	6'3"	265	29		

Use Name	Pos.	Hgt	Wgt	Age	Int	Pts
Hubert Bobo	LB	6'1"	218	26	4	
Jerry Fields	LB	6'1"	222	22		
Jim Furey	LB	6'	228	27		
Larry Grantham	LB	6'	205	22	1	
Johnny Bookman	DB	5'11"	185	26	6	
Dick Felt	DB	6'	180	28	4	6
Don Flynn (from DAL)	DB	6'	205	26	2	
Paul Hynes (from DAL)	DB	6'1"	210	21		
Dainard Paulson	DB	5'11"	190	24	1	
Bert Rechichar	DB	6'1"	210	31		
Lee Riley	DB	6'1"	190	29	4	
Junior Wren	DB	6'	192	31	1	

Use Name	Pos.	Hgt	Wgt	Age	Int	Pts
Don Allard	QB	6'	190	25		
Al Dorow	QB	6'	195	31		24
Dick Jamieson	QB	6'1"	192	25		
Bob Scrabis	QB	6'3"	225	25		6
Jim Apple	HB	6'	200	22		
Dick Christy	HB	5'10"	195	25		30
Bob Renn	HB	6'	180	27		6
Bill Shockley (to BUF)	HB	6'	185	23		25
Mel West (from BOS)	HB	5'9"	190	22		18
Bob Brooks	FB	6'	215	21		
Bill Mathis	FB	6'1"	220	22		48
Don Maynard	FL	6'	185	25		48
Thurlow Cooper	OE	6'4"	228	28		24
Curley Johnson	OE	6'	215	26		
Art Powell	OE	6'3"	212	24		30

BUFFALO BILLS 6-8-0 Buster Ramsey

Scores of Each Game		
10	DENVER	22
41	NEW YORK	31
21	BOSTON	23
11	SAN DIEGO	19
22	Houston	12
27	DALLAS	24
21	Boston	52
16	HOUSTON	28
22	OAKLAND	31
30	Dallas	20
23	Denver	10
14	New York	21
26	Oakland	21
10	San Diego	28

Use Name	Pos.	Hgt	Wgt	Age	Int	Pts
Don Chelf	OT	6'3"	235	26		
Harold Olson	OT	6'3"	260	22		
Ken Rice	OT	6'2"	250	21		
John Dittrich	OG	6'1"	240	28		
Ed Muelhaupt	OG	6'3"	230	25		6
Billy Shaw	OG	6'3"	240	21		
Wayne Wolf	OG	6'2"	243	22		
Al Bemiller	C	6'3"	225	22		
Lavern Torczon	DE	6'2"	235	25		
Mack Yoho	DE	6'2"	240	25	1	
Tom Day	DE	6'2"	245	26		
Chuck McMurtry	DT	6'	285	23		
John Scott	DT	6'4"	260	25		
Jim Sorey	DT	6'4"	280	24		

Use Name	Pos.	Hgt	Wgt	Age	Int	Pts
Stew Barber	OT-LB	6'3"	235	22	3	6
Ralph Felton	LB	5'11"	210	29	2	
Joe Hergert	LB	6'1"	215	25	1	18
Cotton Letner	LB	6'1"	215	24		
Archie Matsos	LB	6'	215	26	2	
Billy Atkins	DB	6'1"	195	26	10	41
Jim Crotty (from WAS-N)	DB	5'11"	190	23	2	
Jack Johnson (to DAL)	DB	6'3"	200	27		
Billy Majors	DB	6'	175	22		
Richie McCabe	DB	6'1"	187	27	1	
Don McDonald	DB	5'11"	185	24		6
Vern Valdez	DB	5'11"	190	25	2	
Jim Wagstaff	DB	6'2"	190	25	3	

Use Name	Pos.	Hgt	Wgt	Age	Int	Pts
Johnny Green	QB	6'3"	198	24		6
Tom O'Connell	QB	5'11"	180	29		
Warren Rabb	QB	6'1"	204	24		2
M. C. Reynolds	QB	6'	195	26		24
Richie Lucas	DB-HB-QB	6'	190	22	2	12
Dewey Bohling (from NY)	HB	5'11"	190	22		18
Fred Brown	HB	5'11"	187	21		12
Wray Carlton	HB	6'2"	210	23		24
Dan Chamberlain	HB	6'4"	200	24		
Elbert Dubenion	HB	6'	190	26		48
Willmer Fowler	HB	5'11"	185	24		
Art Baker	FB	6'	220	23		18
Glenn Bass	OE	6'2"	190	22		18
Monte Crockett	OE	6'3"	210	22		
Perry Richards	OE	6'2"	205	27		18
Tom Rychlec	OE	6'3"	220	27		12

HOUSTON OILERS

RUSHING

Last Name	No.	Yds	Avg	TD
Cannon	200	948	4.7	6
Tolar	157	577	3.7	4
Smith	60	258	4.3	2
King	12	50	4.2	2
Lee	8	36	4.5	0
Hall	7	13	1.9	0
Blanda	7	12	1.7	0
Groman	1	2	2.0	1

RECEIVING

Last Name	No.	Yds	Avg	TD
Hennigan	82	1746	21	12
Groman	50	1175	24	17
Cannon	43	586	14	9
Tolar	24	219	9	1
McLeod	14	172	12	2
White	13	238	18	1
Dewveall	12	200	17	3
Smith	10	131	13	1
King	3	83	28	1
Hall	1	20	20	1
Spence	1	14	14	0
Blanda	1	–16	–16	0

PUNT RETURNS

Last Name	No.	Yds	Avg	TD
Cannon	9	70	8	0
King	7	32	5	0
Smith	1	15	15	0
Hall	2	1	1	0

KICKOFF RETURNS

Last Name	No.	Yds	Avg	TD
Cannon	18	439	24	0
King	8	190	24	0
Hall	6	140	23	0
Dukes	4	57	14	0
Tolar	2	42	21	0
Cline	1	24	24	0
Laraway	1	22	22	0
McLeod	1	13	13	0
Wharton	1	8	8	0
Smith	1	5	5	0

PASSING – PUNTING – KICKING

PASSING	Att	Comp	%	Yds	Yd/Att	TD	Int–%	RK
Blanda	362	187	52	3330	9.2	36	22– 6	1
Lee	127	66	52	1205	9.4	12	6– 5	
Cannon	5	0	0	0	0.0	0	1– 20	
Smith	2	1	50	33	16.5	0	0– 0	
Groman	1	0	0	0	0.0	0	0– 0	
Tolar	1	0	0	0	0.0	0	0– 0	

PUNTING	No	Avg
Norton	48	40.7
Hall	8	29.8

KICKING	XP	Att	%	FG	Att	%
Blanda	64	65	98	16	26	62
Milstead	1	1	100	0	0	0

BOSTON PATRIOTS

RUSHING

Last Name	No.	Yds	Avg	TD
Lott	100	461	4.7	5
Garron	69	389	5.6	2
Burton	82	260	3.2	2
Parilli	38	183	4.8	5
Crawford	41	148	3.6	0
Yewcic	11	51	4.6	1
Songin	8	39	4.9	0
Colclough	3	37	12.3	0
Schwedes	10	14	1.4	0
Washington	1	3	3.0	0

RECEIVING

Last Name	No.	Yds	Avg	TD
Cappelletti	45	768	17	8
Colclough	42	757	18	9
Lott	32	333	10	6
Garron	24	341	14	3
Stephens	19	186	10	2
Burton	13	115	9	0
Crawford	9	85	9	0
Johnson	9	82	9	1
Yewcic	6	56	9	0
Schwedes	1	21	21	0
Shonta	1	9	9	0

PUNT RETURNS

Last Name	No.	Yds	Avg	TD
Burton	8	128	16	0
Bruney	23	109	5	0
Klein	1	23	23	0
Webb	1	20	20	1
Lott	1	8	8	0
Moore	1	0	0	0

KICKOFF RETURNS

Last Name	No.	Yds	Avg	TD
Garron	16	438	27	1
Burton	15	401	27	1
Beach	2	38	19	0
Long	4	24	6	0
Webb	1	21	21	0
Ratkowski	1	17	17	0
Stephens	1	6	6	0
Schwedes	1	0	0	0
Cudzik	1	0	0	0

PASSING – PUNTING – KICKING

PASSING	Att	Comp	%	Yds	Yd/Att	TD	Int–%	RK
Songin	212	98	46	1429	6.7	14	9– 4	3
Parilli	198	104	53	1314	6.7	13	9– 5	2
Yewcic	8	3	38	25	3.1	1	2– 25	
Burton	1	0	0	0	0.0	0	1–100	
Cappelletti	1	1	100	27	27.0	1	0– 0	

PUNTING	No	Avg
Yewcic	62	38.8

KICKING	XP	Att	%	FG	Att	%
Cappelletti	48	50	96	17	32	53

2 POINT XP
Parilli (1)

NEW YORK TITANS

RUSHING

Last Name	No.	Yds	Avg	TD
Mathis	202	846	4.2	7
West	72	322	4.5	3
Dorow	54	317	5.9	4
Christy	81	180	2.2	2
Brooks	15	55	3.7	0
Renn	1	14	14.0	0
Shockley	5	9	1.8	0
Johnson	1	3	3.0	0
Apple	7	2	0.3	0
Scrabis	1	1	1.0	1

RECEIVING

Last Name	No.	Yds	Avg	TD
Powell	71	881	12	5
Maynard	43	629	15	8
Christy	29	521	18	1
Renn	18	268	15	1
Cooper	15	208	14	4
West	13	146	11	0
Mathis	12	42	4	1
Shockley	3	27	9	0
Johnson	1	32	32	0
O'Neil	1	–13	–13	0

PUNT RETURNS

Last Name	No.	Yds	Avg	TD
Christy	18	383	21	2
West	2	51	26	0
Apple	2	12	6	0
Maynard	1	9	9	0
Shockley	2	6	3	0
Cockrell	1	2	2	0

KICKOFF RETURNS

Last Name	No.	Yds	Avg	TD
Christy	15	360	24	0
West	13	306	24	0
Shockley	12	261	22	0
Renn	10	201	20	0
Brooks	8	111	14	0
Johnson	5	84	17	0
Hynes	2	45	23	0
Saidock	2	26	13	0
Ellis	3	25	8	0
Fields	1	10	10	0
Apple	1	16	16	0
Walsh	2	15	8	0
Budrewicz	1	0	0	0
Cooper	1	0	0	0

PASSING – PUNTING – KICKING

PASSING	Att	Comp	%	Yds	Yd/Att	TD	Int–%	RK
Dorow	438	197	45	2651	6.1	19	30– 7	7
Scrabis	21	7	33	82	3.9	1	2– 10	
Christy	1	0	0	0	0.0	0	0– 0	

PUNTING	No	Avg
Johnson	66	42.7
Wren	8	33.9

KICKING	XP	Att	%	FG	Att	%
Guesman	24	26	92	5	15	33
Shockley	13	13	100	4	9	44
Cooper	0	0	0	0	1	0

BUFFALO BILLS

RUSHING

Last Name	No.	Yds	Avg	TD
Baker	152	498	3.3	3
Carlton	101	311	3.1	4
Brown	53	192	3.6	1
Dubenion	17	173	10.2	2
Bohling	55	153	2.8	2
Reynolds	30	142	4.7	4
Atkins	2	87	43.5	1
Rabb	13	47	3.6	0
Lucas	10	15	1.5	0
Green	14	15	1.1	1
Bass	2	8	4.0	0
Fowler	1	2	2.0	0
Rychlec	1	–18	–18.0	0

RECEIVING

Last Name	No.	Yds	Avg	TD
Bass	50	765	15	3
Rychlec	33	405	12	2
Dubenion	31	461	15	6
Crockett	20	325	16	0
Richards	19	285	15	3
Carlton	17	193	11	0
Bohling	13	217	17	1
Baker	6	73	12	0
Lucas	6	69	12	0
Chamberlain	1	16	16	0
Brown	1	11	11	0

PUNT RETURNS

Last Name	No.	Yds	Avg	TD
Bass	8	75	9	0
Wagstaff	1	35	35	0
Valdez	1	30	30	0
Atkins	2	30	15	0
Brown	2	14	7	0
Dubenion	1	3	3	0
Bohling	4	0	0	0

KICKOFF RETURNS

Last Name	No.	Yds	Avg	TD
Dubenion	16	329	21	0
Baker	12	281	23	0
Bohling	10	246	25	0
Lucas	7	126	18	0
Brown	2	105	53	1
Carlton	4	60	15	0
Rice	2	13	7	0
Richards	1	10	10	0
Crockett	1	0	0	0

PASSING – PUNTING – KICKING

PASSING	Att	Comp	%	Yds	Yd/Att	TD	Int–%	RK
Reynolds	181	83	46	1004	5.6	2	13– 7	9
Green	126	56	44	903	7.2	6	5– 4	
Rabb	74	34	46	586	7.9	5	2– 3	
Lucas	50	20	40	282	5.6	2	4– 8	
O'Connell	5	1	20	11	2.2	0	1– 20	
Carlton	2	0	0	0	0.0	0	0– 0	
Bohling	1	0	0	0	0.0	0	0– 0	

PUNTING	No	Avg
Atkins	84	45.0

KICKING	XP	Att	%	FG	Att	%
Atkins	29	31	94	2	6	33
Hergert	0	0	0	6	14	43
Yoho	0	0	0	0	4	0

2 POINT XP
Lucas (3)
Rabb (1)

SAN DIEGO CHARGERS 12-2-0 Sid Gillman

Scores of Each Game		
26	Dallas	10
44	OAKLAND	0
34	HOUSTON	24
19	Buffalo	11
38	Boston	27
25	New York	10
41	Oakland	10
37	DENVER	0
48	NEW YORK	13
19	Denver	16
24	DALLAS	14
13	Houston	33
28	BUFFALO	10
0	BOSTON	41

Use Name	Pos.	Hgt	Wgt	Age	Int	Pts
Sam DeLuca	OT	6'2"	245	25		
Ron Mix	OT	6'4"	245	23		
Sherman Plunkett	OT	6'4"	285	27		
Ernie Wright	OT	6'4"	270	20		
Ernie Barnes	OG	6'3"	260	22		
Orlando Ferrante	OG	6'	230	28		
Gene Selawski	OT-OG	6'4"	252	25		
Geroge Belotti (from HOU)	C	6'4"	250	26		
Don Rogers	C	6'2"	250	24		
Earl Faison	DE	6'5"	256	22	2	
Ron Nery	DE	6'6"	230	26		
Bill Hudson	DT	6'4"	270	25	1	6
Ernie Ladd	DT	6'9"	315	22		
Henry Schmidt	DT	6'4"	260	24		
Chuck Allen	LB	6'1"	218	21	5	6
Emil Karas	LB	6'3"	230	27	3	
Paul Maguire	LB	6'	215	23	1	
Maury Schleicher	LB	6'3"	240	24		
Bob Laraba	HB-LB	6'3"	195	28	5	19
George Blair	DB	5'11"	190	23	2	81
Claude Gibson	DB	6'1"	190	22	5	2
Dick Harris	DB	5'11"	175	24	7	18
Charley McNeil	DB	5'11"	175	25	9	12
Bud Whitehead	DB	6'	180	22	1	
Bob Zeman	DB	6'1"	203	24	8	6
Hunter Enis	QB	6'2"	190	24		12
Jack Kemp	QB	6'1"	200	27		36
Keith Lincoln	HB	6'2"	205	22		18
Paul Lowe	HB	6'	180	24		54
Bo Roberson	HB	6'1"	185	26		18
Charlie Flowers	FB	6'1"	220	24		18
Bob Scarpitto	FL	5'11"	185	22		12
Howard Clark	OE	6'2"	215	26		
Luther Hayes	OE	6'4"	200	22		18
Dave Kocourek	OE	6'5"	230	24		24
Don Norton	OE	6'1"	185	23		36
Jacque Mackinnon	OG-OE	6'4"	240	22		

DALLAS TEXANS 6-8-0 Hank Stram

Scores of Each Game		
10	SAN DIEGO	26
42	Oakland	35
26	HOUSTON	21
19	Denver	12
24	Buffalo	27
7	Houston	38
17	BOSTON	18
21	Boston	28
20	BUFFALO	30
14	San Diego	24
43	OAKLAND	11
7	New York	28
49	DENVER	21
35	NEW YORK	24

Use Name	Pos.	Hgt	Wgt	Age	Int	Pts
Jerry Cornelison	OT	6'3"	250	24		
Charley Diamond	OT	6'2"	235	25		
Jim Tyrer	OT	6'6"	292	22		
John Cadwell	OG	6'3"	230	22		
Sid Fournet	OG	6'	240	28		
Billy Krisher	OG	6'1"	235	25		
Al Reynolds	OG	6'3"	235	23		
Marvin Terrell	OG	6'1"	235	23		
Jon Gilliam	C	6'2"	225	22		
Mel Branch	DE	6'2"	230	24		
Luther Jeralds	DE	6'3"	235	23		
Paul Miller	DE	6'2"	240	29		
Ray Collins	DT	5'11"	250	33		
Jerry Mays	DT	6'4"	245	21	1	
Walter Napier	DT	6'4"	270	25		
Paul Rochester	DT	6'2"	250	24		
Ted Greene	LB	6'1"	230	27	1	
Sherrill Headrick	LB	6'2"	215	24	2	12
E. J. Holub	LB	6'4"	230	23	1	
Smokey Stover	LB	6'	230	22	2	
Dave Grayson	DB	5'10"	180	22	3	6
Ed Kelley	DB	6'2"	195	26		
Doyle Nix	DB	6'1"	195	28	3	
Dave Webster	DB	6'4"	220	23	5	
Duane Wood	DB	6'1"	190	25	4	
Cotton Davidson	QB	6'1"	185	28		26
Randy Duncan	QB	6'	185	23		
Tom Greene	QB	6'1"	190	23		
Abner Haynes	HB	6'	180	23		78
Frank Jackson	HB	6'1"	182	21		30
Johnny Robinson	HB	6'	195	22		42
Bo Dickenson	FB	6'2"	210	26		34
Billy Pricer	FB	5'10"	215	26		
Jack Spikes	FB	6'2"	225	23		54
Charley Barnes	OE	6'5"	230	24		
Max Boydston	OE	6'2"	210	28		6
Chris Burford	OE	6'3"	210	23		30
Tony Romeo	OE	6'2"	215	22		
Ben Agajanian (to GB-N)	K	6'	220	42		16

DENVER BRONCOS 3-11-0 Frankie Filchock

Scores of Each Game		
22	Buffalo	10
17	Boston	45
28	New York	35
19	Oakland	33
12	DALLAS	19
27	OAKLAND	24
27	NEW YORK	10
0	San Diego	37
14	HOUSTON	55
16	SAN DIEGO	19
10	BUFFALO	23
14	Houston	45
24	BOSTON	28
21	Dallas	49

Use Name	Pos.	Hgt	Wgt	Age	Int	Pts
Eldon Danenhauer	OT	6'4"	235	25		
Jerry Sturm	FB-OT	6'3"	235	24		
Ken Adamson	OG	6'2"	225	22		
Buzz Guy (from HOU)	OG	6'3"	250	26		
Carl Larpenter	OG	6'4"	235	24		
Jim Barton	C	6'5"	250	26		
Mike Nichols	C	6'3"	225	22		
John Cash	DE	6'3"	230	25		
Chuck Gavin	DE	6'1"	240	27		6
Bob Konovsky	DE	6'2"	250	27		
Joe Young	DE	6'3"	245	26		
Art Hauser	DT	6'	240	30		
Gordy Holz	DT	6'4"	270	27		
Jack Mattox	DT	6'4"	240	22		
Bud McFadin	DT	6'3"	280	33		
Jim Eifrid	LB	6'1"	240	23		
Bob Griffin (to STL-N)	LB	6'3"	250	32		
Bob Hudson	LB	6'4"	235	31	3	
Pat Lamberti (from NY)	LB	6'2"	225	23	1	
Wahoo McDaniel	LB	6'	240	24		
Bill Roehnelt	LB	6'1"	225	25		
Jackie Simpson	LB	6'1"	230	24		
Jerry Stalcup	LB	6'	240	23		
Goose Gonsoulin	DB	6'3"	205	23	6	
Jim McMillin	DB	5'11"	180	23	5	
Bob McNamara	DB	6'	190	27	3	
Phil Nugent	DB	6'2"	195	22	7	
John Pyeatt	DB	6'3"	204	27		
Jimmy Sears	DB	5'11"	187	30		
Dan Smith	DB	5'10"	180	26		
George Herring	QB	6'2"	200	26		12
Frank Tripucka	QB	6'2"	205	33		
Buddy Allen	HB	5'10"	190	23		
Al Carmichael	HB	6'1"	195	31		
Dale Evans	HB	6'3"	210	22		
Al Frazier	HB	5'11"	180	26		50
Jack Hill	HB	6'1"	185	27		31
Gene Mingo	HB	6'1"	200	22		32
Donnie Stone	HB	6'2"	205	24		48
Jerry Traynham	HB	5'10"	190	22		
Dave Ames (from NY)	DB-HB	6'	185	24	1	
Fred Bukaty	FB	5'11"	195	22		32
Jim Stinnette	LB-FB	6'1"	230	23	1	6
Gene Prebola	OE	6'3"	215	23		8
Lionel Taylor	OE	6'2"	214	25		24

OAKLAND RAIDERS 2-12-0 Marty Feldman

Scores of Each Game		
0	Houston	55
0	San Diego	44
35	DALLAS	42
33	DENVER	19
24	Denver	27
10	SAN DIEGO	41
6	NEW YORK	14
31	Buffalo	22
12	New York	23
17	Boston	20
11	Dallas	43
21	BUFFALO	26
21	BOSTON	35
16	HOUSTON	47

Use Name	Pos.	Hgt	Wgt	Age	Int	Pts
Jim Brewington	OT	6'6"	280	22		
Cliff Roberts	OT	6'3"	260	26		
Ron Sabal	OT	6'2"	245	24		
Jack Stone	OT	6'2"	245	24		
Wayne Hawkins	OG	6'	235	23		
Herb Roedel	OG	6'3"	230	22		
Willie Smith	OG	6'2"	255	23		
Jim Otto	C	6'2"	240	23		
Jon Jelacic	DE	6'3"	255	24		
Charley Powell	DE	6'2"	245	29		
George Fields	DT	6'3"	245	25		
Gary Finneran	DT	6'3"	240	27		
Harry Jagielski (from BOS)	DT	6'	260	29	1	
Volney Peters	DT	6'4"	245	32		
Hal Smith	DT	6'5"	250	26		
Bob Voight	DT	6'5"	265	24		
Al Bansavage	LB	6'2"	220	23		
Bob Dougherty	LB	6'	240	27	2	
Tom Louderback	LB	6'2"	235	27	1	6
Riley Morris	LB	6'2"	230	24	3	6
Alex Bravo	DB	6'	190	29	2	
Joe Cannavino	DB	5'11"	185	25	5	
Bob Garner	DB	5'10"	190	26	2	
John Harris	DB	6'1"	195	28	3	
Fred Williamson	DB	6'2"	205	23	5	
Tom Flores	QB	6'1"	190	24		6
Nick Papac	QB	5'11"	190	26		6
Wayne Crow	HB	6'	205	23		14
Clem Daniels	HB	6'1"	220	24		12
George Fleming	HB	5'11"	188	22		63
Charley Fuller	HB	5'11"	176	22		12
Jack Larschied	HB	5'6"	162	27		
Jim Jones	FB	6'1"	212	25		
Walt Kowalczyk	FB	6'	216	26		
Alan Miller	FB	6'	197	23		42
Doug Asad	OE	6'3"	205	23		12
Jerry Burch	OE	6'1"	195	21		6
Bob Coolbaugh	OE	6'3"	200	21		26
Charley Hardy	OE	6'	185	27		24

SAN DIEGO CHARGERS

RUSHING

Last Name	No.	Yds	Avg	TD
Lowe	175	767	4.4	9
Roberson	58	275	4.7	3
Flowers	51	177	3.5	3
Lincoln	41	150	3.7	0
Kemp	43	105	2.4	6
Enis	16	13	0.8	2
Laraba	5	5	1.0	1

RECEIVING

Last Name	No.	Yds	Avg	TD
Kocourek	55	1055	19	4
Norton	47	816	17	6
Lowe	17	103	6	0
Flowers	16	175	11	0
Hayes	14	280	20	3
Lincoln	12	208	17	2
Clark	11	182	17	0
Scarpitto	9	163	18	2
Roberson	6	81	14	0
MacKinnon	3	58	19	0

PUNT RETURNS

Last Name	No.	Yds	Avg	TD
Gibson	14	209	15	0
Lincoln	7	150	21	1
Scarpitto	4	47	12	0
Zeman	2	47	24	1
Selawski	1	5	5	0
Lowe	1	0	0	0

KICKOFF RETURNS

Last Name	No.	Yds	Avg	TD
Lowe	10	240	24	0
Roberson	13	207	16	0
Lincoln	4	98	25	0
Scarpitto	3	50	17	0
Schmidt	1	22	22	0
Gibson	3	17	6	0
Karas	1	5	5	0
Blair	1	2	2	0
Selawski	1	1	1	0
Mix	1	0	0	0
Ferrante	1	0	0	0

PASSING – PUNTING – KICKING

PASSING	Att	Comp	%	Yds	Yd/Att	TD	Int–%	RK
Kemp	364	165	45	2686	7.4	15	22– 6	5
Enis	55	23	42	365	6.6	2	3– 5	
Lowe	4	2	50	70	17.5	0	0– 0	

PUNTING	No	Avg
Maguire	62	42.2

KICKING	XP	Att	%	FG	Att	%
Blair	42	47	89	13	27	48
Laraba	1	2	50	0	0	0
Lincoln	0	1	0	0	0	0

2 POINT XP
Gibson (1)

DALLAS TEXANS

RUSHING

Last Name	No.	Yds	Avg	TD
Haynes	179	841	4.7	9
Jackson	65	386	5.9	3
Spikes	39	334	8.6	5
Dickinson	71	263	3.7	3
Robinson	52	200	3.9	2
Davidson	21	123	5.9	1
Duncan	5	42	8.5	0
Pricer	5	13	2.6	0
Gilliam	1	–6	–6.0	0
Burford	1	–13	–13.0	0

RECEIVING

Last Name	No.	Yds	Avg	TD
Burford	51	850	17	5
Robinson	35	601	17	5
Haynes	34	558	16	3
Dickinson	14	209	15	2
Jackson	13	171	13	2
Boydston	12	167	14	1
Spikes	8	136	17	0
Romeo	7	89	13	0
Pricer	2	21	11	0
Barnes	1	13	13	0

PUNT RETURNS

Last Name	No.	Yds	Avg	TD
Haynes	19	196	10	0
Mays	1	12	12	0
Headrick	2	5	3	0
Robinson	2	4	2	0
Jackson	1	2	2	0
Miller	1	0	0	0

KICKOFF RETURNS

Last Name	No.	Yds	Avg	TD
Grayson	16	453	28	0
Jackson	24	645	27	0
Haynes	8	270	34	1
Gilliam	1	23	23	0
Pricer	1	19	19	0
Stover	1	15	15	0
Mays	1	13	13	0

PASSING – PUNTING – KICKING

PASSING	Att	Comp	%	Yds	Yd/Att	TD	Int–%	RK
Davidson	330	151	46	2445	7.4	17	23– 7	5
Duncan	67	25	37	361	5.4	1	3– 4	
Jackson	2	1	50	9	4.5	0	1– 50	

PUNTING	No	Avg
Davidson	61	40.6

KICKING	XP	Att	%	FG	Att	%
Davidson	20	20	100	0	2	0
Spikes	10	13	77	4	13	31
Agajanian	7	7	100	3	9	33

2 POINT XP
Dickinson (2)
Spikes (1)

DENVER BRONCOS

RUSHING

Last Name	No.	Yds	Avg	TD
Stone	127	505	4.0	4
Bukaty	76	187	2.5	5
Ames	19	114	6.0	0
Frazier	23	110	4.8	0
Herring	15	74	4.9	2
Mingo	18	51	2.8	0
Sturm	8	31	3.9	0
Carmichael	15	24	1.6	0
Traynham	6	12	2.0	0
Stinnette	19	8	0.4	0
Allen	3	–4	–1.3	0
Tripucka	4	–8	–2.0	0

RECEIVING

Last Name	No.	Yds	Avg	TD
Taylor	100	1176	13	4
Frazier	47	799	17	6
Stone	38	344	9	4
Prebola	29	349	12	1
Bukaty	14	94	7	0
Stinnette	11	58	5	1
Mingo	8	110	14	2
Ames	6	20	3	0
Carmichael	5	23	5	0
Hill	4	33	8	0
Sturm	2	–1	–1	0
Traynham	1	–1	–1	0

PUNT RETURNS

Last Name	No.	Yds	Avg	TD
Frazier	18	231	13	1
Carmichael	7	58	8	0
Gavin	1	45	45	1
McNamara	4	17	4	0
Ames	2	17	9	0
Mingo	1	1	1	0

KICKOFF RETURNS

Last Name	No.	Yds	Avg	TD
Frazier	18	504	28	1
Carmichael	16	310	19	0
Ames	12	240	20	0
Stone	9	215	24	0
Mingo	4	120	30	0
Bukaty	3	41	14	0
Gonsoulin	1	34	34	0
Hill	1	23	23	0
Prebola	1	8	8	0
Stinnette	1	6	6	0

PASSING – PUNTING – KICKING

PASSING	Att	Comp	%	Yds	Yd/Att	TD	Int–%	RK
Tripucka	344	167	49	1690	4.9	10	21– 6	8
Herring	211	93	44	1160	5.5	5	22– 10	10
Mingo	8	4	50	136	17.0	2	0– 0	
Stone	2	1	50	18	9.0	1	0– 0	
Taylor	2	0	0	0	0.0	0	1– 50	
Frazier	1	0	0	0	0.0	0	1–100	

PUNTING	No	Avg
Herring	80	39.4

KICKING	XP	Att	%	FG	Att	%
Hill	16	16	100	5	15	33
Mingo	11	11	100	3	10	30

2 POINT XP
Bukaty (1)
Frazier (1)
Prebola (1)

OAKLAND RAIDERS

RUSHING

Last Name	No.	Yds	Avg	TD
Crow	119	490	4.1	2
Miller	85	255	3.0	3
Daniels	31	154	5.1	2
Fuller	38	134	3.5	0
Fleming	31	112	3.6	1
Flores	23	36	1.6	1
Papac	6	28	4.7	1
Kowalczyk	10	28	2.8	0
Larschied	6	3	0.5	0

RECEIVING

Last Name	No.	Yds	Avg	TD
Asad	36	501	14	2
Miller	36	315	9	4
Coolbaugh	32	435	14	4
Hardy	24	337	14	4
Crow	23	196	9	0
Burch	18	235	13	1
Daniels	13	150	12	0
Fuller	12	277	23	2
Fleming	10	49	5	0
Kowalczyk	3	8	3	0
Larschied	2	11	6	0

PUNT RETURNS

Last Name	No.	Yds	Avg	TD
Fuller	4	52	13	0
Daniels	5	34	7	0
Fleming	3	24	8	0
Garner	2	5	3	0
H. Smith	1	2	2	0

KICKOFF RETURNS

Last Name	No.	Yds	Avg	TD
Fleming	29	588	20	0
Daniels	13	276	21	0
Larschied	9	254	28	0
Fuller	8	155	19	0
Miller	6	66	11	0
Kowalczyk	1	19	19	0
Coolbaugh	1	15	15	0
Asad	1	10	10	0

PASSING – PUNTING – KICKING

PASSING	Att	Comp	%	Yds	Yd/Att	TD	Int–%	RK
Flores	366	190	52	2176	6.0	15	19– 5	3
Papac	44	13	30	173	3.9	2	7– 16	
Crow	10	6	60	165	16.5	0	0– 0	
Fleming	1	0	0	0	0.0	0	1–100	
Fuller	1	0	0	0	0.0	0	0– 0	
Larschied	1	0	0	0	0.0	0	1–100	

PUNTING	No	Avg
Crow	61	42.8
Burch	11	28.6

KICKING	XP	Att	%	FG	Att	%
Fleming	24	25	96	11	26	42

2 POINT XP
Coolbaugh (1)
Crow (1)

1962 N.F.L. Millions from the Stay-at-Homes

It was a year of renewal, consolidation, innovation, and departures. Commissioner Pete Rozelle renewed the NFL's television contract with CBS at a new rate of $4.65 million per year, and the club owners rewarded Rozelle with a new five-year contract with a hefty raise. The consolidation took place in Los Angeles, where full control of the Rams was reacquired by Dan Reeves. After taking in Edwin Pauley and Fred Levy as partners, Reeves fell to feuding with his co-owners in recent years, so Rozelle arranged for the submission of secret bids for the controlling interest in the team, which Reeves won. Innovation brought the league a new rule against grabbing another player's face mask, ground-breaking for a Hall of Fame in Canton, Ohio, and a fabulously popular pre-season doubleheader in Cleveland. And leaving the NFL stage this year, by death, were Mrs. Violet Bidwill Wolfner and James Clark, owners of the Cardinals and Eagles, and, by pink slips, long-time coaches Paul Brown and Weeb Ewbank.

EASTERN CONFERENCE

New York Giants—After fourteen years of professional football, thirty-five-year-old Y. A. Tittle became an overnight sensation as the Giant quarterback. Tittle set a new NFL record of thirty-three touchdown passes in a season, including seven in one game against the Redskins, but his style captivated New York fans more than his passing. He would retreat to his protective pocket and calmly survey the field, a thin, middle-aged man defying the behemoths rushing at him. He would back-pedal with tacklers closing in on him and flip an unexpected screen pass to Alex Webster behind a covey of blockers. Near the goal line he often ran the ball in on the bootleg play, outsprinting the deceived defenders on his aged legs. With a strong cast of players surrounding Tittle, the Giants got to the championship game by winning their last nine games.

Pittsburgh Steelers—Bobby Layne had reason to smile after his final NFL season. He wound up his career with 196 touchdown passes, surpassing Sammy Baugh's old mark of 186, and he led the Steelers to three straight wins at the end of the year to capture second place in the East. Other oldsters besides Layne turned in key performances, such as John Henry Johnson, Ernie Stautner, and Big Daddy Lipscomb. Holdover receiver Buddy Dial starred as a deep threat, and newcomer Lou Michaels excelled as a place-kicker. Perhaps the most important job was coach Buddy Parker's patch-up of the defense after injuries wiped out all his linebackers and personal differences elbowed Johnny Sample into disfavor.

Cleveland Browns—The Paul Brown era crashed to an end in a year of disappointment and tragedy. Brown had traded fleet Bobby Mitchell to Washington for the draft rights to Heisman Trophy winner Ernie Davis of Syracuse. Davis, a powerful halfback, was expected to team with Jimmy Brown in a strong running duo, but leukemia struck the rookie down before he ever played a professional game. With no good running halfbacks to divert the enemy's forces, fullback Brown for the first time ever failed to win the league rushing crown. After a lackluster campaign in which the Browns were never contenders, owner Art Modell shocked the football world by firing the most successful coach in pro-football history.

Washington Redskins—The Redskins fielded their first black players this year in Bobby Mitchell, John Nisby, Leroy Jackson, and Ron Hatcher, and the club's fortunes immediately rocketed upward. Mitchell, obtained from Cleveland for the draft rights to Ernie Davis, set the league on fire with his spectacular receiving from his new flanker position, and with quarterback Norm Snead getting good protection from the bolstered offensive line, an all-out passing attack brought the Skins four wins and two ties in their first six contests before their running game and loose pass defense caught up with them.

Dallas Cowboys—Coach Tom Landry had been a great defensive player, but his coaching genius was in a different direction. The Dallas offense was the second best in the league, trailing only the Packers in points scored, but the Dallas defense was the second worst in the league, with only Minnesota allowing more points. Landry got good mileage out of quarterbacks Eddie LeBaron and Don Meredith by shuffling them in and out of the lineup on every play. But once LeBaron was injured in mid-season and Meredith had to go it alone at quarterback, the attack slipped and the Cowboys dropped five of their last six matches.

St. Louis Cardinals—Although Wally Lemm turned out a losing squad in his first year on the job, he did uncover a fine young passer in Charley Johnson. After sitting on the bench last year and beginning this season as Sam Etcheverry's back-up, Johnson won the quarterback job four games into the season. During the remaining stretch he learned by experience and threw a lot of passes to his complementary receivers, speedster Sonny Randle and sure-handed Bobby Joe Conrad. But even with strong running from John David Crow, the attack never caught fire, due to a mediocre line.

Philadelphia Eagles—The fair Philadelphia defense had sufficed when the offense was churning out points at a furious pace, but injuries this year crippled the attack and sent the Eagles tumbling into last place. Quarterback Sonny Jurgensen, still bothered by a shoulder separation suffered in last season's Playoff Bowl, found himself throwing the ball to a bunch of strangers. Only Tommy McDonald stayed healthy among the receivers, as Pete Retzlaff, Bobby Walston, and Dick Lucas all broke arms and Hopalong Cassady broke a leg, while runner Ted Dean joined the parade with a broken foot.

WESTERN CONFERENCE

Green Bay Packers—Even with Paul Hornung below par physically, the Packers overwhelmed the league with All-Pro performances. Fullback Jim Taylor, whose strong point was neither size nor speed but meanness, took the rushing title away from Jimmy Brown and also led the league in scoring with nineteen touchdowns. Bart Starr compiled the best passing record in the circuit, while Willie Wood intercepted the most aerials. The wire service All-Pro teams were overloaded with Packers as fullback Taylor, end Ron Kramer, offensive linemen Forrest Gregg, Jerry Kramer, Fuzzy Thurston, and Jim Ringo, defensive linemen Willie Davis and Henry Jordan, linebackers Bill Forester and Dan Currie, and cornerback Herb Adderley all won honors.

Detroit Lions—Eleven wins are usually good enough for a championship, but the Lions had to settle for second place in the West behind the stampeding Green Bay Packers. The Lions did expose Vince Lombardi's supermen as mere mortals, however, in their Thanksgiving Day meeting in Detroit. The unbeaten Packers that day ran up against a fired-up Detroit defense that turned in an almost perfect performance. Tackle Roger Brown constantly blasted into the Green Bay backfield, linebacker Joe Schmidt blitzed Packer quarterback Bart Starr into the ground, and the defensive unit kept the Packers scoreless until late in the 26-14 upset victory.

Chicago Bears—Like the Packers and Lions, the Bears had a tough defense at the core of the team. The front four and secondary were solid if not spectacular, but the linebacking corps of Joe Fortunato, Bill George, and Larry Morris ranked with the NFL's best. Offensively, coach George Halas had to scramble around for runners when injuries sidelined Rick Casares and Willie Galimore. Ex-Ram Joe Marconi did a yeoman's job at fullback, while freshman Ronnie Bull hustled enough to win Rookie of the Year honors. The air attack moved well on Billy Wade's passes to Mike Ditka and Johnny Morris, but the defense dominated the Bears, as a bruising 3-0 victory over the Lions to close the season underlined.

Baltimore Colts—The last few seasons had been lackluster, and a 7-7 record this season brought coach Weeb Ewbank's regime to an end. Quarterback Johnny Unitas still was the consummate passer and signal-caller, but his supporting cast was looking slightly worn. The running attack was weak, the offensive line was aging, and the place-kicking was unsure. Strong points included a competent defense and a pair of good receivers in Jimmy Orr and Ray Berry, but not enough to save coach Ewbank's job.

San Francisco '49ers—Before the season started, coach Red Hickey called this club the best football team he had ever coached. But once the schedule began, injuries turned the '49ers into a very ordinary team. Tackle Bob St. Clair, the team's best offensive lineman, went to the sidelines with an injured Achilles tendon, and halfback Billy Kilmer, an exciting runner, passer, and blocker, missed the final three games after breaking a leg in a car accident. The defense also slipped a notch, as too much youth subverted the secondary and too much age cut down on tackle Leo Nomellini's quickness.

Minnesota Vikings—The Vikings couldn't match the three wins of their first campaign, but coach Norm Van Brocklin was gathering good young players who would later make Minnesota a title contender. Free agent Mick Tingelhoff won the center's job, rookie linebacker Roy Winston showed promise, and cornerback Ed Sharockman had a good NFL debut after missing 1961 with a broken leg. Aside from these three freshmen, improvement came from youngsters already on the roster, such as quarterback Fran Tarkenton, halfback Tommy Mason, tackle Grady Alderman, defensive end Jim Marshall, and middle linebacker Rip Hawkins.

Los Angeles Rams—Dan Reeves bought out partners Edwin Pauley and Fred Levy, thus ending the front-office bickering that had plagued the team in recent years. But while the ownership picture cleared up, the squad on the field collapsed in a wreck. The Rams won only one game all season, with their offense the worst in the league. Head coach Bob Waterfield tired of all the losing and quit after eight games, leaving the battered team to assistant Harland Svare. But even this season, the worst in Ram history, turned up two bright spots in rookies Merlin Olsen and Roman Gabriel.

FINAL TEAM STATISTICS

OFFENSE

	BALT.	CHI.	CLEVE.	DALLAS	DET.	G.BAY	L.A.	MINN.	N.Y.	PHIL.	PITT.	ST.L.	S.F.	WASH.
FIRST DOWNS:														
Total	251	228	252	246	243	281	201	223	267	235	261	268	239	241
by Rushing	94	88	105	101	103	145	84	102	92	76	133	109	112	59
by Passing	145	128	133	136	124	120	107	107	150	146	112	138	112	156
by Penalty	12	12	14	9	16	16	10	14	25	13	16	21	15	26
RUSHING:														
Numbers	448	386	414	434	489	518	376	426	430	324	572	416	460	371
Yards	1601	1489	1772	2040	1922	2460	1689	1864	1698	1155	2333	1698	1873	1088
Average Yards	3.6	3.9	4.3	4.7	3.9	4.7	4.5	4.4	3.9	3.6	4.1	4.1	4.1	2.9
Touchdowns	9	17	18	16	14	36	10	7	11	13	17	20	15	10
PASSING:														
Attempts	423	430	370	380	379	311	372	348	411	428	319	434	323	428
Completions	237	229	200	200	211	187	189	170	215	228	160	220	185	223
Completion Pct.	56.0	53.3	54.1	52.6	55.7	60.1	50.8	48.9	52.3	53.3	50.2	50.7	57.3	52.1
Passing Yardage	3330	3286	2747	3115	2827	2621	2524	2699	3446	3632	2419	3388	2491	3532
Avg. Yds per Att.	7.9	7.6	7.4	8.2	7.5	8.4	6.8	7.8	8.4	8.5	7.6	7.8	7.7	8.3
Avg. Yds per Comp.	14.1	14.3	13.7	15.6	13.4	14.0	13.4	15.9	16.0	15.9	15.1	15.4	13.5	15.8
Yards Lost Tackled	265	226	213	243	246	290	348	483	139	247	350	288	423	309
Net Yards	3065	3060	2534	2872	2581	2331	2176	2216	3307	3385	2069	3100	2068	3223
Touchdowns	27	20	17	31	19	14	14	22	35	23	14	18	19	27
Interceptions	25	28	16	17	24	13	19	31	22	31	23	30	19	27
Pct. Intercepted	5.9	6.5	4.3	4.5	6.3	4.2	5.1	8.9	5.4	7.2	7.2	6.9	5.9	6.3
PUNTING:														
Number	58	69	45	57	53	50	87	65	55	64	60	59	48	63
Average Distance	41.5	43.7	42.8	45.4	45.3	40.9	45.5	40.3	40.6	42.9	40.0	38.3	45.6	34.5
PUNT RETURNS:														
Number	34	39	20	17	39	31	27	34	17	14	19	20	27	29
Yards	272	281	111	81	502	290	252	374	58	95	169	134	207	184
Average Yards	8.0	7.2	5.6	4.8	12.9	9.4	9.3	11.0	3.4	6.8	8.9	6.7	7.7	6.3
Touchdowns	0	1	0	0	0	0	0	0	0	0	0	0	1	0
KICKOFF RETURNS:														
Number	55	53	46	59	46	30	60	67	54	61	62	64	62	61
Yards	1263	1129	983	1207	1124	716	1447	1522	1405	1385	1350	1495	1739	1720
Average Yards	23.0	21.3	21.4	20.5	24.4	23.9	24.1	22.7	26.0	22.7	21.8	23.4	28.0	28.2
Touchdowns	0	0	0	1	0	1	0	0	1	1	0	0	0	1
INTERCEPTION RETURNS:														
Number	23	23	24	20	24	31	19	25	26	26	28	16	12	28
Yards	331	468	352	366	269	452	261	280	332	289	318	229	127	285
Average Yards	14.4	20.3	14.7	18.3	11.2	14.6	13.7	11.2	12.8	11.1	11.4	14.3	10.6	10.2
Touchdowns	0	2	0	1	2	1	2	1	0	0	2	1	0	0
PENALTIES:														
Number	63	69	66	62	62	60	71	44	62	58	45	58	63	62
Yards	675	776	600	639	624	617	704	447	601	619	427	655	636	663
FUMBLES:														
Number	26	29	24	32	26	29	26	37	24	25	24	36	24	31
Number Lost	19	16	17	19	18	15	16	23	14	13	13	21	14	17
POINTS:														
Total	293	321	291	398	315	415	220	254	398	282	312	287	282	305
PAT Attempts	37	41	36	51	38	53	27	31	49	38	33	39	36	39
PAT Made	31	36	33	50	37	52	26	31	47	36	32	38	36	38
FG Attempts	28	27	31	27	34	21	20	25	28	19	42	14	23	25
FG Made	12	13	14	14	14	15	10	11	19	6	26	5	10	11
Percent FG Made	42.9	48.1	45.2	51.9	41.2	71.4	50.0	44.0	67.9	31.6	61.9	35.7	43.5	44.0
Safeties	2	0	0	0	4	0	1	2	0	0	2	0	0	0

DEFENSE

	BALT.	CHI.	CLEVE.	DALLAS	DET.	G.BAY	L.A.	MINN.	N.Y.	PHIL.	PITT.	ST.L.	S.F.	WASH.
FIRST DOWNS:														
Total	226	228	263	274	180	191	256	266	256	275	250	251	240	280
by Rushing	91	108	122	93	62	88	119	119	100	128	78	93	107	95
by Passing	119	101	125	166	105	94	124	139	136	129	157	141	113	165
by Penalty	16	19	16	15	13	9	13	8	20	18	15	17	20	20
RUSHING:														
Numbers	423	438	466	387	353	404	501	463	413	526	363	452	464	411
Yards	1504	2073	1940	1510	1231	1531	2092	1978	1677	2126	1419	1724	2241	1636
Average Yards	3.6	4.7	4.2	3.9	3.5	3.8	4.2	4.3	4.1	4.0	3.9	3.8	4.8	4.0
Touchdowns	17	17	17	17	6	4	14	20	13	23	13	18	22	12
PASSING:														
Attempts	381	363	341	437	367	355	379	397	450	363	438	377	296	412
Completions	206	170	189	233	187	187	217	214	223	198	223	196	164	247
Completion Pct.	54.1	46.8	55.4	53.3	51.0	52.7	57.3	53.9	49.6	54.5	50.9	52.0	55.4	60.0
Passing Yardage	2975	2460	2277	3904	2441	2084	3144	3365	3238	3023	3490	3302	2494	3860
Avg. Yds per Att.	7.8	6.8	6.7	8.9	6.7	5.9	8.3	8.5	7.2	8.3	8.0	8.8	8.4	9.4
Avg. Yds per Comp.	14.4	14.5	12.0	16.8	13.1	11.1	14.5	15.7	14.5	15.3	15.7	16.8	15.2	15.6
Yards Lost Tackled	356	386	293	230	455	338	255	242	369	103	284	315	186	258
Net Yards	2619	2074	1984	3674	1986	1746	2889	3123	2869	2920	3206	2987	2308	3602
Touchdowns	19	14	15	33	11	10	25	29	21	16	34	21	17	35
Interceptions	23	23	24	20	24	31	19	25	26	26	28	16	12	28
Pct. Intercepted	6.0	6.3	7.0	4.6	6.5	8.7	5.0	6.3	5.8	7.2	6.4	4.2	4.1	6.8
PUNTING:														
Number	67	71	56	63	70	58	56	52	65	42	62	61	61	49
Average Distance	42.7	41.8	40.6	40.6	44.1	43.2	45.5	43.3	38.8	38.2	40.7	40.6	44.6	42.4
PUNT RETURNS:														
Number	23	32	15	28	31	20	55	32	24	24	18	26	32	7
Yards	182	308	121	190	326	183	567	261	138	174	119	122	285	34
Average Yards	7.9	9.6	8.1	6.8	10.5	9.2	10.3	8.2	5.8	7.3	6.6	4.7	8.9	4.9
Touchdowns	0	0	0	0	0	1	1	0	0	0	0	0	0	0
KICKOFF RETURNS:														
Number	52	60	49	63	55	76	50	52	63	56	54	41	51	58
Yards	1433	1514	1098	1604	1379	1524	1211	1149	1700	1459	1151	870	1140	1253
Average Yards	27.6	25.2	22.4	25.5	25.1	20.1	24.2	22.1	27.0	26.1	21.3	21.2	22.4	21.6
Touchdowns	1	0	0	1	0	0	0	0	0	1	0	0	0	2
INTERCEPTION RETURNS:														
Number	25	28	16	17	24	13	19	31	22	31	23	30	19	27
Yards	386	328	161	263	352	122	293	445	182	555	257	389	334	292
Average Yards	15.4	11.7	10.1	15.5	14.7	9.4	15.4	14.4	8.3	17.9	11.2	13.0	17.6	10.8
Touchdowns	0	1	0	1	0	1	2	1	0	2	0	1	3	0
PENALTIES:														
Number	71	65	53	56	51	54	52	68	58	48	53	63	57	83
Yards	792	643	547	569	527	611	592	633	636	479	581	584	626	863
FUMBLES:														
Number	32	37	23	33	34	28	30	30	30	22	21	23	22	28
Number Lost	19	24	13	16	23	19	18	18	13	13	10	15	14	20
POINTS:														
Total	288	287	257	402	177	148	334	410	283	356	363	361	331	376
PAT Attempts	37	34	34	52	19	17	42	52	35	43	48	44	42	49
PAT Made	35	31	32	49	19	17	38	51	34	41	48	43	39	46
FG Attempts	22	31	14	25	25	22	33	30	27	37	19	33	20	26
FG Made	9	16	7	13	14	9	14	15	13	19	9	18	12	12
Percent FG Made	40.9	51.6	50.0	52.0	56.0	40.9	42.4	50.0	48.1	51.4	47.4	54.5	60.0	46.2
Safeties	2	2	0	1	1	1	1	1	0	0	0	0	2	0

1962 NFL
CHAMPIONSHIP GAME
December 30, at New York
(Attendance 64,892)

A Dismal Homecoming

A bone-chilling thirty-five-mile-per-hour wind lanced through Yankee Stadium, where the temperature was 20 degrees at game time and dropped steadily all afternoon. The Giants were out to avenge last year's loss to the Packers but fell short in a bitterly contested, hard-hitting ground game. The wind and cold made passing close to impossible, so the game was fought out primarily between the opposing lines and power runners. One particularly brutal pairing was Packer fullback Jim Taylor and Giant linebacker Sam Huff, the two of them butting heads constantly all game long. The Packers punched out yardage behind the crisp blocking of their offensive line and scored in the opening period on a 26-yard Jerry Kramer field goal. The Packers got a break in the second quarter when Dan Currie's hard tackle knocked the football loose from Phil King on the Giant 28-yard line. On the first play after the recovery, Paul Hornung passed 21 yards to Boyd Dowler on the halfback option, and Jim Taylor blasted through the line for the last seven yards on the next play. The Packers led 10-0 at halftime, but the Giants finally scored in the third period when Erich Barnes blocked Max McGee's punt and Jim Collier fell on it in the end zone for a touchdown. On the next series of downs, the Packers again punted, but New York's Sam Horner fumbled the ball and Green Bay recovered on the Giant 40-yard line. After that, the Packers never lost momentum, and two more Kramer field goals made the final score 16-7.

TEAM STATISTICS

N. Y.		G. B.
18	First Downs – Total	18
5	First Downs – Rushing	11
11	First Downs – Passing	6
2	First Downs – Penalty	1
7	Punts – Number	6
42.0	Punts – Average Distance	25.5
0	Punt Return Yardage	36
0	Interception Returns – Number	1
0	Interception Return – Yards	30
3	Fumbles – Number	2
2	Fumbles – Number Lost	0
4	Penalties – Number	5
62	Yards – Penalized	44
3	Giveaways	0
0	Takeaways	3
−3	Difference	+3

SCORING

NEW YORK	0	0	7	0– 7
GREEN BAY	3	7	3	3–16

First Quarter
G.B. J. Kramer, 26 yard field goal 7:11

Second Quarter
G.B. Taylor, 7 yard rush 12:21
PAT – J. Kramer (kick)

Third Quarter
N.Y. Collier, recovered blocked punt in the end zone. 7:26
PAT – Chandler (kick)
G.B. J. Kramer, 29 yard field goal 11:00

Fourth Quarter
G.B. J. Kramer, 30 yard field goal 13:10

INDIVIDUAL STATISTICS

RUSHING

NEW YORK	No	Yds	Avg.	GREEN BAY	No	Yds	Avg.
Webster	15	56	3.7	Taylor	31	85	2.7
King	11	38	3.5	Hornung	8	35	4.4
	26	94	3.6	Moore	6	24	4.0
				Starr	1	4	4.0
					46	148	3.2

RECEIVING

NEW YORK	No	Yds	Avg.	GREEN BAY	No	Yds	Avg.
Walton	5	75	15.0	Dowler	4	48	12.0
Shofner	5	69	13.8	Taylor	3	20	6.7
Gifford	4	34	8.5	R. Kramer	2	25	12.5
King	2	14	7.0	McGee	1	13	13.0
Webster	1	5	5.0		10	106	10.6
Morrison	1	0	0.0				
	18	197	10.9				

PASSING

	Att	Comp	Comp Pct.	Yds	Int	Yds/ Att.	Yds/ Comp
NEW YORK							
Tittle	41	18	43.9	197	1	4.8	10.9
GREEN BAY							
Starr	21	9	42.9	85	0	4.0	9.4
Hornung	1	1	100.0	21	0	21.0	21.0
	22	10	45.5	106	0	4.8	10.6

NEW YORK GIANTS 12-2-0 Allie Sherman

Scores of Each Game		
7	Cleveland	17
29	Philadelphia	13
31	Pittsburgh	27
31	St. Louis	14
17	PITTSBURGH	20
17	DETROIT	14
49	WASHINGTON	34
31	ST. LOUIS	28
41	Dallas	10
42	Washington	24
19	PHILADELPHIA	14
26	Chicago	24
17	CLEVELAND	13
41	DALLAS	31

Use Name	Pos.	Hgt	Wgt	Age	Int	Pts
Rosey Brown	OT	6'3"	255	29		
Jack Stroud	OT	6'1"	250	33		
Reed Bohovich	OG-OT	6'3"	260	21		
Bookie Bolin	OG	6'2"	235	22		
Darrell Dess	OG	6'	245	26		
Greg Larson	C-OG	6'2"	245	23		
Ray Wietecha	C	6'1"	230	33		
Ken Byers	DE	6'1"	240	22		
Jim Katcavage	DE	6'3"	240	27	1	
Andy Robustelli	DE	6'1"	235	36		
Rosey Grier	DT	6'5"	290	29		
Chuck Janerette	DT	6'3"	250	23		
Dick Modzelewski	DT	6'	260	31		
Sam Huff	LB	6'1"	230	27	1	
Dick Lasse	LB	6'2"	225	26		
Tom Scott	LB	6'2"	220	32	1	
Mickey Walker	LB	6'	230	22		
Bill Winter	LB	6'3"	220	22		
Erich Barnes	DB	6'2"	198	27	6	
Sam Horner	DB	6'	198	24		
Dick Lynch	DB	6'1"	205	26	5	12
Jimmy Patton	DB	6'	185	30	7	
Dick Pesonen	DB	6'	190	24	2	
Allan Webb	DB	5'11"	180	27	3	
Ralph Gugliemi	QB	6'1"	195	29		
Y. A. Tittle	QB	6'	195	35		12
Johnny Counts	HB	5'10"	170	23		6
Paul Dudley	HB	6'	185	22		6
Phil King	HB	6'4"	225	26		12
Joe Morrison	DB-HB	6'1"	212	24		18
Alex Webster	FB	6'3"	225	31		54
Frank Gifford	FL	6'1"	190	32		48
Jim Collier	OE	6'2"	195	23		
Del Shofner	OE	6'3"	185	26		72
Aaron Thomas (from SF)	OE	6'3"	208	24		
Joe Walton	OE	5'11"	200	27		54
Don Chandler	K	6'2"	210	27		104

PITTSBURGH STEELERS 9-5-0 Buddy Parker

Scores of Each Game		
7	Detroit	45
30	Dallas	28
27	NEW YORK	31
13	PHILADELPHIA	7
20	New York	17
27	DALLAS	42
14	CLEVELAND	41
39	MINNESOTA	31
26	St. Louis	17
23	WASHINGTON	21
14	Cleveland	35
19	ST. LOUIS	7
26	Philadelphia	17
27	Washington	24

Use Name	Pos.	Hgt	Wgt	Age	Int	Pts
Charlie Bradshaw	OT	6'6"	255	26		
Dan James	OT	6'4"	280	25		
Ray Lemek	OG	6'	240	28		
Mike Sandusky	OG	6'	230	29		
Ron Stehouwer	OG	6'2"	230	25		
Buzz Nutter	C	6'4"	230	31		
Lou Michaels	DE	6'2"	235	26		110
Ernie Stautner	DE	6'1"	230	37	1	2
John Kenerson (to NY-A)	DT	6'3"	255	23		
Joe Krupa	DT	6'2"	225	29		
Big Daddy Lipscomb	DT	6'6"	288	31		
George Strugar (to NY-A)	DT	6'5"	258	27		
Lou Cordileone (from LA)	DE-DT	6'	245	25		
Myron Pottios - Broken Arm						
Tom Bettis	LB	6'2"	225	29		
Rudy Hayes	LB	6'	215	27		
Ken Kirk	LB	6'2"	230	24		
John Reger	LB	6'	230	31	1	
Bob Schmitz	LB	6'1"	235	24	3	6
Bob Simms (from NY)	LB	6'1"	230	24		
George Tarasovic	LB	6'4"	245	33	4	
Willie Daniel	DB	5'11"	185	24	5	6
Glenn Glass	DB	6'	190	25		
Dick Haley	DB	5'10"	195	26	4	
Brady Keys	DB	6'	185	26	3	
Johnny Sample	DB	6'1"	200	25		
Jackie Simpson	DB	5'10"	185	28		
Clendon Thomas	DB	6'2"	192	25	7	
Ed Brown	QB	6'2"	210	33		
Bobby Layne	QB	6'1"	210	35		6
Terry Nofsinger	QB	6'4"	205	24		
Gary Ballman	HB	6'	190	22		
Dick Hoak	HB	5'11"	190	23		24
Tom Tracy	HB	5'9"	205	30		
Joe Womack	HB	5'9"	210	25		30
Bob Ferguson	FB	5'11"	220	21		
John Henry Johnson	FB	6'2"	215	32		54
Buddy Dial	FL	6'1"	195	25		36
Red Mack	FL	5'10"	185	25		12
John Burrell	OE	6'3"	188	22		
Preston Carpenter	OE	6'2"	190	28		24
Harlon Hill (to DET)	OE	6'3"	200	30		
John Powers	OE	6'2"	215	21		

CLEVELAND BROWNS 7-6-1 Paul Brown

Scores of Each Game		
17	NEW YORK	7
16	WASHINGTON	17
7	Philadelphia	35
19	DALLAS	10
14	BALTIMORE	36
34	St. Louis	7
41	Pittsburgh	14
14	PHILADELPHIA	14
9	Washington	17
38	ST. LOUIS	14
35	PITTSBURGH	14
21	Dallas	45
13	New York	17
13	San Francisco	10

Use Name	Pos.	Hgt	Wgt	Age	Int	Pts
John Brown	OT	6'2"	245	23		
Mike McCormack	OT	6'4"	250	35		
Dick Schafrath	OT	6'3"	255	26		
Gene Hickerson	OG	6'3"	248	27		
Jim Ray Smith	OG	6'3"	245	31		
John Wooten	OG	6'2"	250	27		
John Morrow	C	6'3"	248	29		
Frank Morze	C	6'4"	264	28		
Bill Glass	DE	6'5"	255	26		
Jim Houston	DE	6'2"	235	25		
Paul Wiggin	DE	6'3"	245	28		
Bob Gain	DT	6'3"	260	34		
Frank Parker	DT	6'5"	250	22		
Floyd Peters	DT	6'4"	255	27	1	
Vince Costello	LB	6'	232	30	3	6
Galen Fiss	LB	6'	227	32	4	
Mike Lucci	LB	6'2"	220	22		
Sam Tidmore	LB	6'1"	220	23		
Ross Fichtner	DB	6'	185	24	7	
Don Fleming	DB	6'	188	25	2	
Bobby Franklin	DB	5'11"	182	26	1	
Bernie Parrish	DB	5'11"	195	27	2	
Jim Shofner	DB	6'2"	190	26	4	
Jim Shorter	DB	5'11"	180	21		
John Furman	QB	6'4"	205	22		
Jim Ninowski	QB	6'1"	200	26		
Frank Ryan	QB	6'3"	200	26		6
Ernie Green	HB	6'2"	205	23		6
Charlie Scales	HB	5'11"	215	23		18
Tom Wilson	FB-HB	6'	204	29		6
Jimmy Brown	FB	6'2"	228	26		108
Ray Renfro	FL	6'1"	192	31		24
Johnny Brewer	OE	6'4"	225	25		12
Leon Clarke	OE	6'4"	235	29		
Gary Collins	OE	6'4"	208	21		12
Bob Crespino	OE	6'4"	217	24		
Rich Kreitling	OE	6'2"	208	27		18
Lou Groza	K	6'3"	248	38		75

WASHINGTON REDSKINS 5-7-2 Bill McPeak

Scores of Each Game		
35	Dallas	35
17	Cleveland	16
24	ST. LOUIS	14
20	LOS ANGELES	14
17	St. Louis	17
27	Philadelphia	21
34	New York	49
10	DALLAS	38
17	CLEVELAND	9
21	Pittsburgh	23
24	NEW YORK	42
14	PHILADELPHIA	37
21	Baltimore	34
24	PITTSBURGH	27

Use Name	Pos.	Hgt	Wgt	Age	Int	Pts
Fran O'Brien	OT	6'1"	250	27		
Riley Mattson	OT	6'4	248	23		
Bob Khayat	OG	6'2	230	24		71
Charlie Moore	OG	6'5"	230	22		
John Nisby	OG	6'1"	247	29		
Vince Promuto	OG	6'1"	243	24		
Fred Hageman	C	6'4"	244	24		
Gene Cronin	DE	6'2"	228	29		
Ed Khayat	DE	6'3"	248	27		
John Paluck	DE	6'2"	240	29		
Andy Stynchula	DE	6'3"	257	23		
Ben Davidson	DT	6'8"	275	22		
Joe Rutgens	DT	6'2"	265	23		
Bob Toneff	DT	6'3"	275	32		
Rod Breedlove	LB	6'2"	225	24	3	
Gorden Kelley	LB	6'3	230	24	2	
Al Miller	LB	6'	220	22		
Bob Pellegrini	LB	6'2"	225	27	4	
Claude Crabb	DB	6'	190	22	6	
Doug Elmore	DB	6'	188	22	2	
Bobby Freeman	DB	6'1"	200	29	3	
Dale Hackbart	DB	6'3"	210	26	3	
Jim Kerr	DB	6'	195	23	1	
Jim Steffen	DB	6'	195	25	4	6
Ron Hatcher	FB-DB	5'11"	215	23		
Galen Hall	QB	5'10"	205	23	6	
George Izo	QB	6'3	214	25		
Norm Snead	QB	6'4"	215	22		18
Billy Barnes	HB	5'11"	202	27		18
Leroy Jackson	HB	6'	190	22		6
Dick James	HB	5'9"	175	28		30
Don Bosseler	FB	6'1"	212	26		12
Jim Cunningham	FB	5'11"	220	23		12
Bobby Mitchell	FL	6'	192	27		72
Bill Anderson	OE	6'2"	214	26		12
Fred Dugan	OE	6'3"	198	28		30
Steve Junker	OE	6'3"	217	27		12
Hugh Smith	OE	6'4"	215	24		

DALLAS COWBOYS 5-8-1 Tom Landry

Scores of Each Game		
35	WASHINGTON	35
28	PITTSBURGH	30
27	Los Angeles	17
10	Cleveland	19
41	PHILADELPHIA	19
42	Pittsburgh	27
24	ST. LOUIS	28
38	Washington	10
10	NEW YORK	41
33	CHICAGO	34
14	Philadelphia	28
45	CLEVELAND	21
20	St. Louis	52
31	New York	41

Use Name	Pos.	Hgt	Wgt	Age	Int	Pts
Clyde Brock	OT	6'5"	268	22		
Monte Clark	OT	6'6"	260	25		
Bob Fry	OT	6'4"	240	31		
Dale Memmelaar	OT	6'2"	245	25		
Andy Cvercko	OG	6'	243	25		
Joe Bob Isbell	OG	6'1"	225	22		
Mike Connelly	C	6'3"	235	26		
Lynn Hoyem	C	6'4"	225	22		
George Andrie	DE	6'7"	247	22		
Bob Lilly	DE	6'4"	248	23		
Ken Frost	DT	6'4"	245	23		
John Meyers	DT	6'6"	267	22		
Guy Reese	DT	6'5"	238	22		
Mike Dowdle	LB	6'3"	210	24	1	
Chuck Howley	LB	6'3"	230	26	2	
Bob Lang	LB	6'3"	235	28		
Don Talbert	LB	6'5"	225	22		
Jerry Tubbs	LB	6'2"	220	27	4	
Don Bishop	DB	6'2"	204	27	6	6
Mike Gaechter	DB	6'	190	22	5	6
Cornell Green	DB	6'4"	210	22		
Warren Livingston	DB	5'10"	180	24		
Dick Nolan	DB	6'1"	185	30		
Jerry Norton	DB	5'11"	195	32	2	6
John Houser — Injury						
Ed Nutting — Injury						
Buddy Humphrey	QB	6'1"	200	26		
Eddie LeBaron	QB	5'9"	160	32		
Don Meredith	QB	6'2"	198	24		
Amos Bullocks	HB	6'1"	197	23		18
Don Perkins	HB	5'10"	198	24		42
J. W. Lockett	FB	6'2"	230	25		18
Amos Marsh	FB	6'1"	208	23		54
Frank Clarke	FL	6'	215	29		84
Donnie Davis	FL	6'4"	214	22		
Lee Folkins	OE	6'5"	220	23		36
Billy Howton	OE	6'2"	194	32		36
Pettis Norman	OE	6'3"	215	22		
Glynn Gregory	DB-OE	6'2"	200	23		
Sam Baker	K	6'2"	217	30		92

NEW YORK GIANTS

RUSHING

Last Name	No.	Yds	Avg	TD
Webster	207	743	3.6	5
King	108	460	4.3	2
Morrison	35	146	4.2	1
Tittle	17	108	6.4	2
Dudley	27	100	3.7	0
Counts	14	55	3.9	0
Guglielmi	11	40	3.6	0
Gifford	2	18	9.0	1
Shofner	1	4	4.0	0
Thomas	1	−9	−9.0	0
Chandler	1	−11	−11.0	0

RECEIVING

Last Name	No.	Yds	Avg	TD
Shofner	53	1133	21	12
Webster	47	477	10	4
Gifford	39	796	20	7
Walton	33	406	12	9
King	15	186	12	0
Dudley	9	112	12	1
Morrison	6	107	18	2
Thomas	4	80	20	0
Counts	4	62	16	0
Collier	1	27	27	0
Robustelli	1	26	26	0

PUNT RETURNS

Last Name	No.	Yds	Avg	TD
Counts	8	33	4	0
Morrison	5	22	4	0
Horner	3	3	1	0
Patton	1	0	0	0

KICKOFF RETURNS

Last Name	No.	Yds	Avg	TD
Counts	26	784	30	1
Horner	11	242	22	0
Dudley	8	229	29	0
Morrison	5	113	23	0
King	2	37	19	0
Collier	1	0	0	0
Walker	1	0	0	0

PASSING – PUNTING – KICKING

PASSING	Att	Comp	%	Yds	Yd/Att	TD	Int–	%	RK
Tittle	375	200	53	3224	8.6	33	20–	5	2
Guglielmi	31	14	45	210	6.8	2	1–	3	
Gifford	2	1	50	12	6.0	0	0–	0	
Dudley	1	0	0	0	0.0	0	1–	100	

PUNTING	No	Avg
Chandler	55	40.6

KICKING	XP	Att	%	FG	Att	%
Chandler	47	48	98	19	28	68

PITTSBURGH STEELERS

RUSHING

Last Name	No.	Yds	Avg	TD
Johnson	251	1141	4.5	7
Womack	128	468	3.7	5
Hoak	117	442	3.8	4
Tracy	20	116	5.8	0
Hill	7	72	10.3	0
Burrell	6	38	6.3	0
Ferguson	20	37	1.9	0
Layne	15	25	1.7	1
Ballman	3	7	2.3	0
Mack	2	−2	−1.0	0
Carpenter	1	−3	−3.0	0
Brown	2	−8	−4.0	0

RECEIVING

Last Name	No.	Yds	Avg	TD
Dial	50	981	20	6
Carpenter	36	492	14	4
Johnson	32	226	7	2
Hoak	9	133	15	0
Mack	8	203	25	2
Burrell	8	193	24	0
Hill	7	101	14	0
Womack	6	57	10	0
Tracy	2	11	6	0
Powers	1	16	16	0
Ferguson	1	6	6	0

PUNT RETURNS

Last Name	No.	Yds	Avg	TD
Carpenter	7	109	16	0
Keys	7	46	7	0
Haley	1	13	13	0
Sample	4	1	0	0

KICKOFF RETURNS

Last Name	No.	Yds	Avg	TD
Keys	28	667	24	0
Glass	16	396	25	0
Haley	7	105	15	0
Sample	2	52	26	0
Hoak	2	40	20	0
Ferguson	2	30	15	0
Carpenter	1	29	29	0
Womack	1	16	16	0
Michaels	2	15	8	0
Sandusky	1	0	0	0

PASSING – PUNTING – KICKING

PASSING	Att	Comp	%	Yds	Yd/Att	TD	Int–	%	RK
Layne	233	116	50	1686	7.2	9	17–	7	15
Brown	84	43	51	726	8.6	5	6–	7	
Hoak	1	0	0	0	0.0	0	0–	0	
Tracy	1	1	100	7	7.0	0	0–	0	

PUNTING	No	Avg
Brown	60	40.0

KICKING	XP	Att	%	FG	Att	%
Michaels	32	33	97	26	42	62

CLEVELAND BROWNS

RUSHING

Last Name	No.	Yds	Avg	TD
Jimmy Brown	230	996	4.3	13
Ryan	42	242	5.8	1
Scales	56	239	4.3	3
Wilson	46	141	3.1	1
Green	31	139	4.5	0
Ninowski	9	15	1.7	0

RECEIVING

Last Name	No.	Yds	Avg	TD
Jimmy Brown	47	517	11	5
Kreitling	44	659	15	3
Renfro	31	638	21	4
Brewer	22	290	13	2
Green	17	194	11	1
Collins	11	153	14	2
Clarke	10	106	11	0
Wilson	8	110	14	0
Scales	8	67	8	0
Crespino	2	13	7	0

PUNT RETURNS

Last Name	No.	Yds	Avg	TD
Shofner	8	33	4	0
Green	5	31	6	0

KICKOFF RETURNS

Last Name	No.	Yds	Avg	TD
Wilson	11	307	28	0
Green	13	250	19	0
Scales	9	154	17	0
Tidmore	2	39	20	0
Collins	1	0	0	0

PASSING – PUNTING – KICKING

PASSING	Att	Comp	%	Yds	Yd/Att	TD	Int–	%	RK
Ryan	194	112	58	1541	7.9	10	7–	4	4
Ninowski	173	87	50	1178	6.8	7	8–	5	14
Jimmy Brown	2	1	50	28	14.0	0	0–	0	
Scales	1	0	0	0	0.0	0	1–	100	

PUNTING	No	Avg
Collins	45	42.8

KICKING	XP	Att	%	FG	Att	%
Groza	33	35	94	14	31	45

WASHINGTON REDSKINS

RUSHING

Last Name	No.	Yds	Avg	TD
Barnes	159	492	3.1	3
Bosseler	93	336	3.6	2
Cunningham	35	144	4.1	1
Jackson	49	112	2.3	0
James	9	13	1.4	0
Snead	20	10	0.5	3
Mitchell	1	5	5.0	0
Hall	2	2	1.0	1
Izo	1	−3	−3.0	0
Dugan	1	−9	−9.0	0
Elmore	1	−14	−14	0

RECEIVING

Last Name	No.	Yds	Avg	TD
Mitchell	72	1384	19	11
Dugan	36	466	13	5
Bosseler	32	258	8	0
Anderson	23	386	17	2
James	19	373	20	5
Barnes	14	220	16	0
Junker	11	149	14	2
Jackson	10	253	25	1
Cunningham	6	43	7	1

PUNT RETURNS

Last Name	No.	Yds	Avg	TD
James	19	145	8	0
Steffen	6	30	5	0
Mitchell	3	7	2	0
Kerr	1	2	2	0

KICKOFF RETURNS

Last Name	No.	Yds	Avg	TD
James	32	889	28	0
Mitchell	12	398	33	1
Jackson	10	272	27	0
Steffen	4	107	27	0
Cunningham	2	54	27	0
Miller	1	0	0	0

PASSING – PUNTING – KICKING

PASSING	Att	Comp	%	Yds	Yd/Att	TD	Int–	%	RK
Snead	354	184	52	2926	8.3	22	22–	6	8
Izo	37	17	46	284	7.7	3	4–	11	
Hall	32	19	59	274	8.6	2	1–	3	
Barnes	4	3	75	48	12.0	0	0–	0	
Elmore	1	0	0	0	0.0	0	0–	0	

PUNTING	No	Avg
Elmore	54	34.4
Anderson	7	33.6
Hackbart	2	39.0

KICKING	XP	Att	%	FG	Att	%
B. Khayat	38	38	100	11	25	44

DALLAS COWBOYS

RUSHING

Last Name	No.	Yds	Avg	TD
Perkins	222	945	4.3	7
Marsh	144	802	5.6	6
Bullocks	33	196	5.9	2
Meredith	21	74	3.5	0
Lockett	8	24	3.0	1
LeBaron	6	−1	−0.2	0

RECEIVING

Last Name	No.	Yds	Avg	TD
Howton	49	706	14	6
Clarke	47	1043	22	14
Folkins	39	536	14	6
Marsh	35	467	13	2
Perkins	13	104	8	0
Lockett	7	78	11	2
Gregory	3	70	23	0
Bullocks	3	46	15	1
Norman	2	34	17	0
Davis	2	31	16	0

PUNT RETURNS

Last Name	No.	Yds	Avg	TD
Lockett	8	45	6	0
Gaechter	6	32	5	0
Marsh	3	4	1	0

KICKOFF RETURNS

Last Name	No.	Yds	Avg	TD
Marsh	29	725	25	1
Bullocks	14	265	19	0
Lockett	6	130	22	0
Davis	4	66	17	0
Gaechter	1	16	16	0
Norman	2	5	3	0
Cverko	1	0	0	0
Memmelaar	1	0	0	0
Talbert	1	0	0	0

PASSING – PUNTING – KICKING

PASSING	Att	Comp	%	Yds	Yd/Att	TD	Int–	%	RK
Meredith	212	105	50	1679	7.9	15	8–	4	10
LeBaron	166	95	57	1436	8.7	16	9–	5	3
Baker	1	0	0	0	0.0	0	0–	0	
Lockett	1	0	0	0	0.0	0	0–	0	

PUNTING	No	Avg
Baker	57	45.4

KICKING	XP	Att	%	FG	Att	%
Baker	50	51	98	14	27	52

EASTERN CONFERENCE – Continued

ST. LOUIS CARDINALS 4-9-1 Wally Lemm

Scores of Each Game			Use Name	Pos.	Hgt	Wgt	Age	Int	Pts
27	Philadelphia	21	Ed Cook	OT	6'2"	240	30		
0	Green Bay	17	Fate Echols	OT	6'1"	255	23		
14	Washington	24	Irv Goode	OT	6'4"	235	21		
14	NEW YORK	31	Ernie McMillan	OT	6'6"	255	24		
17	WASHINGTON	17	Ken Panfil	OT	6'6"	255	31		
7	CLEVELAND	34	Ken Gray	OG	6'2"	240	26		
28	Dallas	24	Mike McGee	OG	6'1"	230	24		
28	New York	31	Jerry Perry	OG	6'4"	240	31		53
17	PITTSBURGH	26	Tom Redmond	OG	6'5"	240	25		
14	Cleveland	38	Bob DeMarco	C	6'3"	240	24		
17	SAN FRANCISCO	24	Ed Henke	DE	6'3"	230	34		
7	Pittsburgh	19	Luke Owens	DE	6'2"	255	29		
52	DALLAS	20	Joe Robb	DE	6'3"	230	25		
45	PHILADELPHIA	35	Frank Fuller	DT	6'4"	245	33		
			George Hultz	DT	6'4"	250	23		
			Don Owens	DT	6'5"	255	30		

Use Name	Pos.	Hgt	Wgt	Age	Int	Pts
Ted Bates	LB	6'3"	220	26		
Garland Boyette	LB	6'1"	225	22		
Bill Koman	LB	6'2"	230	28		
Dale Meinert	LB	6'2"	220	29	1	
Marion Rushing	LB	6'2"	210	25		
Roland Jackson	FB-LB	6'	210	22		
Norm Beal	DB	5'11"	170	22		
Pat Fischer	DB	5'10"	165	22	3	
Jimmy Hill	DB	6'2"	190	33	2	
Billy Stacy	DB	6'1"	190	26	6	
Larry Wilson	DB	6'	187	24	2	6
Don Gillis – Injury						
Monte Lee – Military Service						

Use Name	Pos.	Hgt	Wgt	Age	Int	Pts
Sam Etcheverry	QB	5'11"	190	32		
Charley Johnson	QB	6'	190	25		18
Joe Childress	HB	6'	200	28		6
John David Crow	HB	6'2"	215	27		102
Prentice Gautt	FB	6'	200	24		12
Bill Triplett	DB-HB	6'2"	212	23	1	
Mal Hammack	FB	6'2"	205	29		6
Bobby Joe Conrad	FL	6'	195	27		24
Taz Anderson	OE	6'2"	200	23		18
Chuck Bryant	OE	6'2"	220	21		
Jack Elwell	OE	6'3"	200	22		
Hugh McInnis	OE	6'3"	220	24		
Sonny Randle	OE	6'2"	187	26		42
Jim Bakken	K	6'	200	21		

PHILADELPHIA EAGLES 3-10-1 Nick Skorich

Scores of Each Game			Use Name	Pos.	Hgt	Wgt	Age	Int	Pts
21	ST. LOUIS	27	Jim McCusker	OT	6'2"	245	26		
13	NEW YORK	29	J. D. Smith	OT	6'5"	250	26		
35	CLEVELAND	7	Bob Butler	OG	6'1"	235	21		
7	Pittsburgh	13	Pete Case	OG	6'3"	230	21		
19	Dallas	41	Roy Hord (from LA)	OG	6'4"	250	27		
21	WASHINGTON	27	John Wittenborn	OG	6'2"	240	26		6
21	Minnesota	31	Jim Schrader	C	6'2"	252	30		
14	Cleveland	14	Howard Keys	OT-OG-C	6'3"	240	27		
0	GREEN BAY	49	John Baker	DE	6'6"	290	27		
14	New York	19	Bobby Richards	DE	6'2"	225	23		
28	DALLAS	14	Gene Gossage	OG-DE	6'3"	240	27		
37	Washington	14	Dick Stafford	DT-DE	6'4"	235	22		
17	PITTSBURGH	26	Jim Beaver	DT	6'1"	235	23		
35	St. Louis	45	Riley Gunnels	DT	6'3"	250	25		
			John Kapele (from PIT)	DT	6'	240	25		
			Joe Lewis	DT	6'2"	250	27		
			Dan Oakes	DT	6'3"	245	24		

Use Name	Pos.	Hgt	Wgt	Age	Int	Pts
Maxie Baughan	LB	6'1"	226	24	1	
Chuck Bednarik	LB	6'3"	235	37		
Bob Harrison	LB	6'2"	220	25	2	
John Nocera	LB	6'1"	220	28	1	
Mike Woulfe	LB	6'2"	225	23		
Don Burroughs	DB	6'4"	190	31	7	
Jimmy Carr	DB	6'1"	210	29	3	
Irv Cross	DB	6'1"	190	23	5	
Mike McClellan	DB	6'1"	185	23	3	
Ben Scotti	DB	6'1"	186	25	4	

Use Name	Pos.	Hgt	Wgt	Age	Int	Pts
King Hill	QB	6'3"	213	26		6
Sonny Jurgensen	QB	5'11"	200	28		12
Timmy Brown	HB	5'10"	190	25		78
Ted Dean	HB	6'2"	210	24		
Don Jonas	HB	5'11"	195	23		
Theron Sapp	HB	6'1"	205	27		12
Clarence Peaks	FB	6'1"	220	26		18
Merrill Douglas	HB-FB	6'	204	26		
Frank Budd	FL	5'10"	187	23		6
Hopalong Cassady (from CLE)	FL	5'10"	185	28		12
Tommy McDonald	FL	5'10"	172	28		60
Ken Gregory	OE	6'	190	25		
Dick Lucas	OE	6'2"	216	28		6
Pete Retzlaff	OE	6'1"	210	31		18
Ralph Smith	OE	6'2"	205	23		
Bobby Walston	OE	6'	195	33		48

WESTERN CONFERENCE

GREEN BAY PACKERS 13-1-0 Vince Lombardi

Scores of Each Game			Use Name	Pos.	Hgt	Wgt	Age	Int	Pts
34	MINNESOTA	7	Forrest Gregg	OT	6'4"	250	29		
17	ST. LOUIS	0	Norm Masters	OT	6'2"	250	29		
49	CHICAGO	0	Bob Skoronski	OT	6'3"	250	29		
9	DETROIT	7	Ed Blaine	OG	6'2"	240	22		
48	Minnesota	21	Jerry Kramer	OG	6'3"	250	27		65
31	SAN FRANCISCO	13	Fuzzy Thurston	OG	6'1"	250	29		
17	Baltimore	6	Ken Iman	C	6'1"	230	23		
38	Chicago	7	Jim Ringo	C	6'1"	235	31		
49	Philadelphia	0	Willie Davis	DE	6'3"	240	29		6
17	BALTIMORE	13	Bill Quinlan	DE	6'3"	250	30	1	
14	Detroit	26	Ron Gassert	DT	6'3"	250	22		
41	LOS ANGELES	10	Dave Hanner	DT	6'2"	260	33	1	
31	San Francisco	21	Henry Jordan	DT	6'3"	250	27	1	
20	Los Angeles	17	Ron Kostelnik	DT	6'4"	260	22		

Use Name	Pos.	Hgt	Wgt	Age	Int	Pts
Dan Currie	LB	6'3"	240	28		
Bill Forester	LB	6'3"	240	31		
Ray Nitschke	LB	6'3"	235	26	4	
Nelson Toburen	LB	6'3"	235	23		
Herb Adderley	DB	6'1"	205	23	7	12
Hank Gremminger	DB	6'1"	205	29	5	
Johnny Symank	DB	5'11"	180	27		
Jesse Whittenton	DB	6'	195	28	3	
Howie Williams	DB	6'2"	190	25		
Willie Wood	DB	5'10"	185	26	9	

Use Name	Pos.	Hgt	Wgt	Age	Int	Pts
John Roach	QB	6'4"	200	29		
Bart Starr	QB	6'1"	200	29		6
Paul Hornung	HB	6'2"	215	26		74
Tom Moore	HB	6'2"	215	24		42
Elijah Pitts	HB	6'1"	200	23		12
Earl Gros	FB	6'3"	220	21		12
Jim Taylor	FB	6'	215	30		114
Lew Carpenter	FL	6'1"	215	30		
Boyd Dowler	FL	6'5"	220	25		12
Gary Barnes	OE	6'4"	210	27		
Gary Knafelc	OE	6'4"	220	30		
Ron Kramer	OE	6'3"	230	27		42
Max McGee	OE	6'3"	205	30		18

DETROIT LIONS 11-3-0 George Wilson

Scores of Each Game			Use Name	Pos.	Hgt	Wgt	Age	Int	Pts
45	PITTSBURGH	7	Dan LaRose	OT	6'5"	250	22		
45	SAN FRANCISCO	24	John Lomakoski	OT	6'4"	250	21		
29	Baltimore	20	Dick Mills	OG	6'3"	240	22		
7	Green Bay	9	Harley Sewell	OG	6'1"	230	31		
13	LOS ANGELES	10	John Gordy	OT-OG	6'3"	250	26		
14	New York	17	Bob Whitlow	C	6'1"	236	26		
11	CHICAGO	3	Bob Scholtz	OT-C	6'4"	250	24		
12	Los Angeles	3	Darris McCord	DE	6'4"	250	29		2
38	San Francisco	24	Leo Sugar	DE	6'1"	230	33		
17	Minnesota	6	Sam Williams	DE	6'5"	235	31	1	12
26	GREEN BAY	14	Roger Brown	DT	6'5"	300	25		4
21	BALTIMORE	14	Mike Bundra	DT	6'3"	250	23		
37	MINNESOTA	23	John Gonzaga	DT	6'3"	250	29		
0	Chicago	3	Alex Karras	DT	6'2"	245	26	1	2
			Paul Ward	DT	6'3"	247	25		

Use Name	Pos.	Hgt	Wgt	Age	Int	Pts
Carl Brettschneider	LB	6'1"	225	30	2	
Max Messner	LB	6'3"	225	24		
Joe Schmidt	LB	6'1"	220	30	1	
Wayne Walker	LB	6'2"	225	25	1	64
Dave Lloyd	C-LB	6'3"	248	26		
Night Train Lane	DB	6'1"	200	34	4	
Dick LeBeau	DB	6'1"	185	25	4	12
Gary Lowe	DB	5'11"	195	28	2	
Yale Lary	DB	6'	190	31	8	
Bruce Maher	HB-DB	5'11"	190	25		
Tom Hall	OE-DB	6'1"	195	21		
Jim Martin – Voluntarily Retired						

Use Name	Pos.	Hgt	Wgt	Age	Int	Pts
Earl Morrall	QB	6'1"	206	28		6
Milt Plum	QB	6'1"	205	28		21
Dick Compton	HB	6'1"	190	22		
Dan Lewis	HB	6'1"	200	26		42
Tom Watkins	HB	6'1"	195	25		18
Nick Pietrosante	FB	6'2"	225	25		24
Ken Webb	FB	5'11"	205	27		6
Terry Barr	FL	6'	190	27		18
Pat Studstill	FL	6'1"	180	24		24
Gail Cogdill	OE	6'2"	195	25		48
Jim Gibbons	OE	6'2"	220	26		12
Larry Vargo	OE	6'3"	200	22		

CHICAGO BEARS 9-5-0 George Halas

Scores of Each Game			Use Name	Pos.	Hgt	Wgt	Age	Int	Pts
30	San Francisco	14	Art Anderson	OT	6'3"	244	25		
27	Los Angeles	23	Jim Cadile	OT	6'3"	230	21		
0	Green Bay	49	Herm Lee	OT	6'4"	247	31		
13	Minnesota	0	Bob Wetoska	OT	6'3"	240	24		
27	SAN FRANCISCO	34	Roger Davis	OG	6'3"	235	24		
35	BALTIMORE	15	Stan Jones	OG	6'1"	250	31		
3	Detroit	11	Ted Karras	OG	6'1"	243	29		
7	GREEN BAY	38	Mike Pyle	C	6'3"	240	23		
31	MINNESOTA	30	Doug Atkins	DE	6'8"	255	32		
34	Dallas	33	Ed O'Bradovich	DE	6'3"	255	22		
57	Baltimore	0	Maury Youmans	DE	6'6"	260	25		
24	NEW YORK	26	Stan Fanning	DT	6'6"	270	24		
30	LOS ANGELES	14	Bob Kilcullen	DT	6'3"	245	26		
3	DETROIT	0	Earl Leggett	DT	6'3"	250	28		
			Fred Williams	DT	6'4"	248	32		

Use Name	Pos.	Hgt	Wgt	Age	Int	Pts
Joe Fortunato	LB	6'	225	32	3	
Bill George	LB	6'2"	235	31	2	
Roger LeClerc	LB	6'3"	235	24		75
Larry Morris	LB	6'2"	230	27	2	
J. C. Caroline	DB	6'1"	190	29	2	
Bennie McRae	DB	6'1"	180	21	1	
Don Mullins	DB	6'1	195	23		
Tommy Neck	DB	5'11"	190	23		
Richie Petitbon	DB	6'3"	205	24	6	6
Rosey Taylor	DB	5'11"	186	23	2	12
Dave Whitsell	DB	6'	190	26	5	

Use Name	Pos.	Hgt	Wgt	Age	Int	Pts
Rudy Bukich	QB	6'1"	205	31		
Billy Wade	QB	6'2"	210	31		30
Charlie Bivins	HB	6'2"	212	23		6
Ronnie Bull	HB	6'	200	22		6
Willie Galimore	HB	6'1"	187	27		12
Billy Martin	HB	5'11"	197	24		6
Rick Casares	FB	6'2"	225	31		18
Joe Marconi	FB	6'2"	225	28		36
Johnny Morris	FL	5'10	180	27		30
John Adams	OE	6'3"	235	25		18
Angie Coia	OE	6'2"	202	24		24
Mike Ditka	OE	6'3"	230	22		36
Jim Dooley	OE	6'4"	198	32		
Bo Farrington	OE	6'3"	217	26		6
Bobby Joe Green	K	5'11"	175	24		

EASTERN CONFERENCE—Continued

ST. LOUIS CARDINALS

RUSHING

Last Name	No.	Yds	Avg	TD
Crow	192	751	3.9	14
Gautt	114	470	4.1	2
Childress	37	162	4.4	0
Hammack	38	160	4.2	1
Johnson	25	138	5.5	3
Triplett	2	12	6.0	0
Etcheverry	8	5	0.6	0

RECEIVING

Last Name	No.	Yds	Avg	TD
Randle	63	1158	18	7
Conrad	62	954	15	4
Anderson	35	535	15	3
Crow	23	246	11	3
Gautt	16	240	15	0
Childress	15	207	14	1
Hammack	4	27	7	0
Elwell	1	11	11	0
McInnis	1	10	10	0

PUNT RETURNS

Last Name	No.	Yds	Avg	TD
Beal	7	46	7	0
Fischer	4	37	9	0
Stacy	5	35	7	0
Conrad	2	10	5	0
Crow	2	6	3	0

KICKOFF RETURNS

Last Name	No.	Yds	Avg	TD
Triplett	24	608	25	0
Beal	16	394	25	0
Fischer	7	187	27	0
Gautt	6	124	21	0
Stacy	5	121	24	0
Hammack	2	36	18	0
Childress	3	19	6	0
Anderson	1	6	6	0

PASSING – PUNTING – KICKING

PASSING	Att	Comp	%	Yds	Yd/Att	TD	Int–	%	RK
Johnson	308	150	49	2440	7.9	16	20–	7	13
Etcheverry	106	58	55	707	6.7	2	10–	9	
Crow	20	12	60	241	12.1	0	0–	0	

PUNTING	No	Avg
Etcheverry	59	38.3

KICKING	XP	Att	%	FG	Att	%
Perry	38	39	97	5	12	42
Bakken	0	0	0	0	1	0
Conrad	0	0	0	0	1	0

PHILADELPHIA EAGLES

RUSHING

Last Name	No.	Yds	Avg	TD
Brown	137	545	4.0	5
Peaks	137	447	3.3	3
Sapp	23	53	2.3	2
Jurgensen	17	44	2.6	2
Hill	4	40	10.0	1
Smith	1	13	13.0	0
Douglas	4	7	1.8	0
Cassady	1	6	6.0	0

RECEIVING

Last Name	No.	Yds	Avg	TD
McDonald	58	1146	20	10
Brown	52	849	16	6
Peaks	39	347	9	0
Retzlaff	30	584	19	3
Lucas	19	236	12	1
Cassady	14	188	13	2
Sapp	6	80	13	0
Budd	5	130	26	1
Walston	4	43	11	0
Smith	1	29	29	0

PUNT RETURNS

Last Name	No.	Yds	Avg	TD
Brown	6	81	14	0
Cassady	8	49	6	0
McDonald	5	8	2	0
Cross	1	2	2	0
Smith	1	2	2	0

KICKOFF RETURNS

Last Name	No.	Yds	Avg	TD
Brown	30	831	28	1
Cassady	24	482	20	0
Douglas	6	136	23	0
Dean	4	83	21	0
Cross	2	72	36	0
Baughan	3	9	3	0
Woulfe	2	5	3	0

PASSING – PUNTING – KICKING

PASSING	Att	Comp	%	Yds	Yd/Att	TD	Int–	%	RK
Jurgensen	366	196	54	3261	8.9	22	26–	7	5
Hill	61	31	51	361	5.9	0	5–	8	
McDonald	1	1	100	10	10.0	1	0–	0	

PUNTING	No	Avg
Hill	64	42.9

KICKING	XP	Att	%	FG	Att	%
Walston	36	38	95	4	15	27
Wittenborn	0	0	0	2	4	50

WESTERN CONFERENCE

GREEN BAY PACKERS

RUSHING

Last Name	No.	Yds	Avg	TD
Taylor	**272**	**1474**	5.4	**19**
Moore	112	377	3.4	7
Hornung	57	219	3.8	5
Gros	29	155	5.3	2
Pitts	22	110	5.0	2
Starr	21	72	3.4	1
McGee	3	52	17.3	0
Roach	1	5	5.0	0
R. Kramer	1	–4	–4.0	0

RECEIVING

Last Name	No.	Yds	Avg	TD
McGee	49	820	17	3
Dowler	49	724	15	2
R. Kramer	37	555	15	7
Taylor	22	106	5	0
Moore	11	100	9	0
Hornung	9	168	19	2
Carpenter	7	104	15	0
Pitts	3	44	15	0

PUNT RETURNS

Last Name	No.	Yds	Avg	TD
Wood	23	273	12	0
Pitts	7	17	2	0
Kostelnik	1	0	0	0

KICKOFF RETURNS

Last Name	No.	Yds	Avg	TD
Adderley	15	418	28	1
Moore	13	284	22	0
Gros	1	7	7	0
Nitschke	1	7	7	0

PASSING – PUNTING – KICKING

PASSING	Att	Comp	%	Yds	Yd/Att	TD	Int–	%	RK
Starr	285	178	**62**	2438	8.6	12	9–	3	1
Roach	12	3	25	33	2.8	0	0–	0	
Hornung	6	4	67	80	13.3	0	2–	33	
Moore	5	2	40	70	14.0	2	1–	20	
Pitts	2	0	0	0	0.0	0	0–	0	
McGee	1	0	0	0	0.0	0	1–	100	

PUNTING	No	Avg
Dowler	36	43.1
McGee	14	35.4

KICKING	XP	Att	%	FG	Att	%
J. Kramer	38	39	97	9	11	82
Hornung	14	14	100	6	10	60

DETROIT LIONS

RUSHING

Last Name	No.	Yds	Avg	TD
Lewis	120	488	4.1	6
Watkins	113	485	4.3	3
Pietrosante	134	445	3.3	2
Webb	70	267	3.8	1
Plum	29	170	5.9	1
Morrall	17	65	3.8	1
Maher	3	8	2.7	0
Compton	1	3	3.0	0
Cogdill	1	2	2.0	0
Studstill	1	–11	–11.0	0

RECEIVING

Last Name	No.	Yds	Avg	TD
Cogdill	53	991	19	7
Studstill	36	479	13	4
Gibbons	33	318	10	2
Pietrosante	26	251	10	2
Barr	25	425	17	3
Lewis	16	158	10	1
Watkins	12	85	7	0
Webb	10	120	12	0

PUNT RETURNS

Last Name	No.	Yds	Avg	TD
Studstill	**29**	**457**	**16**	0
Watkins	8	42	5	0
Maher	2	3	2	0

KICKOFF RETURNS

Last Name	No.	Yds	Avg	TD
Studstill	20	511	26	0
Watkins	17	452	27	0
Maher	7	141	20	0
Hall	1	16	16	0
Cogdill	1	4	4	0

PASSING – PUNTING – KICKING

PASSING	Att	Comp	%	Yds	Yd/Att	TD	Int–	%	RK
Plum	325	179	55	2378	7.3	15	20–	6	11
Morrall	52	32	62	449	8.6	4	4–	8	
Lary	1	0	0	0	0.0	0	0–	0	
Lewis	1	0	0	0	0.0	0	0–	0	

PUNTING	No	Avg
Lary	52	45.3
Morrall	1	48.0

KICKING	XP	Att	%	FG	Att	%
Walker	37	37	100	9	22	41
Plum	0	0	0	5	12	42

CHICAGO BEARS

RUSHING

Last Name	No.	Yds	Avg	TD
Marconi	89	406	4.6	5
Bull	113	363	3.2	1
Casares	75	255	3.4	2
Galimore	43	233	5.4	2
Wade	40	146	3.7	5
Bivins	14	44	3.1	1
Martin	9	28	3.1	1
Anderson	1	7	7.0	0
J. Morris	2	7	3.5	0

RECEIVING

Last Name	No.	Yds	Avg	TD
Ditka	58	904	16	5
J. Morris	58	889	15	5
Bull	31	331	11	0
Marconi	23	306	13	1
Coia	22	361	16	4
Farrington	13	197	15	1
Casares	10	71	7	1
Adams	5	111	22	3
Galimore	5	56	11	0
Bivins	3	52	17	0
Martin	1	8	8	0

PUNT RETURNS

Last Name	No.	Yds	Avg	TD
J. Morris	20	208	10	0
Martin	17	62	4	0
Taylor	2	11	6	1

KICKOFF RETURNS

Last Name	No.	Yds	Avg	TD
Martin	25	515	21	0
Bivins	12	243	20	0
Bull	9	235	26	0
Taylor	4	98	25	0
Marconi	2	30	15	0
O'Bradovich	1	8	8	0

PASSING – PUNTING – KICKING

PASSING	Att	Comp	%	Yds	Yd/Att	TD	Int–	%	RK
Wade	**412**	**225**	55	3172	7.7	18	24–	6	9
Bukich	13	3	23	79	6.1	1	4–	31	
Bull	3	0	0	0	0.0	0	0–	0	
Casares	2	1	50	35	17.5	1	0–	0	

PUNTING	No	Avg
Green	69	43.7

KICKING	XP	Att	%	FG	Att	%
Leclerc	36	40	90	13	27	48

WESTERN CONFERENCE – Continued

BALTIMORE COLTS 7-7-0 Weeb Ewbank

Scores of Each Game			Use Name	Pos.	Hgt	Wgt	Age	Int	Pts	Use Name	Pos.	Hgt	Wgt	Age	Int	Pts	Use Name	Pos.	Hgt	Wgt	Age	Int	Pts
30	LOS ANGELES	27	Tom Gilburg	OT	6'5"	245	23			Jackie Burkett	LB	6'4"	230	25	2		Lamar McHan	QB	6'1"	205	30		
34	Minnesota	7	George Preas	OT	6'2"	250	30			Bill Pellington	LB	6'2"	238	33	2		Johnny Unitas	QB	6'1"	194	29		
20	DETROIT	29	Dan Sullivan	OT	6'3"	250	23			Bill Saul	LB	6'4"	225	21		2	Bob Clemens	HB	6'1"	208	23		
13	SAN FRANCISCO	21	Jim Parker	OG-OT	6'3"	275	28			Don Shinnick	LB	6'	235	27	5		Alex Hawkins	HB	6'1"	190	25		24
36	Cleveland	14	Wiley Feagin	OG	6'2"	235	25			Dave Yohn	LB	6'	220	24			Tom Matte	HB	6'	192	23		18
15	Chicago	35	Bill Kirchiro	OG	6'1"	235	21			Wendell Harris	DB	5'11"	190	21	2	9	Lenny Moore	HB	6'1"	190	29		24
6	GREEN BAY	17	Palmer Pyle	OG	6'2"	250	25			Lenny Lyles	DB	6'2"	202	26			Joe Perry	FB	6'	195	35		
22	San Francisco	3	Alex Sandusky	OG	6'1"	242	30			Andy Nelson	DB	6'1"	180	29	4		Mark Smolinski	FB	6'	222	23		12
14	Los Angeles	2	Dick Szymanski	C	6'3"	235	30			Jim Welch	DB	6'	190	24	1		Jimmy Orr	FL	5'11"	180	26		66
13	Green Bay	17	Ordell Braase	DE	6'4"	242	30			Bobby Boyd	HB-DB	5'10"	190	24	7		Bake Turner	FL	6'	180	22		6
0	CHICAGO	57	Gino Marchetti	DE	6'4"	245	36										Ray Berry	OE	6'2"	190	29		18
14	Detroit	21	Don Thompson	DE	6'4"	225	23			Jerry Hill – Injury							Dick Bielski	OE	6'1"	227	30		70
34	WASHINGTON	21	Jim Colvin	DT	6'2"	250	25										Dee Mackey	OE	6'5"	236	26		24
42	MINNESOTA	17	John Diehl	DT	6'7"	285	26										R. C. Owens	OE	6'3"	195	27		12
			Billy Ray Smith	DT	6'4"	235	27																

SAN FRANCISCO FORTY NINERS 6-8-0 Red Hickey

Scores of Each Game			Use Name	Pos.	Hgt	Wgt	Age	Int	Pts	Use Name	Pos.	Hgt	Wgt	Age	Int	Pts	Use Name	Pos.	Hgt	Wgt	Age	Int	Pts
14	CHICAGO	30	Leon Donahue	OT	6'4"	245	23			Matt Hazeltine	LB	6'1"	220	29	2		John Brodie	QB	6'1"	186	27		24
24	Detroit	45	Roland Lakes	OT	6'4"	247	22			Carl Kammerer	LB	6'3"	237	25	1		Bob Waters	QB	6'2"	184	24		
21	MINNESOTA	7	Bob St. Clair	OT	6'9"	265	31			Ed Pine	LB	6'4"	230	22	2		Billy Kilmer	HB-QB	6'	190	23		36
21	BALTIMORE	13	John Sutro	OT	6'4"	245	21			Karl Rubke	LB	6'4"	240	26			Bob Gaiters (from NY)	HB	5'11"	210	24		
34	Chicago	27	Bruce Bosley	OG	6'2"	240	28			John Thomas	LB	6'4"	246	27			J. D. Smith	FB-HB	6'1"	200	29		42
13	Green Bay	31	Ted Connolly	OG	6'3"	242	30			Eddie Dove	DB	6'2"	180	25	1		Dale Messer	DB-HB	5'10"	175	25	1	
14	LOS ANGELES	28	Mike Magac	OG	6'3"	240	24			Elbert Kimbrough	DB	5'11"	195	23			Bill Cooper	FB	6'1"	215	23		
3	Baltimore	22	John Mellekas	C	6'3"	255	29			Jerry Mertens	DB	6'	183	26	2		C. R. Roberts	FB	6'3"	197	26		
24	DETROIT	38	Dan Colchico	DE	6'4"	236	25			Jimmy Ridlon	DB	6'1"	177	27	1		Jim Vollenweider	FB	6"1"	210	22		
35	Los Angeles	17	Clark Miller	DE	6'5"	245	23			Abe Woodson	DB	5'11"	188	27	2	12	Lloyd Winston	FB	6'2"	215	22		
24	St. Louis	17	Len Rohde	DE	6'4"	240	24										Bernie Casey	FL	6'4"	215	23		36
24	Minnesota	12	Charlie Krueger	DT	6'4"	245	26			Dave Baker – Military Service							Jim Johnson	FL	6'2"	190	24		24
21	GREEN BAY	31	Leo Nomellini	DT	6'3"	262	37										Kay McFarland	FL	6'2"	180	23		
10	CLEVELAND	13															Clyde Conner	OE	6'2"	190	29		24
																	Monte Stickles	OE	6'4"	230	24		18
																	Tommy Davis	K	6'	212	27		66

MINNESOTA VIKINGS 2-11-1 Norm Van Brocklin

Scores of Each Game			Use Name	Pos.	Hgt	Wgt	Age	Int	Pts	Use Name	Pos.	Hgt	Wgt	Age	Int	Pts	Use Name	Pos.	Hgt	Wgt	Age	Int	Pts
7	Green Bay	34	Grady Alderman	OT	6'2"	235	23			Jim Christopherson	LB	6'	215	24	1	61	John McCormick	QB	6'1"	210	26		
7	BALTIMORE	34	Errol Linden	OT	6'5"	260	25			Rip Hawkins	LB	6'3"	230	23	1	2	Fran Tarkenton	QB	6'1"	190	22		12
7	San Francisco	21	Frank Youso	OT	6'4"	260	26			Cliff Livingston	LB	6'3"	215	32			Tommy Mason	HB	6'	195	23		48
0	CHICAGO	13	Larry Bowie	OG	6'2"	235	22			Clancy Osborne	LB	6'3"	217	27			Hugh McElhenny	HB	6'1"	198	33		
21	GREEN BAY	48	Jerry Huth	OG	6'	228	29			Roy Winston	LB	6'1"	225	22			Bob Reed	HB	5'11"	187	22		6
38	Los Angeles	14	Mike Rabold	OG	6'2"	238	25			Bill Butler	DB	5'10"	194	25	5	6	Bill Brown	FB	5'11"	218	24		6
31	PHILADELPHIA	21	Mick Tingelhoff	C	6'1"	230	22			Dean Derby	DB	6'	190	28	4		Doug Mayberry	FB	6'1"	225	25		12
31	Pittsburgh	39	Bob Denton	DE	6'4"	240	28			Tom Franckhauser	DB	6'	196	25	4		Mel Triplett	FB	6'1"	215	30		18
30	Chicago	31	Jim Leo	DE	6'1"	225	24		2	Chuck Lamson	DB	6'	185	23	1		Oscar Donahue	FL	6'3"	195	24		6
6	DETROIT	17	Jim Marshall	DE	6'3"	230	24			Ed Sharockman	DB	6'	195	2.	6	6	Tom Adams	OE	6'5"	210	22		
24	LOS ANGELES	24	Paul Dickson	DT	6'5"	250	25			Charlie Sumner	DB	6'1"	195	32	3		Charley Ferguson	OE	6'5"	212	22		36
12	SAN FRANCISCO	35	Jim Prestel	DT	6'5"	250	25										Jerry Reichow	OE	6'2"	220	27		18
23	Detroit	37															Gordon Smith	OE	6'2"	200	23		6
17	Baltimore	42															Steve Stonebreaker	OE	6'3"	220	24		6
																	Mike Mercer	K	6'	220	26		3

LOS ANGELES RAMS 1-12-1 Bob Waterfield Harland Svare

Scores of Each Game			Use Name	Pos.	Hgt	Wgt	Age	Int	Pts	Use Name	Pos.	Hgt	Wgt	Age	Int	Pts	Use Name	Pos.	Hgt	Wgt	Age	Int	Pts
27	Baltimore	30	Jim Boeke	OT	6'5"	245	23			Mike Henry	LB	6'2"	215	26	1		Zeke Bratkowski	QB	6'2"	203	30		
23	CHICAGO	27	Joe Carollo	OT	6'2"	258	22			Bill Jobko	LB	6'2"	220	26			Roman Gabriel	QB	6'4"	220	22		
17	DALLAS	27	Frank Varrichione	OT	6'1"	235	30			Marlin McKeever	LB	6'1"	230	22	2		Ron Miller	QB	6'	190	23		
14	Washington	20	Charley Cowan	OG	6'4"	250	24			Jack Pardee	LB	6'2"	225	26		8	Jon Arnett	HB	5'11"	194	27		12
10	Detroit	13	Duane Putnam	OG	6'	233	34			Les Richter	LB	6'3"	235	31			Dick Bass	FB-HB	5'10"	200	25		48
14	MINNESOTA	38	Joe Scibelli	OG	6'1"	250	23			Larry Hayes	C-LB	6'3"	230	27			Ollie Matson	FB	6'2"	210	32		6
28	San Francisco	14	Art Hunter	C	6'4"	248	29			Charley Britt	DB	6'2"	185	24	3		Art Perkins	FB	6'	220	22		12
3	DETROIT	12	Deacon Jones	DE	6'5"	240	23			Lindon Crow	DB	6'1"	200	29	5	6	Glen Shaw	FB	6'1"	217	23		
2	BALTIMORE	14	Lamart Lundy	DE	6'7"	235	27			Alvin Hall	DB	6'	193	29	1		Pervis Atkins	HB-FL	6'1"	195	26		6
17	SAN FRANCISCO	24	Larry Stephens	DE	6'4"	260	24			Ed Meador	DB	5'11"	185	25	1		Duane Allen	OE	6'4"	210	24		12
24	Minnesota	24	John Lovetere	DT	6'4"	280	26			Carver Shannon	DB	6'1"	198	24	4		Carroll Dale	OE	6'1"	195	24		18
10	Green Bay	41	Merlin Olsen	DT	6'5"	265	21	1	6	Bobby Smith	DB	6'	185	24	1		Karl Finch	OE	6'3"	195	23		
14	Chicago	30															Jim Phillips	OE	6'1"	198	25		30
17	GREEN BAY	20															Danny Villanueva	K	5'11"	200	24		56

WESTERN CONFERENCE—Continued

BALTIMORE COLTS

RUSHING

Last Name	No.	Yds	Avg	TD
Moore	106	470	4.4	2
Perry	94	359	3.8	0
Smolinski	85	265	3.1	1
Matte	74	226	3.1	2
Unitas	50	137	2.7	0
Hawkins	29	87	3.0	4
Turner	1	17	17.0	0
Orr	1	14	14.0	0
Boyd	2	13	6.5	0
Clemens	2	9	4.5	0
McHan	4	4	1.0	0

RECEIVING

Last Name	No.	Yds	Avg	TD
Orr	55	974	18	11
Berry	51	687	13	3
Mackey	25	396	16	4
Owens	25	307	12	2
Perry	22	194	9	0
Moore	18	215	12	2
Bielski	15	200	13	2
Smolinski	13	128	10	1
Matte	8	81	10	1
Hawkins	4	37	9	0
Turner	1	*111	111	1

*Includes lateral

PUNT RETURNS

Last Name	No.	Yds	Avg	TD
Turner	10	95	10	0
Harris	8	61	8	0
Hawkins	11	42	4	0
Boyd	3	23	8	0
Nelson	2	22	11	0
Shinnick	0	29	0	0

KICKOFF RETURNS

Last Name	No.	Yds	Avg	TD
Matte	27	613	23	0
Turner	20	504	25	0
Harris	3	86	29	0
Hawkins	2	35	18	0
Smolinski	2	20	10	0
Diehl	1	5	5	0

PASSING – PUNTING – KICKING

PASSING	Att	Comp	%	Yds	Yd/Att	TD	Int–	%	RK
Unitas	389	222	57	2967	7.6	23	23–	6	7
McHan	20	10	50	278	13.9	3	2–	10	
Matte	13	5	38	85	6.5	1	0–	0	
Hawkins	1	0	0	0	0.0	0	0–	0	

PUNTING	No	Avg
Gilburg	57	41.8
McHan	1	22.0

KICKING	XP	Att	%	FG	Att	%
Bielski	25	28	89	11	25	44
Harris	6	9	67	1	3	33

SAN FRANCISCO FORTY NINERS

RUSHING

Last Name	No.	Yds	Avg	TD
Smith	258	907	3.5	6
Kilmer	93	478	5.1	5
Brodie	37	258	7.0	4
Gaiters	43	193	4.5	0
Waters	12	42	3.5	0
Vollenweider	11	37	3.4	0
Roberts	9	19	2.1	0
Cooper	2	−2	−1.0	0
Winston	1	−15	−15.0	0

RECEIVING

Last Name	No.	Yds	Avg	TD
Casey	53	819	15	6
Johnson	34	627	18	4
Conner	24	240	10	4
Stickles	22	366	17	3
Smith	21	197	9	1
Kilmer	16	152	10	1
Gaiters	5	47	9	0
Vollenweider	4	21	5	0
Messer	3	30	10	0
McFarland	3	24	8	0
Roberts	2	0	0	0
Winston	1	2	2	0

PUNT RETURNS

Last Name	No.	Yds	Avg	TD
Woodson	19	179	9	1
Dove	5	21	4	0
Messer	3	7	2	0

KICKOFF RETURNS

Last Name	No.	Yds	Avg	TD
Woodson	37	1157	31	0
Gaiters	11	273	25	0
Vollenweider	6	113	19	0
Messer	4	112	28	0
Winston	3	67	22	0
Cooper	1	17	17	0

PASSING – PUNTING – KICKING

PASSING	Att	Comp	%	Yds	Yd/Att	TD	Int–	%	RK
Brodie	304	175	58	2272	7.5	18	16–	5	6
Kilmer	13	8	62	191	14.7	1	3–	23	
Waters	6	2	33	28	4.7	0	0–	0	
Gaiters	2	0	0	0	0.0	0	0–	0	

PUNTING	No	Avg
Davis	48	45.6

KICKING	XP	Att	%	FG	Att	%
Davis	36	36	100	10	23	43

MINNESOTA VIKINGS

RUSHING

Last Name	No.	Yds	Avg	TD
Mason	167	740	4.4	2
Tarkenton	41	361	8.8	2
Mayberry	74	274	3.7	1
McElhenny	50	200	4.0	0
Triplett	52	160	3.1	2
Brown	34	103	3.0	0
Reed	6	22	3.7	0
McCormick	2	4	2.0	0

RECEIVING

Last Name	No.	Yds	Avg	TD
Reichow	39	561	14	3
Mason	36	603	17	6
Donahue	16	285	18	1
McElhenny	16	191	12	0
Ferguson	14	364	26	6
Stonebreaker	12	227	19	1
Mayberry	11	100	9	1
Brown	10	124	12	1
Smith	7	138	20	1
Reed	4	37	9	1
Adams	3	51	17	0
Triplett	2	30	15	1
Tarkenton	0	−12	0	0

PUNT RETURNS

Last Name	No.	Yds	Avg	TD
Butler	12	169	14	0
Reed	9	82	9	0
Mason	6	52	9	0
McElhenny	5	43	9	0
Sharockman	1	16	16	0
Franckhauser	1	12	12	0

KICKOFF RETURNS

Last Name	No.	Yds	Avg	TD
Butler	26	588	23	0
Reed	13	337	26	0
Mason	12	301	25	0
McElhenny	7	160	23	0
Sharockman	3	71	24	0
Prestel	2	29	15	0
Denton	1	17	17	0
Stonebreaker	1	12	12	0
Bowie	2	7	4	0

PASSING – PUNTING – KICKING

PASSING	Att	Comp	%	Yds	Yd/Att	TD	Int–	%	RK
Tarkenton	329	163	50	2595	7.9	22	25–	8	12
McCormick	18	7	39	104	5.8	0	5–	28	
Mason	1	0	0	0	0.0	0	1–	100	

PUNTING	No	Avg
McCormick	46	39.0
Mercer	19	43.5

KICKING	XP	Att	%	FG	Att	%
Christopherson	28	28	100	11	20	55
Mercer	3	3	100	0	5	0

LOS ANGELES RAMS

RUSHING

Last Name	No.	Yds	Avg	TD
Bass	196	1033	5.3	6
Arnett	76	238	3.1	2
Perkins	48	181	3.8	2
Gabriel	18	93	5.2	0
Shaw	18	76	4.2	0
Miller	3	27	9.0	0
Atkins	7	19	2.7	0
Bratkowski	7	14	2.0	0
Richter	0	8	0.0	0
Matson	3	0	0.0	0

RECEIVING

Last Name	No.	Yds	Avg	TD
Phillips	60	875	15	5
Atkins	35	393	11	1
Bass	30	262	9	2
Dale	29	584	20	3
Perkins	14	83	6	0
Arnett	12	137	11	0
Allen	3	90	30	2
Shaw	3	51	17	0
Matson	3	49	16	1

PUNT RETURNS

Last Name	No.	Yds	Avg	TD
Atkins	11	94	9	0
Bass	6	81	14	0
Arnett	5	49	10	0
Hall	4	21	5	0
Smith	1	7	7	0

KICKOFF RETURNS

Last Name	No.	Yds	Avg	TD
Atkins	28	676	24	0
Bass	19	446	23	0
Hall	8	178	22	0
Arnett	2	87	44	0
Smith	2	60	30	0
Jones	1	0	0	0

PASSING – PUNTING – KICKING

PASSING	Att	Comp	%	Yds	Yd/Att	TD	Int–	%	RK
Bratkowski	219	110	50	1541	7.0	9	16–	7	16
Gabriel	101	57	56	670	6.6	3	2–	2	
Miller	43	17	40	250	5.8	1	1–	2	
Arnett	5	3	60	28	5.6	1	0–	0	
Bass	3	1	33	22	7.3	0	0–	0	
Matson	1	1	100	13	13.0	0	0–	0	

PUNTING	No	Avg
Villanueva	87	45.5

KICKING	XP	Att	%	FG	Att	%
Villanueva	26	27	96	10	20	50

1962 A.F.L. Wismer's Rubbery Titans

The near collapse of the New York franchise was the league's biggest headache this year. A sports truism says that no circuit can be big league without a healthy New York franchise, but the media there had practically ignored the Titans. Owner Harry Wismer's boisterous outbursts against Commissioner Joe Foss, head coach Sammy Baugh, and the NFL Giants had stripped the club of most of its dignity and left it a local joke in New York. The Titans became a ghost team, playing its games before empty stands in the shadows of the old, decrepit Polo Grounds. But Wismer's verbal antics paled in the face of his financial ills, and the joke almost turned into an obituary. Wismer had been losing money in a steady outflow since the league began, and the till finally ran dry in November. When the players' paychecks bounced, the word was out that Wismer was broke. To keep the Titans going, Commissioner Foss stepped in and ran the club with league funds, thus averting the embarrassment of the New York franchise folding in mid-season. While league intervention kept the ship from sinking this year, new skippers for the franchise would be needed for next year.

Dallas owner Lamar Hunt was far from broke, but the situation in that city was a failing one for the AFL. Hunt had been an original founder of the new league when his bid for an NFL franchise for Dallas was turned down in the late 1950s. Once it was certain that the AFL would get off the ground, the NFL had put an expansion team in Dallas. Fans flocked to see the NFL Cowboys play, while the AFL Texans starved in a land full of football fans. Even with the team on the road to a championship this season, attendance stayed low, so Hunt started shopping around for a new place to settle his team.

But attendance in general around the circuit took a sharp turn upward. The number of paid fans at league games increased 20 percent over last year, filling both the stands and the team's coffers very pleasantly. Seats with fans in them looked much better than empty bleachers on ABC's national broadcasts, which still provided the league with enough money to keep the circuit solvent.

A less favorable development was the decision against the anti-trust suit against the NFL. The United States District Court in Baltimore ruled against the suit, and the team owners voted to appeal the decision and keep the legal process moving.

But fans are concerned less with lawsuits, attendance figures, and league maneuvering than with the playing on the field. The Dallas Texans blossomed into the league's top team, a colorful bunch of youngsters who swept through the league behind Len Dawson, a cool quarterback with six years of non-activity in the NFL behind him. The Eastern Division race came down to a tight struggle between the Houston Oilers and the Boston Patriots that kept interest in the league alive through the end of the schedule. The clubs in New York, Oakland, and Denver faired very poorly and definitely needed help to become competitive in the near future, but the level of competition in general was markedly improved over the past. The crowning achievement of the season was the championship game between the Texans and Oilers, played before a full house in Houston. The game ran into the second overtime period before Dallas' Tommy Brooker won it on a field goal. The longest game ever played up until then, this match kept television viewers glued to their TV sets well into the evening, convincing some of them that perhaps the AFL had something going for itself.

EASTERN DIVISION

Houston Oilers—When Oiler coach Wally Lemm resigned to head up the NFL St. Louis Cardinals, Houston owner Bud Adams replied by hiring deposed St. Louis coach Pop Ivy. Although Ivy was reputed to be an offensive genius, the Houston attack bogged down in the early part of the season. A bad back made Billy Cannon a shadow of his former self, quarterback George Blanda started serving up interceptions at a generous rate, and end Bill Groman suddenly wasn't getting open for passes any more. But like last year, the Oilers caught fire after a slow start. With squat Charley Tolar leading the way with his running, the Oilers won their last seven games, sweeping into first place by beating Boston on November 18 and winning every game the rest of the way.

Boston Patriots—Coach Mike Holovak's collection of unknown veterans and youngsters from local colleges battled Houston tooth and nail for the Eastern crown. The defense, led by Larry Eisenhauer, Houston Antwine, and rookie Nick Buoniconti, was more impressive as a unit than as individuals, while the offense scratched out points on Babe Parilli's passing, Ron Burton's running, and Gino Cappelletti's kicking. The Oilers recovered from a slow start to climb right behind the first-place Patriots, and the top spot rode on their November 18 meeting in Houston. Boston not only lost the game 21-17 and first place; they also lost quarterback Parilli with a broken collarbone. Reserve passer Tom Yewcic led the Pats to victories the rest of the way until stumbling 20-0 in the final game against Oakland and thus conceding the Eastern crown to Houston.

Buffalo Bills—The Bills had always had a tough defense, and now coach Lou Saban was building an offense that could score points. The main addition was fullback Cookie Gilchrist, a Canadian League veteran who turned out to be the best power runner in the league. Saban also picked up a fine quarterback when he claimed Jack Kemp off the San Diego waiver list. Kemp had a broken hand at the time, but Saban carried him on the roster until he healed in time to star in the last three games of the year. The defense also got an injection of new blood when rookies Tom Sestak, Mike Stratton, Ray Abruzzese, Booker Edgerson, and Carl Charon all won starting positions. The new players needed time to jell, as the Bills lost their first five games, but seven wins and a tie in the last nine games showed Buffalo fans and coach Saban that he had built a winner.

New York Titans—The front-office situation was so chaotic that the Titans were lucky to finish out the year. Owner Harry Wismer was broke by November, no longer able even to pay his players. With attendance microscopic, the team's image laughable, and the players clamoring for money, the league office stepped in and ran the team the rest of the year. The Titans stayed surprisingly competitive on the field through all the commotion. Coach Bulldog Turner discovered a good quarterback in ex-giant Lee Grosscup, and when injuries kayoed Grosscup, Turner came up with another passer in ex-Bill Johnny Green. Art Powell, Dick Christy, and Don Maynard were the principal targets for these passers, and with fullback Bill Mathis injured most of the season, the pass again was New York's sole offensive threat. Even with good seasons from Larry Grantham and Lee Riley, the defense leaked profusely and condemned the Titans to last place in the East.

WESTERN DIVISION

Dallas Texans—Hank Stram had coached Len Dawson when both were at Purdue, and when the Cleveland Browns cut the quarterback before the season started, Stram immediately invited him to join the Texans. Dawson made up for the six years he sat on NFL benches by passing for twenty-nine touchdowns and leading the Texans to the AFL championship. Runners-up to San Diego the past two years, the Texans dethroned the Chargers by adding Dawson and key rookies Curtis McClinton, Fred Arbanas, Bobby Hunt, Bill Hull, Bill Miller, Bobby Ply, and Tommy Brooker. Stram got All-Pro performances from holdovers Abner Haynes, Chris Burford, Jim Tyrer, Mel Branch, Jerry Mays, E. J. Holub, and Sherrill Headrick, and the Texans swept to the Western crown while the stands stayed clean of paying customers.

Denver Broncos—The Broncos put all their chips on their passing attack and got away with it for two months. With ancient quarterback Frank Tripuka throwing bushels of passes to Lionel Taylor, Bo Dickinson, Gene Prebola, and Bob Scarpitto, the Broncos won seven of their first nine contests to contend for the Western title for the first time ever. But since Denver had no running game and a mediocre defense, the rest of the league wised up to its unbalanced attack over the second half of the season. The Broncos lost their last five games and wound up at a 7-7 mark, but the season was an exciting one for Denver fans and new coach Jack Faulkner. Three of the Broncos won individual league titles, Lionel Taylor in receiving, Gene Mingo in scoring and field goals, and Jim Fraser in punting.

San Diego Chargers—After two years as champs in the West, the Chargers suddenly had problems fielding a healthy team. Linebacker Bob Laraba was killed in an off-season car accident, and an amazing string of injuries left the Chargers an empty shell of their winning teams. Halfback Paul Lowe started the parade by breaking his arm in a pre-season game, and a string of teammates fell in line behind him. Rookie flanker Lance Alworth, linebacker Chuck Allen, defensive back Charley McNeil, and center Wayne Frazier all missed large portions of the schedule with various ailments, and a total of eleven starters were knocked out for seven or more games. To make this season a total loss, quarterback Jack Kemp broke his hand, and when coach Sid Gillman tried to slip him through on waivers to the reserve list, Buffalo claimed him for the $100 waiver price. With rookies and substitutes playing out the schedule, the Chargers lost eight of their last nine games to sink out of contention in the West.

Oakland Raiders—The Raiders were no great football team, as the six-game losing streak left over from last year testified, but the lung infection that sidelined quarterback Tom Flores for the season left the Raiders in desperate straits. They began the year with M. C. Reynolds and Don Heinrich, a pair of old NFL rejects, as passers, but coach Marty Feldman decided to go shopping for another quarterback after only one game. He bought Cotton Davidson from Dallas, and Davidson played out the Oakland schedule with a bad shoulder. The rest of the Raider squad contained little quality outside of Jim Otto, Clem Daniels, and Fred Williamson, and the team proceeded to lose its first thirteen games to run its losing streak to a record nineteen games. On the last day of the season they treated their fans in Frank Youell Field, their temporary home in Oakland, to a 20-0 victory over Boston, their first triumph in over a year.

FINAL TEAM STATISTICS

OFFENSE

	BOSTON	BUFFALO	DALLAS	DENVER	HOUSTON	NEW YORK	OAKLAND	SAN DIEGO
FIRST DOWNS:								
Total	230	238	259	**270**	266	206	187	217
by Rushing	100	**119**	**119**	72	95	60	72	82
by Passing	114	96	125	**177**	157	131	100	113
by Penalty	16	**23**	15	21	14	15	15	22
RUSHING:								
Number	432	**501**	479	322	457	317	367	410
Yards	1970	**2480**	2407	1298	1742	1213	1392	1647
Average Yards	4.6	5.0	**5.0**	4.0	3.8	3.8	3.8	4.0
Touchdowns	11	20	**21**	12	15	9	14	13
PASSING:								
Attempts	382	351	322	**559**	475	505	446	416
Completions	195	150	195	**292**	227	242	175	168
Completion Percentage	51.0	42.7	**60.6**	52.2	47.8	47.9	39.2	40.4
Passing Yards	2930	2181	2824	**3739**	3323	3161	2671	2686
Average Yards per Attempt	7.7	6.2	**8.8**	6.7	7.0	6.3	6.0	6.5
Average Yards per Completion	15.0	14.5	14.5	12.8	14.6	13.1	15.3	**16.0**
Times Tackled Attempting to Pass	23	23	41	30	**11**	54	44	28
Yards Lost Attempting to Pass	164	197	369	335	**94**	419	376	252
Net Yards	2766	1984	2455	**3404**	3229	2742	2295	2434
Touchdowns	25	15	29	21	**32**	20	11	23
Interceptions	**13**	26	17	40	48	35	29	34
Percent Intercepted	**3.4**	7.4	5.3	7.2	10.1	6.9	6.5	8.2
PUNTING:								
Number	69	76	54	60	56	78	**83**	79
Average Distance	38.5	38.8	35.8	**42.9**	41.0	41.0	37.4	41.6
PUNT RETURNS:								
Number	26	28	27	19	28	25	**34**	29
Yards	138	196	236	128	**314**	308	257	278
Average Yards	5.3	7.0	8.7	6.7	11.2	**12.3**	7.6	9.6
Touchdowns	0	1	0	0	1	**3**	0	0
KICKOFF RETURNS:								
Number	53	52	37	57	48	**73**	65	67
Yards	1200	1176	955	1210	1245	1579	1425	**1585**
Average Yards	22.6	22.6	25.8	21.2	**25.9**	21.6	21.9	23.7
Touchdowns	1	**2**	0	0	0	0	1	1
INTERCEPTION RETURNS:								
Number	25	**36**	32	27	35	29	29	29
Yards	365	**505**	395	483	340	356	390	340
Average Yards	14.6	14.0	12.3	**17.9**	9.7	12.3	13.4	11.7
Touchdowns	3	3	0	**4**	2	1	1	1
PENALTIES:								
Number	52	74	66	64	63	84	69	**88**
Yards	456	**797**	644	613	633	771	695	768
FUMBLES:								
Number	37	27	26	28	**17**	35	31	24
Number Lost	20	12	14	14	**9**	20	20	14
POINTS:								
Total	346	309	**389**	353	387	278	213	314
PAT (kick) Attempts	40	40	**49**	36	**49**	32	23	35
PAT (kick) Made	38	34	47	34	**48**	31	20	31
PAT (Rush or Pass) Attempts	1	1	1	3	1	2	**4**	3
PAT (Rush or Pass) Made	1	1	0	1	1	1	**2**	**2**
FG Attempts	37	23	27	**39**	26	27	27	20
FG Made	20	9	14	**27**	11	13	9	17
Percent FG Made	54.1	39.1	51.9	69.2	42.3	48.1	33.3	**85.0**
Safeties	0	0	0	1	**2**	1	0	0

DEFENSE

	BOSTON	BUFFALO	DALLAS	DENVER	HOUSTON	NEW YORK	OAKLAND	SAN DIEGO
FIRST DOWNS:								
Total	220	229	234	234	**217**	253	233	248
by Rushing	**68**	89	76	88	75	103	115	105
by Passing	136	129	143	131	126	122	**106**	120
by Penalty	16	**11**	20	15	16	28	12	23
RUSHING:								
Number	393	373	**351**	439	362	453	477	437
Yards	1426	1687	**1250**	1868	1569	2049	2397	1903
Average Yards	3.6	4.5	**3.6**	4.3	4.3	4.5	5.0	4.4
Touchdowns	14	**10**	14	11	**10**	19	21	16
PASSING:								
Attempts	450	440	467	423	486	417	**371**	402
Completions	216	215	239	202	213	194	**169**	196
Completion Percentage	48.0	48.9	51.2	47.8	**43.8**	46.5	45.6	48.8
Passing Yards	3435	2996	2953	2894	2865	2929	**2517**	2926
Average Yards per Attempt	7.6	6.8	6.3	6.8	**5.9**	7.0	6.8	7.3
Average Yards per Completion	15.9	13.9	**12.4**	14.3	13.5	15.1	14.9	14.9
Times Tackled Attempting to Pass	34	32	28	25	32	36	23	**44**
Yards Lost Attempting to Pass	**327**	254	252	224	304	323	211	311
Net Yards	3108	2742	2701	2670	2561	2606	**2306**	2615
Touchdowns	19	24	**13**	24	18	28	21	29
Interceptions	25	**36**	32	27	35	29	29	29
Percent Intercepted	5.6	**8.2**	6.9	6.4	7.2	7.0	7.8	7.2
PUNTING:								
Number	**79**	70	63	66	72	70	67	68
Average Distance	38.5	38.1	41.2	41.5	38.9	**37.9**	40.9	40.7
PUNT RETURNS:								
Number	**11**	33	26	27	28	31	34	26
Yards	**54**	202	219	245	259	295	352	229
Average Yards	**4.9**	6.1	8.4	9.1	9.3	9.5	10.4	8.8
Touchdowns	**0**	**0**	1	**0**	2	**0**	1	1
KICKOFF RETURNS:								
Number	64	56	72	64	55	46	**39**	56
Yards	1697	1177	1559	1401	1155	1194	**961**	1231
Average Yards	26.5	21.0	21.7	21.9	**21.0**	26.0	24.6	22.0
Touchdowns	1	1	**0**	**0**	1	1	**0**	1
INTERCEPTION RETURNS:								
Number	**13**	26	17	40	48	35	29	34
Yards	**55**	299	113	421	725	544	509	508
Average Yards	**4.2**	11.6	6.6	10.5	15.1	15.5	17.6	14.9
Touchdowns	1	**0**	**0**	5	2	3	3	1
PENALTIES:								
Number	62	**80**	64	76	65	73	75	65
Yards	554	**786**	660	678	559	711	720	709
FUMBLES:								
Number	26	26	29	**34**	25	30	25	30
Number Lost	10	14	16	**19**	17	16	18	13
POINTS:								
Total	295	272	**233**	334	270	423	370	392
PAT (kick) Attempts	33	33	**27**	38	32	51	46	44
PAT (kick) Made	32	30	**24**	36	30	46	44	41
PAT (Rush or Pass) Attempts	3	2	2	3	1	1	**0**	4
PAT (Rush or Pass) Made	1	1	1	1	**0**	1	**0**	4
FG Attempts	26	**20**	28	27	31	31	32	31
FG Made	15	**10**	11	16	14	21	16	17
Percent FG Made	57.7	50.0	**39.3**	59.3	45.2	67.7	50.0	54.8
Safeties	**0**	**0**	**0**	1	**0**	**0**	1	2

SCORING

HOUSTON	0	0	7	10	0	0–17
DALLAS	3	14	0	0	0	3–20

First Quarter
- Dall. Brooker, 16 yard field goal — 10:32

Second Quarter
- Dall. Haynes, 28 yard pass from Dawson — 0:27
  PAT–Brooker (kick)
- Dall. Haynes, 2 yard rush — 11:21
  PAT–Brooker (kick)

Third Quarter
- Hous. Dewveall, 15 yard pass from Blanda — 3:10
  PAT–Blanda (kick)

Fourth Quarter
- Hous. Blanda, 31 yard field goal — 3:53
- Hous. Tolar, 1 yard rush — 9:22
  PAT–Blanda (kick)

Second Overtime (Sixth Quarter)
- Dall. Brooker, 25 yard field goal — 2:54

TEAM STATISTICS

DALLAS		HO
19	First Downs–Total	21
10	First Downs–Rushing	6
5	First Downs–Passing	15
4	First Downs–Penalty	0
2	Fumbles–Number	0
1	Fumbles–Number Lost	0
6	Penalties–Number	6
42	Yards Penalized	50
1	Giveaways	5
5	Takeaways	1
+4	Difference	–4

1962 AFL CHAMPIONSHIP GAME

December 23, at Houston
(Attendance 37,981)

The Longest Afternoon

Houston had won its third straight Eastern title, but the Dallas Texans, making their first title-game appearance, almost blew the Oilers off the field in the first half, running up a 17-0 score on two Abner Haynes touchdowns and a Tommy Brooker field goal. The Oilers came out for the second half in top gear, however, and quickly fought back into the game. George Blanda passed to Willard Dewveall for 15 yards and Houston's first points early in the third quarter. With their backs against the wall, the Oilers rallied to tie the score in the fourth period. Blanda kicked a 31-yard field goal early in the period, and Charley Tolar scored on a one-yard plunge with five minutes left in the game. Blanda's extra point tied the score at 17-17, and regulation time ran out without any further scoring. As the teams readied for overtime, the captains met at mid-field for the coin toss for the next periods. Instructed to take advantage of the wind, Dallas' Abner Haynes blundered by electing to kick off, thus giving the Oilers the advantage of both receiving and having the wind at their backs. The Oilers couldn't score, however, and the Texans took the ball at mid-field near the end of the first overtime period on a Bill Hull interception. With Jack Spikes carrying and receiving the ball on key plays, the Texans moved down to the Houston 19-yard line. Tommy Brooker then booted a 25-yard field goal which ended Houston's championship reign and pro football's longest game.

INDIVIDUAL STATISTICS

HOUSTON	No.	Yds.	Avg.	DALLAS	No.	Yds.	Avg.
RUSHING							
Tolar	17	58	3.4	Spikes	11	77	7.0
Cannon	11	37	3.4	McClinton	24	70	2.9
Smith	2	3	1.5	Dawson	5	26	5.2
	30	98	3.3	Haynes	14	26	1.9
					54	199	3.7
RECEIVING							
Dewveall	6	95	15.8	Haynes	3	45	15.0
Cannon	6	54	9.0	Spikes	2	24	12.0
McLeod	5	70	14.0	Arbanas	2	21	10.5
Hennigan	3	37	11.3	McClinton	1	4	4.0
Tolar	1	8	8.0	Bishop	1	–6	–6.0
Smith	1	6	6.0		9	88	9.8
Jamison	1	–9	–9.0				
	23	261	11.3				
PUNTING							
Norton	3		39.3	Wilson	6		32.0
				Saxton	2		29.0
					8		31.2
PUNT RETURNS							
Jancik	1	0	0.0	Jackson	1	0	0.0
KICKOFF RETURNS							
Jancik	5	139	27.8	Grayson	3	64	21.3
				Haynes	1	22	22.0
					4	86	21.5
INTERCEPTION RETURNS							
None				Robinson	2	50	25.0
				Holub	1	43	43.0
				Hull	1	23	23.0
				Grayson	1	20	20.0
					5	136	27.2

PASSING

HOUSTON	Att.	Comp.	Comp. Pct.	Yds.	Int.	Yds/ Att.	Yds/ Comp.	Yards Lost Tackled
Blanda	46	23	50.0	261	5	5.7	11.3	0
DALLAS								
Dawson	14	9	64.3	88	0	6.3	9.8	6–50

HOUSTON OILERS 11-3-0 Pop Ivy

Scores of Each Game		
28	Buffalo	23
21	Boston	34
42	San Diego	17
17	BUFFALO	14
56	NEW YORK	17
10	Denver	20
7	DALLAS	31
14	Dallas	6
28	Oakland	20
21	BOSTON	17
33	SAN DIEGO	27
34	DENVER	17
32	OAKLAND	17
44	New York	10

Use Name	Pos.	Hgt	Wgt	Age	Int	Pts
Al Jamison	OT	6'5"	250	25		
Rich Michael	OT	6'3"	242	23		
Walt Suggs	OT	6'5"	245	23		
John Frongillo	OG	6'3"	250	22		
Bob Talamini	OG	6'1"	255	23		
Bill Wegener	OG	5'10"	245	21		
Hogan Wharton	OG	6'2"	250	26		
Bob Schmidt	C	6'4"	250	26		
Gary Cutsinger	DE	6'4"	240	21	1	
Don Floyd	DE	6'4"	247	23	4	6
Dan Lanphear	DE	6'2"	230	24		
Ron McDole	DE	6'3"	255	23		
Ed Culpepper	DT	6'1"	260	28		
Bill Herchman	DT	6'2"	255	29		
Ed Husmann	DT	6'	245	31		
Bob Kelly	DT	6'3"	250	22		
Bill Miller	DT	6'4"	270	24		
Doug Cline	LB	6'2"	230	23	2	
Mike Dukes	LB	6'3"	230	26	2	
Tom Goode	LB	6'3"	235	23		
Larry Onesti	LB	6'	205	23		
Gene Babb	FB-LB	6'3"	220	27	2	6
Tony Banfield	DB	6'1"	185	23	6	6
Freddy Glick	DB	6'1"	190	25	3	
Bobby Jancik	DB	5'11"	178	22	2	
Mark Johnston	DB	6'2"	200	24	4	
Jim Norton	DB	6'3"	195	23	8	
Bob Suci	DB	5'10"	178	24	1	
George Blanda	QB	6'1"	212	34		81
Jacky Lee	QB	6'1"	185	23		
Billy Cannon	HB	6'1"	215	25		80
Dave Smith	FB	6'1"	210	25		18
Charley Tolar	HB-FB	5'7"	198	24		48
Charley Hennigan	FL	6'	187	26		48
Willard Dewveall	OE	6'4"	230	25		30
Charley Frazier	OE	6'	160	23		6
Bill Groman	OE	6'	200	26		18
Bob McCleod	OE	6'5"	240	23		36

BOSTON PATRIOTS 9-4-1 Mike Holovak

Scores of Each Game		
28	Dallas	42
34	HOUSTON	21
41	DENVER	16
43	New York	14
7	DALLAS	27
24	SAN DIEGO	20
26	OAKLAND	16
28	Buffalo	28
33	Denver	29
17	Houston	21
21	BUFFALO	10
24	NEW YORK	17
20	San Diego	14
0	Oakland	20

Use Name	Pos.	Hgt	Wgt	Age	Int	Pts
Milt Graham	OT	6'6"	235	28		
Dick Klein	OT	6'4"	254	28		
Charley Long	OT	6'3"	230	24		
Charlie Leo	OG	6'	240	27		
Billy Neighbors	OG	5'11"	240	22		
Tony Sardisco	OG	6'2"	230	29		
Walt Cudzik	C	6'2"	235	29		
Bob Yates	C	6'3"	230	23		
Bob Dee	DE	6'3"	240	29		
Larry Eisenhauer	DE	6'5"	230	22		
Jim Hunt	DE	5'11"	245	23		
Houston Antwine	DT	6'	250	23		
Jess Richardson	DT	6'2"	265	32		
Tom Addison	LB	6'3"	230	26	5	6
Nick Buoniconti	LB	5'11"	220	21	2	
Harry Jacobs	LB	6'2"	235	25		
Rommie Loudd	LB	6'3"	225	28		
Jack Rudolph	LB	6'3"	230	24		
Fred Bruney	DB	5'10"	190	31	3	6
Dick Felt	DB	6'	185	29	5	
Ron Hall	DB	6'	190	25	3	6
Ross O'Hanley	DB	6'	185	23	5	
Chuck Shonta	DB	6'	190	24	2	
Don Webb	HB-DB	5'10"	200	23		
Don Allard	QB	6'	188	26		
Babe Parilli	QB	6'1"	190	32		12
Tom Yewcic	QB	5'11"	185	30		12
Ron Burton	HB	5'10"	190	25		42
Jim Crawford	HB	6'1"	200	26		26
Claude King	HB	5'11"	195	23		6
Larry Garron	FB	6'	215	25		36
Billy Lott	FB	6'	205	27		
Gino Capelletti	FL	6'	190	28		128
Jim Colclough	OE	6'	185	26		60
Tony Romeo	OE	6'2"	220	23		6
Tom Stephens	OE	6'1"	220	26		

Oscar Lofton – Military Service
George McGee – Military Service

BUFFALO BILLS 7-6-1 Lou Saban

Scores of Each Game		
23	HOUSTON	28
20	DENVER	23
6	NEW YORK	17
21	Dallas	41
14	Houston	17
35	SAN DIEGO	10
14	OAKLAND	6
45	Denver	38
28	BOSTON	28
40	San Diego	20
10	Oakland	6
10	Boston	21
23	DALLAS	14
20	New York	3

Use Name	Pos.	Hgt	Wgt	Age	Int	Pts
Stew Barber	OT	6'3"	242	23		
Jerry DeLucca	OT	6'3"	250	26		
Harold Olson	OT	6'3"	258	23		
Tom Day	OG	6'2"	245	27		
George Flint	OG	6'4"	245	24		
Billy Shaw	OG	6'3"	240	22		
Al Bemiller	C	6'3"	238	23		
Frank Jackunas	C	6'3"	225	21		
Nate Borden	DE	6'	238	30		
Leroy Moore (from BOS)	DE	6'	232	26	1	6
Mack Yoho	DE	6'2"	238	26		23
Don Healy	DT	6'3"	264	26		
Tom Saidock	DT	6'5"	260	30		
Tom Sestak	DT	6'5"	267	26	1	6
Jim Sorey	DT	6'4"	285	25		
Sid Youngelman	DT	6'3"	256	30		
Ralph Felton	LB	5'11"	210	30		
Tom Louderback	LB	6'2"	235	28		
Archie Matsos	LB	6'	220	27		
Marv Matuszak	LB	6'3"	230	31	6	
Mike Stratton	LB	6'3"	225	20	6	
John Tracey	OE-LB	6'3"	225	28		
Ray Abruzzese	DB	6'1"	190	24	3	
Joe Cannavino	DB	5'11"	187	26	1	
Carl Charon	DB	5'10"	185	21	7	12
Jim Crotty	DB	5'11"	190	24		
Booker Edgerson	DB	5'10"	178	23	6	
Carl Taseff	DB	5'11"	193	33	2	
Willie West	DB	5'10"	193	24	3	
John Yaccino	DB	6'	190	24		
Al Dorow	QB	6'	195	32		
Jack Kemp (from SD)	QB	6'1"	205	28		12
Warren Rabb	QB	6'1"	205	25		20
Manch Wheeler	QB	6'	190	23		
Wayne Crow	HB	6'	205	24		12
Elbert Dubenion	HB	6'	197	27		36
Carey Henley	HB	5'10"	200	23		
Art Baker	FB	6'	220	24		6
Wray Carlton	HB-FB	6'2"	220	24		12
Cookie Gilchrist	FB	6'3"	246	27		128
Willie Jones	FB	5'11"	208	22		
Glenn Bass	OE	6'2"	197	23		24
Monte Crockett	OE	6'3"	218	23		
Tom Rychlec	OE	6'3"	220	28		6
Ernie Warlick	OE	6'4"	235	30		12

Ken Rice – Knee Injury

NEW YORK TITANS 5-9-0 Bulldog Turner

Scores of Each Game		
28	Oakland	17
14	San Diego	40
17	Buffalo	6
10	DENVER	32
14	BOSTON	43
17	Houston	56
17	Dallas	20
23	SAN DIEGO	3
31	OAKLAND	21
31	DALLAS	52
46	Denver	45
17	Boston	24
3	BUFFALO	20
10	HOUSTON	44

Use Name	Pos.	Hgt	Wgt	Age	Int	Pts
Fran Morelli	OT	6'2"	258	23		
Alex Kroll	C-OT	6'3"	230	24		
Moses Gray	DT-OT	6'3"	260	24		
Gene Cockrell	DE-OT	6'3"	247	29		
Sid Fournet	OG	6'	240	29		
Bob Mischak	OG	6'	240	29		
Mike Hudock	C	6'2"	245	27		
Karl Kaimer	DE	6'3"	230	23		
John Kenerson (from PIT-N)	DE	6'3"	255	23		
Nick Mumley	DE	6'6"	255	26		
Lavern Torczon (from BUF)	DE	6'2"	235	26		
Bob Watters	DE	6'4"	250	26		
Dick Guesman	DT	6'4"	255	26		2
Proverb Jacobs	DT	6'4"	260	27		
George Struger (from PIT-N)	DT	6'5"	258	27		
Hubert Bobo	LB	6'1"	220	27	1	
Ed Cooke	LB	6'4"	250	27	1	6
Roger Ellis	LB	6'3"	233	24		
Jerry Fields	LB	6'1"	222	23		
Larry Grantham	LB	6'	200	23	2	6
Billy Atkins	DB	6'1"	196	27	4	
Wayne Fontes	DB	6'	190	22	4	6
Paul Hynes	DB	6'1"	210	22	2	
Dainard Paulson	DB	5'11"	190	25	3	
Lee Riley	DB	6'1"	195	30	11	
Ed Kovac	HB-DB	6'	200	24	1	
Johnny Green	QB	6'3"	208	25		18
Lee Grosscup	QB	6'1"	187	25		
Dean Look	QB	5'11"	185	25		
Bob Scrabis	QB	6'3"	225	26		
Butch Songin	QB	6'2"	205	38		
Harold Stephens	QB	5'11"	175	23		
Dick Christy	HB	5'10"	192	26		48
Curley Johnson	HB	6'	215	27		
Bill Shockley	HB	6'	185	24		68
Jim Tiller	HB	5'9"	165	23		
Mel West	HB	5'9"	190	23		
Charlie Flowers	FB	6'1"	217	25		
Bobby Fowler	FB	5'11"	212	26		
Bill Mathis	FB	6'1"	220	23		18
Don Maynard	FL	6'	185	26		48
Thurlow Cooper	OE	6'4"	228	29		8
Art Powell	OE	6'3"	212	25		48
Perry Richards	OE	6'2"	205	28		

HOUSTON OILERS

RUSHING

Last Name	No.	Yds	Avg	TD
Tolar	244	1012	4.1	7
Cannon	147	474	3.2	7
Smith	56	249	4.4	1
Blanda	3	6	2.0	0
Lee	4	1	0.3	0
Babb	3	0	0.0	0

RECEIVING

Last Name	No.	Yds	Avg	TD
Hennigan	54	867	16	8
McLeod	33	578	18	6
Dewveall	33	576	17	5
Cannon	32	451	14	6
Tolar	30	251	8	1
Groman	21	328	16	3
Smith	17	117	7	2
Frazier	7	155	22	1

PUNT RETURNS

Last Name	No.	Yds	Avg	TD
Jancik	14	164	12	0
Glick	12	79	7	0
Banfield	2	71	36	1

KICKOFF RETURNS

Last Name	No.	Yds	Avg	TD
Jancik	24	726	30	0
Cannon	18	442	25	0
Smith	2	37	19	0
Glick	1	22	22	0
Tolar	2	18	9	0
McLeod	1	0	0	0

PASSING – PUNTING – KICKING

PASSING	Att	Comp	%	Yds	Yd/Att	TD	Int–%	RK
Blanda	418	197	47	2810	6.7	27	42– 10	5
Lee	50	26	52	433	8.7	4	5– 10	
Cannon	3	2	67	46	15.3	1	0– 0	
Smith	3	2	67	34	11.3	0	0– 0	
Tolar	1	0	0	0	0.0	0	1–100	

PUNTING	No	Avg
Norton	55	41.7

KICKING	XP	Att	%	FG	Att	%
Blanda	48	49	98	11	26	42

2 POINT XP
Cannon (1)

BOSTON PATRIOTS

RUSHING

Last Name	No.	Yds	Avg	TD
Burton	134	548	4.0	2
Crawford	139	459	3.3	2
Garron	67	392	5.8	2
Yewcic	33	215	6.5	2
Parilli	28	169	6.0	2
King	21	144	6.8	1
Lott	8	34	4.2	0
Colclough	1	14	14.0	0
Cappelletti	1	–5	–5.0	0

RECEIVING

Last Name	No.	Yds	Avg	TD
Colclough	40	868	22	10
Burton	40	461	12	4
Romeo	34	608	18	1
Cappelletti	34	479	14	5
Crawford	22	224	10	2
Garron	18	236	8	3
King	5	42	8	0
Webb	1	11	11	0
Lott	1	1	1	0

PUNT RETURNS

Last Name	No.	Yds	Avg	TD
Burton	21	122	6	0
Bruney	3	8	3	0
Buoniconti	1	8	8	0
Hall	1	0	0	0

KICKOFF RETURNS

Last Name	No.	Yds	Avg	TD
Garron	24	686	29	1
Burton	13	238	18	0
King	9	177	20	0
Stephens	2	46	23	0
Crawford	2	24	12	0
Loudd	1	15	15	0
Dee	1	14	14	0
Jacobs	1	0	0	0

PASSING – PUNTING – KICKING

PASSING	Att	Comp	%	Yds	Yd/Att	TD	Int–%	RK
Parilli	253	140	55	1988	7.9	18	8– 3	2
Yewcic	126	54	43	903	7.2	7	5– 4	
Garron	3	1	33	39	13.0	0	0– 0	

PUNTING	No	Avg
Yewcic	68	38.7

KICKING	XP	Att	%	FG	Att	%
Cappelletti	38	40	95	20	37	54

2 POINT XP
Crawford (1)

BUFFALO BILLS

RUSHING

Last Name	No.	Yds	Avg	TD
Gilchrist	214	1096	5.1	13
Crow	110	589	5.4	1
Carlton	94	530	5.6	2
Kemp	20	84	4.2	2
Rabb	37	77	2.1	3
Dorow	15	57	3.8	0
Dubenion	7	40	5.7	0
Jones	4	17	4.2	0
Baker	2	9	4.5	0
Wheeler	3	7	2.3	0
Henley	3	2	0.6	0

RECEIVING

Last Name	No.	Yds	Avg	TD
Warlick	35	482	14	2
Dubenion	33	571	17	5
Bass	32	555	17	4
Gilchrist	24	319	13	2
Crow	8	80	10	1
Carlton	7	54	8	0
Rychlec	6	66	11	1
Baker	3	12	4	0
Tracey	1	28	28	0
Crockett	1	14	14	0

PUNT RETURNS

Last Name	No.	Yds	Avg	TD
West	14	112	8	0
Rychlec	1	24	24	0
Taseff	4	18	5	0
Abruzzese	3	17	6	0
Moore	2	12	6	0
Sestak	2	6	3	0
Cannavino	1	3	3	0
Edgerson	1	1	1	0
Charon	0	3	0	1

KICKOFF RETURNS

Last Name	No.	Yds	Avg	TD
Jones	14	287	21	0
Dubenion	7	231	33	1
Baker	7	220	31	1
Abruzzese	10	194	19	0
Gilchrist	7	150	21	0
Henley	5	90	18	0
Flint	1	4	4	0
DeLucca	1	0	0	0

PASSING – PUNTING – KICKING

PASSING	Att	Comp	%	Yds	Yd/Att	TD	Int–%	RK
Rabb	177	67	38	1196	6.8	10	14– 8	6
Kemp	139	64	46	928	6.7	5	6– 4	
Dorow	75	30	40	333	4.4	2	7– 9	
Crow	4	2	50	18	4.0	0	1– 25	
Taseff	1	0	0	0	0.0	0	0– 0	

PUNTING	No	Avg
Crow	75	39.0

KICKING	XP	Att	%	FG	Att	%
Yoho	20	24	83	1	3	33
Gilchrist	14	16	88	8	20	40

2 POINT XP
Rabb (1)

NEW YORK TITANS

RUSHING

Last Name	No.	Yds	Avg	TD
Christy	114	535	4.6	3
Mathis	71	245	3.4	3
Johnson	26	114	4.3	0
Flowers	21	78	3.7	0
Grosscup	8	62	7.7	0
Tiller	31	43	1.3	0
Green	17	35	2.1	3
Stephens	6	33	5.5	0
Fowler	5	27	5.4	0
West	9	16	1.7	0
Songin	4	11	2.7	0
Look	2	9	4.5	0
Kovac	3	5	1.6	0

RECEIVING

Last Name	No.	Yds	Avg	TD
Powell	64	1130	18	8
Christy	62	538	9	3
Maynard	56	1041	19	8
Johnson	14	62	4	0
Tiller	13	108	8	0
Cooper	12	122	10	1
Flowers	7	55	8	0
Richards	6	69	12	0
Mathis	6	32	5	0
Kovac	1	3	3	0
West	1	1	1	0

PUNT RETURNS

Last Name	No.	Yds	Avg	TD
Christy	15	250	17	2
Tiller	9	47	5	0
Cooke	1	11	11	1

KICKOFF RETURNS

Last Name	No.	Yds	Avg	TD
Christy	38	824	22	0
Tiller	22	462	21	0
West	3	131	44	0
Shockley	3	73	24	0
Kovac	4	72	18	0
Johnson	1	14	14	0
Cooper	1	3	3	0
Fournet	1	0	0	0

PASSING – PUNTING – KICKING

PASSING	Att	Comp	%	Yds	Yd/Att	TD	Int–%	RK
Green	258	128	50	1741	6.8	10	18– 7	4
Grosscup	126	57	45	855	6.8	8	8– 6	
Songin	90	42	47	442	4.9	2	7– 8	
Stephens	22	15	68	123	5.6	0	0– 0	
Christy	6	0	0	0	0.0	0	0– 0	
Scrabis	2	0	0	0	0.0	0	1– 50	
Look	1	0	0	0	0.0	0	1–100	

PUNTING	No	Avg
Johnson	50	39.9
Atkins	21	46.1
Green	3	40.3
Paulson	3	37.7

KICKING	XP	Att	%	FG	Att	%
Shockley	29	29	100	13	26	50
Guesman	2	3	67	0	1	0

2 POINT XP
Cooper (1)

DALLAS TEXANS 11-3-0 Hank Stram

Scores of Each Game			
42	BOSTON	28	
26	Oakland	16	
41	BUFFALO	21	
28	San Diego	32	
27	Boston	7	
20	NEW YORK	17	
31	Houston	7	
6	HOUSTON	14	
52	New York	31	
24	Denver	3	
35	OAKLAND	7	
14	Buffalo	23	
17	DENVER	10	
26	SAN DIEGO	17	

Use Name	Pos.	Hgt	Wgt	Age	Int	Pts
Jerry Cornelison	OT	6'3"	250	25		
Charley Diamond	OT	6'2"	262	26		
Jim Tyrer	OT	6'6"	290	23		
Carl Larpenter	OG-OT	6'4"	240	25		
Sonny Bishop	OG	6'2"	235	22		
Curt Merz	OG	6'4"	250	24		
Al Reynolds	OG	6'3"	235	24		
Marvin Terrell	OG	6'1"	235	24		
Jon Gilliam	C	6'2"	240	23		
Mel Branch	DE	6'2"	230	25		
Dick Davis	DE	6'2"	230	23		
Bill Hull	DE	6'6"	245	21		
Paul Rochester	DT	6'2"	260	25		
Jerry Mays	DE-DT	6'4"	247	22		
Walt Corey	LB	6'	220	24		
Ted Greene	LB	6'1"	230	28		
Sherrill Headrick	LB	6'2"	215	25	3	
Smokey Stover	LB	6'	235	23		
E. J. Holub	C-LB	6'4"	225	24	2	
Dave Grayson	DB	5'10"	180	23	4	
Bobby Hunt	DB	6'1"	180	22	8	
Ed Kelley	DB	6'2"	195	27		
Bobby Ply	DB	6'1"	190	21	7	
Duane Wood	DB	6'1"	200	26	4	
Johnny Robinson	HB-DB	6'	198	23	4	
Len Dawson	QB	6'	190	28		18
Eddie Wilson	QB	6'	190	22		
Abner Haynes	HB	6'	190	24		114
Frank Jackson	HB	6'1"	182	22		24
Jimmy Saxton	HB	5'11"	173	21		
Curtis McClinton	FB	6'3"	232	23		12
Jack Spikes	FB	6'2"	220	24		7
Fred Arbanas	OE	6'3"	236	23		36
Tommy Brooker	OE	6'2"	225	22		87
Chris Burford	OE	6'3"	215	24		72
Bill Miller	OE	6'	190	20		
Tom Pennington	K	6'2"	210	22		19

Dave Webster – Injury

DENVER BRONCOS 7-7-0 Jack Faulkner

Scores of Each Game			
30	SAN DIEGO	21	
23	Buffalo	20	
16	Boston	41	
32	New York	10	
44	OAKLAND	7	
23	Oakland	6	
20	HOUSTON	10	
38	BUFFALO	45	
23	San Diego	20	
29	BOSTON	33	
3	DALLAS	24	
45	NEW YORK	46	
17	Houston	34	
10	Dallas	17	

Use Name	Pos.	Hgt	Wgt	Age	Int	Pts
Eldon Danenhauer	OT	6'4"	245	26		
Jim Perkins	OT	6'5"	250	23		
Jerry Sturm	OT	6'3"	245	25		
Ken Adamson	OG	6'2"	225	23		
John Denvir	OG	6'4"	245	24		
Bob McCullough	OG	6'2"	240	21		
Jim Barton	C	6'5"	250	27		
John Cash	DE	6'3"	240	26	1	
Chuck Gavin	DE	6'1"	245	28	1	
Larry Jordan	DE	6'6"	230	24		
Don Joyce	DE	6'3"	260	32		
Gordy Holz	DT	6'4"	260	28		
Ike Lassiter	DE-DT	6'5"	270	21		
Bud McFadin	DG	6'3"	270	34	6	
Tom Erlandson	LB	6'3"	220	22	1	
Jim Fraser	LB	6'3"	240	26	1	2
Wahoo McDaniel	LB	6'	240	25	4	
Bill Roehnelt	LB	6'1"	230	26		
Jerry Stalcup	LB	6'	230	24		
Goose Gonsoulin	DB	6'3"	210	24	7	6
Chuck Marshall	DB	6'	180	23		
John McGeever	DB	6'1"	195	23	2	6
Jim McMillin	DB	5'11"	190	24	4	12
Tom Minter (to BUF)	DB	5'10"	178	22		
Justin Rowland	DB	6'2"	190	24		
Bob Zeman	DB	6'1"	203	25	6	6
George Shaw	QB	6'1"	185	29		6
Frank Tripucka	QB	6'2"	208	34		6
Al Frazier	HB	5'11"	180	27		18
Gene Mingo	HB	6'1"	200	23		137
Donnie Stone	HB	6'2"	205	25		30
Jerry Tarr	HB	6'	190	22		12
Bo Dickinson	FB	6'2"	220	27		24
Johnny Olszewski	FB	5'11"	202	31		6
Jim Stinnette	FB	6'1"	230	24		6
Bob Scarpitto	FL	5'11"	195	23		36
Gene Prebola	OE	6'3"	225	24		8
Lionel Taylor	OE	6'2"	215	26		24

SAN DIEGO CHARGERS 4-10-0 Sid Gillman

Scores of Each Game			
21	Denver	30	
40	NEW YORK	14	
17	HOUSTON	42	
42	Oakland	33	
32	DALLAS	28	
10	Buffalo	35	
20	Boston	24	
3	New York	23	
20	DENVER	23	
20	BUFFALO	40	
27	Houston	33	
31	OAKLAND	21	
14	BOSTON	20	
17	Dallas	26	

Use Name	Pos.	Hgt	Wgt	Age	Int	Pts
Jack Klotz (from NY)	OT	6'5"	260	28		
Sherman Plunkett	OT	6'4"	297	28		
Ernie Wright	OT	6'4"	265	21		
Ron Mix	OG-OT	6'4"	245	24		
Ernie Barnes	OG	6'3"	247	23		
Pat Shea	OG	6'1"	230	23		
Dick Hudson	OT-OG	6'4"	260	22		
Sam Gruneisen	LB-OG	6'1"	232	21		
Don Rogers	OG-C	6'2"	250	25		
Wayne Frazier	LB-C	6'2"	235	22		
Earl Faison	DE	6'5"	256	23	1	
Paul Miller	DE	6'2"	240	30		
Ron Nery	DE	6'6"	244	27		
Bill Hudson	DT	6'4"	277	26		
Ernie Ladd	DT	6'9"	317	23		
Henry Schmidt	DE-DT	6'4"	246	25		
Chuck Allen	LB	6'1"	220	22	1	
Frank Buncom	LB	6'1"	225	22	4	
Emil Karas	LB	6'3"	230	28	2	
Paul Maguire	LB	6'	223	24	1	
Bob Mitinger	LB	6'2"	222	22		
Maury Schleicher	LB	6'3"	240	25		
Bob Bethune	DB	5'11"	190	23	3	
George Blair	DB	5'11"	197	24	2	82
Claude Gibson	DB	6'1"	193	23	8	6
Dick Harris	DB	5'11"	175	25	5	
Charley McNeil	DB	5'11"	180	26	1	
Bud Whitehead	DB	6'	180	23	1	
John Hadl	QB	6'2"	205	22		6
Val Keckin	QB	6'4"	215	25		
Dick Wood (to DEN)	QB	6'5"	200	26		
Keith Lincoln	HB	6'2"	205	23		24
Bert Coan	HB	6'4"	215	22		
Fred Gillett	HB	6'3"	225	24		
Hez Braxton	FB	6'2"	227	26		8
Bobby Jackson	FB	6'3"	227	27		42
Jacque Mackinnon	FB	6'4"	240	23		12
Gerry McDougall	FB	6'2"	225	27		18
Lance Alworth	OE	6'	183	22		18
Reg Carolan	OE	6'6"	225	22		6
Dave Kocourek	OE	6'5"	230	25		26
Don Norton	OE	6'1"	185	24		42
Jerry Robinson	OE	5'11"	190	23		18

Bob Laraba – died Feb. 16, 1962 – auto accident
Sam DeLuca – Voluntarily Retired
Paul Lowe – Broken Arm

OAKLAND RAIDERS 1-13-0 Marty Feldman Red Conkright

Scores of Each Game			
17	NEW YORK	28	
16	DALLAS	26	
33	SAN DIEGO	42	
7	Denver	44	
6	DENVER	23	
6	Buffalo	14	
16	Boston	26	
21	New York	31	
20	HOUSTON	28	
6	BUFFALO	10	
7	Dallas	35	
21	San Diego	31	
17	Houston	32	
20	BOSTON	0	

Use Name	Pos.	Hgt	Wgt	Age	Int	Pts
Charley Brown	OT	6'4"	245	25		
Pete Nicklas	OT	6'4"	240	22		
Jim Norris	OT	6'4"	235	22		
Jack Stone	OT	6'2"	245	25		
Stan Campbell	OG	6'	230	32		
Dan Ficca	OG	6'1"	230	23		
Wayne Hawkins	OG	6'	235	24		
Jim Otto	C	6'2"	240	24		
Dalva Allen	DE	6'5"	245	26		
Dan Birdwell	DE	6'4"	232	21		
Jon Jelacic	DE	6'3"	255	25	1	
Riley Morris	DE	6'2"	230	25		
Joe Novsek	DE	6'4"	237	22		
Chuck McMurtry	DT	6'	280	24		
George Shirkey	DT	6'4"	255	25		
Orville Trask	DT	6'4"	260	27		
Bob Dougherty	LB	6'	240	28		
Charley Rieves	LB	5'11"	215	23		
Jackie Simpson	LB	6'1"	225	25	3	15
George Boynton	DB	5'11"	190	24		
Bob Garner	DB	5'10"	175	27	3	
Mel Montalbo	DB	6'1"	190	23		
Tom Morrow	DB	5'11"	180	24	10	
Rich Mostardi	DB	5'11"	188	24		
Henry Rivera	DB	5'11"	180	22		
Vern Valdez	DB	5'11"	190	26	4	
Fred Williamson	DB	6'2"	208	24	8	6
Cotton Davidson (from DAL)	QB	6'1"	187	29		25
Hunter Enis (from DEN)	QB	6'2"	195	25		
Chan Gallegos	QB	5'9"	175	22		
Don Heinrich	QB	6'	180	30		
M. C. Reynolds	QB	6'	195	27		
Dobie Craig	HB	6'4"	200	23		24
Clem Daniels	HB	6'1"	220	25		48
Charley Fuller	HB	5'11"	175	23		
Harold Lewis	HB	6'	204	26		
Bo Roberson	HB	6'1"	197	27		44
Gene White	HB	6'1"	197	22		8
Alan Miller	FB	6'	205	24		6
Willie Simpson	FB	6'	218	23		
Max Boydston	OE	6'2"	220	29		
Dick Dorsey	OE	6'3"	200	24		12
Charley Hardy	OE	6'	185	28		
Ben Agajanian	K	6'	220	43		25

Tom Flores – Illness (tuberculosis)

DALLAS TEXANS

RUSHING

Last Name	No.	Yds	Avg	TD
Haynes	221	1049	4.7	13
McClinton	111	604	5.4	2
Dawson	38	252	6.6	3
Jackson	47	251	5.3	3
Spikes	57	232	4.0	0
Burford	1	13	13.0	0
Wilson	1	5	5.0	0
Saxton	3	1	0.3	0

RECEIVING

Last Name	No.	Yds	Avg	TD
Burford	45	645	14	12
Haynes	39	573	15	6
Arbanas	29	469	16	6
McClinton	29	333	11	0
Miller	23	277	12	0
Jackson	10	177	18	1
Spikes	10	132	13	1
Saxton	5	64	13	0
Brooker	4	138	35	3
Robinson	1	16	16	0

PUNT RETURNS

Last Name	No.	Yds	Avg	TD
Haynes	15	119	8	0
Jackson	11	117	11	0
Grayson	1	0	0	0

KICKOFF RETURNS

Last Name	No.	Yds	Avg	TD
Grayson	18	535	30	0
Jackson	10	254	25	0
Saxton	4	77	19	0
McClinton	2	32	16	0
Spikes	2	30	15	0
Haynes	1	27	27	0

PASSING – PUNTING – KICKING

PASSING	Att	Comp	%	Yds	Yd/Att	TD	Int–%	RK
Dawson	310	189	61	2759	8.9	29	17– 5	1
Wilson	11	6	55	65	5.9	0	0– 0	
Haynes	1	0	0	0	0.0	0	0– 0	

PUNTING	No	Avg
Wilson	47	35.8
Saxton	3	46.3

KICKING	XP	Att	%	FG	Att	%
Brooker	33	33	100	12	22	55
Pennington	13	15	87	2	5	40
Spikes	1	1	100	0	0	0

DENVER BRONCOS

RUSHING

Last Name	No.	Yds	Avg	TD
Stone	94	360	3.8	3
Mingo	43	287	5.3	4
Dickinson	73	247	3.3	0
Frazier	39	168	4.2	2
Olszewski	33	114	3.4	0
Stinnette	21	87	4.1	1
Taylor	2	26	13.0	0
Shaw	4	10	2.5	1
Tripucka	2	−1	−0.5	1

RECEIVING

Last Name	No.	Yds	Avg	TD
Taylor	77	908	12	4
Dickinson	60	554	9	4
Prebola	41	599	15	1
Scarpitto	35	667	19	6
Stone	20	223	11	2
Mingo	14	107	8	0
Olszewski	13	150	12	1
Stinnette	13	109	8	0
Frazier	11	211	19	1
Tarr	8	211	26	2

PUNT RETURNS

Last Name	No.	Yds	Avg	TD
Zeman	5	59	12	0
Mingo	7	36	5	0
Frazier	5	32	6	0
Minter	2	1	1	0

KICKOFF RETURNS

Last Name	No.	Yds	Avg	TD
Frazier	19	388	20	0
Minter	10	227	23	0
Tarr	8	217	27	0
McGeever	5	143	29	0
Mingo	6	99	17	0
Olszewski	3	66	22	0
Stinnette	2	27	14	0
Dickinson	2	26	13	0
Danenhauer	1	11	11	0
McMillin	1	6	6	0

PASSING – PUNTING – KICKING

PASSING	Att	Comp	%	Yds	YdTAtt	TD	Int–%	RK
Tripucka	440	240	55	2917	6.6	17	25– 6	3
Shaw	110	49	45	783	7.1	4	14– 13	
Stone	3	1	33	13	4.3	0	0– 0	
Mingo	2	1	50	18	9.0	0	1– 50	
Taylor	2	0	0	0	0.0	0	0– 0	

PUNTING	No	Avg
Fraser	54	44.4
McDaniel	5	34.6

KICKING	XP	Att	%	FG	Att	%
Mingo	32	34	94	27	39	69
Fraser	2	2	100	0	0	0

2 POINT XP
Prebola (1)

SAN DIEGO CHARGERS

RUSHING

Last Name	No.	Yds	Avg	TD
Lincoln	117	574	4.8	2
Jackson	106	411	3.8	5
MacKinnon	59	240	4.0	0
McDougall	43	197	4.5	3
Hadl	40	139	3.4	1
Braxton	17	35	2.1	1
Alworth	1	17	17.0	0
Robinson	2	10	5.0	0
Coan	12	10	0.8	0
Gillett	2	8	4.0	0
Keckin	1	3	3.0	0
Wood	1	0	0.0	0

RECEIVING

Last Name	No.	Yds	Avg	TD
Norton	48	771	16	7
Kocourek	39	688	18	4
Robinson	21	391	19	3
Lincoln	16	214	13	1
Jackson	13	136	10	2
Alworth	10	226	23	3
MacKinnon	9	125	14	2
McDougall	4	27	7	0
Braxton	4	17	4	0
Carolan	3	39	13	1
Coan	1	52	52	0

PUNT RETURNS

Last Name	No.	Yds	Avg	TD
Harris	7	95	14	0
Lincoln	11	94	9	0
Gibson	10	89	9	0
Braxton	1	0	0	0

KICKOFF RETURNS

Last Name	No.	Yds	Avg	TD
Robinson	32	748	23	0
Lincoln	14	398	28	1
Bethune	12	251	21	0
McDougall	3	71	24	0
Gibson	2	55	28	0
Coan	2	31	16	0
Jackson	1	16	16	0
Klotz	1	15	15	0

PASSING – PUNTING – KICKING

PASSING	Att	Comp	%	Yds	Yd/Att	TD	Int–%	RK
Hadl	260	107	41	1632	6.3	15	24– 9	7
Wood	97	41	42	655	6.8	4	7– 7	
Keckin	9	5	56	64	7.1	0	1– 11	
Lincoln	5	2	40	43	8.6	2	0– 0	

PUNTING	No	Avg
Maguire	79	41.6

KICKING	XP	Att	%	FG	Att	%
Blair	31	35	89	17	20	85

2 POINT XP
Braxton (1)
Kocourek (1)

OAKLAND RAIDERS

RUSHING

Last Name	No.	Yds	Avg	TD
Daniels	161	766	4.7	7
Roberson	89	270	3.0	3
Miller	65	182	2.8	1
Davidson	25	54	2.1	3
W. Simpson	10	32	3.2	0
Gallegos	3	25	8.3	0
Enis	2	24	12.0	0
Lewis	9	18	2.0	0
Reynolds	1	9	9.0	0
Craig	1	8	8.0	0
Heinrich	1	4	4.0	0

RECEIVING

Last Name	No.	Yds	Avg	TD
Boydston	30	374	12	0
Roberson	29	583	20	3
Craig	27	492	18	4
Daniels	24	318	13	1
Dorsey	21	344	16	2
Miller	20	259	13	0
Lewis	7	53	8	0
White	6	101	17	1
Hardy	6	80	13	0
Fuller	5	67	13	0

PUNT RETURNS

Last Name	No.	Yds	Avg	TD
Garner	20	162	8	0
Lewis	9	65	7	0
Valdez	2	14	7	0
Morrow	2	13	7	0
Williamson	1	3	3	0

KICKOFF RETURNS

Last Name	No.	Yds	Avg	TD
Roberson	27	748	28	1
Daniels	24	530	22	0
Lewis	3	65	22	0
Miller	6	45	8	0
Dougherty	1	20	20	0
Garner	1	8	8	0
W. Simpson	1	7	7	0
Norris	1	2	2	0
Novsek	1	0	0	0

PASSING – PUNTING – KICKING

PASSING	Att	Comp	%	Yds	Yd/Att	TD	Int–%	RK
Davidson	321	119	37	1977	6.2	7	23– 7	8
Enis	51	27	53	225	4.4	1	1– 2	
Gallegos	35	18	51	298	8.5	2	3– 9	
Heinrich	29	10	34	156	5.4	1	2– 7	
Roberson	6	0	0	0	0.0	0	0– 0	
Reynolds	5	2	40	23	4.6	0	0– 0	
Daniels	1	0	0	0	0.0	0	0– 0	

PUNTING	No	Avg
Morrow	45	36.7
Davidson	40	39.2

KICKING	XP	Att	%	FG	Att	%
Agajanian	10	11	91	5	14	36
J. Simpson	6	6	100	3	10	30
Davidson	4	5	80	1	2	50
Birdwell	0	0	0	0	1	0

2 POINTS XP
Roberson (1)
White (1)

1963 N.F.L. The Best Bet: No Bet

Commissioner Pete Rozelle dropped a bombshell when he announced that certain players had been betting on NFL games. Although none of the men had bet against their own teams, Rozelle decided that players must be above suspicion. Stars Paul Hornung of Green Bay and Alex Karras of Detroit were suspended indefinitely by Rozelle for placing a series of bets on league games, while five other members of the Detroit club were fined $2,000 apiece for betting on the championship game. Another touchy decision by Rozelle was to play the regular slate of games on November 24, a day of mourning for the assassinated President John F. Kennedy. Another tragedy was the death on May 10 of "Big Daddy" Lipscomb, one of the greatest defensive tackles of all time. He was found dead of an overdose of heroin, although many people believe that Lipscomb was drunk and was given the fatal dose after being knocked out in a robbery attempt. On the plus side, though, was the opening of the Hall of Fame in Canton, with seventeen charter members inducted.

EASTERN CONFERENCE

New York Giants—Two losses in the first five games created doubts over the aging Giants, but the team looked pleasantly ripe rather than overage by the end of the season. Winning nine of their last ten games, the Giants captured the Eastern crown for the third straight time. The New York offense, relying heavily on Y. A. Tittle's passes to split end Del Shofner, included such aged stars as Tittle, Frank Gifford, Rosey Brown, and Jack Stroud, while the defense numbered gaffers like Andy Robustelli, Dick Modzelewski, and Tom Scott as starters. But the Giants were old pros, winning all the games they needed to win and keeping their mistakes to a minimum.

Cleveland Browns—With Blanton Collier now the head coach, fullback Jimmy Brown came to camp in a much better state of mind. Brown ran wild once the regular season began, carrying the ball like a workhorse without ever looking tired. After eight games he was already over 1,000 yards for the campaign, and by the end of the season he had set a new record of 1,863 yards. Brown's running kept the Browns in the Eastern race until the Lions knocked them out one week from the end of the season. But in falling short of the title, the Browns did uncover in Frank Ryan their best quarterback since Otto Graham.

St. Louis Cardinals—Young Charley Johnson's passing was the spectacular element in the Cardinal attack, but the running game showed the greatest versatility and depth. Both John David Crow and Prentice Gautt went out with injuries, leaving the Cards without their regular running backs. To replace the injured men, coach Wally Lemm shifted Bill Triplett from defensive back to offensive halfback, and he promoted veteran Joe Childress to a starter's position after several seasons of sitting on the bench. Both runners placed in the top ten in the NFL rushing statistics and provided a fine complement to Johnson's passes to Sonny Randle and Bobby Joe Conrad.

Pittsburgh Steelers—The Steelers had played three ties during the season, so that they could win the title with the best percentage although winning fewer games than the Giants. This constitutional crisis of sorts was averted when the Giants crushed Pittsburgh 33-17. Still, the Steelers surprised most observers by getting as far as they did, relying on players whose futures seemed behind them. The attack depended on power running from John Henry Johnson and Dick Hoak, while the defense was a hardnosed outfit that compensated well for the absence of Big Daddy Lipscomb, who died tragically before the season began.

Dallas Cowboys—Although considered an outside contender for the Eastern crown, the Cowboys never got off the ground after losing their first two games. But although the defense still needed major work and the offensive line needed some shoring up, the Cowboys were still adding good young players to their core. Two rookies made good impressions, Lee Roy Jordan at outside linebacker and Tony Liscio at offensive tackle. In addition, Don Meredith assumed full-time duties at quarterback while Bob Lilly blossomed into a great defensive lineman after being shifted from end to tackle.

Washington Redskins—The long suit in the Redskin attack was the passing game, headed up by young quarterback Norm Snead. Better at the long pass than the short pass, Snead operated a long-range attack with passes to Bobby Mitchell, Fred Dugan, Bill Anderson, and rookie Pat Richter. Mitchell remained the star of the team, the most dangerous receiver in the league after he caught the ball. The running backs were slow and brittle, however, and the defense needed patching up.

Philadelphia Eagles—Winless in their last nine games, the Eagles did not even have injuries as an excuse for their last-place finish. What they could blame was poor morale on a team with better talent than the record indicated. The problems began in training camp when both Sonny Jurgensen and King Hill walked out in a joint holdout for more money. Left without a quarterback, the Eagles gave in to their demands, only to have Jurgensen bothered by various injuries during the season. Coach Nick Skorich got no production out of his fullbacks, had problems in the offensive line, and lost several mediocre defensive linemen with leg problems.

WESTERN CONFERENCE

Chicago Bears—A brutally effective defense brought coach George Halas his first championship in seventeen years. Assistant coach George Allen had installed a zone pass defense that made the Chicago unit the toughest in the league. Allowing only 10 points per game, the Bear defense grew famous around the league as it began to win games with minimal help from the offense. Doug Atkins, Ed O'Bradovich, Bill George, Joe Fortunato, Larry Morris, Richie Petitbon, and Rosey Taylor shone the brightest on defense, while the offense, led by Billy Wade, Johnny Morris, and Mike Ditka, was programmed to stick with safe running plays and short passes without any probability of interception.

Green Bay Packers—Paul Hornung was hardly missed, but the loss of quarterback Bart Starr for four games with a broken hand cost the Packers dearly. Tommy Moore and Elijah Pitts filled in admirably for Hornung at halfback, and guard Jerry Kramer handled the placekicking duties with style. An opening 10-3 loss to the Bears was written off as a fluke, but when Chicago kept winning, first place in the West was on the line in the November 17 rematch at Chicago. By that time, however, Starr was out of action, and Zeke Bratkowski was running the Packer attack. The Bears swept the Pack out of Wrigley Field in taking a 26-7 victory, thus ending Green Bay domination.

Baltimore Colts—New coach Don Shula's regime began with five losses in the first eight games, hardly a reason for enthusiasm, but a fine stretch run served notice that the Colts were still title contenders. Shula had Johnny Unitas, Jim Parker, Ray Berry, Gino Marchetti, and some other veterans of the 1958-59 championship squads, but he also started blending in new talent of his own. Jerry Hill was promoted to starting fullback, and Tom Matte took over at halfback when Lenny Moore missed most the campaign with an appendectomy and a head injury. Two future stars joined the offensive line when tight end John Mackey and tackle Bob Vogel, both rookies, won starting jobs in the forward wall, and two more freshmen, Fred Miller and Johnny Logan, made the defensive unit.

Detroit Lions—The suspension of Alex Karras by Commissioner Rozelle sorely hurt the defensive line, and injuries further ripped up the once impregnable Detroit defense. Three starting defensive backs went out of the lineup with injuries, Yale Lary and Night Train Lane with bad knees and Gary Lowe with a sheared tendon, and Darris McCord and Joe Schmidt stayed on the field even though below par physically. The offense received an unexpected boost when Earl Morrall developed into a first-class quarterback in beating Milt Plum out of the starting job. But the Detroit attack was not strong enough to carry the club, while the defense was no longer healthy enough to lead the way.

Minnesota Vikings—The three-year-old Vikings were quickly losing their image as an expansion club as the young men in the lineup began maturing and blending together. The Vikings won five games and tied one, with the tie coming against the bruising Chicago Bears in a key December contest. Two other games resulted in near misses for the Vikings. They had the Packers beat with under two minutes left in the game, but a ten-yard field goal was blocked by Green Bay's Herb Adderley to thwart Minnesota's bid. The Vikings also had the Colts licked until Johnny Unitas drove his team 88 yards in forty-five seconds to a winning touchdown.

Los Angeles Rams—When the Rams dropped their first five games, fans expected a repeat of last year's disastrous season. Starting in mid-season, however, the team put together an improved offense with a sturdy defense to win five of its last nine games. The offensive upswing came from the confident play of quarterback Roman Gabriel, the fine running and blocking of rookie fullback Ben Wilson, and an improved offensive line. The defensive front four of Deacon Jones, Lamar Lundy, Merlin Olsen, and Roosevelt Grier combined size and quickness, while linebacker Jack Pardee and cornerback Eddie Meador held the back lines of the defense together.

San Francisco '49ers—Abe Woodson brought three kickoffs back for touchdowns and caused so much commotion with his speed that opposing teams resorted to squib kickoffs late in the year. Woodson was the only offense the '49ers had, as the attack lost quarterback John Brodie with a broken arm, leaving the signal-calling up to journeyman Lamar McHan. The defense also suffered losses, as Charlie Krueger, Jerry Mertens, Walt Rock, and Floyd Dean all missed most of the season with knee injuries. When the team went completely flat, dissension spread through the club, and coach Red Hickey was fired in mid-season in favor of the younger Jack Christiansen.

FINAL TEAM STATISTICS

OFFENSE

	BALT.	CHI.	CLEVE.	DALLAS	DET.	G.BAY	L.A.	MINN.	N.Y.	PHIL.	PITT.	ST.L.	S.F.	WASH.
FIRST DOWNS:														
Total	257	257	252	248	230	258	209	223	**278**	203	272	254	183	244
by Rushing	95	108	**135**	105	91	114	80	97	95	78	122	105	87	81
by Passing	149	117	100	132	124	126	117	112	**164**	114	129	134	87	140
by Penalty	13	**32**	17	11	15	18	12	14	19	11	21	15	9	23
RUSHING:														
Number	396	487	460	420	415	504	405	445	453	376	**578**	423	406	344
Yards	1642	1679	**2639**	1795	1601	2248	1393	1842	1777	1438	2136	1839	1454	1289
Average Yards	4.1	3.4	**5.7**	4.3	3.9	4.5	3.4	4.1	3.9	3.8	3.7	4.3	3.6	3.7
Touchdowns	11	15	15	18	11	**22**	14	17	12	8	14	10	8	15
PASSING:														
Attempts	433	404	322	375	406	345	384	355	426	380	368	**438**	349	430
Completions	**248**	221	164	200	202	179	186	197	243	193	170	228	156	204
Completion Pct.	**57.3**	54.7	50.9	53.3	49.8	51.9	48.4	55.5	57.0	50.8	46.2	52.1	44.7	47.4
Passing Yards	**3605**	2670	2449	2799	2997	2711	2558	2687	3558	2666	3028	3403	2090	3525
Avg. Yds per Att.	8.3	6.6	7.6	7.5	7.4	7.9	6.7	7.6	**8.4**	7.0	8.2	7.8	6.0	8.2
Avg. Yds. per Comp.	14.5	12.1	14.9	14.0	14.8	15.1	13.8	13.6	14.6	13.8	**17.8**	14.9	13.4	17.3
Times Tackled	44	**20**	25	43	33	**20**	59	51	35	27	30	40	35	43
Yds. Lost Tackled	309	**177**	232	331	274	178	481	518	311	252	251	372	263	391
Net Yards	**3296**	2493	2217	2468	2723	2533	2077	2169	3247	2414	2777	3031	1827	3134
Touchdowns	20	18	27	20	26	22	11	16	**39**	22	21	30	13	17
Interceptions	**12**	14	20	21	26	21	22	17	21	31	20	21	22	34
Pct. Intercepted	**2.8**	3.5	6.2	5.6	6.4	6.1	5.7	4.8	4.9	8.2	5.4	4.8	6.3	7.9
PUNTING:														
Number	56	64	54	71	66	51	**85**	70	59	69	59	65	73	53
Average Distance	41.0	**46.5**	40.0	44.2	44.6	44.7	44.7	38.7	44.9	43.1	39.4	40.7	45.4	41.7
PUNT RETURNS:														
Number	53	30	25	23	**57**	26	31	35	40	26	31	26	18	30
Yards	485	277	285	177	**635**	229	206	405	364	226	281	166	99	391
Average Yards	9.2	9.2	11.4	7.7	11.1	8.8	6.6	11.6	9.1	8.7	9.1	6.4	5.5	**13.0**
Touchdowns	0	0	0	0	1	0	0	1	0	0	0	0	0	0
KICKOFF RETURNS:														
Number	52	26	50	48	45	46	**70**	69	46	61	49	52	62	64
Yards	1114	424	1099	1100	949	1122	1651	1556	1018	1527	1312	1070	1659	**1718**
Average Yards	21.4	16.3	22.0	22.9	21.1	24.4	23.6	22.6	22.1	25.0	26.8	20.6	26.8	**26.8**
Touchdowns	0	0	0	0	0	1	1	1	0	1	1	0	**3**	1
INTERCEPTION RETURNS:														
Number	15	**36**	22	26	24	22	19	11	34	15	25	18	14	21
Yards	174	537	343	**549**	470	312	182	200	546	210	330	383	221	357
Average Yards	11.6	14.9	15.6	21.1	19.6	14.2	9.6	18.2	16.1	14.0	13.2	**21.3**	15.8	17.0
Touchdowns	2	4	1	0	3	0	0	2	**5**	1	1	2	0	2
PENALTIES:														
Number	77	**92**	52	67	60	53	70	58	67	53	51	69	61	74
Yards	**823**	804	609	627	531	517	788	627	755	558	495	692	439	736
FUMBLES:														
Number	35	**16**	25	29	26	30	30	45	28	30	25	29	25	32
Number Lost	25	**11**	17	15	14	20	17	18	13	16	13	18	8	19
POINTS:														
Total	316	301	343	305	326	369	210	309	**448**	242	321	341	198	279
PAT Attempts	35	37	43	40	42	46	26	39	**57**	32	37	44	24	35
PAT Made	32	35	40	38	42	43	25	39	**52**	29	34	44	24	33
FG Attempts	39	33	23	20	26	34	17	24	29	15	**41**	21	31	26
FG Made	**24**	14	15	9	10	16	9	12	18	7	21	11	10	12
Percent FG Made	61.5	42.4	65.2	45.0	38.5	47.1	52.9	50.0	62.1	46.7	51.2	52.4	32.3	46.2
Safeties	1	1	0	0	1	1	1	0	0	0	1	0	0	0

DEFENSE

	BALT.	CHI.	CLEVE.	DALLAS	DET.	G.BAY	L.A.	MINN.	N.Y.	PHIL.	PITT.	ST.L.	S.F.	WASH.
FIRST DOWNS:														
Total	228	196	242	266	194	**193**	244	258	213	266	244	235	304	285
by Rushing	89	**82**	99	114	74	92	100	103	89	125	90	105	121	110
by Passing	118	96	129	139	109	**87**	126	143	106	131	132	107	168	154
by Penalty	21	18	14	13	11	14	18	12	18	**10**	22	23	15	21
RUSHING:														
Number	434	412	423	455	**405**	428	431	410	411	466	419	461	488	469
Yards	1794	**1442**	1651	2094	1564	1586	1785	1733	1669	1985	1728	1802	2076	1863
Average Yards	4.1	**3.5**	3.9	4.6	3.9	3.7	4.1	4.2	4.1	4.3	4.1	3.9	4.3	4.0
Touchdowns	16	**7**	10	12	12	11	14	12	14	17	14	19	20	12
PASSING:														
Attempts	**348**	353	408	403	378	378	379	404	368	375	384	370	450	417
Completions	181	**164**	208	202	183	180	208	233	176	211	191	180	244	230
Completion Pct.	52.0	**46.5**	51.0	50.1	48.4	47.6	54.9	57.7	47.8	56.3	49.7	48.6	54.2	55.2
Passing Yards	2589	**2045**	2718	3392	2597	2340	3025	3362	2588	3106	3400	2519	3581	3484
Avg. Yds per Att.	7.4	**5.8**	6.7	8.4	6.9	6.2	8.0	8.3	7.0	8.3	8.9	6.8	8.0	8.4
Avg. Yds. per Comp.	14.3	**12.5**	13.1	16.8	14.2	13.0	14.5	14.4	14.7	14.7	17.8	14.0	14.7	15.1
Times Tackled	45	36	29	20	45	39	27	45	**57**	29	34	41	25	33
Yds. Lost Tackled	347	311	243	161	400	327	272	364	**499**	270	299	367	210	270
Net Yards	2242	**1734**	2475	3231	2197	2013	2753	2998	2089	2836	3101	2152	3371	3214
Touchdowns	19	10	16	31	17	**9**	25	31	22	28	21	13	27	33
Interceptions	15	**36**	22	26	24	22	19	11	34	15	25	18	14	21
Pct. Intercepted	4.3	**10.2**	5.4	6.5	6.3	5.8	5.0	2.7	9.2	4.0	6.5	4.9	3.1	5.0
PUNTING:														
Number	72	73	57	50	**83**	59	61	60	71	57	66	74	55	57
Average Distance	43.5	43.2	43.7	43.2	45.5	43.4	42.5	43.9	40.4	**39.1**	44.5	40.1	43.1	44.5
PUNT RETURNS:														
Number	**19**	34	22	36	29	29	60	27	32	34	29	25	50	25
Yards	**119**	277	216	176	319	220	681	155	283	451	287	294	587	161
Average Yards	6.3	8.1	9.8	**4.9**	11.0	7.6	11.4	5.7	8.8	13.3	9.9	11.8	11.7	6.4
Touchdowns	**0**	**0**	**0**	**0**	**0**	**0**	**0**	**0**	**0**	**0**	**0**	**0**	2	**0**
KICKOFF RETURNS:														
Number	66	52	58	47	56	69	44	48	69	**31**	53	51	37	59
Yards	1520	1261	1424	1125	1206	1331	1076	1342	1816	**727**	1133	1279	816	1263
Average Yards	23.0	24.3	24.6	23.9	21.5	**19.3**	24.5	28.0	26.3	23.5	21.4	25.1	22.1	21.4
Touchdowns	**0**	**0**	1	**0**	**0**	**0**	2	3	1	**0**	**0**	1	**0**	1
INTERCEPTION RETURNS:														
Number	**12**	14	20	21	26	21	22	17	21	31	20	21	22	34
Yards	**161**	216	317	437	393	297	369	168	379	516	316	284	283	678
Average Yards	13.4	15.4	15.9	20.8	15.1	14.1	16.8	**9.9**	18.0	16.6	15.8	13.5	12.9	19.9
Touchdowns	1	1	1	5	3	1	2	2	1	1	1	**0**	1	3
PENALTIES:														
Number	58	78	63	52	57	59	63	59	66	54	78	51	73	**83**
Yards	685	718	592	479	624	568	558	621	617	598	780	577	667	**917**
FUMBLES:														
Number	32	36	13	23	24	31	25	**50**	38	23	31	32	27	20
Number Lost	17	18	10	11	11	21	13	**31**	16	15	19	19	13	10
POINTS:														
Total	285	**144**	262	378	265	206	350	390	280	381	295	285	391	398
PAT Attempts	36	**18**	30	48	32	23	43	50	39	47	36	34	51	50
PAT Made	33	**18**	29	45	30	23	39	49	37	42	34	34	50	47
FG Attempts	27	17	35	33	24	33	35	22	**14**	31	22	26	27	33
FG Made	12	6	17	15	13	15	17	13	**3**	19	15	15	11	17
Percent FG Made	44.4	35.3	48.6	45.5	54.2	45.5	48.6	59.1	**21.4**	61.3	68.2	57.7	40.7	51.1
Safeties	**0**	**0**	1	**0**	2	**0**	1	1	**0**	**0**	**0**	**0**	1	**0**

1963 NFL CHAMPIONSHIP GAME
December 29, at Chicago
(Attendance 45,801)

Shofner's Hands and Tittle's Knee

The Bears and Giants, long-time rivals in the NFL, met in the eight-degree cold of Wrigley Field to decide the league championship. The two clubs played with contrasting styles, as the Giants depended heavily on Y. A. Tittle's passes, while the Bears relied on a fierce defense to force the enemy into mistakes. The Bears, however, made the first mistake when quarterback Billy Wade fumbled the ball away on the New York 17-yard line. The Giants then marched 83 yards, with a Tittle-to-Gifford pass counting for six points. After Don Chandler added the extra point, neither team could move the ball until Chicago's Willie Galimore fumbled on his own 31. On the next play, Del Shofner got free in the end zone but had a perfect Tittle pass bounce off his frigid hands. The Bear defense then took matters into hand, as Larry Morris picked off a Tittle screen pass and ran the ball back to the New York 5. Two plays later, Wade's quarterback sneak tied the score. The Giants added three points on a Chandler field goal to make the halftime score 10-7, New York. Tittle had twisted his knee in the second quarter, and he had trouble planting his feet while throwing after that. Late in the third period Ed O'Bradovich intercepted another Tittle screen pass, bringing it back to the New York 14. Three plays later, Wade snuck across the goal line to put the Bears ahead for the first time in the game. Tittle kept throwing the ball through the fourth quarter, but the Chicago defense intercepted two passes and protected the 14-10 margin of victory.

TEAM STATISTICS

CHIC.		N.Y.
14	First Downs – Total	17
6	First Downs – Rushing	8
7	First Downs – Passing	9
1	First Downs – Penalty	0
7	Punts – Number	4
41.0	Punts – Average Distance	43.3
5	Punt Return – Yards	21
5	Interception Returns – Number	0
71	Interception Return – Yards	0
2	Fumbles – Number	2
2	Fumbles – Lost Ball	1
5	Penalties – Number	3
35	Yards Penalized	25
2	Giveaways	6
6	Takeaways	2
+4	Difference	4

SCORING

CHICAGO	7	0	7	0–14
NEW YORK	7	3	0	0–10

First Quarter
N.Y. Gifford, 14 yard pass from Tittle 7:22
PAT – Chandler (kick)
CHI. Wade, 2 yard rush 14:44
PAT – Jencks (kick)

Second Quarter
N.Y. Chandler, 13 yard field goal 5:11

Third Quarter
CHI. Wade, 1 yard rush 12:48
PAT – Jencks (kick)

INDIVIDUAL STATISTICS

CHICAGO	No	Yds	Avg.	NEW YORK	No	Yds	Avg.
RUSHING							
Bull	13	42	3.2	Morrison	18	61	3.4
Wade	8	34	4.5	King	9	39	4.3
Galimore	7	12	1.7	McElhenny	7	19	2.7
Marconi	3	5	1.7	Webster	3	7	2.3
	31	93	3.0	Tittle	1	2	2.0
					38	128	3.4
RECEIVING							
Marconi	3	64	21.3	Gifford	3	45	15.0
Ditka	3	38	12.7	Morrison	3	18	6.0
J. Morris	2	19	9.5	Thomas	2	46	23.0
Coia	1	22	22.0	McElhenny	2	20	10.0
Bull	1	–5	–5.0	Webster	1	18	18.0
	10	138	13.8		11	147	13.4

PASSING

CHICAGO	Att	Comp	Comp Pct.	Yds	Int	Yds/ Att.	Yds/ Comp	Yards Lost Tackled
Wade	28	10	35.7	138	0	4.9	13.4	9
NEW YORK								
Tittle	29	11	37.9	147	5	5.1	13.4	7
Griffing	1	0	0.0	0	0	–	–	0
	30	11	36.7	147	5	4.9	13.4	7

NEW YORK GIANTS 11-3-0 Allie Sherman

Scores of Each Game		
37	Baltimore	28
0	Pittsburgh	31
37	Philadelphia	14
24	Washington	14
24	CLEVELAND	35
37	DALLAS	21
33	Cleveland	6
38	St. Louis	21
42	PHILADELPHIA	14
48	SAN FRANCISCO	14
17	ST. LOUIS	24
34	Dallas	27
44	WASHINGTON	14
33	PITTSBURGH	17

Use Name	Pos.	Hgt	Wgt	Age	Int	Pts
Rosey Brown	OT	6'3"	255	30		
Lou Kirouac	OT	6'3"	230	23		
Jack Stroud	OT	6'1"	250	34		
Lane Howell	DT-OT	6'5"	255	22		
Bookie Bolin	OG	6'2"	235	23		
Darrell Dess	OG	6'	245	27		
Ken Byers	DE-OG	6'1"	240	23		
Greg Larson	C	6'2"	245	24		
Jim Katcavage	DE	6'3"	240	28		6
Andy Robustelli	DE	6'1"	235	37		
John Lovetere	DT	6'4"	283	27		
Dick Modzelewski	DT	6'	260	32		
Bob Taylor	DE-DT	6'3"	235	23		

Use Name	Pos.	Hgt	Wgt	Age	Int	Pts
Al Gursky	LB	6'1"	210	22		
Jerry Hillebrand	LB	6'3"	240	23	5	6
Sam Huff	LB	6'1"	230	28	4	6
Tom Scott	LB	6'2"	220	33		
Mickey Walker	LB	6'	230	23		
Bill Winter	LB	6'3"	220	23	1	
Erich Barnes	DB	6'2"	198	28	3	
Eddie Dove (from SF)	DB	6'2"	180	26	2	
Dick Lynch	DB	6'1"	205	27	9	18
Jimmy Patton	DB	6'	185	31	6	
Dick Pesonen	DB	6'	190	25	1	
Allan Webb	DB	5'11"	180	28	3	
Louis Guy	FL-DB	6'	185	22		

Use Name	Pos.	Hgt	Wgt	Age	Int	Pts
Glynn Griffing	QB	6'1"	200	21		
Y. A. Tittle	QB	6'	195	36		12
Bob Anderson	HB	6'2"	210	26		
Johnny Counts	HB	5'10"	170	24		
Charlie Killett	HB	6'1"	205	22		
Phil King	HB	6'4"	225	27		48
Hugh McElhenny	HB	6'1"	190	34		12
Joe Morrison	FL-HB	6'1"	212	25		60
Alex Webster	FB	6'3"	225	32		24
Frank Gifford	FL	6'1"	190	33		42
Aaron Thomas	OE-FL	6'3"	208	25		18
Del Shofner	OE	6'3"	185	27		54
Joe Walton	OE	5'11"	200	28		36
Don Chandler	K	6'2"	210	28		106

CLEVELAND BROWNS 10-4-0 Blanton Collier

Scores of Each Game		
37	WASHINGTON	14
41	Dallas	24
20	LOS ANGELES	6
35	PITTSBURGH	23
35	New York	24
37	PHILADELPHIA	7
6	NEW YORK	33
23	Philadelphia	17
7	Pittsburgh	9
14	St. Louis	20
27	DALLAS	17
24	St. Louis	10
10	Detroit	38
27	Washington	20

Use Name	Pos.	Hgt	Wgt	Age	Int	Pts
John Brown	OT	6'2"	248	24		
Monte Clark	OT	6'6"	265	26		
Jim McCusker	OT	6'2"	245	27		
Dick Schafrath	OT	6'3"	255	27		
Roger Shoals	OT	6'4"	255	24		
Ted Connolly	OG	6'3"	242	31		
Gene Hickerson	OG	6'3"	248	28		
John Wooten	OG	6'2"	250	28		
John Morrow	C	6'3"	248	30		
Frank Morze	C	6'4"	280	29		
Bill Glass	DE	6'5"	255	27		
Paul Wiggin	DE	6'3"	245	29	1	
Bob Gain	DT	6'3"	260	35		
Jim Kanicki	DT	6'4"	270	21		
Frank Parker	DT	6'5"	255	23		

Use Name	Pos.	Hgt	Wgt	Age	Int	Pts
Vince Costello	LB	6'	228	31	7	
Galen Fiss	LB	6'	227	33	2	
Tom Goosby	LB	6'	235	24		
Jim Houston	LB	6'2"	240	26	1	
Mike Lucci	LB	6'2"	223	23		
Stan Sczurek	LB	5'11"	225	24		
Sam Tidmore	LB	6'1"	225	24		
Walter Beach	DB	6'	185	28		
Larry Benz	DB	5'11"	185	22	7	
Ross Fichtner	DB	6'	185	25	2	6
Bernie Parrish	DB	5'11"	195	28		
Jim Shofner	DB	6'2"	192	27		
Jim Shorter	DB	5'11"	186	22		
Bobby Franklin	HB-DB	5'11"	182	27	2	

Don Fleming – killed in construction accident, June 4, 1963

Use Name	Pos.	Hgt	Wgt	Age	Int	Pts
Jim Ninowski	QB	6'1"	207	27		
Frank Ryan	QB	6'3"	200	27		12
Ernie Green	HB	6'2"	205	24		18
Charlie Scales	HB	5'11"	215	24		6
Ken Webb	HB	5'11"	205	28		
Jimmy Brown	FB	6'2"	228	27		90
Gary Collins	FL	6'4"	208	22		78
Ray Renfro	FL	6'1"	192	32		6
Johnny Brewer	OE	6'4"	235	26		
Bob Crespino	OE	6'4"	225	25		6
Tom Hutchinson	OE	6'1"	190	22		
Rich Kreitling	OE	6'2"	208	28		36
Lou Groza	K	6'3"	250	39		85

ST. LOUIS CARDINALS 9-5-0 Wally Lemm

Scores of Each Game		
34	Dallas	7
28	Philadelphia	24
10	Pittsburgh	23
56	Minnesota	14
24	PITTSBURGH	23
7	GREEN BAY	30
21	Washington	7
21	NEW YORK	38
24	WASHINGTON	20
20	Cleveland	14
24	New York	17
10	CLEVELAND	24
38	PHILADELPHIA	14
24	DALLAS	28

Use Name	Pos.	Hgt	Wgt	Age	Int	Pts
Irv Goode	OT	6'4"	245	22		
Ernie McMillan	OT	6'6"	255	25		
Bob Reynolds	OT	6'6"	256	22		
Ed Cook	OG-OT	6'2"	240	31		
Ken Gray	OG	6'2"	240	27		
John Houser	OG	6'3"	242	27		
Bob DeMarco	C	6'3"	240	25		
Don Brumm	DE	6'3"	225	20		
Ed Henke	DE	6'3"	230	35		
Tom Redmond	DE	6'5"	240	26		
Joe Robb	DE	6'3"	230	26		
Fate Echols	DT	6'1"	260	24		
Don Owens	DT	6'5"	255	31		
Luke Owens	DT	6'2"	255	30		
Sam Silas	DT	6'4"	250	20		

Use Name	Pos.	Hgt	Wgt	Age	Int	Pts
Garland Boyette	LB	6'1"	225	23		
Bill Koman	LB	6'2"	230	29		
Dave Meggyesy	LB	6'1"	215	21		
Dale Meinert	LB	6'2"	220	30		
Marion Rushing	LB	6'2"	210	26		
Larry Stallings	LB	6'2"	225	21		
Jimmy Burson	DB	6'	180	21		
Pat Fischer	DB	5'10"	165	23	8	
Jimmy Hill	DB	6'2"	190	34	3	6
Billy Stacy	DB	6'1"	190	27	1	
Johnny Symank	DB	5'11"	180	28	1	6
Jerry Stovall	DB	6'2"	195	21	1	
Larry Wilson	DB	6'	185	25	4	12

John Wittenborn – Injury

Use Name	Pos.	Hgt	Wgt	Age	Int	Pts
Buddy Humphrey	QB	6'1"	197	27		
Charley Johnson	QB	6'	190	26		6
John David Crow	HB	6'2"	215	28		
Bob Paremore	HB	5'11"	190	23		12
Bill Triplett	HB	6'2"	210	24		48
Joe Childress	FB-HB	6'	200	29		24
Prentice Gautt	FB	6'	200	25		
Bill Thornton	FB	6'1"	205	23		6
Mal Hammack	OE-FB	6'2"	205	30		
Bobby Joe Conrad	FL	6'	195	28		60
Taz Anderson	OE	6'2"	200	24		
Billy Gambrell	OE	5'10"	175	21		
Sonny Randle	OE	6'2"	187	27		72
Jackie Smith	OE	6'4"	205	22		12
Jim Bakken	K	6'	200	22		77

PITTSBURGH STEELERS 7-4-3 Buddy Parker

Scores of Each Game		
21	Philadelphia	21
31	NEW YORK	0
23	ST. LOUIS	10
23	Cleveland	35
23	St. Louis	24
38	WASHINGTON	27
27	DALLAS	21
14	Green Bay	33
9	CLEVELAND	7
34	Washington	28
17	CHICAGO	17
20	PHILADELPHIA	20
24	Dallas	19
17	New York	33

Use Name	Pos.	Hgt	Wgt	Age	Int	Pts
Art Anderson	OT	6'3"	244	26		
Charlie Bradshaw	OT	6'6"	255	27		
Dan James	OT	6'4"	260	26		
Ray Lemek	OG	6'	240	29		
Mike Sandusky	OG	6'	230	30		
Ron Stehouwer	OG	6'2"	230	26		
Buzz Nutter	C	6'4"	230	32		
John Baker	DE	6'6"	270	28		
Lou Michaels	DE	6'2"	235	27	1	95
Ernie Stautner	DT-DE	6'1"	230	38		
Frank Atkinson	DT	6'3"	240	22		
Lou Cordileone	DT	6'	250	26		
Joe Krupa	DT	6'2"	235	30		

Use Name	Pos.	Hgt	Wgt	Age	Int	Pts
Myron Pottios	LB	6'2"	240	23	4	
John Reger	LB	6'	230	32	1	
Bob Rowley	LB	6'2"	225	21		
Andy Russell	LB	6'3"	210	21	3	
Bob Schmitz	LB	6'1"	230	25		2
George Tarasovic (to PHI)	LB	6'4"	245	34		
Jim Bradshaw	DB	6'1"	190	24	1	
Willie Daniel	DB	5'11"	185	25		
Glenn Glass	DB	6'	190	26	1	
Dick Haley	DB	5'10"	190	27	6	6
Brady Keys	DB	6'	185	27		
Clendon Thomas	DB	6'2"	195	26	8	

Big Daddy Lipscomb – died May 10

Use Name	Pos.	Hgt	Wgt	Age	Int	Pts
Ed Brown	QB	6'2"	210	34		12
Bill Nelsen	QB	6'	195	22		
Terry Nofsinger	QB	6'4"	205	25		
Dick Hoak	HB	5'11"	190	24		42
Theron Sapp (from PHI)	HB	6'1"	200	28		6
Tom Tracy (to WAS)	HB	5'9"	205	31		8
Bob Ferguson (to MIN)	FB	5'11"	220	22		6
John Henry Johnson	FB	6'2"	215	33		30
Gary Ballman	FL	6"	195	23		36
Roy Curry	FL	6'1"	195	23		6
John Burrell	OE	6'3"	188	23		
Preston Carpenter	OE	6'2"	190	29		6
Buddy Dial	OE	6'1"	195	26		54
Red Mack	OE	5'10"	185	26		18
John Powers	OE	6'2"	210	22		

DALLAS COWBOYS 4-10-0 Tom Landry

Scores of Each Game		
7	ST. LOUIS	34
24	CLEVELAND	41
17	Washington	21
21	Philadelphia	24
17	DETROIT	14
21	New York	37
21	Pittsburgh	27
35	WASHINGTON	20
24	San Francisco	31
27	PHILADELPHIA	20
17	Cleveland	27
27	NEW YORK	34
19	PITTSBURGH	24
28	St. Louis	24

Use Name	Pos.	Hgt	Wgt	Age	Int	Pts
Bob Fry	OT	6'4"	232	32		
Tony Liscio	OT	6'5"	240	23		
Ed Nutting	OT	6'4"	246	24		
Ray Schoenke	OT	6'3"	234	21		
Joe Bob Isbell	OG	6'1"	225	23		
Dale Memmelaar	OG	6'2"	245	26		
Lance Poimbeouf	OG	6'3"	225	23		
Jim Ray Smith	OT-OG	6'3"	245	32		
Mike Connelly	C	6'3"	242	27		
Lynn Hoyem	OG-C	6'4"	240	23		
George Andrie	DE	6'7"	248	23		
Larry Stephens	DE	6'4"	260	25		
Bob Lilly	DT-DE	6'4"	250	24		6
John Meyers	DT	6'6"	267	23		
Guy Reese	DT	6'5"	258	23		

Use Name	Pos.	Hgt	Wgt	Age	Int	Pts
Dave Edwards	LB	6'3"	215	24	1	
Harold Hays	LB	6'3"	235	22		
Chuck Howley	LB	6'3"	223	27	2	
Lee Roy Jordan	LB	6'2"	210	22	3	
Jerry Tubbs	LB	6'2"	215	28	2	
Don Bishop	DB	6'2"	210	28	5	
Mike Gaechter	DB	6'	196	23	3	
Cornell Green	DB	6'4"	216	23	7	6
Warren Livingston	DB	5'10"	185	25	3	
Jerry Overton	DB	6'2"	190	22		
Jimmy Ridlon	DB	6'1"	177	28		

Maury Youmans – Injury
Dan Talbert – Military Service

Use Name	Pos.	Hgt	Wgt	Age	Int	Pts
Eddie LeBaron	QB	5'9"	170	33		
Don Meredith	QB	6'2"	200	25		18
Amos Bullocks	HB	6'1"	202	24		12
Wendell Hays	HB	6'2"	210	22		
Amos Marsh	HB	6'1"	223	24		30
Jim Stiger	HB	5'11"	190	22		6
Don Perkins	FB	5'10"	196	25		42
Frank Clarke	FL	6'	215	30		60
Gary Barnes	OE	6'4"	210	23		
Lee Folkins	OE	6'5"	220	24		24
Billy Howton	OE	6'2"	194	33		18
Pettis Norman	OE	6'3"	210	23		18
Sam Baker	K	6'2"	220	31		65

NEW YORK GIANTS

RUSHING

Last Name	No.	Yds	Avg	TD
King	161	613	3.8	3
Morrison	119	568	4.8	3
Webster	75	255	3.4	4
McElhenny	55	175	3.2	0
Tittle	18	99	5.5	2
Killett	11	36	3.3	0
Griffing	5	20	4.0	0
Gifford	4	10	2.5	0
Chandler	1	0	0.0	0
Anderson	1	−2	−2.0	0

RECEIVING

Last Name	No.	Yds	Avg	TD
Shofner	64	1181	18	9
Gifford	42	657	16	7
King	32	377	12	5
Morrison	31	284	9	7
Walton	26	371	14	6
Thomas	22	469	21	3
Webster	15	128	9	0
McElhenny	11	91	8	2

PUNT RETURNS

Last Name	No.	Yds	Avg	TD
Dove	17	198	12	0
McElhenny	13	74	6	0
Pesonen	7	47	7	0
Webb	3	45	15	0

KICKOFF RETURNS

Last Name	No.	Yds	Avg	TD
Killett	14	332	24	0
Pesonen	8	197	25	0
McElhenny	6	136	23	0
Counts	5	107	21	0
Morrison	4	75	19	0
Webb	3	62	21	0
Dove	3	56	19	0
Guy	3	44	15	0
Scott	0	9	0	0

PASSING – PUNTING – KICKING

PASSING	Att	Comp	%	Yds	Yd/Att	TD	Int–	%	RK
Tittle	367	221	60	3145	8.6	36	14–	4	1
Griffing	40	16	40	306	7.7	3	4–	10	
Morrison	2	1	50	18	9.0	0	0–	0	

PUNTING	No	Avg
Chandler	59	44.9

KICKING	XP	Att	%	FG	Att	%
Chandler	52	56	93	18	29	62

CLEVELAND BROWNS

RUSHING

Last Name	No.	Yds	Avg	TD
Jim Brown	291	1863	6.4	12
Green	87	526	6.0	0
Ryan	62	224	3.6	2
Webb	12	58	4.8	0
Scales	2	−3	−1.5	1
Franklin	1	−10	−10.0	0
Ninowski	5	−19	−3.8	0

RECEIVING

Last Name	No.	Yds	Avg	TD
Collins	43	674	16	13
Brewer	29	454	16	0
Green	28	305	11	3
Jim Brown	24	268	11	3
Kreitling	22	386	18	6
Hutchinson	9	244	27	0
Renfro	4	82	21	1
Crespino	2	22	11	1
Webb	2	2	1	0
Scales	1	13	13	0
Ryan	0	−1	0	0

PUNT RETURNS

Last Name	No.	Yds	Avg	TD
Shorter	7	134	19	0
Green	6	79	13	0
Shofner	9	41	5	0
Parrish	3	31	10	0

KICKOFF RETURNS

Last Name	No.	Yds	Avg	TD
Scales	16	432	27	0
Green	18	394	22	0
Shorter	9	219	24	0
Franklin	2	33	17	0
Webb	1	12	12	0
Tidmore	1	5	5	0
Morrow	1	4	4	0
Benz	1	0	0	0
Shofner	1	0	0	0

PASSING – PUNTING – KICKING

PASSING	Att	Comp	%	Yds	Yd/Att	TD	Int–	%	RK
Ryan	256	135	53	2026	7.9	25	13–	5	4
Ninowski	61	29	48	423	6.9	2	6–	10	
Jim Brown	4	0	0	0	0.0	0	0–	0	
Groza	1	0	0	0	0.0	0	1–	100	

PUNTING	No	Avg
Collins	54	40.0

KICKING	XP	Att	%	FG	Att	%
Groza	40	43	93	15	23	65

ST. LOUIS CARDINALS

RUSHING

Last Name	No.	Yds	Avg	TD
Childress	174	701	4.0	2
Triplett	134	652	4.9	5
Johnson	41	143	3.5	1
Thornton	19	111	5.8	1
Paremore	36	107	3.0	0
Wilson	2	38	19.0	1
Crow	9	34	3.8	0
Stovall	1	32	32.0	0
Hammack	3	16	5.3	0
Gautt	3	5	1.7	0
Conrad	1	0	0.0	0

RECEIVING

Last Name	No.	Yds	Avg	TD
Conrad	73	967	13	10
Randle	51	1014	20	12
Triplett	31	396	13	3
Smith	28	445	16	2
Childress	25	354	14	2
Paremore	6	89	15	1
Anderson	5	47	9	0
Thornton	4	10	3	0
Gambrell	3	63	21	0
Hammack	1	15	15	0
Gautt	1	3	3	0

PUNT RETURNS

Last Name	No.	Yds	Avg	TD
Gambrell	11	111	10	0
Fischer	9	25	3	0
Paremore	4	23	6	0
Stacy	1	6	6	0
Conrad	1	1	1	0

KICKOFF RETURNS

Last Name	No.	Yds	Avg	TD
Stovall	15	419	28	0
Paremore	12	292	24	0
Triplett	14	229	16	0
Thornton	4	70	18	0
Hammack	4	60	15	0
Goode	1	0	0	0
Gray	1	0	0	0
Redmond	1	0	0	0

PASSING – PUNTING – KICKING

PASSING	Att	Comp	%	Yds	Yd/Att	TD	Int–	%	RK
Johnson	423	222	52	3280	7.8	28	21–	5	5
Humphrey	11	4	36	96	8.7	1	0–	0	
Crow	3	2	67	27	9.0	1	0–	0	
Gautt	1	0	0	0	0.0	0	8–	0	

PUNTING	No	Avg
Stovall	65	40.7

KICKING	XP	Att	%	FG	Att	%
Bakken	44	44	100	11	21	52

PITTSBURGH STEELERS

RUSHING

Last Name	No.	Yds	Avg	TD
Johnson	186	773	4.2	4
Hoak	216	679	3.1	6
Sapp	104	452	4.3	1
Ferguson	46	172	3.7	1
Tracy	29	61	2.1	1
Ballman	8	59	7.4	0
Brown	15	20	1.3	2
Mack	2	1	0.5	0
Carpenter	1	−3	−3.0	0
Nelsen	1	−6	−6.0	0

RECEIVING

Last Name	No.	Yds	Avg	TD
Dial	60	1295	22	9
Ballman	26	492	19	5
Mack	25	618	25	3
Johnson	21	145	7	1
Carpenter	17	233	14	1
Hoak	11	118	11	1
Tracy	7	112	16	0
Sapp	4	36	9	0
Ferguson	3	7	2	0
Burrell	2	27	14	0
Curry	1	31	31	1

PUNT RETURNS

Last Name	No.	Yds	Avg	TD
Keys	13	198	15	0
Haley	12	59	5	0
Thomas	6	24	4	0

KICKOFF RETURNS

Last Name	No.	Yds	Avg	TD
Ballman	22	698	32	1
Thomas	12	286	24	0
Keys	9	219	24	0
Sapp	5	58	12	0
Glass	2	46	23	0
Curry	1	27	27	0
Cordileone	1	18	18	0

PASSING – PUNTING – KICKING

PASSING	Att	Comp	%	Yds	Yd/Att	TD	Int–	%	RK
Brown	362	168	46	2982	8.2	21	20–	6	9
Tracy	4	1	25	23	5.8	0	0–	0	
Nofsinger	3	2	67	46	15.3	0	0–	0	
Nelsen	2	0	0	0	0.0	0	0–	0	

PUNTING	No	Avg
Brown	57	39.6
J. Bradshaw	2	35.0

KICKING	XP	Att	%	FG	Att	%
Michaels	32	35	91	21	41	51
Tracy	2	2	100	0	0	0

DALLAS COWBOYS

RUSHING

Last Name	No.	Yds	Avg	TD
Perkins	149	614	4.1	7
Marsh	99	483	4.9	5
Bullocks	96	341	3.6	2
Meredith	41	185	4.5	3
Stiger	31	140	4.5	1
Baker	1	15	15.0	0
Clarke	1	12	12.0	0
LeBaron	2	5	2.5	0

RECEIVING

Last Name	No.	Yds	Avg	TD
Clarke	43	833	19	10
Howton	33	514	16	3
Folkins	31	407	13	4
Marsh	26	224	9	0
Norman	18	341	19	3
Barnes	15	195	13	0
Perkins	14	84	6	0
Stiger	13	131	10	0
Bullocks	7	70	10	0

PUNT RETURNS

Last Name	No.	Yds	Avg	TD
Stiger	14	141	10	0
Overton	5	32	6	0
Gaechter	2	2	1	0
Howley	1	2	2	0
Norman	1	0	0	0

KICKOFF RETURNS

Last Name	No.	Yds	Avg	TD
Bullocks	19	453	24	0
Stiger	18	432	24	0
Marsh	9	167	19	0
Hays	2	48	24	0

PASSING – PUNTING – KICKING

PASSING	Att	Comp	%	Yds	Yd/Att	TD	Int–	%	RK
Meredith	310	167	54	2381	7.7	17	18–	6	10
LeBaron	65	33	51	418	6.4	3	3–	5	

PUNTING	No	Avg
Baker	71	44.2

KICKING	XP	Att	%	FG	Att	%
Baker	38	38	100	9	20	45

LASTERN CONFERENCE – Continued

WASHINGTON REDSKINS 3-11-0 Bill McPeak

Scores of Each Game		
14	Cleveland	37
37	Los Angeles	14
21	DALLAS	17
14	NEW YORK	24
24	PHILADELPHIA	37
27	Pittsburgh	38
7	ST. LOUIS	21
20	Dallas	35
20	St. Louis	24
28	PITTSBURGH	34
13	Philadelphia	10
20	BALTIMORE	36
14	New York	44
20	CLEVELAND	27

Use Name	Pos.	Hgt	Wgt	Age	Int	Pts
Fran O'Brien	OT	6'1"	260	28		
Riley Mattson	OT	6'4"	257	24		
Andy Cvercko (from CLE)	OG	6'	243	26		
Wiley Feagin	OG	6'2"	235	26		
John Nisby	OG	6'1"	247	30		
Vince Promuto	OG	6'1"	240	25		
Fred Hageman	C	6'4"	242	25		
John Paluck	DE	6'2"	252	30	1	
Ron Snidow	DE	6'4"	245	21		
Andy Stynchula	DE	6'3"	257	24		
Ben Davidson	DT	6'8"	275	23		
Ed Khayat	DT	6'3"	245	28		
Joe Rutgens	DT	6'2"	265	24		
Bob Toneff	DT	6'3"	275	33		

Use Name	Pos.	Hgt	Wgt	Age	Int	Pts
Rod Breedlove	LB	6'2"	227	25	1	
Harry Butsko	LB	6'3"	220	22		
Carl Kammerer	LB	6'3"	237	26	2	
Gorden Kelley	LB	6'3"	230	25		
Al Miller	LB	6'	228	23		
Bob Pellegrini	LB	6'2"	235	28	2	
Claude Crabb	DB	6'	197	23	3	6
Dale Hackbart	DB	6'3"	208	27	1	
Ted Rzempoluch	DB	6'1"	195	22		
Johnny Sample	DB	6'1"	200	26	1	
Lonnie Sanders	DB	6'3"	200	21	3	
Jim Steffen	DB	6'	200	26	5	6

Use Name	Pos.	Hgt	Wgt	Age	Int	Pts
George Izo	QB	6'3"	214	26		
Norm Snead	QB	6'4"	215	23		12
Billy Barnes	HB	5'11"	195	28		36
Leroy Jackson	HB	6'	190	23		
Dick James	DB-HB	5'9"	180	29	2	36
Don Bosseler	FB	6'1"	212	27		12
Jim Cunningham	FB	5'11"	224	24		6
Dave Francis	FB	6'1"	210	22		
Frank Budd	FL	5'10"	187	24		
Bobby Mitchell	FL	6'	195	28		48
Bill Anderson	OE	6'3"	215	27		6
Jim Collier	OE	6'2"	195	24		
Fred Dugan	OE	6'3"	194	29		18
Pat Richter	OE	6'5"	230	22		18
Bob Khayat	K	6'2"	230	25		69

PHILADELPHIA EAGLES 2-10-2 Nick Skorich

Scores of Each Game		
21	PITTSBURGH	21
24	ST. LOUIS	28
14	NEW YORK	37
24	DALLAS	21
37	Washington	24
7	Cleveland	37
7	Chicago	16
17	CLEVELAND	23
14	New York	42
20	Dallas	27
10	WASHINGTON	13
20	Pittsburgh	20
14	St. Louis	38
13	MINNESOTA	34

Use Name	Pos.	Hgt	Wgt	Age	Int	Pts
Dave Graham	OT	6'3"	240	24		
J. D. Smith	OT	6'5"	250	27		
Howard Keys	OG-C-OT	6'3"	240	28		
Ed Blaine	OG	6'2"	240	23		
Bill Byrne	OG	6'	240	22		
Pete Case	OG	6'3"	237	22		
Jim Skaggs	OG	6'2"	230	23		
Jim Schrader	C	6'2"	250	31		
Jerry Mazzanti	DE	6'3"	240	23		
Bill Quinlan	DE	6'3"	250	31		
Bobby Richards	DE	6'2"	240	24		
Dick Stafford	DE	6'4"	270	23		
Frank Fuller	DT	6'4"	250	34		
Riley Gunnels	DT	6'3"	250	26		
Ray Mansfield	DT	6'3"	250	22		
John Mellekas	DT	6'3"	255	30		

Use Name	Pos.	Hgt	Wgt	Age	Int	Pts
Maxie Baughan	LB	6'1"	226	25	1	
Lee Roy Caffey	LB	6'3"	230	23	1	6
Bob Harrison	LB	6'2"	220	26		
Ralph Heck	LB	6'2"	220	22		
Dave Lloyd	LB	6'3"	248	27	3	
Don Burroughs	DB	6'4"	190	32	4	
Jimmy Carr	DB	6'1"	205	30	1	
Irv Cross	DB	6'1"	192	24	2	
Mike McClellan	DB	6'1"	185	24	1	
Nate Ramsey	DB	6'1"	195	22	1	
Ben Scotti	DB	6'1"	186	26	1	

Mike Woulfe – Injury
Gene Gossage – Canadian Football League

Use Name	Pos.	Hgt	Wgt	Age	Int	Pts
Ralph Guglielmi (from NY)	QB	6'1"	195	30		
King Hill	QB	6'3"	213	27		
Sonny Jurgensen	QB	5'11"	200	29		6
Timmy Brown	HB	5'10"	190	26		66
Paul Dudley	HB	6'	185	23		
Tom Woodeshick	HB	6'	210	21		
Ted Dean	FB-HB	6'2"	210	25		
Clarence Peaks	FB	6'1"	220	27		12
Ron Goodwin	FL	6'	170	21		24
Tommy McDonald	FL	5'10"	172	29		48
Gary Henson	OE	6'3"	200	23		
Dick Lucas	OE	6'2"	215	29		
Pete Retzlaff	OE	6'1"	210	32		24
Ralph Smith	OE	6'2"	203	24		6
Mike Clark	K	6'1"	200	22		50

WESTERN CONFERENCE

CHICAGO BEARS 11-1-2 George Halas

Scores of Each Game		
10	Green Bay	3
28	Minnesota	7
37	Detroit	21
10	BALTIMORE	3
52	Los Angeles	14
14	San Francisco	20
16	PHILADELPHIA	7
17	Baltimore	7
6	LOS ANGELES	0
26	GREEN BAY	7
17	Pittsburgh	17
17	MINNESOTA	17
27	SAN FRANCISCO	7
24	DETROIT	14

Use Name	Pos.	Hgt	Wgt	Age	Int	Pts
Steve Barnett	OT	6'1"	255	22		
Herm Lee	OT	6'4"	247	32		
Bob Wetoska	OT	6'3"	240	25		
Jim Cadile	OG	6'3"	230	22		
Roger Davis	OG	6'3"	235	25		
Ted Karras	OG	6'1"	243	30		
Mike Pyle	C	6'3"	245	24		
Doug Atkins	DE	6'8"	255	33	1	2
Bob Kilcullen	DE	6'3"	245	27		
Ed O'Bradovich	DE	6'3"	255	23		
John Johnson	DT	6'5"	260	22		
Stan Jones	DT	6'1"	250	32		
Earl Leggett	DT	6'3"	250	29		
Fred Williams	DT	6'4"	248	33		

Use Name	Pos.	Hgt	Wgt	Age	Int	Pts
Tom Bettis	LB	6'2"	235	30		
Joe Fortunato	LB	6'	225	33	2	
Bill George	LB	6'2"	235	32	1	
Roger LeClerc	LB	6'3"	235	25	1	39
Larry Morris	LB	6'2"	230	28		
J. C. Caroline	DB	6'1"	190	30	1	
Larry Glueck	DB	6'	190	21	1	
Bennie McRae	DB	6'1"	180	22	6	6
Richie Petitbon	DB	6'3"	205	25	8	6
Rosey Taylor	DB	5'11"	186	24	9	6
Dave Whitsell	DB	6'	190	27	6	6

Use Name	Pos.	Hgt	Wgt	Age	Int	Pts
Rudy Bukich	QB	6'1"	205	32		6
Billy Wade	QB	6'2"	205	32		36
Charlie Bivins	HB	6'2"	212	24		
Ronnie Bull	HB	6'	200	23		18
Willie Galimore	HB	6'1"	187	28		30
Billy Martin	HB	5'11"	196	25		
Rick Casares	FB	6'2"	225	32		6
Joe Marconi	FB	6'2"	225	29		24
Johnny Morris	FL	5'10"	180	28		12
Angie Coia	OE	6'2"	202	25		6
Mike Ditka	OE	6'3"	230	23		48
Bo Farrington	OE	6'3"	217	27		12
Bob Jencks	OE	6'5"	227	22		38
Bobby Joe Green	K	5'11"	175	25		

GREEN BAY PACKERS 11-2-1 Vince Lombardi

Scores of Each Game		
3	CHICAGO	10
31	DETROIT	10
31	BALTIMORE	20
42	LOS ANGELES	10
37	Minnesota	28
30	St. Louis	7
34	Baltimore	20
33	PITTSBURGH	14
28	MINNESOTA	7
7	Chicago	26
28	SAN FRANCISCO	10
13	Detroit	13
31	Los Angeles	14
21	San Francisco	17

Use Name	Pos.	Hgt	Wgt	Age	Int	Pts
Forrest Gregg	OT	6'4"	250	30		
Norm Masters	OT	6'2"	250	30		
Bob Skoronski	C-OT	6'3"	250	30		
Dan Grimm	OG	6'3"	240	22		
Jerry Kramer	OG	6'3"	255	28		91
Fuzzy Thurston	OG	6'1"	250	30		
Ken Iman	C	6'1"	230	24		
Jim Ringo	C	6'1"	235	32		
Lionel Aldridge	DE	6'4"	240	21		
Willie Davis	DE	6'3"	240	30		2
Urban Henry	DT-DE	6'4"	265	28		
Dave Hanner	DT	6'2"	260	34	1	
Ron Kostelnik	DT	6'4"	260	23		
Henry Jordan	DE-DT	6'3"	250	28		

Use Name	Pos.	Hgt	Wgt	Age	Int	Pts
Dan Currie	LB	6'3"	240	29	1	
Bill Forester	LB	6'3"	240	32	1	
Ed Holler	LB	6'2"	230	23		
Ray Nitschke	LB	6'3"	235	27	2	
Dave Robinson	LB	6'3"	240	22		
Herb Adderley	DB	6'1"	205	24	5	6
Hank Gremminger	DB	6'1"	205	30	3	6
Jerry Norton	DB	5'11"	195	33		
Jesse Whittenton	DB	6'	195	29	4	
Willie Wood	DB	5'10"	190	27	5	

Paul Hornung – Suspended by commissioner

Use Name	Pos.	Hgt	Wgt	Age	Int	Pts
John Roach	QB	6'4"	200	30		
Bart Starr	QB	6'1"	200	30		
Lew Carpenter	HB	6'1"	215	31		
Tom Moore	HB	6'2"	215	25		48
Elijah Pitts	HB	6'1"	200	24		36
Earl Gros	FB	6'3"	230	22		12
Frank Mestnik	FB	6'2"	220	25		
Jim Taylor	FB	6'	215	28		60
Boyd Dowler	FL	6'5"	225	26		36
Bob Jeter	FL	6'1"	190	25		
Jan Barrett (to OAK-A)	OE	6'3"	230	22		
Marv Fleming	OE	6'4"	225	21		12
Ron Kramer	OE	6'3"	240	28		24
Max McGee	OE	6'3"	205	31		36

BALTIMORE COLTS 8-6-0 Don Shula

Scores of Each Game		
28	NEW YORK	37
20	San Francisco	14
20	Green Bay	31
3	Chicago	10
20	SAN FRANCISCO	3
25	Detroit	21
20	GREEN BAY	34
7	CHICAGO	17
24	DETROIT	21
37	Minnesota	34
16	Los Angeles	17
36	Washington	20
41	MINNESOTA	10
19	LOS ANGELES	16

Use Name	Pos.	Hgt	Wgt	Age	Int	Pts
Tom Gilburg	OT	6'5"	245	24		
George Preas	OT	6'2"	250	31		
Bob Vogel	OT	6'5"	232	21		
Dan Sullivan	OG-OT	6'3"	250	24		
Jim Parker	OG	6'3"	275	29		
Palmer Pyle	OG	6'2"	250	26		
Alex Sandusky	OG	6'1"	242	31		
Dick Szymanski	C	6'3"	235	31		
Ordell Braase	DE	6'4"	242	31		
Gino Marchetti	DE	6'4"	245	37		6
Don Thompson	DE	6'4"	225	24		
Jim Colvin	DT	6'2"	255	26		2
John Diehl	DT	6'7"	285	27		
Fred Miller	DT	6'3"	240	22		

Use Name	Pos.	Hgt	Wgt	Age	Int	Pts
Jackie Burkett	LB	6'4"	230	26		
Jim Maples	LB	6'4"	225	22		
Bill Pellington	LB	6'2"	238	34		
Bill Saul	LB	6'4"	225	22		
Don Shinnick	LB	6'	235	28	2	
Bobby Boyd	DB	5'10"	190	25	3	6
Wendell Harris	DB	5'11"	190	22		
Jerry Logan	DB	6'1"	185	22	1	
Lenny Lyles	DB	6'2"	202	27	2	6
Andy Nelson	DB	6'1"	180	30	3	6
Jim Welch	DB	6'	190	25	4	

Billy Ray Smith – Injury

Use Name	Pos.	Hgt	Wgt	Age	Int	Pts
Gary Cuozzo	QB	6'1"	190	22		
Johnny Unitas	QB	6'1"	194	30		
Tom Matte	HB	6'	195	24		30
Lenny Moore	HB	6'1"	190	30		24
Alex Hawkins	OE-HB	6'1"	190	26		
Nate Craddock	FB	6'	220	20		
Jerry Hill	FB	5'11"	210	23		36
J. W. Lockett	FB	6'2"	230	26		6
Jimmy Orr	FL	5'11"	175	27		30
Willie Richardson	FL	6'2"	198	23		
Ray Berry	OE	6'2"	190	30		18
Dick Bielski	OE	6'1"	225	31		
John Mackey	OE	6'3"	220	21		42
R. C. Owens	OE	6'3"	195	28		
Butch Wilson	OE	6'2"	210	21		
Jim Martin	K	6'2"	230	39		104

EASTERN CONFERENCE—Continued

WASHINGTON REDSKINS

RUSHING

Last Name	No.	Yds	Avg	TD
James	105	384	3.7	4
Barnes	93	374	4.0	5
Bosseler	79	290	3.7	2
Snead	23	100	4.3	2
Cunningham	16	33	2.1	1
Jackson	3	30	10.0	0
Mitchell	3	24	8.0	0
Izo	3	4	1.3	0

RECEIVING

Last Name	No.	Yds	Avg	TD
Mitchell	69	1436	21	7
Richter	27	383	14	3
Bosseler	25	289	12	0
Dugan	20	288	14	3
James	15	302	20	2
Barnes	15	256	17	1
Anderson	14	288	21	1
Cunningham	8	86	11	0
Budd	5	106	21	0

PUNT RETURNS

Last Name	No.	Yds	Avg	TD
James	16	214	13	0
Steffen	5	83	17	0
Mitchell	6	49	8	0
Sample	2	45	23	0
Barnes	1	0	0	0

KICKOFF RETURNS

Last Name	No.	Yds	Avg	TD
James	30	830	28	0
Mitchell	9	343	38	1
Budd	10	252	25	0
Jackson	5	113	23	0
Cunningham	6	96	16	0
Steffen	3	84	28	0
Snidow	1	0	0	

PASSING – PUNTING – KICKING

PASSING	Att	Comp	%	Yds	Yd/Att	TD	Int–	%	RK
Snead	363	175	48	3043	8.4	13	27–	7	11
Izo	58	25	43	378	6.5	3	6–	10	
Barnes	4	3	75	81	20.3	1	0–	0	
Anderson	1	0	0	0	0.0	0	1–	100	
James	1	0	0	0	0.0	0	0–	0	

PUNTING	No	Avg
Richter	53	41.7

KICKING	XP	Att	%	FG	Att	%
B. Khayat	33	35	94	12	26	46

PHILADELPHIA EAGLES

RUSHING

Last Name	No.	Yds	Avg	TD
Brown	192	841	4.4	6
Dean	79	268	3.4	0
Peaks	64	212	3.3	1
Jurgensen	13	38	2.9	1
Guglielmi	4	23	5.8	0
Dudley	11	21	1.9	0
Woodeshick	5	18	3.6	0
Hill	3	–1	–0.3	0

RECEIVING

Last Name	No.	Yds	Avg	TD
Retzlaff	57	895	16	4
McDonald	41	731	18	8
Brown	36	487	14	4
Peaks	22	167	8	1
Goodwin	15	215	14	4
Dean	14	108	8	0
R. Smith	5	63	13	1
Dudley	1	8	8	0
Woodeshick	1	–3	–3	0

PUNT RETURNS

Last Name	No.	Yds	Avg	TD
Brown	16	152	10	0
Dean	10	74	7	0

KICKOFF RETURNS

Last Name	No.	Yds	Avg	TD
Brown	33	945	29	1
Dean	16	425	27	0
Woodeshick	3	72	24	0
Henson	3	21	7	0
R. Smith	2	18	9	0
Caffey	1	6	6	0

PASSING – PUNTING – KICKING

PASSING	Att	Comp	%	Yds	Yd/Att	TD	Int–	%	RK
Hill	186	91	49	1213	6.5	10	17–	9	14
Jurgensen	184	99	54	1413	7.7	11	13–	7	12
Guglielmi	24	7	29	118	4.9	0	3–	13	
Brown	3	1	33	11	3.7	1	1–	33	

PUNTING	No	Avg
Hill	69	43.1

KICKING	XP	Att	%	FG	Att	%
Clark	29	32	91	7	15	47

WESTERN CONFERENCE

CHICAGO BEARS

RUSHING

Last Name	No.	Yds	Avg	TD
Marconi	118	446	3.8	2
Bull	117	404	3.5	1
Galimore	85	321	3.8	5
Casares	65	277	4.3	0
Wade	45	132	2.9	6
Bivins	44	104	2.4	0
J. Morris	1	10	10.0	0
Coia	2	2	1.0	0
Bukich	7	1	0.1	1
Whitsell	1	–8	–8.0	0
Green	2	–10	–5.0	0

RECEIVING

Last Name	No.	Yds	Avg	TD
Ditka	59	794	13	8
J. Morris	47	705	15	2
Marconi	28	335	12	2
Farrington	21	335	16	2
Bull	19	132	7	2
Casares	19	94	5	1
Galimore	13	131	10	0
Coia	11	116	11	1
Bivins	3	22	7	0
Jencks	1	6	6	0

PUNT RETURNS

Last Name	No.	Yds	Avg	TD
J. Morris	16	164	10	0
Martin	2	62	31	0
Taylor	12	51	4	0

KICKOFF RETURNS

Last Name	No.	Yds	Avg	TD
Taylor	6	118	20	0
Bull	7	105	15	0
Martin	4	99	25	0
Bivins	2	40	20	0
Galimore	1	19	19	0
Casares	2	18	9	0
Marconi	2	15	8	0
Johnson	1	10	10	0
Pyle	1	0	0	0

PASSING – PUNTING – KICKING

PASSING	Att	Comp	%	Yds	Yd/Att	TD	Int–	%	RK
Wade	356	192	54	2301	6.5	15	12–	3	8
Bukich	43	29	67	369	8.6	3	2–	5	
Bull	3	0	0	0	0.0	0	0–	0	
Green	1	0	0	0	0.0	0	0–	0	
LeClerc	1	0	0	0	0.0	0	0–	0	

PUNTING	No	Avg
Green	64	46.5

KICKING	XP	Att	%	FG	Att	%
Jencks	35	37	95	1	10	10
LeClerc	0	0	0	13	23	57

GREEN BAY PACKERS

RUSHING

Last Name	No.	Yds	Avg	TD
Taylor	248	1018	4.1	9
Moore	132	658	5.0	6
Pitts	54	212	3.9	5
Gros	48	203	4.2	2
Starr	13	116	8.9	0
Roach	3	31	10.3	0
Carpenter	2	8	4.0	0
Mestnik	1	4	4.0	0
Norton	2	0	0.0	0

RECEIVING

Last Name	No.	Yds	Avg	TD
Dowler	53	901	17	6
McGee	39	749	19	6
R. Kramer	32	537	17	4
Moore	23	237	10	2
Taylor	13	68	5	1
Pitts	9	54	6	1
Fleming	7	132	19	2
Gros	1	19	19	0
Carpenter	1	12	12	0
Jeter	1	2	2	0

PUNT RETURNS

Last Name	No.	Yds	Avg	TD
Wood	19	169	9	0
Pitts	7	60	9	0

KICKOFF RETURNS

Last Name	No.	Yds	Avg	TD
Adderley	20	597	30	1
Gros	17	430	25	0
Carpenter	5	75	15	0
Wood	1	20	20	0
Fleming	1	0	0	0
J. Kramer	1	0	0	0
Mestnik	1	0	0	0

PASSING – PUNTING – KICKING

PASSING	Att	Comp	%	Yds	Yd/Att	TD	Int–	%	RK
Starr	244	132	54	1855	7.6	15	10–	4	7
Roach	84	38	45	620	7.4	4	8–	10	
Moore	4	3	75	99	24.8	1	0–	0	
Pitts	2	2	100	41	20.5	1	0–	0	

PUNTING	No	Avg
Norton	51	44.7

KICKING	XP	Att	%	FG	Att	%
J. Kramer	43	46	93	16	34	47

BALTIMORE COLTS

RUSHING

Last Name	No.	Yds	Avg	TD
Matte	133	541	4.1	4
Hill	100	440	4.4	5
Lockett	81	273	3.4	0
Unitas	47	224	4.8	0
Moore	27	136	5.0	2
Cuozzo	3	26	8.7	0
Mackey	1	3	3.0	0
Craddock	1	1	1.0	0
Hawkins	3	–2	–0.7	0

RECEIVING

Last Name	No.	Yds	Avg	TD
Matte	48	466	10	1
Berry	44	703	16	3
Orr	41	708	17	5
Mackey	35	726	21	7
Hill	22	304	14	1
Moore	21	288	14	2
Richardson	17	204	12	0
Lockett	16	158	10	0
Hawkins	3	41	14	0
Owens	1	7	7	0

PUNT RETURNS

Last Name	No.	Yds	Avg	TD
Logan	28	279	10	0
Hawkins	17	156	9	0
Richardson	5	43	9	0
Moore	2	7	4	0
Hill	1	0	0	0

KICKOFF RETURNS

Last Name	No.	Yds	Avg	TD
Matte	16	331	21	0
Mackey	9	271	30	0
Harris	8	198	25	0
Logan	8	170	21	0
Lockett	3	52	17	0
Hill	2	32	16	0
Gilburg	3	29	10	0
Richardson	1	16	16	0
Parker	1	15	15	0
Bielski	1	0	0	0

PASSING – PUNTING – KICKING

PASSING	Att	Comp	%	Yds	Yd/Att	TD	Int–	%	RK
Unitas	410	237	58	3481	8.5	20	12–	3	2
Cuozzo	17	10	59	104	6.1	0	0–	0	
Matte	5	1	20	20	4.0	0	0–	0	

PUNTING	No	Avg
Gilburg	52	41.8
Logan	4	30.3

KICKING	XP	Att	%	FG	Att	%
Martin	32	35	91	24	39	62

WESTERN CONFERENCE – Continued

DETROIT LIONS 5-8-1 George Wilson

Scores of Each Game		
23	Los Angeles	2
10	Green Bay	31
21	CHICAGO	37
26	SAN FRANCISCO	3
14	Dallas	17
21	BALTIMORE	25
28	MINNESOTA	10
45	San Francisco	7
21	Baltimore	24
21	LOS ANGELES	28
31	Minnesota	34
13	GREEN BAY	13
38	CLEVELAND	10
14	Chicago	24

Use Name	Pos.	Hgt	Wgt	Age	Int	Pts
Daryl Sanders	OT	6'5"	240	21		
Lucien Reeberg	OT	6'4"	308	22		
Dan LaRose	OG-OT	6'5"	250	23		
John Gordy	OG	6'3"	250	27		
John Gonzaga	OT-OG	6'3"	250	30		
Bob Whitlow	C	6'1"	236	27		
Bob Scholtz	OT-C	6'4"	250	25		
Darris McCord	DE	6'4"	250	30	1	6
Sam Williams	DE	6'5"	235	32		
Jim Simon	LB-DE	6'5"	225	22		
Roger Brown	DT	6'5"	300	26	1	
Mike Bundra	DT	6'3"	260	24		
Floyd Peters	DT	6'4"	255	28		
Carl Brettschneider	LB	6'1"	225	31		
Ernie Clark	LB	6'1"	220	25		
Dennis Gaubatz	LB	6'2"	205	22	1	
Monte Lee	LB	6'4"	220	25		
Max Messner	LB	6'3"	225	25		
Joe Schmidt	LB	6'1"	220	31		
Wayne Walker	LB	6'2"	225	26	1	56
Larry Vargo	OE-LB	6'3"	215	23	1	6
Night Train Lane	DB	6'1"	200	35	5	
Dick LeBeau	DB	6'1"	185	26	5	6
Gary Lowe	DB	5'11"	195	29	2	
Bruce Maher	DB	5'11"	190	26	1	2
Dick Compton	HB-DB	6'1"	195	23	1	
Yale Lary	DB	6'	190	32	2	6
Tom Hall	OE-DB	6'1"	195	22	3	6
Earl Morrall	QB	6'1"	206	29		6
Milt Plum	QB	6'1"	205	29		16
Hopalong Cassady	HB	5'10"	185	29		
Larry Ferguson	HB	5'10"	185	22		
Dan Lewis	HB	6'1"	200	27		12
Tom Watkins	HB	6'1"	195	26		24
Nick Pietrosante	FB	6'2"	225	26		30
Nick Ryder	FB	6'	205	22		6
Ollie Matson	HB-FB	6'2"	210	33		
Terry Barr	FL	6'	190	28		78
Gail Cogdill	OE	6'2"	195	26		60
Jim Gibbons	OE	6'2"	220	27		6
Al Greer	OE	6'4"	190	22		

Alex Karras – Suspended by commissioner

Pat Studstill – Injury

MINNESOTA VIKINGS 5-8-1 Norm Van Brocklin

Scores of Each Game		
24	San Francisco	20
7	CHICAGO	28
45	SAN FRANCISCO	14
14	ST. LOUIS	56
28	GREEN BAY	37
24	Los Angeles	27
10	Detroit	28
21	LOS ANGELES	13
7	Green Bay	28
34	BALTIMORE	37
34	DETROIT	31
17	Chicago	17
10	Baltimore	41
34	Philadelphia	13

Use Name	Pos.	Hgt	Wgt	Age	Int	Pts
Grady Alderman	OT	6'2"	245	24		
Errol Linden	OT	6'5"	260	26		
Jim Battle	OG	6'1"	240	25		
Larry Bowie	OG	6'2"	245	23		
Jerry Huth	OG	6'	228	30		
Dave O'Brien	OG	6'3"	235	22		
Mick Tingelhoff	C	6'1"	235	23		
Bob Denton	DE	6'4"	240	29		
Don Hultz	DE	6'3"	220	22	1	6
Jim Marshall	DE	6'3"	235	25		6
Paul Dickson	DT	6'5"	255	26		
Jim Prestel	DT	6'5"	260	26		
Pat Russ	DT	6'4"	255	23		
John Campbell	LB	6'3"	215	24		
Rip Hawkins	LB	6'3"	230	24	1	
Bill Jobko	LB	6'2"	220	27		
Steve Stonebreaker	LB	6'3"	220	25		
Roy Winston	LB	6'1"	225	23	1	6
Lee Calland	DB	6'	190	22		
Terry Dillon	DB	6'	193	22		
Tom Franckhauser	DB	6'	196	26	2	
Karl Kassulke	DB	6'	193	21		
Terry Kosens	DB	6'3"	195	21		
Chuck Lamson	DB	6'	185	24	1	
Ed Sharockman	DB	6'	200	23	5	6
Fran Tarkenton	QB	6'1"	190	23		6
Ron Vander Kelen	QB	6'1"	185	23		
Bill Butler	HB	5'10"	194	26		6
Tommy Mason	HB	6'	196	24		54
Bob Reed	HB	5'11"	187	23		
Tom Wilson	HB	6'	204	30		24
Bill Brown	FB	5'11"	218	25		48
Jim Boylan	FL	6'1"	185	24		6
Leon Clarke	FL	6'4"	235	30		
Ray Poage	FL	6'4"	203	22		12
Paul Flatley	OE	6'1"	187	22		24
Jerry Reichow	OE	6'2"	220	28		18
Gordon Smith	OE	6'2"	215	24		12
Fred Cox	K	5'10"	205	24		75

LOS ANGELES RAMS 5-9-0 Harland Svare

Scores of Each Game		
2	DETROIT	23
14	WASHINGTON	37
6	Cleveland	20
10	Green Bay	42
14	CHICAGO	52
27	MINNESOTA	24
28	SAN FRANCISCO	21
13	Minnesota	21
0	Chicago	6
28	Detroit	21
17	BALTIMORE	16
21	San Francisco	17
14	GREEN BAY	31
16	Baltimore	19

Use Name	Pos.	Hgt	Wgt	Age	Int	Pts
Jim Boeke	OT	6'5"	245	24		
Joe Carollo	OT	6'2"	260	23		
Frank Varrichione	OT	6'1"	237	31		
Don Chuy	OG	6'1"	255	22		
Charley Cowan	OG	6'4"	255	25		
Joe Scibelli	OG	6'1"	250	24		
Harley Sewell	OG	6'1"	230	32		
Larry Hayes	C	6'3"	230	28		
Art Hunter	C	6'4"	248	30		
Stan Fanning	DE	6'6"	270	25		
Deacon Jones	DE	6'5"	250	24	1	
Lamar Lundy	DE	6'7"	235	28		
Rosey Grier	DT	6'5"	290	30		
Merlin Olsen	DT	6'5"	265	22		
Mike Henry	LB	6'2"	220	27	5	
Cliff Livingston	LB	6'3"	215	33	1	
Jack Pardee	LB	6'2"	225	27	2	
Bill Swain	LB	6'2"	228	22		
Ken Kirk	C-LB	6'2"	225	25		
Charley Britt	DB	6'2"	185	25	1	
Lindon Crow	DB	6'1"	200	30		2
John Griffin	DB	6'1"	190	23		
Alvin Hall	DB	6'	198	30		
Bobby Smith	DB	6'	190	25	2	
Nat Whitmyer	DB	6'	183	22	1	
Ed Meador	DB	5'11"	193	26	6	
Carver Shannon	HB-DB	6'1"	198	25		6
Terry Baker	QB	6'3"	195	22		
Zeke Bratkowski (to GB)	QB	6'2"	203	31		
Roman Gabriel	QB	6'4"	255	23		18
Jon Arnett	HB	5'11"	194	28		12
Pervis Atkins	HB	6'1"	195	27		6
Dick Bass	HB	5'10"	200	26		30
Art Perkins	FB	6'	225	23		24
Ben Wilson	FB	6'	225	23		12
Jim Phillips	FL	6'1"	198	26		6
John Adams	OE	6'3"	235	26		
Duane Allen	OE	6'4"	225	25		
Carroll Dale	OE	6'1"	195	25		42
Marlin McKeever	OE	6'1"	235	23		
Danny Villanueva	K	5'11"	200	25		52

SAN FRANCISCO FORTY NINERS 2-12-0 Red Hickey Jack Christiansen

Scores of Each Game		
20	MINNESOTA	24
14	BALTIMORE	20
14	Minnesota	45
3	Detroit	26
3	Baltimore	20
20	CHICAGO	14
21	Los Angeles	28
7	DETROIT	45
31	DALLAS	24
14	New York	48
10	Green Bay	28
17	LOS ANGELES	21
7	Chicago	27
17	GREEN BAY	21

Use Name	Pos.	Hgt	Wgt	Age	Int	Pts
Clyde Brock (from DAL)	OT	6'5"	268	23		
Len Rohde	OT	6'4"	240	25		
Bob St. Clair	OT	6'9"	265	32		
Leon Donahue	OG	6'4"	245	24		
Mike Magac	OG	6'3"	240	25		
John Thomas	OG	6'4"	246	28		
Bruce Bosley	OG-C	6'2"	240	29		
Karl Rubke	DE-C	6'4"	240	27		
Clark Miller	DE	6'5"	245	24		
Dan Colchico	DE	6'4"	236	26		
Roland Lakes	DT-DE	6'4"	273	23		
Charlie Krueger	DT	6'4"	245	27		
Leo Nomellini	DT	6'3"	262	38		
Walt Rock	DT	6'5"	240	22		
Chuck Sieminski	DT	6'4"	245	23		
Roy Williams	DT	6'7"	265	25		
Bill Cooper	LB	6'1"	215	24		
Mike Dowdle	LB	6'3"	237	25	2	
Matt Hazeltine	LB	6'1"	220	30		
Ed Pine	LB	6'4"	230	23	1	
Kermit Alexander	DB	5'11"	186	22	5	
Elbert Kimbrough	DB	5'11"	190	24	1	
Howie Williams (from GB)	DB	6'2"	190	26		
Abe Woodson	DB	5'11"	188	28	3	18
Jim Johnson	FL-HB	6'2"	190	25	2	
John Brodie	QB	6'1"	186	28		
Lamar McHan (from BAL)	QB	6'1"	205	31		
Bob Waters	QB	6'2"	184	25		
Don Lisbon	HB	6'	190	22		12
Dale Messer	HB	5'10"	175	26		
Jim Vollenweider	HB	6'1"	210	23		12
Mike Lind	FB	6'2"	215	23		
Joe Perry	FB	6'	200	36		
J. D. Smith	FB	6'1"	200	30		36
Lloyd Winston	FB	6'2"	215	23		6
Bernie Casey	FL	6'4"	215	24		42
Kay McFarland	FL	6'2"	180	24		6
Clyde Conner	OE	6'2"	190	30		
Gary Knafelc	OE	6'4"	220	31		12
Monte Stickles	OE	6'4"	230	25		
Tommy Davis	K	6'	212	28		54

Billy Kilmer – Broken Leg

Jerry Mertens – Knee Injury

Dave Baker – Military Service

WESTERN CONFERENCE–Continued

DETROIT LIONS

RUSHING

Last Name	No.	Yds	Avg	TD
Lewis	133	528	4.0	2
Watkins	97	423	4.4	2
Pietrosante	112	418	3.7	5
Morrall	26	105	4.0	1
Lary	1	26	26.0	0
Plum	9	26	2.9	0
Ryder	10	23	2.3	1
Ferguson	13	23	1.8	0
Matson	13	20	1.5	0
Barr	1	9	9.0	0

RECEIVING

Last Name	No.	Yds	Avg	TD
Barr	66	1086	16	13
Cogdill	48	945	20	10
Gibbons	32	412	13	1
Pietrosante	16	173	11	0
Watkins	16	168	11	1
Lewis	15	115	8	0
Hall	3	29	10	1
Compton	2	41	21	0
Matson	2	20	10	0
Ferguson	2	8	4	0

PUNT RETURNS

Last Name	No.	Yds	Avg	TD
Watkins	32	399	12	1
Ferguson	11	108	10	0
Hall	10	107	11	0
Compton	2	11	6	0
Cassady	1	7	7	0
Maher	1	3	3	0

KICKOFF RETURNS

Last Name	No.	Yds	Avg	TD
Watkins	21	447	21	0
Ferguson	9	231	26	0
Hall	6	143	24	0
Matson	3	61	20	0
Ryder	3	33	11	0
Clark	1	13	13	0
Compton	1	13	13	0
Vargo	1	8	8	0

PASSING – PUNTING – KICKING

PASSING	Att	Comp	%	Yds	Yd/Att	TD	Int–	%	RK
Morrall	328	174	53	2621	8.0	24	14–	4	3
Plum	77	27	35	339	4.4	2	12–	16	
Pietrosante	1	1	100	37	37.0	0	0–	0	

PUNTING	No	Avg
Lary	35	48.9
Morrall	29	39.4
Compton	2	42.5

KICKING	XP	Att	%	FG	Att	%
Walker	29	29	100	9	22	41
Plum	13	13	100	1	4	25

MINNESOTA VIKINGS

RUSHING

Last Name	No.	Yds	Avg	TD
Mason	166	763	4.6	7
Brown	128	445	3.5	5
Wilson	73	282	3.9	4
Tarkenton	28	162	5.8	1
Reed	21	88	4.2	0
Vander Kelen	8	65	8.1	0
Butler	17	48	2.8	0
Reichow	1	–12	–12.0	0

RECEIVING

Last Name	No.	Yds	Avg	TD
Flatley	51	867	17	4
Mason	40	365	9	2
Reichow	35	479	14	3
Brown	17	109	6	2
Poage	15	354	24	2
Reed	13	137	11	0
Wilson	7	48	7	0
Smith	6	177	30	2
Boylan	6	78	13	1
Butler	4	39	10	0
Clarke	3	34	11	0

PUNT RETURNS

Last Name	No.	Yds	Avg	TD
Butler	21	220	10	1
Reed	9	91	10	0
Mason	4	63	16	0
Kassulke	1	31	31	0

KICKOFF RETURNS

Last Name	No.	Yds	Avg	TD
Butler	33	713	22	0
Reed	13	367	28	0
Sharockman	7	139	20	0
Brown	3	105	35	1
Franckhauser	4	94	24	0
Mason	3	61	20	0
Calland	2	45	23	0
Smith	2	24	12	0
Campbell	1	8	8	0
Bowie	1	0	0	0

PASSING – PUNTING – KICKING

PASSING	Att	Comp	%	Yds	Yd/Att	TD	Int–	%	RK
Tarkenton	297	170	57	2311	7.8	15	15–	5	6
Vander Kelen	58	27	47	376	6.5	1	2–	3	

PUNTING	No	Avg
Cox	70	38.7

KICKING	XP	Att	%	FG	Att	%
Cox	39	39	100	12	24	50

LOS ANGELES RAMS

RUSHING

Last Name	No.	Yds	Avg	TD
Bass	143	520	3.6	5
Wilson	109	394	3.6	1
Arnett	58	208	3.6	1
Gabriel	39	132	3.4	3
Perkins	37	70	1.9	4
Baker	9	46	5.1	0
Dale	1	12	12.0	0
Atkins	5	11	2.2	0
Meador	1	1	1.0	0
Bratkowski	4	–3	–0.8	0

RECEIVING

Last Name	No.	Yds	Avg	TD
Phillips	54	793	15	1
Dale	34	638	19	7
Bass	30	348	12	0
Arnett	15	119	8	1
Atkins	14	174	12	1
McKeever	11	152	14	0
Wilson	9	173	19	1
Adams	9	93	10	0
Perkins	8	61	8	0
Shannon	2	7	4	0

PUNT RETURNS

Last Name	No.	Yds	Avg	TD
Shannon	15	132	9	0
Atkins	12	36	3	0
Smith	2	20	10	0
Bass	1	11	11	0
Arnett	1	7	7	0

KICKOFF RETURNS

Last Name	No.	Yds	Avg	TD
Shannon	28	823	29	1
Atkins	19	429	23	0
Arnett	12	279	23	0
Whitmyer	3	80	27	0
Wilson	1	17	17	0
Perkins	1	15	15	0
McKeever	2	8	4	0
Cowan	2	0	0	0
Hall	1	0	0	0
Olsen	1	0	0	0

PASSING – PUNTING – KICKING

PASSING	Att	Comp	%	Yds	Yd/Att	TD	Int–	%	RK
Gabriel	281	130	46	1947	6.9	8	11–	4	13
Bratkowski	93	49	53	567	6.1	4	9–	10	
Baker	19	11	58	140	7.4	0	4–	21	
Arnett	1	0	0	0	0.0	0	1–	100	
Bass	1	0	0	0	0.0	0	0–	0	

PUNTING	No	Avg
Villanueva	81	45.4
Adams	4	30.3

KICKING	XP	Att	%	FG	Att	%
Villanueva	25	26	96	9	17	53

SAN FRANCISCO FORTY NINERS

RUSHING

Last Name	No.	Yds	Avg	TD
Smith	162	560	3.5	5
Lisbon	109	399	3.7	0
Winston	27	127	4.7	1
Vollenweider	47	124	2.6	2
Perry	24	98	4.1	0
Brodie	7	63	9.0	0
McHan	17	59	3.5	0
Lind	8	26	3.3	0
Waters	5	–2	–0.4	0

RECEIVING

Last Name	No.	Yds	Avg	TD
Casey	47	762	16	7
Lisbon	21	259	12	2
Knafelc	18	221	12	2
Smith	17	196	12	1
Conner	16	247	15	0
Stickles	11	152	14	0
McFarland	11	126	11	1
Johnson	6	63	11	0
Perry	4	12	3	0
Lind	2	13	7	0
Winston	2	13	7	0
Vollenweider	1	26	26	0

PUNT RETURNS

Last Name	No.	Yds	Avg	TD
Woodson	13	95	7	0
Messer	5	4	1	0

KICKOFF RETURNS

Last Name	No.	Yds	Avg	TD
Woodson	29	935	32	3
Alexander	24	638	27	0
Vollenweider	4	75	19	0
Cooper	2	8	4	0
St. Clair	2	3	2	0
Stickles	1	0	0	0

PASSING – PUNTING – KICKING

PASSING	Att	Comp	%	Yds	Yd/Att	TD	Int–	%	RK
McHan	196	83	42	1243	6.3	8	11–	6	15
Waters	88	42	48	435	4.9	1	6–	7	
Brodie	61	30	49	367	6.0	3	4–	7	
Lisbon	2	1	50	45	22.5	1	0–	0	
Davis	1	0	0	0	0.0	0	0–	0	
Perry	1	0	0	0	0.0	0	0–	0	
Vollenweider	1	0	0	0	0.0	0	1–	100	

PUNTING	No	Avg
Davis	73	45.4

KICKING	XP	Att	%	FG	Att	%
Davis	24	24	100	10	31	32

1963 A.F.L. Approaching Pay Dirt

Three AFL franchises found secure footing this season after three years of tenuous existence. The Dallas Texans, the 1962 league champions, defended their title as the Kansas City Chiefs, as owner Lamar Hunt tired of losing money and playing second banana to the Cowboys in Dallas. With an attractive young team, the Chiefs sold 15,000 season tickets and made money in their first season in the Midwest. On the East Coast, the New York Titans became the New York Jets and left behind the laughable image of the Harry Wismer years. New owner Sonny Werblin and new coach Weeb Ewbank could not immediately produce a winning club, but they did give the AFL a major-league operation in New York. On the West Coast, young Al Davis took charge of the Oakland Raiders and built them from doormats into an exciting club that barely missed a divisional crown. All three of these clubs enjoyed big increases in attendance, and each of them would use their new revenues to sign top rookies for next year—a cycle that could only lead upward for the league.

EASTERN DIVISION

Boston Patriots—When the television coverage of the Eastern Division playoff between the Patriots and Bills began, viewers saw not players warming up but bulldozers scraping Buffalo's War Memorial Stadium clear of snow. The Patriots had made it to this frigid showdown with a solid defense, a scrappy offense, and a clutch field-goal kicker in Gino Cappelletti. Larry Eisenhauer, Houston Antwine, and Tom Addison steadied the defense, while middle linebacker Nick Buoniconti added the spice with his frequent blitzes. Don Webb, the team's best defensive back, sat out the whole season on the disabled list, but his platoon covered for him better than the offense covered for Ron Burton. With Burton sidelined for the entire schedule with a bad back, the Patriot attack lost most of its speed. But the collapse of the Oilers, the reorganization of the Jets, and the poor start by the Bills kept the Patriots in the divisional race all season. The Patriots and Bills finished in a tie for first place, and in the winter cold of Buffalo the Patriots' old pros won the title 26-8.

Buffalo Bills—Favored by many experts to win the Eastern Division, the Bills fell flat on their face in September. Their first four games netted them three losses and a tie, dropping them into last place before they finally jelled in the month of October. Showing an ability to win close games, the Bills then took seven of their last ten games to catch Boston in a tie for the Eastern title. Quarterback Jack Kemp hit Elbert Dubenion and Bill Miller with pinpoint passes, while Cookie Gilchrist carried the running chores without much help from the halfbacks. The two leading halfbacks were knocked out with hurts, Wray Carolton with a groin injury and Roger Kochman with a leg injury that ended his career after only eight professional games. Gilchrist kept plowing ahead despite little injuries, and he set a new record of 243 yards rushing in one game, on December 8 against New York. The defense was strong up front but vulnerable in the backfield.

Houston Oilers—After three years atop the Eastern Division, the Oilers learned the hard reality of how the other half lives by falling to third place. The defending champs lost their last four straight and five of their last six games, looking more often like a routed army than like a respected football team. Injuries took a hand in the collapse, as a bad back forced tackle Al Jamison into retirement, a pulled thigh muscle kept halfback Billy Cannon on the bench most of the season, and a broken jaw sidelined defensive end Don Floyd for half the schedule. Without Jamison and Cannon, the Houston pass blocking was atrocious, subjecting thirty-six-year-old George Blanda to a rush unfit for a man his age. Cannon's absence also put the whole rushing load on fullback Charley Tolar, who got little help from rookie halfback Bill Tobin. The defense put up no pass rush without Floyd, leaving enemy passers free to spot their receivers in leisure. With all their wounded, the Oilers still managed to stay in the Eastern race until the Patriots demolished them 45-3 on November 1.

New York Jets—New general manager and head coach Weeb Ewbank completely overhauled the team, shuffling players in and out of the pre-season training camp in a steady flow. Looking to shore up the barren New York roster, Ewbank signed free agents cut loose by NFL teams. He especially pounced on players cut from his old Baltimore team, picking up from this source Dee Mackey, Mark Smolinski, Bake Turner, Dave Yohn, and rookies Winston Hill and Bill Baird. For a quarterback, Ewbank discovered Dick Wood, a strong-armed young passer cut loose most recently by the Denver Broncos. Although Wood could throw perfect long passes, his bad knees made him totally immobile, so Ewbank tailored his blocking solely to protect his passer. Billy Mathis and Mark Smolinski won starting backfield jobs on their ability to block, and the offensive line, led by 297-pound Sherman Plunkett, shielded Wood from most enemy interference.

WESTERN DIVISION

San Diego Chargers—In winning their third Western title in four years, the Chargers fielded a backfield as exciting as any in pro football. They had a good veteran quarterback in Tobin Rote, back in the United States after three seasons in the Canadian League, and a good young quarterback in John Hadl. For runners they had Paul Lowe and Keith Lincoln, both quick, slashing runners who could get through the smallest openings in the line. The flanker was Lance Alworth, who came back from an injury-plagued rookie season to tantalize crowds with his leaping grabs and streaking deep patterns. With these talents operating behind a solid line, the San Diego offense put more points on the board than any other attack in the league, but coach Sid Gillman's riches did not end there. The defense also was both colorful and efficient, with Earl Faison, Ernie Ladd, Chuck Allen, and Dick Harris the stars of the unit. Avoiding the string of injuries that ruined the past season, the Chargers found their greatest challenge for the divisional crown not from the defending champion Kansas City team but instead from the surprising Oakland Raiders. Twice the Raiders beat the Chargers, pulling within one game of the top with a 41-27 victory with two weeks left in the season, but the Chargers won both their remaining contests to salt away the championship.

Oakland Raiders—Leaving a comfortable assistantship in San Diego to take over as head coach in Oakland, Al Davis blended holdovers from the disastrous 1962 season with free agents cut loose by other clubs and came up with an exciting team. Davis signed split end Art Powell, who had played out his option in New York, got Tom Flores back from illness, and coaxed several useful players away from other teams at a minimal cost. The offense relied on the passing of quarterbacks Flores and Cotton Davidson to receivers Powell and Bo Roberson and on the running of Clem Daniels to pile up points. Daniels combined speed and power to set a new AFL rushing record with 1,099 yards, and he was also a dangerous deep pass receiving threat coming out of the backfield. The defense had few recognizable names, but terrorized opponents with a dazzling array of blitzes. End Dalva Allen and rookie tackle Dave Costa anchored the forward wall, ex-Bill Archie Matsos starred at middle linebacker, and holdover backs Fred Williamson and Tom Morrow prospered in Davis' new setup. After starting out the season with two wins, the Raiders lost four straight games to Eastern opponents, but then the miracle began. Oakland started winning and never stopped, taking their last eight contests to finish one game behind the Chargers.

Kansas City Chiefs—A fatal injury to rookie Stone Johnson in a preseason game started the Chiefs' season on a foreboding note and dampened the club's enthusiasm. After beating Denver 59-7 to open the season, the Chiefs then won only once in their next ten games. The defense, bolstered by rookies Buck Buchanan and Bobby Bell, stayed tough, but a breakdown in blocking short-circuited the offense. Enemy defenses constantly rushed quarterback Len Dawson with blitzes that his blockers could not pick up, and backs Curtis McClinton and Abner Haynes both fell off from their 1963 performances. Haynes, the AFL's first star, slipped so much that he was restricted to returning kicks for a time. The mid-season drought ended any hopes of repeating as Western champions, and the Chiefs hit the bottom when the New York Jets shut them out 17-0 in a November meeting in New York. After that point, however, the Chiefs put the abundant talent on their roster to full use as they won their last three games.

Denver Broncos—When the Broncos at last uncovered a major-league runner, their passing attack fell apart. The Broncos had always lived and died on the passing of Frank Tripuka, relying on the air game to overcome the lack of any ground attack. Rookie fullback Billy Joe gave the club its first running threat, someone who could break tackles and pick up vital first-down yardage, but Tripuka's arm was no longer up to the weekly strain. After two games, both of which the Broncos lost, Tripuka quit, leaving rookie Mickey Slaughter the only quarterback on the roster. Coach Jack Faulkner then signed ex-Viking John McCormick, and after only four days of practice with the team McCormick led the Broncs to a 14-0 victory over Boston. Next came a 50-34 ambushing of the San Diego Chargers, in which McCormick directed the Denver offense with the precision of a surgeon. With better days obviously on the way, the Broncos suffered a loss from which they never recovered when the Houston Oilers tore up McCormick's knee on the way to a 33-24 victory.

FINAL TEAM STATISTICS

Note: Only offensive totals are available

	BOSTON	BUFFALO	DENVER	HOUSTON	KANSAS CITY	NEW YORK	OAKLAND	SAN DIEGO
FIRST DOWNS:								
by Rushing	100	107	84	68	94	52	85	**112**
by Passing	107	147	133	**169**	141	121	142	124
RUSHING:								
Number	437	**455**	384	341	400	306	359	395
Yards	1618	1838	1508	1209	1697	969	1595	**2201**
Average Yards	3.7	4.0	3.9	3.5	4.2	3.2	4.4	**5.6**
Touchdowns	17	**21**	10	11	12	8	11	20
PASSING:								
Attempts	410	457	453	**501**	439	480	442	357
Completions	184	227	217	**261**	231	209	191	202
Percentage	44.9	49.7	47.9	52.1	52.6	43.5	43.2	**56.6**
Net Yards	2547	3057	2487	**3210**	2651	2530	2926	2950
Touchdowns	17	16	23	26	30	21	**31**	28
Interceptions	29	24	28	33	**22**	29	24	24
Percent Intercepted	7.1	5.3	6.2	6.6	**5.0**	6.0	5.4	6.7
PUNTING:								
Number	75	62	**81**	65	62	72	76	61
Average Distance	38.4	40.2	**44.3**	42.9	43.1	42.1	39.5	37.9
PUNT RETURNS:								
Number	**40**	37	30	36	26	17	36	22
Yards	373	316	387	339	259	202	**395**	261
Average Yards	9.3	8.5	**12.9**	9.4	10.0	11.9	11.0	11.9
Touchdowns	0	0	0	0	0	1	**2**	0
KICKOFF RETURNS:								
Number	52	52	**78**	69	47	74	53	52
Yards	1109	1133	1801	**1821**	1172	1463	1008	1168
Average Yards	21.3	21.8	23.1	**26.4**	24.9	19.8	19.0	22.5
Touchdowns	0	0	**1**	0	**1**	0	0	0
INTERCEPTION RETURNS:								
Number	30	22	15	**36**	26	21	35	29
Yards	**662**	156	170	453	450	284	389	316
Average Yards	**22.1**	7.1	11.3	12.6	17.3	13.5	11.1	10.9
Touchdowns	**3**	1	1	2	1	0	2	1
POINTS:								
Total	327	304	301	302	347	249	363	**399**
PAT (kick) Attempts	36	37	35	39	44	30	47	**48**
PAT (kick) Made	35	32	35	39	43	30	**47**	44
PAT (2-pt) Attempts	1	**2**	1	0	1	**2**	1	**2**
PAT (2-pt) Made	0	**2**	1	0	1	0	0	**2**
FG Attempts	**38**	23	29	22	28	24	19	27
FG Made	**22**	10	16	9	8	9	8	17
Percent FG Made	57.9	43.5	55.2	40.9	28.6	37.5	42.1	**63.0**
Safeties	**2**	**2**	0	0	1	0	**2**	0

1963 AFL CHAMPIONSHIP GAME

January 5, at San Diego
(Attendance 30,127)

Boston's Buttery Defense

SCORING

SAN DIEGO	21	10	7	13	–51
BOSTON	7	3	0	0	–10

First Quarter
- S.D. Rote, 2 yard rush
  PAT–Blair (kick)
- S.D. Lincoln, 67 yard rush
  PAT–Blair (kick)
- Bos. Garron, 7 yard rush
  PAT–Cappelletti (kick)
- S.D. Lowe, 58 yard rush
  PAT–Blair (kick)

Second Quarter
- S.D. Blair, 11 yard field goal
- Bos. Cappelletti, 15 yard field goal
- S.D. Norton, 14 yard pass from Rote
  PAT–Blair (kick)

Third Quarter
- S.D. Alworth, 48 yard pass from Rote
  PAT–Blair (kick)

Fourth Quarter
- S.D. Lincoln, 25 yard pass from Hadl
  PAT–Pass (No Good)
- S.D. Hadl, 1 yard rush
  PAT–Blair (kick)

TEAM STATISTICS

S.D.		BOS.
21	First Downs–Total	14
11	First Downs–Rushing	6
9	First Downs–Passing	8
1	First Downs–Penalty	0
1	Fumbles–Number	1
1	Fumbles–Lost Ball	0
6	Penalties–Number	1
30	Yards Penalized	18
1	Giveaways	2
2	Takeaways	1
+1	Difference	–1

In the fourth AFL championship game, San Diego's famous offense made mincemeat out of Boston's heralded defense. On the second play from scrimmage of the game, Keith Lincoln took a handoff and burst through the middle of the Boston defense for a 56-yard gain; Tobin Rote's quarterback sneak seven plays later gave San Diego a quick 7-0 lead. As soon as the Chargers got the ball back, Lincoln headed around end for a 67-yard touchdown run, making the score 14-0. The Patriots came back with a quick touchdown, but a 58-yard touchdown run by Paul Lowe, the third long run of the first quarter for the Chargers, made the score 21-7. George Blair and Gino Cappelletti exchanged field goals early in the second quarter, but Don Norton scored on a 14-yard pass play to give the Chargers a 31-10 lead at halftime. The Patriot attack got nowhere in the second half, as the San Diego line rushed quarterback Babe Parilli ferociously every time he dropped back to pass. The Chargers, however, kept adding points against the Boston defense. Lance Alworth, the Chargers' chief pass receiver, scored in the third period on a 48-yard pass from Rote, and Lincoln added his third touchdown on a 25-yard pass from reserve quarterback John Hadl in the fourth quarter. Hadl then scored on a one-yard plunge with less than two minutes remaining in the game, and George Blair's kick made the final score a lopsided 51-10. Although not even close, the game helped the AFL by showcasing an exciting offensive team in the Chargers, a direct contrast with the defense-oriented NFL champions, the Chicago Bears.

INDIVIDUAL STATISTICS

SAN DIEGO	No	Yds	Avg.	BOSTON	No	Yds	Avg.
RUSHING							
Lincoln	13	206	15.8	Crump	7	18	2.6
Lowe	12	94	7.8	Garron	3	15	5.0
Rote	4	15	3.8	Lott	3	15	5.0
McDougall	1	2	2.0	Yewcic	1	14	14.0
Hadl	1	1	1.0	Parilli	1	10	10.0
Jackson	1	0	0.0	Burton	1	3	3.0
	32	218	6.8		16	75	4.7
RECEIVING							
Lincoln	7	123	17.6	Burton	4	12	3.0
Alworth	4	77	19.3	Colclough	3	26	8.7
MacKinnon	2	52	26.0	Cappelletti	2	72	36.0
Norton	2	44	22.0	Graham	2	68	34.0
Kocourek	1	5	5.0	Crump	2	28	14.0
McDougall	1	4	4.0	Lott	2	16	8.0
	17	305	17.9	Garron	2	6	3.0
					17	228	13.4
PUNTING							
Maguire	2		43.5	Yewcic	7		46.9
KICKOFF RETURNS							
Alworth	2	47	23.5	Crump	2	31	15.5
Lowe	1	23	23.0	Burton	2	27	13.5
	3	70	23.3	Garron	2	22	11.0
				Suci	1	18	18.0
				Romeo	1	9	9.0
				Yates	1	5	5.0
					9	112	12.4
INTERCEPTION RETURNS							
Maguire	1	10	10.0	None			
Mitinger	1	5	5.0				
	2	15	7.5				

PASSING

	Att.	Comp.	Comp. Pct.	Yds.	Int.	Yds/ Att.	Yds/ Comp.
SAN DIEGO							
Rote	15	10	66.7	173	0	11.5	17.3
Hadl	10	6	60.0	112	0	11.2	18.7
Lincoln	1	1	100.0	20	0	20.0	20.0
	26	17	65.4	305	0	11.7	17.9
BOSTON							
Parilli	29	14	48.3	189	1	6.5	13.5
Yewcic	8	3	37.5	39	1	4.9	13.0
	37	17	45.9	228	2	6.2	13.4

BOSTON PATRIOTS 7-6-1 Mike Holovak

Scores of Each Game		
38	NEW YORK	14
13	San Diego	17
20	Oakland	14
10	Denver	14
24	New York	31
20	OAKLAND	14
40	DENVER	21
21	Buffalo	28
45	HOUSTON	3
6	SAN DIEGO	7
24	KANSAS CITY	24
17	BUFFALO	7
46	Houston	28
3	Kansas City	35
	EAST Playoff	
26	Buffalo	8

Use Name	Pos.	Hgt	Wgt	Age	Int	Pts
Don Oakes	OT	6'3"	255	25		
Bob Yates	OT	6'3"	230	24		
Charley Long	OG	6'3"	250	25		
Billy Neighbors	OG	5'11"	240.	23		
Dave Watson	OG	6'1"	220	22		
Walt Cudzik	C	6'2"	235	30		
Bob Dee	DE	6'3"	240	30		
Larry Eisenhauer	DE	6'5"	245	23	1	
Jim Hunt	DE	5'11"	245	24	1	6
Houston Antwine	DT	6'	250	24		
Jerry DeLucca (from BUF)	DT	6'3"	250	27		
Milt Graham	DT	6'6"	235	29		
Bill Hudson	DT	6'4"	255	27		
Jess Richardson	DT	6'2"	265	33		

Use Name	Pos.	Hgt	Wgt	Age	Int	Pts
Tom Addison	LB	6'3"	230	27	4	
Nick Buoniconti	LB	5'11"	220	22	3	
Don McKinnon	LB	6'3"	215	21		
Jack Rudolph	LB	6'3"	230	25		
Dick Felt	DB	6'	185	30	3	
Ron Hall	DB	6'	190	26	3	
Ross O'Hanley	DB	6'	185	24	3	
Chuck Shonta	DB	6'	200	25	3	
Bob Suci	DB	5'10"	185	25	8	12
Tom Stephens	OE-DB	6'1"	215	27	1	
Don Webb – Injury						

Use Name	Pos.	Hgt	Wgt	Age	Int	Pts
Babe Parilli	QB	6'1"	190	33		30
Tom Yewcic	QB	5'11"	185	31		6
*Ron Burton	HB	5'10"	190	26		
Jim Crawford	HB	6'1"	200	27		6
Tom Neumann	HB	5'11"	205	22		6
Harry Crump	FB	6'	205	22		30
Larry Garron	FB	6'	215	26		24
Billy Lott	FB	6'	205	28		24
Jim Colclough	FL	6'	185	27		18
Gino Cappelletti	OE	6'	190	29		113
Art Graham	OE	6'1"	205	22		30
Tony Romeo	OE	6'2"	220	24		18

*Played only in playoffs

BUFFALO BILLS 7-6-1 Lou Saban

Scores of Each Game		
10	San Diego	14
17	Oakland	35
27	KANSAS CITY	27
20	HOUSTON	31
12	OAKLAND	0
35	Kansas City	26
14	Houston	28
28	BOSTON	21
30	Denver	28
27	DENVER	17
13	SAN DIEGO	23
7	Boston	17
45	NEW YORK	14
19	New York	10
	EAST Playoff	
8	BOSTON	26

Use Name	Pos.	Hgt	Wgt	Age	Int	Pts
Stew Barber	OT	6'3"	250	24		
Dave Behrman	OT	6'5"	260	21		
Ken Rice	OG-OT	6'2"	250	23		
Tom Day	OG	6'2"	262	28		
George Flint	OG	6'4"	246	25		
Dick Hudson	OG	6'4"	264	23		
Charlie Leo	OG	6'	240	28		
Billy Shaw	OG	6'3"	250	23		
Al Bemiller	C	6'3"	235	24		
Ron McDole	DE	6'3"	250	23		
Leroy Moore	DE	6'	232	27		
Mack Yoho	DE	6'2"	238	27		62
Jim Dunaway	DT	6'4"	270	21		
Tom Sestak	DT	6'5"	270	27		
Sid Youngelman	DT	6'3"	260	31		

Use Name	Pos.	Hgt	Wgt	Age	Int	Pts
Harry Jacobs	LB	6'2"	230	26	1	
Marv Matuszak	LB	6'3"	230	32		
Herb Paterra	LB	6'1"	222	22		
Mike Stratton	LB	6'3"	230	21	3	6
John Tracey	LB	6'3"	225	29	5	2
Ray Abruzzese	DB	6'1"	194	25	3	
Carl Charon	DB	5'10"	194	22		6
Booker Edgerson	DB	5'10"	177	24	1	
Henry Rivera	DB	5'11"	180	23		
Gene Sykes	DB	6'1"	200	22		
Willie West	DB	5'10"	193	25	5	
George Saimes	HB-DB	5'10"	192	21	4	

Use Name	Pos.	Hgt	Wgt	Age	Int	Pts
Jack Kemp	QB	6'1"	200	29		48
Daryle Lamonica	QB	6'2"	216	22		2
Glenn Bass	HB	6'2"	195	24		6
Hez Braxton	HB	6'2"	227	27		
Fred Brown	HB	5'11"	190	23		6
Wray Carlton	HB	6'2"	220	25		
Wayne Crow	HB	6'	205	25		
Roger Kochman	HB	6'2"	205	21		6
Ed Rutkowski	HB	6'1"	200	22		6
Cookie Gilchrist	FB	6'3"	250	28		84
Jesse Murdock (from OAK)	FB	6'2"	203	24		
Elbert Dubenion	FL	6'	188	28		24
Charley Ferguson	OE	6'5"	215	23		18
Bill Miller	OE	6'	200	21		18
Ernie Warlick	OE	6'4"	232	31		6

HOUSTON OILERS 6-8-0 Pop Ivy

Scores of Each Game		
13	OAKLAND	24
20	DENVER	14
17	New York	24
31	Buffalo	20
7	Kansas City	28
33	Denver	24
28	BUFFALO	14
28	KANSAS CITY	7
3	Boston	45
31	NEW YORK	27
0	San Diego	27
28	BOSTON	46
14	SAN DIEGO	20
49	Oakland	52

Use Name	Pos.	Hgt	Wgt	Age	Int	Pts
Bob Kelly	OT	6'3"	260	23		
Rich Michael	OT	6'3"	238	24		
Walt Suggs	OT	6'5"	255	24		
Bob Talamini	OG	6'1"	250	24		
Bill Wegener	OG	5'10"	245	22		
Hogan Wharton	OG	6'2"	250	27		
John Frongillo	OG	6'3"	255	23		
Bob Schmidt	C	6'4"	250	27		
Gary Cutsinger	DE	6'4"	245	22		
Don Floyd	DE	6'4"	245	24		
Willis Perkins	DE	6'	260	26		
Ed Culpepper	DT	6'1"	250	29		
Ed Husmann	DT	6'	245	32		
Dudley Meredith	DT	6'4"	275	28		

Use Name	Pos.	Hgt	Wgt	Age	Int	Pts
Johnny Baker	LB	6'3"	220	22		
Danny Brabham	LB	6'4"	235	22	1	
Doug Cline	LB	6'2"	227	24	3	
Mike Dukes	LB	6'3"	230	27	1	
Tom Goode	LB	6'3"	235	24		
Larry Onesti	LB	6'	195	24		
Gene Babb	FB-LB	6'3"	220	28	2	
Tony Banfield	DB	6'1"	185	24	7	
Freddy Glick	DB	6'1"	190	26	12	6
Bobby Jancik	DB	5'11"	178	23	3	
Mark Johnston	DB	6'	200	25	1	6
Jim Norton	DB	6'3"	190	24	6	

Use Name	Pos.	Hgt	Wgt	Age	Int	Pts
George Blanda	QB	6'1"	215	35		64
Jacky Lee	QB	6'1"	187	24		
Bobby Brezina	HB	6'	200	21		
Billy Cannon	HB	6'1"	210	26		
Bill Tobin	HB	5'11"	210	21		32
Dave Smith	FB	6'1"	210	26		30
Charley Tolar	FB	5'7"	200	25		18
Charley Hennigan	FL	6'	187	27		60
Randy Kerbow	FL	6'1"	190	21		
Willard Dewveall	OE	6'4"	225	26		42
Charley Frazier	OE	6'	162	24		6
Bob McLeod	OE	6'5"	230	24		30

NEW YORK JETS 5-8-1 Weeb Ewbank

Scores of Each Game		
14	Boston	38
24	HOUSTON	17
10	OAKLAND	7
31	BOSTON	24
20	San Diego	24
26	Oakland	49
35	DENVER	35
7	SAN DIEGO	53
27	Houston	31
14	Denver	9
17	KANSAS CITY	0
14	Buffalo	45
10	BUFFALO	19
0	Kansas City	48

Use Name	Pos.	Hgt	Wgt	Age	Int	Pts
Winston Hill	OT	6'4"	275	21		
Jack Klotz	OT	6'5"	250	29		
Sherman Plunkett	OT	6'4"	297	29		
Bob Butler	OG	6'1"	230	22		
Dan Ficca	OG	6'1"	245	24		
Sid Fournet	OG	6'	240	30		
Roy Hord	OG	6'4"	245	28		
Pete Perreault	OG	6'3"	245	24		
Mike Hudock	C	6'2"	245	28		
Lavern Torczon	DE	6'2"	238	27	1	
Bob Watters	DE	6'4"	245	27		
Ed Cooke	LB-DE	6'4"	250	28		
Dick Guesman	DT	6'4"	255	27		57
Chuck Janerette	DT	6'3"	250	24	1	
Bob McAdams	DT	6'3"	250	23		
George Strugar	DT	6'5"	260	28		

Use Name	Pos.	Hgt	Wgt	Age	Int	Pts
Ted Bates	LB	6'3"	220	26		
Roger Ellis	LB	6'3"	233	25		
Larry Grantham	LB	6'	200	24	3	6
Walt Michaels	LB	6'	240	34		
Jim Price	LB	6'2"	225	22	1	
Dave Yohn	LB	6'	225	25		
Billy Atkins (to BUF)	DB	6'1"	196	28		
Bill Baird	DB	5'10"	180	24	6	6
Dainard Paulson	DB	5'11"	190	26	6	
Marsh Starks	DB	6'	190	24		6
Tony Stricker	DB	6'	185	22	1	
Clyde Washington	DB	6'	206	25	2	
Dave West	DB	6'3"	190	25		
Bill Wood	DB	5'11"	190	24		

Use Name	Pos.	Hgt	Wgt	Age	Int	Pts
Ed Chlebek	QB	5'11"	175	22		
Johnny Green	QB	6'3"	208	26		
Galen Hall	QB	5'10"	205	23		6
Dick Wood	QB	6'5"	205	27		6
Dick Christy	HB	5'10"	195	27		6
Bill Mathis	HB	6'1"	220	24		12
Bill Perkins	HB	6'2"	225	22		
Curley Johnson	FB	5'7"	210	28		
Mark Smolinski	FB	6'	222	24		30
Don Maynard	FL	6'	185	27		54
Ken Gregory	OE	6'	190	26		
Gene Heeter	OE	6'4"	235	22		6
Dee Mackey	OE	6'5"	236	27		18
Bake Turner	OE	6'	180	23		36

BOSTON PATRIOTS

RUSHING

Last Name	No.	Yds	Avg	TD
Garron	179	750	4.1	2
Crawford	71	233	3.3	1
Yewcic	22	161	7.3	1
Neumann	44	148	3.4	0
Parilli	36	126	3.5	5
Crump	49	120	2.5	5
Lott	35	78	2.2	3
Cappelletti	1	2	2.0	0

RECEIVING

Last Name	No.	Yds	Avg	TD
Colclough	42	693	17	3
Cappelletti	34	493	15	2
Romeo	31	438	14	3
Garron	26	418	16	2
A. Graham	21	550	26	5
Crawford	10	84	8	0
Neumann	10	48	5	1
Lott	3	61	20	1
Crump	3	19	6	0

PUNT RETURNS

Last Name	No.	Yds	Avg	TD
Suci	25	233	9	0
Stephens	14	117	8	0
Garron	1	23	23	0

KICKOFF RETURNS

Last Name	No.	Yds	Avg	TD
Garron	28	693	25	0
Suci	17	360	21	0
Crump	3	33	11	0
Romeo	1	9	9	0
Watson	1	9	9	0
Yates	2	5	3	0

PASSING – PUNTING – KICKING

PASSING	Att	Comp	%	Yds	Yd/Att	TD	Int–%	RK
Parilli	337	153	45	2345	7.0	13	24– 7	9
Yewcic	70	29	41	444	6.3	4	5– 7	
Crawford	2	2	100	27	13.5	0	0– 0	
Garron	1	0	0	0	0.0	0	0– 0	

PUNTING	No	Avg
Yewcic	73	39.4

KICKING	XP	Att	%	FG	Att	%
Cappelletti	35	36	97	22	38	58

BUFFALO BILLS

RUSHING

Last Name	No.	Yds	Avg	TD
Gilchrist	232	979	4.2	12
Kochman	47	232	4.9	0
Kemp	52	226	4.3	8
Rutowski	48	144	3.0	0
Carlton	29	125	4.3	0
Bass	14	59	4.2	0
Saimes	12	41	3.4	0
Brown	6	18	3.0	1
Lamonica	9	8	0.9	0
Crow	6	6	1.0	0

RECEIVING

Last Name	No.	Yds	Avg	TD
Miller	69	860	12	3
Dubenion	54	970	18	4
Warlick	24	479	20	1
Gilchrist	24	211	9	2
Rutkowski	19	264	14	1
Ferguson	9	181	20	3
Bass	9	153	17	1
Saimes	6	12	2	0
Crow	5	69	14	0
Kochman	4	148	37	1
Brown	2	7	4	0
Stratton	1	19	19	0
Carlton	1	9	9	0

PUNT RETURNS

Last Name	No.	Yds	Avg	TD
Abruzzese	17	152	9	0
West	11	86	8	0
Rutkowski	8	67	8	0
Kochman	1	11	11	0

KICKOFF RETURNS

Last Name	No.	Yds	Avg	TD
Rutkowski	13	396	30	0
Dubenion	13	333	26	0
Saimes	7	140	20	0
Abruzzese	6	118	20	0
West	6	56	9	0
Brown	2	40	20	0
Tracey	1	21	21	0
Rivera	1	20	20	0
Murdock	1	17	17	0
Barber	1	9	9	0
Paterra	1	0	0	0
Matuszak	1	17	17	0

PASSING – PUNTING – KICKING

PASSING	Att	Comp	%	Yds	Yd/Att	TD	Int–%	RK
Kemp	384	193	50	2910	7.6	13	20– 5	4
Lamonica	71	33	46	437	6.1	3	4– 6	
Gilchrist	1	1	100	35	35.0	0	0– 0	
Rutkowski	1	0	0	0	0.0	0	0– 0	

PUNTING	No	Avg
Lamonica	51	40.6
Crow	10	42.4

KICKING	XP	Att	%	FG	Att	%
Yoho	32	37	86	10	23	43

2 POINT XP
Lamonica
Tracey

HOUSTON OILERS

RUSHING

Last Name	No.	Yds	Avg	TD
Tolar	194	659	3.4	3
Tobin	75	270	3.6	4
Smith	50	202	4.0	3
Cannon	13	45	3.4	0
Norton	1	15	15.0	0
Lee	2	9	4.5	0
Babb	1	7	7.0	0
Blanda	4	1	0.2	0

RECEIVING

Last Name	No.	Yds	Avg	TD
Hennigan	61	1051	17	10
Dewveall	58	752	13	7
Tolar	41	275	7	0
McLeod	33	530	16	5
Smith	24	270	11	2
Frazier	16	269	17	1
Tobin	13	272	13	1
Kerbow	5	61	12	0
Cannon	5	39	8	0

PUNT RETURNS

Last Name	No.	Yds	Avg	TD
Glick	19	171	9	0
Jancik	13	145	11	0
Norton	4	23	6	0

KICKOFF RETURNS

Last Name	No.	Yds	Avg	TD
Jancik	45	1317	29	0
Glick	20	451	23	0
Cannon	2	39	20	0
Tobin	1	10	10	0
Tolar	1	4	4	0

PASSING – PUNTING – KICKING

PASSING	Att	Comp	%	Yds	Yd/Att	TD	Int–%	RK
Blanda	423	224	53	3003	7.0	24	25– 6	4
Lee	75	37	49	475	6.3	2	8–11	
Smith	2	0	0	0	0.0	0	0– 0	
Cannon	1	0	0	0	0.0	0	0– 0	

PUNTING	No	Avg
Norton	65	42.9

KICKING	XP	Att	%	FG	Att	%
Blanda	39	39	100	9	22	41

2 POINT XP
Tobin

NEW YORK JETS

RUSHING

Last Name	No.	Yds	Avg	TD
Smolinski	150	561	3.7	4
Mathis	107	268	2.5	1
Christy	26	88	3.4	1
Hall	9	24	2.7	1
D. Wood	7	17	2.4	1
Perkins	3	8	2.6	0
Maynard	2	6	3.0	0
Johnson	2	6	3.0	0

RECEIVING

Last Name	No.	Yds	Avg	TD
Turner	71	1007	14	6
Maynard	38	780	21	9
Smolinski	34	278	8	1
Mackey	23	263	11	3
Mathis	18	177	10	1
Gregory	9	90	10	0
Heeter	8	160	20	1
Christy	8	73	9	0

PUNT RETURNS

Last Name	No.	Yds	Avg	TD
Baird	4	143	36	1
Christy	9	46	5	0
Starks	3	7	2	0
Maynard	1	6	6	0

KICKOFF RETURNS

Last Name	No.	Yds	Avg	TD
Christy	24	585	24	0
Starks	19	336	18	0
Turner	14	299	21	0
Stricker	4	90	23	0
Johnson	6	77	13	0
Perkins	4	55	14	0
Mathis	1	11	11	0
Smolinski	1	10	10	0
Mackey	1	0	0	0

PASSING – PUNTING – KICKING

PASSING	Att	Comp	%	Yds	Yd/Att	TD	Int–%	RK
D. Wood	351	160	46	2202	6.3	18	18– 5	6
Hall	118	45	38	611	5.2	3	9– 8	
Green	6	2	33	10	1.7	0	1– 17	
Chlebek	4	2	50	5	1.3	0	0– 0	
Mathis	1	0	0	0	0.0	0	1–100	

PUNTING	No	Avg
Johnson	71	42.6

KICKING	XP	Att	%	FG	Att	%
Guesman	30	30	100	9	24	31

SAN DIEGO CHARGERS 11-3-0 Sid Gillman

Scores of Each Game		
14	BUFFALO	10
17	BOSTON	13
24	KANSAS CITY	10
34	Denver	50
24	NEW YORK	20
38	Kansas City	17
33	OAKLAND	34
53	New York	7
7	Boston	6
23	Buffalo	13
27	HOUSTON	0
27	Oakland	41
20	Houston	14
58	DENVER	20

Use Name	Pos.	Hgt	Wgt	Age	Int	Pts
Ron Mix	OT	6'4"	250	25		
Ernie Park	OT	6'3"	240	21		
Ernie Wright	OT	6'4"	265	22		
Sam DeLuca	OG	6'2"	242	27		
Sam Gruneisen	OG	6'[illegible]"	252	22		
Pat Shea	OG	6'1"	243	24		
Walt Sweeney	OG	6'3"	260	22		
Don Rogers	C	6'2"	245	26		
Earl Faison	DE	6'5"	262	24		2
Bob Petrich	DE	6'4"	252	22		
George Gross	DT	6'3"	260	22		
Ernie Ladd	DT	6'9"	321	24		
Henry Schmidt	DT	6'4"	254	26		
Chuck Allen	LB	6'1"	225	23	5	6
Frank Buncom	LB	6'1"	235	23		
Emil Karas	LB	6'3"	235	29	2	
Bobby Lane	LB	6'2"	222	23		
Paul Maguire	LB	6'	225	25	4	
Bob Mitinger	LB	6'2"	235	23	3	
George Blair	DB	5'11"	195	25	1	95
Gary Glick	DB	6'2"	200	32	1	
Dick Harris	DB	5'11"	187	26	8	6
Charley McNeil	DB	5'11"	180	27	4	
Dick Westmoreland	DB	6'1"	180	22		
Bud Whitehead	DB	6'	185	24	1	
Keith Kinderman	FB-DB	6'	208	23		
John Hadl	QB	6'2"	205	23		
Tobin Rote	QB	6'3"	220	35		12
Paul Lowe	HB	6'	205	26		60
Bobby Jackson	FB	6'3"	238	23		24
Keith Lincoln	FB	6'2"	212	24		48
Gerry McDougall	FB	6'2"	225	28		6
Lance Alworth	FL	6'	185	23		66
Reg Carolan	OE	6'6"	235	23		
Dave Kocourek	OE	6'5"	245	26		32
Jacque MacKinnon	OE	6'4"	250	24		24
Don Norton	OE	6'1"	195	25		6
Jerry Robinson	OE	5'11"	190	24		12

OAKLAND RAIDERS 10-4-0 Al Davis

Scores of Each Game		
24	Houston	13
35	BUFFALO	17
14	BOSTON	20
7	New York	10
0	Buffalo	12
14	Boston	20
49	NEW YORK	26
34	San Diego	33
10	KANSAS CITY	7
22	Kansas City	7
26	Denver	10
41	SAN DIEGO	27
35	DENVER	31
52	HOUSTON	49

Use Name	Pos.	Hgt	Wgt	Age	Int	Pts
Proverb Jacobs	OT	6'4"	260	28		
Dick Klein	OT	6'4"	255	29		
Frank Youso	OT	6'4"	255	27		
Sonny Bishop	OG	6'2"	240	23		
Wayne Hawkins	OG	6'	240	25		
Ollie Spencer	OG	6'2"	240	32		
Bob Mischak	OE-OG	6'	240	30		
Jim Otto	C	6'2"	240	25		
Dalva Allen	DE	6'5"	240	27		
Dan Birdwell	DE	6'4"	240	22		
Jon Jelacic	DE	6'3"	255	26	1	12
Dave Costa	DT	6'3"	245	21		
Chuck McMurtry	DT	6'	270	25		
Jim Norris	DT	6'4"	235	23		
Bob Dougherty	LB	6'	240	29		
Archie Matsos	LB	6'	212	28	4	
Clancy Osborne	LB	6'3"	218	28	2	
Charley Rieves	LB	5'11"	218	24		
Jackie Simpson	LB	6'1"	225	26	2	
Claude Gibson	DB	6'1"	190	24	3	12
Joe Krakoski	DB	6'2"	195	26	4	
Jim McMillin	DB	5'11"	190	25	4	6
Tom Morrow	DB	5'11"	187	25	9	
Warren Powers	DB	6'	188	22		
Fred Williamson	DB	6'2"	215	25	6	
Herm Urenda	OE-DB	5'11"	170	23		
Cotton Davidson	QB	6'1"	180	30		24
Tom Flores	QB	6'1"	196	26		
Clem Daniels	HB	6'1"	220	26		48
Mike Somner	HB	5'11"	192	28		
Doug Mayberry	FB	6'1"	220	26		
Alan Miller	FB	6'	205	25		30
Glen Shaw	FB	6'1"	225	24		12
Bo Roberson	HB-FL	6'1"	197	28		18
Jan Barrett (from GB-N)	OE	6'3"	230	22		
Dobie Craig	OE	6'4"	200	24		12
Ken Herock	OE	6'2"	230	22		18
Art Powell	OE	6'3"	212	26		96
Mike Mercer	K	6'	200	27		71

KANSAS CITY CHIEFS 5-7-2 Hank Stram

Scores of Each Game		
59	Denver	7
27	Buffalo	27
10	San Diego	24
28	HOUSTON	7
26	BUFFALO	35
17	SAN DIEGO	38
7	Houston	28
7	Oakland	10
7	OAKLAND	22
24	Boston	24
0	New York	17
52	DENVER	21
35	BOSTON	3
48	NEW YORK	0

Use Name	Pos.	Hgt	Wgt	Age	Int	Pts
Charley Diamond	OT	6'2"	262	27		
Dave Hill	OT	6'5"	255	22		
Jim Tyrer	OT	6'6"	290	24		
Denny Biodrowski	OG	6'1"	255	23		
Ed Budde	OG	6'5"	260	22		
Bill Diamond	OG	6'	240	23		
Al Reynolds	OG	6'3"	235	25		
Marvin Terrell	OG	6'1"	240	25		
Jon Gilliam	C	6'2"	240	24		
Mel Branch	DE	6'2"	230	26		
Jerry Mays	DE	6'4"	247	23		6
Curt Merz	OG-DE	6'4"	250	25		
Buck Buchanan	DT	6'7"	276	23		
Curt Farrier	DT	6'6"	270	22		
Paul Rochester (to NY)	DT	6'2"	260	26		
Bobby Bell	LB	6'4"	228	23	1	
Walt Corey	LB	6'	220	25		
Sherrill Headrick	LB	6'2"	215	26	2	6
Smokey Stover	LB	6'	235	24		
E. J. Holub	C-LB	6'4"	225	25	5	
Dave Grayson	DB	5'10"	184	24	5	6
Bobby Hunt	DB	6'1"	180	23	6	
Bobby Ply	DB	6'1"	190	22		
Johnny Robinson	DB	6'	195	24	3	
Charley Warner	DB	5'11"	180	23	1	
Duane Wood	DB	6'1"	200	27	3	6
Len Dawson	QB	6'	190	29		12
Eddie Wilson	QB	6'	190	23		
Bert Coan	HB	6'4"	220	23		
Abner Haynes	HB	6'	190	25		36
Jerrel Wilson	LB-HB	6'4"	225	21		
Curtis McClinton	FB	6'3"	232	24		36
Jack Spikes	FB	6'2"	220	25		47
Frank Jackson	FL	6'1"	190	23		54
Fred Arbanas	OE	6'3"	240	24		36
Tommy Brooker	OE	6'2"	230	23		38
Chris Burford	OE	6'3"	210	25		56
Dick Johnson	OE	6'4"	220	24		6

DENVER BRONCOS 2-11-1 Jack Faulkner

Scores of Each Game		
7	KANSAS CITY	59
14	Houston	20
14	BOSTON	10
50	SAN DIEGO	34
24	HOUSTON	33
21	Boston	40
35	New York	35
28	BUFFALO	30
17	Buffalo	27
9	NEW YORK	14
10	OAKLAND	26
21	Kansas City	52
31	Oakland	35
20	San Diego	58

Use Name	Pos.	Hgt	Wgt	Age	Int	Pts
Eldon Danenhauer	OT	6'4"	245	27		
Harold Olson	OT	6'3"	255	24		
Jim Perkins	OT	6'5"	250	24		
Ernie Barnes	OG	6'3"	243	24		
Bob McCullough	OG	6'2"	245	22		
Tom Nomina	OG	6'5"	270	21		
Frank Jackunas	C	6'3"	225	22		
Jerry Sturm	C	6'3"	245	26		
Chuck Gavin	DE	6'1"	250	29		
Ray Jacobs	DE	6'3"	275	23		
Ike Lassiter	DE	6'5"	270	22		
Ron Nery (to HOU)	DE	6'6"	244	28		
Gordy Holz	DT	6'4"	260	29	1	
Bud McFadin	DT	6'3"	280	35		6
Anton Peters	DT	6'3"	250	21		
Tom Erlandson	LB	6'3"	235	23		
Jim Fraser	LB	6'3"	236	27		
Jerry Hopkins	LB	6'2"	235	22	1	
Wahoo McDaniel	LB	6'	238	26	2	
John Nocera	LB	6'1"	230	29		
Leon Simmons	LB	6'	225	24		
Willie Brown	DB	6'1"	190	22	1	
Goose Gonsoulin	DB	6'3"	210	25	6	6
Tom Janik	DB	6'3"	200	22	2	
John McGeever	DB	6'1"	195	24		
John Sklopan	DB	5'11"	190	22		
Bruce Starling	DB	6'1"	186	21		
Bob Zeman	DB	6'1"	203	26	1	
Don Breaux	QB	6'1"	205	23		
John McCormick	QB	6'1"	210	26		
Mickey Slaughter	QB	6'	190	21		6
Frank Tripucka	QB	6'2"	208	35		
Hewritt Dixon	HB	6'2"	215	23		12
Bob Gaiters	HB	5'11"	210	25		6
Gene Mingo	HB	6'1"	200	24		83
Donnie Stone	HB	6'2"	205	26		24
Clarence Walker	HB	6'1"	205	24		
Charley Mitchell	DB-HB	5'11"	185	23	1	6
Bo Dickinson (to HOU)	FB	6'2"	220	28		6
Billy Joe	FB	6'2"	250	22		30
Don Coffey	FL	6'3"	190	23		
Al Frazier	FL	5'11"	180	28		
Bill Groman	FL	6'	190	27		18
Bob Scarpitto	FL	5'11"	196	24		30
Gene Prebola	OE	6'3"	225	25		14
Tom Rychlec	OE	6'3"	225	29		
Lionel Taylor	OE	6'2"	215	27		60

SAN DIEGO CHARGERS

RUSHING

Last Name	No.	Yds	Avg	TD
Lowe	177	1010	5.7	8
Lincoln	128	826	6.5	5
McDougall	38	199	5.2	1
Jackson	18	64	3.6	4
Rote	24	62	2.6	2
Hadl	8	26	3.3	0
Alworth	2	14	7.0	0

RECEIVING

Last Name	No.	Yds	Avg	TD
Alworth	61	1205	20	11
Lowe	26	191	7	2
Lincoln	24	325	14	3
Kocourek	23	359	16	5
Norton	21	281	13	1
Robinson	18	315	18	1
MacKinnon	11	262	24	4
McDougall	10	115	12	0
Jackson	8	85	11	0

PUNT RETURNS

Last Name	No.	Yds	Avg	TD
Alworth	11	120	11	0
Lincoln	7	98	14	0
Harris	4	43	11	0

KICKOFF RETURNS

Last Name	No.	Yds	Avg	TD
Lincoln	17	439	26	0
Alworth	10	216	22	0
Westmoreland	10	204	20	0
Lowe	5	132	26	0
McDougall	3	77	26	0
Harris	2	34	17	0
Robinson	2	27	14	0
Sweeney	1	18	18	0
Jackson	1	16	16	0
Maguire	1	5	5	0

PASSING – PUNTING – KICKING

PASSING	Att	Comp.	%	Yds	Yd/Att	TD	Int–%	RK
Rote	286	170	59	2510	8.7	20	17– 6	1
Hadl	64	28	44	502	7.8	6	6– 9	
Lowe	4	2	50	100	25.0	1	1– 25	
Lincoln	1	0	0	0	0.0	0	0– 0	
McDougall	1	1	100	11	11.0	1	0– 0	
Norton	1	1	100	15	15.0	0	0– 0	

PUNTING	No	Avg.
Maguire	58	38.6
Hadl	2	37.5

KICKING	XP	Att	%	FG	Att	%
Blair	44	48	92	17	27	63

2 POINT XP
Faison
Kocourek

OAKLAND RAIDERS

RUSHING

Last Name	No.	Yds	Avg	TD
Daniels	214	1099	5.1	3
Miller	62	270	4.4	3
Davidson	26	115	4.4	4
Roberson	19	47	2.2	0
Shaw	20	46	2.3	1
Sommer	5	21	4.2	0
Flores	11	2	0.2	0
Mercer	1	–5	–5.0	0

RECEIVING

Last Name	No.	Yds	Avg	TD
Powell	73	1304	18	16
Miller	34	404	12	2
Daniels	30	685	23	5
Roberson	25	407	16	3
Herock	15	269	18	2
Craig	7	205	29	2
Shaw	2	64	32	1
Mischak	2	25	13	0
Sommer	1	24	24	0
Barrett	1	9	9	0

PUNT RETURNS

Last Name	No.	Yds	Avg	TD
Gibson	26	307	12	2
Sommer	4	44	11	0
Roberson	2	34	17	0
Krakoski	4	10	3	0

KICKOFF RETURNS

Last Name	No.	Yds	Avg	TD
Roberson	38	809	21	0
Sommer	5	102	20	0
McMillin	1	23	23	0
Shaw	2	19	10	0
Simpson	1	11	11	0
Gibson	2	10	5	0
Klein	1	7	7	0
Birdwell	1	7	7	0
Herock	1	3	3	0

PASSING – PUNTING – KICKING

PASSING	Att	Comp	%	Yds	Yd/Att	TD	Int–%	RK
Flores	247	113	46	2101	8.5	20	13– 5	3
Davidson	194	77	40	1276	6.5	11	10– 5	8
Daniels	1	1	100	10	10.0	0	0– 0	

PUNTING	No	Avg
Mercer	75	40.0

KICKING	XP	Att	%	FG	Att	%
Mercer	47	47	100	8	19	42

KANSAS CITY CHIEFS

RUSHING

Last Name	No.	Yds	Avg	TD
McClinton	142	568	4.0	3
Haynes	99	352	3.6	4
Dawson	37	272	7.4	2
Spikes	84	257	3.1	2
Coan	17	100	5.9	0
Jackson	3	52	17.3	1
E. Wilson	8	45	5.6	0
J. Wilson	9	41	4.6	0
Burford	1	10	10.0	0

RECEIVING

Last Name	No.	Yds	Avg	TD
Burford	68	824	12	9
Jackson	50	785	16	8
Arbanas	34	373	11	6
Haynes	33	470	14	2
McClinton	27	301	11	3
Spikes	11	125	11	1
Coan	2	35	18	0
Brooker	2	32	16	0
J. Wilson	2	21	11	0
Johnson	2	17	9	1

PUNT RETURNS

Last Name	No.	Yds	Avg	TD
Jackson	11	95	9	0
Haynes	6	57	10	0
Grayson	2	39	20	0
Warner	4	25	6	0
Wood	1	18	18	0
Robinson	1	16	16	0
Headrick	1	9	9	0

KICKOFF RETURNS

Last Name	No.	Yds	Avg	TD
Grayson	20	570	29	1
Haynes	12	317	26	0
Warner	9	215	24	0
Jackson	1	20	20	0
J. Wilson	1	20	20	0
Stover	2	18	9	0
Spikes	2	12	6	0

PASSING – PUNTING – KICKING

PASSING	Att	Comp	%	Yds	Yd/Att	TD	Int–%	RK
Dawson	352	190	54	2389	6.7	26	19– 5	2
E. Wilson	82	39	48	537	6.5	3	2– 2	
Haynes	2	1	50	24	12.0	0	0– 0	
McClinton	2	1	50	33	16.5	1	0– 0	
Spikes	1	0	0	0	0.0	0	1–100	

PUNTING	No	Avg
J. Wilson	60	43.8
E. Wilson	1	43.0

KICKING	XP	Att	%	FG	Att	%
Spikes	23	24	96	2	13	15
Brooker	20	20	100	6	15	40

2 POINT XP
Burford

DENVER BRONCOS

RUSHING

Last Name	No.	Yds	Avg	TD
Joe	154	649	4.2	4
Stone	96	382	3.9	3
Slaughter	32	124	3.9	1
Dixon	23	105	4.5	2
Mingo	24	90	3.7	0
Breaux	10	51	5.1	0
Mitchell	23	45	2.0	0
Dickinson	6	32	5.3	0
Gaiters	9	20	2.2	0
Walker	2	14	7.0	0
Barnes	0	2	0.0	0
McCormick	3	–5	–1.7	0

RECEIVING

Last Name	No.	Yds	Avg	TD
Taylor	78	1101	14	10
Prebola	30	471	16	2
Groman	27	437	16	3
Stone	22	208	9	1
Scarpitto	21	463	22	5
Joe	15	90	6	1
Dixon	10	130	13	0
Mitchell	8	71	9	0
Dickinson	6	57	10	0
Mingo	3	11	4	0
Gaiters	1	74	74	1
Rychlec	1	9	9	0

PUNT RETURNS

Last Name	No.	Yds	Avg	TD
Mitchell	12	141	12	0
Mingo	7	85	12	0
Dixon	3	58	19	0
Frazier	3	42	14	0
Zeman	2	32	16	0
Brown	3	29	10	0

KICKOFF RETURNS

Last Name	No.	Yds	Avg	TD
Mitchell	37	954	26	1
Gaiters	11	225	20	0
Dixon	9	195	22	0
Frazier	7	185	24	0
Mingo	7	151	22	0
Brown	3	70	23	0
Scarpitto	1	8	8	0
Olson	2	0	0	0
Fraser	1	0	0	0
Groman	0	9	0	0
Gonsoulin	0	4	0	0

PASSING – PUNTING – KICKING

PASSING	Att	Comp	%	Yds	Yd/Att	TD	Int–%	RK
Slaughter	223	112	50	1689	7.5	12	14– 6	7
Breaux	138	70	51	935	6.7	7	6– 4	
McCormick	72	28	39	417	5.7	4	3– 4	
Tripucka	15	7	47	31	2.1	0	5– 33	
Stone	3	0	0	0	0.0	0	0– 0	
Mingo	1	0	0	0	0.0	0	0– 0	
Taylor	1	0	0	0	0.0	0	0– 0	

PUNTING	No	Avg
Fraser	78	46.1

KICKING	XP	Att	%	FG	Att	%
Mingo	35	35	100	16	29	55

2 POINT XP
Prebola

1964 N.F.L. A Blue-Chip Business

The war between the leagues was going nicely for the NFL, as all but two NFL teams made a profit during 1964. Only St. Louis and Dallas lost money, and neither had the excuse of direct AFL competition. Franchises now were blue-chip investments, with price tags well into the millions of dollars. Two of the franchises changed hands this year: William Clay Ford purchased the Detroit Lions and Jerry Wolman headed a syndicate that bought the Philadelphia Eagles. The leagues were still at war, but the NFL owners worried very little at this point.

EASTERN CONFERENCE

Cleveland Browns—The Browns added a little variety to their attack to win their first conference title since 1957. Jimmy Brown still was the ultimate runner, but he got some help in the ball-carrying department from halfback Ernie Green. For the first time in years the Browns also launched a dangerous passing game, with Gary Collins and rookie Paul Warfield providing quarterback Frank Ryan with two fine receivers. Led by tackle Dick Schafrath, the offensive line both cleared paths for the runners and protected quarterback Ryan with equal expertise. The defense had problems defending against the pass, but ex-Giant Dick Modzelewski made the line very tough against the run.

St. Louis Cardinals—Coach Wally Lemm put together a marvelously balanced team, only to have it fall apart on three embarrassing occasions. In a four-week span in mid-season, the Cards lost 47-27 to Baltimore, dropped a 31-13 decision to Dallas, and were beaten 34-17 by the collapsing New York Giants. But before and after this cold spell, the Cardinals showed a versatile offense and spirited defense. Quarterback Charley Johnson had a propensity for throwing interceptions, but he usually made up for his errant tosses with long gainers. The strong offensive line cleared the way for runners John David Crow, Joe Childress, and Willie Crenshaw, while the defense combined a small but quick line with steady linebackers and an aggressive secondary featuring Pat Fischer and Larry Wilson.

Washington Redskins—Quarterback Sonny Jurgensen, obtained in a trade with the Eagles, had few peers as a passer, and receivers Bobby Mitchell, Angelo Coia, and Preston Carpenter gave him an abundance of open receivers. Rookie halfback Charley Taylor injected speed into the running attack. But the Washington offense also had a big hole at fullback and a spotty front line of blockers, making it difficult for Jurgensen, Taylor, and Mitchell to shine their brightest. Even with a defense bolstered by ex-Giant Sam Huff and rookie Paul Krause, the Redskins lost their first four games with poor offensive performances. But after rookies Len Hauss and George Seals were thrust into the offensive line, the Skins revived and won six of their next eight games.

Philadelphia Eagles—Joe Kuharich signed a fifteen-year contract as coach and general manager and immediately dived into the trading market to rebuild the Eagles. In a blinding series of deals, he obtained Norm Snead from Washington, Earl Gros and Jim Ringo from Green Bay, Ollie Matson and Floyd Peters from Detroit, Sam Baker from Dallas, and Ray Poage and Don Hultz from Minnesota. Add three good rookies in Bob Brown, Mike Morgan, and Joe Scarpati, and solid holdovers like Pete Retzlaff, Maxie Baughan, Don Burroughs, and Irv Cross, and the Eagles had the makings of a good football team.

Dallas Cowboys—Even after the Cowboys obtained star wide receivers Tommy McDonald and Buddy Dial, the offense had problems scoring points. One cause of the trouble was Don Meredith's leg injury, which had him hobbling through a sub-par season, and another was the erratic kicking of rookie Dick Van Raaphorst. Given the field-goal kicking job after Sam Baker was dealt to Philadelphia, Van Raaphorst cost the Cowboys several games by blowing easy kicks. Although Don Perkins and Frank Clarke kept up their good work, the Dallas offense fell off from its 1963 performance. The defense, however, suddenly blended together into a strong unit.

Pittsburgh Steelers—Coach Buddy Parker had an intricate plan to improve the Steelers this year. He drafted University of Pittsburgh star Paul Martha as a flanker, and then traded incumbent flanker Buddy Dial to Dallas for the draft rights to All-American defensive lineman Scott Appleton from the University of Texas. The whole maneuver failed miserably when Appleton signed with the AFL Houston Oilers, and Martha was a king-sized bust as a pass receiver. Rookies Ben McGee and Chuck Hinton took up the slack in the defensive line, but no one could fill Dial's vacated receiver spot opposite Gary Ballman.

New York Giants—The New York dynasty crashed heavily to pieces this season. Coach Allie Sherman had traded off Sam Huff and Dick Modzelewski during the off season, hoping to fill their spots with younger men, but none of the replacements came close to the steadiness of the two departed defenders. To add to Sherman's headaches, veterans Y. A. Tittle, Alex Webster, Frank Gifford, Del Shofner, Jack Stroud, and Andy Robustelli all showed signs of advanced old age.

WESTERN CONFERENCE

Baltimore Colts—Coach Don Shula had tried to trade Lenny Moore all summer but had found no takers. Moore had lost his halfback job to Tom Matte and was coming off two injury-plagued seasons which cut his market value down to nothing. Once the regular season started, though, Moore won back his job and set a new NFL record with twenty touchdowns. Moore, Tony Lorick, and Jerry Hill provided tough running, and the Baltimore passing attack was even more effective than usual. The defense responded to the offensive improvement by playing better than anyone could expect, with veterans Gino Marchetti, Bill Pellington, and Bob Boyd the core around which a group of average defenders clustered into a solid unit. With a proper mixture of veterans and youngsters, the Colts captured the conference crown.

Green Bay Packers—Paul Hornung rejoined the Packers after his year's suspension but left his kicking eye behind. The Pack lost three games because of easy kicks Hornung missed, such as the 21-20 loss to the Colts in which Hornung missed an extra point. Outside of this one serious flaw, the Packers still were a solid, precise football team. Bart Starr and Jim Taylor starred in the backfield, and the offensive line graded out well despite the trading of Jim Ringo to Philadelphia and the loss of Jerry Kramer to stomach surgery. No one moved the ball easily against the Green Bay defense, which boasted of four All-Pros in Willie Davis, Henry Jordan, Ray Nitschke, and Willie Wood.

Minnesota Vikings—With three straight wins to end the year, the Vikings jumped up into a second-place tie in the West with the Packers. The Vikings had caught up with Green Bay after only four years in existence, and the main stepladder to progress was the Minnesota offense. At quarterback the Vikings had Fran Tarkenton, the original and best scrambler in the league. The halfback was Tommy Mason, the team's breakaway threat, and the fullback was Bill Brown, a squat young man equally adept at running, receiving, and blocking. The offensive line was not spectacular but good enough to allow the backs to star, while the Minnesota defense was making slower but sure progress.

Detroit Lions—Age was cutting heavily into the vaunted Detroit defense. Night Train Lane was thirty-six and bothered by a bad knee, Yale Lary was thirty-three, Joe Schmidt was thirty-two with a bad shoulder, and Sam Williams was thirty-three. When all these veterans could play at top form, the Lion defense still was one of the league's best, but the days where one or more of them had to sit the game out were growing more frequent. The offense was still a rather plodding unit, with flanker Terry Barr the only speedster on the attack. With neither Milt Plum nor Earl Morrall able to take over at quarterback, the offense was far from ready to pick up the slack left by the aging defense.

Los Angeles Rams—Despite a late-season slump which saw them go winless in their last five games, the Rams developed two solid lines this year. The offensive line of Joe Wendryhoski, Joe Scibelli, Don Chuy, Joe Carollo, and Frank Varricheone was quietly efficient, while the defensive front four of Deacon Jones, Merlin Olsen, Roosevelt Grier, and Lamar Lundy won attention for their speed and violence. The backfields were less settled, as two rookies started in the defensive secondary and three freshman won jobs in the offensive backfield. Bucky Pope surprised everyone with his deep pass receiving as a flanker, and Les Josephson filled in well for the sore-kneed Dick Bass. Rookie Bill Munson won the quarterback job, giving the Rams a second good young quarterback to go along with Roman Gabriel.

Chicago Bears—The Chicago offense had been nothing to write home about last year, but when injuries cut the marvelous defense down to life size, the Bears plummeted into the depths of the Western Conference. When the Bears lost three of their first four games, one of them to the Colts by 52-0, hopes for a repeat championship fluttered away. To get some additional punch from the offense, which had been crippled by the pre-season deaths of Willie Galimore and Bo Farrington in an auto accident, coach George Halas used strong-armed Rudy Bukich more often at quarterback and geared his attack around passes to Johnny Morris and Mike Ditka. Although the passes were successful often enough to place Morris and Ditka one-two in the league receiving statistics and to give Morris a new NFL season's record of ninety-three receptions, the Bear season was a huge disappointment.

San Francisco '49ers—When all their running backs were knocked out with injuries, the '49ers couldn't find enough offensive dynamite in the rest of the lineup to ignite the attack. Although Bernie Casey, Monte Stickles, and rookie Dave Parks were a fine trio of receivers, quarterback John Brodie was not a great enough passer to overcome the lack of any ground attack. The defense gave up no easy yardage, with Charlie Krueger, Clark Miller, Matt Hazeltine, rookie Dave Wilcox, and converted flanker Jim Johnson the main ribs of the unit.

FINAL TEAM STATISTICS

OFFENSE

	BALT.	CHI.	CLEVE.	DALLAS	DET.	G.BAY	L.A.	MINN.	N.Y.	PHIL.	PITT.	ST.L.	S.F.	WASH.
FIRST DOWNS:														
Total	245	248	255	230	221	250	208	258	240	243	233	275	233	193
by Rushing	100	83	119	89	87	133	78	124	81	100	110	95	76	70
by Passing	129	141	118	119	115	106	104	115	140	126	105	152	136	116
by Penalty	16	24	18	22	19	11	26	19	19	17	18	28	21	7
RUSHING:														
Number	456	356	435	421	412	495	400	519	435	430	516	456	383	366
Yards	2007	1166	2163	1691	1414	2276	1629	2183	1404	1922	2102	1770	1332	1237
Average Yards	4.4	3.3	5.0	4.0	3.4	4.6	4.1	4.2	3.2	4.5	4.1	3.9	3.5	3.4
Touchdowns	29	5	14	15	7	23	11	14	12	16	14	12	11	11
PASSING:														
Attempts	345	494	344	404	386	321	368	326	431	397	323	422	461	415
Completions	176	282	181	192	206	186	173	179	217	199	141	223	225	214
Completion Pct.	51.0	57.1	52.6	47.5	53.4	57.9	47.0	54.9	50.3	50.1	43.7	52.8	48.8	51.6
Passing Yards	3045	3056	2542	2516	2890	2474	2769	2614	2848	2746	2308	3045	2990	3071
Avg. Yds per Att.	8.8	6.2	7.4	6.2	7.5	7.7	7.5	8.0	6.6	6.9	7.2	7.2	6.5	7.4
Avg. Yds per Comp.	17.3	10.8	14.0	13.1	14.0	13.3	16.0	14.6	13.1	13.8	16.4	13.7	13.3	14.4
Times Tackled	39	30	28	68	37	47	65	48	45	35	51	37	27	44
Yards Lost Tackled	273	215	219	503	332	369	490	491	373	268	450	298	249	350
Net Yards	2772	2841	2323	2013	2558	2105	2279	2123	2475	2478	1858	2747	2741	2721
Touchdowns	22	25	28	10	23	16	18	23	16	19	14	21	18	25
Interceptions	9	21	19	24	21	6	20	12	26	18	24	24	22	16
Pct. Intercepted	2.6	4.3	5.5	5.9	5.4	1.9	5.4	3.7	6.0	4.5	7.4	5.7	4.8	3.9
PUNTING:														
Number	59	71	49	78	68	56	82	72	74	73	62	56	79	91
Average Distance	41.8	44.5	41.9	38.9	45.7	42.2	44.1	46.4	45.4	41.7	43.2	40.9	45.6	41.2
PUNT RETURNS:														
Number	48	30	20	40	35	34	34	35	28	28	30	24	43	32
Yards	453	219	303	459	411	443	181	306	193	201	238	251	322	230
Average Yards	9.4	7.3	15.2	11.5	11.7	13.0	5.3	8.7	6.9	7.2	7.9	10.5	7.5	7.2
Touchdowns	0	0	1	1	2	1	0	0	0	0	0	1	1	0
KICKOFF RETURNS:														
Number	39	58	57	46	57	45	56	53	67	59	56	63	57	52
Yards	926	1314	1323	1102	1327	1160	1258	1130	1688	1365	1356	1424	1393	1097
Average Yards	23.7	22.7	23.2	24.0	23.3	25.8	22.5	21.3	25.2	23.1	24.2	22.6	24.4	21.1
Touchdowns	0	1	0	0	0	0	0	0	1	0	0	0	0	0
INTERCEPTION RETURNS:														
Number	23	10	19	18	22	16	17	19	15	17	12	25	15	34
Yards	366	258	444	316	267	263	487	224	179	272	96	388	155	317
Average Yards	15.9	25.8	23.4	17.6	12.1	16.4	28.6	11.8	11.9	16.0	8.0	15.5	10.3	9.3
Touchdowns	1	0	3	2	0	1	3	4	1	2	1	5	0	3
PENALTIES:														
Number	74	96	60	97	75	50	76	71	65	42	59	64	79	87
Yards	785	817	611	952	674	576	803	787	532	450	615	579	741	825
FUMBLES:														
Number	31	19	15	38	23	25	40	37	44	33	28	29	42	27
Number Lost	10	12	7	19	13	17	19	18	23	22	17	16	24	17
POINTS:														
Total	428	260	415	250	280	342	283	355	241	312	253	357	236	307
PAT Attempts	54	32	50	30	34	44	33	42	30	38	31	40	30	39
PAT Made	53	29	49	28	32	42	31	40	28	36	28	40	30	35
FG Attempts	35	23	33	29	25	39	24	33	20	26	25	38	25	28
FG Made	17	13	22	14	14	12	18	21	9	16	13	25	8	12
Pct. FG Made	48.6	56.5	66.7	48.3	56.0	30.8	75.0	63.6	45.0	61.5	52.0	65.8	32.0	42.9
Safeties	0	0	0	0	1	0	0	0	0	0	0	1	1	1

DEFENSE

	BALT.	CHI.	CLEVE.	DALLAS	DET.	G.BAY	L.A.	MINN.	N.Y.	PHIL.	PITT.	ST.L.	S.F.	WASH.
FIRST DOWNS:														
Total	242	248	275	211	241	197	235	216	247	234	253	235	255	243
by Rushing	93	99	119	71	92	95	92	94	101	93	109	96	90	101
by Passing	121	121	137	121	128	91	131	105	127	128	121	128	138	125
by Penalty	28	28	19	19	21	11	12	17	19	13	23	11	27	17
RUSHING:														
Number	422	436	465	439	429	417	419	389	468	445	454	414	443	440
Yards	1798	1863	2012	1504	1638	1532	1501	1616	1919	1746	1994	1800	1560	1813
Average Yards	4.3	4.3	4.3	3.4	3.8	3.7	3.6	4.2	4.1	3.9	4.4	4.0	3.5	4.1
Touchdowns	13	19	18	6	10	15	14	10	15	15	15	13	11	20
PASSING:														
Attempts	385	366	401	377	406	318	435	375	361	406	378	389	434	406
Completions	217	188	230	172	226	173	213	182	188	202	185	193	232	193
Completion Pct.	56.4	51.4	57.4	45.6	55.7	54.4	49.0	48.5	52.1	49.8	48.9	49.6	53.5	47.5
Passing Yards	2621	2897	2932	2571	2906	1980	3094	2993	2799	2950	2582	2848	3141	2600
Avg. Yds per Att.	6.8	7.9	7.3	6.8	7.2	6.2	7.1	8.0	7.8	7.3	6.8	7.3	7.2	6.4
Avg. Yds per Comp.	12.1	15.4	12.7	14.9	12.9	11.4	14.5	16.4	14.9	14.6	14.0	14.8	13.5	13.5
Times Tackled	57	30	28	45	50	45	49	36	44	47	42	42	43	43
Yards Lost Tackled	489	275	222	325	482	333	400	269	355	379	345	356	297	353
Net Yards	2132	2622	2710	2246	2424	1647	2694	2724	2444	2571	2237	2492	2844	2247
Touchdowns	14	27	18	22	14	11	27	23	28	18	16	21	23	16
Interceptions	23	10	19	18	22	16	17	19	15	17	12	25	15	34
Pct. Intercepted	6.0	2.7	4.7	4.8	5.4	5.0	3.9	5.1	4.2	4.2	3.2	6.4	3.5	8.4
PUNTING:														
Number	73	62	57	80	66	72	73	71	59	80	67	67	76	67
Average Distance	44.0	46.6	39.7	43.5	44.0	43.5	45.1	43.8	42.2	40.5	39.5	43.5	45.8	42.1
PUNT RETURNS:														
Number	25	35	20	19	33	31	43	30	40	35	24	26	50	50
Yards	175	436	183	52	243	397	360	247	559	333	172	151	540	362
Average Yards	7.0	12.5	15.3	2.7	7.4	12.8	8.4	8.2	14.0	9.5	7.2	5.8	10.8	7.2
Touchdowns	1	0	0	0	0	2	0	0	2	0	0	0	2	0
KICKOFF RETURNS:														
Number	70	47	75	50	48	60	58	57	45	55	40	63	37	60
Yards	1490	1183	1517	1090	1052	1320	1544	1324	990	1319	989	1663	883	1499
Average Yards	21.3	25.2	20.2	21.8	21.9	22.0	26.6	23.2	22.0	24.0	24.7	26.4	23.9	25.0
Touchdowns	0	0	0	0	0	0	0	2	0	0	0	0	0	0
INTERCEPTION RETURNS:														
Number	9	21	19	24	21	6	20	12	26	18	24	24	22	16
Yards	119	260	154	370	247	58	452	149	332	273	465	302	530	321
Average Yards	13.2	12.4	8.1	15.4	11.8	9.7	22.6	10.6	12.8	15.2	19.4	12.6	24.1	20.1
Touchdowns	0	1	0	4	3	0	2	0	2	3	6	0	2	3
PENALTIES:														
Number	59	84	64	75	83	56	70	70	75	71	81	71	76	60
Yards	641	743	643	781	805	521	675	708	674	748	706	695	783	624
FUMBLES:														
Number	28	32	30	26	29	34	28	32	42	27	24	24	33	42
Number Lost	18	20	21	20	8	25	13	16	18	12	14	14	14	21
POINTS:														
Total	225	379	293	289	260	245	339	296	399	313	315	331	330	305
PAT Attempts	28	47	36	34	29	30	44	36	49	40	39	36	40	39
PAT Made	27	46	32	32	29	29	42	33	46	40	36	34	39	36
FG Attempts	24	26	23	29	38	23	27	28	39	26	25	34	34	27
FG Made	10	17	15	17	19	12	11	13	19	11	15	27	17	11
Pct. FG Made	41.7	65.4	65.2	58.6	50.0	52.2	40.7	46.4	48.7	42.3	60.0	79.4	50.0	40.7
Safeties	0	0	0	1	0	0	0	1	1	0	0	0	0	1

1964 NFL CHAMPIONSHIP GAME
December 27, at Cleveland
(Attendance 79,544)

Whitewashing the Aerialists

The Colts came into the game as heavy favorites, but the Cleveland defense effectively shut off the famous Baltimore passing attack as the Browns themselves made several big plays through the air. Neither club scored in the first half, as quarterbacks Johnny Unitas and Frank Ryan both used conservative plays to feel out the enemy. Early in the third quarter, however, a 29 yard punt by Baltimore's Tom Gilburg gave the Browns good field position and led to Lou Groza's 43-yard field goal, which finally broke the scoreless deadlock. As soon as the Browns got the ball back, they sprang Jimmy Brown loose on a pitchout good for 46 yards; in short order, Ryan hit Gary Collins with an 18-yard scoring pass. Then, just before the end of the quarter, Ryan stunned the Colts by throwing a 42-yard bomb to Collins, which, along with the extra point, ran the score up to 17-0. The Colts, in a state of shock over this sudden Cleveland outburst, tried to fight their way back into the game but could make no headway against the charged-up Brown defense. The Browns added a nine-yard Groza field goal early in the final period to run their lead to 20-0, and Ryan threw a 51-yard scoring pass to Gary Collins, the third touchdown of the afternoon for the tall flanker, to make the final score a decisive 27-0 to give Cleveland their first championship since 1955.

TEAM STATISTICS

CLEVE.		BALT.
20	First Downs – Total	11
8	First Downs – Rushing	5
9	First Downs – Passing	4
3	First Downs – Penalty	2
3	Punts – Number	4
44.0	Punts – Average Distance	33.8
1	Punt Returns – Number	2
13	Punt Returns – Yards	18
2	Interception Returns – Number	1
10	Interception Returns – Yards	14
0	Fumbles – Number	2
0	Fumbles – Lost Ball	2
7	Penalties – Number	5
59	Yards Penalized	48
1	Giveaways	4
4	Takeaways	1
+3	Difference	–3

SCORING

CLEVELAND	0	0	17	10–27
BALTIMORE	0	0	0	0– 0

Third Quarter
- Cle. Groza, 43 yard field goal
- Cle. Collins, 18 yard pass from Ryan
  PAT – Groza (kick)
- Cle. Collins, 42 yard pass from Ryan
  PAT – Groza (kick)

Fourth Quarter
- Cle. Groza, 9 yard field goal
- Cle. Collins, 51 yard pass from Ryan
  PAT – Groza (kick)

INDIVIDUAL STATISTICS

RUSHING

CLEVELAND	No	Yds	Avg.	BALTIMORE	No	Yds	Avg.
Brown	27	114	4.2	Moore	9	40	4.4
Green	10	29	2.9	Hill	9	31	3.4
Ryan	3	2	0.7	Unitas	6	30	5.0
Warfield	1	–3	–3.0	Boyd	1	–9	–9.0
	41	142	3.5		25	92	3.7

RECEIVING

CLEVELAND	No	Yds	Avg.	BALTIMORE	No	Yds	Avg.
Collins	5	130	26.0	Berry	3	38	12.7
Brown	3	37	12.3	Lorick	3	18	6.0
Brewer	2	26	13.0	Orr	2	31	15.5
Warfield	1	13	13.0	Moore	2	4	2.0
	11	206	18.7	Mackey	1	2	2.0
				Hill	1	2	2.0
					12	95	7.9

PASSING

	Att	Comp	Comp Pct.	Yds	Int	Yds/ Att.	Yds/ Comp	Yards Lost Tackled
CLEVELAND								
Ryan	18	11	61.6	206	1	11.4	18.7	9
BALTIMORE								
Unitas	20	12	60.0	95	2	4.8	7.9	6

CLEVELAND BROWNS 10-3-1 Blanton Collier

Scores of Each Game		
27	Washington	13
33	ST. LOUIS	33
28	Philadelphia	20
27	DALLAS	6
7	PITTSBURGH	23
20	Dallas	16
42	NEW YORK	20
30	Pittsburgh	17
34	WASHINGTON	24
37	DETROIT	21
21	Green Bay	28
38	PHILADELPHIA	24
19	St. Louis	28
52	New York	20

Use Name	Pos.	Hgt	Wgt	Age	Int	Pts
John Brown	OT	6'2"	248	25		
Monte Clark	OT	6'6"	265	27		
Dick Schafrath	OT	6'3"	255	28		
Roger Shoals	OG-OT	6'4"	255	25		6
Gene Hickerson	OG	6'3"	248	29		
Dale Memmelaar	OG	6'2"	248	27		
John Wooten	OG	6'2"	250	29		
John Morrow	C	6'3"	248	31		
Bill Glass	DE	6'5"	255	28		
Paul Wiggin	DE	6'3"	245	30		6
Sid Williams	DE	6'2"	235	22		6
Mike Bundra (from MIN)	DT	6'3"	260	25		
Bob Gain	DT	6'3"	260	36		
Jim Kanicki	DT	6'4"	270	22		
Dick Modzelewski	DT	6'	260	33		
Frank Parker	DT	6'5"	255	24		

Use Name	Pos.	Hgt	Wgt	Age	Int	Pts
Ed Bettridge	LB	6'1"	235	24		
Vince Costello	LB	6'	228	32	2	
Galen Fiss	LB	6'	227	34	1	
Jim Houston	LB	6'2"	240	27	2	6
Mike Lucci	LB	6'2"	233	24		
Stan Sczurek	LB	5'11"	230	25		
Walter Beach	DB	6'	185	29	4	6
Larry Benz	DB	5'11"	185	23	4	
Lowell Caylor	DB	6'3"	205	23		
Ross Fichtner	DB	6'	185	26	2	
Bobby Franklin	DB	5'11"	182	28		
Bernie Parrish	DB	5'11"	195	29	4	6
Dave Raimey	DB	5'10"	195	23		

Use Name	Pos.	Hgt	Wgt	Age	Int	Pts
Jim Ninowski	QB	6'1"	207	28		
Frank Ryan	QB	6'3"	200	28		6
Ernie Green	HB	6'2"	205	25		60
Leroy Kelly	HB	6'	195	22		6
Jimmy Brown	FB	6'2"	228	28		54
Charlie Scales	FB	5'11"	215	25		6
Gary Collins	FL	6'4"	208	23		48
Clifton McNeil	FL	6'2"	185	24		6
Walter Roberts	FL	5'10"	175	22		6
Johnny Brewer	OE	6'4"	235	27		18
Tom Hutchinson	OE	6'1"	190	23		
Paul Warfield	OE	6'	188	21		54
Lou Groza	K	6'3"	250	40		115

ST. LOUIS CARDINALS 9-3-2 Wally Lemm

Scores of Each Game		
16	Dallas	6
33	Cleveland	33
23	San Francisco	13
23	Washington	17
27	Baltimore	47
38	WASHINGTON	24
13	DALLAS	31
17	New York	34
34	PITTSBURGH	30
10	NEW YORK	10
38	Philadelphia	13
21	Pittsburgh	20
28	CLEVELAND	19
36	PHILADELPHIA	34

Use Name	Pos.	Hgt	Wgt	Age	Int	Pts
Ernie McMillan	OT	6'6"	255	26		
Bob Reynolds	OT	6'6"	265	23		
Ed Cook	OG-OT	6'2"	250	32		
Irv Goode	OG	6'4"	250	23		
Ken Gray	OG	6'2"	250	28		
Rick Sortun	OG	6'2"	225	21		
Herschel Turner	OT-OG	6'3"	230	22		
Bob DeMarco	C	6'3"	240	26		
Don Brumm	DE	6'3"	245	21		
Tom Redmond	DE	6'5"	240	27		
Joe Robb	DE	6'3"	245	27		
Chuck Walker	DE	6'2"	235	23		
Ken Kortas	DT	6'2"	290	22		
Luke Owens	DT	6'2"	260	31		
Sam Silas	DT	6'4"	250	21		

Use Name	Pos.	Hgt	Wgt	Age	Int	Pts
Bill Koman	LB	6'2"	230	30	2	
Dave Meggyesy	LB	6'1"	220	22		
Dale Meinert	LB	6'2"	220	31	2	6
Marion Rushing	LB	6'2"	230	27		2
Larry Stallings	LB	6'2"	230	22	2	
Monk Bailey	DB	6'	175	26		
Jimmy Burson	DB	6'	180	22	3	6
Pat Fischer	DB	5'10"	180	24	10	18
Jimmy Hill	DB	6'2"	195	35		
Jerry Stovall	DB	6'2"	205	22	3	6
Larry Wilson	DB	6'	190	26	3	6

Bill Triplett – Illness

Use Name	Pos.	Hgt	Wgt	Age	Int	Pts
Buddy Humphrey	QB	6'1"	200	28		
Charley Johnson	QB	6'	190	27		12
Joe Childress	HB	6'	210	30		12
Bob Paremore	HB	5'11"	190	24		
John David Crow	FB-HB	6'2"	220	29		48
Willie Crenshaw	FB	6'2"	215	23		6
Prentice Gautt	FB	6'	205	26		12
Bill Thornton	FB	6'1"	220	24		6
Bobby Joe Conrad	FL	6'	195	29		36
Taz Anderson	OE	6'2"	215	25		
Billy Gambrell	OE	5'10"	175	22		12
Sonny Randle	OE	6'2"	190	28		30
Jackie Smith	OE	6'4"	210	23		24
Mal Hammack	LB-OE	6'2"	210	31		
Jim Bakken	K	6'	200	23		115

PHILADELPHIA EAGLES 6-8-0 Joe Kuharich

Scores of Each Game		
38	NEW YORK	7
24	SAN FRANCISCO	28
20	CLEVELAND	28
21	PITTSBURGH	7
20	Washington	35
23	New York	17
34	Pittsburgh	10
10	WASHINGTON	21
10	Los Angeles	20
17	Dallas	14
13	ST. LOUIS	38
24	Cleveland	38
24	DALLAS	14
34	St. Louis	36

Use Name	Pos.	Hgt	Wgt	Age	Int	Pts
Bob Brown	OT	6'4"	280	21		
Dave Graham	OT	6'3"	250	25		
Jim Skaggs	OT	6'2"	230	24		
Ed Blaine	OG	6'2"	240	24		
Pete Case	OG	6'3"	243	23		
Lynn Hoyem	C	6'4"	240	24		
Jim Ringo	C	6'1"	230	33		
Jim Schrader	C	6'2"	250	32		
Riley Gunnels	DE	6'3"	253	27		
Don Hultz	DE	6'3"	235	23		
Bobby Richards	DE	6'2"	245	25		
George Tarasovic	DE	6'4"	245	35		
Don Thompson	DE	6'4"	240	25		
Ed Khayat	DT	6'3"	245	29		
John Meyers	DT	6'6"	267	24		
Floyd Peters	DT	6'4"	255	29		

Use Name	Pos.	Hgt	Wgt	Age	Int	Pts
Maxie Baughan	LB	6'1"	230	26		
Ralph Heck	LB	6'2"	224	23		
Dave Lloyd	LB	6'3"	248	28	3	
Mike Morgan	LB	6'4"	232	22		6
Don Burroughs	DB	6'4"	187	33	2	
Irv Cross	DB	6'1"	195	25	3	6
Glenn Glass	DB	6'	190	27	1	
Nate Ramsey	DB	6'1"	200	23	5	
Joe Scarpati	DB	5'10"	185	22	3	6
Claude Crabb	FL-DB	6'	197	24		

Jerry Mazzanti – Military Service
Mike McClellan – Military Service
Fate Echols – Canadian Football League

Use Name	Pos.	Hgt	Wgt	Age	Int	Pts
Jack Concannon	QB	6'3"	195	21		6
King Hill	QB	6'3"	213	28		
Norm Snead	QB	6'4"	215	24		12
Timmy Brown	HB	5'10"	200	27		60
Roger Gill	HB	6'1"	200	23		
Ollie Matson	HB	6'2"	210	34		30
Earl Gros	FB	6'3"	230	23		12
Izzy Lang	FB	6'1"	230	21		
Tom Woodeshick	FB	6'	205	22		12
Red Mack	FL	5'10"	185	27		6
Ron Goodwin	OE-FL	6'	184	22		18
Ray Poage	OE	6'4"	203	23		6
Pete Retzlaff	OE	6'1"	214	33		48
Ralph Smith	DB-OE	6'2"	213	25		
Sam Baker	K	6'2"	220	32		84

WASHINGTON REDSKINS 6-8-0 Bill McPeak

Scores of Each Game		
13	CLEVELAND	27
18	Dallas	24
10	New York	13
17	ST. LOUIS	23
35	PHILADELPHIA	20
24	St. Louis	38
27	CHICAGO	20
21	Philadelphia	10
24	Cleveland	34
30	Pittsburgh	0
28	DALLAS	16
36	NEW YORK	21
7	PITTSBURGH	14
17	Baltimore	45

Use Name	Pos.	Hgt	Wgt	Age	Int	Pts
Steve Barnett	OT	6'1"	255	23		
Riley Mattson	OT	6'4"	254	25		
Fran O'Brien	OT	6'1"	255	29		
John Nisby	OG	6'1"	238	31		
Vince Promuto	OG	6'1"	245	26		
George Seals	OG	6'2"	250	21		
Fred Hageman	C	6'4"	242	26		
Len Hauss	C	6'2"	220	22		
Carl Kammerer	DE	6'3"	237	27		
John Paluck	DE	6'2"	245	32		2
Ron Snidow	DE	6'4"	250	22		
Joe Rutgens	DT	6'2"	255	25		
Bob Toneff	DT	6'3"	257	34		
Fred Williams	DT	6'4"	248	34		

Use Name	Pos.	Hgt	Wgt	Age	Int	Pts
Rod Breedlove	LB	6'2"	227	23		
Jimmy Carr	LB	6'1"	210	31	2	
Sam Huff	LB	6'1"	230	29	4	
Bob Pellegrini	LB	6'2"	237	29		
John Reger	LB	6'	230	33	3	6
Paul Krause	DB	6'3"	198	22	12	6
Johnny Sample	DB	6'1"	200	27	4	6
Lonnie Sanders	DB	6'3"	210	22	2	
Jim Shorter	DB	5'11"	186	23	1	
Jim Steffen	DB	6'	196	27	4	
Tom Walters	DB	6'2"	195	22	2	

Use Name	Pos.	Hgt	Wgt	Age	Int	Pts
George Izo	QB	6'3"	218	27		
Sonny Jurgensen	QB	5'11"	200	30		18
Dick Shiner	QB	6'	190	22		
Pervis Atkins	HB	6'1"	217	28		6
Charley Taylor	HB	6'3"	215	23		60
Tom Tracy	HB	5'9"	205	32		6
Don Bosseler	FB	6'1"	214	28		
J.W. Lockett	FB	6'2"	226	27		18
Ozzie Clay	FL	6'	190	22		
Joe Hernandez	FL	6'2"	180	24		
Bobby Mitchell	FL	6'	196	29		60
Preston Carpenter	OE	6'2"	190	30		18
Angie Coia	OE	6'2"	202	26		30
Pat Richter	OE	6'5"	230	23		
Jim Martin	K	6'2"	238	40		71

DALLAS COWBOYS 5-8-1 Tom Landry

Scores of Each Game		
6	ST. LOUIS	16
24	WASHINGTON	18
17	Pittsburgh	23
6	Cleveland	27
13	NEW YORK	13
16	CLEVELAND	20
31	St. Louis	13
24	Chicago	10
31	New York	21
14	PHILADELPHIA	17
16	Washington	28
21	GREEN BAY	45
14	Philadelphia	24
17	PITTSBURGH	14

Use Name	Pos.	Hgt	Wgt	Age	Int	Pts
Jim Boeke	OT	6'5"	255	25		
Bill Frank	OT	6'5"	255	26		
Bob Fry	OT	6'4"	238	33		
Tony Liscio	OT	6'5"	240	24		
Ray Schoenke	OT	6'3"	234	22		
Jim Ray Smith	OG-OT	6'3"	245	33		
Joe Bob Isbell	OG	6'1"	250	24		
Jake Kupp	OG	6'3"	215	22		
Mike Connelly	C	6'3"	242	28		
Dave Manders	C	6'2"	240	22		
George Andrie	DE	6'7"	264	24		
Larry Stephens	DE	6'4"	260	26		
Maury Youmans	DE	6'6"	260	27		
Jim Colvin	DT	6'2"	253	27		
Bob Lilly	DT	6'4"	250	25		

Use Name	Pos.	Hgt	Wgt	Age	Int	Pts
Dave Edwards	LB	6'3"	213	25	1	
Harold Hays	LB	6'3"	235	23		
Chuck Howley	LB	6'3"	223	28	2	
Lee Roy Jordon	LB	6'2"	215	23	1	
Jerry Tubbs	LB	6'2"	215	29	2	
Don Bishop	DB	6'2"	215	29		
Mike Gaechter	DB	6'	196	24		
Cornell Green	DB	6'4"	220	24		
Warren Livingston	DB	5'10"	185	26	1	6
Mel Renfro	DB	6'	190	22	7	12
Jimmy Ridlon	DB	6'1"	180	29	4	12

Jerry Overton – Off-season accident
Don Talbert – Military Service

Use Name	Pos.	Hgt	Wgt	Age	Int	Pts
Billy Lothridge	QB	6'1"	185	20		6
Don Meredith	QB	6'2"	205	26		24
John Roach	QB	6'4"	200	31		
Amos Bullocks	HB	6'1"	202	25		
Perry Lee Dunn	HB	6'2"	200	21		6
Amos Marsh	HB	6'1"	225	25		12
Jim Stiger	FB-HB	5'11"	190	23		12
Don Perkins	FB	5'10"	196	26		36
Frank Clarke	FL	6'	215	31		30
Buddy Dial	FL	6'1"	195	27		
Tommy McDonald	FL	5'10"	172	30		12
Lee Folkins	OE	6'5"	220	25		
Pete Gent	OE	6'4"	215	21		
Pettis Norman	OE	6'3"	223	24		12
Dick Van Raaphorst	K	5'11"	215	21		70

CLEVELAND BROWNS

RUSHING

Last Name	No.	Yds	Avg	TD
Jimmy Brown	**280**	**1446**	5.2	7
Green	109	491	4.5	6
Ryan	37	217	5.9	1
Kelly	6	12	2.0	0
Scales	2	5	2.5	0
Ninowski	1	–8	–8.0	0

RECEIVING

Last Name	No.	Yds	Avg	TD
Warfield	52	920	18	9
Jimmy Brown	36	340	9	2
Collins	35	544	16	8
Brewer	25	338	14	3
Green	25	283	11	4
McNeil	4	69	17	1
Hutchinson	3	24	8	0
Roberts	1	24	24	1

PUNT RETURNS

Last Name	No.	Yds	Avg	TD
Kelly	9	171	19	1
Roberts	10	132	13	0
Williams	1	0	0	0

KICKOFF RETURNS

Last Name	No.	Yds	Avg	TD
Roberts	24	661	28	0
Kelly	24	582	24	0
Scales	5	75	15	0
Warfield	1	4	4	0
Franklin	1	1	1	0
Clark	1	0	0	0
Williams	1	0	0	0

PASSING – PUNTING – KICKING

PASSING	Att	Comp	%	Yds	Yd/Att	TD	Int–	%	RK
Ryan	334	174	52	2404	7.2	**25**	19–	6	6
Ninowski	9	6	67	125	13.9	2	0–	0	
Jimmy Brown	1	1	100	13	13.0	1	0–	0	

PUNTING	No	Avg
Collins	48	42.0
Franklin	1	36.0

KICKING	XP	Att	%	FG	Att	%
Groza	49	50	98	22	33	67

ST. LOUIS CARDINALS

RUSHING

Last Name	No.	Yds	Avg	TD
Crow	163	554	3.4	7
Childress	102	413	4.0	0
Crenshaw	60	297	5.0	1
Thornton	39	236	6.1	1
Gautt	59	191	3.2	1
Johnson	31	93	3.0	2
Wilson	2	–14	–7.0	0

RECEIVING

Last Name	No.	Yds	Avg	TD
Conrad	61	780	13	6
Smith	47	657	14	4
Randle	25	517	21	5
Gambrell	24	398	17	2
Crow	23	257	11	1
Childress	12	203	17	2
Gautt	9	72	8	1
Crenshaw	8	58	7	0
Anderson	7	60	9	0
Thornton	7	43	6	0

PUNT RETURNS

Last Name	No.	Yds	Avg	TD
Gambrell	12	126	11	0
Bruson	12	125	10	1

KICKOFF RETURNS

Last Name	No.	Yds	Avg	TD
Stovall	24	566	24	0
Crenshaw	13	340	26	0
Paremore	9	192	21	0
Gautt	5	104	21	0
Gambrell	4	92	23	0
Hammack	2	61	31	0
Burson	2	38	19	0
Conrad	1	26	26	0
Thornton	1	5	5	0
Gray	2	0	0	0

PASSING – PUNTING – KICKING

PASSING	Att	Comp	%	Yds	Yd/Att	TD	Int–	%	RK
Johnson	**420**	**223**	53	**3045**	7.3	21	24–	6	7
Crow	1	0	0	0	0.0	0	0–	0	
Humphrey	1	0	0	0	0.0	0.	0–	0	

PUNTING	No	Avg
Smith	41	40.4
Stovall	15	42.1

KICKING	XP	Att	%	FG	Att	%
Bakken	40	40	**100**	**25**	**38**	66

PHILADELPHIA EAGLES

RUSHING

Last Name	No.	Yds	Avg	TD
Gros	154	748	4.9	2
Matson	96	404	4.2	4
T. Brown	90	356	4.0	5
Woodeshick	37	180	4.9	2
Concannon	16	134	8.4	1
Snead	16	59	3.7	2
Lang	12	37	3.1	0
Hill	8	27	3.4	0
Goodwin	1	–23	–23.0	0

RECEIVING

Last Name	No.	Yds	Avg	TD
Retzlaff	51	855	17	8
Poage	37	479	13	1
Gros	29	234	8	0
Goodwin	23	335	15	3
Matson	17	242	14	1
T. Brown	15	244	16	5
Mack	8	169	21	1
Lang	6	69	12	0
Gill	4	58	15	0
Smith	4	35	9	0
Woodeshick	4	12	3	0
Crabb	1	14	14	0

PUNT RETURNS

Last Name	No.	Yds	Avg	TD
T. Brown	10	96	10	0
Gill	6	61	10	0
Lang	6	26	4	0
Matson	2	10	5	0
Scarpati	1	6	6	0
Hultz	1	2	2	0
Glass	1	0	0	0
Mack	1	0	0	0

KICKOFF RETURNS

Last Name	No.	Yds	Avg	TD
T. Brown	30	692	23	0
Lang	13	352	27	0
Gill	7	167	24	0
Matson	3	104	35	0
Gros	2	38	19	0
Glass	1	12	12	0
Morgan	2	0	0	0
Thompson	1	0	0	0

PASSING – PUNTING – KICKING

PASSING	Att	Comp	%	Yds	Yd/Att	TD	Int–	%	RK
Snead	283	138	49	1906	6.7	14	12–	4	11
Hill	88	49	56	641	7.3	3	4–	5	
Concannon	23	12	52	199	8.7	2	1–	4	
T. Brown	2	0	0	0	0.0	0	1–	50	
Gros	1	0	0	0	0.0	0	0–	0	

PUNTING	No	Avg
Baker	49	42.3
Hill	24	40.3

KICKING	XP	Att	%	FG	Att	%
Baker	36	37	97	16	26	62

WASHINGTON REDSKINS

RUSHING

Last Name	No.	Yds	Avg	TD
Taylor	199	755	3.8	5
Lockett	63	175	2.8	1
Atkins	25	98	3.9	1
Tracy	24	67	2.8	1
Jurgensen	27	57	2.1	3
Bosseler	22	46	2.1	0
Mitchell	2	33	16.5	0
Shiner	2	8	4.0	0
Carpenter	1	7	7.0	0
Richter	1	–9	–9.0	0

RECEIVING

Last Name	No.	Yds	Avg	TD
Mitchell	60	904	15	**10**
Taylor	53	814	15	5
Carpenter	31	466	15	3
Coia	29	500	17	5
Lockett	20	204	10	2
Atkins	8	35	4	0
Bosseler	6	56	9	0
Richter	4	49	12	0
Tracy	2	25	13	0
Hernandez	1	18	18	0

PUNT RETURNS

Last Name	No.	Yds	Avg	TD
Atkins	13	138	11	0
Hernandez	5	49	10	0
Shorter	6	19	3	0
Carpenter	2	19	10	0
Clay	4	5	1	0
Carr	1	0	0	0
Kammerer	1	0	0	0

KICKOFF RETURNS

Last Name	No.	Yds	Avg	TD
Clay	19	482	25	0
Atkins	14	319	23	0
Shorter	5	81	16	0
Lockett	3	72	24	0
Mitchell	3	58	19	0
Mattson	3	30	10	0
Taylor	1	20	20	0
Hernandez	1	19	19	0
Snidow	1	16	16	0
Carr	1	0	0	0
Pellegrini	1	0	0	0

PASSING – PUNTING – KICKING

PASSING	Att	Comp	%	Yds	Yd/Att	TD	Int–	%	RK
Jurgensen	385	207	54	2934	7.6	24	13–	3	3
Izo	18	5	28	83	4.6	1	2–	11	
Taylor	10	2	20	54	5.4	0	1–	10	
Carpenter	1	0	0	0	0.0	0	0–	0	
Shiner	1	0	0	0	0.0	0	0–	0	

PUNTING	No	Avg
Richter	**91**	41.2

KICKING	XP	Att	%	FG	Att	%
Martin	35	39	90	12	28	43

DALLAS COWBOYS

RUSHING

Last Name	No.	Yds	Avg	TD
Perkins	174	768	4.4	6
Marsh	100	401	4.0	2
Stiger	68	280	4.1	1
Dunn	26	103	4.0	1
Meredith	32	81	2.5	4
Clarke	10	46	4.6	0
Roach	8	9	1.1	0
Folkins	1	9	9.0	0
Lothridge	2	–6	–3.0	1

RECEIVING

Last Name	No.	Yds	Avg	TD
Clarke	65	973	15	5
McDonald	46	612	13	2
Norman	24	311	13	2
Perkins	15	155	10	0
Marsh	15	131	9	0
Dial	11	178	16	0
Stiger	9	85	9	1
Folkins	5	41	8	0
Dunn	2	30	15	0

PUNT RETURNS

Last Name	No.	Yds	Avg	TD
Renfro	**32**	**418**	13	1
Gaechter	5	24	5	0
McDonald	2	17	9	0
Stiger	1	0	0	0

KICKOFF RETURNS

Last Name	No.	Yds	Avg	TD
Renfro	**40**	**1017**	25	0
Dunn	2	333	17	0
Gaechter	1	31	31	0
Bullocks	1	19	19	0
Marsh	1	2	2	0
Folkins	1	0	0	0

PASSING – PUNTING – KICKING

PASSING	Att	Comp	%	Yds	Yd/Att	TD	Int–	%	RK
Meredith	323	158	49	2143	6.6	9	16–	5	15
Roach	68	32	47	349	5.1	1	6–	9	
Lothridge	9	2	22	24	2.7	0	2–	22	
Dunn	2	0	0	0	0.0	0	0–	0	
Clarke	1	0	0	0	0.0	0	0–	0	
Stiger	1	0	0	0	0.0	0	0–	0	

PUNTING	No	Avg
Lothridge	62	40.3
Folkins	15	33.1
Howley	1	37.0

KICKING	XP	Att	%	FG	Att	%
Van Raaphorst	28	29	97	14	29	48

EASTERN CONFERENCE – Continued

PITTSBURGH STEELERS 5-9-0 Buddy Parker

Scores of Each Game		
14	LOS ANGELES	26
27	NEW YORK	24
23	DALLAS	17
7	Philadelphia	21
23	Cleveland	7
10	Minnesota	30
10	PHILADELPHIA	34
17	CLEVELAND	30
30	St. Louis	34
0	WASHINGTON	30
44	New York	17
20	ST. LOUIS	21
14	Washington	7
14	Dallas	17

Use Name	Pos.	Hgt	Wgt	Age	Int	Pts
Charlie Bradshaw	OT	6'6"	255	28		
Dan James	OT	6'4"	250	27		
Ray Lemek	OG	6'	240	30		
Mike Sandusky	OG	6'	230	31		
Ron Stehouwer	OG	6'2"	230	27		
Buzz Nutter	C	6'4"	230	33		
John Baker	DE	6'6"	270	29		
Dan LaRose	DE	6'5"	250	24		
Ben McGee	DE	6'2"	250	22		
Urban Henry	DT	6'4"	265	29		
Chuck Hinton	DT	6'5"	235	25	1	6
Joe Krupa	DT	6'2"	235	31		
Ray Mansfield	DT	6'3"	255	23		
Bob Harrison	LB	6'2"	225	27		
Max Messner (from NY)	LB	6'3"	225	26		
Myron Pottios	LB	6'2"	240	24	1	
Bill Saul	LB	6'4"	225	23	1	
Bob Schmitz	LB	6'1"	230	26		
Bob Soleau	LB	6'2"	235	23		
Ed Holler	LB	6'2"	235	24	1	
Jim Bradshaw	DB	6'1"	190	25	1	12
Willie Daniel	DB	5'11"	185	26	2	
Dick Haley	DB	5'10"	190	28	2	
Brady Keys	DB	6'	190	28	2	
Bob Sherman	DB	6'2"	195	22		
Ed Brown	QB	6'2"	210	35		12
Bill Nelsen	QB	6'	195	23		
Terry Nofsinger	QB	6'4"	205	26		
Tom Wade	QB	6'2"	195	22		
Dick Hoak	HB	5'11"	190	25		30
Phil King	HB	6'4"	218	28		12
Theron Sapp	HB	6'1"	200	29		
Marv Woodson	HB	6'	195	21		
John Henry Johnson	FB	6'2"	215	34		48
Clarence Peaks	FB	6'1"	212	28		12
Gary Ballman	OE-FL	6'	195	24		42
Paul Martha	OE-FL	6'	185	21		
John Burrell	OE	6'3"	190	24		
Jim Kelly	OE	6'2"	215	22		6
Chuck Logan	OE	6'4"	210	21		
John Powers	OE	6'2"	210	23		
Clendon Thomas	DB-OE	6'2"	195	27	1	6
Mike Clark	K	6'1"	200	23		67

Andy Russell – Military Service

NEW YORK GIANTS 2-10-2 Allie Sherman

Scores of Each Game		
7	Philadelphia	38
24	Pittsburgh	27
13	WASHINGTON	10
3	Detroit	26
13	Dallas	13
17	PHILADELPHIA	23
20	Cleveland	42
34	ST. LOUIS	17
21	DALLAS	31
10	St. Louis	10
17	PITTSBURGH	44
21	Washington	36
21	MINNESOTA	30
20	CLEVELAND	52

Use Name	Pos.	Hgt	Wgt	Age	Int	Pts
Roger Anderson	OT	6'5"	255	21		
Rosey Brown	OT	6'3"	255	31		
Lane Howell	OT	6'5"	255	23		
Frank Lasky	OT	6'2"	265	22		
Jack Stroud	OT	6'1"	250	35		
Bookie Bolin	OG	6'2"	240	24		
Ken Byers (to MIN)	OG	6'1"	240	24		
Darrell Dess	OG	6'	245	28		
Mickey Walker	C-OG	6'	235	24		
Greg Larson	C	6'2"	250	25		
Jim Katcavage	DE	6'3"	240	29		
Andy Robustelli	DE	6'1"	235	38		
Andy Stynchula	DT	6'3"	250	25		1
Bob Taylor	DE	6'3"	240	24		
John Contoulis	DT	6'4"	260	23		
John Lovetere	DT	6'4"	285	28		
Jim Moran	DT	6'5"	255	21		
Tom Costello	LB	6'3"	220	23		
Jerry Hillebrand	LB	6'3"	240	24	1	
Tom Scott	LB	6'2"	220	34	2	
Lou Slaby	LB	6'3"	235	22	2	
Bill Winter	LB	6'3"	220	24		
Erich Barnes	DB	6'2"	198	29	2	12
Dick Lynch	DB	6'1"	205	28	4	
Andy Nelson	DB	6'1"	180	31	1	
Jimmy Patton	DB	6'	185	32	2	
Dick Pesonen	DB	6'	190	26		
Allan Webb	DB	5'11"	180	29	1	
Henry Schictle	QB	6'2"	190	21		
Y.A. Tittle	QB	6'	195	37		6
Gary Wood	QB	5'11"	188	21		18
Dick James	DB-HB	5'9"	182	30		24
Steve Thurlow	HB	6'3"	210	21		6
Clarence Childs	HB	6'	180	25		6
Alex Webster	FB	6'3"	220	33		18
Ernie Wheelwright	FB	6'3"	220	27		18
Frank Gifford	FL	6'1"	190	34		24
Homer Jones	FL	6'2"	205	23		
R. C. Owens	FL	6'3"	195	29		
Joe Morrison	HB-FL-OE	6'1"	212	26		18
Bob Crespino	OE	6'4"	225	26		
Del Shofner	OE	6'3"	185	28		
Aaron Thomas	FL-OE	6'3"	210	26		36
Don Chandler	K	6'2"	210	29		54

Joe Walton – Injury

WESTERN CONFERENCE

BALTIMORE COLTS 12-2-0 Don Shula

Scores of Each Game		
24	Minnesota	34
21	Green Bay	20
52	CHICAGO	0
35	LOS ANGELES	20
47	ST. LOUIS	27
24	GREEN BAY	21
34	Detroit	0
37	SAN FRANCISCO	7
40	Chicago	24
17	MINNESOTA	14
24	Los Angeles	7
14	San Francisco	3
14	DETROIT	31
45	WASHINGTON	17

Use Name	Pos.	Hgt	Wgt	Age	Int	Pts
George Preas	OT	6'2"	250	32		
Tom Gilburg	OT	6'5"	245	25		
Lou Kirouac	OT	6'3"	240	24		
Bob Vogel	OT	6'5"	250	22		
Jim Parker	OG	6'3"	275	30		
Alex Sandusky	OG	6'1"	242	32		
Dan Sullivan	OT-OG	6'3"	250	25		
Dick Szymanski	C	6'3"	235	32		
Ordell Braase	DE	6'4"	242	32		
Gino Marchetti	DE	6'4"	245	38		
Lou Michaels	DE	6'2"	235	28		104
John Diehl	DT	6'7"	275	28		
Fred Miller	DT	6'3"	245	23		
Guy Reese	DT	6'5"	258	24		
Billy Ray Smith	DT	6'4"	240	29		
Jackie Burkett	LB	6'4"	228	27		
Ted Davis	LB	6'1"	225	22		
Bill Pellington	LB	6'2"	238	35	2	
Don Shinnick	LB	6'	235	29	3	
Steve Stonebreaker	LB	6'3"	220	26		6
Wendell Harris	DB	5'11"	190	23	1	
Alvin Haymond	DB	6'	190	22		
Jerry Logan	DB	6'1"	185	23	6	6
Lenny Lyles	DB	6'2"	202	28	2	
Jim Welch	DB	6'	190	26		
Bobby Boyd	HB-DB	5'10"	190	26	9	
Gary Cuozzo	QB	6'1"	195	23		
Johnny Unitas	QB	6'1"	194	31		12
Tom Matte	HB	6'	205	25		6
Lenny Moore	HB	6'1"	190	31		120
Jerry Hill	FB	5'11"	210	24		36
Joe Don Looney	FB	6'1"	230	21		12
Tony Lorick	FB	6'1"	203	22		24
Jimmy Orr	FL	5'11"	175	28		36
Willie Richardson	FL	6'2"	198	24		
Ray Berry	OE	6'2"	187	31		36
Alex Hawkins	OE	6'1"	190	27		6
John Mackey	OE	6'3"	217	22		12
Neal Petties	OE	6'2"	198	23		6
Butch Wilson	OE	6'2"	218	22		6

GREEN BAY PACKERS 8-5-1 Vince Lombardi

Scores of Each Game		
23	CHICAGO	12
20	BALTIMORE	21
14	Detroit	10
23	MINNESOTA	24
24	SAN FRANCISCO	14
21	Baltimore	24
17	LOS ANGELES	27
42	Minnesota	13
30	DETROIT	7
14	San Francisco	24
28	CLEVELAND	21
45	Dallas	21
17	Chicago	3
24	Los Angeles	24

Use Name	Pos.	Hgt	Wgt	Age	Int	Pts
Forrest Gregg	OT	6'4"	250	31		
Steve Wright	OT	6'6"	250	22		
Norm Masters	OT	6'2"	250	31		
Bob Skoronski	C-OT	6'3"	250	31		
Dan Grimm	OG	6'3"	245	23		
Fuzzy Thurston	OG	6'1"	245	31		
Jerry Kramer	OG	6'3"	245	29		
John McDowell	OT-OG	6'3"	260	21		
Ken Bowman	C	6'3"	230	21		
Lionel Aldridge	DE	6'4"	245	22		6
Willie Davis	DE	6'3"	245	31		
Lloyd Voss	DE	6'4"	245	22		
Dave Hanner	DT	6'2"	260	35		
Henry Jordan	DT	6'3"	250	29		6
Ron Kostelnik	DT	6'4"	260	24		
Gene Breen	LB	6'2"	225	23		
Lee Roy Caffey	LB	6'3"	240	24	1	
Dan Currie	LB	6'3"	240	30	2	
Ray Nitschke	LB	6'3"	240	28	2	
Dave Robinson	LB	6'3"	245	23		
Tommy Crutcher	FB-LB	6'3"	220	22		
Herb Adderley	DB	6'1"	210	25	4	
Tom Brown	DB	6'1"	190	23	1	
Hank Gremminger	DB	6'1"	200	31	1	
Doug Hart	DB	6'	190	25	1	
Jerry Norton	DB	5'11"	195	34		
Jesse Whittenton	DB	6'	195	30	1	
Willie Wood	DB	5'10"	190	28	3	7
Zeke Bratkowski	QB	6'2"	200	32		
Dennis Claridge	QB	6'3"	225	22		
Bart Starr	QB	6'1"	200	31		18
Paul Hornung	HB	6'2"	215	27		107
Tom Moore	HB	6'2"	210	26		24
Elijah Pitts	HB	6'1"	205	25		12
Jim Taylor	FB	6'	215	29		90
Boyd Dowler	FL	6'5"	225	27		30
Bob Long	FL	6'3"	190	23		
Bob Jeter	OE-FL	6'1"	205	26		
Marv Fleming	OE	6'4"	230	22		
Ron Kramer	OE	6'3"	240	29		
Max McGee	OE	6'3"	205	32		42

Ken Iman – Broken Hand

MINNESOTA VIKINGS 8-5-1 Norm Van Brocklin

Scores of Each Game		
34	BALTIMORE	24
28	CHICAGO	34
13	Los Angeles	22
24	Green Bay	23
20	DETROIT	24
30	PITTSBURGH	10
27	San Francisco	22
13	GREEN BAY	42
24	SAN FRANCISCO	7
14	Baltimore	17
23	Detroit	23
34	LOS ANGELES	13
30	New York	21
41	Chicago	14

Use Name	Pos.	Hgt	Wgt	Age	Int	Pts
Grady Alderman	OT	6'2"	245	25		
Errol Linden	OT	6'5"	260	27		
Larry Bowie	OG	6'2"	245	24		
Palmer Pyle	OG	6'2"	250	27		
Milt Sunde	OG	6'2"	222	21		
Mick Tingelhoff	C	6'1"	235	24		
Bob Denton	DE	6'4"	244	30		
Carl Eller	DE	6'6"	247	22		6
Jim Marshall	DE	6'3"	235	26		
Howard Simpson	DE	6'5"	230	21		
Paul Dickson	DT	6'5"	255	27		
Dave O'Brien	DT	6'3"	247	23		
Jim Prestel	DT	6'5"	275	27	1	6
John Campbell	LB	6'3"	215	25		
Rip Hawkins	LB	6'3"	230	25	2	12
Bill Jobko	LB	6'2"	225	28		
John Kirby	LB	6'3"	222	22		
Bill Swain	LB	6'2"	228	23		
Roy Winston	LB	6'1"	230	24	3	
Lee Calland	DB	6'	190	23		
Karl Kassulke	DB	6'	193	22	3	
George Rose	DB	5'11"	190	21	6	6
Ed Sharockman	DB	6'	200	24	1	
Bill Butler	HB-DB	5'10"	200	27	2	
Larry Vargo	OE-DB	6'3"	215	24	1	
Fran Tarkenton	QB	6'1"	190	24		12
Ron Vander Kelen	QB	6'1"	185	24		
Ted Dean	HB	6'2"	213	26		
Tommy Mason	HB	6'	196	25		30
Tom Michel	HB	6'	210	23		
Bill Brown	FB	5'11"	220	26		96
Darrell Lester	FB	6'2"	225	23		
Bill McWatters	FB	6'	225	22		6
Tom Hall	FL	6'1"	195	23		12
Hal Bedsole	OE	6'4"	230	22		30
Paul Flatley	OE	6'1"	187	23		18
Bob Lacey	OE	6'3"	205	22		
Jerry Reichow	OE	6'2"	220	29		12
Gordon Smith	OE	6'2"	220	25		6
Fred Cox	K	5'10"	200	25		103
Bobby Walden	K	6'	195	26		

Chuck Lamson – Injury
Terry Dillon – Accidentally Drowned in May

EASTERN CONFERENCE—Continued

PITTSBURGH STEELERS

RUSHING

Last Name	No.	Yds	Avg	TD
Johnson	235	1048	4.5	7
Peaks	118	503	4.3	2
Hoak	84	258	3.1	2
Brown	26	110	4.2	2
King	26	71	2.7	1
Ballman	11	43	3.9	0
Nelsen	3	17	5.7	0
Sapp	4	15	3.8	0
Martha	4	12	3.0	0
Powers	2	10	5.0	0
Holler	1	8	8.0	0
Thomas	2	7	3.5	0

RECEIVING

Last Name	No.	Yds	Avg	TD
Ballman	47	935	20	7
Thomas	17	334	20	1
Johnson	17	69	4	1
Hoak	12	137	11	3
Peaks	12	113	9	0
Kelly	10	186	19	1
Powers	8	193	24	0
Martha	6	145	24	0
Burrell	6	113	19	0
King	4	32	8	1
Sapp	1	44	44	0
Logan	1	7	7	0

PUNT RETURNS

Last Name	No.	Yds	Avg	TD
Keys	14	172	12	0
Martha	13	64	5	0
J. Bradshaw	1	2	2	0
Baker	1	0	0	0
Woodson	1	0	0	0

KICKOFF RETURNS

Last Name	No.	Yds	Avg	TD
Ballman	14	386	28	0
Peaks	12	326	27	0
Woodson	5	178	36	0
Thomas	7	171	24	0
Keys	7	168	24	0
Sapp	4	43	11	0
King	2	27	14	0
Martha	1	26	26	0
Lemek	1	19	19	0
Kelly	1	12	12	0
Burrell	2	0	0	0

PASSING – PUNTING – KICKING

PASSING	Att	Comp	%	Yds	Yd/Att	TD	Int–	%	RK
Brown	272	121	44	1990	7.3	12	19–	7	14
Nelsen	42	16	38	276	6.6	2	3–	7	
Nofsinger	4	3	75	35	8.8	0	1–	25	
Wade	3	1	33	7	2.3	0	0–	0	
Ballman	1	0	0	0	0.0	0	1–	100	
Hoak	1	0	0	0	0.0	0	0–	0	

PUNTING	No	Avg
Brown	31	43.4
Holler	31	43.0

KICKING	XP	Att	%	FG	Att	%
Clark	28	31	90	13	25	52

NEW YORK GIANTS

RUSHING

Last Name	No.	Yds	Avg	TD
Wheelwright	100	402	4.0	0
Webster	76	210	2.8	3
Thurlow	64	210	3.3	0
James	55	189	3.4	3
Wood	39	158	4.1	3
Morrison	45	138	3.1	1
Childs	40	102	2.6	0
Gifford	1	2	2.0	1
Tittle	15	−7	−0.5	1

RECEIVING

Last Name	No.	Yds	Avg	TD
Thomas	43	624	15	6
Morrison	40	505	13	2
Gifford	29	429	15	3
Shofner	22	323	15	0
Webster	19	199	10	0
Wheelwright	14	204	15	3
Crespino	12	165	14	0
James	12	101	8	1
Childs	11	97	9	0
Thurlow	7	74	11	1
Jones	4	82	21	0
Owens	4	45	11	0

PUNT RETURNS

Last Name	No.	Yds	Avg	TD
James	21	153	7	0
Childs	6	40	7	0
Barnes	1	0	0	0

KICKOFF RETURNS

Last Name	No.	Yds	Avg	TD
Childs	34	987	29	1
James	23	515	22	0
Jones	6	111	19	0
Morrison	4	75	19	0

PASSING – PUNTING – KICKING

PASSING	Att	Comp	%	Yds	Yd/Att	TD	Int–	%	RK
Tittle	281	147	52	1798	6.4	10	22–	8	16
Wood	143	66	46	952	6.7	6	3–	2	13
Thurlow	5	3	60	65	13.0	0	0–	0	
Gifford	1	1	100	33	33.0	0	0–	0	
James	1	0	0	0	0.0	0	1–	100	

PUNTING	No	Avg
Chandler	73	45.6
James	1	35.0

KICKING	XP	Att	%	FG	Att	%
Chandler	27	29	93	9	20	45
Stynchula	1	1	100	0	0	

WESTERN CONFERENCE

BALTIMORE COLTS

RUSHING

Last Name	No.	Yds	Avg	TD
Moore	157	584	3.7	16
Lorick	100	513	5.1	4
Hill	88	384	4.4	5
Matte	42	215	5.1	1
Unitas	37	162	4.4	2
Looney	23	127	5.5	1
Boyd	1	25	25.0	0
Mackey	1	−1	−1.0	0
Cuozzo	7	−2	−0.3	0

RECEIVING

Last Name	No.	Yds	Avg	TD
Berry	43	663	15	6
Orr	40	867	22	6
Mackey	22	406	18	2
Moore	21	472	22	3
Hill	14	113	8	1
Lorick	11	164	15	0
Matte	10	169	17	0
Wilson	7	86	12	1
Richardson	3	42	14	0
Hawkins	2	42	21	1
Petties	2	20	10	1
Looney	1	1	1	1

PUNT RETURNS

Last Name	No.	Yds	Avg	TD
Harris	17	214	13	0
Hawkins	16	122	8	0
Logan	13	111	9	0
Haymond	1	6	6	0
Davis	1	0	0	0

KICKOFF RETURNS

Last Name	No.	Yds	Avg	TD
Lorick	13	385	30	0
Looney	14	345	25	0
Hill	4	85	21	0
Matte	3	71	24	0
Gilburg	1	19	19	0
Davis	1	12	12	0
Petties	1	9	9	0
Boyd	1	0	0	0
Haymond	1	0	0	0

PASSING – PUNTING – KICKING

PASSING	Att	Comp	%	Yds	Yd/Att	TD	Int–	%	RK
Unitas	305	158	52	2824	9.3	19	6–	2	4
Cuozzo	36	15	42	163	4.5	2	3–	8	
Matte	4	3	75	58	14.5	1	0–	0	

PUNTING	No	Avg
Looney	32	42.4
Gilburg	27	41.0

KICKING	XP	Att	%	FG	Att	%
Michaels	53	54	98	17	35	49

GREEN BAY PACKERS

RUSHING

Last Name	No.	Yds	Avg	TD
Taylor	235	1169	5.0	12
Hornung	103	415	4.0	5
Moore	102	371	3.6	2
Starr	24	165	6.9	3
Pitts	27	127	4.7	1
Norton	1	24	24.0	0
Crutcher	1	5	5.0	0
Bratkowski	2	0	0.0	0

RECEIVING

Last Name	No.	Yds	Avg	TD
Dowler	45	623	14	5
Taylor	38	354	9	3
R. Kramer	34	551	16	0
McGee	31	592	19	6
Moore	17	140	8	2
Hornung	9	98	11	0
Pitts	6	38	6	0
Fleming	4	36	9	0
Jeter	1	23	23	0
Long	1	19	19	0

PUNT RETURNS

Last Name	No.	Yds	Avg	TD
Wood	19	252	13	0
Pitts	15	191	13	1

KICKOFF RETURNS

Last Name	No.	Yds	Avg	TD
Adderly	19	508	27	0
Moore	16	431	27	0
Brown	7	167	24	0
Crutcher	2	54	27	0
Caffey	1	0	0	0

PASSING – PUNTING – KICKING

PASSING	Att	Comp	%	Yds	Yd/Att	TD	Int–	%	RK
Starr	272	163	60	2144	7.9	15	4–	1	1
Bratkowski	36	19	53	277	7.7	1	1–	3	
Hornung	10	3	30	25	2.5	0	1–	10	
Moore	3	1	33	28	9.3	0	0–	0	

PUNTING	No	Avg
Norton	56	42.2

KICKING	XP	Att	%	FG	Att	%
Hornung	41	43	95	12	38	32
Wood	1	1	100	0	1	0

MINNESOTA VIKINGS

RUSHING

Last Name	No.	Yds	Avg	TD
Brown	226	866	3.8	7
Mason	169	691	4.1	4
Tarkenton	50	330	6.6	2
Michel	39	129	3.3	0
McWatters	14	60	4.3	1
Dean	5	30	6.0	0
Lester	4	18	4.5	0
Walden	1	18	18.0	0
Butler	5	11	2.2	0
Vander Kelen	1	10	10.0	0
Smith	1	2	2.0	0
Hall	4	−4	−1.0	0
Alderman	0	22	0.0	0

RECEIVING

Last Name	No.	Yds	Avg	TD
Brown	48	703	15	9
Flatley	28	450	16	3
Mason	26	239	9	1
Hall	23	325	14	2
Reichow	20	284	14	2
Bedsole	18	295	16	5
Smith	10	211	21	1
McWatters	2	−1	−1	0
Butler	1	58	58	0
Dean	1	23	23	0
Michel	1	14	14	0
Vargo	1	13	13	0

PUNT RETURNS

Last Name	No.	Yds	Avg	TD
Butler	22	156	7	0
Mason	10	150	15	0
Dean	2	0	0	0
Kassulke	1	0	0	0

KICKOFF RETURNS

Last Name	No.	Yds	Avg	TD
Butler	26	597	23	0
Michel	8	192	24	0
Rose	8	180	23	0
Brown	5	68	14	0
Dean	3	50	17	0
Mason	2	36	18	0
McWatters	1	7	7	0

PASSING – PUNTING – KICKING

PASSING	Att	Comp	%	Yds	Yd/Att	TD	Int–	%	RK
Tarkenton	306	171	56	2506	8.2	22	11–	4	2
Vander Kelen	19	7	37	78	4.1	0	1–	5	
Mason	1	1	100	30	30.0	1	0–	0	

PUNTING	No	Avg
Walden	72	46.4

KICKING	XP	Att	%	FG	Att	%
Cox	40	42	95	21	33	64

WESTERN CONFERENCE—Continued

DETROIT LIONS 7-5-2 George Wilson

Scores of Each Game			Use Name	Pos.	Hgt	Wgt	Age	Int	Pts
26	San Francisco	17	Daryl Sanders	OT	6'5"	250	22		
17	Los Angeles	17	J. D. Smith	OT	6'5"	250	28		
10	GREEN BAY	14	John Gonzaga	OG-OT	6'3"	250	31		
26	NEW YORK	3	John Gordy	OG	6'3"	250	28		
24	Minnesota	20	Jim Simon	OG	6'5"	235	23		
10	Chicago	0	Wally Hilgenberg	LB-OG	6'3"	225	21		
0	BALTIMORE	34	Bob Whitlow	C	6'1"	236	28		
37	LOS ANGELES	17	Bob Schlotz	OT-C	6'4"	250	26		
7	Green Bay	30	Darris McCord	DE	6'4"	250	31		
21	Cleveland	37	Bill Quinlan	DE	6'3"	240	32	1	
23	MINNESOTA	23	Sam Williams	DE	6'5"	235	33		6
24	CHICAGO	27	Roger Brown	DT	6'5"	300	27		
31	Baltimore	14	Alex Karras	DT	6'2"	245	28	2	
24	SAN FRANCISCO	7	Roger LaLonde	DT	6'3"	255	22		

Use Name	Pos.	Hgt	Wgt	Age	Int	Pts
Ernie Clark	LB	6'1"	220	26		
Dennis Gaubatz	LB	6'2"	220	23	1	2
Monte Lee	LB	6'4"	220	26		
Joe Schmidt	LB	6'1"	220	32		
Wayne Walker	LB	6'2"	225	27	1	74
Night Train Lane	DB	6'1"	200	36	1	
Dick LeBeau	DB	6'1"	185	27	5	
Bruce Maher	DB	5'11"	190	27	2	
Wayne Rasmussen	DB	6'2"	180	22		
Bobby Thompson	DB	5'10"	175	24	3	
Dick Compton	HB-DB	6'1"	195	24		
Yale Lary	DB	6'	190	33	6	
Gary Lowe	HB-DB	5'11"	195	30		

Lucian Reeberg—Died Jan. 31, 1964 of Uremia

Use Name	Pos.	Hgt	Wgt	Age	Int	Pts
Sonny Gibbs	QB	6'7"	230	23		
Earl Morrall	QB	6'1"	206	30		
Milt Plum	QB	6'1"	205	30		6
Dan Lewis	HB	6'1"	200	28		12
Hugh McElhenny	HB	6'1"	190	35		
Tom Watkins	HB	6'1"	195	27		24
Pat Batten	FB	6'2"	225	22		
Nick Pietrosante	FB	6'2"	225	27		24
Nick Ryder	FB	6'	210	23		6
Terry Barr	FL	6'	190	29		54
Pat Studstill	FL	6'1"	175	26		6
Gail Cogdill	OE	6'2"	195	27		18
Jim Gibbons	OE	6'2"	220	28		48
Hugh McInnis	OE	6'3"	220	26		
Warren Wells	OE	6'1"	195	21		

LOS ANGELES RAMS 5-7-2 Harland Svare

Scores of Each Game			Use Name	Pos.	Hgt	Wgt	Age	Int	Pts
26	Pittsburgh	14	Joe Carollo	OT	6'2"	262	24		
17	DETROIT	17	Frank Varrichione	OT	6'1"	237	32		
22	MINNESOTA	13	Charley Cowan	OG-OT	6'4"	267	26		
20	Baltimore	35	Don Chuy	OG	6'1"	255	23		
17	Chicago	38	Roger Davis	OG	6'3"	235	26		
42	SAN FRANCISCO	14	Joe Scibelli	OG	6'1"	260	25		
27	Green Bay	17	Fred Whittingham	OG	6'1"	240	25		
17	Detroit	37	Art Hunter	C	6'4"	248	31		
20	PHILADELPHIA	10	Joe Wendryhoski	C	6'2"	245	25		
24	CHICAGO	34	Deacon Jones	DE	6'5"	267	25		
7	BALTIMORE	24	Lamar Lundy	DE	6'7"	250	29	1	6
13	Minnesota	34	Rosey Grier	DT	6'5"	290	31		
7	San Francisco	28	Gary Larsen	DT	6'5"	245	24		
24	GREEN BAY	24	Merlin Olsen	DT	6'5"	275	23		

Use Name	Pos.	Hgt	Wgt	Age	Int	Pts
Marv Harris	LB	6'1"	225	22		
Mike Henry	LB	6'2"	227	28		
Cliff Livingston	LB	6'3"	215	34		
Jack Pardee	LB	6'2"	230	28	1	
Andy Von Sonn	LB	6'2"	223	23		
Frank Budka	DB	6'	195	22	2	
Lindon Crow	DB	6'	200	31	1	
Aaron Martin	DB	6'	185	23	2	6
Ed Meador	DB	5'11"	198	27	3	
Jerry Richardson	DB	6'3"	190	21	5	
Bobby Smith	DB	6'	197	26	2	12

Use Name	Pos.	Hgt	Wgt	Age	Int	Pts
Roman Gabriel	QB	6'4"	220	24		6
Bill Munson	QB	6'2"	187	22		
Terry Baker	HB	6'3"	200	23		
Carver Shannon	HB	6'1"	206	26		
Ben Wilson	HB	6'	225	24		36
Dick Bass	FB	5'10"	200	27		12
Les Josephson	FB	6'	210	22		24
Willie Brown	FL	6'	186	21		
Jim Phillips	FL	6'1"	195	27		12
Duane Allen	OE	6'4"	225	26		6
Carroll Dale	OE	6'1"	195	26		12
Marlin McKeever	OE	6'1"	235	24		6
Bucky Pope	FL	6'5"	195	21		60
Billy Truax	OE	6'5"	240	21		
Bruce Gossett	K	6'2"	225	21		85
Danny Villanueva	K	5'11"	213	26		

CHICAGO BEARS 5-9-0 George Halas

Scores of Each Game			Use Name	Pos.	Hgt	Wgt	Age	Int	Pts
12	Green Bay	23	George Burman	OT	6'3"	240	21		
34	Minnesota	28	Herm Lee	OT	6'4"	247	33		
0	Baltimore	52	Bob Wetoska	OT	6'3"	240	26		
21	San Francisco	31	Jim Cadile	OG	6'3"	240	23		
38	LOS ANGELES	17	Dick Evey	OG	6'2"	225	23		
0	DETROIT	10	Ted Karras	OG	6'1"	243	31		
20	Washington	27	Mike Rabold	OG	6'2"	238	27		
10	DALLAS	24	Mike Pyle	C	6'3"	245	25		
24	BALTIMORE	40	Doug Atkins	DE	6'8"	255	34		
34	Los Angeles	24	Bob Kilcullen	DE	6'3"	245	28		
23	SAN FRANCISCO	21	Ed O'Bradovich	DE	6'3"	255	24		
27	Detroit	24	John Johnson	DT	6'5"	260	23		
3	GREEN BAY	17	Stan Jones	DT	6'1"	250	33		
14	MINNESOTA	41	Earl Leggett	DT	6'3"	250	30		

Use Name	Pos.	Hgt	Wgt	Age	Int	Pts
Joe Fortunato	LB	6'	225	34		
Bill George	LB	6'2"	235	33	2	
Roger LeClerc	LB	6'3"	235	26		30
Larry Morris	LB	6'2"	230	29		
Jim Purnell	LB	6'2"	205	22		
Mike Reilly	LB	6'2"	210	21		
J. C. Caroline	DB	6'1"	190	31	2	
Larry Glueck	DB	6'	190	22		
Bennie McRae	DB	6'1"	180	23	2	
Richie Petitbon	DB	6'3"	205	26		
John Sisk	DB	6'3"	195	22		
Rosey Taylor	DB	5'11"	186	25	2	
Dave Whitsell	HB-DB	6'	190	28	2	

Bo Farrington, Willie Galimore } Died in auto accident during training camp, July 26, 1964

Use Name	Pos.	Hgt	Wgt	Age	Int	Pts
Rudy Bukich	QB	6'1"	205	33		
Larry Rakestraw	QB	6'2"	195	22		
Billy Wade	QB	6'2"	205	33		6
Jon Arnett	HB	5'11"	203	29		18
Charlie Bivins	HB	6'2"	212	25		6
Ronnie Bull	HB	6'	200	24		6
Andy Livingston	HB	6'	234	19		6
Billy Martin	HB	5'11"	196	26		
Rick Casares	FB	6'2"	225	33		12
Joe Marconi	FB	6'2"	225	30		30
Johnny Morris	FL	5'10"	180	29		60
Gary Barnes	OE-FL	6'4"	210	24		
Mike Ditka	OE	6'3"	230	24		36
Bob Jencks	OE	6'5"	227	23		38
Rich Kreitling	OE	6'2"	208	29		12
Bill Martin	OE	6'4"	240	21		
Bobby Joe Green	K	5'11"	175	26		

SAN FRANCISCO FORTY NINERS 4-10-0 Jack Christiansen

Scores of Each Game			Use Name	Pos.	Hgt	Wgt	Age	Int	Pts
17	DETROIT	26	Walt Rock	OT	6'5"	245	23		
28	Philadelphia	24	Len Rohde	OT	6'4"	240	26		
13	ST. LOUIS	23	Leon Donahue	OG	6'4"	245	25		
31	CHICAGO	21	Mike Magac	OG	6'3"	240	26		
14	Green Bay	24	Howard Mudd	OG	6'3"	240	22		
14	Los Angeles	42	John Thomas	OG	6'4"	246	29		
22	MINNESOTA	27	Bruce Bosley	C	6'2"	240	30		
7	Baltimore	37	Frank Morze	C	6'4"	280	30		
7	Minnesota	24	Dan Colchico	DE	6'4"	245	27		
24	GREEN BAY	14	Clark Miller	DE	6'5"	245	25		
21	Chicago	23	Karl Rubke	DE	6'4"	240	28		
3	BALTIMORE	14	Charlie Krueger	DT	6'4"	250	28		
28	LOS ANGELES	7	Roland Lakes	DT	6'4"	263	24		
7	Detroit	24	Chuck Sieminski	DT	6'4"	255	24		

Use Name	Pos.	Hgt	Wgt	Age	Int	Pts
Bill Cooper	LB	6'1"	215	25		
Floyd Dean	LB	6'4"	245	24		
Mike Dowdle	LB	6'3"	230	26	1	
Matt Hazeltine	LB	6'1"	230	31	1	
Ed Pine	LB	6'4"	235	24		
Dave Wilcox	LB	6'3"	230	21	1	
Kermit Alexander	DB	5'11"	186	23	5	6
Charley Britt (from MIN)	DB	6'2"	180	26		
Jim Johnson	DB	6'2"	190	26	3	
Elbert Kimbrough	DB	5'11"	190	25	2	
Jerry Mertens	DB	6'	185	28		
Ben Scotti	DB	6'1"	181	27		
Abe Woodson	DB	5'11"	188	29	2	

Bob St. Clair – Heel Injury

Use Name	Pos.	Hgt	Wgt	Age	Int	Pts
John Brodie	QB	6'1"	200	29		12
George Mira	QB	5'11"	183	22		
Billy Kilmer	HB-QB	6'	190	24		
Rudy Johnson	HB	5'1"	190	22		6
Dave Kopay	HB	6'2"	206	22		12
Don Lisbon	HB	6'	197	23		6
Gary Lewis	FB	6'3"	215	22		6
Mike Lind	FB	6'2"	215	24		42
J. D. Smith	FB	6'1"	210	31		
Bernie Casey	FL	6'4"	215	25		24
Dale Messer	FL	5'10"	175	27		
Kay McFarland	OE	6'2"	180	25		
Dave Parks	OE	6'2"	195	22		48
Bob Poole	OE	6'4"	216	22		
Monte Stickles	OE	6'4"	230	26		18
Tommy Davis	K	6'	212	29		54

WESTERN CONFERENCE—Continued

DETROIT LIONS

RUSHING

Last Name	No.	Yds	Avg	TD
Pietrosante	147	536	3.6	4
Lewis	122	463	3.8	1
Watkins	80	218	2.7	1
Morrall	10	70	7.0	0
McElhenny	22	48	2.2	0
Barr	2	31	15.5	0
Plum	12	28	2.3	1
Lary	2	11	5.5	0
Ryder	11	11	1.0	0
Compton	3	2	0.7	0
Cogdill	1	–4	–4.0	0

RECEIVING

Last Name	No.	Yds	Avg	TD
Barr	57	1030	18	9
Cogdill	45	665	15	2
Gibbons	45	605	13	8
Pietrosante	19	152	8	0
Lewis	11	129	12	1
Watkins	10	125	13	1
Studstill	7	102	15	1
McElhenny	5	16	3	0
Ryder	4	30	8	1
Wells	2	21	11	0
McInnis	1	15	15	0

PUNT RETURNS

Last Name	No.	Yds	Avg	TD
Watkins	16	238	15	2
Studstill	17	137	8	0
Thompson	1	27	27	0
McElhenny	1	0	0	0
Maher	0	9	0	0

KICKOFF RETURNS

Last Name	No.	Yds	Avg	TD
Studstill	29	708	24	0
Watkins	16	368	23	0
McElhenny	3	72	24	0
Ryder	2	37	19	0
Clark	2	29	15	0
Lee	1	25	25	0
Thompson	1	24	24	0
Rasmussen	1	20	20	0
Hilgenberg	1	2	2	0
Simon	1	0	0	0
Compton	0	42	0	0

PASSING – PUNTING – KICKING

PASSING	Att	Comp	%	Yds	Yd/Att	TD	Int–	%	RK
Plum	287	154	54	2241	7.8	18	15–	5	5
Morrall	91	50	55	588	6.5	4	3–	3	
Gibbs	3	1	33	3	1.0	0	1–	33	
Barr	1	0	0	0	0.0	0	0–	0	
Lewis	1	0	0	0	0.0	0	0–	0	
Lowe	1	0	0	0	0.0	0	1–	100	
Pietrosante	1	0	0	0	0.0	0	1–	100	
Watkins	1	1	100	58	58.0	1	0–	0	

PUNTING	No	Avg
Lary	67	46.3
Morrall	1	8.0

KICKING	XP	Att	%	FG	Att	%
Walker	32	34	94	14	25	56

LOS ANGELES RAMS

RUSHING

Last Name	No.	Yds	Avg	TD
Wilson	159	553	3.5	5
Josephson	96	451	4.7	3
Bass	72	342	4.8	2
Munson	19	150	7.9	0
Baker	24	82	3.4	0
Shannon	17	35	2.1	0
Pope	2	11	5.5	0
Gabriel	11	5	0.5	1

RECEIVING

Last Name	No.	Yds	Avg	TD
McKeever	41	582	14	1
Dale	32	544	17	2
Pope	25	786	31	10
Josephson	21	269	13	1
Phillips	17	245	14	2
Wilson	15	116	8	1
Bass	9	83	9	0
Baker	8	92	12	0
Allen	2	29	15	1
Shannon	2	4	2	0
Brown	1	19	19	0

PUNT RETURNS

Last Name	No.	Yds	Avg	TD
Shannon	15	81	5	0
Smith	12	68	6	0
Brown	4	23	6	0
Meador	2	9	5	0
Bass	1	0	0	0

KICKOFF RETURNS

Last Name	No.	Yds	Avg	TD
Smith	20	489	24	0
Shannon	18	442	25	0
Meador	6	148	25	0
Brown	6	122	20	0
Bass	1	25	25	0
Martin	2	18	9	0
Larsen	2	14	7	0
Harris	1	0	0	0

PASSING – PUNTING – KICKING

PASSING	Att	Comp	%	Yds	Yd/Att	TD	Int–	%	RK
Munson	223	108	48	1533	6.9	9	15–	7	17
Gabriel	143	65	45	1236	8.6	9	5–	3	9
Baker	1	0	0	0	0.0	0	0–	0	
Meador	1	0	0	0	0.0	0	0–	0	

PUNTING	No	Avg
Villanueva	82	44.1

KICKING	XP	Att	%	FG	Att	%
Gossett	31	33	94	18	24	75

CHICAGO BEARS

RUSHING

Last Name	No.	Yds	Avg	TD
Arnett	119	400	3.4	1
Bull	86	320	3.7	1
Casares	35	123	3.5	0
Marconi	46	98	2.1	2
Wade	24	96	4.0	1
Bivins	29	92	3.2	0
Bukich	12	28	2.3	0
Whitsell	1	14	14.0	0
Green	2	–2	–1.0	0
Livingston	2	–3	–1.5	0

RECEIVING

Last Name	No.	Yds	Avg	TD
J. Morris	93	1200	13	10
Ditka	75	897	12	5
Arnett	25	223	9	2
Kreitling	20	185	9	2
Marconi	20	181	9	3
Bull	15	35	2	0
Casares	14	113	8	2
Bivins	11	59	5	1
Barnes	4	61	15	0
Bill Martin	3	93	31	0
Billy Martin	1	9	9	0
Livingston	1	0	0	0

PUNT RETURNS

Last Name	No.	Yds	Avg	TD
Arnett	19	188	10	0
Billy Martin	11	31	3	0

KICKOFF RETURNS

Last Name	No.	Yds	Avg	TD
Billy Martin	24	534	22	0
Arnett	15	331	22	0
Bivins	8	218	27	0
Livingston	6	167	28	1
Bull	2	44	22	0
Marconi	2	12	6	0
Purnell	1	8	8	0

PASSING – PUNTING – KICKING

PASSING	Att	Comp	%	Yds	Yd/Att	TD	Int–	%	RK
Wade	327	182	56	1944	5.9	13	14–	4	10
Bukich	160	99	62	1099	6.8	12	7–	4	8
Arnett	4	0	0	0	0.0	0	0–	0	
Bull	3	1	33	13	4.3	0	0–	0	

PUNTING	No	Avg
Green	71	44.5

KICKING	XP	Att	%	FG	Att	%
Jencks	29	32	91	3	7	43
LeClerc	0	0	0	10	16	63

SAN FRANCISCO FORTY NINERS

RUSHING

Last Name	No.	Yds	Avg	TD
Kopay	75	271	3.6	0
Lind	100	256	2.6	7
Mira	18	177	9.8	0
Lisbon	55	162	2.9	0
Brodie	27	135	5.0	2
Lewis	43	115	2.7	1
Kilmer	36	113	3.1	0
Smith	13	55	4.2	0
R. Johnson	16	48	3.0	1

RECEIVING

Last Name	No.	Yds	Avg	TD
Casey	58	808	14	4
Stickles	40	685	17	3
Parks	36	703	20	8
Lind	25	178	7	0
Kopay	20	135	7	2
Lisbon	13	104	8	1
Kilmer	11	136	12	0
Lewis	7	73	10	0
McFarland	5	67	13	0
R. Johnson	5	21	4	0
Messer	4	72	18	0
Poole	1	8	8	0

PUNT RETURNS

Last Name	No.	Yds	Avg	TD
Alexander	21	189	9	1
Woodson	22	133	6	0

KICKOFF RETURNS

Last Name	No.	Yds	Avg	TD
Woodson	32	880	28	0
Alexander	20	483	24	0
Kopay	2	30	15	0
Lewis	1	0	0	0
Pine	1	0	0	0
Thomas	1	0	0	0

PASSING – PUNTING – KICKING

PASSING	Att	Comp	%	Yds	Yd/Att	TD	Int–	%	RK
Brodie	392	193	49	2498	6.4	14	16–	4	12
Mira	53	23	43	331	6.3	2	5–	9	
Kilmer	14	8	57	92	6.6	1	1–	7	
Kopay	1	0	0	0	0.0	0	0–	0	
Lind	1	1	100	69	69.0	1	0–	0	

PUNTING	No	Avg
Davis	79	45.6

KICKING	XP	Att	%	FG	Att	%
Davis	30	30	100	8	25	32

1964 A.F.L. TV and New York, An Unbeatable Combination

"People have now stopped asking me if we are going to make it," said Commissioner Joe Foss after signing a new television contract with the National Broadcasting Company. Starting in 1965, NBC would handle the national TV coverage of AFL games and pay the league $36 million for five seasons from 1965 to 1969. With all clubs sharing equally in the television pot, Foss no longer had any worries about any teams going bankrupt. He also had no worries over job security, as the team owners extended him a new three-year contract with a sizable raise in salary.

One of the most gratifying developments for Foss was the sudden popularity of the New York Jets. Only two years before they were the bankrupt Titans, playing in an ancient ball park and living off league funds. Now they played in the new Shea Stadium, set a single-game attendance record three times during this season, and had solid ownership led by Sonny Werblin. With the New York team healthy and strong, the whole league found new respect coming from the East Coast media.

EASTERN DIVISION

Buffalo Bills—The heart of the Bills, the AFL's first great ball-control team, was a powerful fullback and a bruising defensive line. Cookie Gilchrist as usual took care of the heavy-duty running chores, leading the league in rushing despite the lack of an accomplished running mate at halfback. The Bills passed the ball less frequently than the other AFL clubs, as Jack Kemp ran the offense quite conservatively. But when the attack bogged down, coach Lou Saban could send young Daryle Lamonica in at quarterback. A second-year pro with a liking for the long pass, Lamonica relieved Kemp in several games and pulled out victories with deep bombs to Elbert Dubenion and Glenn Bass. Supporting the offense was a strong line featuring Billy Shaw and Stew Barber. The defensive unit also boasted of a strong line, as Ron McDole, Jim Dunaway, Tom Sestak, and Tom Day jelled into the league's best front four, and a tight group of linebackers and backs played well enough behind this line to make the Buffalo defense the stingiest in allowing points. The Bills won games by outplaying opponents in the line, by blocking and tackling better, and if the offense ever needed a three-point boost, coach Saban unveiled pro football's first soccer-style place-kicker in Pete Gogolak, a Hungarian refugee who kicked the ball sideways accurately enough to score 102 points. With a full pantry of hard-nosed ball players, the Bills swept their first nine games and put down a late Boston challenge to win the Eastern crown.

Boston Patriots—Closing with a rush, the Patriots just missed repeating as Eastern champion. Starting with a November 6 win over Houston, they won five straight games to pull within a half game of the first-place Bills before their season-closing showdown on December 20. The Pats had won last year's playoff game in frigid Buffalo, but the Bills turned the tables this year by winning this key game 24-14 in a snowstorm in Boston. The Patriots got as far as they did with little help from rookies, as coach Mike Holovak continued to depend on his shopworn veterans. Thirty-three-year-old Babe Parilli won his first All-Pro honors by passing for thirty-one touchdowns, while slow-footed Gino Cappelletti caught seven TD passes and scored a league-leading 155 points on his receiving and kicking. The defense was still the Patriots' long suit, bailing the team out in victories of 17-14 over Oakland and 12-7 over Denver. The front four of Larry Eisenhauer, Bob Dee, Houston Antwine, and Jim Hunt stood firm against enemy runners, while linebacker Nick Buoniconti blitzed opposing quarterbacks to distraction. But time was growing short for the Patriots, who would soon have to replace such oldsters as Parilli, Cappelletti, and Dee.

New York Jets—With their move into spanking new Shea Stadium, the Jets immediately became the attendance sensation of the league. Their first game in the new park drew an AFL record crowd of 45,665, the second game attracted 47,746, and the November 8 match with Buffalo brought out 60,300 fans. Several factors contributed to the Jets' sudden popularity, such as the new stadium, the scarcity of available tickets for Giant games, the scheduling of games on Saturday nights, and a close identification with the colorful baseball Mets. The fans who did come out saw a team rapidly improving with good young talent. This year's rich rookie class included Matt Snell, a talented all-around fullback; Gerry Philbin and Bert Wilder, a pair of strong defensive ends; Ralph Baker, who won a starting linebacker spot; John Schmitt and Dave Herman, two reserve offensive linemen who would star in later years; and place-kicker Jim Turner. Another newcomer won a large following, as middle linebacker Wahoo McDaniel became a folk hero with New York fans with his violent tackles. Holdovers such as Larry Grantham, Bill Mathis, Don Maynard, Bake Turner, Winston Hill, and Dainard Paulson formed the nucleus of a good club, but any championships would have to wait until a top quarterback was acquired.

Houston Oilers—Hopes that 1963 was just an isolated bad year for the Oilers faded as they lost nine straight games in the center of the schedule. Sammy Baugh was this year's head coach, with Pop Ivy disposed of for not winning a championship last season, and Baugh would get the ax after this losing campaign. The Oiler roster carried heavy doses of both rookies and aging veterans. Of the several freshmen to make the squad, Sid Blanks, Scott Appleton, Pete Jacquess, W. K. Hicks, Benny Nelson, and Willie Frazier saw considerable action. At the other end of the spectrum, thirty-six-year-old George Blanda, thirty-six-year-old Bud McFadin, and thirty-four-year-old Ed Hussman held down starting posts in the Houston lineup. In between the two extremes of age came players in their prime—Charley Hennigan, Freddy Glick, Bob Talamini, and Doug Cline. Hennigan, who was Blanda's favorite pass receiver, hauled in 101 passes to set a new professional record. But not enough Oiler players were at the peak of their powers, and the team hung all its hopes on this year's youngsters improving in the near future.

WESTERN DIVISION

San Diego Chargers—Tobin Rote's old arm had few passes left in it, so John Hadl assumed the bulk of the quarterbacking duties and took the Chargers back to the championship game. The road was a little rockier this year, though. After beating Houston to open the season, the Chargers lost to Boston and Buffalo and just managed a tie with New York. With none of the Western teams very hot in the early going, San Diego then rocketed out to a comfortable lead by winning their next six games. Even a late-season slump, in which they lost three of their last four games, could not bring the Chargers back to the pack. But despite their streaky play, the Chargers boasted of one of the deepest squads in the league. They had good runners in Keith Lincoln and Paul Lowe, pro football's most exciting receiver in Lance Alworth, fine offensive linemen in Ron Mix and Walt Sweeney, and good defenders in Earl Faison, Ernie Ladd, Chuck Allen, Frank Buncom, and Dick Westmoreland. The only thing missing from the San Diego arsenal was a consistent field-goal kicker. The Chargers tried Keith Lincoln, Herb Travenio, Ben Agajanian, and George Blair at the spot during the season. But that lack was not enough to keep the Chargers away from their fourth Western crown in five years.

Kansas City Chiefs—On paper, the Chiefs looked unbeatable; on the field, the Chiefs were a .500 club. They looked like the best team in the league when they beat the Chargers 49-6 and dismantled the Jets 24-7, but they looked like scrubs while losing 33-27 to the lowly Broncos. No one could figure out how a team with good offensive and defensive units could lose seven games, but the Chiefs complicated coach Hank Stram's life by doing that. Len Dawson sparked the attack with thirty touchdown passes despite a trio of slow receivers, while the Kansas City running corps was brimming with talent. Abner Haynes was less consistent but still dangerous at halfback, rookie Mack Lee Hill bulled his way into the starting lineup, and Curtis McClinton, Jack Spikes, and Bert Coan provided unheard-of depth. The defense was one of the league's best, with two superb linemen in Jerry Mays and Buck Buchanan, a trio of fine linebackers in E. J. Holub, Sherrill Headrick, and Bobby Bell, and top backs in Dave Grayson, Duane Wood, Bobby Hunt, and Johnny Robinson. But the Chiefs found ways to lose that defied the heavy weight of their roster.

Oakland Raiders—The miraculous finish of 1963 wore off as the Raiders lost their first five games, but Al Davis' men came back in the second half of the schedule to prove that they were indeed a solid football team. The final five games brought four wins and a tie to Oakland, and among the defeated teams were San Diego and Buffalo, the teams headed for the championship game. The Raiders no longer had the element of surprise on their side, as the rest of the league had seen their blitzes last year and no longer took them lightly, but they resorted to a more settled style of play with fine results in the back stretch. Clem Daniels got off to a slow start, but the powerful halfback recovered to star during the Raiders' late drive. Helping Daniels with strong blocking was Billy Cannon, obtained from Houston to fill the gap at fullback. The defense was strengthened by the addition of end Ben Davidson, a huge lineman cut by the NFL Washington Redskins, and rookie linebacker Dan Conners—and despite the disappointing third-place finish, coach Davis was happy about adding new talent to his future champions.

Denver Broncos—Coach Jack Faulkner resorted to lend lease to get himself a quarterback, sending defensive tackle Bud McFadin to Houston in exchange for quarterback Jacky Lee, who was to return to Houston after two seasons. The deal won press space but few ball games, as Lee was a distinct disappointment in leading the attack. The offensive line was a shambles, however, and few passers could have accomplished much behind it. The poor blocking wasted some good offensive talent, such as split end Lionel Taylor, tight end Hewritt Dixon, halfback Charley Mitchell, and fullback Billy Joe. The defense was easy to march through but did cause enemy quarterbacks some pain with a late-season blitzing campaign; the best performances were turned in by Ray Jacobs, Jerry Hopkins, Willie Brown, and Goose Gonsoulin. The Broncos went into the season with no title hopes, but when they were massacred in the first four games, coach Faulkner got the ax and assistant Mac Speedie took over as head man.

FINAL TEAM STATISTICS

OFFENSE

	BOSTON	BUFFALO	DENVER	HOUSTON	K. CITY	NEW YORK	OAKLAND	SAN DIEGO
FIRST DOWNS:								
Total	226	**255**	207	**284**	250	209	270	254
by Rushing	66	**114**	78	80	90	79	63	85
by Passing	144	130	116	**186**	148	108	**186**	156
by Penalty	16	11	13	18	12	**22**	21	13
RUSHING:								
Number	381	**492**	391	327	415	384	331	392
Yards	1361	**2040**	1311	1347	1825	1457	1480	1522
Average Yards	3.6	4.1	3.4	4.1	4.4	3.8	**4.5**	3.9
Touchdowns	9	**25**	10	14	14	11	9	14
PASSING:								
Attempts	476	397	456	**592**	412	451	521	445
Completions	229	174	230	**299**	228	201	253	224
Completion Percentage	48.1	43.8	50.4	50.5	**55.3**	44.6	48.6	50.3
Passing Yardage	3467	3422	2541	3734	3321	2694	**3886**	3363
Average Yards per Attempt	7.3	**8.6**	5.6	6.3	8.1	6.0	7.5	7.6
Average Yards per Completion	15.1	**19.7**	11.0	12.5	14.6	13.4	15.4	15.0
Times Tackled Attempting to Pass	29	35	61	23	44	27	56	**22**
Yards Lost Attempting to Pass	301	256	520	**207**	446	262	464	221
Net Yards	3166	3166	2021	**3527**	2875	2432	3422	3142
Touchdowns	31	19	14	19	**32**	19	28	28
Interceptions	27	34	32	29	**21**	33	33	30
Percent Intercepted	5.7	8.6	7.0	**4.9**	5.1	7.3	6.3	6.7
PUNTING:								
Number	78	65	**83**	55	79	79	59	63
Average Distance	38.0	42.7	**43.4**	41.2	42.5	41.3	41.5	39.3
PUNT RETURNS:								
Number	38	**46**	25	19	40	38	33	34
Yards	276	421	259	252	400	283	**447**	283
Average Yards	7.3	9.2	10.4	13.3	10.0	7.4	**13.5**	8.3
Touchdowns	0	**1**	**1**	**1**	0	0	0	0
KICKOFF RETURNS:								
Number	58	48	**76**	66	57	54	61	53
Yards	1167	1018	**1758**	1559	1261	1088	1525	1288
Average Yards	20.1	21.2	23.1	23.6	22.1	20.1	**25.0**	24.3
Touchdowns	0	0	0	**1**	0	0	0	0
INTERCEPTION RETURNS:								
Number	31	28	32	30	28	**34**	26	30
Yards	427	470	459	437	408	477	430	**487**
Average Yards	13.8	**16.8**	14.3	14.6	14.6	14.0	16.5	16.2
Touchdowns	1	2	1	3	1	**4**	0	2
PENALTIES:								
Number					Not Available			
Yards								
FUMBLES:								
Number	23	32	27	24	36	**15**	30	30
Number Lost	12	18	8	15	20	**7**	18	16
POINTS:								
Total	365	**400**	240	310	366	278	303	341
PAT (kick) Attempts	36	**46**	25	38	**46**	33	34	43
PAT (kick) Made	36	45	22	37	**46**	33	34	39
PAT (Rush or Pass) Attempts	5	2	3	1	3	1	2	1
PAT (Rush or Pass) Made	3	2	**3**	0	1	0	0	1
FG Attempts	**39**	29	34	29	17	27	24	26
FG Made	**25**	19	14	13	8	13	15	12
Percent FG Made	64.1	**65.5**	41.2	44.8	47.1	48.1	62.5	46.2
Safeties	1	**3**	1	0	0	1	1	0

DEFENSE

	BOSTON	BUFFALO	DENVER	HOUSTON	K. CITY	NEW YORK	OAKLAND	SAN DIEGO
FIRST DOWNS:								
Total	243	**206**	271	276	211	245	255	248
by Rushing	63	**48**	100	103	77	79	103	82
by Passing	165	145	148	159	**124**	152	134	147
by Penalty	15	13	23	14	**10**	14	18	19
RUSHING:								
Number	356	**300**	424	438	390	410	396	399
Yards	1143	**913**	2064	1961	1315	1675	1750	1522
Average Yards	3.2	**3.0**	4.9	4.5	3.4	4.1	4.4	3.8
Touchdowns	10	**4**	21	18	9	14	20	10
PASSING:								
Attempts	530	517	440	**433**	440	473	**433**	484
Completions	261	241	215	229	218	228	**206**	240
Completion Percentage	49.2	**46.6**	48.9	52.9	49.5	48.2	47.6	49.6
Passing Yardage	3645	3361	3353	3469	**2910**	3472	3292	2926
Average Yards per Attempt	6.9	6.5	7.6	8.0	6.6	7.3	7.6	**6.0**
Average Yards per Completion	14.0	13.9	15.6	15.1	13.3	15.2	16.0	**12.2**
Times Tackled Attempting to Pass	47	**50**	44	25	28	28	37	38
Yards Lost Attempting to Pass	428	396	**447**	189	279	231	299	408
Net Yards	3217	2965	2906	3280	2631	3241	2993	**2518**
Touchdowns	23	24	29	24	25	22	**21**	22
Interceptions	31	28	32	30	28	**34**	26	30
Percent Intercepted	5.8	5.4	**7.3**	6.9	6.4	7.2	6.0	6.2
PUNTING:								
Number	82	**87**	59	56	78	71	66	62
Average Distance	41.5	41.9	41.4	**39.1**	40.7	40.5	41.7	41.3
PUNT RETURNS:								
Number	**24**	**24**	40	33	36	43	41	32
Yards	**185**	250	526	295	251	426	272	416
Average Yards	7.7	10.4	13.2	8.9	7.0	9.9	**6.6**	13.0
Touchdowns	**0**	**0**	1	**0**	**0**	1	**0**	1
KICKOFF RETURNS:								
Number	70	59	**44**	53	64	53	64	66
Yards	1637	1385	1166	**978**	1459	1236	1239	1564
Average Yards	23.4	23.5	26.5	**18.5**	22.8	23.3	19.4	23.7
Touchdowns	1	**0**	**0**	**0**	**0**	**0**	**0**	**0**
INTERCEPTION RETURNS:								
Number	27	34	32	29	**21**	33	33	30
Yards	485	406	441	496	**228**	448	713	378
Average Yards	18.0	11.9	13.8	17.1	**10.9**	13.6	21.6	12.6
Touchdowns	1	**0**	1	3	3	1	4	1
PENALTIES:								
Number					Not Available			
Yards								
FUMBLES:								
Number	33	24	**40**	21	29	19	19	32
Number Lost	17	15	**21**	8	18	10	10	15
POINTS:								
Total	297	**242**	438	355	306	315	350	300
PAT (kick) Attempts	33	**23**	52	43	36	38	43	33
PAT (kick) Made	32	**22**	52	41	34	36	43	32
PAT (Rush or Pass) Attempts	3	5	**0**	2	2	1	2	3
PAT (Rush or Pass) Made	2	2	**0**	1	1	**0**	1	3
FG Attempts	27	27	25	30	**20**	27	34	32
FG Made	15	14	22	14	14	15	**11**	14
Percent FG Made	50.0	51.9	88.0	46.7	70.0	55.6	**32.3**	43.8
Safeties	**0**	**0**	1	**0**	**0**	**0**	1	2

1964 AFL CHAMPIONSHIP GAME

December 26, at Buffalo
(Attendance 40,242)

SCORING

BUFFALO	**3**	**10**	**0**	**7**	**—20**
SAN DIEGO	**7**	**0**	**0**	**0**	**— 7**

First Quarter
- S.D. Kocourek, 26 yard pass from Rote
  PAT—Lincoln (kick)
- BUF. Gogolak, 12 yard field goal

Second Quarter
- BUF. Carlton, 4 yard rush
  PAT—Gogolak (kick)
- BUF. Gogolak, 17 yard field goal

Fourth Quarter
- BUF. Kemp, 1 yard rush
  PAT—Gogolak (kick)

TEAM STATISTICS

BUFF.		S.D.
21	First Downs—Total	15
12	First Downs—Rushing	7
8	First Downs—Passing	7
1	First Downs—Penalty	1
0	Fumbles—Number	1
0	Fumbles—Number Lost	0
3	Penalties—Number	3
45	Yards Penalized	20
0	Missed Field Goals	0

No Instant Replay

The San Diego Chargers started fast in defending their AFL title, but the sturdy Buffalo defense caught up and turned the game around before the first half ended. The first time the Chargers got their hands on the ball they drove 80 yards in four plays; Keith Lincoln, the star of last year's championship game, ran 38 yards on one play, and Tobin Rote found Dave Kocourek with a pass good for 26 yards and the first touchdown of the game. Lincoln's extra point made the score 7-0, and some fans expected the Chargers to turn the game into a rout as they had the year before. On the Chargers' next drive, however, the Bills made the key play of the game. When Lincoln caught a short pass in the flat, Buffalo linebacker Mike Stratton leveled him with a crunching tackle that knocked the ball loose and broke one of Lincoln's ribs. With their star back out of action, the Chargers never again could move the ball against the Buffalo defense. Pete Gogolak scored the Bills' first three points on a 12-yard field goal, and 10 second-quarter points gave Buffalo a 13-7 lead at halftime. The third period was scoreless, but the differences in the teams showed through clearly. The San Diego running attack missed the injured Lincoln dearly, while Cookie Gilchrist blasted into the Chargers' line with jackhammer force and regularity. While the San Diego attack withered in the face of the Buffalo pass rush, the Bills added a final touchdown when a Jack Kemp-to-Glenn Bass pass covering 48 yards brought the ball down to the one-yard line before Kemp went over for the 20-7 victory and Buffalo's first major-league sports championship.

INDIVIDUAL STATISTICS

BUFFALO	No	Yds	Avg.	SAN DIEGO	No	Yds	Avg.
RUSHING							
Gilchrist	16	122	7.6	Lincoln	3	47	15.7
Carlton	18	70	3.9	Lowe	7	34	4.9
Kemp	5	16	3.2	MacKinnon	1	17	17.0
Dubenion	1	9	9.0	Kinderman	4	14	3.5
Lamonica	1	2	2.0	Hadl	1	13	13.0
	41	219	5.3	Rote	1	6	6.0
				Norton	1	−7	−7.0
					18	124	6.9
RECEIVING							
Dubenion	3	36	12.0	Kinderman	4	52	13.0
Bass	2	70	35.0	MacKinnon	3	12	4.0
Warlick	2	41	20.5	Kocourek	2	52	26.0
Gilchrist	2	22	11.0	Lowe	2	9	4.5
Ross	1	−1	−1.0	Norton	1	13	13.0
	10	168	16.8	Lincoln	1	11	11.0
					13	149	11.5
PUNTING							
Maguire	5		46.8	Hadl	5		36.4
PUNT RETURNS							
Clarke	1	6	6.0	Robinson	1	30	30.0
				Duncan	1	28	28.0
					2	58	29.0
KICKOFF RETURNS							
Rutkowski	1	27	27.0	Duncan	3	147	49.0
Warner	1	17	17.0	Warren	1	28	28.0
	2	44	22.0		4	175	43.8
INTERCEPTION RETURNS							
Warner	1	8	8.0	None			
Byrd	1	0	0.0				
Stratton	1	0	0.0				
	3	8	2.7				

PASSING

	Att.	Comp.	Comp. Pct.	Yds.	Int.	Yds/ Att.	Yds/ Comp.
BUFFALO							
Kemp	20	10	50.0	168	0	8.4	16.8
SAN DIEGO							
Rote	26	10	38.5	118	2	4.5	11.8
Hadl	10	3	30.0	31	1	3.1	10.3
	36	13	36.1	149	3	4.1	11.5

1964 A.F.L. — Eastern Division

BUFFALO BILLS 12-2-0 Lou Saban

Scores of Each Game			Use Name	Pos.	Hgt	Wgt	Age	Int	Pts	Use Name	Pos.	Hgt	Wgt	Age	Int	Pts	Use Name	Pos.	Hgt	Wgt	Age	Int	Pts
34	KANSAS CITY	17	Stew Barber	OT	6'3"	250	25			Harry Jacobs	LB	6'2"	225	27	2		Jack Kemp	QB	6'1"	200	30		30
30	DENVER	13	Dick Hudson	OT	6'4"	272	24			Paul Maguire	LB	6'	220	26			Daryle Lamonica	QB	6'2"	215	23		40
30	SAN DIEGO	3	Joe O'Donnell	OT	6'2"	246	22			Mike Stratton	LB	6'3"	240	22	1		Joe Auer	HB	6'1"	205	22		18
23	OAKLAND	20	Al Bemiller	OG	6'3"	260	25			John Tracey	LB	6'3"	225	30	3		Wray Carlton	HB	6'2"	216	26		6
48	Houston	17	George Flint	OG	6'4"	244	26			Ray Abbruzzese	DB	6'1"	194	26			Bobby Smith	HB	6'	203	22		24
35	Kansas City	22	Billy Shaw	OG	6'3"	248	24			Butch Byrd	DB	6'	211	22	7	6	Cookie Gilchrist	FB	6'3"	250	29		36
34	NEW YORK	24	Walt Cudzik	C	6'2"	240	31			Hagood Clarke	DB	6'	188	22		6	Willie Ross	FB	5'10"	200	23		6
24	HOUSTON	10	Tom Day	DE	6'2"	250	29			Ollie Dobbins	DB	5'11"	185	22			Elbert Dubenion	FL	6'	187	29		60
20	New York	7	Ron McDole	DE	6'3"	264	24	1		Booker Edgerson	DB	5'10"	180	25	4		Ed Rutkowski	FL	6'1"	208	23		6
28	BOSTON	36	Jim Dunaway	DT	6'4"	276	22			George Saimes	DB	5'10"	195	22	6		Glenn Bass	OE	6'2"	206	25		42
27	San Diego	24	Tom Keating	DT	6'3"	242	21			Gene Sykes	DB	6'1"	195	23	2		Bill Groman	OE	6'	195	28		6
13	Oakland	16	Dudley Meredith	DT	6'4"	275	29										Ernie Warlick	OE	6'4"	235	32		
30	Denver	19	Tom Sestak	DT	6'5"	270	28	1	6	Charley Ferguson – Injury							Pete Gogolak	K	6'2"	200	22		102
24	Boston	14																					

BOSTON PATRIOTS 10-3-1 Mike Holovak

Scores of Each Game			Use Name	Pos.	Hgt	Wgt	Age	Int	Pts	Use Name	Pos.	Hgt	Wgt	Age	Int	Pts	Use Name	Pos.	Hgt	Wgt	Age	Int	Pts
17	Oakland	14	Don Oakes	OT	6'3"	255	26			Tom Addison	LB	6'3"	230	28	2		Babe Parilli	QB	6'1"	190	34		12
33	San Diego	28	Bob Schmidt	OT	6'4"	250	28			Nick Buoniconti	LB	5'11"	220	23	5		Tom Yewcic	QB	5'11"	185	32		
26	NEW YORK	10	Bob Yates	OT	6'3"	230	25			Mike Dukes	LB	6'3"	235	28	1		Ron Burton	HB	5'10"	190	27		30
39	Denver	10	Charley Long	OG	6'3"	250	26			Lonnie Farmer	LB	6'	220	23			J. D. Garrett	HB	5'11"	195	22		12
17	SAN DIEGO	26	Billy Neighbors	OG	5'11"	240	24			Jack Rudolph	LB	6'3"	230	26			Jim Crawford	FB	6'1"	205	28		
43	OAKLAND	43	Dave Watson	OG	6'1"	230	23			Don McKinnon	C-LB	6'3"	230	22			Larry Garron	FB	6'	195	27		54
24	KANSAS CITY	7	Jon Morris	C	6'4"	240	21			Dave Cloutier	DB	6'	195	25			Jim Colclough	FL	6'	185	28		34
14	New York	35	Bob Dee	DE	6'3"	240	31			Dick Felt	DB	6'	185	31	2		Al Snyder	FL	6'	195	22		
25	HOUSTON	24	Larry Eisenhauer	DE	6'5"	250	24			Ron Hall	DB	6'	190	27	11		Gino Cappelletti	OE	6'	190	30		155
36	Buffalo	28	Jim Hunt	DE-DT	5'11"	245	25			Ross O'Hanley	DB	6'	185	25	3	6	Art Graham	OE	6'1"	205	23		36
12	DENVER	7	Len St. Jean	DE	6'1"	240	22			Chuck Shonta	DB	6'	200	26	1		Tony Romeo	OE	6'2"	230	25		24
34	Houston	17	Houston Antwine	DT	6'	270	25			Don Webb	DB	5'10"	200	25	6								
31	Kansas City	24	Jerry DeLucca	DT	6'3"	250	28			Tom Stephens	OE-DB	6'1"	215	28									
14	BUFFALO	24	Jess Richardson	DT	6'2"	265	34																

NEW YORK JETS 5-8-1 Weeb Ewbank

Scores of Each Game			Use Name	Pos.	Hgt	Wgt	Age	Int	Pts	Use Name	Pos.	Hgt	Wgt	Age	Int	Pts	Use Name	Pos.	Hgt	Wgt	Age	Int	Pts
30	DENVER	6	Winston Hill	OT	6'4"	275	22			Ralph Baker	LB	6'3"	235	22	2		Mike Taliaferro	QB	6'2"	210	22		
10	Boston	26	Jim McCusker	OT	6'2"	250	28			Ed Cummings	LB	6'2"	232	23	1		Dick Wood	QB	6'5"	205	28		6
17	SAN DIEGO	17	Sherman Plunkett	OT	6'4"	295	30			Larry Grantham	LB	6'	206	25	2		Pete Liske	DB-QB	6'2"	195	23		
35	OAKLAND	13	Sam DeLuca	OG	6'2"	250	28			Wahoo McDaniel	LB	6'	240	27	3	6	Curley Johnson	HB	6'	215	29		
24	HOUSTON	21	Dan Ficca	OG	6'1"	250	25			Bob Rowley	LB	6'2"	225	22			Bill Mathis	HB	6'1"	220	25		24
24	Buffalo	34	Dave Herman	OG	6'2"	255	22			Mark Johnston (from OAK)	DB	6'	200	26	1		Mark Smolinski	FB	6'	215	25		6
35	BOSTON	14	Pete Perreault	OG	6'3"	245	25			Bill Pashe	DB	5'11"	185	23			Matt Snell	FB	6'2"	220	22		36
7	BUFFALO	20	Mike Hudock	C	6'2"	245	29			Dainard Paulson	DB	5'11"	190	27	12	6	Jim Evans	FL	6'1"	190	24		
16	Denver	20	John Schmitt	C	6'4"	265	21			Bill Rademacher	DB	6'1"	190	22	1		Al Lawson	FL	5'11"	190	22		
26	Oakland	35	Gerry Philbin	DE	6'2"	245	23			Marsh Starks	DB	6'	190	25	1		Don Maynard	FL	6'	185	28		48
27	KANSAS CITY	14	Lavern Torczon	DE	6'2"	250	28	1	6	Vince Turner	DB	5'11"	190	21	1		Gene Heeter	OE	6'4"	235	23		6
3	San Diego	38	Bob Watters	DE	6'4"	245	28			Clyde Washington	DB	6'	206	26			Dee Mackey	OE	6'5"	225	28		
17	Houston	33	Bert Wilder	DE	6'3"	245	24			Bill Baird	HB-DB	5'10"	180	25	8	6	Bake Turner	OE	6'	185	24		54
7	Kansas City	24	Gordy Holz	DT	6'4"	260	30										Jim Turner	K	6'2"	205	23		72
			Bob McAdams	DT	6'3"	250	24																
			Paul Rochester	DT	6'2"	250	27																

HOUSTON OILERS 4-10-0 Sammy Baugh

Scores of Each Game			Use Name	Pos.	Hgt	Wgt	Age	Int	Pts	Use Name	Pos.	Hgt	Wgt	Age	Int	Pts	Use Name	Pos.	Hgt	Wgt	Age	Int	Pts
21	San Diego	27	Staley Faulkner	OT	6'3"	245	23			Danny Brabham	LB	6'4"	240	23			George Blanda	QB	6'1"	215	36		76
42	OAKLAND	28	Jerry Fowler	OT	6'3"	255	23			Doug Cline	LB	6'2"	230	25			Don Trull	QB	6'1"	180	22		
38	Denver	17	Bob Kelly	OT	6'3"	260	24			Sammy Odom	LB	6'2"	235	22	2		Sid Blanks	HB	6'	198	23		42
7	Kansas City	28	Jack Klotz	OT	6'5"	250	30			Larry Onesti	LB	6'	200	25			Ode Burrell	HB	6'	185	24		6
17	BUFFALO	48	Walt Suggs	OT	6'5"	260	25			Charley Rieves	LB	5'11"	218	25	1		Dalton Hoffman	FB	6'	207	22		6
21	New York	24	Sonny Bishop	OG	6'2"	245	24			Johnny Baker	OE-LB	6'3"	225	23	1	6	Dave Smith	FB	6'1"	210	27		
17	SAN DIEGO	20	John Frongillo	OG	6'3"	250	24			Freddy Glick	DB	6'1"	190	27	5		Charley Tolar	FB	5'7"	200	26		24
10	Buffalo	24	Bob Talamini	OG	6'1"	255	25			W. K. Hicks	DB	6'1"	185	21	5		Charley Hennigan	FL	6'	187	28		48
24	Boston	25	John Wittenborn	OG	6'2"	240	28			Pete Jaquess	DB	6'	180	22	8	6	Dobie Craig	OE	6'4"	200	25		6
10	Oakland	20	Tom Goode	C	6'3"	250	25			Benny Nelson	DB	6'	185	22	1	6	Willard Dewveall	OE	6'4"	230	27		24
19	KANSAS CITY	28	Gary Cutsinger	DE	6'4"	245	23			Jim Norton	DB	6'3"	190	25	2		Charley Frazier	OE	6'	175	25		12
17	BOSTON	34	Don Floyd	DE	6'4"	247	25		6	Bobby Jancik	FL-DB	5'11"	178	24	3	6	Willie Frazier	OE	6'4"	225	21		6
33	NEW YORK	17	Scott Appleton	DT	6'3"	250	22	2									Bob McLeod	OE	6'5"	230	25		12
34	DENVER	15	Ed Husmann	DT	6'	245	34			Rich Michael – Injury													
			Bud McFadin	DT	6'3"	270	36																

BUFFALO BILLS

RUSHING

Last Name	No.	Yds	Avg	TD
Gilchrist	230	981	4.3	6
Smith	62	306	4.9	4
Lamonica	55	289	5.3	6
Auer	63	191	3.0	2
Kemp	37	124	3.4	5
Carlton	39	114	2.9	1
Dubenion	1	20	20.0	0
Ross	4	14	3.5	1
Hudson	1	1	1.0	0

RECEIVING

Last Name	No.	Yds	Avg	TD
Bass	43	897	21	7
Dubenion	42	1139	27	10
Gilchrist	30	345	12	0
Warlick	23	478	21	0
Rutkowski	13	234	18	1
Auer	11	166	15	0
Smith	6	72	12	0
Groman	4	68	17	1
Carlton	2	23	12	0

PUNT RETURNS

Last Name	No.	Yds	Avg	TD
Clarke	33	317	10	1
Rutkowski	8	45	6	0
Byrd	2	4	2	0

KICKOFF RETURNS

Last Name	No.	Yds	Avg	TD
Rutkowski	21	498	24	0
Clarke	16	330	21	0
Smith	3	68	23	0
Barber	2	0	0	0
Maguire	1	0	0	0
Auer	0	1	0	0

PASSING – PUNTING – KICKING

PASSING	Att	Comp	%	Yds	Yd/Att	TD	Int–%	RK
Kemp	269	119	44	2285	8.5	13	26– 10	6
Lamonica	128	55	43	1137	8.9	6	8– 6	

PUNTING	No	Avg
Maguire	65	42.7

KICKING	XP	Att	%	FG	Att	%
Gogolak	45	46	98	19	29	66

2 POINT XP
Lamonica (2)

BOSTON PATRIOTS

RUSHING

Last Name	No.	Yds	Avg	TD
Garron	183	585	3.2	2
Burton	102	340	3.3	3
Garrett	56	259	4.6	2
Parilli	34	168	4.9	2
Cappelletti	1	7	7.0	0
Yewcic	5	2	0.4	0

RECEIVING

Last Name	No.	Yds	Avg	TD
Cappelletti	49	865	18	7
Graham	45	720	16	6
Garron	40	350	9	7
Colclough	32	657	21	5
Burton	27	306	11	2
Romeo	26	445	17	4
Garrett	8	101	13	0
Snyder	1	12	12	0
Crawford	1	11	11	0

PUNT RETURNS

Last Name	No.	Yds	Avg	TD
Cloutier	20	136	7	0
Burton	11	78	7	0
Stephens	5	34	7	0
Garrett	2	28	14	0

KICKOFF RETURNS

Last Name	No.	Yds	Avg	TD
Garrett	32	749	23	0
Garron	10	198	20	0
Burton	7	131	19	0
Cloutier	1	46	46	0
Dukes	2	33	17	0
Stephens	2	5	3	0
Romeo	1	5	5	0
Oakes	1	0	0	0
Watson	1	0	0	0
Yates	1	0	0	0

PASSING – PUNTING – KICKING

PASSING	Att	Comp	%	Yds	Yd/Att	TD	Int–%	RK
Parilli	473	228	48	3465	7.3	31	27– 6	3
Garron	2	0	0	0	0.0	0	0– 0	
Yewcic	1	1	100	2	2.0	0	0– 0	

PUNTING	No	Avg
Yewcic	72	38.7
Parilli	5	36.0

KICKING	XP	Att	%	FG	Att	%
Cappelletti	36	36	100	25	39	64

2 POINT XP
Cappelletti
Colclough (2)

NEW YORK JETS

RUSHING

Last Name	No.	Yds	Avg	TD
Snell	215	948	4.4	5
Mathis	105	305	2.9	4
Smolinski	34	117	3.4	1
Taliaferro	9	45	5.0	0
Johnson	6	22	3.7	0
Baird	1	8	8.0	0
Wood	9	6	0.7	1
Maynard	3	3	1.0	0
J. Turner	1	3	3.0	0
Liske	1	0	0.0	0

RECEIVING

Last Name	No.	Yds	Avg	TD
B. Turner	58	974	17	9
Snell	56	393	7	1
Maynard	46	847	18	8
Mackey	14	213	15	0
Heeter	13	153	12	1
Evans	7	56	8	0
Mathis	4	39	10	0
Smolinski	3	19	6	0

PUNT RETURNS

Last Name	No.	Yds	Avg	TD
Baird	18	170	9	0
Starks	5	36	7	0
Paulson	8	34	4	0
Pashe	4	28	7	0
Rademacher	1	3	3	0
V. Turner	2	2	1	0
Rowley	0	10	0	0

KICKOFF RETURNS

Last Name	No.	Yds	Avg	TD
Evans	13	259	20	0
Baird	11	240	22	0
Starks	7	183	26	0
Snell	7	158	23	0
Johnson	4	62	16	0
V. Turner	1	25	25	0
Smolinski	2	19	10	0
Heeter	1	0	0	0
Mathis	1	0	0	0
McCusker	1	0	0	0
Perreault	1	0	0	0

PASSING – PUNTING – KICKING

PASSING	Att	Comp	%	Yds	Yd/Att	TD	Int–%	RK
Wood	358	169	47	2298	6.4	17	25– 7	6
Taliaferro	73	23	32	341	4.7	2	5– 7	
Liske	18	9	50	55	3.1	0	2– 11	
Johnson	1	0	0	0	0.0	0	0– 0	
Snell	1	0	0	0	0.0	0	1–100	

PUNTING	No	Avg
Johnson	77	42.4

KICKING	XP	Att	%	FG	Att	%
J. Turner	33	33	100	13	27	48

HOUSTON OILERS

RUSHING

Last Name	No.	Yds	Avg	TD
Blanks	145	756	5.2	6
Tolar	139	515	3.7	4
Trull	12	42	3.5	0
Smith	8	16	2.0	0
Burrell	8	10	1.3	0
Hoffman	2	3	1.5	1
Blanda	4	–2	–0.5	0
C. Frazier	1	–4	–4.0	0

RECEIVING

Last Name	No.	Yds	Avg	TD
Hennigan	101	1546	15	8
Blanks	56	497	9	1
Dewveall	38	552	15	4
Tolar	35	244	7	0
C. Frazier	31	423	14	2
W. Frazier	9	208	23	1
McLeod	8	81	10	2
Smith	7	38	5	0
Burrell	5	73	15	0
Craig	4	46	12	1
Baker	2	18	9	0
Jancik	1	14	14	0
Hoffman	1	1	1	0
Bishop	1	0	0	0
Blanda	0	–7	0	0

PUNT RETURNS

Last Name	No.	Yds	Avg	TD
Jancik	12	220	18	1
Glick	6	32	5	0
Burrell	1	0	0	0

KICKOFF RETURNS

Last Name	No.	Yds	Avg	TD
Jancik	21	488	23	0
Burrell	17	449	26	1
Nelson	13	304	23	0
Blanks	9	207	23	0
Hoffman	2	52	26	0
Glick	1	27	27	0
W. Frazier	1	0	0	0

PASSING – PUNTING – KICKING

PASSING	Att	Comp	%	Yds	Yd/Att	TD	Int–%	RK
Blanda	505	262	52	3287	6.5	17	27– 5	3
Trull	86	36	42	439	5.1	1	2– 2	
Blanks	1	1	100	8	8.0	1	0– 0	

PUNTING	No	Avg
Norton	53	42.8

KICKING	XP	Att	%	FG	Att	%
Blanda	37	38	97	13	29	45

SAN DIEGO CHARGERS 8-5-1 Sid Gillman

Scores of Each Game		
27	HOUSTON	21
28	BOSTON	33
3	Buffalo	30
17	New York	17
26	Boston	17
42	DENVER	14
20	Houston	17
31	OAKLAND	17
31	Denver	20
28	Kansas City	14
24	BUFFALO	27
38	NEW YORK	3
6	KANSAS CITY	49
20	Oakland	21

Use Name	Pos.	Hgt	Wgt	Age	Int	Pts
Gary Kirner	OT	6'3"	245	22		
Ron Mix	OT	6'4"	250	26		
Ernie Park	OT	6'3"	253	22		
Ernie Wright	OT	6'4"	265	24		
Sam Gruneisen	OG	6'1"	255	23		
Lloyd McCoy	OG	6'1"	245	22		
Pat Shea	OG	6'1"	245	25		
Walt Sweeney	OG	6'3"	255	23		
Don Rogers	C	6'2"	245	27		
Earl Faison	DE	6'5"	270	25	1	6
Bob Mitinger	DE	6'2"	245	24		
Bob Petrich	DE	6'4"	257	23	1	
George Gross	DT	6'3"	270	23		
Ernie Ladd	DT	6'9"	295	25		
Fred Moore	DT	6'3"	255	24		
Henry Schmidt	DT	6'4"	270	27	1	6
Chuck Allen	LB	6'1"	225	24	4	
Frank Buncom	LB	6'1"	235	24	1	
Ron Carpenter	LB	6'2"	230	23	1	
Bob Horton	LB	6'2"	230	21		
Emil Karas	LB	6'3"	235	30		
Bobby Lane	LB	6'2"	222	24		
George Blair	DB	5'11"	195	26		14
Speedy Duncan	DB	5'10"	180	21	1	
Kenny Graham	DB	6'	200	22	4	
Dick Harris	DB	5'11"	187	27	3	
Charley McNeil	DB	5'11"	180	28	2	
Jimmy Warren	DB	5'11"	185	25	2	
Dick Westmoreland	DB	6'1"	190	23	6	
Bud Whitehead	FL-DB	6'	185	25	3	
John Hadl	QB	6'2"	210	24		6
Tobin Rote	QB	6'3"	220	36		
Paul Lowe	HB	6'	205	27		30
Mario Mendez	HB	5'11"	200	22		
Keith Kinderman	FB	6'	215	24		
Keith Lincoln	FB	6'2"	213	25		67
Gerry McDougall	FB	6'2"	225	29		14
Lance Alworth	FL	6'	185	24		90
Dave Kocourek	OE	6'5"	245	27		30
Don Norton	OE	6'1"	195	26		36
Jerry Robinson	OE	5'11"	200	25		
Jacque MacKinnon	FB-OE	6'4"	250	25		12
Ben Agajanian	K	6'	225	45		14
Herb Travenio	K	6'	218	33		16

KANSAS CITY CHIEFS 7-7-0 Hank Stram

Scores of Each Game		
17	Buffalo	34
21	Oakland	9
28	HOUSTON	7
27	Denver	33
22	BUFFALO	35
7	Boston	24
49	DENVER	39
42	OAKLAND	7
14	SAN DIEGO	28
28	Houston	19
14	New York	27
24	BOSTON	31
49	San Diego	6
24	NEW YORK	7

Use Name	Pos.	Hgt	Wgt	Age	Int	Pts
Jerry Cornelison	OT	6'3"	250	27		
Dave Hill	OT	6'5"	260	23		
Jim Tyrer	OT	6'6"	292	25		
Denny Biodrowski	OG	6'1"	255	24		
Ed Budd	OG	6'5"	260	23		
Curt Merz	OG	6'4"	250	26		
Al Reynolds	OG	6'3"	235	26		
Jon Gilliam	C	6'2"	240	25		
Mel Branch	DE	6'2"	230	27		
Ed Lothamer	DE	6'5"	240	21		
Jerry Mays	DT-DE	6'4"	250	24		
Buck Buchanan	DT	6'7"	280	24		
Curt Farrier	DT	6'6"	245	23		
John Maczuzak	DT	6'5"	250	21		
Hatch Rosdahl (from BUF)	DT	6'5"	250	21		
Walt Corey	LB	6'	242	26	1	
Sherrill Headrick	LB	6'2"	215	27	1	
E. J. Holub	LB	6'4"	225	26		
Smokey Stover	LB	6'	232	25	2	
Bobby Bell	DE-LB	6'4"	228	24	1	6
Dave Grayson	DB	5'10"	184	25	7	
Bobby Hunt	DB	6'1"	190	24	7	6
Willie Mitchell	DB	6'1"	185	22	1	
Bobby Ply	DB	6'1"	190	23	1	
Johnny Robinson	DB	6'	195	25	2	
Charley Warner (to BUF)	DB	5'11"	180	24	1	
Duane Wood	DB	6'1"	200	28	5	
Pete Beathard	QB	6'2"	205	22		
Len Dawson	QB	6'	190	30		12
Eddie Wilson	QB	6'	190	24		6
Bert Coan	HB	6'4"	220	24		12
Abner Haynes	HB	6'	190	26		48
Jerrel Wilson	HB	6'4"	225	22		
Mack Lee Hill	FB	5'11"	225	22		36
Curtis McClinton	FB	6'3"	232	25		20
Jack Spikes (to SD)	FB	6'2"	220	26		
Frank Jackson	FL	6'1"	190	24		54
Fred Arbanas	OE	6'3"	240	25		48
Tommy Brooker	OE	6'2"	230	24		70
Chris Burford	OE	6'3"	210	26		42
Reg Carolan	OE	6'6"	232	24		6

OAKLAND RAIDERS 5-7-2 Al Davis

Scores of Each Game		
14	BOSTON	17
28	Houston	42
9	KANSAS CITY	21
20	Buffalo	23
13	New York	35
43	Boston	43
40	DENVER	7
17	San Diego	31
7	Kansas City	42
20	HOUSTON	10
35	NEW YORK	26
20	Denver	20
16	BUFFALO	13
21	SAN DIEGO	20

Use Name	Pos.	Hgt	Wgt	Age	Int	Pts
Proverb Jacobs	OT	6'4"	260	29		
Dick Klein	OT	6'4"	250	30		
Ken Rice	OT	6'2"	240	24		
Frank Youso	OT	6'4"	250	28		
Wayne Hawkins	OG	6'	240	26		
Bob Mischak	OG	6'	230	31		
Jim Otto	C	6'2"	240	26		
Dalva Allen	DE	6'5"	245	28		
Ben Davidson	DE	6'8"	265	24		
Jon Jelacic	DE	6'3"	255	27		
Dan Birdwell	DT	6'4"	250	23	2	
Doug Brown	DT	6'4"	250	24		
Dave Costa	DT	6'2"	250	22		
Rex Mirich	DT	6'4"	250	23		
Jim Norris	DT	6'4"	235	24	2	
Bill Budness	LB	6'1"	215	21	2	
Dan Conners	LB	6'1"	230	22		
Archie Matsos	LB	6'	212	29	2	
Clancy Osborne	LB	6'3"	220	29		
Jackie Simpson	LB	6'1"	225	27		
J. R. Williamson	LB	6'2"	220	22		
Claude Gibson	DB	6'1"	190	25	2	
Louis Guy	DB	6'	190	23		
Joe Krakoski	DB	6'2"	195	27		
Tom Morrow	DB	5'11"	187	26	4	
Warren Powers	DB	6'	185	23	5	
Howie Williams	DB	6'2"	185	27	1	
Fred Williamson	DB	6'2"	215	26	6	
Cotton Davidson	QB	6'1"	180	32		12
Tom Flores	QB	6'1"	190	27		
Billy Cannon	FB-HB	6'1"	225	27		48
Clem Daniels	HB	6'1"	220	27		48
Bo Dickinson	FB	6'2"	220	29		
Bobby Jackson (from HOU)	FB	6'3"	225	24		18
Glen Shaw	FB	6'1"	225	25		12
Bo Roberson	FL	6'1"	190	29		6
Jan Barrett	OE	6'3"	222	23		12
Fred Gillett	OE	6'3"	220	26		
Ken Herock	OE	6'2"	230	23		12
Bill Miller	OE	6'	190	22		
Art Powell	OE	6'3"	212	27		66
Mike Mercer	K	6'	200	28		79

Alan Miller – Injury

DENVER BRONCOS 2-11-1 Jack Faulkner Mac Speedie

Scores of Each Game		
6	New York	30
13	Buffalo	30
17	HOUSTON	38
10	BOSTON	39
33	KANSAS CITY	27
14	San Diego	42
7	Oakland	40
39	Kansas City	49
20	SAN DIEGO	31
20	NEW YORK	16
7	Boston	12
20	OAKLAND	20
19	BUFFALO	30
15	Houston	34

Use Name	Pos.	Hgt	Wgt	Age	Int	Pts
Eldon Danenhauer	OT	6'4"	245	28		
Harold Olson	OT	6'3"	255	25		
Jim Perkins	OT	6'5"	250	25		
Ernie Barnes	OG	6'3"	243	25		
Bob McCullough	OG	6'2"	245	23		
Tom Nomina	OG	6'5"	270	22		
Don Shackleford	OG	6'4"	255	21		
Jerry Sturm	C-OG	6'3"	260	27		
Ray Kubala	C	6'4"	245	22		
Ed Cooke	DE	6'4"	250	29		6
Stan Fanning (from HOU)	DE	6'6"	270	26		
Ike Lassiter	DE	6'5"	270	23		
Leroy Moore	DE	6'	230	28	1	
Dick Guesman	DT	6'4"	255	28		31
Ray Jacobs	DT	6'3"	265	24		
Chuck Janerette	DT	6'3"	265	25		
Tom Erlandson	LB	6'3"	235	24		
Jim Fraser	LB	6'3"	236	28	1	
Jerry Hopkins	LB	6'2"	235	23	2	
Larry Jordan	LB	6'6"	230	26		
Marv Matuszak	LB	6'3"	240	33	2	
Jim Price	LB	6'2"	230	23		
Billy Atkins	DB	6'1"	195	29		
Norm Bass	DB	6'3"	210	25		
Willie Brown	DB	6'1"	190	23	9	
Goose Gonsoulin	DB	6'3"	210	26	7	
John Griffin	DB	6'1"	190	24		
Tom Janik	DB	6'3"	200	23	1	6
John McGeever	DB	6'1"	195	25	6	
Jim McMillin (from OAK)	DB	5'11"	195	26	1	6
Willie West (to NY)	DB	5'10"	193	26	2	
Jim Wright	DB	5'11"	190	25	1	
Jacky Lee	QB	6'1"	187	25		18
Mickey Slaughter	QB	6'	190	22		2
Gene Mingo (to OAK)	HB	6'1"	190	25		39
Charley Mitchell	HB	5'11"	185	24		36
Billy Joe	FB	6'2"	250	23		14
Donnie Stone	FB	6'2"	205	27		
Al Denson	FL	6'2"	208	22		8
Bob Scarpitto	FL	5'11"	196	25		24
Odell Barry	OE	5'10"	180	22		6
Matt Snorton	OE	6'5"	250	21		
Lionel Taylor	OE	6'2"	215	28		42
Hewritt Dixon	HB-OE	6'2"	217	24		6

John McCormick – Knee Injury
Bob Zeman – Injury

SAN DIEGO CHARGERS

RUSHING

Last Name	No.	Yds	Avg	TD
Lincoln	155	632	4.1	4
Lowe	130	496	3.8	3
MacKinnon	24	124	5.2	2
Kinderman	24	111	4.6	0
McDougall	23	73	3.2	2
Hadl	20	70	3.5	1
Alworth	3	60	20.0	2
Robinson	1	10	10.0	0
Rote	10	–12	–1.2	0

RECEIVING

Last Name	No.	Yds	Avg	TD
Alworth	61	1235	20	13
Norton	49	669	14	6
Lincoln	34	302	9	2
Kocourek	33	593	18	5
Lowe	14	182	13	2
MacKinnon	10	177	18	0
Robinson	10	93	9	0
McDougall	8	106	13	0
Kinderman	3	21	7	0
Whitehead	1	–4	–4	0
Rote	1	–11	–11	0

PUNT RETURNS

Last Name	No.	Yds	Avg	TD
Alworth	18	189	11	0
Robinson	7	41	6	0
Graham	2	24	12	0
Duncan	4	19	5	0
Westmoreland	2	10	5	0
Warren	1	0	0	0

KICKOFF RETURNS

Last Name	No.	Yds	Avg	TD
Westmoreland	18	360	20	0
Warren	13	353	27	0
Duncan	9	318	35	0
Graham	7	172	25	0
Robinson	3	70	23	0
Carpenter	1	15	15	0
Norton	1	0	0	0
Wright	1	0	0	0

PASSING – PUNTING – KICKING

PASSING	Att	Comp	%	Yds	Yd/Att	TD	Int–%	RK
Hadl	274	147	54	2157	7.9	18	15– 6	2
Rote	163	74	45	1156	7.1	9	15– 9	11
Lincoln	4	2	50	61	15.3	1	0– 0	
Lowe	2	0	0	0	0.0	0	0– 0	
Alworth	1	1	100	–11	–11.0	0	0– 0	
Kinderman	1	0	0	0	0.0	0	0– 0	

PUNTING	No	Avg
Hadl	62	39.5
Whitehead	1	30.0

KICKING	XP	Att	%	FG	Att	%
Lincoln	16	17	94	5	12	42
Travenio	10	12	83	2	5	40
Agajanian	8	8	100	2	4	50
Blair	5	6	83	3	5	60

2 POINT XP
McDougall

KANSAS CITY CHIEFS

RUSHING

Last Name	No.	Yds	Avg	TD
Haynes	139	697	5.0	4
M. Hill	105	576	5.5	4
McClinton	73	252	3.5	1
Spikes	34	112	3.3	0
Dawson	40	89	2.2	0
Coan	11	56	5.1	2
Beathard	4	43	10.8	0
E. Wilson	6	5	0.8	1
Jackson	2	5	2.5	0
J. Wilson	1	–10	–10.0	0

RECEIVING

Last Name	No.	Yds	Avg	TD
Jackson	62	943	15	9
Burford	51	675	13	7
Haynes	38	562	15	3
Arbanas	34	686	20	8
M. Hill	19	144	8	2
McClinton	13	221	17	2
Spikes	5	17	3	0
Carolan	3	54	18	1
Coan	2	8	4	0
J. Wilson	1	11	11	0

PUNT RETURNS

Last Name	No.	Yds	Avg	TD
Warner	12	165	14	0
Mitchell	18	160	9	0
Jackson	11	103	9	0
Robinson	1	16	16	0
Haynes	1	11	11	0

KICKOFF RETURNS

Last Name	No.	Yds	Avg	TD
Grayson	30	679	23	0
Warner	12	301	25	0
Haynes	12	278	23	0
Coan	5	124	25	0
Lothamer	1	0	0	0
Rosdahl	1	0	0	0
Stover	1	0	0	0

PASSING – PUNTING – KICKING

PASSING	Att	Comp	%	Yds	Yd/Att	TD	Int–%	RK
Dawson	354	199	56	2879	8.1	30	18– 5	1
E. Wilson	47	25	53	392	8.3	1	1– 2	
Beathard	9	4	44	50	5.6	1	2– 22	
Haynes	1	0	0	0	0.0	0	0– 0	
Spikes	1	0	0	0	0.0	0	0– 0	

PUNTING	No	Avg
J. Wilson	78	42.6
E. Wilson	1	32.0

KICKING	XP	Att	%	FG	Att	%
Brooker	46	46	100	8	17	47

2 POINT XP
McClinton

OAKLAND RAIDERS

RUSHING

Last Name	No.	Yds	Avg	TD
Daniels	173	824	4.8	2
Cannon	89	338	3.8	3
C. Davidson	29	167	5.8	2
Jackson	23	64	2.8	3
Flores	11	64	5.8	0
Shaw	9	26	2.9	2
Dickinson	4	8	2.0	0
Roberson	1	–4	–4.0	0
Youso	0	4	0.0	0

RECEIVING

Last Name	No.	Yds	Avg	TD
Powell	76	1361	18	11
Roberson	44	624	14	1
Daniels	42	696	17	6
Cannon	37	454	12	5
Herock	23	360	16	2
Barrett	12	212	18	2
Jackson	10	81	8	0
Shaw	3	31	10	0
Dickinson	3	20	7	0
Miller	2	29	15	0

PUNT RETURNS

Last Name	No.	Yds	Avg	TD
Gibson	29	419	14	0
Roberson	1	20	20	0
Krakoski	1	8	8	0
Morrow	1	0	0	0

KICKOFF RETURNS

Last Name	No.	Yds	Avg	TD
Roberson	36	975	27	0
Cannon	21	518	25	0
Jackson	2	32	16	0
Daniels	1	32	32	0
Conners	1	0	0	0
Dickinson	1	0	0	0
Klein	1	0	0	0

PASSING – PUNTING – KICKING

PASSING	Att	Comp	%	Yds	Yd/Att	TD	Int–%	RK
C. Davidson	320	155	48	2497	7.8	21	19– 6	5
Flores	200	98	49	1389	7.0	7	14– 7	6
Daniels	1	0	0	0	0.0	0	0– 0	

PUNTING	No	Avg
Mercer	58	42.1

KICKING	XP	Att	%	FG	Att	%
Mercer	34	34	100	15	24	63

DENVER BRONCOS

RUSHING

Last Name	No.	Yds	Avg	TD
Mitchell	177	590	3.3	5
Joe	112	415	3.7	2
Lee	42	163	3.9	3
Slaughter	20	54	2.7	0
Stone	12	26	2.2	0
Mingo	6	26	4.3	0
Dixon	18	25	1.4	0
Barry	3	7	2.3	0
Scarpitto	1	5	5.0	0

RECEIVING

Last Name	No.	Yds	Avg	TD
Taylor	76	873	11	7
Dixon	38	585	15	1
Scarpitto	35	375	11	4
Mitchell	33	225	7	1
Denson	25	383	15	1
Joe	12	16	1	0
Stone	4	38	10	0
Barry	4	31	8	0
Mingo	4	25	6	1

PUNT RETURNS

Last Name	No.	Yds	Avg	TD
Barry	16	149	9	1
Mitchell	9	110	12	0

KICKOFF RETURNS

Last Name	No.	Yds	Avg	TD
Barry	47	1245	27	0
Mitchell	10	221	22	0
Mingo	8	163	20	0
West	5	142	28	0
Dixon	6	89	15	0
Olson	2	27	14	0
Shackleford	1	13	13	0
Jordan	1	0	0	0
Sturm	1	0	0	0

PASSING – PUNTING – KICKING

PASSING	Att	Comp	%	Yds	Yd/Att	TD	Int–%	RK
Lee	265	133	50	1611	6.1	11	20– 8	10
Slaughter	189	97	51	930	4.9	3	11– 6	9
Mitchell	1	0	0	0	0.0	0	0– 0	
Taylor	1	0	0	0	0.0	0	1–100	

PUNTING	No	Avg
Fraser	72	44.7
Janik	10	37.4

KICKING	XP	Att	%	FG	Att	%
Guesman	13	15	87	6	22	27
Mingo	9	10	90	8	12	67

2 POINT XP
Denson
Joe
Slaughter

1965 N.F.L. Passing Pioneers and Hello, Dixie

The league lost two long-standing members when Curly Lambeau and Jack Mara died in June. Lambeau had founded the Green Bay Packers in 1919 and coached them through 1949, molding them into NFL powers until a postwar slump set in. Mara had for years run the New York Giants, founded by his father Tim Mara, and his death put his younger brother Wellington at the head of the New York organization. But life went on as usual in the league, with a hot Western Division race, new stars in Gale Sayers, Bob Hayes, and Dick Butkus, and the usual assortment of injuries, errors, and great plays. To spread the riches around—and also rake in some more money—the league voted to expand into Atlanta starting in 1966, reaching into the Deep South for the first time.

EASTERN CONFERENCE

Cleveland Browns—Even with Paul Warfield sidelined for most of the year by a shoulder injury and the defense saddled with the weight of advancing years, the Browns still ran away with the Eastern crown. Coach Blanton Collier had some of the finest offensive assets in the division, including a solid line, a reliable flanker in Gary Collins, a steady quarterback in Frank Ryan, and the incomparable Jimmy Brown at fullback, and the patchwork defense held up well enough to win eleven games. The Browns counted their riches even in the specialists' department, with forty-one-year-old Lou Groza an accurate place-kicker, Leroy Kelly a good punt returner, Walter Roberts a dangerous kickoff returner, and Gary Collins a fine punter in addition to his pass-catching chores.

Dallas Cowboys—The Cowboys failed to break the .500 barrier, but they did uncover one of the league's most exciting performers in rookie end Bob Hayes. A world-record-holding sprinter, Hayes terrorized defensive backs with his pure speed, streaking away from them with no possibility of being caught from behind once in the clear. While Hayes scored thirteen touchdowns, tackle Ralph Neely went unnoticed by all but the coaches with a fine rookie season. Coach Tom Landry added several other freshmen who would contribute to the strong Dallas teams of the next few years in Dan Reeves, Jethro Pugh, Craig Morton, and Obert Logan.

New York Giants—After losing all five of their pre-season games, the Giants obtained quarterback Earl Morrall from Detroit and finished in a surprising tie for second place in the East. Morrall gave the team a steady hand at the head of the offense and threw for twenty-two touchdowns. Joining Morrall in the backfield was a collection of young runners known collectively in the press as the Baby Bulls. Tucker Frederickson, Steve Thurlow, Ernie Koy, and Chuck Mercein all ground out hard overland yardage despite a lack of speed, and split end Homer Jones gave the Giants all the speed they needed in a pass receiver. Even with only a faint knowledge of pass patterns, Jones picked up over 700 yards as a receiver on only twenty-six catches after breaking into the starting lineup in mid-season.

Washington Redskins—The Redskins lost their first five games with a poor offensive show that improved only a little over the season. The Washington running attack was the league's worst, as there still was no full-time fullback, and halfback Charley Taylor came nowhere near duplicating his fine rookie season. The passing offense also slumped, as Bobby Mitchell alone among the receivers consistently got open for Sonny Jurgensen's passes. The Washington defense was a competent unit but was hurt when cornerback Johnny Sample was suspended late in the season for insubordination.

Philadelphia Eagles—Joe Kuharich had traded the Eagles into respectability last year, but progress came more slowly this season. The big trouble spot was the defensive line, which put no pressure at all on enemy passers. The Eagles resorted to frequent blitzing to compensate for the weak line, but this just made them vulnerable to quick passes. The offense was sound throughout, starting with the Bob Brown-led line. Timmy Brown starred at halfback, using his quickness to best advantage on runs and passes, Earl Gros complemented Brown with his power at fullback, and Norm Snead showed progress at quarterback.

St. Louis Cardinals—Tied with the Browns for first place in the East on October 17, the Cards swan-dived out of contention by losing eight of the next nine games and their last six contests straight. Injuries to Charley Johnson, Larry Wilson, and Jerry Stovall contributed to the collapse, and the trading of John David Crow to San Francisco hurt the club more than had been expected. Crow had been a clutch runner, the man to give the ball to when vital yardage was needed, and his departure left the Cards without a leader in the backfield.

Pittsburgh Steelers—Head coach Buddy Parker quit two weeks before the season opener, saying, "I can't win with this bunch of stiffs." On that pleasant note, assistant Mike Nixon took over as head man for a brutal 2-12 season. Nixon benched veteran quarterback Ed Brown and replaced him with Bill Nelsen, who played most of the season on a bad knee, which made him a sitting duck for enemy pass-rushers. The running attack lost its best man when John Henry Johnson was sidelined by a bad knee, and the receiving corps was so thin that the starting split end, Clendon Thomas, was a converted defensive back. When Parker had quit as coach of the Detroit Lions before the 1957 season, the Lions went on to win the championship. This time, Parker knew what he was doing.

WESTERN CONFERENCE

Green Bay Packers—The return of guard Jerry Kramer from stomach surgery, the purchase of kicker Don Chandler from New York, and the development of Marv Fleming, Doug Hart, and Tom Brown into starters plastered over the few cracks in the Packers' solid front. After battling the Colts all season for the Western Conference lead, the Packers blew a chance to clinch the championship by managing only a tie with San Francisco in the final regular-season game. Baltimore and Green Bay finished with identical 10-3-1 records and squared off in a playoff for the Western crown. The Colts came into the playoff game with no experienced quarterback, but their fired-up defense knocked the ball loose from Bill Anderson on the first play from scrimmage, and Don Shinnick ran the fumble 25 yards for a Baltimore touchdown. Quarterback Bart Starr was shaken up on the play and missed most of the game, but the Packers fought back against the spirited Colts to tie the score at 10-10 with a Chandler field goal late in the game. For the second time in history, a pro-football game went into overtime, and another Chandler field goal, which the Colts and many observers claimed went wide, gave the Packers the victory after 13:39 of overtime play.

Baltimore Colts—Driving along to a repeat Western championship, the Colts suddenly lost both their quarterbacks, with Johnny Unitas ripping up a knee in the twelfth game and Gary Cuozzo dislocating a shoulder one week later. Coach Don Shula put halfback Tom Matte into the signal caller's spot, equiping him with a wrist band with some basic plays written on it. Relying on roll-out passes, quarterback keepers, pitchouts, and a fanatical defense, the Colts beat the Rams 20-17 in their final game to get into a Western Conference playoff with the Packers.

Chicago Bears—One of the Bears' three first-round draft picks, defensive end Steve DeLong got away to the AFL, but George Halas opened his wallet wide to sign the other two. Halfback Gale Sayers and linebacker Dick Butkus immediately rewarded Halas' genorosity with All-Pro rookie seasons. Sayers burst on the national consciousness like a comet, slamming through holes at top speed and eluding defensive backs by outdodging and outrunning them. Starring as a kick returner and pass receiver as well as a runner, Sayers scored a record twenty-two touchdowns in the season. While Sayers souped up the Bear offense, Butkus helped return the defense to a high peak with his ferocity at middle linebacker.

San Francisco '49ers—With John Brodie suddenly putting all his talent together in a marvelous season, the '49er offense suddenly blossomed into the league's most explosive. Wide receivers Bernie Casey and Dave Parks gave Brodie two fine targets to hit, and the offensive line gave him good protection against enemy pass rushes. The running game improved immensely over last year with the addition of two new hard-chargers, rookie fullback Ken Willand and ex-Cardinal halfback John David Crow. The defense, however, was as undistinguished as the attack was dynamic.

Minnesota Vikings— The Viking offense still put on a good show, but the defense failed to show the expected progress, seven times getting burned for 35 or more points. This so frustrated head coach Norm Van Brocklin that he resigned in mid-season, only to be talked out of it after a couple of days by the front office. One of Van Brocklin's biggest problems was a growing tension between himself and quarterback Fran Tarkenton. The coach kept trying to make a strict pocket passer out of Tarkenton, while the quarterback stuck to his free-wheeling, scrambling style.

Detroit Lions—Owner William Clay Ford started the year by firing all of head coach George Wilson's assistants, a warning to Wilson to win or face the same fate. Wilson throught it over for a couple of days and handed in his resignation. Harry Gilmer took over as head man and ran into a flood of injuries that weighted the club down in sixth place. One of Gilmer's first decisions was to rely on one quarterback, so he kept Milt Plum and traded Earl Morrall to New York. The only problem was, Plum had a poor year, while Morrall rejuvenated the Giants with his fine passing. With the offense erratic, the Detroit defense no longer was strong enough to carry the team.

Los Angeles Rams—The front four of Deacon Jones, Merlin Olsen, Rosie Grier, and Lamar Lundy became the league's most famous defensive line and often carried the rest of the Los Angeles defense, which was ladened with as many as five rookie starters at one point. The running attack was weak, but the blocking and receiving gave quarterbacks Bill Munson and Roman Gabriel something to work with. Munson started the first ten games and led the club to only one win despite frequent flashes of talent, and Gabriel headed the attack for the final four games after Munson hurt a knee.

FINAL TEAM STATISTICS

OFFENSE

	BALT.	CHI.	CLEVE.	DALLAS	DET.	G.BAY	L.A.	MINN.	N.Y.	PHIL.	PITT.	ST.L.	S.F.	WASH.
FIRST DOWNS:														
Total	266	257	257	211	204	201	251	277	230	267	194	251	292	210
by Rushing	94	132	133	87	93	85	76	130	91	94	71	90	97	69
by Passing	144	110	97	108	93	103	153	126	112	149	104	143	172	125
by Penalty	28	15	27	16	18	13	22	21	27	24	19	18	23	16
RUSHING:														
Number	445	479	476	416	453	432	378	505	423	404	407	431	428	354
Yards	1593	2131	2331	1608	1469	1488	1464	2278	1651	1824	1378	1619	1783	1037
Average Yards	3.6	4.4	4.9	3.9	3.2	3.4	3.9	4.5	3.9	4.5	3.4	3.8	4.2	2.9
Touchdowns	13	27	19	8	16	14	8	19	12	21	10	10	13	7
PASSING:														
Attempts	399	361	329	362	374	306	445	372	342	434	354	448	454	427
Completions	222	201	160	168	170	166	230	189	171	223	161	221	272	220
Completion Pct.	55.6	55.7	48.6	46.4	45.5	54.2	51.7	50.8	50.0	51.4	45.5	49.3	59.9	51.5
Passing Yards	3330	3020	2339	2756	2083	2508	3059	2861	2685	3442	2503	3222	3633	2908
Avg. Yds per Att.	8.3	8.4	7.1	7.6	5.6	8.2	6.9	7.7	7.9	7.9	7.1	7.2	8.0	6.8
Avg. Yds per Comp.	15.0	15.0	14.6	16.4	12.3	15.1	13.3	15.1	15.7	15.4	15.5	14.6	13.4	13.2
Tackled Att. to Pass	43	30	31	55	26	43	45	35	31	33	62	30	19	39
Yards Lost Tackled	325	254	272	369	249	395	344	315	255	254	527	279	146	337
Net Yards	3005	2766	2067	2387	1834	2113	2715	2546	2430	3188	1976	2943	3487	2571
Touchdowns	31	22	23	25	14	19	22	21	23	22	10	20	35	20
Interceptions	17	12	16	18	26	14	19	12	16	26	35	25	21	20
Pct. Intercepted	4.3	3.3	4.9	5.0	7.0	4.6	4.3	3.2	4.7	6.0	9.9	5.6	4.6	4.7
PUNTS:														
Number	56	58	69	73	78	74	66	51	61	56	78	67	54	70
Average Distance	39.6	42.7	45.7	41.3	42.8	42.9	39.7	42.1	41.6	42.2	45.1	40.4	45.8	42.1
PUNT RETURNS:														
Number	45	29	36	39	34	22	32	22	24	21	33	23	38	39
Yards	421	289	427	312	358	65	225	115	35	183	259	27	283	415
Average Yards	9.4	10.0	11.9	8.0	10.5	3.0	7.0	5.2	1.5	8.7	7.8	1.2	7.4	10.6
Touchdowns	0	1	2	0	0	0	0	1	0	1	0	0	0	1
KICKOFF RETURNS:														
Number	52	45	53	44	52	50	53	67	60	60	61	55	59	49
Yards	1242	1146	1209	1166	1416	1040	1351	1524	1303	1438	1238	1287	1276	1011
Average Yards	23.9	25.5	22.8	26.5	27.2	20.8	25.5	22.7	21.7	24.0	20.3	23.4	21.6	20.6
Touchdowns	0	1	0	1	0	0	0	1	0	0	0	0	0	0
INTERCEPTION RETURNS:														
Number	22	20	24	18	26	27	11	19	16	25	12	17	13	27
Yards	318	307	349	198	343	561	224	286	249	313	282	328	97	535
Average Yards	14.5	15.4	14.5	11.0	13.2	20.8	20.4	15.1	15.6	12.5	23.5	19.3	7.5	19.8
Touchdowns	4	2	1	2	3	4	1	2	1	3	2	1	0	2
PENALTIES:														
Number	69	98	84	68	77	48	61	76	61	61	40	45	79	81
Yards	616	826	976	710	767	529	560	771	618	686	326	458	785	692
FUMBLES:														
Number	31	33	20	31	27	18	40	41	31	21	42	15	33	41
Number Lost	19	16	9	17	15	12	22	25	14	10	22	7	19	21
POINTS:														
Total	389	409	363	325	257	316	269	383	270	363	202	296	421	257
PAT Attempts	48	54	45	40	33	38	32	44	37	48	25	33	53	33
PAT Made	48	52	45	37	33	37	30	44	34	45	19	33	52	29
FG Attempts	28	26	25	27	22	26	26	35	25	25	19	31	27	22
FG Made	17	11	16	16	8	17	15	23	4	10	11	21	17	10
Percent FG Made	60.7	42.3	64.0	59.3	36.4	65.4	57.7	65.7	16.0	40.0	57.9	67.7	63.0	45.5
Safeties	1	0	0	0	1	0	1	3	1	0	0	1	0	0

DEFENSE

	BALT.	CHI.	CLEVE.	DALLAS	DET.	G.BAY	L.A.	MINN.	N.Y.	PHIL.	PITT.	ST.L.	S.F.	WASH.
FIRST DOWNS:														
Total	233	244	265	240	210	240	208	242	266	243	243	238	259	237
by Rushing	78	87	104	80	84	115	82	99	108	100	122	89	94	100
by Passing	131	136	135	138	104	111	113	120	140	129	109	133	139	101
by Penalty	24	21	26	22	22	14	13	23	18	14	12	16	26	36
RUSHING:														
Number	410	400	412	422	409	480	417	408	447	419	483	433	405	486
Yards	1483	1530	1866	1444	1460	1988	1409	1755	1956	1582	2080	1813	1535	1753
Average Yards	3.6	3.8	4.5	3.4	3.6	4.1	3.4	4.3	4.4	3.8	4.3	4.2	3.8	3.6
Touchdowns	11	11	11	13	9	10	16	17	20	11	19	11	20	18
PASSING:														
Attempts	400	444	419	426	344	383	349	357	393	393	353	380	448	318
Completions	213	217	204	205	190	187	205	187	208	215	173	184	225	161
Completion Pct.	53.3	48.9	48.7	48.1	55.2	48.8	58.7	52.4	52.9	54.7	49.0	48.4	50.2	50.6
Passing Yards	2903	3086	3153	3063	2508	2316	2884	2692	3251	3123	2703	2826	3302	2539
Avg. Yds per Att.	7.3	7.0	7.5	7.2	7.3	6.0	8.3	7.5	8.3	7.9	7.7	7.4	7.4	8.0
Avg. Yds per Comp.	13.6	14.2	15.5	14.9	13.2	12.4	14.1	14.4	15.6	14.5	15.6	15.4	14.7	15.8
Tackled Att. to Pass	39	40	38	39	49	44	32	23	39	37	33	39	25	45
Yards Lost Tackled	341	348	307	315	411	335	270	199	294	287	253	342	197	422
Net Yards	2562	2738	2846	2748	2097	1981	2614	2493	2957	2836	2450	2484	3105	2117
Touchdowns	22	18	31	17	21	11	22	31	18	28	25	24	24	15
Interceptions	22	20	24	18	26	27	11	19	16	25	12	17	13	27
Pct. Intercepted	5.5	4.5	5.7	4.2	7.6	7.0	3.2	5.3	4.1	6.4	3.4	4.5	2.9	8.5
PUNTS:														
Number	71	65	69	71	74	60	66	64	45	54	76	65	62	69
Average Distance	43.9	42.3	41.1	42.9	42.9	42.1	45.4	38.4	42.7	41.8	42.2	43.3	41.9	43.4
PUNT RETURNS:														
Number	26	22	36	26	39	36	25	29	22	37	44	32	33	30
Yards	198	123	259	139	318	290	176	261	137	263	437	267	408	138
Average Yards	7.6	5.6	7.2	5.3	8.2	8.1	7.0	9.0	6.2	7.1	9.9	8.3	12.4	4.6
Touchdowns	0	0	0	1	1	0	1	0	0	0	2	0	1	0
KICKOFF RETURNS:														
Number	63	72	58	63	43	52	54	62	54	58	30	50	59	42
Yards	1346	1583	1334	1229	858	1216	1364	1557	1175	1531	684	1228	1566	976
Average Yards	21.4	22.0	23.0	19.5	20.0	23.4	25.3	25.1	21.8	26.4	22.8	24.6	26.5	23.2
Touchdowns	1	0	0	0	0	0	0	1	0	0	0	0	1	0
INTERCEPTION RETURNS:														
Number	17	12	16	18	26	14	19	12	16	26	35	25	21	20
Yards	341	219	275	268	515	209	156	215	182	476	646	465	232	191
Average Yards	20.1	18.3	17.2	14.9	19.8	14.9	8.2	17.9	11.4	18.3	18.5	18.6	11.0	9.6
Touchdowns	1	3	1	0	2	1	0	1	1	6	6	1	3	2
PENALTIES:														
Number	80	68	62	50	61	67	70	66	83	66	58	70	71	74
Yards	786	611	586	483	637	677	566	643	848	653	615	750	727	738
FUMBLES:														
Number	33	33	13	37	33	37	27	25	32	32	28	29	34	31
Number Lost	14	24	8	20	20	23	15	11	20	11	15	15	17	15
POINTS:														
Total	284	275	325	280	295	224	328	403	338	359	397	309	402	301
PAT Attempts	35	33	43	33	36	22	40	53	41	47	53	37	52	38
PAT Made	35	30	40	29	36	22	40	52	40	44	49	36	48	37
FG Attempts	23	24	18	30	22	33	32	20	29	26	26	32	27	22
FG Made	13	15	9	17	13	22	16	11	16	11	10	17	14	12
Percent FG Made	56.5	62.5	50.0	56.7	59.1	66.7	50.0	55.0	55.2	42.3	38.5	53.1	51.9	54.5
Safeties	0	1	0	1	2	2	0	0	2	0	0	0	0	0

1965 NFL CHAMPIONSHIP GAME
January 2, at Green Bay
(Attendance 50,777)

Bulldozing the Defense

After two years as Western Division runners-up, the Green Bay Packers returned to the NFL championship game they had won in 1961 and 1962. The Cleveland Browns, the defending NFL champions, came into Lambeau Field to furnish the opposition. The playing field was muddy and footing uncertain, making straight-ahead running plays the best bets of the afternoon. The Packer defense gave Green Bay a decisive edge by dogging Cleveland fullback Jimmy Brown all afternoon, while Packer runners Jim Taylor and Paul Hornung followed strong blocking to eat up yardage on the ground. Packer quarterback Bart Starr crossed up the Browns on the first series of downs by throwing the ball; he hit Carroll Dale with a long pass that gave the Packers a quick 7-0 lead. The Browns retaliated by moving steadily downfield and scoring on a Frank Ryan-to-Gary Collins pass. The extra point went awry, however, and the Packers still led 7-6. A Lou Groza field goal gave the Browns a 9-7 lead at the end of the first quarter, and three second-period field goals, one by Groza and two by Green Bay's Don Chandler, made the halftime score 13-12 in favor of the Packers. Coach Vince Lombardi stressed ball control to his players, and the Packer offense came out for the second half ready to grind out difficult yardage. Using off-tackle blasts and power sweeps with Taylor and Hornung carrying the ball, the Packers drove 90 yards on 11 plays in the third quarter, eating up seven minutes of the clock while putting seven more points on the scoreboard. Whenever the Browns got the ball in the second half, they couldn't move against the Green Bay defense; whenever the Packers had the ball, they would hold onto it for several precious minutes before giving it up. In all, the Green Bay offensive line contributed the most to the Packer victory by constantly knocking the Cleveland defenders back to make room for Taylor and Hornung in the 20-12 victory.

SCORING

GREEN BAY	7	6	7	3	–23
CLEVELAND	9	3	0	0	–12

First Quarter
- G.B. Dale, 47 yard pass from Starr
  PAT – Chandler (kick)
- Cle. Collins, 17 yard pass from Ryan
  PAT – No Good
- Cle. Groza, 24 yard field goal

Second Quarter
- G.B. Chandler, 15 yard field goal
- G.B Chandler, 23 yard field goal
- Cle. Groza, 28 yard field goal

Third Quarter
- G.B. Hornung, 13 yard rush
  PAT – Chandler (kick)

Fourth Quarter
- G.B. Chandler, 29 yard field goal

TEAM STATISTICS

G. B.		CLEVE.
21	First Downs – Total	8
10	First Downs – Rushing	2
9	First Downs – Passing	5
2	First Downs – Penalty	1
3	Punts – Number	4
38.3	Punts - Average Distance	46.0
2	Punt Returns – Number	1
–10	Punt Returns – Yards	11
2	Interception Returns – Number	1
15	Interception Returns – Yards	0
0	Fumbles – Number	0
3	Penalties – Number	2
35	Yards Penalized	20
1	Giveaways	2
2	Takeaways	1
+1	Difference	–1

INDIVIDUAL STATISTICS

RUSHING

GREEN BAY	No.	Yds.	Avg.	CLEVELAND	No.	Yds.	Avg.
Hornung	18	105	5.8	Brown	12	50	4.2
Taylor	27	96	3.6	Ryan	3	9	3.0
Moore	2	3	1.5	Green	3	5	1.7
	47	204	4.3		18	64	3.6

RECEIVING

GREEN BAY	No.	Yds.	Avg.	CLEVELAND	No.	Yds.	Avg.
Dowler	5	59	11.8	Brown	3	44	14.7
Dale	2	60	30.0	Collins	3	41	13.7
Taylor	2	20	10.0	Warfield	2	30	15.0
Hornung	1	8	8.0		8	115	14.4
	10	147	14.7				

PASSING

	Att	Comp	Comp Pct.	Yds	Int	Yds/ Att.	Yds/ Comp	Yards Lost Tackled
GREEN BAY								
Starr	18	10	55.6	147	1	8.2	14.7	
Hornung	1	0	0.0	0	0	–	–	
	19	10	52.6	147	1	7.7	14.7	19
CLEVELAND								
Ryan	18	8	44.4	115	2	6.4	14.4	18

CLEVELAND BROWNS 11-3-0 Blanton Collier

Scores of Each Game		
17	Washington	7
13	ST. LOUIS	49
35	Philadelphia	17
24	PITTSBURGH	19
23	DALLAS	17
38	New York	14
17	MINNESOTA	27
38	PHILADELPHIA	34
34	NEW YORK	21
24	Dallas	17
42	Pittsburgh	21
24	WASHINGTON	16
7	Los Angeles	42
27	St. Louis	24

Use Name	Pos.	Hgt	Wgt	Age	Int	Pts
John Brown	OT	6'2"	248	26		
Monte Clark	OT	6'6"	265	28		
Dick Schafrath	OT	6'3"	255	29		
Gene Hickerson	OG	6'3"	248	30		
Dale Memmelaar	OG	6'2"	248	28		
John Wooten	OG	6'2"	250	30		
John Morrow	C	6'3"	248	32		
Jim Garcia	DE	6'4"	240	21		
Bill Glass	DE	6'5"	255	29	1	
Paul Wiggin	DE	6'3"	245	31		
Walter Johnson	DT	6'3"	265	22		
Jim Kanicki	DT	6'4"	270	23		
Dick Modzelewski	DT	6'	260	34		
Vince Costello	LB	6'	228	33	3	
Galen Fiss	LB	6'	227	35	1	
Jim Houston	LB	6'2"	240	28	2	
Dale Lindsey	LB	6'3"	220	22	1	
Stan Sczurek	LB	5'11"	230	26	1	
Sid Williams	LB	6'2"	235	23	1	
Erich Barnes	DB	6'2"	198	30	1	
Walter Beach	DB	6'	185	30		
Larry Benz	DB	5'11"	185	24	5	
Ross Fichtner	DB	6'	185	27	4	6
Bobby Franklin	DB	5'11"	182	29		
Mike Howell	DB	6'1"	187	22		
Bernie Parrish	DB	5'11"	195	30	4	
Frank Parker – Operation						
Jim Ninowski	QB	6'1"	207	29		
Frank Ryan	QB	6'3"	200	29		
Ernie Green	HB	6'2"	205	26		24
Leroy Kelly	HB	6'	195	23		12
Jimmy Brown	FB	6'2"	228	29		126
Jamie Caleb	FB	6'1"	210	28		
Charlie Scales	FB	5'11"	215	26		
Gary Collins	FL	6'4"	208	24		60
Clifton McNeil	FL	6'2"	185	25		
Johnny Brewer	TE	6'4"	235	28		6
Ralph Smith	TE	6'2"	215	26		
Tom Hutchinson	OE	6'1"	190	24		12
Walter Roberts	OE	5'10"	175	23		24
Paul Warfield	OE	6'	188	22		
Lou Groza	K	6'3"	250	41		93

DALLAS COWBOYS 7-7-0 Tom Landry

Scores of Each Game		
31	NEW YORK	2
27	WASHINGTON	7
13	St. Louis	20
24	PHILADELPHIA	35
17	Cleveland	23
3	Green Bay	13
13	Pittsburgh	22
39	SAN FRANCISCO	31
24	PITTSBURGH	17
17	CLEVELAND	24
31	Washington	34
21	Philadelphia	19
27	ST. LOUIS	13
38	New York	20

Use Name	Pos.	Hgt	Wgt	Age	Int	Pts
Jim Boeke	OT	6'5"	255	26		
Ralph Neely	OT	6'5"	257	21		
Don Talbert	OT	6'5"	240	25		
Mike Connelly	OG	6'3"	248	29		
Leon Donahue (from SF)	OG	6'4"	245	26		
Mitch Johnson	OG	6'4"	245	23		
Jake Kupp	OG	6'3"	233	23		
Dave Manders	C	6'2"	240	23		
George Andrie	DE	6'7"	255	25		6
Garry Porterfield	DE	6'3"	223	22		
Jethro Pugh	DE	6'6"	255	21		
Maury Youmans	DE	6'6"	253	28		
Larry Stephens	DT-DE	6'4"	250	27		
Jim Colvin	DT	6'2"	255	28		
John Diehl (to OAK-A)	DT	6'7"	250	29		
Bob Lilly	DT	6'4"	255	26	1	6
Dave Edwards	LB	6'3"	226	26	2	
Harold Hays	LB	6'3"	223	24		
Chuck Howley	LB	6'3"	223	29		
Lee Roy Jordan	LB	6'2"	216	24		
Jerry Tubbs	LB	6'2"	222	30	2	
Russell Wayt	LB	6'4"	235	22		
Don Bishop	DB	6'2"	216	30		
Mike Gaechter	DB	6'	190	25	2	6
Cornell Green	DB	6'4"	215	25	3	6
Warren Livingston	DB	5'10"	190	27	3	
Obert Logan	DB	5'10"	180	23	3	6
Mel Renfro	HB-DB	6'	195	23	2	12
Joe Bob Isbell – Injury						
Tony Liscio – Injury						
Don Meredith	QB	6'2"	206	27		6
Craig Morton	QB	6'4"	216	22		
Jerry Rhome	QB	6'	180	23		
Perry Lee Dunn	HB	6'2"	200	22		18
Dan Reeves	HB	6'1"	203	21		18
Don Perkins	FB	5'10"	206	27		
J. D. Smith	FB	6'1"	210	32		18
A. D. Whitfield	FB	5'10"	200	21		
Buddy Dial	FL	6'1"	195	28		6
Pete Gent	FL	6'4"	210	22		12
Pettis Norman	TE	6'3"	223	25		18
Frank Clarke	OE	6'	210	32		24
Bob Hayes	OE	6'	190	22		78
Colin Ridgway	K	6'5"	211	26		
Danny Villanueva	K	5'11"	200	27		85

NEW YORK GIANTS 7-7-0 Allie Sherman

Scores of Each Game		
2	Dallas	31
16	Philadelphia	14
23	Pittsburgh	13
14	Minnesota	40
35	PHILADELPHIA	27
14	CLEVELAND	38
14	ST. LOUIS	10
7	WASHINGTON	23
21	Cleveland	34
28	St. Louis	15
14	CHICAGO	35
35	PITTSBURGH	10
27	Washington	10
20	DALLAS	38

Use Name	Pos.	Hgt	Wgt	Age	Int	Pts
Rosey Brown	OT	6'3"	255	32		
Frank Lasky	OT	6'2"	265	23		
John McDowell	OT	6'3"	260	22		
Bookie Bolin	OG	6'2"	240	25		
Pete Case	OG	6'3"	243	24		
Roger Davis	OG	6'3"	240	27		
Mickey Walker	OG	6'	235	25		
Greg Larson	C	6'2"	250	26		
Bob Scholtz	C	6'4"	250	27		
Glen Condren	DE	6'2"	225	23		
Rosey Davis	DE	6'5"	260	23		
Jim Katcavage	DE	6'3"	240	30		2
Andy Stynchula	DE	6'3"	250	26		21
Roger Anderson	DT	6'5"	265	22		
Mike Bundra	DT	6'3"	260	26		
Roger LaLonde	DT	6'3"	255	23		
John Lovetere	DT	6'4"	285	29		
Dave O'Brien	DT	6'3"	247	24		
Jim Carroll	LB	6'1"	225	22	1	
Tom Costello	LB	6'3"	220	24		
Jerry Hillebrand	LB	6'3"	240	25	2	6
Bill Swain	LB	6'2"	228	24		
Olen Underwood	LB	6'1"	210	23	1	
Lou Slaby	DT-LB	6'3"	235	23		
Henry Carr	DB	6'3"	205	22	2	
Clarence Childs	DB	6'	180	26		
Spider Lockhart	DB	6'2"	185	22	4	
Dick Lynch	DB	6'1"	198	29	4	6
Jimmy Patton	DB	6'	185	33	1	
Allan Webb	DB	5'11"	180	30		
Willie Williams	DB	6'	190	22	1	
Jim Moran – Broken Leg						
Earl Morrall	QB	6'1"	206	31		
Bob Timberlake	QB	6'4"	220	22		24
Gary Wood	QB	5'11"	188	22		1
Tucker Frederickson	FB-HB	6'3"	220	22		36
Ernie Koy	HB	6'2"	225	22		
Smith Reed	HB	6'	215	23		
Steve Thurlow	HB	6'3"	216	22		30
Chuck Mercein	FB	6'3"	230	22		12
Ernie Wheelwright	FB	6'3"	240	28		
Bob Crespino	TE	6'4"	225	27		24
Aaron Thomas	FL-TE	6'3"	210	27		30
Homer Jones	FL	6'2"	205	24		36
Joe Morrison	FL	6'1"	212	27		30
Bob Lacey	OE	6'3"	205	23		
Del Shofner	OE	6'3"	185	29		12

WASHINGTON REDSKINS 6-8-0 Bill McPeak

Scores of Each Game		
7	CLEVELAND	17
7	Dallas	27
10	Detroit	14
16	ST. LOUIS	37
7	BALTIMORE	38
24	St. Louis	20
23	PHILADELPHIA	21
23	New York	7
14	Philadelphia	21
31	Pittsburgh	3
34	DALLAS	31
16	Cleveland	24
10	NEW YORK	27
35	PITTSBURGH	14

Use Name	Pos.	Hgt	Wgt	Age	Int	Pts
Fran O'Brien	OT	6'1"	255	30		
Jim Snowden	DE-OT	6'3"	255	23		
Don Croftcheck	OG	6'1"	230	22		
Darrell Dess	OG	6'	245	29		
Vince Promuto	OG	6'1"	245	27		
Robert Reed	OG	6'1"	250	22		
Dave Crossan	C	6'3"	245	25		
Len Hauss	C	6'2"	235	23		
Carl Kammerer	DE	6'3"	243	28		
John Paluck	DE	6'2"	245	32		
Bill Quinlan	DE	6'3"	250	33		
Ron Snidow	DE	6'4"	250	23	1	
Joe Rutgens	DT	6'2"	255	26		
Fred Williams	DT	6'4"	256	35		
Willie Adams	LB	6'2"	235	23		
Jimmy Carr	LB	6'1"	225	32		
Chris Hanburger	LB	6'2"	218	24	1	
Sam Huff	LB	6'1"	230	30	2	
Bob Pellegrini	LB	6'2"	242	30		6
John Reger	LB	6'	220	34		
Rickie Harris	DB	6'	182	22	1	12
Johnny Sample	DB	6'1"	205	28	6	
Lonnie Sanders	DB	6'3"	207	23	4	
Jim Shorter	DB	5'11"	185	24	2	6
Jim Steffen	DB	6'	196	28	3	
Tom Walters	DB	6'2"	195	23	1	6
Paul Krause	FL-DB	6'3"	195	23	6	6
Sonny Jurgensen	QB	5'11"	205	31		12
Dick Shiner	QB	6'	197	23		
Pervis Atkins (to OAK-A)	HB	6'1"	210	29		
George Hughley	HB	6'2"	223	26		6
Dan Lewis	HB	6'1"	200	29		24
Charley Taylor	HB	6'3"	210	24		36
Bob Briggs	FB	6'1"	228	22		
Rick Casares	FB	6'2"	225	34		
Bobby Mitchell	FL	6'	196	30		36
Bill Hunter	DB-FL	6'1"	185	22		6
Fred Mazurek	DB-FL	5'11"	192	22		
Jerry Smith	TE	6'2"	208	22		12
Preston Carpenter	OE	6'2"	208	31		
Angie Coia	OE	6'2"	196	27		18
Bob Jencks	OE	6'5"	227	24		59
Pat Richter	OE	6'5"	230	24		12
John Seedborg	K	6'	227	22		

PHILADELPHIA EAGLES 5-9-0 Joe Kuharich

Scores of Each Game		
34	ST. LOUIS	27
14	NEW YORK	16
17	CLEVELAND	35
35	Dallas	24
27	New York	35
14	PITTSBURGH	20
21	Washington	23
34	Cleveland	38
21	WASHINGTON	14
24	Baltimore	34
28	St. Louis	24
19	DALLAS	21
47	Pittsburgh	13
28	DETROIT	35

Use Name	Pos.	Hgt	Wgt	Age	Int	Pts
Bob Brown	OT	6'4"	276	22		
Dave Graham	OT	6'3"	250	26		
Lane Howell	OT	6'5"	255	24		
Ed Blaine	OG	6'2"	240	25		
Jim Skaggs	OT-OG	6'2"	250	25		
Lynn Hoyem	C-OG	6'4"	253	25		
Dave Recher	C	6'1"	240	22		
Jim Ringo	C	6'1"	230	34		
Bobby Richards	DE	6'2"	245	26		
George Tarasovic	DE	6'4"	248	36	1	12
Don Hultz	LB-DE	6'3"	235	24	1	
Ed Khayat	DT	6'3"	250	30		
John Meyers	DT	6'6"	276	25	2	
Floyd Peters	DT	6'4"	255	30		
Erwin Will	DT	6'5"	270	22		
Maxie Baughan	LB	6'1"	227	27	1	6
Ralph Heck	LB	6'2"	230	24		
Dave Lloyd	LB	6'3"	248	29	2	10
Mike Morgan	LB	6'4"	242	23	1	
Harold Wells	LB	6'2"	223	26		
Irv Cross	DB	6'1"	190	26	3	
Al Nelson	DB	5'11"	180	21	2	
Jim Nettles	DB	5'9"	175	23	3	6
Nate Ramsey	DB	6'1"	200	24	6	
Bob Shann	DB	6'1"	187	22		6
Joe Scarpati	HB-DB	5'10"	185	23	3	
Claude Crabb	FL-DB	6'	190	25		
Jerry Mazzanti – Military Service						
Mike McClellan – Military Service						
Jack Concannon	QB	6'3"	195	22		
King Hill	QB	6'3"	213	29		12
Norm Snead	QB	6'4"	205	25		18
Timmy Brown	HB	5'10"	198	28		54
Ollie Matson	HB	6'2"	210	35		18
Earl Gros	FB	6'3"	220	24		54
Izzy Lang	FB	6'1"	230	22		6
Tom Woodeshick	FB	6'	220	23		
Glenn Glass	FL	6'	203	28		
Ron Goodwin	OE-FL	6'	180	23		6
Roger Gill	TE	6'1"	200	24		
Bill Cronin	TE	6'4"	220	22		
Jim Kelly	TE	6'2"	215	23		
Pete Retzlaff	TE	6'1"	214	34		60
Fred Hill	OE	6'2"	215	22		
Ray Poage	OE	6'4"	200	24		30
Sam Baker	K	6'2"	218	33		65

CLEVELAND BROWNS

Rushing

Last Name	No.	Yds	Avg	TD
Jimmy Brown	289	1544	5.3	17
Green	111	436	3.9	2
Kelly	37	139	3.8	0
Ryan	19	72	3.8	0
Scales	11	59	5.4	0
Ninowski	4	46	11.5	0
Roberts	3	30	10.0	0
Collins	1	16	16.0	0
Franklin	1	−11	−11.0	0

Receiving

Last Name	No.	Yds	Avg	TD
Collins	50	884	18	10
Jimmy Brown	34	328	10	4
Green	25	298	12	2
Roberts	16	314	20	4
Brewer	13	174	13	1
Kelly	9	122	14	0
Hutchinson	6	113	19	2
McNeil	3	69	23	0
Warfield	3	30	10	0
Scales	1	7	7	0

Punt Returns

Last Name	No.	Yds	Avg	TD
Kelly	17	265	16	2
Roberts	18	162	9	0
Scales	1	0	0	0

Kickoff Returns

Last Name	No.	Yds	Avg	TD
Kelly	24	621	26	0
Roberts	18	493	27	0
Scales	4	88	22	0
Green	1	4	4	0
Howell	2	3	2	0
Hutchinson	2	0	0	0
Franklin	1	0	0	0
Lindsey	1	0	0	0

Passing – Punting – Kicking

PASSING	Att	Comp	%	Yds	Yd/Att	TD	Int–%	RK
Ryan	243	119	49	1751	7.2	18	13– 5	12
Ninowski	83	40	48	549	6.6	4	3– 4	
Jimmy Brown	2	1	50	39	19.5	1	0– 0	
Groza	1	0	0	0	0.0	0	0– 0	

PUNTING	No	Avg
Collins	65	46.7
Franklin	4	29.5

KICKING	XP	Att	%	FG	Att	%
Groza	45	45	100	16	25	64

DALLAS COWBOYS

Rushing

Last Name	No.	Yds	Avg	TD
Perkins	177	690	3.9	0
Smith	86	295	3.4	2
Meredith	35	247	7.1	1
Dunn	54	171	3.2	2
Reeves	33	102	3.1	2
Clarke	8	58	7.3	0
Rhome	4	11	2.8	0
Whitfield	1	0	0.0	0
Hayes	4	−8	−2.0	1
Morton	3	−8	−2.7	0

Receiving

Last Name	No.	Yds	Avg	TD
Hayes	46	1003	22	12
Clarke	41	682	17	4
Dial	17	283	17	1
Gent	16	233	15	2
Perkins	14	142	10	0
Norman	11	110	10	3
Reeves	9	210	23	1
Dunn	8	74	9	1
Smith	5	10	2	1

Punt Returns

Last Name	No.	Yds	Avg	TD
Hayes	12	153	13	0
Renfro	24	145	6	0

Kickoff Returns

Last Name	No.	Yds	Avg	TD
Renfro	21	630	30	1
Hayes	17	450	26	0
Reeves	2	45	23	0
Neely	2	13	7	0

Passing – Punting – Kicking

PASSING	Att	Comp	%	Yds	Yd/Att	TD	Int–%	RK
Meredith	305	141	46	2415	7.9	22	13– 4	8
Morton	34	17	50	173	5.1	2	4– 12	
Rhome	21	9	43	157	7.5	1	1– 5	
Reeves	2	1	50	11	5.5	0	0– 0	

PUNTING	No	Avg
Villanueva	60	41.8
Ridgway	13	39.2

KICKING	XP	Att	%	FG	Att	%
Villanueva	37	38	97	16	27	59

NEW YORK GIANTS

Rushing

Last Name	No.	Yds	Avg	TD
Frederickson	195	659	3.4	5
Thurlow	106	440	4.2	4
Koy	35	174	5.0	0
Wheelwright	24	96	4.0	0
Reed	19	70	3.7	0
Wood	5	68	13.6	0
Mercein	18	55	3.1	2
Morrall	17	52	3.1	0
Morrison	3	20	6.7	1
Jones	1	17	17.0	0

Receiving

Last Name	No.	Yds	Avg	TD
Morrison	41	574	14	4
Thomas	27	631	23	5
Jones	26	709	27	6
Frederickson	24	177	7	1
Shofner	22	388	18	2
Thurlow	9	54	6	1
Crespino	7	57	8	4
Reed	6	42	7	0
Koy	4	22	6	0
Mercein	3	14	5	0
Wheelwright	2	17	9	0

Punt Returns

Last Name	No.	Yds	Avg	TD
Williams	18	28	2	0
Carr	4	13	3	0
Lockhart	2	−6	−3	0

Kickoff Returns

Last Name	No.	Yds	Avg	TD
Childs	29	718	25	0
Koy	21	401	19	0
Williams	5	113	23	0
Webb	2	48	24	0
Thurlow	1	19	19	0
Mercein	1	4	4	0
Brown	1	0	0	0

Passing – Punting – Kicking

PASSING	Att	Comp	%	Yds	Yd/Att	TD	Int–%	RK
Morrall	302	155	51	2446	8.1	22	12– 4	5
Wood	36	15	42	190	5.3	1	2– 6	
Koy	2	0	0	0	0.0	0	1– 50	
Frederickson	1	0	0	0	0.0	0	1–100	
Thurlow	1	1	100	49	49.0	0	0– 0	

PUNTING	No	Avg
Koy	56	41.2
Lockhart	6	44.5

KICKING	XP	Att	%	FG	Att	%
Timberlake	21	22	95	1	15	7
Stynchula	12	13	92	3	7	43
Wood	1	1	100	0	0	0
Hillebrand	0	0	0	0	1	0
Mercein	0	0	0	0	2	0

WASHINGTON REDSKINS

Rushing

Last Name	No.	Yds	Avg	TD
Taylor	145	402	2.8	3
Lewis	117	343	2.9	2
Hughley	37	175	4.7	0
Atkins	18	44	2.4	0
Shiner	12	35	2.9	0
Jurgensen	17	23	1.4	2
Briggs	6	10	1.7	0
Casares	2	5	2.5	0

Receiving

Last Name	No.	Yds	Avg	TD
Mitchell	60	867	14	6
Taylor	40	577	14	3
Lewis	25	276	11	2
Carpenter	23	298	13	0
Smith	19	257	14	2
Coia	18	240	13	3
Richter	16	189	12	2
Hughley	9	93	10	1
Briggs	3	40	13	0
Jencks	2	20	10	0
Krause	2	17	9	0
Hunter	1	29	29	1
Casares	1	5	5	0
Atkins	1	0	0	0

Punt Returns

Last Name	No.	Yds	Avg	TD
Harris	31	377	12	1
Mitchell	1	15	15	0
Hughley	2	12	6	0
Atkins	3	11	4	0
Mazurek	1	0	0	0
Pellegrini	1	0	0	0

Kickoff Returns

Last Name	No.	Yds	Avg	TD
Hunter	18	432	24	0
Hughley	13	295	23	0
Mitchell	5	106	21	0
Harris	5	96	19	0
Walters	2	30	15	0
Atkins	1	15	15	0
Taylor	1	15	15	0
Kammerer	1	14	14	0
Briggs	2	8	4	0
Hanburger	1	0	0	0

Passing – Punting – Kicking

PASSING	Att	Comp	%	Yds	Yd/Att	TD	Int–%	RK
Jurgensen	356	190	53	2367	6.7	15	16– 5	10
Shiner	65	28	43	470	7.2	3	4– 6	
Taylor	4	1	25	45	11.3	1	0– 0	
Lewis	2	1	50	26	13.0	1	0– 0	

PUNTING	No	Avg
Richter	54	43.8
Snidow	9	37.3
Seedburg	7	35.3

KICKING	XP	Att	%	FG	Att	%
Jencks	29	33	88	10	22	46

PHILADELPHIA EAGLES

Rushing

Last Name	No.	Yds	Avg	TD
T. Brown	158	861	5.4	6
Gros	145	479	3.3	7
Woodeshick	28	145	5.2	0
Concannon	9	104	11.6	0
Matson	22	103	4.7	2
Snead	24	81	3.4	3
Lang	10	25	2.5	1
K. Hill	7	20	2.9	2
Scarpati	1	6	6.0	0

Receiving

Last Name	No.	Yds	Avg	TD
Retzlaff	66	1190	18	10
T. Brown	50	682	14	3
Poage	31	612	20	5
Gros	29	271	9	2
Goodwin	18	252	14	1
Glass	15	201	13	1
Woodeshick	6	86	14	0
Crabb	2	41	21	0
Lang	2	30	15	0
Matson	2	29	15	1
Gill	1	27	27	0
F. Hill	1	21	21	0

Punt Returns

Last Name	No.	Yds	Avg	TD
Cross	14	79	6	0
Shann	1	63	63	1
Gill	2	28	14	0
T. Brown	4	13	3	0

Kickoff Returns

Last Name	No.	Yds	Avg	TD
Nelson	26	683	26	0
Cross	25	662	26	0
T. Brown	3	46	15	0
Lang	3	36	12	0
Wells	1	8	8	0
Morgan	1	3	3	0
Gill	1	0	0	0

Passing – Punting – Kicking

PASSING	Att	Comp	%	Yds	Yd/Att	TD	Int–%	RK
Snead	288	150	52	2346	8.2	15	13– 5	7
K. Hill	113	60	53	857	7.6	5	10– 9	
Concannon	29	12	41	176	6.1	1	3– 10	
Gros	2	1	50	63	31.5	1	0– 0	
T. Brown	1	0	0	0	0.0	0	0– 0	
Poage	1	0	0	0	0.0	0	0– 0	

PUNTING	No	Avg
Baker	37	41.9
K. Hill	19	42.8

KICKING	XP	Att	%	FG	Att	%
Baker	38	40	95	9	23	39
Lloyd	7	7	100	1	2	50

Scores of Each Game			Use Name	Pos.	Hgt	Wgt	Age	Int	Pts	Use Name	Pos.	Hgt	Wgt	Age	Int	Pts	Use Name	Pos.	Hgt	Wgt	Age	Int	Pts

EASTERN CONFERENCE – Continued

ST. LOUIS CARDINALS 5-9-0 Wally Lemm

27	Philadelphia	34	Ernie McMillan	OT	6'6"	260	27			Bill Koman	LB	6'2"	230	31	1		Buddy Humphrey	QB	6'1"	200	29		
49	Cleveland	13	Bob Reynolds	OT	6'6"	265	24			Dave Meggyesy	LB	6'1"	220	23			Charley Johnson	QB	6'	190	28		6
20	DALLAS	13	Ed Cook	OG-OT	6'2"	250	33			Dale Meinert	LB	6'1"	220	32			Terry Nofsinger	QB	6'4"	215	27		6
37	Washington	16	Irv Goode	OG	6'4"	250	24			Marion Rushing	LB	6'2"	230	28			Prentice Gautt	HB	6'	210	27		12
20	Pittsburgh	7	Ken Gray	OG	6'2"	250	29			Dave Simmons	LB	6'4"	245	22			Bill Triplett	HB	6'2"	210	26		42
20	WASHINGTON	24	Rick Sortun	OG	6'2"	235	22			Larry Stallings	LB	6'2"	230	23		6	Joe Childress	FB	6'	210	31		
10	New York	14	Herschel Turner	OT-OG	6'3"	230	23			Monk Bailey	DB	6'	180	27			Willie Crenshaw	FB	6'2"	230	24		6
21	PITTSBURGH	17	Mike Alford	C	6'3"	230	22			Jimmy Burson	DB	6'	180	23	5		Bill Thornton	FB	6'1"	215	25		
13	Chicago	34	Bob DeMarco	C	6'3"	240	27			Pat Fischer	DB	5'10"	170	25	3		Bobby Joe Conrad	FL	6'	195	30		30
15	NEW YORK	28	Don Brumm	DE	6'3"	245	22		6	Carl Silvestri	DB	6'	195	22			Mal Hammack	TE	6'2"	210	32		
24	PHILADELPHIA	28	Mike Melinkovich	DE	6'4"	240	23			Jerry Stovall	DB	6'2"	205	23	2		Chuck Logan	TE	6'4"	210	22		
3	LOS ANGELES	27	Tom Redmond	DE	6'5"	250	28			Larry Wilson	DB	6'	190	27	6	6	Jackie Smith	TE	6'4"	215	24		12
13	Dallas	27	Joe Robb	DE	6'3"	245	28			Abe Woodson	DB	5'11"	190	30			Billy Gambrell	OE	5'10"	175	23		12
24	CLEVELAND	27	Ed McQuarters	DT	6'1"	250	22										Ray Ogden	OE	6'5"	225	22		
			Luke Owens	DT	6'2"	255	32										Sonny Randle	OE	6'2"	190	29		54
			Sam Silas	DT	6'4"	250	22										Jim Bakken	K	6'	200	24		96
			Chuck Walker	DT	6'2"	245	24																

PITTSBURGH STEELERS 2-12-0 Mike Nixon

9	GREEN BAY	41	Charlie Bradshaw	OT	6'6"	260	29			Rod Breedlove	LB	6'2"	227	27			Ed Brown (to BAL)	QB	6'2"	220	36		
17	San Francisco	27	Dan James	OT	6'4"	250	28			Gene Breen	LB	6'2"	230	24			Bill Nelsen	QB	6'	195	24		6
13	NEW YORK	23	Bob Nichols	OT	6'3"	250	22			John Campbell	LB	6'3"	225	26		6	Tom Wade	QB	6'2"	195	23		
19	Cleveland	24	Ray Lemek	OG	6'	240	31			Max Messner	LB	6'3"	225	27	1		Cannonball Butler	HB	5'10"	195	22		6
7	ST. LOUIS	20	Mike Magac	OG	6'3"	240	27			Ed Pine	LB	6'4"	235	25			Dick Hoak	HB	5'11"	190	26		36
20	Philadelphia	14	Mike Sandusky	OG	6'	235	32			Myron Pottios	LB	6'2"	240	25			John Henry Johnson	FB	6'2"	205	35		
22	DALLAS	13	Ed Adamchik (from NY)	C	6'2"	235	23			Bob Schmitz	LB	6'1"	240	27			Mike Lind	FB	6'2"	225	25		12
17	St. Louis	21	Ken Henson	C	6'6"	260	22			Jim Bradshaw	DB	6'1"	205	26	5	6	Clarence Peaks	FB	6'1"	215	29		
17	Dallas	24	Art Hunter	C	6'4"	247	32			Willie Daniel	DB	5'11"	185	27	1	6	Theron Sapp	FB	6'1"	210	30		
3	WASHINGTON	31	John Baker	DE	6'6"	270	30			Bob Hohn	DB	6'	190	24			Red Mack	FL	5'10"	185	28		
21	CLEVELAND	42	Ben McGee	DE	6'2"	225	23			Brady Keys	DB	6'	198	29	1		Paul Martha	HB-FL	6'	185	22		
10	New York	35	Fran Mallick	DT-DE	6'3"	245	24			Bob Sherman	DB	6'2"	195	23	1		Gary Ballman	OE-FL	6'	200	25		48
13	PHILADELPHIA	47	Riley Gunnels	DT	6'3"	253	28			Marv Woodson	DB	6'	195	22	3	6	John Hilton	TE	6'5"	220	23		
14	Washington	35	Chuck Hinton	DT	6'5"	260	26										John Powers	LB-TE	6'2"	210	24		
			Ken Kortas	DT	6'2"	280	23			Andy Russell – Military Service							Duane Allen (to BAL)	OE	6'4"	225	27		
			Ray Mansfield	DT	6'3"	250	24										Lee Folkins	TE	6'5"	215	26		6
																	Roy Jefferson	OE	6'2"	195	21		6
																	Jerry Simmons	OE	6'1"	190	22		
																	Clendon Thomas	DB-OE	6'2"	205	28		6
																	Mike Clark	K	6'1"	205	24		52
																	Frank Lambert	K	6'3"	200	22		

WESTERN CONFERENCE

GREEN BAY PACKERS 10-3-1 Vince Lombardi

41	Pittsburgh	9	Steve Wright	OT	6'6"	250	23			Lee Roy Caffey	LB	6'3"	250	25	1	6	Zeke Bratkowski	QB	6'2"	200	33		
20	BALTIMORE	17	Bob Skoronski	OT	6'3"	250	32			Tommy Crutcher	LB	6'3"	230	23	1		Dennis Claridge	QB	6'3"	225	23		
23	CHICAGO	14	Forrest Gregg	OG-OT	6'4"	250	32			Ray Nitschke	LB	6'3"	240	29	1		Bart Starr	QB	6'1"	200	32		6
27	SAN FRANCISCO	10	Dan Grimm	OG	6'3"	245	24			Dave Robinson	LB	6'3"	245	24	3		Junior Coffey	HB	6'1"	210	23		
31	Detroit	21	Jerry Kramer	OG	6'3"	245	30			Herb Adderley	DB	6'1"	210	26	6	18	Paul Hornung	HB	6'2"	215	28		48
13	DALLAS	3	Fuzzy Thurston	OG	6'1"	245	32			Tom Brown	DB	6'1"	190	24	3		Allen Jacobs	FB	6'1"	215	24		
10	Chicago	31	Ken Bowman	C	6'3"	230	22			Hank Gremminger	DB	6'1"	200	32			Tom Moore	HB	6'2"	210	27		6
7	DETROIT	12	Bill Curry	C	6'2"	235	22			Doug Hart	DB	6'	190	26	4	6	Elijah Pitts	HB	6'1"	205	26		30
6	LOS ANGELES	3	Lionel Aldridge	DE	6'4"	245	24			Bob Jeter	DB	6'1"	205	27	1		Jim Taylor	FB	6'	215	30		24
38	Minnesota	13	Willie Davis	DE	6'3"	245	32	1		Willie Wood	DB	5'10"	190	29	6		Carroll Dale	FL	6'1"	200	27		12
10	Los Angeles	21	Lloyd Voss	DE	6'4"	260	23										Bob Long	FL	6'3"	190	24		24
24	MINNESOTA	19	Henry Jordan	DT	6'3"	250	30										Bill Anderson	TE	6'3"	215	29		6
42	Baltimore	27	Ron Kostelnik	DT	6'4"	260	25										Marv Fleming	TE	6'4"	235	23		12
24	San Francisco	24	Bud Marshall	DT	6'5"	270	23										Boyd Dowler	OE	6'5"	225	28		24
	Playoff																Max McGee	OE	6'3"	205	33		6
13	BALTIMORE	10															Don Chandler	K	6'2"	210	30		88

BALTIMORE COLTS 10-3-1 Don Shula

35	MINNESOTA	16	Tom Gilburg	OT	6'5"	245	26			Jackie Burkett	LB	6'4"	228	28			Gary Cuozzo	QB	6'1"	195	24		
17	Green Bay	20	George Preas	OT	6'2"	250	33			Ted Davis	LB	6'1"	225	23			Johnny Unitas	QB	6'1"	194	32		6
27	SAN FRANCISCO	24	Bob Vogel	OT	6'5"	250	23			Dennis Gaubatz	LB	6'2"	220	24	1		Lenny Moore	HB	6'1"	190	32		48
31	DETROIT	7	Jim Parker	OG	6'3"	275	31			Monte Lee	LB	6'4"	220	27			Tom Matte	QB-HB	6'	205	26		6
38	Washington	7	Alex Sandusky	OG	6'1"	242	33			Don Shinnick	LB	6'	235	30	1		Jerry Hill	FB	5'11"	210	25		30
35	LOS ANGELES	20	Dan Sullivan	OG	6'3"	250	26			Steve Stonebreaker	LB	6'3"	222	27	1		Tony Lorick	FB	6'1"	215	23		18
34	San Francisco	28	Buzz Nutter	C	6'4"	240	34			Mike Curtis	FB-LB	6'2"	225	22			Jimmy Orr	FL	5'11"	175	29		60
26	Chicago	21	Dick Szymanski	C	6'3"	235	33			Bobby Boyd	DB	5'10"	190	27	9	6	Willie Richardson	FL	6'2"	198	25		6
41	Minnesota	21	Ordell Braase	DE	6'4"	242	33			Wendell Harris	DB	5'11"	185	24	3		John Mackey	TE	6'3"	217	23		42
34	PHILADELPHIA	24	Roy Hilton	DE	6'6"	225	20			Alvin Haymond	DB	6'	190	23	3	6	Butch Wilson	TE	6'2"	218	23		
24	Detroit	24	Lou Michaels	DE	6'2"	240	29		101	Jerry Logan	DB	6'1"	185	24	2	12	Ray Berry	OE	6'2"	187	32		42
0	CHICAGO	13	Fred Miller	DT	6'3"	245	24			Lenny Lyles	DB	6'2"	202	29	1		Alex Hawkins	FL-OE	6'1"	186	28		6
27	GREEN BAY	42	Guy Reese	DT	6'5"	260	25			Jim Welch	DB	6'	190	27			Neal Petties	FL-OE	6'2"	198	24		
20	Los Angeles	17	Billy Ray Smith	DT	6'4"	240	30	1															
			Glenn Ressler	C-DT	6'3"	235	21			Lou Kirouac – Injury							Gino Marchetti – Voluntarily Retired						
	Playoff																						
10	Green Bay	13																					

CHICAGO BEARS 9-5-0 George Halas

24	San Francisco	52	Herm Lee	OT	6'4"	247	34			Dick Butkus	LB	6'3"	240	21	5		Rudy Bukich	QB	6'1"	205	34		18
28	Los Angeles	30	Dick Leeuwenberg	OT	6'5"	242	21			Joe Fortunato	LB	6'	225	35	2		Billy Wade	QB	6'2"	205	34		
14	Green Bay	23	Bob Wetoska	OT	6'3"	240	27			Bill George	LB	6'2"	235	34			Jon Arnett	HB	5'11"	203	30		30
31	LOS ANGELES	6	Jim Cadile	OG	6'3"	240	24			Roger LeClerc	LB	6'3"	235	27		85	Charlie Bivins	HB	6'2"	212	26		12
45	Minnesota	37	Mike Rabold	OG	6'2"	238	28			Larry Morris	LB	6'2"	230	30			Ronnie Bull	HB	6'	200	25		24
38	DETROIT	10	George Seals	DT-OG	6'2"	260	22			Jim Purnell	LB	6'2"	205	23			Gale Sayers	HB	6'	198	22		132
31	GREEN BAY	10	Mike Pyle	C	6'3"	250	26			Mike Reilly	LB	6'2"	238	22			Ralph Kurek	FB	6'2"	210	22		
21	BALTIMORE	26	Doug Atkins	DE	6'8"	255	35	1		J. C. Caroline	DB	6'1"	190	32			Andy Livingston	FB	6'	234	20		12
34	ST. LOUIS	13	Dick Evey	DE	6'2"	225	24	1		Larry Glueck	DB	6'	190	23			Joe Marconi	FB	6'2"	225	31		
17	Detroit	10	Bob Kilcullen	DE	6'3"	245	29			Bennie McRae	DB	6'1"	180	24	4	6	Johnny Morris	FL	5'10"	180	30		24
35	New York	14	Ed O'Bradovich	DE	6'3"	255	25			Richie Petitbon	DB	6'3"	205	27	2		Mike Ditka	TE	6'3"	230	25		12
13	Baltimore	0	John Johnson	DT	6'5"	260	24			Ron Smith	DB	6'1"	185	22			Billy Martin	TE	6'4"	240	22		
61	SAN FRANCISCO	20	Stan Jones	DT	6'1"	250	34			Rosey Taylor	DB	5'11"	186	26	1	6	Dick Gordon	OE	5'11"	190	20		18
17	MINNESOTA	24	Earl Leggett	DT	6'3"	265	31			Dave Whitsell	DB	6'	190	29	4	6	Jim Jones	OE	6'2"	187	21		24
			Dennis Murphy	DT	6'1"	250	21										Bobby Joe Green	K	5'11"	175	27		
										Riley Mattson – Injury													
										Palmer Pyle – Injury													

EASTERN CONFERENCE – Continued

ST. LOUIS CARDINALS

RUSHING

Last Name	No.	Yds	Avg	TD
Triplett	174	617	3.5	6
Crenshaw	127	437	3.4	0
Thornton	31	188	6.1	0
Gautt	44	175	4.0	2
Childress	19	94	4.9	0
Johnson	25	60	2.4	1
Bakken	1	28	28.0	0
Gambrell	4	15	3.8	0
Humphrey	2	4	2.0	0
Nofsinger	4	1	0.3	1

RECEIVING

Last Name	No.	Yds	Avg	TD
Conrad	58	909	16	5
Randle	51	845	17	9
Smith	41	648	16	2
Triplett	26	256	10	1
Crenshaw	23	232	10	1
Gambrell	9	171	19	2
Gautt	9	128	14	0
Childress	3	27	9	0
Thornton	1	6	6	0

PUNT RETURNS

Last Name	No.	Yds	Avg	TD
Silvestri	3	21	7	0
Woodson	18	7	0	0
Burson	1	0	0	0
Gambrell	1	–1	–1	0

KICKOFF RETURNS

Last Name	No.	Yds	Avg	TD
Woodson	27	665	25	0
Gambrell	9	216	24	0
Stovall	7	198	28	0
Silvestri	4	96	24	0
Ogden	2	55	28	0
Hammack	3	34	11	0
Crenshaw	2	23	12	0
Koman	1	0	0	0

PASSING – PUNTING – KICKING

PASSING	Att	Comp	%	Yds	Yd/Att	TD	Int–%	RK
Johnson	322	155	48	2439	7.6	18	15– 5	11
Humphrey	105	58	55	736	7.0	1	9– 9	
Nofsinger	20	8	40	47	2.4	1	1– 5	
Gautt	1	0	0	0	0.0	0	0– 0	

PUNTING	No	Avg
Smith	39	39.3
Bakken	26	42.2
Stovall	2	40.0

KICKING	XP	Att	%	FG	Att	%
Bakken	33	33	100	21	31	**68**

PITTSBURGH STEELERS

RUSHING

Last Name	No.	Yds	Avg	TD
Hoak	131	426	3.3	5
Lind	111	375	3.4	1
Peaks	47	230	4.9	0
Butler	46	108	2.3	0
Nelsen	26	84	3.2	1
Sapp	14	54	3.9	0
Ballman	17	46	2.7	3
Wade	8	43	5.4	0
Johnson	3	11	3.7	0
Martha	2	3	1.5	0
Jefferson	1	–1	–1.0	0
Brown	2	–3	–1.5	0

RECEIVING

Last Name	No.	Yds	Avg	TD
Ballman	40	859	21	5
Thomas	25	431	17	1
Lind	25	236	9	1
Hoak	19	228	12	1
Jefferson	13	287	22	1
Martha	11	171	16	0
Butler	9	117	13	1
Folkins	5	58	12	0
Hilton	4	32	8	0
Mack	3	41	14	0
Peaks	3	22	7	0
Simmons	2	16	8	0
Sapp	1	10	10	0
Nelsen	1	–5	–5	0

PUNT RETURNS

Last Name	No.	Yds	Avg	TD
Jefferson	13	100	8	0
Keys	10	77	8	0
J. Bradshaw	5	73	15	0
Thomas	5	9	2	0

KICKOFF RETURNS

Last Name	No.	Yds	Avg	TD
Butler	25	509	20	0
Peaks	20	429	21	0
Ballman	8	150	19	0
Sapp	5	77	15	0
Woodson	2	45	23	0
Simmons	1	28	28	0

PASSING – PUNTING – KICKING

PASSING	Att	Comp	%	Yds	Yd/Att	TD	Int–%	RK
Nelsen	270	121	45	1917	7.1	8	17– 6	15
Wade	66	33	50	463	7.0	2	13– 20	
Brown	23	10	44	204	8.9	1	5– 22	

PUNTING	No	Avg
Lambert	78	45.1
Brown	2	40.0

KICKING	XP	Att	%	FG	Att	%
Clark	19	24	79	11	19	58

WESTERN CONFERENCE

GREEN BAY PACKERS

RUSHING

Last Name	No.	Yds	Avg	TD
Taylor	207	734	3.5	4
Hornung	89	299	3.4	5
Starr	18	169	9.4	1
Moore	51	124	2.4	0
Pitts	54	122	2.3	4
Chandler	1	27	27.0	0
Coffey	3	12	4.0	0
Jacobs	3	5	1.7	0
Bratkowski	4	–1	–0.3	0
Claridge	2	–3	–1.5	0

RECEIVING

Last Name	No.	Yds	Avg	TD
Dowler	44	610	14	4
Dale	20	382	19	2
Taylor	20	207	10	0
Hornung	19	336	18	3
Fleming	14	141	10	2
Long	13	304	23	4
Pitts	11	182	17	1
McGee	10	154	15	1
Anderson	8	105	13	1
Moore	7	87	12	1

PUNT RETURNS

Last Name	No.	Yds	Avg	TD
Wood	13	38	3	0
Pitts	8	27	3	0
Adderley	1	0	0	0

KICKOFF RETURNS

Last Name	No.	Yds	Avg	TD
Pitts	20	396	20	0
Moore	15	361	24	0
Adderley	10	221	22	0
Crutcher	3	53	18	0
Coffey	1	9	9	0
Grimm	1	0	0	0

PASSING – PUNTING – KICKING

PASSING	Att	Comp	%	Yds	Yd/Att	TD	Int–%	RK
Starr	251	140	56	2055	8.2	16	9– 4	4
Bratkowski	48	21	44	348	7.3	3	4– 8	
Moore	2	2	100	22	11.0	0	0– 0	
Hornung	2	1	50	19	9.5	0	1– 50	
Pitts	2	1	50	51	25.5	0	0– 0	
Claridge	1	1	100	13	13.0	0	0– 0	

PUNTING	No	Avg
Chandler	74	42.9

KICKING	XP	Att	%	FG	Att	%
Chandler	37	38	97	17	26	65

BALTIMORE COLTS

RUSHING

Last Name	No.	Yds	Avg	TD
Hill	147	516	3.5	5
Moore	133	464	3.5	5
Lorick	63	296	4.7	1
Matte	69	235	3.4	1
Unitas	17	68	4.0	1
Cuozzo	6	8	1.3	0
Mackey	1	7	7.0	0
Curtis	6	1	0.2	0

RECEIVING

Last Name	No.	Yds	Avg	TD
Berry	58	739	13	7
Orr	45	847	19	10
Mackey	40	814	20	7
Moore	27	414	15	3
Hill	20	112	6	0
Lorick	15	184	12	2
Matte	12	131	11	0
Hawkins	2	32	16	1
Wilson	1	38	38	0
Richardson	1	14	14	1
Curtis	1	5	5	0

PUNT RETURNS

Last Name	No.	Yds	Avg	TD
Haymond	**41**	**403**	10	0
Hawkins	4	18	5	0

KICKOFF RETURNS

Last Name	No.	Yds	Avg	TD
Haymond	20	614	31	0
Lorick	9	211	23	0
Matte	8	211	26	0
Curtis	2	10	5	0
Hill	1	3	3	0
Hawkins	2	0	0	0

PASSING – PUNTING – KICKING

PASSING	Att	Comp	%	Yds	Yd/Att	TD	Int–%	RK
Unitas	282	164	58	2530	**9.0**	23	12– 4	2
Cuozzo	105	54	51	700	6.7	7	4– 4	
Matte	7	1	14	19	2.7	0	1– 14	

PUNTING	No	Avg
Gilburg	54	39.6

KICKING	XP	Att	%	FG	Att	%
Michaels	48	48	100	17	28	61

CHICAGO BEARS

RUSHING

Last Name	No.	Yds	Avg	TD
Sayers	166	867	5.2	14
Bull	91	417	4.6	3
Livingston	63	363	5.8	2
Arnett	102	363	3.6	5
Marconi	19	47	2.5	0
Bukich	28	33	1.2	3
Wade	5	18	3.6	0
J. Jones	2	13	6.5	0
Gordon	2	10	5.0	0
Kurek	1	0	0.0	0

RECEIVING

Last Name	No.	Yds	Avg	TD
J. Morris	53	846	16	4
Ditka	36	454	13	2
Sayers	29	507	17	6
J. Jones	21	350	17	4
Bull	16	186	12	1
Gordon	13	279	21	3
Livingston	12	134	11	0
Arnett	12	114	10	0
Bivins	4	108	27	2
Marconi	4	43	11	0
Martin	1	–1	–1	0

PUNT RETURNS

Last Name	No.	Yds	Avg	TD
Sayers	16	238	15	1
Arnett	11	52	5	0
Smith	1	2	2	0
Gordon	1	–3	–3	0

KICKOFF RETURNS

Last Name	No.	Yds	Avg	TD
Sayers	21	660	31	1
Gordon	14	242	17	0
Arnett	5	150	30	0
Livingston	2	66	33	0
Smith	1	17	17	0
Kurek	1	11	11	0
LeClerc	1	0	0	0

PASSING – PUNTING – KICKING

PASSING	Att	Comp	%	Yds	Yd/Att	TD	Int–%	RK
Bukich	312	176	56	2641	8.5	20	9– 3	1
Wade	41	20	49	204	5.0	0	2– 5	
Bull	3	2	67	63	21.0	0	0– 0	
Sayers	3	2	67	53	17.7	1	1– 33	
Arnett	2	1	50	59	29.5	1	0– 0	

PUNTING	No	Avg
Green	58	42.7

KICKING	XP	Att	%	FG	Att	%
LeClerc	**52**	**52**	**100**	11	26	42

WESTERN CONFERENCE – Continued

SAN FRANCISCO FORTY NINERS 7-6-1 Jack Christiansen

Scores of Each Game		
52	CHICAGO	24
27	PITTSBURGH	17
24	Baltimore	27
10	Green Bay	27
45	Los Angeles	21
41	MINNESOTA	42
28	BALTIMORE	34
31	Dallas	39
27	Detroit	21
30	LOS ANGELES	27
45	Minnesota	24
17	DETROIT	14
20	Chicago	61
24	GREEN BAY	24

Use Name	Pos.	Hgt	Wgt	Age	Int	Pts
Jim Norton	OT	6'4"	255	22		
Walt Rock	OT	6'5"	245	24		
Len Rohde	OT	6'4"	245	27		
Howard Mudd	OG	6'3"	240	23		
John Thomas	OG	6'4"	246	30		
Jim Wilson	OG	6'3"	255	24		
Bruce Bosley	C	6'2"	240	31		
Joe Cerne	C	6'2"	235	22		
Dan Colchico	DE	6'4"	245	28		
Dan LaRose	DE	6'5"	250	25		
Clark Miller	DE	6'5"	245	26		6
Karl Rubke	DE	6'4"	240	29		
Charlie Krueger	DT	6'4"	254	29		6
Roland Lakes	DT	6'4"	263	25		
Chuck Sieminski	DT	6'4"	265	25		
Ed Beard	LB	6'2"	245	25		
Jack Chapple	LB	6'2"	227	22		6
Floyd Dean	LB	6'4"	245	25		
Mike Dowdle	LB	6'3"	235	27		
Bob Harrison	LB	6'2"	225	28		
Matt Hazeltine	LB	6'1"	230	32	1	
Dave Wilcox	LB	6'3"	230	22	1	6
Kermit Alexander	DB	5'11"	186	24	3	
George Donnelly	DB	6'3"	205	22		
Jim Johnson	DB	6'2"	190	27	6	
Elbert Kimbrough	DB	5'11"	190	26	2	
Jerry Mertens	DB	6'	185	29		
Wayne Swinford	DB	6'	190	22		
John Brodie	QB	6'1"	200	30		6
George Mira	QB	5'11"	190	23		
John David Crow	HB	6'2"	215	30		54
Rudy Johnson	HB	5'11"	190	23		
Dave Kopay	HB	6'2"	217	23		24
Gary Lewis	FB	6'3"	230	23		18
Ken Willard	FB	6'2"	230	22		54
Bernie Casey	FL	6'4"	215	26		48
Dale Messer	FL	5'10"	175	28		
Bob Poole	TE	6'4"	216	23		
Monte Stickles	TE	6'4"	230	27		6
Vern Burke	OE	6'4"	200	24		6
Kay McFarland	OE	6'2"	180	26		6
Dave Parks	OE	6'2"	195	23		72
Tommy Davis	K	6'	212	30		103

MINNESOTA VIKINGS 7-7-0 Norm Van Brocklin

Scores of Each Game		
16	Baltimore	35
29	DETROIT	31
38	Los Angeles	35
40	NEW YORK	14
37	CHICAGO	45
42	San Francisco	41
27	Cleveland	17
24	LOS ANGELES	13
21	BALTIMORE	41
13	GREEN BAY	38
24	SAN FRANCISCO	45
19	Green Bay	24
29	Detroit	7
24	Chicago	17

Use Name	Pos.	Hgt	Wgt	Age	Int	Pts
Grady Alderman	OT	6'2"	240	26		
Errol Linden	OT	6'5"	260	28		
Archie Sutton	OT	6'4"	262	22		
Larry Bowie	OG	6'2"	250	25		
Ken Byers	OG	6'1"	240	25		
Milt Sunde	C-OG	6'2"	234	22		
Mick Tingelhoff	C	6'1"	237	25		
Carl Eller	DE	6'6"	255	23		2
Jim Marshall	DE	6'3"	235	27		
Paul Dickson	DT	6'5"	255	28		
Gary Larsen	DT	6'5"	250	25		
Jim Prestel	DT	6'5"	275	28		2
Rip Hawkins	LB	6'3"	235	26	3	6
Bill Jobko	LB	6'2"	235	29		
John Kirby	LB	6'3"	222	23		
Lonnie Warwick	LB	6'3"	225	23		6
Roy Winston	LB	6'1"	230	25		
Lee Calland	DB	6'	190	24		
Gary Hill	DB	6'	200	21		
Jeff Jordan	DB	6'4"	190	21	4	
Karl Kassulke	DB	6'	193	23	2	
Earsell Mackbee	DB	6'1"	195	24		
George Rose	DB	5'11"	190	22	1	
Ed Sharockman	DB	6'	200	25	6	6
Larry Vargo	DB	6'3"	215	25	3	
Bob Berry	QB	5'11"	190	23		
Fran Tarkenton	QB	6'1"	190	25		6
Ron Vander Kelen	QB	6'1"	185	25		
Billy Barnes	HB	5'11"	202	30		
Dick James	HB	5'9"	185	31		
Phil King	HB	6'4"	220	29		6
Tommy Mason	HB	6'	196	26		66
Dave Osborn	HB	6'	205	22		12
Jim Young	HB	6'	205	22		
Bill Brown	FB	5'11"	230	27		42
Jim Phillips	FL	6'1"	195	28		6
Lance Rentzel	HB-FL	6'2"	210	21		6
Tom Hall	OE-FL	6'1"	195	24		12
Hal Bedsole	TE	6'4"	230	23		18
Paul Flatley	OE	6'1"	187	24		42
Gordon Smith	OE	6'2"	220	26		30
Fred Cox	K	5'10"	200	26		113
Bobby Walden	K	6'	195	27		

DETROIT LIONS 6-7-1 Harry Gilmer

Scores of Each Game		
20	LOS ANGELES	0
31	Minnesota	29
14	WASHINGTON	10
7	Baltimore	31
21	GREEN BAY	31
10	Chicago	38
31	Los Angeles	7
12	Green Bay	7
21	SAN FRANCISCO	27
10	CHICAGO	17
24	BALTIMORE	24
14	San Francisco	17
7	MINNESOTA	29
35	Philadelphia	28

Use Name	Pos.	Hgt	Wgt	Age	Int	Pts
Daryl Sanders	OT	6'5"	250	23		
Roger Shoals	OT	6'4"	255	26		
John Gonzaga	OG-OT	6'3"	250	32		
John Gordy	OG	6'3"	250	29		
Ted Karras	OG	6'1"	243	32		
Jim Simon	OG	6'5"	235	24		
Ed Flanagan	C	6'3"	250	21		
Bob Whitlow	C	6'1"	236	29		
Larry Hand	DE	6'4"	245	25		
Darris McCord	DE	6'4"	250	32		
Sam Williams	DE	6'5"	235	34		
Roger Brown	DT	6'5"	300	28		2
Alex Karras	DT	6'2"	245	29		
Jerry Rush	DT	6'4"	255	33		
Ernie Clark	LB	6'1"	220	27	1	
Wally Hilgenburg	LB	6'3"	225	22		
Mike Lucci	LB	6'2"	223	25		
Joe Schmidt	LB	6'1"	220	33	4	
Wayne Walker	LB	6'2"	225	28	2	57
Jimmy Hill	DB	6'2"	195	36	1	
Jim Kearney	DB	6'2"	200	22		
Night Train Lane	DB	6'1"	200	37		
Dick LeBeau	DB	6'1"	185	28	7	6
Bruce Maher	DB	5'11"	190	28	4	
Wayne Rasmussen	DB	6'2"	180	23	5	12
Bobby Thompson	DB	5'10"	175	25	2	
Tom Vaughn	DB	5'11"	195	22		
George Izo	QB	6'3"	218	28		
Tom Myers	QB	6'	188	21		
Milt Plum	QB	6'1"	205	31		18
Bobby Felts (from BAL)	HB	6'2"	205	22		
Joe Don Looney	HB	6'1"	230	22		36
Amos Marsh	HB	6'1"	220	26		48
Tom Watkins	HB	6'1"	195	28		
Tom Nowatzke	FB	6'3"	228	22		12
Nick Pietrosante	FB	6'2"	225	28		6
Terry Barr	FL	6'	190	30		18
Pat Studstill	FL	6'1"	175	27		18
Jim Gibbons	TE	6'2"	220	29		12
Ron Kramer	TE	6'3"	240	30		6
Gail Cogdill	OE	6'2"	195	28		
John Henderson	OE	6'3"	190	22		6

J. D. Smith – Injury
Warren Wells – Military Service

LOS ANGELES RAMS 4-10-0 Harland Svare

Scores of Each Game		
0	Detroit	20
30	CHICAGO	28
35	MINNESOTA	38
6	Chicago	31
21	SAN FRANCISCO	45
20	Baltimore	35
7	DETROIT	31
13	Minnesota	24
3	Green Bay	6
27	San Francisco	30
21	GREEN BAY	10
27	St. Louis	3
42	CLEVELAND	7
17	BALTIMORE	20

Use Name	Pos.	Hgt	Wgt	Age	Int	Pts
Joe Carollo	OT	6'2"	263	25		
Charley Cowan	OT	6'4"	275	27		
Roger Pillath	OT	6'4"	255	23		
Frank Varrichione	OT	6'1"	237	33		
Don Chuy	OG	6'1"	256	24		
Joe Scibelli	OG	6'1"	264	26		
Joe Wendryhoski	C-OG	6'2"	245	26		
Ken Iman	C	6'1"	235	26		
Frank Marchlewski	C	6'2"	226	21		
Deacon Jones	DE	6'5"	260	26		2
Lamar Lundy	DE	6'7"	260	30		
Tim Powell	DE	6'4"	248	21		
Rosey Grier	DT	6'5"	290	32		
Frank Molden	DT	6'5"	285	23	1	6
Merlin Olsen	DT	6'5"	276	24		
Fred Brown	LB	6'5"	223	22		
Mack Byrd	LB	6'	215	22		
Dan Currie	LB	6'3"	240	31		
Tony Guillory	LB	6'4"	220	22		
Cliff Livingston	LB	6'3"	212	35	1	
Mike Strofolino (to BAL)	LB	6'2"	240	21		
Doug Woodlief	LB	6'3"	235	21		
Chuck Lamson	DB	6'	190	26	2	
Aaron Martin	DB	6'	185	24	2	6
Dan McIlhany	DB	6'1"	195	22	2	
Jerry Richardson	DB	6'3"	190	22	1	
Bobby Smith (to DET)	DB	6'	197	27		
Ed Meador	DB	5'11"	203	28	2	6
Clancy Williams	HB-DB	6'2"	198	22		
Roman Gabriel	QB	6'4"	225	25		12
Bill Munson	QB	6'2"	197	23		6
Ron Smith	QB	6'5"	220	23		
Terry Baker	HB	6'3"	200	24		18
Les Josephson	HB	6'	210	23		
Willie Brown	FL-HB	6'	185	22		6
Dick Bass	FB	5'10"	198	28		24
Jim Stiger (from DAL)	FB	5'11"	214	24		
Ben Wilson	FB	6'	225	25		6
Tommy McDonald	FL	5'10"	175	31		54
Marlin McKeever	TE	6'1"	227	25		24
Billy Truax	TE	6'5"	240	22		6
Steve Heckard	OE	6'1"	195	22		
Jack Snow	OE	6'2"	210	22		18
Jon Kilgore	K	6'1"	200	21		
Bruce Gossett	K	6'2"	230	22		75
Billy Lothridge	K	6'1"	194	21		

Bucky Pope – Knee Injury
Jack Pardee – Voluntarily Retired

WESTERN CONFERENCE – Continued

SAN FRANCISCO FORTY NINERS

RUSHING

Last Name	No.	Yds	Avg	TD
Willard	189	778	4.1	5
Crow	132	514	3.9	2
Lewis	52	256	4.9	3
Kopay	28	81	2.9	2
Mira	5	64	12.8	0
Brodie	15	60	4.0	1
Davis	1	21	21.0	0
R. Johnson	6	9	1.5	0

RECEIVING

Last Name	No.	Yds	Avg	TD
Parks	**80**	**1344**	17	12
Casey	59	765	13	8
Stickles	35	343	10	1
Willard	32	253	8	4
Crow	28	493	18	7
Kopay	11	147	13	1
Lewis	10	25	3	0
McFarland	8	106	13	1
R. Johnson	3	49	16	0
Messer	2	41	21	0
Burke	2	38	19	1
Poole	2	29	15	0

PUNT RETURNS

Last Name	No.	Yds	Avg	TD
Alexander	35	262	7	0
Swinford	2	18	9	0
Lewis	1	3	3	0

KICKOFF RETURNS

Last Name	No.	Yds	Avg	TD
Alexander	32	741	23	0
Lewis	15	355	24	0
R. Johnson	4	71	18	0
Swinford	4	61	15	0
Messer	1	27	27	0
Kopay	1	21	21	0
Cerne	1	0	0	0
Rubke	1	0	0	0

PASSING – PUNTING – KICKING

PASSING	Att	Comp	%	Yds	Yd/Att	TD	Int–%	RK
Brodie	**391**	**242**	62	**3112**	8.0	**30**	16– 4	3
Mira	58	28	48	460	7.9	4	3– 5	
Crow	4	2	50	61	15.3	1	1– 25	
Willard	1	0	0	0	0.0	0	1–100	

PUNTING	No	Avg
Davis	54	45.8

KICKING	XP	Att	%	FG	Att	%
Davis	52	53	98	17	27	63

MINNESOTA VIKINGS

RUSHING

Last Name	No.	Yds	Avg	TD
Brown	160	699	4.4	6
Mason	141	597	4.2	10
Tarkenton	56	356	6.4	1
King	72	356	4.9	0
Barnes	48	148	3.1	0
Osborn	20	106	5.3	2
Vander Kelen	4	13	3.3	0
Young	3	4	1.3	0
Rentzel	1	–1	–1.0	0

RECEIVING

Last Name	No.	Yds	Avg	TD
Flatley	50	896	18	7
Brown	41	503	12	1
Smith	22	431	20	5
Mason	22	321	15	1
Hall	15	287	19	2
Phillips	15	185	12	1
King	12	96	8	1
Bedsole	8	123	15	3
Barnes	3	15	5	0
Osborn	1	4	4	0

PUNT RETURNS

Last Name	No.	Yds	Avg	TD
Mason	9	63	7	0
Hall	3	21	7	0
Warwick	1	10	10	1
Rentzel	4	9	2	0
Young	4	7	2	0
James	1	5	5	0

KICKOFF RETURNS

Last Name	No.	Yds	Avg	TD
Rentzel	23	602	26	1
Osborn	18	422	23	0
James	11	212	19	0
Hall	4	93	23	0
Young	4	78	20	0
Mason	3	66	22	0
Barnes	3	37	12	0
King	1	14	14	0

PASSING – PUNTING – KICKING

PASSING	Att	Comp	%	Yds	Yd/Att	TD	Int–%	RK
Tarkenton	329	171	52	2609	7.9	19	11– 3	6
Vander Kelen	40	18	45	252	6.3	2	0– 0	
Berry	2	0	0	0	0.0	0	0– 0	
Mason	1	0	0	0	0.0	0	1–100	

PUNTING	No	Avg
Walden	51	42.1

KICKING	XP	Att	%	FG	Att	%
Cox	44	44	100	**23**	**35**	66

DETROIT LIONS

RUSHING

Last Name	No.	Yds	Avg	TD
Marsh	131	495	3.8	6
Pietrosante	107	374	3.5	1
Looney	114	356	3.1	5
Watkins	29	95	3.3	0
Nowatzke	27	73	2.7	1
Felts	22	58	2.6	0
Plum	21	37	1.8	3
Sanders	1	2	2.0	0
Studstill	1	–4	–4.0	0
Izo	1	–5	–5.0	0
Barr	1	–12	–12.0	0

RECEIVING

Last Name	No.	Yds	Avg	TD
Studstill	28	389	14	3
Barr	24	433	18	3
Cogdill	20	247	12	0
Kramer	18	206	11	1
Pietrosante	18	163	9	0
Marsh	17	159	9	2
Gibbons	12	111	9	2
Looney	12	109	9	1
Henderson	8	140	18	1
Watkins	5	53	11	0
Nowatzke	5	45	9	1
Felts	3	28	9	0

PUNT RETURNS

Last Name	No.	Yds	Avg	TD
Watkins	23	234	10	0
Vaughn	2	50	25	0
Studstill	5	47	9	0
Felts	3	27	9	0

KICKOFF RETURNS

Last Name	No.	Yds	Avg	TD
Watkins	17	584	**34**	0
Felts	18	422	23	0
Vaughn	13	316	24	0
Studstill	10	257	26	0
Nowatzke	2	12	6	0
Lucci	1	0	0	0

PASSING – PUNTING – KICKING

PASSING	Att	Comp	%	Yds	Yd/Att	TD	Int–%	RK
Plum	308	143	46	1710	5.6	12	19– 6	14
Izo	59	24	41	357	6.1	2	6– 10	
Myers	5	3	60	16	3.2	0	1– 20	
Felts	1	0	0	0	0.0	0	0– 0	
Marsh	1	0	0	0	0.0	0	0– 0	

PUNTING	No	Avg
Studstill	**78**	42.8

KICKING	XP	Att	%	FG	Att	%
Walker	33	33	100	8	22	36

LOS ANGELES RAMS

RUSHING

Last Name	No.	Yds	Avg	TD
Bass	121	549	4.5	2
Josephson	71	225	3.2	0
Wilson	60	189	3.2	1
Munson	26	157	6.0	1
W. Brown	44	133	3.0	0
Baker	25	82	3.3	1
Gabriel	23	79	3.4	2
Stiger	14	62	4.4	0
Meador	2	35	17.5	1
Williams	3	3	1.0	0

RECEIVING

Last Name	No.	Yds	Avg	TD
McDonald	67	1036	15	9
McKeever	44	542	12	4
Snow	38	559	15	3
Baker	22	210	10	2
Bass	21	230	11	2
Josephson	18	169	9	0
Wilson	9	110	12	0
Truax	6	108	18	1
W. Brown	4	91	23	1
Stiger	1	9	9	0
Heckard	1	4	4	0

PUNT RETURNS

Last Name	No.	Yds	Avg	TD
Stiger	16	120	8	0
W. Brown	9	63	7	0
B. Smith	10	56	6	0
Bass	1	0	0	0

KICKOFF RETURNS

Last Name	No.	Yds	Avg	TD
W. Brown	24	615	26	0
B. Smith	18	475	26	0
Williams	9	213	24	0
Wilson	3	66	22	0
Stiger	2	28	14	0

PASSING – PUNTING – KICKING

PASSING	Att	Comp	%	Yds	Yd/Att	TD	Int–%	RK
Munson	267	144	54	1701	6.4	10	14– 5	13
Gabriel	173	83	48	1321	7.6	11	5– 3	9
Josephson	2	1	50	15	7.5	1	0– 0	
Baker	1	1	100	14	14.0	0	0– 0	
Meador	1	0	0	0	0.0	0	0– 0	
Wilson	1	1	100	8	8.0	0	0– 0	

PUNTING	No	Avg
Lothridge	42	38.5
Kilgore	24	41.6

KICKING	XP	Att	%	FG	Att	%
Gossett	30	32	94	15	26	58

1965 A.F.L. Sonny and Joe and John

After years in show business, New York Jet owner Sonny Werblin was a firm believer in the star system, of the gate pull of a big-name star. Werblin set out with checkbook in hand and bagged two of college football's biggest names, Alabama's Joe Namath and Notre Dame's John Huarte, with astronomical contracts that dwarfed the pacts of even the biggest veteran stars. Some people talked about the two fine young quarterbacks Werblin had signed, some talked about the misplaced values of a society that rewarded football players with small fortunes while grossly underpaying schoolteachers, but the important thing was that they talked. They talked about Joe Namath, they talked about the New York Jets, and they talked about the AFL. They stopped talking about whether the AFL would survive; they talked more now of when the leagues would be on a par.

When the league schedule started, a lot of those talking people came out to the games. Opening day in Houston saw a crowd of 52,680 turn out to see the lowly Oilers beat the Jets, with Joe Namath glued to the bench all afternoon. One week later, 53,658 fans filled Shea Stadium in New York to welcome Namath to the big city. Namath's development into a fine passer by mid-season furthered his publicity value and made Werblin's move look like a stroke of genius.

The league was feeling confident enough to vote for expansion in 1966, setting up a new team in Miami, which had flopped as a pro-football town in 1946 but was now a fast-growing metropolis. Only a few years ago, the league had been more worried about franchises folding than in creating new outposts for the AFL.

EASTERN DIVISION

Buffalo Bills—The trade of Cookie Gilchrist to Denver took most of the punch out of the running game, and injuries to Elbert Dubenion and Glenn Bass robbed the team of its starting wide receivers, but the Bills coasted to another Eastern title on a stone-wall defense and Pete Gogolak's strong right leg. Anonymous people manned the defense, but although Ron McDole, Tom Day, Tom Sestak, Jim Dunaway, Mike Stratton, Harry Jacobs, John Tracey, Butch Byrd, Hagood Clarke, George Saimes, and Charley Warner were short on reputation as individuals, respect for them as a unit was universal. The offense began with a strong line but lacked the backs and ends to take full advantage of the blocking. Gilchrist had been dealt off because of recurring feuds with coach Lou Saban, but replacement Billy Joe was no match for Cookie as a runner, receiver, or blocker. The other runners—Wray Carlton, Bobby Smith, and Donnie Stone—were pedestrian pluggers. With Dubenion and Bass sidelined, journeymen Bo Roberson and Charley Ferguson filled the wide receiver spots, but quarterback Jack Kemp orchestrated this collection of odds and ends into a steady unit which headed for their third straight championship game in Lou Saban's last year before returning to college coaching.

New York Jets—Owner Sonny Werblin set the football world on its ear by signing the two most glamorous rookie quarterbacks to expensive contracts. Joe Namath to a $400,000 pact and Heisman Trophy winner John Huarte to a $200,000 pact. Huarte missed training camp because of the College All-Star Game and spent the year on the taxi squad, but Namath made a big splash right from the start. After sitting out the first few games, Namath took over the quarterback job and showed a quick release that triggered a strong passing arm. In addition, his sudden affluence and swinging bachelor's lifestyle made the newspapers constantly and proved to be a bonanza of publicity for the Jets and the AFL. But if Namath and Huarte attracted all the attention, other rookies made the Jets a stronger club down the second half of the season. George Sauer, playing tight end out of necessity, middle linebacker Al Atkinson, defensive end Verlon Biggs, defensive tackle Jim Harris, and defensive backs Jim Hudson and Cornell Gordon all put in solid freshman years for the improved New Yorkers who won five of their last eight games.

Boston Patriots—Head coach Mike Holovak had never paid much attention to pre-season games, expecting his team to start playing for real once the starting bell rang. The Patriots lost all five of their exhibition games this year, but then kept losing right into October. Winless in the first seven games, the Pats made a comeback in the second half of the schedule, but their horrid start killed any chances of challenging Buffalo for first place. Holovak had never gone all out to sign prestigious college seniors, relying instead on veterans and rookies from small and local schools, and now this policy was showing up in the deterioration of the team. The defense, long the club's strong point, began to creak with age, while the offense suffered because of Babe Parilli's off season. The thirty-four-year-old Parilli gave up twenty-six interceptions, a sign that his arm was losing its old zip. The Pats did sign two big-name rookie runners, Jim Nance and Joe Bellino, but neither had a good freshman season. Nance played overweight all year, while Bellino, making his pro debut after three years in the Navy, did not have the size to be a consistent ground-gainer.

Houston Oilers—With the exception of W. K. Hicks, the Oilers were using the same men in the defensive secondary that staffed the championship Houston teams in the early years of the AFL. Enemy passers burned the Oiler secondary for twenty-seven touchdown passes, a sign of the improvement in AFL play and of the lack of foresight in the Houston management. With the worst defense in the league, head coach Hugh Taylor was fortunate to pick up four wins in his year at the helm. The offense was in no shape to carry the team, as it had weaknesses in all sectors. The offensive line needed help, and the receiving fell off because of Charley Hennigan's bad knee. Halfback Sid Blanks missed the season with a knee injury, and fullback Charley Tolar had slowed up considerably, throwing the brunt of the running chores on 185-pound Ode Burrell. At quarterback, thirty-seven-year-old George Blanda was plagued with a flood of interceptions, but young Don Trull still saw little action. But even with all their problems, the Oilers did put together some good games, like a 19-17 upset of Buffalo and a 31-10 pasting of Boston.

WESTERN DIVISION

San Diego Chargers—Although the San Diego defense ranked with Buffalo's at the top of the league, the offense still won most of the headlines for the Chargers. The versatile attack boasted of stars in all quarters. Linemen Ron Mix and Walt Sweeney were among the AFL's best, and flanker Lance Alworth gained a phenomenal 1,602 yards with a variety of leaping, diving, and streaking catches which netted him fourteen touchdowns. Quarterback John Hadl developed into a top-flight pro as a passer and play-caller. Halfback Paul Lowe hustled his way to a new league rushing record of 1,121 yards, and Keith Lincoln combined with rookie Gene Foster to provide punch at the fullback slot. But the San Diego defense bailed out the offense on its rare off days, as in a 13-13 tie with Boston and a 10-10 tie with the Chiefs. Earl Faison and Ernie Ladd still stacked up runners and passers, but both star linemen expressed dissatisfaction with the organization and were playing out their option. Fitting right in with the veterans were several newcomers to the unit, rookies Rick Redman, Steve DeLong, Dick Degan, and Speedy Duncan—enough to give the Chargers their fifth Western crown in six years.

Oakland Raiders—Head coach and general manager Al Davis kept building the Raiders with top rookie talent. This year's batch of Oakland freshmen included wide receiver Fred Biletnikoff, cornerback Kent McCloughan, linebacker Gus Otto, and offensive tackles Bob Svihus and Harry Schuh. The Raiders now had sufficient depth to compensate for injuries, as Tom Flores and Dick Wood handled the quarterbacking in fine fashion with Cotton Davidson out for most of the year with an injury. The offense, with Clem Daniels and Art Powell the main guns, performed quite well, and the defense had two solid rookie starters in Otto and McCloughan and an All-Pro cornerback in Dave Grayson. An inability to beat San Diego and Buffalo killed the Oakland title chances, as the Raiders dropped all four of their contests with the divisional champions-to-be.

Kansas City Chiefs—With one of the deepest rosters in pro football, the Chiefs seemed to be playing in the shadow of an evil star. Since the team moved to Kansas City in 1963, serious injury or death struck four Chief players. Stone Johnson suffered a fatal neck injury in a 1963 pre-season game, Ed Budde almost died from a blow on the head when attacked on the street in 1964, Fred Arbanas lost most of the vision in his left eye from an off-the-field altercation, and fullback Mack Lee Hill died on the operating table of complications following knee surgery midway through this season. On the field, the Chiefs had a habit of winning some games in impressive fashion, then going flat and losing to a weaker team. The Kansas City offense still was a top-flight unit, with the receiving strengthened by rookie Otis Taylor and the running game weakened by the trade of Abner Haynes and the tragic death of Hill. The defense had no problems with men like Jerry Mays, Buck Buchanan, E. J. Holub, Sherrill Headrick, Bobby Bell, Fred Williamson, and Johnny Robinson in the lineup.

Denver Broncos—For the first time in their history, the Broncos relied on the running game as their main offensive threat. Trades brought fullback Cookie Gilchrist and halfback Abner Haynes, both legendary AFL runners, to Denver during the summer, and while Gilchrist still bulled over tackles at peak form, Haynes lost his starting job to rookie Wendell Hayes. At any rate, the depth in the running-back slots kept the attack alive despite severe uncertainty at quarterback. Coach Mac Speedie used John McCormick, Mickey Slaughter, and Jacky Lee in the passer's spot and was satisfied with none of them. Lionel Taylor got open for enough passes from the three quarterbacks to lead the league in receiving, his fifth pass-catching title in the AFL's six years of play, but none of the other receivers on the team made much of a dent on enemy defenses.

FINAL TEAM STATISTICS

OFFENSE

	BOSTON	BUFFALO	DENVER	HOUSTON	K. CITY	NEW YORK	OAKLAND	SAN DIEGO
FIRST DOWNS:								
Total	214	206	255	227	232	213	225	268
by Rushing	55	69	111	63	101	77	72	127
by Passing	130	119	117	140	121	121	134	127
by Penalty	29	18	27	24	10	15	19	14
RUSHING:								
Number	373	392	453	324	418	367	390	486
Yards	1117	1288	1829	1175	1752	1476	1538	1998
Average Yards	3.0	3.3	4.0	3.6	4.2	4.0	3.9	4.1
Touchdowns	8	16	14	10	15	11	8	13
PASSING:								
Attempts	473	461	482	550	395	459	431	401
Completions	193	208	222	224	199	209	195	203
Completion Percentage	40.8	45.1	46.1	40.7	50.4	45.5	45.2	50.6
Passing Yards	2854	2744	2848	3070	2894	2751	2713	3379
Average Yards Per Attempt	6.0	6.0	5.9	5.6	7.3	6.0	6.3	8.4
Average Yards Per Completion	14.8	13.2	12.8	13.7	14.5	13.2	13.9	16.6
Times Tackled Attempting to Pass	37	29	24	31	37	17	33	27
Yards Lost Attempting to Pass	347	283	208	257	351	162	253	276
Net Yards	2507	2461	2640	2813	2543	2589	2460	3103
Touchdowns	19	13	18	25	22	21	22	23
Interceptions	29	24	30	35	20	22	17	26
Percent Intercepted	6.1	5.2	6.2	6.4	5.1	4.8	3.9	6.5
PUNTING:								
Number	82	80	68	85	72	72	75	70
Average Distance	40.1	43.0	42.3	43.7	44.6	45.3	41.1	40.0
PUNT RETURNS:								
Number	27	36	37	28	38	29	34	38
Yards	152	389	355	189	419	166	365	508
Average Yards	5.6	10.8	9.6	6.8	11.0	5.7	10.7	13.4
Touchdowns	0	0	1	0	1	0	1	2
KICKOFF RETURNS:								
Number	60	45	71	77	48	54	46	50
Yards	1191	1022	1731	1669	1080	1107	990	1028
Average Yards	19.9	22.7	24.4	21.7	22.5	20.5	21.5	20.6
Touchdowns	0	2	0	0	0	0	0	0
INTERCEPTION RETURNS:								
Number	21	32	25	27	20	26	24	28
Yards	233	393	465	416	342	235	482	377
Average Yards	11.1	12.3	18.6	15.4	17.1	9.0	20.1	13.5
Touchdowns	0	1	3	0	2	0	4	3
PENALTIES:								
Number	58	78	69	76	70	58	69	84
Yards	537	685	750	856	744	684	661	929
FUMBLES:								
Number	24	28	29	23	34	27	17	22
Number Lost	12	14	16	11	20	18	9	13
POINTS:								
Total	244	313	303	298	322	285	298	340
PAT (Kick) Attempts	27	31	32	34	37	31	35	40
PAT (Kick) Made	27	31	32	34	37	31	35	40
PAT (Rush or Pass) Attempts	0	2	6	3	3	1	0	1
PAT (Rush or Pass) Made	0	0	2	2	3	1	0	0
FG Attempts	27	46	29	23	30	34	34	30
FG Made	17	28	13	12	13	20	17	18
Percent FG Made	63.0	60.9	44.8	52.2	43.3	58.8	50.0	60.0
Safeties	2	0	0	1	0	0	1	0

DEFENSE

	BOSTON	BUFFALO	DENVER	HOUSTON	K. CITY	NEW YORK	OAKLAND	SAN DIEGO
FIRST DOWNS:								
Total	232	226	244	271	207	235	235	190
by Rushing	92	65	87	132	69	85	90	55
by Passing	127	141	138	111	113	136	125	118
by Penalty	13	20	19	28	25	14	20	17
RUSHING:								
Number	425	360	384	508	381	432	407	306
Yards	1531	1114	1337	2683	1376	1551	1487	1094
Average Yards	3.6	3.1	3.5	5.3	3.6	3.6	3.7	3.6
Touchdowns	10	5	24	17	12	10	10	7
PASSING:								
Attempts	431	502	440	416	451	472	466	474
Completions	206	227	202	177	216	220	199	206
Completion Percentage	47.8	45.2	45.9	42.5	47.9	46.6	42.7	43.5
Passing Yards	2891	3416	3265	2643	2711	2900	2947	2480
Average Yards Per Attempt	6.7	6.8	7.4	6.4	6.0	6.1	6.3	5.2
Average Yards Per Completion	14.0	15.0	16.2	14.9	12.6	13.2	14.8	12.0
Times Tackled Attempting to Pass	30	28	26	22	39	22	30	38
Yards Lost Attempting to Pass	291	246	305	173	326	238	246	312
Net Yards	2600	3170	2960	2470	2385	2662	2701	2168
Touchdowns	17	19	23	27	18	22	27	17
Interceptions	21	32	25	27	20	26	24	28
Percent Intercepted	4.9	6.4	5.7	6.5	4.4	5.5	5.2	5.9
PUNTING:								
Number	78	76	73	59	83	78	77	80
Average Distance	42.1	40.2	45.9	42.5	44.1	39.8	42.1	43.4
PUNT RETURNS:								
Number	33	30	26	48	29	40	34	27
Yards	232	222	343	494	401	352	257	242
Average Yards	7.0	7.4	13.2	10.3	13.8	8.8	7.6	9.0
Touchdowns	0	0	1	2	2	0	0	0
KICKOFF RETURNS:								
Number	41	60	58	48	56	60	62	66
Yards	946	1449	1197	995	1173	1421	1227	1410
Average Yards	23.1	24.2	20.6	20.7	20.9	23.7	19.8	21.4
Touchdowns	1	0	0	0	0	1	0	0
INTERCEPTION RETURNS:								
Number	29	24	30	35	20	22	17	26
Yards	365	467	426	471	238	339	186	451
Average Yards	12.6	19.5	14.2	13.5	11.9	15.4	10.9	17.3
Touchdowns	4	1	2	3	0	2	0	1
PENALTIES:								
Number	72	69	86	67	60	77	69	62
Yards	658	832	836	701	623	865	666	665
FUMBLES:								
Number	17	33	27	31	24	25	23	24
Number Lost	9	25	14	13	13	12	14	13
POINTS:								
Total	302	226	392	429	285	303	239	227
PAT (Kick) Attempts	28	21	50	48	33	33	29	25
PAT (Kick) Made	28	21	50	48	33	33	29	25
PAT (Rush or Pass) Attempts	6	4	0	2	1	2	1	0
PAT (Rush or Pass) Made	2	4	0	2	0	0	0	0
FG Attempts	40	30	24	43	28	34	20	34
FG Made	22	15	14	25	16	20	10	16
Percent FG Made	55.0	50.0	58.3	58.1	57.1	58.8	50.0	47.1
Safeties	0	1	0	1	0	0	0	2

1965 AFL CHAMPIONSHIP GAME

December 26, at San Diego
(Attendance 30,361)

Stubbornly Brilliant

The San Diego weather was mild compared with last year's chill in Buffalo, but the Bills' defense played the same hard-hitting game and again would up as victors. Buffalo's strong front four and tight pass defense completely handcuffed the favored Chargers, as they never could get past the Buffalo 24-yard line. Through the first quarter and the first ten minutes of the second quarter, both defenses kept the scoreboard empty, but the Bills scored on a Jack Kemp-to-Ernie Warlick pass with five minutes left before intermission. The Chargers then punted the ball back to the Bills, and Butch Byrd returned the kick 74 yards down the sideline for another Buffalo score. The two quick touchdowns gave the Bills a 14-0 lead to take into the clubhouse at halftime, while the Chargers had to ponder on the goose egg on their side of the scoreboard. Going back to last year's championship game, the Chargers now were scoreless in their last five quarters against the Buffalo defense. The second half proved no more pleasant for the Chargers, as John Hadl, Keith Lincoln, Paul Lowe, and Lance Alworth could not get the ball across the Buffalo goal line. Jack Kemp, meanwhile, guided the Bills' offense steadily against the stubborn San Diego defense. Pete Gogolak booted a pair of field goals in the third quarter to give the Bills some breathing room, and his 32-yarder in the fourth quarter ran the final score to 23-0. Quarterback Kemp, a former Charger, won the game MVP award for his surgical precision in running the attack.

SCORING

SAN DIEGO	0	0	0	0	– 0
BUFFALO	0	14	6	3	–23

Second Quarter
Buf. Warlick, 18 yard pass from Kemp
PAT–Gogolak (kick)
Buf. Byrd, 74 yard punt return
PAT–Gogolak (kick)

Third Quarter
Buf. Gogolak, 11 yard field goal
Buf. Gogolak, 39 yard field goal

Fourth Quarter
Buf. Gogolak, 32 yard field goal

TEAM STATISTICS

S.D.		BUF.
12	First Downs–Total	23
5	First Downs–Rushing	13
7	First Downs–Passing	9
0	First Downs–Penalty	1
7	Punts–Number	4
40.7	Punts–Average Distance	46.3
3	Penalties–Number	2
41	Yards–Penalized	21
2	Missed Field Goals	2

INDIVIDUAL STATISTICS

SAN DIEGO	No.	Yds.	Avg.	BUFFALO	No.	Yds.	Avg.
RUSHING							
Lowe	12	57	4.8	Carlton	16	63	3.9
Hadl	8	24	3.0	Joe	16	35	2.2
Lincoln	4	16	4.0	Stone	3	5	1.7
Foster	2	9	4.5	Smith	1	5	5.0
Breaux	1	–2	–2.0		36	108	3.0
	27	104	3.9				
RECEIVING							
Alworth	4	82	20.5	Roberson	3	88	29.3
Lowe	3	3	1.0	Warlick	3	35	11.7
Norton	1	35	35.0	Costa	2	32	16.0
Farr	1	24	24.0	Tracy	1	12	12.0
MacKinnon	1	10	10.0		9	167	18.6
Lincoln	1	7	7.0				
Kocourek	1	3	3.0				
	12	164	13.7				
PUNT RETURNS							
Duncan	1	12	12.0	Byrd	3	87	29.0
KICKOFF RETURNS							
Duncan	2	62	31.0	Warner	1	17	17.0
Farr	1	35	35.0				
	3	97	32.3				
INTERCEPTION RETURNS							
Warren	1	0	0.0	Byrd	1	24	24.0
				Jacobs	1	12	12.0
					2	36	18.0

PASSING

SAN DIEGO	Att.	Comp.	Comp. Pct.	Yds.	Int.	Yds/ Att.	Yds/ Comp.	Yards Lost Tackled
Hadl	23	11	47.8	140	2	6.1	12.7	
Breaux	2	1	50.0	24	0	12.0	24.0	
	25	12	48.0	164	2	6.6	13.7	45
BUFFALO								
Kemp	19	8	42.1	155	1	8.2	19.4	
Lamonica	1	1	100.0	12	0	12.0	12.0	
	20	9	45.0	167	1	8.4	18.6	15

BUFFALO BILLS 10-3-1 Lou Saban

Scores of Each Game		
24	BOSTON	7
30	Denver	15
33	NEW YORK	21
17	OAKLAND	12
3	SAN DIEGO	34
23	Kansas City	7
31	DENVER	13
17	HOUSTON	19
23	Boston	7
17	Oakland	14
20	San Diego	20
29	Houston	18
34	KANSAS CITY	25
12	New York	14

Use Name	Pos.	Hgt	Wgt	Age	Int	Pts
Stew Barber	OT	6'3"	250	26		
Dick Hudson	OT	6'4"	272	25		
Joe O'Donnell	OT	6'2"	246	23		
Al Bemiller	OG	6'3"	260	26		
George Flint	OG	6'4"	244	27		
Billy Shaw	OG	6'3"	248	25		
Dave Behrman	C	6'5"	260	23		
Tom Day	DE	6'2"	250	30	1	
Ron McDole	DE	6'3"	264	25	1	
Jim Dunaway	DT	6'4"	276	23		
Tom Keating	DT	6'3"	242	22		
Dudley Meredith	DT	6'4"	275	30		
Henry Schmidt	DT	6'4"	270	28		
Tom Sestak	OT-DT	6'5"	270	29		
Harry Jacobs	LB	6'2"	225	28	1	
Bill Laskey	LB	6'2"	250	22		
Paul Maguire	LB	6'	220	27		
Marty Schottenheimer	LB	6'3"	225	22		
Mike Stratton	LB	6'3"	240	23	2	
John Tracey	OE-LB	6'3"	225	31	1	
Butch Byrd	DB	6'	211	23	5	
Hagood Clarke	DB	6'	188	23	7	
Booker Edgerson	DB	5'10"	180	26	5	
Tom Janik	DB	6'3"	200	24		
George Saimes	DB	5'10"	195	23	4	6
Gene Sykes	DB	6'1"	195	24		
Charley Warner	HB-DB	5'11"	180	25	5	24
Jack Kemp	QB	6'1"	200	31		24
Daryle Lamonica	QB	6'2"	215	24		6
Joe Auer	HB	6'1"	205	23		
Wray Carlton	HB	6'2"	216	27		42
Bobby Smith	HB	6'	203	24		6
Billy Joe	FB	6'2"	250	24		36
Donnie Stone	FB	6'2"	205	28		
Elbert Dubenion	FL	6'	187	30		6
Floyd Hudlow	FL	5'11"	185	21		
Bo Roberson (from OAK)	FL	6'1"	190	30		18
Ed Rutkowski	FL	6'1"	208	24		6
Glenn Bass	OE	6'2"	206	26		6
Paul Costa	OE	6'4"	240	23		
Charley Ferguson	OE	6'5"	215	25		12
Bill Groman	OE	6'	195	29		
Pete Mills	OE	5'11"	180	22		
Ernie Warlick	OE	6'4"	235	33		6
Pete Gogolak	K	6'2"	200	23		115

NEW YORK JETS 5-8-1 Weeb Ewbank

Scores of Each Game		
21	Houston	27
10	KANSAS CITY	14
21	Buffalo	33
13	Denver	16
24	OAKLAND	24
9	SAN DIEGO	34
45	DENVER	10
13	Kansas City	10
30	Boston	20
41	HOUSTON	14
23	BOSTON	27
7	San Diego	38
14	Oakland	24
14	BUFFALO	12

Use Name	Pos.	Hgt	Wgt	Age	Int	Pts
Nick DeFelice	OT	6'3"	250	25		
Winston Hill	OT	6'4"	275	23		
Sherman Plunkett	OT	6'4"	295	31		
Sam DeLuca	OG	6'2"	250	29		
Dan Ficca	OG	6'1"	250	26		
Dave Herman	OG	6'2"	255	23		
Pete Perreault	OG	6'3"	245	26		
Mike Hudock	C	6'2"	245	30		
John Schmitt	C	6'4"	265	22		
Gerry Philbin	DE	6'2"	245	24		
Lavern Torczon	DE	6'2"	250	29		
Bert Wilder	DE	6'3"	245	25		
Verlon Biggs	DT-DE	6'4"	250	22	1	
Jim Harris	DT	6'4"	265	21		
Paul Rochester	DT	6'2"	250	28		
Arnie Simkus	DT	6'4"	240	22		
Al Atkinson	LB	6'1"	225	22	1	
Ralph Baker	LB	6'3"	235	23	2	
Larry Grantham	LB	6'	206	26	1	
Wahoo McDaniel	LB	6'	240	28	1	
Jim O'Mahoney	LB	6'1"	233	24		
Ray Abbruzzese	DB	6'1"	200	27	2	
Bill Baird	DB	5'10"	180	26	3	
Cornell Gordon	DB	6'	185	24	2	
Dainard Paulson	DB	5'11"	190	28	7	
Bill Rademacher	DB	6'1"	190	23		
Clyde Washington	DB	6'	206	27		
Willie West	DB	5'10"	185	27	6	
Jim Hudson	HB-DB	6'2"	210	22		
Joe Namath	QB	6'2"	194	22		
Mike Taliaferro	QB	6'2"	210	23		
Charley Browning	HB	6'	220	22		
Kern Carson (from SD)	HB	6'	202	23		12
Cosmo Iacavazzi	HB	5'11"	200	22		
Curley Johnson	HB	6'	215	30		6
Bill Mathis	HB	6'1"	220	26		36
Bob Schweickert	HB	6'1"	195	22		
Mark Smolinski	FB	6'	215	26		
Matt Snell	FB	6'2"	220	23		24
Jim Evans	FL	6'1"	190	25		
Don Maynard	FL	6'	185	29		84
Gene Heeter	OE	6'4"	235	24		
Dee Mackey	OE	6'5"	225	29		8
Jerry Robinson	OE	5'11"	200	26		
George Sauer	OE	6'1"	206	21		12
Bake Turner	OE	6'	185	25		12
Jim Turner	K	6'2"	205	24		91

BOSTON PATRIOTS 4-8-2 Mike Holovak

Scores of Each Game		
7	Buffalo	24
10	Houston	31
10	DENVER	27
17	Kansas City	27
10	OAKLAND	24
13	SAN DIEGO	13
21	Oakland	30
22	San Diego	6
7	BUFFALO	23
20	NEW YORK	30
10	KANSAS CITY	10
27	New York	23
28	Denver	20
42	HOUSTON	14

Use Name	Pos.	Hgt	Wgt	Age	Int	Pts
Tom Neville	OT	6'4"	230	22		
Don Oakes	OT	6'3"	255	27		
Bob Schmidt	OT	6'4"	250	29		
Bob Yates	OT	6'3"	230	26		
Justin Canale	OG	6'2"	230	21		
Charley Long	OG	6'3"	250	27		
Billy Neighbors	OG	5'11"	240	25		
Jon Morris	C	6'4"	240	22		
Bob Dee	DE	6'3"	240	32		
Larry Eisenhauer	DE	6'5"	250	25		
Jim Hunt	DE	5'11"	245	26		
Len St. Jean	DE	6'1"	240	23		
Bill Dawson	OE-DE	6'3"	240	21		
Houston Antwine	DT	6'	270	26	1	
George Pyne	DT	6'4"	285	22		
Tom Addison	LB	6'3"	230	29	1	
Nick Buoniconti	LB	5'11"	220	24	3	
Mike Dukes (to NY)	LB	6'3"	235	29	1	
Lonnie Farmer	LB	6'	220	24	1	
Ed Meixler	LB	6'3"	245	22		
Jack Rudolph	LB	6'3"	230	27		
Jay Cunningham	DB	5'10"	180	22	2	
Dick Felt	DB	6'	185	32		
White Graves	DB	6'	185	22	2	
Ron Hall	DB	6'	190	28	3	
Tom Hennessey	DB	6'	180	25	2	
Ross O'Hanley	DB	6'	185	26	1	
Chuck Shonta	DB	6'	200	27	2	
Don Webb	DB	5'10"	200	26	2	
Babe Parilli	QB	6'1"	190	35		
Eddie Wilson	QB	6'	190	25		
Tom Yewcic	QB	5'11"	185	33		
Joe Bellino	HB	5'9"	187	27		
Ron Burton	HB	5'10"	190	28		18
J. D. Garrett	HB	5'11"	195	23		18
Larry Garron	FB	6'	195	28		12
Jim Nance	FB	6'1"	250	22		30
Jim Colclough	FL	6'	185	29		18
Ellis Johnson	HB-FL	6'2"	190	21		
Gino Cappelletti	OE	6'	190	31		132
Art Graham	OE	6'1"	205	24		
Tony Romeo	OE	6'2"	230	26		12
Jim Whalen	OE	6'2"	210	21		

HOUSTON OILERS 4-10-0 Hugh Taylor

Scores of Each Game		
27	NEW YORK	21
31	BOSTON	10
17	Oakland	21
14	San Diego	31
17	Denver	28
38	KANSAS CITY	36
19	Buffalo	17
21	OAKLAND	33
21	DENVER	31
14	New York	41
21	Kansas City	52
18	BUFFALO	29
26	SAN DIEGO	37
14	Boston	42

Use Name	Pos.	Hgt	Wgt	Age	Int	Pts
Norm Evans	OT	6'5"	235	22		
Rich Michael	OT	6'3"	245	26		
Walt Suggs	OT	6'5"	260	26		
Maxie Williams	OT	6'4"	242	25		
Sonny Bishop	OG	6'2"	245	25		
John Frongillo	OG	6'3"	250	25		
Bob Talamini	OG	6'1"	255	26		
John Wittenborn	OG	6'2"	240	29		
Wayne Frazier	C	6'2"	245	25		
Tom Goode	C	6'3"	250	26		
Gary Cutsinger	DE	6'4"	245	24	1	
Bob Evans	DE	6'3"	250	23		6
Don Floyd	DE	6'4"	247	26		
George Kinney	DE	6'4"	250	22		
Ray Straham	DE	6'6"	250	22		
Scott Appleton	DT	6'3"	250	23		
Jim Hayes	DT	6'4"	265	24		
Ed Husmann	DT	6'	245	34		
Bud McFadin	DT	6'3"	270	37		
Johnny Baker	LB	6'3"	225	24		
Danny Brabham	LB	6'4"	240	24		
Doug Cline	LB	6'2"	230	26		
Bobby Maples	LB	6'3"	230	22	1	
Larry Onesti	LB	6'	200	26		6
Charley Rieves	LB	5'11"	218	26		
Tony Banfield	DB	6'1"	185	26	3	
Freddy Glick	DB	6'1"	190	28	2	
W. K. Hicks	DB	6'1"	185	22	9	
Bobby Jancik	DB	5'11"	178	25	4	
Pete Jaquess	DB	6'	180	23		
Jim Norton	DB	6'3"	190	26	7	
George Blanda	QB	6'1"	215	37		61
Don Trull	QB	6'1"	180	23		12
Ode Burrell	HB	6'	185	25		46
B. W. Cheeks	HB	6'1"	230	23		
Dalton Hoffman	FB	6'	207	23		
Harry Hooligan	FB	6'2"	225	27		
Bobby Jackson	FB	6'3"	238	25		12
Keith Kinderman	FB	6'	215	25		
Jack Spikes	FB	6'2"	220	27		27
Charley Tolar	FB	5'7"	200	27		
Charley Hennigan	FL	6'	187	29		24
Sammy Weir	FL	5'9"	170	23		
Dick Compton	OE	6'1"	195	25		12
Charley Frazier	OE	6'	175	26		36
Willie Frazier	OE	6'4"	225	22		48
Bob McLeod	OE	6'5"	230	26		6

Sid Blanks – Knee Injury

BUFFALO BILLS

RUSHING

Last Name	No.	Yds	Avg	TD
Carlton	156	592	3.8	6
Joe	123	377	3.1	4
Smith	43	137	3.2	1
Stone	19	61	3.2	0
Kemp	36	49	1.4	4
Lamonica	10	30	3.0	1
Maguire	1	21	21.0	0
Auer	3	19	6.3	0
Warner	1	2	2.0	0
Roberson	1	–4	–4.0	0

RECEIVING

Last Name	No.	Yds	Avg	TD
Roberson	46	703	15	3
Joe	27	271	10	2
Carlton	24	196	8	1
Costa	21	401	19	0
Ferguson	21	262	12	2
Bass	18	299	17	1
Dubenion	18	281	16	1
Rutkowski	18	247	14	1
Smith	12	116	10	0
Warlick	8	112	14	1
Stone	6	29	5	0
Mills	1	43	43	0
Warner	1	11	11	1
Tracey	1	2	2	0
Kemp	1	–9	–9	0

PUNT RETURNS

Last Name	No.	Yds	Avg	TD
Byrd	22	220	10	0
Rutkowski	11	127	12	0
Warner	1	16	16	0
Clarke	1	13	13	0
Hudlow	1	12	12	0
Saimes	0	1	0	0

KICKOFF RETURNS

Last Name	No.	Yds	Avg	TD
Warner	32	825	26	2
Roberson	16	318	20	0
Rutkowski	5	97	19	0
Hudlow	2	36	18	0
Maguire	1	5	5	0
Dunaway	1	0	0	0

PASSING – PUNTING – KICKING

PASSING	Att	Comp	%	Yds	Yd/Att	TD	Int–%	RK
Kemp	391	179	46	2368	6.1	10	18– 5	6
Lamonica	70	29	41	376	5.4	3	6– 9	

PUNTING	No	Avg
Maguire	80	43.0

KICKING	XP	Att	%	FG	Att	%
Gogolak	31	31	100	28	46	61

NEW YORK JETS

RUSHING

Last Name	No.	Yds	Avg	TD
Snell	169	763	4.5	4
Mathis	147	604	4.1	5
Smolinski	24	59	2.5	0
Carson	7	25	3.6	2
Namath	8	19	2.4	0
McDaniel	1	13	13.0	0
Taliaferro	7	4	0.6	0
Johnson	2	3	1.5	0
Maynard	1	2	2.0	0

RECEIVING

Last Name	No.	Yds	Avg	TD
Maynard	68	1218	18	14
Snell	38	264	7	0
B. Turner	31	402	13	2
Sauer	29	301	10	2
Mathis	17	242	14	1
Mackey	16	255	16	1
Smolinski	6	25	4	0
Evans	2	24	12	0
Heeter	1	14	14	0
Johnson	1	6	6	1

PUNT RETURNS

Last Name	No.	Yds	Avg	TD
Baird	14	88	6	0
Robinson	3	36	12	0
West	10	34	3	0
Carson	1	7	7	0
B. Turner	1	1	1	0

KICKOFF RETURNS

Last Name	No.	Yds	Avg	TD
B. Turner	18	402	22	0
Carson	17	355	21	0
Robinson	7	164	23	0
Smolinski	6	98	16	0
Baird	2	50	25	0
Browning	1	31	31	0
Sauer	1	20	20	0
Abruzzese	1	16	16	0
O'Mahoney	1	15	15	0
DeFelice	1	0	0	0
Hudson	1	0	0	0
Paulson	1	0	0	0

PASSING – PUNTING – KICKING

PASSING	Att	Comp	%	Yds	Yd/Att	TD	Int–%	RK
Namath	340	164	48	2220	6.5	18	15– 4	3
Taliaferro	119	45	38	531	4.5	3	7– 6	

PUNTING	No	Avg
Johnson	72	45.3

KICKING	XP	Att	%	FG	Att	%
J. Turner	31	31	100	20	34	59

2 POINT XP
Mackey

BOSTON PATRIOTS

RUSHING

Last Name	No.	Yds	Avg	TD
Nance	111	321	2.9	5
Garron	74	259	3.5	1
Parilli	50	200	4.0	0
Garrett	42	147	3.5	1
Burton	45	108	2.4	1
Bellino	24	49	2.0	0
Johnson	19	29	1.5	0
Wilson	8	4	0.5	0

RECEIVING

Last Name	No.	Yds	Avg	TD
Colclough	40	677	17	3
Cappelletti	37	680	18	9
Graham	25	316	13	0
Whalen	22	381	17	0
Garron	15	222	15	1
Romeo	15	203	14	2
Nance	12	83	7	0
Burton	10	127	13	2
Garrett	7	49	7	2
Bellino	5	74	15	0
Johnson	4	29	7	0
Yewcic	1	13	13	0

PUNT RETURNS

Last Name	No.	Yds	Avg	TD
Burton	15	61	4	0
Cunningham	5	35	7	0
Hennessey	5	21	4	0
Garrett	1	19	19	0
Nance	1	16	16	0

KICKOFF RETURNS

Last Name	No.	Yds	Avg	TD
Cunningham	17	374	22	0
Garrett	12	232	19	0
Burton	7	188	27	0
Garron	5	141	28	0
Bellino	7	138	20	0
Dukes	3	45	15	0
Nance	3	40	13	0
Johnson	2	29	15	0
Rudolph	1	4	4	0
Canale	2	0	0	0
Pyne	1	0	0	0

PASSING – PUNTING – KICKING

PASSING	Att	Comp	%	Yds	Yd/Att	TD	Int–%	RK
Parilli	426	173	41	2597	6.1	18	26– 6	7
Wilson	46	20	44	257	5.6	1	3– 7	
Yewcic	1	0	0	0	0.0	0	0– 0	

PUNTING	No	Avg
Yewcic	74	41.8
E. Wilson	5	38.8

KICKING	XP	Att	%	FG	Att	%
Cappelletti	27	27	100	17	27	63

HOUSTON OILERS

RUSHING

Last Name	No.	Yds	Avg	TD
Burrell	130	528	4.1	3
Tolar	73	230	3.2	0
Spikes	47	173	3.7	3
Trull	29	145	5.0	2
Jackson	37	85	2.3	2
Hoffman	1	11	11.0	0
C. Frazier	1	10	10.0	0
Compton	1	2	2.0	0
Blanda	4	–6	–1.5	0

RECEIVING

Last Name	No.	Yds	Avg	TD
Burrell	55	650	12	4
Hennigan	41	578	14	4
C. Frazier	38	717	19	6
Wil. Frazier	37	521	14	8
Tolar	25	138	6	0
McLeod	15	226	15	1
Spikes	8	57	7	0
Compton	3	140	47	2
Jackson	1	31	31	0
Weir	1	12	12	0

PUNT RETURNS

Last Name	No.	Yds	Avg	TD
Jancik	12	85	7	0
Glick	7	44	6	0
Burrell	3	39	13	0
Jaquess	4	17	4	0
Hicks	1	4	4	0
Weir	1	0	0	0

KICKOFF RETURNS

Last Name	No.	Yds	Avg	TD
Jancik	18	430	24	0
Jaquess	13	280	22	0
Weir	10	215	22	0
Burrell	8	202	25	0
Hicks	7	181	26	0
Glick	4	84	21	0
Kinderman	4	72	18	0
Compton	4	68	17	0
Spikes	4	41	10	0
Jackson	2	39	20	0
Williams	1	23	23	0
Cheeks	1	19	19	0
Maples	1	15	15	0

PASSING – PUNTING – KICKING

PASSING	Att	Comp	%	Yds	Yd/Att	TD	Int–%	RK
Blanda	442	186	42	2542	5.8	20	30– 7	8
Trull	107	38	36	528	4.9	5	5– 5	
Tolar	1	0	0	0	0.0	0	0– 0	

PUNTING	No	Avg
Norton	84	44.2

KICKING	XP	Att	%	FG	Att	%
Blanda	28	28	100	11	21	52
Spikes	6	6	100	1	2	50

2 POINT XP
Burrell (2)

SAN DIEGO CHARGERS 9-2-3 Sid Gillman

Scores of Each Game		
34	DENVER	31
17	Oakland	6
10	KANSAS CITY	10
31	HOUSTON	14
34	Buffalo	3
13	Boston	13
34	New York	9
6	BOSTON	22
35	Denver	21
7	Kansas Ciry	31
20	BUFFALO	20
38	NEW YORK	7
37	Houston	26
24	OAKLAND	14

Use Name	Pos.	Hgt	Wgt	Age	Int	Pts
Gary Kirner	OT	6'3"	245	23		
Ron Mix	OT	6'4"	250	27		
Ernie Park	OT	6'3"	253	25		
Ernie Wright	OT	6'4"	265	26		
John Farris	OG	6'4"	245	24		
Ed Mitchell	OG	6'2"	265	23		
Pat Shea	OG	6'1"	245	26		
Walt Sweeney	OG	6'3"	255	24		
Sam Gruneisen	C	6'1"	255	24		
Steve DeLong	DE	6'3"	245	22		
Earl Faison	DE	6'5"	270	26	1	6
Howard Kindig	DE	6'6"	250	24		
Bob Petrich	DE	6'4"	257	24		
George Gross	DT	6'3"	270	24		
Ernie Ladd	DT	6'9"	295	26		
Fred Moore	DT	6'3"	255	25		

Use Name	Pos.	Hgt	Wgt	Age	Int	Pts
Chuck Allen	LB	6'1"	225	25	1	
Frank Buncom	LB	6'1"	235	25		
Ron Carpenter	LB	6'2"	230	24		
Dick Degen	LB	6'1"	225	23	2	
Bob Horton	LB	6'2"	230	22		
Rick Redman	LB	5'11"	220	22	1	
Speedy Duncan	DB	5'10"	180	22	4	12
Kenny Graham	DB	6'	200	23	5	6
Dick Harris	DB	5'11"	187	28	1	
Jack Jacobson	DB	6'2"	200	24		
Jimmy Warren	DB	5'11"	185	26	5	
Dick Westmoreland	DB	6'1"	190	24	1	
Bud Whitehead	DB	6'	185	26	7	6
Bob Zeman	DB	6'1"	195	28		

Use Name	Pos.	Hgt	Wgt	Age	Int	Pts
Don Breaux	QB	6'1"	200	25		
John Hadl	QB	6'2"	210	25		6
Steve Tensi	QB	6'5"	207	22		
Gene Foster	FB-HB	5'11"	200	22		12
Paul Lowe	HB	6'	205	28		48
Jim Allison	FB	6'	225	22		
Keith Lincoln	FB	6'2"	212	26		42
Lance Alworth	FL	6'	185	25		84
Sammy Taylor	FL	6'	190	25		
Dave Kocourek	OE	6'5"	245	28		12
Jacque MacKinnon	OE	6'4"	250	26		
Don Norton	OE	6'1"	195	27		12
Herb Travenio	K	6'	218	34		94

OAKLAND RAIDERS 8-5-1 Al Davis

Scores of Each Game		
37	KANSAS CITY	10
6	SAN DIEGO	17
21	HOUSTON	17
12	Buffalo	17
24	Boston	10
24	New York	24
30	BOSTON	21
7	Kansas City	14
33	Houston	21
14	BUFFALO	17
28	Denver	20
24	DENVER	13
24	NEW YORK	14
14	San Diego	24

Use Name	Pos.	Hgt	Wgt	Age	Int	Pts
Harry Schuh	OG-OT	6'2"	260	22		
Bob Svihus	OT	6'4"	245	22		
Frank Youso	OT	6'4"	250	29		
Rich Zecher	OT	6'2"	240	22		
Wayne Hawkins	OG	6'	240	27		
Marv Marinovich	OG	6'3"	250	26		
Bob Mischak	OG	6'	230	32		
Ken Rice	OG	6'2"	240	25		
Jim Otto	C	6'2"	240	27		
Ben Davidson	DE	6'8"	265	25		
Ike Lassiter	DE	6'5"	270	24		
Carleton Oats	DE	6'2"	235	22		
Dan Birdwell	DT	6'4"	250	24		
Dave Costa	DT	6'2"	250	23		
John Diehl (from DAL-N)	DT	6'7"	250	29		
Rex Mirich	DT	6'4"	250	24		

Use Name	Pos.	Hgt	Wgt	Age	Int	Pts
Bill Budness	LB	6'1"	215	22	1	
Dan Conners	LB	6'1"	230	23		
Dick Herman	LB	6'2"	215	22		
Archie Matsos	LB	6'	212	30	3	
Gus Otto	LB	6'2"	220	22	3	12
J. R. Williamson	LB	6'2"	220	23		
Dave Grayson	DB	5'10"	185	26	3	12
Claude Gibson	DB	6'1"	190	26	4	6
Joe Krakoski	DB	6'2"	195	28		
Kent McCloughan	DB	6'1"	190	22	3	
Warren Powers	DB	6'	185	24	5	
Howie Williams	DB	6'2"	185	28	2	

Use Name	Pos.	Hgt	Wgt	Age	Int	Pts
Cotton Davidson	QB	6'1"	180	33		
Tom Flores	QB	6'1"	190	28		
Dick Wood	QB	6'5"	200	29		6
Clem Daniels	HB	6'1"	220	28		72
Gene Mingo	HB	6'1"	190	26		24
Larry Todd	HB	6'1"	185	22		
Roger Hagberg	FB	6'2"	220	26		6
Alan Miller	FB	6'	210	27		24
Fred Biletnikoff	FL	6'1"	190	22		
Pervis Atkins (from WAS-N)	OE	6'1"	195	29		
Billy Cannon	OE	6'1"	225	28		
Ken Herock	OE	6'2"	230	24		
Art Powell	OE	6'3"	212	28		72
Mike Mercer	K	6'	200	29		62

KANSAS CITY CHIEFS 7-5-2 Hank Stram

Scores of Each Game		
10	Oakland	37
14	New York	10
10	San Diego	10
27	BOSTON	17
31	Denver	23
7	BUFFALO	23
36	Houston	38
14	OAKLAND	7
10	NEW YORK	13
31	SAN DIEGO	7
10	Boston	10
52	HOUSTON	21
25	Buffalo	34
45	DENVER	35

Use Name	Pos.	Hgt	Wgt	Age	Int	Pts
Jerry Cornelison	OT	6'3"	250	28		
Dave Hill	OT	6'5"	260	24		
Jim Tyrer	OT	6'6"	292	26		
Denny Biodrowski	OG	6'1"	255	25		
Ed Budde	OG	6'5"	260	24		
Curt Merz	OG	6'4"	250	27		
Al Reynolds	OG	6'3"	235	27		
Jon Gilliam	C	6'2"	240	26		
Mel Branch	DE	6'2"	230	28		
Chuck Hurston	DE	6'6"	227	22		
Ed Lothamer	DE	6'5"	240	22		
Buck Buchanan	DT	6'7"	280	25		
Al Dotson	DT	6'4"	255	22		
Curt Farrier	DT	6'6"	245	24		
Jerry Mays	DT	6'4"	250	25		
Hatch Rosdahl	DT	6'5"	250	22		

Use Name	Pos.	Hgt	Wgt	Age	Int	Pts
Ronnie Caveness	LB	6'1"	215	22		
Walt Corey	LB	6'	242	27		
Jim Fraser	LB	6'3"	236	29		
Sherrill Headrick	LB	6'2"	215	28	1	
E. J. Holub	LB	6'4"	225	27	1	
Smokey Stover	LB	6'	232	26		
Bobby Bell	DE-LB	6'4"	228	25	4	6
Bobby Hunt	DB	6'1"	190	25	1	
Willie Mitchell	DB	6'1"	185	23	2	12
Bobby Ply	DB	6'1"	190	24		
Johnny Robinson	DB	6'	195	26	5	
Fred Williamson	DB	6'2"	215	27	6	

Use Name	Pos.	Hgt	Wgt	Age	Int	Pts
Pete Beathard	QB	6'2"	205	23		26
Len Dawson	QB	6'	190	31		12
Soloman Brannan	HB	6'1"	188	23		
Bert Coan	HB	6'4"	220	25		18
*Mack Lee Hill	HB	5'11"	225	23		18
Jerrel Wilson	HB	6'4"	225	23		2
Curtis McClinton	FB	6'3"	232	26		54
Frank Jackson	FL	6'1"	190	25		6
Frank Pitts	FL	6'2"	190	21		
Fred Arbanas	OE	6'3"	240	26		24
Tommy Brooker	OE	6'2"	230	25		76
Chris Burford	OE	6'3"	210	27		36
Reg Carolan	OE	6'6"	232	25		2
Otis Taylor	OE	6'2"	215	22		30

*Died Dec. 14, 1965 after knee surgery

DENVER BRONCOS 4-10-0 Mac Speedie

Scores of Each Game		
31	San Diego	34
15	BUFFALO	30
27	Boston	10
16	NEW YORK	13
23	KANSAS CITY	31
28	HOUSTON	17
13	Buffalo	31
10	New York	45
21	SAN DIEGO	35
31	Houston	21
20	OAKLAND	28
13	Oakland	24
20	BOSTON	28
35	Kansas City	45

Use Name	Pos.	Hgt	Wgt	Age	Int	Pts
Lee Bernet	OT	6'2"	245	21		
Bob Breitenstein	OT	6'3"	250	22		
Eldon Danenhauer	OT	6'4"	245	29		
Jon Hohman	OG	6'1"	240	22		
Bob McCullough	OG	6'2"	245	24		
Tom Nomina	OG	6'5"	270	23		
Charlie Parker	OG	6'1"	245	23		
Jerry Sturm	OG	6'3"	260	28		
Ray Kubala	C	6'4"	245	23		
Ed Cooke	DE	6'4"	250	30	3	
Leroy Moore	DE	6'	230	29		
Ray Jacobs	DT	6'3"	265	25		
Chuck Janerette	DT	6'3"	265	26	1	
Max Leetzow	DT	6'4"	240	22		
Jim Thompson	DT	6'3"	255	24		

Use Name	Pos.	Hgt	Wgt	Age	Int	Pts
John Bramlett	LB	6'2"	210	24	1	12
Ed Cummings	LB	6'2"	228	24		
Tom Erlandson	LB	6'3"	235	25	1	
Jerry Hopkins	LB	6'2"	235	24	1	
Gene Jeter	LB	6'3"	230	23		
Jim Thibert	LB	6'3"	230	25		
Willie Brown	DB	6'1"	190	24	2	
Gerry Bussell	DB	6'	185	22		
Miller Farr (to SD)	DB	6'1"	188	22	2	
Goose Gonsoulin	DB	6'3"	210	27	6	2
John Griffin	DB	6'1"	190	25	4	12
Gary Kroner	DB	6'1"	200	24		71
John McGeever	DB	6'1"	195	26	1	
Jim McMillin	DB	5'11"	195	27		
Nemiah Wilson	DB	6'	180	22	3	6

Use Name	Pos.	Hgt	Wgt	Age	Int	Pts
Jacky Lee	QB	6'1"	187	26		
John McCormick	QB	6'1"	210	28		
Mickey Slaughter	QB	6'	190	23		
Paul Carmichael	HB	6'	200	20		
Wendell Hayes	HB	6'2"	195	24		44
Abner Haynes	HB	6'	190	27		36
Charley Mitchell	HB	5'11"	185	25		
Cookie Gilchrist	FB	6'3"	250	30		42
Darrell Lester	FB	6'2"	225	24		
Al Denson	FL	6'2"	208	23		
Bob Scarpitto	FL	5'11"	196	26		30
Odell Barry	OE	5'10"	180	23		
Hewritt Dixon	OE	6'2"	217	25		12
Lionel Taylor	OE	6'2"	215	29		36

SAN DIEGO CHARGERS

RUSHING

Last Name	No.	Yds	Avg	TD
Lowe	222	1121	5.1	7
Foster	121	469	3.9	2
Lincoln	74	302	4.1	3
Allison	29	100	3.5	0
Hadl	28	91	3.3	1
MacKinnon	3	17	5.7	0
Breaux	1	−1	−1.0	0
Shea	1	−5	−5.0	0
Norton	1	−5	−5.0	0
Alworth	3	−12	−4.0	0
Sweeney	0	8	0.0	0

RECEIVING

Last Name	No.	Yds	Avg	TD
Alworth	69	1602	23	14
Norton	34	485	14	2
Kocourek	28	363	13	2
Lincoln	23	376	16	4
Foster	17	199	12	0
Lowe	17	126	7	1
Allison	8	109	13	0
Mackinnon	6	106	18	0
Taylor	1	13	13	0

PUNT RETURNS

Last Name	No.	Yds	Avg	TD
Duncan	30	464	15	2
Graham	5	36	7	0
Harris	3	8	3	0

KICKOFF RETURNS

Last Name	No.	Yds	Avg	TD
Duncan	26	612	24	0
Foster	5	108	22	0
Allison	4	80	20	0
Lincoln	2	46	23	0
Harris	1	15	15	0
Kirner	1	0	0	0
Mackinnon	1	0	0	0

PASSING – PUNTING – KICKING

PASSING	Att	Comp	%	Yds	Yd/Att	TD	Int–%	RK
Hadl	348	174	50	2798	8.0	20	21– 6	2
Breaux	43	22	51	404	9.4	2	4– 9	
Lowe	4	3	75	81	20.3	0	0– 0	
Foster	3	2	67	31	10.3	0	0– 0	
Lincoln	3	2	67	65	21.7	1	1– 33	

PUNTING	No	Avg
Hadl	38	40.7
Redman	29	39.5
Allison	2	36.0
Whitehead	1	40.0

KICKING	XP	Att	%	FG	Att	%
Travenio	40	40	100	18	30	60

OAKLAND RAIDERS

RUSHING

Last Name	No.	Yds	Avg	TD
Daniels	219	884	4.0	5
Miller	73	272	3.7	1
Todd	32	183	5.7	0
Hagberg	48	171	3.6	1
Flores	11	32	2.9	0
Wood	4	16	4.0	1
Mercer	1	−1	−1.0	0

RECEIVING

Last Name	No.	Yds	Avg	TD
Powell	52	800	15	12
Daniels	36	568	16	7
Biletnikoff	24	331	14	0
Miller	21	208	10	3
Herock	18	221	12	0
Hagberg	12	121	10	0
Todd	8	106	13	0
Cannon	7	127	18	0
Atkins	1	6	6	0
Mingo	1	5	5	0

PUNT RETURNS

Last Name	No.	Yds	Avg	TD
Gibson	31	357	12	1
Krakoski	2	5	3	0
Hagberg	1	3	3	0

KICKOFF RETURNS

Last Name	No.	Yds	Avg	TD
Todd	20	461	23	0
Gibson	9	186	21	0
Hagberg	3	50	17	0
Grayson	1	34	34	0
Herman	1	0	0	0

PASSING – PUNTING – KICKING

PASSING	Att	Comp	%	Yds	Yd/Att	TD	Int–%	RK
Flores	269	122	45	1593	5.9	14	11– 4	5
Wood	157	69	44	1003	6.4	8	6– 4	4
Daniels	2	2	100	95	47.5	0	0– 0	
C. Davidson	1	1	100	8	8.0	0	0– 0	
Mercer	1	1	100	14	14.0	0	0– 0	
Todd	1	0	0	0	0.0	0	0– 0	

PUNTING	No	Avg
Mercer	75	41.1

KICKING	XP	Att	%	FG	Att	%
Mercer	35	35	100	9	15	60
Mingo	0	0	0	8	19	42

KANSAS CITY CHIEFS

RUSHING

Last Name	No.	Yds	Avg	TD
McClinton	175	661	3.8	6
M. Hill	125	627	5.0	2
Dawson	43	142	3.3	2
Beathard	25	138	5.5	4
Coan	45	137	3.0	1
Jackson	1	26	26.0	0
Taylor	2	17	8.5	0
Wilson	2	4	2.0	0

RECEIVING

Last Name	No.	Yds	Avg	TD
Burford	47	575	12	6
McClinton	37	590	16	3
Jackson	28	440	16	1
Taylor	26	446	17	5
Arbanas	24	418	17	4
M. Hill	21	264	13	1
Coan	9	85	9	2
Carolan	6	65	11	0
Pitts	1	11	11	0

PUNT RETURNS

Last Name	No.	Yds	Avg	TD
Mitchell	19	242	13	1
Jackson	13	163	13	0
Brannan	5	10	2	0
Pitts	1	4	4	0

KICKOFF RETURNS

Last Name	No.	Yds	Avg	TD
Coan	19	479	25	0
Jackson	9	260	29	0
Brannan	9	226	25	0
Pitts	5	100	20	0
Stover	3	7	2	0
Fraser	1	5	5	0
Mays	2	3	2	0

PASSING – PUNTING – KICKING

PASSING	Att	Comp	%	Yds	Yd/Att	TD	Int–%	RK
Dawson	305	163	53	2262	7.4	21	14– 5	1
Beathard	89	36	41	632	7.1	1	6– 7	
McClinton	1	0	0	0	0.0	0	0– 0	

PUNTING	No	Avg
Wilson	68	46.1
Fraser	3	27.0

KICKING	XP	Att	%	FG	Att	%
Brooker	37	37	100	13	30	43

2 POINT XP
Beathard
Carolan
Wilson

DENVER BRONCOS

RUSHING

Last Name	No.	Yds	Avg	TD
Gilchrist	252	954	3.8	6
Hayes	130	526	4.1	5
Haynes	41	166	4.1	3
Scarpitto	4	94	23.5	0
Slaughter	20	75	3.8	0
Barry	2	19	9.5	0
Lee	2	1	0.5	0
McCormick	1	−2	−2.0	0
Denson	1	−4	−4.0	0

RECEIVING

Last Name	No.	Yds	Avg	TD
Taylor	85	1131	13	6
Scarpitto	32	585	18	5
Haynes	26	216	8	2
Dixon	25	354	14	2
Hayes	24	294	12	2
Gilchrist	18	154	9	1
Denson	9	102	11	0
Barry	2	11	6	0
McCullough	1	1	1	0

PUNT RETURNS

Last Name	No.	Yds	Avg	TD
Barry	21	210	10	0
Haynes	14	121	9	1
Bussell	2	24	12	0

KICKOFF RETURNS

Last Name	No.	Yds	Avg	TD
Haynes	34	901	27	0
Barry	26	611	24	0
Farr	7	123	18	0
Bussell	5	103	21	0
Hayes	4	93	23	0
Carmichael	1	15	15	0
Dixon	1	8	8	0

PASSING – PUNTING – KICKING

PASSING	Att	Comp	%	Yds	Yd/Att	TD	Int–%	RK
McCormick	253	103	41	1292	5.1	7	14– 6	10
Slaughter	147	75	51	864	5.9	6	12– 8	9
Lee	80	44	55	692	8.7	5	3– 4	
Hayes	1	0	0	0	0.0	0	1–100	
Haynes	1	0	0	0	0.0	0	0– 0	

PUNTING	No	Avg
Scarpitto	67	42.3
McCormick	1	45.0

KICKING	XP	Att	%	FG	Att	%
Kroner	32	32	100	13	29	45

2 POINT XP
Gunsoulin
Hayes

1966 N.F.L. Closing the Checkbook

The war between the two leagues was getting very expensive. To sign heralded rookies Donny Anderson, Jim Grabowski, and Tommy Nobis, NFL clubs had to give each of them contracts more lucrative than that given to Joe Namath by the AFL Jets last year. But after the New York Giants signed kicker Pete Gogolak away from the AFL Buffalo Bills, the heat of battle became unbearable. Considering the signing of Gogolak as a direct slap, the AFL owners went all out to pirate away established NFL stars. With John Brodie, Roman Gabriel, and Mike Ditka on the verge of jumping and other NFL stars thinking it over, the established league sat down with the upstarts to discuss terms of peace. In June, officials of both leagues announced a merger that would change the organizational set-up of pro football. With Pete Rozelle as Commissioner over both leagues, the NFL and AFL would conduct a common draft of college players starting next year and would finish this season with the first Super Bowl between the two league champions.

EASTERN CONFERENCE

Dallas Cowboys—With Don Meredith at quarterback, the Dallas offense was the league's most versatile and explosive. Bob Hayes used his sprinter's speed to gain 1,232 yards on passes, while Dan Reeves succeeded at halfback despite his slowness afoot. Signed two years ago as a free agent, Reeves hustled his way to sixteen touchdowns, eight each by running and receiving, and was a threat to throw the option pass on sweeps. Ralph Neely led the blocking in a strong offensive line. The defense, loaded with quality players, led the league in sacking enemy quarterbacks and gave up yardage with extreme reluctance. Coach Tom Landry had been collecting talent for years and now all the pieces had fit together.

Cleveland Browns—Jimmy Brown had retired to become an actor, but no one could blame replacement Leroy Kelly for Cleveland's slip to second place. Kelly had distinguished himself for two years as a kick returner, and when he was thrust into Brown's vacant shoes at fullback, he surprised the league by rushing for 1,141 yards, second only to Gale Sayers in the NFL. Kelly relied more on speed than did Brown, leaving the power running to Ernie Green. Paul Warfield returned from last year's shoulder injury to join Gary Collins in the wide receiving duo, and Frank Ryan found his targets often enough to throw for twenty-nine touchdowns. The Browns' fatal flaw this season was a slow start in which they lost two of their first three games.

Philadelphia Eagles—Despite a weak passing attack, the Eagles reached third place with their best record in five years. Behind a good offensive line, the running corps of Timmy Brown, Earl Gros, Tom Woodeshick, and Izzy Lang ate up large chunks of yardage, and Brown also doubled as the team's top kickoff returner, bringing two kickoffs back for touchdowns in one game against the Cowboys. The lack of quality receivers and Norm Snead's poor season hurt the attack, but the defense showed enough strength to carry the team.

St. Louis Cardinals—The Cards had a new coach in Charley Winner but the same old problem with injuries. Battling with Dallas for first place in the East, the Cards lost quarterback Charley Johnson with a knee injury and they scored only fifty-two points in their last five games, losing four of them, to fall to fourth place. Injuries also stripped end Sonny Randle, offensive linemen Bob DeMarco, Ken Gray, and Irv Goode, and cornerback Pat Fischer from the active rolls for varying lengths of time.

Washington Redskins—The Redskins brought former Cleveland great Otto Graham back to pro football as head coach, and Graham as expected put the emphasis in the Washington attack on the pass. The air game worked fine, with Sonny Jurgensen doing the pitching and Charley Taylor, converted from halfback to end in mid-season, Bobby Mitchell, and Jerry Smith doing most of the catching. Even without a legitimate running attack, the Redskins could put points on the scoreboard. But the defense needed time to jell, with seven new faces in the starting lineup.

Pittsburgh Steelers—Coach Bill Austin took the Steelers to five wins despite some severe problems on offense. The line blocked poorly, rookie Willie Asbury was the only effective runner, and the quarterback situation was unstable. Bill Nelsen hurt his knee in the second game of the year, and Ron Smith, let go by the Packers, filled in at quarterback for most of the season. The defense carried the club through the body of the schedule, but Nelsen returned to action for the last three games and beat New York 47-28 and Atlanta 57-33 to end the year.

Atlanta Falcons—The Falcons lost their first nine NFL games but came back to win three of their last five contests to escape the cellar in their first season in the league. Junior Coffey, obtained from Green Bay in the expansion draft, developed into a fine runner, but most of the impressive performances were turned in by rookies such as linebacker Tommy Nobis, quarterback Randy Johnson, and defensive backs Bob Riggle, Nick Rassas, and Ken Reaves.

New York Giants—With Tucker Frederickson out all year with a bad knee, Earl Morrall sidelined for the last half of the schedule with a broken wrist, and the defense a horrendous hodgepodge of journeymen and youth, the Giants suffered through the worst season in their history. They beat the Redskins 13-10 in mid-October for their only win of the year, and the rematch in late November resulted in a 72-41 embarrassment.

WESTERN CONFERENCE

Green Bay Packers—The Packers shelled out about $1,000,000 to sign All-American runners Donny Anderson and Jim Grabowski, but Vince Lombardi kept his Green Bay machine running with old pros and a few key replacement parts. With Paul Hornung bothered by a neck injury, Elijah Pitts did most of the playing at halfback, while ex-Ram Carroll Dale slipped past Max McGee into the starting lineup as a wide receiver. On defense, quick Bob Jeter switched from offensive end to capture a cornerback slot. The heart of the Packers, however, was still the troop of seasoned veterans who had grown used to the taste of winning, and that was good enough to bring the Packers home first in the West.

Baltimore Colts—The Colts lost the opening game of the season to the Packers and struggled futilely to catch up the rest of the year. With a veteran team that was approaching old age all at once, the Colts had solid units both on defense and offense. The defensive line relied on quickness and got some size late in the year when Gino Marchetti came out of retirement; the linebacking was strengthened by the conversion of Mike Curtis from fullback to a corner linebacker; and Bobby Boyd, Lenny Lyles, Alvin Haymond, Jerry Logan, and Jim Welch blanketed enemy pass receivers from their deep spots. The offense moved on the arm of Johnny Unitas, but the Colts lost twice to the Packers and had to settle for second place behind them.

Los Angeles Rams—The Rams had to go to court to get George Allen to be their head coach, but the results proved well worth the trouble. Allen rebuilt the Los Angeles defense into one of the league's best. He inherited a great front four in Deacon Jones, Lamar Lundy, Merlin Olsen, and Rosie Grier, but he completely overhauled the linebacking. He talked Jack Pardee out of retirement, signed Bill George as a free agent after the Bears cut him, and traded for Maxie Baughan from the Eagles and Myron Pottios from the Steelers. To tighten up the secondary, he brought in Irv Cross from Philadelphia. Although the offense lacked flair, the improved defense carried the club to its first winning season since 1958.

San Francisco '49ers—With the Houston Oilers trying to lure him into the AFL, John Brodie bargained himself into a multiyear contract worth over $900,000. With his financial future secure, Brodie did nothing to show that he could lead a team to a championship. With a good line, punishing runners in Ken Willard and John David Crow, and fine wide receivers like Bernie Casey and Dave Parks, the San Francisco attack ran in spurts, running up big scores against Detroit, Chicago, and Atlanta and losing 28-3 to Minnesota and 34-3 to Los Angeles.

Chicago Bears—With George Halas taking George Allen into court to keep him from resigning as an assistant coach, with Doug Atkins and Mike Ditka openly critical of Halas, with Rudy Bukich suffering through a miserable campaign, and with Johnny Morris sidelined with a bad knee, Bear fans found Gale Sayers' superb season a pleasant diversion from the Bears' problems. Sayers improved on his rookie season by leading the NFL in rushing, catching thirty-four passes and breaking off two touchdowns in pacing the league in kickoff returning. Adding together his rushing, receiving, and returning totals, Sayers gained 2,440 yards, a new record.

Detroit Lions—Problems at quarterback made the Detroit offense a plodding affair. Milt Plum began the year as signal-caller but went out of service with a mid-season injury. Karl Sweetan, who had spent last season with the semi-pro Pontiac Arrows, stepped in and did a creditable job as a passer but could not ignite the attack into steady fireworks. On one play, however, Sweetan got the offense moving, passing to Pat Studstill for a 99-yard touchdown against the Colts on October 16. Studstill was one of the league's sensations, developing into a dangerous pass receiver despite his small size and very ordinary speed. Another player to attract attention was Garo Yepremian, a soccer-style place-kicker from Cyprus who was signed in mid-season and booted a record six field goals against the Vikings on November 13.

Minnesota Vikings—Expecting to move up into championship status for the last few seasons, the Vikings simply were not improving with their current team. The defense was not getting much better, halfback Tommy Mason was spending more time hurt than healthy, and quarterback Fran Tarkenton was hardly on speaking terms with coach Norm Van Brocklin. Once in a while the potential would show through in big victories such as the 20-17 triumph over Green Bay, but this promising team kept losing without much promise of winning.

FINAL TEAM STATISTICS

OFFENSE

	ATL.	BALT.	CHI.	CLEV.	DALL.	DET.	G.B.	L.A.	MINN.	N.Y.	PHIL.	PITT.	ST.L.	S.F.	WASH.
FIRST DOWNS:															
Total	211	237	196	278	**287**	216	231	255	279	236	231	207	212	282	225
by Rushing	85	82	96	117	124	73	98	103	**126**	80	112	65	88	101	78
by Passing	104	142	85	142	139	126	115	133	132	129	104	117	108	**153**	130
by Penalty	22	13	15	19	24	17	18	19	21	27	15	25	16	**28**	17
RUSHING:															
Number	405	418	463	415	471	394	475	448	**551**	380	478	375	458	422	356
Yards	1519	1556	1927	**2166**	2122	1429	1673	1742	2091	1457	1859	1092	1601	1790	1377
Average Yards	3.8	3.7	4.2	**5.2**	4.5	3.6	3.5	3.9	3.8	3.8	3.9	2.9	3.5	4.2	3.9
Touchdowns	11	7	12	18	**24**	13	18	12	15	7	19	13	10	12	9
PASSING:															
Attempts	381	401	338	402	413	456	318	450	417	424	378	401	386	**500**	443
Completions	175	221	159	212	214	239	193	249	216	208	179	188	180	**261**	255
Completion Percentage	45.9	55.1	47.0	52.7	51.8	52.4	**60.7**	55.3	51.8	49.1	47.4	46.9	46.6	52.2	57.6
Passing Yards	2362	3172	2016	3142	**3331**	2752	2831	2891	2932	2999	2159	2877	2292	3239	3230
Average Yards per Attempt	6.2	7.9	5.0	7.8	8.1	6.0	**8.9**	6.4	7.0	7.1	5.7	7.2	5.9	6.5	7.3
Average Yards per Completion	13.5	14.4	12.7	14.8	**15.6**	11.5	14.7	11.6	13.6	14.4	12.1	15.3	12.7	12.4	12.7
Times Tackled Attempting to Pass	38	30	29	29	42	35	31	54	45	62	35	66	38	30	**27**
Yards Lost Tackled Attempting to Pass	345	242	244	237	308	328	229	351	384	524	259	523	352	247	**216**
Net Yards	2017	2930	1772	2905	**3023**	2424	2602	2540	2548	2475	1900	2354	1940	2992	3014
Touchdowns	14	26	10	**33**	27	8	18	12	18	20	14	18	13	21	28
Interceptions	27	27	23	15	14	28	**5**	17	22	31	22	22	19	26	20
Percent Intercepted	7.1	6.7	6.8	3.7	3.4	6.1	**1.6**	3.8	5.3	7.3	5.8	5.5	4.9	5.2	4.5
PUNTS:															
Number	73	49	80	57	55	72	62	71	60	53	65	78	**81**	70	68
Average Distance	40.7	**45.6**	42.0	39.0	39.2	41.1	41.0	42.8	41.1	38.9	39.8	42.1	35.6	40.6	42.4
PUNT RETURNS:															
Number	18	**45**	25	24	41	38	37	**45**	31	22	31	21	40	**45**	29
Yards	100	357	97	146	258	**396**	215	341	129	120	162	43	316	238	201
Average Yards	5.6	7.9	3.9	6.1	6.3	**10.4**	5.8	7.6	4.2	5.5	5.2	2.0	7.9	5.3	6.9
Touchdowns	0	0	0	0	0	1	1	0	0	0	1	0	1	1	1
KICKOFF RETURNS:															
Number	**82**	51	48	54	44	58	42	42	52	80	64	64	57	56	69
Yards	**1737**	1094	1341	1111	1086	1316	903	1015	987	1616	1419	1384	1348	1326	1435
Average	21.2	21.5	**27.9**	20.6	22.9	22.7	21.5	24.2	19.0	20.2	22.2	21.6	23.6	23.7	20.8
Touchdowns	0	0	**2**	0	1	0	0	0	0	1	**2**	1	1	0	0
INTERCEPTION RETURNS:															
Number	19	22	15	**30**	17	24	28	26	14	17	20	24	21	18	23
Yards	177	267	155	408	303	366	**547**	362	230	217	345	280	330	379	369
Average Yards	9.3	12.1	10.3	13.6	17.8	15.3	19.5	13.9	16.4	12.8	17.3	11.7	15.7	**21.1**	16.0
Touchdowns	1	2	0	1	3	1	**6**	4	1	2	1	2	3	3	1
PENALTIES:															
Number	79	64	80	69	63	82	57	72	67	57	63	75	67	**86**	64
Yards	753	617	714	747	824	**931**	544	651	787	602	666	768	586	819	591
FUMBLES:															
Number	30	19	26	**17**	23	33	23	25	33	29	32	34	26	26	27
Number Lost	17	12	12	**10**	**10**	21	19	12	14	13	17	17	18	12	15
POINTS:															
Total	204	314	234	403	**445**	206	335	289	292	263	326	316	264	320	351
PAT Attempts	26	36	26	54	**56**	23	43	29	34	31	39	36	28	39	41
PAT Made	21	35	24	52	**56**	23	41	29	34	29	38	35	27	38	39
FG Attempts	19	39	30	23	31	30	28	**49**	33	28	25	32	40	31	34
FG Made	9	21	18	9	17	15	12	**28**	18	16	18	21	23	16	22
Percent FG Made	47.4	53.8	60.0	39.1	54.8	50.0	42.9	57.1	54.5	57.1	**72.0**	65.6	57.5	51.6	64.7
Safeties	0	0	0	0	1	0	0	1	0	0	0	1	0	0	0

DEFENSE

	ATL.	BALT.	CHI.	CLEV.	DALL.	DET.	G.B.	L.A.	MINN.	N.Y.	PHIL.	PITT.	ST.L	S.F.	WASH.
FIRST DOWNS:															
Total	295	245	239	255	221	240	211	**196**	213	273	249	238	209	238	261
by Rushing	126	94	102	113	**64**	109	90	**64**	85	122	90	107	68	88	106
by Passing	151	134	116	124	140	108	106	114	116	137	139	**105**	109	126	134
by Penalty	18	17	21	18	17	23	15	18	**12**	14	20	26	32	24	21
RUSHING:															
Number	472	460	466	450	**356**	479	446	401	412	480	390	468	377	414	438
Yards	2172	1733	1604	1894	**1176**	2006	1644	1302	1686	2053	1693	1786	1192	1629	1831
Average Yards	4.6	3.8	3.4	4.2	3.3	4.2	3.7	3.2	4.1	4.3	4.3	3.8	**3.2**	3.9	4.2
Touchdowns	20	7	13	12	**6**	16	9	10	15	23	13	11	11	15	19
PASSING:															
Attempts	396	425	406	406	457	363	390	406	391	**357**	446	397	443	414	411
Completions	227	240	202	221	212	210	202	**190**	206	194	226	192	197	206	224
Completion Percentage	57.3	56.5	49.8	54.4	46.4	57.9	51.8	46.8	52.7	54.3	50.7	48.4	**44.5**	49.8	54.5
Passing Yards	3376	2759	2600	2650	2802	2702	**2316**	2830	2426	3086	2964	2849	2733	2895	3237
Average Yards per Attempt	8.5	6.5	6.4	6.5	6.1	7.4	**5.9**	7.0	6.2	8.6	6.6	7.2	6.2	7.0	7.9
Average Yards per Completion	14.9	11.5	12.9	12.0	13.2	12.9	**11.5**	14.9	11.8	15.9	13.1	14.8	13.9	14.1	14.5
Times Tackled Attempting to Pass	34	47	29	35	**60**	34	47	45	25	26	34	38	52	40	45
Yards Lost Tackled Attempting to Pass	276	401	233	278	420	294	357	361	190	194	287	344	**433**	345	376
Net Yards	3100	2358	2367	2372	2382	2408	**1959**	2469	2236	2892	2677	2505	2300	2550	2861
Touchdowns	26	14	13	14	17	19	**7**	13	13	36	23	27	15	22	21
Interceptions	19	22	15	**30**	17	24	28	26	14	17	20	24	21	18	23
Percent Intercepted	4.8	5.2	3.7	**7.4**	3.7	6.6	7.2	6.4	3.6	4.8	4.5	6.0	4.7	4.3	5.6
PUNTS:															
Number	38	71	71	56	79	71	69	73	72	58	60	64	**85**	76	61
Average Distance	38.6	40.6	42.4	39.7	42.4	41.1	41.3	43.8	40.6	39.8	39.9	**37.8**	40.7	41.2	38.4
PUNT RETURNS:															
Number	35	30	46	**23**	26	27	30	49	28	27	31	42	25	33	40
Yards	197	130	250	111	108	**98**	171	269	250	218	300	242	159	368	248
Average Yards	5.6	4.3	5.4	4.3	4.2	**3.6**	5.7	5.5	8.9	8.1	9.7	5.8	6.4	11.2	6.2
Touchdowns	1	**0**	1	**0**	1	**0**	**0**	**0**	**0**	1	1	**0**	**0**	1	**0**
KICKOFF RETURNS:															
Number	**44**	63	49	68	78	45	52	58	50	49	65	63	50	59	70
Yards	**362**	1320	1055	1501	1699	1004	1213	1329	1203	1085	1330	1485	1021	1343	1488
Average	21.9	21.0	21.5	22.1	21.8	22.3	23.3	22.9	24.1	22.1	20.5	23.6	**20.4**	22.8	21.3
Touchdowns	**0**	**0**	**0**	2	3	**0**	**0**	**0**	**0**	1	1	**0**	**0**	1	**0**
INTERCEPTION RETURNS:															
Number	27	27	23	15	14	28	**5**	17	22	31	22	22	19	26	20
Yards	385	438	426	**68**	274	409	75	338	337	465	380	319	236	334	251
Average Yards	14.3	16.2	18.5	**4.5**	19.6	14.7	15.0	19.9	15.3	15.0	17.3	14.5	12.4	12.8	12.6
Touchdowns	3	3	6	**0**	1	3	**0**	2	2	4	3	1	1	1	1
PENALTIES:															
Number	66	69	71	61	63	61	67	76	67	83	63	82	83	**91**	62
Yards	588	704	636	563	778	564	745	704	667	788	703	835	761	**938**	626
FUMBLES:															
Number	24	25	35	24	23	19	26	**37**	24	19	30	**37**	20	24	36
Number Lost	13	18	**23**	19	14	11	14	20	8	7	15	16	10	11	20
POINTS:															
Total	437	226	272	259	239	317	**163**	212	304	501	340	347	265	325	355
PAT Attempts	52	25	34	29	29	38	**17**	26	33	66	40	42	28	40	42
PAT Made	48	25	32	28	29	38	**16**	26	32	64	40	38	28	37	40
FG Attempts	41	33	29	28	31	31	27	**22**	41	23	30	33	41	31	31
FG Made	25	17	12	19	12	17	15	**10**	24	13	20	19	23	16	21
Percent FG Made	61.0	51.5	41.4	67.9	**38.7**	54.8	55.6	45.5	58.5	56.5	66.7	57.6	56.1	51.6	67.7
Safeties	1	**0**	**0**	**0**	**0**	**0**	**0**	**0**	1	1	**0**	**0**	**0**	**0**	**0**

Super-bound

A trip to the first Super Bowl awaited the winner of this NFL championship game, which featured the Packers and the Cowboys. The Packers took an early lead on a Bart Starr-to-Elijah Pitts touchdown pass and immediately added on another touchdown when Mel Renfro fumbled the kickoff and Jim Grabowski ran the recovery in from 17 yards out. The Cowboys, one of pro football's exciting young teams, came right back with two touchdowns to tie the score, 14-14, at the end of one quarter. The Packers scored in the second period on a long Bart Starr-to-Carroll Dale pass, while the Cowboys answered only with a Danny Villanueva field goal. Another Villanueva three-pointer lowered the Packer lead to 21-20 in the third quarter, but touchdown passes to Boyd Dowler and Max McGee ran the score to 34-20 and seemingly put the game on ice. The Cowboys fought back, however, scoring on a long pass from Don Meredith to Frank Clarke. In the final minutes, Dallas drove for the winning touchdown, only to fall short when Meredith's fourth-down pass was intercepted in the end zone by Tom Brown

1966 NFL CHAMPIONSHIP GAME

January 1, at Dallas (Attendance 74,152)

SCORING

DALLAS	14	3	3	7	–27
GREEN BAY	14	7	7	6	–34

First Quarter
- GB Pitts, 17 yd pass by Starr (Chandler – kick)
- GB Grabowski, 18 yd Fumble recovery return (Chandler – kick)
- DA Reeves, 3 yd rush (Villanueva – kick)
- DA Perkins, 23 yd rush (Villanueva – kick)

Second Quarter
- GB Dale, 51 yd pass by Starr (Chandler – kick)
- DA Villanueva, 11 yd field goal

Third Quarter
- DA Villanueva, 32 yd field goal
- GB Dowler, 16 yd pass by Starr (Chandler – kick)

Fourth Quarter
- GB McGee, 28 yd pass by Starr (Kick Blocked)
- DA Clarke, 68 yd pass by Meredith (Villanueva – kick)

TEAM STATISTICS

	DALL.	G.B.
First Downs – Total	23	19
First Downs – Rushing	12	3
First Downs – Passing	10	14
First Downs – Penalty	1	2
Punts – Number	4	4
Punts – Average Distance	32.2	40.0
Punt Returns – Number	3	0
Punt Returns – Yards	–9	0
Interception Ret – Number	0	1
Interception Ret – Yards	0	0
Fumbles – Number	3	1
Fumbles – Lost Ball	1	1
Penalties – Number	6	2
Yards Penalized	29	23
Offensive Plays	73	57
Net Yards	231	367
Average Gain	3.2	6.4
Giveaways	2	1
Takeaways	1	2
Difference	–1	+1

INDIVIDUAL STATISTICS

RUSHING

DALLAS	No	Yds	Avg.	GREEN BAY	No	Yds	Avg.
Perkins	17	108	6.4	Pitts	12	66	5.5
Reeves	17	47	2.8	Taylor	10	37	3.7
Meredith	4	22	5.5	Starr	2	–1	–0.5
Norman	2	10	5.0		24	102	4.3
	40	187	4.7				

RECEIVING

DALLAS	No	Yds	Avg.	GREEN BAY	No	Yds	Avg.
Reeves	4	77	19.3	Dale	5	128	25.6
Norman	4	30	7.5	Taylor	5	23	4.6
Clarke	3	102	34.0	Fleming	3	50	16.7
Gent	3	28	9.3	Dowler	3	49	16.3
Hayes	1	1	3.0	McGee	1	28	28.0
	15	238	15.9	Pitts	1	17	17.0
				Long	1	9	9.0
					19	304	16.0

PASSING

	Att	Comp	Comp Pct.	Yds	Int	Yds/ Att.	Yds/ Comp	Yds Lost Tackled
DALLAS								
Meredith	31	15	48.4	238	1	7.7	15.9	2– 7
GREEN BAY								
Starr	28	19	67.9	304	0	10.9	16.0	5–39

DALLAS COWBOYS 10-3-1 Tom Landry

Scores of Each Game		
52	NEW YORK	7
28	MINNESOTA	17
47	Atlanta	14
56	PHILADELPHIA	7
10	St. Louis	10
21	Clevleand	30
52	PITTSBURGH	21
23	Philadelphia	24
31	Washington	30
20	Pittsburgh	7
26	CLEVELAND	14
31	ST. LOUIS	17
31	WASHINGTON	34
17	New York	7

Use Name	Pos.	Hgt	Wgt	Age	Int	Pts
Jim Boeke	OT	6'5"	255	27		
Ralph Neely	OT	6'5"	257	22		
Tony Liscio	OG-OT	6'5"	255	26		
Leon Donahue	OG	6'4"	245	27		
John Niland	OG	6'4"	250	22		
Mike Connelly	OT-OG	6'3"	248	30		
Dave Manders	C	6'2"	240	24		
Malcolm Walker	OT-C	6'4"	245	23		
George Andrie	DE	6'7"	255	26	1	6
Larry Stephens	DE	6'4"	250	28		
Jethro Pugh	DT-DE	6'6"	250	22		
John Wilbur	DT-DE	6'3"	250	23		
Jim Colvin	DT	6'2"	255	29		
Bob Lilly	DT	6'4"	255	27		
Bill Sandeman	DT	6'6"	250	23		
Willie Townes	DE-DT	6'5"	265	23		2
Dave Edwards	LB	6'3"	226	27	1	
Harold Hays	LB	6'3"	223	25		
Chuck Howley	LB	6'3"	223	30		6
Lee Roy Jordan	LB	6'2"	216	25	1	6
Jerry Tubbs	LB	6'2"	222	31	1	
Dick Daniels	DB	5'9"	180	20		
Mike Gaechter	DB	6'	190	26	3	
Cornell Green	DB	6'4"	215	26	4	6
Mike Johnson	DB	5'10"	186	22		
Warren Livingston	DB	5'10"	190	28	2	
Obert Logan	DB	5'10"	180	24	2	
Mel Renfro	HB-DB	6'	195	24	2	6
Jim Steffen – Injury						
Don Meredith	QB	6'2"	206	28		30
Craig Morton	QB	6'4"	216	23		
Jerry Rhome	QB	6'	187	24		
Dan Reeves	HB	6'1"	203	22		96
Les Shy	HB	6'1"	210	22		6
Walt Garrison	FB-HB	6'	200	22		6
Don Perkins	FB	5'10"	206	28		48
J. D. Smith	FB	6'1"	210	33		6
Buddy Dial	FL	6'1"	195	29		6
Pete Gent	FL	6'4"	210	23		6
Frank Clarke	TE	6'	210	33		24
Pettis Norman	TE	6'3"	223	26		
Bob Hayes	OE	6'	190	23		78
Danny Villanueva	K	5'11"	200	28		107

PHILADELPHIA EAGLES 9-5-0 Joe Kuharich

Scores of Each Game		
13	St. Louis	16
23	ATLANTA	10
35	NEW YORK	17
10	ST. LOUIS	41
7	Dallas	56
31	Pittsburgh	14
31	New York	3
13	WASHINGTON	27
24	DALLAS	23
7	Cleveland	27
35	San Francisco	34
27	PITTSBURGH	23
33	CLEVELAND	21
37	Washington	28

Use Name	Pos.	Hgt	Wgt	Age	Int	Pts
Bob Brown	OT	6'4"	276	23		
Dave Graham	OT	6'3"	250	27		
Lane Howell	OT	6'5"	270	25		
Ray Rissmiller	OT	6'4"	250	24		
Ed Blaine	OG	6'2"	240	26		
Jim Skaggs	OG	6'2"	250	26		
Bruce Van Dyke	OG	6'2"	235	22		
Lynn Hoyem	C-OG	6'4"	253	26		
Dave Recher	C	6'1"	245	23		
Jim Ringo	C	6'1"	230	35		
Randy Beisler	DE	6'4"	245	21		
Don Hultz	DE	6'3"	235	25		
Gary Pettigrew	DE	6'4"	245	21		
Dave Cahill	DT	6'3"	238	24		
John Meyers	DT	6'6"	276	26		
Floyd Peters	DT	6'4"	255	31		
Ike Kelley	LB	5'11"	225	22		
Dave Lloyd	LB	6'3"	248	30	3	
Mike Morgan	LB	6'4"	242	24	1	
Arunas Vasys	LB	6'2"	225	23		
Harold Wells	LB	6'2"	220	27	1	6
Fred Whittingham	LB	6'1"	240	27	1	
Aaron Martin	DB	6'	185	25	1	6
Ron Medved	DB	6'1"	210	22		
Al Nelson	DB	5'11"	186	22	1	6
Jim Nettles	DB	5'9"	180	24	3	6
Nate Ramsey	DB	6'1"	200	25	1	
Joe Scarpati	DB	5'10"	185	24	8	
Fred Brown – Knee Injury						
Frank Molden – Knee Injury						
Ray Poage – Knee Injury						
Bob Shann – Injury						
Jack Concannon	QB	6'3"	195	23		12
King Hill	QB	6'3"	213	30		
Norm Snead	QB	6'4"	205	26		6
Timmy Brown	HB	5'10"	198	29		48
Ollie Matson	HB	6'2"	210	36		12
Earl Gros	FB	6'3"	220	25		54
Izzy Lang	FB	6'1"	230	23		6
Tom Woodeshick	HB-FB	6'	220	24		30
Willie Brown	FL	6'	185	23		
T.J. Jackson	FL	6'	180	23		
Ron Goodwin	OE-FL	6'	180	24		6
Pete Retzlaff	TE	6'1"	214	35		36
Dave Lince	TE	6'6"	250	22		
Fred Hill	OE	6'2"	215	23		
Ben Hawkins	FL-OE	6'	180	22		
Sam Baker	K	6'2"	218	34		92

CLEVELAND BROWNS 9-5-0 Blanton Collier

Scores of Each Game		
38	Washington	14
20	GREEN BAY	21
28	ST. LOUIS	34
28	New York	7
41	PITTSBURGH	10
30	DALLAS	21
49	Atlanta	17
6	Pittsburgh	16
27	PHILADELPHIA	7
14	WASHINGTON	3
14	Dallas	26
49	NEW YORK	40
21	Philadelphia	33
38	St. Louis	10

Use Name	Pos.	Hgt	Wgt	Age	Int	Pts
Jim Battle	OT	6'4"	235	25		
John Brown	OT	6'2"	248	27		
Monte Clark	OT	6'6"	265	29		
Dick Schafrath	OT	6'3"	255	30		
Gene Hickerson	OG	6'3"	248	31		
Joe Bob Isbell	OG	6'1"	250	26		
John Wooten	OG	6'2"	250	31		
Fred Hoaglin	C	6'4"	240	22		
John Morrow	C	6'3"	248	33		
Bill Glass	DE	6'5"	255	30		6
Paul Wiggin	DE	6'3"	245	32	1	
Walter Johnson	DT	6'3"	265	23		
Jim Kanicki	DT	6'4"	270	24		
Dick Modzelewski	DT	6'	260	35		
Frank Parker	DT	6'5"	270	26		
Johnny Brewer	LB	6'4"	235	29	1	
Vince Costello	LB	6'	228	34	1	
Galen Fiss	LB	6'	227	36		
Dale Lindsey	LB	6'3"	220	23		
Sid Williams	LB	6'2"	235	24		
Jim Houston	TE-LB	6'2"	240	29	2	7
Erich Barnes	DB	6'2"	198	31	4	
Walter Beach	DB	6'	185	31	1	
Ross Fichtner	DB	6'	185	28	8	6
Bobby Franklin	DB	5'11"	182	30		
Mike Howell	DB	6'1"	187	23	8	
Ernie Kellerman	DB	6'	183	22	3	
Bernie Parrish (to HOU-A)	DB	5'11"	195	31	1	
Gary Lane	QB	6'1"	210	23		
Jim Ninowski	QB	6'1"	207	30		
Frank Ryan	QB	6'3"	200	30		
Leroy Kelly	HB	6'	195	24		96
Randy Schultz	FB-HB	5'11"	210	22		
Ernie Green	FB	6'2"	205	27		54
Charlie Harraway	FB	6'2"	230	21		
Nick Pietrosante	FB	6'2"	225	29		
Gary Collins	FL	6'4"	208	25		72
Clifton McNeil	FL	6'2"	185	26		12
Milt Morin	TE	6'4"	250	24		18
Ralph Smith	TE	6'2"	215	27		18
Paul Warfield	OE	6'	188	23		36
Walter Roberts	FL-OE	5'10"	163	24		
Lou Groza	K	6'3"	250	42		78

ST. LOUIS CARDINALS 8-5-1 Charley Winner

Scores of Each Game		
16	PHILADELPHIA	13
23	WASHINGTON	7
34	Cleveland	28
41	Philadelphia	10
24	NEW YORK	19
10	DALLAS	10
20	Washington	26
24	CHICAGO	17
20	New York	17
9	Pittsburgh	30
6	PITTSBURGH	3
17	Dallas	31
10	Atlanta	16
10	CLEVELAND	38

Use Name	Pos.	Hgt	Wgt	Age	Int	Pts
John McDowell	OT	6'3"	260	23		
Ernie McMillan	OT	6'6"	260	28		
Bob Reynolds	OT	6'6"	265	25		
Dave O'Brien	OG-OT	6'3"	247	25		
Ken Gray	OG	6'2"	250	30		
Frank Roy	OG	6'2"	230	23		
Rick Sortun	OG	6'2"	235	23		
Irv Goode	C-OG	6'4"	250	25		
Bob DeMarco	C	6'3"	240	28		
Dick Kasperek	C	6'3"	225	22		
Don Brumm	DE	6'3"	245	23		
Mike Melinkovich	DE	6'4"	245	24		
Joe Robb	DE	6'3"	245	29		
Dave Long	DT-DE	6'4"	235	21		
Sam Silas	DT	6'4"	250	23		
Chuck Walker	DT	6'2"	245	25		
Fred Heron	DE-DT	6'4"	250	21		
Bill Koman	LB	6'2"	230	32		
Dave Meggyesy	LB	6'1"	220	24		
Dale Meinert	LB	6'2"	220	33		
Dave Simmons	LB	6'4"	245	23		
Larry Stallings	LB	6'2"	230	24	1	
Mike Strofolino	LB	6'2"	230	22		
Jimmy Burson	DB	6'	180	24	2	
Pat Fischer	DB	5'10"	170	26	1	
Jim Heidel	DB	6'1"	185	22		
Jerry Stovall	DB	6'2"	205	24	3	6
Bobby Williams	DB	6'1"	185	24		
Larry Wilson	DB	6'	190	28	10	12
Abe Woodson	DB	5'11"	190	31	4	
Bill Thornton – Injury						
Jim Hart	QB	6'2"	195	22		
Charley Johnson	QB	6'	190	29		12
Terry Nofsinger	QB	6'4"	215	28		12
Charlie Bryant	HB	6'1"	207	25		
Roy Shivers	HB	6'	200	24		6
Bill Triplett	HB	6'2"	210	27		
Johnny Roland	FB-HB	6'2"	207	23		36
Willie Crenshaw	FB	6'2"	230	25		
Prentice Gautt	HB-FB	6'	210	28		12
Bobby Joe Conrad	FL	6'	195	31		12
Mal Hammack	TE	6'2"	210	33		
Ray Ogden	TE	6'5"	225	23		
Jackie Smith	TE	6'4"	215	25		18
Sonny Randle	OE	6'2"	190	30		12
Billy Gambrell	FL-OE	5'10"	175	24		30
Jim Bakken	K	6'	200	25		96

WASHINGTON REDSKINS 7-7-0 Otto Graham

Scores of Each Game		
14	CLEVELAND	38
7	St. Louis	23
33	Pittsburgh	27
24	PITTSBURGH	10
33	ATLANTA	20
10	New York	13
26	ST. LOUIS	20
27	Philadelphia	13
10	Blatimore	37
30	DALLAS	31
3	Cleveland	14
72	NEW YORK	41
34	Dallas	31
28	PHILADELPHIA	37

Use Name	Pos.	Hgt	Wgt	Age	Int	Pts
Mitch Johnson	OT	6'4"	245	24		
John Kelly	OT	6'3"	256	22		
Jim Snowden	OT	6'3"	255	24		
Tom Goosby	OG	6'	235	27		
Jake Kupp	OG	6'3"	233	24		
Vince Promuto	OG	6'1"	245	28		
Ray Schoenke	OG	6'3"	234	24		
Don Croftcheck	LB-OG	6'1"	230	23		
Dave Crossan	C	6'3"	245	26		
Len Hauss	C	6'2"	235	24		
Willie Adams	DE	6'2"	235	24		
Bill Briggs	DE	6'3"	250	22		
Carl Kammerer	DE	6'3"	243	29		
Ron Snidow	DE	6'4"	250	24		
Walt Barnes	DT	6'3"	250	22		
Stan Jones	DT	6'1"	250	35		
Joe Rutgens	DT	6'2"	255	27		
Jim Carroll (from NY)	LB	6'1"	230	23	1	
Chris Hanburger	LB	6'2"	218	25	1	
Sam Huff	LB	6'1"	230	31	1	
Steve Jackson	LB	6'1"	225	23	1	
John Reger	LB	6'	220	35	3	6
Billy Clay	DB	6'1"	192	22	1	
Rickie Harris	DB	6'	182	23	1	6
Paul Krause	DB	6'3"	195	24	2	
Brig Owens	DB	5'11"	190	23	7	12
Lonnie Sanders	DB	6'3"	207	24		
Jim Shorter	DB	5'11"	185	25	5	
Tom Walters	DB	6'2"	195	24		
John Seedborg – Military Service						
Sonny Jurgensen	QB	5'11"	205	32		
Dick Shiner	QB	6'	197	24		
Ron Rector (to ATL)	HB	6'	200	22		
Steve Thurlow (from NY)	HB	6'3"	216	23		
Tom Barrington	FB-HB	6'1"	218	22		
Joe Kantor	FB	6'1"	217	23		
A. D. Whitfield	FB	5'10"	200	22		18
Joe Don Looney (from DET)	HB-FB	6'1"	230	23		24
John Burrell	FL	6'3"	195	26		
Fred Mazurek	FL	5'11"	192	23		
Bobby Mitchell	FL	6'	196	31		60
Jim Avery	TE	6'2"	235	22		
Pat Richter	TE	6'5"	230	25		
Jerry Smith	TE	6'2"	208	23		36
Pat Hodgson	OE	6'2"	190	22		
Charley Taylor	HB-OE	6'3"	210	25		90
Charlie Gogolak	K	5'10"	165	21		105

DALLAS COWBOYS

RUSHING

Last Name	No.	Yds	Avg	TD
Reeves	175	757	4.3	8
Perkins	186	726	3.9	8
Meredith	38	242	6.4	5
Shy	17	118	6.9	1
Garrison	16	62	3.9	1
Renfro	8	52	6.5	0
Morton	7	50	7.1	0
Clarke	8	49	6.1	0
Rhome	7	37	5.3	0
Villanueva	1	23	23.0	0
Smith	7	7	1.0	1
Hayes	1	−1	−1.0	0

RECEIVING

Last Name	No.	Yds	Avg	TD
Hayes	64	1232	19	13
Reeves	41	557	14	8
Gent	27	474	18	1
Clarke	26	355	14	4
Perkins	23	231	10	0
Dial	14	252	18	1
Norman	12	144	12	0
Renfro	4	65	16	0
Garrison	2	18	9	0
Smith	1	3	3	0

PUNT RETURNS

Last Name	No.	Yds	Avg	TD
Renfro	21	123	6	0
Hayes	17	106	6	0
Howley	1	30	30	0
Reeves	2	−1	−1	0

KICKOFF RETURNS

Last Name	No.	Yds	Avg	TD
Renfro	19	487	26	1
Garrison	20	445	22	0
Reeves	3	56	19	0
Neely	2	18	9	0

PASSING – PUNTING – KICKING

PASSING	Att	Comp	%	Yds	Yd/Att	TD	Int–%	RK
Meredith	344	177	51	2805	8.2	24	12– 3	4
Rhome	36	21	58	253	7.0	0	1– 3	
Morton	27	13	48	225	8.3	3	1– 4	
Reeves	6	3	50	48	8.0	0	0– 0	

PUNTING	No	Avg
Villanueva	65	39.2

KICKING	XP	Att	%	FG	Att	%
Villanueva	56	56	100	17	31	55

PHILADELPHIA EAGLES

RUSHING

Last Name	No.	Yds	Avg	TD
T. Brown	161	548	3.4	3
Gros	102	396	3.9	7
Woodeshick	85	330	3.9	4
Lang	52	239	4.6	1
Concannon	25	195	7.8	2
Matson	29	101	3.5	1
Snead	15	32	2.1	1
Baker	1	15	15.0	0
F. Hill	1	5	5.0	0
K. Hill	7	−2	−0.3	0

RECEIVING

Last Name	No.	Yds	Avg	TD
Retzlaff	40	653	16	6
T. Brown	33	371	11	3
F. Hill	29	304	10	0
Gros	18	214	12	2
Goodwin	16	212	13	1
Hawkins	14	143	10	0
Lang	12	107	9	0
Woodeshick	10	118	12	1
Matson	6	30	5	1
Concannon	1	7	7	0

PUNT RETURNS

Last Name	No.	Yds	Avg	TD
Martin	11	118	11	1
Hawkins	9	47	5	0
Concannon	2	3	2	0
Nelson	1	3	3	0
T. Brown	1	0	0	0
W. Brown	5	−1	0	0
Scarpati	2	−8	−4	0

KICKOFF RETURNS

Last Name	No.	Yds	Avg	TD
T. Brown	20	562	28	2
Matson	26	544	21	0
Martin	4	132	33	0
W. Brown	4	58	15	0
Nelson	2	34	17	0
Whittingham	2	33	17	0
Beisler	1	17	17	0
Jackson	1	16	16	0
Lince	1	13	13	0
Medved	2	10	5	0
Hawkins	1	0	0	0

PASSING – PUNTING – KICKING

PASSING	Att	Comp	%	Yds	Yd/Att	TD	Int–%	RK
Snead	226	103	46	1275	5.6	8	11– 5	16
K. Hill	97	53	55	571	5.9	5	7– 7	
Concannon	51	21	41	262	5.1	1	4– 8	
Lang	3	2	67	51	17.0	0	0– 0	
Gros	1	0	0	0	0.0	0	0– 0	

PUNTING	No	Avg
Baker	42	41.1
K. Hill	23	37.5

KICKING	XP	Att	%	FG	Att	%
Baker	38	39	97	18	25	72

CLEVELAND BROWNS

RUSHING

Last Name	No.	Yds	Avg	TD
Kelly	209	1141	5.5	15
Green	144	750	5.2	3
Ryan	36	156	4.3	0
Harraway	7	40	5.7	0
Collins	2	38	19.0	0
Schultz	7	32	4.6	0
Pietrosante	7	20	2.9	0
Ninowski	3	−11	−3.7	0

RECEIVING

Last Name	No.	Yds	Avg	TD
Collins	56	946	17	12
Green	45	445	10	6
Warfield	36	741	21	5
Kelly	32	366	11	1
Morin	23	333	14	3
Smith	13	183	14	3
McNeil	2	94	47	2
Roberts	2	19	10	0
Pietrosante	1	12	12	0
Houston	1	10	10	1
Costello	1	−7	−7	0

PUNT RETURNS

Last Name	No.	Yds	Avg	TD
Kelly	13	104	8	0
Roberts	11	42	4	0

KICKOFF RETURNS

Last Name	No.	Yds	Avg	TD
Roberts	20	454	23	0
Kelly	19	403	21	0
Harraway	9	193	21	0
Schultz	3	52	17	0
Pietrosante	2	9	5	0
Smith	1	0	0	0

PASSING – PUNTING – KICKING

PASSING	Att	Comp	%	Yds	Yd/Att	TD	Int–%	RK
Ryan	382	200	52	2974	7.8	29	14– 4	3
Ninowski	18	11	61	175	9.7	4	1– 6	
Groza	1	1	100	−7	−7.0	0	0– 0	
Kelly	1	0	0	0	0.0	0	0– 0	

PUNTING	No	Avg
Collins	57	39.0

KICKING	XP	Att	%	FG	Att	%
Groza	51	52	98	9	23	39
Houston	1	1	100	0	0	0

ST. LOUIS CARDINALS

RUSHING

Last Name	No.	Yds	Avg	TD
Roland	192	695	3.6	5
Gautt	110	370	3.4	1
Crenshaw	94	360	3.8	0
Johnson	20	39	2.0	2
Bryant	5	31	6.2	0
Gambrell	3	26	8.7	0
Nofsinger	18	25	1.4	2
Triplett	13	25	1.9	0
Stovall	1	17	17.0	0
Smith	1	8	8.0	0
Shivers	1	5	5.0	0

RECEIVING

Last Name	No.	Yds	Avg	TD
Smith	45	810	18	3
Conrad	34	388	11	2
Gambrell	24	409	17	5
Roland	21	213	10	0
Randle	17	218	13	2
Gautt	16	114	7	1
Crenshaw	15	46	3	0
Shivers	5	81	16	0
Triplett	2	6	3	0
Sortun	1	7	7	0

PUNT RETURNS

Last Name	No.	Yds	Avg	TD
Roland	20	221	11	1
Shivers	16	49	3	0
Gambrell	4	46	12	0

KICKOFF RETURNS

Last Name	No.	Yds	Avg	TD
Shivers	27	762	28	1
Roland	15	347	23	0
Williams	7	132	19	0
Bryant	2	70	35	0
Gambrell	1	16	16	0
Roy	2	10	5	0
Long	1	9	9	0
Melinkovich	1	2	2	0
Ogden	1	0	0	0

PASSING – PUNTING – KICKING

PASSING	Att	Comp	%	Yds	Yd/Att	TD	Int–%	RK
Johnson	205	103	50	1334	6.5	10	11– 5	9
Nofsinger	162	68	42	799	4.9	2	8– 5	18
Hart	11	4	36	29	2.6	0	0– 0	
Roland	8	5	63	130	16.3	1	0– 0	

PUNTING	No	Avg
Smith	47	37.9
Bakken	29	33.1
Stovall	5	27.8

KICKING	XP	Att	%	FG	Att	%
Bakken	27	28	96	23	40	58

WASHINGTON REDSKINS

RUSHING

Last Name	No.	Yds	Avg	TD
Whitfield	93	472	5.1	2
Taylor	87	262	3.0	3
Thurlow	80	260	3.3	0
Looney	63	220	3.5	4
Mitchell	13	141	10.8	1
Rector	9	40	4.4	0
Barrington	10	37	3.7	0
Jurgensen	12	14	1.2	0
Shiner	1	10	10.0	0
Kantor	1	2	2.0	0

RECEIVING

Last Name	No.	Yds	Avg	TD
Taylor	72	1119	16	12
Mitchell	58	905	16	9
Smith	54	686	13	6
Thurlow	23	165	7	0
Whitfield	18	101	6	1
Looney	12	49	4	0
Richter	7	100	14	0
Kupp	4	28	7	0
Mazurek	2	28	14	0
Barrington	2	23	12	0
Rector	2	9	5	0
Burrell	1	9	9	0
Johnson	1	1	1	0

PUNT RETURNS

Last Name	No.	Yds	Avg	TD
Harris	18	108	6	1
Taylor	5	63	13	0
Mitchell	4	21	5	0
Mazurek	2	9	5	0

KICKOFF RETURNS

Last Name	No.	Yds	Avg	TD
Mazurek	21	505	24	0
Harris	20	405	20	0
Looney	13	265	20	0
Taylor	3	98	33	0
Rector	3	65	22	0
Barrington	2	39	20	0
Croftcheck	2	36	18	0
Kantor	2	35	18	0
Jackson	2	26	13	0
Johnson	2	22	11	0
Barnes	1	14	14	0
Goosby	1	0	0	0

PASSING – PUNTING – KICKING

PASSING	Att	Comp	%	Yds	Yd/Att	TD	Int–%	RK
Jurgensen	436	254	58	3209	7.4	28	19– 4	2
Shiner	5	0	0	0	0.0	0	1– 20	
Barrington	1	0	0	0	0.0	0	0– 0	
Mitchell	1	1	100	21	21.0	0	0– 0	

PUNTING	No	Avg
Richter	68	42.4

KICKING	XP	Att	%	FG	Att	%
Gogolak	39	41	95	22	34	65

EASTERN CONFERENCE – Continued

PITTSBURGH STEELERS 5-8-1 Bill Austin

Scores of Each Game		
34	NEW YORK	34
17	DETROIT	3
27	WASHINGTON	33
10	Washington	24
10	Cleveland	41
14	PHILADELPHIA	31
21	Dallas	52
16	CLEVELAND	6
30	ST. LOUIS	9
7	DALLAS	20
3	St. Louis	6
23	Philadelphia	27
47	New York	28
57	Atlanta	33

Use Name	Pos.	Hgt	Wgt	Age	Int	Pts
Charlie Bradshaw	OT	6'6"	260	30		
Dan James	OT	6'4"	250	29		
Fran O'Brien (from WAS)	OT	6'1"	255	30		
Roger Pillath	OT	6'4"	242	24		
Larry Gagner	OG	6'3"	240	22		
Mike Magac	OG	6'3"	240	28		
Eli Strand	OG	6'2"	250	23		
Ralph Wenzel	OG	6'3"	240	23		
Pat Killorin	C	6'2"	220	22		
Ray Mansfield	C	6'3"	250	25		
John Baker	DE	6'6"	270	31		
Ben McGee	DE	6'2"	225	24		
Tim Powell	DE	6'4"	248	22		
Riley Gunnels	DT	6'3"	253	29	1	
Chuck Hinton	DT	6'5"	260	27		
Ken Kortas	DT	6'2"	280	24		
Lloyd Voss	DT	6'4"	260	24		
Rod Breedlove	LB	6'2"	227	28	2	
Gene Breen	LB	6'2"	230	25		
John Campbell	LB	6'3"	225	27	2	
Andy Russell	LB	6'3"	215	24		7
Bill Saul	LB	6'4"	225	25	2	
Bob Schmitz (to MIN)	LB	6'1"	240	28		
Jim Bradshaw	DB	6'1"	205	27	4	6
Willie Daniel	DB	5'11"	185	28		
Bob Hohn	DB	6'	190	25		
Brady Keys	DB	6'	198	30	4	
Paul Martha	DB	6'	185	23	3	
Clendon Thomas	DB	6'2"	205	29	2	6
Marv Woodson	DB	6'	195	23	4	6
Theron Sapp – Injury						
George Izo	QB	6'3"	218	29		
Ron Meyer	QB	6'4"	205	22		
Bill Nelsen	QB	6'	195	25		
Ron Smith	QB	6'5"	220	24		
Amos Bullocks	HB	6'1"	202	27		12
Cannonball Butler	HB	5'10"	185	23		24
Dick Hoak	HB	5'11"	190	27		6
Bobby Smith	HB	6'	203	24		
Dick Leftridge	FB	6'2"	240	21		12
Mike Lind	FB	6'2"	225	26		
Willie Asbury	FB	6'1"	230	23		54
Roy Jefferson	FL	6'2"	195	22		24
John Hilton	TE	6'5"	220	24		24
Tony Jeter	TE	6'3"	220	22		
Steve Smith	TE	6'5"	240	22		
Jerry Simmons	OE	6'1"	190	23		6
J. R. Wilburn	OE	6'2"	190	23		
Gary Ballman	FL-OE	6'	200	26		30
Mike Clark	K	6'1"	205	25		97
Frank Lambert	K	6'3"	200	23		

ATLANTA FALCONS 3-11-0 Norb Hecker

Scores of Each Game		
14	LOS ANGELES	19
10	Philadelphia	23
10	Detroit	28
14	DALLAS	47
20	Washington	33
7	SAN FRANCISCO	44
3	Green Bay	56
17	CLEVELAND	49
7	BALTIMORE	19
27	New York	16
6	Chicago	23
20	Minnesota	13
16	ST. LOUIS	10
33	PITTSBURGH	57

Use Name	Pos.	Hgt	Wgt	Age	Int	Pts
Rich Koeper	OT	6'4"	245	23		
Errol Linden	OT	6'5"	260	29		
Jim Simon	OT	6'5"	235	25		
Don Talbert	OT	6'5"	240	26		
Lou Kirouac	OG	6'3"	240	25		46
Ed Cook	OG	6'2"	250	34		
Dan Grimm	OG	6'3"	245	25		
Frank Marchlewski	C	6'2"	238	22		
Bob Whitlow	C	6'1"	236	30		
Bobby Richards	DE	6'2"	247	27		
Sam Williams	DE	6'5"	235	35		
Karl Rubke	DE	6'4"	244	30		
Jerry Jones	DT-DE	6'3"	277	22		
Bud Marshall (from WAS)	DT	6'5"	270	24		
Guy Reese	DT	6'5"	260	26		
Chuck Sieminski	DT	6'4"	265	26		
Joe Szczercko	DT	6'	245	24		
Ralph Heck	LB	6'2"	230	25		
Bill Jobko	LB	6'2"	235	30	2	
Larry Morris	LB	6'2"	230	31		
Tommy Nobis	LB	6'2"	230	22		
Marion Rushing	LB	6'2"	230	29	3	
Lee Calland	DB	6'	190	25	3	
Nick Rassas	DB	6'	190	22		
Ken Reaves	DB	6'3"	200	21	1	
Jerry Richardson	DB	6'3"	190	23	5	
Bob Riggle	DB	6'1"	200	22	3	6
Carl Silvestri	DB	6'	195	23		
Tommy Tolleson	DB	6'	185	23		
Ron Smith	HB-DB	6'1"	180	23	2	
Dennis Claridge	QB	6'3"	225	24		
Randy Johnson	QB	6'3"	195	22		24
Steve Sloan	QB	6'1"	185	22		
Junior Coffey	HB	6'1"	210	24		30
Perry Lee Dunn	HB	6'2"	200	23		
Rudy Johnson	HB	5'11"	190	24		
Preston Ridlehuber	HB	6'2"	215	22		12
Jimmy Sidle	TE-HB	6'2"	215	23		
Charlie Scales	FB	5'11"	215	27		
Ernie Wheelwright	FB	6'3"	240	29		36
Bill Wolski	FB	5'11"	203	22		
Glenn Glass (to DEN-A)	FL	6'	203	29		
Bob Sherlag	FL	6'	197	23		6
Gary Barnes	OE-FL	6'4"	210	26		6
Alex Hawkins	OE-FL	6'1"	186	29		12
Taz Anderson	TE	6'2"	215	27		18
Billy Martin	TE	6'4"	240	23		
Hugh McInnis	TE	6'3"	220	28		
Vern Burke	OE	6'4"	202	25		6
Angie Coia	OE	6'2"	196	28		
Tom Hutchinson	OE	6'1"	190	25		
Billy Lothridge	K	6'1"	194	22		
Wade Traynham	K	6'2"	218	24		2

NEW YORK GIANTS 1-12-1 Allie Sherman

Scores of Each Game		
34	Pittsburgh	34
7	Dallas	52
17	Philadelphia	35
7	CLEVELAND	28
19	St. Louis	24
13	WASHINGTON	10
3	PHILADELPHIA	31
17	ST. LOUIS	20
14	Los Angeles	55
16	ATLANTA	27
41	Washington	72
40	Cleveland	49
28	PITTSBURGH	47
7	DALLAS	17

Use Name	Pos.	Hgt	Wgt	Age	Int	Pts
Roger Davis	OT	6'3"	240	28		
Francis Peay	OT	6'5"	250	22		
Willie Young	OT	6'	247	23		
Bob Scholtz	C-OT	6'4"	250	28		
Bookie Bolin	OG	6'2"	240	26		
Pete Case	OG	6'3"	245	25		
Darrell Dess (from WAS)	OG	6'	245	30		
Charlie Harper	OG	6'2"	248	22		
Greg Larson	C	6'2"	250	27		
Joe Wellborn	C	6'2"	215	20		
Glen Condren	DE	6'2"	250	24		
Rosey Davis	DE	6'5"	260	24		
Jim Garcia	DE	6'4"	250	22		
Jim Katcavage	DE	6'3"	240	31		
Bill Matan	DE	6'4"	240	22		
Don Davis	DT	6'6"	260	22		
Jim Moran	DT	6'5"	270	23		
Jim Prestel	DT	6'5"	275	29		
Mike Ciccolella	LB	6'1"	235	22		
Jerry Hillebrand	LB	6'3"	240	26	1	6
Stan Sczurek	LB	5'11"	230	27		
Jeff Smith	LB	6'	237	22	1	
Larry Vargo	LB	6'3"	215	26	1	
Henry Carr	DB	6'3"	195	23	4	6
Clarence Childs	DB	6'	180	27	2	6
Phil Harris	DB	6'	195	21		
Wendell Harris	DB	5'11"	185	25	1	6
Spider Lockhart	DB	6'2"	175	23	6	
Dick Lynch	DB	6'1"	198	30		
Jimmy Patton	DB	6'	185	34	1	
Tucker Frederickson – Knee Injury						
Bill Swain – Knee Injury						
Tom Kennedy	QB	6'1"	200	27		
Earl Morrall	QB	6'1"	206	32		
Gary Wood	QB	5'11"	188	23		18
Steve Bowman	HB	6'	195	21		
Allen Jacobs	FB	6'1"	215	25		6
Dan Lewis	HB	6'1"	200	30		6
Smith Reed	HB	6'	215	24		
Ernie Koy	FB-HB	6'2"	230	23		
Chuck Mercein	FB	6'3"	230	23		
Pep Menefee	FL	6'1"	198	24		
Joe Morrison	HB-FB-FL	6'1"	212	28		48
Bob Crespino	TE	6'4"	225	28		12
Aaron Thomas	TE	6'3"	210	28		24
Freeman White	LB-TE	6'5"	225	22		
Del Shofner	OE	6'3"	185	30		
Homer Jones	FL-OE	6'2"	205	25		48
Pete Gogolak	K	6'2"	200	24		77

WESTERN CONFERENCE

GREEN BAY PACKERS 12-2-0 Vince Lombardi

Scores of Each Game		
24	BALTIMORE	3
21	Cleveland	20
24	LOS ANGELES	13
23	DETROIT	14
20	San Francisco	21
17	Chicago	0
56	ATLANTA	3
31	Detroit	7
17	MINNESOTA	20
13	CHICAGO	6
28	Minnesota	16
20	SAN FRANCISCO	7
14	Baltimore	10
27	Los Angeles	23

Use Name	Pos.	Hgt	Wgt	Age	Int	Pts
Bob Skoronski	OT	6'3"	250	33		
Steve Wright	OT	6'6"	250	24		
Forrest Gregg	OG-OT	6'4"	250	33		
Gale Gillingham	OG	6'3"	250	22		
Jerry Kramer	OG	6'3"	245	31		
Fuzzy Thurston	OG	6'1"	245	33		
Ken Bowman	C	6'3"	230	23		
Bill Curry	C	6'2"	235	23		
Lionel Aldridge	DE	6'4"	245	24		
Bob Brown	DE	6'5"	270	26		
Willie Davis	DE	6'3"	245	33		
Henry Jordan	DT	6'3"	250	31		
Ron Kostelnik	DT	6'4"	260	26		
Jim Weatherwax	DT	6'7"	275	23		
Lee Roy Caffey	LB	6'3"	250	26	3	6
Tommy Crutcher	LB	6'3"	230	24	1	
Ray Nitschke	LB	6'3"	240	30	2	
Dave Robinson	LB	6'3"	245	25	5	
Phil Vandersea	LB	6'3"	225	23		
Herb Adderley	DB	6'1"	210	27	4	6
Tom Brown	DB	6'1"	190	25	4	
Doug Hart	DB	6'	190	27	1	6
Dave Hathcock	DB	6'	190	23		
Bob Jeter	DB	6'1"	205	28	5	12
Willie Wood	DB	5'10"	190	30	3	6
Zeke Bratkowski	QB	6'2"	200	34		
Bart Starr	QB	6'1"	200	33		12
Donny Anderson	HB	6'3"	220	23		18
Paul Hornung	HB	6'2"	215	29		30
Elijah Pitts	HB	6'1"	205	27		60
Jim Grabowski	FB	6'2"	225	22		6
Jim Taylor	FB	6'	215	31		36
Carroll Dale	FL	6'1"	200	28		42
Bob Long	FL	6'3"	190	25		
Red Mack (from ATL)	FL	5'10"	185	29		
Bill Anderson	TE	6'3"	216	30		
Allen Brown	TE	6'5"	240	23		
Marv Fleming	TE	6'4"	235	24		12
Boyd Dowler	OE	6'5"	225	29		
Max McGee	OE	6'3"	205	34		6
Don Chandler	K	6'2"	210	31		77

BALTIMORE COLTS 9-5-0 Don Shula

Scores of Each Game		
3	Green Bay	24
38	Minnesota	23
36	SAN FRANCISCO	14
17	Chicago	27
45	DETROIT	14
20	MINNESOTA	17
17	Los Angeles	3
37	WASHINGTON	10
19	Atlanta	7
14	Detroit	20
7	LOS ANGELES	23
21	CHICAGO	16
10	GREEN BAY	14
30	San Francisco	14

Use Name	Pos.	Hgt	Wgt	Age	Int	Pts
Sam Ball	OT	6'4"	240	22		
Jim Parker	OT	6'3"	275	32		
Bob Vogel	OT	6'5"	250	24		
Glenn Ressler	C-OT	6'3"	235	22		
Dale Memmelaar	OG	6'2"	248	29		
Alex Sandusky	OG	6'1"	242	34		
Dan Sullivan	OG	6'3"	250	27		
Dick Szymanski	C	6'3"	235	34		
Ordell Braase	DE	6'4"	242	34		
Roy Hilton	DE	6'6"	240	21		
Gino Marchetti	DE	6'4"	245	40		
Lou Michaels	DE	6'2"	250	30		98
Fred Miller	DT	6'3"	245	25		
Billy Ray Smith	DT	6'4"	250	31		
Andy Stynchula	DE-DT	6'3"	250	27		
Barry Brown	LB	6'3"	230	23	1	
Jackie Burkett	LB	6'4"	228	29		
Mike Curtis	LB	6'2"	232	23		6
Ted Davis	LB	6'1"	232	24	1	
Dennis Gaubatz	LB	6'2"	232	25	2	
Don Shinnick	LB	6'	228	31	3	
Steve Stonebreaker	LB	6'3"	228	28	1	
Tom Bleick	DB	6'2"	200	23		
Bobby Boyd	DB	5'10"	190	28	6	6
George Harold	DB	6'3"	205	24		
Alvin Haymond	DB	6'	190	24	4	6
Jerry Logan	DB	6'1"	185	25	3	
Lenny Lyles	DB	6'2"	202	30	1	
Jim Welch	DB	6'	190	28		
Gary Cuozzo	QB	6'1"	195	25		
Johnny Unitas	QB	6'1"	194	33		6
Jerry Allen	HB	6'1"	205	25		
Tom Matte	HB	6'	205	27		18
Lenny Moore	FL-HB	6'1"	190	33		18
Bob Baldwin	FB-HB	6'1"	225	23		
Jerry Hill	FB	5'11"	210	26		
Tony Lorick	FB	6'1"	215	24		18
Jimmy Orr	FL	5'11"	185	30		18
Willie Richardson	FL	6'2"	198	26		12
John Mackey	TE	6'3"	217	24		54
Butch Wilson	TE	6'2"	228	24		12
Ray Berry	OE	6'2"	187	33		42
Neal Petties	OE	6'2"	198	25		
David Lee	K	6'4"	215	22		

EASTERN CONFERENCE—Continued

PITTSBURGH STEELERS

RUSHING

Last Name	No.	Yds	Avg	TD
Asbury	169	544	3.2	7
Hoak	81	212	2.6	1
Butler	46	114	2.5	2
B. Smith	24	93	3.9	0
Bullocks	29	83	2.9	1
Jefferson	2	36	18.0	0
Nelsen	6	18	3.0	0
Leftridge	8	17	2.1	2
Lind	3	4	1.3	0
Meyer	1	−2	−2.0	0
R. Smith	4	−9	−2.3	0
Izo	2	−18	−9.0	0

RECEIVING

Last Name	No.	Yds	Avg	TD
Hilton	46	603	13	4
Ballman	41	663	16	5
Jefferson	32	772	24	4
Hoak	23	239	10	0
Asbury	19	228	12	2
Wilburn	7	103	15	0
Simmons	6	68	11	1
Bullocks	5	64	13	1
Butler	4	93	23	1
B. Smith	3	26	9	0
Jeter	2	18	9	0

PUNT RETURNS

Last Name	No.	Yds	Avg	TD
Jefferson	12	29	2	0
Keys	5	11	2	0
J. Bradshaw	2	3	2	0
Simmons	2	0	0	0

KICKOFF RETURNS

Last Name	No.	Yds	Avg	TD
Ballman	20	477	24	0
Butler	17	454	27	1
Simmons	10	196	20	0
Woodson	6	113	19	0
Martha	2	39	20	0
Saul	2	35	18	0
Keys	1	18	18	0
Campbell	1	15	15	0
Lind	1	15	15	0
Russell	2	12	6	0
Leftridge	1	10	10	0
Hilton	1	0	0	0

PASSING

Last Name	Att	Comp	%	Yds	Yd/Att	TD	Int–%	RK
R. Smith	181	79	44	1249	6.9	8	12– 7	12
Nelsen	112	63	56	1122	10.0	7	1– 1	
Izo	81	35	43	360	4.4	2	8– 10	
Meyer	19	7	37	59	3.1	0	1– 5	
Hoak	6	4	67	87	14.5	1	0– 0	
Asbury	1	0	0	0	0.0	0	0– 0	
Bullocks	1	0	0	0	0.0	0	0– 0	

PUNTING

Last Name	No	Avg
Lambert	78	42.1

KICKING

Last Name	XP	Att	%	FG	Att	%
Clark	34	34	100	21	32	66
Russell	1	1	100	0	0	0

ATLANTA FALCONS

RUSHING

Last Name	No.	Yds	Avg	TD
Coffey	199	722	3.6	4
Wheelwright	121	458	3.8	3
Ran. Johnson	35	142	4.1	4
Dunn	22	52	2.4	0
Scales	10	38	3.8	0
Ridlehuber	4	23	5.8	0
Lothridge	1	22	22.0	0
Claridge	5	15	3.0	0
Sidle	1	12	12.0	0
Rud. Johnson	3	3	1.0	0

RECEIVING

Last Name	No.	Yds	Avg	TD
Hawkins	44	661	15	2
Martin	29	330	11	0
Burke	28	348	12	1
Coffey	15	182	12	1
Wheelwright	15	137	9	3
Barnes	12	173	14	1
Anderson	10	195	20	3
Dunn	5	45	9	0
Coia	4	93	23	0
Ridlehuber	4	84	21	2
Sherlag	4	53	13	1
Scales	3	16	5	0
Hutchinson	1	28	28	0
Sidle	1	16	16	0
Marchlewski	0	1	0	0

PUNT RETURNS

Last Name	No.	Yds	Avg	TD
Smith	11	80	7	0
Rassas	4	10	3	0
Sherlag	2	8	4	0
Reaves	1	2	2	0

KICKOFF RETURNS

Last Name	No.	Yds	Avg	TD
Smith	43	1013	24	0
Rassas	8	203	25	0
Sidle	6	117	20	0
Scales	5	101	20	0
Reaves	4	85	21	0
Rushing	2	52	26	0
Morris	5	50	10	0
Dunn	2	36	18	0
Hawkins	1	30	30	0
Wolski	1	21	21	0
Coffey	1	18	18	0
Glass	1	11	11	0
Heck	1	0	0	0
Martin	1	0	0	0
Sherlag	1	0	0	0

PASSING

Last Name	Att	Comp	%	Yds	Yd/Att	TD	Int–%	RK
Ran. Johnson	295	129	44	1795	6.1	12	21– 7	17
Claridge	70	40	57	471	6.7	2	2– 3	
Sloan	13	6	46	96	7.4	0	2– 15	
Dunn	2	0	0	0	0.0	0	2–100	
Lothridge	1	0	0	0	0.0	0	0– 0	

PUNTING

Last Name	No	Avg
Lothridge	73	40.7

KICKING

Last Name	XP	Att	%	FG	Att	%
Kirouac	19	24	79	9	18	50
Traynham	2	2	100	0	1	0

NEW YORK GIANTS

RUSHING

Last Name	No.	Yds	Avg	TD
Mercein	94	327	3.5	0
Morrison	67	275	4.1	2
Jacobs	77	273	3.5	1
Wood	28	196	7.0	3
Lewis	32	164	5.1	1
Koy	66	146	2.2	0
Jones	5	43	8.6	0
Kennedy	5	16	3.2	0
Morrall	5	12	2.4	0
Larson	0	−2	0.0	0

RECEIVING

Last Name	No.	Yds	Avg	TD
Jones	48	1044	22	8
Morrison	46	724	16	6
Thomas	43	683	16	4
Mercein	27	152	6	0
Crespino	16	167	10	2
Jacobs	10	69	7	0
Koy	8	43	5	0
Lewis	6	87	15	0
Shofner	3	19	6	0
Menefee	1	11	11	0

PUNT RETURNS

Last Name	No.	Yds	Avg	TD
Lockhart	17	113	7	0
P. Harris	5	7	1	0

KICKOFF RETURNS

Last Name	No.	Yds	Avg	TD
Childs	34	855	25	1
P. Harris	22	480	22	0
Lewis	13	214	16	0
Koy	3	20	7	0
Jacobs	2	18	9	0
White	2	14	7	0
W. Harris	1	9	9	0
Young	2	6	3	0
Rog. Davis	1	0	0	0

PASSING

Last Name	Att	Comp	%	Yds	Yd/Att	TD	Int–%	RK
Wood	170	81	48	1142	6.7	6	13– 8	15
Morrall	151	71	47	1105	7.3	7	12– 8	14
Kennedy	100	55	55	748	7.5	7	6– 6	
Koy	2	0	0	0	0.0	0	0– 0	
Lewis	1	1	100	4	4.0	0	0– 0	

PUNTING

Last Name	No	Avg
Koy	49	39.4
Lockhart	4	32.8

KICKING

Last Name	XP	Att	%	FG	Att	%
Gogolak	29	31	94	16	28	57

WESTERN CONFERENCE

GREEN BAY PACKERS

RUSHING

Last Name	No.	Yds	Avg	TD
Taylor	204	705	3.5	4
Pitts	115	393	3.4	7
Hornung	76	200	2.6	2
Grabowski	29	127	4.4	1
Starr	21	104	5.0	2
D. Anderson	25	104	4.2	2
Chandler	1	33	33.0	0
Bratkowski	4	7	1.8	0

RECEIVING

Last Name	No.	Yds	Avg	TD
Taylor	41	331	8	2
Dale	37	876	24	7
Fleming	31	361	12	2
Dowler	29	392	14	0
Pitts	26	460	18	3
Hornung	14	192	14	3
McGee	4	91	23	1
Grabowski	4	13	3	0
Long	3	68	23	0
D. Anderson	2	33	17	0
B. Anderson	2	14	7	0

PUNT RETURNS

Last Name	No.	Yds	Avg	TD
D. Anderson	6	124	21	1
Wood	22	82	4	0
Pitts	7	9	1	0
T. Brown	2	0	0	0

KICKOFF RETURNS

Last Name	No.	Yds	Avg	TD
D. Anderson	23	533	23	0
Adderley	14	320	23	0
Vandersea	3	50	17	0
Pitts	1	0	0	0
Wood	1	0	0	0

PASSING

Last Name	Att	Comp	%	Yds	Yd/Att	TD	Int–%	RK
Starr	251	156	62	2257	9.0	14	3– 1	1
Bratkowski	64	36	56	569	8.9	4	2– 3	
Pitts	2	0	0	0	0.0	0	0– 0	
Hornung	1	1	100	5	5.0	0	0– 0	

PUNTING

Last Name	No	Avg
Chandler	60	40.9
D. Anderson	2	44.5

KICKING

Last Name	XP	Att	%	FG	Att	%
Chandler	41	43	95	12	28	43

BALTIMORE COLTS

RUSHING

Last Name	No.	Yds	Avg	TD
Lorick	143	524	3.7	3
Hill	104	395	3.8	0
Matte	86	381	4.4	0
Moore	63	209	3.3	3
Unitas	20	44	2.2	1
Cuozzo	1	9	9.0	0
Mackey	1	−6	−6.0	0

RECEIVING

Last Name	No.	Yds	Avg	TD
Berry	56	786	14	7
Mackey	50	829	17	9
Orr	37	618	17	3
Matte	23	307	13	3
Moore	21	260	12	0
Richardson	14	246	18	2
Lorick	12	81	7	0
Hill	5	18	4	0
Wilson	3	27	9	2

PUNT RETURNS

Last Name	No.	Yds	Avg	TD
Haymond	40	347	9	0
Davis	2	7	4	0
Logan	1	3	3	0
Allen	1	0	0	0
Matte	1	0	0	0

KICKOFF RETURNS

Last Name	No.	Yds	Avg	TD
Moore	18	453	25	0
Haymond	10	223	22	0
Lorick	10	214	21	0
Curtis	3	64	21	0
Matte	3	55	18	0
Allen	3	53	18	0
Baldwin	2	18	9	0
Brown	2	14	7	0

PASSING

Last Name	Att	Comp	%	Yds	Yd/Att	TD	Int–%	RK
Unitas	348	195	56	2748	7.9	22	24– 7	5
Cuozzo	50	26	52	424	8.5	4	2– 4	
Matte	3	0	0	0	0.0	0	1– 33	

PUNTING

Last Name	No	Avg
Lee	49	45.6

KICKING

Last Name	XP	Att	%	FG	Att	%
Michaels	35	36	97	21	39	54

WESTERN CONFERENCE – Continued

LOS ANGELES RAMS 8-6-0 George Allen

Scores of Each Game			Use Name	Pos.	Hgt	Wgt	Age	Int	Pts	Use Name	Pos.	Hgt	Wgt	Age	Int	Pts	Use Name	Pos.	Hgt	Wgt	Age	Int	Pts
19	Atlanta	14	Joe Carollo	OT	6'2"	263	26			Maxie Baughan	LB	6'1"	227	28	2		Roman Gabriel	QB	6'4"	225	26		18
31	CHICAGO	17	Charley Cowan	OT	6'4"	275	28			Dan Currie	LB	6'3"	240	32			Bill Munson	QB	6'2"	197	24		
13	Green Bay	24	Bob Nichols	OT	6'3"	250	23			Bill George	LB	6'2"	235	35			Tom Moore	HB	6'	210	28		24
34	SAN FRANCISCO	3	Don Chuy	OG	6'1"	256	25			Jack Pardee	LB	6'2"	230	30	2		Les Josephson	HB	6'	210	24		6
14	Detroit	7	Ted Karras	OG	6'1"	243	33			Myron Pottios	LB	6'2"	240	26			Jim Stiger	FB-HB	5'11"	214	25		6
7	Minnesota	35	Joe Scibelli	OG	6'1"	264	27			Doug Woodlief	LB	6'3"	235	22			Dick Bass	FB	5'10"	198	29		48
10	Chicago	17	Tom Mack	OG	6'3"	245	22			Irv Cross	DB	6'1"	190	27	1	6	Henry Dyer	FB	6'2"	225	21		
3	BALTIMORE	17	Ken Iman	C	6'1"	235	27			Hank Gremminger	DB	6'1"	200	33	1		Tommy McDonald	FL	5'10"	175	32		12
13	San Francisco	21	Joe Wendryhoski	C	6'2"	245	27			Chuck Lamson	DB	6'	190	27	5	6	Marlin McKeever	TE	6'1"	227	26		6
55	NEW YORK	14	Bruce Anderson	DE	6'4"	230	22			Clancy Williams	DB	6'2"	198	23	8	6	Dave Pivec	TE	6'3"	240	22		
21	MINNESOTA	6	Deacon Jones	DE	6'5"	260	27	1		George Youngblood	DB	6'3"	200	21			Billy Truax	TE	6'5"	240	23		6
23	Baltimore	7	Lamar Lundy	DE	6'7"	260	31	1	6	Ed Meador	DB	5'11"	203	29	5		Steve Heckard	OE	6'1"	195	23		
23	DETROIT	3	Rosey Grier	DT	6'5"	290	33		2	Claude Crabb	FL-DB	6'	190	26			Bucky Pope	FL-OE	6'5"	195	23		6
23	GREEN BAY	27	Earl Leggett	DT	6'3"	265	32										Jack Snow	OE	6'2"	212	23		18
			Merlin Olsen	DT	6'5"	276	25			Tony Guillory – Injury							Bruce Gossett	K	6'2"	230	23		113
																	Jon Kilgore	K	6'1"	200	22		

SAN FRANCISCO FORTY NINERS 6-6-2 Jack Christiansen

Scores of Each Game			Use Name	Pos.	Hgt	Wgt	Age	Int	Pts	Use Name	Pos.	Hgt	Wgt	Age	Int	Pts	Use Name	Pos.	Hgt	Wgt	Age	Int	Pts
20	MINNESOTA	20	Dave McCormick	OT	6'6"	250	23			Ed Beard	LB	6'2"	225	26			John Brodie	QB	6'1"	210	31		18
14	Baltimore	36	Walt Rock	OT	6'5"	257	25			Mike Dowdle	LB	6'3"	248	28	1	6	Billy Kilmer	QB	6'	204	26		
3	Los Angeles	34	Len Rohde	OT	6'4"	255	28			Bob Harrison	LB	6'2"	225	29			George Mira	QB	5'11"	192	24		
21	GREEN BAY	20	Howard Mudd	OG	6'3"	263	24			Matt Hazeltine	LB	6'1"	230	33	1	6	John David Crow	HB	6'2"	224	31		24
44	Atlanta	7	John Thomas	OG	6'4"	250	31			Dave Wilcox	LB	6'3"	234	23			Bob Daugherty	HB	6'2"	205	24		
27	DETROIT	24	Jim Wilson	OG	6'3"	255	25			Kermit Alexander	DB	5'11"	186	25	4	12	Jim Jackson	HB	6'	180	22		6
3	Minnesota	28	Bruce Bosley	C	6'2"	246	32			George Donnelly	DB	6'3"	205	23	2		Dave Kopay	HB	6'2"	225	24		12
21	LOS ANGELES	13	Joe Cerne	C	6'2"	235	23			Jim Johnson	DB	6'2"	187	28	4	6	Gary Lewis	FB	6'3"	230	24		18
30	Chicago	30	Stan Hindman	DE	6'3"	232	22			Elbert Kimbrough	DB	5'11"	196	27	3		Ken Willard	FB	6'2"	230	23		42
34	PHILADELPHIA	35	Clark Miller	DE	6'5"	245	27			Mel Phillips	DB	6'	188	24			Bernie Casey	FL	6'4"	210	27		6
41	Detroit	14	Jim Norton	DT-DE	6'4"	255	23			Al Randolph	DB	6'2"	190	22	3	6	Kay McFarland	FL	6'2"	186	27		6
7	Green Bay	20	Charlie Johnson	DT	6'2"	266	22										Dick Witcher	FL	6'3"	210	21		6
41	CHICAGO	14	Charlie Krueger	DT	6'4"	267	30										Kent Kramer	TE	6'5"	230	22		18
14	BALTIMORE	30	Roland Lakes	DT	6'4"	285	26										Monte Stickles	TE	6'4"	235	28		12
																	Dave Parks	OE	6'2"	207	24		30
																	Wayne Swinford	OE	6'	200	23		
																	Tommy Davis	K	6'	220	31		86

CHICAGO BEARS 5-7-2 George Halas

Scores of Each Game			Use Name	Pos.	Hgt	Wgt	Age	Int	Pts	Use Name	Pos.	Hgt	Wgt	Age	Int	Pts	Use Name	Pos.	Hgt	Wgt	Age	Int	Pts
3	Detroit	14	Herm Lee	OT	6'4"	247	35			Doug Buffone	LB	6'1"	218	22			Rudy Bukich	QB	6'1"	205	35		12
17	Los Angeles	31	Riley Mattson	OT	6'4"	255	27			Dick Butkus	LB	6'3"	245	22	1		Larry Rakestraw	QB	6'2"	195	24		
13	Minnesota	10	Bob Wetoska	OT	6'3"	240	28			Joe Fortunato	LB	6'	225	36	1	6	Billy Wade	QB	6'2"	205	35		
27	BALTIMORE	17	Jim Cadile	OG	6'3"	240	25			Jim Purnell	LB	6'2"	225	24			Jon Arnett	HB	5'11"	203	31		6
0	GREEN BAY	17	Mike Rabold	OG	6'2"	238	29			Mike Reilly	LB	6'2"	238	23			Gale Sayers	HB	6'	198	23		72
17	LOS ANGELES	10	George Seals	OT-OG	6'2"	260	23			Charlie Brown	DB	6'1"	193	23			Brian Piccolo	FB-HB	6'	205	22		
17	St. Louis	24	Roger LeClerc	C	6'3"	235	28		78	Curtis Gentry	DB	6'	187	25	1		Ralph Kurek	FB	6'2"	210	23		6
10	DETROIT	10	Mike Pyle	C	6'3"	250	27			Benny McRae	DB	6'1"	180	25	3		Joe Marconi	FB	6'2"	225	32		
30	SAN FRANCISCO	30	Doug Atkins	DE	6'8"	255	36	1		Richie Petitbon	DB	6'3"	205	28	4		Ronnie Bull	HB-FB	6'	200	26		
6	Green Bay	13	Ed O'Bradovich	DE	6'3"	255	26		6	Rosey Taylor	DB	5'11"	186	27	1		Johnny Morris	FL	5'10"	180	31		
23	ATLANTA	6	Brian Schweda	DE	6'3"	240	23			Dave Whitsell	DB	6'	190	30	3		Duane Allen	TE	6'4"	225	28		
16	Baltimore	21	Frank Cornish	DT	6'6"	285	22										Charlie Bivins	TE	6'2"	212	27		
14	San Francisco	41	Dick Evey	DT	6'2"	225	25			Andy Livingston - Knee Injury							Mike Ditka	TE	6'3"	230	26		12
41	MINNESOTA	28	John Johnson	DT	6'5"	260	25										Dick Gordon	OE	5'11"	190	21		6
			Bob Kilcullen	DT	6'3"	245	30										Jim Jones	OE	6'2"	187	22		30
																	Bobby Joe Green	K	5'11"	175	28		

DETROIT LIONS 4-9-1 Harry Gilmer

Scores of Each Game			Use Name	Pos.	Hgt	Wgt	Age	Int	Pts	Use Name	Pos.	Hgt	Wgt	Age	Int	Pts	Use Name	Pos.	Hgt	Wgt	Age	Int	Pts
14	CHICAGO	3	Daryl Sanders	OT	6'5"	250	24			Ernie Clark	LB	6'1"	220	28	1		Tom Myers	QB	6'	188	22		
3	Pittsburgh	17	Roger Shoals	OT	6'4"	255	27			Bill Cody	LB	6'1"	220	22			Milt Plum	QB	6'1"	205	32		1
28	ATLANTA	10	J. D. Smith	OT	6'5"	250	30			Wally Hilgenberg	LB	6'3"	225	23			Karl Sweetan	QB	6'1"	210	23		6
14	Green Bay	23	John Gordy	OG	6'3"	250	30			Mike Lucci	LB	6'2"	223	26	5	6	Bobby Felts	HB	6'2"	202	23		12
7	LOS ANGELES	14	Bob Kowalkowski	OG	6'3"	245	22			Lou Slaby	LB	6'3"	235	24			Amos Marsh	HB	6'1"	220	27		18
14	Baltimore	45	Doug Van Horn	OG	6'2"	245	22			Wayne Walker	LB	6'2"	225	29	1	17	Bruce McLenna	HB	6'3"	225	24		
24	San Francisco	27	Mike Alford	C	6'3"	235	23			Jim Kearney	DB	6'2"	200	23			Jim Todd	HB	5'11"	195	23		
7	GREEN BAY	31	Ed Flanagan	C	6'3"	250	22			Dick LeBeau	DB	6'1"	185	29	4		Tom Nowatzke	FB	6'3"	233	23		42
10	Chicago	10	Larry Hand	DE	6'4"	245	26			Bruce Maher	DB	5'11"	190	29	5		Pat Studstill	FL	6'1"	175	28		30
32	Minnesota	31	Jerry Mazzanti	DE	6'3"	240	26			Wayne Rasmussen	DB	6'2"	180	24	3		Willie Walker	FL	6'3"	200	23		
20	BALTIMORE	14	Darris McCord	DE	6'4"	250	33			Bobby Smith	DB	6'	197	28			Johnnie Robinson	DB-FL	6'3"	205	21		6
14	SAN FRANCISCO	41	Roger Brown	DT	6'5"	300	29			Bobby Thompson	DB	5'10"	175	26	4		Jim Gibbons	TE	6'2"	220	30		6
3	Los Angeles	23	Alex Karras	DT	6'2"	245	30			Tom Vaughn	DB	5'11"	195	23	1		Ron Kramer	TE	6'3"	240	31		
16	MINNESOTA	28	Jerry Rush	DT	6'4"	270	24										Gail Cogdill	OE	6'2"	195	29		6
										Tom Watkins – Operation							Bill Malinchak	OE	6'1"	190	22		
										Warren Wells – Military Service							John Henderson	FL-OE	6'3"	190	23		
																	Garo Yepremian	K	5'8"	160	22		50

MINNESOTA VIKINGS 4-9-1 Norm Van Brocklin

Scores of Each Game			Use Name	Pos.	Hgt	Wgt	Age	Int	Pts	Use Name	Pos.	Hgt	Wgt	Age	Int	Pts	Use Name	Pos.	Hgt	Wgt	Age	Int	Pts
20	San Francisco	20	Doug Davis	OT	6'4"	240	22			Don Hansen	LB	6'3"	226	22			Bob Berry	QB	5'11"	190	24		
23	BALTIMORE	38	Chuck Arrobio	OT	6'4"	250	22			John Kirby	LB	6'3"	222	24			Fran Tarkenton	QB	6'1"	190	26		24
17	Dallas	28	Grady Alderman	OT	6'2"	240	27			Dave Tobey	LB	6'3"	230	23			Ron Vander Kelen	QB	6'1"	185	26		
10	CHICAGO	13	Archie Sutton	OT	6'4"	262	23			Lonnie Warwick	LB	6'3"	225	24	2		Billy Barnes	HB	5'11"	202	31		6
35	LOS ANGELES	7	Larry Bowie	OG	6'2"	250	26			Roy Winston	LB	6'1"	230	26			Jim Lindsey	HB	6'2"	200	21		18
17	Baltimore	20	Milt Sunde	OG	6'2"	234	23			Mike Fitzgerald	DB	5'10"	180	25	1		Tommy Mason	HB	6'	196	27		18
28	SAN FRANCISCO	3	Jim Vellone	OG	6'2"	255	22			Dale Hackbart	DB	6'3"	210	30	5	6	Dave Osborn	HB	6'	205	23		18
20	Green Bay	17	Mick Tinglehoff	C	6'1"	237	26			Jeff Jordan	DB	6'4"	190	22			Jeff Williams	HB	6'1"	210	22		
31	DETROIT	32	Carl Eller	DE	6'6"	255	24			Karl Kassulke	DB	6'	193	24	2		Jim Young	HB	6'	205	23		
6	Los Angeles	21	Jim Marshall	DE	6'3"	235	28			Earsell Mackbee	DB	6'1"	195	25	2		Bill Brown	FB	5'11"	230	28		36
16	GREEN BAY	28	Paul Dickson	DT	6'5"	255	29			George Rose	DB	5'11"	190	23	1		Phil King	HB-FB	6'4"	220	30		6
13	ATLANTA	20	Gary Larsen	DT	6'5"	250	26			Ed Sharockman	DB	6'	200	26	1		Jim Phillips	FL	6'1"	195	29		18
28	Detroit	16	Jerry Shay	DT	6'3"	240	22										Lance Rentzel	OE-FL	6'2"	210	22		
28	Chicago	41	Mike Tilleman	DT	6'5"	260	22			Ken Byers – Injury							Hal Bedsole	TE	6'4"	230	24		
																	Preston Carpenter (from WAS)	TE	6'2"	208	32		24
																	John Powers	TE	6'2"	210	25		
																	Paul Flatley	OE	6'1"	187	25		18
																	Tom Hall	FL-OE	6'1"	195	25		12
																	Fred Cox	K	5'10"	200	27		88
																	Bobby Walden	K	6'	195	28		

WESTERN CONFERENCE – Continued

LOS ANGELES RAMS

RUSHING

Last Name	No.	Yds	Avg	TD
Bass	248	1090	4.4	8
Moore	104	272	2.6	1
Gabriel	52	176	3.4	3
Josephson	14	97	6.9	0
Stiger	24	95	4.0	0
Meador	1	7	7.0	0
Munson	4	3	0.8	0
Iman	1	2	2.0	0

RECEIVING

Last Name	No.	Yds	Avg	TD
Moore	60	433	7	3
McDonald	55	714	13	2
Snow	34	634	19	3
Bass	31	274	9	0
Truax	29	314	11	0
McKeever	23	277	12	1
Stiger	8	72	9	1
Heckard	5	102	20	0
Josephson	2	10	5	1
Crabb	1	47	47	0
Pope	1	14	14	1

PUNT RETURNS

Last Name	No.	Yds	Avg	TD
Stiger	33	259	8	0
Cross	12	82	7	0

KICKOFF RETURNS

Last Name	No.	Yds	Avg	TD
Williams	15	420	28	0
Cross	12	348	29	0
Stiger	7	150	21	0
Dyer	5	61	12	0
Currie	1	25	25	0
McKeever	1	8	8	0
Lamson	1	3	3	0

PASSING – PUNTING – KICKING

PASSING	Att	Comp	%	Yds	Yd/Att	TD	Int–%	RK
Gabriel	397	217	55	2540	6.4	10	16– 4	7
Munson	50	30	60	284	5.7	2	1– 2	
Kilgore	1	1	100	47	47.0	0	0– 0	
Meador	1	0	0	0	0.0	0	0– 0	
Moore	1	1	100	20	20.0	0	0– 0	

PUNTING	No	Avg
Kilgore	71	42.8

KICKING	XP	Att	%	FG	Att	%
Gossett	29	29	100	28	49	57

SAN FRANCISCO FORTY NINERS

RUSHING

Last Name	No.	Yds	Avg	TD
Willard	191	763	4.0	5
Crow	121	477	3.9	1
Kopay	47	204	4.3	1
Lewis	36	130	3.6	2
Mira	10	103	10.3	0
Davis	3	43	14.3	0
Casey	1	23	23.0	0
Kilmer	3	23	7.7	0
Brodie	5	18	3.6	3
Jackson	4	7	1.8	0
Parks	1	–1	–1.0	0

RECEIVING

Last Name	No.	Yds	Avg	TD
Parks	66	974	15	5
Casey	50	669	13	1
Willard	42	351	8	2
Crow	30	341	11	3
Stickles	27	315	12	2
McFarland	13	219	17	1
Witcher	10	115	12	1
Kopay	10	67	7	1
Lewis	7	44	6	1
Kramer	5	81	16	3
Jackson	1	63	63	1

PUNT RETURNS

Last Name	No.	Yds	Avg	TD
Alexander	30	198	7	1
Kopay	4	28	7	0
Swinford	8	12	2	0
Jackson	2	0	0	0
Donnelly	1	0	0	0

KICKOFF RETURNS

Last Name	No.	Yds	Avg	TD
Alexander	37	984	27	0
Jackson	8	162	20	0
Swinford	4	73	18	0
Lewis	3	65	22	0
Kopay	2	20	10	0
Phillips	1	20	20	0
Hindman	1	2	2	0

PASSING – PUNTING – KICKING

PASSING	Att	Comp	%	Yds	Yd/Att	TD	Int–%	RK
Brodie	427	232	54	2810	6.6	16	22– 5	8
Mira	53	22	42	284	5.4	5	2– 4	
Kilmer	16	5	31	84	5.3	0	1– 6	
Crow	4	2	50	61	15.3	0	1– 25	

PUNTING	No	Avg
Davis	63	41.4
Kilmer	7	33.4

KICKING	XP	Att	%	FG	Att	%
Davis	38	39	97	16	31	52

CHICAGO BEARS

RUSHING

Last Name	No.	Yds	Avg	TD
Sayers	229	1231	5.4	8
Bull	100	318	3.2	0
Kurek	52	179	3.4	1
Arnett	55	178	3.2	1
Bukich	18	14	0.8	2
Piccolo	3	12	4.0	0
Marconi	3	5	1.7	0
Gordon	1	2	2.0	0
Rakestraw	1	–5	–5.0	0
Jones	1	–7	–7.0	0

RECEIVING

Last Name	No.	Yds	Avg	TD
Sayers	34	447	13	2
Ditka	32	378	12	2
Jones	28	504	18	5
Bull	20	174	9	0
Gordon	15	210	14	1
Kurek	10	178	18	0
Arnett	10	42	4	0
Morris	5	49	10	0
Allen	3	28	9	0
Bivins	2	6	3	0

PUNT RETURNS

Last Name	No.	Yds	Avg	TD
Arnett	15	58	4	0
Sayers	6	44	7	0
Gordon	4	–5	–1	0

KICKOFF RETURNS

Last Name	No.	Yds	Avg	TD
Sayers	23	718	31	2
Gordon	19	521	27	0
Arnett	2	39	20	0
Butkus	3	32	11	0
Taylor	1	3	3	0
Brown	0	28	0	0

PASSING – PUNTING – KICKING

PASSING	Att	Comp	%	Yds	Yd/Att	TD	Int–%	RK
Bukich	309	147	48	1858	6.0	10	21– 7	13
Wade	21	9	43	79	3.8	0	1– 5	
Sayers	6	2	33	58	9.7	0	1– 17	
Arnett	1	0	0	0	0.0	0	0– 0	
Bull	1	1	100	21	21.0	0	0– 0	

PUNTING	No	Avg
Green	80	42.0

KICKING	XP	Att	%	FG	Att	%
Leclerc	24	25	96	18	30	60

DETROIT LIONS

RUSHING

Last Name	No.	Yds	Avg	TD
Nowatzke	151	512	3.4	6
Marsh	134	433	3.2	3
Sweetan	34	219	6.4	1
Felts	34	83	2.4	2
Plum	12	59	4.9	0
McLenna	16	51	3.2	0
Studstill	2	20	10.0	0
Todd	2	6	3.0	0
Wil. Walker	1	4	4.0	0

RECEIVING

Last Name	No.	Yds	Avg	TD
Studstill	67	1266	19	5
Nowatzke	54	316	6	1
Cogdill	47	411	9	1
Kramer	37	432	12	0
Marsh	12	111	9	0
Henderson	6	121	20	0
Malinchak	5	34	7	0
McLenna	3	13	4	0
Felts	2	1	1	0
Wil. Walker	1	21	21	0
Gibbons	1	2	2	1

PUNT RETURNS

Last Name	No.	Yds	Avg	TD
Robinson	13	185	14	1
Vaughn	18	179	10	0
Felts	2	20	10	0
Todd	5	12	2	0

KICKOFF RETURNS

Last Name	No.	Yds	Avg	TD
Vaughn	23	595	26	0
Felts	20	392	20	0
Robinson	6	127	21	0
Todd	3	105	35	0
Slaby	1	14	14	0
Mazzanti	1	8	8	0
Alford	1	0	0	0

PASSING – PUNTING – KICKING

PASSING	Att	Comp	%	Yds	Yd/Att	TD	Int–%	RK
Sweetan	309	157	51	1809	5.9	4	14– 5	11
Plum	146	82	56	943	6.5	4	13– 9	10
Myers	1	0	0	0	0.0	0	1–100	

PUNTING	No	Avg
Studstill	72	41.1

KICKING	XP	Att	%	FG	Att	%
Yepremian	11	11	100	13	22	59
Way. Walker	11	11	100	2	8	25
Plum	1	1	100	0	0	0

MINNESOTA VIKINGS

RUSHING

Last Name	No.	Yds	Avg	TD
Brown	251	829	3.3	6
Tarkenton	62	376	6.1	4
Osborn	87	344	4.0	1
Mason	58	235	4.1	2
Lindsey	57	146	2.6	1
Walden	5	82	16.4	0
King	17	40	2.4	0
Vender Kelen	4	19	4.8	0
Barnes	5	16	3.2	1
Berry	3	12	4.0	0
Williams	1	2	2.0	0
Carpenter	1	–10	–10.0	0

RECEIVING

Last Name	No.	Yds	Avg	TD
Flatley	50	777	16	3
Brown	37	359	10	0
Phillips	32	554	17	3
Carpenter	30	518	17	4
Hall	23	271	12	2
Lindsey	20	250	13	2
Osborn	15	141	9	2
Mason	7	39	6	1
King	2	24	12	1
Rentzel	2	10	5	0
Barnes	1	20	20	0

PUNT RETURNS

Last Name	No.	Yds	Avg	TD
Sharockman	9	95	11	0
Rentzel	11	16	1	0
Mason	3	9	3	0
Young	2	7	4	0
Lindsey	2	4	2	0
Williams	4	–2	–1	0

KICKOFF RETURNS

Last Name	No.	Yds	Avg	TD
Fitzgerald	14	301	22	0
Rentzel	9	181	20	0
Hall	7	141	20	0
Young	5	105	21	0
Lindsey	4	79	20	0
King	6	78	13	0
Williams	3	61	20	0
Rose	1	20	20	0
Osborn	1	19	19	0
Winston	1	2	2	0
Sunde	1	0	0	0

PASSING – PUNTING – KICKING

PASSING	Att	Comp	%	Yds	Yd/Att	TD	Int–%	RK
Tarkenton	358	192	54	2561	7.2	17	16– 4	6
Berry	37	13	35	215	5.8	1	5– 14	
Vander Kelen	20	10	50	147	7.4	0	1– 5	
Brown	1	0	0	0	0.0	0	0– 0	
King	1	1	100	9	9.0	0	0– 0	

PUNTING	No	Avg
Walden	60	41.1

KICKING	XP	Att	%	FG	Att	%
Cox	34	34	100	18	33	55

1966 A.F.L. Peace and the Super Bowl

After the New York Giants signed kicker Pete Gogolak away from the Buffalo Bills, the AFL owners decided to declare full-scale war against the NFL. Al Davis, the energetic young leader of the Oakland franchise, was put in charge of the war effort as Commissioner of the League, replacing Joe Foss in April, and an all-out effort was launched to steal star NFL players. Quarterbacks were special targets, with John Brodie and Roman Gabriel considered likely candidates to jump. With the bidding war for graduating collegians already costing clubs heavily, financial competition for established players would make bankruptcy a possibility for some teams. The two leagues sat down to put an end to the suicidal war, and the merger agreement was unveiled in June. Pete Rozelle became Commissioner over both leagues, the AFL agreed to pay reparations to the NFL teams, and a championship game—soon dubbed the Super Bowl—was arranged for the two league champions. By 1970, the AFL would be absorbed into the NFL, with all franchises to remain intact in their present locations. With peace at hand, Al Davis left the AFL office to return to Oakland as managing partner, just in time to preside over the opening of the new Oakland-Alameda County Coliseum. Milt Woodard took over as league president and would guide the league well up until its absorption into the NFL in 1970.

EASTERN DIVISION

Buffalo Bills—Head coach Lou Saban was looking for new challenges after winning two straight AFL championships, so he resigned to become top man at the University of Maryland. Assistant Coach Joe Collier took over the top spot and kept the Bills exactly as Saban had molded them, a tough defensive team with a ball-control offense. With a bad knee bothering Tom Sestak, Jim Dunaway and Ron McDole provided leadership in the defensive line, while the tight linebacking crew of Mike Stratton, Harry Jacobs, and John Tracey held the defense together. In the secondary, Butch Byrd, George Saimes, Hagood Clarke, and Tom Janik strangled enemy passing attacks. The Buffalo offense got help from rookies Bobby Burnett and Bobby Crockett. Burnett joined with Wray Carlton in providing the running necessary for the methodical Buffalo attack, while Crockett won the starting split-end job. The team surpassed last year's squad on paper, but lost twice to Boston during the season and headed into the final weekend a half game behind the Patriots. The Jets did their part by beating the Pats 38-28, and the Bills capitalized by defeating Denver to take their third straight Eastern title.

Boston Patriots—Jim Nance cut down on his weight and set the league on fire with his rushing in his second pro year. Using pure power plus surprising speed, Nance pounded away at defenses in work-horse fashion, gaining an AFL record 1,458 yards and eleven touchdowns for his troubles. Quarterback Babe Parilli used Nance to set up his passes, and receivers Art Graham, Gino Cappelletti, and Jim Whalen gave him targets to hit when not handing off to Nance. Parilli ran the attack so well that John Huarte, the Heisman Trophy winner obtained from the New York Jets, rarely took his warm-up wraps off. The Boston defense stuck to the same lines as in recent years, with a strong front four, a lot of blitzing from middle linebacker Nick Buoniconti, and a lukewarm secondary. With Cappelletti in top form as a place-kicker, the Pats had a final ace whenever their offense stalled in enemy territory. Coach Mike Holovak prepared his team well for the schedule, and the team twice beat the Bills during the year to take a slight lead into the final game of the year against New York, but dropped a 38-28 decision as Parilli passed for 379 yards.

New York Jets—With a wealth of young offensive talent, the Jets made an early run at the Eastern title with four straight wins to open the season. Joe Namath, Matt Snell, George Sauer, Emerson Boozer, Pete Lammons, Winston Hill, Dave Herman, and John Schmitt were all twenty-five years old or less, and veterans like Billy Mathis, Sherman Plunkett, Don Maynard, and Sam DeLuca added stability to this dynamic attack. The defense contained players of widely varied talents. Verlon Biggs, Gerry Philbin, and Al Atkinson were good young talents, but only Larry Grantham had a good season among the veterans. After the good start, several factors caught up with the Jets and dragged them back into third place. The defense had problems stopping enemy passers, Namath had problems with interceptions, and the Jets had problems winning away from Shea Stadium, beating only weak Denver and Miami teams on the road.

Houston Oilers—After losing his job with the St. Louis Cardinals, Wally Lemm returned to the Oilers as head coach for the second time. In his previous term in Texas he had taken the Oilers to a divisional crown in 1961 after being promoted to the top spot in mid-season. This year he went along mostly with the same veterans who had won for him five years ago, but the results were different, only three wins and a tie for fourth place with the fledgling Dolphins. George Blanda, Charley Hennigan, Rich Michael, Don Floyd, Freddy Glick, Bob McLeod, Jim Norton, and Bob Talamini started this year after starting for Lemm in his first regime. Veteran NFL players such as John Henry Johnson and Bernie Parrish further added to the age on the team but contributed little on the field. After opening the season with a 45-7 win over Denver and a 31-0 thumping of Oakland, the Oilers lost most of their games the rest of the way.

Miami Dolphins—The Dolphins had problems at almost every position in their first year, but nowhere more than at quarterback. Of the two passers taken in the expansion draft, Eddie Wilson hurt a knee in training camp and missed the season, while Dick Wood had very little left in his arm. Rookie Rick Norton went out with a fractured jaw in mid-season, leaving coach George Wilson with George Wilson, Jr., his son, as the starting quarterback. Not one to be accused of nepotism, coach Wilson promoted John Stofa from the North American Football League for the last few games, and Stofa came through with four touchdown passes in the season-ending victory over Houston. Stocked mostly with over-the-hill veterans, the Dolphins got their existence off to an auspicious start when Joe Auer returned the opening kickoff of their first game all the way for a touchdown.

WESTERN DIVISION

Kansas City Chiefs—The first AFL Super Bowl representatives swept through their schedule with a powerful offense and well-coordinated defense. The Chiefs had shelled out a lot of money to halfback Mike Garrett in a pre-merger signing, and the short halfback gave the Chiefs a dangerous breakaway runner in the backfield. Curtis McClinton and Bert Coan also pitched in with hard work as ball carriers, making it hard for defenses to watch for Len Dawson passes. Chris Burford continued to run his precise patterns from the split end position, and Otis Taylor provided a deep threat at flanker with a fine sophomore season. Jim Tyrer and Ed Budde starred in the offensive line, but their comrades there showed considerably less consistency. The attack got by on the brilliance of the backs and ends, but the defense got by with a few stars and some mediocre talents.

Oakland Raiders—During Al Davis' two-month term as AFL Commissioner, the Raiders hired Johnny Rauch as their new head coach, and when Davis returned to Oakland as managing partner, some observers expected a conflict between the two men. Davis and Rauch got along well, but the Raiders finished in second place for the third time in four years. The Raiders won four of six meetings with Western opponents but lost three times to Eastern teams to kill their title chances. Despite top performances from Clem Daniels and Art Powell, the attack was a mediocre unit, but the defense played consistently well with flashes of brilliance. Tom Keating, obtained from the Buffalo Bills, used his extraordinary quickness to put a strong rush on enemy passers, and defensive ends Ben Davidson and Ike Lassiter added size to the line. The linebacking showed improvement as the young starters gained experience. The secondary was perhaps the league's best, with Dave Grayson, Kent McCloughan, and Rodger Bird each an individual star. Still, the Raiders needed a little more experience on defense and a little more punch on offense.

San Diego Chargers—The Chargers underwent a lot of changes this year, including a drop out of first place. The team's ownership changed hands in August when Barron Hilton sold the club to a group headed by Eugene Klein and Sam Schulman, and head coach Sid Gillman also sent a group of veteran players into exile. Salary disputes sent defensive linemen Ernie Ladd to Houston and Earl Faison to Miami, and the expansion draft to stock the Dolphins siphoned off defensive backs Jim Warren and Dick Westmoreland. A broken ankle sidelined middle linebacker Chuck Allen for most of the campaign, making the defense a patchwork quilt. Two veterans on offense, halfback Paul Lowe and tackle Ron Mix, suffered through off seasons, but a strong passing attack kept the Chargers rolling. Rookie Gary Garrison joined flanker Lance Alworth in a devastating receiving combo, giving quarterback John Hadl many opportunities to throw the ball. Even with all their problems, the Chargers kept the winning habit by taking their first four games, but once enemy offenses learned they could run on the San Diego line, the Chargers limped home to third place.

Denver Broncos—The Broncos scored the fewest points of any team in pro football, with problems in all sectors of the offense. Quarterbacks came and went on the Denver roster all season. John McCormick started for most of the campaign but showed very little; Mickey Slaughter, an occasional starter for the last three years, rarely got off the bench; veteran Tobin Rote came out of retirement, threw eight passes, and went right back into retirement; and rookies Max Chaboian and Scotty Glacken got late-season starting shots. With the revolving door at quarterback, end Lionel Taylor's catches fell off to thirty-five, his lowest since the AFL began. The running corps was hurt by the absence of Cookie Gilchrist, who held out into the season and was dealt to Miami, and Eldon Danehauer's injury took the best blocker out of the line. The best offense on the Broncos this year came from the kick returners, as Goldie Sellers and Nemiah Wilson scored three times on kickoff returns and Abner Haynes had the second highest average in the league for punt returns. The defense changed personnel less often than the offense but got little better results. The whole situation prompted head coach Mac Speedie to quit after two games, and assistant Ray Malavasi guided the team the rest of the way.

FINAL TEAM STATISTICS

OFFENSE

	BOSTON	BUFFALO	DENVER	HOUSTON	K. CITY	MIAMI	NEW YORK	OAKLAND	SAN DIEGO
FIRST DOWNS:									
Total	243	255	171	246	**266**	200	254	226	230
by Rushing	100	**110**	61	76	106	75	81	70	77
by Passing	121	126	95	144	140	103	**145**	144	137
by Penalty	22	19	15	26	20	22	**28**	12	16
RUSHING:									
Number	**471**	455	376	413	439	394	376	363	361
Yards	1963	1892	1173	1515	**2274**	1410	1442	1427	1537
Average Yards	4.2	4.2	3.1	3.7	**5.2**	3.6	3.8	3.9	4.3
Touchdowns	17	**19**	6	11	**19**	5	15	13	9
PASSING:									
Attempts	393	473	402	485	377	454	**514**	450	434
Completions	186	199	166	226	199	179	**251**	212	224
Completion Percentage	47.3	42.1	41.3	46.6	**52.8**	39.4	48.8	47.1	51.6
Passing Yards	2784	3000	2351	3168	3123	2374	**3556**	3425	3347
Avg. Yards per Attempt	7.1	6.3	5.8	6.5	**8.3**	5.2	6.9	7.6	7.7
Avg. Yards per Completion	15.0	15.1	14.2	14.0	15.7	13.3	14.2	**16.2**	14.9
Times Tackled Att. to Pass	25	16	37	28	30	36	**9**	34	32
Yards Lost Tackled	211	144	356	271	283	326	**92**	281	331
Net Yards	2573	2856	1995	2897	2840	2048	**3464**	3144	3016
Touchdowns	20	15	12	29	**31**	16	21	26	29
Interceptions	21	21	30	28	**15**	32	29	26	**15**
Percent Intercepted	5.3	4.4	7.5	5.8	4.0	7.0	5.6	5.8	**3.5**
PUNTING:									
Number	76	69	77	69	62	**82**	62	74	66
Average Distance	36.5	41.2	**45.2**	42.2	43.8	39.4	42.5	41.6	37.0
PUNT RETURNS:									
Number	24	**43**	26	23	31	21	36	41	21
Yards	143	**411**	235	159	276	204	260	367	257
Average Yards	6.0	9.6	9.0	6.9	8.9	9.7	7.2	9.0	**12.2**
Touchdowns	0	**2**	0	0	**2**	0	0	0	1
KICKOFF RETURNS:									
Number	54	51	58	64	54	**65**	62	60	55
Yards	1145	1064	**1558**	1514	1148	1507	1300	1191	1282
Average Yards	21.2	20.9	**26.9**	23.7	21.3	23.2	21.0	19.9	23.3
Touchdowns	0	1	**3**	0	0	1	1	0	0
INTERCEPTION RETURNS:									
Number	22	29	13	18	**33**	31	21	23	27
Yards	348	472	109	259	408	**522**	218	380	359
Average Yards	15.8	16.3	8.4	14.4	12.4	**16.8**	10.4	16.5	13.3
Touchdowns	0	**4**	0	0	0	**4**	1	1	1
PENALTIES:									
Number	64	62	66	71	61	73	64	**80**	68
Yards	601	637	**771**	682	680	660	682	752	667
FUMBLES:									
Number	25	27	36	19	21	29	19	22	**17**
Number Lost	13	15	17	12	16	10	9	12	**7**
POINTS:									
Total	315	358	196	335	**448**	213	322	315	335
PAT (kick) Attempts	36	42	20	40	**52**	23	35	40	40
PAT (kick) Made	35	41	20	39	**48**	23	34	39	39
PAT (Rush or Pass) Attempts	2	1	2	1	**3**	**3**	**3**	0	1
PAT (Rush or Pass) Made	**2**	0	1	0	**2**	**2**	**2**	0	0
FG Attempts	32	**38**	25	30	28	22	35	30	31
FG Made	16	19	14	16	**22**	10	18	12	16
Percent FG Made	50.0	50.0	56.0	53.3	**78.6**	45.5	51.4	40.0	51.6
Safeties	0	**1**	0	**1**	0	0	**1**	0	**1**

DEFENSE

	BOSTON	BUFFALO	DENVER	HOUSTON	K.CITY	MIAMI	NEW YORK	OAKLAND	SAN DIEGO
FIRST DOWNS:									
Total	243	**192**	251	244	222	237	231	211	260
by Rushing	68	**49**	101	88	75	83	81	84	127
by Passing	153	131	122	131	125	140	131	**106**	116
by Penalty	22	**12**	28	25	22	14	19	21	17
RUSHING:									
Number	369	**344**	441	422	353	416	388	418	497
Yards	1135	**1051**	2029	1833	1356	1510	1524	1792	2403
Average Yards	3.1	**3.1**	4.6	4.3	3.8	3.6	3.9	4.3	4.8
Touchdowns	7	**6**	17	10	10	15	14	16	19
PASSING:									
Attempts	509	466	396	438	494	425	467	405	**382**
Completions	247	205	192	209	226	198	212	183	**170**
Completion Percentage	48.5	**44.0**	48.5	47.7	45.8	46.6	45.4	45.2	44.5
Passing Yards	3565	3307	2819	3390	2876	3281	3064	2440	**2386**
Avg. Yards per Attempt	7.0	7.1	7.1	7.7	**5.8**	7.7	6.6	6.0	6.2
Avg. Yards per Completion	14.4	16.1	14.7	16.2	**12.7**	16.6	14.5	13.3	14.0
Times Tackled Att. to Pass	22	32	33	21	26	16	35	**36**	26
Yards Lost Tackled	209	249	304	228	262	180	310	**322**	231
Net Yards	3356	3058	2515	3162	2614	3101	2754	**2118**	2155
Touchdowns	26	22	26	35	18	25	19	15	**13**
Interceptions	22	29	13	18	**33**	31	21	23	27
Percent Intercepted	4.3	6.2	3.3	4.1	6.7	**7.3**	4.5	5.7	7.1
PUNTING:									
Number	**86**	84	60	68	69	64	81	73	52
Average Distance	**38.5**	39.6	42.7	40.0	41.3	43.9	40.4	41.3	43.0
PUNT RETURNS:									
Number	20	20	38	37	36	40	24	35	[illegible]
Yards	127	301	296	269	359	412	121	343	**84**
Average Yards	6.4	15.1	7.8	7.3	10.0	10.3	**5.0**	9.8	5.3
Touchdowns	1	2	**0**	**0**	1	1	**0**	**0**	**0**
KICKOFF RETURNS:									
Number	46	65	**43**	60	84	46	57	56	66
Yards	988	1329	1000	1385	2045	**939**	1368	1268	1387
Average Yards	21.5	20.4	23.3	23.1	24.3	**20.4**	24.0	22.6	21.0
Touchdowns	**0**	**0**	**0**	2	1	1	1	1	**0**
INTERCEPTION RETURNS:									
Number	21	21	30	28	**15**	32	29	26	**15**
Yards	**204**	303	545	448	225	370	297	405	278
Average Yards	**9.7**	14.4	18.2	16.0	15.0	11.6	10.2	15.6	18.5
Touchdowns	2	1	2	3	2	1	2	**0**	**0**
PENALTIES:									
Number	76	55	75	69	56	79	**85**	54	60
Yards	757	546	576	725	592	852	**883**	614	527
FUMBLES:									
Number	30	19	**35**	25	21	25	15	28	17
Number Lost	15	9	**18**	13	8	15	8	17	8
POINTS:									
Total	283	**225**	381	396	276	362	312	288	284
PAT (kick) Attempts	36	**28**	46	49	**28**	42	36	31	32
PAT (kick) Made	34	**28**	46	49	**28**	38	34	30	31
PAT (Rush or Pass) Attempts	**0**	3	1	1	4	2	1	3	1
PAT (Rush or Pass) Made	**0**	1	1	1	1	1	1	2	1
FG Attempts	26	**22**	40	30	28	36	28	30	31
FG Made	**11**	13	17	15	18	18	18	16	17
Percent FG Made	**42.3**	59.1	42.5	50.0	64.3	50.0	64.3	53.3	54.8
Safeties	**0**	**0**	**0**	**0**	**0**	2	**0**	1	1

1966 AFL CHAMPIONSHIP GAME

January 1, at Buffalo
(Attendance 42,080)

SCORING

BUFFALO	7	0	0	0– 7
KANSAS CITY	7	10	0	14–31

First Quarter
K.C. Arbanas, 29 yard pass from Dawson
PAT – Mercer (kick)
BUFF. Dubenion, 69 yard pass from Kemp
PAT – Lusteg (kick)

Second Quarter
K.C. Taylor, 29 yard pass from Dawson
PAT – Mercer (kick)
K.C. Mercer, 32 yard Field goal

Fourth Quarter
K.C. Garrett, 1 yard rush
PAT – Mercer (kick)
K.C. Garrett, 18 yard rush
PAT – Mercer (kick)

TEAM STATISTICS

BUFF.		K.C.
9	First Downs – Total	14
2	First Downs – Rushing	6
7	First Downs – Passing	8
0	First Downs – Penalty	0
8	Punts – Number	6
39.3	Punts – Average Distance	42.3
3	Penalties – Number	4
23	Yards Penalized	40
0	Missed Field Goals	1

Super Reps

This year's AFL title was the most desirable in the league's short history, for this year's champion would get the chance to play the NFL champion in the first Super Bowl. The Buffalo Bills had won the last two AFL titles, but the Kansas City Chiefs solved the tough Buffalo defense and scored a decisive 31-7 victory. Len Dawson passed the Chiefs into a quick 7-0 lead with a 29-yard pass to Fred Arbanas early in the game. The Bills came back to tie the score on a surprise long pass to Elbert Dubenion from Jack Kemp, but the Chiefs moved ahead 14-7 with a second-quarter touchdown pass from Dawson to Otis Taylor. Toward the end of the first half Buffalo appeared on the verge of tying the game, but a key interception spelled disaster for the Bills. With Buffalo driving and but ten yards from a touchdown, Kemp's pass was intercepted in the end zone by Johnny Robinson, who ran the ball back 72 yards to set up a 32-yard field goal by Mike Mercer and run the score to 17-7 at halftime. The third quarter passed without any scoring, and the Chiefs put the game out of reach with a pair of fourth-quarter touchdowns. Mike Garrett, the star rookie halfback, scored from the one-yard line and the 18-yard line on running plays. The Bills remained scoreless and as a result of the Kansas City defense outshining the more famous Buffalo unit, the front four completely stifling the Bills' running game and putting a strong rush on Kemp when he dropped back to pass, the Chiefs became the AFL's first Super Bowl representatives.

INDIVIDUAL STATISTICS

BUFFALO	No	Yds	Avg.	KANSAS CITY	No	Yds	Avg.
RUSHING							
Carlton	9	31	3.4	Garrett	13	39	3.0
Burnett	3	6	2.0	McClinton	11	38	3.5
Kemp	1	3	3.0	Dawson	5	28	5.6
	13	40	3.1	Coan	2	6	3.0
				Eu. Thomas	2	2	1.0
					33	113	3.4
RECEIVING							
Burnett	6	127	21.2	Taylor	5	78	15.6
Dubenion	2	79	39.5	Burford	4	76	19.0
Bass	2	26	13.0	Garrett	4	16	4.0
Crockett	1	16	16.0	Arbanas	2	44	22.0
Carlton	1	5	5.0	McClinton	1	13	13.0
	12	253	21.1		16	227	14.2
PUNT RETURNS							
Byrd	3	0	0.0	Garrett	3	37	12.3
Rutkowski	2	16	8.0				
	5	16	3.2				
KICKOFF RETURNS							
Warner	5	91	18.2	Coan	1	35	35.0
Meredith	1	8	8.0	Garrett	1	3	3.0
	6	99	16.5		2	38	19.0
INTERCEPTION RETURNS							
None				Robinson	1	72	72.0
				Em. Thomas	1	26	26.0
					2	98	49.0

PASSING

	Att	Comp	Comp Pct.	Yds	Int	Yds/ Att.	Yds/ Comp	Yards Lost Tackled
BUFFALO								
Kemp	27	12	44.4	253	2	9.4	21.1	38
KANSAS CITY								
Dawson	24	16	66.7	227	0	9.5	14.2	63

BUFFALO BILLS 9-4-1 Joe Collier

Scores of Each Game		
7	San Diego	27
20	KANSAS CITY	42
58	MIAMI	24
27	HOUSTON	20
29	Kansas City	14
10	BOSTON	20
17	SAN DIEGO	17
33	New York	23
29	Miami	0
14	NEW YORK	3
42	Houston	20
31	Oakland	10
3	Boston	14
38	DENVER	21

Use Name	Pos.	Hgt	Wgt	Age	Int	Pts
Stew Barber	OT	6'3"	250	27		
Wayne DeSutter	OT	6'4"	250	22		
Dick Hudson	OT	6'4"	265	26		
Joe O'Donnell	OG	6'2"	252	24		
Remi Prudhomme	OG	6'4"	240	24		
Billy Shaw	OG	6'3"	260	26		
Bob Schmidt	OT-C	6'4"	250	30		
Al Bemiller	OG-C	6'3"	240	27		
Tom Day	DE	6'2"	250	31		
Ron McDole	DE	6'3"	275	26	1	
Dave Costa	DT	6'2"	250	24		
Jim Dunaway	DT	6'4"	280	24		6
Dudley Meredith	DT	6'4"	285	31		
Tom Sestak	DT	6'5"	270	30		

Use Name	Pos.	Hgt	Wgt	Age	Int	Pts
Paul Guidry	LB	6'3"	225	22		
Harry Jacobs	LB	6'2"	226	29	2	
Paul Maguire	LB	6'	228	28		
Marty Schottenheimer	LB	6'3"	225	23	1	
Mike Stratton	LB	6'3"	235	24	3	6
John Tracey	LB	6'3"	228	32	1	
Butch Byrd	DB	6'	211	24	6	12
Hagood Clarke	DB	6'	203	24	5	6
Booker Edgerson	DB	5'10"	188	27		
Tom Janik	DB	6'3"	200	25	8	12
Charlie King	DB	6'	185	23	1	
George Saimes	DB	5'10"	185	24	1	
Charley Warner	DB	5'11"	170	26		6

Use Name	Pos.	Hgt	Wgt	Age	Int	Pts
Jack Kemp	QB	6'1"	200	32		30
Daryle Lamonica	QB	6'2"	218	25		6
Bobby Burnett	HB	6'2"	208	23		48
Allen Smith	HB	6'	200	23		
Wray Carlton	FB	6'2"	230	28		36
Doug Goodwin	FB	6'2"	228	24		
Jack Spikes	FB	6'2"	220	28		24
Elbert Dubenion	FL	6'	190	31		12
Paul Costa	TE	6'4"	255	24		18
Glenn Bass	OE	6'2"	206	27		
Bobby Crockett	OE	6'	195	23		18
Charley Ferguson	OE	6'5"	224	26		6
Pete Mills	OE	5'11"	180	23		
Ed Rutkowski	OE	6'1"	208	25		12
Booth Lusteg	K	5'11"	190	25		98

BOSTON PATRIOTS 8-4-2 Mike Holovak

Scores of Each Game		
0	San Diego	24
24	Denver	10
24	KANSAS CITY	43
24	NEW YORK	24
20	Buffalo	10
35	SAN DIEGO	17
24	OAKLAND	21
10	DENVER	17
27	HOUSTON	21
27	Kansas City	27
20	Miami	14
14	BUFFALO	3
38	Houston	14
28	New York	38

Use Name	Pos.	Hgt	Wgt	Age	Int	Pts
Tom Neville	OT	6'4"	230	23		
Don Oakes	OT	6'3"	255	28		
Karl Singer	OT	6'3"	246	22		
Justin Canale	OG	6'2"	230	22		
Charley Long	OG	6'3"	250	28		
Len St. Jean	OG	6'1"	240	24		
Joe Avezzano	C	6'2"	235	22		
Jon Morris	C	6'4"	240	23		
Jim Boudreaux	DE	6'4"	245	21		
Bob Dee	DE	6'3"	240	33		
Larry Eisenhauer	DE	6'5"	250	26		
Houstine Antwine	DT	6'	270	27		
Jim Hunt	DT	5'11"	245	27		6
Ed Khayat	DT	6'3"	250	31		
John Mangum	DT	6'3"	275	22		

Use Name	Pos.	Hgt	Wgt	Age	Int	Pts
Tom Addison	LB	6'3"	230	30		
Nick Buoniconti	LB	5'11"	220	25	4	
Lonnie Farmer	LB	6'	220	25		
Jim Fraser	LB	6'3"	235	30	1	
Doug Satcher	LB	6'	222	21		
Jay Cunningham	DB	5'10"	180	23		
Dick Felt	DB	6'	185	33	2	
White Graves	DB	6'	185	23	1	
Ron Hall	DB	6'	190	29	6	
Tom Hennessey	DB	6'	185	26	6	
Billy Johnson	DB	5'11"	180	23		
Vic Purvis	DB	5'11"	200	22		
Chuck Shonta	DB	6'	200	28	1	
Don Webb	DB	5'10"	200	27	1	

Use Name	Pos.	Hgt	Wgt	Age	Int	Pts
John Huarte	QB	6'	190	22		
Babe Parilli	QB	6'1"	190	36		6
Tom Yewcic	QB	5'11"	185	34		
J. D. Garrett	HB	5'11"	195	24		
Larry Garron	HB	6'	195	29		54
Bob Cappadonna	FB	6'1"	230	22		8
Jim Nance	FB	6'1"	235	23		66
Joe Bellino	FL	5'9"	185	28		6
Gino Cappelletti	FL	6'	190	32		119
Tony Romeo	TE	6'2"	230	27		2
Jim Whalen	TE	6'2"	210	22		24
Jim Colclough	OE	6'	185	30		
Art Graham	OE	6'1"	205	25		24
Ellis Johnson	OE	6'2"	190	22		

NEW YORK JETS 6-6-2 Weeb Ewbank

Scores of Each Game		
19	Miami	14
52	HOUSTON	13
16	Denver	7
24	Boston	24
17	SAN DIEGO	16
0	Houston	24
21	OAKLAND	24
23	BUFFALO	33
3	Buffalo	14
30	MIAMI	13
24	KANSAS CITY	32
28	Oakland	28
27	San Diego	42
38	BOSTON	28

Use Name	Pos.	Hgt	Wgt	Age	Int	Pts
Nick DeFelice	OT	6'3"	250	26		
Mitch Dudek	OT	6'4"	245	22		
Winston Hill	OT	6'4"	274	24		
Sherman Plunkett	OT	6'4"	300	32		
Steve Chomyszak	C-OT	6'5"	265	21		
Sam DeLuca	OG	6'2"	250	30		
Dan Ficca	OG	6'1"	245	27		
Dave Herman	OG	6'2"	255	24		
Pete Perreault	OG	6'3"	245	27		
John Schmitt	C	6'4"	265	23		
Jim Waskiewicz	C	6'4"	227	22		
Verlon Biggs	DE	6'4"	253	23		
Gerry Philbin	DE	6'2"	245	25		
Bill Yearby	DE	6'3"	235	22		
Bert Wilder	DT-DE	6'3"	245	26		
Bob Werl	OG-DE	6'3"	240	23		
Jim Harris	DT	6'4"	280	22		
Paul Rochester	DT	6'2"	250	29		
Henry Schmidt	DT	6'4"	255	29		

Use Name	Pos.	Hgt	Wgt	Age	Int	Pts
Al Atkinson	LB	6'1"	230	23	4	
Ralph Baker	LB	6'3"	228	24		
Paul Crane	LB	6'2"	205	22		
Larry Grantham	LB	6'	206	27	1	
Jim O'Mahoney	LB	6'1"	228	25		
Ray Abruzzese	DB	6'1"	194	28	2	
Bill Baird	DB	5'10"	180	27	5	6
Cornell Gordon	DB	6'	185	25		
Jim Gray	DB	6'	180	24		
Pat Gucciardo	DB	5'11"	185	22		
Sherman Lewis	DB	5'10"	180	24		
Dainard Paulson	DB	5'11"	190	29		
Johnny Sample	DB	6'1"	205	29	6	
Jim Hudson	DB	6'2"	210	23	3	
Dee Mackey – Injury						

Use Name	Pos.	Hgt	Wgt	Age	Int	Pts
Joe Namath	QB	6'2"	190	23		12
Mike Taliaferro	QB	6'2"	205	24		2
Emerson Boozer	HB	5'11"	215	23		36
Earl Christy	HB	5'11"	190	23		
Bill Mathis	HB	6'1"	220	27		18
Allen Smith	HB	5'11"	195	22		
Mark Smolinski	FB	6'	215	27		18
Matt Snell	FB	6'2"	220	24		48
Don Maynard	FL	6'	180	30		30
Sammy Weir	FL	5'9"	170	24		
Pete Lammons	TE	6'3"	235	22		24
Bill Rademacher	OE	6'1"	190	24		
George Sauer	OE	6'1"	206	22		32
Bake Turner	OE	6'	180	26		
Curley Johnson	K	6'	215	31		6
Jim Turner	K	6'2"	205	25		88

HOUSTON OILERS 3-11-0 Wally Lemm

Scores of Each Game		
45	DENVER	7
31	OAKLAND	0
13	New York	52
20	Buffalo	27
38	Denver	40
24	NEW YORK	0
13	MIAMI	20
23	Kansas City	48
23	Oakland	38
21	Boston	27
20	BUFFALO	42
22	SAN DIEGO	28
14	BOSTON	38
28	Miami	29

Use Name	Pos.	Hgt	Wgt	Age	Int	Pts
George Allen	OT	6'7"	270	22		
Glen Ray Hines	OT	6'5"	255	22		
Rich Michael	OT	6'3"	242	27		
Walt Suggs	OT	6'5"	245	27		
Sonny Bishop	OG	6'2"	245	26		
Bob Talamini	OG	6'1"	255	27		
John Wittenborn	OG	6'2"	240	30		
John Frongillo	C	6'3"	255	26		
Gary Cutsinger	DE	6'4"	245	25		
Don Floyd	DE	6'4"	250	27		
Ed Scrutchins	DE	6'3"	260	25		
Scott Appleton	DT	6'3"	255	24		
Jim Hayes	DT	6'4"	260	25		
Pat Holmes	DT	6'5"	270	26		
Ernie Ladd	DT	6'9"	295	27		
George Rice	OG-DT	6'3"	267	22		

Use Name	Pos.	Hgt	Wgt	Age	Int	Pts
Johnny Baker	LB	6'3"	238	25	1	
Garland Boyette	LB	6'1"	238	26		
Danny Brabham	LB	6'4"	233	25		
John Carrell	LB	6'3"	227	23		
Ronnie Caveness	LB	6'1"	225	23	1	
Doug Cline (to SD)	LB	6'2"	230	27	1	6
Bobby Maples	LB	6'3"	245	23		
John Meyer	LB	6'1"	225	24		
Olen Underwood	LB	6'1"	230	24		
Freddy Glick	DB	6'1"	190	29	4	
W. K. Hicks	DB	6'1"	185	23	3	
Bobby Jancik	DB	5'11"	178	26	2	
Jim Norton	DB	6'3"	190	27	4	
Bernie Parrish	DB	5'11"	195	31	2	
Mickey Sutton	DB	6'	190	23		
Allen Trammell	DB	6'	190	24		
Theo Viltz	DB	6'2"	190	23		

Use Name	Pos.	Hgt	Wgt	Age	Int	Pts
George Blanda	QB	6'1"	220	38		87
Buddy Humphrey	QB	6'1"	200	30		
Jacky Lee	QB	6'1"	190	27		
Don Trull	QB	6'1"	190	24		42
Sid Blanks	HB	6'	205	25		12
Ode Burrell	HB	6'	185	26		30
Hoyle Granger	FB-HB	6'1"	225	22		12
John Henry Johnson	FB	6'2"	225	36		18
Donnie Stone	FB	6'2"	205	29		
Charley Tolar	FB	5'7"	200	28		
Larry Elkins	FL	6'1"	190	23		18
Charley Hennigan	FL	6'	187	30		18
Bob McLeod	TE	6'5"	230	27		18
Bob Poole	TE	6'4"	215	24		
Charley Frazier	OE	6'	175	27		72

MIAMI DOLPHINS 3-11-0 George Wilson

Scores of Each Game		
14	OAKLAND	23
14	NEW YORK	19
24	Buffalo	58
10	San Diego	44
10	Oakland	21
24	DENVER	7
20	Houston	13
0	BUFFALO	29
16	Kansas City	34
13	New York	30
14	BOSTON	20
7	Denver	17
18	KANSAS CITY	19
29	HOUSTON	28

Use Name	Pos.	Hgt	Wgt	Age	Int	Pts
Norm Evans	OT	6'5"	235	23		
Ernie Park	OT	6'3"	253	24		
Maxie Williams	OT	6'4"	240	26		
Billy Neighbors	OG	5'11"	245	26		
Ken Rice	OG	6'2"	240	26		
Jim Higgins	OT-OG	6'1"	250	24		
Tom Goode	C	6'3"	240	27		
Mike Hudock	C	6'2"	245	31		
Mel Branch	DE	6'2"	230	29		
Whit Canale	DE	6'3"	245	24		
Ed Cooke	DE	6'4"	250	31		
Earl Faison (from SD)	DE	6'5"	265	27	1	
John Holmes	DE	6'2"	248	22		
Lavern Torczon	DE	6'2"	250	30		
Al Dotson	DT	6'4"	255	23		
Tom Nomina	DT	6'5"	270	24		
Rich Zecher	DT	6'2"	240	23		

Use Name	Pos.	Hgt	Wgt	Age	Int	Pts
Bob Bruggers	LB	6'1"	225	22		
Frank Emanuel	LB	6'3"	225	23	1	
Tom Erlandson	LB	6'3"	235	26	3	6
Wahoo McDaniel	LB	6'	230	29	2	
Jack Rudolph	LB	6'3"	225	28	1	
Jack Thornton	LB	6'1"	230	21		
Pete Jaquess	DB	6'	185	24	3	6
John McGeever	DB	6'1"	195	27	2	
Bob Neff	DB	6'1"	185	22	1	
Bob Petrella	DB	6'	185	21		
Hal Wantland	DB	6'	195	22		
Jimmy Warren	DB	5'11"	185	27	5	6
Willie West	DB	5'10"	187	28	8	
Dick Westmoreland	DB	6'1"	195	25	4	6
Ross O'Hanley – Injury						
Eddie Wilson – Knee Injury						

Use Name	Pos.	Hgt	Wgt	Age	Int	Pts
Rick Norton	QB	6'1"	198	22		
John Stofa	QB	6'3"	210	24		
George Wilson	QB	6'1"	190	23		2
Dick Wood	QB	6'5"	200	30		6
Joe Auer	HB	6'1"	200	24		54
Bill Hunter	HB	6'1"	180	23		
Gene Mingo	HB	6'1"	190	27		53
Sam Price	FB-HB	5'11"	215	22		
Rick Casares	FB	6'2"	233	35		6
George Chesser	FB	6'2"	225	23		
Cookie Gilchrist	FB	6'3"	250	31		6
Billy Joe	FB	6'2"	236	25		8
Frank Jackson	FL	6'1"	190	26		12
Bo Roberson	FL	6'1"	190	31		12
John Roderick	FL	6'1"	180	22		6
Bill Cronin	TE	6'4"	230	23		6
Dave Kocourek	TE	6'5"	240	29		12
Wes Mathews	OE	5'10"	180	22		
Stan Mitchell	OE	6'2"	220	22		
Doug Moreau	OE	6'2"	193	21		
Karl Noonan	OE	6'3"	185	22		6
Howard Twilley	OE	5'10"	180	22		

BUFFALO BILLS

RUSHING

Last Name	No.	Yds	Avg	TD
Burnett	187	766	4.1	4
Carlton	156	696	4.5	6
Smith	31	148	4.8	0
Kemp	40	130	3.3	5
Spikes	28	119	4.3	3
Dubenion	3	16	5.3	0
Rutkowski	1	10	10.0	0
Lamonica	9	6	0.7	1
P. Costa	0	1	0.0	0

RECEIVING

Last Name	No.	Yds	Avg	TD
Dubenion	50	747	15	2
Burnett	34	419	12	4
Crockett	31	533	17	3
P. Costa	27	400	15	3
Carlton	21	280	13	0
Ferguson	16	293	18	1
Bass	10	130	13	0
Rutkowski	6	150	25	1
Spikes	2	45	23	1
O'Donnell	1	2	2	0
Smith	1	1	1	0

PUNT RETURNS

Last Name	No.	Yds	Avg	TD
Rutkowski	18	209	12	1
Byrd	23	186	8	1
Clarke	2	12	6	0
Stratton	0	4	0	0

KICKOFF RETURNS

Last Name	No.	Yds	Avg	TD
Warner	33	846	26	1
Rutkowski	6	121	20	0
Mills	4	76	19	0
Prudhomme	1	16	16	0
Schmidt	1	2	2	0
DeSutter	2	0	0	0
Ferguson	2	0	0	0
D. Costa	1	0	0	0
Maguire	1	0	0	0
O'Donnell	0	3	0	0

PASSING – PUNTING – KICKING Statistics

PASSING	Att	Comp	%	Yds	Yd/Att	TD	Int–%	RK
Kemp	389	166	43	2451	6.3	11	16– 4	7
Lamonica	84	33	39	549	6.5	4	5– 6	

PUNTING	No	Avg
Maguire	69	41.2

KICKING	XP	Att	%	FG	Att	%
Lusteg	41	42	98	19	38	50

BOSTON PATRIOTS

RUSHING

Last Name	No.	Yds	Avg	TD
Nance	299	1458	4.9	11
Garron	101	319	3.2	4
Cappadonna	22	88	4.0	1
Parilli	28	42	1.5	1
Huarte	7	40	5.7	0
Garrett	13	21	1.6	0
Yewcic	1	–5	–5.0	0

RECEIVING

Last Name	No.	Yds	Avg	TD
Graham	51	673	13	4
Cappelletti	43	676	16	6
Garron	30	416	14	5
Whalen	29	502	17	4
Colclough	16	284	18	0
Nance	8	103	13	0
Bellino	6	77	13	1
Romeo	2	46	23	0
Garrett	1	7	7	0

PUNT RETURNS

Last Name	No.	Yds	Avg	TD
Purvis	5	43	9	0
Hennessey	7	39	6	0
B. Johnson	7	37	5	0
Bellino	4	19	5	0
Graves	1	5	5	0

KICKOFF RETURNS

Last Name	No.	Yds	Avg	TD
Bellino	18	410	23	0
Cunningham	17	371	22	0
Purvis	8	185	23	0
Garron	2	49	25	0
Cappadonna	3	46	15	0
E. Johnson	2	45	23	0
Singer	1	27	27	0
Mangum	1	8	8	0
Colclough	1	2	2	0
B. Johnson	1	2	2	0

PASSING – PUNTING – KICKING Statistics

PASSING	Att	Comp	%	Yds	Yd/Att	TD	Int–%	RK
Parilli	382	181	47	2721	7.1	20	20– 5	6
Huarte	11	5	46	63	5.7	0	1– 9	

PUNTING	No	Avg
Fraser	53	38.6
Yewcic	20	36.6

KICKING	XP	Att	%	FG	Att	%
Cappelletti	35	36	97	16	32	50

2 POINT XP
Cappadonna
Romeo

NEW YORK JETS

RUSHING

Last Name	No.	Yds	Avg	TD
Snell	178	644	3.6	4
Boozer	97	455	4.7	5
Mathis	72	208	2.9	2
Smolinski	21	69	3.3	2
Namath	6	42	7.0	2
Johnson	2	24	12.0	0

RECEIVING

Last Name	No.	Yds	Avg	TD
Sauer	63	1079	17	5
Maynard	48	840	18	5
Snell	48	346	7	4
Lammons	31	565	14	4
Mathis	22	379	17	1
Smolinski	11	74	7	1
Boozer	8	133	17	0
B. Turner	7	115	16	0
Johnson	1	18	18	1
Weir	1	4	4	0
Rademacher	1	3	3	0

PUNT RETURNS

Last Name	No.	Yds	Avg	TD
Lewis	7	76	11	0
B. Turner	10	60	6	0
Weir	8	48	6	0
Baird	5	35	7	0
Christy	5	23	5	0
Hudson	1	18	18	0

KICKOFF RETURNS

Last Name	No.	Yds	Avg	TD
Boozer	26	659	25	1
Christy	10	203	20	0
Weir	6	121	20	0
Lewis	5	121	24	0
Gray	5	77	15	0
Smolinski	6	59	10	0
B. Turner	2	50	25	0
Wilder	1	6	6	0
Johnson	1	4	4	0

PASSING – PUNTING – KICKING Statistics

PASSING	Att	Comp	%	Yds	Yd/Att	TD	Int–%	RK
Namath	471	232	49	3379	7.2	19	27– 6	4
Taliaferro	41	19	46	177	4.3	2	2– 5	
Hudson	1	0	0	0	0.0	0	0– 0	
Snell	1	0	0	0	0.0	0	0– 0	

PUNTING	No	Avg
Johnson	62	42.5

KICKING	XP	Att	%	FG	Att	%
J. Turner	34	35	97	18	35	51

2 POINT XP
Sauer
Taliaferro

HOUSTON OILERS

RUSHING

Last Name	No.	Yds	Avg	TD
Burrell	122	406	3.3	0
Granger	56	388	6.9	1
Blanks	71	235	3.3	0
Johnson	70	226	3.2	3
Trull	38	139	3.7	7
Tolar	46	105	2.3	0
Stone	6	18	3.0	0
Blanda	3	1	0.3	0
Lee	1	–3	–3.0	0

RECEIVING

Last Name	No.	Yds	Avg	TD
Frazier	57	1129	20	12
Burrell	33	400	12	5
Hennigan	27	313	12	3
McLeod	23	339	15	3
Elkins	21	283	13	3
Blanks	19	234	12	2
Tolar	13	68	5	0
Poole	12	131	11	0
Granger	12	104	9	1
Johnson	8	150	19	0
Stone	1	17	17	0

PUNT RETURNS

Last Name	No.	Yds	Avg	TD
Burrell	8	78	10	0
Jancik	10	62	6	0
Trammell	5	19	4	0

KICKOFF RETURNS

Last Name	No.	Yds	Avg	TD
Jancik	34	875	26	0
Blanks	21	487	23	0
Trammell	3	63	21	0
Boyette	3	42	14	0
Hayes	2	31	16	0
Burrell	1	16	16	0

PASSING – PUNTING – KICKING Statistics

PASSING	Att	Comp	%	Yds	Yd/Att	TD	Int–%	RK
Blanda	271	122	45	1764	6.5	17	21– 8	9
Trull	172	84	49	1200	7.0	10	5– 3	4
Humphrey	32	15	47	168	5.3	2	1– 3	
Lee	8	4	50	27	3.4	0	1– 13	
Burrell	1	1	100	9	9.0	0	0– 0	
Tolar	1	0	0	0	0.0	0	0– 0	

PUNTING	No	Avg
Norton	69	42.2

KICKING	XP	Att	%	FG	Att	%
Blanda	39	40	98	16	30	53

MIAMI DOLPHINS

RUSHING

Last Name	No.	Yds	Avg	TD
Auer	121	416	3.4	4
Gilchrist	72	262	3.6	0
Joe	71	232	3.3	0
Wilson	27	137	5.1	0
Casares	43	135	3.1	0
Price	31	107	3.5	0
Chesser	16	74	4.6	0
Jackson	2	22	11.0	0
Stofa	3	17	5.7	0
Wood	5	6	1.2	1
Norton	3	2	0.7	0

RECEIVING

Last Name	No.	Yds	Avg	TD
Kocourek	27	320	12	2
Roberson	26	519	20	2
Auer	22	263	12	4
Noonan	17	224	13	1
Jackson	16	317	20	2
Joe	13	116	9	1
Gilchrist	13	110	8	1
Roderick	11	156	14	1
Twilley	10	128	13	0
Casares	8	45	6	1
Cronin	7	83	12	1
Mingo	3	40	13	0
Moreau	2	15	8	0
Price	2	14	7	0
Matthews	1	20	20	0
Chesser	1	4	4	0

PUNT RETURNS

Last Name	No.	Yds	Avg	TD
Auer	5	99	20	0
Neff	10	60	6	0
Matthews	4	38	10	0
Jackson	2	7	4	0

KICKOFF RETURNS

Last Name	No.	Yds	Avg	TD
Auer	28	698	25	1
Neff	15	376	25	0
Matthews	5	109	22	0
Jackson	4	105	26	0
Hunter	5	84	17	0
Jaquess	5	77	15	0
Roderick	1	17	17	0
Branch	1	15	15	0
Bruggers	1	3	3	0
Noonan	0	23	0	0

PASSING – PUNTING – KICKING Statistics

PASSING	Att	Comp	%	Yds	Yd/Att	TD	Int–%	RK
Wood	230	83	36	993	4.3	4	14– 6	10
Wilson	112	46	41	764	6.8	5	10– 9	
Stofa	57	29	51	425	7,5	4	2– 4	
Norton	55	21	38	192	3.5	3	6– 11	

PUNTING	No	Avg
Wilson	42	42.1
McDaniel	32	38.2
Chesser	7	33.3

KICKING	XP	Att	%	FG	Att	%
Mingo	23	23	100	10	22	46

2 POINT XP
Joe
Wilson

KANSAS CITY CHIEFS 11-2-1 Hank Stram

Scores of Each Game		
42	Buffalo	20
32	Oakland	10
43	Boston	24
14	BUFFALO	29
37	DENVER	10
13	OAKLAND	34
56	Denver	10
48	HOUSTON	23
24	SAN DIEGO	14
34	MIAMI	16
27	BOSTON	27
32	New York	24
19	Miami	18
27	San Diego	17

Use Name	Pos.	Hgt	Wgt	Age	Int	Pts
Tony DiMidio	OT	6'3"	250	24		
Dave Hill	OT	6'5"	254	25		
Jim Tyrer	OT	6'6"	292	27		
Denny Biodrowski	OG	6'1"	255	26		
Ed Budde	OG	6'5"	260	25		
Curt Merz	OG	6'4"	267	28		
Al Reynolds	OG	6'3"	250	28		
Hatch Rosdahl	OG	6'5"	250	23		
Wayne Frazier	C	6'2"	245	26		
Jon Gilliam	C	6'2"	240	27		
Aaron Brown	DE	6'5"	250	22		
Chuck Hurston	DE	6'6"	230	23		
Jerry Mays	DE	6'4"	252	26		
Buck Buchanan	DT	6'7"	287	26		
Ed Lothamer	DT	6'5"	270	23		
Andy Rice	DT	6'3"	266	24		
Bud Abell	LB	6'3"	220	25		
Bobby Bell	LB	6'4"	228	26	2	6
Walt Corey	LB	6'	233	28		
Sherrill Headrick	LB	6'2"	240	29	2	
E. J. Holub	LB	6'4"	236	28		
Smokey Stover	LB	6'	227	27	1	
Solomon Brannan	DB	6'1"	188	24		
Jimmy Hill	DB	6'2"	198	37		
Bobby Hunt	DB	6'1"	193	26	10	
Willie Mitchell	DB	6'1"	185	24	3	6
Bobby Ply	DB	6'1"	190	25	1	
Johnny Robinson	DB	6'	205	27	10	6
Fletcher Smith	DB	6'2"	188	22		2
Emmitt Thomas	DB	6'2"	190	23		
Fred Williamson	DB	6'2"	210	28	4	
Pete Beathard	QB	6'2"	210	24		6
Len Dawson	QB	6'	190	32		
Bert Coan	HB	6'4"	220	26		54
Mike Garrett	HB	5'9"	195	22		48
Gene Thomas	HB	6'1"	210	23		6
Curtis McClinton	FB	6'3"	227	28		54
Jerrel Wilson	FB	6'4"	222	24		2
Otis Taylor	FL	6'2"	211	23		48
Fred Arbanas	TE	6'3"	240	27		26
Chris Burford	OE	6'3"	210	28		48
Reg Carolan	OE	6'6"	238	26		18
Frank Pitts	OE	6'2"	190	22		6
Tommy Brooker	K	6'2"	235	26		19
Mike Mercer (from OAK)	K	6'	210	30		98

Curt Farrier – Injury

OAKLAND RAIDERS 8-5-1 Johnny Rauch

Scores of Each Game		
23	Miami	14
0	Houston	31
10	KANSAS CITY	32
20	SAN DIEGO	29
21	MIAMI	10
34	Kansas City	13
24	New York	21
21	Boston	24
38	HOUSTON	23
41	San Diego	19
17	Denver	3
10	BUFFALO	31
28	NEW YORK	28
28	DENVER	10

Use Name	Pos.	Hgt	Wgt	Age	Int	Pts
Jim Harvey	OT	6'5"	245	23		
Harry Schuh	OT	6'2"	260	23		
Bob Svihus	OT	6'4"	245	23		
Wayne Hawkins	OG	6'	240	28		
Palmer Pyle	OG	6'2"	245	29		
Dick Tyson	OG	6'2"	245	22		
Jim Otto	C	6'2"	240	28		
Ben Davidson	DE	6'8"	265	26		
Greg Kent	DE	6'6"	275	23		
Ike Lassiter	DE	6'5"	270	25	1	
Carleton Oats	DT-DE	6'2"	235	23		
Dan Birdwell	DT	6'4"	250	25	1	
Dave Daniels	DT	6'3"	245	25		
Tom Keating	DT	6'3"	247	23		
Rex Mirich	DT	6'4"	250	25		
Bill Budness	LB	6'1"	215	23		
Dan Conners	LB	6'1"	240	24	2	6
Rich Jackson	LB	6'2"	230	25		
Bill Laskey	LB	6'2"	240	23		
Gus Otto	LB	6'2"	220	23		
Ray Schmautz	LB	6'1"	225	23		
J. R. Williamson	LB	6'2"	220	24		
Rodger Bird	DB	5'11"	195	23	4	
Dave Grayson	DB	5'10"	185	27	3	
Joe Krakoski	DB	6'2"	195	29		
Kent McCloughan	DB	6'1"	190	23	4	
Warren Powers	DB	6'	190	25	5	
Howie Williams	DB	6'2"	187	29	3	
Willie Williams	DB	6'	190	23		
Cotton Davidson	QB	6'1"	180	34		
Tom Flores	QB	6'1"	190	29		6
Charlie Green	QB	6'	190	23		
Pervis Atkins	HB	6'1"	195	30		
Pete Banaszak	HB	5'11"	200	22		
Clem Daniels	HB	6'1"	218	29		60
Roger Hagberg	FB	6'2"	215	27		6
Hewritt Dixon	HB-FB	6'2"	225	26		54
Fred Biletnikoff	FL	6'1"	190	23		18
Billy Cannon	TE	6'1"	215	29		12
Tom Mitchell	TE	6'2"	235	22		6
Bill Miller	OE	6'	190	24		
Art Powell	OE	6'3"	212	29		66
Larry Todd	OE	6'1"	185	23		6
Mike Eischeid	K	6'	190	25		70

George Flint – Injury

SAN DIEGO CHARGERS 7-6-1 Sid Gillman

Scores of Each Game		
27	BUFFALO	7
24	BOSTON	0
29	Oakland	20
44	MIAMI	10
16	New York	17
17	Buffalo	17
17	Boston	35
24	DENVER	17
14	Kansas City	24
19	OAKLAND	41
17	Denver	20
28	Houston	22
42	NEW YORK	27
17	KANSAS CITY	27

Use Name	Pos.	Hgt	Wgt	Age	Int	Pts
Gary Kirner	OT	6'3"	248	24		
Ron Mix	OT	6'4"	250	28		
Terry Owens	OT	6'6"	240	22		
Ernie Wright	OT	6'4"	265	26		
Don Estes	OG	6'2"	250	23		
John Farris	OG	6'4"	245	25		
Ed Mitchell	OG	6'2"	280	24		
Walt Sweeney	OG	6'3"	250	25		
Sam Gruneisen	C	6'1"	240	25		
Paul Latzke	C	6'4"	245	24		
Jim Griffin	DE	6'3"	255	24		
Howard Kindig	DE	6'6"	255	25	1	
Fred Moore	DE	6'3"	255	26		
Bob Petrich	DE	6'4"	250	25		
Houston Ridge	DE	6'4"	232	22		
Steve DeLong	DT	6'3"	252	23		
George Gross	DT	6'3"	258	25		
Larry Martin	DT	6'2"	270	24		
Chuck Allen	LB	6'1"	225	26	1	
Frank Buncom	LB	6'1"	240	26		
Dick Degen	LB	6'1"	220	24	1	
Tom Good	LB	6'	230	22		
Emil Karas	LB	6'3"	230	32		
Mike London	LB	6'2"	230	21		
John Milks	LB	6'	222	22	1	
Bob Mitinger	LB	6'2"	230	26		
Rick Redman	LB	5'11"	225	23	2	6
Joe Beauchamp	DB	6'	185	22	2	
Speedy Duncan	DB	5'10"	175	23	7	6
Miller Farr	DB	6'1"	192	23	3	
Kenny Graham	DB	6'	195	24	5	6
Dave Plump	DB	6'1"	195	23		
Jim Tolbert	DB	6'3"	207	22	1	
Bud Whitehead	DB	6'	185	27	2	
Nat Whitmyer	DB	6'	180	25		
Bob Zeman	DB	6'1"	205	29		
John Hadl	QB	6'2"	215	26		12
Dan Henning	QB	6'	195	24		
Steve Tensi	QB	6'5"	215	23		
Paul Lowe	HB	6'	205	29		18
Gene Foster	FB-HB	5'11"	212	23		18
Jim Allison	FB	6'	220	23		12
Keith Lincoln	FB	6'2"	215	27		18
John Travis	FB	6'1"	216	23		
Lance Alworth	FL	6'	180	26		78
Willie Frazier	TE	6'4"	235	23		12
Jacque MacKinnon	TE	6'4"	250	27		36
Gary Garrison	OE	6'1"	195	22		24
Don Norton	OE	6'1"	195	28		
Dick Van Raaphorst	K	5'11"	215	23		87

Pat Shea – Injury

DENVER BRONCOS 4-10-0 Mac Speedie Ray Malavasi

Scores of Each Game		
7	Houston	45
10	BOSTON	24
7	NEW YORK	16
40	HOUSTON	38
10	Kansas City	37
7	Miami	24
10	KANSAS CITY	56
17	San Diego	24
17	Boston	10
3	OAKLAND	17
20	SAN DIEGO	17
17	MIAMI	7
10	Oakland	28
21	Buffalo	38

Use Name	Pos.	Hgt	Wgt	Age	Int	Pts
Lee Bernet	OT	6'2"	245	22		
Bob Breitenstein	OT	6'3"	270	23		
Sam Brunelli	OG	6'1"	240	23		
John Gonzaga	OG	6'3"	250	33		
Jon Hohman	OG	6'1"	245	23		
Bill Keating	OG	6'2"	236	21		
Pat Matson	OG	6'1"	250	22		
Jerry Sturm	OG	6'3"	260	29		
Larry Kaminski	C	6'2"	240	21		
Ray Kubala	C	6'4"	245	24		
Marvin Davis	DE	6'4"	252	22		
Dan LaRose	DE	6'5"	250	26		
Max Leetzow	DE	6'4"	240	23		
George Tarasovic	DE	6'4"	250	37		
Larry Cox	DT	6'2"	250	22		
Jerry Inman	DT	6'3"	255	26		
Ray Jacobs	DT	6'3"	275	26		
Bob Young	DT	6'2"	275	23		
John Bramlett	LB	6'2"	220	25	1	6
Don Gulseth	LB	6'1"	240	24		
Jerry Hopkins	LB	6'2"	235	25	2	
Gene Jeter	LB	6'3"	230	24		
Archie Matsos (to SD)	LB	6'	212	31	3	
Ron Sbranti	LB	6'2"	230	21		
Willie Brown	DB	6'1"	190	25	3	
Billy Fletcher	DB	5'10"	190	22		
Goose Gonsoulin	DB	6'3"	210	28		
John Griffin	DB	6'1"	190	26		
Bob Richardson	DB	6'1"	180	22		
Lew Scott	DB	5'10"	173	23		
Goldie Sellers	DB	6'2"	198	24	3	12
Nemiah Wilson	DB	6'	165	23	1	6
Lonnie Wright	DB	6'2"	205	22	1	
Eric Crabtree	OE-DB	5'11"	190	21		
Max Choboian	QB	6'4"	205	24		12
Scotty Glacken	QB	6'	190	21		
John McCormick	QB	6'1"	190	29		
Tobin Rote	QB	6'3"	220	38		
Mickey Slaughter	QB	6'	190	25		
Abner Haynes	HB	6'	190	28		18
Charley Mitchell	HB	5'11"	185	26		12
Mike Kellogg	FB	6'	220	23		
Darrell Lester	FB	6'2"	220	25		6
Wendell Hayes	HB-FB	6'2"	195	25		6
Bob Scarpitto	FL	5'11"	196	27		32
Al Denson	TE	6'2"	208	24		18
Max Wettstein	TE	6'3"	217	22		
Jason Franci	OE	6'1"	210	22		
Glenn Glass	OE	6'	203	29		
Lionel Taylor	OE	6'2"	215	30		6
Gary Kroner	K	6'1"	200	25		62

Eldon Danenhauer – Injury

KANSAS CITY CHIEFS

RUSHING

Last Name	No.	Yds	Avg	TD
Garrett	147	801	5.5	6
McClinton	140	540	3.9	4
Coan	96	521	5.4	7
Dawson	24	167	7.0	0
Beathard	20	152	7.6	1
G. Thomas	7	53	7.6	1
Taylor	2	33	16.5	0
Wilson	3	7	2.3	0

RECEIVING

Last Name	No.	Yds	Avg	TD
Taylor	58	1297	22	8
Burford	58	758	13	8
Arbanas	22	305	14	4
McClinton	19	285	15	5
Coan	18	131	7	2
Garrett	15	175	12	1
Carolan	7	154	22	3
Pitts	1	11	11	0
Wilson	1	7	7	0

PUNT RETURNS

Last Name	No.	Yds	Avg	TD
Garrett	17	139	8	1
E. Thomas	9	56	6	0
Brown	1	43	43	0
Pitts	1	21	21	1
Williamson	1	10	10	0
Mitchell	1	7	7	0
Ply	1	0	0	0

KICKOFF RETURNS

Last Name	No.	Yds	Avg	TD
E. Thomas	29	673	23	0
Garrett	14	323	23	0
G. Thomas	3	62	21	0
Brannan	1	24	24	0
Coan	1	22	22	0
Brown	1	6	6	0
Stover	3	0	0	0
Taylor	2	0	0	0
Pitts	0	38	0	0

PASSING – PUNTING – KICKING

PASSING	Att	Comp	%	Yds	Yd/Att	TD	Int–%	RK
Dawson	284	159	56	2527	8.9	26	10– 4	1
Beathard	90	39	43	578	6.4	4	4– 4	
Coan	1	1	100	18	18.0	1	0– 0	
Garrett	1	0	0	0	0.0	0	0– 0	
Taylor	1	0	0	0	0.0	0	1–100	

PUNTING	No	Avg
Wilson	61	44.5
Mercer	9	41.4

KICKING	XP	Att	%	FG	Att	%
Mercer	35	38	92	21	30	70
Brooker	13	13	100	2	2	100
Smith	2	4	50	0	0	0

2 POINT XP
Arbanas
Wilson

OAKLAND RAIDERS

RUSHING

Last Name	No.	Yds	Avg	TD
C. Daniels	204	801	3.9	7
Hagberg	62	282	4.6	0
Dixon	68	277	4.1	5
Flores	5	50	10.0	1
Banaszak	4	18	4.5	0
Atkins	14	10	0.7	0
C. Davidson	6	–11	–1.8	0

RECEIVING

Last Name	No.	Yds	Avg	TD
Powell	53	1026	19	11
C. Daniels	40	652	16	3
Dixon	29	345	12	4
Mitchell	23	301	13	1
Hagberg	21	248	12	1
Biletnikoff	17	272	16	3
Cannon	14	436	31	2
Todd	14	134	10	1
Banaszak	1	11	11	0

PUNT RETURNS

Last Name	No.	Yds	Avg	TD
Bird	37	323	9	0
Krakoski	2	19	10	0
Atkins	1	13	13	0
Cannon	1	12	12	0

KICKOFF RETURNS

Last Name	No.	Yds	Avg	TD
Atkins	29	608	21	0
Bird	19	390	21	0
Grayson	6	128	21	0
W. Williams	2	52	26	0
Hagberg	1	13	13	0
Mirich	2	0	0	0
Powers	1	0	0	0

PASSING – PUNTING – KICKING

PASSING	Att	Comp	%	Yds	Yd/Att	TD	Int–%	RK
Flores	306	151	49	2638	8.6	24	14– 5	3
C. Davidson	139	59	42	770	5.5	2	11– 8	
C. Daniels	3	0	0	0	0.0	0	1– 33	
Green	2	2	100	17	8.5	0	0– 0	

PUNTING	No	Avg
Eischeid	64	42.3

KICKING	XP	Att	%	FG	Att	%
Eischeid	37	37	100	11	26	42

SAN DIEGO CHARGERS

RUSHING

Last Name	No.	Yds	Avg	TD
Lowe	146	643	4.4	3
Foster	81	352	4.4	1
Lincoln	58	214	3.7	1
Allison	31	213	6.9	2
Hadl	38	95	2.5	2
Redman	2	14	7.0	0
Alworth	3	10	3.3	0
Tensi	1	–1	–1.0	0
Garrison	1	–3	–3.0	0

RECEIVING

Last Name	No.	Yds	Avg	TD
Alworth	73	1383	19	13
Garrison	46	642	14	4
MacKinnon	26	477	18	6
Foster	26	260	10	2
Lincoln	14	264	19	2
Allison	12	99	8	0
Lowe	12	41	3	0
Frazier	9	144	16	2
Norton	4	50	13	0
Hadl	2	–13	–7	0

PUNT RETURNS

Last Name	No.	Yds	Avg	TD
Duncan	18	238	13	1
Graham	2	15	8	0
Plump	1	4	4	0

KICKOFF RETURNS

Last Name	No.	Yds	Avg	TD
Duncan	25	642	26	0
Plump	15	345	23	0
Lowe	7	167	24	0
Beauchamp	4	64	16	0
Farr	2	54	27	0
Whitmyer	1	10	10	0
Gruneisen	1	0	0	0

PASSING – PUNTING – KICKING

PASSING	Att	Comp	%	Yds	Yd/Att	TD	Int–%	RK
Hadl	375	200	53	2846	7.6	23	14– 4	2
Tensi	52	21	40	405	7.8	5	1– 2	
Lincoln	4	2	50	71	17.8	1	0– 0	
Lowe	3	1	33	25	8.3	0	0– 0	

PUNTING	No	Avg
Redman	66	37.0

KICKING	XP	Att	%	FG	Att	%
Van Raaphorst	20	40	08	16	31	62

DENVER BRONCOS

RUSHING

Last Name	No.	Yds	Avg	TD
Hayes	105	417	4.0	1
Haynes	129	304	2.4	2
Mitchell	70	199	2.8	0
Scarpitto	4	110	27.5	1
Lester	34	84	2.5	0
Choboian	21	45	2.1	2
Slaughter	1	10	10.0	0
Kellogg	6	3	0.5	0
McCormick	4	2	0.5	0
Glacken	2	–1	–0.5	0

RECEIVING

Last Name	No.	Yds	Avg	TD
Haynes	46	480	10	1
Denson	36	725	20	3
Taylor	35	448	13	1
Scarpitto	21	335	16	4
Mitchell	14	239	17	2
Hayes	8	49	6	0
Lester	2	26	13	1
Crabtree	1	38	38	0
Franci	1	8	8	0
Kellogg	1	5	5	0
Wright	1	–2	–2	0

PUNT RETURNS

Last Name	No.	Yds	Avg	TD
Haynes	10	119	12	0
Scott	7	56	8	0
Sellers	6	49	8	0
Wilson	2	10	5	0
Lester	1	1	1	0

KICKOFF RETURNS

Last Name	No.	Yds	Avg	TD
Sellers	19	541	28	2
Wilson	10	309	31	1
Scott	9	282	31	0
Haynes	9	229	25	0
Crabtree	5	129	26	0
Mitchell	3	55	18	0
Lester	1	11	11	0
Sturm	1	2	2	0
Inman	1	0	0	0

PASSING – PUNTING – KICKING

PASSING	Att	Comp	%	Yds	Yd/Att	TD	Int–%	RK
McCormick	193	68	35	993	5.1	6	15– 8	11
Choboian	163	82	50	1110	6.8	4	12– 7	8
Slaughter	25	7	28	124	5.0	1	0– 0	
Glacken	11	6	55	84	7.6	1	0– 0	
Rote	8	3	38	40	5.0	0	1– 13	
Haynes	2	0	0	0	0.0	0	2–100	

PUNTING	No	Avg
Scarpitto	76	45.8

KICKING	XP	Att	%	FG	Att	%
Kroner	20	20	100	14	25	56

2 POINT XP
Scarpitto

Super Bowl I

January 15, at Los Angeles
(Attendance 61,946)

Thirty Minutes of Equality

It seemed somehow unreal. The Green Bay Packers and the Kansas City Chiefs had always been parts of different universes in the world of sports. But here they were, the champions of the NFL and the AFL, meeting on the field in a confrontation many thought was years away.

Until recently, the NFL had not even recognized that the AFL was there. The established league considered the newer league an inferior and annoying upstart, worthy only of contempt when it first began. But while AFL scores were never posted in NFL stadia, NFL owners felt the AFL's presence directly when the new league began signing a fair share of top players and driving player salaries up in general. Despite the icy external show, fans knew that the NFL people wanted nothing better than the death of the AFL.

The AFL people, however, had never denied the NFL's existence; in fact, they used the older league as an open measure of their own league. NFL games were reported right along with AFL games on the scoreboard, as if both belonged on an equal footing, and AFL clubs were measured by the hypothetical situation of how they would do against a good NFL team. Ultimate success for the AFL would be standing shoulder to shoulder with the NFL.

The war between the leagues had been fought in courtrooms and the press, with subpoenas and checkbooks. The NFL looked down on the new league with utter disdain at first, but as the rich men who owned AFL clubs bid up player salaries and threatened to lure away established NFL stars, the officials of the older league decided to swallow some pride and look for a way to end the war between the circuits.

Negotiations in the spring brought about a peace agreement between the leagues that changed the structure of pro football as it had been in the 1960s. The NFL and AFL agreed to end their financial war by holding a common draft of college seniors and respecting each other's player contracts, and although the AFL clubs had to pay reparations, the clubs of both leagues now were coequal members of a joint structure. By the end of the decade, the AFL would be absorbed completely into an expanded NFL.

But the biggest dividend for the football fan was the establishment of an NFL-AFL championship game between the two league champions. Unofficially dubbed "The Super Bowl" by the media, this game would bring together the top teams in two leagues which had never played each other. This year's game would be unprecedented.

Older fans, of course, remembered the startling entry of the Cleveland Browns into the NFL in 1950. The Browns had completely dominated the AAFC during its four-year existence, but many fans and reporters looked on that circuit as an inferior league. The Browns relished the chance to prove that *they* were not inferior, and they decisively defeated the defending champion Philadelphia Eagles in their first confrontation with NFL competition. The Browns went on to take the league title in that first season, and some fans liked the chances of the AFL team in the Super Bowl because of the Browns' example.

Emerging as the AFL champion and Super Bowl representative were the Kansas City Chiefs, a team which had played three years in Dallas before moving to Missouri. Owned by Lamar Hunt and coached from the beginning by Hank Stram, the Chiefs had compiled an 11-2-1 record during the season and dissected a strong Buffalo team in the AFL championship game. Len Dawson, who had been waived out of the NFL after five years of bench-sitting, had found himself as a quarterback in the AFL, excelling both as a passer and a play-caller. Otis Taylor, Mike Garrett, Ed Budde, Jim Tyrer, and Buck Buchanan were all talented young pros who obviously could make most teams in the NFL. For the rest of the Kansas City offense and most of the defense, a lingering doubt remained. How well would these men, all solid AFL players, make out against the best the NFL could offer?

That best, for the fourth time in the last six years, was the Green Bay Packers, that hard-hitting precision machine hand-built by coach Vince Lombardi. Although the parts were aging, Lombardi's machine still was a multifaceted wonder. His offensive line was quietly but constantly effective in moving people aside, and the running backs were the hard-nosed types who thrived on power sweeps and off-tackle smashes. At the heart of the attack was quarterback Bart Starr, a marvelous football tactician with a penchant for throwing very few interceptions. The Packer defense had set standards for all pro-football teams. Green Bay's mobile front four, big yet fast linebackers, and ball-hawking man-to-man pass defenders had written the book on modern defense. Presiding over it all and adding the special edge was coach Lombardi, the inspirational leader, the tough disciplinarian, the devout Catholic and family man, and a football theorist who set a tone for pro football which still is strong. Lombardi believed that the team that blocks and tackles best wins, and he drilled his teams to block crisply, to tackle hard, and to win.

So, on a warm January day in Los Angeles, the champions of two different leagues who played the same game but had never met came together on the same field. At first it was strange to see these two teams at the same time, but the fans and teams themselves soon settled into a very important football game for a lot of money plus the title of champion of all professional football.

The Chiefs fought the Packers to a standstill for most of the first period, but Green Bay got onto the scoreboard with a 37-yard pass from Bart Starr to Max McGee. Filling in for the injured Boyd Dowler, the thirty-four-year-old McGee would haul in seven passes today; eased out of the starting lineup this past season, he had caught only three passes during the regular campaign.

The Packers, however, were giving the Chiefs their first taste of what NFL teams had had to put up with for years. The only AFL fullback who had ever run with the ferocity of Jim Taylor was Cookie Gilchrist, who now was past his prime. The AFL had never produced as violent and perceptive a middle linebacker as Ray Nitschke, or as devastating a pair of corner linebackers as Dave Robinson and Lee Roy Caffey. The first quarter ended with the score only 7-0, but the Packers seemed to be on the verge of blowing the game wide open.

Far from folding, however, the Chiefs played their best football of the afternoon in the second period. Dawson's passes seemingly were finding gaps in the Packers' pass defense. Throwing both to his ends and backs, Dawson methodically moved the Chiefs downfield until they had the ball on the Green Bay seven-yard line. A short pass to fullback Curtis McClinton carried the ball into the end zone and marked the first time an AFL team had scored on an NFL team; some experts had freely predicted a Green Bay shutout in this contest. Seconds after the touchdown, Mike Mercer's extra-point kick knotted the score at 7-7.

With all expectations of an easy rout laid to rest, the Packers went to work on the next series of downs. Mixing passes and running plays, Starr drove the Packers deep into Kansas City territory, keying on several weak points he had discovered in the Chiefs' defense. He found that the Packers could run at end Chuck Hurston and tackle Andy Rice and throw against Sherrill Headrick, Fred Williamson, and Willie Mitchell; these men had held up against AFL competition but seemed out of their depth against the Packers. Green Bay especially enjoyed throwing against Williamson, since he had bragged that his hammer tackle, which was really only a forearm smash, would wreak havoc with the Packers. In the second half, Williamson himself would be carried from the field unconscious, the victim of a Green Bay "hammer tackle" of sorts.

Moving fairly easy through the Chiefs, the Packers scored their second touchdown on a 14-yard run by Jim Taylor, who simply ran over several Chiefs on the way to the end zone. Don Chandler's kick made the score 14-7, but the Chiefs were not yet ready to give up. Dawson responded with his own passing attack, and a 31-yard Mercer field goal cut the Green Bay lead to 14-10 at halftime.

The Chiefs had stayed surprisingly close to the Packers in the first half, and a good final thirty minutes of play could have brought them an upset victory. Beginning the second half with high hopes, the Chiefs quickly met with a misfortune which let all the air out of them. Dawson dropped back to pass but was surrounded by a strong Green Bay pass rush; instead of eating the ball and taking the loss, he heaved the ball downfield. Willie Wood of the Packers picked it off and brought it back all the way to the Kansas City five-yard line. Elijah Pitts carried it over from there, and the game was never the same afterward. The Packers oozed confidence the rest of the afternoon, while the Chiefs simply looked outmanned.

Dawson found it much harder to move the ball in the second half, and the Chiefs never threatened to score in the final two periods. The Packers, meanwhile, took firm control of the game with good blocking and tackling. Max McGee's second touchdown catch of the day built the Packer lead up to 28-10 after three quarters, and Elijah Pitts' second touchdown run made the final score 35-10.

The Chiefs came away beaten but not disgraced. Although the Green Bay steamroller eventually ground them down, the Chiefs never gave up, and their first-half showing proved that an AFL club could hold its own with a top NFL club—at least for thirty minutes. Coach Stram did learn from the game which of his players could be exploited by a strong club, and he was making plans to replace certain men before a week had passed after the game.

For Vince Lombardi and the Packers, the victory added one more trophy to their collection. Green Bay had won several NFL titles in the 1960s, and now they had won the Super Bowl, a distinct product of this decade.

Some people claimed that Super Bowl I proved the inferiority of the AFL. Probably closer to the truth was the statement that the Chiefs were not inferior to the NFL, only to the Green Bay Packers.

KANSAS CITY		GREEN BAY
	OFFENSE	
Burford	LE	Dale
Tyrer	LT	Skoronski
Budde	LG	Thurston
Frazier	C	Curry
Merz	RG	Kramer
Hill	RT	Gregg
Arbanas	RE	Fleming
Dawson	QB	Starr
O. Taylor	FL	Dowler
Garrett	HB	E. Pitts
McClinton	FB	J. Taylor
	DEFENSE	
Mays	LE	Davis
Rice	LT	Kostelnik
Buchanan	RT	Jordan
Hurston	RE	Aldridge
Bell	LLB	D. Robinson
Headrick	MLB	Nitschke
Holub	RLB	Coffey
Williamson	LCB	Adderley
Mitchell	RCB	Jeter
Hunt	LS	T. Brown
J. Robinson	RS	Wood

SUBSTITUTES

KANSAS CITY

Offense

Beathard	Gilliam
Biodrowski	F. Pitts
Carolan	Reynolds
Coan	G. Thomas
DiMidio	

Defense

Abell	Smith
A. Brown	Stover
Corey	E. Thomas
Ply	

Kickers

Mercer	Wilson

GREEN BAY

Offense

B. Anderson	Long
D. Anderson	Mack
Bowman	McGee
Bratkowski	Vandersea
Gillingham	Wright
Grabowski	

Defense

B. Brown	Heathcock
Crutcher	Weatherwax
Hart	

Kicker

Chandler

SCORING

KANSAS CITY	0	10	0	0	–10
GREEN BAY	7	7	14	7	–35

First Quarter
G.B. McGee, 37 yard pass from Starr
PAT – Chandler (kick)

Second Quarter
K.C. McClinton, 17 yard pass from Dawson PAT – Mercer (kick)
G.B. Taylor, 14 yard rush
PAT – Chandler (kick)
K.C. Mercer, 31 yard field goal

Third Quarter
G.B. Pitts, 5 yard rush
PAT – Chandler (kick)
G.B. McGee, 13 yard pass from Starr
PAT – Chandler (kick)

Fourth Quarter
G.B. Pitts, 1 yard rush
PAT – Chandler (kick)

TEAM STATISTICS

K. C.		G.B.
17	First Downs – Total	21
4	First Downs – Rushing	10
12	First Downs – Passing	11
1	First Downs – Penalty	0
1	Fumbles – Number	1
0	Fumbles – Lost Ball	0
4	Penalties – Number	4
26	Yards Penalized	40
64	Total Offensive Plays	64
239	Total Net Yards	358
3.7	Average Gain	5.6
1	Missed Field Goals	0
1	Giveaways	1
1	Takeaways	1
0	Difference	0

* includes Punts

INDIVIDUAL STATISTICS

RUSHING

KANSAS CITY	No	Yds	Avg.	GREEN BAY	No	Yds	Avg.
Dawson	3	24	8.0	Taylor	16	53	3.3
Garrett	6	17	2.8	Pitts	11	45	4.1
McClinton	6	16	2.7	D. Anderson	4	30	7.5
Beathard	1	14	14.0	Grabowski	2	2	1.0
Coan	3	1	0.3		33	130	3.9
	19	72	3.8				

RECEIVING

KANSAS CITY	No	Yds	Avg.	GREEN BAY	No	Yds	Avg.
Burford	4	67	16.8	McGee	7	138	19.7
Taylor	4	57	14.3	Dale	4	59	14.8
Garrett	3	28	9.3	Pitts	2	32	16.0
McClinton	2	34	17.0	Fleming	2	22	11.0
Arbanas	2	30	15.0	Taylor	1	–1	–1.0
Carolan	1	7	7.0		16	250	15.6
Coan	1	5	5.0				
	17	228	13.4				

PUNTING

KANSAS CITY	No	Yds	Avg.	GREEN BAY	No	Yds	Avg.
Wilson	7		45.3	Chandler	3		43.3
				D. Anderson	1		43.0
					4		43.3

PUNT RETURNS

KANSAS CITY	No	Yds	Avg.	GREEN BAY	No	Yds	Avg.
Garrett	2	17	9.5	D. Anderson	3	25	8.3
E. Thomas	1	2	2.0	Wood	1	–2	–2.0
	3	19	6.3		4	23	5.8

KICKOFF RETURNS

KANSAS CITY	No	Yds	Avg.	GREEN BAY	No	Yds	Avg.
Coan	4	87	21.8	Adderley	2	40	20.0
Garrett	2	43	21.5	D. Anderson	1	25	25.0
	6	130	21.7		3	65	21.7

INTERCEPTION RETURNS

KANSAS CITY	No	Yds	Avg.	GREEN BAY	No	Yds	Avg.
Mitchell	1	0	0.0	Wood	1	50	50.0

PASSING

KANSAS CITY	Att	Comp	Comp Pct.	Yds	Int	Yds/ Att.	Yds/ Comp	Yards Lost Tackled
Dawson	27	16	59.3	211	1	7.8	13.2	43
Beathard	5	1	20.0	17	0	3.4	17.0	18
	32	17	53.1	228	1	7.1	13.4	6–61
GREEN BAY								
Starr	23	16	69.6	250	1	10.9	15.6	3–22
Bratkowski	1	0	0.0	0	0	–	–	0
	24	16	66.7	250	1	10.4	15.6	3–22

1967 N.F.L. Four Crowns and Then Some

With expansion to New Orleans bringing league membership to sixteen clubs, the NFL revamped its post-season playoff system by dividing the Eastern and Western conferences into four four-team divisions. The champions of the Coastal and Central divisions would meet for the Western crown, and the champions of the Capitol and Century divisions would meet for the Eastern crown; the winners of these matches then would clash for the NFL championship. This new arrangement expanded post-season title play to three weeks, with conference championships, the league championship, and the Super Bowl.

EASTERN CONFERENCE — CAPITOL DIVISION

Dallas Cowboys—Injuries to Don Meredith, Dan Reeves, and Dave Manders slowed the offense up, but the Cowboys still had more than enough power to take the Capitol Division crown. The Cowboys had depth few teams could match, so that coach Tom Landry could find adequate replacements for his wounded troops. When quarterback Meredith missed three games, young Craig Morton filled in well, and Mike Connelly took over for Manders at center. The Dallas defense kept its fine edge, with Bob Lilly, Chuck Howley, and Cornell Green winning All-Pro honors.

Philadelphia Eagles—A disappointing season had fans calling for coach Joe Kuharich's ouster at the end of the year. The Eagles hoped to challenge the Cowboys after obtaining receivers Gary Ballman and Mike Ditka, but with their rash of injuries the Eagles were lucky to hold onto second place. Timmy Brown, Bob Brown, Lane Howell, Al Nelson, Ditka, and Ballman all missed stretches of the schedule. Despite poor protection, quarterback Norm Snead had a good year, with flanker Ben Hawkins his chief pass receiver. The Eagle defense, however, could be blamed more on a lack of talent in the line than on injuries.

Washington Redskins—Three Redskin receivers finished in the top four in the receiving statistics, and Sonny Jurgensen won the league passing title, yet the Skins finished in third place in the Capitol Division. The running and kicking games gave the passing attack little support, so opposing defenses knew the Redskins would come out throwing. Coach Otto Graham thought he had found a good fullback in first-draft choice Ray McDonald, but the big freshman was a big disappointment.

New Orleans Saints—Coach Tom Fears stocked his team liberally with veterans, with Billy Kilmer, Jim Taylor, Ray Poage, Dough Atkins, Earl Leggett, Lou Cordileone, Jackie Burkett, and Dave Whitsell all key men. The Saints did uncover two good rookies in Dan Abramowicz, a slow-footed receiver with good moves, and defensive tackle Dave Rowe, but the team relied mostly on oldsters whose best days were behind them.

CENTURY DIVISION

Cleveland Browns—A bad arm troubled quarterback Frank Ryan, defensive ends Paul Wiggin and Bill Glass slumped off in their early thirties, Erich Barnes was slowing up at cornerback, and forty-three-year-old Lou Groza was not getting the old zip into his kicks. The Browns still had top performers in Leroy Kelly, Paul Warfield, Gary Collins, Dick Schafrath, Gene Hickerson, Jim Houston and other veterans at their peak, and with the other clubs in the Century Division experiencing problems, the Browns coasted to the title without much of a challenge.

New York Giants—The Giants sent a bundle of draft choices to Minnesota for quarterback Fran Tarkenton, and the scrambling quarterback immediately injected an element of excitement back into the team. Tarkenton found a kindred spirit in split end Homer Jones, a fast receiver who ran around until he got open rather than execute precise pass patterns; Tarkenton found Jones in the open often enough for Jones to gain 1,209 yards and score thirteen touchdowns.

St. Louis Cardinals—The Cards had some of the league's best talent, a flashy blitzing defense, and a top place-kicker in Jim Bakken, but head coach Charlie Winner had his hands full of problems this season. Before the regular season even started, quarterback Charley Johnson was drafted into the Army, leaving inexperienced Jim Hart at the throttle; the youngster showed a strong arm and a tendency to throw interceptions. By the end of the year, racial tension burst into the open, with black players claiming that not enough of them were used on defense.

Pittsburgh Steelers—Bill Nelsen's bad knees again forced the Steelers to field a substitute quarterback for part of the season, and this year's emergency passer was Kent Nix, former Green Bay taxi-squader. The Pittsburgh offense frightened few opponents, but the defense was a solid, hard-working unit that kept the Steelers in most of their games. The club won only four games, but their losses included a 27-24 decision to New York and a 15-10 defeat by Washington.

WESTERN CONFERENCE — CENTRAL DIVISION

Green Bay Packers—Coach Vince Lombardi thought he was well covered at running back despite the departure of both Jim Taylor and Paul Hornung from the roster, but injuries sent him scurrying in all directions for healthy ball-carriers. Elijah Pitts and Jim Grabowski missed the late-season games with physical ills, leaving Lombardi with only Donny Anderson from the regular runners. To flesh out the backfield, Lombardi picked up journeymen Ben Wilson and Chuck Mercein and started playing rookie Travis Williams at halfback. Williams was the talk of the league with his blistering kickoff returning, and now he combined with the other substitute Packer ball-carriers in a backfield that didn't look good but punched out the necessary yardage to win.

Chicago Bears—The Bear defense regularly held opponents under 20 points, but the offense rarely capitalized on this during the first half of the schedule. Over the last seven games, however, the offense generated enough points to win five and tie one. Gale Sayers shone as usual throughout the year, but other players helped him move the ball down the stretch. Jack Concannon, the scrambling quarterback obtained from Philadelphia for Mike Ditka, settled comfortably into the Chicago system after October, hustling Brian Piccolo provided a running threat besides Sayers, and Dick Gordon developed into a dangerous receiver. After this flourishing finish, seventy-three-year-old George Halas called it quits as a coach.

Detroit Lions—The team had problems in the passing and kicking departments, but two gilt-edge rookies entertained fans all season. Halfback Mel Farr ran for 860 yards to give the Lions their first running threat in years. In the defensive secondary, rookie Lem Barney covered the league's best receivers without giving anything away, and once he got his hands on an errant enemy pass he threatened to sprint away to a touchdown.

Minnesota Vikings—Gone were coach Norm Van Brocklin, Fran Tarkenton, and Tommy Mason, and coming down from Canada were new head coach Bud Grant and quarterback Joe Kapp. The trade of Tarkenton to New York gave the Vikings some extra high draft choices, so their rookie class was a rich one, including Alan Page. Gene Washington, Clint Jones, John Beasley, and Bob Grim.

COASTAL DIVISION

Los Angeles Rams—Myron Pottios took over for the retired Bill George at middle linebacker, and big Roger Brown was purchased from Detroit to replace the injured Rosie Grier, but the defense continued to play with an almost perfect teamwork. Quarterback Roman Gabriel ran a ball-control offense that scored enough points to win eleven games and lose only one during the season. The Baltimore Colts stayed right with the Rams in the standings, but Los Angeles took the Coastal title by outscoring Baltimore in their two meetings.

Baltimore Colts—Even while replacing some old veterans, the Colts still swept to a 11-1-2 record. Receivers Ray Berry and Jimmy Orr went out with injuries, and subs Willie Richardson and Alex Hawkins filled in in fine fashion. Offensive tackle Jim Parker retired in mid-season with physical ills, and Sam Ball effectively plugged the hole in the line. Two rookies, huge tackle Bubba Smith and safety Rick Volk, saved a lot of action on defense. But Johnny Unitas and the tough Colt defense kept the Colts strong during all the changes.

San Francisco '49ers—Quarterback John Brodie was inconsistent, split end Dave Parks was hurt, and the team lost three of four games with the Rams and Colts. The defense developed into a solid unit, with a strong pass rush, a top linebacker in Dave Wilcox, and two good cornerbacks in Jim Johnson and Kermit Alexander, but the offense lacked the firepower to move the club above the .500 mark.

Atlanta Falcons—The rookie crop brought little help, leaving the Falcons with the same top men as last year. Tommy Nobis, Randy Johnson, and Junior Coffey continued the strong play of their rookie seasons, but coach Norb Hecker could augment his squad only with castoffs from other clubs as defensive tackle Jim Norton, split end Jerry Simmons, and veteran flanker Tommy McDonald helped out among the bargain acquisitions.

FINAL TEAM STATISTICS

OFFENSE

	ATL.	BALT.	CHI.	CLEV.	DALL.	DET.	G.B.	L.A.	MINN.	N.O.	N.Y.	PHIL.	PITT.	ST.L.	S.F.	WASH.
FIRST DOWNS:																
Total	180	**289**	175	238	261	215	243	262	199	220	274	239	252	248	242	280
by Rushing	68	105	98	**119**	109	104	115	106	91	67	115	69	83	97	101	82
by Passing	95	159	62	102	141	92	112	133	85	135	135	146	145	131	121	**177**
by Penalty	17	**25**	15	17	11	19	16	23	23	18	24	24	24	20	20	21
RUSHING:																
Number	344	443	489	444	477	473	474	**490**	454	334	436	328	431	472	434	345
Yards	1303	1645	1852	**2139**	1900	1907	1915	1906	1811	1192	1864	1250	1397	1839	1764	1247
Average Yards	3.8	3.7	3.8	**4.8**	4.0	4.0	4.0	3.9	4.0	3.6	4.3	3.8	3.2	3.9	4.1	3.6
Touchdowns	6	**21**	12	15	13	14	18	16	10	9	16	12	13	15	16	13
PASSING:																
Attempts	370	457	268	333	417	351	331	390	336	478	406	445	442	431	469	**527**
Completions	179	265	131	160	210	160	182	206	150	237	221	244	214	204	228	**301**
Completion Percentage	48.4	**58.0**	48.9	48.0	50.4	45.6	55.0	52.8	44.6	49.6	54.4	54.8	48.4	47.3	48.6	57.1
Passing Yards	2144	3561	1673	2314	3093	1826	2758	2947	1951	2989	3382	3463	2781	3170	2862	**3887**
Average Yards per Attempt (Gross)	5.8	7.8	6.2	6.9	7.4	5.2	**8.3**	7.6	5.8	6.3	8.3	7.8	6.3	7.4	6.1	7.4
Average Yards per Completion (Gross)	12.0	13.4	12.8	14.5	14.7	11.4	15.2	14.3	13.0	12.6	15.3	14.2	13.0	**15.5**	12.6	12.9
Times Tackled Attempting to Pass	49	25	27	44	42	24	41	25	35	52	37	49	30	24	26	**19**
Yards Lost Tackled Attempting to Pass	434	198	232	372	294	195	394	213	284	391	342	369	270	229	208	**157**
Net Yards	1710	3363	1441	1942	2799	1631	2364	2734	1667	2598	3040	3094	2511	2941	2654	**3730**
Touchdowns	13	22	9	22	28	14	15	28	11	13	**33**	30	19	20	16	31
Interceptions	25	17	18	18	28	19	27	**16**	24	23	20	24	29	35	26	17
Percent Intercepted	6.8	3.7	6.7	5.4	6.7	5.4	8.2	4.1	7.1	4.8	4.9	5.4	6.6	8.1	5.5	**3.2**
PUNTS:																
Number	**87**	49	79	67	67	83	66	68	75	74	55	61	72	62	73	72
Average Distance	**43.7**	42.3	42.9	37.1	40.4	40.5	36.5	42.2	41.0	42.9	36.0	38.3	38.1	40.8	37.6	41.3
PUNT RETURNS:																
Number	25	42	22	35	33	34	39	**50**	35	23	22	29	30	34	35	34
Yards	94	323	194	**357**	320	97	157	328	107	79	102	158	143	198	314	203
Average Yards	3.8	7.7	8.8	**10.2**	9.7	2.9	4.0	6.6	3.1	3.4	4.6	5.4	4.8	5.8	9.0	6.0
Touchdowns	0	**1**	**1**	**1**	**1**	0	0	0	0	0	0	0	0	0	0	0
KICKOFF RETURNS:																
Number	69	42	47	55	48	50	46	43	53	**72**	69	62	58	66	56	61
Yards	1471	988	1157	1396	1014	1145	1241	1033	1215	**1739**	1363	1246	1221	1372	1326	1330
Average Yards	21.3	23.5	24.6	25.4	21.1	22.9	**27.0**	24.0	22.9	24.2	19.8	20.1	21.1	20.8	23.7	21.8
Touchdowns	1	0	3	1	0	0	**4**	0	1	2	0	0	0	0	0	1
INTERCEPTION RETURNS:																
Number	17	**32**	28	22	29	23	26	**32**	16	22	17	21	26	19	16	20
Yards	343	453	334	375	331	343	284	**476**	316	333	209	274	264	205	198	183
Average Yards	**20.2**	14.2	11.9	17.0	11.4	14.9	10.9	14.9	19.8	15.1	12.3	13.0	10.2	10.8	12.4	9.2
Touchdowns	2	3	2	3	3	**6**	2	4	2	2	0	2	1	1	0	1
PENALTIES:																
Number	**88**	52	98	72	81	65	48	85	**100**	76	80	77	68	65	89	67
Yards	**866**	458	953	773	785	712	531	854	**1075**	785	842	830	759	720	931	588
FUMBLES:																
Number	20	**13**	25	24	26	32	19	32	23	21	21	22	33	23	20	26
Number Lost	14	**8**	14	17	14	21	10	13	13	14	10	16	16	11	10	14
POINTS:																
Total	175	394	239	334	342	260	332	**398**	233	233	369	351	281	333	273	347
PAT Attempts	22	48	29	43	45	34	39	48	26	27	**49**	45	35	36	33	47
PAT Made	22	46	26	43	41	33	39	**48**	26	27	45	45	35	36	33	42
FG Attempts	18	37	26	23	23	21	29	**43**	33	32	21	19	22	39	33	26
FG Made	7	20	13	11	9	7	19	20	17	14	10	12	12	**27**	14	7
Percent FG Made	38.9	54.1	50.0	47.8	39.1	33.3	65.5	46.5	51.5	43.8	47.6	63.2	54.5	**69.2**	42.4	26.9
Safeties	0	0	0	0	**2**	1	1	1	0	1	0	0	0	0	0	1

DEFENSE

	ATL.	BALT.	CHI.	CLEV.	DALL.	DET.	G.B.	L.A.	MINN.	N.O.	N.Y.	PHIL.	PITT.	ST.L.	S.F.	WASH.
FIRST DOWNS:																
Total	294	208	215	281	236	205	**183**	200	217	276	261	286	228	216	237	274
by Rushing	124	78	91	115	**64**	98	98	75	105	114	113	105	80	79	92	98
by Passing	152	116	98	153	145	85	**78**	104	90	138	125	161	128	117	128	153
by Penalty	18	14	26	13	27	22	**7**	21	22	24	23	20	20	20	17	23
RUSHING:																
Number	504	387	419	459	**339**	471	443	361	500	469	416	434	418	410	407	431
Yards	2139	1411	1531	1767	**1081**	1795	1923	1119	2104	2092	1799	1741	1377	1502	1698	1852
Average Yards	4.2	3.6	3.7	3.8	3.2	3.8	4.3	**3.1**	4.2	4.5	4.3	4.0	3.3	3.7	4.2	4.3
Touchdowns	18	**5**	11	15	11	15	7	6	12	22	20	16	12	13	17	19
PASSING:																
Attempts	421	395	384	454	482	**312**	337	445	314	410	389	480	397	360	403	468
Completions	238	221	164	250	260	**143**	155	212	149	207	195	255	201	169	212	261
Completion Percentage	56.5	55.9	**42.7**	55.1	53.9	45.8	46.0	47.6	47.5	50.5	50.1	53.1	50.6	46.9	52.6	55.8
Passing Yards	3588	2678	2146	3231	3167	2089	**1644**	2694	2071	3035	2731	3382	2854	3023	2755	3713
Average Yards per Attempt (Gross)	8.5	6.8	5.6	7.1	6.6	6.7	**4.9**	6.1	6.6	7.4	7.0	7.0	7.2	8.4	6.8	7.9
Average Yards per Completion (Gross)	15.1	12.1	13.1	12.9	12.2	14.6	**10.6**	12.7	13.9	14.7	14.0	13.3	14.2	17.9	13.0	14.2
Times Tackled Attempting to Pass	21	36	30	41	45	39	29	43	36	23	31	23	29	37	**48**	38
Yards Lost Tackled Attempting to Pass	196	246	271	332	377	356	267	287	319	199	246	151	276	340	**409**	310
Net Yards	3392	2432	1875	2899	2790	1733	**1377**	2407	1752	2836	2485	3231	2578	2683	2346	3403
Touchdowns	31	13	14	19	21	**11**	13	14	17	25	25	29	22	26	19	25
Interceptions	17	**32**	28	22	29	23	26	**32**	16	22	17	21	26	19	16	20
Percent Intercepted	4.0	**8.1**	7.3	4.8	6.0	7.4	7.7	7.2	5.1	5.4	4.4	4.4	6.5	5.3	4.0	4.3
PUNTS:																
Number	49	69	77	62	72	79	75	**86**	79	63	56	50	70	81	70	72
Average Distance	39.9	39.4	41.3	39.9	42.5	39.3	41.6	40.8	38.9	39.9	39.7	**38.8**	38.9	39.0	43.8	40.1
PUNT RETURNS:																
Number	54	21	41	29	37	38	**13**	33	39	35	21	33	39	24	29	36
Yards	408	144	168	70	266	323	**22**	240	163	261	214	130	277	79	175	234
Average Yards	7.6	6.9	4.1	2.4	7.2	8.5	**1.7**	7.3	4.2	7.5	10.2	3.9	7.1	3.3	6.0	6.5
Touchdowns	**0**	**0**	**0**	**0**	**0**	1	**0**	**0**	**0**	**0**	**0**	**0**	1	1	1	**0**
KICKOFF RETURNS:																
Number	**38**	65	52	59	59	43	59	66	48	51	69	59	56	65	54	54
Yards	**889**	1483	1064	1288	1350	959	1276	1414	1076	1166	1511	1466	1300	1481	1311	1223
Average Yards	23.4	22.8	**20.5**	21.8	22.9	22.3	21.6	21.4	22.4	22.9	21.9	24.8	23.2	22.8	24.3	22.6
Touchdowns	**0**	1	**0**	2	**0**	1	**0**	2	**0**	**0**	1	2	1	1	1	1
INTERCEPTION RETURNS:																
Number	25	17	18	13	28	19	27	**16**	24	23	20	24	29	35	26	17
Yards	326	272	246	290	353	235	370	**186**	315	303	216	429	368	469	292	251
Average Yards	13.0	16.0	13.7	15.1	12.6	12.4	13.7	11.6	13.1	13.2	**10.8**	17.9	12.7	13.4	11.2	14.8
Touchdowns	4	2	1	1	3	2	3	**0**	4	**0**	1	3	1	5	3	1
PENALTIES:																
Number	87	82	82	57	64	73	55	**91**	90	83	68	67	73	89	64	86
Yards	853	**927**	782	655	717	822	482	912	906	824	774	715	833	782	596	882
FUMBLES:																
Number	26	17	23	23	27	13	23	18	**38**	21	28	28	26	19	24	21
Number Lost	10	8	16	14	**19**	10	14	13	**19**	10	15.	14	13	13	13	14
POINTS:																
Total	422	198	218	297	268	259	209	**196**	294	379	379	409	320	356	337	353
PAT Attempts	53	**21**	27	37	35	32	24	23	34	48	48	52	39	46	41	46
PAT Made	52	**21**	26	36	34	31	23	22	34	46	47	52	36	42	40	45
FG Attempts	39	28	26	25	23	29	28	26	31	29	21	32	30	**19**	35	24
FG Made	16	17	10	13	**8**	12	14	12	18	15	14	15	16	12	17	10
Percent FG Made	41.0	60.7	38.5	52.0	**34.8**	41.4	50.0	46.2	58.1	51.7	66.7	46.9	53.3	63.2	48.6	41.7
Safeties	2	**0**	**0**	**0**	**0**	**0**	**0**	**0**	1	**0**	1	**0**	1	1	**0**	1

CONFERENCE PLAYOFFS

December 23, at Milwaukee (Attendance 49,861)

Milwaukee (Attendance 49,861)

SCORING

GREEN BAY	0	14	7	7	–28
LOS ANGELES	7	0	0	0	– 7

First Quarter
L.A. Casey, 28 yard pass from Gabriel
PAT–Gossett (kick)

Second Quarter
G.B. Williams, 46 yard rush
PAT–Chandler (kick)
G.B. Dale, 18 yard pass from Starr
PAT–Chandler (kick)

Third Quarter
G.B. Mercein, 6 yard rush
PAT–Chandler (kick)

Fourth Quarter
G.B. Williams, 2 yard rush
PAT–Chandler (kick)

TEAM STATISTICS

G.B.		L.A.
20	First Downs–Total	12
11	First Downs–Rushing	2
8	First Downs–Passing	9
1	First Downs–Penalty	1
1	Times Tackled Passing	5
11	Yards Lost–Tackled	44
3	Fumbles–Number	0
3	Fumbles–Lost Ball	0
7	Penalties–Number	3
44	Yards Penalized	25
5	Punts–Number	6
32.6	Punts–Average Distance	39.3
3	Punt Returns–Number	1
44	Punt Returns–Yards	0
2	Kickoff Returns–Number	4
19	Kickoff Returns–Yards	80
1	Interception Returns–Number	1
20	Interception Returns–Yards	24
4	Giveaways	1
1	Takeaways	4
–3	Difference	+3

INDIVIDUAL STATISTICS

GREEN BAY	No	Yds	Avg.	LOS ANGELES	No	Yds	Avg.
RUSHING							
Williams	18	88	4.9	Bass	14	40	2.9
Anderson	12	52	4.3	Jo'phson	9	16	1.8
Mercein	12	13	1.1	Gabriel	3	6	2.0
Starr	2	8	4.0	Mason	2	13	6.5
Wilson	1	2	2.0		28	75	2.7
	45	163	3.6				
RECEIVING							
Dale	6	109	18.2	Casey	5	82	16.4
Dowler	3	35	11.7	Traux	2	45	22.5
Fleming	3	30	10.0	Jo'phson	2	30	15.0
Anderson	2	30	15.0	Snow	1	17	17.0
Mercein	2	10	5.0	Pope	1	12	12.0
Williams	1	8	8.0		11	186	16.9
	17	222	13.1				

PASSING

	Att.	Cmp.	Comp. Pct.	Yds.	Int.	Yds/ Att.	Yds/ Comp.
G.B.							
Starr	23	17	73.9	222	1	9.7	13.1
L.A.							
Gabriel	31	11	35.5	186	1	6.0	16.9

December 24, at Dallas (Attendance 70,786)

DALLAS	14	10	21	7	–52
CLEVELAND	0	7	0	7	–14

First Quarter
Dal. Baynham, 3 yard pass from Meredith
PAT–Villanueva (kick)
Dal. Perkins, 4 yard rush
PAT–Villanueva (kick)

Second Quarter
Dal. Hayes, 86 yard pass from Meredith
PAT–Villanueva (kick)
Dal. Villanueva, 10 yard field goal
Cle. Morin, 13 yard pass from Ryan
PAT–Groza (kick)

Third Quarter
Dal. Baynham, 1 yard rush
PAT–Villanueva (kick)
Dal. Perkins, 1 yard rush
PAT–Villanueva (kick)
Dal. Green, 60 yard interception return
PAT–Villanueva (kick)

Fourth Quarter
Dal. Baynham, 1 yard rush
PAT–Villanueva (kick)
Cle. Warfield, 75 yard pass from Ryan
PAT–Groza (kick)

TEAM STATISTICS

DAL.		CLE.
22	First Downs–Total	15
13	First Downs–Rushing	4
7	First Downs–Passing	10
2	First Downs–Penalty	1
1	Times Tackled Passing	5
2	Yards Lost Tackled	31
2	Fumbles–Number	0
1	Fumbles–Lost Ball	0
2	Penalties–Number	2
10	Yards Penalized	18
2	Punts–Number	7
44.5	Punts–Average Distance	39.8
4	Punt Returns–Number	2
155	Punt Returns–Yards	11
1	Kickoff Returns–Number	7
4	Kickoff Returns–Yards	112
1	Interception Returns–Number	1
60	Interception Returns–Yards	0
2	Giveaways	1
1	Takeaways	2
–1	Difference	+1

INDIVIDUAL STATISTICS

DALLAS	No	Yds	Avg.	CLEVELAND	No	Yds	Avg.
RUSHING							
Perkins	18	74	4.1	Kelly	15	96	6.4
Baynham	13	50	3.8	Green	10	49	4.9
Garrison	9	33	3.6	Ryan	2	14	7.0
Clarke	1	8	8.0		27	159	5.9
Reeves	3	7	2.3				
Meredith	2	6	3.0				
	46	178	3.9				
RECEIVING							
Hayes	5	144	28.8	Kelly	4	39	9.8
Rentzel	3	65	21.7	Warf'ld	3	99	33.9
Reeves	1	9	9.0	Morin	3	35	11.7
Perkins	1	4	4.0	Green	3	18	6.0
Baynham	1	3	3.0	Collins	1	3	3.0
	11	225	20.5		14	194	13.9

PASSING

DALL.	Att	Cmp	Pct	Yds	Int	Yd/A	Yd/C
Meredith	12	10	83.3	212	0	17.7	21.2
Morton	3	1	33.3	13	1	4.3	13.0
	15	11	73.3	225	1	15.0	20.5
CLEVE.							
Ryan	30	14	46.7	194	1	6.5	13.9

CAPITOL DIVISION

DALLAS COWBOYS 9-5-0 Tom Landry

Scores of Each Game		
21	Cleveland	14
38	NEW YORK	24
13	LOS ANGELES	35
17	Washington	14
14	NEW ORLEANS	10
24	Pittsburgh	21
14	Philadelphia	21
37	ATLANTA	7
27	New Orleans	10
20	WASHINGTON	27
46	ST. LOUIS	21
17	Baltimore	23
38	PHILADELPHIA	17
16	San Francisco	24

Use Name	Pos.	Hgt	Wgt	Age	Int	Pts
Jim Boeke	OT	6'5"	260	28		
Ralph Neely	OT	6'5"	265	23		
Tony Liscio	OT	6'5"	255	27		
Leon Donahue	OG	6'4"	245	28		
John Niland	OG	6'4"	245	23		
John Wilbur	OG	6'3"	240	24		
Mike Connelly	C	6'3"	248	31		
Malcolm Walker	OT-C	6'4"	250	24		
George Andrie	DE	6'7"	250	27		
Larry Stephens	DE	6'4"	250	29		
Willie Townes	DE	6'5"	260	24		
Ron East	DT	6'4"	242	24		
Bob Lilly	DT	6'4"	260	28		
Jethro Pugh	DT	6'6"	260	23		2
Dave Edwards	LB	6'3"	228	28	3	6
Harold Hays	LB	6'3"	225	26		
Chuck Howley	LB	6'3"	225	31	1	6
Lee Roy Jordan	LB	6'2"	225	26	3	8
Phil Clark	DB	6'2"	207	22	1	
Dick Daniels	DB	5'9"	180	21		
Mike Gaechter	DB	6'	190	27	2	
Cornell Green	DB	6'4"	208	27	7	
Mike Johnson	DB	5'10"	184	23	5	
Mel Renfro	DB	6'	190	25	7	
Buddy Dial — Injury						
Dave Manders — Injury						
Don Meredith	QB	6'2"	205	29		
Craig Morton	QB	6'4"	216	24		
Jerry Rhome	QB	6'	185	25		
Craig Baynham	HB	6'1"	200	23		6
Dan Reeves	HB	6'1"	200	23		66
Les Shy	HB	6'1"	200	23		
Don Perkins	FB	5'10"	200	29		36
Walt Garrison	HB-FB	6'	205	23		
Pete Gent	FL	6'4"	205	24		6
Lance Rentzel	OE-FL	6'2"	200	23		48
Frank Clarke	TE	6'	210	34		12
Pettis Norman	TE	6'3"	225	27		12
Rayfield Wright	TE	6'7"	235	22		
Bob Hayes	OE	6'	185	24		66
Sims Stokes	OE	6'1"	198	23		
Harold Deters	K	6'	200	23		12
Danny Villanueva	K	5'11"	200	29		56

PHILADELPHIA EAGLES 6-7-1 Joe Kuharich

Scores of Each Game		
35	WASHINGTON	24
6	BALTIMORE	38
34	PITTSBURGH	24
38	Atlanta	7
27	SAN FRANCISCO	28
14	St. Louis	48
21	DALLAS	14
24	New Orleans	31
17	Los Angeles	33
48	NEW ORLEANS	21
7	New York	44
35	Washington	35
17	Dallas	38
28	CLEVELAND	24

Use Name	Pos.	Hgt	Wgt	Age	Int	Pts
Bob Brown	OT	6'4"	295	24		
Lane Howell	OT	6'5"	272	26		
Randy Beisler	DE-OT	6'4"	245	22		
Dick Hart	OG	6'2"	250	24		
Jim Skaggs	OG	6'2"	252	27		
Bill Stetz	OG	6'3"	250	23		
Gordon Wright	OG	6'3"	245	23		
Lynn Hoyem	C-OG	6'4"	253	27		
Dave Recher	C	6'1"	246	24		
Jim Ringo	C	6'1"	230	36		
Don Hultz	DE	6'3"	242	26	1	6
Gary Pettigrew	DE	6'4"	245	22		
Mel Tom	DE	6'4"	243	26		
Dean Wink	DE	6'4"	246	22		
John Meyers	DT	6'6"	276	27		
Floyd Peters	DT	6'4"	255	32	1	
Fred Brown	LB	6'5"	232	24	2	
Ike Kelley	LB	5'11"	225	23	1	
Dave Lloyd	LB	6'3"	248	31	1	
Mike Morgan	LB	6'4"	242	25	1	
Arunas Vasys	LB	6'2"	235	24		
Harold Wells	LB	6'2"	220	28	1	
Jim Gray	DB	6'	182	25		
Aaron Martin	DB	6'	190	26	2	
Ron Medved	DB	6'1"	210	23	2	
Jim Nettles	DB	5'9"	177	25	4	6
Al Nelson	DB	5'11"	186	23		
Nate Ramsey	DB	6'1"	200	26		
Taft Reed	DB	6'2"	200	25		
Joe Scarpati	DB	5'10"	185	25	4	6
Bob Shann	DB	6'1"	190	24	1	
Dave Graham — Injury						
Frank Molden — Knee Injury						
Benjy Dial	QB	6'1"	185	24		
King Hill	QB	6'3"	216	31		
Norm Snead	QB	6'4"	215	27		12
Timmy Brown	HB	5'10"	198	30		12
Harry Jones	HB	6'2"	205	22		
Harry Wilson	HB	5'11"	204	22		
Izzy Lang	FB	6'1"	232	24		30
Tom Woodeshick	HB-FB	6'	220	25		60
Chuck Hughes	FL	5'11"	172	24		
Ron Goodwin	OE-FL	6'	180	25		
Ben Hawkins	OE-FL	6'	180	23		60
Mike Ditka	TE	6'3"	235	27		12
Pete Emelianchik	TE	6'2"	220	24		
Jim Kelly	TE	6'2"	218	25		24
Dave Lince	TE	6'6"	265	23		
Fred Hill	OE	6'2"	215	24		
Gary Ballman	FL-OE	6'	205	27		42
Sam Baker	K	6'2"	218	35		81

WASHINGTON REDSKINS 5-6-3 Otto Graham

Scores of Each Game		
24	Philadelphia	35
30	New Orleans	10
38	NEW YORK	34
14	DALLAS	17
20	Atlanta	20
28	Los Angeles	28
13	BALTIMORE	17
21	ST. LOUIS	27
31	SAN FRANCISCO	28
27	Dallas	20
37	Cleveland	42
35	PHILADELPHIA	35
15	Pittsburgh	10
14	NEW ORLEANS	30

Use Name	Pos.	Hgt	Wgt	Age	Int	Pts
Mitch Johnson	OT	6'4"	250	25		
John Kelly	OT	6'3"	250	23		
Jim Snowden	OT	6'3"	255	25		
Don Bandy	OG	6'3"	250	22		
Vince Promuto	OG	6'1"	245	29		
Ray Schoenke	OG	6'3"	250	25		
Dave Crossan	C	6'3"	245	27		
Len Hauss	C	6'2"	235	25		
Heath Wingate	C	6'2"	240	25		
Bill Briggs	DE	6'3"	250	23		
Carl Kammerer	DE	6'3"	243	25		
Ron Snidow	DE	6'4"	250	25		
Walt Barnes	DT	6'3"	250	23		
Spain Musgrave	DT	6'4"	275	22		
Jim Prestel	DT	6'5"	275	30		
Joe Rutgens	DT	6'2"	255	28		
Ed Breding	LB	6'4"	235	22		2
Jim Carroll	LB	6'1"	230	24	1	
Chris Hanburger	LB	6'2"	218	26		
Larry Hendershot	LB	6'3"	240	22		
Sam Huff	LB	6'1"	230	32	2	
Steve Jackson	LB	6'1"	225	24		
Sid Williams	LB	6'2"	235	25		
Rickie Harris	DB	6'	182	24	1	
Paul Krause	DB	6'3"	195	25	8	
Brig Owens	DB	5'11"	190	24	1	8
Lonnie Sanders	DB	6'3"	207	25		
Jim Shorter	DB	5'11"	185	26	4	
Tom Walters	DB	6'2"	195	25		
Dick Smith	OE-DB	6'	205	23	3	
Sonny Jurgensen	QB	5'11"	203	33		12
Jim Ninowski	QB	6'1"	207	31		
Jerry Allen	HB	6'1"	205	26		24
Pete Larson	HB	6'1"	200	23		6
Steve Thurlow	HB	6'3"	222	24		
Joe Don Looney	FB-HB	6'1"	230	24		6
Ray McDonald	FB	6'4"	248	23		24
A. D. Whitfield	FB	5'10"	200	23		18
John Burrell	FL	6'3"	195	27		
T. J. Jackson	DB-FL	6'	180	24		
John Love	DB-FL	5'11"	185	22		34
Bobby Mitchell	HB-FL	6'	196	32		42
Pat Richter	TE	6'5"	230	26		
Jerry Smith	TE	6'2"	208	24		72
Charley Taylor	OE	6'3"	210	26		54
Bruce Alford	K	6'	185	22		3
Charlie Gogolak	K	5'10"	165	22		6
Gene Mingo (from MIA-A)	K	6'1"	190	28		32

NEW ORLEANS 3-11-0 Tom Fears

Scores of Each Game		
13	LOS ANGELES	27
10	WASHINGTON	30
7	CLEVELAND	42
21	New York	27
10	Dallas	14
13	San Francisco	27
10	PITTSBURGH	14
31	PHILADELPHIA	24
10	DALLAS	27
21	Philadelphia	48
27	ATLANTA	24
20	St. Louis	31
10	Baltimore	30
30	Washington	14

Use Name	Pos.	Hgt	Wgt	Age	Int	Pts
Dick Anderson	OT	6'5"	245	22		2
George Harvey	OT	6'4"	245	21		
Jerry Jones	OT	6'3"	270	23		
Dave McCormick	OT	6'6"	250	24		
Ray Rissmiller	OT	6'4"	250	25		
Jerry Sturm	OT	6'3"	260	30		
Roy Schmidt	OG	6'3"	250	25		
Eli Strand	OG	6'2"	250	24		
Del Williams	OG	6'2"	245	21		
Joe Wendryhoski	C	6'2"	245	28		
Doug Atkins	DE	6'8"	270	37		
Jim Garcia	DE	6'4"	250	23		
Brian Schweda	DE	6'3"	240	24		
Lou Cordileone	DT	6'	250	30		
Earl Leggett	DT	6'3"	265	33		
Dave Rowe	DT	6'6"	265	22		
Mike Tilleman	DT	6'5"	260	23		
Jackie Burkett	LB	6'4"	228	30	3	
Bill Cody	LB	6'1"	220	23		
Ted Davis	LB	6'1"	232	25		
Les Kelley	LB	6'3"	233	22		
Dave Simmons	LB	6'4"	245	24	1	
Steve Stonebreaker	LB	6'3"	228	29		
Phil Vandersea	LB	6'3"	225	24		
Fred Whittingham	LB	6'1"	240	28	1	
Bo Burris	DB	6'3"	195	22		
Bruce Cortez	DB	6'	175	21		
John Douglas	DB	6'1"	195	22	1	
Ben Hart	DB	6'2"	205	21	1	
Jim Heidel	DB	6'1"	185	23	1	
Obert Logan	DB	5'10"	180	25	3	
George Rose	DB	5'11"	190	24	1	
Dave Whitsell	DB	6'	190	31	10	12
Gary Cuozzo	QB	6'1"	195	26		6
Billy Kilmer	QB	6'	204	27		6
Gary Wood	QB	5'11"	188	24		
Tom Barrington	HB	6'1"	213	23		
Charlie Brown	HB	5'10"	187	21		12
John Gilliam	HB	6'1"	190	22		12
Jimmy Jordan	HB	6'1"	200	23		
Don McCall	HB	5'11"	195	22		12
Randy Schultz	FB-HB	5'11"	210	23		12
Jim Taylor	FB	6'	215	32		12
Ernie Wheelwright (from ATL)	FB	6'3"	236	30		6
Elijah Nevett	FL	6'	185	23		
Walter Roberts	FL	5'10"	163	25		30
Tom Hall	OE-FL	6'1"	195	26		
Vern Burke	TE	6'4"	202	26		
Jim Hester	TE	6'4"	225	22		
Kent Kramer	TE	6'5"	235	23		12
Dan Abramowicz	OE	6'1"	197	22		36
Ray Poage	OE	6'4"	205	26		
Charlie Durkee	K	5'11"	165	23		69
Tom McNeill	K	6'1"	195	25		

CAPITOL DIVISION

DALLAS COWBOYS

RUSHING

Last Name	No.	Yds	Avg	TD
Perkins	201	823	4.1	6
Reeves	173	603	3.5	5
Garrison	24	146	6.1	0
Norman	9	91	10.1	0
Meredith	28	84	3.0	0
Clarke	4	72	18.0	1
Shy	17	59	3.5	0
Morton	15	42	2.8	0
Baynham	3	6	2.0	1
Rhome	2	–11	–5.5	0
Villanueva	1	–15	–15.0	0

RECEIVING

Last Name	No.	Yds	Avg	TD
Rentzel	58	996	17	8
Hayes	49	998	20	10
Reeves	39	490	13	6
Norman	20	220	11	2
Perkins	18	116	6	0
Clarke	9	119	13	1
Gent	9	88	10	1
Shy	3	36	12	0
Baynham	3	13	4	0
Garrison	2	17	9	0

PUNT RETURNS

Last Name	No.	Yds	Avg	TD
Hayes	24	276	12	1
Rentzel	6	45	18	0
Renfro	3	–1	0	0

KICKOFF RETURNS

Last Name	No.	Yds	Avg	TD
Garrison	20	366	18	0
Baynham	12	331	28	0
Renfro	5	112	22	0
Shy	5	96	19	0
Stokes	4	92	23	0
Hayes	1	17	17	0
East	1	0	0	0

PASSING – PUNTING – KICKING

PASSING	Att	Comp	%	Yds	Yd/Att	TD	Int–%	RK
Meredith	255	128	50	1834	7.2	16	16– 6	8
Morton	137	69	50	978	7.1	10	10– 7	
Rhome	18	9	50	86	4.8	0	1– 6	
Reeves	7	4	57	195	27.9	2	1–14	

PUNTING	No	Avg
Villanueva	67	40.4

KICKING	XP	Att	%	FG	Att	%
Villanueva	32	34	94	8	19	42
Deters	9	10	90	1	4	25

PHILADELPHIA EAGLES

RUSHING

Last Name	No.	Yds	Avg	TD
Woodeshick	155	670	4.3	6
Lang	101	336	3.3	2
T. Brown	53	179	3.4	1
Snead	9	30	3.3	2
Jones	8	17	2.1	0
Ballman	1	17	17.0	1
Goodwin	1	1	1.0	0

RECEIVING

Last Name	No.	Yds	Avg	TD
Hawkins	59	1265	21	10
Ballman	36	524	15	6
Woodeshick	34	391	12	4
Ditka	26	274	11	2
Lang	26	201	8	3
T. Brown	22	202	9	1
Kelly	21	345	16	4
F. Hill	9	144	16	0
Goodwin	6	65	11	0
Jones	3	32	11	0
Wilson	2	20	10	0

PUNT RETURNS

Last Name	No.	Yds	Avg	TD
Martin	20	128	6	0
Shann	3	17	6	0
Hughes	3	11	4	0
Scarpati	1	2	2	0
Lince	1	0	0	0
Reed	1	0	0	0

KICKOFF RETURNS

Last Name	No.	Yds	Avg	TD
T. Brown	13	301	23	0
Hawkins	10	250	25	0
Wilson	7	150	21	0
Hughes	7	126	18	0
Shann	6	133	22	0
Reed	5	111	22	0
Lince	3	46	15	0
Ballman	2	43	22	0
Jones	2	32	16	0
Gray	1	30	30	0
F. Brown	1	17	17	0
Medved	1	7	7	0
Beisler	1	0	0	0
Kelley	1	0	0	0
Ramsey	1	0	0	0
Vasys	1	0	0	0

PASSING – PUNTING – KICKING

PASSING	Att	Comp	%	Yds	Yd/Att	TD	Int–%	RK
Snead	434	240	55	3399	7.8	29	24– 6	5
K. Hill	7	2	29	33	4.7	1	0– 0	
Dial	3	1	33	5	1.7	0	0– 0	
Lang	1	1	100	26	26.0	0	0– 0	

PUNTING	No	Avg
Baker	61	38.3

KICKING	XP	Att	%	FG	Att	%
Baker	45	45	100	12	19	63

WASHINGTON REDSKINS

RUSHING

Last Name	No.	Yds	Avg	TD
Whitfield	91	384	4.2	1
Allen	77	262	3.4	3
McDonald	52	223	4.3	4
Mitchell	61	189	3.1	1
Larson	25	84	3.4	1
Jurgensen	15	46	3.1	2
Thurlow	13	33	2.5	0
Looney	11	26	2.4	1

RECEIVING

Last Name	No.	Yds	Avg	TD
Taylor	70	990	14	9
J. Smith	67	849	13	12
Mitchell	60	866	14	6
Whitfield	36	494	14	2
Love	17	248	15	1
Allen	11	101	9	1
Thurlow	10	95	10	0
McDonald	10	60	6	0
Burrell	9	95	11	0
Larson	8	45	6	0
Richter	1	31	31	0
Looney	1	12	12	0
Hanburger	1	1	1	0

PUNT RETURNS

Last Name	No.	Yds	Avg	TD
Harris	23	208	9	0
Love	11	–5	–1	0

KICKOFF RETURNS

Last Name	No.	Yds	Avg	TD
Harris	25	580	23	0
Love	17	422	25	1
T. Jackson	7	131	19	0
D. Smith	4	120	30	0
Looney	2	42	21	0
Kelly	2	19	10	0
Allen	1	13	13	0
Burrell	1	2	2	0
Briggs	1	1	1	0
McDonald	1	0	0	0

PASSING – PUNTING – KICKING

PASSING	Att	Comp	%	Yds	Yd/Att	TD	Int–%	RK
Jurgenson	508	288	57	3747	7.4	31	16– 3	1
Ninowski	18	12	67	123	6.8	0	1– 6	
Mitchell	1	1	100	17	17.0	0	0– 0	

PUNTING	No	Avg
Richter	72	41.3

KICKING	XP	Att	%	FG	Att	%
Mingo	20	22	91	4	10	40
Love	10	11	91	2	7	29
Alford	3	4	75	0	2	0
Gogolak	3	3	100	1	4	25
Owens	2	3	67	0	2	0

NEW ORLEANS SAINTS

RUSHING

Last Name	No.	Yds	Avg	TD
Taylor	130	390	3.0	2
Wheelwright	80	241	3.0	1
Kilmer	20	142	7.1	1
Barrington	34	121	3.6	0
Schultz	32	117	3.7	2
McCall	21	86	4.1	1
Cuozzo	19	43	2.3	1
Gilliam	7	41	5.9	0
McNeill	4	38	9.5	0
Brown	8	16	2.0	2

RECEIVING

Last Name	No.	Yds	Avg	TD
Abramowicz	50	721	14	6
Taylor	38	251	7	0
Poage	24	380	16	0
Gilliam	22	264	12	1
Kramer	20	207	10	2
Hall	19	249	13	0
Roberts	17	384	23	3
Schultz	14	186	13	0
Wheelwright	13	107	8	0
Burke	8	84	11	0
McCall	4	75	19	1
Barrington	4	50	13	0
Brown	3	23	8	0
Hester	2	10	5	0

PUNT RETURNS

Last Name	No.	Yds	Avg	TD
Roberts	11	50	5	0
Douglas	2	15	8	0
Gilliam	7	13	2	0
Brown	3	1	0	0

KICKOFF RETURNS

Last Name	No.	Yds	Avg	TD
Roberts	28	737	26	1
Gilliam	16	481	30	1
McCall	7	198	28	0
Barrington	7	113	16	0
Brown	5	103	21	0
Jordan	3	56	19	0
Rose	1	21	21	0
Douglas	1	17	17	0
Vandersea	1	13	13	0
Logan	1	0	0	0
Nevett	1	0	0	0
Sturm	1	0	0	0

PASSING – PUNTING – KICKING

PASSING	Att	Comp	%	Yds	Yd/Att	TD	Int–%	RK
Cuozzo	260	134	52	1562	6.0	7	12– 5	9
Kilmer	204	97	48	1341	6.6	6	11– 5	15
Wood	11	5	46	62	5.6	0	0– 0	
Barrington	2	0	0	0	0.0	0	0– 0	
McNeill	1	1	100	24	24.0	0	0– 0	

PUNTING	No	Avg
McNeill	74	42.9

KICKING	XP	Att	%	FG	Att	%
Durkee	27	27	100	14	32	44

CENTURY DIVISION

CLEVELAND BROWNS 9-5-0 Blanton Collier

Scores of Each Game		
14	DALLAS	21
14	Detroit	31
42	New Orleans	7
21	PITTSBURGH	10
20	ST. LOUIS	16
24	CHICAGO	0
34	New York	38
34	Pittsburgh	14
7	Green Bay	55
14	MINNESOTA	10
42	WASHINGTON	37
24	NEW YORK	14
20	St. Louis	16
24	Philadelphia	28

Use Name	Pos.	Hgt	Wgt	Age	Int	Pts
Monte Clark	OT	6'6"	255	30		
John Demarie	OT	6'3"	250	22		
Dick Schafrath	OT	6'3"	255	31		
Jim Copeland	OG	6'2"	230	22		
Gene Hickerson	OG	6'3"	248	32		
Joe Taffoni	OG	6'3"	245	22		
John Wooten	OG	6'2"	250	32		
Fred Hoaglin	C	6'4"	240	23		
Bill Glass	DE	6'5"	255	31	1	
Jack Gregory	DE	6'6"	245	22		
Paul Wiggin	DE	6'3"	245	33		
Walter Johnson	DT	6'3"	270	24		
Jim Kanicki	DT	6'4"	270	25		
Frank Parker	DT	6'5"	270	27		
Billy Andrews	LB	6'	225	22		
Johnny Brewer	LB	6'4"	235	30	2	6
Jim Houston	LB	6'2"	245	30	3	12
Dale Lindsey	LB	6'3"	225	24	1	
Bob Matheson	LB	6'4"	240	22	1	
Erich Barnes	DB	6'2"	198	32	4	
Ben Davis	DB	5'11"	185	21	1	6
Ross Fichtner	DB	6'	185	29	4	
Mike Howell	DB	6'1"	187	24	3	
Ernie Kellerman	DB	6'	183	23	1	
Carl Ward	DB	5'9"	180	23	1	6
George Youngblood (to NO)	DB	6'3"	205	22		
Gary Lane	QB	6'1"	210	24		
Frank Ryan	QB	6'3"	200	31		
Dick Shiner	QB	6'	197	25		
Leroy Kelly	HB	6'	200	25		78
Larry Conjar	FB	6'	215	21		
Ernie Green	FB	6'2"	205	28		36
Charlie Harraway	FB	6'2"	230	22		
Nick Pietrosante	FB	6'2"	225	30		
Eppie Barney	FL	6'	198	23		
Gary Collins	FL	6'4"	215	26		42
Ron Green	FL	6'1"	200	23		
Clifton McNeil	FL	6'2"	185	27		12
Ron Duncan	TE	6'6"	255	24		
Milt Morin	TE	6'4"	250	25		
Ralph Smith	TE	6'2"	220	28		12
Paul Warfield	OE	6'	188	24		48
Lou Groza	K	6'3"	250	43		76

NEW YORK GIANTS 7-7-0 Allie Sherman

Scores of Each Game		
37	St. Louis	20
24	Dallas	38
34	Washington	38
27	NEW ORLEANS	21
27	Pittsburgh	24
21	GREEN BAY	48
38	CLEVELAND	34
24	Minnesota	27
7	Chicago	34
28	PITTSBURGH	20
44	PHILADELPHIA	7
14	Cleveland	24
7	DETROIT	30
37	ST. LOUIS	14

Use Name	Pos.	Hgt	Wgt	Age	Int	Pts
Francis Peay	OT	6'5"	250	23		
Willie Young	OT	6'	250	24		
Bookie Bolin	OG	6'2"	240	27		
Pete Case	OG	6'3"	245	26		
Darrell Dess	OG	6'	245	31		6
Andy Gross	OG	6'	230	21		
Charlie Harper	OG	6'2"	250	23		
Chuck Hinton	C	6'2"	235	24		
Greg Larson	C	6'2"	250	28		
Glen Condren	DE	6'2"	250	25		
Rosey Davis	DE	6'5"	260	25		
Jim Katcavage	DE	6'3"	240	32		
Randy Staten	DE	6'1"	225	23		
Bruce Anderson	DT	6'4"	250	23		
Roger Anderson	DT	6'5"	265	24		
Jim Colvin	DT	6'2"	245	30		
Bob Lurtsema	DT	6'6"	250	25		
Jim Moran	DT	6'5"	275	24		
Ken Avery	LB	6'1"	220	23		
Mike Ciccolella	LB	6'1"	235	23		
Vince Costello	LB	6'	228	35	4	
Dick Kotite	LB	6'3"	234	24		
Bill Swain	LB	6'2"	230	26	1	
Ed Weisacosky	LB	6'	236	23		
Freeman White	DB-LB	6'5"	225	23	2	
Henry Carr	DB	6'3"	195	24	1	
Clarence Childs	DB	6'	180	28		
Wendell Harris	DB	5'11"	185	26	1	2
Dave Hathcock	DB	6'	195	24		
Spider Lockhart	DB	6'2"	175	24	5	
Bobby Post	DB	6'1"	195	22		
Willie Williams	DB	6'	190	24	1	
Scott Eaton	DB	6'3"	195	23	2	
Earl Morrall	QB	6'1"	206	33		6
Fran Tarkenton	QB	6'1"	190	27		12
Allen Jacobs	HB	6'1"	215	26		
Randy Minniear	HB	6'	200	23		12
Bill Triplett	HB	6'2"	210	28		12
Ernie Koy	FB-HB	6'2"	230	24		30
Tucker Frederickson	FB	6'3"	230	24		12
Joe Morrison	HB-FB-FL	6'1"	212	29		54
Bob Crespino	TE	6'4"	225	29		6
Aaron Thomas	TE	6'3"	210	29		54
Del Shofner	OE	6'3"	190	31		6
Homer Jones	FL-OE	6'2"	215	26		84
Pete Gogolak	K	6'2"	200	25		46
Les Murdock	K	6'3"	245	23		25

Don Davis – Injury
Tom Kennedy – Injury

Jeff Smith – Knee Injury
Larry Vargo – Knee Injury
Smith Reed – Military Service

ST. LOUIS CARDINALS 6-7-1 Charlie Winner

Scores of Each Game		
20	NEW YORK	37
28	Pittsburgh	14
38	DETROIT	28
34	Minnesota	24
16	Cleveland	20
48	PHILADELPHIA	14
23	GREEN BAY	31
27	Washington	21
14	PITTSBURGH	14
3	Chicago	30
21	Dallas	46
31	NEW ORLEANS	20
16	CLEVELAND	20
14	New York	37

Use Name	Pos.	Hgt	Wgt	Age	Int	Pts
Ernie McMillan	OT	6'6"	260	29		
Bob Reynolds	OT	6'6"	265	26		
Clyde Williams	OT	6'2"	255	27		
Dave O'Brien	OG-OT	6'3"	245	26		
Ken Gray	OG	6'2"	250	31		
Ed Marcontell (to HOU-A)	OG	6'	260	23		
Rick Sortun	OG	6'2"	235	24		
Irv Goode	C-OG	6'4"	250	26		
Bob DeMarco	C	6'3"	240	29		
Dick Kasperek	C	6'3"	225	23		
Don Brumm	DE	6'3"	245	24		
Joe Robb	DE	6'3"	245	30		
Bob Rowe	DE	6'4"	255	22		
Dave Long	DT-DE	6'4"	235	22		
Sam Silas	DT	6'4"	250	24		
Chuck Walker	DT	6'2"	245	26		
Fred Heron	DE-DT	6'4"	250	22		
Jerry Hillebrand	LB	6'3"	240	27		
Bill Koman	LB	6'2"	230	33		
Dave Meggyesy	LB	6'1"	220	25		
Dale Meinert	LB	6'2"	220	34	1	
Larry Stallings	LB	6'2"	230	25		
Mike Strofolino	LB	6'2"	230	23		
Mike Barnes	DB	6'3"	205	22		
Jimmy Burson	DB	6'	180	25	2	
Pat Fischer	DB	5'10"	170	27	4	6
Chuck Latourette	DB	6'	190	22		
Phil Spiller	DB	6'	195	22	2	
Jerry Stovall	DB	6'2"	205	25	4	
Bobby Williams	DB	6'1"	185	25	2	
Larry Wilson	DB	6'	190	29	4	
Jim Hart	QB	6'2"	195	23		18
Charley Johnson	QB	6'	190	30		
Charlie Bryant	HB	6'1"	207	26		
Roy Shivers	HB	6'	200	25		6
Johnny Roland	FB-HB	6'2"	207	24		66
Willie Crenshaw	FB	6'2"	230	26		
Bill Thornton	FB	6'1"	215	27		
Prentice Gautt	HB-FB	6'	210	29		12
Bobby Joe Conrad	FL	6'	195	32		12
Dave Williams	FL	6'2"	205	22		30
Chuck Logan	TE	6'4"	220	24		
Jackie Smith	TE	6'4"	215	26		54
Ted Wheeler	TE	6'3"	230	21		
Billy Gambrell	FL-OE	5'10"	175	25		12
Jim Bakken	K	6'	200	26		117

PITTSBURGH STEELERS 4-9-1 Bill Austin

Scores of Each Game		
41	CHICAGO	13
14	ST. LOUIS	28
24	Philadelphia	34
10	Cleveland	21
24	NEW YORK	27
21	DALLAS	24
14	New Orleans	10
14	CLEVELAND	34
14	St. Louis	14
20	New York	28
27	MINNESOTA	41
24	Detroit	14
10	WASHINGTON	15
24	Green Bay	17

Use Name	Pos.	Hgt	Wgt	Age	Int	Pts
John Brown	OT	6'2"	248	28		
Mike Haggerty	OT	6'4"	230	21		
Fran O'Brien	OT	6'1"	265	31		
Larry Gagner	OG	6'3"	240	23		
Bruce Van Dyke	OG	6'2"	235	23		
Ralph Wenzel	OG	6'3"	240	24		
Sam Davis	OT-OG	6'1"	245	23		
Ray Mansfield	C	6'3"	250	26		
John Baker	DE	6'6"	270	32	1	
Jerry Mazzanti	DE	6'3"	240	27		
Ben McGee	DE	6'2"	260	25	1	6
Lloyd Voss	DE	6'4"	260	25	1	
Dick Arndt	DT	6'5"	265	23		
Chuck Hinton	DT	6'5"	260	28		6
Ken Kortas	DT	6'2"	280	25		6
Rod Breedlove	LB	6'2"	225	29		
John Campbell	LB	6'3"	225	28	2	
Ray May	LB	6'1"	230	22		
Andy Russell	LB	6'3"	215	25	3	
Bill Saul	LB	6'4"	226	26	1	
Jim Bradshaw	DB	6'1"	205	28		
John Foruria	DB	6'2"	205	22		
Bob Hohn	DB	6'	185	26	2	
Paul Martha	DB	6'	185	24	4	
Bobby Morgan	DB	6'	205	27		
Clendon Thomas	DB	6'2"	200	30	2	
Marv Woodson	DB	6'	195	24	7	
Rich Bader	QB	6'1"	190	24		
Bill Nelsen	QB	6'	195	26		
Kent Nix	QB	6'1"	195	23		12
Charlie Bivins (to BUF-A)	HB	6'2"	212	28		6
Cannonball Butler	HB	5'10"	185	24		
Dick Hoak	HB	5'11"	190	28		12
Don Shy	HB	6'1"	215	21		30
Willie Asbury	FB	6'1"	230	24		24
Earl Gros	FB	6'3"	230	26		6
Roy Jefferson	FL	6'2"	195	23		24
Jerry Marion	FL	5'10"	175	22		
Chet Anderson	TE	6'3"	245	22		12
John Hilton	TE	6'5"	220	25		30
Dick Compton	OE	6'1"	195	27		6
Marshall Cropper	OE	6'3"	210	23		
J. R. Wilburn	OE	6'2"	190	24		30
Mike Clark	K	6'1"	200	26		71
Jim Elliott	K	5'11"	184	24		

Wally Hilgenburg – Injury

CENTURY DIVISION

CLEVELAND BROWNS

Rushing

Last Name	No.	Yds	Avg	TD
Kelly	**235**	**1205**	**5.1**	**11**
E. Green	145	710	4.9	4
Conjar	20	78	3.9	0
Pietrosante	10	73	7.3	0
Ryan	22	57	2.6	0
Lane	2	21	10.5	0
Warfield	2	10	5.0	0
Collins	1	6	6.0	0
Shiner	2	−7	−3.5	0
Harraway	5	−14	−2.8	0

Receiving

Last Name	No.	Yds	Avg	TD
E. Green	39	369	9	2
Warfield	32	702	22	8
Collins	32	500	16	7
Kelly	20	282	14	2
Smith	14	211	15	1
Morin	7	90	13	0
Conjar	6	68	11	0
Pietrosante	6	56	9	0
McNeil	3	33	11	2
Barney	1	3	3	0

Punt Returns

Last Name	No.	Yds	Avg	TD
Davis	18	229	**13**	**1**
Ward	6	62	10	0
Kelly	9	59	7	0
Harraway	1	7	7	0
Youngblood	1	0	0	0

Kickoff Returns

Last Name	No.	Yds	Avg	TD
Davis	27	708	26	0
Ward	22	546	25	1
Kelly	5	131	26	0
Barney	1	11	11	0

Passing – Punting – Kicking

PASSING	Att	Comp	%	Yds	Yd/Att	TD	Int–%	RK
Ryan	280	136	49	2026	7.2	20	16– 6	7
Lane	43	21	49	254	5.9	2	1– 2	
Shiner	9	3	33	34	3.8	0	1–11	
Kelly	1	0	0	0	0.0	0	0– 0	

PUNTING	No	Avg
Collins	57	36.5
Kelly	10	40.7

KICKING	XP	Att	%	FG	Att	%
Groza	43	43	100	11	23	48

NEW YORK GIANTS

Rushing

Last Name	No.	Yds	Avg	TD
Koy	146	704	4.8	4
Frederickson	97	311	3.2	2
Tarkenton	44	306	7.0	2
Triplett	58	171	2.9	2
Morrison	36	161	4.5	2
Minniear	35	98	2.8	1
Jones	5	60	12.0	1
Jacobs	11	23	2.1	0
Morrall	4	11	2.8	1
Case	0	16	0.0	0
Young	0	2	0.0	0
Dess	0	1	0.0	1

Receiving

Last Name	No.	Yds	Avg	TD
Thomas	51	877	17	9
Jones	49	1209	**25**	**13**
Morrison	37	524	14	7
Koy	32	212	7	1
Frederickson	19	153	8	0
Crespino	10	125	13	1
Minniear	8	49	6	1
Shofner	7	146	21	1
Triplett	7	69	10	0
Eaton	1	18	18	0

Punt Returns

Last Name	No.	Yds	Avg	TD
Lockhart	7	54	8	0
Williams	6	28	5	0
Minniear	4	13	3	0
Hathcock	3	7	2	0
Harris	2	0	0	0

Kickoff Returns

Last Name	No.	Yds	Avg	TD
Childs	29	603	21	0
Hathcock	14	315	23	0
Triplett	7	139	20	0
Minniear	6	98	16	0
Jones	2	38	19	0
Frederickson	1	19	19	0
Koy	1	18	18	0
Crespino	1	7	7	0
Lurtsema	1	7	7	0
Post	1	0	0	0

Passing – Punting – Kicking

PASSING	Att	Comp	%	Yds	Yd/Att	TD	Int–%	RK
Tarkenton	377	204	54	3088	8.2	29	19– 5	3
Morrall	24	13	54	181	7.5	3	1– 4	
Koy	4	3	75	101	25.3	1	0– 0	
Morrison	1	1	100	12	12.0	0	0– 0	

PUNTING	No	Avg
Koy	40	37.7
Morrall	15	31.5

KICKING	XP	Att	%	FG	Att	%
Gogolak	28	29	97	6	10	60
Murdock	13	15	87	4	9	44
Harris	2	2	100	0	1	0

ST. LOUIS CARDINALS

Rushing

Last Name	No.	Yds	Avg	TD
Roland	234	876	3.7	10
Gautt	142	573	4.0	1
Crenshaw	44	149	3.4	0
Smith	9	86	9.6	0
Shivers	20	64	3.2	1
Hart	13	36	2.8	3
Latourette	2	23	11.5	0
Bryant	3	16	5.3	0
Thornton	4	9	2.3	0
D. Williams	1	7	7.0	0

Receiving

Last Name	No.	Yds	Avg	TD
Smith	56	1205	22	9
Conrad	47	637	14	2
D. Williams	28	405	14	5
Gambrell	28	398	14	2
Roland	20	269	13	1
Gautt	15	202	13	1
Crenshaw	6	30	5	0
Shivers	3	15	5	0
Thornton	1	9	9	0

Punt Returns

Last Name	No.	Yds	Avg	TD
Spiller	15	124	8	0
Shivers	9	36	4	0
Latourette	6	21	4	0
Roland	3	17	6	0
C. Williams	1	0	0	0

Kickoff Returns

Last Name	No.	Yds	Avg	TD
B. Williams	24	583	24	0
Bryant	14	324	23	0
Spiller	10	219	22	0
Shivers	9	160	18	0
Stallings	2	39	20	0
Roland	2	33	17	0
Crenshaw	2	14	7	0
Barnes	1	0	0	0
Fischer	1	0	0	0
Sortun	1	0	0	0

Passing – Punting – Kicking

PASSING	Att	Comp	%	Yds	Yd/Att	TD	Int–%	RK
Hart	397	192	48	3008	7.6	19	30– 8	10
Johnson	29	12	41	162	5.6	1	3– 10	
Roland	4	0	0	0	0.0	0	1– 25	
Smith	1	0	0	0	0.0	0	1–100	

PUNTING	No	Avg
Latourette	62	40.8

KICKING	XP	Att	%	FG	Att	%
Bakken	36	36	100	**27**	39	**69**

PITTSBURGH STEELERS

Rushing

Last Name	No.	Yds	Avg	TD
Shy	99	341	3.4	4
Asbury	80	315	3.9	4
Butler	90	293	3.3	0
Gros	72	252	3.5	1
Hoak	52	142	2.7	1
Nix	15	45	3.0	2
Bivins	7	23	3.3	1
Hilton	1	15	15.0	0
Compton	1	1	1.0	0
Jefferson	5	−11	−2.2	0
Nelsen	9	−19	−2.1	0

Receiving

Last Name	No.	Yds	Avg	TD
Wilburn	51	767	15	5
Compton	42	507	12	1
Jefferson	29	459	16	4
Hilton	26	343	13	5
Gros	19	175	9	0
Hoak	17	111	7	1
Shy	12	152	13	1
Anderson	8	141	18	2
Butler	4	23	6	0
Asbury	3	52	17	0
Bivins	1	24	24	0
Marion	1	16	16	0
Cropper	1	11	11	0

Punt Returns

Last Name	No.	Yds	Avg	TD
Bradshaw	16	97	6	0
Thomas	9	34	4	0
Jefferson	1	10	10	0
Marion	1	2	2	0
Shy	1	−5	−5	0

Kickoff Returns

Last Name	No.	Yds	Avg	TD
Shy	21	473	23	0
Martha	18	403	22	0
Butler	10	223	22	0
Russell	6	97	16	0
Campbell	1	25	25	0
Hilton	1	0	0	0
May	1	0	0	0

Passing – Punting – Kicking

PASSING	Att	Comp	%	Yds	Yd/Att	TD	Int–%	RK
Nix	268	136	51	1587	5.9	8	19– 7	13
Nelsen	165	74	45	1125	6.8	10	9– 5	12
Hoak	8	4	50	69	8.6	1	1–13	
Clark	1	0	0	0	0.0	0	0– 0	

PUNTING	No	Avg
Elliott	72	38.1

KICKING	XP	Att	%	FG	Att	%
Clark	35	35	100	12	22	55

CENTRAL DIVISION

GREEN BAY PACKERS 9-4-1 Vince Lombardi

Scores of Each Game		
17	DETROIT	17
13	CHICAGO	10
23	ATLANTA	0
27	Detroit	17
7	MINNESOTA	10
48	New York	21
31	St. Louis	23
10	Baltimore	13
55	CLEVELAND	7
13	SAN FRANCISCO	0
17	Chicago	13
30	Minnesota	27
24	Los Angeles	27
17	PITTSBURGH	24

Use Name	Pos.	Hgt	Wgt	Age	Int	Pts
Forest Gregg	OT	6'4"	250	34		
Bob Skoronski	OT	6'3"	245	34		
Steve Wright	OT	6'6"	250	25		
Gale Gillingham	OG	6'3"	255	23		
Jerry Kramer	OG	6'3"	245	32		
Fuzzy Thurston	OG	6'1"	245	34		
Ken Bowman	C	6'3"	230	24		
Bob Hyland	OG-C	6'5"	250	22		
Lionel Aldridge	DE	6'4"	245	25		
Bob Brown	DE	6'5"	260	27		
Willie Davis	DE	6'3"	245	34		2
Henry Jordan	DT	6'3"	250	32		
Ron Kostelnik	DT	6'4"	260	27		
Jim Weatherwax	DT	6'7"	260	24		

Use Name	Pos.	Hgt	Wgt	Age	Int	Pts
Lee Roy Caffey	LB	6'3"	250	27	2	
Tommy Crutcher	LB	6'3"	230	25		
Jim Flanigan	LB	6'3"	230	22		
Ray Nitschke	LB	6'3"	240	31	3	6
Dave Robinson	LB	6'3"	240	26	4	
Herb Adderley	DB	6'1"	200	28	4	6
Tom Brown	DB	6'1"	190	26	1	
Doug Hart	DB	6'	190	28		
Bob Jeter	DB	6'1"	205	29	8	
John Rowser	DB	6'1"	180	23		
Willie Wood	DB	5'10"	190	31	4	

Use Name	Pos.	Hgt	Wgt	Age	Int	Pts
Zeke Bratkowski	QB	6'2"	210	35		
Don Horn	QB	6'2"	195	22		
Bart Starr	QB	6'1"	190	34		
Donny Anderson	HB	6'3"	210	24		54
Elijah Pitts	HB	6'1"	205	28		36
Travis Williams	HB	6'1"	210	21		36
Jim Grabowski	FB	6'2"	220	23		18
Chuck Mercein (from NY)	FB	6'3"	230	24		8
Ben Wilson	FB	6'	225	27		12
Carroll Dale	FL	6'1"	200	29		30
Bob Long	FL	6'3"	205	26		
Claudis James	HB-FL	6'2"	190	23		
Allen Brown	TE	6'5"	235	24		
Dick Capp	TE	6'3"	235	23		
Marv Fleming	TE	6'4"	235	25		6
Boyd Dowler	OE	6'5"	225	30		24
Max McGee	OE	6'3"	210	35		
Don Chandler	K	6'2"	210	32		96

CHICAGO BEARS 7-6-1 George Halas

Scores of Each Game		
13	Pittsburgh	41
10	Green Bay	13
17	Minnesota	7
3	BALTIMORE	24
14	DETROIT	3
0	Cleveland	24
17	LOS ANGELES	28
27	Detroit	13
34	NEW YORK	7
30	ST. LOUIS	3
13	GREEN BAY	17
28	San Francisco	14
10	MINNESOTA	10
23	Atlanta	14

Use Name	Pos.	Hgt	Wgt	Age	Int	Pts
Randy Jackson	OT	6'5"	245	23		
Dan James	OT	6'4"	250	30		
Bob Pickens	OT	6'4"	258	24		
George Seals	OT	6'2"	260	24		
Bob Wetoska	OT	6'3"	240	29		
Jim Cadile	OG	6'3"	240	26		
Don Croftcheck	OG	6'1"	230	24		
Doug Kriewald	OG	6'4"	245	23		
Mike Rabold	OG	6'2"	250	30		
Mike Pyle	C	6'3"	250	28		
Marty Amsler	DE	6'5"	260	24	1	
Ed O'Bradovich	DE	6'3"	255	27		
Loyd Phillips	DE	6'3"	230	22		
Frank Cornish	DT	6'6"	270	23	2	
Dick Evey	DT	6'2"	245	26		
John Johnson	DT	6'5"	260	26		
Frank McRae	DT	6'7"	270	23		

Use Name	Pos.	Hgt	Wgt	Age	Int	Pts
Doug Buffone	LB	6'1"	230	23	3	6
Dick Butkus	LB	6'3"	245	23	1	
Rudy Kuechenberg	LB	6'2"	215	24		
Jim Purnell	LB	6'2"	238	25		
Mike Reilly	LB	6'2"	230	24		
Charlie Brown	DB	6'1"	193	24	1	
Al Dodd	DB	6'	180	22		
Curtis Gentry	DB	6'	185	26	4	
Bennie McRae	DB	6'1"	180	26	5	12
Richie Petitbon	DB	6'3"	205	29	5	
Joe Taylor	DB	6'2"	195	26	1	
Rosey Taylor	DB	5'11"	186	28	5	6

Use Name	Pos.	Hgt	Wgt	Age	Int	Pts
Rudy Bukich	QB	6'1"	205	36		
Jack Concannon	QB	6'3"	205	24		18
Larry Rakestraw	QB	6'2"	195	25		12
Gale Sayers	HB	6'	198	24		72
Ronnie Bull	FB-HB	6'	200	27		6
Ralph Kurek	FB	6'2"	210	24		
Andy Livingston	FB	6'	234	22		
Brian Piccolo	HB-FB	6'	205	23		
Johnny Morris	FL	5'10"	180	32		6
Duane Allen	TE	6'4"	225	29		
Austin Denney	TE	6'2"	230	23		
Terry Stoepel	TE	6'4"	235	22		
Dick Gordon	OE	5'11"	190	22		30
Bob Jones	OE	6'4"	195	22		6
Jim Jones	OE	6'2"	187	23		
Bobby Joe Green	K	5'11"	175	29		
Mac Percival	K	6'4"	217	27		65

DETROIT LIONS 5-7-2 Joe Schmidt

Scores of Each Game		
17	Green Bay	17
31	CLEVELAND	14
28	St. Louis	38
17	GREEN BAY	27
3	Chicago	14
24	ATLANTA	3
45	San Francisco	3
13	CHICAGO	27
10	Minnesota	10
7	Baltimore	41
7	LOS ANGELES	31
14	PITTSBURGH	24
30	New York	7
14	MINNESOTA	3

Use Name	Pos.	Hgt	Wgt	Age	Int	Pts
Charlie Bradshaw	OT	6'6"	260	31		
Bill Cottrell	OT	6'3"	265	22		
Roger Shoals	OT	6'4"	255	28		
Randy Winkler	OT	6'5"	260	24		
Frank Gallagher	OG	6'2"	240	24		
John Gordy	OG	6'3"	250	31		
Bob Kowalkowski	OG	6'3"	245	23		
Chuck Walton	OG	6'3"	250	26		
Ed Flanagan	C	6'3"	250	23		
Larry Hand	DE	6'4"	245	27	2	12
Lew Kamanu	DE	6'4"	245	23		
John McCambridge	DE	6'4"	245	21		
Darris McCord	DE	6'4"	250	34	1	
Mike Melinkovich	DE	6'4"	245	25		
Alex Karras	DT	6'2"	245	31		
Denis Moore	DT	6'5"	230	23		
Jerry Rush	DT	6'4"	270	25		

Use Name	Pos.	Hgt	Wgt	Age	Int	Pts
Ernie Clark	LB	6'1"	220	29	1	
Ron Goovert	LB	5'11"	225	23		
Mike Lucci	LB	6'2"	230	27	2	6
Paul Naumoff	LB	6'1"	210	22		
Wayne Walker	LB	6'2"	225	30		26
Lem Barney	DB	6'	202	21	10	18
Mike Bass	DB	6'	190	22		
Dick LeBeau	DB	6'1"	185	30	4	
Bruce Maher	DB	5'11"	190	30	2	2
Wayne Rasmussen	DB	6'2"	180	25		
Bobby Thompson	DB	5'10"	175	27		
Tom Vaughn	DB	5'11"	195	24	1	
Mike Weger	DB	6'2"	195	21		
Johnnie Robinson – Injury						

Use Name	Pos.	Hgt	Wgt	Age	Int	Pts
Milt Plum	QB	6'1"	205	33		
Karl Sweetan	QB	6'1"	200	24		6
Mel Farr	HB	6'2"	208	22		36
Bobby Felts	HB	6'2"	202	24		
Tom Watkins	HB	6'1"	195	30		30
Amos Marsh	FB	6'1"	220	28		18
Tom Nowatzke	FB	6'3"	222	24		36
Pat Studstill	FL	6'1"	175	29		12
John Henderson	OE-FL	6'3"	190	24		
Jim Gibbons	TE	6'2"	220	31		
Ron Kramer	TE	6'3"	240	32		
Jerry Zawadzkas	TE	6'4"	220	20		
Gail Cogdill	OE	6'2"	195	30		6
Bill Malinchak	OE	6'1"	190	23		24
Garo Yepremian	K	5'8"	160	23		28

MINNESOTA VIKINGS 3-8-3 Bud Grant

Scores of Each Game		
21	SAN FRANCISCO	27
3	Los Angeles	39
7	CHICAGO	17
24	ST. LOUIS	34
10	Green Bay	7
20	BALTIMORE	20
20	Atlanta	21
27	NEW YORK	24
10	DETROIT	10
10	Cleveland	14
41	Pittsburgh	27
27	GREEN BAY	30
10	Chicago	10
3	Detroit	14

Use Name	Pos.	Hgt	Wgt	Age	Int	Pts
Grady Alderman	OT	6'2"	240	28		
Bob Breitenstein (from DEN)	OT	6'3"	267	24		
Doug Davis	OT	6'4"	250	23		
Archie Sutton	OT	6'4"	265	24		
Larry Bowie	OG	6'2"	255	27		
John Pentecost	OG	6'2"	250	23		
Milt Sunde	OG	6'2"	250	24		
Jim Vellone	OT-OG	6'2"	255	23		
Mick Tingelhoff	C	6'1"	237	27		
Carl Eller	DE	6'6"	265	25		
Jim Marshall	DE	6'3"	235	29		
Archie Simkus	DE	6'4"	250	24		
Paul Dickson	DT	6'5"	255	30		
Gary Larsen	DT	6'5"	255	27		
Alan Page	DT	6'5"	255	22		
Jerry Shay	DT	6'3"	245	23		

Use Name	Pos.	Hgt	Wgt	Age	Int	Pts
Paul Faust	LB	6'	220	23		
Don Hansen	LB	6'3"	228	23		
Jim Hargrove	LB	6'3"	230	22	1	6
John Kirby	LB	6'3"	235	25		
Dave Tobey	LB	6'3"	230	24		
Lonnie Warwick	LB	6'3"	235	25	2	
Roy Winston	LB	6'1"	230	27		
Al Coleman	DB	6'1"	195	22		
Mike Fitzgerald (to NY-ATL)	DB	5'10"	180	26		
Dale Hackbart	DB	6'3"	210	31	2	6
Jeff Jordan	DB	6'4"	190	23		
Karl Kassulke	DB	6'	195	25	2	
Brady Keys (from PIT)	DB	6'	185	31	3	
Earsell Mackbee	DB	6'1"	195	26	5	12
Ed Sharockman	DB	6'	200	27	3	

Use Name	Pos.	Hgt	Wgt	Age	Int	Pts
Bob Berry	QB	5'11"	190	25		
Joe Kapp	QB	6'2"	212	29		12
Ron Vander Kelen	QB	6'1"	190	27		6
Earl Denny	HB	6'1"	200	22		
Clint Jones	HB	6'	206	22		6
Jim Lindsey	HB	6'2"	200	22		
Dave Osborn	HB	6'	205	24		18
Pete Tatman	HB	6'1"	220	22		
Bill Brown	FB	5'11"	230	29		30
Jim Phillips	FL	6'1"	195	30		18
Bob Grim	DB-FL	6'	197	22		6
John Beasley	TE	6'3"	228	22		24
Marlin McKeever	TE	6'1"	235	27		
Paul Flatley	OE	6'1"	187	26		
Gene Washington	OE	6'3"	216	23		12
Fred Cox	K	5'10"	200	28		77
Bobby Walden	K	6'	190	29		

CENTRAL DIVISION

GREEN BAY PACKERS

RUSHING

Last Name	No.	Yds	Avg	TD
Grabowski	120	466	3.9	2
Wilson	103	453	4.4	2
Anderson	97	402	4.1	6
Pitts	77	247	3.2	6
Williams	35	188	5.4	1
Starr	21	90	4.3	0
Mercein	14	46	4.0	1
Dale	1	9	9.0	0
Bratkowski	5	6	1.2	0
Horn	1	–2	–2.0	0

RECEIVING

Last Name	No.	Yds	Avg	TD
Dowler	54	836	15	4
Dale	35	738	21	5
Anderson	22	331	15	3
Pitts	15	210	14	0
Wilson	14	88	6	0
Grabowski	12	171	14	1
Fleming	10	126	13	1
Long	8	96	12	0
Williams	5	80	16	1
A. Brown	3	43	14	0
McGee	3	33	11	0
Mercein	1	6	6	0

PUNT RETURNS

Last Name	No.	Yds	Avg	TD
Anderson	9	98	11	0
T. Brown	9	40	4	0
Pitts	9	16	2	0
Wood	12	3	0	0

KICKOFF RETURNS

Last Name	No.	Yds	Avg	TD
Williams	18	739	41	4
Anderson	11	226	21	0
Adderley	10	207	21	0
Crutcher	3	48	16	0
A. Brown	1	13	13	0
Hart	1	8	8	0
Robinson	1	0	0	0
Wood	1	0	0	0

PASSING – PUNTING – KICKING

PASSING	Att	Comp	%	Yds	Yd/Att	TD	Int–%	RK
Starr	210	115	55	1823	8.7	9	17– 8	6
Bratkowski	94	53	56	724	7.7	5	9–10	
Horn	24	12	50	171	7.1	1	1– 4	
Anderson	2	1	50	19	9.5	0	0– 0	
Pitts	1	1	100	21	21.0	0	0– 0	

PUNTING	No	Avg
Anderson	65	36.6
Chandler	1	31.0

KICKING	XP	Att	%	FG	Att	%
Chandler	39	39	100	19	29	66
Mercein	2	3	67	0	1	0

CHICAGO BEARS

RUSHING

Last Name	No.	Yds	Avg	TD
Sayers	186	880	4.7	7
Piccolo	87	317	3.6	0
Concannon	67	279	4.2	3
Bull	61	176	2.9	0
Kurek	37	112	3.0	0
Rakestraw	11	42	3.8	2
Livingston	28	41	1.5	0
J. Jones	4	19	4.8	0
Morris	1	6	6.0	0
Gordon	3	–7	–2.3	0
Bukich	4	–13	–3.3	0

RECEIVING

Last Name	No.	Yds	Avg	TD
Gordon	31	534	17	5
Morris	20	231	12	1
Bull	18	250	14	1
Sayers	16	126	8	1
Piccolo	13	103	8	0
Denny	12	113	9	0
J. Jones	7	138	20	0
Livingston	5	62	12	0
Kurek	5	30	6	0
B. Jones	3	80	27	1
Stoepel	1	6	6	0

PUNT RETURNS

Last Name	No.	Yds	Avg	TD
Gordon	12	82	7	0
Sayers	3	80	27	1
Morris	4	24	6	0
Dodd	3	8	3	0

KICKOFF RETURNS

Last Name	No.	Yds	Avg	TD
Sayers	16	603	38	3
Gordon	16	397	25	0
Kurek	5	81	16	0
Dodd	3	34	11	0
Brown	2	34	17	0
J. Taylor	1	8	8	0
Jackson	1	0	0	0
Kriewald	1	0	0	0
Kuechenberg	1	0	0	0
Stoepel	1	0	0	0

PASSING – PUNTING – KICKING

PASSING	Att	Comp	%	Yds	Yd/Att	TD	Int–%	RK
Concannon	186	92	49	1260	6.8	6	14– 8	17
Rakestraw	44	21	48	228	5.2	3	2– 5	
Bukich	33	18	55	185	5.6	0	2– 6	
Sayers	5	0	0	0	0.0	0	0– 0	

PUNTING	No	Avg
Green	79	42.9

KICKING	XP	Att	%	FG	Att	%
Percival	26	29	90	13	26	50

DETROIT LIONS

RUSHING

Last Name	No.	Yds	Avg	TD
Farr	206	860	4.2	3
Watkins	106	361	3.4	4
Nowatzke	70	288	4.1	4
Marsh	58	229	3.9	2
Sweetan	17	93	5.5	1
Felts	10	66	6.6	0
Plum	6	5	0.8	0
Flanagan	0	5	0.0	0

RECEIVING

Last Name	No.	Yds	Avg	TD
Farr	39	317	8	3
Malinchak	26	397	15	4
Cogdill	21	322	15	1
Nowatzke	21	145	7	2
Henderson	13	144	11	0
Studstill	10	162	16	2
Gibbons	10	107	11	0
Watkins	8	93	12	1
Marsh	7	103	15	1
Kramer	4	40	10	0
Walton	1	–4	–4	0

PUNT RETURNS

Last Name	No.	Yds	Avg	TD
Watkins	15	57	4	0
Thompson	9	20	2	0
Barney	4	14	4	0
Vaughn	4	7	2	0
Weger	1	0	0	0
Felts	1	–1	–1	0

KICKOFF RETURNS

Last Name	No.	Yds	Avg	TD
Vaughn	16	446	28	0
Watkins	20	411	21	0
Thompson	4	134	34	0
Barney	5	87	17	0
Goovert	2	40	20	0
Weger	2	27	14	0
Zawadzkas	1	0	0	0

PASSING – PUNTING – KICKING

PASSING	Att	Comp	%	Yds	Yd/Att	TD	Int–%	RK
Sweetan	177	74	42	901	5.1	10	11– 6	18
Plum	172	86	50	925	5.4	4	8– 5	14
Farr	2	0	0	0	0.0	0	0– 0	

PUNTING	No	Avg
Barney	47	37.4
Studstill	36	44.5

KICKING	XP	Att	%	FG	Att	%
Yepremian	22	23	96	2	6	33
Walker	11	11	100	5	15	33

MINNESOTA VIKINGS

RUSHING

Last Name	No.	Yds	Avg	TD
Osborn	215	972	4.5	2
Brown	185	610	3.3	5
Kapp	27	167	6.2	2
Jones	13	23	1.8	0
Grim	1	20	20.0	0
Lindsey	4	10	2.5	0
Vander Kelen	9	9	1.0	1

RECEIVING

Last Name	No.	Yds	Avg	TD
Osborn	34	272	8	1
Flatley	23	232	10	0
Brown	22	263	12	0
Phillips	21	352	17	3
McKeever	14	184	13	0
Washington	13	384	30	2
Beasley	13	120	9	4
Grim	6	108	18	1
Lindsey	4	36	9	0

PUNT RETURNS

Last Name	No.	Yds	Avg	TD
Grim	25	101	4	0
Keys	7	7	1	0
Fitzgerald	2	4	2	0
Sharockman	4	0	0	0

KICKOFF RETURNS

Last Name	No.	Yds	Avg	TD
Jones	25	597	24	1
Grim	22	493	22	0
Fitzgerald	12	240	20	0
Lindsey	3	71	24	0
Sharockman	1	22	22	0
Denny	1	18	18	0
Tatman	1	14	14	0

PASSING – PUNTING – KICKING

PASSING	Att	Comp	%	Yds	Yd/Att	TD	Int–%	RK
Kapp	214	102	48	1386	6.5	8	17– 8	19
Vander Kelen	115	45	39	522	4.5	3	7– 6	
Berry	7	3	43	43	6.1	0	0– 0	

PUNTING	No	Avg
Walden	75	41.6

KICKING	XP	Att	%	FG	Att	%
Cox	26	26	100	17	33	52

COASTAL DIVISION

LOS ANGELES RAMS 11-1-2 George Allen

Scores of Each Game		
27	New Orleans	13
39	MINNESOTA	3
35	Dallas	13
24	SAN FRANCISCO	27
24	Baltimore	24
28	WASHINGTON	28
28	Chicago	17
17	San Francisco	7
33	PHILADELPHIA	17
31	Atlanta	3
31	Detroit	7
20	ATLANTA	3
27	GREEN BAY	24
34	BALTIMORE	10

Use Name	Pos.	Hgt	Wgt	Age	Int	Pts
Joe Carollo	OT	6'2"	258	27		
Charley Cowan	OT	6'4"	265	29		
Bob Nichols	OT	6'3"	250	24		
Don Chuy	OG	6'1"	255	26		
Tom Mack	OG	6'3"	245	23		
Joe Scibelli	OG	6'1"	255	28		
Ken Iman	C	6'1"	240	28		
George Burman	OG-C	6'3"	255	24		
Deacon Jones	DE	6'5"	260	28		2
Lamar Lundy	DE	6'7"	260	32		
Gregg Schumacher	DE	6'2"	240	25		
Roger Brown	DT	6'5"	300	30		
Merlin Olsen	DT	6'5"	276	26		
Diron Talbert	DT	6'5"	238	23		
Dave Cahill	DE-DT	6'3"	238	25		
Maxie Baughan	LB	6'1"	230	29	4	
Gene Breen	LB	6'2"	230	26		
Tony Guillory	LB	6'4"	236	24		
Jack Pardee	LB	6'2"	230	31	6	12
Myron Pottios	LB	6'2"	240	27	1	
Doug Woodlief	LB	6'3"	230	23	2	
Claude Crabb	DB	6'	192	27	1	
Irv Cross	DB	6'1"	195	28	2	
Willie Daniel	DB	5'11"	190	29	2	
Chuck Lamson	DB	6'	195	28	2	
Ed Meador	DB	5'11"	200	30	8	12
Clancy Williams	DB	6'2"	198	24	4	
Kelton Winston	DB	6'	195	26		
Hal Bedsole – Injury						
Henry Dyer – Injury						
Rosey Grier – Injury						
Roman Gabriel	QB	6'4"	230	27		36
Bill Munson	QB	6'2"	200	25		
Willie Ellison	HB	6'1"	207	22		
Les Josephson	HB	6'	220	25		48
Tommy Mason	HB	6'	190	28		
Dick Bass	FB	5'10"	195	30		42
Jim Stiger	FB	5'11"	214	26		
Bernie Casey	FL	6'4"	210	28		48
Billy Truax	TE	6'5"	235	24		24
Dave Pivec	LB-TE	6'3"	240	23		6
Bucky Pope	OE	6'5"	205	24		12
Jack Snow	OE	6'2"	195	24		48
Wendell Tucker	OE	5'10"	185	23		
Bruce Gossett	K	6'2"	230	24		108
Jon Kilgore	K	6'1"	205	23		

BALTIMORE COLTS 11-1-2 Don Shula

Scores of Each Game		
38	ATLANTA	31
38	Philadelphia	6
41	SAN FRANCISCO	7
24	Chicago	3
24	LOS ANGELES	24
20	Minnesota	20
17	Washington	13
13	GREEN BAY	10
49	Atlanta	7
41	DETROIT	7
26	San Francisco	9
23	DALLAS	17
30	NEW ORLEANS	10
10	Los Angeles	34

Use Name	Pos.	Hgt	Wgt	Age	Int	Pts
Sam Ball	OT	6'4"	240	23		
Jim Parker	OT	6'3"	275	33		
Bob Vogel	OT	6'5"	250	25		
Norman Davis	OG	6'3"	250	22		
Dale Memmelaar	OG	6'2"	246	30		
Glenn Ressler	OG	6'3"	250	23		
Dan Sullivan	OG	6'3"	250	28		
Dick Szymanski	C	6'3"	235	35		
Bill Curry	LB-C	6'2"	235	24		
Ordell Braase	DE	6'4"	245	35		6
Roy Hilton	DE	6'6"	240	22		
Lou Michaels	DE	6'2"	250	31		106
Bubba Smith	DE	6'7"	295	22		
Fred Miller	DT	6'3"	250	26		
Billy Ray Smith	DT	6'4"	250	32		
Andy Stynchula	DE-DT	6'3"	250	28		
Barry Brown	LB	6'3"	235	24		
Mike Curtis	LB	6'2"	232	24	1	
Dennis Gaubatz	LB	6'2"	232	26	2	
Ron Porter	LB	6'3"	232	22	1	
Don Shinnick	LB	6'	228	32	3	
Bobby Boyd	DB	5'10"	192	29	6	6
George Harold	DB	6'3"	194	25		
Alvin Haymond	DB	6'	194	25	2	
Jerry Logan	DB	6'1"	190	26	4	6
Lenny Lyles	DB	6'2"	204	31	5	6
Preston Pearson	DB	6'1"	190	22		
Charlie Stukes	DB	6'3"	212	23	2	
Rick Volk	DB	6'3"	195	22	6	6
Jim Welch	HB-DB	6'	196	29		
Johnny Unitas	QB	6'1"	196	34		
Jim Ward	QB	6'2"	195	23		
Tom Matte	HB	6'	214	28		72
Lenny Moore	HB	6'1"	198	34		24
Jerry Hill	FB	5'11"	215	27		12
Tony Lorick	FB	6'1"	217	25		36
Don Alley	FL	6'2"	200	21		
Jimmy Orr	FL	5'11"	185	31		6
Willie Richardson	FL	6'2"	198	27		48
John Mackey	TE	6'3"	224	25		18
Butch Wilson	TE	6'2"	228	25		
Ray Berry	OE	6'2"	190	34		6
Ray Perkins	OE	6'	183	25		12
Alex Hawkins (from ATL)	FL-OE	6'1"	186	30		24
David Lee	K	6'4"	215	23		

SAN FRANCISCO FORTY-NINERS 7-7-0 Jack Christiansen

Scores of Each Game		
27	Minnesota	21
38	ATLANTA	7
7	Baltimore	41
27	Los Angeles	24
28	Philadelphia	27
27	NEW ORLEANS	13
3	DETROIT	45
7	LOS ANGELES	17
28	Washington	31
0	Green Bay	13
9	BALTIMORE	26
14	CHICAGO	28
34	Atlanta	28
24	DALLAS	16

Use Name	Pos.	Hgt	Wgt	Age	Int	Pts
Dave Hettema	OT	6'4"	247	25		
Walt Rock	OT	6'5"	255	26		
Len Rohde	OT	6'4"	250	29		
Elmer Collett	OG	6'4"	230	22		
Howard Mudd	OG	6'3"	254	25		
Don Parker	OG	6'3"	235	22		
John Thomas	OG	6'4"	250	32		
Bruce Bosley	C	6'2"	244	33		
Joe Cerne	C	6'2"	240	24		
Stan Hindman	DE	6'3"	232	23		
Tom Holzer	DE	6'4"	250	22		
Walter Johnson	DE	6'4"	225	23		
Clark Miller	DE	6'5"	247	28	1	
Charlie Johnson	DT	6'2"	265	23		
Charlie Krueger	DT	6'4"	260	31		
Roland Lakes	DT	6'4"	280	27		
Ed Beard	LB	6'2"	226	27		
Bob Harrison	LB	6'2"	228	30		
Matt Hazeltine	LB	6'1"	230	34		
Frank Nunley	LB	6'2"	220	21	1	
Dave Wilcox	LB	6'3"	234	24	2	
Kermit Alexander	DB	5'11"	180	26	5	
George Donnelly	DB	6'3"	210	24		
Goose Gonsoulin	DB	6'3"	210	29	3	
Jim Jackson	DB	6'	193	23	1	
Jim Johnson	DB	6'2"	187	29	2	
Mel Phillips	DB	6'	192	25	1	
Al Randolph	DB	6'2"	192	23		
Wayne Trimble	DB	6'3"	203	21		
Kay McFarland – Injury						
John Brodie	QB	6'1"	210	32		6
George Mira	QB	5'11"	190	25		
Steve Spurrier	QB	6'2"	203	22		
John David Crow	HB	6'2"	224	32		30
Doug Cunningham	HB	5'11"	185	21		12
Dave Kopay	HB	6'2"	218	25		
Bill Tucker	FB-HB	6'2"	222	23		
Gary Lewis	FB	6'3"	230	25		42
Ken Willard	FB	6'2"	230	24		36
Chip Myers	FL	6'4"	185	22		
Wayne Swinford	FL	6'	192	24		
Dick Witcher	TE-FL	6'3"	204	22		18
Dave Olerich	TE	6'1"	220	22		
Monte Stickles	TE	6'4"	235	29		
Bob Windsor	TE	6'4"	223	24		18
Dave Parks	OE	6'2"	207	25		12
Sonny Randle	OE	6'2"	190	31		24
Tommy Davis	K	6'	220	32		75

ATLANTA FALCONS 1-12-1 Norb Hecker

Scores of Each Game		
31	Baltimore	38
7	San Francisco	38
0	Green Bay	23
7	PHILADELPHIA	38
20	WASHINGTON	20
3	Detroit	24
21	MINNESOTA	20
7	Dallas	37
7	BALTIMORE	49
3	LOS ANGELES	31
24	New Orleans	27
3	Los Angeles	20
28	SAN FRANCISCO	34
14	CHICAGO	23

Use Name	Pos.	Hgt	Wgt	Age	Int	Pts
Errol Linden	OT	6'5"	260	30		
Bill Sandeman (from NO)	OT	6'6"	250	24		
Don Talbert	OT	6'5"	255	27		
Jim Simon	OG-OT	6'5"	240	26		
Ed Cook	OG	6'2"	250	35		
Dan Grimm	OG	6'3"	245	26		
Tom Harmon	OG	6'4"	238	25		
Lou Kirouac	OG	6'3"	240	26		
Jake Kupp (to NO)	OG	6'3"	233	25		
Jim Wilson	OG	6'3"	258	26		
Frank Marchlewski	C	6'2"	238	23		
Karl Rubke	DT-C	6'4"	244	31		
Bob Hughes	DE	6'4"	255	22		
Bobby Richards	DE	6'2"	245	28		
Sam Williams	DE	6'5"	245	36		
Bo Wood	DE	6'3"	225	21		
Jim Norton	DT	6'4"	254	24	1	
Chuck Sieminski	DT	6'4"	270	27		
Joe Szczecko	DT	6'	245	25		
Dick Absher (from WAS)	LB	6'4"	227	23		4
Andy Bowling	LB	6'3"	235	22		
Ralph Heck	LB	6'2"	230	26		
Tommy Nobis	LB	6'2"	235	23	3	6
Marion Rushing	LB	6'2"	230	30	1	
Bob Sanders	LB	6'3"	235	24		
Tom Bleick	DB	6'2"	200	24		
Lee Calland	DB	6'	190	26	3	6
Floyd Hudlow	DB	5'11"	195	23	2	
Nick Rassas	DB	6'	190	23		
Ken Reaves	DB	6'3"	205	22	7	
Jerry Richardson	DB	6'3"	190	24		
Bob Riggle	DB	6'1"	200	23		
Randy Johnson	QB	6'3"	196	23		6
Terry Nofsinger	QB	6'4"	215	29		
Steve Sloan	QB	6'	185	23		
Perry Lee Dunn	HB	6'2"	215	24		
Tom Moore	HB	6'2"	210	29		
Ron Rector	HB	6'	200	23		
Junior Coffey	FB	6'1"	210	25		30
Jim Mankins	FB	6'1"	235	23		
Tommy McDonald	FL	5'10"	175	33		24
Ron Smith	DB-FL	6'1"	192	24		6
Taz Anderson	TE	6'2"	215	28		6
Billy Martin	TE	6'4"	235	24		18
Ray Ogden (from NO)	TE	6'5"	225	24		6
Gary Barnes	OE	6'4"	210	27		6
Jerry Simmons (from NO)	OE	6'1"	190	24		12
Billy Lothridge	K	6'1"	195	23		
Wade Traynham	K	6'2"	218	25		43

COASTAL DIVISION

LOS ANGELES RAMS

RUSHING

Last Name	No.	Yds	Avg	TD
Josephson	178	800	4.5	4
Bass	187	627	3.4	6
Mason	63	213	3.4	0
Gabriel	43	198	4.6	6
Ellison	14	84	6.0	0
Stiger	3	6	2.0	0
Munson	2	−22	−11.0	0

RECEIVING

Last Name	No.	Yds	Avg	TD
Casey	53	871	16	8
Truax	37	487	13	4
Josephson	37	400	11	4
Snow	28	735	26	8
Bass	27	212	8	1
Mason	13	70	5	0
Pope	8	152	19	2
Pivec	2	2	1	1
Ellison	1	18	18	0

PUNT RETURNS

Last Name	No.	Yds	Avg	TD
Cross	17	136	8	0
Meador	21	131	6	0
Tucker	6	40	7	0
Winston	1	12	12	0
Stiger	4	9	2	0
Crabb	1	0	0	0

KICKOFF RETURNS

Last Name	No.	Yds	Avg	TD
Ellison	13	340	26	0
Tucker	11	242	22	0
Williams	7	161	23	0
Cross	4	134	34	0
Josephson	5	91	18	0
Winston	3	65	22	0

PASSING – PUNTING – KICKING

PASSING	Att	Comp	%	Yds	Yd/Att	TD	Int–%	RK
Gabriel	371	196	53	2779	7.5	25	13– 4	4
Munson	10	5	50	38	3.8	1	2–20	
Josephson	5	2	40	47	9.4	0	1–20	
Mason	3	2	67	65	21.7	1	0– 0	
Meador	1	1	100	18	18.0	1	0– 0	

PUNTING	No	Avg
Kilgore	68	42.2

KICKING	XP	Att	%	FG	Att	%
Gossett	48	48	100	20	43	47

BALTIMORE COLTS

RUSHING

Last Name	No.	Yds	Avg	TD
Matte	147	636	4.3	9
Lorick	133	436	3.3	6
Hill	90	311	3.5	2
Moore	42	132	3.1	4
Unitas	22	89	4.0	0
Ward	5	23	4.6	0
Hawkins	2	12	6.0	0
Welch	2	6	3.0	0

RECEIVING

Last Name	No.	Yds	Avg	TD
Richardson	63	860	14	8
Mackey	55	686	12	3
Matte	35	496	14	3
Hawkins	27	469	17	4
Lorick	22	189	9	0
Hill	19	156	8	0
Perkins	16	302	19	2
Moore	13	153	12	0
Berry	11	167	15	1
Orr	3	72	24	1
Alley	1	11	11	0

PUNT RETURNS

Last Name	No.	Yds	Avg	TD
Haymond	26	155	6	0
Volk	11	88	8	0
Logan	5	80	16	1

KICKOFF RETURNS

Last Name	No.	Yds	Avg	TD
Moore	16	392	25	0
Haymond	13	326	25	0
Lorick	8	212	27	0
Stukes	1	19	19	0
Logan	2	17	9	0
Matte	1	14	14	0
Davis	1	8	8	0

PASSING – PUNTING – KICKING

PASSING	Att	Comp	%	Yds	Yd/Att	TD	Int–%	RK
Unitas	436	255	58	3428	7.9	20	16– 4	2
Ward	16	9	56	115	7.2	2	1– 6	
Matte	5	1	20	18	3.6	0	0– 0	

PUNTING	No	Avg
Lee	49	42.3

KICKING	XP	Att	%	FG	Att	%
Michaels	46	48	96	20	37	54

SAN FRANCISCO FORTY NINERS

RUSHING

Last Name	No.	Yds	Avg	TD
Willard	169	510	3.0	5
Crow	113	479	4.2	2
Lewis	67	342	5.1	6
Cunningham	43	212	4.9	2
Brodie	20	147	7.4	1
Mira	7	23	3.3	0
Kopay	6	21	3.5	0
Spurrier	5	18	3.6	0
Windsor	1	7	7.0	0
Tucker	3	5	1.7	0

RECEIVING

Last Name	No.	Yds	Avg	TD
Witcher	46	705	15	3
Randle	33	502	15	4
Crow	31	373	12	3
Parks	26	313	12	2
Willard	23	242	11	1
Windsor	21	254	12	2
Lewis	21	218	10	1
Cunningham	13	121	9	0
Stickles	7	86	12	0
Tucker	2	22	11	0
Myers	2	13	7	0
Kopay	2	11	6	0
Olerich	1	2	2	0

PUNT RETURNS

Last Name	No.	Yds	Avg	TD
Cunningham	27	249	9	0
Alexander	6	64	11	0
Tucker	1	1	1	0
Gonsoulin	1	0	0	0

KICKOFF RETURNS

Last Name	No.	Yds	Avg	TD
Cunningham	31	826	27	0
Tucker	9	199	22	0
Lewis	9	190	21	0
Swinford	2	51	26	0
Kopay	1	21	21	0
Windsor	1	21	21	0
Alexander	1	18	18	0
Nunley	2	0	0	0

PASSING – PUNTING – KICKING

PASSING	Att	Comp	%	Yds	Yd/Att	TD	Int–%	RK
Brodie	349	168	48	2013	5.8	11	16– 5	11
Mira	65	35	54	592	9.1	5	3– 5	
Spurrier	50	23	46	211	4.2	0	7–14	
Crow	5	2	40	46	9.2	0	0– 0	

PUNTING	No	Avg
Spurrier	73	37.6

KICKING	XP	Att	%	FG	Att	%
Davis	33	33	100	14	33	42

ATLANTA F[illegible]ONS

RUSHING

Last Name	No.	Yds	Avg	TD
Coffey	180	722	4.0	4
Johnson	24	144	6.0	1
Rector	24	127	5.3	0
Moore	53	104	2.0	0
Dunn	27	63	2.3	0
Smith	8	42	5.3	0
Nofsinger	3	33	11.0	0
Lothridge	1	16	16.0	0
Mankins	2	7	3.5	0
Sloan	1	2	2.0	0

RECEIVING

Last Name	No.	Yds	Avg	TD
McDonald	33	436	13	4
Coffey	30	196	7	1
Simmons	23	312	14	2
Ogden	20	327	16	1
Martin	15	182	12	3
Dunn	13	111	9	0
Smith	11	227	21	0
Barnes	10	154	15	1
Moore	10	74	7	0
Anderson	8	99	12	1
Rector	4	13	3	0
Mankins	1	11	11	0

PUNT RETURNS

Last Name	No.	Yds	Avg	TD
Smith	20	92	5	0
Hudlow	1	2	2	0
Simmons	3	0	0	0

KICKOFF RETURNS

Last Name	No.	Yds	Avg	TD
Smith	39	976	25	1
Dunn	7	128	18	0
Hudlow	2	56	28	0
Rassas	2	51	26	0
Ogden	3	41	14	0
Simmons	2	38	19	0
Linden	3	37	12	0
Mankins	1	12	12	0
Wood	1	9	9	0
Talbert	1	2	2	0
Martin	1	0	0	0
Sandeman	1	0	0	0

PASSING – PUNTING – KICKING

PASSING	Att	Comp	%	Yds	Yd/Att	TD	Int–%	RK
Johnson	288	142	49	1620	5.6	10	21– 7	16
Nofsinger	60	30	50	352	5.9	1	2– 3	
Sloan	18	4	22	38	2.1	0	2–11	
Dunn	2	1	50	32	16.0	1	0– 0	
Moore	2	2	100	102	51.0	1	0– 0	

PUNTING	No	Avg
Lothridge	87	43.7

KICKING	XP	Att	%	FG	Att	%
Traynham	22	22	100	7	18	39
Absher	4	4	100	0	1	0

1967 A.F.L. Coming Up to Equal Footing

The AFL wasn't ready yet to win a Super Bowl, but the clubs in the newer league won some respect with their showing in interleague pre-season games. The games were far more competitive than had been expected, and the AFL drew first blood when the Denver Broncos beat the Detroit Lions 13-7 in the first interleague contest. The two leagues battled on even lines through the late-summer games, but the AFL administered the worst beating when the Chiefs, still smarting from their Super Bowl loss to Green Bay, crushed the Chicago Bears 66-27. The pre-season series seemed to prove that AFL teams could play on a par with average NFL teams but that time was needed to catch up with NFL powers like the Packers.

Time was on the AFL's side, however, as the common draft assured a steady flow of young talent into the league. Teams like Boston and Denver, which had never done well in signing its draft choices, now had an easier time coming to terms with graduating collegiate talent. The AFL teams also were moving into better stadia, with the San Diego Chargers this year setting up shop in a new municipal stadium.

EASTERN DIVISION

Houston Oilers—A 3-11 team only a year ago, the Oilers used a fine rookie class and a revitalized defense to capture their first divisional crown since 1962. Every adjustment head coach Wally Lemm made in the defense worked out splendidly; he moved veterans around and inserted rookies with the touch of a chess grandmaster. Pat Holmes, a disappointment last year as a tackle, caught fire as an end. Second-year man George Rice took over a tackle spot and drew compliments around the league. Rookie linebacker George Webster combined size, speed, and sound football sense in an All-Pro freshman season, and his linebacking mates were Garland Boyette, playing the middle for the first time, and Olen Underwood. W. K. Hicks and Jim Norton held onto their secondary posts, but joining them were newcomers Miller Farr, a quick cornerback picked up in a trade from San Diego, and rookie strong safety Ken Houston. This rebuilt unit allowed only eighteen touchdowns all year. The leading lights of the offense were fullback Hoyle Granger, quarterback Pete Beathard, who was picked up in mid-season from Kansas City, and star guard Bob Talamini.

New York Jets—As usual, the Jets looked like a sure title winner until December, and then, as usual, they fell apart. Ending November with a 7-2-1 record and a one-game lead over the coming Houston Oilers, the Jets started December by losing to Denver, Kansas City, and Oakland. They straightened out in time to beat San Diego in the season's finale, but by then the Oilers had locked up first place. The Jet pass defense contributed heavily to this year's late slump, as the line failed to rush enemy passers consistently and the secondary was not airtight. The Jets also had offensive problems, although Joe Namath and receivers George Sauer and Don Maynard bombed enemy defenses regularly. Fullback Matt Snell, the team's workhorse, ripped up a knee in the opening game and didn't return to action until mid-November; by then, halfback Emerson Boozer had gone out with an injured knee of his own.

Buffalo Bills—The Buffalo defensive unit stayed strong despite the loss of middle linebacker Harry Jacobs for the last seven games with a broken elbow, but the offense, never too robust to begin with, broke down completely under a rash of knee injuries. Bobby Crockett, last year's rookie receiving threat, sat out the entire year with a bad knee, while running back Bobby Burnett, veteran guard Billy Shaw, and split end Art Powell missed at least half the schedule with their knee injuries. Quarterback Jack Kemp's bad season further hurt the attack, and only newcomer Keith Lincoln, picked up in a swap with San Diego, kept the offense alive with his running and receiving. With all the injuries, the Bills scored more than 20 points in only three games all year—not nearly enough for a fourth straight championship.

Miami Dolphins—By mid-season rookie Bob Griese had taken over as the starting quarterback. Showing a strong arm and unshakable poise, Griese hooked up with rookie split end Jack Clancy in an effective passing combination. Outside of these two rookies, however, the Miami offense gave fans little to cheer about. Halfback Abner Haynes was long past his prime and was shipped out to New York before the year ended. The line had huge gaps, and flanker Howard Twilley had neither size nor speed. The defense, though not one of the league's best, did field several representative ball players.

Boston Patriots—Jim Nance still dominated the team with his powerful ball-carrying, but the supporting cast on the Patriots slipped, and they fell to last place in the East. With no speed at halfback or in the receivers, and with Babe Parilli showing advanced symptoms of old age, defenses waited for Nance's smashes into the line, yet the big fullback from Syracuse still bowled over the expectant defenders for 1,216 yards.

WESTERN DIVISION

Oakland Raiders—In a daring trade, the Raiders sent quarterback Tom Flores and split end Art Powell, both established starters, to Buffalo for quarterback Daryle Lamonica and Glenn Bass. Bass didn't make the team, but Lamonica developed into a fine long passer. End Bill Miller came from Buffalo at little cost and gave Lamonica a steady target. Willie Brown came over from Denver and beat All-Pro Dave Grayson out of a cornerback position. Thirty-nine-year-old George Blanda signed aboard after being released by Houston; the old-timer backed up Lamonica and led the league in scoring with his steady place-kicking. The rookie crop turned up guard Gene Upshaw, who immediately ranked among the league's best offensive linemen, and linebacker Duane Benson, who played on the special teams with zeal. Of course, the Raiders already had some top-notch players, with Billy Cannon, Jim Otto, Ben Davidson, Tom Keating, and Kent McCloughan winning All-League honors among the returning veterans. The Raiders' depth showed when halfback Clem Daniels broke his ankle late in the year and Pete Banaszak filled in with no noticeable drop in quality. Thus, the Raiders easily swept the Western Division title.

Kansas City Chiefs—AFL clubs learned well the lesson taught by the Green Bay Packers in the first Super Bowl. The Packers had singled out certain weak links in the Kansas City defense and ruthlessly exploited them, and now the AFL clubs found success in directing their attacks right at the same people. Enemy offenses singled out for special treatment, linebackers Chuck Hurston and Sherrill Headrick and cornerbacks Fred Williamson and Willie Mitchell, and by the time coach Hank Stram could readjust his defense the Chiefs had lost all four of their meetings with Oakland and San Diego and all chances for a repeat title in the West. But Stram did substitute some young talent into the lineup, and after Bud Abell, Emmitt Thomas, Fletcher Smith, and rookies Jim Lynch and Willie Lanier got their bearings, the Kansas City linebacking and secondary were a lot tougher. Aside from closing out the season with three straight wins, the high point of the year was the unveiling of two spectacular special team rookies: Norwegian place-kicker Jan Stenerud, and kick returner Noland Smith.

San Diego Chargers—The Chargers got off to a fast start and had high hopes of regaining the Western Division title, only to lose their last four games and slip back into a third-place finish. Coach Sid Gillman's biggest headache was his defense, which disintegrated down the stretch. Despite high-priced talents like Scott Appleton and Steve DeLong, the line put practically no pressure at all on enemy passers, and, given time, opposing quarterbacks found the San Diego secondary easy to pick apart. The offense kept the title drive alive until late in the season and kept the fans filing into the new San Diego Stadium. Enemy defenses had to worry first about flanker Lance Alworth, pro football's premier deep pass receiver, but if they paid too much attention to him, quarterback John Hadl simply threw to ends Gary Garrison and Willie Frazier, both fine pass catchers in their own right. The line was one of the best in pro football, especially at protecting the passer, and the San Diego running attack got a quick shot of energy in the form of Dickie Post and Brad Hubbert, a pair of rookie backs.

Denver Broncos—Lou Saban returned to pro football as head coach and general manager of the Broncos and immediately ripped the club apart to get a fresh start in building a winner. At times during the season Saban was starting fifteen rookies on the two platoons, a sign of his willingness to go with youth now to build a winner later. The team's biggest problems came in pass defense, where a rookie-laden secondary and linebacking corps could not handle good air attacks. The defensive line showed more stability as veteran Dave Costa, obtained from Buffalo for a draft pick, starred at a tackle post and youngsters Rich Jackson and Pete Duranko showed promise at the ends. Saban rebuilt the offense into a creditable unit, although the line was manned by and large with inexperienced or mediocre players. Saban got himself a quarterback by trading two first-round draft choices to San Diego for Steve Tensi, a promising young passer who learned as he played in Denver. Two fine wide receivers surfaced in Al Denson, last year's tight end, and Eric Crabtree, one of last year's bench warmers, while the running game improved immensely with the arrival of rookie halfback Floyd Little.

FINAL TEAM STATISTICS

OFFENSE

	BOSTON	BUFFALO	DENVER	HOUSTON	K.CITY	MIAMI	NEW YORK	OAKLAND	SAN DIEGO
FIRST DOWNS:									
Total	219	203	172	207	251	212	282	250	259
by Rushing	80	65	65	111	116	65	82	79	88
by Passing	120	119	91	86	117	123	180	154	150
by Penalty	19	19	16	10	18	24	20	17	21
RUSHING									
Number	391	371	420	476	462	326	389	458	417
Yards	1604	1271	1265	2122	2018	1323	1307	1928	1715
Average Yards	4.1	3.4	3.0	4.5	4.4	4.1	3.4	4.2	4.1
Touchdowns	10	9	10	12	18	10	17	19	14
PASSING:									
Attempts	434	434	374	332	382	480	515	464	463
Completions	191	183	150	143	213	229	271	236	230
Completion Percentage	44.0	42.2	40.1	43.1	55.8	47.7	52.6	50.9	49.7
Passing Yards	2784	2763	2190	1532	2773	2741	4128	3541	3517
Avg. Yards per Attempt	6.4	6.4	5.9	4.6	7.3	5.7	8.0	7.6	7.6
Avg. Yards per Completion	14.6	15.1	14.6	10.7	13.0	12.0	15.2	15.0	15.3
Time Tackled Att. to Pass	45	45	58	20	32	41	28	40	11
Yards Lost Tackled	361	446	508	151	301	405	283	353	107
Net Yards	2423	2317	1682	1381	2472	2336	3845	3188	3410
Touchdowns	20	14	17	11	26	16	27	33	26
Interceptions	32	34	18	20	19	28	29	23	24
Percent Intercepted	7.4	7.8	4.8	6.0	5.0	5.8	5.6	5.0	5.2
PUNTS:									
Number	65	77	105	71	61	70	65	76	63
Average Distance	40.5	43.1	44.9	42.6	41.3	41.6	42.1	44.3	37.5
PUNT RETURNS:									
Number	43	47	26	20	33	25	48	51	39
Yards	412	199	351	255	245	128	326	642	480
Average Yards	9.6	4.2	13.5	12.8	7.4	5.1	6.8	12.6	12.3
Touchdowns	0	0	1	0	0	0	0	0	0
KICKOFF RETURNS:									
Number	73	51	60	44	53	67	57	45	54
Yards	1436	1113	1518	1020	1245	1443	1144	962	1239
Average Yards	19.7	21.8	25.3	23.2	23.5	21.5	20.1	21.4	22.9
Touchdowns	0	0	0	1	1	0	0	0	0
INTERCEPTION RETURNS:									
Number	17	27	28	28	31	28	27	30	13
Yards	257	401	413	676	578	402	322	404	274
Average Yards	15.1	14.9	14.8	26.0	18.6	14.4	11.9	13.5	21.1
Touchdowns	2	3	3	6	4	1	1	4	2
PENALTIES:									
Number	59	74	48	61	68	53	64	71	72
Yards	520	828	512	698	680	490	691	768	817
FUMBLES:									
Number	37	32	30	17	28	36	15	19	18
Number Lost	22	13	12	7	8	16	8	13	10
POINTS:									
Total	280	237	256	258	408	219	371	468	360
PAT (kick) Attempts	31	26	30	30	45	28	40	57	45
PAT (kick) Made	30	25	28	30	45	27	36	56	45
PAT (2 Point) Attempts	2	1	1	1	4	0	6	1	0
PAT (2 Point) Made	0	1	1	0	2	0	4	1	0
FG Attempts	31	27	28	28	36	18	32	30	30
FG Made	16	16	12	14	21	8	17	20	15
Percent	51.6	59.3	42.9	50.0	58.3	44.4	53.1	66.7	50.0
Safeties	2	0	2	0	1	0	0	1	0

DEFENSE

	BOSTON	BUFFALO	DENVER	HOUSTON	K.CITY	MIAMI	NEW YORK	OAKLAND	SAN DIEGO
FIRST DOWNS:									
Total	219	201	276	233	221	269	203	182	251
by Rushing	61	73	115	86	73	115	80	60	88
by Passing	138	106	143	126	132	133	111	103	148
by Penalty	20	22	18	21	16	21	12	19	15
RUSHING									
Number	417	437	444	424	343	466	386	352	441
Yards	1350	1622	2076	1637	1408	2145	1633	1129	1553
Average Yards	3.2	3.7	4.7	3.9	4.1	4.6	4.2	3.2	3.5
Touchdowns	12	11	21	7	10	18	14	9	17
PASSING:									
Attempts	423	377	459	461	462	349	424	459	464
Completions	211	162	214	228	229	188	195	189	230
Completion Percentage	49.9	43.0	46.6	49.5	49.6	53.9	46.0	41.2	49.6
Passing Yards	3123	2191	3289	2619	2890	3082	2489	2831	3455
Avg. Yards per Attempt	7.4	5.8	7.2	5.7	6.3	8.8	5.9	6.2	7.5
Avg. Yards per Completion	14.8	13.5	15.4	11.5	12.6	16.4	12.8	15.0	15.0
Time Tackled Att. to Pass	31	43	18	25	38	28	39	67	31
Yards Lost Tackled	267	366	164	201	354	247	347	666	303
Net Yards	2856	1825	3125	2418	2536	2835	2142	2165	3152
Touchdowns	28	17	27	10	13	31	20	18	26
Interceptions	17	27	28	26	31	28	27	30	13
Percent Intercepted	4.0	7.2	6.1	5.6	6.7	8.0	6.4	6.5	2.8
PUNTS:									
Number	73	74	65	63	64	52	79	111	72
Average Distance	41.9	41.0	41.5	41.0	43.0	41.1	43.2	41.9	45.2
PUNT RETURNS:									
Number	31	33	61	41	31	41	36	37	21
Yards	252	301	718	383	331	268	311	250	224
Average Yards	8.1	9.1	11.8	9.3	10.7	6.5	8.6	6.8	10.7
Touchdowns	0	0	0	0	0	0	1	0	0
KICKOFF RETURNS:									
Number	45	56	42	51	55	46	64	82	63
Yards	946	1292	1046	950	1207	1079	1387	1707	1506
Average Yards	21.0	23.1	24.9	18.6	21.9	23.5	21.7	20.8	23.9
Touchdowns	0	0	1	0	1	0	0	0	0
INTERCEPTION RETURNS:									
Number	32	34	18	20	19	28	29	23	24
Yards	640	554	262	156	471	395	711	209	329
Average Yards	20.0	16.3	14.6	7.8	24.8	14.1	24.5	9.1	13.7
Touchdowns	7	2	2	1	5	3	5	0	1
PENALTIES:									
Number	70	51	58	59	76	59	67	69	61
Yards	722	507	628	614	757	691	717	702	666
FUMBLES:									
Number	26	26	23	29	34	19	24	29	22
Number Lost	17	9	13	13	18	8	6	15	10
POINTS:									
Total	389	285	409	199	254	407	329	233	352
PAT (kick) Attempts	46	33	50	14	28	50	40	27	44
PAT (kick) Made	44	32	48	14	28	47	39	26	44
PAT (2 Point) Attempts	2	0	2	4	2	3	1	2	0
PAT (2 Point) Made	0	0	2	3	1	0	1	2	0
FG Attempts	31	38	31	42	25	26	26	14	27
FG Made	19	17	15	23	14	14	14	9	14
Percent	61.3	44.7	48.4	54.8	56.0	53.8	53.8	64.3	51.9
Safeties	0	2	0	1	1	0	0	1	1

HOUSTON OILERS 9-4-1 Wally Lemm

Scores of Each Game		
20	KANSAS CITY	25
20	Buffalo	3
3	San Diego	13
10	DENVER	6
28	New York	28
24	Kansas City	19
10	BUFFALO	3
7	Boston	18
20	Denver	18
27	BOSTON	6
17	MIAMI	14
7	OAKLAND	19
24	SAN DIEGO	17
41	Miami	10

Use Name	Pos.	Hgt	Wgt	Age	Int	Pts
Glen Ray Hines	OT	6'5"	270	23		
Walt Suggs	OT	6'5"	265	28		
Sonny Bishop	OG	6'2"	245	27		
Ed Marcontell (from StL-N)	OG	6'	260	23		
Tom Regner	OG	6'1"	255	23		
Bob Talamini	OG	6'1"	255	28		
Bobby Maples	C	6'3"	245	24		
Don Floyd	DE	6'4"	245	28		
Pat Holmes	DE	6'5"	260	27		
Willie Jones	DE	6'2"	260	25		
Carel Stith	DE	6'5"	270	22		
Bud Marshall	DT	6'5"	270	25		
Willie Parker	DT	6'2"	270	22		
Andy Rice (from KC)	DT	6'3"	266	25		
George Rice	DT	6'3"	260	23		
Pete Barnes	LB	6'3"	245	22		
Garland Boyette	LB	6'1"	240	27		
Danny Brabham	LB	6'4"	233	26		
Ronnie Caveness	LB	6'1"	225	24		
Olen Underwood	LB	6'1"	230	25	1	
George Webster	LB	6'4"	223	21	1	
Larry Carwell	DB	6'1"	187	23		
Miller Farr	DB	6'1"	188	24	10	18
W. K. Hicks	DB	6'1"	190	24	3	
Ken Houston	DB	6'3"	190	22	4	18
Bobby Jancik	DB	5'11"	178	27	1	
Pete Johns	DB	6'3"	188	22		
Zeke Moore	DB	6'2"	190	23		6
Jim Norton	DB	6'3"	180	28	6	6
Billy Anderson	QB	6'1"	195	26		
Pete Beathard (from KC)	QB	6'2"	210	25		6
Bob Davis	QB	6'3"	202	21		
Jacky Lee (to KC)	QB	6'1"	188	28		
Sid Blanks	HB	6'	208	26		12
Woody Campbell	HB	5'11"	205	22		36
Hoyle Granger	FB	6'1"	225	23		54
Roy Hopkins	FB	6'1"	227	22		
Glenn Bass	FL	6'2"	206	28		6
Ode Burrell	FL	6'	195	27		
Larry Elkins	FL	6'1"	195	24		
Bob Poole	TE	6'4"	215	25		
Alvin Reed	TE	6'5"	228	23		6
Charley Frazier	OE	6'	188	28		6
Lionel Taylor	OE	6'2"	215	31		6
John Wittenborn	K	6'2"	240	31		72

Gary Cutsinger – Back Injury

NEW YORK JETS 8-5-1 Weeb Ewbank

Scores of Each Game		
17	Buffalo	20
38	Denver	24
29	MIAMI	7
27	OAKLAND	14
28	HOUSTON	28
33	Miami	14
30	BOSTON	23
18	Kansas City	42
20	BUFFALO	10
29	Boston	24
24	DENVER	33
7	KANSAS CITY	21
29	Oakland	38
42	San Diego	31

Use Name	Pos.	Hgt	Wgt	Age	Int	Pts
Winston Hill	OT	6'4"	275	25		
Sherman Plunkett	OT	6'4"	330	33		
Jim Harris	OT	6'4"	280	23		
Paul Seiler	OG-OT	6'4"	255	21		
Dave Herman	OG	6'2"	255	25		
Pete Perreault	OG	6'3"	245	28		
Randy Rasmussen	OG	6'2"	255	22		
Jeff Richardson	OG	6'3"	260	22		
John Matlock	C	6'4"	246	22		
John Schmitt	C	6'4"	245	24		
Verlon Biggs	DE	6'4"	260	24		
Gerry Philbin	DE	6'2"	248	26		
Bert Wilder	DT-DE	6'3"	245	27		
Dennis Randall	DT	6'6"	245	21		
Paul Rochester	DT	6'2"	255	30		
John Elliott	LB-DE-DT	6'4"	245	22		
Al Atkinson	LB	6'1"	228	24	5	
Ralph Baker	LB	6'3"	228	25	1	
Paul Crane	LB	6'2"	205	23		
Larry Grantham	LB	6'	206	28	5	
Carl McAdams	LB	6'3"	240	23		
Jim Waskiewicz	OT-LB	6'4"	235	23		
Bill Baird	DB	5'10"	180	28	3	
Randy Beverly	DB	5'11"	185	23	4	
Solomon Brannan	DB	6'1"	185	25		
Cornell Gordon	DB	6'	187	26	1	
Jim Hudson	DB	6'2"	210	24	4	
Henry King	DB	6'4"	205	22		
Sherman Lewis	DB	5'10"	180	25		
Bill Rademacher	DB	6'1"	190	25		
Johnny Sample	DB	6'1"	208	30	4	6
Joe Namath	QB	6'2"	195	24		6
Mike Taliaferro	QB	6'2"	205	25		
Jim Turner	QB	6'2"	205	26		87
Emerson Boozer	HB	5'11"	207	24		78
Earl Christy	HB	5'11"	195	24		
Bill Mathis	HB	6'1"	220	28		46
Billy Joe	FB	6'2"	236	26		12
Mark Smolinski	FB	6'	215	28		24
Matt Snell	FB	6'2"	220	25		
Don Maynard	FL	6'	180	31		62
Bob Schweickert	FL	6'1"	190	24		
Curley Johnson	TE	6'	215	32		
Pete Lammons	TE	6'3"	228	23		12
George Sauer	OE	6'1"	195	23		38
Bake Turner	OE	6'	180	27		

BUFFALO BILLS 4-10-0 Joe Collier

Scores of Each Game		
20	NEW YORK	17
3	HOUSTON	20
0	BOSTON	23
17	SAN DIEGO	37
17	Denver	16
20	OAKLAND	24
3	Houston	10
35	MIAMI	13
10	New York	20
20	DENVER	21
14	Miami	17
13	Kansas City	23
44	Boston	16
21	Oakland	28

Use Name	Pos.	Hgt	Wgt	Age	Int	Pts
Stew Barber	OT	6'3"	252	28		
Dick Cunningham	OT	6'2"	242	22		
Dick Hudson	OT	6'4"	265	27		
Gary Bugenhagen	OG	6'2"	248	22		
Joe O'Donnell	OG	6'2"	252	25		
Billy Shaw	OG	6'3"	258	27		
Al Bemiller	C	6'3"	246	28		
Bob Schmidt	C	6'4"	250	31		
Ron McDole	DE	6'4"	270	27	1	
Bob Petrich	DE	6'4"	250	26		
Remi Prudhomme	DE	6'4"	263	25		
Jim Dunaway	DT	6'4"	280	25	1	
Dudley Meredith	DT	6'4"	285	32	1	
Tom Sestak	DT	6'5"	260	31		6
Paul Guidry	LB	6'3"	234	23		
Harry Jacobs	LB	6'2"	244	30		
Jim LeMoine	LB	6'2"	245	22		
Paul Maguire	LB	6'	230	29		
Marty Schottenheimer	LB	6'3"	225	24	3	6
Mike Stratton	LB	6'3"	244	25	1	
John Tracey	TE-LB	6'3"	228	33	1	
Butch Byrd	DB	6'	208	25	5	
Hagood Clarke	DB	6'	195	25		
Booker Edgerson	DB	5'10"	183	28	2	
Tom Janik	DB	6'3"	190	26	10	12
Charlie King	DB	6'	185	24		
John Pitts	DB	6'4"	218	22		
George Saimes	DB	5'10"	188	25	2	
Tom Flores	QB	6'1"	200	30		
Jack Kemp	QB	6'1"	204	33		14
Teddy Bailey	HB	6'	220	23		
Charlie Bivins (from PIT-N)	HB	6'2"	212	28		
Bobby Burnett	HB	6'2"	208	24		
Gene Donaldson	HB	6'2"	225	25		
Allen Smith	HB	6'	200	24		
Keith Lincoln	FB-HB	6'2"	216	28		54
Jack Spikes	FB	6'2"	220	29		
Wray Carlton	HB-FB	6'2"	224	29		18
Elbert Dubenion	FL	6'	187	32		
Tony King	FL	6'1"	194	23		
Monte Ledbetter (from HOU)	FL	6'2"	185	24		12
Ed Rutkowski	FL	6'1"	198	26		
Paul Costa	TE	6'4"	246	25		12
Bill Masters	TE	6'5"	235	23		12
Art Powell	OE	6'3"	214	30		24
Mike Mercer	K	6'	217	31		73

Bobby Crockett – Knee Injury

Charley Ferguson – Injury
George Flint – Injury

MIAMI DOLPHINS 4-10-0 George Wilson

Scores of Each Game		
35	DENVER	21
0	KANSAS CITY	24
7	New York	29
0	Kansas City	41
10	Boston	41
14	NEW YORK	33
13	Buffalo	35
0	San Diego	24
17	Oakland	31
17	BUFFALO	14
14	Houston	17
41	SAN DIEGO	24
41	BOSTON	32
10	HOUSTON	41

Use Name	Pos.	Hgt	Wgt	Age	Int	Pts
Norm Evans	OT	6'5"	250	24		
Jack Pyburn	OT	6'6"	240	22		
Charlie Fowler	OG-OT	6'2"	260	23		
Billy Neighbors	OG	5'11"	250	27		
Ken Rice	OG	6'2"	240	27		
Freddie Woodson	OG	6'2"	250	23		
Maxie Williams	OT-OG	6'4"	250	27		
Tom Goode	C	6'3"	245	28		
Mel Branch	DE	6'2"	235	30		
Ed Cooke	DE	6'4"	250	32		
Jim Riley	DE	6'4"	240	22		
Claude Brownlee	DT	6'4"	265	23		
Ray Jacobs	DT	6'3"	285	27		
Tom Nomina	DT	6'5"	260	25		
John Richardson	DT	6'2"	250	22		
Rich Zecher (to BUF)	DT	6'2"	240	24		
John Bramlett	LB	6'2"	220	26	4	
Bob Bruggers	LB	6'1"	225	23	1	
Frank Emanuel	LB	6'3"	225	24	1	
Tom Erlandson	LB	6'3"	220	27	1	
Jerry Hopkins	LB	6'2"	235	26		
Wahoo McDaniel	LB	6'	230	30	1	
Pete Jaquess (to DEN)	DB	6'	184	25		
Mack Lamb	DB	6'1"	188	23		
Bob Neff	DB	6'	180	23	1	
Bob Petrella	DB	6'	185	22	3	
Jimmy Warren	DB	5'11"	175	28	4	6
Willie West	DB	5'10"	187	29	1	
Dick Westmoreland	DB	6'1"	190	26	10	6
Tom Beier	FL-DB	5'11"	198	22	1	
Bob Griese	QB	6'1"	190	22		6
Rick Norton	QB	6'1"	190	23		
Archie Roberts	QB	6'	193	24		
John Stofa	QB	6'3"	210	25		6
Joe Auer	HB	6'1"	205	25		18
Jack Harper	HB	5'11"	190	22		24
Abner Haynes (to NY)	HB	6'	190	29		12
Larry Seiple	HB	6'	200	22		
George Chesser	FB	6'2"	220	24		
Stan Mitchell	FB	6'2"	220	23		24
Sam Price	HB-FB	5'11"	215	23		12
Jack Clancy	FL	6'1"	195	23		12
Frank Jackson	FL	6'1"	185	27		6
John Roderick	FL	6'1"	180	23		
Preston Carpenter	TE	6'2"	208	33		
Doug Moreau	TE	6'2"	205	22		18
Karl Noonan	OE	6'3"	190	23		6
Howard Twilley	OE	5'10"	180	23		12
Booth Lusteg	K	5'11"	190	26		39
Gene Mingo (to WAS-N)	K	6'1"	190	28		12

BOSTON PATRIOTS 3-10-1 Mike Holovak

Scores of Each Game		
21	Denver	26
14	San Diego	28
7	Oakland	35
23	Buffalo	0
31	SAN DIEGO	31
41	MIAMI	10
14	OAKLAND	48
23	New York	30
18	HOUSTON	7
10	KANSAS CITY	33
24	NEW YORK	29
6	Houston	27
16	BUFFALO	44
32	Miami	41

Use Name	Pos.	Hgt	Wgt	Age	Int	Pts
Jim Boudreaux	OT	6'4"	245	22		
Tom Neville	OT	6'4"	255	24		
Don Oakes	OT	6'3"	255	29		
Karl Singer	OT	6'3"	250	23		
Justin Canale	OG	6'2"	250	23		1
Charley Long	OG	6'3"	250	29		
Len St. Jean	OG	6'1"	240	25		
Jon Morris	C	6'4"	240	24		
Bob Dee	DE	6'3"	250	34		
Larry Eisenhauer	DE	6'5"	255	27		
Tom Fussell	DE	6'3"	245	21		
Houston Antwine	DT	6'	270	28		
Jim Hunt	DT	5'11"	255	28		2
John Mangum	DT	6'3"	270	23		
Mel Witt	DT	6'3"	265	21		
Ed Toner	LB-DT	6'3"	250	22		
Tom Addison	LB	6'3"	230	31		
Nick Buoniconti	LB	5'11"	220	26	4	2
Ray Ilg	LB	6'1"	220	21		
Ed Philpott	LB	6'3"	240	21		
Doug Satcher	LB	6'	220	22		
John Charles	DB	6'1"	200	23	1	6
Jay Cunningham	DB	5'10"	180	24	1	6
White Graves	DB	6'	185	24		
Ron Hall	DB	6'	190	30	1	
Billy Johnson	DB	5'11"	175	24		
Leroy Mitchell	DB	6'2"	200	22	3	
Vic Purvis	DB	5'11"	200	23		
Chuck Shonta	DB	6'	200	29	3	
Don Webb	DB	5'10"	200	28	4	
John Huarte	QB	6'	190	23		
Babe Parilli	QB	6'1"	190	37		
Don Trull (from HOU)	QB	6'1"	190	25		18
Joe Bellino	HB	5'9"	185	29		
J. D. Garrett	HB	5'11"	195	25		6
Larry Garron	HB	6'1"	195	30		30
Bobby Leo	HB	5'10"	180	22		6
Jim Nance	FB	6'1"	240	24		48
Bob Cappadona	FB	6'1"	230	23		6
Gino Cappelletti	FL	6'	190	33		95
Bobby Nichols	TE	6'2"	220	23		
Tony Romeo	TE	6'2"	230	28		
Jim Whalen	TE	6'2"	210	23		30
Jim Colclough	OE	6'	185	31		
Art Graham	OE	6'1"	205	26		24
Terry Swanson	K	6'	210	22		

HOUSTON OILERS

RUSHING

Last Name	No.	Yds	Avg	TD
Granger	236	1194	5.1	6
Campbell	110	511	4.6	4
Blanks	66	206	3.1	1
Beathard	32	133	4.2	1
Hopkins	13	42	3.2	0
Davis	5	32	6.4	0
Elkins	2	19	9.5	0
Lee	6	−3	−0.5	0
Burrell	3	−3	−1.0	0
Norton	1	−7	−7.0	0

RECEIVING

Last Name	No.	Yds	Avg	TD
Granger	31	300	10	3
Frazier	23	253	11	1
Taylor	18	233	13	1
Campbell	17	136	8	2
Burrell	12	193	16	0
Reed	11	144	13	1
Blanks	11	93	8	1
Bass	5	42	8	1
Poole	4	55	14	0
Elkins	3	32	11	0
Hopkins	3	9	3	0
Lee	1	−1	−1	0

PUNT RETURNS

Last Name	No.	Yds	Avg	TD
Carwell	9	154	17	0
Moore	5	82	16	0
Jancik	6	19	3	0

KICKOFF RETURNS

Last Name	No.	Yds	Avg	TD
Moore	14	405	**29**	**1**
Jancik	16	349	22	0
Carwell	8	164	21	0
Houston	2	40	20	0
Hopkins	1	26	26	0
Campbell	1	19	19	0
Farr	1	17	17	0
Reed	1	0	0	0

PASSING – PUNTING – KICKING

PASSING	Att	Comp	%	Yds	Yd/Att	TD	Int–%	RK
Beathard	231	94	41	1114	4.8	9	14– 6	9
Lee	91	42	46	414	4.6	3	6– 7	
Davis	19	9	47	71	3.7	0	2–11	
Campbell	1	0	0	0	0.0	0	0– 0	

PUNTING	No	Avg
Norton	71	42.6

KICKING	XP	Att	%	FG	Att	%
Wittenborn	30	30	100	14	28	50

NEW YORK JETS

RUSHING

Last Name	No.	Yds	Avg	TD
Boozer	119	442	3.7	**10**
Mathis	78	243	3.1	4
Snell	61	207	3.4	0
Joe	37	154	4.2	2
Smolinski	64	139	2.2	1
Taliaferro	2	20	10.0	0
Maynard	4	18	4.5	0
Namath	6	14	2.3	0
Schweickert	1	1	1.0	0
Sauer	1	−3	−3.0	0

RECEIVING

Last Name	No.	Yds	Avg	TD
Sauer	**75**	1189	16	6
Maynard	71	**1434**	**20**	10
Lammons	45	515	11	2
Mathis	25	429	17	3
Smolinski	21	177	8	3
Boozer	12	205	17	3
Snell	11	54	5	0
Joe	8	85	11	0
B. Turner	3	40	13	0

PUNT RETURNS

Last Name	No.	Yds	Avg	TD
Baird	25	219	9	0
Christy	16	83	5	0
Lewis	7	24	3	0

KICKOFF RETURNS

Last Name	No.	Yds	Avg	TD
Christy	23	521	23	0
Boozer	11	213	19	0
Brannan	9	204	23	0
B. Turner	4	40	10	0
Lewis	1	22	22	0
McAdams	1	16	16	0
Smolinski	1	3	3	0
Waskiewicz	2	0	0	0
Wilder	1	0	0	0

PASSING – PUNTING – KICKING

PASSING	Att	Comp	%	Yds	Yd/Att	TD	Int–%	RK
Namath	**491**	**258**	53	**4007**	**8.2**	26	28– 6	3
Taliaferro	20	11	55	96	4.8	1	1– 5	
J. Turner	4	2	50	25	6.3	0	0– 0	

PUNTING	No	Avg
Johnson	65	42.1

KICKING	XP	Att	%	FG	Att	%
J. Turner	36	39	92	17	32	53

2 POINT XP
Mathis (2)
Maynard
Sauer

BUFFALO BILLS

RUSHING

Last Name	No.	Yds	Avg	TD
Lincoln	159	601	3.8	4
Carlton	107	467	4.4	3
Burnett	45	96	2.1	0
Bivins	15	58	3.9	0
Kemp	36	58	1.6	2
Spikes	4	9	2.3	0
Donaldson	3	−1	−0.3	0
Dubenion	2	−17	−8.5	0

RECEIVING

Last Name	No.	Yds	Avg	TD
Lincoln	41	558	14	5
Costa	39	726	19	2
Dubenion	25	384	15	0
Powell	20	346	17	4
Masters	20	274	14	2
Ledbetter	13	204	16	2
Burnett	11	114	10	0
Carlton	9	97	11	0
Rutkowski	6	59	10	0
Donaldson	1	20	20	0
Tracey	1	15	15	0
Spikes	1	9	9	0

PUNT RETURNS

Last Name	No.	Yds	Avg	TD
Byrd	30	142	5	0
Rutkowski	15	43	3	0
C. King	1	12	12	0
Edgerson	1	2	2	0

KICKOFF RETURNS

Last Name	No.	Yds	Avg	TD
Bivins	16	380	24	0
Smith	16	346	22	0
C. King	12	316	26	0
Rutkowski	3	71	24	0
Meredith	3	0	0	0
Guidry	1	0	0	0

PASSING – PUNTING – KICKING

PASSING	Att	Comp	%	Yds	Yd/Att	TD	Int–%	RK
Kemp	369	161	44	2503	6.8	14	26– 7	8
Flores	64	22	34	260	4.1	0	8–13	
Rutkowski	1	0	0	0	0.0	0	0– 0	

PUNTING	No	Avg
Maguire	77	43.1

KICKING	XP	Att	%	FG	Att	%
Mercer	25	25	100	16	27	59

2 POINT XP
Kemp

MIAMI DOLPHINS

RUSHING

Last Name	No.	Yds	Avg	TD
Haynes	72	346	4.8	2
Mitchell	83	269	3.2	3
Harper	41	197	4.8	1
Price	46	179	3.9	1
Griese	37	157	4.2	1
Auer	44	128	2.9	1
Seiple	3	58	19.3	0
Jackson	1	48	48.0	0
Norton	7	14	2.0	0
Chesser	2	3	1.5	0
Stofa	2	2	1.0	1
Moreau	1	−2	−2.0	0
Clancy	3	−4	−1.3	0

RECEIVING

Last Name	No.	Yds	Avg	TD
Clancy	67	868	13	2
Moreau	34	410	12	3
Twilley	24	314	13	2
Auer	18	218	12	2
Mitchell	18	133	7	1
Haynes	16	100	6	0
Noonan	12	141	12	1
Harper	11	212	19	3
Carpenter	10	127	13	0
Jackson	9	122	14	1
Price	8	56	7	1
Seiple	1	21	21	0
Beier	1	19	19	0

PUNT RETURNS

Last Name	No.	Yds	Avg	TD
Auer	9	42	5	0
Haynes	6	37	6	0
Neff	6	34	6	0
Harper	4	15	4	0

KICKOFF RETURNS

Last Name	No.	Yds	Avg	TD
Haynes	26	569	22	0
Auer	21	441	21	0
Neff	15	351	23	0
Carpenter	3	87	29	0
Roderick	4	63	16	0
Mitchell	2	57	29	0

PASSING – PUNTING – KICKING

PASSING	Att	Comp	%	Yds	Yd/Att	TD	Int–%	RK
Griese	331	166	50	2005	6.1	15	18– 5	5
Norton	133	53	40	596	4.5	1	9– 7	
Roberts	10	5	50	11	1.1	0	1–10	
Seiple	2	2	100	61	30.5	0	0– 0	
Stofa	2	2	100	51	25.5	0	0– 0	
Clancy	1	1	100	17	17.0	0	0– 0	
Lusteg	1	0	0	0	0.0	0	0– 0	

PUNTING	No	Avg
Seiple	70	41.6

KICKING	XP	Att	%	FG	Att	%
Lusteg	18	18	100	7	12	58
Mingo	9	9	100	1	6	17

BOSTON PATRIOTS

RUSHING

Last Name	No.	Yds	Avg	TD
Nance	**269**	**1216**	4.5	7
Garron	46	163	3.5	0
Cappadona	28	100	3.6	0
Parilli	14	61	4.4	0
Trull	22	30	1.4	3
Bellino	6	15	2.5	0
Garrett	5	7	1.4	0
Leo	1	7	7.0	0
Huarte	2	5	2.5	0
Graham	1	−5	−5.0	0

RECEIVING

Last Name	No.	Yds	Avg	TD
Graham	41	606	15	4
Whalen	39	651	17	5
Cappelletti	35	397	11	3
Garron	30	507	17	5
Nance	22	196	9	1
Colclough	14	263	19	0
Cappadona	6	104	17	1
Leo	1	25	25	1
Nichols	1	19	19	0
Garrett	1	12	12	0
Romeo	1	4	4	0

PUNT RETURNS

Last Name	No.	Yds	Avg	TD
Bellino	15	129	9	0
Johnson	6	124	21	0
Cunningham	17	105	6	0
Leo	5	54	11	0

KICKOFF RETURNS

Last Name	No.	Yds	Avg	TD
Cunningham	30	627	21	0
Bellino	18	357	20	0
Leo	11	232	21	0
Garrett	4	73	18	0
Garron	3	73	24	0
Singer	2	29	15	0
Cappadona	3	26	9	0
Ilg	1	10	10	0
Johnson	1	9	9	0

PASSING – PUNTING – KICKING

PASSING	Att	Comp	%	Yds	Yd/Att	TD	Int–%	RK
Parilli	344	161	47	2317	6.7	19	24– 7	6
Trull	92	31	34	480	5.2	1	7– 8	
Huarte	9	3	33	25	2.8	0	1–11	

PUNTING	No	Avg
Swanson	65	40.5

KICKING	XP	Att	%	FG	Att	%
Cappelletti	29	30	97	16	31	52
Canale	1	1	100	0	0	0

OAKLAND RAIDERS 13-1-0 Johnny Rauch

Scores of Each Game		
51	DENVER	0
35	BOSTON	7
23	KANSAS CITY	21
14	New York	27
24	Buffalo	20
48	Boston	14
51	SAN DIEGO	10
21	Denver	17
31	MIAMI	17
44	Kansas City	22
41	San Diego	21
19	Houston	7
38	NEW YORK	29
28	BUFFALO	21

Use Name	Pos.	Hgt	Wgt	Age	Int	Pts
Harry Schuh	OT	6'2"	260	24		
Bob Svihus	OT	6'4"	245	24		
Dan Archer	OG-OT	6'5"	245	22		
Jim Harvey	OG	6'5"	245	24		
Wayne Hawkins	OG	6'	240	29		
Bob Kruse	OG	6'2"	250	25		
Gene Upshaw	OT-OG	6'5"	255	22		
Jim Otto	C	6'2"	240	29		
Ben Davidson	DE	6'8"	265	27		
Ike Lassiter	DE	6'5"	270	26		
Carleton Oats	DE	6'2"	235	24		6
Dan Birdwell	DT	6'4"	250	26	1	2
Tom Keating	DT	6'3"	247	24		
Richard Sligh	DT	7'	300	22		
Duane Benson	LB	6'2"	215	22		
Bill Budness	LB	6'1"	215	24		
Dan Conners	LB	6'1"	230	25	3	12
Bill Fairband	LB	6'3"	228	21		
Bill Laskey	LB	6'2"	235	24		
Gus Otto	LB	6'2"	220	24	1	
J. R. Williamson	LB	6'2"	220	25	2	
Rodger Bird	DB	5'11"	195	24		
Willie Brown	DB	6'1"	190	26	7	6
Dave Grayson	DB	5'10"	185	28	4	
Kent McCloughan	DB	6'1"	190	24	2	
Warren Powers	DB	6'	190	26	6	12
Howie Williams	DB	6'2"	186	30	4	
George Blanda	QB	6'1"	215	39		116
Daryle Lamonica	QB	6'2"	215	26		24
Pete Banaszak	HB	5'11"	200	23		12
Estes Banks	HB	6'1"	200	22		
Clem Daniels	HB	6'1"	218	30		36
Larry Todd	HB	6'1"	185	24		12
Roger Hagberg	FB	6'2"	215	28		18
Hewritt Dixon	HB-FB	6'2"	220	27		42
Fred Biletnikoff	FL	6'1"	190	24		30
Rod Sherman	FL	6'	190	22		6
Billy Cannon	TE	6'1"	215	30		60
Dave Kocourek	TE	6'5"	240	30		2
Ken Herock	OE	6'2"	230	26		
Bill Miller	OE	6'	190	25		36
Warren Wells	OE	6'1"	190	24		36
Mike Eischeid	K	6'	190	26		

Charley Warner – Injury

KANSAS CITY CHIEFS 9-5-0 Hank Stram

Scores of Each Game		
25	Houston	20
24	Miami	0
21	Oakland	23
41	MIAMI	0
31	San Diego	45
19	HOUSTON	24
52	DENVER	9
42	NEW YORK	18
33	Boston	10
16	SAN DIEGO	17
22	OAKLAND	44
23	BUFFALO	13
21	New York	7
38	Denver	24

Use Name	Pos.	Hgt	Wgt	Age	Int	Pts
Dave Hill	OT	6'5"	260	26		
Bob Kelly	OT	6'3"	265	27		
Jim Tyrer	OT	6'6"	292	28		
Tony DiMidio	C-OT	6'3"	250	25		
Denny Biodrowski	OG	6'1"	255	27		
Ed Budde	OG	6'5"	260	26		
Curt Merz	OG	6'4"	267	29		
Al Reynolds	OG	6'3"	250	29		
Wayne Frazier (to BUF)	C	6'2"	245	27		
Jon Gilliam	C	6'2"	240	28		
Mike Hudock	C	6'2"	245	32		
Jerry Mays	DE	6'4"	252	27		
Gene Trosch	DT-DE	6'7"	277	22		
Buck Buchanan	DT	6'7"	287	27		
Ernie Ladd (from HOU)	DT	6'9"	292	28		
Ed Lothamer	DE-DT	6'5"	260	24		
Bud Abell	LB	6'3"	220	26		
Bobby Bell	LB	6'4"	228	27	4	6
Sherrill Headrick	LB	6'2"	240	30	1	
Chuck Hurston	LB	6'6"	240	24		
Willie Lanier	LB	6'1"	245	22		
Jim Lynch	LB	6'1"	235	22	1	
E. J. Holub	C-LB	6'4"	236	29		
Bobby Hunt	DB	6'1"	193	27	5	
Jim Kearney	DB	6'2"	206	24		
Sam Longmire	DB	6'3"	195	24		
Willie Mitchell	DB	6'1"	185	25	4	6
Johnny Robinson	DB	6'	205	28	5	
Fletcher Smith	DB	6'2"	188	23	6	
Emmitt Thomas	DB	6'2"	192	24	4	6
Fred Williamson	DB	6'2"	210	29	1	6
Len Dawson	QB	6'	190	33		
Bert Coan	HB	6'4"	220	27		24
Mike Garrett	HB	5'9"	200	23		60
Gene Thomas	HB	6'1"	210	24		18
Curtis McClinton	FB	6'3"	227	29		20
Jerrel Wilson	FB	6'4"	222	25		
Gloster Richardson	FL	6'	200	24		12
Noland Smith	FL	5'6"	154	23		6
Otis Taylor	FL	6'2"	215	24		72
Fred Arbanas	TE	6'3"	240	28		30
Reg Carolan	TE	6'6"	240	27		2
Chris Burford	OE	6'3"	210	29		18
Frank Pitts	OE	6'2"	200	23		12
Jan Stenerud	K	6'2"	187	24		108
Wayne Walker	K	6'2"	215	22		

Aaron Brown – Thigh Injury

SAN DIEGO CHARGERS 8-5-1 Sid Gillman

Scores of Each Game		
28	BOSTON	14
13	HOUSTON	3
37	Buffalo	17
31	Boston	31
45	KANSAS CITY	31
38	Denver	21
10	Oakland	51
24	MIAMI	0
17	Kansas City	16
24	DENVER	20
21	OAKLAND	41
24	Miami	41
17	Houston	24
31	NEW YORK	42

Use Name	Pos.	Hgt	Wgt	Age	Int	Pts
Harold Akin	OT	6'5"	262	22		
Gary Kirner	OT	6'3"	248	25		
Ron Mix	OT	6'4"	250	29		
Terry Owens	OT	6'6"	240	23		
Ernie Wright	OT	6'4"	265	27		
Ed Mitchell	OG	6'2"	280	25		
Walt Sweeney	OG	6'3"	255	26		
Larry Little	DT-OG	6'1"	265	21		
Sam Gruineisen	C	6'1"	240	26		
Paul Latzke	C	6'4"	240	25		
Tom Day	DE	6'2"	262	32		
Jim Griffin	DE	6'3"	255	25		
Howard Kindig (to BUF)	DE	6'6"	255	26		
Scott Appleton	DT	6'3"	256	25		6
Ron Billingsley	DT	6'8"	265	22		
Steve DeLong	DT	6'3"	252	24		
George Gross	DT	6'3"	258	26		
Houston Ridge	DT	6'4"	235	23		
Chuck Allen	LB	6'1"	225	27	2	
Johnny Baker	LB	6'3"	238	26		
Frank Buncom	LB	6'1"	240	27		
Bernie Erickson	LB	6'2"	238	22	1	
Ron McCall	LB	6'2"	245	22		
Bob Print	LB	6'	220	23		
Rick Redman	LB	5'11"	225	24	2	
Jeff Staggs	LB	6'2"	248	23		
Joe Beauchamp	DB	6'	185	23	3	
Speedy Duncan	DB	5'10"	175	24	2	18
Kenny Graham	DB	6'	195	25	2	6
Bob Howard	DB	6'1"	190	22		
Frank Marsh	DB	6'2"	205	26		
Jim Tolbert	DB	6'3"	207	23	1	
Bud Whitehead	HB-DB	6'	185	28		
John Hadl	QB	6'2"	215	27		18
Kay Stephenson	QB	6'1"	205	22		
Gene Foster	HB	5'11"	212	24		
Paul Lowe	HB	6'	205	30		6
Dickie Post	HB	5'9"	190	21		48
Jim Allison	FB	6'	220	24		
Brad Hubbert	FB	6'1"	227	26		24
Russ Smith	HB-FB	6'1"	225	23		6
Lance Alworth	FL	6'	180	27		54
Willie Frazier	TE	6'4"	225	24		60
Jacque MacKinnon	TE	6'4"	250	28		12
Ollie Cordill	OE	6'2"	180	24		
Gary Garrison	OE	6'1"	195	23		12
Steve Newell	OE	6'1"	186	22		
Dick Van Raaphorst	K	5'11"	215	24		90

Nat Whitmyer – Injury

DENVER BRONCOS 3-11-0 Lou Saban

Scores of Each Game		
26	BOSTON	21
0	Oakland	51
21	Miami	35
24	NEW YORK	38
6	Houston	10
16	BUFFALO	17
21	SAN DIEGO	38
9	Kansas City	52
17	OAKLAND	21
18	HOUSTON	20
21	Buffalo	20
20	San Diego	24
33	New York	24
24	KANSAS CITY	38

Use Name	Pos.	Hgt	Wgt	Age	Int	Pts
Dave Behrman	OT	6'5"	260	25		
Bob Breitenstein (to MIN-N)	OT	6'3"	267	24		
Sam Brunelli	OT	6'1"	255	24		
Tom Cichowski	OT	6'4"	250	22		
Mike Current (from MIA)	OT	6'4"	250	21		
Pat Matson	OG	6'1"	250	23		
Ernie Park	OG	6'3"	240	25		
Don Smith	OG	6'4"	240	24		
Dick Tyson	OG	6'2"	245	23		
Bob Young	OG	6'2"	260	24		
George Goeddeke	C-OG	6'3"	240	22		
Larry Kaminski	C	6'2"	240	22		
Ray Kubala	C	6'4"	245	25		
Roger LeClerc	C	6'3"	245	29		5
Pete Duranko	DE	6'2"	240	23		
Rich Jackson	DE	6'2"	255	26		2
Rex Mirich	DE	6'4"	250	26		
Dave Costa	DT	6'2"	265	25		
Larry Cox	DT	6'2"	250	23		
Jerry Inman	DT	6'3"	255	27		
Bill Keating (to MIA)	DT	6'2"	236	22		
Lou Andrus	LB	6'6"	255	24		
Carl Cunningham	LB	6'3"	240	23	1	
John Huard	LB	6'	220	23	2	
Gene Jeter	LB	6'3"	230	25		
Chip Myrtle	LB	6'2"	215	22	1	
Frank Richter	LB	6'3"	230	22	2	
Henry Sorrell	LB	6'1"	215	23		
Jack Lentz	DB	6'	195	22	4	
Bobby Ply (from KC-BUF)	DB	6'1"	190	26		
Errol Prisby	DB	5'10"	184	24		
Goldie Sellers	DB	6'2"	198	25	7	6
Jim Summers	DB	5'10"	175	21		
Gene Sykes	DB	6'1"	195	26	2	
Nemiah Wilson	DB	6'	165	24	4	12
Lonnie Wright	DB	6'2"	205	23	4	
Tom Cassese	HB-DB	6'1"	197	21	1	
Scotty Glacken	QB	6'	190	22		
Jim LeClair	QB	6'1"	208	23		6
Steve Tensi	QB	6'5"	215	24		
Floyd Little	HB	5'10"	195	25		12
Fran Lynch	HB	6'1"	210	21		
Charley Mitchell	HB	5'11"	185	27		
Cookie Gilchrist	FB	6'3"	250	32		
Wendell Hayes	FB	6'2"	220	26		26
Bo Hickey	FB	5'11"	225	21		30
Mike Kellogg	FB	6'	220	24		
Al Denson	FL	6'2"	208	25		66
Bob Scarpitto	FL	5'11"	196	28		
Tom Beer	TE	6'4"	235	22		
Andre White	TE	6'5"	225	22		2
Eric Crabtree	OE	5'11"	182	22		30
Neal Sweeney	OE	6'2"	170	22		
Rick Duncan	K	6'	208	26		9
Dick Humphreys	K	6'1"	240	27		39
Gary Kroner	K	6'1"	200	26		11

Max Leetzow – Injury

OAKLAND RAIDERS

RUSHING

Last Name	No.	Yds	Avg	TD
Daniels	130	575	4.4	4
Dixon	153	559	3.7	5
Banaszak	68	376	5.5	1
Hagberg	44	146	3.3	2
Todd	29	116	4.0	2
Lamonica	22	110	5.0	4
Banks	10	26	2.6	0
Sherman	1	13	13.0	1
Wells	1	7	7.0	0

RECEIVING

Last Name	No.	Yds	Avg	TD
Dixon	59	563	10	2
Biletnikoff	40	876	22	5
Miller	38	537	14	6
Cannon	32	629	20	10
Daniels	16	222	14	2
Banaszak	16	192	12	1
Wells	13	302	23	6
Hagberg	11	114	10	1
Sherman	5	61	12	0
Todd	4	42	11	0
Kocourek	1	4	4	0
Herock	1	−1	−1	0

PUNT RETURNS

Last Name	No.	Yds	Avg	TD
Bird	46	612	13	0
Powers	2	19	10	0
Grayson	3	11	4	0

KICKOFF RETURNS

Last Name	No.	Yds	Avg	TD
Grayson	19	405	21	0
Sherman	12	279	23	0
Bird	6	143	24	0
Todd	5	123	25	0
Hagberg	2	12	6	0
Benson	1	0	0	0

PASSING – PUNTING – KICKING

PASSING	Att	Comp	%	Yds	Yd/Att	TD	Int–%	RK
Lamonica	425	220	52	3228	7.6	30	20– 5	1
Blanda	38	15	39	285	7.5	3	3– 8	
Daniels	1	1	100	28	28.0	0	0– 0	

PUNTING	No	Avg
Eischeid	76	44.3

KICKING	XP	Att	%	FG	Att	%
Blanda	56	57	98	20	30	67

2 POINT XP
Kocourek

KANSAS CITY CHIEFS

RUSHING

Last Name	No.	Yds	Avg	TD
Garrett	236	1087	4.6	9
McClinton	97	392	4.0	2
Coan	63	275	4.4	4
G. Thomas	35	133	3.8	1
Dawson	20	68	3.4	0
Taylor	5	29	5.8	1
Pitts	3	19	6.3	1
Wilson	1	10	10.0	0
N. Smith	1	8	8.0	0

RECEIVING

Last Name	No.	Yds	Avg	TD
Taylor	59	958	16	11
Garrett	46	261	6	1
McClinton	26	219	8	1
Burford	25	389	16	3
Arbanas	20	295	15	5
G. Thomas	13	99	8	2
Richardson	12	312	26	2
Coan	5	41	8	0
Pitts	4	131	33	1
Carolan	2	26	13	0
N. Smith	1	42	42	0

PUNT RETURNS

Last Name	No.	Yds	Avg	TD
N. Smith	26	212	8	0
Garrett	4	22	6	0
E. Thomas	2	8	4	0
Robinson	1	3	3	0

KICKOFF RETURNS

Last Name	No.	Yds	Avg	TD
N. Smith	41	1148	28	1
G. Thomas	6	56	9	0
Coan	1	29	29	0
Carolan	1	2	2	0
Lanier	1	1	1	0
Buchanan	1	0	0	0
Hill	1	0	0	0
Lothamer	1	0	0	0
Pitts	0	9	0	0

PASSING – PUNTING – KICKING

PASSING	Att	Comp	%	Yds	Yd/Att	TD	Int–%	RK
Dawson	357	206	58	2651	7.4	24	17– 5	2
Garrett	4	1	25	17	4.3	1	0– 0	

PUNTING	No	Avg
Wilson	41	42.4
Walker	19	38.7
Carolan	1	42.0

KICKING	XP	Att	%	FG	Att	%
Stenerud	45	45	100	21	36	58

2 POINT XP
Carolan
McClinton

SAN DIEGO CHARGERS

RUSHING

Last Name	No.	Yds	Avg	TD
Post	161	663	4.1	7
Hubbert	116	643	5.5	2
Smith	22	115	5.2	1
Hadl	37	107	2.9	3
Foster	38	78	2.1	0
Lowe	28	71	2.5	1
Allison	10	34	3.4	0
Stephenson	2	11	5.5	0
Alworth	1	5	5.0	0
Garrison	1	1	1.0	0
Redman	1	−13	−13.0	0

RECEIVING

Last Name	No.	Yds	Avg	TD
Frazier	57	922	16	10
Alworth	52	1010	19	9
Garrison	44	772	18	2
Post	32	278	9	1
Hubbert	19	214	11	2
Foster	9	46	5	0
Mackinnon	7	176	25	2
Newell	7	68	10	0
Lowe	2	25	13	0
Smith	1	6	6	0

PUNT RETURNS

Last Name	No.	Yds	Avg	TD
Duncan	36	434	12	0
Graham	3	46	15	0

KICKOFF RETURNS

Last Name	No.	Yds	Avg	TD
Tolbert	18	441	25	0
Post	15	371	25	0
Duncan	9	231	26	0
Lowe	8	145	18	0
Smith	3	61	17	0
Erickson	1	0	0	0

PASSING – PUNTING – KICKING

PASSING	Att	Comp	%	Yds	Yd/Att	TD	Int–%	RK
Hadl	427	217	51	3365	7.9	24	22– 5	4
Stephenson	26	11	42	117	4.5	2	2– 8	
Post	6	1	17	9	1.5	0	0– 0	
Alworth	1	0	0	0	0.0	0	0– 0	
Foster	1	0	0	0	0.0	0	0– 0	
Lowe	1	1	100	26	26.0	0	0– 0	
Whitehead	1	0	0	0	0.0	0	0– 0	

PUNTING	No	Avg
Redman	68	37.0
Cordill	3	48.3
Hadl	2	35.0

KICKING	XP	Att	%	FG	Att	%
Van Raaphorst	45	45	100	15	30	50

DENVER BRONCOS

RUSHING

Last Name	No.	Yds	Avg	TD
Little	130	381	2.9	1
Mitchell	82	308	3.8	0
Hickey	73	263	3.6	4
Hayes	85	255	3.0	4
Gilchrist	10	21	2.1	0
Glacken	1	10	10.0	0
Lynch	2	7	3.5	0
LeClair	8	6	0.8	1
Cassese	1	5	5.0	0
Scarpitto	1	5	5.0	0
Tensi	24	4	0.2	0
Crabtree	2	2	1.0	0
Denson	1	−2	−2.0	0

RECEIVING

Last Name	No.	Yds	Avg	TD
Denson	46	899	20	11
Crabtree	46	716	16	5
Hayes	13	125	10	0
Beer	11	155	14	0
Hickey	7	36	5	1
Mitchell	7	15	2	0
Little	7	11	2	0
Sweeney	6	136	23	0
White	5	87	17	0
Scarpitto	1	14	14	0
Gilchrist	1	−4	−4	0

PUNT RETURNS

Last Name	No.	Yds	Avg	TD
Little	16	270	17	1
Sellers	4	24	6	0
Crabtree	2	24	12	0
Huard	1	19	19	0
Cassese	3	14	5	0

KICKOFF RETURNS

Last Name	No.	Yds	Avg	TD
Little	35	942	27	0
Mitchell	8	164	21	0
Sellers	6	120	20	0
Wilson	4	106	27	0
Hayes	3	104	35	0
Lynch	1	27	27	0
Crabtree	1	26	26	0
Cassese	1	19	19	0
Beer	1	10	10	0

PASSING – PUNTING – KICKING

PASSING	Att	Comp	%	Yds	Yd/Att	TD	Int–%	RK
Tensi	325	131	40	1915	5.9	16	17– 5	7
LeClair	45	19	42	275	6.1	1	1– 2	
Glacken	4	0	0	0	0.0	0	0– 0	

PUNTING	No	Avg
Scarpitto	105	44.9

KICKING	XP	Att	%	FG	Att	%
Humphreys	18	19	95	7	15	47
Kroner	5	6	83	2	2	100
Duncan	3	3	100	2	5	40
LeClerc	2	2	100	1	6	17

2 POINT XP
Hayes

NFL CHAMPIONSHIP GAME
December 31, at Green Bay
(Attendance 50,861)

SCORING

GREEN BAY	7	7	0	7–21
DALLAS	0	10	0	7–17

First Quarter
G.B. Dowler, 8 yard pass from Starr
PAT – Chandler (kick)

Second Quarter
G.B. Dowler, 43 yard pass from Starr
PAT – Chandler (kick)
Dal. Andrie, 7 yard fumble return (by Starr)
PAT – Villanueva (kick)
Dal. Villanueva, 21 yard field goal

Fourth Quarter
Dal. Rentzel, 50 yard pass from Reeves
PAT – Villanueva (kick)
G.B. Starr, 1 yard rush
PAT – Chandler (kick)

TEAM STATISTICS

G. B.		DAL.
18	First Downs – Total	11
5	First Downs – Rushing	4
10	First Downs – Passing	6
3	First Downs – Penalty	1
1	Interception Returns – Number	0
15	Interception Returns – Yards	0
3	Fumbles – Number	3
2	Fumbles – Lost Ball	1
2	Penalties – Number	7
10	Yards Penalized	58
2	Giveaways	2
2	Takeaways	2
0	Difference	0

Green Bay's Golden Gamble

Last year's game between the Packers and Cowboys had been an NFL classic, but their rematch this season ranked among the most memorable football games of all time. Both clubs had won conference playoffs to get this far, with Green Bay beating the Rams 28-7 and Dallas clobbering the Browns 52-14, and they clashed for the NFL title in a titanic struggle under nightmarish conditions.

At game time the temperature in Green Bay was 13 degrees below zero, and a fifteen-mile-per-hour wind made it almost unbearable for player and spectator alike. Somewhat better acclimated to the cold than the Cowboys, the Packers mounted a 14-0 lead by early in the second quarter. The Dallas defense, however, took matters into its own hands. Willie Townes hit Starr attempting to pass, and when the ball squirted loose George Andrie picked it up and ran it into the end zone. When Willie Wood fumbled a punt a short time later, the Cowboys added a field goal to cut the score to 14-10 at halftime.

In the fourth period, the Cowboys went ahead on the first play when halfback Dan Reeves surprised the Packer secondary by throwing a long option pass to Lance Rentzel. With their backs to the wall, the Pack still trailed 17-14 when they took over the ball on their own 31-yard line with 4:50 left in the game. Mixing running plays and passes to his backs, Starr moved the Packers quickly downfield until they had a first down on the Dallas one-yard line with under a minute left on the clock. Twice Donny Anderson tried to run it in, twice he failed, and twice Starr called time out. With no time outs remaining and twenty seconds on the clock, the Packers snubbed a field-goal try and put all their chips on one last running play. At the snap, guard Jerry Kramer pushed Jethro Pugh out of the way, and Starr plunged through the gap for the winning touchdown.

INDIVIDUAL STATISTICS

GREEN BAY	No	Yds	Avg.	DALLAS	No	Yds	Avg.
RUSHING							
Anderson	18	35	1.9	Perkins	17	51	3.0
Mercein	6	20	3.3	Reeves	13	42	3.2
Williams	4	13	3.3	Meredith	1	9	9.0
Wilson	3	11	3.7	Baynham	1	−2	−2.0
Starr	1	1	1.0	Clarke	1	−8	−8.0
	32	80	2.5		33	92	2.8
RECEIVING							
Dowler	4	77	19.3	Hayes	3	16	5.3
Anderson	4	44	11.0	Reeves	3	11	3.7
Dale	3	44	14.7	Rentzel	2	61	30.5
Mercein	2	22	11.0	Clarke	2	24	12.0
Williams	1	4	4.0	Baynham	1	−3	−3.0
	14	191	13.6		11	109	9.9
PUNTING							
Anderson	8		29.0	Villanueva	8		39.1
PUNT RETURNS							
Wood	4	21	5.3	None			
Brown	1	−2	−2.0				
	5	19	3.8				
KICKOFF RETURNS							
Caffey	1	7	7.0	Stevens	2	15	7.5
Crutcher	1	3	3.0	Stokes	1	28	28.0
Weatherwax	1	0	0.0		3	43	14.3
	3	10	3.3				

PASSING

GREEN BAY	Att	Comp	Comp Pct.	Yds	Int	Yds/ Att.	Yds/ Comp	Yards Lost Tackled
Starr	24	14	58.3	191	0	8.0	13.6	8–76
DALLAS								
Meredith	25	10	40.0	59	1	2.4	5.9	1– 9
Reeves	1	1	100.0	50	0	50.0	50.0	0– 0
	26	11	42.3	109	1	4.2	9.9	1– 9

AFL CHAMPIONSHIP GAME
December 31, at Oakland
(Attendance 53,330)

SCORING

OAKLAND	3	14	10	13–40
HOUSTON	0	0	0	7– 7

First Quarter
Oak. Blanda, 37 yard field goal

Second Quarter
Oak. Dixon, 69 yard rush
PAT – Blanda (kick)
Oak. Kocourek, 17 yard pass from Lamonica
PAT – Blanda (kick)

Third Quarter
Oak. Lamonica, 1 yard rush
PAT – Blanda (kick)
Oak. Blanda, 40 yard field goal

Fourth Quarter
Oak. Blanda, 42 yard field goal
Hous. Frazier, 5 yard pass from Beathard
PAT – Wittenborn (kick)
Oak. Blanda, 36 yard field goal
Oak. Miller, 12 yard pass from Lamonica
PAT – Blanda (kick)

TEAM STATISTICS

OAK.		HOUS.
18	First Downs – Total	11
11	First Downs – Rushing	4
6	First Downs – Passing	6
1	First Downs – Penalty	1
0	Fumbles – Number	4
0	Fumbles – Lost Ball	2
4	Penalties – Number	7
69	Yards Penalized	45
2	Missed Field Goals	0
0	Giveaways	3
3	Takeaways	0
+3	Difference	−3

Lamonica's Field-Goal Touchdown

The Oilers had won the Eastern Division title because of their strong defense, but the Raiders had no problems moving the ball in this championship game. With guard Gene Upshaw leading a fired-up Oakland offensive line, the Raiders attacked the Oilers on the ground, with Hewritt Dixon and Pete Banaszak steadily eating up the yardage all afternoon. George Blanda, whom the Oilers had put on waivers before the season, opened the scoring with a 37-yard field goal, and a 69-yard touchdown run around left end by Dixon gave Oakland more momentum. With eighteen seconds left in the half, the Raiders lined up for a close field-goal attempt, only to have holder Daryle Lamonica jump up and throw a touchdown pass to tight end Dave Kocourek.

Trailing 17-0 and getting nowhere against the Oakland defense, the Oilers needed some fireworks at the start of the second half to get back into the game. Instead, Zeke Moore fumbled the kickoff and gave the ball back to the Raiders deep in Houston territory. The Raiders needed seven plays to reach the end zone, with Lamonica sneaking over from the 1 for the score.

Once the score reached 24-0, all the steam leaked out of the Oilers. Fullback Hoyle Granger, the key to the Houston ground attack, never got untracked all day, and quarterback Pete Beathard had no success passing against the swarming Oakland secondary.

After three periods, the score had risen to 27-0, but the Oilers finally got on the scoreboard with a touchdown pass from Beathard to Charley Frazier plus John Whittenborn's extra point. That was the only Houston score of the day, however, and before the final gun sounded, the Raiders added ten points on a Blanda field goal and a scoring pass from Lamonica to Bill Miller. The 40-7 victory put the Raiders into the Super Bowl, but an Achilles tendon injury suffered by defensive tackle Tom Keating would hobble him for that upcoming match.

INDIVIDUAL STATISTICS

OAKLAND	No	Yds	Avg.	HOUSTON	No	Yds	Avg.
RUSHING							
Dixon	21	144	6.9	Granger	14	19	1.4
Banaszak	15	116	7.7	Campbell	6	15	2.5
Lamonica	5	22	4.4	Blanks	1	6	6.0
Hagberg	2	−1	−0.5	Beathard	1	−2	−2.0
Todd	4	−8	−2.0		22	38	1.7
Biletnikoff	1	−10	−10.0				
	48	263	5.5				
RECEIVING							
Miller	3	32	10.7	Frazier	7	81	11.6
Cannon	2	31	15.5	Reed	4	60	15.0
Biletnikoff	2	19	9.5	Campbell	2	5	2.5
Kocourek	1	17	17.0	Taylor	1	6	6.0
Dixon	1	8	8.0	Granger	1	−10	−10.0
Banaszak	1	4	4.0		15	142	9.5
	10	111	11.1				
PUNTING							
Eischeid	4		44.3	Norton	11		38.5
PUNT RETURNS							
Bird	5	49	9.8	None			
Sherman	1	−2	−2.0				
	6	47	7.8				
KICKOFF RETURNS							
Grayson	1	47	47.0	Jancik	4	100	25.0
Todd	1	32	32.0	Moore	3	87	29.0
	2	79	39.5	Burrell	1	28	28.0
				Suggs	1	0	0.0
					9	215	23.9
INTERCEPTION RETURNS							
Brown	1	2	2.0	None			

PASSING

OAKLAND	Att	Comp	Comp Pct.	Yds	Int	Yds/ Att.	Yds/ Comp	Yards Lost Tackled
Lamonica	24	10	41.7	111	0	4.6	11.1	
Blanda	2	0	0.0	0	0	–	–	
	26	10	38.5	111	0	4.3	11.1	10
HOUSTON								
Beathard	35	15	40.5	142	1	4.1	9.5	34

SUPER BOWL II
January 14, at Miami
(Attendance: 75,546)

The Errors of Youth

The Packers might naturally have suffered a mental letdown after their cliff-hanging NFL championship match with the Dallas Cowboys, but the knowledge that this was Vince Lombardi's last game as head coach gave the team all the incentive it needed against the AFL champion Oakland Raiders. In his nine seasons at Green Bay, Lombardi had turned the Packers from chronic losers to perennial champions, and his players were determined that he go out a winner.

The Oakland Raiders, on the other hand, had just won their first AFL crown by severely thrashing the Houston Oilers in the championship game. Like the Kansas City Chiefs last year, the Raiders had several players obviously good enough for any league, but other Oakland players would have to prove themselves against the Packers. They did, but what hurt the Raiders this day were mistakes, the sort of errors that plague young teams in any league.

The first quarter went fairly evenly, with the only scoring coming on Don Chandler's 39-yard field goal. Another Chandler three-pointer upped the score to 6-0 in the second quarter, and then the Raiders made their first costly mistake. The Packers had the ball on their own 38-yard line when Bart Starr dropped back to pass. Someone in the Raider secondary missed his assignment and left Boyd Dowler all alone downfield; Starr hit him with a perfect pass, which he carried to the end zone. With the extra point making the score 13-0, the Raiders seemed close to early death in this contest.

Daryle Lamonica revived his team's failing spirits, however, by driving the Raiders downfield and hitting Bill Miller with a 23-yard touchdown pass. The Oakland defense then stopped the Packer offense, but Rodger Bird, normally a sure-handed punt returner, called for a fair catch and fumbled the ball. The Packers recovered near mid-field and converted the break into another Chandler field goal and a 16-7 halftime lead.

Using their ball-control offense, the Packers nursed their lead through the second half and built it up to 33-14 on a Donny Anderson touchdown, a Chandler field goal, and Herb Adderley's return of an interception for a touchdown. Lamonica threw another touchdown pass to Miller in the fourth quarter, but that only made the final score a clear-cut 33-14. Vince Lombardi, retiring to the front office, was going out a winner.

GREEN BAY		OAKLAND
	OFFENSE	
Dowler	LE	Miller
Skoronski	LT	Svihus
Gillingham	LG	Upshaw
Bowman	C	J. Otto
Kramer	RG	Hawkins
Gregg	RT	Schuh
Fleming	RE	Cannon
Starr	QB	Lamonica
Dale	FL	Biletnikoff
Anderson	HB	Banaszak
Wilson	FB	Dixon
	DEFENSE	
Davis	LE	Lassiter
Kostelnik	LT	Birdwell
Jordan	RT	Keating
Aldridge	RE	Davidson
Robinson	LLB	Laskey
Nitschke	MLB	Connors
Caffey	RLB	G. Otto
Adderley	LCB	McCloughan
Jeter	RCB	W. Brown
T. Brown	LS	Powers
Wood	RS	H. Williams

SUBSTITUTES

GREEN BAY

Offense

Bratkowski	McGee
Capp	Mercein
Hyland	Thurston
Long	T. Williams

Defense

B. Brown	Hart
Crutcher	Rowser
Flanigan	Weatherwax

Kicker

Chandler

OAKLAND

Offense

Archer	Kocourek
Hagberg	Kruse
Harvey	Todd
Herock	Wells

Defense

Bird	Oates
Benson	Sligh
Budness	Williamson
Grayson	

Kickers

Blanda	Eischeid

SCORING

GREEN BAY	3	13	10	7–33
OAKLAND	0	7	0	7–14

First Quarter
G.B. Chandler, 39 yard field goal

Second Quarter
G.B. Chandler, 20 yard field goal
G.B. Dowler, 62 yard pass from Starr PAT – Chandler (kick)
Oak. Miller, 23 yard pass from Lamonica PAT – Blanda (kick)
G.B. Chandler, 43 yard field goal

Third Quarter
G.B. Anderson, 2 yard rush PAT – Chandler (kick)
G.B. Chandler, 31 yard field goal

Fourth Quarter
G.B. Adderley, 60 yard interception return PAT – Chandler (kick)
Oak. Miller, 23 yard pass from Lamonica PAT – Blanda (kick)

TEAM STATISTICS

G. B.		OAK.
19	First Downs – Total	16
11	First Downs – Rushing	5
7	First Downs – Passing	10
1	First Downs – Penalties	1
0	Fumbles – Number	3
0	Fumbles – Lost Ball	2
1	Penalties – Number	4
12	Yards Penalized	31
69	Total Offensive Plays	57
322	Total Net Yards	293
4.7	Average Gain	5.1
0	Missed Field Goals	1
0	Giveaways	3
3	Takeaways	0
+3	Difference	–3

INDIVIDUAL STATISTICS

GREEN BAY	No	Yds	Avg.	OAKLAND	No	Yds	Avg.
RUSHING							
Wilson	17	62	3.6	Dixon	12	54	4.5
Anderson	14	48	3.4	Todd	2	37	18.5
Williams	8	36	4.5	Banaszak	6	16	2.7
Starr	1	14	14.0		20	107	5.4
Mercein	1	0	0.0				
	41	160	3.9				
RECEIVING							
Dale	4	43	10.8	Miller	5	84	16.8
Fleming	4	35	8.8	Banaszak	4	69	17.3
Dowler	2	71	35.5	Cannon	2	25	12.5
Anderson	2	18	9.0	Biletnikoff	2	10	5.0
McGee	1	35	35.0	Wells	1	17	17.0
	13	202	15.5	Dixon	1	3	3.0
					15	208	13.9
PUNTING							
Anderson	6		39.0	Eischeid	6		44.0
PUNT RETURNS							
Wood	5	35	7.0	Bird	2	12	6.0
KICKOFF RETURNS							
Adderley	1	24	14.0	Todd	3	63	21.0
Williams	1	18	18.0	Grayson	2	61	30.5
Crutcher	1	7	7.0	Hawkins	1	3	3.0
	3	49	16.3	Kocourek	1	0	0.0
					7	127	18.1
INTERCEPTION RETURNS							
Adderley	1	60	60.0	None			

PASSING

GREEN BAY	Att	Comp	Comp Pct.	Yds	Int	Yds/ Att.	Yds/ Comp	Yards Lost Tackled
Starr	24	13	54.2	202	0	8.4	15.5	4–30
OAKLAND								
Lamonica	34	15	44.1	208	1	6.1	13.9	3–22

1968 N.F.L. Eleven Missing Monuments

A lot of familiar faces were missing from NFL playing fields this season. Retired from active duty were Ray Berry, Jim Parker, Lenny Moore, Lou Groza, Sam Huff, Del Shofner, Jim Ringo, Jim Taylor, and Don Chandler, all of them top-notch performers in the league since the 1950s. Berry left with a record 631 lifetime receptions, Groza with records of twenty-one active professional seasons and 1,608 points scored, and Ringo left with an appearance record streak of 182 consecutive games, a streak still running at his retirement. Also tucked away in front-office positions out of the public's eye were George Halas and Vince Lombardi, two of the most famous coaches in pro-football history. Age prompted Halas to leave the sidelines, while Lombardi quit because he had accomplished everything in his nine years as Packer head coach.

EASTERN CONFERENCE — CAPITOL DIVISION

Dallas Cowboys—Depth was the key to the Cowboys' continued stay atop the Capitol Division. When quarterback Don Meredith needed a rest, young Craig Morton filled in and kept the offense rolling smoothly. When halfback Dan Reeves hurt his knee in the season's fourth game, substitute runners Craig Baynham and Walt Garrison filled the breach. Other top reserves on this team were Malcolm Walker, Rayfield Wright, Larry Cole, and Blaine Nye, each of whom could have started on most NFL teams.

New York Giants—The aerial circus of Fran Tarkenton to Homer Jones kept the attack alive, but the rest of the team needed shoring up. The running backs were slow, the defensive line couldn't mount an effective pass rush, and the linebacking was inexperienced and easily fooled. They did beat Dallas, but that was more a fluke than a true reading of the team.

Washington Redskins—Combined with the retirement of Sam Huff, a pair of decisions that backfired helped bring Otto Graham's pro coaching career to an end. Graham sent a first-draft pick to Los Angeles for rookie quarterback Gary Beban, last year's Heisman Trophy winner at UCLA. After signing with the Redskins for a lucrative salary, Beban flopped in training camp as a quarterback, spent most of the year on the taxi squad, and flopped late in the season as a running back. Another Graham move that didn't work out was the trading of safety Paul Krause to Minnesota.

Philadelphia Eagles—Norm Snead broke his leg in the first pre-season game, the Eagles lost their first eleven regular season games, owner Jerry Wolman went bankrupt, and coach Joe Kuharich heard hometown crowds screaming for his head. The Eagles ended their losing streak by beating Detroit 12-0 on four Sam Baker field goals, and a second win one week later gave the club some dignity but removed all chances of landing O. J. Simpson next year. At the end of the year, Leonard Tose bought the team from Wolman and canned Kuharich, fifteen-year contract and all.

CENTURY DIVISION

Cleveland Browns—When the Browns dropped two of their first three games with a meager offensive output, coach Blanton Collier benched quarterback Frank Ryan in favor of ex-Steeler Bill Nelsen. Playing behind the solid Cleveland line, Nelsen stayed healthy all season and put some life in the Browns' attack. With Nelsen, Leroy Kelly, and Paul Warfield leading the way, the Browns began an eight-game winning streak on October 20 by beating the undefeated Colts. The streak came to an end only on the final Sunday of the season, when a meaningless loss to St. Louis tightened the final standings.

St. Louis Cardinals—The Cards beat the Browns twice, but Cleveland finished ahead by half a game. With a strong, balanced squad, the Cards had severe problems with Western opponents, losing to the Rams, Colts, and 49ers and just barely beating the Falcons 17-12. Despite the near miss at the title, several developments pleased coach Charley Winner. Quarterback Jim Hart improved considerably in his second year at the helm, cutting his interceptions from 30 down to 18. The defense replaced retired linebackers Dale Meinert and Bill Koman without a hitch, and rookie Chuck Latourette put on a good show as a kick returner, punter and sometimes defensive back.

New Orleans Saints—Although the Saints won four games, their move up to third place was due more to the Steelers' deterioration than to their own improvement. Coach Tom Fears improved his offense by signing end Dave Parks after he played out his option at San Francisco. He had to pay a steep price, however, when Commissioner Pete Rozelle deemed rookie tackle Kevin Hardy and next year's number-one draft pick as San Francisco's just renumeration.

Pittsburgh Steelers—The Steelers combined a poor offense with a limp defense in an irresistible combination for defeat, and head coach Bill Austin found himself discharged after the debacle ended. Dick Hoak and Roy Jefferson turned in good offensive performances, but they were hardly noticeable admidst the mediocrity.

WESTERN CONFERENCE — CENTRAL DIVISION

Minnesota Vikings—The Vikings won the Central Division title with a defense as rugged as the Minnesota weather in December. The front line of Carl Eller, Jim Marshall, Alan Page, and Gary Larsen now ranked with Los Angeles' Fearsome Foursome as the top defensive lines in the league, and the linebacking and secondary were without weakness. The acquisition of safety Paul Krause from the Redskins was the knot that tied the Vikings' pass defense together. Although the offense ranked fourteenth in the league in total yardage and dead last in passing, quarterback Joe Kapp won as many headlines as the defensive people with his intense competitiveness and wobbling passes which often hit their mark in clutch situations.

Chicago Bears—Head coach Jim Dooley lost his first two games and then beat the Vikings at a terrible cost. In that game, Jack Concannon went out with a fractured collarbone and Rudy Bukich with a shoulder separation. After third-stringer Larry Rakestraw failed to move the team, Dooley gave rookie Virgil Carter a shot at quarterback. Carter drove the Bears to four straight wins before more injuries ended the team's title hopes. In the victory over San Francisco, a tackle by Kermit Alexander ripped ligaments and cartilage in Gale Sayers' right knee. One week later, a broken ankle ended Carter's fine rookie season.

Green Bay Packers—Vince Lombardi had quit as head coach, confining himself to the general manager's desk, and the Packers, under Phil Bengston, dropped to a 6-7-1 mark. Age was catching up on the players of the championship teams of the early 1960s, and replacements were not turning up. A bad arm kept quarterback Bart Starr out of action for almost half the season, and Don Chandler retired, leaving the Packers with no reliable place-kicker.

Detroit Lions—Last year's top newcomers had been Mel Farr and Lem Barney; this year's pair were wide receiver Earl McCullough and tight end Charlie Sanders. These two rookies joined with newcomers Bill Munson and Billy Gambrell to make the Detroit passing game a genuine threat to enemy defenses. Injuries plagued the running corps, however, and the reconstructed Lions needed more time together to play as a team.

COASTAL DIVISION

Baltimore Colts—A few weeks before their season's opener, the Colts had a solid team everywhere but at quarterback. Johnny Unitas was bothered by a bad elbow, so coach Don Shula sent a fourth-round draft pick and reserve end Butch Wilson to New York for journeyman quarterback Earl Morrall. Shula expected Morrall to fill in while Unitas recuperated, but while Unitas sat out most of the season, Morrall used his pinpoint passing and poised signal calling to lead the Colts to a 13-1 season. Morrall's job was made easier by the running of Tom Matte, the blocking and receiving of John Mackey, and the line play of Bob Vogel, while the defense made life miserable for heralded enemy quarterbacks.

Los Angeles Rams—Despite a string of injuries, the Rams fought their way to a 10-3-1 record. But after the season ended, owner Dan Reeves fired George Allen. Personality differences and Allen's practice of trading off draft picks for older pros convinced Reeves that he'd be better off with a different coach, but the Ram players immediately raised an outcry in favor of their deposed coach. The protests had some effect, because when Reeves held a press conference to name the new coach, he announced the return of Allen.

San Francisco '49ers—New head coach Dick Nolan took over a talent squad in his first head assignment, but he couldn't get his team past the Colts and Rams in the Coastal Division. With three losses and a tie against these two rivals, the '49ers had the misfortune of playing in pro football's strongest division. The '49ers did well against the rest of the league, with a steady attack their chief weapon. Bolstered by Nolan's confidence in him, quarterback John Brodie took firm charge of the offense, finding ex-Brown Clifton McNeil a most congenial pass receiver.

Atlanta Falcons—When the Falcons lost their first three games of the season, coach Norb Hecker was canned and ex-Viking head man Norm Van Brocklin given the job, and he tore the club apart in search of a winning combination. After a 30-7 loss to Cleveland, he put five starting players on waivers. He gave a starting safetyman's job to Billy Lothridge, a punting specialist with only one kidney. He dropped promising Randy Johnson from the starting lineup and promoted Bob Berry, whom he had coached in Minnesota to starting quarterback.

FINAL TEAM STATISTICS

OFFENSE

	ATL.	BALT.	CHI.	CLEV.	DALL.	DET.	G.B.	L.A.	MINN.	N.O.	N.Y.	PHIL.	PITT.	ST.L.	S.F.	WASH.
FIRST DOWNS:																
Total	174	258	219	248	297	221	240	245	223	224	256	197	245	245	260	223
by Rushing	71	110	121	104	135	87	96	111	114	80	119	78	91	117	98	67
by Passing	94	131	78	123	143	119	130	115	89	122	114	100	137	107	141	132
by Penalty	9	17	20	21	19	15	14	19	20	22	23	19	17	21	21	24
RUSHING:																
Number	366	463	500	447	480	433	450	503	500	409	474	369	399	463	443	360
Yards	1305	1809	2377	2031	2091	1702	1749	1932	1921	1527	1882	1411	1721	1996	1784	1164
Average Yards	3.6	3.9	4.8	4.5	4.4	3.9	3.9	3.8	3.8	3.7	4.0	3.8	4.3	4.3	4.0	3.2
Touchdowns	9	16	14	20	22	6	12	14	19	7	13	3	7	22	11	6
PASSING:																
Attempts	326	359	343	363	399	377	318	384	282	439	366	380	451	385	417	408
Completions	158	196	158	184	217	204	188	189	154	210	195	194	211	169	239	227
Completion Percentage	48.5	54.6	46.1	50.7	54.4	54.1	59.1	49.2	54.6	47.8	53.3	51.1	46.8	43.9	57.3	55.6
Passing Yards	2386	3094	1868	3039	3295	2649	2651	2413	1995	2549	2715	2357	2764	2389	3107	2824
Average Yards per Attempt	7.3	8.6	5.4	8.4	8.3	7.0	8.3	6.3	7.1	5.8	7.4	6.2	6.1	6.2	7.5	6.9
Average Yards per Completion	15.1	15.8	11.8	16.5	15.2	13.0	14.1	12.8	13.0	12.1	13.9	12.1	13.1	14.1	13.0	12.4
Times Tackled Attempting to Pass	70	29	24	21	34	45	41	28	35	33	30	26	41	23	27	37
Yards Lost Tackled Attempting to Pass	527	222	187	181	269	329	376	241	310	213	273	207	285	202	182	340
Net Yards	1859	2872	1681	2858	3026	2320	2275	2172	1685	2336	2442	2150	2479	2187	2925	2484
Touchdowns	9	28	10	27	25	17	21	20	11	17	21	16	22	16	24	23
Interceptions	24	22	21	16	18	15	15	17	17	29	17	29	26	20	23	18
Percent Intercepted	7.4	6.1	6.1	4.4	4.5	4.0	4.7	4.4	6.0	6.6	4.6	7.6	5.8	5.2	5.5	4.4
PUNTS:																
Number	75	49	66	63	59	71	59	81	61	75	57	60	68	65	68	76
Average Distance	44.3	39.5	38.0	37.3	40.9	40.4	40.0	39.6	39.3	37.6	36.0	41.3	40.4	41.6	39.0	43.3
PUNT RETURNS:																
Number	16	42	19	24	30	19	43	44	30	34	20	24	38	31	36	29
Yards	66	350	81	96	405	89	238	307	250	153	101	264	308	356	120	194
Average Yards	4.1	8.3	4.3	4.0	13.5	4.7	5.5	7.0	8.3	4.5	5.1	11.0	8.1	11.5	3.3	6.7
Touchdowns	0	0	0	0	2	0	1	0	1	1	0	1	1	1	0	0
KICKOFF RETURNS:																
Number	68	38	58	54	39	54	48	45	52	53	62	61	70	56	60	64
Yards	1273	1003	1370	974	841	1247	1007	1024	1049	1149	1110	1379	1502	1404	1064	1410
Average Yards	18.7	26.4	23.6	18.0	21.6	23.1	21.0	22.8	20.2	21.7	17.9	22.6	21.5	25.1	17.7	22.0
Touchdowns	0	2	0	0	0	1	0	1	0	0	0	1	0	0	0	0
INTERCEPTION RETURNS:																
Number	14	29	18	32	26	24	17	25	16	16	26	13	17	13	20	21
Yards	330	483	226	386	275	242	244	220	267	268	388	51	151	65	367	225
Average Yards	23.6	16.7	12.6	12.1	10.6	10.1	14.4	8.8	16.7	16.8	14.9	3.9	8.9	5.0	18.4	10.7
Touchdowns	2	4	1	2	3	1	0	2	1	1	2	0	1	0	3	1
PENALTIES:																
Number	63	75	113	74	77	70	64	74	65	82	67	63	46	66	90	65
Yards	659	655	1194	841	751	810	653	760	692	843	608	666	479	708	794	643
FUMBLES:																
Number	26	23	28	23	21	26	31	21	22	19	17	19	26	24	26	29
Number Lost	15	12	16	14	15	17	18	12	14	11	13	13	14	11	14	19
POINTS:																
Total	170	402	250	394	431	207	281	312	282	246	294	202	244	325	303	249
PAT Attempts	20	50	25	49	54	26	35	37	32	27	36	21	32	40	39	32
PAT Made	17	48	25	46	54	24	32	37	31	27	36	17	28	40	36	30
FG Attempts	21	28	36	24	29	29	29	31	29	37	24	30	21	24	24	19
FG Made	11	18	25	18	17	9	13	17	19	19	14	19	8	15	11	9
Percent FG Made	52.4	64.3	69.4	75.0	58.6	31.0	44.8	54.8	65.5	51.4	58.3	63.3	38.1	62.5	45.8	47.4
Safeties	0	0	0	0	1	0	0	1	1	0	0	1	0	0	0	0

DEFENSE

	ATL.	BALT.	CHI.	CLEV.	DALL.	DET.	G.B.	L.A.	MINN.	N.O.	N.Y.	PHIL.	PITT.	ST.L.	S.F.	WASH.
FIRST DOWNS:																
Total	302	207	240	259	202	214	213	190	210	228	263	256	244	238	250	259
by Rushing	129	71	102	110	61	92	105	66	98	97	125	128	92	90	111	122
by Passing	157	119	102	130	123	105	92	104	98	109	121	111	131	131	124	118
by Penalty	16	17	36	19	18	17	16	20	14	22	17	17	21	17	15	19
RUSHING:																
Number	518	375	427	423	369	457	476	397	432	439	425	515	441	423	445	497
Yards	2235	1339	1704	1842	1195	1680	1800	1305	1903	2105	2001	2141	1624	1558	1776	2194
Average Yards	4.3	3.6	4.0	4.4	3.2	3.7	3.8	3.3	4.4	4.8	4.7	4.2	3.7	3.7	4.0	4.4
Touchdowns	17	6	17	11	2	13	11	9	8	13	22	18	14	10	12	18
PASSING:																
Attempts	389	432	333	439	428	337	327	353	315	366	364	327	413	399	416	359
Completions	248	224	172	213	220	157	157	158	185	153	191	182	220	210	201	202
Completion Percentage	63.8	51.9	51.7	48.5	51.4	46.6	48.0	44.8	58.7	41.8	52.5	55.7	53.3	52.6	48.3	56.3
Passing Yards	3306	2405	2893	2447	2838	2448	2031	2196	2162	2483	2498	2557	3360	3261	2548	2662
Average Yards per Attempt	8.5	5.6	8.7	5.6	6.6	7.3	6.2	6.2	6.9	6.8	6.9	7.8	8.1	8.2	6.1	7.4
Average Yards per Completion	13.3	10.7	16.8	11.5	12.9	15.6	12.9	13.9	11.7	16.2	13.1	14.0	15.3	15.5	12.7	13.2
Times Tackled Attempting to Pass	29	45	30	26	51	36	28	51	44	34	21	21	28	44	35	21
Yards Lost Tackled Attempting to Pass	221	367	226	199	400	291	235	383	307	297	158	184	199	400	304	173
Net Yards	3085	2038	2667	2248	2438	2157	1796	1813	1855	2186	2340	2373	3161	2861	2244	2489
Touchdowns	30	9	25	19	20	12	14	12	16	25	18	20	29	23	19	16
Interceptions	14	29	18	32	26	24	17	25	16	16	26	13	17	13	20	21
Percent Intercepted	3.6	6.7	5.4	7.3	6.1	7.1	5.2	7.1	5.1	4.4	7.1	4.0	4.1	3.3	4.8	5.8
PUNTS:																
Number	45	78	66	60	77	66	77	88	64	69	47	55	66	70	68	57
Average Distance	41.5	40.8	40.1	39.9	40.4	40.7	39.6	40.0	38.4	40.8	40.0	38.9	40.0	38.1	40.9	39.6
PUNT RETURNS:																
Number	46	19	28	21	25	32	19	30	29	30	23	33	32	36	31	45
Yards	286	62	120	120	125	139	66	206	204	320	174	270	297	266	238	485
Average Yards	6.2	3.3	4.3	5.7	5.0	4.3	3.5	6.9	7.1	10.7	7.6	8.2	9.3	7.4	7.7	10.8
Touchdowns	0	0	0	0	0	0	0	1	0	1	1	0	2	1	0	2
KICKOFF RETURNS:																
Number	42	71	54	64	68	44	56	62	56	57	51	45	49	56	56	51
Yards	799	391	968	1417	1326	1017	1211	1262	1291	1134	1344	1030	1154	1303	1163	996
Average Yards	19.0	19.6	17.9	22.1	19.5	23.1	21.6	20.4	23.1	19.9	26.4	22.9	23.6	23.3	20.8	19.5
Touchdowns	0	0	0	0	0	1	0	1	0	0	1	0	0	1	1	0
INTERCEPTION RETURNS:																
Number	24	22	21	16	18	15	15	17	17	29	17	29	26	20	23	18
Yards	326	192	260	152	331	150	150	286	360	294	120	408	404	173	390	192
Average Yards	13.6	8.7	12.4	9.5	18.4	10.0	10.0	16.8	21.2	10.1	7.1	14.1	15.5	8.7	17.0	10.7
Touchdowns	2	1	1	1	1	1	0	2	2	2	0	2	5	0	1	3
PENALTIES:																
Number	63	72	91	61	54	76	60	88	74	74	62	76	79	71	71	82
Yards	628	799	896	620	657	658	541	806	875	757	579	843	844	728	646	879
FUMBLES:																
Number	30	29	20	20	21	22	28	31	29	33	21	18	16	19	22	22
Number Lost	16	12	12	14	15	12	17	19	22	26	14	7	9	8	11	14
POINTS:																
Total	389	144	333	273	186	241	227	200	242	327	325	351	397	289	310	358
PAT Attempts	49	16	43	33	23	28	25	25	27	42	43	40	50	35	35	41
PAT Made	47	15	40	33	21	28	24	23	26	37	37	39	49	34	34	41
FG Attempts	30	19	31	26	22	29	26	17	27	27	23	35	26	33	32	32
FG Made	16	11	11	14	9	15	17	9	18	12	10	24	16	15	22	23
Percent FG Made	53.3	57.9	35.5	53.8	40.9	51.7	65.4	52.9	66.7	44.4	43.5	68.6	61.5	45.5	68.8	71.9
Safeties	0	0	1	0	0	0	1	0	0	1	0	0	0	0	0	1

CONFERENCE PLAYOFFS

EASTERN---December 21, at Cleveland (Attendance 81,497)

SCORING

CLEVELAND	3	7	14	7	–31
DALLAS	7	3	3	7	–20

First Quarter
- Cle. Cockroft, 38 yard field goal
- Dal. Howley, 44 yard fumble return
  - PAT – Clark (kick)

Second Quarter
- Dal. Clark, 16 yard field goal
- Cle. Kelly, 46 yard pass from Nelsen
  - PAT – Cockroft (kick)

Third Quarter
- Cle. Lindsey, 27 yd interception return
  - PAT – Cockroft (kick)
- Cle. Kelly, 35 yard run
  - PAT – Cockroft (kick)
- Dal. Clark, 47 yard field goal

Fourth Quarter
- Cle. E.Green, 2 yard rush
  - PAT – Cockroft (kick)
- Dal. Garrison, 2 yard pass from Morton
  - PAT – Clark (kick)

TEAM STATISTICS

CLE.		DAL.
12	First Downs – Total	13
4	First Downs – Rushing	5
8	First Downs – Passing	8
0	First Downs – Penalty	0
1	Times Tackled Passing	2
5	Yards Lost – Tackled	25
1	Fumbles – Number	1
1	Fumbles – Lost Ball	0
6	Penalties – Number	4
40	Yards Penalized	20
7	Punts – Number	5
36.1	Punts – Average Distance	41.0
3	Punt Returns – Number	0
6	Punt Returns – Yards	0
4	Kickoff Returns – Number	5
67	Kickoff Returns – Yards	72
4	Interception Returns – Number	1
52	Interception Returns – Yards	6
0	Missed Field Goals	2
2	Giveaways	4
4	Takeaways	2
+2	Difference	–2

INDIVIDUAL STATISTICS

RUSHING

CLEVELAND	No	Yds	Avg.	DALLAS	No	Yds	Avg.
Kelly	20	87	4.4	Perkins	14	51	3.6
Harraway	5	12	2.4	Morton	2	14	7.0
E.Green	3	5	1.7	Baynham	10	7	0.7
Nelsen	2	–2	–1.0	Garrison	1	6	6.0
	30	102	3.4	Meredith	1	5	5.0
				Shy	2	3	1.5
					30	86	2.9

RECEIVING

CLEVELAND	No	Yds	Avg.	DALLAS	No	Yds	Avg.
Warfield	4	86	21.5	Hayes	5	83	16.6
Morin	4	47	11.8	Rentzel	3	75	25.0
Kelly	2	46	23.0	Garrison	2	8	4.0
Collins	2	26	13.0	Baynham	1	34	34.0
Harraway	1	–2	–2.0	Norman	1	5	5.0
	13	203	15.6		12	205	17.1

PASSING

	Att	Cmp	Pct.	Yds	Int	Yd/A	Yd/C
Nelsen	25	13	52.0	203	1	8.1	15.6
Morton	23	9	39.1	163	1	7.1	18.1
Meredith	9	3	33.3	42	3	4.7	14.0
	32	12	37.5	205	4	6.4	17.1

WESTERN---December 22, at Baltimore (Attendance 60,238)

SCORING

BALTIMORE	0	7	14	3	–24
MINNESOTA	0	0	0	14	–14

Second Quarter
- Bal. Mitchell, 3 yd pass from Morrall
  - PAT – Michaels (kick)

Third Quarter
- Bal. Mackey, 49 yard pass from Morrall
  - PAT – Michaels (kick)
- Bal. Curtis, 60 yard fumble return
  - PAT – Michaels (kick)

Fourth Quarter
- Min. Martin, 1 yard pass from Kapp
  - PAT – Cox (kick)
- Bal. Michaels, 33 yard field goal
- Min. Brown, 7 yard pass from Kapp
  - PAT – Cox (kick)

TEAM STATISTICS

BAL.		MIN.
15	First Downs – Total	22
2	First Downs – Rushing	4
12	First Downs – Passing	17
1	First Downs – Penalty	1
4	Times Tackled Passing	3
35	Yards Lost – Tackled	21
1	Fumbles – Number	2
1	Fumbles – Lost Ball	1
2	Penalties – Number	4
38	Yards Penalized	30
5	Punts – Number	6
40.4	Punts – Average Distance	39.6
2	Punt Returns – Number	3
11	Punt Returns – Yards	7
3	Kickoff Returns – Number	5
54	Kickoff Returns – Yards	113
2	Interception Returns – Number	1
44	Interception Returns – Yards	21
1	Missed Field Goals	0
2	Giveaways	3
3	Takeaways	2
+1	Difference	–1

INDIVIDUAL STATISTICS

RUSHING

BALTIMORE	No	Yds	Avg.	MINNESOTA	No	Yds	Avg.
Matte	14	31	2.2	Kapp	10	52	5.2
J. Hill	8	10	1.3	Brown	10	30	3.0
Mackey	1	9	9.0	Osborn	5	4	0.8
Pearson	4	0	0.0	Jones	2	0	0.0
	27	50	1.9	Lindsey	1	–1	–1.0
					28	85	3.0

RECEIVING

BALTIMORE	No	Yds	Avg.	MINNESOTA	No	Yds	Avg.
Rich'son	6	148	24.7	Brown	8	82	10.3
Mackey	2	92	46.0	Wash'ton	5	95	19.0
Orr	2	36	18.0	Beasley	5	69	13.8
Mitchell	1	3	3.0	Henderson	5	33	6.6
Pearson	1	1	1.0	Lindsey	1	9	9.0
	12	180	23.3	Martin	1	1	1.0
				Osborn	1	–2	–2.0
					26	287	11.0

PASSING

	Att	Cmp	Pct.	Yds	Int	Yd/A	Yd/C
Morrall	22	13	59.1	280	1	12.7	21.5
Kapp	44	26	59.1	287	2	6.5	11.0

CAPITOL DIVISION

DALLAS COWBOYS 12-2-0 Tom Landry

Scores of Each Game		
59	DETROIT	13
28	CLEVELAND	7
45	Philadelphia	13
27	St. Louis	10
34	PHILADELPHIA	14
20	Minnesota	7
17	GREEN BAY	28
17	New Orleans	3
21	NEW YORK	27
44	Washington	24
34	Chicago	3
29	WASHINGTON	20
28	PITTSBURGH	7
28	New York	10

Use Name	Pos.	Hgt	Wgt	Age	Int	Pts
Tony Liscio	OT	6'5"	255	28		
Ralph Neely	OT	6'5"	265	24		
Rayfield Wright	TE-OT	6'7"	243	23		6
John Niland	OG	6'4"	245	24		
Blaine Nye	OG	6'4"	255	22		
John Wilbur	OG	6'3"	240	25		
Dave Manders	C	6'2"	250	26		
Malcolm Walker	OT-C	6'4"	250	25		
George Andrie	DE	6'7"	250	28		
Larry Cole	DE	6'4"	230	21	1	12
Willie Townes	DE	6'5"	260	25		6
Andy Stynchula	DT-DE	6'3"	250	29		
Ron East	DT	6'4"	242	25		
Bob Lilly	DT	6'4"	260	29		
Jethro Pugh	DT	6'6'	260	24		2

Use Name	Pos.	Hgt	Wgt	Age	Int	Pts
Jackie Burkett	LB	6'4"	228	31		
Dave Edwards	LB	6'3"	228	29		
Chuck Howley	LB	6'3"	225	32	6	6
Lee Roy Jordan	LB	6'2"	225	27	3	
D. D. Lewis	LB	6'2"	210	22		
Dave Simmons	LB	6'4"	245	25	1	
Phil Clark	DB	6'2"	210	23		
Dick Daniels	DB	5'9"	180	22	2	
Mike Gaechter	DB	6'	190	28	3	
Cornell Green	DB	6'4"	208	28	4	6
Mike Johnson	DB	5'10"	184	24	3	
Mel Renfro	DB	6'	190	26	3	

Buddy Dial – Injury
Leon Donohue – Injury

Use Name	Pos.	Hgt	Wgt	Age	Int	Pts
Don Meredith	QB	6'2"	205	30		6
Craig Morton	QB	6'4"	216	25		12
Craig Baynham	HB	6'1"	206	24		48
Dan Reeves	HB	6'1"	200	24		30
Les Shy	HB	6'1"	200	24		6
Walt Garrison	FB	6'	205	24		30
Don Perkins	FB	5'10"	200	30		36
Bob Hayes	WR	6'	185	25		72
Dennis Homan	WR	6'1"	180	22		6
Dave McDaniels	WR	6'4"	200	23		
Sonny Randle (from SF)	WR	6'2"	190	32		6
Lance Rentzel	WR	6'2"	200	24		36
Pete Gent	TE	6'4"	205	25		
Pettis Norman	TE	6'3"	225	28		6
Mike Clark	K	6'1"	200	27		105
Ron Widby	K	6'4"	210	23		

NEW YORK GIANTS 7-7-0 Allie Sherman

Scores of Each Game		
34	Pittsburgh	20
34	Philadelphia	25
48	WASHINGTON	21
33	NEW ORLEANS	21
21	Atlanta	24
10	SAN FRANCISCO	26
13	Washington	10
0	BALTIMORE	26
27	Dallas	21
7	PHILADELPHIA	6
21	Los Angeles	24
10	Cleveland	45
21	ST. LOUIS	28
10	DALLAS	28

Use Name	Pos.	Hgt	Wgt	Age	Int	Pts
Rich Buzin	OT	6'4"	250	22		
Charlie Harper	OT	6'2"	250	24		
Steve Wright	OT	6'6"	250	26		
Willie Young	OT	6'	250	25		
Pete Case	OG	6'3"	245	27		
Darrell Dess	OG	6'	245	32		
Andy Gross	OG	6'	230	22		
Doug Van Horn	OG	6'2"	245	24		
Chuck Hinton	C	6'2"	235	25		
Greg Larson	C	6'2"	250	29		
Bruce Anderson	DE	6'4"	250	24		
McKinley Boston	DE	6'2"	245	22		
Jim Katcavage	DE	6'3"	240	33		
Roger Anderson	DT	6'5"	265	25	1	
Bob Lurtsema	DT	6'6"	250	26	1	
Sam Silas	DT	6'4"	250	25		

Use Name	Pos.	Hgt	Wgt	Age	Int	Pts
Ken Avery	LB	6'1"	220	24		
Barry Brown	LB	6'3"	235	25		
Mike Ciccolella	LB	6'1"	235	24	1	
Vince Costello	LB	6'	228	36		
Tommy Crutcher	LB	6'3"	230	26		
Henry Davis	LB	6'3"	235	25		
Scott Eaton	DB	6'3"	195	24	4	
Jim Holifield	DB	6'3"	195	22		
Spider Lockhart	DB	6'2"	175	25	8	12
Bruce Maher	DB	5'11"	190	31	1	
Willie Williams	DB	6'	190	25	10	
Freeman White	TE-DB	6'5"	225	24		

Smith Reed – Military Service

Use Name	Pos.	Hgt	Wgt	Age	Int	Pts
Gary Lane	QB	6'1"	210	25		
Fran Tarkenton	QB	6'1"	190	28		18
Gary Wood	QB	5'11"	188	25		
Ronnie Blye	HB	5'11"	185	24		6
Bobby Duhon	HB	6'	190	21		24
Randy Minniear	HB	6'	200	24		12
Ernie Koy	FB-HB	6'2"	230	25		24
Tucker Frederickson	FB	6'3"	230	25		18
Homer Jones	WR	6'2"	220	27		42
Joe Koontz	WR	6'1"	192	23		
Joe Morrison	WR	6'1"	212	30		36
Bob Crespino	TE-WR	6'4"	225	30		
Butch Wilson	TE	6'2"	228	26		
Aaron Thomas	WR-TE	6'3"	210	30		24
Pete Gogolak	K	6'2"	185	26		78

WASHINGTON REDSKINS 5-9-0 Otto Graham

Scores of Each Game		
38	Chicago	28
17	New Orleans	37
21	New York	48
17	PHILADELPHIA	14
16	PITTSBURGH	13
14	St. Louis	41
10	NEW YORK	13
14	Minnesota	27
16	Philadelphia	10
24	DALLAS	44
7	GREEN BAY	27
20	Dallas	29
21	CLEVELAND	24
14	DETROIT	3

Use Name	Pos.	Hgt	Wgt	Age	Int	Pts
Walt Rock	OT	6'5"	255	27		
Jim Snowden	OT	6'3"	255	26		
Fred Washington	OT	6'5"	268	23		
Ray Schoenke	OG-OT	6'3"	250	26		
Don Bandy	OG	6'3"	250	23		
Willie Banks	OG	6'2"	237	22		
Vince Promuto	OG	6'1"	245	30		
John Wooten	OG	6'2"	250	33		
Dave Crossan	C	6'3"	245	28		
Len Hauss	C	6'2"	235	26		
Carl Kammerer	DE	6'3"	243	31		
Spain Musgrove	DT-DE	6'4"	275	23		
Walt Barnes	DT	6'3"	250	24		
Frank Bosch	DT	6'4"	246	22		
Dennis Crane	DT	6'6"	260	23		
Joe Rutgens	DT	6'2"	255	29		

Use Name	Pos.	Hgt	Wgt	Age	Int	Pts
Ed Breding	LB	6'4"	235	23		
Jim Carroll	LB	6'1"	230	25		
Chris Hanburger	LB	6'2"	218	27	2	6
Mike Morgan	LB	6'4"	242	26	2	
Tom Roussel	LB	6'3"	235	23		
Pat Fischer	DB	5'10"	170	28	2	
George Harold	DB	6'3"	194	26		
Rickie Harris	DB	6'	182	25	2	
Aaron Martin	DB	6'	190	27	4	
Brig Owens	DB	5'11"	190	25	8	
Jim Smith	DB	6'3"	195	21		6
Dick Smith	HB-DB	6'	205	24	1	

John Love – Military Service
Sam Huff – Voluntarily Retired
Joe Don Looney – Military Service

Use Name	Pos.	Hgt	Wgt	Age	Int	Pts
Sonny Jurgensen	QB	5'11"	203	34		6
Jim Ninowski	QB	6'1"	207	32		
Harry Theofiledes	QB	5'10"	180	24		
Gary Beban	HB-QB	6'1"	195	22		
Jerry Allen	HB	6'1"	205	27		30
Bob Brunet	HB	6'1"	205	22		6
Pete Larson	HB	6'1"	200	24		12
Ray McDonald	FB	6'4"	248	24		
Steve Thurlow	FB	6'3"	222	25		
A. D. Whitfield	FB	5'10"	200	24		
Charley Taylor	WR	6'3"	210	27		30
Bobby Mitchell	WR	6'	196	33		
Jerry Smith	TE-WR	6'2"	208	25		36
Ken Barefoot	TE	6'5"	228	22		6
Marlin McKeever	TE	6'1"	235	28		
Pat Richter	TE	6'5"	230	27		54
Mike Bragg	K	5'11"	186	21		
Charlie Gogolak	K	5'10"	165	23		57

PHILADELPHIA EAGLES 2-12-0 Joe Kuharich

Scores of Each Game		
13	Green Bay	30
25	NEW YORK	34
13	DALLAS	45
14	Washington	17
14	Dallas	34
16	CHICAGO	29
3	Pittsburgh	6
17	ST. LOUIS	45
10	WASHINGTON	16
6	New York	7
13	Cleveland	47
12	Detroit	0
29	NEW ORLEANS	17
17	MINNESOTA	24

Use Name	Pos.	Hgt	Wgt	Age	Int	Pts
Bob Brown	OT	6'4"	295	25		
Dave Graham	OT	6'3"	250	29		
Lane Howell	OT	6'5"	272	27		
Mike Dirks	OG	6'2"	250	22		
Dick Hart	OG	6'2"	250	25		
Mark Nordquist	OG	6'4"	235	22		
Gene Ceppetelli	C	6'2"	247	26		
Mike Evans	C	6'5"	250	21		
Dave Recher	C	6'1"	246	25		
Don Hultz	DE	6'3"	242	27		
Gary Pettigrew	DE	6'4"	245	23		
Tim Rossovich	DE	6'4"	245	22		
Mel Tom	DE	6'4"	248	27		
Frank Molden	DT	6'5"	280	26		
Floyd Peters	DT	6'4"	255	33	1	
Dean Wink	DT	6'4"	246	23		
Randy Beisler	DE-DT	6'4"	245	23	1	

Use Name	Pos.	Hgt	Wgt	Age	Int	Pts
Fred Brown	LB	6'5"	232	25		
Wayne Colman	LB	6'1"	230	22		
Dave Lloyd	LB	6'3"	248	32		
Arunas Vasys	LB	6'2"	235	25		
Harold Wells	LB	6'2"	220	29	2	
Adrian Young	LB	6'1"	225	22		
Alvin Haymond	DB	6'	194	26	1	12
John Mallory	DB	6'	180	22		6
Ron Medved	DB	6'1"	210	24	1	
Al Nelson	DB	5'11"	186	24	3	
Jim Nettles	DB	5'9"	177	26		
Nate Ramsey	DB	6'1"	200	27	2	
Joe Scarpati	HB-DB	5'10"	185	26	2	

Ike Kelley – Knee Injury
Jim Skaggs – Knee Injury
Harry Wilson – Injury

Use Name	Pos.	Hgt	Wgt	Age	Int	Pts
John Huarte	QB	6'	190	24		
Norm Snead	QB	6'4"	215	28		
Izzy Lang	HB	6'1"	232	25		6
Harry Jones	HB	6'2"	205	23		
Cyril Pinder	HB	6'2"	222	21		
Larry Conjar	FB	6'	214	22		2
Tom Woodeshick	FB	6'	220	26		18
Gary Ballman	WR	6'	205	28		24
Ron Goodwin	WR	6'	180	26		
Ben Hawkins	WR	6'	180	24		30
Chuck Hughes	WR	5'11"	170	25		
Mike Ditka	TE	6'3"	235	28		12
Fred Hill	TE	6'2"	215	25		18
Sam Baker	K	6'2"	218	36		74
Rick Duncan	K	6'	208	27		

CAPITOL DIVISION

DALLAS COWBOYS

RUSHING

Last Name	No.	Yds	Avg	TD
Perkins	191	836	4.4	4
Baynham	103	438	4.3	5
Garrison	45	271	6.0	5
Shy	64	179	2.8	1
Reeves	40	178	4.5	4
Meredith	22	123	5.6	1
Norman	4	51	12.8	0
Morton	4	28	7.0	2
Hayes	4	2	0.5	0
Gent	2	−5	−2.5	0
Wright	1	−10	−10.0	0

RECEIVING

Last Name	No.	Yds	Avg	TD
Rentzel	54	1009	19	6
Hayes	53	909	17	10
Baynham	29	380	13	3
Norman	18	204	11	1
Perkins	17	180	11	2
Gent	16	194	12	0
Shy	10	105	11	0
Garrison	7	111	16	0
Reeves	7	84	12	1
Homan	4	92	23	1
Randle	4	56	14	1
Wright	1	15	15	1

PUNT RETURNS

Last Name	No.	Yds	Avg	TD
Hayes	15	312	21	2
Rentzel	14	93	7	0
Homan	1	0	0	0

KICKOFF RETURNS

Last Name	No.	Yds	Avg	TD
Baynham	23	590	26	0
Daniels	9	193	21	0
Homan	2	21	11	0
Hayes	1	20	20	0
Neely	3	17	6	0
Norman	1	0	0	0

PASSING – PUNTING – KICKING

PASSING	Att	Comp	%	Yds	Yd/Att	TD	Int–	%	RK
Meredith	309	171	55	2500	8.1	21	12–	4	2
Morton	85	44	52	752	8.9	4	6–	7	
Reeves	4	2	50	43	10.8	0	0–	0	
Baynham	1	0	0	0	0.0	0	0–	0	

PUNTING	No	Avg
Widby	59	40.9

KICKING	XP	Att	%	FG	Att	%
M. Clark	54	54	100	17	29	59

NEW YORK GIANTS

RUSHING

Last Name	No.	Yds	Avg	TD
Frederickson	142	486	3.4	1
Koy	89	394	4.4	3
Duhon	101	362	3.6	3
Tarkenton	57	301	5.3	3
Blye	53	243	4.6	1
Minniear	14	38	2.7	2
Morrison	9	28	3.1	0
Jones	3	18	6.0	0
Thomas	2	14	7.0	0
Wood	2	0	0.0	0
Young	2	−2	−1.0	0

RECEIVING

Last Name	No.	Yds	Avg	TD
Jones	45	1057	23	7
Morrison	37	425	11	6
Duhon	37	373	10	1
Thomas	29	449	15	4
Koy	12	59	5	1
Blye	10	91	9	0
Frederickson	10	64	6	2
Crespino	7	130	19	0
Wilson	4	34	9	0
Minniear	4	32	8	0
Larson	0	1	0	0

PUNT RETURNS

Last Name	No.	Yds	Avg	TD
Lockhart	13	69	5	0
Duhon	7	32	5	0

KICKOFF RETURNS

Last Name	No.	Yds	Avg	TD
Blye	35	734	21	0
Duhon	13	214	16	0
Holifield	7	111	16	0
Frederickson	2	13	7	0
Koontz	1	13	13	0
Hinton	1	12	12	0
Lurtsema	1	11	11	0
Eaton	1	2	2	0
Williams	1	0	0	0

PASSING – PUNTING – KICKING

PASSING	Att	Comp	%	Yds	Yd/att	TD	Int–	%	RK
Tarkenton	337	182	54	2555	7.6	21	12–	4	5
Wood	24	9	38	123	5.1	0	5–	21	
Koy	3	2	67	13	4.3	0	0–	0	
Duhon	2	2	100	24	12.0	0	0–	0	

PUNTING	No	Avg
Koy	44	37.5
Williams	10	29.1
Lockhart	3	36.7

KICKING	XP	Att	%	FG	Att	%
Gogolak	30	30	100	14	24	58

WASHINGTON REDSKINS

RUSHING

Last Name	No.	Yds	Avg	TD
Allen	123	399	3.2	4
Brunet	71	227	3.2	0
Thurlow	51	184	3.6	0
Larson	44	132	3.0	1
Whitfield	37	125	3.4	0
Mitchell	10	46	4.6	0
Jurgensen	8	21	2.6	1
Beban	5	18	3.6	0
Ninowski	2	13	6.5	0
D. Smith	3	5	1.7	0
Theofiledes	3	0	0.0	0
Taylor	2	−3	−1.5	0
Bragg	1	−3	−3.0	0

RECEIVING

Last Name	No.	Yds	Avg	TD
Taylor	48	650	14	5
Jerry Smith	45	626	14	6
Richter	42	533	13	9
Allen	21	294	14	1
Brunet	18	160	9	1
Mitchell	14	130	9	0
Whitfield	13	107	8	0
Thurlow	12	151	13	0
Larson	12	146	12	1
D. Smith	1	15	15	0
Beban	1	12	12	0

PUNT RETURNS

Last Name	No.	Yds	Avg	TD
Harris	19	144	8	0
Jim Smith	6	38	6	0
Martin	2	12	6	0
Mitchell	1	0	0	0
Owens	1	0	0	0

KICKOFF RETURNS

Last Name	No.	Yds	Avg	TD
Harris	23	579	25	0
Mitchell	11	235	21	0
D. Smith	10	228	23	0
Larson	6	151	25	0
Martin	7	146	21	0
Jim Smith	3	61	20	0
Rock	2	10	5	0
Barnes	1	0	0	0
McKeever	1	0	0	0

PASSING – PUNTING – KICKING

PASSING	Att	Comp	%	Yds	Yd/Att	TD	Int–	%	RK
Jurgensen	292	167	57	1980	6.8	17	11–	4	8
Ninowski	95	49	52	633	6.7	4	6–	6	
Theofiledes	20	11	55	211	10.6	2	1–	5	
Beban	1	0	0	0	0.0	0	0–	0	

PUNTING	No	Avg
Bragg	76	43.3

KICKING	XP	Att	%	FG	Att	%
Gogolak	30	31	97	9	19	47

PHILADELPHIA EAGLES

RUSHING

Last Name	No.	Yds	Avg	TD
Woodeshick	217	947	4.4	3
Lang	69	235	3.4	0
Pinder	40	117	2.9	0
Ballman	1	30	30.0	0
Snead	9	27	3.0	0
Jones	22	24	1.1	0
Conjar	8	21	2.6	0
Huarte	2	9	4.5	0

RECEIVING

Last Name	No.	Yds	Avg	TD
Hawkins	42	707	17	5
Woodeshick	36	328	9	0
F. Hill	30	370	12	3
Ballman	30	341	11	4
Lang	17	147	9	1
Pinder	16	166	10	0
Ditka	13	111	9	2
Jones	5	87	17	0
Hughes	3	39	13	0
Mallory	1	58	58	1
Baker	1	3	3	0

PUNT RETURNS

Last Name	No.	Yds	Avg	TD
Haymond	15	201	13	1
Mallory	4	46	12	0
Scarpati	5	17	3	0

KICKOFF RETURNS

Last Name	No.	Yds	Avg	TD
Haymond	28	677	24	1
Nelson	11	308	28	0
Hawkins	12	254	21	0
Mallory	6	94	16	0
Rossovich	2	20	10	0
Jones	1	18	18	0
Graham	1	8	8	0

PASSING – PUNTING – KICKING

PASSING	Att	Comp	%	Yds.	Yd/Att	TD	Int–	%	RK
Snead	291	152	52	1655	5.7	11	21–	7	15
Huarte	15	7	47	110	7.3	1	2–	13	
Scarpati	2	1	50	3	1.5	0	0–	0	
Baker	1	1	100	58	58.0	1	0–	0	

PUNTING	No	Avg
Baker	55	40.9
Duncan	5	45.6

KICKING	XP	Att	%	FG	Att	%
Baker	17	21	81	19	30	63

CENTURY DIVISION

CLEVELAND BROWNS 10-4-0 Blanton Collier

Scores of Each Game		
24	New Orleans	10
7	Dallas	28
6	LOS ANGELES	24
31	PITTSBURGH	24
21	ST. LOUIS	27
30	Baltimore	20
30	ATLANTA	7
33	San Francisco	21
35	NEW ORLEANS	17
45	Pittsburgh	24
47	PHILADELPHIA	13
45	NEW YORK	10
24	Washington	21
16	St. Louis	27

Use Name	Pos.	Hgt	Wgt	Age	Int	Pts
Monte Clark	OT	6'6"	255	31		
Dick Schafrath	OT	6'3"	255	32		
Joe Taffoni	OT	6'3"	250	23		
Jim Copeland	OG	6'2"	245	23		
John Demarie	OG	6'3"	255	23		
Gene Hickerson	OG	6'3"	248	33		
Fred Hoaglin	C	6'4"	240	24		
Bob Whitlow	C	6'1"	236	32		
Bill Glass	DE	6'5"	255	32	2	6
Jack Gregory	DE	6'6"	250	23		
Ron Snidow	DE	6'4"	250	26		
Marv Upshaw	DE	6'3"	245	21		
Walter Johnson	DT	6'3"	270	25		
Jim Kanicki	DT	6'4"	270	26		
Bill Sabatino	DT	6'3"	245	23		
Billy Andrews	LB	6'	225	23		
John Garlington	LB	6'1"	225	22	1	
Jim Houston	LB	6'2"	245	31	3	
Dale Lindsey	LB	6'3"	225	25	1	
Bob Matheson	LB	6'4"	240	23	2	
Wayne Meylan	LB	6'1"	240	22		
Erich Barnes	DB	6'2"	198	33	3	6
Ben Davis	DB	5'11"	185	22	8	
Mike Howell	DB	6'1"	187	25	6	
Nate James	DB	6'1"	195	23		
Ernie Kellerman	DB	6'	183	24	6	
Alvin Mitchell	DB	6'3"	195	24		
Carl Ward	DB	5'9"	180	24		
Bill Nelsen	QB	6'	195	27		6
Frank Ryan	QB	6'3"	200	32		
Leroy Kelly	HB	6'	200	26		120
Reece Morrison	HB	6'	205	22		12
Ernie Green	FB	6'2"	205	29		12
Charlie Harraway	FB	6'2"	230	23		6
Charlie Leigh	FB	5'11"	205	22		6
Eppie Barney	WR	6'	204	24		12
Gary Collins	WR	6'4"	215	27		
Ron Green	WR	6'1"	200	24		
Tommy McDonald	WR	5'10"	175	34		6
Paul Warfield	WR	6'	188	25		72
Milt Morin	TE	6'4"	250	26		30
Ralph Smith	TE	6'2"	220	29		
Don Cockroft	K	6'1"	185	23		100

ST. LOUIS CARDINALS 9-4-1 Charlie Winner

Scores of Each Game		
13	LOS ANGELES	24
17	San Francisco	35
21	New Orleans	20
10	DALLAS	27
27	Cleveland	21
41	WASHINGTON	14
31	NEW ORLEANS	17
45	Philadelphia	17
28	PITTSBURGH	28
0	Baltimore	27
17	ATLANTA	12
20	Pittsburgh	10
28	New York	21
27	CLEVELAND	16

Use Name	Pos.	Hgt	Wgt	Age	Int	Pts
Bob Duncum	OT	6'3"	250	24		
Ernie McMillan	OT	6'6"	260	30		
Bob Reynolds	OT	6'6"	265	27		
Clyde Williams	OG-OT	6'2"	255	28		
Ken Gray	OG	6'2"	250	32		
Rick Sortun	OG	6'2"	235	25		
Ted Wheeler	OG	6'3"	245	22		
Irv Goode	C-OG	6'4"	250	27		
Bob DeMarco	C	6'3"	240	30		
Dick Kasperek	C	6'3"	225	24		
Don Brumm	DE	6'3"	245	25		6
Dave Long	DE	6'4"	235	23		
Chuck Walker	DE	6'2"	245	27		
Fred Heron	DT	6'4"	250	23		
Bob Rowe	DT	6'4"	260	23		
Joe Schmiesing	DE-DT	6'4"	243	23		
Ernie Clark	LB	6'1"	230	30	1	
Dave Meggyesy	LB	6'1"	220	26		
Jamie Rivers	LB	6'2"	235	22	2	
Rocky Rosema	LB	6'2"	220	22		
Larry Stallings	LB	6'2"	230	26		
Mike Strofolino	LB	6'2"	230	24		
Bob Atkins	DB	6'3"	212	22	2	
Mike Barnes	DB	6'3"	205	23		
Brady Keys	DB	6'	185	32	1	
Chuck Latourette	DB	6'	190	23		6
Lonnie Sanders	DB	6'3"	207	26	3	
Mac Sauls	DB	6'	185	23		
Jerry Stovall	DB	6'2"	205	26		
Larry Wilson	DB	6'	190	30	4	
Jim Hart	QB	6'2"	195	24		36
Charley Johnson	QB	6'	190	31		
MacArthur Lane	HB	6'	220	26		
Johnny Roland	HB	6'2"	207	25		12
Roy Shivers	HB	6'	200	26		42
Willie Crenshaw	FB	6'2"	230	27		42
Cid Edwards	FB	6'2"	230	24		6
Bobby Joe Conrad	WR	6'	195	33		24
Jerry Daanen	WR	6'	190	23		
Freddie Hyatt	WR	6'3"	212	22		
Bob Lee	WR	6'3"	200	23		
Dave Williams	WR	6'2"	205	23		36
Chuck Logan	TE	6'4"	220	25		
Jackie Smith	TE	6'4"	215	27		30
Jim Bakken	K	6'	200	27		85

NEW ORLEANS SAINTS 4-9-1 Tom Fears

Scores of Each Game		
10	CLEVELAND	24
37	WASHINGTON	17
20	ST. LOUIS	21
21	New York	38
20	MINNESOTA	17
16	Pittsburgh	12
17	St. Louis	31
3	DALLAS	17
17	Cleveland	35
7	Green Bay	29
20	Detroit	20
17	CHICAGO	23
17	Philadelphia	29
24	PITTSBURGH	14

Use Name	Pos.	Hgt	Wgt	Age	Int	Pts
Jim Boeke	OT	6'5"	260	29		
Jerry Jones	OT	6'3"	265	24		
Dave McCormick	OT	6'6"	250	25		
Jerry Sturm	OT	6'3"	260	31		
Jake Kupp	OG	6'3"	233	26		
Ross Gwinn	OG	6'3"	273	24		
Roy Schmidt	OG	6'3"	250	26		
Del Williams	OG	6'2"	245	22		
Joe Wendryhoski	C	6'2"	245	29		
Doug Atkins	DE	6'8"	270	38		
Brian Schweda	DE	6'3"	240	25		
Tom Carr	DT	6'3"	267	26		
Lou Cordileone	DT	6'	250	31	1	
Earl Leggett	DT	6'3"	265	34		
Dave Rowe	DT	6'6"	265	23		
Mike Tilleman	DE-DT	6'5"	280	24		
Johnny Brewer	LB	6'4"	235	31		
Bill Cody	LB	6'1"	220	24		
Ted Davis	LB	6'1"	232	26		
Jim Ferguson	LB	6'4"	240	25		
Les Kelley	LB	6'3"	233	23	1	
Steve Stonebreaker	LB	6'3"	225	30		
Fred Whittingham	LB	6'1"	240	29	1	
Bo Burris	DB	6'3"	195	23	3	6
John Douglas	DB	6'1"	195	23		
Ross Fichtner	DB	6'	195	30		
Gene Howard	DB	6'	190	21	3	
Elbert Kimbrough	DB	5'11"	197	29	1	
Elijah Nevett	DB	6'	185	24		
Dave Whitsell	DB	6'	190	32	6	6
George Youngblood	DB	6'3"	205	23		
Billy Kilmer	QB	6'	204	28		12
Ronnie South	QB	6'1"	195	23		
Karl Sweetan	QB	6'1"	200	25		
Charlie Brown	HB	5'10"	187	22		6
Don McCall	HB	5'11"	195	23		36
Tom Barrington	FB-HB	6'1"	213	24		6
Tony Baker	FB	5'11"	230	23		
Tony Lorick	FB	6'1"	217	26		18
Ernie Wheelwright	FB	6'3"	236	31		6
Randy Schultz	HB-FB	5'11"	210	24		
Dan Abramowicz	WR	6'1"	195	23		42
John Gilliam	WR	6'1"	190	23		
Dave Parks	WR	6'2"	203	26		
Dave Szymakowski	WR	6'2"	198	22		
Jim Hester	TE	6'4"	225	23		12
Ray Poage	TE	6'4"	205	27		
Monte Stickles	TE	6'4"	235	30		12
Charlie Durkee	K	5'11"	165	24		84
Jim Fraser	K	6'3"	235	32		
Tom McNeill	K	6'1"	195	26		

PITTSBURGH STEELERS 2-11-1 Bill Austin

Scores of Each Game		
20	NEW YORK	34
10	Los Angeles	45
7	BALTIMORE	41
24	Cleveland	31
13	Washington	16
12	NEW ORLEANS	16
6	PHILADELPHIA	3
41	Atlanta	21
28	St. Louis	28
24	CLEVELAND	45
28	SAN FRANCISCO	45
10	ST. LOUIS	20
7	Dallas	28
14	New Orleans	24

Use Name	Pos.	Hgt	Wgt	Age	Int	Pts
John Brown	OT	6'2"	248	29		
Mike Haggerty	OT	6'4"	230	22		
Fran O'Brien	OT	6'1"	265	32		
Ernie Ruple	OT	6'4"	256	22		
Mike Taylor	OT	6'4"	247	23		
Sam Davis	OG	6'1"	245	24		
Larry Gagner	OG	6'3"	240	24		
Bruce Van Dyke	OG	6'2"	235	24		
Ralph Wenzel	OG	6'3"	240	25		
Mike Connelly	C	6'3"	248	32		
Ray Mansfield	C	6'3"	250	27		
Ben McGee	DE	6'2"	260	26		
Lloyd Voss	DE	6'4"	260	26		
Dick Arndt	DT	6'5"	265	24		
Chuck Hinton	DT	6'5"	260	29		
Ken Kortas	DT	6'2"	280	26		
Frank Parker	DT	6'5"	270	28		
John Campbell	LB	6'3"	225	29	1	
Dick Capp	LB	6'3"	235	24		
John Foruria	LB	6'2"	205	23		
Jerry Hillebrand	LB	6'3"	240	28	2	
Ray May	LB	6'1"	230	23	3	6
Andy Russell	LB	6'3"	215	26	2	
Bill Saul	LB	6'4"	225	27		
Lou Harris	DB	6'	180	22		
Bob Hohn	DB	6'	185	27		
Paul Martha	DB	6'	185	25	3	6
Clendon Thomas	DB	6'2"	200	31	3	
Bob Wade	DB	6'2"	200	23		
Marv Woodson	DB	6'	195	25	3	
Kent Nix	QB	6'1"	195	24		
Dick Shiner	QB	6'	197	26		
Rocky Bleier	HB	5'11"	190	22		
Dick Hoak	HB	5'11"	190	29		24
Don Shy	HB	6'1"	210	22		6
Tom Watkins	HB	6'1"	195	31		
Willie Asbury	FB	6'1"	230	25		
Earl Gros	FB	6'3"	230	27		36
Dick Compton	WR	6'1"	200	28		6
Marshall Cropper	WR	6'3"	210	24		
Ken Hebert	WR	6'	200	23		
Roy Jefferson	WR	6'2"	195	24		72
J. R. Wilburn	WR	6'2"	190	25		18
Jon Henderson	DB-WR	6'	195	23		
John Hilton	TE	6'5"	220	26		6
Tony Jeter	TE	6'3"	223	21		
Dick Kotite	TE	6'3"	235	25		12
Booth Lusteg	K	5'11"	190	27		50
Bill Shockley	K	6'	185	30		2
Bobby Walden	K	6'	190	30		

CENTURY DIVISION

CLEVELAND BROWNS

RUSHING

Last Name	No.	Yds	Avg	TD
Kelly	248	1239	5.0	16
Harraway	91	334	3.7	0
E. Green	41	152	3.7	0
Leigh	23	144	6.3	1
Ryan	11	64	5.8	0
Morrison	18	39	2.2	1
Nelsen	13	30	2.3	1
Smith	1	13	13.0	0
Morin	1	8	8.0	0
Barney	0	8	0.0	1

RECEIVING

Last Name	No.	Yds	Avg	TD
Warfield	50	1067	21	12
Morin	43	792	18	5
Kelly	22	297	14	4
Barney	18	189	11	1
E. Green	16	142	9	2
Harraway	12	162	14	1
Collins	9	230	26	0
McDonald	7	113	16	1
Leigh	3	−4	−1	0
Morrison	2	40	20	1
Smith	2	11	6	0

PUNT RETURNS

Last Name	No.	Yds	Avg	TD
Leigh	14	76	5	0
Davis	9	11	1	0
Kelly	1	9	9	0

KICKOFF RETURNS

Last Name	No.	Yds	Avg	TD
Leigh	14	322	23	0
Ward	13	236	18	0
James	8	166	21	0
Davis	8	152	19	0
Morrison	4	85	21	0
Kelly	1	10	10	0
Smith	1	3	3	0
Andrews	1	0	0	0
Barnes	1	0	0	0
Copeland	1	0	0	0
Houston	1	0	0	0
Howell	1	0	0	0

PASSING – PUNTING – KICKING

PASSING	Att	Comp	%	Yds	Yd/Att	TD	Int–	%	RK
Nelsen	293	152	52	2366	8.1	19	10–	3	6
Ryan	66	31	47	639	9.7	7	6–	9	
Kelly	4	1	25	34	8.5	1	0–	0	

PUNTING	No	Avg
Cockroft	61	37.7
Collins	2	26.0

KICKING	XP	Att	%	FG	Att	%
Cockroft	46	48	96	18	24	75

ST. LOUIS CARDINALS

RUSHING

Last Name	No.	Yds	Avg	TD
Crenshaw	203	813	4.0	6
Roland	121	455	3.8	2
Edwards	31	214	6.9	1
Shivers	44	184	4.2	4
Smith	12	163	13.6	3
Lane	23	74	3.2	0
D. Williams	3	47	15.7	0
Hart	19	20	1.1	6
Latourette	1	15	15.0	0
Wilson	1	12	12.0	0
Johnson	5	−1	−0.2	0

RECEIVING

Last Name	No.	Yds	Avg	TD
Smith	49	789	16	2
D. Williams	43	682	16	6
Conrad	32	449	14	4
Crenshaw	23	232	10	1
Shivers	9	103	11	3
Roland	8	97	12	0
Daanen	4	35	9	0
Edwards	1	2	2	0

PUNT RETURNS

Last Name	No.	Yds	Avg	TD
Latourette	28	345	12	1
Roland	3	11	4	0

KICKOFF RETURNS

Last Name	No.	Yds	Avg	TD
Latourette	46	1237	27	0
Crenshaw	6	104	17	0
Roland	3	63	21	0
Long	1	0	0	0

PASSING – PUNTING – KICKING

PASSING	Att	Comp	%	Yds	Yd/Att	TD	Int–	%	RK
Hart	316	140	44	2059	6.5	15	18–	6	14
Johnson	67	29	43	330	4.9	1	1–	1	
Latourette	1	0	0	0	0.0	0	0–	0	
Roland	1	0	0	0	0.0	0	1–	100	

PUNTING	No	Avg
Latourette	65	41.6

KICKING	XP	Att	%	FG	Att	%
Bakken	40	40	100	15	24	63

NEW ORLEANS SAINTS

RUSHING

Last Name	No.	Yds	Avg	TD
McCall	155	637	4.1	4
Lorick	104	344	3.3	0
Schultz	43	152	3.5	0
Barrington	45	111	2.5	0
Wheelwright	21	99	4.7	1
Kilmer	21	97	4.6	2
Gilliam	2	36	18.0	0
Abramowicz	2	27	13.6	0
Poage	1	22	22.0	0
South	4	5	1.3	0
Baker	4	2	0.5	0
McNeill	2	1	0.5	0
Whitsell	1	−1	−1.0	0
Sweetan	4	−5	−1.3	0

RECEIVING

Last Name	No.	Yds	Avg	TD
Abramowicz	54	890	16	7
Lorick	26	272	10	3
McCall	26	270	10	2
Parks	25	258	10	0
Gilliam	24	284	11	0
Hester	17	300	18	2
Stickles	15	206	14	2
Schultz	12	34	3	0
Barrington	9	33	4	1
Poage	1	11	11	0
Wheelwright	1	−9	−9	0

PUNT RETURNS

Last Name	No.	Yds	Avg	TD
Gilliam	15	60	4	0
Brown	8	60	8	1
Howard	8	42	5	0
Nevett	3	−9	−3	0

KICKOFF RETURNS

Last Name	No.	Yds	Avg	TD
Howard	23	533	23	0
Gilliam	15	328	22	0
Brown	8	137	17	0
Nevett	2	94	47	0
Stonebreaker	1	22	22	0
Kelley	1	20	20	0
Douglas	1	10	10	0
Jones	1	5	5	0
Whitsell	1	0	0	0

PASSING – PUNTING – KICKING

PASSING	Att	Comp	%	Yds	Yd/Att	TD	Int–	%	RK
Kilmer	315	167	53	2060	6.5	15	17–	5	10
Sweetan	78	27	35	318	4.1	1	9–	12	
South	38	14	37	129	3.4	1	3–	8	
Barrington	6	2	33	42	7.0	0	0–	0	
McCall	1	0	0	0	0.0	0	0–	0	
Parks	1	0	0	0	0.0	0	0–	0	

PUNTING	No	Avg
McNeill	49	41.0
South	14	27.6
Fraser	11	35.5
Lorick	1	36.0

KICKING	XP	Att	%	FG	Att	%
Durkee	27	27	100	19	37	51

PITTSBURGH STEELERS

RUSHING

Last Name	No.	Yds	Avg	TD
Hoak	175	858	4.9	3
Gros	151	579	3.8	3
Shy	35	106	3.0	1
Jefferson	6	57	9.5	0
Shiner	14	53	3.8	0
Bleier	6	39	6.5	0
Nix	6	15	2.5	0
Asbury	4	9	2.3	0
Walden	2	5	2.5	0

RECEIVING

Last Name	No.	Yds	Avg	TD
Jefferson	58	1074	19	11
Wilburn	39	514	13	3
Hoak	28	253	9	1
Gros	27	211	8	3
Hilton	20	285	14	1
Shy	13	106	8	0
Kotite	6	65	11	2
Compton	5	45	9	1
Cropper	4	54	14	0
Bleier	3	68	23	0
Asbury	3	27	9	0
Henderson	3	26	9	0
Hillebrand	1	27	27	0
Jeter	1	9	9	0

PUNT RETURNS

Last Name	No.	Yds	Avg	TD
Jefferson	28	274	10	1
Harris	6	21	4	0
Bleier	2	13	7	0
Watkins	2	0	0	0

KICKOFF RETURNS

Last Name	No.	Yds	Avg	TD
Shy	28	682	24	0
Henderson	29	589	20	0
Bleier	6	119	20	0
Cropper	3	53	8	0
Watkins	1	22	22	0
Harris	1	19	19	0
Hilton	1	9	9	0
Taylor	1	9	9	0

PASSING – PUNTING – KICKING

PASSING	Att	Comp	%	Yds	Yd/Att	TD	Int–	%	RK
Shiner	304	148	49	1856	6.1	18	17–	6	12
Nix	130	56	43	720	5.5	4	8–	6	
Hoak	16	7	44	188	11.8	0	1–	6	
Walden	1	0	0	0	0.0	0	0–	0	

PUNTING	No	Avg
Walden	68	40.4

KICKING	XP	Att	%	FG	Att	%
Lusteg	26	29	90	8	20	40
Shockley	2	3	67	0	1	0

CENTRAL DIVISION

MINNESOTA VIKINGS 8-6-0 Bud Grant

Scores of Each Game		
47	ATLANTA	7
26	Green Bay	13
17	CHICAGO	27
24	DETROIT	10
17	New Orleans	20
7	DALLAS	20
24	Chicago	26
27	WASHINGTON	14
14	GREEN BAY	10
13	Detroit	6
9	Baltimore	21
3	LOS ANGELES	31
30	San Francisco	20
24	Philadelphia	17

Use Name	Pos.	Hgt	Wgt	Age	Int	Pts
Grady Alderman	OT	6'2"	240	29		
Doug Davis	OT	6'4"	250	24		
Ron Yary	OT	6'6"	265	22		
Bookie Bolin	OG	6'2"	240	28		
Larry Bowie	OG	6'2"	255	28		
Milt Sunde	OG	6'2"	250	25		
Jim Vellone	OG	6'2"	255	24		
Mick Tingelhoff	C	6'1"	237	28		
Carl Eller	DE	6'6"	265	26		
Jim Marshall	DE	6'3"	235	30		2
Steve Smith	DE	6'5"	240	24		
Paul Dickson	DT	6'5"	255	31		
Gary Larsen	DT	6'5"	255	28		
Alan Page	DT	6'5"	265	23		

Use Name	Pos.	Hgt	Wgt	Age	Int	Pts
Jim Hargrove	LB	6'3"	230	22		
Wally Hilgenberg	LB	6'3"	225	25		
John Kirby	LB	6'3"	235	26		
Mike McGill	LB	6'2"	237	21		
Lonnie Warwick	LB	6'3"	235	26		
Roy Winston	LB	6'1"	230	28		
Bobby Bryant	DB	6'	175	24	2	6
Dale Hackbart	DB	6'3"	210	32		
Karl Kassulke	DB	6'	195	26	1	
Paul Krause	DB	6'3"	195	26	7	
Earsell Mackbee	DB	6'1"	195	27	2	
Ed Sharockman	DB	6'	200	28	4	
Charlie West	DB	6'1"	190	22		6

Don Hansen – Knee Injury

Use Name	Pos.	Hgt	Wgt	Age	Int	Pts
Gary Cuozzo	QB	6'1"	198	27		
King Hill (from PHI)	QB	6'3"	216	32		
Joe Kapp	QB	6'2"	212	30		18
Earl Denny	HB	6'1"	200	23		
Clint Jones	HB	6'	206	23		6
Dave Osborn	HB	6'	205	25		
Jim Lindsey	FB-HB	6'2"	200	23		24
Bill Brown	FB	5'11"	230	30		84
Oscar Reed	HB-FB	5'11"	220	24		
Bob Goodridge	WR	6'2"	202	22		
Bob Grim	WR	6'	197	23		
Tom Hall	WR	6'1"	195	27		6
John Henderson	WR	6'3"	190	25		
Art Powell	WR	6'3"	214	31		
Gene Washington	WR	6'3"	218	24		36
John Beasley	TE	6'3"	228	23		
Billy Martin	TE	6'4"	235	25		6
Fred Cox	K	5'10"	200	29		88

CHICAGO BEARS 7-7-0 Jim Dooley

Scores of Each Game		
28	WASHINGTON	38
0	Detroit	42
27	Minnesota	17
7	Baltimore	28
10	DETROIT	28
29	Philadelphia	16
26	MINNESOTA	24
13	Green Bay	10
27	SAN FRANCISCO	19
13	ATLANTA	16
3	DALLAS	34
23	New Orleans	17
17	Los Angeles	16
27	GREEN BAY	28

Use Name	Pos.	Hgt	Wgt	Age	Int	Pts
Randy Jackson	OT	6'5"	245	24		
Wayne Mass	OT	6'4"	245	22		
Bob Pickens	OT	6'4"	258	25		
Bob Wetoska	C-OT	6'3"	240	30		
Jim Cadile	OG	6'3"	240	27		
Doug Kriewald	OG	6'4"	245	23		
George Seals	OG	6'2"	260	25		
Mike Pyle	C	6'3"	250	29		
Ed O'Bradovich	DE	6'3"	255	28		
Loyd Phillips	DE	6'3"	240	23	2	
Willie Holman	DT-DE	6'4"	250	23		
Frank Cornish	DT	6'6"	285	24		
Dick Evey	DT	6'2"	245	27	1	
John Johnson	DT	6'5"	260	27		

Use Name	Pos.	Hgt	Wgt	Age	Int	Pts
Doug Buffone	LB	6'1"	230	24	1	
Dick Butkus	LB	6'3"	245	24	3	
Rudy Kuechenberg	LB	6'2"	215	25		
Dan Pride	LB	6'3"	225	26		
Jim Purnell	LB	6'2"	238	26		
Mike Reilly	LB	6'2"	230	25		
Clarence Childs	DB	6'	180	29		
Curtis Gentry	DB	6'	185	27	1	
Major Hazelton	DB	6'1"	185	23		
Bennie McRae	DB	6'1"	180	27	4	
Richie Petitbon	DB	6'3"	205	30	2	
Joe Taylor	DB	6'2"	200	27	1	
Rosey Taylor	DB	5'11"	186	29	3	6

Marty Amsler – Injury
Terry Stoepel – Military Service

Use Name	Pos.	Hgt	Wgt	Age	Int	Pts
Rudy Bukich	QB	6'1"	205	37		
Virgil Carter	QB	6'1"	185	22		24
Jack Concannon	QB	6'3"	205	25		12
Larry Rakestraw	QB	6'2"	195	26		
Garry Lyle	HB	6'2"	198	22		
Gale Sayers	HB	6'1"	205	25		12
Brian Piccolo	HB	6'	205	24		12
Ralph Kurek	FB	6'2"	210	25		6
Andy Livingston	FB	6'	234	23		
Ronnie Bull	HB-FB	6'	200	28		18
Mike Hull	TE-FB	6'3"	220	23		
Dick Gordon	WR	5'11"	190	23		24
Bob Jones	WR	6'4"	196	23		
Cecil Turner	WR	5'10"	170	24		12
Bob Wallace	WR	6'3"	211	22		12
Austin Denney	TE	6'2"	230	24		12
Emilio Vallez	TE	6'2"	210	22		
Bobby Joe Green	K	5'11"	175	30		
Jon Kilgore	K	6'1"	205	24		
Mac Percival	K	6'4"	217	28		100

GREEN BAY PACKERS 6-7-1 Phil Bengtson

Scores of Each Game		
30	PHILADELPHIA	13
13	MINNESOTA	26
17	DETROIT	23
38	Atlanta	7
14	LOS ANGELES	16
14	Detroit	14
28	Dallas	17
10	CHICAGO	13
10	Minnesota	14
29	NEW ORLEANS	7
27	Washington	7
20	San Francisco	27
3	BALTIMORE	16
28	Chicago	27

Use Name	Pos.	Hgt	Wgt	Age	Int	Pts
Forrest Gregg	OT	6'4"	250	35		
Dick Himes	OT	6'4"	244	22		
Francis Peay	OT	6'5"	250	24		
Bob Skoronski	OT	6'3"	245	35		
Gale Gillingham	OG	6'3"	255	24		
Jerry Kramer	OG	6'3"	245	33		21
Bill Lueck	OG	6'3"	235	22		
Ken Bowman	C	6'3"	230	25		
Bob Hyland	OG-C	6'5"	250	23		
Lionel Aldridge	DE	6'4"	245	26		
Leo Carroll	DE	6'7"	250	24		
Willie Davis	DE	6'3"	245	35		
Francis Winkler	DE	6'3"	230	21		
Leon Crenshaw	DT	6'6"	280	25		
Henry Jordan	DT	6'3"	250	33		
Ron Kostelnik	DT	6'4"	260	28		
Bob Brown	DE-DT	6'5"	260	28		

Use Name	Pos.	Hgt	Wgt	Age	Int	Pts
Lee Roy Caffey	LB	6'3"	250	28		
Fred Carr	LB	6'5"	238	22		
Jim Flanigan	LB	6'3"	240	23		
Ray Nitschke	LB	6'3"	240	32	2	
Dave Robinson	LB	6'3"	240	27	2	
Phil Vandersea	TE-LB	6'3"	225	25		
Herb Adderley	DB	6'1"	200	29	3	
Tom Brown	DB	6'1"	190	27	4	12
Doug Hart	DB	6'1"	190	29	1	
Bob Jeter	DB	6'1"	205	30	3	
John Rowser	DB	6'1"	180	24		
Gordon Rule	DB	6'2"	180	22		
Willie Wood	DB	5'10"	190	32	2	

Jim Weatherwax – Knee Injury
Ben Wilson– Knee Injury

Use Name	Pos.	Hgt	Wgt	Age	Int	Pts
Zeke Bratkowski	QB	6'2"	210	36		
Don Horn	QB	6'2"	195	23		
Bart Starr	QB	6'1"	190	34		6
Bill Stevens	QB	6'3"	195	23		
Donny Anderson	HB	6'3"	210	25		36
Elijah Pitts	HB	6'1"	205	29		12
Travis Williams	HB	6'1"	210	22		
Jim Grabowski	FB	6'2"	220	24		24
Chuck Mercein	FB	6'3"	230	25		19
Carroll Dale	WR	6'1"	200	30		48
Boyd Dowler	WR	6'5"	225	31		36
Claudis James	WR	6'2"	190	24		12
Bucky Pope	WR	6'5"	200	25		
Marv Fleming	TE	6'4"	235	26		18
Errol Mann	K	6'	203	27		4
Mike Mercer (from BUF-A)	K	6'	217	32		33

DETROIT LIONS 4-8-2 Joe Schmidt

Scores of Each Game		
13	Dallas	59
42	CHICAGO	0
23	Green Bay	17
10	Minnesota	24
28	Chicago	10
14	GREEN BAY	14
7	SAN FRANCISCO	14
7	Los Angeles	10
10	BALTIMORE	27
6	MINNESOTA	13
20	NEW ORLEANS	20
0	PHILADELPHIA	12
24	Atlanta	7
3	Washington	14

Use Name	Pos.	Hgt	Wgt	Age	Int	Pts
Charlie Bradshaw	OT	6'6"	260	32		
Bill Cottrell	OT	6'3"	250	23		
Rocky Freitas	OT	6'6"	258	22		
Greg Kent	OT	6'6"	265	25		
Roger Shoals	OT	6'4"	255	29		
Frank Gallagher	OG	6'2"	240	25		
Bob Kowalkowski	OG	6'3"	245	24		
Chuck Walton	OG	6'3"	250	27		
Ed Flanagan	C	6'3"	250	24		
John Baker	DE	6'6"	270	33		
Larry Hand	DE	6'4"	245	28		
Lew Kamanu	DE	6'4"	245	24		
Joe Robb	DE	6'3"	245	31		
Alex Karras	DT	6'2"	255	32		
Denis Moore	DT	6'5"	255	25		
Jerry Rush	DT	6'4"	260	26		
Chuck Sieminski	DT	6'4"	270	28		

Use Name	Pos.	Hgt	Wgt	Age	Int	Pts
Mike Lucci	LB	6'2"	230	28	1	
Ed Mooney	LB	6'2"	238	23		
Paul Naumoff	LB	6'1"	225	23	1	
Bill Swain	LB	6'2"	230	27	1	6
Wayne Walker	LB	6'2"	225	31	1	24
Lem Barney	DB	6'	185	22	7	12
Dick LeBeau	DB	6'1"	185	31	5	
Wayne Rasmussen	DB	6'2"	175	26		
Bobby Rasmussen	DB	5'10"	185	28		
Tom Vaughn	DB	5'11"	190	25	3	
Mike Weger	DB	6'2"	185	22	5	
Jim Welch	HB-DB	6'	196	30		

Use Name	Pos.	Hgt	Wgt	Age	Int	Pts
Greg Landry	QB	6'4"	205	21		6
Bill Munson	QB	6'2"	200	26		6
Mike Campbell	HB	5'11"	200	23		
Nick Eddy	HB	6'1"	205	24		
Mel Farr	HB	6'2"	205	23		42
Dave Kopay	FB-HB	6'2"	225	26		
Tom Nowatzke	FB	6'3"	230	25		6
Bill Triplett	HB-FB	6'2"	210	29		
Billy Gambrell	WR	5'10"	175	26		42
Bill Malinchak	WR	6'1"	200	24		
Earl McCullouch	WR	5'11"	172	22		30
Phil Odle	WR	5'11"	187	25		
Jim Gibbons	TE	6'2"	230	32		
Charlie Sanders	TE	6'4"	215	22		6
Jerry DePoyster	K	6'1"	200	22		27

CENTRAL DIVISION

MINNESOTA VIKINGS

RUSHING

Last Name	No.	Yds	Avg	TD
Brown	222	805	3.6	11
Jones	128	536	4.2	1
Kapp	50	269	5.4	3
Lindsey	53	152	2.9	4
Osborn	42	140	3.3	0
Denny	2	9	4.5	0
Reed	2	6	3.0	0
Cuozzo	1	4	4.0	0
Hill	1	1	1.0	0

RECEIVING

Last Name	No.	Yds	Avg	TD
Washington	46	756	16	6
Brown	31	329	11	3
Beasley	23	289	13	0
Hall	19	268	14	1
Lindsey	15	148	10	0
Martin	10	101	10	1
Henderson	4	42	11	0
Jones	4	26	7	0
Powell	1	31	31	0
Goodridge	1	5	5	0

PUNT RETURNS

Last Name	No.	Yds	Avg	TD
West	20	201	10	1
Bryant	10	49	5	0

KICKOFF RETURNS

Last Name	No.	Yds	Avg	TD
West	22	576	26	0
Bryant	19	373	20	0
Jones	4	60	15	0
Denny	3	19	6	0
Sharockman	1	14	14	0
Lindsey	1	7	7	0
Alderman	1	0	0	0
Martin	1	0	0	0

PASSING – PUNTING – KICKING

PASSING	Att	Comp	%	Yds	Yd/Att	TD	Int–	%	RK
Kapp	248	129	52	1695	6.8	10	17–	7	13
Hill	71	33	47	531	7.5	3	6–	8	
Cuozzo	33	24	73	297	9.0	1	0–	0	
Brown	1	1	100	3	3.0	0	0–	0	

PUNTING	No	Avg
Hill	33	41.0
Martin	28	37.4

KICKING	XP	Att	%	FG	Att	%
Cox	31	32	97	19	29	66

CHICAGO BEARS

RUSHING

Last Name	No.	Yds	Avg	TD
Sayers	138	856	6.2	2
Bull	107	472	4.4	3
Piccolo	123	450	3.7	2
Carter	48	265	5.5	4
Concannon	28	104	3.7	2
Kurek	17	95	5.6	1
Wallace	3	29	9.7	0
Lyle	4	28	7.0	0
Livingston	7	25	3.6	0
Hull	12	22	1.8	0
Turner	2	16	8.0	0
Rakestraw	9	12	1.3	0
Green	1	4	4.0	0
Denney	1	–1	–1.0	0

RECEIVING

Last Name	No.	Yds	Avg	TD
Gordon	29	477	16	4
Piccolo	28	291	10	0
Denney	23	247	11	2
Wallace	19	281	15	2
Bull	17	145	9	0
Sayers	15	117	8	0
Turner	14	208	15	2
Lyle	5	32	6	0
Kurek	4	50	13	0
Hull	4	20	5	0

PUNT RETURNS

Last Name	No.	Yds	Avg	TD
Sayers	2	29	15	0
Wallace	6	27	5	0
Turner	9	19	2	0
Gordon	1	5	5	0
Hazelton	1	1	1	0

KICKOFF RETURNS

Last Name	No.	Yds	Avg	TD
Sayers	17	461	27	0
Turner	20	363	18	0
Childs	8	291	36	0
Gordon	3	97	32	0
Wallace	3	80	27	0
Kurek	4	48	12	0
Butkus	2	30	15	0
Kuechenburg	1	0	0	0

PASSING – PUNTING – KICKING

PASSING	Att	Comp	%	Yds	Yd/Att	TD	Int–	%	RK
Concannon	143	71	50	715	5.0	5	9–	6	16
Carter	122	55	45	769	6.3	4	5–	4	
Rakestraw	67	30	45	361	5.4	1	7–	10	
Bukich	7	2	29	23	3.3	0	0–	0	
Sayers	2	0	0	0	0.0	0	0–	0	
Bull	1	0	0	0	0.0	0	0–	0	
Kilgore	1	0	0	0	0.0	0	0–	0	

PUNTING	No	Avg
Kilgore	35	35.2
Green	27	42.3
Lyle	4	33.5

KICKING	XP	Att	%	FG	Att	%
Percival	25	25	100	25	36	69

GREEN BAY PACKERS

RUSHING

Last Name	No.	Yds	Avg	TD
Anderson	170	761	4.5	5
Grabowski	135	518	3.8	3
Pitts	72	264	3.7	2
Williams	33	63	1.9	0
Starr	11	62	5.6	1
Mercein	17	49	2.9	1
Bratkowski	8	24	3.0	0
James	1	15	15.0	0
Horn	3	–7	–2.3	0

RECEIVING

Last Name	No.	Yds	Avg	TD
Dowler	45	668	15	6
Dale	42	818	19	8
Anderson	25	333	13	1
Fleming	25	278	11	3
Grabowski	18	210	12	0
Pitts	17	142	8	0
James	8	148	19	2
Williams	5	48	10	0
Mercein	3	6	2	0

PUNT RETURNS

Last Name	No.	Yds	Avg	TD
Wood	26	126	5	0
T. Brown	16	111	7	1
Pitts	1	1	1	0

KICKOFF RETURNS

Last Name	No.	Yds	Avg	TD
Williams	28	599	21	0
Adderley	14	331	24	0
Pitts	2	40	20	0
Robinson	2	29	15	0
Vandersea	1	8	8	0
Winkler	1	0	0	0

PASSING – PUNTING – KICKING

PASSING	Att	Comp	%	Yds	Yd/Att	TD	Int–	%	RK
Starr	171	109	64	1617	9.5	15	8–	5	4
Bratkowski	126	68	54	835	6.6	3	7–	6	
Horn	16	10	63	187	11.7	2	0–	0	
Anderson	3	1	33	12	4.0	1	0–	0	
Stevens	2	0	0	0	0.0	0	0–	0	

PUNTING	No	Avg
Anderson	59	40.0

KICKING	XP	Att	%	FG	Att	%
Mercer	12	14	86	7	12	58
Kramer	9	9	100	4	9	44
Mercein	7	7	100	2	5	40
Mann	4	4	100	0	3	0

DETROIT LIONS

RUSHING

Last Name	No.	Yds	Avg	TD
Farr	128	597	4.7	3
Triplett	120	384	3.2	0
Kopay	53	207	3.9	0
Eddy	48	176	3.7	0
Nowatzke	36	116	3.2	1
Munson	25	109	4.4	1
Landry	7	39	5.6	1
Campbell	7	24	3.4	0
DePoyster	1	20	20.0	0
Welch	3	14	4.7	0
McCullouch	3	13	4.3	0
Sanders	2	3	1.5	0

RECEIVING

Last Name	No.	Yds	Avg	TD
McCullouch	40	680	17	5
Sanders	40	533	13	1
Gambrell	28	492	18	7
Triplett	28	135	5	0
Farr	24	375	16	4
Kopay	18	130	7	0
Eddy	8	91	11	0
Odle	6	71	12	0
Nowatzke	4	6	2	0
Gibbons	2	38	19	0
Campbell	2	15	8	0
Malinchak	1	41	41	0

PUNT RETURNS

Last Name	No.	Yds	Avg	TD
Barney	13	79	6	0
Eddy	4	10	3	0
Vaughn	2	0	0	0

KICKOFF RETURNS

Last Name	No.	Yds	Avg	TD
Barney	25	670	27	1
Thompson	17	363	21	0
Vaughn	5	128	26	0
Nowatzke	3	34	11	0
Kopay	2	29	15	0
Gambrell	1	12	12	0
Mooney	1	11	11	0

PASSING – PUNTING – KICKING

PASSING	Att	Comp	%	Yds	Yd/Att	TD	Int–	%	RK
Munson	329	181	55	2311	7.0	15	8–	2	7
Landry	48	23	48	338	7.0	2	7–	15	

PUNTING	No	Avg
DePoyster	71	40.4

KICKING	XP	Att	%	FG	Att	%
DePoyster	18	20	90	3	15	20
Walker	6	6	100	6	14	43

COASTAL DIVISION

BALTIMORE COLTS 13-1-0 Don Shula

Scores of Each Game	
27 SAN FRANCISCO	10
28 Atlanta	20
41 Pittsburgh	7
28 CHICAGO	7
42 San Francisco	14
20 CLEVELAND	30
27 LOS ANGELES	10
26 New York	0
27 Detroit	10
27 ST. LOUIS	0
21 MINNESOTA	9
44 ATLANTA	0
16 Green Bay	3
28 Los Angeles	24

Use Name	Pos.	Hgt	Wgt	Age	Int	Pts
Sam Ball	OT	6'4"	240	24		
Bob Vogel	OT	6'5"	250	26		
Cornelius Johnson	OG	6'2"	245	25		
Glen Ressler	OG	6'3"	250	24		
Dan Sullivan	OG	6'3"	250	29		
Bill Curry	C	6'2"	235	25		
Dick Szymanski	C	6'3"	235	36		
Ordell Braase	DE	6'4"	245	36		
Roy Hilton	DE	6'6"	240	23	1	6
Lou Michaels	DE	6'2"	250	32		102
John Williams	DE	6'3"	256	22		
Fred Miller	DT	6'3"	250	27		
Billy Ray Smith	DT	6'4"	250	33		
Bubba Smith	DE-DT	6'7"	295	23		
Mike Curtis	LB	6'2"	232	25	2	6
Dennis Gaubatz	LB	6'2"	232	27	2	
Bob Grant	LB	6'2"	225	21		
Ron Porter	LB	6'3"	232	23		
Don Shinnick	LB	6'	228	33	1	
Sid Williams	LB	6'2"	235	26		
Ocie Austin	DB	6'3"	200	21		
Bobby Boyd	DB	5'10"	192	30	8	6
Jerry Logan	DB	6'1"	190	27	3	
Lenny Lyles	DB	6'2"	204	32	5	
Charlie Stukes	DB	6'3"	212	24	1	6
Rick Volk	DB	6'3"	195	23	6	
Earl Morrall	QB	6'1"	206	34		6
Johnny Unitas	QB	6'1"	196	35		
Jim Ward	QB	6'2"	195	24		
Timmy Brown	HB	5'10"	198	31		12
Tom Matte	HB	6'	214	29		60
Preston Pearson	HB	6'1"	190	23		24
Terry Cole	FB	6'1"	220	23		18
Jerry Hill	FB	5'11"	215	28		12
Gail Cogdill (from DET)	WR	6'2"	195	31		
Alex Hawkins	WR	6'1"	186	31		
Jimmy Orr	WR	5'11"	185	32		36
Ray Perkins	WR	6'	183	26		6
Willie Richardson	WR	6'2"	198	28		48
John Mackey	TE	6'3"	224	26		30
Tom Mitchell	TE	6'2"	215	24		24
David Lee	K	6'4"	215	24		

LOS ANGELES RAMS 10-3-1 George Allen

Scores of Each Game	
24 St. Louis	13
45 PITTSBURGH	10
24 Cleveland	6
24 SAN FRANCISCO	10
16 Green Bay	14
27 ATLANTA	14
10 Baltimore	27
10 DETROIT	7
17 Atlanta	10
20 San Francisco	20
24 NEW YORK	21
31 Minnesota	3
16 CHICAGO	17
24 BALTIMORE	28

Use Name	Pos.	Hgt	Wgt	Age	Int	Pts
Joe Carollo	OT	6'2"	258	28		
Charley Cowan	OT	6'4"	265	30		
Jim Wilson	OT	6'3"	258	27		
Don Chuy	OG	6'1"	255	27		
Tom Mack	OG	6'3"	250	24		
Joe Scibelli	OG	6'1"	255	29		
George Burman	C-OG	6'3"	255	25		
Ken Iman	C	6'1"	240	29		
Frank Marchlewski (from ATL)	C	6'2"	238	24		
Deacon Jones	DE	6'5"	260	29		
Lamar Lundy	DE	6'7"	260	33		
Gregg Schumacher	DE	6'2"	240	26		
Coy Bacon	DT	6'4"	270	26		
Roger Brown	DT	6'5"	300	31		
Merlin Olsen	DT	6'5"	276	27		
Diron Talbert	DT	6'5"	238	24		
Maxie Baughan	LB	6'1"	230	30	4	
Gene Breen	LB	6'2"	230	27		
Tony Guillory	LB	6'4"	236	25		
Dean Halverson	LB	6'2"	220	22		
Jack Pardee	LB	6'2"	230	32	2	12
Myron Pottios	LB	6'2"	235	28		
Doug Woodlief	LB	6'3"	230	24		
Claude Crabb	DB	6'	192	28		
Irv Cross	DB	6'1"	195	29	3	
Willie Daniel	DB	5'11"	190	30		
Ed Meador	DB	5'11"	200	31	6	
Ron Smith	DB	6'1"	192	25	3	6
Clancy Williams	DB	6'2"	203	25	7	
Kelton Winston	DB	6'	195	27		
Roman Gabriel	QB	6'4"	230	28		24
Milt Plum	QB	6'1"	205	34		
Mike Dennis	HB	6'1"	207	24		
Willie Ellison	HB	6'1"	207	23		42
Vilnis Ezerins	FB-HB	6'1"	217	23		
Tommy Mason	FB-HB	6'	200	29		18
Dick Bass	FB	5'10"	195	31		18
Henry Dyer	FB	6'2"	235	23		6
Bernie Casey	WR	6'4"	212	29		30
Harold Jackson	WR	5'10"	175	22		
Jack Snow	WR	6'2"	195	25		18
Pat Studstill	WR	6'1"	175	30		6
Wendell Tucker	WR	5'10"	185	24		24
Dave Pivic	TE	6'3"	240	24		2
Billy Truax	TE	6'5"	235	25		18
Bruce Gossett	K	6'2"	230	25		88

Dave Cahill – Knee Injury
Chuck Lamson – Injury
Les Josephson – Foot Injury

SAN FRANCISCO FORTY NINERS 7-6-1 Dick Nolan

Scores of Each Game	
10 Baltimore	27
35 ST. LOUIS	17
28 ATLANTA	13
10 Los Angeles	24
14 BALTIMORE	42
26 New York	10
14 Detroit	7
21 CLEVELAND	33
19 Chicago	27
20 LOS ANGELES	20
45 Pittsburgh	28
27 GREEN BAY	20
20 MINNESOTA	30
14 Atlanta	12

Use Name	Pos.	Hgt	Wgt	Age	Int	Pts
Cas Banaszek	OT	6'3"	235	22		
Forrest Blue	OT	6'5"	248	22		
Lance Olssen	OT	6'5"	257	21		
Len Rohde	OT	6'4"	250	30		
Elmer Collett	OG	6'4"	244	23		
Howard Mudd	OG	6'3"	254	26		
Woody Peoples	OG	6'2"	247	25		
Bruce Bosley	C	6'2"	244	34		
Bill Belk	DE	6'3"	242	22	1	6
Stan Hindman	DE	6'3"	232	24	1	6
Clark Miller	DE	6'5"	247	29		
Charlie Johnson	DT	6'2"	265	24		
Charlie Krueger	DT	6'4"	260	32		
Roland Lakes	DT	6'4"	280	28		
Kevin Hardy	DE-DT	6'5"	287	23		
Ed Beard	LB	6'2"	226	28	2	
Tommy Hart	LB	6'3"	212	23		
Harold Hays	LB	6'3"	225	27		
Matt Hazeltine	LB	6'1"	230	35		
Frank Nunley	LB	6'2"	230	22		
Dave Wilcox	LB	6'3"	234	25		
Kermit Alexander	DB	5'11"	180	27	9	6
Johnny Fuller	DB	6'	175	22	2	
Jim Johnson	DB	6'2"	187	30	1	
Mel Phillips	DB	6'	192	26		
Al Randolph	DB	6'2"	192	24	4	
John Woitt	DB	5'11"	174	22		
John Brodie	QB	6'1"	210	33		
George Mira	QB	5'11"	190	26		
Steve Spurrier	QB	6'2"	203	23		
Doug Cunningham	HB	5'11"	193	22		
Clem Daniels	HB	6'1"	218	31		
Gary Lewis	HB	6'3"	230	26		24
Ken Willard	FB	6'2"	230	25		42
Bill Tucker	TE-FB	6'2"	220	24		42
Kay McFarland	WR	6'2"	186	29		6
Clifton McNeil	WR	6'2"	185	28		42
Dick Witcher	WR	6'3"	204	23		12
Dave Olerich	TE	6'1"	220	23		
Bob Windsor	TE	6'4"	224	25		12
John David Crow	HB-TE	6'2"	224	33		30
Tommy Davis	K	6'	220	33		53
Dennis Patera	K	6'	225	22		16

George Donnelly – Injury

Tom Holzer – Injury
George Rose – Injury
Don Parker – Knee Injury
John Thomas – Knee Injury
Dave Hettema – Military Service

ATLANTA FALCONS 2-12-0 Norb Hecker Norm Van Brocklin

Scores of Each Game	
7 Minnesota	47
20 BALTIMORE	28
13 San Francisco	28
7 GREEN BAY	38
24 NEW YORK	21
14 Los Angeles	27
7 Cleveland	30
21 PITTSBURGH	41
10 LOS ANGELES	17
16 Chicago	13
12 St. Louis	17
0 Baltimore	44
7 DETROIT	24
12 SAN FRANCISCO	14

Use Name	Pos.	Hgt	Wgt	Age	Int	Pts
Errol Linden	OT	6'5"	260	31		
Bill Sandeman	OT	6'6"	250	25		
Don Talbert	OT	6'5"	255	28		
Steve Duich	OG	6'3"	248	22		
Dan Grimm	OG	6'3"	245	27		
Jim Simon	OG	6'5"	240	27		
Randy Winkler	OT-OG	6'5"	255	25		
Joe Cerne	C	6'2"	240	25		
Phil Sobocinski	C	6'3"	235	22		
Rick Cash	DE	6'5"	260	23		
Claude Humphrey	DE	6'5"	255	24		
Jim Garcia	DT-DE	6'4"	250	24		
Carlton Dabney	DT	6'5"	250	21	1	
Jim Norton (to PHI)	DT	6'4"	254	25		
Jerry Shay	DT	6'3"	245	24		
Art Strahan	DT	6'5"	266	25		
Joe Szczecko	DT	6'	245	26		
Dick Absher	LB	6'4"	227	24		
Ron Acks	LB	6'2"	225	23		
Grady Allen	LB	6'3"	215	22		
Greg Brezina	LB	6'2"	220	22		
Ralph Heck	LB	6'2"	230	27	1	
Tommy Nobis	LB	6'2"	235	24	1	
Marion Rushing (to HOU-A)	LB	6'2"	230	31		
Jimmy Burson	DB	6'	185	26	4	6
Lee Calland	DB	6'	190	27	2	
Ollie Cordill	DB	6'2"	180	25		
Mike Freeman	DB	5'11"	190	24		
Floyd Hudlow	DB	5'11"	195	24		
Billy Lothridge	DB	6'1"	195	24	3	
Nick Rassas	DB	6'	190	24	1	
Ken Reaves	DB	6'3"	205	23	1	6
Phil Spiller (to CIN-A)	DB	6'	195	23		
Larry Suchy	DB	5'11"	180	22		
Bob Berry	QB	5'11"	190	26		12
Randy Johnson	QB	6'3"	196	24		6
Bruce Lemmerman	QB	6'1"	196	22		
Joe Auer	HB	6'1"	205	26		
Charlie Bryant	HB	6'1"	207	27		
Cannonball Butler	HB	5'10"	185	25		12
Perry Lee Dunn	HB	6'2"	215	25		18
Billy Harris	HB	6'	195	22		6
Dwight Lee (from SF)	HB	6'2"	198	22		
Doug Goodwin	FB	6'2"	228	26		
Brendan McCarthy (to DEN-A)	FB	6'3"	220	23		6
Harmon Wages	HB-FB	6'1"	210	22		6
Dave Dunaway (from GB)	WR	6'2"	205	23		
Rick Eber	WR	6'	173	23		
Paul Flatley	WR	6'1"	187	27		
Bob Long	WR	6'3"	205	27		24
Jerry Simmons	WR	6'1"	190	25		
John Wright	WR	6'	195	22		
Mike Donohoe	TE	6'3"	227	23		6
Ray Ogden	TE	6'5"	225	25		12
Bob Etter	K	5'11"	152	23		50

Junior Coffey – Knee Injury

Bob Sanders – Injury

COASTAL DIVISION

BALTIMORE COLTS

RUSHING

Last Name	No.	Yds	Avg	TD
Matte	183	662	3.6	9
Cole	104	418	4.0	3
Hill	91	360	4.0	1
Brown	39	159	4.1	2
MacKey	10	103	10.3	0
Pearson	19	78	4.1	0
Morrall	11	18	1.6	1
Lee	3	12	4.0	0
Unitas	3	−1	−0.3	0

RECEIVING

Last Name	No.	Yds	Avg	TD
Mackey	45	644	14	5
Richardson	37	698	19	8
Orr	29	743	26	6
Matte	25	275	11	1
Hill	18	161	9	1
Perkins	15	227	15	1
Cole	13	75	6	0
Mitchell	6	117	20	4
Brown	4	53	13	0
Cogdill	3	42	14	0
Pearson	2	70	35	2
Hawkins	2	31	16	0

PUNT RETURNS

Last Name	No.	Yds	Avg	TD
Volk	25	198	8	0
Brown	16	125	8	0
Logan	1	27	27	0

KICKOFF RETURNS

Last Name	No.	Yds	Avg	TD
Pearson	15	527	35	2
Brown	15	298	20	0
Cole	5	123	25	0
Matte	1	22	22	0
Porter	1	19	19	0
Logan	1	14	14	0

PASSING – PUNTING – KICKING

PASSING	Att	Comp	%	Yds	Yd/Att	TD	Int–	%	RK
Morrall	317	182	57	2909	9.2	26	17–	5	1
Unitas	32	11	34	139	4.3	2	4	13	
Ward	9	3	33	46	5.1	0	1–	11	
Matte	1	0	0	0	0.0	0	0–	0	

PUNTING	No	Avg
Lee	49	39.5

KICKING	XP	Att	%	FG	Att	%
Michaels	48	50	96	18	28	64

LOS ANGELES RAMS

RUSHING

Last Name	No.	Yds	Avg	TD
Ellison	151	616	4.1	5
Bass	121	494	4.1	1
Mason	108	395	3.7	3
Gabriel	34	139	4.1	4
Dennis	29	136	4.7	0
Dyer	55	136	2.5	1
Meador	1	11	11.0	0
Plum	2	3	1.5	0
Ezerins	2	2	1.0	0

RECEIVING

Last Name	No.	Yds	Avg	TD
Truax	35	417	12	3
Casey	29	565	19	5
Snow	29	500	17	3
Bass	27	195	7	2
Ellison	20	248	12	2
Mason	15	144	10	0
Dennis	8	53	7	0
Dyer	8	37	5	0
Tucker	7	124	18	4
Studstill	7	108	15	1
Pivec	3	27	9	0
Gabriel	1	−5	−5	0

PUNT RETURNS

Last Name	No.	Yds	Avg	TD
Smith	27	171	6	0
Meador	17	138	8	0

KICKOFF RETURNS

Last Name	No.	Yds	Avg	TD
Smith	26	718	28	1
Ellison	12	268	22	0
Meador	1	20	20	0
Williams	1	16	16	0
Dennis	2	2	1	0
Pivec	2	0	0	0
Ezerins	1	0	0	0

PASSING – PUNTING – KICKING

PASSING	Att	Comp	%	Yds	Yd/Att	TD	Int–	%	RK
Gabriel	366	184	50	2364	6.5	19	16–	4	9
Plum	12	5	42	49	4.1	1	1–	8	
Dennis	2	0	0	0	0.0	0	0–	0	
Mason	2	0	0	0	0.0	0	0–	0	
Ellison	1	0	0	0	0.0	0	0–	0	
Studstill	1	0	0	0	0.0	0	0–	0	

PUNTING	No	Avg
Studstill	81	39.6

KICKING	XP	Att	%	FG	Att	%
Gossett	37	37	100	17	31	55

SAN FRANCISCO FORTY NINERS

RUSHING

Last Name	No.	Yds	Avg	TD
Willard	227	967	4.3	7
Lewis	141	573	4.1	1
Tucker	30	136	4.6	3
Brodie	18	71	3.9	0
Daniels	12	37	3.1	0
Cunningham	6	7	1.2	0
Mira	1	5	5.0	0
Crow	4	4	1.0	0
McNeil	1	−1	−1.0	0
Spurrier	1	−15	−15.0	0

RECEIVING

Last Name	No.	Yds	Avg	TD
McNeil	71	994	14	7
Witcher	39	531	14	1
Willard	36	232	6	0
Crow	31	531	17	5
Lewis	27	244	9	3
Tucker	15	197	13	4
Windsor	8	146	18	2
McFarland	5	140	28	1
Cunningham	2	25	13	0
Daniels	2	23	12	0

PUNT RETURNS

Last Name	No.	Yds	Avg	TD
Alexander	24	87	4	0
Fuller	12	33	3	0

KICKOFF RETURNS

Last Name	No.	Yds	Avg	TD
Alexander	20	360	18	0
Cunningham	14	286	20	0
Daniels	10	206	21	0
Tucker	5	103	21	0
Fuller	1	23	23	0
Hays	2	21	11	0
Banaszek	1	15	15	0
Olerich	1	4	4	0
Hart	1	3	3	0
Nunley	2	0	0	0
Peoples	1	0	0	0

PASSING – PUNTING – KICKING

PASSING	Att	Comp	%	Yds	Yd/Att	TD	Int–	%	RK
Brodie	404	234	58	3020	7.5	22	21–	5	3
Mira	11	4	36	44	4.0	1	1–	9	
McNeil	2	1	50	43	21.5	1	1–	50	

PUNTING	No	Avg
Spurrier	68	39.0

KICKING	XP	Att	%	FG	Att	%
Davis	26	26	100	9	16	56
Patera	10	12	83	2	8	25

ATLANTA FALCONS

RUSHING

Last Name	No.	Yds	Avg	TD
Butler	94	365	3.9	2
Dunn	72	219	3.0	3
Wages	59	211	3.6	0
Harris	53	144	2.7	0
Berry	26	139	5.3	2
Johnson	11	97	8.8	1
McCarthy	31	86	2.8	1
Bryant	9	29	3.2	0
Auer	3	19	6.3	0
Ogden	1	12	12.0	0
Lee	6	7	1.2	0
Lemmerman	1	0	0.0	0
Simmons	1	−6	−6.0	0
Lothridge	1	−16	−16.0	0

RECEIVING

Last Name	No.	Yds	Avg	TD
Simmons	28	479	17	0
Ogden	25	452	18	2
Long	22	484	22	4
Flatley	20	305	15	0
Wages	16	121	8	1
Butler	15	127	8	0
McCarthy	13	119	9	0
Dunn	9	118	13	0
Donohoe	6	52	9	1
Harris	3	118	39	1
Bryant	1	11	11	0

PUNT RETURNS

Last Name	No.	Yds	Avg	TD
Burson	11	56	5	0
Rassas	4	10	3	0
Spiller	1	0	0	0

KICKOFF RETURNS

Last Name	No.	Yds	Avg	TD
Butler	37	799	22	0
Rassas	10	180	18	0
Bryant	5	112	22	0
Lee	3	63	21	0
Auer	2	31	16	0
Talbert	3	30	10	0
Wages	1	23	23	0
Donohoe	1	22	22	0
Szczecko	3	18	6	0
Spiller	1	18	18	0
Harris	1	16	16	0
Grimm	1	4	4	0
Allen	1	0	0	0
Cerne	1	0	0	0

PASSING – PUNTING – KICKING

PASSING	Att	Comp	%	Yds	Yd/Att	TD	Int–	%	RK
Johnson	156	73	47	892	5.7	2	10–	6	17
Berry	153	81	53	1433	9.4	7	13–	8	11
Lemmerman	15	3	20	40	2.7	0	1–	7	
Wages	2	1	50	21	10.5	0	0–	0	

PUNTING	No	Avg
Lothridge	75	44.3

KICKING	XP	Att	%	FG	Att	%
Etter	17	19	89	11	21	52

1968 A.F.L. The Jets, Heidi, and Howls

Heidi, the Swiss mountain girl from the storybooks, had football fans flooding telephone lines with cries of protest on November 17. With the Jets beating Oakland 32-29 with two minutes left in the game, NBC television was faced with a dilemma; it could either continue coverage of the football game to its conclusion or it could broadcast a special dramatization of "Heidi" at its scheduled hour and leave the football game before time ran out. NBC opted for "Heidi," and football fans poured calls of protest into the television station for taking the game off the air. To add fuel to the fire, the Raiders scored two touchdowns in those last minutes to take the game 43-32. NBC tried to make amends by showing films of the final two minutes of action on the late news shows, and the network promised never again to get burned with such a decision.

EASTERN DIVISION

New York Jets—There was no December collapse for the Jets this year, as they won their last three games from Miami, Cincinnati, and Miami, both easy marks. In first place heading into the final month, the Jets this year held onto the top spot right to the end. The New York offense was too much for the rest of the Eastern Division, with Joe Namath riding herd on one of pro football's most explosive attacks. Continuing to hit George Sauer and Don Maynard with bullet passes at regular intervals, Namath also blossomed into a top diagnostician, deftly sending runners Matt Snell and Emerson Boozer into the line at the right time more often than not. Much had been expected of the New York offense, and it delivered in style; but the New York defense, consistently downgraded by opponents and the press, hung together in a unit which jumped on every enemy mistake. Even place-kicker Jim Turner, aided by new holder Babe Parilli, had a good year. With the Eastern title in their pockets, the Jets headed for a post-season date with destiny.

Houston Oilers—The Oilers caught lightning in a bottle in their surprise 1967 Eastern title, but they dropped this year to a 7-7 mark more typical of a young club still in the midst of rebuilding. Paced by two of the league's top defensive players in George Webster and Miller Farr, the Oilers still surrendered points grudgingly, but the Houston attack frightened few opponents. Fullback Hoyle Granger ran well behind a strong line, but neither he nor Woody Campbell had game-breaking speed. The receiving was strengthened by rookies Mac Haik and Jim Beirne and the development of Alvin Reed into a top tight end, but quarterback problems made the Oiler passing game extremely erratic. Pete Beathard displayed a strong arm and periods of inaccuracy before an appendectomy shelved him late in the year, and Don Trull, picked up after the Patriots cut him, was not a permanent answer.

Miami Dolphins—Fullback Larry Csonka needed time to get used to pro football but showed unmistakable power as a runner. Catching on more quickly was halfback Jim Kiick, a fifth-round draft pick who was a reliable runner and receiver. The defense was shored up by freshmen Manny Fernandez and Dick Anderson; Fernandez, signed as a free agent, provided the team's only pass-rushing, while safetyman Anderson had a flair for both tackling and intercepting. Another rookie, tackle Doug Crusan, won a starting job in the offensive line. Of course, some of the veterans also turned in good performances, with quarterback Bob Griese leading the way. The second-year passer had a good season despite poor protection and the loss of Jack Clancy, his favorite receiver, to knee surgery. Split end Karl Noonan, a slow but meticulous receiver, filled in for Clancy and hauled in fifty-eight passes.

Boston Patriots—Coach Mike Holovak made a break with the past by trading veteran quarterback Babe Parilli to New York for young Mike Taliaferro, but the Boston attack suffered for the change. Taliaferro could not ignite the offense and lost his job to rookie Tom Sherman. Other veteran Patriot players endured poor seasons. A bad ankle robbed Jim Nance of much of his effectiveness, and bad knees put defensive end Larry Eisenhauer and middle linebacker Nick Buoniconti out of action for several games. Coach Holovak got good work from cornerback Leroy Mitchell, tight end Jim Whalen, center Jon Morris, and defensive tackle Houston Antwine, but the Patriots needed a complete overhauling.

Buffalo Bills—The Bills' quarterback ills started when veterans Jack Kemp and Tom Flores were both injured before the regular season began. Coach Joel Collier started the year with rookie Dan Darragh as the signal-caller, but with the offensive line thinned out by injuries and age, Darragh soon was racked up enough by enemy defenses that his knee gave out. Next on the firing line was Kay Stephenson, a young man picked up from San Diego, and he lasted a couple of games before going out with a broken collarbone. Ed Rutkowski, a veteran utility man who had last played quarterback at Notre Dame six years ago, then stepped in and stayed healthy while guiding the Bills to the end of the season. The team scored the least points in the league but did have the satisfaction of beating the Jets 37-35 for their only victory of the season. The Bills had been a championship team only two years before, so coach Collier paid with his head two games into the campaign.

WESTERN DIVISION

Oakland Raiders—The Raiders were hit with a long string of injuries, yet still charged to a 12-2 record and a tie for the Western title. Defensive tackle Tom Keating missed the entire season with an Achilles-tendon injury suffered in last year's AFL championship game, but Carleton Oats filled in competently and Dan Birdwell compensated with his best year ever. When linebacker Bill Laskey also hurt his Achilles tendon, rookie Chip Oliver stepped into the starting lineup with a fine performance. When a knee injury shelved cornerback Kent McCloughan in mid-season, the Raiders had an exciting substitute in rookie Butch Atkinson. The offense avoided injuries but found two new starters in wide receiver Warren Wells and halfback Charlie Smith. With the title on the line, Daryle Lamonica threw five touchdown passes to win the playoff game 41-6.

Kansas City Chiefs—The Chiefs came back from last year's poor season to tie for first place in the West with a 12-2 record. The Kansas City defense allowed the fewest points in the league, with top players in all departments. Jerry Mays and Buck Buchanan starred in the line, the linebacking trio of Bobby Bell, Willie Lanier, and Jim Lynch was tops in the league, and safety Johnny Robinson steadied a secondary with several new starters. The offense matched the defense in efficiency, although an injury to Otis Taylor put more emphasis on a ball-control attack. Rookie fullback Robert Holmes, an unknown fourteenth-round draft pick, surprised everyone with his dogged ball-carrying, while veterans Mike Garrett and Curtis McClinton were bothered by injuries.

San Diego Chargers—The Chargers made the Western pennant race a three-way affair until dropping three of their last four games. Before home-town audiences, the Chargers lost 37-15 to New York, 40-3 to Kansas City, and 34-27 to Oakland, shooting all their title hopes to pieces. The Chargers had to be ranked among the league powers, but they could not beat the other top teams like the Jets, Chiefs, and Raiders. The biggest problem for coach Sid Gillman was his defense. The front four of Steve DeLong, Scott Appleton, Russ Washington, and Houston Ridge had good college press clippings but rarely got to the enemy passer, the linebacking was no better than adequate, and the secondary was solid only at Kenny Graham's strong safety spot. The San Diego attack as always found ways to put points on the scoreboard regularly. Quarterback John Hadl, operating behind an excellent offensive line, kept receivers Lance Alworth and Gary Garrison busy catching passes, and although fullback Brad Hubbert missed most of the season with a knee injury, halfback Dickie Post kept up the fine running of his rookie year.

Denver Broncos—The Broncos embarrassed themselves by losing 24-10 to the new Cincinnati Bengals on opening day, but they jelled into a respectable team after losing their first three games. In a five-week stretch from October 6 to November 3, Denver beat the Bengals, Jets, Dolphins, and Patriots while losing only to the Chargers. The key to this hot streak was the heavy pressure put on opposing passers by the Bronco defensive line, with end Rich Jackson developing into an All-Pro performer and tackle Dave Costa providing steady play against the run. The linebacking and secondary still was in a state of flux, but the strong pressure exerted by the line prevented passers from exploiting these weak spots. The Denver attack moved the ball well until quarterback Steve Tensi and split end Al Denson both went out in mid-season with broken collarbones, but rookie Marlin Briscoe, the first black ever to play regularly at T-formation quarterback in the pro ranks, kept the club interesting to the end with his scrambling and clutch passing.

Cincinnati Bengals—Paul Brown had built the Cleveland Browns into a powerhouse by signing poised players returning from World War II, but he set a different course for the new Cincinnati Bengals. Brown threw his lineup open to rookies and young players who had not fit in elsewhere. With so many inexperienced players in the lineup, most clubs would have suffered through a dismal season of hard learning, but Brown drilled his young Bengals so that they learned and played competitive football right from the start.

FINAL TEAM STATISTICS

OFFENSE

	BOSTON	BUFFALO	CIN.	DENVER	HOUSTON	K.C.	MIAMI	N.Y.	OAKLAND	S.D.
FIRST DOWNS:										
Total	181	159	171	217	240	223	247	249	287	270
by Rushing	69	71	85	75	99	123	78	80	97	93
by Passing	94	72	73	124	128	89	144	144	162	164
by Penalty	18	16	13	18	13	11	25	25	28	13
RUSHING:										
Number	421	400	421	411	462	537	417	467	471	428
Yards	1362	1527	1807	1614	1804	2227	1704	1608	2168	1765
Average Yards	3.1	3.8	4.3	3.9	3.9	4.1	4.1	3.4	4.6	4.1
Touchdowns	8	9	14	11	16	16	12	22	16	12
PASSING:										
Attempts	409	405	313	427	414	270	423	436	468	472
Completions	160	168	167	179	191	156	216	217	237	225
Completion Percentage	39.1	41.5	53.4	41.9	46.1	57.8	51.1	49.8	50.6	47.7
Passing Yards	2121	1714	1896	2826	2864	2492	2843	3574	3771	3813
Average Yards per Att.	5.2	4.2	6.1	6.6	6.9	9.2	6.7	8.2	8.1	8.1
Average Yards per Comp.	13.3	10.2	11.4	15.8	15.0	16.0	13.2	16.5	15.9	16.9
Tackled Att. to pass	38	39	38	51	29	24	52	18	29	18
Yards Lost Tackled	356	371	277	469	316	216	441	135	243	190
Net Yards	1765	1343	1619	2357	2548	2276	2402	3439	3528	3623
Touchdowns	16	7	8	20	17	20	21	20	31	29
Interceptions	33	28	11	27	25	11	22	19	18	33
Percent Intercepted	8.1	6.9	3.5	6.3	6.0	4.1	5.2	4.4	3.8	7.0
PUNTS:										
Number	96	100	84	96	73	65	75	68	64	56
Average Distance	39.9	41.8	40.9	42.7	41.2	45.3	40.6	43.8	43.6	40.7
PUNT RETURNS:										
Number	37	44	30	38	52	31	28	36	55	39
Yards	197	301	196	332	443	450	205	286	666	292
Average Yards	5.3	6.8	6.5	8.7	8.5	14.5	7.3	7.9	12.1	7.5
Touchdowns	0	1	0	1	0	2	0	0	2	1
KICKOFF RETURNS:										
Number	71	69	54	60	53	38	50	46	49	51
Yards	1442	1537	1068	1361	1235	736	1134	995	1092	1065
Average Yards	20.3	22.3	19.8	22.7	23.3	19.9	22.7	21.6	22.3	20.9
Touchdowns	0	1	0	0	0	0	0	0	0	0
INTERCEPTION RETURNS:										
Number	23	22	10	20	20	37	22	28	25	20
Yards	220	475	144	165	396	469	386	456	424	275
Average Yards	9.6	21.6	14.4	8.3	19.8	12.7	17.5	16.3	17.0	13.8
Touchdowns	1	4	2	0	5	2	1	2	4	2
PENALTIES:										
Number	67	67	55	73	61	66	48	76	81	72
Yards	682	687	586	772	644	650	485	742	958	654
FUMBLES:										
Number	28	23	27	28	28	26	17	19	34	20
Number Lost	20	14	10	13	13	16	8	9	21	12
POINTS:										
Total	229	199	215	255	303	371	276	419	453	382
PAT (kick) Attempts	26	19	24	32	38	40	36	43	54	43
PAT (kick) Made	26	19	24	31	37	39	36	43	54	40
PAT (2-Point) Attempts	0	3	1	0	0	0	0	2	1	2
PAT (2-Point) Made	0	2	0	0	0	0	0	1	1	2
FG Attempts	27	28	27	23	29	40	19	46	34	32
FG Made	15	14	13	10	12	30	8	34	21	22
Percent FG Made	55.6	50.0	48.1	43.5	41.4	75.0	42.1	73.9	61.8	68.8
Safeties	1	1	1	1	1	1	0	1	2	1

DEFENSE

	BOSTON	BUFFALO	CIN.	DENVER	HOUSTON	K.C.	MIAMI	N.Y.	OAKLAND	S.D.
FIRST DOWNS:										
Total	237	210	275	251	198	215	240	178	215	225
by Rushing	86	85	116	94	89	52	116	59	83	90
by Passing	123	103	140	145	96	140	112	104	113	118
by Penalty	28	22	19	12	13	23	12	15	19	17
RUSHING:										
Number	479	505	473	457	462	365	445	368	442	439
Yards	1825	2021	2097	1861	1704	1266	2172	1195	1804	1641
Average Yards	3.8	4.0	4.4	4.1	3.7	3.5	4.9	3.2	4.1	3.7
Touchdowns	22	15	13	20	9	4	19	9	12	13
PASSING:										
Attempts	416	340	411	429	359	461	342	403	446	430
Completions	200	143	212	217	158	214	179	187	189	217
Completion Percentage	48.1	42.1	51.6	50.6	44.0	46.4	52.3	46.4	42.4	50.5
Passing Yards	2826	2477	2903	3419	2003	3262	2904	2567	2657	2896
Average Yards per Att.	6.8	7.3	7.1	8.0	5.6	7.1	8.5	6.4	6.0	6.7
Average Yards per Comp.	14.1	17.3	13.7	15.8	12.7	15.2	16.2	13.7	14.1	13.3
Tackled Att. to pass	27	31	32	31	33	45	21	43	49	24
Yards Lost Tackled	236	273	283	256	332	439	192	399	400	204
Net Yards	2590	2204	2620	3163	1671	2823	2712	2168	2257	2692
Touchdowns	20	19	25	25	13	14	23	17	13	20
Interceptions	23	22	10	20	20	37	22	28	25	20
Percent Intercepted	5.5	6.5	2.4	4.7	5.6	8.0	6.4	6.9	5.6	4.7
PUNTS:										
Number	81	75	63	76	88	73	55	98	94	74
Average Distance	40.5	39.7	44.2	43.0	44.1	42.8	43.4	38.4	42.3	42.3
PUNT RETURNS:										
Number	59	45	41	46	40	31	28	39	40	21
Yards	502	521	252	282	379	220	250	531	211	220
Average Yards	8.5	11.6	6.1	6.1	9.5	7.1	8.9	13.6	5.3	10.5
Touchdowns	1	1	0	0	1	0	0	3	0	1
KICKOFF RETURNS:										
Number	40	49	40	29	58	54	54	82	75	60
Yards	901	1062	977	704	1302	1044	1108	1664	1652	1251
Average Yards	22.5	21.7	24.4	24.3	22.4	19.3	20.5	20.3	22.0	20.9
Touchdowns	0	0	1	0	0	0	0	0	0	0
INTERCEPTION RETURNS:										
Number	33	28	11	27	25	11	22	19	18	33
Yards	510	472	79	328	326	119	432	455	155	534
Average Yards	15.5	16.9	7.2	12.1	13.0	10.8	19.6	23.9	8.6	16.2
Touchdowns	3	6	0	3	2	0	3	4	0	2
PENALTIES:										
Number	70	66	62	64	54	62	70	65	90	63
Yards	874	540	632	750	526	564	655	695	932	692
FUMBLES:										
Number	37	24	19	24	17	22	28	29	24	26
Number Lost	17	13	9	12	10	12	18	15	15	15
POINTS:										
Total	406	367	329	404	248	170	355	280	233	310
PAT (kick) Attempts	49	41	39	47	25	18	44	34	23	35
PAT (kick) Made	49	40	37	47	25	18	43	33	22	35
PAT (2-Point) Attempts	0	0	0	1	1	0	1	2	3	1
PAT (2-Point) Made	0	0	0	1	1	0	1	2	1	0
FG Attempts	31	48	35	34	30	27	24	17	28	31
FG Made	21	27	18	21	21	14	12	9	17	19
Percent FG Made	67.7	56.3	51.4	61.8	70.0	51.9	50.0	52.9	60.7	61.3
Safeties	0	0	2	2	1	1	2	0	1	1

WESTERN DIVISION PLAYOFF

December 22 at Oakland
(Attendance 53,605)

SCORING

OAKLAND	21	7	0	13	–41
KANSAS CITY	0	6	0	0	– 6

First Quarter
- Oak. Biletnikoff, 24 yard pass from Lamonica
  PAT–Blanda (kick)
- Oak. Wells, 23 yard pass from Lamonica
  PAT–Blanda (kick)
- Oak. Biletnikoff, 44 yard pass from Lamonica
  PAT–Blanda (kick)

Second Quarter
- K.C. Stenerud, 10 yard field goal
- K.C. Stenerud, 8 yard field goal
- Oak. Biletnikoff, 54 yard pass from Lamonica
  PAT–Blanda (kick)

Fourth Quarter
- Oak. Wells, 35 yard pass from Lamonica
  PAT–Blanda (kick)
- Oak. Blanda, 41 yard field goal
- Oak. Blanda, 40 yard field goal

TEAM STATISTICS

OAK.		K.C.
22	First Downs–Total	13
7	First Downs–Rushing	3
14	First Downs–Passing	9
1	First Downs–Penalty	1
1	Fumbles–Number	2
0	Fumbles–Lost Ball	0
1	Penalties–Number	2
2	Yards Penalized	20
0	Missed Field Goals	1
70	Offensive Plays–Total	61
454	Net Yards	312
6.5	Average Gain	5.1
0	Giveaways	4
4	Takeaways	0
+4	Difference	–4

INDIVIDUAL STATISTICS

OAKLAND	No.	Yds.	Avg.	KANSAS CITY	No.	Yds.	Avg.
RUSHING							
Smith	13	74	5.7	Holmes	13	46	3.5
Banaszak	3	19	6.3	Hayes	3	10	3.3
Dixon	10	13	1.3	Dawson	2	9	4.5
Hagberg	4	12	3.0	Garrett	6	5	0.8
	30	118	3.9		24	70	2.9
RECEIVING							
Biletnikoff	7	180	25.7	Pitts	5	56	11.2
Smith	5	52	10.4	Taylor	4	117	29.3
Wells	4	93	23.3	Garrett	4	31	7.8
Cannon	2	15	7.5	Richardson	3	57	19.0
Dixon	1	7	7.0	Holmes	1	–8	–8.0
	19	347	18.3		17	253	14.9
PUNTING							
Eischeid	5		45.4	Wilson	6		50.3
PUNT RETURNS							
Bird	3	29	9.7	Smith	2	–9	–4.5
KICKOFF RETURNS							
Atkinson	1	34	34.0	Smith	5	73	14.6
				Mitchell	2	46	23.0
				Lanier	1	0	0.0
					8	119	14.9
INTERCEPTION RETURNS							
Wilson	1	14	14.0	None			
Hopkins	1	7	7.0				
Connors	1	5	5.0				
Brown	1	0	0.0				
	4	26	6.5				

PASSING

	Att.	Comp.	Comp. Pct.	Yds.	Int.	Yds/ Att.	Yds/ Comp.	Yards Lost Tackled
OAKLAND								
Lamonica	39	19	48.7	347	0	8.9	18.3	1–11
KANSAS CITY								
Dawson	36	17	47.2	253	4	7.0	14.9	1–11

NEW YORK JETS 11-3-0 Weeb Ewbank

Scores of Each Game		
20	Kansas City	19
47	Boston	31
35	Buffalo	37
23	SAN DIEGO	20
13	DENVER	21
20	Houston	14
48	BOSTON	14
25	BUFFALO	21
26	HOUSTON	7
32	Oakland	43
37	San Diego	15
35	MIAMI	17
27	CINCINNATI	14
31	Miami	7

Use Name	Pos.	Hgt	Wgt	Age	Int	Pts
Winston Hill	OT	6'4"	280	26		
Sam Walton	OT	6'5"	270	25		
Jeff Richardson	C-OT	6'3"	250	23		
Randy Rasmussen	OG	6'2"	255	23		
Bob Talamini	OG	6'1"	255	29		
Dave Herman	OT-OG	6'2"	255	26		
John Schmitt	C	6'4"	245	25		
Paul Crane	LB-C	6'2"	205	24		2
Verlon Biggs	DE	6'4"	270	25		
Gerry Philbin	DE	6'2"	245	27		
Steve Thompson	DE	6'5"	245	23		
John Elliott	DT	6'4"	245	23		
Ray Hayes	DT	6'5"	245	21		
Karl Henke	DT	6'4"	245	23		
Paul Rochester	DT	6'2"	255	31		
Carl McAdams	DE-DT	6'3"	240	24		

Use Name	Pos.	Hgt	Wgt	Age	Int	Pts
Al Atkinson	LB	6'1"	230	25	2	
Ralph Baker	LB	6'3"	235	26	3	
Larry Grantham	LB	6'	210	29		
Mike Stromberg	LB	6'2"	235	23		
Bill Baird	DB	5'10"	180	29	4	
Randy Beverly	DB	5'11"	185	24	4	6
Earl Christy	DB	5'11"	195	25	1	
Mike D'Amato	DB	6'2"	204	25		
John Dockery	DB	6'	186	23		
Cornell Gordon	DB	6'	187	27	2	
Jim Hudson	DB	6'2"	210	25	5	
Jim Richards	DB	6'1"	180	21		
Johnny Sample	DB	6'1"	208	31	7	6

Paul Seiler – Military Service

Use Name	Pos.	Hgt	Wgt	Age	Int	Pts
Joe Namath	QB	6'2"	195	25		12
Babe Parilli	QB	6'1"	190	38		6
Jim Turner	QB	6'2"	205	27		145
Emerson Boozer	HB	5'11"	204	25		30
Bill Mathis	HB	6'1"	220	29		38
Billy Joe	FB	6'2"	236	27		18
Matt Snell	FB	6'2"	220	26		42
Lee White	FB	6'4"	240	22		
Mark Smolinski	TE-FB	6'	215	29		6
Don Maynard	WR	6'1"	180	32		60
Harvey Nairn	WR	6'1"	178	22		
Bill Rademacher	WR	6'1"	190	26		
George Sauer	WR	6'1"	195	24		18
Bake Turner	WR	6'	180	28		12
Curley Johnson	TE	6'	215	33		
Pete Lammons	TE	6'3"	228	24		18

HOUSTON OILERS 7-7-0 Wally Lemm

Scores of Each Game		
21	KANSAS CITY	26
24	Miami	10
14	San Diego	30
15	OAKLAND	24
7	MIAMI	24
16	Boston	0
14	NEW YORK	20
30	Buffalo	7
27	Cincinnati	17
7	New York	26
38	DENVER	17
10	Kansas City	24
35	BUFFALO	6
45	BOSTON	17

Use Name	Pos.	Hgt	Wgt	Age	Int	Pts
Glen Ray Hines	OT	6'5"	265	24		
Bob Robertson	OT	6'4"	246	21		
Walt Suggs	OT	6'5"	265	29		
Sonny Bishop	OG	6'2"	245	28		
Tom Regner	OG	6'1"	255	24		
Dick Swatland	OG	6'3"	245	22		
Bobby Maples	C	6'3"	245	25		
Steve Quinn	C	6'1"	225	22		
Elvin Bethea	DE	6'3"	250	22		
Gary Cutsinger	DE	6'4"	245	27		
Pat Holmes	DE	6'5"	250	28		
Bud Marshall	DT	6'5"	275	26		
Dudley Meredith (from BUF)	DT	6'4"	285	33		
Willie Parker	DT	6'2"	265	23		
George Rice	DT	6'3"	260	24		
Carel Stith	DT	6'5"	265	23		
Tom Domres	DE-DT	6'3"	255	21		

Use Name	Pos.	Hgt	Wgt	Age	Int	Pts
Pete Barnes	LB	6'3"	245	23		
Garland Boyette	LB	6'1"	245	28	1	
Ronnie Caveness	LB	6'1"	225	25		
Marion Rushing (from ATL-N)	LB	6'2"	230	31		
Rich Stotter	LB	6'	225	23		
Olen Underwood	LB	6'1"	230	26	1	2
George Webster	LB	6'4"	223	22	1	
Larry Carwell	DB	6'1"	190	24	4	6
Miller Farr	DB	6'1"	190	25	3	12
W. K. Hicks	DB	6'1"	195	25	3	
Ken Houston	DB	6'3"	192	23	5	12
Pete Johns	DB	6'3"	190	23		
Zeke Moore	DB	6'2"	198	24		
Jim Norton	DB	6'3"	180	29	2	
Bob Smith	DB	6'	180	23		

Use Name	Pos.	Hgt	Wgt	Age	Int	Pts
Pete Beathard	QB	6'2"	207	26		12
Bob Davis	QB	6'3"	208	22		6
Don Trull	QB	6'1"	196	26		
Sid Blanks	HB	6'	210	27		
Ode Burrell	HB	6'	192	28		
Woody Campbell	HB	5'11"	202	23		36
Hoyle Granger	FB	6'1"	225	24		42
Roy Hopkins	FB	6'1"	225	23		
Glenn Bass	WR	6'2"	210	29		
Jim Beirne	WR	6'2"	196	21		24
Charley Frazier	WR	6'	184	29		
Mac Haik	WR	6'1"	196	22		48
Lionel Taylor	WR	6'2"	215	32		
Jim LeMoine	TE	6'2"	245	23		
Alvin Reed	TE	6'5"	230	24		30
Wayne Walker	K	6'2"	215	23		50
John Wittenborn	K	6'2"	240	32		23

MIAMI DOLPHINS 5-8-1 George Wilson

Scores of Each Game		
10	HOUSTON	24
21	OAKLAND	47
3	KANSAS CITY	48
24	Houston	7
14	BUFFALO	14
24	Cincinnati	22
14	Denver	21
28	San Diego	34
21	Buffalo	17
21	CINCINNATI	38
34	Boston	10
17	New York	35
38	BOSTON	7
7	NEW YORK	31

Use Name	Pos.	Hgt	Wgt	Age	Int	Pts
Doug Crusan	OT	6'5"	255	22		
Norm Evans	OT	6'5"	250	25		
Jack Pyburn	OT	6'6"	250	23		
Charlie Fowler	OG	6'2"	260	24		
Billy Neighbors	OG	5'11"	250	28		
Maxie Williams	OG	6'4"	250	28		
Freddie Woodson	DE-OG	6'2"	255	24		
Tom Goode	C	6'3"	250	29		
Mel Branch	DE	6'2"	235	31		
Manny Fernandez	DE	6'2"	250	22		
Bob Joswick	DE	6'5"	250	22		
Jim Riley	DE	6'4"	255	23		
Ray Jacobs	DT	6'3"	285	28		
Tom Nomina	DT	6'5"	260	26		
John Richardson	DT	6'2"	260	23		
Jim Urbanek	DT	6'4"	270	23		

Use Name	Pos.	Hgt	Wgt	Age	Int	Pts
Rudy Barber	LB	6'1"	255	23		
John Bramlett	LB	6'2"	210	27	2	
Bob Bruggers (to SD)	LB	6'1"	230	24		
Randy Edmunds	LB	6'2"	220	22	1	
Frank Emanuel	LB	6'3"	225	25	2	6
Jimmy Keyes	LB	6'2"	225	24		51
Wahoo McDaniel	LB	6'	230	31		
Ed Weisacosky	LB	6'	230	24		
Dick Anderson	DB	6'2"	205	22	8	6
Mack Lamb	DB	6'1"	188	24	1	
Bob Neff	DB	6'	180	24		
Bob Petrella	DB	6'	185	23	1	
Jimmy Warren	DB	5'11"	175	29	2	
Dick Washington	DB	6'1"	205	23		
Willie West	DB	5'10"	187	30	4	6
Dick Westmoreland	DB	6'1"	195	27	1	

Jack Clancy – Knee Injury

Use Name	Pos.	Hgt	Wgt	Age	Int	Pts
Bob Griese	QB	6'1"	190	23		6
Kim Hammond	QB	6'1"	192	23		
Rick Norton	QB	6'1"	190	24		
Jack Harper	HB	5'11"	190	23		
Jim Kiick	HB	5'11"	215	22		24
Sam Price	HB	5'11"	215	24		
Gary Tucker	HB	5'11"	195	23		
Larry Seiple	TE-HB	6'	213	23		6
Larry Csonka	FB	6'3"	240	21		42
Stan Mitchell	HB-FB	6'2"	225	24		24
Bill Darnall	WR	6'2"	197	24		
Gene Milton	WR	5'10"	170	23		6
Karl Noonan	WR	6'3"	190	24		66
Howard Twilley	WR	5'10"	180	24		6
Jim Cox	TE	6'2"	227	24		
Doug Moreau	TE	6'2"	215	23		27

BOSTON PATRIOTS 4-10-0 Mike Holovak

Scores of Each Game		
16	Buffalo	7
31	NEW YORK	47
20	Denver	17
10	Oakland	41
0	HOUSTON	16
23	BUFFALO	6
14	New York	48
14	DENVER	35
17	SAN DIEGO	27
17	Kansas City	31
10	MIAMI	34
33	CINCINNATI	14
7	Miami	38
17	Houston	45

Use Name	Pos.	Hgt	Wgt	Age	Int	Pts
Jim Boudreaux	OT	6'4"	245	23		
Paul Feldhausen	OT	6'6"	270	22		
Tom Funchess	OT	6'5"	260	23		
Tom Neville	OT	6'4"	255	25		
Don Oakes	OT	6'3"	255	30		
Karl Singer	OT	6'3"	255	24		
Justin Canale	OG	6'2"	250	24		
Charley Long	OG	6'3"	250	30		
Len St. Jean	OG	6'1"	245	26		
Jon Morris	C	6'4"	240	25		
J. R. Williamson	LB-C	6'2"	220	26		
Dennis Byrd	DE	6'4"	260	21		
Larry Eisenhauer	DE	6'5"	255	28		
Mel Witt	DE	6'3"	265	22	1	6
Houston Antwine	DT	6'	270	29		
Whit Canale	DT	6'3"	245	26		
Jim Hunt	DT	5'11"	255	29		
Ed Toner	DT	6'3"	250	23		

Use Name	Pos.	Hgt	Wgt	Age	Int	Pts
Nick Buoniconti	LB	5'11"	220	27	3	
Jim Cheyunski	LB	6'2"	225	22	1	
Ray Ilg	LB	6'1"	220	22		
Ed Koontz	LB	6'2"	230	21		
Ed Philpott	LB	6'3"	240	22	4	6
Doug Satcher	LB	6'	220	23	1	2
John Charles	DB	6'1"	200	24	1	
Billy Johnson	DB	5'11"	180	25	2	
Daryle Johnson	DB	5'11"	190	22	1	
Art McMahon	DB	5'11"	185	22	2	
Leroy Mitchell	DB	6'2"	190	23	7	
Willie Porter	DB	5'11"	195	22		
Don Webb	DB	5'10"	195	29		

Use Name	Pos.	Hgt	Wgt	Age	Int	Pts
King Corcoran	QB	6'	200	26		
Tom Sherman	QB	6'	190	22		
Mike Taliaferro	QB	6'2"	205	26		
Larry Garron	HB	6'	195	31		6
Gene Thomas (to OAK)	HB	6'1"	210	25		12
R. C. Gamble	FB-HB	6'3"	220	21		12
Preston Johnson	FB	6'2"	230	23		
Jim Nance	FB	6'1"	240	25		24
Gino Cappelletti	WR	6'	190	34		83
Jim Colclough	WR	6'	185	32		
Art Graham	WR	6'1"	205	27		6
Bobby Leo	WR	5'10"	180	23		
Aaron Marsh	WR	6'1"	190	23		24
Bill Murphy	WR	6'1"	185	21		
Bob Scarpitto	WR	5'11"	190	29		6
Bobby Nichols	TE	6'2"	220	24		
Jim Whalen	TE	6'2"	210	24		42
Terry Swanson	K	6'	210	23		

BUFFALO BILLS 1-12-1 Joe Collier

Scores of Each Game		
7	BOSTON	16
6	OAKLAND	48
23	Cincinnati	34
37	NEW YORK	35
7	KANSAS CITY	18
14	Miami	14
6	Boston	23
7	HOUSTON	30
21	New York	25
17	MIAMI	21
6	SAN DIEGO	21
32	Denver	34
10	Oakland	13
6	Houston	35

Use Name	Pos.	Hgt	Wgt	Age	Int	Pts
Stew Barber	OT	6'3"	248	29		
Dick Cunningham	OT	6'2"	244	23		
Ray Rissmiller	OT	6'4"	250	26		
Mike McBath	DE-OT	6'4"	248	22		
George Flint	OG	6'4"	240	30		
Bob Kalsu	OG	6'3"	235	23		
Billy Shaw	OG	6'3"	252	28		
Al Bemiller	C	6'3"	243	29		
Jack Frantz	C	6'3"	230	21		
Tom Day	DE	6'2"	265	33		
Ron McDole	DE	6'3"	270	28	2	
Howard Kindig	C-DE	6'6"	264	27		
Jim Dunaway	DT	6'4"	282	26		
Tom Sestak	DT	6'5"	262	32		
Bob Tatarek	DT	6'4"	255	22		

Use Name	Pos.	Hgt	Wgt	Age	Int	Pts
Edgar Chandler	LB	6'3"	222	22		
Paul Guidry	LB	6'3"	228	24	1	
Harry Jacobs	LB	6'2"	226	31		
Paul Maguire	LB	6'	228	30		
Marty Schottenheimer	LB	6'3"	224	25	1	
Mike Stratton	LB	6'3"	230	26	1	
Butch Byrd	DB	6'	196	26	6	6
Hagood Clarke	DB	6'	192	26		6
Booker Edgerson	DB	5'10"	183	29	4	12
Tom Janik	DB	6'3"	195	27	3	6
Jerry Lawson	DB	5'11"	192	23		
John Pitts	DB	6'4"	215	23	2	
George Saimes	DB	5'10"	185	26	2	
Charlie Brown	HB-DB	6'1"	195	25		

Jack Kemp – Knee Injury
Joe O'Donnell – Knee Injury
Charley Ferguson – Injury

Use Name	Pos.	Hgt	Wgt	Age	Int	Pts
Dan Darragh	QB	6'3"	196	21		
Tom Flores	QB	6'1"	202	31		
Benny Russell	QB	6'1"	190	24		
Kay Stephenson	QB	6'1"	210	23		
Ed Rutkowski	WR-QB	6'1"	200	27		6
Max Anderson	HB	5'8"	180	23		18
Gary McDermott	HB	6'1"	211	22		26
Charley Mitchell	HB	5'11"	185	28		
Ben Gregory	FB-HB	6'3"	220	21		6
Bob Cappadonna	FB	6'1"	230	24		20
Wayne Patrick	FB	6'2"	225	22		
Keith Lincoln (to SD)	HB-FB	6'2"	216	29		
Bobby Crockett	WR	6'	200	25		
Elbert Dubenion	WR	6'	187	33		
Monte Ledbetter	WR	6'2"	185	25		6
Haven Moses	WR	6'3"	200	22		12
Richard Trapp	WR	6'1"	174	21		
Bill Masters	TE	6'5"	225	24		
Paul Costa	OT-TE	6'4"	248	26		12
Bruce Alford	K	6'	185	23		57
Mike Mercer (to GB-N)	K	6'	217	32		4

NEW YORK JETS

RUSHING

Last Name	No.	Yds	Avg	TD
Snell	179	747	4.2	6
Boozer	143	441	3.1	5
Mathis	74	208	2.8	5
Joe	42	186	4.4	3
Sauer	2	21	10.5	0
Smolinski	12	15	1.3	0
Namath	5	11	2.2	2
Parilli	7	−2	−0.3	1
Johnson	2	−6	−3.0	0
Rademacher	1	−13	−13.0	0

RECEIVING

Last Name	No.	Yds	Avg	TD
Sauer	66	1141	17	3
Maynard	57	1297	23	10
Lammons	32	400	13	3
Snell	16	105	7	1
Boozer	12	101	8	0
B. Turner	10	241	24	2
Mathis	9	149	17	1
Smolinski	6	40	7	0
Johnson	5	78	16	0
Joe	2	11	6	0
Rademacher	2	11	6	0

PUNT RETURNS

Last Name	No.	Yds	Avg	TD
Christy	13	116	9	0
Baird	18	111	6	0
Richards	4	57	14	0
Philbin	1	2	2	0

KICKOFF RETURNS

Last Name	No.	Yds	Avg	TD
Christy	25	599	24	0
B. Turner	14	319	23	0
D'Amato	1	32	32	0
Snell	3	28	9	0
Smolinski	1	17	17	0
Rademacher	1	0	0	0

PASSING – PUNTING – KICKING

PASSING	Att	Comp	%	Yds	Yd/Att	TD	Int–%	RK
Namath	380	187	49	3147	8.3	15	17– 4	3
Parilli	55	29	53	401	7.3	5	2– 4	
Snell	1	1	100	26	26.0	0	0– 0	

PUNTING	No	Avg
Johnson	68	43.8

KICKING	XP	Att	%	FG	Att	%
J. Turner	43	43	100	34	46	74

2 POINT XP
Mathis

HOUSTON OILERS

RUSHING

Last Name	No.	Yds	Avg	TD
Granger	202	848	4.2	7
Campbell	115	436	3.8	6
Blanks	63	169	2.7	0
Hopkins	31	104	3.4	0
Davis	15	91	6.1	1
Beathard	18	79	4.4	2
Trull	14	47	3.4	0
Norton	1	20	20.0	0
Haik	2	7	3.5	0
Beirne	1	3	3.0	0

RECEIVING

Last Name	No.	Yds	Avg	TD
Reed	46	747	16	5
Haik	32	584	18	8
Beirne	31	474	15	4
Granger	26	361	14	0
Campbell	21	234	11	0
Blanks	13	184	14	0
Frazier	9	123	14	0
Taylor	6	90	15	0
Hopkins	4	40	10	0
Burrell	2	35	18	0
Wittenborn	1	−8	−8	0

PUNT RETURNS

Last Name	No.	Yds	Avg	TD
Carwell	27	227	8	0
Blanks	22	179	8	0
Burrell	2	26	13	0
Moore	1	11	11	0

KICKOFF RETURNS

Last Name	No.	Yds	Avg	TD
Moore	32	787	25	0
Carwell	15	335	22	0
Burrell	2	70	35	0
Hopkins	1	21	21	0
Houston	1	13	13	0
Robertson	2	9	5	0

PASSING – PUNTING – KICKING

PASSING	Att	Comp	%	Yds	Yd/Att	TD	Int–%	RK
Beathard	223	105	47	1559	7.0	7	16– 7	8
Trull	105	53	50	864	8.2	10	3– 3	
Davis	86	33	38	441	5.1	0	6– 7	

PUNTING	No	Avg
Norton	73	41.2

KICKING	XP	Att	%	FG	Att	%
Walker	26	26	100	8	16	50
Wittenborn	11	11	100	4	13	31

MIAMI DOLPHINS

RUSHING

Last Name	No.	Yds	Avg	TD
Kiick	165	621	3.8	4
Csonka	138	540	3.9	6
Griese	42	230	5.5	1
Mitchell	54	176	3.3	1
Milton	2	46	23.0	0
Seiple	5	42	8.4	0
Price	5	27	5.4	0
Tucker	4	13	3.3	0
Norton	1	9	9.0	0
Hammond	1	0	0.0	0

RECEIVING

Last Name	No.	Yds	Avg	TD
Noonan	58	760	13	11
Kiick	44	422	10	0
Twilley	39	604	15	1
Moreau	27	365	14	3
Cox	11	147	13	0
Csonka	11	118	11	1
Milton	9	143	16	1
Mitchell	8	190	24	3
Seiple	7	69	10	1
Darnall	2	25	13	0

PUNT RETURNS

Last Name	No.	Yds	Avg	TD
Neff	8	71	9	0
Milton	6	55	9	0
Tucker	5	40	8	0
Anderson	5	18	4	0
Washington	1	15	15	0
Harper	1	7	7	0
Warren	2	−1	−1	0

KICKOFF RETURNS

Last Name	No.	Yds	Avg	TD
Milton	18	408	23	0
Warren	10	227	23	0
Neff	5	190	38	0
Anderson	6	106	18	0
Tucker	3	54	18	0
Kiick	1	28	28	0
Price	1	22	22	0
Harper	1	18	18	0
Urbanek	2	15	8	0
Richardson	1	1	1	0
Woodson	1	0	0	0
Cox	0	41	0	0

PASSING – PUNTING – KICKING

PASSING	Att	Comp	%	Yds	Yd/Att	TD	Int–%	RK
Griese	355	186	52	2473	7.0	21	16– 5	4
Norton	41	17	41	254	6.2	0	4– 10	
Hammond	26	13	50	116	4.5	0	2– 8	
Kiick	1	0	0	0	0.0	0	0– 0	

PUNTING	No	Avg
Seiple	75	40.6

KICKING	XP	Att	%	FG	Att	%
Keyes	30	30	100	7	16	44
Moreau	6	6	100	1	3	33

BOSTON PATRIOTS

RUSHING

Last Name	No.	Yds	Avg	TD
Nance	177	593	3.4	4
Gamble	78	311	4.0	1
Thomas	88	215	2.4	2
Garron	36	97	2.7	1
Sherman	25	80	3.2	0
Taliaferro	8	51	6.4	0
Marsh	4	8	2.0	0
P. Johnson	2	6	3.0	0
Cappelletti	1	2	2.0	0
Whalen	1	0	0.0	0
Corcoran	1	−1	−1.0	0

RECEIVING

Last Name	No.	Yds	Avg	TD
Whalen	47	718	15	7
Marsh	19	331	17	4
Murphy	18	268	15	0
Graham	16	242	15	1
Nance	14	51	4	0
Cappelletti	13	182	14	2
Gamble	11	55	5	1
Thomas	10	85	9	0
Colclough	8	136	17	0
Scarpitto	2	49	25	1
Garron	1	4	4	0
J. Canale	1	0	0	0

PUNT RETURNS

Last Name	No.	Yds	Avg	TD
Porter	22	135	6	0
B. Johnson	10	34	3	0
Leo	2	12	6	0
Graham	2	11	6	0
D. Johnson	1	5	5	0

KICKOFF RETURNS

Last Name	No.	Yds	Avg	TD
Porter	36	812	23	0
B. Johnson	22	442	20	0
Marsh	4	74	19	0
D. Johnson	3	63	21	0
Thomas	1	22	22	0
Long	2	20	10	0
Graham	1	9	9	0
Cheyunski	1	0	0	0
Gamble	1	0	0	0

PASSING – PUNTING – KICKING

PASSING	Att	Comp	%	Yds	Yd/Att	TD	Int–%	RK
Sherman	226	90	40	1199	5.3	12	16– 7	9
Taliaferro	176	67	38	889	5.1	4	15– 9	11
Corcoran	7	3	43	33	4.7	0	2– 29	

PUNTING	No	Avg
Swanson	62	39.5
Scarpitto	34	40.6

KICKING	XP	Att	%	FG	Att	%
Cappelletti	26	26	100	15	27	56

BUFFALO BILLS

RUSHING

Last Name	No.	Yds	Avg	TD
Anderson	147	525	3.6	2
Gregory	52	283	5.4	1
Cappadona	73	272	3.7	1
McDermott	47	102	2.2	3
Rutkowski	20	96	4.8	1
Lincoln	26	84	3.2	0
Masters	6	70	11.7	0
Brown	3	39	13.0	0
Stephenson	4	30	7.5	0
Costa	2	11	5.5	1
Darragh	13	11	0.8	0
Maguire	1	6	6.0	0
Patrick	1	2	2.0	0
Moses	5	−4	−0.8	0

RECEIVING

Last Name	No.	Yds	Avg	TD
Moses	42	633	15	2
Trapp	24	235	10	0
Anderson	22	140	6	0
McDermott	20	115	6	1
Cappadona	18	92	5	2
Costa	15	172	11	1
Masters	8	101	13	0
Crockett	6	76	13	0
Gregory	5	21	4	0
Ledbetter	4	94	24	1
Rutkowski	1	27	27	0
Patrick	1	5	5	0
Lincoln	1	3	3	0
Bemiller	1	0	0	0

PUNT RETURNS

Last Name	No.	Yds	Avg	TD
Clarke	29	241	8	1
Trapp	5	26	5	0
Rutkowski	8	23	3	0
Byrd	2	11	6	0

KICKOFF RETURNS

Last Name	No.	Yds	Avg	TD
Anderson	39	971	25	1
Brown	12	274	23	0
Mitchell	5	98	20	0
Rutkowski	5	87	17	0
Costa	5	68	14	0
Lincoln	2	37	19	0
McDermott	1	16	16	0
Maguire	1	5	5	0
Barber	1	0	0	0
Ledbetter	0	18	0	0

PASSING – PUNTING – KICKING

PASSING	Att	Comp	%	Yds	Yd/Att	TD	Int–%	RK
Darragh	215	92	43	917	4.3	3	14– 7	10
Rutkowski	100	41	41	380	3.8	0	6– 6	
Stephenson	79	29	37	364	4.6	4	7– 9	
Flores	5	3	60	15	3.0	0	1– 20	
McDermott	3	2	67	35	11.7	0	0– 0	
Russell	2	1	50	3	1.5	0	0– 0	
Anderson	1	0	0	0	0.0	0	0– 0	

PUNTING	No	Avg
Maguire	100	41.8

KICKING	XP	Att	%	FG	Att	%
Alford	15	15	100	14	24	58
Mercer	4	4	100	0	4	0

2 POINT XP
Cappadona
McDermott

OAKLAND RAIDERS 12-2-0 Johnny Rauch

Scores of Each Game		
48	Buffalo	6
47	Miami	21
24	Houston	15
41	BOSTON	10
14	SAN DIEGO	23
10	Kansas City	24
31	CINCINNATI	10
38	KANSAS CITY	21
43	Denver	7
43	NEW YORK	32
34	Cincinnati	0
13	BUFFALO	10
33	DENVER	27
34	San Diego	27
	Playoff	
41	KANSAS CITY	6

Use Name	Pos.	Hgt	Wgt	Age	Int	Pts
Harry Schuh	OT	6'2"	260	25		
Art Shell	OT	6'5"	255	21		
Bob Svihus	OT	6'4"	245	25		
Jim Harvey	OG-OT	6'5"	245	25		
Wayne Hawkins	OG	6'	240	30		
Bob Kruse	OG	6'2"	250	26		
Gene Upshaw	OG	6'5"	255	23		
Jim Otto	C	6'2"	248	30		
Ben Davidson	DE	6'8"	275	28		
Ike Lassiter	DE	6'5"	270	27		
Carleton Oats	DE	6'2"	260	25		
Dan Birdwell	DT	6'4"	250	27		
Al Dotson	DT	6'4"	260	25		
Karl Rubke	C-DT	6'4"	234	32		
Tom Keating – Foot Injury						
Bill Laskey – Foot Injury						
Duane Benson	LB	6'2"	215	23		
Bill Budness	LB	6'1"	215	25		
Dan Conners	LB	6'1"	230	26	2	
Bill Fairband	LB	6'3"	228	22		
Jerry Hopkins	LB	6'2"	238	27		
Dave Ogas	LB	6'3"	240	22		
Chip Oliver	LB	6'2"	220	22		
Gus Otto	LB	6'2"	220	25		
Butch Atkinson	DB	6'	180	21	4	18
Rodger Bird	DB	5'11"	195	25	3	6
Willie Brown	DB	6'1"	190	27	2	6
Dave Grayson	DB	5'10"	185	29	10	6
Kent McCloughan	DB	6'1"	190	25	1	
Warren Powers	DB	6'	190	27	1	
Howie Williams	DB	6'2"	190	31	2	
Nemiah Wilson	DB	6'	165	25		
George Blanda	QB	6'1"	215	40		117
Cotton Davidson	QB	6'1"	180	36		
Daryle Lamonica	QB	6'2"	215	27		6
Pete Banaszak	HB	5'11"	200	24		30
Preston Ridlehuber	HB	6'2"	215	24		6
Charlie Smith	HB	6'1"	205	22		42
Larry Todd	HB	6'1"	185	25		12
Hewritt Dixon	FB	6'2"	230	28		26
Roger Hagberg	FB	6'2"	215	29		12
Fred Biletnikoff	WR	6'1"	190	25		42
Eldridge Dickey	WR	6'2"	198	22		
John Eason	WR	6'2"	220	23		
Bill Miller	WR	6'	190	26		6
John Roderick	WR	6'1"	180	24		
Warren Wells	WR	6'1"	190	25		72
Billy Cannon	TE	6'1"	215	31		36
Dave Kocourek	TE	6'5"	235	31		6
Mike Eischeid	K	6'	190	27		

KANSAS CITY CHIEFS 12-2-0 Hank Stram

Scores of Each Game		
26	Houston	21
19	NEW YORK	20
34	DENVER	2
48	Miami	3
18	Buffalo	7
13	CINCINNATI	3
24	OAKLAND	10
27	SAN DIEGO	20
21	Oakland	38
16	Cincinnati	9
31	BOSTON	17
24	HOUSTON	10
40	San Diego	3
30	Denver	7
	Playoff	
6	Oakland	41

Use Name	Pos.	Hgt	Wgt	Age	Int	Pts
Dave Hill	OT	6'5"	260	27		
Jim Tyrer	OT	6'6"	275	29		
Ed Budde	OG	6'5"	260	27		
George Daney	OG	6'3"	240	32		
Curt Merz	OG	6'4"	267	30		
Mo Moorman	OG	6'5"	252	24		
E. J. Holub	C	6'4"	236	30		
Aaron Brown	DE	6'5"	265	24		
Jerry Mays	DE	6'4"	252	28		
Remi Prudhomme	DT-DE	6'4"	250	26		
Buck Buchanan	DT	6'7"	287	28	1	2
Ernie Ladd	DT	6'9"	290	29	1	
Ed Lothamer	DT	6'5"	270	25		
Curley Culp	OG-DT	6'1"	265	22		
Bud Abell	LB	6'3"	220	27	2	
Bobby Bell	LB	6'4"	228	28	5	
Chuck Hurston	LB	6'6"	240	25		
Willie Lanier	LB	6'1"	245	23	4	6
Jim Lynch	LB	6'1"	235	23	3	6
Dave Martin	LB	6'	215	21		
Caesar Belser	DB	6'	212	23		
Jim Kearney	DB	6'2"	206	25	3	
Willie Mitchell	DB	6'1"	185	26	5	
Johnny Robinson	DB	6'	205	29	6	
Goldie Sellers	DB	6'2"	198	26	3	6
Emmitt Thomas	DB	6'2"	192	25	4	
Gene Trosch – Injury						
Len Dawson	QB	6'	190	34		
Jacky Lee	QB	6'1"	185	29		
Mike Livingston	QB	6'3"	205	22		
Bert Coan	HB	6'4"	220	28		6
Mike Garrett	HB	5'9"	200	24		36
Paul Lowe (from SD)	HB	6'	205	31		
Wendell Hayes	FB-HB	6'2"	220	27		30
Robert Holmes	FB	5'9"	220	22		42
Curtis McClinton	FB	6'3"	227	30		
Jack Gehrke	WR	6'	178	22		
Sam Longmire	WR	6'3"	195	25		
Frank Pitts	WR	6'2"	200	24		36
Gloster Richardson	WR	6'	200	25		36
Noland Smith	WR	5'6"	154	24		6
Otis Taylor	WR	6'2"	215	25		30
Fred Arbanas	TE	6'3"	240	29		
Reg Carolan	TE	6'6"	240	28		
Jan Stenerud	K	6'2"	187	25		129
Jerrel Wilson	K	6'4"	222	26		

SAN DIEGO CHARGERS 9-5-0 Sid Gillman

Scores of Each Game		
29	CINCINNATI	13
30	HOUSTON	14
31	Cincinnati	10
20	New York	23
23	Oakland	14
55	DENVER	24
20	Kansas City	27
34	MIAMI	28
27	Boston	17
21	Buffalo	6
15	NEW YORK	37
47	Denver	23
3	KANSAS CITY	40
27	OAKLAND	34

Use Name	Pos.	Hgt	Wgt	Age	Int	Pts
Harold Akin	OT	6'5"	260	23		
Ron Mix	OT	6'4"	250	30		
Terry Owens	OT	6'6"	270	24		
Bob Wells	OT	6'4"	270	23		
Gary Kirner	OG	6'3"	255	26		
Larry Little	OG	6'1"	270	22		
Jim Schmedding	OG	6'2"	250	22		
Walt Sweeney	OG	6'3"	260	27		
Sam Gruneisen	C	6'1"	250	27		
Paul Latzke	C	6'4"	240	26		
Bill Lenkaitis	C	6'3"	250	22		
Marty Baccaglio (to CIN)	DE	6'3"	245	23		
Steve DeLong	DE	6'3"	252	25		
Houston Ridge	DE	6'4"	245	24		
Ron Billingsley	DT-DE	6'8"	265	23		
Scott Appleton	DT	6'3"	260	26		
Bob Briggs	DT	6'4"	270	23		
Russ Washington	DT	6'6"	290	21		
Chuck Allen	LB	6'1"	225	28	1	
Bernie Erickson (to CIN)	LB	6'2"	240	23		
Tom Erlandson	LB	6'3"	220	28	2	
Jim Fetherston	LB	6'2"	225	23	1	
Curtis Jones	LB	6'2"	245	25		
Ron McCall	LB	6'2"	245	23		
Bob Mitinger	LB	6'2"	230	28		
Bob Print	LB	6'	220	24		
Rick Redman	LB	5'11"	225	25		
Jeff Staggs	LB	6'2"	240	24	2	
Joe Beauchamp	DB	6'	185	24	5	12
Speedy Duncan	DB	5'10"	175	25	1	6
Dick Farley	DB	6'	185	22		
Kenny Graham	DB	6'	205	26	5	
Bob Howard	DB	6'1"	190	23	1	
Dick Speights	DB	5'11"	175	22		
Jim Tolbert	DB	6'3"	207	24	2	
Bud Whitehead	DB	6'	185	29		
Ken Dyer	WR-DB	6'3"	185	22		6
Jon Brittenum	QB	6'	185	24		
John Hadl	QB	6'2"	215	28		12
Dickie Post	HB	5'9"	190	22		18
Russ Smith	HB	6'1"	209	24		24
Jim Allison	FB	6'	215	25		
Gene Foster	FB	5'11"	220	25		6
Brad Hubbert	FB	6'1"	227	27		12
Gerry McDougall	FB	6'2"	225	33		
Lance Alworth	WR	6'	180	28		62
Lane Fenner	WR	6'5"	210	23		
Gary Garrison	WR	6'1"	195	24		60
Phil Tuckett	WR	6'	180	23		
Willie Frazier	TE	6'4"	235	25		18
Jacque MacKinnon	TE	6'4"	240	29		38
Andre White (from CIN)	TE	6'5"	225	23		
Dennis Partee	K	6'2"	208	22		106

DENVER BRONCOS 5-9-0 Lou Saban

Scores of Each Game		
10	Cincinnati	24
2	Kansas City	34
17	BOSTON	20
10	CINCINNATI	7
21	New York	13
24	San Diego	55
21	MIAMI	14
35	Boston	14
7	OAKLAND	43
17	Houston	38
34	BUFFALO	32
23	SAN DIEGO	47
27	Oakland	33
7	KANSAS CITY	30

Use Name	Pos.	Hgt	Wgt	Age	Int	Pts
Sam Brunelli	OT	6'1"	270	25		
Tom Cichowski	OT	6'4"	250	23		
Mike Current	OT	6'4"	260	22		
Wallace Dickey	OT	6'3"	260	27		
George Gaiser	OT	6'4"	255	23		
George Goeddeke	OG	6'3"	245	23		
Buzz Highsmith	OG	6'4"	230	25		
Bob Vaughn	OG	6'4"	240	23		
Bob Young	OG	6'2"	260	25		
Jay Bachman	C	6'3"	250	22		
Larry Kaminski	C	6'2"	245	23		
Pete Duranko	DE	6'2"	252	24		
Rich Jackson	DE	6'2"	255	27		
Paul Smith	DE	6'3"	245	23		
Dave Costa	DT	6'2"	265	26		
Larry Cox	DT	6'2"	250	24		
Jerry Inman	DT	6'3"	255	28		
Rex Mirich	DT	6'4"	250	27		
Carl Cunningham	LB	6'3"	240	24	1	
Fred Forsberg	LB	6'1"	235	24	1	
John Huard	LB	6'	220	24	2	
Gordon Lambert	LB	6'5"	245	23		
Frank Richter	LB	6'3"	230	23		
Dave Tobey	LB	6'3"	230	25		
Chip Myrtle	TE-LB	6'2"	225	23		2
Drake Garrett	DB	5'9"	183	23	2	
Charlie Greer	DB	6'	205	22	4	
Gus Holloman	DB	6'3"	195	22	1	
Pete Jaquess	DB	6'	182	26	5	
Jack Lentz	DB	6'	195	23	1	
Hal Lewis	DB	6'2"	188	25		
Tommy Luke	DB	6'	190	26		
Alex Moore	DB	6'	195	23		
Tom Oberg	DB	6'	185	23	3	
Jesse Stokes	DB	6'	190	24		
Marlin Briscoe	QB	5'10"	177	22		18
Joe DiVito	QB	6'2"	205	22		
Jim LeClair	QB	6'1"	208	24		
John McCormick	QB	6'1"	190	31		
Steve Tensi	QB	6'5"	215	25		
Terry Erwin	HB	6'	190	21		
Hub Lindsey	HB	5'11"	196	22		
Floyd Little	HB	5'10"	195	26		30
Fran Lynch	HB	6'1"	194	22		24
Garrett Ford	FB	6'2"	230	22		6
Brendan McCarthy (from ATL-N)	FB	6'3"	220	23		12
Eric Crabtree	WR	5'11"	182	23		30
Al Denson	WR	6'2"	208	23		30
Mike Haffner	WR	6'2"	205	26		6
Jim Jones	WR	6'2"	195	24		12
Bobby Moten	WR	6'4"	212	25		
Bill Van Heusen	WR	6'1"	200	22		18
Tom Beer	TE	6'4"	230	23		6
Dave Washington	TE	6'4"	228	27		
Bobby Howfield	K	5'9"	180	31		57
Bob Humphreys	K	6'1"	240	28		4

CINCINNATI BENGALS 3-11-0 Paul Brown

Scores of Each Game		
13	San Diego	29
24	DENVER	10
34	BUFFALO	23
10	SAN DIEGO	31
7	Denver	10
3	Kansas City	13
22	MIAMI	24
10	Oakland	31
17	HOUSTON	27
9	KANSAS CITY	16
38	Miami	21
0	OAKLAND	34
14	Boston	33
14	New York	27

Use Name	Pos.	Hgt	Wgt	Age	Int	Pts
Howard Fest	OT	6'6"	265	22		
Bob Kelly	OT	6'3"	270	28		
Ernie Wright	OT	6'4"	270	28		
Dan Archer	OG-OT	6'5"	245	23		
Pat Matson	OG	6'1"	245	24		
Dave Middendorf	OG	6'3"	260	22		
Pete Perreault	OG	6'3"	248	29		
Bob Johnson	C	6'5"	260	22		
John Matlock	OT-C	6'4"	255	23		
Jim Griffin	DE	6'3"	265	26		6
Harry Gunner	DE	6'6"	250	23	1	2
Willie Jones	DE	6'2"	260	26		
Dennis Randall	DE	6'6"	240	22		
Steve Chomyszak	DT	6'5"	280	23		
Bill Kindricks	DT	6'3"	268	22		
Andy Rice	DT	6'3"	268	26		
Bill Staley	DT	6'3"	250	21		
Al Beauchamp	LB	6'2"	236	24	2	6
Danny Brabham	LB	6'4"	233	27		
Frank Buncom	LB	6'1"	245	28		
Paul Elzey	LB	6'3"	235	22		
Sherrill Headrick	LB	6'2"	240	31	1	
Mike Hibler	LB	6'1"	235	22		
Wayne McClure	LB	6'1"	225	22		
John Neidert (to NY)	LB	6'2"	230	22		
Curt Frazier	DB	5'11"	193	23		
White Graves	DB	6'	185	25		
Rex Keeling	DB	6'3"	220	24		
Charlie King	DB	6'	184	25	1	6
Bill Scott	DB	6'	188	24		
Fletcher Smith	DB	6'2"	178	24	1	
Phil Spiller (from ATL-N)	DB	6'	195	23		
Bobby Hunt	HB-DB	6'1"	190	28	1	6
Jess Phillips	HB-DB	6'1"	205	21	3	
John Stofa	QB	6'3"	210	26		
Dewey Warren	QB	6'	205	23		
Sam Wyche	QB	6'4"	210	23		
Essex Johnson	HB	5'9"	190	21		18
Paul Robinson	HB	6'	200	23		54
Ted Washington	HB	5'11"	210	22		
Estes Banks	FB	6'1"	220	23		6
Ron Lamb (from DEN)	FB	6'2"	225	24		
Tom Smiley	FB	6'1"	235	24		6
Saint Saffold	WR	6'4"	202	24		
Rod Sherman	WR	6'	190	23		10
Monk Williams	WR	5'7"	155	23		
Warren McVea	HB-WR	5'10"	182	22		18
Ken Herock	TE	6'2"	230	27		
Bill Peterson	TE	6'3"	230	23		
Bob Trumpy	WR-TE	6'6"	220	23		18
Dale Livingston	K	6'	210	23		59

OAKLAND RAIDERS

RUSHING

Last Name	No.	Yds	Avg	TD
Dixon	206	865	4.2	2
Smith	95	504	3.6	5
Banaszak	91	362	4.0	4
Hagberg	39	164	4.2	1
Lamonica	19	98	5.2	1
Todd	13	89	6.8	2
Eischeid	2	41	20.5	0
Wells	2	38	19.0	1
Ridlehuber	4	7	1.8	0

RECEIVING

Last Name	No.	Yds	Avg	TD
Biletnikoff	61	1037	17	6
Wells	53	1137	21	11
Dixon	38	360	9	2
Cannon	23	360	16	6
Smith	22	321	15	2
Banaszak	15	182	12	1
Miller	9	176	20	1
Hagberg	8	78	10	1
Todd	4	40	10	0
Kocourek	3	46	15	1
Dickey	1	34	34	0

PUNT RETURNS

Last Name	No.	Yds	Avg	TD
Atkinson	**36**	**490**	14	**2**
Bird	11	128	12	0
Dickey	6	48	8	0
Shell	1	0	0	0
Wilson	1	0	0	0

KICKOFF RETURNS

Last Name	No.	Yds	Avg	TD
Atkinson	32	802	**25**	0
Smith	8	167	21	0
Wilson	4	84	21	0
Hagberg	1	21	21	0
Dickey	1	17	17	0
Kruse	1	1	1	0
Hopkins	1	0	0	0
G. Otto	1	0	0	0

PASSING – PUNTING – KICKING

PASSING	Att	Comp	%	Yds	Yd/Att	TD	Int–%	RK
Lamonica	416	206	50	3245	7.8	25	15– 4	2
Blanda	49	30	61	522	10.7	6	2– 4	
C. Davidson	2	1	50	4	2.0	0	0– 0	
Banaszak	1	0	0	0	0.0	0	1–100	

PUNTING	No	Avg
Eischeid	64	43.6

KICKING	XP	Att	%	FG	Att	%
Blanda	**54**	**54**	100	21	34	62

2 POINT XP
Dixon

KANSAS CITY CHIEFS

RUSHING

Last Name	No.	Yds	Avg	TD
Holmes	174	866	5.0	7
Garrett	164	564	3.4	3
Hayes	85	340	4.0	4
Coan	40	160	4.0	1
McClinton	24	107	4.5	0
Pitts	11	107	9.7	0
Taylor	5	41	8.2	1
Dawson	20	40	2.0	0
Arbanas	3	14	4.7	0
Livingston	2	2	1.0	0
Wilson	5	1	0.2	0
Lowe	2	−1	−0.5	0
Smith	2	−2	−1.0	0
Richardson	1	−3	−3.0	0

RECEIVING

Last Name	No.	Yds	Avg	TD
Garrett	33	359	11	3
Pitts	30	655	22	6
Richardson	22	494	22	6
Taylor	20	420	21	4
Holmes	19	201	11	0
Hayes	12	108	9	1
Arbanas	11	189	17	0
McClinton	3	−4	−1	0
Carolan	2	26	13	0
Coan	2	15	8	0
Smith	1	15	15	0
Wilson	1	14	14	0

PUNT RETURNS

Last Name	No.	Yds	Avg	TD
Smith	18	270	**15**	1
Sellers	7	129	18	1
Robinson	2	26	13	0
Mitchell	1	21	21	0
Garrett	2	4	2	0
Belser	1	0	0	0

KICKOFF RETURNS

Last Name	No.	Yds	Avg	TD
Smith	23	549	24	0
Coan	5	100	20	0
Sellers	2	40	20	0
Belser	4	38	10	0
Kearney	1	9	9	0
Abell	1	0	0	0
Daney	1	0	0	0
Prudhomme	1	0	0	0

PASSING – PUNTING – KICKING

PASSING	Att	Comp	%	Yds	Yd/Att	TD	Int–%	RK
Dawson	224	131	**59**	2109	**9.4**	17	9– 4	**1**
Lee	45	25	56	383	8.5	3	1– 2	
Garrett	1	0	0	0	0.0	0	1–100	

PUNTING	No	Avg
Wilson	63	**45.1**
Carolan	2	50.5

KICKING	XP	Att	%	FG	Att	%
Stenerud	39	40	98	30	40	75

SAN DIEGO CHARGERS

RUSHING

Last Name	No.	Yds	Avg	TD
Post	151	758	**5.0**	3
Smith	88	426	4.8	4
Foster	109	394	3.6	1
Hubbert	28	119	4.3	2
Allison	23	31	1.3	0
Alworth	3	18	6.0	0
Hadl	23	14	0.6	2
Brittenum	2	−4	−2.0	0

RECEIVING

Last Name	No.	Yds	Avg	TD
Alworth	**68**	**1312**	19	10
Garrison	52	1103	21	10
MacKinnon	33	646	20	6
Foster	23	224	10	0
Post	18	165	9	0
Frazier	16	237	15	3
Smith	7	71	10	0
Hubbert	5	11	2	0
Allison	2	22	11	0
White	2	18	9	0
Dyer	1	22	22	0

PUNT RETURNS

Last Name	No.	Yds	Avg	TD
Duncan	18	206	11	1
Graham	13	61	5	0
Smith	8	25	3	0

KICKOFF RETURNS

Last Name	No.	Yds	Avg	TD
Duncan	25	586	23	0
Post	10	199	20	0
Allison	7	121	17	0
Whitehead	2	81	41	0
Speights	1	21	21	0
Smith	1	20	20	0
Baccaglio	2	0	0	0
Latzke	1	0	0	0

PASSING – PUNTING – KICKING

PASSING	Att	Comp	%	Yds	Yd/Att	TD	Int–%	RK
Hadl	**440**	**208**	47	**3473**	7.9	**27**	32– 7	5
Brittenum	17	9	53	125	7.4	1	1– 6	
Foster	7	6	86	169	24.1	0	0– 0	
Post	4	1	25	23	5.8	0	0– 0	
Smith	3	0	0	0	0.0	1	0– 0	
Allison	1	1	100	23	23.0	1	0– 0	

PUNTING	No	Avg
Partee	56	40.7

KICKING	XP	Att	%	FG	Att	%
Partee	40	43	93	22	32	69

2 POINT XP
Alworth
MacKinnon

DENVER BRONCOS

RUSHING

Last Name	No.	Yds	Avg	TD
Little	158	584	3.7	3
Briscoe	41	308	7.5	3
Lynch	66	221	3.3	4
Ford	41	186	4.5	1
McCarthy	28	89	3.2	0
Erwin	24	76	3.2	0
LeClair	12	40	3.3	0
Moore	4	22	5.5	0
Lindsey	4	17	4.3	0
Van Heusen	1	6	6.0	0
Tensi	6	2	0.3	0
Haffner	2	2	1.0	0
DiVito	1	−1	−1.0	0
Jones	1	−1	−1.0	0

RECEIVING

Last Name	No.	Yds	Avg	TD
Crabtree	35	601	17	5
Denson	34	586	17	5
Beer	20	276	14	1
Van Heusen	19	353	19	3
Little	19	331	17	1
Jones	13	190	15	2
Haffner	12	232	19	1
McCarthy	7	69	10	2
Ford	6	40	7	0
Lynch	4	52	13	0
Moore	3	35	12	0
Erwin	2	21	11	0
Myrtle	1	18	18	0
Washington	1	12	12	0

PUNT RETURNS

Last Name	No.	Yds	Avg	TD
Little	24	261	11	1
Greer	9	53	6	0
Luke	3	13	4	0
Jaquess	2	5	3	0

KICKOFF RETURNS

Last Name	No.	Yds	Avg	TD
Little	26	649	25	0
Holloman	7	194	28	0
Stokes	5	106	21	0
Garrett	3	77	26	0
Moore	4	74	19	0
Lindsey	3	72	24	0
Erwin	3	55	18	0
Greer	2	41	21	0
Luke	2	34	17	0
Crabtree	1	30	30	0
Forsberg	2	16	8	0
Dickey	1	13	13	0
Jaquess	1	0	0	0

PASSING – PUNTING – KICKING

PASSING	Att	Comp	%	Yds	Yd/Att	TD	Int–%	RK
Briscoe	224	93	42	1589	7.1	14	13– 6	7
Tensi	119	48	40	709	6.0	5	8– 7	
LeClair	54	27	50	401	7.4	1	5– 9	
McCormick	19	8	42	89	4.7	0	1– 5	
DiVito	6	1	17	16	2.7	0	0– 0	
Little	2	0	0	0	0.0	0	0– 0	
Lynch	2	1	50	4	2.0	0	0– 0	
Haffner	1	1	100	18	18.0	0	0– 0	

PUNTING	No	Avg
Van Heusen	88	43.8
DiVito	8	30.3

KICKING	XP	Att	%	FG	Att	%
Howfield	30	30	100	9	18	50
Humphreys	1	1	100	1	5	20

CINCINNATI BENGALS

RUSHING

Last Name	No.	Yds	Avg	TD
Robinson	**238**	**1023**	4.3	**8**
E. Johnson	26	178	6.8	3
Smiley	63	146	2.3	1
McVea	9	133	14.8	1
Banks	34	131	3.9	0
Lamp	39	107	2.7	0
Wyche	12	74	6.2	0
Saffold	1	21	21.0	0
Warren	4	17	4.3	0
Livingston	1	11	11.0	0
Keeling	1	10	10.0	0
Phillips	1	7	7.0	0
Hunt	1	5	5.0	1
Washington	1	4	4.0	0
Sherman	1	3	3.0	0
Stofa	10	1	0.1	0
Trumpy	1	−1	−1.0	0

RECEIVING

Last Name	No.	Yds	Avg	TD
Trumpy	37	639	17	3
Sherman	31	374	12	1
Robinson	24	128	5	1
McVea	21	264	13	2
Smiley	19	86	5	0
Saffold	16	172	11	0
Lamb	7	87	12	0
Herock	6	75	13	0
Banks	4	15	4	1
E. Johnson	1	33	33	0
Peterson	1	10	10	0
Wyche	1	5	5	0

PUNT RETURNS

Last Name	No.	Yds	Avg	TD
E. Johnson	22	111	5	0
Spiller	2	51	26	0
Phillips	2	16	8	0
Williams	2	14	7	0
King	1	3	3	0
Robinson	1	1	1	0

KICKOFF RETURNS

Last Name	No.	Yds	Avg	TD
McVea	14	310	22	0
E. Johnson	14	266	19	0
Banks	6	106	18	0
Williams	5	112	22	0
Spiller	5	91	18	0
Peterson	3	80	27	0
Robinson	3	58	19	0
Lamb	1	24	24	0
Phillips	1	23	23	0
McClure	1	11	11	0
Randall	1	11	11	0
Neidert	1	0	0	0
Saffold	1	0	0	0

PASSING – PUNTING – KICKING

PASSING	Att	Comp	%	Yds	Yd/Att	TD	Int–%	RK
Stofa	177	85	48	896	5.1	5	5– 3	6
Warren	80	47	59	506	6.3	1	4– 5	
Wyche	55	35	64	494	9.0	2	2– 4	
Keeling	1	0	0	0	0.0	0	0– 0	

PUNTING	No	Avg
Livingston	70	43.4
Smith	8	28.8
Keeling	6	28.3

KICKING	XP	Att	%	FG	Att	%
Livingston	20	20	100	13	26	50
Sherman	4	4	100	0	1	0

1968 Championship Games

NFL CHAMPIONSHIP GAME

December 29, at Cleveland
(Attendance 80,628)

Evening a Past Account

The conference playoffs had produced one expected result and one upset. The Baltimore Colts beat the Minnesota Vikings 24-14 as they had been picked to do, but the Cleveland Browns had surprised the Dallas Cowboys by knocking them off 31-20 in Don Meredith's playing farewell.

The Colts and Browns had met for the NFL title four years ago, with the Browns stunning Baltimore with a 27-0 upset. The Colts again were favored this year, but their stifling defense smothered the Cleveland attack and evened the score from 1964.

The Browns had the first scoring opportunity of the game when Don Cockroft attempted a 41-yard field goal, but Bubba Smith blocked the kick. With Bill Nelsen rushed incessantly and Leroy Kelly hounded every time he touched the ball, the Browns rarely crossed into Baltimore territory all afternoon.

The first period ended without a score, but a Lou Michaels field goal gave Baltimore a 3-0 lead early in the second period. With the Colt blockers beating the Cleveland front four regularly, the Colts put together a sixty-yard, ten-play drive which ended in Tom Matte's plunge into the end zone. When the Browns tried to come back with a pass, Mike Curtis intercepted and gave the ball to his offense on the Cleveland 33. Matte ran for twelve yards on the first play, then Jerry Hill carried for nine, and Matte finally covered the last twelve yards with a dodging run through the Cleveland secondary. The halftime score was 17-0, and the Browns looked like a beaten team.

The Colts stuck to the ground in the second half, eating up yardage and time with Matte and Hill running the ball. A time-consuming drive led to Matte's third touchdown of the day in the third quarter, and ten more points in the final period ran the final score up to 34-0. After this one-sided affair ended a quick survey of the press box uncovered not one writer who gave the New York Jets a chance against the Colts in the Super Bowl.

SCORING

CLEVELAND	0	0	0	0–	0
BALTIMORE	0	17	7	10–	34

Second Quarter
- Bal. Michaels, 28 yard field goal
- Bal. Matte, 1 yard rush — PAT–Michaels (kick)
- Bal. Matte, 12 yard rush — PAT–Michaels (kick)

Third Quarter
- Bal. Matte, 2 yard rush — PAT–Michaels (kick)

Fourth Quarter
- Bal. Michaels, 10 yard field goal
- Bal. Brown, 4 yard run — PAT–Michaels (Kick)

TEAM STATISTICS

CLE.		BAL.
12	First Downs–Total	22
2	First Downs–Rushing	13
8	First Downs–Passing	8
2	First Downs–Penalty	1
2	Fumbles–Number	2
1	Fumbles–Lost Ball	1
7	Penalties–Number	3
54	Yards Penalized	15
2	Missed Field Goals	0
3	Giveaways	2
2	Takeaways	3
–1	Difference	+1

INDIVIDUAL STATISTICS

CLEVELAND	No	Yds	Avg.	BALTIMORE	No	Yds	Avg.
RUSHING							
Kelly	13	28	2.2	Matte	17	88	5.2
Harraway	6	26	4.3	Hill	11	60	5.5
Green	1	2	2.0	Brown	5	18	3.6
	20	56	2.8	Cole	3	14	4.7
				Mackey	2	4	2.0
				Morrall	1	0	0.0
					39	184	4.7
RECEIVING							
Harraway	4	40	10.0	Richardson	3	78	26.0
Morin	3	41	13.7	Mackey	2	34	17.0
Kelly	3	27	9.0	Orr	2	33	16.5
Warfield	2	30	15.0	Matte	2	15	7.5
Collins	1	13	13.0	Mitchell	1	7	7.0
	13	151	11.6	Cole	1	2	2.0
					11	169	15.4
PUNTING							
Cockroft	5		33.4	Lee	2		37.0
PUNT RETURNS							
Davis	1	4	4.0	Brown	1	0	0.0
KICKOFF RETURNS							
Morrison	3	51	19.0	Pearson	1	21	21.0
Davis	3	40	13.3				
	6	91	15.2				
INTERCEPTION RETURNS							
Davis	1	0	0.0	Volk	1	26	26.0
				Curtis	1	0	0.0
					2	26	13.0

PASSING

CLEVELAND	Att.	Comp.	Comp. Pct.	Yds.	Int.	Yds/ Att.	Yds/ Comp.	Yards Lost Tackled
Nelsen	26	11	42.3	132	2	5.1	12.0	
Ryan	6	2	33.3	19	0	3.3	8.5	
	32	13	40.6	151	2	4.7	11.6	4–34
BALTIMORE								
Morrall	25	11	44.4	169	1	6.8	15.4	0– 0

AFL CHAMPIONSHIP GAME

December 29, at New York
(Attendance 62,627)

Down and Up, but Never Sideways

After beating the Chiefs in a Western Division playoff, the Oakland Raiders came to New York to face the brash, young New York Jets for the AFL title. Joe Namath came out throwing, and after only 3:39 of the opening period, the Jets had scored on a Namath-to-Don Maynard pass. Jim Turner later added a field goal to give the Jets a 10-0 lead after one quarter. Oakland wide receiver Fred Biletnikoff started getting open in the second quarter, however, and Daryle Lamonica hit him with a touchdown pass early in the period. Before the half ended, Jim Turner and George Blanda each kicked a three-pointer to make the score 13-10 in favor of the Jets.

Early in the second half, Lamonica's long bombs to Biletnikoff and Warren Wells gave the Raiders a first down on the New York 6-yard line. Three plays moved the ball only to the 1-yard line, so Blanda kicked a short field goal to knot the score at 13-13.

Late in the third period it was New York's turn to move. Namath mixed his plays well in driving the Jets 80 yards to a touchdown, with the final 20 yards coming on a pass to tight end Pete Lammons. Turner's kick made the count 20-13 with one period left.

The Raiders struck deep into New York territory early in the quarter, but had to settle for another Blanda field goal. Trailing 20-16, the Raiders turned the game around when George Atkinson picked off a Namath pass and returned it 32 yards to the New York 5. Pete Banaszak scored on the next play to put the Raiders ahead for the first time. Less than a minute later, a 52-yard pass play from Namath to Maynard brought the Jets into striking range of the Oakland end zone, and another pass to Maynard took the ball across the goal line and put New York on top 27-23. The Raiders drove right back into New York territory, but the Jets got the ball by recovering a loose lateral pass which the Raiders thought was an incomplete forward pass. After that, the Jets just hung on for their Super Bowl destiny.

SCORING

NEW YORK	10	3	7	7–	27
OAKLAND	0	10	3	10–	23

First Quarter
- N.Y. Maynard, 14 yard pass from Namath — PAT–J. Turner (kick)
- N.Y. J. Turner, 33 yard field goal

Second Quarter
- Oak. Biletnikoff, 29 yard pass from Lamonica — PAT–Blanda (kick)
- N.Y. J. Turner, 36 yard field goal
- Oak. Blanda, 26 yard field goal

Third Quarter
- Oak. Blanda, 9 yard field goal
- N.Y. Lammons, 20 yard pass from Namath — PAT–J. Turner (kick)

Fourth Quarter
- Oak. Blanda, 20 yard field goal
- Oak. Banaszak, 4 yard rush — PAT–Blanda (kick)
- N.Y. Maynard, 6 yard pass from Namath — PAT–J. Turner (kick)

TEAM STATISTICS

N.Y.		OAK.
25	First Downs–Total	18
9	First Downs–Rushing	3
15	First Downs–Passing	14
1	First Downs–Penalty	1
1	Fumbles–Number	2
1	Fumbles–Lost Ball	0
4	Penalties–Number	2
26	Yards Penalized	23
1	Missed Field Goals	1
2	Giveaways	0
0	Takeaways	2
–2	Difference	+2

INDIVIDUAL STATISTICS

NEW YORK	No	Yds	Avg.	OAKLAND	No	Yds	Avg.
RUSHING							
Snell	19	71	3.7	Dixon	8	42	5.3
Boozer	11	51	4.6	Banaszak	3	6	2.0
Namath	1	14	14.0	Lamonica	3	1	0.3
Mathis	3	8	2.7	Smith	5	1	0.2
	34	144	4.2		19	50	2.6
RECEIVING							
Sauer	7	70	10.0	Biletnikoff	7	190	11.2
Maynard	6	118	19.7	Dixon	5	48	9.6
Lammons	4	52	13.0	Cannon	4	69	17.3
Snell	1	15	15.0	Wells	3	83	27.7
Boozer	1	11	11.0	Banaszak	1	11	11.0
	19	266	14.0		20	401	20.1
PUNTING							
Johnson	10		41.5	Eischeid	7		42.7
PUNT RETURNS							
Baird	2	8	4.0	Atkinson	2	11	5.5
Christy	1	0	0.0	Bird	2	6	3.0
	3	8	2.7		4	17	4.3
KICKOFF RETURNS							
Christy	3	86	28.7	Atkinson	4	112	28.0
B. Turner	1	24	24.0	Smith	1	17	17.0
	4	110	27.5		5	129	25.8
INTERCEPTION RETURNS							
None				Atkinson	1	32	32.0

PASSING

NEW YORK	Att.	Comp.	Comp. Pct.	Yds.	Int.	Yds/ Att.	Yds/ Comp.	Yards Lost Tackled
Namath	49	19	38.8	266	1	5.4	14.0	10
OAKLAND								
Lamonica	47	20	42.6	401	0	8.5	20.1	8

SUPER BOWL III
January 12, at Miami
(Attendance 75,377)

The Ironclad Guarantee

When Joe Namath, three days before the game, said, "I think we'll win it; in fact, I'll guarantee it," people snickered. The New York Jets were close to three-touchdown underdogs against the Baltimore Colts, and everyone expected to see the Colts, an establishment NFL team, clobber the long-haired Jets and shut the mouth of their free-spirit quarterback. Coached by Don Shula, the Colts had a feared defense that mixed zone pass coverage and frequent blitzes and a poised offense led by quarterback Earl Morrall, who had substituted spectacularly during the season for the sore-armed Johnny Unitas.

On offense, the Colts did everything in the first half except score. They drove to the New York 20-yard line only to lose the ball on an interception. They recovered a fumble on the New York 12 only to have Lou Michaels miss a close-range field goal. They sprang Tom Matte loose on a 58-yard run only to suffer another interception to kill the drive. The play that typified the Colts' frustration the best came in the second quarter. On a razzle-dazzle play, Earl Morrall handed the ball off, got it back on a lateral, and looked downfield for a receiver. He never noticed Jimmy Orr free in the end zone, so alone that he was jumping up and down and waving his arms to get attention. Morrall instead threw the ball down the middle right into the arms of New York's Jim Hudson.

The Jets, meanwhile, unexpectedly used the off-tackle smash as their main offensive weapon. With Winston Hill leading the way, fullback Matt Snell repeatedly picked up five and six yards through the right side of the Colt line. Whenever the Colts threw their blitz at Namath, he somehow smelled it out and beat it by shooting a quick pass to George Sauer. Mixing his plays well, Namath led the Jets on an 80-yard drive in twelve plays, with Snell carrying the ball into the end zone from the four-yard line. At halftime, the Jets were ahead 7-0.

The script stayed the same in the second half. The Jets ground out the yardage slowly, scoring on three Jim Turner field goals, while Morrall could not get the Colts on the scoreboard. Johnny Unitas, sore arm and all, took over at quarterback in the final period, and although he drove the Colts to a touchdown, it was too little too late. The Jets had won the Super Bowl 16-7; the AFL had finally triumphed.

NEW YORK JETS		BALTIMORE
	OFFENSE	
Sauer	LE	Orr
W. Hill	LT	Vogel
Talamini	LG	Ressler
Schmitt	C	Curry
Rasmussen	RG	Sullivan
Herman	RT	Ball
Lammons	TE	Mackey
Namath	QB	Morrall
Maynard	FL	W. Richardson
Boozer	RB	Matte
Snell	RB	J. Hill
	DEFENSE	
Philbin	LE	B. Smith
Rochester	LT	B. R. Smith
Elliot	RT	Miller
Biggs	RE	Braase
Baker	LLB	Curtis
Atkinson	MLB	Gaubatz
Grantham	RLB	Shinnick
Sample	LHB	Boyd
Beverly	RHB	Lyles
Hudson	LS	Logan
Baird	FS	Volk

SUBSTITUTES

NEW YORK

Offense

Crane	J. Richardson
Mathis	Smolinski
Parilli	B. Turner
Rademacher	Walton

Defense

Christy	McAdams
D'Amato	Neidert
Dockery	Richards
Gordon	Thompson

Kickers

Johnson	J. Turner

BALTIMORE

Offense

Brown	Pearson
Cole	Perkins
Hawkins	Szymanski
Johnson	Unitas
Mitchell	J. Williams

Defense

Austin	Porter
Hilton	Stukes
Michaels	S. Williams

Kicker

Lee

SCORING

NEW YORK JETS	0	7	6	3	16
BALTIMORE	0	0	0	7	7

Second Quarter
N.Y. Snell, 4 yard rush — 5:57
PAT – Turner (kick)

Third Quarter
N.Y. Turner, 32 yd field goal — 4:52
N.Y. Turner, 30 yd field goal — 11:02

Fourth Quarter
N.Y. Turner, 9 yard field goal — 1:34
Balt. Hill, 1 yard rush — 11:41
PAT – Michaels (kick)

TEAM STATISTICS

N. Y.		BALT.
21	First Downs – Total	18
10	First Downs – Rushing	7
10	First Downs – Passing	9
1	First Downs – Penalty	2
1	Fumbles – Number	1
1	Fumbles – Lost Ball	1
5	Penalties – Number	3
28	Yards Penalized	23
74	Total Offensive Plays	64
337	Total Net Yards	324
4.6	Average Gain	5.1
2	Field Goals Missed	2
1	Giveaways	5
5	Takeaways	1
+4	Difference	–4

INDIVIDUAL STATISTICS

RUSHING

NEW YORK JETS	No	Yds	Avg.	BALTIMORE	No	Yds	Avg.
Snell	30	121	4.0	Matte	11	116	10.5
Boozer	10	19	1.9	Hill	9	29	3.2
Mathis	3	2	0.7	Unitas	1	0	0.0
	43	142	3.3	Morrall	2	–2	–1.0
					23	143	6.2

RECEIVING

NEW YORK JETS	No	Yds	Avg.	BALTIMORE	No	Yds	Avg.
Sauer	8	133	16.6	Richardson	6	58	9.7
Snell	4	40	10.0	Orr	3	42	14.0
Mathis	3	20	6.7	Mackey	3	35	11.7
Lammons	2	13	6.5	Matte	2	30	15.0
	17	206	12.1	Hill	2	1	0.5
				Mitchell	1	15	15.0
					17	181	10.6

PUNTING

NEW YORK JETS	No	Yds	Avg.	BALTIMORE	No	Yds	Avg.
Johnson	4		38.8	Lee	3		44.3

PUNT RETURNS

NEW YORK JETS	No	Yds	Avg.	BALTIMORE	No	Yds	Avg.
Baird	1	0	0.0	Brown	4	34	8.5

KICKOFF RETURNS

NEW YORK JETS	No	Yds	Avg.	BALTIMORE	No	Yds	Avg.
Christy	1	25	25.0	Pearson	2	59	29.5
				Brown	2	45	22.5
					4	104	26.0

INTERCEPTION RETURNS

NEW YORK JETS	No	Yds	Avg.	BALTIMORE	No	Yds	Avg.
Beverly	2	0	0.0	None			
Hudson	1	9	9.0				
Sample	1	0	0.0				
	4	9	2.3				

PASSING

	Att	Comp	Comp Pct.	Yds	Int	Yds/ Att.	Yds/ Comp	Yards Lost Tackled
NEW YORK								
Namath	28	17	60.7	206	0	7.4	12.1	2–11
Parilli	1	0	0.0	0	0	–	–	0
	29	17	58.6	206	0	7.1	12.1	2–11
BALTIMORE								
Morrall	17	6	35.3	71	3	4.2	11.8	0
Unitas	24	11	45.8	110	1	4.6	10.0	0
	41	17	41.5	181	4	4.4	10.6	0

1969 N.F.L. Equalizing the Competition

It took a thirty-five-hour, forty-five minute meeting to do it, but the NFL came up with a blueprint for next year's merger of the two leagues. Commissioner Pete Rozelle announced on May 17 that both leagues would be part of the NFL next year and that the Baltimore Colts, Cleveland Browns, and Pittsburgh Steelers had agreed to join the present ten AFL clubs in the American Conference, while the thirteen remaining old-line NFL clubs would form the National Conference. Each conference would be parted into Eastern, Central, and Western divisions, and interconference play would begin in the regular season. In other words, this would be the last year in which the NFL and AFL would be separate, distinctive entries.

EASTERN CONFERENCE—CAPITAL DIVISION

Dallas Cowboys— D n Meredith and Don Perkins both retired this year, but the Cowboys came up with an entire new backfield and kept on winning without a hitch. Craig Morton moved up into the starting quarterback spot, Walt Garrison, a rodeo cowboy in the summer, took over at fullback, and rookie Calvin Hill, a product of the Ivy League, led the league in rushing all season only to lose the title when sidelined with an injury for the final game of the year. All the other parts of the Cowboy machine were in fine order. Bob Hayes and Lance Rentzel provided speed at wide receiver, the offensive line was both strong and deep, and the defense pressured quarterbacks unmercifully whenever they attempted to pass.

Washington Redskins—In search of new challenges, Vince Lombardi packed his bags and moved to Washington as the head coach and general manager of the Redskins. The results were immediate, as the Skins had their first winning season since 1955. Lombardi had a good passing attack left over from the previous regime, and he constructed a solid running game with rookie halfback Larry Brown and ex-Brown fullback Charlie Harraway. On defense, Lombardi concentrated on the pass defense, rigging up a tight secondary of Pat Fischer, Mike Bass, Brig Owens, and Rickie Harris.

New Orleans Saints—Billy Kilmer was no glamorous quarterback, but he was a fine leader who moved the team well. The strength of the attack was the stable of receivers; Dan Abramowicz, Al Dodd, and Dave Parks had few peers as a group. Coach Tom Fears added a running game to the offense by coming up with Andy Livingston and Tony Baker as his new running backs. Livingston came over from the Bears, and Baker came off of last year's taxi squad; both ran with power and speed. The defense was a trouble area, although tackles Dave Rowe and Mike Tilleman played well.

Philadelphia Eagles—The Eagles began a rebuilding program under the new leadership of general manager Pete Retzlaff and head coach Jerry Williams this year. The team still finished in last place, but emphasis was placed on developing young players for the future. Williams gave plenty of playing time to rookies Leroy Keyes, Ernie Calloway, and Bill Bradley, and young veterans like Ben Hawkins, Harold Jackson, Mike Evans, Gary Pettigrew, and Tim Rossovich all were handed full-time starting jobs.

CENTURY DIVISION

Cleveland Browns—The Browns were loaded with offensive talent, such as quarterback Bill Nelsen, runner Leroy Kelly, receivers Gary Collins, Paul Warfield, and Milt Morin, and blockers Dick Schafrath and Gene Hickerson. The defense, however, featured several young Turks amidst some overage and mediocre players. Jack Gregory developed into a strong pass-rusher toward the end of the season, rookie Walt Sumner filled in well for the injured Ben Davis at cornerback, and Ernie Kellerman kept up his good work at strong safety, but problems arose at middle linebacker, where Dale Lindsey was barely adequate, and cornerback, where thirty-four-year-old Erich Barnes was playing on borrowed time.

New York Giants—When the Giants lost all their pre-season games, owner Wellington Mara canned coach Allie Sherman, long-term contract and all, and elevated assistant Alex Webster. The Giants responded to the switch by beating the Vikings. Things leveled off after that, with the Giants winning some and losing some as befits a mediocre team. One of the biggest enigmas of the year was Homer Jones, who found his way into the end zone only once all year.

St. Louis Cardinals—Injuries to Jerry Stovall, Bob Atkins, and Jamie Rivers made the Cards vulnerable to the pass; the New Orleans Saints exploited this weakness to win a 52-41 decision. The offense could produce points in a hurry, with a good line, good receivers in John Gilliam, Dave Williams, and Jackie Smith and powerful runners in Cid Edwards and Johnny Roland. Charley Johnson and Jim Hart split the quarterbacking chores, but neither could provide leadership.

Pittsburgh Steelers—New head coach Chuck Noll won only one game all year but still felt that progress was made in several areas. The defensive line was upgraded by ferocious rookie tackle Joe Greene, the secondary found a hard-hitting safety in Chuck Beatty, and the offensive line improved with the development of young veterans Larry Gagner, Bruce Van Dyke, and Ray Mansfield. Noll also got good seasons out of veterans Roy Jefferson, Ben McGee, and Andy Russell but was disappointed by a poor rookie season for Terry Hanratty.

WESTERN CONFERENCE — CENTRAL DIVISION

Minnesota Vikings—Although the heart of the Vikings was their defense, the biggest star on the team was a quarterback who had problems passing. Joe Kapp, whose passes wobbled ominously but often found the mark, set the tone of the Vikings with actions, such as his scrambling runs which included hurdling over defenders and bulling through tacklers. The Viking attack was unrelenting but unspectacular, leading the league in points scored primarily because the defense kept giving it the ball.

Detroit Lions—Just as when he had played, coach Joe Schmidt's Lions relied on the defense to carry the club. The front four was anchored by Alex Karras, the linebacking trio of Paul Naumoff, Mike Lucci, and Wayne Walker combined mobility and strength, and cornerbacks Lem Barney and Dick LeBeau made passing a difficult task for enemy quarterbacks. The Lion quarterback situation was unsettled, however, as Bill Munson and Greg Landry split the job with indifferent results, and injuries to Mel Farr and Nick Eddy hurt the running game.

Green Bay Packers—The Packers remained a tough team despite several problems. Bart Starr missed the last four games with a shoulder injury, Jerry Kramer and Bob Skoronski retired, and age was creeping up on the defensive line. The most damaging deficiency, however, was the lack of a reliable place-kicker. Coach Phil Bengtson started the year with Mike Mercer, who hit on only five of seventeen field-goal attempts, and then switched to Booth Lusteg, whose one-for-five record was no improvement.

Chicago Bears—Gale Sayers recaptured his old form after a hesitant start and rocketed to the NFL rushing crown. Outside of that, the Bears endured a campaign of unbroken gloom. The team lost its first seven games, beat the just as miserable Pittsburgh Steelers, then went on to lose their last six games. Coach Jim Dooley juggled his quarterbacks to get some life into the passing attack, but all he got for his troubles were some unhappy passers. Jack Concannon started the year at the controls, but when he couldn't move the team, Dooley put rookie Bobby Douglass into the lineup.

COASTAL DIVISION

Los Angeles Rams—Old pros like Deacon Jones, Merlin Olsen, Jack Pardee, Maxie Baughan, Clancy Williams, and Eddie Meador made few errors on defense, the hallmark of a George Allen team, and the Roman Gabriel-led offense rarely turned the ball over without holding onto it for a stretch. Operating behind a superb line of Bob Brown, Charlie Cowan, Tom Mack, Joe Scibelli, and Ken Iman, Gabriel ground out yardage with handoffs to rookie Larry Smith, Les Josephson, and Tommy Mason and with quick passes to Jack Snow, Wendell Tucker, and Billy Truax. The Rams' ball-control tactics worked so well that they won their first eleven games.

Baltimore Colts—The ill omen of their Super Bowl defeat followed the Colts through this season. Ordell Braase, Don Shinnick, and Bobby Boyd retired after the loss to the Jets, and Jerry Hill, Terry Cole, Willie Richardson, John Mackey, Lou Michaels, Dennis Gaubatz, and Lenny Lyles suffered through sub-par seasons. Thus, one year after winning the NFL championship, the Colts had a completely different look. Ted Hendricks, Roy Hilton, Bob Grant, Charlie Stukes, and Tommy Maxwell were new starters on defense, with Mike Curtis having to learn the middle linebacker spot. Johnny Unitas reclaimed the quarterback position but showed little fire.

Atlanta Falcons—Coach Norm Van Brocklin fielded two strong defensive ends in Claude Humphrey and John Zook, a top cornerback in Ken Reaves, a good tight end in Jim Mitchell, and a potential All-Pro tackle in George Kunz. One of Van Brocklin's biggest problems, however, was that his offensive line, with four rookie starters, could not pass-block.

San Francisco '49ers—Injuries cut down Kevin Hardy, John Brodie, Stan Hindman, Ed Beard, and Johnny Fuller, retirement erased Matt Hazeltine, and the '49ers fell back into the basement in the Coastal Division. Coach Dick Nolan had veteran talent in such as Ken Willard, Elmer Collett, Charlie Krueger, Dave Wilcox, Jim Johnson, and mid-season pickup Rosey Taylor, and he had rookie talent in Gene Washington, Skip Vanderbundt, Ted Kwalick, and Earl Edwards, but the '49ers persisted as one of pro football's top enigmas.

FINAL TEAM STATISTICS

OFFENSE

	ATL.	BALT.	CHI.	CLEV.	DALL.	DET.	G.B.	L.A.	MINN.	N.O.	N.Y.	PHIL.	PITT.	ST.L.	S.F.	WASH.
FIRST DOWNS:																
Total	209	255	237	250	275	198	242	209	239	282	235	231	210	224	253	256
by Rushing	97	99	120	97	133	83	95	75	102	93	91	83	81	83	84	84
by Passing	89	140	97	138	125	93	122	114	117	158	133	132	115	125	153	149
by Penalty	23	16	20	15	17	22	25	20	20	31	11	16	14	16	16	23
RUSHING:																
Number	455	417	462	447	532	474	432	382	489	399	397	395	400	382	391	377
Yards	2058	1490	2078	1788	2276	1755	1692	1413	1850	1705	1593	1563	1542	1446	1536	1532
Average Yards	4.5	3.6	4.5	4.0	4.3	3.7	3.9	3.7	3.8	4.3	4.0	4.0	3.9	3.8	3.9	4.1
Touchdowns	9	16	14	17	17	11	11	8	15	12	8	10	8	17	13	11
PASSING:																
Attempts	282	429	384	378	355	329	319	416	346	453	435	458	391	430	496	444
Completions	149	225	193	199	189	165	182	222	176	245	234	216	176	216	278	275
Completion Percentage	52.8	52.4	50.3	52.6	53.2	50.2	57.1	53.4	50.9	54.1	53.8	47.2	45.0	50.2	56.0	61.9
Passing Yards	2230	3143	1929	2830	3212	1958	2678	2650	2498	3215	3076	3022	2458	2940	3379	3106
Average Yards per Attempt	7.9	7.3	5.0	7.5	9.0	6.0	8.4	6.4	7.2	7.1	7.1	6.6	6.3	6.8	6.8	7.0
Average Yards per Completion	15.0	14.0	10.0	14.2	17.0	11.9	14.7	11.9	14.2	13.1	13.1	14.0	14.0	13.6	12.2	11.3
Times Tackled Attempting to Pass	63	19	55	20	44	42	34	17	34	27	37	29	52	21	27	40
Yards Lost Tackled Attempting to Pass	477	156	439	190	366	358	302	129	252	241	301	240	374	201	221	322
Net Yards	1753	2987	1490	2640	2846	1600	2376	2521	2246	2974	2775	2782	2084	2739	3158	2784
Touchdowns	20	17	11	24	24	12	20	25	24	22	24	20	17	19	22	22
Interceptions	12	27	21	21	18	18	17	7	18	20	8	28	29	25	26	16
Percent Intercepted	4.3	6.3	5.5	5.6	5.1	5.5	5.3	1.7	5.2	4.4	1.8	6.1	7.4	5.8	5.2	3.6
PUNTS:																
Number	69	57	76	60	63	74	59	80	67	49	73	74	77	73	71	70
Average Distance	41.2	45.3	39.0	37.5	43.3	33.9	40.1	40.7	40.0	41.4	37.6	39.8	42.3	37.6	40.5	42.2
PUNT RETURNS:																
Number	26	37	30	32	38	21	32	58	45	30	15	36	37	38	22	26
Yards	82	192	164	183	273	230	287	556	266	217	50	219	165	201	63	190
Average Yards	3.2	5.2	5.5	5.7	7.2	11.0	9.0	9.6	5.9	7.2	3.3	6.1	4.5	5.3	2.9	7.3
Touchdowns	0	0	0	0	0	1	1	0	0	0	0	0	0	0	0	1
KICKOFF RETURNS:																
Number	52	51	52	46	36	42	50	53	33	62	56	63	60	68	47	60
Yards	1104	1290	1132	985	718	1017	1165	1107	774	1455	1075	1258	1241	1507	908	1268
Average Yards	21.2	25.3	21.8	21.4	19.9	24.2	23.3	20.9	23.5	23.5	19.2	20.0	20.7	22.2	19.3	21.1
Touchdowns	1	1	0	0	0	1	2	0	0	0	0	0	1	1	0	0
INTERCEPTION RETURNS:																
Number	19	15	16	19	24	21	19	26	30	12	19	15	25	15	20	16
Yards	200	106	132	217	339	207	428	424	459	73	221	179	257	245	194	246
Average Yards	10.5	7.1	8.3	11.4	14.1	9.9	22.5	16.3	15.3	6.1	11.6	11.9	10.3	16.3	9.7	15.4
Touchdowns	0	0	1	3	1	0	2	3	2	0	1	3	0	1	1	1
PENALTIES:																
Number	63	62	89	58	81	71	63	95	67	83	70	80	67	72	85	74
Yards	601	561	940	603	840	734	602	994	744	943	777	843	659	765	845	756
FUMBLES:																
Number	37	23	27	26	28	18	31	23	17	20	22	18	36	24	25	23
Number Lost	19	12	17	14	12	12	21	11	12	12	15	11	20	10	12	10
POINTS:																
Total	276	279	210	351	369	259	269	320	379	311	264	279	218	314	277	307
PAT Attempts	33	34	26	45	44	26	36	36	43	35	33	33	26	40	37	37
PAT Made	33	33	26	45	43	26	35	36	43	33	33	31	26	38	35	35
FG Attempts	30	31	21	23	36	37	22	34	37	41	21	30	26	24	21	27
FG Made	15	14	8	12	20	25	6	22	26	22	11	16	12	12	6	16
Percent FG Made	50.0	45.2	38.1	52.2	55.6	67.6	27.3	64.7	70.3	53.7	52.4	53.3	46.2	50.0	28.6	59.3
Safeties	0	0	2	0	1	1	0	1	0	1	0	1	0	0	1	1

DEFENSE

	ATL.	BALT.	CHI.	CLEV.	DALL.	DET.	G.B.	L.A.	MINN.	N.O.	N.Y.	PHIL.	PITT.	ST.L.	S.F.	WASH.
FIRST DOWNS:																
Total	254	256	208	257	203	182	224	242	158	242	243	268	260	289	242	277
by Rushing	120	70	89	120	52	64	103	84	55	88	120	111	101	83	91	149
by Passing	120	164	98	121	141	101	107	125	88	131	103	136	142	185	128	110
by Penalty	14	22	21	16	10	17	14	33	15	23	20	21	17	21	23	18
RUSHING:																
Number	475	399	440	417	313	372	485	415	337	419	466	467	455	438	422	511
Yards	2032	1400	1900	1990	1050	1223	1982	1475	1089	1835	2053	1909	1732	1644	1704	2299
Average Yards	4.3	3.5	4.3	4.8	3.4	3.3	4.1	3.6	3.2	4.4	4.4	4.1	3.8	3.8	4.0	4.5
Touchdowns	14	8	17	18	3	7	7	8	4	15	14	15	17	10	14	26
PASSING:																
Attempts	383	459	296	387	458	350	360	430	410	382	340	444	410	465	402	369
Completions	225	271	150	202	235	167	177	202	213	200	171	243	227	260	205	192
Completion Percentage	58.7	59.0	50.7	52.2	51.3	47.7	49.2	47.0	52.0	52.4	50.3	54.7	55.4	55.9	51.0	52.0
Passing Yards	2536	3499	2239	2787	3109	2238	2133	2919	2035	3382	2430	3250	2973	3752	2726	2316
Average Yards per Attempt	6.6	7.6	7.6	7.2	6.8	6.4	5.9	6.8	5.0	8.9	7.1	7.3	7.3	8.1	6.8	6.3
Average Yards per Completion	11.3	12.9	14.9	13.8	13.2	13.4	12.1	14.5	9.6	16.9	14.2	13.4	13.1	14.4	13.3	12.1
Times Tackled Attempting to Pass	30	33	33	37	55	46	36	50	49	21	32	25	33	33	30	18
Yards Lost Tackled Attempting to Pass	251	250	258	323	452	377	288	393	404	199	275	181	304	220	255	139
Net Yards	2285	3249	1981	2464	2657	1861	1845	2526	1631	3183	2155	3069	2669	3532	2471	2177
Touchdowns	13	20	23	19	23	15	13	18	8	32	18	23	27	38	22	11
Interceptions	19	15	16	19	24	21	19	26	30	12	19	15	25	15	20	16
Percent Intercepted	5.0	3.3	5.4	4.9	5.5	6.0	5.3	6.0	7.3	3.1	5.6	3.4	6.1	3.2	5.0	4.3
PUNTS:																
Number	56	69	63	64	82	70	72	77	100	58	53	69	65	67	65	62
Average Distance	38.8	38.4	41.4	40.5	42.2	40.0	39.7	41.0	36.8	41.6	38.9	40.9	40.1	40.4	40.4	40.7
PUNT RETURNS:																
Number	38	35	28	20	43	31	18	36	34	27	41	21	41	35	39	36
Yards	171	182	106	72	305	133	62	181	237	176	449	93	396	158	293	324
Average Yards	4.5	5.2	3.8	3.6	7.1	4.3	3.4	5.0	7.0	6.5	11.0	4.4	9.7	4.5	7.5	9.0
Touchdowns	0	0	0	0	0	0	0	0	0	0	2	0	1	0	0	0
KICKOFF RETURNS:																
Number	52	55	38	56	64	59	51	56	70	48	45	51	46	49	43	48
Yards	1132	1135	917	1166	1242	1242	1078	1208	1453	935	1100	1043	962	1007	1186	1198
Average Yards	21.8	20.6	24.1	20.8	19.4	21.1	21.1	21.6	20.8	19.5	24.4	20.5	20.9	20.6	27.6	25.0
Touchdowns	2	0	1	0	0	0	1	0	1	0	0	0	1	0	1	0
INTERCEPTION RETURNS:																
Number	12	27	21	21	18	18	17	7	18	20	8	28	29	25	26	16
Yards	233	394	271	275	167	168	256	40	208	265	78	343	535	202	304	188
Average Yards	19.4	14.6	12.9	13.1	9.3	9.3	15.1	5.7	11.6	13.3	9.8	12.3	18.4	8.1	11.7	11.8
Touchdowns	2	3	0	1	1	1	1	0	2	0	0	3	3	0	1	1
PENALTIES:																
Number	73	74	66	72	58	90	65	88	69	81	62	79	79	71	70	83
Yards	762	848	612	746	680	857	733	709	795	773	601	950	793	773	671	904
FUMBLES:																
Number	37	18	21	32	23	24	23	33	24	20	23	31	25	19	26	19
Number Lost	27	10	11	22	11	21	7	12	12	10	14	14	16	12	11	10
POINTS:																
Total	268	268	339	300	223	188	221	243	133	393	298	377	404	389	319	319
PAT Attempts	32	32	43	38	28	23	23	26	16	49	35	44	50	48	39	38
PAT Made	32	31	42	36	28	23	23	25	16	47	32	44	49	47	38	38
FG Attempts	27	34	31	22	25	29	34	26	18	29	29	37	26	31	36	27
FG Made	14	15	13	12	9	9	20	20	7	16	18	23	17	18	15	17
Percent FG Made	51.9	44.1	41.9	54.5	36.0	31.0	58.8	78.9	38.9	55.2	62.1	62.2	65.4	58.1	41.7	63.0
Safeties	1	0	0	0	0	0	0	1	0	2	1	0	2	0	1	1

CONFERENCE PLAYOFFS

SCORING

MINNESOTA 7 0 7 9–23
LOS ANGELES 7 10 0 3–20

First Quarter
LA Klein, 3 yard pass from Gabriel
PAT–Gossett (kick)
Mn. Osborn, 1 yard rush
PAT–Cox (kick)

Second Quarter
LA Gossett, 20 yard field goal
LA Truax, 2 yard pass from Gabriel
PAT–Gossett (kick)

Third Quarter
Mn. Osborn, 1 yard rush
PAT–Cox (kick)

Fourth Quarter
LA Gossett, 27 yard field goal
Mn. Kapp, 2 yard rush
PAT–Cox (kick)
Mn. Eller, Safety-tackled Gabriel in end zone.

TEAM STATISTICS

MINN.		L.A.
18	First Downs–Total	19
7	First Downs–Rushing	10
10	First Downs–Passing	9
1	First Downs–Penalty	0
2	Times Tackled Passing	3
18	Yards Lost–Tackled	21
3	Fumbles–Number	1
1	Fumbles–Lost Ball	0
4	Penalties–Number	4
36	Yards Penalized	37
3	Punts–Number	3
39.3	Punts–Average Distance	36.3
1	Punt Returns–Number	2
6	Punt Returns–Yards	8
6	Kickoff Returns–Number	4
111	Kickoff Returns–Yards	69
1	Interception Returns–Number	2
29	Interception Returns–Yards	19
0	Missed Field Goals	1
3	Giveaways	1
1	Takeaways	3
–2	Difference	+2

INDIVIDUAL STATISTICS

RUSHING

MINNESOTA	No	Yds	Avg.	LOS ANGELES	No	Yds	Avg.
Kapp	7	42	6.0	Smith	11	60	5.5
Osborn	13	30	2.3	Gabriel	4	26	6.5
Brown	8	22	2.8	Ellison	4	22	5.5
Reed	1	3	3.0	Josephson	10	16	1.6
	29	97	3.3	Mason	1	2	2.0
					30	126	4.2

RECEIVING

Washington	4	90	22.5	Josephson	7	41	5.9
Henderson	4	68	17.0	Smith	6	36	6.0
Brown	2	20	10.0	Truax	5	47	9.4
Reed	2	18	9.0	Tucker	3	23	7.7
	12	196	16.3	Klein	1	3	3.0
					22	150	6.8

PASSING

MINN.	Att.	Cmp.	Pct.	Yds.	Int.	Yd/A	Yd/C
Kapp	19	12	63.2	196	2	10.3	16.3
L.A.							
Gabriel	32	22	62.5	150	1	4.7	6.8

December 28, at Dallas (Attendance 69,321)

SCORING

DALLAS 0 0 7 7–14
CLEVELAND 7 10 7 14–38

First Quarter
Cle Scott, 2 yard rush
PAT–Cockroft (kick)

Second Quarter
Cle. Morin, 6 yard pass from Nelsen
PAT–Cockroft (kick)
Cle. Cockroft, 29 field goal

Third Quarter
Cle. Scott, 2 yard rush
PAT–Cockroft (kick)
Dal. Morton, 2 yard rush
PAT–Clark (kick)

Fourth Quarter
Cle. Kelly, 1 yard rush
PAT–Cockroft (kick)
Cle. Sumner, 88 yard interception return PAT–Cockroft (kick)
Dal. Rentzel, 5 yard pass from Staubach
PAT–Clark (kick)

TEAM STATISTICS

DAL.		CLE.
17	First Downs–Total	22.
9	First Downs–Rushing	4
6	First Downs–Passing	17
2	First Downs–Penalty	1
3	Times Tackled Passing	1
19	Yards Lost–Tackled	7
2	Fumbles–Number	1
1	Fumbles–Lost Ball	0
6	Penalties–Number	6
51	Yards Penalized	50
5	Punts–Number	1
36.2	Punts–Average Distance	34.0
1	Punt Returns–Number	2
0	Punt Returns–Yards	11
5	Kickoff Returns–Number	3
106	Kickoff Returns–Yards	56
0	Interception Returns–Number	2
0	Interception Returns–Yards	123
0	Missed Field Goals	1
3	Giveaways	0
0	Takeaways	3
–3	Difference	+3

INDIVIDUAL

RUSHING

DALLAS				CLEVELAND			
Garrison	9	49	5.4	Kelly	19	66	3.5
Staubach	3	22	7.3	Scott	11	33	3.0
Hill	8	17	2.1	Morrison	2	3	1.5
Morton	4	12	3.0	Cockroft	1	0	0.0
Shy	1	0	0.0	Johnson	2	–5	–2.5
	25	100	4.0		35	97	2.8

RECEIVING

Hayes	4	44	11.0	Warfield	8	99	11.4
Rentzel	3	41	13.7	Morin	4	52	13.0
Garrison	2	15	7.5	Scott	2	39	19.5
Norman	1	26	26.0	Collins	2	19	9.5
Hill	1	7	7.0	Kelly	2	10	5.0
Reeves	1	3	3.0	Morrison	1	18	18.0
	12	136	11.3	Jones	1	17	17.0
					20	254	12.7

PASSING

DALLAS	Att.	Cmp.	Pct.	Yds.	Int.	Yd/A	Yd/C
Morton	24	8	33.3	92	2	3.8	11.5
Staubach	5	4	80.0	44	0	8.8	11.0
	29	12	41.4	136	2	4.7	11.3
CLEVE.							
Nelsen	27	18	66.7	219	0	8.1	12.2
Rhome	2	2	100.0	35	0	17.5	17.5
	29	20	69.0	254	0	8.8	12.7

CAPITOL DIVISION

DALLAS COWBOYS 11-2-1 Tom Landry

Scores of Each Game		
24	ST. LOUIS	3
21	New Orleans	17
38	Philadelphia	7
24	Atlanta	17
49	PHILADELPHIA	14
25	NEW YORK	3
10	Cleveland	42
33	NEW ORLEANS	17
41	Washington	28
23	Los Angeles	24
24	SAN FRANCISCO	24
10	Pittsburgh	7
27	BALTIMORE	10
20	WASHINGTON	10

Use Name	Pos.	Hgt	Wgt	Age	Int	Pts
Tony Liscio	OT	6'5"	255	29		
Ralph Neely	OT	6'5"	265	25		
Rayfield Wright	TE-OT	6'7"	250	24		
John Niland	OG	6'4"	245	25		
Blaine Nye	OG	6'4"	250	23		
John Wilbur	OG	6'3"	240	26		
Dave Manders	C	6'2"	250	27		
Malcolm Walker	C	6'4"	250	26		
George Andrie	DE	6'7"	250	29		2
Larry Cole	DE	6'4"	255	22	1	6
Halvor Hagen	OT-DE	6'5"	250	22		
Ron East	DT	6'4"	242	26		
Bob Lilly	DT	6'4"	260	30		6
Jethro Pugh	DT	6'6"	260	25		
Jackie Burkett	LB	6'4"	228	32		
Dave Edwards	LB	6'3"	228	30	1	
Chuck Howley	LB	6'3"	225	33	2	
Lee Roy Jordan	LB	6'2"	220	28	2	
Tom Stincic	LB	6'2"	226	22		
Fred Whittingham	LB	6'1"	240	30		
Otto Brown	DB	6'1"	188	22	1	
Phil Clark	DB	6'2"	210	24	2	
Mike Gaechter	DB	6'	190	29	3	
Cornell Green	DB	6'4"	208	29	2	
Mike Johnson	DB	5'10"	184	25		
Mel Renfro	DB	6'	190	27	10	
D. D. Lewis – Military Service						
Willie Townes – Injury						
Bob Belden	QB	6'2"	210	22		
Craig Morton	QB	6'4"	214	26		6
Roger Staubach	QB	6'2"	195	27		6
Craig Baynham	HB	6'1"	206	25		
Calvin Hill	HB	6'3"	230	22		48
Les Shy	HB	6'1"	200	25		12
Dan Reeves	FB-HB	6'1"	200	25		30
Walt Garrison	FB	6'	205	25		12
Claxton Welch	HB-FB	5'11"	200	22		
Bobby Joe Conrad	WR	6'	195	34		
Richmond Flowers	WR	6'	183	22		
Bob Hayes	WR	6'	185	26		24
Dennis Homan	WR	6'1"	180	23		
Lance Rentzel	WR	6'2"	202	25		78
Mike Ditka	TE	6'3"	225	29		18
Pettis Norman	TE	6'3"	220	29		18
Mike Clark	K	6'1"	205	28		103
Ron Widby	K	6'4"	210	24		

WASHINGTON REDSKINS 7-5-2 Vince Lombardi

Scores of Each Game		
26	New Orleans	20
23	Cleveland	27
17	San Francisco	17
33	ST. LOUIS	17
20	NEW YORK	14
14	Pittsburgh	7
17	Baltimore	41
28	PHILADELPHIA	28
28	DALLAS	41
27	ATLANTA	20
13	LOS ANGELES	24
34	Philadelphia	29
17	NEW ORLEANS	14
10	Dallas	20

Use Name	Pos.	Hgt	Wgt	Age	Int	Pts
Walt Rock	OT	6'5"	255	28		
Jim Snowden	OT	6'3"	255	27		
Ray Schoenke	C-OT	6'3"	250	27		
Willie Banks	OG	6'2"	237	23		
Steve Duich	OG	6'3"	248	23		
Vince Promuto	OG	6'1"	245	31		
Dave Crossan	C	6'3"	245	29		
Len Hauss	C	6'2"	235	27		
Leo Carroll	DE	6'7"	250	25		
John Hoffman	DE	6'7"	260	26		6
Carl Kammerer	DE	6'3"	243	32		
Clark Miller	DE	6'5"	246	30		
Frank Bosch	DT	6'4"	246	23		
Dennis Crane	DT	6'6"	260	24		
Spain Musgrave	DT	6'4"	275	24		
Jim Norton	DT	6'4"	254	26		
Joe Rutgens	DT	6'2"	255	30		
Chris Hanburger	LB	6'2"	218	28		6
Sam Huff	LB	6'1"	230	34	3	6
Marlin McKeever	LB	6'1"	235	29	1	
Harold McLinton	LB	6'2"	235	22		
Tom Roussel	LB	6'3"	235	24		
John Didion	C-LB	6'4"	245	21		
Mike Bass	DB	6'	190	24	3	
Tom Brown	DB	6'1"	195	28		
Pat Fischer	DB	5'10"	170	29	2	
Rickie Harris	DB	6'	182	26	4	6
Brig Owens	DB	5'11"	190	26	3	
Ted Vactor	DB	6'	185	25		
Bob Wade	DB	6'2"	200	24		
Sonny Jurgensen	QB	5'11"	203	35		6
Frank Ryan	QB	6'3"	207	33		
Jerry Allen	HB	6'1"	200	28		
Larry Brown	HB	5'11"	195	21		24
Dave Kopay	FB-HB	6'2"	225	27		
Henry Dyer	FB	6'2"	230	24		6
Charlie Harraway	FB	6'2"	215	24		54
Chuck Mercein	FB	6'3"	220	26		
Gary Beban	WR	6'1"	195	23		
Bob Long	WR	6'3"	205	28		6
Walter Roberts	WR	5'10"	163	27		
Charley Taylor	WR	6'3"	210	28		48
Pat Richter	TE	6'5"	230	28		
Jerry Smith	TE	6'2"	208	26		54
Mike Bragg	K	5'11"	186	22		
Curt Knight	K	6'1"	190	26		83

NEW ORLEANS SAINTS 5-9-0 Tom Fears

Scores of Each Game		
20	WASHINGTON	26
17	DALLAS	21
17	Los Angeles	36
17	CLEVELAND	27
10	BALTIMORE	30
10	Philadelphia	13
51	St. Louis	42
17	Dallas	33
25	New York	24
43	SAN FRANCISCO	38
26	PHILADELPHIA	17
17	Atlanta	45
14	Washington	17
27	PITTSBURGH	24

Use Name	Pos.	Hgt	Wgt	Age	Int	Pts
Jerry Jones	OT	6'3"	265	25		
Errol Linden	OT	6'5"	250	32		
Don Talbert	OT	6'5"	255	29		
Norman Davis	OG	6'3"	245	24		
Jake Kupp	OG	6'3"	246	27		
John Shinners	OG	6'2"	254	22		
Del Williams	OG	6'2"	245	23		
Jerry Sturm	C	6'3"	265	32		
Doug Atkins	DE	6'8"	275	39		
Dan Colchico	DE	6'4"	245	32		
Dave Long	DE	6'4"	245	24		
Richard Neal	DE	6'3"	254	21		
Mike Rengel	DT	6'5"	260	22		
Dave Rowe	DT	6'6"	280	24		
Mike Tilleman	DT	6'5"	280	25		
Dick Absher	LB	6'4"	227	25	1	
Johnny Brewer	LB	6'4"	235	32		
Bill Cody	LB	6'1"	227	25		
Ted Davis	LB	6'1"	232	27		
Les Kelley	LB	6'3"	233	24		
Mike Morgan	LB	6'4"	242	27		
Bill Saul	LB	6'4"	225	28		
Bo Burris	DB	6'3"	195	24	1	
Ollie Cordill	DB	6'2"	180	26		
Gene Howard	DB	6'	190	22	2	
Elijah Nevett	DB	6'	185	25	3	
Steve Preece	DB	6'1"	195	22	1	6
Bobby Thompson	DB	5'10"	188	29	1	
Carl Ward	DB	5'9"	180	25		
Dave Whitsell	DB	6'	185	33	3	
Lou Cordileone – Knee Injury						
Edd Hargett	QB	5'11"	186	22		
Billy Kilmer	QB	6'	204	29		
Jim Ninowski	QB	6'1"	207	33		
Joe Don Looney	HB	6'1"	230	26		
Don Shy	HB	6'1"	205	23		12
Tony Baker	FB-HB	5'11"	230	24		12
Tom Barrington	FB-HB	6'1"	213	25		6
Andy Livingston	FB	6'	234	24		48
Tony Lorick	FB	6'1"	217	27		
Ernie Wheelwright	FB	6'3"	236	32		30
Dan Abramowicz	WR	6'1"	195	24		42
Al Dodd	WR	6'	180	24		6
Dave Parks	TE-WR	6'2"	203	27		18
Jim Hester	TE	6'4"	250	24		6
Ray Poage	TE	6'4"	215	28		24
Tom Dempsey	K	6'1"	264	28		99
Tom McNeill	K	6'1"	195	27		

PHILADELPHIA EAGLES 4-9-1 Jerry Williams

Scores of Each Game		
20	CLEVELAND	27
41	PITTSBURGH	27
7	DALLAS	38
20	Baltimore	24
14	Dallas	49
13	NEW ORLEANS	10
23	New York	20
28	Washington	28
17	LOS ANGELES	23
34	St. Louis	30
17	New Orleans	26
29	WASHINGTON	34
3	ATLANTA	27
13	San Francisco	14

Use Name	Pos.	Hgt	Wgt	Age	Int	Pts
Joe Carollo	OT	6'2"	258	29		
Dave Graham	OT	6'3"	250	30		
Lane Howell	OT	6'5"	272	28		
Don Chuy	OG	6'1"	255	28		
Dick Hart	OG	6'2"	255	26		
Jim Skaggs	OG	6'2"	252	29		
Mark Nordquist	C-OG	6'4"	242	23		
Gene Ceppetelli (to NY)	C	6'2"	247	27		
Mike Evans	C	6'5"	250	22		
Don Hultz	DE	6'3"	242	28		
Tim Rossovich	DE	6'4"	260	23		
Mel Tom	DE	6'4"	250	28		2
Ernie Calloway	DT	6'6"	240	21		
Mike Dirks	DT	6'2"	246	23		
Floyd Peters	DT	6'4"	255	34		
Gary Pettigrew	DE-DT	6'4"	255	24		
Wayne Colman (to NO)	LB	6'1"	230	23	1	
Tony Guillory	LB	6'4"	235	26		
Bill Hobbs	LB	6'	213	23		
Jay Johnson	LB	6'3"	230	23		
Ike Kelley	LB	5'11"	222	25		
Dave Lloyd	LB	6'3"	248	33	2	
Ron Porter (from BAL)	LB	6'3"	232	24		
Adrian Young	LB	6'1"	225	23	1	
Bill Bradley	DB	5'11"	190	22	1	6
Irv Cross	DB	6'1"	195	30	1	
Ron Medved	DB	6'1"	195	25		
Al Nelson	DB	5'11"	186	25	3	
Nate Ramsey	DB	6'1"	200	28	2	6
Jimmy Raye	DB	6'	185	23		
Joe Scarpati	DB	5'10"	185	27	4	6
George Mira	QB	5'11"	190	27		
Norm Snead	QB	6'4"	215	29		12
Ronnie Blye	HB	5'11"	185	25		
Harry Jones	HB	6'2"	205	24		
Leroy Keyes	HB	6'3"	208	22		18
Harry Wilson	HB	5'11"	204	24		
Cyril Pinder	FB-HB	6'2"	222	22		6
Tom Woodeschick	FB	6'	225	27		24
Gary Ballman	WR	6'	205	29		12
Ben Hawkins	WR	6'	180	25		48
Chuck Hughes	WR	5'11"	175	26		
Harold Jackson	WR	5'10"	175	23		54
Kent Lawrence	WR	5'11"	175	22		
Fred Brown	TE	6'5"	237	26		
Fred Hill	TE	6'2"	215	26		6
Sam Baker	K	6'2"	218	37		7[illegible]

CAPITOL DIVISION

DALLAS COWBOYS

RUSHING

Last Name	No.	Yds	Avg	TD
Hill	204	942	4.6	8
Garrison	176	818	4.6	2
Reeves	59	173	2.9	4
Shy	42	154	3.7	1
Morton	16	62	3.9	1
Staubach	15	60	4.0	1
Welch	6	21	3.5	0
Norman	5	20	4.0	0
Hayes	4	17	4.3	0
Rentzel	2	11	5.5	0
Baynham	3	−2	−0.7	0

RECEIVING

Last Name	No.	Yds	Avg	TD
Rentzel	43	960	22	12
Hayes	40	746	19	4
Hill	20	232	12	0
Reeves	18	187	10	1
Ditka	17	268	16	3
Norman	13	238	18	3
Garrison	13	131	10	0
Homan	12	240	20	0
Shy	8	124	16	1
Conrad	4	74	19	0
Wright	1	12	12	0

PUNT RETURNS

Last Name	No.	Yds	Avg	TD
Hayes	18	179	10	0
Renfro	15	80	5	0
Rentzel	4	14	4	0
Johnson	1	0	0	0

KICKOFF RETURNS

Last Name	No.	Yds	Avg	TD
Flowers	11	238	22	0
Hill	4	125	31	0
Baynham	6	114	19	0
Welch	5	112	22	0
Hayes	3	80	27	0
Shy	3	47	16	0
Garrison	1	2	2	0
Green	2	0	0	0
Johnson	1	0	0	0

PASSING – PUNTING – KICKING

PASSING	Att	Comp	%	Yds	Yd/Att	TD	Int–	%	RK
Morton	302	162	54	2619	8.7	21	15–	5	5
Staubach	47	23	49	421	9.0	1	2–	4	
Hill	3	3	100	137	45.7	2	0–	0	
Reeves	3	1	33	35	11.7	0	1–	33	

PUNTING	No	Avg
Widby	63	43.3

KICKING	XP	Att	%	FG	Att	%
M. Clark	43	44	98	20	36	56

WASHINGTON REDSKINS

RUSHING

Last Name	No.	Yds	Avg	TD
L. Brown	202	888	4.4	4
Harraway	141	428	3.0	6
Jurgensen	17	156	9.2	1
Taylor	3	24	8.0	0
Dyer	6	18	3.0	0
Smith	3	8	2.7	0
Kopay	3	4	1.3	0
Allen	1	3	3.0	0
Bragg	1	3	3.0	0

RECEIVING

Last Name	No.	Yds	Avg	TD
Taylor	71	883	12	8
Harraway	55	489	9	3
Smith	54	682	13	9
Long	48	533	11	1
L. Brown	34	302	9	0
Kopay	6	60	10	0
Roberts	4	66	17	0
Dyer	2	86	43	1
Allen	1	5	5	0

PUNT RETURNS

Last Name	No.	Yds	Avg	TD
Harris	14	158	11	1
Roberts	12	32	3	0

KICKOFF RETURNS

Last Name	No.	Yds	Avg	TD
Harris	19	458	24	0
Roberts	17	383	23	0
Dyer	11	207	19	0
Kopay	9	187	21	0
McKeever	2	31	16	0
Snowden	1	2	2	0
Richter	1	0	0	0

PASSING – PUNTING – KICKING

PASSING	Att	Comp	%	Yds	Yd/Att	TD	Int–%		RK
Jurgensen	442	274	62	3102	7.0	22	15–	3	1
Ryan	1	1	100	4	4.0	0	0–	0	
Knight	1	0	0	0	0.0	0	1–	100	

PUNTING	No	Avg
Bragg	70	42.2

KICKING	XP	Att	%	FG	Att	%
Knight	35	36	97	16	27	59

NEW ORLEANS SAINTS

RUSHING

Last Name	No.	Yds	Avg	TD
Livingston	181	761	4.2	5
Baker	134	642	4.8	1
Wheelwright	25	85	3.4	4
Shy	21	75	3.6	1
Abramowicz	3	61	20.3	0
Barrington	7	33	4.7	1
Kilmer	11	18	1.6	0
Hargett	5	15	3.0	0
Dodd	3	12	4.0	0
Lorick	5	11	2.2	0
Poage	1	−3	−3.0	0
Looney	3	−5	−1.7	0

RECEIVING

Last Name	No.	Yds	Avg	TD
Abramowicz	73	1015	14	7
Dodd	37	600	16	1
Baker	34	352	10	1
Parks	31	439	14	3
Livingston	28	278	10	3
Poage	18	236	13	4
Shy	9	141	16	1
Wheelwright	8	68	9	1
Barrington	4	42	11	0
Hester	3	44	15	1

PUNT RETURNS

Last Name	No.	Yds	Avg	TD
Dodd	15	106	7	0
Howard	9	73	8	0
Thompson	4	25	6	0
Barrington	1	8	8	0
Ward	1	5	5	0

KICKOFF RETURNS

Last Name	No.	Yds	Avg	TD
Shy	16	447	28	0
Barrington	17	394	23	0
Howard	9	227	25	0
Dodd	8	171	21	0
Thompson	5	101	20	0
Ward	3	58	19	0
Nevett	2	53	27	0
Hester	1	4	4	0
Preece	1	0	0	0

PASSING – PUNTING – KICKING

PASSING	Att	Comp	%	Yds	Yd/Att	TD	Int–	%	RK
Kilmer	360	193	54	2532	7.0	20	17–	5	8
Hargett	52	31	60	403	7.8	0	0–	0	
Ninowski	34	17	50	227	6.7	1	2–	6	
Livingston	4	3	75	38	9.5	1	1–	25	
Barrington	2	1	50	15	7.5	0	0–	0	
Looney	1	0	0	0	0.0	0	0–	0	

PUNTING	No	Avg
Cordill	42	40.9
McNeill	7	44.6

KICKING	XP	Att	%	FG	Att	%
Dempsey	33	35	94	22	41	54

PHILADELPHIA EAGLES

RUSHING

Last Name	No.	Yds	Avg	TD
Woodeshick	186	831	4.5	4
Keyes	121	361	3.0	3
Pinder	60	309	5.2	1
Blye	8	25	3.1	0
Mira	3	16	5.3	0
Jackson	2	10	5.0	0
Wilson	4	7	1.8	0
Bradley	1	5	5.0	0
Snead	8	2	0.3	2
Jones	1	0	0.0	0
Hawkins	1	−3	−3.0	0

RECEIVING

Last Name	No.	Yds	Avg	TD
Jackson	65	1116	17	9
Hawkins	43	761	18	8
Ballman	31	492	16	2
Keyes	29	276	10	0
Woodeshick	22	177	8	0
Pinder	12	77	6	0
Hill	6	64	11	1
Hughes	3	29	10	0
Blye	2	−6	−3	0
Brown	1	20	20	0
Lawrence	1	10	10	0
Wilson	1	6	6	0

PUNT RETURNS

Last Name	No.	Yds	Avg	TD
Bradley	28	181	6	0
Lawrence	2	26	13	0
Scarpati	4	6	2	0
Hawkins	1	6	6	0
Hughes	1	0	0	0

KICKOFF RETURNS

Last Name	No.	Yds	Avg	TD
Bradley	21	467	22	0
Blye	19	370	19	0
Keyes	9	200	22	0
Lawrence	5	97	19	0
Nelson	3	63	21	0
Pinder	4	56	14	0
Graham	2	5	3	0

PASSING – PUNTING – KICKING

PASSING	Att	Comp	%	Yds	Yd/Att	TD	Int–	%	RK
Snead	379	190	50	2768	7.3	19	23–	6	12
Mira	76	25	33	240	3.2	1	5–	7	
Keyes	2	1	50	14	7.0	0	0–	0	
Bradley	1	0	0	0	0.0	0	0–	0	

PUNTING	No	Avg
Bradley	74	39.8

KICKING	XP	Att	%	FG	Att	%
Baker	31	31	100	16	30	53

CENTURY DIVISION

CLEVELAND BROWNS 10-3-1 Blanton Collier

Scores of Each Game		
27	Philadelphia	20
27	WASHINGTON	23
21	DETROIT	28
27	New Orleans	17
42	PITTSBURGH	31
21	ST. LOUIS	21
42	DALLAS	10
3	Minnesota	51
24	Pittsburgh	3
28	NEW YORK	17
28	Chicago	24
20	GREEN BAY	7
27	St. Louis	21
14	New York	27

Use Name	Pos.	Hgt	Wgt	Age	Int	Pts
Monte Clark	OT	6'6"	250	32		
Bob Oliver	OT	6'3"	240	22		
Dick Schafrath	OT	6'3"	248	33		
Joe Taffoni	OT	6'3"	250	24		
Jim Copeland	OG	6'2"	245	24		
John Demarie	OG	6'3"	255	24		
Gene Hickerson	OG	6'3"	248	34		
Chuck Reynolds	OG	6'2"	240	22		
Fred Hoaglin	C	6'4"	250	25		
Jack Gregory	DE	6'6"	250	24	1	
Ron Snidow	DE	6'4"	250	27		
Marv Upshaw	DT-DE	6'3"	245	22	1	
Walter Johnson	DT	6'3"	275	26		6
Jim Kanicki	DT	6'4"	270	27		
Joe Righetti	DT	6'3"	253	21		
Al Jenkins	DE-DT	6'2"	255	23		

Use Name	Pos.	Hgt	Wgt	Age	Int	Pts
Billy Andrews	LB	6'	225	24		
John Garlington	LB	6'1"	225	23	2	
Jim Houston	LB	6'2"	240	32		
Dale Lindsey	LB	6'3"	225	26	1	
Bob Matheson	LB	6'4"	240	24		
Wayne Meylan	LB	6'1"	235	23		
Erich Barnes	DB	6'2"	212	34	1	6
Dean Brown	DB	5'10"	170	22		
Mike Howell	DB	6'1"	190	26	6	
Ernie Kellerman	DB	6'	185	25	3	6
Alvin Mitchell	DB	6'3"	195	25		
Freddie Summers	DB	6'1"	180	22		
Walt Sumner	DB	6'1"	180	22	4	6

Ben Davis – Knee Injury

Use Name	Pos.	Hgt	Wgt	Age	Int	Pts
Bill Nelsen	QB	6'	195	28		
Jerry Rhome	QB	6'	185	27		
Ron Johnson	HB	6'1"	205	21		42
Reece Morrison	HB	6'	205	23		6
Bo Scott	FB	6'3"	210	26		
Charlie Leigh	FB	5'11"	205	23		
Leroy Kelly	HB-FB	6'	200	27		60
Gary Collins	WR	6'4"	220	28		66
Fair Hooker	WR	6'1"	193	22		
Dave Jones	WR	6'2"	185	22		
Paul Warfield	WR	6'	188	26		60
Chip Glass	TE	6'4"	236	22		12
Milt Morin	TE	6'4"	250	27		
Don Cockroft	K	6'1"	185	24		81

NEW YORK GIANTS 6-8-0 Allie Sherman

Scores of Each Game		
24	MINNESOTA	23
0	Detroit	24
28	CHICAGO	24
10	PITTSBURGH	7
14	Washington	20
3	Dallas	25
20	PHILADELPHIA	23
17	St. Louis	42
24	NEW ORLEANS	25
17	Cleveland	28
10	Green Bay	20
49	ST. LOUIS	6
21	Pittsburgh	17
27	CLEVELAND	14

Use Name	Pos.	Hgt	Wgt	Age	Int	Pts
Rich Buzin	OT	6'4"	250	23		
Steve Wright	OT	6'6"	250	27		
Willie Young	OT	6'	265	26		
Pete Case	OG	6'3"	245	28		
Darrell Dess	OG	6'	245	33		
Doug Van Horn	OG	6'2"	245	25		
Charlie Harper	OT-OG	6'2"	250	25		
Chuck Hinton	C	6'2"	235	26		
Greg Larson	C	6'2"	250	30		
Bruce Anderson	DE	6'4"	250	25		
Fred Dryer	DE	6'6"	235	23		
John Johnson	DT	6'5"	260	28		
Tim McCann	DT	6'5"	265	22		
Frank Molden	DT	6'5"	280	27		
Frank Parker	DT	6'5"	270	29		
Joe Szczecko	DT	6'	245	27		
Bob Lurtsema	DE-DT	6'6"	250	27		

Use Name	Pos.	Hgt	Wgt	Age	Int	Pts
McKinley Boston	LB	6'2"	245	23		
Tommy Crutcher	LB	6'3"	230	27	1	
Henry Davis	LB	6'3"	235	26		
Ralph Heck	LB	6'2"	230	28	2	
Ray Hickl	LB	6'2"	210	22		
John Kirby (from MIN)	LB	6'3"	235	27		
Harold Wells	LB	6'2"	220	30		
Al Brenner	DB	6'1"	200	21		
Scott Eaton	DB	6'3"	195	25	2	6
Jim Holifield	DB	6'3"	195	23	1	
Spider Lockhart	DB	6'2"	175	26	2	
Tom Longo	DB	6'1"	198	25	2	
Bruce Maher	DB	5'11"	185	32	5	
Willie Williams	DB	6'	190	26	4	

Bobby Duhon – Injury

Use Name	Pos.	Hgt	Wgt	Age	Int	Pts
Milt Plum	QB	6'1"	205	35		
Frank Tarkenton	QB	6'1"	190	29		
Gary Wood	QB	5'11"	188	26		
John Fuqua	HB	5'11"	200	22		
Randy Minniear	HB	6'	210	25		6
Ernie Koy	FB-HB	6'2"	230	26		36
Joe Morrison	WR-HB	6'1"	212	31		66
Junior Coffey (from ATL)	FB	6'1"	210	27		30
Tucker Frederickson	FB	6'3"	220	26		6
Dave Dunaway	WR	6'2"	205	24		
Don Herrmann	WR	6'2"	195	22		30
Rich Houston	WR	6'2"	197	23		
Homer Jones	WR	6'2"	215	28		6
Dick Kotite	TE	6'3"	235	26		6
Freeman White	TE	6'5"	225	25		6
Butch Wilson	TE	6'2"	228	27		
Aaron Thomas	WR-TE	6'3"	210	31		18
Pete Gogolak	K	6'2"	185	27		66
Curley Johnson	K	6'	215	34		

ST. LOUIS CARDINALS 4-9-1 Charlie Winner

Scores of Each Game		
3	Dallas	24
20	CHICAGO	17
27	Pittsburgh	14
17	Washington	33
10	MINNESOTA	27
21	Cleveland	21
42	NEW ORLEANS	51
42	NEW YORK	17
0	Detroit	20
30	PHILADELPHIA	34
47	PITTSBURGH	10
6	New York	49
21	CLEVELAND	27
28	Green Bay	45

Use Name	Pos.	Hgt	Wgt	Age	Int	Pts
Vern Emerson	OT	6'5"	260	23		
Ernie McMillan	OT	6'6"	260	31		
Bob Reynolds	OT	6'6"	265	28		
Clyde Williams	OT	6'2"	250	29		
Irv Goode	OG	6'4"	250	28		
Ken Gray	OG	6'2"	250	33		
Rick Sortun	OG	6'2"	240	26		
Bob DeMarco	C	6'3"	245	31		
Wayne Mulligan	C	6'2"	245	22		
Don Brumm	DE	6'3"	245	26		
Rolf Krueger	DE	6'4"	245	22		
Cal Snowden	DE	6'4"	235	22		
Chuck Walker	DE	6'2"	250	28		
Fred Heron	DT	6'4"	255	24		
Bob Rowe	DT	6'4"	255	24	2	6
Joe Schmiesing	DT	6'4"	245	24		

Use Name	Pos.	Hgt	Wgt	Age	Int	Pts
Chip Healy	LB	6'3"	230	22		
Dave Meggyesy	LB	6'1"	230	27		
Dave Olerich	LB	6'1"	220	24		
Jamie Rivers	LB	6'2"	235	23		
Rocky Rosema	LB	6'2"	230	23	1	
Larry Stallings	LB	6'2"	230	27		6
Bob Atkins	DB	6'3"	212	23	3	
Lonnie Sanders	DB	6'3"	205	27		
Mac Sauls	DB	6'	185	24		
Jerry Stovall	DB	6'2"	195	27	1	
Roger Wehrli	DB	6'1"	185	21	3	
Larry Wilson	DB	6'	190	31	2	6
Mike Wilson	DB	5'11"	185	22		
Terry Brown	WR-DB	6'1"	205	22	1	

Use Name	Pos.	Hgt	Wgt	Age	Int	Pts
Jim Hart	QB	6'2"	205	25		12
King Hill	QB	6'3"	216	33		
Charley Johnson	QB	6'	190	32		6
MacArthur Lane	HB	6'1"	220	27		6
Johnny Roland	HB	6'2"	215	26		36
Roy Shivers	HB	6'	200	27		18
Willie Crenshaw	FB	6'2"	230	28		18
Cid Edwards	FB	6'2"	230	25		18
Jerry Daanen	WR	6'	190	24		
John Gilliam	WR	6'1"	190	24		60
Freddie Hyatt	WR	6'3"	212	23		
Dave Williams	WR	6'2"	205	24		42
Bob Brown	TE	6'3"	225	26		
Jackie Smith	TE	6'4"	230	28		6
Jim Bakken	K	6'	200	28		74

PITTSBURGH STEELERS 1-13-0 Chuck Noll

Scores of Each Game		
16	DETROIT	13
27	Philadelphia	41
14	ST. LOUIS	27
7	New York	10
31	Cleveland	42
7	WASHINGTON	14
34	GREEN BAY	38
7	Chicago	38
3	CLEVELAND	24
14	Minnesota	52
10	St. Louis	47
7	DALLAS	10
17	NEW YORK	21
24	New Orleans	27

Use Name	Pos.	Hgt	Wgt	Age	Int	Pts
John Brown	OT	6'2"	255	30		
Mike Haggerty	OT	6'4"	240	23		
Mike Taylor (to NO)	OT	6'4"	245	24		
Sam Davis	OG	6'1"	245	25		
Larry Gagner	OG	6'3"	240	25		
Bruce Van Dyke	OG	6'2"	246	25		
Ralph Wenzel	OG	6'3"	236	26		
Jon Kolb	C	6'2"	220	22		
Ray Mansfield	C	6'3"	240	28		
L. C. Greenwood	DE	6'5"	240	22		
Ben McGee	DE	6'2"	250	27		
Lloyd Voss	DE	6'4"	256	27		
Dick Arndt	DT	6'5"	265	25		
Joe Greene	DT	6'4"	270	22		
Chuck Hinton	DT	6'5"	258	30	1	
Clarence Washington	DT	6'3"	265	22		

Use Name	Pos.	Hgt	Wgt	Age	Int	Pts
John Campbell (to BAL)	LB	6'3"	225	30		
Doug Fisher	LB	6'1"	225	22		
Jerry Hillebrand	LB	6'3"	240	29	1	
Ray May	LB	6'1"	230	24	2	
Andy Russell	LB	6'3"	225	27	2	
Brian Stenger	LB	6'4"	220	22	3	
Sid Williams	LB	6'2"	235	27		
Chuck Beatty	DB	6'2"	207	23		
Lee Calland (from CHI)	DB	6'	190	28	2	
Bob Hohn	DB	6'	185	28	5	
Paul Martha	DB	6'	187	26	5	
Clancy Oliver	DB	6'1"	180	21		
Jim Shorter	DB	5'11"	180	28	3	
Marv Woodson (to NO)	DB	6'	195	26	1	

Rocky Bleier – Military Service

Use Name	Pos.	Hgt	Wgt	Age	Int	Pts
Terry Hanratty	QB	6'1"	200	21		
Kent Nix	QB	6'1"	195	25		
Dick Shiner	QB	6'	197	27		6
Bob Campbell	HB	6'	195	22		
Dick Hoak	HB	5'11"	195	30		18
Don McCall	HB	5'11"	195	24		6
Warren Bankston	FB	6'4"	226	22		6
Earl Gros	FB	6'3"	220	28		42
Don Alley	WR	6'2"	200	23		
Marshall Cropper	WR	6'3"	200	25		
Jon Henderson	WR	6'	195	24		18
Roy Jefferson	WR	6'2"	190	25		54
J. R. Wilburn	WR	6'2"	190	26		
Erwin Williams	WR	6'5"	215	22		6
Bob Adams	TE	6'2"	225	23		
John Hilton	TE	6'5"	222	27		
Gene Mingo	K	6'1"	216	30		62
Bobby Walden	K	6'	190	30		

CENTURY DIVISION

CLEVELAND BROWNS

RUSHING

Last Name	No.	Yds	Avg	TD
Kelly	196	817	4.2	9
R. Johnson	137	471	3.4	7
Morrison	60	301	5.0	1
Scott	44	157	3.6	0
Morin	2	30	15.0	0
Warfield	2	23	11.5	0
Rhome	1	0	0.0	0
Nelsen	5	−11	−2.2	0

RECEIVING

Last Name	No.	Yds	Avg	TD
Collins	54	786	15	11
Warfield	42	886	21	10
Morin	37	495	13	0
R. Johnson	24	164	7	0
Kelly	20	267	13	1
Morrison	6	71	12	0
Scott	6	25	4	0
Glass	4	91	23	2
Jones	2	33	17	0
Hooker	2	21	11	0
Leigh	2	−9	−5	0

PUNT RETURNS

Last Name	No.	Yds	Avg	TD
Sumner	9	88	10	0
Morrison	11	49	4	0
Kelly	7	28	4	0
Leigh	5	18	4	0

KICKOFF RETURNS

Last Name	No.	Yds	Avg	TD
Scott	25	722	29	0
Morrison	9	155	17	0
Brown	2	45	23	0
R. Johnson	1	31	31	0
Kelly	2	26	13	0
Leigh	2	6	3	0
Howell	1	0	0	0
Jenkins	1	0	0	0
Kanicki	1	0	0	0
Mathesen	1	0	0	0
Mitchell	1	0	0	0

PASSING – PUNTING – KICKING

PASSING	Att	Comp	%	Yds	Yd/Att	TD	Int–	%	RK
Nelson	352	190	54	2743	7.8	23	19–	5	6
Rhome	19	7	37	35	1.8	0	2–	11	
Kelly	5	1	20	36	7.2	1	0–	0	
Morrison	1	1	100	16	16.0	0	0–	0	
R. Johnson	1	0	0	0	0.0	0	0–	0	

PUNTING	No	Avg
Cockroft	57	37.5
Collins	3	37.3

KICKING	XP	Att	%	FG	Att	%
Cockroft	45	45	100	12	23	52

NEW YORK GIANTS

RUSHING

Last Name	No.	Yds	Avg	TD
Coffey	131	511	3.9	2
Morrison	107	387	3.6	4
Koy	76	300	3.9	2
Tarkenton	37	172	4.6	0
Minniear	35	141	4.0	1
Frederickson	33	136	4.1	0
Fuqua	20	89	4.5	0
Houston	1	11	11.0	0
Jones	3	8	2.7	0
Dunaway	1	4	4.0	0
Wood	1	3	3.0	0
Plum	1	−1	−1.0	0

RECEIVING

Last Name	No.	Yds	Avg	TD
Morrison	44	647	15	7
Jones	42	744	18	1
Herrmann	33	423	13	5
White	29	315	11	1
Thomas	22	348	16	3
Koy	19	152	8	4
Frederickson	14	95	7	1
Coffey	14	89	6	3
Wilson	10	132	13	0
Minniear	6	68	11	0
Fuqua	3	11	4	0
Houston	2	69	35	0
Dunaway	2	37	19	0
Young	1	8	8	0
Kotite	1	2	2	1

PUNT RETURNS

Last Name	No.	Yds	Avg	TD
Lockhart	10	29	3	0
Minniear	3	15	5	0
Brenner	2	6	3	0

KICKOFF RETURNS

Last Name	No.	Yds	Avg	TD
Fuqua	20	399	20	0
Houston	12	252	21	0
Holifield	8	156	20	0
Williams	6	96	16	0
Minniear	5	83	17	0
Brenner	2	39	20	0
Longo	2	31	16	0
Lockhart	1	19	19	0

PASSING – PUNTING – KICKING

PASSING	Att	Comp	%	Yds	Yd/Att	TD	Int–	%	RK
Tarkenton	409	220	54	2918	7.1	23	8–	2	3
Wood	16	10	63	106	6.6	1	0–	0	
Plum	9	3	33	37	4.1	0	0–	0	
Koy	1	1	100	15	15.0	0	0–	0	

PUNTING	No	Avg
Koy	26	35.9
C. Johnson	22	37.4
Dunaway	13	38.2
Gogolak	12	40.9

KICKING	XP	Att	%	FG	Att	%
Gogolak	33	33	100	11	21	52

ST. LOUIS CARDINALS

RUSHING

Last Name	No.	Yds	Avg	TD
Edwards	107	504	4.7	3
Roland	138	498	3.6	5
Crenshaw	55	172	3.1	3
Shivers	27	115	4.3	2
Lane	25	93	3.7	1
Johnson	17	51	3.0	1
Hart	7	16	2.3	2
D. Williams	1	1	1.0	0
Smith	4	0	0.0	0
Gilliam	1	−4	−4.0	0

RECEIVING

Last Name	No.	Yds	Avg	TD
D. Williams	56	702	13	7
Gilliam	52	997	19	9
Smith	43	561	13	1
Edwards	23	309	13	0
Roland	12	136	11	1
Crenshaw	11	94	9	0
Lane	9	61	7	0
Shivers	7	61	9	1
Daanen	2	12	6	0
T. Brown	1	7	7	0

PUNT RETURNS

Last Name	No.	Yds	Avg	TD
Wehrli	13	65	5	0
Roland	10	53	5	0
Shivers	9	44	5	0
T. Brown	6	39	7	0

KICKOFF RETURNS

Last Name	No.	Yds	Avg	TD
Lane	20	523	26	0
Gilliam	11	339	31	1
T. Brown	15	320	21	0
Shivers	10	205	21	0
M. Wilson	4	66	17	0
Crenshaw	4	34	9	0
Wehrli	1	18	18	0
Olerich	2	2	1	0
C. Williams	1	0	0	0

PASSING – PUNTING – KICKING

PASSING	Att	Comp	%	Yds	Yd/Att	TD	Int–	%	RK
Johnson	260	131	50	1847	7.1	13	13–	5	13
Hart	169	84	50	1086	6.4	6	12–	7	18
Hill	1	1	100	7	7.0	0	0–	0	

PUNTING	No	Avg
Hill	73	37.6

KICKING	XP	Att	%	FG	Att	%
Bakken	38	40	95	12	24	50

PITTSBURGH STEELERS

RUSHING

Last Name	No.	Yds	Avg	TD
Hoak	151	531	3.5	2
Gros	116	343	3.0	4
Bankston	62	259	4.2	1
Hanratty	10	106	10.6	0
McCall	30	98	3.3	0
Nix	10	70	7.0	0
Shiner	14	55	3.9	1
Jefferson	4	46	11.5	0
Wilburn	2	29	14.5	0
B. Campbell	1	5	5.0	0

RECEIVING

Last Name	No.	Yds	Avg	TD
Jefferson	67	1079	16	9
Wilburn	20	373	19	0
Hoak	20	190	10	1
Gros	17	131	8	3
Hilton	12	231	19	0
Henderson	12	188	16	3
Cropper	9	116	13	0
Adams	6	80	13	0
Bankston	6	6	1	0
E. Williams	3	14	5	1
McCall	2	2	1	0
B. Campbell	1	32	32	0
Alley	1	16	16	0

PUNT RETURNS

Last Name	No.	Yds	Avg	TD
B. Campbell	28	133	5	0
Jefferson	4	23	6	0
Hoak	1	9	9	0
Martha	3	0	0	0
Davis	1	0	0	0

KICKOFF RETURNS

Last Name	No.	Yds	Avg	TD
McCall	21	532	25	1
B. Campbell	26	522	20	0
Bankston	4	89	22	0
Jefferson	4	80	20	0
Woodson	1	18	18	0
Davis	3	0	0	0
Kolb	1	0	0	0

PASSING – PUNTING – KICKING

PASSING	Att	Comp	%	Yds	Yd/Att	TF	Int–	%	RK
Shiner	209	97	46	1422	6.8	7	10–	5	15
Hanratty	126	52	41	716	5.7	8	13–	10	
Nix	53	25	47	290	5.5	2	6–	11	
Hoak	3	2	67	30	10.0	0	0–	0	

PUNTING	No	Avg
Walden	77	42.3

KICKING	XP	Att	%	FG	Att	%
Mingo	26	26	100	12	26	46

CENTRAL DIVISION

MINNESOTA VIKINGS 12-2-0 Bud Grant

Scores of Each Game		
23	New York	24
52	BALTIMORE	14
19	GREEN BAY	7
31	Chicago	0
27	St. Louis	10
24	DETROIT	10
31	CHICAGO	14
51	CLEVELAND	3
9	Green Bay	7
52	PITTSBURGH	14
27	Detroit	0
20	Los Angeles	13
10	SAN FRANCISCO	7
3	Atlanta	10

Use Name	Pos.	Hgt	Wgt	Age	Int	Pts
Grady Alderman	OT	6'2"	242	30		
Doug Davis	OT	6'4"	255	25		
Ron Yary	OT	6'6"	265	23		
Bookie Bolin	OG	6'2"	250	29		
Milt Sunde	OG	6'2"	250	26		
Jim Vellone	OG	6'2"	255	25		
Ed White	OG	6'2"	252	22		
Mick Tingelhoff	C	6'1"	237	29		
Carl Eller	DE	6'6"	265	27		
Jim Marshall	DE	6'3"	260	31	1	
Steve Smith	DE	6'5"	240	25		
Paul Dickson	DT	6'5"	257	32		
Gary Larsen	DT	6'5"	260	29		
Alan Page	DT	6'5"	260	24		6
Jim Hargrove	LB	6'3"	232	24		
Wally Hilgenberg	LB	6'3"	235	26		
Mike McGill	LB	6'2"	237	22		
Mike Reilly	LB	6'2"	235	26		6
Lonnie Warwick	LB	6'3"	237	27	4	
Roy Winston	LB	6'1"	230	29	3	
Bobby Bryant	DB	6'	175	25	8	
Karl Kassulke	DB	6'	195	27	2	
Paul Krause	DB	6'3"	195	27	5	6
Earsell Mackbee	DB	6'1"	195	28	6	
Ed Sharockman	DB	6'	200	29	1	
Charlie West	DB	6'1"	190	23		
Dale Hackbart	LB-DB	6'3"	214	33		
Gary Cuozzo	QB	6'1"	195	28		
Joe Kapp	QB	6'2"	215	31		
Bob Lee	QB	6'2"	195	23		
Billy Harris	HB	6'	190	23		
Clint Jones	HB	6'	206	24		18
Dave Osborn	HB	6'	205	26		48
Bill Brown	FB	5'11"	230	31		18
Jim Lindsey	HB-FB	6'2"	212	24		12
Oscar Reed	HB-FB	5'11"	222	25		18
Bob Grim	WR	6'	197	24		6
Tom Hall	WR	6'1"	195	28		
John Henderson	WR	6'3"	190	26		30
Gene Washington	WR	6'3"	218	25		54
John Beasley	TE	6'3"	230	24		30
Kent Kramer	TE	6'5"	235	25		6
Fred Cox	K	5'10"	200	30		121

DETROIT LIONS 9-4-1 Joe Schmidt

Scores of Each Game		
13	Pittsburgh	16
24	NEW YORK	0
28	Cleveland	21
17	GREEN BAY	28
13	CHICAGO	7
10	Minnesota	24
26	San Francisco	14
27	ATLANTA	21
20	ST. LOUIS	0
16	Green Bay	10
0	MINNESOTA	27
17	Baltimore	17
28	LOS ANGELES	0
20	Chicago	3

Use Name	Pos.	Hgt	Wgt	Age	Int	Pts
Rocky Freitas	OT	6'6"	260	23		
Roger Shoals	OT	6'4"	255	30		
Jim Yarbrough	OT	6'6"	250	22		
Frank Gallagher	OG	6'2"	240	26		
Bob Kowalkowski	OG	6'3"	245	25		
Rocky Rasley	OG	6'3"	248	22		
Chuck Walton	OG	6'3"	250	28		
Ed Flanagan	C	6'3"	250	25		
Bill Cottrell	OG-C	6'3"	250	24		
Larry Hand	DE	6'4"	245	29		
Joe Robb	DE	6'3"	245	32		
Denis Moore	DT-DE	6'5"	255	25		
Alex Karras	DT	6'2"	255	33	1	
Jerry Rush	DT	6'4"	260	27		
Dan Goich	DE-DT	6'4"	265	25		
Mike Lucci	LB	6'2"	230	29		
Ed Mooney	LB	6'2"	240	24		
Paul Naumoff	LB	6'1"	225	24		
Tom Nowatzke	LB	6'3"	230	26		
Bill Swain	LB	6'2"	230	28		
Wayne Walker	LB	6'2"	225	32	1	
Lem Barney	DB	6'	185	23	8	6
Dick LeBeau	DB	6'1"	185	32	6	
Wayne Rasmussen	DB	6'2"	175	27		
Tom Vaughn	DB	5'11"	190	26	2	
Mike Weger	DB	6'2"	185	23	3	
Bobby Williams	DB	6'1"	205	27		6
Greg Barton	QB	6'2"	195	23		
Greg Landry	QB	6'4"	205	22		6
Bill Munson	QB	6'2"	200	27		
Nick Eddy	HB	6'1"	205	25		18
Mel Farr	HB	6'2"	205	24		24
Altie Taylor	HB	5'10"	196	21		
Bill Triplett	FB	6'2"	210	30		24
Larry Watkins	FB	6'2"	215	22		6
Bill Malinchak	WR	6'1"	200	25		
Earl McCullouch	WR	5'11"	180	23		30
Phil Odle	WR	5'11"	190	26		
Larry Walton	WR	5'11"	180	22		
John Wright	WR	6'	197	23		18
Craig Cotton	TE	6'4"	222	22		
Charlie Sanders	TE	6'4"	215	23		18
Rick Duncan	K	6'	208	28		
Errol Mann	K	6'	200	28		101

GREEN BAY PACKERS 8-6-0 Phil Bengtson

Scores of Each Game		
17	CHICAGO	0
14	SAN FRANCISCO	7
7	Minnesota	19
28	Detroit	17
21	Los Angeles	34
28	ATLANTA	10
38	Pittsburgh	34
6	Baltimore	14
7	MINNESOTA	9
10	DETROIT	16
20	NEW YORK	10
7	Cleveland	20
21	Chicago	3
45	ST. LOUIS	28

Use Name	Pos.	Hgt	Wgt	Age	Int	Pts
Forrest Gregg	OT	6'4"	250	36		
Bill Hayhoe	OT	6'8"	258	22		
Dick Himes	OT	6'4"	244	23		
Francis Peay	OT	6'5"	250	25		
Dave Bradley	OG	6'4"	245	22		
Gale Gillingham	OG	6'3"	255	25		
Bill Lueck	OG	6'3"	235	23		
Ken Bowman	C	6'3"	230	26		
Bob Hyland	OG-C	6'5"	250	24		
Lionel Aldridge	DE	6'4"	245	27		
Willie Davis	DE	6'3"	245	36	1	
Phil Vandersea	DE	6'3"	235	26		
Francis Winkler	DE	6'3"	230	22		
Bob Brown	DT	6'5"	260	29		
Henry Jordan	DT	6'3"	250	34		
Rich Moore	DT	6'6"	285	22		
Jim Weatherwax	DT	6'7"	260	21		
Lee Roy Caffey	LB	6'3"	250	29	2	
Fred Carr	LB	6'5"	238	23		
Jim Flanigan	LB	6'3"	240	24		
Ray Nitschke	LB	6'3"	235	33		2
Dave Robinson	LB	6'3"	240	28		
Herb Adderley	DB	6'1"	200	30	5	6
Doug Hart	DB	6'	190	30	3	6
Bob Jeter	DB	6'1"	205	31	3	
John Rowser	DB	6'1"	180	25		
Gordon Rule	DB	6'2"	180	23		
Willie Wood	DB	5'10"	190	33	3	
Don Horn	QB	6'2"	195	24		6
Bart Starr	QB	6'1"	190	36		
Bill Stevens	QB	6'3"	195	24		
Donny Anderson	HB	6'3"	210	26		12
Elijah Pitts	HB	6'1"	205	30		6
Travis Williams	HB	6'1"	210	23		54
Jim Grabowski	FB	6'2"	220	25		12
Perry Williams	FB	6'2"	220	22		
Dave Hampton	HB-FB	6'	210	22		42
Carroll Dale	WR	6'1"	200	31		36
Boyd Dowler	WR	6'5"	225	32		24
John Spilis	WR	6'3"	205	21		
Marv Fleming	TE	6'4"	235	27		12
Ron Jones	TE	6'3"	220	22		
Booth Lusteg	K	5'11"	190	28		15
Mike Mercer	K	6'	217	33		38

Zeke Bratkowski – Voluntarily Retired

CHICAGO BEARS 1-13-0 Jim Dooley

Scores of Each Game		
0	Green Bay	17
17	St. Louis	20
24	New York	28
0	MINNESOTA	31
7	Detroit	13
7	LOS ANGELES	9
14	Minnesota	31
38	PITTSBURGH	7
31	Atlanta	48
21	BALTIMORE	24
24	CLEVELAND	28
21	San Francisco	42
3	GREEN BAY	21
3	DETROIT	20

Use Name	Pos.	Hgt	Wgt	Age	Int	Pts
Randy Jackson	OT	6'5"	245	25		
Wayne Mass	OT	6'4"	245	23		
Rufus Mayes	OT	6'5"	255	21		
Bob Pickens	OT	6'4"	258	26		
Bob Wetoska	C-OT	6'3"	240	31		
Jim Cadile	OG	6'3"	240	28		
Howard Mudd (from SF)	OG	6'3"	252	27		
George Seals	OG	6'2"	260	26		
Jim Ferguson (from ATL)	C	6'4"	240	26		
Mike Pyle	C	6'3"	250	30		
Marty Amsler	DE	6'5"	255	26		
Dave Hale	DE	6'7"	230	22		
Willie Holman	DE	6'4"	250	24		
Ed O'Bradovich	DE	6'3"	255	29		2
Loyd Phillips	DE	6'3"	240	24		
Frank Cornish	DT	6'6"	300	25		
Dick Evey	DT	6'2"	245	28		2
Ken Kortas	DT	6'2"	280	27		
Doug Buffone	LB	6'1"	230	25	2	
Dick Butkus	LB	6'3"	245	25	2	2
Tim Casey (to DEN-A)	LB	6'1"	225	25		
Rudy Kuechenberg	LB	6'2"	215	26		
Dave Martin	LB	6'1"	225	22		
Dan Pride	LB	6'3"	225	27	1	
Dick Daniels	DB	5'9"	180	23	3	
Major Hazelton	DB	6'1"	185	24		
Bennie McRae	DB	6'1"	180	28	1	
Joe Taylor	DB	6'2"	200	28	3	
George Youngblood	DB	6'3"	205	24	3	6
Garry Lyle	HB-DB	6'2"	198	23	1	
Virgil Carter	QB	6'1"	185	23		
Jack Concannon	QB	6'3"	205	26		6
Bobby Douglass	QB	6'3"	215	22		12
Gale Sayers	HB	6'	198	26		48
Brian Piccolo	FB-HB	6'	205	25		18
Ronnie Bull	FB	6'	200	29		
Mike Hull	FB	6'3"	220	24		6
Ralph Kurek	FB	6'2"	210	26		
Ross Montgomery	FB	6'3"	220	22		
Ron Copeland	WR	6'4"	196	22		
Dick Gordon	WR	5'11"	190	24		24
Bob Jones	WR	6'4"	196	24		
Jerry Simmons (from ATL)	WR	6'1"	190	26		
Cecil Turner	WR	5'10"	170	25		
Bob Wallace	WR	6'3"	211	23		30
Austin Denney	TE	6'2"	230	25		6
Emilio Vallez	TE	6'2"	210	23		
Ray Odgen	WR-TE	6'5"	225	26		
Bobby Joe Green	K	5'11	175	31		
Mac Percival	K	6'4"	220	29		50

Terry Stoepel – Military Service

CENTRAL DIVISION

MINNESOTA VIKINGS

RUSHING

Last Name	No.	Yds	Avg	TD
Osborn	186	643	3.5	7
Brown	126	430	3.4	3
Reed	83	393	4.7	1
Jones	54	241	4.5	3
Kapp	22	104	4.7	0
Lindsey	6	21	3.5	1
Harris	6	13	2.2	0
Lee	3	9	3.0	0
Cuozzo	3	–4	–1.3	0

RECEIVING

Last Name	No.	Yds	Avg	TD
Washington	39	821	21	9
Henderson	34	553	16	5
Beasley	33	361	11	4
Osborn	22	236	11	1
Brown	21	183	9	0
Grim	10	155	16	1
Reed	7	59	8	2
Jones	3	23	8	0
Lindsey	2	45	23	1
Kramer	2	37	19	1
Harris	2	13	7	0
Hall	1	12	12	0

PUNT RETURNS

Last Name	No.	Yds	Avg	TD
West	39	245	6	0
Grim	4	12	3	0
Bryant	2	9	5	0

KICKOFF RETURNS

Last Name	No.	Yds	Avg	TD
Jones	17	444	26	0
West	9	240	27	0
Reed	1	38	38	0
Lindsey	2	26	13	0
Harris	1	23	23	0
Smith	1	3	3	0
Alderman	1	0	0	0
Sunde	1	0	0	0

PASSING – PUNTING – KICKING

PASSING	Att	Comp	%	Yds	Yd/Att	TD	Int–	%	RK
Kapp	237	120	51	1726	7.3	19	13–	5	10
Cuozzo	98	49	50	693	7.1	4	5–	5	
Lee	11	7	64	79	7.2	1	0–	0	

PUNTING	No	Avg
Lee	67	40.0

KICKING	XP	Att	%	FG	Att	%
Cox	43	43	100	26	37	70

DETROIT LIONS

RUSHING

Last Name	No.	Yds	Avg	TD
Triplett	111	377	3.4	3
Taylor	118	348	2.9	0
Eddy	78	272	3.5	2
Farr	58	245	4.2	4
Landry	33	243	7.4	1
Watkins	62	201	3.2	1
Barney	3	36	12.0	0
Munson	7	31	4.4	0
L. Walton	2	6	3.0	0
McCullouch	1	4	4.0	0
Sanders	1	–8	–8.0	0

RECEIVING

Last Name	No.	Yds	Avg	TD
Sanders	42	656	16	3
McCullouch	33	529	16	5
Triplett	13	141	11	1
Farr	13	94	7	0
Watkins	13	87	7	0
Taylor	13	86	7	0
Wright	12	130	11	2
L. Walton	12	109	9	0
Eddy	10	78	8	1
Malinchak	2	24	12	0
Odle	2	24	12	0

PUNT RETURNS

Last Name	No.	Yds	Avg	TD
Barney	9	191	21	1
L. Walton	9	24	3	0
Vaughn	2	10	5	0
Eddy	1	5	5	0

KICKOFF RETURNS

Last Name	No.	Yds	Avg	TD
Williams	17	563	33	1
L. Walton	12	230	19	0
Barney	7	154	22	0
Vaughn	2	44	22	0
Nowatzke	1	14	14	0
Mooney	2	12	6	0
Yarbrough	1	0	0	0

PASSING – PUNTING – KICKING

PASSING	Att	Comp	%	Yds	Yd/Att	TD	Int–	%	RK
Munson	166	84	51	1062	6.4	7	8–	5	14
Landry	160	80	50	853	5.3	4	10–	6	20
Barton	1	0	0	0	0.0	0	0–	0	
Farr	1	0	0	0	0.0	0	0–	0	
L. Walton	1	1	100	43	43.0	1	0–	0	

PUNTING	No	Avg
Barney	66	34.1
Malinchak	5	36.8
Duncan	3	25.7

KICKING	XP	Att	%	FG	Att	%
Mann	26	26	100	25	37	68

GREEN BAY PACKERS

RUSHING

Last Name	No.	Yds	Avg	TD
T. Williams	129	536	4.2	4
Hampton	80	365	4.6	4
Anderson	87	288	3.3	1
Grabowski	73	261	3.6	1
Pitts	35	134	3.8	0
Starr	7	60	8.6	0
P. Williams	18	55	3.1	0
Horn	3	7	2.3	1

RECEIVING

Last Name	No.	Yds	Avg	TD
Dale	45	879	20	6
Dowler	31	477	15	4
T. Williams	27	275	10	3
Fleming	18	226	13	2
Hampton	15	216	14	2
Anderson	14	308	22	1
Grabowski	12	98	8	1
Pitts	9	47	5	1
Spilis	7	89	13	0
P. Williams	4	63	16	0

PUNT RETURNS

Last Name	No.	Yds	Avg	TD
T. Williams	8	189	24	1
Pitts	16	60	4	0
Wood	8	38	5	0

KICKOFF RETURNS

Last Name	No.	Yds	Avg	TD
Hampton	22	582	26	1
T. Williams	21	517	25	1
Robinson	3	31	10	0
Pitts	1	22	22	0
Gillingham	1	13	13	0
Hyland	1	0	0	0
P. Williams	1	0	0	0

PASSING – PUNTING – KICKING

PASSING	Att	Comp	%	Yds	Yd/Att	TD	Int–	%	RK
Horn	168	89	53	1505	9.0	11	11–	7	11
Starr	148	92	62	1161	7.8	9	6–	4	2
Stevens	3	1	33	12	4.0	0	0–	0	

PUNTING	No	Avg
Anderson	58	40.2
Dowler	1	34.0

KICKING	XP	Att	%	FG	Att	%
Mercer	23	23	100	5	17	29
Lusteg	12	12	100	1	5	20

CHICAGO BEARS

RUSHING

Last Name	No.	Yds	Avg	TD
Sayers	236	1032	4.4	8
Douglass	51	408	8.0	2
Bull	44	187	4.3	0
Piccolo	45	148	3.3	2
Hull	29	81	2.8	1
Concannon	22	62	2.8	1
Montgomery	15	52	3.5	0
Gordon	2	28	14.0	0
Kurek	8	24	3.0	0
Carter	4	19	4.8	0
Green	1	17	17.0	0
Wallace	4	16	4.0	0
Denney	1	4	4.0	0

RECEIVING

Last Name	No.	Yds	Avg	TD
Wallace	47	553	12	5
Gordon	36	414	12	4
Denney	22	203	9	1
Piccolo	17	143	8	1
Sayers	17	116	7	0
Simmons	14	182	13	0
Bull	14	91	7	0
Hull	12	63	5	0
Ogden	7	100	14	0
Kurek	4	30	8	0
Montgomery	2	8	4	0
Turner	1	19	19	0
Lyle	1	11	11	0

PUNT RETURNS

Last Name	No.	Yds	Avg	TD
Lyle	12	78	7	0
Piccolo	9	43	5	0
Turner	8	32	4	0
Gordon	1	11	11	0

KICKOFF RETURNS

Last Name	No.	Yds	Avg	TD
Sayers	14	339	24	0
Turner	10	326	33	0
Lyle	11	248	23	0
Gordon	6	105	18	0
Kurek	4	66	17	0
Butkus	3	28	9	0
Seals	2	20	10	0
Holman	1	0	0	0
Kuechenberg	1	0	0	0

PASSING – PUNTING – KICKING

PASSING	Att	Comp	%	Yds	Yd/Att	TD	Int–	%	RK
Concannon	160	87	54	783	4.9	4	8–	5	16
Douglass	148	68	46	773	5.2	5	8–	5	19
Carter	71	36	51	343	4.8	2	5–	7	
Green	2	2	100	30	15.0	0	0–	0	
Sayers	2	0	0	0	0.0	0	0–	0	
Bull	1	0	0	0	0.0	0	0–	0	

PUNTING	No	Avg
Green	76	39.0

KICKING	XP	Att	%	FG	Att	%
Percival	26	26	100	8	21	38

COASTAL DIVISION

LOS ANGELES RAMS 11-3-0 George Allen

Scores of Each Game		
27	Baltimore	20
17	ATLANTA	7
36	NEW ORLEANS	17
27	San Francisco	21
34	GREEN BAY	21
9	Chicago	7
38	Atlanta	6
41	SAN FRANCISCO	30
23	Philadelphia	17
24	DALLAS	23
24	Washington	13
13	MINNESOTA	20
0	Detroit	28
7	BALTIMORE	13

Use Name	Pos.	Hgt	Wgt	Age	Int	Pts
Bob Brown	OT	6'4"	275	26		
Charley Cowan	OT	6'4"	265	31		
Mitch Johnson	OT	6'4"	250	27		
Mike LaHood	OG	6'3"	248	24		
Tom Mack	OG	6'3"	250	25		
Joe Scibelli	OG	6'1"	255	30		
George Burman	C-OG	6'3"	255	26		
Ken Iman	C	6'1"	240	30		
Frank Marchlewski	C	6'2"	240	25		
Rick Cash	DE	6'5"	260	24		
Deacon Jones	DE	6'5"	250	30		
Lamar Lundy	DE	6'7"	250	34		
Diron Talbert	DE	6'5"	245	25		
Coy Bacon	DT	6'4"	270	27		
Roger Brown	DT	6'5"	285	32		
Merlin Olsen	DT	6'5"	270	28		
Maxie Gaughan	LB	6'1"	230	31		
Jack Pardee	LB	6'2"	225	33	1	
John Pergine	LB	6'1"	225	22		
Myron Pottios	LB	6'2"	232	29	1	
Jim Purnell	LB	6'2"	238	27		
Doug Woodlief	LB	6'3"	225	25	4	
Willie Daniel	DB	5'11"	190	31	1	
Alvin Haymond	DB	6'	194	27		
Ed Meador	DB	5'11"	190	32	5	12
Jim Nettles	DB	5'9"	177	27	2	
Richie Petitbon	DB	6'3"	208	31	5	
Nate Shaw	DB	6'2"	205	24		
Ron Smith	DB	6'1"	192	26	3	6
Clancy Williams	DB	6'2"	194	26	4	
Roman Gabriel	QB	6'4"	220	29		30
Karl Sweetan	QB	6'1"	200	26		
Mike Dennis	HB	6'1"	207	25		
Willie Ellison	HB	6'1"	200	24		12
Larry Smith	HB	6'3"	220	21		18
Dick Bass	FB	5'10"	195	32		
Les Josephson	FB	6'	207	26		12
Izzy Lang	FB	6'1"	232	26		
Tommy Mason	HB-FB	6'	195	30		12
David Ray	WR	6'	195	24		
Jack Snow	WR	6'2"	190	26		36
Pat Studstill	WR	6'1"	175	31		
Wendell Tucker	WR	5'10"	185	25		42
Pat Curran	TE	6'3"	238	23		
Bob Klein	TE	6'5"	235	22		6
Billy Truax	TE	6'5"	235	26		30
Bruce Gossett	K	6'2"	230	26		102

Jim Wilson – Injury

BALTIMORE COLTS 8-5-1 Don Shula

Scores of Each Game		
20	LOS ANGELES	27
14	Minnesota	52
21	Atlanta	14
24	PHILADELPHIA	20
30	New Orleans	10
21	SAN FRANCISCO	24
41	WASHINGTON	17
14	GREEN BAY	6
17	San Francisco	20
24	Chicago	21
13	ATLANTA	6
17	DETROIT	17
10	Dallas	27
13	Los Angeles	7

Use Name	Pos.	Hgt	Wgt	Age	Int	Pts
Sam Ball	OT	6'4"	240	25		
Bob Vogel	OT	6'5"	250	27		
Dan Grimm (to WAS)	OG	6'3"	245	28		
Cornelius Johnson	OG	6'2"	245	26		
Glenn Ressler	OG	6'3"	250	25		
Dan Sullivan	OG	6'3"	250	30		
John Williams	OG	6'3"	256	23		
Bill Curry	C	6'2"	235	26		
Carl Mauck	C	6'3"	240	22		
Roy Hilton	DE	6'6"	240	24		
Lou Michaels	DE	6'2"	250	33		75
Bubba Smith	DE	6'7"	295	24		
Ron Kostelnik	DT	6'4"	260	29		
Fred Miller	DT	6'3"	250	28		
Billy Ray Smith	DT	6'4"	250	34		
Mike Curtis	LB	6'2"	232	26		
Dennis Gaubatz	LB	6'2"	232	28	1	
Bob Grant	LB	6'2"	225	23	3	
Ted Hendricks	LB	6'7"	215	21		
Butch Riley	LB	6'2"	220	22		
Don Shinnick	LB	6'	228	34		
Ocie Austin	DB	6'3"	200	22	2	
Jim Duncan	DB	6'2"	200	23		6
Jerry Logan	DB	6'1"	190	28	1	
Lenny Lyles	DB	6'2"	204	33		
Tommy Maxwell	DB	6'2"	195	22	3	
Charlie Stukes	DB	6'3"	212	25	1	
Rick Volk	DB	6'3"	195	24	4	
Earl Morrall	QB	6'1"	206	35		
Johnny Unitas	QB	6'1"	196	36		
Tom Matte	HB	6'	214	30		78
Preston Pearson	HB	6'1"	190	24		
Terry Cole	FB	6'1"	220	24		18
Larry Conjar	FB	6'	214	23		
Perry Lee Dunn	FB	6'2"	215	26		
Jerry Hill	FB	5'11"	215	29		12
Eddie Hinton	WR	6'	200	22		6
Jimmy Orr	WR	5'11"	185	33		12
Ray Perkins	WR	6'	183	27		18
Willie Richardson	WR	6'2"	198	29		18
Sam Havrilak	DB-WR	6'2"	195	21		6
John Mackey	TE	6'3"	224	27		12
Tom Mitchell	TE	6'2"	215	25		18
Roland Moss	TE	6'3"	215	22		
David Lee	K	6'4"	230	25		

ATLANTA FALCONS 6-8-0 Norm Van Brocklin

Scores of Each Game		
24	SAN FRANCISCO	12
7	Los Angeles	17
14	BALTIMORE	21
17	DALLAS	24
21	San Francsico	7
10	Green Bay	28
6	LOS ANGELES	38
21	Detroit	27
48	CHICAGO	31
20	Washington	27
6	Baltimore	13
45	NEW ORLEANS	17
27	Philadelphia	3
10	MINNESOTA	3

Use Name	Pos.	Hgt	Wgt	Age	Int	Pts
Bob Kelly	OT	6'3"	270	29		
George Kunz	OT	6'5"	245	22		
Bill Sandeman	OT	6'6"	250	26		
Bob Breitenstein	OG-OT	6'3"	267	26		
Dick Enderle	OG	6'1"	247	21		
Mal Snider	OG	6'4"	235	22		6
Roy Schmidt	OT-OG	6'3"	250	27		
Bruce Bosley	C	6'2"	244	35		
Jim Waskiewicz	C	6'4"	240	25		
Bob Hughes	DE	6'4"	250	24		
Claude Humphrey	DE	6'5"	255	25		6
John Zook	DE	6'5"	240	21	2	
Dave Cahill	DT	6'3"	245	27		
Glen Condren	DT	6'2"	250	27		
Bill Sabatino	DT	6'3"	245	24		
Jerry Shay	DT	6'3"	245	25		
Ron Acks	LB	6'2"	225	24		6
Grady Allen	LB	6'3"	225	23	1	
Greg Brezina	LB	6'2"	220	23	1	
Ted Cottrell	LB	6'1"	232	22		
Fritz Greenlee	LB	6'2"	230	25		
Don Hansen	LB	6'3"	228	25	2	
Tommy Nobis	LB	6'2"	235	25	1	
Jeff Van Note	LB	6'2"	230	23		
Mike Freeman	DB	5'11"	190	25		
Al Lavan	DB	6'1"	194	22	2	
John Mallory	DB	6'	190	23	1	
Ken Reaves	DB	6'3"	205	24	3	
Rudy Redmond	DB	6'	185	22	5	
Jim Weatherford	DB	5'10"	180	23	1	6
Nate Wright (to STL)	DB	5'11"	180	21	2	
Bob Berry	QB	5'11	190	27		
Randy Johnson	QB	6'3"	196	25		6
Bruce Lemmerman	QB	6'1"	196	23		6
Cannonball Butler	HB	5'10"	185	26		30
Gary McDermott	HB	6'1"	211	23		
Jeff Stanceil	HB	6'	192	22		
Paul Gipson	FB-HB	6'	205	23		6
Harmon Wages	FB	6'1"	210	23		18
Charlie Bryant	HB-FB	6'1"	207	28		
Gail Cogdill	WR	6'2"	200	32		30
Paul Flatley	WR	6'1"	187	28		36
Bob Lee	WR	6'3"	200	24		
Monte Ledbetter (From BUF-A)	WR	6'2"	185	26		
Tom McCauley	WR	6'3"	184	22		
Jim Mitchell	TE	6'2"	224	21		24
Ralph Smith	TE	6'2"	220	30		
Bob Etter	K	5'11"	152	24		78
Billy Lothridge	K	6'1"	190	25		

Randy Winkler – Military Service

SAN FRANCISCO FORTY NINERS 4-8-2 Dick Nolan

Scores of Each Game		
12	Atlanta	24
7	Green Bay	14
17	WASHINGTON	17
21	LOS ANGELES	27
7	ATLANTA	21
24	Baltimore	21
14	DETROIT	26
30	Los Angeles	41
20	BALTIMORE	17
38	New Orleans	43
24	Dallas	24
42	CHICAGO	21
7	Minnesota	10
14	PHILADELPHIA	13

Use Name	Pos.	Hgt	Wgt	Age	Int	Pts
Cas Banaszek	OT	6'3"	240	23		
Lance Olssen	OT	6'5"	267	22		
Len Rohde	OT	6'4"	250	31		
Elmer Collett	OG	6'4"	244	24		
Woody Peoples	OG	6'2"	247	26		
Randy Beisler	OT-OG	6'4"	255	24		
Forrest Blue	C	6'5"	248	23		
Bill Belk	DE	6'3"	242	23		
Tommy Hart	DE	6'3"	235	24		
Stan Hindman	DE	6'3"	237	25		
Earl Edwards	DT-DE	6'6"	276	23		
Charlie Krueger	DT	6'4"	270	33	1	
Roland Lakes	DT	6'4"	265	29		6
Sam Silas	DE-DT	6'4"	255	26		
Ed Beard	LB	6'2"	220	29		
Harold Hays	LB	6'3"	225	28		
Frank Nunley	LB	6'2"	230	23	1	
Jim Sniadecki	LB	6'2"	220	22		
Skip Vanderbundt	LB	6'3"	240	22		
Dave Wilcox	LB	6'3"	237	26	2	
Kermit Alexander	DB	5'11"	186	28	5	
Johnny Fuller	DB	6'	175	23	1	
Jim Johnson	DB	6'2"	187	31	5	
Mel Phillips	DB	6'	192	27		
Al Randolph	DB	6'2"	204	25	2	
Rosey Taylor (from CHI)	DB	5'11"	186	30	2	
John Woitt	DB	5'11"	170	23	1	6
John Brodie	QB	6'1"	204	34		
Steve Spurrier	QB	6'2"	203	24		
Doug Cunningham	HB	5'11"	190	23		18
Gene Moore	HB	6'	208	22		
Noland Smith (From KC-A)	HB	5'6"	156	25		
Jimmy Thomas	HB	6'1"	216	22		36
Gary Lewis	FB-HB	6'3"	230	27		
Ken Willard	FB	6'2"	225	26		60
Bill Tucker	FB	6'2"	226	25		24
Lee Johnson	WR	6'1"	204	24		
Clifton McNeil	WR	6'2"	185	29		18
Gene Washington	WR	6'1"	186	22		18
Dick Witcher	WR	6'3"	204	24		18
Bill Wondolowski	WR	5'10"	168	22		
Ted Kwalick	TE	6'4"	230	22		6
Bob Windsor	TE	6'4"	230	26		12
Tommy Davis	K	6'	225	34		22
Momcilo Gavric	K	5'10"	167	31		31
Jon Kilgore	K	6'1"	205	25		

Kevin Hardy – Knee Injury
Dave Hettema – Military Service
Matt Hazeltine –Voluntary Retirement

COASTAL DIVISION

LOS ANGELES RAMS

RUSHING

Last Name	No.	Yds	Avg	TD
L. Smith	166	599	3.6	1
Josephson	124	461	3.7	0
Gabriel	35	156	4.5	5
Mason	33	135	4.1	1
Ellison	20	56	2.8	1
Meador	1	5	5.0	0
Bass	1	1	1.0	0
Lang	1	1	1.0	0
Sweetan	1	−1	−1.0	0

RECEIVING

Last Name	No.	Yds	Avg	TD
Snow	49	734	15	6
L. Smith	46	300	7	2
Tucker	38	629	17	7
Truax	37	431	12	5
Josephson	32	295	9	2
Mason	11	185	17	1
Ellison	4	31	8	1
Studstill	3	28	9	0
Klein	2	17	9	1

PUNT RETURNS

Last Name	No.	Yds	Avg	TD
Haymond	33	435	13	0
R. Smith	23	122	5	0
Pergine	1	0	0	0
Meador	1	−1	−1	0

KICKOFF RETURNS

Last Name	No.	Yds	Avg	TD
R. Smith	27	585	22	0
Haymond	16	375	23	0
Lang	4	70	18	0
Ellison	2	38	19	0
Curran	2	28	14	0
Burman	1	11	11	0
Klein	1	0	0	0

PASSING – PUNTING – KICKING

PASSING	Att	Comp	%	Yds	Yd/Att	TD	Int–	%	RK
Gabriel	399	217	54	2549	6.4	24	7–	2	4
Sweetan	13	5	38	101	7.8	1	0–	0	
Ellison	2	0	0	0	0.0	0	0–	0	
Meador	1	0	0	0	0.0	0	0–	0	
L. Smith	1	0	0	0	0.0	0	0–	0	

PUNTING	No	Avg
Studstill	80	40.7

KICKING	XP	Att	%	FG	Att	%
Gossett	36	36	100	22	34	65

BALTIMORE COLTS

RUSHING

Last Name	No.	Yds	Avg	TD
Matte	235	909	3.9	11
Cole	73	204	2.8	2
Hill	49	143	2.9	2
Pearson	24	81	3.4	0
Havrilak	5	49	9.8	1
Dunn	13	45	3.5	0
Perkins	3	36	12.0	0
Unitas	11	23	2.1	0
Mackey	2	3	1.5	0
Conjar	1	0	0.0	0
Hinton	1	−3	−3.0	0

RECEIVING

Last Name	No.	Yds	Avg	TD
Richardson	43	646	15	3
Matte	43	513	12	2
Mackey	34	443	13	2
Perkins	28	391	14	3
Orr	25	474	19	2
Hinton	13	269	21	1
Hill	11	44	4	0
Mitchell	9	199	22	3
Cole	9	65	7	1
Dunn	5	30	6	0
Pearson	4	64	16	0
Havrilak	1	5	5	0

PUNT RETURNS

Last Name	No.	Yds	Avg	TD
Volk	10	58	6	0
Havrilak	13	58	4	0
Logan	8	41	5	0
Pearson	6	37	6	0

KICKOFF RETURNS

Last Name	No.	Yds	Avg	TD
Pearson	31	706	23	0
Duncan	19	560	29	1
Hinton	1	24	24	0

PASSING – PUNTING – KICKING

PASSING	Att	Comp	%	Yds	Yd/Att	TD	Int–	%	RK
Unitas	327	178	54	2342	7.2	12	20–	6	9
Morrall	99	46	46	755	7.6	5	7–	7	
Matte	3	1	33	46	15.3	0	0–	0	

PUNTING	No	Avg
Lee	57	45.3

KICKING	XP	Att	%	FG	Att	%
Michaels	33	34	97	14	31	45

ATLANTA FALCONS

RUSHING

Last Name	No.	Yds	Avg	TD
Butler	163	655	4.0	3
Wages	72	375	5.2	2
Gipson	62	303	4.9	1
Bryant	50	246	4.9	0
Mitchell	5	77	15.4	0
Berry	20	68	3.4	0
Lemmerman	10	57	5.7	1
Johnson	11	55	5.0	1
McCauley	2	49	24.5	0
McDermott	7	6	0.9	0
Stanceil	4	−1	−0.3	0

RECEIVING

Last Name	No.	Yds	Avg	TD
Flatley	45	834	19	6
Cogdill	24	374	16	5
Mitchell	22	339	15	4
Wages	22	228	10	1
Butler	17	297	17	2
Gipson	4	33	8	0
Smith	2	17	9	0
Bryant	2	15	8	0
Ledbetter	1	16	16	0
Brezina	1	9	9	0

PUNT RETURNS

Last Name	No.	Yds	Avg	TD
Mallory	13	42	3	0
Freeman	4	30	8	0
Wright	4	21	5	0
Cahill	1	0	0	0
McCauley	4	−11	−3	0

KICKOFF RETURNS

Last Name	No.	Yds	Avg	TD
Bryant	21	407	19	0
Butler	13	405	31	0
Gipson	9	145	16	0
Wages	6	76	13	0
Snider	1	48	48	1
Kunz	1	13	13	0
Stanceil	1	10	10	0

PASSING – PUNTING – KICKING

PASSING	Att	Comp	%	Yds	Yd/Att	TD	Int–	%	RK
Berry	124	71	57	1087	8.8	10	2–	2	
Johnson	93	51	55	788	8.5	8	5–	5	
Lemmerman	62	25	40	330	5.3	1	4–	6	
Gipson	1	0	0	0	0.0	0	1–	100	
Lothridge	1	1	100	9	9.0	0	0–	0	
Wages	1	1	100	16	16.0	1	0–	0	

PUNTING	No	Avg
Lothridge	69	41.2

KICKING	XP	Att	%	FG	Att	%
Etter	33	33	100	15	30	50

SAN FRANCISCO FORTY NINERS

RUSHING

Last Name	No.	Yds	Avg	TD
Willard	171	557	3.3	7
Cunningham	147	541	3.7	3
Thomas	23	190	8.3	1
Tucker	20	72	3.6	2
Brodie	11	62	5.6	0
Spurrier	5	49	9.8	0
Windsor	5	39	7.8	0
Davis	2	21	10.5	0
Lewis	4	5	1.3	0
Moore	2	4	2.0	0
Washington	1	−4	−4.0	0

RECEIVING

Last Name	No.	Yds	Avg	TD
Washington	51	711	14	3
Cunningham	51	484	9	0
Windsor	49	597	12	2
Willard	36	326	9	3
Witcher	33	435	13	3
Thomas	18	364	20	5
McNeil	17	255	15	3
Tucker	14	104	7	2
L. Johnson	4	42	11	0
Kwalick	2	32	16	1
Moore	2	28	14	0
Edwards	1	1	1	0

PUNT RETURNS

Last Name	No.	Yds	Avg	TD
Smith	10	46	5	0
Cunningham	3	23	8	0
Fuller	5	12	2	0
Alexander	4	−18	−5	0

KICKOFF RETURNS

Last Name	No.	Yds	Avg	TD
Smith	14	315	23	0
Cunningham	9	207	23	0
Fuller	8	155	19	0
Lewis	5	155	31	0
Alexander	3	47	16	0
Taylor	1	16	16	0
Wilcox	1	10	10	0
Edwards	3	3	1	0
Kwalick	1	0	0	0
Sniadecki	1	0	0	0
Tucker	1	0	0	0

PASSING – PUNTING – KICKING

PASSING	Att	Comp	%	Yds	Yd/Att	TD	Int–	%	RK
Brodie	347	194	56	2405	6.9	16	15–	4	7
Spurrier	146	81	55	926	6.3	5	11–	8	17
Cunningham	3	3	100	48	16.0	1	0–	0	

PUNTING	No	Avg
Kilgore	36	40.3
Davis	23	41.5
Spurrier	12	39.0

KICKING	XP	Att	%	FG	Att	%
Gavric	22	24	92	3	11	27
Davis	13	13	100	3	10	30

1969 A.F.L. Losing One Status to Gain Another

With the announcement of the realignment of pro football for 1970, the AFL learned that this was its last season in existence. None of the league officials grieved very heavily, since all ten clubs would be part of the NFL's American Conference next year, but some fans and players openly mourned the passing of the AFL as a separate organization. With two distinct leagues, the Super Bowl had much of the flavor of baseball's World Series, but some people expected the excitement to pale with the amalgamation into one league.

Twenty players from the premier season of 1960 still were active in 1969. George Blanda, Billy Cannon, Gino Cappelletti, Tom Flores, Larry Grantham, Wayne Hawkins, Jim Hunt, Harry Jacobs, Jack Kemp, Jacky Lee, Paul Lowe, Paul Maguire, Billy Mathis, Don Maynard, Ron Mix, Jim Otto, Babe Parilli, Johnny Robinson, Paul Rochester, and Ernie Wright all followed different paths into the new league, and each of them stuck around for ten years to watch the AFL progress from an inferior product in fancy settings to a top-notch league on a par with the long-established NFL.

The AFL went out not with a whisper but with the trumpets of victory. The Kansas City Chiefs, who won the league championship in a new playoff setup which pitted first- and second-place finishers in the opposite divisions against each other in an opening round before the championship game, won a final triumph for the AFL by beating the Minnesota Vikings 23-7 in the Super Bowl.

EASTERN DIVISION

New York Jets—The Jets coasted to another divisional title, beating every Eastern opponent they met during the season. Their four losses to Western teams, however, pointed out weak spots in the defending champions' club. The New York secondary folded against a good passing attack. Last year's starting cornerbacks, Johnny Sample and Randy Beverly, both fell out of favor with coach Weeb Ewbank, and the younger replacements couldn't handle top-notch receivers. A strong pass rush and good linebacking compensated for the leaky secondary to some extent, with Gerry Philbin, John Elliott, and Larry Grantham key men in the front lines. The Jet offense still put a lot of points on the scoreboard, with Joe Namath, Matt Snell, Emerson Boozer, Don Maynard, George Sauer, and Pete Lammons moving the ball against the best of defenses.

Houston Oilers—The Houston defense played so well that the team won half its games with little help from the offense. Elvin Bethea, George Webster, Miller Farr, and Ken Houston all ranked with the AFL's top defenders, and Zeke Moore, Garland Boyette, and W. K. Hicks were quality players who stood up to any attack in the league. Not even the absence of Leroy Mitchell, the fine cornerback obtained from Boston who suffered a broken neck in training camp, seriously hurt the Oilers' defense. The offense, however, creaked and groaned with pain in several spots. Hoyle Granger and Roy Hopkins, the starting runners, both were fullback types, strong on straight-ahead plays but not fast enough to make outside plays work. Pete Beathard compounded the unit's problems by failing to ignite an effective passing attack; after leading the club to a divisional crown in 1967, the twenty-seven-year-old passer had made little progress since.

Boston Patriots—New head coach Clive Rush found instant unpopularity with the fans and press when the Patriots lost their first seven games of the season, but his charges found themselves and won four of their next five matches. They shut out Houston 24-0, beat Cincinnati, Buffalo, and Miami, and lost to Miami 17-16 when Rush elected to gamble for a two-point conversion which failed. The Boston defense, stripped of stars Nick Buoniconti and Leroy Mitchell in off-season trades, had no charismatic players or exciting standouts, but the unit grew tighter with each game. The offense got a boost from rookies Carl Garrett, Ron Sellers, and Mike Montler and veterans Mike Taliaferro and Jim Nance, both rebounding from off-seasons.

Buffalo Bills—Head coach Johnny Rauch quit the Oakland Raiders to come to Buffalo, and he lost more games in this one year than he had in three years in Oakland. But the big story of the season was the arrival of O. J. Simpson. The Heisman Trophy winner from USC had openly expressed reluctance about playing in Buffalo, but once he signed with the Bills, he gave the team a much-needed running threat in the backfield. Simpson gained 697 yards rushing despite playing behind a porous line and under a head coach who built his offense around passing.

Miami Dolphins—The Dolphins slipped back into last place in the East, and head coach George Wilson paid for it with his job. Wilson, however, left behind a solid core of quality players for the next regime. Guard Larry Little and linebacker Nick Buoniconti had joined the team this year in trades which cost Miami very little, and rookies Lloyd Mumford, Bill Stanfill, and Mercury Morris further swelled the ranks of top players on the team. Already on the Miami scene were Bob Griese, Larry Csonka, Jim Kiick, Manny Fernandez, and Howard Twilley—enough talent to change Miami's future fortunes.

WESTERN DIVISION

Oakland Raiders—Throwing for thirty-four touchdowns, Lamonica won the league MVP award for the second time in the past three seasons. On the other end of Lamonica's passes were two complementary wide receivers, Warren Wells, whose strong point was speed, and Fred Biletnikoff, who relied on good moves and sure hands to make fifty-four catches. With the running attack a secondary feature, the offensive line spent most of its time expertly shielding Lamonica from enemy rushers. On defense, the Raiders got better the farther back you went. The line was adequate; Tom Keating recovered from his Achilles tendon injury, but Dan Birdwell missed most of the season with a bad knee. The linebacking corps of Dan Conners, Gus Otto, and Chip Oliver used the excellent mobility to fine advantage, and the secondary of Willie Brown, Nemiah Wilson, Dave Grayson, and George Atkinson had few peers in the pro ranks. With new coach John Madden blending all the pieces together into a harmonious whole, the Raiders edged the Chiefs out for first place in the West by beating them twice during the season.

Kansas City Chiefs—While the Raiders moved the ball primarily on passes, the Chiefs stuck to the ground on offense. Quarterbacks Len Dawson and Mike Livingston had a deep contingent of running backs to call on; Mike Garrett and Warren McVea provided speed from the halfback slot, and Robert Holmes and Wendell Hayes gave the Chiefs power at fullback. These four handled the running chores so well that coach Hank Stram moved Curtis McClinton to tight end and used rookie Ed Podolak exclusively as a kick returner. The Chiefs reversed Oakland's strategy and used the pass only to loosen enemy defenses for the run. The Kansas City defensive unit was brimming with talented players. Jerry Mays and Buck Buchanan had long starred in the line, and Aaron Brown and Curley Culp had fit in since the championship season of 1966. The linebacking trio of Bobby Bell, Willie Lanier, and Jim Lynch had everything. The secondary of Emmitt Thomas, rookie Jim Marsalis, Johnny Robinson, and Jim Kearney left few enemy receivers unattended.

San Diego Chargers—Five games from the end of the season, a bad case of ulcers forced Sid Gillman to give up the coaching reign and concentrate on his general manager's duties. Of course, the Chargers' 4-5-0 record at the time may have contributed to Gillman's decision and to his ulcers. Assistant Charlie Waller moved up to head coach, and after the Chargers lost their first game for him, the team won its last four outings. The talent on the roster was deep enough to make winning an expected event, not just a late-season occurrence. Halfback Dickie Post, receivers Lance Alworth and Gary Garrison, and guard Walt Sweeney all stood out for excellence, but the Chargers were let down by John Hadl's poor season and Ron Mix's injury-plagued campaign. The defense got good years out of Steve DeLong, Pete Barnes, Rick Redman, Jim Hill, Bob Howard, and Kenny Graham, but the rest of the unit needed patching up.

Denver Broncos—The Broncos began the season with impressive victories over the Patriots and Jets, but injuries took most of the steam out of the offense by mid-season. Quarterback Steve Tensi was bothered by a bad knee, receivers Mike Haffner and Bill Van Heusen missed the last month of the season with injured knees, and runner Floyd Little missed five games with shoulder and knee problems. Little's absence particularly hurt the team, as he had developed into a top runner before getting hurt. Inexperience rather than injuries troubled the defense, but this young unit came up with occasional sterling performances like a 13-0 shutout of the Chargers. The strength of the defense lay up front, where Rich Jackson and Dave Costa were two of the league's top linemen. The linebackers and deep backs all were young players, with speedy rookie cornerback Bill Thompson one of the most exciting newcomers in the AFL.

Cincinnati Bengals—Paul Brown's youth parade brought Greg Cook, Speedy Thomas, Horst Muhlmann, Bill Bergey, Royce Berry, and Ken Riley to Cincinnati as freshman starters this year, with Cook an immediate sensation at quarterback. After starring in the College All-Star game, the blond, handsome Cook reported to the Bengal's training camp and took right over as the offensive leader. On opening day, he threw two touchdown passes in leading the team to a victory over Miami. One week later, he threw three scoring passes and ran for another six points in engineering an upset over San Diego, and he helped beat the Chiefs in their third game. Cook then sat out a month of action with a sore passing arm, but he returned to beat Oakland.

FINAL TEAM STATISTICS

OFFENSE

	BOSTON	BUFFALO	CIN.	DENVER	HOUSTON	K.C.	MIAMI	NEW YORK	OAKLAND	S.D.
FIRST DOWNS:										
Total	166	224	172	243	256	258	224	252	261	**275**
by Rushing	64	83	66	87	95	**129**	73	98	84	119
by Passing	87	122	95	130	146	125	131	130	**153**	131
by Penalty	15	19	11	**26**	15	4	20	24	24	25
RUSHING:										
Number	367	384	363	394	440	**522**	401	469	459	455
Yards	1489	1522	1523	1637	1706	**2220**	1513	1782	1765	1985
Average Yards	4.1	4.0	4.2	4.2	3.9	4.3	3.8	3.8	3.8	**4.4**
Touchdowns	11	7	10	12	12	**19**	12	14	4	18
PASSING:										
Attempts	338	442	308	403	**489**	351	424	394	439	444
Completions	162	215	163	192	**239**	196	201	203	227	208
Completion Percentage	47.9	48.6	52.9	47.6	48.9	**55.8**	47.4	51.5	51.7	46.8
Passing Yards	2191	2716	2720	2835	3147	2638	2558	2939	**3375**	2927
Average Yards per Att.	6.5	6.1	**8.8**	7.0	6.4	7.5	6.0	7.5	7.7	6.6
Average Yards per Comp.	13.5	12.6	**16.7**	14.8	13.2	13.5	12.7	14.5	14.9	14.1
Tackled Att. to Pass	24	42	57	44	36	26	53	16	**12**	33
Yards Lost Tackled	261	371	375	311	322	251	481	138	**104**	301
Net Yards	1930	2345	2345	2524	2825	2387	2077	2801	**3271**	2626
Touchdowns	19	17	22	23	15	16	12	21	**36**	13
Interceptions	18	30	**15**	23	31	20	29	20	26	21
Percent Intercepted	5.3	6.8	4.9	5.7	6.3	5.7	6.8	5.1	5.9	**4.7**
PUNTS:										
Number	70	78	**85**	72	70	68	**85**	56	69	71
Average Distance	41.5	44.5	38.8	40.1	38.9	44.4	40.6	44.3	42.7	**44.6**
PUNT RETURNS:										
Number	23	31	23	37	43	32	**45**	39	39	31
Yards	212	187	135	**450**	391	251	266	256	225	300
Average Yards	9.2	6.0	5.9	**12.2**	9.1	7.8	5.9	6.6	5.8	9.7
Touchdowns	0	0	0	0	0	0	0	0	0	0
KICKOFF RETURNS:										
Number	54	**62**	55	56	49	41	60	46	42	39
Yards	1247	**1475**	1165	1323	1141	1090	1383	985	996	842
Average Yards	23.1	23.8	21.2	23.6	23.3	**26.6**	23.1	21.4	23.7	21.6
Touchdowns	0	0	0	0	0	**1**	**1**	0	0	0
INTERCEPTION RETURNS:										
Number	20	19	21	14	23	**32**	18	29	26	31
Yards	326	251	362	228	335	**595**	317	348	484	444
Average Yards	16.3	13.2	17.2	16.3	14.6	18.6	17.6	12.0	**18.6**	14.3
Touchdowns	1	1	1	2	2	2	2	1	**4**	3
PENALTIES:										
Number	77	67	50	80	70	62	53	61	**100**	63
Yards	837	632	556	753	730	757	631	725	**1274**	731
FUMBLES:										
Number	**15**	35	30	**15**	24	34	27	19	17	27
Number Lost	10	21	23	8	17	19	13	13	**7**	13
POINTS:										
Total	266	230	280	297	278	359	233	353	**377**	288
PAT (kick) Attempts	29	24	33	37	29	38	27	33	**45**	34
PAT (kick) Made	26	23	32	36	29	38	26	33	**45**	33
PAT (2-Point) Attempts	3	2	0	0	2	2	1	**4**	0	1
PAT (2-Point) Made	1	0	0	0	2	1	0	1	0	0
FG Attempts	34	26	24	29	40	35	22	**47**	37	28
FG Made	14	17	16	13	19	27	13	**32**	20	15
Percent FG Made	41.2	65.4	66.7	44.8	47.5	**77.1**	59.1	68.1	54.1	53.6
Safeties	**2**	0	1	0	1	0	0	0	1	0

DEFENSE

	BOSTON	BUFFALO	CIN.	DENVER	HOUSTON	K.C.	MIAMI	NEW YORK	OAKLAND	S.D.
FIRST DOWNS:										
Total	278	236	278	276	183	**181**	206	229	232	232
by Rushing	142	106	135	95	77	**53**	66	63	90	71
by Passing	115	118	130	151	**93**	111	126	151	107	148
by Penalty	21	**12**	13	30	13	17	14	15	35	13
RUSHING:										
Number	528	454	523	436	430	**314**	422	343	438	366
Yards	2359	1858	2651	1709	1556	**1091**	1489	1326	1661	1442
Average Yards	4.5	4.1	5.1	3.9	3.6	**3.5**	3.5	3.9	3.8	3.9
Touchdowns	18	17	13	15	10	**6**	9	7	13	11
PASSING:										
Attempts	**348**	368	396	437	371	426	404	437	422	423
Completions	203	175	205	223	167	200	196	232	**164**	241
Completion Percentage	58.3	47.6	51.8	51.0	45.0	46.9	48.5	53.1	**38.9**	57.0
Passing Yards	2610	2772	2866	3295	2495	**2491**	2845	3086	2511	3075
Average Yards per Att.	7.5	7.5	7.2	7.5	6.7	**5.8**	7.0	7.1	6.0	7.3
Average Yards per Comp.	12.9	15.8	14.0	14.8	14.9	**12.5**	14.5	13.3	15.3	12.8
Tackled Att. to Pass	22	31	16	45	32	**48**	25	42	47	35
Yards Lost Tackled	159	296	180	363	278	**419**	208	330	402	280
Net Yards	2451	2476	2686	2932	2217	**2072**	2637	2756	2109	2795
Touchdowns	18	21	24	19	18	**10**	25	22	15	22
Interceptions	20	19	21	14	23	**32**	18	29	26	31
Percent Intercepted	5.7	5.2	5.3	3.2	6.2	**7.5**	4.5	6.6	6.2	7.3
PUNTS:										
Number	55	62	55	71	85	84	80	69	**87**	76
Average Distance	**38.6**	42.7	41.4	43.1	43.1	43.0	44.1	39.8	41.8	40.3
PUNT RETURNS:										
Number	**19**	45	39	35	37	43	30	28	37	30
Yards	**114**	466	297	246	196	502	130	280	151	291
Average Yards	6.0	10.4	7.6	7.0	5.3	11.7	4.3	10.0	**4.1**	9.7
Touchdowns	0	0	0	0	0	0	0	0	0	0
KICKOFF RETURNS:										
Number	56	55	39	**21**	38	59	47	72	64	53
Yards	1068	1322	1065	**471**	792	1431	1073	1669	1518	1238
Average Yards	**19.1**	24.0	27.3	22.4	20.8	24.3	22.8	23.2	23.7	23.4
Touchdowns	0	0	1	1	0	0	0	0	0	0
INTERCEPTION RETURNS:										
Number	18	30	**15**	23	31	20	29	20	26	21
Yards	**225**	449	239	421	441	325	596	380	349	265
Average Yards	**12.5**	15.0	15.9	18.3	14.2	16.3	20.6	19.0	13.4	12.6
Touchdowns	1	2	**0**	4	3	3	3	2	1	**0**
PENALTIES:										
Number	69	71	72	**84**	61	39	66	69	81	71
Yards	810	719	824	901	592	443	840	788	**918**	791
FUMBLES:										
Number	**33**	25	13	24	27	25	27	25	25	13
Number Lost	14	**18**	15	14	17	15	13	16	16	6
POINTS:										
Total	316	359	367	344	279	**177**	332	269	242	276
PAT (kick) Attempts	38	40	42	38	33	**17**	33	28	27	33
PAT (kick) Made	37	39	41	38	33	**16**	32	28	26	31
PAT (2-Point) Attempts	**0**	**0**	**0**	2	**0**	2	4	4	2	1
PAT (2-Point) Made	**0**	**0**	**0**	**0**	**0**	**0**	1	2	**0**	1
FG Attempts	28	41	46	32	30	27	36	27	30	**25**
FG Made	17	26	24	22	16	15	24	15	14	**13**
Percent FG Made	60.7	63.4	52.2	68.8	53.3	55.6	66.7	55.6	**46.7**	52.0
Safeties	**0**	1	1	**0**	**0**	1	2	**0**	**0**	**0**

INTER-DIVISIONAL PLAYOFFS

December 20, at New York (Attendance 62,977)

SCORING

NEW YORK	**3**	**0**	**0**	**3– 6**
KANSAS CITY	**0**	**3**	**3**	**7–13**

First Quarter
N.Y. J. Turner, 27 yard field goal

Second Quarter
K.C. Stenerud, 23 yard field goal

Third Quarter
K.C. Stenerud, 25 yard field goal

Fourth Quarter
N.Y. J. Turner, 7 yard field goal
K.C. Richardson, 19 yard pass from Dawson PAT–Stenerud (kick)

TEAM STATISTICS

N.Y.		K.C.
19	First Downs–Total	14
5	First Downs–Rushing	3
11	First Downs–Passing	9
3	First Downs–Penalty	2
1	Fumbles–Number	0
1	Fumbles–Lost Ball	0
3	Penalties–Number	5
15	Yards Penalized	63
0	Missed Field Goals	3
64	Offensive Plays–Total	59
235	Net Yards	276
3.7	Average Gain	4.7
4	Giveaways	0
0	Takeaways	4
–4	Difference	+4

INDIVIDUAL STATISTICS

NEW YORK	No	Yds	Avg.	KANSAS CITY	No	Yds	Avg.
RUSHING							
Snell	12	61	5.1	Garrett	18	67	3.7
Boozer	3	14	4.7	Hayes	10	32	3.2
Mathis	6	11	1.8	Holmes	1	0	0.0
Namath	1	1	1.0	McVea	1	0	0.0
	22	87	4.0		30	99	3.3
RECEIVING							
Sauer	5	61	12.2	Hayes	5	46	9.2
Lammons	3	37	12.3	Taylor	2	74	37.0
B. Turner	2	25	12.5	Arbanas	2	39	19.5
Maynard	1	18	18.0	Holmes	1	29	29.0
Boozer	1	10	10.0	Richardson	1	19	19.0
Snell	1	9	9.0	Pitts	1	–6	–6.0
Mathis	1	4	4.0		12	201	16.8
	14	164	11.7				
PUNTING							
O'Neal	5		37.2	Wilson	6		33.5
PUNT RETURNS							
Battle	2	10	5.0	Garrett	1	10	10.0
				Mitchell	1	4	4.0
					2	14	7.0
KICKOFF RETURNS							
Battle	3	64	21.3	Holmes	2	33	16.5
Nock	1	33	33.0	Hayes	1	31	31.0
	4	97	24.3		3	64	21.3
INTERCEPTION RETURNS							
None				Marsalis	2	42	21.0
				Thomas	1	0	0.0
					3	42	14.0

PASSING

	Att.	Comp.	Comp. Pct.	Yds.	Int.	Yds/ Att.	Yds/ Comp.	Yds Lost Tkld.
NEW YORK								
Namath	40	14	35.0	164	3	4.1	11.7	2–16
KANSAS CITY								
Dawson	27	12	44.4	201	0	7.4	16.8	2–24

December 21, at Oakland (Attendance 53,539)

SCORING

OAKLAND	**28**	**7**	**14**	**7–56**
HOUSTON	**0**	**0**	**0**	**7– 7**

First Quarter
Oak. Biletnikoff, 13 yard pass from Lamonica PAT–Blanda (kick)
Oak. Atkinson, 57 yard interception return PAT–Blanda (kick)
Oak. Sherman, 24 yard pass from Lamonica PAT–Blanda (kick)
Oak. Biletnikoff, 31 yard pass from Lamonica PAT–Blanda (kick)

Second Quarter
Oak. Smith, 60 yard pass from Lamonica PAT–Blanda (kick)

Third Quarter
Oak. Sherman, 23 yard pass from Lamonica PAT–Blanda (kick)
Oak. Gannon, 3 yard pass from Lamonica PAT–Blanda (kick)

Fourth Quarter
Hou. Reed, 8 yard pass from Beathard PAT–Gerela (kick)
Oak. Hubbard, 4 yard rush PAT–Blanda (kick)

TEAM STATISTICS

OAK.		HOUS.
17	First Downs–Total	14
5	First Downs–Rushing	1
11	First Downs–Passing	10
1	First Downs–Penalty	3
3	Fumbles–Number	3
1	Fumbles–Lost Ball	2
7	Penalties–Number	3
63	Yards Penalized	48
0	Missed Field Goals	0
60	Offensive Plays–Total	71
412	Net Yards	197
6.9	Average Gain	2.8
4	Giveaways	5
5	Takeaways	4
+1	Difference	–1

INDIVIDUAL STATISTICS

OAKLAND	No	Yds	Avg.	HOUSTON	No	Yds	Avg.
RUSHING							
Dixon	13	48	3.7	Granger	14	29	2.1
Todd	8	31	3.9	LeVias	1	4	4.0
Hubbard	6	19	3.2	Campbell	1	0	0.0
Hagberg	2	9	4.5	Beathard	3	–5	–1.7
Smith	8	3	0.4		19	28	1.5
	37	110	3.0				
RECEIVING							
Smith	4	103	25.8	Reed	7	81	11.6
Sherman	4	60	15.0	Beirne	5	48	9.6
Biletnikoff	3	70	23.3	Granger	3	31	10.3
Todd	1	40	40.0	Haik	2	42	21.0
Hubbard	1	33	33.0	LeVias	1	7	7.0
Cannon	1	3	3.0		18	209	11.6
	14	309	22.1				
PUNTING							
Eischeid	5		42.0	Burrell	11		41.4
PUNT RETURNS							
Atkinson	2	19	9.5	LeVias	2	4	2.0
Sherman	1	8	8.0				
	3	27	9.0				
KICKOFF RETURNS							
Atkinson	1	38	38.0	LeVias	4	69	17.3
Sherman	1	26	26.0	Burrell	3	61	20.3
	2	64	32.0		7	130	18.6
INTERCEPTION RETURNS							
Atkinson	1	57	57.0	Farr	1	0	0.0
Brown	1	15	15.0	Moore	1	0	0.0
Wilson	1	0	0.0	Peacock	1	0	0.0
	3	72	24.0		3	0	0.0

PASSING

	Att.	Cmp.	Comp. Pct.	Yds.	Int.	Yds/ Att.	Yds/ Comp.	Lost Tkld.
OAKLAND								
Lamonica	17	13	76.5	276	1	16.2	21.2	
Blanda	5	1	20.0	33	2	6.6	33.0	
	22	14	63.6	309	3	14.0	22.1	1– 7
HOUSTON								
Beathard	46	18	39.1	209	3	4.5	11.6	6–40

NEW YORK JETS 10-4-0 Weeb Ewbank

Scores of Each Game		
33	Buffalo	19
19	Denver	21
27	San Diego	34
23	Boston	14
21	Cincinnati	7
26	HOUSTON	17
23	BOSTON	17
34	MIAMI	31
16	BUFFALO	6
16	KANSAS CITY	34
40	CINCINNATI	7
14	OAKLAND	27
34	Houston	26
27	Miami	9

Use Name	Pos.	Hgt	Wgt	Age	Int	Pts
Winston Hill	OT	6'4"	280	27		
Sam Walton	OT	6'5"	270	26		
Roger Finnie	OT	6'3"	245	23		
Paul Seiler	C-OT	6'4"	255	23		
Dave Herman	OG	6'2"	255	27		
Pete Perreault	OG	6'3"	248	30		
Randy Rasmussen	OG	6'2"	255	24		
Gordon Wright	OG	6'3"	245	25		
John Schmitt	C	6'4"	245	26		
Paul Crane	LB-C	6'2"	205	25	3	12
Verlon Biggs	DE	6'4"	270	26		
Jimmie Jones	DE	6'3"	215	22		
Gerry Philbin	DE	6'2"	245	28	1	
John Elliott	DT	6'4"	245	24		
Carl McAdams	DT	6'3"	240	25		
Paul Rochester	DT	6'2"	255	32		
Steve Thompson	DT	6'5"	245	24		
Al Atkinson	LB	6'1"	230	26	2	
Ralph Baker	LB	6'3"	235	27	1	
Jim Carroll	LB	6'1"	230	26		
Larry Grantham	LB	6'	210	30		
John Neidert	LB	6'2"	230	23		
Bill Baird	DB	5'10"	180	30	5	
Mike Battle	DB	6'1"	175	23	1	
Randy Beverly	DB	5'11"	185	25	2	
John Dockery	DB	6'	186	24	5	
Cornell Gordon	DB	6'	187	28	4	
Jim Hudson	DB	6'2"	210	26	2	
Cecil Leonard	DB	5'11"	170	23		
Jim Richards	DB	6'1"	180	22	3	
Harvey Nairn – Military Service						
Joe Namath	QB	6'2"	195	26		12
Babe Parilli	QB	6'1"	190	39		
Jim Turner	QB	6'2"	205	28		129
Al Woodall	QB	6'5"	210	23		
Emerson Boozer	HB	5'11"	204	26		24
Bill Mathis	HB	6'1"	220	30		30
George Nock	HB	5'10"	200	23		
Matt Snell	FB	6'2"	220	27		30
Lee White	FB	6'4"	240	23		
Don Maynard	WR	6'	180	33		38
Steve O'Neal	WR	6'3"	185	23		
George Sauer	WR	6'1"	195	25		48
Bake Turner	WR	6'	180	29		18
Pete Lammons	TE	6'3"	228	25		12
Wayne Stewart	TE	6'7"	202	22		

HOUSTON OILERS 6-6-2 Wally Lemm

Scores of Each Game		
17	Oakland	21
17	Buffalo	3
22	MIAMI	10
28	BUFFALO	14
0	Kansas City	24
17	New York	26
24	DENVER	21
0	Boston	24
31	CINCINNATI	31
20	Denver	20
32	Miami	7
17	SAN DIEGO	21
26	NEW YORK	34
27	BOSTON	23

Use Name	Pos.	Hgt	Wgt	Age	Int	Pts
Elbert Drungo	OT	6'5"	250	26		
Glen Ray Hines	OT	6'5"	265	25		
Walt Suggs	OT	6'5"	260	30		
Sonny Bishop	OG	6'2"	245	29		
Jim LeMoine	OG	6'2"	245	24		
Tom Regner	OG	6'1"	255	25		
Hank Autry	C	6'3"	230	22		
Bobby Maples	C	6'3"	245	26		
Elvin Bethea	DE	6'3"	250	23		2
Pat Holmes	DE	6'5"	250	29		
Glenn Woods	DE	6'4"	250	23		
Ben Mayes	DT-DE	6'5"	265	24		
Tom Domres	DT	6'3"	255	22		6
Willie Parker	DT	6'2"	265	24		
George Rice	DT	6'3"	260	25		
Carel Stith	DT	6'5"	265	24		
Garland Boyette	LB	6'1"	245	29		
Ron Pritchard	LB	6'1"	222	22		
Olen Underwood	LB	6'1"	230	27	1	
Loyd Wainscott	LB	6'1"	235	22		
Ed Watson	LB	6'2"	222	24		
George Webster	LB	6'4"	223	23	2	
John Douglas	DB	6'1"	195	24		
Miller Farr	DB	6'1"	190	26	6	
W. K. Hicks	DB	6'1"	195	26	4	
Ken Houston	DB	6'3"	192	24	4	6
Zeke Moore	DB	6'2"	198	25	4	6
Johnny Peacock	DB	6'2"	205	22	2	6
Leroy Mitchell – Broken Neck						
Pete Beathard	QB	6'2"	207	27		12
Bob Davis	QB	6'3"	208	23		
Don Trull	QB	6'1"	196	27		12
Ode Burrell	HB	6'	192	29		
Woody Campbell	HB	5'11"	202	24		6
Mike Richardson	HB	5'11"	185	22		2
Hoyle Granger	FB-HB	6'1"	225	25		24
Roy Hopkins	FB	6'1"	225	24		30
Rich Johnson	HB-FB	6'1"	210	22		6
Jim Beirne	WR	6'2"	196	22		26
Mac Haik	WR	6'1"	196	23		6
Charlie Joiner	WR	5'11"	185	21		
Jerry LeVias	WR	5'10"	175	22		30
Paul Zaeske	WR	6'2"	200	23		
Ed Carrington	TE	6'4"	225	25		
Alvin Reed	TE	6'5"	230	25		12
Roy Gerela	K	5'10"	185	21		86

BOSTON PATRIOTS 4-10-0 Clive Rush

Scores of Each Game		
7	Denver	35
0	KANSAS CITY	31
23	OAKLAND	38
14	NEW YORK	23
16	Buffalo	23
10	SAN DIEGO	13
17	New York	23
24	HOUSTON	0
16	MIAMI	17
25	Cincinnati	14
35	BUFFALO	21
38	Miami	23
18	San Diego	28
23	Houston	27

Use Name	Pos.	Hgt	Wgt	Age	Int	Pts
Tom Funchess	OT	6'5"	260	24		
Ezell Jones	OT	6'4"	255	22		2
Tom Neville	OT	6'4"	255	26		
Charley Long	OG	6'3"	250	31		
Len St. Jean	OG	6'1"	245	27		
Mike Montler	C-OG	6'4"	270	25		
Jon Morris	C	6'4"	240	26		
J. R. Williamson	LB-C	6'2"	220	27		
Ron Berger	DE	6'8"	275	25		
Johnny Cagle	DE	6'3"	260	22		
Larry Eisenhauer	DE	6'5"	255	29		
Mel Witt	DE	6'3"	265	23		
Karl Henke	DT-DE	6'4"	245	24		
Houston Antwine	DT	6'	270	30		
Jim Hunt	DT	5'11"	255	30		
Ray Jacobs	DT	6'3"	285	29		
Ed Toner	DT	6'3"	250	24		
John Bramlett	LB	6'2"	210	28	1	
Jim Cheyunski	LB	6'2"	220	23	1	
Ed Philpott	LB	6'3"	240	23	4	
Marty Schottenheimer	LB	6'3"	224	26	1	
Larry Carwell	DB	6'1"	190	25	4	
John Charles	DB	6'1"	200	25	4	6
Tom Janik	DB	6'3"	195	28	1	
Daryle Johnson	DB	5'11"	190	23	2	8
Art McMahon	DB	5'11"	185	23		
John Outlaw	DB	5'10"	180	24		
Clarence Scott	DB	6'2"	205	25		
Don Webb	DB	5'10"	195	30	2	
Kim Hammond	QB	6'1"	192	24		2
Mike Taliaferro	QB	6'2"	205	27		
Teddy Bailey	HB	6'	200	25		
Sid Blanks	HB	6'	210	28		
Carl Garrett	HB	5'11"	210	22		42
Bob Gladieux	HB	5'11"	190	22		
Jim Nance	FB	6'1"	240	26		36
R. C. Gamble	HB-FB	6'3"	220	22		
Gino Cappelletti	WR	6'	190	35		68
Charley Frazier	WR	6'	184	30		42
Aaron Marsh	WR	6'1"	190	24		
Bill Rademacher	WR	6'1"	190	27		18
Tom Richardson	WR	6'2"	195	24		
Ron Sellers	WR	6'4"	198	22		36
Ken Herock	TE	6'2"	230	28		
Jim Whalen	TE	6'2"	210	25		6
Barry Brown	LB-TE	6'3"	220	26		

BUFFALO BILLS 4-10-0 Johnny Rauch

Scores of Each Game		
19	NEW YORK	33
3	HOUSTON	17
41	DENVER	28
14	Houston	28
23	BOSTON	16
21	Oakland	50
6	Miami	24
7	KANSAS CITY	29
6	New York	16
28	MIAMI	3
21	Boston	35
16	CINCINNATI	13
19	Kansas City	22
6	San Diego	45

Use Name	Pos.	Hgt	Wgt	Age	Int	Pts
Stew Barber	OT	6'3"	248	30		
Paul Costa	OT	6'4"	248	27		
Howard Kindig	OT	6'6"	264	28		
Mike Richey	OT	6'5"	250	22		
George Flint	OG	6'4"	240	31		
Billy Shaw	OG	6'3"	252	29		
Angelo Loukas	OG	6'3"	250	22		
Joe O'Donnell	OG	6'2"	252	26		
Al Bemiller	C	6'3"	243	30		
Mike McBath	DE	6'4"	248	23		
Ron McDole	DE	6'3"	270	29		
Julian Nunamaker	DE	6'3"	250	23		
Chuck DeVleigher	DT	6'4"	265	22		
Jim Dunaway	DT	6'4"	282	27		
Waddey Harvey	DT	6'4"	270	22		
Bob Kruse	DT	6'2"	250	27		
Bob Tatarek	DT	6'4"	255	23		
Edgar Chandler	LB	6'3"	222	23		
Jerald Collins	LB	6'1"	220	22		
Paul Guidry	LB	6'3"	228	25	2	
Harry Jacobs	LB	6'2"	226	32	2	
Paul Maguire	LB	6'	228	31		
Dave Ogas	LB	6'3"	240	23		
Mike Stratton	LB	6'3"	230	27		
Butch Byrd	DB	6'	196	27	7	6
Hilton Crawford	DB	6'	198	24		
Booker Edgerson	DB	5'10"	183	30	1	6
John Pitts	DB	6'4"	215	24	2	
Pete Richardson	DB	6'1"	205	22	2	
George Saimes	DB	5'10"	185	27	3	
Robert James	WR-DB	6'1"	177	22		
Bob Kalsu – Military Service						
Dan Darragh	QB	6'3"	196	22		
James Harris	QB	6'3"	215	22		
Jack Kemp	QB	6'1"	204	35		
Tom Sherman (from BOS)	QB	6'	190	23		
Max Anderson	HB	5'8"	180	24		6
Preston Ridlehuber	HB	6'2"	215	25		
O. J. Simpson	HB	6'2"	204	22		30
Bill Enyart	FB	6'4"	236	22		18
Wayne Patrick	FB	6'2"	225	23		18
Marlin Briscoe	WR	5'10"	177	23		30
Bobby Crockett	WR	6'	200	26		
Monte Ledbetter (to ATL-N)	WR	6'2"	185	26		
Haven Moses	WR	6'3"	200	23		30
Roy Reeves	WR	5'11"	182	23		
Bubba Thornton	WR	6'	175	22		
Charley Ferguson	TE	6'5"	224	29		
Willie Grate	TE	6'4"	225	23		6
Bill Masters	TE	6'5"	225	25		6
Bruce Alford	K	6'	185	24		74

MIAMI DOLPHINS 3-10-1 George Wilson

Scores of Each Game		
21	Cincinnati	27
17	Oakland	20
10	Houston	22
20	OAKLAND	20
14	SAN DIEGO	21
10	Kansas City	17
24	BUFFALO	6
31	New York	34
17	Boston	16
3	Buffalo	28
7	HOUSTON	32
23	BOSTON	38
27	DENVER	24
9	NEW YORK	27

Use Name	Pos.	Hgt	Wgt	Age	Int	Pts
John Boynton	OT	6'4"	255	23		
Doug Crusan	OT	6'5"	255	23		
Norm Evans	OT	6'5"	250	26		
Billy Neighbors	OG	5'11"	250	29		
Maxie Williams	OG	6'4"	250	29		
Larry Little	OT-OG	6'1"	270	23		
Tom Goode	C	6'3"	250	30		
Jeff Richardson	OT-C	6'3"	250	24		
Norm McBride	DE	6'3"	235	22		
Jim Riley	DE	6'4"	255	24		
Bill Stanfill	DE	6'5"	250	22	2	12
Bob Joswick	DT-DE	6'5"	250	23		
Manny Fernandez	DT	6'2"	250	23		
Bob Heinz	DT	6'6"	265	22		
John Richardson	DT	6'2"	260	24		
Freddie Woodson	OG-DT	6'2"	255	25		
Nick Buoniconti	LB	5'11"	220	28	3	
Randy Edmunds	LB	6'2"	220	23		
Frank Emanuel	LB	6'3"	225	26		
Jimmy Keyes	LB	6'2"	225	25		
Dale McCullers	LB	6'1"	215	21		
Jesse Powell	LB	6'1"	212	22		
Ed Weisacosky	LB	6'	230	25	3	
Dick Anderson	DB	6'2"	205	23	3	
Tom Beier	DB	5'11"	198	24	1	
Garry Grady	DB	5'11"	180	22		
Lloyd Mumphord	DB	5'11"	180	22	5	
Willie Pearson	DB	6'	190	22		
Bob Petralla	DB	6'	185	24	1	
Jimmy Warren	DB	5'11"	175	30		
Dick Westmoreland	DB	6'1"	195	28		
Bob Griese	QB	6'1"	190	24		
Rick Norton	QB	6'1"	190	25		
John Stofa (From CIN)	QB	6'3"	210	27		
Jim Kiick	HB	5'11"	215	23		60
Mercury Morris	HB	5'10"	185	22		12
Barry Pryor	HB	6'	215	23		
Larry Csonka	FB	6'3"	240	22		18
Stan Mitchell	FB	6'2"	225	25		
Jack Clancy	WR	6'1"	195	25		6
Bill Darnall	WR	6'2"	197	25		
Jimmy Hines	WR	6'	175	22		
Gene Milton	WR	5'10"	170	24		6
Karl Noonan	WR	6'3"	190	25		18
Howard Twilley	WR	5'10"	180	25		6
Tommy Boutwell	QB-WR	6'2"	205	22		
Jim Mertens	TE	6'3"	235	22		
Doug Moreau	TE	6'2"	215	24		
Larry Seiple	TE	6'	213	24		30
Karl Kremser	K	6'	180	24		65

NEW YORK JETS

RUSHING

Last Name	No.	Yds	Avg	TD
Snell	191	695	3.6	4
Boozer	130	604	4.6	4
Mathis	96	355	3.7	4
White	28	88	3.1	0
Namath	11	33	3.0	2
Woodall	4	13	3.3	0
Sauer	1	5	5.0	0
Parilli	3	4	1.3	0
B. Turner	1	−4	−4.0	0
Nock	3	−5	−1.7	0
Maynard	1	−6	−6.0	0

RECEIVING

Last Name	No.	Yds	Avg	TD
Maynard	47	938	20	6
Sauer	45	745	17	8
Lammons	33	400	12	2
Snell	22	187	9	1
Boozer	20	222	11	0
Mathis	18	183	10	1
B. Turner	11	221	20	3
Stewart	5	39	8	0
Dockery	1	6	6	0
White	1	−2	−2	0

PUNT RETURNS

Last Name	No.	Yds	Avg	TD
Battle	34	235	7	0
Baird	4	21	5	0
Leonard	1	0	0	0

KICKOFF RETURNS

Last Name	No.	Yds	Avg	TD
Battle	31	750	24	0
Leonard	7	120	17	0
B. Turner	3	74	25	0
Richards	2	36	18	0
White	1	5	5	0
Carroll	1	0	0	0
Sauer	1	0	0	0

PASSING

Last Name	Att	Comp	%	Yds	Yd/Att	TD	Int–	%	RK
Namath	361	185	51	2734	7.6	19	17–	5	2
Parilli	24	14	58	138	5.8	2	1–	4	
Woodall	9	4	44	67	7.4	0	2–	22	

PUNTING

Last Name	No	Avg
O'Neal	54	44.3
B. Turner	2	44.5

KICKING

Last Name	XP	Att	%	FG	Att	%
J. Turner	33	33	100	32	47	68

2 POINT XP

Maynard

HOUSTON OILERS

RUSHING

Last Name	No.	Yds	Avg	TD
Granger	186	740	4.0	3
Hopkins	131	473	3.6	4
Burrell	41	147	3.6	0
Campbell	28	98	3.5	1
Beathard	19	89	4.7	2
Richardson	5	51	10.2	0
Johnson	11	42	3.8	0
Trull	8	25	3.1	2
Haik	2	21	10.5	0
LeVias	6	18	3.0	0
Davis	3	2	0.7	0

RECEIVING

Last Name	No.	Yds	Avg	TD
Reed	51	664	13	2
LeVias	42	696	17	5
Beirne	42	540	13	4
Hopkins	29	338	12	1
Haik	27	375	14	1
Granger	27	330	12	1
Campbell	7	82	12	0
Joiner	7	77	11	0
Burrell	5	28	6	0
Johnson	2	17	9	1

PUNT RETURNS

Last Name	No.	Yds	Avg	TD
LeVias	35	292	8	0
Richardson	7	93	13	0
Burrell	1	6	6	0

KICKOFF RETURNS

Last Name	No.	Yds	Avg	TD
LeVias	38	940	25	0
Burrell	5	101	20	0
Joiner	3	73	24	0
Reed	3	0	0	0
Houston	0	27	0	0

PASSING

Last Name	Att	Comp	%	Yds	Yd/Att	TD	Int–	%	RK
Beathard	370	180	49	2455	6.6	10	21–	6	8
Trull	75	34	45	469	6.3	3	6–	8	
Davis	42	25	60	223	5.3	2	4–	10	
LeVias	2	0	0	0	0.0	0	0–	0	

PUNTING

Last Name	No	Avg
Gerela	41	40.4
Burrell	29	36.8

KICKING

Last Name	XP	Att	%	FG	Att	%
Gerela	29	29	100	19	40	48

2 POINT XP

Beirne
Richardson

BOSTON PATRIOTS

RUSHING

Last Name	No.	Yds	Avg	TD
Nance	193	750	3.9	6
Garrett	137	691	5.0	5
Gamble	16	35	2.2	0
Blanks	7	30	4.3	0
Frazier	2	−1	−0.5	0
Taliaferro	12	−16	−1.3	0

RECEIVING

Last Name	No.	Yds	Avg	TD
Garrett	29	267	9	2
Nance	29	168	6	0
Sellers	27	705	26	6
Frazier	19	306	16	7
Rademacher	17	217	13	3
Whalen	16	235	15	1
Marsh	8	108	14	0
Gamble	7	74	11	0
Brown	6	69	12	0
Blanks	2	16	8	0
Cappelletti	1	21	21	0
Richardson	1	5	5	0

PUNT RETURNS

Last Name	No.	Yds	Avg	TD
Garrett	12	159	13	0
Carwell	5	43	9	0
Blanks	5	10	2	0
Janik	1	0	0	0

KICKOFF RETURNS

Last Name	No.	Yds	Avg	TD
Garrett	28	792	28	0
Marsh	8	136	23	0
Blanks	6	131	22	0
Gladieux	4	61	15	0
Scott	6	43	7	0
Carwell	1	28	28	0
Gamble	1	23	23	0
Berger	1	20	20	0
Schott'nhmer	1	13	13	0

PASSING

Last Name	Att	Comp	%	Yds	Yd/Att	TD	Int–	%	RK
Taliaferro	331	160	48	2160	6.5	19	18–	5	11
Hammond	6	2	33	31	5.2	0	0–	0	
Garrett	1	0	0	0	0.0	0	0–	0	

PUNTING

Last Name	No	Avg
Janik	70	41.5

KICKING

Last Name	XP	Att	%	FG	Att	%
Cappelletti	26	27	96	14	34	41

2 POINT XP

Hammond

BUFFALO BILLS

RUSHING

Last Name	No.	Yds	Avg	TD
Simpson	181	697	3.9	2
Patrick	83	361	4.3	3
Enyart	47	191	4.1	1
Kemp	37	124	3.4	0
Anderson	13	74	5.7	1
Ridlehuber	4	25	6.3	0
Harris	10	25	2.5	0
Sherman	2	14	7.0	0
Darragh	6	14	2.3	0
Masters	1	−3	−3.0	0

RECEIVING

Last Name	No.	Yds	Avg	TD
Moses	39	752	19	5
Patrick	35	229	7	0
Masters	33	387	12	1
Briscoe	32	532	17	5
Simpson	30	343	11	3
Enyart	19	186	10	2
Thornton	14	134	10	0
Anderson	7	65	9	0
Crockett	4	50	13	0
Grate	1	19	19	1
James	1	19	19	0

PUNT RETURNS

Last Name	No.	Yds	Avg	TD
Anderson	19	142	7	0
Byrd	7	37	5	0
Reeves	2	3	2	0
Ridlehuber	1	3	3	0
James	1	2	2	0
Richardson	1	0	0	0

KICKOFF RETURNS

Last Name	No.	Yds	Avg	TD
Thornton	30	749	25	0
Simpson	21	529	25	0
Anderson	4	86	22	0
Crawford	3	74	25	0
Collins	2	14	7	0
Enyart	1	12	12	0
Harvey	1	11	11	0

PASSING

Last Name	Att	Comp	%	Yds	Yd/Att	TD	Int–	%	RK
Kemp	344	170	49	1981	5.8	13	22–	6	9
Darragh	52	24	46	365	7.0	1	6–	12	
Harris	36	15	42	270	7.5	1	1–	3	
Sherman	2	2	100	20	10.0	1	0–	0	
Briscoe	1	0	0	0	0.0	0	1–	100	
Maguire	1	1	100	19	19.0	0	0–	0	
Ridlehuber	1	1	100	45	45.0	1	0–	0	

PUNTING

Last Name	No	Avg
Maguire	78	44.5

KICKING

Last Name	XP	Att	%	FG	Att	%
Alford	23	24	96	17	26	65

MIAMI DOLPHINS

RUSHING

Last Name	No.	Yds	Avg	TD
Kiick	180	575	3.2	9
Csonka	131	566	4.3	2
Morris	23	110	4.8	1
Griese	21	102	4.9	0
Mitchell	28	80	2.9	0
Milton	7	62	8.9	0
Norton	8	16	2.0	0
Hines	1	7	7.0	0
Seiple	1	6	6.0	0
Noonan	1	−11	−11.0	0

RECEIVING

Last Name	No.	Yds	Avg	TD
Seiple	41	577	14	5
Kiick	29	443	15	1
Noonan	29	307	11	3
Clancy	21	289	14	1
Csonka	21	183	9	1
Milton	12	179	15	0
Twilley	10	158	16	1
Mitchell	10	125	13	0
Moreau	10	136	14	0
Morris	6	65	11	0
Boutwell	4	29	7	0
Mertens	2	26	13	0
Hines	2	23	12	0
Pryor	2	−3	−2	0
Darnall	1	13	13	0
Anderson	1	8	8	0

PUNT RETURNS

Last Name	No.	Yds	Avg	TD
Morris	25	172	7	0
Anderson	12	82	7	0
Beier	5	8	2	0
Milton	1	4	4	0
McCullers	1	0	0	0
Twilley	1	0	0	0

KICKOFF RETURNS

Last Name	No.	Yds	Avg	TD
Morris	43	1136	26	1
Milton	8	166	21	0
Beier	4	58	15	0
Hines	1	22	22	0
Mertens	2	1	1	0
Mumphord	1	0	0	0
Warren	1	0	0	0

PASSING

Last Name	Att	Comp	%	Yds	Yd/Att	TD	Int–	%	RK
Griese	252	121	48	1695	6.7	10	16–	6	10
Norton	148	65	44	709	4.8	2	11–	7	12
Stofa	23	14	61	146	6.4	0	2–	9	
Seiple	1	1	100	8	8.0	0	0–	0	

PUNTING

Last Name	No	Avg
Seiple	80	40.8
Anderson	5	37.6

KICKING

Last Name	XP	Att	%	FG	Att	%
Kremser	26	27	96	13	22	59

OAKLAND RAIDERS 12-1-1 John Madden

Scores of Each Game		
21	HOUSTON	17
20	MIAMI	17
38	Boston	23
20	Miami	20
24	Denver	14
50	BUFFALO	21
24	San Diego	12
17	Cincinnati	31
41	DENVER	10
21	SAN DIEGO	16
27	Kansas City	24
27	New York	14
37	CINCINNATI	17
10	KANSAS CITY	6

Use Name	Pos.	Hgt	Wgt	Age	Int	Pts
Harry Schuh	OT	6'2"	260	26		
Art Shell	OT	6'5"	255	22		
Bob Svihus	OT	6'4"	245	26		
George Buehler	OG	6'2"	260	22		
Jim Harvey	OG	6'5"	245	26		
Wayne Hawkins	OG	6'	240	31		
Gene Upshaw	OG	6'5"	255	24		
Jim Otto	C	6'2"	248	31		
Ben Davidson	DE	6'8"	275	29		
Ike Lassiter	DE	6'5"	270	28		
Carleton Oats	DT-DE	6'2"	260	26		
Dan Birdwell	DT	6'4"	250	28		
Al Dotson	DT	6'4"	260	26		2
Tom Keating	DT	6'3"	247	26		
Art Thoms	DT	6'5"	250	22		
Duane Benson	LB	6'2"	215	24		
Bill Budness	LB	6'1"	215	26		
Dan Conners	LB	6'1	230	27	1	12
Bill Laskey	LB	6'2"	235	26	3	
Chip Oliver	LB	6'2"	220	23	1	6
Gus Otto	LB	6'2"	220	26	2	
Jackie Allen	DB	6'1"	187	21		
Butch Atkinson	DB	6'	180	22	2	6
Willie Brown	DB	6'1"	190	28	5	
Dave Grayson	DB	5'10"	185	30	8	6
Kent McCloughan	DB	6'1"	190	26		
Howie Williams	DB	6'2"	190	32	2	
Nemiah Wilson	DB	6'	165	26	2	
George Blanda	QB	6'1"	215	41		105
Daryle Lamonica	QB	6'2"	215	28		6
Charlie Smith	HB	6'1"	205	23		24
Larry Todd	HB	6'1"	185	26		12
Pete Banaszak	FB-HB	5'11"	200	25		18
Hewritt Dixon	FB	6'2"	230	29		6
Marv Hubbard	FB	6'1"	215	23		
Fred Biletnikoff	WR	6'1"	190	26		72
Drew Buie	WR	6'2"	178	22		
Rod Sherman	WR	6'	190	24		
Warren Wells	WR	6'1"	190	26		84
Billy Cannon	TE	6'1"	215	32		12
Lloyd Edwards	TE	6'3"	248	22		
Roger Hagberg	TE	6'2"	215	30		6
Mike Eischeid	K	6'	190	28		

KANSAS CITY CHIEFS 11-3-0 Hank Stram

Scores of Each Game		
27	San Diego	9
31	Boston	0
19	Cincinnati	24
26	Denver	13
24	HOUSTON	0
17	MIAMI	10
42	CINCINNATI	22
29	Buffalo	7
27	SAN DIEGO	3
34	New York	16
24	OAKLAND	27
31	DENVER	17
22	BUFFALO	19
6	Oakland	10

Use Name	Pos.	Hgt	Wgt	Age	Int	Pts
Dave Hill	OT	6'5"	260	28		
Jim Tyrer	OT	6'6"	275	30		
Ed Budde	OG	6'5"	260	28		
George Daney	OG	6'3"	240	22		6
Mo Moorman	OG	6'5"	252	25		
E. J. Holub	C	6'4"	236	31		
Remi Prudhomme	C	6'4"	250	27		
Aaron Brown	DE	6'5"	265	25		
Jerry Mays	DE	6'4"	252	29		
Gene Trosch	DE	6'7"	277	24		
Buck Buchanan	DT	6'7"	287	29		
Curley Culp	DT	6'1"	265	23		
Ed Lothamer	DT	6'5"	270	26		
Bobby Bell	LB	6'4"	228	29		6
Chuck Hurston	LB	6'6"	240	26		
Willie Lanier	LB	6'1"	245	24	4	
Jim Lynch	LB	6'1"	235	24	3	
Bob Stein	LB	6'2"	235	21		
Caesar Belser	DB	6'	212	24		
Jim Kearney	DB	6'2"	206	26	5	6
Jim Marsalis	DB	5'11"	194	23	2	
Willie Mitchell	DB	6'1"	185	27	1	
Johnny Robinson	DB	6'	205	30	8	
Goldie Sellers	DB	6'2"	198	27		6
Emmitt Thomas	DB	6'2"	192	26	9	6
Len Dawson	QB	6'	190	35		
Tom Flores (from BUF)	QB	6'1"	202	32		
Jacky Lee	QB	6'1"	185	30		
Mike Livingston	QB	6'3"	205	23		
Mike Garrett	HB	5'9"	200	25		48
Paul Lowe	HB	6'	205	32		
Warren McVea	HB	5'10"	182	23		42
Ed Podolak	HB	6'1"	204	22		
Noland Smith (to SF-N)	HB	5'6"	156	25		
Wendell Hayes	FB	6'2"	220	28		24
Robert Holmes	FB	5'9"	220	23		30
Frank Pitts	WR	6'2"	200	25		12
Gloster Richardson	WR	6'	200	26		12
Otis Taylor	WR	6'2"	215	26		42
Mickey McCarty	TE	6'5"	255	22		
Curtis McClinton	TE	6'3"	227	31		
Morris Stroud	TE	6'10"	235	23		
Fred Arbanas	OT-TE	6'3"	240	30		
Jan Stenerud	K	6'2"	187	26		119
Jerrel Wilson	K	6'4"	222	27		

SAN DIEGO CHARGERS 8-6-0 Sid Gillman Charlie Waller

Scores of Each Game		
9	KANSAS CITY	27
20	Cincinnati	34
34	NEW YORK	27
21	CINCINNATI	14
21	Miami	14
13	Boston	10
12	OAKLAND	24
0	Denver	13
3	Kansas City	27
16	Oakland	21
45	DENVER	24
21	Houston	17
28	BOSTON	18
45	BUFFALO	6

Use Name	Pos.	Hgt	Wgt	Age	Int	Pts
Gene Ferguson	OT	6'7"	306	21		6
Ron Mix	OT	6'4"	250	31		
Terry Owens	OT	6'6"	270	25		
Bob Wells	OT	6'4"	270	24		
Gary Kirner	OG	6'3"	255	27		
Jim Schmedding	OG	6'2"	250	23		
Walt Sweeney	OG	6'3"	260	28		
Sam Gruneisen	C	6'1"	250	28		
Bill Lenkaitis	OG-C	6'3"	250	23		
Ron Billingsley	DE	6'8"	265	24		
Steve DeLong	DE	6'3"	252	26		
Houston Ridge	DE	6'4"	245	25		
Bob Briggs	DT	6'4"	270	24		
LevertCarr	DT	6'5"	250	25		
Dan Sartin	DT	6'1"	245	23		
Russ Washington	DT	6'6"	290	22		
Chuck Allen	LB	6'1"	225	29		
Pete Barnes	LB	6'3"	245	24	5	
Bob Bruggers	LB	6'1"	230	25	1	
Jim Campbell	LB	6'3"	218	23	1	
Jim Fetherston	LB	6'2"	225	24		
Rick Redman	LB	5'11"	225	26	1	
Jeff Staggs	LB	6'2"	240	25		
Joe Beauchamp	DB	6'	185	25		
Speedy Duncan	DB	5'10"	175	26	6	6
Dick Farley	DB	6'	185	23		
Kenny Graham	DB	6'	205	27	4	12
Jim Hill	DB	6'2"	192	22	7	
Bob Howard	DB	6'1"	190	24	6	
Gene Huey	DB	5'11"	190	22		
Larry Rentz	DB	6'1"	170	22		
Jim Tolbert	DB	6'3"	207	25		
Marty Domres	QB	6'3"	212	22		24
John Hadl	QB	6'2"	215	29		12
Dickie Post	HB	5'9"	190	23		36
Ron Sayers	HB	6'1"	202	22		
Russ Smith	FB-HB	6'1"	209	25		12
Gene Foster	FB	5'11"	220	26		6
Brad Hubbert	FB	6'1"	227	28		24
Lance Alworth	WR	6'	180	29		24
Rick Eber	WR	6'	185	24		6
Gary Garrison	WR	6'1"	195	25		42
Richard Trapp	WR	6'1"	174	22		
Willie Frazier	TE	6'4"	235	26		
Jacque MacKinnon	TE	6'4"	240	30		
Jeff Queen	TE	6'1"	230	23		
Dennis Partee	K	6'2"	208	23		78

DENVER BRONCOS 5-8-1 Lou Saban

Scores of Each Game		
35	BOSTON	7
21	NEW YORK	19
28	Buffalo	41
13	KANSAS CITY	26
14	OAKLAND	24
30	Cincinnati	23
21	Houston	24
13	SAN DIEGO	0
10	Oakland	41
20	HOUSTON	20
24	San Diego	45
17	Kansas City	31
24	Miami	27
27	CINCINNATI	16

Use Name	Pos.	Hgt	Wgt	Age	Int	Pts
Sam Brunelli	OT	6'1"	270	26		
Mike Current	OT	6'4"	260	23		
Wallace Dickey	OT	6'3"	260	28		
George Goeddeke	OG	6'3"	253	24		
Buzz Highsmith	OG	6'4"	230	26		
Mike Schnitker	OG	6'3"	235	22		
Bob Young	OG	6'2"	260	26		
Jay Bachman	C	6'3"	250	23		
Larry Kaminski	C	6'2"	245	24		
Walt Barnes	DE	6'3"	250	25		
Pete Duranko	DE	6'2"	252	25		
Rich Jackson	DE	6'2"	255	28		
Dave Costa	DT	6'2"	265	27		
Jerry Inman	DT	6'3"	255	29		
Rex Mirich	DT	6'4"	250	28		
Paul Smith	DT	6'3"	245	24		
Tim Casey (from CHI-N)	LB	6'1"	225	25		
Gary Crane	LB	6'4"	230	22		
Ken Criter	LB	5'11"	223	22		
Carl Cunningham	LB	6'3"	240	25	2	
John Huard	LB	6'	220	25	2	
Gordon Lambert	LB	6'5"	245	24		
Chip Myrtle	LB	6'2"	225	24		
Frank Richter	LB	6'3"	230	24		
Phil Brady	DB	6'2"	211	26		
George Burrell	DB	5'10"	180	21	2	6
Grady Cavness	DB	5'11"	187	22	2	
Charlie Greer	DB	6'	205	23	2	
Gus Holloman	DB	6'3"	195	23	1	
Pete Jaquess	DB	6'	182	27		
Tom Oberg	DB	6'	185	24		
Jimmy Smith	DB	6'3"	190	24		
Bill Thompson	DB	6'1"	200	22	3	6
Ted Alfen	HB-DB	6'	195	22		
Pete Liske	QB	6'2"	185	28		
Al Pastrana	QB	6'1"	190	24		
Steve Tensi	QB	6'5"	215	26		
Bobby Burnett	HB	6'2"	208	26		
Floyd Little	HB	5'10"	195	27		42
Frank Quayle	HB	5'10"	195	22		
Wandy Williams	HB	6'1"	193	23		6
Henry Jones	FB	6'2"	235	23		
Brendan McCarthy	FB	6'3"	220	24		
Tom Smiley	FB	6'1"	235	25		24
Fran Lynch	HB-FB	6'1"	194	23		12
Al Denson	WR	6'2"	208	27		60
John Embree	WR	6'4"	207	25		30
Mike Haffner	WR	6'2"	205	27		30
Bill Van Heusen	WR	6'1"	200	23		
Tom Beer	TE	6'4"	230	24		
Tom Buckman	TE	6'4"	230	22		6
Dave Pivec	TE	6'3"	240	25		
Bobby Howfield	K	5'9"	180	32		75

CINCINNATI BENGALS 4-9-1 Paul Brown

Scores of Each Game		
27	MIAMI	21
34	SAN DIEGO	20
24	KANSAS CITY	19
14	San Diego	21
7	NEW YORK	21
23	DENVER	30
22	Kansas City	42
31	OAKLAND	17
31	Houston	31
14	BOSTON	25
7	New York	40
13	Buffalo	16
17	Oakland	37
16	Denver	27

Use Name	Pos.	Hgt	Wgt	Age	Int	Pts
Howard Fest	OT	6'6"	265	23		
Frank Peters	OT	6'4"	250	21		
Ernie Wright	OT	6'4"	270	29		
Ernie Park	OG-OT	6'3"	240	27		
Justin Canale	OG	6'2"	250	25		
Guy Dennis	OG	6'2"	255	22		
Pat Matson	OG	6'1"	245	25		
Dave Middendorf	OG	6'3"	260	23		
Mike Wilson	OG	6'1"	240	21		
Bob Johnson	C	6'5"	260	23		
Marty Baccaglio	DE	6'3"	245	24		
Royce Berry	DE	6'3"	242	23		
Harry Gunner	DE	6'6"	250	24	1	6
Steve Chomyszak	DT	6'5"	280	24		
Andy Rice	DT	6'3"	268	27		
Bill Staley	DT	6'3"	250	22		
Ken Avery	LB	6'1"	225	25		
Al Beauchamp	LB	6'2"	236	25	1	
Bill Bergey	LB	6'2"	240	24	2	
Tim Buchanan	LB	6'	233	23		
Ed Harmon	LB	6'4"	230	22		
Bill Peterson	LB	6'3"	230	24	4	
Al Coleman	DB	6'1"	183	24		
Ken Dyer	DB	6'3"	185	23		
John Guillory	DB	5'10"	190	24	1	
Bobby Hunt	DB	6'1"	190	29	4	
Charlie King	DB	6'	184	26		
Ken Riley	DB	6'	182	22	4	
Fletcher Smith	DB	6'2"	178	25	4	
Jim Williams	DB	6'1"	190	23		
Greg Cook	QB	6'3"	212	22		6
Sam Wyche	QB	6'4"	210	24		6
Essex Johnson	HB	5'9"	190	22		
Paul Robinson	HB	6'	200	24		24
Ron Lamb	FB	6'2"	225	25		
Clem Turner	FB	6'1"	245	24		
Jess Phillips	HB-FB	6'1"	205	22		18
Eric Crabtree	WR	5'11"	182	24		42
Jack Gehrke	WR	6'	178	23		
Chip Myers	WR	6'4"	200	24		12
Tommie Smith	WR	6'4"	190	25		
Speedy Thomas	WR	6'1"	175	22		24
Bruce Coslet	TE	6'3"	225	23		6
Bob Trumpy	WR-TE	6'6"	220	24		54
Dale Livingston	K	6'	210	24		
Horst Muhlman	K	6'1"	210	29		80
Terry Swanson	K	6'	210	24		

Frank Buncom –Died Sept. 14, 1969 from pulmonary embolism

OAKLAND RAIDERS

RUSHING

Last Name	No.	Yds	Avg	TD
Smith	177	600	3.4	2
Dixon	107	398	3.7	0
Banaszak	88	377	4.3	0
Todd	47	198	4.2	1
Hubbard	21	119	5.7	0
Lamonica	13	36	2.8	1
Wells	3	24	8.0	0
Eischeid	1	10	10.0	0
Hagberg	1	3	3.0	0
Blanda	1	0	0.0	0

RECEIVING

Last Name	No.	Yds	Avg	TD
Biletnikoff	54	837	15	12
Wells	47	1260	27	14
Dixon	33	275	8	1
Smith	30	322	11	2
Cannon	21	262	12	2
Banaszak	17	119	7	3
Todd	16	149	9	1
Hagberg	6	84	14	1
Hubbard	2	30	15	0
Buie	1	37	37	0

PUNT RETURNS

Last Name	No.	Yds	Avg	TD
Atkinson	25	153	6	0
Sherman	9	46	5	0
Grayson	4	28	7	0
Allen	1	−2	−2	0

KICKOFF RETURNS

Last Name	No.	Yds	Avg	TD
Atkinson	16	382	24	0
Sherman	12	300	25	0
Smith	10	247	25	0
Allen	3	67	22	0
Benson	1	0	0	0

PASSING – PUNTING – KICKING

PASSING	Att	Comp	%	Yds	Yd/Att	TD	Int–	%	RK
Lamonica	426	221	52	3302	7.8	34	25–	6	3
Blanda	13	6	46	73	5.6	2	1–	8	

PUNTING	No	Avg
Eischeid	69	42.7

KICKING	XP	Att	%	FG	Att	%
Blanda	45	45	100	20	37	54

KANSAS CITY CHIEFS

RUSHING

Last Name	No.	Yds	Avg	TD
Garrett	168	732	4.4	6
Holmes	150	612	4.1	2
McVea	106	500	4.7	7
Hayes	62	208	3.4	4
Livingston	15	102	6.8	0
Lowe	10	33	3.3	0
Pitts	5	28	5.6	0
Dawson	1	3	3.0	0
Lee	1	3	3.0	0
Arbanas	1	1	1.0	0
Flores	1	0	0.0	0
Taylor	2	−2	−1.0	0

RECEIVING

Last Name	No.	Yds	Avg	TD
Garrett	43	432	10	2
Taylor	41	696	17	7
Pitts	31	470	15	2
Holmes	26	266	10	3
Richardson	23	381	17	2
Arbanas	16	258	16	0
Hayes	9	64	7	0
McVea	7	71	10	0

PUNT RETURNS

Last Name	No.	Yds	Avg	TD
Smith	9	107	12	0
Mitchell	13	101	8	0
Garrett	8	28	4	0
Sellers	2	15	8	0

KICKOFF RETURNS

Last Name	No.	Yds	Avg	TD
McVea	13	318	24	0
Mitchell	7	178	25	0
Podolak	7	165	24	0
Smith	4	125	31	0
Lowe	5	116	23	0
Hayes	2	81	41	0
Holmes	2	54	27	0
Bell	1	53	53	1

PASSING – PUNTING – KICKING

PASSING	Att	Comp	%	Yds	Yd/Att	TD	Int–	%	RK
Dawson	166	98	59	1323	8.0	9	13–	8	6
Livingston	161	84	52	1123	7.0	4	6–	4	4
Lee	20	12	60	109	5.5	1	1–	5	
Flores	6	3	50	49	8.2	1	0–	0	
McVea	3	1	33	50	16.7	1	0–	0	

PUNTING	No	Avg
Wilson	68	44.4

KICKING	XP	Att	%	FG	Att	%
Stenerud	38	38	100	27	35	77

SAN DIEGO CHARGERS

RUSHING

Last Name	No.	Yds	Avg	TD
Post	182	873	4.8	6
Hubbert	94	333	3.5	4
Foster	64	236	3.7	0
Smith	51	211	4.1	2
Domres	19	145	7.6	4
Hadl	26	109	4.2	2
Sayers	14	53	3.8	0
Alworth	5	25	5.0	0

RECEIVING

Last Name	No.	Yds	Avg	TD
Alworth	64	1003	16	4
Garrison	40	804	20	7
Post	24	235	10	0
Frazier	17	205	12	0
Foster	14	83	6	1
Hubbert	11	43	4	0
Queen	10	148	15	0
Smith	10	144	14	0
Eber	9	141	16	1
MacKinnon	7	82	12	0
Trapp	2	39	20	0

PUNT RETURNS

Last Name	No.	Yds	Avg	TD
Duncan	27	280	10	0
Graham	3	15	5	0
Smith	1	5	5	0

KICKOFF RETURNS

Last Name	No.	Yds	Avg	TD
Duncan	21	587	28	0
Smith	6	138	23	0
Post	4	74	19	0
Sayers	2	42	21	0
Foster	1	1	1	0
Fetherston	3	0	0	0
Briggs	1	0	0	0
Huey	1	0	0	0

PASSING – PUNTING – KICKING

PASSING	Att	Comp	%	Yds	Yd/Att	TD	Int–	%	RK
Hadl	324	158	49	2253	7.0	10	11–	3	5
Domres	112	47	42	631	5.6	2	10–	9	
Foster	5	2	40	39	7.8	1	0–	0	
Post	2	1	50	4	2.0	0	0–	0	
Hubbert	1	0	0	0	0.0	0	0–	0	

PUNTING	No	Avg
Partee	71	44.6

KICKING	XP	Att	%	FG	Att	%
Partee	33	33	100	15	28	54

DENVER BRONCOS

RUSHING

Last Name	No.	Yds	Avg	TD
Little	146	729	5.0	6
Lynch	96	407	4.2	2
Quayle	57	183	3.2	0
Smiley	56	166	3.0	3
Tensi	12	63	5.3	0
Liske	10	50	5.0	0
Williams	10	18	1.8	1
Denson	1	9	9.0	0
Burnett	5	9	1.8	0
Jones	1	3	3.0	0

RECEIVING

Last Name	No.	Yds	Avg	TD
Denson	53	809	15	10
Haffner	35	563	16	5
Embree	29	469	16	5
Little	19	218	11	1
Quayle	11	167	15	0
Beer	9	200	22	0
Pivic	9	117	13	0
Lynch	9	86	10	0
Williams	5	56	11	0
Smiley	5	23	5	1
Buckman	4	48	12	1
Van Heusen	3	64	21	0
Pastrana	1	15	15	0

PUNT RETURNS

Last Name	No.	Yds	Avg	TD
Thompson	25	288	12	0
Little	6	70	12	0
Burrell	5	56	11	0
Greer	1	36	36	0

KICKOFF RETURNS

Last Name	No.	Yds	Avg	TD
Williams	23	574	25	0
Thompson	18	513	29	0
Burrell	6	108	18	0
Little	3	81	27	0
Criter	3	31	10	0
Barnes	1	16	16	0
Hollomon	1	0	0	0
Myrtle	1	0	0	0

PASSING – PUNTING – KICKING

PASSING	Att	Comp	%	Yds	Yd/Att	TD	Int–	%	RK
Tensi	286	131	46	1990	7.0	14	12–	4	7
Liske	115	61	53	845	7.4	9	11–	10	
Little	2	0	0	0	0.0	0	0–	0	

PUNTING	No	Avg
Holloman	47	39.7
Van Heusen	25	40.8

KICKING	XP	Att	%	FG	Att	%
Howfield	36	37	97	13	29	45

CINCINNATI BENGALS

RUSHING

Last Name	No.	Yds	Avg	TD
Phillips	118	578	4.9	3
Robinson	160	489	3.1	4
Cook	25	148	5.9	1
Wyche	12	107	8.9	1
Turner	23	105	4.6	0
E. Johnson	15	54	3.6	0
Livingston	1	18	18.0	0
Thomas	4	16	4.0	1
Lamb	5	8	1.6	0

RECEIVING

Last Name	No.	Yds	Avg	TD
Crabtree	40	855	21	7
Trumpy	37	835	23	9
Thomas	33	481	15	3
Robinson	20	104	5	0
Phillips	13	128	10	0
Myers	10	205	21	2
Turner	5	14	3	0
Riley	2	15	8	0
T. Smith	1	41	41	0
Coslet	1	39	39	1
E. Johnson	1	3	3	0

PUNT RETURNS

Last Name	No.	Yds	Avg	TD
E. Johnson	17	85	5	0
Thomas	4	15	4	0
Coleman	1	0	0	0
Guillory	1	0	0	0
King	0	35	0	0

KICKOFF RETURNS

Last Name	No.	Yds	Avg	TD
E. Johnson	16	362	23	0
Riley	14	334	24	0
Guillory	8	170	21	0
Robinson	5	168	34	0
Lamb	5	64	13	0
Phillips	3	52	17	0
Turner	3	15	15	0
Gunner	1	0	0	0

PASSING – PUNTING – KICKING

PASSING	Att	Comp	%	Yds	Yd/Att	TD	Int–	%	RK
Cook	197	106	54	1854	9.4	15	11–	6	1
Wyche	108	54	50	838	7.8	7	4–	4	
Livingston	2	2	100	15	7.5	0	0–	0	
Gehrke	1	1	100	13	13.0	0	0–	0	

PUNTING	No	Avg
Livingston	70	39.6
Swanson	12	38.3
Muhlmann	2	19.0
Lamb	1	29.0

KICKING	XP	Att	%	FG	Att	%
Muhlmann	32	33	97	16	24	67

1969 NFL CHAMPIONSHIP GAME

January 4, 1970 at Minnesota
(Attendance 46,503)

SCORING

MINNESOTA	14	10	3	0	–27
CLEVELAND	0	0	0	7	– 7

First Quarter		
Min.	Kapp, 7 yard rush PAT–Cox (kick)	3:48
Min.	Washington, 75 yard pass from Kapp PAT–Cox (kick)	7:07
Second Quarter		
Min.	Cox, 30 yard field goal	1:07
Min.	Osborn, 20 yard rush PAT–Cox (kick)	10:15
Third Quarter		
Min.	Cox, 32 yard field goal	11:18
Fourth Quarter		
Cle.	Collins, 3 yard pass from Nelsen PAT–Cockroft (kick)	1:24

TEAM STATISTICS

MINN.		CLEVE.
18	First Downs–Total	14
13	First Downs–Rushing	4
5	First Downs–Passing	10
0	First Downs–Penalty	0
0	Fumbles–Number	2
0	Fumbles–Lost Ball	1
3	Penalties–Number	1
33	Yards Penalized	5
0	Giveaways	3
3	Takeaways	0
+3	Difference	–3

Viking Heat

The Browns had beaten the Cowboys 38-14 in the first round of the playoffs with a tight pass defense and sharp passing by Bill Nelsen, and they hoped to pull another upset over the Vikings in the NFL title match. The Vikings had crushed the Browns 51-3 in a regular-season meeting and had disposed of the powerful Los Angeles Rams 23-20 with a fourth-quarter rally in last week's opening playoff game, and their superb defense made them favorites for this game.

Conditions for the game were typical of Minnesota in January. Snow ringed the field, and 8-degree temperature chilled the spectators through their layers of clothing. The Browns suffered from the cold, resorting to heaters and special footgear to combat it, but the Vikings used no heaters at all. Coach Bud Grant said, "we generate our own heat."

On the first series of the game, the Browns showed their discomfort in this weather. Cornerback Walt Sumner slipped and fell while covering Viking receiver Gene Washington, and Joe Kapp hit his man with a pass good for 33 yards down to the Cleveland 24-yard line. The Vikings moved down to the 7-yard line, and Kapp scored on a play characteristic of his rough style. He bumped into fullback Bill Brown in his backfield, then stormed straight ahead and broke several tackles on his way to the end zone. Several minutes later, Cleveland cornerback Erich Barnes lost his footing and fell while covering Washington, and Kapp whipped a pass which the end carried 75 yards for a second Minnesota touchdown. Trailing 14-0 and fully aware that the Minnesota defense allowed its opponents an average of only ten points a game, the Browns looked like a beaten team before the first quarter had ended. With the Viking defense keeping the Cleveland attack bottled up all afternoon, Minnesota won the game 27-7 and the NFL championship in the team's ninth year of operation.

INDIVIDUAL STATISTICS

MINNESOTA	No	Yds	Avg.	CLEVELAND	No	Yds	Avg.
RUSHING							
Osborn	18	108	6.0	Kelly	15	80	5.3
Kapp	8	57	7.1	Scott	6	17	2.8
Brown	12	43	3.6		21	97	4.6
Reed	5	7	1.4				
Jones	2	7	3.5				
	45	222	4.9				
RECEIVING							
Washington	3	120	40.0	Scott	5	56	11.2
Henderson	2	17	8.5	Collins	5	43	8.6
Brown	1	20	20.0	Warfield	4	47	11.8
Beasley	1	12	12.0	Kelly	2	17	8.5
	7	169	24.1	Morin	1	18	18.0
					17	181	10.6
PUNTING							
Lee	3		41.0	Cockroft	3		33.0
PUNT RETURNS							
West	1	1	1.0	Kelly	2	10	5.0
				Morrison	1	11	11.0
					3	21	7.0
KICKOFF RETURNS							
West	1	22	22.0	Scott	4	60	15.0
Jones	1	20	20.0	Morrison	1	23	23.0
	2	42	21.0		5	83	16.6
INTERCEPTION RETURNS							
Hilgenberg	1	0	0.0	None			
Krause	1	0	0.0				
	2	0	0.0				

PASSING

	Att.	Comp.	Comp. Pct.	Yds.	Int.	Yds/ Att.	Yds/ Comp.	Yards Lost Tackled
MINNESOTA								
Kapp	13	7	53.8	169	0	13.0	24.1	1– 8
CLEVELAND								
Nelsen	33	17	51.5	181	2	5.5	10.6	2–10

1969 AFL CHAMPIONSHIP GAME

January 4, 1970 at Oakland
(Attendance 53,564)

SCORING

OAKLAND	7	0	0	0	– 7
KANSAS CITY	0	7	7	3	–17

First Quarter		
Oak.	Smith, 3 yard rush PAT–Blanda (kick)	14:14
Second Quarter		
K.C.	Hayes, 1 yard rush PAT–Stenerud (kick)	13:10
Third Quarter		
K.C.	Holmes, 5 yard rush PAT–Stenerud (kick)	11:17
Fourth Quarter		
K.C.	Stenerud, 22 yard field goal	10:12

TEAM STATISTICS

OAK.		K.C.
18	First Downs–Total	13
6	First Downs–Rushing	5
10	First Downs–Passing	6
2	First Downs–Penalty	2
1	Fumbles–Number	5
0	Fumbles–Lost Ball	4
5	Penalties–Number	5
45	Yards Penalized	43
4	Giveaways	4
4	Takeaways	4
0	Difference	0

Finishing First When It Counts

The AFL installed a new playoff system for its final season, pitting the first-place finishers against the runners-up in the opposite division, with the winners playing for the league crown. The result was that two Western clubs met in the title game, as the first-place Raiders clobbered Houston 56-7 while the second-place Chiefs upset the New York Jets 13-6.

While the Raiders took a 7-0 lead on Charlie Smith's touchdown late in the first period, Kansas City passer Len Dawson found the Oakland defense hard to crack, as he missed on seven straight passes. Late in the second quarter, however, he hit Frank Pitts with a 41-yard bomb which brought the ball to the Oakland 1-yard line. From there, Wendell Hayes smashed over, and the Chiefs took a 7-7 tie into the locker room at halftime.

Early in the second half, Lamonica hurt his passing hand against the helmet of Aaron Brown and could not grip the ball properly the rest of the game. George Blanda relieved Lamonica at quarterback but had no miracles up his sleeve today. In addition to missing three field-goal attempts, he could not stand up under the Kansas City pass rush and saw one of his passes intercepted in the end zone. After intercepting Blanda's pass, Emmitt Thomas had run it out to the 6-yard line. Dawson then moved his team downfield through the air. Otis Taylor and Robert Holmes caught passes for long gains, and a pass interference penalty on the Raiders gave the Chiefs a first down on the Oakland 7. Holmes carried the ball three straight times to reach the end zone and put the Chiefs ahead 14-7.

Sore hand and all, Lamonica returned to the lineup in the final period, but three of his crippled passes were picked off by the Chiefs, who won the game 17-7 and headed off to the Super Bowl despite finishing second behind the Raiders in the regular season.

INDIVIDUAL STATISTICS

OAKLAND	No	Yds	Avg.	KANSAS CITY	No	Yds	Avg.
RUSHING							
Dixon	12	36	3.0	Hayes	8	35	4.4
Smith	12	31	2.6	Garrett	7	19	2.7
Banaszak	2	8	4.0	Holmes	18	14	0.8
Todd	2	4	2.0	McVea	3	13	4.3
	28	79	2.8	Dawson	3	5	1.7
					39	86	2.2
RECEIVING							
Smith	8	86	10.8	Taylor	3	62	20.7
Sherman	3	45	15.0	Holmes	2	16	8.0
Cannon	2	22	11.0	Pitts	1	41	41.0
Banaszak	2	13	6.5	Arbanas	1	10	10.0
Wells	1	24	24.0		7	129	18.4
Dixon	1	1	1.0				
	17	191	11.2				
PUNTING							
Eischeid	6		48.5	Wilson	8		42.9
PUNT RETURNS							
Atkinson	2	–1	–0.5	Garrett	4	9	2.3
KICKOFF RETURNS							
Atkinson	3	95	31.7	Holmes	1	26	26.0
Sherman	1	17	17.0	Hill	1	0	0.0
	4	112	28.0	Hayes	Lat	17	–
					2	43	21.5
INTERCEPTION RETURNS							
None				Thomas	2	69	34.5
				Marsalis	1	23	23.0
				Kearney	1	17	17.0
					4	109	27.3

PASSING

	Att.	Comp.	Comp. Pct.	Yds.	Int.	Yds/ Att.	Yds/ Comp.	Yards Lost Tackled
OAKLAND								
Lamonica	39	15	38.5	167	3	4.3	11.1	
Blanda	6	2	33.3	24	1	4.0	12.0	
	45	17	37.8	191	4	4.2	11.2	4–37
KANSAS CITY								
Dawson	17	7	41.2	129	0	7.6	18.4	1– 8

SUPER BOWL IV

January 11, at New Orleans

(Attendance 80,562)

An Upsetting Farewell

All of the Kansas City Chiefs wore a patch on their jerseys saying "AFL-10." This referred to the ten-year existence of the AFL, which would fade into oblivion after this game and the AFL All-Star Game a week later. As things turned out, the Chiefs took the AFL out in style by handily beating the NFL champion Minnesota Vikings.

It didn't figure. The Vikings had bullied their way through the NFL with a frightening defense, led by the front four of Jim Marshall, Carl Eller, Alan Page, and Gary Larsen and a ball-control attack paced by tough quarterback Joe Kapp. Odds-makers branded the Vikings as two-touchdown favorites to return the Super Bowl title to the NFL after a year in the possession of the AFL New York Jets.

The Chiefs had been to the Super Bowl before, however, and knew how to prepare better for the fanfare. While the Vikings were awed by the hubbub in New Orleans during the week before the game, the Chiefs seriously set about to avenge their loss to Green Bay in Super Bowl I.

The "I" formation that Kansas City used, concealing the position of their backs until the last moment before the play, gave the Minnesota defense some problems right from the start. The Chiefs assigned two men each to block Marshall and Eller, and this move gave the Kansas City backs room to run. Quarterback Len Dawson also found the Viking zone pass coverage less difficult than had been imagined, and he would complete twelve of seventeen passes through the afternoon.

The Kansas City defensive linemen, meanwhile, were putting hot pressure on Joe Kapp, forcing him to hurry his passes. While the defense harassed Kapp in the first period, Jan Stenerud booted a 48 yard field goal to put the Chiefs ahead 3-0.

The second quarter went no better for the Viking attack as the Chiefs scored 13 points to break the game open. Stenerud kicked another field goal, Mike Garrett scored a touchdown after the Vikings had fumbled deep in their own territory, and Stenerud's third field goal made the score 16-0 at halftime.

The Vikings came out for the second half ready to climb back into the game, and Kapp immediately led them on a 69-yard drive that led to the Vikings' first touchdown. But the Vikes could not score again, and Otis Taylor's brilliant 46-yard run with a short pass made the final score only a little worse, 23-7, in favor of the Chiefs and, for the final time, the AFL.

KANSAS CITY		MINNESOTA
	OFFENSE	
Pitts	WR	Washington
Tyrer	LT	Alderman
Budde	LG	Vellone
Holub	C	Tingelhoff
Moorman	RG	Sunde
Hill	RT	Yary
Arbanas	TE	Beasley
Taylor	WR	Henderson
Dawson	QB	Kapp
Garrett	RB	Osborn
Holmes	RB	B. Brown
	DEFENSE	
Mays	LE	Eller
Culp	LT	Larsen
Buchanan	RT	Page
A. Brown	RE	Marshall
Bell	LLB	Winston
Lanier	MLB	Warwick
Lynch	RLB	Hilgenberg
Marsalis	LCB	Mackbee
Thomas	RCB	Sharockman
Kearney	LS	Kassulke
Robinson	RS	Krause

SUBSTITUTES

KANSAS CITY

Offense

Daney	McVea
Hayes	Podolak
Livingston	Prudhomme
McClinton	Richardson

Defense

Belser	Sellers
Hurston	Stein
Lothamer	Trosch
Mitchell	

Kickers

Stenerud	Wilson

MINNESOTA

Offense

Cuozzo	Lee
Grim	Lindsey
Harris	Reed
Jones	Smith
Kramer	White

Defense

Dickson	McGill
Hackbart	West
Hargrove	

Kicker

Cox

SCORING

KANSAS CITY	3	13	7	0–23
MINNESOTA	0	0	7	0– 7

First Quarter

K.C.	Stenerud, 48 yard field goal

Second Quarter

K.C.	Stenerud, 32 yard field goal
K.C.	Stenerud, 25 yard field goal
K.C.	Garrett, 5 yard rush
	PAT – Stenerud (kick)

Third Quarter

Minn.	Osborn, 4 yard rush
	PAT – Cox (kick)
K.C.	Taylor, 46 yard pass from Dawson
	PAT – Stenerud (kick)

TEAM STATISTICS

K. C.		MINN.
18	First Downs – Total	13
8	First Downs – Rushing	2
7	First Downs – Passing	10
3	First Downs – Penalty	1
0	Fumbles – Number	3
0	Fumbles – Lost Ball	2
4	Penalties – Number	6
47	Yards Penalized	67
62	Total Offensive Plays	50
273	Total Net Yards	239
4.4	Average Gain	4.8
0	Missed Field Goals	1
1	Giveaways	5
5	Takeaways	1
+4	Difference	–4

INDIVIDUAL STATISTICS

KANSAS CITY	No	Yds	Avg.	MINNESOTA	No	Yds	Avg.
RUSHING							
Garrett	11	39	3.5	Brown	6	26	4.3
Pitts	3	37	12.3	Reed	4	17	4.3
Hayes	8	31	3.9	Osborn	7	15	2.1
McVea	12	26	2.2	Kapp	2	9	4.5
Dawson	3	11	3.7		19	67	3.5
Holmes	5	7	1.4				
	42	151	3.6				
RECEIVING							
Taylor	6	81	13.5	Henderson	7	111	15.9
Pitts	3	33	11.0	Brown	3	11	3.7
Garrett	2	25	12.5	Beasley	2	41	20.5
Hayes	1	3	3.0	Reed	2	16	8.0
	12	142	11.8	Osborn	2	11	5.5
				Washington	1	9	9.0
					17	199	11.7
PUNTING							
Wilson	4		48.5	Lee	3		37.0
PUNT RETURNS							
Garrett	1	0	0.0	West	2	18	9.0
KICKOFF RETURNS							
Hayes	2	36	18.0	West	3	46	15.3
				Jones	1	33	33.0
					4	79	19.8
INTERCEPTION RETURNS							
Lanier	1	9	9.0	Krause	1	0	0.0
Robinson	1	9	9.0				
Thomas	1	6	6.0				
	3	24	8.0				

PASSING

KANSAS CITY	Att	Comp	Comp Pct.	Yds	Int	Yds/ Att.	Yds/ Comp	Yards Lost Tackled
Dawson	17	12	70.6	142	1	8.4	11.8	3–20
MINNESOTA								
Kapp	25	16	64.0	183	2	7.3	11.4	
Cuozzo	3	1	33.3	16	1	5.3	16.0	
	28	17	60.7	199	3	7.1	11.7	3–27

Use Name (Nicknames) – Positions	Team by Year	See Section	Hgt	Wgt	College	Int	Pts
Abell, Bud LB	66-68KC-A		6'3"	220	Missouri	2	
Abruzzese, Ray DB	62-64BufA 65-66NY-A		6'1"	194	Alabama	10	
Absher, Dick LB	67Was 67-68Atl 69-71NO 72Phi		6'4"	231	Maryland	3	4
Adamchik, Ed C	65NYG 65Pit		6'2"	235	Pittsburgh		
Adams, John FB-OE	59-62ChiB 63LA	2	6'3"	235	Los Angeles State		24
Adams, Tom OE	62Min		6'5"	210	Minnesota-Duluth		
Adams, Willie LB-DE	65-66Was		6'2"	235	New Mexico State		
Adamson, Ken OG	60-62DenA		6'2"	222	Notre Dame		
Adderly, Herb DB	61-69GB 70-72Dal	3	6'1"	204	Michigan State	48	54
Addison, Tom LB	60-67BosA		6'3"	231	South Carolina	16	6
Akin, Howard OT	67-68SD-A		6'5"	261	Oklahoma State		
Alderman, Grady OT-OG	60Det 61-74Min		6'2"	242	Detroit		
Aldridge, Lionel DE	63-71GB 72-73SD		6'4"	245	Utah State		6
Alexander, Kermit DB	63-69SF 70-71LA 72-73Phi	3	5'11"	185	U.C.L.A.	43	36
Alfen, Ted HB	69DenA		6'	195	Springfield		
Alford, Bruce K	67Was 68-69BufA	5	6'	185	Texas Christian		134
Alford, Mike C	65StL 66Det		6'3"	233	Auburn		
Allard, Don QB	61NY-A 61BosA		6'	189	Boston College		
Allen, Buddy HB	61DenA		5'10"	190	Utah State		
Allen, Chuck LB	61-69SD-A 70-71Pit 72Phi		6'1"	224	Washington	28	12
Allen, Dalva DE	60-61HouA 62-64OakA		6'5"	224	Houston	1	
Allen, Don FB	60DenA	2	6'	200	Texas		6
Allen, Duane OE-TE	61-64LA 65Pit 65Bal 66-67ChiB	2	6'4"	221	Santa Ana J.C.		30
Allen, George OT	66HouA		6'7"	270	West Texas State		
Allen, Jerry HB	66Bal 67-69Was	2	6'1"	204	Nebraska-Omaha		54
Alley, Don WR-FL	67Bal 69Pit		6'2"	200	Adams State		
Allison, Jim FB	65-68SD-A	2	6'	220	San Diego State		12
Alliston, Vaughan LB	60DenA		6'	218	Mississippi	1	
Alworth, Lance (Bambi) FL-WR-OE	62-69SD-A 70SD 71-72Dal	23	6'	182	Arkansas		524
Amerson, Glen DB	61Phi		6'1"	186	Texas Tech		
Ames, Dave HB-DB	61NY-A 61DenA		6'	185	Richmond	1	
Amsler, Marty DE	67ChiB 68JJ 69ChiB 70GB		6'5"	257	Indiana, Evansville	1	
Anderson, Art OT	61-62ChiB 63Pit		6'3"	244	Idaho		
Anderson, Bill OE-TE	58-63Was 65-66GB	2	6'3"	211	Tennessee		90
Anderson, Billy QB	67HouA		6'1"	195	Tulsa		
Anderson, Bob HB	63NYG		6'2"	210	Army		
Anderson, Bruce DE-DT	66LA 67-69NYG 70Was		6'4"	246	Williamette		
Anderson, Chet TE	67Pit		6'3"	245	Minnesota		12
Anderson, Dick OT	67NO		6'5"	245	Ohio State		2
Anderson, Max HB	68-69BufA 70KJ 71Buf	23	5'8"	180	Arizona State		24
Anderson, Ralph OE	58ChiB 60LA-A	2	6'4"	223	Los Angeles State		36
died Nov. 26, 1960—diabetes							
Anderson, Roger DT-OT	64-65NYG 66CFL 67-68NYG		6'5"	263	Virginia Union	1	
Anderson, Taz OE-TE	61-64StL 66-67Atl	2	6'2"	208	Georgia Tech		60
Andrie, George DE	62-72Dal		6'7"	252	Marquette	1	14
Andrus, Lou LB	67DenA		6'6"	255	Brigham Young		
Antwine, Houston DT	61-69BosA 70Bos 71NE 72Phi		6'	265	Southern Illinois	1	
Apple, Jim HB	61NY-A		6'	200	Upsala		
Appleton, Scott DT	64-66HouA 67-68SD-A		6'3"	254	Texas	2	6
Arbanas, Fred TE-OE	62DalA 63-69KC-A 70KC	2	6'3"	240	Michigan State		206
Archer, Dan OG-OT	67OakA 68CinA		6'5"	245	Oregon		
Armstrong, Ray DT	60OakA		6'1"	235	Texas Christian		
Arndt, Dick DT	67-70Pit		6'5"	265	Idaho		
Arnett, Jon HB-FL-OE	57-63LA 64-66ChiB	123	5'11"	197	Southern Calif.		234
Arrobio, Chuck OT	66Min		6'4"	250	Southern Calif.		
Asad, Doug OE	60-61OakA	2	6'3"	203	Northwestern		18
Asbury, Willie FB	66-68Pit	2	6'1"	230	Kent State		78
Atchason, Jack OE	60BosA 60HouA		6'4"	215	Western Illinois		6
Atkins, Billy DB-HB	58-59SF 60-61BufA	45	6'1"	196	Auburn	20	86
	62-63NY-A 63BufA 64DenA						
Atkins, Doug DE	53-54Cle 55-66ChiB 67-69NO		6'8"	257	Tennessee	3	2
Atkins, Pervis HB-FL-OE	61-63LA 64-65Was 65-66OakA	23	6'1"	200	New Mexico State		18
Atkinson, Frank DT	63Pit		6'3"	240	Stanford		
Auer, Joe HB	64-65BufA 66-67MiaA 68Atl	23	6'1"	204	Georgia Tech		
Autry, Hank C	69HouA 70Hou		6'3"	233	Southern Miss.		
Aveni, John OE-K	59-60ChiB 61Was	5	6'3"	212	Indiana		144
Avery, Jim TE	68Was		6'2"	235	Northern Illinois		
Avezzano, Joe C	66BosA		6'2"	235	Florida State		
Babb, Gene FB-LB	57-58SF 60-61Dal 62-63HouA	2	6'3"	216	Austin	4	30
Baccaglio, Marty DE	68SD-A 68-69CinA 70Cin		6'3"	245	San Jose State		
Bachman, Jay C	68-69DenA 70-71Den		6'3"	250	Cincinnati		
Badar, Rich QB	67Pit		6'1"	190	Indiana		
Bailey, Monk DB	64-65StL		6'	178	Utah		
Bailey, Teddy HB	67BufA 69BosA		6'	210	Cincinnati		
Baird, Bill DB-HB	63-69NY-A	3	5'10"	180	San Fran. State	34	18
Baker, Art FB	61-62BufA	2	6'	220	Syracuse		24
Baker, Dave DB	59-61SF 62-63MS		6'	192	Oklahoma	21	
Baker, John DE-DT-OT	58-61LA 62Phi 63-67Pit 68Det		6'6"	279	N. Car. Central	2	
Baker, Johnny LB-DE	63-66HouA 67SD-A		5'3"	229	Mississippi State	2	6
Baker, Larry OT	60NY-A		6'2"	240	Bowling Green		
Baker, Ralph LB	64-69NY-A 70-74NYJ		6'3"	232	Penn State	19	13
Baker, Sam FB-K	53Was 54-55MS 56-59Was	2 45	6'2"	217	Oregon State		977
	60-61Cle 62-63Dal 64-69Phi						
Baker, Terry HB-QB	63-65LA	2	6'3"	198	Oregon State		18
Bakken, Jim K	62-78StL	45	6'	199	Wisconsin		1380
Baldwin, Bob HB-FB	66Bal		6'1"	225	Clemson		
Ball, Sam OT	66-70Bal		6'4"	240	Kentucky		
Ballman, Gary WR-FL-OE-TE-HB	62-66Pit 67-72Phi	23	6'	203	Michigan State		252
	72NYG 73Min						
Bandy, Don OG	67-68Was		6'3"	250	Tulsa		
Banfield, Tony DB	60-63,65HouA		6'1"	185	Oklahoma State	27	6
Banks, Estes FB-HB	67OakA 68CinA	2	6'1"	210	Colorado		
Bansavage, Al LB	60LA-A 61OakA		6'2"	225	Southern Calif.		
Barbee, Joe DT	60OakA		6'3"	250	Kent State		
Barber, Rudy LB	68MiaA		6'1"	255	Bethune-Cookman		
Barber, Stew OT-LB	61-69BufA		6'3"	247	Penn State	3	6
Barefoot, Ken TE	68Was		6'5"	228	Virginia Tech		6
Barnes, Billy HB	57-61Phi 62-63Was 65-66Min	12	5'11"	201	Wake Forest		228
Barnes, Charlie OE	61DalA		6'5"	230	Northeast La.		
Barnes, Erich DB	58-60ChiB 61-64NYG 65-71Cle		6'2"	201	Purdue	45	60
Barnes, Ernie OG-OT	60NY-A 61-62SD-A 63-64DenA		6'3"	250	N. Car. Central		
Barnes, Gary OE-FL	62GB 63Dal 64ChiB 66-67Atl	2	6'4"	210	Clemson		12
Barnes, Mike DB	67-68StL		6'3"	205	Texas-Arlington		
Barnes, Walt DE-DT	66-68Was 69DenA 70-71Den 72JJ		6'3"	250	Nebraska		
Barnett, Steve OT	63ChiB 64Was		6'1"	255	Oregon		
Barney, Eppie WR-FL	67-68Cle	2	6'	201	Iowa State		12
Barr, Terry FL-DB-HB	57-65Det	23	6'	189	Michigan	5	228
Barrett, Bob OE	60BufA		6'3"	200	Baldwin-Wallace		
Barrett, Jan OE	63GB 63-64OakA	2	6'3"	226	Fresno State		12
Barrington, Tom HB-FB	66Was 67-70NO	23	6'1"	214	Ohio State		24
Barry, Odell OE	64-65DenA	3	5'10"	180	Findlay		6
Barton, Greg QB	69Det 71-72CFL 74WFL		6'2"	195	Tulsa		
Barton, Jim C	60DalA 61-62DenA		6'5"	250	Marshall		
Bass, Dick FB-HB	60-69LA	23	5'10"	197	U. of Pacific		252
Bass, Glenn OE-HB-FL-WR	61-66BufA 67-68HouA	2	6'2"	202	East Carolina		102
Bass, Norm DB	64DenA		6'3"	210	U. of Pacific		
61-63 played major league baseball							
Bates, Ted LB	59ChiC 60-62StL 63NY-A		6'3"	219	Oregon State		
Batten, Pat FB	64Det		6'2"	225	Hardin-Simmons		
Battle, Jim OG	63Min		6'1"	240	Southern Illinois		
Battle, Jim OT	66Cle		6'4"	235	Southern U.		
Battle, Mike DB	69NY-A 70NYJ	3	6'1"	175	Southern Calif.	1	
Baughan, Maxie LB	60-65Phi 66-70LA		6'1"	227	Georgia Tech	18	6
Baynham, Craig HB	67-69Dal 70ChiB 71JJ 72StL	23	6'1"	204	Georgia Tech		54
Beach, Walter DB	60-61BosA 63-66Cle		6'	184	Central Michigan	6	12
Beal, Norm DB	62StL		5'11"	170	Missouri		
Beans, Byron OT-DT	59-60Pit 61HouA		6'6"	249	Notre Dame		
Beard, Ed LB	65-72SF		6'2"	225	Tennessee	3	
Beathard, Pete QB	64-67KC-A 67-69HouA 70-71StL	12	6'2"	205	Southern Calif.		68
	72LA 73KC 74-75WFL 75Oak						
Beaver, Jim DT	62Phi		6'1"	235	Florida		
Beban, Gary QB-HB-WR	68-69Was		6'1"	195	U.C.L.A.		
Bedsole, Hal TE-OE	64-66Min 67JJ	2	6'4"	230	Southern Calif.		48
Beer, Tom TE-OG	67-69DenA 70Bos 71-72NE	2	6'4"	232	Houston		24
Behrman, Dave OT-C	63,65BufA 67DenA		6'5"	260	Michigan State		
Beier, Tom DB-FL	67,69MiaA		5'11"	198	Georgia Tech	2	
Beldon, Bob QB	69-70Dal		6'2"	208	Notre Dame		
Bell, Bobby LB-DE	63-69KC-A 70-74KC		6'4"	228	Minnesota	26	54
Bell Henry HB	60DenA	2	5'10"	210	none		
Bellino, Joe HB-FL	65-67BosA	23	5'9"	186	Navy		
Belotti, George C	60-61HouA 61SD-A		6'4"	253	Southern Calif.		
Bemiller, Al C-OG	61-69BufA		6'3"	243	Syracuse		
Bengston, Phil	HC68-70GB				Minnesota		
Bennett, Phil LB	60BosA		6'3"	225	Miami (Fla.)		
Benz, Larry DB	63-65Cle		5'11"	185	Northwestern	16	
Bercich, Bob DB	60-61Dal		6'1"	198	Michigan State	5	
Bernet, Lee OT	65-66DenA		6'2"	245	Wisconsin		
Berry, Raymond OE	55-67Bal HC84-89NE	2	6'2"	189	S.M.U.		408
Bethune, Bob DB	62SD-A		5'11"	190	Mississippi State	3	
Bettridge, Ed LB	64Cle		6'1"	235	Bowling Green		
Beverly, Randy DB	67-69NY-A 70Bos 71NE		5'11"	189	Colorado State	12	6
Biodrowski, Denny OG	63-67KC-A		6'1"	255	Memphis State		
Bird, Rodger DB	66-68OakA	3	5'11"	195	Kentucky	7	6
Birdwell, Dan DT-DE	62-69OakA		6'4"	247	Houston	4	2
Bishop, Don DB-FL-HB	58-59Pit 59ChiB 60-65Dal		6'2"	209	Los Angeles City C.	22	6
Bishop, Sonny OG	62DalA 63OakA 64-69HouA		6'2"	243	Fresno State		
Bivins, Charlie HB-TE	60-66ChiB 67Pit 67BufA	23	6'2"	212	Morris Brown		36
Blaine, Ed OG	62GB 63-66Phi		6'2"	240	Missouri		
Blair, George DB	61-64SD-A	5	5'11"	194	Mississippi	5	272
Blanda, George QB-DB-LB-K	49-58ChiB 60-66HouA	12 5	6'1"	210	Kentucky	1	2000
	67-69OakA 70-75Oak						
Blanks, Sid HB	64HouA 65KJ 66-68HouA 69BosA 70Bos	23	6'	206	Texas A & I		66
Blazer, Phil OG	60BufA		6'1"	235	North Carolina		
Bleick, Tom DB	66Bal 67Atl		6'2"	200	Georgia Tech		
Blye (born Bliey), Ronnie HB	68NYG 69Phi	23	5'11"	185	Notre Dame, Florida A&M		6
Bobo, Hubert LB	60LA-A 61-62NY-A		6'1"	217	Ohio State		5
Boeke, Jim OT	60-63LA 64-67Dal 68NO		6'5"	250	Heidelberg		
Bohling, Dewey HB	60-61NY-A 61BufA	2	5'11"	190	Hardin-Simmons		54
Bohovich, Reed OG-OT	62NYG		6'3"	260	Lehigh		
Bolin, Bookie OG	62-67NYG 68-69Min		6'2"	240	Mississippi		
Bookman, Johnny DB	57NYG 60DalA 61NY-A		5'11"	182	Miami (Fla.)	13	6
Bosch, Frank DT	68-70Was		6'4"	246	Colorado		
Bosley, Bruce OG-C-DE	56-68SF 69Atl		6'2"	241	West Virginia		
Bosseler, Don FB	57-64Was	2	6'1"	212	Miami (Fla.)		138
Boston, McKinley DE-LB	68-69NYG		6'2"	245	Minnesota		
Botchan, Ron LB	60LA-A 61HouA		6'1"	234	Occidental	2	
Boudreaux, Jim OT-DE	66-68BosA		6'4"	245	Louisiana Tech		
Boutwell, Tommy WR-QB	69MiaA		6'2"	205	Southern Miss.		
Bowie, Larry OG	62-68Min		6'2"	247	Purdue		
Bowling, Andy LB	67Atl		6'3"	235	Virginia Tech		
Bowman, Ken C	64-73GB 74XJ		6'3"	230	Wisconsin		
Bowman, Steve HB	66NYG		6'	195	Alabama		
Boyd, Bobby DB-HB	60-68Bal		5'10"	190	Oklahoma	57	30
Boyette, Garland LB	62-63StL 66-69HouA 70-72Hou		6'1"	237	Grambling	2	6
Boylan, Jim FL	63Min		6'1"	185	Washington State		6
Boynton, George DB	62OakA		5'11"	190	East Texas State		
Boynton, John OT	69MiaA		6'4"	255	Tennessee		
Braase, Ordell DE	57-68Bal		6'4"	240	South Dakota		
Brabham, Danny LB	63-67HouA, 68CinA		6'4"	236	Arkansas	1	
Bradfute, Byron OT	60-61Dal		6'3"	243	Southern Miss.		
Bradshaw, Charlie OT	58-60LA 61-66Pit 67-68Det		6'6"	255	Baylor		
Bradshaw, Jim DB	63-67Pit		6'1"	199	Tenn.-Chatanooga	11	24
Brady, Phil DB	69DenA		6'2"	211	Brigham Young		
Bramlett, John LB	65-66DenA 67-68MiaA		6'2"	216	Memphis State	10	18
	69BosA 70Bos 71Atl						
Branch, Mel DE	60-62DalA 63-65KC-A 66-68MiaA		6'2"	231	Louisiana State		
Brannen, Solomon DB-HB	65-66KC-A 67NY-A		6'1"	188	Morris Brown		
Bratkowski, Zeke QB	54ChiB 55-56MS 57-60ChiB	12 4	6'4"	204	Georgia		30
	61-63LA 64-68GB 69-70VR 71GB						
Bravo, Alex DB	57-58LA 60-61OakA		6'	190	Cal. Poly-Pomona	6	
Braxton, Hez FB-HB	62SD-A 63BufA		6'2"	227	Virginia Union		8
Breaux, Don QB	63DenA 65SD-A	1	6'1"	203	McNeese State		
Breding, Ed LB	67-68Was		6'4"	235	Texas A&M		2
Breedlove, Rod LB	65-67Pit		6'2"	225	Maryland	11	
Breen, Gene LB	64GB 65-66Pit 67-68LA		6'2"	229	Virginia Tech		

Use Name (Nicknames) – Positions	Team by Year	See Section	Hgt	Wgt	College	Int	Pts
Breitenstein, Bob OT-OG	65-67DenA 67Min 69-70Atl		6'3"	264	Tulsa		
Brenner, Al DB	69-70NYG		6'1"	200	Michigan State		
Brewer, Billy DB	60Was		6'	190	Mississippi		
Brewer, Johnny LB-OE-TE-DE	61-67Cle 68-70NO	2	6'4"	233	Mississippi	3	42
Brewington, Jim OT	61OakA		6'6"	280	N. Car. Central		
Brezina, Bobby HB	63HouA		6'	200	Houston		
Briggs, Bill DE	66-67Was		6'3"	250	Iowa		
Briggs, Bob FB	65Was		6'1"	228	Central St.-Okla.		
Britt, Charley DB	60-63LA 64Min 64SF		6'2"	183	Georgia	14	6
Brittenum, Jon QB	68SD-A		6'	185	Arkansas		
Brock, Clyde OT	62-63Dal 63SF		6'5"	268	Utah State		
Brodhead, Bob QB	60BufA	1	6'2"	207	Duke		2
Brodie, John QB	57-73SF	12	6'1"	198	Stanford		132
Brodnax, J. W. FB	60DenA		6'	208	Louisiana State		6
Brooker, Tommy OE-K	63DalA 63-66KC-A	5	6'2"	230	Alabama		290
Brooks, Bob FB	61NY-A		6'	215	Ohio U.		
Brown, Allen TE	66-67GB		6'5"	238	Mississippi		
Brown, Barry LB-TE	66-67Bal 68NYG 69BosA 70Bos	2	6'3"	228	Florida	1	
Brown, Bill LB	60BosA		6'1"	230	Syracuse	1	
Brown, Bill FB	61ChiB 62-74Min	2	5'11"	225	Illinois		456
Brown, Bob OT	64-68Phi 69-70LA 71-73Oak		6'4"	284	Nebraska		
Brown, Charley OT	62OakA		6'4"	245	Houston		
Brown, Charlie DB-HB	66-67ChiB 68BufA		6'1"	194	Syracuse	1	
Brown, Charlie HB	67-68NO		5'10"	187	Missouri		18
Brown, Don HB	60HouA		6'1"	205	Houston		
Brown, Doug DT	64OakA		6'4"	250	Fresno State		
Brown, Fred HB	61,63BufA	2	5'11"	189	Georgia		18
Brown, Fred LB-TE	65LA 66KJ 67-69Phi		6'5"	231	Miami (Fla.)	2	
Brown, Jimmie FB	56-65Cle	23	6'2"	228	Syracuse		756
Brown, John OT	62-66Cle 67-71Pit 72JJ		6'2"	250	Syracuse		
Brown, Roger DT	60-66Det 67-69LA		6'5"	298	Md. Eastern Shore	2	6
Brown, Timmy HB	59GB 60-67Phi 68Bal	23	5'10"	195	Ball State		384
Brown, Tom DB	64-68GB 69Was	3	6'1"	191	Maryland	13	12
63 played major league baseball							
Brown, Willie FL-HB	64-65LA 66Phi		6'	185	Southern Calif.		
Brown, Willie DB	63-66DenA 67-69OakA 70-78Oak		6'1"	195	Grambling	54	12
Browning, Charley HB	65NY-A		6'	220	Washington		
Brownlee, Claude DT	67MiaA		6'4"	265	Benedict		
Bruggers, Bob LB	66-68MiaA 68-69SD-A 70-71SD		6'1"	220	Minnesota	2	
Brumm, Don DE	63-69StL 70-71Phi 72StL		6'3"	243	Purdue		
Brunelli, Sam OT-OG	66-69DenA 70-71Den 72JJ		6'1"	263	Colorado State		
Bryant, Bob OE	60DalA		6'5"	230	Texas		
Bryant, Charlie HB-FB	66-67StL 68-69Atl	23	6'1"	207	Allen		
Bryant, Chuck OE	62StL		6'2"	220	Ohio State		
Buchanan, Buck DT	63-69KC-A 70-75KC		6'7"	279	Grambling	3	2
Buchanan, Tim LB	69CinA		6'	233	Hawaii		
Buckman, Tom TE	69DenA 71JJ		6'4"	230	Texas A&M		6
Budd, Frank FL	62Phi 63Was	2	5'10"	187	Villanova		6
Budde, Ed OG	63-69KC-A 70-76 KC		6'5"	261	Michigan State		
Budka, Frank DB	64LA		6'	195	Notre Dame	2	
Budness, Bill LB	62-69OakA 70Oak		6'1"	215	Boston U.	3	
Budrewicz, Tom OG	61NY-A		6'2"	245	Brown		
Bugenhagen, Gary OG-OT	67BufA 70Bos		6'2"	249	Syracuse		
Bukaty, Fred FB	61DenA	2	5'11"	195	Kansas		32
Bukich, Rudy QB	53LA 54-55MS 56LA 57-58Was	12	6'1"	202	Southern Calif.		54
	58-59ChiB 60-61Pit 62-68ChiB						
Bull, Ronnie HB-FB	62-70ChiB 71Phi	2	6'	200	Baylor		84
Bullocks, Amos HB	62-64Dal 66Pit	23	6'1"	201	Southern Illinois		42
Buncom, Frank LB	62-67SD-A 68CinA		6'1"	236	Southern Calif.	5	
died Sept. 14, 1969 – pulmonary embolism							
Bundra, Mike DT	62-63Det 64Min 64Cle 65Bal		6'3"	258	Southern Calif.		
Buoniconti, Nick LB	62-68BosA 69MiaA 70-74Mia 75BG		5'11"	220	Notre Dame	32	8
	76Mia						
Burch, Jerry OE	61OakA	2	6'1"	195	Georgia Tech		6
Burford, Chris OE	60-62DalA 63-67KC-A	2	6'3"	211	Stanford		332
Burke, Vern OE-TE	65SF 66Atl 67NO	2	6'4"	201	Oregon State		12
Burkett, Jackie LB-C	61-66Bal 67NO 68-69Dal 70NO		6'4"	229	Auburn	10	
Burman, George C-OG-OT	64ChiB 67-70LA 71-72Was		6'3"	253	Northwestern		
Burnett, Bobby HB	66-67BufA 68JJ 69DenA	2	6'2"	208	Arkansas		48
Burnett, Len DB	61Pit		6'1"	195	Oregon		
Burrell, George DB	69DenA		5'10"	180	Pennsylvania	2	6
Burrell, John OE-FL	62-64Pit 66-67Was	2	6'3"	191	Rice		
Burrell, Ode HB-FL	64-69HouA	234	6'	189	Mississippi State		82
Burris, Bo DB	67-69NO		6'3"	195	Houston	4	6
Burroughs, Don DB	55-59LA 60-64Phi		6'4"	185	Colorado State	50	
Burson, Jimmy DB	63-67StL 68Atl		6'	181	Auburn	16	12
Burton, Leon HB	60NY-A	3	5'9"	172	Arizona		18
Burton, Ron HB	60-65BosA	23	5'10"	190	Northwestern		114
Bussell, Jerry DB	65DenA		6'	185	Georgia Tech		
Butkus, Dick LB-C	65-73ChiB		6'3"	244	Illinois	22	10
Butler, Bill DB-HB	59GB 60Dal 61Pit 62-64Min	23	5'10"	189	Tenn.-Chatanooga	11	24
Butler, Bob OG	62Phi 63NY-A		6'1"	233	Kentucky		
Butler, Cannonball HB	65-67Pit 68-71Atl 72StL 73JJ	23	5'10"	191	Edward Waters		102
Butsko, Harry LB	63Was		6'3"	220	Maryland		
Buzyniski, Bernie LB	60BufA		6'3"	228	Holy Cross	1	
Byers, Ken OG-DE	62-63NYG 64-65Min 66JJ		6'1"	240	Cincinnati		
Byrd, Butch DB	63-69BufA 70Buf 71Den	3	6'	203	Boston U.	40	36
Byrd, Dennis DE	68BosA		6'4"	260	N. Carolina State		
Byrd, Mack LB	65LA		6'	215	Southern Calif.		
Byrne, Bill OG	63Phi		6'	240	Boston College		
Cadile, Jim OG-OT	62-72ChiB		6'3"	239	San Jose State		
Cadwell, John OG	61DalA		6'3"	230	Oregon State		
Caffey, Lee Roy LB	63Phi 64-69GB 70ChiB 71Dal 72SD		6'3"	247	Texas A&M	11	18
Cagle, Johnny DE	69BosA		6'3"	260	Clemson		
Cahill, Dave DT-DE	66Phi 67LA 68KJ 69Atl		6'3"	240	Arizona State		
Caleb, Jamie HB-FB	60Cle 61Min 62CFL 65Cle	3	6'1"	210	Grambling		6
Callahan, Dan OG	60NY-A		6'	230	Wooster		
Calland, Lee DB	63-65Min 66-68Atl 69ChiB 69-72Pit		6'	190	Louisville	19	6
Campbell, Bob HB	69Pit	3	6'	195	Penn State		
Campbell, Jim LB	69SD-A		6'3"	218	West Texas State	1	
Campbell, John LB	63-64Min 65-69Pit 69Bal		6'3"	222	Minnesota	5	6
Campbell, Ken OE	60NY-A		6'1"	213	West Chester		
Campbell, Mike HB	68Det		5'11"	200	Lenoir Rhyne		

Use Name (Nicknames) – Positions	Team by Year	See Section	Hgt	Wgt	College	Int	Pts
Campbell, Woody HB	67-69HouA 70-71Hou	2	5'1"	205	Northwestern		90
Canale, Justin OG	65-68BosA 69CinA		6'2"	242	Mississippi State		1
Canale, Whit DE-DT	66MiaA 68BosA		6'3"	245	Tennessee		
Cannavino, Joe DB	60-61OakA 62BufA		5'11"	186	Ohio State	10	
Cannon, Billy TE-HB-FB-OE	60-63HouA 64-69OakA 70KC	23	6'1"	216	Louisiana State		392
Capp, Dick LB-TE	67GB 68Pit		6'3"	235	Boston College		
Cappadonna, Bob FB	66-67BosA 68BufA	2	6'1"	230	Northeastern		34
Cappelletti, Gino FL-WR-OE-DB	60-69BosA 70Bos	2 5	6'	190	Minnesota	4	1130
Carlton, Wray HB-FB	60-67BufA	2	6'2"	218	Duke		204
Carmichael, Paul HB	65DenA		6'	200	El Camino J.C.		
Carclan, Reg OE-TE	62-63SD-A 64-68KC-A	2	6'6"	235	Toledo		34
Caroline, J. C. DB-HB	56-65ChiB	2	6'1"	190	Illinois	24	36
Carollo, Joe OT	62-68LA 69-70Phi 71LA 72-73Cle		6'2"	262	Notre Dame		
Carothers, Don OE	60DenA		6'5"	225	Bradley		
Carpenter, Preston OE-TE-HB	56-59Cle 60-63Pit	23	6'2"	197	Arkansas		144
Carpenter, Ron LB	64-65SD-A		6'2"	230	Texas A&M	1	
Carr, Henry DB	65-67NYG		6'3"	198	Arizona State	7	6
Carr, Jimmy DB-LB-HB	55,57ChiC 59-63Phi 64-65Was	2	6'1"	206	Charleston	15	6
Carr, Tom DT	68NO		6'3"	267	Morgan State		
Carrell, John LB	66HouA		6'3"	227	Texas Tech		
Carrington, Ed TE	68KJ 69HouA		6'4	225	Virginia		
Carroll, Jim LB	65-66NYG 66-68Was 69NY-A		6'1"	229	Notre Dame	3	
Carroll, Leo DE	67KJ 68GB 69-70Was 71JJ		6'7"	250	San Diego State		
Carson, Kern HB	65SD-A 65NY-A		6'	202	San Diego State		12
Carwell, Larry DB	67-68HouA 69BosA 70Bos 71-72NE	3	6'1"	191	Iowa State	14	18
Casares, Rick FB	55-64ChiB 65Was 66MiaA	2	6'2	226	Florida		360
Case, Pete OG	62-64Phi 65-70NYG		6'3"	242	Georgia		
Casey, Bernie FL-WR-OE	61-66SF 67-68LA	2	6'4"	213	Bowling Green		240
Casey, Tim LB	69ChiB 69DenA		6'1"	225	Oregon		
Cash, John DE	61-62DenA		6'3"	235	Allen	1	
Cassesse, Tom DB-HB	67DenA		6'1"	197	C. W. Post	1	
Cavalli, Carmen DE	60OakA		6'4"	245	Richmond		
Caveness, Ronnie LB	65KC-A 66-68HouA		6'1"	223	Arkansas	1	
Cavness, Grady DB	69DenA 70Atl		5'11"	190	Texas-El Paso	2	
Caylor, Lowell DB	64Cle		6'3"	205	Miami-Ohio		
Ceppetelli, Gene C	68-69Phi 69NYG		6'2"	247	Villanova		
Cernel, Joe C	65-67SF 68Atl		6'2"	238	Northwestern		
Chamberlain, Dan OE-HB	60-61BufA	2	6'4"	200	Sacramento State		24
Chandler, Don HB-K	56-64NYG 65-67GB	45	6'2"	208	Florida		530
Chapple, Jack LB	65SF		6'2"	227	Stanford		6
Charon, Carl DB	62-63BufA		5'10"	190	Michigan State	7	18
Cheeks, B. W. HB	65HouA		6'1"	230	Texas Southern		
Chelf, Don OG-OT	60-61BufA		6'3"	235	Iowa		
Chesser, George FB	66-67MiaA		6'2"	223	Delta State		
Childress, Joe HB-FB	56-59ChiC 60StL	2	6'	202	Auburn		96
	61JJ 62-65StL						
Childs, Clarence DB-HB	64-67NYG 68ChiB	23	6'	180	Florida A&M	2	12
Chlebek, Ed QB	63NY-A		5'11"	175	Western Michigan		
Choboian, Max QB	66DenA	1	6'4"	205	San Fran. State		12
Christopherson, Jim LB	62Min	5	6'	215	Concordia (Minn.)	1	61
Christy, Dick HB	58Pit 60BosA 61-63NY-A	23	5'10"	191	N. Carolina State		120
Christy, Earl HB-DB	66-68NY-A	3	5'11"	193	Md. Eastern Shore	1	1
Chuy, Don OG	63-68LA 69Phi		6'1"	255	Clemson		
Ciccolella, Mike LB	66-68NYG		6'1"	235	Dayton	1	
Cichowski, Tom OT	67-68DenA		6'4"	250	Maryland		
Clancy, Jack WR-FL	67MiaA 68KJ 69MiaA 70GB	2	6'1"	295	Michigan		30
Claridge, Dennis QB	64-65GB 66Atl	1	6'3"	225	Nebraska		
Clark, Ernie LB	63-67Det 68StL		6'1"	222	Michigan State	4	
Clark, Howard DE	60LA-A 61SD-A	2	6'2"	210	Tenn.-Chattanooga		
Clark, Mike K	63Phi 64-67Pit 68-71Dal 72JJ 73Dal	5	6'1"	203	Texas A&M		724
Clark, Monte OT-DT-DE	59-61SF 62Dal 63-69Cle		6'6"	260	Southern Calif.		
	HC76SF HC78-84Det						
Clark, Phil DB	67-69Dal 70ChiB 71NE		6'2"	209	Northwestern	4	
Clarke, Frank OE-FL-TE	57-59Cle 60-67Dal	2	6'	211	Colorado		306
Clarke, Hagood DB	64-68BufA	3	6'	193	Florida	12	18
Clay, Billy DB	66Was		6'1"	192	Mississippi	1	
Clay, Ozzie FL	64Was		6'	190	Iowa State		
Clemens, Bob HB	62Bal		6'1"	208	Pittsburgh		
Clement, Henry OE	61Pit		6'2"	200	North Carolina		
Cline, Doug LB-FB	60-66HouA 66SD-A	2	6'2"	225	Clemson	7	30
Cloutier, Dave DB	64BosA		6'	195	Maine		
Coan, Bert HB	62SD-A 63-68KC-A	23	6'4"	219	Kansas		114
Cockrell, Gene OT-DE	60-62NY-A		6'3"	247	Hardin-Simmons		
Cody, Bill LB	66Det 67-70NO 72Phi		6'1"	225	Auburn		
Coffey, Don FL	63DenA		6'3"	190	Memphis State		
Coffey, Junior FB-HB	65GB 66-67Atl 68KJ	2	6'1"	211	Washington		90
	69Atl 69NYG 70KJ 71NYG						
Cogdill, Gail OE-WR	60-68Det 68Bal 69-70Atl	2	6'2"	195	Washington State		216
Cohen, Abe OG	60BosA		5'11"	230	Tenn.-Chattanooga		
Coia, Angie OE	60-63ChiB 64-65Was 66Atl	2	6'2"	202	Southern Calif.		120
Colchico, Dan DE	60-65SF 69NO		6'4"	240	San Jose State		
Colclough, Jim OE-FL-WR	60-68BosA	2	6'	185	Boston College		238
Cole, Fred OG	60LA-A		5'11"	226	Maryland		
Cole, Terry FB	68-69Bal 70Pit 71Mia	2	6'1"	220	Indiana		36
Collier, Blanton	HC63-70Cle				Georgetown (Ky.)		
Collier, Jim OE	62NYG 63Was		6'2"	195	Arkansas		
Collier, Joel	HC66-68BufA				Northwestern		
Collins, Gary FL-WR-OE	62-71Cle	2 4	6'4"	211	Maryland		420
Colvin, Jim DT-DE-OG	60-63Bal 64-66Dal 67NYG		6'2"	250	Houston		2
Compton, Dick OE-DB-HB-WR	62-64Det 65HouA 67-68Pit	2	6'1"	195	McMurry	1	24
Concannon, Jack QB	64-66Phi 67-71ChiB 74GB 75Det	12	6'3"	201	Boston College		72
Condren, Glen DT-DE	65-67NYG 69-72Atl		6'2"	246	Oklahoma		
Conjar, Larry FB	65Cle 68Phi 69-70Bal	2	6'	214	Notre Dame		2
Connelly, Mike C-OG-OT	60-67Dal 68Pit		6'3"	242	Utah State		
Conners, Dan LB	64-69OakA 70-74Oak		6'1"	231	Miami (Fla.)	15	30
Conrad, Bobby Joe FL-HB-WR-DB	58-59ChiC	23 5	6'	194	Texas A&M	4	389
	60-68StL 69Dal						
Contoulis, John DT	64NYG		6'4"	260	Connecticut		
Cook, Ed OT-OG	58-59ChiC 60-65StL 66-67Atl		6'2"	245	Notre Dame		
Cook, Greg QB	69CinA 70-72SJ 73Cin	12	6'3"	214	Cincinnati		6
Cooke, Ed DE-LB	58ChiB 58Phi 60-63NY-A		6'4"	248	Maryland	7	12
	64-65DenA 66-67MiaA						
Coolbaugh, Bob OE	61OakA	2	6'3"	200	Richmond		26
Cooper, Bill FB-LB	61-64SF		6'1"	215	Muskingum		6

Use Name (Nicknames) – Positions	Team by Year	See Section	Hgt	Wgt	College	Int	Pts
Cooper, Thurlow OE-DE	60-62NY-A	2	6'4"	228	Maine		52
Copeland, Ron WR	69ChiB		6'4"	196	U.C.L.A.		
Corcoran, King QB	68BosA		6'	200	Maryland		
Cordileone, Lou DT-DE-OG	60NYG 61SF 62LA		6'	247	Clemson	1	
	62-63Pit 67-68NO 69KJ						
Cordill, Ollie DB-OE	67SD-A 68Atl 69NO	4	6'2"	180	Memphis State		
Corey, Walt LB	60,62DalA 63-66KC-A		6'	229	Miami (Fla.)	4	
Cornelison, Jerry OT	60-62DalA 64-65KC-A		6'3"	250	S.M.U.		
Cornish, Frank DT	66-70ChiB 70-71Mia 72Buf		6'6"	285	Grambling	2	
Coronado, Bob OE	61Pit		6'1"	195	U. of Pacific		
Cortez, Bruce DB	67NO		6'	175	Parsons		
Costa, Dave DT-DE	63-65OakA 66BufA 67-69DenA		6'2"	257	Utah		2
	70-71Den 72-73SD 74Buf						
Costa, Paul OT-TE-OE	65-69BufA 70-72Buf	2	6'4"	252	Notre Dame		42
Costello, Tom LB	64-65NYG		6'3"	220	Dayton		
Costello, Vince LB	57-66Cle 67-68NYG		6'	228	Ohio U.	22	12
Cottrell, Bill OT-C-OG	67-70Det 71JJ 72Den		6'3"	255	Delaware Valley		
Cottrell, Ted LB	69-70AtL		6'1"	233	Delaware Valley		
Counts, Johnny HB	62-63NYG	3	5'10"	170	Illinois		6
Cowan, Charley OT-OG	61-75LA		6'4"	264	N. Mex. Highlands		
Cox, Jim TE	68MiaA	2	6'2"	227	Miami (Fla.)		
Cox, Larry DT	66-68DenA		6'2"	250	Abilene Christian		
Coyle, Russ DB	61LA		6'2"	195	Oklahoma		
Crabb, Claude DB-FL	62-63Was 64-65Phi 66-68LA		6'	193	Colorado	10	6
Crabtree, Eric WR-OE-DB	66 68DenA 69CinA	2	5'11"	184	Pittsburgh		132
	70-71Cin 71NE						
Craddock, Nate FB	63Bal		6'	220	Parsons		
Craig, Dobie OE-HB	62-63OakA 64HouA	2	6'4"	200	Howard Payne		42
Crane, Dennis DT-OT	68-69Was 70NYG		6'6"	260	Southern Calif.		
Crane, Gary LB	69DenA		6'4"	230	Arkansas State		
Crane, Paul LB-C	66-69NY-A 70-72NYJ		6'2"	208	Alabama	5	14
Crawford, Bill OG	60NYG		6'1"	235	British Columbia		
Crawford, Hilton DB	69BufA		6'	198	Grambling		
Crawford, Jim FB-HB	60-64BosA	2	6'1"	203	Wyoming		46
Crenshaw, Leon DT	68GB		6'6"	280	Tuskegee		
Crenshaw, Willie FB	64-69StL 70Den	23	6'2"	228	Kansas State		108
Crespino, Bob OE-TE-WR	61-64Cle 64-68NYG	2	6'4"	223	Mississippi		54
Crockett, Bobby WR-OE	66BufA 67KJ 68-69BufA	2	6'	198	Arkansas		18
Crockett, Monte OE	60-62BufA	2	6'3"	213	N. Mex. Highlands		6
Croftcheck, Don OG-LB	65-66Was 67ChiB		6'1"	230	Indiana		
Cronin, Bill TE	65Phi 66MiaA		6'4"	225	Boston College		6
Cropper, Marshall WR-OE	67-69Pit	2	6'3"	207	Md. Eastern Shore		
Cross, Irv DB	61-65Phi 66-68LA 69Phi	3	6'1"	192	Northwestern	22	12
Crossan, Dave C	65-69Was		6'3"	245	Maryland		
Crotty, Jim DB	60-61Was 61-62BufA		5'11"	192	Notre Dame	3	
Crouthamel, Jake HB	60BosA		5'11"	195	Dartmouth		
Crow, Al DT	60BosA		6'6"	260	William & Mary		
Crow, John David HB-FB-TE	58-59ChiC	12	6'2"	218	Texas A&M		444
	60-64StL 65-68SF						
Crow, Wayne HB-DB	60-61OakA 62-63BufA	2 4	6'	205	California	4	26
Crump, Harry FB	63BosA	2	6'	205	Boston College		30
Crutcher, Tommy LB-FB	64-67GB 68-69NYG		6'3"	229	Texas Christian	3	
	70KJ 71-72GB						
Cudzik, Walt C-LB	54Was 60-63BosA 64BufA		6'2"	231	Purdue		
Culpepper, Ed DT	58-59ChiC 60StL 61Min 62-63HouA		6'1"	255	Alabama		
Cummings, Ed LB	64NY-A 65DenA		6'2"	230	Stanford	1	
Cunningham, Carl LB	67-69DenA 70Den 71NO		6'3"	240	Houston	4	
Cunningham, Jay DB	65-67BosA	3	5'10"	180	Bowling Green	3	6
Cunningham, Jim FB	61-63Was	2	5'11"	221	Pittsburgh		30
Cuozzo, Gary QB	63-66Bal 67NO 68-71Min 72StL	12	6'1"	195	Virginia		6
Currie, Dan LB	58-64GB 65-66LA		6'3"	239	Michigan State	11	6
Curry, Bill C-LB	65-66GB 67-72Bal 73Hou 74LA		6'2"	235	Georgia Tech		
Curry, Ray FL	63Pit		6'1"	195	Jackson State		6
Cutsinger, Gary DE	62-66HouA 67XJ 68HouA		6'4"	244	Oklahoma State		
Cvercko, Andy OG	60GB 61-62Dal 63Cle 63Was		6'	242	Northwestern		
Daanen, Jerry WR	68-70StL		6'	190	Miami (Fla.)		
Dabney, Carlton DT	68Atl 69-70XJ		6'5"	250	Morgan State	1	
Dale, Carroll WR-OE-FL	60-64LA 65-72GB 73Min	2	6'1"	198	Virginia Tech		312
D'Amato, Mike DB	68NY-A		6'2"	204	Hofstra		
Danenhauer, Bill DE	60DenA 60BosA		6'4"	245	Emporia State		
Danenhauer, Eldon OT	60-65DenA 66KJ		6'4"	242	Pittsburg State		
Daniel, Willie DB	61-66Pit 67-69LA		5'11"	187	Mississippi State	14	12
Daniels, Clem HB-DB	60DalA 61-67OakA 68SF	23	6'1"	219	Prairie View	3	324
Daniels, Dave DT	66OakA		6'3"	245	Florida A&M		
Daniels, Dick DB	68-69Dal 69-70ChiB 71JJ		5'9"	180	Pacific (Ore.)	7	
Darnall, Bill WR	68-69MiaA 70JJ		6'2"	197	North Carolina		
Darragh, Dan QB	68-69BufA 70Buf	1	6'3"	196	William & Mary		
Darre, Bernie OG	61Was		6'2"	230	Tulane		
Daugherty, Bob HB	66SF		6'2"	205	Tulsa		
Davidson, Ben DE-DT	61GB 62-63Was 64-69OakA		6'8"	272	Washington		
	70-71Oak 72FJ						
Davidson, Cotton QB	54Bal 55-56MS 57Bal 58CFL	12 45	6'1"	182	Baylor		104
	60-62DalA 62-66OakA 67JJ 68OakA						
Davidson, Pete DT	60HouA		6'5"	255	The Citadel		
Davis, Al	HC63-65OakA				Syracuse		
Davis, Dick DE	62DalA		6'2"	230	Kansas		
Davis, Don DT	66NYG 67JJ		6'6"	260	Los Angeles State		
Davis, Donnie FL-TE	62Dal 70Hou		6'4"	220	Southern U.		
Davis, Doug OT	66-72Min		6'4"	250	Kentucky		
Davis, Glenn OE	60-61Det	2	6'	180	Ohio State		
Davis, Jack OG	60BosA		6'	226	Maryland		
Davis, Jack OG	60DenA		6'2"	235	Arizona		
Davis, Marvin DE	66DenA		6'4"	252	Wichita State		
Davis, Norman OG	67Bal 69NO 70Phi		6'3"	247	Grambling		
Davis, Roger OG-OT	60-63ChiB 64LA 65-66NYG		6'3"	236	Syracuse		
Davis, Rosey DE	65-67NYG		6'5"	260	Tennessee State		
Davis, Sonny LB	61Dal		6'2"	220	Baylor		
Davis, Ted LB	64-66Bal 67-69NO 70Mia		6'1"	230	Georgia Tech	2	
Davis, Tommy K	59-69SF	45	6'	215	Louisiana State		738
Davis, Willie DE-OT	58-59Cle 60-69GB		6'3"	243	Grambling	2	16
Dawson, Bill DE-OE	65BosA		6'3"	240	Florida State		
Dawson, Len QB	57-59Pit 60-61Cle 62DalA	12	6'	190	Purdue		54
	63-69KC-A 70-75KC						
Day, Al LB	60DenA		6'2"	216	Eastern Michigan		
Day, Eagle QB	59-60Was	1 4	6'	183	Mississippi		
Day, Tom DE-OG-DT-OT	60StL 61-66BufA 67SD-A 68BufA		6'2"	252	N. Carolina A&T	1	
Dean, Floyd LB	64-65SF		6'4"	245	Florida		
Dean, Ted HB-FB	60-63Phi 64Min	23	6'2"	211	Wichita State		36
Dee, Bob DE-DT	57-58Was 60-67BosA		6'3"	248	Holy Cross	1	
DeFelice, Mick OT	65-66NY-A		6'3"	250	Southern Conn. St.		
Degen, Dick LB	65-66SD-A		6'1"	223	Long Beach State	3	
DeLong, Steve DT-DE	65-69SD-A 70-71SD 72ChiB		6'3"	251	Tennessee	1	
DeLuca, Sam OG-OT	60LA-A 61SD-A 62VR		6'2"	247	South Carolina		
	63SD-A 64-66NY-A						
DeLuca, Jerry OT-DT	59Phi 60-61BosA 62-63BufA		6'3"	249	Middle Tenn. St.		
	63-64BosA						
DeMarco, Bob C-OG	61-69StL 70-71Mia 72-74Cle 75LA		6'3"	243	Dayton		
Demko, George DE	61Pit		6'3"	240	Appalachian State		
Denney, Austin TE	67-69ChiB 70-71 Buf	2	6'2"	230	Tennessee		18
Dennis, Mike HB	68-69LA	2	6'1"	207	Mississippi		
Denny, Earl HB	67-68Min		6'1"	200	Missouri		
Denson, Al WR-FL-TE	64-69DenA 70Den 71Min	2	6'2"	208	Florida A&M		194
Denton, Bob DE-OT	60Cle 61-64Min		6'4"	241	U. of Pacific		
Denvir, John OG	62DenA		6'4"	245	Colorado		
Deskins, Don OG	60OakA		6'3"	240	Michigan		
Dess, Darrell OG-OT	58Pit 59-64NYG 65-66Was		6'	243	N. Carolina State		6
	66-69NYG						
DeSutter, Wayne OT	66BufA		6'4"	250	Western Illinois		
Deters, Harold K	67Dal	5	6'	200	N. Carolina State		12
DeVleigher, Chuck DT	69BufA		6'4"	265	Memphis State		
Dewveall, Willard OE	59-60ChiB 61-64HouA	2	6'4"	224	S.M.U.		162
Dial, Benjy QB	67Phi		6'1"	185	East. New Mexico		
Dial, Buddy FL-OE	59-63Pit 64-66Dal 67-68JJ	2	6'1"	194	Rice		264
Diamond, Bill OG	63KC-A		6'	240	Miami (Fla.)		
Diamond, Charley OT	60-62DalA 63KC-A		6'2"	249	Miami (Fla.)		
Dickey, Eldridge WR	68OakA 71Oak		6'2"	198	Tennessee State		6
Dickey, Wallace OT	68-69DenA		6'3"	260	SW Texas State		
Dickinson, Bo FB	60-61DalA 62-63DenA	2	6'2"	218	Southern Miss.		70
	63HouA 64OakA						
Dickson, Paul DT-OT	59LA 60Dal 61-70Min 71StL		6'5"	252	Baylor		
Diehl, John DT	61-64Bal 65Dal 65OakA		6'7"	276	Virginia		
Dillon, Terry DB	63Min		6'	193	Montana		
died May, 1964 – accidental drowing							
DiMidio, Tony OT-C	66-67KC-A		6'3"	250	West Chester		
Dimitroff, Tom QB	60BosA		5'11"	200	Miami - Ohio		
Dirks, Mike DT-OG	68-71Phi		6'2"	247	Wyoming		6
Discenzo, Tony OT	60BosA 60BufA		6'5"	240	Michigan State		
Ditka, Mike TE	61-66Chi 67-68Phi 69-72Dal HC83-90Chi	2	6'3"	229	Pittsburgh		270
DiVito, Joe QB	68DenA		6'2"	205	Boston College		
Dixon, Hewritt FB-HB-OE	63-65DenA 66-69OakA	2	6'2"	223	Florida A&M		170
	70Oak 71JJ						
Dobbins, Ollie DB	64BufA		5'11"	185	Morgan State		
Doelling, Fred DB	60Dal		5'10"	190	Pennsylvania		
Donahue, Oscar FL	62Min	2	6'3"	195	San Jose State		
Donaldson, Gene FB	67BufA		6'2"	225	Purdue		
Donnahoo, Roger DB	60NY-A		6'	185	Michigan State	5	12
Donnell, Ben DE	60LA-A		6'5"	248	Vanderbilt		
Donnelly, George DB	65-67SF		6'3"	207	Illinois	2	
Donohue, Leon OG-OT	62-65SF 65-67Dal 68JJ		6'4"	245	San Jose State		
Dorsey, Dick OE	62OakA	2	6'3"	200	Southern Calif., Oklahoma		12
Dotson, Al DT	65KC-A 66MiaA 68-69OakA 70Oak		6'4"	258	Grambling		2
Dougherty, Bob LB	57LA 58Pit 60-63OakA		6'	238	Cincinnati, Kentucky	3	
Douglas, John DB	67-68NO 69HouA 70JJ		6'1"	195	Texas Southern	1	
Douglas, Merrill FB-HB	58-60ChiB 61Dal 62Phi	2	6'	204	Utah		12
Dove, Eddie DB	59-63SF 63NYG	3	6'2"	181	Colorado	10	
Dowdle, Mike LB-FB	60-62Dal 63-66SF		6'3"	226	Texas	6	6
Dowler, Boyd FL-OE-WR	59-69GB 70VR 71Was	2 4	6'5"	224	Colorado		240
Driskill, Joe DB	60-61StL		6'1"	195	Northeast La.		
Dubenion, Elbert FL-HB-WR	60-68BufA	23	6'	189	Bluffton		234
Dudek, Mitch OT	66NY-A		6'4"	245	Xavier - Ohio		
Dudley, Paul HB	62NYG 63Phi	2	6'	185	Arkansas		6
Dugan, Fred OE	58-59SF 60Dal 61-63Was	2	6'3"	197	Dayton		78
Duich, Steve OG	68Atl 69Was		6'3"	248	San Diego State		
Dukes, Mike LB	60-63HouA 64-65BosA 65NY-A		6'3"	231	Clemson	9	
Dumbrowski, Leon LB	60NY-A		6'	215	Delaware		
Dunaway, Dave WR	68GB 68Atl 69NYG		6'2"	205	Duke		
Dunaway, Jim DT	63-69BufA 70-71Buf 72Mia 73JJ		6'4"	278	Mississippi	1	6
Duncan, Randy QB	61DalA	1	6'	185	Iowa		
Duncan, Rick K	67DenA 68Phi 69Det		6'	208	Eastern Montana		9
Duncan, Ron TE	67Cle		6'6"	255	Wittenberg		
Duncan, Speedy DB	64-69SD-A 70SD 71-74Was	3	5'10"	177	Jackson State	24	54
Duncom, Bob OT	68StL		6'3"	250	West Texas State		
Dunn, Perry Lee HB-FB	64-65Dal 66-68Atl 69Bal	2	6'2"	208	Mississippi		42
Dupre, Charlie DB	60NY-A		6'1"	195	Baylor		
Durkee, Charlie K	67-68,71-72NO	5	5'11'	165	Oklahoma State		243
Dyer, Henry FB	66LA 67JJ 68LA 69-70Was	2	6'2"	230	Grambling		12
Dyer, Ken DB-WR	68SD-A 69CinA 70-71Cin		6'3"	187	Arizona State	3	6
Eason, John WR	68OakA		6'2"	220	Florida A&M		
Eaton, Scott DB	67-71NYG 72JJ		6'3"	199	Oregon State	11	6
Eber, Rick WR	68Atl 69SD-A 70SD 71JJ	2	6'	181	Tulsa		6
Echols, Fate OT-DT	62-63StL 64CFL		6'1"	258	Northwestern		
Eddy, Nick HB	68-70Det 71KJ 72Det	2	6'1"	207	Notre Dame		
Edgerson, Booker DB	62-69BufA 70Den		5'10"	182	Western Illinois	23	2
Edmunds, Randy LB	68-69MiaA 71NE 72Bal		6'2"	223	Georgia Tech	1	
Edwards, Dave LB	63-75Dal		6'3"	224	Auburn	13	6
Edwards, Lloyd TE	69OakA		6'3"	248	San Diego State		
Eifrid, Jim LB	61DenA		6'	240	Colorado State		
Eisenhauer, Larry DE	61-69BosA		6'5"	247	Boston College	1	
Elkins, Larry FL	66-67HouA 69JJ	2	6'1"	193	Baylor		18
Ellersick, Don DB	60LA		6'1"	193	Washington State	2	
Elliott, Jim K	67Pit	4	5'11"	184	Presbyterian		
Ellis, Roger LB-C	60-63NY-A		6'3"	233	Maine	1	
Ellzey, Charley C-LB	60-61StL		6'3"	243	Southern Miss.		
Elmore, Doug DB	62Was	4	6'	188	Mississippi	2	
Elwell, Jack OE	62StL		6'3"	200	Purdue		
Elzey, Paul LB	68CinA		6'3"	235	Toledo		
Emanuel, Frank LB	66-69MiaA 70NO		6'3"	225	Tennessee	4	6
Embree, John WR	69DenA 70Den 71JJ	2	6'4"	201	Compton C.C.		30

Use Name (Nicknames) – Positions	Team by Year	See Section	Hgt	Wgt	College	Int	Pts
Emelianchik, Pete TE	67Phi		6'2"	220	Richmond		
Enis, Hunter QB	60DalA 61SD-A 62DenA 62OakA	12	6'2"	192	Texas Christian		30
Epperson, Pat OE	60DenA	2	6'3"	225	Adams State		
Erdelatz, Eddie	HC60OakA				St. Mary's		
Erickson, Bernie LB	67-68SD-A 68CinA		6'2"	239	Abilene Christian	1	
Erlandson, Tom LB	62-65DenA 66-67MiaA 68SD-A		6'3"	229	Washington State	8	6
Erwin, Terry HB	68DenA		6'	190	Boston College		
Estes, Don OG	66SD-A		6'2"	250	Louisiana State		
Etcheverry, Sam QB	61-62StL	12 4	5'11"	190	Denver		
Etter, Bob K	68-69Atl	5	5'11"	152	Georgia		128
Evans, Bob DE	65HouA		6'3"	250	Texas A&M		
Evans, Dale HB	61DenA		6'3"	210	Kansas State		
Evans, Jim FL	64-65NY-A		6'1"	190	Texas-El Paso		
Evey, Dick DT-DE-OG	64-69ChiB 70LA 71Det		6'2"	238	Tennessee	2	
Ewbank, Weeb	HC54-62Bal HC63-69NY-A HC70-73NYJ				Miami-Ohio		
Ezerins, Vilnis HB-FB	68LA		6'1"	217	Wis.-Whitewater		
Fairband, Bill LB	67-68OakA		6'3"	228	Colorado		
Faison, Earl DE	61-66SD-A 66MiaA		6'5"	263	Indiana	6	14
Falls, Mike OG	60-61Dal		6'1"	240	Minnesota		
Fanning, Stan OT-DE-DT	60-62ChiB 63LA 64HouA 64DenA		6'6"	267	Idaho		
Farley, Dick DB	68-69SD-A		6'	185	Boston U.		
Farmer, Lonnie LB	64-66BosA		6'	220	Tenn.-Chatanooga	1	
Farr, Miller DB	65DenA 65-66SD-A 67-69HouA 70-72StL 73Det		6'1"	190	Wichita State	35	36
Farrier, Curt DT	63-65KC-A 66JJ		6'6"	253	Montana State		
Farrington, Bo OE	60-63ChiB	2	6'3"	217	Prairie View		42
killed in auto accident at 1964 training camp							
Farris, John OG	65-66SD-A		6'4"	245	San Diego State		
Faulkner, Jack	HC62-64DenA				Miami (Fla.)		
Faulkner, Staley OT	64HouA		6'3"	245	Texas		
Faust, Paul LB	67Min		6'	220	Minnesota		
Feagin, Wiley OG	61-62Bal 63Was		6'2"	236	Houston		
Feldhausen, Paul OT	68BosA		6'6"	270	Northland		
Feldman, Marty	HC61-62OakA				Stanford		
Felt, Dick DB	60-61NY-A 62-66BosA		6'	184	Brigham Young	18	6
Felts, Bobby HB	65Bal 65-67Det	23	6'2"	203	Florida A&M		12
Fenner, Lane WR	68SD-A		6'5"	210	Florida State		
Ferguson, Bob FB	62-63Pit 63Min	2	5'11"	220	Ohio State		6
Ferguson, Charley OE-TE	61Cle 62Min 63BufA 64JJ 65-66BufA 67-68JJ 69BufA	2	6'5"	218	Tennessee State		78
Ferguson, Jim C-LB	68NO 69Atl 69ChiB 71JJ		6'4"	240	Southern Calif.		
Ferguson, Larry HB	63Det		5'10"	185	Iowa		
Ferrante, Orlando OG	60LA-A 61SD-A		6'	230	Southern Calif.		
Fetherston, Jim LB	68-69SD-A		6'2"	225	California	1	
Ficca, Dan OG	62OakA 63-66NY-A		6'1"	244	Southern Calif.		
Fichtner, Ross DB	60-67Cle 68NO		6'	186	Purdue	27	18
Fields, George DE-DT	60-61OakA		6'3"	245	Bakersfield State	2	
Fields, Jerry LB	61-62NY-A		6'1"	222	Ohio State		
Finch, Karl OE	62LA		6'3"	195	Cal. Poly-Pomona		
Finneran, Gary DT	60LA-A 61OakA		6'3"	240	Southern Calif.		
Fischer, Pat (Mouse) DB-HB	61-67StL 68-77Was	3	5'10"	170	Nebraska	56	30
Fisher, Doug LB	69-70Pit		6'1"	225	San Diego State		
Fiss, Galen LB	56-66Cle		6'	226	Kansas	13	
Fitzgerald, Mike DB	66-67Min 67NYG 67Atl	3	5'10"	180	Iowa State	1	
Flanigan, Jim LB	67-70GB 71NO		6'3"	238	Pittsburgh	1	
Flatley, Paul OE-WR	63-67Min 68-70Atl	2	6'1"	187	Northwestern		144
Fleming, Don DB	60-62Cle		6'	187	Florida	10	
died June 4, 1963 – construction accident							
Fleming, George HB	61OakA	23 5	5'11"	188	Washington		63
Fleming, Marv TE-OE	63-69GB 70-74Mia	2	6'4"	233	Utah		96
Fletcher, Billy DB	66DenA		5'10"	190	Memphis State		
Flint, George OG	62-65BufA 66JJ 67-69BufA		6'4"	243	Arizona State		
Flores, Tom QB	60-61OakA 62IL 63-66OakA 67-69BufA 69KC-A HC79-81Oak HC82-87Raid	12	6'1"	194	U. of Pacific		30
Flowers, Charlie FB	60LA-A 61SD-A 62NY-A	2	6'1"	215	Mississippi		30
Floyd, Don DE	60-67HouA		6'4"	242	Texas Christian	4	12
Flynn, Don DB	60-61DalA 61NY-A		6'	205	Houston	5	6
Folkins, Lee TE-DE	61GB 62-64Dal 65Pit	2	6'5"	219	Washington		66
Fontes, Wayne DB	62NY-A HC88-90Det		6'	190	Michigan State	4	6
Ford, Fred HB	60BufA 60LA-A	2	5'8"	180	Cal. Poly-Pomona		12
Ford, Garrett FB	68DenA	2	6'2"	230	West Virginia		6
Fortunato, Joe LB-FB	55-66ChiB		6'	225	Mississippi State	16	18
Foruria, John DB-HB	67-68Pit	2	6'2"	205	Idaho		
Foster, Gene FB-HB	65-69SD-A 70SD	2	5'11"	214	Arizona State		46
Fournet, Sid OG-LB-DE	55-56LA 57Pit 60-61DalA 62-63NY-A		6'	235	Louisiana State	1	
Fowler, Bobby FB	62NY-A		5'11"	212	Martin C.C.		
Fowler, Charlie OG-OT	67-68MiaA		6'2"	260	Houston		
Fowler, Jerry OT	64HouA		6'3"	255	Northwestern La.		
Fowler, Willmer HB	60-61BufA	2	5'11"	185	Northwestern		6
Franci, Jason OE	66DenA		6'1"	210	Cal.-Santa Barbara		
Francis, Dave FB	63Was		6'1"	210	Ohio State		
Frankhauser, Tom DB	59LA 60-61Dal 62-63Min	3	6'	195	Purdue	13	
Frank, Bill OT	64Dal		6'5"	255	Colorado		
Franklin, Bobby DB-HB	60-66Cle		5'11"	182	Mississippi	13	18
Frantz, Jack C	68BufA		6'3"	230	California		
Fraser, Jim LB-K	62-64DenA 65KC-A 66BosA 68NO	4	6'3"	236	Wisconsin	3	2
Frazier, Al HB-FL	61-63DenA	23	5'11"	180	Florida A&M		68
Frazier, Charley OE-WR	62-68HouA 69BosA 70Bos	2	6'	177	Texas Southern		180
Frazier, Curt DB	68CinA		5'11"	183	Fresno State		
Frazier, Wayne C-LB	62SD-A 65HouA 66-67KC-A 67BufA		6'2"	243	Auburn		
Frazier, Willie TE-OE	64-66HouA 66-69SD-A 70SD 71Hou 71-72KC 74-75WFL 75Hou 76KJ	2	6'4"	235	Ark.-Pine Bluff		222
Fredrickson, Tucker FB-HB	65NYG 66KJ 67-71NYG	2	6'3"	233	Auburn		102
Freeman, Bobby DB-HB	57-58Cle 59GB 60-61Phi 62Was		6'1"	202	Auburn	15	
Freeman, Mike DB	68-70Atl		5'11"	187	Fresno State	1	
Frey, Dick DE-OG	60DalA 61HouA		6'2"	233	Texas A&M		
Fritsch, Ernie C-LB	60StL		6'	230	Detroit		
Frongillo, John OG-C	62-66HouA		6'3"	252	Baylor		
Frost, Ken DT	61-62Dal		6'4"	245	Tennessee	1	
Fuller, Charley HB	61-62OakA	2	5'11"	176	San Fran. State		12
Furey, Jim LB	60NY-A		6'	228	Kansas State		
Furman, John QB	62Cle		6'4"	205	Texas-El Paso		
Fussell, Tom DE	67BosA		6'3"	245	Louisiana State		

Use Name (Nicknames) – Positions	Team by Year	See Section	Hgt	Wgt	College	Int	Pts
Gabriel, Roman QB	62-72LA 73-77Phi	12	6'4"	225	N. Carolina State		180
Gaechter, Mike DB	62-69Dal		6'	192	Oregon	21	12
Gagner, Larry OG	66-69Pit 70JJ 72KC		6'3"	246	Florida		
Gaiser, George OT	68DenA		6'4"	255	S.M.U.		
Gaiters, Bob HB	61-62NYG 62SF 63DenA	23	5'11"	210	New Mexico State		48
Galimore, Willie HB	57-63ChiB	23	6'1"	187	Florida A&M		222
killed in auto accident at 1964 training camp							
Gamble, R. C. HB-FB	68-69BosA	2	6'3"	220	S. Carolina State		12
Gambrell, Billy OE-FL-WR	63-67StL 68Det	23	5'10"	175	South Carolina		105
Garcia, Jim DE-DT	65Cle 66NYG 67NO 68Atl		6'4"	248	Purdue		
Garner, Bob DB	60LA-A 61-62OakA	3	5'10"	185	Fresno State	7	
Garrett, Drake QB	68DenA 70Den		5'9"	183	Michigan State	2	
Garrett, J.D. HB	64-67DenA	23	5'11"	195	Grambling		36
Garrett, Mike HB	66-69KC-A 70KC 70-73SD	23	5'9"	199	Southern Calif.		294
Garron, Larry HB-FB	60-68BosA	23	6'	199	Western Illinois		252
Gassert, Ron DT	62GB		6'3"	250	Virginia		
Gaubatz, Dennis LB	63-64Det 65-69Bal		6'2"	225	Louisiana State	10	2
Gault, Billy LB	61Min		6'1"	185	Texas Christian		
Gault, Prentice HB-FB-LB	60Cle 61-67StL	2	6'	204	Oklahoma		102
Gavin, Chuck DE	60-63DenA		6'1"	243	Tennessee State	1	6
Gavric, Momcilo K	69SF	5	5'10"	167	none		31
Gehrke, Jack WR	68KC-A 69CinA 71Dan 72JJ	2	6'	178	Utah		
Gent, Pete FL-TE-OE	64-68Dal	2	6'4"	209	Michigan State		24
Gentry, Curtis DB	66-68ChiB		6'	186	Md. Eastern Shore	6	
Gibbons, Jim OE-TE	58-68Det	2	6'2"	220	Iowa		120
Gibbs, Sonny QB	64Det		6'7"	230	Texas Christian		
Gibson, Claude DB	61-62SD-A 63-65OakA	3	6'1"	191	N. Carolina State	22	26
Gilburg, Tom OT	61-65Bal	4	6'5"	245	Syracuse		
Gilchrist, Cookie FB	62-64BufA 65DenA 66MiaA 67DenA	2 5	6'3"	249	none		296
Gill, Roger HB-TE	64-65Phi		6'1"	200	Texas Tech		
Gillett, Fred HB-OE	62SD-A 64OakA		6'3"	228	Los Angeles State		
Gilliam, Jon C	61-62DalA 63-67KC-A		6'2"	238	East Texas State		
Gillis, Don C	58-59ChiC 60-61StL 62JJ		6'3"	245	Rice		
Gillman, Sid	HC55-59LA HC60LA-A HC61-69SD-A HC71SD HC73-74Hou				Ohio State		
Glacken, Scotty QB	66-67DenA		6'	190	Duke		
Glass, Bill DE-C-OT	58-61Det 62-68Cle		6'5"	252	Baylor	4	12
Glass, Glenn DB-FL-OE	62-63Pit 64-65Phi 66Atl 66DenA	2	6'	197	Tennessee	2	
Glenn, Howard OG	60NY-A		6'	235	Linfield		
died Oct. 9, 1960 – broken neck							
Glick, Freddie DB	59ChiC 60StL 61-66HouA	3	6'1"	189	Colorado State	31	6
Glueck, Larry DB	63-65ChiB		6'	190	Villanova	1	
Goeddeke, George OG-OT-C	67-69DenA 70-72Den 73JJ		6'3"	250	Notre Dame		
Gogolak, Charlie K	66-68Was 70Bos 71-72NE	5	5'10"	168	Princeton		270
Gogolak, Pete K	64-65BufA 66-74NYG	5	6'2"	193	Cornell		863
Goldstein, Al OE	60OakA	2	6'	204	North Carolina		12
Gonsoulin, Goose DB	60-66DenA 67SF		6'3"	209	Baylor	46	14
Gonzaga, John OT-OG-DT-DE	56-59SF 60Dal 61-65Det 66DenA		6'3"	247	none		
Good, Tom LB	66SD-A		6'	230	Marshall		
Goode, Tom C-LB	62-65HouA 66-69MiaA 70Bal		6'3"	244	Mississippi State		
Goodridge, Bob WR	68Min		6'2"	202	Vanderbilt		
Goodwin, Doug FB	66BufA 68Atl		6'2"	228	Md. Eastern Shore		
Goodwin, Ron OE-FL-WR	63-68Phi	2	6'	180	Baylor		54
Goosby, Tom OG-LB	63Cle 66Was		6'	235	Baldwin-Wallace		
Goovert, Ron LB	67Det		5'11"	225	Michigan State		
Gordon, Cornell DB	65-69NY-A 70-72Den		6'	187	N. Carolina A&T	14	
Gordy, John OG-OT	57Det 58VR 59-67Det		6'3"	248	Tennessee		
Gossage, Gene DE-OG-DT	60-62Phi 63CFL		6'3"	239	Northwestern		
Gossett, Bruce K	64-69LA 70-74SF	5	6'2"	229	Richmond		1031
Grabosky, Gene DT	60BufA		6'5"	275	Syracuse		
Grabowski, Jim FB	66-70GB 71ChiB	2	6'2"	221	Illinois		66
Grady, Garry DB	69MiaA		5'11"	180	Eastern Michigan		
Graham, Art OE-WR	63-68BosA	2	6'1"	205	Boston College		120
Graham, Dave OT	63-66Phi 67JJ 68-69Phi 70JJ		6'3"	248	Virginia		
Graham, Kenny DB	64-69SD-A 70Cin 70Pit	3	6'	201	Washington State	28	30
Graham, Milt OT-DT	61-63BosA		6'6"	235	Colgate		
Granderson, Rufus DT	60DalA		6'5"	277	Prairie View		
Granger, Charley OT	61Dal 61StL		6'2"	240	Southern U.		
Granger, Hoyle FB-HB	66-69HouA 70Hou 71NO 72Hou	2	6'1"	225	Mississippi State		144
Grantham, Larry LB	60-69NY-A 70-73NYJ		6'	204	Mississippi	24	18
Grate, Willie TE	69BufA 70Buf		6'4"	225	S. Carolina State		18
Graves, White DB	65-67BosA 68CinA		6'	185	Louisiana State	3	
Gray, Jim DB	66NY-A 67Phi		6'	181	Toledo		
Gray, Ken OG-LB	58-59ChiC 60-69StL 70Hou		6'2"	245	Howard Payne		
Gray, Moses OT-DT	61-62NY-A		6'3"	260	Indiana		
Grayson, Dave DB	61-62DalA 63-64KC-A 65-69OakA 70Oak	3	5'10"	184	Oregon	48	36
Greaves, Gary OT	60HouA		6'3"	235	Miami (Fla.)		
Grecni, Dick LB	61Min		6'1"	230	Ohio U.	1	
Green, Allen K	61Dal	45	6'2"	215	Mississippi		34
Green, Bobby Joe K	60-61Pit 62-73ChiB		5'11"	175	Florida		
Green, Charlie QB	66OakA		6'	190	Wittenberg		
Green, Cornell DB	62-74Dal		6'4"	211	Utah State	34	24
Green, Ernie HB-FB	62-68Cle	23	6'2"	205	Louisville		210
Green, Jerry HB	68BosA		6'	190	Georgia Tech		
Green, Johnny QB	60-61BufA 62-63NY-A	12	6'3"	203	Tenn.-Chatanooga		36
Green, Ron FL-WR	67-68Cle		6'1"	200	North Dakota		
Greene, Ted LB	60-62DalA		6'1"	230	Tampa	4	
Greene, Tom QB	60BosA 61DalA	12 4	6'1"	190	Holy Cross		
Greenlee, Fritz LB	69SF		6'2"	230	Arizona State		
Greer, Al OE	63Det		6'4"	180	Jackson State		
Greer, Jim OE	60DenA		6'3"	215	Elizabeth City St.		6
Gregg, Forrest OT-OG-DT	56GB 57MS 58-70GB 71Dal HC75-77Cle HC80-83Cin HC84-87GB		6'4"	249	S.M.U.		
Gregory, Ben HB-FB	68BufA	2	6'3"	220	Nebraska		6
Gregory, Glynn OE-DB	61-62Dal		6'2"	200	S.M.U.	1	
Gregory, Ken OE	61Bal 62Phi 63NY-A		6'	190	Whittier		
Gremminger, Hank DB	56-65GB 66LA		6'1"	201	Baylor	29	6
Grier, Rosey DT-DE	55-56NYG 57MS 58-62NYG 63-66LA 67JJ		6'5"	284	Penn State		4
Griffin, Jim DE	66-67SD-A 68CinA		6'3"	258	Grambling		6
Griffin, John DB	63LA 64-66DenA		6'1"	190	Memphis State	4	12
Griffing, Glynn QB	63NYG	1	6'1"	200	Mississippi		
Grimm, Dan OG	63-65GB 66-68Atl 69Bal 69Was		6'3"	244	Colorado		

Use Name (Nicknames) – Positions	Team by Year	See Section	Hgt	Wgt	College	Int	Pts
Groman, Bill OE-FL	60-62HouA 63DenA 64-65BufA	2	6'	195	Heidelberg		222
Gros, Earl FB	62-63GB 64-66Phi 67-69Pit 70NO	2	6'3"	224	Louisiana State		228
Grosscup, Lee QB	60-61NYG 62NY-A	1	6'1"	186	Utah		
Grottkau, Bob OG	59-60Det 61Dal		6'4"	228	Oregon		
Gruneisen, Sam C-OG-LB	62-69SD-A 70-72SD 73Hou		6'1"	248	Villanova		
Gucciardo, Pat DB	66NY-A		5'11"	185	Kent State		
Guesman, Dick DT	62-63NY-A 64DenA	5	6'4"	255	West Virginia		129
Gugliemi, Ralph QB	55Was 56-57MS 58-60Was 61StL 62-63NYG 63Phi	12	6'1"	196	Notre Dame		12
Guidry, Paul LB	66-69BufA 70-72Buf 73Hou		6'3"	229	McNeese State	5	
Guillory, John DB	69CinA 70Cin		5'10"	190	Stanford	1	
Guillory, Tony LB	65LA 66JJ 67-68LA 69Phi		6'4"	232	Lamar		
Gulseth, Don LB	66DenA		6'1"	240	North Dakota		
Gunnels, Riley DT-DE	60-64Phi 65-66Pit		6'3"	250	Georgia	1	
Gunner, Harry DE	68-69CinA 70ChiB		6'6"	250	Oregon State	2	8
Gursky, Al LB	63NYG		6'1"	210	Penn State		
Guy, Louis DB-FL	63NYG 64OakA		6'	188	Mississippi		
Guzik, John LB-OG	59-60LA 61HouA		6'3"	231	Pittsburgh		
Gwinn, Ross OG	68NO		6'3"	273	Northwestern La.		
Hackbart, Dale DB	60GB 61-63Was 64-65CFL 66-70Min 71-72StL 73Den		6'3"	210	Minnesota	19	24
Hadl, John QB	62-69SD-A 70-72SD 73-74LA 74-75GB 76-77Hou	12 4	6'2"	213	Kansas		96
Haffner, Mike WR	68-69DenA 70Den 71Cin	2	6'2"	205	U.C.L.A.		42
Hagberg, Roger FB-TE	65-69OakA	2	6'2"	216	Minnesota		48
Hageman, Fred C	61-64Was		6'4"	243	Kansas		
Haggerty, Mike OT	67-70Pit 71NE 72Det		6'4"	239	Miami (Fla.)		
Haik, Mac WR	68-69HouA 70-71Hou	2	6'1"	196	Mississippi		54
Hale, Dave DT-DE	67-71ChiB 72JJ 73ChiB		6'7"	251	Ottawa (Kan.)		
Haley, Dick DB-HB-FL-OE	59-60Was 61Min 61-64Atl	3	5'10"	193	Pittsburgh	14	12
Hall, Alvin DB	61-63LA		6'	195	none	1	
Hall, Galen QB	62Was 63NY-A	1	5'10"	200	Penn State		12
Hall, Ken HB	59ChiC 60-61HouA 61StL	23	6'1"	205	Texas A&M		24
Hall, Pete OE	61NYG		6'2"	200	Marquette		
Hall, Ron DB	59Pit 60MS 61-67BosA		6'	190	Missouri Valley	30	6
Hall, Tom FL-OE-WR-DB	62-63Det 64-66Min 67NO 68-69Min	2	6'1"	195	Minnesota	3	48
Hammack, Mal FB-OE-TE-LB	55ChiB 56MS 57-59ChiB 60-66StL	2	6'2"	205	Florida		48
Hammond, Kim QB	68MiaA 69BosA		6'1"	192	Florida State		2
Hardy, Charley OE	60-62OakA	2	6'	184	San Jose State		42
Harmon, Ed LB	69CinA		6'4"	230	Louisville		
Harmon, Tom OG	67Atl		6'4"	238	Gustavus Adolphus		
Harold, George DB	66-67Bal 68Was		6'3"	198	Allen		
Harper, Charlie OG-OT-DT	66-72NYG		6'2"	250	Oklahoma State		
Harper, Darrell HB	60BufA		6'1"	195	Michigan		7
Harper, Jack HB	67-68MiaA	2	5'11"	190	Florida		24
Harris, Billy HB	68Atl 69Min 70JJ 71NO	2	6'	196	Colorado		6
Harris, Dick DB	60LA-A 61-65SD-A	3	6'	185	Ouachita Baptist	12	
Harris, Jim DT	65-67NY-A		6'4"	275	Utah State		
Harris, John DB-HB	60-61OakA		6'1"	195	Santa Monica J.C.	3	
Harris, Lou DB	68Pit		6'	180	Kent State		
Harris, Marv LB	64LA		6'1"	225	Stanford		
Harris, Phil DB	66NYG		6'	195	Texas		
Harris, Rickie DB	65-70Was 71-72NE	3	6'	182	Arizona	15	24
Harris, Wendell DB	62-65Bal 66-67NYG	3 5	5'11"	188	Louisiana State	8	17
Harrison, Bob LB	59-61SF 62-63Phi 64Pit 65-67SF		6'2"	223	Oklahoma	5	
Harrison, Bob DB	61Bal		5'11"	187	Ohio U.	3	
Hart, Ben DB	67NO		6'2"	205	Oklahoma	1	
Hart, Dick OG	67-70Phi 71JJ 72Buf		6'2"	250	none		
Hart, Doug DB	64-71GB		6'	190	Texas-Arlington	15	32
Hart, Pete FB	60NY-A	2	5'9"	190	Hardin-Simmons		
Harvey, George OT	67NO		6'4"	245	Kansas		
Harvey, Jim OG-OT	66-69OakA 70-71Oak		6'5"	247	Mississippi		
Harvey, Waddey DT	69BufA 70Buf		6'4"	276	Virginia Tech		
Hatcher, Ron DB-FB	62Was		5'11"	215	Michigan State		
Hathcock, Dave DB	66GB 67NYG		6'	193	Memphis State		
Hawkins, Alex HB-OE-FL-WR	59-65Bal 66-67Atl 67-68Bal	23	6'1"	188	South Carolina		132
Hawkins, Ben WR-FL-OE	66-73Phi 74Cle	2	6'	180	Arizona State		198
Hawkins, Rip LB	61-65Min		6'3"	231	North Carolina	12	20
Hawkins, Wayne OG	60-69OakA		6'	239	U. of Pacific		
Hayes, Jim DT	65-66HouA		6'4"	263	Jackson State		
Hayes, Larry C-LB	61NYG 62-63LA		6'3"	230	Vanderbilt		6
Hayes, Luther DE	61SD-A	2	6'4"	200	Southern Calif.		18
Hayes, Ray FB	61Min	2	6'3"	235	Central St.-Okla.		12
Hayes, Ray DT	68NY-A		6'5"	248	Toledo		
Hayes, Rudy LB	59-60,62Pit		6'	217	Clemson		
Hayes, Wendell FB-HB	63Dal 65-67DenA 68-69KC-A 70-74KC	2	6'2"	215	Humboldt State		214
Haymond, Alvin DB	64-67Bal 68Phi 69-71LA 72Was 73Hou	3	6'	193	Southern U.	10	30
Haynes, Abner HB	60-62DalA 63-64KC-A 65-66DenA 67MiaA 67NY-A	23	6'	188	North Texas		414
Hays, Harold LB	68-69SF		6'3"	227	Southern Miss.		
Hazeltine, Matt LB	55-68SF 69VR 70NYG		6'1"	220	California	13	18
Hazelton, Major DB	68-69ChiB 70NO		6'1"	185	Florida A&M		
Headrick, Sherrill LB	60-62DalA 63-67KC-A 68CinA		6'2"	223	Texas Christian	15	18
Healy, Chip LB	69-70StL		6'3"	233	Vanderbilt		
Healy, Don DT-OG	58-59ChiB 60-61Dal 62BufA		6'3"	259	Maryland	1	
Hebert, Ken WR	68Pit		6'	200	Houston		
Heck, Ralph LB	63-65Phi 66-68Atl 69-71NYG		6'2"	228	Colorado	5	6
Heckard, Steve OE	65-66LA		6'1"	195	Davidson		
Hector, Willie OT	61LA		6'2"	220	U. of Pacific		
Heenan, Pat DB-OE	60Was		6'1"	190	Notre Dame	1	
Heeter, Gene OE	63-65NY-A	2	6'4"	235	West Virginia		12
Heidel, Jim DB	66StL 67NO		6'1"	185	Mississippi	1	
Hendershot, Larry LB	67Was		6'3"	240	Arizona State		
Henderson, John WR-OE-FL	65-67Det 68-72Min	2	6'3"	191	Michigan		60
Henderson, Jon WR-DB	68-69Pit 70Was	23	6'	198	Colorado State		36
Henke, Karl DT-DE	68NY-A 69BosA		6'4"	245	Tulsa		
Henley, Carey HB	62BufA		5'10"	200	Tenn.-Chatanooga		
Hennessey, Tom DB	65-66BosA		6'	183	Holy Cross	8	
Hennigan, Charley FL-OE	60-66HouA	2	6'	187	Northwestern La.		306
Henning, Dan QB	66SD-A HC83-84Atl		6'	195	William & Mary		

Use Name (Nicknames) – Positions	Team by Year	See Section	Hgt	Wgt	College	Int	Pts
Henry, Mike LB	59-61Pit 62-64LA		6'2"	220	Southern Calif.		
Henry, Urban DT-DE	61LA 63GB 64Pit		6'4"	265	Georgia Tech		
Henson, Gary DE	63Phi		6'3"	200	Colorado		
Henson, Ken C	65Pit		6'6"	260	Texas Christian		
Hergert, Joe LB	60-61BufA	5	6'1"	216	Florida	2	30
Herman, Dave OG-OT	64-69NY-A 70-73NYJ		6'2"	255	Michigan State		
Herman, Dick LB	65OakA		6'2"	215	Florida State		
Hernandez, Joe FL	64Was		6'2"	180	Arizona		
Herndon, Don HB	60NY-A		6'	195	Tampa		6
Herock, Ken OE-TE	63-65,67OakA 68CinA 69BosA	2	6'2"	230	West Virginia		30
Heron, Fred DT-DE	66-72StL		6'4"	255	San Jose State		
Herring, George QB	60-61DenA	1 4	6'2"	200	Southern Miss.		12
Hester, Jim TE	67-69NO 70ChiB		6'4"	238	North Dakota		18
Hettema, Dave OT	67SF 68-69MS 70Atl		6'4"	249	New Mexico		
Hibler, Mike LB	68CinA		6'1"	235	Stanford		
Hickerson, Gene OG	58-60Cle 61BL 62-73Cle		6'3"	248	Mississippi		
Hickey, Bo FB	67DenA	2	5'11"	225	Maryland		30
Hickl, Ray LB	69-70NYG		6'2"	215	Texas A&I		
Hickman, Harry FB	59ChiC 60GB		6'2"	227	Baylor		
Hicks, W. K. DB	64-69HouA 70-72NYJ		6'1"	191	Texas Southern	40	
Higgins, Jim OG	66MiaA		6'1"	250	Xavier-Ohio		
Highsmith, Buzz OG-OT-C	68-69DenA 72Hou		6'4"	238	Florida A&M		
Hill, Dave OT	63-69KC-A 70-74KC		6'5"	259	Auburn		
Hill, Fred TE-OE-WR	65-71Phi	2	6'2"	215	Southern Calif.		30
Hill, Gary DB	65Mia		6'	200	Southern Calif.		
Hill, Jack HB	61DenA	5	6'1"	185	Utah State		31
Hill, Jerry FB-HB	61Bal 62JJ 63-70Bal	2	5'11"	212	Wyoming		150
Hill, Jimmy DB	55-57ChiC 58AJ 59ChiC 60-64StL 65Det 66KC-A		6'2"	192	Sam Houston St.	20	18
Hill, King QB	58-59ChiC 60StL 61-68Phi 68Min 69StL	12 4	6'3"	212	Rice		54
Hill, Mack Lee HB-FB	64-65KC-A died Dec. 14, 1965 after knee surgery	2	5'11"	225	Southern U.		54
Hill, Winston OT	63-69NY-A 70-76NYJ 77LA		6'4"	278	Texas Southern		
Hillebrand, Jerry LB	63-66NYG 67StL 68-70Pit		6'3"	240	Colorado	14	18
Hilton, John TE	65-69Pit 70GB 71Min 72-73Det 74WFL	2	6'5"	222	Richmond		96
Hindman, Stan DE-DT	66-71,74SF		6'3"	236	Mississippi	1	6
Hines, Glen Ray OT	66-69HouA 71-72NO 73Pit		6'5"	264	Arkansas		
Hines, Jimmy WR	69MiaA		6'	175	Texas Southern		
Hinton, Chuck DT	64-71Pit 71NYJ 72Bal		6'5"	257	N. Car. Central	2	12
Hinton, Chuck C	67-69NYG		6'2"	235	Mississippi		
Hoak, Dick HB	61-70Pit	12	5'11"	191	Penn State		198
Hodgson, Pat OE	66Was		6'2"	190	Georgia		
Hoffman, Dalton FB	64-65HouA		6'	207	Baylor		6
Hohman, John OG	65-66DenA		6'1"	243	Wisconsin		
Hohn, Bob DB	65-69Pit		6'	187	Nebraska	7	
Hoisington, Al OE	60OakA 60BufA		6'3"	200	Pasadena City		12
Holifield, Jim DB	68-69NYG		6'3"	195	Jackson State	1	
Holler, Ed LB	63GB 64Pit	4	6'2"	233	South Carolina	1	
Holmes, John DE	66MiaA		6'2"	248	Florida A&M		
Holmes, Pat DE-DT	66-69HouA 70-72Hou 73KC		6'5"	254	Texas Tech	1	
Holub, E. J. LB-C	61-62DalA 63-69KC-A 70KC		6'4"	231	Texas Tech	9	
Holz, Gordy DT-OT	60-63DenA 64NY-A		6'4"	264	Minnesota	1	
Holzer, Tom DE	67SF 68JJ		6'4"	250	Louisville		
Hooligan, Harry FB	65HouA		6'2"	225	Bishop		
Hopkins, Jerry LB	63-66DenA 67MiaA 68OakA		6'2"	236	Texas A&M	6	
Hopkins, Roy FB	67-69HouA 70Hou 71JJ	2	6'1"	233	Texas Southern		48
Hord, Roy OG	60-62LA 62Phi 63NY-A		6'4"	244	Duke		
Horner, Sam HB-DB	60-61Was 62NYG	234	6'	197	V.M.I.		6
Hornung, Paul (The Golden Boy) HB-FB	57-62GB 63SL 64-66GB	12 5	6'2"	215	Notre Dame		760
Horton, Bob LB	64-65SD-A		6'2"	230	Boston U.		
Houser, John OG-C	57-59LA 60-61Dal 62JJ 63StL		6'3"	239	Redlands		
Houston, Jim LB-DE-TE	60-72Cle		6'2"	239	Ohio State	14	25
Howell, Lane OT-DT	63-64NYG 65-69Phi		6'5"	264	Grambling		
Howell, Mike DB	65-72Cle 72Mia		6'1"	189	Grambling	27	
Howley, Chuck LB	58-59ChiB 60JJ 61-73Dal		6'3"	228	West Virginia	25	
Hoyem, Lynn C-OG	62-63Dal 64-67Phi		6'4"	244	Long Beach State		
Huard, John LB	67-69DenA 70-71JJ		6'	220	Maine	6	
Huarte, John QB	66-67BosA 68Phi 70-71KC 72ChiB	1	6'	188	Notre Dame		
Hubbert, Brad FB	67-69SD-A 70SD	2	6'1"	230	Arizona		66
Hudlow, Floyd DB-FL	65BufA 67-68Atl		5'11"	192	Arizona	2	
Hudock, Mike C	60-65NY-A 66MiaA 67KC-A		6'1"	245	Miami (Fla.)		
Hudson, Bill DT	61-62SD-A 63BosA		6'4"	267	Clemson	1	6
Hudson, Dick OT-OG	62SD-A 63-67BufA		6'4"	266	Memphis State		
Hudson, Jim DB	65-69NY-A 70NYJ		6'2"	210	Texas	14	
Huey, Gene DB	69SD-A		5'11"	190	Wyoming		
Huff, Sam LB	56-63NYG 64-67Was 68VR 69Was		6'1"	230	West Virginia	30	30
Hughes, Bob DE	67,69Atl		6'4"	253	Jackson State		
Hughes, Chuck WR	67-69Phi 70-71Det died Oct. 24, 1971 – heart attack	2	5'11"	173	Texas-El Paso		
Hughley, George HB	65Was	2	6'2"	223	Central St.-Okla.		6
Hull, Bill DE	62DalA		6'6"	245	Wake Forest		
Hultz, Don DE-DT-LB	63Min 64-73Phi 74ChiB		6'3"	238	Southern Miss.	4	12
Hultz, George DT	62StL		6'4"	250	Southern Miss.		
Humphrey, Buddy QB	59-60LA 61-62Dal 63-65StL 66HouA	1	6'1"	198	Baylor		
Humphreys, Bob K	67-68DenA	5	6'1"	240	Wichita State		43
Hunt, Bobby DB-HB	62DalA 63-67KC-A 68-69CinA		6'1"	188	Auburn	42	12
Hunt, Jim (Earthquake) DT-DE	60-69BosA 70Bos		5'11"	249	Prairie View	1	14
Hunter, Art C-OT-DT-DE	54GB 55MS 56-59Cle 60-64LA 65Pit		6'4"	243	Notre Dame		
Hunter, Bill FL-HB-DB	65Was 66MiaA		6'1"	183	Syracuse		6
Hurston, Chuck LB-DE	65-69KC-A 70KC 71Buf		6'6"	237	Auburn		
Husmann, Ed DT-OG-LB-DE	53ChiC 54-55MS 56-59ChiC 60Dal 61-65HouA		6'	235	Nebraska		
Hutchinson, Tom OE	66Atl	2	6'1"	190	Kentucky		12
Huth, Jerry OG	56NYG 57-58MS 59-60Phi 61-63Min		6'	226	Wake Forest		6
Hynes, Paul DB	61DalA 61-62NY-A		6'1"	210	Louisiana Tech	2	
Iacovazzi, Cosmo HB	65NY-A		5'11"	200	Princeton		
Ilg, Ray LB	67-68BosA		6'1"	220	Colgate		
Iman, Ken C	60-63GB 64BH 65-74LA		6'1"	236	SE Missouri St.		
Inman, Jerry DT	66-69DenA 70-71Den 72JJ 73Den		6'3"	255	Oregon		
Isbell, Joe Bob OG	62-64Dal 65JJ 66Cle		6'1"	238	Houston		
Izo, George QB	60StL 61-64Was 65Det 66Pit	1	6'3"	218	Notre Dame		

Use Name (Nicknames) – Positions	Team by Year	See Section	Hgt	Wgt	College	Int	Pts
Jackson, Bobby DB	60Phi 61ChiB		6'1"	190	Alabama		
Jackson, Bobby FB	62-63SD-A 64HouA 64OakA 65HouA	2	6'3"	232	New Mexico State		96
Jackson, Frank FL-HB	61-62DalA 63-65KC-A 66-67MiaA	23	6'1"	187	S.M.U.		186
Jackson, Jim DB-HB	66-67SF		6'	187	Western Illinois	1	6
Jackson, Leroy HB	62-63Was	2	6'	190	Western Illinois		6
Jackson, Rich DE-LB	66OakA 67-69DenA 70-72Den 72Cle		6'2"	252	Southern U.		2
Jackson, Roland FB-LB	62StL		6'	210	Rice		
Jackson, Steve LB	66-67Was		6'1"	225	Texas-Arlington	1	
Jackson, T. J. FL-DB	66Phi 67Was		6'	180	none		
Jackunas, Frank C	62BufA 63DenA		6'3"	225	Detroit		
Jacobs, Allen FB-HB	65GB 66-67NYG	2	6'1"	215	Utah		6
Jacobs, Harry LB-DE	60-62BosA 63-69BufA 72NO		6'2"	228	Bradley	12	
Jacobs, Proverb DT-OT	58Phi 61NYG 61-62NY-A 63-64OakA		6'4"	258	California		
Jacobs, Ray DT-DE	63-66DenA 67-68MiaA 69BosA		6'3"	276	Howard Payne		
Jacobson, Jack DB	65SD-A		6'2"	200	Oklahoma State		
Jagielski, Harry DT-OT	56ChiC 56Was 60-61BosA 61OakA		6'	257	Indiana	1	
James, Claudis WR-HB-FL	67-68GB		6'2"	190	Jackson State		
James, Dan OT-C	60-66Pit 67ChiB		6'4"	262	Ohio State		
James, Dick HB-DB	56-63Was 64NYG 65Min	23	5'9"	179	Oregon	12	204
James, Nate DB	68Cle		6'1"	195	Florida A&M		
Jamieson, Al OT	60-62HouA		6'5"	245	Colgate		
Jamieson, Dick QB	60-61NY-A	1	6'1"	191	Bradley		
Janick, Bobby DB-FL	62-67HouA	3	5'11"	178	Lamar	15	6
Janerette, Chuck DT-OT-OG	60LA 61-62NYG 63NY-A 64-65DenA		6'3"	253	Penn State	2	
Janik, Tom DB	63-64DenA 65-68BufA 69BosA 70Bos 71NE	4	6'3"	198	Texas A&I	25	36
Jaquess, Pete DB	64-65HouA 66-67MiaA 67-69DenA 70Den		6'	182	East. New Mexico	16	12
Jelacic, Jon DE-OG	58NYG 61-64OakA		6'3"	250	Minnesota	2	12
Jencks, Bob OE	63-64ChiB 65Was	5	6'5"	227	Miami-Ohio		135
Jeralds, Luther DE	61DalA		6'3"	235	N. Car. Central		
Jeter, Bob DB-FL-OE	63-70GB 71-73ChiB		6'1"	203	Iowa	26	12
Jeter, Gene LB	65-67DenA		6'3"	230	Ark.-Pine Bluff		
Jeter, Tony TE	66,68Pit		6'3"	222	Nebraska		
Jobko, Bill LB	58-62LA 63-65Min 66Atl		6'2"	224	Ohio State	5	
Joe, Billy FB	63-64DenA 65BufA 66MiaA 67-68NY-A	2	6'2"	243	Villanova		118
Johns, Pete DB	67-68HouA		6'3"	189	Tulane		
Johnson, Billy DB	66-68BosA		5'11"	178	Nebraska	2	
Johnson, Charley QB	61-69StL 70-71Hou 72-75Den	12	6'	191	New Mexico State		60
Johnson, Charlie DT	66-68SF		6'2"	266	Louisville		
Johnson, Curley HB-TE-OE-FB-K	60DalA 61-68NY-A 69NYG	2 4	6'	215	Houston		26
Johnson, Daryle DB	68-69BosA 70Bos		5'11"	190	Morgan State	5	8
Johnson, Dick OE	63KC-A		6'4"	220	Minnesota		6
Johnson, Ellis HB-FL-OE	65-66BosA		6'2"	190	Southeastern La.		
Johnson, Gene DB	59-60Phi 61Min 61NYG		6'	187	Cincinnati	4	
Johnson, Jay LB	69-70Phi		6'3"	230	East Texas State		
Johnson, Jim DB-FL	61-76SF	2	6'2"	188	U.C.L.A.	47	38
Johnson, John DT	63-68ChiB 69NYG		6'5"	260	Indiana		
Johnson, John Henry FB-HB-DB	54-56SF 57-59Det 60-65Pit 66HouA	2	6'2"	210	St. Mary's, Arizona State		330
Johnson, Lee WR	69-70SF		6'1"	204	Tennessee State		
Johnson, Mike DB	66-69Dal		5'10"	185	Kansas	8	
Johnson, Mitch OT-OG	65Dal 66-67Was 69-70LA 71Cle 72Was		6'4"	249	U.C.L.A.		
Johnson, Preston FB	68BosA		6'2"	230	Florida A&M		
Johnson, Rich HB-FB	69HouA		6'1"	210	Illinois		6
Johnson, Rudy HB	64-65SF 66Atl	2	5'11"	190	Nebraska		6
Johnson, Walter DE	67SF		6'4"	225	Tuskegee		
Johnston, Mark DB	60-63HouA 64OakA 64NY-A		6'	201	Northwestern	13	12
Johnston, Rex HB	60Pit		6'1"	195	Southern Calif.		
64 played major league baseball							
Jonas, Don HB	62Phi		5'11"	195	Penn State		
Jones, Bob WR-OE	67-69ChiB		6'1"	194	Virginia Union		
Jones, Curtis LB	68SD-A		6'2"	245	Missouri		
Jones, Dave WR	69-71Cle		6'2"	185	Kansas State		
Jones, Deacon DE	61-71LA 72-73SD 74Was		6'5"	254	S. Carolina State	2	3
Jones, Ezell OT	69BosA 70Bos		6'4"	255	Minnesota		
Jones, Gene LB	61HouA		6'	200	Rice		
Jones, Harry HB	67-70Phi 71JJ	2	6'2"	205	Arkansas		
Jones, Henry FB	69DenA		6'2"	235	Grambling		
Jones, Homer WR-FL-OE	64-69NYG 70Cle	23	6'2"	211	Texas Southern		228
Jones, Jerry OT-DT-DE	66Atl 67-69NO		6'3"	269	Bowling Green		
Jones, Jim OE-WR	65-67ChiB 68DenA	2	6'2"	189	Wisconsin		66
Jones, Ron TE	69GB		6'3"	220	Texas-El Paso		
Jones, Stan OG-DT-OT	54-65ChiB 66Was		6'1"	252	Maryland		
Jones, Willie FB	62BufA		5'11"	208	Purdue		
Jones, Willie DT-DE	67HouA 68CinA 70-71Cin		6'2"	260	Kansas State		
Jordan, Henry DT-DE	57-58Cle 59-69GB		6'3"	249	Virginia	1	6
Jordan, Jeff DB	65-67Min		6'4"	190	Tulsa	4	
Jordan, Jimmy HB	67NO		6'1"	200	Florida		
Jordan, Larry LB-DE	62,64DenA		6'6"	230	Youngstown State		
Jordan, Lee Roy LB	63-76Dal		6'2"	219	Alabama	32	20
Josephson, Les FB-HB	64-67LA 68FJ 69-74LA	2	6'	209	Augustana (S.D.)		168
Joswick, Bob DE-DT	68-69MiaA		6'5"	250	Tulsa		
Joyner, L. C. DB	60OakA		6'1"	197	none		
Julian, Fred DB	60NY-A		5'9"	185	Michigan	6	
Junker, Steve OE	57Det 58KJ 59-60Det 61-62Was	2	6'3"	217	Xavier-Ohio		36
Jurgensen, Sonny QB	57-63Phi 64-74Was	12	5'11"	202	Duke		90
Kalmer, Karl DE	62NY-A		6'3"	230	Boston U.		
Kalsu, Bob OG	68BufA 69MS		6'3"	235	Oklahoma		
Killed in action in Viet Nam 1970							
Kamanu, Lew DE	67-68Det		6'4"	245	Weber State		
Kammerer, Carl DE-LB	61-62SF 63-69Was		6'3"	240	U. of Pacific	3	
Kanicki, Jim DT	63-69Cle 70-71NYG 72KJ		6'4"	270	Michigan State		
Kantor, Joe FB	66Was		6'1"	217	Notre Dame		
Kapele, John DE-OT-DT	60-62Pit 62Phi		6'	240	Brigham Young		
Kapp, Joe QB	67-69Min 70Bos 71HO	12	6'2"	214	California		30
Karas, Emil LB-DE	59Was 60LA-A 61-64, 66SD-A		6'3"	230	Dayton	8	
Karras, Alex DT	58-62Det 63SL 64-70Det		6'2"	248	Iowa	4	2

Use Name (Nicknames) – Positions	Team by Year	See Section	Hgt	Wgt	College	Int	Pts
Karras, Ted OG-OT-LB	58-59Pit 60-64ChiB 65Det 66LA		6'1"	240	Indiana		
Kasperek, Dick C	66-68StL		6'3"	225	Iowa State		
Kassulke, Karl DB	63-72Min		6'	194	Drake	19	
1973 paralyzed in motorcycle accident							
Katcavage, Jim DE-DT	56-68NYG		6'3"	237	Dayton	1	12
Katcik, Joe DT	60NY-A		6'9"	290	Notre Dame		
Keating, Bill OG-OT	66-67DenA 67MiaA		6'2"	236	Michigan		
Keckin, Val QB	62SD-A		6'4"	215	Southern Miss.		
Keeling, Rex DB	68CinA		6'3"	220	Samford		
Kellerman, Ernie DB	66-71Cle 72Cin 73Buf		6'	184	Miami-Ohio	19	6
Kelley, Ed DB	61-62DalA		6'2"	195	Texas		
Kelley, Gordon LB	60-61SF 62-63Was		6'3"	230	Georgia	5	
Kelley, Ike LB	66-67Phi 68KJ 69-71Phi 72JJ		5'11"	224	Ohio State	1	
Kelley, Les LB	67-69NO		6'3"	233	Alabama	1	
Kellogg, Mike FB	66-67DenA		6'	220	Santa Clara		
Kelly, Bob OT-DT	61-64HouA 67KC-A 68CinA 69Atl		6'3"	261	New Mexico State		
Kelly, Leroy HB-FB	64-73Cle	23	6'	199	Morgan State		540
Kemp, Jack QB	57Pit 58CFL 60LA-A 61-62SD-A 62-67BufA 68KJ 69BufA	12	6'1"	201	Occidental		242
Kempinski, Charlie OG	60LA-A		6'	235	Mississippi		
Kendall, Charlie DB	60HouA		6'2"	185	U.C.L.A.	2	
Kennerson, John DE-OT	60LA 62Pit 62NY-A		6'3"	255	Kentucky State		
Kennedy, Tom QB	66NYG 67JJ	1	6'1"	200	Los Angeles State		
Kent, Greg OT-DE	66OakA 67CFL 68Det		6'6"	270	Utah		
Kerbow, Randy FL	63HouA		6'1"	190	Rice		
Kerr, Jim DB	61-62Was		6'	195	Penn State	8	
Keyes, Bob HB	60OakA		5'10"	183	San Diego State		
Keyes, Jimmy LB	68-69MiaA	5	6'2"	225	Mississippi		51
Keys, Brady DB-HB	61-67Pit 67Min 68StL	3	6'	189	Colorado State	16	
Keys, Howard C-OT-OG	60-63Phi		6'3"	239	Oklahoma State		
Khayat, Bob OG-C-K	60,62-63Was	5	6'2"	230	Mississippi		204
Khayat, Ed DT-DE-OT	57Was 58-61Phi 62-63Was 64-65Phi 66BosA HC71-72Phi		6'3"	240	Tulane	1	
Kilcullen, Bob DE-OT-DT	57-58ChiB 59MS 60-66ChiB		6'3"	245	Texas Tech		
Kilgore, John K	65-67LA 68ChiB 69SF	4	6'1"	203	Auburn		
Killett, Charlie HB	63NYG		6'1"	205	Memphis State		
Killorin, Pat C	66Pit		6'2"	220	Syracuse		
Kimber, Bill OE	59-60NYG 61BosA		6'2"	192	Florida State		
Kimbrough, Elbert DB	61LA 62-66SF 68NO		5'11"	193	Northwestern	9	
Kinderman, Keith FB-DB	63-64SD-A 65HouA		6'	213	Florida State		
Kindig, Howard DE-OT-C	65-66SD-A 67-69BufA 70-71Buf 72Mia 73JJ 74NYJ		6'6"	260	Los Angeles State	1	
Kindricks, Bill DT	68CinA		6'3"	268	Alabama A&M		
King, Charlie DB	66-67BufA 68-69CinA		6'	185	Purdue	2	6
King, Claude HB	61HouA 62BosA	2	5'11"	190	Houston		24
King, Henry DB	67NY-A		6'4"	205	Utah State		
King, Phil (Chief) HB-FB	58-63NYG 64Pit 65-66Min	23	6'4"	223	Vanderbilt		96
King, Tony FL	67BufA		6'1"	194	Findlay		
Kinney, George DE	65HouA		6'4"	250	Wiley		
Kirby, John LB	64-69Min 69-70NYG		6'3"	229	Nebraska		
Kirchiro, Bill OG	62Bal		6'1"	235	Maryland		
Kirk, Len LB-C	60-61ChiB 62Pit 63LA		6'2"	229	Mississippi		
Kirner, Gary OT-OG	64-69SD-A		6'3"	249	Southern Calif.		
Kirouac, Lou OG-OT	63NYG 64Bal 65JJ 66-67Atl	5	6'3"	238	Boston College		46
Klein, Dick OT	58-59ChiB 60Dal 61Pit 61-62BosA 63-64OakA		6'4"	254	Iowa		
Klotz, Jack OT	60-62NY-A 62SD-A 63NY-A 64HouA		6'5"	256	Widener		
Kochman, Roger HB	63BufA	2	6'2"	205	Penn State		6
Kocourek, Dave OE-TE	60LA-A 61-65SD-A 66MiaA 67-68OakA	2	6'5"	237	Wisconsin		150
Koeper, Rich OT	66Atl		6'4"	245	Oregon State		
Koman, Bill LB	56Bal 57-58Phi 59ChiC 60-67StL		6'2"	229	North Carolina	7	
Kompara, John DT	60LA-A		6'2"	245	South Carolina		
Koontz, Ed LB	68BosA		6'2"	230	Catawba		
Koontz, Joe WR	68NYG		6'1"	192	San Fran. State		
Kopay, Dave HB-FB	64-67SF 68Det 69-70Was 72NO 72GB	2	6'2"	220	Washington		48
Kortas, Ken DT	64StL 65-68Pit 69ChiB		6'2"	282	Louisville		6
Kosens, Terry DB	63Min		6'3"	195	Hofstra		
Kostelnik, Ron DT	61-68GB 69Bal		6'4"	260	Cincinnati		
Kotite, Dick TE-LB	67NYG 68Pit 69,71-72NYG	2	6'3"	233	Wagner		30
Kovac, Ed HB-DB	60Bal 62NY-A		6'	199	Cincinnati	1	
Kowalczyk, Walt FB-DB	58-59Phi 60Dal 61OakA	2	6'	208	Michigan State	1	18
Koy, Ernie HB-FB	65-70NYG	234	6'2"	228	Texas		90
Krakoski, Joe DB	61Was 63-66OakA		6'2"	196	Illinois	8	
Kramer, Jerry OG	58-68GB	5	6'3"	246	Idaho		177
Kramer, Ron OE-TE	57GB 58MS 59-64GB 65-67Det	2	6'3"	234	Michigan		96
Kreitling, Rich OE	59-63Cle 64ChiB	2	6'2"	208	Illinois		102
Kremser, Karl K	69MiaA 70Mia	5	6'	178	Army, Tennessee		67
Kriewald, Doug OG	67-68ChiB		6'4"	245	West Texas State		
Krisher, Billy OG	58Pit 60-61DalA		6'1"	233	Oklahoma		
Kroll, Alex C-OT	62NY-A		6'3"	230	Rutgers		
Kroner, Gary DB-K	65-67DenA	5	6'1"	200	Wisconsin		144
Krueger, Charlie DT-DE	59-73SF		6'4"	256	Texas A&M	1	12
Krupa, Joe DT	56-64Pit		6'2"	232	Purdue		
Kruse, Bob OG-OT	67-68OakA 69BufA		6'2"	250	Colorado State, Wayne State-Neb.		
Kubala, Ray C	64-67DenA		6'4"	245	Texas A&M		
Kuechenberg, Rudy LB	67-69ChiB 70GB 71Atl		6'2"	215	Indiana		
Kulbachi, Joe HB	60BufA	2	6'	185	Purdue		6
Kurek, Ralph FB	65-70ChiB	2	6'2"	210	Wisconsin		12
Lacey, Bob OE	64Min 65NYG		6'3"	205	North Carolina		
Ladd, Ernie DT	61-65SD-A 66-67HouA 67-68KC-A		6'9"	302	Grambling	1	
Lage, Dick OE	61StL		6'4"	222	Lenoir Rhyne		
Lakes, Roland DT-OT-DE	61-70SF 71NYG		6'4"	267	Wichita State		6
LaLonde, Roger DT	64Det 65NYG		6'3"	255	Muskingum		
Lamb, Mack DB	67-68MiaA		6'1"	188	Tennessee State	1	
Lambert, Frank K	65-66Pit	4	6'3"	200	Mississippi		
Lambert, Gordon (Pig) B	68-69DenA		6'5"	245	West Virginia, Tennessee-Martin		
Lamberti, Pat LB	61NY-A 61DenA		6'2"	225	Richmond	1	
Lammons, Pete TE	67-69NY-A 70-71NYJ 72GB	2	6'3"	229	Texas		84
Lamonica, Daryle QB	63-66BufA 67-69OakA 70-74Oak	12 4	6'2"	215	Notre Dame		90
Lamson, Chuck DB	62-63Min 64JJ 65-67LA 68JJ		6'	189	Wyoming	11	6
Lane, Bobby LB	63-64SD-A		6'2"	222	Baylor		
Lane, Gary QB	66-67Cle 68NYG	1	6'1"	210	Missouri		

Use Name (Nicknames) – Positions	Team by Year	See Section	Hgt	Wgt	College	Int	Pts
Lang, Izzy FB-HB	64-68Phi 69LA	2	6'1"	231	Tennessee State		48
Lanphear, Dan DE	60,62HouA		6'2"	225	Wisconsin		
Laphan, Bill C	60Phi 61Min		6'3"	250	Iowa		
Laraba, Bob LB-QB-HB	60LA-A 61SD-A		6'3"	195	Texas-El Paso	6	19
died Feb. 16, 1962 auto accident							
Laraway, Jack LB	60BufA 61HouA		6'1"	218	Purdue	1	
LaRose, Dan DE-OT-OG	61-63Det 64Pit 65SF 66DenA		6'5"	250	Missouri		
Larpenter, Carl OG-OT	61-62DenA 62DalA		6'4"	237	Texas		
Larscheid, Jack HB	60-61OakA	23	5'6"	162	U. of Pacific		12
Larsen, Gary DT	64LA 65-74Min		6'5"	256	Concordia (Minn.)		
Larson, Bill FB	60BosA		5'10"	190	Illinois Wesleyan		
Larson, Greg C-OG-OT	61-73NYG		6'2"	249	Minnesota		
Larson, Pete HB	67-68Was	2	6'1"	200	Cornell		18
Lasky, Frank OT	64-65NYG		6'2"	265	Florida		
Lasse, Dick LB	58-59Pit 60-61Was 62NYG		6'2"	222	Syracuse	3	
Lassiter, Ike DE-DT	62-64DenA 65-69OakA 70Bos 71NE		6'5"	270	St. Augustine	1	
Latourette, Chuck DB-WR	67-68,70-71StL	34	6'	190	Rice		12
Latzke, Paul C	66-68SD-A		6'4"	242	U. of Pacific		
Lavan, Al DB	69-70Atl		6'1"	194	Colorado State	5	
Lawrence, Don DT-OG-OT	59-61Was		6'1"	245	Notre Dame		
Lawrence, Kent WR	69Phi 70Atl		5'11"	175	Georgia		
Lawson, Al FL	64NY-A		5'11"	190	Delaware State		
Lawson, Jerry DB	68BufA		5'11"	192	Utah		
LeBeau, Dick DB	59-72Det		6'1"	185	Ohio State	62	14
LeClair, Jim QB	67-68DenA	1	6'1"	208	C. W. Post		6
LeClerc, Roger LB-C-DT	60-66ChiB 67DenA	5	6'3"	236	Trinity (Conn.)		382
Ledbetter, Monte WR-FL	67HouA 67-69BufA 69Atl	2	6'2"	185	Northwestern La.		18
Lee, Bob OG	60BosA		6'1"	245	Missouri		
Lee, Bob WR	68StL 69Atl		6'3"	200	Minnesota		
Lee, Dwight HB	68SF 68Atl		6'2"	198	Michigan State		
Lee, Herm OT-OG	57Pit 58-66ChiB		6'4"	244	Florida A&M		
Lee, Jacky QB	60-63HouA 64-65DenA 66-67HouA	12	6'1"	186	Cincinnati		18
	67-69KC-A						
Lee, Monte LB	61StL 62MS 63-64Det 65Bal		6'4"	221	Texas	1	
Leetzow, Max DE-DT	65-66DenA 67JJ		6'4"	240	Idaho		
Leeuwenberg, Dick OT	65ChiB		6'5"	242	Stanford		
Leftridge, Dick FB	66Pit		6'2"	240	West Virginia		12
Leggett, Earl DT-DE	57-60ChiB 61KJ 62-65ChiB		6'3"	254	Louisiana State	1	2
	66LA 67-68NO						
Lemek, Ray OT-OG	57-61Was 62-65Pit		6'	238	Notre Dame		
Lemm, Wally	HC61HouA HC62-65StL				Carroll (Wis.)		
	HC66-69HouA HC70Hou						
Lemmerman, Bruce QB	68-69Atl	1	6'1"	196	Northridge State		
LeMoine, Jim OG-LB-TE	67BufA 68-69HouA		6'2"	245	Utah State		
Lentz, Jack DB	67-68DenA		6'	195	Holy Cross	5	
Leo Bobby HB-WR	67-68BosA		5'10"	180	Harvard		6
Leo, Charlie OG	60-62BosA 63BufA		6'	238	Indiana		
Leo, Jim DE-LB	60NYG 61-62Min		6'1"	222	Cincinnati		2
Lester, Darrell FB	64Min 65-66DenA	2	6'2"	223	McNeese State		6
Letner, Cotton LB	61BufA		6'1"	215	Tennessee		
Lewis, Dan HB	58-64Det 65Was 66NYG	23	6'1"	199	Wisconsin		144
Lewis, Gary FB-HB	64-69SF 70NO	23	6'3"	228	Arizona State		108
Lewis, Hal DB	68DenA		6'2"	188	Arizona State		
Lewis, Harold HB-DB	59Bal 60BufA 62OakA		6'	200	Houston		
Lewis, Joe DT	58-60Pit 61Bal 62Phi		6'2"	256	Compton C.C.	1	6
Lewis, Sherman DB	66-67NY-A		5'10"	180	Michigan State		
Lilly, Bob DT-DE	61-74Dal		6'4"	256	Texas Christian	1	24
Lince, Dave TE	66-67Phi		6'6"	258	North Dakota		
Lincoln, Keith HB-FB	61-66SD-A 67-68BufA 68SD-A	23 5	6'2"	212	Washington State		271
Lind, Mike DB	63-64SF 65-66Pit	2	6'2"	220	Notre Dame		54
Linden, Errol OT	61Cle 62-65Min 66-68Atl 69-70NO		6'5"	258	Houston		
Lindquist, Paul DT	61BosA		6'3"	265	New Hampshire		
Lindsey, Dale LB	65-72Cle 73NO		6'3"	224	Western Kentucky	8	6
Lindsey, Hub HB	68DenA		5'11"	196	Wyoming		
Lindsey, Jim HB-FB	66-72Min	2	6'2"	206	Arkansas		66
Linne, Aubrey OE	61Bal		6'7"	235	Texas Christian		
Lisbon, Don HB	63-64SF	2	6'	194	Bowling Green		18
Liscio, Tony OT-OG	63-64Dal 65JJ 66-71Dal		6'5"	251	Tulsa		
Liske, Pete QB	64NY-A 65-68CFL 69DenA 70Den 71-72Phi	12	6'2"	199	Penn State		12
Livingston, Andy FB-HB	64-65ChiB 66KJ	2	6'	234	none		66
	67-68ChiB 69-70NO						
Livingston, Cliff LB-DE	54-61NYG 62Min 63-65LA		6'3"	212	U.C.L.A.	8	6
Livingston, Dale K	68-69CinA 70GB	45	6'	210	Western Michigan		123
Livingston, Walt HB	60BosA		6'	185	Heidelberg		
Livingston, Warren DB	61-66Dal		5'10"	185	Arizona	10	6
Lloyd, Dave LB-C	59-61Cle 62Det 63-70Phi		6'3"	247	Georgia	14	10
Lockett, J. W. FB	61SF 61-62Dal 63Bal 64Was	2	6'2"	229	Central St.-Okla.		60
Locklin, Billy LB	60OakA		6'2"	225	New Mexico State		
Lofton, Oscar OE	60BosA 61-62MS	2	6'6"	218	Southeastern La.		24
Logan, Chuck TE-OE	64Pit 65,67-68StL		6'4"	215	Northwestern		
Logan, Jerry DB	63-72Bal	3	6'1"	188	West Texas State	34	36
Logan, Obert DB	65-66Dal 67NO		5'10"	180	Trinity (Texas)	8	6
Lomakoski, John OT	62Det		6'4"	250	Western Michigan		
Lombardi, Vince	HC59-67GB HC69-70Was				Fordham		
died Sept. 3, 1970 – cancer							
London, Mike LB	66SD-A		6'2"	230	Wisconsin		
Long, Bob FL-WR	64-67GB 68Atl 69Was 70LA	2	6'3"	199	Wichita State		60
Long, Charley OG-OT	61-69BosA		6'3"	247	Tenn.-Chattanooga		
Long, Dave DE-DT	66-68StL 69-72NO		6'4"	241	Iowa		
Long, Mike OE	60BosA		6'	188	Brandeis		
Longenecker, Ken DT	60Pit		6'4"	285	Lebanon Valley		
Longmire, Sam DB-WR	67-68KC-A		6'3"	195	Purdue		
Look, Dean QB	62NY-A		5'11"	185	Michigan State		
61 played major league baseball							
Looney, Joe Don FB-HB	64Bal 65-66Det 66-67Was	234	6'1"	230	Texas, Texas Christian		78
	68MS 69NO				Oklahoma		
Lopasky, Bill OG	61SF		6'2"	235	West Virginia		
Lorick, Tony FB	64-67Bal 68-69NO	23	6'1"	214	Arizona State		114
Lothamer, Ed DT-DE	64-69KC-A 71-72KC		6'5"	261	Michigan State		
Lothridge, Billy QB-DB-K	64Dal 65LA 66-71Atl 72Mia	4	6'1"	194	Georgia Tech	3	6
Lott, Billy FB-HB-DB	58NYG 60OakA 61-63BosA	2	6'	203	Mississippi		128
Loudd, Rommie LB	60LA-A 61-62BosA		6'3"	227	U.C.L.A.	4	
Louderback, Tom LB-C-OG	58-59Phi 60-61OakA 62BufA		6'2"	235	San Jose State	3	6
Loukas, Angelo OG-OT	69BufA 70Bos		6'3"	250	Northwestern		
Love, John FL-WR-DB	67Was 68MS 72LA	23 5	5'11"	185	North Texas State		40

Use Name (Nicknames) – Positions	Team by Year	See Section	Hgt	Wgt	College	Int	Pts
Lovetere, John DT	59-62LA 63-65NYG		6'4"	280	Compton C.C.		6
Lowe, Gary DB-HB	56-57Was 57-64Det		5'11"	196	Michigan State	20	2
Lowe, Paul HB	60LA-A 61SD-A 62BA 63-67SD-A	23	6'	200	Oregon State		282
	68-69KC-A						
Lucas, Dick OE	58Pit 60-63Phi	2	6'2"	213	Boston College		36
Lucas, Richie QB-HB-DB	60-61BufA	12	6'	190	Penn State	2	30
Lucci, Mike LB	62-64Cle 65-73Det		6'2"	230	Tennessee	21	24
Luce, Lew HB	61Was		6'	187	Penn State		
Luke, Tommy DB	68DenA		6'	190	Mississippi		
Lundy, Lamar DE-OE	57-69LA	2	6'7"	245	Purdue	3	54
Lusteg, Booth K	66BufA 67MiaA 68Pit 69GB	5	5'11"	190	none		202
Lyles, Lenny DB-HB	58Bal 59-60SF 61-69Bal	23	6'2"	202	Louisville	16	48
Lynch, Dick DB	58Was 59-66NYG		6'1"	202	Notre Dame	37	42
Mack, Red FL-OE-HB	61-63Pit 64Phi	2	5'10"	185	Notre Dame		48
	65Pit 66Atl 66GB						
Mackbee, Earsell DB	65-69Min		6'1"	195	Utah State	15	12
Mackey, Dee OE	60SF 61-62Bal 63-66NY-A	2	6'5"	232	East Texas State		50
Mackey, John TE-OE	63-71Bal 72SD	2	6'3"	222	Syracuse		228
MacKinnon, Jacque TE-OE-FB-OG	61-69SD-A 70Oak	2	6'4"	245	Colgate		134
Maczuzak, John DT	64KC-A		6'5"	250	Pittsburgh		
Magac, Mike OG	60-64SF 65-66Pit		6'3"	240	Missouri		
Maguire, Paul LB-DE-OE-K	60LA-A 61-63SD-A	4	6'	224	The Citadel	9	6
	64-69BufA 70Buf						
Maher, Bruce DB-HB	60-67Det 68-69NYG		5'11"	190	Detroit	22	6
Majors, Billy DB	61BufA		6'	175	Tennessee		
Mallick, Fran DE-DT	65Pit		6'3"	245	none		
Mallory, John DB	68Phi 69-71Atl	3	6'	188	West Virginia	2	24
Manders, Dave C	64-66Dal 67JJ 68-74Dal		6'2"	247	Michigan State		
Mangum, John DT	66-67BosA		6'3"	273	Southern Miss.		
Mankins, Jim FB	67Atl		6'1"	235	Florida State		
Manning, Pete DB	60-61ChiB		6'3"	208	Wake Forest		
Manoukian, Don OG	60OakA		5'9"	242	Stanford		
Maples, Jim LB	63Bal		6'4"	225	Baylor		
Marchlewski, Frank C	65LA 66-68Atl 68-69LA 70Buf		6'2"	237	Minnesota		
Marconi, Joe FB-HB	56-61LA 62-66ChiB	2	6'2"	225	West Virginia		234
Marcontell, Ed OG	67StL 67HouA		6'	220	Lamar		
Marinovich, Marv OG	65OakA		6'3"	250	Southern Calif.		
Marion, Jerry FL	67Pit		5'10"	175	Wyoming		
Marques, Bob LB	60NY-A		6'	220	Boston U.		
Marsh, Aaron WR	68-69BosA	2	6'	190	Eastern Kentucky		24
Marsh, Amos HB-FB	61-64Dal 65-67Det	23	6'	218	Oregon State		198
Marsh, Frank DB	67SD-A		6'2"	205	Oregon State		
Marshall, Bud DT	65GB 66Was 66Atl 67-68HouA		6'5"	271	S.F. Austin State		
Marshall, Chuck DB	62DenA		6'	180	Oregon State		
Marshall, Jim DE	60Cle 61-79Min		6'3"	239	Ohio State	1	8
Martha, Paul DB-FL-OE-HB	64-69Pit 70Den	2	6'	186	Pittsburgh	21	6
Martin, Aaron DB	64-65LA 66-67Phi 68Was	3	6'	187	N. Car. Central		
Martin, Billy (Bill) TE-OE	64-65ChiB	2 4	6'4"	238	Georgia Tech		24
	66-67Atl 68Min						
Martin, Billy HB	62-64ChiB	3	5'11"	196	Minnesota		6
Martin, Blanche FB	60NY-A 60LA-A		6'	195	Michigan State		6
Martin, Dave LB	68KC-A 69ChiB		6'	220	Notre Dame		
Martin, Larry DT	66SD-A		6'2"	270	San Diego State		
Mason, Tommy HB-FB	61-66Min 67-70LA 71Was 72JJ	23	6'	195	Tulane		270
Masters, Norm OT	57-64GB		6'2"	249	Michigan State		
Matan, Bill DE	66NYG		6'4"	240	Kansas State		
Mathis, Bill HB-FB	60-69NY-A	2	6'1"	219	Clemson		282
Matsos, Archie LB	60-62BufA 63-65OakA		6'	215	Michigan State	22	6
	66DenA 66SD-A						
Matte, Tom HB-QB	61-72Bal	123	6'	207	Ohio State		342
Matthews, Wes OE	66MiaA		5'10"	180	Northeastern Okla.		
Mattox, Jack DT	61DenA		6'4"	240	Fresno State		
Matson, Riley OT	61-64Was 65JJ 66ChiB		6'4"	252	Oregon		
Mayberry, Doug FB	61-62Min 63OakA	2	6'1"	223	Utah State		12
Mayes, Ben DE-DT	69HouA		6'5"	265	Duke		
Maynard, Don FL-WR-OE-HB	58NYG 60-69NY-A	23	6'	180	Texas-El Paso		532
	70-72NYJ 73StL						
Mays, Jerry DE-DT	61-62DalA 63-69KC-A 70KC		6'4"	250	S.M.U.	1	6
Mazurek, Fred FL-DB	65-66Was		5'11"	192	Pittsburgh		
Mazzanti, Jerry DE	63Phi 64-65MS 66Det 67Pit		6'3"	240	Arkansas		
McAdams, Bob DT	63-64NY-A		6'3"	250	N. Car. Central		
McAdams, Carl LB-DT-DE	67-69NY-A		6'3"	240	Oklahoma		
McBride, Norm DE	69MiaA 70Mia		6'3"	240	Utah		
McCall, Don HB	67-68NO 69Pit 70NO	23	5'11"	195	Southern Calif.		60
McCall, Ron LB	67-68SD-A		6'2"	245	Weber State		
McCambridge, John DE	67Det		6'4"	245	Northwestern		
McCann, Tim DT	69NYG		6'5"	265	Princeton		
McCarthy, Brendan FB	68Atl 68-69DenA	2	6'3"	220	Boston College		18
McCarty, Mickey TE	69KC-A		6'5"	255	Texas Christian		
McClellan, Mike DB	62-63Phi 64-65MS		6'1"	185	Oklahoma	4	
McClinton, Curtis FB-TE	62DalA 63-69KC-A	2	6'3"	230	Kansas		196
McCloughan, Kent DB	65-69OakA 70Oak		6'1"	190	Nebraska	15	
McClure, Wayne LB	68CinA 70Cin		6'1"	225	Mississippi		
McComb, Don DE	60BosA		6'4"	240	Villanova		
McCord, Darris DE-DT-OT	55-67Det		6'4"	247	Tennessee	3	8
McCormick, Dave OT	66SF 67-68NO		6'6"	250	Louisiana State		
McCormick, John QB	62Min 63DenA 64KJ	1 4	6'1"	201	Massachusetts		
	65-66,68DenA						
McCoy, Lloyd OG	64SD-A		6'1"	245	San Diego State		
McCreery, Bob OT	61Bal		6'5"	256	Wake Forest		
McCullers, Dale LB	69MiaA		6'1"	215	Florida State		
McCullough, Bob OG	62-65DenA		6'5"	244	Colorado		
McCuster, Jim OT	58ChiC 59-62Phi 63Cle 64NY-A		6'2"	246	Pittsburgh		
McDaniel, Wahoo LB-OG	60HouA 61-63DenA	4	6'	235	Oklahoma	13	6
	64-65NY-A 66-68MiaA						
McDaniels, Dave WR	68Dal		6'4"	200	Miss. Valley St.		
McDermott, Gary HB	68BufA 69Atl	2	6'1"	211	Tulsa		26
McDole, Ron DE-DT	61StL 62HouA 63-69BufA		6'3"	266	Nebraska	11	14
	70Buf 71-77Was						
McDonald, Don DB	61BufA		5'11"	185	Houston		
McDonald, Ray FB	67-68Was	2	6'4"	248	Idaho		24
McDonald, Tommy FL-HB-WR	57-63Phi 64Dal 65-66LA	23	5'10"	176	Oklahoma		510
	67Atl 68Cle						
McDougall, Gerry FB	62-64,68SD-A	2	6'2"	225	U.C.L.A.		38
McDowell, John OT-OG	64GB 65NYG 66StL		6'3"	260	St. John's-Minn.		
McFadin, Bud DT-DG-OG-LB	52-56LA 60-63DenA		6'3"	260	Texas	1	24
	64-65HouA						

Use Name (Nicknames) – Positions	Team by Year	See Section	Hgt	Wgt	College	Int	Pts
McFarland, Kay FL-OE-WR	62-66SF 67JJ 68SF	2	6'2"	182	Colorado State		24
McFarlane, Nyle HB	60OakA		6'2"	205	Brigham Young		12
McGee, Ben DE-DT	64-72Pit		6'2"	255	Jackson State	1	6
McGee, George OT	60BosA 61-62MS		6'2"	259	Southern U.		
McGee, Max OE	54GB 55-56MS 57-67GB	2 4	6'3"	205	Tulane		306
McGee, Mike OG	60-62StL		6'1"	230	Duke		
McGeever, John DB	62-65DenA 66MiaA		6'1"	195	Auburn	11	6
McGrew, Dan C	60BufA		6'2"	250	Purdue		
McIlhany, Dan DB	65LA		6'1"	195	Texas A&M	2	
McInnis, Hugh OE-TE	60-62StL 64Det 66Atl	2	6'3"	219	Southern Miss.		
McKeever, Marlin LB-TE-OE	61-66LA 67Min	2	6'1"	233	Southern Calif.	9	36
	68-70Was 71-72LA 73Phi						
McKinnon, Don LB-C	63-64BosA		6'3"	223	Dartmouth		
McLenna, Bruce HB	66Det		6'3"	225	Hillsdale		
McLeod, Bob OE-TE	61-66HouA	2	6'5"	231	Abilene Christian		114
McMahon, Art DB	68-69BosA 70Bos 72NE		5'11"	188	N. Carolina State	3	
McMillan, Ernie OT	61-74StL 75GB		6'6"	258	Illinois		
McMillan, Jim DB	61-62DenA 63-64OakA 64-65DenA		5'11"	190	Colorado State	14	24
McMullen, John OG	60-61NY-A		6'	244	Notre Dame		
McMurtry, Chuck DT	60-61BufA 62-63OakA		6'	286	Whittier		
McNamara, Bob DB-HB	60-61DenA		6'	189	Minnesota	7	12
McNeil, Charley DB	60LA-A 61-64SD-A		5'11"	179	Compton C.C.	19	12
McNeil, Clifton WR-FL	64-67Cle 68-69SF 70-71NYG	2	6'2"	186	Grambling		138
	71-72Was 73Hou						
McQuarters, Ed DT	65StL		6'1"	250	Oklahoma		
McRae, Bennie DB	62-70ChiB 71NYG		6'1"	180	Michigan	27	24
McRae, Frank DT	67ChiB		6'7"	270	Tennessee State		
McWaters, Bill FB	64Min		6'	225	North Texas		
Meador, Ed DB	59-70LA	3	5'11"	193	Arkansas Tech	46	36
Medved, Ron DB	66-70Phi		6'1"	205	Washington	3	
Meggysey, Dave LB	63-69StL		6'1"	221	Syracuse		
Meinert, Dale LB-OG-OT	58-59ChiC 60-67StL		6'2"	219	Oklahoma State	9	6
Meixler, Ed LB	65BosA		6'3"	245	Boston U.		
Melinkovich, Mike DE	65-66StL 67Det		6'4"	243	Grays Harbor J.C.		
Mellekas, John C-DT-OT	56ChiB 57MS 58-61ChiB		6'3"	255	Arizona		
	62SF 63Phi						
Memmelaar, Dale OG-OT	59ChiC 60-61StL 62-63Dal		6'2"	247	Wyoming		
	64-65Cle 66-67Dal						
Mendez, Mario HB	64SD-A		5'11"	200	San Diego State		
Menefee, Pep FL	66NYG		6'1"	108	New Mexico State		
Mercein, Chuck FB	65-67NYG 67-68GB 69Was 70NYJ	2 5	6'3"	227	Yale		45
Mercer, Mike K	61-62Min 63-66OakA 66KC-A	45	6'	208	Arizona State		594
	67-68BufA 68-69GB 70SD						
Meredith, Don (Dandy Don) QB	60-68Dal	12	6'2"	202	S.M.U.		
Meredith, Dudley DT	63HouA 64-68BufA 68HouA		6'4"	280	Lamar	1	
Mertens, Jerry DB	58-62SF 63KJ 64-65SF		6'	184	Drake	8	6
Mertens, Jim TE	69MiaA		6'3"	235	Fairmont State		
Merz, Curt OG-DE	62DalA 63-68KC-A		6'4"	257	Iowa		
Messer, Dale HB-FL-DB	61-65SF	2	5'10"	175	Fresno State	1	
Messner, Max LB	60-63Det 64NYG 64-65Pit		6'3"	225	Cincinnati	2	
Mestnik, Frank FB	60-61StL 63GB	2	6'2"	200	Marquette		30
Meyer, Ed OT	60BufA		6'2"	240	West Texas State		
Meyer, John LB	66HouA		6'1"	225	Notre Dame		
Meyer, Ron QB	66Pit		6'4"	205	S. Dakota State		
Meyers, John DT	62-63Dal 64-67Phi		6'6"	272	Washington	2	
Meylan, Wayne LB	68-69Cle 70Min		6'1"	237	Nebraska		
Michael, Rich OT	60-63HouA 64JJ 65-66HouA		6'3"	238	Ohio State		
Michaels, Lou DE-K	58-60LA 61-63Pit	5	6'2"	243	Kentucky		955
	64-69Bal 71GB						
Michel, Tom HB	64Min	2	6'	210	East Carolina		
Middendorf, Dave OG	68-69CinA 70NYJ		6'3"	260	Washington State		
Milks, John LB	66SD-A		6'	222	San Diego State	1	
Miller, Al LB	62-63Was		6'	224	Ohio U.		
Miller, Alan FB	60BosA 61-63OakA 64JJ 65OakA	2	6'	202	Boston College		120
Miller, Bill DT	62HouA		6'4"	270	N. Mex. Highlands		
Miller, Bill OE-WR	62DalA 63BufA 64,66-68OakA	2	6'	192	Miami (Fla.)		60
Miller, Clark DE	62-68SF 69Was 70LA		6'5"	246	Utah State	1	6
Miller, Fred DT	63-72Bal		6'3"	248	Louisiana State		
Miller, Ron QB	62LA	1	6'	190	Wisconsin		
Mills, Dick OG	61-62Det		6'3"	240	Pittsburgh		
Mills, Pete OE	65-66BufA		5'11"	180	Wichita State		
Milstead, Charlie QB-DB	60-61HouA	4	6'2"	190	Texas A&M	2	1
Milton, Gene WR	68-69MiaA	23	5'10"	170	Florida A&M		12
Mingo, Gene HB-K	60-63DenA 64-65OakA	23 5	6'1"	199	none		629
	66-67MiaA 67Was 69-70Pit						
Minnicar, Randy HB	67-69NYG 70Cle	2	6'	205	Purdue		36
Minter, Tom DB	62DenA 62BufA		5'10"	178	Baylor		
Mira, George QB	64-68SF 69Phi 71Mia	12	5'11"	190	Miami (Fla.)		
Mirich, Rex DT-DE	64-66OakA 67-69DenA 70Bos		6'4"	251	Arizona State		
Mischak, Bob OG	58NYG 60-62NY-A 63-65OakA		6'	237	Army		
Mitchell, Alvin DB-WR	68-69Cle 70Den		6'3"	195	Morgan State		
Mitchell, Bobby FL-HB-WR	58-61Cle 62-68Was	23	6'	192	Illinois		546
Mitchell, Charley HB-DB	63-67DenA 68BufA	23	5'11"	185	Washington	1	54
Mitchell, Ed OG	65-67SD-A		6'2"	275	Southern U.		
Mitchell, Stan FB-HB-OE	66-69MiaA 70Mia 71JJ	2	6'2"	220	Tennessee		54
Mitchell, Willie DB	64-69KC-A 70KC	3	6'1"	185	Tennessee State	16	24
Mitinger, Bob LB-DE	62-64,66,68SD-A		6'2"	232	Penn State	3	
Mix, Ron OT-OG	60LA-A 61-69SD-A 70VR 71Oak		6'4"	249	Southern Calif.		
Molden, Frank DT	65LA 66-67KJ 68Phi 69NYG		6'5"	282	Jackson State	1	6
Montalbo, Mel DB	62OakA		6'1"	190	Utah State		
Moore, Alex DB	68DenA		6'	195	Norfolk State		
Moore, Charlie OG	62Was		6'5"	230	Arkansas		
Moore, Denis DT-DE	67-69Det		6'5"	247	Southern Calif.		
Moore, Fred DT-DE	64-66SD-A		6'4"	260	Oklahoma	1	
Moore, Gene HB	69SF		6'	208	Occidental		
Moore, Lenny HB-FL	56-67Bal	23	6'1"	191	Penn State		678
Moore, Leroy DE	60BufA 61-62BosA 62-63BufA		6'	231	Ft. Valley State	2	6
	64-65DenA						
Moore, Rich DT	69-70GB		6'6"	285	Villanova		
Moore, Tom HB	60-65GB 66LA 67Atl	23	6'2"	213	Vanderbilt		186
Mooty, Jim DB	60Dal		5'11"	177	Arkansas		
Moran, Jim DT	64NYG 65BL 66-67NYG		6'5"	260	Idaho		
Moreau, Doug TE-OE	66-69MiaA	2	6'2"	207	Louisiana State		45
Morelli, Fran OT	62NY-A		6'2"	258	Colgate		
Morgan, Bobby DB	67Pit		6'	205	New Mexico		

Use Name (Nicknames) – Positions	Team by Year	See Section	Hgt	Wgt	College	Int	Pts
Morgan, Mike LB	64-67Phi 68Was 69-70NO 71JJ		6'4"	241	Louisiana State	6	12
Morrall, Earl QB	56SF 57-58Pit 58-64Det	12 4	6'1"	205	Michigan State		48
	65-67NYG 68-71Bal 72-76Mia						
Morris, Dennit LB	58SF 60-61HouA		6'1"	228	Oklahoma	5	
Morris, Johnny FL-HB	58-67ChiB	23	5'10"	180	Cal.-Santa Barbara		222
Morris, Larry LB-HB	55-57LA 59-64ChiB 66Atl	2	6'2"	226	Georgia Tech	6	12
Morris, Riley LB-DE	60-62OakA		6'2"	230	Florida A&M	3	6
Morrison, Joe HB-FL-WR-FB-DB-OE	59-72NYG	23	6'1"	210	Cincinnati		390
Morrow, John C-OG-DE	56LA 57MS 58-59LA 60-66Cle		6'3"	244	Michigan		
Morrow, Tom DB	62-64OakA	4	5'11"	185	Southern Miss.	23	
Morze, Frank C-DT	57-61SF 62-63Cle 64SF		6'4"	272	Boston College		
Mostardi, Rich DB	60Cle 61Min 62OakA		5'11"	188	Kent State	2	
Moten, Bobby WR	68DenA		6'4"	212	Bishop		
Mudd, Howard OG	64-69SF 69-70ChiB		6'3"	251	Hillsdale		
Muelhaupt, Ed OG	60-61BufA		6'3"	230	Iowa State		
Mullins, Don DB	61-62ChiB		6'1"	195	Houston		
Mumley, Nick DE-OT	60-62NY-A		6'6"	252	Purdue	1	6
Murchison, Lee OE	61Dal		6'3"	205	U. of Pacific		
Murdock, Jesse HB-FB	63OakA 63BufA		6'2"	203	Calif. Western		
Murdock, Les K	67NYG	5	6'3"	245	Florida State		25
Murphy, Bill WR	68BosA	2	6'1"	185	Cornell		
Murphy, Dennis DT	65ChiB		6'1"	250	Florida		
Murphy, Fred OE	60Cle 61Min		6'3"	205	Georgia Tech		
Musgrove, Spain DT-DE	67-69Was 70Hou		6'4"	275	Utah State		
Myers, Tom QB	65-66Det		6'	188	Northwestern		
Nairn, Harvey WR	68NY-A 69MS		6'1"	178	Southern U.		
Nance, Jim FB	65-69Bos A 70Bos 71NE 73NYJ	2	6'1"	241	Syracuse		276
Napier, Walter DT	60-61DalA		6'4"	275	Paul Quinn		
Neck, Tommy DB	62ChiB		5'11"	190	Louisiana State		
Neff, Bob DB	66-68MiaA	3	6'	182	S.F. Austin State	2	
Neidert, John (J.T.) LB	68CinA 68-69NY-A 70ChiB		6'2"	230	Louisville		
Neighbors, Billy OG	62-65BosA 66-69MiaA		5'11"	244	Alabama		
Nelsen, Bill QB	63-67Pit 68-72Cle	12	6'	195	Southern Calif.		12
Nelson, Al DB	65-73Phi	3	5'11"	185	Cincinnati	13	18
Nelson, Andy (Bones) DB	57-63Bal 64NYG		6'1"	180	Memphis State	33	18
Nelson, Benny DB	64HouA		6'	185	Alabama	1	6
Nery, Ron DE	60LA-A 61-62SD-A 63DenA 63HouA		6'6"	236	Kansas State		
Nettles, Jim DB	65-68Phi 69-72LA		5'9"	177	Wisconsin	26	24
Neumann, Tom HB	63BosA	2	5'11"	205	Northern Michigan		6
Nevett, Elijah DB-FL	67-70NO		6'	185	Clark-Ga.	6	
Newell, Steve OE	67SD-A		6'1"	186	Long Beach State		
Nichols, Bob OT	65Pit 66-67LA		6'3"	250	Stanford		
Nichols, Bobby TE	66-67BosA		6'2"	220	Boston U.		
Nichols, Mike C	60-61DenA		6'3"	225	Ark.-Pine Bluff		
Nicklas, Pete OT	62OakA		6'4"	240	Baylor		
Ninowski, Jim QB	58-59Cle 60-61Det 62-66Cle	12	6'1"	206	Michigan State		60
	67-68Was 69NO						
Nisby, John OG	57-61Pit 62-64Was		6'1"	235	Pacific (Ore.)		
Nitschke, Ray LB	58-72GB		6'3"	235	Illinois	25	12
Nocera, John LB	59-62Phi 63DenA		6'1"	220	Iowa	1	
Nofsinger, Terry QB	61-64Pit 65-66StL 67Atl	12	6'4"	209	Utah		18
Nomina, Tom DT-OG	63-65DenA 66-68MiaA		6'5"	267	Miami-Ohio		
Noonan, Karl WR-OE	66-69MiaA 70-71Mia 72KJ	2	6'3"	193	Iowa		102
Norman, Dick QB	61ChiB		6'3"	210	Stanford		
Norman, Pettis TE-OE	62-70Dal 71-73SD	2	6'3"	220	Johnson C. Smith		90
Norris, Jim DT-OT	62-64OakA		6'4"	235	Houston	2	
Norris, Trusse OE	60LA-A		6'1"	190	U.C.L.A.		
Norton, Don OE	60LA-A 61-66SD-A	2	6'1"	190	Iowa		162
Norton, Jim DB	60-68HouA	4	6'3"	187	Idaho	45	
Norton, Jim DT-OT-OE	65-66SF 67-68Atl 68Phi		6'4"	254	Washington	1	
	69Was 70NYG						
Norton, Ray HB	60-61SF		6'2"	184	San Jose State		
Norton, Rick QB	66-69MiaA 70GB	1	6'1"	192	Kentucky		
Novsek, Joe DE	62OakA		6'4"	237	Tulsa		
Nowatzke, Tom FB-LB	65-69Det 70-72Bal	2	6'3"	229	Indiana	1	102
Nugent, Phil DB	61DenA		6'2"	195	Tulane	7	
Nunnery, R. B. OT	60DalA		6'4"	275	Louisiana State		
Nutting, Ed OT	61Cle 62JJ 63Dal		6'4"	246	Georgia Tech		
Oakes, Don OT-DT	61-62Phi 63-68BosA		6'3"	253	Virginia Tech		
Oates, Carlton DE-DT	65-69OakA 70-72Oak 73GB		6'2"	252	Florida A&M		6
Oberg, Tom DB	68-69DenA		6'	185	Portland State	3	
O'Bradovich, Ed DE	62-71ChiB		6'3"	255	Illinois		8
O'Brien, Dave DT-OT-OG	63-64Min 65NYG 66-67StL		6'3"	244	Boston College		
O'Brien, Fran OT-OG-DE	59Cle 60-66Was 66-68Pit		6'1"	253	Michigan State		
Odle, Phil WR	68-70Det		5'11"	191	Brigham Young		
Odom, Sammy LB	64HouA		6'2"	235	Northwestern La.	2	
O'Donnell, Joe OG-OT	64-67BufA 68KJ 69BufA 70-71Buf		6'2"	253	Michigan		
Ogas, Dave LB	68OakA 69BufA		6'3"	240	San Diego State		
Ogden, Ray TE-WR-OE	65-66StL 67NO	2	6'5"	225	Alabama		24
	67-68Atl 69-71ChiB						
Oglesby, Paul DT	60OakA		6'4"	235	U.C.L.A.		
O'Hanley, Ross DB	60-65BosA 66JJ		6'	183	Boston College	15	6
Oliver, Bob OT	69Cle		6'3"	240	Abilene Christian		
Oliver, Chip LB	68-69OakA		6'2"	220	Southern Calif.	1	6
Oliver, Clancy DB	69-70Pit		6'1"	180	San Diego State		
Olsen, Merlin DT	62-76LA		6'5"	270	Utah State	1	6
Olson, Harold OT	60-62BufA 63-64DenA		6'3"	259	Clemson		
Olssen, Lance OT	68-69SF		6'5"	262	Purdue		
O'Mahoney, Jim LB	65-66NY-A		6'1"	231	Miami (Fla.)		
Onesti, Larry LB	62-65HouA		6'	200	Northwestern		6
Orr, Jimmy FL-OE-WR	58-60Pit 61-70Bal	2 4	5'11"	185	Georgia		396
Osborne, Clancy LB	59-60SF 61-62Min 63-64OakA		6'3"	218	Arizona State	6	
Osborne, Tom OE	60-61Was	2	6'3"	190	Hastings		12
Otto, Gus LB	65-69OakA 70-73Oak		6'2"	220	Missouri	6	12
Otto, Jim C	60-69OakA 70-74Oak		6'2"	244	Miami (Fla.)		
Overton, Jerry DB	63Dal		6'2"	190	Utah		
injured in accident before 1964 season							
Owens, Don DT-OT	57Was 58-60Phi 60-63StL		6'5"	255	Southern Miss.		6
Owens, Luke DE-DT-OT	57Bal 58-59ChiC 60-65StL		6'2"	254	Kent State		2
Owens, R. C. (Alley Oop) OE-FL	57-61SF 62-63Bal 64NYG	2	6'3"	197	Coll. of Idaho		138
Pagliei, Joe FB	59Phi 60NY-A	4	6'	220	Clemson		6
Paluck, John DE-DT	56Was 57-58MS 59-65Was		6'2"	241	Pittsburgh	2	8
Papac, Nick QB	61OakA	1	5'11"	190	Fresno State		6

Use Name (Nicknames) – Positions	Team by Year	See Section	Hgt	Wgt	College	Int	Pts
Pardee, Jack LB	57-64LA 65VR 66-70LA 71-72Was HC75-77ChiB HC78-80Was HC90Hou		6'2"	224	Texas A&M	22	38
Paremore, Bob HB	63-64StL	2	5'11"	190	Florida A&M		12
Parilli, Babe QB	52-53GB 54-55MS 56Cle 57-58GB 59CFL 60OakA 61-67BosA 68-69NY-A	12	6'1"	190	Kentucky		146
Park, Ernie OT-OG	63-65SD-A 66MiaA 67DenA 69CinA		6'3"	247	McMurry		
Parker, Charlie OG	65DenA		6'1"	245	Southern Miss.		
Parker, Don OG	67SF 68KJ		6'3"	235	Virginia		
Parker, Frank DT	62-64Cle 65IL 66-67Cle 68Pit 69NYG		6'5"	263	Oklahoma State		
Parker, Jim OT-OG	57-67Bal		6'3"	273	Ohio State		
Parker, Willie DT	68-69HouA 70Hou		6'2"	266	Ark.–Pine Bluff		
Parks, Dave OE-TE-WR	64-67SF 68-72NO 73Hou	2	6'2"	202	Texas Tech		264
Parrish, Bernie DB	59-66Cle 66HouA		5'11"	194	Florida	31	24
Pashe, Bill DB	64NY-A		5'11"	185	George Washington		
Patera, Dennis K	68SF	5	6'	225	Brigham Young		16
Patera, Herb LB	63BufA		6'1"	222	Michigan State		
Patton, Jimmy DB	55-66NYG	3	6'	183	Mississippi	52	24
Paulson, Dainard DB	61-66NY-A		5'11"	190	Oregon State	29	6
Peacock, Johnny DB	69HouA 70Hou		6'2"	203	Houston	5	12
Peaks, Clarence FB	57-63Phi 64-65Pit	23	6'1"	218	Michigan State		144
Pearson, Willie DB	69MiaA		6'	190	N. Carolina A&T		
Pellegrini, Bob LB-OG	56, 58-61Phi 62-65Was		6'2"	233	Maryland	13	6
Pennington, Tom K	62DalA	5	6'2"	210	Georgia		19
Pentecost, John OG	67 Min		6'2"	250	U.C.L.A.		
Perkins, Art FB	62-63LA	2	6'	223	North Texas State		36
Perkins, Bill HB	63NY-A		6'2"	225	Iowa		
Perkins, Don FB-HB	61-68Dal	2	5'10"	200	New Mexico		270
Perkins, Jim OT	62-64DenA		6'5"	250	Colorado		
Perkins, Ray WR-OE	67-71Bal HC79-82NG HC87-90TB	2	6'	183	Alabama		66
Perkins, Willis OG-DE	61HouA 61BosA 63HouA		6'	250	Texas Southern		
Perlo, Phil LB	60 HouA		6'	220	Maryland		
Perreault, Pete OG-OT	63-67NY-A 68CinA 69NY-A 70NYJ 71Min		6'3"	246	Boston U.		
Pesonen, Dick DB	60GB 61Min 62-64NYG		6'	190	Minnesota-Duluth	4	
Peters, Anton DT	63DenA		6'3"	250	Florida		
Peters, Floyd DT	59-62Cle 63Det 64-69Phi 70Was		6'4"	254	San Fran. State	3	
Peters, Frank OT	69CinA		6'4"	250	Ohio U.		
Peterson, Ken OG	61 Min		6'2"	235	Utah		
Petitbon, Richie LB	59-68ChiB 69-70LA 71-73Was		6'3"	206	Tulane	48	18
Petrella, Bob DB	66-69MiaA 70-71Mia		6'	186	Tennessee	5	
Petrich, Bob DE	63-66SD-A 67BufA		6'4"	253	West Texas State	1	
Petties, Neal OE-FL	64-66Bal		6'2"	198	San Diego State		6
Philbin, Gerry DE	64-69NY-A 70-72NYJ 73Phi 74WFL		6'2"	245	Buffalo State	1	
Phillips Jim (Red) OE-FL	58-64LA 65-67Min	2	6'1"	197	Auburn		204
Phillips, Loyd DE	67-69ChiB		6'3"	237	Arkansas	3	
Philpott, Ed LB	67-69BosA 70Bos 71NE		6'3"	240	Miami-Ohio	9	6
Piccolo, Brian HB-FB died June 16, 1970-cancer	66-69ChiB	2	6'	205	Wake Forest		30
Pirkens, Bob OT	67-69ChiB		6'4"	258	Nebraska		
Pietrosante, Nick FB	59-65Det 66-67Cle	2	6'2"	225	Notre Dame		180
Pillath, Roger OT	65LA 66Pit		6'4"	249	Wisconsin		
Pine, Ed LB	62-64SF 65Pit		6'4"	233	Utah	3	
Pitts, Elijah HB	61-69GB 70LA 70NO 71GB	23	6'1"	204	Philander Smith		210
Pivec, Dave TE-LB	66-68LA 69DenA	2	6'3"	240	Notre Dame		8
Plum, Milt QB	57-61Cle 62-67Det 68LA 69NYG	12 5	6'1"	205	Penn State		112
Plump, Dave DB	66SD-A		6'1"	195	Fresno State		
Plunkett, Sherman (Tank) OT	58-60Bal 61-62SD-A 63-67NY-A		6'4"	290	Md. Eastern Shore		
Ply, Bobby DB	62DalA 63-67KC-A 67BufA 67DenA		6'1"	190	Baylor	9	
Poage, Ray TE-OE-FL	63Min 64-65Phi 66KJ 67-70NO 71Atl	2	6'4"	208	Texas		78
Poimbeouf, Lance OG	63Dal		6'3"	225	Southwestern La.		
Poole, Bob TE-OE-FL	64-65SF 66-67HouA	2	6'4"	216	Clemson		
Pope, Bucky OE-WR	64LA 65KJ 66-67LA 68GB	2	6'5"	199	Catawba		78
Porter, Willie DB	68BosA	3	5'11"	195	Texas Southern		
Porterfield, Garry DE	65Dal		6'3"	223	Tulsa		
Post, Bobby DB	67NYG		6'1"	195	Kings Point		
Post, Dickie HB	67-69SD-A 70SD 71Den 71Hou	23	5'9"	190	Houston		114
Pottios, Myron LB	61Pit 62BA 63-65Pit 66-70LA 71-73Was		6'2"	236	Notre Dame	12	
Powell, Art OE-DB-WR	59Phi 60-62NY-A 63-66OakA 67BufA 68Min	2	6'3"	211	San Jose State	3	492
Powell, Preston FB	61Cle		6'2"	225	Grambling		
Powell, Tim DE	65LA 66Pit		6'4"	248	Northwestern		
Powers, John OE-TE-LB	62-65Pit 66Min		6'2"	211	Notre Dame		
Powers, Warren DB	63-68OakA		6'	188	Nebraska	22	12
Preas, George OT-OG-LB	55-65Bal		6'2"	244	Virginia Tech		
Prebola, Gene OE	60OakA 61-63DenA	2	6'3"	220	Boston U.		42
Prestell, Jim DT	60Cle 61-66Min 66NYG 67Was		6'5"	264	Idaho	1	8
Price, Jim LB	63NY-A 64DenA		6'2"	228	Auburn	1	
Price, Sam HB-FB	66-68MiaA	2	5'11"	215	Illinois		12
Pride, Dan LB	68-69ChiB		6'3"	225	Jackson State	1	
Print, Bob LB	67-68SD-A		6'	220	Dayton		
Prisby, Errol DB	67DenA		5'10"	184	Cincinnati		
Promuto, Vince OG	60-70 Was		6'1"	244	Holy Cross		
Prudhomme, Remi C-OG-DE-DT	66-67BufA 68-69KC-A 70JJ 71-72NO 72Buf		6'4"	251	Louisiana State		
Pryor, Barry HB	69MiaA 70Mia		6'1"	215	Boston U.		
Purnell, Jim LB	64-68ChiB 69-72GB		6'2"	229	Wisconsin	3	
Purvis, Vic DB	66-67BosA		5'11"	200	Southern Miss.		
Pyburn, Jack OT	67-68MiaA		6'6"	245	Texas A&M		
Pyeatt, John DB	60-61DenA		6'3"	204	none	4	6
Pyle, Mike C	61-69ChiB		6'3"	247	Yale		
Pyle, Palmer OG	60-63Bal 64Min 65JJ 66OakA		6'2"	248	Michigan State		
Pyne, George DT	65BosA		6'4"	285	Olivet		
Quayle, Frank HB	69DenA	2	5'10"	195	Virginia		
Quinlan, Bill DE	57-58Cle 59-62GB 63Phi 64Det 65Was		6'3"	248	Michigan	3	
Quinn, Steve C	68HouA		6'1"	225	Notre Dame		
Rabb, Warren QB	60Det 61-62BufA	12	6'1"	202	Louisiana State		22
Rabold, Mike OG	59Det 60StL 61-62Min 64-67ChiB		6'2"	239	Indiana		
Rademacher, Bill WR-DB-OE	64-68NY-A 69BosA 70Bos	2	6'1"	190	Northern Michigan	1	18
Raimey, Dave DB	64Cle		5'10"	195	Michigan		
Rakestraw, Larry QB	64, 66-68ChiB	1	6'2"	195	Georgia		12
Ramsey, Nate DB	63-72Phi 73NO		6'1"	200	Indiana	21	6
Randall, Dennis DE-DT	67NY-A 68CinA		6'6"	243	Oklahoma State		

Use Name (Nicknames) – Positions	Team by Year	See Section	Hgt	Wgt	College	Int	Pts
Randle, Sonny OE-WR	59ChiC 60-66StL 67-68SF 68Dal	2	6'2"	189	Virginia		390
Rasmussen, Wayne DB	64-72Det 73JJ		6'2"	179	S. Dakota State	16	12
Rassas, Nick DB	66-68Atl		6'	190	Notre Dame	1	
Ratkowski, Ray HB	61BosA		6'	195	Notre Dame		
Raye, Jimmy DB	69Phi		6'	185	Michigan State		
Recher, Dave C	65-68Phi		6'1"	244	Iowa		
Rector, Ron HB	66Was 66-67Atl	2	6'	200	Northwestern		
Redman, Rick LB	65-69SD-A 70-73SD	4	5'11"	225	Washington	9	6
Redmond, Tom DE-OG-OT	60-65StL		6'5"	243	Vanderbilt		
Reeberg, Lucian OT died Jan. 31, 1964–uremia	63Det		6'4"	308	Hampton U.		
Reed, Bob HB	62-63Min	23	5'11"	187	U. of Pacific		6
Reed, Leo OG-OT	61HouA 61DenA		6'4"	240	Colorado State		
Reed, Robert OG	65Was		6'1"	250	Tennessee State		
Reed, Smith HB	65-66NYG 67-68MS		6'	215	Alcorn State		
Reed, Taft DB	67Phi		6'2"	200	Jackson State		
Reese, Guy DT	62-63Dal 64-65Bal 66Atl		6'5"	255	S.M.U.		
Reeves, Dan HB-FB	65-72Dal HC81-90Den	12	6'1"	201	South Carolina		253
Reeves, Roy WR	69BufA		5'11"	182	South Carolina		
Reger, John LB-OG	55-63 Pit 64-66 Was		6'	225	Pittsburgh	15	18
Regner, Tom OG	67-69HouA 70-72Hou		6'1"	255	Notre Dame		
Reichow, Jerry OE-QB	56-57Det 58KJ 59Det 60Phi 61-64Min	12	6'2"	217	Iowa		144
Reifsnyder, Bob DE	60-61NY-A		6'2"	255	Navy		
Reilly, Mike LB	64-68ChiB 69Min		6'2"	230	Iowa		6
Remmert, Dennis LB	60BufA		6'3"	215	Iowa State		
Rengel, Mike DT	69NO 70JJ		6'5"	260	Hawaii		
Renn, Bob HB	61NY-A	2	6'	180	Florida State		6
Rentz, Larry DB	69SD-A		6'1"	170	Florida		
Rentzel, Lance WR-FL-OE-HB	65-66Min 67-70Dal 71-72LA 73SL 74LA	23	6'2"	203	Oklahoma		248
Retzlaff, Pete OE-TE-FL	56-66Phi	2	6'1"	211	S. Dakota State		282
Reynolds, Al OG	60-62DalA 63-67KC-A		6'3"	238	Tarkio		
Reynolds, Bob OT	63-71StL 72-73NE 73StL		6'6"	264	Bowling Green		
Reynolds, Chuck C-OG	69-70Cle		6'2"	240	Tulsa		2
Reynolds, M.C. (Chief) QB	58-59ChiC 60Was 60StL 61BufA 62OakA	12	6'	193	Louisiana State		24
Rhome, Jerry QB	65-67Dal 69Cle 70Hou 71LA	12	6'	186	Tulsa		6
Rice, George DT-OG	66-69HouA		6'3"	262	Louisiana State		
Rice, Ken OG-OT	61BufA 62KJ 63BufA 64-65OakA 66-67MiaA		6'2"	243	Auburn		
Richards, Bobby DE	62-65 Phi 66-67Atl		6'2"	241	Louisiana State		
Richards, Jim DB	68-69NY-A 70-71MS		6'1"	180	Virginia Tech	3	
Richards, Perry OE	57Pit 58Det 59ChiC 60StL 61BufA 62NY-A	2	6'2"	205	Detroit		24
Richardson, Al DE	60BosA		6'3"	250	Grambling		
Richardson, Bob (Red) DB	66DenA		6'1"	180	U.C.L.A.		
Richardson, Jeff OT-C-OG	67-68NY-A 69MiaA		6'3"	253	Michigan State		
Richardson, Jerry (The Razor) FL-OE-HB	59-60Bal	2	6'3"	185	Wofford		24
Richardson, Jerry DB	64-65LA 66-67Atl		6'3"	190	West Texas State	11	
Richardson, Tom WR	69BosA 70Bos		6'2"	195	Jackson State		
Richardson, Willie FL-WR	63-69Bal 70Mia 71Bal	2	6'2"	198	Jackson State		150
Richey, Mike OT	69BufA 70NO		6'5"	257	North Carolina		
Richter, Frank LB	67-69DenA		6'3"	230	Georgia	2	
Richter, Pat OE-TE	63-70Was	2 4	6'5"	230	Wisconsin		84
Ridge, Houston DE-DT	66-69SD-A 70JJ		6'4"	239	San Diego State		
Ridgeway, Colin K	65 Dal		6'5"	211	Lamar		
Ridlehuber, Preston HB	66Atl 68OakA 69BufA		6'2"	215	Georgia		18
Ridlon, Jimmy DB	57-62SF 63-64Dal		6'1"	181	Syracuse	9	12
Rieves, Charley LB	62-63OakA 64-65HouA		5'11"	217	Houston	1	
Riggle, Bob DB	66-67Atl 68JJ		6'1"	200	Penn State	3	6
Righetti, Joe DT	69-70Cle		6'3"	253	Waynesburg		
Riley, Butch LB	69Bal		6'2"	220	Texas A&I		
Riley, Jim DE	67-69MiaA 70-71Mia 72KJ		6'4"	252	Oklahoma		
Ringo, Jim C	53-63GB 64-67Phi HC76-77Buf		6'1"	232	Syracuse		
Rissmiller, Ray OT	66Phi 67NO 68BufA		6'4"	250	Georgia		
Rivera, Henry DB	62OakA 63BufA		5'11"	180	Oregon State		
Roach, Johnny QB-DB	56ChiC 57-58MS 59ChicC 60StL 61-63GB 64Dal	12	6'4"	197	S.M.U.		12
Robb, Joe DE-LB	59-60Phi 61-67StL 68-71Det		6'3"	238	Texas Christian	1	
Roberson, Bo FL-HB	61SD-A 62-65OakA 65BufA 66MiaA	23	6'1"	192	Cornell		116
Roberts, Archie QB	67MiaA		6'1"	193	Columbia		
Roberts, Cliff OT	61OakA		6'3"	260	Illinois		
Roberts, C. R. FB	59-62SF	2	6'3"	202	Southern Calif.		24
Roberts, Walter (The Flea) FL-WR-OE	64-66Cle 67NO 69-70Was	23	5'10"	167	San Jose State		66
Robertson, Bob OT	68HouA		6'4"	246	Illinois		
Robinson, Dave LB	63-72GB 73-74Was		6'3"	243	Penn State	27	6
Robinson, Jerry OE	62-64SD-A 65NY-A	23	5'11"	195	Grambling		30
Robinson, Johnnie DB-FL	66Det 67JJ		6'3"	205	Tennessee State		6
Robinson, Johnny DB-HB	60-62DalA 63-69KC-A 70-71KC HC83-84LA	2	6'	200	Louisiana State	57	108
Robotti, Frank LB	61BosA		6'	220	Boston College	2	
Rochester, Paul DT	60-62DalA 63KC-A 63-69NY-A		6'2"	254	Michigan State		
Rock, Walt OT-DT	63-67SF 68-73Was		6'5"	252	Maryland		
Roderick, John FL-WR	66-67MiaA 68OakA	2	6'1"	180	S.M.U.		6
Rosdel, Herb OG	61OakA		6'3"	230	Marquette		
Roehnelt, Bill LB	58-59ChiB 60Was 61-62DenA		6'1"	227	Bradley		
Rogers, Don C-OG	60LA-A 61-64SD-A		6'2"	245	South Carolina		
Rohde, Len OT-DE	60-74SF		6'4"	246	Utah State		
Roland, Johnny HB-FB	66-72StL 73NYG	23	6'2"	213	Missouri		216
Rolle, Dave FB	60DenA	2	6'	215	Oklahoma		18
Romeo, Tony OE-TE	61DalA 62-67BosA	2	6'2"	225	Florida State		62
Rosdahl, Hatch DT-OG-DE	64BufA 64-66KC-A		6'5"	250	Penn State		
Rose, George DB	64-66Min 67NO 68JJ		5'11"	190	Auburn	9	6
Rosema, Rocky LB	68-71StL		6'2"	228	Michigan	1	
Ross, Dave OE	60NY-A	2	6'3"	210	Los Angeles State		6
Ross, Willie FB	64BufA		5'10"	200	Nebraska		6
Rowland, Justin DB	60ChiB 61Min 62DenA		6'2"	189	Texas Christian	1	
Rowley, Bob LB	63Pit 64NY-A		6'2"	225	Virginia		
Roy, Frank OG	66StL		6'2"	230	Utah		
Rubke, Karl LB-DE-C-DT	57-60SF 61Min 62-65SF 66-67Atl 68OakA		6'4"	240	Southern Calif.	2	
Rudolph, Jack LB	60, 62-65BosA 66MiaA		6'3"	228	Georgia Tech	3	
Rule, Gordon DB	68-69GB		6'2"	180	Dartmouth		
Ruple, Ernie DT	68Pit		6'4"	256	Arkansas		
Rush, Jerry DT	65-71Det		6'4"	264	Michigan State		
Rushing, Marion LB	59ChicC 62-65StL 66-68Atl 68HouA		6'2"	223	Southern Illinois	4	2

Use Name (Nicknames) – Positions	Team by Year	See Section	Hgt	Wgt	College	Int	Pts
Russ, Pat DT	63Min		6'4"	255	Purdue		
Russell, Benny QB	68BufA		6'1"	190	Louisville		
Rutgens, Joe DT	61-69Was		6'2"	258	Illinois		
Rutkowski, Charlie DE	60BufA		6'3"	248	Ripon		
Rutkowski, Ed FL-HB-DE-QB-WR	63-68BufA	123	6'1"	204	Notre Dame		36
Ryan, Frank QB	58-61LA 62-68Cle 69-70Was	12	6'3"	199	Rice		42
Ryan, Joe DE	60NY-A		6'2"	235	Villanova		
Rychlec, Tom OE	58Det 60-62BufA 63DenA	2	6'3"	220	American Inter.		18
Ryder, Nick FB	63-64Det		6'	208	Miami (Fla.)		12
Rzempolich, Ted DB	63Was		6'1"	195	Virginia		
Sabel, Ron OT-OG	60-61OakA		6'2"	238	Purdue		
Sabatino, Bill DT	68Cle 69Atl		6'3"	245	Colorado		
Safford, Saint WR	68CinA	2	6'4"	202	San Jose State		
Saidock, Tom DT	59Phi 58JJ 60-61NY-A 62BufA		6'5"	261	Michigan State		
Saimes, George DB-HB	63-69BufA 70-72Den		5'10"	188	Michigan State	22	6
St. Jean, Len OG-DE	64-69BosA 70Bos 71-73NE		6'1"	244	Northern Michigan		
Sample, Johnny DB-HB	58-60Bal 61-62Pit 63-65Was 66-68NY-A	3	6'1"	203	Md. Eastern Shore	41	36
Sandeman, Bill OT-DT	66Dal 67NO 67-73Atl		6'6"	254	U. of Pacific		
Sanders, Bob LB	67Atl 68JJ		6'3"	235	North Texas		
Sanders, Daryl OT	63-63Det		6'5"	248	Ohio State		
Sanders, Lonnie DB	63-67Was 68-69StL		6'3"	206	Michigan State	12	
Sandusky, Alex OG	54-66Bal		6'1"	235	Clarion		
Sandusky, Mike OG	57-65Pit		6'	231	Maryland		
Sapienza, Rick DB-HB	60NY-A		5'11"	185	Villanova		
Sapp, Theron HB-FB	59-63Phi 63-65Pit 66JJ	2	6'1"	203	Georgia		30
Sardisco, Tony OG-LB	56Was 56SF 60-62BosA		6'2"	226	Tulane		
Sartin, Dan DT	69SD-A		6'1"	245	Mississippi		
Satcher, Doug LB	66-68BosA		6'	221	Southern Miss.	1	2
Sauer, George WR-OE	65-69NY-A 70NYJ	2	6'1"	199	Texas		172
Saul, Bill LB	62-63Bal 64,66-68Pit 69NO 70Det		6'4"	225	Penn State	4	2
Sauls, Mac DB	68-69Atl		6'	185	SW Texas State		
Saxton, Jimmy HB	62DalA		5'11"	173	Texas		
Sayers, Gale HB	65-71ChiB	23	6'	199	Kansas		336
Sayers, Ron HB	69SD-A		6'1"	202	Nebraska-Omaha		
Sbranti, Ron LB	66DenA		6'2"	230	Utah State		
Scales, Charlie FB-HB	60-61Pit 62-65Cle 66Atl	23	5'11"	214	Indiana		30
Scarpati, Joe DB-HB	64-69Phi 70NO 71JJ		5'10"	185	N. Carolina State	25	18
Scarpitto, Bob FL-WR	61SD-A 62-67DenA 68BosA	2 4	5'11"	194	Notre Dame		170
Schaffer, Joe LB	60BufA		6'	210	Tennessee	1	
Schafrath, Dick OT-OG-DE	57-71Cle		6'3"	253	Ohio State		
Schick, Doyle LB	61Was		6'1"	210	Kansas		
Schichtle, Henry QB	64NYG		6'2"	190	Wichita State		
Schleicher, Maury LB-DE	59ChiC 60LA-A 61-62SD-A		6'3"	238	Penn State	1	
Schmautz, Ray LB	66OakA		6'1"	225	San Diego State		
Schmedding, Jim OG	68-69SD-A 70SD		6'2"	250	Weber State		
Schmidt, Bob C-OT-OG	59-60NYG 61-63HouA 64-65BosA 66-67BufA		6'4"	248	Minnesota		
Schmidt, Henry DT-DE	59-60SF 61 64SD-A 65BufA 66NY-A		6'4"	258	Southern Calif., Trinity (Texas)	1	6
Schmidt, Roy OG-OT	67-68NO 69Atl 70Was 71Min		6'3"	250	Long Beach State		
Schmitt, John C	64-69NY-A 70-73NYJ 74GB		6'4"	253	Hofstra		
Schmitz, Bob LB	61-66Pit 66Min		6'1"	235	Montana State	3	8
Schoenke, Ray OG-OT-C	63-64Dal 66-75Was		6'3"	246	S.M.U.		
Scholtz, Bob C-OG	60-64Det 65-66NYG		6'4"	250	Notre Dame		
Schottenheimer, Marty LB	65-68BufA 69BosA 70Bos HC84-88Cle 89-90KC		6'3"	225	Pittsburgh	6	6
Schuh, Harry OT-OG	65-69OakA 70Oak 71-73LA 74GB		6'2"	260	Memphis State		
Schultz, Randy HB-FB	66Cle 67-68NO	2	5'11"	210	Iowa State		12
Schumacher, Gregg DE	67-68LA		6'2"	240	Illinois		
Schweda, Brian DE	66ChiB 67-68NO		6'3"	240	Kansas		
Schwedes, Ger HB	60-61BosA		6'1"	205	Syracuse		
Schweickert, Bob HB-FL	65,67NY-A		6'1"	193	Virginia Tech		
Scibelli, Joe OG	61-75LA		6'1"	256	Notre Dame		
Scott, Bill DB	68DenA		6'	188	Idaho		
Scott, John DT	60-61BufA		6'4"	260	Ohio State		
Scott, Lew DB	66DenA		5'10"	173	Oregon State		
Scott, Wilbert LB	61Pit		6'	215	Indiana		
Scotti, Ben DB	59-61Was 62-63Phi 64SF		6'1"	185	Maryland	10	
Scrabis, Bob QB	60-62NY-A	1	6'3"	223	Penn State		6
Scrutchins, Ed DE	66HouA		6'3"	260	Toledo		
Sczurek, Stan LB	63-65Cle 66NYG		5'11"	229	Purdue	1	
Seals, George DT-OG-OT	64Was 65-71ChiB 72-73KC		6'2"	259	Missouri	1	6
Sedlock, Bob OT	60BufA		6'4"	295	Georgia		
Seedborg, John K	65Was 66MS		6'	227	Arizona State		
Selawski, Gene OT-OG	59LA 60Cle 61SD-A		6'4"	252	Purdue		
Sellers, Goldie DB	66-67DenA 68-69KC-A 70LJ	3	6'2"	198	Grambling	13	30
Sestak, Tom DT-OT	62-68BufA		6'5"	267	McNeese State	2	18
Shackleford, Don OG	64DenA		6'4"	255	U. of Pacific		
Shann, Bob DB	65Phi 66JJ 67Phi		6'1"	189	Boston College	1	6
Shannon, Carver DB-HB	62-64LA	3	6'1"	201	Southern Illinois	4	6
Sharockman, Ed DB	62-72Min		6'	200	Pittsburgh	40	36
Shaw, Billy OG	61-69BufA		6'3"	250	Georgia Tech		
Shaw, Glen FB-HB	60ChiB 62LA 63-64OakA	2	6'1"	221	Kentucky		24
Shaw, Nate LB	69-70LA		6'2"	205	Southern Calif.		
Shaw, Jerry DT	66-67Min 68-69Atl 70-71NYG		6'3"	244	Purdue		
Shea, Pat OG	62-65SD-A 66JJ		6'1"	241	Southern Calif.		
Sherer, Dave OE	59Bal 60Dal	4	6'3"	218	S.M.U.		
Sherlag, Bob FL	66Atl		6'	197	Memphis State		6
Sherman, Bob DB	64-65Pit		6'2"	195	Iowa	1	
Sherman, Tom QB	68-69BosA 69BufA	12	6'	190	Penn State		
Shields, Lebron DE-OT	60Bal 61Min		6'4"	243	Tennessee		2
Shiner, Dick QB	64-66Was 67Cle 68-69Pit 70NYG 71,73Atl 73-74NE	12	6'	197	Maryland		12
Shinnick, Don LB	57-69Bal		6'	232	U.C.L.A.	37	
Shirkey, George DT	60-61HouA 62OakA		6'4"	252	Austin		
Shivers, Roy HB	66-72StL	23	6'	200	Utah State		90
Shoals, Roger OT-OG	63-64Cle 65-70Det 71Den		6'4"	256	Maryland		6
Shockley, Bill HB-K	60-61NY-A 61BufA 62NY-A 68Pit	23 5	6'	185	West Chester		181
Shofner, Del OE-DB	57-60LA 61-67NYG	2 4	6'3"	186	Baylor	3	306
Shofner, Jim DB	58-63Cle HC90Cle	3	6'2"	191	Texas Christian	20	
Shonta, Chuck DB	60-67BosA		6'	196	Eastern Michigan	15	6
Shorter, Jim DB	62-63Cle 64-67Was 69Pit		5'11"	184	Detroit	15	6

Use Name (Nicknames) – Positions	Team by Year	See Section	Hgt	Wgt	College	Int	Pts
Shy, Les HB	68-69Dal 70NYG	23	6'1"	202	Long Beach State		24
Sidle, Jimmy TE-HB	66Atl		6'2"	215	Auburn		
Sieminski, Chuck DT	63-65SF 66-67Atl 68Det		6'4"	262	Penn State		
Silas, Sam DT-DE	63-67StL 68NYG 69-70SF		6'4"	251	Southern Illinois		
Silvestri, Carl DB	65StL 66Atl		6'	195	Wisconsin		
Simkus, Arnie DT-DE	65NY-A 67Min		6'4"	245	Michigan		
Simmons, Dave LB	65-66StL 67NO 68Dal		6'4"	245	Georgia Tech	2	
Simmons, Jerry WR-OE	65-67Pit 67NO 67-69Atl 69ChiB 71-74Den	2	6'1"	190	Bethune-Cookman		54
Simmons, Leon LB	63DenA		6'	225	Grambling		
Simms, Bob LB-OE-DE	60-61NYG 62Pit		6'1"	223	Rutgers		
Simon, Jim OG-OT-DE-LB	63-65Det 66-68Atl		6'5"	235	Miami (Fla.)		
Simpson, Howard DE	64Min		6'5"	230	Auburn		
Simpson, Jackie DB	58-60Bal 61-62Pit		5'10"	183	Florida	2	
Simpson, Jackie LB	61DenA 62-64OakA	5	6'1"	226	Mississippi	5	15
Simpson, Willie FB	62OakA		6'	218	San Fran. State		
Singer, Karl OT	66-68BosA		6'3"	250	Purdue		
Sisk, John DB	64ChiB		6'3"	195	Miami (Fla.)		
Skaggs, Jim OG-OT	63-67Phi 68KJ 69-72Phi		6'2"	246	Washington		
Sklopan, John DB	63DenA		5'11"	190	Southern Miss.		
Skoronski, Bob OT-C	56GB 57-58MS 59-69GB		6'3"	249	Indiana		
Slaby, Lou LB-DT	64-65NYG 66Det		6'3"	235	Pittsburgh		
Slaughter, Mickey QB	63-66DenA	12	6'	190	Louisiana Tech		8
Sligh, Richard DT	67OakA		7'	300	N.Car. Central		
Sloan, Steve QB	66-67Atl	1	6'	185	Alabama		
Smiley, Tom FB	68CinA 69DenA 70Hou	2	6'1"	235	Lamar		30
Smith, Allen HB	66NY-A		5'11"	195	Findlay		
Smith, Allen HB	66-67BufA	2	6'	200	Ft. Valley State		
Smith, Billy Ray DT-DE	57LA 58-60Pit 61-62Bal 63JJ 64-70Bal		6'4"	240	Arkansas	1	
Smith, Bob DB	68HouA		6'	180	Miami-Ohio		
Smith, Bobby DB	62-65LA 65-66Det	3	6'	193	U.C.L.A.	5	12
Smith, Bobby HB	64-65BufA 66Pit	2	6'	203	North Texas		30
Smith, Carl FB	60BufA		6'	200	Tennessee		6
Smith, Dan DB	61DenA		5'10"	180	Northeastern Okla.		
Smith, Dave FB	60-64HouA		6'1"	209	Ripon		108
Smith, Dick DB-HB-OE	67-68Was		6'	205	Northwestern	4	
Smith, Don OG	67DenA		6'4"	240	Florida A&M		
Smith, Fletcher DB	66-67KC-A 68-69CinA 70-71Cin		6'2"	182	Tennessee State	15	2
Smith, Gordon OE	61-65Min	2	6'2"	211	Missouri		78
Smith, Hal DT	60BosA 60DenA 61OakA		6'5"	250	U.C.L.A.		
Smith, Hugh OE	62Was		6'4"	215	Kansas		
Smith, Jackie TE-OE	63-77StL 78Dal	2 4	6'4"	225	Northwestern La.		258
Smith, J. D. FB-HB-DB	56ChiB 56-64SF 65-66Dal	2	6'1"	205	N. Carolina A&T	2	276
Smith, J. D. OT	59-63Phi 64Det 65JJ 66Det		6'5"	250	Rice		6
Smith, J. D. (Jet Stream) FB-HB	60OakA 61ChiB	2	6'	215	Compton C.C.		
Smith, Jeff LB	66NYG 67KJ		6'	237	Southern Calif.	1	
Smith, Jim DB	68Was		6'3"	195	Oregon		6
Smith, Jimmy DB	69DenA		6'3"	190	Utah State		
Smith, Jim Ray OG-OT-DE	56-62Cle 63-64Dal		6'3"	241	Baylor		
Smith, Noland (Super Gnat) WR-FL-HB	67-69KC-A 69SF	3	5'6"	155	Tennessee State		12
Smith, Ralph (Catfish) TE-OE-DB	62-64Phi 65-68Cle 69Atl	2	6'2"	214	Mississippi		36
Smith, Ron QB	65LA 66Pit	1	6'5"	220	Richmond		
Smith, Russ HB-FB	67-69SD-A 70SD	2	6'1"	214	Miami (Fla.)		60
Smith, Tommie WR	69CinA		6'4"	180	San Jose State		
Smith, Willie OG-OT	60DenA 61OakA		6'2"	255	Michigan		
Smith, Zeke OG-DE-LB	60Bal 61NYG		6'2"	233	Auburn		
Smolinski, Mark FB-TE	61-62Bal 63-68NY-A	2	6'	218	Wyoming		102
Snead, Norm QB	61-63Was 64-70Phi 71Min 72-74NYG 74-75SF 76NYG	12	6'4"	215	Wake Forest		138
Snell, Matt FB	64-69NY-A 70-72NYJ	2	6'2"	220	Ohio State		186
Snidow, Ron DE-DT	63-67Was 68-72Cle		6'4"	249	Oregon	1	2
Snorton, Matt OE	64DenA		6'5"	250	Michigan State		
Snowden, Jim OT-DE	65-71Was 72JJ		6'3"	255	Notre Dame		
Snyder, Al FL	64BosA		6'	195	Holy Cross		
Soborinski, Phil C	68Atl		6'3"	235	Wisconsin		
Soleau, Bob LB	64Pit		6'2"	235	William & Mary		
Soltis, Bob DB	60-61BosA		6'2"	205	Minnesota	2	
Sommer, Mike HB-DB	58-59Was 59-61Bal 61Was 63OakA	2	5'11"	190	George Washington		12
Songin, Butch QB	60-61BosA 62NY-A	12	6'2"	200	Boston College		18
Sorey, Jim DT	60-62BufA		6'4"	278	Texas Southern		
Sorrell, Henry LB	67DenA		6'1"	215	Tenn.-Chattanooga		
Sortun, Rick OG	64-69StL		6'2"	234	Washington		
South, Ronnie QB	68NO	1	6'1"	195	Arkansas		
Speights, Dick DB	68SD-A		5'11"	175	Wyoming		
Spence, Julian (Sus) DB-FL	56ChiC 57SF 60-61HouA		5'11"	170	Sam Houston St.	6	
Spikes, Jack FB	60-62DalA 63-64KC-A 64SD-A 65HouA 66-67BufA	2 5	6'2"	221	Texas Christian		262
Spiller, Phil DB	67StL 68Atl 68CinA		6'	195	Los Angeles State	2	
Stacy, Billy DB-HB	59ChiC 60-63StL	23	6'1"	191	Mississippi State	20	42
Stafford, Dick DE-DT	62-63Phi		6'4"	253	Texas Tech		
Stalcup, Jerry LB-OG	60LA 61-62DenA		6'	230	Wisconsin	1	
Stallings, Don DT-DE-OT	60Was		6'4"	250	North Carolina		
Stallings, Larry LB	63-76StL		6'2"	230	Georgia Tech	9	18
Stanciel, Jeff HB	69Atl		6'	192	Miss. Valley St.		
Stanton, Jack HB	61Pit		6'1"	190	N. Carolina State		
Starks, Marsh DB	63-64NY-A	3	6'	190	Illinois	1	6
Starling, Bruce DB	63DenA		6'1"	186	Florida		
Starr, Bart QB	56-71GB HC75-83GB	12	6'1"	197	Alabama		90
Staten, Randy DE	67NYG		6'1"	225	Minnesota		
Steffen, Jim DB	59-61Det 61-65Was 66GJ	3	6'	196	Occidental, UCLA	17	12
Stenhouwer, Ron OG-OT	60-64Pit		6'2"	232	Colorado State		
Stephens, Harold QB	62NY-A		5'11"	175	Hardin-Simmons		
Stephens, Larry DE-DT	60-61Cle 62LA 63-67Dal		6'4"	245	Texas	1	6
Stephens, Tom OE-DB	60-64BosA	2	6'1"	207	Syracuse	1	36
Stephenson, Kay QB	67SD-A 68BufA HC83-85Buf	1	6'1"	208	Florida		
Stetz, Bill OG	67Phi		6'3"	250	Boston College		
Stevens, Bill QB	68-69GB		6'3"	195	Texas-El Paso		
Stickles, Monte OE-TE	60-67SF 68NO	2	6'4"	232	Notre Dame		96
Stiger, Jim HB-FB	63-65Dal 65-67LA	23	5'11"	204	Washington		24
Stinnette, Jim FB-LB	61-62DenA	2	6'1"	230	Oregon State	1	12
Stith, Carel DT-DE	67-69HouA		6'5"	267	Nebraska		

Use Name (Nicknames) – Positions	Team by Year	See Section	Hgt	Wgt	College	Int	Pts
Stoepel, Terry TE	67ChiB 68-69MS 70Hou		6'4"	235	Tulsa		
Stofa, John QB	66-67MiaA 68-69CinA 69MiaA 70Mia	1	6'3"	210	Buffalo State		6
Stokes, Jesse DB	68DenA		6'	190	Corpus Christi		
Stokes, Sims OE	67Dal		6'1"	198	Northern Arizona		
Stone, Donnie HB-FB	61-64DenA 65BufA 66HouA	2	6'2"	205	Arkansas		102
Stone, Jack OT	60DalA 61-62OakA		6'2"	245	Oregon		
Stonebraker, Steve LB-OE	62-63Min 64-66Bal 67-68NO	2	6'3"	223	Detroit	2	12
Stotter, Rich LB	68HouA		6'	225	Houston		
Stovall, Jerry DB	63-71StL	34	6'2"	201	Louisiana State	18	12
Stover, Smokey LB	60-62DalA 63-66KC-A		6'	229	Northeast La.	6	
Strahan, Art DT	68Atl		6'5"	266	Texas Southern		
Strahan, Ray DE	65HouA		6'6"	250	Texas Southern		
Stram, Hank HC60-62DalA HC63-69KC-A HC70-74KC HC76-77NO					Purdue		
Strand, Eli OG	66Pit 67NO		6'2"	250	Iowa State		
Stransky, Bob HB	60DenA	2	6'1"	180	Colorado		
Stratton, Mike LB	62-69BufA 70-72Buf 73SD		6'3"	236	Tennessee	21	12
Stricker, Tony DB	63NY-A		6'	185	Colorado	1	
Strickland, Dave OG	60DenA		6'	220	Memphis State		
Strofolino, Mike LB	65LA 65Bal 66-68StL		6'2"	223	Villanova		
Stromberg, Mike LB	68NY-A		6'2"	235	Temple		
Struger, George DT	57-61LA 62Pit 62-63NY-A		6'5"	259	Washington	1	
Studstill, Pat FL-WR	61-62Det 63JJ 64-67Det 68-71LA 72NE	234	6'1"	176	Houston		114
Sturm, Jerry C-OT-OG-FB	61-66DenA 67-70NO 71Hou 72Phi		6'3"	257	Illinois		
Stynchula, Andy DE-DT-C	60-63Was 64-65NYG 66-67Bal 68Dal	5	6'3"	252	Penn State		22
Suchy, Larry DB	68Atl		5'11"	180	Mississippi Coll.		
Suci, Bob DB	62HouA 63BosA	3	5'10'	182	Michigan State	9	12
Suggs, Walt OT-C	62-69HouA 70-71Hou		6'5"	257	Mississippi State		
Sullivan, Dan OG-OT	62-72Bal		6'3"	250	Boston College		
Summers, Jim DB	67DenA		5'10"	175	Michigan State		
Sunde, Milt OG-C	64-74Min		6'2"	245	Minnesota		
Sutro, John OT	62SF		6'4"	245	San Jose State		
Sutton, Archie OT	65-67Min		6'4"	263	Illinois		
Sutton, Mickey DB	66HouA		6'	190	Auburn		
Svihus, Bob OT-OG	65-69OakA 70Oak 71-73NYJ		6'4"	245	Southern Calif.		
Swain, Bill LB	63LA 64Min 65NYG 66KJ 67 NYG 68-69Det		6'2"	229	Oregon	2	6
Swanson, Terry K	67-68BosA 69CinA	4	6'	210	Massachusetts		
Swatland, Dick OG	68HouA		6'3"	245	Notre Dame		
Sweeney, Neal OE	67DenA		6'2"	170	Tulsa		
Sweeney, Walt OG	63-69SD-A 70-73SD 74-75Was 76KJ		6'3"	256	Syracuse		
Sweetan, Karl QB	66-67Det 68NO 69-70LA	12	6'1"	203	Wake Forest		12
Swinford, Wayne DB-OE-FL	65-67SF		6'	194	Georgia		
Swink, Jim HB	60DalA		6'1"	185	Texas Christian		
Sykes, Gene DB	63-65BufA 67DenA		6'1"	196	Louisiana State	4	
Symank, Johnny DB	57-62GB 63StL		5'11"	180	Florida	19	6
Szczecko, Joe DT	66-68Atl 69NYG		6'	245	Northwestern		
Szymakowski, Dave WR	68NO		6'2"	198	West Texas State		
Szymanski, Dick C-LB	55Bal 56MS 57-68Bal		6'3"	233	Notre Dame	6	6
Talamini, Bob OG	60-67HouA 68NY-A		6'1"	249	Kentucky		
Talbert, Don OT-LB	62Dal 63-64MS 65Dal 66-68Atl 69-70NO 71Dal		6'5"	248	Texas		
Taliferro, Mike QB	64-67NY-A 68-69BosA 70Bos 71NE 72Buf	12	6'2"	206	Illinois		2
Tarasovic, George DE-LB-C	52-53Pit 54-55MS 56-63Pit 63-65Phi 66DenA		6'4"	245	Louisiana State	7	18
Tarbox, Bruce OG	61LA		6'2"	230	Syracuse		
Tarkenton, Fran QB	61-66Min 67-71NYG 72-78Min	12	6'1"	190	Georgia		192
Tarr, Jerry HB	62DenA		6'	190	Oregon		12
Tatman, Pete HB	67Min		6'1"	220	Nebraska		
Taylor, Bob DE-DT	63-64NYG		6'3"	238	Md. Eastern Shore		
Taylor, Jim FB	58-66GB 67NO	2	6'	214	Louisiana State		558
Taylor, Lionel OE-WR-FL	59ChiB 60-66DenA 67-68HouA	2	6'2"	215	N. Mex. Highlands		270
Taylor, Rosey DB	61-69ChiB 69-71SF 72Was 73JJ	3	5'11"	186	Grambling	32	36
Taylor, Sammy FL	65SD-A		6'	190	Grambling		
Tensi, Steve QB	65-66SD-A 67-69DenA 70Den	12	6'5"	213	Florida State		
Teresa, Tony HB	58SF 60OakA	2	5'9"	188	San Jose State		60
Terrell, Marvin OG	60-62DalA 63KC-A		6'1"	236	Mississippi		
Tharp, Corky DB	60NY-A		5'10"	180	Alabama	2	
Theofiledes, Harry QB	68Was		5'10"	180	Waynesburg		
Thibert, Jim LB	65DenA		6'3"	230	Toledo		
Thomas, Aaron TE-OE-FL-WR	61-62SF 62-70NYG	2	6'3"	209	Oregon State		222
Thomas, Clendon DB-OE-FL-HB	58-61LA 62-68Pit	2	6'2"	196	Oklahoma	27	30
Thomas, Gene HB	66-67KC-A 68BosA 68OakA	2	6'1"	210	Florida A&M		36
Thomas, John OG-OT-LB	58-67SF 68JJ		6'4"	246	U. of Pacific		
Thompson, Bobby DB	64-68Det 69NO	3	5'10"	179	Arizona	10	
Thompson, Don DE	62-63Bal 64Phi		6'4"	230	Richmond		
Thompson, Jim DT	65DenA		6'3"	255	Southern Illinois		
Thornton, Bill FB	63-65StL 66JJ 67StL	2	6'1"	214	Nebraska		12
Thornton, Bubba WR	69BufA	23	6'	175	Texas Christian		
Thornton, Jack LB	66MiaA		6'1"	230	Auburn		
Thurlow, Steve HB-FB	64-66NYG 66-68Was	2	6'3"	217	Stanford		36
Thurston, Fuzzy OG	58Bal 59-67GB		6'1"	247	Valparaiso		
Tidmore, Sam LB	62-63Cle		6'1"	223	Ohio State		
Tiller, Jim HB	62NY-A	2	5'9"	165	Purdue		
Timberlake, Bob QB	65NYG	5	6'4"	220	Michigan		24
Tingelhoff, Mick C	62-78Min		6'1"	237	Nebraska		
Tobey, Dave LB	66-67Min 68DenA		6'3"	230	Oregon		
Tobin, Bill HB	63HouA	2	5'11"	210	Missouri		32
Toburen, Nelson LB	61-62GB		6'3"	235	Wichita State		
Todd, Jim HB	66Det		5'11"	195	Ball State		
Todd, Larry HB	65-69OakA 70Oak	23	6'1"	185	Arizona State		42
Tolar, Charley FB-HB	60-66HouA	2	5'7"	199	Northwestern La.		138
Tolleson, Tommy DB	66Atl		6'	185	Alabama		
Toner, Ed DT-LB	67-69BosA 70JJ		6'3"	250	Massachusetts		
Torczon, Lavern DE	60-62BufA 62-65NY-A 66MiaA		6'2"	243	Nebraska	2	6
Townes, Willie DE-DT	66-68Dal 69JJ 70NO		6'5"	263	Tulsa		8
Towns, Bobby DB-DE-HB	60StL 61BosA		6'1"	180	Georgia		
Tracey, John (Jack) LB-OE-TE	59ChiC 60StL 61Phi 62-67BufA	2	6'3"	225	Texas A&M	12	4
Tracy, Tom (Tom the Bomb) HB-FB	56-57Det 58-63Pit 63-64Was	12	5'9"	205	Tennessee		199

Use Name (Nicknames) – Positions	Team by Year	See Section	Hgt	Wgt	College	Int	Pts
Trammell, Allen DB	66HouA		6'	190	Florida		
Trapp, Richard WR	68BufA 69SD-A	2	6'1"	174	Florida		
Trask, Orville DT	60-61HouA 62OakA		6'4"	260	Rice	1	
Travenio, Herb K	64-65SD-A	5	6'	218	none		110
Travis, John FB	66SD-A		6'1"	216	San Jose State		
Traynham, Jerry HB	61DenA		5'10"	190	Southern Calif.		
Traynham, Wade K	66-67Atl	5	6'2"	218	Frederick		45
Trimble, Wayne DB	67SF		6'3"	203	Alabama		
Triplett, Bill HB-FB-DB	62-63StL 64IL 65-66StL 67NYG 68-72Det	23	6'2"	212	Miami-Ohio	1	132
Tripucka, Frank QB	49Det 50-52ChiC 52Dal 53-59CFL 60-63DenA	12 4	6'2"	192	Notre Dame		36
Trosch, Gene DE-DT	67KC-A 68JJ 69KC-A 70LJ		6'7"	277	Miami (Fla.)		
Truax, Billy TE-OE	64-70LA 71-73Dal	2	6'5"	238	Louisiana State		108
Truax, Dalton OT	60OakA		6'2"	235	Tulane		
Trull, Don QB	64-67HouA 67BosA 68-69HouA	12	6'1"	189	Baylor		84
Tubbs, Jerry LB-C	57-58ChiC 58-59SF 60-66Dal		6'2"	221	Oklahoma	17	
Tucker, Bill FB-HB-TE	67-70SF 71ChiB	23	6'2"	221	Tennessee State		78
Tucker, Gary HB	68MiaA		5'11"	195	Tenn.-Chatanooga		
Tucker, Wendell WR-OE	67-70LA	2	5'10"	185	S. Carolina State		66
Tuckett, Phil WR	68SD-A		6'	180	Weber State		
Turner, Bake OE-WR-FL	62Bal 63-69NY-A 70Bos	23	6'	180	Texas Tech		150
Turner, Herschel OG-OT	64-65StL		6'3"	230	Kentucky		
Turner, Vince DB	64NY-A		5'11"	190	Missouri	1	
Tyrer, Jim OT	61-62DalA 63-69KC-A 70-73KC 74Was		6'6"	283	Ohio State		
Tyson, Dick OG	66OakA 67DenA		6'2"	245	Tulsa		
Underwood, Olen LB	65NYG 66-69HouA 70Hou 71Den		6'1"	224	Texas	5	2
Unitas, Johnny QB	56-72Bal 73SD	12	6'1"	194	Louisville		78
Urbanek, Jim DT	68MiaA		6'4"	270	Mississippi		
Urenda, Herm DB-OE	63OakA		5'11"	170	U. of Pacific		
Valdez, Vern DB	60LA 61BufA 62OakA		5'11"	190	Cal.-San Diego	7	
Vallez, Emilio TE	68-69ChiB		6'2"	210	New Mexico		
Vander Kelen, Ron QB	63-67Min	12	6'1"	186	Wisconsin		6
Vandersea, Phil LB-DE-TE	66GB 67NO 68-69GB		6'3"	228	Massachusetts		
Van Raaphorst, Dick K	64Dal 66-67SD-A	5	5'11"	215	Ohio State		247
Vargo, Larry DB-OE-LB	62-63Det 64-65Min 66NYG 67KJ		6'3"	212	Detroit	6	6
Varrichione, Frank OT	55-60Pit 61-65LA		6'1"	234	Notre Dame		
Vasys, Aruras HB	66-68Phi		6'2"	232	Notre Dame		
Vaughn, Bob OG	68DenA		6'4"	240	Mississippi		
Vaughn, Tom DB	65-71Det	3	5'11"	192	Iowa State	9	
Vellone, Jim OG-OT	66-70Min 71IL		6'2"	255	Southern Calif.		
Vereb, Ed HB	60Was		6'	190	Maryland		
Villanueva, Danny K	60-64LA 65-67Dal	45	5'11"	202	New Mexico State		491
Viltz, Theo DB	66HouA		6'2"	190	Southern Calif.		
Vogel, Bob OT	63-72Bal		6'5"	248	Ohio State		
Voight, Bob DT	61OakA		6'5"	265	Los Angeles State		
Vollenweider, Jim HB-FB	62-63SF	2	6'1"	210	Miami (Fla.)		12
Von Sonn, Andy LB	64LA		6'2"	223	U.C.L.A.		
Voss, Lloyd DE-DT-OT	64-65GB 66-71Pit 72Den		6'4"	256	Nebraska	1	
Wade, Billy QB	54-60LA 61-66ChiB	12	6'2"	204	Vanderbilt		144
Wade, Bob DB	68Pit 69Was 70Den		6'2"	200	Morgan State	1	
Wade, Tom QB	64-65Pit	1	6'2"	195	Texas		
Wagstaff, Jim DB	59ChiC 60-61BufA		6'2"	192	Idaho State	9	6
Wainscott, Loyd LB	69HouA 70Hou		6'1"	235	Texas		
Walker, Clarence HB	63DenA		6'1"	205	Southern Illinois		
Walker, Malcolm C-OT	66-69Dal 70GB		6'4"	249	Rice		
Walker, Mickey OG-LB-C	61-65NYG		6'	232	Michigan State		
Walker, Wayne LB	58-72Det	5	6'2"	225	Idaho	14	345
Walker, Wayne K	67KC-A 68HouA	5	6'2"	215	Northwestern La.		50
Walker, Willie FL	66Det		6'3"	200	Tennessee State		
Wallace, Henry DB	60LA-A		6'	195	U. of Pacific		
Waller, Charlie	HC69SD-A HC70SD				Georgia		
Walsh, Ed OT	61NY-A		6'4"	243	Widener		
Walters, Tom DB	64-67Was		6'2"	195	Southern Miss.	3	6
Walton, Joe OE-DE	57-60Was 61-63NYG 64XJ HC83-89NYJ	2	5'11"	202	Pittsburgh	1	168
Walton, Sam OT	68-69NY-A 71Hou		6'5"	270	East Texas State		
Wantland, Hal DB	66MiaA		6'	195	Tennessee		
Ward, Carl DB	67-68Cle 69NO	3	5'9"	180	Michigan	1	6
Ward, Jim QB	67-68Bal 71Phi 72JJ	1	6'2"	197	Gettysburg		
Ward, Paul DT	61-62Det		6'3"	247	Whitworth		
Warlick, Ernie DE	62-65BufA	2	6'4"	234	N. Car. Central		24
Warner, Charley DB-HB	63-64KC-A 64-66BufA 67JJ	3	5'11"	178	Prairie View	7	30
Warren, Dewey QB	68CinA	1	6'	205	Tennessee		
Warren, Jimmy DB	64-65SD-A 66-69MiaA 70-74,77Oak	3	5'11"	178	Illinois	25	24
Warwick, Lonnie LB	65-72Min 73-74Atl 75WFL		6'3"	235	Tennessee Tech	12	6
Warzeka, Ron DT	60OakA		6'4"	250	Montana State		
Washington, Clarence DT	69-70Pit 71JJ		6'3"	265	Ark.-Pine Bluff		
Washington, Clyde DB-HB	60-61BosA 63-65NY-A		6'	202	Purdue	9	
Washington, Dave TE	68DenA		6'4"	228	Southern Calif.		
Washington, Dick DB	68MiaA		6'1"	205	Bethune-Cookman		
Washington, Fred OT	68Was		6'5"	268	North Texas		
Washington, Ted HB	68CinA		5'11"	210	San Diego State		
Waskiewicz, Jim C-OT-LB	66-67NY-A 69Atl		6'4"	237	Wichita State		
Waters, Bob QB	60-63SF	12	6'2"	184	Presbyterian		18
Watkins, Tom HB	61Cle 62-65Det 66JJ 67Det 68Pit	23	6'1"	195	Iowa State		102
Watson, Dave OG	63-64BosA		6'1"	225	Georgia Tech		
Watson, Ed LB	69HouA		6'2"	222	Grambling		
Watters, Bob DE	62-64NY-A		6'4"	247	Lincoln (Mo.)		
Wayt, Russell LB	65Dal		6'4"	235	Rice		
Weatherford, Jim DB	69Atl		5'10"	180	Tennessee	1	6
Weatherwax, Jim DT	66-67GB 68KJ 69GB		6'7"	265	Los Angeles State		
Webb, Allan DB-HB	61-65NYG		5'11"	180	Arnold	7	
Webb, Bob HB-DB	61-62BosA 63JJ 64-69BosA 70Bos 71NE		5'10"	196	Iowa State	21	24
Webb, Ken HB-FB	58-62Det 63Cle	23	5'11"	207	Presbyterian		54
Webster, Dave DB	60-61DalA 62JJ		6'4"	218	Prairie View	11	18
Wegener, Bill OG	62-63HouA		5'10"	245	Missouri		
Weir, Sammy FL	65HouA 66NY-A		5'9"	170	Arkansas State		
Weisacosky, Ed LB	67NYG 68-69MiaA 70Mia 71-72NE		6'	228	Miami (Fla.)	3	

Use Name (Nicknames) – Positions	Team by Year	See Section	Hgt	Wgt	College	Int	Pts
Welch, Jim DB-HB	60-67Bal 68Det		6'	191	S.M.U.	5	6
Wellborn, Joe C	66NYG		6'2"	215	Texas A&M		
Wells, Bob OT	68-69SD-A 70SD		6'4"	273	Johnson C. Smith		
Wells, Harold LB	65-68Phi 69NYG		6'2"	221	Purdue	4	6
Wells, Joel HB	61NYG	2	6'1"	198	Clemson		12
Wells, Warren WR-OE	64Det 65-66MS 67-69OakA 70Oak	2	6'1"	191	Texas Southern		258
71—Declared ineligible to play pro football							
Wendryhoski, Joe C-OG	64-66LA 67-68NO		6'2"	245	Illinois		
Wenzel, Ralph OG	66-70Pit 72-73SD		6'3"	244	San Diego State		
Werl, Bob OG-DE	66NY-A		6'3"	240	Miami (Fla.)		
West, Dave DB	63NY-A		6'3"	190	Central St.-Ohio		
West, Mel HB	61BosA 61-62NY-A	2	5'9"	190	Missouri		18
West, Willie DB-HB	60-61StL 62-63BufA	3	5'10"	188	Oregon	30	12
	64DenA 64-65NY-A 66-68MiaA						
Westmoreland, Dick DB	63-65SD-A 66-69MiaA	3	6'1"	191	N. Carolina A&T	22	12
Wetoska, Bob OT-OG-C	60-69ChiB		6'3"	241	Notre Dame		
Wettstein, Max TE	66DenA		6'3"	217	Florida State		
Whalen, Jim TE-OE	65-69BosA 70-71Den 71Phi	2	6'2"	210	Boston College		120
Wharton, Hogan OG	60-63HouA		6'2"	248	Houston		
Wheeler, Manuch QB	62BufA		6'	190	Maine		
Wheeler, Ted OG-TE	67-68StL 70ChiB		6'3"	240	West Texas State		
Wheelwright, Ernie FB	64-65NYG 66-67Atl 67-70NO	2	6'3"	235	Southern Illinois		96
White, Andre TE	67DenA 68CinA 68SD-A		6'5"	225	Florida A&M		2
White, Bob FB	60HouA		6'2"	220	Ohio State		
White, Freeman TE-DB-LB	66-69NYG	2	6'5"	225	Nebraska	2	6
White, Gene HB	62OakA		6'1"	197	Florida A&M		8
White, Harvey QB	60BosA		6'1"	190	Clemson		
White, John OE	60-61HouA	2	6'4"	230	Texas Southern		6
Whitehead, Bud DB-FL-HB	61-68SD-A		6'	184	Florida State	15	6
Whitfield, A.D. FB	65Dal 66-68Was	2	5'10"	200	North Texas		36
Whitley, Hall LB	60NY-A		6'2"	225	Texas A&I		
Whitlow, Bob C-OG	60-61Was 61-65Det 66Atl 68Cle		6'1"	236	Arizona		
Whitmyer, Nat DB	63LA 66SD-A 67JJ		6'	182	Washington	1	
Whitsell, Dave DB-HB	58-60Det 61-66ChiB 67-69NO		6'	189	Indiana	46	30
Whittenton, Jesse DB	56-57LA 58-64GB		6'	193	Texas El-Paso	24	12
Whittingham, Fred LB-OG	64LA 66Phi 67-68NO		6'1"	240	Cal. Poly-Pomona	3	
	69Dal 70Bos 71Phi						
Wiggin, Paul DE	57-67Cle HC75-77KC		6'3"	242	Stanford	3	12
Wilbur, John OG-DE-DT	66-69Dal 70LA 71-73Was		6'3"	245	Stanford		
Wilburn, J. R. WR-OE	66-70Pit	2	6'2"	190	South Carolina		48
Wilcox, Dave LB	64-74SF		6'3"	235	Oregon	14	12
Wilcox, John OT-DE	60Phi		6'5"	230	Oregon		
Wilder, Bert DE-DT	64-67NY-A		6'3"	245	N. Carolina State		
Will, Erwin DT	65Phi		6'5"	270	Dayton		
Willard, Ken FB	65-73SF 74StL	2	6'2"	225	North Carolina		372
Williams, A.D. OE-FL	59GB 60Cle 61Min	2	6'2"	210	U. of Pacific		6
Williams, Bobby DB	66-67StL 69-71Det	3	6'1"	195	Central Okla.	3	12
Williams, Clancy DB-HB	65-72LA	3	6'2"	197	Washington State	28	12
Williams, Clyde OT-OG	67-71StL		6'2"	252	Southern U.		
Williams, Erwin WR	69Pit		6'5"	215	Md. Eastern Shore		6
Williams, Frank FB	61LA		6'2"	215	Pepperdine		
Williams, Howie DB	62-63GB 63SF 64-69OakA		6'2"	188	Howard C.C.	14	
Williams, Jeff HB	66Min		6'1"	210	Oklahoma State		
Williams, Jim DB	69CinA		6'1"	190	Alcorn State		
Williams, Maxie OG-OT	65HouA 66-69MiaA 70Mia		6'4"	247	Southeastern La.		
Williams, Monk WR	68CinA		5'7"	155	Ark.-Pine Bluff		
Williams, Ray DT	63SF		6'7"	265	U. of Pacific		
Williams, Sam DE-OE-LB	59LA 60-65Det 66-67Atl		6'5"	235	Michigan State	1	20
Williams, Sid LB-DE	64-66Cle 67Was 68Bal 69Pit		6'2"	235	Southern U.	1	6
Williams, Travis HB	67-70GB 71LA 72KJ	23	6'1"	210	Arizona State		100
Williams, Wandy HB	69DenA 70Den		6'	192	Kansas, Hofstra		6
Williams, Willie DB	65NYG 66OakA 67-73NYG		6'	190	Grambling	35	
Williamson, Fred (The Hammer) DB	60Pit 61-64OakA		6'2"	210	Northwestern	36	12
	65-67KC-A						
Williamson, J. R. LB-C	64-67OakA 68-69BosA		6'2"	220	Louisiana Tech	3	
	70Bos 71JJ						
Willsey, Ray	HC61StL				California		
Wilson, Ben FB-HB	63-65LA 67GB 68KJ	2	6'	225	Southern Calif.		66
Wilson, Butch TE-OE	63-67Bal 68-69NYG	2	6'2"	223	Alabama		18
Wilson, Eddie QB	62DalA 63-64KC-A 65BosA 66KJ	1 4	6'	190	Arizona		6

Use Name (Nicknames) – Positions	Team by Year	See Section	Hgt	Wgt	College	Int	Pts
Wilson, George QB	66MiaA	12 4	6'1"	190	Xavier-Ohio		2
Wilson, Harry HB	67Phi 68JJ 69Phi		5'11"	204	Nebraska		
Wilson, Jerrel HB-FB-LB-K	63-69KC-A 70-77KC 78NE	4	6'4"	222	Southern Miss.	4	4
Wilson, Jim OG-OT	65-66SF 67Atl 68LA 69-71JJ		6'3"	257	Georgia		
Wilson, Larry DB	60-72StL HC79StL		6'	190	Utah	52	50
Wilson, Mike DB	69StL		5'11"	185	Western Illinois		
Wingate, Heath C	67Was		6'2"	240	Bowling Green		
Wink, Dean DE-DT	67-68Phi		6'4"	246	Yankton		
Winkler, Francis DE	68-69GB		6'3"	230	Memphis State		
Winkler, Randy OG-OT	67Det 68Atl 69-70MS 71GB		6'5"	258	Tarleton State		
Winner, Charlie	HC66-70StL HC74-75NYJ				SE Missouri St., Washington-St.L		
Winslow, Paul HB	60GB		5'11"	200	N. Car. Central		6
Winslow, Kelton DB	67-68LA		6'	195	Wiley		
Winston, Lloyd FB	62-63SF	2	6'2"	215	Southern Calif.		6
Winston, Roy LB	62-76Min		6'1"	226	Louisiana State	12	20
Winter, Bill LB	62-64NYG		6'4"	220	St. Olaf		
Wisener, Gary DB-OE	60Dal 61HouA		6'1"	206	Baylor		
Witcher, Al OE-DE	60HouA		6'1"	200	Baylor	1	6
Witcher, Dick WR-TE-FL	66-73SF	2	6'3"	205	U.C.L.A.		90
Witt, Mel DE-DT	67-69BosA 70Bos		6'3"	261	Texas-Arlington	1	6
Wittenborn, John OG-K	58-60SF 60-62Phi 63JJ	5	6'2"	238	SE Missouri St.		101
Woitt, John DB	68-69SF		5'11"	172	Mississippi State	1	6
Wolff, Wayne OG	61BufA		6'2"	243	Wake Forest		
Wolski, Bill FB	66Atl		5'11"	203	Notre Dame		
Womack, Joe HB	62Pit	2	5'9"	210	Los Angeles State		30
Wondolowski, Bill WR	69SF		5'10"	168	Eastern Montana		
Wood, Bill DB	63NY-A		5'11"	190	West Va. Wesleyan		
Wood, Bo DE	67Atl		6'3"	225	North Carolina		
Wood, Dick QB	62SD-A 62DenA 63-64NY-A	12	6'5"	202	Auburn		24
	65OakA 66MiaA						
Wood, Duane DB	60-62DalA 63-64KC-A		6'1"	196	Oklahoma State	20	12
Wood, Gary QB	64-66NYG 67NO 68-69NYG	12	5'11"	188	Cornell		37
Wood, Willie DB	60-71GB	3	5'10"	189	Southern Calif.	48	25
Woodeshick, Tom FB-HB	63-71Phi 72StL	2	6'	219	West Virginia		162
Woodlief, Doug LB	65-69LA 70JJ		6'3"	231	Memphis State	6	
Woods, Glenn DE	69HouA		6'4"	250	Prairie View		
Woodson, Abe DB-HB	58-64SF 65-66StL	3	5'11"	188	Illinois	19	48
Woodson, Freddie OG-DE-DT	67-69MiaA		6'2"	253	Florida A&M		
Woodson, Marv DB-HB	64-69Pit 69NO		6'	195	Indiana	18	12
Woulfe, Mike LB	62Phi 63JJ		6'2"	225	Colorado		
Wright, Ernie OT	60LA-A 61-67SD-A 68-69CinA		6'4"	268	Ohio State		
	70-71Cin 72SD						
Wright, Gordon OG	67Phi 69NY-A		6'3"	245	Delaware State		
Wright, Jim DB	64DenA		5'11"	190	Memphis State	1	
Wright, John WR	68Atl 69Det 70JJ	2	6'	196	Illinois		18
Wright, Lonnie DB	66-67DenA		6'2"	205	Colorado State	5	
67-72 played in A.B.A.							
Wright, Steve OT-DE	64-67GB 68-69NYG 70Was		6'6"	250	Alabama		
	71ChiB 72StL						
Wulff, Jim DB-HB	60-61Was		6'1"	185	Michigan State	3	
Yaccino, John DB	62BufA		6'	190	Pittsburgh		
Yates, Bob OT-C-DT	60-65BosA		6'3"	233	Syracuse		
Yearby, Bill DE	66NY-A		6'3"	235	Michigan		
Yelverton, Bill DE	60DenA		6'4"	220	Mississippi	1	6
Yewcic, Tom QB-HB	61-66BosA	12 4	5'11"	186	Michigan State		24
57 played major league baseball							
Yohn, Dave LB	62Bal 63NY-A		6'	223	Gettysburg		
Yoho, Mack DE	60-63BufA	5	6'2"	239	Miami-Ohio	2	97
Youmans, Maury DE-DT	60-62ChiB 63JJ 64-65Dal		6'6"	253	Syracuse		
Young, Jim HB	65-66Min		6'	205	Queens (Ont.)		
Young, Joe DE	60-61DenA		6'3"	245	Arizona		
Youngblood, George DB	66LA 67Cle 67-68NO 69ChiB		6'3"	204	Los Angeles State	3	6
Youso, Frank OT	58-60NYG 61-62Min 63-65OakA		6'4"	257	Minnesota		
Zaeske, Paul WR	69HouA 70Hou		6'2"	200	North Park		
Zaruba, Carroll DB	60DalA		5'9"	210	Nebraska		
Zawadzkas, Jerry TE	67Det		6'4"	220	Columbia		
Zecher, Rich DT-OT	65OakA 66-67MiaA 67BufA		6'2"	240	Utah State		
Zeman, Bob DB	60LA-A 61SD-A 62-63DenA		6'1"	202	Wisconsin	17	12
	64JJ 65-66SD-A						

Lifetime Statistics - 1960-1969 Players Section 1 - **PASSING**
(All men with 25 or more passing attempts)

Name	Years	Att.	Comp.	Comp. Pct.	Yards	Yds./ Att.	TD	Int.	Pct. Int.
Jon Arnett	57-66	33	8	24.2	147	4.5	2	2	6.1
Billy Barnes	57-63,65-66	25	10	40.0	233	9.3	4	4	16.0
Pete Beathard	64-73,75	1282	575	44.9	8176	6.4	43	84	6.6
George Blanda	49-58,60-74	4007	1911	47.7	26920	6.7	236	277	6.9
Zeke Bratkowski	54,57-68,71	1484	762	51.3	10345	7.0	65	122	8.2
Don Breaux	63,65	181	92	50.8	1339	7.4	9	10	5.5
Bob Brodhead	60	25	7	28.0	75	3.0	0	3	12.0
John Brodie	57-73	4491	2469	55.0	31548	7.0	214	224	5.0
Rudy Bukich	53,56-68	1190	626	52.6	8433	7.1	61	74	6.2
Max Chaboian	66	163	82	50.3	1110	6.8	4	12	7.4
Dennis Claridge	64-66	71	41	57.7	484	6.8	2	2	2.8
Jack Concannon	64-71,74-75	1110	560	50.5	6270	5.6	36	63	5.7
Greg Cook	69,73	200	107	53.5	1865	9.3	15	11	5.5
John David Crow	58-68	70	33	47.1	759	10.8	5	5	7.1
Garry Cuozzo	63-72	1182	584	49.4	7402	6.3	43	55	4.7
Dan Darragh	68-70	296	127	42.9	1352	4.6	4	22	7.4
Cotton Davidson	54,57,60-66,68	1752	770	43.9	11760	6.7	73	108	6.2
Len Dawson	57-75	3741	2136	57.1	28711	7.7	239	183	4.9
Eagle Day	59-60	32	15	46.9	194	6.1	0	2	6.2
Randy Duncan	61	67	25	37.3	361	6.4	1	3	4.6
Hunter Enis	60-62	160	80	50.0	947	5.9	4	6	3.7
Sam Etcheverry	61-62	302	154	51.0	1982	6.6	16	21	7.0
Tom Flores	60-61,63-69	1715	838	48.9	11959	7.0	93	92	5.4
Roman Gabriel	62-77	4498	2366	52.6	29444	6.5	201	149	3.3
Chan Gallegos	62	35	18	51.4	298	8.5	2	3	8.6
Johnny Green	60-63	618	275	44.5	3921	6.3	26	34	5.5
Tom Greene	60-61	63	27	42.9	251	4.0	1	6	9.5
Glynn Griffing	63	40	16	40.0	306	7.7	3	4	10.0
Lee Grosscup	60-62	173	73	42.2	1086	6.3	10	12	6.9
Ralph Gugliemi	55,58-63	626	292	46.6	4119	6.6	24	52	8.3
John Hadl	62-77	4637	2363	50.4	33503	7.1	244	268	5.7
Galen Hall	62-63	150	64	42.7	885	5.9	5	10	6.7
Kim Hammond	68-69	32	15	46.9	147	4.6	0	2	6.3
George Herring	60-61	233	102	43.8	1297	5.6	5	23	9.9
King Hill	58-69	881	429	48.7	5553	6.3	37	71	8.1
Dick Hoak	61-70	40	20	50.0	427	10.7	4	3	7.5
Paul Hornung	57-62,64-66	55	24	43.6	383	7.0	5	4	7.3
John Huarte	66-68,70-72	48	19	39.6	230	4.8	1	5	10.4
Buddy Humphrey	59-66	175	87	49.7	1094	6.3	4	12	6.9
George Izo	60-66	317	132	41.6	1791	5.6	12	32	10.1
Dick Jamieson	60-61	70	35	50.0	586	8.4	6	2	2.9
Charley Johnson	61-75	3392	1737	51.2	24410	7.2	170	181	5.3
Sonny Jurgensen	57-74	4262	2433	57.1	32224	7.6	255	189	4.4
Joe Kapp	67-70	918	449	48.9	5911	6.4	40	64	7.0
Jack Kemp	57,60-67,69	3073	1436	46.7	21218	6.9	114	183	6.0
Tom Kennedy	66	100	55	55.0	748	7.5	7	6	6.0
Daryle Lamonica	63-74	2601	1288	49.5	19154	7.4	164	138	5.3
Gary Lane	66-68	43	21	48.8	254	5.9	2	1	2.3
Jim LeClair	67-68	99	46	46.5	676	6.8	2	6	6.1
Jacky Lee	60-69	838	430	51.3	6191	7.4	46	57	6.8
Bruce Lemmerman	68-69	77	28	36.4	370	4.8	1	5	6.5
Pete Liske	64,69-72	778	396	50.9	5170	6.6	30	46	5.9
Richie Lucas	60-61	99	43	43.4	596	6.0	4	7	7.1
Tom Matte	61-72	42	12	28.6	246	5.9	2	2	4.8
John McCormick	62-63,65-66,68	555	214	38.6	2895	5.2	17	38	6.8
Don Meredith	60-68	2308	1170	50.7	17199	7.5	135	111	4.8
Ron Miller	62	43	17	39.5	250	5.8	1	1	2.3
George Mira	64-69,71	346	148	42.8	2109	6.1	19	20	5.8
Earl Morrall	56-76	2689	1379	51.3	20809	7.7	161	148	5.5
Bill Nelsen	63-72	1905	963	50.6	14165	7.4	98	101	5.3
Jim Ninowski	58-69	1048	513	49.0	7133	6.8	34	67	6.4
Terry Nofsinger	61-67	260	118	45.4	1357	5.2	4	12	4.6
Rick Norton	66-70	382	159	41.6	1815	4.8	7	30	7.9
Nick Papac	61	44	13	29.5	173	3.9	2	7	15.8
Babe Parilli	52-53,56-58,60-69	3330	1552	46.6	22681	6.8	178	220	6.6
Milt Plum	57-69	2419	1306	54.0	17536	7.2	122	127	5.3
Warren Rabb	60-62	251	101	40.2	1782	7.1	15	16	6.4
Larry Rakestraw	64,66-68	111	51	45.9	589	5.3	4	9	8.1
Dan Reeves	65-72	32	14	43.8	370	11.6	2	4	12.5
Jerry Reichow	56-57,59-64	38	12	31.6	187	4.9	0	4	10.5
M. C. Reynolds	58-62	450	222	49.3	2932	6.5	17	28	6.2
Jerry Rhome	65-67,69-71	280	139	49.6	1628	5.8	7	14	5.0
Johnny Roach	56,59-64	413	182	44.1	2765	6.7	24	37	9.0
Ed Rutkowski	63-68	102	41	40.2	380	3.7	0	6	5.9
Frank Ryan	58-70	2133	1090	51.1	16042	7.5	149	111	5.2
Bob Scrabis	60-62	26	7	26.9	82	3.2	1	3	11.5
Tom Sherman	68-69	228	92	40.4	1219	5.3	16	16	7.0
Dick Shiner	64-71,73-74	736	354	48.1	4801	6.5	36	43	5.8
Mickey Slaughter	63-66	584	291	49.8	3607	6.3	22	37	6.3
Steve Sloan	66-67	31	10	32.3	134	4.3	0	4	12.9
Ron Smith	65-66	181	79	43.6	1249	6.9	8	12	6.6
Norm Snead	61-76	4353	2276	52.2	30797	7.1	196	257	5.9
Butch Songin	60-62	694	327	47.1	4347	6.3	38	31	4.5
Ronnie South	68	38	14	36.8	129	3.4	1	3	7.9
Bart Starr	56-71	3149	1808	57.4	24718	7.8	152	138	4.4
Kay Stephenson	67-68	105	40	38.1	481	4.6	6	9	8.6
John Stofa	66-70	312	146	46.8	1758	5.6	12	11	3.5
Karl Sweetan	66-70	590	269	45.6	3210	5.4	17	34	5.8
Mike Taliaferro	64-72	966	419	43.4	5241	5.4	36	63	6.5
Fran Tarkenton	61-78	6467	3686	57.0	47003	7.3	342	266	4.1
Steve Tensi	65-70	862	369	42.8	5558	6.4	43	46	5.3
Tom Tracy	56-64	67	24	35.8	854	12.7	6	5	7.5
Frank Tripucka	49-52,60-63	1745	879	50.4	10282	5.9	59	124	7.1
Don Trull	64-69	617	276	44.7	3980	6.5	30	28	4.5
Johnny Unitas	56-73	5186	2830	54.6	40239	7.8	290	253	4.9
Ron Vander Kelen	63-67	252	107	42.5	1375	5.5	6	11	4.4
Billy Wade	54-66	2523	1370	54.3	18530	7.3	124	134	5.3
Tom Wade	64-65	69	34	49.3	470	6.8	2	13	18.8
Jim Ward	67-68,71	26	13	50.0	165	6.3	2	2	7.7
Dewey Warren	68	80	47	58.8	506	6.3	1	4	5.0
Bob Waters	60-63	124	59	47.6	707	5.7	3	8	6.5
Eddie Wilson	62-65	186	90	48.4	1251	6.7	5	6	3.2
George Wilson	66	112	46	41.1	764	6.8	5	10	8.9
Dick Wood	62-66	1193	522	43.8	7151	6.0	51	70	5.9
Gary Wood	64-69	400	186	46.5	2575	6.4	14	23	5.7
Tom Yewcic	61-66	206	87	42.2	1374	6.7	12	12	5.8

Lifetime Statistics - 1960-1969 Players Section 2 - **RUSHING and RECEIVING**
(All men with 25 or more rushing attempts or 10 or more receptions)

		RUSHING				RECEIVING			
Name	Years	Att.	Yards	Avg.	TD	Rec.	Yards	Avg.	TD
John Adams	59-63	41	99	2.4	1	21	264	12.6	3
Don Allen	60	30	18	0.6	1	5	34	6.8	0
Duane Allen	61-67					10	227	22.7	5
Jerry Allen	66-69	201	664	3.3	7	33	400	12.1	2
Jim Allison	65-68	93	378	4.1	2	22	230	10.5	0
Lance Alworth	62-72	24	129	5.4	2	542	10267	18.9	85
Bill Anderson	58-63,65-66	4	11	2.8	0	168	3048	18.1	15
Max Anderson	68-69,71	160	599	3.7	3	29	205	7.1	0
Ralph Anderson	58,60					55	791	14.4	6
Taz Anderson	61-64,66-67					87	1335	15.3	9
Fred Arbanas	62-70	4	15	3.8	0	218	3101	14.2	34
Jon Arnett	57-66	964	3833	4.0	26	222	2290	10.3	10
Doug Asad	60-61					50	698	14.0	3
Willie Asbury	66-68	253	868	3.4	11	25	307	12.2	2
Pervis Atkins	61-66	74	201	2.7	1	64	675	10.5	2
Joe Auer	64-68	234	773	3.3	7	51	647	12.7	6
Gene Babb	57-58,60-63	152	461	3.0	3	33	281	8.5	1
Art Baker	61-62	154	507	3.3	3	9	85	9.4	0
Sam Baker	53,56-69	49	234	4.8	2	7	59	8.4	0
Terry Baker	63-65	58	210	3.6	1	30	302	10.1	2
Gary Ballman	62-73	41	202	4.9	4	323	5366	16.6	37
Estes Banks	67-68	44	157	3.6	0	4	15	3.8	1
Billy Barnes	57-63,65-66	994	3421	3.4	29	153	1786	11.7	9
Gary Barnes	62-64,66-67					41	583	14.2	2
Eppie Barney	67-68	0	8	–	1	19	192	10.1	1
Terry Barr	57-65	32	151	4.7	2	227	3810	16.8	35
Jan Barrett	63-64					13	221	17.0	2
Tom Barrington	66-70	168	530	3.2	3	41	278	6.8	1
Dick Bass	60-69	1218	5417	4.4	34	204	1841	9.0	7
Glenn Bass	60-68	16	67	4.2	0	167	2841	17.0	17
Craig Baynham	67-70,72	152	553	3.6	6	45	466	10.4	3
Pete Beathard	64-73,75	131	680	5.2	11				
Hal Bedsole	64-66					26	418	16.1	8
Harry Bell	60	42	238	5.5	0	2	13	6.5	0
Joe Bellino	65-67	30	64	2.1	0	11	153	13.9	1
Ray Berry	55-67					631	9275	14.7	68
Charles Bivins	60-67	153	498	3.3	3	28	262	9.4	3
George Blanda	49-58,60-75	144	268	1.9	9	1	-16	-16.0	0
Sid Blanks	64-70	365	1440	3.9	7	106	1073	10.1	4
Ronnie Blye	68-69	61	268	4.4	1	12	85	7.1	0
Dewey Bohling	60-61	178	584	3.3	4	43	485	11.3	5
Don Bosseler	57-64	775	3112	4.0	22	136	1083	8.0	1
Zeke Bratkowski	54,57-68,71	92	308	3.3	5				
Johnny Brewer	61-70					89	1256	14.1	6
John Brodie	57-73	235	1167	5.0	22				
Barry Brown	66-70					21	214	10.2	0
Bill Brown	61-74	1649	5838	3.5	52	286	3183	11.1	23
Fred Brown	61,63	59	210	3.6	2	3	18	6.0	0
Jimmy Brown	57-65	2359	12312	5.2	106	262	2499	9.5	20
Timmy Brown	59-68	889	3862	4.3	31	235	3399	14.5	26
Willie Brown	64-66	44	133	3.0	0	5	110	22.0	1
Charlie Bryant	66-69	67	322	4.8	0	3	26	8.7	0
Frank Budd	62-63					10	236	23.6	1
Fred Bukaty	61	76	187	2.5	5	15	94	6.7	0
Rudy Bukich	53,56-68	112	109	1.0	9				
Ronnie Bull	62-71	881	3222	3.7	9	172	1479	8.6	5
Amos Bullocks	62-64,66	158	620	3.9	5	15	180	12.0	2
Jerry Burch	61					18	235	13.1	1
Chris Burford	60-67	3	10	3.3	0	391	5505	14.1	55
Vern Burke	65-67					38	470	12.4	2

Lifetime Statistics - 1960-1969 Players Section 2 - **RUSHING AND RECEIVING** (continued)
(All men with 25 or more rushing attempts or 10 or more receptions)

		RUSHING				RECEIVING			
Name	**Years**	**Att.**	**Yards**	**Avg.**	**TD**	**Rec.**	**Yards**	**Avg.**	**TD**
Bobby Burnett	66-67,69	237	871	3.7	4	45	533	11.8	4
John Burrell	62-64,66-67	6	38	6.3	0	26	437	16.8	0
Ode Burrell	64-69	304	1088	3.6	3	112	1379	12.3	9
Ron Burton	60-65	429	1536	3.6	9	111	1205	10.9	8
Bill Butler	59-64	29	108	3.7	0	6	95	15.8	0
Cannonball Butler	65-72	797	2768	3.5	9	89	959	10.8	7
Woody Campbell	67-71	408	1493	3.7	13	80	709	8.9	2
Billy Cannon	60-70	602	2455	4.1	17	236	3656	15.5	47
Bob Cappadonna	66-68	123	460	3.7	2	24	196	8.2	3
Gino Cappelletti	60-70	4	6	1.5	0	292	4589	15.7	42
Wray Carlton	60-67	819	3368	4.1	29	110	1329	12.1	5
Reg Carolan	62-68					23	364	15.8	5
J.C. Caroline	56-65	68	263	3.9	2	6	111	18.5	1
Preston Carpenter	56-67	223	884	4.0	1	305	4457	14.6	23
Jimmy Carr	55,57,59-65	30	115	3.8	0	9	157	17.4	0
Rick Casares	55-66	1431	[illegible]	[illegible]	49	191	1588	8.3	11
Bernie Casey	61-68	1	23	23.0	0	359	5444	15.2	40
Dan Chamberlain	60-61					18	295	16.4	4
Joe Childress	56-60,62-65	530	2210	4.2	3	121	1700	14.0	13
Clarence Childs	64-68	40	102	2.6	0	11	97	8.8	0
Dick Christy	58,60-63	337	1267	3.8	10	132	1473	11.2	6
Jack Clancy	67,69-70	3	-4	-1.3	0	104	1401	13.5	5
Howard Clark	60-61					38	613	16.1	0
Franke Clarke	57-67	32	231	7.2	1	291	5426	18.6	50
Doug Cline	60-66	37	105	2.8	2	4	15	3.8	0
Bert Coan	62-68	284	1259	4.4	15	39	367	9.4	4
Junior Coffey	65-67,69,71	535	2037	3.8	10	64	487	7.6	5
Gail Cogdill	60-70	2	-2	-1.0	0	356	5696	16.0	34
Angie Coia	60-66	5	-2	-0.4	0	121	2037	16.8	20
Jim Colclough	60-68	4	51	12.8	0	283	[illegible]	[illegible]	39
Terry Cole	68-71	189	641	3.4	5	25	171	6.8	1
Gary Collins	62-71	8	60	15.0	0	331	5299	16.0	70
Dick Compton	62-65,67-68	6	8	1.3	0	52	733	14.1	14
Jack Concannon	64-71,74-75	217	1026	4.7	12				
Larry Coniar	67-70	30	102	3.4	0	6	68	11.3	0
Bobby Joe Conrad	58-69	118	441	3.7	2	422	5902	14.0	38
Greg Cook	69,73	25	148	5.9	1				
Bob Coolbaugh	61					32	435	13.6	4
Thurlow Cooper	60-62					36	491	13.6	8
Paul Costa	65-72	2	12	6.0	1	102	1699	16.7	6
Jim Cox	68					11	147	13.4	0
Eric Crabtree	66-71	8	37	4.6	0	164	2663	16.2	22
Dobie Craig	62-64	1	8	8.0	0	38	743	19.6	7
Jim Crawford	60-64	302	1078	3.6	5	52	496	9.5	2
Willie Crenshaw	64-70	652	2428	3.7	15	104	797	7.7	3
Bob Crespino	61-68					58	741	12.8	9
Bobby Crockett	66,68-69					41	659	16.1	3
Monte Crockett	60-62					35	512	14.6	1
Marshall Cropper	67-69					14	181	12.9	0
John David Crow	58-68	1157	4963	4.3	38	258	3699	14.3	35
Wayne Crow	60-63	235	1085	4.6	3	36	345	9.6	1
Harry Crump	63	49	120	2.5	5	3	19	6.3	0
Jim Cunningham	61-63	120	337	2.8	3	26	219	8.4	2
Gary Cuozzo	63-72	16	176	2.3	1				
Carroll Dale	60-73	4	30	7.5	0	438	8277	18.9	52
Clem Daniels	60-68	1146	5138	4.5	30	203	3314	16.3	24
Cotton Davidson	54,57,60-66,68	149	357	2.4	11				
Glenn Davis	60-61					10	132	13.2	0
Len Dawson	57-75	294	1293	4.4	9				
Ted Dean	60-64	263	923	3.5	2	51	684	13.4	4
Austin Denney	67-71	2	3	1.5	0	71	764	10.8	3
Mike Dennis	68-69	29	136	4.7	0	8	53	6.6	0
Al Denson	64-71	4	3	0.8	0	260	4275	16.4	32
Willard Dewveall	59-64					204	3304	16.2	27
Buddy Dial	59-66	4	14	3.5	0	261	5436	20.8	44
Bo Dickinson	60-64	189	693	3.7	4	86	886	10.3	6
Mike Ditka	61-72	2	2	1.0	0	427	5812	13.6	43
Hewitt Dixon	63-70	772	3090	4.0	15	263	[illegible]	10.7	13
Oscar Donahue	62					16	285	17.8	1
Mike Dorsey	62					21	344	16.4	2
Merrill Douglas	58-62	54	213	3.9	2	4	26	6.5	0
Boyd Dowler	59-69,71	2	28	14.0	0	474	7270	15.3	40
Elbert Dubenion	60-68	46	326	7.1	3	[illegible]	[illegible]	[illegible]	35
Paul Dudley	62-63	38	121	3.2	0	10	120	12.0	1
Fred Dugan	58-63	1	-9	-9	0	153	2226	14.5	13
Perry Lee Dunn	64-69	214	653	3.1	6	42	408	9.7	1
Henry Dyer	66,68-70	82	256	3.1	1	14	160	11.4	1
Rick Eder	68-70					11	184	16.7	1
Nick Eddy	68-70,72	152	523	3.4	3	24	237	9.9	2
Larry Elkins	66-67	2	19	9.5	0	24	315	13.1	3
John Embree	69-70					33	519	15.7	5
Hunter Enis	60-62	30	25	0.8	5				
Pat Epperson	60					11	99	9.0	0
Sam Etcheverry	61-62	41	78	1.9	0				
Bo Farrington	60-63	1	-2	-2.0	0	55	881	16.0	7
Bobby Felts	65-67	66	207	3.1	2	5	29	5.8	0
Bob Ferguson	62-63	66	209	3.2	1	4	13	3.3	0
Charley Ferguson	61-63,65-66,68-69					62	1168	18.8	13
Paul Flatley	63-70					306	4905	16.0	24
George Fleming	61	31	112	3.6	1	10	49	4.9	0
Marv Fleming	63-74					157	1823	11.6	16
Tom Flores	60-61,63-69	101	142	1.4	5				
Charlie Flowers	60-62	111	416	3.7	4	35	383	10.9	1
Lee Folkins	61-65	1	9	9.0	0	80	1042	13.0	10
Fred Ford	60	38	194	5.1	2	1	5	5.0	0

		RUSHING				RECEIVING			
Name	**Years**	**Att.**	**Yards**	**Avg.**	**TD**	**Rec.**	**Yards**	**Avg.**	**TD**
Garrett Ford	68	41	186	4.5	1	6	40	6.7	0
Gene Foster	65-70	445	1613	3.6	4	99	904	9.1	3
Willmer Fowler	60-61	94	372	4.0	1	10	99	9.9	0
Al Frazier	61-63	62	278	4.5	2	58	1010	17.4	7
Charley Frazier	62-70	4	5	1.3	0	209	3461	16.6	30
Willie Frazier	64-72,75	6	118	19.7	1	207	3069	14.8	35
Tucker Frederickson	65,67-71	651	2209	3.4	9	128	1011	7.9	8
Charley Fuller	61-62	38	134	3.5	0	17	344	20.2	2
Roman Gabriel	62-77	354	1302	3.7	30	1	-5	-5.0	0
Bob Gaiters	61-63	168	673	4.0	6	17	175	10.3	2
Willie Galimore	57-63	670	2985	4.5	26	87	1201	13.8	10
R.C. Gamble	68-69	94	346	3.7	1	18	129	7.2	1
Billy Gambrell	63-68	7	41	5.9	0	116	1931	16.6	18
J.D. Garrett	64-67	116	434	3.7	3	17	169	9.9	2
Mike Garrett	66-73	1308	5481	4.2	35	238	2010	8.4	13
Larry Garron	60-68	763	2981	3.9	14	185	2502	13.5	26
Prentice Gault	60-67	629	2466	3.9	11	79	901	11.4	6
Jack Gehrke	68-69,71-72	1	2	2.0	0	14	254	18.1	0
Pete Gent	64-68	2	-5	-2.5	0	68	989	14.5	4
Jim Gibbons	58-68					287	3561	12.4	20
Cookie Gilchrist	62-67	1010	4293	4.3	37	110	1135	10.3	6
Glenn Glass	62-66					15	201	13.4	0
Al Goldstein	60	3	-2	-0.7	1	27	354	13.1	1
Ron Goodwin	63-68	2	-22	-11.0	0	78	1079	13.8	9
Jim Grabowski	66-71	475	1731	3.6	8	82	675	8.2	3
Art Graham	63-68	1	-5	-5.0	0	199	3107	15.6	20
Hoyle Granger	66-72	805	3653	4.5	19	134	1339	10.0	5
Ernie Green	62-68	668	3204	4.8	15	195	2036	10.4	20
Johnny Green	60-63	77	-106	-1.4	6	1	0	0.0	0
Tom Greene	60-61	16	-27	-1.7	0				
Jim Greer	60					22	284	12.9	1
Ben Gregory	68	52	283	5.4	1	5	21	4.2	0
Bill Groman	60-65	1	2	2.0	1	174	3481	20.0	36
Earl Gros	62-70	821	3157	3.8	28	142	1255	8.8	10
Ralph Guglielmi	55,58-63	177	633	3.6	2				
John Hadl	62-77	351	1112	3.2	16	3	-9	-3.0	0
Mike Haffner	68-71	3	3	1.0	0	59	991	16.8	7
Roger Hagberg	66-69	194	766	3.9	4	58	645	11.1	4
Mac Haik	67-71	4	28	7.0	0	76	1149	15.1	9
Ken Hall	59-61	51	212	4.2	0	8	118	14.8	2
Tom Hall	62-69	4	-4	-1.0	0	103	1441	14.0	8
Mal Hammack	55,57-66	320	1278	4.0	7	27	255	9.4	0
Charley Hardy	60-62					54	840	15.6	7
Jack Harper	67-68	41	197	4.8	1	11	212	19.3	3
Billy Harris	68-69,71	60	158	2.6	0	5	131	26.2	1
Pete Hart	60	25	113	4.5	0	3	19	6.3	0
Alex Hawkins	59-68	208	787	3.8	10	129	1751	13.6	12
Ben Hawkins	66-73	10	8	0.8	0	261	4764	18.3	32
Luther Hayes	61					14	280	20.0	3
Ray Hayes	61	73	319	4.4	2	16	121	8.1	0
Wendell Hayes	63,65-74	988	3758	3.8	28	161	1461	9.1	7
Abner Haynes	60-67	1036	4630	4.5	46	287	3535	12.3	20
Gene Heeter	63-65					22	327	14.9	2
John Henderson	65-72					108	1735	16.1	10
Jon Henderson	68-70					28	390	13.9	0
Charley Hennigan	60-66					410	6823	16.6	51
Ken Herock	63-69					63	924	14.7	4
Bo Hickey	67	73	263	3.6	4	7	36	5.1	1
Fred Hill	65-71	1	5	5.0	0	85	1005	11.8	5
Jerry Hill	61,63-70	606	2668	4.4	22	117	970	8.3	3
King Hill	58-69	88	306	3.5	9				
Mack Lee Hill	64-65	230	1203	5.2	6	40	408	10.2	3
John Hilton	65-73	1	15	15.0	0	144	2047	14.2	16
Dick Hoak	61-70	1132	3965	3.5	25	146	1452	9.9	8
Roy Hopkins	67-70	232	826	3.6	7	50	529	10.6	1
Sam Horner	60-62	118	355	3.0	0	17	219	12.9	1
Paul Hornung	57-62,64-66	893	3711	4.2	50	130	1480	11.4	12
Brad Hubbert	67-70	287	1270	4.4	9	42	312	7.4	2
Chuck Hughes	67-71					15	262	17.5	0
George Hughley	65	37	175	4.7	0	9	93	10.3	1
Tom Hutchinson	63-66					19	409	21.5	2
Bobby Jackson	62-65	184	624	3.4	14	32	333	10.4	2
Frank Jackson	61-67	121	790	6.5	7	188	2955	15.7	24
Leroy Jackson	62-63	52	142	2.7	0	10	253	25.3	0
Allen Jacobs	65-67	91	301	3.3	1	10	69	6.9	0
Dick James	56-65	502	1930	3.8	19	104	1669	16.0	15
Billy Joe	63-68	539	2013	3.7	15	77	589	7.6	4
Charley Johnson	61-75	196	539	2.8	10				
Curley Johnson	60-69	64	209	3.3	1	32	370	11.6	3
Jim Johnson	61-75					40	690	17.3	4
John Henry Johnson	54-66	1571	6803	4.3	48	186	1478	7.9	7
Rudy Johnson	64-66	25	60	2.4	1	8	70	8.8	0
Harry Jones	67-70	44	85	1.9	0	9	131	14.6	0
Homer Jones	64-70	17	146	8.6	1	224	4986	22.3	36
Jim Jones	65-68	8	24	3.0	0	69	1182	17.1	11
Les Josephson	64-67,69-74	797	3407	4.3	17	194	1970	10.2	11
Steve Junker	57,59-62					48	639	13.3	6
Sonny Jurgensen	57-74	181	493	2.7	15	1	-3	-3.0	0
Joe Kapp	67-70	119	611	5.1	5				
Jim Kelly	64-65,67					31	531	17.1	5
Leroy Kelly	64-73	1727	7274	4.2	74	190	2281	12.0	13
Jack Kemp	57,60-67,69	394	796	2.0	40				
Claude King	61-62	33	194	5.9	3	8	125	15.6	1
Phil King	58-66	569	2192	3.9	7	86	951	11.1	9

Lifetime Statistics - 1960-1969 Players Section 2 - **RUSHING AND RECEIVING** (continued)
(All men with 25 or more rushing attempts or 10 or more receptions)

Name	Years	RUSHING Att.	Yards	Avg.	TD	RECEIVING Rec.	Yards	Avg.	TD
Roger Kochman	63	47	232	4.9	0	4	148	37.0	1
Dave Kocourek	60-68					249	4090	16.4	24
Dave Kopay	64-72	235	876	3.7	3	77	593	7.7	4
Dick Kotite	67-69,71-72					17	213	12.5	5
Walt Kowalczyk	58-61	103	264	2.6	2	34	256	7.5	1
Ernie Koy	65-70	414	1723	4.2	9	76	498	6.6	6
Ron Kramer	57,59-67	6	9	1.5	0	229	3272	14.3	16
Rich Kreitling	59-64	2	−13	−6.5	0	123	1775	14.4	17
Joe Kulbacki	60	41	108	2.6	1	2	9	4.5	0
Ralph Kurek	65-70	121	434	3.6	2	26	299	11.5	0
Pete Lammons	66-72	0	3	–	0	185	2364	12.8	14
Daryle Lamonica	63-74	166	640	3.9	14				
Izzy Lang	64-69	245	873	3.6	4	63	554	8.8	4
Jack Larscheid	60-61	100	400	4.0	1	24	198	8.3	1
Pete Larson	67-68					20	191	9.6	1
Monte Ledbetter	67-69					18	314	17.4	3
Jacky Lee	60-69	82	150	1.8	3	1	−1	−1.0	0
Darrell Lester	64-66	38	102	2.7	0	2	26	13.0	1
Dan Lewis	58-66	800	3205	4.0	19	99	1162	11.7	5
Gary Lewis	64-70	343	1421	4.1	13	72	604	8.4	5
Keith Lincoln	61-68	758	3383	4.5	19	165	2250	13.6	19
Mike Lind	63-66	222	661	3.0	8	52	427	8.2	1
Jim Lindsey	66-72	178	566	3.2	6	56	632	11.3	4
Don Lisbon	63-64	164	561	3.4	0	34	363	10.7	3
Pete Liske	64,69-72	38	141	3.7	2				
Andy Livingston	64-65,67-70	291	1216	4.2	7	46	474	10.3	3
J.W. Lockett	61-64	229	170	3.4	3	62	589	9.5	7
Oscar Lofton	60					19	360	18.9	4
Bob Long	64-70					98	1539	15.7	10
Joe Don Looney	64-67,69	214	724	3.4	11	26	171	6.6	2
Tony Lorick	64-69	548	2124	3.9	14	86	890	10.3	5
Billy Lott	58,60-63	246	1123	4.6	13	85	919	10.8	8
John Love	67,72					18	267	14.8	2
Paul Lowe	60-61,63-69	1026	4995	4.9	40	111	1045	9.4	7
Dick Lucas	58,60-63					34	384	11.3	6
Richie Lucas	60-61	56	105	1.9	2	11	127	11.5	1
Lamar Lundy	57-69					35	584	16.7	6
Lenny Lyles	58-69	35	69	2.0	2	8	57	7.1	1
Red Mack	61-66	4	−1	−0.3	0	52	1159	22.3	8
Dee Mackey	60-65					94	1352	14.4	8
John Mackey	63-72	19	127	6.7	0	331	5236	15.8	38
Jacques MacKinnon	61-70	86	377	4.4	2	112	2109	18.8	20
Joe Marconi	56-66	673	2771	4.1	30	136	1326	9.8	9
Aaron Marsh	68-69	4	8	2.0	0	27	439	16.3	4
Amos Marsh	61-67	750	3222	4.3	25	133	1384	10.4	7
Paul Martha	64-70	6	15	2.5	0	17	316	18.6	0
Billy Martin	64-68					58	705	12.2	4
Tommy Mason	61-71	1040	4203	4.0	32	214	2324	10.9	13
Bill Mathis	60-69	1044	3589	3.4	37	149	1775	11.9	9
Tom Matte	61-72	1200	4646	3.9	45	249	2869	11.5	12
Doug Mayberry	61-63	87	314	3.6	1	13	118	9.1	1
Don Maynard	58,60-73	24	70	2.9	0	633	11834	18.7	88
Don McCall	67-70	229	884	3.9	6	37	390	10.5	3
Brendan McCarthy	68-69	59	175	3.0	1	20	184	9.2	2
Curtis McClinton	62-69	762	3124	4.1	18	154	1945	12.6	14
Gary McDermott	68-69	54	108	2.0	3	20	115	5.8	1
Roy McDonald	67-68	52	223	4.3	4	10	60	6.0	0
Tommy McDonald	57-68	17	22	1.3	0	495	8410	17.0	84
Gerry McDougall	62-64,68	104	469	4.5	6	22	248	11.3	0
Kay McFarland	62-66,68					45	682	15.2	4
Max McGee	54,57-67	12	121	10.1	0	345	6346	18.4	50
Hugh McInnis	60-62,64,66	4	30	7.5	0	22	392	17.8	0
Marlin McKeever	61-73					133	1737	13.1	6
Bob McLeod	61-66					126	1926	15.3	19
Clifton McNeil	64-73	5	6	1.2	0	181	2734	15.1	22
Chuck Mercein	65-70	163	531	3.3	4	37	205	5.5	1
Don Meredith	60-68	242	1216	5.0	15				
Dale Messer	61-65					12	176	14.7	0
Frank Mestnik	60-61,63	200	767	3.8	4	15	53	3.5	1
Tom Michel	64	39	129	3.3	0	1	14	14.0	0
Alan Miller	60-63,65	386	1395	3.6	9	130	1470	11.3	11
Bill Miller	62-64,66-68					141	1879	13.3	10
Gene Milton	68-69	9	108	12.0	0	21	322	15.3	1
Gene Mingo	60-70	185	777	4.2	8	52	454	8.7	4
Randy Minniear	67-70	96	316	3.3	5	19	148	7.8	1
George Mira	60-64,71	50	379	7.6	0				
Bobby Mitchell	58-68	513	2735	5.3	18	521	7954	15.3	65
Charley Mitchell	63-68	352	1142	3.2	5	62	650	8.9	3
Stan Mitchell	60-70	173	548	3.2	4	42	533	12.7	5
Lenny Moore	56-67	1069	5174	4.8	63	363	6039	16.6	48
Tom Moore	60-67	660	2445	3.7	21	141	1152	8.2	10
Doug Moreau	66-69	1	−2	−2.0	0	73	926	12.7	6
Earl Morrall	56-75	235	878	3.7	8				
Johnny Morris	58-67	224	1040	4.6	5	356	5059	14.2	31
Larry Morris	55-57,59-66	40	148	3.7	1				
Joe Morrison	59-72	677	2474	3.7	18	395	4993	12.6	47
Bill Murphy	68					18	268	14.9	0
Jim Nance	65-71,73	1341	5401	4.0	45	133	870	6.5	1
Bill Nelsen	63-72	84	89	1.1	2	1	−5	−5.0	0
Tom Neumann	63	44	148	3.4	0	10	48	4.8	0
Jim Ninowski	58-69	92	367	4.0	10				
Terry Nofsinger	61-67	31	65	2.1	3				
Karl Noonan	66-71	2	−20	−10.0	0	136	1798	13.2	17
Pettis Norman	62-73	23	198	8.6	0	183	2492	13.6	15
Don Norton	60-66	2	−3	−1.5	0	228	3486	15.3	27
Tom Nowatzke	65-72	361	1249	3.5	13	100	605	6.1	4

Name	Years	RUSHING Att.	Yards	Avg.	TD	RECEIVING Rec.	Yards	Avg.	TD
Ray Ogden	65-73	1	12	12.0	0	53	885	16.7	4
Jimmy Orr	58-70	15	122	8.1	0	400	7914	19.8	66
Tom Osborne	60-61					29	343	11.8	2
R.C. Owens	57-64	1	23	23.0	1	206	3285	15.9	22
Bob Paremore	63-64	36	107	3.0	0	6	89	14.8	1
Babe Parilli	52-53,56-58,60-69	394	1416	3.6	24				
Dave Parks	64-73	4	−10	−2.5	0	360	5619	15.6	44
Clarence Peaks	57-65	951	3660	3.8	21	190	1793	9.4	3
Art Perkins	62-63	85	251	3.0	6	22	144	6.5	0
Don Perkins	61-68	1500	6217	4.1	42	146	1310	9.0	3
Ray Perkins	67-71	10	77	7.7	0	93	1538	16.5	11
Jim Phillips	58-67					401	6044	15.1	34
Brian Piccolo	66-69	258	927	3.6	4	58	537	9.3	1
Nick Pietrosante	59-67	955	4026	4.2	28	131	1391	10.6	2
Elijah Pitts	61-71	514	1788	3.5	28	104	1265	12.0	6
Dave Pivec	66-69					14	146	10.4	1
Milt Plum	57-69	217	531	2.4	13	1	20	20.0	0
Ray Poage	63-65,67-71	3	32	10.7	0	145	2309	15.9	13
Bob Poole	64-67					19	223	11.7	0
Bucky Pope	64,66-68	2	11	5.5	0	34	952	28.0	13
Dickie Post	67-71	608	2605	4.3	17	96	903	9.4	2
Art Powell	59-68					479	8046	16.8	81
Gene Prebola	60-63					133	1823	13.7	6
Sam Price	66-68	82	213	3.8	1	10	70	7.0	1
Frank Quayle	69	57	183	3.2	0	11	167	15.2	0
Warren Rabb	60-62	50	124	2.5	3				
Bill Rademacher	64-70	1	−13	−13.0	0	24	282	11.8	3
Sonny Randle	59-68					365	5996	16.4	65
Ron Rector	66-67	33	167	5.1	0	6	22	3.7	0
Bob Reed	62-63	27	110	4.1	0	17	174	10.2	1
Dan Reeves	65-72	535	1990	3.7	25	129	1693	13.1	17
Jerry Reichow	56-57,59-64	20	105	5.3	0	172	2579	15.0	24
Bob Renn	61	1	14	14.0	0	18	268	14.9	1
Lance Rentzel	65-72,74	26	196	7.5	2	268	4826	18.0	38
Pete Retzlaff	56-66	6	−4	−0.7	0	452	7412	16.4	47
M.C. Reynolds	58-62	88	419	4.8	4				
Jerry Rhome	65-67,69-71	26	91	3.5	1				
Perry Richards	57-62					39	558	14.3	4
Jerry Richardson	59-60					15	171	11.4	4
Willie Richardson	63-71	2	27	13.5	0	195	2950	15.1	25
Pat Richter	63-70	1	−9	−9.0	0	99	1315	13.3	14
Johnny Roach	56,59-64	42	99	2.4	2				
Bo Roberson	61-66	168	584	3.5	6	176	2917	16.6	12
C.R. Roberts	59-62	155	637	4.1	4	21	132	6.3	0
Walter Roberts	64-67,69-70	5	45	9.0	0	67	1218	18.2	9
Jerry Robinson	62-65	3	20	6.7	0	49	799	16.3	4
Johnny Robinson	60-71	150	658	4.4	6	77	1228	15.9	9
John Roderick	66-68					11	156	14.2	1
Johnny Roland	66-74	1015	3750	3.7	28	153	1430	9.3	6
Dave Rolle	60	130	501	3.9	2	21	122	5.8	1
Tony Romeo	61-67					116	1833	15.8	10
Dave Ross	60					10	122	12.2	1
Ed Rutkowski	63-68	69	250	3.6	1	63	981	15.6	4
Frank Ryan	58-70	310	1358	4.4	6	0	31	–	1
Tom Rychlec	58,60-63	1	−18	−18.0	0	87	1091	12.5	3
Saint Saffold	68	1	21	21.0	0	16	172	10.8	0
Theron Sapp	59-65	202	763	3.8	5	23	247	10.7	0
George Sauer	65-70	4	23	5.8	0	309	4965	16.1	28
Gale Sayers	65-71	991	4956	5.0	39	112	1307	11.7	9
Charlie Scales	60-66	157	603	3.8	4	21	144	6.9	0
Bob Scarpitto	61-68	10	214	21.4	1	156	2651	17.0	27
Randy Schultz	66-68	82	301	3.7	2	26	220	8.5	0
Glen Shaw	60,62-64	47	148	3.1	3	8	146	18.3	1
Tom Sherman	68-69	27	94	3.5	0				
Dick Shiner	64-71,73-74	58	161	2.8	2				
Roy Shivers	66-72	176	680	3.9	10	38	400	10.5	4
Bill Shockley	60-62,68	42	165	3.9	0	31	96	8.7	2
Del Shofner	57-67	4	1	0.3	0	349	6470	18.5	51
Les Shy	66-70	144	523	3.6	3	23	273	11.9	1
Jerry Simmons	65-69,71-74	3	−3	−1.0	0	138	2105	15.3	9
Mickey Slaughter	63-66	73	263	3.6	1				
Tom Smiley	68-70	120	312	2.6	4	24	109	4.5	1
Allen Smith	66-67	31	148	4.8	0	1	1	1.0	0
Bobby Smith	64-66	129	536	4.2	5	21	214	10.2	0
Dave Smith	60-64	328	1368	4.2	11	80	772	9.7	7
Gordon Smith	61-65	1	2	2.0	0	57	1277	22.4	13
Jackie Smith	63-78	38	327	8.6	3	480	7918	16.5	40
J.D. Smith	56-66	1100	4672	4.2	40	127	1122	8.8	6
J.D. Smith	60-61	66	220	3.3	6	17	194	11.4	1
Ralph Smith	62-69	2	26	13.0	0	41	549	13.4	5
Russ Smith	67-70	213	915	4.3	10	23	265	11.5	0
Mark Smolinski	61-68	421	1323	3.1	9	103	841	8.2	7
Norm Snead	61-75	209	522	2.5	23				
Matt Snell	64-72	1057	4285	4.1	24	193	1375	7.1	7
Mike Sommer	58-61,63	78	253	3.2	2	9	166	18.4	0
Butch Songin	60-62	48	−90	−1.9	2				
Jack Spikes	60-67	408	1693	4.1	18	56	679	12.1	3
Billy Stacy	59-63					12	241	20.1	1
Bart Starr	56-71	247	1308	5.3	15				
Tom Stephens	60-64					41	506	12.3	5
Monte Stickles	60-68					222	3199	14.4	16
Jim Stiger	63-67	140	583	4.2	2	31	297	9.6	2
Jim Stinnette	61-62	40	95	2.4	1	24	167	7.0	1
Donnie Stone	61-66	354	1352	3.8	10	91	859	9.4	7
Steve Stonebraker	62-68					12	227	18.9	1

Lifetime Statistics - 1960-1969 Players Section 2 - **RUSHING and RECEIVING** (continued)
(All men with 25 or more rushing attempts or 10 or more receptions)

		RUSHING				RECEIVING			
Name	**Years**	**Att.**	**Yards**	**Avg.**	**TD**	**Rec.**	**Yards**	**Avg.**	**TD**
Bob Stransky	60	28	78	2.8	0	3	11	3.7	0
Pat Studstill	61-62,64-72	6	39	6.5	0	181	2840	15.7	18
Kark Sweetan	66-70	56	307	5.5	2				
Mike Taliaferro	64-72	46	134	2.9	0				
Fran Tarkenton	61-78	675	3674	5.4	32	0	-12	–	0
Jim Taylor	58-67	1941	8597	4.4	83	225	1756	7.8	10
Lionel Taylor	59-68	4	20	5.0	0	567	7195	12.7	45
Steve Tensi	65-70	47	82	1.7	0				
Tony Teresa	58,60	139	608	4.4	6	35	393	11.2	4
Aaron Thomas	61-70	4	-10	-2.5	0	262	4554	17.4	37
Clendon Thomas	58-68	18	70	3.9	0	60	1046	17.4	4
Gene Thomas	66-68	130	401	3.1	4	23	184	8.0	2
Bill Thornton	63-65,67	93	544	5.8	2	13	68	5.2	0
Bubba Thornton	69					14	134	9.6	0
Steve Thurlow	64-68	314	1127	3.6	4	61	539	8.8	2
Jim Tiller	62	31	43	1.3	0	13	108	8.3	0
Bill Tobin	63	75	270	3.6	4	13	172	13.2	1
Larry Todd	65-70	138	625	4.5	5	51	522	10.2	2
Charley Tolar	60-66	907	3277	3.6	21	175	1266	7.2	2
John Tracey	59-67					20	303	15.2	0
Tom Tracy	56-64	808	2912	3.6	17	113	1468	13.0	14
Richard Trapp	68-69					26	274	10.5	0
Bill Triplett	62-63,65-72	681	2446	3.6	17	113	1055	9.3	5
Frank Tripucka	49-52,60-63	70	-125	-1.8	6				
Billy Truax	64-73					199	2458	12.4	17
Don Trull	64-69	123	428	3.5	14				
Bill Tucker	67-71	127	431	3.4	6	59	496	8.4	7
Wendell Tucker	67-70					57	983	17.2	11
Bake Turner	62-70	2	13	6.5	0	220	3539	16.1	25
Johnny Unitas	56-73	450	1777	3.9	13	1	1	1.0	0
Ron Vander Kelen	63-67	26	116	4.5	1				
Jim Vollenweider	62-63	58	161	2.8	2	5	47	9.4	0
Billy Wade	54-66	318	1334	4.2	24	0	10	–	0
Joe Walton	57-63					178	2628	14.8	28
Ernie Warlick	62-65					90	1551	17.2	4
Bob Waters	60-63	65	281	4.3	3				
Tom Watkins	61-65,67-68	468	1791	3.8	10	55	590	10.7	4
Ken Webb	58-63	264	891	3.4	8	46	483	10.5	1
Joel Wells	61	65	216	3.3	1	6	31	5.2	1
Warren Wells	64,67-70	9	103	11.4	1	158	3655	23.1	42
Mel West	61-62	81	338	4.2	3	14	147	10.5	0
Jim Whelan	65-71	1	0	0.0	0	197	3155	16.0	20
Ernie Wheelwright	64-70	387	1426	3.7	9	54	531	9.8	7
Freeman White	66-69					29	315	10.9	1
John White	60-61					14	256	18.3	1
A. D. Whitfield	65-68	222	981	4.4	3	67	702	10.5	3
J. R. Wilburn	66-70	7	54	7.7	0	123	1834	14.9	8
Ken Willard	65-74	1622	6105	3.8	45	277	2184	7.9	17
A. D. Williams	59-61					15	190	12.7	1
Travis Williams	67-71	289	1166	4.0	6	52	598	11.5	5
Ben Wilson	63-65,67	431	1589	3.7	9	47	487	10.4	2
Butch Wilson	63-69					25	317	12.7	3
George Wilson	66	27	137	5.1	0				
Lloyd Winston	62-63	28	112	4.0	1	3	15	5.0	0
Dick Witcher	66-73					172	2359	13.7	14
Joe Womack	62	128	468	3.7	5	6	57	9.5	0
Dick Wood	62-66	26	45	1.7	4				
Gary Wood	64-69	75	419	5.6	6				
Tom Woodeshick	63-72	836	3577	4.3	21	126	1175	9.3	6
John Wright	68-69					12	130	10.8	2
Tom Yewcic	61-66	72	424	5.9	4	7	69	9.9	0

Lifetime Statistics - 1960-1969 Players Section 3 - **PUNT RETURNS and KICKOFF RETURNS**
(All men with 25 or more Punt Returns or 25 or more Kickoff Returns)

		PUNT RETURNS				KICKOFF RETURNS			
Name	**Year**	**No.**	**Yards**	**Avg.**	**TD**	**No.**	**Yards**	**Avg.**	**TD**
Herb Adderley	61-72	1	0	0.0	0	120	3080	25.7	2
Kermit Alexander	63-73	133	835	6.3	2	153	3586	23.4	0
Lance Alworth	62-72	29	309	10.7	0	10	216	21.6	0
Max Anderson	68-69,71	19	142	7.5	0	43	1057	24.6	1
Jon Arnett	57-66	120	981	8.2	1	126	3110	24.7	2
Pervis Atkins	61-66	40	292	7.3	0	95	2124	22.4	0
Joe Auer	64-68	14	141	10.1	0	51	1171	23.0	1
Bill Baird	63-69	88	787	8.9	1	13	290	22.3	0
Gary Ballman	62-73					66	1754	26.6	1
Terry Barr	57-65	50	262	5.2	0	26	655	25.2	1
Tom Barrington	66-70	1	8	8.0	0	32	675	21.1	0
Odell Barry	64-65	37	359	9.7	1	73	1856	25.4	0
Dick Bass	60-69	24	263	11.0	1	54	1415	26.2	0
Mike Battle	69-70	53	352	6.6	0	71	1041	23.1	0
Craig Baynham	67-70,72					41	1035	25.2	0
Joe Bellino	65-67	19	148	7.8	0	43	905	21.0	0
Roger Bird	66-68	94	283	5.4	0	25	533	21.3	0
Charlie Bivins	60-67					78	1911	24.5	0
Sid Blanks	64-70	36	272	7.6	0	43	977	22.7	0
Ronnie Blye	68-69					54	1104	20.4	0
Jimmie Brown	57-65					29	648	22.3	0
Timmy Brown	59-68	71	639	9.0	1	184	4781	26.0	5
Tom Brown	64-69	27	151	5.6	1	7	167	23.9	0
Willie Brown	64-66	18	85	4.7	0	34	795	23.4	0
Charlie Bryant	66-69					42	913	21.7	0
Amos Bullocks	62-64,66					34	737	21.7	0
Ode Burrell	64-69	15	149	9.9	0	33	838	25.4	1
Leon Burton	60	12	93	7.8	0	31	897	28.9	2
Ron Burton	60-65	56	389	6.9	0	46	1119	24.3	1
Bill Butler	59-64	88	850	9.7	2	132	2886	21.9	0
Cannonball Butler	65-72					133	2931	22.0	1
Butch Byrd	64-71					86	600	7.0	1
Jamie Caleb	60-61,65	1	8	8.0	0	27	594	22.0	0
Bob Campbell	69	28	133	4.8	0	26	522	20.1	0
Billy Cannon	60-70	14	178	12.7	0	67	1704	25.4	1
Preston Carpenter	56-67	26	284	10.9	0	29	752	25.9	0
Larry Carwell	67-72	49	474	9.7	0	25	557	22.3	0
Clarence Childs	64-68	6	40	6.7	0	134	3454	25.8	2
Dick Christy	58,60-65	67	905	13.5	4	117	2770	23.7	0
Earl Christy	66-68	34	222	6.5	0	58	1323	22.8	0
Hagood Clarke	64-68	65	583	9.0	2	16	330	20.6	0
Bert Coan	62-68					33	785	23.9	0
Bobby Joe Conrad	58-69	51	462	9.1	2	33	813	24.6	0
Johnny Counts	62-63	8	33	4.1	0	31	891	28.7	1
Willie Crenshaw	64-70					27	515	19.1	0
Irv Cross	61-69	51	376	7.4	0	44	1227	27.9	0
Jay Cunningham	65-67	22	140	6.4	0	64	1372	21.4	0
Clem Daniels	60-68	8	103	12.9	0	57	1206	21.2	0
Ted Dean	60-64	46	279	6.1	0	70	1553	22.2	0
Eddie Dove	59-63	61	437	7.2	0	3	56	18.7	0
Elbert Dubenion	60-68	3	9	3.0	0	40	961	24.0	1
Speedy Duncan	64-74	202	2201	10.9	4	180	4539	25.2	0
Bobby Felts	65-67	6	46	7.7	0	38	814	21.4	0
Pat Fischer	61-77	17	80	4.7	0	26	613	24.5	0
Mike Fitzgerald	66-67	2	4	2.0	0	26	541	20.8	0
George Fleming	61	3	24	8.0	0	60	1634	27.2	0
Tom Frankhauser	59-63	3	19	6.3	0	30	620	20.7	0
Al Frazier	61-63	26	305	11.7	1	44	1077	24.5	1
Bob Gaiters	61-63					33	786	23.8	0
Willie Galimore	57-63					43	1100	25.6	1
Billy Gambrell	63-68	28	282	10.1	0	15	336	22.4	0
Bob Garner	60-63	28	252	9.0	0	1	8	8.0	0
J. D. Garrett	64-67	3	47	15.7	0	48	1054	22.0	0
Mike Garrett	66-73	39	235	6.0	1	14	323	23.1	0
Larry Garron	60-68	1	23	23.0	0	89	2299	25.8	2
Claude Gibson	61-65	110	1381	12.6	3	17	268	15.8	0
Freddie Glick	59-66	44	326	7.4	0	26	584	22.5	0
Kenny Graham	64-70	29	238	8.2	0	7	172	24.6	0
Dave Grayson	61-70	10	78	7.8	0	110	2804	25.5	1
Ernie Green	62-68	11	110	10.0	0	32	648	20.3	0
Dick Haley	59-64	20	87	4.4	0	37	729	19.7	0
Ken Hall	59-61	11	164	14.9	1	31	833	26.9	1
Dick Harris	60-65	27	251	9.3	0	3	49	16.3	0
Rickie Harris	65-72	128	1029	8.0	3	102	2326	22.8	0
Wendell Harris	62-67	27	275	10.2	0	12	293	24.4	0
Alex Hawkins	59-68	52	358	6.9	0	6	86	14.3	0
Alvin Haymond	64-73	253	2148	8.5	1	170	4438	26.1	2
Abner Haynes	60-67	85	875	10.3	1	121	3025	25.0	1
Jon Henderson	68-70					30	589	19.6	0
Sam Horner	60-62	6	19	3.2	0	39	828	21.2	0
Frank Jackson	61-67	49	487	9.9	0	48	1284	26.8	0
Dick James	56-65	120	952	7.9	0	189	4676	24.7	0
Bobby Jancik	62-67	67	695	10.4	1	158	4185	26.5	0
Homer Jones	64-70					37	888	24.0	1
Leroy Kelly	64-73	94	990	10.5	3	76	1784	23.5	0
Brady Keys	61-68	65	646	9.9	0	47	1113	23.7	0
Phil King	58-66					30	592	19.7	0
Ernie Koy	65-70					25	439	17.6	0
Jack Larscheid	60-61	12	106	8.8	0	39	1106	28.4	0
Chuck Latourette	67-68,70-71	64	537	8.4	1	59	1491	25.3	0
Dan Lewis	58-66					30	535	17.8	0
Gary Lewis	64-70	1	3	3.0	0	32	784	24.5	0
Keith Lincoln	61-68	25	342	13.7	1	39	1018	26.1	1
Jerry Logan	63-72	62	577	9.3	1	12	217	18.1	0
Joe Don Looney	64-67,69					29	652	22.5	0
Tony Lorick	64-69					40	1022	25.6	0
John Love	67,72	21	34	1.6	0	25	589	23.6	1
Paul Lowe	60-61,63-69	2	0	0.0	0	63	1411	22.4	0
Lenny Lyles	58-69					81	2161	26.7	3
John Mallory	68-71	39	294	7.5	1	6	94	15.7	0
Amos Marsh	61-67	17	75	4.4	0	65	1561	24.0	1
Aaron Martin	64-68	33	258	7.8	1	13	296	22.8	0
Billy Martin	62-64	30	155	5.2	0	53	1148	21.7	0
Tommy Mason	61-71	46	483	10.5	0	45	1067	23.7	0
Tom Matte	61-72	1	0	0.0	0	62	1367	22.0	0
Don Maynard	58,60-73	26	132	5.1	0	14	343	24.5	0
Don McCall	67-70					29	756	26.1	1
Tommy McDonald	57-68	73	404	5.5	1	51	1055	20.7	0
Ed Meador	59-70	43	275	6.4	0	7	168	24.0	0
Gene Milton	68-69	7	59	8.4	0	26	574	22.1	0

Lifetime Statistics – 1960-1969 Players Section 3 – PUNT RETURNS and KICKOFF RETURNS (continued)
(All men with 25 or more Punt Returns or 25 or more Kickoff Returns)

Name	Years	Punt Returns No.	Yards	Avg.	TD	Kickoff Returns No.	Yards	Avg.	TD
Gene Mingo	60-70	18	214	11.9	1	34	742	21.8	0
Bobby Mitchell	58-68	69	699	10.1	3	102	2690	26.4	5
Charley Mitchell	63-68	21	251	12.0	0	63	1492	23.7	1
Willie Mitchell	64-70	56	564	10.1	1	7	178	25.4	0
Lenny Moore	56-67	14	56	4.0	0	49	1180	24.1	1
Tom Moore	60-67					71	1882	26.5	0
Johnny Morris	58-67	104	893	8.6	1	54	1267	23.5	0
Joe Morrison	59-72	23	79	3.4	0	30	640	21.3	0
Bob Neff	66-68	24	165	6.9	0	35	917	26.2	0
Al Nelson	65-73	1	3	3.0	0	101	2625	26.0	0
Jimmy Patton	55-66	27	143	5.3	1	28	735	26.3	1
Clarence Peaks	57-65					39	882	22.6	0
Elijah Pitts	61-71	75	394	5.3	1	28	535	19.1	0
Willie Porter	68	22	135	6.1	0	36	812	22.6	0
Dickie Post	67-71					34	760	22.4	0
Bob Reed	62-63	18	173	9.6	0	26	704	27.1	0
Lance Rentzel	65-72,74	48	217	4.5	0	32	783	24.5	1
Bo Roberson	61-66	3	54	18.0	0	130	3057	23.5	1
Walter Roberts	64-67,69-70	72	446	6.2	0	107	2728	25.5	1
Jerry Robinson	62-65	10	77	7.7	0	44	1009	22.9	0
Johnny Roland	66-73	49	452	9.2	2	25	507	20.3	0
Ed Rutkowski	63-68	68	514	7.6	1	53	1270	24.0	0
Johnny Sample	58-68	68	559	8.2	1	60	1560	26.0	1
Gale Sayers	65-71	27	391	14.5	2	91	2781	30.6	6
Charlie Scales	60-66	1	0	0.0	0	46	991	21.5	0
Goldie Sellers	66-69	19	217	11.4	1	27	701	26.0	2
Carver Shannon	62-64	30	213	7.1	0	46	1265	27.5	1
Roy Shivers	66-72	34	129	3.8	0	48	1162	24.2	1
Bill Shockley	60-62,68	5	18	3.6	0	32	745	23.3	0
Jim Shofner	58-63	46	308	6.7	0	1	0	0.0	0
Les Shy	66-70					29	687	23.7	0
Bobby Smith	62-66	25	151	6.0	0	40	1024	25.6	0
Noland Smith	67-69	63	635	10.1	1	82	2137	26.1	1
Billy Stacy	59-63	54	393	7.3	2	26	607	23.3	0
Marsh Starks	63-64	8	43	5.4	0	26	519	20.0	0
Jim Steffen	59-66	47	349	7.4	0	44	1107	25.2	0
Jim Stiger	63-67	68	529	7.8	0	27	610	22.6	0
Jerry Stovall	63-71					46	1183	25.7	0
Pat Studstill	61-62,64-72	59	716	12.1	0	75	1924	25.7	1
Bob Suci	62-63	25	233	9.3	0	17	360	21.2	0
Rosey Taylor	61-72	15	66	4.4	1	26	614	23.6	0
Bobby Thompson	64-69	14	72	5.1	0	27	622	23.0	0
Bubba Thornton	69					30	749	25.0	0
Larry Todd	65-70					25	584	23.3	0
Bill Triplett	62-63,65-72					49	1058	21.6	0
Bill Tucker	67-71	1	1	1.0	0	40	879	22.0	0
Bake Turner	62-70	21	156	7.4	0	75	1688	22.5	0
Tom Vaughn	65-71	33	298	9.0	0	62	1595	25.7	0
Carl Ward	67-69	7	67	9.6	0	38	840	22.1	1
Charley Warner	63-66	17	206	12.1	0	86	2187	25.4	3
Jimmy Warren	64-74,77	4	-1	-0.3	0	30	684	22.8	0
Tom Watkins	61-65,67-68	96	970	10.1	3	101	2510	24.9	0
Ken Webb	58-63					27	561	20.8	0
Willie West	60-68	51	388	7.6	0	40	908	22.7	0
Dick Westmoreland	63-69	2	10	5.0	0	28	564	20.1	0
Bobby Williams	66-67,69-71					77	1934	25.1	2
Clancy Williams	65-72					32	810	25.3	0
Travis Williams	67-71	13	213	16.4	1	102	2801	27.5	6
Willie Wood	60-71	187	1391	7.4	2	3	20	6.7	0
Abe Woodson	58-66	123	956	7.8	2	193	5538	28.7	5

Lifetime Statistics – 1960-1969 Players Section 4 – PUNTING
(All men with 25 or more Punts)

Name	Years	No.	Avg.
Billy Atkins	58-64	219	42.0
Sam Baker	53,56-69	701	42.7
Jim Bakken	62-77	61	37.5
Zeke Bratkowski	54,57-68,71	90	38.7
Ode Burrell	64-69	29	36.8
Don Chandler	56-67	660	43.5
Gary Collins	62-71	336	41.0
Ollie Cordill	67-69	45	41.4
Wayne Crow	60-63	222	40.2
Cotton Davidson	54,57,60-66,68	278	38.4
Tommy Davis	56-69	511	44.7
Eagle Day	59-60	59	42.0
Boyd Dowler	59-69,71	93	42.9
Jim Elliott	67	72	38.1
Doug Elmore	62	54	34.4
Sam Etcheverry	61-62	59	38.3
Jim Fraser	62-66,68	271	43.3
Tom Gilburg	61-65	232	41.4
Allen Green	61	61	36.7
Bobby Joe Green	60-73	970	42.6
Tom Greene	60-61	59	37.9
John Hadl	62-77	105	39.7
George Herring	60-61	150	38.4
King Hill	58-69	368	41.3
Ed Holler	63-64	31	43.0
Sam Horner	60-62	64	38.4
Tom Janik	63-71	253	39.1
Curley Johnson	60-69	556	42.5
John Kilgore	65-69	234	41.0
Ernie Koy	65-70	225	38.5
Frank Lambert	65-66	156	43.6
Daryle Lamonica	63-74	51	40.6
Chuck Latourette	67-68,70-71	248	40.5
Dale Livingston	68-70	146	41.1
Joe Don Looney	64-67,69	32	42.4
Billy Lothridge	64-72	532	41.0
Paul Maguire	60-70	794	41.7
Billy Martin	64-68	28	37.4
John McCormick	62-63,65-66,68	47	39.1
Wahoo McDaniel	60-68	37	37.7
Max McGee	54,57-67	256	41.6
Mike Mercer	61-70	307	40.6
Charley Milstead	60-61	66	35.8
Earl Morrall	56-76	106	37.7
Tom Morrow	62-64	45	36.7
Jim Norton	60-68	518	42.4
Jimmy Orr	58-70	59	39.4
Joe Paglieri	59-60	49	37.3
Rick Redman	65-73	153	37.5
Pat Richter	63-70	338	42.0
Bob Scarpito	61-68	282	44.0
Dave Sherer	59-60	102	42.2
Del Shofner	57-67	153	42.0
Jackie Smith	63-77	86	38.5
Jerry Stovall	63-71	87	40.2
Pat Studstill	61-62,64-72	560	40.7
Terry Swanson	67-69	139	39.8
Frank Tripucka	49-52,60-63	93	38.8
Danny Villanueva	60-67	488	42.7
Eddie Wilson	62-65	54	36.1
George Wilson	66	42	42.1
Jerrel Wilson	63-78	1069	43.2
Tom Yewcic	61-66	369	39.4

Lifetime Statistics – 1960-1969 Players Section 5 – KICKING
(All men with 10 or more PAT or Field Goal attempts)

Name	Years	PAT	PAT Att.	PAT Pct.	FG	FG Att.	FG Pct.
Bruce Alford	67-69	41	43	95	31	52	60
Billy Atkins	58-64	56	63	89	8	19	42
John Aveni	59-61	72	80	90	22	63	35
Sam Baker	53,56-69	428	444	96	179	316	57
Jim Bakken	62-78	534	553	97	282	447	63
George Blair	61-64	122	136	90	50	79	63
George Blanda	49-58,60-75	941	957	98	335	638	53
Tommy Brooker	62-66	149	149	100	41	86	48
Gino Cappelletti	60-70	342	353	97	176	333	53
Don Chandler	56-67	248	258	96	94	161	58
Jim Christopherson	62	28	28	100	11	20	55
Mike Clark	63-71,73	325	338	96	133	232	57
Bobby Joe Conrad	58-69	95	99	96	14	33	42
Cotton Davidson	54,57,60-66,68	32	33	97	2	5	40
Tommy Davis	59-69	348	350	99	130	276	47
Harold Deters	67	9	10	90	1	4	25
Charlie Durkee	67-68,71-72	87	88	99	52	101	51
Bob Etter	68-69	50	52	96	26	51	51
George Fleming	61	24	25	96	11	26	42
Momcilo Gavric	69	22	24	92	3	11	27
Cookie Gilchrist	62-67	14	16	88	8	20	40
Charlie Gogolak	66-68,70-72	114	117	97	52	93	56
Pete Gogolak	64-74	344	354	97	173	294	59
Bruce Gossett	64-74	374	383	98	219	360	61
Allen Green	61	19	19	100	5	15	33
Dick Guesman	60-64	69	74	93	20	62	32
Wendell Harris	60-67	8	11	73	1	4	25
Joe Hergert	60-61				8	18	44
Jack Hill	61	16	16	100	5	15	23
Paul Hornung	57-62,64-66	190	194	98	66	140	47
Bob Humphreys	67-68	19	20	95	8	20	40
Bob Jencks	63-65	93	102	91	14	39	36
Jimmy Keyes	68-69	30	30	100	7	16	44
Bob Khayat	60,62-63	90	92	98	38	74	51
Lou Kirouac	63-64,66-67	19	24	79	9	18	50
Jerry Kramer	58-68	90	94	96	29	54	54
Karl Kremser	69-70	28	29	97	13	23	57
Gary Kroner	65-67	57	58	98	29	56	52
Roger LeClerc	60-67	154	160	96	76	152	50
Keith Lincoln	61-68	16	18	89	5	12	42
Dale Livingston	68-70	39	41	95	28	54	52
John Love	67,72	10	11	91	2	7	29
Booth Lusteg	66-69	97	101	96	35	75	47
Chuck Mercein	65-70	9	10	90	2	8	25
Mike Mercer	61-70	288	295	98	102	193	53
Lou Michaels	58-69,71	386	402	96	187	341	55
Gene Mingo	60-70	215	223	96	112	219	51
Les Murdock	67	13	15	87	4	9	44
Dennis Patera	68	10	12	83	2	8	25
Tom Pennington	62	13	15	87	2	5	40
Milt Plum	57-69	16	16	100	6	16	38
Bill Shockley	60-62,68	91	95	96	26	57	46
Jackie Simpson	61-64	6	6	100	3	10	30
Jack Spikes	60-67	74	80	93	20	59	34
Andy Stynchula	60-68	13	14	93	3	7	43
Bob Timberlake	65	21	22	95	1	15	7
Herb Travenio	64-65	50	52	96	20	35	57
Wade Traynham	66-67	24	24	100	7	19	37
Dick Van Raaphorst	64,66-67	112	114	98	45	90	50
Danny Villanueva	60-67	236	241	98	85	160	53
Wayne Walker	67-68	26	26	100	8	16	50
Wayne Walker	58-72	172	175	98	53	131	40
John Wittenborn	58-62,64-68	41	41	100	20	45	44
Mack Yoho	60-63	52	61	85	13	35	37

1970-1979

1970-1979
BIG DOLLARS — BIG PROBLEMS

On February 1, 1970 they made it official. As agreed upon three years and eight months before, the National and American Football Leagues entered into marriage. Their courtship was rocky to the very end. As late as January, the important matter of the older NFL's divisional realignment remained unsettled. But by March 16, the biggest problem faced by a "competition committee" of Tex Schramm, Vince Lombardi, Paul Brown and Al Davis upon convening in Honolulu was whether or not to allow the AFL's two-point option for touchdowns. After deciding to stick to the NFL's single-point rule, all that was left for the committee to take care of were minor matter regarding things such as putting players' names on jerseys and the type of football that would be used.

The two leagues officially became the American and National Football Conference of the National Football League, with Kansas City Chiefs owner Lamar Hunt and Chicago Bears owner George Halas selected as their respective figurehead presidents. In their first draft under one roof in February, the first player chosen was Terry Bradshaw, a strong-armed signal caller from Louisiana Tech, by Pittsburgh. Bradshaw went on to live up to his high rating and was only one of the many wise draft selections that enabled the Steelers to become an AFC powerhouse after years of mediocrity in the old NFL.

Dynasties and Diversity

In September 1970, just a few weeks before the regular season began, Vince Lombardi, the dominant force in the '60's as head coach of the mighty Green Bay Packers, died of stomach cancer. His influence lived on, however, as bone-crunching defenses and conservative but powerful running attacks were what most head coaches felt that they needed to win games. In the very first interconference struggle on the first week of the '70 season, Bud Grant's Minnesota Vikings avenged their previous season's Super Bowl loss to Hank Stram's Kansas City Chiefs, defeating them 27-10 with a heavy dependence on ball control and an opportunistic defense. Grant said, "We proved that the defense of the 1960's can beat the offense of the '70's." Further proof was provided by Don Shula's Miami Dolphins, a team that went on to become the '70's first true dynasty, with three successive Super Bowl trips beginning in 1971.

After losing 24-3 to the Dallas Cowboys and Duane Thomas in Super Bowl VI, the stage was set for professional football's most impressive team performance, a perfect 17-0 season in '72. Behind the unspectacular but effective running of Larry Csonka, Jim Kiick and Mercury Morris, the smooth, calculated quarterbacking of Bob Griese and Earl Morrall and a defense that had "no names" but plenty of quickness and savvy, the Dolphins wrote 1972's biggest and most colorful story. Miami's 14-7 win over Washington in Super Bowl VII left them 17-0, including playoffs, the first NFL team to ever accomplish such a feat. In '73 the Dolphins finally lost (in their second game) but remained the league's best through their 24-7 rout of Minnesota in Super Bowl VIII.

Other NFL coaches quickly copied Shula's recipe, devising complicated defenses and run-oriented offenses. High scoring, pass-laden games, the kind that epitomized the AFL in its early days, became rare. Field position, zone defenses and cautious play selection that guaranteed a minimum of turnovers tended to eliminate some of the game's most exciting elements.

The Pittsburgh Steelers, the decade's second dynasty, won four Super Bowls in six years with an offense that depended on the running of Franco Harris and Rocky Bleier, spiced with occasional long passes from Bradshaw to Lynn Swann and John Stallworth. The strength of the team was its' impregnable defense, led by Mean Joe Greene, Jack Lambert, Jack Ham, L.C. Greenwood, and Mel Blount.

Two other teams of the decade could be considered near-dynasties for their consistent fine play: the Dallas Cowboys and the Oakland Raiders. Although both boasted sometimes spectacular offenses, their victories were rooted in crunching defensive work.

New Rules

In general, rule changes during the decade were aimed at encouraging more offense and scoring. Before the 1972 season began, a rule changed that was designed to open the passing game by moving the hashmarks closer to the middle of the field, but it actually resulted in much greater success for "outside" running attacks. For Miami, this allowed the speedy Morris to provide a perfect complement to Csonka's inside strength. By season's end, both players were 1,000-yard runners, and the Dolphins had a new NFL rushing record with 2,960 yards. In '73, O. J. Simpson became the first player to rush for over 2,000 yards in a season.

The powers of the league realized there was nothing overly exciting about games like the '73 Super Bowl in which Miami lulled the Vikings — and numerous fans everywhere — to sleep. The recognized enough staleness in their product to warrant some more changes before the '74 season began. Pressure produced by the formation of the World Football League that same year further necessitated a new look. At a meeting in New York, NFL owners laid down the following rule changes:

■ Overtime. In an effort to do away with ties, a 15-minute, sudden-death extra period was introduced for preseason and regular-season games. If a score remained even at the completion of the extra period, the game would then be declared a tie.

■ Kicking. The goalposts were moved back 10 yards for the goal line to the end line to do away with an over-reliance on easy field goals. In addition, kickoffs were moved back five yards to the 35-yard line, and missed field goals would be returned to the line of scrimmage or the 20-yard line, whichever was further from the goal line. This meant the punter would become more important, with his placement and coffin-corner kicking ability outweighing the distance that he kicked he the ball. Finally, players on a team kicking a field goal or punting could not cross the line of scrimmage until the ball was kicked. This meant a punter's "hang time" would also become significant.

■ Passing. Roll-blocking and the cutting down of wide receivers was eliminated to take away what had become a distinct advantage for defenses. Also, downfield defenders were allowed to make contact only once with potential receivers, and wide receivers blocking back toward the ball three yards from the line of scrimmage could not block below the waist.

■ Penalties. Infractions for offensive holding, illegal use of hands and tripping were reduced for 15 to 10 yards when they occurred in the area of the line of scrimmage to three yards beyond it.

In 1978, the NFL went to a 16-game schedule and added a second wild-card team to its playoffs, both moves calculated to increase revenue. To open up the passing game and make the product more appealing, defensive backs were further limited in their aggressive bumping tactics against receivers, and the head slap by defensive linemen was made illegal in 1977 and the following year offensive blocking rules were liberalized to allow greater use of the hands. By extending the season and handle new advantages to the passing attack, the rulemakers made the 300-yard game and the 3,000 yard season commonplace for the NFL throwers.

A Rival League

In 1974, the NFL faced a new rival, the World Football League. The WFL opened on July 10 with 12 franchises, six of them in cities already occupied by NFL teams. It planned a 20-week regular season of what was being billed as wide-open football with 10 "revolutionary" rule changes (kickoffs from the 30-yard line to insure more runbacks, goal posts moved back to the back of the end zone, missed field goals returned to the line of scrimmage except when attempted inside the 20-yard line, an optional two-point conversion attempt, receivers needing just one foot in bounds for a completion, a fifth quarter split into two 7 1/2-minute segments to break ties, a restriction on fair catches of punts, motion permitted by an offensive back toward the line of scrimmage before the snapping of the ball, hashmarks moved in toward the center of the field, and the return of any incomplete pass into the end zone on fourth down to the previous line of scrimmage instead of being automatically returned to the 20-yard line).

The commissioner of the WFL was Gary L. Davidson, an attorney who founded the World Hockey Association. He resigned in '73 as president of the WHA to devote his full time and energy to the organization of the WFL. The 12 initial franchises were the Birmingham Americans, Chicago Fire, Detroit Wheels, the Hawaiians, Houston Texans, Jacksonville Sharks, Memphis Southmen, Southern California Sun and Florida Blazers. Games were scheduled primarily on Wednesdays and Thursdays, and a TV package with the independent TVS network was hoped to net in excess of $1 million for the clubs, with weekly telecasts aired live on Thursday nights on more than 135 stations across the country.

But what really made the NFL and sports fans take notice was the shocking announcement in the spring of '74 that Miami's Csonka, Kiick and wide receiver Paul Warfield planned to leave the team they helped make a dynasty after fulfilling the final year of their Dolphin contracts and jump to the WFL Toronto franchise (that was switched to Memphis before the season began to avoid conflict with the Canadian Football League). The combined offer to the trio from Toronto millionaire owner John Bassett came to $3.5 million.

But the WFL would have to depend on lesser-known players for the most part in its first year. On July 24, the Birmingham Americans pleased a legitimately large home-town crowd with a 58-33 victory over Memphis. NFL reject quarterbacks George Mira (Birmingham) and John Huarte (Memphis) engaged in the kind of barnburning passing battle that any football fan could savor. But in Philadelphia, doctored attendance figures gave the league its first real dose of adverse publicity. It was reported in mid-August that the Bell's actual paid attendance at its first home game was only 13,800 — a far cry from the 55,534 figure it threw out for public consumption. After the announced attendance of 64,719 for its second home game turned out to be a paltry 6,200 paid, Bells president John B. Kelly Jr., abruptly resigned from his post. It quickly become apparent that most of the league's teams were desperately under-capitalized. Franchises began moving or folding on a near-weekly basis. In early November, an emergency session was called in Chicago that ended with Davidson resigning as commissioner. Facing over-all debts reported as high as $20 million in its first season, the WFL no longer posed a serious threat to the NFL.

Under the direction of Chris Hemmeter, the original owner of the Hawaiian franchise, the league attempted to play the '75 season under a clever reorganizational plan built around shared profits. But even with the "Hemmeter Plan," a new $12 million deficit was incurred by the time the season was 10 weeks old, and in late October 1975, the league officially went under.

TV Calls the Tune

Enhancing the merger of the two leagues in 1970 was a splendid wedding present from ABC-TV. For slightly more than $8 million each season, ABC agreed to telecast 13 prime-time games on Monday nights. The risk of professional football over-exposing itself the way boxing did was offset by an overall TV bill to the three major networks that came to about $150 million, including the three-year Monday night package. Divided out, it meant that each of the 26 NFL teams would receive approximately $1.7 million in 1970 — $500,000 more than what each NFL team got on 1969 and $800,00 more than each of the eight AFL franchises received.

Meanwhile, the NFL's viewing audience was multiplying rapidly every week. Before the '73 season began, Congress lifted the TV blackout on home games sold out 72 hours in advance, thanks mainly to the efforts of Massachusets Senator Torbert MacDonald. Rozelle, who claimed only seven NFL teams were assured of weekly sellouts, gloomily predicted disaster. But the Capital Hill politicians, at a time when Watergate was tarnishing their image, were anxious to provide a popular victory for fans. But the real victors were the TV people. Future TV contracts, not ticket-buying customers, would provide the game's main meal ticket. The number of "no shows" at games became a meaningful statistic, but the game didn't suffer so badly at the gate as to argue for a return of the blackout.

By 1978, industry sources called the NFL's contract the largest television package ever. In January of that year, a Louis Harris Sports survey found that 70 percent of the nation's sports fans said they followed football, compared to 54 percent who followed baseball. There seemed to be no limit.

Trouble With the Troops

With once undreamed-of money pouring in from TV, the players quite naturally expected to join in the benefits. Before the merger season of 1970 even got underway, NFL players rallied together in early July and displayed surprisingly strong union strength by threatening to sit out the season unless management could settle a list of grievances, the biggest of which had to do with their pension fund. Peace was assured in August, as the players received a pension fund increase of roughly $11 million, and although neither side was entirely satisfied with the settlement, a contract agreement that extended to the 1974 season enabled the emphasis in the decade's first three yards to be placed mainly in the game itself.

But, in 1974 it was time to negotiate a new contract with the NFL Players' Association. Renewed strike threats and legal hassles began early in 1974 and continued right up to the night of February 16, 1977, when NFLPA executive director Ed Garvey and Sargent Karch, management's main negotiator, finally reached a new contract agreement.

The three-year negotiation period was marked by preseason strikes in 1974 and '75 and by bitterness over the Rozelle Rule. That rule provided that the commissioner would decide the type of compensation a team would receive after losing a free agent. Such strong power in Rozelle's hands discouraged teams for signing free agents, fearing that the commissioner would set a stiff price that would wipe out any benefit. Negotiations made progress after a federal court found that the Rozelle Rule was illegal under antitrust laws. The agreement, which was struck in 1977, created a new free-agent system in which the losing team would receive draft choices from the signing team, with the player's salary determining the exact package. Although less restrictive than the Rozelle Rule, this new system still kept players shackled to one club, as teams were reluctant to give up key draft picks. The contract also preserve the college draft and increased some financial benefits for the players, while limiting some of the commissioner's lesser powers.

N.F.C. 1970 The Monday-Night Circus

The TV gridiron fan found a new addiction this season: Monday-night football. The American Broadcasting Company telecast a game every Monday night of the season, with Howard Cosell, Don Meredith and Keith Jackson the men behind the mikes. For the first time ever, the game itself became secondary to the show put on by the announcers in the press box. Cosell, the verbose ex-labor lawyer who had built a reputation by being highly critical of almost everything, commented on each game in highly dramatic tones, while ex-Dallas Cowboy quarterback Don Meredith, dubbed "Dandy Don" by Cosell, mixed his analysis with homespun country witticisms. The interplay between these two, sometimes veering off into mutual needling, delighted some and drove others to turn the sound off on their sets. Jackson, the member of the trio who concentrated on reporting the game, was rewarded after the season by being dropped from the series.

EASTERN DIVISION

Dallas Cowboys—The Cowboys had so much talent, some coaches would have been delighted to trade their starters for the Dallas second-stringers. With two good running backs already in the fold in Calvin Hill and Walt Garrison, the Cowboys this year added rookie Duane Thomas, an uncommunicative man who did his talking by running over people while carrying a football. Herb Adderley was obtained from Green Bay to further strengthen the secondary, and when Lance Rentzel sat out the last weeks of the season with personal problems, rookie Reggie Rucker filled in capably. Although the offensive line had always been strong, Dave Manders, Blaine Nye, and Rayfield Wright all rose up from the second string to win starting jobs. Even at quarterback, coach Tom Landry had his pick of a good pocket passer in Craig Morton or a top roll-out passer in Roger Staubach.

New York Giants—Quarterback Fran Tarkenton ran the attack with imagination, Ron Johnson developed into a superb runner and receiver after coming over from Cleveland, Tucker Fredericksson shook the injury hex for this year, Clifton McNeil grabbed Tarkenton's passes, and the offensive line matured into a sturdy unit. The defense was less impressive, but aces Fred Dryer, Jim Files, and Spider Lockhart held the platoon together. After beating St. Louis one week from the end, the Giants held a share of first place with Dallas heading into their final game before losing 31-3 to the Rams.

St. Louis Cardinals—The Cards sailed into December with an 8-2-1 record and first place in the East was theirs for the taking. Twice during the year the Cards had beaten the Cowboys, laying a 38-0 drubbing on them in their meeting in Dallas. MacArthur Lane, Ernie McMillan, Larry Stallings, Roger Wehrli, and Larry Wilson all turned in All-Pro performances, while a host of other Cards all enjoyed good seasons. But just when the team seemed about to capture its first title since moving to St. Louis in 1960, the roof caved in. First the Detroit Lions beat them, then the New York Giants clubbed them 34-17 to knock them out of first place. Then, with the title a fleeting dream, the Cards dropped their finale 28-27 to the Redskins.

Washington Redskins—When training camp opened, head coach Vince Lombardi wasn't there; he was in the hospital, terminally ill with cancer. Assistant Bill Austin took over as head man until Lombardi got out of the hospital, but the all-time great coach died on September 3, two weeks before the start of the regular season. Austin guided the club through the season, but the team never really recovered from Lombardi's death. The only bright spot of the year was the development of runner Larry Brown into a star. Using his blockers well and fighting for every yard, Brown became the first Redskin to rush 1,000 yards.

Philadelphia Eagles—A flabby defense and an injury to fullback Tom Woodeshick shackled the Eagles into last place in the Eastern Division, but the team did have talent in several areas. The trio of Gary Ballman, Harold Jackson, and Ben Hawkins provided top-notch receiving, and Cyril Pinder ran well at halfback. The linebacking corps had three solid players in Adrian Young, Tim Rossovich, and Ron Porter; Rossovich had other skills in addition to his talents on the field. The curly-haired, mustachioed Rossovich would occasionally do unusual things, such as walking into a party with his hair on fire.

CENTRAL DIVISION

Minnesota Vikings—The Vikings still had that marvelous defense, but they lacked that extra inspirational spark when quarterback Joe Kapp sat out the early games over a salary dispute and then was sold to Boston. Carl Eller, Alan Page, Paul Krause, and the other members of the defense smothered enough enemy offenses to win twelve games, while the offense operated just enough under Gary Cuozzo to make it back to first place this year. Place kicker Fred Cox could be counted on to make good on three-pointers within the 40-yard line to bail out the offense. But although Cuozzo passed the ball better than Kapp, the fanatical leadership Kapp provided was missing.

Detroit Lions—Even without a clear-cut starter at quarterback, the Lion attack still blossomed into a steady point-producing outfit. Bill Munson and Greg Landry split the passer's spot, although Landry played more as the season went on, and both found good runners in Mel Farr and Altie Taylor and good receivers in Earl McCullough, Larry Walton, and Charlie Sanders. The line gave both quarterbacks good protection and figured highly in the offense's performance. On defense, the linebacking and secondary corps were full with top players, with Dick LeBeau and Paul Naumoff of All-Pro quality, but the front four needed some new blood, as Alex Karras no longer was rushing quarterbacks as he once had.

Chicago Bears—Gale Sayers, the once incomparable runner, hurt his knee and went out of action early in the season for surgery. Brian Piccolo fell fatally ill with cancer. Quarterback Bobby Douglass threw four touchdown passes in his first starting assignment of the year, but broke his wrist late in the game and missed the rest of the year. Pre-season trades for Elijah Pitts, Lee Roy Caffey, and Craig Baynham didn't work out. But the Bears did win six games, and did uncover an exciting player in little Cecil Turner, who returned four kickoffs all the way to tie the NFL record.

Green Bay Packers—The Packers kept dropping veterans of the Lombardi years and suffered through another losing season. Willie Davis, Henry Jordan, and Boyd Dowler all retired, Elijah Pitts, Lee Roy Caffey, and Bob Hyland were dealt to Chicago, and Herb Adderley and Marv Fleming went to Dallas and Miami in trades. Of those staying on the scene, a sore arm hampered quarterback Bart Starr, a torn Achilles tendon sidelined linebacker Dave Robinson, and age started catching up on middle linebacker Ray Nitschke.

WESTERN DIVISION

San Francisco '49ers—After years of near misses and disappointing finishes, the '49ers finally put everything together and won the Western crown. The offense, always respected, blossomed into one of pro football's best with fine seasons from John Brodie, Gene Washington, Forrest Blue, and Cas Banaszek. The entire front line had a good year, allowing Brodie to be dropped only eight times all season. The defense, however, surprised most experts by turning in a superb performance. Coach Dick Nolan rotated the front four spots and thus kept fresh men in the game at all times. Dave Wilcox starred at linebacker, and the secondary of Jim Johnson, rookie Bruce Taylor, Rosey Taylor, and Al Randolph discouraged enemy passers. The acquisition of place kicker Bruce Gossett from Los Angeles nicely rounded out the picture.

Los Angeles Rams—Coach George Allen kept adding veterans to the squad, this year bringing in Kermit Alexander, but the Rams fell just short of the Western title. The defense as usual made life difficult for enemy offenses, and the Los Angeles attack again moved slowly but surely under the direction of Roman Gabriel. The rise of the '49ers gave the Rams competition for the divisional crown, however, and a 28-23 loss to Detroit on the final Monday-night game of the year knocked the Rams out of first place for good. The team recovered to beat New York to end the season, but that was to be George Allen's last game with the Rams. Owner Dan Reeves, already dying with cancer, fired Allen after the season despite his 49-17-4 record.

Atlanta Falcons—After improving for several seasons, the Falcons fell back for the first time under coach Norm Van Brocklin's regime. One weight on the team's progress was a remarkably unexciting offense, with an unsettled quarterback situation, no speed in the running back and receiving spots, and chaos in the front line. The defense had three star players in end Claude Humphrey, middle linebacker Tommy Nobis, and cornerback Ken Reaves, but most of the other positions lacked a quality occupant.

New Orleans Saints—The Saints' roster was like a revolving door, with players joining and leaving the squad in steady flows all season. Head coach Tom Fears was one of the mid-season departures, with J. D. Roberts promoted from a minor-league team to take charge of the Saints. The Saints had a few good players who put out consistently good performances, but they were almost buried amidst the chaos and mediocrity which ruined the season for the team. Flanker Dan Abramowicz and defensive tackle Dave Rowe played well, but the hero of the club was place kicker Tom Dempsey, a man born without a right hand and without toes on his right foot. Using a special kicking shoe, Dempsey was an erratic kicker but made the record books by booting a 63-yard three-pointer to beat the Detroit Lions.

FINAL TEAM STATISTICS

OFFENSE

	ATL.	CHI.	DALL.	DET.	G.B.	L.A.	MINN.	N.O.	N.Y.G.	PHIL.	ST.L.	S.F.	WASH.
FIRST DOWNS:													
Total	199	179	229	243	194	224	225	183	257	229	226	237	249
by Rushing	76	55	119	113	69	93	98	55	94	81	110	86	122
by Passing	110	104	95	107	110	120	111	112	150	126	104	125	100
by Penalty	13	20	15	23	15	11	16	16	13	22	12	26	27
RUSHING:													
Number	431	353	522	514	453	430	508	371	465	450	429	471	444
Yards	1600	1092	2300	2127	1595	1763	1634	1215	1799	1539	1998	1580	2021
Average Yards	3.7	3.1	4.4	4.1	3.5	4.1	3.2	3.3	3.9	3.4	4.7	3.4	4.6
Touchdowns	4	3	16	16	8	12	16	4	11	11	18	13	11
PASSING:													
Attempts	342	422	297	294	351	426	344	415	403	410	390	383	342
Completions	197	210	149	167	177	218	173	213	230	218	178	226	203
Completion Percentage	57.6	49.8	50.2	56.8	50.4	51.2	50.3	51.3	57.1	53.2	45.6	59.0	59.4
Passing Yards	2262	2431	2445	2121	2196	2658	2378	2690	2892	2651	2689	2990	2357
Avg. Yards per Attempt	6.6	5.8	8.2	7.2	6.3	6.2	6.9	6.5	7.2	6.5	6.9	7.8	6.9
Avg. Yards per Complet.	11.5	11.6	16.4	12.7	12.4	12.2	13.7	12.6	12.6	12.2	15.1	13.2	11.6
Times Tackled Passing	53	33	39	36	43	23	29	28	37	23	26	8	29
Yards Lost Tackled	431	258	296	264	382	150	197	232	258	200	216	67	249
Net Yards	1831	2173	2149	1857	1814	2508	2181	2458	2634	2451	2473	2923	2108
Touchdowns	18	21	18	19	11	17	12	11	19	16	16	25	23
Interceptions	21	22	16	12	24	13	15	22	12	23	19	10	10
Percent Intercepted	6.1	5.2	5.4	4.1	6.8	3.1	4.4	5.3	3.0	5.6	4.9	2.6	2.9
PUNTS:													
Number	76	84	69	62	87	67	61	77	54	71	65	75	61
Average Distance	38.7	40.8	41.3	40.0	40.2	39.1	37.9	42.5	38.3	36.6	40.9	38.4	40.9
PUNT RETURNS:													
Number	34	57	32	34	25	62	35	29	29	32	41	48	27
Yards	356	246	237	306	98	418	216	214	193	100	315	550	45
Average Yards	10.5	4.3	7.4	9.0	3.9	6.7	6.2	7.4	6.7	3.1	7.7	11.5	1.7
Touchdowns	2	0	0	1	0	0	0	0	1	0	1	0	0
KICKOFF RETURNS:													
Number	47	56	37	43	63	47	36	53	52	59	47	49	61
Yards	916	1472	888	959	1422	1236	842	1044	1157	1252	926	967	1223
Average Yards	19.5	26.3	24.0	22.3	22.6	26.3	23.4	19.7	22.3	21.2	19.7	19.7	20.0
Touchdowns	0	4	1	1	2	1	0	0	0	0	0	0	0
INTERCEPTION RETURNS:													
Number	19	17	24	28	20	19	28	22	17	10	21	22	15
Yards	191	129	307	417	398	280	412	260	223	102	255	308	240
Average Yards	10.1	7.6	12.8	14.9	19.9	14.7	14.7	11.8	13.1	10.2	12.1	14.0	16.0
Touchdowns	0	0	0	4	1	2	2	0	0	0	2	2	0
PENALTIES:													
Number	76	94	87	58	76	88	60	91	71	73	84	88	65
Yards	807	853	934	659	691	959	631	1029	641	799	896	997	613
FUMBLES:													
Number	24	29	29	26	34	27	25	27	28	26	24	24	26
Number Lost	17	13	12	15	17	17	16	18	14	16	14	15	14
POINTS:													
Total	206	256	299	347	196	325	335	172	301	241	325	352	297
PAT Attempts	26	28	35	41	22	34	35	17	32	29	38	41	34
PAT Made	23	28	35	41	19	34	35	16	32	25	37	39	33
FG Attempts	25	34	27	29	28	45	46	34	41	25	32	31	27
FG Made	9	20	18	20	15	29	30	18	25	14	20	21	20
Percent FG Made	36.0	58.8	66.7	69.0	53.6	64.4	65.2	52.9	61.0	56.0	62.5	67.7	74.1
Safeties	0	0	0	0	0	0	0	0	1	0	0	2	0

DEFENSE

	ATL.	CHI.	DALL.	DET.	G.B.	L.A.	MINN.	N.O.	N.Y.G.	PHIL.	ST.L.	S.F.	WASH.
FIRST DOWNS:													
Total	211	234	205	186	202	195	168	263	223	213	242	213	266
by Rushing	93	83	87	61	88	64	68	100	98	102	96	81	125
by Passing	98	133	105	112	102	113	89	150	110	95	116	110	125
by Penalty	20	18	13	13	12	18	11	13	15	16	30	22	16
RUSHING:													
Number	479	459	415	362	453	395	398	469	419	457	472	425	468
Yards	1722	1471	1656	1152	1829	1359	1365	1891	1692	2064	1762	1799	2068
Average Yards	3.6	3.2	4.0	3.2	4.0	3.4	3.4	4.0	4.0	4.5	3.7	4.2	4.4
Touchdowns	14	11	10	7	14	6	4	15	11	16	10	12	19
PASSING:													
Attempts	348	394	399	371	369	378	367	430	364	313	382	384	374
Completions	191	233	193	194	177	196	195	238	186	161	183	185	205
Completion Percentage	54.9	59.1	48.4	52.3	48.0	51.9	53.1	55.3	51.1	51.4	47.9	48.2	54.8
Passing Yards	2397	2925	2226	2491	2496	2615	1798	3197	2650	2176	2416	2434	2434
Avg. Yards per Attempt	6.9	7.4	5.6	6.7	6.8	6.9	4.9	7.4	7.3	7.0	6.3	6.3	6.5
Avg. Yards per Complet.	12.5	12.6	11.5	12.8	14.1	13.3	9.2	13.4	14.2	13.5	13.2	13.2	11.9
Times Tackled Passing	30	42	41	23	32	53	49	17	35	34	40	30	24
Yards Lost Tackled	243	329	313	195	270	426	360	136	279	287	309	261	169
Net Yards	2154	2596	1913	2296	2226	2189	1438	3061	2371	1889	2107	2173	2265
Touchdowns	11	18	10	14	13	15	6	19	19	16	16	19	14
Interceptions	19	17	24	28	20	19	28	22	17	10	21	22	15
Percent Intercepted	5.5	4.3	6.0	7.5	5.4	5.0	7.6	5.1	4.7	3.2	5.5	5.7	4.0
PUNTS:													
Number	60	87	74	70	71	88	84	56	62	62	80	82	56
Average Distance	41.2	37.6	41.1	39.1	40.1	37.8	37.5	40.4	39.7	39.1	40.0	40.4	39.3
PUNT RETURNS:													
Number	40	40	38	29	40	32	38	41	21	22	26	38	35
Yards	267	268	281	113	338	181	322	434	61	163	90	180	259
Average Yards	6.7	6.7	7.4	3.9	8.5	5.7	8.5	10.6	2.9	7.4	3.5	4.7	7.4
Touchdowns	0	0	1	0	0	0	1	1	0	1	0	0	0
KICKOFF RETURNS:													
Number	41	47	60	67	36	71	69	35	57	50	54	58	49
Yards	983	935	1142	1427	888	1278	1514	735	1359	1030	1262	1362	1181
Average Yards	24.0	19.9	19.0	21.3	24.7	18.0	21.9	21.0	23.8	20.6	23.4	23.5	24.1
Touchdowns	1	0	0	0	0	0	3	0	1	1	1	0	1
INTERCEPTION RETURNS:													
Number	21	22	16	12	24	13	15	22	12	23	19	10	10
Yards	283	251	259	174	421	92	175	256	172	461	276	95	181
Average Yards	13.5	11.4	16.2	14.5	17.5	7.1	11.7	11.6	14.3	20.0	14.5	9.5	18.1
Touchdowns	1	1	1	1	3	0	0	1	0	2	0	0	1
PENALTIES:													
Number	93	76	70	90	63	77	58	79	71	90	68	87	87
Yards	897	826	732	805	686	825	586	875	675	991	659	965	930
FUMBLES:													
Number	22	27	25	30	29	28	27	26	31	25	20	35	22
Number Lost	16	14	15	16	17	16	16	16	13	18	14	20	13
POINTS:													
Total	261	261	221	202	293	202	143	347	270	332	228	267	314
PAT Attempts	29	31	24	22	30	22	14	40	32	36	27	32	37
PAT Made	27	27	24	22	29	22	14	38	30	35	27	30	36
FG Attempts	40	29	26	26	42	25	27	34	29	39	26	24	26
FG Made	20	16	17	16	28	16	15	23	16	27	13	15	18
Percent FG Made	50.0	55.2	65.4	61.5	66.7	64.0	55.6	67.6	55.2	69.2	50.0	62.5	69.2
Safeties	0	0	1	0	0	0	0	0	0	0	0	0	1

CONFERENCE PLAYOFFS

December 28, at Dallas
(Attendance 69,613)

SCORING

DALLAS	3	0	0	2–5
DETROIT	0	0	0	0–0

First Quarter
Dal. Clark, 26 yard field goal

Fourth Quarter
Dal. Andrie, Safety-tackled Landry

TEAM STATISTICS

DALLAS		DETR.
19	First Downs—Total	7
11	First Downs—Rushing	2
8	First Downs—Passing	5
0	First Downs—Penalty	0
0	Fumbles—Number	3
0	Fumbles—Lost Ball	2
6	Penalties—Number	0
47	Yards Penalized	0
0	Missed Field Goals	0
69	Offensive Plays—Total	50
231	Net Yards	156
3.3	Average Gain	3.1
1	Giveaways	3
3	Takeaways	1
+2	Difference	–2

INDIVIDUAL STATISTICS

DALLAS	No.	Yds.	Avg.	DETROIT	No.	Yds.	Avg.
RUSHING							
Thomas	30	135	4.5	Farr	12	31	2.6
Garrison	17	72	4.2	Taylor	9	16	1.8
Morton	3	2	0.7	Landry	3	15	5.0
	50	209	4.2	Owens	2	9	4.5
				Walton	1	5	5.0
					27	76	2.8
RECEIVING							
Garrison	2	8	4.0	Walton	3	39	13.0
Hayes	1	20	20.0	Taylor	2	7	3.5
Norman	1	10	10.0	McCullough	1	39	39.0
	4	38	9.5	Owens	1	7	7.0
					7	92	13.1
PUNTING							
Widby	8		44.7	Weaver	8		48.8
PUNT RETURNS							
Renfro	4	23	5.8	Barney	5	20	4.0
				Vaughan	1	1	1.0
					6	21	3.5
KICKOFF RETURNS							
Hayes	1	16	16.0	Williams	1	24	24.0
Waters	1	9	9.0	Maxwell	1	13	13.0
	2	25	12.5		2	37	18.5
INTERCEPTION RETURNS							
Renfro	1	13	13.0	Weger	1	31	31.0

PASSING

	Att.	Comp.	Comp. Pct.	Yds.	Int.	Yds/ Att.	Yds/ Comp.	Yds Lost Tkld.
DALLAS								
Morton	18	4	22.2	38	1	2.1	9.5	1–16
DETROIT								
Landry	12	5	41.7	48	0	4.0	9.6	
Munson	8	2	25.0	44	1	5.5	22.0	
	20	7	35.0	92	1	4.8	13.1	3–12

December 27, at Bloomington
(Attendance 45,103)

SCORING

MINNESOTA	7	0	0	7–14
SAN FRANCISCO	7	3	0	7–17

First Quarter
Min. Krause, 22 yard fumble return
PAT—Cox (kick)
S.F. Witcher, 24 yard pass from Brodie
PAT—Gossett (kick)

Second Quarter
S.F. Gossett, 40 yard field goal

Fourth Quarter
S.F. Brodie, 1 yard rush
PAT—Gossett (kick)
Min. Washington, 24 yard pass from Cuozzo
PAT—Cox (kick)

TEAM STATISTICS

MINN.		S.F.
14	First Downs—Total	14
7	First Downs—Rushing	5
6	First Downs—Passing	8
1	First Downs—Penalty	1
3	Fumbles—Number	5
2	Fumbles—Lost Ball	3
1	Penalties—Number	3
5	Yards Penalized	37
2	Missed Field Goals	1
60	Offensive Plays—Total	71
241	Net Yards	289
4.1	Average Gain	4.1
4	Giveaways	3
3	Takeaways	4
–1	Difference	+1

INDIVIDUAL STATISTICS

MINNESOTA	No.	Yds.	Avg.	SAN FRANCISCO	No	Yds	Avg.
RUSHING							
Jones	15	60	4.0	Willard	27	85	3.1
Osborn	12	41	3.4	Tucker	7	5	0.7
Cuozzo	1	11	11.0	Brodie	2	3	1.5
Brown	2	5	2.5	Kwalick	1	2	2.0
	30	117	3.9	Cunningham	1	0	0.0
					38	95	2.5
RECEIVING							
Henderson	5	80	16.0	Tucker	6	48	8.0
Grim	2	37	18.5	Witcher	4	45	11.3
Washington	1	24	24.0	Kwalick	3	45	15.0
Jones	1	5	5.0	Washington	2	45	22.5
	9	146	16.2	Willard	1	18	18.0
					16	201	12.6
PUNTING							
McNeill	7		39.4	Spurrier	8		33.8
PUNT RETURNS							
None				B. Taylor	5	69	13.8
KICKOFF RETURNS							
Jones	3	49	16.3	Beard	1	17	17.0
Brown	1	23	23.0	Tucker	1	13	13.0
	4	72	18.0	Hoskins	1	0	0.0
					3	30	10.0
INTERCEPTION RETURNS							
None				Sniadecki	1	5	5.0
				B. Taylor	1	0	0.0
					2	5	2.5

PASSING

	Att.	Comp.	Comp. Pct.	Yds.	Int.	Yds/ Att.	Yds/ Comp.	Yds Lost Tkld.
MINNESOTA								
Cuozzo	27	9	33.3	146	2	5.4	16.2	3–22
SAN FRANCISCO								
Brodie	32	16	50.0	201	0	6.3	12.6	1– 8

DALLAS COWBOYS 10-4-0 Tom Landry

Score	Scores of Each Game	Opp.
17	Philadelphia	7
28	N. Y. GIANTS	10
7	St. Louis	20
13	ATLANTA	0
13	Minnesota	54
27	Kansas City	16
21	PHILADELPHIA	17
20	N. Y. Giants	23
0	ST. LOUIS	38
45	Washington	21
16	GREEN BAY	3
34	WASHINGTON	0
6	Cleveland	2
52	HOUSTON	10

Use Name	Pos.	Hgt	Wgt	Age	Int	Pts
Bob Asher	OT	6'5"	250	22		
Tony Liscio	OT	6'5"	255	30		
Ralph Neely	OT	6'5"	265	26		
Rayfield Wright	OT	6'7"	255	25		
John Niland	OG	6'4"	245	26		
Blaine Nye	OG	6'4"	250	24		
Halvor Hagen	C-OG	6'5"	253	23		
Dave Manders	C	6'2"	250	28		
George Andrie	DE	6'7"	250	30		
Larry Cole	DE	6'4"	255	23		
Pat Toomay	DE	6'5"	244	25		
Ron East	DT	6'4"	242	27		
Bob Lilly	DT	6'4"	260	31		
Jethro Pugh	DT	6'6"	260	26	1	
Dave Edwards	LB	6'3"	225	31	2	
Chuck Howley	LB	6'3"	225	34	2	
Lee Roy Jordan	LB	6'2"	220	29	1	
Steve Kiner	LB	6'	218	23	1	
D. D. Lewis	LB	6'2"	225	24		
Tom Stincic	LB	6'2"	230	23	1	
Herb Adderley	DB	6'1"	200	31	3	
Richmond Flowers	DB	6'	180	23		
Cornell Green	DB	6'4"	208	30	1	
Cliff Harris	DB	6'	184	21	2	
Mel Renfro	DB	6'	190	28	4	
Mark Washington	DB	5'10"	188	22	1	6
Charlie Waters	DB	6'1"	193	21	5	
Bob Belden	QB	6'2"	205	23		
Craig Morton	QB	6'4"	214	27		
Roger Staubach	QB	6'2"	197	28		
Dan Reeves	HB	6'1"	200	26		12
Claxton Welch	HB	5'11"	203	23		6
Calvin Hill	FB-HB	6'3"	227	23		24
Duane Thomas	FB-HB	6'1"	220	23		30
Walt Garrison	FB	6'	205	26		30
Margene Atkins	WR	5'10"	183	23		
Bob Hayes	WR	6'	185	27		66
Dennis Homan	WR	6'1"	180	24		
Lance Rentzel	WR	6'2"	202	26		30
Reggie Rucker	WR	6'2"	190	22		6
Mike Ditka	TE	6'3"	225	30		
Pettis Norman	TE	6'3"	220	30		
Mike Clark	K	6'1"	205	29		89
Ron Widby	K	6'4"	210	25		

NEW YORK GIANTS 9-5-0 Alex Webster

Score	Scores of Each Game	Opp.
16	CHICAGO	24
10	Dallas	28
10	New Orleans	14
30	PHILADELPHIA	23
16	Boston	0
35	ST. LOUIS	17
22	N. Y. Jets	10
23	DALLAS	20
35	WASHINGTON	33
20	Philadelphia	23
27	Washington	24
20	BUFFALO	6
34	St. Louis	17
3	LOS ANGELES	31

Use Name	Pos.	Hgt	Wgt	Age	Int	Pts
Rich Buzin	OT	6'4"	250	24		
Dennis Crane	OT	6'6"	260	25		
Willie Young	OT	6'	265	27		
Charlie Harper	OG-OT	6'2"	250	26		
Willie Banks	OG	6'2"	237	24		
Pete Case	OG	6'3"	245	29		
Doug Van Horn	OG	6'2"	245	26		
Len Johnson	C-OG	6'2"	250	24		
Pat Hughes	C	6'2"	240	23		
Greg Larson	C	6'2"	250	31		
John Baker	DE	6'5"	260	28		
Fred Dryer	DE	6'6"	240	24		
Bob Lurtsema	DE	6'6"	250	28		
Jim Kanicki	DT	6'4"	270	28		
Jim Norton	DT	6'4"	254	27		
Jerry Shay	DT	6'3"	245	26		
John Douglas	LB	6'2"	225	25		
Jim Files	LB	6'4"	240	22	1	2
Matt Hazeltine	LB	6'1"	225	37	1	
Ralph Heck	LB	6'2"	230	29	1	
Ray Hickl	LB	6'2"	220	23		
John Kirby	LB	6'3"	232	28		
Al Brenner	DB	6'1"	200	22		
Otto Brown	DB	6'1"	188	23		
Scott Eaton	DB	6'3"	205	26	2	
Joe Green	DB	5'11"	195	23		
Spider Lockhart	DB	6'2"	175	27	4	
Tom Longo	DB	6'1"	200	26	2	
Kenny Parker	DB	6'1"	190	24		
Willie Williams	DB	6'	190	27	6	
Dick Shiner	QB	6'	197	28		
Fran Tarkenton	QB	6'1"	190	30		12
Bobby Duhon	HB	6'	195	23		6
Ron Johnson	HB	6'1"	205	22		72
Les Shy	HB	6'1"	200	26		
Joe Morrison	FB-WR-HB	6'1"	212	32		
Tucker Frederickson	FB	6'3"	220	27		24
Ernie Koy	HB-FB	6'2"	225	27		
Don Herrmann	WR	6'2"	195	23		12
Rich Houston	WR	6'2"	197	24		
Clifton McNeil	WR	6'2"	187	30		30
Bob Tucker	TE	6'3"	230	25		30
Aaron Thomas	WR-TE	6'3"	210	32		6
Pete Gogolak	K	6'2"	190	28		107
Bill Johnson	K	6'2"	208	26		

Junior Coffey – Knee Injury
Tommy Crutcher – Knee Injury

ST. LOUIS CARDINALS 8-5-1 Charlie Winner

Score	Scores of Each Game	Opp.
13	Los Angeles	34
27	WASHINGTON	17
20	DALLAS	7
24	NEW ORLEANS	17
35	Philadelphia	20
17	N. Y. Giants	35
44	HOUSTON	0
31	BOSTON	0
38	Dallas	0
6	Kansas City	6
23	PHILADELPHIA	14
3	Detroit	16
17	N. Y. GIANTS	34
27	Washington	28

Use Name	Pos.	Hgt	Wgt	Age	Int	Pts
Vern Emerson	OT	6'5"	260	24		
Ernie McMillan	OT	6'6"	255	32		
Bob Reynolds	OT	6'6"	265	29		
Clyde Williams	OG-OT	6'2"	250	30		
Irv Goode	OG	6'4"	255	29		
Chuck Hutchison	OG	6'3"	240	21		
Mike LaHood	OG	6'3"	250	25		
Wayne Mulligan	C	6'2"	245	23		
Rolf Krueger	DE	6'4"	250	23		
Cal Snowden	DE	6'4"	250	23		
Chuck Walker	DE	6'2"	250	29		
Joe Schmiesing	DT-DE	6'4"	250	25		
Fred Heron	DT	6'4"	260	25		
Bob Rowe	DT	6'4"	255	25		
Mike Siwok	DT	6'3"	260	22		
Chip Healy	LB	6'3"	235	23		
Dave Olerich	LB	6'1"	225	25		
Don Parish	LB	6'1"	220	22	1	6
Jamie Rivers	LB	6'2"	235	24		
Rocky Romesa	LB	6'2"	230	24		
Larry Stallings	LB	6'2"	230	28	1	
Terry Brown	DB	6'1"	210	23		
Miller Farr	DB	6'1"	190	27	5	6
Chuck Latourette	DB	6'	190	25		6
Tony Plummer	DB	5'11"	190	23		
Jerry Stovall	DB	6'2"	195	28	2	
Roger Wehrli	DB	6'1"	195	22	6	
Larry Wilson	DB	6'	195	32	5	
Nate Wright	DB	5'11"	180	22	1	
Pete Beathard	QB	6'2"	210	28		
Jim Hart	QB	6'2"	205	26		
Charlie Pittman	HB	6'1"	200	22		
Roy Shivers	HB	6'	200	28		12
Paul White	HB	6'	200	22		
MacArthur Lane	FB-HB	6'	220	28		78
Cid Edwards	FB	6'2"	230	26		12
Johnny Roland	HB-FB	6'2"	215	27		30
Jerry Daanen	WR	6'	190	25		
John Gilliam	WR	6'1"	195	25		36
Freddie Hyatt	WR	6'3"	210	24		
Dave Williams	WR	6'2"	210	25		18
Bob Brown	TE	6'3"	225	27		
Jim McFarland	TE	6'5"	225	22		
Jackie Smith	TE	6'4"	235	29		24
Jim Bakken	K	6'	195	29		97

WASHINGTON REDSKINS 6-8-0 Bill Austin

Score	Scores of Each Game	Opp.
17	San Francisco	26
17	St. Louis	27
33	Philadelphia	21
31	DETROIT	10
20	Oakland	34
20	CINCINNATI	0
19	Denver	3
10	MINNESOTA	19
33	N. Y. Giants	35
21	DALLAS	45
24	N. Y. GIANTS	27
0	Dallas	34
24	PHILADELPHIA	6
28	ST. LOUIS	27

Use Name	Pos.	Hgt	Wgt	Age	Int	Pts
Walt Rock	OT	6'5"	255	29		
Jim Snowden	OT	6'3"	255	28		
Steve Wright	OT	6'6"	250	28		
Paul Laaveg	OG	6'4"	245	21		
Vince Promuto	OG	6'1"	245	32		
Roy Schmidt	OG	6'3"	250	28		
Ray Schoenke	OG	6'3"	250	28		
Gene Hamlin	C	6'3"	245	24		
Len Hauss	C	6'2"	235	28		
Bruce Anderson	DE	6'4"	250	26		
Bill Brundige	DE	6'5"	270	21		
Leo Carroll	DE	6'7"	250	26		
Terry Hermeling	DE	6'5"	255	24		
John Hoffman	DE	6'7"	260	27		
Frank Bosch	DT	6'4"	246	24		
Floyd Peters	DT	6'4"	255	35		
Manny Sistrunk	DT	6'5"	265	23		
Chris Hanburger	LB	6'2"	218	29	1	
Marlin McKeever	LB	6'1"	235	30		
Harold McLinton	LB	6'2"	235	23		
Tom Roussel	LB	6'3"	235	25		
Rusty Tillman	LB	6'2"	230	24		
John Didion	C-LB	6'4"	245	22		
Mike Bass	DB	6'	190	25	4	
Pat Fischer	DB	5'10"	170	30	2	
Jim Harris	DB	5'11"	173	24		
Rickie Harris	DB	6'	182	27	3	
Jon Jaqua	DB	6'	190	22	1	
Brig Owens	DB	5'11"	190	27	4	
Ted Vactor	DB	6'	185	26		
Sonny Jurgensen	QB	5'11"	203	36		6
Frank Ryan	QB	6'3"	207	34		
Larry Brown	HB	5'11"	195	22		42
Bob Brunet	HB	6'1"	205	24		
Danny Pierce	FB-HB	6'3"	216	22		
Henry Dyer	FB	6'2"	230	25		
Charlie Harraway	FB	6'2"	215	25		30
Dave Kopay	HB-FB	6'2"	225	28		
Jon Henderson	WR	6'	200	25		18
Bill Malinchak	WR	6'1"	200	26		
Walter Roberts	WR	5'10"	163	28		6
Charley Taylor	WR	6'3"	210	29		48
Mack Alston	TE	6'2"	230	23		
Pat Richter	TE	6'5"	230	29		
Jerry Smith	TE	6'2"	208	27		54
Mike Bragg	K	5'11"	186	23		
Curt Knight	K	6'1"	190	27		93

PHILADELPHIA EAGLES 3-10-1 Jerry Williams

Score	Scores of Each Game	Opp.
7	DALLAS	17
16	Chicago	20
21	WASHINGTON	33
23	N. Y. Giants	30
20	ST. LOUIS	35
17	Green Bay	30
17	Dallas	21
24	MIAMI	17
13	ATLANTA	13
23	N. Y. GIANTS	20
14	St. Louis	23
10	Baltimore	29
6	Washington	24
30	PITTSBURGH	20

Use Name	Pos.	Hgt	Wgt	Age	Int	Pts
Joe Carollo	OT	6'2"	265	30		
Wade Key	OT	6'4"	245	23		
Dick Stevens	OT	6'4"	240	22		
Norman Davis	OG	6'3"	245	25		
Dick Hart	OG	6'2"	250	27		
Jim Skaggs	OG	6'2"	250	30		
Mark Nordquist	C-OG	6'4"	246	24		
Mike Evans	C	6'5"	250	23		
Calvin Hunt	C	6'3"	243	22		
Don Brumm	DE	6'3"	245	27		
Ernie Calloway	DE	6'6"	240	22		
Mel Tom	DE	6'4"	250	29		
Mike Dirks	DT	6'2"	246	24		6
Gary Pettigrew	DT	6'4"	255	25		
Don Hultz	DE-DT	6'3"	240	29		
Carl Gersbach	LB	6'1"	230	23		
Bill Hobbs	LB	6'	220	24		
Jay Johnson	LB	6'3"	230	24		
Ike Kelley	LB	5'11"	224	26		
Dave Lloyd	LB	6'3"	248	34		
Ron Porter	LB	6'3"	232	25		
Tim Rossovich	LB	6'4"	250	24		
Adrian Young	LB	6'1"	232	24	2	
Bill Bradley	DB	5'11"	190	23		
Richard Harvey	DB	6'2"	190	24		
Ed Hayes	DB	6'1"	185	24	1	
Ray Jones	DB	6'	187	22	2	
Ron Medved	DB	6'1"	200	26		
Al Nelson	DB	5'11"	186	26	2	
Steve Preece	DB	6'1"	195	23	2	6
Nate Ramsey	DB	6'1"	200	29	1	
Jim Throner	DB	6'2"	194	21		
Rick Arrington	QB	6'2"	185	23		6
Norm Snead	QB	6'4"	215	30		18
Harry Jones	HB	6'2"	205	25		
Leroy Keyes	HB	6'3"	208	23		
Cyril Pinder	HB	6'2"	222	23		12
Larry Watkins	FB-HB	6'2"	215	23		6
Lee Bougess	FB	6'2"	210	22		24
Tom Woodeshick	FB	6'	222	28		12
Ben Hawkins	WR	6'	180	26		24
Harold Jackson	WR	5'10"	175	24		30
Billy Walik	WR	5'11"	180	22		
Steve Zabel	TE	6'4"	235	22		6
Gary Ballman	WR-TE	6'	205	30		18
Fred Hill	WR-TE	6'2"	215	27		6
Mark Moseley	K	5'11"	182	22		67

Dave Graham – Injury

DALLAS COWBOYS

RUSHING

Last Name	No.	Yds	Avg	TD
Thomas	151	803	5.3	5
Hill	153	577	3.8	4
Garrison	126	507	4.0	3
Staubach	27	221	8.2	0
Reeves	35	84	2.4	2
Morton	16	37	2.3	0
Hayes	4	34	8.5	1
Norman	2	16	8.0	0
Welch	5	13	2.6	1
Rentzel	1	11	11.0	0
Homan	2	−3	−1.5	0

RECEIVING

Last Name	No.	Yds	Avg	TD
Hayes	34	889	26	10
Rentzel	28	556	20	5
Garrison	21	205	10	2
Hill	13	95	7	0
Reeves	12	140	12	0
Thomas	10	73	7	0
Rucker	9	200	22	1
Ditka	8	98	12	0
Homan	7	105	15	0
Norman	6	70	12	0
Kiner	1	14	14	0

PUNT RETURNS

Last Name	No.	Yds	Avg	TD
Hayes	15	116	8	0
Renfro	13	77	6	0
Adkins	4	44	11	0

KICKOFF RETURNS

Last Name	No.	Yds	Avg	TD
Thomas	19	416	22	0
Washington	5	242	48	1
Adkins	7	149	21	0
Kiner	3	50	17	0
Harris	1	22	22	0
Waters	1	6	6	0
Flowers	1	3	3	0

PASSING – PUNTING – KICKING

PASSING	Att	Comp	%	Yds	Yd/Att	TD	Int–	%	RK
Morton	207	102	49	1819	8.8	15	7–	3	5
Staubach	82	44	54	542	6.6	2	8–	10	
Hill	4	1	25	12	3.0	0	0–	0	
Reeves	3	1	33	14	4.7	0	1–	33	
Rentzel	1	1	100	58	58.0	1	0–	0	

PUNTING	No	Avg
Widby	69	41.3

KICKING	XP	Att	%	FG	Att	%
Clark	35	35	100	18	27	67

NEW YORK GIANTS

RUSHING

Last Name	No.	Yds	Avg	TD
R. Johnson	263	1027	3.9	8
Frederickson	120	375	3.1	1
Tarkenton	43	236	5.5	2
Duhon	18	111	6.2	0
Morrison	11	25	2.3	0
Shy	4	13	3.3	0
McNeil	4	7	1.8	0
Koy	2	5	2.5	0

RECEIVING

Last Name	No.	Yds	Avg	TD
McNeil	50	764	15	4
R. Johnson	48	487	10	4
Tucker	40	571	14	5
Frederickson	40	408	10	3
Herrmann	24	290	12	2
Morrison	11	136	12	0
Thomas	6	92	15	1
Houston	4	68	17	0
Duhon	4	58	15	0
Shy	2	8	4	0
Koy	1	10	10	0

PUNT RETURNS

Last Name	No.	Yds	Avg	TD
Duhon	19	157	8	1
Lockhart	9	31	3	0
Brenner	1	5	5	0

KICKOFF RETURNS

Last Name	No.	Yds	Avg	TD
Shy	21	544	26	0
Duhon	14	255	18	0
Houston	8	173	22	0
R. Johnson	5	140	28	0
Green	2	26	13	0
Douglas	1	16	16	0
Hughes	1	3	3	0

PASSING – PUNTING – KICKING

PASSING	Att	Comp	%	Yds	Yd/Att	TD	Int–	%	RK
Tarkenton	389	219	56	2777	7.1	19	12–	3	3
Shiner	12	9	75	87	7.3	0	0–	0	
Duhon	2	2	100	28	14.0	0	0–	0	

PUNTING	No	Avg
B. Johnson	43	39.5
Koy	11	33.5

KICKING	XP	Att	%	FG	Att	%
Gogalak	32	32	100	25	41	61

ST. LOUIS CARDINALS

RUSHING

Last Name	No.	Yds	Avg	TD
Lane	206	977	4.7	11
Roland	94	392	4.2	3
Edwards	70	350	5.0	1
Shivers	24	98	4.1	2
Gilliam	5	68	13.6	1
Smith	5	43	8.6	0
Latourette	2	38	19.0	0
Hart	18	18	1.0	0
B. Brown	1	8	8.0	0
Pittman	2	4	2.0	0
Beathard	2	2	1.0	0

RECEIVING

Last Name	No.	Yds	Avg	TD
Gilliam	45	952	21	5
Smith	37	687	19	4
Lane	32	365	11	2
D. Williams	23	364	16	3
Edwards	19	150	8	1
Roland	17	96	6	1
Shivers	3	44	15	0
Daanen	2	31	16	0

PUNT RETURNS

Last Name	No.	Yds	Avg	TD
Latourette	30	171	6	0
Roland	10	140	14	1
Wehrli	1	4	4	0

KICKOFF RETURNS

Last Name	No.	Yds	Avg	TD
Latourette	13	254	20	0
Pittman	10	237	24	0
Wright	8	156	20	0
Gilliam	5	107	21	0
White	3	65	22	0
Roland	3	40	13	0
Shivers	2	35	18	0
T. Brown	2	32	16	0
Wilson	1	0	0	0

PASSING – PUNTING – KICKING

PASSING	Att	Comp	%	Yds	Yd/Att	TD	Int–	%	RK
Hart	373	171	46	2575	6.9	14	18–	5	9
Beathard	17	7	41	114	6.7	2	1–	6	

PUNTING	No	Avg
Latourette	65	40.9

KICKING	XP	Att	%	FG	Att	%
Bakken	37	38	97	20	32	63

WASHINGTON REDSKINS

RUSHING

Last Name	No.	Yds	Avg	TD
Brown	237	1125	4.7	5
Harraway	146	577	4.0	5
Dyer	21	102	4.9	0
Kopay	13	49	3.8	0
Jurgensen	6	39	6.5	1
Brunet	9	37	4.1	0
Smith	2	29	14.5	0
Bragg	2	25	12.5	0
Taylor	1	17	17.0	0
Roberts	2	15	7.5	0
Pierce	5	6	1.2	0

RECEIVING

Last Name	No.	Yds	Avg	TD
Smith	43	575	13	9
Taylor	42	593	14	8
Brown	37	341	9	2
Roberts	27	411	15	1
Harraway	24	136	6	0
Henderson	13	176	14	3
Kopay	7	24	3	0
Dyer	4	37	9	0
Brunet	3	28	9	0
Richter	2	30	15	0
Pierce	1	6	6	0

PUNT RETURNS

Last Name	No.	Yds	Avg	TD
Roberts	10	28	3	0
R. Harris	14	10	1	0
Vactor	2	7	4	0
Kopay	1	0	0	0

KICKOFF RETURNS

Last Name	No.	Yds	Avg	TD
Vactor	28	700	25	0
R. Harris	10	208	21	0
J. Harris	9	172	19	0
Dyer	5	78	16	0
Hanburger	2	33	17	0
McKeever	1	21	21	0
Tillman	1	10	10	0
Brundige	1	1	1	0
Richter	2	0	0	0
Bass	1	0	0	0
Henderson	1	0	0	0

PASSING – PUNTING – KICKING

PASSING	Att	Comp	%	Yds	Yd/Att	TD	Int–	%	RK
Jurgensen	337	202	60	2354	7.0	23	10–	3	2
Ryan	4	1	25	3	0.8	0	0–	0	
Bragg	1	0	0	0	0.0	0	0–	0	

PUNTING	No	Avg
Bragg	61	40.9

KICKING	XP	Att	%	FG	Att	%
Knight	33	34	97	20	27	74

PHILADELPHIA EAGLES

RUSHING

Last Name	No.	Yds	Avg	TD
Pinder	166	657	4.0	2
Bouggess	159	401	2.5	2
Woodeshick	52	254	4.9	2
Watkins	32	96	3.0	1
H. Jones	13	44	3.4	0
Snead	18	35	1.9	3
Arrington	4	33	8.3	1
Bradley	1	14	14.0	0
Keyes	2	7	3.5	0
Hawkins	2	3	1.5	0
Jackson	1	−5	−5.0	0

RECEIVING

Last Name	No.	Yds	Avg	TD
Bouggess	50	401	8	2
Ballman	47	601	13	2
Jackson	41	613	15	5
Hawkins	30	612	20	4
Pinder	28	249	9	0
Zabel	8	119	15	1
Woodeshick	6	28	5	0
Hill	3	10	3	1
Watkins	3	6	2	0
H. Jones	1	12	12	0
Walik	1	0	0	0

PUNT RETURNS

Last Name	No.	Yds	Avg	TD
Walik	20	78	4	0
Hawkins	10	16	2	0
Hayes	2	6	3	0

KICKOFF RETURNS

Last Name	No.	Yds	Avg	TD
Walik	32	805	25	0
Nelson	10	187	19	0
Hayes	6	107	18	0
R. Jones	6	97	16	0
H. Jones	2	23	12	0
Rossovich	1	22	22	0
Pettigrew	1	11	11	0
Hawkins	1	0	0	0

PASSING – PUNTING – KICKING

PASSING	Att	Comp	%	Yds	Yd/Att	TD	Int–	%	RK
Snead	335	181	54	2323	6.9	15	20–	6	7
Arrington	73	37	51	328	4.5	1	3–	4	
Ballman	1	0	0	0	0.0	0	0–	0	
Bouggess	1	0	0	0	0.0	0	0–	0	

PUNTING	No	Avg
Bradley	61	36.8
Moseley	10	35.0

KICKING	XP	Att	%	FG	Att	%
Moseley	25	28	89	14	25	56

1970 N.F.C. — Central Division

MINNESOTA VIKINGS 12-2-0 Bud Grant

Scores of Each Game		
27	KANSAS CITY	10
26	NEW ORLEANS	0
10	Green Bay	13
24	Chicago	0
54	DALLAS	13
13	LOS ANGELES	3
30	Detroit	17
19	Washington	10
24	DETROIT	20
10	GREEN BAY	3
10	N. Y. Jets	20
16	CHICAGO	13
35	Boston	14
37	Atlanta	7

Use Name	Pos.	Hgt	Wgt	Age	Int	Pts
Grady Alderman	OT	6'2"	245	31		
Doug Davis	OT	6'4"	255	26		
Steve Smith	OT	6'5"	250	26		
Ron Yary	OT	6'6"	255	24		
Milt Sunde	OG	6'2"	250	27		
Jim Vellone	OG	6'2"	255	26		
Ed White	OG	6'2"	260	23		
Mick Tingelhoff	C	6'1"	237	30		
Carl Eller	DE	6'6"	250	28		
Jim Marshall	DE	6'3"	248	32		
John Ward	DE	6'4"	260	22		
Paul Dickson	DT	6'5"	250	33		
Gary Larsen	DT	6'5"	260	30		
Alan Page	DT	6'5"	245	25	1	6
Jim Hargrove	LB	6'3"	235	25		
Wally Hilgenberg	LB	6'3"	230	27	2	
Mike McGill	LB	6'2"	235	23		6
Wayne Meylan	LB	6'1"	235	24		
Lonnie Warwick	LB	6'3"	237	28	3	
Roy Winston	LB	6'1"	228	30	1	6
Bobby Bryant	DB	6'	170	26	3	6
John Charles	DB	6'1"	200	26	1	
Dale Hackbart	DB	6'3"	205	34		
Karl Kassulke	DB	6'	195	28	3	
Paul Krause	DB	6'3"	188	28	6	
Ted Provost	DB	6'2"	195	22		
Ed Sharockman	DB	6'	200	30	7	18
Charlie West	DB	6'1"	190	24	1	
Bill Cappleman	QB	6'3"	210	23		
Gary Cuozzo	QB	6'1"	195	29		
Bob Lee	QB	6'2"	195	24		6
Clint Jones	HB	6'	206	25		54
Dave Osborn	HB	6'	205	27		36
Bill Brown	FB	5'11"	230	32		12
Jim Lindsey	HB-FB	6'2"	210	25		6
Oscar Reed	HB-FB	5'11"	222	26		6
Bob Grim	WR	6'	200	25		
John Henderson	WR	6'3"	190	27		12
Gene Washington	WR	6'3"	208	26		24
John Beasley	TE	6'3"	233	25		12
Kent Kramer	TE	6'5"	235	26		
Stu Voigt	TE	6'1"	220	22		
Fred Cox	K	5'10"	200	31		125
Tom McNeill	K	6'1"	195	28		

Billy Harris – Injury

DETROIT LIONS 10-4-0 Joe Schmidt

Scores of Each Game		
40	Green Bay	0
38	CINCINNATI	3
28	CHICAGO	14
10	Washington	31
41	Cleveland	24
16	Chicago	10
17	MINNESOTA	30
17	New Orleans	19
20	Minnesota	24
28	SAN FRANCISCO	7
28	OAKLAND	14
16	ST. LOUIS	3
28	Los Angeles	23
20	GREEN BAY	0

Use Name	Pos.	Hgt	Wgt	Age	Int	Pts
Rocky Freitas	OT	6'6"	280	24		
Roger Shoals	OT	6'4"	260	31		
Jim Yarbrough	OT	6'6"	250	23		
Frank Gallagher	OG	6'2"	245	27		
Bob Kowalkowski	OG	6'3"	240	26		
Rocky Rasley	OG	6'3"	250	23		
Chuck Walton	OG	6'3"	255	29		
Bill Cottrell	C	6'3"	255	25		
Ed Flanagan	C	6'3"	245	26		
Larry Hand	DE	6'4"	250	30	1	6
Jim Mitchell	DE	6'3"	245	21		
Joe Robb	DE	6'3"	245	33		
Dan Goich	DT	6'4"	265	26		
Dave Haverdick	DT	6'4"	245	22		
Alex Karras	DT	6'2"	245	34		
Jerry Rush	DT	6'4"	265	28		
Mike Lucci	LB	6'2"	230	30	2	
Ed Mooney	LB	6'2"	225	25		
Paul Naumoff	LB	6'1"	215	25		
Bill Saul	LB	6'4"	225	29		
Wayne Walker	LB	6'2"	228	33		
Lem Barney	DB	6'	188	24	7	18
Dick LeBeau	DB	6'1"	185	33	9	
Wayne Rasmussen	DB	6'2"	180	28	2	
Tom Vaughn	DB	5'11"	190	27	1	
Mike Weger	DB	6'2"	200	24	5	6
Bobby Williams	DB	6'1"	200	28	1	6
Greg Landry	QB	6'4"	205	23		6
Bill Munson	QB	6'2"	210	28		
Nick Eddy	HB	6'1"	207	26		6
Altie Taylor	HB	5'10"	196	22		24
Mel Farr	FB-HB	6'2"	210	25		66
Steve Owens	FB	6'2"	220	22		12
Bill Triplett	FB	6'2"	215	31		6
Bruce Maxwell	HB-FB	6'1"	220	23		
Charlie Brown	WR	6'2"	195	21		
Chuck Hughes	WR	5'11"	175	27		
Earl McCullouch	WR	5'11"	175	24		24
Phil Odle	WR	5'11"	195	27		
Larry Walton	WR	5'11"	180	23		30
John Wright	WR	6'	197	23		
Craig Cotton	TE	6'4"	222	23		
Charlie Sanders	TE	6'4"	235	24		36
Errol Mann	K	6'	200	29		101
Herman Weaver	K	6'4"	210	21		

CHICAGO BEARS 6-8-0 Jim Dooley

Scores of Each Game		
24	N. Y. Giants	16
20	PHILADELPHIA	16
14	Detroit	28
0	MINNESOTA	24
7	SAN DIEGO	20
10	DETROIT	16
23	Atlanta	14
16	SAN FRANCISCO	37
19	Green Bay	20
31	BUFFALO	13
20	Baltimore	21
13	Minnesota	16
35	GREEN BAY	17
24	New Orleans	3

Use Name	Pos.	Hgt	Wgt	Age	Int	Pts
Jeff Curchin	OT	6'6"	265	22		
Randy Jackson	OT	6'5"	245	26		
Wayne Mass	OT	6'4"	240	24		
Jim Cadile	OG	6'3"	240	29		
Glenn Holloway	OG	6'3"	245	21		
Howard Mudd	OG	6'3"	252	28		
Ted Wheeler	OG	6'3"	245	24		
Bob Hyland	C	6'5"	250	25		
Harry Gunner	DE	6'6"	250	25		
Ed O'Bradovich	DE	6'3"	255	26		
Willie Holman	DT-DE	6'4"	250	25		
Dave Hale	DT	6'7"	260	23		
George Seals	DT	6'2"	260	27	1	
Bill Staley	DT	6'3"	248	23		
Ross Brupbacher	LB	6'3"	215	22	2	
Doug Buffone	LB	6'1"	225	26	4	
Dick Butkus	LB	6'3"	245	26	3	
Lee Roy Caffey	LB	6'3"	250	30		
Jimmy Gunn	LB	6'1"	220	21		
John Neidert	LB	6'2"	230	24		
Phil Clark	DB	6'2"	208	25	1	
Dick Daniels	DB	5'9"	180	24	2	
Butch Davis	DB	5'11"	183	22	1	
Bennie McRae	DB	6'1"	180	29	1	
Ron Smith	DB	6'1"	192	27		
Joe Taylor	DB	6'2"	200	29	2	
Garry Lyle	HB-DB	6'2"	198	24		
Jack Concannon	QB	6'3"	205	27		12
Bobby Douglass	QB	6'3"	215	23		
Kent Nix	QB	6'1"	195	26		
Craig Baynham	HB	6'1"	203	26		
Gale Sayers	HB	6'	198	27		
Don Shy (from NO)	HB	6'1"	205	24		6
Ronnie Bull	FB-HB	6'	200	30		
Mike Hull	FB	6'3"	220	25		
Ralph Kurek	FB	6'2"	210	27		
Ross Montgomery	FB	6'3"	220	23		
Linzy Cole	WR	5'11"	170	22		
George Farmer	WR	6'4"	210	22		12
Dick Gordon	WR	5'11"	190	25		78
Jim Seymour	WR	6'4"	210	23		24
Cecil Turner	WR	5'10"	170	26		24
Jim Hester	TE	6'4"	250	25		
Ray Ogden	TE	6'5"	225	27		6
Bob Wallace	TE	6'3"	211	24		
Rich Coady	C-TE	6'3"	238	25		6
Bobby Joe Green	K	5'11'	175	32		
Mac Percival	K	6'4"	220	30		88

Brian Piccolo – Died 6-16-70 – cancer

GREEN BAY PACKERS 6-8-0 Phil Bengtson

Scores of Each Game		
0	DETROIT	40
27	ATLANTA	24
13	MINNESOTA	10
22	San Diego	20
21	LOS ANGELES	31
30	PHILADELPHIA	17
10	San Francisco	26
10	BALTIMORE	13
20	CHICAGO	19
3	Minnesota	10
3	Dallas	16
20	Pittsburgh	12
17	Chicago	35
0	Detroit	20

Use Name	Pos.	Hgt	Wgt	Age	Int	Pts
Forrest Gregg	OT	6'4"	250	37		
Bill Hayhoe	OT	6'8"	258	23		
Dick Himes	OT	6'4"	244	24		
Francis Peay	OT	6'5"	250	26		
Dave Bradley	OG	6'4"	245	23		
Gale Gillingham	OG	6'3"	255	26		
Bill Lueck	OG	6'3"	235	24		
Ken Bowman	C	6'3"	230	27		
Malcolm Walker	OT-C	6'4"	250	27		
Lionel Aldridge	DE	6'4"	245	28		
Marty Amsler	DE	6'5"	255	27		
Bob Brown	DE	6'5"	260	30		
Clarence Williams	DE	6'5"	255	23		
Kevin Hardy	DT	6'5"	260	25		
Mike McCoy	DT	6'5"	284	21		
Rich Moore	DT	6'6"	285	23		
Fred Carr	LB	6'5"	238	24	2	
Jim Carter	LB	6'3"	235	21		
Jim Flanigan	LB	6'3"	240	25		
Rudy Kuechenberg	LB	6'2"	215	27		
Ray Nitschke	LB	6'3"	235	34		
Dave Robinson	LB	6'3"	240	29	2	
Cleo Walker	C-LB	6'3"	220	22		
Ken Ellis	DB	5'10"	190	22	3	
Lee Harden	DB	5'11"	195	23		
Doug Hart	DB	6'	190	31	3	6
Ervin Hunt	DB	6'2"	190	23		
Bob Jeter	DB	6'1"	205	32	3	
Al Matthews	DB	5'11"	190	22		
Willie Wood	DB	5'10"	190	34	7	
Don Horn	QB	6'2"	195	25		
Rick Norton	QB	6'1"	190	26		
Frank Patrick	QB	6'7"	225	23		
Bart Starr	QB	6'1"	190	37		6
Donny Anderson	HB	6'3"	210	27		30
Larry Krause	HB	6'	208	22		6
Travis Williams	HB	6'1"	210	24		12
Jim Grabowski	FB	6'2"	220	26		6
Perry Williams	FB	6'2"	220	23		
Dave Hampton	HB-FB	6'	210	23		6
Mike Carter	WR	6'1"	210	22		
Jack Clancy	WR	6'1"	195	26		12
Carroll Dale	WR	6'1"	200	32		12
John Spilis	WR	6'3"	205	22		
John Hilton	TE	6'5"	225	28		24
Rich McGeorge	TE	6'4"	235	21		12
Dale Livingston	K	6'	210	25		64

Zeke Bratkowski – Voluntarily Retired
Boyd Dowler – Voluntarily Retired

MINNESOTA VIKINGS

RUSHING

Last Name	No.	Yds	Avg	TD
Osborn	207	681	3.3	5
Jones	120	369	3.1	9
Brown	101	324	3.2	0
Reed	42	132	3.1	1
Cuozzo	17	61	3.6	0
Lindsey	11	47	4.3	0
Lee	10	20	2.0	1

RECEIVING

Last Name	No.	Yds	Avg	TD
Washington	44	702	16	4
Henderson	31	527	17	2
Grim	23	287	12	0
Osborn	23	202	9	1
Beasley	17	237	14	2
Brown	15	149	10	2
Jones	9	117	13	0
Reed	6	53	9	0
Lindsey	4	94	24	1
Kramer	1	10	10	0

PUNT RETURNS

Last Name	No.	Yds	Avg	TD
West	29	169	6	0
Grim	5	46	9	0
Dickson	1	1	1	0

KICKOFF RETURNS

Last Name	No.	Yds	Avg	TD
Jones	19	452	24	0
West	11	319	29	0
Reed	5	71	14	0
Smith	1	0	0	0

PASSING – PUNTING – KICKING

PASSING	Att	Comp	%	Yds	Yd/Att	TD	Int–	%	RK
Cuozzo	257	128	50	1720	6.7	7	10–	4	9
Lee	79	40	51	610	7.7	5	5–	6	
Cappleman	7	4	57	49	7.0	0	0–	0	
Cox	1	1	100	–1	–1.0	0	0–	0	

PUNTING	No	Avg
McNeill	61	37.9

KICKING	XP	Att	%	FG	Att	%
Cox	35	35	100	30	46	65

DETROIT LIONS

RUSHING

Last Name	No.	Yds	Avg	TD
Farr	166	717	4.3	9
Taylor	198	666	3.4	2
Landry	35	350	10.0	1
Triplett	48	156	3.3	1
Owens	36	122	3.4	2
Eddy	18	47	2.6	1
Munson	9	33	3.7	0
L. Walton	2	20	10.0	0
Maxwell	1	9	9.0	0
McCullouch	1	7	7.0	0

RECEIVING

Last Name	No.	Yds	Avg	TD
Sanders	40	544	14	6
L. Walton	30	532	18	5
Farr	29	213	7	2
Taylor	27	261	10	2
McCullouch	15	278	19	4
Hughes	8	162	20	0
Triplett	6	52	9	0
Eddy	4	22	6	0
Owens	4	21	5	0
Brown	2	38	19	0
Cotton	1	6	6	0
Freitas	1	–8	–8	0

PUNT RETURNS

Last Name	No.	Yds	Avg	TD
Barney	25	259	10	1
Eddy	4	25	6	0
Vaughn	3	22	7	0
L. Walton	2	0	0	0

KICKOFF RETURNS

Last Name	No.	Yds	Avg	TD
Williams	25	544	22	1
Eddy	7	168	24	0
Barney	2	96	48	0
Vaughn	3	66	22	0
Owens	1	26	26	0
L. Walton	1	21	21	0
Maxwell	1	20	20	0
Mooney	1	12	12	0
Naumoff	2	6	3	0

PASSING – PUNTING – KICKING

PASSING	Att	Comp	%	Yds	Yd/Att	TD	Int–	%	RK
Munson	158	84	53	1049	6.6	10	7–	4	8
Landry	136	83	61	1072	7.9	9	5–	4	

PUNTING	No	Avg
Weaver	62	40.0

KICKING	XP	Att	%	FG	Att	%
Mann	41	41	100	20	29	69

CHICAGO BEARS

RUSHING

Last Name	No.	Yds	Avg	TD
Montgomery	62	229	3.7	0
Shy	79	227	2.9	1
Bull	68	214	3.1	0
Concannon	42	136	3.2	2
Hull	32	99	3.1	0
Baynham	26	68	2.6	0
Sayers	23	52	2.3	0
Kurek	6	24	4.0	0
Douglass	7	22	3.1	0
Gordon	4	17	4.3	0
Green	1	7	7.0	0
Turner	3	–3	–1.0	0

RECEIVING

Last Name	No.	Yds	Avg	TD
Gordon	71	1026	14	13
Farmer	31	496	16	2
Wallace	15	160	11	0
Montgomery	14	75	5	0
Bull	13	60	5	0
Hull	13	44	3	0
Baynham	12	43	4	0
Shy	10	149	15	0
Hester	7	54	8	0
Seymour	6	145	24	4
Coady	6	44	7	1
Cole	3	47	16	0
Kurek	3	11	4	0
Turner	2	53	27	0
Percival	1	19	19	0
Ogden	1	6	6	1
Lyle	1	5	5	0
Sayers	1	–6	–6	0

PUNT RETURNS

Last Name	No.	Yds	Avg	TD
Smith	33	126	4	0
Cole	14	83	6	0
Lyle	9	37	4	0
Turner	1	0	0	0

KICKOFF RETURNS

Last Name	No.	Yds	Avg	TD
Turner	23	752	33	4
Smith	28	651	23	0
Montgomery	4	69	17	0
Butkus	1	0	0	0

PASSING – PUNTING – KICKING

PASSING	Att	Comp	%	Yds	Yd/Att	TD	Int–	%	RK
Concannon	385	194	50	2130	5.5	16	18–	5	9
Douglass	30	12	40	218	7.3	4	3–	10	
Bull	4	2	50	46	11.5	1	1–	25	
Green	2	2	100	37	18.5	0	0–	0	
Nix	1	0	0	0	0.0	0	0–	0	

PUNTING	No	Avg
Green	83	40.9
Lyle	1	29.0

KICKING	XP	Att	%	FG	Att	%
Percival	28	28	100	20	34	59

GREEN BAY PACKERS

RUSHING

Last Name	No.	Yds	Avg	TD
Anderson	222	853	3.8	5
T. Williams	74	276	3.7	1
Grabowski	67	210	3.1	1
Hampton	48	115	2.4	0
Starr	12	62	5.2	1
P. Williams	17	44	2.6	0
Krause	2	13	6.5	0
Dale	2	9	4.5	0
Patrick	2	5	2.5	0
Horn	5	4	0.8	0
McGeorge	1	3	3.0	0
Livingston	1	1	1.0	0

RECEIVING

Last Name	No.	Yds	Avg	TD
Dale	49	814	17	2
Anderson	36	414	12	0
Hilton	25	350	14	4
Grabowski	19	83	4	0
Clancy	16	244	15	2
T. Williams	12	127	11	1
Hampton	7	23	3	0
Spilis	6	76	13	0
P. Williams	3	11	4	0
McGeorge	2	32	16	2
Krause	2	22	11	0

PUNT RETURNS

Last Name	No.	Yds	Avg	TD
Wood	11	58	5	0
Ellis	7	27	4	0
T. Williams	4	20	5	0
C. Williams	1	0	0	0
Harden	2	–7	–4	0

KICKOFF RETURNS

Last Name	No.	Yds	Avg	TD
Krause	18	513	29	1
Ellis	22	451	21	0
T. Williams	10	203	20	0
Hampton	6	188	31	1
McCoy	3	22	7	0
Gregg	2	21	11	0
P. Williams	1	20	20	0
Himes	1	4	4	0

PASSING – PUNTING – KICKING

PASSING	Att	Comp	%	Yds	Yd/Att	TD	Int–	%	RK
Starr	255	140	55	1645	6.5	3	13–	5	1
Horn	76	28	37	428	5.6	2	10–	13	
Patrick	14	6	43	59	4.2	0	1–	7	
Norton	5	3	60	64	12.8	1	0–	0	
Anderson	1	0	0	0	0.0	0	0–	0	

PUNTING	No	Avg
Anderson	81	40.8
Livingston	6	33.2

KICKING	XP	Att	%	FG	Att	%
Livingston	19	21	90	15	28	54

SAN FRANCISCO FORTY NINERS 10-3-1 Dick Nolan

Scores of Each Game		
26	WASHINGTON	17
34	CLEVELAND	31
20	Atlanta	21
20	Los Angeles	6
20	NEW ORLEANS	20
19	DENVER	14
26	GREEN BAY	10
37	Chicago	16
30	Houston	20
7	Detroit	28
13	LOS ANGELES	30
24	ATLANTA	20
38	New Orleans	27
38	Oakland	7

Use Name	Pos.	Hgt	Wgt	Age	Int	Pts
Cas Banaszek	OT	6'3"	250	24		
Len Rohde	OT	6'4"	250	32		
Randy Beisler	OG-OT	6'4"	255	25		
Elmer Collett	OG	6'4"	240	25		
Bob Hoskins	OG	6'2"	235	24		
Woody Peoples	OG	6'2"	247	27		
Forrest Blue	C	6'5"	260	24		
Bill Belk	DE	6'3"	254	24		
Cedrick Hardman	DE	6'3"	255	21		
Tommy Hart	DE	6'3"	250	25	1	
Stan Hindman	DE	6'3"	235	26		
Earl Edwards	DT	6'6"	265	24		
Charlie Krueger	DT	6'4"	270	34		
Roland Lakes	DT	6'4"	268	30		
Sam Silas	DE-DT	6'4"	255	27		

Use Name	Pos.	Hgt	Wgt	Age	Int	Pts
Ed Beard	LB	6'2"	220	30		
Carter Campbell	LB	6'3"	214	22		
Frank Nunley	LB	6'2"	230	24	3	
Jim Sniadecki	LB	6'2"	220	23		
Skip Vanderbundt	LB	6'3"	234	23	3	
Dave Wilcox	LB	6'3"	237	27	2	
Johnny Fuller	DB	6'	175	24	1	
Jim Johnson	DB	6'2"	184	32	2	8
Mel Phillips	DB	6'	192	28	3	6
Al Randolph	DB	6'2"	200	26	1	2
Mike Simpson	DB	5'11"	175	23		
Bruce Taylor	DB	6'	180	22	3	6
Rosey Taylor	DB	5'11"	186	31	3	

Use Name	Pos.	Hgt	Wgt	Age	Int	Pts
John Brodie	QB	6'1"	203	35		12
Steve Spurrier	QB	6'2"	203	25		
Doug Cunningham	HB	5'11"	190	24		18
John Isenbarger	HB	6'3"	205	22		6
Jim Strong	HB	6'1"	204	23		
Jimmy Thomas	WR-HB	6'1"	216	23		18
Ken Willard	FB	6'2"	225	27		60
Bill Tucker	HB-FB	6'2"	216	26		12
Lee Johnson	WR	6'1"	204	25		
Preston Riley	WR	6'	180	22		
Gene Washington	WR	6'1"	186	23		72
Dick Witcher	WR	6'3"	204	25		12
Ted Kwalick	TE	6'4"	230	23		6
Bob Windsor	TE	6'4"	230	27		12
Bruce Gossett	K	6'2"	225	27		102

LOS ANGELES RAMS 9-4-1 George Allen

Scores of Each Game		
34	ST. LOUIS	13
19	Buffalo	0
37	SAN DIEGO	10
6	SAN FRANCISCO	20
31	Green Bay	21
3	Minnesota	13
30	New Orleans	17
10	ATLANTA	10
20	N.Y. JETS	31
17	Atlanta	7
30	San Francisco	13
34	NEW ORLEANS	16
23	DETROIT	28
31	N.Y. Giants	3

Use Name	Pos.	Hgt	Wgt	Age	Int	Pts
Bob Brown	OT	6'4"	290	27		
Charley Cowan	OT	6'4"	265	32		
Mitch Johnson	OT	6'4"	250	28		
Tom Mack	OG	6'3"	250	26		
Joe Scibelli	OG	6'1"	255	31		
John Wilbur	OG	6'3"	240	27		
Ken Iman	C	6'1"	240	31		
George Burman	OG-C	6'3"	255	27		
Coy Bacon	DE	6'4"	270	28		6
Rick Cash	DE	6'5"	260	25		
Deacon Jones	DE	6'5"	250	31		
Clark Miller	DE	6'5"	246	31		
Dick Evey	DT	6'2"	245	29		
Merlin Olsen	DT	6'5"	270	29		
Diron Talbert	DT	6'5"	255	26		

Use Name	Pos.	Hgt	Wgt	Age	Int	Pts
Maxie Baughan	LB	6'1"	230	32	1	
Jack Pardee	LB	6'2"	225	34	1	
John Pergine	LB	6'1"	225	23		
Myron Pottios	LB	6'2"	232	30	2	
Jim Purnell	LB	6'2"	238	28		
Jack Reynolds	LB	6'1"	232	22		
Rich Saul	LB	6'3"	235	22		
Kermit Alexander	DB	5'11"	186	29	4	6
Alvin Haymond	DB	6'	194	28		6
Ed Meador	DB	5'11"	190	33	2	
Jim Nettles	DB	5'9"	177	28	3	
Richie Petitbon	DB	6'3"	208	32	1	
Nate Shaw	DB	6'2"	205	25		
Clancy Williams	DB	6'2"	194	27	5	6

Doug Woodlief — Injury
Jim Wilson — Injury

Use Name	Pos.	Hgt	Wgt	Age	Int	Pts
Roman Gabriel	QB	6'4"	220	30		6
Karl Sweetan	QB	6'1"	205	27		
Willie Ellison	HB	6'1"	200	25		42
Larry Smith	HB	6'3"	220	22		12
Tommy Mason	FB-HB	6'	195	31		6
Pat Curran	FB	6'3"	238	24		6
Les Josephson	FB	6'	207	27		30
Jeff Jordan	HB-FB	6'1"	215	25		
Bob Long	WR	6'3"	205	29		6
David Ray	WR	6'	195	25		121
Jack Snow	WR	6'2"	190	27		42
Pat Studstill	WR	6'1"	175	32		12
Wendell Tucker	WR	5'10"	185	26		
Donnie Williams	WR	6'3"	210	22		
Bob Klein	TE	6'5"	235	23		
Billy Truax	TE	6'5"	235	27		18

ATLANTA FALCONS 4-8-2 Norm Van Brocklin

Scores of Each Game		
14	New Orleans	3
24	Green Bay	27
21	SAN FRANCISCO	20
0	Dallas	13
10	Denver	24
32	NEW ORLEANS	14
14	CHICAGO	23
10	Los Angeles	10
13	Philadelphia	13
7	LOS ANGELES	17
7	MIAMI	20
20	San Francisco	24
27	PITTSBURGH	16
7	MINNESOTA	37

Use Name	Pos.	Hgt	Wgt	Age	Int	Pts
Dave Hettema	OT	6'4"	250	28		
George Kunz	OT	6'5"	245	23		
Bill Sandeman	OT	6'6"	260	27		
Mal Snider	OT	6'4"	250	23		
Dick Enderle	OG	6'1"	258	22		
Andy Mauer	OG	6'3"	257	21		
Gary Roberts	OG	6'2"	242	23		
Bob Breitenstein	OT-OG	6'3"	267	27		
John Matlock	C	6'4"	250	25		
Jeff Van Note	C	6'2"	244	24		
Claude Humphrey	DE	6'5"	244	26	1	
Randy Marshall	DE	6'5"	237	23		6
John Zook	DE	6'5"	240	22	1	
Glen Condren	DT	6'2"	247	28		
Greg Lens	DT	6'5"	260	25		
Jim Sullivan	DE-DT	6'4"	240	26		

Greg Brezina — Injury

Use Name	Pos.	Hgt	Wgt	Age	Int	Pts
Ron Acks	LB	6'2"	225	25		
Grady Allen	LB	6'3"	230	24	1	
Ted Cottrell	LB	6'1"	233	23		
Dean Halverson	LB	6'2"	220	24		
Don Hansen	LB	6'3"	220	26	1	
Tommy Nobis	LB	6'2"	237	26	2	
John Small	LB	6'5"	254	23		
Grady Cavness	DB	5'11"	192	23		
Mike Freeman	DB	5'11"	180	26	1	
Al Lavan	DB	6'1"	194	23	3	
John Mallory	DB	6'	198	24	1	12
Tom McCauley	DB	6'3"	184	23	1	6
Ken Reaves	DB	6'3"	202	25	6	
Rudy Redmond	DB	6'	190	23	1	

Carlton Dabney — Back Injury
Randy Winkler — Military Service

Use Name	Pos.	Hgt	Wgt	Age	Int	Pts
Bob Berry	QB	5'11"	190	28		
Randy Johnson	QB	6'3"	210	26		
Cannonball Butler	HB	5'10"	195	27		6
Sonny Campbell	HB	5'11"	192	22		12
Paul Gipson	FB-HB	6'	205	24		18
Harmon Wages	FB	6'1"	215	24		18
Art Malone	HB-FB	5'11"	209	22		6
Mike Brunson	WR	6'1"	187	23		
Gail Cogdill	WR	6'2"	200	33		6
Paul Flatley	WR	6'1"	190	29		6
Kent Lawrence	WR	5'11"	175	23		
Todd Snyder	WR	6'2"	184	21		12
Mike Donohoe	TE	6'3"	227	25		6
Jim Mitchell	TE	6'2"	235	22		42
Billy Lothridge	K	6'1"	190	26		
Kenny Vinyard	K	5'10"	190	23		50

NEW ORLEANS SAINTS 2-11-1 Tom Fears J. D. Roberts

Scores of Each Game		
3	ATLANTA	14
0	Minnesota	26
14	N.Y. GIANTS	10
17	St. Louis	24
20	San Francisco	20
14	Atlanta	32
17	LOS ANGELES	30
19	DETROIT	17
10	Miami	21
6	DENVER	31
6	Cincinnati	26
16	Los Angeles	34
27	SAN FRANCISCO	38
3	CHICAGO	24

Use Name	Pos.	Hgt	Wgt	Age	Int	Pts
Errol Linden	OT	6'5"	250	33		
Mike Richey	OT	6'5"	263	23		
Don Talbert	OT	6'5"	255	30		
Mike Taylor	OT	6'4"	245	25		
Jake Kupp	OG	6'3"	248	28		
John Shinners	OG	6'2"	254	23		
Doug Sutherland	OG	6'3"	250	22		
Jerry Sturm	C-OT-OG	6'3"	265	33		
Del Williams	C	6'2"	240	24		
Larry Estes	DE	6'6"	260	23		
Dave Long	DE	6'4"	245	25		
Richard Neal	DE	6'3"	254	22		
Willie Townes	DT-DE	6'5"	265	27		
Dave Rowe	DT	6'6"	280	25		
Clovis Swinney	DT	6'3"	240	25		
Mike Tilleman	DT	6'5"	280	26		

Use Name	Pos.	Hgt	Wgt	Age	Int	Pts
Dick Absher	LB	6'4"	235	26		
Johnny Brewer	LB	6'4"	235	33		
Jackie Burkett	LB	6'4"	228	33	4	
Bill Cody	LB	6'1"	230	26		
Wayne Colman	LB	6'1"	230	24		
Frank Emanuel	LB	6'3"	225	27		
Hap Farber (from MIN)	LB	6'1"	220	22		
Harry Jacobs	LB	6'2"	226	33		
Mike Morgan	LB	6'4"	242	28	1	6
Major Hazelton	DB	6'1"	185	25		
Hugo Hollas	DB	6'1"	190	25	5	
Gene Howard	DB	6'	190	23		
Delles Howell	DB	6'3"	195	23	3	
Dicky Lyons	DB	6'	190	23	1	
Elijah Nevett	DB	6'	185	26	3	
Joe Scarpati	DB	5'10"	185	28	1	
Doug Wyatt	DB	6'1"	195	23	4	

Mike Rengel — Injury

Use Name	Pos.	Hgt	Wgt	Age	Int	Pts
Edd Hargett	QB	5'11"	185	23		
Billy Kilmer	QB	6'	204	30		
Steve Ramsey	QB	6'2"	210	22		
Bill Dusenbery	HB	6'2"	198	21		
Don McCall	HB	5'11"	195	25		6
Vic Nyvall	HB	5'10"	185	22		
Elijah Pitts (from LA)	HB	6'1"	205	31		
Tony Baker	FB-HB	5'11"	225	25		6
Tom Barrington	FB-HB	6'1"	213	26		12
Dick Davis (from DEN)	FB-HB	5'11"	215	23		
Earl Gros	FB	6'3"	220	29		
Andy Livingston	FB	6'	235	25		
Jim Otis	FB	6'	220	22		
Ernie Wheelwright	FB	6'3"	235	33		
Gary Lewis	HB-FB	6'3"	230	28		
Dan Abramowicz	WR	6'1"	195	25		30
Ken Burrough	WR	6'4"	212	22		12
Al Dodd	WR	6'	180	25		12
Bob Shaw	WR	6'	194	21		
Dave Parks	TE	6'2"	203	28		12
Ray Poage	TE	6'4"	215	29		6
Tom Dempsey	K	6'1"	264	29		70
Julian Fagan	K	6'3"	205	22		

SAN FRANCISCO FORTY NINERS

RUSHING

Last Name	No.	Yds	Avg	TD
Willard	236	789	3.3	7
Cunningham	128	443	3.5	3
Tucker	42	137	3.3	1
Thomas	31	89	2.9	0
Kwalick	3	65	21.7	0
Isenbarger	18	43	2.4	0
Brodie	9	29	3.2	2
Strong	2	3	1.5	0
Spurrier	2	−18	−9.0	0

RECEIVING

Last Name	No.	Yds	Avg	TD
Washington	53	1100	21	12
Cunningham	35	209	6	0
Windsor	31	363	12	2
Willard	31	259	8	3
Witcher	22	288	13	2
Tucker	17	108	6	1
Thomas	12	221	18	3
Kwalick	10	148	15	1
Isenbarger	8	158	20	1
Riley	7	136	19	0

PUNT RETURNS

Last Name	No.	Yds	Avg	TD
B. Taylor	43	516	12	0
Fuller	4	29	7	0
Riley	1	5	5	0

KICKOFF RETURNS

Last Name	No.	Yds	Avg	TD
Tucker	25	577	23	0
B. Taylor	12	190	16	0
Thomas	6	177	30	0
Beard	2	8	4	0
Fuller	1	8	8	0
Belk	1	7	7	0
Riley	1	0	0	0
Windsor	1	0	0	0

PASSING – PUNTING – KICKING

PASSING	Att	Comp	%	Yds	Yd/Att	TD	Int–	%	RK
Brodie	378	223	59	2941	7.8	24	10–	3	1
Spurrier	4	3	75	49	12.3	1	0–	0	
Isenbarger	1	0	0	0	0.0	0	0–	0	

PUNTING	No	Avg
Spurrier	75	38.4

KICKING	XP	Att	%	FG	Att	%
Gossett	39	41	95	21	31	68

LOS ANGELES RAMS

RUSHING

Last Name	No.	Yds	Avg	TD
Josephson	150	640	4.3	5
Ellison	90	381	4.2	5
Smith	77	338	4.4	1
Mason	44	123	2.8	0
Gabriel	28	104	3.7	1
Curran	25	92	3.7	0
Jordan	10	50	5.0	0
Studstill	1	23	23.0	0
Petitbon	1	3	3.0	0
Johnson	1	1	1.0	0

RECEIVING

Last Name	No.	Yds	Avg	TD
Snow	51	859	17	7
Josephson	44	427	10	0
Truax	36	420	12	3
Smith	24	164	7	1
Studstill	18	252	14	2
Tucker	12	230	19	0
Mason	12	127	11	1
Ellison	10	84	8	2
Long	3	35	12	1
Curran	3	25	8	0
Klein	2	20	10	0
Ray	1	11	11	0
D. Williams	1	9	9	0
Jordan	1	−5	−5	0

PUNT RETURNS

Last Name	No.	Yds	Avg	TD
Haymond	53	376	7	0
Alexander	7	38	5	0
Nettles	2	4	2	0

KICKOFF RETURNS

Last Name	No.	Yds	Avg	TD
Haymond	35	1022	29	1
Alexander	7	126	18	0
Curran	3	51	17	0
Ellison	1	20	20	0
Johnson	1	17	17	0

PASSING – PUNTING – KICKING

PASSING	Att	Comp	%	Yds	Yd/Att	TD	Int–	%	RK
Gabriel	407	211	52	2552	6.3	16	12–	3	6
Sweetan	13	6	46	81	6.2	1	0–	0	
Curran	2	0	0	0	0.0	0	1–	50	
Smith	2	0	0	0	0.0	0	0–	0	
Josephson	1	1	100	25	25.0	0	0–	0	
Studstill	1	0	0	0	0.0	0	0–	0	

PUNTING	No	Avg
Studstill	67	39.1

KICKING	XP	Att	%	FG	Att	%
Ray	34	34	100	29	45	64

ATLANTA FALCONS

RUSHING

Last Name	No.	Yds	Avg	TD
Butler	166	636	3.8	0
Wages	119	422	3.5	1
Gipson	52	177	3.4	0
Malone	40	136	3.4	0
Campbell	28	116	4.1	2
Berry	13	60	4.6	0
Mitchell	5	23	4.6	1
Johnson	7	21	3.0	0
Brunson	1	9	9.0	0

RECEIVING

Last Name	No.	Yds	Avg	TD
Mitchell	44	650	15	6
Flatley	39	544	14	1
Wages	26	153	6	2
Butler	24	151	6	1
Snyder	23	311	14	2
Gipson	16	186	12	3
Malone	9	38	4	1
Cogdill	7	101	14	1
Campbell	7	92	13	0
Donohoe	2	36	18	1

PUNT RETURNS

Last Name	No.	Yds	Avg	TD
Mallory	17	203	12	1
McCauley	14	138	10	1
Freeman	3	15	5	0

KICKOFF RETURNS

Last Name	No.	Yds	Avg	TD
Butler	14	284	20	0
Campbell	10	230	23	0
Gipson	8	189	24	0
Malone	5	66	13	0
Cavness	3	61	20	0
Brunson	4	54	14	0
Wages	1	22	22	0
Lavan	1	10	10	0
Freeman	1	0	0	0

PASSING – PUNTING – KICKING

PASSING	Att	Comp	%	Yds	Yd/Att	TD	Int–	%	RK
Berry	269	156	58	1806	6.7	16	13–	5	4
Johnson	72	40	56	443	6.2	2	8–	11	
Wages	1	1	100	13	13.0	0	0–	0	

PUNTING	No	Avg
Lothridge	76	38.7

KICKING	XP	Att	%	FG	Att	%
Vinyard	23	26	88	9	25	36

NEW ORLEANS SAINTS

RUSHING

Last Name	No.	Yds	Avg	TD
Baker	82	337	4.1	1
Barrington	72	228	3.2	2
Otis	71	211	3.0	0
Pitts	35	104	3.0	0
Davis	27	94	3.5	0
McCall	23	63	2.7	1
Wheelwright	16	45	2.8	0
Kilmer	12	42	3.5	0
Dodd	5	31	6.2	0
Livingston	10	29	2.9	0
Poage	1	13	13.0	0
Abramowicz	1	7	7.0	0
Hargett	4	7	1.8	0
Dusenbery	4	6	1.5	0
Nyvall	5	6	1.2	0
Burrough	1	4	4.0	0
Gros	4	2	0.5	0
Fagan	1	−6	−6.0	0

RECEIVING

Last Name	No.	Yds	Avg	TD
Abramowicz	55	906	16	5
Dodd	28	484	17	1
Parks	26	447	17	2
Barrington	22	130	6	0
Otis	20	124	6	0
Poage	15	166	11	1
Burrough	13	196	15	2
Baker	12	47	4	0
Pitts	7	63	9	0
McCall	5	43	9	0
Davis	4	29	7	0
Gros	2	0	0	0
Nyvall	2	−1	−1	0
Shaw	1	49	49	0
Wheelwright	1	7	7	0

PUNT RETURNS

Last Name	No.	Yds	Avg	TD
Dodd	14	129	9	0
Lyons	5	34	7	0
Hollas	4	22	6	0
Wyatt	1	15	15	0
Howard	5	14	3	0

KICKOFF RETURNS

Last Name	No.	Yds	Avg	TD
Dodd	15	319	21	0
Burrough	15	298	20	0
Dusenbery	10	183	18	0
Barrington	6	129	22	0
McCall	1	26	26	0
Otis	2	22	11	0
Pitts	1	22	22	0
Lyons	1	20	20	0
Lewis	1	19	19	0
Poage	1	6	6	0

PASSING – PUNTING – KICKING

PASSING	Att	Comp	%	Yds	Yd/Att	TD	Int–	%	RK
Kilmer	237	135	57	1557	6.6	6	17–	7	12
Hargett	175	78	45	1133	6.5	5	5–	3	12
Ramsey	2	0	0	0	0.0	0	0–	0	
Dodd	1	0	0	0	0.0	0	0–	0	

PUNTING	No	Avg
Fagan	77	42.5

KICKING	XP	Att	%	FG	Att	%
Dempsey	16	17	94	18	34	53

1970 A.F.C. New League, Old Faces

In their first season in the NFL, the old AFL clubs found things rougher than they expected. In interconference games, the NFC came out on top in two thirds of them. An AFC team did win the Super Bowl, but that was the Baltimore Colts, an old-line NFL club which had moved over to the AFC this season along with Cleveland and Pittsburgh. Nevertheless, the ten clubs which had made up the AFL placed a good share of players on all All-Pro teams, and the two expansion teams which came out of the AFL gave good reason for the former members to be proud. The Miami Dolphins and Cincinnati Bengals, both created in the mid 1960s, each made the playoffs. The Atlanta Falcons and New Orleans Saints, NFL expansion teams from the same period, came nowhere near matching the record of these two.

EASTERN DIVISION

Baltimore Colts—Soft-Spoken Don McCafferty took over as head coach after Don Shula quit to go to Miami, and the Colts rewarded him with a championship in his first season on the job. The Baltimore offense scored the most points in the conference, yet went through some mid-season changes. John Williams moved into the starting lineup at guard after an embarrassing 44-24 loss to Kansas City, hustling Tom Nowatzke filled in as running back when injuries kayoed Tom Matte, and oldsters Johnny Unitas and Earl Morrall occasionally relieved each other at quarterback. The defense, however, was a picture of stability, with stars Bubba Smith, Mike Curtis, Ted Hendricks, Rick Volk, and Jerry Logan leading a quick and mobile unit.

Miami Dolphins—The Dolphins had to pay highly to get Don Shula, including a first-draft choice which went to Baltimore as compensation, but the results proved the new coach's worth. Under Shula's direction, Bob Griese matured as a quarterback, Larry Csonka, Jim Kiick, and Mercury Morris developed into top runners, and the offensive line meshed into a fine unit, with Larry Little blossoming into a star. On defense, however, Shula did his best job, turning an indifferent unit into the conference's best. Five rookies started on defense, Mike Kolen, Doug Swift, Tim Foley, Curtis Johnson, and Jake Scott. The veteran pillars on the platoon were Manny Fernandez, Nick Buoniconti, and Dick Anderson.

New York Jets—Injuries destroyed the Jets' chances of defending their divisional title. Joe Namath's broken wrist robbed the offense of its leader, and a torn Achilles tendon took fullback Matt Snell out of the lineup just when he was running better than at any time in his career. Emerson Boozer, Don Maynard, and Roger Finnie also missed a lot of time in sick bay, forcing wholesale replacements on the offensive unit. Although Al Woodall, George Nock, and Rich Caster were capable substitutes, they could not replace the firepower lost in Namath, Snell, and Maynard. Injuries also hurt the defense, with Steve Thompson and Jim Hudson the major casualties, but that unit held together well and kept the Jets respectable in their worst moments.

Buffalo Bills—Rookie Dennis Shaw won the starting quarterback job and showed the potential to become a fine passer, while receiver Marlin Briscoe caught enough Shaw passes to lead the league in receiving. On the defensive unit, Al Cowlings, Edgar Chandler, and Bobby James showed talent and enthusiasm to make up for their inexperience. Unfortunate events of the year included O. J. Simpson's knee injury which sidelined him for the second half of the season, Mike Stratton's Achilles tendon injury, and Wayne Patrick's separated shoulder.

Boston Patriots—The Patriots shelled out a bundle to pick up quarterback Joe Kapp from Minnesota in mid-season, but Kapp was out of shape and unfamiliar with the Boston system; the result was a season in which he threw three touchdown passes and seventeen interceptions. Kapp's poor season fit in well with the entire situation on the Patriots. Running backs Jim Nance and Carl Garrett seemed apathetic at times, Gino Cappelletti continued to regress as a place kicker, the offensive line never lived up to its potential, and the defense lost Jim Cheyunski and rookie Phil Olsen to injuries. By mid-season, John Mazur had replaced Clive Rush as head coach.

CENTRAL DIVISION

Cincinnati Bengals—Even with quarterback Greg Cook out of action with a bad shoulder, the Bengals still stormed into the playoffs and delighted coach 'Paul Brown by beating the Browns out for first place in the Central Division. The Cincinnati defense had been strengthened by rookies Mike Reid, Ron Carpenter, and Lemar Parrish, but the offense started out slowly under new quarterback Virgil Carter. After losing six of their first seven games, the Bengals suddenly jelled; they beat Buffalo, Cleveland, Pittsburgh, and their other four remaining opponents to streak past the rival Browns from upstate. Starring along the way were runners Jess Phillips and Paul Robinson, receiver Chip Myers, center Bob Johnson, kicker Horst Muhlmann, linebacker Bill Bergey, and rookies Reid, Carpenter, and Parrish.

Cleveland Browns—Aside from Leroy Kelly's bad season and a chaotic linebacking situation, two off-season trades contributed the most to Cleveland's slump this year. With Bill Nelsen's bad knees making him a constant question mark, the Browns traded star receiver Paul Warfield to Miami for their first-draft pick, which Cleveland used to take Purdue quarterback Mike Phipps. Then the Browns shipped Ron Johnson, Jim Kanicki, and Wayne Meylan to New York for receiver Homer Jones. While Warfield and Johnson starred in their new surroundings, Phipps showed that he needed plenty more seasoning and Jones failed to even win a starting job.

Pittsburgh Steelers—Even with Terry Bradshaw not delivering as expected, the Steelers did make a mid-season run at the Central Division crown before slumping off into five losses in their last six games. The big improvement in the Steelers came on defense, where Mean Joe Greene and Andy Russell stood out on a unit with eleven solid starters. Less impressive was the offense, where coach Chuck Noll fielded a complete new set of runners and receivers to go with his rookie quarterback.

Houston Oilers—Coach Wally Lemm announced before the season that this was his final year with the Oilers, but his team gave him very little in the way of a going-away gift, as they dropped into last place in the AFC Central Division. Injuries hurt the team, as quarterback Charley Johnson, newly acquired from St. Louis, linebacker George Webster, guard Tom Regner, and fullback Hoyle Granger all suffered disabling wounds. But even without the injuries, the Oilers had too few good players to challenge seriously for the title in their weak division.

WESTERN DIVISION

Oakland Raiders—Old George Blanda, playing his twenty-first season of pro football, made a specialty out of pulling games out of the fire at the last second as he saved five games in a row with late heroics. He filled in for the injured Daryle Lamonica and threw a pair of touchdown passes to beat Pittsburgh 31-14, he kicked a 48-yard field goal with three seconds left to tie Kansas City 17-17, he kicked a 52-yarder to beat Cleveland 23-20 in the last three seconds, he came off the bench to drive the Raiders to the winning touchdown in a 24-19 victory over Denver, and he kicked a field goal with four seconds left to beat San Diego 20-17—all of which helped Oakland to take first place in the West.

Kansas City Chiefs—The spark which had moved the club last year was missing, especially on offense; the Kansas City attack virtually ignored long-gaining plays and confined itself to short passes and inside running plays. The overconservative offense wasted the talents of Otis Taylor, who scored only three touchdowns all year, and Ed Podolak, who scored only four times after breaking into the starting lineup. Coach Hank Stram made only two substitutions in last year's lineup, replacing Mike Garrett at halfback with Podolak and promoting Jack Rudnay to starting center over sore-kneed E. J. Holub.

San Diego Chargers—With a flabby pass rush and a secondary that picked off only five enemy passes all year, the defense gave head coach Charlie Walker his biggest headache in his first full season on the job. The front four contained heralded ex-collegians in Steve DeLong, Ron Billingsley, and Gene Ferguson, but the best work came from unknown rookie Joe Owens. While Pete Barnes and Bob Babich solidified the linebacking, the secondary of Bob Howard, Joe Beauchamp, Jim Hill, and Jim Tolbert was remarkably undistinguished. Injuries to Dickie Post and Brad Hubbert hurt the running attack, but a strong passing game kept the offense in business.

Denver Broncos—The Broncos charged out of the starting gate with a 4-1 record, but problems at quarterback eventually caught up with the team. Steve Tensi missed most of the campaign with injuries and Pete Liske played quarterback most of the way. Although Liske had leadership ability and skill at reading defenses, the ex-Canadian League star did not have a strong enough arm to hold the job. By the end of the year, coach Lou Saban was playing rookie Al Pastrana at the spot with dismal results. The high point of the season for Saban was the development of Floyd Little into an All-Pro workhorse runner and the good showing of rookie Bobby Anderson.

FINAL TEAM STATISTICS

OFFENSE

	BALT.	BOS.	BUFF.	CIN.	CLEV.	DENV.	HOUS.	K.C.	MIAMI	N.Y.J.	OAK.	PITT.	S.D.
FIRST DOWNS:													
Total	242	184	203	210	239	217	232	183	228	230	270	206	231
by Rushing	70	63	71	100	87	84	88	83	106	90	107	84	83
by Passing	148	98	120	97	134	112	126	86	100	122	139	97	119
by Penalty	24	23	12	13	18	21	18	14	22	18	24	25	29
RUSHING:													
Number	411	334	367	461	462	436	419	448	492	463	471	432	395
Yards	1336	1040	1465	2057	1579	1802	1556	1858	2082	1653	1964	1715	1450
Average Yards	3.3	3.1	4.0	4.5	3.4	4.1	3.7	4.1	4.2	3.6	4.2	4.0	3.7
Touchdowns	9	11	8	16	14	17	10	11	14	11	7	13	9
PASSING:													
Attempts	416	392	402	339	392	403	470	289	299	386	418	384	387
Completions	219	176	213	172	190	183	238	154	159	193	210	150	192
Completion Percentage	52.6	44.9	53.0	50.7	48.5	45.4	50.6	53.3	53.2	50.0	50.2	39.1	49.6
Passing Yards	3087	1975	2916	2097	2752	2358	2768	2038	2284	2592	3029	2312	2936
Avg. Yards per Attempt	7.4	5.0	7.3	6.2	7.0	5.9	5.9	7.1	7.6	6.7	7.2	6.0	7.6
Avg. Yards per Complet.	14.1	11.2	13.7	12.2	14.5	12.9	11.6	13.2	14.4	13.4	14.4	15.4	15.3
Times Tackled Passing	33	42	53	31	16	44	33	38	36	35	19	28	57
Yards Lost Tackled	289	389	486	227	170	333	262	319	327	285	164	275	433
Net Yards	2798	1586	2430	1870	2582	2025	2506	1719	1957	2307	2865	2037	2503
Touchdowns	23	7	13	12	17	11	12	13	15	14	28	12	24
Interceptions	22	28	26	11	24	28	23	16	19	22	21	32	19
Percent Intercepted	5.3	7.1	6.5	3.2	6.1	6.9	4.9	5.5	6.4	5.7	5.0	8.3	4.9
PUNTS:													
Number	63	86	83	79	71	87	84	76	58	73	79	78	74
Average Distance	44.7	39.1	38.9	46.2	42.6	42.9	42.4	44.9	41.2	40.1	39.5	44.2	42.8
PUNT RETURNS:													
Number	36	32	45	37	34	63	41	31	30	26	37	51	31
Yards	351	305	298	327	236	556	257	371	295	150	308	281	173
Average Yards	9.8	9.5	6.6	8.8	6.9	8.8	6.3	12.0	9.8	5.8	8.3	5.5	5.6
Touchdowns	1	0	0	1	0	0	0	0	1	0	1	0	0
KICKOFF RETURNS:													
Number	45	62	62	39	44	49	55	44	48	56	44	40	42
Yards	1161	1275	1244	1002	1001	1114	1168	997	1036	1106	1017	997	813
Average Yards	25.8	20.6	20.1	25.7	22.8	22.7	21.2	22.7	21.6	19.8	23.1	24.9	19.4
Touchdowns	1	0	2	1	1	0	0	0	1	0	0	0	0
INTERCEPTION RETURNS:													
Number	25	8	11	23	19	16	18	31	23	23	19	23	9
Yards	408	184	179	180	324	220	242	395	414	281	112	266	90
Average Yards	16.3	23.0	16.3	7.8	17.1	13.8	13.4	12.7	18.0	12.2	5.9	11.6	10.0
Touchdowns	3	0	2	0	3	0	0	1	1	2	0	1	0
PENALTIES:													
Number	71	88	99	71	65	94	78	83	77	88	92	82	79
Yards	708	849	1108	831	634	887	833	888	834	1022	1021	835	852
FUMBLES:													
Number	25	18	37	22	24	23	26	26	24	20	21	30	19
Number Lost	14	13	26	12	14	13	15	15	11	11	9	16	6
POINTS:													
Total	321	149	204	312	286	253	217	272	297	255	300	210	282
PAT Attempts	38	18	25	34	35	28	23	26	33	28	36	26	35
PAT Made	36	17	24	33	34	27	23	26	33	28	36	24	34
FG Attempts	34	22	19	37	22	32	32	42	30	35	29	28	19
FG Made	19	8	10	25	12	18	18	30	22	19	16	10	12
Percent FG Made	55.9	36.4	52.6	67.6	54.5	56.3	56.3	71.4	73.3	54.3	55.2	35.7	63.2
Safeties	0	0	0	0	3	2	1	0	0	1	0	0	1

DEFENSE

	BALT.	BOS.	BUFF.	CIN.	CLEVE	DENV.	HOUS.	K.C.	MIAMI	N.Y.J.	OAK.	PITT.	S.D.
FIRST DOWNS:													
Total	214	242	213	236	236	199	227	226	226	216	223	225	245
by Rushing	79	115	87	87	104	67	85	83	82	65	90	91	106
by Passing	120	105	103	131	120	118	115	111	128	122	104	120	117
by Penalty	15	22	23	18	12	14	27	32	16	29	29	14	22
RUSHING:													
Number	390	503	484	418	451	409	466	418	387	408	460	487	480
Yards	1439	2074	1718	1543	2006	1351	1793	1657	1453	1283	2027	1679	1967
Average Yards	3.7	4.1	3.5	3.7	4.4	3.3	3.8	4.0	3.8	3.1	4.4	3.4	4.1
Touchdowns	6	20	16	11	10	7	16	10	8	7	10	8	15
PASSING:													
Attempts	452	334	338	428	357	379	344	408	403	383	339	393	365
Completions	238	177	157	209	186	191	164	195	234	165	157	191	207
Completion Percentage	52.7	53.0	46.4	48.8	52.1	50.4	47.7	47.8	58.1	43.1	46.3	48.6	56.7
Passing Yards	2780	2430	2334	2885	2528	2810	2851	2280	2708	2680	2386	2555	2422
Avg. Yards per Attempt	6.2	7.3	6.9	6.7	7.1	7.4	8.3	5.6	6.7	7.0	7.0	6.5	6.6
Avg. Yards per Complet.	11.7	13.7	14.9	13.8	13.6	14.7	17.4	11.7	11.6	16.2	15.2	13.4	11.7
Times Tackled Passing	41	28	31	28	34	50	30	35	18	35	39	26	27
Yards Lost Tackled	374	243	246	250	290	456	246	270	157	308	297	238	207
Net Yards	2406	2187	2088	2635	2238	2354	2605	2010	2551	2372	2089	2317	2215
Touchdowns	16	19	15	18	16	20	25	15	17	20	22	21	13
Interceptions	25	8	11	23	19	16	18	31	23	23	19	23	9
Percent Intercepted	5.5	2.4	3.3	5.4	5.3	4.2	5.2	7.6	5.7	6.0	5.6	5.9	2.5
PUNTS:													
Number	78	63	76	80	66	89	77	79	63	68	80	85	64
Average Distance	38.4	43.8	44.0	43.8	42.4	44.9	44.4	43.4	41.7	38.9	41.6	41.9	44.1
PUNT RETURNS:													
Number	38	42	42	48	23	56	52	51	20	42	40	51	34
Yards	365	303	291	392	83	416	441	414	241	380	303	304	312
Average Yards	9.6	7.2	6.9	8.2	3.6	7.4	8.5	8.1	12.1	9.0	7.6	6.0	9.2
Touchdowns	1	1	2	2	0	0	0	0	1	1	0	1	0
KICKOFF RETURNS:													
Number	58	41	46	33	39	24	32	45	55	58	54	49	52
Yards	1237	841	1112	774	956	544	741	1128	1142	1210	1233	1068	1153
Average Yards	21.3	20.5	24.2	23.5	24.5	22.7	23.2	25.1	20.8	20.9	22.8	21.8	22.2
Touchdowns	0	2	1	0	0	0	0	0	1	2	0	1	0
INTERCEPTION RETURNS:													
Number	22	28	26	11	24	28	23	16	19	22	21	32	19
Yards	283	302	334	150	399	213	334	195	258	397	303	318	235
Average Yards	12.9	10.8	12.8	13.6	16.6	7.6	14.5	12.2	13.6	18.0	14.4	9.9	12.4
Touchdowns	1	2	0	0	4	0	2	0	1	3	1	1	0
PENALTIES:													
Number	101	101	73	81	88	82	76	77	68	70	87	76	89
Yards	1032	1096	814	784	871	817	833	817	704	655	1148	790	998
FUMBLES:													
Number	14	33	23	28	28	35	22	22	24	22	17	29	21
Number Lost	9	17	15	16	12	16	8	12	15	11	8	15	15
POINTS:													
Total	234	361	337	255	265	264	352	244	228	286	293	272	278
PAT Attempts	25	44	35	31	32	28	44	26	28	33	33	32	30
PAT Made	25	44	35	31	31	27	44	25	27	32	32	29	29
FG Attempts	37	28	46	24	26	36	30	28	22	32	31	32	40
FG Made	19	17	30	12	14	23	14	21	11	18	21	15	23
Percent FG Made	51.4	60.7	65.2	50.0	53.8	63.9	46.7	75.0	50.0	56.3	67.7	46.9	57.5
Safeties	1	1	1	1	0	0	1	0	0	1	0	3	0

CONFERENCE PLAYOFFS

December 27, at Oakland
(Attendance 52,594)

SCORING

OAKLAND	0	7	7	7	–21
MIAMI	0	7	0	7	–14

Second Quarter
Mia. Warfield, 16 yard pass from Griese
PAT–Yepremian (kick)
Oak. Biletnikoff, 22 yard pass from Lamonica PAT–Blanda (kick)

Third Quarter
Oak. Brown, 50 yard interception return
PAT–Blanda (kick)

Fourth Quarter
Oak. Sherman, 82 yard pass from Lamonica
PAT–Blanda (kick)
Mia. Richardson, 7 yard pass from Griese
PAT–Yepremian (kick)

TEAM STATISTICS

OAK.		MIAMI
12	First Downs–Total	16
5	First Downs–Rushing	5
7	First Downs–Passing	9
0	First Downs–Penalty	2
4	Fumbles–Number	2
2	Fumbles–Lost Ball	0
4	Penalties–Number	0
30	Yards Penalized	0
1	Missed Field Goals	2
52	Offensive Plays–Total	63
301	Net Yards	242
5.8	Average Gain	3.8
2	Giveaways	1
1	Takeaways	2
–1	Difference	+1

INDIVIDUAL STATISTICS

OAKLAND	No.	Yds.	Avg.	MIAMI	No.	Yds.	Avg.
RUSHING							
Hubbard	18	58	3.2	Kiick	14	64	6.0
Smith	9	37	4.1	Morris	8	29	3.6
Dixon	8	31	3.9	Csonka	10	23	2.3
Banaszak	1	–6	–6.0	Griese	1	2	2.0
	36	120	3.3		33	118	3.6
RECEIVING							
Biletnikoff	3	46	15.3	Warfield	4	62	15.5
Chester	2	47	23.5	Kiick	4	34	8.5
Sherman	1	82	82.0	Richardson	2	30	15.0
Smith	1	9	9.0	Morris	2	15	7.5
Dixon	1	3	3.0	Twilley	1	14	14.0
	8	187	23.4		13	155	11.9
PUNTING							
Eischeid	4		32.2	Seiple	5		39.2
PUNT RETURNS							
Atkinson	1	–1	–1.0	Scott	1	–1	–1.0
				Anderson	1	–4	–4.0
					2	–5	–2.5
KICKOFF RETURNS							
Sherman	1	22	22.0	Ginn	2	27	13.5
Atkinson	1	19	19.0	Morris	1	21	21.0
Budness	1	0	0.0	Seiple	1	8	8.0
	3	41	13.7		4	56	14.0

PASSING

OAKLAND	Att.	Comp.	Comp. Pct.	Yds.	Int.	Yds/ Att.	Yds/ Comp.	Yards Lost Tkld.
Lamonica	16	8	50.0	187	0	11.7	23.4	0– 0
MIAMI								
Griese	27	13	48.1	155	1	5.7	11.9	3–31

December 26, at Baltimore
(Attendance 49,694)

SCORING

BALTIMORE	7	3	0	7	–17
CINCINNATI	0	0	0	0	– 0

First Quarter
Bal. Jefferson, 45 yard pass from Unitas
PAT–O'Brien (kick)

Second Quarter
Bal. O'Brien, 44 yard field goal

Fourth Quarter
Bal. Hinton, 53 yard pass from Unitas
PAT–O'Brien (kick)

TEAM STATISTICS

BALT.		CIN.
15	First Downs–Total	7
12	First Downs–Rushing	2
3	First Downs–Passing	5
0	First Downs–Penalty	0
0	Fumbles–Number	1
0	Fumbles–Lost Ball	0
6	Penalties–Number	1
63	Yards Penalized	5
2	Missed Field Goals	1
66	Offensive Plays–Total	46
299	Net Yards	139
4.5	Average Gain	3.0
0	Giveaways	1
1	Takeaways	0
+1	Difference	–1

INDIVIDUAL STATISTICS

BALTIMORE	No.	Yds.	Avg.	CINCINNATI	No.	Yds.	Avg.
RUSHING							
Bulaich	25	116	4.6	Robinson	5	25	5.0
Nowatzke	10	25	2.5	Carter	2	16	8.0
Unitas	2	18	9.0	Phillips	10	12	1.2
Hill	3	11	3.7	Lewis	3	10	3.3
Jefferson	3	5	1.7	Johnson	2	0	0.0
Havrilak	3	0	0.0		22	63	2.9
Hinton	1	–5	–5.0				
	47	170	3.6				
RECEIVING							
Hinton	3	86	28.7	Myers	4	66	16.5
Jefferson	2	51	25.5	Phillips	2	12	6.0
Mackey	1	8	8.0	Thomas	1	9	9.0
	6	145	24.2	Johnson	1	6	6.0
					8	93	11.6
PUNTING							
Lee	6		38.3	Lewis	8		39.1
PUNT RETURNS							
Gardin	7	28	4.0	Parrish	2	6	3.0
KICKOFF RETURNS							
Nowatzke	1	0	0.0	Robinson	2	29	14.5
				Lamb	1	17	17.0
					3	46	15.3
INTERCEPTION RETURNS							
M. Curtis	1	0	0.0	None			

PASSING

BALTIMORE	Att.	Comp.	Comp. Pct.	Yds.	Int.	Yds/ Att.	Yds/ Comp.	Yds Lost Tkld
Unitas	17	6	35.3	145	0	8.5	24.2	2–16
CINCINNATI								
Carter	20	7	35.0	64	1	3.2	9.1	
Wyche	1	1	100.0	29	0	29.0	29.0	
	21	8	38.1	93	1	4.4	11.6	3–17

BALTIMORE COLTS 11-2-1 Don McCafferty

Scores of Each Game		
16	San Diego	14
24	KANSAS CITY	44
14	Boston	6
24	Houston	20
29	N.Y. Jets	22
27	BOSTON	3
35	MIAMI	0
13	Green Bay	10
17	BUFFALO	17
17	Miami	34
21	CHICAGO	20
29	PHILADELPHIA	10
20	Buffalo	14
35	N.Y. JETS	20

Use Name	Pos.	Hgt	Wgt	Age	Int	Pts
Sam Ball	OT	6'4"	240	26		
Dennis Nelson	OT	6'5"	260	24		
Bob Vogel	OT	6'5"	250	28		
Cornelius Johnson	OG	6'2"	245	27		
Glenn Ressler	OG	6'3"	250	26		
Dan Sullivan	OG	6'3"	250	31		
John Williams	OG	6'3"	256	24		
Bill Curry	C	6'2"	235	27		
Tom Goode	C	6'3"	245	31		
Roy Hilton	DE	6'6"	240	25		
Billy Newsome	DE	6'4"	240	22		
Bubba Smith	DE	6'7"	295	25		
Jim Bailey	DT	6'5"	245	22		
Fred Miller	DT	6'3"	250	29		
Billy Ray Smith	DT	6'4"	250	35		
George Wright	DT	6'3"	260	23		
Mike Curtis	LB	6'2"	232	27	5	
Bob Grant	LB	6'2"	225	24	2	6
Ted Hendricks	LB	6'7"	215	22	1	6
Ray May	LB	6'1"	230	25	1	
Robbie Nichols	LB	6'3"	220	23		
Tom Curtis	DB	6'1"	196	22	1	
Jim Duncan	DB	6'2"	220	24	2	6
Ron Gardin	DB	5'11"	180	25		6
Jerry Logan	DB	6'1"	190	29	6	12
Tommy Maxwell	DB	6'2"	195	23		
Charlie Stukes	DB	6'3"	212	26	3	
Rick Volk	DB	6'3"	195	25	4	
Earl Morrall	QB	6'1"	206	36		
Johnny Unitas	QB	6'1"	196	37		
Sam Havrilak	HB	6'2"	195	22		
Jack Maitland	HB	6'1"	210	22		12
Tom Matte	HB	6'	214	31		
Norm Bulaich	FB-HB	6'1"	218	23		18
Larry Conjar	FB	6'	214	24		
Jerry Hill	FB	5'11"	217	30		12
Tom Nowatzke	FB	6'3"	230	27		6
Eddie Hinton	WR	6'	200	23		42
Roy Jefferson	WR	6'2"	190	26		42
Jim O'Brien	WR	6'	195	23		93
Jimmy Orr	WR	5'11"	185	34		12
Ray Perkins	WR	6'	183	28		6
John Mackey	TE	6'3"	224	28		18
Tom Mitchell	TE	6'2"	215	26		24
David Lee	K	6'4"	230	26		

MIAMI DOLPHINS 10-4-0 Don Shula

Scores of Each Game		
14	Boston	27
20	Houston	10
20	OAKLAND	13
20	N.Y. Jets	6
33	Buffalo	14
0	CLEVELAND	28
0	Baltimore	35
17	Philadelphia	24
21	NEW ORLEANS	10
34	BALTIMORE	17
20	Atlanta	7
37	BOSTON	20
16	N.Y. JETS	10
45	BUFFALO	7

Use Name	Pos.	Hgt	Wgt	Age	Int	Pts
Doug Crusan	OT	6'5"	260	24		
Norm Evans	OT	6'5"	250	27		
Wayne Moore	OT	6'6"	265	25		
Bob Kuechenberg	OG	6'3"	255	22		
Jim Langer	OG	6'2"	240	22		
Larry Little	OG	6'1"	270	24		
Maxie Williams	OG	6'4"	250	30		
Bob DeMarco	C	6'3"	245	32		
Carl Mauck	C	6'3"	240	23		
Norm McBride	DE	6'3"	245	23		
Jim Riley	DE	6'4"	260	25		
Bill Stanfill	DE	6'5"	250	23		
Frank Cornish (from CHI)	DT	6'6"	285	26		
Manny Fernandez	DT	6'2"	250	24		
Bob Heinz	DT	6'6"	290	23		
John Richardson	DT	6'2"	260	25		
Nick Buoniconti	LB	5'11"	220	29		
Ted Davis	LB	6'1"	232	28	1	
Mike Kolen	LB	6'2"	215	22		
Dick Palmer	LB	6'2"	220	22		
Jesse Powell	LB	6'1"	215	23		
Doug Swift	LB	6'3"	230	21		
Ed Weisacosky	LB	6'	230	26		
Dick Anderson	DB	6'2"	200	24	8	
Dean Brown	DB	5'10"	170	23	1	
Tim Foley	DB	6'	195	22		
Curtis Johnson	DB	6'2"	200	22	3	
Lloyd Mumphord	DB	5'11"	180	23	5	12
Bob Petrella	DB	6'	185	25		
Jake Scott	DB	6'	188	25	5	6
Bill Darnall–Injury						
Bob Griese	QB	6'1"	190	25		12
John Stofa	QB	6'3"	210	28		
Hubert Ginn	HB	5'11"	190	23		
Jim Kiick	HB	5'11"	220	24		36
Mercury Morris	HB	5'10"	190	23		6
Barry Pryor	HB	6'	215	24		
Larry Csonka	FB	6'3"	250	23		36
Stan Mitchell	FB	6'2"	210	26		6
Karl Noonan	WR	6'3"	205	26		6
Willie Richardson	WR	6'2"	198	30		6
Howard Twilley	WR	5'10"	180	26		30
Paul Warfield	WR	6'	190	27		36
Marv Fleming	TE	6'4"	235	28		
Jim Mandich	TE	6'3"	225	21		6
Larry Seiple	TE	6'	220	25		
Karl Kremser	K	6'	175	25		2
Garo Yepremian	K	5'8"	172	26		97

NEW YORK JETS 4-10-0 Weeb Ewbank

Scores of Each Game		
21	Cleveland	31
31	Boston	21
31	Buffalo	34
6	MIAMI	20
22	BALTIMORE	29
6	BUFFALO	10
10	N.Y. GIANTS	22
17	Pittsburgh	21
31	Los Angeles	20
17	BOSTON	3
20	MINNESOTA	10
13	OAKLAND	14
10	Miami	16
20	Baltimore	35

Use Name	Pos.	Hgt	Wgt	Age	Int	Pts
Dave Foley	OT	6'5"	255	22		
Winston Hill	OT	6'4"	285	28		
Roger Finnie	OG-OT	6'3"	245	24		
Tom Bayless	OG	6'3"	240	22		
Dave Herman	OG	6'2"	255	28		
Dave Middendorf	OG	6'3"	260	24		
Randy Rasmussen	OG	6'2"	255	25		
Pete Perreault	OT-OG	6'3"	248	31		
John Schmitt	C	6'4"	250	27		
Paul Crane	LB-C	6'2"	212	26		
Verlon Biggs	DE	6'4"	270	27		
Jimmie Jones	DE	6'3"	215	23		
Gerry Philbin	DE	6'2"	245	29		
Mark Lomas	DT-DE	6'4"	230	22		
John Elliott	DT	6'4"	244	25		2
John Little	DE-DT	6'3"	220	23		
Steve Thompson	DE-DT	6'5"	245	25		
Al Atkinson	LB	6'1"	230	27	3	
Ralph Baker	LB	6'3"	235	28	2	
John Ebersole	LB	6'3"	240	21		
Larry Grantham	LB	6'	210	31	3	6
Dennis Onkotz	LB	6'1"	220	22		
Mike Battle	DB	6'1"	175	24		
John Dockery	DB	6'	186	25		
W.K. Hicks	DB	6'1"	195	27	8	
Gus Holloman	DB	6'3"	195	24	3	
Jim Hudson	DB	6'2"	210	27		
Cecil Leonard	DB	5'11"	160	24		
Steve Tannen	DB	6'1"	194	22	2	6
Earlie Thomas	DB	6'1"	190	24	2	6
Jim Richards–Military Service						
Paul Seiler–Injury						
Bob Davis	QB	6'3"	205	25		
Joe Namath	QB	6'2"	200	27		
Jim Turner	QB	6'2"	215	29		85
Al Woodall	QB	6'5"	205	24		
Emerson Boozer	HB	5'11"	195	27		30
Cliff McClain	HB	6'	217	22		
George Nock	HB	5'10"	200	24		36
Chuck Mercein	FB	6'3"	222	27		6
Matt Snell	FB	6'2"	220	28		6
Lee White	FB	6'4"	235	24		6
Eddie Bell	WR	5'10"	160	22		12
Rich Caster	WR	6'5"	222	21		18
Don Maynard	WR	6'	180	34		
Steve O'Neal	WR	6'3"	185	24		
George Sauer	WR	6'1"	195	26		24
Gary Arthur	TE	6'5"	230	22		
Pete Lammons	TE	6'3"	230	26		12
Wayne Stewart	TE	6'7"	213	23		

BUFFALO BILLS 3-10-1 Johnny Rauch

Scores of Each Game		
10	DENVER	25
0	LOS ANGELES	19
34	N.Y. JETS	31
10	Pittsburgh	23
14	MIAMI	33
10	N.Y. Jets	6
45	Boston	10
14	CINCINNATI	43
17	Baltimore	17
13	Chicago	31
10	BOSTON	14
6	N.Y. Giants	20
14	BALTIMORE	20
7	Miami	45

Use Name	Pos.	Hgt	Wgt	Age	Int	Pts
Levert Carr	OT	6'5"	260	26		
Paul Costa	OT	6'4"	255	28		
Jerry Gantt	OT	6'4"	266	21		
Art Laster	OT	6'4"	280	22		
Howard Kindig	C-OT	6'6"	264	29		
Richard Cheek	OG	6'3"	266	22		
Joe O'Donnell	OG	6'2"	262	27		
Jim Reilly	OG	6'2"	260	22		
Wayne Fowler	C	6'3"	260	21		
Frank Marchlewski	C	6'2"	240	26		
Al Cowlings	DE	6'5"	258	23		
Mike McBath	DE	6'4"	248	24		
Ron McDole	DE	6'3"	288	30		
Jim Dunaway	DT	6'4"	277	28		
Waddey Harvey	DT	6'4"	282	23		
Julian Nunamaker	DT	6'3"	252	24		
Bob Tatarek	DT	6'4"	260	24		
Al Andrews	LB	6'3"	216	26		
Edgar Chandler	LB	6'3"	235	24	1	6
Jerald Collins	LB	6'1"	220	23		
Dick Cunningham	LB	6'2"	244	25		
Paul Guidry	LB	6'3"	233	26		
Mike McCaffrey	LB	6'3"	235	24		
Mike Stratton	LB	6'3"	240	28		
Jackie Allen	DB	6'1"	187	22		
Butch Byrd	DB	6'	196	28	4	6
Ike Hill	DB	5'10"	180	23		
Robert James	DB	6'1"	177	23		
Tommy Pharr	DB	5'10"	187	23		
John Pitts	DB	6'4"	223	25	1	
Pete Richardson	DB	6'1"	193	23	5	
Max Anderson – Knee Injury						
Dan Darragh	QB	6'3"	196	23		
James Harris	QB	6'3"	215	23		
Dennis Shaw	QB	6'2"	210	23		
Greg Jones	HB	6'1"	200	22		12
Lloyd Pate	HB	6'1"	205	24		6
O. J. Simpson	HB	6'2"	204	23		36
Bill Enyart	FB	6'4"	236	23		6
Wayne Patrick	FB	6'2"	254	24		6
Glenn Alexander	WR	6'3"	205	23		
Marlin Briscoe	WR	5'10"	177	24		48
Clyde Glosson	WR	5'11"	175	23		
Haven Moses	WR	6'3"	205	24		12
Austin Denney	TE	6'2"	230	26		
Willie Grate	TE	6'4"	225	24		12
Roland Moss (from SD)	HB-TE	6'3"	215	23		
Grant Guthrie	K	6'	210	22		54
Paul Maguire	K	6'	232	32		

BOSTON PATRIOTS 2-12-0 Clive Rush John Mazur

Scores of Each Game		
27	MIAMI	14
21	N.Y. JETS	31
6	Baltimore	14
10	Kansas City	23
0	N.Y. GIANTS	16
3	BALTIMORE	27
10	BUFFALO	45
0	St. Louis	31
14	SAN DIEGO	16
3	N.Y. Jets	17
14	Buffalo	10
20	Miami	37
14	MINNESOTA	35
7	Cincinnati	45

Use Name	Pos.	Hgt	Wgt	Age	Int	Pts
Tom Funchess	OT	6'5"	260	25		
Ezell Jones	OT	6'4"	255	23		
Tom Neville	OT	6'4"	255	27		
Len St. Jean	OG	6'1"	245	28		
Gary Bugenhagen	OT-OG	6'2"	250	25		
Angelo Loukas	OT-OG	6'3"	250	23		
Jon Morris	C	6'4"	255	27		
Mike Montler	OG-C	6'4"	270	26		
Ron Berger	DE	6'8"	275	26		
Ike Lassiter	DE	6'5"	270	29		
Dennis Wirgowski	DE	6'5"	255	22		
Mel Witt	DE	6'3"	250	24		
Houston Antwine	DT	6'	270	31		
Jim Hunt	DT	5'11"	255	31		
Rex Mirich	DT	6'4"	258	29		
Mike Ballou	LB	6'3"	235	22		
John Bramlett	LB	6'2"	220	29	1	
Jim Cheyunski	LB	6'2"	220	24		
Ed Philpott	LB	6'3"	240	24	1	
Marty Schottenheimer	LB	6'3"	225	27		
Fred Whittingham	LB	6'1"	240	31		
J.R. Williamson	LB	6'2"	220	28	1	
Randy Beverly	DB	5'11"	185	26		
Larry Carwell	DB	6'1"	190	26		
Tom Janik	DB	6'3"	200	29		
Daryle Johnson	DB	5'11"	190	24	2	
Art McMahon	DB	5'11"	190	24	1	
John Outlaw	DB	5'10"	180	25		
Clarence Scott	DB	6'2"	205	26	1	
Don Webb	DB	5'10"	195	31	1	
Ed Toner – Injury						
Joe Kapp	QB	6'2"	215	32		
Mike Taliaferro	QB	6'2"	205	28		
Sid Blanks	HB	6'	205	29		
Carl Garrett	HB	5'11"	210	23		24
Bob Gladieux (to BUF)	HB	5'11"	190	23		
Odell Lawson	HB	6'2"	218	22		
Jim Nance	FB	6'1"	240	27		42
Eddie Ray	TE-FB	6'1"	230	23		
Gino Cappelletti	WR	6'	190	36		30
Charley Frazier	WR	6'	190	31		
Gayle Knief	WR	6'3"	205	23		6
Bill Rademacher	WR	6'1"	190	28		
Tom Richardson	WR	6'2"	195	25		
Ron Sellers	WR	6'4"	195	23		24
Bake Turner	WR	6'	180	30		12
Tom Beer	TE	6'4"	228	25		
Barry Brown	TE	6'3"	220	27		
Charlie Gogolak	K	5'10"	170	25		11

BALTIMORE COLTS

RUSHING

Last Name	No.	Yds	Avg	TD
Bulaich	139	426	3.1	3
Nowatzke	73	248	3.4	1
Maitland	74	209	2.8	1
Havrilak	54	159	2.9	0
Hill	36	115	3.2	2
Hinton	5	58	11.6	2
Jefferson	4	47	11.8	0
Matte	12	43	3.6	0
Unitas	9	16	1.8	0
Morrall	2	6	3.0	0
Perkins	2	6	3.0	0
Conjar	1	3	3.0	0

RECEIVING

Last Name	No.	Yds	Avg	TD
Hinton	47	733	16	5
Jefferson	44	749	17	7
Mackey	28	435	16	3
Mitchell	20	261	13	4
Nowatzke	16	93	6	0
Havrilak	14	141	10	0
Bulaich	11	123	11	0
Orr	10	199	20	2
Perkins	10	194	19	1
Maitland	9	67	7	1
Hill	8	62	8	0
O'Brien	1	28	28	0
Matte	1	2	2	0

PUNT RETURNS

Last Name	No.	Yds	Avg	TD
Gardin	28	330	12	1
Volk	3	15	5	0
Logan	2	4	2	0
T. Curtis	3	2	1	0

KICKOFF RETURNS

Last Name	No.	Yds	Avg	TD
Duncan	20	707	35	1
Gardin	11	265	24	0
Nowatzke	7	93	13	0
Havrilak	2	36	18	0
Maitland	1	28	28	0
Grant	1	21	21	0
Jefferson	1	11	11	0
Newsome	1	0	0	0
Stukes	1	0	0	0

PASSING – PUNTING – KICKING

PASSING	Att	Comp	%	Yds	Yd/Att	TD	Int–	%	RK
Unitas	321	166	52	2213	6.9	14	18–	6	6
Morrall	93	51	55	792	8.5	9	4–	4	
Havrilak	2	2	100	82	41.0	0	0–	0	

PUNTING	No	Avg
Lee	63	44.7

KICKING	XP	Att	%	FG	Att	%
O'Brien	36	38	95	19	34	56

MIAMI DOLPHINS

RUSHING

Last Name	No.	Yds	Avg	TD
Csonka	193	874	4.5	6
Kiick	191	658	3.4	6
Morris	60	409	6.8	0
Griese	26	89	3.4	2
Mitchell	8	23	2.9	0
Seiple	2	21	10.5	0
Warfield	2	13	6.5	0
Stofa	2	5	2.5	0
Pryor	2	0	0.0	0
Ginn	5	–1	–0.2	0
Noonan	1	–9	–9.0	0

RECEIVING

Last Name	No.	Yds	Avg	TD
Kiick	42	497	12	0
Warfield	28	703	25	6
Twilley	22	281	13	5
Fleming	18	205	11	0
Morris	12	149	12	0
Csonka	11	94	9	0
Noonan	10	186	19	1
W. Richardson	7	67	10	1
Mitchell	6	85	14	1
Seiple	2	14	7	0
Mandich	1	3	3	1

PUNT RETURNS

Last Name	No.	Yds	Avg	TD
Scott	27	290	11	1
Anderson	1	6	6	0
Morris	2	–1	–1	0

KICKOFF RETURNS

Last Name	No.	Yds	Avg	TD
Morris	28	812	29	1
Scott	4	117	29	0
Ginn	5	59	12	0
Mitchell	4	35	9	0
Anderson	1	8	8	0
Seiple	2	5	3	0
Mandich	2	0	0	0
Brown	1	0	0	0
Foley	1	0	0	0

PASSING – PUNTING – KICKING

PASSING	Att	Comp	%	Yds	Yd/Att	TD	Int–	%	RK
Griese	245	142	58	2019	8.2	12	17–	7	4
Stofa	53	16	30	240	4.5	3	2–	4	
Kiick	1	1	100	25	25.0	0	0–	0	

PUNTING	No	Avg
Seiple	58	41.2

KICKING	XP	Att	%	FG	Att	%
Yepremian	31	31	100	22	29	76
Kremser	2	2	100	0	1	0

NEW YORK JETS

RUSHING

Last Name	No.	Yds	Avg	TD
Boozer	139	581	4.2	5
Nock	135	402	3.0	5
Snell	64	281	4.4	1
White	70	215	3.1	0
Woodall	28	110	3.9	0
Mercein	20	44	2.2	0
O'Neal	1	16	16.0	0
Davis	2	11	5.5	0
Turner	1	1	1.0	0
Namath	1	1	1.0	0
Bell	2	–7	–3.5	0

RECEIVING

Last Name	No.	Yds	Avg	TD
Maynard	31	525	17	0
Sauer	31	510	16	4
Boozer	28	258	9	0
Lammons	25	316	13	2
Bell	21	246	12	2
Caster	19	393	21	3
Nock	18	146	8	1
White	12	125	10	1
Mercein	3	27	9	1
Snell	2	26	13	0
McClain	1	11	11	0
Stewart	1	7	7	0
Battle	1	2	2	0

PUNT RETURNS

Last Name	No.	Yds	Avg	TD
Battle	19	117	6	0
Bell	7	33	5	0

KICKOFF RETURNS

Last Name	No.	Yds	Avg	TD
Battle	40	891	22	0
McClain	4	70	18	0
Bell	3	61	20	0
Leonard	1	35	35	0
Mercein	4	32	8	0
Nock	1	18	18	0
Caster	1	0	0	0
Onkotz	1	0	0	0
Tannen	1	–1	–1	0

PASSING – PUNTING – KICKING

PASSING	Att	Comp	%	Yds	Yd/Att	TD	Int–	%	RK
Woodall	188	96	51	1265	6.7	9	9–	5	9
Namath	179	90	50	1259	7.0	5	12–	7	13
Davis	17	6	35	66	3.9	0	0–	0	
Bell	1	0	0	0	0.0	0	1–	100	
O'Neal	1	1	100	2	2.0	0	0–	0	

PUNTING	No	Avg
O'Neal	73	40.1

KICKING	XP	Att	%	FG	Att	%
Turner	28	28	100	19	35	54

BUFFALO BILLS

RUSHING

Last Name	No.	Yds	Avg	TD
Simpson	120	488	4.1	5
Patrick	66	259	3.9	1
Shaw	39	210	5.4	0
Enyart	58	196	3.4	0
Pate	46	162	3.5	1
Jones	31	113	3.6	1
Darragh	1	26	26.0	0
Briscoe	3	19	6.3	0
Harris	3	–8	–2.7	0

RECEIVING

Last Name	No.	Yds	Avg	TD
Briscoe	57	1036	18	8
Moses	39	726	19	2
Enyart	35	235	7	1
Pate	19	103	5	0
Patrick	16	142	9	0
Denney	14	201	14	0
Simpson	10	139	14	0
Jones	8	89	11	0
Grate	7	147	21	2
Alexander	4	51	13	0
Moss	2	31	16	0
Glosson	2	16	8	0

PUNT RETURNS

Last Name	No.	Yds	Avg	TD
Pharr	23	184	8	0
Hill	19	102	5	0
Allen	2	10	5	0
Alexander	1	2	2	0

KICKOFF RETURNS

Last Name	No.	Yds	Avg	TD
Simpson	7	333	48	1
Alexander	12	204	17	0
Hill	9	165	18	0
Jones	7	162	23	1
Moss	7	131	19	0
Glosson	4	61	15	0
Enyart	3	60	20	0
Patrick	3	38	13	0
Pate	1	21	21	0
Collins	2	17	9	0
Andrews	1	16	16	0
McCaffrey	2	15	8	0
Laster	2	8	4	0
McBath	1	7	7	0
Pharr	1	6	6	0
Costa	1	0	0	0

PASSING – PUNTING – KICKING

PASSING	Att	Comp	%	Yds	Yd/Att	TD	Int–	%	RK
Shaw	321	178	55	2507	7.8	10	20–	6	4
Harris	50	24	48	338	6.8	3	4–	8	
Darragh	29	11	38	71	2.5	0	2–	7	
Simpson	2	0	0	0	0.0	0	0–	0	

PUNTING	No	Avg
Maguire	83	38.9

KICKING	XP	Att	%	FG	Att	%
Guthrie	24	25	96	10	19	53

BOSTON PATRIOTS

RUSHING

Last Name	No.	Yds	Avg	TD
Nance	145	522	3.6	7
Garrett	88	272	3.1	4
Lawson	56	99	1.8	0
Kapp	20	71	3.6	0
Blanks	13	44	3.4	0
Ray	5	13	2.6	0
Taliaferro	3	11	3.7	0
Gladieux	4	8	2.0	0

RECEIVING

Last Name	No.	Yds	Avg	TD
Sellers	38	550	14	4
Turner	28	428	15	2
Garrett	26	216	8	0
Nance	26	148	6	0
Brown	15	145	10	0
Beer	11	150	14	0
Lawson	11	113	10	0
Frazier	9	86	10	0
Blanks	5	49	10	0
Rademacher	4	51	13	0
Knief	3	39	13	1

PUNT RETURNS

Last Name	No.	Yds	Avg	TD
Garrett	17	168	10	0
Blanks	9	83	9	0
Carwell	3	48	16	0
Johnson	2	6	3	0
Lawson	1	0	0	0

KICKOFF RETURNS

Last Name	No.	Yds	Avg	TD
Lawson	25	546	22	0
Garrett	24	511	21	0
Blanks	7	152	22	0
Carwell	1	30	30	0
Whittingham	1	24	24	0
Schottenheimer	1	8	8	0
Beer	1	4	4	0
Beverly	1	0	0	0
Brown	1	0	0	0

PASSING – PUNTING – KICKING

PASSING	Att	Comp	%	Yds	Yd/Att	TD	Int–	%	RK
Kapp	219	98	45	1104	5.0	3	17–	8	17
Taliaferro	173	78	45	871	5.0	4	11–	6	16

PUNTING	No	Avg
Janik	86	39.1

KICKING	XP	Att	%	FG	Att	%
Cappelletti	12	13	92	6	15	40
Gogolak	5	5	100	2	7	29

CINCINNATI BENGALS 8-6-0 Paul Brown

Scores of Each Game			Use Name	Pos.	Hgt	Wgt	Age	Int	Pts
31	OAKLAND	21	Howard Fest	OT	6'6"	268	24		
3	Detroit	38	Rufus Mayes	OT	6'5"	255	22		
13	HOUSTON	20	Ernie Wright	OT	6'4"	270	30		
27	Cleveland	30	Guy Dennis	OG	6'2"	255	23		
19	KANSAS CITY	27	Pat Matson	OG	6'1"	245	26		
0	Washington	20	Mike Wilson	OT-OG	6'1"	240	22		
10	Pittsburgh	21	Bob Johnson	C	6'5"	265	24		
43	Buffalo	14	Marty Baccaglio	DE	6'3"	245	25		
14	CLEVELAND	10	Royce Berry	DE	6'3"	248	24		12
34	PITTSBURGH	7	Ron Carpenter	DE	6'4"	260	22		
26	NEW ORLEANS	6	Nick Roman	DE	6'3"	230	22		
17	San Diego	14	Steve Chomyszak	DT	6'5"	265	25		
30	Houston	20	Willie Jones	DT	6'2"	260	28		
45	BOSTON	7	Mike Reid	DT	6'3"	258	23		

Use Name	Pos.	Hgt	Wgt	Age	Int	Pts
Ken Avery	LB	6'1"	225	26	1	
Al Beauchamp	LB	6'2"	236	26	1	6
Bill Bergey	LB	6'2"	240	25	3	
Larry Ely	LB	6'1"	230	22		
Wayne McClure	LB	6'1"	225	24		
Bill Peterson	LB	6'3"	230	25		
Al Coleman	DB	6'1"	183	25		
Sandy Durko	DB	6'1"	185	22		
Ken Dyer	DB	6'3"	186	24	3	
Kenny Graham (to PIT)	DB	6'	205	28	3	
John Guillory	DB	5'10"	190	25		
Lemar Parrish	DB	5'11"	185	22	5	18
Ken Riley	DB	6'	184	23	4	
Fletcher Smith	DB	6'2"	180	26	3	

Greg Cook–Shoulder Injury

Use Name	Pos.	Hgt	Wgt	Age	Int	Pts
Virgil Carter	QB	6'1"	200	24		12
Dave Lewis	QB	6'2"	210	24		
Sam Wyche	QB	6'4"	210	25		12
Essex Johnson	HB	5'9"	200	23		24
Paul Robinson	HB	6'	200	25		42
Paul Dunn	FB-HB	6'	210	22		
Doug Dressler	FB	6'3"	220	22		
Ron Lamb	FB	6'2"	230	26		
Jess Phillips	HB-FB	6'1"	210	23		30
Eric Crabtree	WR	5'11"	182	25		12
Chip Myers	WR	6'4"	200	25		6
Speedy Thomas	WR	6'1"	178	23		12
Bruce Coslet	TE	6'3"	230	24		6
Mike Kelly	TE	6'4"	215	22		
Bob Trumpy	TE	6'6"	225	25		12
Horst Muhlmann	K	6'1"	210	30		108

CLEVELAND BROWNS 7-7-0 Blanton Collier

Scores of Each Game			Use Name	Pos.	Hgt	Wgt	Age	Int	Pts
31	N.Y. JETS	21	Al Jenkins	OT	6'2"	255	24		
31	San Francisco	34	Bob McKay	OT	6'5"	260	22		
15	PITTSBURGH	7	Dick Schafrath	OT	6'3"	258	34		
30	CINCINNATI	27	Joe Taffoni	OT	6'3"	250	25		
24	DETROIT	41	Jim Copeland	OG	6'2"	245	25		
28	Miami	0	John Demarie	OG	6'3"	255	25		
10	SAN DIEGO	27	Gene Hickerson	OG	6'3"	248	35		
20	Oakland	23	Fred Hoaglin	C	6'4"	250	26		
10	Cincinnati	14	Chuck Reynolds	C	6'2"	240	23		2
28	HOUSTON	14	Jack Gregory	DE	6'6"	250	25		
9	Pittsburgh	28	Joe Jones	DE	6'6"	246	22		
21	Houston	10	Ron Snidow	DE	6'4"	250	28		2
2	DALLAS	6	Walter Johnson	DT	6'3"	275	27	1	2
27	Denver	13	Joel Righetti	DT	6'3"	253	22		
			Jerry Sherk	DT	6'4"	253	22		
			Bill Yanchar	DT	6'3"	250	22		

Use Name	Pos.	Hgt	Wgt	Age	Int	Pts
Billy Andrews	LB	6'	225	25	1	6
Tom Beutler	LB	6'1"	232	23		
John Garlington	LB	6'1"	225	24	1	
Jim Houston	LB	6'2"	240	33	1	
Dale Lindsey	LB	6'3"	225	27	2	6
Bob Matheson	LB	6'4"	240	25	1	
Erich Barnes	DB	6'2"	212	35	5	6
Ben Davis	DB	5'11"	185	24	1	
Mike Howell	DB	6'1"	190	27	1	
Ernie Kellerman	DB	6'	185	26	1	
Tom Schoen	DB	5'11"	185	24		
Rickey Stevenson	DB	5'11"	188	22		
Freddie Summers	DB	6'1"	180	23		
Walt Sumner	DB	6'1"	180	23	4	

Use Name	Pos.	Hgt	Wgt	Age	Int	Pts
Don Gault	QB	6'2"	190	24		
Bill Nelsen	QB	6'	195	29		
Mike Phipps	QB	6'2"	207	22		
Ken Brown	HB	5'10"	205	24		
Leroy Kelly	HB	6'	200	28		48
Randy Minniear	HB	6'	210	26		6
Reece Morrison	HB	6'	205	24		6
Bo Scott	FB	6'3"	210	27		66
Steve Engel	HB-FB	6'1"	218	22		
Gary Collins	WR	6'4"	210	29		24
Fair Hooker	WR	6'1"	193	23		12
Dave Jones	WR	6'2"	185	23		
Homer Jones	WR	6'2"	215	29		12
Chip Glass	TE	6'4"	236	23		12
Milt Morin	TE	6'4"	240	28		6
Don Cockroft	K	6'1"	190	25		70

PITTSBURGH STEELERS 5-9-0 Chuck Noll

Scores of Each Game			Use Name	Pos.	Hgt	Wgt	Age	Int	Pts
7	HOUSTON	19	John Brown	OT	6'2"	255	31		
13	Denver	16	Mike Haggerty	OT	6'4"	240	24		
7	Cleveland	15	Rick Sharp	OT	6'3"	262	22		
23	BUFFALO	10	Sam Davis	OG	6'1"	245	26		
7	Houston	3	Bruce Van Dyke	OG	6'2"	225	26		
14	Oakland	31	Ralph Wenzel	OG	6'3"	250	27		
21	CINCINNATI	10	Ray Mansfield	C	6'3"	240	29		
21	N.Y. JETS	17	Jon Kolb	OT-C	6'2"	220	23		
14	KANSAS CITY	31	L. C. Greenwood	DE	6'5"	240	23		
7	Cincinnati	34	Ben McGee	DE	6'2"	250	28		
28	CLEVELAND	9	Lloyd Voss	DE	6'4"	256	28		
12	GREEN BAY	20	Dick Arndt	DT	6'5"	265	26		
16	Atlanta	27	Joe Greene	DT	6'4"	270	23		
20	Philadelphia	30	Chuck Hinton	DT	6'5"	248	31		
			Clarence Washington	DT	6'3"	265	23		

Rocky Bleier – Wounded in Military Service

Use Name	Pos.	Hgt	Wgt	Age	Int	Pts
Chuck Allen	LB	6'1"	225	30	4	
Carl Crennel	LB	6'1"	230	21		
Henry Davis	LB	6'3"	235	27		
Doug Fisher	LB	6'1"	225	23		
Jerry Hillebrand	LB	6'3"	240	30	2	
Andy Russell	LB	6'3"	225	28	3	
Brian Stenger	LB	6'4"	220	23		
Ocie Austin	DB	6'3"	200	23	1	
Fred Barry	DB	5'10"	184	22		
Chuck Beatty	DB	6'2"	200	24	2	6
Mel Blount	DB	6'3"	205	22	1	
Lee Calland	DB	6'	190	29	7	
Clancy Oliver	DB	6'1"	180	22		
John Rowser	DB	6'1"	180	26	3	
John Sodaski	DB	6'1"	197	22		

Larry Gagner–Injury from automobile accident

Use Name	Pos.	Hgt	Wgt	Age	Int	Pts
Terry Bradshaw	QB	6'3"	218	21		6
Terry Hanratty	QB	6'1"	200	22		
Dick Hoak	HB	5'11"	190	31		6
Preston Pearson	HB	6'1"	190	25		12
John Fugua	FB-HB	5'11"	200	23		54
Warren Bankston	FB	6'4"	225	23		12
Terry Cole	FB	6'1"	220	25		
Hubie Bryant	WR	5'10"	175	24		
Dave Kalina	WR	6'3"	205	23		
Ron Shanklin	WR	6'1"	180	23		24
Dave Smith	WR	6'2"	205	23		12
Jon Staggers	WR	5'10"	186	21		6
J. R. Wilburn	WR	6'2"	190	27		
Bob Adams	TE	6'2"	225	24		
Dennis Hughes	TE	6'1"	220	22		18
Gene Mingo	K	6'1"	210	31		32
Bobby Walden	K	6'	190	32		
Allen Watson	K	5'10"	165	25		22

HOUSTON OILERS 3-10-1 Wally Lemm

Scores of Each Game			Use Name	Pos.	Hgt	Wgt	Age	Int	Pts
19	Pittsburgh	7	Elbert Drungo	OT	6'5"	250	27		
10	MIAMI	20	Glen Ray Hines	OT	6'5"	265	26		
20	Cincinnati	13	Walt Suggs	OT	6'5"	260	31		
20	BALTIMORE	24	Ken Gray	OG	6'2"	250	34		
3	PITTSBURGH	7	Tom Regner	OG	6'1"	255	26		
31	San Diego	31	Ron Saul	OG	6'2"	255	22		
0	St. Louis	44	Doug Wilkerson	OG	6'2"	245	23		
9	Kansas City	24	Hank Autry	C	6'3"	235	23		
20	SAN FRANCISCO	30	Bobby Maples	C	6'3"	245	27		
14	Cleveland	28	Elvin Bethea	DE	6'3"	255	24		
31	DENVER	21	Pat Holmes	DE	6'5"	250	30		
10	CLEVELAND	21	Spain Musgrove	DT-DE	6'4"	275	25		
20	CINCINNATI	30	Lee Brooks	DT	6'5"	266	22		
10	Dallas	52	Tom Domres	DT	6'3"	255	23		
			Willie Parker	DT	6'2"	265	25		

Use Name	Pos.	Hgt	Wgt	Age	Int	Pts
Garland Boyette	LB	6'1"	245	30	1	
Claude Harvey	LB	6'4"	225	22		
Jess Lewis	LB	6'1"	230	23		
Ron Pritchard	LB	6'1"	235	23	2	2
Olen Underwood	LB	6'1'	220	28		
Loyd Wainscott	LB	6'1"	235	23		
George Webster	LB	6'4"	223	24		
Bob Atkins	DB	6'3"	215	24	1	
Ken Houston	DB	6'3"	195	25	3	
Benny Johnson	DB	5'11"	178	22		
Leroy Mitchell	DB	6'2"	190	25	2	
Zeke Moore	DB	6'2"	198	26	6	
Johnny Peacock	DB	6'2"	200	23	3	6

John Douglas–Injury

Use Name	Pos.	Hgt	Wgt	Age	Int	Pts
Charley Johnson	QB	6'	190	33		
Bob Naponic	QB	6'	190	23		
Jerry Rhome	QB	6'	188	28		6
Woody Campbell	HB	5'11"	208	25		6
Mike Richardson	HB	5'11"	198	23		18
Joe Dawkins	FB-HB	5'11"	220	22		12
Hoyle Granger	FB	6'1"	225	26		6
Roy Hopkins	FB	6'1"	215	25		18
Tom Smiley	FB	6'1"	235	26		
Jim Beirne	WR	6'2"	196	23		6
Mac Haik	WR	6'1"	196	24		
Charlie Joiner	WR	5'11"	185	22		18
Jerry LeVias	WR	5'10"	175	23		30
Paul Zaeske	WR	6'2"	200	24		
Donnie Davis	TE	6'4"	225	30		
Alvin Reed	TE	6'5"	230	26		12
Terry Stoepel	TE	6'4"	235	25		
Roy Gerela	K	5'10"	185	22		77
Spike Jones	K	6'2"	190	23		

CINCINNATI BENGALS

RUSHING

Last Name	No.	Yds	Avg	TD
Phillips	163	648	4.0	4
Robinson	149	622	4.2	6
E. Johnson	65	273	4.2	2
Carter	34	246	7.2	2
Wyche	19	118	6.2	2
Dressler	18	77	4.3	0
Lamb	6	35	5.8	0
Crabtree	3	23	7.7	0
Lewis	2	8	4.0	0
Thomas	2	7	3.5	0

RECEIVING

Last Name	No.	Yds	Avg	TD
Myers	32	542	17	1
Phillips	31	124	4	1
Trumpy	29	480	17	2
Thomas	21	257	12	2
Crabtree	19	231	12	2
Robinson	17	175	10	1
E. Johnson	15	190	13	2
Coslet	8	98	12	1

PUNT RETURNS

Last Name	No.	Yds	Avg	TD
Parrish	23	194	8	1
E. Johnson	7	72	10	0
Graham	1	41	41	0
Thomas	4	20	5	0
Robinson	1	0	0	0
Smith	1	0	0	0

KICKOFF RETURNS

Last Name	No.	Yds	Avg	TD
Parrish	16	482	30	1
Robinson	14	363	26	0
E. Johnson	3	68	23	0
Dressler	4	48	12	0
Lamb	2	41	21	0

PASSING – PUNTING – KICKING

PASSING	Att	Comp	%	Yds	Yd/Att	TD	Int–	%	RK
Carter	278	143	51	1647	5.9	9	9–	3	7
Wyche	57	26	46	411	7.2	3	2–	4	
Lewis	4	3	75	39	9.8	0	0–	0	

PUNTING	No	Avg
Lewis	79	46.2

KICKING	XP	Att	%	FG	ATT	%
Muhlman	33	33	100	25	37	68

CLEVELAND BROWNS

RUSHING

Last Name	No.	Yds	Avg	TD
Kelly	206	656	3.2	6
Scott	151	625	4.1	7
Morrison	73	175	2.4	0
Phipps	11	94	8.5	0
Minniear	12	39	3.3	1
Morin	1	2	2.0	0
Nelsen	7	−4	−0.6	0
Brown	1	−8	−8.0	0

RECEIVING

Last Name	No.	Yds	Avg	TD
Scott	40	351	9	4
Morin	37	611	17	1
Hooker	28	490	18	2
Collins	26	351	14	4
Kelly	24	311	13	2
Glass	19	403	21	2
H. Jones	10	141	14	1
Morrison	5	95	19	1
Minniear	1	−1	−1	0

PUNT RETURNS

Last Name	No.	Yds	Avg	TD
Morrison	15	133	9	0
Sumner	8	70	9	0
Schoen	8	18	2	0
Kelly	2	15	8	0
Jenkins	1	0	0	0

KICKOFF RETURNS

Last Name	No.	Yds	Avg	TD
H. Jones	29	739	25	1
Morrison	7	153	22	0
Brown	2	44	22	0
Schoen	1	27	27	0
Matheson	2	21	11	0
Righetti	1	17	17	0
Glass	1	0	0	0
Morin	1	0	0	0

PASSING – PUNTING – KICKING

PASSING	Att	Comp	%	Yds	Yd/Att	TD	Int–	%	RK
Nelsen	313	159	51	2156	6.9	16	16–	5	8
Phipps	60	29	48	529	8.8	1	5–	8	
Gault	19	2	11	67	3.5	0	3–	16	

PUNTING	No	Avg
Cockroft	71	42.6

KICKING	XP	Att	%	FG	Att	%
Cockroft	34	35	97	12	22	55

PITTSBURGH STEELERS

RUSHING

Last Name	No.	Yds	Avg	TD
Fuqua	138	691	5.0	7
Pearson	173	503	2.9	2
Bradshaw	32	233	7.3	1
Bankston	26	122	4.7	2
Hoak	40	115	2.9	1
Bryant	3	25	8.3	0
Wilburn	5	25	5.0	0
Cole	9	8	0.9	0
Smith	1	6	6.0	0
Hanratty	4	−5	−1.3	0
Hughes	1	−8	−8.0	0

RECEIVING

Last Name	No.	Yds	Avg	TD
Shanklin	30	691	23	4
Smith	30	458	15	2
Hughes	24	332	14	3
Fuqua	23	289	13	2
Bryant	8	154	19	0
Bankston	7	30	4	0
Staggers	6	118	20	1
Wilburn	6	77	13	0
Pearson	6	71	12	0
Hoak	4	25	6	0
Adams	3	36	12	0
Cole	3	31	10	0

PUNT RETURNS

Last Name	No.	Yds	Avg	TD
Bryant	37	159	4	0
Staggers	13	70	5	0
Blount	1	52	52	0

KICKOFF RETURNS

Last Name	No.	Yds	Avg	TD
Blount	18	535	30	0
Staggers	14	333	24	0
Pearson	4	114	29	0
Sharp	1	9	9	0
Wenzel	1	6	6	0
Calland	1	0	0	0
Washington	1	0	0	0

PASSING – PUNTING – KICKING

PASSING	Att	Comp	%	Yds	Yd/Att	TD	Int–	%	RK
Bradshaw	218	83	38	1410	6.5	6	24–	11	15
Hanratty	163	64	39	842	5.2	5	8–	5	14
Hoak	2	2	100	40	20.0	1	0–	0	
Walden	1	1	100	20	20.0	0	0–	0	

PUNTING	No	Avg
Walden	75	45.2
Bradshaw	3	17.3

KICKING	XP	Att	%	FG	Att	%
Mingo	17	17	100	5	18	28
Watson	7	8	88	5	10	50

HOUSTON OILERS

RUSHING

Last Name	No.	Yds	Avg	TD
Dawkins	124	517	4.2	2
Richardson	103	368	3.6	2
Hopkins	57	207	3.6	3
Campbell	59	189	3.2	1
Granger	51	169	3.3	1
Rhome	9	54	6.0	1
LeVias	7	37	5.3	0
Naponic	3	12	4.0	0
C. Johnson	5	3	0.6	0
Smiley	1	0	0.0	0

RECEIVING

Last Name	No.	Yds	Avg	TD
Reed	47	604	13	2
LeVias	41	529	13	5
Richardson	34	381	11	1
Joiner	28	416	15	3
Haik	17	190	11	0
Beirne	16	216	14	1
Dawkins	15	94	6	0
Campbell	15	78	5	0
Hopkins	14	142	10	0
Granger	11	118	11	0

PUNT RETURNS

Last Name	No.	Yds	Avg	TD
LeVias	25	213	9	0
Richardson	10	30	3	0
Houston	4	13	3	0
Beirne	1	1	1	0
Dawkins	1	0	0	0

KICKOFF RETURNS

Last Name	No.	Yds	Avg	TD
LeVias	26	598	23	0
B. Johnson	15	320	21	0
Moore	7	190	27	0
Drungo	1	25	25	0
Hopkins	1	20	20	0
Lewis	1	15	15	0
Davis	2	0	0	0
Granger	1	0	0	0
Reed	1	0	0	0

PASSING – PUNTING – KICKING

PASSING	Att	Comp	%	Yds	Yd/Att	TD	Int–	%	RK
C. Johnson	281	144	51	1652	5.9	7	12–	4	10
Rhome	168	88	52	1031	6.1	5	8–	5	11
Naponic	20	6	30	85	4.3	0	2–	10	
LeVias	0	0	0	0	0.0	0	1–	100	

PUNTING	No	Avg
Jones	84	42.4

KICKING	XP	Att	%	FG	Att	%
Gerela	23	23	100	18	32	56

OAKLAND RAIDERS 8-4-2 John Madden

Scores of Each Game		
21	Cincinnati	31
27	San Diego	27
13	Miami	20
35	DENVER	23
34	WASHINGTON	20
31	PITTSBURGH	14
17	Kansas City	17
23	CLEVELAND	20
24	Denver	19
20	SAN DIEGO	17
14	Detroit	28
14	N.Y. Jets	13
20	KANSAS CITY	6
7	SAN FRANCISCO	38

Use Name	Pos.	Hgt	Wgt	Age	Int	Pts
Harry Schuh	OT	6'2"	260	27		
Art Shell	OT	6'5"	255	23		
Bob Svihus	OT	6'4"	245	27		
George Buehler	OG	6'2"	260	23		
Jim Harvey	OG	6'5"	250	27		
Gene Upshaw	OG	6'5"	255	25		
Jim Otto	C	6'2"	248	32		
Tony Cline	DE	6'2"	230	22	1	
Ben Davidson	DE	6'8"	280	30		
Carleton Oats	DT-DE	6'2"	260	27		
Al Dotson	DT	6'4"	260	27		
Tom Keating	DT	6'3"	247	27		
Art Thoms	DT	6'5"	250	23		
Duane Benson	LB	6'2"	215	25	1	
Bill Budness	LB	6'1"	215	27		
Dan Conners	LB	6'1"	230	28		
Gerald Irons	LB	6'2"	230	23		
Bill Laskey	LB	6'2"	235	27	1	
Gus Otto	LB	6'2"	220	27		
Carl Weathers	LB	6'2"	220	22		
Butch Atkinson	DB	6'	180	23	3	
Willie Brown	DB	6'1"	190	29	3	
Dave Grayson	DB	5'10"	187	31	1	
Kent McCloughan	DB	6'1"	190	27	5	
Jimmy Warren	DB	5'11"	175	31	2	
Nemiah Wilson	DB	6'	160	27	2	
Alvin Wyatt	DB	5'10"	185	22		6
George Blanda	QB	6'1"	215	42		84
Daryle Lamonica	QB	6'2"	215	29		
Ken Stabler	QB	6'3"	194	24		
Pete Banaszak	HB	5'11"	200	26		12
Don Highsmith	HB	6'	200	22		
Charlie Smith	HB	6'1"	205	24		30
Larry Todd	HB	6'1"	185	27		
Hewritt Dixon	FB	6'2"	230	30		12
Marv Hubbard	FB	6'1"	215	24		6
Fred Biletnikoff	WR	6'1"	190	27		42
Drew Buie	WR	6'2"	178	23		
Rod Sherman	WR	6'	190	25		
Warren Wells	WR	6'1"	190	27		66
Ray Chester	TE	6'3"	220	22		42
Ted Koy	TE	6'1"	210	22		
Jacque MacKinnon	TE	6'4"	240	31		
Mike Eischeid	K	6'	190	29		

Roger Hagberg – died April 15, 1970 Auto Accident

KANSAS CITY CHIEFS 7-5-2 Hank Stram

Scores of Each Game		
10	Minnesota	27
44	Baltimore	24
13	Denver	26
23	BOSTON	10
27	Cincinnati	19
16	DALLAS	27
17	OAKLAND	17
24	HOUSTON	9
31	Pittsburgh	14
6	ST. LOUIS	6
26	SAN DIEGO	14
16	DENVER	0
6	Oakland	20
13	San Diego	31

Use Name	Pos.	Hgt	Wgt	Age	Int	Pts
Dave Hill	OT	6'5"	260	29		
Sid Smith	OT	6'4"	260	22		
Jim Tyrer	OT	6'6"	270	31		
Ed Budde	OG	6'5"	260	29		
George Daney	OG	6'3"	240	23		
Mo Moorman	OG	6'5"	252	26		
E. J. Holub	C	6'4"	236	32		
Mike Oriard	C	6'4"	223	22		
Jack Rudnay	C	6'3"	240	22		
Aaron Brown	DE	6'5"	265	26		
Jerry Mays	DE	6'4"	250	30		
Marv Upshaw	DE	6'3"	245	23		
Buck Buchanan	DT	6'7"	275	30		
Curley Culp	DT	6'1"	265	24		
Bob Liggett	DT	6'2"	255	23		
Bobby Bell	LB	6'4"	228	30	3	6
Chuck Hurston	LB	6'6"	240	27		
Willie Lanier	LB	6'1"	245	25	2	
Jim Lynch	LB	6'1"	235	25	3	
Bob Stein	LB	6'2"	235	22		
Clyde Werner	LB	6'4"	225	22		
Ceasar Belser	DB	6'	212	25		
Dave Hadley	DB	5'9"	186	21		
Jim Kearney	DB	6'2"	206	27	4	
Jim Marsalis	DB	5'11"	194	24	4	
Willie Mitchell	DB	6'1"	185	28		
Johnny Robinson	DB	6'	205	31	10	6
Emmitt Thomas	DB	6'2"	192	27	5	
Len Dawson	QB	6'	190	36		
John Huarte	QB	6'	185	26		
Mike Livingston	QB	6'3"	212	24		
Warren McVea	HB	5'10"	182	24		
Ed Podolak	HB	6'1"	204	23		24
Wendell Hayes	FB	6'2"	220	29		30
Robert Holmes	FB	5'9"	220	24		24
Frank Pitts	WR	6'2"	200	26		12
Otis Taylor	WR	6'2"	215	27		18
Lewis Porter	WR	5'11"	178	23		
Gloster Richardson	WR	6'	200	27		12
Fred Arbanas	TE	6'3"	245	31		6
Billy Cannon	TE	6'1"	215	33		12
Morris Stroud	TE	6'10"	245	24		6
Jan Stenerud	K	6'2"	187	27		116
Jerrel Wilson	K	6'4"	222	28		

Remi Prudhomme–Injury
Goldie Sellers–Thigh Injury
Gene Trosch–Thigh Injury

SAN DIEGO CHARGERS 5-6-3 Charlie Waller

Scores of Each Game		
14	BALTIMORE	16
27	OAKLAND	27
10	Los Angeles	37
20	GREEN BAY	22
20	Chicago	7
31	HOUSTON	31
27	Cleveland	10
24	DENVER	21
16	Boston	14
17	Oakland	20
14	Kansas City	26
14	CINCINNATI	17
17	Denver	17
31	KANSAS CITY	13

Use Name	Pos.	Hgt	Wgt	Age	Int	Pts
Terry Owens	OT	6'6"	275	26		
Russ Washington	OT	6'6"	295	23		
Bob Wells	OT	6'4"	280	25		
Ira Gordon	OG	6'3"	268	22		
Bill Lenkaitis	OG	6'3"	265	24		
Jim Schmedding	OG	6'2"	250	24		
Walt Sweeney	OG	6'3"	256	29		
Sam Gruneisen	C	6'1"	250	29		
Cal Withrow	C	6'	240	25		
Bob Briggs	DE	6'4"	276	25		
Joe Owens	DE	6'2"	235	23		2
Jeff Staggs	DE	6'2"	246	26		
Ron Billingsley	DT	6'8"	290	25		
Steve DeLong	DT	6'3"	252	27	1	
Gene Ferguson	DT	6'7"	300	22		
Andy Rice	DT	6'3"	268	28		
Tom Williams	DT	6'4"	250	22		
Bob Babich	LB	6'2"	230	23		
Pete Barnes	LB	6'3"	247	25	3	
Bob Bruggers	LB	6'1"	224	26		
Jack Protz	LB	6'1"	218	22		
Rick Redman	LB	5'11"	230	27		
Joe Beauchamp	DB	6'	185	26	1	
Chuck Detwiler	DB	6'	185	23		6
Speedy Duncan	DB	5'10"	175	27		
Chris Fletcher	DB	5'11"	185	21		
Jim Hill	DB	6'2"	190	23		
Bob Howard	DB	6'1"	190	25	2	
Jim Tolbert	DB	6'3"	207	26	2	
Wayne Clark	QB	6'2"	200	23		
Marty Domres	QB	6'3"	215	23		
John Hadl	QB	6'2"	218	30		6
Mike Garrett (from KC)	HB	5'9"	200	26		12
Dickie Post	HB	5'9"	190	24		6
Dave Smith	HB	6'1"	210	22		
Russ Smith	FB-HB	6'1"	212	26		18
Brad Hubbert	FB	6'1"	240	29		6
Jeff Queen	FB	6'1"	220	24		12
Gene Foster	HB-FB	5'11"	220	27		
Lance Alworth	WR	6'	180	30		24
Rick Eber	WR	6'	185	25		
Gary Garrison	WR	6'1"	193	26		72
Walker Gillette	WR	6'5"	198	23		
Willie Frazier	TE	6'4"	250	27		48
Art Strozier	TE	6'2"	220	24		
Mike Mercer	K	6'	215	34		70
Dennis Partee	K	6'2"	218	24		

Ron Mix– Voluntarily Retired
Houston Ridge– Injury

DENVER BRONCOS 5-8-1 Lou Saban

Scores of Each Game		
25	Buffalo	10
16	PITTSBURGH	13
26	KANSAS CITY	13
23	Oakland	35
24	ATLANTA	10
14	San Francisco	19
3	WASHINGTON	19
21	San Diego	24
19	OAKLAND	24
31	New Orleans	6
21	Houston	31
0	Kansas City	16
17	SAN DIEGO	17
13	CLEVELAND	27

Use Name	Pos.	Hgt	Wgt	Age	Int	Pts
Sam Brunelli	OT	6'1"	270	27		
Mike Current	OT	6'4"	274	24		
Steve Alexakos	OG	6'2"	260	23		
George Goeddeke	OG	6'3"	253	25		
Mike Schnitker	OG	6'3"	245	23		
Bob Young	OG	6'2"	256	27		
Jay Bachman	C	6'3"	250	24		
Larry Kaminski	C	6'2"	245	25		
Walt Barnes	DE	6'3"	250	26		
Pete Duranko	DE	6'2"	250	26		
Rich Jackson	DE	6'2"	255	29		
Alden Roche	DE	6'4"	255	25		
Dave Costa	DT	6'2"	260	28		
Jerry Inman	DT	6'3"	256	30		
Paul Smith	DT	6'3"	256	25		
Bill Butler	LB	6'4"	226	26		
Ken Criter	LB	5'11"	223	23		
Carl Cunningham	LB	6'3"	240	26		
Fred Forsberg	LB	6'1"	235	26		
Bill McKoy	LB	6'3"	235	22		
Chip Myrtle	LB	6'2"	225	25		
Dave Washington	LB	6'5"	215	21		2
Booker Edgerson	DB	5'10"	183	31		
Drake Garrett	DB	5'9"	183	24		
Cornell Gordon	DB	6'	187	29	3	
Charlie Greer	DB	6'	205	24	4	
Pete Jaquess	DB	6'	182	28		
Paul Martha	DB	6'	187	27	6	
George Saimes	DB	5'10"	185	28		
Bill Thompson	DB	6'1"	200	23	2	
Bob Wade	DB	6'2"	200	25	1	
Alvin Mitchell	WR-DB	6'3"	195	26		
Pete Liske	QB	6'2"	206	29		6
Al Pastrana	QB	6'1"	190	25		6
Steve Tensi	QB	6'5"	210	27		
Floyd Little	HB	5'10"	196	28		18
Wandy Williams	HB	6'1"	190	24		
Bobby Anderson	FB-HB	6'	208	22		24
Willie Crenshaw	FB	6'2"	230	29		36
Clem Turner	FB	6'1"	236	25		12
Fran Lynch	HB-FB	6'1"	205	24		6
Al Denson	WR	6'2"	208	28		12
John Embree	WR	6'4"	194	26		
Mike Haffner	WR	6'2"	205	28		6
Jerry Hendren	WR	6'2"	187	22		
Bill Van Heusen	WR	6'1"	200	24		12
Bill Masters	TE	6'5"	240	26		12
Jim Whalen	TE	6'2"	210	26		18
Bobby Howfield	K	5'9"	180	33		81

John Huard–Injury

OAKLAND RAIDERS

RUSHING

Last Name	No.	Yds	Avg	TD
Dixon	197	861	4.4	1
Smith	168	681	4.1	3
Hubbard	51	246	4.8	1
Banaszak	21	75	3.6	2
Todd	17	39	2.3	0
Wells	3	34	11.3	0
Lamonica	8	24	3.0	0
Blanda	2	4	2.0	0
Sherman	1	2	2.0	0
Highsmith	2	2	1.0	0
Stabler	1	–4	–4.0	0

RECEIVING

Last Name	No.	Yds	Avg	TD
Biletnikoff	45	768	17	7
Wells	43	935	22	11
Chester	42	556	13	7
Dixon	31	207	7	1
Smith	23	173	8	2
Sherman	18	285	16	0
Todd	5	51	10	0
Buie	2	52	26	0
Banaszak	1	2	2	0

PUNT RETURNS

Last Name	No.	Yds	Avg	TD
Wyatt	25	231	9	1
Sherman	8	65	8	0
Atkinson	4	12	3	0

KICKOFF RETURNS

Last Name	No.	Yds	Avg	TD
Atkinson	23	574	25	0
Wyatt	13	286	22	0
Warren	2	47	24	0
Hubbard	2	41	21	0
Sherman	2	39	20	0
Thoms	2	30	15	0

PASSING – PUNTING – KICKING

PASSING	Att	Comp	%	Yds	Yd/Att	TD	Int–	%	RK
Lamonica	356	179	50	2516	7.1	22	15–	4	1
Blanda	55	29	53	461	8.4	5	5–	9	
Stabler	7	2	29	52	7.4	0	1–	14	

PUNTING	No	Avg
Eischeid	79	39.5

KICKING	XP	Att	%	FG	Att	%
Blanda	36	36	100	16	29	55

KANSAS CITY CHIEFS

RUSHING

Last Name	No.	Yds	Avg	TD
Podolak	168	749	4.5	3
Hayes	109	381	3.5	5
McVea	61	260	4.3	0
Holmes	63	206	3.3	3
Pitts	5	84	16.8	0
Dawson	11	46	4.2	0
Livingston	3	26	8.7	0
Porter	2	21	10.5	0
Taylor	3	13	4.3	0
Cannon	1	6	6.0	0
Richardson	1	4	4.0	0

RECEIVING

Last Name	No.	Yds	Avg	TD
Taylor	34	618	18	3
Podolak	26	307	12	1
Hayes	26	219	8	0
Holmes	23	173	8	1
Pitts	11	172	16	2
Arbanas	8	108	14	1
Cannon	7	125	18	2
Richardson	5	171	34	2
McVea	5	26	5	0
Stroud	4	86	22	1
Porter	1	29	29	0

PUNT RETURNS

Last Name	No.	Yds	Avg	TD
Podolak	23	311	14	0
Mitchell	4	33	8	0
Porter	1	–3	–3	0

KICKOFF RETURNS

Last Name	No.	Yds	Avg	TD
Holmes	19	535	28	0
Podolak	17	348	20	0
McVea	3	57	19	0
Stein	3	23	8	0
Porter	1	22	22	0
Smith	1	12	12	0

PASSING – PUNTING – KICKING

PASSING	Att	Comp	%	Yds	Yd/Att	TD	Int–	%	RK
Dawson	262	141	54	1876	7.2	13	14–	5	3
Livingston	22	11	50	122	5.6	0	1–	5	
Huarte	2	0	0	0	0.0	0	1–	50	
Podolak	2	2	100	40	20.0	0	0–	0	
McVea	1	0	0	0	0.0	0	0–	0	

PUNTING	No	Avg
Wilson	76	44.9

KICKING	XP	Att	%	FG	Att	%
Stenerud	26	26	100	30	42	71

SAN DIEGO CHARGERS

RUSHING

Last Name	No.	Yds	Avg	TD
Queen	77	261	3.4	1
Post	74	225	3.0	1
Garrett	67	208	3.1	1
Hadl	28	188	6.7	1
Hubbert	49	175	3.6	1
R. Smith	52	163	3.1	3
Frazier	5	120	24.0	1
Foster	32	84	2.6	0
D. Smith	14	42	3.0	0
Domres	14	39	2.8	0
Garrison	4	7	1.8	0

RECEIVING

Last Name	No.	Yds	Avg	TD
Garrison	44	1006	23	12
Frazier	38	497	13	6
Alworth	35	608	17	4
Queen	20	236	12	1
Garrett	14	131	9	0
Post	13	113	9	0
Foster	10	92	9	0
Hubbert	7	44	6	0
R. Smith	5	44	9	0
D. Smith	4	66	16	0
Eber	2	43	22	0
Strozier	2	40	20	0
Gillette	2	21	11	0

PUNT RETURNS

Last Name	No.	Yds	Avg	TD
Fletcher	16	137	9	0
R. Smith	9	31	3	0
Garrett	3	30	10	0
Duncan	5	10	2	0
Detwiler	1	5	5	0

KICKOFF RETURNS

Last Name	No.	Yds	Avg	TD
Duncan	19	410	22	0
Fletcher	17	382	22	0
Queen	1	12	12	0
R. Smith	1	9	9	0
Beauchamp	1	0	0	0
Hill	1	0	0	0
T. Owens	1	0	0	0

PASSING – PUNTING – KICKING

PASSING	Att	Comp	%	Yds	Yd/Att	TD	Int–	%	RK
Hadl	327	162	50	2388	7.3	22	15–	5	2
Domres	55	28	51	491	8.9	2	4–	7	
Foster	3	1	33	9	3.0	0	0–	0	
Clark	2	1	50	48	24.0	0	0–	0	

PUNTING	No	Avg
Partee	65	43.9
Mercer	8	35.4
Hadl	1	30.0

KICKING	XP	Att	%	FG	Att	%
Mercer	34	35	97	12	19	63

DENVER BRONCOS

RUSHING

Last Name	No.	Yds	Avg	TD
Little	**209**	**901**	4.3	3
Anderson	83	368	4.4	4
Crenshaw	69	200	2.9	5
Turner	29	106	3.7	2
Pastrana	14	89	6.4	1
Lynch	20	81	4.1	1
Liske	7	42	6.0	1
Tensi	4	14	3.5	0
Haffner	1	1	1.0	0

RECEIVING

Last Name	No.	Yds	Avg	TD
Denson	47	646	14	2
Whalen	36	503	14	3
Crenshaw	18	105	6	1
Little	17	161	9	0
Van Heusen	16	382	24	2
Haffner	12	196	16	1
Anderson	9	140	16	0
Masters	9	83	9	2
Turner	8	23		0
Lynch	7	6		0
Embree	4			0

PUNT RETURNS

Last Name	No.	Yds	Avg	TD
Thompson	23	233	10	0
Little	22	187	9	0
Greer	14	123	9	0
Jaquess	4	13	3	0

KICKOFF RETURNS

Last Name	No.	Yds	Avg	TD
Anderson	21	520	25	0
Hendren	8	197	25	0
Thompson	9	188	21	0
Little	6	126	21	0
Turner	1	31	31	0
Criter	2	20	10	0
Washington	1	20	20	0
Myrtle	1	1	1	0
Lynch	0	11	0	0

PASSING – PUNTING – KICKING

PASSING	Att	Comp	%	Yds	Yd/Att	TD	Int–	%	RK
Liske	238	112	47	1340	5.6	7	11–	5	12
Tensi	80	38	48	539	6.7	3	8–	10	
Pastrana	75	29	39	420	5.6	1	9–	12	
Anderson	7	4	57	59	8.4	0	0–	0	
Little	2	0	0	0	0.0	0	0–	0	
Van Heusen	1	0	0	0	0.0	0	0–	0	

PUNTING	No	Avg
Van Heusen	87	42.9

KICKING	XP	Att	%	FG	Att	%
Howfield	27	28	96	18	32	56

1970 Championship Games

NFC CHAMPIONSHIP GAME

January 3, at San Francisco
(Attendance 59,364)

Two Interceptions Too Many

SCORING

SAN FRANCISCO	3	0	7	0–10
DALLAS	0	3	14	0–17

First Quarter
- S.F. — Gossett, 16 yard field goal

Second Quarter
- Dal. — Clark, 21 yard field goal

Third Quarter
- Dal. — Thomas, 13 yard rush; PAT–Clark (kick)
- Dal. — Garrison, 5 yard pass from Morton; PAT–Clark (kick)
- S.F. — Witcher, 26 yard pass from Brodie; PAT–Gossett (kick)

TEAM STATISTICS

S.F.		DALLAS
15	First Downs–Total	22
2	First Downs–Rushing	16
12	First Downs–Passing	5
1	First Downs–Penalty	1
1	Fumbles–Number	4
0	Fumbles–Lost Ball	1
5	Penalties–Number	7
51	Yards Penalized	75
1	Missed Field Goals	2
61	Offensive Plays–Total	75
307	Net Yards	319
5.0	Average Gain	4.3
2	Giveaways	1
1	Takeaways	2
–1	Difference	+1

The opening round of the first NFC playoffs had produced two interesting games, as the Cowboys had beaten the Lions 5-0 on a field as muddy as a pigsty and the '49ers had edged the tough Vikings 17-14. In the conference championship, the Cowboys and '49ers would use different offensive styles with different results.

Dallas quarterback Craig Morton had a sore arm and could not match the passing ability of San Francisco's John Brodie, but the Cowboys did have two strong runners in rookie Duane Thomas and Walt Garrison, plus a top-notch offensive line to block for them. Neither offense did much in the first quarter, as Bruce Gossett of San Francisco booted a 16-yard field goal while Dallas' Mike Clark missed from the 40. The defensive deadlock continued into the second period, with Clark hitting on a 21 yard field goal to knot the first half score at 3-3.

The Cowboys got the first big break of the game in the third period. With Dallas end Larry Cole putting heavy pressure on him, Brodie rushed a pass over the middle which Lee Roy Jordan picked off at the San Francisco 13-yard line. Duane Thomas covered the ground to the end zone on the very next play, and Clark's extra point made the score 10-3. The '49ers drove right back into Dallas territory, but Mel Renfro intercepted a Brodie pass on the 18-yard line to extinguish that threat. The Cowboys then pounded their way downfield on the running of Thomas and Garrison, with a swing pass from Morton to Garrison covering the final five yards to the goal line.

Brodie then led his team on a 73-yard drive capped by a 26-yard scoring pitch to Dick Witcher; with Gossett's extra point, the '49ers trailed 17-10 with fifteen minutes left to play. The Dallas defense stood firm for the rest of the day, however, and the Cowboys headed off to the Super Bowl after failing in four previous playoff tries.

INDIVIDUAL STATISTICS

SAN FRANCISCO	No	Yds	Avg.	DALLAS	No	Yds	Avg.
RUSHING							
Willard	13	42	3.2	Thomas	27	143	5.3
Cunningham	5	14	2.8	Garrison	17	71	4.2
Thomas	1	5	5.0	Welch	5	27	5.4
	19	61	3.2	Reeves	2	–12	–6.0
					51	229	4.5
RECEIVING							
Washington	6	88	14.7	Garrison	3	51	17.0
Cunningham	4	34	8.5	Thomas	2	24	12.0
Windsor	3	70	23.3	Rucker	1	21	21.0
Witcher	3	41	13.7	Ditka	1	5	5.0
Willard	2	22	11.0		7	101	14.4
Kwalick	1	7	7.0				
	19	262	13.8				
PUNTING							
Spurrier	5		41.0	Widby	6		40.2
PUNT RETURNS							
B. Taylor	2	5	2.5	Hayes	1	8	8.0
				Reeves	1	0	0.0
					2	8	4.0
KICKOFF RETURNS							
Thomas	3	66	22.0	Washington	1	20	20.0
Tucker	1	23	23.0	Waters	1	16	16.0
	4	89	22.3	Kiner	1	10	10.0
					3	46	15.3
INTERCEPTION RETURNS							
None				Renfro	1	19	19.0
				Jordan	1	4	4.0
					2	23	11.5

PASSING

SAN FRANCISCO	Att.	Comp.	Comp. Pct.	Yds.	Int.	Yds/ Att.	Yds/ Comp.	Yards Lost Tackled
Brodie	30	19	47.5	262	2	6.6	13.8	2–16
DALLAS								
Morton	22	7	31.8	101	0	4.6	14.4	2–11

AFC CHAMPIONSHIP GAME

January 3, at Baltimore
(Attendance 54,799)

Two Old Men and One Crown

SCORING

BALTIMORE	3	7	10	7–27
OAKLAND	0	3	7	7–17

First Quarter
- Balt. — O'Brien, 16 yard field goal

Second Quarter
- Balt. — Bulaich, 2 yard rush; PAT–O'Brien (kick)
- Oak. — Blanda, 48 yard field goal

Third Quarter
- Oak. — Biletnikoff, 38 yard pass from Blanda; PAT–Blanda (kick)
- Balt. — O'Brien, 23 yard field goal
- Balt. — Bulaich, 11 yard rush; PAT–O'Brien (kick)

Fourth Quarter
- Oak. — Wells, 15 yard pass from Blanda; PAT–Blanda (kick)
- Balt. — Perkins, 68 yard pass from Unitas; PAT–O'Brien (kick)

TEAM STATISTICS

BALT.		OAK.
18	First Downs–Total	16
7	First Downs–Rushing	5
11	First Downs–Passing	10
0	First Downs–Penalty	1
0	Fumbles–Number	1
0	Fumbles–Lost Ball	1
2	Penalties–Number	2
10	Yards Penalized	20
2	Missed Field Goals	0
71	Offensive Plays–Total	63
363	Net Yards	336
5.1	Average Gain	5.3
0	Giveaways	4
4	Takeaways	0
+4	Difference	–4

One old AFL team and one old NFL team squared off in the first AFC championship match. The Oakland Raiders got this far by beating the upcoming Miami Dolphins 21-14 in the first playoff round, while the Baltimore Colts arrived at this game fresh from a 17-0 whitewash of the Cincinnati Bengals. Before the game was over, it had developed into a duel of two of pro football's oldest quarterbacks, Johnny Unitas and George Blanda.

Baltimore scored the only points of the first quarter on Jim O'Brien's 16-yard field goal, as neither Unitas nor Oakland's Daryle Lamonica could spark the offense. Early in the second quarter, however, Lamonica pulled a thigh muscle when hit by Bubba Smith, so the forty-three-year-old Blanda had to take over at quarterback. By the time he entered the game, Baltimore had run its lead to 10-0 on a Norm Bulaich touchdown that Unitas had set up with a key pass to Eddie Hinton. When Blanda could drive his team only to the Baltimore 40-yard line, he simply kicked a field goal to net three points and drop the halftime score to 10-3.

The Raiders tied the score in the third quarter when Blanda hit Fred Biletnikoff with a 38-yard touchdown pass. Coolly directing his offense, Unitas brought the Colts back close enough for O'Brien to kick a field goal, and he engineered another long drive late in the period which Bulaich capped with his second touchdown.

Blanda responded in the final period by driving the Raiders 80 yards, with the final 15 yards coming on a pass to Warren Wells. The Raiders now trailed 20-17, but the Baltimore defense came through with clutch plays when needed. The Raiders twice were in scoring range of the Baltimore goal line, but both drives ended with Blanda passes getting intercepted in the end zone. The Colts finally iced the victory away when Unitas hit Ray Perkins, one of four wide receivers in on the play, with a 68-yard scoring pass which lengthened the final score to 27-17.

INDIVIDUAL STATISTICS

BALTIMORE	No	Yds	Avg.	OAKLAND	No	Yds	Avg.
RUSHING							
Bulaich	22	71	3.2	Dixon	10	51	5.1
Nowatzke	8	32	4.0	Smith	9	44	4.9
Hill	5	12	2.4	Hubbard	3	12	4.0
Unitas	2	9	4.5		22	107	4.9
Havrilak	1	2	2.0				
	38	126	3.3				
RECEIVING							
Hinton	5	115	23.0	Wells	5	108	21.6
Jefferson	3	36	12.0	Biletnikoff	5	92	18.4
Perkins	2	80	40.0	Dixon	3	15	5.0
Mackey	1	14	14.0	Chester	2	36	18.0
	11	245	22.3	Smith	2	21	10.5
				Hubbard	1	5	5.0
					18	277	15.4
PUNTING							
Lee	6		45.3	Eischeid	5		40.0
PUNT RETURNS							
Gardin	2	1	0.5	Atkinson	2	10	5.0
KICKOFF RETURNS							
Duncan	4	105	26.3	Atkinson	2	37	18.5
				Sherman	1	23	23.0
					3	60	20.0
INTERCEPTION RETURNS							
Logan	1	16	16.0	None			
May	1	0	0.0				
Volk	1	0	0.0				
	3	16	5.3				

PASSING

BALTIMORE	Att.	Comp.	Comp. Pct.	Yds.	Int.	Yds/ Att.	Yds/ Comp.	Yards Lost Taclked
Unitas	30	11	36.7	245	0	8.2	22.3	3– 8
OAKLAND								
Blanda	32	17	53.0	271	3	8.5	15.9	
Lamonica	4	1	25.0	6	0	1.5	6.0	
	36	18	50.0	277	3	7.7	15.4	5–48

SUPER BOWL V

January 17, at Miami

(Attendance 80.055)

Follow the Bouncing Ball

The first Super Bowl under the new merger arrangement ended in high drama after being, for most of the afternoon, a comedy of errors. Both the Dallas Cowboys and Baltimore Colts took turns giving the game away, but neither team would take it until the final seconds of play.

The strong defenses of both clubs dominated the first-quarter action, although the Cowboys did score on a 14-yard Mike Clark field goal. Another Clark field goal made the score 6-0 in the second quarter when the Colts tied the score on a fluke play. Baltimore quarterback Johnny Unitas threw a long pass down the center of the field to wide receiver Eddie Hinton; the ball bounced off Hinton's hands, back up into the air, grazed the fingertips of Dallas cornerback Mel Renfro, and came right down to the surprised John Mackey. Taking the ball around mid-field, Mackey sprinted the rest of the way to the end zone. The Cowboys blocked the Baltimore extra point, however, so the score remained tied at 6-6.

On the next Baltimore offensive series, a hard tackle by George Andrie forced Unitas to fumble the ball on his own 29-yard line and sent him out of the game with bruised ribs. Cowboy quarterback Craig Morton, operating with a sore arm, then moved his team down to the 7-yard line, from where a short pass to Duane Thomas scored the only Dallas touchdown of the day. Clark's conversion ran the score to 13-6, and neither offense could score again before the end of the half.

The Colts kept up the parade of mistakes when Jim Duncan fumbled the opening kickoff deep in Baltimore territory. The Cowboys then drove from the 31-yard line to the two-yard line on five plays, with Thomas' hard running the key element. With the ball in the shadows of the goal posts, Thomas took a handoff and fumbled the ball, the Colts recovering on the one-foot line.

With the threat erased, the third quarter settled into a pattern of offensive futility, with neither Morton nor Earl Morrall, filling in for the injured Unitas, able to ignite an attack. With only eight minutes left in the game, the Cowboys still clung to their 13-6 lead.

At that point, however, a Morton pass bounced off the fingers of fullback Walt Garrison into the hands of Colt safety Rick Volk, who returned the ball 17 yards to the Dallas three-yard line. In short order, Tom Nowatzke smashed over for the touchdown, and Jim O'Brien added the tying extra point.

Overtime seemed imminent late in the final quarter, but another Morton pass was intercepted with 1:09 left in the game. Mike Curtis stole the pass on the Dallas 41 and returned it to the 28. Two running plays ran the clock down, and then Jim O'Brien, Baltimore's rookie kicker, booted a 32-yard three-pointer to give the Colts an artistically flawed but nonetheless satisfying 16-13 victory.

BALTIMORE		DALLAS
	OFFENSE	
Hinton	WR	Hayes
Vogel	LT	Neely
Ressler	LG	Niland
Curry	C	Manders
Williams	RG	Nye
Sullivan	RT	Wright
Mackey	TE	Norman
Jefferson	WR	Rucker
Unitas	QB	Morton
Bulaich	RB	Thomas
Nowatzke	RB	Garrison
	DEFENSE	
Bubba Smith	LE	Cole
B. R. Smith	LT	Pugh
Miller	RT	Lilly
Hilton	RE	Andrie
May	LLB	Edwards
Curtis	MLB	Jordan
Hendricks	RLB	Howley
Stukes	LCB	Adderley
Duncan	RCB	Renfro
Logan	LS	Green
Volk	RS	Waters

SUBSTITUTES

BALTIMORE

Offense

Ball	Maitland
Goode	Mitchell
Havrilak	Morrall
J. Hill	Perkins
Johnson	

Defense

Gardin	Newsome
Grant	Nichols
Maxwell	

Kickers

O'Brien	Lee

DALLAS

Offense

Asher	Homan
Ditka	Reeves
C. Hill	Welch

Defense

East	Lewis
Flowers	Stincic
Harris	Toomay
Kiner	Washington

Kickers

Clark	Widby

SCORING

BALTIMORE	0	6	0	10	–16
DALLAS	3	10	0	0	–13

First Quarter
- Dall. Clark, 14 yard field goal

Second Quarter
- Dall. Clark, 30 yard field goal
- Balt. Mackey, 75 yard pass from Unitas
  - PAT – O'Brien (kick–blocked)
- Dall. Thomas, 7 yard pass from Morton
  - PAT – Clark (kick)

Fourth Quarter
- Balt. Nowatzke, 2 yard rush
  - PAT – O'Brien (kick)
- Balt. O'Brien, 32 yard field goal

TEAM STATISTICS

BALT.		DALLAS
14	First Downs – Total	10
4	First Downs – Rushing	4
6	First Downs – Passing	5
4	First Downs – Penalty	1
5	Fumbles – Number	1
3	Fumbles – Lost Ball	1
4	Penalties – Number	10
31	Yards Penalized	133
1	Missed Field Goals	0
56	Offensive Plays	59
329	Net Yards	215
5.9	Average Gain	3.7
6	Giveaways	4
4	Takeaways	6
–2	Difference	+2

INDIVIDUAL STATISTICS

BALTIMORE	No	Yds	Avg.	DALLAS	No	Yds	Avg.
			RUSHING				
Nowatzke	10	33	3.3	Garrison	12	65	5.4
Bulaich	18	28	1.6	Thomas	18	35	1.9
Unitas	1	4	4.0	Morton	1	2	2.0
Havrilak	1	3	3.0		31	102	3.3
Morrall	1	1	1.0				
	31	69	2.2				
			RECEIVING				
Jefferson	3	52	17.3	Reeves	5	46	9.2
Mackey	2	80	40.0	Thomas	4	21	5.3
Hinton	2	51	25.5	Garrison	2	19	9.5
Havrilak	2	27	13.5	Hayes	1	41	41.0
Nowatzke	1	45	45.0		12	127	10.6
Bulaich	1	5	5.0				
	11	260	23.6				
			PUNTING				
Lee	4		41.5	Widby	9		41.9
			PUNT RETURNS				
Gardin	4	4	1.0	Hayes	3	9	3.0
Logan	1	8	8.0				
	5	12	2.4				
			KICKOFF RETURNS				
Duncan	4	90	22.5	Harris	1	18	18.0
				Hill	1	14	14.0
				Lewis	1	2	2.0
					3	34	11.1
			INTERCEPTION RETURNS				
Volk	1	30	30.0	Howley	2	22	11.0
Logan	1	14	14.0	Renfro	1	0	0.0
Curtis	1	13	13.0		3	22	7.3
	3	57	19.0				

PASSING

BALTIMORE	Att	Comp	Comp Pct.	Yds.	Int	Yds/ Att.	Yds/ Comp	Yards Lost Tackled
Morrall	15	7	46.7	147	1	9.8	21.0	0– 0
Unitas	9	3	33.3	88	2	9.8	29.3	0– 0
Havrilak	1	1	100.0	25	0	25.0	25.0	0– 0
	25	11	44.0	260	3	10.4	23.6	0– 0
DALLAS								
Morton	26	12	46.2	127	3	4.9	10.6	2–14

1971 N.F.C. With a Little Offensive Help

The long bomb and frequent passing had enlivened the game ever since Don Hutson and Sammy Baugh made their debuts in the 1930s and had become a way of offensive life since the days of Otto Graham and Bob Waterfield in the late 1940s. This year, however, defense had caught up. With most teams rigging up complex zone defenses which rendered long-passing quarterbacks impotent, scoring dropped and the field-goal kicker replaced the deep receiver as pro football's glamorous point producer. To counter the new defenses, pro offenses employed big, strong running backs and quarterbacks who could throw on the roll-out play and carry the ball occasionally. But a rule of thumb for this season was that the team with the better defense usually won; indeed, all four teams which made the playoffs had outstanding defenses which often overshadowed their offensive platoons.

EASTERN DIVISION

Dallas Cowboys—For the first half of the season, coach Tom Landry alternated Craig Morton and Roger Staubach at quarterback; the Cowboys won four games and lost three. But starting with the eighth game, Landry gave the job full time to Staubach, and the team won its last seven games to move past the Redskins into first place. Both Dallas quarterbacks were fine passers, but Staubach gave the defense something extra to worry about by often running with the ball. By mid-season, defenses also had to worry about Duane Thomas running the ball. After sitting out the early games over a salary dispute, Thomas returned to the team in a sullen mood, but his ball-carrying fit right into the Dallas scheme of things.

Washington Redskins—When George Allen was hired as head coach, he immediately set out to trade for veteran players who would make no mistakes on the field. The resulting collection of football oldsters became known as the Over the Hill Gang. In a dazzling array of trades, Allen picked up Billy Kilmer, Roy Jefferson, Boyd Dowler, Clifton McNeil, Ron McDole, Verlon Biggs, Diron Talbert, Jack Pardee, Myron Pottios, Richie Petitbon, John Wilbur, and Speedy Duncan. Allen rigged together a defense which indeed made no errors, which delighted in forcing enemy offenses into fumbles and interceptions. The Washington attack started out fast but slumped when injuries erased Sonny Jurgensen, Charley Taylor, and Jerry Smith from the lineup and cut down on Larry Brown's effectiveness.

Philadelphia Eagles—Apparently on the way to another dismal season after losing their first three games, the Eagles fired head coach Jerry Williams and replaced him with young Ed Khayat. The Eagles lost their first two games under Khayat, but then went on to a 7-2 record. The defense triggered the reversal by jelling into one of the league's top units. On this surprising platoon, only Tim Rossovich and Bill Bradley had recognizable names; the others were parts of a nameless horde which swarmed over enemy players. The Eagles' offense, on the other hand, was feeble.

St. Louis Cardinals—Bob Hollway's first season as head coach flattened out into a 4-9-1 record and a disappointing fourth-place finish in the East. Hollway had coached the magnificent Viking defense as an assistant at Minnesota, but the St. Louis defense this season suffered from a variety of injuries and a slow adjustment to Hollway's new system. The Cardinal offense also sputtered, with neither Jim Hart nor Pete Beathard taking charge at quarterback.

New York Giants—The Giants had the worst defense in the NFC, totally unable to put pressure on enemy passers, while the secondary suffered from injuries and Bennie McRae's advanced years. Ron Johnson's knee injury ripped the heart out of the Giant running attack. In the passing department, quarterback Fran Tarkenton found tight end Bob Tucker a congenial target, but there was no deep threat to replace the traded Homer Jones.

CENTRAL DIVISION

Minnesota Vikings—The Vikings' great defense again won first place in the Central Division, but the Minnesota offense just didn't have the power or direction to make the Vikings a complete team. At the quarterback spot, Gary Cuozzo, Bob Lee, and Norm Snead all rotated without any of them igniting a spark in the attack. Injuries to receivers Gene Washington and John Beasley also hurt the passing game, although Bob Grim rebounded from years of injuries to become a legitimate deep threat. Clint Jones, Dave Osborn, Jim Lindsey, Oscar Reed, and Bill Brown all were short-yardage runners, adept at grinding out yards behind the strong Viking front wall.

Detroit Lions—Blossoming into stardom in his fourth pro season was quarterback Greg Landry, a man with a strong passing arm plus the size and strength of a fullback in carrying the ball. Landry set a record for quarterbacks this season with 530 yards rushing. Second in the entire NFC in rushing yardage was Lion fullback Steve Owens, the powerful Heisman Trophy winner who had suffered through an injury-ruined rookie season last year. With Altie Taylor also picking up yardage on the ground, the Lions had the best running attack in the conference. The defense held the Lions back this season, with the front four unable to mount a pass rush now that Alex Karras had passed his prime and was cut loose before the season started. One tragic note of the season was the death of Chuck Hughes, who collapsed of a heart attack on the field in full view of millions.

Chicago Bears—Even with Gale Sayers still out with his bad knee, the Bears got off to a strong start. Middle linebacker Dick Butkus held the defense together with his outstanding play, and reserve quarterback Kent Nix was the offensive hero in the early going. After mid-season, however, both Nix and Jack Concannon were injured, leaving the entire quarterbacking load on Bobby Douglass' shoulders. The Bears dropped six of their last seven, and coach Jim Dooley got the ax at the end of the season.

Green Bay Packers—Dan Devine, who left the University of Missouri to take over as head coach in Green Bay, suffered through a trying professional debut as his Packers blew an early lead and lost to the Giants 42-40 on opening day. To make matters worse, several players smashed into Devine on an out-of-bounds play and broke his leg. Getting through the rest of the season with the help of a crutch, Devine found little pleasing in the Packers' drop to last place in the Central Division. His hardest decision was to bench all-time great Ray Nitschke, and his greatest pleasure was the play of rookie fullback John Brockington, who led the NFC in rushing 1,105 yards.

WESTERN DIVISION

San Francisco '49ers—Even with John Brodie suffering through an erratic season, the '49ers still had enough talent on both platoons to beat out the surprising Los Angeles Rams for first place in the West. Operating behind a top-notch offensive line, the '49ers running game prospered with Ken Willard's good year and a fine rookie performance from speedster Vic Washington. This took the pressure off Brodie, who still had Gene Washington, Ted Kwalick, and Dick Witcher to throw to. On defense, coach Dick Nolan stuck with one set of linemen and was rewarded with excellent seasons from Cedrick Hardman, Charlie Krueger, Earl Edwards, and Tommy Hart.

Los Angeles Rams—Long-time UCLA coach Tommy Prothro moved into the professional ranks by rebuilding the Rams and almost winning a divisional title. Prothro traded away Diron Talbert, Jack Pardee, Myron Pottios, Maxie Baughan, Richie Petitbon, Tommy Mason, Bob Brown, Wendell Tucker, and Billy Truax from last year's team and replaced them with younger players. The defense had eight new starters, with only Deacon Jones, Merlin Olsen, and Coy Bacon returning, but the new unit hung together well. On the offense, key new starters were Willie Ellison, who ran for a record 247 yards against New Orleans on December 5, Lance Rentzel, Bob Klein, and Harry Schuh.

Atlanta Falcons—The Falcons enjoyed their first season ever with an aggressive defense and a patchwork offense. The front four fielded two top linemen in Claude Humphrey and John Zook, linebacker Don Hansen's fine season made up for the loss of Tommy Nobis to a knee injury, and Ken Reaves starred in an underrated secondary which allowed the least passing yards in the Conference. On offense, the line improved into a good unit, with George Kunz and Mal Snider the top performers. The running attack lost its speed when a knee injury sidelined rookie Joe Profit, but Cannonball Butler, Art Malone, Harmon Wages, and free agent rookie Willie Belton ground out the yardage with straight-ahead power plays. Both of the wide receivers were rookies, Ken Burrow and Wes Chesson, but at quarterback the Falcons could field only journeymen Bob Berry and Dick Shiner.

New Orleans Saints—Rookie quarterback Archie Manning made a fine professional debut by scoring a touchdown on the last play of the game to beat the Rams 24-20 on opening day. Foot and leg problems kept him on the bench for much of the campaign, but Manning did show a strong arm and a talent for running with the ball. With Manning or Ed Hargett at quarterback, the New Orleans offense showed new punch. The line was improved with the addition of Glen Ray Hines, Don Morrison, and John Didion, and the receiving corps had always been the Saints' strongest department. At running back, second-year man Jim Strong, picked up from San Francisco, and rookies Bob Gresham and James Ford handled most of the running chores.

FINAL TEAM STATISTICS

OFFENSE

	ATL.	CHI.	DALL.	DET.	G.B.	L.A.	MINN.	N.O.	N.Y.G.	PHIL.	ST.L.	S.F.	WASH.
FIRST DOWNS:													
Total	221	189	288	269	208	234	198	242	236	201	212	257	212
by Rushing	99	75	135	131	115	105	89	105	86	65	86	113	77
by Passing	108	99	144	104	87	111	95	106	140	119	109	122	112
by Penalty	14	15	9	34	6	18	14	31	10	17	17	22	23
RUSHING:													
Number	494	365	512	532	500	460	484	452	394	407	417	498	477
Yards	1703	1434	2249	2376	2229	2139	1695	1711	1461	1248	1530	2129	1757
Average Yards	3.4	3.9	4.4	4.5	4.5	4.7	3.5	3.8	3.7	3.1	3.7	4.3	3.7
Touchdowns	12	6	25	15	18	15	14	18	11	6	8	12	8
PASSING:													
Attempts	285	443	361	299	254	370	334	387	462	390	385	391	334
Completions	167	186	206	157	121	185	157	182	268	200	170	209	182
Completion Percentage	58.6	42.0	57.1	52.5	47.6	50.0	47.0	47.0	58.0	51.3	44.2	53.5	54.5
Passing Yards	2495	2294	3037	2453	1842	2304	1910	2355	3062	2552	2656	2688	2391
Avg. Yards per Attempt	8.8	5.4	8.4	8.2	7.3	6.2	5.7	6.1	6.6	6.5	6.9	6.9	7.2
Avg. Yards per Complet.	14.9	12.3	14.7	15.6	15.2	12.5	12.2	12.9	11.4	12.8	15.6	12.9	13.1
Times Tackled Passing	31	49	32	31	18	26	28	50	40	26	19	11	17
Yards Lost Tackled	239	392	251	252	157	210	255	400	348	229	185	111	118
Net Yards	2256	1902	2786	2201	1685	2094	1655	1955	2714	2323	2471	2677	2273
Touchdowns	16	12	22	17	12	18	9	12	14	13	14	18	13
Interceptions	21	28	14	14	24	11	18	14	25	20	26	24	15
Percent Intercepted	7.4	6.3	3.9	4.7	9.4	3.0	5.4	3.6	5.4	5.1	6.8	6.1	4.5
PUNTS:													
Number	60	77	56	42	56	70	89	77	66	75	61	51	58
Average Distance	36.9	40.2	41.6	41.7	40.0	41.4	39.5	41.4	40.6	41.9	38.8	38.7	40.5
PUNT RETURNS:													
Number	37	36	31	23	38	35	27	16	19	24	30	39	45
Yards	174	262	248	194	177	172	164	100	122	172	234	268	427
Average Yards	4.7	7.3	8.0	8.4	4.7	4.9	6.1	6.3	6.4	7.2	7.8	6.9	9.5
Touchdowns	0	0	0	0	0	0	0	0	0	0	0	0	0
KICKOFF RETURNS:													
Number	59	59	50	51	58	54	41	56	63	49	58	46	43
Yards	1477	1325	1376	1233	1546	1322	960	1143	1416	1183	1363	1075	913
Average Yards	25.0	22.5	27.5	24.2	26.7	24.5	23.4	20.4	22.5	24.1	23.5	23.4	21.2
Touchdowns	0	0	2	2	1	1	0	0	1	0	1	0	0
INTERCEPTION RETURNS:													
Number	20	22	26	22	16	27	27	20	15	22	17	14	29
Yards	180	267	402	295	205	452	572	342	227	374	191	186	480
Average Yards	9.0	12.1	15.5	13.4	12.8	16.7	21.2	17.1	15.1	17.0	11.2	13.3	16.6
Touchdowns	1	0	0	3	0	2	1	1	1	1	1	0	5
PENALTIES:													
Number	79	78	94	69	61	79	70	85	77	81	66	88	80
Yards	723	746	952	738	568	642	661	869	640	838	643	961	801
FUMBLES:													
Number	39	28	30	35	29	32	25	29	37	21	35	33	32
Number Lost	15	18	21	19	20	18	12	11	20	15	20	18	20
POINTS:													
Total	274	185	406	341	274	313	245	266	228	221	231	300	276
PAT Attempts	34	20	50	39	33	37	25	31	30	24	24	33	27
PAT Made	29	20	50	39	32	37	25	29	30	23	24	33	27
FG Attempts	21	33	33	37	26	29	32	28	17	37	32	36	40
FG Made	13	15	18	22	14	18	22	17	6	18	21	23	29
Percent FG Made	61.9	45.5	54.5	59.5	53.8	62.1	68.8	60.7	35.3	48.6	65.6	63.9	59.2
Safeties	1	0	1	1	1	0	2	0	0	0	0	0	0

DEFENSE

	ATL.	CHI.	DALL.	DET.	G.B.	L.A.	MINN.	N.O.	N.Y.G.	PHIL.	ST.L.	S.F.	WASH.
FIRST DOWNS:													
Total	237	234	200	210	230	239	194	260	228	251	244	199	213
by Rushing	114	99	59	97	104	91	88	129	104	104	109	80	73
by Passing	106	117	125	99	110	129	88	110	112	129	120	96	119
by Penalty	17	18	16	14	16	19	18	21	12	18	15	23	21
RUSHING:													
Number	500	509	353	432	489	455	447	495	449	450	486	408	408
Yards	2149	2116	1144	1842	1707	1658	1600	2200	2059	1962	1985	1668	1396
Average Yards	4.3	4.2	3.2	4.3	3.5	3.6	3.6	4.4	4.6	4.4	4.1	4.1	3.4
Touchdowns	19	14	8	15	7	11	2	18	12	16	10	4	7
PASSING:													
Attempts	343	362	421	306	353	387	405	333	333	407	375	341	411
Completions	164	192	209	163	186	200	206	175	173	220	212	152	191
Completion Percentage	47.8	53.0	49.6	53.3	52.7	51.7	50.9	52.6	52.0	54.1	56.5	44.6	46.5
Passing Yards	1895	2607	2660	2163	2469	2693	2022	2472	2458	2971	2546	2309	2448
Avg. Yards per Attempt	5.5	7.2	6.3	7.1	7.0	7.0	5.0	7.4	7.4	7.3	6.8	6.8	6.0
Avg. Yards per Complet.	11.6	13.6	12.7	13.3	13.3	13.5	9.8	14.1	14.2	13.5	12.0	15.2	12.8
Times Tackled Passing	31	28	43	18	19	37	27	24	18	32	20	38	36
Yards Lost Tackled	257	203	336	146	168	314	216	234	151	311	166	298	321
Net Yards	1638	2404	2324	2017	2301	2379	1806	2238	2307	2660	2380	2011	2127
Touchdowns	9	12	15	17	21	15	10	20	25	16	12	17	11
Interceptions	20	22	26	22	16	27	27	20	15	22	17	14	29
Percent Intercepted	5.8	6.1	6.2	7.2	4.5	7.0	6.7	6.1	4.5	5.4	4.5	4.1	7.1
PUNTS:													
Number	63	67	65	58	61	66	78	50	61	57	58	73	77
Average Distance	41.4	40.2	41.5	41.2	40.1	39.4	40.0	41.2	39.8	40.5	40.4	39.7	41.2
PUNT RETURNS:													
Number	26	31	26	18	23	27	47	43	50	40	24	19	17
Yards	117	172	231	111	169	67	336	251	319	372	160	44	87
Average Yards	4.5	5.5	8.9	6.2	7.3	2.5	7.1	5.8	6.4	9.3	6.7	2.3	5.1
Touchdowns	0	0	0	0	0	0	0	0	0	0	1	0	0
KICKOFF RETURNS:													
Number	52	32	70	70	56	57	49	54	45	48	54	61	61
Yards	1228	817	1681	1627	1248	1176	1077	1326	1063	1101	1318	1467	1066
Average Yards	23.6	25.5	24.0	23.2	22.3	20.6	22.0	24.6	23.6	22.9	24.4	24.0	17.5
Touchdowns	1	1	0	0	0	1	0	2	0	1	1	0	0
INTERCEPTION RETURNS:													
Number	21	28	14	14	24	11	18	14	25	20	26	24	15
Yards	242	465	304	207	449	83	204	171	377	359	358	385	284
Average Yards	11.5	16.6	21.7	14.8	18.7	7.5	11.3	12.2	15.1	18.0	13.8	16.0	18.9
Touchdowns	0	1	1	1	2	1	1	1	4	1	0	1	1
PENALTIES:													
Number	61	78	61	97	60	62	57	98	69	94	79	75	93
Yards	614	819	647	942	514	665	615	967	730	908	831	610	720
FUMBLES:													
Number	32	36	40	23	33	22	34	39	29	34	28	31	22
Number Lost	18	23	25	11	16	7	18	25	15	25	16	16	12
POINTS:													
Total	277	276	222	286	298	260	139	347	362	302	279	216	190
PAT Attempts	31	29	25	35	34	30	14	44	42	36	29	23	20
PAT Made	31	28	24	35	32	29	13	44	42	35	28	21	19
FG Attempts	23	41	25	25	37	32	32	26	32	33	39	33	33
FG Made	20	24	16	13	20	17	14	13	22	17	25	19	17
Percent FG Made	87.0	58.5	64.0	52.0	54.1	53.1	43.8	50.0	68.8	51.5	64.1	57.6	51.5
Safeties	0	1	0	1	1	0	0	0	1	0	1	0	0

CONFERENCE PLAYOFFS

December 25 at Bloomington
(Attendance 47,307)

SCORING

MINNESOTA	0	3	0	9–12
DALLAS	3	3	14	0–20

First Quarter
Dal. Clark, 26 yard field goal

Second Quarter
Min. Cox, 27 yard field goal
Dal. Clark, 44 yard field goal

Third Quarter
Dal. Thomas, 13 yard rush
PAT–Clark (kick)
Dal. Hayes, 9 yard pass from Staubach
PAT–Clark (kick)

Fourth Quarter
Min. Page, safety tackled Staubach in end zone
Min. Voigt, 6 yard pass from Cuozzo
PAT–Cox (kick)

TEAM STATISTICS

MINN.		DALLAS
17	First Downs–Total	10
5	First Downs–Rushing	5
12	First Downs–Passing	5
0	First Downs–Penalty	0
1	Fumbles–Number	0
1	Fumbles–Lost Ball	0
2	Penalties–Number	2
18	Yards Penalized	10
2	Missed Field Goals	0
64	Offensive Plays–Total	55
311	Net Yards	183
4.9	Average Gain	3.3
5	Giveaways	0
0	Takeaways	5
–5	Difference	+5

INDIVIDUAL STATISTICS

MINNESOTA	No.	Yds.	Avg.	DALLAS	No.	Yds.	Avg.
RUSHING							
Jones	15	52	3.5	D. Thomas	21	66	3.1
Lee	3	28	9.3	Hill	14	28	2.0
Osborn	6	13	2.2	Garrison	2	2	1.0
Lindsey	1	6	6.0	Staubach	2	2	1.0
Grim	1	2	2.0		39	98	2.5
	26	101	3.9				
RECEIVING							
Washington	5	70	14.0	Hayes	3	31	10.3
Grim	4	74	18.5	Alworth	2	33	16.5
Voigt	4	46	11.5	Ditka	2	18	9.0
Reed	4	–3	–0.8	Hill	2	14	7.0
Lindsey	1	25	25.0	D. Thomas	1	3	3.0
White	1	–2	–2.0		10	99	9.9
	19	210	11.1				
PUNTING							
Lee	4		43.5	Widby	7		37.0
PUNT RETURNS							
West	2	6	3.0	Waters	2	37	18.5
KICKOFF RETURNS							
Jones	2	75	37.5	I. Thomas	2	31	15.5
West	2	74	37.0	Harris	1	21	21.0
Bryant	1	22	22.0		3	52	17.3
Brown	1	17	17.0				
	6	188	31.3				
INTERCEPTION RETURNS							
None				Harris	1	30	30.0
				Howley	1	26	26.0
				Adderly	1	8	8.0
				Jordan	1	5	5.0
					4	69	17.3

PASSING

MINNESOTA	Att.	Comp.	Comp. Pct.	Yds.	Int.	Yds/ Att.	Yds/ Comp.	Yds. Lost Tkld.
Cuozzo	22	12	54.5	124	2	5.6	10.3	0– 0
Lee	16	7	43.8	86	2	5.4	12.3	0– 0
	38	19	50.0	210	4	5.5	11.1	0– 0
DALLAS								
Staubach	14	10	71.4	99	0	7.1	9.9	2–14

December 26, at San Francisco
(Attendance 45,327)

SCORING

SAN FRANCISCO	0	3	14	7–24
WASHINGTON	7	3	3	7–20

First Quarter
Was. Smith, 5 yard pass from Kilmer
PAT–Knight (kick)

Second Quarter
S.F. Gossett, 23 yard field goal
Was. Knight, 40 yard field goal

Third Quarter
S.F. G. Washington, 78 yard pass from Brodie PAT–Gossett (kick)
S.F. Windsor, 2 yard pass from Brodie
PAT–Gossett (kick)
Was. Knight, 36 yard field goal

Fourth Quarter
S.F. Hoskins, recovered fumble in end zone
PAT–Gossett (kick)
Was. Brown, 16 yard pass from Kilmer
PAT–Knight (kick)

TEAM STATISTICS

S.F.		WASH.
11	First Downs–Total	13
2	First Downs–Rushing	6
9	First Downs–Passing	5
0	First Downs–Penalty	2
0	Fumbles – Number	3
0	Fumbles Lost Ball	2
3	Penalties–Number	4
41	Yards Penalized	55
0	Missed Field Goals	1
59	Offensive Plays–Total	67
285	Net Yards	192
4.8	Average Gain	2.9
0	Giveaways	3
3	Takeaways	0
+3	Difference	–3

INDIVIDUAL STATISTICS

SAN FRANCISCO	No.	Yds.	Avg.	WASHINGTON	No.	Yds.	Avg.
RUSHING							
V. Washington	16	59	3.7	Brown	27	84	3.1
Willard	19	46	2.4	Harraway	10	28	2.8
Schreiber	4	7	1.8	Kilmer	1	0	0.0
	39	112	2.8	Jefferson	1	–13	–13.0
					39	99	2.5
RECEIVING							
Kwalick	3	26	8.7	Brown	6	62	10.3
Witcher	2	28	14.0	Smith	3	32	10.7
G. Washington	1	78	78.0	Mason	1	8	8.0
Schreiber	1	22	22.0	Harraway	1	4	4.0
V. Washington	1	10	10.0		11	106	9.6
Willard	1	10	10.0				
Windsor	1	2	2.0				
	10	176	17.6				
PUNTING							
Spurrier	10		33.7	Bragg	5		46.0
PUNT RETURNS							
Fuller	1	8	8.0	Duncan	2	11	5.5
Simpson	1	4	4.0	Vactor	1	47	47.0
B. Taylor	1	1	1.0		3	58	19.3
	3	13	4.3				
KICKOFF RETURNS							
V. Washington	4	79	19.8	Duncan	3	170	56.7
Cunningham	1	0	0.0	McLinton	1	19	19.0
	5	79	15.8		4	189	47.3
INTERCEPTION RETURNS							
R. Taylor	1	17	17.0	None			

PASSING

SAN FRANCISCO	Att.	Cmp.	Comp. Pct.	Yds.	Int.	Yds/ Att.	Yds/ Comp.	Yds Lost Tkld.
Brodie	19	10	52.6	176	0	9.3	17.6	1– 3
WASHINGTON								
Kilmer	27	11	40.7	106	1	3.9	9.6	1–13

DALLAS COWBOYS 11-3-0 Tom Landry

Scores of Each Game		
49	Buffalo	37
42	Philadelphia	7
16	WASHINGTON	20
20	N.Y. GIANTS	13
14	New Orleans	24
44	NEW ENGLAND	21
19	Chicago	23
16	St. Louis	13
20	PHILADELPHIA	7
13	Washington	0
28	LOS ANGELES	21
52	N.Y. JETS	10
42	N.Y. Giants	14
31	ST. LOUIS	12

Use Name	Pos.	Hgt	Wgt	Age	Int	Pts
Forrest Gregg	OT	6'4"	250	38		
Tony Liscio	OT	6'5"	255	31		
Ralph Neely	OT	6'5"	265	27		
Don Talbert	OT	6'5"	255	31		
Rayfield Wright	OT	6'7"	255	26		
John Niland	OG	6'4"	245	27		
Blaine Nye	OG	6'4"	250	25		
Rodney Wallace	OG	6'5"	255	22		
John Fitzgerald	C	6'5"	250	23		
Dave Manders	C	6'2"	250	29		
George Andrie	DE	6'7"	250	31		
Larry Cole	DE	6'4"	255	24		
Tody Smith	DE	6'5"	245	22		
Pat Toomay	DE	6'5"	244	26		
Bill Gregory	DT	6'5"	255	21		
Bob Lilly	DT	6'4"	260	32		6
Jethro Pugh	DT	6'6"	260	27		
Lee Roy Caffey	LB	6'3"	250	31		
Dave Edwards	LB	6'3"	225	32	2	
Chuck Howley	LB	6'3"	225	35	5	
Lee Roy Jordan	LB	6'2"	220	30	2	
D. D. Lewis	LB	6'2"	225	25	1	
Tom Stincic	LB	6'2"	230	24		
Herb Adderley	DB	6'1"	200	32	6	
Cornell Green	DB	6'4"	208	31	2	
Cliff Harris	DB	6'	184	22	2	
Mel Renfro	DB	6'	190	29	4	
Ike Thomas	DB	6'2"	193	23		12
Mark Washington	DB	5'10"	183	23		
Charlie Waters	DB	6'1"	193	22	2	
Bob Asher – Injury						
Craig Morton	QB	6'4"	214	28		6
Roger Staubach	QB	6'2"	197	29		12
Dan Reeves	HB	6'1"	200	27		1
Claxton Welch	HB	5'11"	203	24		8
Joe Williams	HB	6'	195	24		6
Calvin Hill	FB-HB	6'3"	235	24		66
Duane Thomas	FB-HB	6'1"	210	24		78
Walt Garrison	FB	6'	205	27		12
Margene Adkins	WR	5'10"	183	24		
Lance Alworth	WR	6'	180	31		12
Bob Hayes	WR	6'	185	28		48
Gloster Richardson	WR	6'	200	28		18
Mike Ditka	TE	6'3"	225	31		6
Billy Truax	TE	6'5"	235	28		6
Mike Clark	K	6'1"	205	30		86
Toni Fritsch	K	5'7"	185	26		17
Ron Widby	K	6'4"	210	26		

WASHINGTON REDSKINS 9-4-1 George Allen

Scores of Each Game		
24	ST. LOUIS	17
30	N.Y. Giants	3
20	Dallas	16
22	HOUSTON	13
20	ST. LOUIS	0
20	Kansas City	27
24	NEW ORLEANS	14
7	PHILADELPHIA	7
15	Chicago	16
0	DALLAS	13
20	Philadelphia	13
23	N.Y. GIANTS	7
38	Los Angeles	24
13	CLEVELAND	20

Use Name	Pos.	Hgt	Wgt	Age	Int	Pts
Terry Hermeling	OT	6'5"	255	25		
Walt Rock	OT	6'5"	255	30		
Jim Snowden	OT	6'3"	255	29		
Mike Taylor	OT	6'4"	245	26		
Paul Laaveg	OG	6'4"	245	22		
Ray Schoenke	OG	6'3"	250	29		
John Wilbur	OG	6'3"	250	28		
George Burman	C-OG	6'3"	255	28		
Len Hauss	C	6'2"	235	29		
Verlon Biggs	DE	6'4"	270	28		
Jimmie Jones	DE	6'3"	215	24		
Ron McDole	DE	6'3"	288	31	3	6
Bill Brundige	DT	6'5"	270	22		
Manny Sistrunk	DT	6'5"	265	24		
Diron Talbert	DT	6'5"	255	27		
Bob Grant	LB	6'2"	225	25		
Chris Hanburger	LB	6'2"	218	30	1	6
Harold McLinton	LB	6'2"	235	24		
Jack Pardee	LB	6'2"	225	35	5	6
Myron Pottios	LB	6'2"	232	31	1	
Rusty Tillman	LB	6'2"	230	25		
Mike Bass	DB	6'	190	26	8	6
Speedy Duncan	DB	5'10"	175	28	1	6
Pat Fischer	DB	5'10"	170	31	3	6
Jon Jaqua	DB	6'	190	23		
Brig Owens	DB	5'11"	190	28	2	
Richie Petitbon	DB	6'3"	208	33	5	
Ted Vactor	DB	6'	185	27		
Sonny Jurgensen	QB	5'11"	203	37		
Billy Kilmer	QB	6'	204	31		12
Sam Wyche	QB	6'4"	210	26		
Larry Brown	HB	5'11"	195	23		36
Bob Brunet	HB	6'1"	205	25		
Tommy Mason	FB-HB	6'	195	32		
Charlie Harraway	FB	6'2"	215	26		12
Mike Hull	FB	6'3"	220	26		
Jeff Jordan	HB-FB	6'1"	215	26		
Boyd Dowler	WR	6'5"	225	34		
Roy Jefferson	WR	6'2"	195	27		24
Bill Malinchak	WR	6'1"	200	27		
Clifton McNeil (from NYG)	WR	6'2"	187	31		18
Charley Taylor	WR	6'3"	210	30		24
Mack Alston	TE	6'2"	230	24		
Jerry Smith	TE	6'2"	208	28		6
Mike Bragg	K	5'11"	186	24		
Curt Knight	K	6'1"	190	28		114

PHILADELPHIA EAGLES 6-7-1 Jerry Williams Ed Khayat

Scores of Each Game		
14	Cincinnati	37
7	DALLAS	42
3	SAN FRANCISCO	31
0	MINNESOTA	13
10	Oakland	34
23	N.Y. GIANTS	7
17	DENVER	16
7	Washington	7
7	Dallas	20
37	St. Louis	20
13	WASHINGTON	20
23	Detroit	20
19	ST. LOUIS	7
41	N.Y. Giants	28

Use Name	Pos.	Hgt	Wgt	Age	Int	Pts
Wayde Key	OT	6'4"	245	24		
Steve Smith	OT	6'5"	250	27		6
Dick Stevens	OT	6'4"	240	23		
Henry Allison	OG	6'2"	255	24		
Jim Skaggs	OG	6'2"	250	31		
Tuufuli Uperesa	OG	6'3"	255	23		
Mike Evans	C	6'5"	250	24		
Mark Nordquist	OG-C	6'4"	245	25		
Don Brumm	DE	6'3"	245	28		
Richard Harris	DE	6'4"	260	23		
Mel Tom	DE	6'4"	250	30		
Mike Dirks	DT	6'2"	245	25		
Don Hultz	DT	6'3"	240	30	1	
Gary Pettigrew	DT	6'4"	255	26		
Ernie Calloway	DE-DT	6'6"	240	23		
Dick Hart – Injury						
Harry Jones – Injury						
Bob Creech	LB	6'3"	222	22		
Bill Hobbs	LB	6'	220	25		6
Ike Kelley	LB	5'11"	224	27		
Ron Porter	LB	6'3"	232	26		
Tim Rossovich	LB	6'4"	240	25	1	
Fred Whittingham	LB	6'1"	240	32		
Adrian Young	LB	6'1"	232	25		
Steve Zabel	TE-LB	6'4"	235	23	1	12
Bill Bradley	DB	5'11"	190	24	11	
Vern Davis	DB	6'4"	208	21		
Leroy Keyes	DB	6'3"	208	24	6	
Al Nelson	DB	5'11"	186	27	2	12
Steve Preece	DB	6'1"	195	24		
Nate Ramsey	DB	6'1"	200	30		
Jack Smith	DB	6'4"	204	23		
Jim Thrower	DB	6'2"	194	22		
Greg Barton – Canadian Football League						
Rich Arrington	QB	6'2"	190	24		
Pete Liske	QB	6'2"	200	30		6
Jim Ward	QB	6'2"	200	27		
Tom Bailey	HB	6'2"	211	22		6
Ronnie Bull	FB-HB	6'	200	31		6
Sonny Davis	FB-HB	5'11"	215	23		6
Larry Watkins	FB-HB	6'2"	215	24		6
Lee Bouggess	FB	6'2"	210	23		18
Tom Woodeshick	FB	6'	222	29		6
Tony Baker (from NO)	FB	5'11"	225	26		6
Harold Carmichael	WR	6'7"	225	21		
Ben Hawkins	WR	6'	180	27		30
Harold Jackson	WR	5'10"	175	25		18
Billy Walik	WR	5'11"	180	23		
Kent Kramer	TE	6'5"	235	27		6
Gary Ballman	WR-TE	6'	210	31		
Fred Hill	WR-TE	6'2"	215	28		
Tom Dempsey	K	6'1"	264	30		49
Happy Feller	K	5'11"	185	22		28
Tom McNeill	K	6'1"	195	29		

ST. LOUIS CARDINALS 4-9-1 Bob Hollway

Scores of Each Game		
17	WASHINGTON	24
17	N.Y. JETS	10
20	N.Y. GIANTS	21
26	Atlanta	9
0	Washington	20
14	SAN FRANCISCO	26
28	Buffalo	23
13	DALLAS	16
17	San Diego	20
20	PHILADELPHIA	37
24	N.Y. Giants	7
16	GREEN BAY	16
7	Philadelphia	19
12	Dallas	31

Use Name	Pos.	Hgt	Wgt	Age	Int	Pts
Vern Emerson	OT	6'5"	260	25		
Ernie McMillan	OT	6'6"	255	33		
Bob Reynolds	OT	6'6"	265	30		
Dan Dierdorf	OG-OT	6'4"	265	22		
Irv Goode	OG	6'4"	255	30		
Chuck Hutchison	OG	6'3"	240	22		
Clyde Williams	OG	6'2"	250	31		
Tom Banks	C	6'1"	240	23		
Wayne Mulligan	C	6'2"	245	24		
Joe Schmiesing	DE	6'4"	260	26		
Chuck Walker	DE	6'2"	250	30		
Ron Yankowski	DE	6'5"	225	24		
Rolf Krueger	DT-DE	6'4"	250	24		
Paul Dickson	DT	6'5"	250	34		
Fred Heron	DT	6'4"	260	26		
Bob Rowe	DT	6'4"	260	26		
Terry Brown – Injury						
Jim Hargrove	LB	6'3"	223	26		
Mike McGill	LB	6'2"	235	24	1	
Terry Miller	LB	6'2"	225	25		
Rick Ogle	LB	6'3"	230	22		
Jamie Rivers	LB	6'2"	235	25		
Rocky Rosema	LB	6'2"	230	24		
Larry Stallings	LB	6'2"	230	29	1	6
Jeff Allen	DB	5'11"	190	23		
Miller Farr	DB	6'1"	190	28	2	
Dale Hackbart	DB	6'3"	220	35	1	
George Hoey	DB	5'10"	170	24		6
Tom Longo	DB	6'1"	200	27		
Ted Provost	DB	6'2"	195	23		
Jerry Stovall	DB	6'2"	195	29	2	
Norm Thompson	DB	6'1"	175	23	4	
Roger Wehrli	DB	6'1"	195	23	2	
Larry Willingham	DB	6'1"	190	22		
Larry Wilson	DB	6'	195	33	4	
Pete Beathard	QB	6'2"	200	29		
Jim Hart	QB	6'2"	200	27		
Roy Shivers	HB	6'	200	29		6
Larry Stegent	HB	6'1"	200	23		
Paul White	HB	6'	200	23		
MacArthur Lane	FB-HB	6'	220	29		18
Cid Edwards	FB	6'2"	230	27		24
Johnny Roland	HB-FB	6'2"	215	28		
John Gilliam	WR	6'1"	195	26		18
Mel Gray	WR	5'9"	170	22		24
Freddie Hyatt	WR	6'3"	200	25		
Chuck Latourette	WR	6'	190	26		
Dave Williams	WR	6'2"	210	26		6
Jim McFarland	TE	6'5"	225	23		12
Jackie Smith	TE	6'4"	235	30		24
Jim Bakken	K	6'	195	30		87

NEW YORK GIANTS 4-10-0 Alex Webster

Scores of Each Game		
42	Green Bay	40
3	WASHINGTON	30
21	St. Louis	20
13	Dallas	20
7	BALTIMORE	31
7	Philadelphia	23
10	MINNESOTA	17
35	SAN DIEGO	17
21	Atlanta	17
13	Pittsburg	17
7	ST. LOUIS	24
7	Washington	23
14	DALLAS	42
28	PHILADELPHIA	41

Use Name	Pos.	Hgt	Wgt	Age	Int	Pts
Willie Young	OT	6'	265	28		
Charlie Harper	OG-OT	6'2"	250	27		
Bob Hyland	OG-OT	6'5"	250	26		
Steve Alexakos	OG	6'2"	260	24		
Doug Van Horn	OG	6'2"	245	27		
Wayne Walton	OG	6'5"	245	22		
Greg Larson	C	6'2"	250	32		
Fred Dryer	DE	6'6"	240	25		
Bob Lurtsema	DE	6'6"	250	29		
Henry Reed	DE	6'3"	230	22	1	
Dave Tipton	DE	6'6"	240	22		
Dick Hanson	DT	6'6"	280	22		
Jim Kanicki	DT	6'4"	270	29		
Roland Lakes	DT	6'4"	263	31		
Dave Roller	DT	6'2"	240	21		
Jerry Shay	DT	6'3"	245	27		
Vern Vanoy	DT	6'8"	270	25		
John Douglas	LB	6'2"	225	26		
Jim Files	LB	6'4"	240	23	1	
Ralph Heck	LB	6'2"	230	30	1	6
Ron Hornsby	LB	6'3"	232	22		
Pat Hughes	LB	6'2"	240	24		
Pete Athas	WR-DB	5'11"	185	23	2	6
Otto Brown	DB	6'1"	183	24		6
Scott Eaton	DB	6'3"	205	27	1	
Richmond Flowers (from DAL)	DB	6'	180	24	1	
Joe Green	DB	5'11"	195	24		6
Spider Lockhart	DB	6'2"	175	28	3	
Bennie McRae	DB	6'1"	180	30		
Willie Williams	DB	6'	190	28		5
Randy Johnson	QB	6'3"	205	27		
Fran Tarkenton	QB	6'1"	190	31		18
Bobby Duhon	HB	6'	195	24		6
Ron Johnson	HB	6'1"	205	23		6
Rocky Thompson	HB	5'11"	200	23		12
Charlie Evans	FB	6'1"	215	23		30
Tucker Frederickson	FB	6'3"	220	28		6
Junior Coffey	HB-FB	6'1"	215	29		
Don Herrmann	WR	6'2"	195	24		6
Rich Houston	WR	6'2"	197	25		24
Coleman Zeno	WR	6'4"	210	24		
Joe Morrison	HB-FB-WR	6'1"	212	33		6
Dick Kotite	TE	6'3"	230	28		12
Bob Tucker	TE	6'3"	230	26		24
Tom Blanchard	K	6'	190	23		
Pete Gogolak	K	6'2"	190	29		48

DALLAS COWBOYS

RUSHING

Last Name	No.	Yds	Avg	TD
D. Thomas	175	793	4.5	11
Hill	106	468	4.4	8
Garrison	127	429	3.4	1
Staubach	41	343	8.4	2
Reeves	17	79	4.6	0
Williams	21	67	3.2	1
Welch	14	51	3.6	1
Hayes	3	18	6.0	0
Morton	4	9	2.3	1
Ditka	2	2	1.0	0
Alworth	2	–10	–5.0	0

RECEIVING

Last Name	No.	Yds	Avg	TD
Garrison	40	396	10	1
Hayes	35	840	24	8
Alworth	34	487	14	2
Ditka	30	360	12	1
Hill	19	244	13	3
Truax	15	232	15	1
D. Thomas	13	153	12	2
Richardson	8	170	21	3
Adkins	4	53	13	0
Williams	3	59	20	0
Reeves	3	25	8	0
Welch	1	–1	–1	0

PUNT RETURNS

Last Name	No.	Yds	Avg	TD
Harris	17	129	8	0
Waters	9	109	12	0
Adkins	4	5	1	0
Hayes	1	5	5	0

KICKOFF RETURNS

Last Name	No.	Yds	Avg	TD
Harris	29	823	28	0
I. Thomas	7	295	42	2
Welch	4	105	26	0
D. Thomas	2	64	32	0
Ditka	3	30	10	0
Waters	1	18	18	0
Lewis	1	15	15	0
Hayes	1	14	14	0
Williams	1	12	12	0
Green	1	0	0	0

PASSING – PUNTING – KICKING

PASSING	Att	Comp	%	Yds	Yd/Att	TD	Int–	%	RK
Staubach	211	126	60	1882	8.9	15	4–	2	1
Morton	143	76	55	1131	7.9	7	8–	6	7
Reeves	5	2	40	24	4.8	0	1–	20	
Hill	1	0	0	0	0.0	0	1–	100	
D. Thomas	1	0	0	0	0.0	0	0–	0	

PUNTING	No	Avg
Widby	56	41.6

KICKING	XP	Att	%	FG	Att	%
Clark	47	47	100	13	25	52
Fritsch	2	2	100	5	8	63
Reeves	1	1	100	0	0	0

WASHINGTON REDSKINS

RUSHING

Last Name	No.	Yds	Avg	TD
Brown	253	948	3.7	4
Harraway	156	635	4.1	2
Mason	31	85	2.7	0
Jurgensen	3	29	9.7	0
Brunet	10	27	2.7	0
Jefferson	2	13	6.5	0
Hull	2	8	4.0	0
Kilmer	17	5	0.3	2
Smith	1	5	5.0	0
Wyche	1	4	4.0	0
Petitbon	1	–2	–2.0	0

RECEIVING

Last Name	No.	Yds	Avg	TD
Jefferson	47	701	15	4
McNeil	30	453	15	3
Dowler	26	352	14	0
C. Taylor	24	370	15	4
Harraway	20	121	6	0
Smith	16	227	14	1
Brown	16	176	11	2
Mason	12	109	9	0
Alston	5	87	17	0
Brunet	2	4	2	0

PUNT RETURNS

Last Name	No.	Yds	Avg	TD
Duncan	22	233	11	0
Vactor	23	194	8	0

KICKOFF RETURNS

Last Name	No.	Yds	Avg	TD
Duncan	27	724	27	0
Jaqua	6	78	13	0
Bass	4	61	15	0
McLinton	5	46	9	0
Tillman	1	4	4	0

PASSING – PUNTING – KICKING

PASSING	Att	Comp	%	Yds	Yd/Att	TD	Int–	%	RK
Kilmer	306	166	54	2221	7.3	13	13–	4	3
Jurgensen	28	16	57	170	7.1	0	2–	7	

PUNTING	No	Avg
Bragg	58	40.5

KICKING	XP	Att	%	FG	Att	%
Knight	27	27	100	29	49	59

PHILADELPHIA EAGLES

RUSHING

Last Name	No.	Yds	Avg	TD
Bull	94	351	3.7	0
Bouggess	97	262	2.7	2
Woodeshick	66	188	2.8	0
Baker	46	174	3.8	0
S. Davis	47	163	3.5	1
Watkins	35	98	2.8	1
Bailey	5	41	1.8	1
Jackson	23	41	8.2	0
Liske	13	29	2.2	1
Arrington	5	23	4.6	0
Hawkins	4	8	2.0	0
Zabel	1	–5	–5.0	0

RECEIVING

Last Name	No.	Yds	Avg	TD
Jackson	47	716	15	3
Hawkins	37	650	18	4
Bouggess	24	170	7	1
Carmichael	20	288	14	0
Ballman	13	238	18	0
S. Davis	11	46	4	0
Baker	10	80	8	1
Bull	9	75	8	1
Hill	7	92	13	0
Bailey	7	55	8	0
Kramer	6	65	11	1
Watkins	6	40	7	0
Woodeshick	6	36	6	1
Zabel	2	4	2	2

PUNT RETURNS

Last Name	No.	Yds	Avg	TD
Bradley	18	118	7	0
Walik	5	48	10	0
Hawkins	1	6	6	0

KICKOFF RETURNS

Last Name	No.	Yds	Avg	TD
Walik	14	369	26	0
Nelson	13	358	28	0
Thrower	12	299	25	0
Jackson	2	48	24	0
S. Davis	2	44	22	0
Pettigrew	2	37	19	0
Harris	2	28	14	0
Kramer	1	0	0	0
Zabel	1	0	0	0

PASSING – PUNTING – KICKING

PASSING	Att	Comp	%	Yds	Yd/Att	TD	Int–	%	RK
Liske	269	143	53	1957	7.3	11	15–	6	9
Arrington	118	55	47	576	4.9	2	5–	4	
Bull	1	1	100	15	15.0	0	0–	0	
S. Davis	1	0	0	0	0.0	0	0–	0	
Ward	1	1	100	4	4.0	0	0–	0	

PUNTING	No	Avg
McNeill	73	42.0
Bradley	2	38.0

KICKING	XP	Att	%	FG	Att	%
Dempsey	13	14	93	12	17	71
Feller	10	10	100	6	20	30

ST. LOUIS CARDINALS

RUSHING

Last Name	No.	Yds	Avg	TD
Lane	150	592	3.9	3
Edwards	108	316	2.9	4
Roland	78	278	3.6	0
Shivers	55	202	3.7	1
Gray	2	56	28.0	0
Beathard	4	29	7.3	0
Latourette	3	19	6.3	0
Gilliam	2	16	8.0	0
Smith	1	10	10.0	0
Hart	13	9	0.7	0
White	1	3	3.0	0

RECEIVING

Last Name	No.	Yds	Avg	TD
Gilliam	42	837	20	3
Lane	29	298	10	0
Smith	21	379	18	4
Gray	18	534	30	4
Roland	15	108	7	0
D. Williams	12	182	15	1
Edwards	12	122	10	0
Shivers	10	76	8	0
McFarland	5	54	11	2
Hyatt	4	58	15	0
Stegent	1	12	12	0
Reynolds	1	–4	–4	0

PUNT RETURNS

Last Name	No.	Yds	Avg	TD
Willingham	10	84	8	0
Wehrli	9	84	9	0
Thompson	5	27	5	0
Gilliam	1	21	21	0
Roland	3	10	3	0
Stallings	1	8	8	0
Dickson	1	0	0	0

KICKOFF RETURNS

Last Name	No.	Yds	Avg	TD
Gray	30	740	25	0
Hoey	9	251	28	1
Thompson	7	182	26	0
Willingham	6	125	21	0
Edwards	2	41	21	0
Roland	2	24	12	0
Dierdorf	1	0	0	0
Stegent	1	0	0	0

PASSING – PUNTING – KICKING

PASSING	Att	Comp	%	Yds	Yd/Att	TD	Int–	%	RK
Hart	243	110	45	1626	6.7	8	14–	6	13
Beathard	141	60	43	1030	7.3	6	12–	9	15
Shivers	1	0	0	0	0.0	0	0–	0	

PUNTING	No	Avg
Latourette	56	38.5
Bakken	5	41.4

KICKING	XP	Att	%	FG	Att	%
Bakken	24	24	100	21	32	66

NEW YORK GIANTS

RUSHING

Last Name	No.	Yds	Avg	TD
Duhon	93	344	3.7	1
Frederickson	64	242	3.8	0
Thompson	54	177	3.3	1
Evans	48	171	3.6	5
Ron Johnson	32	156	4.9	1
Morrison	38	131	3.4	0
Tarkenton	30	111	3.7	3
Coffey	22	70	3.2	0
Randy Johnson	6	29	4.8	0
Zeno	2	10	5.0	0
Athas	1	3	3.0	0
Houston	2	2	1.0	0
Tucker	1	1	1.0	0

RECEIVING

Last Name	No.	Yds	Avg	TD
Tucker	59	791	13	4
Morrison	40	411	10	1
Herrmann	27	297	11	1
Duhon	25	266	11	0
Houston	24	426	18	4
Frederickson	21	114	5	1
Thompson	16	85	5	0
Evans	13	144	11	0
Kotite	10	146	15	2
Ron Johnson	6	47	8	0
Zeno	5	97	19	0
Coffey	5	20	4	0

PUNT RETURNS

Last Name	No.	Yds	Avg	TD
Duhon	12	77	6	0
Lockhart	4	24	6	0
Athas	3	21	7	0

KICKOFF RETURNS

Last Name	No.	Yds	Avg	TD
Thompson	36	947	26	1
Duhon	11	200	18	0
Flowers	8	156	20	0
Green	5	106	21	0
Douglas	1	7	7	0
Dryer	1	0	0	0
Walton	1	0	0	0

PASSING – PUNTING – KICKING

PASSING	Att	Comp	%	Yds	Yd/Att	TD	Int–	%	RK
Tarkenton	386	226	59	2567	6.7	11	21–	5	8
Ran. Johnson	74	41	55	477	6.5	3	3–	4	
Blanchard	1	1	100	18	18.0	0	0–	0	
Duhon	1	0	0	0	0.0	0	1–	100	

PUNTING	No	Avg
Blanchard	66	40.6

KICKING	XP	Att	%	FG	Att	%
Gogolak	30	30	100	6	17	35

MINNESOTA VIKINGS 11-3-0 Bud Grant

Scores of Each Game		
16	Detroit	13
17	CHICAGO	20
19	BUFFALO	0
13	Philadelphia	0
24	Green Bay	13
10	BALTIMORE	3
17	N.Y. Giants	10
9	SAN FRANCISCO	13
3	GREEN BAY	0
23	New Orleans	10
24	ATLANTA	7
14	San Diego	30
29	DETROIT	10
27	Chicago	10

Use Name	Pos.	Hgt	Wgt	Age	Int	Pts
Grady Alderman	OT	6'2"	247	32		
Doug Davis	OT	6'4"	250	27		
Ron Yary	OT	6'6"	255	25		
Pete Perreault	OG-OT	6'3"	248	32		
Roy Schmidt	OG	6'3"	250	29		
Milt Sunde	OG	6'2"	250	28		
Doug Sutherland	OG	6'3"	250	23		
Ed White	OG	6'2"	262	24		
Mick Tingelhoff	C	6'1"	237	31		
Godfrey Zaunbrecher	C	6'2"	235	23		
Carl Eller	DE	6'6"	247	29		
Jim Marshall	DE	6'3"	248	33		
John Ward	DE	6'4"	260	23		
Gary Larsen	DT	6'5"	260	31		
Alan Page	DT	6'5"	245	26		
Jerry Patton	DT	6'3"	260	25		

Use Name	Pos.	Hgt	Wgt	Age	Int	Pts
Carl Gersbach	LB	6'1"	230	24		
Wally Hilgenberg	LB	6'3"	230	28	2	
Noel Jenke	LB	6'1"	218	24		
Lonnie Warwick	LB	6'3"	238	29		
Carl Winfrey	LB	6'	230	22		
Roy Winston	LB	6'1"	222	31	1	6
Bobby Bryant	DB	6'	170	27	3	
Karl Kassulke	DB	6'	195	29	2	
Paul Krause	DB	6'3"	200	29	6	
Ed Sharockman	DB	6'	200	31	6	
Charlie West	DB	6'1"	197	25	7	
Jeff Wright	DB	5'11"	190	22		
Nate Wright	DB	5'11"	180	23		

John Beasley – Injury
Jim Vellone – Hodgkin's Disease

Use Name	Pos.	Hgt	Wgt	Age	Int	Pts
Gary Cuozzo	QB	6'1"	195	30		
Bob Lee	QB	6'2"	195	25		6
Norm Snead	QB	6'4"	215	31		6
Clint Jones	HB	6'	205	26		24
Dave Osborn	HB	6'	208	28		36
Bill Brown	FB	5'11"	230	33		12
Leo Hayden	HB-FB	6'	212	23		
Jim Lindsey	HB-FB	6'2"	210	26		6
Oscar Reed	HB-FB	5'11"	222	27		6
Al Denson	WR	6'2"	208	29		
Bob Grim	WR	6'	195	26		42
John Henderson	WR	6'3"	195	28		
Gene Washington	WR	6'3"	208	27		
Bob Brown	TE	6'3"	225	28		
John Hilton	TE	6'5"	225	29		
Stu Voigt	TE	6'1"	220	23		6
Fred Cox	K	5'10"	200	32		91

DETROIT LIONS 7-6-1 Joe Schmidt

Scores of Each Game		
13	MINNESOTA	16
34	New England	7
[illegible]	ATLANTA	38
[illegible]	GREEN BAY	28
31	Houston	7
23	CHICAGO	28
14	Green Bay	14
24	Denver	20
13	LOS ANGELES	21
28	Chicago	3
32	KANSAS CITY	21
20	PHILADELPHIA	23
10	Minnesota	29
27	San Francisco	31

Use Name	Pos.	Hgt	Wgt	Age	Int	Pts
Rocky Freitas	OT	6'6"	280	25		
Ray Parson	OT	6'4"	250	24		
Jim Yarbrough	OT	6'6"	250	24		
Frank Gallagher	OG	6'2"	245	28		
Bob Kowalkowski	OG	6'3"	240	27		
Chuck Walton	OG	6'3"	255	30		
Dave Thompson	C-OG	6'4"	275	22		
Ed Flanagan	C	6'3"	245	27		
Larry Hand	DE	6'4"	250	31		
Jim Mitchell	DE	6'3"	245	22		
Joe Robb	DE	6'3"	245	34		
Bob Bell	DT	6'4"	250	23		6
Dick Evey	DT	6'2"	245	30		
Jerry Rush	DT	6'4"	265	29		
Larry Woods	DT	6'6"	260	23		

Use Name	Pos.	Hgt	Wgt	Age	Int	Pts
Ken Lee	LB	6'4"	230	22		
Mike Lucci	LB	6'2"	230	31	5	12
Ed Mooney	LB	6'2"	225	26		
Paul Naumoff	LB	6'1"	215	26		
Wayne Walker	LB	6'2"	228	34	2	2
Charlie Weaver	LB	6'2"	218	22		
Lem Barney	DB	6'	188	25	3	6
Al Clark	DB	6'	180	23		
Dick LeBeau	DB	6'1"	185	34	6	
Wayne Rasmussen	DB	6'2"	180	29	4	
Tom Vaughn	DB	5'11"	190	28	1	
Mike Weger	DB	6'2"	200	25	1	6
Bobby Williams	DB	6'1"	200	29		

Charlie Brown – Injury
Bill Cottrell – Injury
Nick Eddy – Knee Injury

Use Name	Pos.	Hgt	Wgt	Age	Int	Pts
Greg Landry	QB	6'4"	205	24		18
Bill Munson	QB	6'2"	210	29		
Altie Taylor	HB	5'10"	196	23		30
Mickey Zofko	HB	6'3"	195	21		
Mel Farr	FB-HB	6'2"	210	26		6
Paul Gipson	FB-HB	6'	210	25		
Steve Owens	FB	6'2"	220	23		60
Bill Triplett	FB	6'2"	215	32		
*Chuck Hughes	WR	5'11"	175	28		
Ron Jessie	WR	6'	183	23		14
Earl McCullouch	WR	5'11"	175	25		18
Larry Walton	WR	5'11"	180	24		30
Craig Cotton	TE	6'4"	222	24		
Charlie Sanders	TE	6'4"	235	25		30
Errol Mann	K	6'	200	30		103
Herman Weaver	K	6'4"	210	22		

*Died Oct. 24, 1971 – Heart Attack

CHICAGO BEARS 6-8-0 Jim Dooley

Scores of Each Game		
17	PITTSBURGH	15
20	Minnesota	17
3	Los Angeles	17
35	NEW ORLEANS	14
0	San Francisco	13
28	Detroit	23
23	DALLAS	19
14	GREEN BAY	17
16	WASHINGTON	15
3	DETROIT	28
3	Miami	34
3	Denver	6
10	Green Bay	31
10	MINNESOTA	27

Use Name	Pos.	Hgt	Wgt	Age	Int	Pts
Jeff Curchin	OT	6'6"	255	23		
Randy Jackson	OT	6'5"	245	27		
Steve Wright	OT	6'6"	250	29		
Jim Cadile	OG	6'3"	240	30		
Glenn Holloway	OG	6'3"	245	22		
Bob Newton	OT-OG	6'4"	250	22		
Rich Coady	C	6'3"	238	26		
Gene Hamlin	C	6'3"	245	25		
John Hoffman	DE	6'7"	260	28		
Willie Holman	DE	6'4"	250	26		
Tony McGee	DE	6'4"	250	22		
Ed O'Bradovich	DE	6'3"	255	31		
Dave Hale	DT	6'7"	260	24		
George Seals	DT	6'2"	260	28		6
Bill Staley	DT	6'3"	248	24		

Use Name	Pos.	Hgt	Wgt	Age	Int	Pts
Ross Brupbacher	LB	6'3"	215	23	2	6
Doug Buffone	LB	6'1"	225	27	2	
Dick Butkus	LB	6'3"	245	27	4	1
Jimmy Gunn	LB	6'1"	215	22	1	
Larry Rowden	LB	6'2"	220	21		
Charlie Ford	DB	6'3"	185	22	5	
Cliff Hardy	DB	6'	187	24		
Bob Jeter	DB	6'1"	205	33	1	
Garry Lyle	DB	6'2"	198	25	1	
Jerry Moore	DB	6'3"	208	21		
Ron Smith	DB	6'1"	192	28	3	
Joe Taylor	DB	6'2"	200	30	3	

Craig Baynham – Injury

Use Name	Pos.	Hgt	Wgt	Age	Int	Pts
Jack Concannon	QB	6'3"	205	28		
Bobby Douglass	QB	6'3"	215	24		19
Kent Nix	QB	6'1"	195	27		
Joe Moore	HB	6'1"	205	22		
Cyril Pinder	HB	6'2"	222	24		6
Gale Sayers	HB	6'	198	28		
Don Shy	HB	6'1"	210	27		12
Jim Grabowski	FB	6'2"	220	27		
Jim Harrison	FB	6'4"	235	22		
Bill Tucker	FB	6'2"	220	27		
George Farmer	WR	6'4"	210	23		30
Dick Gordon	WR	5'11"	190	26		30
Jim Seymour	WR	6'4"	210	24		
Cecil Turner	WR	5'10"	170	27		
Ray Ogden	TE	6'5"	225	28		
Earl Thomas	TE	6'3"	224	22		
Bob Wallace	TE	6'3"	211	25		12
Bobby Joe Green	K	5'11"	175	33		
Mac Percival	K	6'4"	220	31		63

GREEN BAY PACKERS 4-8-2 Dan Devine

Scores of Each Game		
40	N.Y. GIANTS	42
34	DENVER	13
20	CINCINNATI	17
28	Detroit	31
13	MINNESOTA	24
13	Los Angeles	30
14	DETROIT	14
17	Chicago	14
0	Minnesota	3
21	Atlanta	28
21	NEW ORLEANS	29
16	St. Louis	16
31	CHICAGO	10
6	Miami	27

Use Name	Pos.	Hgt	Wgt	Age	Int	Pts
Bill Hayhoe	OT	6'8"	258	24		
Dick Himes	OT	6'4"	244	25		
Francis Peay	OT	6'5"	250	27		
Dave Bradley	OG	6'4"	245	24		
Gale Gillingham	OG	6'3"	255	27		
Bill Lueck	OG	6'3"	235	25		
Randy Winkler	OG	6'5"	260	28		
Ken Bowman	C	6'3"	230	28		
Wimpy Winther	C	6'4"	260	23		
Cal Withrow	C	6'	240	26		
Lionel Aldridge	DE	6'4"	245	29		
Alden Roche	DE	6'4"	255	26		
Donnell Smith	DE	6'4"	245	22		
Clarence Williams	DE	6'5"	255	24		
Bob Brown	DT	6'5"	260	31		
Jim DeLisle	DT	6'4"	254	22		
Mike McCoy	DT	6'5"	284	22		

Use Name	Pos.	Hgt	Wgt	Age	Int	Pts
Fred Carr	LB	6'5"	238	25		
Jim Carter	LB	6'3"	235	22	1	
Tommy Crutcher	LB	6'3"	235	29		
Ray Nitschke	LB	6'3"	235	35	1	
Dave Robinson	LB	6'3"	245	30	3	
Ken Ellis	DB	5'10"	190	23	6	6
Charlie Hall	DB	6'1"	195	22		
Doug Hart	DB	6'	190	32	2	8
Al Matthews	DB	5'11"	190	23	1	
Al Randolph	DB	6'2"	196	27	1	
Willie Wood	DB	5'10"	190	35	1	

Use Name	Pos.	Hgt	Wgt	Age	Int	Pts
Zeke Bratkowski	QB	6'2"	215	39		6
Scott Hunter	QB	6'2"	205	23		24
Frank Patrick	QB	6'7"	225	24		
Bart Starr	QB	6'1"	190	38		6
Donny Anderson	HB	6'3"	210	28		36
Larry Krause	HB	6'	208	23		
Elijah Pitts	HB	6'1"	210	32		
Dave Hampton	FB-HB	6'	210	24		30
John Brockington	FB	6'	225	22		30
Perry Williams	FB	6'2"	220	24		
Carroll Dale	WR	6'1"	200	33		24
Dave Davis	WR	6'	175	23		
John Spilis	WR	6'3"	205	23		6
Len Garrett	TE	6'3"	230	22		
Rich McGeorge	TE	6'4"	235	22		24
Dave Conway	K	6'	195	25		5
Ken Duncan	K	6'2"	210	26		
Lou Michaels	K	6'2"	250	35		43
Tim Webster	K	6'	195	21		26

MINNESOTA VIKINGS

RUSHING

Last Name	No.	Yds	Avg	TD
Jones	180	675	3.8	4
Osborn	123	349	2.8	5
Lindsey	46	182	4.0	0
Reed	50	182	3.6	1
Bill Brown	46	136	3.0	2
Grim	6	127	21.2	0
Cuozzo	15	24	1.6	0
Lee	11	14	1.3	1
Snead	6	6	1.0	1
Denson	1	0	0.0	0

RECEIVING

Last Name	No.	Yds	Avg	TD
Grim	45	691	15	7
Osborn	25	195	8	1
Voigt	15	214	14	1
Reed	15	138	9	0
Washington	12	165	14	0
Denson	10	125	13	0
Bill Brown	10	94	9	0
Jones	9	98	11	0
Lindsey	8	31	4	0
Bob Brown	6	141	24	0
Henderson	2	18	9	0

PUNT RETURNS

Last Name	No.	Yds	Avg	TD
West	18	94	5	0
Grim	7	44	6	0
Bryant	2	26	13	0

KICKOFF RETURNS

Last Name	No.	Yds	Avg	TD
West	24	556	23	0
Jones	12	329	27	0
Grim	3	52	17	0
Bryant	1	23	23	0
Voigt	1	0	0	0

PASSING – PUNTING – KICKING

PASSING	Att	Comp	%	Yds	Yd/Att	TD	Int–	%	RK
Cuozzo	168	75	45	842	5.0	6	8–	5	14
Lee	90	45	50	598	6.6	2	4–	4	
Snead	75	37	49	470	6.3	1	6–	8	
Grim	1	0	0	0	0.0	0	0–	0	

PUNTING	No	Avg
Lee	89	39.5

KICKING	XP	Att	%	FG	Att	%
Cox	25	25	100	22	32	69

DETROIT LIONS

RUSHING

Last Name	No.	Yds	Avg	TD
Owens	246	1035	4.2	8
Taylor	174	736	4.2	4
Landry	76	530	7.0	3
Farr	22	64	2.9	0
Gipson	4	12	3.0	0
Munson	3	9	3.0	0
Triplett	4	4	1.0	0
Jessie	1	0	0.0	0
McCullouch	1	–7	–7.0	0
L. Walton	1	–7	–7.0	0

RECEIVING

Last Name	No.	Yds	Avg	TD
Owens	32	350	11	2
Sanders	31	502	16	5
L. Walton	30	491	16	5
Taylor	26	270	10	1
McCullouch	21	552	26	3
Cotton	6	88	15	0
Farr	5	60	12	1
Jessie	4	87	22	0
Hughes	1	32	32	0
Gipson	1	21	21	0

PUNT RETURNS

Last Name	No.	Yds	Avg	TD
Barney	14	122	9	0
L. Walton	6	38	6	0
Vaughn	2	30	15	0
Thompson	1	4	4	0

KICKOFF RETURNS

Last Name	No.	Yds	Avg	TD
Jessie	16	470	29	2
Barney	9	222	25	0
Clark	8	216	27	0
Williams	4	112	28	0
Gipson	5	105	21	0
Triplett	3	70	23	0
Parson	2	26	13	0
Mooney	2	8	4	0
Cotton	1	4	4	0
Rasmussen	1	0	0	0

PASSING – PUNTING – KICKING

PASSING	Att	Comp	%	Yds	Yd/Att	TD	Int–	%	RK
Landry	261	136	52	2237	8.6	16	13–	5	2
Munson	38	21	55	216	5.7	1	1–	3	

PUNTING	No	Avg
H. Weaver	42	41.7

KICKING	XP	Att	%	FG	Att	%
Mann	37	37	100	22	37	60
Walker	2	2	100	0	0	0

CHICAGO BEARS

RUSHING

Last Name	No.	Yds	Avg	TD
Shy	116	420	3.6	2
Pinder	63	311	4.9	1
Douglass	39	284	7.3	3
Grabowski	51	149	2.9	0
Joe Moore	29	90	3.1	0
Tucker	32	82	2.6	0
Sayers	13	38	2.9	0
Buffone	1	19	19.0	0
Harrison	5	13	2.6	0
Nix	9	12	1.3	0
Farmer	1	11	11.0	0
Concannon	5	5	1.0	0
Wallace	1	0	0.0	0

RECEIVING

Last Name	No.	Yds	Avg	TD
Farmer	46	737	16	5
Gordon	43	610	14	5
Wallace	27	400	15	2
Shy	19	163	9	0
Grabowski	17	100	6	0
Tucker	11	65	6	0
Pinder	10	51	5	0
Seymour	5	75	15	0
Thomas	3	40	13	0
Joe Moore	2	22	11	0
Harrison	2	18	9	0
Turner	1	13	13	0

PUNT RETURNS

Last Name	No.	Yds	Avg	TD
Smith	26	194	7	0
Turner	9	63	7	0
Lyle	1	5	5	0

KICKOFF RETURNS

Last Name	No.	Yds	Avg	TD
Smith	26	671	26	0
Turner	31	639	21	0
Butkus	2	15	8	0

PASSING – PUNTING – KICKING

PASSING	Att	Comp	%	Yds	Yd/Att	TD	Int–	%	RK
Douglass	225	91	40	1164	5.2	5	15–	7	16
Nix	137	51	37	760	5.6	6	10–	7	
Concannon	77	42	55	334	4.3	0	3–	4	
Green	2	1	50	13	6.5	0	0–	0	
Shy	1	1	100	23	23.0	1	0–	0	
Wallace	1	0	0	0	0.0	0	0–	0	

PUNTING	No	Avg
Green	77	40.2

KICKING	XP	Att	%	FG	Att	%
Percival	18	18	100	15	33	46
Butkus	1	1	100	0	0	0
Douglass	1	1	100	0	0	0

GREEN BAY PACKERS

RUSHING

Last Name	No.	Yds	Avg	TD
Brockington	216	1105	5.1	4
Anderson	186	757	4.1	5
Hampton	67	307	4.6	3
Hunter	21	50	2.4	4
Starr	3	11	3.7	1
P. Williams	3	4	1.3	0
Bratkowski	1	1	1.0	1
Krause	3	–6	–2.0	0

RECEIVING

Last Name	No.	Yds	Avg	TD
Dale	31	598	19	4
McGeorge	27	463	17	4
Anderson	26	306	12	1
Spilis	14	281	20	1
Brockington	14	98	7	1
Davis	6	59	10	0
Hampton	3	37	12	1

PUNT RETURNS

Last Name	No.	Yds	Avg	TD
Ellis	22	107	5	0
Davis	6	36	6	0
Wood	4	21	5	0
Pitts	5	13	3	0
Randolph	1	0	0	0

KICKOFF RETURNS

Last Name	No.	Yds	Avg	TD
Hampton	46	1314	29	1
Krause	5	101	20	0
Pitts	2	41	21	0
P. Williams	2	41	21	0
Davis	1	22	22	0
Ellis	1	22	22	0
Carter	1	5	5	0

PASSING – PUNTING – KICKING

PASSING	Att	Comp	%	Yds	Yd/Att	TD	Int–	%	RK
Hunter	163	75	46	1210	7.4	7	17–	10	11
Starr	45	24	53	286	6.4	0	3–	7	
Bratkowski	37	19	51	298	8.1	4	3–	8	
Patrick	5	1	20	39	7.8	0	1–	20	
Anderson	4	2	50	9	2.3	1	0–	0	

PUNTING	No	Avg
Anderson	50	40.4
Duncan	6	36.0

KICKING	XP	Att	%	FG	Att	%
Michaels	19	20	95	8	14	57
Webster	8	8	100	6	11	55
Conway	5	5	100	0	1	0

SAN FRANCISCO FORTY NINERS 9-5-0 Dick Nolan

Scores of Each Game		
17	Atlanta	20
38	New Orleans	20
31	Philadelphia	3
13	LOS ANGELES	20
13	CHICAGO	0
26	St. Louis	14
27	NEW ENGLAND	10
13	Minnesota	9
20	NEW ORLEANS	26
6	Los Angeles	17
24	N.Y. Jets	21
17	KANSAS CITY	26
24	ATLANTA	3
31	DETROIT	27

Use Name	Pos.	Hgt	Wgt	Age	Int	Pts
Cas Banaszek	OT	6'3"	250	25		
Len Rohde	OT	6'4"	250	33		
John Watson	OT	6'4"	248	22		
Randy Beisler	OG	6'4"	255	26		
Elmer Collett	OG	6'4"	240	26		
Bob Hoskins	OG	6'2"	235	25		
Woody Peoples	OG	6'2"	247	28		
Forrest Blue	C	6'5"	260	25		6
Bill Belk	DE	6'3"	258	25		
Cedrick Hardman	DE	6'3"	255	22		
Tommy Hart	DE	6'3"	257	26		6
Earl Edwards	DT	6'6"	272	25		
Charlie Krueger	DT	6'4"	260	35		
Stan Hindman	DE-DT	6'3"	235	27		
Ed Beard	LB	6'2"	220	31		
Frank Nunley	LB	6'2"	232	25	1	
Jim Sniadecki	LB	6'2"	220	24		
Skip Vanderbundt	LB	6'3"	230	24	1	
Dave Wilcox	LB	6'3"	235	28		
Johnny Fuller	DB	6'	185	25	2	
Tony Harris	DB	6'2"	190	22		
Jim Johnson	DB	6'2"	185	33	3	
Mel Phillips	DB	6'	196	29		
Mike Simpson	DB	5'11"	175	24	1	
Bruce Taylor	DB	6'	180	23	3	6
Rosey Taylor	DB	5'11"	186	32	3	
John Brodie	QB	6'1"	203	36		18
Steve Spurrier	QB	6'2"	200	26		
Doug Cunningham	HB	5'11"	192	25		6
John Isenbarger	HB	6'3"	205	23		
Vic Washington	HB	5'10"	196	25		42
Ken Willard	FB	6'2"	225	28		30
Larry Schreiber	HB-FB	6'	200	24		7
Preston Riley	WR	6'	180	23		
Gene Washington	WR	6'1"	185	24		24
Dick Witcher	WR	6'3"	204	26		18
Jimmy Thomas	HB-WR	6'1"	214	24		6
Ted Kwalick	TE	6'4"	220	24		30
Bob Windsor	TE	6'4"	230	28		
Bruce Gossett	K	6'2"	235	28		101
Jim McCann	K	6'2"	170	22		

LOS ANGELES RAMS 8-5-1 Tommy Prothro

Scores of Each Game		
20	New Orleans	24
20	ATLANTA	20
17	CHICAGO	3
20	San Francisco	13
24	Atlanta	16
30	GREEN BAY	13
14	MIAMI	20
17	Baltimore	24
21	Detroit	13
17	SAN FRANSCISCO	6
21	Dallas	28
45	NEW ORLEANS	28
24	WASHINGTON	38
23	Pittsburgh	14

Use Name	Pos.	Hgt	Wgt	Age	Int	Pts
Rich Buzin	OT	6'4"	250	25		
Joe Carollo	OT	6'2"	265	31		
Charley Cowan	OT	6'4"	265	33		
Harry Schuh	OT	6'2"	260	28		
Mike LaHood	OG	6'3"	250	26		
Tom Mack	OG	6'3"	250	27		
Joe Scibelli	OG	6'1"	255	32		
Ken Iman	C	6'1"	240	32		
Rich Saul	OG-C	6'3"	235	23		
Deacon Jones	DE	6'5"	250	32		
Jack Youngblood	DE	6'4"	248	21		
Coy Bacon	DT-DE	6'4"	270	29	1	
Bill Nelson	DT	6'7"	270	23		
Merlin Olsen	DT	6'5"	270	30		
Phil Olsen	DT	6'5"	265	23		
Greg Wojcik	DT	6'6"	268	25		
Ken Geddes	LB	6'3"	235	23		
Dean Halverson	LB	6'2"	212	25		
Marlin McKeever	LB	6'1"	235	31	4	
Don Parish (from STL)	LB	6'1"	220	23		
John Pergine	LB	6'1"	225	24		
Jim Purnell	LB	6'2"	238	29	2	
Jack Reynolds	LB	6'1"	232	23		
Isiah Robertson	LB	6'3"	225	22	4	
Kermit Alexander	DB	5'11"	186	30	3	6
Dave Elmendorf	DB	6'1"	195	22	2	
Alvin Haymond	DB	6'	194	29		
Gene Howard	DB	6'	190	24	6	6
Jim Nettles	DB	5'9"	177	29	5	6
Clancy Williams	DB	6'2"	194	28		
Jim Wilson – Injury						
Jim Ferguson – Injury						
Roman Gabriel	QB	6'4"	220	31		12
Jerry Rhome	QB	6'	188	29		
Willie Ellison	HB	6'1"	200	26		24
Larry Smith	HB	6'3"	220	23		30
Bob Thomas	HB	5'10"	200	22		
Travis Williams	HB	6'1"	210	25		6
Les Josephson	FB	6'	207	28		30
Lee White	FB	6'4"	235	25		
Matt Maslowski	WR	6'3"	210	21		6
David Ray	WR	6'	195	26		91
Lance Rentzel	WR	6'2"	202	27		36
Jack Snow	WR	6'2"	190	28		30
Pat Studstill	WR	6'1"	175	33		
Roger Williams	WR	5'10"	180	25		
Pat Curran	TE	6'3"	238	25		6
Bob Klein	TE	6'5"	235	24		24

ATLANTA FALCONS 7-6-1 Norm Van Brocklin

Scores of Each Game		
20	SAN FRANCISCO	17
20	Los Angeles	20
38	Detroit	41
9	ST. LOUIS	26
16	LOS ANGELES	24
28	NEW ORLEANS	6
31	Cleveland	14
9	Cincinnati	6
17	N.Y. GIANTS	21
28	GREEN BAY	21
7	Minnesota	24
24	OAKLAND	13
3	San Francisco	24
24	New Orleans	20

Use Name	Pos.	Hgt	Wgt	Age	Int	Pts
George Kunz	OT	6'5"	256	24		
Bill Sandeman	OT	6'6"	256	28		
Mal Snider	OT	6'4"	252	24		
Dick Enderle	OG	6'1"	248	23		
Andy Mauer	OG	6'3"	257	22		
Jim Miller	OG	6'3"	240	22		
John Matlock	C	6'4"	250	26		
Jeff Van Note	C	6'2"	244	25		
Claude Humphrey	DE	6'5"	248	27		
Mike Lewis	DE	6'3"	223	22		
Randy Marshall	DE	6'5"	237	24		
John Zook	DE	6'5"	248	23		2
Glen Condren	DT	6'2"	250	29		
Greg Lens	DT	6'5"	260	26		
John Small	LB-DT	6'5"	254	24		
Ron Acks	LB	6'2"	220	26	1	
Grady Allen	LB	6'3"	230	25		
John Bramlett	LB	6'2"	220	30		
Greg Brezina	LB	6'2"	226	25	3	
Don Hansen	LB	6'3"	220	27	3	6
Rudy Kuechenberg	LB	6'2"	215	28		
Tommy Nobis	LB	6'2"	237	27		
Cleo Walker	LB	6'3"	220	23		
Ray Brown	DB	6'2"	198	22	3	
Tom Hayes	DB	6'1"	193	25	3	18
John Mallory	DB	6'	184	25		6
Tom McCauley	DB	6'3"	193	24	1	
Tony Plummer	DB	5'11"	190	24		
Ken Reaves	DB	6'3"	203	26	6	
Rudy Redmond	DB	6'	190	24		
Larry Shears	DB	5'10"	185	22		
Bob Berry	QB	5'11"	190	29		
Leo Hart	QB	6'4"	203	22		
Dick Shiner	QB	6'	195	29		6
Willie Belton	HB	5'11"	196	22		6
Cannonball Butler	HB	5'10"	200	28		24
Sonny Campbell	HB	5'11"	192	23		
Joe Profit	HB	6'	204	22		6
Art Malone	FB	5'11"	209	23		48
Harmon Wages	FB	6'1"	222	25		12
Ken Burrow	WR	6'	190	23		36
Wes Chesson	WR	6'2"	190	22		
Ray Jarvis	WR	5'11"	193	22		
Todd Snyder	WR	6'2"	184	22		
Mike Donohoe	TE	6'3"	228	26		
Jim Mitchell	TE	6'2"	225	23		36
Ray Poage	TE	6'4"	215	30		
Bill Bell	K	6'1"	190	23		68
Billy Lothridge	K	6'1"	200	27		

NEW ORLEANS SAINTS 4-8-2 J. D. Roberts

Scores of Each Game		
24	LOS ANGELES	20
20	SAN FRANCISCO	38
13	Houston	13
14	Chicago	35
24	DALLAS	14
6	Atlanta	28
14	Washington	24
21	OAKLAND	21
26	San Francisco	20
10	MINNESOTA	23
29	Green Bay	21
28	Los Angeles	45
17	CLEVELAND	21
20	ATLANTA	24

Use Name	Pos.	Hgt	Wgt	Age	Int	Pts
Glen Ray Hines	OT	6'5"	265	27		
Sam Holden	OT	6'3"	258	24		
Don Morrison	OT	6'5"	255	21		
Jake Kupp	OG	6'3"	248	29		
John Shinners	OG	6'2"	254	24		
Remi Pudhomme	C-OG	6'4"	250	29		
John Didion	C	6'4"	245	23		
Del Williams	C	6'2"	240	25		
Larry Estes	DE	6'6"	260	24		
Richard Neal	DE	6'3"	254	23		
Joe Owens	DE	6'2"	235	24		
Mike Walker	DE	6'4"	235	21		
Dan Goich	DT	6'4"	265	27		
Dave Long	DT	6'4"	245	26		
Bob Pollard	DT	6'3"	245	22		
Doug Mooers	DE-DT	6'6"	265	24		
Dick Absher	LB	6'4"	235	27	1	
Wayne Colman	LB	6'1"	230	25	1	
Carl Cunningham	LB	6'3"	240	27		
Jim Flanigan	LB	6'3"	240	26	1	
Ray Hester	LB	6'2"	215	22		
Tom Roussel	LB	6'3"	235	26		
Richard Harvey	DB	6'2"	190	25		
Hugo Hollas	DB	6'1"	190	26	5	
Delles Howell	DB	6'3"	195	24	5	
Bivian Lee	DB	6'3"	200	23		
Dee Martin	DB	6'1"	190	22	3	
Reynaud Moore	DB	6'2"	190	21		
Doug Wyatt	DB	6'1"	195	24	4	6
Leo Carroll – Injury						
John Huard – Injury						
Mike Morgan – Injury						
Joe Scarpati – Injury						
Edd Hargett	QB	5'11"	185	24		6
Archie Manning	QB	6'3"	204	22		24
Bob Gresham	HB	5'11"	193	23		36
Billy Harris	HB	6'	204	25		
Virgil Robinson	HB	5'11"	195	23		12
James Ford	FB-HB	6'	205	21		12
Hoyle Granger	FB	6'1"	225	27		6
Dave Kopay	HB-FB	6'2"	218	29		
Jim Strong	HB-FB	6'1"	204	22		18
Dan Abramowicz	WR	6'1"	195	26		30
Al Dodd	WR	6'	185	26		
Bob Newland	WR	6'2"	190	22		
Carlos Bell	TE	6'5"	238	22		
Don Burchfield	TE	6'2"	227	22		
Dave Parks	TE	6'2"	203	29		30
Skip Butler (to NYG)	K	6'2"	200	23		8
Charlie Durkee	K	5'11"	165	27		72
Julian Fagan	K	6'3"	205	23		

SAN FRANCISCO FORTY NINERS

RUSHING

Last Name	No.	Yds	Avg	TD
Willard	216	855	4.0	4
V. Washington	191	811	4.2	3
Schreiber	34	180	5.3	0
Cunningham	25	98	3.9	1
Kwalick	6	62	10.3	0
Brodie	14	45	3.2	3
Thomas	3	36	12.0	1
Isenberger	5	34	6.8	0
Windsor	1	21	21.0	0
Spurrier	1	2	2.0	0
McCann	2	–15	–7.5	0

RECEIVING

Last Name	No.	Yds	Avg	TD
Kwalick	52	664	13	5
G. Wash'gton	46	884	19	4
V. Wash'gton	36	317	9	4
Willard	27	202	7	1
Cunningham	19	188	10	0
Witcher	18	250	14	3
Schreiber	3	79	26	1
Riley	3	39	13	0
Thomas	3	33	11	0
Windsor	2	32	16	0

PUNT RETURNS

Last Name	No.	Yds	Avg	TD
B. Taylor	34	235	7	0
Fuller	3	31	10	0
Riley	1	2	2	0
Vanderbundt	1	0	0	0

KICKOFF RETURNS

Last Name	No.	Yds	Avg	TD
V. Wash'gton	33	858	26	0
Cunningham	6	121	20	0
Windsor	4	66	17	0
Beard	1	21	21	0
Kwalick	2	9	5	0

PASSING – PUNTING – KICKING

PASSING	Att	Comp	%	Yds	Yd/Att	TD	Int–	%	RK
Brodie	387	208	54	2642	6.8	18	24–	6	6
Spurrier	4	1	25	46	11.5	0	0–	0	

PUNTING	No	Avg
McCann	49	38.7
Spurrier	2	38.5

KICKING	XP	Att	%	FG	Att	%
Gossett	32	32	100	23	36	64
Schreiber	1	1	100	0	0	0

LOS ANGELES RAMS

RUSHING

Last Name	No.	Yds	Avg	TD
Ellison	211	1000	4.7	4
Josephson	99	449	4.5	3
Smith	91	404	4.4	5
Rentzel	14	113	8.1	1
T. Williams	18	103	5.7	0
Gabriel	18	48	2.7	2
Klein	3	21	7.0	0
White	2	11	5.5	0
Rhome	3	0	0.0	0
Snow	1	–10	–10.0	0

RECEIVING

Last Name	No.	Yds	Avg	TD
Rentzel	38	534	14	5
Snow	37	666	18	5
Ellison	32	238	7	0
Smith	31	324	10	0
Josephson	26	230	9	2
Klein	14	160	11	4
Maslowski	3	82	27	1
T. Williams	3	68	23	0
Curran	1	2	2	1

PUNT RETURNS

Last Name	No.	Yds	Avg	TD
Haymond	24	123	5	0
Rentzel	9	40	4	0
Alexander	1	5	5	0
T. Williams	1	4	4	0

KICKOFF RETURNS

Last Name	No.	Yds	Avg	TD
T. Williams	25	743	30	1
Haymond	9	207	23	0
Howard	7	164	23	0
R. Williams	4	100	25	0
Youngblood	2	36	18	0
Curran	3	35	12	0
LaHood	1	25	25	0
Thomas	1	12	12	0
Josephson	1	0	0	0
Saul	1	0	0	0

PASSING – PUNTING – KICKING

PASSING	Att	Comp	%	Yds	Yd/Att	TD	Int–	%	RK
Gabriel	352	180	51	2238	6.4	17	10–	3	5
Rhome	18	5	28	66	5.6	1	1–	6	

PUNTING	No	Avg
Studstill	70	41.4

KICKING	XP	Att	%	FG	Att	%
Ray	37	37	100	18	29	62

ATLANTA FALCONS

RUSHING

Last Name	No.	Yds	Avg	TD
Butler	186	594	3.2	2
Malone	120	438	3.7	6
Wages	64	266	4.2	1
Belton	56	237	4.2	1
Campbell	29	79	2.7	0
Berry	19	31	1.6	0
Mitchell	4	25	6.3	0
Jarvis	1	13	13.0	0
Profit	3	10	3.3	1
Shiner	10	9	0.9	1
Burrow	1	5	5.0	0
Chesson	1	–4	–4.0	0

RECEIVING

Last Name	No.	Yds	Avg	TD
Malone	34	380	11	2
Burrow	33	741	22	6
Mitchell	33	593	18	5
Chesson	20	224	11	0
Wages	19	249	13	1
Butler	15	143	10	2
Poage	4	71	18	0
Campbell	3	40	13	0
Belton	3	22	7	0
Mallory	1	27	27	0
Brezina	1	3	3	0
Kunz	1	2	2	0

PUNT RETURNS

Last Name	No.	Yds	Avg	TD
Belton	30	163	5	0
McCauley	1	8	8	0
Mallory	5	3	1	0
Brown	1	0	0	0

KICKOFF RETURNS

Last Name	No.	Yds	Avg	TD
Belton	28	706	25	0
Butler	13	372	29	0
Profit	10	247	25	0
Campbell	4	95	24	0
Wages	1	21	21	0
Enderle	1	20	20	0
Small	1	12	12	0
Matlock	1	4	4	0

PASSING – PUNTING – KICKING

PASSING	Att	Comp	%	Yds	Yd/Att	TD	Int–	%	RK
Berry	226	136	60	2005	8.9	11	16–	7	4
Shiner	57	30	53	463	8.1	5	5–	9	
Hart	1	0	0	0	0.0	0	0–	0	
Lothridge	1	1	100	27	27.0	0	0–	0	

PUNTING	No	Avg
Lothridge	44	37.3
Bell	16	36.1

KICKING	XP	Att	%	FG	Att	%
Bell	29	33	88	13	21	62

NEW ORLEANS SAINTS

RUSHING

Last Name	No.	Yds	Avg	TD
Strong	95	404	4.3	3
Gresham	127	383	3.0	6
Ford	93	379	4.1	2
Manning	33	172	5.2	4
Granger	32	139	4.3	1
Robinson	29	96	3.3	1
Hargett	9	24	2.7	1
Dodd	1	7	7.0	0
Harris	1	1	1.0	0
Parks	2	–2	–1.0	0
Fagan	1	–17	–17.0	0

RECEIVING

Last Name	No.	Yds	Avg	TD
Abramowicz	37	657	18	5
Parks	35	568	16	5
Newland	21	319	15	0
Gresham	17	203	12	0
Strong	16	78	5	0
Dodd	15	298	20	0
Robinson	12	53	4	1
Granger	12	52	4	0
Ford	7	54	8	0
Burchfield	3	36	12	0
Manning	1	–7	–7	0

PUNT RETURNS

Last Name	No.	Yds	Avg	TD
Dodd	13	88	7	0
Moore	2	12	6	0
Abramowicz	1	0	0	0

KICKOFF RETURNS

Last Name	No.	Yds	Avg	TD
Robinson	19	443	23	0
Dodd	12	252	21	0
Moore	11	246	22	0
Strong	9	134	15	0
Gresham	3	60	20	0
Burchfield	1	5	5	0
Absher	1	3	3	0

PASSING – PUNTING – KICKING

PASSING	Att	Comp	%	Yds	Yd/Att	TD	Int–	%	RK
Hargett	210	96	46	1191	5.7	6	5–	2	10
Manning	177	86	49	1164	6.6	6	9–	5	11

PUNTING	No	Avg
Fagan	77	41.4

KICKING	XP	Att	%	FG	Att	%
Durkee	24	25	96	16	23	70
Butler	5	6	83	1	5	20

1971 A.F.C. Aerial Oneupmanship

The old American Football League had never had an abundant supply of good quarterbacks, but the AFC now held the edge in that department over the NFC. The AFC had good veterans like Johnny Unitas and Len Dawson, men in their peak years like Joe Namath, John Hadl, Bob Griese, and Daryle Lamonica, and promising young passers like Jim Plunkett, Terry Bradshaw, Mike Phipps, and Dan Pastorini. After five years of the common draft, the AFC had picked the quarterback plums from the college crop, while the only exciting young passers in the NFC were Roger Staubach, Greg Landry, and Archie Manning.

EASTERN DIVISION

Miami Dolphins— Although the Miami defense played surprisingly strong, the pride of the Dolphins was their versatile offense. Enemy defenses had to contend with an unheralded but solid line, a great deep receiver in Paul Warfield, a good short receiver in Howard Twilley, two relentless runners in Larry Csonka and Jim Kiick, a breakaway runner in Mercury Morris, and an enormously resourceful quarterback in young Bob Griese. Whenever the attack stalled, place kicker Garo Yepremian was deadly within the 50-yard line. With all this offensive firepower, the Dolphins raced evenly with the Colts through most of the season. Although assured of at least a wild-card berth in the playoffs, the Dolphins seemed to have conceded first place by losing to Baltimore on the next to last weekend, but a victory over Green Bay, plus the Colts' upset loss to New England, let the Dolphins slip into first place on the final day of the season.

Baltimore Colts—The Colts won the wild-card playoff spot on the strength of the conference's best defense and a strong offense. The defense had some problems at one cornerback slot, but the presence of stars Bubba Smith, Ted Hendricks, Mike Curtis, Ray May, Charlie Stukes, Rick Volk, and Jerry Logan glossed over any shortcomings in the other positions. The offense went with Earl Morrall at quarterback for the first half of the schedule, but Johnny Unitas recovered from an off-season Achilles tendon injury to reclaim the starting spot down the stretch. Although his arm was not what it once had been, Unitas still had enough guile to maneuver his way through the best defenses in the league.

New England Patriots—The Patriots had a brand-new name, a brand-new stadium in Foxboro, Massachusetts, to play in, and a talented new quarterback in rookie Jim Plunkett. In his professional debut, Plunkett threw two touchdown passes in leading the Patriots to a 20-6 upset victory over the Oakland Raiders, and the big rookie continued to impress friend and foe alike all season with his arm and poise. To catch Plunkett's passes, the Patriots signed little Randy Vataha, Plunkett's college teammate who had been cut by the Rams early in training camp. Other newcomers who made a good impression were rookie defensive tackle Julius Adams and ex-Dallas linebacker Steve Kiner.

New York Jets—The Jets again went through the season with many of their regulars missing from action. Injuries sidelined Joe Namath, Matt Snell, Gerry Philbin, and John Elliott for long stretches of time, George Sauer and Steve Thompson both quit football at their physical prime for other interests, and Verlon Biggs played out his option and signed with the Washington Redskins. Injuries so decimated the defensive line that coach Weeb Ewbank at one point talked Clovis Swinney out of his job selling cars to help the Jets out.

Buffalo Bills—For the second time in the last four years, scout Harvey Johnson stepped in as interim head coach under dismal conditions. This year, Johnny Rauch resigned before the season began, leaving Johnson to guide the dispirited Bills through a horrendous 1-13-0 campaign. Major problems during the year were injuries in the offensive line, where Johnson was forced to start five rookies and a second-year man, quarterback Dennis Shaw's serious regression from his good rookie showing, and a disorganized defense.

CENTRAL DIVISION

Cleveland Browns—With Mike Phipps still not ready to take over as starting quarterback, Bill Nelsen took his aching knees into battle once more and took the Browns to the championship of the NFL's weakest division. The road to first place was a rocky one, with the Browns losing four straight mid-season games before going on a five-game winning streak. On paper, the Browns looked like a team evenly balanced between strengths and weaknesses. Leroy Kelly, Bo Scott, Milt Morin, Clarence Scott, Jack Gregory, and Walter Johnson fit comfortably into the asset column, but under the deficit heading were listed disorganization in the linebacking and secondary, advanced age in several offensive linemen, and the lack of a clutch wide receiver.

Pittsburgh Steelers—Dave Smith won a place on the roster of famous bloopers with his bonehead play of October 18. Sprinting to the end zone with a pass, Smith mistook the 5-yard line for the goal line and slammed the ball down on the ground, thinking that he had scored a touchdown. The referee noticed full well that Smith had never carried the ball across the goal line, and when the ball rolled through the end zone, he ruled it a touchback, gave the ball to Kansas City, and erased six points that Smith and the Steelers were already counting. But aside from that play, Smith enjoyed a fine season, as did fellow wide receiver Ron Shanklin and quarterback Terry Bradshaw.

Houston Oilers—Owner Bud Adams hired Ed Hughes, a man highly respected around the league, as his new head coach, but Adams quickly lost confidence in the coach and put him on the spot by firing one of his assistants in mid-season with no notice. The players rallied around Hughes late in the year and won their final three games after a very slow start. One of Hughes' moves during the season was to bench quarterback Charley Johnson and try rookies Lynn Dickey and Dan Pastorini at the position. Pastorini finally nailed down the starting job, showing good potential despite taking a steady pounding from defenders who sliced right through the porous Houston front wall.

Cincinnati Bengals—The Bengals slumped back into last place in the Central Division. Six of those losses, however, were by four points or less, so the Bengals were not nearly as lame as their record indicated. The Cincinnati attack again relied heavily on the run, with rookie Fred Willis and Essex Johnson taking over from Jess Phillips and Paul Robinson as the heavy-duty ball carriers. The need for a strong ground game was underlined by the weakened situation at quarterback. Greg Cook, the rookie marvel of 1970, still was out of action with a bad shoulder, and Virgil Carter missed several games with injuries.

WESTERN DIVISION

Kansas City Chiefs—The Chiefs opened up their offense and won first place in the Western Division. Morris Stroud and rookie Elmo Wright developed into good receivers, giving Len Dawson two new targets to throw at and also taking some of the defense's attention away from Otis Taylor. No longer the only receiving threat on the team, Taylor enjoyed his best year as a pro, leading the NFL in yards gained on receptions. Ed Podolak spearheaded the running game and also contributed in the receiving and kick-returning departments. On defense, Jerry Mays' retirement weakened the front four, but the linebacking trio of Bobby Bell, Willie Lanier, and Jim Lynch plus the talented secondary kept the unit in fine condition.

Oakland Raiders—The Raiders finished out of first place for the first time in five years, but they still compiled a winning record despite several sizable difficulties. First of all, Warren Wells, who was Daryle Lamonica's favorite deep receiver, ran afoul of the law and had to sit the season out. Then Hewritt Dixon and Charlie Smith, both starting running backs, went out of action with injuries, and the advancing years started cutting down in Tom Keating's and Ben Davidson's effectiveness in the defensive line. To remedy all these problems, Madden inserted rookie receiver Mike Siani into the lineup to team up with Fred Biletnikoff on the flanks, he promoted subs Marv Hubbard and Pete Banaszak to starters with fine results, and he rejuvenated the defense by giving lots of playing time to youngsters Tony Cline, Art Thoms, Harold Rice, Horace Jones, and Phil Villapiano.

San Diego Chargers—The San Diego management had a new look at the start of the season as Sid Gillman decided to resume his coaching duties and Harland Svare came in as general manager. By mid-season, however, Gillman got into a disagreement with owner Eugene Klein and found himself out of work. Svare, meanwhile, found himself back on the field as head coach for the final four games. As usual, the San Diego defense leaked profusely, while the offense cranked out points at a rapid clip. The trade of Lance Alworth to Dallas gave the attack a new look, with rookie Billy Parks filling in with great results until he broke his arm late in the year.

Denver Broncos—Floyd Little's strong running cheered Lou Saban somewhat, but assorted other troubles made the coach's final half season a vexing one. Injuries erased starters Rich Jackson, Pete Duranko, Larry Kaminski, and Sam Brunelli and exposed the thinness of the Denver bench. None of the wide receivers on the team took up the slack left by the trade of Al Denson to Minnesota, and the quarterback situation was a highly unhealthy one. After several injury-filled seasons, quarterback Steve Tensi packed it all in, leaving ex-Packer Don Horn at the starting quarterback. After a lackluster first half, Horn went out with an injury, leaving only inexperienced Steve Ramsey as a passer. Nine games were enough for Saban this year, and assistant Jerry Smith took over as head man for the final five games.

FINAL TEAM STATISTICS

OFFENSE

	BALT.	BUFF.	CIN.	CLEV.	DENV.	HOUS.	K.C.	MIAMI	N.ENG.	N.Y.J.	OAK.	PITT.	S.D.
FIRST DOWNS:													
Total	242	185	236	231	217	201	240	232	190	202	258	226	264
by Rushing	123	68	109	89	102	62	108	121	85	115	128	98	86
by Passing	104	96	115	127	105	117	119	94	94	67	110	111	147
by Penalty	15	21	12	15	10	22	13	17	11	20	20	17	31
RUSHING:													
Number	512	320	462	461	512	361	487	486	419	485	473	416	390
Yards	2149	1337	2142	1558	2093	1106	1843	2429	1669	1888	2130	1758	1604
Average Yards	4.2	4.2	4.6	3.4	4.1	3.1	3.8	5.0	4.0	3.9	4.5	4.2	4.1
Touchdowns	23	6	14	19	9	10	14	11	7	12	19	10	11
PASSING:													
Attempts	344	401	365	376	358	423	337	293	330	278	348	414	450
Completions	176	202	214	188	175	194	183	156	159	119	174	214	244
Completion Percentage	51.2	50.4	58.6	50.0	48.9	45.9	54.3	53.2	48.2	42.8	50.0	51.7	54.2
Passing Yards	2152	2410	2427	2521	2243	2643	2694	2248	2206	1556	2363	2446	3305
Avg. Yards per Attempt	6.3	6.0	6.6	6.7	6.3	6.2	8.0	7.7	6.7	5.6	6.8	5.9	7.3
Avg. Yards per Complet.	12.2	11.9	11.3	13.4	12.8	13.6	14.7	14.4	13.9	13.1	13.6	11.4	13.5
Times Tackled Passing	27	49	40	22	22	31	35	25	36	23	24	37	19
Yards Lost Tackled	230	421	303	222	178	234	347	265	319	177	235	322	171
Net Yards	1922	1989	2124	2299	2065	2409	2347	1983	1887	1379	2128	2124	3134
Touchdowns	10	12	15	14	8	12	15	20	19	15	21	15	23
Interceptions	21	32	11	27	27	37	13	10	16	16	26	26	28
Percent Intercepted	6.1	8.0	3.0	7.2	7.5	8.7	3.9	3.4	4.8	5.8	7.5	6.3	6.2
PUNTS:													
Number	62	75	73	67	76	75	64	52	87	78	62	79	55
Average Distance	41.0	40.9	44.7	39.9	41.8	40.6	44.8	40.1	37.3	38.8	39.9	43.7	43.5
PUNT RETURNS:													
Number	43	44	25	40	41	32	33	41	31	25	29	35	37
Yards	351	343	145	359	320	198	150	432	181	155	182	264	215
Average Yards	8.2	7.8	5.8	9.0	7.8	6.2	4.5	10.5	5.8	6.2	6.3	7.5	5.8
Touchdowns	0	2	0	0	0	0	0	0	0	0	0	1	0
KICKOFF RETURNS:													
Number	32	74	43	46	44	59	47	32	64	55	54	49	49
Yards	679	1673	863	1065	960	1409	1031	806	1354	1168	1234	1120	1000
Average Yards	21.2	22.6	20.1	23.2	21.8	23.9	21.9	25.2	21.2	21.2	22.9	22.9	20.4
Touchdowns	0	0	0	0	0	0	0	1	0	0	0	0	0
INTERCEPTION RETURNS:													
Number	28	11	27	24	20	23	27	17	15	13	23	17	22
Yards	367	93	273	283	288	456	403	143	229	136	453	246	317
Average Yards	13.1	8.5	10.1	11.3	14.4	19.8	14.9	8.4	15.3	10.5	19.7	14.5	14.4
Touchdowns	1	0	2	0	1	5	3	0	2	0	2	1	2
PENALTIES:													
Number	57	74	82	68	67	91	72	65	67	70	81	88	81
Yards	529	691	921	612	781	856	734	632	657	672	869	898	895
FUMBLES:													
Number	26	33	29	29	25	24	23	22	26	30	26	37	30
Number Lost	11	16	12	18	12	14	13	13	16	10	13	16	15
POINTS:													
Total	313	184	284	285	203	251	302	315	238	212	344	246	311
PAT Attempts	36	21	32	34	18	29	32	33	29	27	43	28	37
PAT Made	35	20	32	34	18	26	32	33	28	26	41	27	36
FG Attempts	29	25	36	28	38	28	45	40	21	19	22	27	29
FG Made	20	12	20	15	25	17	26	28	12	8	15	17	17
Percent FG Made	69.0	48.0	55.6	53.6	65.8	60.7	57.8	70.0	57.1	42.1	68.2	63.0	58.6
Safeties	1	1	0	1	1	0	0	0	0	0	0	0	1

DEFENSE

	BALT.	BUFF.	CIN.	CLEV.	DENV.	HOUS.	K.C.	MIAMI	N.ENG.	N.Y.J.	OAK.	PITT.	S.D.
FIRST DOWNS:													
Total	166	250	213	232	206	237	223	214	237	235	242	225	272
by Rushing	60	135	93	115	90	117	73	93	106	118	100	81	143
by Passing	95	101	102	100	91	97	125	111	111	101	122	132	114
by Penalty	11	14	18	17	25	23	25	10	20	16	20	12	15
RUSHING:													
Number	352	562	446	484	426	489	367	403	481	472	480	440	493
Yards	1113	2496	1778	2227	1834	1723	1300	1661	1918	2302	1751	1482	2296
Average Yards	3.2	4.4	4.0	4.6	4.3	3.5	3.5	4.1	4.0	4.9	3.6	3.4	4.7
Touchdowns	8	21	11	14	11	22	9	10	14	18	14	13	25
PASSING:													
Attempts	361	303	335	339	356	354	418	363	350	342	359	408	347
Completions	185	157	157	156	150	180	209	206	170	163	184	235	193
Completion Percentage	51.2	51.8	46.9	46.0	42.1	50.8	50.0	56.7	48.6	47.7	51.3	57.6	55.6
Passing Yards	2027	2333	2382	2170	2420	2416	2703	2293	2403	2285	2609	3060	2439
Avg. Yards per Attempt	5.6	7.7	7.1	6.4	6.8	6.8	6.5	6.3	6.9	6.7	7.3	7.5	7.0
Avg. Yards per Complet.	11.0	14.9	15.2	13.9	16.1	13.4	12.9	11.1	14.1	14.0	14.2	13.0	12.6
Times Tackled Passing	33	30	30	25	44	37	28	34	25	27	32	33	19
Yards Lost Tackled	288	225	254	203	435	344	235	293	249	230	223	294	177
Net Yards	1739	2108	2128	1967	1985	2072	2468	2000	2154	2055	2386	2766	2262
Touchdowns	9	20	19	12	18	11	11	10	16	17	15	16	15
Interceptions	28	11	27	24	20	23	27	17	15	13	23	17	22
Percent Intercepted	7.8	3.6	8.1	7.1	5.6	6.5	6.5	4.7	4.3	3.8	6.4	4.2	6.3
PUNTS:													
Number	88	66	73	66	67	76	67	72	66	65	59	77	67
Average Distance	38.9	39.0	40.9	42.4	45.7	42.2	40.7	40.7	38.8	38.1	41.7	41.5	43.7
PUNT RETURNS:													
Number	40	40	41	26	45	39	40	26	36	41	26	45	20
Yards	267	446	304	227	468	304	286	106	279	359	168	319	40
Average Yards	6.7	11.2	7.4	8.7	10.4	7.8	7.2	4.1	7.8	8.8	6.5	7.1	2.0
Touchdowns	0	0	1	0	0	0	0	0	1	0	0	0	0
KICKOFF RETURNS:													
Number	62	42	39	55	43	41	47	59	49	34	55	45	55
Yards	1345	971	1024	1252	1059	862	1071	1180	1427	906	1155	1002	1245
Average Yards	21.7	23.1	26.3	22.8	24.6	20.8	22.8	20.0	29.1	26.6	21.0	22.3	22.6
Touchdowns	0	0	0	0	0	0	0	0	1	1	0	0	0
INTERCEPTION RETURNS:													
Number	21	32	11	27	27	37	13	10	16	16	26	26	28
Yards	220	418	219	453	432	505	167	166	157	279	267	350	339
Average Yards	10.5	13.1	19.9	16.8	16.0	13.6	12.8	16.6	9.8	17.4	10.3	13.5	12.1
Touchdowns	1	3	1	2	2	3	0	1	1	1	0	1	4
PENALTIES:													
Number	67	89	72	86	78	75	71	62	60	81	80	81	84
Yards	687	883	722	772	771	916	751	569	559	814	832	784	887
FUMBLES:													
Number	22	17	21	31	36	31	16	38	35	35	26	27	27
Number Lost	13	11	12	16	20	14	6	14	14	14	17	18	10
POINTS:													
Total	140	394	265	273	275	330	208	174	325	299	278	292	341
PAT Attempts	18	45	32	30	32	37	21	21	35	37	30	32	44
PAT Made	17	45	31	30	32	36	20	21	34	35	30	30	44
FG Attempts	18	30	22	31	35	35	32	21	36	25	34	35	24
FG Made	5	25	14	21	17	24	20	9	27	14	22	22	11
Percent FG Made	27.8	65.8	63.6	67.7	48.6	68.9	62.5	42.9	75.0	56.0	64.7	62.9	45.8
Safeties	0	2	0	0	0	0	1	0	0	0	1	2	0

CONFERENCE PLAYOFFS

December 25, at Kansas City
(Attendance 45,822)

SCORING

KANSAS CITY	10	0	7	7	0	0	—24
MIAMI	0	10	7	7	0	3	—27

First Quarter
- K.C. Stenerud, 24 yard field goal
- K.C. Podolak, 7 yard pass from Dawson PAT—Stenerud (kick)

Second Quarter
- Mia. Csonka, 1 yard rush PAT—Yepremian (kick)
- Mia. Yepremian, 14 yard field goal

Third Quarter
- K.C. Otis, 1 yard rush PAT—Stenerud (kick)
- Mia. Kiick, 1 yard rush PAT—Yepremian (kick)

Fourth Quarter
- K.C. Podolak, 3 yard rush PAT—Stenerud (kick)
- Mia. Fleming, 5 yard pass from Griese PAT—Yepremian (kick)

Second Overtime Period
- Mia. Yepremian, 37 yard field goal 7:40

TEAM STATISTICS

K.C.		MIAMI
23	First Downs—Total	22
13	First Downs—Rushing	6
10	First Downs—Passing	14
0	First Downs—Penalty	2
2	Fumbles—Number	0
2	Fumbles—Lost Ball	0
6	Penalties—Number	5
44	Yards Penalized	26
3	Missed Field Goals	1
71	Offensive Plays—Total	78
451	Net Yards	407
6.4	Average Gain	5.2
4	Giveaways	2
2	Takeaways	4
−2	Difference	+2

INDIVIDUAL STATISTICS

KANSAS CITY	No.	Yds.	Avg.	MIAMI	No.	Yds.	Avg.
RUSHING							
Hayes	22	100	4.5	Csonka	24	86	3.6
Podolak	17	85	5.0	Kiick	15	56	3.7
Wright	2	15	7.5	Griese	2	9	4.5
Otis	3	13	4.3	Warfield	2	−7	−3.5
	44	213	4.8		43	144	3.3
RECEIVING							
Podolak	8	110	13.8	Warfield	7	140	20.0
Wright	3	104	34.7	Twilley	5	58	11.6
Taylor	3	12	4.0	Fleming	4	37	9.3
Hayes	3	6	2.0	Kiick	3	24	8.0
Frazier	1	14	14.0	Mandich	1	4	4.0
	18	246	13.7		20	263	13.2
PUNTING							
Wilson	2		51.0	Seiple	6		40.0
PUNT RETURNS							
Podolak	2	1	0.5	Scott	1	18	18.0
KICKOFF RETURNS							
Podolak	3	154	52.0	Morris	2	61	30.5
INTERCEPTION RETURNS							
Lanier	1	17	17.0	Scott	1	13	13.0
Lynch	1	0	0.0	Johnson	1	0	0.0
	2	17	8.5		2	13	6.5

PASSING

KANSAS CITY	Att.	Comp.	Comp. Pct.	Yds.	Int.	Yds/ Att.	Yds/ Comp.	Yds Lost Tkld.
Dawson	26	18	69.2	246	2	9.5	13.7	1–8
Podolak	1	0	0.0	0	0	–	–	
	27	18	66.7	246	2	9.1	13.7	1–8
MIAMI								
Griese	35	20	57.1	263	2	7.5	13.2	0–0

December 26, at Cleveland
(Attendance 70,734)

SCORING

CLEVELAND	0	0	3	0	— 3
BALTIMORE	0	14	3	3	—20

Second Quarter
- Balt. Nottingham, 1 yard rush PAT—O'Brien (kick)
- Balt. Nottingham, 7 yard rush PAT—O'Brien (kick)

Third Quarter
- Cle. Cockroft, 14 yard field goal
- Balt. O'Brien, 42 yard field goal

Fourth Quarter
- Balt. O'Brien, 15 yard field goal

TEAM STATISTICS

CLE.		BALT.
11	First Downs—Total	16
5	First Downs—Rushing	7
5	First Downs—Passing	8
1	First Downs—Penalty	1
6	Fumbles—Number	2
2	Fumbles—Lost Ball	2
3	Penalties—Number	5
18	Yards Penalized	43
2	Missed Field Goals	0
56	Offensive Plays—Total	64
165	Net Yards	271
2.9	Average Gain	4.2
5	Giveaways	3
3	Takeaways	5
−2	Difference	+2

INDIVIDUAL STATISTICS

CLEVELAND	No.	Yds.	Avg.	BALTIMORE	No.	Yds.	Avg.
RUSHING							
Kelly	14	49	3.5	Nottingham	23	92	4.0
Bo Scott	8	25	3.1	Matte	16	26	1.6
Nelsen	2	−5	−2.5	McCauley	3	9	3.0
	24	69	2.9	Nowatzke	1	1	1.0
					43	128	3.0
RECEIVING							
Bo Scott	5	41	8.2	Mitchell	5	73	14.6
Kelly	4	24	6.0	Matte	3	22	7.3
Hooker	1	39	39.0	Hinton	2	30	15.0
Morin	1	16	16.0	Perkins	1	10	10.0
Glass	1	11	11.0	Nottingham	1	5	5.0
	12	131	10.9	Havrilak	1	3	3.0
					13	143	11.0
PUNTING							
Cockroft	5		40.8	Lee	6		37.2
PUNT RETURNS							
Kelly	3	71	23.7	Volk	4	27	6.8
D. Jones	1	3	3.0				
	4	74	18.5				
KICKOFF RETURNS							
S. Brown	2	34	17.0	Pittman	1	25	25.0
Bo Scott	1	30	30.0				
Morrison	1	19	19.0				
Dieken	1	15	15.0				
	5	98	19.6				
INTERCEPTION RETURNS							
Snidow	1	1	1.0	Volk	2	56	28.0
C. Scott	Lat	22	–	Stukes	1	23	23.0
	1	23	23.0		3	89	29.7

PASSING

CLEVE.	Att.	Cmp.	Pct.	Yds.	Int.	Yd/A	Yd/C	Tkld
Nelsen	21	9	42.9	104	3	5.0	11.6	
Phipps	6	3	50.0	27	0	4.5	9.0	
	27	12	44.4	131	3	4.9	10.9	5–35
BALT.								
Unitas	21	13	61.9	143	1	6.8	11.0	0– 0

MIAMI DOLPHINS 10-3-1 Don Shula

Scores of Each Game		
10	Denver	10
29	Buffalo	14
10	N.Y. JETS	14
23	Cincinnati	13
41	NEW ENGLAND	3
30	N.Y. Jets	14
20	Los Angeles	14
34	BUFFALO	0
24	PITTSBURGH	21
17	BALTIMORE	14
34	CHICAGO	3
13	New England	34
3	Baltimore	14
27	GREEN BAY	6

Use Name	Pos.	Hgt	Wgt	Age	Int	Pts
Doug Crusan	OT	6'5"	250	25		
Norm Evans	OT	6'5"	252	28		
Wayne Mass	OT	6'4"	240	25		
Bob Kuechenberg	OG	6'3"	247	23		
Jim Langer	OG	6'2"	250	23		
Larry Little	OG	6'1"	265	25		
Bob DeMarco	C	6'3"	250	33		
Vern Den Herder	DE	6'6"	250	22		
Jim Riley	DE	6'4"	250	26		
Bill Stanfill	DE	6'5"	250	24		
Frank Cornish	DT	6'6"	285	27		
Manny Fernandez	DT	6'2"	248	25		
John Richardson	DT	6'2"	248	26		
Bob Heinz	DE-DT	6'6"	270	24		

Dick Palmer–Injury

Use Name	Pos.	Hgt	Wgt	Age	Int	Pts
Nick Buoniconti	LB	5'11"	220	30	1	
Dale Farley	LB	6'3"	235	22		
Mike Kolen	LB	6'2"	220	23		
Bob Matheson	LB	6'4"	240	26		
Jesse Powell	LB	6'1"	215	24		
Doug Swift	LB	6'3"	228	22	1	
Dick Anderson	DB	6'2"	196	25	2	
Tim Foley	DB	6'	194	23	4	
Curtis Johnson	DB	6'2"	196	23	2	6
Ray Jones	DB	6'	187	23		
Lloyd Mumphord	DB	5'11"	180	24		
Bob Petrella	DB	6'	190	26		
Jake Scott	DB	6'	188	26	7	

Dean Brown–Injury
Dick Daniels–Injury
Stan Mitchell–Injury

Use Name	Pos.	Hgt	Wgt	Age	Int	Pts
Bob Griese	QB	6'1"	190	26		
George Mira	QB	5'11"	192	29		
Hubert Ginn	HB	5'11"	188	24		
Jim Kiick	HB	5'11"	215	25		18
Mercury Morris	HB	5'10"	190	24		12
Terry Cole	FB	6'1"	220	26		
Larry Csonka	FB	6'3"	237	24		48
Charlie Leigh	FB	5'11"	205	25		
Karl Noonan	WR	6'3"	198	27		
Otto Stowe	WR	6'2"	188	22		6
Howard Twilley	WR	5'10"	185	27		24
Paul Warfield	WR	6'	185	28		66
Marv Fleming	TE	6'4"	235	29		12
Jim Mandich	TE	6'3"	224	23		6
Larry Seiple	TE	6'	215	26		
Garo Yepremian	K	5'8"	165	27		117

BALTIMORE COLTS 10-4-0 Don McCafferty

Scores of Each Game		
22	N.Y. JETS	0
13	CLEVELAND	14
23	New England	3
43	Buffalo	0
31	N.Y. Giants	7
3	Minnesota	10
34	PITTSBURGH	21
24	LOS ANGELES	17
14	N.Y. Jets	13
14	Miami	17
37	Oakland	14
24	BUFFALO	0
14	MIAMI	3
17	NEW ENGLAND	21

Use Name	Pos.	Hgt	Wgt	Age	Int	Pts
Lynn Larson	OT	6'4"	254	23		
Dennis Nelson	OT	6'5"	260	25		
Bob Vogel	OT	6'5"	250	29		
Cornelius Johnson	OG	6'2"	245	28		
Glenn Ressler	OG	6'3"	250	27		
Dan Sullivan	OG	6'3"	250	32		
John Williams	OG	6'3"	256	25		
Bill Curry	C	6'2"	236	28		
Ken Mendenhall	C	6'3"	235	23		
Roy Hilton	DE	6'6"	240	26		
Billy Newsome	DE	6'4"	240	23	2	6
Bubba Smith	DE	6'7"	295	26		
Jim Bailey	DT		245	23		
Rusty Ganas	DT	6'4"	257	21		
Fred Miller	DT	6'3"	250	30		
George Wright	DT	6'3"	260	24		

Use Name	Pos.	Hgt	Wgt	Age	Int	Pts
Tom Beutler	LB	6'1"	232	24		
Mike Curtis	LB	6'2"	232	28	3	
Ted Hendricks	LB	6'7"	215	23	5	6
Bill Laskey	LB	6'2"	235	28		
Ray May	LB	6'1"	230	26	1	
Robbie Nichols	LB	6'3"	220	24		
Tom Nowatzke	FB-LB	6'3"	230	28	1	
Tom Curtis	DB	6'1"	196	23		
Jim Duncan	DB	6'2"	200	25		
Lenny Dunlap	DB	6'1"	195	22		
Lonnie Hepburn	DB	5'11"	185	22		
Rex Kern	DB	5'11"	190	22		
Jerry Logan	DB	6'1"	190	30	4	
Charlie Stukes	DB	6'3"	212	27	8	
Rick Volk	DB	6'3"	195	26	4	

Use Name	Pos.	Hgt	Wgt	Age	Int	Pts
Earl Morrall	QB	6'1"	206	37		
Johnny Unitas	QB	6'1"	196	38		
Tom Matte	HB	6'	214	32		48
Don McCauley	HB	6'1"	207	22		12
Charlie Pittman	HB	6'1"	200	23		
Don Nottingham	FB	5'10"	210	22		36
Norm Bulaich	HB-FB	6'1"	218	24		60
Sam Havrilak	WR	6'2"	195	23		
Eddie Hinton	WR	6'	200	24		12
Jim O'Brien	WR	6'	195	24		95
Ray Perkins	WR	6'	183	29		24
Willie Richardson	WR	6'2"	198	31		12
John Mackey	TE	6'3"	224	29		
Tom Mitchell	TE	6'2"	215	27		
David Lee	K	6'4"	230	27		

NEW ENGLAND PATRIOTS 6-8-0 John Mazur

Scores of Each Game		
20	OAKLAND	6
7	DETROIT	34
3	BALTIMORE	23
20	N.Y. JETS	0
3	Miami	41
21	Dallas	44
10	San Francisco	27
28	HOUSTON	20
38	BUFFALO	33
7	Cleveland	27
20	Buffalo	27
34	MIAMI	13
6	N.Y. Jets	13
21	Baltimore	17

Use Name	Pos.	Hgt	Wgt	Age	Int	Pts
Mike Haggerty	OT	6'4"	250	25		
Mike Montler	OT	6'4"	270	27		
Tom Neville	OT	6'4"	255	28		
Bill Lenkaitis	OG	6'3"	265	25		
Len St. Jean	OG	6'1"	245	29		
Halvor Hagen	C-OG	6'5"	253	24		
Jon Morris	C	6'4"	255	28		
Ike Lassiter	DE	6'5"	270	30		
Art May	DE	6'3"	245	22		
Dennis Wirgowski	DE	6'5"	255	23		
Ron Berger	DT-DE	6'8"	275	27		
Julius Adams	DT	6'3"	258	23		
Houston Antwine	DT	6'	270	32		
Dave Rowe	DT	6'6"	280	26		
Bill Atessis	DE-DT	6'3"	240	22		

Rick Cash–Injury
Joe Kapp–Holdout
J. R. Williamson–Injury

Use Name	Pos.	Hgt	Wgt	Age	Int	Pts
Jim Cheyunski	LB	6'2"	220	25	1	
Dennis Coleman	LB	6'3"	225	22		
Randy Edmunds	LB	6'2"	225	25		
Steve Kiner	LB	6'	219	24	4	
Ed Philpott	LB	6'3"	240	25		
Ed Weisacosky	LB	6'	220	27		
Randy Beverly	DB	5'11"	205	27	2	
Larry Carwell	DB	6'1"	200	27	5	6
Phil Clark	DB	6'2"	208	26		
Rickie Harris	DB	6'	182	28		
Tom Janik	DB	6'3"	200	30		
Irv Mallory	DB	6'1"	196	22		
John Outlaw	DB	5'10"	175	26	3	6
Perry Pruett	DB	6'1"	190	22		
Clarence Scott	DB	6'2"	205	27		
Don Webb	DB	5'10"	185	32		
Ron Gardin (from BAL)	WR-DB	5'11"	180	26		

Use Name	Pos.	Hgt	Wgt	Age	Int	Pts
Jim Plunkett	QB	6'3"	220	23		
Mike Taliaferro	QB	6'2"	205	29		
Carl Garrett	HB	5'11"	210	24		12
Bob Gladieux	HB	5'11"	190	24		
Jack Maitland	HB	6'1"	210	23		6
Odell Lawson	FB	6'2"	218	23		
Jim Nance	FB	6'1"	240	28		30
Hubie Bryant	WR	5'10"	168	25		6
Eric Crabtree (from CIN)	WR	5'11"	185	26		18
Reggie Rucker (from DAL-NYG)	WR	6'2"	190	23		6
Ron Sellers	WR	6'4"	195	24		18
Eric Stolberg	WR	6'2"	180	22		
Al Sykes	WR	6'3"	180	24		
Randy Vataha	WR	5'10"	180	22		54
Roland Moss	TE	6'3"	215	24		12
Tom Beer	OG-TE	6'4"	235	26		18
Charlie Gogolak	K	5'10"	170	26		64

NEW YORK JETS 6-8-0 Weeb Ewbank

Scores of Each Game		
0	Baltimore	22
10	St. Louis	17
14	Miami	10
0	New England	20
28	BUFFALO	17
14	MIAMI	30
21	San Diego	49
13	KANSAS CITY	10
13	BALTIMORE	14
20	Buffalo	7
21	SAN FRANCISCO	24
10	Dallas	52
13	NEW ENGLAND	6
35	CINCINNATI	21

Use Name	Pos.	Hgt	Wgt	Age	Int	Pts
Winston Hill	OT	6'4"	285	29		
John Mooring	OT	6'6"	255	24		
Bob Svihus	OT	6'4"	245	28		
Dave Foley	C-OT	6'5"	255	23		
Dave Herman	OG	6'2"	255	29		
Roy Kirksey	OG	6'1"	265	23		
Randy Rasmussen	OG	6'2"	255	26		
John Schmitt	C	6'4"	250	28		
Paul Crane	LB-C	6'2"	212	27	1	
Mark Lomas	DE	6'4"	230	23		
Gerry Philbin	DE	6'2"	245	30		
John Little	DT-DE	6'3"	220	24		
Steve Thompson	DT-DE	6'5"	245	25		
John Elliott	DT	6'4"	244	26		
Roger Finnie	DT	6'3"	245			
Chuck Hinton (from PIT)	DT	6'5"	264	32		
Scott Palmer	DT	6'3"	245	23		
Clovis Swinney	DT	6'3"	240	26		

Use Name	Pos.	Hgt	Wgt	Age	Int	Pts
Al Atkinson	LB	6'1"	230	28	2	
Ralph Baker	LB	6'3"	235	29		1
Larry Grantham	LB	6'	210	32	1	
John Ebersole	LB	6'3"	240	22		
Bill Zapalac	DE-LB	6'4"	225	23		
John Dockery	DB	6'	186	26	2	
Chris Farasopoulos	DB	5'11"	190	22		
W.K. Hicks	DB	6'1"	195	28		4
Gus Holloman	DB	6'3"	195	25	2	
Rich Sowells	DB	6'	175	22		
Steve Tannen	DB	6'1"	194	23		
Earlie Thomas	DB	6'1"	190	25		
Phil Wise	DB	6'	190	22	1	

Jim Richards–Military Service

Use Name	Pos.	Hgt	Wgt	Age	Int	Pts
Bob Davis	QB	6'3"	205	26		6
Joe Namath	QB	6'2"	200	28		
Al Woodall	QB	6'5"	205	25		
Emerson Boozer	HB	5'11"	195	28		36
George Nock	HB	5'10"	200	25		30
Cliff McClain	FB-HB	6'	217	23		12
John Riggins	FB	6'2"	237	22		18
Matt Snell	FB	6'2"	220	29		
Steve Harkey	HB-FB	6'	215	22		
Eddie Bell	WR	5'10"	160	23		6
Rich Caster	WR	6'5"	222	22		36
Don Maynard	WR	6'	180	35		12
Steve O'Neal	WR	6'3"	185	25		
Vern Studdard	WR	5'11"	175	23		
Gary Arthur	TE	6'5"	230	23		
Pete Lammons	TE	6'3"	230	27		6
Wayne Stewart	TE	6'7"	213	24		
Bobby Howfield	K	5'9"	180	34		49

BUFFALO BILLS 1-13-0 Harvey Johnson

Scores of Each Game		
37	DALLAS	49
14	MIAMI	29
0	Minnesota	19
0	BALTIMORE	43
17	N.Y. Jets	28
3	San Diego	20
23	ST. LOUIS	28
0	Miami	34
33	New England	38
7	N.Y. JETS	20
27	NEW ENGLAND	20
0	Baltimore	24
14	HOUSTON	20
9	Kansas City	22

Use Name	Pos.	Hgt	Wgt	Age	Int	Pts
Paul Costa	OT	6'4"	255	29		
Donnie Green	OT	6'7"	270	23		
Willie Young	OT	6'4"	270	23		
Bob Hews	DE-OT	6'5"	240	22		
Joe O'Donnell	OG	6'2"	262	28		
Mike Wilson	OG	6'1"	240	23		
Levert Carr	OT-OG	6'5"	260	27		
Bruce Jarvis	C	6'7"	246	22		
Howard Kindig	OT-C	6'6"	265	30		
Mike McBath	DE	6'4"	248	25		
Al Cowlings	DE	6'5"	258	24		
Louis Ross	DE	6'6"	238	24		
Cal Snowden	DE	6'4"	242	24		
Bill McKinley	LB-DE	6'3"	240	22		
Jim Dunaway	DT	6'4"	277	29		
Bob Tatarek	DT	6'4"	260	25		

Use Name	Pos.	Hgt	Wgt	Age	Int	Pts
Al Andrews	LB	6'3"	216	27	1	
Edgar Chandler	LB	6'3"	235	25	1	2
Jerald Collins	LB	6'1"	220	24		
Dick Cunningham	LB	6'2"	232	26		
Paul Guidry	LB	6'3"	233	27	1	
Mike Stratton	LB	6'3"	240	29		
Chuck Hurston	LB	6'6"	240	28		
Jackie Allen	DB	6'1"	187	23		
Tim Beamer	DB	5'11"	185	23		
Tony Greene	DB	5'10"	170	22		
Robert James	DB	6'1"	185	24	4	6
John Pitts	DB	6'4"	223	26	2	
Pete Richardson	DB	6'1"	193	24	1	
Alvin Wyatt	DB	5'10"	185	23	1	6

Richard Cheek – Knee Injury
Julian Nunamaker – Injury
Jim Reilly – Illness

Use Name	Pos.	Hgt	Wgt	Age	Int	Pts
James Harris	QB	6'3"	215	24		
Dennis Shaw	QB	6'2"	210	24		
Max Anderson	HB	5'8"	180	26		
Greg Jones	HB	6'1"	200	23		6
O.J. Simpson	HB	6'2"	214	24		30
Jim Braxton	FB	6'2"	226	22		
Wayne Patrick	FB	6'2"	254	25		6
Marlin Briscoe	WR	5'10"	178	25		30
Bob Chandler	WR	6'	180	22		
J.D. Hill	WR	6'1"	193	22		12
Haven Moses	WR	6'3"	205	25		12
Ike Hill	DB-WR	5'10"	180	24		12
Austin Denney	TE	6'2"	230	27		
Ted Koy	TE	6'1"	210	23		6
Jan White	TE	6'2"	215	22		
Dave Chappie	K	6'	180	24		
Grant Guthrie	K	6'	210	23		17
Spike Jones	K	6'2"	190	24		
John Leypoldt	K	6'2"	224	25		39

MIAMI DOLPHINS

RUSHING

Last Name	No.	Yds	Avg	TD
Csonka	195	1051	5.4	7
Kiick	162	738	4.6	3
Morris	57	315	5.5	1
Warfield	9	115	12.8	0
Ginn	22	97	4.4	0
Griese	26	82	3.2	0
Leigh	5	15	3.0	0
Seiple	1	14	14.0	0
Cole	3	11	3.7	0
Mira	6	–9	–1.5	0

RECEIVING

Last Name	No.	Yds	Avg	TD
Warfield	43	996	23	11
Kiick	40	338	8	0
Twilley	23	349	15	4
Fleming	13	137	11	2
Csonka	13	113	9	1
Noonan	10	180	18	0
Stowe	5	68	14	1
Morris	5	16	3	0
Mandich	3	19	6	1
Seiple	1	32	32	0

PUNT RETURNS

Last Name	No.	Yds	Avg	TD
Scott	33	318	10	0
Anderson	8	114	14	0

KICKOFF RETURNS

Last Name	No.	Yds	Avg	TD
Morris	15	423	28	1
Ginn	10	252	25	0
Leigh	4	99	25	0
Matheson	3	32	11	0

PASSING – PUNTING – KICKING

PASSING	Att	Comp	%	Yds	Yd/Att	TD	Int–	%	RK
Griese	263	145	55	2089	7.9	19	9–	3	1
Mira	30	11	37	158	5.3	1	1–	3	

PUNTING	No	Avg
Seiple	52	40.1

KICKING	XP	Att	%	FG	Att	%
Yepremian	33	33	100	28	40	70

BALTIMORE COLTS

RUSHING

Last Name	No.	Yds	Avg	TD
Bulaich	152	741	4.9	8
Matte	173	607	3.5	8
Nottingham	95	388	4.1	5
McCauley	58	246	4.2	2
Hinton	4	56	14.0	0
Perkins	5	35	7.0	0
Richardson	2	27	13.5	0
Mackey	3	18	6.0	0
Morrall	6	13	2.2	0
Mitchell	2	9	4.5	0
Unitas	9	5	0.6	0
Pittman	2	3	1.5	0
Nowatzke	1	1	1.0	0

RECEIVING

Last Name	No.	Yds	Avg	TD
Mitchell	33	402	12	0
Matte	29	239	8	0
Hinton	25	436	17	2
Bulaich	25	229	9	2
Perkins	24	424	18	4
Nottingham	15	88	6	0
Mackey	11	143	13	0
Richardson	10	173	17	2
McCauley	3	6	2	0
Havrilak	1	12	12	0

PUNT RETURNS

Last Name	No.	Yds	Avg	TD
Volk	22	118	5	0
Dunlap	8	112	14	0
Kern	3	19	6	0
T. Curtis	7	15	2	0
Logan	1	12	12	0

KICKOFF RETURNS

Last Name	No.	Yds	Avg	TD
Pittman	14	330	24	0
McCauley	8	194	24	0
Duncan	3	102	34	0
Dunlap	1	28	28	0
Logan	1	16	16	0
Stukes	1	8	8	0
Nowatzke	1	1	1	0
T. Curtis	1	0	0	0
Matte	1	0	0	0
Mitchell	1	0	0	0

PASSING – PUNTING – KICKING

PASSING	Att	Comp	%	Yds	Yd/Att	TD	Int–	%	RK
Unitas	176	92	52	942	5.4	3	9–	5	10
Morrall	167	84	50	1210	7.3	7	12–	7	9
Matte	1	0	0	0	0.0	0	0–	0	

PUNTING	No	Avg
Lee	62	41.0

KICKING	XP	Att	%	FG	Att	%
O'Brien	35	36	97	20	29	69

NEW ENGLAND PATRIOTS

RUSHING

Last Name	No.	Yds	Avg	TD
Garrett	181	784	4.3	1
Nance	129	463	3.6	5
Plunkett	45	210	4.7	0
Gladieux	37	175	4.7	0
Maitland	13	25	1.9	1
Crabtree	3	12	4.0	0
Lawson	8	8	1.0	0
Bryant	4	1	0.3	0
Rucker	1	14	14.0	0
Neville	0	–8	0.0	0

RECEIVING

Last Name	No.	Yds	Avg	TD
Vataha	51	872	17	9
Crabtree	23	222	10	3
Garrett	22	265	12	1
Nance	18	95	5	0
Sellers	14	222	16	3
Bryant	14	212	15	1
Beer	12	191	16	3
Moss	9	124	14	1
Gladieux	6	60	10	0
Rucker	4	52	13	1
Sykes	1	15	15	0
Maitland	1	6	6	0

PUNT RETURNS

Last Name	No.	Yds	Avg	TD
Garrett	8	124	16	0
Gardin	6	89	15	0
Bryant	10	24	2	0
Harris	5	19	4	0
Gladieux	4	0	0	0

KICKOFF RETURNS

Last Name	No.	Yds	Avg	TD
Garrett	24	538	22	0
Gardin	14	321	23	0
Bryant	10	252	25	0
Gladieux	6	85	14	0
Lawson	2	47	24	0
Rucker	2	45	23	0
Maitland	2	40	20	0
Mallory	1	19	19	0
Hagen	1	7	7	0
Janik	1	0	0	0
Webb	1	0	0	0

PASSING – PUNTING – KICKING

PASSING	Att	Comp	%	Yds	Yd/Att	TD	Int–	%	RK
Plunkett	328	158	48	2158	6.6	19	16–	5	5
Gladieux	2	1	50	48	24.0	0	0–	0	

PUNTING	No	Avg
Janik	87	37.3

KICKING	XP	Att	%	FG	Att	%
Gogolak	28	28	100	12	21	57

NEW YORK JETS

RUSHING

Last Name	No.	Yds	Avg	TD
Riggins	180	769	4.3	1
Boozer	188	618	3.3	5
Davis	18	154	8.6	1
Nock	48	137	2.9	3
McClain	12	108	9.0	2
Harkey	20	62	3.1	0
Woodall	13	26	2.0	0
Caster	2	10	5.0	0
Maynard	1	2	2.0	0
Namath	3	–1	–0.3	0
Lammons	0	3	0.0	0

RECEIVING

Last Name	No.	Yds	Avg	TD
Riggins	36	231	6	2
Caster	26	454	17	6
Maynard	21	408	19	2
Boozer	11	120	11	1
Lammons	8	149	19	1
Nock	6	44	7	2
Bell	5	110	22	1
Harkey	5	28	6	0
Arthur	1	12	12	0

PUNT RETURNS

Last Name	No.	Yds	Avg	TD
Farasopoulos	19	155	8	0
Studdard	4	3	1	0
Hicks	1	0	0	0
Bell	1	–3	–3	0

KICKOFF RETURNS

Last Name	No.	Yds	Avg	TD
Farasopoulos	25	545	22	0
Studdard	15	329	22	0
Wise	8	210	26	0
Nock	5	71	14	0
McClain	1	11	11	0
Harkey	1	2	2	0

PASSING – PUNTING – KICKING

PASSING	Att	Comp	%	Yds	Yd/Att	TD	Int–	%	RK
Davis	121	49	40	624	5.2	10	8–	7	
Woodall	97	42	43	395	4.1	0	2–	2	
Namath	59	28	47	537	9.1	5	6–	10	
O'Neal	1	0	0	0	0.0	0	0–	0	

PUNTING	No	Avg
O'Neal	78	38.8

KICKING	XP	Att	%	FG	Att	%
Howfield	25	26	96	8	19	42
Baker	1	1	100	0	0	0

BUFFALO BILLS

RUSHING

Last Name	No.	Yds	Avg	TD
Simpson	183	742	4.1	5
Patrick	79	332	4.2	1
Braxton	21	84	4.0	0
Shaw	14	82	5.9	0
G. Jones	16	53	3.3	0
Harris	6	42	7.0	0
J. D. Hill	1	2	2.0	0

RECEIVING

Last Name	No.	Yds	Avg	TD
Briscoe	44	603	14	5
Patrick	36	327	9	0
Moses	23	470	20	2
Simpson	21	162	8	0
Braxton	18	141	8	0
G. Jones	16	113	7	1
White	13	130	10	0
J. D. Hill	11	216	20	2
Koy	10	133	13	1
B. Chandler	5	60	12	0
I. Hill	5	55	11	1

PUNT RETURNS

Last Name	No.	Yds	Avg	TD
Wyatt	23	188	8	1
I. Hill	14	133	10	1
Beamer	7	22	3	0

KICKOFF RETURNS

Last Name	No.	Yds	Avg	TD
Wyatt	30	762	25	0
Beamer	20	394	20	0
I. Hill	12	280	23	0
Simpson	4	107	27	0
Braxton	5	90	18	0
G. Jones	1	24	24	0
Kindig	2	16	8	0

PASSING – PUNTING – KICKING

PASSING	Att	Comp	%	Yds	Yd/Att	TD	Int–	%	RK
Shaw	291	149	51	1813	6.2	11	26–	9	11
Harris	103	51	50	512	5.0	1	6–	6	
Braxton	3	1	33	49	16.3	0	0–	0	
Briscoe	2	1	50	36	18.0	0	0–	0	
Simpson	2	0	0	0	0.0	0	0–	0	

PUNTING	No	Avg
S. Jones	72	41.2
Chapple	3	33.7

KICKING	XP	Att	%	FG	Att	%
Leypoldt	12	12	100	9	15	60
Guthrie	8	9	89	3	10	30

CLEVELAND BROWNS 9-5-0 Nick Skorich

Scores of Each Game		
31	HOUSTON	0
14	Baltimore	13
20	OAKLAND	34
27	PITTSBURG	17
27	Cincinnati	24
0	DENVER	27
14	ATLANTA	31
9	Pittsburgh	26
7	Kansas City	13
27	NEW ENGLAND	7
37	Houston	24
31	CINCINNATI	27
21	New Orleans	17
20	Washington	13

Use Name	Pos.	Hgt	Wgt	Age	Int	Pts
Doug Dieken	OT	6'5"	237	22		2
Mitch Johnson	OT	6'4"	250	29		
Bob McKay	OT	6'5"	260	23		
Dick Schrafrath	OT	6'3"	258	35		
Jim Copeland	OG	6'2"	245	26		
John Demarie	OG	6'3"	255	26		
Gene Hickerson	OG	6'3"	248	36		
Mike Sikich	OG	6'2"	243	22		
Fred Hoaglin	C	6'4"	250	27		
Jack Gregory	DE	6'6"	250	26		
Joe Jones	DE	6'6'	246	23		
Bob Briggs	DT-DE	6'4"	276	26		
Walter Johnson	DT	6'3"	275	28		6
Jerry Sherk	DT	6'4"	253	23	2	
Ron Snidow	DT	6'4"	250	29		
Billy Andrews	LB	6'	225	26	3	
John Garlington	LB	6'1"	225	25	1	
Charlie Hall	LB	6'3"	215	22		
Jim Houston	LB	6'2"	240	34		
Rick Kingrea	LB	6'1"	233	22		
Dale Lindsey	LB	6'3"	225	28	2	
Erich Barnes	DB	6'2"	212	36		
Ben Davis	DB	5'11"	186	25	2	
Mike Howell	DB	6'1"	190	28	2	
Ernie Kellerman	DB	6'	185	27	3	
Clarence Scott	DB	6'	175	22	4	
Freddie Summers	DB	6'1"	180	24		
Walt Sumner	DB	6'1"	180	24	5	
Bill Nelson	QB	6'	195	30		
Mike Phipps	QB	6'2"	207	23		
Ken Brown	HB	5'10"	205	25		
Leroy Kelly	HB	6'	200	29		72
Reece Morrison	HB	6'	205	25		
Bo Scott	FB	6'3"	210	28		60
Bo Cornell	FB	6'1"	217	22		
Stan Brown	WR	5'9"	184	22		
Gary Collins	WR	6'4"	210	30		18
Fair Hooker	WR	6'1"	193	24		6
Dave Jones	WR	6'2"	185	24		
Frank Pitts	WR	6'2"	200	27		24
Chip Glass	TE	6'4"	236	24		6
Milt Morin	TE	6'4"	240	29		12
Don Cockroft	K	6'1"	190	26		79

PITTSBURGH STEELERS 6-8-0 Chuck Noll

Scores of Each Game		
15	Chicago	17
21	CINCINNATI	10
21	SAN DIEGO	17
17	Cleveland	27
16	Kansas Ctiy	38
23	HOUSTON	16
21	Baltimore	34
26	CLEVELAND	9
21	Miami	24
17	N.Y. GIANTS	13
10	DENVER	22
3	Houston	29
21	Cincinnati	13
14	LOS ANGELES	23

Use Name	Pos.	Hgt	Wgt	Age	Int	Pts
John Brown	OT	6'2"	255	32		
Rick Sharp	OT	6'3"	265	23		
Jon Kolb	C-OT	6'2"	262	24		
Sam Davis	OG	6'1"	255	27		
Mel Holmes	OG	6'3"	250	21		
Gerry Mullins	OG	6'3"	235	22		
Bruce Van Dyke	OG	6'2"	255	27		
Jim Clack	C	6'3"	250	23		
Ray Mansfield	C	6'3"	255	30		
Bobby Maples	C	6'3"	245	28		
Bert Askson	DE	6'3"	220	25		
L.C. Greenwood	DE	6'5"	240	24		
Dwight Write	DE	6'4"	250	22		
Ben McGee	DT-DE	6'2"	260	29		
Joe Greene	DT	6'4"	280	24		
Lloyd Voss	DT	6'4"	255	29		
Chuck Allen	LB	6'1"	227	31	3	
Henry Davis	LB	6'3"	235	28		
Jačk Ham	LB	6'3"	220	22	2	
Andy Russell	LB	6'3"	225	29		
Brian Stenger	LB	6'4"	230	24		
Ralph Anderson	DB	6'2"	180	22	1	
Ocie Austin	DB	6'3"	200	24		
Chuck Beatty	DB	6'2"	200	25		
Mel Blount	DB	6'3"	205	23	2	
Lee Calland	DB	6'	190	30	2	
Glen Edwards	DB	6'	185	24	1	
John Rowser	DB	6'1"	185	27	4	6
Mike Wagner	DB	6'1"	196	22	2	
Terry Bradshaw	QB	6'3"	218	22		30
Terry Hanratty	QB	6'1"	210	23		6
Bob Leahy	QB	6'2"	205	25		
Rocky Bleier	HB	5'11"	205	25		
Jim Brumfield	HB	6'1"	195	24		
Preston Pearson	HB	6'1"	190	26		18
John Fuqua	FB-HB	5'11"	200	24		30
Warren Bankston	FB	6'4"	230	24		
Frank Lewis	WR	6'1"	196	24		
Ron Shanklin	WR	6'1"	180	24		36
Dave Smith	WR	6'2"	205	24		30
Jon Staggers	WR	5'10"	186	22		6
Al Young	WR	6'1"	195	22		
Bob Adams	TE	6'2"	225	25		
Larry Brown	TE	6'4"	225	22		6
Dennis Hughes	TE	6'1"	220	23		
Roy Gerela	K	5'10"	185	23		78
Bobby Walden	K	6'	190	33		

Clarence Washington—Injury

HOUSTON OILERS 4-9-1 Ed Hughes

Scores of Each Game		
0	Cleveland	31
16	KANSAS CITY	20
13	NEW ORLEANS	13
13	Washington	22
7	DETROIT	31
16	Pittsburgh	23
10	CINCINNATI	6
20	New England	28
21	Oakland	41
13	Cincinnati	28
24	CLEVELAND	37
29	PITTSBURGH	3
20	Buffalo	14
49	SAN DIEGO	33

Use Name	Pos.	Hgt	Wgt	Age	Int	Pts
Tom Funchess	OT	6'5"	260	26		
Sam Walton	OT	6'5"	270	28		
Gene Ferguson	OT	6'7"	300	23		
Walt Suggs	C-OT	6'5"	250	32		
Elbert Drungo	OG	6'5"	250	28		
Tom Regner	OG	6'1"	255	27		
Ron Saul	OG	6'2"	255	23		
Bob Young	OG	6'2"	256	28		
Jerry Sturm	C	6'3"	265	34		
Allen Aldridge	DE	6'6"	260	26		
Elvin Bethea	DE	6'3"	262	25		
Pat Holmes	DE	6'5"	250	31		
Scott Lewis	DE	6'6"	260	21		
Ron Billingsley	DT	6'8"	290	26		
Lee Brooks	DT	6'5"	266	23	1	
Tom Domres (to DEN)	DT	6'3"	260	24		
Mike Tilleman	DT	6'5"	280	27		
Garland Boyette	LB	6'1"	235	31		6
Phil Croyle	LB	6'3"	220	23		
Dave Olerich	LB	6'1"	225	26		
Ron Pritchard	LB	6'1"	235	24		
George Webster	LB	6'4"	223	25		
Willie Alexander	DB	6'2"	195	21	4	
Bob Atkins	DB	6'3"	210	25	1	6
John Charles	DB	6'1"	200	27	5	
Ken Houston	DB	6'3"	196	26	9	30
Leroy Howard	DB	5'11"	175	22		
Benny Johnson	DB	5'11"	178	23		
Zeke Moore	DB	6'2"	196	27	3	
Lynn Dickey	QB	6'4"	218	21		
Charley Johnson	QB	6'	190	34		
Dan Pastorini	QB	6'3"	220	22		18
Woody Campbell	HB	5'11"	208	26		6
Andy Hopkins	HB	5'10"	187	22		
Dickie Post (from DEN)	HB	5'9"	190	25		6
Mike Richardson	HB	5'11"	196	24		
Ward Walsh	HB	6'	215	22		6
Robert Holmes (from KC)	FB	5'9"	220	25		24
Leroy Sledge	FB	6'2"	230	25		6
Joe Dawkins (to DEN)	HB-FB	5'11"	222	23		12
Jim Beirne	WR	6'2"	196	24		6
Ken Burrough	WR	6'4"	210	23		6
Linzy Cole	WR	5'11"	170	23		
Mac Haik	WR	6'1"	195	25		
Charlie Joiner	WR	5'11"	188	23		42
Alvin Reed	TE	6'5"	230	27		6
Floyd Rice	TE	6'3"	220	22		
Braden Beck	K	6'2"	200	27		4
Mark Moseley	K	5'11"	182	23		73

Roy Hopkins – Injury

CINCINNATI BENGALS 4-10-0 Paul Brown

Scores of Each Game		
37	PHILADELPHIA	14
10	Pittsburgh	21
17	Green Bay	20
13	MIAMI	23
24	CLEVELAND	27
27	Oakland	31
6	Houston	10
6	ATLANTA	9
24	Denver	10
28	HOUSTON	13
31	SAN DIEGO	0
27	Cleveland	31
13	PITTSBURGH	21
21	N.Y. JETS	35

Use Name	Pos.	Hgt	Wgt	Age	Int	Pts
Howard Fest	OT	6'6"	268	25		
Vern Holland	OT	6'5"	270	23		
Rufus Mayes	OT	6'5"	255	23		
Ernie Wright	OT	6'4"	270	31		
Guy Dennis	OG	6'2"	255	24		
Steve Lawson	OG	6'3"	265	22		
Pat Matson	OG	6'1"	245	27		
Bob Johnson	C	6'5"	265	25		
Royce Berry	DE	6'3"	248	25		
Ron Carpenter	DE	6'4"	260	23		
Ken Johnson	DE	6'5"	262	24		
Nick Roman	DE	6'3"	230	23		
Steve Chomyszak	DT	6'5"	265	26		
Willie Jones	DT	6'2"	260	29		
Mike Reid	DT	6'3"	258	24		
Doug Adams	LB	6'	223	22		
Ken Avery	LB	6'1"	225	27		
Al Beauchamp	LB	6'2"	236	27	6	6
Bill Bergey	LB	6'2"	240	26	1	
Larry Ely	LB	6'1"	230	23		
Bill Peterson	LB	6'3"	230	26	1	
Al Coleman	DB	6'1"	183	26	1	
Neal Craig	DB	6'1"	185	23	1	
Sandy Durko	DB	6'1"	185	23	4	
Ken Dyer	DB	6'3"	190	25		
Jim Harris	DB	5'11"	173	25		
Lemar Parrish	DB	5'11"	185	23	7	12
Ken Riley	DB	6'	184	24	5	
Fletcher Smith	DB	6'2"	180	27	1	
Ken Anderson	QB	6'1"	202	22		6
Virgil Carter	QB	6'1"	200	25		1
Dave Lewis	QB	6'2"	210	25		
Essex Johnson	HB	5'9"	195	24		36
Paul Robinson	HB	6'	200	26		6
Jess Phillips	HB	6'1"	210	24		6
Doug Dressler	FB	6'3"	220	23		6
Ron Lamb	FB	6'2"	230	27		
Fred Willis	FB	6'	215	23		42
Mike Haffner	WR	6'2"	205	29		
Ed Marshall	WR	6'5"	200	23		
Chip Myers	WR	6'4"	200	26		6
Speedy Thomas	WR	6'1"	178	24		12
Bruce Coslet	TE	6'3"	230	25		24
Mike Kelley	TE	6'4"	215	23		
Bob Trumpy	TE	6'6"	225	26		18
Horst Muhlmann	K	6'1"	210	31		91

Greg Cook—Shoulder Injury

CLEVELAND BROWNS

RUSHING

Last Name	No.	Yds	Avg	TD
Kelly	234	865	3.7	10
B. Scott	179	606	3.4	9
K. Brown	11	47	4.3	0
Phipps	6	35	5.8	0
Cornell	11	12	1.1	0
Cockroft	1	12	12.0	0
Morin	1	1	1.0	0
Morrison	5	−2	−0.4	0
Nelsen	13	−18	−1.4	0

RECEIVING

Last Name	No.	Yds	Avg	TD
Hooker	45	649	14	1
Morin	40	581	15	2
B. Scott	30	233	8	1
Pitts	27	487	18	4
Kelly	25	252	10	2
Collins	15	231	15	3
D. Jones	4	66	17	0
Cornell	1	18	18	0
Glass	1	4	4	1

PUNT RETURNS

Last Name	No.	Yds	Avg	TD
Kelly	30	292	10	0
D. Jones	9	63	7	0
Kellerman	1	4	4	0

KICKOFF RETURNS

Last Name	No.	Yds	Avg	TD
K. Brown	15	330	22	0
Morrison	9	267	30	0
Pitts	9	238	26	0
S. Brown	7	157	22	0
Houston	1	21	21	0
Cornell	1	19	19	0
Dieken	1	16	16	0
Kelly	1	11	11	0
Kellerman	1	5	5	0
Glass	1	1	1	0

PASSING – PUNTING – KICKING

PASSING	Att	Comp	%	Yds	Yd/Att	TD	Int–	%	RK
Nelsen	325	174	54	2319	7.1	13	23–	7	5
Phipps	47	13	28	179	3.8	1	4	9	
Kelly	4	1	25	23	5.8	0	0–	0	

PUNTING	No	Avg
Cockroft	62	40.5
Collins	5	32.4

KICKING	XP	Att	%	FG	Att	%
Cockroft	34	34	100	15	28	54

PITTSBURGH STEELERS

RUSHING

Last Name	No.	Yds	Avg	TD
Fuqua	155	625	4.0	4
Pearson	131	605	4.6	0
Bankston	70	274	3.9	0
Bradshaw	53	247	4.7	5
Walden	1	14	14.0	0
Staggers	1	5	5.0	0
Hanratty	1	3	3.0	1
Shanklin	2	1	0.5	0
Leahy	1	−6	−6.0	0
Smith	1	−10	−10.0	0

RECEIVING

Last Name	No.	Yds	Avg	TD
Shanklin	49	652	13	6
Fuqua	49	427	9	1
Smith	47	663	14	5
Pearson	20	246	12	2
Adams	20	160	8	0
Bankston	17	148	9	0
Staggers	8	103	13	0
Lewis	3	44	15	0
L. Brown	1	3	3	1

PUNT RETURNS

Last Name	No.	Yds	Avg	TD
Staggers	31	262	8	1
Wagner	2	2	1	0
Edwards	1	0	0	0
Fuqua	1	0	0	0

KICKOFF RETURNS

Last Name	No.	Yds	Avg	TD
Brumfield	12	271	23	0
Staggers	10	261	26	0
Pearson	7	205	29	0
Edwards	9	198	22	0
Bankston	5	76	15	0
Blount	4	76	19	0
Bleier	1	21	21	0
Clack	1	12	12	0

PASSING – PUNTING – KICKING

PASSING	Att	Comp	%	Yds	Yd/Att	TD	Int–	%	RK
Bradshaw	373	203	54	2259	6.1	13	22–	6	8
Hanratty	29	7	24	159	5.5	2	3–	10	
Leahy	11	3	27	18	1.6	0	1–	9	
Walden	1	1	100	10	10.0	0	0–	0	

PUNTING	No	Avg
Walden	79	43.7

KICKING	XP	Att	%	FG	Att	%
Gerela	27	27	100	17	27	63

HOUSTON OILERS

RUSHING

Last Name	No.	Yds	Avg	TD
R. Holmes	112	323	2.9	4
Campbell	96	259	2.7	1
Pastorini	26	140	5.4	3
Dawkins	42	135	3.2	2
Walsh	38	129	3.4	0
Post	40	86	2.2	0
Sledge	24	74	3.1	0
Richardson	17	33	1.9	0
Dickey	1	4	4.0	0
Hopkins	2	2	1.0	0
C. Johnson	2	0	0.0	0

RECEIVING

Last Name	No.	Yds	Avg	TD
Beirne	38	550	14	1
Joiner	31	681	22	7
Reed	25	408	16	1
Burrough	25	370	15	1
Campbell	20	179	9	0
R. Holmes	19	154	8	0
Post	9	112	12	1
Dawkins	9	53	6	0
Walsh	6	36	6	1
Sledge	6	32	5	1
Richardson	4	17	4	0

PUNT RETURNS

Last Name	No.	Yds	Avg	TD
Cole	14	107	8	0
Houston	16	91	6	0
Rice	2	0	0	0

KICKOFF RETURNS

Last Name	No.	Yds	Avg	TD
Cole	32	834	26	0
R. Holmes	12	300	25	0
Moore	10	214	21	0
Burrough	8	157	20	0
Post	5	116	23	0
Dawkins	2	34	17	0
Richardson	1	26	26	0
Joiner	1	25	25	0
Walsh	1	24	24	0
Rice	1	0	0	0

PASSING – PUNTING – KICKING

PASSING	Att	Comp	%	Yds	Yd/Att	TD	Int–	%	RK
Pastorini	270	127	47	1702	6.3	7	21–	8	12
C. Johnson	94	46	49	592	6.3	3	7–	7	
Dickey	57	19	33	315	5.5	0	9–	16	
Campbell	2	2	100	34	17.0	2	0–	0	

PUNTING	No	Avg
Pastorini	75	40.6

KICKING	XP	Att	%	FG	Att	%
Moseley	25	27	93	16	26	62
Beck	1	2	50	1	2	50

CINCINNATI BENGALS

RUSHING

Last Name	No.	Yds	Avg	TD
Willis	135	590	4.4	7
E. Johnson	85	522	6.1	4
Phillips	94	420	4.5	0
Robinson	49	213	4.3	1
Dressler	54	204	3.8	1
Anderson	22	125	5.7	1
Carter	8	42	5.3	0
Lamb	5	13	2.6	0
Durko	1	7	7.0	0
Lewis	6	6	1.0	0
Thomas	2	−1	−0.5	0

RECEIVING

Last Name	No.	Yds	Avg	TD
Trumpy	40	531	13	3
Myers	27	286	11	1
Willis	24	223	9	0
Thomas	22	327	15	2
Phillips	22	125	6	1
Coslet	21	356	17	4
Dressler	19	145	8	0
E. Johnson	14	258	18	2
Robinson	8	47	6	0
Marshall	2	18	9	0
Kelly	1	9	9	0

PUNT RETURNS

Last Name	No.	Yds	Avg	TD
Parrish	12	93	8	0
E. Johnson	3	28	9	0
Durko	6	14	2	0
Thomas	4	10	3	0

KICKOFF RETURNS

Last Name	No.	Yds	Avg	TD
Robinson	18	335	19	0
Parrish	13	296	23	0
Willis	4	81	20	0
Phillips	2	49	25	0
Lamb	2	42	21	0
E. Johnson	2	40	20	0
Dressler	1	20	20	0
Kelly	1	0	0	0

PASSING – PUNTING – KICKING

PASSING	Att	Comp	%	Yds	Yd/Att	TD	Int–	%	RK
Carter	222	138	62	1624	7.3	10	7–	3	3
Anderson	131	72	55	777	5.9	5	4–	3	
Lewis	10	3	30	18	1.8	0	0–	0	
Willis	2	1	50	8	4.0	0	0–	0	

PUNTING	No	Avg
Lewis	72	44.8
Dressler	1	34.0

KICKING	XP	Att	%	FG	Att	%
Muhlmann	31	31	100	20	36	56
Carter	1	1	100	0	0	0

KANSAS CITY CHIEFS 10-3-1 Hank Stram

Scores of Each Game		
14	San Diego	21
20	Houston	16
16	Denver	3
31	SAN DIEGO	10
38	PITTSBURGH	16
27	WASHINGTON	20
20	Oakland	20
10	N.Y. Jets	13
13	CLEVELAND	7
28	DENVER	10
21	Detroit	32
26	San Francisco	17
16	OAKLAND	14
22	BUFFALO	9

Use Name	Pos.	Hgt	Wgt	Age	Int	Pts
Dave Hill	OT	6'5"	260	30		
Sid Smith	OT	6'4"	260	23		
Jim Tyrer	OT	6'6"	270	32		
Ed Budde	OG	6'5"	260	30		
George Daney	OG	6'3"	240	24		
Mo Moorman	OG	6'5"	252	27		
Mike Oriard	C	6'4"	223	23		
Jack Rudnay	C	6'3"	240	23		
Bruce Bergey	DE	6'4"	240	24		
Aaron Brown	DE	6'5"	265	27	1	6
Marv Upshaw	DE	6'3"	245	24		
Buck Buchanan	DT	6'7"	275	31	1	
Curley Culp	DT	6'1"	265	25		
Ed Lothamer	DT	6'5"	270	28		
Wilbur Young	DT	6'6"	305	22	1	

Use Name	Pos.	Hgt	Wgt	Age	Int	Pts
Bobby Bell	LB	6'4"	228	31	1	6
Willie Lanier	LB	6'1"	245	26	2	
Jim Lynch	LB	6'1"	235	26	1	
Bob Stein	DE-LB	6'2"	235	23	1	
Nate Allen	DB	5'10"	170	23		
Caesar Belser	DB	6'	212	26		
Dave Hadley	DB	5'9"	186	22	1	
Jim Kearney	DB	6'2"	206	28	3	
Jim Marsalis	DB	5'11"	194	25	3	
Kerry Reardon	DB	5'11"	180	22		
Johnny Robinson	DB	6'	205	32	4	
Mike Sensibaugh	DB	5'11"	192	22		
Emmitt Thomas	DB	6'2"	192	28	8	6

Clyde Werner—Knee Injury

Use Name	Pos.	Hgt	Wgt	Age	Int	Pts
Len Dawson	QB	6'	190	37		
John Huarte	QB	6'	185	27		
Mike Livingston	QB	6'3"	212	25		
Mike Adamle	HB	5'9"	197	21		6
Warren McVea	HB	5'10"	182	25		18
Ed Podolak	HB	6'1"	202	24		54
Glenn Ellison	HB-FB	6'1"	215	22		
Wendell Hayes	FB	6'2"	220	30		12
Jim Otis	WR	6'	220	23		12
Dennis Homan	WR	6'1"	180	25		
Bruce Jankowski	WR	5'11"	185	22		
Otis Taylor	WR	6'2"	215	28		48
Elmo Wright	WR	6'	190	22		18
Willie Frazier (from HOU)	TE	6'4"	250	28		
Morris Stroud	TE	6'10"	255	25		6
Jan Stenerud	K	6'2"	187	28		110
Jerrel Wilson	K	6'4"	222	29		

OAKLAND RAIDERS 8-4-2 John Madden

Scores of Each Game		
6	New England	20
34	San Diego	0
34	Cleveland	20
27	Denver	16
34	PHILADELPHIA	10
31	CINCINNATI	27
20	KANSAS CITY	20
21	New Orleans	21
41	HOUSTON	21
34	SAN DIEGO	33
14	BALTIMORE	37
13	Atlanta	24
14	Kansas City	16
21	DENVER	13

Use Name	Pos.	Hgt	Wgt	Age	Int	Pts
Bob Brown	OT	6'4"	290	28		
Ron Mix	OT	6'4"	250	33		
Art Shell	OT	6'5"	255	24		
Paul Seiler	C-OT	6'4"	260	25		
George Buehler	OG	6'2"	260	24		
Jim Harvey	OG	6'5"	250	28		
Gene Upshaw	OG	6'5"	255	26		
Warren Koegel	C	6'3"	250	21		
Jim Otto	C	6'2"	248	33		
Tony Cline	DE	6'2"	230	31		
Ben Davidson	DE	6'8"	280	31		
Horace Jones	DE	6'3"	240	22		
Harold Rice	DE	6'2"	230	26		
Tom Gibson	DT	6'6"	290	23		
Tom Keating	DT	6'3"	247	28		
Carleton Oats	DT	6'2"	260	28		
Art Thomas	DT	6'5"	250	24		

Use Name	Pos.	Hgt	Wgt	Age	Int	Pts
Duane Benson	LB	6'2"	215	26		
Dan Conners	LB	6'1"	230	29	3	
Gerald Irons	LB	6'2"	230	24		
Terry Mendenhall	LB	6'1"	210	22		
Gus Otto	LB	6'2"	220	28		
Greg Slough	LB	6'3"	230	23		
Phil Villapiano	LB	6'1"	210	22	2	
Carl Weathers	LB	6'2"	220	23		
Butch Atkinson	DB	6'	180	24	4	6
Willie Brown	DB	6'1"	190	30	2	
Tommy Maxwell	DB	6'2"	195	24		
Jack Tatum	DB	5'10"	200	22	4	
Jimmy Warren	DB	5'11"	175	32	2	12
Nemiah Wilson	DB	6'	160	28	5	

Hewitt Dixon – Injury

Warren Wells – Legal probation – ineligible to play pro football.

Use Name	Pos.	Hgt	Wgt	Age	Int	Pts
George Blanda	QB	6'1"	215	43		86
Daryle Lamonica	QB	6'2"	215	30		
Ken Stabler	QB	6'3"	194	25		12
Clarence Davis	HB	5'10"	190	22		12
Don Highsmith	HB	6'	200	23		6
Charlie Smith	HB	6'1"	205	25		6
Pete Banaszak	FB-HB	5'11"	210	27		48
Bill Enyart	FB	6'4"	235	24		
Marv Hubbard	FB	6'1"	215	25		36
Fred Biletnikoff	WR	6'1"	190	28		54
Drew Buie	WR	6'2"	178	24		12
Eldridge Dickey	WR	6'2"	198	25		6
Rod Sherman	WR	6'	190	26		6
Ray Chester	TE	6'3"	220	23		42
Bob Moore	TE	6'3"	220	22		
Jerry DePoyster	K	6'1"	205	25		
Mike Eischeid	K	6'	190	30		

SAN DIEGO CHARGERS 6-8-0 Sid Gillman Harland Svare

Scores of Each Game		
21	KANSAS CITY	14
0	OAKLAND	34
17	Pittsburg	21
10	Kansas City	31
16	Denver	20
20	BUFFALO	3
49	N.Y. JETS	21
17	N.Y. Giants	35
20	St. LOUIS	17
33	Oakland	34
0	Cincinnati	31
30	MINNESOTA	14
45	DENVER	17
33	Houston	49

Use Name	Pos.	Hgt	Wgt	Age	Int	Pts
Terry Owens	OT	6'6"	275	27		
Russ Washington	OT	6'6"	295	24		
Ira Gordon	OG-OT	6'3"	268	23		
Harris Jones	OG	6'4"	233	26		
Walt Sweeney	OG	6'3"	256	30		
Doug Wilkerson	OG	6'2"	245	24		
Sam Gruneisen	C	6'1"	250	30		
Carl Mauck	C	6'3"	234	24		
Jack Porter	C	6'4"	255	23		
West Grant (from BUF)	DE	6'3"	245	24		
Jeff Staggs	DE	6'2"	246	27		
Lee Thomas	DE	6'5"	246	24		
Steve DeLong	DT-DE	6'3"	252	28		
Ron East	DT	6'4"	242	28		
Kevin Hardy	DT	6'5"	260	26		
Andy Rice	DT	6'3"	268	29		
Gary Nowak	DT	6'5"	247	22		
Tom Williams	DT	6'4"	250	23		

Use Name	Pos.	Hgt	Wgt	Age	Int	Pts
Bob Babich	LB	6'2"	230	24		6
Pete Barnes	LB	6'3"	247	26	2	6
Bob Bruggers	LB	6'1"	224	27		
Rick Redman	LB	5'11"	230	28	1	
Mel Rogers	LB	6'2"	230	24		
John Tanner	LB	6'4"	222	26		
Ray White	LB	6'1"	225	22		2
Joe Beauchamp	DB	6'	185	27	4	
Chuck Detwiler	DB	6'	185	24		
Chris Fletcher	DB	5'11"	185	22	3	6
Jim Hill	DB	6'2"	190	24	2	
Bob Howard	DB	6'1"	190	26	4	
Bryant Salter	DB	6'4"	200	21	6	
Jim Tolbert	DB	6'3"	207	27		

Rick Eber—Injury

Use Name	Pos.	Hgt	Wgt	Age	Int	Pts
Marty Domres	QB	6'3"	215	24		
John Hadl	QB	6'2"	218	31		6
Mike Garrett	HB	5'9"	200	27		42
Mike Montgomery	HB	6'2"	202	22		18
Leon Burns	FB	6'2"	223	26		6
Jeff Queen	FB	6'1"	220	25		42
Eddie Ray	FB	6'1"	230	24		
Chuck Dicus	WR	6'	172	22		6
Gary Garrison	WR	6'1"	193	27		36
Walker Gillette	WR	6'5"	198	24		12
Jerry LeVias	WR	5'10"	178	24		6
Billy Parks	WR	6'1"	185	23		24
Pettis Norman	TE	6'3"	220	31		6
Art Strozier	TE	6'2"	220	25		
Dennis Partee	K	6'2"	218	25		87

DENVER BRONCOS 4-9-1 Lou Saban Jerry Smith

Scores of Each Game		
10	MIAMI	10
13	Green Bay	34
3	KANSAS CITY	16
16	OAKLAND	27
20	SAN DIEGO	16
27	Cleveland	0
16	Philadelphia	17
20	DETROIT	24
10	CINCINNATI	24
10	Kansas City	28
22	Pittsburg	10
6	CHICAGO	3
17	San Diego	45
13	Oakland	21

Use Name	Pos.	Hgt	Wgt	Age	Int	Pts
Sam Brunelli	OT	6'1"	270	28		
Mike Current	OT	6'4"	274	25		
Marv Montgomery	OT	6'6"	255	23		
Roger Shoals	OT	6'4"	260	32		
George Goeddeke	OG	6'3"	253	26		
Mike Schitkner	OG	6'3"	245	24		
Larron Jackson	OT-OG	6'3"	270	22		
Jay Bachman	C	6'3"	250	25		
Larry Kaminski	C	6'2"	245	26		
Tommy Lyons	C	6'2"	228	23		
Lyle Alzado	DE	6'3"	252	22		
Walt Barnes	DE	6'3"	250	27		
Rich Jackson	DE	6'2"	255	30		
Dave Costa	DT	6'2"	260	29		
Jerry Inman	DT	6'3"	256	31		
Paul Smith	DT	6'3"	256	26		

Use Name	Pos.	Hgt	Wgt	Age	Int	Pts
Carter Campbell	LB	6'3"	232	23		
Ken Criter	LB	5'11"	223	24		
Fred Forsberg	LB	6'1"	235	27	3	6
Bill McKoy	LB	6'3"	235	23		
Chip Myrtle	LB	6'2"	225	26	3	
Olen Underwood	LB	6'1"	220	29	1	
Dave Washington	LB	6'5"	215	23	1	
Butch Byrd	DB	6'	196	29		
Cornell Gordon	DB	6'	187	30	2	
Charlie Greer	DB	6'	205	25	3	
Leroy Mitchell	DB	6'2"	190	26	2	
Randy Montgomery	DB	5'11"	182	24		
George Saimes	DB	5'10"	183	29		
Bill Thompson	DB	6'1"	200	24	5	

Tom Buckman – Injury

Pete Duranko – Injury

Use Name	Pos.	Hgt	Wgt	Age	Int	Pts
Don Horn	QB	6'2"	195	26		
Steve Ramsey	QB	6'2"	210	23		
Floyd Little	HB	5'10"	196	29		36
Fran Lynch	FB-HB	6'1"	205	25		8
Clem Turner	FB	6'1"	236	26		6
Bobby Anderson	HB-FB	6'	208	23		24
Gordon Bowdell	WR	6'2"	203	22		
Jack Gehrke	WR	6'	178	25		
Dwight Harrison	WR	6'1"	178	22		12
Jerry Simmons	WR	6'1"	190	28		6
Bill Van Huesen	WR	6'1"	200	25		
Bill Masters	TE	6'5"	240	27		6
John Mosier	TE	6'3"	220	23		
Jim Whalen (to PHI)	TE	6'2"	210	27		
Jim Turner	K	6'2"	205	30		93

John Embree—Injury

KANSAS CITY CHIEFS

RUSHING

Last Name	No.	Yds	Avg	TD
Podolak	184	708	3.8	9
Hayes	132	537	4.1	1
McVea	68	288	4.2	3
Otis	49	184	3.8	0
Adamle	13	43	3.3	0
Taylor	1	25	25.0	1
Dawson	12	24	2.0	0
Livingston	5	11	2.2	0
Frazier	1	−2	−2.0	0
Wright	1	−10	−10.0	0

RECEIVING

Last Name	No.	Yds	Avg	TD
Taylor	57	1110	19	7
Podolak	36	252	7	0
Wright	26	528	20	3
Stroud	22	454	21	1
Hayes	16	150	9	1
Otis	13	81	6	2
Frazier	10	154	15	0
McVea	5	−3	−1	0
Homan	2	47	24	0
Smith	1	12	12	0
Adamle	1	6	6	1

PUNT RETURNS

Last Name	No.	Yds	Avg	TD
Podolak	14	84	6	0
Homan	10	61	6	0
Reardon	3	5	2	0
Belser	1	2	2	0
Sensibaugh	5	−2	0	0

KICKOFF RETURNS

Last Name	No.	Yds	Avg	TD
Reardon	12	308	26	0
McVea	9	177	20	0
Adamle	7	149	21	0
Hayes	4	75	19	0
Sensibaugh	4	71	18	0
Podolak	3	65	22	0
Bergey	1	15	15	0

PASSING – PUNTING – KICKING

PASSING	Att	Comp	%	Yds	Yd/Att	TD	Int–	%	RK
Dawson	301	167	55	2504	8.3	15	13–	4	2
Livingston	28	12	43	130	4.6	0	0–	0	
Huarte	6	2	33	18	3.0	0	0–	0	
Podolak	2	2	100	42	21.0	0	0–	0	

PUNTING	No	Avg
Wilson	64	44.8

KICKING	XP	Att	%	FG	Att	%
Stenerud	32	32	100	26	44	59
Stein	0	0	0	0	1	0

OAKLAND RAIDERS

RUSHING

Last Name	No.	Yds	Avg	TD
Hubbard	181	867	4.8	5
Banaszak	137	563	4.1	8
Davis	54	321	5.9	2
Highsmith	76	307	4.0	1
Buie	2	32	16.0	0
Stabler	4	29	7.3	2
Lamonica	4	16	4.0	0
Chester	3	5	1.7	0
Smith	11	4	0.4	1
DePoyster	1	−14	−14.0	0

RECEIVING

Last Name	No.	Yds	Avg	TD
Biletnikoff	61	929	15	9
Chester	28	442	16	7
Hubbard	22	167	8	1
Davis	15	97	6	0
Banaszak	13	128	10	0
Sherman	12	187	16	1
Highsmith	10	109	11	0
Buie	5	133	27	2
Dickey	4	78	20	1
Smith	2	67	34	0
Moore	2	26	13	0

PUNT RETURNS

Last Name	No.	Yds	Avg	TD
Atkinson	20	159	8	0
Maxwell	6	21	4	0
Sherman	2	2	1	0
Highsmith	1	0	0	0

KICKOFF RETURNS

Last Name	No.	Yds	Avg	TD
Davis	27	734	27	0
Highsmith	21	454	22	0
Hubbard	3	46	15	0
Banaszak	1	0	0	0
Seiler	1	0	0	0
Smith	1	0	0	0

PASSING – PUNTING – KICKING

PASSING	Att	Comp	%	Yds	Yd/Att	TD	Int–	%	RK
Lamonica	242	118	49	1717	7.1	16	16–	7	7
Blanda	58	32	55	378	6.5	4	6–	10	
Stabler	48	24	50	268	5.6	1	4	8	

PUNTING	No	Avg
DePoyster	51	39.5
Eischeid	11	41.9

KICKING	XP	Att	%	FG	Att	%
Blanda	41	42	98	15	22	68

SAN DIEGO CHARGERS

RUSHING

Last Name	No.	Yds	Avg	TD
Garrett	140	591	4.2	4
Queen	95	318	3.3	4
Montgomery	60	226	3.8	1
Burns	61	223	3.7	1
Parks	5	77	15.4	0
Hadl	18	75	4.2	1
LeVias	4	73	18.3	0
Ray	2	15	7.5	0
Partee	1	7	7.0	0
Norman	1	1	1.0	0
Domres	1	0	0.0	0
Garrison	1	0	0.0	0
Dicus	1	−2	−2.0	0

RECEIVING

Last Name	No.	Yds	Avg	TD
Garrison	42	889	21	6
Parks	41	609	15	4
Garrett	41	283	7	3
Montgomery	28	361	13	2
Norman	27	358	13	1
Queen	23	270	12	3
LeVias	21	265	13	1
Gillette	10	147	15	2
Dicus	6	89	15	1
Burns	3	22	7	0
Strozier	1	6	6	0
Tanner	1	6	6	0

PUNT RETURNS

Last Name	No.	Yds	Avg	TD
LeVias	22	145	7	0
Fletcher	12	68	6	0
Garrett	3	2	1	0

KICKOFF RETURNS

Last Name	No.	Yds	Avg	TD
LeVias	24	559	23	0
Fletcher	11	217	20	0
Salter	8	172	22	0
Rogers	1	20	20	0
Burns	2	19	10	0
Sweeney	1	13	13	0
Thomas	1	0	0	0
Wilkerson	1	0	0	0

PASSING – PUNTING – KICKING

PASSING	Att	Comp	%	Yds	Yd/Att	TD	Int–	%	RK
Hadl	431	233	54	3075	7.1	21	25–	6	4
Domres	12	7	58	97	8.1	1	3–	25	
Montgomery	6	3	50	80	13.3	1	0–	0	
Garrett	1	1	100	53	53.0	0	0–	0	

PUNTING	No	Avg
Partee	55	43.5

KICKING	XP	Att	%	FG	Att	%
Partee	36	37	97	17	29	59

DENVER BRONCOS

RUSHING

Last Name	No.	Yds	Avg	TD
Little	284	1133	4.0	6
Anderson	139	533	3.8	3
Lynch	26	162	6.2	0
Masters	7	71	10.1	0
C. Turner	17	43	2.5	0
Harrison	5	36	7.2	0
Mosier	4	31	7.8	0
Horn	6	15	2.5	0
Van Heusen	1	10	10.0	0
Simmons	1	7	7.0	0
Ramsey	3	6	2.0	0
Gehrke	1	2	2.0	0

RECEIVING

Last Name	No.	Yds	Avg	TD
Anderson	37	353	10	1
Masters	27	382	14	1
Little	26	255	10	0
Simmons	25	403	16	1
Harrison	19	265	14	2
Gehrke	14	254	18	0
Whalen	8	165	21	0
C. Turner	7	65	9	1
Mosier	3	36	12	0
Lynch	2	42	21	1
Bowdell	1	19	19	0
Van Heusen	1	10	10	0
Washington	1	0	0	0
Schnitker	1	−11	−11	0

PUNT RETURNS

Last Name	No.	Yds	Avg	TD
Thompson	29	274	9	0
Greer	11	46	4	0
Mitchell	1	0	0	0

KICKOFF RETURNS

Last Name	No.	Yds	Avg	TD
Little	7	199	28	0
Anderson	8	187	23	0
Thompson	5	105	21	0
C. Turner	5	100	20	0
Criter	5	81	16	0
R. Montgomery	4	80	20	0
Bachman	2	20	10	0
Forsberg	1	19	19	0
Lynch	0	19	0	0

PASSING – PUNTING – KICKING

PASSING	Att	Comp	%	Yds	Yd/Att	TD	Int–	%	RK
Ramsey	178	84	47	1120	6.3	15	13–	7	13
Horn	173	89	51	1056	6.1	3	14–	8	14
Anderson	3	1	33	48	16.0	0	0–	0	
Gehrke	2	1	50	19	9.5	0	0–	0	
Little	1	0	0	0	0.0	0	0–	0	
Van Heusen	1	0	0	0	0.0	0	0–	0	

PUNTING	No	Avg
Van Heusen	76	41.8

KICKING	XP	Att	%	FG	Att	%
J. Turner	18	18	100	25	38	66

1971 Championship Games

NFC CHAMPIONSHIP GAME

January 2, at Dallas
(Attendance 63,409)

Brodie's Mistake and Dallas' Defense

SCORING

DALLAS	0	7	0	7–14
SAN FRANCISCO	0	0	3	0– 3

Second Quarter
Dall. Hill, 1 yard rush
PAT–Clark (kick)

Third Quarter
S.F. Gossett, 28 yard field goal

Fourth Quarter
Dall. D. Thomas, 2 yard rush
PAT–Clark (kick)

TEAM STATISTICS

DALLAS		S.F.
16	First Downs–Total	9
9	First Downs–Rushing	2
7	First Downs–Passing	7
0	First Downs–Penalty	0
2	Fumbles–Number	0
1	Fumbles–Lost Ball	0
2	Penalties–Number	1
30	Yards Penalized	12
3	Missed Field Goals	1
70	Offensive Plays–Total	47
244	Net Yards	239
3.5	Average Gain	5.1
1	Giveaways	3
3	Takeaways	1
+2	Difference	–2

The Cowboys and '49ers both won a return trip to the conference title game on the strength of a strong defense. Dallas had beaten the Vikings 20-12 to begin the playoffs, while the '49ers topped Washington 24-20 in the opening round, and the defensive units would decide the game today as they had last week.

Quarterbacks Roger Staubach and John Brodie made no headway against the psyched-up defenses in the first quarter. In the second period, however, Brodie committed a fatal error that the Cowboys capitalized on. Deep in his own territory, Brodie aimed a short screen pass to fullback Ken Willard without noticing Dallas' George Andrie lurking ominously on the scene. Once the ball was in the air, Andrie stepped in front of Willard, grabbed it, and lumbered down to the 1-yard line before being stopped. Calvin Hill carried the ball in, and Mike Clark's kick gave the Cowboys a 7-0 lead. Bruce Gossett put the '49ers on the scoreboard with a 28-yard field goal late in the period that cut the halftime Dallas lead down to 7-3.

The defensive units continued to dominate in the third period, and the slender Dallas lead looked as though it might hold up. In the fourth quarter, however, Roger Staubach went to work on some insurance points. Taking over on their own 20-yard line, the Cowboys drove downfield in a drive in which they converted four third-down situations into first downs. Staubach kept the drive alive with his scrambling, often creating time for his receivers to get open or finding room to run the ball himself. One key third-down play saw coach Tom Landry send tight end Mike Ditka into the lineup after '49er safety Mel Phillips was injured; Ditka promptly caught a clutch third-down pass against substitute safety Johnny Fuller. Duane Thomas sprinted around end for the final two yards, and the Dallas defense never let up for a second in preserving the 14-3 victory.

INDIVIDUAL STATISTICS

DALLAS	No	Yds	Avg.	SAN FRANCISCO	No	Yds	Avg.
RUSHING							
Staubach	8	55	6.9	V. Washington	10	58	5.8
Garrison	14	52	3.7	Willard	6	3	0.5
D. Thomas	15	44	2.9		16	61	3.8
Hill	9	21	2.3				
	46	172	3.7				
RECEIVING							
Truax	2	43	21.5	G. Washington	4	88	22.0
Hayes	2	22	11.0	Kwalick	4	52	13.0
Alworth	1	17	17.0	V. Washington	3	28	9.3
Reeves	1	17	17.0	Willard	1	6	6.0
D. Thomas	1	7	7.0	Witcher	1	6	6.0
Ditka	1	5	5.0	Cunningham	1	4	4.0
Garrison	1	–8	–8.0		14	184	13.1
	9	103	11.4				
PUNTING							
Widby	6		45.0	Spurrier	6		38.2
PUNT RETURNS							
Hayes	1	3	3.0	Fuller	2	10	5.0
Harris	1	1	1.0	Taylor	1	0	0.0
	2	4	2.0		3	10	3.3
KICKOFF RETURNS							
Harris	1	19	19.0	V. Washington	2	35	17.5
				Cunningham	1	21	21.0
					3	56	18.7
INTERCEPTION RETURNS							
Jordan	1	23	23.0	None			
Andrie	1	7	7.0				
Harris	1	2	2.0				
	3	32	10.7				

PASSING

	Att.	Comp.	Comp. Pct.	Yds.	Int.	Yds/ Att.	Yds/ Comp.	Yards Lost Tackled
DALLAS								
Staubach	18	9	50.0	103	0	5.7	11.4	6–31
SAN FRANCISCO								
Brodie	30	14	46.7	184	3	6.1	13.1	1– 6

AFC CHAMPIONSHIP GAME

January 2, at Miami
(Attendance 76,622)

Good Strategy, Wrong Target

SCORING

MIAMI	7	0	7	7–21
BALTIMORE	0	0	0	0– 0

First Quarter
Miami Warfield, 75 yard pass from Griese
PAT–Yepremian (kick)

Third Quarter
Miami Anderson, 62 yard interception return
PAT–Yepremian (kick)

Fourth Quarter
Miami Csonka, 5 yard rush
PAT–Yepremian (kick)

TEAM STATISTICS

MIAMI		BALT.
13	First Downs–Total	16
8	First Downs–Rushing	6
4	First Downs–Passing	10
1	First Downs–Penalty	0
0	Fumbles–Number	1
0	Fumbles–Lost Ball	0
1	Penalties–Number	2
12	Yards Penalized	20
0	Missed Field Goals	3
45	Offensive Plays–Total	68
286	Net Yards	302
6.4	Average Gain	4.4
1	Giveaways	3
3	Takeaways	1
+2	Difference	–2

The Dolphins had to guard against a letdown in this game as they were coming off an exhausting victory in the opening round of the playoffs. The Chiefs and Dolphins had battled back and forth all afternoon, with regulation time ending in a 24-24 tie. The two clubs fought through almost eighteen minutes of overtime before Garo Yepremian ended football's longest game with a 37-yard field goal.

The Colts, on the other hand, were coming off an easy 20-3 triumph over the Browns, so they were well rested physically and emotionally. Coach Don McCafferty planned to use a ball-control offense and a tight defense to defeat the Dolphins, but a 75-yard touchdown pass from Bob Griese to Paul Warfield early in the first quarter put Miami ahead 7-0 and put the pressure on Johnny Unitas and the Baltimore offense. But with starting backs Tom Matte and Norm Bulaich out of action with injuries, the Colts could not grind the yardage out against the quick Miami defense. The Colt defense also held up after the early Miami touchdown, and the half ended with the score 7-0.

With their ground attack getting no place against the Miami defense, the Colts went to the air in the third period. But while Griese had scored on a long bomb in the opening period, Unitas met disaster when he went for the bomb in the third quarter. Throwing deep for Eddie Hinton, Unitas undershot his man and instead hit Miami safety Dick Anderson. With his mates throwing blocks like experienced offensive players, Anderson weaved 62 yards with the ball for the second Miami touchdown.

Unitas had no luck crossing the Miami goal line for the rest of the afternoon, while the Dolphins scored a third touchdown on Larry Csonka's five-yard run which had been set up by a 50-yard pass to Warfield.

INDIVIDUAL STATISTICS

MIAMI	No	Yds	Avg.	BALTIMORE	No	Yds	Avg.
RUSHING							
Kiick	18	66	3.7	McCauley	15	50	3.3
Csonka	15	63	4.2	Nottingham	11	33	3.0
Griese	1	12	12.0	Nowatzke	2	5	2.5
Morris	1	3	3.0	Unitas	1	5	5.0
	35	144	4.1		29	93	3.2
RECEIVING							
Warfield	2	125	62.5	Hinton	6	98	16.3
Twilley	2	33	16.5	Nottingham	4	26	6.5
	4	158	39.5	Perkins	3	19	6.3
				Havrilak	2	31	15.5
				McCauley	2	24	12.0
				Mitchell	1	14	14.0
				Mackey	1	6	6.0
				Matte	1	6	6.0
					20	224	11.2
PUNTING							
Seiple	6		42.7	Lee	3		45.3
PUNT RETURNS							
Scott	2	20	10.0	Volk	5	20	4.0
KICKOFF RETURNS							
Morris	1	22	22.0	Pittman	2	58	29.0
INTERCEPTION RETURNS							
Anderson	1	62	62.0	Logan	1	0	0.0
Kolen	1	11	11.0				
Scott	1	0	0.0				
	3	73	24.3				

PASSING

	Att.	Comp.	Comp. Pct.	Yds.	Int.	Yds/ Att.	Yds/ Comp.	Yards Lost Tackled
MIAMI								
Griese	8	4	50.0	158	1	19.8	39.5	2–16
BALTIMORE								
Unitas	36	20	55.6	224	3	6.3	11.2	3–15

SUPER BOWL VI

January 16, at New Orleans

(Attendance 80,591)

Finally Lassoing the Championship

The Cowboys had ended every season since 1966 with a loss in the playoffs, before finally losing last year in the Super Bowl to Baltimore. But now they were hopeful of kicking that habit with a new quarterback in charge of the offense. Since Roger Staubach had replaced Craig Morton as the starting passer halfway through the season, the Cowboys had won seven straight regular-season games and two playoff games. To end the doubts about their ability to win the big games, the Cowboys would have to beat the Miami Dolphins, an up-and-coming young team masterfully built by head coach Don Shula.

The young Dolphins made their first mistake in the opening period when fullback Larry Csonka muffed a handoff from quarterback Bob Griese on the Dallas 48-yard line. After Dallas recovered the fumble, Staubach led the Cowboys deep into Miami territory before settling for a Mike Clark field goal.

Even in the first quarter, Dallas consistently ate up yardage on the ground, with Duane Thomas and Walt Garrison carrying the ball through gaping holes cut open by Cowboy linemen. The Dallas defense, meanwhile, completely shut off the Miami running attack of Csonka and Jim Kiick. The Cowboys also mixed passes into their attack, and a seven-yard touchdown pass from Staubach to Lance Alworth capped a long Dallas drive in the second period. Although the Dolphins scored on a Garo Yepremian field goal, the Cowboys dominated the first half and took a 10-3 lead into the clubhouse at halftime.

After taking the second-half kickoff, the Cowboys ate up five minutes of the clock with a ball-control drive that featured strong running by Duane Thomas. A pitchout to Thomas for three yards scored the touchdown and opened the Dallas lead to 17-3.

Trailing by two touchdowns after three periods, the Dolphins desperately needed some offensive fireworks in the fourth quarter. Instead, they ran into disaster. With his team finally on the march, Griese lashed a pass at Kiick at mid-field. Cowboy linebacker Chuck Howley had been knocked down when the pass was thrown, but he jumped up and picked it off in front of Kiick. With a convoy of blockers in front of him, Howley chugged downfield with the ball before running out of gas on the Miami 9. Two running plays moved the ball to the 7, and then Staubach hit Mike Ditka in the end zone with a pass to put the game out of reach for the Dolphins. Mike Clark's extra point made the score 24-3, and although the Dolphins launched a drive deep into Dallas territory, a fumble by Griese ended the last Miami scoring threat of the day.

DALLAS		MIAMI
	OFFENSE	
Hayes	WR	Warfield
Liscio	LT	Crusan
Niland	LG	Kuechenberg
Manders	C	DeMarco
Nye	RG	Little
Wright	RT	Evans
Ditka	TE	Fleming
Alworth	WR	Twilley
Staubach	QB	Griese
D. Thomas	RB	Kiick
Garrison	RB	Csonka
	DEFENSE	
L. Cole	LE	Riley
Pugh	LT	Fernandez
Lillie	RT	Heinz
Andrie	RE	Stanfill
Edwards	LLB	Swift
Jordan	MLB	Buoniconti
Howley	RLB	Kolen
Adderley	LCB	Foley
Renfro	RCB	Johnson
Green	LS	Anderson
Harris	RS	Scott

SUBSTITUTES

DALLAS

Offense

Fitzgerald	Truax
Hill	Welch
Reeves	Williams

Defense

Gregory	I. Thomas
Lewis	Toomay
Smith	Waters
Stincic	

Kickers

Clark	Widby

MIAMI

Offense

T. Cole	Moore
Ginn	Morris
Langer	Noonan
Mandich	Stowe

Defense

Cornish	Mumphord
Den Herder	Petrella
Matheson	Powell

Kickers

Yepremian	Seiple

SCORING

DALLAS	3	7	7	7–24
MIAMI	0	3	0	0– 3

First Quarter

Dallas — Clark, 9 yard field goal

Second Quarter

Dallas — Alworth, 7 yard pass from Staubach PAT – Clark (kick)

Miami — Yepremian, 31 yard field goal

Third Quarter

Dallas — D. Thomas, 3 yard rush PAT – Clark (kick)

Fourth Quarter

Dallas — Ditka, 7 yard pass from Staubach PAT – Clark (kick)

TEAM STATISTICS

DALLAS		MIAMI
23	First Downs – Total	10
15	First Downs – Rushing	3
8	First Downs – Passing	7
0	First Downs – Penalty	0
1	Fumbles – Number	2
1	Fumbles – Lost Ball	2
3	Penalties – Number	0
15	Yards Penalized	0
0	Missed Field Goals	1
69	Offensive Plays	44
352	Net Yards	185
5.1	Average Gain	4.2
1	Giveaways	3
3	Takeaways	1
+2	Difference	–2

INDIVIDUAL STATISTICS

RUSHING

DALLAS	No	Yds	Avg.	MIAMI	No	Yds	Avg.
D. Thomas	19	95	5.0	Csonka	9	40	4.4
Garrison	14	74	5.3	Kiick	10	40	4.0
Hill	7	25	3.6	Griese	1	0	0.0
Staubach	5	18	3.6		20	80	4.0
Ditka	1	17	17.0				
Hayes	1	16	16.0				
Reeves	1	7	7.0				
	48	252	5.3				

RECEIVING

DALLAS	No	Yds	Avg.	MIAMI	No	Yds	Avg.
D. Thomas	3	17	5.7	Warfield	4	39	9.8
Alworth	2	28	14.0	Kiick	3	21	7.0
Ditka	2	28	14.0	Csonka	2	18	9.0
Hayes	2	23	11.5	Fleming	1	27	27.0
Garrison	2	11	5.5	Twilley	1	20	20.0
Hill	1	12	12.0	Mandich	1	9	9.0
	12	119	9.9		12	134	11.2

PUNTING

DALLAS	No	Yds	Avg.	MIAMI	No	Yds	Avg.
Widby	5		37.2	Seiple	5		40.0

PUNT RETURNS

DALLAS	No	Yds	Avg.	MIAMI	No	Yds	Avg.
Hayes	1	–1	–1.0	Scott	1	21	21.0

KICKOFF RETURNS

DALLAS	No	Yds	Avg.	MIAMI	No	Yds	Avg.
I. Thomas	1	32	32.0	Morris	4	90	22.5
Waters	1	11	11.0	Ginn	1	32	32.0
	2	43	21.5		5	122	24.4

INTERCEPTION RETURNS

DALLAS	No	Yds	Avg.	MIAMI
Howley	1	41	41.0	None

PASSING

	Att	Comp	Comp Pct.	Yds	Int	Yds/ Att.	Yds/ Comp	Yards Lost Tackled
DALLAS								
Staubach	19	12	63.2	119	0	6.3	9.9	2–19
MIAMI								
Griese	23	12	52.2	134	1	5.8	11.2	1–29

1972 N.F.C. Grounded but Not Stopped

In modern offensive football, the wide receiver was fast becoming an ornamental decoy, while the quarterback's main function was no longer passing the ball but handing it off. A record number of ten rushers carried the ball for 1,000 yards this year as the running back now was pro football's chief offensive weapon. The development of zone pass defenses had cut down on the air game's potency, so clubs more and more decided to move the ball on the ground in three- and four-yard chunks rather than going for twenty or thirty yards at a time with pass plays. An ever-increasing number of teams found that the best offense against a zone defense was two strong running backs and a strong-legged place kicker. Fading away into history were the days when long bombers like Van Brocklin, Unitas, and Lamonica captivated crowds and captured headlines with spectacular heaves.

EASTERN DIVISION

Washington Redskins—George Allen's collection of misfits and rejects, known collectively as the Over the Hill Gang, stayed at a high level of enthusiasm all season and knocked the Dallas Cowboys out of first place in the Eastern Division for the first time since 1965. Allen's pride and joy was his defensive unit, which allowed the fewest points of any defense in the conference. The offense moved the ball well despite the absence of Sonny Jurgensen for most of the season with injuries; most of the time, substitute quarterback Bill Kilmer had only to hand off to halfback Larry Brown to keep the Skins on the march. Running at top speed and using his blockers well, Brown piled up a conference-leading total of 1,216 yards rushing despite sitting out the last two games of the season with an injury.

Dallas Cowboys—The Cowboys still had one of the deepest rosters in the NFL, but they dropped to second place in the East because they lacked the fine competitive edge they had last year. They lost to the Packers, Redskins, and '49ers during the season, and with a chance to take first place on the final day of the season they lost a listless 23-3 decision to New York and settled for the wild-card spot in the playoffs. The Cowboys did have several personnel problems. Duane Thomas' non-relations with his teammates forced the team to trade him to San Diego, a shoulder injury sidelined quarterback Roger Staubach for most of the season, a bad back took George Andrie out of the defensive line, and Bob Lilly's back hurt him all through the season.

New York Giants—Comebackers and newcomers led the Giants to a surprising winning season. The chief comeback was by halfback Ron Johnson, rebounding from a 1971 knee injury to carry the ball with his old authority and flair. Kicker Pete Gogolak also came back from a poor 1971 season to give the Giants a consistent three-point threat within the 40-yard line. Newcomers to the New York squad more than made up for the traded Fran Tarkenton and Fred Dryer. Quarterback Norm Snead led the NFC in passing statistics, but his main value was as a steady leader on offense. The defensive line improved immensely with the addition of end Jack Gregory from the Browns and rookie tackles John Mendenhall and Larry Jacobson.

St. Louis Cardinals—Despite top talent in some positions, the Cards stumbled through a season in which Gary Cuozzo, Tim Van Galder, and Jim Hart took turns as the starting quarterback, in which the defensive line had problems rushing opposing passers, and in which injuries sidelined linebackers Jamie Rivers, Jeff Staggs, and Mike McGill. Even though the Cards won their final two games, coach Bob Holloway got the ax after the season; departing of his own accord was safety Larry Wilson, retiring after a great thirteen-year pro career.

Philadelphia Eagles—The tough defense coach Ed Khayat had built last year was weakened by the trade of Tim Rossovich to San Diego because of a personality clash with the coach and by injuries to Ernie Calloway and Steve Zabel. The offensive had great receivers in Harold Jackson, Ben Hawkins, and Harold Carmichael but didn't have a quarterback who could consistently get the ball to them. Veteran Pete Liske had all the qualifications except a strong arm, while rookie John Reaves had a great arm but also the chronic rookie problem of inexperience. Rookie Po James played well at halfback, but the Eagles lacked the great back necessary in this era of running football.

CENTRAL DIVISION

Green Bay Packers—In his second year as coach, Dan Devine took the Packers back to the top in the Central Division with a grinding defense and a methodical ball-control offense. The pride of the defense was the secondary of Ken Ellis, rookie Willie Buchanon, Jim Hill, and Al Matthews, four young speedsters who minimized the effect of Willie Wood's retirement. The Packers didn't have any stars like Willie Davis or Henry Jordan or a younger Ray Nitschke in the front lines, but the rebuilt front four and linebacking constantly frustrated enemy running attacks. Bart Starr's retirement left Scott Hunter in charge of the offense, although Starr remained as an assistant coach and called all the plays for Hunter. Even though his arm was not strong, Hunter kept the attack moving simply by handing off to back John Brockington and MacArthur Lane.

Detroit Lions—The Detroit offense steadily turned out points, ranking second in the league in point production, but the defense could not compete with the other units in Green Bay and Minnesota. Coach Joe Schmidt was swimming in offensive talents—a fine quarterback in Greg Landry, good runners in Steve Owens and Altie Taylor, a star receiver in Charlie Sanders, and one of the best offensive lines in the NFL. The chief defensive shortcoming was the lack of a strong pass rush. Despite taking defensive linemen Bob Bell and Herb Orvis as their first draft choices the last two years, the Lions had not rebuilt their line into a top unit. At the end of the year coach Schmidt resigned and defensive stars Wayne Walker and Dick LeBeau retired.

Minnesota Vikings—The Vikings solved their quarterback problems by getting Fran Tarkenton back from the Giants in a trade, but the defense slumped off from the super level it had been playing at. Injuries nagged Carl Eller, Alan Page, and Gary Larsen and made the Minnesota front four less fearsome than usual. Middle linebacker Lonnie Warwick missed eight games on the disabled list, and rookie Jeff Siemon showed much promise and made many mistakes. On offense, Tarkenton gave the team a major-league passer, but the receiving corps suffered because of Gene Washington's second straight injury-plagued season. The Viking running backs were all good for sure short yardage, but none of them ever threatened to break loose a long run.

Chicago Bears—The Bears had a completely schizophrenic offense, first in the NFL in rushing, last in passing. Quarterback Bobby Douglass was a big, strong lad who set a new record of 968 yards gained rushing by a quarterback, but his passes came infrequently and often shot wide of the intended receiver. Douglass, fullback Jim Harrison, and halfbacks Don Shy and Cyril Pinder moved the ball well on the ground, but enemy defenses paid a minimum of attention to the Chicago air game. For a while the all-out running attack worked, but once opposing teams got wise to the Bear game plan, Chicago lost six of their last seven games. Coach Abe Gibron's first year on the job saw Gale Sayers retire with a bad knee and Dick Butkus continue to play up to All-Pro standards with a knee that hurt him more and more with each game.

WESTERN DIVISION

San Francisco '49ers—Heisman Trophy winner Steve Spurrier had done little else but punt in his past five seasons as a pro, but he stepped in for the injured John Brodie in mid-season and quarterbacked the '49ers to first place in the West. With a solid line to protect him and two great receivers in Gene Washington and Ted Kwalick to throw to, Spurrier engineered five San Francisco victories in the final six games, reaching his personal peak with five touchdown passes on November 19 against the Bears. On defense, the '49ers launched a ferocious pass rush despite disabling injuries to Cedrick Hardman and Earl Edwards; Tommy Hart and Charley Krueger responded with superior seasons to pick up the slack. The '49er playoff hopes soared in their final game when Brodie returned from the injured list to spark the team to a 20-17 victory over Minnesota.

Atlanta Falcons—The Falcons were strong at every position except quarterback, kicker, and defensive tackle, but these flaws kept the club from doing better than second place in the West. Quarterback Bob Berry had made the best of his limited talent, but coach Norm Van Brocklin had lost confidence in his ability to lead the Falcons to a title. Neither did kicker Bill Bell nor defensive tackles Glen Condren and Mike Lewis satisfy the coach. The Falcons did have a liberal supply of All-Stars in Claude Humphrey, John Zook, Tommy Nobis, Ken Reaves, George Kunz, Jim Mitchell, and Dave Hampton. Picked up from Green Bay, Hampton gained his 1,000th yard rushing of the year late in the final game. The game was stopped and the ball presented to Hampton. On his next carry Hampton lost five yards to finish at 995 yards for the year. Hampton, however, kept the ball.

Los Angeles Rams—With the death of owner Dan Reeves in April 1971, his family operated the club for a year and then sold the Rams to Robert Irsay. Before the 1972 season began, however, Irsay traded the Rams to Carroll Rosenbloom for his ownership of the Colts. Rosenbloom had grown accustomed to excellence from his Colt teams, but his first Ram squad disappointed him by finishing below .500 and in third place. Coach Tommy Prothro had daringly traded off Deacon Jones during the summer and replaced him with ex-Giant Fred Dryer, but leaks in the secondary hurt the defense more than the rebuilt front four. Quarterback Roman Gabriel's sore arm put a crimp in the offense, and five losses in the last six games cost Prothro his job.

New Orleans Saints—While the mid-1960s expansion teams in Atlanta, Miami, and Cincinnati had all achieved respectability, the Saints still had a look of a patchwork team created out of odds and ends. Coach J.D. Roberts had some topnotch players in quarterback Archie Manning, receiver Danny Abramowicz, tackle Glen Ray Hines, and rookie middle linebacker Joe Federspiel, but most of the roster was made up of journeymen and inexperienced youngsters. The distinguishing marks of the Saints this year were an uncanny ability to lose the ball on fumbles and interceptions and a morale problem in which the players expected one another to make errors and lose games.

FINAL TEAM STATISTICS

OFFENSE

	ATL.	CHI.	DALL.	DET.	G.B.	L.A.	MINN.	N.O.	N.Y.	PHIL.	ST.L.	S.F.	WASH.
FIRST DOWNS:													
Total	231	190	256	240	195	238	235	226	265	203	181	234	235
by Rushing	113	124	118	120	109	113	95	83	120	78	68	87	110
by Passing	101	54	126	97	72	108	127	123	124	110	102	129	106
by Penalty	17	12	12	23	14	17	13	20	21	15	11	18	19
RUSHING:													
Number	500	536	499	473	544	472	472	337	524	398	361	445	513
Yards	2092	2360	2124	2021	2127	2209	1740	1230	2022	1393	1229	1616	2082
Average Yards	4.2	4.4	4.3	4.3	3.9	4.7	3.7	3.6	3.9	3.5	3.4	3.6	4.1
Touchdowns	16	15	17	20	17	17	11	5	16	2	9	11	17
PASSING:													
Attempts	296	205	367	305	237	371	385	449	344	375	363	380	284
Completions	157	78	196	155	101	184	218	230	206	184	171	217	159
Completion Percentage	53.0	38.0	53.4	50.8	42.6	49.6	56.6	51.2	59.9	49.1	47.1	57.1	56.0
Passing Yards	2202	1283	2580	2283	1536	2282	2726	2781	2537	2527	2259	2888	2281
Avg. Yards per Attempt	7.4	6.3	7.0	7.5	6.5	6.2	7.1	6.2	7.4	6.7	6.2	7.6	8.0
Avg. Yards per Complet.	14.0	16.4	13.2	14.7	15.2	12.4	12.5	12.1	12.3	13.7	13.2	13.3	14.3
Times Tackled Passing	41	32	31	26	17	16	26	43	10	53	30	22	11
Yards Lost Tackled	283	175	238	149	124	136	203	347	76	457	221	153	88
Net Yards	1919	1108	2342	2134	1412	2146	2523	2434	2461	2070	2038	2735	2193
Touchdowns	13	9	16	19	7	13	19	18	20	10	11	27	21
Interceptions	15	13	23	18	9	22	13	21	15	20	23	24	15
Percent Intercepted	5.1	4.3	6.3	5.9	3.8	5.9	3.4	4.7	4.4	5.3	6.3	6.3	5.3
PUNTS:													
Number	61	67	51	43	65	53	62	71	47	63	73	64	59
Average Distance	42.8	41.2	38.2	40.3	41.8	44.2	42.8	40.8	42.7	40.3	39.4	39.7	38.5
PUNT RETURNS:													
Number	27	28	28	18	25	33	26	16	18	27	16	44	34
Yards	194	178	134	100	364	347	159	43	125	179	61	373	159
Average Yards	7.2	6.4	4.8	5.6	14.6	10.5	6.1	2.7	6.9	6.6	3.8	8.5	4.7
Touchdowns	0	0	0	0	2	0	0	0	0	0	0	0	0
KICKOFF RETURNS:													
Number	52	52	50	52	49	56	42	62	50	59	53	44	48
Yards	1039	1528	1080	1304	1141	1287	989	1312	1262	1375	1152	1041	1133
Average Yards	20.0	29.4	21.6	25.1	23.3	23.0	23.5	21.2	25.2	23.3	21.7	23.7	23.6
Touchdowns	0	2	0	0	0	0	0	0	1	0	0	1	0
INTERCEPTION RETURNS:													
Number	18	21	16	12	17	16	26	14	23	19	11	19	17
Yards	205	193	213	184	223	251	365	141	205	164	118	146	287
Average Yards	11.4	9.2	13.3	15.3	13.1	15.7	14.0	10.1	8.9	8.6	10.7	7.7	16.9
Touchdowns	1	0	1	1	1	1	2	0	2	0	0	3	1
PENALTIES:													
Number	73	74	90	48	63	78	51	69	57	76	64	73	78
Yards	650	574	841	417	610	648	440	585	512	690	582	664	721
FUMBLES: Number	42	40	27	17	22	24	32	33	32	37	43	30	27
Number Lost	19	22	15	7	10	9	19	16	14	18	16	13	11
POINTS:													
Total	269	225	319	339	304	291	301	215	331	145	193	353	336
PAT Attempts	31	27	36	40	29	31	34	26	39	12	22	43	42
PAT Made	31	27	36	39	29	31	34	24	34	11	19	41	40
FG Attempts	30	24	36	29	48	41	33	25	31	35	22	29	30
FG Made	16	12	21	20	33	24	21	11	21	20	14	18	14
Percent FG Made	53.3	50.0	58.3	69.0	68.8	58.5	63.6	44.0	67.7	57.1	63.6	62.1	46.7
Safeties	2	0	2	0	1	1	0	1	0	1	0	0	1

DEFENSE

	ATL.	CHI.	DALL.	DET.	G.B.	L.A.	MINN.	N.O.	N.Y.	PHIL.	ST.L.	S.F.	WASH.
FIRST DOWNS:													
Total	221	224	217	239	209	235	200	251	218	268	276	221	223
by Rushing	122	96	81	126	85	101	103	107	101	137	119	96	95
by Passing	83	108	113	103	109	110	82	129	111	117	138	105	108
by Penalty	16	20	23	10	15	24	15	15	6	14	19	20	20
RUSHING:													
Number	504	476	428	491	443	438	454	482	402	544	548	446	427
Yards	2063	1751	1515	2204	1517	1762	2002	2089	1855	2266	2189	1847	1733
Average Yards	4.1	3.7	3.5	4.5	3.4	4.0	4.4	4.3	4.6	4.2	4.0	4.1	4.1
Touchdowns	16	11	7	14	14	9	13	15	9	22	11	12	12
PASSING:													
Attempts	301	342	382	312	340	363	331	367	333	318	365	366	367
Completions	137	180	187	171	174	181	169	213	182	175	221	169	186
Completion Percentage	45.5	52.6	49.0	54.8	51.2	49.9	51.1	58.0	54.7	55.0	60.5	46.2	50.7
Passing Yards	1911	2345	2508	2146	2209	2472	1791	2596	2571	2615	2733	2582	2130
Avg. Yards per Attempt	6.3	6.9	6.6	6.9	6.5	6.8	5.4	7.1	7.7	8.2	7.5	7.1	5.8
Avg. Yards per Complet.	13.9	13.0	13.4	12.5	12.7	13.7	10.6	12.2	14.1	14.9	12.4	15.3	11.5
Times Tackled Passing	24	23	32	21	29	42	21	24	37	17	22	46	35
Yards Lost Tackled	207	173	268	142	252	327	92	194	232	143	183	403	268
Net Yards	1704	2172	2240	2004	1957	2145	1699	2402	2339	2472	2550	2179	1862
Touchdowns	13	16	18	18	7	20	13	21	19	20	15	14	10
Interceptions	18	21	16	12	17	16	26	14	23	19	11	19	17
Percent Intercepted	6.0	6.1	4.2	3.8	5.0	4.4	7.9	3.8	6.9	6.0	3.0	5.2	4.6
PUNTS:													
Number	56	62	65	46	66	71	62	52	47	54	48	72	69
Average Distance	41.8	43.0	40.6	38.8	41.4	41.2	41.5	39.3	38.1	40.5	39.4	43.4	40.1
PUNT RETURNS:													
Number	30	24	15	26	32	22	35	36	27	26	37	20	19
Yards	239	126	41	321	225	54	317	281	171	137	144	70	39
Average Yards	8.0	5.3	2.7	12.3	7.0	2.5	9.1	7.8	6.3	5.3	3.9	3.5	2.1
Touchdowns	0	0	0	1	0	0	0	0	0	0	0	0	0
KICKOFF RETURNS:													
Number	48	42	52	68	46	54	62	50	63	41	40	66	53
Yards	1076	1025	1272	1593	932	999	1373	1129	1516	886	1037	1530	1191
Average Yards	22.4	24.4	24.5	23.4	20.3	18.5	22.1	22.6	24.1	21.6	25.9	23.2	22.5
Touchdowns	1	0	0	1	0	0	0	0	0	0	1	0	0
INTERCEPTION RETURNS:													
Number	15	13	23	23	9	22	13	21	15	20	23	24	15
Yards	206	104	302	294	69	439	116	349	192	198	289	240	160
Average Yards	13.7	8.0	13.1	16.3	7.7	20.0	8.9	16.6	12.8	9.9	12.6	10.0	10.7
Touchdowns	1	1	1	0	2	3	0	1	1	0	3	1	1
PENALTIES:													
Number	61	69	59	86	50	60	47	78	66	72	68	81	64
Yards	555	644	586	703	446	553	490	711	641	637	645	677	568
FUMBLES: Number	23	37	40	32	35	25	27	27	31	30	31	40	28
Number Lost	15	14	17	15	19	11	14	13	15	8	16	17	15
POINTS:													
Total	274	275	240	290	226	286	252	361	247	352	303	249	218
PAT Attempts	32	31	28	34	26	34	27	38	28	43	31	28	23
PAT Made	31	30	27	32	25	32	24	38	25	42	31	28	23
FG Attempts	31	27	34	34	27	30	35	43	29	25	47	29	33
FG Made	17	19	15	18	15	16	22	31	18	16	28	17	19
Percent FG Made	54.8	70.4	44.1	52.9	55.6	53.3	62.9	72.1	62.1	64.0	59.6	58.6	57.6
Safeties	0	1	0	0	0	1	0	1	0	2	1	1	0

CONFERENCE PLAYOFFS

December 23, at San Francisco (Attendance 59,746)

SCORING

SAN FRANCISCO	7	14	7	0	–28
DALLAS	3	10	0	17	–30

First Quarter
- S.F. V. Washington, 97 yard kickoff return–PAT–Gossett (kick)
- DAL. Fritsch, 37 yard field goal

Second Quarter
- S.F. Schreiber, 1 yard rush PAT–Gossett (kick)
- S.F. Schreiber, 1 yard rush PAT–Gossett (kick)
- DAL. Fritsch, 45 yard field goal
- DAL. Alworth, 28 yard pass from Morton–PAT–Fritsch (kick)

Third Quarter
- S.F. Schreiber, 1 yard rush PAT–Gossett (kick)

Fourth Quarter
- DAL. Fritsch, 27 yard field goal
- DAL. Parks, 20 yard pass from Staubach–PAT–Fritsch (kick)
- DAL. Sellers, 10 yard pass from Staubach–PAT–Fritsch (kick)

TEAM STATISTICS

S.F.		DAL.
13	First Downs–Total	22
7	First Downs–Rushing	5
6	First Downs–Passing	15
0	First Downs–Penalty	2
5	Fumbles–Number	4
1	Fumbles–Lost Ball	3
7	Penalties–Number	3
56	Yards Penalized	35
2	Missed Field Goals	0
59	Offensive Plays	77
261	Net Yards	402
4.4	Average Gain	5.2
3	Giveaways	5
5	Takeaways	3
+2	Difference	–2

INDIVIDUAL STATISTICS

SAN FRANCISCO	No.	Yds.	Avg.	DALLAS	No.	Yds.	Avg.
RUSHING							
V. Washington	10	56	5.6	Hill	18	125	6.9
Schreiber	26	52	2.0	Staubach	3	23	7.7
Thomas	1	3	3.0	Garrison	9	15	1.7
	37	111	3.0	Morton	1	2	2.0
					31	165	5.3
RECEIVING							
Riley	4	41	10.3	Parks	7	125	16.9
G. Washington	3	76	25.3	Garrison	3	24	8.0
Schreiber	3	20	6.7	Alworth	2	50	25.0
V. Washington	1	8	8.0	Sellers	2	21	10.5
Kwalick	1	5	5.0	Montgomery	2	19	9.5
	12	150	12.5	Hayes	1	13	13.0
				Ditka	1	9	9.0
				Hill	1	6	6.0
				Truax	1	3	3.0
					20	270	13.5
PUNTING							
McCann	6		37.3	Bateman	6		41.8
PUNT RETURNS							
Taylor	1	5	5.0	Waters	1	2	2.0
KICKOFF RETURNS							
V. Washington	3	136	45.3	Harris	3	83	27.7
Beard	1	5	5.0				
McGill	1	5	5.0				
	5	146	29.2				
INTERCEPTION RETURNS							
Vanderbundt	2	4	2.0	Waters	2	12	6.0

PASSING

SAN FRANCISCO	Att.	Comp.	Comp. Pct.	Yds.	Int.	Yds/ Att.	Yds/ Comp.	Yards Lost Tackled
Brodie	22	12	54.5	150	2	6.8	12.5	0– 0
DALLAS								
Morton	21	8	38.1	96	2	4.6	12.0	
Staubach	20	12	60.0	174	0	8.7	14.5	
	41	20	48.8	270	2	6.6	13.5	5–33

December 24, at Washington (Attendance 52,321)

SCORING

WASHINGTON	0	10	0	6	–16
GREEN BAY	0	3	0	0	– 3

Second Quarter
- G.B. Marcol, 17 yard field goal
- WASH. Jefferson, 32 yard pass from Kilmer–PAT–Knight (kick)
- WASH. Knight, 42 yard field goal

Fourth Quarter
- WASH. Knight, 35 yard field goal
- WASH. Knight, 46 yard field goal

TEAM STATISTICS

WASH.		G.B.
13	First Downs–Total	10
6	First Downs–Rushing	2
4	First Downs–Passing	8
3	First Downs–Penalty	0
1	Fumbles–Number	0
1	Fumbles–Lost Ball	0
4	Penalties–Number	6
39	Yards Penalized	54
0	Missed Field Goals	1
51	Offensive Plays	55
232	Net Yards	211
4.5	Average Gain	3.8
1	Giveaways	1
1	Takeaways	1
0	Difference	0

INDIVIDUAL STATISTICS

WASHINGTON	No.	Yds.	Avg.	GREEN BAY	No.	Yds.	Avg.
RUSHING							
Brown	25	101	4.0	Lane	14	56	4.0
Harraway	10	34	3.4	Hunter	2	13	6.5
Kilmer	1	3	3.0	Brockington	13	9	0.7
	36	138	3.8		29	78	2.7
RECEIVING							
Jefferson	5	84	16.8	Lane	4	42	10.5
Taylor	2	16	8.0	Dale	2	28	14.0
	7	100	14.3	Glass	2	23	11.5
				Brockington	2	17	8.5
				Staggers	1	23	23.0
				Garrett	1	17	17.0
					12	150	12.5
PUNTING							
Bragg	6		46.5	Widby	8		36.6
PUNT RETURNS							
Haymond	2	4	2.0	Staggers	3	20	6.7
Vactor	1	15	15.0	Ellis	1	13	13.0
	3	19	6.3		4	33	8.3
KICKOFF RETURNS							
Mul-Key	2	60	30.0	Thomas	3	50	16.7
				Hudson	1	12	12.0
					4	62	15.5
INTERCEPTION RETURNS							
Hanburger	1	15	15.0	None			

PASSING

WASHINGTON	Att.	Comp.	Comp. Pct.	Yds.	Int.	Yds/ Att.	Yds/ Comp.	Yards Lost Tackled
Kilmer	14	7	50.0	100	0	7.1	14.3	1– 6
GREEN BAY								
Hunter	24	12	50.0	150	1	6.3	12.5	2–17

WASHINGTON REDSKINS 11-3-0 George Allen

Scores of Each Game		
24	Minnesota	21
24	ST. LOUIS	10
23	New England	24
14	PHILADELPHIA	0
33	St. Louis	3
24	DALLAS	20
23	N.Y. Giants	16
35	N.Y. Jets	17
27	N.Y. GIANTS	13
24	ATLANTA	13
21	GREEN BAY	16
23	Philadelphia	7
24	Dallas	34
17	BUFFALO	24

Use Name	Pos.	Hgt	Wgt	Age	Int	Pts
Terry Hermeling	OT	6'5"	255	26		
Mitch Johnson	OT	6'4"	250	30		
Walt Rock	OT	6'5"	255	31		
Paul Laaveg	OG	6'4"	245	23		
John Wilbur	OG	6'3"	250	29		
Ray Schoenke	OT-OG	6'3"	250	30		
Len Hauss	C	6'2"	235	30		
George Burman	OG-C	6'3"	255	29		
Verlon Biggs	DE	6'4"	275	29		6
Mike Fanucci	DE	6'4"	225	22		
Jimmie Jones	DE	6'3"	215	25		
Ron McDole	DT-DE	6'3"	265	32		
Bill Brundige	DT	6'5"	270	23		
Manny Sistrunk	DT	6'5"	265	25		
Diron Talbert	DT	6'5"	255	28		
Jim Snowden – Injury						
Chris Hamburger	LB	6'2"	218	31	4	6
Harold McLinton	LB	6'2"	235	25	2	
Jack Pardee	LB	6'2"	225	36		
Myron Pottios	LB	6'2"	232	32		
Rusty Tillman	LB	6'2"	230	26		
Mike Bass	DB	6'	190	27	3	6
Speedy Duncan	DB	5'10"	180	29	1	
Pat Fischer	DB	5'10"	170	32	4	
Alvin Haymond	DB	6'	194	30		
Jon Jaqua	DB	6'	190	24		
Brig Owens	DB	5'11"	190	29	1	
Richie Petitbon	DB	6'3"	208	34		
Jeff Severson	DB	6'1"	180	22		
Rosey Taylor	DB	5'11"	186	33	1	
Ted Vactor	DB	6'	185	28	1	
Tommy Mason – Injury						
Sonny Jurgensen	QB	5'11"	203	38		
Billy Kilmer	QB	6'	204	32		
Sam Wyche	QB	6'4"	218	27		
Larry Brown	HB	5'11"	195	24		72
Bob Brunet	HB	6'1"	205	26		12
Herb Mul-Key	HB	6'	190	22		6
George Nock	HB	5'10"	200	26		
Charlie Harraway	FB	6'2"	215	27		36
Mike Hull	FB	6'3"	220	27		
Jeff Jordan	HB-FB	6'1"	215	27		
Roy Jefferson	WR	6'2"	195	28		18
Bill Malinchak	WR	6'1"	200	28		8
Clifton McNeil	WR	6'2"	187	32		
Charley Taylor	WR	6'3"	210	31		42
Mack Alston	TE	6'2"	230	25		
Jerry Smith	TE	6'2"	208	29		42
Mike Bragg	K	5'11"	186	25		
Curt Knight	K	6'1"	190	29		82

DALLAS COWBOYS 10-4-0 Tom Landry

Scores of Each Game		
28	PHILADELPHIA	6
23	N.Y. Giants	14
13	Green Bay	16
17	PITTSBURGH	13
21	Baltimore	0
20	Washington	24
28	DETROIT	24
34	San Diego	28
33	ST. LOUIS	24
28	Philadelphia	7
10	SAN FRANCISCO	31
27	St. Louis	6
34	WASHINGTON	24
3	N.Y. GIANTS	23

Use Name	Pos.	Hgt	Wgt	Age	Int	Pts
Ralph Neely	OT	6'5"	265	28		
Rayfield Wright	OT	6'7"	255	27		
Rodney Wallace	OG-OT	6'5"	255	23		
John Niland	OG	6'4"	245	28		6
Blaine Nye	OG	6'4"	250	26		
John Fitzgerald	C-OG	6'5"	250	24		
Dave Manders	C	6'2"	250	30		
George Andrie	DE	6'7"	250	32		
Larry Cole	DE	6'4"	250	25		
Tody Smith	DE	6'5"	245	23		
Pat Toomay	DE	6'5"	244	27		
Bill Gregory	DT	6'5"	255	22		
Bob Lilly	DT	6'4"	260	33		
Jethro Pugh	DT	6'6"	260	28		
John Babinecz	LB	6'1"	222	22		
Ralph Coleman	LB	6'4"	216	22		
Dave Edwards	LB	6'3"	225	33		
Chuck Howley	LB	6'3"	225	36	1	
Lee Roy Jordan	LB	6'2"	220	31	2	
Mike Keller	LB	6'4"	220	21		
D. D. Lewis	LB	6'2"	225	26	1	
Herb Adderly	DB	6'1"	200	33		
Benny Barnes	DB	6'1"	190	21		
Cornell Green	DB	6'4"	208	32	2	
Cliff Harris	DB	6'	184	23	3	
Mel Renfro	DB	6'	190	30	1	
Mark Washington	DB	5'10"	188	24		2
Charlie Waters	DB	6'1"	193	23	6	6
Craig Morton	QB	6'4"	214	29		12
Roger Staubach	QB	6'2"	197	30		
Mike Montgomery	HB	6'2"	210	23		18
Dan Reeves	HB	6'1"	200	28		
Calvin Hill	FB-HB	6'3"	227	25		54
Robert Newhouse	FB-HB	5'10"	202	22		6
Walt Garrison	FB	6'	205	28		60
Bill Thomas	FB	6'2"	225	22		
Lance Alworth	WR	6'	180	32		12
Bob Hayes	WR	6'	185	29		
Billy Parks	WR	6'1"	185	24		6
Ron Sellers	WR	6'4"	195	25		30
Mike Ditka	TE	6'3"	225	32		6
Jean Fugett	TE	6'3"	220	20		
Billy Truax	TE	6'5"	240	29		
Marv Bateman	K	6'4"	213	22		
Toni Fritsch	K	5'7"	185	27		99

NEW YORK GIANTS 8-6-0 Alex Webster

Scores of Each Game		
16	Detroit	30
14	DALLAS	23
27	Philadelphia	12
45	NEW ORLEANS	21
23	San Francisco	17
27	ST. LOUIS	21
16	WASHINGTON	23
29	DENVER	17
13	Washington	27
13	St. Louis	7
62	PHILADELPHIA	10
10	Cincinnati	13
13	MIAMI	23
23	Dallas	3

Use Name	Pos.	Hgt	Wgt	Age	Int	Pts
Joe Taffoni	OT	6'3"	255	27		
Willie Young	OT	6'	265	29		
John Hill	C-OT	6'2"	245	22		
Mark Ellison	OG	6'2"	250	23		
Dick Enderle	OG	6'1"	250	24		
Doug Van Horn	OG	6'2"	245	28		
Bob Hyland	C-OT-OG	6'5"	255	27		
Greg Larson	C	6'2"	250	33		
Jack Gregory	DE	6'6"	250	27		
Henry Reed	DE	6'3"	230	23		
Larry Jacobsen	DT-DE	6'6"	260	22		
Dan Goich	DT	6'4"	250	28		
John Mendenhall	DT	6'1"	255	23		
Charlie Harper	DT	6'2"	250	28		
Dave Tipton	DE-DT	6'	240	23		
Carter Campbell	LB	6'3"	240	24		
John Douglas	LB	6'2"	228	27	1	
Jim Files	LB	6'4"	240	24	2	6
Ron Hornsby	LB	6'3"	232	23		
Pat Hughes	LB	6'2"	240	25	2	
Pete Athas	DB	5'11"	185	24	4	
Otto Brown	DB	6'1"	188	25	1	
Chuck Crist	DB	6'2"	205	21	1	
Richmond Flowers	DB	6'	180	25	4	
Spider Lockhart	DB	6'2"	175	29	4	6
Eldridge Small	DB	6'1"	190	22		
Willie Williams	DB	6'	190	29	4	
Scott Eaton – Injury						
Jim Kanicki – Knee Injury						
Randy Johnson	QB	6'3"	205	28		6
Norm Snead	QB	6'4"	215	32		
Bobby Duhon	HB	6'	195	25		
Ron Johnson	HB	6'1"	205	24		84
Rocky Thompson	HB	5'11"	200	24		6
Vin Clements	FB	6'3"	210	23		
Charlie Evans	FB	6'1"	220	24		30
Joe Orduna	HB-FB	6'	195	24		12
Bob Grim	WR	6'	200	27		6
Don Herrmann	WR	6'2"	205	25		30
Rich Houston	WR	6'2"	195	26		18
Joe Morrison	HB-FB-WR	6'1"	212	34		
Dick Kotite	TE	6'3"	230	29		
Bob Tucker	TE	6'3"	230	27		30
Tom Gatewood	WR-TE	6'3"	215	21		
Tom Blanchard	K	6'	190	24		
Pete Gogolak	K	6'2"	190	30		97

ST. LOUIS CARDINALS 4-9-1 Bob Holloway

Scores of Each Game		
10	Baltimore	3
10	Washington	24
19	PITTSBURGH	25
19	Minnesota	17
3	WASHINGTON	33
21	N.Y. Giants	27
10	CHICAGO	27
6	Philadelphia	6
24	Dallas	33
7	N.Y. GIANTS	13
10	Miami	31
6	DALLAS	27
24	LOS ANGELES	14
24	PHILADELPHIA	23

Use Name	Pos.	Hgt	Wgt	Age	Int	Pts
Ernie McMillan	OT	6'6"	255	34		
Steve Wright	OT	6'6"	250	30		
Dan Dierdorf	OG-OT	6'4"	265	23		
Dave Bradley	OG	6'4"	245	25		
Conrad Dobler	OG	6'3"	250	21		
Chuck Hutchison	OG	6'3"	240	23		
Bob Young	OG	6'2"	260	29		
Wayne Mulligan	C	6'2"	245	25		
Tom Banks	OG-C	6'1"	240	24		
Tom Beckman	DE	6'5"	250	21		
Don Brumm	DE	6'3"	245	29		
Martin Imhof	DE	6'6"	255	22		
Ron Yankowski	DE	6'5"	225	25		
Fred Heron	DT	6'4"	240	27		
Scott Palmer	DT	6'3"	245	24		
John Richardson	DT	6'2"	250	28		
Bob Rowe	DT	6'4"	260	27		
Mark Arneson	LB	6'2"	220	22		
Steve Conley (from CIN)	LB	6'2"	225	23		
Jim Hargrove	LB	6'3"	225	27		
Mike McGill	LB	6'2"	235	25	2	
Terry Miller	LB	6'2"	225	26		
Jamie Rivers	LB	6'2"	235	26		
Jeff Staggs	LB	6'2"	240	28	1	
Larry Stallings	LB	6'2"	230	30		
Miller Farr	DB	6'1"	190	29	3	
Dale Hackbart	DB	6'3"	210	36	1	
Norm Thompson	DB	6'1"	175	24	1	12
Eric Washington	DB	6'2"	190	22		
Roger Wehrli	DB	6'1"	195	24		
Larry Willingham	DB	6'1"	190	23		
Larry Wilson	DB	6'	195	34	3	
Jeff Allen – Injury						
Larry Stegent – Injury						
Gary Cuozzo	QB	6'1"	195	31		
Jim Hart	QB	6'2"	200	28		
Tim Van Galder	QB	6'1"	190	28		
Danny Anderson	HB	6'3"	210	29		36
Craig Baynham	HB	6'1"	205	28		
Cannonball Butler	HB	5'10"	200	29		
Roy Shivers	HB	6'	200	30		
Leo Hayden	FB-HB	6'	210	24		6
Don Heater	FB-HB	6'2"	205	22		
Leon Burns	FB	6'2"	235	27		12
Tom Woodeshick	FB	6'	222	30		
Johnny Roland	HB-FB	6'2"	215	29		24
Walker Gillette	WR	6'5"	200	25		12
Mel Gray	WR	5'9"	170	23		
Freddie Hyatt	WR	6'3"	200	26		
Bobby Moore	WR	6'2"	210	22		18
Bob Wicks	WR	6'3"	195	22		
Jim McFarland	TE	6'5"	225	24		
Ara Person	TE	6'2"	220	23		
Jackie Smith	TE	6'4"	235	31		12
Jim Bakken	K	6'	195	31		61

PHILADELPHIA EAGLES 2-11-1 Ed Khayat

Scores of Each Game		
6	Dallas	28
17	CLEVELAND	27
12	N.Y. GIANTS	27
0	Washington	14
3	LOS ANGELES	34
21	Kansas City	20
3	New Orleans	21
6	ST. LOUIS	6
18	Houston	17
7	DALLAS	28
10	N.Y. Giants	62
7	WASHINGTON	23
12	CHICAGO	21
23	St. Louis	24

Use Name	Pos.	Hgt	Wgt	Age	Int	Pts
Wade Key	OT	6'4"	245	25		
Wayne Mass (from NE)	OT	6'4"	245	26		
Steve Smith	OT	6'5"	250	28		
Dick Stevens	OT	6'4"	240	24		
Henry Allison	OG	6'2"	255	25		
Tom Luken	OG	6'3"	253	22		
Jim Skaggs	OG	6'2"	250	32		
Vern Winfield	OG	6'2"	248	23		
Mark Nordquist	C-OG	6'4"	246	26		
Mike Evans	C	6'5"	250	26		
Jerry Sturm	C	6'3"	260	35		
Larry Estes	DE	6'6"	250	25		
Richard Harris	DE	6'4"	260	24		
Mel Tom	DE	6'4"	250	31		
Houston Antwine	DT	6'	270	33		
Don Hultz	DT	6'3"	240	31		
Gary Pettigrew	DT	6'4"	255	27		
Ernie Calloway	DE-DT	6'6"	255	24		
Dick Absher	LB	6'4"	235	28	1	
Chuck Allen	LB	6'1"	225	32	1	
John Bunting	LB	6'1"	220	22	1	
Bill Cody	LB	6'1"	230	28		
Bob Creech	LB	6'3"	228	23		
Bill Overmeyer	LB	6'3"	220	23		
Ron Porter	LB	6'3"	232	27	2	
John Sodaski	LB	6'2"	222	24		
Steve Zabel	LB	6'4"	235	24		
Kermit Alexander	DB	5'11"	186	31		
Jackie Allen	DB	6'1"	187	24		
Bill Bradley	DB	5'11"	190	25	9	
Al Coleman	DB	6'1"	183	27		2
Pat Gibbs	DB	5'10"	188	22		
Leroy Keyes	DB	6'3"	208	25	2	
Al Nelson	DB	5'11"	186	28		
Nate Ramsey	DB	6'1"	200	31	3	
Jim Thrower	DB	6'2"	194	23		
Lee Bouggess – Injury						
Ike Kelly – Injury						
Rick Arrington	QB	6'2"	185	25		
Pete Liske	QB	6'2"	200	31		
John Reaves	QB	6'3"	210	22		6
Larry Crowe	HB	6'1"	198	22		
Po James	HB	6'1"	202	23		6
Tom Sullivan	HB	6'	190	22		
Sonny Davis	FB-HB	5'11"	215	24		
Tony Baker	FB	5'11"	225	27		
Larry Watkins	FB	6'2"	230	25		6
Tom Bailey	HB-FB	6'2"	211	23		
Harold Carmichael	WR	6'7"	225	22		12
Ben Hawkins	WR	6'	180	28		6
Harold Jackson	WR	5'10"	175	26		24
Billy Walik	WR	5'11"	180	24		6
Clark Hoss	TE	6'8"	235	23		
Kent Kramer	TE	6'5"	235	28		6
Gary Ballman	WR-TE	6'	215	32		
Tom Dempsey	K	6'1"	255	31		71
Tom McNeil	K	6'1"	195	30		

WASHINGTON REDSKINS

RUSHING

Last Name	No.	Yds	Avg	TD
Brown	285	1216	4.3	8
Harraway	148	567	3.8	6
Mul-Key	33	155	4.7	1
Brunet	30	82	2.7	2
C. Taylor	3	39	13.0	0
Nock	6	22	3.7	0
Smith	1	9	9.0	0
Kilmer	3	–3	–1.0	0
Jurgensen	4	–5	–1.3	0

RECEIVING

Last Name	No.	Yds	Avg	TD
C. Taylor	49	673	14	7
Jefferson	35	550	16	3
Brown	32	473	15	4
Smith	21	353	17	7
Harraway	15	105	7	0
Mul-Key	4	66	17	0
Alston	2	53	27	0
Brunet	1	8	8	0

PUNT RETURNS

Last Name	No.	Yds	Avg	TD
Vactor	17	88	5	0
Duncan	11	70	6	0
Haymond	6	1	0	0

KICKOFF RETURNS

Last Name	No.	Yds	Avg	TD
Duncan	15	364	24	0
Haymond	10	291	29	0
Mul-Key	8	209	26	0
Brunet	8	190	24	0
Bass	2	22	11	0
Vactor	1	21	21	0
Fanucci	1	15	15	0
McLinton	1	15	15	0
Tillman	2	6	3	0

PASSING – PUNTING – KICKING

PASSING	Att	Comp	%	Yds	Yd/Att	TD	Int–	%	RK
Kilmer	225	120	53	1648	7.3	19	11–	5	4
Jurgensen	59	39	66	633	10.7	2	4–	7	

PUNTING	No	Avg
Bragg	59	38.5

KICKING	XP	Att	%	FG	Att	%
Knight	40	41	98	14	30	47

DALLAS COWBOYS

RUSHING

Last Name	No.	Yds	Avg	TD
Hill	245	1036	4.2	6
Garrison	167	784	4.7	7
Newhouse	28	116	4.1	1
Montgomery	35	81	2.3	1
Staubach	6	45	7.5	0
Morton	8	26	3.3	2
Reeves	3	14	4.7	0
Neely	1	10	10.0	0
Hayes	2	8	4.0	0
Alworth	1	2	2.0	0
Fugett	3	2	0.7	0

RECEIVING

Last Name	No.	Yds	Avg	TD
Hill	43	364	8	3
Garrison	37	390	11	3
Sellers	31	653	21	5
Parks	18	298	17	1
Ditka	17	198	12	1
Hayes	15	200	13	0
Alworth	15	195	13	2
Montgomery	8	131	16	1
Fugett	7	94	13	0
Truax	4	49	12	0
Newhouse	1	8	8	0

PUNT RETURNS

Last Name	No.	Yds	Avg	TD
Harris	19	78	4	0
Waters	9	56	6	0

KICKOFF RETURNS

Last Name	No.	Yds	Avg	TD
Harris	26	615	24	0
Newhouse	18	382	21	0
Thomas	2	50	25	0
Waters	2	18	9	0
Montgomery	1	15	15	0
Fugett	1	0	0	0

PASSING – PUNTING – KICKING

PASSING	Att	Comp	%	Yds	Yd/Att	TD	Int–	%	RK
Morton	339	185	55	2396	7.1	15	21–	6	8
Staubach	20	9	45	98	4.9	0	2–	10	
Hill	3	1	33	55	18.3	1	0–	0	
Montgomery	3	1	33	31	10.3	0	0–	0	
Reeves	2	0	0	0	0.0	0	0–	0	

PUNTING	No	Avg
Bateman	51	38.2

KICKING	XP	Att	%	FG	Att	%
Fritsch	36	36	100	21	36	58

NEW YORK GIANTS

RUSHING

Last Name	No.	Yds	Avg	TD
Ron Johnson	298	1182	4.0	9
Evans	91	317	3.5	4
Clements	46	221	4.8	0
Orduna	36	129	3.6	1
Morrison	9	36	4.0	0
Thompson	9	35	3.9	0
Randy Johnson	9	26	2.9	1
Duhon	9	23	2.6	0
Snead	10	21	2.1	0
Blanchard	1	17	17.0	0
Herrmann	3	9	3.0	0
Tucker	3	6	2.0	1

RECEIVING

Last Name	No.	Yds	Avg	TD
Tucker	55	764	14	4
Ron Johnson	45	451	10	5
Herrmann	28	422	15	5
Houston	27	468	17	3
Evans	26	182	7	1
Clements	9	118	13	0
Grim	5	67	13	1
Morrison	5	39	8	0
Orduna	4	6	2	1
Duhon	2	20	10	0

PUNT RETURNS

Last Name	No.	Yds	Avg	TD
Athas	8	95	12	0
Duhon	2	20	10	0
Grim	7	10	1	0
Mendenhall	1	0	0	0

KICKOFF RETURNS

Last Name	No.	Yds	Avg	TD
Thompson	29	821	28	1
Orduna	12	244	20	0
Small	1	100	100	0
Duhon	2	47	24	0
Douglas	4	43	11	0
Crist	1	7	7	0
Enderle	1	0	0	0

PASSING – PUNTING – KICKING

PASSING	Att	Comp	%	Yds	Yd/Att	TD	Int–	%	RK
Snead	325	196	60	2307	7.1	17	12–	4	2
Ron Johnson	17	10	59	230	13.5	3	3–	18	
Blanchard	1	0	0	0	0.0	0	0–	0	
Ron Johnson	1	0	0	0	0.0	0	0–	0	

PUNTING	No	Avg
Blanchard	47	42.7

KICKING	XP	Att	%	FG	Att	%
Gogolak	34	38	89	21	31	68

ST. LOUIS CARDINALS

RUSHING

Last Name	No.	Yds	Avg	TD
Anderson	153	536	3.5	4
Roland	105	414	3.9	2
Burns	26	69	2.7	2
Moore	9	44	4.9	0
Baynham	17	43	2.5	0
Smith	5	31	6.2	0
Van Galder	9	28	3.1	0
Hart	9	17	1.9	0
Woodeshick	5	14	2.8	0
Shivers	5	12	2.4	0
Hayden	8	11	1.4	1
Cuozzo	4	7	1.8	0
Butler	6	3	0.5	0
Conley	3	8	2.7	0

RECEIVING

Last Name	No.	Yds	Avg	TD
Roland	38	321	8	2
Gillette	33	550	17	2
Moore	29	500	17	3
Anderson	28	298	11	2
Smith	26	407	16	2
Burns	6	24	4	0
Gray	3	62	21	0
Hyatt	2	32	16	0
Shivers	1	20	20	0
Hayden	1	17	17	0
Baynham	1	10	10	0
Butler	1	8	8	0
Wicks	1	8	8	0
Woodeshick	1	2	2	0

PUNT RETURNS

Last Name	No.	Yds	Avg	TD
Willingham	9	41	5	0
Wehrli	5	24	5	0
Gray	2	–4	–2	0

KICKOFF RETURNS

Last Name	No.	Yds	Avg	TD
Moore	20	437	22	0
Gray	17	378	22	0
Willingham	9	194	22	0
Butler	4	85	21	0
Hyatt	1	41	41	0
Wehrli	1	10	10	0
Burns	1	7	7	0

PASSING – PUNTING – KICKING

PASSING	Att	Comp	%	Yds	Yd/Att	TD	Int–	%	RK
Cuozzo	158	69	44	897	5.7	5	11–	7	13
Hart	119	60	50	857	7.2	5	5–	4	
Van Galder	79	40	51	434	5.5	1	7–	9	
Anderson	3	2	67	71	23.7	0	0–	0	
Smith	2	0	0	0	0.0	0	0–	0	
Wilson	2	0	0	0	0.0	0	0–	0	

PUNTING	No	Avg
Anderson	72	39.5
Bakken	1	26.0

KICKING	XP	Att	%	FG	Att	%
Bakken	19	21	90	14	22	64

PHILADELPHIA EAGLES

RUSHING

Last Name	No.	Yds	Avg	TD
James	182	565	3.1	0
Baker	90	322	3.6	0
Watkins	67	262	3.9	1
Reaves	18	109	6.1	1
Jackson	9	76	8.4	0
Bailey	7	22	3.1	0
Liske	7	20	2.9	0
Sullivan	13	13	1.0	0
Arrington	1	2	2.0	0
Crowe	1	2	2.0	0
Hawkins	3	0	0.0	0

RECEIVING

Last Name	No.	Yds	Avg	TD
Jackson	62	1048	17	4
Hawkins	30	512	17	1
Carmichael	20	276	14	2
James	20	156	8	1
Baker	16	114	7	0
Kramer	11	176	16	1
Ballman	9	183	20	0
Watkins	6	–2	0	0
Bailey	5	32	6	0
Sullivan	4	17	4	0
Walik	1	15	15	1

PUNT RETURNS

Last Name	No.	Yds	Avg	TD
Bradley	22	155	7	0
Winfield	1	12	12	0
Gibbs	1	8	8	0
Walik	3	4	1	0

KICKOFF RETURNS

Last Name	No.	Yds	Avg	TD
Nelson	25	728	29	0
Walik	21	466	22	0
Sullivan	3	72	24	0
Gibbs	3	61	20	0
Bradley	2	22	11	0
Pettigrew	1	17	17	0
Winfield	3	9	3	0
Overmyer	1	0	0	0

PASSING – PUNTING – KICKING

PASSING	Att	Comp	%	Yds	Yd/Att	TD	Int–	%	RK
Reaves	224	108	48	1508	6.7	7	12–	5	10
Liske	138	71	51	973	7.1	3	7–	5	
Arrington	13	5	38	46	3.5	0	1–	8	

PUNTING	No	Avg
Bradley	56	40.2
McNeill	7	41.4

KICKING	XP	Att	%	FG	Att	%
Dempsey	11	12	92	20	35	57

GREEN BAY PACKERS 10-4-0 Dan Devine

Scores of Each Game		
26	Cleveland	10
14	OAKLAND	20
16	DALLAS	13
20	CHICAGO	17
24	Detroit	23
9	ATLANTA	10
13	MINNESOTA	27
34	SAN FRANCISCO	24
23	Chicago	17
23	Houston	10
16	Washington	21
33	DETROIT	7
23	Minnesota	7
30	New Orleans	20

Use Name	Pos.	Hgt	Wgt	Age	Int	Pts
Bill Hayhoe	OT	6'8"	258	25		
Dick Himes	OT	6'4"	244	26		
Kevin Hunt	OT	6'5"	260	23		
Francis Peay	OT	6'5"	250	28		
Bill Lueck	OG	6'3"	235	26		
Mal Snider	OG	6'4"	250	25		
Keith Wortman	OG	6'2"	245	22		
Ken Bowman	C	6'3"	230	29		
Cal Withrow	C	6'	240	27		
Dave Pureifory	DE	6'1"	260	22		
Alden Roche	DE	6'4"	255	27		
Clarence Williams	DE	6'5"	255	25		6
Bob Brown	DT	6'5"	260	32		2
Gale Gillingham	DT	6'3"	255	28		
Mike McCoy	DT	6'5"	284	23		
Vern Vanoy	DT	6'8"	270	26		
Fred Carr	LB	6'5"	238	26		
Jim Carter	LB	6'3"	235	23	1	
Tommy Crutcher	LB	6'3"	230	30		
Larry Hefner	LB	6'2"	215	23		
Ray Nitschke	LB	6'3"	235	36		
Dave Robinson	LB	6'3"	245	31	2	
Willie Buchanon	DB	6'	190	21	4	6
Ken Ellis	DB	5'10"	190	24	4	12
Paul Gibson	DB	6'2"	195	24		
Charlie Hall	DB	6'1"	195	23		
Jim Hill	DB	6'2"	190	25	4	
Bob Kroll	DB	6'1"	195	22		
Al Matthews	DB	5'11"	190	24	2	
Ike Thomas	DB	6'2"	193	24		
Larry Krause – Injury						
Scott Hunter	QB	6'2"	205	24		30
Frank Patrick	QB	6'7"	225	25		
Jerry Tagge	QB	6'2"	220	22		6
Bob Hudson	HB	5'11"	210	24		
MacArthur Lane	HB	6'	220	30		18
Dave Kopay	FB-HB	6'2"	218	30		
John Brockington	FB	6'1"	225	23		54
Perry Williams	FB	6'2"	220	25		
Carroll Dale	WR	6'1"	200	34		6
Dave Davis	WR	6'	175	24		6
Leland Glass	WR	6'	185	22		6
Jon Staggers	WR	5'10"	186	23		12
Len Garrett	TE	6'3"	230	23		
Pete Lammons	TE	6'3"	228	28		
Rich McGeorge	TE	6'4"	235	23		12
Chester Marcol	K	6'	190	23		128
Ron Widby	K	6'4"	210	27		

DETROIT LIONS 8-5-1 Joe Schmidt

Scores of Each Game		
30	N.Y. GIANTS	16
10	MINNESOTA	34
38	Chicago	24
26	Atlanta	23
23	GREEN BAY	24
34	SAN DIEGO	20
24	Dallas	28
14	CHICAGO	0
14	Minnesota	16
27	NEW ORLEANS	14
37	N.Y. JETS	20
7	Green Bay	33
21	Buffalo	21
34	Los Angeles	17

Use Name	Pos.	Hgt	Wgt	Age	Int	Pts
Rocky Freitas	OT	6'6"	270	26		
Gordon Jolley	OT	6'5"	230	23		
Jim Yarbrough	OT	6'6"	265	25		
Frank Gallagher	OG	6'2"	245	29		
Bob Kowalkowski	OG	6'3"	240	28		
Rocky Rasley	OG	6'3"	250	25		
Chuck Walton	OG	6'3"	255	31		
Ed Flanagan	C	6'3"	245	28		
Dave Thompson	OT-C	6'4"	275	23		
Gene Hamlin	C	6'3"	245	26		
Larry Hand	DE	6'4"	250	32		
Jim Mitchell	DE	6'3"	245	23	1	
Herb Orvis	DE	6'5"	240	25		
Ken Sanders	DE	6'5"	225	22		
Bob Bell	DT	6'4"	250	24		
John Gordon	DT	6'6"	260	24		
Joe Schmiesing	DT	6'4"	260	27		
Bob Tatarek (from BUF)	DT	6'4"	270	26		
Larry Woods	DT	6'6"	260	24		
Mike Lucci	LB	6'2"	230	32	2	
Paul Naumoff	LB	6'1"	215	27	1	
Rick Ogle	LB	6'3"	230	23		
Wayne Walker	LB	6'2"	228	35		
Charlie Weaver	LB	6'2"	218	23	1	
Adrian Young (from PHI)	LB	6'1"	232	26		
Lem Barney	DB	6'	188	26	3	
Leon Jenkins	DB	5'11"	165	22		
Dick LeBeau	DB	6'1"	185	35		
Charlie Potts	DB	6'3"	210	23		
Al Randolph	DB	6'2"	205	28		
Wayne Rasmussen	DB	6'2"	180	30	2	
Rudy Redmond	DB	6'	195	25	2	6
Mike Weger	DB	6'2"	200	26		
Sonny Campbell – Injury						
Ed Mooney – Injury						
Greg Landry	QB	6'4"	210	25		54
Bill Munson	QB	6'2"	210	30		
Nick Eddy	HB	6'1"	210	28		6
Mel Farr	HB	6'2"	210	27		18
Altie Taylor	HB	5'10"	200	24		36
Mickey Zofko	HB	6'3"	195	22		1
Steve Owens	FB	6'2"	215	24		24
Bill Triplett	FB	6'2"	215	33		
Al Barnes	WR	6'1"	170	23		6
Ron Jessie	WR	6'	183	24		24
Earl McCullouch	WR	5'11"	175	26		6
Larry Walton	WR	5'11"	180	25		36
Craig Cotton	TE	6'4"	222	25		6
John Hilton	TE	6'5"	225	30		6
Charlie Sanders	TE	6'4"	225	26		12
Errol Mann	K	6'	200	31		98
Herman Weaver	K	6'4"	210	23		

MINNESOTA VIKINGS 7-7-0 Bud Grant

Scores of Each Game		
21	WASHINGTON	24
34	Detroit	10
14	MIAMI	16
17	ST. LOUIS	19
23	Denver	20
10	Chicago	13
27	Green Bay	13
37	NEW ORLEANS	6
16	DETROIT	14
45	Los Angeles	41
10	Pittsburgh	23
23	CHICAGO	10
7	GREEN BAY	23
17	San Francisco	20

Use Name	Pos.	Hgt	Wgt	Age	Int	Pts
Grady Alderman	OT	6'2"	247	33		
Doug Davis	OT	6'4"	250	28		
Ron Yary	OT	6'6"	255	26		
Ed White	OG	6'2"	262	25		
Milt Sunde	C-OG	6'2"	250	29		
John Ward	DE-OG	6'4"	250	24		
Mick Tingelhoff	C	6'1"	237	32		
Godfrey Zaunbrecher	C	6'2"	240	24		
Carl Eller	DE	6'6"	247	30		
Jim Marshall	DE	6'3"	248	34		
Bob Lurtsema	DT-DE	6'6"	250	30		
Gary Larsen	DT	6'5"	260	32		
Alan Page	DT	6'5"	245	27		
Doug Sutherland	DE-DT	6'3"	250	24		
Carl Gersbach	LB	6'1"	230	25		
Wally Hilgenberg	LB	6'3"	230	29	1	6
Amos Martin	LB	6'3"	228	23		
Jeff Siemon	LB	6'2"	230	22	2	
Lonnie Warwick	LB	6'3"	238	30	1	
Roy Winston	LB	6'1"	222	32	3	
Terry Brown	DB	6'1"	205	25		
Bobby Bryant	DB	6'	170	28	4	6
Karl Kassulke	DB	6'	195	30	2	
Paul Krause	DB	6'3"	200	30	6	12
Ed Sharockman	DB	6'	200	32		
Charlie West	DB	6'1"	197	26	3	
Jeff Wright	DB	5'11"	190	23	2	
Nate Wright	DB	5'11"	180	24	2	
Bob Lee	QB	6'2"	195	26		
Fran Tarkenton	QB	6'1"	190	32		
Clint Jones	HB	6'	205	27		12
Dave Osborn	HB	6'	208	29		18
Ed Marinaro	FB-HB	6'2"	212	22		6
Bill Brown	FB	5'11"	228	34		48
Oscar Reed	HB-FB	5'11"	222	28		12
Jim Lindsey	HB-FB	6'2"	210	27		
Calvin Demery	WR	6'	190	22		
John Gilliam	WR	6'	195	27		42
John Henderson	WR	6'3"	195	29		12
Gene Washington	WR	6'3"	208	28		12
John Beasley	TE	6'3"	228	27		6
Stu Voigt	TE	6'1"	220	24		12
Fred Cox	K	5'10"	200	33		97
Mike Eischeid	K	6'	190	31		

CHICAGO BEARS 4-9-1 Abe Gibron

Scores of Each Game		
21	ATLANTA	37
13	LOS ANGELES	13
24	DETROIT	38
17	Green Bay	20
17	Cleveland	0
13	MINNESOTA	10
27	St. Louis	10
0	Detroit	14
17	GREEN BAY	23
21	SAN FRANCISCO	34
3	CINCINNATI	13
10	Minnesota	23
21	Philadelphia	12
21	Oakland	28

Use Name	Pos.	Hgt	Wgt	Age	Int	Pts
Lionel Antoine	OT	6'6"	255	22		
Rich Buzin	OT	6'4"	250	26		
Randy Jackson	OT	6'5"	250	28		
Bob Asher	OG-OT	6'5"	250	24		
Jim Cadile	OG	6'3"	250	31		
Glen Holloway	OG	6'3"	250	23		
Ernie Janet	OG	6'4"	250	23		
Bob Newton	OG	6'4"	250	23		
Rich Coady	C	6'3"	245	27		
Steve DeLong	DE	6'3"	254	29		
Willie Holman	DE	6'4"	250	27		
Larry Horton	DT-DE	6'4"	248	23		
Bill Line	DT	6'7"	260	23		
Jim Osborne	DT	6'3"	250	22		
Andy Rice	DT	6'3"	268	30		
Bill Staley	DT	6'3"	250	25		
Tony McGee	DE-DT	6'4"	250	23		
Ross Brupbacher	LB	6'3"	215	24	1	6
Doug Buffone	LB	6'1"	230	28	1	
Jimmy Gunn	LB	6'1"	220	23		
Bill McKinney	LB	6'1"	226	27		
Bob Pifferini	LB	6'2"	226	22		
Larry Rowden	LB	6'2"	220	22		
Dick Butkus	C-LB	6'3"	245	28	2	1
Craig Clemons	DB	5'11"	187	23		
Charlie Ford	DB	6'3"	185	23	7	
Bob Jeter	DB	6'1"	200	34	2	
Garry Lyle	DB	6'2"	198	26	2	
Jerry Moore	DB	6'3"	208	22	1	
Ron Smith	DB	6'1"	195	29	1	6
Joe Taylor	DB	6'2"	200	31	4	
Joe Moore – Injury						
Dave Hale – Injury						
Bobby Douglass	QB	6'3"	225	25		48
John Huarte	QB	6'	185	28		
Cyril Pinder	HB	6'2"	210	25		18
Gary Kosins	FB-HB	6'1"	215	23		6
Don Shy	FB-HB	6'1"	210	26		6
Jim Harrison	FB	6'4"	235	23		18
Roger Lawson	HB-FB	6'2"	215	22		6
George Farmer	WR	6'4"	214	24		12
Jim Seymour	WR	6'4"	210	25		6
Cecil Turner	WR	5'10"	176	28		
Bob Parsons	TE	6'4"	234	22		6
Earl Thomas	TE	6'3"	224	23		24
Bob Wallace	TE	6'3"	220	26		
Bobby Joe Green	K	5'11"	175	34		
Mac Percival	K	6'4"	220	32		62

GREEN BAY PACKERS

RUSHING

Last Name	No.	Yds	Avg	TD
Brockington	274	1027	3.7	8
Lane	177	821	4.6	3
P. Williams	33	139	4.2	0
Hudson	15	62	4.1	0
Kopay	10	39	3.9	0
Hunter	22	37	1.7	5
Glass	2	13	6.5	0
Davis	2	0	0.0	0
Tagge	8	−3	−0.4	1
Staggers	1	−8	−8.0	0

RECEIVING

Last Name	No.	Yds	Avg	TD
Lane	26	285	11	0
Brockington	19	243	13	1
Dale	16	317	20	1
Glass	15	261	17	1
Staggers	8	123	15	1
Davis	4	119	30	1
Garrett	4	66	17	0
McGeorge	4	50	13	2
Kopay	3	19	6	0
Nitschke	1	34	34	0
Lammons	1	19	19	0

PUNT RETURNS

Last Name	No.	Yds	Avg	TD
Ellis	14	215	15	1
Staggers	9	148	16	1
Glass	1	1	1	0
Hudson	1	0	0	0

KICKOFF RETURNS

Last Name	No.	Yds	Avg	TD
Thomas	21	572	27	0
Staggers	11	260	24	0
Hudson	11	247	22	0
Kroll	1	23	23	0
Robinson	1	20	20	0
Ellis	1	10	10	0
P. Williams	1	9	9	0
Garrett	1	0	0	0
Wortman	1	0	0	0

PASSING – PUNTING – KICKING

PASSING	Att	Comp	%	Yds	Yd/Att	TD	Int–	%	RK
Hunter	199	86	43	1252	6.3	6	9–	5	10
Tagge	29	10	34	154	5.3	0	0–	0	
Patrick	4	1	25	9	2.3	0	0–	0	
Lane	2	2	100	19	9.5	0	0–	0	
Widby	2	2	100	102	51.0	1	0–	0	
Staggers	1	0	0	0	0.0	0	0–	0	

PUNTING	No	Avg
Widby	65	41.8

KICKING	XP	Att	%	FG	Att	%
Marcol	29	29	100	33	48	69

PASSING	Att	Comp	%	Yds	Yd/Att	TD	Int–	%	RK

DETROIT LIONS

RUSHING

Last Name	No.	Yds	Avg	TD
Taylor	154	658	4.3	4
Landry	81	524	6.5	9
Owens	143	519	3.6	4
Farr	62	216	3.5	3
Triplett	17	48	2.8	0
Zofko	7	28	4.0	0
Eddy	8	28	3.5	0
Munson	1	0	0.0	0

RECEIVING

Last Name	No.	Yds	Avg	TD
Taylor	29	250	9	2
C. Sanders	27	416	15	2
L. Walton	24	485	20	6
Jessie	24	424	18	4
Owens	15	100	7	0
Farr	10	132	13	0
Cotton	8	129	16	1
Hilton	5	133	27	1
McCullouch	5	96	19	1
Barnes	4	58	15	1
Eddy	2	46	23	1
Zofko	2	14	7	0

PUNT RETURNS

Last Name	No.	Yds	Avg	TD
Barney	15	108	7	0
L. Walton	3	−8	−3	0

KICKOFF RETURNS

Last Name	No.	Yds	Avg	TD
Zofko	26	616	24	0
Jessie	23	558	24	0
Barney	1	17	17	0
Triplett	1	12	12	0
Orvis	1	5	5	0
L. Walton	0	96	0	0

PASSING – PUNTING – KICKING

PASSING	Att	Comp	%	Yds	Yd/Att	TD	Int–	%	RK
Landry	268	134	50	2066	7.7	18	17–	6	6
Munson	35	20	57	194	5.5	1	1–	3	
Jessie	1	0	0	0	0.0	0	0–	0	
McCullouch	1	1	100	23	23.0	0	0–	0	

PUNTING	No	Avg
H. Weaver	43	40.3

KICKING	XP	Att	%	FG	Att	%
Mann	38	39	97	20	29	69
Zofko	1	1	100	0	0	0

MINNESOTA VIKINGS

RUSHING

Last Name	No.	Yds	Avg	TD
Reed	151	639	4.2	2
Bill Brown	82	263	3.2	4
Osborn	82	261	3.2	2
Marinaro	66	223	3.4	0
Tarkenton	27	180	6.7	0
Jones	52	164	3.2	2
Gilliam	8	14	1.8	0
Lindsey	1	8	8.0	0
Voigt	1	1	1.0	1
Krause	1	0	0.0	0
Eischeid	1	−13	−13.0	0

RECEIVING

Last Name	No.	Yds	Avg	TD
Gilliam	47	1035	22	7
Reed	30	205	7	0
Beasley	28	232	8	1
Marinaro	28	218	8	1
Bill Brown	22	298	14	4
Osborn	20	166	8	1
Washington	18	259	14	2
Henderson	10	190	19	2
Voigt	6	50	8	1
Jones	6	42	7	0
Lindsey	3	28	9	0
White	0	3	0	0

PUNT RETURNS

Last Name	No.	Yds	Avg	TD
West	16	111	7	0
Bryant	10	48	5	0

KICKOFF RETURNS

Last Name	No.	Yds	Avg	TD
Gilliam	14	369	26	0
Jones	12	327	27	0
West	9	196	22	0
Bryant	2	41	21	0
Bill Brown	3	37	12	0
Lindsey	1	17	17	0
Voigt	1	2	2	0

PASSING – PUNTING – KICKING

PASSING	Att	Comp	%	Yds	Yd/Att	TD	Int–	%	RK
Tarkenton	378	215	57	2651	7.0	18	13–	3	1
Lee	6	3	50	75	12.5	1	0–	0	
Krause	1	0	0	0	0.0	0	0–	0	

PUNTING	No	Avg
Eischeid	62	42.8

KICKING	XP	Att	%	FG	Att	%
Cox	34	34	100	21	33	64

CHICAGO BEARS

RUSHING

Last Name	No.	Yds	Avg	TD
Douglass	141	968	6.9	8
Harrison	167	622	3.7	2
Shy	91	342	3.8	1
Pinder	87	300	3.4	3
Lawson	33	106	3.2	1
Butkus	1	28	28.0	0
Thomas	5	13	2.6	0
Kosins	3	5	1.7	0
Parsons	1	0	0.0	0
Turner	3	0	0.0	0
Huarte	1	−2	−2.0	0
Seymour	1	−9	−9.0	0
Farmer	2	−13	−6.5	0

RECEIVING

Last Name	No.	Yds	Avg	TD
Thomas	20	365	18	3
Farmer	14	380	27	2
Seymour	10	165	17	1
Shy	10	109	11	0
Lawson	8	120	15	0
Harrison	8	30	4	1
Turner	3	71	24	0
Kosins	2	15	8	1
Pinder	1	13	13	0
Wallace	1	9	9	0
Parsons	1	6	6	1

PUNT RETURNS

Last Name	No.	Yds	Avg	TD
Smith	26	163	6	0
Clemons	2	15	8	0

KICKOFF RETURNS

Last Name	No.	Yds	Avg	TD
Smith	30	924	31	1
Turner	16	409	26	0
Clemons	2	53	27	0
Holloway	1	28	28	0
Butkus	1	15	15	0
Pinder	1	14	14	0
Horton	1	3	3	0
Thomas	0	82	0	1

PASSING – PUNTING – KICKING

PASSING	Att	Comp	%	Yds	Yd/Att	TD	Int–	%	RK
Douglass	198	75	38	1246	6.3	9	12–	6	12
Huarte	5	2	40	14	2.8	0	0–	0	
Green	2	1	50	23	11.5	0	1–	50	

PUNTING	No	Avg
Green	67	41.2

KICKING	XP	Att	%	FG	Att	%
Percival	26	26	100	12	24	50
Butkus	1	1	100	0	0	0

SAN FRANCISCO FORTY NINERS 8-5-1 Dick Nolan

Scores of Each Game		
34	SAN DIEGO	3
20	Buffalo	27
37	New Orleans	2
7	Los Angeles	31
17	N.Y. GIANTS	23
20	NEW ORLEANS	20
49	Atlanta	14
24	Green Bay	34
24	BALTIMORE	21
34	Chicago	21
31	Dallas	10
16	LOS ANGELES	26
20	ATLANTA	0
20	MINNESOTA	17

Use Name	Pos.	Hgt	Wgt	Age	Int	Pts
Len Rohde	OT	6'4"	248	34		
John Watson	OT	6'4"	248	23		
Cas Banaszek	C-OT	6'3"	250	26		
Randy Beisler	OG	6'4"	250	27		
Elmer Collett	OG	6'4"	240	27		
Woody Peoples	OG	6'2"	258	29		
Forrest Blue	C	6'5"	260	26		
Bill Belk	DE	6'3"	253	26		
Cedrick Hardman	DE	6'3"	255	23		
Tommy Hart	DE	6'3"	248	27	1	
Rolf Krueger	DT-DE	6'4"	253	25		
Earl Edwards	DT	6'6"	262	26		
Bob Hoskins	DT	6'2"	253	26		
Charlie Krueger	DT	6'4"	268	36		
Ed Beard	LB	6'2"	220	32	1	
Marty Huff	LB	6'2"	234	23		
Frank Nunley	LB	6'2"	230	26	1	
Dave Olerich	LB	6'1"	220	27		
Jim Sniadecki	LB	6'2"	230	25		
Skip Vanderbundt	LB	6'3"	224	25	2	18
Dave Wilcox	LB	6'3"	240	29	3	
Johnny Fuller	DB	6'	185	26	1	
Windlan Hall	DB	5'11"	178	22	1	
Jim Johnson	DB	6'2"	187	34	4	
Ralph McGill	DB	5'11"	183	22		
Mel Phillips	DB	6'	194	30	1	
Mike Simpson	DB	5'11"	168	25	2	6
Bruce Taylor	DB	6'	187	24	2	
John Brodie	QB	6'1"	203	37		6
Joe Reed	QB	6'1"	195	24		
Steve Spurrier	QB	6'2"	203	27		
John Isenbarger	HB	6'3"	205	24		6
Doug Cunningham	HB	5'11"	190	26		
Jimmy Thomas	HB	6'1"	214	25		6
Vic Washington	HB	5'10"	196	26		30
Ken Willard	FB	6'2"	216	29		30
Larry Schreiber	HB-FB	6'	200	25		18
Terry Beasley	WR	5'10"	184	21		
Preston Riley	WR	6'	180	24		6
Gene Washington	WR	6'1"	185	25		72
Ted Kwalick	TE	6'4"	223	25		54
Dick Witcher	TE	6'3"	204	27		6
Bruce Gossett	K	6'2"	228	29		95
Jim McCann	K	6'2"	163	23		

ATLANTA FALCONS 7-7-0 Norm Van Brocklin

Scores of Each Game		
37	Chicago	21
20	New England	21
31	LOS ANGELES	3
23	DETROIT	26
21	New Orleans	14
10	Green Bay	9
14	SAN FRANCISCO	49
7	Los Angeles	20
36	NEW ORLEANS	20
13	Washington	24
23	DENVER	20
20	HOUSTON	10
0	San Francisco	20
14	KANSAS CITY	17

Use Name	Pos.	Hgt	Wgt	Age	Int	Pts
Len Gotshalk	OT	6'4"	244	22		
George Kunz	OT	6'5"	257	25		
Bill Sandeman	OT	6'6"	252	29		
Dennis Havig	OG	6'2"	245	23		
Andy Mauer	OG	6'3"	265	23		
Jim Miller	OG	6'3"	240	23		
Ted Fritsch	C	6'2"	240	22		
Jeff Van Note	OG-C	6'2"	243	26		
Claude Humphrey	DE	6'5"	252	28		2
John Zook	DE	6'5"	243	24		6
Chuck Walker (from STL)	DT-DE	6'2"	250	31		
Glen Condren	DT	6'2"	250	30		
Rosie Manning	DT	6'5"	256	22		
John Small	DT	6'5"	270	25		
Mike Lewis	DE-DT	6'3"	244	23	1	2
Grady Allen	LB	6'3"	230	26		
Duane Benson	LB	6'2"	215	27		
Greg Brezina	LB	6'2"	226	26		
Don Hansen	LB	6'3"	235	28	1	
Noel Jenke	LB	6'1"	220	25		
Tommy Nobis	LB	6'2"	240	28	3	6
Ray Brown	DB	6'2"	208	23	2	
Ray Easterling	DB	6'	195	22		
Clarence Ellis	DB	5'11"	193	22	3	
Willie Germany	DB	6'	192	23		
Tom Hayes	DB	6'1"	200	26	5	
Tony Plummer	DB	5'11"	188	25		
Ken Reaves	DB	6'3"	210	27	3	
Larry Shears	DB	5'10"	185	23		
Harmon Wages – Knee Injury						
Bob Berry	QB	5'11"	185	30		12
Pat Sullivan	QB	6'0"	198	22		
Willie Belton	HB	5'11"	207	23		
Dave Hampton	HB	6'	210	25		42
Joe Profit	HB	6'	213	23		
Ron Lamb	FB	6'2"	225	28		
Art Malone	FB	5'11"	211	24		60
Eddie Ray	FB	6'1"	240	25		
Ken Burrow	WR	6'	190	24		30
Wes Chesson	WR	6'2"	195	23		6
Ray Jarvis	WR	5'11"	200	23		
Todd Snyder	WR	6'2"	194	23		
Larry Mialik	TE	6'2"	226	22		
Jim Mitchell	TE	6'2"	234	24		24
Bill Bell	K	6'1"	192	24		79
John James	K	6'3"	197	23		

LOS ANGELES RAMS 6-7-1 Tommy Prothro

Scores of Each Game		
34	NEW ORLEANS	14
13	Chicago	13
3	Atlanta	31
31	SAN FRANCISCO	7
34	Philadelphia	3
15	CINCINNATI	12
17	Oakland	45
20	ATLANTA	7
10	DENVER	16
41	MINNESOTA	45
16	New Orleans	19
26	San Francisco	16
14	St. Louis	24
17	DETROIT	34

Use Name	Pos.	Hgt	Wgt	Age	Int	Pts
Charley Cowan	OT	6'4"	250	23		
Harry Schuh	OT	6'2"	260	29		
John Williams	OG-OT	6'3"	256	26		
Mike LaHood	OG	6'3"	250	27		
Tom Mack	OG	6'3"	250	28		
Joe Scibelli	OG	6'1"	255	33		
Ken Iman	C	6'1"	240	33		
Rich Saul	OG-C	6'3"	235	24		
Coy Bacon	DE	6'4"	270	30		
Fred Dryer	DE	6'6"	240	26		
Jack Youngblood	DE	6'4"	250	22		
Larry Brooks	DT	6'3"	255	22		
Bill Nelson	DT	6'7"	270	24		
Merlin Olsen	DT	6'5"	270	31		
Phil Olsen	DT	6'5"	265	24		
Ken Geddes	LB	6'3"	235	24		
Dean Halverson	LB	6'2"	212	26		
Marlin McKeever	LB	6'1"	235	32	2	
John Pergine	LB	6'1"	225	25		
Jim Purnell	LB	6'2"	238	30	1	
Jack Reynolds	LB	6'1"	232	24		
Isiah Robertson	LB	6'3"	225	23		
Al Clark	DB	6'	180	24	1	
Dave Elmendorf	DB	6'1"	195	23	3	
Gene Howard	DB	6'	190	25	3	6
Jim Nettles	DB	5'9"	177	30	6	
Clancy Williams	DB	6'2"	194	29		
Roger Williams	DB	5'10"	180	26		
Travis Williams – Knee Injury						
Pete Beathard	QB	6'2"	200	30		
Roman Gabriel	QB	6'4"	220	32		6
Jim Bertelsen	HB	5'11"	205	22		36
Lawrence McCutcheon	HB	6'1"	205	22		
Larry Smith	HB	6'3"	220	24		18
Bob Thomas	HB	5'10"	200	23		18
Les Josephson	FB	6'	207	29		6
Willie Ellison	HB-FB	6'1"	200	27		36
Dick Gordon	WR	5'11"	190	27		6
John Love	WR	5'11"	185	27		6
David Ray	WR	6'	195	27		103
Lance Rentzel	WR	6'2"	202	28		12
Jack Snow	WR	6'2"	190	29		24
Joe Sweet	WR	6'2"	196	24		8
Pat Curran	TE	6'3"	238	26		
Bob Klein	TE	6'5"	235	25		6
Dave Chapple	K	6'	180	25		

NEW ORLEANS SAINTS 2-11-1 J. D. Roberts

Scores of Each Game		
14	Los Angeles	34
17	KANSAS CITY	20
2	SAN FRANCISCO	37
21	N.Y. Giants	45
14	ATLANTA	21
20	San Francisco	20
21	PHILADELPHIA	3
6	Minnesota	37
20	Atlanta	36
14	Detroit	27
19	LOS ANGELES	16
17	N.Y. Jets	18
10	NEW ENGLAND	17
20	GREEN BAY	30

Use Name	Pos.	Hgt	Wgt	Age	Int	Pts
Glen Ray Hines	OT	6'5"	265	28		
Don Morrison	OT	6'5"	255	22		
Craig Robinson	OT	6'4"	250	23		
Carl Johnson	OG-OT	6'3"	240	22		
Jake Kupp	OG	6'3"	248	30		
Royce Smith	OG	6'3"	245	23		
Del Williams	OG	6'2"	240	26		
John Didion	C	6'4"	245	24		
Bob Kuziel	C	6'4"	255	22		
Wimpy Winther	C	6'4"	260	24		
Mike Crangle	DE	6'4"	243	25		
Richard Neal	DE	6'3"	254	24		6
Joe Owens	DE	6'2"	245	25		2
Faddie Tillman	DT-DE	6'5"	230	23		
Dave Long	DT	6'4"	245	27		
Doug Mooers	DT	6'6"	265	25		
Bob Pollard	DT	6'3"	245	23		
Wayne Coleman	LB	6'1"	230	26		
Joe Federspiel	LB	6'1"	225	22		
Willie Hall	LB	6'2"	217	22		
Ray Hester	LB	6'2"	215	23		
Bill Hobbs	LB	6'	220	26		
Dick Palmer (from BUF)	LB	6'2"	232	24		
Tom Roussel	LB	6'3"	235	27	2	
Tom Stincic	LB	6'2"	230	25		
Billy Hayes	DB	6'1"	175	25		
Hugo Hollas	DB	6'1"	190	27	1	
Delles Howell	DB	6'3"	202	25	1	
Ernie Jackson	DB	5'10"	173	22	3	6
Bivian Lee	DB	6'3"	200	24	4	
Tom Myers	DB	5'11"	184	21	3	
Doug Wyatt	DB	6'1"	195	25		6
Carlos Bell – Injury						
Al Dodd – Injury						
Dee Martin – Knee Injury						
Edd Hargett	QB	5'11"	190	25		
Archie Manning	QB	6'3"	204	23		12
Bob Gresham	HB	5'11"	195	24		18
Virgil Robinson	HB	5'11"	195	24		
Joe Williams	HB	6'	193	25		
James Ford	FB-HB	6'	200	22		
Bill Butler	FB	6'	218	22		12
Jim Strong	FB	6'1"	204	25		
Arthur Green	HB-FB	5'11"	198	24		
Dan Abramowicz	WR	6'1"	195	27		42
Margene Adkins	WR	5'10"	183	25		
Bob Newland	WR	6'2"	190	23		12
Cephus Weatherspoon	WR	6'1"	182	24		
Creston Whitaker	WR	6'2"	187	24		
Bob Brown	TE	6'3"	225	29		6
Dave Parks	TE	6'2"	203	30		36
Charlie Durkee	K	5'11"	165	28		18
Julian Fagan	K	6'3"	205	24		
Happy Feller	K	5'11"	185	23		28
Toni Linhart	K	6'	170	30		11

RUSHING

Last Name	No.	Yds	Avg	TD
SAN FRANCISCO FORTY NINERS				
V. Washington	141	468	3.3	3
Schreiber	118	420	3.6	2
Willard	100	345	3.5	4
Thomas	52	250	4.8	1
Spurrier	11	51	4.6	0
Cunningham	8	32	4.0	0
Reed	4	22	5.5	0
Kwalick	5	11	2.2	0
Isenbarger	3	9	3.0	0
Brodie	3	8	2.7	1
ATLANTA FALCONS				
Hampton	230	995	4.3	6
Malone	180	798	4.4	8
Profit	40	132	3.3	0
Berry	24	86	3.6	2
Ray	8	34	4.3	0
Belton	10	20	2.0	0
Mitchell	2	19	9.5	0
Sullivan	2	8	4.0	0
Burrow	3	3	1.0	0
Bell	1	−3	−3.0	0
LOS ANGELES RAMS				
Ellison	170	764	4.5	5
Bertelsen	123	581	4.7	5
Thomas	77	433	5.6	3
Smith	60	276	4.6	2
Josephson	18	75	4.2	0
Rentzel	7	71	10.1	1
Gabriel	14	16	1.1	1
Sweet	1	1	1.0	0
Beathard	1	−1	−1.0	0
Klein	1	−7	−7.0	0
NEW ORLEANS SAINTS				
Gresham	121	381	3.1	3
Manning	63	351	5.6	2
Butler	54	233	4.3	0
Strong	37	120	3.2	0
J. Williams	31	72	2.3	0
Green	14	51	3.6	0
Ford	11	28	2.5	0
V. Robinson	5	1	0.2	0
Parks	1	−7	−7.0	0

RECEIVING

Last Name	No.	Yds	Avg	TD
SAN FRANCISCO FORTY NINERS				
G. Wash'gton	46	918	20	12
V. Wash'gton	43	393	9	1
Kwalick	40	751	19	9
Schreiber	31	283	9	1
Willard	24	131	5	1
Thomas	15	148	10	0
Riley	11	156	14	1
Isenbarger	3	66	22	1
Witcher	3	22	7	1
Beasley	1	20	20	0
ATLANTA FALCONS				
Malone	50	585	12	2
Burrow	29	492	17	5
Mitchell	28	470	17	4
Hampton	23	244	11	1
Chesson	18	338	19	1
Profit	3	22	7	0
Snyder	1	19	19	0
Jarvis	1	18	18	0
Ray	1	14	14	0
Lamb	1	10	10	0
Belton	1	−1	−1	0
Berry	1	−9	−9	0
LOS ANGELES RAMS				
Snow	30	590	20	4
Bertelsen	29	331	11	1
Klein	29	330	11	1
Rentzel	27	365	14	1
Ellison	23	141	6	1
Smith	15	186	12	1
Josephson	14	170	12	1
Thomas	11	95	9	0
Gordon	3	29	10	1
Sweet	2	26	13	1
Love	1	19	19	1
NEW ORLEANS SAINTS				
Newland	47	579	12	2
Abramowicz	38	668	18	7
Parks	32	542	17	6
Gresham	29	192	7	0
Butler	25	226	9	2
J. Williams	16	116	7	0
Strong	14	123	9	0
Brown	11	175	16	1
Adkins	9	96	11	0
Green	7	49	7	0
Ford	1	9	9	0
Whitaker	1	6	6	0

PUNT RETURNS

Last Name	No.	Yds	Avg	TD
SAN FRANCISCO FORTY NINERS				
McGill	22	219	10	0
Taylor	21	145	7	0
Fuller	1	9	9	0
ATLANTA FALCONS				
Belton	17	110	6	0
Brown	8	71	9	0
Ellis	1	13	13	0
Small	1	0	0	0
LOS ANGELES RAMS				
Bertelson	16	232	15	0
Elmendorf	3	56	19	0
Love	10	39	4	0
Gordon	4	20	5	0
NEW ORLEANS SAINTS				
Myers	9	43	5	0
Adkins	7	0	0	0

KICKOFF RETURNS

Last Name	No.	Yds	Avg	TD
SAN FRANCISCO FORTY NINERS				
V. Washington	27	771	29	1
McGill	10	192	19	0
Schreiber	2	41	21	0
Nunley	1	21	21	0
Hoskins	2	17	9	0
Beard	2	−1	−1	0
ATLANTA FALCONS				
Hampton	25	535	21	0
Belton	21	441	21	0
Malone	2	37	19	0
Plummer	1	21	21	0
Germany	2	5	3	0
Chesson	1	0	0	0
LOS ANGELES RAMS				
Ellison	14	345	25	0
Thomas	8	212	27	0
Love	8	167	21	0
R. Williams	6	141	24	0
Gordon	4	141	35	0
Bertelsen	4	88	22	0
Clark	3	59	20	0
Howard	2	51	26	0
Pergine	3	46	15	0
Curran	4	37	9	0
NEW ORLEANS SAINTS				
Adkins	43	1020	24	0
Green	8	187	23	0
Strong	4	53	13	0
J. Williams	2	23	12	0
Butler	1	14	14	0
Hollas	2	9	5	0
Newland	1	6	6	0

PASSING – PUNTING – KICKING

SAN FRANCISCO FORTY NINERS

PASSING	Att	Comp	%	Yds	Yd/Att	TD	Int–	%	RK
Spurrier	269	147	55	1983	7.4	18	16–	6	4
Brodie	110	70	64	905	8.2	9	8–	7	
Isenbarger	1	0	0	0	0.0	0	0–	0	

PUNTING	No	Avg
McCann	64	39.7

KICKING	XP	Att	%	FG	Att	%
Gossett	41	42	98	18	29	62

ATLANTA FALCONS

PASSING	Att	Comp	%	Yds	Yd/Att	TD	Int–	%	RK
Berry	277	154	56	2158	7.8	13	12–	4	3
Sullivan	19	3	16	44	2.3	0	3–	16	

PUNTING	No	Avg
James	61	42.8

KICKING	XP	Att	%	FG	Att	%
Bell	31	31	100	16	30	53

LOS ANGELES RAMS

PASSING	Att	Comp	%	Yds	Yd/Att	TD	Int–	%	RK
Gabriel	323	165	51	2027	6.3	12	15–	5	9
Beathard	48	19	40	255	5.3	1	7–	15	

PUNTING	No	Avg
Chapple	53	44.2

KICKING	XP	Att	%	FG	Att	%
Ray	31	31	100	24	41	59

NEW ORLEANS SAINTS

PASSING	Att	Comp	%	Yds	Yd/Att	TD	Int–	%	RK
Manning	448	230	51	2781	6.2	18	21–	5	7
Gresham	1	0	0	0	0.0	0	0–	0	

PUNTING	No	Avg
Fagan	71	40.8

KICKING	XP	Att	%	FG	Att	%
Feller	10	11	91	6	11	55
Durkee	9	9	100	3	9	33
Linhart	5	5	100	2	5	40

1972 A.F.C. Perfect From Start to Finish

Vince Lombardi's Packers had never done it. George Halas' Chicago Bears had come close but always fallen short. But Don Shula's Miami Dolphins did it; they went through the season unbeaten and untied and won three more games in the playoffs to finish with a perfect 17-0-0 record. The Bears had finished the 1934 and 1942 regular seasons with unblemished records, but both squads lost in the NFL championship game. Before the NFL split up into divisions, the Canton Bulldogs had gone undefeated in 1922 and 1923 and the Green Bay Packers in 1929, but each of those teams had been tied during the season. Paul Brown's Cleveland Browns breezed through the 1948 AAFC season without a loss or tie, but they had not been able to repeat that achievement after coming over to the NFL. The Dolphins were the first NFL team to compile an absolutely perfect record for a season, and they were a young team which had still not reached full development.

EASTERN DIVISION

Miami Dolphins—Seven years ago the Dolphins had been created out of castoffs from the eight AFL teams; four years ago, they had finished on the bottom of the AFL's Eastern Division. But since Don Shula had taken over as coach in 1970, he had rebuilt, reorganized, and psyched the Dolphins into a powerhouse which rolled undefeated and untied through the 1973 season. The Miami defense was known as the "No-Name Defense," but those anonymous defenders allowed the fewest points in the NFL. After Bob Griese went out with an ankle injury in mid-season, veteran Earl Morrall stepped in at quarterback and kept the offense moving. The five Miami interior linemen—Norm Evans, Wayne Moore, Bob Keuchenberg, Larry Little, and Jim Langer—had all been cut loose by other pro teams, but the Dolphin blocking protected Morrall and cleared the way for runners Larry Csonka, Mercury Morris, and Jim Kiick. Csonka and Morris became the first teammates ever to gain 1,000 yards each in one season.

New York Jets—Quarterback Joe Namath stayed healthy all year and again wreaked havoc on defensive backs with his bullet passing, but the Jets nevertheless finished with a 7-7 record and out of the playoffs. The Jet defense unfortunately allowed points as readily as Namath and the offense could score them. None of the deep backs had a good year, while the front line was hurt by Gerry Philbin's disenchantment with coach Weeb Ewbank and John Elliott's slow recovery from knee surgery. The New York offensive cupboard was full. Running behind a line that was growing shopworn, John Riggins and Emerson Boozer balanced Namath's passing with consistently strong ball-carrying. But when Riggins and Boozer both went out of action late in the year with injuries, the Jet attack lost most of its spark.

Baltimore Colts—New owner Bob Irsay installed Joe Thomas as his general manager, and Thomas began ripping the team apart after it fell out of contention with four losses in the first five games. He fired coach Don McCafferty, ordered interim coach John Sandusky to bench veteran quarterback John Unitas in favor of younger Marty Domres, and one by one disposed of Baltimore veterans who had starred in the late 1960s and early 1970s. Before next season would begin, Thomas had traded off Unitas, Tom Matte, Dan Sullivan, Bill Curry, Bubba Smith, Fred Miller, Jerry Logan, Billy Newsome, Tom Nowatzke, and Norm Bulaich, and Bob Vogel retired.

Buffalo Bills—By the end of the opening game, starting offensive linemen Bruce Jarvis and Jim Reilly were out for the season with injuries. More blockers went onto the disabled list as the season progressed, and the Bills scoured the country for healthy offensive linemen to fill the breach. But even with the patchwork line, O. J. Simpson blossomed into stardom by running for 1,251 yards, the most in the NFL. Helping O. J. to prominence was head coach Lou Saban, who returned to the Bills with an offensive plan of going to Simpson twice as often as he had been used. Saban had quit the Bills after leading them to the AFL championship in 1965, but victories came harder with this Buffalo squad as only Walt Patulski, Don Croft, and Bobby James caused any excitement in the defensive platoon.

New England Patriots—General manager Upton Bell and head coach John Mazur battled with each other all season over how to build the Patriots. When the team won only three games all year, both Bell and Mazur were out of work by the end of the year. The biggest offensive problem was a deteriorating offensive line which exposed quarterback Jim Plunkett to severe punishment from enemy linemen. On defense, only Julius Adams and Jim Cheyunski provided any stability in the line and linebacking. Several veteran Patriots were lopped from the squad this year, as Jim Nance, Houston Antwine, Ron Sellers, and Don Webb all were casualties of a rebuilding program cursed with two dissenting architects. Before the season was over, coach Mazur had quit. In an unusual move to end an unusual season, the San Diego Chargers lent scout Phil Bengtson to the Patriots as interim head coach for the rest of the year.

CENTRAL DIVISION

Pittsburgh Steelers—Pittsburgh fans thoroughly enjoyed the Steelers' drive to their first title of any sort. One group of fans dubbed themselves "Franco's Army" and adopted rookie fullback Franco Harris as their favorite. Harris' power running had given the Pittsburgh attack a new dimension. Another group of fans, known as "Gerela's Gorillas," took place-kicker Roy Gerela as their idol. Appreciated by all Steeler fans were quarterback Terry Bradshaw and the very strong defensive unit. With both platoons playing well, the Steelers held a share of first place until December 3, when a 30-0 thumping of the Browns gave the team complete possession of the top rung in the division.

Cleveland Browns—The Browns' greatest asset was their ability to stay cool in pressure situations. Despite injuries in the defensive line, a chaotic linebacking situation, and problems in the offensive line, the Browns calmly beat the Bengals and Jets in the final two games to win the AFC wild-card berth in the playoffs. The partial retirement of Bill Nelsen put the quarterbacking burden squarely on Mike Phipps' shoulders, and the young passer responded with a season of steady progress as a leader. The Browns had strength at running back, with Leroy Kelly and Bo Scott, and in the secondary, where youngsters Clarence Scott and Tom Darden had become instant stars.

Cincinnati Bengals—The Bengals' season unfolded in three separate stages. First came the good start of four wins in the opening five games, then a mid-season slump of four losses in five games, and finally a late spurt of three wins in the last four games. Playing consistently well throughout the season was the Cincinnati defense, a unit strengthened by the addition of two top rookies in Sherman White and Tommy Casanova. Veteran Bengal defenders Mike Reid, Ron Carpenter, Bill Bergey, and Lemar Parrish shared with the rookies a wealth of talent, but the offense lacked the polished excellence of the defense; too many holes remained to be filled in this platoon. The Bengals needed a powerful running back and a speedy wide receiver, but few people bet against Paul Brown finding them in next year's draft as he had found his defense.

Houston Oilers—Owner Bud Adams used a long-term contract to lure head coach Bill Peterson away from Rice, but the new coach could not stop the deterioration of the Oilers. Outside of an early-season upset of the Jets, the Oilers served as the NFL's punching bag. Mid-season trades brought Fred Willis, Paul Robinson, and Dave Smith to Houston, but they could not help an offensive plagued with a porous line. On defense, the team's two best linemen, Elvin Bethea and Mike Tilleman, demanded to be traded; two starting linebackers, George Webster and Ron Pritchard, were traded in mid-season.

WESTERN DIVISION

Oakland Raiders—The Raiders had a knack for slipping new talent into the lineup while continuing to win without interruption. The defensive line, for instance, had been completely rebuilt in the last two seasons. Veterans like Ben Davidson, Tom Keating, and Carleton Oates had been eased aside in favor of youngsters Horace Jones, Art Thoms, Otis Sistrunk, and Tony Cline. The defense, meanwhile, suffered no letdown at all in stopping the run or pressuring the passer. At linebacker, the Raiders surrounded veteran Dan Conners with young outside men Phil Villipiano and Gerald Irons, and the secondary had veteran cornerbacks in Willie Brown and Nemiah Wilson and young safeties in George Atkinson and Jack Tatum. The offense had the same mixture of experience and youth, while the specialists ranged from rookie punt returner Cliff Branch to forty-four-year-old place-kicker George Blanda.

Kansas City Chiefs—Unable to win regularly at home, the Chiefs thus gave the Raiders only a weak challenge for the Western Division title. After years as an AFC power, the team was starting to crack under the weight of time. Safety Johnny Robinson retired, offensive linemen Ed Budde, Jim Tyrer, and Dave Hill were slowing down, and quarterback Len Dawson needed more rest. Other trouble spots for coach Hank Stram were receiver Elmo Wright's injury, a mediocre showing by the defensive ends, and a disappointing showing by rookie runner Jeff Kinney.

Denver Broncos—The Broncos followed the trend to hiring college coaches by signing John Ralston away from Stanford, but Ralston went out and traded for a veteran quarterback to lead the young Broncos on the field. Charley Johnson came over from Houston and gave the club a top passer and a poised offensive leader. With the Denver passing attack in good order, Floyd Little carried less of the offensive burden but still picked up 859 yards on the ground. Ralston traded away veteran defensive linemen Richard Jackson and Dave Costa, but the new unit of Lyle Alzado, Paul Smith, Pete Duranko, and Lloyd Voss kept pressure on opposing quarterbacks as the Broncos had their highest finish in ten years.

San Diego Chargers—Coach Harland Svare traded for some of the league's most famous oldsters and malcontents, bringing John Mackey, Deacon Jones, Lionel Aldridge, Dave Costa, Cid Edwards, Tim Rossovich, and Duane Thomas to San Diego. The Thomas deal was a complete washout, as Thomas' personal problems put him in no mood to play football. Injuries bothered Rossovich, and age had cut down on Mackey's skills, but the other acquisitions enjoyed good seasons in their new home. The defense suffered, however, when injuries decimated the secondary, and the offense was hurt by a difference in philosophy between quarterback John Hadl and offensive coach Bob Schnelker. Whereas Hadl had always run a wide-open passing attack, Schnelker insisted on a ball-control offense.

FINAL TEAM STATISTICS

OFFENSE

	BALT.	BUFF.	CIN.	CLEV.	DENV.	HOUS.	K.C.	MIAMI	N.ENG.	N.Y.	OAK.	PITT.	S.D.
FIRST DOWNS:													
Total	251	221	255	215	237	183	245	291	236	250	297	228	262
by Rushing	97	104	112	102	87	80	118	170	86	106	145	131	123
by Passing	124	98	122	101	132	88	116	102	126	117	122	79	116
by Penalty	30	19	21	12	18	15	11	19	24	27	30	18	23
RUSHING:													
Number	462	512	491	453	409	397	476	613	386	461	521	497	504
Yards	1894	2132	1996	1793	1838	1518	1915	2960	1532	2010	2376	2520	1995
Average Yards	4.1	4.2	4.1	4.0	4.5	3.8	4.0	4.8	4.0	4.4	4.6	5.1	4.0
Touchdowns	10	11	16	13	17	7	6	26	13	18	20	22	12
PASSING:													
Attempts	381	316	384	337	384	375	384	259	412	347	370	324	377
Completions	203	164	219	158	201	181	217	144	198	172	198	156	192
Completion Percentage	53.3	51.9	57.0	46.9	52.3	48.3	56.5	55.6	48.1	49.6	53.5	48.1	50.9
Passing Yards	2503	2012	2513	2135	2900	2045	2335	2235	2579	2930	2599	1958	2516
Avg. Yards per Attempt	6.6	6.4	6.5	6.3	7.6	5.5	6.1	8.6	6.3	8.4	7.0	6.0	6.7
Avg. Yards per Complet.	12.3	12.3	11.5	13.5	14.4	11.3	10.8	15.5	13.0	17.0	13.1	12.6	13.1
Time Tackled Passing	25	49	24	27	38	45	34	21	44	17	24	32	23
Yards Lost Tackled	210	411	192	219	266	372	297	159	452	153	230	247	212
Net Yards	2293	1601	2321	1916	2634	1673	2038	2076	2127	2777	2369	1711	2304
Touchdowns	15	16	10	13	19	10	20	17	10	21	23	12	15
Interceptions	12	24	11	19	23	23	20	12	28	22	15	12	28
Percent Intercepted	3.1	7.6	2.9	5.6	6.0	6.1	5.2	4.6	6.8	6.3	7.6	3.7	7.4
PUNTS:													
Number	57	80	66	81	60	85	66	44	75	51	55	66	45
Average Distance	42.1	38.8	42.1	43.2	40.1	41.0	44.8	39.4	38.1	39.3	36.9	43.6	40.3
PUNT RETURNS:													
Number	43	25	47	37	28	34	29	40	17	25	24	30	23
Yards	348	164	437	211	310	163	126	329	37	242	66	262	185
Average Yards	8.1	6.6	9.3	5.7	11.1	4.8	4.3	8.2	2.2	9.7	2.8	8.7	8.0
Touchdowns	0	0	2	0	1	0	0	0	0	1	0	0	0
KICKOFF RETURNS:													
Number	47	60	46	41	55	54	46	24	55	56	38	33	60
Yards	1321	1389	1018	933	1256	1093	1057	546	1293	1218	813	760	1273
Average Yards	28.1	23.2	22.1	22.8	22.8	20.2	23.0	22.8	23.5	21.8	21.4	23.0	21.2
Touchdowns	1	0	0	0	1	0	0	0	0	0	0	0	0
INTERCEPTION RETURNS:													
Number	23	23	20	13	10	6	24	26	10	19	25	28	24
Yards	331	369	326	154	109	93	396	286	223	282	328	395	310
Average Yards	14.4	16.0	16.3	11.8	10.9	15.5	16.5	11.0	22.3	14.8	13.1	14.1	12.9
Touchdowns	1	3	3	1	0	0	5	1	0	0	1	1	1
PENALTIES:													
Number	58	87	76	57	89	66	69	68	66	74	84	81	87
Yards	605	900	738	536	827	581	653	714	761	719	757	728	789
FUMBLES:													
Number	37	29	28	21	25	30	23	25	26	21	31	27	40
Number Lost	22	15	18	9	11	10	12	16	10	9	17	14	20
POINTS:													
Total	235	257	299	268	325	164	287	385	192	367	365	343	264
PAT Attempts	28	30	31	29	38	18	32	45	24	41	45	37	30
PAT Made	28	29	30	28	37	17	32	43	24	40	44	35	28
FG Attempts	39	24	40	27	29	21	36	37	16	37	26	41	31
FG Made	13	16	27	22	20	13	21	24	8	27	17	28	18
Percent FG Made	33.3	66.7	67.5	81.5	69.0	61.9	58.3	64.9	50.0	73.0	65.4	68.3	58.1
Safeties	0	0	1	0	0	0	0	0	0	0	0	1	1

DEFENSE

	BALT.	BUFF.	CIN.	CLEV.	DENV.	HOUS.	K.C.	MIAMI	N.ENG.	N.Y.	OAK.	PITT.	S.D.
FIRST DOWNS:													
Total	233	249	207	240	251	263	227	186	288	255	227	228	244
by Rushing	111	125	98	130	102	147	93	76	143	121	97	88	99
by Passing	109	95	92	89	123	100	116	96	124	118	104	116	124
by Penalty	13	29	17	21	26	16	18	14	21	16	26	24	21
RUSHING:													
Number	515	532	406	520	439	546	453	389	548	476	469	445	435
Yards	1989	2241	1815	2333	1668	2591	1805	1548	2717	2072	1764	1715	1673
Average Yards	3.9	4.2	4.5	4.5	3.8	4.7	4.0	4.0	5.0	4.4	3.8	3.9	3.8
Touchdowns	15	26	11	13	15	23	12	8	27	16	9	6	18
PASSING:													
Attempts	313	308	350	310	397	324	368	348	326	363	348	411	358
Completions	178	131	167	160	206	174	186	178	175	186	166	206	201
Completion Percentage	56.9	42.5	47.7	51.6	51.9	53.7	50.5	51.1	53.7	51.2	47.7	50.1	56.1
Passing Yards	2555	2148	2033	1994	2540	2315	2483	2029	2634	2888	2363	2393	2441
Avg. Yards per Attempt	8.2	7.0	5.8	6.4	6.4	7.1	6.7	5.8	8.1	8.0	6.8	5.8	6.8
Avg. Yards per Complet.	14.4	16.4	12.2	12.5	12.3	13.3	13.3	11.4	15.1	15.5	14.2	11.6	12.1
Time Tackled Passing	25	22	38	38	41	24	32	33	15	27	27	40	26
Yards Lost Tackled	232	197	296	258	357	172	261	280	101	251	211	337	233
Net Yards	2323	1951	1737	1736	2183	2143	2222	1749	2533	2637	2152	2056	2208
Touchdowns	15	19	11	14	19	12	17	10	24	18	14	9	18
Interceptions	23	23	20	13	10	6	24	26	10	19	25	28	24
Percent Intercepted	7.3	7.5	5.7	4.2	2.5	1.9	6.5	7.5	3.1	5.2	7.2	6.8	6.7
PUNTS:													
Number	71	65	84	74	66	61	61	68	48	56	56	74	56
Average Distance	39.0	39.5	42.4	40.9	45.2	42.1	40.3	41.1	40.4	39.4	42.5	40.3	38.4
PUNT RETURNS:													
Number	29	39	26	46	28	31	38	17	34	23	28	37	17
Yards	204	329	152	357	249	299	328	67	366	239	215	169	157
Average Yards	7.0	8.4	5.8	7.8	8.9	9.6	8.6	3.9	10.8	10.4	7.7	4.6	9.2
Touchdowns	0	1	0	0	1	1	0	0	1	0	0	0	1
KICKOFF RETURNS:													
Number	50	29	44	50	54	28	43	56	32	47	59	54	53
Yards	1091	644	984	1198	1246	547	1083	1283	784	1386	1393	1190	1225
Average Yards	21.8	22.2	22.4	24.0	23.1	19.5	25.2	22.9	24.5	29.5	23.6	22.0	23.1
Touchdowns	0	0	0	0	0	0	0	0	0	1	1	0	1
INTERCEPTION RETURNS:													
Number	12	24	11	19	23	23	20	12	28	22	15	12	28
Yards	169	305	70	145	441	319	278	249	490	271	178	195	229
Average Yards	14.1	12.7	6.4	7.6	19.2	13.9	13.9	20.8	17.5	12.3	11.9	16.3	8.2
Touchdowns	0	1	0	0	6	3	0	2	2	1	0	1	0
PENALTIES:													
Number	84	72	69	63	83	79	66	70	88	86	83	77	75
Yards	826	685	581	557	784	741	643	659	862	856	801	712	679
FUMBLES:													
Number	22	20	30	39	27	29	35	32	23	21	22	37	26
Number Lost	13	8	9	16	12	18	19	20	14	12	12	20	10
POINTS:													
Total	252	377	229	249	350	380	254	171	446	324	248	175	344
PAT Attempts	30	47	24	27	41	40	30	21	54	37	27	18	41
PAT Made	27	47	23	27	39	39	29	18	54	36	26	17	41
FG Attempts	24	27	29	29	33	40	31	19	36	33	37	27	28
FG Made	15	16	20	20	21	33	15	9	22	22	20	16	19
Percent FG Made	62.5	59.3	69.0	69.0	63.6	82.5	48.4	47.4	61.1	66.7	54.1	59.3	67.9
Safeties	0.	0	1	0	1	1	0	0	1	0	0	1	0

CONFERENCE PLAYOFFS

December 23, at Pittsburgh (Attendance 50,327)

SCORING

PITTSBURGH	0	0	3	10–13
OAKLAND	0	0	0	7– 7

Third Quarter
- PIT. Gerela, 18 yard field goal

Fourth Quarter
- PIT. Gerela, 29 yard field goal
- OAK. Stabler, 30 yard rush PAT–Blanda (kick)
- PIT. Harris, 60 yard pass from Bradshaw PAT–Gerela (kick)

TEAM STATISTICS

PITT.		OAK.
13	First Downs–Total	13
7	First Downs–Rushing	9
6	First Downs–Passing	4
0	First Downs–Penalty	0
0	Fumbles–Number	3
0	Fumbles–Lost Ball	2
1	Penalties–Number	2
5	Yards Penalized	15
1	Missed Field Goals	0
64	Offensive Plays	65
252	Net Yards	216
3.9	Average Gain	3.3
1	Giveaways	4
4	Takeaways	1
+3	Difference	–3

INDIVIDUAL STATISTICS

PITTSBURGH	No.	Yds.	Avg.	OAKLAND	No.	Yds.	Avg.
RUSHING							
Harris	18	64	3.6	Smith	14	57	4.1
Fuqua	16	25	1.6	Hubbard	14	44	3.1
Bradshaw	2	19	9.5	Stabler	1	30	30.0
	36	108	3.0	Davis	2	7	3.5
					31	138	4.5
RECEIVING							
Harris	5	96	19.2	Chester	3	40	13.3
Shanklin	3	55	18.3	Biletnikoff	3	28	9.3
Fuqua	1	11	11.0	Smith	2	8	4.0
McMakin	1	9	9.0	Banaszek	1	12	12.0
Young	1	4	4.0	Siani	1	7	7.0
	11	175	15.9	Otto	1	5	5.0
				Hubbard	1	2	2.0
					12	102	8.5
PUNTING							
Walden	6		48.2	DePoyster	7		45.1
PUNT RETURNS							
Edwards	3	39	13.0	Atkinson	1	37	37.0
KICKOFF RETURNS							
Pearson	1	21	21.0	Davis	1	26	26.0
INTERCEPTION RETURNS							
Ham	1	0	0.0	Wilson	1	7	7.0
Russell	1	0	0.0				
	2	0	0.0				

PASSING

	Att.	Comp.	Comp. Pct.	Yds.	Int.	Yds/ Att.	Yds/ Comp.	Yards Lost Tackled
PITTSBURGH								
Bradshaw	25	11	44.0	175	1	7.0	15.9	3–31
OAKLAND								
Lamonica	18	6	33.0	45	2	2.5	7.5	
Stabler	12	6	50.0	57	0	4.8	9.5	
	30	12	40.0	102	2	3.4	8.5	4–24

December 24, at Miami (Attendance 78,916)

SCORING

MIAMI	10	0	0	10–20
CLEVELAND	0	0	7	7–14

First Quarter
- MIA. Babb, 6 yard return of blocked punt PAT–Yepremiam (kick)
- MIA. Yepremiam, 40 yard field goal

Third Quarter
- CLE. Phipps, 5 yard rush PAT – Cockroft (kick)

Fourth Quarter
- MIA. Yepremiam, 46 yard field goal
- CLE. Hooker, 27 yard pass from Phipps PAT–Cockroft (kick)
- MIA. Kiick, 8 yard rush PAT–Yepremiam (kick)

TEAM STATISTICS

MIAMI		CLEVE.
17	First Downs–Total	15
11	First Downs–Rushing	9
4	First Downs–Passing	6
2	First Downs–Penalty	0
2	Fumbles–Number	2
2	Fumbles–Lost Ball	0
3	Penalties–Number	3
25	Yards Penalized	25
2	Missed Field Goals	0
64	Offensive Plays	57
272	Net Yards	283
4.3	Average Gain	5.0
2	Giveaways	5
5	Takeaways	2
+3	Difference	–3

INDIVIDUAL STATISTICS

MIAMI	No.	Yds.	Avg.	CLEVELAND	No.	Yds.	Avg.
RUSHING							
Morris	15	72	4.8	Scott	16	94	5.9
Kiick	14	50	3.6	Phipps	8	47	5.9
Warfield	2	41	20.5	Brown	4	13	3.3
Csonka	12	32	2.7	Kelly	4	11	2.8
Morrall	4	3	0.8		32	165	5.2
	47	198	4.2				
RECEIVING							
Twilley	3	33	11.0	Scott	4	30	7.5
Warfield	2	50	25.0	Hooker	3	53	17.7
Kiick	1	5	5.0	Kelly	1	27	27.0
	6	88	14.7	Morin	1	21	21.0
					9	131	14.6
PUNTING							
Seiple	5		42.0	Cockroft	6		34.7
PUNT RETURNS							
Scott	1	1	1.0	Darden	1	38	38.0
				Kelley	1	8	8.0
					2	46	23.0
KICKOFF RETURNS							
None				Lefear	3	56	18.7
INTERCEPTION RETURNS							
Swift	2	19	9.5	None			
Anderson	2	12	6.0				
Johnson	1	33	33.0				
	5	64	12.8				

PASSING

	Att.	Comp.	Comp. Pct.	Yds.	Int.	Yds/ Att.	Yds/ Comp.	Yards Lost Tackled
MIAMI								
Morrall	13	6	46.2	88	0	6.8	14.7	4–14
CLEVELAND								
Phipps	23	9	39.1	131	5	5.7	14.6	2–13

MIAMI DOLPHINS 14-0-0 Don Shula

Scores of Each Game			
20	Kansas City	10	
34	HOUSTON	13	
16	Minnesota	14	
27	N.Y. Jets	17	
24	SAN DIEGO	10	
24	BUFFALO	23	
23	Baltimore	0	
30	Buffalo	16	
52	NEW ENGLAND	0	
28	N.Y. JETS	24	
31	ST. LOUIS	10	
37	New England	21	
23	N.Y. Giants	13	
16	BALTIMORE	0	

Use Name	Pos.	Hgt	Wgt	Age	Int	Pts
Doug Crusan	OT	6'5"	250	26		
Norm Evans	OT	6'5"	252	29		
Wayne Moore	OT	6'6"	265	27		
Bob Kuechenberg	OG	6'3"	247	24		
Larry Little	OG	6'1"	265	26		
Al Jenkins	OT-OG	6'2"	245	26		
Jim Langer	C	6'2"	250	24		
Howard Kindig	OT-C	6'6"	260	31		
Vern Den Herder	DE	6'6"	250	23	1	
Bill Stanfill	DE	6'5"	250	25		
Bob Matheson	LB-DE	6'4"	240	27		
Jim Dunaway	DT	6'4"	277	30		
Manny Fernandez	DT	6'2"	248	26		
Baldy Moore	DT	6'5"	265	26		
Bob Heinz	DE-DT	6'6"	270	25		

Use Name	Pos.	Hgt	Wgt	Age	Int	Pts
Larry Ball	LB	6'6"	225	22		
Nick Buoniconti	LB	5'11"	220	31	2	
Mike Kolen	LB	6'2"	220	24	1	
Jesse Powell	LB	6'1"	215	25		
Doug Swift	LB	6'3"	228	23	3	
Dick Anderson	DB	6'2"	196	26	3	6
Charlie Babb	DB	6'	190	22	1	
Tim Foley	DB	6'	194	24	3	
Curtis Johnson	DB	6'2"	196	24	3	
Lloyd Mumphford	DB	5'11"	180	25	4	6
Jake Scott	DB	6'	188	27	5	
Karl Noonan – Knee Injury						
Jim Riley – Knee Injury						

Use Name	Pos.	Hgt	Wgt	Age	Int	Pts
Jim Del Gaizo	QB	6'1"	198	25		
Bob Griese	QB	6'1"	190	27		6
Earl Morrall	QB	6'1"	206	38		6
Hubert Ginn	HB	5'11"	188	25		6
Ed Jenkins	HB	6'2"	210	22		
Jim Kiick	HB	5'11"	215	26		36
Mercury Morris	HB	5'10"	190	25		72
Larry Csonka	FB	6'3"	237	25		36
Charlie Leigh	FB	5'11"	205	26		
Marlin Briscoe	WR	5'10"	178	26		24
Otto Stowe	WR	6'2"	188	23		12
Howard Twilley	WR	5'10"	185	28		18
Paul Warfield	WR	6'	185	29		18
Marv Fleming	TE	6'4"	235	30		6
Jim Mandich	TE	6'3"	224	24		18
Larry Seiple	TE	6'	215	27		
Billy Lothridge	K	6'1"	200	28		
Garo Yepremian	K	5'8"	172	28		115

NEW YORK JETS 7-7-0 Weeb Ewbank

Scores of Each Game			
41	Buffalo	24	
44	Baltimore	34	
20	Houston	26	
17	MIAMI	27	
41	New England	13	
24	BALTIMORE	20	
34	NEW ENGLAND	10	
17	WASHINGTON	35	
41	BUFFALO	3	
24	Miami	28	
20	Detroit	37	
18	NEW ORLEANS	17	
16	Oakland	24	
10	CLEVELAND	26	

Use Name	Pos.	Hgt	Wgt	Age	Int	Pts
Winston Hill	OT	6'4"	270	30		
Bob Svihus	OT	6'4"	245	29		
John Mooring	C-OT	6'6"	255	25		
Roger Finnie	OG	6'3"	245	26		
Dave Herman	OG	6'2"	255	30		
Randy Rasmussen	OG	6'2"	255	27		6
Roy Kirksey	DT-OG	6'1"	265	24		
John Schmitt	C	6'4"	250	29		
Gerry Philbin	DE	6'2"	245	31		
Joey Jackson	DT-DE	6'4"	257	23		
Mark Lomas	DT-DE	6'4"	245	24		
John Elliott	DT	6'4"	244	27		
John Little	DT	6'3"	235	25		
Steve Thompson	DT	6'5"	237	27		
Ed Galigher	DE-DT	6'4"	255	21		

Use Name	Pos.	Hgt	Wgt	Age	Int	Pts
Al Atkinson	LB	6'1"	230	29	1	
Ralph Baker	LB	6'3"	228	30	2	
John Ebersole	LB	6'3"	227	23		
Larry Grantham	LB	6'	210	33		
Mike Taylor	LB	6'1"	230	22	1	
Paul Crane	C-LB	6'2"	212	28	1	
Bill Zapalac	DE-LB	6'4"	225	24		
Chris Farasopoulos	DB	5'11"	190	23	2	6
W. K. Hicks	DB	6'1"	195	29	1	
Gus Holloman	DB	6'3"	195	26	1	
Rich Sowells	DB	6'	175	23	2	
Steve Tannen	DB	6'1"	194	24	7	
Earlie Thomas	DB	6'1"	190	26	1	
Phil Wise	DB	6'	190	23		

Use Name	Pos.	Hgt	Wgt	Age	Int	Pts
Bob Davis	QB	6'3"	205	27		
Joe Namath	QB	6'2"	200	29		
Hank Bjorklund	BH	6'1"	200	22		
Emerson Boozer	HB	5'11"	195	29		84
Cliff McClain	HB	6'	217	24		
John Riggins	FB	6'2"	233	23		48
Matt Snell	FB	6'2"	220	30		
Steve Harkey	HB-FB	6'	215	23		
Jerome Barkum	WR	6'3"	215	22		12
Eddie Bell	WR	5'10"	160	24		12
Don Maynard	WR	6'	180	36		12
Rocky Turner	WR	6'	190	22		
Rich Caster	TE	6'5"	228	23		60
Wayne Stewart	TE	6'7"	213	25		6
Bobby Howfield	K	5'9"	180	35		121
Steve O'Neal	K	6'3"	185	26		

BALTIMORE COLTS 5-9-0 Don McCafferty John Sandusky

Scores of Each Game			
3	ST. LOUIS	10	
34	N.Y. JETS	44	
17	Buffalo	0	
20	SAN DIEGO	23	
0	DALLAS	21	
20	N.Y. Jets	24	
0	MIAMI	23	
24	New England	17	
21	San Francisco	24	
20	Cincinnati	19	
31	NEW ENGLAND	0	
35	BUFFALO	7	
10	Kansas City	24	
0	Miami	16	

Use Name	Pos.	Hgt	Wgt	Age	Int	Pts
Tom Drougas	OT	6'4"	257	22		
Dennis Nelson	OT	6'5"	260	26		
Bob Vogel	OT	6'5"	250	30		
Cornelius Johnson	OG	6'2"	245	29		
Glenn Ressler	OG	6'3"	250	28		
John Shinners	OG	6'2"	254	25		
Dan Sullivan	OG	6'3"	250	33		
Bill Curry	C	6'2"	236	29		
Ken Mendenhall	C	6'3"	235	24		
Dick Amman	DE	6'5"	234	21		
Roy Hilton	DE	6'6"	240	27		
Billy Newsome	DE	6'4"	250	24		
Chuck Hinton	DT	6'5"	264	33		
Fred Miller	DT	6'3"	250	31		
Jim Bailey	DE-DT	6'5"	255	24		

Use Name	Pos.	Hgt	Wgt	Age	Int	Pts
Mike Curtis	LB	6'2"	232	29	4	6
Randy Edmunds	LB	6'2"	225	26		
Ted Hendricks	LB	6'7"	220	24	2	
Bill Laskey	LB	6'2"	235	29		
Ray May	LB	6'1"	230	27	2	
Stan White	LB	6'1"	225	22		
Lonnie Hepburn	DB	5'11"	180	23	1	
Rex Kern	DB	5'11"	190	23		
Bruce Laird	DB	6'	185	22	1	
Jerry Logan	DB	6'1"	190	31	4	
Jack Mildren	DB	6'1"	200	22		
Nelson Munsey	DB	6'1"	185	24		6
Charlie Stukes	DB	6'3"	212	28	5	
Rick Volk	DB	6'3"	195	27	4	
Bubba Smith – Knee Injury						

Use Name	Pos.	Hgt	Wgt	Age	Int	Pts
Marty Domres	QB	6'3"	220	25		6
Johnny Unitas	QB	6'1"	196	39		
Tom Matte	HB	6'	214	33		6
Don McCauley	HB	6'1"	207	23		30
Lydell Mitchell	HB	5'11"	204	23		12
Don Nottingham	FB	5'10"	210	23		18
Tom Nowatzke	FB	6'3"	230	29		
Norm Bulaich	HB-FB	6'1"	218	25		6
Glenn Doughty	WR	6'2"	204	21		
Willie Franklin	WR	6'2"	194	22		
Sam Havrilak	WR	6'2"	195	24		36
Eddie Hinton	WR	6'	200	25		6
Jim O'Brien	WR	6'	195	25		75
Cotton Speyrer	WR	6'	175	23		
Tom Mitchell	TE	6'2"	215	28		24
John Mosier	TE	6'3"	220	24		
David Lee	K	6'4"	230	28		
Boris Shlapak	K	6'	165	22		4

BUFFALO BILLS 4-9-1 Lou Saban

Scores of Each Game			
24	N.Y. JETS	41	
27	SAN FRANCISCO	20	
0	BALTIMORE	17	
38	NEW ENGLAND	14	
16	Oakland	28	
23	Miami	24	
21	PITTSBURGH	38	
16	MIAMI	30	
3	N.Y. Jets	41	
27	New England	24	
10	Cleveland	27	
7	Baltimore	35	
21	DETROIT	21	
24	Washington	17	

Use Name	Pos.	Hgt	Wgt	Age	Int	Pts
Paul Costa	OT	6'4"	268	30		
Dave Foley	OT	6'5"	255	24		
Donnie Green	OT	6'7"	285	24		
Willie Young	OT	6'4"	270	24		
Bill Adams	OG	6'2"	250	22		
Dick Hart	OG	6'2"	250	29		
Reggie McKenzie	OG	6'4"	235	22		
Jeff Curchin	OT-OG	6'6"	255	24		
Remi Prudhomme (from NO)	C-OG	6'4"	250	30		
Tom Beard	C	6'6"	280	23		
Bruce Jarvis	C	6'7"	245	23		
John Matlock	C	6'4"	250	27		
Bobby Penchion	OG-C	6'5"	255	23		
Walt Patulski	DE	6'6"	252	22		
Louis Ross	DE	6'6"	242	25		
Al Cowlings	DT-DE	6'5"	250	25		
Frank Cornish	DT	6'6"	285	28		
Don Croft	DT	6'3"	252	23		
Steve Okoniewski	DT	6'3"	247	23		
Jerry Patton	DT	6'3"	250	26		
Mike McBath	DE-DT	6'4"	250	26		

Use Name	Pos.	Hgt	Wgt	Age	Int	Pts
Edgar Chandler	LB	6'3"	225	26		
Dick Cunningham	LB	6'2"	232	27		
Dale Farley	LB	6'3"	235	23	1	
Paul Guidry	LB	6'3"	233	28	1	
Ken Lee	LB	6'4"	232	23	6	6
Jeff Lyman	LB	6'2"	230	22		
Andy Selfridge	LB	6'4"	218	23		
Mike Stratton	LB	6'3"	240	30	1	
Dave Washington	TE-LB	6'5"	220	23	1	
Leon Garror	DB	6'	180	24		
Tony Greene	DB	5'10"	170	23	3	6
Robert James	DB	6'1"	185	25	1	
John Pitts	DB	6'4"	215	27	1	
John Saunders	DB	6'3"	202	22		
Maurice Tyler	DB	6'	188	22	4	
Alvin Wyatt	DB	5'10"	180	24	4	6
Mike Clark – Injury						
Irv Goode – Knee Injury						

Use Name	Pos.	Hgt	Wgt	Age	Int	Pts
Leo Hart	QB	6'4"	203	23		
Dennis Shaw	QB	6'2"	215	25		
Mike Taliaferro	QB	6'2"	205	30		
Randy Jackson	HB	6'	220	23		6
O. J. Simpson	HB	6'2"	214	25		36
Ted Koy	FB-HB	6'1"	215	24		
Jim Braxton	FB	6'2"	226	23		36
Wayne Patrick	FB	6'2"	245	26		6
Bob Chandler	WR	6'	180	23		30
Linzy Cole (from HOU)	WR	5'11"	170	24		
Dwight Harrison (from DEN)	WR	6'1"	178	23		
J. D. Hill	WR	6'1"	193	23		30
Bob Christiansen	TE	6'4"	230	23		
Jan White	TE	6'2"	216	23		12
Spike Jones	K	6'2"	190	25		
John Leypoldt	K	6'2"	224	26		77
Bill McKinley – Injury						
Jim Reilly – Illness						

NEW ENGLAND PATRIOTS 3-11-0 John Mazur Phil Bengtson

Scores of Each Game			
7	CINCINNATI	31	
21	ATLANTA	20	
24	WASHINGTON	23	
14	Buffalo	38	
13	N.Y. JETS	41	
3	Pittsburgh	33	
10	N.Y. Jets	34	
17	BALTIMORE	24	
0	Miami	52	
24	BUFFALO	27	
0	Baltimore	31	
21	MIAMI	37	
17	New Orleans	10	
21	Denver	45	

Use Name	Pos.	Hgt	Wgt	Age	Int	Pts
Mike Montler	OT	6'4"	255	28		
Tom Neville	OT	6'4"	255	29		
Bob Reynolds	OT	6'6"	265	31		
Sam Adams	OG	6'3"	252	23		
Halvor Hagen	OG	6'5"	253	25		
Len St. Jean	OG	6'1"	250	30		
Bill Lenkaitis	C-OG	6'3"	260	26		
Jon Morris	C	6'4"	254	29		
Ron Berger	DE	6'8"	285	28		
Jim White	DE	6'3"	256	23		
Dennis Wirgowski	DT-DE	6'5"	250	24		
Rick Cash	DT	6'5"	260	26		
Dave Rowe	DT	6'6"	280	27		
Julius Adams	DE-DT	6'3"	260	24		

Use Name	Pos.	Hgt	Wgt	Age	Int	Pts
Ron Acks	LB	6'2"	220	27		
Dick Blanchard	LB	6'3"	225	23	1	
Jim Cheyunski	LB	6'2"	225	26		
Ralph Cindrich	LB	6'1"	228	22		
Ron Kadziel	LB	6'4"	230	23		
Ed Weisacosky	LB	6'	220	28		
Ron Bolton	DB	6'2"	180	22		
Larry Carwell	DB	6'1"	190	28	1	6
Rickie Harris	DB	6'	182	29	3	
George Hoey	DB	5'10"	170	25	1	
Honor Jackson	DB	6'1"	195	23	4	
Art McMahon	DB	5'11"	190	26		
John Outlaw	DB	5'10"	180	27		
Clarence Scott	DB	6'2"	200	28		

Use Name	Pos.	Hgt	Wgt	Age	Int	Pts
Brian Dowling	QB	6'2"	210	25		18
Jim Plunkett	QB	6'3"	220	24		6
Carl Garrett	HB	5'11"	215	25		30
Bob Gladieux	HB	5'11"	195	25		
Jack Maitland	HB	6'1"	210	24		
Henry Matthews	HB	6'3"	203	23		
John Tarver	FB	6'3"	227	23		12
Josh Ashton	HB-FB	6'1"	205	23		24
Hubie Bryant	WR	5'10"	168	26		
Tom Reynolds	WR	6'3"	200	23		12
Reggie Rucker	WR	6'2"	190	24		18
Pat Studstill	WR	6'1"	175	34		
Randy Vataha	WR	5'10"	175	23		12
Tom Beer	TE	6'4"	235	27		
Bob Windsor	TE	6'4"	226	29		6
Charlie Gogolak	K	5'10"	170	27		27
Mike Walker	K	6'	190	22		21

MIAMI DOLPHINS

RUSHING

Last Name	No.	Yds	Avg	TD
Csonka	213	1117	5.2	6
Morris	190	1000	5.3	12
Kiick	137	521	3.8	5
Ginn	27	142	5.3	1
Leigh	21	79	3.8	0
Morrall	17	67	3.9	1
Warfield	4	23	5.8	0
Griese	3	11	3.7	1
DelGaizo	1	0	0.0	0

RECEIVING

Last Name	No.	Yds	Avg	TD
Warfield	29	606	21	3
Kiick	21	147	7	1
Twilley	20	364	18	3
Briscoe	16	279	17	4
Morris	15	168	11	0
Stowe	13	276	21	2
Fleming	13	156	12	1
Mandich	11	168	15	3
Csonka	5	48	10	0
Ginn	1	23	23	0

PUNT RETURNS

Last Name	No.	Yds	Avg	TD
Leigh	22	210	10	0
Scott	13	100	8	0
Anderson	5	19	4	0

KICKOFF RETURNS

Last Name	No.	Yds	Avg	TD
Morris	14	334	24	0
Leigh	6	153	26	0
Matheson	2	34	17	0
Ginn	1	25	25	0
Briscoe	1	0	0	0

PASSING – PUNTING – KICKING

PASSING	Att	Comp	%	Yds	Yd/Att	TD	Int–	%	RK
Morrall	150	83	55	1360	9.1	11	7–	5	1
Griese	97	53	55	638	6.6	4	4–	4	
DelGaizo	9	5	56	165	18.3	2	1–	11	
Briscoe	3	3	100	72	24.0	0	0–	0	

PUNTING	No	Avg
Seiple	36	39.9
Lothridge	4	37.5
Anderson	4	36.8

KICKING	XP	Att	%	FG	Att	%
Yepremian	43	45	96	24	37	65

NEW YORK JETS

RUSHING

Last Name	No.	Yds	Avg	TD
Riggins	207	944	4.6	7
Boozer	120	549	4.6	11
McClain	59	305	5.2	0
Harkey	45	129	2.9	0
Bjorklund	15	42	2.8	0
Davis	6	32	5.3	0
Namath	6	8	1.3	0
Caster	2	6	3.0	0
Bell	1	–5	–5.0	0

RECEIVING

Last Name	No.	Yds	Avg	TD
Caster	39	833	21	10
Bell	35	629	18	2
Maynard	29	510	18	2
Riggins	21	230	11	1
Barkum	16	304	19	2
Boozer	11	142	13	3
Harkey	9	114	13	0
McClain	6	88	15	0
Bjorklund	4	54	14	0
Stewart	2	26	13	1

PUNT RETURNS

Last Name	No.	Yds	Avg	TD
Farasopoulos	17	179	11	1
Turner	5	38	8	0
Hicks	3	25	8	0

KICKOFF RETURNS

Last Name	No.	Yds	Avg	TD
Farasopoulos	26	627	24	0
Wise	9	211	23	0
Bjorklund	7	150	21	0
Hicks	4	73	24	0
Turner	3	57	19	0
McClain	2	45	23	0
Kirksey	2	33	17	0
Snell	1	14	14	0
Zapalac	1	8	8	0
Barkum	1	0	0	0

PASSING – PUNTING – KICKING

PASSING	Att	Comp	%	Yds	Yd/Att	TD	Int–	%	RK
Namath	324	162	50	2816	8.7	19	21–	6	8
Davis	22	10	46	114	5.2	2	1–	5	
McClain	1	0	0	0	0.0	0	0–	0	

PUNTING	No	Avg
O'Neal	51	39.3

KICKING	XP	Att	%	FG	Att	%
Howfield	40	41	98	27	37	73

BALTIMORE COLTS

RUSHING

Last Name	No.	Yds	Avg	TD
McCauley	178	675	3.8	2
Nottingham	123	466	3.8	3
L. Mitchell	45	215	4.8	1
Matte	33	137	4.2	0
Domres	30	137	4.6	1
Bulaich	27	109	4.0	1
Havrilak	12	72	6.0	2
Doughty	2	33	16.5	0
Unitas	3	15	5.0	0
Nowatzke	3	11	3.7	0
O'Brien	3	9	3.0	0
Mildren	3	8	2.7	0
T. Mitchell	0	7	0.0	0

RECEIVING

Last Name	No.	Yds	Avg	TD
T. Mitchell	40	494	12	4
Havrilak	33	571	17	4
McCauley	30	256	9	2
Nottingham	25	191	7	0
L. Mitchell	18	147	8	1
Matte	14	182	13	1
O'Brien	11	263	24	2
Hinton	11	146	13	1
Bulaich	9	55	6	0
Speyrer	8	114	14	0
Doughty	3	31	10	0
Mosier	1	53	53	0

PUNT RETURNS

Last Name	No.	Yds	Avg	TD
Laird	34	303	9	0
Volk	5	25	5	0
Logan	4	20	5	0

KICKOFF RETURNS

Last Name	No.	Yds	Avg	TD
Laird	29	843	29	0
McCauley	13	377	29	1
Bulaich	1	62	62	0
Nottingham	2	38	19	0
Mildren	1	1	1	0
Hendricks	1	0	0	0

PASSING – PUNTING – KICKING

PASSING	Att	Comp	%	Yds	Yd/Att	TD	Int–	%	RK
Domres	222	115	52	1392	6.3	11	6	3	6
Unitas	157	88	56	1111	7.1	4	6–	4	4
Havrilak	1	0	0	0	0.0	0	0–	0	
Mildren	1	0	0	0	0.0	0	0–	0	

PUNTING	No	Avg
Lee	57	42.1

KICKING	XP	Att	%	FG	Att	%
O'Brien	24	24	100	13	31	42
Shlapak	4	4	100	0	8	0

BUFFALO BILLS

RUSHING

Last Name	No.	Yds	Avg	TD
Simpson	291	1251	4.3	6
Braxton	116	453	3.9	5
Shaw	35	138	3.9	0
Patrick	35	130	3.7	0
Jackson	17	57	3.4	0
B. Chandler	3	27	9.0	0
L. Hart	5	19	3.8	0
Taliaferro	5	19	3.8	0
Jones	2	18	9.0	0
Hill	1	11	11.0	0
Harrison	1	9	9.0	0
Koy	1	9	9.0	0

RECEIVING

Last Name	No.	Yds	Avg	TD
Hill	52	754	15	5
B. Chandler	33	528	16	5
Simpson	27	198	7	0
Braxton	24	232	10	1
White	12	148	12	2
Patrick	8	42	5	1
Jackson	2	21	11	1
Harrison	1	16	16	0
Koy	1	9	9	0
Washington	1	4	4	0

PUNT RETURNS

Last Name	No.	Yds	Avg	TD
Wyatt	11	85	8	0
Cole	7	35	5	0
Hill	4	24	6	0
Greene	2	18	9	0
Harrison	1	2	2	0

KICKOFF RETURNS

Last Name	No.	Yds	Avg	TD
Cole	18	456	25	0
Wyatt	17	432	25	0
Greene	15	378	25	0
Koy	5	63	13	0
Selfridge	3	36	12	0
Hill	2	32	16	0
Simpson	1	21	21	0
Braxton	1	12	12	0
Prudhomme	1	0	0	0

PASSING – PUNTING – KICKING

PASSING	Att	Comp	%	Yds	Yd/Att	TD	Int–	%	RK
Shaw	258	136	53	1666	6.5	14	17–	7	9
Taliaferro	33	16	48	176	5.3	1	4–	12	
L. Hart	15	6	40	53	3.5	0	3–	20	
Simpson	8	5	63	113	14.1	1	0–	0	
Jones	2	1	50	4	2.0	0	0–	0	

PUNTING	No	Avg
Jones	80	38.8

KICKING	XP	Att	%	FG	Att	%
Leypoldt	29	30	97	16	24	67

NEW ENGLAND PATRIOTS

RUSHING

Last Name	No.	Yds	Avg	TD
Ashton	128	546	4.3	3
Garrett	131	488	3.7	5
Plunkett	36	230	6.4	1
Tarver	42	132	3.1	1
Gladieux	24	56	2.3	0
Dowling	7	35	5.0	3
Maitland	13	33	2.5	0
Studstill	1	11	11.0	0
Rucker	3	5	1.7	0
Windsor	1	–4	–4.0	0

RECEIVING

Last Name	No.	Yds	Avg	TD
Rucker	44	681	15	3
Windsor	33	383	12	1
Garrett	30	410	14	0
Vataha	25	369	15	2
Ashton	22	207	9	1
Gladieux	19	192	10	0
Tarver	11	112	10	1
T. Reynolds	8	152	19	2
Maitland	4	33	8	0
Beer	2	40	20	0

PUNT RETURNS

Last Name	No.	Yds	Avg	TD
Garrett	6	36	6	0
Harris	4	5	1	0
Carwell	5	2	0	0
Gladieux	2	–6	–3	0

KICKOFF RETURNS

Last Name	No.	Yds	Avg	TD
Garrett	16	410	26	0
Ashton	15	309	21	0
Rucker	8	227	28	0
Hoey	9	210	23	0
Matthews	3	74	25	0
Maitland	3	48	16	0
Beer	1	15	15	0

PASSING – PUNTING – KICKING

PASSING	Att	Comp	%	Yds	Yd/Att	TD	Int–	%	RK
Plunkett	355	169	48	2196	6.2	8	25–	7	14
Dowling	54	29	54	383	7.1	2	1–	2	
Garrett	1	0	0	0	0.0	0	1–100		
Gladieux	1	0	0	0	0.0	0	1–100		
Studstill	1	0	0	0	0.0	0	0–	0	

PUNTING	No	Avg
Studstill	75	38.1

KICKING	XP	Att	%	FG	Att	%
Walker	15	15	100	2	8	25
Gogolak	9	9	100	6	8	75

PITTSBURGH STEELERS 11-3-0 Chuck Noll

Scores of Each Game		
34	OAKLAND	28
10	Cincinnati	15
25	St. Louis	19
13	Dallas	17
24	HOUSTON	7
33	NEW ENGLAND	3
38	Buffalo	21
40	CINCINNATI	17
16	KANSAS CITY	7
24	Cleveland	26
23	MINNESOTA	10
30	CLEVELAND	0
9	Houston	3
24	San Diego	2

Use Name	Pos.	Hgt	Wgt	Age	Int	Pts
Gordon Gravelle	OT	6'5"	250	23		
Jon Kolb	OT	6'2"	262	25		
Gerry Mullins	OG-OT	6'3"	235	23		6
Sam Davis	OG	6'1"	255	28		
Bruce Van Dyke	OG	6'2"	255	28		
Mel Holmes	OT-OG	6'3"	250	22		
Jim Clack	C	6'3"	250	24		
Ray Mansfield	C	6'3"	255	31		
L.C. Greenwood	DE	6'5"	245	25		
Craig Hanneman	DE	6'3"	240	23		
Dwight White	DE	6'4"	250	23		
Steve Furness	DT	6'4"	255	21		
Joe Greene	DT	6'4"	270	25		
Ernie Holmes	DT	6'3"	260	24		
Ben McGee	DT	6'2"	260	30		

Bob Adams – Injury

Use Name	Pos.	Hgt	Wgt	Age	Int	Pts
Ed Bradley	LB	6'2"	240	22		
Henry Davis	LB	6'3"	235	29	2	6
Jack Ham	LB	6'3"	220	23	7	6
Andy Russell	LB	6'3"	225	30		
Brian Stenger	LB	6'4"	230	25		
George Webster (from HOU)	LB	6'4"	223	26		
Carl Winfrey	LB	6'	230	23		
Ralph Anderson	DB	6'2"	180	23	3	2
Chuck Beatty (to STL)	DB	6'2"	205	26	2	
Mel Blount	DB	6'3"	205	24	3	6
Lee Calland	DB	6'	190	31		
John Dockery	DB	6'	186	27		
Glen Edwards	DB	6'	185	25	1	
John Rowser	DB	6'1"	185	28	4	
Mike Wagner	DB	6'1"	196	23	6	

John Brown – Injury

Use Name	Pos.	Hgt	Wgt	Age	Int	Pts
Terry Bradshaw	QB	6'3"	218	23		42
Joe Gilliam	QB	6'2"	187	21		
Terry Hanratty	QB	6'1"	210	24		
Rocky Bleier	HB	5'11"	205	26		
Preston Pearson	HB	6'1"	205	27		
Franco Harris	FB-HB	6'2"	230	22		66
Warren Bankston	FB	6'4"	235	25		
Steve Davis	HB-FB	6'1"	218	22		6
John Fuqua	HB-FB	5'11"	200	25		24
Frank Lewis	WR	6'1"	196	25		30
Barry Pearson	WR	5'11"	185	22		
Ron Shanklin	WR	6'1"	180	25		18
Al Young	WR	6'1"	195	23		
Larry Brown	TE	6'4"	225	23		6
John McMakin	TE	6'3"	232	21		6
Roy Gerela	K	5'10"	185	24		119
Bobby Walden	K	6'	190	34		

CLEVELAND BROWNS 10-4-0 Nick Skorich

Scores of Each Game		
10	GREEN BAY	26
27	Philadelphia	17
27	CINCINNATI	6
7	KANSAS CITY	31
0	CHICAGO	17
23	Houston	17
27	Denver	20
20	HOUSTON	0
21	San Diego	17
26	PITTSBURGH	24
27	BUFFALO	10
0	Pittsburgh	30
27	Cincinnati	24
26	N.Y. Jets	10

Use Name	Pos.	Hgt	Wgt	Age	Int	Pts
Joe Carollo	OT	6'2"	265	32		
Doug Dieken	OT	6'5"	237	23		
Bob McKay	OT	6'5"	260	24		
Chris Morris	OT	6'3"	250	22		
John Demarie	C-OG-OT	6'3"	246	27		
Gene Hickerson	OG	6'3"	252	37		
Bubba Pena	OG	6'2"	250	23		
Craig Wycinsky	OG	6'3"	243	24		
Jim Copeland	C-OG	6'2"	243	27		
Bob DeMarco	C	6'3"	248	34		
Fred Hoaglin	C	6'4"	246	28		
Wes Grant	DE	6'3"	245	25		
Rich Jackson (from DEN)	DE	6'2"	255	31		
Nick Roman	DE	6'3"	235	24	1	6
Ron Snidow	DE	6'4"	247	30		
Bob Briggs	DT-DE	6'4"	258	27	1	6
Cotton Fest	DT	6'2"	255	22		
Walter Johnson	DT	6'3"	263	29	1	
George Wright	DT	6'3"	265	25		
Jerry Sherk	DE-DT	6'4"	258	24		

Use Name	Pos.	Hgt	Wgt	Age	Int	Pts
Billy Andrews	LB	6'	220	27	1	
John Garlington	LB	6'1"	218	26	1	
Charlie Hall	LB	6'3"	220	23	1	
Rick Kingrea	LB	6'1"	233	23		
Dale Lindsey	LB	6'3"	225	29		
Mel Long	LB	6'	228	25		
Jim Houston	DE-LB	6'2"	236	35		
Cliff Brooks	DB	6'1"	190	23		
Thom Darden	DB	6'2"	195	22	3	
Ben Davis	DB	5'11"	180	26	3	
Mike Howell (to MIA)	DB	6'1"	190	29	1	
Bobby Majors	DB	6'1"	193	23		
Clarence Scott	DB	6'	180	23		6
Walt Sumner	DB	6'1"	195	25		

Joe Jones – Knee Injury

Use Name	Pos.	Hgt	Wgt	Age	Int	Pts
Don Horn	QB	6'2"	195	27		
Bill Nelsen	QB	6'	195	31		
Mike Phipps	QB	6'2"	208	24		30
Leroy Kelly	HB	6'	202	30		30
Bill LeFear	HB	5'11"	197	22		
Ken Brown	FB-HB	5'10"	203	26		12
Bo Cornell	FB	6'1"	215	23		
Bo Scott	FB	6'3"	215	29		12
Charlie Brinkman	WR	6'2"	208	23		
Fair Hooker	WR	6'1"	190	25		12
Frank Pitts	WR	6'2"	200	28		48
Gloster Richardson	WR	6'	200	29		
Paul Staroba	WR	6'3"	204	23		6
Chip Glass	TE	6'4"	235	25		
Milt Morin	TE	6'4"	236	30		6
Don Cockroft	K	6'1"	195	27		94

CINCINNATI BENGALS 8-6-0 Paul Brown

Scores of Each Game		
31	New England	7
15	PITTSBURGH	10
6	Cleveland	27
21	DENVER	10
23	Kansas City	16
12	Los Angeles	15
30	HOUSTON	7
17	Pittsburgh	40
14	OAKLAND	20
19	BALTIMORE	20
13	Chicago	3
13	N.Y. GIANTS	10
24	CLEVELAND	27
61	Houston	17

Use Name	Pos.	Hgt	Wgt	Age	Int	Pts
Vern Holland	OT	6'5"	270	24		
Stan Walters	OT	6'6"	270	24		
Rufus Mayes	OG-OT	6'5"	260	24		
Guy Dennis	OG	6'2"	255	25		
Steve Lawson	OG	6'3"	265	23		
Pat Matson	OG	6'1"	245	28		
Howard Fest	OT-OG	6'6"	262	26		
Tom DeLeone	C-OG	6'2"	252	22		
Bob Johnson	C	6'5"	260	26		
Royce Berry	DE	6'3"	250	26		
Ron Carpenter	DE	6'4"	260	24		
Sherman White	DE	6'5"	255	23		2
Steve Chomyszak	DT	6'5"	270	27		
Ken Johnson	DT	6'5"	265	24		
Mike Reid	DT	6'3"	250	25		

Use Name	Pos.	Hgt	Wgt	Age	Int	Pts
Doug Adams	LB	6'	227	23	3	
Ken Avery	LB	6'1"	230	28		
Al Beauchamp	LB	6'2"	237	28	1	
Bill Bergey	LB	6'2"	243	27		
Tim Kearney	LB	6'2"	227	21		
Jim LeClair	LB	6'2"	226	21		
Bill Peterson	LB	6'3"	226	27		
Ron Pritchard (from HOU)	LB	6'1"	235	25		
Tommy Casanova	DB	6'2"	202	22	5	6
Neal Craig	DB	6'1"	190	24	2	6
Bernard Jackson	DB	6'	173	22	1	
Ernie Kellerman	DB	6'	183	28		
Lemar Parrish	DB	5'11"	184	24	5	18
Ken Riley	DB	6'	180	25	3	

Greg Cook – Shoulder Injury
Sandy Durko – Injury

Use Name	Pos.	Hgt	Wgt	Age	Int	Pts
Ken Anderson	QB	6'1"	211	23		18
Virgil Carter	QB	6'1"	198	26		12
Dave Lewis	QB	6'2"	218	26		
Essex Johnson	HB	5'9"	197	25		36
Reece Morrison (from CLE)	HB	6'	207	26		
Doug Dressler	FB	6'3"	226	24		42
Jess Phillips	HB-FB	6'1"	205	25		6
Drew Buie	WR	6'2"	185	25		
Charlie Joiner (from HOU)	WR	5'11"	188	24		12
Chip Myers	WR	6'4"	210	27		18
Speedy Thomas	WR	6'1"	170	25		6
Bruce Coslet	TE	6'3"	220	26		6
Mike Kelly	TE	6'4"	222	24		
Bob Trumpy	TE	6'6"	228	27		12
Pete Watson	TE	6'1"	210	22		
Horst Muhlmann	K	6'1"	220	32		111

HOUSTON OILERS 1-13-0 Bill Peterson

Scores of Each Game		
17	Denver	30
13	Miami	34
26	N.Y. JETS	20
0	OAKLAND	34
7	Pittsburgh	24
17	CLEVELAND	23
7	Cincinnati	30
0	Cleveland	20
17	PHILADELPHIA	18
10	GREEN BAY	23
20	San Diego	34
10	Atlanta	20
3	PITTSBURGH	9
17	CINCINNATI	61

Use Name	Pos.	Hgt	Wgt	Age	Int	Pts
Lavert Carr	OT	6'5"	260	28		
Gene Ferguson	OT	6'7"	300	24		
Tom Funchess	OT	6'5"	265	27		
Buzz Highsmith	C-OT	6'4"	255	29		
Soloman Freelon	OG	6'2"	250	21		
Ralph Miller	OG	6'4"	260	23		
Tom Regner	OG	6'1"	255	28		
Ron Saul	OG	6'2"	255	24		
Calvin Hunt	C	6'3"	245	24		
Guy Murdock	C	6'2"	245	21		
Allen Aldridge	DE	6'6"	260	27		
Elvin Bethea	DE	6'3"	262	26		
Council Rudolph	DE	6'3"	260	22		
Pat Holmes	DT-DE	6'5"	250	32		
Ron Billingsley	DT	6'8"	290	27		
Lee Brooks	DT	6'5"	255	24		
Mike Tilleman	DT	6'5"	280	28		
Greg Sampson	DE-DT	6'6"	260	21		

Use Name	Pos.	Hgt	Wgt	Age	Int	Pts
Garland Boyette	LB	6'1"	235	32		
Phil Croyle	LB	6'3"	220	24		
Rich Lewis	LB	6'3"	220	22		
Floyd Rice	LB	6'3"	225	23		
Guy Roberts	LB	6'1"	215	22		
Willie Alexander	DB	6'2"	195	22	1	
Bob Atkins	DB	6'3"	210	26	2	
John Charles	DB	6'1"	192	28	2	
Ken Houston	DB	6'3"	195	27		
Benny Johnson	DB	5'11"	178	24	1	
Zeke Moore	DB	6'2"	196	28		
Jim Tolbert	DB	6'3"	202	28		

Lynn Dickey – Hip Injury
Elbert Drungo – Knee Injury

Use Name	Pos.	Hgt	Wgt	Age	Int	Pts
Ed Baker	QB	6'2"	198	23		
Kent Nix	QB	6'1"	195	28		
Dan Pastorini	QB	6'3"	215	23		12
Al Johnson	HB	6'	200	22		
Paul Robinson (from CIN)	HB	6'	198	27		18
Willie Rodgers	HB	6'	210	23		12
Ward Walsh (to GB)	HB	6'	210	23		6
Hoyle Granger	FB	6'1"	225	28		
Robert Holmes	FB	5'9"	220	26		
Fred Willis (from CIN)	FB	6'	212	24		12
Lewis Jolley	HB-FB	6'	210	22		
Ken Burrough	WR	6'4"	210	24		24
Rhett Dawson	WR	6'1"	185	23		6
Dave Smith (from PIT)	WR	6'2"	205	25		
Alvin Reed	TE	6'5"	235	28		
Jim Beirne	WR-TE	6'2"	196	25		6
Skip Butler	K	6'2"	200	24		51
Mark Moseley	K	5'11"	182	24		5

PITTSBURGH STEELERS

RUSHING

Last Name	No.	Yds	Avg	TD
Harris	188	1055	5.6	10
Fuqua	150	665	4.4	4
Bradshaw	58	346	6.0	7
P. Pearson	67	264	3.9	0
Steve Davis	20	85	4.3	1
Lewis	3	68	22.7	0
Bankston	7	20	2.9	0
Bleier	1	17	17.0	0
McMakin	1	0	0.0	0
Gilliam	2	0	0.0	0

RECEIVING

Last Name	No.	Yds	Avg	TD
Shanklin	38	669	18	3
Lewis	27	391	14	5
McMakin	21	277	13	1
Harris	21	180	9	1
Fuqua	18	152	8	0
P. Pearson	11	79	7	0
Young	6	86	14	0
Brown	1	13	13	1
Bankston	1	5	5	0
Steve Davis	1	5	5	0
Mullins	1	3	3	1

PUNT RETURNS

Last Name	No.	Yds	Avg	TD
Edwards	22	202	9	0
Lewis	5	56	11	0
Bleier	2	1	1	0
P. Pearson	1	3	3	0

KICKOFF RETURNS

Last Name	No.	Yds	Avg	TD
P. Pearson	13	292	22	0
Steve Davis	7	207	30	0
Harris	8	183	23	0
Bleier	2	40	20	0
Bankston	1	20	20	0
Edwards	1	18	18	0
McMakin	1	0	0	0

PASSING – PUNTING – KICKING

PASSING	Att	Comp	%	Yds	Yd/Att	TD	Int–	%	RK
Bradshaw	308	147	48	1887	6.1	12	12–	4	12
Gilliam	11	7	64	48	4.4	0	0–	0	
Hanratty	4	2	50	23	5.8	0	0–	0	
Walden	1	0	0	0	0.0	0	0–	0	

PUNTING	No	Avg
Walden	65	43.8
Gerela	1	29.0

KICKING	XP	Att	%	FG	Att	%
Gerela	35	36	97	28	41	68

CLEVELAND BROWNS

RUSHING

Last Name	No.	Yds	Avg	TD
Kelly	224	811	3.6	4
B. Scott	123	571	4.6	2
Phipps	60	256	4.3	5
Brown	32	114	3.6	2
Pitts	3	29	9.7	0
Cornell	7	8	1.1	0
Lefear	3	6	2.0	0
Nelsen	1	−2	−2.0	0

RECEIVING

Last Name	No.	Yds	Avg	TD
Pitts	36	620	17	8
Hooker	32	441	14	2
Morin	30	540	18	1
Kelly	23	204	9	1
B. Scott	23	172	8	0
Brown	5	64	13	0
Glass	5	61	12	0
Cornell	2	7	4	0
Staroba	1	19	19	1
Richardson	1	7	7	0

PUNT RETURNS

Last Name	No.	Yds	Avg	TD
Majors	16	96	6	0
Darden	15	61	4	0
Kelly	5	40	8	0
Sumner	1	14	14	0

KICKOFF RETURNS

Last Name	No.	Yds	Avg	TD
Brown	20	473	24	0
Majors	10	222	22	0
Lefear	6	138	23	0
Johnson	2	33	17	0

PASSING – PUNTING – KICKING

PASSING	Att	Comp	%	Yds	Yd/Att	TD	Int–	%	RK
Phipps	305	144	47	1994	6.5	13	16–	5	11
Nelsen	31	14	45	141	4.6	0	3–	10	
Kelly	1	0	0	0	0.0	0	0–	0	

PUNTING	No	Avg
Cockroft	81	43.2

KICKING	XP	Att	%	FG	Att	%
Cockroft	28	29	97	22	27	81

CINCINNATI BENGALS

RUSHING

Last Name	No.	Yds	Avg	TD
E. Johnson	212	825	3.9	4
Dressler	128	565	4.4	6
Phillips	48	207	4.3	1
Anderson	22	94	4.3	3
Carter	12	57	4.8	2
Lewis	1	15	15.0	0
Joiner	3	14	4.7	0
Morrison	1	2	2.0	0

RECEIVING

Last Name	No.	Yds	Avg	TD
Myers	57	792	14	3
Trumpy	44	500	11	2
Dressler	39	348	9	1
E. Johnson	29	420	14	2
Joiner	24	439	18	2
Thomas	17	171	10	1
Phillips	10	50	5	0
Coslet	5	48	10	1
Buie	1	5	5	0

PUNT RETURNS

Last Name	No.	Yds	Avg	TD
Casanova	30	289	10	1
Parrish	15	141	9	1
E. Johnson	2	7	4	0

KICKOFF RETURNS

Last Name	No.	Yds	Avg	TD
Jackson	21	509	24	0
Parrish	15	348	23	0
Joiner	5	88	18	0
Morrison	3	67	22	0
Casanova	1	34	34	0
Lewis	1	15	15	0
E. Johnson	1	13	13	0
Dennis	1	11	11	0
Kelly	1	0	0	0

PASSING – PUNTING – KICKING

PASSING	Att	Comp	%	Yds	Yd/Att	Td	Int–	%	RK
Anderson	301	171	57	1918	6.4	7	7–	2	5
Carter	82	47	57	579	7.1	3	4–	5	

PUNTING	No	Avg
Lewis	66	42.1

KICKING	XP	Att	%	FG	Att	%
Muhlmann	30	31	97	27	40	68

HOUSTON OILERS

RUSHING

Last Name	No.	Yds	Avg	TD
Willis	134	461	3.4	0
Robinson	107	449	4.2	3
Pastorini	38	205	5.4	2
Rodgers	71	204	2.9	2
Granger	42	175	4.2	0
Holmes	43	172	4.0	0
Walsh	8	36	4.5	0
A. Johnson	11	13	1.2	0
Baker	1	9	9.0	0
Nix	3	3	1.0	0

RECEIVING

Last Name	No.	Yds	Avg	TD
Willis	45	297	7	2
Smith	30	316	11	0
Burrough	26	521	20	4
Reed	19	251	13	0
Granger	15	74	5	0
Robinson	14	112	8	0
Beirne	7	95	14	1
Dawson	6	78	13	1
Rodgers	6	61	10	0
Holmes	6	32	5	0
A. Johnson	6	24	4	0
Walsh	4	22	6	0

PUNT RETURNS

Last Name	No.	Yds	Avg	TD
Houston	25	148	6	0
Moore	7	15	2	0
A. Johnson	2	0	0	0

KICKOFF RETURNS

Last Name	No.	Yds	Avg	TD
Rodgers	17	335	20	0
B. Johnson	13	230	18	0
Jolley	11	267	24	0
A. Johnson	7	154	22	0
Holmes	2	39	20	0
Moore	1	22	22	0
Granger	1	5	5	0

PASSING – PUNTING – KICKING

PASSING	Att	Comp	%	Yds	Yd/Att	Td	Int–	%	RK
Pastorini	299	144	48	1711	5.7	7	12–	4	13
Nix	63	33	52	287	4.6	3	6–	9	
Baker	10	4	40	47	4.7	0	4–	40	
Willis	4	1	25	16	4.0	0	1–	25	

PUNTING	No	Avg
Pastorini	82	41.2
Butler	3	35.0

KICKING	XP	Att	%	FG	Att	%
Butler	15	16	94	12	19	63
Moseley	2	2	100	1	2	50

OAKLAND RAIDERS 10-3-1 John Madden

Scores of Each Game		
28	Pittsburgh	34
20	Green Bay	14
17	SAN DIEGO	17
34	Houston	0
28	BUFFALO	16
23	DENVER	30
45	LOS ANGELES	17
14	Kansas City	27
20	Cincinnati	14
37	Denver	20
26	KANSAS CITY	3
21	San Diego	19
24	N.Y. JETS	16
28	CHICAGO	21

Use Name	Pos.	Hgt	Wgt	Age	Int	Pts
Bob Brown	OT	6'4"	280	29		
Art Shell	OT	6'5"	265	25		
Paul Seiler	C-OT	6'4"	260	26		
George Buehler	OG	6'2"	260	25		
Gene Upshaw	OG	6'5"	255	27		
John Vella	OG	6'4"	255	22		
Jim Otto	C	6'2"	255	34		
Dave Dalby	OG-C	6'2"	240	21		
Tony Cline	DE	6'2"	240	24	1	
Horace Jones	DE	6'3"	240	23		
Tom Keating	DT	6'3"	247	29		
Carleton Oats	DT	6'2"	260	29		
Art Thoms	DT	6'5"	250	25	1	
Otis Sistrunk	DE-DT	6'4"	255	24	1	

Ben Davidson – Heel Injury

Use Name	Pos.	Hgt	Wgt	Age	Int	Pts
Joe Carroll	LB	6'1"	220	22		
Dan Conners	LB	6'1"	230	30	1	
Gerald Irons	LB	6'2"	230	25	2	
Terry Mendenhall	LB	6'1"	210	23		
Gus Otto	LB	6'2"	220	29		
Greg Slough	LB	6'3"	230	24		
Phil Villapiano	LB	6'1"	222	23	3	6
Butch Atkinson	DB	6'	180	25	4	
Willie Brown	DB	6'1"	190	31	4	
Tommy Maxwell	DB	6'2"	195	25		
Jack Tatum	DB	5'10"	200	23	4	6
Skip Thomas	DB	6'1"	205	22		
Jimmy Warren	DB	5'11"	175	33		
Nemiah Wilson	DB	6'	165	29	4	

Warren Koegel – Injury

Use Name	Pos.	Hgt	Wgt	Age	Int	Pts
George Blanda	QB	6'1"	215	44		95
Daryle Lamonica	QB	6'2"	215	31		
Ken Stabler	QB	6'3"	215	26		
Clarence Davis	HB	5'10"	190	23		36
Don Highsmith	HB	6'	200	24		6
Charlie Smith	HB	6'1"	205	26		60
Marv Hubbard	FB	6'1"	225	26		24
Peter Banaszak	HB-FB	5'11"	210	28		6
Jeff Queen	TE-FB	6'11"	220	26		
Fred Biletnikoff	WR	6'1"	190	29		42
Cliff Branch	WR	5'11"	170	24		
Mike Siani	WR	6'2"	195	22		30
Ray Chester	TE	6'3"	225	24		48
Bob Moore	TE	6'3"	220	23		6
Jerry DePoyster	K	6'1"	200	26		

KANSAS CITY CHIEFS 8-6-0 Hank Stram

Scores of Each Game		
10	MIAMI	20
20	New Orleans	17
45	Denver	24
31	Cleveland	7
16	CINCINNATI	23
20	PHILADELPHIA	21
26	San Diego	14
27	OAKLAND	14
7	Pittsburgh	16
17	SAN DIEGO	27
3	Oakland	26
24	DENVER	21
24	BALTIMORE	10
17	Atlanta	14

Use Name	Pos.	Hgt	Wgt	Age	Int	Pts
Dave Hill	OT	6'5"	260	31		
Sid Smith	OT	6'4"	260	24		
Jim Tyrer	OT	6'6"	280	33		
Ed Budde	OG	6'5"	265	31		
George Daney	OG	6'3"	240	25		
Larry Gagner	OG	6'3"	268	28		
Mo Moorman	OG	6'5"	252	28		
Mike Oriard	C	6'4"	223	24		
Jack Rudnay	C	6'3"	240	24		
Aaron Brown	DE	6'5"	255	28		
Marv Upshaw	DE	6'3"	260	25		
Wilbur Young	DT-DE	6'6"	285	23		
Buck Buchanan	DT	6'7"	270	32		
Curley Culp	DT	6'1"	265	26		
Ed Lothamer	DT	6'5"	270	29		
George Seals	DT	6'2"	260	29		

Use Name	Pos.	Hgt	Wgt	Age	Int	Pts
Bobby Bell	LB	6'4"	228	32	3	6
Keith Best	LB	6'3"	220	22		
Willie Lanier	LB	6'1"	245	27	2	
Jim Lynch	LB	6'1"	235	27		
Bob Stein	LB	6'2"	235	24		
Clyde Werner	LB	6'4"	225	24	1	
Nate Allen	DB	5'10"	170	24	1	
Jim Kearney	DB	6'2"	206	29	5	24
Jim Marsalis	DB	5'11"	194	26	2	
Larry Marshall	DB	5'10"	195	22		
Kerry Reardon	DB	5'11"	180	23		
Mike Sensibaugh	DB	5'11"	192	23	8	
Emmitt Thomas	DB	6'2"	192	29	2	

Warren McVea–Knee Injury

Use Name	Pos.	Hgt	Wgt	Age	Int	Pts
Len Dawson	QB	6'	190	38		
Mike Livingston	QB	6'3"	212	26		
Mike Adamle	HB	5'9"	197	22		6
Ed Podolak	HB	6'1"	204	25		36
Wendell Hayes	FB	6'2"	220	31		18
Jim Otis	FB	6'	220	24		
Jeff Kinney	HB-FB	6'2"	215	22		6
Dennis Homan	WR	6'1"	180	26		6
Bruce Jankowski	WR	5'11"	185	23		
Otis Taylor	WR	6'2"	215	29		36
Bob West	WR	6'4"	218	21		18
Elmo Wright	WR	6'	190	23		
Willie Frazier	TE	6'4"	234	29		30
Morris Stroud	TE	6'10"	255	26		6
Jan Stenerud	K	6'2"	187	29		95
Jerrel Wilson	K	6'4"	222	30		

DENVER BRONCOS 5-9-0 John Ralston

Scores of Each Game		
30	HOUSTON	17
14	San Diego	37
24	KANSAS CITY	45
10	Cincinnati	21
20	MINNESOTA	23
30	Oakland	23
20	CLEVELAND	27
17	N.Y. Giants	29
16	Los Angeles	10
20	OAKLAND	37
20	Atlanta	23
21	Kansas City	24
38	SAN DIEGO	13
45	NEW ENGLAND	21

Use Name	Pos.	Hgt	Wgt	Age	Int	Pts
Mike Current	OT	6'4"	274	26		
Marv Montgomery	OT	6'6"	255	24	1	
Rick Sharp	OT	6'3"	265	24		
George Goeddeke	OG-OT	6'3"	253	27		
Bill Cottrell	OG	6'3"	255	27		
Larron Jackson	OG	6'3"	270	23		
Mike Schnitker	OG	6'3"	245	25		
Tommy Lyons	C-OG	6'2"	228	24		
Larry Kaminski	C	6'2"	245	27		
Bobby Maples	C	6'3"	250	29		
Lyle Alzado	DE	6'3"	252	23		
John Hoffman (from STL)	DE	6'7"	260	29		
Lloyd Voss	DT-DE	6'4"	255	30		
Tom Domres	DT	6'3"	260	25		
Paul Smith	DT	6'3"	256	27		
Pete Duranko	DE-DT	6'2"	250	28		

Walt Barnes – Injury

Use Name	Pos.	Hgt	Wgt	Age	Int	Pts
Ken Criter	LB	5'11"	223	25		
Fred Forsberg	Lb	6'1"	235	28		
Bob Geddes	LB	6'2"	240	26		
Tom Graham	LB	6'2"	235	22	2	
Bill McKoy	LB	6'3"	235	24		
Chip Myrtle	LB	6'2"	225	27		
Don Parish	LB	6'1"	220	24		
Mike Simone	LB	6'	210	22		
Cornell Gordon	DB	6'	187	31		
Charlie Greer	DB	6'	205	26	2	6
Leroy Mitchell	DB	6'2"	190	27	3	
Randy Montgomery	DB	5'11"	182	25		6
Steve Preece (from PHI)	DB	6'1"	195	25	1	
George Saimes	DB	5'10"	188	30		
Bill Thompson	DB	6'1"	200	25	1	
Bill West	DB	5'10"	185	24		

Sam Brunelli – Injury
Jack Gehrke – Injury

Use Name	Pos.	Hgt	Wgt	Age	Int	Pts
Mike Ernst	QB	6'1"	190	21		
Charley Johnson	QB	6'	190	35		
Steve Ramsey	QB	6'2"	210	24		12
Floyd Little	HB	5'10"	196	30		78
Fran Lynch	FB-HB	6'1"	205	26		12
Clem Turner	FB	6'1"	236	27		
Bobby Anderson	HB-FB	6'	208	24		12
Joe Dawkins	HB-FB	5'11"	223	24		12
Jim Krieg	WR	5'9"	172	23		
Haven Moses (from BUF)	WR	6'3"	205	26		36
Rod Sherman	WR	6'	190	27		18
Jerry Simmons	WR	6'1"	190	29		12
Bill Van Heusen	WR	6'1"	200	26		6
Bill Masters	TE	6'5"	240	28		18
Riley Odoms	TE	6'4"	230	22		6
Jim Turner	K	6'2"	205	31		97

Jerry Inman – Injury

SAN DIEGO CHARGERS 4-9-1 Harland Svare

Scores of Each Game		
3	San Francisco	34
37	DENVER	14
17	Oakland	17
23	Baltimore	20
10	Miami	24
20	Detroit	34
14	KANSAS CITY	26
28	DALLAS	34
17	CLEVELAND	21
27	Kansas City	17
34	HOUSTON	20
19	OAKLAND	21
13	Denver	38
2	PITTSBURGH	24

Use Name	Pos.	Hgt	Wgt	Age	Int	Pts
Ira Gordon	OT	6'3"	268	24		
Terry Owens	OT	6'6"	268	28		
Russ Washington	OT	6'6"	294	25		
Ernie Wright	OT	6'4"	270	32		
Walt Sweeney	OG	6'3"	256	31		
Ralph Wenzel	OG	6'3"	250	29		
Doug Wilkerson	OG	6'2"	250	25		
Sam Gruneisen	C	6'1"	250	31		
Carl Mauck	C	6'3"	245	25		6
Lionel Aldridge	DE	6'4	245	30		
Deacon Jones	DE	6'5"	250	33		
Cal Snowden	DE	6'4"	253	25		
Lee Thomas	DE	6'5"	246	25		
Dave Costa	DT	6'2"	260	30		2
Ron East	DT	6'4"	236	29		
Kevin Hardy	DT	6'5"	276	27		
Greg Wojcik	DT	6'6"	268	26		

Use Name	Pos.	Hgt	Wgt	Age	Int	Pts
John Andrews	LB	6'3"	225	23		
Bob Babich	LB	6'2"	230	25	2	
Pete Barnes	LB	6'3"	240	27	1	
Lee Roy Caffey	LB	6'3"	250	32	1	
Pete Lazetich	LB	6'3"	245	22		
Rick Redman	LB	5'11"	222	29	1	
Tim Rossovich	LB	6'4"	240	26	1	
Ray White	LB	6'1"	242	23		
Joe Beauchamp	DB	6'	182	28	6	6
Reggie Berry	DB	6'	190	23		
Chuck Detwiler	DB	6'	185	24		
Lenny Dunlap	DB	6'1"	195	23	5	
Chris Fletcher	DB	5'11"	185	23		
Bob Howard	DB	6'1"	175	27		
Ray Jones	DB	6'	187	24		
Bryant Salter	DB	6'4"	194	22	7	

Harris Jones – Injury
Mel Rogers – Shoulder Injury

Use Name	Pos.	Hgt	Wgt	Age	Int	Pts
Wayne Clark	QB	6'2"	200	25		
John Hadl	QB	6'2"	214	32		6
Mike Garrett	HB	5'9"	200	28		42
John Sykes	HB	5'11"	195	23		
Jesse Taylor	HB	6'	200	24		6
Oscar Dragon	FB-HB	6'	214	22		
Cid Edwards	FB	6'2"	230	28		42
Lee White	FB	6'4"	240	26		
Mike Carter	WR	6'1"	210	24		
Chuck Dicus	WR	6'	176	23		12
Gary Garrison	WR	6'1"	193	28		42
Jerry LeVias	WR	5'10"	178	25		
Dave Williams	WR	6'2"	200	27		18
John Mackey	TE	6'3"	224	30		
Pettis Norman	TE	6'3"	220	32		
Bill McClard	K	5'10"	202	20		11
Dennis Partee	K	6'2"	230	26		71

Duane Thomas – Holdout

OAKLAND RAIDERS

RUSHING

Last Name	No.	Yds	Avg	TD
Hubbard	219	1100	5.0	4
Smith	170	686	4.0	8
Davis	71	363	5.1	6
Banaszak	30	138	4.6	1
Lamonica	10	33	3.3	0
Stabler	6	27	4.5	0
Highsmith	9	11	1.2	1
Queen	4	10	2.5	0
Branch	1	5	5.0	0
Chester	1	3	3.0	0

RECEIVING

Last Name	No.	Yds	Avg	TD
Biletnikoff	58	802	14	7
Chester	34	576	17	8
Siani	28	496	18	5
Smith	28	353	13	2
Hubbard	22	103	5	0
Banaszak	9	63	7	0
Davis	8	82	10	0
Moore	6	49	8	1
Branch	3	41	14	0
Highsmith	2	34	17	0

PUNT RETURNS

Last Name	No.	Yds	Avg	TD
Atkinson	10	33	3	0
Branch	12	21	2	0
Maxwell	2	12	6	0

KICKOFF RETURNS

Last Name	No.	Yds	Avg	TD
Davis	18	464	26	0
Branch	9	191	21	0
Atkinson	3	75	25	0
Warren	4	57	14	0
Maxwell	1	26	26	0
Seiler	1	0	0	0
Slough	1	0	0	0
Smith	1	0	0	0

PASSING – PUNTING – KICKING

PASSING	Att	Comp	%	Yds	Yd/Att	TD	Int–	%	RK
Lamonica	281	149	53	1998	7.1	18	12–	4	2
Stabler	74	44	60	524	7.1	4	3–	4	
Blanda	15	5	33	77	5.1	1	0–	0	

PUNTING	No.	Avg
DePoyster	55	36.9

KICKING	XP	Att	%	FG	Att	%
Blanda	44	44	100	17	26	65

KANSAS CITY CHIEFS

RUSHING

Last Name	No.	Yds	Avg	TD
Podolak	171	615	3.6	4
Hayes	128	536	4.2	0
Adamle	73	303	4.2	1
Livingston	14	133	9.5	0
Kinney	38	122	3.2	1
Otis	29	92	3.2	0
Dawson	15	75	5.0	0
Wright	1	24	24.0	0
Taylor	5	13	2.6	0
West	2	2	1.0	0

RECEIVING

Last Name	No.	Yds	Avg	TD
Taylor	57	821	14	6
Podolak	46	345	8	2
Hayes	31	295	9	3
Adamle	15	76	5	0
Frazier	13	172	13	5
Homan	12	135	11	1
Otis	12	76	6	0
Wright	11	81	7	0
West	9	165	18	2
Stroud	4	80	20	1
Kinney	4	45	11	0
Jankowski	2	24	12	0
Allen	1	20	20	0

PUNT RETURNS

Last Name	No.	Yds	Avg	TD
Marshall	18	103	8	0
Podolak	8	11	1	0
Homan	2	9	5	0
Reardon	1	3	3	0

KICKOFF RETURNS

Last Name	No.	Yds	Avg	TD
Marshall	23	651	28	0
Adamle	8	185	23	0
Podolak	7	119	17	0
Kinney	4	63	16	0
Reardon	2	35	18	0
Upshaw	1	4	4	0
Kearney	1	0	0	0

PASSING – PUNTING – KICKING

PASSING	Att	Comp	%	Yds	Yd/Att	TD	Int–	%	RK
Dawson	305	175	57	1835	6.0	13	12–	4	7
Livingston	78	41	53	480	6.2	7	8–	10	
Wilson	1	1	100	20	20.0	0	0–	0	

PUNTING	No	Avg
Wilson	66	44.8

KICKING	XP	Att	%	FG	Att	%
Stenerud	32	32	100	21	36	58

DENVER BRONCOS

RUSHING

Last Name	No.	Yds	Avg	TD
Little	216	859	4.0	9
Anderson	72	319	4.4	1
Dawkins	56	243	4.3	2
Lynch	34	164	4.8	2
Van Heusen	3	76	25.3	1
Odoms	5	72	14.4	0
Krieg	1	63	63.0	0
C. Turner	5	16	3.2	0
Ramsey	6	15	2.5	2
Moses	2	11	5.5	0
Ernst	1	4	4.0	0
Sherman	1	2	2.0	0
Johnson	3	0	0.0	0
Masters	3	–15	–5.0	0

RECEIVING

Last Name	No.	Yds	Avg	TD
Sherman	38	661	17	3
Little	28	367	13	4
Masters	25	393	16	3
Anderson	23	215	9	1
Odoms	21	320	15	1
Moses	18	284	16	6
Dawkins	18	242	13	0
Simmons	17	235	14	2
Lynch	7	75	11	0
Krieg	4	99	25	0
Van Heusen	4	59	15	0
C. Turner	1	10	10	0

PUNT RETURNS

Last Name	No.	Yds	Avg	TD
Sherman	10	89	9	0
Thomspson	4	82	21	0
Greer	4	67	17	1
Little	8	64	8	0
Simone	1	5	5	0
Krieg	1	3	3	0

KICKOFF RETURNS

Last Name	No.	Yds	Avg	TD
Montgomery	29	756	26	1
Dawkins	15	357	24	0
Little	3	48	16	0
Lynch	3	45	15	0
C. Turner	1	25	25	0
Krieg	1	18	18	0
Anderson	1	13	13	0
Simone	1	–6	–6	0
Preece	1	0	0	0

PASSING – PUNTING – KICKING

PASSING	Att	Comp	%	Yds	Yd/Att	TD	Int–	%	RK
Johnson	238	132	55	1783	7.5	14	14–	6	3
Ramsey	137	65	47	1050	7.7	3	9–	7	
Ernst	4	1	25	10	2.5	0	0–	0	
Anderson	3	1	33	14	4.7	1	0–	0	
Little	2	2	100	43	21.5	1	0–	0	

PUNTING	No	Avg
Van Heusen	60	40.1

KICKING	XP	Att	%	FG	Att	%
J Turner	37	37	100	20	29	69

SAN DIEGO CHARGERS

RUSHING

Last Name	No.	Yds	Avg	TD
Garrett	272	1031	3.8	6
Edwards	157	679	4.3	5
Hadl	22	99	4.5	1
L. White	23	75	3.3	0
Taylor	13	58	4.5	0
Dragon	9	30	3.3	0
Carter	1	25	25.0	0
Williams	1	14	14.0	0
Norman	1	9	9.0	0
Garrison	2	–6	–3.0	0
Clark	2	–8	–4.0	0
Dicus	1	–11	–11.0	0

RECEIVING

Last Name	No.	Yds	Avg	TD
Garrison	52	744	14	7
Edwards	40	557	14	2
Garrett	31	245	8	1
Norman	19	262	14	0
Dicus	18	227	13	2
Williams	14	315	23	3
Mackey	11	110	10	0
L. White	3	20	7	0
Carter	2	24	12	0
LeVias	1	8	8	0
Hadl	1	4	4	0

PUNT RETURNS

Last Name	No.	Yds	Avg	TD
Dunlap	19	179	9	0
Garrett	2	10	5	0
Taylor	1	0	0	0
LeVias	1	–4	–4	0

KICKOFF RETURNS

Last Name	No.	Yds	Avg	TD
Taylor	31	676	22	0
Dunlap	12	271	23	0
Berry	7	138	20	0
Detwiler	4	94	24	0
Sykes	2	44	22	0
R. Jones	3	41	14	0
Beauchamp	1	0	0	0
Williams	0	9	0	0

PASSING – PUNTING – KICKING

PASSING	Att	Comp	%	Yds	Yd/Att	TD	Int–	%	RK
Hadl	370	190	51	2449	6.6	15	26–	7	10
Clark	6	2	33	67	11.2	0	2–	33	
Garrett	1	0	0	0	0.0	0	0–	0	

PUNTING	No	Avg
Partee	45	40.3

KICKING	XP	Att	%	FG	Att	%
Partee	26	28	93	15	25	60
McClard	2	2	100	3	6	50

1972 Championship Games

NFC CHAMPIONSHIP GAME

December 31, at Washington
(Attendance 53,129)

No Stronger Than Its Weakest Link

SCORING

WASHINGTON	0	10	0	16–26
DALLAS	0	3	0	0– 3

Second Quarter
- Wash. Knight, 18 yard field goal
- Wash. Taylor, 15 yard pass from Kilmer; PAT–Knight (Kick)
- Dall. Fritsch, 35 yard field goal

Fourth Quarter
- Wash. Taylor, 45 yard pass from Kilmer; PAT–Knight (Kick)
- Wash. Knight, 39 yard field goal
- Wash. Knight, 46 yard field goal
- Wash. Knight, 45 yard field goal

TEAM STATISTICS

WASH.		DALLAS
16	First Downs–Total	8
4	First Downs–Rushing	3
11	First Downs–Passing	3
1	First Downs–Penalty	2
2	Fumbles–Number	1
1	Fumbles–Lost Ball	1
4	Penalties–Number	4
38	Yards Penalized	30
0	Missed Field Goals	1
62	Offensive Plays–Total	45
316	Net Yards	169
5.1	Average Gain	3.8
1	Giveaways	1
1	Takeaways	1
0	Difference	0

The Cowboys and Redskins, arch-rivals in the Eastern Division, each made it to the NFC title game with a strong showing in the first round of the playoffs. The Redskins completely stifled the Packer running attack in a 16-3 triumph, while the Cowboys rallied in the fourth quarter to beat the '49ers 30-28. The two clubs had split their meetings during the regular season, and this match would decide the Super Bowl berth.

Roger Staubach, who had sat out most of the season with an injured shoulder but had returned to action in the come-from-behind victory over San Francisco the week before, started at quarterback for the Cowboys in place of Craig Morton. The Washington defense greeted him with a ferocious pass rush that kept him off balance all afternoon and prevented any second-half heroics.

The Washington offensive game plan called for attacking the Cowboys at their weak left cornerback spot, where Charley Waters, normally a safety, had beaten Herb Adderley out of a job. Leading 3-0 in the second quarter, the Redskins went to work on Waters. Charley Taylor beat him to haul in a 51-yard pass, and several plays later Kilmer hit Taylor with a 15-yard scoring pitch. The Cowboys answered with a drive deep into Washington territory, but when Calvin Hill overthrew Walt Garrison in the end zone on an option pass, they had to settle for a Toni Fritsch field goal.

Early in the third period Waters broke an arm, and coach Tom Landry put Mark Washington into the corner position and left the veteran Adderley on the bench. Taylor exploited Washington's inexperience in the fourth quarter by beating him for a 45-yard touchdown pass which gave the Redskins some breathing room. Forced to go to the air, the Cowboys could make no headway against the Redskin defense, and three Curt Knight field goals in the final quarter gave the Redskins a much savored 26-3 victory.

INDIVIDUAL STATISTICS

WASHINGTON	No	Yds	Avg.	DALLAS	No	Yds	Avg.
RUSHING							
Brown	30	88	2.9	Staubach	5	59	11.8
Harraway	11	19	1.7	Hill	9	22	2.4
Kilmer	3	15	5.0	Garrison	7	15	2.1
	44	122	2.8		21	96	4.6
RECEIVING							
Taylor	7	146	20.9	Sellers	2	29	14.5
Harraway	3	13	4.3	Garrison	2	18	9.0
Jefferson	2	19	9.5	Hill	2	11	5.5
Brown	2	16	8.0	Parks	1	21	21.0
	14	194	13.9	Alworth	1	15	15.0
				Ditka	1	4	4.0
					9	98	10.9
PUNTING							
Bragg	4		36.0	Bateman	7		43.1
PUNT RETURNS							
Haymond	4	10	2.5	Waters	3	–5	–1.7
KICKOFF RETURNS							
None				Harris	2	29	14.5
				Newhouse	1	25	25.0
					3	54	18.0

PASSING

	Att.	Comp.	Comp. Pct.	Yds.	Int.	Yds/ Att.	Yds/ Comp.	Yards Lost Tackled
WASHINGTON								
Kilmer	18	14	77.8	194	0	10.8	13.9	0– 0
DALLAS								
Staubach	20	9	45.0	98	0	4.9	10.9	3–25
Hill	1	0	0.0	0	0	–	–	
	21	9	42.9	98	0	4.7	10.9	3–25

AFC CHAMPIONSHIP GAME

December 31, at Pittsburgh
(Attendance 50,845)

Simply Not Enough of Bradshaw

SCORING

PITTSBURGH	7	0	3	7–17
MIAMI	0	7	7	7–21

First Quarter
- Pitt. Mullins, Recovery of Pitt fumble in end zone; PAT–Gerela (kick)

Second Quarter
- Miami Csonka, 9 yard pass from Morrall; PAT–Yepremian (kick)

Third Quarter
- Pitt. Gerela, 14 yard field goal
- Miami Kiick, 2 yard rush; PAT–Yepremian (kick)

Fourth Quarter
- Miami Kiick, 3 yard rush; PAT–Yepremian (kick)
- Pitt. Young, 12 yard pass from Bradshaw; PAT–Gerela (kick)

TEAM STATISTICS

PITT.		MIAMI
13	First Downs–Total	19
6	First Downs–Rushing	11
6	First Downs–Passing	6
1	First Downs–Penalty	2
2	Fumbles–Number	0
0	Fumbles–Lost Ball	0
4	Penalties–Number	2
30	Yards Penalized	19
1	Missed Field Goals	0
48	Offensive Plays–Total	65
250	Net Yards	314
5.2	Average Gain	4.8
2	Giveaways	1
1	Takeaways	2
–1	Difference	+1

The Dolphins came into this game after a miracle season, while the Steelers came in after a miracle play. By beating Cleveland 20-14 last week in the start of the playoffs, the Dolphins ran their record to 15-0 for the season. The Steelers had a less shining record, but their spirits were high after beating the Raiders 13-7 in the opening round of the playoffs. In that game the Steelers scored the winning touchdown with five seconds left on a deflected pass which Franco Harris snagged in mid-air and carried across the goal line.

In the first quarter, after an extended drive into Miami territory, Terry Bradshaw fumbled on the three-yard line and Gerry Mullins fell on the ball as it rolled into the end zone. Although the Steelers took a 7-0 lead, the play was costly, as Bradshaw was knocked dizzy and had to be relieved by Terry Hanratty.

An alert play by punter Larry Seiple helped the Dolphins tie the score in the second quarter. Noticing that all the Steelers had dropped back to block for the return, Seiple crossed the defense up and ran with the ball, gaining 37 yards to the Pittsburgh 12-yard line. Two plays later Morrall hit Csonka with a scoring pass, and Garo Yepremian added the extra point.

As the second half began, Miami coach Don Shula put Bob Griese, out since October with a broken leg, in at quarterback to shake up his offense. The Steelers went ahead 10-7 on a Roy Gerela field goal, but Griese hit Paul Warfield with a 52-yard pass play which put the Dolphins in striking distance. Six plays later, Jim Kiick carried the ball in, and another Kiick touchdown in the fourth quarter lengthened the Miami lead to 21-10. Bradshaw returned to action for the final seven minutes of the game, but after leading the Steelers to one touchdown, he suffered two interceptions in his final three passes.

INDIVIDUAL STATISTICS

PITTSBURGH	No	Yds	Avg.	MIAMI	No	Yds	Avg.
RUSHING							
Harris	16	76	4.8	Morris	16	76	4.8
Fuqua	8	47	5.9	Csonka	24	68	2.8
Bradshaw	2	5	2.5	Seiple	1	37	37.0
	26	128	4.9	Kiick	8	12	1.5
					49	193	3.9
RECEIVING							
Young	4	54	13.5	Fleming	5	50	10.0
Shanklin	2	49	24.5	Warfield	2	63	31.5
Harris	2	3	1.5	Csonka	1	9	9.0
McMakin	1	22	22.0	Mandich	1	5	5.0
Brown	1	9	9.0	Morris	1	–6	–6.0
	10	137	13.7		10	121	12.1
PUNTING							
Walden	4		51.3	Seiple	4		35.5
PUNT RETURNS							
Edwards	1	5	5.0	None			
KICKOFF RETURNS							
P. Pearson	2	63	31.5	Morris	1	23	23.0
S. Davis	1	22	22.0				
	3	85	28.3				
INTERCEPTION RETURNS							
Edwards	1	28	28.0	Buoniconti	1	6	6.0
				Kuler	1	5	5.0
					2	11	5.5

PASSING

	Att.	Comp.	Comp. Pct.	Yds.	Int.	Yds/ Att.	Yds/ Comp.	Yards Lost Tackled
PITTSBURGH								
Bradshaw	10	5	50.0	80	2	8.0	16.0	
Hanratty	10	5	50.0	57	0	5.7	11.4	
	20	10	50.0	137	2	6.9	13.7	2–15
MIAMI								
Morrall	11	7	63.6	51	1	4.6	7.3	
Griese	5	3	60.0	70	0	14.0	23.3	
	16	10	62.5	121	1	7.6	12.1	0– 0

SUPER BOWL VII

January 14, at Los Angeles

(Attendance 90,182)

Super Perfect

The contrasts were interesting. The Miami Dolphins had swept through fourteen regular-season games and two playoff games without a loss and now had a chance to compile a perfect 17-0 record for the year. Under the thorough leadership of head coach Don Shula, the Dolphins had rebounded from last year's Super Bowl loss to Dallas to become a cool, mature, precise club, with programmed brutality on both platoons.

The Washington Redskins had mostly veteran players, but their style was not one of coolness. Coach George Allen strove to whip his men into a frenzy before every game, and he put a fanatical emphasis on this game. A loss in this game would spoil the entire season, he said, and he drilled his troops in Spartan fashion to prepare them for the younger Dolphins.

The Miami defense scuttled the Washington running attack right from the start, a reversal from last year's dissection of the Dolphin front wall by the Cowboys. Larry Brown and Charley Harraway found Miami tackle Manny Fernandez forever in their path, and quarterback Bill Kilmer suffered through a bad afternoon with his passing. The Dolphins picked off three passes, with safety Jake Scott making two of the interceptions.

The Dolphin attack moved well against the heralded Redskin defense, but three penalties prevented any score until late in the period. Just before the end of the quarter Howard Twilley beat Pat Fischer to the outside and hauled in a 28-yard Bob Griese touchdown pass which he carried in from the 5. Leading 7-0, the Dolphins continued to paralyze the Redskin offense in the second period and scored again late in the period. One minute before halftime Jim Kiick capped a long Miami drive by going over from the one-yard line, giving the Dolphins a solid 14-0 lead at intermission.

The Redskins finally got their offense rolling after taking the second-half kickoff. With Brown gaining on the ground and Kilmer completing three passes, the Redskins drove into Miami territory before the drive stalled. Curt Knight then lined up a comparitively easy 32-yard field goal, but his kick sailed wide to the right and the Dolphins took possession.

The Miami defense re-established its superiority through the second half as the Dolphin offense held onto the ball long enough on each possession to eat up valuable time. With two minutes left in the game, Garo Yepremian attempted a 42-yard field goal, only to have it blocked. When the ball bounced back to him, he picked it up and started to run toward the sidelines. With no football experience except kicking, Yepremian then attempted to pass the ball, only to have it slip out of his hands right to Mike Bass of the Redskins. Bass ran 49 yards with the aborted pass for Washington's only score of the day, but the Dolphins hung onto the 14-7 lead the rest of the way and became the first NFL team ever to go through a complete season with all wins.

MIAMI		WASHINGTON
	OFFENSE	
Warfield	WR	C. Taylor
W. Moore	LT	Hermeling
Kuechenberg	LG	Laaveg
Langer	C	Hauss
Little	RG	Wilbur
Evans	RT	Rock
Fleming	TE	Smith
Twilley	WR	Jefferson
Griese	QB	Kilmer
Kiick	RB	Brown
Csonka	RB	Harraway
	DEFENSE	
Den Herder	LE	McDole
Fernandez	LT	Brundige
Heinz	RT	Talbert
Stanfill	RE	Biggs
Swift	LLB	Pardee
Bouniconti	MLB	Pottios
Kolen	RLB	Hanburger
Mumphord	LCB	Fischer
Johnson	RCB	Bass
Anderson	LS	Owens
Scott	RS	R. Taylor

SUBSTITUTES

MIAMI

Offense	
Briscoe	Leigh
Crusan	Mandich
Ginn	Morrall
Jenkins	Morris
Kindig	
Defense	
Babb	M. Moore
Ball	Powell
Matheson	Stuckey
Kickers	
Seiple	Yepremian

WASHINGTON

Offense	
Alston	McNeil
Brunet	Mul-Key
Burman	Wyche
Hull	
Defense	
Fanucci	Severson
Haymond	Sistrunk
Jaqua	Tillman
McLinton	Vactor
Kickers	
Bragg	Knight

SCORING

MIAMI	7	7	0	0	–14
WASHINGTON	0	0	0	7	– 7

First Quarter

Mia.	Twilley, 28 yd pass from Griese PAT – Yepremian (kick)	14:59

Second Quarter

Mia.	Kiick, 1 yard rush PAT – Yepremian (kick)	14:42

Fourth Quarter

Was.	Bass, 49 yard fumble return PAT – Knight	12:53

TEAM STATISTICS

MIAMI		WASH.
12	First Downs – Total	16
7	First Downs – Rushing	9
5	First Downs – Passing	7
0	First Downs – Penalty	0
2	Fumbles – Number	1
1	Fumbles – Lost Ball	0
3	Penalties – Number	3
35	Yards Penalized	25
50	Total Offensive Plays	66
253	Total Net Yards	228
5.1	Average Gain	3.5
1	Missed Field Goals	1
2	Giveaways	3
3	Takeaways	2
+1	Difference	–1

INDIVIDUAL STATISTICS

MIAMI	No	Yds	Avg.	WASHINGTON	No	Yds	Avg.
RUSHING							
Csonka	15	112	7.5	Brown	22	72	3.3
Kiick	12	38	3.2	Harraway	10	37	3.7
Morris	10	34	3.4	Kilmer	2	18	9.0
	37	184	5.0	Taylor	1	8	8.0
				Smith	1	6	6.0
					36	141	3.9
RECEIVING							
Warfield	3	36	12.0	Jefferson	5	50	10.0
Kiick	2	6	3.0	Brown	5	26	5.2
Twilley	1	28	28.0	Taylor	2	20	10.0
Mandich	1	19	19.0	Smith	1	11	11.0
Csonka	1	–1	–1.0	Harraway	1	–3	–3.0
	8	88	11.0		14	104	7.4
PUNTING							
Seiple	7		43.0	Bragg	5		31.2
PUNT RETURNS							
Scott	2	4	2.0	Haymond	4	9	2.3
KICKOFF RETURNS							
Morris	2	33	16.5	Haymond	2	30	15.0
				Mul-Key	1	15	15.0
					3	45	15.0
INTERCEPTION RETURNS							
Scott	2	63	31.5	Owens	1	0	0.0
Buoniconti	1	32	32.0				
	3	95	31.7				

PASSING

	Att	Comp	Comp Pct.	Yds	Int	Yds/ Att.	Yds/ Comp	Yards Lost Tackled
MIAMI								
Griese	11	8	72.7	88	1	8.0	11.0	2–19
WASHINGTON								
Kilmer	28	14	50.0	104	3	3.7	7.4	2–17

1973 N.F.C. Recession at the Concessions

When Congress passed a bill forbidding television blackouts of games sold out forty-eight hours ahead of time, the NFL reluctantly televised home games for the first time in years. This situation gave birth to a new football term, the "no-show," who was a fan holding a ticket for a sold-out game but instead watched it at home on TV. Ticket sales were not affected by the new ruling, but concession profits fell in the parks on days when unpleasant weather made the television set a much more comfortable way to view the game.

EASTERN DIVISION

Dallas Cowboys—The Cowboys had injuries at several key positions but still made the playoffs. When newly acquired flanker Otto Stowe broke an ankle in mid-season, rookie Drew Pearson stepped into the starting lineup and began grabbing passes in all kinds of situations. A bad back made defensive tackle Bob Lilly's season a miserable one, but middle linebacker Lee Roy Jordan took charge of the defense with his first All-Pro season in an eleven-year pro career. Other added assets for coach Tom Landry were quarterback Roger Staubach's staying healthy for the entire season, Bob Hayes's recovery from an off-season to reclaim his starting wide-receiver job, and tight end Billy Joe DuPree's good rookie season.

Washington Redskins—The Over the Hill Gang was far from finished. Coach George Allen added Dave Robinson, Ken Houston, Alvin Reed, and Duane Thomas to his squad through a variety of trades. Robinson and Houston replaced the retired Jack Pardee and Roosevelt Taylor on the defensive unit, while Reed and Thomas gave the Skins all-star depth on offense. Thomas left his personal problems behind him when he reported to the Redskins, working hard to regain his top form of the 1971 season, but the superb running and blocking of backs Larry Brown and Charley Harraway kept Duane on the bench for most of the season. Veteran passing ace Sonny Jurgensen stayed healthy enough to share the quarterback job with Billy Kilmer, and their collective wisdom guided the Redskins attack.

Philadelphia Eagles—New head coach Mike McCormack ripped the Eagles apart and started all over again from scratch. To run the offense, he paid a high price to the Rams for Roman Gabriel, a quarterback who was used to winning. Ex-Colt Norm Bulaich and second-year man Tom Sullivan started at running back, tall Harold Carmichael and rookie Don Zimmerman won the wide-receiver jobs, and rookie Charley Young was an instant All-Pro at tight end. Operating behind a line with two fine rookies in Jerry Sisemore and Guy Morriss, Gabriel picked enemy defenses apart with precision passing and sharp play-calling. Coach McCormack had less success in rebuilding the defense. End Mel Tom was traded to Chicago after an argument with an assistant coach, cornerback Nate Ramsey was cut in mid-season, linebacker Ron Porter was traded to Minnesota, and knee injuries kayoed linebacker Steve Zabel and cornerback Al Nelson.

St. Louis Cardinals—New head coach Don Coryell succeeded in building a fine passing attack, but injuries and a bad defense held the Cards under .500 for the third straight season. Quarterback Jim Hart won the starting position and developed into a top passer, hitting wide receivers Mel Gray and Ahmad Rashad (previously known as Bobby Moore) with long bombs which had grown infrequent in 1970s pro football. But the St. Louis defense had problems stopping even mediocre attacks, despite a good rookie season from massive end Dave Butz. Late-season injuries crippled both platoons, with Hart and most of the offensive line out for the last few games of the year.

New York Giants—A perfect 6-0 record in pre-season play inflated Giant hopes to a vibrating level, but the cruel reality which followed turned the season into a nightmare. After opening with a win and tie in Yankee Stadium, the Giants for all purposes became a road team for the rest of the season. Yankee Stadium was shut for repairs, so the Giants held their practices in Jersey City and played their "home" games in the Yale Bowl in New Haven. The gypsy life disheartened the players, and the team lost seven straight games after leaving the old ball park. Coach Alex Webster announced his resignation before the final game, not a totally unexpected move.

CENTRAL DIVISION

Minnesota Vikings—Fran Tarkenton finally began burying his image as a loser by leading the Vikings into the playoffs with a 12-2 record for the regular season. Aiding Tarkenton considerably was the front four of Carl Eller, Alan Page, Gary Larsen, and Jim Marshall, all of whom stayed healthy and gave the Minnesota defense its old devastating strength. The secondary lost safety Karl Kassulke when he was seriously hurt in a pre-season motorcycle accident, but the quartet of Bobby Bryant, Nate Wright, Paul Krause, and Jeff Wright threw an airtight cover on enemy receivers. The Viking offense had a new weapon in rookie Chuck Foreman, a slashing runner who also caught passes. At wide receiver, John Gilliam made fans forget the traded Gene Washington with his speed and sure hands. The Vikings had always had a defense, but now that they had an offense they outclassed their rivals in the Central Division.

Detroit Lions—High hopes for a divisional title flattened out into a disappointing second-place finish and bitter words from the owner and coach. The Lions compiled a 1-4-1 record in their first six games, with a 29-27 loss to Baltimore on October 21 the bitterest pill to swallow. Coach Don McCafferty said, "If we can't beat the Colts, we can't beat anybody." Owner William Clay Ford added, "I don't think they want to win—at least it doesn't look like it." The Lions responded with a 27-0 shutout of the Packers the next week, but a limp 20-0 loss to Washington on Thanksgiving Day brought another public blast from McCafferty. "We stunk out the joint," said the coach. We've got some losers on this ball club and they won't be around next year."

Green Bay Packers—The Packer defense had carried the team into the playoffs last year, but the one-dimensional Green Bay offense was too much of a load for the defense to carry this season. John Brockington and MacArthur Lane kept eating up the yardage on the ground, with Brockington gaining 1,000 yard for the third time in his three-year pro career. The Green Bay passing attack, however, was next to nonexistent. Coach Dan Devine gave youngsters Scott Hunter, Jim Del Gaizo, and Jerry Tagge each a shot at the quarterback job, but none of them took the pressure off the runners with a consistent passing game. The offensive line enjoyed its greatest success clearing the way for Brockington and Lane, with guard Gale Gillingham bouncing back from an injury-filled 1972 season to win All-Pro honors.

Chicago Bears—Dick Butkus scored the first touchdown of his pro career by falling on a Houston fumble in the end zone on October 28, but a bad knee made it increasingly hard for him to cover pass receivers coming out of the backfield. The problem with the Bears' offense had nothing to do with injuries; quarterback Bobby Douglass was a superior runner but simply could not pass well. Chicago fans singled Douglass out for insults whenever the Bears lost, calling on coach Abe Gibron to stick rookie quarterback Gary Huff into the lineup. Gibron stayed with Douglass until November 18, when he gave Huff his first extended chance. The inexperienced rookie threw four interceptions as the Lions crushed the Bears 30-7; the fans afterward booed Douglass but didn't call for Huff.

WESTERN DIVISION

Los Angeles Rams—Carroll Rosenbloom had given Weeb Ewbank, Don Shula, and Don McCafferty their first head coaching positions while he owned the Colts, and he struck gold again this year with the Rams by hiring Chuck Knox as the head man. Knox led a team supposedly in need of an overhauling to a runaway title in the Western Division and a berth in the playoffs. The Los Angeles passing attack profited from two new faces brought in by Knox. Quarterback John Hadl came over from San Diego and receiver Harold Jackson from Philadelphia in major trades, and both men starred in their new surroundings. Two strong young runners, Larry McCutcheon and Jim Bertelsen, made Hadl's signal-calling task easier, with the excellent offensive line laboring anonymously for both the runners and passers. The defensive unit played up to the standards set by George Allen, although Merlin Olsen was the only starter left from that era. With little expected of them, the Rams won their first six games of the year and ran away from the other teams in the division.

Atlanta Falcons—With solid starters at every position except quarterback, the Falcons opened the season with a smashing triumph over the Saints in which Dick Shiner masterfully engineered the Atlanta attack. Shiner soon regressed into the mediocre form he had shown all his career, and coach Norm Van Brocklin next turned to Bob Lee at the position. An ex-Viking with little experience, Lee sparked the Falcons to a 41-0 victory over San Diego and a mid-season winning streak which made the team a prime candidate for the wild-card spot in the playoffs. December, however, brought bad times to the Falcons, as they lost to Buffalo and St. Louis.

San Francisco '49ers—Disappointment colored the '49ers season as the team finished a distant third in the West. Fullback Ken Willard publicly expressed his disappointment when benched at the start of the season. Bad knees turned receiver Gene Washington and cornerback Jim Johnson into disappointing performers. Quarterback John Brodie endured the bitterest season of all, finding himself on the bench behind Steve Spurrier and Joe Reed after the team got off to a slow start. The thirty-eight-year-old Brodie announced in mid-season that this would be his last campaign, and coach Dick Nolan gave him the starting nod in the season's finale against the Steelers, but a sore arm sent him out of the game in the first half.

New Orleans Saints—John North replaced J. D. Roberts as head coach in training camp, taking over a club that looked like one of the worst in the league. An opening-day trouncing by the Falcons embarrassed the team, but North patiently developed his defense into a good unit. The Saints beat the Bears on October 7 for their first victory, and they won four other games during the season, including an upset of the Washington Redskins. Young veterans Billy Newsome, Joe Owens, Joe Federspiel, Ernie Jackson, and Bivian Lee starred on the improved defensive platoon, while quarterback Archie Manning got some help on offense from end John Beasley, runner Jess Phillips and receiver Jubilee Dunbar, all picked up in trades.

FINAL TEAM STATISTICS
(Other statistics not available at press time)

OFFENSE

	ATL.	CHI.	DALL.	DET.	G.B.	L.A.	MINN.	N.O.	N.Y.	PHIL.	ST.L.	S.F.	WASH.
FIRST DOWNS:													
Total	240	193	281	237	187	**294**	246	207	239	267	238	251	232
by Rushing	123	97	139	122	98	**177**	135	100	83	103	96	97	76
by Passing	100	77	127	104	72	101	99	88	141	**147**	111	127	131
by Penalty	17	19	15	11	17	16	12	19	15	17	**31**	27	25
RUSHING:													
Number	518	496	542	496	527	**659**	538	497	456	417	416	422	459
Yards	2037	1907	2418	2133	1973	**2925**	2275	1842	1478	1791	1671	1743	1439
Average Yards	3.9	3.8	**4.5**	4.3	3.7	4.4	4.2	3.7	3.2	4.3	4.0	4.1	3.1
Touchdowns	**18**	11	17	17	10	**18**	14	5	11	9	13	15	9
PASSING:													
Attempts	320	303	321	325	255	271	298	338	412	**479**	394	466	372
Completions	168	136	192	171	119	144	179	163	230	**275**	210	233	209
Completion Percentage	52.5	44.9	59.8	52.6	46.7	53.1	**60.1**	48.2	55.8	57.4	53.3	50.0	56.2
Passing Yards	2362	1617	2602	2105	1503	2107	2234	1901	2762	**3236**	2592	2645	2560
Avg. Yards per Attempt	7.4	5.3	**8.1**	6.4	5.9	7.8	7.5	5.6	6.7	6.8	6.6	5.7	6.9
Avg. Yards per Complet.	14.1	11.9	13.6	12.3	12.6	**14.6**	12.5	11.7	12.0	11.8	12.3	11.4	12.2
Times Tackled Passing	41	49	43	27	27	**17**	32	37	28	34	27	27	31
Yards Lost Tackled	361	395	269	192	220	**126**	278	242	201	238	209	164	202
Net Yards	2001	1222	2333	1913	1283	1981	1956	1659	2561	**2998**	2383	2481	2358
Touchdowns	14	8	**26**	12	7	22	16	11	14	23	16	9	20
Interceptions	12	16	16	19	17	11	**9**	17	30	13	15	25	14
Percent Intercepted	3.8	5.3	5.0	5.8	6.7	4.1	3.0	5.0	7.3	**2.7**	3.8	5.4	3.8
PUNTS:													
Number	63	**86**	59	54	68	51	66	81	68	64	66	79	64
Average Distance	42.6	39.8	41.5	43.2	41.0	40.8	39.8	41.7	38.8	40.9	37.5	**43.7**	40.3
PUNT RETURNS:													
Number	48	37	28	35	30	**51**	28	22	21	15	27	37	40
Yards	429	204	174	289	137	**478**	140	218	160	116	192	393	331
Average Yards	8.9	5.5	6.2	8.3	4.6	9.4	5.0	9.9	7.6	7.7	7.1	**10.6**	8.3
Touchdowns	0	**1**	0	0	0	0	0	0	0	0	0	0	0
KICKOFF RETURNS:													
Number	53	59	33	50	53	36	35	47	56	**63**	58	**63**	43
Yards	1107	1344	725	1061	1189	915	752	947	1198	**1441**	1369	1301	1118
Average Yards	20.9	22.8	22.0	21.2	22.4	25.4	21.5	20.1	21.4	22.9	23.6	20.7	**26.0**
Touchdowns	0	**1**	0	0	0	**1**	0	0	0	0	**1**	0	**1**
INTERCEPTION RETURNS:													
Number	22	14	18	22	15	20	21	16	20	15	10	17	**26**
Yards	528	176	300	522	220	300	263	126	214	120	71	134	**598**
Average Yards	**24.0**	12.6	16.7	23.7	14.7	15.0	12.5	7.9	10.7	8.0	7.1	7.9	23.0
Touchdowns	2	0	2	1	3	1	2	0	0	1	0	0	**4**
PENALTIES:													
Number	66	86	83	64	68	54	55	58	67	61	61	**93**	81
Yards	598	817	762	584	653	606	482	516	586	566	594	**903**	771
FUMBLES:													
Number	40	40	25	30	23	**21**	29	34	23	41	36	32	32
Number Lost	21	26	12	14	11	**9**	17	17	10	15	14	14	18
POINTS:													
Total	318	195	382	271	202	**388**	296	163	226	310	286	262	325
PAT Attempts	34	22	**46**	30	20	42	33	16	25	34	31	26	37
PAT Made	34	21	**45**	28	19	40	33	16	25	34	31	26	37
FG Attempts	38	24	30	33	35	**47**	35	36	28	40	32	33	42
FG Made	26	14	19	21	21	**30**	21	17	17	24	23	26	22
Percent FG Made	68.4	58.3	63.3	63.6	60.0	63.8	60.0	47.2	60.7	60.0	71.9	**78.8**	52.4
Safeties	1	0	2	0	0	**3**	1	0	0	0	0	1	0

DEFENSE

	ATL.	CHI.	DALL.	DET.	G.B.	L.A.	MINN.	N.O.	N.Y.	PHIL.	ST.L.	S.F.	WASH.
FIRST DOWNS:													
Total	212	247	208	245	230	**173**	220	271	240	286	307	242	233
by Rushing	104	138	83	127	114	**71**	105	131	126	136	135	112	89
by Passing	92	90	106	98	101	**87**	100	119	94	135	157	115	119
by Penalty	16	19	19	20	**15**	**15**	**15**	21	20	**15**	**15**	**15**	25
RUSHING:													
Number	520	563	435	501	506	**366**	450	556	497	513	504	513	480
Yards	2129	2509	1471	2117	1999	**1270**	1974	2402	2174	2423	2120	1963	1603
Average Yards	4.1	4.5	3.4	4.2	4.0	3.5	4.4	4.3	4.4	4.7	4.2	3.8	**3.3**
Touchdowns	12	19	**5**	10	13	**5**	**5**	17	21	22	16	11	8
PASSING:													
Attempts	324	303	352	332	327	328	377	337	**275**	370	417	383	406
Completions	**151**	156	187	173	180	179	198	176	161	219	252	194	203
Completion Percentage	**46.6**	51.5	53.1	52.1	55.0	54.6	52.5	52.2	58.5	59.2	60.4	50.7	50.0
Passing Yards	**1619**	1978	2301	2058	2050	2023	2124	2333	2252	2789	3226	2591	2531
Avg. Yards per Attempt	**5.0**	6.5	6.5	6.2	6.3	6.2	5.6	6.9	8.2	7.5	7.7	6.8	6.2
Avg. Yards per Complet.	10.7	12.7	12.3	11.9	11.4	11.3	**10.7**	13.3	14.0	12.7	12.8	13.4	12.5
Times Tackled Passing	29	32	40	33	25	45	30	24	35	21	29	32	**53**
Yards Lost Tackled	189	304	306	270	228	342	230	155	267	150	197	225	**355**
Net Yards	**1430**	1674	1995	1788	1822	1681	1894	2178	1985	2639	3029	2366	2176
Touchdowns	11	17	15	15	14	10	**8**	15	17	22	23	19	12
Interceptions	22	14	18	22	15	20	21	16	20	15	10	17	**26**
Percent Intercepted	6.8	4.6	5.1	6.6	4.6	6.1	5.6	4.7	**7.3**	4.1	2.4	4.4	6.4
PUNTS:													
Number	80	66	70	65	67	**81**	57	63	52	49	54	72	**81**
Average Distance	42.1	40.5	39.4	41.5	38.9	40.8	41.0	44.5	40.9	39.9	41.4	41.3	**38.4**
PUNT RETURNS:													
Number	30	40	29	30	41	24	41	49	32	35	23	46	**14**
Yards	185	294	152	166	300	261	271	587	379	376	186	367	**104**
Average Yards	6.1	7.4	**5.2**	5.5	7.3	10.9	6.5	11.9	11.8	10.8	8.1	8.0	7.4
Touchdowns	**0**	**0**	1	**0**	**0**	**0**	1	1	**0**	**0**	**0**	**0**	**0**
KICKOFF RETURNS:													
Number	58	**33**	53	59	40	68	58	**33**	43	55	57	52	62
Yards	1369	813	1320	1220	817	1318	1148	**724**	988	1246	1350	1151	1237
Average Yards	23.6	24.6	24.9	20.7	20.4	19.4	**19.1**	22.0	22.7	22.7	23.7	22.1	20.0
Touchdowns	**0**	**0**	**0**	**0**	**0**	**0**	**0**	**0**	**0**	1	1	1	1
INTERCEPTION RETURNS:													
Number	12	16	16	19	17	11	**9**	17	30	13	15	25	14
Yards	**83**	335	151	171	256	103	88	280	525	287	267	379	173
Average Yards	**6.9**	20.9	9.4	9.0	15.1	9.4	9.8	16.5	17.5	22.1	17.8	15.2	12.4
Touchdowns	**0**	1	1	**0**	1	1	**0**	3	3	1	2	1	**0**
PENALTIES:													
Number	58	77	52	68	54	61	58	69	58	73	**95**	77	86
Yards	562	672	516	606	483	566	633	751	484	692	**892**	754	708
FUMBLES:													
Number	29	35	**44**	31	34	29	36	32	32	31	31	23	35
Number Lost	15	19	**23**	11	18	18	15	14	12	15	17	15	18
POINTS:													
Total	224	334	203	247	259	178	**168**	312	362	393	365	319	198
PAT Attempts	24	37	23	26	28	17	**15**	36	42	47	42	32	21
PAT Made	23	35	23	25	28	16	**15**	35	42	45	41	32	21
FG Attempts	28	38	30	31	**27**	**27**	38	34	30	40	34	45	29
FG Made	19	25	**14**	22	19	20	21	19	22	22	24	31	17
Percent FG Made	67.9	65.8	**46.7**	71.0	70.4	74.1	55.3	55.9	73.3	55.0	70.6	68.9	58.6
Safeties	**0**	1	**0**	**0**	3	**0**	**0**	2	1	**0**	**0**	1	**0**

CONFERENCE PLAYOFFS

December 22, at Minnesota (Attendance 45,475)

SCORING

MINNESOTA	0	3	7	17–27
WASHINGTON	0	7	3	10–20

Second Quarter
Minn. Cox, 19 yard field goal
Wash. Brown, 3 yard rush PAT–Knight (kick)

Third Quarter
Minn. Brown, 2 yard rush PAT–Cox (kick)
Wash. Knight, 52 yard field goal

Fourth Quarter
Wash. Knight, 42 yard field goal
Minn. Gilliam, 28 yard pass from Tarkenton PAT–Cox (kick)
Minn. Gilliam, 6 yard pass from Tarkenton PAT–Cox (kick)
Wash. Jefferson, 28 yard pass from Kilmer PAT–Knight (kick)
Minn. Cox, 30 yard field goal

TEAM STATISTICS

MINN.		WASH.
17	First Downs–Total	18
6	First Downs–Rushing	10
11	First Downs–Passing	7
0	First Downs–Penalty	1
2	Fumbles–Number	2
2	Fumbles–Lost Ball	1
2	Penalties–Number	0
9	Yards Penalized	0
0	Missed Field Goals	2
63	Offensive Plays	66
359	Net Yards	314
5.7	Average Gain	4.8
3	Giveaways	2
2	Takeaways	3
–1	Difference	+1

INDIVIDUAL STATISTICS

MINNESOTA	No.	Yds.	Avg.	WASHINGTON	No.	Yds.	Avg.
RUSHING							
Reed	17	95	5.6	Brown	29	115	4.0
Foreman	11	40	3.6	Harraway	13	40	3.1
Marinaro	1	3	3.0		42	155	3.7
Brown	1	2	2.0				
Tarkenton	4	1	0.3				
	34	141	4.1				
RECEIVING							
Reed	5	76	15.2	Jefferson	6	84	14.0
Voigt	3	39	13.0	Taylor	4	56	14.0
Foreman	3	23	7.7	Brown	2	13	6.5
Gilliam	2	36	18.0	Harraway	1	6	6.0
Dale	2	31	15.5		13	159	12.2
Lash	1	17	17.0				
	16	222	13.9				
PUNTING							
Eischeid	6		31.9	Bragg	4		37.3
PUNT RETURNS							
Bryant	2	3	1.5	Duncan	3	8	2.7
				Mul-Key	1	10	10.0
					4	18	4.5
KICKOFF RETURNS							
Gilliam	3	49	16.3	Mul-Key	3	69	23.0
West	2	78	39.0	Brunet	2	35	17.5
	5	127	25.4		5	104	20.8
INTERCEPTION RETURNS							
N. Wright	1	26	26.0	Bass	1	28	28.0

PASSING

MINNESOTA	Att.	Comp.	Comp. Pct.	Yds.	Int.	Yds/ Att.	Yds/ Comp.	Yards Lost Tackled
Tarkenton	28	16	57.1	222	1	7.9	13.9	1–4
WASHINGTON								
Kilmer	24	13	54.2	159	1	6.6	12.2	0–0

December 23, at Irving, Tex. (Attendance 64,291)

SCORING

DALLAS	14	3	0	10–27
LOS ANGELES	0	6	0	10–16

First Quarter
Dall. Hill, 3 yard rush PAT–Fritsch (kick)
Dall. Pearson, 4 yard pass from Staubach PAT–Fritsch (kick)

Second Quarter
Dall. Fritsch, 39 yard field goal
L.A. Ray, 33 yard field goal
L.A. Ray, 37 yard field goal

Fourth Quarter
L.A. Ray, 40 yard field goal
L.A. Baker, 5 yard rush PAT–Ray (kick)
Dall. Pearson, 83 yard pass from Staubach PAT–Fritsch (kick)
Dall. Fritsch, 12 yard field goal

TEAM STATISTICS

DALL.		L.A.
15	First Downs–Total	11
11	First Downs–Rushing	5
4	First Downs–Passing	5
0	First Downs–Penalty	1
2	Fumbles–Number	2
2	Fumbles–Lost Ball	2
5	Penalties–Number	2
44	Yards Penalized	20
0	Missed Field Goals	3
68	Offensive Plays	58
298	Net Yards	192
4.4	Average Gain	3.3
4	Giveaways	3
3	Takeaways	4
–1	Difference	+1

INDIVIDUAL STATISTICS

DALLAS	No.	Yds.	Avg.	LOS ANGELES	No.	Yds.	Avg.
RUSHING							
Hill	25	97	3.9	McCutcheon	13	48	3.7
Staubach	4	30	7.5	Bertelsen	12	37	3.1
Garrison	10	30	3.0	Hadl	2	10	5.0
Newhouse	6	5	0.8	Baker	1	5	5.0
	45	162	3.6	Smith	2	–7	–3.5
					30	93	3.1
RECEIVING							
Pearson	2	87	43.5	Snow	3	77	25.7
Hill	2	21	10.5	Smith	2	13	6.5
Fuggett	1	38	38.0	Jackson	1	40	40.0
Hayes	1	29	29.0	McCutcheon	1	3	3.0
Garrison	1	3	3.0		7	133	19.0
DuPree	1	2	2.0				
	8	180	22.5				
PUNTING							
Bateman	7		46.7	Chapple	5		43.6
PUNT RETURNS							
Richards	2	3	1.5	Bertelsen	4	52	13.0
				Elmendorf	1	1	1.0
					5	53	10.6
KICKOFF RETURNS							
Waters	1	23	23.0	Scribner	4	106	26.5
Harris	1	19	19.0	Clark	2	49	24.5
	2	42	21.0		6	155	25.8
INTERCEPTION RETURNS							
Jordan	1	2	2.0	Reynolds	1	4	4.0
				Elmendorf	1	0	0.0
					2	4	2.0

PASSING

DALLAS	Att.	Comp.	Comp. Pct.	Yds.	Int.	Yds/ Att.	Yds/ Comp.	Yards Lost Tackled
Staubach	16	8	50.0	180	2	11.3	22.5	7–44
LOS ANGELES								
Hadl	23	7	30.4	133	1	5.8	19.0	5–34
McCutcheon	1	0	0.0	0	0	–	–	0– 0
	24	7	29.2	133	1	5.5	19.0	5–34

DALLAS COWBOYS 10-4-0 Tom Landry

Scores of Each Game		
20	Chicago	17
40	NEW ORLEANS	3
45	ST. LOUIS	10
7	Washington	14
31	Los Angeles	37
45	N. Y. GIANTS	28
16	Philadelphia	30
38	CINCINNATI	10
23	N. Y. Giants	10
31	PHILADELPHIA	10
7	MIAMI	14
22	Denver	10
27	WASHINGTON	7
30	St. Louis	3

Use Name	Pos.	Hgt	Wgt	Age	Int	Pts
Ralph Neely	OT	6'5"	265	29		
Rodney Wallace	OT	6'5"	255	24		
Rayfield Wright	OT	6'7"	255	28		
John Niland	OG	6'4"	245	29		
Blaine Nye	OG	6'4"	250	27		
Jim Arneson	C-OG	6'3"	236	22		
Bruce Walton	C-OG	6'6"	250	22		
John Fitzgerald	C	6'5"	250	25		
Dave Manders	C	6'2"	250	31		
Larry Cole	DE	6'4"	250	26		
Harvey Martin	DE	6'5"	262	22		
Pat Toomay	DE	6'5"	244	28	1	
Bill Gregory	DT	6'5"	255	23		
Bob Lilly	DT	6'4"	260	34		
Jethro Puth	DT	6'6"	260	29		

Use Name	Pos.	Hgt	Wgt	Age	Int	Pts
John Babinecz	LB	6'1"	222	23		
Rodrigo Barnes	LB	6'1"	215	23		
Dave Edwards	LB	6'3"	225	34		
Chuck Howley	LB	6'3"	225	27		
Lee Roy Jordan	LB	6'2"	220	32	6	6
Mike Keller	LB	6'4"	220	22		
D. D. Lewis	LB	6'2"	225	27		6
Benny Barnes	DB	6'1"	190	22	1	4
Cornell Green	DB	6'4"	208	33		
Cliff Harris	DB	6'	184	24	2	
Mel Renfro	DB	6'	190	31	2	6
Mark Washington	DB	5'10"	188	25	1	
Charlie Waters	DB	6'1"	193	24	5	

Use Name	Pos.	Hgt	Wgt	Age	Int	Pts
Craig Morton	QB	6'4"	214	30		
Roger Staubach	QB	6'2"	197	31		18
Cyril Pinder	HB	6'2"	210	26		
Les Strayhorn	HB	5'10"	205	22		6
Calvin Hill	FB-HB	6'3"	227	26		36
Walt Garrison	FB	6'	205	29		48
Robert Newhouse	HB-FB	5'10"	202	23		12
Larry Robinson	HB-FB	6'4"	210	22		
Bob Hayes	WR	6'	185	30		18
Mike Montgomery	WR	6'2"	210	24		18
Drew Pearson	WR	6'	175	22		12
Golden Richards	WR	6'	172	22		6
Otto Stowe	WR	6'2"	188	24		36
Billy Joe DuPree	TE	6'4"	225	23		30
Jean Fugett	TE	6'3"	220	21		18
Billy Truax	TE	6'5"	240	30		
Marv Bateman	K	6'4"	213	23		1
Mike Clark	K	6'1"	205	32		4
Toni Fritsch	K	5'7"	185	28		97

WASHINGTON REDSKINS 10-4-0 George Allen

Scores of Each Game		
38	SAN DIEGO	0
27	St. Louis	34
28	Philadelphia	7
14	DALLAS	7
21	N. Y. Giants	3
31	ST. LOUIS	13
3	New Orleans	19
16	Pittsburgh	21
33	SAN FRANCISCO	9
22	BALTIMORE	14
20	Detroit	0
27	N. Y. GIANTS	24
7	Dallas	27
38	PHILADELPHIA	20

Use Name	Pos.	Hgt	Wgt	Age	Int	Pts
Terry Hermeling	OT	6'5"	255	27		
Walt Rock	OT	6'5"	255	32		
George Starke	OT	6'5"	250	25		
Paul Laaveg	OG	6'4"	245	24		
Ray Schoenke	OG	6'3"	250	31		
John Wilbur	OG	6'3"	250	30		
Len Hauss	C	6'2"	235	31		
Dan Ryczek	C	6'3"	250	24		
Verlon Biggs	DE	6'4"	275	30		6
Jimmie Jones	DE	6'3"	215	26		
Ron McDole	DE	6'3"	265	33		
Bill Brundige	DT	6'5"	270	24		
Manny Sistrunk	DT	6'5"	265	26		
Diron Talbert	DT	6'5"	255	29		

Jon Jaqua – Injury

Use Name	Pos.	Hgt	Wgt	Age	Int	Pts
Chris Hanburger	LB	6'2"	218	32	1	
Harold McLinton	LB	6'2"	235	26		
John Pergine	LB	6'1"	225	26		
Myron Pottios	LB	6'2"	232	33		
Dave Robinson	LB	6'3"	245	32	4	6
Rusty Tillman	LB	6'2"	230	27		
Mike Bass	DB	6'	190	28	5	6
Speedy Duncan	DB	5'10"	180	30	1	
Pat Fischer	DB	5'10"	170	33	3	
Ken Houston	DB	6'3"	198	28	6	
Brig Owens	DB	5'11"	190	30	5	12
Richie Petitbon	DB	6'3"	208	35		
Ted Vactor	DB	6'	185	29	1	6
Larry Willis	DB	5'11"	170	24		

Rosey Taylor – Injury

Use Name	Pos.	Hgt	Wgt	Age	Int	Pts
Sonny Jurgensen	QB	5'11"	203	39		
Billy Kilmer	QB	6'	204	33		
Larry Brown	HB	5'11"	195	25		84
Bob Brunet	HB	6'1"	205	27		
Herb Mul-Key	HB	6'	190	23		6
Charlie Harraway	FB	6'2"	215	28		24
Mike Hull	FB	6'3"	220	28		
Duane Thomas	HB-FB	6'1"	215	26		
Frank Grant	WR	5'11"	180	23		6
Roy Jefferson	WR	6'2"	195	29		6
Bill Malinchak	WR	6'1"	200	29		
Charlie Taylor	WR	6'3"	210	32		42
Mike Hancock	TE	6'4"	220	23		12
Alvin Reed	TE	6'5"	235	29		
Jerry Smith	TE	6'2"	208	30		
Mike Bragg	K	5'11"	186	26		
Curt Knight	K	6'1"	190	30		103

PHILADELPHIA EAGLES 5-8-1 Mike McCormack

Scores of Each Game		
23	ST. LOUIS	34
23	N. Y. Giants	23
7	WASHINGTON	28
26	Buffalo	27
27	St. Louis	24
21	Minnesota	28
30	DALLAS	16
24	NEW ENGLAND	23
27	ATLANTA	44
10	Dallas	31
20	N. Y. GIANTS	16
28	San Francisco	38
24	N. Y. JETS	23
20	Washington	38

Use Name	Pos.	Hgt	Wgt	Age	Int	Pts
Jerry Sisemore	OT	6'4"	260	22		
Steve Smith	OT	6'5"	250	29		
Dick Stevens	OT	6'4"	240	25		
Wade Key	OG	6'4"	245	26		
Roy Kirksey	OG	6'1"	265	25		
Tom Luken	OG	6'3"	253	23		
Mark Nordquist	OG	6'4"	246	27		
Vern Winfield	OG	6'2"	248	24		
Mike Evans	C	6'5"	250	27		
Guy Morriss	C	6'4"	255	22		
Gerry Philbin	DE	6'2"	245	32		
Dennis Wirgowski	DE	6'5"	250	25	1	
Will Wynn	DE	6'4"	240	24		6
Bill Dunstan	DT	6'4"	250	24		
Don Hultz	DT	6'3"	240	32		
Gary Pettigrew	DT	6'4"	255	28		
Richard Harris	DE-DT	6'4"	260	25		

Use Name	Pos.	Hgt	Wgt	Age	Int	Pts
John Bunting	LB	6'1"	220	23		
Dick Cunningham	LB	6'2"	238	28		
Dean Halverson	LB	6'2"	225	27		
Marlin McKeever	LB	6'1"	235	33		
Kevin Reilly	LB	6'2"	220	21		
Tom Roussel	LB	6'3"	235	28		
John Sodaski	LB	6'1"	222	25	1	
Steve Zabel	LB	6'4"	235	25	2	
Kermit Alexander	DB	5'11"	186	32		
Bill Bradley	DB	5'11"	190	26	4	
Al Coleman	DB	6'1"	183	28		
Joe Lavender	DB	6'4"	190	24		
Randy Logan	DB	6'1"	195	22	5	
Al Nelson	DB	5'11"	186	29		
John Outlaw	DB	5'10"	180	28	2	6

Use Name	Pos.	Hgt	Wgt	Age	Int	Pts
Roman Gabriel	QB	6'4"	220	33		6
John Reaves	QB	6'3"	210	23		
Po James	HB	6'1"	202	24		6
Greg Oliver	HB	6'	192	24		
Tom Sullivan	HB	6'	190	23		30
Tom Bailey	FB-HB	6'2"	211	24		6
Lee Bouggess	FB	6'2"	210	25		6
Norm Bulaich	HB-FB	6'1"	218	26		24
Harold Carmichael	WR	6'7"	225	23		54
Stan Davis	WR	5'10"	180	23		
Ben Hawkins	WR	6'	180	29		
Bob Picard	WR	6'1"	195	23		
Don Zimmerman	WR	6'3"	195	23		18
Kent Kramer	TE	6'5"	235	29		
Charlie Young	TE	6'4"	230	22		42
Tom Dempsey	K	6'1"	255	32		106
Tom McNeill	K	6'1"	195	31		

ST. LOUIS CARDINALS 4-9-1 Don Coryell

Scores of Each Game		
34	Philadelphia	23
34	WASHINGTON	27
10	Dallas	45
10	OAKLAND	17
24	PHILADELPHIA	27
13	Washington	31
35	N. Y. GIANTS	27
17	DENVER	17
21	Green Bay	25
13	N. Y. Giants	24
24	Cincinnati	42
16	DETROIT	20
32	Atlanta	10
3	DALLAS	30

Use Name	Pos.	Hgt	Wgt	Age	Int	Pts
Dan Dierdorf	OT	6'4"	265	24		
Ernie McMillan	OT	6'6"	255	35		
Mike Taylor	OT	6'4"	255	28		
Tom Banks	OG	6'1"	240	25		
Ron Davis	OG	6'2"	235	22		
Conrad Dobler	OG	6'3"	250	22		
Roger Finnie	OG	6'3"	245	27		
Bob Young	OG	6'2"	260	30		
Tom Brahaney	C	6'2"	225	21		
Warren Koegel	C	6'3"	250	23		
Wayne Mulligan	C	6'2"	245	26		
Council Rudolph	DE	6'3"	260	23		
Ron Yankowski	DE	6'5"	240	26		
Dave Butz	DT-DE	6'7"	290	23		
Lee Brooks	DT	6'5"	265	25		
John Richardson	DT	6'2"	250	27		
Bob Rowe	DT	6'4"	260	28		
Bonnie Sloan	DT	6'5"	260	24		

Use Name	Pos.	Hgt	Wgt	Age	Int	Pts
Mark Arneson	LB	6'2"	220	23	1	
Pete Barnes	LB	6'3"	240	28	1	
Jack LeVeck	LB	6'	225	23		
Terry Miller	LB	6'2"	225	27		
Jamie Rivers	LB	6'2"	235	27	1	
Jeff Staggs	LB	6'2"	240	29		
Larry Stallings	LB	6'2"	230	31	1	
Dwayne Crump	DB	5'11"	180	23		
Chuck Detwiler	DB	6'	185	26	1	
Clarence Duren	DB	6'1"	190	22	2	
Norm Thompson	DB	6'1"	175	25		
Jim Tolbert	DB	6'3"	202	29	2	
Eric Washington	DB	6'2"	190	23		
Roger Wehrli	DB	6'1"	195	25	1	

Leon Burns – Injury

Use Name	Pos.	Hgt	Wgt	Age	Int	Pts
Jim Hart	QB	6'2"	215	29		
Gary Keithley	QB	6'3"	205	22		
Donny Anderson	HB	6'3"	210	30		78
Willie Belton	HB	5'11"	195	24		
Terry Metcalf	HB	5'10"	185	21		12
Eddie Moss	HB	6'	215	24		
Jim Otis	FB	6'	220	25		6
Leo Hayden	HB-FB	6'	210	25		
Don Shy	HB-FB	6'1"	210	27		12
Walker Gillette	WR	6'5"	200	26		6
Mel Gray	WR	5'9"	170	24		42
Don Maynard	WR	6'	180	37		
Marv Owens	WR	5'11"	205	23		
Ahmad Rashad	WR	6'2"	210	23		18
Gary Hammond	HB-WR	5'11"	180	24		
Jim McFarland	TE	6'5"	225	25		6
Jackie Smith	TE	6'4"	235	32		6
Jim Bakken	K	6'	200	32		100

NEW YORK GIANTS 2-11-1 Alex Webster

Scores of Each Game		
34	HOUSTON	14
23	PHILADELPHIA	23
10	Cleveland	12
14	GREEN BAY	16
3	WASHINGTON	21
28	Dallas	45
27	St. Louis	35
0	Oakland	42
10	DALLAS	23
24	St. LOUIS	13
16	Philadelphia	20
24	Washington	27
6	Los Angeles	40
7	MINNESOTA	31

Use Name	Pos.	Hgt	Wgt	Age	Int	Pts
Bart Buetow	OT	6'5"	250	22		
John Hill	OT	6'2"	245	23		
Joe Taffoni	OT	6'3"	255	28		
Willie Young	OT	6'	265	30		
Mark Ellison	OG	6'2"	250	24		
Dick Enderle	OG	6'1"	250	25		
Doug Van Horn	OG	6'2"	245	29		
Bob Hyland	OT-C	6'5"	255	28		
Greg Larson	C	6'2"	250	34		
Carter Campbell	DE	6'3"	240	25		
Jack Gregory	DE	6'6"	250	28		
Dave Tipton	DE	6'6"	240	24		
Rich Glover	DT	6'1"	240	22		
Dan Goich	DT	6'4"	250	29		
Larry Jacobson	DT	6'6"	260	23		
John Mendenhall	DT	6'1"	255	24		

Use Name	Pos.	Hgt	Wgt	Age	Int	Pts
John Douglas	LB	6'2"	228	28	1	
Jim Files	LB	6'4"	240	25	1	
Ron Hornsby	LB	6'3"	232	24		
Pat Hughes	LB	6'2"	240	26	3	
Brian Kelley	LB	6'3"	222	22		
Henry Reed	LB	6'3"	230	24	1	
Brad Van Pelt	LB	6'5"	235	22		
Pete Athas	DB	5'11"	185	27	5	
Otto Brown	DB	6'1"	188	25		
Chuck Crist	DB	6'2"	205	22	2	
Richmond Flowers	DB	6'	180	26	1	
Spider Lockhart	DB	6'2"	175	30	2	
Ron Lumpkin	DB	6'2"	200	22		
Eldridge Small	DB	6'1"	190	23		
Willie Williams	DB	6'	190	30	4	

Use Name	Pos.	Hgt	Wgt	Age	Int	Pts
Randy Johnson	QB	6'3"	205	29		6
Norm Snead	QB	6'4"	215	33		
Ron Johnson	HB	6'1"	205	25		54
Jack Rizzo	HB	5'10"	195	24		
Rocky Thompson	HB	5'11"	200	25		
Joe Orduna	FB-HB	6'	195	25		6
Vin Clements	FB	6'3"	215	24		12
Charlie Evans	FB	6'1"	220	25		6
Johnny Roland	HB-FB	6'2"	220	30		12
Bob Grim	WR	6'	200	28		12
Don Herrmann	WR	6'2"	205	26		12
Rich Houston	WR	6'2"	195	27		
Walt Love	WR	5'9"	180	22		
Gary Ballman (to MIN)	TE	6'	215	33		
Tom Gatewood	TE	6'3"	215	22		
Bob Tucker	TE	6'3"	230	28		30
Tom Blanchard	K	6'	190	25		
Pete Gogolak	K	6'2"	190	31		76
Jim McCann	K	6'2"	163	24		

DALLAS COWBOYS

RUSHING

Last Name	No.	Yds	Avg	TD
Hill	273	1142	4.2	6
Garrison	105	440	4.2	6
Newhouse	84	436	5.2	1
Staubach	46	250	5.4	3
Strayhorn	11	62	5.6	1
Fugett	1	34	34.0	0
Stowe	3	28	9.3	0
Robinson	2	17	8.5	0
Pinder	12	15	1.3	0
Richards	1	2	2.0	0
DuPree	2	2	1.0	0
Morton	2	0	0.0	0
Montgomery	1	-10	-10.0	0

RECEIVING

Last Name	No.	Yds	Avg	TD
Hill	32	290	9	0
DuPree	29	392	14	5
Garrison	26	273	11	2
Stowe	23	389	17	6
Pearson	22	388	18	2
Hayes	22	360	16	3
Montgomery	14	164	12	3
Fugett	9	168	19	3
Newhouse	9	87	10	1
Richards	6	91	15	1

PUNT RETURNS

Last Name	No.	Yds	Avg	TD
Richards	21	139	7	0
Harris	3	20	7	0
Pearson	2	13	7	0
Montgomery	2	2	1	0

KICKOFF RETURNS

Last Name	No.	Yds	Avg	TD
Montgomery	6	175	29	0
Pearson	7	155	22	0
Harris	6	148	25	0
Robinson	4	86	22	0
Newhouse	3	62	21	0
Richards	3	44	15	0
Strayhorn	2	44	22	0
Walton	1	11	11	0
Washington	1	0	0	0

PASSING – PUNTING – KICKING

PASSING	Att	Comp	%	Yds	Yd/Att	TD	Int–%	RK
Staubach	286	179	63	2428	8.5	23	15– 5	2
Morton	32	13	41	174	5.4	3	1– 3	
Garrison	1	0	0	0	0.0	0	0– 0	
Hill	1	0	0	0	0.0	0	0– 0	
Montgomery	1	0	0	0	0.0	0	0– 0	

PUNTING	No	Avg
Bateman	55	41.6
Montgomery	4	39.5

KICKING	XP	Att	%	FG	Att	%
Fritsch	43	43	100	18	28	64
Clark	1	2	50	1	2	50
Bateman	1	1	100	0	0	0

WASHINGTON REDSKINS

RUSHING

Last Name	No.	Yds	Avg	TD
Brown	273	860	3.2	8
Harraway	128	452	3.5	1
Thomas	32	95	3.0	0
Mul-Key	8	20	2.5	0
Kilmer	9	10	1.1	0
Jurgensen	3	7	2.3	0
Brunet	2	4	2.0	0
Jefferson	1	1	1.0	0
Hull	2	-3	-1.5	0
C. Taylor	1	-7	-7.0	0

RECEIVING

Last Name	No.	Yds	Avg	TD
C. Taylor	59	801	14	7
Jefferson	41	595	15	1
Brown	40	482	12	6
Harraway	32	291	9	3
Smith	19	215	11	0
Reed	9	124	14	0
Thomas	5	40	8	0
Hancock	2	3	2	2
Grant	1	12	12	1
Jurgensen	1	-3	-3	0

PUNT RETURNS

Last Name	No.	Yds	Avg	TD
Duncan	28	228	8	0
Mul-Key	11	103	9	0
Smith	1	0	0	0

KICKOFF RETURNS

Last Name	No.	Yds	Avg	TD
Mul-Key	36	1011	28	1
Duncan	4	65	16	0
Tillman	3	42	14	0

PASSING – PUNTING – KICKING

PASSING	Att	Comp	%	Yds	Yd/Att	TD	Int–%	RK
Kilmer	227	122	54	1656	7.3	14	9 – 4	6
Jurgensen	145	87	60	904	6.2	6	5 – 3	

PUNTING	No	Avg
Bragg	64	40.3

KICKING	XP	Att	%	FG	Att	%
Knight	37	37	100	22	42	52

PHILADELPHIA EAGLES

RUSHING

Last Name	No.	Yds	Avg	TD
Sullivan	217	968	4.5	4
Bulaich	106	436	4.1	1
James	36	178	4.9	1
Bailey	20	91	4.6	0
Carmichael	3	42	14.0	0
Bouggess	15	34	2.3	1
Young	4	24	6.0	1
Gabriel	12	10	0.8	1
Oliver	1	6	6.0	0
Reaves	2	2	1.0	0
Bradley	1	0	0.0	0

RECEIVING

Last Name	No.	Yds	Avg	TD
Carmichael	67	1116	17	9
Young	55	854	16	6
Sullivan	50	322	6	1
Bulaich	42	403	10	3
Zimmerman	22	220	10	3
James	17	94	6	0
Bailey	10	80	8	1
Hawkins	6	114	19	0
Bouggess	4	18	5	0
Oliver	1	9	9	0
Davis	1	6	6	0

PUNT RETURNS

Last Name	No.	Yds	Avg	TD
Bradley	8	106	13	0
Alexander	5	10	2	0
Davis	2	0	0	0

KICKOFF RETURNS

Last Name	No.	Yds	Avg	TD
James	16	413	26	0
Sullivan	12	280	23	0
Nelson	11	264	24	0
Davis	10	236	24	0
Alexander	9	189	21	0
Coleman	2	24	12	0
Bailey	2	18	9	0
Oliver	1	17	17	0

PASSING – PUNTING – KICKING

PASSING	Att	Comp	%	Yds	Yd/Att	TD	Int–%	RK
Gabriel	460	270	59	3219	7.0	23	12– 3	1
Reaves	19	5	26	17	0.9	0	1– 5	

PUNTING	No	Avg
McNeill	46	40.9
Bradley	18	40.8

KICKING	XP	Att	%	FG	Att	%
Dempsey	34	34	100	24	40	60

ST. LOUIS CARDINALS

RUSHING

Last Name	No.	Yds	Avg	TD
Anderson	167	679	4.1	10
Metcalf	148	628	4.2	2
Otis	55	234	4.3	1
Shy	16	66	4.1	0
Moss	14	41	2.9	0
Keithley	8	29	3.6	0
Hammond	4	11	2.8	0
Hart	3	-3	-1.0	0
Smith	1	-14	-14.0	0

RECEIVING

Last Name	No.	Yds	Avg	TD
Smith	41	600	15	1
Anderson	41	409	10	3
Metcalf	37	316	9	0
Rashad	30	409	14	3
Gray	29	513	18	7
Gillette	20	244	12	1
Hammond	4	39	10	0
Shy	3	15	5	1
Otis	2	19	10	0
McFarland	2	10	5	0
Maynard	1	18	18	0

PUNT RETURNS

Last Name	No.	Yds	Avg	TD
Wehrli	9	92	10	0
Hammond	11	80	7	0
Thompson	6	18	3	0
Belton	1	2	2	0

KICKOFF RETURNS

Last Name	No.	Yds	Avg	TD
Shy	16	445	28	1
Hammond	12	314	26	0
Metcalf	4	124	31	0
Hayden	5	98	20	0
Belton	3	83	28	0
Moss	4	78	20	0
Gray	4	73	18	0
McFarland	3	57	19	0
Detwiler	3	55	18	0
Butz	1	23	23	0
Owens	1	19	19	0
Wehrli	2	0	0	0

PASSING – PUNTING – KICKING

PASSING	Att	Comp	%	Yds	Yd/Att	TD	Int–%	RK
Hart	320	178	56	2223	7.0	15	10– 3	4
Keithley	73	32	44	369	5.1	1	5 – 7	
Hammond	1	0	0	0	0.0	0	0 – 0	

PUNTING	No	Avg
Keithley	66	37.5

KICKING	XP	Att	%	FG	Att	%
Bakken	31	31	100	23	32	72

NEW YORK GIANTS

RUSHING

Last Name	No.	Yds	Avg	TD
Ron Johnson	260	902	3.5	6
Clements	57	214	3.8	1
Roland	53	142	2.7	1
Orduna	36	104	2.9	1
Evans	34	77	2.3	1
Randy Johnson	4	24	6.0	1
Snead	4	13	3.3	0
Thompson	5	5	1.0	0
Tucker	1	4	4.0	0
Rizzo	1	3	3.0	0
Grim	1	-10	-10.0	0

RECEIVING

Last Name	No.	Yds	Avg	TD
Tucker	50	681	14	5
Herrmann	43	520	12	2
Grim	37	593	16	2
Ron Johnson	32	377	12	3
Roland	22	190	9	1
Clements	15	129	9	1
Evans	13	100	8	0
Houston	8	90	11	0
Orduna	6	44	7	0
Ballman	3	38	13	0
Hyland	1	16	16	0
Rizzo	1	11	11	0
Young	1	-5	-5	0

PUNT RETURNS

Last Name	No.	Yds	Avg	TD
Athas	20	153	8	0
Crist	1	7	7	0

KICKOFF RETURNS

Last Name	No.	Yds	Avg	TD
Love	18	396	22	0
Houston	15	375	25	0
Small	11	207	19	0
Orduna	6	104	17	0
Rizzo	4	86	22	0
Kelley	2	30	15	0

PASSING – PUNTING – KICKING

PASSING	Att	Comp	%	Yds	Yd/Att	TD	Int–%	RK
Snead	235	131	56	1483	6.3	7	22– 9	11
Ran. Johnson	177	99	56	1279	7.2	7	8 – 5	

PUNTING	No	Avg
Blanchard	56	41.9
McCann	12	24.5

KICKING	XP	Att	%	FG	Att	%
Gogolak	25	25	100	17	28	61

MINNESOTA VIKINGS 12-2-0 Bud Grant

Scores of Each Game		
24	OAKLAND	16
22	Chicago	13
11	GREEN BAY	3
23	Detroit	9
17	San Francisco	13
28	PHILADELPHIA	21
10	LOS ANGELES	9
26	CLEVELAND	3
28	DETROIT	7
14	Atlanta	20
31	CHICAGO	13
0	Cincinnati	27
31	Green Bay	7
31	N. Y. Giants	7

Use Name	Pos.	Hgt	Wgt	Age	Int	Pts
Grady Alderman	OT	6'2"	247	34		
Ron Yary	OT	6'6"	255	27		
Charlie Goodrum	OG-OT	6'3"	256	23		
Frank Gallagher (from ATL)	OG	6'2"	245	30		
Steve Lawson	OG	6'3"	265	24		
Milt Sunde	OG	6'2"	250	30		
John Ward	OG	6'4"	260	25		
Ed White	OG	6'2"	262	26		
Mick Tingelhoff	C	6'1"	237	33		
Godfrey Zaunbrecher	C	6'2"	240	25		
Carl Eller	DE	6'6"	247	31		
Jim Marshall	DE	6'3"	248	35		
Bob Lurtsema	DT-DE	6'6"	250	31		
Gary Larsen	DT	6'5"	260	33		
Alan Page	DT	6'5"	245	28		
Doug Sutherland	DT	6'3"	250	25		
Wally Hilgenberg	LB	6'3"	230	30	1	6
Amos Martin	LB	6'3"	228	24		
Ron Porter	LB	6'3"	232	28		
Jeff Siemon	LB	6'2"	230	23	2	
Roy Winston	LB	6'1"	222	33		2
Terry Brown	DB	6'1"	205	26	1	6
Bobby Bryant	DB	6'	170	29	7	6
Paul Krause	DB	6'3"	200	31	4	
Al Randolph	DB	6'2"	205	29		
Charlie West	DB	6'1"	197	27		
Jeff Wright	DB	5'11"	190	24	3	
Nate Wright	DB	5'11"	180	25	3	
Bob Berry	QB	5'11"	185	31		
Fran Tarkenton	QB	6'1"	190	33		6
Brent McClanahan	HB	5'10"	202	22		
Dave Osborn	HB	6'	208	30		
Chuck Foreman	FB-HB	6'2"	216	22		36
Bill Brown	FB	5'11"	222	35		24
Ed Marinaro	HB-FB	6'2"	212	23		24
Oscar Reed	HB-FB	5'11"	222	29		18
Carroll Dale	WR	6'1"	200	35		
Rhett Dawson	WR	6'1"	185	24		
John Gilliam	WR	6'1"	195	28		54
Jim Lash	WR	6'2"	200	21		
Doug Kingswriter	TE	6'2"	222	23		
Stu Voigt	TE	6'1"	220	25		12
Fred Cox	K	5'10"	200	34		96
Mike Eischeid	K	6'	190	32		

Karl Kassulke – Paralyzed in motorcycle accident

DETROIT LIONS 6-7-1 Don McCafferty

Scores of Each Game		
10	Pittsburgh	24
13	Green Bay	13
31	ATLANTA	6
9	MINNESOTA	23
13	New Orleans	20
27	BALTIMORE	29
34	GREEN BAY	0
30	SAN FRANCISCO	20
7	Minnesota	28
30	Chicago	7
0	WASHINGTON	20
20	St. Louis	16
40	CHICAGO	7
7	Miami	34

Use Name	Pos.	Hgt	Wgt	Age	Int	Pts
Rocky Freitas	OT	6'6"	270	27		
Mike Haggerty	OT	6'4"	245	27		
Gordon Jolley	OT	6'5"	250	24		
Jim Yarbrough	OT	6'6"	265	26		
Guy Dennis	OG	6'2"	255	26		
Bob Kowalkowski	OG	6'3"	240	29		
Rocky Rasley	OG	6'3"	250	26		
Chuck Walton	OG	6'3"	255	32		
Ed Flanagan	C	6'3"	245	29		
Dave Thompson	OG-C	6'4"	275	24		
Larry Hand	DE	6'4"	250	33		
Jim Mitchell	DE	6'3"	245	24		
Ken Sanders	DE	6'5"	240	23		
Bob Bell	DT	6'4"	250	25		
Herb Orvis	DT	6'5"	240	26		
Ernie Price	DT	6'4"	255	22		
John Small	DT	6'5"	260	26		
Mike Hennigan	LB	6'2"	210	21		
Jim Laslavic	LB	6'2"	230	21		
Mike Lucci	LB	6'2"	230	33	4	
Paul Naumoff	LB	6'1"	215	28		
Jim Teal	LB	6'3"	225	23		
Charlie Weaver	LB	6'2"	218	24	2	
Lem Barney	DB	6'	188	27	4	
Miller Farr	DB	6'1"	190	30	1	
Willie Germany	DB	6'	192	24		
Dick Jauron	DB	6'	190	22	4	6
Levi Johnson	DB	6'3"	190	22	5	
Jim Thrower	DB	6'2"	194	24		
Mike Weger	DB	6'2"	200	27	2	
Doug Wyatt	DB	6'1"	195	26		
Bill Cappleman	QB	6'3"	210	26		
Greg Landry	QB	6'4"	210	26		12
Bill Munson	QB	6'2"	210	31		
Mel Farr	HB	6'2"	210	28		24
Altie Taylor	HB	5'10"	200	25		30
Mickey Zofko	HB	6'3"	195	23		
Leon Crosswhite	FB	6'2"	215	22		6
Jim Hooks	FB	5'11"	225	21		
Steve Owens	FB	6'2"	215	25		18
Al Barnes	WR	6'1"	170	24		6
Ron Jessie	WR	6'	183	25		24
Earl McCullouch	WR	5'11"	175	27		6
Jim O'Brien	WR	6'	195	26		38
Larry Walton	WR	5'11"	180	26		30
John Hilton	TE	6'5"	225	31		6
Charlie Sanders	TE	6'4"	225	27		12
Errol Mann	K	6'	200	32		53
Herman Weaver	K	6'4"	210	24		

Wayne Rasmussen – Injury
Rudy Redmond – Injury

GREEN BAY PACKERS 5-7-2 Dan Devine

Scores of Each Game		
23	N. Y. JETS	7
13	DETROIT	13
3	Minnesota	11
16	N. Y. Giants	14
10	KANSAS CITY	10
7	Los Angeles	24
0	Detroit	34
17	CHICAGO	31
25	ST. LOUIS	21
24	New England	33
6	San Francisco	20
30	NEW ORLEANS	10
7	MINNESOTA	31
21	Chicago	0

Use Name	Pos.	Hgt	Wgt	Age	Int	Pts
Kent Branstetter	OT	6'3"	260	24		
Bill Hayhoe	OT	6'8"	258	26		
Dick Himes	OT	6'4"	244	27		
Mal Snider	OG-OT	6'4"	250	26		
Gale Gillingham	OG	6'3"	255	29		
Bill Lueck	OG	6'3"	235	27		
Keith Wortman	OG	6'2"	245	23		
Ken Bowman	C	6'3"	230	30		
Larry McCarren	C	6'3"	240	22		
Cal Withrow	C	6'	240	28		
Aaron Brown	DE	6'5"	270	29		
Dave Pureifory	DE	6'1"	260	23		
Alden Roche	DE	6'4"	255	28		
Clarence Williams	DE	6'5"	255	26		
Bob Brown	DT	6'5"	260	33		
Mike McCoy	DT	6'5"	284	24		
Carleton Oats	DT	6'2"	260	30		
Fred Carr	LB	6'5"	238	27		
Jim Carter	LB	6'3"	235	24	3	6
Larry Hefner	LB	6'2"	230	24	1	
Noel Jenke	LB	6'1"	225	26		
Tom MacLeod	LB	6'3"	220	22	2	
Tom Toner	LB	6'3"	225	23	1	
Hise Austin	DB	6'4"	195	22		
Willie Buchanan	DB	6'	190	22		
Ken Ellis	DB	5'10"	190	25	3	6
Charlie Hall	DB	6'1"	195	24		
Jim Hill	DB	6'2"	190	26	3	
Al Matthews	DB	5'11"	190	25	2	6
Perry Smith	DB	6'1"	195	22		
Ike Thomas	WR-DB	6'2"	193	25		
Jim Del Gaizo	QB	6'1"	198	26		
Scott Hunter	QB	6'2"	205	25		6
Jerry Tagge	QB	6'2"	220	23		12
Don Highsmith	HB	6'	200	25		
Larry Krause	HB	6'	208	25		
MacArthur Lane	HB	6'	220	31		12
Ron McBride	HB	6'	200	24		
Les Goodman	FB-HB	5'11"	206	23		6
John Brockington	FB	6'1"	225	24		18
Perry Williams	FB	6'2"	220	26		6
Leland Glass	WR	6'	185	23		
Barry Smith	WR	6'1"	185	22		12
Jon Staggers	WR	5'10"	186	24		24
Paul Staroba	WR	6'3"	204	24		
Mike Donohoe	TE	6'3"	228	28		
Rich McGeorge	TE	6'4"	235	24		6
Chester Marcol	K	6'	190	24		82
Ron Widby	K	6'4"	220	28		

Bob Kroll – Injury

CHICAGO BEARS 3-11-0 Abe Gibron

Scores of Each Game		
17	DALLAS	20
13	MINNESOTA	22
33	Denver	14
16	New Orleans	21
6	Atlanta	46
10	NEW ENGLAND	13
35	HOUSTON	14
31	Green Bay	17
7	Kansas City	19
7	DETROIT	30
13	Minnesota	31
0	LOS ANGELES	26
7	Detroit	40
0	GREEN BAY	21

Use Name	Pos.	Hgt	Wgt	Age	Int	Pts
Lionel Antwine	OT	6'6"	255	23		
Bob Asher	OT	6'5"	250	25		
Randy Jackson	OT	6'5"	250	29		
Steve Kinney	OT	6'5"	255	24		
Glenn Holloway	OG	6'3"	255	24		
Ernie Janet	OG	6'4"	250	24		
Bob Newton	OG	6'4"	250	24		
Rich Coady	C	6'3"	235	28		
Willie Holman (to WAS)	DE	6'4"	250	28		
Gary Hrivnak	DE	6'5"	248	22		
Tony McGee	DE	6'4"	250	24		
Mel Tom (from PHI)	DE	6'4"	250	32		
Wally Chambers	DT	6'6"	250	22		
Dave Hale	DT	6'7"	255	26		
Jim Osborne	DT	6'3"	250	23		
Andy Rice	DT	6'3"	268	31		
Doug Buffone	LB	6'1"	225	29	3	
Dick Butkus	LB	6'3"	245	29	1	6
Gail Clark	LB	6'2"	227	22		
Jimmy Gunn	LB	6'1"	220	24		
Bob Pifferini	LB	6'2"	226	23		
Don Rives	LB	6'2"	215	22		
Adrian Young	LB	6'1"	232	27		
Craig Clemons	DB	5'11"	200	24	2	
Allan Ellis	DB	5'10"	185	22	1	
Charlie Ford	DB	6'3"	185	24	2	
Bob Jeter	DB	6'1"	200	35		
Garry Lyle	DB	6'2"	198	27	5	
Willie Roberts	DB	6'1"	190	25		
Joe Taylor	DB	6'2"	200	32		
Bobby Douglass	QB	6'3"	225	26		30
Gary Huff	QB	6'1"	200	22		
Carl Garrett	HB	5'11"	215	26		30
Joe Moore	HB	6'1"	205	24		
Reggie Sanderson	HB	5'10"	206	22		
Gary Kosins	FB-HB	6'1"	220	24		
Jim Harrison	FB	6'4"	235	24		18
Roger Lawson	HB-FB	6'2"	215	23		
George Farmer	WR	6'4"	214	25		6
Ike Hill	WR	5'10"	180	26		12
Dave Juenger	WR	6'1"	195	22		
Mike Reppond	WR	6'	180	22		
Tom Reynolds	WR	6'3"	200	24		
Cecil Turner	WR	5'10"	176	29		
Craig Cotton	TE	6'4"	222	26		
Bob Parsons	TE	6'4"	234	23		6
Earl Thomas	WR-TE	6'3"	215	24		24
Bobby Joe Green	K	5'11"	175	35		
Mac Percival	K	6'4"	220	33		28
Mirro Roder	K	6'1"	218	29		35

MINNESOTA VIKINGS

RUSHING

Last Name	No.	Yds	Avg	TD
Foreman	182	801	4.4	4
Reed	100	401	4.0	3
Marinaro	95	302	3.2	2
Osborn	48	216	4.5	0
B. Brown	47	206	4.4	3
Tarkenton	41	202	4.9	1
Gilliam	5	71	14.2	1
McClanahan	17	69	4.1	0
Berry	2	5	2.5	0
Voigt	1	2	2.0	0

RECEIVING

Last Name	No.	Yds	Avg	TD
Gilliam	42	907	22	8
Foreman	37	362	10	2
Marinaro	26	196	8	2
Voigt	23	318	14	2
Reed	19	122	6	0
Dale	14	192	14	0
B. Brown	5	22	4	1
Osborn	3	4	1	0
Lash	2	34	17	0
Kingsriter	2	27	14	0
Dawson	2	24	12	0
Ward	1	1	1	0

PUNT RETURNS

Last Name	No.	Yds	Avg	TD
Bryant	25	140	6	0
J. Wright	2	0	0	0
West	1	0	0	0

KICKOFF RETURNS

Last Name	No.	Yds	Avg	TD
McClanahan	16	410	26	0
Gilliam	10	174	17	0
West	3	104	35	0
B. Brown	3	35	12	0
Reed	2	29	15	0
J. Wright	1	0	0	0

PASSING – PUNTING – KICKING

PASSING	Att	Comp	%	Yds	Yd/Att	TD	Int–%	RK
Tarkenton	274	169	62	2113	7.7	15	7– 3	3
Berry	24	10	42	121	5.0	1	2– 8	

PUNTING	No	Avg
Eischeid	66	39.8

KICKING	XP	Att	%	FG	Att	%
Cox	33	33	100	21	35	60

DETROIT LIONS

RUSHING

Last Name	No.	Yds	Avg	TD
Taylor	176	719	4.1	5
Owens	113	401	3.5	3
Mel Farr	97	373	3.8	4
Landry	42	267	6.4	2
Hooks	19	110	5.8	0
L. Walton	4	74	18.5	1
Munson	10	33	3.3	0
Zofko	11	33	3.0	0
Jessie	5	31	6.2	1
Crosswhite	11	30	2.7	1
C. Walton	1	26	26.0	0
H. Weaver	1	18	18.0	0
McCullouch	2	12	6.0	0
Barney	2	0	4.6	0
C. Sanders	1	−1	−1.0	0
Cappleman	1	−2	−2.0	0

RECEIVING

Last Name	No.	Yds	Avg	TD
C. Sanders	28	433	15	2
Taylor	27	252	9	0
Mel Farr	26	183	7	0
Owens	24	232	10	0
L. Walton	21	302	14	4
Jessie	20	364	18	3
McCullouch	9	179	20	1
Hilton	6	70	12	1
Barnes	3	43	14	1
Zofko	2	16	8	0
O'Brien	2	14	7	0
C. Walton	1	7	7	0
Hooks	1	6	6	0
Crosswhite	1	4	4	0

PUNT RETURNS

Last Name	No.	Yds	Avg	TD
Barney	27	231	9	0
Jauron	6	49	8	0
L. Walton	1	9	9	0
Teal	1	0	0	0

KICKOFF RETURNS

Last Name	No.	Yds	Avg	TD
Jauron	17	405	24	0
Taylor	12	295	25	0
Jessie	6	154	26	0
Thrower	3	54	18	0
Hooks	2	52	26	0
Johnson	3	51	17	0
Barney	1	28	28	0
Jolley	1	15	15	0
Zofko	1	7	7	0
Barnes	1	0	0	0
Dennis	1	0	0	0
Germany	1	0	0	0
C. Weaver	1	0	0	0

PASSING – PUNTING – KICKING

PASSING	Att	Comp	%	Yds	Yd/Att	TD	Int–%	RK
Munson	187	95	51	1129	6.0	9	8– 4	12
Landry	128	70	55	908	7.1	3	10– 8	
Cappleman	11	5	45	33	3.0	0	1– 9	
Zofko	1	1	100	35	35.0	0	0– 0	

PUNTING	No	Avg
H. Weaver	54	43.2

KICKING	XP	Att	%	FG	Att	%
Mann	14	14	100	13	19	68
O'Brien	14	14	100	8	14	57

GREEN BAY PACKERS

RUSHING

Last Name	No.	Yds	Avg	TD
Brockington	265	1144	4.3	3
Lane	170	528	3.1	1
Goodman	18	88	4.9	1
P. Williams	32	87	2.7	1
Tagge	15	62	4.1	2
Staggers	4	33	8.3	1
Staroba	1	11	11.0	0
Krause	1	8	8.0	0
Highsmith	7	7	1.0	0
B. Smith	1	5	5.0	0
Hunter	8	3	0.4	1
Del Gaizo	4	1	0.3	0

RECEIVING

Last Name	No.	Yds	Avg	TD
Lane	27	255	9	1
Staggers	25	412	16	3
McGeorge	16	260	16	1
Brockington	16	128	8	0
B. Smith	15	233	16	2
Glass	11	119	11	0
P. Williams	5	44	9	0
Goodman	2	19	10	0
Staroba	1	23	23	0
Donohoe	1	10	10	0

PUNT RETURNS

Last Name	No.	Yds	Avg	TD
Staggers	19	90	5	0
Ellis	11	47	4	0

KICKOFF RETURNS

Last Name	No.	Yds	Avg	TD
Thomas	23	527	23	0
Ellis	12	319	27	0
Krause	11	244	22	0
Lane	2	31	16	0
P. Williams	1	24	24	0
A. Brown	2	19	10	0
Highsmith	1	18	18	0
B. Brown	1	7	7	0

PASSING – PUNTING – KICKING

PASSING	Att	Comp	%	Yds	Yd/Att	TD	Int–%	RK
Tagge	106	56	53	720	6.8	2	7– 7	
Hunter	84	35	42	442	5.3	2	4– 5	
Del Gaizo	62	27	44	318	5.1	2	6–10	
Lane	2	1	50	23	11.5	1	0– 0	
Brockington	1	0	0	0	0.0	0	0– 0	

PUNTING	No	Avg
Widby	56	43.1
Staroba	12	31.1

KICKING	XP	Att	%	FG	Att	%
Marcol	19	20	95	21	35	60

CHICAGO BEARS

RUSHING

Last Name	No.	Yds	Avg	TD
Garrett	175	655	3.7	5
Douglass	94	525	5.6	5
Harrison	100	374	3.7	1
Moore	58	191	3.3	0
Lawson	24	70	2.9	0
Kosins	24	65	2.7	0
Huff	11	22	2.0	0
Sanderson	3	8	2.7	0
Farmer	1	8	8.0	0
Thomas	1	5	5.0	0
Parsons	2	2	1.0	0
Hill	3	−14	−4.7	0

RECEIVING

Last Name	No.	Yds	Avg	TD
Thomas	24	343	14	4
Garrett	23	292	13	0
Harrison	21	200	10	2
Farmer	15	219	15	1
Cotton	13	186	14	0
Hill	10	119	12	0
Lawson	9	60	7	0
Reynolds	7	127	18	0
Sanderson	5	23	5	0
Kosins	4	8	2	0
Moore	3	17	6	0
Parsons	2	23	12	1

PUNT RETURNS

Last Name	No.	Yds	Avg	TD
Hill	36	204	6	1
Moore	1	0	0	0

KICKOFF RETURNS

Last Name	No.	Yds	Avg	TD
Hill	27	637	24	1
Garrett	16	486	30	0
Turner	8	127	16	0
Sanderson	2	44	22	0
Cotton	2	15	8	0
Parsons	2	15	8	0
Holloway	1	8	8	0
Osborne	1	0	0	0
Thomas	0	12	0	0

PASSING – PUNTING – KICKING

PASSING	Att	Comp	%	Yds	Yd/Att	TD	Int–%	RK
Douglass	174	81	47	1057	6.1	5	7– 4	13
Huff	126	54	43	525	4.2	3	8– 6	
Garrett	1	0	0	0	0.0	0	0– 0	
Hill	1	1	100	35	35.0	0	0– 0	
Thomas	1	0	0	0	0.0	0	1–100	

PUNTING	No	Avg
Green	82	40.5
Parsons	4	26.5

KICKING	XP	Att	%	FG	Att	%
Roder	11	12	92	8	16	50
Percival	10	10	100	6	8	75

LOS ANGELES RAMS 12-2-0 Chuck Knox

Scores of Each Game		
23	Kansas City	13
31	ATLANTA	0
40	San Francisco	20
31	Houston	26
37	DALLAS	31
24	GREEN BAY	7
9	Minnesota	10
13	Atlanta	15
29	NEW ORLEANS	7
31	SAN FRANCISCO	13
24	New Orleans	13
26	Chicago	0
40	N. Y. GIANTS	6
30	CLEVELAND	17

Use Name	Pos.	Hgt	Wgt	Age	Int	Pts
Charley Cowan	OT	6'4"	265	35		
Harry Schuh	OT	6'2"	260	30		
John Williams	OT	6'3"	256	27		
Tom Mack	OG	6'3"	250	29		
Joe Scibelli	OG	6'1"	255	34		
Rich Saul	C-OG	6'3"	235	25		
Ken Iman	C	6'1"	240	34		
Fred Dryer	DE	6'6"	240	27		
Jack Youngblood	DE	6'4"	250	23		
Larry Brooks	DT	6'3"	255	23		
Bill Nelson	DT	6'7"	270	25		
Merlin Olsen	DT	6'5"	270	32		
Phil Olsen	DT	6'5"	265	25		

Use Name	Pos.	Hgt	Wgt	Age	Int	Pts
Ken Geddes	LB	6'3"	235	25		
Rick Kay	LB	6'4"	235	23		
Jack Reynolds	LB	6'1"	232	25	2	
Isiah Robertson	LB	6'3"	225	24	3	6
Bob Stein	LB	6'2"	235	25	1	
Jim Youngblood	LB	6'3"	240	23	1	
Cullen Bryant	DB	6'1"	210	22		6
Al Clark	DB	6'	180	25	1	
Dave Elmendorf	DB	6'1"	195	24	1	
Eddie McMillan	DB	6'	180	21	4	
Steve Preece	DB	6'1"	195	26	2	6
Charlie Stukes	DB	6'3"	212	29	5	
Bill Drake	WR-DB	6'1"	195	23		

Use Name	Pos.	Hgt	Wgt	Age	Int	Pts
John Hadl	QB	6'2"	214	33		
James Harris	QB	6'3"	210	26		
Jim Bertelsen	HB	5'11"	205	23		30
Lawrence McCutcheon	HB	6'1"	205	23		30
Rob Scribner	HB	6'	200	22		
Larry Smith	HB	6'3"	220	25		12
Tony Baker	FB	5'11"	225	28		42
Cullen Bryant	FB	6'1"	218	22		
Les Josephson	FB	6'	207	30		12
Dick Gordon (to GB)	WR	5'11"	190	28		
Harold Jackson	WR	5'1"	175	27		78
David Ray	WR	6'	195	28		130
Rod Sherman	WR	6'	190	28		
Jack Snow	WR	6'2"	190	30		12
Joe Sweet	WR	6'2"	196	25		
Pat Curran	TE	6'3"	238	27		
Bob Klein	TE	6'5"	235	26		12
Dave Chapple	K	6'	180	26		

ATLANTA FALCONS 9-5-0 Norm Van Brocklin

Scores of Each Game		
62	New Orleans	7
0	Los Angeles	31
6	Detroit	31
9	SAN FRANCISCO	13
46	CHICAGO	6
41	San Diego	0
17	San Francisco	3
15	LOS ANGELES	13
44	Philadelphia	27
20	MINNESOTA	14
28	N. Y. Jets	20
6	BUFFALO	17
10	ST. LOUIS	32
14	NEW ORLEANS	10

Use Name	Pos.	Hgt	Wgt	Age	Int	Pts
Nick Bebout	OT	6'5"	260	22		
Len Gotshalk	OT	6'4"	260	23		
George Kunz	OT	6'5"	268	26		
Bill Sandeman	OT	6'6"	265	30		
Dennis Havig	OG	6'2"	256	24		
Andy Mauer	OG	6'3"	247	24		
Ted Fritsch	C	6'2"	240	23		
Jeff Van Note	C	6'2"	247	27		
Claude Humphrey	DE	6'5"	265	29	1	
Greg Marx	DE	6'4"	260	23		
John Zook	DE	6'5"	250	25		
Mike Lewis	DT	6'3"	260	24		
Rosie Manning	DT	6'5"	256	23		
Mike Tilleman	DT	6'5"	278	29		
Chuck Walker	DT	6'2"	260	32	1	

Use Name	Pos.	Hgt	Wgt	Age	Int	Pts
Duane Benson	LB	6'2"	215	28		
Greg Brezina	LB	6'2"	226	27	3	
Don Hansen	LB	6'3"	228	29	1	
Ken Mitchell	LB	6'1"	224	25		
Tommy Nobis	LB	6'2"	243	29		
Lonnie Warwick	LB	6'3"	240	31		
Ray Brown	DB	6'2"	202	24	6	
Ray Easterling	DB	6'	195	23		
Clarence Ellis	DB	5'11"	190	23	2	
Tom Hayes	DB	6'1"	198	27	4	12
Rolland Lawrence	DB	5'10"	180	22	1	
Tony Plummer	DB	5'11"	188	26	1	6
Ken Reaves	DB	6'3"	210	28	2	

Use Name	Pos.	Hgt	Wgt	Age	Int	Pts
Bob Lee	QB	6'2"	195	27		
Dick Shiner (to NE)	QB	6'	195	31		
Pat Sullivan	QB	6'	200	23		
Dave Hampton	HB	6'	210	26		30
Joe Washington	HB	5'9"	180	22		
Eddie Ray	FB	6'1"	240	26		66
Art Malone	FB	5'11"	216	25		18
Harmon Wages	FB	6'1"	212	27		6
Ken Burrow	WR	6'	190	25		42
Wes Chesson	WR	6'2"	195	24		6
Al Dodd	WR	6'	178	28		
Tom Geredine	WR	6'2"	195	23		6
Louis Neal	WR	6'4"	215	22		6
Larry Mialik	TE	6'2"	226	23		
Jim Mitchell	TE	6'2"	236	25		
John James	K	6'3"	197	24		
Nick Mike-Mayer	K	5'8"	186	23		112

SAN FRANCISCO FORTY-NINERS 5-9-0 Dick Nolan

Scores of Each Game		
13	Miami	21
36	Denver	34
20	LOS ANGELES	40
13	Atlanta	9
13	MINNESOTA	17
40	NEW ORLEANS	0
3	ATLANTA	17
20	Detroit	30
9	Washington	33
13	Los Angeles	31
20	GREEN BAY	6
38	PHILADELPHIA	28
10	New Orleans	16
14	PITTSBURGH	37

Use Name	Pos.	Hgt	Wgt	Age	Int	Pts
Cas Banaszek	OT	6'3"	250	27		
Len Rohde	OT	6'4"	248	35		
John Watson	OG-OT	6'4"	248	24		
Randy Beisler	OG	6'4"	244	28		
Ed Hardy	OG	6'4"	242	21		
Woody Peoples	OG	6'2"	250	30		
Forrest Blue	C	6'5"	260	27		
Jean Barrett	OT-C	6'6"	254	22		
Bill Belk	DE	6'3"	242	27		
Cedrick Hardman	DE	6'3"	255	24		2
Tommy Hart	DE	6'3"	248	28		
Bob Hoskins	DT	6'2"	250	27		
Charlie Krueger	DT	6'4"	254	37		
Rolf Krueger	DT	6'4"	253	26		

Use Name	Pos.	Hgt	Wgt	Age	Int	Pts
Willie Harper	LB	6'2"	215	23		
Charlie Hunt	LB	6'2"	212	22		
Frank Nunley	LB	6'2"	230	27	1	
Dave Olerich	LB	6'1"	220	28		
Jim Sniadecki	LB	6'2"	228	26	1	
Skip Vanderbundt	LB	6'3"	224	26	1	
Dave Wilcox	LB	6'3"	234	30	2	
Windlan Hall	DB	5'11"	175	23	1	12
Jim Johnson	DB	6'2"	188	35	4	
Ralph McGill	DB	5'11"	186	23		
Mel Phillips	DB	6'	190	31	1	
Mike Simpson	DB	5'11"	170	26		
Bruce Taylor	DB	6'	180	25	6	

Terry Beasley – Shoulder Injury

Use Name	Pos.	Hgt	Wgt	Age	Int	Pts
John Brodie	QB	6'1"	203	38		6
Joe Reed	QB	6'1"	192	25		
Steve Spurrier	QB	6'2"	200	28		12
Dave Atkins	HB	6'1"	202	24		6
Doug Cunningham	HB	5'11"	195	27		6
Jimmy Thomas	HB	6'1"	214	26		6
Vic Washington	HB	5'10"	196	27		48
Ken Willard	FB	6'2"	220	30		12
Randy Jackson	HB-FB	6'	220	24		
Larry Schreiber	HB-FB	6'	210	26		
Dan Abramowicz (from NO)	WR	6'1"	195	28		6
Ed Beverly	WR	5'11"	168	23		
John Isenbarger	WR	6'3"	196	25		
Gene Washington	WR	6'1"	185	26		12
Ted Kwalick	TE	6'4"	226	26		30
Dick Witcher	TE	6'3"	204	28		
Bruce Gossett	K	6'2"	228	30		104
Tom Wittum	K	6'1"	185	23		

NEW ORLEANS SAINTS 5-9-0 John North

Scores of Each Game		
7	ATLANTA	62
3	Dallas	40
10	Baltimore	14
21	CHICAGO	16
20	DETROIT	13
0	San Francisco	40
19	WASHINGTON	3
13	BUFFALO	0
7	Los Angeles	29
14	San Diego	17
13	LOS ANGELES	24
10	Green Bay	30
16	SAN FRANCISCO	10
10	Atlanta	14

Use Name	Pos.	Hgt	Wgt	Age	Int	Pts
Paul Ferson	OT	6'5"	260	23		
Carl Johnson	OT	6'3"	255	23		
Don Morrison	OT	6'5"	255	23		
Craig Robinson	OT	6'4"	250	24		
Jake Kupp	OG	6'3"	248	31		
Royce Smith	OG	6'3"	245	24		
Del Williams	OG	6'2"	240	27		
John Didion	C	6'4"	245	25		
Steve Baumgartner	DE	6'7"	260	22		
Andy Dorris	DE	6'4"	230	22		
Billy Newsome	DE	6'4"	250	26	1	
Joe Owens	DE	6'2"	245	25	1	
Derland Moore	DT	6'4"	260	21	1	
Bob Pollard	DT	6'3"	245	24		
Elex Price	DT	6'3"	260	23		

Use Name	Pos.	Hgt	Wgt	Age	Int	Pts
Wayne Colman	LB	6'1"	230	27		
Bob Creech	LB	6'3"	228	24		
Joe Federspiel	LB	6'1"	225	23	1	
Willie Hall	LB	6'2"	225	23		
Ray Hester	LB	6'2"	215	24		
Rick Kingrea	LB	6'1"	233	24		
Dale Lindsey	LB	6'3"	225	30		
Jim Merlo	LB	6'1"	220	21	3	
Dick Palmer	LB	6'2"	232	25		
Mike Fink	DB	5'11"	180	22		
Johnny Fuller	DB	6'	185	27	1	
Ernie Jackson	DB	5'10"	175	23	3	
Bivian Lee	DB	6'3"	200	25	3	
Jerry Moore	DB	6'3"	208	23		
Tom Myers	DB	5'11"	184	22	3	
Nate Ramsey	DB	6'1"	200	32		

Ron Billingsley – Injury
Hugo Hollas – Knee Injury

Use Name	Pos.	Hgt	Wgt	Age	Int	Pts
Bob Davis	QB	6'3"	205	27		
Archie Manning	QB	6'3"	215	24		12
Bobby Scott	QB	6'1"	200	24		
Henry Matthews	HB	6'3"	203	24		
Joe Profit (from ATL)	HB	6'	213	24		12
Howard Stevens	HB	5'5"	175	23		12
Jess Phillips	FB-HB	6'1"	210	26		
Bill Butler	FB	6'	210	23		18
Odell Lawson	FB	6'2"	205	23		
Lincoln Minor	HB-FB	6'2"	211	23		
Jubilee Dunbar	WR	6'	196	26		24
Freddie Hyatt	WR	6'3"	200	27		
Bob Newland	WR	6'2"	190	24		24
Preston Riley	WR	6'	180	25		
Speedy Thomas	WR	6'1"	170	26		
Doug Winslow	WR	5'11"	180	22		
Bert Askson	TE	6'3"	220	27		
John Beasley (from MIN)	TE	6'3"	228	28		12
Bob Brown	TE	6'3"	225	30		
Len Garrett (from GB)	TE	6'3"	230	24		
Mike Kelly	TE	6'4"	215	25		
Happy Feller	K	5'11"	185	24		19
Bill McClard	K	5'10"	202	21		48
Steve O'Neal	K	6'3"	185	27		

LOS ANGELES RAMS

RUSHING

Last Name	No.	Yds	Avg	TD
McCutcheon	210	1097	5.2	2
Bertelsen	206	854	4.1	4
Baker	85	344	4.0	7
Smith	79	291	3.7	2
Josephson	36	174	4.8	2
Scribner	20	109	5.5	0
Harris	4	29	7.3	0
Gordon	2	15	7.5	0
Preece	1	11	11.0	1
Hadl	14	5	0.4	0
Chapple	1	0	0.0	0
Jackson	2	−8	−4.0	0

RECEIVING

Last Name	No.	Yds	Avg	TD
Jackson	40	874	22	13
McCutcheon	30	289	10	3
Klein	21	277	13	2
Bertelsen	19	267	14	1
Snow	16	252	16	2
Smith	10	65	7	0
Curran	5	56	11	1
Scribner	2	19	10	0
Sherman	1	8	8	0

PUNT RETURNS

Last Name	No.	Yds	Avg	TD
Bertelsen	26	258	10	0
Elmendorf	22	187	9	0
Scribner	3	32	11	0

KICKOFF RETURNS

Last Name	No.	Yds	Avg	TD
Bryant	13	369	28	1
Scribner	11	314	29	0
Clark	2	80	40	0
Gordon	3	68	23	0
Curran	1	24	24	0
Elmendorf	2	23	12	0
Smith	1	16	16	0
Bertelsen	1	15	15	0
McCutcheon	1	6	6	0
Klein	1	0	0	0

PASSING – PUNTING – KICKING

PASSING	Att	Comp	%	Yds	Yd/Att	TD	Int–%	RK
Hadl	258	135	52	2008	7.8	22	11– 4	5
Harris	11	7	64	68	6.2	0	0 – 0	
Smith	2	2	100	31	15.5	0	0 – 0	

PUNTING	No	Avg
Chapple	51	40.8

KICKING	XP	Att	%	FG	Att	%
Ray	40	42	95	30	47	64

ATLANTA FALCONS

RUSHING

Last Name	No.	Yds	Avg	TD
Hampton	263	997	3.8	4
Ray	96	434	4.5	9
Malone	76	336	4.4	2
Lee	29	67	2.3	0
Wages	18	47	2.6	1
Washington	4	36	9.0	0
J. Mitchell	5	34	6.8	0
Sullivan	3	19	6.3	0
Burrow	2	17	8.5	0
Shiner	3	−2	−0.7	0
Geredine	1	−3	−3.0	0

RECEIVING

Last Name	No.	Yds	Avg	TD
J. Mitchell	32	420	13	0
Burrow	31	567	18	7
Hampton	25	273	11	1
Dodd	10	201	15	0
Ray	19	192	10	2
Malone	19	177	9	1
Geredine	12	231	19	1
Neal	5	131	26	1
Chesson	2	36	18	1
Mialik	2	30	15	0
Wages	2	14	7	0

PUNT RETURNS

Last Name	No.	Yds	Avg	TD
Brown	40	360	9	0
Dodd	8	69	9	0

KICKOFF RETURNS

Last Name	No.	Yds	Avg	TD
Washington	20	432	22	0
Hampton	11	258	23	0
Geredine	9	211	23	0
Plummer	5	115	23	0
Lawrence	3	71	24	0
Benson	3	20	7	0
Wages	1	0	0	0

PASSING – PUNTING – KICKING

PASSING	Att	Comp	%	Yds	Yd/Att	TD	Int–%	RK
Lee	230	120	52	1786	7.8	10	8 – 3	7
Shiner	68	36	53	432	6.4	3	4 – 6	
Sullivan	26	14	54	175	6.7	1	0 – 0	

PUNTING	No	Avg
James	63	42.6

KICKING	XP	Att	%	FG	Att	%
Mike-Mayer	34	34	100	26	38	68

SAN FRANCISCO FORTY-NINERS

RUSHING

Last Name	No.	Yds	Avg	TD
V. Washington	151	543	3.5	8
Willard	83	366	4.4	1
Thomas	56	259	4.6	1
Cunningham	44	165	3.8	1
Schreiber	42	163	3.9	0
Reed	15	85	5.7	0
Wittum	1	63	63.0	0
Kwalick	5	37	7.4	0
Spurrier	9	32	3.6	2
Atkins	4	19	4.8	1
Brodie	5	16	3.2	1
Jackson	6	10	1.7	0
Isenbarger	1	−6	−6.0	0

RECEIVING

Last Name	No.	Yds	Avg	TD
Kwalick	47	729	16	5
G. Washington	37	606	16	2
Abramowicz	37	460	12	1
V. Washington	33	238	7	0
Willard	22	160	7	1
Thomas	19	157	8	0
Cunningham	15	118	8	0
Schreiber	12	98	8	0
Isenbarger	10	67	7	0
Jackson	1	20	20	0
Witcher	1	13	13	0
Atkins	1	−3	−3	0

PUNT RETURNS

Last Name	No.	Yds	Avg	TD
Taylor	15	207	14	0
McGill	22	186	8	0

KICKOFF RETURNS

Last Name	No.	Yds	Avg	TD
V. Washington	24	549	23	0
McGill	17	374	22	0
Cunningham	8	173	22	0
Atkins	3	93	31	0
Thomas	5	81	16	0
Olerich	2	17	9	0
Hall	1	14	14	0
Simpson	1	0	0	0
Sniadecki	1	0	0	0
Willard	1	0	0	0

PASSING – PUNTING – KICKING

PASSING	Att	Comp	%	Yds	Yd/Att	TD	Int–%	RK
Brodie	194	98	51	1126	5.8	3	12– 6	15
Spurrier	157	83	53	882	5.6	4	7 – 4	14
Reed	114	51	45	589	5.2	2	6 – 5	
Isenbarger	1	1	100	48	48.0	0	0 – 0	

PUNTING	No	Avg
Wittum	79	43.7

KICKING	XP	Att	%	FG	Att	%
Gossett	26	26	100	26	33	79

NEW ORLEANS SAINTS

RUSHING

Last Name	No.	Yds	Avg	TD
Phillips	198	663	3.3	0
Butler	87	348	4.0	1
Profit	90	329	3.7	2
Manning	63	293	4.7	2
Stevens	45	183	4.1	2
Lawson	6	23	3.8	0
Scott	9	18	2.0	0
Davis	3	10	3.3	0
Minor	3	10	3.3	0
Myers	1	8	8.0	0
Newland	1	6	6.0	0
Matthews	4	4	1.0	0
Dunbar	3	3	1.0	0
O'Neal	2	−1	−0.5	0

RECEIVING

Last Name	No.	Yds	Avg	TD
Beasley	32	283	9	2
Newland	29	489	17	4
Dunbar	23	447	19	4
Phillips	22	169	8	0
Butler	19	125	7	2
Brown	11	132	12	0
Profit	11	108	10	0
Winslow	4	45	11	0
Stevens	4	39	10	0
Garrett	2	30	15	0
Matthews	2	19	10	0
Lawson	2	−5	−3	0
Minor	1	5	5	0

PUNT RETURNS

Last Name	No.	Yds	Avg	TD
Stevens	17	171	10	0
Winslow	5	47	9	0

KICKOFF RETURNS

Last Name	No.	Yds	Avg	TD
Stevens	26	590	23	0
Profit	8	144	18	0
Lawson	7	118	17	0
Fink	5	81	16	0
Moore	1	14	14	0
Jackson	1	0	0	0

PASSING – PUNTING – KICKING

PASSING	Att	Comp	%	Yds	Yd/Att	TD	Int–%	RK
Manning	267	140	52	1642	6.2	10	12– 4	10
Scott	54	18	33	245	4.5	1	3 – 6	
Davis	17	5	29	14	0.8	0	2 –12	

PUNTING	No	Avg
O'Neal	81	41.7

KICKING	XP	Att	%	FG	Att	%
McClard	9	9	100	13	24	54
Feller	7	7	100	4	12	33

1973 A.F.C. The Runningest Buffalo

Just as baseball fans had spent the year counting Hank Aaron's home runs as he closed in on Babe Ruth's one-year home run mark, football fans added up O. J. Simpson's rushing yardage week by week as he went after Jimmy Brown's one-year rushing mark of 1,863 yards. Simpson, the main ingredient in the Buffalo offense, excited the football world by running for a record 250 yards on opening day against New England. After seven games, he already had gained 1,000 yards, a goal coveted by runners for an entire season. With two games left on the schedule, O. J. had 1,584 yards and needed two good days to break the record. A good day of 219 yards against New England put him within shouting distance of the record. Needing 61 yards to set a new mark, Simpson quickly broke the record in the season's finale in cold, rainy New York. With a workhorse performance the rest of the day, he became the first runner ever to gain 2,000 yards in one season.

EASTERN DIVISION

Miami Dolphins—The Dolphins were aiming at a second perfect season, but a tough 12-7 loss to Oakland in their second game brought an end to those hopes. But the Dolphins still had the cold, hard precision and flawless execution which made them the class of professional football. The offense still had Griese, Csonka, Warfield, Little, Langer, and company; the defense boasted of Stanfill, Buoniconti, Anderson, Scott, and the rest of the No Name Defense. Coach Don Shula again made sure that his players were hungry, and except for the loss to Oakland and a 16-3 upset by the Colts after Miami had clinched the Eastern crown, the Dolphins came close to another flawless season.

Buffalo Bills—When O. J. Simpson faced the reporters after breaking Jimmy Brown's single-season rushing mark, he began the meeting by introducing the offensive linemen one by one. They included Mike Montler, Reggie MacKenzie, Donnie Green, Dave Foley, and rookies Joe DeLamielleure and Paul Seymour. They were the reasons for O. J.'s success, so he figured they deserved to share in the flory. Simpson was not the entire story of the Bills' surge to a 9-5 record and second place in the East. Rookie quarterback Joe Ferguson played well, although his main task was handing off to Simpson. J. D. Hill and Bob Chandler gave the team a pair of fine wide receivers, and another receiver, Dwight Harrison, was converted into a starter in the secondary. Earl Edwards came from the '49ers in a trade and beefed up the front line of the defense.

New England Patriots—The defense could not stop a strong running attack, and good clubs simply cranked the yardage out against the Patriots on the ground. O. J. Simpson, for instance, enjoyed his two most productive days of his record season against New England. But even with the defensive problems, coach Chuck Fairbanks' first season was successful because of the fine rookie class the Patriots fielded. Guard John Hannah strengthened the blocking, Darryl Stingley won a starting wide-receiver job, Sam Cunningham added power to the running game, and little Mack Herron excited people on kick returns. Veteran receiver Reggie Rucker provided a bonus by developing into a star, but the kicking game still bothered the Pats, as rookie Jeff White booted a punt for -6 yards in one game and missed an extra point and an 18-yard field goal in a 24-23 loss to Philadelphia.

New York Jets—Weeb Ewbank's final year as head coach before retirement degenerated into a dismal 4-10 season. The defense played well through the campaign, but the offensive unit suffered from age, injury, and turmoil. Flanker Don Maynard was cut in the pre-season, while fullback John Riggins did not sign a contract until just before opening day and never did reach his best form. The offensive line slipped in its pass protection, exposing the Jet quarterbacks to enemy tacklers. Joe Namath went out of action with an injured shoulder against the Colts on September 23, and Al Woodall followed him onto the disabled list two weeks later to leave rookie free-agent Bill Demory as the team's only quarterback.

Baltimore Colts—A thorough housecleaning had swept out many veterans of recent years, as new head coach Howard Schnellenberger suffered through a 4-10 season in which few of his personnel shifts worked out very well. Second-year runner Lydell Mitchell did star in the backfield, but the offense was hurt by ex-Raider tight end Ray Chester's poor showing and by a confused quarterback situation. Rookie Bert Jones began the year as the starter, but veteran Marty Domres took over the position over the back part of the schedule; neither name could ignite much of a passing attack. The Colts enjoyed one moment of glory by beating the Dolphins late in the year.

CENTRAL DIVISION

Cincinnati Bengals—The maturing of quarterback Ken Anderson and the addition of three talented rookies brought the Cincinnati offense up to the level of its topnotch defensive unit. With experience improving his poise, Anderson calmly executed the plays called by coach Paul Brown via messenger guards. Giving Brown and Anderson more to work with were rookies Isaac Curtis, Bobby Clark, and Lenvil Elliott, three swift and powerful freshmen. Curtis gave the Bengals a deep threat at wide receiver, while Clark provided power in the backfield to go along with the speed of veteran Eassex Johnson. When injuries slowed up these two runners late in the season, Elliott broke into the lineup with a flair. The Bengal defense had been solid all along, so the team stormed into first place with a strong finish.

Pittsburgh Steelers—The Pittsburgh offense kept raking in points despite constant injuries to key players. Fullback Franco Harris missed the early going with a bad knee, and by the time he got back into action, halfback Frenchy Fuqua went out with a broken collarbone. Quarterback Terry Bradshaw starred until he suffered a shoulder separation in mid-season; Terry Hanratty then stepped in and kept the attack rolling until injured ribs put him out of commission. With third-stringer Joe Gilliam at quarterback, the Steelers rose up and beat the Washington Redskins 21-16. The defense turned in strong performances week after week, with Joe Greene, L. C. Greenwood, Andy Russell, Jack Ham, and Mike Wagner all candidates for All-Pro honors as the Steelers again made it to the playoffs.

Cleveland Browns—Age had turned the Browns into a mediocre team that finished third in the AFC Central Division. The Cleveland offensive unit especially creaked, with the line laboring under the weight of three thirty-three-year-old members. Fullback Bo Scott's injury and quarterback Mike Phipps' slower-than-expected development further slowed the attack, and the Browns' two first-round draft picks were of very little help. Receiver Steve Holden spent most of the season on the bench, while guard Pete Adams passed his rookie season on the disabled list. The Cleveland defense, however, held together well, aided immensely by ex-Charger Bob Babich's work at middle linebacker, and the Browns posted a winning record.

Houston Oilers—The Oilers had given coach Bill Peterson what was described as a "lifetime" pact to join the team in 1972, but his lifetime as Houston head coach ran out after five games of this season. With Peterson's two-year record at 1-18 after five straight losses this year, general manager Sid Gillman stepped out of the front office to take over as head coach. Hoping to recapture the magic of his years at San Diego, Gillman headed the Oilers for the remainder of the season, but could only manage one victory.

WESTERN DIVISION

Oakland Raiders—The Raiders failed to score a touchdown in their first three games, so coach John Madden decided to bench quarterback Daryle Lamonica and replace him with lefty Ken Stabler. Whereas Lamonica excelled at throwing the long pass, Stabler thrived on running the ball-control offense preferred by coach Madden. With two strong runners in Marv Hubbard and Charlie Smith, two sure-handed receivers in Fred Biletnikoff and Mike Siani, and a superb front line, Stabler found many assets to manipulate in the Oakland attack. The defense had lots of old assets and one big addition in ex-Colt Bubba Smith. The Raider defense kept the team in the Western race early in the year, and the offense came through in victories over Kansas City and Denver in December to win first place and a playoff berth.

Denver Broncos—Bronco fans were amazed to find their club in the fight for first place all season long. In two years on the job, coach John Ralston had built a fine offense around the passing of veteran Charley Johnson and the running of star Floyd Little, with a solid line supporting both the air and ground games. The defense added two stand-out rookies in end Barney Chavous and cornerback Calvin Jones, and Veteran tackle Paul Smith sparked the squad with his All-Pro performance at rushing enemy passers. On the last day of the season the Broncos faced Oakland in a face-to-face duel for the Western title. Trailing 14-10 in the fourth quarter, the Broncos gambled on a fake punt play on fourth down. Bill Van Heusen did not gain the needed yards. The Raiders took the ball over and scored a touchdown as the Broncos had to settle for second place in their first winning season ever.

Kansas City Chiefs—After a poor pre-season, the Kansas City defense played with its accustomed vigor in the regular season, but the offense had problems generating any steam at all. Veteran quarterback Len Dawson suffered from a variety of small hurts which kept him out of the lineup much of the time, and substitute Pete Beathard, in his second tour of duty in Kansas City, could not get the attack moving in early season trials. Coach Hank Stram finally turned to Mickey Livingston, who brought the offense back to life, and the Chiefs suddenly were in first place in late November. A 14-10 loss to Denver, however, knocked them out of first place, and a 37-7 beating at the hands of the Raiders ended any playoffs hopes for this year.

San Diego Chargers—The Chargers' attempt to regain respectability by bringing in old, established players failed miserably this year. Quarterback Johnny Unitas had little zip left in his arm after seventeen years with the Colts, and he wound up on the bench watching rookie Dan Fouts lead the attack. An injury to receiver Gary Garrison further hurt the offense, and coach Harland Svare unexplainedly benched runner Mike Garrett early in the season. Morale on the club plunged, and when receiver Dave Williams was released in mid-season, he called the team "a zoo." Svare resigned as coach after eight games to concentrate on front-office duties as general manager, turning over the reigns to assistant Ron Waller.

FINAL TEAM STATISTICS

(Other statistics not available at press time)

OFFENSE

	BALT.	BUFF.	CIN.	CLEV.	DENV.	HOUS.	K.C.	MIAMI	N.ENG.	N.Y.	OAK.	PITT.	S.D.
FIRST DOWNS:													
Total	218	219	252	200	253	193	208	215	237	222	**288**	217	198
by Rushing	121	**152**	124	107	111	89	106	111	97	95	129	111	88
by Passing	79	60	108	79	127	93	93	91	122	109	**139**	89	93
by Penalty	18	7	**20**	14	15	11	9	13	18	18	**20**	17	17
RUSHING:													
Number	536	**605**	515	506	487	386	511	507	454	453	547	555	431
Yards	2031	**3088**	2236	1968	1954	1388	1793	2521	1612	1864	2510	2143	1814
Average Yards	3.8	**5.1**	4.3	3.9	4.0	3.6	3.5	5.0	3.6	4.1	4.6	3.9	4.2
Touchdowns	9	**20**	13	12	16	9	11	16	15	7	14	12	9
PASSING:													
Attempts	300	213	332	308	378	**411**	313	256	380	373	353	309	363
Completions	137	96	180	152	196	**225**	173	133	195	181	205	140	161
Completion Percentage	45.7	45.1	54.2	49.4	51.9	54.7	55.3	52.0	51.3	48.5	**58.1**	45.3	44.4
Passing Yards	1746	1236	2439	1741	**2706**	2370	2039	1675	2581	2353	2611	2157	2129
Avg. Yards per Attempt	5.8	5.8	7.3	5.7	7.2	5.8	6.5	6.5	6.8	6.3	**7.4**	7.0	5.9
Avg. Yards per Complet.	12.7	12.9	13.6	11.5	13.8	10.5	11.8	12.6	13.2	13.0	12.7	**15.4**	13.2
Times Tackled Passing	32	31	24	45	27	43	39	**13**	37	37	45	30	37
Yards Lost Tackled	271	239	163	368	187	451	296	**93**	350	297	348	230	321
Net Yards	1475	997	2276	1373	**2519**	1919	1743	1582	2231	2056	2263	1927	1808
Touchdowns	14	4	18	10	**22**	11	10	17	13	16	16	20	9
Interceptions	25	14	**12**	20	20	27	13	**12**	17	22	18	26	30
Percent Intercepted	8.3	6.6	**3.6**	6.5	5.3	6.6	4.2	4.7	4.5	5.9	5.1	8.4	8.3
PUNTS:													
Number	62	66	68	82	69	**85**	80	48	61	74	69	62	72
Average Distance	38.7	40.3	41.0	40.5	45.1	38.8	**45.5**	42.3	37.7	37.1	45.3	41.1	41.1
PUNT RETURNS:													
Number	24	32	45	36	40	30	42	37	33	27	46	**52**	33
Yards	129	279	333	308	404	227	279	382	324	165	344	**416**	408
Average Yards	5.4	8.7	7.4	8.6	10.1	7.6	6.6	10.3	9.8	6.1	7.5	8.0	**12.4**
Touchdowns	0	1	0	0	0	0	0	0	0	0	1	0	**2**
KICKOFF RETURNS:													
Number	60	42	39	49	36	**76**	31	24	57	52	39	40	70
Yards	1343	972	876	1084	793	**1799**	725	523	1372	1061	937	843	1597
Average Yards	22.4	23.1	22.5	22.1	22.0	23.7	23.4	21.8	**24.1**	20.4	24.0	21.1	22.8
Touchdowns	1	**2**	0	0	0	1	0	0	1	1	0	0	0
INTERCEPTION RETURNS:													
Number	15	14	18	12	14	17	21	21	13	19	17	**37**	16
Yards	116	224	166	202	220	298	328	335	105	288	162	**673**	205
Average Yards	7.7	16.0	9.2	16.8	15.7	17.5	15.6	16.0	8.1	15.2	9.5	**18.2**	12.8
Touchdowns	1	1	0	1	2	0	1	2	0	2	0	3	1
PENALTIES:													
Number	57	75	83	70	83	**95**	83	52	50	62	82	84	74
Yards	483	744	799	620	745	**900**	797	416	550	575	759	817	628
FUMBLES:													
Number	**16**	27	25	34	21	43	36	22	51	32	29	36	41
Number Lost	13	13	14	17	**9**	25	18	16	25	17	16	14	21
POINTS:													
Total	226	259	286	234	**354**	199	231	343	258	240	292	347	188
PAT Attempts	26	28	32	24	**41**	22	23	38	31	27	32	37	22
PAT Made	22	28	31	24	**40**	22	21	38	25	27	31	36	20
FG Attempts	28	30	31	31	33	24	38	37	29	24	33	**43**	27
FG Made	16	21	21	22	22	15	24	25	15	17	23	**29**	12
Percent FG Made	57.1	70.0	67.7	**71.0**	66.7	62.5	63.2	67.6	51.7	70.8	69.7	67.4	44.4
Safeties	0	0	0	0	1	0	0	1	1	0	0	1	0

DEFENSE

	BALT.	BUFF.	CIN.	CLEV.	DENV.	HOUS.	K.C.	MIAMI	N.ENG.	N.Y.	OAK.	PITT.	S.D.
FIRST DOWNS:													
Total	243	231	219	196	239	274	209	195	215	226	**194**	210	267
by Rushing	104	101	109	102	97	138	90	109	142	116	**88**	95	125
by Passing	123	112	97	79	121	114	95	78	**67**	101	92	91	124
by Penalty	16	18	13	15	21	22	24	8	**6**	9	14	24	18
RUSHING:													
Number	491	455	459	513	455	576	493	511	560	538	**435**	488	559
Yards	2089	1797	1807	2091	1795	2410	1956	1991	2850	2228	**1470**	1652	2264
Average Yards	4.3	3.9	3.9	4.1	3.9	4.2	4.0	3.9	5.1	4.1	**3.4**	3.4	4.1
Touchdowns	15	11	15	7	14	19	11	9	16	12	**5**	8	23
PASSING:													
Attempts	331	368	338	312	387	326	324	320	**240**	296	370	359	341
Completions	199	166	182	144	202	178	157	151	**134**	150	170	164	177
Completion Percentage	60.1	**45.1**	53.8	46.2	52.2	54.6	48.5	47.2	55.8	50.7	45.9	45.7	51.9
Passing Yards	2599	2394	2240	1984	2766	2466	1942	1604	**1600**	2148	1995	1923	2473
Avg. Yards per Attempt	7.9	6.5	6.6	6.4	7.1	7.6	6.0	**5.0**	6.7	7.3	5.4	5.4	7.3
Avg. Yards per Complet.	13.1	14.4	12.3	13.8	13.7	13.9	12.4	**10.6**	11.9	14.3	11.7	11.7	14.0
Times Tackled Passing	25	32	**43**	29	36	27	38	45	32	26	40	33	26
Yards Lost Tackled	200	276	**342**	248	326	229	323	314	262	198	305	251	219
Net Yards	2399	2118	1898	1736	2440	2237	1619	**1290**	1338	1950	1690	1672	2254
Touchdowns	16	12	9	16	15	26	11	**5**	11	18	12	11	18
Interceptions	15	14	18	12	14	17	21	21	13	19	17	**37**	16
Percent Intercepted	4.5	3.8	5.3	3.8	3.6	5.2	6.5	6.6	5.4	6.4	4.6	**10.3**	4.7
PUNTS:													
Number	47	63	77	78	69	62	84	76	62	67	**90**	75	60
Average Distance	**37.4**	39.8	41.7	40.4	43.3	39.6	42.9	38.5	40.5	40.9	43.1	42.4	43.1
PUNT RETURNS:													
Number	27	34	27	44	31	44	48	30	29	36	40	37	35
Yards	280	312	**123**	270	257	343	446	182	152	411	290	308	257
Average Yards	10.4	9.2	**4.6**	6.1	8.3	7.8	9.5	6.1	5.2	11.3	7.3	8.3	7.4
Touchdowns	0	1	0	0	0	0	0	0	0	1	0	0	0
KICKOFF RETURNS:													
Number	42	44	42	48	61	37	40	56	40	44	46	59	**35**
Yards	950	934	1170	1165	1244	**811**	1031	1202	963	1021	981	1357	862
Average Yards	22.6	21.2	27.9	24.3	**20.4**	21.9	25.8	21.5	24.1	23.2	21.4	23.0	24.6
Touchdowns	0	1	1	0	1	1	0	0	1	0	0	0	1
INTERCEPTION RETURNS:													
Number	25	14	**12**	20	20	27	13	**12**	17	22	18	26	30
Yards	336	**149**	198	271	331	357	151	190	385	296	187	512	532
Average Yards	13.4	10.6	16.5	13.6	16.6	13.2	11.6	15.8	22.6	13.5	**10.4**	19.7	17.7
Touchdowns	4	0	1	0	1	4	0	0	1	2	1	2	0
PENALTIES:													
Number	69	53	78	79	84	**90**	63	61	77	86	67	86	68
Yards	684	485	710	738	**824**	811	649	616	693	783	623	757	579
FUMBLES:													
Number	35	30	31	21	26	29	33	29	29	30	35	**41**	31
Number Lost	**22**	19	16	9	15	10	18	8	18	19	16	18	18
POINTS:													
Total	341	230	231	255	296	447	192	**150**	300	306	175	210	386
PAT Attempts	39	25	27	24	31	53	22	**15**	32	34	19	22	46
PAT Made	38	23	27	24	30	52	21	**13**	30	33	19	21	42
FG Attempts	33	34	23	46	35	42	27	27	32	34	30	29	38
FG Made	29	19	14	29	26	25	**13**	15	26	23	14	19	22
Percent FG Made	69.7	55.9	60.9	63.0	74.3	59.5	48.1	55.6	81.3	67.6	**46.7**	65.5	57.9
Safeties	0	0	0	0	1	1	0	1	0	0	0	0	1

CONFERENCE PLAYOFFS

December 22, at Oakland (Attendance 51,110)

SCORING

OAKLAND	7	3	13	10	–33
PITTSBURGH	0	7	0	7	–14

First Quarter
Oak. Hubbard, 1 yard rush PAT–Blanda (kick)

Second Quarter
Oak. Blanda, 25 yard field goal
Pitt. B. Pearson, 4 yard pass from Bradshaw PAT–Gerela (kick)

Third Quarter
Oak. Blanda, 31 yard field goal
Oak. Blanda, 22 yard field goal
Oak. W. Brown, 54 yard interception return PAT–Blanda (kick)

Fourth Quarter
Oak. Blanda, 10 yard field goal
Pitt. Lewis, 26 yard pass from Bradshaw PAT–Gerela (kick)
Oak. Hubbard, 1 yard rush PAT–Blanda (kick)

TEAM STATISTICS

OAK.		PITT.
24	First Downs–Total	15
14	First Downs–Rushing	2
8	First Downs–Passing	10
2	First Downs–Penalty	3
0	Fumbles–Number	1
0	Fumbles–Lost Ball	0
9	Penalties–Number	4
75	Yards Penalized	60
1	Missed Field Goals	0
74	Offensive Plays	46
361	Net Yards	223
4.8	Average Gain	4.8
0	Giveaways	3
3	Takeaways	0
+3	Difference	–3

INDIVIDUAL STATISTICS

OAKLAND	No	Yds	Avg.	PITTSBURGH	No	Yds	Avg.
RUSHING							
Hubbard	20	91	4.6	Harris	10	29	2.9
C. Smith	17	73	4.3	P. Pearson	4	14	3.5
C. Davis	12	48	4.0	Fuqua	3	13	4.3
Banaszak	5	17	3.4	Bradshaw	3	9	3.0
Moore	1	3	3.0		20	65	3.2
	55	232	4.2				
RECEIVING							
Siani	5	68	13.6	Lewis	4	70	17.5
Moore	3	26	8.7	Fuqua	4	52	13.0
C. Smith	2	10	5.0	B. Pearson	2	7	3.5
Hubbard	1	17	17.0	P. Pearson	1	24	24.0
Biletnikoff	1	8	8.0	Williams	1	14	14.0
Banaszak	1	5	5.0		12	167	13.9
	13	134	10.3				
PUNTING							
Guy	2		39.0	Walden	5		41.6
PUNT RETURNS							
Atkinson	2	11	5.5	Edwards	1	20	20.0
KICKOFF RETURNS							
C. Davis	3	58	19.3	P. Pearson	4	79	19.8
				Steve Davis	3	77	25.7
					7	156	22.3
INTERCEPTION RETURNS							
W. Brown	1	54	54.0	None			
Atkinson	1	8	8.0				
Villapiano	1	0	0.0				
	3	62	20.7				

PASSING

	Att.	Comp.	Comp. Pct.	Yds.	Int.	Yds/ Att.	Yds/ Comp.	Yards Lost Tackled
OAKLAND								
Stabler	17	14	82.4	142	0	8.4	10.1	2–13
PITTSBURGH								
Bradshaw	25	12	48.0	167	3	6.7	13.9	1– 9

December 23, at Miami (Attendance 80,047)

SCORING

MIAMI	14	7	10	3	–34
CINCINNATI	3	13	0	0	–16

First Quarter
Mia. Warfield, 13 yard pass from Griese PAT–Yepremian (kick)
Cin. Muhlmann, 24 yard field goal
Mia. Csonka, 1 yard rush PAT–Yepremian (kick)

Second Quarer
Mia. Morris, 4 yard rush PAT–Yepremian (kick)
Cin. Craig, 45 yard interception return PAT–Muhlmann (kick)
Cin. Muhlmann, 46 yard field goal
Cin. Muhlmann, 12 yard field goal

Third Quarter
Mia. Mandich, 7 yard pass from Griese PAT–Yepremian (kick)
Mia. Yepremian, 50 yard field goal

Fourth Quarter
Mia. Yepremian, 46 yard field goal

TEAM STATISTICS

MIAMI		CIN.
27	First Downs–Total	11
18	First Downs–Rushing	5
9	First Downs–Passing	6
0	First Downs–Penalty	0
2	Fumbles–Number	0
1	Fumbles–Lost Ball	0
1	Penalties–Number	2
5	Yards Penalized	19
0	Missed Field Goals	0
71	Offensive Plays	50
400	Net Yards	194
5.6	Average Gain	3.9
3	Giveaways	1
1	Takeaways	3
–2	Difference	+2

INDIVIDUAL STATISTICS

MIAMI	No	Yds	Avg.	CINCINNATI	No	Yds	Avg.
RUSHING							
Morris	20	106	5.3	Clark	7	40	5.7
Csonka	20	71	3.6	Anderson	3	26	8.8
Kiick	10	51	5.1	E. Johnson	2	17	8.5
Leigh	1	8	8.0	Elliott	7	15	2.1
Nottingham	1	5	5.0	Curtis	1	–1	–1.0
	52	241	4.6		20	97	4.9
RECEIVING							
Warfield	4	95	23.8	Elliott	9	53	5.9
Mandich	3	28	9.3	Joiner	2	33	16.5
Kiick	3	19	6.3	Clark	2	18	9.0
Briscoe	1	17	17.0	Curtis	1	9	9.0
	11	159	14.5		14	113	8.1
PUNTING							
Seiple	2		49.0	Lewis	7		36.3
PUNT RETURNS							
Scott	1	4	4.0	Casanova	1	15	15.0
Anderson	1	2	2.0	Parrish	1	11	11.0
	2	6	3.0		2	26	13.0
KICKOFF RETURNS							
Anderson	1	14	14.0	Parrish	1	25	25.0
Morris	1	0	0.0	Jackson	1	17	17.0
	2	14	7.0		2	42	21.0
INTERCEPTION RETURNS							
Anderson	1	19	19.0	Craig	1	45	45.0
				Casanova	1	0	0.0
					2	45	22.5

PASSING

	Att.	Comp.	Comp. Pct.	Yds.	Int.	Yds/ Att.	Yds/ Comp.	Yards Lost Tackled
MIAMI								
Griese	18	11	61.1	159	1	8.8	14.5	
Briscoe	1	0	0.0	0	1	–	–	
	19	11	57.9	159	2	8.4	14.5	0– 0
CINCINNATI								
Anderson	27	14	51.9	113	1	4.2	8.1	3–16

MIAMI DOLPHINS 12-2 Don Shula

Scores of Each Game		
21	SAN FRANCISCO	13
7	Oakland	12
44	NEW ENGLAND	23
31	N. Y. JETS	3
17	Cleveland	9
27	BUFFALO	6
30	New England	14
24	N. Y. Jets	14
44	BALTIMORE	0
17	Buffalo	0
14	Dallas	7
30	PITTSBURGH	26
3	Baltimore	16
34	DETROIT	7

Use Name	Pos.	Hgt	Wgt	Age	Int	Pts
Doug Crusan	OT	6'5"	250	27		
Norm Evans	OT	6'5"	252	30		
Wayne Moore	OT	6'6"	265	28		
Willie Young	OT	6'4"	270	25		
Bob Kuechenberg	OG	6'3"	247	25		
Larry Little	OG	6'1"	265	27		
Ed Newman	OG	6'2"	245	22		
Jim Langer	C	6'2"	250	25		
Irv Goode	OG-C	6'4"	252	32		
Vern Den Herder	DE	6'6"	250	24		
Bill Stanfill	DE	6'5"	250	26		
Bob Heinz	DT-DE	6'6"	270	26		
Manny Fernandez	DT	6'2"	250	27		
Baldy Moore	DT	6'2"	265	27		
Larry Woods	DT	6'6"	260	25		

Use Name	Pos.	Hgt	Wgt	Age	Int	Pts
Larry Ball	LB	6'6"	225	23	1	
Bruce Bannon	LB	6'3"	225	22		
Nick Buoniconti	LB	5'11"	220	32		6
Mike Kolen	LB	6'2"	220	25	2	
Bob Matheson	LB-DE	6'4"	240	28		
Jesse Powell	LB	6'1"	215	26		
Doug Swift	LB	6'3"	228	24	1	
Dick Anderson	DB	6'2"	196	27	8	12
Charlie Babb	DB	6'	190	23		
Tim Foley	DB	6'	194	25	2	12
Curtis Johnson	DB	6'2"	196	25	2	2
Lloyd Mumphord	DB	5'11"	180	26		
Jake Scott	DB	6'	188	28	4	
Henry Stuckey	DB	6'1"	190	23	1	

Jim Dunaway – Injury
Howard Kindig – Injury

Use Name	Pos.	Hgt	Wgt	Age	Int	Pts
Bob Griese	QB	6'1"	190	28		
Earl Morrall	QB	6'1"	206	39		
Jim Kiick	HB	5'11"	215	27		
Mercury Morris	HB	5'10"	190	26		60
Charlie Leigh	FB-HB	5'11"	205	27		6
Larry Csonka	FB	6'3"	237	26		30
Don Nottingham (from BAL)	FB	5'10"	210	24		6
Marlin Briscoe	WR	5'10"	178	27		12
Bo Rather	WR	6'1"	182	22		
Ron Sellers	WR	6'4"	195	26		
Howard Twilley	WR	5'10"	185	29		
Paul Warfield	WR	6'	185	30		66
Marv Fleming	TE	6'4"	235	31		
Jim Mandich	TE	6'3"	224	25		24
Larry Seiple	TE	6'	215	28		
Garo Yepremian	K	5'8"	175	29		113

Ed Jenkins – Injury

BUFFALO BILLS 9-5 Lou Saban

Scores of Each Game		
31	New England	13
7	San Diego	34
9	N. Y. JETS	7
27	PHILADELPHIA	26
31	BALTIMORE	13
6	Miami	27
23	KANSAS CITY	14
0	New Orleans	13
13	CINCINNATI	16
0	MIAMI	17
24	Baltimore	17
17	Atlanta	6
37	NEW ENGLAND	13
34	N. Y. Jets	14

Use Name	Pos.	Hgt	Wgt	Age	Int	Pts
Dave Foley	OT	6'5"	255	25		
Donnie Green	OT	6'7"	272	25		
Mike Montler	C-OT	6'4"	255	29		
Joe DeLamielleure	OG	6'3"	254	22		
Reggie McKenzie	OG	6'4"	235	23		
Bobby Penchion	OG	6'5"	265	24		
Bruce Jarvis	C	6'7"	250	24		
Willie Parker	OG-C	6'3"	240	24		
Earl Edwards	DE	6'6"	262	27		
Halvor Hagen	DE	6'5"	245	26		
Walt Patulski	DE	6'6"	260	23		
Mike Kadish	DT	6'5"	265	23		
Bob Kampa	DT	6'4"	252	22		
Steve Okoniewski	DT	6'3"	247	24		
Jerry Patton	DT	6'3"	265	27		
Jeff Winans	DT	6'5"	265	21		

Use Name	Pos.	Hgt	Wgt	Age	Int	Pts
Jim Cheyunski	LB	6'2"	225	27	3	
Phil Croyle (from HOU)	LB	6'3"	220	25		
Dale Farley	LB	6'3"	235	24		
Fred Forsberg (from DEN)	LB	6'1"	235	29	1	
Merv Krakau	LB	6'2"	242	22		
Rich Lewis	LB	6'3"	220	23		
John Skorupan	LB	6'2"	214	22		
Bill Cahill	DB	5'11"	180	22		6
Leon Garror	DB	6'	180	25	1	
Tony Greene	DB	5'10"	170	24	1	
Dwight Harrison	DB	6'1"	178	24	5	6
Robert James	DB	6'1"	185	26	1	
Ernie Kellerman	DB	6'	183	29	2	
Ken Stone (to WAS)	DB	6'1"	180	22		6
Donnie Walker	DB	6'1"	185	22	1	

Don Croft – Knee Injury

Use Name	Pos.	Hgt	Wgt	Age	Int	Pts
Joe Ferguson	QB	6'1"	190	23		12
Dennis Shaw	QB	6'2"	215	26		
Steve Jones	HB	6'	200	22		
O. J. Simpson	HB	6'2"	214	26		72
Pete Van Valkenberg	HB	6'2"	192	23		
Jim Braxton	FB	6'2"	243	24		24
Bo Cornell	FB	6'1"	215	24		
Larry Watkins	FB	6'2"	230	26		18
Bob Chandler	WR	6'	180	24		19
Wallace Francis	WR	5'11"	188	21		12
J. D. Hill	WR	6'1"	202	24		
Ray Jarvis	WR	5'11"	193	24		
Ted Koy	TE	6'1"	212	25		
Paul Seymour	TE	6'5"	260	23		
Dave Washington	TE	6'5"	220	24		
Spike Jones	K	6'2"	190	26		
John Leypoldt	K	6'2"	230	27		90

NEW ENGLAND PATRIOTS 5-9 Chuck Fairbanks

Scores of Each Game		
13	BUFFALO	31
7	KANSAS CITY	10
23	Miami	44
24	BALTIMORE	16
7	N. Y. JETS	9
13	Chicago	10
14	MIAMI	30
23	Philadelphia	24
13	N. Y. Jets	33
33	GREEN BAY	24
32	Houston	0
30	SAN DIEGO	14
13	Buffalo	37
13	Baltimore	18

Use Name	Pos.	Hgt	Wgt	Age	Int	Pts
Tom Neville	OT	6'4"	255	30		
Leon Gray	OT	6'3"	256	21		
Bob Reynolds (to STL)	OT	6'6"	265	32		
Willie Banks	OG	6'2"	250	27		
Sam Adams	OT-OG	6'3"	252	24		
John Hannah	OG	6'2"	265	22		
Bill Lenkaitis	OG	6'3"	260	27		
Len St. Jean	OG	6'1"	250	31		
Jon Morris	C	6'4"	254	30		
Doug Dumler	C	6'3"	242	22		
Nate Dorsey	DE	6'4"	240	23		
Ray Hamilton	DE	6'1"	232	22		
Donnell Smith	DE	6'4"	245	24		
Julius Adams	DT-DE	6'3"	257	25		
Rick Cash	DT	6'5"	260	27		
Mel Lunsford	DT	6'3"	250	23		
Art Moore	DT	6'5"	253	22		
Dave Rowe	DT	6'6"	280	28		

Use Name	Pos.	Hgt	Wgt	Age	Int	Pts
Ron Acks	LB	6'2"	220	28	1	
Edgar Chandler	LB	6'3"	225	27		
Will Foster	LB	6'2"	230	24		6
Bob Geddes	LB	6'2"	240	27		
Steve Kiner	LB	6'	218	26		2
Steve King	LB	6'4"	255	22		
Brian Stenger	LB	6'4"	230	26		
John Tanner	LB	6'4"	235	28		
Ralph Anderson	DB	6'2"	180	24	2	
Ron Bolton	DB	6'2"	180	23	6	
Greg Boyd	DB	6'2"	200	21		
Sandy Durko	DB	6'1"	185	25	3	
George Hoey	DB	5'10"	170	26		
Honor Jackson (to NYG)	DB	6'1"	195	24	1	
Don Martin	DB	5'11"	187	23		
Dave Mason	DB	6'	200	23		

Wayne Patrick – Knee Injury

Use Name	Pos.	Hgt	Wgt	Age	Int	Pts
Brian Dowling	QB	6'2"	200	26		
Jim Plunkett	QB	6'3"	220	25		30
Josh Ashton	HB	6'1"	205	24		
Mack Herron	HB	5'5"	170	25		24
Bob McCall	HB	6'	205	23		
Claxton Welch	HB	5'11"	203	26		
Paul Gipson	FB-HB	6'	210	26		
Sam Cunningham	FB	6'3"	215	23		30
John Tarver	FB	6'3"	227	24		24
Reggie Rucker	WR	6'2"	190	25		18
Darryl Stingley	WR	6'	190	21		12
Randy Vataha	WR	5'10"	175	24		12
Bob Adams	TE	6'2"	225	27		
John Mosier	TE	6'3"	220	25		
Bob Windsor	TE	6'4"	226	30		24
Bruce Barnes	K	5'11"	215	22		
Bill Bell	K	6'1"	192	25		7
Jeff White	K	5'11"	170	24		63

NEW YORK JETS 4-10 Weeb Ewbank

Scores of Each Game		
7	Green Bay	23
34	Baltimore	10
7	Buffalo	9
3	Miami	31
9	New England	7
14	Pittsburgh	26
28	DENVER	40
14	MIAMI	24
33	NEW ENGLAND	13
14	Cincinnati	20
20	ATLANTA	28
20	BALTIMORE	17
23	Philadelphia	24
14	BUFFALO	34

Use Name	Pos.	Hgt	Wgt	Age	Int	Pts
Winston Hill	OT	6'4"	280	31		
Bob Svihus	OT	6'4"	245	30		
Robert Woods	OT	6'3"	255	23		
John Mooring	C-OT	6'6"	255	26		
Dave Herman	OG	6'2"	255	31		
Randy Rasmussen	OG	6'2"	255	28		
Gary Puetz	OT-OG	6'3"	255	21		
Rick Harrell	C	6'3"	238	22		
John Schmitt	C	6'4"	250	30		
Ed Galigher	DE	6'4"	255	22		
Mark Lomas	DE	6'4"	250	25		
Joey Jackson	DT-DE	6'4"	270	24		
Richard Neal	DT-DE	6'3"	254	25		
John Little	DT	6'3"	250	26		
Steve Thompson	DT	6'5"	250	28		
John Elliott	DE-DT	6'4"	244	28		

Use Name	Pos.	Hgt	Wgt	Age	Int	Pts
Al Atkinson	LB	6'1"	230	30	1	
Ralph Baker	LB	6'3"	228	31	4	6
John Ebersole	LB	6'3"	235	24	1	
Bill Ferguson	LB	6'3"	225	22		
Rob Spicer	LB	6'4"	227	22		
Mike Taylor	LB	6'1"	230	23		
Bill Zapalac	LB	6'4"	225	25		
Chris Farasopoulos	DB	5'11"	190	24	1	
Delles Howell	DB	6'3"	200	26	4	
Burgess Owens	DB	6'2"	200	22	1	6
Rich Sowells	DB	6'	175	24	3	6
Steve Tannen	DB	6'1"	194	25	1	
Earlie Thomas	DB	6'1"	190	27	2	
Phil Wise	DB	6'	190	24		6

Use Name	Pos.	Hgt	Wgt	Age	Int	Pts
Bill Demory	QB	6'2"	195	22		
Joe Namath	QB	6'2"	200	30		
Al Woodall	QB	6'5"	194	27		
Mike Adamle	HB	5'9"	197	23		
Hank Bjorklund	HB	6'1"	200	23		
Emerson Boozer	HB	5'11"	205	30		36
Cliff McClain	HB	6'	217	25		
Jim Nance	FB	6'1"	240	30		
John Riggins	FB	6'2"	230	24		24
Margene Adkins	WR	5'10"	183	26		
Jerome Barkum	WR	6'3"	215	23		36
Eddie Bell	WR	5'10"	160	25		12
David Knight	WR	6'1"	182	22		6
Rocky Turner	DB-WR	6'	200	23		
Dennis Cambal	TE	6'3"	228	24		
Rich Caster	TE	6'5"	228	24		24
Julian Fagan	K	6'3"	205	25		
Bobby Howfield	K	5'9"	180	36		78

BALTIMORE COLTS 4-10 Howard Schnellenberger

Scores of Each Game		
14	Cleveland	24
10	N. Y. JETS	34
14	NEW ORLEANS	10
16	New England	24
13	Buffalo	31
29	Detroit	27
21	OAKLAND	34
27	HOUSTON	31
0	Miami	44
14	Washington	22
17	BUFFALO	24
17	N. Y. Jets	20
16	MIAMI	3
18	NEW ENGLAND	13

Use Name	Pos.	Hgt	Wgt	Age	Int	Pts
Tom Drougas	OT	6'4"	257	23		
Dennis Nelson	OT	6'5"	260	27		
David Taylor	OT	6'4"	254	23		
Elmer Collett	OG	6'4"	240	28		
Cornelius Johnson	OG	6'2"	245	30		
Glenn Ressler	OG	6'3"	250	29		
Fred Hoaglin	C	6'4"	246	29		
Ken Mendenhall	C	6'3"	235	25		
Dan Neal	C	6'4"	240	24		
Mike Barnes	DE	6'6"	255	22		
Roy Hilton	DE	6'6"	240	28		
Dick Amman	DT-DE	6'5"	250	22		
Jim Bailey	DT	6'5"	255	25		
Joe Ehrmann	DT	6'5"	260	24		
Joe Schmiesing	DE-DT	6'4"	260	28		
Bill Windauer	DT	6'3"	245	23		

Use Name	Pos.	Hgt	Wgt	Age	Int	Pts
Stan Cherry	LB	6'5"	200	22		
Mike Curtis	LB	6'2"	232	30	2	
Ted Hendricks	LB	6'7"	220	25	3	6
Mike Kaczmarek	LB	6'4"	235	22	1	
Ed Mooney	LB	6'2"	225	28		
Stan White	LB	6'1"	225	23	4	6
Brian Herosian	DB	6'3"	200	22		
Rex Kern	DB	5'11"	190	24	2	
Bruce Laird	DB	6'	185	23		
Jack Mildren	DB	6'1"	200	23		
Nelson Munsey	DB	6'1"	185	25		
Ray Oldham	DB	6'	200	22	2	
Rick Volk	DB	6'3"	195	28	1	

Use Name	Pos.	Hgt	Wgt	Age	Int	Pts
Marty Domres	QB	6'3"	220	26		12
Bert Jones	QB	6'3"	205	21		
Hubert Ginn (from MIA)	HB	5'11"	188	26		
Lydell Mitchell	HB	5'11"	204	24		12
Bill Olds	FB	6'1"	224	22		12
Don McCauley	HB-FB	6'1"	207	24		12
Glenn Doughty	WR	6'2"	204	22		24
Sam Havrilak	WR	6'2"	195	25		
Ollie Smith	WR	6'2"	195	24		
Cotton Speyrer	WR	6'	175	24		30
Tom Mitchell	TE-WR	6'2"	215	29		24
John Andrews	TE	6'3"	227	24		6
Ray Chester	TE	6'3"	235	25		6
George Hunt	K	6'1"	215	23		70
David Lee	K	6'4"	230	29		

MIAMI DOLPHINS

RUSHING

Last Name	No.	Yds	Avg	TD
Csonka	219	1003	4.6	5
Morris	149	954	6.4	10
Kiick	76	257	3.4	0
Nottingham	52	252	4.8	1
Leigh	22	134	6.1	1
Griese	13	20	1.5	0
Warfield	1	15	15.0	0
Morrall	1	9	9.0	0
Briscoe	2	−5	−2.5	0

RECEIVING

Last Name	No.	Yds	Avg	TD
Briscoe	30	447	15	2
Warfield	29	514	18	11
Kiick	27	208	8	0
Mandich	24	302	13	4
Csonka	7	22	3	0
Morris	4	51	13	0
Leigh	4	9	2	0
Nottingham	3	26	9	0
Fleming	3	22	7	0
Sellers	2	54	27	0
Twilley	2	30	15	0

PUNT RETURNS

Last Name	No.	Yds	Avg	TD
Scott	22	266	12	0
Leigh	9	64	7	0
Anderson	6	52	9	0

KICKOFF RETURNS

Last Name	No.	Yds	Avg	TD
Leigh	9	251	28	0
Morris	11	242	22	0
Scott	2	20	10	0
Nottingham	1	17	17	0
Bannon	1	10	10	0
Seiple	1	0	0	0

PASSING – PUNTING – KICKING

PASSING	Att	Comp	%	Yds	Yd/Att	TD	Int–%	RK
Griese	218	116	53	1422	6.5	17	8– 4	3
Morrall	38	17	45	253	6.7	0	4–11	

PUNTING	No.	Avg
Seiple	48	42.3

KICKING	XP	Att	%	FG	Att	%
Yepremian	38	38	100	25	37	68

BUFFALO BILLS

RUSHING

Last Name	No.	Yds	Avg	TD
Simpson	332	2003	6.0	12
Braxton	108	494	4.6	4
Watkins	98	414	4.2	2
Ferguson	48	147	3.1	2
Van Valkenberg	2	20	10.0	0
Cornell	4	13	3.3	0
Steve Jones	4	9	2.3	0
Shaw	4	2	0.5	0
Chandler	5	−14	−2.8	0

RECEIVING

Last Name	No.	Yds	Avg	TD
Chandler	30	427	14	3
Hill	29	422	15	0
Watkins	12	86	7	1
Seymour	10	114	11	0
Braxton	6	101	17	0
Simpson	6	70	12	0
R. Jarvis	1	12	12	0
Van Valkenberg	1	7	7	0
Ferguson	1	−3	−3	0

PUNT RETURNS

Last Name	No.	Yds	Avg	TD
Walker	25	210	8	0
Cahill	4	73	18	1
Chandler	2	5	3	0
Hill	1	−9	−9	0

KICKOFF RETURNS

Last Name	No.	Yds	Avg	TD
Francis	23	687	30	2
Jones	6	116	19	0
R. Jarvis	5	84	17	0
Cahill	2	42	21	0
Watkins	1	18	18	0
Parker	1	16	16	0
T. Greene	1	7	7	0
Cornell	1	2	2	0
Braxton	1	0	0	0
Van Valkenberg	1	0	0	0

PASSING – PUNTING – KICKING

PASSING	Att	Comp	%	Yds	Yd/Att	TD	Int–%	RK
Ferguson	164	73	45	939	5.7	4	10– 6	13
Shaw	46	22	48	300	6.5	0	4– 9	
Simpson	2	1	50	−3	−1.5	0	0– 0	
Chandler	1	0	0	0	0.0	0	0– 0	

PUNTING	No	Avg
Spike Jones	66	40.3

KICKING	XP	Att	%	FG	Att	%
Leypoldt	27	27	100	21	30	70
Chandler	1	1	100	0	0	0

NEW ENGLAND PATRIOTS

RUSHING

Last Name	No.	Yds	Avg	TD
Cunningham	155	516	3.3	4
Tarver	72	321	4.5	4
Ashton	93	305	3.3	0
Plunkett	44	209	4.8	5
Herron	61	200	3.3	2
Stingley	6	64	10.7	0
McCall	10	15	1.5	0
B. Adams	2	7	3.5	0
Gipson	5	−1	−0.2	0
Rucker	2	−1	−0.5	0
Welch	1	−2	−2.0	0
Windsor	1	−6	−6.0	0
Vataha	2	−15	−7.5	0

RECEIVING

Last Name	No.	Yds	Avg	TD
Rucker	53	743	14	3
Windsor	23	348	15	4
Stingley	23	339	15	2
Vataha	20	341	17	2
Herron	18	265	15	1
Cunningham	15	144	10	1
B. Adams	14	197	14	0
Ashton	11	113	10	0
Tarver	9	41	6	0
Welch	6	22	4	0
McCall	3	18	6	0

PUNT RETURNS

Last Name	No.	Yds	Avg	TD
Herron	27	282	10	0
Durko	3	21	7	0
Stingley	3	31	7	0

KICKOFF RETURNS

Last Name	No.	Yds	Avg	TD
Herron	41	1092	27	1
Stingley	6	143	24	0
Rucker	5	103	21	0
McCall	2	17	9	0
Tarver	1	17	17	0
Hannah	1	0	0	0
Windsor	1	0	0	0

PASSING – PUNTING – KICKING

PASSING	Att	Comp	%	Yds	Yd/Att	TD	Int–%	RK
Plunkett	376	193	51	2550	6.8	13	17– 5	5

PUNTING	No	Avg
Barnes	55	38.8
White	6	27.2

KICKING	XP	Att	%	FG	Att	%
White	21	25	84	14	25	56
Bell	4	5	80	1	4	25

NEW YORK JETS

RUSHING

Last Name	No.	Yds	Avg	TD
Boozer	182	831	4.6	3
Riggins	134	482	3.6	4
Adamle	67	264	3.9	0
Nance	18	78	4.3	0
Bjorkland	22	72	3.3	0
Woodall	13	68	5.2	0
Fagan	2	47	23.5	0
McClain	8	32	4.0	0
Barkum	1	2	2.0	0
Demory	4	−1	−0.3	0
Namath	1	−2	−2.0	0
Caster	1	−9	−9.0	0

RECEIVING

Last Name	No.	Yds	Avg	TD
Barkum	44	810	18	6
Caster	35	593	17	4
Bell	24	319	13	2
Riggins	23	158	7	0
Boozer	22	130	6	3
Adamle	9	63	7	0
Adkins	6	109	18	0
Knight	6	78	13	1
McClain	6	52	9	0
Nance	4	26	7	0
Bjorkland	2	15	8	0

PUNT RETURNS

Last Name	No.	Yds	Avg	TD
Farasopoulos	14	111	8	0
Turner	11	54	5	0
Tannen	2	0	0	0

KICKOFF RETURNS

Last Name	No.	Yds	Avg	TD
Adkins	31	615	20	0
Bjorkland	9	175	19	0
Owens	2	103	52	1
McClain	5	89	18	0
Adamle	5	79	16	0

PASSING – PUNTING – KICKING

PASSING	Att	Comp	%	Yds	Yd/Att	TD	Int–%	RK
Woodall	201	101	50	1228	6.1	9	8– 4	6
Namath	133	68	51	966	7.3	5	6– 5	
Demory	39	12	31	159	4.1	2	8–21	

PUNTING	No	Avg
Fagan	74	37.1

KICKING	XP	Att	%	FG	Att	%
Howfield	27	27	100	17	24	71

BALTIMORE COLTS

RUSHING

Last Name	No.	Yds	Avg	TD
L. Mitchell	253	963	3.8	2
McCauley	144	514	3.6	2
Domres	32	126	3.9	2
Olds	26	100	3.8	2
Doughty	10	96	9.6	0
Jones	18	58	3.2	0
Ginn	16	47	2.9	0
Mildren	2	14	7.0	0
Havrilak	2	9	4.5	0
Chester	1	1	1.0	0
Speyrer	1	1	1.0	0
Smith	1	−3	−3.0	0
Lee	2	−16	−8.0	0
Nelson	0	3	0.0	0

RECEIVING

Last Name	No.	Yds	Avg	TD
Doughty	25	587	23	4
T. Mitchell	25	313	13	4
McCauley	25	186	7	0
Chester	18	181	10	1
Speyrer	17	311	18	4
L. Mitchell	17	113	7	0
Ginn	3	2	1	0
Olds	2	−4	−2	0
Smith	1	37	37	0
Havrilak	1	9	9	0
Andrews	1	1	1	1

PUNT RETURNS

Last Name	No.	Yds	Avg	TD
Laird	15	72	5	0
Volk	7	45	6	0
Kern	2	12	6	0

KICKOFF RETURNS

Last Name	No.	Yds	Avg	TD
Laird	24	547	23	0
Speyrer	17	496	29	1
Ginn	9	198	22	0
White	1	17	17	0
Volk	2	16	8	0
Olds	3	14	5	0
Andrews	1	13	13	0
Munsey	1	13	13	0
McCauley	1	12	12	0

PASSING – PUNTING – KICKING

PASSING	Att	Comp	%	Yds	Yd/Att	TD	Int–%	RK
Domres	191	93	49	1153	6.0	9	13– 7	11
Jones	108	43	40	539	5.0	4	12–11	
Speyrer	1	1	100	54	54.0	1	0– 0	

PUNTING	No	Avg
Lee	62	38.7

KICKING	XP	Att	%	FG	Att	%
Hunt	22	24	92	16	28	57

CINCINNATI BENGALS 10-4-0 Paul Brown

Scores of Each Game		
10	Denver	28
24	HOUSTON	10
20	San Diego	13
10	CLEVELAND	17
9	PITTSBURGH	7
14	KANSAS CITY	6
13	Pittsburgh	20
10	Dallas	38
16	Buffalo	13
20	N. Y. JETS	14
42	ST. LOUIS	24
27	MINNESOTA	0
34	Cleveland	17
27	Houston	24

Use Name	Pos.	Hgt	Wgt	Age	Int	Pts
Vern Holland	OT	6'5"	270	25		
Rufus Mayes	OT	6'5"	260	25		
Stan Walters	OT	6'6"	270	25		
Howard Fest	OG-OT	6'6"	262	27		
Pat Matson	OG	6'1"	245	29		
John Shinners	OG	6'2"	254	26		
Tom DeLeone	C	6'2"	252	23		
Bob Johnson	C	6'5"	260	27		
Royce Berry	DE	6'3"	250	27		
Ken Johnson	DE	6'5"	265	26		
Lee Thomas	DE	6'5"	246	26		
Sherman White	DE	6'5"	255	24		
Ron Carpenter	DT	6'4"	260	25		
Steve Chomyszak	DT	6'5"	265	28		
Mike Reid	DT	6'3"	255	26		
Doug Adams	LB	6'	222	24		
Ken Avery	LB	6'1"	227	29	1	
Al Beauchamp	LB	6'2"	237	29	3	
Bill Bergey	LB	6'2"	243	28	3	
Tim Kearney	LB	6'2"	227	22		
Jim LeClair	LB	6'2"	226	22		
Ron Pritchard	LB	6'1"	235	26		
Lyle Blackwood	DB	6'	190	22		
Tommy Casanova	DB	6'2"	202	23	4	
Neal Craig	DB	6'1"	190	25	2	
Bernard Jackson	DB	6'	173	23	1	
Bob Jones	DB	6'1"	194	22		
Lemar Parrish	DB	5'11"	185	25	2	6
Ken Riley	DB	6'	180	26	2	
Ken Anderson	QB	6'1"	211	24		
Greg Cook	QB	6'3"	215	26		
Mike Ernst	QB	6'1"	190	22		
Lenvil Elliott	HB	6'	200	21		12
Essex Johnson	HB	5'9"	200	26		42
Reece Morrison	HB	6'	207	27		
Booby Clark	FB	6'2"	245	22		48
Joe Wilson	HB-FB	5'10"	210	22		
Isaac Curtis	WR	6'	190	22		54
Tim George	WR	6'5"	225	21		
Charlie Joiner	WR	5'11"	188	25		
Chip Myers	WR	6'4"	210	28		
Bruce Coslet	TE	6'3"	227	27		
Al Chandler	TE	6'2"	233	22		
Bob Trumpy	TE	6'6"	228	28		30
Dave Lewis	K	6'2"	225	27		
Horst Muhlmann	K	6'1"	220	33		94

Virgil Carter – Broken Collarbone
Doug Dressler – Knee Injury

PITTSBURGH STEELERS 10-4-0 Chuck Noll

Scores of Each Game		
24	DETROIT	10
33	CLEVELAND	6
36	Houston	7
38	SAN DIEGO	21
7	Cincinnati	19
26	N. Y. JETS	14
20	CINCINNATI	13
21	WASHINGTON	16
17	Oakland	9
13	DENVER	23
16	Cleveland	21
26	Miami	30
33	HOUSTON	7
37	San Francisco	14

Use Name	Pos.	Hgt	Wgt	Age	Int	Pts
Gordon Gravelle	OT	6'5"	250	24		
Glen Ray Hines	OT	6'5"	265	29		
Jon Kolb	OT	6'2"	262	26		
Sam Davis	OG	6'1"	255	29		
Mel Holmes	OG	6'3"	250	23		
Bruce Van Dyke	OG	6'2"	255	29		
Gerry Mullins	OT-OG	6'3"	244	24		
Jim Clack	C	6'3"	250	25		
Ray Mansfield	C	6'3"	260	32		
L. C. Greenwood	DE	6'5"	245	26		
Dwight White	DE	6'4"	250	24	2	2
Steve Furness	DT-DE	6'4"	255	22		
Joe Greene	DT	6'4"	275	26		
Craig Hanneman	DT	6'3"	240	24		
Ernie Holmes	DT	6'3"	260	25		
Tom Keating	DT	6'3"	247	30		
Ed Bradley	LB	6'2"	240	23		
Henry Davis	LB	6'3"	235	30	2	
Jack Ham	LB	6'3"	225	24	2	6
Andy Russell	LB	6'3"	225	31	3	6
Loren Toews	LB	6'3"	212	21	2	
George Webster	LB	6'4"	223	27		
Mel Blount	DB	6'3"	205	25	4	
John Dockery	DB	6'	186	28	1	
Glen Edwards	DB	6'	185	26	6	6
Dennis Meyer	DB	5'11"	186	22	6	6
John Rowser	DB	6'1"	185	29		
J.T. Thomas	DB	6'2"	196	22	1	
Mike Wagner	DB	6'1"	196	24	8	6
Terry Bradshaw	QB	6'3"	218	24		18
Joe Gilliam	QB	6'2"	187	22		
Terry Hanratty	QB	6'1"	210	25		
Rocky Bleier	HB	5'11"	205	27		
Preston Pearson	HB	6'1"	205	28		24
Franco Harris	FB-HB	6'2"	230	23		18
Steve Davis	HB-FB	6'1"	218	23		18
John Fuqua	HB-FB	5'11"	205	26		12
Dave Davis	WR	6'	175	25		
Frank Lewis	WR	6'1"	196	26		18
Barry Pearson	WR	5'11"	185	23		18
Glenn Scolnik	WR	6'3"	190	22		
Ron Shanklin	WR	6'1"	180	26		60
Larry Brown	TE	6'4"	225	24		
John McMakin	TE	6'3"	232	22		6
Roy Gerela	K	5'10"	185	25		123
Bobby Walden	K	6'	190	35		

Al Young – Illness

CLEVELAND BROWNS 7-5-2 Nick Skorich

Scores of Each Game		
24	BALTIMORE	14
6	Pittsburgh	33
12	N. Y. GIANTS	10
17	Cincinnati	10
9	MIAMI	17
42	HOUSTON	13
16	SAN DIEGO	16
3	Minnesota	26
23	Houston	13
7	Oakland	3
21	PITTSBURGH	16
20	Kansas City	20
17	CINCINNATI	34
17	Los Angeles	30

Use Name	Pos.	Hgt	Wgt	Age	Int	Pts
Joe Carollo	OT	6'2"	265	33		
Doug Dieken	OT	6'5"	254	24		
Bob McKay	OT	6'5"	260	25		
Chris Morris	OT	6'3"	250	23		
John Demarie	OG	6'3"	246	28		
Chuck Hutchison	OG	6'3"	240	24		
Gene Hickerson	OG	6'3"	252	38		
Jim Copeland	C-OG	6'2"	243	28		
Bob DeMarco	C	6'3"	248	35		
Bob Briggs	DE	6'4"	258	28		
Joe Jones	DE	6'6"	250	25		
Nick Roman	DE	6'3"	244	25		
Carl Barisich	DT	6'4"	255	22		
Walter Johnson	DT	6'3"	265	30		
Jerry Sherk	DT	6'4"	255	25		
Billy Andrews	LB	6'	220	28		
Bob Babich	LB	6'2"	230	26	1	
John Garlington	LB	6'1"	218	27	1	
Charlie Hall	LB	6'3"	225	24		
Mel Long	LB	6'	228	26		
Jim Romaniszyn	LB	6'2"	214	21		
Cliff Brooks	DB	6'1"	190	24		
Thom Darden	DB	6'2"	195	23	1	
Ben Davis	DB	5'11"	180	27	2	
Van Green	DB	6'1"	192	22		6
Clarence Scott	DB	6'	180	24	5	6
Jim Stienke	DB	5'11"	188	22		
Walt Sumner	DB	6'1"	195	26	2	
Don Horn	QB	6'2"	195	28		
Mike Phipps	QB	6'2"	205	25		30
Leroy Kelly	HB	6'	202	31		18
Billy LeFear	HB	5'11"	197	23		
Greg Pruitt	HB	5'10"	186	22		30
Hugh McKinnis	FB	6'	225	25		
Bo Scott	FB	6'3"	215	30		6
Ken Brown	HB-FB	5'10"	203	27		
Steve Holden	WR	6'	192	22		
Fair Hooker	WR	6'1"	195	26		12
Frank Pitts	WR	6'2"	200	29		24
Gloster Richardson	WR	6'	200	30		6
Dave Sullivan	WR	5'11"	185	22		
Chip Glass	TE	6'4"	235	26		
Milt Morin	TE	6'4"	236	31		6
Ken Smith	TE	6'4"	225	22		
Don Cockroft	K	6'1"	195	28		90

Bubba Pena – Knee Injury

HOUSTON OILERS 1-13-0 Bill Peterson Sid Gillman

Scores of Each Game		
14	N. Y. Giants	34
10	Cincinnati	24
7	PITTSBURGH	36
26	LOS ANGELES	31
20	DENVER	48
13	Cleveland	42
14	Chicago	35
31	Baltimore	27
13	CLEVELAND	23
14	Kansas City	38
0	NEW ENGLAND	32
6	OAKLAND	17
7	Pittsburgh	33
24	CINCINNATI	27

Use Name	Pos.	Hgt	Wgt	Age	Int	Pts
Levert Carr	OT	6'5"	260	29		
Elbert Drungo	OT	6'5"	265	30		
Tom Funchess	OT	6'5"	270	28		
Kevin Hunt (from NE)	OT	6'5"	260	24		
Soloman Freelon	OG	6'2"	250	22		
Brian Goodman	OG	6'2"	250	24		
Al Jenkins	OG	6'2"	245	27		
Harris Jones	OG	6'4"	245	28		
Ralph Miller	OG	6'4"	260	24		
Ron Saul	OG	6'2"	255	25		
Bill Curry	C	6'2"	236	30		
Sam Gruneisen	C	6'1"	250	32		
Calvin Hunt	C	6'3"	245	25		
Ron Lou	C	6'2"	235	22		
Elvin Bethea	DE	6'3"	262	27		
Mike Fanucci	DE	6'4"	240	23		
Tody Smith	DE	6'5"	245	24		
Wes Grant	DT-DE	6'3"	245	26		
Al Cowlings	DT	6'5"	255	26		
John Matuszak	DT	6'8"	290	22		
Greg Sampson	DT	6'6"	260	22		
Gregg Bingham	LB	6'1"	227	22	2	
Ralph Cindrich	LB	6'1"	228	23		
Paul Guidry	LB	6'3"	233	29		
Brian McConnell	LB	6'4"	207	23		
Guy Roberts	LB	6'1"	215	23	4	
Ted Washington	LB	6'1"	240	25		
Willie Alexander	DB	6'2"	195	23	3	
Bob Atkins	DB	6'3"	210	27		
Joe Blahak	DB	5'9"	182	23	2	
John Charles	DB	6'1"	200	29		
Larry Eaglin	DB	6'3"	195	22		6
Alvin Haymond	DB	6'	194	31		
Benny Johnson	DB	5'11"	178	25		
Zeke Moore	DB	6'2"	196	29		
Jeff Severson	DB	6'1"	180	23	4	
Alvin Wyatt	DB	5'10"	180	25		
Lynn Dickey	QB	6'4"	218	23		1
Edd Hargett	QB	5'11"	190	26		
Dan Pastorini	QB	6'3"	215	24		
Bob Gresham	HB	5'11"	195	25		24
Al Johnson	HB	6'	200	23		
Paul Robinson	HB	6'	195	28		12
George Amundson	FB-HB	6'3"	215	23		
Lewis Jolley	FB-HB	6'	210	23		
Bill Thomas	FB	6'2"	225	23		
Fred Willis	FB	6'	212	25		30
Jim Beirne	WR	6'2"	196	26		
Ken Burrough	WR	6'4"	210	25		18
Eddie Hinton	WR	6'	200	26		
Clifton McNeil	WR	6'2"	187	33		
Billy Parks	WR	6'1"	185	25		6
Dave Parks	TE	6'2"	203	31		6
Mack Alston	TE	6'2"	230	26		24
Ron Mayo	TE	6'3"	223	22		
Skip Butler	K	6'2"	200	25		66
Dave Green (to CIN)	K	5'11"	200	23		

Jim Ford – Leg Injury
Willie Rogers – Knee Injury
Sid Smith – Injury

CINCINNATI BENGALS

RUSHING

Last Name	No.	Yds	Avg	TD
E. Johnson	195	997	5.1	4
Clark	254	988	3.9	8
Elliott	22	122	5.5	1
Anderson	26	97	3.7	0
Wilson	10	39	3.9	0
Morrison	3	11	3.7	0
Lewis	3	–7	–2.3	0
Curtis	2	–11	–5.5	0

RECEIVING

Last Name	No.	Yds	Avg	TD
Curtis	45	843	19	9
Clark	45	347	8	0
Trumpy	29	435	15	5
E. Johnson	28	356	13	3
Joiner	13	214	16	0
Coslet	9	123	14	0
Myers	7	77	11	0
George	2	28	14	0
Elliott	1	12	12	1
Morrison	1	4	4	0

PUNT RETURNS

Last Name	No.	Yds	Avg	TD
Parrish	25	200	8	0
Casanova	15	119	8	0
Blackwood	4	12	3	0
Lewis	1	2	2	0

KICKOFF RETURNS

Last Name	No.	Yds	Avg	TD
Jackson	21	520	25	0
Wilson	8	173	22	0
Parrish	7	143	20	0
Lewis	2	40	20	0
Coslet	1	0	0	0

PASSING – PUNTING – KICKING

PASSING	Att	Comp	%	Yds	Yd/Att	TD	Int–%	RK
Anderson	329	179	54	2428	7.4	18	12– 4	1
Cook	3	1	33	11	3.7	0	0– 0	

PUNTING	No	Avg
Lewis	68	41.0

KICKING	XP	Att	%	FG	Att	%
Muhlmann	31	32	97	21	31	68

PITTSBURGH STEELERS

RUSHING

Last Name	No.	Yds	Avg	TD
Harris	188	698	3.7	3
P. Pearson	132	554	4.2	2
Fugua	117	457	3.9	2
Steve Davis	67	266	4.0	2
Bradshaw	34	145	4.3	3
Gilliam	6	23	3.8	0
Shanklin	3	1	0.3	0
Bleier	3	0	0.0	0
Hanratty	3	0	0.0	0
Walden	1	0	0.0	0
Lewis	1	–1	–1.0	0

RECEIVING

Last Name	No.	Yds	Avg	TD
Shanklin	30	711	24	10
Lewis	23	409	18	3
B. Pearson	23	317	14	3
Fugua	17	150	9	0
McMakin	13	195	15	1
P. Pearson	11	173	16	2
Harris	10	69	7	0
Steve Davis	7	31	4	1
Brown	5	88	18	0
D. Davis	1	14	14	0

PUNT RETURNS

Last Name	No.	Yds	Avg	TD
Edwards	34	336	10	0
Meyer	18	80	4	0

KICKOFF RETURNS

Last Name	No.	Yds	Avg	TD
Steve Davis	15	404	27	0
P. Pearson	16	308	19	0
Bleier	3	47	16	0
Harris	1	23	23	0
Fuqua	1	22	22	0
Hanneman	1	20	20	0
Edwards	1	10	10	0
Webster	1	9	9	0
Mansfield	1	0	0	0

PASSING – PUNTING – KICKING

PASSING	Att	Comp	%	Yds	Yd/Att	TD	Int–%	RK
Bradshaw	180	89	49	1183	6.6	10	15– 8	8
Hanratty	69	31	45	643	9.3	8	5– 7	
Gilliam	60	20	33	331	5.5	2	6–10	

PUNTING	No	Avg
Walden	62	41.1

KICKING	XP	Att	%	FG	Att	%
Gerela	36	37	97	29	43	67

CLEVELAND BROWNS

RUSHING

Last Name	No.	Yds	Avg	TD
Brown	161	537	3.3	0
Phipps	60	395	6.6	5
Kelly	132	389	2.9	3
Pruitt	61	369	6.0	4
LeFear	26	135	5.2	0
Bo Scott	34	79	2.3	0
McKinnis	28	77	2.8	0
Cockroft	1	–3	–3.0	0
Richardson	3	–10	–3.3	0

RECEIVING

Last Name	No.	Yds	Avg	TD
Pitts	31	317	10	4
Morin	26	417	16	1
Brown	22	187	9	0
Hooker	18	196	11	2
Kelly	15	180	12	0
Richardson	12	175	15	1
Pruitt	9	110	12	1
Bo Scott	6	23	4	1
LeFear	5	38	8	0
Holden	3	27	9	0
McKinnis	3	11	4	0
Glass	2	60	30	0

PUNT RETURNS

Last Name	No.	Yds	Avg	TD
Pruitt	16	180	11	0
Darden	9	51	6	0
LeFear	7	51	7	0
Holden	2	19	10	0
Kelly	1	7	7	0
Hall	1	0	0	0

KICKOFF RETURNS

Last Name	No.	Yds	Avg	TD
Pruitt	16	453	28	0
Le Fear	15	337	22	0
Holden	8	172	22	0
Long	6	87	15	0
Romaniszyn	2	21	11	0
Dieken	2	14	7	0

PASSING – PUNTING – KICKING

PASSING	Att	Comp	%	Yds	Yd/Att	TD	Int–%	RK
Phipps	299	148	49	1719	5.8	9	20– 7	9
Horn	8	4	50	22	2.8	1	0– 0	
Pruitt	1	0	0	0	0.0	0	0– 0	

PUNTING	No	Avg
Cockroft	82	40.5

KICKING	XP	Att	%	FG	Att	%
Cockroft	24	24	100	22	31	71

HOUSTON OILERS

RUSHING

Last Name	No.	Yds	Avg	TD
Willis	171	579	3.4	4
Gresham	104	400	3.8	2
Robinson	34	151	4.4	2
Pastorini	31	102	3.3	0
Amundson	15	56	3.7	0
Thomas	10	39	3.9	0
Burrough	5	38	7.6	1
Alston	1	13	13.0	0
Dickey	6	9	1.5	0
Jolley	7	6	0.9	0
Hinton	1	–2	–2.0	0
Johnson	1	–3	–3.0	0

RECEIVING

Last Name	No.	Yds	Avg	TD
Willis	57	371	7	1
B. Parks	43	581	14	1
Burrough	43	577	13	2
Gresham	28	244	9	1
Alston	19	195	10	4
Hinton	13	202	16	1
Amundson	7	60	9	0
Robinson	7	46	7	0
Jolley	3	56	19	0
D. Parks	3	31	10	1
Thomas	1	4	4	0
McNeil	1	3	3	0

PUNT RETURNS

Last Name	No.	Yds	Avg	TD
Severson	16	126	8	0
Haymond	14	101	7	0

KICKOFF RETURNS

Last Name	No.	Yds	Avg	TD
Gresham	27	723	27	0
Haymond	28	703	25	0
Hinton	8	141	18	0
Eaglin	3	76	25	0
Blahak	2	41	21	0
Jolley	2	41	21	0
Fanucci	3	40	13	0
Severson	1	17	17	0

PASSING – PUNTING – KICKING

PASSING	Att	Comp	%	Yds	Yd/Att	TD	Int–%	RK
Pastorini	290	154	53	1482	5.1	5	17– 6	10
Dickey	120	71	59	888	7.4	6	10– 8	
Willis	1	0	0	0	0.0	0	0– 0	

PUNTING	No	Avg
Butler	36	37.3
Pastorini	27	40.3
Green	22	39.5

KICKING	XP	Att	%	FG	Att	%
Butler	21	21	100	15	24	63
Dickey	1	1	100	0	0	0

OAKLAND RAIDERS 9-4-1 John Madden

Scores of Each Game		
16	Minnesota	24
12	MIAMI	7
3	Kansas City	16
17	St. Louis	10
27	SAN DIEGO	17
23	Denver	23
34	Baltimore	21
42	N. Y. GIANTS	0
9	PITTSBURGH	17
3	CLEVELAND	7
31	San Diego	3
17	Houston	6
37	KANSAS CITY	7
21	DENVER	7

Use Name	Pos.	Hgt	Wgt	Age	Int	Pts
Art Shell	OT	6'5"	265	26		
John Vella	OT	6'4"	255	23		
Bob Brown	OT	6'4"	280	30		
Paul Seiler	C-OT	6'4"	260	27		
George Buehler	OG	6'2"	260	26		
Gene Upshaw	OG	6'5"	255	28		
Dave Dalby	C-OG	6'2"	240	22		
Jim Otto	C	6'2"	255	35		
Tony Cline	DE	6'2"	240	25		
Horace Jones	DE	6'3"	255	24		
Bubba Smith	DE	6'7"	265	28		
Kelvin Korver	DT	6'6"	260	24	1	
Otis Sistrunk	DT	6'4"	255	25		
Art Thoms	DT	6'5"	250	26		

Use Name	Pos.	Hgt	Wgt	Age	Int	Pts
Joe Carroll	LB	6'1"	220	23		
Dan Conners	LB	6'1"	230	31		
Gerald Irons	LB	6'2"	230	26	2	
Monte Johnson	LB	6'4"	235	21		
Phil Villapiano	LB	6'1"	222	24	1	
Gary Weaver	LB	6'1"	224	24		
Butch Atkinson	DB	6'	180	26	3	12
Willie Brown	DB	6'1"	190	32	3	
Tommy Maxwell	DB	6'2"	195	26		
Jack Tatum	DB	5'10"	200	24	1	
Skip Thomas	DB	6'1"	205	23	2	
Jimmy Warren	DB	5'11"	175	34	1	
Nemiah Wilson	DB	6'	165	30	3	

Jackie Allen – Injury

Use Name	Pos.	Hgt	Wgt	Age	Int	Pts
George Blanda	QB	6'1"	215	45		100
Daryle Lamonica	QB	6'2"	215	32		
Ken Stabler	QB	6'3"	215	27		
Clarence Davis	HB	5'10"	190	24		24
Bob Hudson	HB	5'11"	205	25		
Charlie Smith	HB	6'1"	205	27		30
Marv Hubbard	FB	6'1"	225	27		36
Pete Banaszak	HB-FB	5'11"	210	29		
Jeff Queen	TE-FB	6'1"	220	27		
Fred Biletnikoff	WR	6'1"	190	30		24
Cliff Branch	WR	5'11"	170	25		18
Mike Siani	WR	6'2"	195	23		18
Steve Sweeney	WR	6'3"	205	22		6
Warren Bankston	TE	6'4"	235	26		
Bob Moore	TE	6'3"	220	24		24
Ray Guy	K	6'3"	190	23		

DENVER BRONCOS 7-5-2 John Ralston

Scores of Each Game		
28	CINCINNATI	10
34	SAN FRANCISCO	36
14	CHICAGO	33
14	Kansas City	16
48	Houston	20
23	OAKLAND	23
40	N. Y. Jets	28
17	St. Louis	17
30	SAN DIEGO	19
23	Pittsburgh	13
14	KANSAS CITY	10
10	DALLAS	22
42	San Diego	28
7	Oakland	21

Use Name	Pos.	Hgt	Wgt	Age	Int	Pts
Mike Askea	OT	6'4"	260	22		
Mike Current	OT	6'4"	274	27		
Larron Jackson	OT	6'3"	270	24		
Marv Montgomery	OT	6'6"	255	25		
Paul Howard	OG	6'3"	260	22		
Tommy Lyons	OG	6'2"	228	25		
Mike Schnitker	OG	6'3"	245	26		
Larry Kaminski	C	6'2"	245	28		
Bobby Maples	C	6'3"	250	30		
Lyle Alzado	DE	6'3"	252	24		
Barney Chavous	DE	6'3"	252	22		
John Grant	DE	6'3"	235	23		
Ed Smith	DE	6'5"	240	23		
Pete Duranko	DT	6'2"	250	29		
Jerry Inman	DT	6'3"	256	33		
Paul Smith	DT	6'3"	256	28		

Use Name	Pos.	Hgt	Wgt	Age	Int	Pts
Ken Criter	LB	5'11"	223	26		2
Tom Graham	LB	6'2"	235	23		
Tom Jackson	LB	5'11"	220	22		
Bill Laskey	LB	6'2"	235	30	2	
Ray May (from BAL)	LB	6'1"	230	28	1	
Jim O'Malley	LB	6'1"	230	22		
Mike Simone	LB	6'	210	23		
Charlie Greer	DB	6'	205	27	1	
Dale Hackbart	DB	6'3"	210	37		
Calvin Jones	DB	5'7"	170	22	4	
Leroy Mitchell	DB	6'2"	190	28		
Randy Montgomery	DB	5'11"	182	26		
John Pitts	DB	6'4"	218	28		
Bill Thompson	DB	6'1"	200	26	3	12
Maurice Tyler	DB	6'	188	23		

Tom Domres – Injury
George Goeddeke – Injury
Chip Myrtle – Injury

Use Name	Pos.	Hgt	Wgt	Age	Int	Pts
Charley Johnson	QB	6'	190	36		
Steve Ramsey	QB	6'2"	210	25		
Bobby Anderson	HB	6'	208	25		6
Otis Armstrong	HB	5'10"	196	22		6
Floyd Little	HB	5'10"	196	31		78
Oliver Ross	FB-HB	6'	210	23		
Joe Dawkins	FB	5'11"	223	25		12
Fran Lynch	HB-FB	6'1"	205	27		
Haven Moses	WR	6'3"	205	27		54
Jerry Simmons	WR	6'1"	190	30		6
Bill Van Heusen	WR	6'1"	200	27		6
Gene Washington	WR	6'3"	205	29		18
Bill Masters	TE	6'5"	240	29		
Riley Odoms	TE	6'4"	230	23		42
Jim Turner	K	6'2"	205	32		106

KANSAS CITY CHIEFS 7-5-2 Hank Stram

Scores of Each Game		
13	LOS ANGELES	23
10	New England	7
16	OAKLAND	3
16	DENVER	14
10	Green Bay	10
6	Cincinnati	14
14	Buffalo	23
19	San Diego	0
19	CHICAGO	7
38	HOUSTON	14
10	Denver	14
20	CLEVELAND	20
7	Oakland	37
33	SAN DIEGO	6

Use Name	Pos.	Hgt	Wgt	Age	Int	Pts
Dave Hill	OT	6'5"	260	32		
Francis Peay	OT	6'5"	250	29		
Jim Tyrer	OT	6'6"	280	34		
Ed Budde	OG	6'5"	265	32		
George Daney	OG	6'3"	240	26		
Mo Moorman	OT-OG	6'5"	252	29		
Wayne Walton	OT-OG	6'5"	255	24		
Jack Rudnay	C	6'3"	240	25		
Mike Oriard	OG-C	6'4"	223	25		
Pat Holmes	DE	6'5"	250	33	1	
John Lohmeyer	DE	6'4"	230	22		6
Marv Upshaw	DE	6'3"	260	26		
Wilbur Young	DE	6'6"	285	24		
Buck Buchanan	DT	6'7"	270	33	1	
Curley Culp	DT	6'1"	265	27		
George Seals	DT	6'2"	260	30		

Use Name	Pos.	Hgt	Wgt	Age	Int	Pts
Bobby Bell	LB	6'4"	228	33	1	
Willie Lanier	LB	6'1"	245	28	3	6
Jim Lynch	LB	6'1"	235	28	1	
Al Palewicz	LB	6'1"	215	23		
Clyde Werner	LB	6'4"	225	25		
Nate Allen	DB	5'10"	170	25	1	
Doug Jones	DB	6'2"	202	23		
Jim Kearney	DB	6'2"	206	30	3	
Jim Marsalis	DB	5'11"	194	27	2	
Larry Marshall	DB	5'10"	195	23		
Kerry Reardon	DB	5'11"	180	24	2	
Mike Sensibaugh	DB	5'11"	192	24	3	
Emmitt Thomas	DB	6'2"	192	30	3	

Cannonball Butler – Injury
Ernie Calloway – Knee Injury

Use Name	Pos.	Hgt	Wgt	Age	Int	Pts
Pete Beathard	QB	6'2"	200	31		6
Len Dawson	QB	6'	190	39		
Mike Livingston	QB	6'3"	212	27		12
Leroy Keyes	HB	6'3"	208	26		
Warren McVea	HB	5'10"	182	27		
Ed Podolak	HB	6'1"	205	26		18
Willie Ellison	FB-HB	6'1"	210	28		12
Wendell Hayes	FB	6'2"	220	32		12
Jeff Kinney	HB-FB	6'2"	215	22		6
Andy Hamilton	WR	6'3"	190	23		
Dan Kratzer	WR	6'3"	194	24		
Dave Smith	WR	6'2"	205	26		
Otis Taylor	WR	6'2"	215	30		24
Bob West	WR	6'4"	218	22		
Elmo Wright	WR	6'	190	24		12
Gary Butler	TE	6'3"	235	22		12
Morris Stroud	TE	6'10"	255	27		12
Jan Stenerud	K	6'2"	187	30		93
Jerrel Wilson	K	6'4"	222	31		

SAN DIEGO CHARGERS 2-11-1 Harland Svare Ron Waller

Scores of Each Game		
0	Washington	38
34	BUFFALO	7
13	CINCINNATI	20
21	Pittsburgh	38
17	Oakland	27
0	ATLANTA	41
16	Cleveland	16
0	KANSAS CITY	19
19	Denver	30
17	NEW ORLEANS	14
3	OAKLAND	31
14	New England	30
28	DENVER	42
6	Kansas City	33

Use Name	Pos.	Hgt	Wgt	Age	Int	Pts
Ira Gordon	OT	6'3"	268	25		
Terry Owens	OT	6'6"	268	29		
Russ Washington	OT	6'6"	290	26		
Al Dennis	OG	6'4"	250	22		
Walt Sweeney	OG	6'3"	256	32		
Ralph Wenzel	OG	6'3"	250	30		
Doug Wilkerson	OG	6'2"	256	26		
Jay Douglas	C	6'6"	242	22		
Carl Mauck	C	6'3"	243	26		
Lionel Aldridge	DE	6'4"	245	31		
Coy Bacon	DE	6'4"	270	31		6
Deacon Jones	DE	6'5"	250	34		
Pete Lazetich	DE	6'3"	225	23		
Cal Snowden	DE	6'4"	253	26		
Dave Costa	DT	6'2"	260	31		
Greg Wojcik	DT	6'4"	243	30		

Use Name	Pos.	Hgt	Wgt	Age	Int	Pts
Carl Gersbach	LB	6'1"	230	26	1	
Rick Redman	LB	5'11"	222	30	1	
Floyd Rice (from HOU)	LB	6'3"	223	24	1	6
Mel Rogers	LB	6'2"	230	26	1	
Tim Rossovich	LB	6'4"	240	27	1	
Mike Stratton	LB	6'3"	240	31	3	
Joe Beauchamp	DB	6'	188	29		
Reggie Berry	DB	6'	190	24		
Lenny Dunlap	DB	6'1"	195	24		
Chris Fletcher	DB	5'11"	185	24		
Bob Howard	DB	6'1"	177	28	5	
Willie McGee	DB	5'11"	175	23		
Bryant Salter	DB	6'4"	196	23	1	
Ron Smith	DB	6'1"	195	30	1	12

Ray White – Injury

Use Name	Pos.	Hgt	Wgt	Age	Int	Pts
Wayne Clark	QB	6'2"	205	26		
Dan Fouts	QB	6'3"	193	22		
Johnny Unitas	QB	6'1"	196	40		
Mike Garrett	HB	5'9"	200	29		6
Clint Jones	HB	6'	205	28		6
Bob Thomas	HB	5'10"	200	24		6
Cid Edwards	FB	6'2"	230	29		6
Robert Holmes	FB	5'9"	220	27		42
Gary Garrison	WR	6'1"	193	29		12
Ron Holliday	WR	5'9"	168	25		1
Jerry LeVias	WR	5'10"	178	26		18
Dave Williams (to PIT)	WR	6'2"	200	28		
Pettis Norman	TE	6'3"	220	33		
Gary Parris	TE	6'2"	226	23		
Jim Thaxton	TE	6'2"	240	24		12
Dennis Partee	K	6'2"	230	27		9
Ray Wersching	K	5'11"	210	23		46

OAKLAND RAIDERS

RUSHING

Last Name	No.	Yds	Avg	TD
Hubbard	193	903	4.7	6
C. Smith	173	682	3.9	4
Davis	116	609	5.3	4
Banaszak	34	198	5.8	0
Stabler	21	101	4.8	0
Guy	1	21	21.0	0
Hudson	4	3	0.8	0
Lamonica	5	−7	−1.4	0

RECEIVING

Last Name	No.	Yds	Avg	TD
Biletnikoff	48	660	14	4
Siani	45	742	16	3
Moore	34	375	11	4
C. Smith	28	260	9	1
Branch	19	290	15	3
Hubbard	15	116	8	0
Davis	7	76	11	0
Banaszak	6	31	5	0
Sweeny	2	52	26	1
Hudson	1	9	9	0

PUNT RETURNS

Last Name	No.	Yds	Avg	TD
Atkinson	41	336	8	1
Maxwell	4	8	2	0
Warren	1	0	0	0

KICKOFF RETURNS

Last Name	No.	Yds	Avg	TD
Davis	19	504	27	0
Hudson	14	350	25	0
Banaszak	3	48	16	0
C. Smith	2	23	12	0
Bankston	1	12	12	0

PASSING – PUNTING – KICKING

PASSING	Att	Comp	%	Yds	Yd/Att	TD	Int–%	RK
Stabler	260	163	63	1997	7.7	14	10– 4	2
Lamonica	93	42	45	614	6.6	2	8– 9	

PUNTING	No	Avg
Guy	69	45.3

KICKING	XP	Att	%	FG	Att	%
Blanda	31	31	100	23	33	70

DENVER BRONCOS

RUSHING

Last Name	No.	Yds	Avg	TD
Little	256	979	3.8	12
Dawkins	160	706	4.4	2
Armstrong	26	90	3.5	0
Anderson	19	61	3.2	1
Odoms	5	53	10.6	0
Van Heusen	4	34	8.5	0
Moses	3	25	8.3	1
Ross	5	21	4.2	0
Johnson	7	−2	−0.3	0
Simmons	1	−4	−4.0	0
Masters	1	−9	−9.0	0

RECEIVING

Last Name	No.	Yds	Avg	TD
Odoms	43	629	15	7
Little	41	423	10	1
Dawkins	30	329	11	0
Moses	28	518	19	8
Anderson	15	153	10	0
Simmons	13	249	19	1
Washington	10	150	15	3
Van Heusen	8	149	19	1
Masters	5	65	13	0
Armstrong	2	43	22	1
Jackson	1	−2	−2	0

PUNT RETURNS

Last Name	No.	Yds	Avg	TD
Thompson	30	366	12	0
Tyler	4	20	5	0
Greer	3	11	4	0
Little	1	7	7	0
Criter	1	0	0	0
Mitchell	1	0	0	0

KICKOFF RETURNS

Last Name	No.	Yds	Avg	TD
Armstrong	20	472	24	0
Dawkins	10	222	22	0
Thompson	1	25	25	0
Tyler	1	23	23	0
Montgomery	1	22	22	0
Lynch	1	14	14	0
Forsberg	1	12	12	0
Simone	1	3	3	0

PASSING – PUNTING – KICKING

PASSING	Att	Comp	%	Yds	Yd/Att	TD	Int–%	RK
Johnson	346	184	53	2465	7.1	20	17– 5	3
Ramsey	27	10	37	194	7.2	2	2– 7	
Anderson	3	2	67	47	15.7	0	0– 0	
Turner	1	0	0	0	0.0	0	1–100	
Van Heusen	1	0	0	0	0.0	0	0– 0	

PUNTING	No	Avg
Van Heusen	69	45.1

KICKING	XP	Att	%	FG	Att	%
Turner	40	40	100	22	33	67

KANSAS CITY CHIEFS

RUSHING

Last Name	No.	Yds	Avg	TD
Podolak	210	721	3.4	3
Ellison	108	411	3.8	2
Hayes	95	352	3.7	2
Kinney	50	128	2.6	1
Livingston	19	94	4.9	2
Dawson	6	40	6.7	0
Wright	5	29	5.8	0
Beathard	6	16	2.7	0
Butler	2	10	5.0	0
McVea	4	6	1.5	0
Keyes	2	1	0.5	0
Taylor	4	−14	−3.5	0

RECEIVING

Last Name	No.	Yds	Avg	TD
Podolak	55	445	8	0
Taylor	34	565	17	4
Hayes	18	134	7	0
Wright	16	252	16	2
Stroud	12	216	18	2
Kinney	11	126	11	0
Ellison	9	64	7	0
Butler	8	124	16	2
West	4	65	16	0
Hamilton	2	35	18	0
Smith	2	20	10	0
Moorman	1	−1	−1	0
Keyes	1	−6	−6	0

PUNT RETURNS

Last Name	No.	Yds	Avg	TD
Marshall	29	180	6	0
Podolak	11	90	8	0
Reardon	2	9	5	0

KICKOFF RETURNS

Last Name	No.	Yds	Avg	TD
Marshall	14	391	28	0
McVea	8	146	18	0
Kinney	5	130	26	0
Reardon	2	45	23	0
Werner	1	13	13	0
West	1	0	0	0

PASSING – PUNTING – KICKING

PASSING	Att	Comp	%	Yds	Yd/Att	TD	Int–%	RK
Livingston	145	75	52	916	6.3	6	7– 5	7
Dawson	101	66	65	725	7.2	2	5– 5	
Beathard	64	31	48	389	6.1	2	1– 2	
Keyes	1	0	0	0	0.0	0	0– 0	
Podolak	1	0	0	0	0.0	0	0– 0	
Wilson	1	1	100	9	9.0	0	0– 0	

PUNTING	No	Avg
Wilson	80	45.5

KICKING	XP	Att	%	FG	Att	%
Stenerud	21	23	91	24	38	63

SAN DIEGO CHARGERS

RUSHING

Last Name	No.	Yds	Avg	TD
Edwards	133	609	4.6	1
Garrett	114	467	4.1	0
Holmes	78	289	3.7	7
C. Jones	55	170	3.1	1
Clark	13	86	6.6	0
Holliday	6	70	11.7	0
Thomas	22	48	2.2	0
LeVias	2	33	16.5	0
Fouts	7	32	4.6	0
Norman	1	10	10.0	0

RECEIVING

Last Name	No.	Yds	Avg	TD
LeVias	30	536	18	3
Edwards	25	164	7	0
Holmes	19	151	8	0
Garrett	15	124	8	1
Garrison	14	292	21	2
Holliday	14	182	13	0
Norman	13	200	15	0
C. Jones	7	126	18	0
Thaxton	7	119	17	2
Dave Williams	7	118	17	0
Thomas	7	51	7	1
McGee	3	67	22	0

PUNT RETURNS

Last Name	No.	Yds	Avg	TD
Smith	27	352	13	2
McGee	6	56	9	0

KICKOFF RETURNS

Last Name	No.	Yds	Avg	TD
Smith	36	947	26	0
McGee	20	423	21	0
C. Jones	10	217	22	0
Rice	2	17	9	0
East	1	8	8	0
Rogers	1	4	4	0
Douglas	1	0	0	0
Wenzel	1	0	0	0
Holliday	0	−2	0	0

PASSING – PUNTING – KICKING

PASSING	Att	Comp	%	Yds	Yd/Att	TD	Int–%	RK
Fouts	194	87	45	1126	5.8	6	13– 7	12
Clark	90	40	44	532	5.9	0	9–10	
Unitas	76	34	45	471	6.2	3	7– 9	
Holliday	2	0	0	0	0.0	0	1–50	
Garrett	1	0	0	0	0.0	0	0– 0	

PUNTING	No	Avg
Partee	72	41.1

KICKING	XP	Att	%	FG	Att	%
Wersching	13	15	87	11	25	44
Partee	6	6	100	1	2	50
Holliday	1	1	100	0	0	0

1973 Championship Games

NFC CHAMPIONSHIP GAME

December 30, at Irving, Texas
(Attendance 60,272)

Tarkenton's Winning Formula

SCORING

DALLAS	0	0	10	0–10
MINNESOTA	3	7	7	10–27

First Quarter
Minn. — Cox, 44 yard field goal

Second Quarter
Minn. — Foreman, 5 yard rush
PAT–Cox (kick)

Third Quarter
Dall. — Richards, 63 yard punt return
PAT–Fritsch (kick)
Minn. — Gilliam, 54 yard pass from Tarkenton
PAT–Cox (kick)
Dall. — Fritsch, 17 yard field goal

Fourth Quarter
Minn. — Bryant, 63 yard interception return
PAT–Cox (kick)
Minn. — Cox, 34 yard field goal

TEAM STATISTICS

DALLAS		MINN.
9	First Downs–Total	20
3	First Downs–Rushing	14
5	First Downs–Passing	6
1	First Downs–Penalty	0
2	Fumbles–Number	4
2	Fumbles–Lost Ball	3
2	Penalties–Number	3
20	Yards Penalized	33
0	Missed Field Goals	0
49	Offensive Plays	72
153	Net Yards	306
3.1	Average Gain	4.3
6	Giveaways	4
4	Takeaways	6
–2	Difference	+2

Fran Tarkenton was in his first playoffs in his thirteen-year career, and he celebrated last week by leading the Vikings to a 27-20 victory over the Redskins. Now he hoped to further destroy his image as a loser by beating the Cowboys, who had defeated the Rams 27-16 in the opening round of the playoffs.

The Vikings established a winning formula on offense in the first half by mixing unexpected passes with a strong running attack. The Minnesota blockers keyed on removing middle linebacker Lee Roy Jordan from all running plays, and with star tackle Bob Lilly out of action with a bad back, the Cowboys could not stop ball carriers Chuck Foreman and Oscar Reed. The Vikings controlled the ball for most of the first half, and their defense foiled the Cowboys whenever they got the ball.

Fred Cox scored Minnesota's first three points with a first-quarter field goal, and the Vikings added a touchdown in the second period on an 86-yard drive capped by Foreman's five-yard run.

The Dallas offense, playing without the injured Calvin Hill, could not crack the Minnesota defense until Golden Richards put the Cowboys on the scoreboard by returning a punt 63 yards for a touchdown. The Cowboys now had the momentum to take the lead, but Tarkenton deflated the Dallas hopes three plays later when he hit John Gilliam with a long bomb that went for a 54-yard touchdown. The Cowboys added a Toni Fritsch field goal late in the period to make the score 17-10 with fifteen minutes left.

Turnovers dominated the final period. The teams took turns giving the ball up until Bobby Bryant intercepted a Staubach pass and returned it 63 yards for a score. Another intercepted pass led to a Cox field goal which lengthened the Viking lead to 27-10. The Cowboys suffered the final indignity late in the game when Walt Garrison fumbled the ball away on the Minnesota two-yard line.

INDIVIDUAL STATISTICS

DALLAS	No	Yds	Avg.	MINNESOTA	No	Yds	Avg.
RUSHING							
Newhouse	14	40	2.9	Foreman	19	76	4.0
Staubach	5	30	6.0	Reed	18	75	4.2
Garrison	5	9	1.8	Osborn	4	27	6.8
Fugett	1	1	1.0	Tarkenton	4	16	4.0
	25	80	3.2	Brown	2	9	4.5
					47	203	4.3
RECEIVING							
Hayes	2	25	12.5	Foreman	4	28	7.0
Pearson	2	24	12.0	Gilliam	2	63	31.5
Montgomery	2	15	7.5	Voigt	2	23	11.5
DuPree	1	20	20.0	Lash	1	11	11.0
Garrison	1	10	10.0	Reed	1	8	8.0
Fugett	1	–1	–1.0		10	133	13.3
Newhouse	1	–4	–4.0				
	10	89	8.9				
PUNTING							
Bateman	4		39.5	Eischeid	3		43.3
PUNT RETURNS							
Richards	1	63	63.0	Bryant	1	0	0.0
KICKOFF RETURNS							
Harris	2	54	27.0	West	2	45	22.5
Waters	1	18	18.0	Gilliam	1	21	21.0
	3	72	24.0		3	66	22.0
INTERCEPTION RETURNS							
Waters	1	1	1.0	Bryant	2	63	31.5
				J. Wright	1	13	13.0
				Siemon	1	0	0.0
					4	76	19.0

PASSING

	Att.	Comp.	Comp. Pct.	Yds.	Int.	Yds/ Att.	Yds/ Comp.	Yards Lost Tackled
DALLAS								
Staubach	21	10	47.6	89	4	4.2	8.9	2–26
MINNESOTA								
Tarkenton	21	10	47.6	133	1	6.3	13.3	4–30

AFC CHAMPIONSHIP GAME

December 30, at Miami
(Attendance 75,105)

Bringing the Raiders Down to Earth

SCORING

MIAMI	7	7	3	10–27
OAKLAND	0	0	10	0–10

First Quarter
Miami — Csonka, 11 yard rush
PAT–Yepremian (kick)

Second Quarter
Miami — Csonka, 2 yard rush
PAT–Yepremian (kick)

Third Quarter
Oak. — Blanda, 21 yard field goal
Miami — Yepremian, 42 yard field goal
Oak. — Siani, 25 yard pass from Stabler
PAT–Blanda (kick)

Fourth Quarter
Miami — Yepremian, 26 yard field goal
Miami — Csonka, 2 yard rush
PAT–Yepremian (kick)

TEAM STATISTICS

MIAMI		OAK.
21	First Downs–Total	15
18	First Downs–Rushing	4
2	First Downs–Passing	8
1	First Downs–Penalty	2
1	Fumbles–Number	1
0	Fumbles–Lost Ball	0
3	Penalties–Number	3
26	Yards Penalized	35
0	Missed Field Goals	1
60	Offensive Plays	49
292	Net Yards	236
4.9	Average Gain	4.8
1	Giveaways	1
1	Takeaways	1
0	Difference	0

The Raiders had used a powerful running attack to beat the Steelers 33-14 in the AFC semifinal match, but the Dolphins, coming off a 34-16 victory over the Bengals, taught the Raiders a lesson about ball control in this AFC title match. Dolphin quarterback Bob Griese passed the ball only six times all game, relying instead on his powerful running backs to grind out the yardage. Larry Csonka and Mercury Morris plowed through gaping holes cut in the Oakland defense by the Miami blockers, and the Dolphins succeeded in eating up both yardage and the clock.

On the first series of the day, the Dolphins drove 64 yards to a touchdown, with the key play of the drive a 27-yard scramble by Griese on third-and-11 on the Oakland 38-yard line. Larry Csonka plowed over from the 11-yard line for the score.

The Raiders threatened in the first period when Ken Stabler hit Mike Siani with a pass deep in Miami territory, but a holding penalty nullified the play and extinguished the threat. The Dolphins, meanwhile, put together another long drive late in the half, and Csonka scored from the 2 after Griese had frozen the Raiders by faking a roll-out.

George Blanda put the Raiders on the scoreboard early in the second half with a 21-yard field goal, but Charley Leigh's 52-yard return of the kickoff led to Garo Yepremian's 42-yard three-pointer to make the score 17-3. Stabler started clicking on short passes late in the period, and his 25-yard scoring pitch to Siani narrowed the Miami lead to 17-10.

The Dolphins gave themselves some breathing room five minutes into the fourth quarter with a Yepremian field goal, and when the defensive unit stopped the Raiders on a fourth-and-inches try, the Miami attack ground out a final touchdown to run the winning margin to 27-10.

INDIVIDUAL STATISTICS

MIAMI	No	Yds	Avg.	OAKLAND	No	Yds	Avg.
RUSHING							
Csonka	29	117	4.0	Hubbard	10	54	5.4
Morris	14	86	6.1	C. Smith	10	35	3.5
Griese	3	39	13.0	C. Davis	4	15	3.8
Kiick	6	12	2.0	Banaszak	2	3	1.5
Nottingham	1	12	12.0		26	107	4.1
	53	266	5.0				
RECEIVING							
Warfield	1	27	27.0	C. Smith	5	43	8.6
Briscoe	1	6	6.0	Siani	3	45	15.0
Kiick	1	1	1.0	Biletnikoff	2	15	7.5
	3	34	11.3	Hubbard	2	11	5.5
				Moore	1	9	4.5
				C. Davis	1	6	6.0
					15	129	8.6
PUNTING							
Seiple	1		39.0	Guy	2		51.0
PUNT RETURNS							
Scott	2	10	5.0	Atkinson	1	0	0.0
KICKOFF RETURNS							
Leigh	1	52	52.0	C. Davis	3	68	22.7
Morris	1	19	19.0	C. Smith	1	21	21.0
Nottingham	1	19	19.0		4	89	22.3
	3	90	30.0				
INTERCEPTION RETURNS							
Matheson	1	29	29.0	W. Brown	1	0	0.0

PASSING

	Att.	Comp.	Comp. Pct.	Yds.	Int.	Yds/ Att.	Yds/ Comp.	Yards Lost Tackled
MIAMI								
Griese	6	3	50.0	34	1	5.7	11.3	1–8
OAKLAND								
Stabler	23	15	65.2	129	1	5.6	8.6	0–0

SUPER BOWL VIII
January 13, at Houston
(Attendance 68,142)

Dolphin Defense and Csonka Crashes

The Dolphins did not enjoy a perfect season this year, but they did play an almost perfect game against the Vikings in the Super Bowl. After receiving the opening kickoff, the Dolphins immediately set the tone of the day with a crunching 62-yard drive. With the Miami line ripping the famous Minnesota front four to shreds, Larry Csonka repeatedly burst through the middle for good yardage. On the tenth play of the drive, Csonka bulled into the end zone from five yards out; the Dolphins now had a 7-0 lead to nurse.

Viking quarterback Fran Tarkenton, a man eager to erase his image as a loser, could make no progress against the swarming Miami defense. The Dolphin line smothered the Minnesota running game, and the Dolphin zone defense made passing a very risky proposition. Tarkenton tried every play in the Viking playbook to no avail.

The Dolphins, meanwhile, did not stop with their seven-point lead. With Bob Griese passing very rarely, the Miami attack continued to move the ball on the ground. The Dolphin linemen habitually beat the Viking front four off the ball, slamming into them before they could react; Minnesota ends Carl Eller and Jim Marshall were taken out of almost every play. The second Dolphin touchdown came late in the opening quarter on a plunge by Jim Kiick, who had not scored all season. Garo Yepremian added the extra point, and the 14-0 lead looked close to impregnable.

Yepremian added a field goal in the second quarter to give the Dolphins a 17-0 halftime edge that understated the one-sidedness of the first half. The Vikings were not making out-and-out blunders; they simply were being beaten by better blocking and tackling. They did make a mistake on the second-half kickoff when a clipping penalty called back a long return by John Gilliam. The momentum which the return had given to the Vikings immediately shifted back to the Dolphins, and within seven minutes Csonka drove into the end zone for the third Miami touchdown.

With the decision no longer in doubt, the Vikings got onto the scoreboard in the fourth quarter on a touchdown run by Tarkenton. After Cox booted the extra point, the Vikings shocked Miami by recovering an on-side kick; once again, however, a penalty nullified the play and nipped a Minnesota rally before it could begin.

By the end of the day, the Dolphins again were undisputed champions of pro football, and Larry Csonka had set a Super Bowl rushing record with 145 hard-fought yards. With two straight championships to their credit, the Dolphins now drew comparisons with the Packers of Vince Lombardi's era. Although Marv Fleming, who played on both clubs, said, "This is the greatest team ever," the question joined the ranks of unanswerable sports fantasies.

LINEUPS

MIAMI		MINNESOTA
	OFFENSE	
Warfield	WR	Dale
W. Moore	LT	Alderman
Kuechenberg	LG	White
Langer	C	Tinglehoff
Little	RG	Gallagher
Evans	RT	Yary
Mandich	TE	Voigt
Briscoe	WR	Gilliam
Griese	QB	Tarkenton
Morris	RB	Foreman
Csonka	RB	Reed
	DEFENSE	
Den Herder	LE	Eller
Fernandez	LT	Larsen
Heinz	RT	Page
Stanfill	RE	Marshall
Swift	LLB	Winston
Buoniconti	MLB	Siemon
Kolen	RLB	Hilgenberg
Mumphord	LCB	N. Wright
Johnson	RCB	Bryant
Anderson	LS	J. Wright
Scott	RS	Krause

SUBSTITUTES

MIAMI

OFFENSE	
Crusan	Morrall
Fleming	Newman
Goode	Nottingham
Kiick	Twilley
DEFENSE	
Babb	Matheson
Ball	M. Moore
Bannon	Stuckey
Foley	
KICKERS	
Seiple	Yepremian

MINNESOTA

OFFENSE	
B. Brown	Lash
Goodrum	Marinaro
Kingsriter	Osborn
DEFENSE	
T. Brown	Porter
Lurtsema	Sutherland
Martin	West
KICKERS	
Cox	Eischeid

SCORING

MIAMI	14	3	7	0	–24
MINNESOTA	0	0	0	7	– 7

First Quarter		
Mia.	Csonka, 5 yard rush	9:33
	PAT – Yepremian (kick)	
Mia.	Kiick, 1 yard rush	13:38
	PAT – Yepremian (kick)	
Second Quarter		
Mia.	Yepremian, 28 yard field goal	8:58
Third Quarter		
Mia.	Csonka, 2 yard rush	6:16
	PAT – Yepremian (kick)	
Fourth Quarter		
Minn.	Tarkenton, 4 yard rush	1:35
	PAT – Cox (kick)	

TEAM STATISTICS

MIAMI		MINN.
21	First Downs – Total	14
13	First Downs – Rushing	5
4	First Downs – Passing	8
4	First Downs – Penalty	1
1	Fumbles – Number	2
0	Fumbles – Lost Ball	1
1	Penalties – Number	7
4	Yards Penalized	65
0	Missed Field Goals	0
61	Offensive Plays	54
259	Net Yards	238
4.2	Average Gain	4.4
0	Giveaways	2
2	Takeaways	0
+2	Difference	–2

INDIVIDUAL STATISTICS

RUSHING

MIAMI	No	Yds	Avg.	MINNESOTA	No	Yds	Avg.
Csonka	33	145	4.4	Reed	11	32	2.9
Morris	11	34	3.1	Foreman	7	18	2.6
Kiick	7	10	1.4	Tarkenton	4	17	4.3
Griese	2	7	3.5	Marinaro	1	3	3.0
	53	196	3.7	B. Brown	1	2	2.0
					24	72	3.0

RECEIVING

MIAMI	No	Yds	Avg.	MINNESOTA	No	Yds	Avg.
Warfield	2	33	16.5	Foreman	5	27	5.4
Mandich	2	21	10.5	Gilliam	4	44	11.0
Briscoe	2	19	9.5	Voigt	3	46	15.3
	6	73	12.2	Marinaro	2	39	19.5
				B. Brown	1	9	9.0
				Kingsriter	1	9	9.0
				Lash	1	9	9.0
				Reed	1	–1	–1.0
					18	182	10.1

PUNTING

MIAMI	No	Yds	Avg.	MINNESOTA	No	Yds	Avg.
Seiple	3		39.6	Eischeid	5		42.2

PUNT RETURNS

MIAMI	No	Yds	Avg.	MINNESOTA	No	Yds	Avg.
Scott	3	20	6.7				

KICKOFF RETURNS

MIAMI	No	Yds	Avg.	MINNESOTA	No	Yds	Avg.
Scott	2	47	23.5	Gilliam	2	41	20.5
				West	2	28	14.0
					4	69	17.3

INTERCEPTION RETURNS

MIAMI	No	Yds	Avg.	MINNESOTA	No	Yds	Avg.
Johnson	1	10	10.0	None			

PASSING

	Att	Comp	Comp Pct.	Yds	Int	Yds/ Att.	Yds/ Comp	Yards Lost Tackled
MIAMI								
Griese	7	6	85.7	73	0	10.4	12.2	1–10
MINNESOTA								
Tarkenton	28	18	64.3	182	1	6.5	10.1	2–16

1974 N.F.C. Internal and External Headaches

The summer was a troubled one for the N.F.L. The Players Association called a strike on July 1 for a variety of reasons, and veteran players spent the early part of training camp walking picket lines and working out in local playgrounds. While the early exhibition games went on with an overwhelming number of rookies and free agents, the World Football League opened shop as the newest alternative to the N.F.L. The twelve W.F.L. teams threw a lot of money around and signed to future contracts such N.F.L. stars as Larry Csonka, Paul Warfield, Jim Kiick, Calvin Hill, Kenny Stabler, Ted Kwalick, Bill Bergey, John Gilliam, Ted Hendricks, Tim Foley, Craig Morton, and Rayfield Wright, all scheduled for delivery in one to three years, after their N.F.L. contracts ran out.

The W.F.L. started play in July with mostly nondescript players and huge crowds in attendance. But by the time the N.F.L. strike ended in August, the W.F.L. was in big trouble. Those huge attendance figures turned out to be padded with thousands of freebies, and club owners found their reserves of capital rapidly shrinking. By September, franchises were shifting cities and clubs were going bankrupt, and players were going without paychecks—strong indications that the W.F.L. was a sinking ship and no threat at all to the established league.

EASTERN DIVISION

St. Louis Cardinals—The Cards didn't figure as a contender this season, but six straight wins at the start of the schedule established them as the Cinderella club of the N.F.C. Coach Don Coryell had rigged together a potent offense last season, but his defense rebounded from a disappointed 1973 campaign to keep the Cards in every game by holding enemy scoring down. Big tackle Dave Butz missed most of the season with a knee injury, but the defense held together around an All-Pro performance by cornerback Roger Wehrli. The heart of the team, however, was the offense, which had breakaway potential both in the air and on the ground. A strong offensive line cleared the way for quick running back Terry Metcalf and protected quarterback Jim Hart while he zeroed in on speedster Mel Gray. The Cards made the playoffs for the first time since 1948, when the club was still based in Chicago.

Washington Redskins—Instead of an experienced, shopworn veteran, coach George Allen's prize acquisition this year was quarterback Joe Theismann, a star at Notre Dame seasoned by play in the Canadian Football League. But Theismann's main duty this season was running back punts, as veterans Billy Kilmer and Sonny Jurgensen continued to pilot the Redskin attack. Jurgensen particularly captured the public's fancy, as this 40-year-old passer with the protruding belly won several games in relief performances. The Redskins relied more than usual on the air game, as the running attack suffered from bad seasons by Larry Brown and Duane Thomas, plus Charlie Harraway's jump to the W.F.L. The defense was as tough as ever and brought the team home in a tie for first place.

Dallas Cowboys—After the Cowboys won their opening game and then lost four straight, fans and writers were saying prayers over the team's dead playoff chances. But the Cowboys didn't count themselves out and started the long fight back to catch the Cardinals and Redskins. One key game on that road was a November 17 confrontation in Washington, where the Redskins roared out to a 28–0 halftime lead; the Cowboys came back, 28–21, but fell short when Drew Pearson dropped a pass in the end zone late in the game. The two clubs met again on Thanksgiving Day, with the Redskins taking a 16–3 lead and knocking quarterback Roger Staubach out of action. Rookie Clint Longley then came into the fray and led the Cowboys to a 24–23 win with a 50-yard touchdown pass to Pearson with only 28 seconds left. But the Cowboys could not overcome their earlier disasters and didn't make the playoffs for the first time in nine years.

Philadelphia Eagles—Coach Mike McCormack had built the Eagles into an offensive power last year, and the addition of middle linebacker Bill Bergey from Cincinnati was expected to tighten up the defense enough to permit a shot at the playoffs. Four wins in the first five games kept the Eagles hot on the heels of first-place St. Louis, but then six straight losses ended any playoff hopes. The defense was much improved, but the offense went flat, with quarterback Roman Gabriel benched for the last three games in favor of rookie Mike Boryla.

New York Giants—The Giants had a new General Manager in former star player Andy Robustelli and a new head coach in Bill Arnsbarger, who designed the famous Miami defense while an assistant under Don Shula. The new management drafted two fine rookie guards in John Hicks and Tom Mullen, and quarterback Craig Morton benefited from their pass protection after coming over from Dallas in an October trade. But despite improvements at some positions, the Giants still came up short at most positions and still had to practice in Jersey City, New Jersey and play home games in the Yale Bowl in New Haven, Connecticut. Without a real home, the Giants suffered through a 2–12 season, including a string of disheartening losses coming late in the fourth quarter.

CENTRAL DIVISION

Minnesota Vikings—The Vikings used a familiar formula to quickly take charge of the Central Division. The blend of an overwhelming defense plus a versatile offense versed at ball-control had won divisional titles before, and again propelled the Vikings into the playoffs this season. The front four of Alan Page, Carl Eller, Jim Marshall, and Doug Sutherland put unrelenting pressure on enemy offenses, and the secondary didn't lose much when cornerback Bobby Bryant broke his arm and was replaced by rookie Jackie Wallace. The Viking offense had stars in all sectors, featuring quarterback Fran Tarkenton, running back Chuck Foreman, wide receiver John Gilliam, and tackle Ron Yary.

Detroit Lions—The season got off to a depressing start when head coach Don McCafferty died of a heart attack in training camp. With assistant Rick Forzano taking over the reigns, the Lions got off to a slow start in the regular season and seemed destined to finish in the lower ranks of the league. But the club righted itself and stayed in contention for a wildcard playoff berth into December before being eliminated. Bill Munson captured the starting quarterback's job in the preseason, but Greg Landry reclaimed the position late in the year when Munson suffered a dislocated shoulder.

Green Bay Packers—The Packer defense, bolstered by the addition of All-Pro linebacker Ted Hendricks from Baltimore, was one of the N.F.L.'s best, but the offense could generate little fireworks. Runners John Brockington and MacArthur Lane punched out less yards than had been expected, and young quarterback Jerry Tagge couldn't ignite a respectable passing attack. An October trade for John Hadl helped the offense somewhat, but not enough to give the Pack a winning season. Rumors of coach Dan Devine's impending dismissal circulated all season, but Devine beat the punch by resigning after the season to become head coach at Notre Dame.

Chicago Bears—The Bears beat Detroit in their opening game, but persistent quarterback problems quickly dragged the Bears down into another losing season. Neither Gary Huff nor Bobby Douglass was successful in putting points on the scoreboard, and coach Abe Gibron was fired after the season. The Bears were such a dull show that a game against the Giants on December 1 drew a crowd of 18,802 and a no-show total of 36,951. With Dick Butkus retired, the Bears simply had no big names to draw a crowd in bad weather.

WESTERN DIVISION

Los Angeles Rams—Experts made the Rams the preseason favorite to reach the Super Bowl, but coach Chuck Knox's club never jelled into a powerhouse. They easily outdistanced the weak competition in the Western Division, but upset losses to clubs like New England and New Orleans belied the shaky base of the team's good record. One major change made by coach Knox was the trade of quarterback John Hadl to Green Bay in October and the elevation of sub James Harris to the starter's slot. The only black starting quarterback in the N.F.C., Harris had fine support from a strong offensive line, good receivers, and great running from Lawrence McCutcheon. The defense was the stingiest in the entire N.F.L. with end Jack Youngblood and tackle Larry Brooks making All-Pro, and with tackle Merlin Olsen still a formidable force.

San Francisco '49ers—The '49er offense sputtered under a veritable parade of quarterbacks. With John Brodie retired, Steve Spurrier was expected to start, but he suffered a shoulder separation in a preseason game. Joe Reed began the season in competent fashion but soon fell apart. Rookie Dennis Morrison then took his turn, and then 13th-draft-choice Tom Owen got a chance and saw considerable action in the latter part of the schedule. Veteran Norm Snead came over in a mid-season trade but could accomplish little more than the others in the parade. Rookie Wilbur Jackson injected some punch into the running game, but the defense suffered from Charlie Krueger's retirement, Jim Johnson's bad toe, and Mel Phillips' broken arm.

New Orleans Saints—Another mediocre season fanned recurrent rumors that quarterback Archie Manning was going to be traded to shore up several other positions. A flurry of quarterback trading in late October in the N.F.C. saw Manning stay in New Orleans, but coach John North was evidently not completely satisfied with his young passer. North sat Manning down for several games and started subs Bobby Scott and Larry Cipa.

Atlanta Falcons—The Falcons seemed ready to move into the playoff ranks for the first time, but instead the club degenerated into a dismal also-ran. Quarterbacks Bob Lee, Pat Sullivan, and Kim McQuilken could not move the offense, and the entire squad bristled under coach Norm Van Brocklin's stern regime. Rumors of the Dutchman's imminent firing ran wild in Atlanta, and a press conference in November saw Van Brocklin challenge a reporter to a fist fight. Van Brocklin was then canned with the team record at 2–6, and Atlanta fans were so disenchanted that there were 48,830 no-shows for the season's finale on December 15 against Green Bay.

FINAL TEAM STATISTICS

OFFENSE

	ATL.	CHI.	DALL.	DET.	G.B.	L.A.	MINN.	N.O.	N.Y.	PHIL.	St.L.	S.F.	WASH
FIRST DOWNS:													
Total	174	203	**295**	211	214	265	264	233	215	244	247	227	249
by Rushing	77	92	**147**	88	87	132	114	117	90	79	120	101	77
by Passing	86	96	129	114	108	112	136	91	107	141	117	104	**156**
by Penalty	11	15	19	9	19	21	14	**25**	18	24	10	22	16
RUSHING:													
Number	400	434	542	397	482	**566**	488	503	441	415	466	477	470
Yards	1493	1480	**2454**	1433	1571	2125	1856	1983	1496	1385	1956	1981	1443
Average Yards	3.7	3.4	**4.5**	3.6	3.3	3.8	3.8	3.9	3.4	3.3	4.2	4.2	3.1
Touchdowns	6	10	**22**	13	10	16	17	9	11	13	12	10	11
PASSING:													
Attempts	356	396	**385**	377	385	338	400	389	393	**461**	391	361	413
Completions	160	185	206	216	187	169	234	185	207	**258**	201	170	254
Completion Percentage	44.9	46.7	53.5	57.3	48.6	50.0	58.5	47.6	52.7	56.0	51.4	47.1	**61.5**
Passing Yards	1781	2079	2856	2475	2162	2368	2909	2037	2349	2531	2492	2281	**2978**
Avg. Yards per Attempt	5.0	5.3	7.4	6.6	5.6	7.0	7.3	5.2	6.0	5.5	6.4	6.3	7.2
Avg. Yards per Complet.	11.1	11.2	13.9	11.5	11.6	**14.0**	12.4	11.0	11.4	9.8	12.4	13.4	11.7
Times Tackled Passing	50	36	47	35	17	21	19	37	20	42	**16**	35	25
Yards Lost Passing	474	359	327	255	**126**	161	154	276	156	319	134	274	176
Net Yards	1307	1720	2529	2220	2036	2207	2755	1761	2193	2212	2358	2007	**2802**
Touchdowns	4	8	14	11	5	16	**22**	10	12	14	20	15	**22**
Interceptions	31	22	15	11	21	13	13	21	26	17	**8**	28	11
Percent Intercepted	8.7	5.6	3.9	2.9	5.5	3.8	3.3	5.4	6.6	3.7	**2.1**	7.8	2.7
PUNTS:													
Number	**96**	91	73	73	69	75	73	91	69	84	81	70	74
Average Distance	40.5	37.7	38.5	38.2	38.4	36.4	36.1	**41.8**	40.1	36.0	38.7	40.8	38.1
PUNT RETURNS:													
Number	51	44	**62**	34	42	53	43	43	41	37	52	44	46
Yards	**635**	248	573	429	416	507	320	415	408	339	512	398	453
Average Yards	12.5	5.6	9.2	**12.6**	9.9	9.6	7.4	9.7	10.0	[illegible]	9.8	9.9	9.8
Touchdowns	1	0	1	0	**2**	0	0	0	0	0	0	1	1
KICKOFF RETURNS:													
Number	60	57	49	**62**	49	40	50	53	59	48	50	51	45
Yards	1296	1256	1071	1293	1022	938	1090	1040	**1458**	1062	1203	1144	1166
Average Yards	21.0	22.0	21.0	20.0	20.9	23.5	21.8	19.6	24.7	22.1	24.1	22.4	**25.9**
Touchdowns	0	0	0	0	0	**1**	0	0	0	0	**1**	0	**1**
INTERCEPTION RETURNS:													
Number	17	18	13	17	23	22	22	16	15	18	16	20	**26**
Yards	210	293	110	266	278	340	282	179	91	176	**372**	247	328
Average Yards	12.4	16.3	8.5	15.6	12.1	15.5	12.8	11.2	6.1	9.8	**23.3**	12.4	13.1
Touchdowns	1	0	0	**2**	1	**2**	0	1	0	1	1	1	**2**
PENALTIES:													
Number	82	**88**	86	86	55	58	56	75	65	76	77	63	78
Yards	636	679	703	719	536	550	501	598	567	**722**	645	606	621
FUMBLES:													
Number	32	35	31	23	25	29	24	26	28	32	37	31	**16**
Number Lost	24	15	16	14	16	14	**9**	12	10	12	**9**	14	**9**
POINTS:													
Total	111	152	297	256	210	263	310	166	195	242	285	226	**320**
PAT Attempts	12	18	38	27	19	35	**40**	20	24	31	36	28	38
PAT Made	12	17	**37**	23	19	26	32	19	21	26	30	25	35
FG Attempts	16	13	21	32	**39**	16	20	16	19	16	22	24	31
FG Made	9	9	10	23	**25**	9	12	9	10	10	13	11	19
Percent FG Made	56.3	69.2	47.6	**71.9**	64.1	56.3	60.0	56.3	52.6	62.5	59.1	45.8	61.3
Safeties	0	0	1	1	1	0	1	0	0	0	0	0	0

DEFENSE

	ATL.	CHI.	DALL.	DET.	G.B.	L.A.	MINN.	N.O.	N.Y.	PHIL.	St.L.	S.F.	WASH.
FIRST DOWNS:													
Total	238	231	199	270	218	**186**	230	226	291	248	249	232	210
by Rushing	140	104	**63**	127	93	66	100	104	134	105	108	113	79
by Passing	**85**	102	110	124	106	109	120	105	142	129	122	101	114
by Penalty	13	25	26	19	19	11	**10**	17	15	14	19	18	17
RUSHING:													
Number	627	519	417	486	465	**381**	437	447	521	460	461	503	414
Yards	2564	1739	1344	2102	1641	**1302**	1605	1758	1916	1797	1888	2033	1439
Average Yards	4.1	3.4	**3.2**	4.3	3.5	3.4	3.7	3.9	3.7	3.9	4.1	4.0	3.5
Touchdowns	19	17	8	17	10	**4**	12	11	15	14	15	13	7
PASSING:													
Attempts	**302**	329	349	405	383	381	396	369	415	434	413	339	399
Completions	**136**	174	178	219	188	194	214	193	245	230	230	178	197
Completion Percentage	**45.0**	52.9	51.0	54.1	49.1	50.9	54.0	52.3	59.0	53.0	55.7	52.5	49.4
Passing Yards	**1847**	2250	2451	2423	2254	2465	2569	2330	2688	2684	2581	2178	2102
Avg. Yards per Attempt	6.1	6.8	7.0	6.0	5.9	6.7	6.5	6.3	6.5	6.2	6.2	6.5	5.3
Avg. Yards per Complet.	13.6	12.9	13.8	11.1	12.0	12.7	12.0	12.1	11.0	11.7	11.2	12.2	**10.7**
Times Tackled Passing	31	25	37	24	28	**44**	31	37	25	28	35	28	31
Yards Lost Passing	275	171	332	187	254	**363**	267	291	147	211	218	247	256
Net Yards	**1572**	2079	2119	2236	2000	2102	2302	2039	2541	2473	2363	1931	1846
Touchdowns	13	12	17	13	10	16	**8**	17	22	9	11	14	13
Interceptions	17	18	13	17	23	22	22	16	15	18	16	20	**25**
Percent Intercepted	5.6	5.5	3.7	4.2	6.0	5.8	5.6	4.3	3.6	4.1	3.9	6.0	6.4
PUNTS:													
Number	84	77	93	62	84	**95**	75	77	65	73	85	74	80
Average Distance	38.3	38.5	39.9	37.2	36.6	41.2	37.1	42.5	**36.2**	39.1	39.2	39.5	38.4
PUNT RETURNS:													
Number	59	58	**31**	37	48	40	45	59	43	37	56	46	50
Yards	658	633	343	275	356	453	345	906	478	**252**	518	491	458
Average Yards	11.2	10.9	11.1	7.4	7.4	11.3	7.7	15.4	11.0	**6.8**	9.3	10.7	9.2
Touchdowns	1	1	1	**0**	**0**	1	**0**	2	**0**	**0**	1	**0**	1
KICKOFF RETURNS:													
Number	**33**	35	61	60	55	58	64	40	45	46	54	51	64
Yards	812	**700**	1194	1256	1156	1232	1116	894	1154	1028	1203	1099	1379
Average Yards	24.6	20.0	19.6	20.9	21.0	21.2	**17.4**	22.4	25.6	22.3	22.3	21.5	21.5
Touchdowns	**0**	**0**	**0**	**0**	**0**	**0**	**0**	**0**	**0**	1	**0**	**0**	**0**
INTERCEPTION RETURNS:													
Number	31	22	15	11	21	13	13	21	26	17	**8**	28	11
Yards	451	225	93	149	289	92	186	268	372	362	**75**	409	**75**
Average Yards	14.5	10.2	**6.2**	13.5	13.8	7.1	14.2	12.3	14.3	21.3	9.4	14.6	6.8
Touchdowns	1	1	**0**	**0**	1	**0**	1	2	2	1	**0**	1	1
PENALTIES:													
Number	54	74	69	71	**88**	82	70	77	80	86	80	85	69
Yards	449	601	657	566	715	772	660	690	616	722	654	**830**	529
FUMBLES:													
Number	26	28	31	23	19	15	25	37	28	36	24	**38**	28
Number Lost	12	14	13	13	12	3	11	19	10	16	9	**20**	15
POINTS:													
Total	271	279	235	270	206	**181**	195	263	299	217	218	236	196
PAT Attempts	34	33	28	30	23	22	**21**	34	39	26	27	29	24
PAT Made	31	29	28	28	**17**	19	18	29	32	25	26	26	22
FG Attempts	28	23	21	32	26	**14**	24	17	24	26	**14**	19	15
FG Made	12	16	13	20	17	**10**	17	**10**	11	12	**10**	12	**10**
Percent FG Made	**42.9**	69.6	61.9	62.5	65.4	71.4	70.7	58.8	45.8	46.2	71.4	63.2	66.7
Safeties	**0**	2	**0**	1	**0**	**0**	**0**	**0**	**0**	**0**	**0**	**0**	**0**

CONFERENCE PLAYOFFS

December 21, at Minnesota (Attendance 44,626)

SCORING

MINNESOTA	0	7	16	7	– 30
ST. LOUIS	0	7	0	7	– 14

Second Quarter
- St.L. Thomas, 13 yard pass from Hart PAT–Bakken (kick)
- Minn. Gilliam, 16 yard pass from Tarkenton PAT–Cox (kick)

Third Quarter
- Minn. Cox, 37 yard field goal
- Minn. N. Wright, 20 yard fumble return PAT–Cox (kick)
- Minn. Gilliam, 38 yard pass from Tarkenton PAT-kick failed

Fourth Quarter
- Minn. Foreman, 4 yard rush PAT–Cox (kick)
- St.L. Metcalf, 11 yard rush PAT–Bakken (kick)

TEAM STATISTICS

MINN.		St.L.
19	First Downs-Total	17
12	First Downs-Rushing	6
7	First Downs-Passing	10
0	First Downs-Penalty	1
0	Fumbles-Number	2
0	Fumbles-Lost Ball	1
4	Penalties-Number	1
39	Yards Penalized	15
0	Missed Field Goals	1
66	Offensive Plays	67
363	Net Yards	284
5.5	Average Gain	4.2
2	Giveaways	2
2	Takeaways	2
0	Difference	0

INDIVIDUAL STATISTICS

MINNESOTA	No.	Yds.	Avg.	ST. LOUIS	No.	Yds.	Avg.
RUSHING							
Foreman	23	114	5.0	Metcalf	15	55	3.7
Osborn	16	67	4.2	Otis	8	35	4.4
Gilliam	1	16	16.0	Hart	1	10	10.0
Tarkenton	2	0	2.0	Willard	1	0	0.0
	42	197	4.7		25	100	4.0
RECEIVING							
Foreman	5	54	10.8	Thomas	6	64	10.7
Osborn	4	36	9.0	Gray	5	77	15.4
Gilliam	2	54	27.0	Metcalf	4	43	10.8
Voigt	2	25	12.5	Hammond	1	10	10.0
	13	169	13.0	Smith	1	7	7.0
				Otis	1	–1	–1.0
					18	200	11.1
PUNTING							
Eischeid	5		38.2	Roberts	7		36.4
PUNT RETURNS							
Wallace	1	3	3.0	Metcalf	3	18	6.0
KICKOFF RETURNS							
McCullum	2	49	24.5	Metcalf	3	85	28.3
Kingswriter	1	0	1.0	Hartle	3	14	4.7
	3	49	16.3		6	99	16.5
INTERCEPTION RETURNS							
J. Wright	1	18	18.0	Wehrli	1	10	10.0
				Arneson	1	7	7.0
					2	17	8.5

PASSING

MINNESOTA	Att.	Comp.	Comp. Pct.	Yds	Int	Yds/ Att.	Yds/ Comp.	Lost Tackled
Tarkenton	23	13	56.5	169	2	7.3	13.0	1–3
ST. LOUIS								
Hart	40	18	45.0	200	1	5.0	11.1	2-16

December 22, at Los Angeles (Attendance 80,118)

SCORING

LOS ANGELES	7	0	3	9–19
WASHINGTON	3	7	0	0–10

First Quarter
- L.A. Klein, 10 yard pass from Harris PAT–Ray (kick)
- Was. Bragg, 35 yard field goal

Second Quarter
- Was. Denson, 1 yard rush PAT–Bragg (kick)

Third Quarter
- L.A. Ray, 37 yard field goal

Fourth Quarter
- L.A. Ray, 26 yard field goal
- L.A. Robertson, 59 yard interception return PAT–bad center pass no attempt made

TEAM STATISTICS

L.A.		WASH.
14	First Downs-Total	13
8	First Downs-Rushing	4
6	First Downs-Passing	7
0	First Downs-Penalty	2
2	Fumbles-Number	3
0	Fumbles-Lost Ball	3
5	Penalties-Number	1
49	Yards Penalized	5
2	Missed Field Goals	0
66	Offensive Plays	58
226	Net Yards	218
3.4	Average Gain	3.8
2	Giveaways	6
6	Takeaways	2
+4	Difference	–4

INDIVIDUAL STATISTICS

LOS ANGELES	No.	Yds.	Avg.	WASHINGTON	No.	Yds.	Avg.
RUSHING							
McCutcheon	26	71	2.7	Brown	18	39	2.2
Bertelsen	6	34	5.7	Denson	7	5	0.7
Harris	6	17	2.8	Kilmer	2	5	2.5
Capelletti	1	5	2.5		27	49	1.8
Baker	2	2	1.0				
Scribner	1	2	2.0				
	42	131	3.1				
RECEIVING							
Jackson	2	35	17.5	Taylor	4	79	19.8
Klein	2	23	11.5	Evans	4	31	7.8
McCutcheon	2	20	10.0	J. Smith	2	35	17.5
Curran	1	12	12.0	Denson	2	17	8.5
Bertelsen	1	5	5.0	Grant	1	15	15.0
	8	95	11.9		13	177	13.6
PUNTING							
Burke	5		43.0	Bragg	5		45.2
PUNT RETURNS							
Bertelsen	1	10	10.0	Theismann	4	22	5.5
Bryant	1	6	6.0	L. Jones	1	9	9.0
	2	16	8.0		5	31	6.2
KICKOFF RETURNS							
Bryant	3	82	27.3	L. Jones	4	76	19.0
				Cunningham	1	19	19.0
					5	95	19.0
INTERCEPTION RETURNS							
Robertson	1	59	59.0	Fischer	1	17	17.0
Reynolds	1	12	12.0	Stone	1	7	7.0
Simpson	1	0	0.0		2	24	12.0
	3	71	23.7				

PASSING

LOS ANGELES	Att.	Comp.	Comp. Pct.	Yds.	Int.	Yds/ Att.	Yds/ Comp.	Yards Lost Tackled
Harris	24	8	33.3	95	2	4.0	11.9	0–0
WASHINGTON								
Kilmer	18	7	38.9	99	0	5.5	14.1	0–0
Jurgensen	12	6	50.0	78	3	6.5	13.0	1–8
	30	13	43.3	177	3	5.9	13.6	1–8

ST. LOUIS CARDINALS 10-4-0 Don Coryell

Scores of Each Game		
7	PHILADELPHIA	3
17	Washington	10
29	CLEVELAND	7
34	San Francisco	9
31	DALLAS	28
31	Houston	27
23	WASHINGTON	20
14	Dallas	17
24	MINNESOTA	28
13	Philadelphia	3
23	N.Y. Giants	21
13	KANSAS CITY	17
10	New Orleans	14
26	N.Y. GIANTS	14

Use Name	Pos.	Hgt	Wgt	Age	Int	Pts
Dan Dierdorf	OT	6'4"	280	25		
Greg Kindle	OT	6'4"	265	23		
Ernie McMillan	OT	6'6"	265	36		
Conrad Dobler	OG	6'3"	255	23		
Bob Young	OG	6'2"	270	31		
Roger Finnie	OT-OG	6'3"	250	28		
Tom Banks	C	6'1"	240	26		
Tom Brahaney	C	6'2"	250	22		
Cal Withrow	C	6'	240	29		
Bob Crum	DE	6'5"	240	23		
Council Rudolph	DE	6'3"	245	24		
Ron Yankowski	DE	6'5"	235	27		6
Lee Brooks	DT-DE	6'5"	240	26		
Bob Bell	DT	6'4"	250	26		
Dave Butz	DT	6'7"	290	24		
Steve George	DT	6'5"	265	23		
Bob Rowe	DT	6'4"	245	29		
Mark Arneson	LB	6'2"	220	24		
Pete Barnes	LB	6'3"	235	29		
Greg Hartle	LB	6'2"	225	23		
Jack LeVeck	LB	6'	220	24		
Terry Miller	LB	6'2"	220	28		
Steve Neils	LB	6'2"	215	23		
Larry Stallings	LB	6'2"	230	32	2	
Dwayne Crump	DB	5'11"	180	24	1	
Clarence Duren	DB	6'1"	190	23	2	
Ken Reaves (from NO)	DB	6'3"	210	29	1	
Hurles Scales (from CHI)	DB	6'1"	200	23		
Scott Stringer	DB	5'11"	180	23		
Norm Thompson	DB	6'1"	180	26	6	6
Jim Tolbert	DB	6'3"	210	30	2	
Roger Wehrli	DB	6'1"	190	26	2	6
Ron Davis – Injury						
Jim Hart	QB	6'2"	210	30		12
Dennis Shaw	QB	6'2"	210	27		
Donny Anderson	HB	6'3"	215	31		36
Willie Belton	HB	5'11"	195	25		
Steve Jones (from BUF)	HB	6'	200	23		
Terry Metcalf	HB	5'10"	185	22		48
Eddie Moss	HB	6'	215	25		
Jim Otis	FB	6'	225	26		6
Ken Willard	FB	6'2"	215	31		6
J. V. Cain	WR	6'4"	225	23		6
Mel Gray	WR	5'9"	170	25		36
Gary Hammond	WR	5'11"	185	25		
Earl Thomas	WR	6'3"	215	25		30
Jim McFarland	TE	6'5"	225	26		
Jackie Smith	TE	6'4"	230	33		18
Sergio Albert	K	6'3"	195	22		
Jim Bakken	K	6'	200	33		69
Hal Roberts	K	6'1"	180	22		

WASHINGTON REDSKINS 10-4-0 George Allen

Scores of Each Game		
13	N.Y. Giants	10
10	St. Louis	17
30	DENVER	3
17	Cincinnati	28
20	MIAMI	17
24	N.Y. GIANTS	3
20	St. Louis	23
17	Green Bay	6
27	Philadelphia	20
28	DALLAS	21
26	PHILADELPHIA	7
23	Dallas	24
23	Los Angeles	17
42	CHICAGO	0

Use Name	Pos.	Hgt	Wgt	Age	Int	Pts
George Starke	OT	6'5"	250	26		
Jim Tyrer	OT	6'6"	270	35		
Paul Laaveg	OG	6'4"	250	25		
Ray Schoenke	OG	6'3"	250	32		
Walt Sweeney	OG	6'3"	254	33		
Fred Sturt	OT-OG	6'4"	255	23		
Len Hauss	C	6'2"	235	32		
Dan Ryczek	C	6'3"	245	25		
Verlon Biggs	DE	6'4"	275	31		
Martin Imhof	DE	6'6"	256	24		
Deacon Jones	DE	6'5"	272	35		1
Ron McDole	DE	6'3"	265	34		
Bill Brundige	DT	6'5"	270	25		
Dennis Johnson	DT	6'4"	260	22		
Manny Sistrunk	DT	6'5"	265	27		
Diron Talbert	DT	6'5"	255	30		
Bob Brunet – Injury						
Terry Hermeling – Injury						
Brad Dusek	LB	6'2"	214	23		
Chris Hanburger	LB	6'2"	218	33	4	6
Harold McLinton	LB	6'2"	235	27	1	6
Stu O'Dell	LB	6'1"	220	22		
John Pergine	LB	6'1"	225	27		
Dave Robinson	LB	6'3"	245	33	2	
Russ Tillman	LB	6'2"	230	28		
Mike Varty	LB	6'1"	220	22		
Mike Bass	DB	6'	190	29	3	6
Speedy Duncan	DB	5'10"	180	31		
Pat Fischer	DB	5'10"	170	34	3	
Ken Houston	DB	6'3"	198	29	2	6
Larry Jones	DB	5'10"	170	23		6
Brig Owens	DB	5'11"	190	31	4	
Bryant Salter	DB	6'4"	196	24	1	
Ken Stone	DB	6'1"	180	23	5	
Ted Vactor – Injury						
Sonny Jurgensen	QB	5'11"	203	40		
Billy Kilmer	QB	6'	204	34		
Joe Theismann	QB	6'	184	24		6
Larry Brown	HB	5'11"	195	26		42
Doug Cunningham	HB	5'11"	195	28		
Herb Mul-Key	HB	6'	190	24		
Larry Smith	HB	6'3"	220	26		6
Moses Denson	FB-HB	6'1"	215	30		12
Charlie Evans	FB	6'1"	220	26		12
Mike Hull	FB	6'3"	220	29		
Duane Thomas	HB-FB	6'1"	215	27		36
Frank Grant	WR	5'11"	180	24		6
Roy Jefferson	WR	6'2"	195	30		24
Bill Malinchak	WR	6'1"	200	30		
Charley Taylor	WR	6'3"	210	33		30
Mike Hancock	TE	6'4"	220	24		
Alvin Reed	TE	6'5"	235	30		6
Jerry Smith	TE	6'2"	208	31		18
Mike Bragg	K	5'11"	186	27		10
Mark Moseley	K	5'11"	205	26		81

DALLAS COWBOYS 8-6-0 Tom Landry

Scores of Each Game		
24	Atlanta	0
10	Philadelphia	13
6	N.Y. GIANTS	14
21	MINNESOTA	23
28	St. Louis	31
31	PHILADELPHIA	24
21	N.Y. Giants	7
17	ST. LOUIS	14
20	SAN FRANCISCO	14
21	Washington	28
10	Houston	0
24	WASHINGTON	23
41	CLEVELAND	17
23	Oakland	27

Use Name	Pos.	Hgt	Wgt	Age	Int	Pts
Ralph Neely	OT	6'5"	255	30		
Bruce Walton	OT	6'6"	252	23		
Rayfield Wright	OT	6'7"	260	29		
Gene Killian	OG	6'4"	250	21		
John Niland	OG	6'4"	255	30		
Blaine Nye	OG	6'4"	255	28		
Jim Arneson	C-OG	6'3"	252	23		
John Fitzgerald	C	6'5"	255	26		
Dave Manders	C	6'2"	250	32		
Larry Cole	DE	6'4"	250	27		
Too Tall Jones	DE	6'9"	260	23		
Harvey Martin	DE	6'5"	252	23		
Pat Toomay	DE	6'5"	250	25		
Bill Gregory	DT	6'5"	252	24		
Bob Lilly	DT	6'4"	260	35		
Jethro Pugh	DT	6'6"	250	30		
Dave Edwards	LB	6'3"	226	35		
Ken Hutcherson	LB	6'1"	220	22		
Lee Roy Jordan	LB	6'2"	226	33	2	
D. D. Lewis	LB	6'2"	218	28	2	
Cal Peterson	LB	6'3"	220	21		
Louie Walker	LB	6'1"	216	22		
Benny Barnes	DB	6'1"	192	23		
Cornell Green	DB	6'4"	212	34	2	
Cliff Harris	DB	6'	190	25	3	
Mel Renfro	DB	6'	192	32	1	
Mark Washington	DB	5'10"	186	26	1	
Charlie Waters	DB	6'1"	193	25	2	
Toni Fritsch – Knee Injury						
Rodney Wallace – Injury						
John Babinecz – Injury						
Clint Longley	QB	6'1"	193	22		
Roger Staubach	QB	6'2"	197	32		18
Doug Dennison	HB	6'1"	195	22		24
Dennis Morgan	HB	5'11"	200	22		6
Les Strayhorn	HB	5'10"	205	23		
Charles Young	HB	6'1"	210	21		
Calvin Hill	FB-HB	6'3"	230	27		42
Walt Garrison	FB	6'	205	30		36
Robert Newhouse	HB-FB	5'10"	205	24		18
Bob Hayes	WR	6'	1[illegible]0	31		6
Bill Houston	WR	6'3"	208	23		
Drew Pearson	WR	6'	183	23		18
Golden Richards	WR	6'	183	23		30
Billy Joe DuPree	TE	6'4"	228	24		24
Jean Fugett	TE	6'3"	226	22		6
Ron Howard	TE	6'4"	215	23		
Duane Carrell	K	5'10"	185	24		
Efren Herrera	K	5'9"	185	23		57
Mac Percival	K	6'4"	220	34		10

PHILADELPHIA EAGLES 7-7-0 Mike McCormack

Scores of Each Game		
3	St. Louis	7
13	DALLAS	10
30	BALTIMORE	10
13	San Diego	7
35	N.Y. GIANTS	7
24	Dallas	31
10	New Orleans	14
0	Pittsburgh	27
20	WASHINGTON	27
3	ST. LOUIS	13
7	Washington	26
36	GREEN BAY	14
20	N.Y. Giants	7
28	DETROIT	17

Use Name	Pos.	Hgt	Wgt	Age	Int	Pts
Herb Dobbins	OT	6'4"	260	23		
Jerry Sisemore	OT	6'4"	250	23		
Steve Smith	OT	6'5"	250	30		
Dick Stevens	OT	6'4"	245	26		
Wade Key	OG	6'4"	245	27		
Roy Kirksey	OG	6'1"	255	26		
Tom Luken	OG	6'3"	253	24		
Mark Nordquist	OG	6'4"	246	28		
Guy Morriss	C	6'4"	245	23		
Willie Cullars	DE	6'5"	250	23		
Joe Jones	DE	6'6"	250	26		
Will Wynn	DE	6'4"	245	25		6
Jim Cagle	DT	6'5"	255	22		
Bill Dunstan	DT	6'4"	250	25		6
Jerry Patton	DT	6'3"	265	28	1	
Mitch Sutton	DT	6'4"	265	23		
Bill Bergey	LB	6'2"	250	29	5	
John Bunting	LB	6'1"	220	24	2	
Dean Halverson	LB	6'2"	230	28	1	
Frank LeMaster	LB	6'2"	224	22		
Kevin Reilly	LB	6'2"	220	22		
Steve Zabel	LB	6'4"	234	26	2	
Bill Bradley	DB	5'11"	190	27	2	
Charlie Ford	DB	6'3"	195	25		
Joe Lavender	DB	6'4"	190	25	1	12
Randy Logan	DB	6'1"	195	23	2	
Larry Marshall (from MIN)	DB	5'10"	195	24		
John Outlaw	DB	5'10"	180	29	2	
Artimus Parker	DB	6'3"	215	22		
Marion Reeves	DB	6'1"	195	22		
Al Coleman – Injury						
Mike Boryla	QB	6'3"	200	23		
Roman Gabriel	QB	6'4"	220	34		
John Reaves	QB	6'3"	210	24		
Po James	HB	6'1"	202	25		12
Greg Oliver	HB	6'	192	25		
Tom Sullivan	HB	6'	190	24		72
Tom Bailey	FB-HB	6'2"	211	25		
Norm Bulaich	FB	6'1"	218	27		
Randy Jackson	FB	6'	220	25		
Harold Carmichael	WR	6'7"	225	24		48
Wes Chesson	WR	6'2"	190	25		
Bob Picard	WR	6'1"	195	24		
Charlie Smith	WR	6'1"	185	24		
Don Zimmerman	WR	6'3"	195	24		12
Kent Kramer	TE	6'5"	235	30		
Charlie Young	TE	6'4"	238	23		18
Tom Dempsey	K	6'1"	265	33		56
Merritt Kersey	K	6'1"	205	24		

NEW YORK GIANTS 2-12-0 Bill Arnsparger

Scores of Each Game		
10	WASHINGTON	13
20	NEW ENGLAND	28
14	Dallas	6
7	ATLANTA	14
7	Philadelphia	35
3	Washington	24
7	DALLAS	21
33	Kansas City	27
20	N.Y. JETS (OT)	26
19	Detroit	20
21	ST. LOUIS	23
13	Chicago	16
7	PHILADELPHIA	20
14	St. Louis	26

Use Name	Pos.	Hgt	Wgt	Age	Int	Pts
John Hill	OT	6'2"	245	24		
Doug Van Horn	OT	6'2"	245	30		
Willie Young	OT	6'	255	31		
Dick Enderle	OG	6'1"	250	26		
John Hicks	OG	6'2"	258	23		
Tom Mullen	OG	6'3"	245	22		
Karl Chandler	C	6'5"	250	22		
Bob Hyland	C	6'5"	255	29		
Rick Dvorak	DE	6'4"	235	22		
Jack Gregory	DE	6'6"	255	29		
Roy Hilton	DE	6'6"	240	29		6
George Hasenohrl	DT	6'1"	260	23		
Larry Jacobson	DT	6'6"	260	24		
John Mendenhall	DT	6'1"	255	25		
Gary Pettigrew	DT	6'4"	255	29		
Jim Pietrzak	DT	6'5"	260	21		
Andy Rice	DT	6'3"	268	32		
Carl Wafer	DT	6'3"	250	23		
Ron Hornsby	LB	6'3"	228	25	1	
Pat Hughes	LB	6'2"	225	27	2	
Brian Kelley	LB	6'3"	222	23	1	
Henry Reed	LB	6'3"	230	25		
Andy Selfridge	LB	6'4"	220	25	1	
Bill Singletary	LB	6'2"	230	23		
Brad Van Pelt	LB	6'5"	235	23	2	
Pete Athas	DB	5'11"	185	26	2	
Bobby Brooks	DB	6'1"	195	23		
Chuck Crist	DB	6'2"	205	23	3	
Honor Jackson	DB	6'1"	195	25		
Spider Lockhart	DB	6'2"	175	31	2	
Clyde Powers	DB	6'1"	195	23		
Eldridge Small	DB	6'1"	190	24	1	
Jim Stienke	DB	5'11"	182	23		
Terry Hermeling – Knee Injury						
Jim DelGaizo	QB	6'1"	190	27		
Craig Morton (from DAL)	QB	6'4"	210	31		
Norm Snead (to SF)	QB	6'4"	215	34		
Carl Summerell	QB	6'4"	208	22		
Steve Crosby	HB	5'11"	205	24		
Ron Johnson	HB	6'1"	205	26		36
Leon McQuay	HB	5'9"	195	24		6
Mickey Zofko (from DET)	HB	6'3"	195	24		
Joe Dawkins	FB	5'11"	220	26		30
Doug Kotar	HB-FB	5'11"	205	23		24
Don Clune	WR	6'3"	195	22		
Walker Gillette	WR	6'5"	200	27		18
Bob Grim	WR	6'	200	29		12
Don Herrmann	WR	6'2"	205	27		
Ray Rhodes	WR	5'11"	185	23		
Chip Glass	TE	6'4"	235	27		
Bob Tucker	TE	6'3"	230	29		12
Pete Gogolak	K	6'2"	190	32		51
Dave Jennings	K	6'4"	205	22		

ST. LOUIS CARDINALS

RUSHING

Last Name	No.	Yds	Avg	TD
Metcalf	152	718	4.7	6
Otis	158	664	4.2	1
Anderson	90	316	3.5	3
Willard	40	175	4.4	0
Belton	12	49	4.1	0
Hart	10	21	2.1	2
Moss	4	13	3.3	0

RECEIVING

Last Name	No.	Yds	Avg	TD
Metcalf	50	377	8	1
Gray	39	770	20	6
Thomas	34	513	15	5
Smith	25	413	17	3
Otis	19	109	6	0
Anderson	15	116	8	3
Cain	13	152	12	1
Willard	4	28	7	1
Hammond	2	14	7	0

PUNT RETURNS

Last Name	No.	Yds	Avg	TD
Metcalf	26	340	13	0
Hammond	17	125	7	0
Wehrli	4	39	10	0
Belton	4	8	2	0
Tolbert	1	0	0	0

KICKOFF RETURNS

Last Name	No.	Yds	Avg	TD
Metcalf	20	623	31	1
Hammond	11	268	24	0
Moss	8	133	17	0
Belton	5	111	22	0
LeVeck	2	32	16	0
Reeves	1	22	22	0
Finnie	1	8	8	0
Cain	1	5	5	0
Crum	1	1	1	0

PASSING – PUNTING – KICKING

PASSING	Att	Comp	%	Yds	Yd/Att	TD	Int–%	RK
Hart	388	200	52	2411	6.2	20	8– 2	5
Metcalf	2	0	0	0	0.0	0	0– 0	
Hammond	1	1	100	81	81.0	0	0– 0	

PUNTING	No	Avg
Roberts	81	38.7

KICKING	XP	Att	%	FG	Att	%
Bakken	30	36	83	13	22	59

WASHINGTON REDSKINS

RUSHING

Last Name	No.	Yds	Avg	TD
Brown	163	430	2.6	3
Denson	103	391	3.8	0
Thomas	95	347	3.7	5
L. Smith	55	149	2.7	0
Evans	32	79	2.5	2
Kilmer	6	27	4.5	0
Cunningham	5	17	3.4	0
Theismann	3	12	4.0	1
J. Smith	1	5	5.0	0
Mul-Key	1	3	3.0	0
Taylor	1	–1	–1.0	0
Jurgensen	4	–6	–1.5	0
Grant	1	–10	–10.0	0

RECEIVING

Last Name	No.	Yds	Avg	TD
Taylor	54	738	14	5
J. Smith	44	554	13	3
Jefferson	43	654	15	4
Brown	37	388	11	4
Denson	26	174	7	2
L. Smith	23	137	6	0
Thomas	10	31	3	1
Grant	9	196	22	1
Reed	4	36	9	1
Evans	2	44	22	0
Cunningham	2	26	13	0

PUNT RETURNS

Last Name	No.	Yds	Avg	TD
Theismann	15	157	11	0
Mul-Key	13	140	11	0
Houston	6	81	14	1
L. Jones	8	54	7	0
Duncan	3	19	6	0
Stone	1	2	2	0

KICKOFF RETURNS

Last Name	No.	Yds	Avg	TD
L. Jones	23	672	29	1
Mul-Key	10	285	29	0
Evans	4	60	15	0
L. Smith	2	57	29	0
Denson	2	49	25	0
Bass	1	22	22	0
Ryczek	1	11	11	0
Tillman	1	10	10	0
Dusek	1	0	0	0

PASSING – PUNTING – KICKING

PASSING	Att	Comp	%	Yds	Yd/Att	TD	Int–%	RK
Kilmer	234	137	59	1632	7.0	10	6– 3	4
Jurgensen	167	107	64	1185	7.1	11	5– 3	1
Theismann	11	9	82	145	13.2	1	0– 0	
Brown	1	1	100	16	16.0	0	0– 0	

PUNTING	No	Avg
Bragg	74	38.1

KICKING	XP	Att	%	FG	Att	%
Moseley	27	29	93	18	30	60
Bragg	7	8	88	1	1	100
D. Jones	1	1	100	0	0	—

DALLAS COWBOYS

RUSHING

Last Name	No.	Yds	Avg	TD
Hill	185	844	4.6	7
Newhouse	124	501	4.0	3
Garrison	113	429	3.8	5
Staubach	47	320	6.8	3
Young	33	205	6.2	0
Strayhorn	11	66	6.0	0
Dennison	16	52	3.3	4
DuPree	4	43	10.8	0
Pearson	3	6	2.0	0
Waters	1	6	6.0	0
Richards	1	–5	–5.0	0
Longley	4	–13	–3.2	0

RECEIVING

Last Name	No.	Yds	Avg	TD
Pearson	62	1087	18	2
Garrison	34	253	7	1
DuPree	29	466	16	4
Richards	26	467	18	5
Hill	12	134	11	0
Young	11	73	7	0
Newhouse	9	67	7	0
Hayes	7	118	17	1
Houston	6	72	12	0
Fugett	4	60	15	1
Dennison	2	23	12	0
Strayhorn	2	12	6	0
Barnes	1	37	37	0
Staubach	1	–13	–13	0

PUNT RETURNS

Last Name	No.	Yds	Avg	TD
Morgan	19	287	15	1
Harris	26	193	7	0
Richards	13	74	6	0
Hayes	2	11	6	0
Waters	1	8	8	0
Renfro	1	0	0	0

KICKOFF RETURNS

Last Name	No.	Yds	Avg	TD
Morgan	35	823	24	0
Young	8	161	20	0
Dennison	3	54	18	0
Strayhorn	2	19	10	0
Harris	1	14	14	0

PASSING – PUNTING – KICKING

PASSING	Att	Comp	%	Yds	Yd/Att	TD	Int–%	RK
Staubach	360	190	53	2552	7.1	11	15– 4	6
Longley	21	12	57	209	10.0	2	0– 0	
Carrell	1	1	100	37	37.0	0	0– 0	
Pearson	1	1	100	46	46.0	1	0– 0	

PUNTING	No	Avg
Carrell	40	39.8

KICKING	XP	Att	%	FG	Att	%
Herrera	33	33	100	8	13	62
Percival	4	5	80	2	8	25

PHILADELPHIA EAGLES

RUSHING

Last Name	No.	Yds	Avg	TD
Sullivan	244	760	3.1	11
James	67	276	4.1	2
Bulaich	50	152	3.0	0
Gabriel	14	76	5.4	0
Young	6	38	6.3	0
Bailey	10	32	3.2	0
Boryla	6	25	4.2	0
Oliver	7	19	2.7	0
Reaves	1	8	8.0	0
Jackson	7	3	0.4	0
Kersey	1	2	2.0	0
Carmichael	2	–6	–3.0	0

RECEIVING

Last Name	No.	Yds	Avg	TD
Young	63	696	11	3
Carmichael	56	649	12	8
Sullivan	39	312	8	1
James	33	230	7	0
Zimmerman	30	368	12	2
Bulaich	28	204	7	0
Bailey	6	27	5	0
Jackson	2	17	9	0
C. Smith	1	28	28	0

PUNT RETURNS

Last Name	No.	Yds	Avg	TD
Bradley	22	248	11	0
Marshall	13	118	9	0
Reaves	3	12	4	0
C. Smith	4	7	2	0

KICKOFF RETURNS

Last Name	No.	Yds	Avg	TD
Marshall	20	468	23	0
Jackson	14	339	24	0
James	12	238	20	0
Kramer	2	39	20	0
Kirksey	1	19	19	0
Bailey	1	14	14	0
Chesson	1	1	1	0
Zimmerman	1	0	0	0

PASSING – PUNTING – KICKING

PASSING	Att	Comp	%	Yds	Yd/Att	TD	Int–%	RK
Gabriel	338	193	57	1867	5.5	9	12– 4	8
Boryla	102	60	59	580	5.7	5	3– 3	
Reaves	20	5	25	84	4.2	0	2–10	
Carmichael	1	0	0	0	0.0	0	0– 0	

PUNTING	No	Avg
Kersey	82	36.1
Bradley	2	33.5

KICKING	XP	Att	%	FG	Att	%
Dempsey	26	30	87	10	16	63

NEW YORK GIANTS

RUSHING

Last Name	No.	Yds	Avg	TD
Dawkins	156	561	3.6	2
Kotar	106	396	3.7	4
McQuay	55	240	4.4	1
Johnson	97	218	2.2	4
Crosby	14	55	3.9	0
Snead	4	29	7.3	0
Del Gaizo	3	15	5.0	0
Summerell	2	8	4.0	0
Zofko	3	6	2.0	0
Morton	4	5	1.3	0
Rhodes	1	–6	–6.0	0

RECEIVING

Last Name	No.	Yds	Avg	TD
Dawkins	46	332	7	3
Tucker	41	496	12	2
Gillette	29	466	16	3
Grim	28	466	17	2
Johnson	24	171	7	2
Herrmann	10	97	10	0
Kotar	10	57	6	0
Rhodes	9	138	15	0
McQuay	5	59	12	0
Glass	3	23	8	0
Zofko	3	15	5	0
Crosby	2	44	22	0

PUNT RETURNS

Last Name	No.	Yds	Avg	TD
Athas	20	180	9	0
Rhodes	10	124	12	0
McQuay	7	81	12	0
Kotar	3	14	5	0
Brooks	1	9	9	0

KICKOFF RETURNS

Last Name	No.	Yds	Avg	TD
McQuay	25	689	28	0
Kotar	15	350	23	0
Dawkins	4	154	39	0
Brooks	5	106	21	0
Crosby	2	47	24	0
Small	2	46	23	0
Zofko	3	33	11	0
Rhodes	1	27	27	0
Kelley	3	29	8	0
Powers	1	0	0	0

PASSING – PUNTING – KICKING

PASSING	Att	Comp	%	Yds	Yd/Att	TD	Int–%	RK
Morton	239	124	52	1522	6.4	9	13– 5	9
Snead	159	97	61	983	6.2	5	8– 5	9
Del Gaizo	32	12	38	165	5.2	0	3– 9	
Summerell	13	6	46	59	4.5	0	3–23	

PUNTING	No	Avg
Jennings	68	39.8
Crosby	1	60.0

KICKING	XP	Att	%	FG	Att	%
Gogolak	21	23	91	10	19	53

MINNESOTA VIKINGS 10-4-0 Bud Grant

Scores of Each Game		
32	Green Bay	17
7	Detroit	6
11	CHICAGO	7
23	Dallas	21
51	HOUSTON	10
16	DETROIT	20
14	NEW ENGLAND	17
17	Chicago	0
28	St. Louis	24
7	GREEN BAY	19
17	Los Angeles	20
29	NEW ORLEANS	9
23	ATLANTA	10
35	Kansas City	15

Use Name	Pos.	Hgt	Wgt	Age	Int	Pts
Grady Alderman	OT	6'2"	247	35		
Charlie Goodrum	OT	6'3"	256	24		
Steve Riley	OT	6'6"	258	21		
Ron Yary	OT	6'6"	255	28		
Steve Lawson	OG	6'3"	265	25		
Andy Mauer (From NO)	OG	6'3"	275	25		
Milt Sunde	OG	6'2"	250	31		
Ed White	OG	6'2"	280	27		
Scott Anderson	C	6'4"	234	23		
Mick Tingelhoff	C	6'1"	240	34		
Dave Boone	DE	6'3"	248	23		
Carl Eller	DE	6'6"	247	32		
Jim Marshall	DE	6'3"	240	36		
Bob Lurtsema	DT-DE	6'6"	250	32		
Gary Larsen	DT	6'5"	255	34		
Alan Page	DT	6'5"	245	29		
Doug Sutherland	DT	6'3"	250	26		

Use Name	Pos.	Hgt	Wgt	Age	Int	Pts
Matt Blair	LB	6'5"	230	23		
Wally Hilgenberg	LB	6'3"	230	31		2
Amos Martin	LB	6'3"	228	25	3	6
Fred McNeill	LB	6'2"	230	22		
Jeff Siemon	LB	6'2"	230	24	2	
Roy Winston	LB	6'1"	222	34		
Joe Blahak	DB	5'9"	188	24		
Terry Brown	DB	6'1"	205	27	2	
Bobby Bryant	DB	6'	170	30		
Paul Krause	DB	6'3"	200	32	2	
Randy Poltl	DB	6'3"	190	22		
Jackie Wallace	DB	6'3"	197	23	1	
Jeff Wright	DB	5'11"	190	25	4	
Nate Wright	DB	5'11"	180	26	6	

John Ward – Injury

Use Name	Pos.	Hgt	Wgt	Age	Int	Pts
Bob Berry	QB	5'11"	185	32		
Fran Tarkenton	QB	6'1"	190	34		12
Brent McClanahan	HB	5'11"	202	23		6
Dave Osborn	HB	6'	208	31		24
Chuck Foreman	FB-HB	6'2"	207	23		90
Bill Brown	FB	5'11"	222	36		
Ed Marinaro	HB-FB	6'2"	212	24		12
Oscar Reed	HB-FB	5'11"	222	30		6
John Gilliam	WR	6'1"	195	29		30
John Holland	WR	6'	190	22		
Jim Lash	WR	6'2"	200	22		
Sam McCullum	WR	6'2"	203	21		18
Steve Craig	TE	6'3"	230	23		6
Doug Kingswriter	TE	6'2"	222	24		
Stu Voigt	TE	6'1"	225	26		30
Fred Cox	K	5'10"	200	35		68
Mike Eischeid	K	6'	190	33		

DETROIT LIONS 7-7-0 Don McCafferty - died of heart attack July 28, 1974 Rick Forzano

Scores of Each Game		
9	Chicago	17
6	MINNESOTA	7
19	Green Bay	21
13	Los Angeles	16
17	SAN FRANCISCO	14
20	Minnesota	16
19	GREEN BAY	17
19	NEW ORLEANS	14
13	Oakland	35
20	N.Y. GIANTS	19
34	CHICAGO	17
27	DENVER	31
23	Cincinnati	19
17	Philadelphia	28

Use Name	Pos.	Hgt	Wgt	Age	Int	Pts
Rocky Freitas	OT	6'6"	270	28		
Gordon Jolley	OT	6'5"	250	25		
Jim Yarbrough	OT	6'6"	265	27		
Bob Kowalkowski	OG	6'3"	240	30		
Chuck Walton	OG	6'3"	256	33		
Daryl White	OG	6'3"	250	22		
Guy Dennis	C-OG	6'2"	255	27		
Ed Flanagan	C	6'3"	245	30		
Fred Rothwell	C	6'3"	240	21		
Larry Hand	DE	6'4"	250	34		
Ken Sanders	DE	6'5"	240	24		
Ernie Price	DT-DE	6'4"	255	23		
Billy Howard	DT	6'4"	245	24		
Herb Orvis	DT	6'5"	240	27		
Jim Mitchell	DE-DT	6'3"	245	25		2
John Small	LB-DT	6'5"	260	27		

Use Name	Pos.	Hgt	Wgt	Age	Int	Pts
Mike Hennigan	LB	6'2"	210	22		
Jim Laslavic	LB	6'2"	230	22	1	
Paul Naumoff	LB	6'1"	215	29	1	
Ed O'Neil	LB	6'3"	245	21		
Charlie Weaver	LB	6'2"	220	25	3	
Lem Barney	DB	6'	190	28	4	
Carl Capria	DB	6'3"	185	22		
Ben Davis	DB	5'11"	180	28	1	
Bill Frohbose	DB	6'	185	22		
Dick Jauron	DB	6'	190	23	1	
Levi Johnson	DB	6'3"	190	23	5	18
Jim Thrower	DB	6'2"	195	25		
Charlie West	DB	6'1"	200	28	1	
Doug Wyatt	DB	6'1"	195	27		

Dick Cunningham – Injury
Mike Weger – Knee Injury

Use Name	Pos.	Hgt	Wgt	Age	Int	Pts
Greg Landry	QB	6'4"	210	27		6
Bill Munson	QB	6'2"	210	32		6
Sam Wyche	QB	6'4"	220	29		
Dexter Bussey	HB	6'1"	195	22		
Jimmie Jones	HB	5'10"	205	24		6
Altie Taylor	HB	5'10"	200	26		36
Leon Crosswhite	FB	6'2"	215	24		6
Jim Hooks	FB	5'11"	225	22		
Steve Owens	FB	6'2"	215	26		18
Ray Jarvis	WR	5'10"	195	25		
Ron Jessie	WR	6'	185	26		24
Bob Pickard	WR	6'	185	21		6
Larry Walton	WR	5'11"	185	27		18
T. C. Blair	TE	6'4"	220	23		
Charlie Sanders	TE	6'4"	225	28		18
Errol Mann	K	6'	200	33		92
Herman Weaver	K	6'4"	210	25		

GREEN BAY PACKERS 6-8-0 Dan Devine

Scores of Each Game		
17	MINNESOTA	32
20	Baltimore	13
21	DETROIT	19
7	BUFFALO	27
17	LOS ANGELES	6
9	Chicago	10
17	Detroit	19
6	WASHINGTON	17
20	CHICAGO	3
19	Minnesota	7
34	SAN DIEGO	0
14	Philadelphia	36
6	San Francisco	7
3	Atlanta	10

Use Name	Pos.	Hgt	Wgt	Age	Int	Pts
Dick Himes	OT	6'4"	260	28		
Lee Nystrom	OT	6'5"	260	23		
Harry Schuh	OT	6'2"	260	31		
Gale Gillingham	OG	6'3"	265	30		
Bill Lueck	OG	6'3"	250	28		
Bruce Van Dyke	OG	6'2"	255	30		
Keith Wortman	OG	6'2"	250	24		
Mal Snider	OT-OG	6'4"	250	27		
Larry McCarren	C	6'3"	248	23		
John Schmitt	C	6'4"	250	31		
Aaron Brown	DE	6'5"	270	30		
Mike Fannuci	DE	6'4"	242	24		
Dave Pureifory	DE	6'1"	255	24		
Alden Roche	DE	6'4"	255	29		
Clarence Williams	DE	6'5"	255	27	1	
Mike McCoy	DT	6'5"	275	25	1	
Steve Okoniewski	DT	6'3"	252	25		

Ken Bowman – Back Injury

Use Name	Pos.	Hgt	Wgt	Age	Int	Pts
Ron Acks	LB	6'2"	225	29		
Fred Carr	LB	6'5"	240	28	1	
Jim Carter	LB	6'3"	245	25	1	
Mark Cooney	LB	6'4"	230	22		
Larry Hefner	LB	6'2"	230	25		
Ted Hendricks	LB	6'7"	220	26	5	2
Noel Jenke	LB	6'1"	225	27		
Willie Buchanon	DB	6'	190	23	4	
Ken Ellis	DB	5'10"	195	26	3	6
Charley Hall	DB	6'1"	190	25	2	
Jim Hill	DB	6'2"	195	27	2	
Dave Mason	DB	6'	195	24		
Al Matthews	DB	5'11"	190	26	3	
Perry Smith	DB	6'1"	195	23		

Bill Hayhoe – Injury
Tom Toner – Collarbone Injury
Ron Widby – Back Injury

Use Name	Pos.	Hgt	Wgt	Age	Int	Pts
Jack Concannon	QB	6'3"	200	31		6
John Hadl (from LA)	QB	6'2"	214	34		
Jerry Tagge	QB	6'2"	215	24		
Larry Krause	HB	6'	208	26		
MacArthur Lane	HB	6'	220	32		36
Eric Torkelson	HB	6'2"	194	21		6
Les Goodman	FB-HB	5'11"	206	24		
Charlie Leigh (from MIA)	FB-HB	5'11"	206	28		
John Brockington	FB	6'1"	225	25		30
Barty Smith	FB	6'4"	240	22		
Steve Odom	WR	5'8"	165	21		18
Ken Payne	WR	6'1"	185	23		
Barry Smith	WR	6'1"	190	23		6
Jon Staggers	WR	5'10"	180	25		6
Mike Donohoe	TE	6'3"	230	29		
Rich McGeorge	TE	6'4"	230	25		
Chester Marcol	K	6'	190	25		94
Randy Walker	K	5'10"	177	22		

CHICAGO BEARS 4-10-0 Abe Gibron

Scores of Each Game		
17	DETROIT	9
21	N.Y. JETS	23
7	Minnesota	11
24	NEW ORLEANS	10
10	Atlanta	13
10	GREEN BAY	9
6	Buffalo	16
0	MINNESOTA	17
3	Green Bay	20
0	SAN FRANCISCO	34
17	Detroit	34
16	N.Y. GIANTS	13
21	San Diego	28
0	Washington	42

Use Name	Pos.	Hgt	Wgt	Age	Int	Pts
Lionel Antoine	OT	6'6"	263	24		
Bob Asher	OT	6'5"	260	26		
Randy Jackson	OT	6'5"	247	30		
Steve Kinney	OT	6'5"	260	25		
Tom Forrest	OG	6'2"	255	22		
Mike Hoban	OG	6'2"	235	22		
Ernie Janet	OG	6'4"	255	25		
Bob Newton	OG	6'4"	260	25		
Rich Coady	C	6'3"	246	29		
Gary Hrivnak	DE	6'5"	254	23		
Mel Tom	DE	6'4"	242	33		
Richard Harris	DT-DE	6'4"	255	26		
Wally Chambers	DT	6'6"	255	23		
Dave Gallagher	DT	6'4"	256	22		
Don Hultz	DT	6'3"	240	33		
Jim Osborne	DT	6'3"	254	24		

Use Name	Pos.	Hgt	Wgt	Age	Int	Pts
Waymond Bryant	LB	6'3"	230	22	2	
Doug Buffone	LB	6'1"	227	30	1	
Jimmy Gunn	LB	6'1"	218	25		
Bob Pifferini	LB	6'2"	226	24		
Don Rives	LB	6'2"	220	23		
Craig Clemons	DB	5'11"	200	25	4	
Allan Ellis	DB	5'10"	182	23	3	
Norm Hodgins	DB	6'1"	190	22		
Bill Knox	DB	5'9"	193	23	2	
Garry Lyle	DB	6'2"	193	28	3	
Randy Montgomery	DB	5'11"	185	27	2	
Joe Taylor	DB	6'2"	197	32	1	

Tom Reynolds – injury

Use Name	Pos.	Hgt	Wgt	Age	Int	Pts
Joe Barnes	QB	5'11"	196	22		
Bobby Douglass	QB	6'3"	228	27		6
Gary Huff	QB	6'1"	194	23		12
Dave Gagnon	HB	5'10"	210	22		
Carl Garrett	HB	5'11"	205	27		12
Ken Grandberry	HB	6'	196	22		12
Clifton Taylor	HB	5'11"	200	22		6
Pete Van Valkenberg (from GB)	HB	6'2"	205	24		
Gary Kosins	FB-HB	6'1"	213	25		6
Jim Harrison	FB	6'4"	238	25		6
Perry Williams	FB	6'2"	222	27		6
George Farmer	WR	6'4"	214	26		
Ike Hill	WR	5'10"	180	27		6
Bo Rather	WR	6'1"	180	23		18
Charlie Wade	WR	5'10"	163	24		6
Wayne Wheeler	WR	6'2"	180	25		6
Jim Kelly	TE	6'4"	210	23		
Fred Pagac	TE	6'	220	22		
Bob Parsons	TE	6'4"	234	24		6
Mirro Roder	K	6'1"	228	30		44

1974 N.F.C. — Central Division

MINNESOTA VIKINGS

RUSHING

Last Name	No.	Yds	Avg	TD
Foreman	199	777	3.9	9
Osborn	131	514	3.9	4
Reed	62	215	3.5	0
Marinaro	44	124	2.8	1
Tarkenton	21	120	5.7	2
B. Brown	19	41	2.2	0
McClanahan	9	41	4.6	1
Gilliam	2	16	8.0	0
Berry	1	8	8.0	0

RECEIVING

Last Name	No.	Yds	Avg	TD
Foreman	53	586	11	6
Lash	32	631	20	0
Voigt	32	268	8	5
Osborn	29	196	7	0
Gilliam	26	578	22	5
Marinaro	17	132	8	1
Reed	15	99	7	1
McCullum	7	138	20	3
Kingsriter	5	89	18	0
Holland	5	84	17	0
B. Brown	5	41	8	0
Craig	4	26	7	1
McClanahan	3	35	12	0
N. Wright	1	6	6	0

PUNT RETURNS

Last Name	No.	Yds	Avg	TD
Wallace	25	191	8	0
McCullum	12	86	7	0
Hilgenberg	1	−2	−2	0

KICKOFF RETURNS

Last Name	No.	Yds	Avg	TD
McClanahan	23	549	24	0
McCullum	12	300	25	0
Gilliam	3	86	29	0
Wallace	2	31	16	0
Foreman	1	30	30	0
B. Brown	3	19	6	0
Osborn	1	14	14	0
Marinaro	1	5	5	0

PASSING – PUNTING – KICKING

PASSING	Att	Comp	%	Yds	Yd/Att	TD	Int–%	RK
Tarkenton	351	199	57	2598	7.4	17	12– 3	3
Berry	48	34	71	305	6.4	5	1– 2	
Eischeid	1	1	100	6	6.0	0	0– 0	

PUNTING	No	Avg
Eischeid	73	36.1

KICKING	XP	Att	%	FG	Att	%
Cox	32	39	82	12	20	60

DETROIT LIONS

RUSHING

Last Name	No.	Yds	Avg	TD
Taylor	150	532	3.5	5
Owens	97	374	3.9	3
Jones	32	147	4.6	1
Hooks	44	143	3.3	0
Landry	22	95	4.3	1
Crosswhite	12	49	4.1	1
Munson	18	40	2.2	1
Bussey	9	22	2.4	0
Jessie	6	17	2.8	1
Pickard	1	5	5.0	0
L. Walton	2	3	1.5	0
Wyche	1	0	0.0	0

RECEIVING

Last Name	No.	Yds	Avg	TD
Jessie	54	761	14	3
C. Sanders	42	532	13	3
L. Walton	31	404	13	3
Taylor	30	293	10	1
Owens	24	158	7	0
Hooks	9	53	6	0
Pickard	8	88	11	1
Jones	4	35	9	0
Bussey	4	24	6	0
Jarvis	3	87	29	0
Crosswhite	3	31	10	0
Munson	1	−6	−6	0

PUNT RETURNS

Last Name	No.	Yds	Avg	TD
Jauron	17	286	17	0
Jarvis	5	62	12	0
Barney	5	37	7	0
West	6	32	5	0
Capria	1	12	12	0

KICKOFF RETURNS

Last Name	No.	Yds	Avg	TD
Jones	38	927	24	0
Jarvis	5	90	18	0
West	4	71	18	0
Bussey	5	59	12	0
Jessie	2	55	28	0
L. Walton	1	22	22	0
Jauron	2	21	11	0
Dennis	1	18	18	0
Crosswhite	1	11	11	0
Johnson	1	0	0	0

PASSING – PUNTING – KICKING

PASSING	Att	Comp	%	Yds	Yd/Att	TD	Int–%	RK
Munson	292	166	57	1874	6.4	8	7– 2	6
Landry	82	49	60	572	7.0	3	3– 4	
L. Walton	2	1	50	29	14.5	0	0– 0	
Wyche	1	0	0	0	0.0	0	1–100	

PUNTING	No	Avg
H. Weaver	72	38.5
Mann	1	18.0

KICKING	XP	Att	%	FG	Att	%
Mann	23	26	88	23	32	72

GREEN BAY PACKERS

RUSHING

Last Name	No.	Yds	Avg	TD
Brockington	266	883	3.3	5
Lane	137	362	2.6	3
Goodman	20	101	5.1	0
Odom	6	66	11.0	1
Torkelson	13	60	4.6	0
Tagge	18	58	3.2	0
Hadl	19	25	1.3	0
Barty Smith	9	19	2.1	0
Walker	1	18	18.0	0
Concannon	3	7	2.3	1
Leigh	1	0	0.0	0

RECEIVING

Last Name	No.	Yds	Avg	TD
Brockington	43	314	7	0
Lane	34	315	9	3
Staggers	32	450	14	0
McGeorge	30	440	15	0
Barty Smith	20	294	15	1
Odom	15	249	17	1
Payne	5	63	13	0
Goodman	5	19	4	0
Torkelson	2	10	5	0
Donohue	1	8	8	0

PUNT RETURNS

Last Name	No.	Yds	Avg	TD
Staggers	22	222	10	1
Odom	15	191	13	1
Ellis	3	3	1	0
Hefner	1	0	0	0
Torkelson	1	0	0	0

KICKOFF RETURNS

Last Name	No.	Yds	Avg	TD
Odom	31	713	23	0
Leigh	11	251	23	0
Goodman	4	49	12	0
Torkelson	1	20	20	0
Okoniewski	2	11	6	0
Krause	1	6	6	0

PASSING – PUNTING – KICKING

PASSING	Att	Comp	%	Yds	Yd/Att	TD	Int–%	RK
Hadl	299	142	48	1752	5.9	8	14– 5	12
Tagge	146	70	48	709	4.9	1	10– 7	15
Concannon	54	28	52	381	7.1	1	3– 6	
Lane	1	0	0	0	0.0	0	0– 0	

PUNTING	No	Avg
Walker	69	38.4

KICKING	XP	Att	%	FG	Att	%
Marcol	19	19	100	25	39	64

CHICAGO BEARS

RUSHING

Last Name	No.	Yds	Avg	TD
Grandberry	144	475	3.3	2
Garrett	96	346	3.6	1
Douglass	36	229	6.4	1
Williams	74	218	2.9	1
Harrison	36	94	2.6	1
Huff	23	37	1.6	2
Kosins	8	30	3.8	1
Barnes	1	19	19.0	0
C. Taylor	9	18	2.0	1
Gagnon	1	15	15.0	0
Rather	2	10	5.0	0
Hodgins	1	3	3.0	0
Rives	1	2	2.0	0
Pagac	1	−1	−1.0	0
Wade	1	−15	−15.0	0

RECEIVING

Last Name	No.	Yds	Avg	TD
Wade	39	683	18	1
Grandberry	30	212	7	0
Rather	29	408	14	3
Williams	25	167	7	0
Garrett	16	132	8	1
Kelly	8	100	13	0
Hill	7	109	16	1
Pagac	6	79	13	0
Wheeler	5	59	12	1
Farmer	5	45	9	0
Harrison	5	38	8	0
Gagnon	4	20	5	0
C. Taylor	3	23	8	0
Parsons	2	9	5	1
Kosins	1	3	3	0

PUNT RETURNS

Last Name	No.	Yds	Avg	TD
Hill	33	183	6	0
Knox	5	35	7	0
Van Valkenburg	4	22	6	0
Hodgins	2	8	4	0

KICKOFF RETURNS

Last Name	No.	Yds	Avg	TD
Grandberry	22	568	26	0
C. Taylor	27	567	21	0
Pagac	3	53	18	0
Van Valkenburg	2	42	21	0
Gagnon	2	32	16	0
Gallagher	1	16	16	0
Kinney	1	0	0	0

PASSING – PUNTING – KICKING

PASSING	Att	Comp	%	Yds	Yd/Att	TD	Int–%	RK
Huff	283	142	50	1663	5.9	62	17– 6	13
Douglass	100	41	41	387	3.9	2	4– 4	
Barnes	9	2	22	29	3.2	0	1–11	
Hill	1	0	0	0	0.0	0	0– 0	
Hodgins	1	0	0	0	0.0	0	0– 0	
Parsons	1	0	0	0	0.0	0	0– 0	
Rather	1	0	0	0	0.0	0	0– 0	

PUNTING	No	Avg
Parsons	90	37.9
Barnes	1	27.0

KICKING	XP	Att	%	FG	Att	%
Roder	17	17	100	9	13	69

1974 N.F.C. — Western Division

LOS ANGELES RAMS 10-4-0 Chuck Knox

Scores of Each Game		
17	Denver	10
24	NEW ORLEANS	0
14	New England	20
16	DETROIT	13
6	Green Bay	17
37	SAN FRANCISCO	14
20	N.Y. Jets	13
15	San Francisco	13
21	ATLANTA	0
7	New Orleans	20
20	MINNESOTA	17
30	Atlanta	7
17	WASHINGTON	23
19	BUFFALO	14

Use Name	Pos.	Hgt	Wgt	Age	Int	Pts
Charlie Cowan	OT	6'4"	265	36		
Tim Stokes	OT	6'5"	252	24		
John Williams	OT	6'3"	256	28		
Tom Mack	OG	6'3"	250	30		
Joe Scibelli	OG	6'1"	255	35		
Rich Saul	C-OG	6'3"	235	26		
Bill Curry	C	6'2"	235	31		
Ken Iman	C	6'1"	240	35		
Fred Dryer	DE	6'6"	240	28		
Jack Youngblood	DE	6'4"	255	24		
Cody Jones	DT-DE	6'5"	240	23		
Larry Brooks	DT	6'3"	255	24		
Bill Nelson	DT	6'7"	270	26		
Merlin Olsen	DT	6'5"	270	33		
Phil Olsen	DT	6'5"	265	26		

Use Name	Pos.	Hgt	Wgt	Age	Int	Pts
Ken Geddes	LB	6'3"	235	26	2	
Jim Peterson	LB	6'5"	240	24		
Jack Reynolds	LB	6'1"	232	26		
Isiah Robertson	LB	6'3"	225	25	2	
Bob Stein	LB	6'2"	235	26		
Jim Youngblood	LB	6'3"	240	24		
Al Clark	DB	6'	185	26		
Bill Drake	DB	6'1"	195	24		
Dave Elmendorf	DB	6'1"	195	25	7	12
Eddie McMillan	DB	6'	190	22		
Tony Plummer	DB	5'11"	190	27		
Steve Preece	DB	6'1"	195	27	3	
Bill Simpson	DB	6'1"	180	22	1	
Charlie Stukes	DB	6'3"	212	30	7	
Rick Kay - Knee Injury						

Use Name	Pos.	Hgt	Wgt	Age	Int	Pts
James Harris	QB	6'3"	210	27		30
Ron Jaworski	QB	6'2"	185	23		6
Jim Bertelsen	HB	5'11"	205	24		12
Larry McCutcheon	HB	6'1"	205	24		30
Bob Scribner	HB	6'	200	23		6
Cullen Bryant	HB	6'1"	218	23		6
Tony Baker	FB	5'11"	215	29		30
Les Josephson	FB	6'	207	31		
John Cappelletti	HB-FB	6'1"	217	22		
Harold Jackson	WR	5'10"	175	28		30
Willie McGee	WR	5'11"	178	24		
Lance Rentzel	WR	6'2"	202	30		6
Jack Snow	WR	6'2"	190	31		18
Pat Curran	TE	6'3"	238	28		
Bob Klein	TE	6'5"	235	27		24
Terry Nelson	TE	6'2"	230	23		
Mike Burke	K	5'10"	188	24		1
Dave Chapple (to NE)	K	6'	195	27		
David Ray	K	6'	195	29		52

SAN FRANCISCO FORTY-NINERS 6-8-0 Dick Nolan

Scores of Each Game		
17	New Orleans	13
16	Atlanta	10
3	CINCINNATI	21
9	ST. LOUIS	34
14	Detroit	17
14	Los Angeles	37
24	OAKLAND	35
13	LOS ANGELES	15
14	Dallas	20
34	Chicago	0
27	ATLANTA	0
0	Cleveland	7
7	GREEN BAY	6
35	NEW ORLEANS	2

Use Name	Pos.	Hgt	Wgt	Age	Int	Pts
Cas Banaszek	OT	6'3"	255	28		
Keith Fahnhorst	OT	6'6"	255	22		
Len Rohde	OT	6'4"	248	36		
Jean Barrett	C-OT	6'6"	254	23		
Bobby Penchion	OG	6'5"	252	25		
Woody Peoples	OG	6'2"	252	31		
Randy Beisler	OT-OG	6'4"	247	29		
John Watson	OT-OG	6'4"	245	25		
Forrest Blue	C	6'5"	265	28		
Cedrick Hardman	DE	6'3"	258	25		
Tommy Hart	DE	6'3"	248	29		
Bill Belk	DT-DE	6'3"	248	28		6
Rolf Krueger	DT-DE	6'4"	253	27		
Mike Raines	DT-DE	6'5"	255	20		
Stan Hindman	DT	6'3"	245	30		
Bob Hoskins	DT	6'2"	250	28		
Bill Sandifer	DT	6'6"	278	22		

Use Name	Pos.	Hgt	Wgt	Age	Int	Pts
Willie Harper	LB	6'2"	220	24		
Tom Hull	LB	6'3"	230	22		
Billy McKoy	LB	6'3"	226	26		
Frank Nunley	LB	6'2"	234	28	4	
Skip Vanderbundt	LB	6'3"	223	27	2	
Dave Wilcox	LB	6'3"	240	31	1	6
Caesar Belser	DB	6'	205	29		
Windlan Hall	DB	5'11"	175	24		
Hugo Hollas	DB	6'1"	190	29		
Mike Holmes	DB	6'2"	193	23	3	
Jim Johnson	DB	6'2"	185	36	3	
Ralph McGill	DB	5'11"	183	24	5	
Mel Phillips	DB	6'	190	32	1	
John Saunders	DB	6'3"	196	24		
Bruce Taylor	DB	6'	190	26	1	
Ed Hardy — Injury						

Use Name	Pos.	Hgt	Wgt	Age	Int	Pts
Dennis Morrison	QB	6'3"	211	23		
Tom Owen	QB	6'1"	194	21		6
Joe Reed	QB	6'1"	195	26		
Steve Spurrier	QB	6'2"	198	29		
Manfred Moore	HB	6'	194	23		12
Del Williams	HB	6'	195	23		18
Wilbur Jackson	HB	6'1"	215	22		12
Sammy Johnson	FB	6'	223	21		12
Larry Schreiber	HB-FB	6'	210	27		24
Danny Abramowicz	WR	6'1"	193	29		6
Terry Beasley	WR	5'10"	182	24		18
Mike Bettiga	WR	6'3"	193	24		
Gene Washington	WR	6'1"	185	27		36
Bob West	WR	6'4"	218	23		
Tom Mitchell	TE	6'2"	215	30		
Ted Kwalick	WR-TE	6'4"	228	27		12
Bruce Gossett	K	6'2"	230	31		58
Tom Wittum	K	6'1"	190	24		

NEW ORLEANS SAINTS 5-9-0 John North

Scores of Each Game		
13	SAN FRANCISCO	17
0	Los Angeles	24
14	ATLANTA	13
10	Chicago	24
17	Denver	33
13	Atlanta	3
14	PHILADELPHIA	10
14	Detroit	19
0	MIAMI	21
20	LOS ANGELES	7
7	PITTSBURGH	28
9	Minnesota	29
14	ST. LOUIS	10
2	San Francisco	35

Use Name	Pos.	Hgt	Wgt	Age	Int	Pts
Phil LaPorta	OT	6'4"	256	21		
John Mooring	OT	6'6"	255	27		
Don Morrison	OT	6'5"	260	24		
Jake Kupp	OG	6'3"	248	32		
Rocky Rasley	OG	6'3"	255	27		
Emanuel Zanders	OG	6'1"	283	23		
John Didion	C	6'4"	255	26		
Dave Thompson	OT-C	6'4"	260	25		
Steve Baumgartner	DE	6'7"	260	23		
Andy Dorris	DE	6'4"	230	23		
Billy Newsome	DE	6'4"	260	26		
Joe Owens	DE	6'2"	250	27		
Derland Moore	DT	6'4"	260	22		
Elex Price	DT	6'3"	260	24		
Bob Pollard	DE-DT	6'3"	250	25		

Use Name	Pos.	Hgt	Wgt	Age	Int	Pts
Don Coleman	LB	6'2"	222	21		
Wayne Colman	LB	6'1"	220	28	1	
Joe Federspiel	LB	6'1"	235	24	1	
Rick Kingrea	LB	6'1"	230	25		
Jim Merlo	LB	6'1"	225	22		
Rick Middleton	LB	6'2"	228	22		
Greg Boyd	DB	6'2"	200	22		
Chris Farasopolous	DB	5'11"	190	25	1	
Johnny Fuller	DB	6'	185	28	1	
Ernie Jackson	DB	5'10"	175	24	4	
Bivian Lee	DB	6'3"	200	26		
Jerry Moore	DB	6'3"	208	24	1	
Tom Myers	DB	5'11"	184	23	3	
Terry Schmidt	DB	6'	180	22	4	6
Mo Spencer (from StL)	DB	6'	175	22		

Use Name	Pos.	Hgt	Wgt	Age	Int	Pts
Larry Cipa	QB	6'3"	209	21		6
Archie Manning	QB	6'3"	215	25		6
Bobby Scott	QB	6'1"	200	25		
Alvin Maxon	HB	5'11"	205	21		18
Howard Stevens	HB	5'5"	165	24		6
Bill Butler	FB-HB	6'	210	24		
Jess Phillips	FB-HB	6'1"	210	27		12
Jack DeGrenier	FB	6'1"	225	22		
Odell Lawson	FB	6'2"	205	26		
Rod McNeill	FB	6'2"	220	23		6
Dave Davis	WR	6'	175	26		
Sam Havrilak	WR	6'2"	195	26		
Earl McCullouch	WR	5'11"	175	28		
Bob Newland	WR	6'2"	190	25		12
Joel Parker	WR	6'5"	212	22		24
Speedy Thomas	WR	6'1"	170	27		
Bob Wicks	WR	6'3"	205	24		
Richard Williams	WR	5'11"	170	22		
John Beasley	TE	6'3"	228	29		
Len Garrett	TE	6'3"	230	25		
Paul Seal	TE	6'4"	222	22		24
Tom Blanchard	K	6'	190	26		
Donnie Gibbs	K	6'2"	205	28		
Bill McClard	K	5'10"	202	22		46

ATLANTA FALCONS 3-11-0 Norm Van Brocklin Marion Campbell

Scores of Each Game		
0	DALLAS	24
10	SAN FRANCISCO	16
3	New Orleans	14
4	N.Y. Giants	7
13	CHICAGO	10
3	NEW ORLEANS	13
17	Pittsburgh	24
7	Miami	42
0	Los Angeles	21
7	BALTIMORE	17
0	San Francisco	27
7	LOS ANGELES	30
10	Minnesota	23
10	GREEN BAY	3

Use Name	Pos.	Hgt	Wgt	Age	Int	Pts
Nick Bebout	OT	6'5"	260	23		
George Kunz	OT	6'5"	268	27		
Dennis Havig	OG	6'2"	256	25		
Jim Miller	OG	6'3"	240	25		
Royce Smith	OG	6'3"	250	25		
Len Gotshalk	OT-OG	6'4"	260	24		
Ted Fritsch	C	6'2"	242	24		
Paul Ryczek	C	6'2"	230	22		
Jeff Van Note	C	6'2"	247	28		
Claude Humphrey	DE	6'5"	265	30		
John Zook	DE	6'5"	250	26	1	
Larry Bailey	DT	6'4"	238	22		
Mike Lewis	DT	6'3"	260	24		
Rosie Manning	DT	6'5"	255	23		
Mike Tilleman	DT	6'5"	278	30		
Chuck Walker	DT	6'2"	260	33		

Use Name	Pos.	Hgt	Wgt	Age	Int	Pts
Greg Brezina	LB	6'2"	220	28	1	
Don Hansen	LB	6'3"	228	30	1	
Ken Mitchell	LB	6'1"	224	26		
Tommy Nobis	LB	6'2"	243	30	1	
Dick Palmer	LB	6'2"	232	28		
Lonnie Warwick	DB	6'3"	240	32		
Ray Brown	DB	6'2"	202	25	8	6
Rick Byas	DB	5'9"	180	23		
Ray Easterling	DB	6'	192	24		
Clarence Ellis	DB	5'11"	190	24	3	
Tom Hayes	DB	6'1"	198	28	1	
Rudy Holmes	DB	5'10"	178	21		
Rolland Lawrence	DB	5'10"	180	23	1	

Use Name	Pos.	Hgt	Wgt	Age	Int	Pts
Bob Lee	QB	6'2"	200	28		6
Kim McQuilken	QB	6'2"	203	23		
Pat Sullivan	QB	6'	200	24		
Dave Hampton	HB	6'	202	27		12
Molly McGee	HB	5'10"	184	21		
Haskel Stanback	HB	6'	210	22		6
Vince Kendrick	FB	6'	223	22		6
Eddie Ray	FB	6'1"	240	27		
Art Malone	HB-FB	5'11"	216	26		12
Ken Burrow	WR	6'	190	26		6
Al Dodd	WR	6'	178	29		6
Tom Geredine	WR	6'2"	190	24		
Louie Neal	WR	6'4"	215	23		
Gerald Tinker	WR	5'9"	170	23		6
Henry Childs (to NO)	TE	6'2"	223	23		
Larry Mialik	TE	6'2"	226	23		
Jim Mitchell	TE	6'2"	236	26		6
John James	K	6'3"	200	25		
Nick Mike-Mayer	K	5'8"	187	24		

LOS ANGELES RAMS

RUSHING

Last Name	No.	Yds	Avg	TD
McCutcheon	236	1109	4.7	3
Bertelsen	127	419	3.3	2
Cappelletti	55	198	3.6	0
Baker	53	135	2.5	5
Harris	42	112	2.7	5
Josephson	11	35	3.2	0
Jaworski	7	34	4.9	1
Bryant	10	24	2.4	0
Scribner	9	24	2.7	0
Snow	1	13	13.0	0
Jackson	1	4	4.0	0
T. Nelson	1	3	3.0	0
Preece	1	–4	–4.0	0
Rentzel	1	–9	–9.0	0

RECEIVING

Last Name	No.	Yds	Avg	TD
McCutcheon	39	408	11	2
Jackson	30	514	17	5
Snow	24	397	17	3
Klein	24	336	14	4
Bertelsen	20	175	9	0
Rentzel	18	396	22	1
Cappelletti	6	35	6	0
Baker	4	65	16	0
Scribner	2	28	14	1
Bryant	2	14	7	0

PUNT RETURNS

Last Name	No.	Yds	Avg	TD
Bryant	17	171	10	0
Elmendorf	17	134	8	0
Bertelsen	11	132	12	0
Scribner	8	70	9	0

KICKOFF RETURNS

Last Name	No.	Yds	Avg	TD
Bryant	23	617	27	1
McGee	12	288	24	0
Cappelletti	2	17	9	0
Curran	1	16	16	0
Scribner	1	0	0	0
Youngblood	1	0	0	0

PASSING – PUNTING – KICKING

PASSING	Att	Comp	%	Yds	Yd/Att	TD	Int–%	RK
Harris	198	106	54	1544	7.8	11	6– 3	2
Jaworski	24	10	42	144	6.0	0	1– 4	
Burke	1	1	0	0	0.0	0	0– 0	

PUNTING	No	Avg
Chapple	55	36.3
Burke	46	37.0

KICKING	XP	Att	%	FG	Att	%
Ray	25	31	81	9	16	56
Burke	1	3	33	0	0	—

SAN FRANCISCO FORTY-NINERS

RUSHING

Last Name	No.	Yds	Avg	TD
Jackson	174	705	4.1	0
Schreiber	174	634	3.6	3
Johnson	44	237	5.4	2
Williams	36	201	5.6	3
Reed	16	107	6.7	0
Owen	16	36	2.3	1
Moore	10	24	2.4	1
Wittum	1	13	13.0	0
Washington	2	4	2.0	0
Morrison	1	0	0.0	0
Mitchell	1	–2	–2.0	0
Beasley	1	–3	–3.0	0

RECEIVING

Last Name	No.	Yds	Avg	TD
Schreiber	30	217	7	1
Washington	29	615	21	6
Abramowicz	25	369	15	1
Jackson	23	190	8	2
Mitchell	19	262	14	0
Beasley	17	253	15	3
Kwalick	13	231	18	2
Johnson	11	106	10	0
Moore	2	29	15	0
Williams	1	9	9	0

PUNT RETURNS

Last Name	No.	Yds	Avg	TD
McGill	20	166	8	0
Moore	5	149	30	1
Holmes	9	45	5	0
Taylor	10	38	4	0

KICKOFF RETURNS

Last Name	No.	Yds	Avg	TD
Holmes	25	612	25	0
Moore	18	398	22	0
Jackson	5	103	21	0
Johnson	2	31	16	0
West	1	0	0	0

PASSING – PUNTING – KICKING

PASSING	Att	Comp	%	Yds	Yd/Att	TD	Int–%	RK
Owen	184	88	48	1327	7.2	10	15– 8	11
Reed	74	29	39	316	4.3	2	7–10	
Morrison	51	21	41	227	4.5	1	5–10	
Spurrier	3	1	33	2	0.7	0	0– 0	
Abramowicz	1	1	100	41	41.0	0	0– 0	

PUNTING	No	Avg
Wittum	68	41.2
Gossett	2	28.0

KICKING	XP	Att	%	FG	Att	%
Gossett	25	27	93	11	24	46

NEW ORLEANS SAINTS

RUSHING

Last Name	No.	Yds	Avg	TD
Maxson	165	714	4.3	2
Phillips	174	556	3.2	2
Manning	28	204	7.3	1
Stevens	43	190	4.4	1
DeGrenier	33	110	3.3	0
McNeil	22	90	4.1	1
Butler	21	74	3.5	0
Cipa	12	35	2.9	1
Seal	2	7	3.5	1
Parker	2	2	1.0	0
Scott	1	1	1.0	0

RECEIVING

Last Name	No.	Yds	Avg	TD
Maxon	42	294	7	1
Parker	41	455	11	4
Seal	32	466	15	3
Newland	27	490	18	2
Stevens	13	81	6	0
Phillips	11	55	5	0
Beasley	5	85	17	0
McNeil	5	64	13	0
DeGrenier	4	13	3	0
Butler	2	3	2	0
Havrilak	1	23	23	0
McCullouch	1	5	5	0
Thomas	1	3	3	0

PUNT RETURNS

Last Name	No.	Yds	Avg	TD
Stevens	37	376	10	0
Farasopoulos	3	36	12	0
Jackson	2	3	2	0
McNeill	1	0	0	0

KICKOFF RETURNS

Last Name	No.	Yds	Avg	TD
Stevens	33	749	23	0
Phillips	7	124	18	0
Jackson	1	27	27	0
Schmidt	1	23	23	0
Kingree	1	22	22	0
Federspeil	2	20	10	0
Lawson	1	20	20	0
Middleton	2	18	9	0
Davis	1	14	14	0
Coleman	2	13	7	0
Butler	1	12	12	0
Spencer	1	–2	–2	0

PASSING – PUNTING – KICKING

PASSING	Att	Comp	%	Yds	Yd/Att	TD	Int–%	RK
Manning	261	134	51	1429	5.5	6	16– 6	14
Scott	71	31	44	366	5.2	4	4– 6	
Cipa	55	20	36	242	4.4	0	0– 0	
McClard	1	0	0	0	0.0	0	1–100	
Parker	1	0	0	0	0.0	0	0– 0	

PUNTING	No	Avg
Blanchard	88	42.1
Gibbs	3	33.0

KICKING	XP	Att	%	FG	Att	%
McClard	19	20	95	9	16	56

ATLANTA FALCONS

RUSHING

Last Name	No.	Yds	Avg	TD
Hampton	127	464	3.7	2
Malone	116	410	3.5	2
Stanback	57	235	4.1	1
Ray	46	139	3.0	0
Lee	19	99	5.2	1
Kendrick	17	71	4.2	0
McGee	7	30	4.3	0
J. Mitchell	3	21	7.0	0
Sullivan	3	19	6.3	0
Tinker	2	5	2.5	0
McQuilken	2	1	0.5	0
Neal	1	–1	–1.0	0

RECEIVING

Last Name	No.	Yds	Avg	TD
Burrow	34	545	16	1
J. Mitchell	30	479	16	1
Malone	28	168	6	0
Hampton	13	111	9	0
Dodd	12	130	11	1
Kendrick	12	86	7	1
Ray	10	43	4	0
Neal	8	99	12	0
Stanback	8	39	5	0
Geredine	4	69	17	0
Tinker	1	12	12	0

PUNT RETURNS

Last Name	No.	Yds	Avg	TD
Dodd	27	344	13	0
Tinker	14	195	14	1
Brown	9	96	11	0
Fritsch	1	0	0	0

KICKOFF RETURNS

Last Name	No.	Yds	Avg	TD
Tinker	29	704	24	0
Geredine	9	219	24	0
McGee	8	167	21	0
Byas	5	136	27	0
Mitchell	4	36	9	0
Easterling	2	34	17	0
Childs	1	0	0	0
Fritsch	1	0	0	0
Ryczek	1	0	0	0

PASSING – PUNTING – KICKING

PASSING	Att	Comp	%	Yds	Yd/Att	TD	Int–%	RK
Lee	172	78	45	852	5.0	3	14– 8	16
Sullivan	105	48	46	556	5.3	1	8– 8	
McQuilken	79	34	43	373	4.7	0	9–11	

PUNTING	No	Avg
James	96	40.5

KICKING	XP	Att	%	FG	Att	%
Mike-Mayer	12	12	100	9	16	56

1974 A.F.C. Same Game, Different Rules

The N.F.L. this year took some steps to return to its games the offensive fireworks that had been so common in the 1950's and 1960's. To promote more passing, the "bump-and-run" method of pass defense was closely regulated. To cut down on the number of field goals and increase the emphasis on touchdowns, the league fathers moved the goal posts back to the rear of the end zone, where they had stood all along in college ball and where they had stood in pro ball until being moved up to the goal line in 1933. Another change brought missed field goals that travel into the end zone back out to the line of scrimmage. And an extra sudden-death period was added for all tie games during the season, a measure heretofore reserved for playoff games. All these moves did produce some additional points and a couple of overtime games, but the main shift in tactics was to a new reliance on coffin-corner punting, with an eye to keeping opponents bottled up in a poor field position all game long.

EASTERN DIVISION

Miami Dolphins—The signing of Larry Csonka, Paul Warfield, Jim Kiick, Tim Foley, and Bob Kuechenberg to future contracts with the new World Football League caused some bitterness in the Dolphin family; but coach Don Shula decided to play his best players regardless of where they might be in the future. When the Dolphins got off to a lack-lustre start, it was injuries, not dissension, at the heart of the team's problems. Csonka, Warfield, Wayne Moore, Doug Swift, Mercury Morris, and Manny Fernandez all suffered through injury-cursed seasons to throw the finely-tuned Dolphin machine out of gear. But subs like Nat Moore, Don Nottingham, and Ben Malone came through when thrown into the breach, and the Dolphins soon were playing in their usual championship style. A 35–28 victory over Buffalo on November 17 put Miami back into first place, and the Dolphins held on to it the rest of the way.

Buffalo Bills—O.J. Simpson couldn't duplicate his record-setting performance of last year, but he still raced for 1125 yards despite a sore knee. The Buffalo attack had an added dimension this season, as young quarterback Joe Ferguson passed the ball much more often to wide receivers like ex-Cardinal Ahmad Rashad. A sound defense featuring backs Bobby James and Tony Greene complemented the powerful offense and helped boost the Bills into first place with a 29–28 win over New England on October 20. Although the Dolphins knocked the Bills out of the top slot one month later, Buffalo still marched into the playoffs as the wild-card team.

New England Patriots—The Pats began the season with a reorganized defense and an almost unbelievable stretch of good football. The Patriots beat the defending champion Dolphins 34–24 on opening day, and chalked up another big upset by upending the highly-touted Rams 20–14 two weeks later. The team's opening spurt brought in four straight wins and six out of the first seven. But then injuries started decimating the New England offense. Darryl Stingley, Reggie Rucker, Bob Windsor, and Sam Cunningham all went out of the lineup, and the crippled Patriot squad faltered badly down the stretch. But aside from the steady work of quarterback Jim Plunkett and defensive tackle Julius Adams, the star of the season was Mack Herron, the diminutive halfback who set a new record for total yardage gained in all categories combined for one season.

New York Jets—Charley Winner succeeded his father-in-law Weeb Ewbank as head coach this year, but a 1–7 start made it debatable if he would be staying very long in New York. But then Joe Namath led his mates to a 26–20 overtime win over the rival Giants, and the Jets suddenly came together. The team won its last six games to reach the .500 level and reclaim some of the dignity lost in the horrendous first part of the schedule.

Baltimore Colts—The year started on a down note, as All-Pro linebacker Ted Hendricks signed a future contract with the W.F.L. and was then traded at a dirt-cheap price to Green Bay by General Manager Joe Thomas. The personnel situation on the Colt roster was even worse than last season, and coach Howard Schnellenberger was fired after three games, with his fate sealed by an argument he had with owner Robert Irsay over whether Marty Domres or Bert Jones should play quarterback. Thomas doubled as coach for the rest of the year but could direct the team to only two wins.

CENTRAL DIVISION

Pittsburgh Steelers—The Steelers' strong 6–0 preseason showing was less surprising than Joe Gilliam's winning the starting quarterback job away from Terry Bradshaw. Gilliam faltered in mid-season and was benched in favor of Bradshaw, but the Steelers had so much talent that they easily captured first place in the Central Division. The Steelers had a solid offensive line, a copious supply of wide receivers, a superb fullback in Franco Harris, and a brutally effective defense featuring Mean Joe Greene, L.C. Greenwood, Andy Russell, and Jack Ham. The biggest bonus of the year was the play of halfback Rocky Bleier, who had recovered well enough from leg injuries suffered in the Vietnam war to claim a starting job in the offensive backfield.

Cincinnati Bengals—Passer Ken Anderson enjoyed a fine season, but a variety of circumstances reduced the Bengals to a 7–7 campaign. The defense never recovered from the loss of All-Pro middle linebacker Bill Bergey, whom coach Paul Brown traded to Philadelphia after he signed a future contract with the W.F.L. Injuries did in the offense. The backfield lost Booby Clark to foot and hand injuries and Essex Johnson to a bad knee, while the line suffered from Vern Holland's broken leg and Bob Johnson's broken ankle.

Houston Oilers—Coach Sid Gillman patched up the pitiful Oilers and turned out a respectable football team. The process needed time to take effect, as the Oilers won their opening game and then dropped five straight. During the early part of the campaign, Gillman also had to endure the efforts of defensive tackle John Matuszak to jump to the W.F.L. He actually did jump to the Houston Texans of that league, but was served with a restraining order right on the field in the middle of his first game. Soon after his return to the Oilers, Gillman sent him off to Kansas City in return for Curley Culp. A defensive front three of Elvin Bethea, Culp, and Tody Smith spearheaded a much improved defense that led the Oilers to six wins in their last eight games, including upsets over the Bills and Steelers. But despite his achievement of turning the Oilers around, Gillman resigned both his coach and General Manager positions after the season in a dispute with owner Bud Adams over how freely Gillman spent the team's money on a variety of "extravagant" arrangements such as an illegally-large taxi squad.

Cleveland Browns—The once-mighty Browns tumbled to their worst season ever, a humbling 4–10 campaign which dumped them ignominiously into the cellar in the Central Division. Five losses in the first six games took the Browns out of any playoff contention, and things improved only slightly the rest of the year. Little Greg Pruitt excited the fans, but the team in general was a dull loser that cost coach Nick Skorich his job.

WESTERN DIVISION

Oakland Raiders—Quarterback Ken Stabler signed a future pact with the W.F.L., but he didn't let it cramp his style with the Raiders this year. The lefty passer guided the N.F.L.'s most explosive offense with the cool of a surgeon, throwing a league-leading 26 touchdown passes. His wide receivers were Fred Biletnikoff, with average speed but extraordinary moves, and Cliff Branch, a small sprinter who broke into the lineup when Mike Siani was injured. Power running came from big Marv Hubbard, and the versatile offensive line had All-Pro candidates in Gene Upshaw and Art Shell. With such an offense, the defense played far better than it had to for the Raiders to nail down the Western Division title. The offensive riches included 46-year-old George Blanda, whose place kicking left little to be desired and who got into the final game of the year at quarterback and threw a touchdown pass.

Denver Broncos—The Broncos hoped to challenge for a playoff berth, but they never climbed above a mediocre level during this season. A noteworthy game of this disappointing campaign was a 35–35 tie with the Pittsburgh Steelers on September 22, the first N.F.L. regular season game to go into overtime; an extra period resulted in no score, and the extra exertion may have contributed to both team's losing the next week. On the positive side for the Broncos, tight end Riley Odoms won All-Pro honors for his play, while second-year running back Otis Armstrong surprisingly blossomed into a dangerous runner, piling up a league-leading total of 1407 yards.

Kansas City Chiefs—The old Kansas City powerhouse that used to battle Oakland for the Western title every season was no more. Age was eating into the talent at almost all the positions, and only a handful of younger players showed a capacity for playing up to the standards of the old Chiefs. Rookie Woody Green did sparkle in his limited performances at running back, but his addition only balanced the mid-season loss of Ed Podolak with a thumb injury. The Chiefs endured their first losing season since 1963, but the gradual slide to this point prompted owner Lamar Hunt to fire Hank Stram, the only coach the team had had since opening shop in Dallas 15 years before.

San Diego Chargers—Preseason training camp saw all-time great quarterback Johnny Unitas come into camp, work out for a few days, and then announce his retirement. New coach Tommy Prothro manned the passer's position with youngsters Dan Fouts and Jesse Freitas, and the young quarterbacks helped the Chargers win five games in a rebuilding season. The sturdiest building block Prothro could find was rookie Don Woods, an exciting runner whom the Green Bay Packers had cut loose on waivers before the season.

FINAL TEAM STATISTICS

OFFENSE

	BALT.	BUFF.	CIN.	CLEV.	DENV	HOUS.	K.C.	MIAMI	N.ENG	N.Y.	OAK.	PITT.	S.D.
FIRST DOWNS:													
Total	244	220	260	223	258	200	224	272	255	234	**284**	251	245
by Rushing	110	118	115	104	120	76	92	134	123	96	127	**136**	113
by Passing	109	85	131	92	118	103	113	118	113	119	**137**	98	117
by Penalty	25	17	14	**27**	20	21	19	20	19	19	20	17	15
RUSHING:													
Number	450	545	445	461	486	421	469	**570**	520	444	561	546	508
Yards	1818	2094	1978	1924	2157	1361	1720	2191	2134	1625	2334	**2417**	2111
Average Yards	4.0	3.8	**4.4**	4.2	4.4	3.2	3.7	3.8	4.1	3.7	4.2	4.4	4.2
Touchdowns	13	11	14	14	20	16	10	**25**	21	12	15	19	15
PASSING:													
Attempts	**425**	251	353	367	329	363	395	283	359	369	335	386	349
Completions	221	128	**224**	179	184	203	211	171	177	194	186	166	165
Completion Percentage	52.0	51.0	**63.5**	48.8	55.9	55.9	53.4	60.4	49.3	52.6	55.5	43.0	47.3
Passing Yards	2424	1728	**2804**	2129	2660	2275	2421	2313	2514	2631	2561	2154	2479
Avg. Yards per Attempt	5.7	6.9	7.9	5.8	8.1	6.3	6.1	**8.2**	7.0	7.1	7.6	5.6	7.1
Avg. Yards per Complet.	11.0	13.5	12.5	11.9	14.5	11.2	11.5	13.5	14.2	13.6	13.8	13.0	**15.0**
Times Tackled Passing	49	33	37	48	46	33	37	31	21	19	24	**18**	23
Yards Lost Tackled	399	236	293	402	332	298	313	229	**174**	195	177	196	175
Net Yards	2025	1492	**2511**	1727	2328	1977	2108	2084	2340	2436	2384	1958	2304
Touchdowns	9	14	18	12	18	12	11	18	19	20	**28**	12	12
Interceptions	24	15	**13**	24	17	19	25	18	23	24	18	21	22
Percent Intercepted	5.7	6.0	**3.7**	6.5	5.2	5.2	6.3	6.4	6.4	6.5	5.4	5.4	6.3
PUNTS:													
Number	71	69	66	**90**	75	79	83	65	71	75	74	78	76
Average Distance	37.1	40.6	40.9	40.5	40.3	39.2	41.7	38.6	36.2	35.9	**42.2**	39.0	40.0
PUNT RETURNS:													
Number	42	56	52	52	43	41	44	46	40	53	45	**67**	37
Yards	253	460	632	523	474	495	296	520	533	425	517	**774**	287
Average Yards	6.0	8.2	12.2	10.1	11.0	12.1	6.7	11.3	**13.3**	8.0	11.5	11.6	7.8
Touchdowns	0	0	**2**	0	0	0	0	0	0	0	0	1	0
KICKOFF RETURNS:													
Number	**66**	50	54	60	54	62	56	49	58	61	50	42	55
Yards	**1489**	1128	1157	1375	1188	1419	1211	1118	1198	1307	1140	901	1142
Average Yards	22.6	22.6	21.4	**22.9**	22.0	22.9	21.6	22.8	20.7	21.4	22.8	21.5	20.8
Touchdowns	0	0	0	**1**	0	0	0	0	0	0	0	0	0
INTERCEPTION RETURNS:													
Number	10	20	9	24	22	21	**28**	16	24	17	27	25	15
Yards	87	413	110	336	311	313	**531**	139	294	278	378	320	273
Average Yards	8.7	**20.7**	12.2	14.0	14.1	14.9	19.0	8.7	12.3	16.4	14.0	12.8	18.2
Touchdowns	0	2	0	2	1	1	**5**	0	2	2	1	2	0
PENALTIES:													
Number	66	79	78	78	76	90	70	69	87	76	92	**104**	74
Yards	587	706	653	767	632	749	515	556	843	600	845	**978**	609
FUMBLES:													
Number	28	32	27	34	23	26	29	25	26	26	**22**	33	24
Number Lost	13	14	18	15	13	14	13	13	15	**8**	10	19	11
POINTS:													
Total	190	264	283	251	302	236	233	327	348	279	**355**	305	212
PAT Attempts	22	30	36	30	39	30	26	43	43	36	**46**	35	28
PAT Made	22	25	32	29	35	29	24	43	42	27	**44**	33	26
FG Attempts	20	**33**	18	16	21	19	24	15	22	18	17	29	16
FG Made	12	19	11	14	11	9	17	8	16	12	11	**20**	6
Percent FG Made	60.0	57.6	61.1	**87.5**	52.4	47.4	**70.8**	**53.3**	72.7	66.7	64.7	69.0	37.5
Safeties	0	1	1	0	0	0	1	1	0	0	1	1	0

DEFENSE

	BALT.	BUFF.	CIN.	CLEV.	DENV	HOUS	K.C.	MIAMI	N.ENG.	N.Y.	OAK.	PITT.	S.D.
FIRST DOWNS:													
Total	237	219	256	247	265	268	267	208	240	267	237	**200**	272
by Rushing	120	96	127	126	109	124	107	**83**	100	132	110	87	128
by Passing	101	97	109	95	135	129	141	117	129	112	106	**83**	127
by Penalty	16	26	20	26	21	15	19	**8**	11	23	21	30	17
RUSHING:													
Number	516	489	497	555	487	474	502	**404**	467	539	459	472	508
Yards	1961	1878	2152	2415	1808	2050	1801	1624	**1587**	2240	2108	1608	2160
Average Yards	3.8	3.8	4.3	4.4	3.7	4.3	3.6	4.0	3.4	4.2	4.6	**3.4**	4.3
Touchdowns	20	19	16	17	17	15	16	**7**	16	20	12	**7**	21
PASSING:													
Attempts	312	311	359	**308**	426	405	408	372	374	347	367	339	367
Completions	180	146	186	**139**	237	231	206	200	210	186	175	147	222
Completion Percentage	57.7	46.9	51.8	45.1	55.6	57.0	50.5	53.8	56.1	53.6	47.7	**43.4**	60.5
Passing Yards	2348	1898	2110	2259	2805	2724	2838	2452	2774	2249	2425	**1872**	2815
Avg. Yards per Attempt	7.5	6.1	5.9	7.3	6.6	6.7	7.0	6.6	7.4	6.5	6.6	**5.5**	7.7
Avg. Yards per Complet.	13.0	13.0	11.3	16.3	11.8	**11.8**	13.8	12.3	13.2	12.1	13.9	12.7	12.7
Times Tackled Passing	21	32	36	28	32	40	26	31	38	25	36	**52**	18
Yards Lost Tackled	183	287	320	234	222	349	175	270	294	192	314	**406**	145
Net Yards	2165	1611	1790	2025	2583	2375	2663	2182	2480	2057	2111	**1466**	2670
Touchdowns	16	**11**	13	22	14	19	22	14	17	14	12	14	13
Interceptions	10	20	9	24	22	21	**28**	16	24	17	27	25	15
Percent Intercepted	3.2	6.4	2.5	**7.8**	5.2	5.2	6.9	4.3	6.4	4.9	7.4	7.4	4.1
PUNTS:													
Number	67	77	81	76	70	70	80	70	75	71	73	**91**	66
Average Distance	38.4	**37.1**	37.8	38.0	42.6	39.1	40.1	39.2	38.4	37.2	39.9	41.2	40.6
PUNT RETURNS:													
Number	46	45	41	68	45	56	55	42	41	**27**	40	47	48
Yards	413	416	457	705	529	500	634	**259**	314	352	283	413	401
Average Yards	9.0	9.2	11.1	10.4	11.8	8.9	11.5	**6.2**	7.7	13.0	7.1	8.8	8.4
Touchdowns	**0**	**0**	**0**	1	**0**	**0**	**0**	**0**	**0**	**0**	**0**	**0**	**0**
KICKOFF RETURNS:													
Number	45	58	55	55	57	51	54	64	64	57	69	56	**39**
Yards	**903**	1345	1198	1345	1369	1111	1333	1222	1678	1395	1455	1275	960
Average Yards	20.1	23.2	21.8	24.5	24.0	21.8	24.7	**19.1**	26.2	24.5	21.1	22.8	24.6
Touchdowns	**0**	**0**	**0**	1	1	**0**	**0**	**0**	1	**0**	**0**	**0**	**0**
INTERCEPTION RETURNS:													
Number	24	15	**13**	24	17	19	25	18	23	24	18	21	22
Yards	384	183	**140**	423	304	238	336	320	331	452	276	222	311
Average Yards	16.0	12.2	10.8	17.6	17.9	12.5	13.4	17.8	14.4	18.8	15.3	**10.6**	14.1
Touchdowns	3	1	**0**	1	3	**0**	1	1	2	4	2	1	1
PENALTIES:													
Number	75	73	77	81	78	**94**	83	67	76	78	61	76	80
Yards	737	597	640	731	595	**872**	811	525	642	684	502	575	751
FUMBLES:													
Number	25	26	23	31	22	26	34	33	29	18	32	**38**	19
Number Lost	14	11	11	16	11	15	16	17	14	9	14	**22**	13
POINTS:													
Total	329	244	259	344	294	282	293	216	289	300	228	**189**	285
PAT Attempts	40	32	30	43	35	34	40	25	37	38	27	**22**	37
PAT Made	38	28	28	38	34	30	**33**	24	32	36	25	21	36
FG Attempts	27	15	22	23	24	23	14	21	18	24	22	17	20
FG Made	17	8	17	14	16	16	**6**	14	11	12	13	12	9
Percent FG Made	63.0	53.3	77.3	60.9	66.7	69.6	**42.9**	66.7	61.1	50.0	59.1	70.6	45.0
Safeties	**0**	**0**	**0**	3	1	**0**	1	**0**	1	**0**	1	**0**	**0**

CONFERENCE PLAYOFFS

December 21, at Oakland (Attendance 52,817)

SCORING

OAKLAND	0	7	7	14	28
MIAMI	7	3	6	10	26

First Quarter
- Mia. N. Moore, 89-yard kickoff return PAT–Yepremian (kick)

Second Quarter
- Oak. C. Smith, 31 yard pass from Stabler PAT–Blanda (kick)
- Mia. Yepremian, 33 yard field goal

Third Quarter
- Oak. Biletnikoff, 13 yard pass from Stabler PAT–Blanda (kick)
- Mia. Warfield, 16 yard pass from Griese PAT–kick missed

Fourth Quarter
- Mia. Yepremian, 46 yard field goal
- Oak. Branch, 72 yard pass from Stabler PAT–Blanda (kick)
- Mia. Malone, 23 yard rush PAT–Yepremian (kick)
- Oak. Davis, 8 yard pass from Stabler PAT–Blanda (kick)

TEAM STATISTICS

OAK.		MIAMI
19	First Downs-Total	18
8	First Downs-Rushing	10
11	First Downs-Passing	6
0	First Downs-Penalty	2
0	Fumbles-Number	0
0	Fumbles-Lost Ball	0
3	Penalties-Number	3
59	Yards Penalized	15
0	Missed Field Goals	0
64	Offensive Plays	57
411	Net Yards	294
6.4	Average Gain	5.2
1	Giveaways	1
1	Takeaways	1
0	Difference	0

INDIVIDUAL STATISTICS

OAKLAND	No.	Yds.	Avg.	MIAMI	No.	Yds.	Avg.
RUSHING							
Davis	12	59	4.9	Csonka	24	114	4.8
Hubbard	14	55	3.9	Malone	14	83	5.9
Banaszak	3	14	4.7	Griese	2	14	7.0
Stabler	3	7	2.3	Kiick	1	2	2.0
	32	135	4.2		41	213	5.2
RECEIVING							
Biletnikoff	8	122	15.3	Warfield	3	47	15.7
Branch	3	84	28.0	N. Moore	2	40	20.0
Moore	3	22	7.3	Nottingham	1	9	9.0
C. Smith	2	35	17.5	Kiick	1	5	5.0
C. Davis	2	16	8.0		7	101	14.4
Hubbard	1	9	9.0				
Pitts	1	5	5.0				
	20	293	14.7				
PUNTING							
Guy	7		42.7	Seiple	6		33.2
PUNT RETURNS							
R. Smith	3	16	5.3	N. Moore	2	5	2.5
KICKOFF RETURNS							
Hart	4	88	22.0	N. Moore	3	137	45.7
R. Smith	2	47	23.5	Ginn	2	46	23.0
	6	135	22.5		5	183	36.6
INTERCEPTION RETURNS							
Villapiano	1	5	5.0				

PASSING

	Att.	Comp.	Comp. Pct.	Yds.	Int.	Yds/ Att.	Yds/ Comp.	Yards Lost Tackled
OAKLAND								
Stabler	30	20	66.7	293	1	9.8	14.7	2–17
MIAMI								
Griese	14	7	50.0	101	0	7.2	14.4	2–20

December 22, at Pittsburgh (Attendance 48,321)

SCORING

PITTSBURGH	3	26	0	3	32
BUFFALO	7	0	7	0	14

First Quarter
- Pitt. Gerela, 21 yard field goal
- Buf. Seymour, 22 yard pass from Ferguson PAT–Leypoldt (kick)

Second Quarter
- Pit. Bleier, 27 yard pass from Bradshaw PAT–kick blocked
- Pit. Harris, 1 yard rush PAT–Gerela (kick)
- Pit. Harris, 4 yard rush PAT–kick blocked
- Pit. Harris, 1 yard rush PAT–Gerela (kick)

Third Quarter
- Buf. Simpson, 3 yard pass from Ferguson PAT–Leypoldt (kick)

Fourth Quarter
- Pit. Gerela, 22 yard field goal

TEAM STATISTICS

PITT.		BUF.
29	First Downs-Total	15
18	First Downs-Rushing	5
9	First Downs-Passing	10
2	First Downs-Penalty	0
2	Fumbles-Number	2
0	Fumbles-Lost Ball	1
2	Penalties-Number	3
10	Yards Penalized	15
0	Missed Field Goals	0
72	Offensive Plays	47
438	Net Yards	264
6.1	Average Gain	5.6
0	Giveaways	1
1	Takeaways	0
+1	Difference	–1

INDIVIDUAL STATISTICS

PITTSBURGH	No.	Yds.	Avg.	BUFFALO	No.	Yds.	Avg.
RUSHING							
Harris	24	74	3.1	Simpson	15	49	3.3
Bradshaw	5	48	9.6	Braxton	5	48	9.6
Bleier	14	45	3.2	Ferguson	1	3	3.0
Steve Davis	5	32	6.4		21	100	4.8
Swann	2	24	12.0				
Gilliam	1	12	12.0				
	51	235	4.6				
RECEIVING							
Swann	3	60	20.0	Hill	4	59	14.8
Bleier	3	54	18.0	Simpson	3	37	12.3
Lewis	2	18	9.0	Seymour	2	35	17.5
Brown	1	29	29.0	Rashad	1	25	25.0
McMakin	1	22	22.0	Braxton	1	8	8.0
Shanklin	1	15	15.0		11	164	14.9
Harris	1	5	5.0				
	12	203	16.9				
PUNTING							
Walden	3		38.7	Bateman	5		39.4
PUNT RETURNS							
Edwards	2	13	6.5	Walker	2	11	5.5
Swann	2	12	6.0				
	4	25	6.3				
KICKOFF RETURNS							
Blount	2	56	28.0	Francis	6	118	19.7
Steve Davis	1	30	30.0				
	3	86	28.7				

PASSING

	Att.	Comp.	Comp. Pct.	Yds	Int.	Yds/ Att.	Yds/ Comp.	Yards Lost Tackled
PITTSBURGH								
Bradshaw	19	12	63.2	203	0	10.7	16.9	0–0
Gilliam	2	0	00.0	0	0	–	–	0–0
	21	12	57.1	203	0	9.7	16.9	0–0
BUFFALO								
Ferguson	26	11	42.3	164	0	6.3	14.9	0–0

MIAMI DOLPHINS 11-3-0 Don Shula

Scores of Each Game		
24	New England	34
24	Buffalo	16
28	San Diego	21
21	N.Y. JETS	17
17	Washington	20
9	KANSAS CITY	3
17	BALTIMORE	7
42	ATLANTA	7
21	New Orleans	0
35	BUFFALO	28
14	N.Y. Jets	17
24	CINCINNATI	3
17	Baltimore	16
34	NEW ENGLAND	27

Use Name	Pos.	Hgt	Wgt	Age	Int	Pts
Doug Crusan	OT	6'5"	250	28		
Norm Evans	OT	6'5"	250	31		
Tom Funchess	OT	6'5"	270	29		
Wayne Moore	OT	6'6"	265	29		
Tom Wickert	OT	6'4"	246	22		
Larry Little	OG	6'1"	265	28		
Ed Newman	OG	6'2"	245	23		
Bob Kuechenberg	OT-OG	6'3"	252	26		
Jim Langer	C	6'2"	253	26		
Irv Goode	OG-C	6'4"	262	33		
Vern Den Herder	DE	6'6"	252	25		
Bill Stanfill	DE	6'5"	252	27		
Don Reese	DT-DE	6'6"	255	22		
Randy Crowder	DT	6'2"	236	22		
Manny Fernandez	DT	6'2"	250	28		
Baldy Moore	DT	6'2"	265	28		
Bob Heinz	DE-DT	6'6"	265	27		
Larry Ball	LB	6'6"	235	24		
Bruce Bannon	LB	6'3"	225	23		
Nick Buoniconti	LB	5'11"	220	33	2	
Mike Kolen	LB	6'2"	222	26	1	
Bob Matheson	LB	6'4"	235	29	1	
Doug Swift	LB	6'3"	226	25		
Dick Anderson	DB	6'2"	196	28	1	
Charlie Babb	DB	6'	190	24		
Tim Foley	DB	6'	194	26	2	2
Curtis Johnson	DB	6'2"	196	26		
Lloyd Mumphrey	DB	5'11"	176	27		
Jake Scott	DB	6'	188	29	8	
Henry Stuckey	DB	6'1"	180	24	1	
Jeris White	DB	5'11"	180	21		
Bob Griese	QB	6'1"	190	29		6
Earl Morrall	QB	6'1"	210	40		
Don Strock	QB	6'5"	216	23		
Hubert Ginn	HB	5'11"	185	27		12
Jim Kiick	HB	5'11"	214	28		12
Benny Malone	HB	5'10"	193	22		18
Mercury Morris	HB	5'10"	192	27		12
Larry Csonka	FB	6'3"	237	27		54
Don Nottingham	FB	5'10"	210	25		48
Melvin Baker	WR	6'	192	24		12
Marlin Briscoe	WR	5'10"	175	28		6
Nat Moore	WR	5'9"	180	22		12
Howard Twilley	WR	5'10"	185	30		12
Paul Warfield	WR	6'	188	31		12
Marv Fleming	TE	6'4"	230	32		6
Jim Mandich	TE	6'3"	224	26		36
Larry Seiple	TE	6'	214	29		
Garo Yepremian	K	5'8"	175	30		67

BUFFALO BILLS 9-5-0 Lou Saban

Scores of Each Game		
21	OAKLAND	20
16	MIAMI	24
16	N.Y. JETS	12
27	Green Bay	7
27	Baltimore	14
30	NEW ENGLAND	28
16	CHICAGO	6
29	New England	28
9	HOUSTON	21
28	Miami	35
15	Cleveland	10
6	BALTIMORE	0
10	N.Y. Jets	20
14	Los Angeles	19

Use Name	Pos.	Hgt	Wgt	Age	Int	Pts
Dave Foley	OT	6'5"	253	26		
Donnie Green	OT	6'7"	272	26		
Halvor Hagen	OT	6'5"	253	27		
Bill Adams	OG	6'2"	254	24		
Joe DeLamielleure	OG	6'3"	245	23		
Reggie McKenzie	OG	6'4"	242	24		
Bruce Jarvis	C	6'7"	250	25		
Nick Nighswander	C	6'	232	22		
Mike Montler	OT-C	6'4"	253	30		
Willie Parker	OG-C	6'3"	245	25		
Dave Costa	DE	6'2"	250	32		
Dave Means	DE	6'4"	235	22		
Walt Patulski	DE	6'6"	260	24		
Don Croft	DT	6'3"	254	25		
Mike Kadish	DT	6'5"	270	24		2
Jeff Yeates	DT	6'3"	240	23		
Earl Edwards	DE-DT	6'6"	256	28		
Doug Allen	LB	6'2"	228	22	1	
Jim Cheyunski	LB	6'2"	220	28	1	
Merv Krakau	LB	6'2"	237	23	1	
Rich Lewis	LB	6'3"	215	24	1	
John Skorupan	LB	6'2"	220	23		
Bo Cornell	FB-LB	6'1"	215	25		
Ted Koy	TE-LB	6'1"	210	26		
Dave Washington	TE-LB	6'5"	223	25	2	12
Bill Cahill	DB	5'11"	170	23		
Neal Craig	DB	6'1"	190	26	1	6
Tony Greene	DB	5'10"	170	25	9	
Dwight Harrison	DB	6'1"	185	25	1	
Robert James	DB	6'1"	184	27	3	
Rex Kern	DB	5'11"	190	25		
Al Randolph	DB	6'2"	205	30		
Donnie Walker	DB	6'1"	180	23		
Jeff Winans – Injury						
Joe Ferguson	QB	6'1"	180	24		12
Scott Hunter	QB	6'2"	205	26		
Gary Marangi	QB	6'1"	196	22		
Don Calhoun	HB	6'	198	22		
Clint Haserlig	HB	6'	190	22		
Gary Hayman	HB	6'1"	198	23		
Ed Jenkins (from NYG, to NE)	HB	6'2"	210	24		
Wayne Mosley	HB	6'	190	21		
O. J. Simpson	HB	6'2"	212	27		24
Jim Braxton	FB	6'2"	240	25		24
Larry Watkins	FB	6'2"	235	27		12
Bob Chandler	WR	6'	180	25		6
Wallace Francis	WR	5'11"	195	22		
J. D. Hill	WR	6'1"	190	25		36
Ahmad Rashad	WR	6'2"	200	24		36
Reuben Gant	TE	6'4"	230	22		
Paul Seymour	TE	6'5"	243	24		12
Marv Bateman (from DAL)	K	6'4"	210	24		
Spike Jones	K	6'2"	195	27		
John Leypoldt	K	6'2"	237	28		82

NEW ENGLAND PATRIOTS 7-7-0 Chuck Fairbanks

Scores of Each Game		
34	MIAMI	24
28	N.Y. Giants	20
20	LOS ANGELES	14
42	BALTIMORE	3
24	N.Y. Jets	0
28	Buffalo	30
17	Minnesota	14
28	BUFFALO	29
14	CLEVELAND	21
16	N.Y. JETS	21
27	Baltimore	17
26	Oakland	41
17	PITTSBURGH	21
27	Miami	34

Use Name	Pos.	Hgt	Wgt	Age	Int	Pts
Allen Gallaher	OT	6'3"	255	23		
Leon Gray	OT	6'3"	256	22		
Tom Neville	OT	6'4"	253	31		
Sam Adams	OG	6'3"	252	25		
Bill DuLac	OG	6'4"	260	23		
John Hannah	OG	6'2"	265	23		6
Doug Dumler	C	6'3"	242	23		
Jon Morris	C	6'4"	248	31		
Bill Lenkaitis	OG-C	6'3"	250	28		
Craig Hanneman	DE	6'3"	245	25		
Tony McGee	DE	6'4"	245	25		
Donnell Smith	DE	6'4"	252	25		
Julius Adams	DT-DE	6'3"	257	26		
Mel Lunsford	DT-DE	6'3"	260	24		
Ray Hamilton	NT	6'1"	246	23		
Art Moore	NT	6'5"	253	23		
Gail Clark	LB	6'2"	225	23		
Kent Carter	LB	6'3"	235	24		
Rodrigo Barnes (from DAL)	LB	6'1"	215	24		
Maury Damkroger	LB	6'2"	230	22		
Bob Geddes	LB	6'2"	240	28	2	6
Sam Hunt	LB	6'1"	240	23	3	
Steve King	LB	6'4"	230	23	1	
Steve Nelson	LB	6'2"	230	23		
John Tanner	TE-LB	6'4"	235	29		6
George Webster	LB	6'4"	230	28		
Ron Bolton	DB	6'2"	170	24	7	
Sandy Durko	DB	6'1"	186	26		
Prentice McCray	DB	6'1"	187	23	3	
Dave McCurry	DB	6'1"	187	23		
Jim Massey	DB	5'11"	198	26		
Jack Mildren	DB	6'1"	200	24	3	
Ken Pope	DB	5'11"	200	22		
Deac Sanders	DB	6'1"	178	24	5	6
Neil Graff	QB	6'3"	200	24		
Jim Plunkett	QB	6'3"	212	26		12
Dick Shiner	QB	6'	210	32		
Josh Ashton	HB	6'1"	202	25		
Noe Gonzalez	HB	6'	210	23		
Mack Herron	HB	5'5"	175	26		72
Andy Johnson	HB	6'	204	21		
Sam Cunningham	FB	6'3"	224	24		66
John Tarver	FB	6'3"	220	25		12
Joe Wilson	HB-FB	5'10"	210	23		
Eddie Hinton	WR	6'	200	27		
Al Marshall	WR	6'2"	190	23		6
Reggie Rucker	WR	6'2"	190	26		24
Steve Schubert	WR	5'10"	185	23		6
Darryl Stingley	WR	6'	195	22		12
Joe Sweet	WR	6'2"	196	26		
Randy Vataha	WR	5'10"	170	25		18
Bob Adams	TE	6'2"	222	28		
Bob Windsor	TE	6'4"	225	31		6
Bruce Barnes	K	5'11"	212	23		
John Smith	K	6'	185	24		90

NEW YORK JETS 7-7-0 Charley Winner

Scores of Each Game		
16	Kansas City	24
23	Chicago	21
12	Buffalo	16
17	Miami	21
0	NEW ENGLAND	24
20	BALTIMORE	35
13	LOS ANGELES	20
22	HOUSTON	27
26	N.Y. Giants (OT)	20
21	New England	16
17	MIAMI	14
27	SAN DIEGO	14
20	BUFFALO	10
45	Baltimore	38

Use Name	Pos.	Hgt	Wgt	Age	Int	Pts
Gordie Browne	OT	6'5"	265	22		
Winston Hill	OT	6'4"	280	32		
Robert Woods	OT	6'3"	255	24		
Roger Bernhardt	OG	6'4"	244	24		
Randy Rasmussen	OG	6'2"	267	29		
Travis Roach	OG	6'2"	260	24		
Gary Puetz	OT-OG	6'4"	255	22		
Howard Kindig	C	6'6"	260	33		
Warren Koegel	C	6'3"	260	24		
Wayne Mulligan	C	6'2"	250	27		
Ed Galigher	DE	6'4"	260	23		
Mark Lomas	DE	6'4"	250	26		
John Little	DT-DE	6'3"	250	27		
Carl Barzilauskas	DT	6'6"	280	23		
Larry Woods	DT	6'6"	270	26		
Richard Neal	DE-DT	6'3"	260	26		
Joe Schmiesing	DE-DT	6'4"	256	29		
Al Atkinson	LB	6'1"	230	31		
Ralph Baker	LB	6'3"	228	32	2	6
John Ebersole	LB	6'3"	235	25	3	
Bill Ferguson	LB	6'3"	225	23		
Steve Reese	LB	6'2"	232	22		
Jamie Rivers	LB	6'2"	245	28	1	
Delles Howell	DB	6'3"	200	27	2	
Burgess Owens	DB	6'2"	200	23	3	12
Rich Sowells	DB	6'	185	25	2	
Steve Tannen	DB	6'1"	194	26	2	
Earlie Thomas	DB	6'1"	190	28		
Phil Wise	DB	6'	190	25		
Roscoe Word	DB	5'11"	170	21	2	
Bill Demory	QB	6'2"	195	23		
Joe Namath	QB	6'2"	200	31		6
Al Woodall	QB	6'5"	194	28		
Mike Adamle	HB	5'9"	193	24		12
Hank Bjorklund	HB	6'1"	200	24		
Emerson Boozer	HB	5'11"	205	31		30
Jazz Jackson	HB	5'8"	167	22		12
Bob Burns	FB	6'3"	212	22		6
John Riggins	FB	6'2"	230	25		42
Jerome Barkum	WR	6'3"	212	24		18
Eddie Bell	WR	5'10"	160	26		6
Dave Knight	WR	6'1"	182	23		24
Marv Owens	WR	5'11"	205	24		
Lou Piccone	WR	5'9"	175	25		
Willie Brister	TE	6'4"	236	22		
Rich Caster	TE	6'5"	228	25		42
Greg Gantt	K	5'11"	188	22		1
Bobby Howfield	K	5'9"	180	37		26
Pat Leahy	K	6'	200	23		36

BALTIMORE COLTS 2-12-0 Howard Schnellenberger Joe Thomas

Scores of Each Game		
0	Pittsburgh	30
13	GREEN BAY	20
10	Philadelphia	30
3	New England	42
14	BUFFALO	27
35	N.Y. Jets	20
7	Miami	17
14	CINCINNATI	24
6	DENVER	17
17	Atlanta	7
17	NEW ENGLAND	27
0	Buffalo	6
16	MIAMI	17
38	N.Y. JETS	45

Use Name	Pos.	Hgt	Wgt	Age	Int	Pts
Dennis Nelson	OT	6'5"	260	28		
Dave Simonson	OT	6'6"	246	22		
David Taylor	OT	6'4"	254	24		
Elmer Collett	OG	6'4"	240	29		
Robert Pratt	OG	6'3"	255	23		
Glenn Ressler	OG	6'3"	250	30		
Bob Van Duyne	OG	6'5"	235	22		
Ken Mendenhall	C	6'3"	240	25		
Dan Neal	C	6'4"	240	25		
Mike Barnes	DE	6'6"	255	23		
Fred Cook	DE	6'4"	235	22		
John Dutton	DE	6'7"	260	23		
Steve Williams	DE	6'6"	260	23		
Jim Bailey	DT	6'5"	255	26		
Joe Ehrmann	DT	6'5"	260	25		
Bill Windauer	DT	6'3"	245	24		
Tony Bertuca	LB	6'2"	225	24		
Mike Curtis	LB	6'2"	232	31	3	
Dan Dickel	LB	6'3"	220	22	1	
Tom MacLeod	LB	6'3"	230	23		
Danny Rhodes	LB	6'2"	220	23		
Stan White	LB	6'1"	225	24	1	
Randy Hall	DB	6'3"	185	22		
Bruce Laird	DB	6'	185	24	1	
Nelson Munsey	DB	6'1"	185	26		
Doug Nettles	DB	6'	177	23	1	
Ray Oldham	DB	6'	200	23	1	
Tim Rudnick	DB	5'10"	185	22		
Rick Volk	DB	6'3"	195	29	2	
Marty Domres	QB	6'3"	222	27		12
Bert Jones	QB	6'3"	205	22		24
Bill Troup	QB	6'5"	220	23		
Lydell Mitchell	HB	5'11"	204	25		42
Joe Orduna	HB	6'	195	26		6
Bill Olds	FB	6'1"	224	23		18
Don McCauley	HB-FB	6'1"	214	25		6
Tim Berra	WR	5'11"	185	22		
Roger Carr	WR	6'3"	200	22		
Glenn Doughty	WR	6'2"	204	23		12
Freddie Scott	WR	6'2"	175	22		
Ollie Smith	WR	6'2"	195	25		
Cotton Speyrer	WR	6'	175	25		6
John Andrews	TE	6'3"	227	25		
Ray Chester	TE	6'3"	235	26		6
Ron Mayo	TE	6'3"	223	23		
David Lee	K	6'4"	230	30		
Toni Linhart	K	6'	178	32		58

MIAMI DOLPHINS

RUSHING

Last Name	No.	Yds	Avg	TD
Csonka	197	749	3.8	9
Malone	117	479	4.1	3
Kiick	86	274	3.2	1
Nottingham	66	273	4.1	8
Morris	56	214	3.8	1
Ginn	26	99	3.8	2
Griese	16	66	4.1	1
Briscoe	1	17	17.0	0
N. Moore	3	16	5.3	0
Morrall	1	11	11.0	0
Strock	1	−7	−7.0	0

RECEIVING

Last Name	No.	Yds	Avg	TD
N. Moore	37	605	16	2
Mandich	33	374	11	6
Warfield	27	536	20	2
Twilley	24	256	11	2
Kiick	18	155	9	1
Briscoe	11	132	12	1
Csonka	7	35	5	0
Baker	4	121	30	2
Nottingham	3	40	13	0
Morris	2	27	14	1
Malone	2	26	13	0
Ginn	2	3	2	0
Fleming	1	3	3	1

PUNT RETURNS

Last Name	No.	Yds	Avg	TD
Scott	31	346	11	0
N. Moore	9	136	15	0
Babb	2	29	15	0
Anderson	3	9	3	0
Stuckey	1	0	0	0

KICKOFF RETURNS

Last Name	No.	Yds	Avg	TD
N. Moore	22	587	27	0
Ginn	12	235	20	0
Malone	6	159	27	0
Matheson	5	65	13	0
Baker	1	22	22	0
Babb	1	0	0	0

PASSING – PUNTING – KICKING

PASSING	Att	Comp	%	Yds	Yd/Att	TD	Int–%	RK
Griese	253	152	60	1968	7.8	16	15– 6	4
Morrall	27	17	63	301	11.1	2	3–11	
Kiick	1	1	100	13	13.0	0	0– 0	
Moore	1	1	100	31	31.0	0	0– 0	
Briscoe	1	0	0	0	0.0	0	0– 0	

PUNTING	No	Avg
Seiple	65	38.6

KICKING	XP	Att	%	FG	Att	%
Yepremian	43	43	100	8	15	53

BUFFALO BILLS

RUSHING

Last Name	No.	Yds	Avg	TD
Simpson	270	1125	4.2	3
Braxton	146	543	3.7	4
Watkins	41	170	4.1	2
Ferguson	54	111	2.1	2
Calhoun	21	88	4.2	0
Hayman	7	31	4.4	0
Marangi	4	20	5.0	0
Mosley	2	6	3.0	0

RECEIVING

Last Name	No.	Yds	Avg	TD
Rashad	36	433	12	4
Hill	32	572	18	6
Braxton	18	171	10	0
Seymour	15	246	16	2
Simpson	15	189	13	1
Chandler	7	88	13	1
Calhoun	2	10	5	0
Jenkins	1	12	12	0
Watkins	1	7	7	0
Green	1	0	0	0

PUNT RETURNS

Last Name	No.	Yds	Avg	TD
Walker	43	384	9	0
Cahill	10	62	6	0
Hayman	2	13	7	0
Kern	1	1	1	0

KICKOFF RETURNS

Last Name	No.	Yds	Avg	TD
Francis	37	947	26	0
Calhoun	6	90	15	0
Cornell	3	45	15	0
Cahill	1	26	26	0
Walker	1	20	20	0
Craig	1	0	0	0
Rashad	1	0	0	0

PASSING – PUNTING – KICKING

PASSING	Att	Comp	%	Yds	Yd/Att	TD	Int–%	RK
Ferguson	232	119	51	1588	6.8	12	12– 5	7
Marangi	18	9	50	140	7.8	2	3–17	
Simpson	1	0	0	0	0.0	0	0– 0	

PUNTING	No	Avg
Bateman	67	40.5
Jones	35	37.3

KICKING	XP	Att	%	FG	Att	%
Leypoldt	25	29	86	19	33	58

NEW ENGLAND PATRIOTS

RUSHING

Last Name	No.	Yds	Avg	TD
Herron	231	824	3.6	7
Cunningham	166	811	4.9	9
Plunkett	30	161	5.4	2
Tarver	41	101	2.5	2
Ashton	26	99	3.8	0
Stingley	5	63	12.6	1
Wilson	15	57	3.8	0
Vataha	3	21	7.0	0
Hinton	1	1	1.0	0
Johnson	2	−4	−2.0	0

RECEIVING

Last Name	No.	Yds	Avg	TD
Herron	38	474	13	5
Rucker	27	436	16	4
Vataha	25	561	22	3
Cunningham	22	214	10	2
B. Adams	17	244	14	0
Windsor	12	127	11	1
Stingley	10	139	14	1
Tarver	9	37	4	0
Johnson	8	147	18	0
Wilson	3	38	13	0
Hinton	2	36	18	0
Tanner	2	23	12	1
Schubert	1	21	21	1
Marshall	1	17	17	1

PUNT RETURNS

Last Name	No.	Yds	Avg	TD
Herron	35	517	15	0
Schubert	3	15	5	0
Durko	1	1	1	0
Hinton	1	0	0	0

KICKOFF RETURNS

Last Name	No.	Yds	Avg	TD
Herron	28	629	23	0
Johnson	15	303	20	0
Schubert	5	112	22	0
Hinton	3	83	28	0
Wilson	2	33	17	0
Hunt	1	21	21	0
Tanner	2	17	9	0
Durko	1	0	0	0
D. Smith	1	0	0	0

PASSING – PUNTING – KICKING

PASSING	Att	Comp	%	Yds	Yd/Att	TD	Int–%	RK
Plunkett	352	173	49	2457	7.0	19	22– 6	9
Shiner	6	3	50	37	6.2	0	1–17	
Graff	1	1	100	20	20.0	0	0– 0	

PUNTING	No	Avg
B. Barnes	45	35.6

KICKING	XP	Att	%	FG	Att	%
J. Smith	42	43	98	16	22	73

NEW YORK JETS

RUSHING

Last Name	No.	Yds	Avg	TD
Riggins	169	680	4.0	5
Boozer	153	563	3.7	4
Burns	40	158	4.0	0
Adamle	28	93	3.3	2
Jackson	20	74	3.7	0
Bjorklund	23	57	2.5	0
Barkum	1	2	2.0	1
Namath	8	1	0.1	1
Woodall	2	−3	−1.5	0

RECEIVING

Last Name	No.	Yds	Avg	TD
Barkum	41	524	13	3
Knight	40	579	15	4
Caster	38	745	20	7
Riggins	19	180	10	2
Boozer	14	161	12	1
Bell	13	126	10	1
Burns	11	83	8	1
Adamle	9	84	9	0
Brister	5	90	18	0
Jackson	2	44	22	1
Bjorklund	2	15	8	0

PUNT RETURNS

Last Name	No.	Yds	Avg	TD
Word	38	301	8	0
Piccone	9	75	8	0
Jackson	6	49	8	0

KICKOFF RETURNS

Last Name	No.	Yds	Avg	TD
Piccone	39	961	25	0
Jackson	4	100	25	0
Bjorklund	4	73	18	0
Word	4	69	17	0
Burns	3	52	17	0
B. Owens	3	35	12	0
Adamle	2	17	9	0
Knight	2	0	0	0

PASSING – PUNTING – KICKING

PASSING	Att	Comp	%	Yds	Yd/Att	TD	Int–%	RK
Namath	361	191	53	2616	7.2	20	22– 6	5
Woodall	8	3	38	15	1.9	0	2–25	

PUNTING	No	Avg
Gantt	75	35.9

KICKING	XP	Att	%	FG	Att	%
Leahy	18	19	95	6	11	55
Howfield	8	12	67	6	7	86
Gantt	1	2	50	0	0	—

BALTIMORE COLTS

RUSHING

Last Name	No.	Yds	Avg	TD
Mitchell	214	757	3.5	5
Olds	129	475	3.7	1
Jones	39	279	7.2	4
Domres	22	145	6.6	2
McCauley	30	90	3.0	0
Doughty	7	51	7.3	0
Scott	2	12	6.0	0
Andrews	5	6	1.2	0
Orduna	2	3	1.5	1

RECEIVING

Last Name	No.	Yds	Avg	TD
Mitchell	72	544	8	2
Chester	37	461	13	1
Doughty	24	300	13	2
Carr	21	405	19	0
Olds	21	153	7	2
Scott	18	317	18	0
McCauley	17	112	7	1
Speyrer	9	110	12	1
Smith	1	14	14	0
Orduna	1	8	8	0

PUNT RETURNS

Last Name	No.	Yds	Avg	TD
Berra	16	114	7	0
Speyrer	8	54	7	0
Scott	3	31	10	0
Laird	11	30	3	0
Rudnick	2	23	12	0
Volk	1	1	1	0
Bertuca	1	0	0	0

KICKOFF RETURNS

Last Name	No.	Yds	Avg	TD
Speyrer	22	539	25	0
Laird	19	499	26	0
Berra	13	259	20	0
Orduna	3	68	23	0
Scott	3	61	20	0
Mayo	2	23	12	0
Andrews	1	18	18	0
McCauley	1	17	17	0
Rudnick	1	5	5	0
Oldham	1	0	0	0

PASSING – PUNTING – KICKING

PASSING	Att	Comp	%	Yds	Yd/Att	TD	Int–%	RK
Jones	270	143	53	1610	6.0	8	12– 4	10
Domres	153	77	50	803	5.2	0	12– 8	15
McCauley	2	1	50	11	5.5	1	0– 0	

PUNTING	No	Avg
Lee	71	37.1

KICKING	XP	Att	%	FG	Att	%
Linhart	22	22	100	12	20	60

PITTSBURGH STEELERS 10-3-1 Chuck Noll

Scores of Each Game		
30	BALTIMORE	0
35	Denver (OT)	35
0	OAKLAND	17
13	Houston	7
34	Kansas City	24
20	CLEVELAND	16
24	ATLANTA	17
27	PHILADELPHIA	0
10	Cincinnati	17
26	Cleveland	16
28	New Orleans	7
10	HOUSTON	13
21	New England	17
27	CINCINNATI	3

Use Name	Pos.	Hgt	Wgt	Age	Int	Pts
Gordon Gravelle	OT	6'5"	250	25		
Jon Kolb	OT	6'2"	262	27		
Dave Reavis	OT	6'5"	250	24		
Rick Druschel	OG-OT	6'2"	248	22		
Sam Davis	OG	6'1"	255	30		
Jim Clack	C-OG	6'3"	250	26		
Gerry Mullins	OT-OG	6'3"	244	25		6
Ray Mansfield	C	6'3"	260	33		
Mike Webster	OG-C	6'1"	232	22		
L. C. Greenwood	DE	6'5"	245	27		2
Dwight White	DE	6'4"	255	25		
Jim Wolf	DE	6'2"	230	22		
Charlie Davis	DT	6'1"	265	22		
Joe Greene	DT	6'4"	275	27	1	
Ernie Holmes	DT	6'3"	260	26		
Steve Furness	DE-DT	6'4"	255	24		

Use Name	Pos.	Hgt	Wgt	Age	Int	Pts
Ed Bradley	LB	6'2"	240	24		
Jack Ham	LB	6'3"	225	25	5	
Marv Kellum	LB	6'2"	225	22	1	
Jack Lambert	LB	6'4"	215	22	2	
Andy Russell	LB	6'3"	225	32	1	
Loren Toews	LB	6'3"	212	22		
Jimmy Allen	DB	6'2"	194	22		
Mel Blount	DB	6'3"	205	26	2	6
Dick Conn	DB	6'	185	23		
Glen Edwards	DB	6'	185	27	5	6
Donnie Shell	DB	5'11"	190	22	1	
J.T. Thomas	DB	6'2"	196	23	5	6
Mike Wagner	DB	6'1"	210	25	2	
Henry Davis – Injury						

Use Name	Pos.	Hgt	Wgt	Age	Int	Pts
Terry Bradshaw	QB	6'3"	218	25		12
Joe Gilliam	QB	6'2"	187	23		6
Terry Hanratty	QB	6'1"	210	26		
Rocky Bleier	HB	5'11"	210	28		12
Preston Pearson	HB	6'1"	205	29		24
Franco Harris	FB-HB	6'2"	230	24		36
Reggie Harrison (from STL)	FB	5'11"	215	24		6
Steve Davis	HB-FB	6'1"	218	24		18
John Fugua	HB-FB	5'11"	195	27		12
Reggie Garrett	WR	6'1"	172	22		
Frank Lewis	WR	6'1"	196	27		24
Ron Shanklin	WR	6'1"	190	27		6
John Stallworth	WR	6'2"	183	22		6
Lynn Swann	WR	6'	178	22		18
Larry Brown	TE	6'4"	230	25		6
Randy Grossman	TE	6'1"	215	20		
John McMakin	TE	6'3"	232	23		
Roy Gerela	K	5'10"	185	26		93
Bobby Walden	K	6'	190	26		

CINCINNATI BENGALS 7-7-0 Paul Brown

Scores of Each Game		
33	CLEVELAND	7
17	SAN DIEGO	20
21	San Francisco	3
28	WASHINGTON	17
34	Cleveland	24
27	Oakland	30
21	HOUSTON	34
24	Baltimore	14
17	PITTSBURGH	10
3	Houston	20
33	KANSAS CITY	6
3	Miami	24
19	DETROIT	23
3	Pittsburgh	27

Use Name	Pos.	Hgt	Wgt	Age	Int	Pts
Vern Holland	OT	6'5"	268	26		
Dave Lapham	OT	6'3"	255	22		
Rufus Mayes	OT	6'5"	258	26		
Stan Walters	OT	6'6"	262	26		
Howard Fest	OG-OT	6'6"	256	28		
Pat Matson	OG	6'1"	245	30		
John Shinners	OG	6'2"	255	27		
Bob Johnson	C	6'5"	262	28		
Royce Berry	DE	6'3"	250	28		
Ken Johnson	DE	6'5"	256	27		
Bob Maddox	DE	6'5"	232	25		6
Sherman White	DE	6'5"	255	25		
Ron Carpenter	DT	6'4"	260	26		2
Bill Kollar	DT	6'3"	255	21		
Mike Reid	DT	6'3"	255	27		

Use Name	Pos.	Hgt	Wgt	Age	Int	Pts
Doug Adams	LB	6'1"	226	25		
Ken Avery	LB	6'1"	227	30		
Al Beauchamp	LB	6'2"	232	30	1	
Evan Jolitz	LB	6'2"	225	22		
Tim Kearney	LB	6'2"	230	23		
Vic Koegel	LB	6'	215	22		
Jim LeClair	LB	6'2"	235	23		
Ron Pritchard	LB	6'1"	230	27		
Lyle Blackwood	DB	6'	190	23		
Tommy Casanova	DB	6'2"	195	24	2	
Bernard Jackson	DB	6'	178	24	1	
Bob Jones	DB	6'1"	194	23		
Lemar Parrish	DB	5'11"	185	26		18
Ken Riley	DB	6'	182	27	5	
Ken Sawyer	DB	6'	192	22		

Use Name	Pos.	Hgt	Wgt	Age	Int	Pts
Ken Anderson	QB	6'1"	211	25		12
Wayne Clark	QB	6'2"	203	27		6
Charlie Davis	HB	5'11"	200	22		
Lenvil Elliott	HB	6'	205	22		12
Essex Johnson	HB	5'9"	200	27		6
Booby Clark	FB	6'2"	245	23		36
Doug Dressler	FB	6'3"	228	26		12
Ed Williams	FB	6'2"	245	24		24
Isaac Curtis	WR	6'	193	23		60
Charlie Joiner	WR	5'11"	188	26		6
John McDaniel	WR	6'1"	193	22		
Chip Myers	WR	6'4"	205	29		6
Al Chandler	TE	6'2"	230	23		
Bruce Coslet	TE	6'3"	227	28		
Bob Trumpy	TE	6'6"	228	29		12
Dave Green	K	5'11"	208	24		
Horst Muhlmann	K	6'1"	220	34		65

HOUSTON OILERS 7-7-0 Sid Gillman

Scores of Each Game		
21	SAN DIEGO	14
7	Cleveland	20
7	KANSAS CITY	17
7	PITTSBURGH	13
10	Minnesota	51
27	ST. LOUIS	31
34	Cincinnati	21
27	N.Y. Jets	22
21	Buffalo	9
20	CINCINNATI	3
0	DALLAS	10
13	Pittsburgh	10
14	Denver	37
28	CLEVELAND	24

Use Name	Pos.	Hgt	Wgt	Age	Int	Pts
Elbert Drungo	OT	6'5"	265	31		
Kevin Hunt	OT	6'5"	260	25		
Greg Sampson	OT	6'6"	260	23		
Ronnie Carroll	OG	6'2"	265	25		
Curley Culp (from KC)	DT-OG	6'1"	265	28		
Soloman Freelon	OG	6'2"	250	23		
Brian Goodman	OG	6'2"	250	25		
Harris Jones	OG	6'4"	245	29		
Ron Saul	OG	6'2"	255	26		
Fred Hoaglin	C	6'4"	250	30		
Sid Smith	OT-C	6'4"	260	26		
Elvin Bethea	DE	6'3"	255	28		6
Ed Fisher	DE	6'3"	245	25		
Tody Smith	DE	6'5"	250	25	1	
Jim White	DE	6'3"	255	25		
Al Cowlings	LB-DT	6'5"	245	27		
Bubba McCollum	DT	6'	250	22		
Ron Lou – injury						

Use Name	Pos.	Hgt	Wgt	Age	Int	Pts
Duane Benson	LB	6'2"	215	29	2	
Gregg Bingham	LB	6'1"	230	23	4	
Ralph Cindrich (to DEN)	LB	6'1"	230	24		
Marvin Davis	LB	6'4"	235	22		
Steve Kiner	LB	6'	220	27	1	
Guy Roberts	LB	6'1"	217	24		
Ted Washington	LB	6'1"	240	26		
Willie Alexander	DB	6'2"	190	24	2	
Bob Atkins	DB	6'3"	210	28	6	
John Charles	DB	6'1"	200	30		
Leonard Fairley	DB	5'11"	200	24		
Al Johnson	DB	6'	200	24		
Tommy Maxwell	DB	6'2"	195	27	2	
Zeke Moore	DB	6'2"	196	30	2	6
Jeff Severson	DB	6'1"	185	24	1	
C. L. Whittington	DB	6'1"	200	22		

Use Name	Pos.	Hgt	Wgt	Age	Int	Pts
Lynn Dickey	QB	6'4"	210	24		
James Foote	QB	6'2"	210	22		
Dan Pastorini	QB	6'3"	205	25		
Ronnie Coleman	HB	5'10"	195	23		6
Bob Gresham	HB	5'11"	195	26		
Willie Rodgers	HB	6'	210	25		30
Vic Washington	HB	5'10"	196	28		12
Terry Wells	HB	5'11"	195	23		
George Amundson	FB	6'3"	215	23		30
Fred Willis	FB	6'	205	26		24
Ken Burrough	WR	6'4"	210	26		12
Billy Johnson	WR	5'9"	170	22		18
Mike Montgomery	WR	6'2"	210	25		6
Billy Parks	WR	6'1"	190	26		6
Mack Alston	TE	6'2"	230	27		18
Jerry Broadnax	TE	6'2"	225	23		
Jeff Queen	TE	6'1"	217	28		6
David Beverly	K	6'2"	180	24		
Skip Butler	K	6'2"	200	26		56

CLEVELAND BROWNS 4-10-0 Nick Skorich

Scores of Each Game		
7	Cincinnati	33
20	HOUSTON	7
7	St. Louis	29
24	OAKLAND	40
24	CINCINNATI	34
16	Pittsburgh	20
23	DENVER	21
25	San Diego	36
21	New England	14
16	PITTSBURGH	26
10	BUFFALO	15
7	SAN FRANCISCO	0
17	Dallas	41
24	Houston	28

Use Name	Pos.	Hgt	Wgt	Age	Int	Pts
Barry Darrow	OT	6'7"	260	24		
Doug Dieken	OT	6'5"	254	25		
Bob McKay	OT	6'5"	260	26		
Gerry Sullivan	OT	6'4"	250	22		
Pete Adams	OG	6'4"	260	23		
Jim Copeland	OG	6'2"	243	29		
John Demarie	OG	6'3"	246	29		
Glen Holloway	OG	6'3"	250	25		
Chuck Hutchison	OG	6'3"	250	25		
Tom DeLeone	C	6'2"	252	24		
Bob DeMarco	C	6'3"	248	36		
Mark Ilgenfritz	DE	6'4"	250	22		
Mike Seifert	DE	6'3"	245	23		
Carl Barisch	DT	6'4"	255	23		
Walter Johnson	DT	6'3"	265	31		
Jerry Sherk	DT	6'4"	255	26		

Use Name	Pos.	Hgt	Wgt	Age	Int	Pts
Billy Andrews	LB	6'	225	29	1	
Bob Babich	LB	6'2"	230	27	1	
John Garlington	LB	6'1"	218	28	2	
Charlie Hall	LB	6'3"	225	25	3	6
Mel Long	LB	6'	228	27		
Jim Romaniszyn	LB	6'2"	224	22		
Preston Anderson	DB	6'1"	183	22		
Cliff Brooks	DB	6'1"	190	25		
Eddie Brown	DB	5'11"	180	22	2	
Thom Darden	DB	6'2"	195	24	8	6
Van Green	DB	6'1"	192	23	2	6
Clarence Scott	DB	6'	180	25	4	
Walt Sumner	DB	6'1"	195	27		
Ken Smith – Injury						

Use Name	Pos.	Hgt	Wgt	Age	Int	Pts
Mike Phipps	QB	6'2"	205	26		6
Brian Sipe	QB	6'1"	195	25		24
Ken Brown	HB	5'10"	203	28		36
Greg Pruitt	HB	5'10"	190	23		30
Billy LeFear	WR-HB	5'11"	197	24		
Hugh McKinnis	FB	6'	215	26		12
Bo Scott	FB	6'3"	215	31		
Jubilee Dunbar	WR	6'	196	27		
Tim George	WR	6'5"	210	22		
Ben Hawkins	WR	6'1"	180	30		
Steve Holden	WR	6'	198	23		18
Fair Hooker	WR	6'1"	195	27		6
Gloster Richardson	WR	6'	200	31		12
Dave Sullivan	WR	5'11"	185	23		
Milt Morin	TE	6'4"	236	32		18
Jim Thaxton (From SD)	TE	6'2"	240	25	1	
Don Cockroft	K	6'1"	195	29		71
Chris Gartner	K	6'	170	24		

PITTSBURGH STEELERS

RUSHING

Last Name	No.	Yds	Avg	TD
Harris	208	1006	4.8	5
Bleier	88	373	4.2	2
Pearson	70	317	4.5	4
Steve Davis	71	246	3.5	2
Bradshaw	34	224	6.6	2
Fuqua	50	156	3.1	2
Gilliam	14	41	2.9	1
Harrison	6	30	5.0	1
Lewis	2	25	12.5	0
Swann	1	14	14.0	0
Hanratty	1	−6	−6.0	0
Stallworth	1	−9	−9.0	0

RECEIVING

Last Name	No.	Yds	Avg	TD
Lewis	30	365	12	4
Harris	23	200	9	1
Shanklin	19	324	17	1
Brown	17	190	11	1
Stallworth	16	269	17	1
Grossman	13	164	13	0
Swann	11	208	19	2
Steve Davis	11	152	14	1
Pearson	11	118	11	0
Bleier	7	87	12	0
Fuqua	6	68	11	0
Mullins	1	7	7	1
Harrison	1	2	2	0

PUNT RETURNS

Last Name	No.	Yds	Avg	TD
Swann	41	577	14	1
Edwards	16	128	8	0
Conn	10	69	7	0

KICKOFF RETURNS

Last Name	No.	Yds	Avg	TD
Steve Davis	12	269	22	0
Pearson	12	258	22	0
Blount	5	152	30	0
Harrison	4	72	18	0
Bleier	3	67	22	0
Conn	1	34	34	0
Edwards	2	31	16	0
Swann	2	11	6	0
Allen	1	7	7	0

PASSING – PUNTING – KICKING

PASSING	Att	Comp	%	Yds	Yd/Att	TD	Int–%	RK
Gilliam	212	96	45	1274	6.0	4	8– 4	12
Bradshaw	148	67	45	785	5.3	7	8– 5	13
Hanratty	26	3	12	95	3.7	1	5–19	

PUNTING	No	Avg
Walden	78	39.0

KICKING	XP	Att	%	FG	Att	%
Gerela	33	35	94	20	29	69

CINCINNATI BENGALS

RUSHING

Last Name	No.	Yds	Avg	TD
Davis	72	375	5.2	0
Elliott	68	345	5.1	1
Anderson	43	314	7.3	2
B. Clark	99	312	3.2	5
Dressler	72	255	3.5	2
Williams	58	238	4.1	3
Curtis	8	62	7.8	0
E. Johnson	19	44	2.3	0
Joiner	4	20	5.0	0
W. Clark	1	8	8.0	1
McDaniel	1	5	5.0	0

RECEIVING

Last Name	No.	Yds	Avg	TD
Myers	32	383	12	1
Curtis	30	633	21	10
Dressler	29	196	7	0
Joiner	24	390	16	1
B. Clark	23	194	8	1
Trumpy	21	330	16	2
Davis	19	171	9	0
Elliott	18	187	10	1
Williams	13	98	8	1
E. Johnson	8	85	11	1
McDaniel	2	79	40	0
Coslet	2	24	12	0
Jackson	1	22	22	0
Chandler	1	9	9	0
Johnson	1	3	3	0

PUNT RETURNS

Last Name	No.	Yds	Avg	TD
Parrish	18	338	19	2
Casanova	24	265	11	0
Blackwood	10	29	3	0

KICKOFF RETURNS

Last Name	No.	Yds	Avg	TD
Jackson	29	682	24	0
Davis	12	243	20	0
McDaniel	3	64	21	0
Casanova	1	48	48	0
Parrish	2	36	18	0
Williams	2	33	17	0
Dressler	3	32	11	0
Blackwood	1	17	17	0
Elliott	1	2	2	0

PASSING – PUNTING – KICKING

PASSING	Att	Comp	%	Yds	Yd/Att	TD	Int–%	RK
Anderson	328	213	65	2667	8.1	18	10– 3	1
W. Clark	22	9	41	98	4.5	0	3–14	
Green	2	1	50	22	11.0	0	0– 0	
Elliott	1	1	100	17	17.0	0	0– 0	

PUNTING	No	Avg
Green	66	40.9

KICKING	XP	Att	%	FG	Att	%
Muhlmann	32	35	91	11	18	61

HOUSTON OILERS

RUSHING

Last Name	No.	Yds	Avg	TD
Rodgers	122	413	3.4	5
V. Washington	74	281	3.8	2
Willis	74	239	3.2	3
Coleman	52	193	3.7	1
Amundson	59	138	2.3	4
B. Johnson	5	82	16.4	1
Dickey	3	7	2.3	0
Queen	2	7	3.5	0
Gresham	3	6	2.0	0
Beverly	1	4	4.0	0
Burrough	1	0	0.0	0
Alston	1	−3	−3.0	0
Pastorini	24	−6	−0.2	0

RECEIVING

Last Name	No.	Yds	Avg	TD
Burrough	36	492	14	2
B. Johnson	29	388	13	2
Willis	25	130	5	1
Rodgers	24	153	6	0
Parks	20	330	17	1
Amundson	18	152	8	1
Alston	17	249	15	3
V. Washington	13	92	7	0
Montgomery	9	170	20	1
Coleman	4	9	2	0
Broadnax	3	69	23	0
Gresham	3	19	6	0
Wells	1	9	9	0
Queen	1	4	4	1

PUNT RETURNS

Last Name	No.	Yds	Avg	TD
B. Johnson	30	409	14	0
Severson	11	86	8	0

KICKOFF RETURNS

Last Name	No.	Yds	Avg	TD
B. Johnson	29	785	27	0
Gresham	9	180	20	0
V. Washington	7	177	25	0
Severson	6	108	18	0
Coleman	3	91	30	0
Whittington	3	37	12	0
Amundson	2	17	9	0
A. Johnson	1	14	14	0
Saul	1	10	10	0
Jones	1	0	0	0

PASSING – PUNTING – KICKING

PASSING	Att	Comp	%	Yds	Yd/Att	TD	Int–%	RK
Pastorini	247	140	57	1571	6.4	10	10– 4	5
Dickey	113	63	56	704	6.2	2	8– 7	
Coleman	2	0	0	0	0.0	0	0– 0	
Amundson	1	0	0	0	0.0	0	1–100	

PUNTING	No	Avg
Beverly	79	39.2

KICKING	XP	Att	%	FG	Att	%
Butler	29	29	100	9	19	47

CLEVELAND BROWNS

RUSHING

Last Name	No.	Yds	Avg	TD
Pruitt	126	540	4.3	3
McKinnis	124	519	4.2	2
K. Brown	125	458	3.7	4
Phipps	39	279	7.2	1
B. Scott	23	86	3.7	0
Sipe	16	44	2.8	4
Holden	1	6	6.0	0
LeFear	6	2	0.3	0
Thaxton	1	−10	−10.0	0

RECEIVING

Last Name	No.	Yds	Avg	TD
McKinnis	32	258	8	0
Holden	30	452	15	3
K. Brown	29	194	7	2
Morin	27	330	12	3
Pruitt	21	274	13	1
Richardson	9	266	30	2
B. Scott	7	22	3	0
Dunbar	6	74	12	0
D. Sullivan	5	92	18	0
Thaxton	4	71	18	0
Hooker	4	48	12	1
LeFear	4	21	5	0
Green	1	27	27	0

PUNT RETURNS

Last Name	No.	Yds	Avg	TD
Pruitt	27	349	13	0
Darden	21	173	8	0
LeFear	2	1	1	0
E. Brown	2	0	0	0

KICKOFF RETURNS

Last Name	No.	Yds	Avg	TD
Pruitt	22	606	28	1
LeFear	26	574	22	0
E. Brown	6	138	23	0
Romaniszyn	5	48	10	0
K. Brown	1	9	9	0

PASSING – PUNTING – KICKING

PASSING	Att	Comp	%	Yds	Yd/Att	TD	Int–%	RK
Phipps	256	117	46	1384	5.4	9	17– 7	14
Sipe	108	59	55	603	5.6	1	7– 7	
Pruitt	2	2	100	115	57.5	2	0– 0	
Cockroft	1	1	100	27	27.0	0	0– 0	

PUNTING	No	Avg
Cockroft	90	40.5

KICKING	XP	Att	%	FG	Att	%
Cockroft	29	30	97	14	16	88

OAKLAND RAIDERS 12-2-0 John Madden

Scores of Each Game		
20	Buffalo	21
27	KANSAS CITY	7
17	Pittsburgh	0
40	Cleveland	24
14	SAN DIEGO	10
30	CINCINNATI	27
35	San Francisco	24
28	Denver	17
35	DETROIT	13
17	San Diego	10
17	DENVER	20
41	NEW ENGLAND	26
7	Kansas City	6
27	DALLAS	23

Use Name	Pos.	Hgt	Wgt	Age	Int	Pts
Henry Lawrence	OT	6'4"	268	22		
Harold Paul	OT	6'5"	245	24		
Art Shell	OT	6'5"	265	27		
John Vella	OT	6'4"	255	24		
George Buehler	OG	6'2"	260	27		
Dan Medlin	OG	6'3"	260	24		
Gene Upshaw	OG	6'5"	255	29		
Jim Otto	C	6'2"	255	36		
Dave Dalby	OG-C	6'2"	240	23		
Tony Cline	DE	6'2"	244	26		
Horace Jones	DE	6'3"	255	25		
Bubba Smith	DE	6'7"	265	29		
Kelvin Korver	DT	6'6"	270	25		
Otis Sistrunk	DT	6'4"	255	26	1	2
Art Thoms	DT	6'5"	260	27		6
Dan Conners	LB	6'1"	230	32	3	
Mike Dennery	LB	6'	222	24		
Gerald Irons	LB	6'2"	230	27	2	
Monte Johnson	LB	6'4"	235	22	1	
Phil Villapiano	LB	6'1"	222	25		
Gary Weaver	LB	6'1"	224	25		
Butch Atkinson	DB	6'	180	26	4	
Willie Brown	DB	6'1"	195	33	1	
Bob Prout	DB	6'1"	190	23		
Ron Smith	DB	6'1"	195	31		
Jack Tatum	DB	5'10"	200	25	4	
Skip Thomas	DB	6'1"	205	24	6	6
Jimmy Warren	DB	5'11"	175	35	2	
Nemiah Wilson	DB	6'	165	31	3	
George Blanda	QB	6'2"	215	46		77
Daryle Lamonica	QB	6'2"	215	33		
Larry Lawrence	QB	6'1"	208	25		
Ken Stabler	QB	6'3"	215	28		6
Clarence Davis	HB	5'10"	195	25		18
Harold Hart	HB	6'	206	21		18
Bob Hudson	HB	5'11"	205	26		
Charlie Smith	HB	6'1"	205	28		12
Mark van Eeghen	FB-HB	6'1"	215	22		
Warren Bankston	FB	6'4"	235	27		
Marv Hubbard	FB	6'1"	225	28		24
Pete Banaszak	HB-FB	5'11"	210	30		30
Fred Biletnikoff	WR	6'1"	190	31		42
Morris Bradshaw	WR	6'	198	21		
Cliff Branch	WR	5'11"	170	26		78
Frank Pitts	WR	6'2"	200	30		
Mike Siani	WR	6'2"	195	24		6
Dave Casper	TE	6'4"	250	22		18
Bob Moore	TE	6'3"	220	25		12
Ray Guy	K	6'3"	190	24		
George Jakowenko	K	5'9"	170	26		

DENVER BRONCOS 7-6-1 John Ralston

Scores of Each Game		
10	LOS ANGELES	17
35	PITTSBURGH (OT)	35
3	Washington	30
17	Kansas City	14
33	NEW ORLEANS	17
27	SAN DIEGO	7
21	Cleveland	23
17	OAKLAND	28
17	Baltimore	6
34	KANSAS CITY	42
20	Oakland	17
31	Detroit	27
37	HOUSTON	14
0	San Diego	17

Use Name	Pos.	Hgt	Wgt	Age	Int	Pts
Mike Current	OT	6'4"	270	28		
Claudie Minor	OT	6'4"	280	23		
Marv Montgomery	OT	6'6"	255	26		
LeFrancis Arnold	OG	6'3"	245	21		
Paul Howard	OG	6'3"	260	23		
Tommy Lyons	OG	6'2"	230	26		
Mike Schnitker	OG	6'3"	245	27		
Larron Jackson	OT-OG	6'3"	260	25		
Bobby Maples	C	6'3"	250	31		
Lyle Alzado	DE	6'3"	265	25		
Barney Chavous	DE	6'3"	252	23		
Steve Coleman	DE	6'4"	252	23		
John Grant	DE	6'3"	235	24		
Ed Smith	DE	6'5"	240	24	1	
Pete Duranko	DT	6'2"	250	30		
Dan Goich	DT	6'4"	250	30		
Bob Kampa (from BUF)	DT	6'4"	245	23		
Paul Smith	DT	6'3"	256	29		
Ken Criter	LB	5'11"	223	27		
Randy Gradishar	LB	6'3"	233	22		
Tom Jackson	LB	5'11"	220	23	1	
Bill Laskey	LB	6'2"	230	31	1	
Ray May	LB	6'1"	230	29	2	
Jim O'Malley	LB	6'1"	230	23		
Joe Rizzo	LB	6'1"	220	23		
Mike Simone	LB	6'	210	24		
Charlie Greer	DB	6'	205	28	1	
Lonnie Hepburn	DB	5'11"	180	25		
Calvin Jones	DB	5'7"	170	23	5	
John Pitts	DB	6'4"	218	29	1	
John Rowser	DB	6'1"	190	30	4	
Bill Thompson	DB	6'1"	200	27	5	6
Maurice Tyler	DB	6'	188	24	1	
John Hufnagel	QB	6'1"	194	23		
Charley Johnson	QB	6'	200	37		
Steve Ramsey	QB	6'2"	210	26		
Otis Armstrong	HB	5'10"	196	23		72
Floyd Little	HB	5'10"	196	32		6
Oliver Ross	HB	6'	210	24		
Jon Keyworth	FB	6'3"	230	23		60
Fran Lynch	HB-FB	6'1"	205	28		
Haven Moses	WR	6'3"	208	28		12
Jerry Simmons	WR	6'1"	190	31		12
Otto Stowe	WR	6'2"	188	25		6
Bill Van Heusen	WR	6'1"	200	28		24
Boyd Brown	TE	6'4"	216	22		
Bill Masters	TE	6'5"	240	30		
Riley Odoms	TE	6'4"	230	24		36
Jim Turner	K	6'2"	205	33		68

Bobby Anderson – Broken Ankle

KANSAS CITY CHIEFS 5-9-0 Hank Stram

Scores of Each Game		
24	N.Y. JETS	16
7	Oakland	27
7	Houston	17
14	DENVER	17
24	PITTSBURGH	34
3	Miami	9
24	San Diego	14
21	N.Y. GIANTS	33
7	SAN DIEGO	14
42	Denver	34
6	Cincinnati	33
17	St. Louis	13
6	OAKLAND	7
15	MINNESOTA	35

Use Name	Pos.	Hgt	Wgt	Age	Int	Pts
Tom Drougas (from DEN)	OT	6'4"	267	24		
Charlie Getty	OT	6'4"	260	22		
Dave Hill	OT	6'5"	260	33		
Jim Nicholson	OT	6'6"	260	24		
Francis Peay	OT	6'5"	250	30		
Wayne Walton	OG-OT	6'5"	255	25		
Ed Budde	OG	6'5"	265	33		
Tom Condon	OG	6'3"	240	21		
George Daney	OG	6'3"	240	27		
Tom Humphrey	C	6'6"	260	24		
Jack Rudnay	C	6'3"	240	26		
Bob Briggs	DE	6'4"	258	29		
Fred DeBernardi	DE	6'6"	250	25		
Marv Upshaw	DE	6'3"	260	27	1	6
Wilbur Young	DE	6'6"	285	25	1	6
Buck Buchanan	DT	6'7"	270	34		
Tom Keating	DT	6'3"	247	31		
John Matuszak	DT	6'8"	275	23		
Bobby Bell	LB	6'4"	228	34	1	6
Tom Graham (from DEN)	LB	6'2"	235	24		
Willie Lanier	LB	6'1"	245	29	2	2
Jim Lynch	LB	6'1"	235	29		
Al Palewicz	LB	6'1"	215	24		
Bob Thornbladh	LB	6'1"	220	22		
Clyde Werner	LB	6'4"	230	26	1	
Nate Allen	DB	5'10"	170	26	1	
Doug Jones	DB	6'2"	202	24	1	
Jim Kearney	DB	6'2"	206	31		
Jim Marsalis	DB	5'11"	194	28		
Willie Osley	DB	6'	195	24		
Kerry Reardon	DB	5'11"	180	25	4	
Mike Sensibaugh	DB	5'11"	192	25	4	
Emmitt Thomas	DB	6'2"	192	31	12	12
Dean Carlson	QB	6'3"	210	24		
Len Dawson	QB	6'	190	40		
David Jaynes	QB	6'2"	212	22		
Mike Livingston	QB	6'3"	212	28		
Woody Green	HB	6'1"	205	23		24
Cleo Miller	HB	5'11"	202	21		
Donnie Joe Morris	HB	5'11"	195	24		
Ed Podolak	HB	6'1"	205	27		18
Willie Ellison	FB-HB	6'1"	210	29		12
Wendell Hayes	FB	6'2"	220	33		12
Bill Thomas	FB	6'2"	225	24		
Jeff Kinney	HB-FB	6'2"	215	24		6
Larry Brunson	WR	5'11"	180	25		12
Andy Hamilton	WR	6'3"	190	24		
Barry Pearson	WR	5'11"	185	24		6
Otis Taylor	WR	6'2"	215	31		12
Elmo Wright	WR	6'	190	25		12
John Strada	TE	6'3"	230	22		
Morris Stroud	TE	6'10"	255	28		12
Jan Stenerud	K	6'2"	187	31		75
Jerrel Wilson	K	6'4"	222	32		

Gary Butler – Knee Injury
John Lohmeyer – Injury

SAN DIEGO CHARGERS 5-9-0 Tommy Prothro

Scores of Each Game		
14	Houston	21
20	Cincinnati	17
21	MIAMI	28
7	PHILADELPHIA	13
10	Oakland	14
7	Denver	27
14	KANSAS CITY	24
36	CLEVELAND	25
14	Kansas City	7
10	OAKLAND	17
0	Green Bay	34
14	N.Y. Jets	27
28	CHICAGO	21
17	DENVER	0

Use Name	Pos.	Hgt	Wgt	Age	Int	Pts
Terry Owens	OT	6'6"	260	30		
Brian Vertefeuille	OT	6'3"	252	23		
Russ Washington	OT	6'6"	290	27		
Mark Markovich	OG	6'5"	256	21		
Doug Wilkerson	OG	6'2"	256	27		
Ira Gordon	OT-OG	6'3"	265	26		
Jay Douglas	C	6'6"	260	23		
Carl Mauck	C	6'3"	243	27		
Coy Bacon	DE	6'4"	270	32		
Raymond Baylor	DE	6'5"	263	27		
Blenda Gay	DE	6'5"	250	24		6
Pete Lazetich	DE	6'3"	245	24		
Dave Tipton	DE	6'6"	240	25		
Bon Boatwright	DT	6'5"	262	22		
Bob Brown	DT	6'5"	290	34		
Dave Rowe	DT	6'6"	265	29		
John Teerlinck	DT	6'5"	245	23		
Charles Anthony	LB	6'1"	230	22	1	
Fred Forsberg	LB	6'1"	225	30		
Carl Gersbach	LB	6'1"	230	27	1	
Don Goode	LB	6'2"	234	23		
Mike Lee	LB	6'	232	23		
Chip Myrtle	LB	6'2"	225	29		
Floyd Rice	LB	6'3"	223	25	3	
Mel Rogers	LB	6'2"	233	27		
Jeff Staggs	LB	6'2"	240	30		
Joe Beauchamp	DB	6'	188	30	1	
Reggie Berry	DB	6'	185	25		
Danny Colbert	DB	5'11"	167	23		
Lenny Dunlap	DB	6'1"	198	25		
Chris Fletcher	DB	5'11"	182	25	4	
George Hoey	DB	5'10"	180	27	1	
Bob Howard	DB	6'1"	177	29	3	
Sam Williams	DB	6'2"	192	22	1	
Dan Fouts	QB	6'3"	193	23		6
Jesse Freitas	QB	6'1"	203	22		
Don Horn	QB	6'2"	195	29		
Glen Bonner	HB	6'2"	202	22		24
Bob Thomas	HB	5'10"	202	25		
Tommy Thompson	HB	6'1"	205	23		
Don Woods	HB	6'1"	210	23		60
Cid Edwards	FB	6'2"	230	30		
Bo Matthews	FB	6'4"	230	22		24
Jim Beirne	WR	6'2"	206	27		
Harrison Davis	WR	6'4"	220	22		12
Gary Garrison	WR	6'1"	195	30		30
Dick Gordon	WR	5'11"	190	29		
Jerry LeVias	WR	5'10"	177	27		
Dave Grannell	TE	6'4"	230	22		
Gary Parris	TE	6'2"	226	24		
Wayne Stewart	TE	6'7"	230	27		6
Dennis Partee	K	6'2"	209	28		29
Ray Wersching	K	5'11"	210	24		15

Clint Jones – Injury
Reece Morrison – Injury

OAKLAND RAIDERS

RUSHING

Last Name	No.	Yds	Avg	TD
Hubbard	188	865	4.6	4
Davis	129	554	4.3	2
Banaszak	80	272	3.4	5
Hart	51	268	5.3	2
C. Smith	64	194	3.0	1
van Eeghen	28	139	5.0	0
L. Lawrence	4	39	9.8	0
Hudson	1	12	12.0	0
Bankston	1	6	6.0	0
Stabler	12	−2	−0.2	1
Lamonica	2	−3	−1.5	0
Pitts	1	−10	−10.0	0

RECEIVING

Last Name	No.	Yds	Avg	TD
Branch	60	1092	18	13
Biletnikoff	42	593	14	7
Moore	30	356	12	2
Davis	11	145	13	1
Hubbard	11	95	9	0
Banaszak	9	64	7	0
C. Smith	8	100	13	1
van Eeghen	4	33	8	0
Casper	4	26	7	3
Siani	3	30	10	1
Pitts	3	23	8	0
Hart	1	4	4	0

PUNT RETURNS

Last Name	No.	Yds	Avg	TD
R. Smith	41	486	12	0
Atkinson	4	31	8	0

KICKOFF RETURNS

Last Name	No.	Yds	Avg	TD
Hart	18	466	26	0
R. Smith	19	420	22	0
Banaszak	8	137	17	0
Davis	3	107	36	0
Bankston	1	10	10	0
Bradshaw	1	0	0	0

PASSING – PUNTING – KICKING

PASSING	Att	Comp	%	Yds	Yd/Att	TD	Int–%	RK
Stabler	310	178	57	2469	8.0	26	12– 4	2
L. Lawrence	11	4	36	29	2.6	0	1– 9	
Lamonica	9	3	33	35	3.9	1	4– 44	
Blanda	4	1	25	28	7.0	1	0– 0	
Guy	1	0	0	0	0.0	0	0–100	

PUNTING	No	Avg
Guy	74	42.2

KICKING	XP	Att	%	FG	Att	%
Blanda	44	46	96	11	17	65

DENVER BRONCOS

RUSHING

Last Name	No.	Yds	Avg	TD
Armstrong	263	1407	5.3	9
Keyworth	81	374	4.6	10
Little	117	312	2.7	1
Odoms	4	25	6.3	0
Hufnagel	2	22	11.0	0
Moses	2	16	8.0	0
Ross	3	8	2.7	0
Stowe	1	1	1.0	0
Van Heusen	1	−1	−1.0	0
Ramsey	5	−2	−0.4	0
Lynch	3	−2	−0.7	0
Johnson	4	−3	−0.7	0

RECEIVING

Last Name	No.	Yds	Avg	TD
Odoms	42	639	15	6
Armstrong	38	405	11	3
Moses	34	559	16	2
Little	29	344	12	0
Van Heusen	16	421	26	4
Keyworth	12	109	9	0
Simmons	10	161	16	2
Stowe	2	9	5	1
Ross	1	13	13	0

PUNT RETURNS

Last Name	No.	Yds	Avg	TD
Thompson	26	350	14	0
Greer	13	90	7	0
Little	4	34	9	0

KICKOFF RETURNS

Last Name	No.	Yds	Avg	TD
Armstrong	16	386	24	0
Thompson	13	325	25	0
Little	8	171	21	0
Ross	7	117	17	0
Keyworth	4	85	21	0
Brown	3	56	19	0
Criter	3	48	16	0

PASSING – PUNTING – KICKING

PASSING	Att	Comp	%	Yds	Yd/Att	TD	Int–%	RK
Johnson	244	136	56	1969	8.1	13	9– 4	3
Ramsey	74	41	55	580	7.8	5	7–10	
Hufnagel	10	6	60	70	7.0	0	1–10	
Van Heusen	1	1	100	41	41.0	0	0– 0	

PUNTING	No	Avg
Van Heusen	75	40.3

KICKING	XP	Att	%	FG	Att	%
Turner	35	38	92	11	21	52

KANSAS CITY CHIEFS

RUSHING

Last Name	No.	Yds	Avg	TD
Green	135	509	3.8	3
Podolak	101	386	3.8	2
Kinney	63	249	4.0	0
Hayes	57	206	3.6	2
Miller	40	186	4.7	0
Ellison	37	114	3.1	2
Livingston	9	28	3.1	0
Dawson	11	28	2.5	0
Wright	3	26	8.7	1
Carlson	2	17	8.5	0
Taylor	1	6	6.0	0
Pearson	1	1	1.0	0
Jaynes	1	0	0.0	0
B. Thomas	3	−3	−1.0	0
Brunson	5	−33	−6.6	0

RECEIVING

Last Name	No.	Yds	Avg	TD
Podolak	43	306	7	1
Pearson	27	387	14	1
Green	26	247	10	1
Taylor	24	375	16	2
Brunson	22	374	17	2
Kinney	18	105	6	1
Miller	14	149	11	0
Wright	13	209	16	1
Stroud	12	141	12	2
Ellison	5	64	13	0
Hayes	4	23	6	0
Hamilton	2	25	13	0
Strada	1	16	16	0

PUNT RETURNS

Last Name	No.	Yds	Avg	TD
Podolak	15	134	9	0
Brunson	19	111	6	0
Reardon	4	30	8	0
Green	5	21	4	0
Morris	1	0	0	0

KICKOFF RETURNS

Last Name	No.	Yds	Avg	TD
B. Thomas	25	571	23	0
Miller	14	310	22	0
Brunson	12	280	23	0
Morris	1	17	17	0
Green	1	16	16	0
Keating	1	10	10	0
Humphrey	1	7	7	0
Jones	1	0	0	0

PASSING – PUNTING – KICKING

PASSING	Att	Comp	%	Yds	Yd/Att	TD	Int–%	RK
Dawson	235	138	59	1573	6.7	7	13– 6	8
Livingston	141	66	47	732	5.2	4	10– 7	16
Carlson	15	7	47	116	7.7	0	1– 7	
Jaynes	2	0	0	0	0.0	0	1–50	
Wilson	2	0	0	0	0.0	0	0– 0	

PUNTING	No	Avg
Wilson	83	41.7

KICKING	XP	Att	%	FG	Att	%
Stenerud	24	26	92	17	24	71

SAN DIEGO CHARGERS

RUSHING

Last Name	No.	Yds	Avg	TD
Woods	227	1162	5.1	7
Matthews	95	328	3.5	4
Edwards	65	261	4.0	0
Bonner	66	199	3.0	3
Fouts	19	63	3.3	1
Thomas	21	56	2.7	0
D. Gordon	1	25	25.0	0
Freitas	6	16	2.7	0
Thompson	6	8	1.3	0
Davis	2	−7	−3.5	0

RECEIVING

Last Name	No.	Yds	Avg	TD
Garrison	41	785	19	5
Woods	26	349	13	3
Stewart	19	283	15	1
Davis	18	432	24	2
Edwards	13	102	8	0
Matthews	12	90	8	0
Bonner	11	101	9	1
LeVias	9	105	12	0
Beirne	7	121	17	0
Grannell	3	51	17	0
Parris	3	36	12	0
D. Gordon	2	15	8	0
Thomas	1	9	9	0

PUNT RETURNS

Last Name	No.	Yds	Avg	TD
Colbert	15	128	9	0
LeVias	5	41	8	0
D. Gordon	8	39	5	0
Hoey	4	38	10	0
Davis	4	34	9	0
Beirne	1	7	7	0

KICKOFF RETURNS

Last Name	No.	Yds	Avg	TD
D. Gordon	14	354	25	0
Thompson	12	242	20	0
Colbert	10	215	22	0
LeVias	6	116	19	0
Hoey	3	73	24	0
Woods	3	61	20	0
Thomas	2	32	16	0
Parris	3	29	10	0
Dunlap	1	19	19	0
Stewart	1	1	1	0

PASSING – PUNTING – KICKING

PASSING	Att	Comp	%	Yds	Yd/Att	TD	Int–%	RK
Fouts	237	115	49	1732	7.3	8	13– 6	11
Freitas	109	49	45	719	6.6	3	8– 7	
Woods	3	1	33	28	9.3	1	1–33	

PUNTING	No	Avg
Partee	76	40.0

KICKING	XP	Att	%	FG	Att	%
Partee	26	28	93	1	5	20
Wersching	0	0	—	5	11	45

1974 Championship Games

NFC CHAMPIONSHIP GAME

December 29, at Minnesota
(Attendance 47,404)

Six Inches Short of Glory

The Vikings were looking for a third trip to the Super Bowl after beating the Cardinals 30–14 in the opening round of the playoffs. The Rams, on the other hand, were looking for their first Super Bowl ticket after beating the Redskins 19–10 for their first playoff victory since 1952. Both clubs rode strong defenses into this title match, but the Vikings had come through the pressure of post-season play before and for that reason were touted as the favorites in this game. Although both defensive units played up to championship standards, the offensive units looked tight under the pressure. Turnovers made the contest a sloppy affair, with the Vikings losing the ball three times and the Rams five times. Neither team could move the ball in the first period, with the Viking defense showing right from the start that it would hold Lawrence McCutcheon, the NFC's leading rusher, to way below his average yardage. The Vikings scored in the second period on a Fran Tarkenton-to-Jim Lash pass, and a David Ray field goal made the score 7–3 in favor of Minnesota at halftime. Minnesota's Mike Eischeid placed a coffin-corner punt out of bounds on the Los Angeles one-yard line early in the third period, and the Rams started a long trek upfield. Five plays later, quarterback James Harris hit Harold Jackson with a long pass that carried the ball 73 yards to the Minnesota 2-yard line, with a clutch tackle by safety Jeff Wright preventing a touchdown. John Cappelletti carried the ball to the six-inch line on the next play, but that was as close as the Rams would come. Guard Tom Mack was called for illegal motion before the next play, and the ball was moved back to around the five yard line. Harris ran for three yards on the next play, but then his pass into the end zone for tight end Pat Curran was tipped away by cornerback Jackie Wallace and picked off by linebacker Wally Hilgenberg. After their 99-yard drive had gone for naught, the Rams never again came close to taking the lead. The Vikings marched 80 yards in the fourth period, with Dave Osborn scoring from the one-yard line on a fourth-down play. A long touchdown pass from Harris to Jackson brought the Rams back to 14–10 late in the game, but the Viking pass rush crumpled the Rams' late attempts to score again.

SCORING

MINNESOTA	0	7	0	7–14
LOS ANGELES	0	3	0	7–10

Second Quarter	Minn.	Lash, 29 yard pass from Tarkenton PAT–Cox (kick)
	L.A.	Ray, 27 yard field goal
Fourth Quarter	Minn.	Osborn, 1 yard rush PAT–Cox (kick)
	L.A.	Jackson, 44 yard pass from Harris PAT–Ray (kick)

TEAM STATISTICS

MINN.		L.A.
18	First Downs–Total	15
9	First Downs–Rushing	5
7	First Downs–Passing	10
2	First Downs–Penalty	0
5	Fumbles–Number	3
2	Fumbles–Lost Ball	3
2	Penalties–Number	7
20	Yards Penalized	70
0	Missed Field Goals	0
69	Offensive Plays	58
269	Net Yards	340
3.9	Average Gain	5.9
3	Giveaways	5
5	Takeaways	3
+2	Difference	–2

INDIVIDUAL STATISTICS

MINNESOTA	No	Yds	Avg.	LOS ANGELES	No	Yds	Avg.
RUSHING							
Foreman	22	80	3.6	Bertelsen	14	65	4.6
Osborn	20	76	3.8	McCutcheon	12	32	2.7
Tarkenton	4	5	1.2	Harris	3	17	5.7
Marinaro	1	3	3.0	Cappelletti	3	8	2.7
	47	164	3.5	Baker	1	–1	–1.0
					33	121	3.7
RECEIVING							
Voigt	4	43	10.8	Bertelsen	5	53	10.6
Lash	2	40	20.0	Jackson	3	139	46.3
Gilliam	2	33	16.5	McCutcheon	2	22	11.0
Marinaro	1	6	6.0	Snow	1	19	19.0
Osborn	1	1	1.0	Klein	1	10	10.0
	10	123	12.3	Cappelletti	1	5	5.0
					13	248	19.1
PUNTING							
Eischeid	6		39.2	Burke	5		43.8
PUNT RETURNS							
McCullum	3	20	6.7	Bryant	3	18	6.0
N. Wright	1	3	3.0	Scribner	1	1	1.0
	4	23	5.6	Bertelsen	1	0	0.0
					5	19	3.8
KICKOFF RETURNS							
McClanahan	2	55	27.5	Bryant	3	57	19.0
McCullum	1	23	23.0				
	3	78	26.0				
INTERCEPTION RETURNS							
Poltl	1	16	16.0	Stukes	1	0	0.0
Hilgenberg	1	0	0.0				
	2	16	8.0				

PASSING

	Att.	Comp.	Comp. Pct.	Yds.	Int.	Yds/ Att.	Yds/ Comp.	Yards Lost Tackled
MINNESOTA								
Tarkenton	20	10	50.0	123	1	6.2	12.3	2–18
LOS ANGELES								
Harris	23	13	56.5	248	2	10.8	19.1	2–29

AFC CHAMPIONSHIP GAME

December 29, at Oakland
(Attendance 53,515)

Near, but Not Far Enough

The Raiders were the popular choice to go on to the Super Bowl, after their fine regular season and then their stirring upset of the Miami Dolphins December 21, taking a 28–26 victory with a Ken Stabler-to-Clarence Davis touchdown pass with 26 seconds left in the game. With the Dolphin dynasty ended, the Raiders seemed the logical heir apparent, but the Steelers, fresh from a 32–14 dissection of Buffalo in the opening playoff round, disputed this line of succession. The key to the game was the Steeler defense, which completely nullified the Raider offense that had led the NFL in points scored. The Raiders found some room to move in the air, but the ground lanes were totally blocked off by the Pittsburgh linemen and linebackers. Conversely, the Oakland defense shut off the Pittsburgh passing game for most of the afternoon, but Steeler runners Franco Harris and Rocky Bleier were able to steadily eat up yardage behind the fine blocking of their offensive line. The Raiders scored in the opening period with George Blanda hitting a 40-yard field goal. Roy Gerela drilled one home from 23 yards in the second period to send the clubs off at halftime tied at 3–3. The Raiders took a 10–3 lead in the third quarter when Stabler whipped a 38-yard touchdown pass to Cliff Branch, one of the swift receiver's nine receptions of the day. The Oakland defense shut the Steelers out in the third period, and the Raiders seemed on the way to their second Super Bowl appearance. The opportunistic Steelers, however, were waiting to pounce on any Oakland errors. The Steelers knotted the game at 10–10 on Franco Harris's eight-yard touchdown carry, and then the defensive unit took over. Pittsburgh linebacker Jack Ham picked off a Stabler pass on the Oakland 33-yard line and carried it back all the way down to the nine yard line. Terry Bradshaw soon capitalized on this break by tossing a six-yard scoring pass to Lynn Swann, and now the Steelers were in charge and the Raiders forced to play "catch up" football. They closed the gap to 17–13 on a Blanda field goal, but Steeler rookie Jack Lambert intercepted a Stabler pass which Franco Harris soon converted into a 22-yard touchdown run, making the final score 24–13.

The frustration for Oakland was neatly summed up by John Madden, the head coach, when he said after the game, "It's really hard to come this far and lose."

SCORING

OAKLAND	3	0	7	3–13
PITTSBURGH	0	3	0	21–24

First Quarter	Oak.	Blanda, 40 yard field goal
Second Quarter	Pitt.	Gerela, 23 yard field goal
Third Quarter	Oak.	Branch, 38 yard pass from Stabler PAT–Blanda (kick)
Fourth Quarter	Pitt.	Harris, 8 yard rush PAT–Gerela (kick)
	Pitt.	Swann, 6 yard pass from Bradshaw PAT–Gerela (kick)
	Oak.	Blanda, 24 yard field goal
	Pitt.	Harris, 21 yard rush PAT–Gerela (kick)

TEAM STATISTICS

OAK.		PITT.
15	First Downs–Total	20
0	First Downs–Rushing	11
13	First Downs–Passing	7
2	First Downs–Penalty	2
0	Fumbles–Number	3
0	Fumbles–Lost Ball	2
5	Penalties–Number	4
60	Yards Penalized	30
1	Missed Field Goals	1
59	Offensive Plays	68
278	Net Yards	305
4.7	Average Gain	4.5
3	Giveaways	3
3	Takeaways	3
0	Difference	0

INDIVIDUAL STATISTICS

OAKLAND	No	Yds	Avg.	PITTSBURGH	No	Yds	Avg.
RUSHING							
C. Davis	10	16	1.6	Harris	29	111	3.8
Banaszak	3	7	2.3	Bleier	18	98	5.4
Hubbard	7	6	0.9	Bradshaw	3	15	5.0
Stabler	1	0	0.0		50	224	4.5
	21	29	1.4				
RECEIVING							
Branch	9	186	20.7	L. Brown	2	37	18.5
Moore	4	32	8.0	Bleier	2	25	12.5
Biletnikoff	3	45	15.0	Swann	2	17	8.5
C. Davis	2	8	4.0	Stallworth	2	16	8.0
Banaszak	1	0	0.0		8	95	11.9
	19	271	4.3				
PUNTING							
Guy	5		43.4	Walden	4		41.0
PUNT RETURNS							
none				Swann	3	30	10.0
				Edwards	1	15	15.0
					4	45	11.3
KICKOFF RETURNS							
Hart	3	63	21.0	S. Davis	3	76	25.3
R. Smith	2	42	21.0	Pearson	1	28	28.0
	5	105	21.0		4	104	26.0
INTERCEPTION RETURNS							
Wilson	1	37	37.0	Ham	2	19	9.5
				Thomas	1	37	37.0
					3	56	18.7

PASSING

	Att.	Comp.	Comp. Pct.	Yds.	Int.	Yds/ Att.	Yds/ Comp.	Yards Lost Tackled
OAKLAND								
Stabler	36	19	52.8	271	3	7.5	14.3	2–22
PITTSBURGH								
Bradshaw	17	8	47.1	95	1	5.6	11.9	1–14

SUPER BOWL IX

January 12, at New Orleans
(Attendance 79,065)

Rooney's 42-Year Reward

This year's Super Bowl matchups included the Minnesota Vikings, twice losers of the NFL's big meal ticket, and the Pittsburgh Steelers, who were enjoying their first trip to the post season event. For the Vikings, already branded as a club unable to win the big one, the game was a matter of professional pride. The Steelers motivation came from the fact that they had finally pocketed their first conference title since 1933, the year the franchise began.

Many of the past Super Bowls have been conservative and relatively dull games, Super Bowl IX was no exception as both teams continued the same offensive pattern of trying to avoid costly mistakes rather than trying to break the game open. In fact, the only score of the first half was a safety, with the Steelers getting two points when Viking quarterback Fran Tarkenton botched a pitch-out deep in his own territory and had to fall on the ball in the end zone. The close 2–0 halftime score belied a key difference in the teams; the Pittsburgh defense, led by Joe Greene, had successfully shut down Viking running star Chuck Foreman, while the Steeler offensive line was opening up constant holes in the Viking front four to allow Franco Harris to go rushing through.

The break that the Steelers were waiting for came on the opening kickoff of the second half, when Minnesota's Bill Brown fumbled the ball and Pittsburgh's Marv Kellum recovered it on the Viking 30-yard line. Harris followed his offensive line the rest of the way, covering 24 yards in one carry and finally going over for the touchdown on a nine-yard sweep around left end. The 9–0 Steeler lead held up through the third period, but the Vikings came back with a strong challenge in the final period. A pass interference call on Mike Wagner gave the Vikes the ball on the Steeler five-yard line, but Foreman fumbled on the next play and Greene recovered for Pittsburgh. Four plays later. Matt Blair blocked Bobby Walden's punt, with Terry Brown falling on it in the end zone for a Viking touchdown. Fred Cox missed the extra point, and the Steeler defense steadfastly refused to let the Vikes close enough to go for the tying field goal. A 65-yard Pittsburgh drive culminating in a four-yard scoring pass from Terry Bradshaw to Larry Brown iced the game away with 3:31 left.

By the time the final gun sounded the Vikings had their third loss in three attempts, and the Steelers had a host of triumphs which included Franco Harris and his record-setting 158 yards rushing and the happiest owner in pro football in Art Rooney who, after 42 frustrating years, finally claimed his dream—a pro football championship.

LINEUP

PITTSBURGH		MINNESOTA
	OFFENSE	
Lewis	WR	Lash
Kolb	LT	Goodrum
Clack	LG	Maurer
Mansfield	C	Tingelhoff
Mullins	RG	White
Gravelle	RT	Yary
L. Brown	TE	Voigt
Shanklin	WR	Gilliam
Bradshaw	QB	Tarkenton
Bleier	RB	Foreman
Harris	RB	Osborn
	DEFENSE	
Greenwood	LE	Eller
Greene	LT	Sutherland
Holmes	RT	Page
White	RE	Marshall
Ham	LLB	Winston
Lambert	MLB	Siemon
Russell	RLB	Hilgenberg
Thomas	LCB	N. Wright
Blount	RCB	Wallace
Wagner	LS	J. Wright
Edwards	RS	Krause

SUBSTITUTES

PITTSBURGH		
	OFFENSE	
Sam Davis		McMakin
Steve Davis		Pearson
Druschel		Reaves
Garrett		Swann
Grossman		Stallworth
Harrison		Webster
	DEFENSE	
Allen		Furness
Bradley		Kellum
Conn		Shell
C. Davis		Toews
	KICKERS	
Gerela		Walden

MINNESOTA		
	OFFENSE	
Alderman		Marinaro
Anderson		McClanahan
B. Brown		McCullum
Craig		Reed
Kingsriter		Sunde
Lawson		
	DEFENSE	
Blair		Martin
T. Brown		McNeill
Larsen		Poltl
Lurtsema		
	KICKERS	
Cox		Eischeid

SCORING

PITTSBURGH	0	2	7	7–16
MINNESOTA	0	0	0	6– 6

Second Quarter		
Pitt.	Safety – Tarkenton tackled in end zone.	7:49
Third Quarter		
Pitt.	Harris, 12 yard rush PAT – Gerela (kick	1:35
Fourth Quarter		
Minn.	T. Brown, Recovered blocked punt in end zone. Kick failed	4:27
Pitt.	L. Brown, 4 yard pass from Bradshaw PAT – Gerela (kick)	11:29

TEAM STATISTICS

PITT.		MINN.
17	First Downs-Total	9
11	First Downs-Rushing	2
5	First Downs-Passing	5
1	First Downs-Penalty	2
4	Fumbles-Number	3
2	Fumbles-Lost Ball	2
8	Penalties-Number	4
122	Yards Penalized	18
1	Missed Field Goals	1
73	Offensive Plays	47
333	Net Yards	119
4.6	Average Gain	2.5
2	Giveaways	5
5	Takeaways	2
+3	Difference	–3

INDIVIDUAL STATISTICS

PITTSBURGH	No.	Yds.	Avg.	MINNESOTA	No.	Yds.	Avg.
RUSHING							
Harris	34	158	4.6	Foreman	12	18	1.5
Bleier	17	65	3.8	Tarkenton	1	0	0.0
Bradshaw	5	33	6.6	Osborn	8	–1	–0.1
Swann	1	–7	–7.0		21	17	0.8
	57	249	4.4				
RECEIVING							
T. Brown	3	40	16.3	Foreman	5	50	10.0
Stallworth	3	24	8.0	Voigt	2	31	15.5
Bleier	2	11	5.5	Osborn	2	7	3.5
Lewis	1	12	12.0	Gilliam	1	16	16.0
	9	96	10.7	Reed	1	–2	–2.0
					11	102	9.3
PUNTING							
Walden	7		34.7	Eischeid	6		37.2
PUNT RETURNS							
Swann	3	34	11.3	McCullum	3	11	3.7
Edwards	2	2	1.0	N. Wright	1	1	1.0
	5	36	7.2		4	12	3.0
KICKOFF RETURNS							
Harrison	2	17	8.5	McCullum	1	26	26.0
Pearson	1	15	15.0	McClanahan	1	22	22.0
	3	32	10.7	B. Brown	1	2	2.0
					3	50	16.7
INTERCEPTION RETURNS							
Wagner	1	26	26.0	none			
Blount	1	10	10.0				
Greene	1	10	10.0				
	3	46	15.3				

PASSING

PITTSBURGH	Att.	Comp.	Comp. Pct.	Yds.	Int.	Yds/ Att.	Yds/ Comp.	Yards Lost Tackled
Bradshaw	14	9	64.3	96	0	6.9	10.7	2–12
MINNESOTA								
Tarkenton	26	11	42.3	102	3	3.9	9.3	0– 0

1975 N.F.C. Striking Toward Freedom

The N.F.L. Players Association had struck during training camp in 1974 over the inability to reach agreement with the club owners on a contract, eventually going back to work without a settlement. In the training camps of 1975, the contract negotiations still dragged on, with Players Association president Ed Garvey unable to maintain a united front among his players. With the Rozelle Rule concerning free agent status the main bone of contention, the New England Patriots took the lead by striking on September 13, the Saturday before their final exhibition game. The Pats sat that game out, and by Wednesday, the Redskins, Jets, Giants, and Lions had joined them in striking. A truce was arranged on Thursday, September 18, so that the regular season got under way without a delay on Sunday. Only after the season did the players' fight to do away with the Rozelle Rule, which limited their freedom of movement in playing out their option, come to fruit. In the winter, federal judge Earl R. Larson ruled that the Rozelle Rule was an illegal monopolistic practice by the N.F.L. The lawyers' bills piled up for the league into 1976, as the owners appealed Larson's ruling and successfully beat back a legal challenge to the college and expansion drafts to be held for the upcoming season.

EASTERN DIVISION

St. Louis Cardinals—The Cards started the season in lacklustre form, with losses to the Cowboys and Redskins among their first four decisions. But quarterback Jim Hart got his explosive offense rolling thereafter and won nine of the remaining ten games on the schedule to recapture first place in the East. The Cards took the top spot directly, beating both the Redskins and Cowboys down the stretch. The Cards trailed the Redskins 17-10 with 20 seconds remaining in the game on November 16 when Hart threw a pass to Mel Gray in the end zone. Gray dropped the ball when hit, but after conferring on the field for three minutes amidst pressure from both teams and the fans, the officials ruled that he had held on to it just long enough to make it a legal catch and a touchdown. Jim Bakken kicked the extra point to send the game into overtime, and he won it 20-17 with a field goal seven minutes into the extra period.

Dallas Cowboys—This was to be a rebuilding year for the Cowboys. After all, they had not made the playoffs last season, and from that squad, Calvin Hill had jumped to the W.F.L. and Bob Lilly, Walt Garrison, and Cornell Green had retired. But the expert observers did not take note of the depth on the Dallas roster and the marvelous collection of rookies that reported to the team. With holdover stars like Roger Staubach and Drew Pearson, a blossoming star like Robert Newhouse, and a serviceable pickup in veteran Preston Pearson, the offense kept rolling along in fine fashion, even spicing things up with an occasional shift into the shotgun formation. Oldsters like Mel Renfro, Lee Roy Jordan, and Jethro Pugh anchored the defense, but youngsters like Too Tall Jones and Harvey Martin provided much of the thunder. The Cowboys got off to a quick start, hit a midseason slump, and finished strong to capture a wildcard spot in the playoffs.

Washington Redskins—The Redskin defensive unit had the same tough veteran look of recent years, but the offense took on a more youthful appearance. Sonny Jurgensen was retired, young Frank Grant took over a wide receiver spot, and rookie Mike Thomas revitalized the running attack with 919 yards. With Jurgensen gone, Billy Kilmer handled almost all the quarterbacking and came through with high grades despite some injury problems. When the Skins won six of their first eight games, including triumphs over St. Louis and Dallas, a playoff berth seemed assured. But losses to St. Louis and Oakland cast a shadow over those hopes, and with the wildcard spot on the line on December 13, the Skins were crushed by the Cowboys 31-10. The dispirited club dropped the season's finale to the Eagles and went home, out of the playoffs for the first time in George Allen's reign. One highpoint of the disappointing campaign was Charley Taylor's moving into first place in the all-time list of pass receivers, surpassing Don Maynard's old mark.

New York Giants—Moving into Shea Stadium as temporary boarders with the Jets, the Giants began their second season under Bill Arnsbarger with a promising 23-14 victory over the Eagles. But the club lapsed back into mediocrity, losing three games, upsetting Buffalo 17-14, and then losing six of the next seven, including a 40-14 humiliation to the Green Bay Packers. The offense lost much of its zip at midseason, and the defense suffered because of John Mendenhall's bad ankle.

Philadelphia Eagles—The Eagles had no draft picks in the first six rounds of the college draft, and with no new help arriving, last year's late-season slump continued into this campaign. The team had top-notch performers at several positions, with tight end Charley Young and middle linebacker Bill Bergey among the very best at their positions. A weak pass rush and other soft spots, however, sent the Eagles to the bottom of the division. They did win four games, including two over the Redskins, and they did battle Dallas and St. Louis furiously before losing close decisions, but this was not enough to save coach Mike McCormick from the chopping block after the season.

CENTRAL DIVISION

Minnesota Vikings—The only Viking weakness on paper seemed to be at wide receiver, where John Gilliam had jumped to the W.F.L. But when Gilliam's Chicago team folded in September, he returned to the Vikes in time for the opening of the N.F.L. schedule. With his return, the Vikings excelled at all positions and ripped off ten straight victories at the start of the campaign to quickly ice away the Central Division title. The defensive unit, led by Carl Eller, Alan Page, Jeff Siemon, and Paul Krause, turned in its usual superb performance, and the offense produced the most points in the N.F.C., thanks greatly to Fran Tarkenton and Chuck Foreman. Tarkenton led the Conference in touchdown passes and moved past Johnny Unitas into first place in the all-time totals. Foreman enjoyed an exceptional season, scoring 22 touchdowns to tie Gale Sayers' old mark which O.J. Simpson also surpassed this year.

Detroit Lions—Pre-season predictions didn't hold out much hope for the Lions. Their top receiver, Ron Jessie, had played out his option and signed with Los Angeles, and the rest of the squad simply didn't measure up to the powers of the Conference. Three victories in the first four games fanned some sparks of hope, but the team faded in a blaze of injuries. Bill Munson and Greg Landry, the two top quarterbacks, both went on the shelf with injuries on October 26, and third-stringer Joe Reed filled in the rest of the way.

Chicago Bears—Jack Pardee came in as head coach, fresh from leading the Florida Blazers into the championship game of the W.F.L. last year. He promised a fresh look, but the same pale complexion showed on both the offensive and defensive units. The most glaring sore spot was quarterback, where Bobby Douglass started the season. He led the team to a 35-7 opening game loss and was soon on waivers. Gary Huff handled the controls through the bulk of the schedule, but rookie Bob Avellini finished the season at the helm, showing promise in a 42-17 triumph over New Orleans. Bright spots were Wally Chambers' great year in the defensive line and the influx of new talent in rookie runners Walter Payton and Roland Harper, rookie defensive end Mike Hartenstein, and tight end Greg Latta, a W.F.L. refugee.

Green Bay Packers—The naming of Bart Starr as head coach beckoned to the championship years of Vince Lombardi, but the old quarterback brought no magic with him this year. The Pack lost its first four games before upsetting Dallas 19-17 to get into the victory column. The Packers won three of their last five contests, but all came over weak opponents. Starr faced the same problem that plagued the departed Dan Devine—how to generate an offense. John Hadl was cursed with interceptions, and fullback John Brockington slipped in production.

WESTERN DIVISION

Los Angeles Rams—The Rams had never jelled into the superpower that people expected, but they still had undeniable quality and depth in all sectors. The defensive unit, featuring Jack Youngblood and Isaiah Robertson, ranked next to the Minnesota outfit in frugality of points allowed. The offense had a solid line led by Tom Mack, fine receivers in Harold Jackson and Ron Jessie, and a stable of hard-charging runners like Larry McCutcheon, Cullen Bryant, Jim Bertelson, and John Cappelletti. James Harris at quarterback was just good enough to lead this club to a runaway victory in the Western Division. Coach Chuck Knox found riches on his bench when Harris injured his shoulder on December 14 and back-up Ron Jaworski took the team to a victory in the finale.

San Francisco 49ers—The early promise of the Dick Nolan regime petered out into the frustration of a lukewarm club with some hot flashes. After a weak start, the 49ers came alive in mid-season with three straight wins, including a 24-23 upset of the Rams. But then the club dropped its last four games of the schedule to slip out of contention for the playoffs and cost Nolan his job. The quarterback position was a recurring problem, with neither Steve Spurrier nor Norm Snead taking charge. Del Williams and Gene Washington provided some offensive flair, but the 49ers needed some new direction to turn their fortunes around.

Atlanta Falcons—The Falcons traded a lot to Baltimore for the first pick in the college draft, using that pick to take quarterback Steve Bartkowski. Bartkowski showed good potential despite an injured elbow and a less-than-sterling offensive unit around him. The main threat was Dave Hampton, who ran for 1002 yards. The defensive unit also had its problems, but had a coming star in cornerback Rolland Lawrence. The fans still seemed turned off after the rising expectations and ultimate turmoil of the Van Brocklin years, and a sparse audience of 29,444 saw the Falcons beat the Saints 14-7 on October 5.

New Orleans Saints—The Saints relapsed into pitifulness this season. They lost their first three games while scoring only 10 points, beat Green Bay 20-19, and then lost their next two games. Coach John North was canned at this point, and Ernie Hefferle took over on an interim basis. He made it look easy when the Saints beat Atlanta 23-7 in his first game in charge, but his club then found its true level and lost its last seven games. The end of the season saw Hank Stram sign on as the new head coach to try to build the Saints into the sort of power that the Kansas City Chiefs had been under him.

FINAL TEAM STATISTICS

OFFENSE

	ATL.	CHI.	DALL.	DET.	G.B.	L.A.	MINN.	N.O.	N.Y.	PHIL.	ST.L.	S.F.	WASH.
FIRST DOWNS:													
Total	225	190	288	241	211	273	314	215	229	237	276	240	272
by Rushing	87	74	132	111	84	134	142	109	95	84	131	86	97
by Passing	118	99	142	111	112	120	156	82	105	134	128	133	150
by Penalty	20	17	14	19	15	19	16	24	29	19	17	21	25
RUSHING:													
Number	465	441	571	532	431	585	556	463	482	461	555	422	444
Yards	1794	1653	2432	2147	1547	2371	2094	1642	1627	1702	2402	1598	1752
Average Yards	3.9	3.7	4.3	4.0	3.6	4.1	3.8	3.5	3.4	3.7	4.3	3.8	3.9
Touchdowns	12	11	17	10	14	18	18	9	17	3	19	12	9
PASSING:													
Attempts	388	356	376	362	394	334	446	392	379	458	355	450	448
Completions	165	191	207	183	212	181	281	181	193	238	187	234	229
Completion Percentage	42.5	53.7	55.1	50.6	53.8	54.2	63.0	46.2	50.9	52.0	52.7	52.0	51.1
Passing Yards	2361	2169	2835	2240	2400	2450	3121	1961	2457	2640	2619	2806	3092
Avg. Yards per Attempt	6.1	6.1	7.5	6.2	6.1	7.3	7.0	5.0	6.5	5.8	7.4	6.2	6.9
Avg. Yards per Complet.	14.3	11.4	13.7	12.2	11.3	13.5	11.1	10.8	12.7	11.1	14.0	12.0	13.5
Times Tackled Passing	32	32	39	41	42	30	29	53	49	30	8	33	27
Yards Lost Passing	294	330	242	323	328	255	260	416	355	200	66	246	175
Net Yards	2067	1839	2593	1917	2072	2195	2861	1545	2102	2440	2553	2560	2917
Touchdowns	18	9	19	15	11	14	27	8	11	19	20	15	28
Interceptions	29	23	17	12	22	17	14	24	18	23	20	19	29
Percent Intercepted	7.5	6.5	4.5	3.3	5.6	5.1	3.1	6.1	4.8	5.0	5.9	4.2	6.5
PUNTS:													
Number	89	94	68	81	95	73	73	92	86	83	64	67	72
Average Distance	41.5	39.0	39.4	41.9	35.8	39.4	41.1	41.0	39.0	38.9	37.7	41.9	40.6
PUNT RETURNS:													
Number	35	51	32	36	30	55	36	47	49	35	40	63	61
Yards	248	512	313	328	190	517	167	372	350	299	410	616	464
Average Yards	7.1	10.0	9.8	9.1	6.3	9.4	4.6	9.1	7.1	8.5	10.3	9.8	7.6
Touchdowns	0	0	1	0	0	0	0	0	1	0	1	0	1
KICKOFF RETURNS:													
Number	66	75	54	52	63	34	36	62	55	59	55	60	58
Yards	1217	1644	1158	1114	1398	764	787	1291	1250	1388	1337	1372	1296
Average Yards	18.4	21.9	21.4	21.4	22.2	22.5	21.9	20.8	22.7	23.5	24.3	22.9	22.3
Touchdowns	0	0	1	0	1	0	0	0	0	0	1	0	0
INTERCEPTION RETURNS:													
Number	25	13	25	20	14	22	28	16	16	26	22	11	18
Yards	342	241	346	315	174	372	404	305	117	344	249	138	335
Average Yards	13.7	18.5	13.8	15.8	12.4	16.9	14.4	19.1	7.3	13.2	11.3	12.5	18.6
Touchdowns	2	2	3	1	0	2	0	0	0	2	1	1	0
PENALTIES:													
Number	78	100	94	95	72	73	90	71	52	81	83	89	78
Yards	635	881	715	838	606	746	708	527	440	744	730	693	723
FUMBLES:													
Number	37	35	25	28	31	26	33	33	44	29	33	44	28
Number Lost	19	17	18	18	16	8	12	16	19	12	19	25	17
POINTS:													
Total	240	191	350	245	226	312	377	165	216	225	356	255	325
PAT Attempts	33	22	41	29	27	36	48	19	29	24	43	31	40
PAT Made	30	18	38	25	22	31	46	18	24	21	41	27	37
FG Attempts	10	23	35	21	17	26	17	21	11	29	24	28	25
FG Made	4	13	22	14	12	21	13	11	6	20	19	14	16
Percent FG Made	40.0	56.5	62.9	66.7	70.6	80.8	76.5	52.4	54.5	69.0	79.2	50.0	64.0
Safeties	0	1	0	2	3	1	2	0	0	0	0	0	0

DEFENSE

	ATL.	CHI.	DALL.	DET.	G.B.	L.A.	MINN.	N.O.	N.Y.	PHIL.	ST.L.	S.F.	WASH.
FIRST DOWNS:													
Total	288	282	234	235	260	204	190	251	264	275	284	253	255
by Rushing	131	118	100	100	132	77	77	105	137	130	118	102	105
by Passing	142	143	113	116	112	103	93	125	120	123	142	130	128
by Penalty	15	21	21	19	16	24	20	21	7	22	24	21	22
RUSHING:													
Number	571	547	474	480	580	423	383	507	555	529	487	518	525
Yards	2277	2070	1699	1929	2339	1533	1532	1930	2422	2233	1925	1829	2047
Average Yards	4.0	3.8	3.6	4.0	4.0	3.6	4.0	3.8	4.4	4.2	4.0	3.5	3.9
Touchdowns	13	25	13	12	14	4	7	15	16	20	16	14	11
PASSING:													
Attempts	437	399	373	360	369	387	360	354	365	424	446	411	389
Completions	227	208	162	181	192	187	175	206	196	226	233	228	217
Completion Percentage	51.9	52.1	43.4	50.3	52.0	48.3	48.6	58.2	53.7	53.3	52.2	55.5	55.8
Passing Yards	2810	2825	2328	2377	2474	2126	1994	2587	2539	2658	2862	2521	2714
Avg. Yards per Attempt	6.4	7.1	6.2	6.6	6.7	5.5	5.5	7.3	6.6	6.3	6.4	6.1	7.0
Avg. Yards per Complet.	12.4	13.6	14.4	13.1	12.9	11.4	11.4	12.6	12.9	11.8	12.3	11.6	13.0
Times Tackled Passing	35	35	41	38	32	43	46	28	26	17	24	40	36
Yards Lost Passing	275	319	288	306	302	337	373	200	172	120	192	324	276
Net Yards	2535	2506	2040	2071	2172	1789	1621	2387	2367	2538	2670	2197	2438
Touchdowns	16	22	19	16	13	11	14	25	20	13	16	15	17
Interceptions	25	13	25	20	14	22	28	16	16	26	22	11	18
Percent Intercepted	5.7	3.0	6.6	5.6	3.8	5.7	7.8	4.5	4.4	6.1	5.0	2.7	4.6
PUNTS:													
Number	71	86	82	80	70	89	89	75	82	65	67	84	87
Average Distance	41.1	41.4	39.6	36.9	39.7	39.7	39.6	42.7	37.6	37.0	40.1	42.1	38.9
PUNT RETURNS:													
Number	52	49	37	41	45	45	51	61	39	58	34	43	38
Yards	389	303	261	524	222	401	419	679	364	530	329	490	240
Average Yards	7.5	6.2	7.1	12.8	4.9	8.9	8.2	11.1	9.3	9.1	9.7	11.4	6.3
Touchdowns	0	0	0	1	0	0	0	1	1	1	0	0	0
KICKOFF RETURNS:													
Number	45	43	66	53	49	64	69	42	46	51	71	48	64
Yards	1038	893	1576	1084	1051	1327	1345	1073	927	1149	1609	1061	1357
Average Yards	23.1	20.8	23.9	20.5	21.4	21.0	19.5	25.5	20.2	22.5	22.7	22.1	21.2
Touchdowns	0	0	0	0	1	0	0	1	0	0	1	0	1
INTERCEPTION RETURNS:													
Number	20	23	17	12	22	17	14	24	18	23	20	19	29
Yards	602	235	203	82	388	204	235	367	214	411	216	212	469
Average Yards	20.8	10.2	11.9	6.8	17.6	12.0	16.8	15.3	11.9	17.9	10.8	11.2	16.2
Touchdowns	1	0	0	0	2	0	0	2	1	2	0	0	4
PENALTIES:													
Number	78	78	63	94	73	85	91	77	97	97	82	86	89
Yards	721	723	639	874	544	626	681	726	755	784	679	702	772
FUMBLES:													
Number	25	29	43	30	44	31	29	43	22	30	26	34	27
Number Lost	12	14	19	17	27	18	13	22	8	18	15	16	19
POINTS:													
Total	289	379	268	262	285	135	180	360	306	302	276	286	276
PAT Attempts	31	48	32	31	32	15	21	48	39	36	33	34	33
PAT Made	28	47	31	26	30	13	19	44	37	32	27	31	27
FG Attempts	38	18	18	23	31	19	13	12	21	27	26	22	30
FG Made	25	14	13	16	21	10	9	8	11	18	15	17	17
Percent FG Made	65.8	77.8	72.2	69.6	67.7	52.6	69.2	66.7	52.4	66.7	57.7	77.3	56.7
Safeties	0	1	0	1	0	1	1	2	1	0	0	0	0

CONFERENCE PLAYOFFS

December 27, at Los Angeles (Attendance 72,650)

SCORING

LOS ANGELES	14	14	0	7	– 35
ST. LOUIS	0	9	7	7	– 23

First Quarter
- L.A. Jaworski, 5 yard rush PAT – Dempsey (kick)
- L.A. Youngblood, 47 yard interception return PAT – Dempsey (kick)

Second Quarter
- L.A. Simpson, 65 yard interception return PAT – Dempsey (kick)
- St.L. Otis, 3 yard rush PAT – Kick failed
- L.A. Jackson, 66 yard pass from Jaworski PAT – Dempsey (kick)
- St.L. Bakken, 29 yard field goal

Third Quarter
- St. L. M. Gray, 11 yard pass from Hart PAT – Bakken (kick)

Fourth Quarter
- L.A. Jessie, 2 yard fumble recovery PAT – Dempsey (kick)
- St.L. Jones, 3 yard rush PAT – Bakken (kick)

TEAM STATISTICS

L.A.		ST.L.
26	First Downs – Total	22
14	First Downs – Rushing	5
10	First Downs – Passing	16
2	First Downs – Penalty	1
5	Fumbles – Number	3
3	Fumbles – Lost Ball	2
5	Penalties – Number	6
38	Yards Penalized	70
1	Missed Field Goals	0
73	Offensive Plays	70
440	Net Yards	363
6.0	Average Gain	5.2
3	Giveaways	5
5	Takeaways	3
+2	Difference	-2

INDIVIDUAL STATISTICS

LOS ANGELES	No.	Yds.	Avg.	ST. LOUIS	No.	Yds.	Avg.
RUSHING							
McCutcheon	37	202	5.5	Otis	12	38	3.2
Scribner	4	16	4.0	Jones	6	28	4.7
Bryant	3	12	4.0	Metcalf	8	27	3.4
Jaworski	8	7	0.9	Latin	1	2	2.0
	52	237	4.6		27	95	3.5
RECEIVING							
Jessie	4	52	13.0	Metcalf	6	94	15.7
McCutcheon	3	8	2.7	Otis	4	52	13.0
Jackson	2	84	42.0	M. Gray	3	52	17.3
Bryant	2	26	13.0	Harris	2	33	16.5
T. Nelson	1	33	33.0	Latin	2	23	11.5
	12	203	16.9	Jones	2	19	9.5
				Cain	2	17	8.5
				Smith	1	1	1.0
					22	291	13.2
PUNTING							
Carrell	5		31.6	West	6		42.7
PUNT RETURNS							
Scribner	1	7	7.0	Metcalf	1	3	3.0
Elmendorf	1	0	0.0				
	2	7	3.5				
KICKOFF RETURNS							
Bryant	3	61	20.3	Metcalf	3	105	35.0
Jessie	1	17	17.0	Hammond	2	36	13.0
Elmendorf	1	12	12.0	Crump	1	28	28.0
	5	90	18.0	Latin	1	22	22.0
					7	191	27.3
INTERCEPTION RETURNS							
Simpson	2	83	41.5	none			
Youngblood	1	47	47.0				
	3	130	43.3				

PASSING

LOS ANGELES	Att.	Comp.	Comp. Pct.	Yds	Int	Yds/ Att.	Yds/ Comp	Yards Lost Tackled
Jaworski	23	12	52.2	203	0	8.8	16.9	0-0
ST. LOUIS								
Hart	41	22	53.7	291	3	7.1	13.2	2-23

December 28, at Minnesota (Attendance 46,425)

SCORING

MINNESOTA	0	7	0	7	– 14
DALLAS	0	0	7	10	– 17

Second Quarter
- Min.. Foreman, 1 yard rush PAT – Cox (kick)

Third Quarter
- Dall. Dennison, 4 yard rush PAT – Fritsch (kick)

Fourth Quarter
- Dall. Fritsch, 24 yard field goal
- Minn. McClanahan, 1 yard rush PAT – Cox (kick)
- Dall. D. Pearson, 50 yard pass from Staubach PAT – Fritsch (kick)

TEAM STATISTICS

MINN.		DALL.
12	First Downs – Total	19
6	First Downs – Rushing	7
6	First Downs – Passing	11
0	First Downs – Penalty	1
2	Fumbles – Number	3
0	Fumbles – Lost Ball	1
7	Penalties – Number	4
60	Yards Penalized	30
1	Missed Field Goals	1
58	Offensive Plays	75
215	Net Yards	356
3.1	Average Gain	4.3
1	Giveaways	1
1	Takeaways	1
0	Difference	0

INDIVIDUAL STATISTICS

MINNESOTA	No.	Yds.	Avg.	DALLAS	No.	Yds.	Avg.
RUSHING							
Foreman	18	56	3.1	Dennison	11	36	3.3
Tarkenton	3	32	10.7	P. Pearson	11	34	3.1
McClanahan	4	22	5.5	Newhouse	12	33	2.8
Marinaro	2	5	2.5	Staubach	7	24	3.4
	27	115	4.3	Fuggett	1	4	4.0
					42	131	3.1
RECEIVING							
Marinaro	5	64	12.8	P. Pearson	5	77	15.4
Foreman	4	42	10.5	D. Pearson	4	91	22.8
Gilliam	1	15	15.0	Newhouse	2	25	12.5
Lash	1	15	15.0	Richards	2	20	10.0
Voigt	1	-1	-1.0	Fuggett	2	13	6.5
	12	135	11.3	DuPree	1	17	17.0
				Dennison	1	3	3.0
					17	246	14.4
PUNTING							
Clabo	7		39.6	Hoopes	6		38.5
PUNT RETURNS							
McCullum	3	4	1.3	Richards	2	13	6.5
Bryant	1	1	1.0	Harris	2	5	2.5
	4	5	1.3		4	18	4.5
KICKOFF RETURNS							
McClanahan	2	38	19.0	P. Pearson	2	26	13.0
McCullum	1	3	3.0	Dennison	1	13	13.0
Osborn	1	0	0.0		3	39	13.0
	4	41	10.3				
INTERCEPTION RETURNS							
none				Renfro	1	0	0.0

PASSING

MINNESOTA	Att.	Comp.	Comp. Pct.	Yds.	Int.	Yds/ Att.	Yds/ Comp	Yards Lost Tackled
Tarkenton	26	12	46.2	135	1	5.2	11.3	4-35
DALLAS								
Staubach	29	17	58.6	256	0	8.8	15.1	5-21

ST. LOUIS CARDINALS 11-3 Don Coryell

Scores of Each Game		
23	ATLANTA	20
31	Dallas	*37
26	N.Y. GIANTS	14
17	Washington	27
31	PHILADELPHIA	20
20	N.Y. Giants	13
24	NEW ENGLAND	17
24	Philadelphia	23
20	WASHINGTON	*17
37	N.Y. Jets	6
14	BUFFALO	32
31	DALLAS	17
34	Chicago	20
24	Detroit	13

Use Name	Pos.	Hgt	Wgt	Age	Int	Pts
Dan Dierdorf	OT	6'4"	280	26		
Greg Kindle	OG-OT	6'4"	265	24		
Roger Finnie	OG-OT	6'3"	250	29		
Henry Allison	OG	6'3"	255	28		
Conrad Dobler	OG	6'3"	255	24		
Bob Young	OG	6'2"	270	32		
Tom Brahaney	C	6'2"	250	23		
Tom Banks	OG-C	6'1"	245	27		
Bob Bell	DE	6'4"	250	27		
Council Rudolph	DE	6'3"	245	25	1	
Ron Yankowski	DE	6'5"	250	28		
Lee Brooks	DT	6'5"	250	27		
Charlie Davis	DT	6'1"	265	23		
Bob Rowe	DT	6'4"	270	30		

Use Name	Pos.	Hgt	Wgt	Age	Int	Pts
Mark Arneson	LB	6'2"	220	25	1	
Pete Barnes	LB	6'3"	240	30	2	
Greg Hartle	LB	6'2"	225	24		
Steve Neils	LB	6'2"	215	24		
Larry Stallings	LB	6'2"	230	33	1	
Ray White	LB	6'1"	220	26		
Dwayne Crump	DB	5'11"	180	25		6
Clarence Duren	DB	6'1"	190	24	1	
Tim Gray	DB	6'1"	200	22		
Ken Reaves	DB	6'3"	210	30	3	
Norm Thompson	DB	6'1"	180	27	7	6
Jim Tolbert	DB	6'3"	210	31		
Roger Wehrli	DB	6'1"	190	27	6	1

Steve George – Knee Injury

Use Name	Pos.	Hgt	Wgt	Age	Int	Pts
Jim Hart	QB	6'2"	210	31		6
Gary Keithley	QB	6'3"	215	24		
Dennis Shaw	QB	6'2"	210	28		
Josh Ashton	HB	6'1"	205	26		
Steve Jones	HB	6'	200	24		18
Jerry Latin	HB	5'10"	190	22		6
Terry Metcalf	HB	5'10"	185	23		78
Eddie Moss	FB	6'	215	26		6
Jim Otis	FB	6'	225	27		36
Mel Gray	WR	5'9"	175	26		66
Gary Hammond	WR	5'11"	185	26		
Ike Harris	WR	6'3"	205	22		
Earl Thomas	WR	6'3"	220	26		12
J.V. Cain	TE	6'4"	225	24		6
Jackie Smith	TE	6'4"	230	34		12
Jeff West	TE	6'3"	220	22		
Jim Bakken	K	6'	200	34		97

DALLAS COWBOYS 10-4 Tom Landry

Scores of Each Game		
18	LOS ANGELES	7
37	ST. LOUIS	*31
36	Detroit	10
13	N.Y. Giants	7
17	GREEN BAY	19
20	Philadelphia	17
24	Washington	*30
31	KANSAS CITY	34
34	New England	31
27	PHILADELPHIA	17
14	N.Y. GIANTS	3
17	St. Louis	31
31	WASHINGTON	10
31	N.Y. Jets	21

Use Name	Pos.	Hgt	Wgt	Age	Int	Pts
Pat Donovan	OT	6'4"	250	22		
Ralph Neely	OT	6'5"	260	31		
Bruce Walton	OT	6'6"	252	24		
Rayfield Wright	OT	6'7"	260	29		
Burton Lawless	OG	6'4"	250	21		
Blaine Nye	OG	6'4"	255	29		
Herbert Scott	OG	6'2"	250	22		
Kyle Davis	C	6'4"	240	22		
John Fitzgerald	C	6'5"	255	27		
Too Tall Jones	DE	6'9"	260	24	1	
Harvey Martin	DE	6'5"	257	24		
Randy White	LB-DT-DE	6'4"	245	22		
Larry Cole	DT	6'4"	250	28		
Bill Gregory	DT	6'5"	252	25	1	
Jethro Pugh	DT	6'6"	250	31		

Use Name	Pos.	Hgt	Wgt	Age	Int	Pts
Bob Breunig	LB	6'2"	227	22		
Warren Capone	LB	6'1"	218	24		
Dave Edwards	LB	6'3"	225	36		
Thomas Henderson	LB	6'2"	220	22		6
Lee Roy Jordan	LB	6'2"	220	34	6	
D.D. Lewis	LB	6'2"	218	29		
Cal Peterson	LB	6'3"	220	22	1	
Benny Barnes	DB	6'1"	185	24		
Cliff Harris	DB	6'	190	25	3	6
Randy Hughes	DB	6'4"	200	22	2	6
Mel Renfro	DB	6'	190	33	4	
Mark Washington	DB	5'10"	186	27	4	
Charlie Waters	DB	6'1"	193	26	3	6
Roland Woolsey	DB	6'1"	182	22		

Use Name	Pos.	Hgt	Wgt	Age	Int	Pts
Clint Longley	QB	6'1"	193	23		
Roger Staubach	QB	6'2"	197	33		24
Preston Pearson	HB	6'1"	205	30		24
Charley Young	HB	6'1"	210	22		18
Doug Dennison	FB-HB	6'1"	195	23		42
Scott Laidlaw	FB	6'	206	22		
Robert Newhouse	FB	5'10"	200	25		12
Percy Howard	WR	6'4"	210	23		
Drew Pearson	WR	6'	180	24		48
Golden Richards	WR	6'	183	24		30
Billy Joe DuPree	TE	6'4"	228	25		6
Ron Howard	TE	6'4"	225	24		
Jean Fugett	WR-TE	6'3"	226	23		18
Toni Fritsch	K	5'7"	195	30		104
Mitch Hoopes	K	6'1"	210	22		

Efren Herrera – Injury

WASHINGTON REDSKINS 8-6 George Allen

Scores of Each Game		
41	NEW ORLEANS	3
49	N.Y. GIANTS	13
10	Philadelphia	26
27	St. Louis	17
10	Houston	13
23	Cleveland	7
30	DALLAS	*24
21	N.Y. Giants	13
17	St. Louis	*20
23	OAKLAND	*26
31	MINNESOTA	30
30	Atlanta	27
10	Dallas	31
3	PHILADELPHIA	26

Use Name	Pos.	Hgt	Wgt	Age	Int	Pts
Terry Hermeling	OT	6'5"	255	29		
George Starke	OT	6'5"	250	27		
Tim Stokes	OT	6'5"	250	25		
Paul Laaveg	OG	6'4"	250	26		
Walt Sweeney	OG	6'3"	254	34		
Ray Schoenke	OT-OG	6'3"	250	33		
Jim Arneson	C-OG	6'3"	252	24		
Len Hauss	C	6'2"	235	33		
Bob Kuziel	C	6'4"	255	25		
Dan Ryzcek	C	6'3"	245	26		
Dave Butz	DE	6'7"	297	25		
Ron McDole	DE	6'3"	265	35		6
Bill Brundige	DT	6'5"	270	26		
Dennis Johnson	DT	6'4"	260	23	1	
Manny Sistrunk	DT	6'5"	265	28		
Diron Talbert	DT	6'5"	255	31		

Use Name	Pos.	Hgt	Wgt	Age	Int	Pts
Brad Dusek	LB	6'2"	214	24		6
Chris Hanburger	LB	6'2"	218	33	3	
Harold McLinton	LB	6'2"	235	28		
John Pergine	LB	6'1"	225	28		6
Russ Tillman	LB	6'2"	230	29		
Pete Wysocki	LB	6'2"	225	26		
Mike Bass	DB	6'	190	30	4	
Eddie Brown (from CLE)	DB	5'11"	185	23	1	
Pat Fischer	DB	5'10"	170	35	3	
Ken Houston	DB	6'3"	198	30	4	
Brig Owens	DB	5'11"	190	32	1	
Bryant Salter	DB	6'4"	196	25	1	
Ken Stone	DB	6'1"	180	24		
Spencer Thomas	DB	6'2"	185	24		

Verlon Biggs – Knee Injury

Use Name	Pos.	Hgt	Wgt	Age	Int	Pts
Randy Johnson	QB	6'3"	205	31		
Billy Kilmer	QB	6'	204	35		6
Joe Theismann	QB	6'	184	25		
Larry Brown	HB	5'11"	195	27		30
Ralph Nelson	HB	6'2"	195	21		6
Mike Thomas	HB	5'11"	190	22		42
Bob Brunet	FB	6'1"	205	29		6
Moses Denson	FB	6'1"	215	31		
Frank Grant	WR	5'11"	180	25		48
Roy Jefferson	WR	6'2"	195	31		12
Larry Jones	WR	5'10"	170	24		6
Charley Taylor	WR	6'3"	210	34		36
Alvin Reed	TE	6'5"	235	31		12
Jerry Smith	TE	6'2"	208	32		18
Mike Bragg	K	5'11"	186	28		
Mark Moseley	K	5'11"	205	27		85

Mike Hancock – Injury
Stu O'Dell – Shoulder Injury

NEW YORK GIANTS 5-9 Bill Arnsparger

Scores of Each Game		
23	Philadelphia	14
13	Washington	49
14	St. Louis	26
7	DALLAS	13
17	Buffalo	14
13	ST. LOUIS	20
35	SAN DIEGO	24
13	WASHINGTON	21
10	PHILADELPHIA	13
14	Green Bay	40
3	Dallas	14
0	BALTIMORE	21
28	NEW ORLEANS	14
26	San Francisco	23

Use Name	Pos.	Hgt	Wgt	Age	Int	Pts
Dave Simonson	OT	6'6"	248	23		
Al Simpson	OT	6'5"	255	24		
Doug Van Horn	OT	6'2"	245	31		
Willie Young	OT	6'	255	32		
Dick Enderle	OG	6'1"	250	27		
John Hicks	OG	6'2"	258	24		
Tom Mullen	OG	6'3"	245	23		
Karl Chandler	C	6'5"	250	23		
Bob Hyland	C	6'5"	255	30		
Rick Dvorak	DE	6'4"	235	23		
Dave Gallagher	DE	6'4"	256	23		
Jack Gregory	DE	6'6"	255	30		
George Martin	DE	6'4"	245	22		
John Mendenhall	DT	6'1"	255	26		
Jim Pietrzak	DT	6'5"	260	22		
Bill Windauer (from MIA)	DT	6'3"	248	25		

Use Name	Pos.	Hgt	Wgt	Age	Int	Pts
Jimmy Gunn (from CHI)	LB	6'1"	218	26	1	
Pat Hughes	LB	6'2"	225	28		
Brian Kelley	LB	6'3"	222	24	3	
Bob Schmit	LB	6'1"	220	25		
Andy Selfridge	LB	6'4"	220	26		
Brad Van Pelt	LB	6'5"	235	24	3	
Bobby Brooks	DB	6'1"	195	24	4	
Rondy Colbert	DB	5'9"	165	21		6
Charlie Ford (from BUF)	DB	6'3"	185	26	1	
Robert Giblin	DB	6'2"	205	22		
Spider Lockhart	DB	6'2"	175	32	1	
Clyde Powers	DB	6'1"	195	24	3	
Jim Stienke	DB	5'11"	182	24	2	
Henry Stuckey	DB	6'1"	180	25		

Larry Jacobson – Broken Ankle

Use Name	Pos.	Hgt	Wgt	Age	Int	Pts
Craig Morton	QB	6'4"	210	32		
Carl Summerell	QB	6'4"	208	23		
Mike Wells	QB	6'5"	225	24		
Steve Crosby	HB	5'11"	205	25		
Ron Johnson	HB	6'1"	205	27		36
Doug Kotar	HB	5'11"	205	24		36
Joe Dawkins	FB	5'11"	220	27		12
Larry Watkins	FB	6'2"	230	28		18
Marsh White	FB	6'2"	220	22		6
Danny Buggs	WR	6'2"	185	22		
Don Clune	WR	6'3"	195	23		
Walker Gillette	WR	6'5"	200	28		12
Ray Rhodes	WR	5'11"	185	24		36
Jim Obradovich	TE	6'2"	225	22		6
Bob Tucker	TE	6'3"	230	30		6
George Hunt	K	6'1"	215	25		42
Dave Jennings	K	6'4"	205	23		

PHILADELPHIA EAGLES 4-10 Mike McCormack

Scores of Each Game		
14	N.Y. GIANTS	23
13	Chicago	15
26	WASHINGTON	10
16	Miami	24
20	St. Louis	31
17	DALLAS	20
3	LOS ANGELES	42
23	ST. LOUIS	24
13	N.Y. Giants	10
17	Dallas	27
27	SAN FRANCISCO	17
0	CINCINNATI	31
10	Denver	25
26	Washington	3

Use Name	Pos.	Hgt	Wgt	Age	Int	Pts
Jeff Bleamer	OT	6'4"	253	22		
Jerry Sisemore	OT	6'4"	260	24		
Stan Walters	OT	6'6"	270	27		
Ernie Janet (from GB)	OG	6'4"	255	26		
Wade Key	OG	6'4"	245	28		
Bill Lueck	OG	6'3"	250	29		
Tom Luken	OG	6'3"	253	25		
John Niland	OG	6'4"	250	31		
Ron Lou	C	6'2"	240	24		
Guy Morriss	C	6'4"	255	24		
Don Ratliff	DE	6'5"	250	25		
Blenda Gay	DE	6'5"	255	25		
Will Wynn	DE	6'4"	245	26		
Bill Dunstan	DT	6'4"	250	26		
Rich Glover	DT	6'1"	244	24		
Mitch Sutton	DT	6'4"	255	24		
Rosie Manning (from ATL)	DT	6'5"	259	24		

Use Name	Pos.	Hgt	Wgt	Age	Int	Pts
Bill Bergey	LB	6'2"	250	30	3	
John Bunting	LB	6'1"	220	25	1	
Steve Colavito	LB	6'	225	24		
Tom Ehlers	LB	6'2"	218	23		
Dean Halverson	LB	6'2"	230	29		
Frank LeMaster	LB	6'2"	230	23	4	6
Jim Opperman	LB	6'3"	220	22		
Bill Bradley	DB	5'11"	190	28	5	
Cliff Brooks	DB	6'1"	190	26		
Joe Lavender	DB	6'4"	190	26	3	6
Randy Logan	DB	6'1"	195	24	1	
Larry Marshall	DB	5'10"	195	25		
John Outlaw	DB	5'10"	180	30	5	
Artimus Parker	DB	6'3"	215	23	4	

Tom Bailey – Knee Injury

Use Name	Pos.	Hgt	Wgt	Age	Int	Pts
Mike Boryla	QB	6'3"	200	24		
Roman Gabriel	QB	6'4"	220	35		6
Bill Troup	QB	6'5"	220	24		
Po James	HB	6'1"	202	26		12
Merritt Kersey	HB	6'1"	205	25		
James McAlister	HB	6'1"	205	23		18
Dennis Morgan	HB	5'11"	195	23		
Tom Sullivan	FB-HB	6'	190	25		
Art Malone	FB	5'11"	216	27		
John Tarver	FB	6'3"	220	26		
George Amundson	HB-FB	6'3"	215	24		
Harold Carmichael	WR	6'7"	225	25		42
Bob Picard	WR	6'1"	195	25		
Charlie Smith	WR	6'1"	185	25		36
Don Zimmerman	WR	6'3"	195	25		
Keith Krepfle	TE	6'3"	225	23		
Charlie Young	TE	6'4"	238	24		18
Spike Jones	K	6'2"	185	28		
Horst Muhlmann	K	6'1"	220	35		81

*Overtime

ST. LOUIS CARDINALS

RUSHING

Last Name	No.	Yds	Avg	TD
Otis	269	1076	4.0	5
Metcalf	165	816	4.9	9
Jones	54	275	5.1	2
Latin	35	165	4.7	1
Ashton	10	44	4.4	0
Hammond	3	13	4.3	0
Moss	4	12	3.0	1
Hart	11	7	0.6	1
M. Gray	1	6	6.0	0
Shaw	3	−12	−4.0	0

RECEIVING

Last Name	No.	Yds	Avg	TD
M. Gray	48	926	19	11
Metcalf	43	378	9	2
Thomas	21	375	18	2
Jones	19	194	10	1
Harris	15	266	18	0
Smith	13	246	19	2
Cain	12	134	11	1
Otis	12	69	6	1
Latin	2	25	13	0
Hammond	2	6	3	0

PUNT RETURNS

Last Name	No.	Yds	Avg	TD
Metcalf	23	285	12	1
Hammond	9	70	8	0
M. Gray	7	53	8	0
Wehrli	1	2	2	0

KICKOFF RETURNS

Last Name	No.	Yds	Avg	TD
Metcalf	35	960	27	1
Hammond	13	254	20	0
Smith	1	25	25	0
Moss	1	21	21	0
Hartle	1	20	20	0
T. Gray	1	20	20	0
Jones	1	18	18	0
Wehrli	1	10	10	0
Reaves	1	9	9	0

PASSING – PUNTING – KICKING

PASSING	Att	Comp	%	Yds	Yd/Att	TD	Int–%	RK
Hart	345	182	53	2507	7.3	19	19– 6	6
Shaw	8	4	50	61	7.6	0	1–13	
Metcalf	2	1	50	51	25.5	1	0– 0	

PUNTING	No	Avg
West	64	37.7

KICKING	XP	Att	%	FG	Att	%
Bakken	40	41	98	19	24	82

DALLAS COWBOYS

RUSHING

Last Name	No.	Yds	Avg	TD
Newhouse	209	930	4.4	2
P. Pearson	133	509	3.8	2
Dennison	111	383	3.5	7
Staubach	55	316	5.7	4
Young	50	225	4.5	2
Richards	3	18	6.0	0
Hoopes	1	13	13.0	0
Longley	3	12	4.0	0
D. Pearson	1	11	11.0	0
Laidlaw	3	10	3.3	0
DuPree	1	3	3.0	0
Fugett	1	2	2.0	0

RECEIVING

Last Name	No.	Yds	Avg	TD
D. Pearson	46	822	18	8
Fugett	38	488	13	3
Newhouse	34	275	8	0
P. Pearson	27	353	13	2
Richards	21	451	22	4
Young	18	184	10	1
Laidlaw	11	100	9	0
DuPree	9	138	15	1
Dennison	2	5	3	0
Breunig	1	21	21	0

PUNT RETURNS

Last Name	No.	Yds	Avg	TD
Richards	28	288	10	1
Woolsey	4	25	6	0

KICKOFF RETURNS

Last Name	No.	Yds	Avg	TD
P. Pearson	16	391	24	0
Dennison	13	262	20	0
Woolsey	12	247	21	0
Henderson	4	130	33	1
Young	3	54	18	0
P. Howard	2	51	26	0
Breunig	2	13	7	0
Peterson	1	10	10	0
Waters	1	0	0	0

PASSING – PUNTING – KICKING

PASSING	Att	Comp	%	Yds	Yd/Att	TD	Int–%	RK
Staubach	348	198	57	2666	7.7	17	16– 5	2
Longley	23	7	30	102	4.4	1	1– 4	
Hoopes	3	1	33	21	7.0	0	0– 0	
Newhouse	2	1	50	46	23.0	1	0– 0	

PUNTING	No	Avg
Hoopes	68	39.4

KICKING	XP	Att	%	FG	Att	%
Fritsch	38	40	95	22	35	63

WASHINGTON REDSKINS

RUSHING

Last Name	No.	Yds	Avg	TD
M. Thomas	235	919	3.9	4
L. Brown	97	352	3.6	3
Denson	56	195	3.5	0
Nelson	31	139	4.5	0
Grant	3	46	15.3	0
Kilmer	11	34	3.1	1
Theismann	3	34	11.3	0
Brunet	6	23	3.8	1
R. Johnson	2	10	5.0	0

RECEIVING

Last Name	No.	Yds	Avg	TD
Taylor	53	744	14	6
Grant	41	776	19	8
M. Thomas	40	483	12	3
Smith	31	391	13	3
L. Brown	25	225	9	2
Jefferson	15	255	17	2
Denson	13	81	6	0
Nelson	5	58	12	1
Pergine	2	41	21	1
Jones	2	33	17	0
Reed	2	5	3	2

PUNT RETURNS

Last Name	No.	Yds	Avg	TD
Jones	53	407	8	1
E. Brown	8	68	9	0
Theismann	2	5	3	0

KICKOFF RETURNS

Last Name	No.	Yds	Avg	TD
Jones	47	1086	23	0
E. Brown	6	126	21	0
Nelson	5	107	21	0
Brunet	5	83	17	0
Tillman	1	4	4	0
Grant	0	16	0	0

PASSING – PUNTING – KICKING

PASSING	Att	Comp	%	Yds	Yd/Att	TD	Int–%	RK
Kilmer	346	178	51	2440	7.1	23	16– 5	3
Johnson	79	41	52	556	7.0	4	10–13	
Theismann	22	10	46	96	4.4	1	3–14	
Anderson	1	0	0	0	0.0	0	0– 0	

PUNTING	No	Avg
Bragg	72	40.6

KICKING	XP	Att	%	FG	Att	%
Moseley	37	39	95	16	25	64

NEW YORK GIANTS

RUSHING

Last Name	No.	Yds	Avg	TD
Dawkins	129	438	3.4	2
Kotar	122	378	3.1	6
Johnson	116	351	3.0	5
Watkins	68	303	4.5	3
White	17	90	5.3	1
Morton	22	72	3.3	0
Summerell	3	4	1.3	0
Buggs	1	0	0.0	0
Rhodes	3	−4	−1.3	0
Tucker	1	−5	−5.0	0

RECEIVING

Last Name	No.	Yds	Avg	TD
Gillette	43	600	14	2
Tucker	34	484	14	1
Johnson	34	280	8	1
Rhodes	26	537	21	6
Dawkins	24	245	10	0
Kotar	9	86	10	0
Obradovich	7	65	9	1
Watkins	7	43	6	0
Clune	5	97	19	0
White	3	15	5	0
Hicks	1	5	5	0

PUNT RETURNS

Last Name	No.	Yds	Avg	TD
Colbert	27	238	9	1
Buggs	19	93	5	0
Lockhart	2	14	7	0
Kotar	1	5	5	0

KICKOFF RETURNS

Last Name	No.	Yds	Avg	TD
Colbert	17	408	24	0
Kotar	17	405	24	0
Buggs	16	353	22	0
Obradovich	2	38	19	0
Dawkins	1	32	32	0
Crosby	1	14	14	0
Selfridge	1	0	0	0

PASSING – PUNTING – KICKING

PASSING	Att	Comp	%	Yds	Yd/Att	TD	Int–%	RK
Morton	363	186	51	2359	6.5	11	16– 4	8
Summerell	16	7	44	98	6.1	0	2–13	

PUNTING	No	Avg
Jennings	76	40.9
Hunt	9	24.2
Crosby	1	28.0

KICKING	XP	Att	%	FG	Att	%
Hunt	24	29	83	6	11	55

PHILADELPHIA EAGLES

RUSHING

Last Name	No.	Yds	Avg	TD
Sullivan	173	632	3.7	0
McAlister	103	335	3.3	1
Malone	101	325	3.2	0
James	43	196	4.6	1
Smith	9	85	9.4	0
Gabriel	13	70	5.4	1
Boryla	8	33	4.1	0
Tarver	7	20	2.9	0
Carmichael	1	6	6.0	0
Young	2	1	0.5	0
Jones	1	−1	−1.0	0

RECEIVING

Last Name	No.	Yds	Avg	TD
Young	49	659	13	3
Carmichael	49	639	13	7
Smith	37	515	14	6
James	32	267	8	1
Sullivan	28	276	10	0
Malone	20	120	6	0
McAlister	17	134	8	2
Tarver	5	14	3	0
Krepfle	1	16	16	0

PUNT RETURNS

Last Name	No.	Yds	Avg	TD
Marshall	23	235	10	0
Morgan	8	60	8	0
Bradley	4	4	1	0

KICKOFF RETURNS

Last Name	No.	Yds	Avg	TD
Marshall	22	557	25	0
James	13	311	24	0
McAlister	12	278	23	0
Morgan	7	170	24	0
Sullivan	3	42	14	0
Opperman	1	15	15	0
Sisemore	1	15	15	0

PASSING – PUNTING – KICKING

PASSING	Att	Comp	%	Yds	Yd/Att	TD	Int–%	RK
Gabriel	292	151	52	1644	5.6	13	11– 4	7
Boryla	166	87	52	996	6.0	6	12– 7	14

PUNTING	No	Avg
Jones	68	40.3
Kersey	15	32.6

KICKING	XP	Att	%	FG	Att	%
Muhlmann	21	24	88	20	29	69

1975 N.F.C. — Central Division

MINNESOTA VIKINGS 12-2 Bud Grant

Scores of Each Game		
27	SAN FRANCISCO	17
42	Cleveland	10
28	CHICAGO	3
29	N.Y. JETS	21
25	DETROIT	19
13	Chicago	9
28	Green Bay	17
38	ATLANTA	0
20	New Orleans	7
28	SAN DIEGO	13
30	Washington	31
24	GREEN BAY	3
10	Detroit	17
35	Buffalo	13

Use Name	Pos.	Hgt	Wgt	Age	Int	Pts
Charlie Goodrum	OT	6'3"	256	25		
Steve Riley	OT	6'6"	258	22		
Ron Yary	OT	6'6"	255	29		
Steve Lawson	OG	6'3"	265	26		
Andy Mauer	OG	6'3"	275	26		
Ed White	OG	6'2"	270	28		
Mick Tingelhoff	C	6'1"	240	35		
John Ward	OG-C	6'4"	250	27		
Carl Eller	DE	6'6"	247	33	1	
Jim Marshall	DE	6'3"	240	37		
Mark Mullaney	DE	6'6"	242	22		
Alan Page	DT	6'5"	245	30		
Doug Sutherland	DT	6'3"	250	27		
Bob Lurtsema	DE-DT	6'6"	250	33		
Matt Blair	LB	6'5"	230	24	1	
Wally Hilgenberg	LB	6'3"	230	32	1	
Amos Martin	LB	6'3"	228	26		
Fred McNeill	LB	6'2"	230	23	1	
Jeff Siemon	LB	6'2"	237	25	3	
Bob Stein (from SD)	LB	6'2"	235	27		
Roy Winston	LB	6'1"	222	35		
Pete Athas (from CLE)	DB	5'11"	185	27	1	
Autry Beamon	DB	6'	190	21	1	2
Joe Blahak	DB	5'9"	188	24	1	2
Terry Brown	DB	6'1"	205	28	2	6
Bobby Bryant	DB	6'	170	31	6	
Paul Krause	DB	6'3"	200	33	10	6
Jeff Wright	DB	5'11"	190	26		
Nate Wright	DB	5'11"	180	27		
Bob Berry	QB	5'11"	185	33		
Bob Lee	QB	6'2"	195	29		
Fran Tarkenton	QB	6'1"	190	35		12
Chuck Foreman	HB	6'2"	207	24		132
Ed Marinaro	FB-HB	6'2"	212	25		24
Brent McClanahan	FB-HB	5'10"	202	24		6
Robert Miller	FB	5'11"	204	22		6
Dave Osborn	FB	6'	208	32		6
John Gilliam	WR	6'1"	195	30		42
Clint Haslerig (from BUF)	WR	6'	194	23		
Jim Lash	WR	6'2"	200	23		24
Sam McCullum	WR	6'2"	203	22		
Steve Craig	TE	6'3"	230	24		
Doug Kingsriter	TE	6'2"	222	25		
Stu Voight	TE	6'1"	225	27		24
Neil Clabo	K	6'2"	200	22		
Fred Cox	K	5'10"	200	36		85

DETROIT LIONS 7-7 Rick Forzano

Scores of Each Game		
30	GREEN BAY	16
17	Atlanta	14
10	DALLAS	36
27	CHICAGO	7
19	Minnesota	25
8	Houston	24
28	San Francisco	17
21	CLEVELAND	10
13	GREEN BAY	10
21	Kansas City	*24
0	LOS ANGELES	20
21	Chicago	25
17	MINNESOTA	10
13	ST. LOUIS	24

Use Name	Pos.	Hgt	Wgt	Age	Int	Pts
Rocky Freitas	OT	6'6"	275	29		
Craig Hertwig	OT	6'8"	270	23		
Jim Yarbrough	OT	6'6"	265	28		
Lynn Boden	OG	6'5"	270	22		
Bob Kowalkowski	OG	6'3"	245	31		
Gordon Jolley	OT-OG	6'5"	245	26		
Guy Dennis	C-OG	6'2"	250	28		
Richard Hicks	C	6'4"	250	24		
Jon Morris	C	6'4"	250	32		
Ernie Price	DE	6'4"	245	24		2
Ken Sanders	DE	6'5"	245	25		
Larry Hand	DT-DE	6'4"	245	35	1	
Doug English	DT	6'5"	245	22		
Herb Orvis	DT	6'5"	245	28		
Billy Howard	DE-DT	6'4"	255	25		
Jim Mitchell	DE-DT	6'3"	250	26		
Larry Ball	LB	6'6"	235	25		
Mike Hennigan	LB	6'2"	225	23		6
Jim Laslavic	LB	6'2"	240	23	2	
Paul Naumoff	LB	6'1"	215	30	2	
Ed O'Neil	LB	6'3"	235	22		6
Charlie Weaver	LB	6'2"	225	26	1	
Lem Barney	DB	6'	190	29	5	
Ben Davis	DB	5'11"	180	29	1	6
Lenny Dunlap	DB	6'1"	200	26		
Dick Jauron	DB	6'	190	24	4	
Levi Johnson	DB	6'3"	200	24	3	6
Mike Weger	DB	6'2"	200	29	1	
Charlie West	DB	6'1"	195	29		
Jack Concannon	QB	6'3"	200	32		
Greg Landry	QB	6'4"	205	28		
Bill Munson	QB	6'2"	200	33		
Joe Reed	QB	6'1"	195	27		6
Dexter Bussey	HB	6'1"	210	23		24
Altie Taylor	HB	5'10"	200	27		24
Bobby Thompson	HB	5'11"	195	28		6
Jim Hooks	FB	5'11"	225	23		
Horace King	FB	5'10"	210	22		12
Marlin Briscoe (from SD)	WR	5'10"	180	29		24
George Farmer (from CHI)	WR	6'4"	214	27		
Dennis Franklin	WR	6'1"	185	22		
Ray Jarvis	WR	5'11"	190	26		24
Jon Staggers	WR	5'10"	185	26		12
Leonard Thompson	WR	5'10"	190	23		
John McMakin	TE	6'3"	225	24		
Charlie Sanders	TE	6'4"	230	29		18
Errol Mann	K	6'	205	34		67
Alan Pringle	K	6'	195	23		
Herman Weaver	K	6'4"	210	26		

Steve Ownes – Knee Injury
Larry Walton – Knee Injury
Jim Thrower – Knee Injury

GREEN BAY PACKERS 4-10 Bart Starr

Scores of Each Game		
16	DETROIT	30
13	Denver	23
7	MIAMI	31
19	New Orleans	20
19	Dallas	17
13	PITTSBURGH	16
17	MINNESOTA	28
14	Chicago	27
10	Detroit	13
40	N.Y. GIANTS	14
28	CHICAGO	7
3	Minnesota	24
5	Los Angeles	22
22	ATLANTA	13

Use Name	Pos.	Hgt	Wgt	Age	Int	Pts
Ernie McMillan	OT	6'6"	265	37		
Dick Himes	OT	6'4"	260	29		
Bill Bain	OG	6'4"	270	23		
Pat Matson	OG	6'1"	245	31		
Bruce Van Dyke	OG	6'2"	255	31		
Keith Wortman	OG	6'2"	250	25		
Robert McCaffrey	C	6'2"	245	23		
Larry McCarren	C	6'3"	248	24		
Bill Cooke	DE	6'5"	250	24		
Dave Pureifory	DE	6'1"	255	25		4
Alden Roche	DE	6'4"	255	30		
Clarence Williams	DE	6'5"	255	28		
Mike McCoy	DT	6'5"	275	26		6
Steve Okoniewski	DT	6'3"	272	26		
Dave Roller	DT	6'2"	270	25		
Ron Acks	LB	6'2"	225	30		
Fred Carr	LB	6'5"	240	29	3	
Jim Carter	LB	6'3"	245	26		
Larry Hefner	LB	6'2"	230	26		
Tom Hull	LB	6'3"	230	23		
Tom Toner	LB	6'3"	235	25	1	2
Gary Weaver	LB	6'1"	224	26		
Willie Buchanon	DB	6'	190	24		
Ken Ellis	DB	5'10"	195	27	1	
Johnnie Gray	DB	5'11"	185	21	1	
Charlie Hall	DB	6'1"	190	26		
Steve Luke	DB	6'2"	205	21		
Al Matthews	DB	5'11"	190	27	2	
Hurles Scales	DB	6'1"	200	24		
Perry Smith	DB	6'1"	195	24	6	
Carlos Brown	QB	6'3"	210	23		
John Hadl	QB	6'2"	214	35		
Don Milan	QB	6'3"	196	26		
Will Harrell	HB	5'8"	182	22		18
Eric Torkelson	HB	6'2"	195	22		12
Terry Wells	HB	5'11"	195	24		
John Brockington	FB	6'1"	225	26		48
Barty Smith	FB	6'4"	240	23		30
Kent Gaydos	WR	6'6"	228	25		
Steve Odom	WR	5'8"	174	22		30
Ken Payne	WR	6'1"	185	24		
Barry Smith	WR	6'1"	190	24		6
Gerald Tinker (from ATL)	WR	5'9"	175	24		12
Charlie Wade	WR	5'10"	163	25		
Bert Askson	TE	6'3"	225	29		
Rich McGeorge	TE	6'4"	230	26		6
David Beverly (from HOU)	K	6'2"	182	25		
Steve Broussard	K	6'	200	26		
Joe Danelo	K	5'9"	166	21		53
Chester Marcol	K	6'	190	26		3

Bill Hayhoe – Broken Leg

Norm Hodgkins – Injury
Larry Krause – Shoulder Injury

CHICAGO BEARS 4-10 Jack Pardee

Scores of Each Game		
7	BALTIMORE	35
15	PHILADELPHIA	13
3	Minnesota	28
7	Detroit	27
3	Pittsburgh	34
9	MINNESOTA	13
13	MIAMI	46
27	GREEN BAY	14
3	San Francisco	31
10	Los Angeles	38
7	Green Bay	28
25	DETROIT	21
20	ST. LOUIS	34
42	New Orleans	17

Use Name	Pos.	Hgt	Wgt	Age	Int	Pts
Lionel Antoine	OT	6'6"	263	25		
Bob Asher	OT	6'5"	260	27		
Jeff Sevy	OT	6'5"	250	24		
Noah Jackson	OG	6'2"	263	24		
Bob Newton	OG	6'4"	260	26		
Revie Sorey	OG	6'2"	260	21		
Mark Nordquist	C-OG	6'4"	246	29		
Dan Neal	C	6'4"	240	26		
Dan Peiffer	C	6'3"	250	24		
Richard Harris	DE	6'4"	255	27		
Mike Hartenstine	DE	6'3"	250	22		2
Gary Hrivnak	DE	6'5"	254	24		
Mel Tom	DE	6'4"	242	34		
Wally Chambers	DT	6'6"	255	24		
Jim Osborne	DT	6'3"	254	25		
Ron Rydalch	DT	6'4"	260	23		
Roger Stillwell	DT	6'5"	265	23		
John Babinecz	LB	6'1"	222	25	1	
Waymond Bryant	LB	6'3"	230	23		
Doug Buffone	LB	6'1"	227	31	1	
Larry Ely	LB	6'1"	230	27	1	
Carl Gersbach	LB	6'1"	230	28	1	
Bob Pifferini	LB	6'2"	226	25		
Don Rives	LB	6'2"	220	24		
Craig Clemons	DB	5'11"	200	26	2	6
Earl Douthit	DB	6'2"	188	22		
Allan Ellis	DB	5'10"	182	24	2	
Bill Knox	DB	5'9"	193	24		
Virgil Livers	DB	5'8"	176	23	2	6
Doug Plank	DB	6'	197	22	2	
Ted Vactor	DB	6'	185	31		
Nemiah Wilson	DB	6'	165	32		
Bob Avellini	QB	6'2"	197	22		6
Virgil Carter (from SD)	QB	6'1"	185	29		
Gary Huff	QB	6'1"	194	24		
Roland Harper	HB	5'11"	194	22		6
Johnny Musso	HB	5'11"	205	25		
Walter Payton	HB	5'11"	200	21		42
Mike Adamle	FB-HB	5'9"	193	25		6
Tom Donchez	FB	6'2"	216	22		
Cid Edwards	FB	6'2"	230	31		6
Bob Grim	WR	6'	200	30		12
Bo Rather	WR	6'1"	180	24		12
Steve Schubert	WR	5'10"	185	24		
Ron Shanklin	WR	6'1"	190	28		
Gary Butler	TE	6'3"	235	24		
Greg Latta	TE	6'3"	226	22		18
Bob Parsons	TE	6'4"	234	25		6
Bob Thomas	K	5'10"	178	23		57

*Overtime

MINNESOTA VIKINGS

RUSHING

Last Name	No.	Yds	Avg	TD
Foreman	280	1070	3.8	13
Marinaro	101	358	3.5	1
McClanahan	92	336	3.7	0
Tarkenton	16	108	6.8	2
Osborn	32	94	2.9	1
Miller	30	93	3.1	1
Gilliam	3	35	11.7	0
Berry	1	0	0.0	0
Lee	1	0	0.0	0

RECEIVING

Last Name	No.	Yds	Avg	TD
Foreman	73	691	10	9
Marinaro	54	462	9	3
Gilliam	50	777	16	7
Lash	37	535	15	3
Voigt	34	363	11	4
McClanahan	18	141	8	1
Craig	6	68	11	0
Miller	4	35	9	0
Haslerig	2	28	14	0
McCullum	2	25	13	0
Osborn	1	−4	−4	0

PUNT RETURNS

Last Name	No.	Yds	Avg	TD
Bryant	19	125	7	0
McCullum	12	22	2	0
J. Wright	1	22	22	0
Athas	6	37	6	0
Beamon	1	0	0	0
Blair	2	−2	−1	0

KICKOFF RETURNS

Last Name	No.	Yds	Avg	TD
McClanahan	17	360	21	0
McCullum	9	221	25	0
Athas	6	95	16	0
Miller	5	93	19	0
Marinaro	5	71	14	0
Osborn	1	38	38	0
Foreman	1	4	4	0

PASSING – PUNTING – KICKING

PASSING	Att	Comp	%	Yds	Yd/Att	TD	Int–%	RK
Tarkenton	425	273	64	2994	7.0	25	13– 3	1
Lee	14	5	36	103	7.4	2	1– 7	
Berry	6	3	50	24	4.0	0	0– 0	
Lash	1	0	0	0	0.0	0	0– 0	

PUNTING	No	Avg
Clabo	73	41.1

KICKING	XP	Att	%	FG	Att	%
Cox	46	48	96	13	17	76

DETROIT LIONS

RUSHING

Last Name	No.	Yds	Avg	TD
Bussey	157	696	4.4	2
Taylor	195	638	3.3	4
B. Thompson	51	268	5.3	1
King	61	260	4.3	2
Reed	34	193	5.7	1
Landry	20	92	4.6	0
Staggers	2	26	13.0	0
Jarvis	1	0	0.0	0
Munson	4	−3	−0.8	0
Briscoe	2	−3	−1.5	0
Hooks	4	−8	−2.0	0
L. Thompson	1	−12	−12.0	0

RECEIVING

Last Name	No.	Yds	Avg	TD
Sanders	37	486	13	3
Jarvis	29	501	17	4
Briscoe	24	372	16	4
Taylor	21	111	5	0
B. Thompson	19	122	6	0
Bussey	14	175	13	2
Staggers	14	174	12	2
King	13	81	6	0
Farmer	8	118	15	0
Franklin	5	109	22	0
McMakin	2	43	22	0
Hooks	1	5	5	0

PUNT RETURNS

Last Name	No.	Yds	Avg	TD
West	22	219	10	0
Barney	8	80	10	0
Jauron	6	29	5	0

KICKOFF RETURNS

Last Name	No.	Yds	Avg	TD
B. Thompson	22	565	26	0
L. Thompson	12	271	23	0
King	6	117	20	0
Weger	3	42	14	0
West	2	41	21	0
Bussey	2	38	19	0
Hooks	2	8	4	0
Dunlap	1	19	19	0
Hennigan	1	13	13	0
Dennis	1	0	0	0

PASSING – PUNTING – KICKING

PASSING	Att	Comp	%	Yds	Yd/Att	TD	Int–%	RK
Reed	191	86	45	1181	6.2	9	10– 5	10
Munson	109	65	60	626	5.7	5	2– 2	
Landry	56	31	55	403	7.2	1	0– 0	
Concannon	2	1	50	30	15.0	0	0– 0	
Briscoe	2	0	0	0	0.0	0	0– 0	
King	1	0	0	0	0.0	0	0– 0	
H. Weaver	1	0	0	0	0.0	0	0– 0	

PUNTING	No	Avg
H. Weaver	80	42.0
Mann	1	34.0

KICKING	XP	Att	%	FG	Att	%
Mann	25	29	86	14	21	67

GREEN BAY PACKERS

RUSHING

Last Name	No.	Yds	Avg	TD
Brockington	144	434	3.0	7
Harrell	121	359	3.0	1
Barty Smith	60	243	4.1	4
Torkelson	42	226	5.4	2
Wells	33	139	4.2	0
Odom	5	55	11.0	0
Hadl	20	47	2.4	0
Milan	4	41	10.3	0
Tinker	1	5	5.0	0
Payne	1	−2	−2.0	0

RECEIVING

Last Name	No.	Yds	Avg	TD
Payne	58	766	13	0
Harrell	34	261	8	2
Brockington	33	242	8	1
McGeorge	32	458	14	1
Barty Smith	16	140	9	1
Odom	15	299	20	4
Barry Smith	6	77	13	1
Torkelson	6	37	6	0
Wells	6	11	2	0
Tinker	4	84	21	1
Askson	2	25	13	0

PUNT RETURNS

Last Name	No.	Yds	Avg	TD
Harrell	21	136	7	0
Ellis	6	27	5	0
Gray	1	27	27	0
Hall	1	0	0	0
Odom	1	0	0	0

KICKOFF RETURNS

Last Name	No.	Yds	Avg	TD
Odom	42	1034	25	1
Luke	6	91	15	0
Torkelson	5	89	18	0
Harrell	3	78	26	0
Barty Smith	4	63	13	0
Wells	1	26	26	0
McGeorge	1	17	17	0
Bain	1	10	10	0

PASSING – PUNTING – KICKING

PASSING	Att	Comp	%	Yds	Yd/Att	TD	Int–%	RK
Hadl	353	191	54	2095	5.9	6	21– 6	13
Milan	32	15	47	181	5.7	1	1– 3	
Harrell	5	3	60	61	12.2	3	0– 0	
Brown	4	3	75	63	15.8	1	0– 0	

PUNTING	No	Avg
Beverly	78	37.7
Broussard	29	31.8

KICKING	XP	Att	%	FG	Att	%
Danelo	20	23	87	11	16	69

CHICAGO BEARS

RUSHING

Last Name	No.	Yds	Avg	TD
Payton	196	679	3.5	7
Harper	100	453	4.5	1
Adamle	94	353	3.8	1
Edwards	27	73	2.7	0
Musso	6	33	5.5	0
Rather	4	24	6.0	0
Huff	5	7	1.4	0
Avellini	4	−3	−0.8	1

RECEIVING

Last Name	No.	Yds	Avg	TD
Rather	39	685	18	2
Payton	33	213	7	0
Grim	28	374	13	2
Harper	27	191	7	0
Latta	16	202	13	3
Adamle	15	111	7	0
Parsons	13	184	14	1
Edwards	11	86	8	1
Schubert	5	68	14	0
Jackson	1	17	17	0
Sevy	1	6	6	0

PUNT RETURNS

Last Name	No.	Yds	Avg	TD
Livers	42	456	11	0
Schubert	6	33	6	0
Plank	3	23	8	0
Knox	1	0	0	0

KICKOFF RETURNS

Last Name	No.	Yds	Avg	TD
Livers	26	529	20	0
Payton	14	444	32	0
Douthitt	13	333	26	0
Schubert	9	146	16	0
Knox	4	67	17	0
Harper	4	67	17	0
Adamle	1	27	27	0
Vactor	1	25	25	0
Rather	1	6	6	0
Osborne	1	0	0	0

PASSING – PUNTING – KICKING

PASSING	Att	Comp	%	Yds	Yd/Att	TD	Int–%	RK
Huff	205	114	56	1083	5.3	3	9– 4	12
Avellini	126	67	53	942	7.5	6	11– 9	
Carter	5	3	60	24	4.8	0	1–20	
Adamle	2	2	100	57	28.5	0	0– 0	
Grim	1	0	0	0	0.0	0	0– 0	
Parsons	1	0	0	0	0.0	0	0– 0	
Payton	1	0	0	0	0.0	0	1–100	

PUNTING	No	Avg
Parsons	93	39.0
Payton	1	39.0

KICKING	XP	Att	%	FG	Att	%
Thomas	18	22	82	13	23	57

LOS ANGELES RAMS 12-2 Chuck Knox

Scores of Each Game		
7	Dallas	18
23	San Francisco	14
24	BALTIMORE	13
13	San Diego	*10
22	ATLANTA	7
38	NEW ORLEANS	14
42	Philadelphia	3
23	SAN FRANCISCO	24
16	Atlanta	7
38	CHICAGO	10
20	Detroit	0
14	New Orleans	7
22	GREEN BAY	5
10	PITTSBURGH	3

Use Name	Pos.	Hgt	Wgt	Age	Int	Pts
Charlie Cowan	OT	6'4"	265	37		
Doug France	OT	6'5"	260	22		
John Williams	OT	6'3"	256	29		
Dennis Harrah	OG	6'5"	257	22		
Tom Mack	OG	6'3"	250	31		
Joe Scibelli	OG	6'1"	255	36		
Bob DeMarco	C	6'3"	245	37		
Rich Saul	C	6'3"	235	27		
Al Cowlings	DE	6'5"	245	28		
Fred Dryer	DE	6'6"	240	29	1	6
Mike Fanning	DE	6'6"	260	22		
Jack Youngblood	DE	6'4"	255	25		2
Larry Brooks	DT	6'3"	255	25		
Cody Jones	DT	6'5"	240	24		
Bill Nelson	DT	6'7"	270	27		
Merlin Olsen	DT	6'5"	270	34		
Ken Geddes	LB	6'3"	235	27	1	
Rick Kay	LB	6'4"	235	25		
Jim Peterson	LB	6'5"	240	25		6
Jack Reynolds	LB	6'1"	232	27	1	
Isiah Robertson	LB	6'3"	225	26	4	6
Jim Youngblood	LB	6'3"	240	25		
Al Clark	DB	6'	185	26		
Dave Elmendorf	DB	6'1"	195	26	4	
Monte Jackson	DB	5'11"	190	22	2	6
Eddie McMillan	DB	6'	190	23	3	
Rod Perry	DB	5'9"	170	21		
Steve Preece	DB	6'1"	195	28		
Bill Simpson	DB	6'1"	180	23	6	
James Harris	QB	6'3"	210	28		6
Ron Jaworski	QB	6'2"	185	24		12
John Cappelletti	HB	6'1"	217	23		36
Larry McCutcheon	HB	6'1"	205	25		18
Rob Scribner	HB	6'	200	24		12
Jim Bertelsen	FB	5'11"	205	25		18
Cullen Bryant	FB	6'1"	240	24		12
Rod Phillips	TE-FB	6'	220	22		
Harold Jackson	WR	5'10"	175	29		42
Ron Jessie	WR	6'	185	27		18
Willie McGee	WR	5'11"	178	25		
Jack Snow	WR	6'2"	190	32		6
Bob Klein	TE	6'5"	235	28		12
Terry Nelson	TE	6'2"	230	23		
Duane Carrell	K	5'10"	185	25		
Tom Dempsey	K	6'1"	260	34		94

Charlie Stukes – Knee Injury

SAN FRANCISCO FORTY-NINERS 5-9 Dick Nolan

Scores of Each Game		
17	Minnesota	27
14	LOS ANGELES	23
20	Kansas City	3
3	ATLANTA	17
35	NEW ORLEANS	21
16	New England	24
17	DETROIT	28
24	Los Angeles	23
31	CHICAGO	3
16	New Orleans	6
17	Philadelphia	27
13	HOUSTON	27
9	Atlanta	31
23	N.Y. GIANTS	26

Use Name	Pos.	Hgt	Wgt	Age	Int	Pts
Cas Banaszek	OT	6'3"	255	29		
Keith Fahnhorst	OT	6'6"	265	23		
Jeff Hart	OT	6'5"	266	21		
Bobby Penchion	OG	6'5"	252	26		
Woody Peoples	OG	6'2"	252	32		
John Watson	OT-OG	6'4"	245	26		
Bill Reid	C	6'1"	242	23		
Jean Barrett	OG-C	6'6"	254	24		
Cleveland Elam	DE	6'3"	254	23		
Cedrick Hardman	DE	6'3"	258	26		
Tommy Hart	DE	6'3"	244	30		6
Wayne Baker	DT	6'6"	270	22		
Bob Haskins	DT	6'2"	250	29		
Bill Sandifer	DT	6'6"	278	23		
Jimmy Webb	DT	6'5"	248	23		
Greg Collins	LB	6'2"	234	22		
Willie Harper	LB	6'2"	220	25		
Frank Nunley	LB	6'2"	234	29	1	
Skip Vanderbundt	LB	6'3"	223	28	2	
Dave Washington	LB	6'5"	223	26		6
Nate Allen	DB	5'10"	170	27	1	6
Tim Anderson	DB	6'	192	26		
Windlan Hall	DB	5'11"	175	25		
Jim Johnson	DB	6'2"	185	37	2	
Ralph McGill	DB	5'11"	183	25	1	6
Mel Phillips	DB	6'	190	33	1	
John Saunders	DB	6'3"	196	25		
Bruce Taylor	DB	6'	190	27	3	
Tom Owen	QB	6'1"	194	22		
Norm Snead	QB	6'4"	215	35		6
Steve Spurrier	QB	6'2"	198	30		
Wilbur Jackson	HB	6'1"	215	23		
Kermit Johnson	HB	6'	200	23		
Manfred Moore	HB	6'	194	24		
Del Williams	HB	6'	195	24		24
Sammy Johnson	FB	6'	223	22		18
Larry Schreiber	FB	6'	209	28		36
Terry Beasley	WR	5'10"	182	25		
Bob Hayes	WR	6'	185	32		
Mike Holmes	WR	6'2"	193	24		6
Gene Washington	WR	6'1"	185	28		54
Len Garrett (from NO)	TE	6'3"	230	26		
Bill Larson	TE	6'4"	225	21		
Tom Mitchell	TE	6'2"	215	31		18
Steve Mike-Mayer	K	6'	178	27		69
Tom Wittum	K	6'1"	190	25		

ATLANTA FALCONS 4-10 Marion Campbell

Scores of Each Game		
20	St. Louis	23
14	DETROIT	17
14	NEW ORLEANS	7
17	San Francisco	3
7	Los Angeles	22
14	CINCINNATI	21
7	New Orleans	23
0	Minnesota	38
7	LOS ANGELES	16
35	DENVER	21
34	Oakland	*37
27	WASHINGTON	30
31	SAN FRANCISCO	9
13	Green Bay	22

Use Name	Pos.	Hgt	Wgt	Age	Int	Pts
Brent Adams	OT	6'5"	256	23		
Nick Bebout	OT	6'5"	267	24		
Len Gotshalk	OT	6'4"	253	25		
Dennis Havig	OG	6'2"	254	26		
Larron Jackson	OG	6'3"	260	26		
Royce Smith	OG	6'3"	260	26		
Paul Ryczek	C	6'2"	238	23		
Jeff Van Note	C	6'2"	252	29		
John Zook	DE	6'5"	248	27		
Roy Hilton	DE	6'6"	250	30		
Mike Lewis	DT	6'3"	258	25		
Jeff Merrow	DT	6'4"	230	22		
Mike Tilleman	DT	6'5"	273	31		
Chuck Walker	DT	6'2"	250	33		
Greg Brezina	LB	6'2"	220	29	4	
Don Hansen	LB	6'3"	226	31	1	
Fulton Kuykendall	LB	6'5"	225	22		
Tommy Nobis	LB	6'2"	232	31		
Ralph Ortega	LB	6'2"	220	22		
Carl Russ	LB	6'2"	227	22		
Ray Brown	DB	6'2"	208	26	4	6
Rick Byas	DB	5'9"	172	24		
Ray Easterling	DB	6'	186	25	3	
Tom Hayes	DB	6'1"	196	29	4	
Bob Jones	DB	6'1"	193	24		
Rolland Lawrence	DB	5'10"	174	24	9	6
Ron Mabra	DB	5'10"	164	24		
Steve Bartkowski	QB	6'4"	213	22		12
Kim McQuilken	QB	6'2"	200	24		
Pat Sullivan	QB	6'	200	25		
Larry Crowe	HB	6'1"	198	25		
Dave Hampton	HB	6'	206	28		36
Mack Herron (from NE)	HB	5'5"	175	27		
Haskel Stanback	HB	6'	210	23		30
Brad Davis	FB	5'11"	208	22		
Monroe Eley	FB	6'2"	210	23		
Woody Thompson	FB	6'1"	228	23		
Oscar Reed	HB-FB	5'11"	222	31		
Ken Burrow	WR	6'	188	27		12
Wallace Francis	WR	5'11"	185	23		24
Alfred Jenkins	WR	5'10"	155	23		36
Frank Pitts	WR	6'2"	200	31		
Greg McCrary	TE	6'3"	230	23		
Jim Mitchell	TE	6'2"	235	27		30
John James	K	6'3"	197	26		
Nick Mike-Mayer	K	5'8"	185	25		42

Claude Humphrey – Knee Injury

Ted Fritsch – Knee Injury
Vince Kendrick – Knee Injury
Jim Miller – Knee Injury

NEW ORLEANS SAINTS 2-12 John North Ernie Hefferle

Scores of Each Game		
3	Washington	41
0	CINCINNATI	21
7	Atlanta	14
20	GREEN BAY	19
21	San Francisco	35
14	Los Angeles	38
23	ATLANTA	7
10	Oakland	48
7	MINNESOTA	20
6	SAN FRANCISCO	16
16	Cleveland	17
7	LOS ANGELES	14
14	N.Y. Giants	28
17	CHICAGO	42

Use Name	Pos.	Hgt	Wgt	Age	Int	Pts
John Hill	OT	6'2"	245	25		
Phil LaPorta	OT	6'4"	256	22		
Chris Morris	OT	6'3"	250	25		
Don Morrison	OT	6'5"	260	25		
Kurt Schumacher	OT	6'3"	260	22		
Dave Thompson	C-OT	6'4"	260	26		
Jake Kupp	OG	6'3"	248	33		
Emanuel Zanders	OG	6'1"	260	24		
Tom Wickert	OT-OG	6'4"	246	23		
Sylvester Croom	C	6'	235	20		
Lee Gross	C	6'3"	245	22		
Steve Baumgartner	DE	6'7"	260	24		
Andy Dorris	DE	6'4"	240	24		
Elois Grooms	DE	6'4"	240	22		
Joe Owens	DE	6'2"	250	28		
Derland Moore	DT	6'4"	260	23		
Bob Pollard	DT	6'3"	250	26		
Elex Price	DT	6'3"	260	25		
Rusty Chambers	LB	6'1"	215	21		6
Don Coleman	LB	6'2"	222	22		
Joe Federspiel	LB	6'1"	235	25		
Rick Kingrea	LB	6'1"	230	26	1	
Rick Middleton	LB	6'2"	228	23	1	
Greg Westbrooks	LB	6'2"	215	22	1	
Chuck Crist	DB	6'2"	205	24	3	
Jim DeRatt	DB	6'	203	22		
Johnny Fuller	DB	6'	185	29		
Ernie Jackson	DB	5'10"	175	25	2	
Bivian Lee	DB	6'3"	200	27	2	
Tom Myers	DB	5'11"	184	24	5	6
Terry Schmidt	DB	6'	177	23	1	
Mo Spencer	DB	6'	175	23		
Larry Cipa	QB	6'3"	209	22		
Archie Manning	QB	6'3"	207	26		6
Bobby Scott	QB	6'1"	200	26		
Alvin Maxson	HB	5'11"	205	22		18
Steve Rogers	HB	6'2"	200	22		
Mike Strachan	HB	6'	195	22		12
Andrew Jones	FB	6'2"	213	22		6
Morris LaGrand (from KC)	FB	6'1"	220	22		6
Rod McNeill	FB	6'2"	220	24		24
Larry Burton	WR	6'1"	190	23		12
Gil Chapman	WR	5'9"	180	22		
Andy Hamilton	WR	6'3"	190	25		
Don Herrmann	WR	6'2"	205	28		6
Joel Parker	WR	6'5"	212	23		12
Henry Childs	TE	6'2"	223	24		
Paul Seal	TE	6'4"	222	23		6
Tom Blanchard	K	6'	180	27		
Bill McClard	K	5'10"	202	23		4
Richie Szaro	K	5'11"	205	27		47

Wayne Colman – Broken Arm
Dave Davis – Ankle Injury
Jim Merlo – Injury
Bob Newland – Injury

*—Overtime

LOS ANGELES RAMS

RUSHING

Last Name	No.	Yds	Avg	TD
McCutcheon	213	911	4.3	2
Bryant	117	467	4.0	2
Bertelsen	116	457	3.9	3
Scribner	42	216	5.1	2
Cappelletti	48	158	3.3	6
Phillips	17	69	4.1	0
Harris	18	45	2.5	1
Jaworski	12	33	2.8	2
Jessie	2	15	7.5	0

RECEIVING

Last Name	No.	Yds	Avg	TD
H. Jackson	43	786	18	7
Jessie	41	547	13	3
McCutcheon	31	230	7	1
Bryant	20	229	12	0
Klein	16	237	15	2
Bertelsen	14	208	15	0
McGee	6	83	14	0
Snow	4	86	22	1
Scribner	2	28	14	0
Phillips	2	10	5	0
Nelson	1	5	5	0
Cowan	1	1	1	0

PUNT RETURNS

Last Name	No.	Yds	Avg	TD
Scribner	26	205	8	0
Bertelsen	11	143	13	0
Elmendorf	15	125	8	0
Bryant	2	47	24	0
Simpson	1	−3	−3	0

KICKOFF RETURNS

Last Name	No.	Yds	Avg	TD
McGee	17	404	24	0
Bryant	12	280	23	0
Cappelletti	3	39	13	0
Scribner	1	24	24	0
Bertelsen	1	17	17	0

PASSING – PUNTING – KICKING

PASSING	Att	Comp	%	Yds	Yd/Att	TD	Int–%	RK
Harris	285	157	55	2148	7.5	14	15– 5	4
Jaworski	48	24	50	302	6.3	0	2– 4	
McCutcheon	1	0	0	0	0.0	0	0– 0	

PUNTING	No	Avg
Carrell	73	39.4

KICKING	XP	Att	%	FG	Att	%
Dempsey	31	36	86	21	26	81

SAN FRANCISCO FORTY-NINERS

RUSHING

Last Name	No.	Yds	Avg	TD
D. Williams	117	631	5.4	3
Schreiber	134	337	2.5	5
Jackson	78	303	3.9	0
S. Johnson	55	185	3.4	3
Spurrier	15	91	6.1	0
Snead	9	30	3.3	1
K. Johnson	4	25	6.3	0
Moore	3	10	3.3	0
Beasley	1	5	5.0	0
Owen	1	1	1.0	0
Hayes	2	−2	−1.0	0
Holmes	1	−4	−4.0	0
Washington	1	−4	−4.0	0
Wittum	1	−10	−10.0	0

RECEIVING

Last Name	No.	Yds	Avg	TD
Washington	44	735	17	9
Schreiber	40	289	7	1
Williams	34	370	11	1
Mitchell	25	366	15	3
S. Johnson	23	177	8	0
Beasley	20	297	15	0
Jackson	17	128	8	0
Holmes	16	220	14	1
Hayes	6	119	20	0
Larson	5	64	13	0
Wittum	2	29	15	0
Moore	1	11	11	0
Fahnhorst	1	1	1	0

PUNT RETURNS

Last Name	No.	Yds	Avg	TD
McGill	31	290	9	0
Taylor	16	166	10	0
Moore	16	160	10	0

KICKOFF RETURNS

Last Name	No.	Yds	Avg	TD
Moore	26	650	25	0
S. Johnson	17	400	24	0
K. Johnson	6	135	23	0
Holmes	2	59	30	0
Baker	4	45	11	0
Hart	2	28	14	0
Williams	1	24	24	0
Hall	1	18	18	0
Fahnhorst	1	13	13	0

PASSING – PUNTING – KICKING

PASSING	Att	Comp	%	Yds	Yd/Att	TD	Int–%	RK
Spurrier	207	102	49	1151	5.6	5	7– 3	9
Snead	189	108	57	1337	7.1	9	10– 5	5
Owen	51	24	47	318	6.2	1	2– 4	
S. Johnson	2	0	0	0	0.0	0	0– 0	
Washington	1	0	0	0	0.0	0	0 0	

PUNTING	No	Avg
Wittum	67	41.9

KICKING	XP	Att	%	FG	Att	%
Mike-Mayer	27	31	87	14	28	50

ATLANTA FALCONS

RUSHING

Last Name	No.	Yds	Avg	TD
Hampton	250	1002	4.0	5
Stanback	105	440	4.2	5
Herron	62	274	4.4	0
Thompson	68	247	3.6	0
Reed	14	40	2.9	0
McQuilken	4	26	6.5	0
Bartkowski	14	15	1.1	2
Francis	2	12	6.0	0
Sullivan	6	9	1.5	0
Tinker	1	5	5.0	0
Ely	1	3	3.0	0

RECEIVING

Last Name	No.	Yds	Avg	TD
Jenkins	38	767	20	6
J. Mitchell	34	536	16	4
Burrow	25	323	13	2
Hampton	21	195	9	1
Stanback	14	116	8	0
Thompson	14	92	7	0
Francis	13	270	21	4
Tinker	7	121	17	2
Herron	5	50	10	0
Reed	2	1	1	0
Jones	1	25	25	0

PUNT RETURNS

Last Name	No.	Yds	Avg	TD
Herron	22	183	8	0
Eley	7	61	9	0
Jenkins	6	38	6	0
Tinker	6	23	4	0
Mabra	4	20	5	0
Brown	2	12	6	0

KICKOFF RETURNS

Last Name	No.	Yds	Avg	TD
Tinker	13	307	24	0
Francis	14	265	19	0
Herron	13	264	20	0
Eley	8	131	16	0
Byas	5	94	19	0
Lawrence	4	80	20	0
Thompson	4	62	16	0
McCrary	3	48	16	0
Jenkins	1	24	24	0
Reed	2	17	9	0
Davis	1	0	0	0

PASSING – PUNTING – KICKING

PASSING	Att	Comp	%	Yds	Yd/Att	TD	Int–%	RK
Bartkowski	255	115	45	1662	6.5	13	15– 6	11
Sullivan	70	28	40	380	5.4	3	5– 7	
McQuilken	61	20	33	253	4.2	1	9–15	
James	1	1	100	25	25.0	0	0– 0	
Stanback	1	1	100	41	41.0	1	0– 0	

PUNTING	No	Avg
James	89	41.5

KICKING	XP	Att	%	FG	Att	%
Mike-Mayer	30	33	91	4	10	40

NEW ORLEANS SAINTS

RUSHING

Last Name	No.	Yds	Avg	TD
Strachan	161	668	4.1	2
Maxson	139	371	2.7	3
McNeill	61	206	3.4	2
Manning	33	186	5.6	1
Jones	42	108	2.6	1
Rogers	17	62	3.6	0
LaGrand	13	38	2.9	1
Seal	1	10	10.0	0
Burton	2	8	4.0	0
Cipa	6	2	0.3	0

RECEIVING

Last Name	No.	Yds	Avg	TD
Maxson	41	234	6	0
Strachan	30	224	8	0
Seal	28	414	15	1
McNeill	18	138	8	2
Burton	16	305	19	2
Hamilton	12	210	18	0
Childs	10	179	18	0
Jones	10	52	5	0
Parker	9	123	14	2
Herrmann	3	47	16	1
Chapman	1	7	7	0
Rogers	1	2	2	0
LaGrand	1	−1	−1	0

PUNT RETURNS

Last Name	No.	Yds	Avg	TD
Chapman	17	207	12	0
Schmidt	11	76	7	0
Myers	10	70	7	0
DeRatt	2	17	9	0
Spencer	1	0	0	0

KICKOFF RETURNS

Last Name	No.	Yds	Avg	TD
Chapman	28	614	22	0
McNeill	10	276	28	0
Maxson	6	103	17	0
Rogers	6	98	16	0
Strachan	5	91	18	0
Spencer	5	68	14	0
Schmidt	2	54	27	0
Chambers	1	15	15	0

PASSING – PUNTING – KICKING

PASSING	Att	Comp	%	Yds	Yd/Att	TD	Int–%	RK
Manning	338	159	47	1683	5.0	7	20– 6	15
Cipa	37	14	38	182	4.9	1	3– 8	
Scott	17	8	47	96	5.7	0	1– 6	

PUNTING	No	Avg
Blanchard	92	41.0

KICKING	XP	Att	%	FG	Att	%
Szaro	17	17	100	10	16	63

1975 A.F.C. Closing The Marketplace

The World Football League began its second year of play with some impressive new assets. Larry Csonka, Paul Warfield, and Jim Kiick reported to the Memphis club amidst much publicity, Calvin Hill and Ted Kwalick joined the Hawaii team, and John Gilliam played in the Chicago lineup. But other N.F.L. stars such as Kenny Stabler, L.C. Greenwood, and Curly Culp made haste to cancel their future contracts with W.F.L. clubs, and some of last year's stars of the new league, such as Tony Adams and Greg Latta, jumped at the chance to sign with N.F.L. teams. These departing players had taken an accurate reading of the league's pulse, for the massively bad publicity from last season carried over into 1975 and plunged the once-optimistic circuit into a new round of staggering debts and defaulted contracts. On October 22, 11 weeks into its 20-week schedule, the W.F.L. closed its doors and went out of business. Attendance for this second season averaged 13,371 per game and was fading, while new debts accumulated this year totaled up to about $10 million.

EASTERN DIVISION

Baltimore Colts—The Colts seemed headed for another dismal season when they dropped four of their first five games, but they then beat the Jets 45-28 and roared through the rest of the schedule with the momentum of a runaway boulder. New coach Ted Marchibroda found the young talent under his command suddenly jelling into a top-flight unit in mid-season. Quarterback Bert Jones blossomed into one of the N.F.L.'s dangerous young passers, while Lydell Mitchell starred as a runner and receiver out of the backfield. The offensive line, bolstered by All-Pro tackle George Kunz from the Falcons, played far better than expected, and the defensive front four of Fred Cook, John Dutton, Joe Ehrmann, and Mike Barnes sacked quarterbacks with amazing regularity. The turnabout was so sudden that observers had to wonder when Cinderella was going to turn back into a pumpkin. On November 10, the Colts came back from a 21-0 deficit to beat the Bills 42-35. They upset the Dolphins in Miami 33-17 on November 23, and three weeks later climbed into a first-place tie by beating the Dolphins in Baltimore 10-7 in overtime. A 34-21 victory over New England in the final game clinched a playoff spot for the surprise team of the year.

Miami Dolphins—Coach Don Shula had other worries besides the defection of Larry Csonka, Paul Warfield, and Jim Kiick to the W.F.L. Injuries played havoc with his defensive platoon, striking down Dick Anderson, Nick Buoniconti, Bob Heinz, Manny Fernandez, and Bill Stanfill. But Shula managed to plug all the holes, getting good seasons out of odds and ends like Norm Bulaich, Don Nottingham, and Charlie Babb. After beating Buffalo 35-30 on October 26, the Dolphins looked home free for another divisional title. But the Oilers upset them 20-19 on November 16, and the Colts clobbered them 33-17 the next week. But worse than losing the game to the Colts was losing Bob Griese in that contest for the rest of the season with a toe injury. Forty-one year old Earl Morrall played well in leading the Dolphins to a 20-7 decision over New England but hurt his knee in the process. That left third-stringer Don Strock at quarterback. He engineered a 31-21 victory over Buffalo, but the red-hot Colts then took the 10-7 decision in an epic overtime contest. With two losses to the Colts, the Dolphins incredibly found themselves out of the playoffs.

Buffalo Bills—O.J. Simpson had reached the stage where he was in a class only with the greats of the past. Running behind the great Buffalo offensive line, the Juice rushed for 1817 yards and set a new record with 23 touchdowns scored for the season. Quarterback Joe Ferguson found it easier to pass against defenses keying on the running of Simpson and Jim Braxton. The only fly in the ointment was a defensive backfield which was decimated by injuries. After the Bills won five of their first six games, opponents began scoring points as fast as O.J. and company could put them on the board. Midseason losses to the Colts, Bengals, and Dolphins put an end to the playoff hopes for this year.

New York Jets—Two victories in the first three games fueled hopes for the Jets, but the defensive unit suddenly fell to pieces. After the promising start, the Jets lost to the Vikings 29-21, to the Dolphins 43-0, and to the Colts 45-28. Losses to the Bills and Vikings were followed by a 52-19 slaughter at the hands of the Colts, during which two Jets players broke into a fist fight on the sidelines. Coach Charley Winner got the axe and was replaced on an interim basis by Ken Shipp. One victory in five games was all Shipp could coax out of this squad with massive defensive problems and a mediocre season out of Joe Namath.

New England Patriots—The bad vibrations started with the strike in the final week of training camp and carried throughout the season. Jim Plunkett twice separated his shoulder, robbing the attack of leadership right at the start of the campaign. After the second injury, rookie Steve Grogan played so well that fans at Schaeffer Stadium booed Plunkett when he returned to the lineup. Mack Herron symbolized the turnaround in Patriot fortunes. After setting a record last season for total yardage, Herron fell out of favor with coach Chuck Fairbanks, found himself benched, and was waived to Atlanta late in the season.

CENTRAL DIVISION

Pittsburgh Steelers—Despite a 37-0 triumph over San Diego to start the season, the Steelers looked better and better as the campaign wore on. After losing to Buffalo in their second game, the Steelers then tore through the league with 11 straight victories. The Pittsburgh defense smothered enemy attacks week after week, even while losing Joe Greene for a time with neck and groin injuries. Franco Harris led the offense with 1246 yards on the ground, but the performances of Terry Bradshaw, Lynn Swann, and the yeoman line ranked as high in excellence. The Steelers beat back challenges from the Oilers and Bengals to brand themselves the team to beat in the playoffs.

Cincinnati Bengals—Even with All-Pro defensive lineman Mike Reid retired to a career as a pianist, the Bengals had talent enough to threaten the Steelers in the Central Division. Paul Brown's men ran out to six quick wins but then lost 30-24 to the Steelers on November 2 to fall into a first place tie. They then dropped into second place by losing to the Browns the next week. Although they beat back the challenging Oilers 23-9 on November 30, the attempt to recapture first place failed by again bowing to the Steelers 35-14 on December 13. But a 47-17 shellacking of San Diego in the final game clinched a wildcard berth in the playoffs.

Houston Oilers—Bum Phillips thoroughly enjoyed his first year as head coach as the Oilers made a surprise run at a playoff berth. The Oilers won six of their first seven games, but inability to beat either the Steelers or Bengals condemned them to being an exciting also-ran. The defensive front three of Elvin Bethea, Curly Culp, and Tody Smith had new comfort in Robert Brazile, an excellent rookie linebacker. Operating behind a surprisingly strong line, quarterback Dan Pastorini got off lots of passes to Ken Burrough, while Ronnie Coleman and rookie Don Hardeman crunched out the yardage on the ground. The real star of the season, however, was Billy Johnson, a flashy little wide receiver and kick returner whose wobbly-leg victory dance after touchdowns turned on the fans and threatened spiking with extinction.

Cleveland Browns—The Browns had fallen on hardtimes, and the hiring of Forrest Gregg as head coach had no immediate effect on the situation. Nine losses at the start of the campaign horrified fans who had known only success until recently. An upset 35-23 victory over state-rival Cincinnati soothed some of the hurt, but few people would deny that the Browns were weaker at more positions than they were strong. Greg Pruitt and Reggie Rucker stood out as offensive threats among the rubble, while Jerry Sherk and rookie Mack Mitchell worked hard in the defensive line.

WESTERN DIVISION

Oakland Raiders—The depth on the Raiders was such that the second unit could probably have played winning ball in the N.F.L. Despite Jim Otto's retirement and a bad knee which hobbled Kenny Stabler, the Oakland offensive machine rolled on with a strong line, five good running backs, and a complementary set of wide receivers in Cliff Branch and Fred Biletnikoff. The defense had a new recruit in All-Pro linebacker Ted Hendricks who was so strong that Bubba Smith was cut. George Blanda and Ray Guy gave Oakland an edge in kicking, while the specialty teams sparkled with kickoff returner Harold Hart and rookie punt receiver Neal Colzie. As expected, the Raiders easily captured the Western Division crown, but their plans to go all the way through the playoffs to the Super Bowl were soon thwarted by the Steelers.

Denver Broncos—The Broncos opened the season with two victories, but then fell into a rut which sank them below the .500 level. The ground game suffered when Otis Armstrong was injured, although second-year man Jon Keyworth assumed the heavy-duty running chores with some flair. At quarterback, veteran Charley Johnson failed to ignite the offense, lost his job to Steve Ramsey, then broke his collarbone after getting back into the lineup. At the end of this disappointing campaign, Johnson and Denver favorite Floyd Little retired after distinguished careers.

Kansas City Chiefs—New coach Paul Wiggins had to suffer through three straight losses at the start of the schedule, but the 42-10 upset over Oakland on national television got the Chiefs into the win column with a vengeance. The Chiefs did make a long-shot run at a playoff berth before dropping their last four games. Without a long string of injuries, the Chiefs might have stayed in the thick of the race. The offensive line was hurt and then Otis Taylor went out with a bad knee, and both Mickey Livingston and Len Dawson were kayoed with injuries, leaving W.F.L. ex-patriot Tony Adams running the offense at the end. Wiggins could look back on good performances from Willie Lanier, Emmitt Thomas, Jack Rudnay, and Woody Green, and count on better things to come from his spirited squad.

San Diego Chargers—Experts speculated as December began whether the Chargers would complete their schedule at 0-14, the first team ever to reach that mark. With a perfect record of 11 losses, the Chargers beat the Chiefs and ruined their chance at the record book. The Chargers had no offense at all, with the running game wiped out by injuries to Don Woods and Bo Matthews and with quarterbacks Don Fouts and Jesse Freitas unable to ignite any attack. The Chargers presented such a dull show that only 24,349 fans showed up on November 9 to see them lose to New England.

FINAL TEAM STATISTICS

OFFENSE

	BALT.	BUFF.	CIN.	CLEV.	DENV.	HOUS.	K.C.	MIAMI	N.ENG.	N.Y.	OAK.	PITT.	S.D.
FIRST DOWNS:													
Total	266	**318**	295	247	268	234	261	266	253	266	315	288	198
by Rushing	131	**162**	107	109	109	121	110	136	94	126	159	149	98
by Passing	114	132	**166**	114	137	90	128	108	133	111	139	125	89
by Penalty	21	24	22	24	22	23	23	22	26	**29**	17	14	11
RUSHING:													
Number	536	588	499	440	490	526	487	594	472	501	**643**	581	434
Yards	2217	**2974**	1819	1850	1993	2068	1847	2500	1845	2079	2573	2633	1801
Average Yards	4.1	**5.1**	3.6	4.2	4.1	3.9	3.8	4.2	3.9	4.1	4.0	4.5	4.1
Touchdowns	**28**	26	20	14	9	14	14	26	14	15	**28**	22	14
PASSING:													
Attempts	354	354	433	**437**	427	347	395	279	401	384	350	337	337
Completions	211	182	**255**	220	210	165	217	170	193	174	196	191	165
Completion Percentage	59.6	51.4	58.9	50.3	49.2	47.6	54.9	**60.9**	48.1	45.3	56.0	56.7	49.0
Passing Yards	2606	2661	**3497**	2297	2900	2099	2785	2196	2768	2468	2625	2544	1998
Avg. Yards per Attempt	7.4	7.5	**8.1**	5.3	7.0	6.0	7.1	7.8	6.9	6.4	7.5	6.7	5.9
Avg. Yards per Complet.	12.4	**14.6**	13.7	10.4	13.7	12.7	12.8	12.9	14.3	14.2	13.4	13.3	12.1
Times Tackled Passing	38	**22**	34	38	47	27	53	23	39	34	26	31	50
Yards Lost Passing	325	**168**	256	340	359	230	425	187	330	317	234	290	388
Net Yards	2281	2493	**3241**	1957	2541	1869	2360	2009	2438	2151	2391	2254	1610
Touchdowns	19	**28**	23	7	15	14	15	19	16	16	19	21	7
Interceptions	**8**	19	14	23	34	17	16	17	28	33	28	12	17
Percent Intercepted	**2.3**	5.4	3.2	5.3	8.0	4.9	4.1	6.1	7.0	8.6	8.0	3.6	5.0
PUNTS:													
Number	**86**	61	68	82	63	74	72	65	83	59	68	69	79
Average Distance	39.6	41.6	39.0	40.5	39.9	39.3	39.3	38.6	38.8	36.5	**43.8**	39.4	36.7
PUNT RETURNS:													
Number	42	33	48	40	41	43	37	43	33	22	**58**	54	38
Yards	439	278	267	294	570	620	303	509	262	116	**688**	548	442
Average Yards	10.5	8.4	5.6	7.4	11.5	**14.4**	8.2	11.8	7.9	5.3	11.9	10.1	11.6
Touchdowns	0	0	0	0	0	**3**	0	1	0	0	0	0	1
KICKOFF RETURNS:													
Number	52	62	46	67	59	54	62	40	66	**74**	51	38	69
Yards	1190	1457	1042	1526	1446	1144	1350	949	1250	**1704**	1324	815	1482
Average Yards	22.9	23.5	22.7	22.8	24.5	21.2	21.8	23.7	23.0	23.0	**26.0**	21.4	21.5
Touchdowns	0	0	0	0	0	1	0	0	1	0	1	1	0
INTERCEPTION RETURNS:													
Number	29	25	22	10	16	24	20	21	13	15	**35**	27	20
Yards	**493**	376	410	107	293	425	388	183	165	98	450	421	223
Average Yards	17.0	15.0	18.6	10.7	18.3	17.7	**19.4**	8.7	12.7	6.5	12.9	15.6	11.2
Touchdowns	**4**	2	2	1	1	0	0	0	1	0	0	0	0
PENALTIES:													
Number	80	90	88	85	92	100	82	74	89	99	**101**	89	84
Yards	760	748	783	851	790	849	658	575	719	799	**951**	756	705
FUMBLES:													
Number	**18**	24	31	35	28	28	38	20	43	24	31	34	32
Number Lost	10	15	20	14	14	17	18	9	22	**8**	20	20	12
POINTS:													
Total	395	**420**	340	218	254	293	282	357	258	258	375	373	189
PAT Attempts	52	**57**	45	24	28	34	31	46	33	32	48	46	22
PAT Made	**51**	**51**	40	21	23	31	30	40	33	27	44	44	21
FG Attempts	18	16	21	23	29	30	**32**	16	17	21	21	21	24
FG Made	10	9	10	17	21	18	**22**	13	9	13	13	17	12
Percent FG Made	55.6	56.3	47.6	73.9	72.4	60.0	68.8	**81.3**	52.9	61.9	61.9	80.9	50.0
Safeties	1	0	0	1	0	**2**	0	1	0	0	**2**	1	0

DEFENSE

	BALT.	BUFF.	CIN.	CLEV.	DENV.	HOUS.	K.C.	MIAMI	N.ENG.	N.Y.	OAK.	PITT.	S.D.
FIRST DOWNS:													
Total	242	300	241	274	247	264	289	224	254	308	242	**214**	312
by Rushing	101	124	115	124	119	104	149	92	118	155	99	**91**	154
by Passing	124	151	107	125	106	137	121	113	120	133	113	**97**	139
by Penalty	17	25	19	25	22	23	19	19	**16**	20	30	26	19
RUSHING:													
Number	453	480	473	544	526	498	562	443	555	574	475	**431**	606
Yards	1821	1993	2194	2032	1974	**1680**	2724	1768	2220	2737	1785	1825	2442
Average Yards	4.0	4.2	4.6	3.7	3.8	**3.4**	4.8	4.0	4.0	4.8	3.8	4.2	4.0
Touchdowns	17	21	15	21	19	13	24	14	20	25	15	**8**	21
PASSING:													
Attempts	393	431	389	361	348	409	325	375	368	**316**	398	396	390
Completions	193	237	175	202	181	235	186	200	213	180	**171**	183	237
Completion Percentage	49.1	55.0	45.0	56.0	52.0	57.5	57.2	53.3	57.9	57.0	**43.0**	46.2	60.8
Passing Yards	2317	3355	**2001**	2889	2245	2800	2703	2335	2515	2860	2318	2194	2719
Avg. Yards per Attempt	5.9	7.6	**5.1**	8.0	6.5	6.9	8.3	6.2	6.8	9.1	5.8	5.5	7.0
Avg. Yards per Complet.	12.0	14.1	**11.4**	14.3	12.4	11.9	14.5	11.7	11.8	15.9	13.6	12.0	11.5
Times Tackled Passing	**59**	30	27	34	27	45	28	40	33	19	55	43	26
Yards Lost Passing	**496**	275	272	298	213	343	191	314	271	141	474	358	209
Net Yards	1821	3080	**1729**	2591	2032	2457	2512	2021	2244	2719	1844	1836	2510
Touchdowns	17	25	11	25	14	14	18	**9**	18	26	14	**9**	16
Interceptions	29	25	22	10	16	24	20	21	13	15	**35**	27	20
Percent Intercepted	7.4	5.8	5.7	2.8	4.6	5.9	6.2	5.6	3.5	4.7	**8.8**	6.8	5.1
PUNTS:													
Number	83	59	77	73	76	73	61	72	77	56	86	**90**	56
Average Distance	38.6	40.7	40.8	38.5	42.1	41.0	40.7	39.9	39.5	**33.7**	38.7	40.1	39.8
PUNT RETURNS:													
Number	51	29	42	45	39	47	36	34	42	**22**	35	36	48
Yards	513	**179**	386	469	534	356	503	373	513	208	265	199	373
Average Yards	10.1	6.2	9.2	10.4	13.7	7.6	14.0	11.0	12.2	9.5	7.6	**5.5**	7.8
Touchdowns	**0**	**0**	1	**0**	**0**	**0**	**0**	1	1	1	**0**	**0**	**0**
KICKOFF RETURNS:													
Number	70	64	66	48	57	61	59	65	46	52	68	64	**40**
Yards	1655	1496	1560	1279	1273	1355	1334	1549	1142	1203	1262	1304	**1101**
Average Yards	23.6	23.4	23.6	26.6	22.3	22.2	22.6	23.8	24.8	23.1	**18.6**	20.4	27.5
Touchdowns	1	**0**	**0**	1	**0**	**0**	**0**	1	**0**	**0**	**0**	**0**	**0**
INTERCEPTION RETURNS:													
Number	**8**	19	14	23	34	17	16	17	28	33	28	12	17
Yards	111	262	244	340	447	186	179	214	388	538	549	**47**	171
Average Yards	13.9	13.8	17.4	14.8	13.2	10.9	11.2	12.6	13.9	16.3	19.6	**3.9**	10.0
Touchdowns	**0**	**0**	1	1	1	**0**	1	1	1	4	2	**0**	1
PENALTIES:													
Number	79	80	91	89	88	91	99	82	**103**	93	63	85	81
Yards	700	651	821	735	779	892	**934**	716	759	798	527	700	686
FUMBLES:													
Number	29	**42**	40	26	37	38	40	23	31	25	14	22	34
Number Lost	12	20	**22**	16	16	19	**22**	9	16	13	6	10	14
POINTS:													
Total	269	355	246	372	307	226	341	222	358	433	255	**162**	345
PAT Attempts	36	47	30	48	35	27	44	27	42	57	32	**19**	40
PAT Made	35	46	26	45	34	21	40	25	37	53	30	**15**	35
FG Attempts	**10**	16	15	21	28	21	22	20	35	16	20	18	34
FG Made	**6**	9	12	13	21	13	11	11	23	12	11	11	22
Percent FG Made	60.0	56.3	80.0	61.9	75.0	61.9	**50.0**	55.0	65.7	75.0	55.0	61.1	64.7
Safeties	**0**	**0**	2	**0**	**0**	2	2	1	**0**	1	**0**	**0**	2

CONFERENCE PLAYOFFS

December 27, at Pittsburgh (Attendance 49,053)

SCORING

PITTSBURGH	7	0	7	14	– 28
BALTIMORE	0	7	3	0	– 10

First Quarter
- Pitt. Harris, 8 yard rush PAT – Gerela (kick)

Second Quarter
- Balt. Doughty, 5 yard pass from Domres PAT – Linhart (kick)

Third Quarter
- Balt. Linhart, 21 yard field goal
- Pitt. Bleier, 7 yard rush PAT – Gerela (kick)

Fourth Quarter
- Pitt. Bradshaw, 2 yard rush PAT – Gerela (kick)
- Pitt. Russell, 93 yard fumble return PAT – Gerela (kick)

TEAM STATISTICS

PITT.		BALT.
16	First Downs – Total	10
13	First Downs – Rushing	4
3	First Downs – Passing	4
0	First Downs – Penalty	2
3	Fumbles – Number	2
3	Fumbles – Lost Ball	1
5	Penalties – Number	6
45	Yards Penalized	53
0	Missed Field Goals	0
59	Offensive Plays	68
287	Net Yards	154
4.9	Average Gain	2.3
5	Giveaways	3
3	Takeaways	5
-2	Difference	+2

INDIVIDUAL STATISTICS

PITTSBURGH	No.	Yds.	Avg.	BALTIMORE	No.	Yds.	Avg.
RUSHING							
Harris	27	153	5.7	Mitchell	20	63	2.4
Bleier	12	28	2.3	Domres	4	17	4.3
Bradshaw	3	22	7.3	Olds	5	6	1.2
Collier	1	8	8.0	Jones	2	6	3.0
	43	211	4.9	McCauley	3	3	1.0
				Carr	1	-13	-13.0
					41	82	2.0
RECEIVING							
Lewis	3	65	31.7	Mitchell	4	20	5.0
Swann	2	15	7.5	Doughty	2	63	31.5
Bleier	2	14	7.0	McCauley	1	9	9.0
L. Brown	1	9	9.0	Kennedy	1	8	8.0
	8	103	12.9		8	100	12.5
PUNTING							
Walden	4		39.8	Lee	9		40.1
PUNT RETURNS							
Edwards	2	22	11.0	Stevens	3	30	10.0
Collier	1	17	17.0	Volk	1	0	0.0
D. Brown	1	7	7.0		4	30	7.5
	4	46	11.5				
KICKOFF RETURNS							
D. Brown	2	53	26.5	Laird	4	86	21.5
Harrison	1	21	21.0	McCauley	1	17	17.0
	3	74	24.7		5	103	20.6
INTERCEPTION RETURNS							
Blount	1	20	20.0	Mumphord	2	67	33.5
Ham	1	6	6.0				
	2	26	13.0				

PASSING

PITTSBURGH	Att.	Comp.	Comp. Pct.	Yds.	Int.	Yds/ Att.	Yds/ Comp.	Yards Lost Tackled
Bradshaw	13	8	61.6	103	2	7.9	12.9	3-27
BALTIMORE								
Jones	11	6	54.5	91	0	8.3	11.4	
Domres	11	2	18.1	9	2	0.8	4.5	
	22	8	36.4	100	2	4.5	12.5	5-28

December 28, at Oakland (Attendance 53,039)

SCORING

OAKLAND	3	14	7	7	– 31
CINCINNATI	0	7	7	14	– 28

First Quarter
- Oak. Blanda, 27 yard field goal

Second Quarter
- Oak. Siani, 9 yard pass from Stabler PAT – Blanda (kick)
- Cin. Fritts, 1 yard rush PAT – Green (kick)
- Oak. Moore, 8 yard pass from Stabler PAT – Blanda (kick)

Third Quarter
- Oak. Banaszak, 6 yard rush PAT – Blanda (kick)
- Cin. Elliott, 6 yard rush PAT – Green (kick)

Fourth Quarter
- Oak. Casper, 2 yard pass from Stabler PAT – Blanda (kick)
- Cin. Joiner, 25 yard pass from Anderson PAT – Green (kick)
- Cin. Curtis, 14 yard pass from Anderson PAT – Green (kick)

TEAM STATISTICS

OAK.		CIN.
27	First Downs – Total	17
9	First Downs – Rushing	8
15	First Downs – Passing	6
3	First Downs – Penalty	3
2	Fumbles – Number	1
1	Fumbles – Lost Ball	0
7	Penalties – Number	5
64	Yards Penalized	37
2	Missed Field Goals	0
75	Offensive Plays	57
358	Net Yards	258
4.8	Average Gain	4.5
2	Giveaways	0
0	Takeaways	2
-2	Difference	+2

INDIVIDUAL STATISTICS

OAKLAND	No.	Yds.	Avg.	CINCINNATI	No.	Yds.	Avg.
RUSHING							
C. Davis	16	63	3.9	B. Clark	8	46	5.8
Banaszak	17	62	3.6	Elliott	4	25	6.3
Hubbard	12	33	2.8	Fritts	6	14	2.3
J. Phillips	3	16	5.3	Anderson	3	12	4.0
van Eeghen	1	3	3.0	Johnson	3	0	0.0
Stabler	2	-4	-2.0	Williams	1	0	0.0
	51	173	3.4		25	97	3.9
RECEIVING							
Moore	6	57	9.5	B. Clark	4	38	9.5
Branch	5	89	17.8	Myers	3	67	22.3
Siani	3	35	11.7	Joiner	3	60	20.0
C. Davis	2	16	8.0	Curtis	3	20	6.7
Casper	1	2	2.0	Coslet	2	14	7.0
	17	199	11.7	Elliott	1	9	9.0
				Trumpy	1	-7	-7.0
					17	201	11.8
PUNTING							
Guy	1		38.0	D. Green	6		35.8
PUNT RETURNS							
Colzie	4	64	16.0	Blackwood	1	7	7.0
KICKOFF RETURNS							
C. Davis	4	93	23.3	B. Jackson	2	43	21.5
Hart	1	28	28.0	Elliott	1	18	18.0
	5	121	24.2	Parish	1	10	10.0
					4	71	17.8
INTERCEPTION RETURNS							
none				K. Riley	1	34	34.0

PASSING

OAKLAND	Att.	Comp.	Comp. Pct.	Yds.	Int.	Yds/ Att.	Yds/ Comp.	Yards Lost Tackled
Stabler	23	17	73.9	199	1	8.7	11.7	4-14
CINCINNATI								
Anderson	27	17	63.0	201	0	7.4	11.8	5-40

BALTIMORE COLTS 10-4 Ted Marchibroda

Scores of Each Game		
35	Chicago	7
20	OAKLAND	31
13	Los Angeles	24
31	BUFFALO	38
10	New England	21
45	N.Y. Jets	28
21	CLEVELAND	7
42	Buffalo	35
52	N.Y. JETS	19
33	Miami	17
28	KANSAS CITY	14
21	N.Y. Giants	0
10	MIAMI	7
34	NEW ENGLAND	21

Use Name	Pos.	Hgt	Wgt	Age	Int	Pts
Ed George	OT	6'4"	270	29		
George Kunz	OT	6'5"	266	28		
David Taylor	OT	6'4"	257	25		
Elmer Collett	OG	6'4"	246	30		
Ken Huff	OG	6'4"	260	22		
Robert Pratt	OG	6'3"	248	24		
Bob Van Duyne	OG	6'5"	245	23		
Forrest Blue	C	6'5"	265	29		
Ken Mendenhall	C	6'3"	250	26		
Fred Cook	DE	6'4"	247	23	1	6
John Dutton	DE	6'7"	268	23		
Glenn Robinson	DE	6'6"	236	24		
Mike Barnes	DT	6'6"	260	24		
Joe Ehrmann	DT	6'5"	254	26		
Dave Pear	DT	6'2"	242	22		
Jim Cheyunski	LB	6'2"	220	29	2	
Mike Curtis	LB	6'2"	232	32	1	
Dan Dickel	LB	6'3"	230	23		
Derrel Luce	LB	6'3"	224	22		
Tom MacLeod	LB	6'3"	228	24	1	
Mike Varty	LB	6'1"	225	23		
Stan White	LB	6'1"	220	25	8	6
Bruce Laird	DB	6'	198	25	3	2
Lloyd Mumphord	DB	5'11"	176	28	4	
Nelson Munsey	DB	6'1"	198	27	3	6
Doug Nettles	DB	6'	178	24		
Ray Oldham	DB	6'	190	24	2	
Rick Volk	DB	6'3"	195	30		
Jackie Wallace	DB	6'3"	197	24	4	12
Marty Domres	QB	6'3"	230	28		6
Bert Jones	QB	6'3"	212	23		18
Marshall Johnson	HB	6'1"	190	22		12
Lydell Mitchell	HB	5'11"	195	26		90
Howard Stevens	HB	5'5"	165	25		
Roosevelt Leaks	FB	5'10"	220	22		6
Bill Olds	FB	6'1"	222	24		24
Don McCauley	HB-FB	6'1"	216	26		66
Roger Carr	WR	6'3"	193	23		12
Glenn Doughty	WR	6'2"	202	24		24
Freddie Scott	WR	6'2"	170	23		
Ray Chester	TE	6'3"	236	27		18
Jimmie Kennedy	TE	6'3"	233	23		6
David Lee	K	6'4"	220	31		
Toni Linhart	K	6'	180	33		81

Randy Hall – Foot Injury

MIAMI DOLPHINS 10-4 Don Shula

Scores of Each Game		
21	OAKLAND	31
22	New England	14
31	Green Bay	7
24	PHILADELPHIA	16
43	N.Y. Jets	0
35	Buffalo	30
46	Chicago	13
27	N.Y. JETS	7
19	Houston	20
17	BALTIMORE	33
20	NEW ENGLAND	7
31	BUFFALO	21
7	Baltimore	10
14	DENVER	13

Use Name	Pos.	Hgt	Wgt	Age	Int	Pts
Darryl Carlton	OT	6'6"	260	22		
Norm Evans	OT	6'5"	250	32		
Wayne Moore	OT	6'6"	265	30		
Tom Drougas	OG-OT	6'4"	255	25		
Bob Kuechenberg	OG	6'3"	252	27		
Larry Little	OG	6'1"	265	29		
Ed Newman	OG	6'2"	245	24		
Jim Langer	C	6'2"	253	27		
Vern Den Herder	DE	6'6"	252	26		
Don Reese	DE	6'6"	255	23		2
Bill Stanfill	DE	6'5"	252	28		
Randy Crowder	DT	6'2"	236	23		
Manny Fernandez	DT	6'2"	250	29		
John Andrews	DE-DT	6'6"	250	23		
Rodrigo Barnes (from NE)	LB	6'1"	215	25		
Bruce Elia	LB	6'1"	222	22		
Mike Kolen	LB	6'2"	222	27	1	
Bob Matheson	LB	6'4"	235	30	3	
Earnest Rhone	LB	6'2"	212	22	2	
Doug Swift	LB	6'3"	226	26		
Steve Towle	LB	6'2"	233	21	1	
Charlie Babb	DB	6'	190	25	4	
Tim Foley	DB	6'	194	27		
Barry Hill	DB	6'3"	185	22		
Curtis Johnson	DB	6'2"	196	27	4	
Jake Scott	DB	6'	188	30	6	
Jeris White	DB	5'11"	180	22		
Jim Del Gaizo	QB	6'1"	190	28		
Bob Griese	QB	6'1"	190	30		6
Earl Morrall	QB	6'1"	210	41		
Don Strock	QB	6'5"	216	24		6
Hubert Ginn	HB	5'11"	185	28		
Benny Malone	HB	5'10"	193	23		18
Mercury Morris	HB	5'10"	192	28		24
Larry Seiple	HB	6'	214	30		
Norm Bulaich	FB	6'1"	220	28		60
Don Nottingham	FB	5'10"	210	26		72
Stan Winfrey	FB	5'11"	223	22		
Nat Moore	WR	5'9"	180	23		24
Morris Owens	WR	6'	190	22		
Cotton Speyrer	WR	6'	175	26		
Howard Twilley	WR	5'10"	185	31		24
Freddie Solomon	HB-WR	5'11"	180	22		18
Jim Mandich	TE	6'3"	224	27		24
Jim McFarland	TE	6'5"	225	27		
Andre Tillman	TE	6'5"	230	22		
Garo Yepremian	K	5'8"	175	31		79

Bob Heinz – Knee Injury

Dick Anderson – Knee Injury
Nick Buoniconti – Broken Finger

BUFFALO BILLS 8-6 Lou Saban

Scores of Each Game		
42	N.Y. JETS	14
30	Pittsburgh	21
38	DENVER	10
38	Baltimore	31
14	N.Y. GIANTS	17
30	MIAMI	35
24	N.Y. Jets	23
35	BALTIMORE	42
24	Cincinnati	33
45	NEW ENGLAND	31
32	St. Louis	14
21	Miami	31
34	New England	14
13	MINNESOTA	35

Use Name	Pos.	Hgt	Wgt	Age	Int	Pts
Dave Foley	OT	6'5"	247	27		
Donnie Green	OT	6'7"	252	27		
Halvor Hagen	OT	6'5"	260	28		
Bill Adams	OG	6'2"	246	25		
Joe DeLamielleure	OG	6'3"	248	24		
Reggie McKenzie	OG	6'4"	244	25		
Mike Montler	C	6'4"	245	31		
Willie Parker	C	6'3"	252	26		
Mark Johnson	DE	6'2"	240	22		
Dave Means	DE	6'4"	235	23		
Walt Patulski	DE	6'6"	260	25		
Pat Toomay	DE	6'5"	244	30	1	6
Jeff Winans	DE	6'5"	260	23		
Don Croft	DT	6'3"	260	26		
Earl Edwards	DT	6'6"	254	29		
Mike Kadish	DT	6'5"	270	25		6
Jeff Yeates	DT	6'3"	250	24		
Doug Allen	LB	6'2"	228	23		
Bo Cornell	LB	6'1"	222	26		
Merv Krakau	LB	6'2"	233	24	1	
John McCrumbly	LB	6'1"	245	23		
Bob Nelson	LB	6'4"	232	22		
Tom Ruud	LB	6'2"	223	22		
John Skorupan	LB	6'2"	225	24	1	
Steve Freeman	DB	5'11"	185	22	2	6
Tony Greene	DB	5'10"	170	26	6	
Dwight Harrison	DB	6'1"	186	26	8	
Ed Jones	DB	6'	185	23	3	
Royce McKinney	DB	6'1"	190	21		
Frank Oliver	DB	6'1"	189	23		
Ike Thomas	DB	6'2"	195	27	2	
Joe Ferguson	QB	6'1"	184	25		6
Gary Marangi	QB	6'1"	203	23		
Gary Hayman	HB	6'1"	202	24		
O.J. Simpson	HB	6'2"	212	28		138
Jim Braxton	FB	6'2"	242	26		78
Steve Schnarr	FB	6'2"	218	22		
Dan Abramowicz	WR	6'1"	193	30		
Bob Chandler	WR	6'	180	26		36
J. D. Hill	WR	6'1"	185	26		42
John Holland	WR	6'	190	23		6
Vic Washington	DB-WR	5'10"	196	29		
Reuben Gant	TE	6'4"	230	23		12
Paul Seymour	TE	6'5"	246	25		6
Marv Bateman	K	6'4"	214	25		
John Leypoldt	K	6'2"	226	29		78

Robert James – Knee Injury
Doug Jones – Knee Injury

Ahmad Rashad – Knee Injury

NEW ENGLAND PATRIOTS 3-11 Chuck Fairbanks

Scores of Each Game		
0	HOUSTON	7
14	MIAMI	22
7	N.Y. Jets	36
10	Cincinnati	27
21	BALTIMORE	10
24	SAN FRANCISCO	16
17	St. Louis	24
33	San Diego	19
31	DALLAS	34
31	Buffalo	45
7	Miami	20
28	N.Y. JETS	30
14	BUFFALO	34
21	Baltimore	34

Use Name	Pos.	Hgt	Wgt	Age	Int	Pts
Leon Gray	OT	6'3"	256	23		
Shelby Jordan	OT	6'7"	260	23		
Sam Adams	OG	6'3"	252	26		
Steve Corbett	OG	6'4"	248	24		
Bill Du Lac	OG	6'4"	260	24		
John Hannah	OG	6'2"	265	24		
Doug Dumler	C	6'3"	242	24		
Bill Lenkaitis	C	6'3"	250	29		
Julius Adams	DE	6'3"	260	27		
Craig Hanneman	DE	6'3"	245	26		
Mel Lunsford	DE	6'3"	260	25		
Tony McGee	DE	6'4"	245	26		
Martin Imhoff	DE	6'6"	256	25		
Pete Cusick	NT	6'1'	255	22		
Ray Hamilton	NT	6'1"	245	24		6
Jerry Patton	DT	6'3"	255	29		
Dave Tipton (to SD)	DT	6'1"	255	21		
Maury Damkroger	LB	6'2"	230	23		
Bob Geddes	LB	6'2"	240	29		
Sam Hunt	LB	6'1"	240	24		
Steve King	LB	6'4"	230	24		
Steve Nelson	LB	6'2"	230	24	2	
Kevin Reilly	LB	6'2"	220	23	1	
Rod Shoate	LB	6'1"	211	22		
George Webster	LB	6'4"	230	29	1	
Steve Zabel	LB	6'4"	230	27		
Ron Bolton	DB	6'2"	170	25	5	
Dick Conn	DB	6'	185	24		
Bob Howard	DB	6'1"	177	30	3	6
Durwood Keeton	DB	5'10"	180	23		
Jim Massey	DB	5'11"	198	27		
Prentice McCray	DB	6'1"	187	24		
Deac Sanders	DB	6'1"	178	25	1	
Neil Graff	QB	6'3"	200	25		
Steve Grogan	QB	6'4"	200	22		18
Jim Plunkett	QB	6'3"	212	27		6
Don Calhoun (from BUF)	HB	6'	198	23		12
Andy Johnson	HB	6'	204	22		24
Leon McQuay	HB	5'9"	195	25		
Bobby Anderson	FB-HB	6'	208	27		
Allen Carter	FB	5'11"	208	22		6
Sam Cunningham	FB	6'3"	224	25		48
Steve Burks	WR	6'5"	211	22		
Darryl Stingley	WR	6'	195	23		12
Randy Vataha	WR	5'10"	170	26		36
Elmo Wright (from HOU)	WR	6'	190	26		
Russ Francis	TE	6'6"	240	22		24
Bob Windsor	TE	6'4"	225	32		
Mike Patrick	K	6'	213	22		
John Smith	K	6'	185	25		60

Arthur Moore – Knee Injury
Joe Wilson – Ankle Injury

Al Marshall – Knee Injury
Tom Neville – Broken Leg

Leon Crosswhite – Foot Injury

NEW YORK JETS 3-11 Charley Winner Ken Shipp

Scores of Each Game		
14	Buffalo	42
30	Kansas City	24
36	NEW ENGLAND	7
21	Minnesota	29
0	MIAMI	43
28	BALTIMORE	45
23	BUFFALO	24
7	Miami	27
19	Baltimore	52
6	ST. LOUIS	37
7	PITTSBURGH	20
30	New England	28
16	San Diego	24
21	DALLAS	31

Use Name	Pos.	Hgt	Wgt	Age	Int	Pts
Gordie Browne	OT	6'5"	265	23		
Winston Hill	OT	6'4"	280	33		
Robert Woods	OT	6'3"	255	25		
Gary Puetz	OG	6'4"	265	23		
Randy Rasmussen	OG	6'2"	267	30		
Darrell Austin	OT-OG	6'4"	250	23		
Wayne Mulligan	C	6'2"	250	28		
Joe Fields	OG-C	6'2"	240	21		
Richard Neal	DE	6'3"	260	27		
Billy Newsome	DE	6'4"	246	27		
Jim Bailey	DT	6'5"	255	27	1	
Carl Barzilauskas	DT	6'6"	280	24		
Ed Galigher	DT	6'4"	253	24		
Larry Woods	DT	6'6"	270	27		
Ken Bernich	LB	6'2"	250	23		
John Ebersole	LB	6'3"	227	26	2	
Rich Lewis	LB	6'3"	215	25		
Steve Reese	LB	6'2"	232	23		
Jamie Rivers	LB	6'2"	245	29		
Godwin Turk	LB	6'3"	230	24	2	
Richard Wood	LB	6'2"	215	22		
Carl Capria	DB	6'3"	185	23		
Jerry Davis	DB	5'11"	182	24		
George Hoey (from DEN)	DB	5'10"	180	28		
Delles Howell	DB	6'3"	200	28	2	
Burgess Owens	DB	6'2"	200	24	3	
Bob Prout	DB	6'1"	183	24	1	
Rich Sowells	DB	6'	180	26	1	
Ed Taylor	DB	6'	170	22		
Donnie Walker	DB	6'1"	180	24		
Phil Wise	DB	6'	190	26	2	
Roscoe Word	DB	5'11"	170	22	1	
John Jones	QB	6'1"	180	23		
Joe Namath	QB	6'2"	200	32		
Emerson Boozer	HB	5'11"	205	32		6
Carl Garrett	HB	5'11"	205	28		36
Bob Gresham	HB	5'11"	195	27		6
Jazz Jackson	HB	5'8"	167	23		
John Riggins	FB	6'2"	225	26		54
Steve Davis	HB-FB	6'1"	218	25		6
Jerome Barkum	WR	6'3"	212	25		30
Eddie Bell	WR	5'10"	160	27		24
David Knight	WR	6'1"	175	24		
Lou Piccone	WR	5'9"	175	26		
Willie Brister	TE	6'4"	236	23		6
Rich Caster	TE	6'5"	228	26		24
Greg Gantt	K	5'11"	188	23		
Pat Leahy	K	6'	200	24		66

Al Atkinson – Knee Injury
Mark Lomas – Foot Injury
Steve Tannen – Shoulder Injury

Al Woodall – Knee Injury

BALTIMORE COLTS

RUSHING

Last Name	No.	Yds	Avg	TD
Mitchell	289	1193	4.1	11
Jones	47	321	6.8	3
Olds	94	281	3.0	2
McCauley	60	196	3.3	10
Leaks	41	175	4.3	1
Domres	4	46	11.5	1
Doughty	1	5	5.0	0

RECEIVING

Last Name	No.	Yds	Avg	TD
Mitchell	60	544	9	4
Doughty	39	666	17	4
Chester	38	457	12	3
Olds	30	194	7	2
Carr	23	517	23	2
McCauley	14	93	7	1
Johnson	4	115	29	2
Kennedy	2	15	8	1
Leaks	1	5	5	0

PUNT RETURNS

Last Name	No.	Yds	Avg	TD
Stevens	36	396	11	0
Wallace	6	43	7	0

KICKOFF RETURNS

Last Name	No.	Yds	Avg	TD
Laird	31	799	26	0
Johnson	7	134	19	0
McCauley	4	86	22	0
Stevens	3	71	24	0
Pratt	4	64	16	0
Kennedy	2	36	18	0
Wallace	1	0	0	0

PASSING – PUNTING – KICKING

PASSING	Att	Comp	%	Yds	Yd/Att	TD	Int–%	RK
Jones	344	203	59	2483	7.2	18	8– 2	3
Domres	10	8	80	123	12.3	1	0– 0	

PUNTING	No	Avg
Lee	86	39.6

KICKING	XP	Att	%	FG	Att	%
Linhart	51	52	98	10	18	56

MIAMI DOLPHINS

RUSHING

Last Name	No.	Yds	Avg	TD
Morris	219	875	4.0	4
Nottingham	168	718	4.3	12
Bulaich	78	309	4.0	5
Malone	65	220	3.4	3
Solomon	4	87	21.8	0
Ginn	21	78	3.7	0
Moore	8	69	8.6	0
Griese	17	59	3.5	1
Strock	6	38	6.3	1
Morrall	4	33	8.3	0
Winfrey	3	10	3.3	0
Seiple	1	4	4.0	0

RECEIVING

Last Name	No.	Yds	Avg	TD
Moore	40	705	18	4
Bulaich	32	276	9	5
Twilley	24	366	15	4
Solomon	22	339	15	2
Mandich	21	217	10	4
Seiple	10	84	8	0
Nottingham	9	66	7	0
Tillman	5	60	12	0
Ginn	3	21	7	0
Malone	2	47	24	0
Morris	2	15	8	0

PUNT RETURNS

Last Name	No.	Yds	Avg	TD
Solomon	26	320	12	1
Babb	7	95	14	0
Moore	8	80	10	0
Scott	1	10	10	0
Ginn	1	4	4	0

KICKOFF RETURNS

Last Name	No.	Yds	Avg	TD
Solomon	17	348	21	0
Moore	9	243	27	0
Ginn	9	235	26	0
Nottingham	3	80	27	0
Winfrey	1	25	25	0
Malone	1	18	18	0

PASSING – PUNTING – KICKING

PASSING	Att	Comp	%	Yds	Yd/Att	TD	Int–%	RK
Griese	191	118	62	1693	8.9	14	13– 7	5
Strock	45	26	58	230	5.1	2	2– 4	
Morrall	43	26	61	273	6.4	3	2– 5	

PUNTING	No	Avg
Seiple	65	38.6

KICKING	XP	Att	%	FG	Att	%
Yepremian	40	46	87	13	16	81

BUFFALO BILLS

RUSHING

Last Name	No.	Yds	Avg	TD
Simpson	329	1817	5.5	16
Braxton	186	823	4.4	9
Ferguson	23	82	3.6	1
Marangi	7	78	11.1	0
Washington	9	49	5.4	0
Hayman	10	30	3.0	0
Haslerig	2	9	4.5	0
Chandler	2	5	2.5	0
Hill	1	1	1.0	0

RECEIVING

Last Name	No.	Yds	Avg	TD
Chandler	55	746	14	6
Hill	36	667	19	7
Simpson	28	426	15	7
Braxton	26	282	11	4
Seymour	19	268	14	1
Gant	9	107	12	2
Holland	7	144	21	1
Washington	2	21	11	0

PUNT RETURNS

Last Name	No.	Yds	Avg	TD
Hayman	25	216	9	0
Holland	7	53	8	0
Jones	1	9	9	0

KICKOFF RETURNS

Last Name	No.	Yds	Avg	TD
Washington	35	923	26	0
Hayman	8	179	22	0
McKinney	6	151	25	0
Schnarr	4	80	20	0
Holland	4	67	17	0
Cornell	3	38	13	0
McKenzie	1	15	15	0
Ruud	1	4	4	0

PASSING – PUNTING – KICKING

PASSING	Att	Comp	%	Yds	Yd/Att	TD	Int–%	RK
Ferguson	321	169	53	2426	7.6	25	17– 5	6
Marangi	33	13	39	235	7.1	3	2– 6	

PUNTING	No	Avg
Bateman	61	41.6

KICKING	XP	Att	%	FG	Att	%
Leypoldt	51	57	89	9	16	56

NEW ENGLAND PATRIOTS

RUSHING

Last Name	No.	Yds	Avg	TD
Cunningham	169	666	3.9	6
Johnson	117	488	4.2	3
Calhoun	42	184	4.4	1
Grogan	30	110	3.7	3
Carter	22	95	4.3	0
McQuay	33	47	1.4	0
Stingley	6	39	6.5	0
Plunkett	4	7	1.8	1
Vataha	1	4	4.0	0
Graff	2	2	1.0	0
Anderson	1	1	1.0	0

RECEIVING

Last Name	No.	Yds	Avg	TD
Vataha	46	720	16	6
Francis	35	636	18	4
Cunningham	32	253	8	2
Johnson	26	294	11	1
Stingley	21	378	18	2
Burks	6	158	26	0
Windsor	6	57	10	0
Calhoun	5	111	22	1
Wright	4	46	12	0
McQuay	4	27	7	0
Carter	2	39	20	0

PUNT RETURNS

Last Name	No.	Yds	Avg	TD
Stingley	15	113	8	0
Johnson	6	60	10	0

KICKOFF RETURNS

Last Name	No.	Yds	Avg	TD
Carter	32	879	28	1
McQuay	15	252	17	0
Johnson	10	188	19	0
Burks	4	65	16	0
Stingley	2	44	22	0
Calhoun	1	17	17	0

PASSING – PUNTING – KICKING

PASSING	Att	Comp	%	Yds	Yd/Att	TD	Int–%	RK
Grogan	274	139	51	1976	7.2	11	18– 7	11
Plunkett	92	36	39	571	6.2	3	7– 8	
Graff	35	18	51	221	6.3	2	3– 9	

PUNTING	No	Avg
Patrick	83	38.8

KICKING	XP	Att	%	FG	Att	%
Smith	33	33	100	9	17	53

NEW YORK JETS

RUSHING

Last Name	No.	Yds	Avg	TD
Riggins	238	1005	4.2	8
Garrett	122	566	4.6	5
S. Davis	70	290	4.1	1
Gresham	25	98	3.9	1
Jones	9	59	6.6	0
Boozer	20	51	2.6	0
Jackson	6	11	1.8	0
Namath	10	6	0.6	0
Barkum	1	−7	−7.0	0

RECEIVING

Last Name	No.	Yds	Avg	TD
Caster	47	820	17	4
Barkum	36	549	15	5
Riggins	30	363	12	1
Bell	20	344	17	4
Garrett	19	180	10	1
Piccone	7	79	11	0
S. Davis	6	56	9	0
Jackson	5	54	11	0
Gresham	2	4	2	0
Boozer	1	16	16	1
Brister	1	3	3	0

PUNT RETURNS

Last Name	No.	Yds	Avg	TD
Piccone	18	74	4	0
Bell	2	42	21	0
Jackson	1	0	0	0
Sowells	1	0	0	0

KICKOFF RETURNS

Last Name	No.	Yds	Avg	TD
Piccone	26	637	25	0
S. Davis	20	483	24	0
Garrett	7	159	23	0
Gresham	7	153	22	0
Taylor	7	151	22	0
Wood	3	27	9	0
Jackson	2	52	26	0
Word	1	22	22	0
Wise	1	20	20	0

PASSING – PUNTING – KICKING

PASSING	Att	Comp	%	Yds	Yd/Att	TD	Int–%	RK
Namath	326	157	48	2286	7.0	15	28– 9	13
Jones	57	16	28	181	3.2	1	5– 9	
Gantt	1	1	100	1	1.0	0	0– 0	

PUNTING	No	Avg
Gantt	59	36.5

KICKING	XP	Att	%	FG	Att	%
Leahy	27	30	90	13	21	62

PITTSBURGH STEELERS 12-2 Chuck Noll

Scores of Each Game		
37	San Diego	0
21	BUFFALO	30
42	Cleveland	6
20	DENVER	9
34	CHICAGO	3
16	Green Bay	13
30	Cincinnati	24
24	HOUSTON	17
28	KANSAS CITY	3
32	Houston	9
20	N.Y. Jets	7
31	CLEVELAND	17
35	CINCINNATI	14
3	Los Angeles	10

Use Name	Pos.	Hgt	Wgt	Age	Int	Pts
Gordon Gravelle	OT	6'5"	255	26		
Jon Kolb	OT	6'2"	262	28		
Dave Reavis	OT	6'5"	254	25		
Sam Davis	OG	6'1"	250	31		
Gerry Mullins	OT-OG	6'3"	240	26		6
Jim Clack	C-OG	6'3"	250	27		
Ray Mansfield	C	6'3"	260	34		
Mike Webster	OG-C	6'1"	245	23		
John Banaszak	DE	6'3"	232	25		
L. C. Greenwood	DE	6'5"	245	28		
Dwight White	DE	6'4"	255	26		2
Joe Greene	DT	6'4"	275	28		
Ernie Holmes	DT	6'3"	260	27		
Steve Furness	DE-DT	6'4"	255	25		

Use Name	Pos.	Hgt	Wgt	Age	Int	Pts
Ed Bradley	LB	6'2"	232	25		
Jack Ham	LB	6'3"	225	26	1	
Marv Kellum	LB	6'2"	225	23		
Jack Lambert	LB	6'4"	220	23	2	
Andy Russell	LB	6'3"	220	33		
Loren Toews	LB	6'3"	222	23		
Jimmy Allen	DB	6'2"	194	23	2	
Mel Blount	DB	6'3"	200	27	11	
Dave Brown	DB	6'1"	200	22		
Glen Edwards	DB	6'	185	28	3	
Donnie Shell	DB	5'11"	195	23	1	
J. T. Thomas	DB	6'2"	196	24	3	6
Mike Wagner	DB	6'1"	210	26	4	

Use Name	Pos.	Hgt	Wgt	Age	Int	Pts
Terry Bradshaw	QB	6'3"	210	26		18
Joe Gilliam	QB	6'2"	187	24		
Terry Hanratty	QB	6'1"	205	27		
Rocky Bleier	HB	5'11"	210	29		12
Mike Collier	HB	5'11"	200	21		24
John Fuqua	HB	5'11"	200	28		6
Franco Harris	FB	6'2"	230	25		66
Reggie Harrison	FB	5'11"	215	25		18
Reggie Garrett	WR	6'1"	175	23		6
Frank Lewis	WR	6'1"	196	28		12
John Stallworth	WR	6'2"	185	23		24
Lynn Swann	WR	6'	180	23		66
Larry Brown	TE	6'4"	230	26		6
Randy Grossman	TE	6'1"	215	21		6
Roy Gerela	K	5'10"	190	27		95
Bobby Walden	K	6'	197	37		

CINCINNATI BENGALS 11-3 Paul Brown

Scores of Each Game		
24	CLEVELAND	17
21	New Orleans	0
21	Houston	19
27	NEW ENGLAND	10
14	OAKLAND	10
21	Atlanta	14
24	PITTSBURGH	30
17	Denver	16
33	BUFFALO	24
23	Cleveland	35
23	HOUSTON	19
31	Philadelphia	0
14	Pittsburgh	35
47	SAN DIEGO	17

Use Name	Pos.	Hgt	Wgt	Age	Int	Pts
Vern Holland	OT	6'5"	268	27		
Al Krevis	OT	6'6"	263	23		
Rufus Mayes	OT	6'5"	265	27		
Howard Fest	OG	6'6"	262	29		
Dave Lapham	OG	6'3"	258	23		
John Shinners	OG	6'2"	255	28		
Bob Johnson	C	6'5"	255	29		
Ken Johnson	DE	6'5"	260	28		
Sherman White	DE	6'5"	250	26		
Bob Brown	DT	6'5"	290	35		
Ron Carpenter	DT	6'4"	260	27		
Bill Kollar	DT	6'3"	250	22		
Baldy Moore	DT	6'5"	265	29		

Royce Berry – Dislocated Wrist

Use Name	Pos.	Hgt	Wgt	Age	Int	Pts
Al Beauchamp	LB	6'2"	232	31		
Glenn Cameron	LB	6'2"	230	22		
Brad Cousino	LB	6'	220	22		
Chris Devlin	LB	6'3"	222	21		
Bo Harris	LB	6'3"	230	22		
Jim LeClair	LB	6'2"	235	24	3	
Ron Pritchard	LB	6'1"	230	28		
Lyle Blackwood	DB	6'	192	24	2	
Tommy Casanova	DB	6'2"	195	25		
Marvin Cobb	DB	6'	185	22	4	6
Ricky Davis	DB	6'1"	182	22	1	
Bernard Jackson	DB	6'	178	25	5	
Lemar Parrish	DB	5'11"	185	27	1	
Ken Riley	DB	6'	182	28	6	6

Use Name	Pos.	Hgt	Wgt	Age	Int	Pts
Ken Anderson	QB	6'1"	211	26		12
John Reaves	QB	6'3"	210	25		12
Lenvil Elliott	HB	6'	205	23		24
Stan Fritts	HB	6'1"	215	22		60
Essex Johnson	HB	5'9"	200	28		12
Booby Clark	FB	6'2"	245	24		24
Harold Henson	FB	6'3"	240	22		
Ed Williams	FB	6'2"	245	25		18
Isaac Curtis	WR	6'	193	24		42
Charlie Joiner	WR	5'11"	189	27		30
Chip Myers	WR	6'4"	205	30		18
John McDaniel	WR	6'1"	193	23		
Bruce Coslet	TE	6'3"	227	29		
Jack Novak	TE	6'4"	242	22		
Bob Trumpy	TE	6'6"	228	30		6
Dave Green	K	5'11"	208	25		70

Charlie Davis – Knee Injury

HOUSTON OILERS 10-4 Bum Phillips

Scores of Each Game		
7	New England	0
33	SAN DIEGO	17
19	CINCINNATI	21
40	Cleveland	10
13	WASHINGTON	10
24	DETROIT	8
17	Kansas City	13
17	Pittsburgh	24
20	MIAMI	19
9	PITTSBURGH	32
19	Cincinnati	23
27	San Francisco	13
27	Oakland	26
21	CLEVELAND	10

Use Name	Pos.	Hgt	Wgt	Age	Int	Pts
Elbert Drungo	OT	6'5"	265	32		
Kevin Hunt	OT	6'5"	260	26		
Greg Sampson	OT	6'6"	270	24		
Ed Fisher	OG	6'3"	245	26		
Conway Hayman	OG	6'3"	262	22		
Ron Saul	OG	6'2"	250	27		
Fred Hoaglin	C	6'4"	250	31		
Carl Mauck	C	6'3"	245	28		
Curley Culp	DG	6'1"	265	29		6
Elvin Bethea	DE	6'3"	255	29		2
Tody Smith	DE	6'5"	250	26		
Jim White	DE	6'3"	255	26		
Bubba Smith	DT-DE	6'7"	265	30		
John Little	DE-DT	6'3"	250	28		

Ronnie Carroll – Injury
Al Johnson – Ankle Injury
Lee Thomas – Injury

Use Name	Pos.	Hgt	Wgt	Age	Int	Pts
Duane Benson	LB	6'2"	220	30		
Gregg Bingham	LB	6'1"	230	24	4	
Robert Brazile	LB	6'4"	235	22		
Ralph Cindrich	LB	6'1"	230	25		
Steve Kiner	LB	6'	220	28	2	
Guy Roberts	LB	6'1"	220	25		
Ted Thompson	LB	6'1"	215	22		
Ted Washington	LB	6'1"	240	27	3	
Willie Alexander	DB	6'2"	190	25	3	
Bob Atkins	DB	6'3"	210	29	4	
Mark Cotney	DB	5'11"	200	23		
Willie Germany	DB	6'	192	26	2	6
Zeke Moore	DB	6'2"	197	31	5	
Greg Stemrick	DB	5'11"	185	23		
C. L. Whittington	DB	6'1"	200	23	1	

Use Name	Pos.	Hgt	Wgt	Age	Int	Pts
Lynn Dickey	QB	6'4"	210	25		
Dan Pastorini	QB	6'3"	205	26		6
Ronnie Coleman	HB	5'10"	195	24		30
Willie Rogers	HB	6'	210	26		8
Don Hardeman	FB	6'2"	235	23		30
Robert Holmes	FB	5'9"	220	29		
Fred Willis	FB	6'	205	27		12
Jim Beirne	WR	6'2"	206	28		
Ken Burrough	WR	6'4"	210	27		48
Emmett Edwards	WR	6'1"	187	23		
Nate Hawkins	WR	6'1"	190	25		
Billy Johnson	WR	5'9"	170	23		30
Billy Parks	WR	6'1"	190	27		
Mack Alston	TE	6'2"	230	28		24
Willie Frazier	TE	6'4"	235	32		
John Sawyer	TE	6'2"	230	22		6
Skip Butler	K	6'2"	200	27		85

CLEVELAND BROWNS 3-11 Forrest Gregg

Scores of Each Game		
17	Cincinnati	24
10	MINNESOTA	42
6	PITTSBURGH	42
10	HOUSTON	40
15	Denver	16
7	WASHINGTON	23
7	Baltimore	21
10	Detroit	21
17	Oakland	38
35	CINCINNATI	23
17	NEW ORLEANS	16
17	Pittsburgh	31
40	KANSAS CITY	14
10	Houston	21

Use Name	Pos.	Hgt	Wgt	Age	Int	Pts
Barry Darrow	OT	6'7"	260	25		
Doug Dieken	OT	6'5"	252	26		
Robert Jackson	OT	6'5"	245	22		
Gerry Sullivan	OT	6'4"	250	23		
Chuck Hutchison	OG	6'3"	250	26		
Bob McKay	OG	6'5"	265	27		
Tom DeLeone	C	6'2"	248	25		
John Demarie	C	6'3"	248	30		
Joe Jones (from PHI)	DE	6'6"	250	27		
Ron East	DE	6'4"	250	32		2
Stan Lewis	DE	6'4"	240	21		
Mack Mitchell	DE	6'7"	245	23		
Carl Barisich	DT	6'4"	255	24		
Walter Johnson	DT	6'3"	265	32		
Jerry Sherk	DT	6'4"	250	27		

Use Name	Pos.	Hgt	Wgt	Age	Int	Pts
Dick Ambrose	LB	6'	235	22		
Bob Babich	LB	6'2"	230	28		
John Garlington	LB	6'1"	220	29		
Dave Graf	LB	6'2"	215	22	1	
Charlie Hall	LB	6'3"	230	26	2	6
Jack LeVeck	LB	6'	225	25		
Neal Craig	DB	6'1"	190	27	1	
Van Green	DB	6'1"	192	24	1	
Jim Hill	DB	6'2"	195	28	1	6
Tony Peters	DB	6'1"	192	22	1	
John Pitts (from DEN)	DB	6'4"	218	30	1	
Clarence Scott	DB	6'	180	26	2	

Pete Adams – Knee Injury
Thom Darden – Knee Injury

Use Name	Pos.	Hgt	Wgt	Age	Int	Pts
Will Cureton	QB	6'3"	200	25		
Mike Phipps	QB	6'2"	205	27		
Brian Sipe	QB	6'1"	190	26		
Ken Brown	HB	5'10"	203	29		6
Cleo Miller (from KC)	HB	5'11"	202	22		6
Larry Poole	HB	6'	195	23		
Greg Pruitt	HB	5'10"	190	24		54
Henry Hynoski	FB	6'	210	22		
Hugh McKinnis	FB	6'	220	27		24
Billy Pritchett	FB	6'3"	230	24		
Steve Holden	WR	6'	194	24		
Billy Lefear	WR	5'11"	197	25		
Willie Miller	WR	5'9"	172	28		6
Reggie Rucker	WR	6'2"	190	27		18
Milt Morin	TE	6'4"	240	33		
Garry Parris	TE	6'2"	226	25		
Oscar Roan	TE	6'6"	214	28		18
Don Cockroft	K	6'1"	195	30		72

PITTSBURGH STEELERS

RUSHING

Last Name	No.	Yds	Avg	TD
Harris	262	1246	4.8	10
Bleier	140	528	3.8	2
Fuqua	74	285	3.9	1
Bradshaw	35	210	6.0	3
Harrison	43	191	4.4	3
Collier	21	124	5.9	3
Lewis	2	36	18.0	0
Swann	3	13	4.3	0
Hanratty	1	0	0.0	0

RECEIVING

Last Name	No.	Yds	Avg	TD
Swann	49	781	16	11
Harris	28	214	8	1
Stallworth	20	423	21	4
Fuqua	18	146	8	0
Lewis	17	308	18	2
L. Brown	16	244	15	1
Bleier	15	65	4	0
Garrett	13	178	14	1
Grossman	11	135	12	1
Shell	2	39	20	0
Collier	1	7	7	0
Harrison	1	4	4	0

PUNT RETURNS

Last Name	No.	Yds	Avg	TD
Edwards	25	267	11	0
D. Brown	22	217	10	0
Swann	7	64	9	0

KICKOFF RETURNS

Last Name	No.	Yds	Avg	TD
Collier	22	523	24	1
Blount	8	139	17	0
D. Brown	6	126	21	0
Harris	1	27	27	0
Fuqua	1	0	0	0

PASSING – PUNTING – KICKING

PASSING	Att	Comp	%	Yds	Yd/Att	TD	Int–%	RK
Bradshaw	286	165	58	2055	7.2	18	9– 3	4
Gilliam	48	24	50	450	9.4	3	3– 6	
Walden	3	2	67	39	13.0	0	0– 0	

PUNTING	No	Avg
Walden	69	39.4

KICKING	XP	Att	%	FG	Att	%
Gerela	44	46	96	17	21	81

CINCINNATI BENGALS

RUSHING

Last Name	No.	Yds	Avg	TD
Clark	167	594	3.6	4
Fritts	94	375	4.0	8
Elliott	71	308	4.3	1
Anderson	49	188	3.8	2
E. Johnson	58	177	3.1	1
Williams	35	136	3.9	2
Henson	11	38	3.5	0
Reaves	6	13	2.2	2
Coslet	1	1	1.0	0
McDaniel	1	–2	–2.0	0
Curtis	6	–9	–1.5	0

RECEIVING

Last Name	No.	Yds	Avg	TD
Curtis	44	934	21	7
Clark	42	334	8	0
Joiner	37	726	20	5
Myers	36	527	15	3
E. Johnson	25	196	8	1
Trumpy	22	276	13	1
Elliott	20	196	10	3
Coslet	10	117	12	0
Williams	10	96	10	1
Fritts	6	63	11	2
Novak	2	34	17	0
Hensen	1	–2	–2	0

PUNT RETURNS

Last Name	No.	Yds	Avg	TD
Blackwood	23	123	5	0
Parrish	13	83	6	0
Casanova	11	60	6	0
Cobb	1	1	1	0

KICKOFF RETURNS

Last Name	No.	Yds	Avg	TD
Jackson	25	587	24	0
Elliott	13	272	21	0
Parrish	4	114	29	0
McDaniel	3	69	23	0
Cobb	1	0	0	0
Cousino	1	0	0	0

PASSING – PUNTING – KICKING

PASSING	Att	Comp	%	Yds	Yd/Att	TD	Int–%	RK
Anderson	377	228	61	3169	8.4	21	11– 3	1
Reaves	51	25	49	297	5.8	2	3– 6	
Fritts	4	2	50	31	7.8	0	0– 0	
Green	1	0	0	0	0.0	0	0– 0	

PUNTING	No	Avg
Green	68	39.0

KICKING	XP	Att	%	FG	Att	%
Green	40	45	89	10	21	48

HOUSTON OILERS

RUSHING

Last Name	No.	Yds	Avg	TD
Coleman	175	790	4.5	5
Hardeman	166	648	3.9	5
Willis	118	420	3.6	2
Pastorini	23	97	4.2	1
Rodgers	18	55	3.1	1
Holmes	19	42	2.2	0
Johnson	5	17	3.4	0
Dickey	1	3	3.0	0
Edwards	1	–4	–4.0	0

RECEIVING

Last Name	No.	Yds	Avg	TD
Burrough	53	1063	20	8
Johnson	37	393	11	1
Willis	20	104	5	0
Alston	18	165	9	4
Coleman	18	129	7	0
Sawyer	7	144	21	1
Hardeman	5	10	2	0
Edwards	2	22	11	0
Hawkins	1	32	32	0
Reirne	1	15	15	0
Frazier	1	9	9	0
Parks	1	8	8	0
Holmes	1	5	5	0

PUNT RETURNS

Last Name	No.	Yds	Avg	TD
Johnson	40	612	15	3
Cotney	2	8	4	0
Coleman	1	0	0	0

KICKOFF RETURNS

Last Name	No.	Yds	Avg	TD
Johnson	33	798	24	1
Cotney	10	189	19	0
Coleman	8	149	19	0
Rodgers	1	13	13	0
Whittington	1	0	0	0
Thompson	1	–5	–5	0

PASSING – PUNTING – KICKING

PASSING	Att	Comp	%	Yds	Yd/Att	TD	Int–%	RK
Pastorini	342	163	48	2053	6.0	14	16– 5	10
Dickey	4	2	50	46	11.5	0	1–25	
Coleman	1	0	0	0	0.0	0	0– 0	

PUNTING	No	Avg
Pastorini	62	39.5

KICKING	XP	Att	%	FG	Att	%
Butler	31	34	91	18	30	60

CLEVELAND BROWNS

RUSHING

Last Name	No.	Yds	Avg	TD
Pruitt	217	1067	4.9	8
McKinnis	71	259	3.6	4
Pritchett	75	199	2.7	0
Poole	17	114	6.7	0
Phipps	18	70	3.9	0
Sipe	9	60	6.7	0
K. Brown	16	45	2.8	1
Hynoski	7	38	5.4	0
C. Miller	13	23	1.8	1
Cureton	1	1	1.0	0
W. Miller	1	–2	–2.0	0
Holden	2	–4	–2.0	0

RECEIVING

Last Name	No.	Yds	Avg	TD
Rucker	60	770	13	3
Pruitt	44	299	7	1
Roan	41	463	11	3
Holden	21	320	15	0
McKinnis	17	155	9	0
Pritchett	16	109	7	0
W. Miller	7	57	8	0
Hynoski	4	31	8	0
Brown	2	23	12	0
C. Miller	2	20	10	0
Morin	1	19	19	0
Lefear	1	14	14	0
Parris	1	12	12	0
Poole	1	5	5	0
Craig	1	1	1	0
Green	1	–1	–1	0

PUNT RETURNS

Last Name	No.	Yds	Avg	TD
Pruitt	13	130	10	0
W. Miller	10	47	5	0
Poole	6	35	6	0
Hynoski	2	16	8	0
Lefear	1	14	14	0
Green	1	0	0	0

KICKOFF RETURNS

Last Name	No.	Yds	Avg	TD
Lefear	13	412	32	0
Pruitt	14	302	22	0
C. Miller	12	241	20	0
Hynoski	8	194	24	0
K. Brown	7	126	18	0
W. Miller	4	94	24	0
Poole	2	65	33	0
McKinnis	3	39	13	0
Ambrose	1	3	3	0

PASSING – PUNTING – KICKING

PASSING	Att	Comp	%	Yds	Yd/Att	TD	Int–%	RK
Phipps	313	162	52	1749	5.6	4	19– 6	14
Sipe	88	45	51	427	4.9	1	3– 3	
Cureton	32	10	31	95	3.0	1	1– 3	
Cockroft	2	2	100	0	0.0	0	0– 0	
Hynoski	1	0	0	0	0.0	0	0– 0	
W. Miller	1	1	100	26	26.0	1	0– 0	

PUNTING	No	Avg
Cockroft	82	40.5

KICKING	XP	Att	%	FG	Att	%
Cockroft	21	24	88	17	23	74

OAKLAND RAIDERS 11-3 John Madden

Scores of Each Game		
31	Miami	21
31	Baltimore	20
6	San Diego	0
10	KANSAS CITY	42
10	Cincinnati	14
25	SAN DIEGO	0
42	Denver	17
48	NEW ORLEANS	10
38	CLEVELAND	17
26	Washington	*23
37	ATLANTA	*34
17	DENVER	10
26	Houston	27
28	Kansas City	20

Use Name	Pos.	Hgt	Wgt	Age	Int	Pts
Henry Lawrence	OT	6'4"	278	23		
Art Shell	OT	6'5"	265	28		
John Vella	OT	6'4"	260	25		
George Buehler	OG	6'2"	270	28		
Dan Medlin	OG	6'3"	252	25		
Gene Upshaw	OG	6'5"	255	30		
Dave Dalby	C	6'2"	250	24		
Steve Sylvester	OG-C	6'4"	262	22		
Tony Cline	DE	6'2"	244	27		
Horace Jones	DE	6'3"	260	26		
Dave Rowe (from SD)	DT	6'6"	270	30		
Kelvin Korver	DT	6'6"	270	26		
Otis Sistrunk	DT	6'4"	273	27		
Art Thoms	DT	6'5"	250	28	1	

Use Name	Pos.	Hgt	Wgt	Age	Int	Pts
Mike Dennery	LB	6'	226	25		
Willie Hall	LB	6'2"	220	25		2
Ted Hendricks	LB	6'7"	220	27	2	2
Gerald Irons	LB	6'2"	236	28	1	
Monte Johnson	LB	6'4"	240	23	1	
Phil Villapiano	LB	6'1"	222	26	2	
Butch Atkinson	DB	6'	185	27	4	
Willie Brown	DB	6'1"	210	34	4	
Neal Colzie	DB	6'2"	205	22	4	
Charlie Phillips	DB	6'2"	215	22	6	
Jack Tatum	DB	5'10"	206	26	4	
Skip Thomas	DB	6'1"	205	25	6	

Use Name	Pos.	Hgt	Wgt	Age	Int	Pts
George Blanda	QB	6'2"	215	47		83
Pete Beathard	QB	6'2"	205	33		
David Humm	QB	6'2"	184	23		
Larry Lawrence	QB	6'1"	208	26		
Ken Stabler	QB	6'3"	215	29		
Pete Banaszak	HB	5'11'	210	31		96
Louis Carter	HB	5'11"	200	22		
Clarence Davis	HB	5'10"	195	26		30
Harold Hart	HB	6'	206	22		24
Jess Phillips	FB-HB	6'1"	208	28		6
Marv Hubbard	FB	6'1"	235	29		12
Mark van Eeghen	FB	6'1"	225	23		18
Fred Biletnikoff	WR	6'1"	190	32		12
Morris Bradshaw	WR	6'	195	22		24
Cliff Branch	WR	5'11"	170	27		54
Mike Siani	WR	6'2"	195	25		
Dave Casper	TE	6'4"	228	23		6
Ted Kwalick	TE	6'4"	226	28		
Bob Moore	TE	6'3"	220	26		
Warren Bankston	FB-TE	6'4"	235	28		6
Ray Guy	K	6'3"	195	25		

DENVER BRONCOS 6-8 John Ralston

Scores of Each Game		
37	KANSAS CITY	33
23	GREEN BAY	13
14	Buffalo	38
9	Pittsburgh	20
16	CLEVELAND	15
13	Kansas City	26
17	OAKLAND	42
16	CINCINNATI	17
27	San Diego	17
21	Atlanta	35
13	SAN DIEGO	*10
10	Oakland	17
25	PHILADELPHIA	10
13	Miami	14

Use Name	Pos.	Hgt	Wgt	Age	Int	Pts
Mike Current	OT	6'4"	258	29		
Claudie Minor	OT	6'4"	285	24		
Marv Montgomery	OT	6'6"	255	27		
Stan Rogers	OT	6'4"	255	23		
Brian Goodman	OG	6'2"	250	26		
Paul Howard	OG	6'3"	260	24		
Tommy Lyons	OG	6'2"	230	27		
Carl Schaukowitch	OG	6'2"	237	24		
Bobby Maples	C	6'3"	250	32		
Phil Olsen	DT-C	6'5"	260	27		
Barney Chavous	DE	6'3"	252	24		
Lyle Alzado	DT-DE	6'3"	265	26		
John Grant	DT-DE	6'3"	235	25		
Rubin Carter	DT	6'	256	22		
Paul Smith	DT	6'3"	256	30	6	

Ed Smith – Knee Injury

Use Name	Pos.	Hgt	Wgt	Age	Int	Pts
Randy Gradishar	LB	6'3"	235	23	3	6
Tom Jackson	LB	5'11"	220	24	2	
Mike Lemon (from NO)	LB	6'2"	215	24		
Ray May	LB	6'1"	230	30	1	
Jim O'Malley	LB	6'1"	230	24	1	
Joe Rizzo	LB	6'1"	220	24		
Bob Swenson	LB	6'3"	220	22	1	
Steve Haggerty	DB	5'10"	175	22		
Calvin Jones	DB	5'7"	170	24	1	
Randy Poltl	DB	6'3"	190	23		
John Rowser	DB	6'1"	190	31	1	
Jeff Severson	DB	6'1"	185	25		
Earlie Thomas	DB	6'1"	190	29	2	
Bill Thompson	DB	6'1"	200	28	2	
Louis Wright	DB	6'2"	195	22	2	

Clarence Ellis – Knee Injury

Use Name	Pos.	Hgt	Wgt	Age	Int	Pts
John Hufnagel	QB	6'1"	194	24		
Charley Johnson	QB	6'	190	38		
Steve Ramsey	QB	6'2"	210	27		
Otis Armstrong	HB	5'10"	196	24		
Floyd Little	HB	5'10"	195	33		24
Fran Lynch	FB-HB	6'1"	205	29		24
Mike Franckowiak	FB	6'3"	220	22		
Al Haywood	FB	5'11"	215	27		
Jon Keyworth	FB	6'3"	230	23		24
Oliver Ross	HB-FB	6'	210	25		
Jack Dolbin	WR	5'10"	180	26		24
Haven Moses	WR	6'3"	208	29		12
Rick Upchurch	WR	5'10"	170	23		18
Bill Van Heusen	WR	6'1"	200	29		6
Bob Adams	TE	6'2"	220	29		
Boyd Brown	TE	6'4"	216	23		
Riley Odoms	TE	6'4"	230	25		24
Jim Turner	K	6'2"	205	34		86

KANSAS CITY CHIEFS 5-9 Paul Wiggin

Scores of Each Game		
33	Denver	37
24	N.Y. JETS	30
3	SAN FRANCISCO	20
42	OAKLAND	10
12	San Diego	10
26	DENVER	13
13	HOUSTON	17
34	Dallas	31
3	Pittsburgh	28
24	DETROIT	*21
14	Baltimore	28
20	SAN DIEGO	28
14	Cleveland	40
20	Oakland	28

Use Name	Pos.	Hgt	Wgt	Age	Int	Pts
Gary Palmer	OT	6'4"	255	24		
Charlie Getty	OT	6'4"	260	23		
Jim Nicholson	OT	6'6"	260	25		
Bill Story	OT	6'3"	245	23		
Randy Beisler	OG	6'4"	244	30		
Roger Bernhardt	OG	6'4"	244	25		
Ed Budde	OG	6'5"	265	34		
Tom Condon	OG	6'3"	240	22		
Rocky Rasley	OG	6'3"	255	28		
Mike Wilson	OG	6'1"	250	27		
Charlie Ane	C	6'1"	233	23		
Jack Rudnay	C	6'3"	240	27		
John Lohmeyer	DE	6'4"	230	24		
Bob Maddox	DE	6'5"	232	26		
John Matuszak	DE	6'8"	275	24		6
Louis Ross	DE	6'6"	265	28		
Wilbur Young	DE	6'6"	285	26		
Buck Buchanan	DT	6'7"	270	35		
Larry Estes	DT	6'6"	250	28		
Tom Keating	DT	6'3"	247	32		
Marv Upshaw	DT	6'3"	260	28		

Use Name	Pos.	Hgt	Wgt	Age	Int	Pts
Ken Avery	LB	6'1"	227	31		
Tim Kearney	LB	6'2"	230	24		
Willie Lanier	LB	6'1"	245	30	5	
Jim Lynch	LB	6'1"	225	30		
Al Palewicz	LB	6'1"	215	25		
Bill Peterson	LB	6'3"	225	30		
Hise Austin	DB	6'4"	187	24		
Jim Kearney	DB	6'2"	206	32		
Jim Marsalis	DB	5'11"	190	29	1	
Don Martin	DB	5'11"	185	25		
Kerry Reardon	DB	5'11"	180	26	3	
Mike Sensibaugh	DB	5'11"	192	26	5	
Emmitt Thomas	DB	6'2"	192	32	6	

Clyde Werner – Tendon Injury

Use Name	Pos.	Hgt	Wgt	Age	Int	Pts
Tony Adams	QB	6'	198	25		
Wayne Clark	QB	6'2"	203	28		
Len Dawson	QB	6'	190	41		
Mike Livingston	QB	6'3"	212	29		12
Woody Green	HB	6'1"	205	24		36
Ed Podolak	HB	6'1"	205	28		30
Charlie Thomas	HB	5'9"	180	24		
Doug Dressler (from NE)	FB	6'3"	228	27		6
MacArthur Lane	FB	6'	220	33		12
Jeff Kinney	HB-FB	6'2"	215	25		12
Larry Brunson	WR	5'11"	180	26		12
Reggie Craig	WR	6'	187	22		
Barry Pearson	WR	5'11"	185	25		18
Otis Taylor	WR	6'2"	215	32		
Bill Masters	TE	6'5"	240	31		18
Walter White	TE	6'3"	208	24		18
Jim McCann	K	6'2"	165	26		
Jan Stenerud	K	6'2"	187	32		96
Jerrel Wilson	K	6'4"	222	33		

SAN DIEGO CHARGERS 2-12 Tommy Prothro

Scores of Each Game		
0	PITTSBURGH	37
17	Houston	33
0	OAKLAND	6
10	LOS ANGELES	*13
10	KANSAS CITY	12
0	Oakland	25
24	N.Y. Giants	35
19	NEW ENGLAND	33
17	DENVER	27
13	Minnesota	28
10	Denver	*13
28	Kansas City	20
24	N.Y. JETS	16
17	Cincinnati	47

Use Name	Pos.	Hgt	Wgt	Age	Int	Pts
Terry Owens	OT	6'6"	264	31		
Billy Shields	OT	6'7"	260	22		
Russ Washington	OT	6'6"	285	28		
Booker Brown	OG	6'2"	257	22		
Ira Gordon	OG	6'3"	283	27		
Ralph Perretta	OG	6'2"	252	22		
Doug Wilkerson	OG	6'2"	262	28		
Ed Flanagan	C	6'3"	245	31		
Mark Markovich	C	6'5"	256	22		
Coy Bacon	DE	6'4"	278	33		
Fred Dean	DE	6'3"	220	23		
Gary Johnson	DT	6'2"	262	23		
Louie Kelcher	DT	6'5"	282	22		
John Teerlinck	DT	6'5"	250	24		
Greg Wojcik	DT	6'6"	270	32		

Use Name	Pos.	Hgt	Wgt	Age	Int	Pts
Billy Andrews	LB	6'	220	30		
Don Goode	LB	6'2"	225	24	1	
Tom Graham	LB	6'2"	235	25	2	
Drew Mehalic	LB	6'4"	225	22	1	
Floyd Rice	LB	6'3"	225	26	1	
Frank Tate	LB	6'3"	225	23		
Joe Beauchamp	DB	6'	184	31	1	
Danny Colbert	DB	5'11"	176	24	2	
Chris Fletcher	DB	5'11"	190	26	6	
Mike Fuller	DB	5'9"	195	22	1	6
Hal Stringert	DB	5'11"	180	23		
Maurice Tyler	DB	6'	190	25		
Mike Williams	DB	5'10"	180	21	4	
Sam Williams	DB	6'2"	186	23	1	

Charles Anthony – Broken Leg
Jim Harrison – Injury
Ken Hutcherson – Leg Injury

Use Name	Pos.	Hgt	Wgt	Age	Int	Pts
Dan Fouts	QB	6'3"	204	24		12
Jesse Freitas	QB	6'1"	192	23		
Bobby Douglass (from CHI)	HB-QB	6'2"	228	28		6
Dave Atkins	HB	6'1"	208	26		
Glen Bonner	HB	6'2"	202	23		
Charlie Smith	HB	6'1"	205	29		
Don Woods	HB	6'1"	214	24		12
Rickey Young	HB	6'2"	193	21		36
Tony Baker	FB	5'11"	215	30		6
Bo Matthews	FB	6'4"	230	23		18
Sam Scarber	FB	6'2"	232	27		12
Melvin Baker (from NO-NE)	WR	6'	192	25		
Gary Garrison	WR	6'1"	194	31		12
Dwight McDonald	WR	6'2"	187	24		18
Joe Sweet	WR	6'2"	193	27		
Chuck Bradley	TE	6'6"	232	24		
Craig Cotton	TE	6'4"	222	27		
Pat Curran	TE	6'3"	238	29		1
Denniss Partee	K	6'2"	225	29		
Ray Wersching	K	5'11"	222	25		56

*Overtime

OAKLAND RAIDERS

RUSHING

Last Name	No.	Yds	Avg	TD
Banaszak	187	672	3.6	16
van Eeghen	136	597	4.4	2
Davis	112	486	4.3	4
J. Phillips	63	298	4.7	1
Hubbard	60	294	4.9	2
Hart	56	173	3.1	3
Carter	11	27	2.5	0
Humm	7	21	3.0	0
Branch	2	18	9.0	0
Lawrence	2	−3	−1.5	0
Stabler	6	−5	−0.8	0
Bradshaw	1	−5	−5.0	0

RECEIVING

Last Name	No.	Yds	Avg	TD
Branch	51	893	18	9
Biletnikoff	43	587	14	2
Moore	19	175	9	0
Siani	17	294	17	0
van Eeghen	12	42	4	1
Davis	11	126	12	1
Banaszak	10	64	6	0
Bradshaw	7	180	26	4
Hubbard	7	81	12	0
Hart	6	27	5	0
Casper	5	71	14	1
J. Phillips	4	25	6	0
Carter	2	39	20	0
Bankston	2	21	11	1

PUNT RETURNS

Last Name	No.	Yds	Avg	TD
Colzie	48	655	14	0
Atkinson	8	33	4	0
Phillips	2	0	0	0

KICKOFF RETURNS

Last Name	No.	Yds	Avg	TD
Hart	17	518	31	1
J. Phillips	12	310	26	0
Davis	9	268	30	0
van Eeghen	7	112	16	0
Atkinson	2	60	30	0
Banaszak	2	24	12	0
Bankston	1	19	19	0
Carter	1	13	13	0

PASSING – PUNTING – KICKING

PASSING	Att	Comp	%	Yds	Yd/Att	TD	Int–%	RK
Stabler	293	171	58	2296	7.8	16	24– 8	8
Humm	38	18	47	246	6.5	3	2– 5	
Lawrence	15	5	33	50	3.3	0	1– 7	
Blanda	3	1	33	11	3.7	0	1–33	
Guy	1	1	100	22	22.0	0	0– 0	

PUNTING	No	Avg
Guy	68	43.8

KICKING	XP	Att	%	FG	Att	%
Blanda	44	48	96	13	21	62

DENVER BRONCOS

RUSHING

Last Name	No.	Yds	Avg	TD
Keyworth	182	725	4.0	3
Little	125	445	3.6	2
Lynch	57	218	3.8	3
Armstrong	31	155	5.0	0
Ross	42	121	2.9	0
Upchurch	16	97	6.1	1
Dolbin	5	72	14.4	0
Hufnagel	8	47	5.9	0
Ramsey	6	38	6.3	0
Odoms	5	27	5.4	0
Van Heusen	2	26	13.0	0
Johnson	10	21	2.1	0
Franckowiak	1	1	1.0	0

RECEIVING

Last Name	No.	Yds	Avg	TD
Keyworth	42	314	8	1
Odoms	40	544	14	3
Moses	29	505	17	2
Little	29	308	11	2
Dolbin	22	421	19	3
Upchurch	18	436	24	2
Van Heusen	15	246	16	1
Ross	7	69	10	0
Lynch	6	33	6	1
Brown	1	[illegible]	14	0
Armstrong	1	10	10	0

PUNT RETURNS

Last Name	No.	Yds	Avg	TD
Upchurch	27	312	12	0
Thompson	13	158	12	0
Lynch	1	0	0	0

KICKOFF RETURNS

Last Name	No.	Yds	Avg	TD
Upchurch	40	1084	27	0
Little	16	307	19	0
Ross	1	20	20	0
Severson	1	20	20	0
Maples	1	15	15	0

PASSING – PUNTING – KICKING

PASSING	Att	Comp	%	Yds	Yd/Att	TD	Int–%	RK
Ramsey	233	128	55	1562	6.7	9	14– 6	9
Johnson	142	65	46	1021	7.2	5	12– 9	15
Hufnagel	51	16	31	287	5.6	1	8–16	
Van Heusen	1	1	100	30	30.0	0	0– 0	

PUNTING	No	Avg
Van Heusen	63	39.9

KICKING	XP	Att	%	FG	Att	%
Turner	23	26	88	21	28	75

KANSAS CITY CHIEFS

RUSHING

Last Name	No.	Yds	Avg	TD
Green	167	611	3.7	5
Podolak	102	351	3.4	3
Lane	79	311	3.9	2
Kinney	85	304	3.6	2
Brunson	2	89	44.5	0
Livingston	13	68	5.2	1
Adams	8	42	5.3	0
Dressler	6	24	4.0	0
Dawson	5	7	1.4	0
White	3	−10	−3.3	0

RECEIVING

Last Name	No.	Yds	Avg	TD
Podolak	37	332	9	2
Pearson	36	608	17	3
Lane	25	202	8	0
Masters	24	314	13	3
White	23	559	24	3
Brunson	23	398	17	2
Green	23	215	9	1
Kinney	21	148	7	0
Dressler	3	6	2	1
Craig	1	10	10	0
LaGrand	1	−1	−1	0
Adams	1	−7	−7	0

PUNT RETURNS

Last Name	No.	Yds	Avg	TD
Thomas	12	112	9	0
Podolak	13	96	7	0
Reardon	5	41	8	0
Pearson	2	31	16	0
Craig	4	19	5	0
Brunson	1	4	4	0

KICKOFF RETURNS

Last Name	No.	Yds	Avg	TD
Thomas	22	516	24	0
Green	16	343	21	0
Craig	10	247	25	0
Kinney	2	39	20	0
Dressler	1	18	18	0
Brunson	1	8	8	0
Peterson	1	8	8	0

PASSING – PUNTING – KICKING

PASSING	Att	Comp	%	Yds	Yd/Att	TD	Int–%	RK
Livingston	176	88	50	1245	7.1	8	6– 3	7
Dawson	140	93	66	1095	7.8	5	4– 3	2
Adams	77	36	47	445	5.8	2	4– 5	
Podolak	1	0	0	0	0.0	0	1–100	
White	1	0	0	0	0.0	0	1–100	

PUNTING	No	Avg
Wilson	54	41.4
McCann	14	35.2
Dressler	4	25.0

KICKING	XP	Att	%	FG	Att	%
Stenerud	30	31	97	22	32	69

SAN DIEGO CHARGERS

RUSHING

Last Name	No.	Yds	Avg	TD
Young	138	577	4.2	5
Woods	87	317	3.6	2
Matthews	71	254	3.6	3
Fouts	23	170	7.4	2
T. Baker	42	131	3.1	1
Bonner	28	120	4.3	0
Scarber	15	68	4.5	1
Freitas	11	56	5.1	0
Douglass	10	42	4.2	0
Douglass	5	34	6.8	1
Garrison	3	30	10.0	0
Curran	3	21	7.0	0
Carter	2	11	5.5	0
M. Baker	1	21	21.0	0
Atkins	1	4	4.0	0

RECEIVING

Last Name	No.	Yds	Avg	TD
Curran	45	619	14	0
Garrison	27	438	16	2
Young	21	166	8	1
McDonald	19	298	16	3
Woods	13	101	8	0
Scarber	12	68	6	1
Matthews	9	59	7	0
Sweet	8	147	18	0
T. Baker	6	27	5	0
M. Baker	2	26	13	0
Bonner	2	8	4	0
Bradley	1	42	42	0

PUNT RETURNS

Last Name	No.	Yds	Avg	TD
Fuller	36	410	11	1
Colbert	2	32	16	0

KICKOFF RETURNS

Last Name	No.	Yds	Avg	TD
Fuller	31	725	23	0
Young	15	323	22	0
Smith	8	222	28	0
Andrews	6	93	16	0
Colbert	5	91	18	0
Curran	3	28	9	0
Markovich	1	0	0	0

PASSING – PUNTING – KICKING

PASSING	Att	Comp	%	Yds	Yd/Att	TD	Int–%	RK
Fouts	195	106	54	1396	7.2	2	10– 5	12
Freitas	110	49	45	525	4.8	5	5– 5	
Douglass	47	15	32	140	3.0	0	3– 6	

PUNTING	No	Avg
Partee	79	36.8

KICKING	XP	Att	%	FG	Att	%
Wersching	20	21	95	12	24	50

1975 Championship Games

NFC CHAMPIONSHIP GAME
January 4, 1976 at Los Angeles
(Attendance 84,483)

A Study in Contrasts

In the NFC semifinal match Los Angeles won easily over St. Louis, 35-23. By contrast, Dallas, the wild-card team, came back from a 14-10 deficit with 24 seconds left to play (a 50-yard TD bomb from Roger Staubach to Drew Pearson) to astonish Minnesota 17-14. But past performances went out the window in this championship game as the Cowboys totally humiliated the favorite Rams 37-7.

The game was one of the most lopsided ever staged in the playoffs, and represented a drastic difference in playing styles. While coach Chuck Knox's Rams played it close to the vest and suffered for it as a consequence, coach Tom Landry did just the opposite with Dallas. Leading 14-0 in the second quarter as the result of two touchdown passes by Staubach, Landry had the Cowboys go for broke rather than cautiously sit on the lead. Staubach connected to Preston Pearson on a 15-yard pass to run the score to 21-0 and then called several time outs to try and get into field goal range as the half ran out. The Rams play on the other hand was best typified by their choice on the first series of downs when the game opened. Facing third down and 15 from their 30, they elected to run a sweep. It was unsuccessful and they punted the ball away.

Dallas ran the score to 34-0 in the third quarter behind Staubach's fourth TD pass of the day, and two field goals by Toni Fritsch. In the 4th quarter the Rams scored a touchdown to avoid their first home field shutout in 30 years. Fritsch then added another field goal to make the final score 37-7.

Part of the Rams fall from grace following a 12-2 regular season was the inability of All-Pro ends Jack Youngblood and Fred Dryer to penetrate Staubach even once, and for Lawrence McCutcheon, Pro Bowl running back, to gain ten yards in 11 rushes. Also stopped cold was All-Pro wide receiver Harold Jackson, who had no completions for the day. As a final capper, last year's Pro Bowl Most Valuable Player, quarterback James Harris, suffering from an injured shoulder, was yanked early in the first quarter after throwing an interception.

SCORING

LOS ANGELES	0	0	0	7– 7
DALLAS	7	14	13	3–37

First Quarter
Dall. P.Pearson, 18 yard pass from Staubach
PAT–Fritsch (kick)

Second Quarter
Dall. Richards, 4 yard pass from Staubach
PAT–Fritsch (kick)
Dall. P. Pearson, 15 yard pass from Staubach
PAT–Fritsch (kick)

Third Quarter
Dall. P. Pearson, 19 yard pass from Staubach
PAT–Fritsch (kick)
Dall. Fritsch, 40 yard field goal
Dall. Fritsch, 26 yard field goal

Fourth Quarter
L.A. Cappelletti, 1 yard rush
PAT–Dempsey (kick)
Dall. Fritsch, 26 yard field goal

TEAM STATISTICS

L.A.		DALLAS
9	First Downs – Total	24
1	First Downs – Rushing	8
7	First Downs – Passing	15
1	First Downs – Penalty	1
1	Fumbles – Number	1
0	Fumbles – Lost Ball	0
4	Penalties – Number	5
25	Yards Penalized	59
2	Missed Field Goals	0
45	Offensive Plays	78
118	Net Yards	441
2.6	Average Gain	5.7
3	Giveaways	1
1	Takeaways	3
–2	Difference	+2

INDIVIDUAL STATISTICS

LOS ANGELES	No.	Yds	Avg.	DALLAS	No	Yds	Avg.
RUSHING							
Jaworski	2	12	6.0	Newhouse	16	64	4.0
McCutcheon	11	10	0.9	Staubach	7	54	7.7
Cappelletti	1	1	1.0	Dennison	13	35	2.7
Scribner	1	1	1.0	P. Pearson	7	20	2.9
Bryant	1	–2	–2.0	Young	6	17	2.8
	16	22	1.4	Fuggett	1	5	5.0
					50	195	3.9
RECEIVING							
Jessie	4	52	13.0	P. Pearson	7	123	17.6
McCutcheon	3	39	13.0	D. Pearson	5	46	9.2
Nelson	3	28	9.3	Richards	2	46	23.0
Bryant	1	28	28.0	Fuggett	2	5	2.5
	11	147	13.4	Young	1	15	15.0
				Dennison	1	11	11.0
					18	246	13.7
PUNTING							
Carrell	7		35.4	Hoopes	4		34.8
PUNT RETURNS							
Scribner	2	3	1.5	Richards	3	17	5.7
				Harris	1	9	9.0
					4	26	6.5
KICKOFF RETURNS							
McGee	5	103	20.6	Dennison	2	47	23.5
Bryant	2	49	24.5				
Jessie	1	15	15.0				
	8	167	20.9				
INTERCEPTION RETURNS							
Simpson	1	37	37.0	Lewis	2	20	10.0
				C. Harris	1	22	22.0
					3	42	14.0

PASSING

LOS ANGELES	Att	Comp	Comp Pct.	Yds	Int	Yds/ Att.	Yds/ Comp	Yards Lost Tackled
Jaworski	22	11	50.0	147	2	6.7	13.4	5–51
J. Harris	2	0	00.0	0	1	–	–	–
	24	11	45.8	147	3	6.1	13.4	5–51
DALLAS								
Staubach	26	16	61.5	220	1	8.5	13.8	0–0
Longley	2	2	100.0	26	0	13.0	13.0	0–0
	28	18	64.3	246	1	8.8	13.7	0–0

AFC CHAMPIONSHIP GAME
January 4, 1976 at Pittsburgh)
(Attendance 49,103)

A Cold Reception

Oakland had done everything they could to prepare for Pittsburgh in the AFC Championship game. They went through the season with a 11-3 record and then held off Cincinnati 31-28 in the semifinal game. But they were met with an ice-covered and snow swept field and bone-chilling winds, plus the nearly impregnable defense of the Steelers. When the long afternoon came to a close they found themselves on the short end of a 16-10 score and another summer in which to think of the Super Bowl again.

Pittsburgh got ready for their second Super Bowl try by going through a 12-2 campaign and then stopping the Baltimore resurgence 28-10. The big plus for the Steelers was the return to fulltime duty after eight weeks of a hurting, defensive tackle Joe Greene.

When the first half came to a close, Pittsburgh led 3-0 as the result of a 36-yard field goal by Roy Gerela. In the third quarter the hard-hitting defensive battle continued with both teams unable to reach the scoreboard. Then, within a six minutes stretch of the final quarter Pittsburgh's Franco Harris bruised his way for 25 yards into the end zone, Oakland quarterback Ken Stabler hit Mike Siani with a 14-yard pass, and Terry Bradshaw, the Steeler's quarterback, hit John Stallworth with a 20-yard pass. Gerela's kick failed, and the score stood at 16-7.

By the time Oakland got on the board again there were 12 seconds left to play. Stabler had taken over the ball with 1:31 on the clock and drove his club from the Oakland 35 to the Pittsburgh 24. Ageless George Blanda, who had reached an NFL milestone during the season by scoring his 2000th career point, booted a 41-yard field goal to put the score at 16-10.

On the ensuing kickoff to Pittsburgh, Oakland went for the miracle by attempting a dribbler. Marv Hubbard recovered the ball for Oakland with seven seconds left. Stabler, at his own 45, threw a long bomb which hit Cliff Branch on the 15. But the Steelers were there to stop him as the season ran out for Oakland.

SCORING

PITTSBURGH	0	3	0	13–16
OAKLAND	0	0	0	10–10

Second Quarter
Pit. Gerela, 36 yard field goal

Fourth Quarter
Pit. Harris, 25 yard rush
PAT–Gerela (kick)
Oak. Siani, 14 yard pass from Stabler
PAT–Blanda (kick)
Pit. Stallworth, 20 yard fass from Bradshaw
PAT–Kick no good
Oak. Blanda, 41 yard field goal.

TEAM STATISTICS

PIT.		OAK.
16	First Downs – Total	18
5	First Downs – Rushing	3
10	First Downs – Passing	13
1	First Downs – Penalty	2
5	Fumbles – Number	4
5	Fumbles – Lost Ball	3
3	Penalties – Number	4
32	Yards Penalized	40
2	Missed Field Goals	1
64	Offensive Plays	76
332	Net Yards	321
5.2	Average Gain	4.2
8	Giveaways	5
5	Takeaways	8
–3	Difference	+3

INDIVIDUAL STATISTICS

PITTSBURGH	No	Yds	Avg.	OAKLAND	No	Yds	Avg.
RUSHING							
Harris	27	79	2.9	Banaszak	8	33	4.1
Bradshaw	2	22	11.0	Hubbard	10	30	3.0
Bleier	10	16	1.6	Davis	13	29	2.2
	39	117	3.0	Phillips	1	1	1.0
					32	93	2.9
RECEIVING							
Harris	5	58	11.6	Siani	5	80	18.0
Grossman	4	36	9.0	Casper	5	67	13.4
Swann	2	45	22.5	Branch	2	56	28.0
Stallworth	2	30	15.0	Banaszak	2	12	6.0
Lewis	1	33	33.0	Moore	2	12	6.0
L. Brown	1	13	13.0	Hart	1	16	16.0
	15	215	14.3	Davis	1	3	3.0
					18	246	13.7
PUNTING							
Walden	4		38.5	Guy	8		37.8
PUNT RETURNS							
D. Brown	2	28	14.0	Siani	1	0	0.0
Collier	1	0	0.0				
	3	28	9.3				
KICKOFF RETURNS							
Collier	2	57	28.5	Davis	3	56	18.7
Harrison	1	2	2.0	Banaszak	1	15	15.0
	3	59	19.7		4	71	17.8
INTERCEPTION RETURNS							
Wagner	2	34	17.0	Tatum	2	8	4.0
				M. Johnson	1	11	11.0
					3	19	6.3

PASSING

PITTSBURGH	Att	Comp	Comp Pct.	Yds	Int	Yds/ Att.	Yds/ Comp	Yards Lost Tackled
Bradshaw	25	15	60.0	215	3	8.6	14.3	0–0
OAKLAND								
Stabler	42	18	42.9	246	2	5.9	13.7	2–18

SUPER BOWL X
January 18, at Miami
(Attendance: 80,187)

Swann's Song

Unlike past Super Bowl efforts, which had more fanfare off the field than on, this year's edition featured enough excitement to compete with the pre-game show. Favorite Pittsburgh, returning for the second time in two years, was facing Dallas, the first wildcard team to ever reach the NFL finals.

Through the first three quarters Dallas held a 10-7 lead. Then, at 3:32 of the final quarter, Reggie Harrison, a Pittsburgh reserve running back who plays on special teams, blocked a punt by Mitch Hoopes at the Dallas 9. The ball bounced off Harrison's face hard enough to wind up in the Dallas end zone, good enough for a two-point safety and run the score to 10-9. It was a play which was considered the turning point of the game. Roy Gerela put Pittsburgh in front for the first time with a 36-yard field at 6:19. A few minutes later Mike Wagner intercepted a Roger Staubach pass and returned it 19 yards to the Dallas 7. Terry Bradshaw was unable to get the touchdown, but Gerela booted an 18-yard field goal.

With the score 15-10, the game's hero, Lynn Swann, took a 59-yard pass from Bradshaw and ran it 5 yards into the end zone at 11:58. The kick failed and the stage was set for the final dramatics. The Cowboys drove 80 yards in five plays with under two minutes to play to make the score 21-17. On the drive, two passes of 30 and 11 yards from Staubach to Drew Pearson proved the key. Terry Hanratty replaced Bradshaw, who had been shaken up on his 64-yard pass to Swann, for Pittsburgh's last offensive series and found himself with fourth down and 9 to go on the Dallas 41. Only 1:28 was left to play and coach Chuck Noll decided to gamble, owing to the fact that Dallas had no time outs left. Rather than punt and risk the run back, he had the Steelers go for the run. They got two yards and Dallas took possession. Five plays later the game was over and Pittsburgh had its second straight Super Bowl triumph.

Dallas coach Tom Landry blamed the defeat on the blocked punt by Harrison, which he said changed the momentum of the game around. He may have been right, but Swann's performance—which earned him the game's Most Valuable Player award—was momentum enough for the Steelers. Hospitalized only two weeks earlier with a concussion, and dropping passes in practice, the fleet-footed receiver returned to catch four passes for an astonishing total of 161 yards—a Super Bowl record certain to stand for many years.

LINEUPS

PITTSBURGH		DALLAS
OFFENSE		
Stallworth	WR	Richards
Kolb	LT	Neely
Clack	LG	Lawless
Mansfield	C	Fitzgerald
Mullins	RG	Nye
Gravelle	RT	Wright
L. Brown	TE	Fugett
Swann	WR	D. Pearson
Bradshaw	QB	Staubach
Bleier	RB	P. Pearson
F. Harris	RB	Newhouse
DEFENSE		
Greenwood	LE	Jones
Green	LT	Pugh
Holmes	RT	Cole
D. White	RE	Martin
Ham	LLB	D. Edwards
Lambert	MLB	Jordan
Russell	RLB	Lewis
Thomas	LCB	Washington
Blount	RCB	Renfro
Wagner	LS	Waters
G. Edwards	RS	C. Harris

SUBSTITUTES

PITTSBURGH

OFFENSE	
Collier	Hanratty
S. Davis	Harrison
Fuqua	Lewis
Garrett	Reavis
Grossman	Webster
DEFENSE	
Allen	Furness
Banaszak	Kellum
Bradley	Shell
D. Brown	Toews
KICKERS	
Gerela	Walden

DALLAS

OFFENSE	
K. Davis	P. Howard
Dennison	R. Howard
Donovan	Scott
DuPree	Young
DEFENSE	
Barnes	Hughes
Breunig	Peterson
Capone	R. White
Gregory	Woolsey
Henderson	
Kickers	
Fritsch	Hoopes

SCORING

PITTSBURGH	7	0	0	14–21
DALLAS	7	3	0	7–17

First Quarter		
Dall.	D. Pearson, 29 yard pass from Staubach	4:36
	PAT – Fritsch (kick)	
Pitt.	Grossman, 7 yard pass from Bradshaw	3:03
	PAT – Gerela (kick)	
Second Quarter		
Dall.	Fritsch, 36 yard field goal	0:15
Fourth Quarter		
Pitt.	Safety – Harrison blocked punt out of end zone	3:32
Pitt.	Gerela, 36 yard field goal	6:19
Pitt.	Gerela, 18 yard field goal	8:23
Pitt.	Swann, 64 yard pass from Bradshaw	11:58
	PAT – Gerela (kick – failed)	
Dall.	P. Howard, 34 yard pass from Staubach	13:12
	PAT – Fritsch (kick)	

TEAM STATISTICS

PITT.		DALL.
13	First Downs – Total	14
7	First Downs – Rushing	6
6	First Downs – Passing	8
0	First Downs – Penalty	0
4	Fumbles – Number	4
0	Fumbles – Lost Ball	0
0	Penalties – Number	2
0	Yards Penalized	20
2	Missed Field Goals	0
67	Offensive Plays	62
339	Net Yards	270
5.1	Average Gain	4.4
0	Giveaways	3
3	Takeaways	0
+3	Difference	-3

INDIVIDUAL STATISTICS

PITTSBURGH	No	Yds	Avg.	DALLAS	No	Yds	Avg.
RUSHING							
F. Harris	27	82	3.0	Newhouse	16	56	3.5
Bleier	15	51	3.4	Staubach	5	22	4.4
Bradshaw	4	16	4.0	Dennison	5	16	3.2
	46	149	3.2	P. Pearson	5	14	2.8
					31	108	3.5
RECEIVING							
Swann	4	161	40.3	P. Pearson	5	53	10.6
Stallworth	2	8	4.0	Young	3	31	10.3
F. Harris	1	26	26.0	D. Pearson	2	59	29.5
L. Brown	1	7	7.0	Newhouse	2	12	6.0
Grossman	1	7	7.0	P. Howard	1	34	34.0
	9	209	23.2	Fugett	1	9	9.0
				Dennison	1	6	6.0
					15	204	13.6
PUNTING							
Walden	4		39.8	Hoopes	7		35.0
PUNT RETURNS							
D. Brown	3	14	4.7	Richards	1	3	3.0
G. Edwards	2	17	8.5				
	5	31	6.2				
KICKOFF RETURNS							
Blount	3	64	21.3	P. Pearson	4	48	12.0
Collier	1	25	25.0	Henderson	*0	48	–
	4	89	22.3	* = lateral	4	96	24.0
INTERCEPTION RETURNS							
Thomas	1	35	35.0	none			
G. Edwards	1	35	35.0				
Wagner	1	19	19.0				
	3	89	29.7				

PASSING

	Att	Comp	Comp Pct.	Yds.	Int	Yds/ Att.	Yds/ Comp	Yards Lost Tackled
PITTSBURGH								
Bradshaw	19	9	47.4	209	0	11.0	23.2	2–19
DALLAS								
Staubach	24	15	62.5	204	3	8.5	13.6	7–42

1976 N.F.C. THE VIKES — Bridesmaids, Again

EASTERN DIVISION

Dallas Cowboys — Providing themselves beyond expectations with a trip to the Super Bowl the previous year, the Pokes rung up 11 victories and eight Pro Bowl selections (more than any team except Pittsburgh) on the way to a first-place finish that was tarnished by their first-round playoff failure against Los Angeles. Dallas' offense scored just 13 TD's in its last eight games, however, as the need for a breakaway running threat became more evident. While the pass catching chores appeared to be in good hands as Drew Pearson led the NFC in receptions and Billy Joe DuPree set a club record for catches by a tight end (42), only twice did a Cowboy rusher gain over 100 yards in a game.

Washington Redskins — After making four major trades and spending a bundle on free agents John Riggins, Calvin Hill and Jean Fugett before the season began, the pressure was on Head Coach George Allen to produce a winner. The Skins squeaked past St. Louis for the NFC "Wild Card" spot before Minnesota humiliated them in the playoffs. Critics remained divided all year on the question of who between Billy Kilmer and Joe Theismann should be the starting QB, but the feisty Kilmer emerged as the No. 1 man after engineering clutch victories down the stretch. As usual, the Skins' special teams were magnificent as Eddie Brown fell just a few yards short of an NFL punt return record and PK Mark Moseley led the NFC in scoring.

St. Louis Cardinals — Despite leading the league in offense and featuring three All-Pros in their offensive line, the 10-4 Cards failed to make the playoffs because of their two losses to conference rival Washington, also 10-4 for the year. The "Cardiac" crew won eight of its 10 games by seven points or less, four of them coming after halftime deficits. Their most dramatic victory came in Week No. 10 when they rallied from 15 points behind in the second half to nip the Rams 30-28 on Jim Bakken's 25-yard FG with four seconds left. But the next week at home against the Skins, the Cards suffered a costly emotional letdown, losing 16-10 after usually reliable WR Mel Gray dropped a last-minute endzone pass that would have won the game. After losing 19-14 the next week in Dallas, one play again stood out—an apparent pass interference penalty against TE J.V. Cain in the endzone with a minute remaining that was never called.

Philadelphia Eagles — Well-aware of the long-range drafting deficiencies caused by earlier trades for Roman Gabriel, Mike Boryla and Bill Bergey, rookie Head Coach Dick Vermeil announced at the beginning of the season it would take at least five years to turn things around in Philly. After Gabriel had trouble coming back from off-season knee surgery and Boryla finished the year with the lowest passing average per play among starting NFL QB's, the stage was set for the deal with L.A. that brought in strong-armed Ron Jaworski before the '77 season began. Each of the Eagles' four wins were against losing teams, and at one point in the second half of the season, they lost five straight and scored only 17 points.

New York Giants — Equipped with a flashy new stadium in New Jersey, the Giants couldn't help but be associated with the ill-fated WFL. In April they signed FB Larry Csonka, and after an 0-7 start, they replaced Head Coach Bill Arnsparger with Zonk's WFL mentor in Memphis, John McVay. The Giants finished 3-4 under McVay, good enough to win him a two-year contract. They finally won their first game the 10th week, upsetting Washington 12-9 behind a strong defense led by LB's Brad Van Pelt and Harry Carson. The offense, particularly the line, was weak all year, however, as Craig Morton's mediocre quarterbacking signalled his departure to Denver and Csonka and OT Tom Mullen were knocked out late in the season with knee injuries.

CENTRAL DIVISION

Minnesota Vikings — Fighting off repeated claims that they were too old, the Vikes had another banner year, grabbing their eighth straight division title. After WR John Gilliam and RB Ed Marinaro became free agents and left the team, newcomer WR's Ahmad Rashad and Sammy White, the latter a brilliant rookie, picked up the slack offensively with more than 50 catches apiece. Multi-purpose RB Chuck Foreman led the team in receiving and rushing while Fran Tarkenton continued to capture all of the NFL's major passing records. But after their fourth frustrating Super Bowl loss, Foreman threatened not to return unless his salary increased and Tarkenton said he might retire to become another jock-turned-TV broadcaster.

Chicago Bears — Jack Pardee was named NFC Coach of the Year for piloting the Bears to a 7-7 finish, their best since '68. With a demanding schedule forcing them to take on six playoff qualifiers, they responded with two victories among the six—33-7 over Washington and 14-13 over Minnesota—as well as tough one-point losses to Oakland and Minnesota that would have been wins if not for faulty kicking. But aside from Walter Payton's 1,390 rushing yards, tops in the NFC, the Bears' offense remained unimaginative. The verdict was still out on second-year QB Bob Avellini, especially after he finished the season with a two-for 17 passing performance in a 28-14 loss to Denver. Sid Gillman, one of the game's great free-thinkers, was lured out of retirement after the season ended to become offensive coordinator.

Detroit Lions — Dissension and a rough 1-3 start cost Rick Forzano his head coaching job. Replacement Tommy Hudspeth got off on the right foot by opening up the offense with a double-wing, double-WR formation that shocked New England 30-10 the fifth week. But a pitiful offensive line and a dismal 1-6 road record that included losses to New Orleans and the New York Giants did little to secure Hudspeth's future. Behind OLB Charlie Weaver, the team's MVP, and linemen Jim Mitchell and Ken Sanders, the Lions' stunting defense remained strong, allowing the NFL's third lowest yardage total despite losing three tackles to surgery.

Green Bay Packers — Blessed with decent draft picks for the first time since '72, the Pack showed a very slight improvement, one more victory than '75, in Bart Starr's second season at the helm, and still needed help at almost every position when the year ended. Green Bay's five wins were all against sub-.500 teams, and it had to come from behind in the second half in four of them. QB Lynn Dickey, obtained from Houston before the season began in exchange for QB John Hadl and CB Ken Ellis, was respectable until a shoulder separation knocked him out of the last four games.

WESTERN DIVISION

Los Angeles Rams — On the way to their fourth straight division title, the Rams featured a season-long battle among James Harris, Ron Jaworski and Pat Haden for the starting QB job. While nagging injuries continually hampered his competitors, Haden finally emerged as L.A.'s No. 1 man with five regular-season games left. A bountiful rushing attack headed by Lawrence McCutcheon and John Cappelletti was the key factor in the NFC's highest-scoring offense. Defensively, CB Monte Jackson's league-leading 10 interceptions spearheaded a sterling secondary that received strong assistance from a tough defensive line anchored by LT Merlin Olsen in his last season. The team's individual highlight was Harris' fourth-week, 436-yard passing performance in a 31-28 victory over Miami, the second-best ever by a Ram QB.

San Francisco 49ers — With Monte Clark replacing Dick Nolan as head coach, the Niners were the NFL's biggest surprise the first half of the season with a 6-1 record. They fell to 2-5 the second half, but finished the year with the conference's best defense, led by All-Pro DE Tommy Hart and his sack-happy cohorts, and a productive ground game featuring Delvin Williams and Wilbur Jackson. Monday night victories over L.A. and Minnesota were the strongest indicators of what appeared to be a long and happy coaching career in S.F. for Clark, but his falling out with the team's new owners after the season cut it short and paved the way for a strife-torn '77 campaign conducted by new GM Joe Thomas.

New Orleans Saints — New Head Coach Hank Stram had "Thunder and Lightning" in his offense in the form of rookie runners Tony Galbreath and Chuck Muncie, but a porous front wall offset their effectiveness as the Saints finished 4-10, two victories better than '75. QB's Bobby Scott and Bobby Douglass took over for Archie Manning, on the sidelines all season with tendonitis in his passing shoulder.

Atlanta Falcons — The Falcs lost four of their first five games, at which point GM Pat Peppler abruptly replaced Marion Campbell as head coach. A crucial blow to their offense was the knee injury that knocked QB Steve Bartowski out of the lineup for nine games. The high point of their dreary 4-10 season came in the 11th week when they scored 17 points in the fourth quarter to upset playoff-bound Dallas 17-10. John James provided excellent punting all season while tiny WR Alfred Jenkins remained a constant long-range threat.

Seattle Seahawks — In their first season, the Seattle expansionites fared much better than their Tampa Bay counterparts, winning two games against the Bucs and Atlanta and coming up with close calls against Minnesota, St. Louis and Green Bay. On offense, QB Jim Zorn displayed great potential at times but threw too many interceptions while Steve Largent and Sherm Smith were pleasant surprises at WR and RB, respectively. The defense was a mess, however, giving up about 400 yards and 30 points a game.

FINAL TEAM STATISTICS

OFFENSE

	ATL.	CHI.	DALL.	DET.	G.B.	L.A.	MINN.	N.O.	N.Y.	PHIL.	ST.L.	S.F.	SEA.	WASH.
FIRST DOWNS:														
Total	191	201	269	259	210	265	294	226	216	220	**307**	242	239	255
by Rushing	78	115	111	123	99	143	125	92	98	109	**140**	131	75	114
by Passing	93	67	140	120	94	111	**150**	111	97	91	142	91	141	122
by Penalty	20	19	18	16	17	11	19	23	21	20	**25**	20	23	19
RUSHING:														
Number	470	578	538	516	485	**613**	540	431	530	505	580	576	374	548
Yards	1689	2363	2147	2213	1722	**2528**	2003	1775	1904	2080	2301	2447	1416	2111
Average Yards	3.6	4.1	4.0	**4.3**	3.6	4.1	3.7	4.1	3.6	4.1	4.0	4.2	3.8	3.9
Touchdowns	10	20	16	9	15	**23**	18	16	11	8	17	14	14	10
PASSING:														
Attempts	354	278	390	356	357	315	442	403	326	369	392	306	**480**	370
Completions	157	123	222	201	164	171	**270**	206	175	182	220	155	229	187
Completion Pct.	44.4	44.2	56.9	56.5	45.9	54.3	**61.1**	51.1	53.7	49.3	56.1	50.7	47.7	50.5
Passing Yards	1809	1705	2967	2630	2105	2629	**3117**	2353	2104	1844	2967	1963	2874	2288
Avg. Yds. per Att.	5.1	6.1	7.6	7.4	5.9	**8.3**	7.1	5.8	6.5	5.0	7.6	6.4	6.0	6.2
Avg. Yds per Comp.	11.5	13.9	13.4	13.1	12.8	**15.4**	11.5	11.4	12.0	10.1	13.5	12.7	12.6	12.2
Times Tackled	44	24	30	67	41	32	31	51	44	43	**17**	34	28	38
Yds Lost Tackled	395	225	230	490	375	288	262	369	312	352	**132**	325	225	303
Net Yards	1414	1480	2737	2140	1730	2341	**2855**	1984	1792	1492	2835	1638	2649	1985
Touchdowns	10	9	17	**20**	10	17	17	8	9	11	18	15	13	**20**
Interceptions	24	15	13	12	22	15	**10**	14	24	18	13	21	30	20
Pct. Intercepted	6.8	5.4	3.3	3.4	6.2	4.8	**2.2**	3.5	7.4	4.9	3.3	6.9	6.3	5.4
PUNTS:														
Number	**101**	100	74	85	84	79	69	**101**	77	97	66	91	82	90
Average Distance	**42.1**	37.3	37.0	38.8	36.6	38.1	38.8	39.3	39.7	35.5	35.3	39.9	37.4	38.9
PUNT RETURNS:														
Number	60	43	45	31	40	52	40	42	41	41	36	**65**	37	52
Yards	385	269	489	207	300	476	271	375	197	425	350	557	246	**688**
Average Yards	6.4	6.3	10.9	6.7	7.5	9.2	6.8	8.9	4.8	10.4	9.7	8.6	6.6	**13.2**
Touchdowns	0	0	0	0	0	0	0	0	0	0	0	**2**	0	1
KICKOFF RETURNS:														
Number	60	51	42	47	65	44	42	62	53	58	54	38	**79**	50
Yards	1269	1087	1027	987	1361	1027	859	1173	1044	1148	1102	777	**1605**	1066
Average Yards	21.2	21.3	**24.5**	21.0	20.9	23.3	20.5	18.9	19.7	19.8	20.4	20.4	20.3	21.3
Touchdowns	0	0	0	0	0	**1**	0	0	0	0	0	0	0	0
INTERCEPTION RET:														
Number	18	24	16	24	11	**32**	19	12	12	9	19	9	15	26
Yards	207	215	133	**445**	197	376	213	212	62	195	243	93	218	190
Average Yards	11.5	9.0	8.3	18.5	17.9	11.8	11.2	17.7	5.2	**21.7**	12.8	10.3	14.5	7.3
Touchdowns	0	2	0	**3**	2	**3**	0	**3**	0	0	1	0	1	0
PENALTIES:														
Number	84	**114**	94	97	87	83	77	103	86	91	84	102	80	90
Yards	714	**984**	761	819	791	764	615	901	734	722	683	848	684	868
FUMBLES:														
Number	30	**24**	26	38	37	29	33	32	27	33	44	30	30	36
Number Lost	17	13	16	21	23	21	19	18	**12**	14	24	**12**	18	23
POINTS:														
Total	172	253	296	262	218	**351**	305	253	170	165	309	270	229	291
PAT Attempts	20	31	34	32	27	44	36	29	21	19	36	32	29	32
PAT Made	20	27	34	28	24	**36**	32	25	20	18	33	26	26	31
FG Attempts	21	25	23	24	19	26	31	23	21	16	27	28	16	**34**
FG Made	10	12	18	14	10	17	19	18	8	11	20	16	9	**22**
Percent FG Made	47.6	48.0	**78.3**	58.3	52.6	65.4	61.3	**78.3**	38.1	68.8	74.1	57.1	56.3	64.7
Safeties	1	**2**	**2**	0	1	0	0	0	0	0	0	**2**	1	1

DEFENSE

	ATL.	CHI.	DALL.	DET.	G.B.	L.A.	MINN.	N.O.	N.Y.	PHIL.	ST.L.	S.F.	SEA.	WASH.
FIRST DOWNS:														
Total	257	250	246	**191**	262	213	207	275	251	262	239	218	323	215
by Rushing	143	104	113	94	132	**79**	103	129	120	113	111	94	166	109
by Passing	95	128	111	**76**	107	118	91	121	119	129	105	102	136	91
by Penalty	19	18	22	21	23	16	13	25	**12**	20	23	22	21	15
RUSHING:														
Number	574	522	484	496	546	**429**	487	554	560	532	491	487	614	555
Yards	2577	1984	1821	1901	2288	**1564**	2096	2288	2203	2053	1979	1786	2876	2205
Average Yards	4.5	3.8	3.8	3.8	4.2	**3.6**	4.3	4.1	3.9	3.9	4.0	3.7	4.7	4.0
Touchdowns	22	**10**	12	13	17	11	14	22	14	16	19	**10**	20	12
PASSING:														
Attempts	340	401	391	**313**	354	397	323	367	330	404	342	374	367	354
Completions	184	200	187	**137**	196	199	158	200	189	237	176	180	223	146
Completion Pct.	54.1	49.9	47.8	43.8	55.4	50.1	48.9	54.5	57.3	58.7	51.5	48.1	60.8	**41.2**
Passing Yards	2276	2612	2236	1904	2192	2487	**1887**	2514	2230	2688	2358	2349	2770	2241
Avg. Yds. per Att.	6.7	6.5	**5.7**	6.1	6.2	6.3	5.9	6.9	6.8	6.7	6.9	6.3	7.5	6.3
Avg. Yds per Comp.	12.4	13.1	12.0	13.9	**11.2**	12.5	12.0	12.6	11.8	11.3	13.4	13.1	12.4	15.4
Times Tackled	35	49	44	28	43	45	45	39	31	19	31	**61**	27	44
Yds Lost Tackled	275	395	327	218	357	395	322	312	242	138	248	**573**	246	324
Net Yards	2001	2217	1909	1686	1835	2092	**1575**	2202	1988	2550	2110	1776	2524	1917
Touchdowns	14	15	12	11	13	11	**8**	18	11	17	13	13	27	11
Interceptions	18	24	16	24	11	**32**	19	12	12	9	19	9	15	26
Pct. Intercepted	5.3	6.0	4.1	7.7	3.1	**8.1**	5.9	3.3	3.6	2.2	5.6	2.4	4.1	7.3
PUNTS:														
Number	87	85	95	84	77	95	79	88	78	86	71	**108**	65	93
Average Distance	38.5	36.3	38.7	40.1	38.5	41.2	37.1	39.4	37.0	37.9	38.8	40.1	**35.0**	38.9
PUNT RETURNS:														
Number	52	44	**28**	39	48	39	40	64	45	53	33	52	56	44
Yards	360	346	**252**	278	268	281	286	742	500	405	304	351	537	323
Average Yards	6.9	7.9	9.0	7.1	**5.6**	7.2	7.2	11.6	11.1	7.6	9.2	6.8	9.6	7.3
Touchdowns	**0**	**0**	**0**	**0**	**0**	**0**	**0**	1	**0**	**0**	1	**0**	1	**0**
KICKOFF RETURNS:														
Number	**38**	54	62	55	44	70	66	54	39	44	66	46	47	63
Yards	934	969	1275	1188	784	1383	1209	1359	**725**	912	1623	924	1041	1028
Average Yards	24.6	17.9	20.6	21.6	17.8	19.8	18.3	25.2	18.6	20.7	24.6	20.1	22.1	**16.3**
Touchdowns	**0**	**0**	**0**	**0**	**0**	**0**	**0**	**0**	**0**	**0**	1	**0**	**0**	**0**
INTERCEPTION RET:														
Number	24	15	13	12	22	15	**10**	14	24	18	13	21	30	20
Yards	469	213	155	**121**	362	211	185	140	249	189	134	253	388	149
Average Yards	19.5	14.2	11.9	10.1	16.5	14.1	**18.5**	10.0	10.4	10.5	10.3	12.0	12.9	**7.5**
Touchdowns	4	**0**	1	**0**	3	**0**	**0**	1	1	1	**0**	2	4	**0**
PENALTIES:														
Number	102	86	71	88	104	82	76	**105**	104	105	83	94	**108**	95
Yards	868	699	643	696	914	747	653	**883**	835	907	708	906	**926**	818
FUMBLES:														
Number	30	37	32	27	27	31	24	**38**	32	31	32	37	24	**38**
Number Lost	20	23	12	15	15	16	13	**27**	15	15	20	16	11	21
POINTS:														
Total	312	216	194	220	299	190	**176**	346	250	286	267	190	429	217
PAT Attempts	40	25	25	25	34	22	22	44	27	35	34	25	53	23
PAT Made	32	25	23	25	29	20	**14**	36	26	33	31	20	51	22
FG Attempts	17	25	**12**	28	33	20	25	17	31	24	20	21	30	30
FG Made	12	13	7	15	22	12	10	14	20	13	10	**6**	20	19
Percent FG Made	70.6	52.0	58.3	53.6	66.7	60.0	40.0	82.4	64.5	54.2	50.0	**28.6**	66.7	63.3
Safeties	2	1	**0**	**0**	**0**	1	**0**	2	1	2	1	1	**0**	**0**

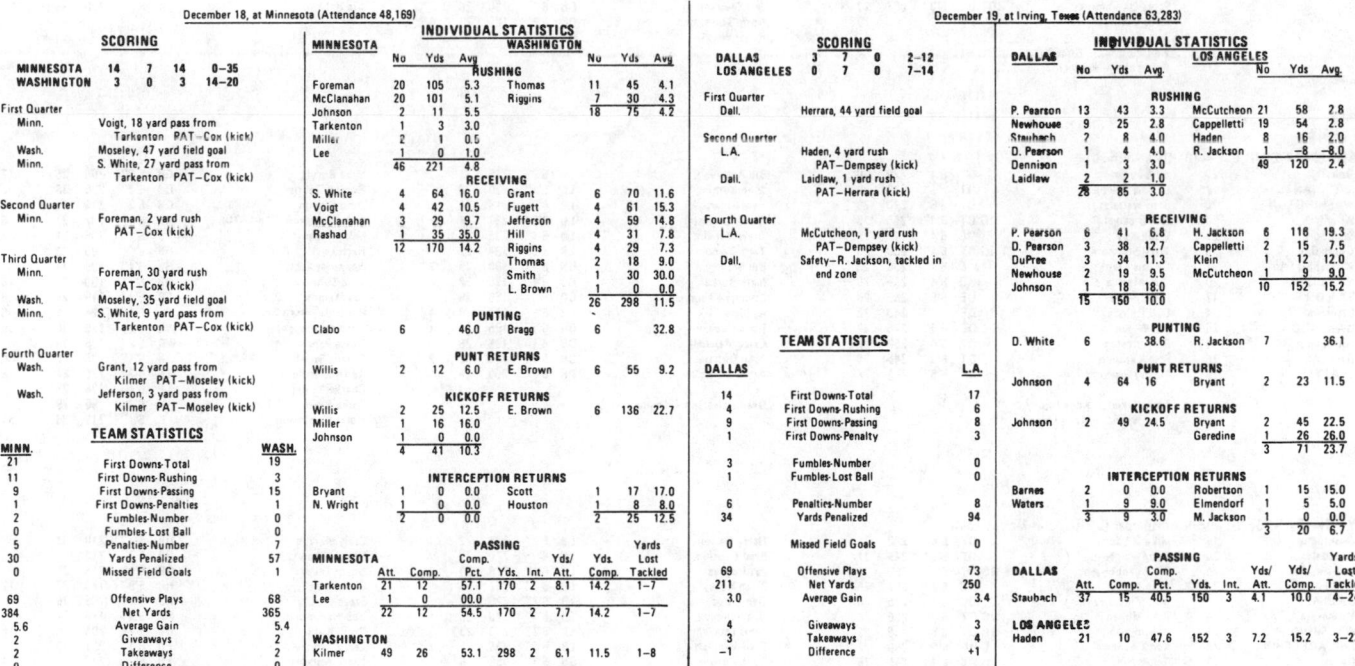

December 18, at Minnesota (Attendance 48,169)

SCORING

MINNESOTA	14	7	14	0–35
WASHINGTON	3	0	3	14–20

First Quarter
- Minn. Voigt, 18 yard pass from Tarkenton PAT–Cox (kick)
- Wash. Moseley, 47 yard field goal
- Minn. S. White, 27 yard pass from Tarkenton PAT–Cox (kick)

Second Quarter
- Minn. Foreman, 2 yard rush PAT–Cox (kick)

Third Quarter
- Minn. Foreman, 30 yard rush PAT–Cox (kick)
- Wash. Moseley, 35 yard field goal
- Minn. S. White, 9 yard pass from Tarkenton PAT–Cox (kick)

Fourth Quarter
- Wash. Grant, 12 yard pass from Kilmer PAT–Moseley (kick)
- Wash. Jefferson, 3 yard pass from Kilmer PAT–Moseley (kick)

TEAM STATISTICS

MINN.		WASH.
21	First Downs-Total	19
11	First Downs-Rushing	3
9	First Downs-Passing	15
1	First Downs-Penalties	1
2	Fumbles-Number	0
0	Fumbles-Lost Ball	0
5	Penalties-Number	7
30	Yards Penalized	57
0	Missed Field Goals	1
69	Offensive Plays	68
384	Net Yards	365
5.6	Average Gain	5.4
2	Giveaways	2
2	Takeaways	2
0	Difference	0

INDIVIDUAL STATISTICS

MINNESOTA	No	Yds	Avg	WASHINGTON	No	Yds	Avg
RUSHING							
Foreman	20	105	5.3	Thomas	11	45	4.1
McClanahan	20	101	5.1	Riggins	7	30	4.3
Johnson	2	11	5.5		18	75	4.2
Tarkenton	1	3	3.0				
Miller	2	1	0.5				
Lee	1	0	1.0				
	46	221	4.8				
RECEIVING							
S. White	4	64	16.0	Grant	6	70	11.6
Voigt	4	42	10.5	Fugett	4	61	15.3
McClanahan	3	29	9.7	Jefferson	4	59	14.8
Rashad	1	35	35.0	Hill	4	31	7.8
	12	170	14.2	Riggins	4	29	7.3
				Thomas	2	18	9.0
				Smith	1	30	30.0
				L. Brown	1	0	0.0
					26	298	11.5
PUNTING							
Clabo	6		46.0	Bragg	6		32.8
PUNT RETURNS							
Willis	2	12	6.0	E. Brown	6	55	9.2
KICKOFF RETURNS							
Willis	2	25	12.5	E. Brown	6	136	22.7
Miller	1	16	16.0				
Johnson	1	0	0.0				
	4	41	10.3				
INTERCEPTION RETURNS							
Bryant	1	0	0.0	Scott	1	17	17.0
N. Wright	1	0	0.0	Houston	1	8	8.0
	2	0	0.0		2	25	12.5

PASSING

MINNESOTA	Att.	Comp.	Comp. Pct.	Yds.	Int.	Yds/ Att.	Yds. Comp.	Yards Lost Tackled
Tarkenton	21	12	57.1	170	2	8.1	14.2	1–7
Lee	1	0	00.0					
	22	12	54.5	170	2	7.7	14.2	1–7
WASHINGTON								
Kilmer	49	26	53.1	298	2	6.1	11.5	1–8

December 19, at Irving, Texas (Attendance 63,283)

SCORING

DALLAS	3	7	0	2–12
LOS ANGELES	0	7	0	7–14

First Quarter
- Dall. Herrara, 44 yard field goal

Second Quarter
- L.A. Haden, 4 yard rush PAT–Dempsey (kick)
- Dall. Laidlaw, 1 yard rush PAT–Herrara (kick)

Fourth Quarter
- L.A. McCutcheon, 1 yard rush PAT–Dempsey (kick)
- Dall. Safety–R. Jackson, tackled in end zone

TEAM STATISTICS

DALLAS		L.A.
14	First Downs-Total	17
4	First Downs-Rushing	6
9	First Downs-Passing	8
1	First Downs-Penalty	3
3	Fumbles-Number	0
1	Fumbles-Lost Ball	0
6	Penalties-Number	8
34	Yards Penalized	94
0	Missed Field Goals	0
69	Offensive Plays	73
211	Net Yards	250
3.0	Average Gain	3.4
4	Giveaways	3
3	Takeaways	4
–1	Difference	+1

INDIVIDUAL STATISTICS

DALLAS	No	Yds	Avg.	LOS ANGELES	No	Yds	Avg.
RUSHING							
P. Pearson	13	43	3.3	McCutcheon	21	58	2.8
Newhouse	9	25	2.8	Cappelletti	19	54	2.8
Staubach	2	8	4.0	Haden	8	16	2.0
D. Pearson	1	4	4.0	R. Jackson	1	–8	–8.0
Dennison	1	3	3.0		49	120	2.4
Laidlaw	2	2	1.0				
	28	85	3.0				
RECEIVING							
P. Pearson	6	41	6.8	H. Jackson	6	116	19.3
D. Pearson	3	38	12.7	Cappelletti	2	15	7.5
DuPree	3	34	11.3	Klein	1	12	12.0
Newhouse	2	19	9.5	McCutcheon	1	9	9.0
Johnson	1	18	18.0		10	152	15.2
	15	150	10.0				
PUNTING							
D. White	6		38.6	R. Jackson	7		36.1
PUNT RETURNS							
Johnson	4	64	16	Bryant	2	23	11.5
KICKOFF RETURNS							
Johnson	2	49	24.5	Bryant	2	45	22.5
				Geredine	1	26	26.0
					3	71	23.7
INTERCEPTION RETURNS							
Barnes	2	0	0.0	Robertson	1	15	15.0
Waters	1	9	9.0	Elmendorf	1	5	5.0
	3	9	3.0	M. Jackson	1	0	0.0
					3	20	6.7

PASSING

DALLAS	Att.	Comp.	Comp. Pct.	Yds.	Int.	Yds/ Att.	Yds/ Comp.	Yards Lost Tackled
Staubach	37	15	40.5	150	3	4.1	10.0	4–24
LOS ANGELES								
Haden	21	10	47.6	152	3	7.2	15.2	3–22

DALLAS COWBOYS 11-3 Tom Landry

Scores of Each Game		
27	PHILADELPHIA	7
24	New Orleans	6
30	BALTIMORE	27
28	Seattle	13
24	N.Y. Giants	14
17	St. Louis	21
31	CHICAGO	21
20	Washington	7
9	N.Y. GIANTS	3
17	BUFFALO	10
10	Atlanta	17
19	ST. LOUIS	14
26	Philadelphia	7
14	WASHINGTON	27

Use Name	Pos.	Hgt.	Wgt.	Age	Int	Pts.
Pat Donovan	OT	6'4"	250	23		
Ralph Neely	OT	6'5"	255	32		
Rayfield Wright	OT	6'7"	255	31		
Jim Eidson	OG-C	6'3"	264	22		
Burton Lawless	OG	6'4"	250	22		
Blaine Nye	OG	6'4"	255	30		
Tom Rafferty	OG-C	6'3"	250	22		
Herbert Scott	OG	6'2"	250	23		
John Fitzgerald	C	6'5"	252	28		
Too Tall Jones	DE	6'9"	265	25		
Harvey Martin	DE	6'5"	252	25	1	
Greg Schaum	DE	6'4"	246	22		
Larry Cole	DT	6'4"	250	29		
Bill Gregory	DT	6'5"	252	26		
Jethro Pugh	DT	6'6"	248	32		
Bob Breunig	LB	6'2"	228	23		
Mike Hegman	LB	6'1"	221	23		
Tim Henderson	LB	6'2"	223	23	2	
Lee Roy Jordon	LB	6'2"	220	35		
D.D. Lewis	LB	6'2"	215	30		
Randy White	LB	6'4"	240	23		
Benny Barnes	DB	6'1"	190	25	1	
Cliff Harris	DB	6'	190	27	3	
Randy Hughes	DB	6'4"	210	23	1	
Aaron Kyle	DB	5'11"	181	22	2	
Beasley Reece	DB	6'1"	186	22		
Mel Renfro	DB	6'	190	34	3	
Mark Washington	DB	5'10"	186	28	4	
Charlie Waters	DB	6'1"	195	27	3	
Roger Staubach	QB	6'2"	197	34		18
Danny White	QB	6'2"	180	24		
Doug Dennison	HB-FB	6'1"	208	24		36
Preston Pearson	HB	6'1"	208	31		18
Charley Young	HB	6'1"	220	23		6
Jim Jensen	FB	6'3"	230	22		
Scott Laidlaw	FB	6'	206	23		24
Robert Newhouse	FB-HB	5'10"	205	26		18
Butch Johnson	WR	6'1"	187	22		12
Drew Pearson	WR	6'	185	25		42
Golden Richards	WR	6'	190	25		18
Billy Joe DuPree	TE	6'4"	230	26		12
Jay Saldi	TE	6'3"	217	21		
Efren Herrera	K	5'9"	190	25		88

Kyle Davis – Knee Injury

Percy Howard – Injured

WASHINGTON REDSKINS 10-4 George Allen

Scores of Each Game		
19	N.Y. GIANTS	17
31	SEATTLE	7
20	Philadelphia	*17
7	Chicago	33
30	KANSAS CITY	33
20	DETROIT	7
20	ST. LOUIS	10
7	DALLAS	20
24	San Francisco	21
9	N.Y. Giants	12
16	St. Louis	10
24	PHILADELPHIA	0
37	N.Y. Jets	16
27	Dallas	24

Use Name	Pos.	Hgt.	Wgt.	Age	Int	Pts.
Terry Hermeling	OT	6'5"	255	30		
George Starke	OT	6'5"	249	28		
Tim Stokes	OT	6'5"	252	26		
Dan Nugent	OG	6'3"	250	23		
Ron Saul	OG	6'2"	254	28		
Ted Fritsch	C	6'2"	242	26		
Len Hauss	C	6'2"	235	34		
Bob Kuziel	C	6'5"	255	26		
Dallas Hickman	DE	6'6"	235	24		
Karl Lorch	DE	6'3"	260	26		
Ron McDole	DE	6'3"	265	36		2
Bill Brundige	DT-DE	6'5"	270	27		
Dave Butz	DT	6'7"	285	26		
Dennis Johnson	DT	6'4"	260	24	1	
Diron Talbert	DT	6'5"	255	32		
Brad Dusek	LB	6'2"	214	25	1	6
Chris Hanburger	LB	6'2"	218	35	1	
Harold McLinton	LB	6'2"	235	29	1	
Stu O'Dell	LB	6'1"	220	24		
Russ Tillmann	LB	6'2"	230	30		
Pete Wysocki	LB	6'2"	225	27		
Eddie Brown	DB	5'11"	190	24	1	6
Pat Fischer	DB	5'10"	170	36	5	
Ken Houston	DB	6'3"	198	31	4	
Joe Lavender	DB	6'4"	190	27	8	
Brig Owens	DB	5'11"	190	33		
Jake Scott	DB	6'	188	31	4	
Gerard Williams	DB	6'1"	184	24		
Billy Kilmer	QB	6'	204	36		
Joe Theismann	QB	6'	184	26		6
Larry Brown	HB	5'11"	195	28		
Bob Brunet	HB	6'1"	205	30		
Mike Thomas	HB	5'11"	190	23		54
Calvin Hill	FB	6'3"	227	29		6
John Riggins	FB	6'2"	230	27		24
Danny Buggs (from NYG)	WR	6'2"	185	23		
Brian Fryer	WR	6'1"	185	23		
Frank Grant	WR	5'11"	181	26		30
Roy Jefferson	WR	6'2"	195	32		12
Larry Jones	WR	5'10"	170	25		
Bill Malinchak	WR	6'1"	200	32		
Doug Winslow	WR	5'11"	181	25		
Jean Fugett	TE	6'3"	226	24		36
Jerry Smith	TE	6'2"	208	33		12
Mike Bragg	K	5'11"	186	29		
Mark Moseley	K	5'11"	205	28		97

Paul Laaveg – Knee Injury
Ernie Janet – Groin Injury
Walt Sweeney – Knee Injury

Charley Taylor – Shoulder Injury

ST. LOUIS CARDINALS 10-4 Don Coryell

Scores of Each Game		
30	Seattle	24
29	GREEN BAY	0
24	San Diego	43
27	N.Y. GIANTS	21
33	PHILADELPHIA	14
21	DALLAS	17
10	Washington	20
23	SAN FRANCISCO	*20
17	Philadelphia	14
30	Los Angeles	28
10	WASHINGTON	16
14	Dallas	19
24	BALTIMORE	17
17	N.Y. Giants	14

Use Name	Pos.	Hgt.	Wgt.	Age	Int	Pts.
Dan Dierdorf	OT	6'4"	280	27		
Roger Finnie	OT-OG	6'3"	250	30		
Brad Oates	OT	6'6"	270	22		
Henry Allison	OG	6'3"	255	29		
Conrad Dobler	OG	6'3"	255	25		
Keith Wortman	OG	6'2"	248	26		
Bob Young	OG	6'2"	270	33		
Tom Banks	C-OG	6'1"	245	28		
Tom Brahaney	C	6'2"	250	24		
Bob Bell	DE	6'4"	250	28		
Ron Yankowski	DE	6'5"	250	29		
John Zook	DE	6'5"	250	28		
Lee Brooks	DT	6'5"	250	28		
Charlie Davis	DT	6'1"	265	24		
Mike Dawson	DT	6'4"	270	22		
Steve Okoniewski	DT-DE	6'3"	267	27		
Marv Upshaw	DT	6'3"	260	29		
Mark Arneson	LB	6'2"	220	26	1	
Al Beauchamp	LB	6'2"	235	32		
Carl Gersbach	LB	6'1"	230	29		
Greg Hartle	LB	6'2"	225	25		
Tim Kearney (from TB)	LB	6'2"	228	25	1	
Mike McDonald	LB	6'2"	215	23		
Mike McGraw	LB	6'2"	225	22		
Steve Neils	LB	6'2"	215	25		
Larry Stallings	LB	6'2"	230	34		
Ray White	LB	6'1"	220	27	2	
Dwayne Crump	DB	5'11"	180	26		
Clarence Duren	DB	6'1"	190	25	1	
Lee Nelson	DB	5'10"	185	22		
Ken Reaves	DB	6'3"	210	31	2	
Mike Sensibaugh	DB	5'11"	190	27	4	6
Jeff Severson	DB	6'1"	185	26		
Norm Thompson	DB	6'1"	180	28	4	
Roger Wehrli	DB	6'1"	190	28		
Billy Donckers	QB	6'1"	205	25		
Jim Hart	QB	6'2"	210	32		
Steve Jones	HB	6'	200	25		54
Jerry Latin	HB	5'10"	190	23		6
Terry Metcalf	HB	5'10"	185	24		42
Wayne Morris	HB	6'	200	22		24
Eddie Moss	FB	6'	215	27		
Jim Otis	FB	6'	225	28		12
J.V. Cain	WR	6'4"	225	25		30
Mel Gray	WR	5'9"	175	27		30
Gary Hammond	WR	5'11"	185	27		
Ike Harris	WR	6'3"	205	25		6
Pat Tilley	WR	5'10"	175	23		6
Terry Joyce	TE	6'6"	230	22		
Jackie Smith	TE	6'4"	230	35		
Jim Bakken	K	6'	200	35		93

Walt Patulski – Knee Injury
Bob Rowe – Back Injury

PHILADELPHIA EAGLES 4-10 Dick Vermeil

Scores of Each Game		
7	Dallas	27
20	N.Y. GIANTS	7
17	WASHINGTON	*20
14	Atlanta	13
14	St. Louis	33
13	Green Bay	28
12	MINNESOTA	31
10	N.Y. Giants	0
14	ST. LOUIS	17
3	Cleveland	24
7	OAKLAND	26
0	Washington	24
7	DALLAS	26
27	SEATTLE	10

Use Name	Pos.	Hgt.	Wgt.	Age	Int	Pts.
Ed George	OT	6'4"	270	30		
Dennis Nelson	OT	6'5"	260	30		
Stan Walters	OT	6'6"	270	28		
Jeff Bleamer	OG-OT	6'4"	253	23		
Wade Key	OG	6'4"	245	29		
Jerry Sisemore	OG-OT	6'4"	260	25		
Dennis Franks	C	6'1"	236	23		
Guy Morriss	C	6'4"	255	25		
Blenda Gay	DE	6'5"	255	25		
Carl Hairston	DE	6'3"	245	23		
Bill Wynn	DE	6'4"	245	27		
Bill Dunstan	DT	6'4"	250	27		
Pete Lazetich	DT	6'3"	245	26		
Manny Sistrunk	DT	6'5"	275	29		
Bill Bergey	LB	6'2"	250	31	2	
John Bunting	LB	6'1"	220	26		
Tom Ehlers	LB	6'2"	218	24	1	
Frank LeMaster	LB	6'2"	231	24		
Drew Mahalic	LB	6'4"	228	23		
Terry Tautolo	LB	6'2"	234	22		
Bill Bradley	DB	5'11"	190	29	2	
Mark Burke	DB	6'1"	175	22		
Tommy Campbell	DB	6'	188	26		
Al Clark	DB	6'	185	28	1	
Randy Logan	DB	6'1"	195	25	1	
Larry Marshall	DB	5'10"	195	26		
John Outlaw	DB	5'10"	180	30	2	
Artimus Parker	DB	6'3"	200	24		
Mike Boryla	QB	6'3"	200	25		12
Roman Gabriel	QB	6'4"	220	36		
John Walton	QB	6'2"	210	28		
Dave Hampton (from ATL)	HB	6'	202	29		6
Mike Hogan	HB-FB	6'2"	205	21		
Herb Lusk	HB	6'	190	23		
James McAlister	HB	6'1"	205	24		
Tom Sullivan	HB	6'	190	26		18
Art Malone	FB	5'11"	216	28		6
Bill Olds (from SEA)	FB	6'1"	224	25		6
Harold Carmichael	WR	6'7"	225	26		30
Vince Papale	WR	6'2"	195	30		
Charlie Smith	WR	6'1"	185	26		30
Keith Krepfle	TE	6'3"	225	24		6
Charlie Young	TE	6'4"	238	25		
Spike Jones	K	6'2"	195	29		
Horst Muhlmann	K	6'1"	219	36		51

Tom Luken – Knee Injury
John Niland – Knee Injury

Dean Halverson – Injured

NEW YORK GIANTS 3-11 Bill Arnsparger (0-7), John McVay (3-4)

Scores of Each Game		
17	Washington	19
7	Philadelphia	20
10	Los Angeles	24
21	St. Louis	27
14	DALLAS	24
7	Minnesota	24
0	PITTSBURGH	27
0	PHILADELPHIA	10
3	Dallas	9
12	WASHINGTON	9
13	Denver	14
28	SEATTLE	16
24	DETROIT	10
14	ST. LOUIS	17

Use Name	Pos.	Hgt.	Wgt.	Age	Int	Pts.
Mike Gibbons	OT	6'4"	262	25		
Doug Van Horn	OT	6'2"	245	32		
Bill Ellenboggen	OG-OT	6'4"	260	25		
John Hicks	OG	6'2"	258	25		
Ron Mikolajczyk	OG	6'3"	275	26		
Tom Mullen	OG-OT	6'3"	250	24		
Al Simpson	OG-OT	6'5"	255	25		
Karl Chandler	C-OG	6'5"	250	24		
Ralph Hill	C	6'1"	245	26		
Troy Archer	DE	6'4"	250	21		
Rick Dvorak	DE	6'4"	245	24		
Jack Gregory	DE	6'6"	250	31		
George Martin	DE	6'4"	245	23		
Dave Gallagher	DT	6'4"	256	24	1	
John Mendenhall	DT	6'1"	255	27	1	
Harry Carson	LB	6'2"	228	22		
Brad Cousino	LB	6'	220	23		
Pat Hughes	LB	6'2"	225	29	1	
Brian Kelley	LB	6'3"	222	25		
Dan Lloyd	LB	6'3"	225	22		
Bob Schmit	LB	6'1"	220	26		
John Tate	LB	6'2"	230	23		
Brad Van Pelt	LB	6'5"	235	25	2	
Bobby Brooks	DB	6'1"	195	25	1	
Bill Bryant	DB	5'11"	195	25		
Rondy Colbert	DB	5'9"	165	22		
Larry Mallory	DB	5'11"	185	24	1	
Clyde Powers	DB	6'1"	195	25	1	
Jim Stienke	DB	5'11"	182	25	2	6
Henry Stuckey	DB	6'1"	180	26		
Rick Volk	DB	6'3"	195	31	2	
Craig Morton	QB	6'4"	210	33		
Dennis Shaw	QB	6'2"	215	29		
Norm Snead	QB	6'4"	215	36		
Gordon Bell	HB	5'9"	180	22		12
Steve Crosby	HB	5'11"	205	26		
Bob Hammond	HB	5'9"	175	24		
Doug Kotar	HB	5'11"	205	25		18
Larry Csonka	FB	6'3"	237	29		24
Larry Watkins	FB	6'2"	230	29		6
Marsh White	FB	6'2"	220	23		6
Walker Gillette	WR	6'5"	200	29		12
Ed Marshall (from NYJ)	WR	6'4"	198	28		18
Ray Rhodes	WR	5'11"	185	25		6
Jim Robinson	WR	5'9"	170	23		6
Roger Wallace	WR	5'11"	180	24		
Gary Shirk	TE	6'1"	220	26		6
Bob Tucker	TE	6'3"	230	31		6
Joe Danelo	K	5'9"	166	22		44
Dave Jennings	K	6'4"	205	24		

Jim Pietrzak – Back Injury

Charlie Ford – Knee Injury
Robert Giblin – Shoulder Injury

* – Overtime

DALLAS COWBOYS

RUSHING

Last Name	No.	Yds	Avg	TD
Dennison	153	542	3.5	6
Newhouse	116	450	3.9	3
Laidlaw	94	424	4.5	3
P. Pearson	68	233	3.4	1
Young	48	208	4.3	0
Staubach	43	184	4.3	3
DuPree	7	50	7.1	0
D. Pearson	2	20	10.0	0
Saldi	1	19	19.0	0
D. White	6	17	2.8	0

RECEIVING

Last Name	No.	Yds.	Avg	TD
D. Pearson	58	806	14	6
DuPree	42	680	16	2
Laidlaw	38	325	9	1
P. Pearson	23	316	14	2
Richards	19	414	22	3
Newhouse	15	86	6	0
Young	11	134	12	1
Dennison	8	67	8	0
Johnson	5	84	17	2
Barnes	1	43	43	0
Reece	1	6	6	0
Saldi	1	6	6	0

PUNT RETURNS

Last Name	No.	Yds	Avg	TD
Johnson	45	489	11	0

KICKOFF RETURNS

Last Name	No.	Yds	Avg	TD
Johnson	28	693	25	0
Jensen	13	313	24	0
Saldi	1	9	9	0
Henderson	0	12	0	0

PASSING – PUNTING – KICKING

PASSING	Att	Comp	%	Yds	Yd/Att	TD	Int–%	RK
Staubach	369	208	56	2715	7.4	14	11– 3	5
D. White	20	13	65	213	10.7	2	2– 10	
D. Pearson	1	1	100	39	39.0	1	0– 0	

PUNTING	No	Avg
D. White	70	38.4
Herrera	2	24.5

KICKING	XP	Att	%	FG	Att	%
Herrera	34	34	100	18	23	78

WASHINGTON REDSKINS

RUSHING

Last Name	No.	Yds	Avg	TD
Thomas	254	1101	4.3	5
Riggins	162	572	3.5	3
Hill	79	301	3.8	1
Theismann	17	97	5.7	1
L. Brown	20	56	2.8	0
Fugett	2	0	0.0	0
Kilmer	13	–7	–0.5	0
Grant	1	–9	–9.0	0

RECEIVING

Last Name	No.	Yds.	Avg	TD
Grant	50	818	16	5
Thomas	28	290	10	4
Jefferson	27	364	13	2
Fugett	27	334	12	6
Riggins	21	172	8	1
L. Brown	17	98	6	0
Hill	7	100	14	0
Smith	7	75	11	2
Buggs	2	25	13	0
Malinchak	1	12	12	0

PUNT RETURNS

Last Name	No.	Yds	Avg	TD
E. Brown	48	646	13	1
Scott	3	27	9	0
Jones	1	15	15	0

KICKOFF RETURNS

Last Name	No.	Yds	Avg	TD
E. Brown	30	738	25	0
Fryer	9	166	18	0
Brunet	4	85	21	0
Winslow	2	32	16	0
Jones	1	16	16	0
Owens	1	15	15	0
Tillman	1	14	14	0
Lorch	1	0	0	0
Wysocki	1	0	0	0

PASSING – PUNTING – KICKING

PASSING	Att	Comp	%	Yds	Yd/Att	TD	Int–%	RK
Kilmer	206	108	52	1252	6.1	12	10– 5	6
Theismann	163	79	49	1036	6.4	8	10– 6	9
Hill	1	0	0	0	0.0	0	0– 0	

PUNTING	No	Avg
Bragg	90	38.9

KICKING	XP	Att	%	FG	Att	%
Moseley	31	32	97	22	34	65

ST. LOUIS CARDINALS

RUSHING

Last Name	No.	Yds	Avg	TD
Otis	233	891	3.8	2
Metcalf	134	537	4.0	3
Jones	113	451	4.0	8
Morris	64	292	4.6	3
Latin	25	115	4.6	1
Wehrli	2	8	4.0	0
Hart	8	7	0.9	0
Joyce	1	0	0.0	0

RECEIVING

Last Name	No.	Yds.	Avg	TD
Harris	52	782	15	1
Gray	36	686	19	5
Metcalf	33	388	12	4
Jones	29	152	5	1
Tilley	26	407	16	1
Cain	26	400	15	5
Morris	8	75	9	1
Latin	4	35	9	0
Smith	3	22	7	0
Otis	2	15	8	0
Hammond	1	5	5	0

PUNT RETURNS

Last Name	No.	Yds	Avg	TD
Metcalf	17	188	11	0
Tilley	15	146	10	0
Hammond	3	16	5	0
Neils	1	0	0	0

KICKOFF RETURNS

Last Name	No.	Yds	Avg	TD
Latin	10	[illegible]	22	0
Metcalf	16	325	20	0
Morris	9	181	20	0
Smith	3	63	21	0
Crump	3	57	19	0
Hammond	2	36	18	0
Nelson	1	43	43	0
McGraw	1	13	13	0
Oates	1	12	12	0
Okoniewski	1	12	12	0
Severson	1	3	3	0

PASSING – PUNTING – KICKING

PASSING	Att	Comp	%	Yds	Yd/Att	TD	Int–%	RK
Hart	388	218	56	2946	7.6	18	13– 3	4
Donckers	1	1	100	16	16.0	0	0– 0	
Metcalf	1	0	0	0	0.0	0	0– 0	
Wehrli	1	0	0	0	0.0	0	0– 0	

PUNTING	No	Avg
Joyce	64	36.4

KICKING	XP	Att	%	FG	Att	%
Bakken	33	35	94	20	27	74

PHILADELPHIA EAGLES

RUSHING

Last Name	No.	Yds	Avg	TD
Hogan	123	561	4.6	0
Sullivan	99	399	4.0	2
Hampton	83	291	3.5	1
McAlister	68	265	3.9	0
Lusk	61	254	4.2	0
Boryla	29	166	5.7	2
Olds	38	129	3.4	1
Smith	9	25	2.8	1
Malone	2	14	7.0	1
Young	1	6	6.0	0
Gabriel	4	2	0.5	0
Walton	2	1	0.5	0

RECEIVING

Last Name	No.	Yds.	Avg	TD
Carmichael	42	503	12	5
Young	30	374	12	0
Smith	27	412	15	4
Hogan	15	89	6	0
Sullivan	14	116	8	1
Lusk	13	119	9	0
McAlister	12	72	6	0
Hampton	12	57	5	0
Olds	9	29	3	0
Krepfle	6	80	13	1
Malone	1	–3	–3	0
LeMaster	1	–4	–4	0

PUNT RETURNS

Last Name	No.	Yds	Avg	TD
Marshall	27	290	11	0
Bradley	9	64	7	0
Clark	4	57	14	0
Burke	1	14	14	0

KICKOFF RETURNS

Last Name	No.	Yds	Avg	TD
Marshall	30	651	22	0
McAlister	9	172	19	0
Lusk	7	155	22	0
Sullivan	5	108	22	0
Hampton	3	46	15	0
Olds	1	11	11	0
Ehlers	1	8	8	0
Bleamer	1	0	0	0
Smith	1	–3	–3	0

PASSING – PUNTING – KICKING

PASSING	Att	Comp	%	Yds	Yd/Att	TD	Int–%	RK
Boryla	246	123	50	1247	5.1	9	14– 6	12
Gabriel	92	46	50	476	5.2	2	2– 2	
Walton	28	12	43	125	4.5	0	2– 7	
Carmichael	2	0	0	0	0.0	0	0– 0	
Jones	1	1	100	–4	–4.0	0	0– 0	

PUNTING	No	Avg
Jones	94	36.6

KICKING	XP	Att	%	FG	Att	%
Muhlmann	18	19	95	11	16	69

NEW YORK GIANTS

RUSHING

Last Name	No.	Yds	Avg	TD
Kotar	185	731	4.0	3
Csonka	160	569	3.6	4
Bell	67	233	3.5	2
White	69	223	3.2	1
Watkins	26	96	3.7	1
Morton	15	48	3.2	0
Rhodes	2	10	5.0	0
Mallory	1	0	0.0	0
Snead	3	–1	–0.3	0
Crosby	1	–1	–1.0	0
Gillette	1	–4	–4.0	0

RECEIVING

Last Name	No.	Yds.	Avg	TD
Tucker	42	498	12	1
Kotar	36	319	9	0
Bell	25	198	8	0
Robinson	18	249	14	1
Rhodes	16	305	19	1
Gillette	16	263	16	2
Marshall	8	166	21	3
Csonka	6	39	7	0
Shirk	4	52	13	1
Watkins	2	8	4	0
White	2	7	4	0

PUNT RETURNS

Last Name	No.	Yds	Avg	TD
Robinson	24	106	4	0
Colbert	13	72	6	0
Stienke	3	18	6	0
Bell	1	1	1	0

KICKOFF RETURNS

Last Name	No.	Yds	Avg	TD
Robinson	20	444	22	0
Bell	18	352	20	0
Shirk	6	109	18	0
Kotar	3	39	13	0
Hammond	2	44	22	0
Colbert	2	42	21	0
Watkins	1	9	9	0
Carson	1	5	5	0

PASSING – PUNTING – KICKING

PASSING	Att	Comp	%	Yds	Yd/Att	TD	Int–%	RK
Morton	284	153	54	1865	6.6	9	20– 7	11
Snead	42	22	52	239	5.7	0	4– 10	

PUNTING	No	Avg
Jennings	74	41.3

KICKING	XP	Att	%	FG	Att	%
Danelo	20	21	95	8	21	38

MINNESOTA VIKINGS 11-2-1 Bud Grant

Scores of Each Game		
40	New Orleans	9
10	LOS ANGELES	*10
10	Detroit	9
17	PITTSBURGH	6
20	CHICAGO	19
24	N.Y. GIANTS	7
31	Philadelphia	12
13	Chicago	14
31	DETROIT	23
27	SEATTLE	21
17	Green Bay	10
16	San Francisco	20
20	GREEN BAY	9
29	Miami	7

Use Name	Pos.	Hgt.	Wgt.	Age	Int	Pts
Bart Buetow	OT	6'5"	250	25		
Charlie Goodrum	OT	6'3"	256	26		
Steve Riley	OT	6'6"	258	23		
Ron Yary	OT	6'6"	255	30		
Wes Hamilton	OG	6'3"	255	23		
Ed White	OG	6'2"	270	29		
Mick Tingelhoff	C	6'1"	240	36		
Scott Anderson	C	6'4"	250	25		
Doug Dumler	C	6'3"	245	25		
Carl Eller	DE	6'6"	247	34		
Jim Marshall	DE	6'3"	240	39		
Mark Mullaney	DE	6'6"	242	23		
Alan Page	DT	6'5"	245	31		
Doug Sutherland	DT	6'3"	250	28		
James White	DT	6'3"	263	22		
Matt Blair	LB	6'5"	229	25	2	
Wally Hilgenberg	LB	6'3"	229	33		
Amos Martin	LB	6'3"	228	27		
Fred McNeill	LB	6'2"	229	24		
Jeff Siemon	LB	6'2"	237	26	1	
Roy Winston	LB	6'1"	222	36		
Nate Allen	DB	5'10"	174	28	3	6
Autry Beamon	DB	6'1"	190	22	1	
Bobby Bryant	DB	6'	170	32	2	
Windlan Hall	DB	5'11"	175	26		
Paul Krause	DB	6'3"	200	34	2	
Jeff Wright	DB	5'11"	190	27	1	
Nate Wright	DB	5'11"	180	28	7	
Bob Berry	QB	5'11"	185	34		
Bob Lee	QB	6'2"	195	30		
Fran Tarkenton	QB	6'1"	190	36		6
Chuck Foreman	HB	6'2"	207	25		84
Brent McClanahan	HB-FB	5'10"	202	25		30
Robert Miller	HB	5'11"	204	23		6
Bob Groce	FB	6'2"	210	22		
Sammy Johnson (from SF)	FB	6'	217	23		12
Mark Kellar	FB	6'	225	24		
Willie Spencer	FB	6'3"	235	23		
Bob Grim	WR	6'	188	31		
Ahmad Rashad	WR	6'2"	200	26		18
Sammy White	WR	5'11"	189	22		60
Leonard Willis	WR	5'10"	180	23		
Steve Craig	TE	6'3"	231	25		
Stu Voigt	TE	6'1"	225	28		6
Neil Clabo	K	6'2"	200	23		
Fred Cox	K	5'10"	200	37		89

CHICAGO BEARS 7-7 Jack Pardee

Scores of Each Game		
10	DETROIT	3
19	San Francisco	12
0	ATLANTA	10
33	WASHINGTON	7
19	Minnesota	20
12	Los Angeles	20
21	Dallas	31
14	MINNESOTA	13
27	OAKLAND	28
24	GREEN BAY	13
10	Detroit	14
16	Green Bay	10
34	Seattle	7
14	DENVER	28

Use Name	Pos.	Hgt.	Wgt.	Age	Int	Pts
Lionel Antoine	OT	6'6"	266	26		
Dan Jiggetts	OT	6'4"	274	22		
Dennis Lick	OT	6'3"	271	22		
Jeff Sevy	OT-OG	6'5"	260	25		
Noah Jackson	OG	6'2"	265	25		
Revie Sorey	OG	6'2"	270	22		
John Ward (from TB)	OG-C	6'4"	269	28		
Dan Neal	C-OG	6'4"	257	27		
Don Peiffer	C	6'3"	254	25		
Royce Berry	DE	6'3"	239	30		
Mike Hartenstine	DE	6'3"	256	23		6
Jerry Meyers	DE	6'4"	245	22		
Roger Stillwell	DE	6'5"	254	24		
Wally Chambers	DT	6'6"	250	25	1	
Jim Osborne	DT	6'3"	248	26		
Ron Rydalch	DT	6'4"	262	24		
Ross Brupbacher	LB	6'3"	220	28	7	
Waymond Bryant	LB	6'3"	239	24	2	
Doug Buffone	LB	6'1"	229	32		
Tom Hicks	LB	6'4"	235	23		
Larry Muckensturm	LB	6'4"	226	22		
Jerry Muckensturm	LB	6'2"	230	25		
Craig Clemons	DB	5'11"	195	27	1	
Allan Ellis	DB	5'10"	180	25	6	6
Gary Fencik	DB	6'1"	190	22		
Bill Knox	DB	5'9"	190	25		
Virgil Livers	DB	5'9"	176	24	3	
Doug Plank	DB	6'	198	23	4	
Terry Schmidt	DB	6'	175	24		
Bob Avellini	QB	6'2"	211	23		6
Virgil Carter	QB	6'1"	190	30		
Gary Huff	QB	6'1"	199	25		
Mike Adamle	HB-FB	5'9"	198	26		8
Roland Harper	HB-FB	6'	215	23		18
Johnny Musso	HB	5'11"	201	26		26
Walter Payton	HB	5'11"	203	22		78
Larry Schreiber	FB-HB	6'	205	29		
Brian Baschnagel	WR-DB	6'	195	22		
Randy Burks	WR	6'2"	170	23		6
Bo Rather	WR	6'1"	188	25		
Steve Schubert	WR	5'10"	187	25		
James Scott	WR	6'1"	185	24		36
Ron Shanklin	WR	6'1"	187	28		
Bob Bruer	TE	6'5"	230	23		
Gary Butler	TE	6'3"	235	25		
Greg Latta	TE	6'3"	228	23		
Bob Parsons	TE	6'4"	241	26		
Bob Thomas	K	5'10"	177	24		63

Gary Hrivnak – Injury

DETROIT LIONS 6-8 Rick Forzano (1-3), Tommy Hudspeth (5-5)

Scores of Each Game		
3	Chicago	10
24	ATLANTA	10
9	MINNESOTA	10
14	Green Bay	24
30	NEW ENGLAND	10
7	Washington	20
41	Seattle	14
27	GREEN BAY	6
23	Minnesota	31
16	New Orleans	17
14	CHICAGO	10
27	BUFFALO	14
10	N.Y. Giants	24
17	LOS ANGELES	20

Use Name	Pos.	Hgt.	Wgt.	Age	Int	Pts
Russ Bolinger	OT	6'5"	255	21		
Rocky Freitas	OT	6'6"	275	30		
Craig Hertwig	OT	6'8"	270	24		
Jim Yarbrough	OT	6'6"	265	29		
Lynn Boden	OG	6'5"	270	23		
Bob Kowalkowski	OG	6'3"	245	32		
Ken Long	OG	6'3"	265	23		
Mark Markovich	C	6'5"	255	23		
Jon Morris	C	6'4"	250	33		
Billy Howard	DE	6'4"	255	26		
Jim Mitchell	DE	6'3"	250	27		
Ernie Price	DE	6'4"	245	25		
Ken Sanders	DE	6'5"	245	26		
Don Croft	DT	6'3"	258	27		
Doug English	DT	6'5"	245	23		
Larry Hand	DT	6'4"	245	36	1	
Herb Orvis	DT	6'5"	245	29		
Jim Laslavic	LB	6'2"	240	24	2	
Paul Naumoff	LB	6'1"	215	31		
Ed O'Neil	LB	6'3"	235	23	1	6
Garth Ten Napel	LB	6'1"	210	22		
Charlie Weaver	LB	6'2"	225	27	2	
John Woodcock	LB	6'3"	240	22		
Lem Barney	DB	6'	190	30	2	6
Ben Davis	DB	5'11"	180	30		6
James Hunter	DB	6'3"	195	22	7	6
Dick Jauron	DB	6'	190	25	2	
Levi Johnson	DB	6'3"	200	25	6	6
Maurice Tyler	DB	6'	188	26		
Charlie West	DB	6'1"	190	30	1	
Gary Danielson	QB	6'2"	195	24		
Greg Landry	QB	6'4"	205	29		6
Joe Reed	QB	6'1"	195	28		6
Andy Bolton (from SEA)	HB	6'1"	205	22		
Dexter Bussey	HB	6'1"	210	24		18
Bobby Thompson	HB	5'11"	195	29		
Lawrence Gaines	FB	6'1"	240	22		30
Jim Hooks	FB	5'11"	225	24		
Horace King	FB	5'10"	210	23		
Dennis Franklin	WR	6'1"	185	23		
J.D. Hill	WR	6'1"	185	27		
Ray Jarvis	WR	5'11"	190	27		30
Bob Picard (from PHI.)	WR	6'1"	198	26		
Leonard Thompson	WR	5'10"	190	24		
Larry Walton	WR	6'	185	29		18
David Hill	TE	6'2"	220	22		30
Charlie Sanders	TE	6'4"	230	30		30
Benny Ricardo (from BUF)	K	5'9"	175	22		54
Herman Weaver	K	6'4"	210	27		

GREEN BAY PACKERS 5-9 Bart Starr

Scores of Each Game		
14	SAN FRANCISCO	26
0	St. Louis	29
7	Cincinnati	28
24	DETROIT	14
27	SEATTLE	20
28	PHILADELPHIA	13
14	Oakland	18
6	Detroit	27
32	NEW ORLEANS	27
13	Chicago	24
10	MINNESOTA	17
10	CHICAGO	16
9	Minnesota	20
24	Atlanta	20

Use Name	Pos.	Hgt.	Wgt.	Age	Int	Pts
Dick Himes	OT	6'4"	260	30		
Mark Koncar	OT	6'5"	271	23		
Dick Enderle (from S.F.)	OG	6'1"	250	28		
Gale Gillingham	OG	6'3"	265	32		
Melvin Jackson	OG	6'1"	267	22		
Steve Knutson	OG	6'3"	254	24		
Bruce Van Dyke	OG	6'2"	255	32		
Bob Hyland	C	6'5"	255	31		
Larry McCarren	C	6'3"	248	24		
Bob Barber	DE	6'3"	240	24		
Dave Pureifory	DE	6'1"	255	27		
Alden Roche	DE	6'4"	255	31		
Clarence Williams	DE	6'5"	255	29		
Mike McCoy	DT	6'5"	275	27		
Dave Roller	DT	6'2"	270	26		
Ron Acks	LB	6'2"	225	31		
Fred Carr	LB	6'5"	240	30	1	6
Jerry Dandridge	LB	6'1"	222	22		
Jim Gueno	LB	6'2"	220	22		
Don Hansen (from SEA)	LB	6'3"	228	32		
Bob Lally	LB	6'2"	230	24		
Tom Perko	LB	6'3"	233	22		
Tom Toner	LB	6'3"	235	26	1	
Gary Weaver	LB	6'1"	225	27		
Willie Buchanan	DB	6'	190	25	2	
Jim Burrow	DB	5'11"	181	22		
Johnnie Gray	DB	5'11"	185	22	4	6
Charlie Hall	DB	6'1"	190	28		
Steve Luke	DB	6'2"	205	22	2	
Mike McCoy	DB	5'11"	183	23		
Perry Smith	DB	6'1"	195	25	1	
Steve Wagner	DB	6'2"	198	22		
Carlos Brown	QB	6'3"	210	24		
Lynn Dickey	QB	6'4"	220	26		6
Randy Johnson (from WAS)	QB	6'3"	205	32		6
Will Harrell	HB	5'9"	182	23		24
Dave Osborn	HB	6'	208	33		
Clifton Taylor	HB	6'	195	24		6
Eric Torkelson	HB	6'2"	194	24		12
John Brockington	FB	6'1"	225	27		12
Barty Smith	FB	6'4"	240	24		30
Ken Starch	FB	5'11"	210	22		
Jessie Green	WR	6'3"	185	22		
Steve Odom	WR	5'8"	174	23		12
Ken Payne	WR	6'1"	185	25		24
Ollie Smith	WR	6'2"	200	27		6
Don Zimmerman (from PHI.)	WR	6'3"	195	26		
Bert Askon	TE	6'3"	225	30		6
Rich McGeorge	TE	6'4"	230	27		6
Randy Beverly	K	6'2"	180	26		
Chester Marcol	K	6'	190	26		54

Jim Carter – Broken Arm

Don Milan – Broken Wrist
Gerald Tinker – Knee Injury

* – Overtime

MINNESOTA VIKINGS

RUSHING

Last Name	No.	Yds	Avg	TD
Foreman	278	1155	4.2	13
McClanhan	130	382	2.9	4
Miller	67	286	4.3	0
Johnson	41	150	3.7	2
Tarkenton	27	45	1.7	1
Kellar	7	25	3.6	0
Groce	3	18	6.0	0
Lee	2	2	1.0	0
Spencer	4	2	0.5	0
S. White	5	–10	– 2.0	0

RECEIVING

Last Name	No.	Yds	Avg	TD
Foreman	55	567	10	1
Rashad	53	671	13	3
S.White	51	906	18	10
McClanahan	40	252	6	1
Voigt	28	303	11	1
Miller	23	181	8	1
Grim	9	108	12	0
Johnson	7	74	11	0
Craig	3	33	11	0
Kellar	2	22	11	0

PUNT RETURNS

Last Name	No.	Yds	Avg	TD
Willis	30	207	7	0
Beamon	7	19	3	0
S.White	3	45	15	0

KICKOFF RETURNS

Last Name	No.	Yds	Avg	TD
Willis	24	552	23	0
S. White	9	173	19	0
Miller	5	77	15	0
Johnson	2	35	18	0
Kellar	1	22	22	0
Blair	1	0	0	0

PASSING – PUNTING – KICKING

PASSING	Att	Comp	%	Yds	Yd/Att	TD	Int–%	RK
Tarkenton	412	255	62	2961	7.2	17	8– 2	3
Lee	30	15	50	156	5.2	0	2– 7	

PUNTING	No	Avg
Clabo	69	38.8

KICKING	XP	Att	%	FG	Att	%
Cox	32	36	89	19	31	61

CHICAGO BEARS

RUSHING

Last Name	No.	Yds	Avg	TD
Payton	311	1390	4.5	13
Harper	147	625	4.3	2
Musso	57	200	3.5	4
Adamle	33	93	2.8	0
Avellini	18	58	3.2	1
Schreiber	4	15	3.8	0
Rather	1	4	4.0	0
Parsons	1	2	2.0	0
Carter	1	0	0.0	0
Scott	2	–4	–2.0	0
Latta	2	–8	–4.0	0
Baschnagel	1	–12	–12.0	0

RECEIVING

Last Name	No.	Yds	Avg	TD
Harper	29	291	10	1
Scott	26	512	20	6
Latta	18	254	14	0
Payton	15	149	10	0
Baschnagel	13	226	17	0
Rather	5	33	7	0
Schubert	4	74	19	0
Adamle	4	28	7	1
Musso	4	26	7	0
Shanklin	2	32	16	0
Burks	1	55	55	1
Schreiber	1	16	16	0
Parsons	1	9	9	0

PUNT RETURNS

Last Name	No.	Yds	Avg	TD
Livers	28	205	7	0
Schubert	11	60	5	0
Baschnagel	2	2	1	0
Adamle	1	2	2	0
Knox	1	0	0	0

KICKOFF RETURNS

Last Name	No.	Yds	Avg	TD
Baschnagel	29	754	26	0
Adamle	11	179	16	0
Harper	6	119	20	0
Musso	2	18	9	0
Livers	1	14	14	0
Schubert	1	3	3	0
Payton	1	0	0	0

PASSING – PUNTING – KICKING

PASSING	Att	Comp	%	Yds	Yd/Att	TD	Int–%	RK
Avellini	271	118	44	1580	5.8	8	15– 6	14
Carter	5	3	60	77	15.4	1	0– 0	
Parsons	2	2	100	48	24.0	0	0– 0	

PUNTING	No	Avg
Parsons	99	37.6

KICKING	XP	Att	%	FG	Att	%
Thomas	27	30	90	12	25	48

DETROIT LIONS

RUSHING

Last Name	No.	Yds	Avg	TD
Bussey	196	858	4.4	3
Gaines	155	659	4.3	4
King	93	325	3.5	0
Landry	43	234	5.4	1
Bolton	15	71	4.7	0
Reed	11	63	5.7	1
B.Thompson	13	42	3.2	0
Walton	1	5	5.0	0
L.Thompaon	1	0	0.0	0
H.Weaver	1	0	0.0	0

RECEIVING

Last Name	No.	Yds	Avg	TD
Jarvis	39	822	21	5
C.Sanders	35	545	16	5
Bussey	28	218	8	0
Gaines	23	130	6	1
King	21	163	8	0
Walton	20	293	15	3
D.Hill	19	249	13	5
B.Thompson	10	108	11	0
L.Thompson	3	52	17	0
O'Neil	1	32	32	1
Franklin	1	16	16	0
J.D. Hill	1	2	2	0

PUNT RETURNS

Last Name	No.	Yds	Avg	TD
Barney	23	191	8	0
Hunter	4	7	2	0
West	3	9	3	0
Ten Napel	1	0	0	0

KICKOFF RETURNS

Last Name	No.	Yds	Avg	TD
B. Thompson	22	431	20	0
Hunter	14	375	27	0
Bolton	15	280	19	0
L.Thompson	5	86	17	0
King	3	63	21	0
Long	2	18	9	0
Bussey	1	14	14	0

PASSING – PUNTING – KICKING

PASSING	Att	Comp	%	Yds	Yd/Att	TD	Int–%	RK
Landry	291	168	58	2191	7.5	17	8– 3	2
Reed	62	32	52	425	6.9	3	3– 5	
H. Weaver	2	1	50	14	7.0	0	0– 0	
D. Hill	1	0	0	0	0.0	1	1–100	

PUNTING	No	Avg
H. Weaver	83	39.5
Ricardo	1	16.0

KICKING	XP	Att	%	FG	Att	%
Ricardo	21	23	91	11	18	61

GREEN BAY PACKERS

RUSHING

Last Name	No.	Yds	Avg	TD
Harrell	130	435	3.3	3
Brockington	117	406	3.5	2
B.Smith	97	355	3.7	5
Torkelson	88	289	3.3	2
Odom	4	78	19.5	0
Brown	12	49	4.1	0
Taylor	14	47	3.4	1
Johnson	5	25	5.0	1
Dickey	11	19	1.7	1
Osborn	6	16	2.7	0
Zimmerman	1	3	3.0	0

RECEIVING

Last Name	No.	Yds	Avg	TD
Payne	33	467	14	4
McGeorge	24	278	12	1
Odom	23	456	20	2
O.Smith	20	364	18	1
Torkelson	19	140	7	0
Harrell	17	201	12	1
B.Smith	11	88	8	0
Brockington	11	49	4	0
Taylor	2	21	11	0
Hall	1	18	18	0
Zimmerman	1	13	13	0
Jackson	1	8	8	0
Askon	1	2	2	1

PUNT RETURNS

Last Name	No.	Yds	Avg	TD
Gray	37	307	8	0
Harrell	3	–7	–2	0

KICKOFF RETURNS

Last Name	No.	Yds	Avg	TD
Odom	29	610	21	0
M.C. McCoy	18	457	25	0
Torkelson	6	123	21	0
Taylor	3	59	20	0
Hyland	3	31	10	0
Osborn	3	19	6	0
Wagner	1	27	27	0
Gray	1	23	23	0
O.Smith	1	12	12	0

PASSING – PUNTING – KICKING

PASSING	Att	Comp	%	Yds	Yd/Att	TD	Int–%	RK
Dickey	243	115	47	1465	6.0	7	14– 6	13
Brown	74	26	35	333	4.5	2	6– 8	
Johnson	35	21	60	249	7.1	0	1– 3	
Harrell	4	1	25	40	10.0	1	1– 25	
Beverly	1	1	100	18	18.0	0	0– 0	

PUNTING	No	Avg
Beverly	83	37.0

KICKING	XP	Att	%	%	Att	%
Marcol	24	27	89	10	19	53

LOS ANGELES RAMS 10-3-1 Chuck Knox

Scores of Each Game		
30	Atlanta	14
10	Minnesota	*10
24	N.Y. GIANTS	10
31	Miami	28
0	SAN FRANCISCO	16
20	CHICAGO	12
16	New Orleans	10
45	SEATTLE	6
12	Cincinnati	20
28	ST. LOUIS	30
23	San Francisco	3
33	NEW ORLEANS	14
59	ATLANTA	0
20	Detroit	17

Use Name	Pos.	Hgt.	Wgt.	Age	Int	Pts
Doug France	OT	6'5"	260	23		
Jackie Slater	OT	6'4"	252	22		
John Williams	OT	6'3"	256	30		
Dennis Harrah	OG	6'5"	257	23		
Greg Horton	OG	6'4"	245	25		
Tom Mack	OG	6'3"	250	32		
Geoff Reece	C	6'4"	247	24		
Rich Saul	C	6'3"	250	28		
Fred Dryer	DE	6'6"	240	30		
Mike Fanning	DE	6'6"	260	23		
Jack Youngblood	DE	6'4"	255	26		
Larry Brooks	DT	6'3"	255	26		
Cody Jones	DT	6'5"	240	25		
Merlin Olsen	DT	6'5"	270	35		
Carl Ekern	LB	6'3"	220	22		
Rick Kay	LB	6'4"	235	26	1	
Kevin McLain	LB	6'2"	238	21		
Jack Reynolds	LB	6'1"	232	28		
Isiah Robertson	LB	6'3"	225	27	4	
Mel Rogers	LB	6'2"	230	29		
Jim Youngblood	LB	6'3"	239	26	2	
Dave Elmendorf	DB	6'1"	195	27	2	
Monte Jackson	DB	5'11"	189	23	10	18
Rod Perry	DB	5'9"	170	22	8	
Steve Preece	DB	6'1"	195	29	1	
Bill Simpson	DB	6'1"	180	24	4	
Pat Thomas	DB	5'9"	180	22		
Pat Haden	QB	5'11"	182	23		24
James Harris	QB	6'3"	210	29		12
Ron Jaworski	QB	6'2"	185	25		6
John Cappelletti	HB-FB	6'1"	217	24		12
Lawrence McCutcheon	HB	6'1"	205	26		66
Rob Scribner	HB	6'	200	25		6
Jim Bertelsen	FB	5'11"	205	26		12
Cullen Bryant	FB	6'1"	235	25		18
Rod Phillips	FB	6'	220	23		6
Tom Geredine	WR	6'2"	189	26		6
Harold Jackson	WR	5'10"	175	30		30
Ron Jessie	WR	6'	185	28		36
Freeman Johns	WR	6'1"	175	22		
Dwight Scales	WR	6'2"	170	23		6
Bob Klein	TE	6'5"	235	29		6
Terry Nelson	TE	6'2"	230	25		
Tom Dempsey	K	6'1"	260	35		87
Rusty Jackson	K	6'2"	190	25		

SAN FRANCISCO FORTY NINERS 8-6 Monte Clark

Scores of Each Game		
26	Green Bay	14
12	CHICAGO	19
37	Seattle	21
17	N.Y. JETS	6
16	Los Angeles	0
33	NEW ORLEANS	3
15	ATLANTA	0
20	St. Louis	*23
21	WASHINGTON	24
16	Atlanta	21
3	LOS ANGELES	23
20	MINNESOTA	16
7	San Diego	*13
27	New Orleans	7

Use Name	Pos.	Hgt.	Wgt.	Age	Int	Pts
Cas Banaszek	OT	6'3"	247	30		
Jean Barrett	OT-C	6'6"	248	25		
Bill Cooke	OT	6'5"	250	25		
Keith Fahnhorst	OT	6'6"	256	24		
Steve Lawson	OG	6'3"	265	27		
Andy Mauer	OG	6'3"	275	27		
Mark Nordquist (from CHI.)	OG-C	6'4"	255	30		
John Watson	OG	6'4"	244	27		
Randy Cross	C	6'3"	247	22		
Tony Cline	DE	6'2"	244	28		
Cedrick Hardman	DE	6'3"	244	27		
Tommy Hart	DE	6'3"	249	31		2
Bill Sandifer	DE-DT	6'6"	260	24		
Cleveland Elam	DT	6'4"	252	24		6
Jimmy Webb	DT	6'4"	247	24		
Bruce Elia	LB	6'1"	217	23		
Willie Harper	LB	6'2"	208	26		
Dale Mitchell	LB	6'3"	223	23		
Frank Nunley	LB	6'2"	221	30	1	
Skip Vanderbundt	LB	6'3"	222	29	2	
Dave Washington	LB	6'5"	228	27		
Jim Johnson	DB	6'2"	187	38	1	
Tony Leonard	DB	5'11"	170	23		6
Eddie Lewis	DB	6'	177	22		
Ralph McGill	DB	5'11"	178	26		6
Mel Phillips	DB	6'	184	34	2	
Bruce Rhodes	DB	6'	187	22	3	
Bruce Taylor	DB	6'	186	28		
Bob Hoskins – Illness						
Woody Peoples – Knee Injury						
Bill Reid – Knee Injury						
Scott Bull	QB	6'5"	211	23		12
Marty Domres	QB	6'4"	220	29		
Jim Plunkett	QB	6'3"	219	28		
Paul Hofer	HB	6'	195	24		6
Kermit Johnson	HB	6'	202	24		6
Del Williams	HB	6'	197	25		54
Bob Ferrell	FB-HB	6'	208	23		6
Wilbur Jackson	FB	6'1"	219	24		12
Kenny Harrison	WR	6'	170	22		
Jim Lash (from MIN)	WR	6'2"	199	24		
Willie McGee	WR	5'11"	187	26		24
Steve Rivera	WR	5'11"	184	22		
Gene Washington	WR	6'1"	187	29		36
Tom Mitchell	TE	6'2"	226	32		6
Jim Obradovich	TE	6'2"	225	23		
Steve Mike-Mayer	K	6'	179	28		74
Tom Wittum	K	6'1"	191	26		

ATLANTA FALCONS 4-10 Marion Campbell (1-4) Pat Peppler (3-6)

Scores of Each Game		
14	LOS ANGELES	30
10	Detroit	24
10	Chicago	0
13	PHILADELPHIA	14
0	New Orleans	30
17	CLEVELAND	20
0	San Francisco	15
23	NEW ORLEANS	20
13	Seattle	30
21	SAN FRANCISCO	16
17	DALLAS	10
14	Houston	20
0	Los Angeles	59
20	GREEN BAY	24

Use Name	Pos.	Hgt.	Wgt.	Age	Int	Pts
Brent Adams	OT	6'5"	256	24		
Greg Kindle	OT	6'4"	265	25		
Phil McKinnely	OT	6'4"	248	22		
Dave Scott	OT	6'4"	285	22		
Len Gotshalk	OG	6'4"	259	26		
Larron Jackson	OG	6'3"	260	27		
Royce Smith	OG	6'3"	250	27		
Paul Ryczek	C	6'2"	230	24		
Jeff Van Note	C	6'2"	247	30		
Jim Weatherly	C	6'3"	245	24		
Jim Bailey	DE	6'5"	255	28		
Claude Humphrey	DE	6'5"	265	32		2
Jeff Merrow	DE-DT	6'4"	230	23		
Ron East	DT	6'4"	250	33		
Steve George	DT	6'6"	265	25		
Mike Lewis	DT	6'3"	261	27		
Mike Tilleman	DT	6'5"	278	32		
Bill Windauer	DT	6'3"	250	26		
Greg Brezina	LB	6'1"	221	30		
Jim Cope	LB	6'1"	235	23		
Fulton Kuykendall	LB	6'5"	225	23		
Dewey McClain	LB	6'3"	236	22	1	
Tommy Nobis	LB	6'2"	243	32	1	
Ralph Ortega	LB	6'2"	220	23		
Guy Roberts	LB	6'1"	220	26	1	
Ray Brown	DB	6'2"	202	27	3	
Rick Byas	DB	5'9"	180	25		
Ray Easterling	DB	6'	192	26	3	
Bob Jones	DB	6'2"	193	25		
Rolland Lawrence	DB	5'10"	179	25	6	
Ron Mabra	DB	5'10"	170	25		
Frank Reed	DB	5'11"	193	22	3	
Monroe Eley – Injury						
Greg McCrary – Leg Injury						
Steve Bartkowski	QB	6'4"	213	23		6
Scott Hunter	QB	6'2"	205	28		6
Kim McQuilken	QB	6'2"	203	25		
Bubba Bean	HB	5'11"	195	22		18
Sonny Collins	HB	6'1"	196	23		
Mike Esposito	HB	6'	185	23		
Haskel Stanback	HB	6'	210	24		24
Brad Davis	FB	5'10"	200	23		
Billy Pritchett	FB	6'3"	233	25		6
Woody Thompson	FB	6'1"	228	24		
Karl Farmer	WR	5'11"	165	22		
Wallace Francis	WR	5'11"	190	24		
John Gilliam	WR	6'1"	187	31		12
Al Jenkins	WR	5'10"	172	24		36
Scott Piper	WR	6'1"	179	22		
Bob Adams	TE	6'2"	218	30		
Jim Mitchell	TE	6'2"	236	28		
John James	K	6'3"	200	27		
Nick Mike-Mayer	K	5'8"	187	26		50

NEW ORLEANS SAINTS 4-10 Hank Stram

Scores of Each Game		
9	MINNESOTA	40
6	DALLAS	24
27	Kansas City	17
26	HOUSTON	31
30	ATLANTA	0
3	San Francisco	33
10	LOS ANGELES	16
20	Atlanta	23
27	Green Bay	32
17	DETROIT	16
51	Seattle	27
14	Los Angeles	33
6	New England	27
7	SAN FRANCISCO	27

Use Name	Pos.	Hgt.	Wgt.	Age	Int	Pts
Jeff Hart	OT	6'5"	252	22		
Marv Montgomery (from DEN)	OT	6'6"	255	28		
Don Morrison	OT	6'5"	250	26		
Kurt Schumacher	OT	6'3"	246	23		
Terry Stieve	OG	6'2"	242	22		
Tom Wickert	OG-OT	6'4"	252	24		
Emanuel Zanders	OG	6'1"	248	25		
Lee Gross	C	6'3"	235	23		
John Hill	C	6'2"	246	26		
Steve Baumgartner	DE	6'7"	255	25		
Andy Dorris	DE	6'4"	240	25		
Elois Grooms	DE	6'4"	250	23		
Jeff Winans (from OAK)	DE	6'5"	260	24		
Derland Moore	DT	6'4"	253	24		
Bob Pollard	DT	6'3"	251	27		
Elex Price	DT	6'3"	253	26	1	6
Ken Bordelon	LB	6'4"	236	22		
Warren Capone	LB	6'1"	220	25		6
Wayne Colman	LB	6'1"	215	30		
Joe Federspiel	LB	6'1"	230	26		
Rick Kingrea	LB	6'1"	222	27		
Jim Merlo	LB	6'1"	220	24	4	12
Greg Westbrooks	LB	6'2"	217	23		
Pete Athas	DB	5'11"	185	28	2	
Chuck Crist	DB	6'2"	205	25	1	
Ernie Jackson	DB	5'10"	176	26	2	
Benny Johnson	DB	5'11"	178	28		
Jim Kearney	DB	6'2"	196	33		
Tom Myers	DB	5'11"	170	25	1	6
Mo Spencer	DB	6'	176	24	1	
Archie Manning – Shoulder Injury						
Joel Parker – Injury						
Louis Ross – Injury						
Bob Stein – Injury						
Bobby Douglass	QB	6'3"	228	29		12
Bobby Scott	QB	6'1"	197	27		6
Alvin Maxson	HB	5'11"	201	24		6
Leon McQuay	HB	5'9"	200	26		
Mike Strachan	HB	6'	200	23		12
Tony Galbreath	FB-HB	6'	220	22		48
Andrew Jones	FB	6'2"	218	23		
Kim Jones	FB	6'4"	238	24		
Chuck Muncie	FB	6'3"	220	23		12
Larry Burton	WR	6'1"	193	24		12
Clarence Chapman	WR	5'10"	185	22		
Don Herrmann	WR	6'2"	193	29		
Tinker Owens	WR	5'11"	170	21		6
Henry Childs	TE	6'2"	220	25		24
Paul Seal	TE	6'4"	223	24		
Jim Thaxton	TE	6'2"	240	27		6
Tom Blanchard	K	6'	187	28		
Richie Szaro	K	5'11"	204	28		79

SEATTLE SEAHAWKS 2-12 Jack Patera

Scores of Each Game		
24	ST. LOUIS	30
7	Washington	31
21	SAN FRANCISCO	37
13	DALLAS	28
20	Green Bay	27
13	Tampa Bay	10
14	DETROIT	41
6	Los Angeles	45
30	ATLANTA	13
21	Minnesota	27
27	NEW ORLEANS	51
16	N.Y. Giants	28
7	CHICAGO	34
10	Philadelphia	27

Use Name	Pos.	Hgt.	Wgt.	Age	Int	Pts
Nick Bebout	OT	6'5"	260	25		
Norm Evans	OT	6'5"	250	33		
Gordon Jolley	OT-OG	6'5"	245	27		
Dave Simonson (from HOU)	OT	6'6"	250	24		
Ron Coder	OG	6'4"	250	22		
John Demarie	OG	6'3"	248	31		
Bob Newton	OG	6'4"	260	27		
Bobby Penchion	OG	6'5"	252	27		
Fred Hoaglin	C	6'4"	250	32		
Art Kuehn	C	6'3"	270	23		
Richard Harris	DE	6'4"	258	28		
Bob Lurtsema (from MIN.)	DE-DT	6'6"	250	34		
Dave Tipton	DE	6'6"	246	27		
Carl Barisich	DT	6'4"	255	25		
Steve Niehaus	DT	6'4"	270	21		
Larry Woods	DT	6'6"	268	28		
Ed Bradley	LB	6'2"	239	26	1	
Randy Coffield	LB	6'3"	215	22		
Greg Collins	LB	6'3"	227	23		
Mike Curtis	LB	6'2"	232	33	2	
Ken Geddes	LB	6'3"	235	28		
Sammy Green	LB	6'2"	228	21		
Lyle Blackwood	DB	6'	190	25		
Dave Brown	DB	6'1"	190	23	4	2
Don Dufek	DB	6'	195	22		
Ernie Jones	DB	6'3"	180	23		
Al Matthews	DB	5'11"	190	28	3	6
Eddie McMillan	DB	6'	190	24	1	
Roland Woolsey	DB	6'1"	182	23	4	
Ken Hutcherson – Injury						
Bill Munson	QB	6'2"	205	34		
Steve Myer	QB	6'2"	188	22		
Jim Zorn	QB	6'2"	200	23		24
Ralph Nelson	HB	6'2"	195	22		6
Oliver Ross	HB-FB	6'	210	26		
Hugh McKinnis	FB	6'	219	28		24
Sherman Smith	FB	6'4"	217	21		30
Don Testerman	FB	6'2"	230	23		12
Don Clune	WR	6'3"	195	24		
Steve Largent	WR	5'11"	184	21		24
Sam McCullum	WR	6'2"	203	23		24
Steve Raible	WR	6'2"	195	22		12
Ron Howard	TE	6'4"	225	25		
John McMakin	TE	6'3"	225	25		12
Don Bitterlich	K	5'7"	166	22		10
Rick Engles	K	5'11"	170	22		
John Leypoldt (from BUF)	K	6'2"	230	30		46

* – Overtime

LOS ANGELES RAMS

RUSHING Last Name	No.	Yds	Avg	TD
McCutcheon	291	1168	4.0	9
Cappelletti	177	688	3.9	1
Phillips	34	206	6.1	1
Bertelsen	42	155	3.7	2
Haden	25	84	3.4	4
Harris	12	76	6.3	2
Bryant	21	64	3.0	2
Jessie	4	37	9.3	0
H. Jackson	1	15	15.0	0
Jaworski	2	15	7.5	1
Scribner	2	12	6.0	1
Geredine	1	8	8.0	0
Preece	1	0	0.0	0

RECEIVING Last Name	No.	Yds	Avg	TD
H. Jackson	39	751	19	5
Jessie	34	779	23	6
Cappelletti	30	302	10	1
McCutcheon	28	305	11	2
Klein	20	229	11	1
Bertelsen	6	33	6	0
Nelson	4	48	12	0
Phillips	4	23	6	0
Scales	3	105	35	1
Bryant	2	28	14	0
Geredine	1	23	23	1
Harrah	0	3	0	0

PUNT RETURNS Last Name	No.	Yds	Avg	TD
Bryant	29	321	11	0
Bertelsen	10	55	6	0
Scribner	8	54	7	0
Scales	4	46	12	0
Johns	1	0	0	0

KICKOFF RETURNS Last Name	No.	Yds	Avg	TD
Bryant	16	459	29	1
Geredine	9	181	20	0
Thomas	7	140	20	0
Scales	7	136	19	0
Scribner	3	54	18	0
Johns	2	56	28	0
Nelson	0	1	0	0

PASSING	Att	Comp	%	Yds	Yd/Att	TD	Int–%	RK
Harris	158	91	58	1460	9.2	8	6– 4	1
Haden	105	60	57	896	8.5	8	4– 4	
Jaworski	52	20	39	273	5.3	1	5– 10	

PUNTING	No	Avg
R. Jackson	77	39.0

KICKING	XP	Att	%	FG	Att	%
Dempsey	36	44	82	17	26	65

SAN FRANCISCO FORTY NINERS

RUSHING Last Name	No.	Yds	Avg	TD
Williams	248	1203	4.9	7
Jackson	200	792	4.0	1
K. Johnson	32	99	3.1	1
Plunkett	19	95	5.0	0
Hofer	18	74	4.1	0
Bull	15	66	4.4	2
Ferrell	9	28	3.1	1
Domres	4	18	4.5	0
McGee	3	12	4.0	0
Lash	3	5	1.7	0
G. Washington	1	3	3.0	0

RECEIVING Last Name	No.	Yds	Avg	TD
G. Washington	33	457	14	6
Jackson	33	324	10	1
Williams	27	283	10	2
T. Mitchell	20	240	12	1
Lash	17	242	14	0
McGee	13	269	21	4
Hofer	4	45	11	1
Harris	3	65	22	0
K. Johnson	1	11	11	0
O'Bradovich	1	11	11	0
Ferrell	1	9	9	0
Rivera	1	7	7	0

PUNT RETURNS Last Name	No.	Yds	Avg	TD
Leonard	35	293	8	1
Rhodes	16	142	9	0
McGill	10	103	10	1
Taylor	3	16	5	0
Rivera	1	3	3	0

KICKOFF RETURNS Last Name	No.	Yds	Avg	TD
Leonard	26	553	21	0
Hofer	5	91	18	0
K. Johnson	4	114	29	0
T. Mitchell	2	7	4	0
Ferrell	1	12	12	0

PASSING	Att	Comp	%	Yds	Yd/Att	TD	Int–%	RK
Plunkett	243	126	52	1592	6.6	13	16– 7	8
Bull	48	21	44	252	5.3	2	4– 8	
Domres	14	7	50	101	7.2	0	1– 7	
Williams	1	1	100	18	18.0	0	0– 0	

PUNTING	No	Avg
Wittum	89	40.8

KICKING	XP	Att	%	FG	Att	%
Mike-Mayer	26	30	87	16	28	57

ATLANTA FALCONS

RUSHING Last Name	No.	Yds	Avg	TD
Bean	124	428	3.5	2
Stanback	95	324	3.4	3
Collins	91	319	3.5	0
Esposito	60	317	5.3	2
Thompson	42	152	3.6	0
Pritchett	14	74	5.3	1
Hunter	14	41	2.9	1
McQuilken	9	26	2.9	0
Mitchell	1	−6	−6.0	0
Bartkowski	8	−10	−1.3	1

RECEIVING Last Name	No.	Yds	Avg	TD
Jenkins	41	710	17	6
Gilliam	21	292	14	2
Stanback	21	174	8	1
Mitchell	17	209	12	0
Esposito	17	88	5	0
Bean	16	148	9	1
Thompson	16	111	7	0
Collins	4	37	9	0
Francis	2	24	12	0
Bob Adams	1	15	15	0
Pritchett	1	1	1	0

PUNT RETURNS Last Name	No.	Yds	Avg	TD
Lawrence	54	372	7	0
Byas	1	8	8	0
Esposito	1	6	6	0
Farmer	1	0	0	0
Mabra	1	0	0	0
Roberts	1	0	0	0
Jones	1	−1	−1	0

KICKOFF RETURNS Last Name	No.	Yds	Avg	TD
Lawrence	21	521	25	0
Byas	12	270	23	0
Francis	9	156	17	0
Collins	7	141	20	0
Mabra	3	61	20	0
Bean	2	38	19	0
Jones	1	22	22	0
Bob Adams	1	21	21	0
Stanback	1	18	18	0
Esposito	1	12	12	0
Ortega	1	9	9	0
Roberts	1	0	0	0

PASSING	Att	Comp	%	Yds	Yds/Att	TD	Int–%	RK
McQuilken	121	48	40	450	3.7	2	10– 8	
Bartkowski	120	57	48	677	5.6	2	9– 8	
Hunter	110	51	46	633	5.8	6	4– 4	
Bean	1	1	100	49	49.0	1	0– 0	
Esposito	1	0	00	0	0.0	0	0– 0	
Jenkins	1	0	00	0	0.0	0	1–100	

PUNTING	No	Avg
James	101	42.1

KICKING	XP	Att	%	FG	Att	%
Mike-Mayer	20	20	100	10	21	48

NEW ORLEANS SAINTS

RUSHING Last Name	No.	Yds	Avg	TD
Muncie	149	659	4.4	2
Galbreath	136	570	4.2	7
Strachan	66	258	3.9	2
Maxson	34	120	3.5	1
Douglass	21	92	4.4	2
Scott	12	48	4.0	1
K. Jones	6	21	3.5	0
Childs	1	16	16.0	1
A. Jones	1	2	2.0	0
Burton	3	−4	−1.3	0
Seal	2	−7	−3.5	0

RECEIVING Last Name	No.	Yds	Avg	TD
Galbreath	54	420	8	1
Herrmann	34	535	16	0
Muncie	31	272	9	0
Childs	26	349	13	3
Burton	18	297	17	2
Owens	12	241	20	1
Seal	9	72	8	0
Thaxton	7	112	16	0
Maxson	7	21	3	0
Strachan	6	22	4	0
K. Jones	1	14	14	0
Douglass	1	−2	−2	0

PUNT RETURNS Last Name	No.	Yds	Avg	TD
Athas	35	332	9	0
Myers	2	22	11	0
Galbreath	2	8	4	0
McQuay	2	5	3	0
Crist	1	8	8	0

KICKOFF RETURNS Last Name	No.	Yds	Avg	TD
Galbreath	20	399	20	0
Maxson	11	191	17	0
Thaxton	8	185	23	0
McQuay	8	151	19	0
Muncie	3	69	23	0
Chapman	3	63	21	0
Athas	2	68	34	0
Schumacher	2	17	9	0
Capone	2	0	0	0
Hart	1	12	12	0
K. Jones	1	12	12	0
Childs	1	6	6	0

PASSING	Att	Comp	%	Yds	Yd/Att	TD	Int–%	RK
Scott	190	103	54	1065	5.6	4	6– 3	7
Douglass	213	103	48	1288	6.0	4	8– 4	10

PUNTING	No	Avg
Blanchard	101	39.3

KICKING	XP	Att	%	FG	Att	%
Szaro	25	29	86	18	23	78

SEATTLE SEAHAWKS

RUSHING Last Name	No.	Yds	Avg	TD
Smith	119	537	4.5	4
Zorn	52	246	4.7	4
Testerman	67	246	3.7	1
Nelson	52	173	3.3	1
McKinnis	46	105	2.3	4
Engles	3	37	12.3	0
Ross	13	23	1.8	0
Munson	1	6	6.0	0
Howard	1	2	2.0	0
Raible	1	2	2.0	0
Largent	4	−14	−3.5	0

RECEIVING Last Name	No.	Yds	Avg	TD
Largent	54	705	13	4
Howard	37	422	11	0
Smith	36	384	11	1
McCullum	32	506	16	4
Testerman	25	232	9	1
McKinnis	13	148	11	0
Nelson	12	96	8	0
McMakin	9	158	18	2
Raible	4	126	32	1
Clune	4	67	17	0
Ross	2	22	11	0
Blackwood	1	8	8	0

PUNT RETURNS Last Name	No.	Yds	Avg	TD
Blackwood	19	132	7	0
Brown	11	74	7	0
Largent	4	36	9	0
Woolsey	2	5	3	0
McMillan	1	−1	−1	0

KICKOFF RETURNS Last Name	No.	Yds	Avg	TD
Ross	30	655	22	0
Blackwood	10	230	23	0
Dufek	9	177	20	0
Largent	8	156	20	0
Smith	5	78	16	0
Testerman	2	29	15	0

PASSING	Att	Comp	%	Yds	Yds/Att	TD	Int–%	RK
Zorn	439	208	47	2571	5.9	12	27– 6	15
Munson	37	20	54	295	8.0	1	3– 8	
Smith	2	0	0	0	0.0	0	0– 0	
Engles	1	1	100	8	8.0	0	0– 0	
Largent	1	0	0	0	0.0	0	0– 0	

PUNTING	No	Avg
Engles	80	38.3

KICKING	XP	Att	%	FG	Att	%
Leypoldt	22	25	88	8	15	53
Bitterlich	7	7	100	1	4	25

1976 A.F.C. The Pats "Cinderella team" Almost Took It All

EASTERN DIVISION

Baltimore Colts — The season started in turmoil with Coach Ted Marchibroda resigning just before the opener in a power struggle with GM Joe Thomas. When several assistants threatened to follow Marchibroda's lead and QB Bert Jones spoke publicly in his coach's defense, Thomas and Owner Bob Irsay quickly made amends with the coach. That was the beginning of the end for master builder Thomas, who was fired at the end of the season after five years at Baltimore. The Colts won eight of their first nine games and finished 11-3, edging New England for the division crown on the basis of a better intra-division record. Jones had a super year, passing for 24 TD's and a 102.6 rating. WR Roger Carr provided the deep threat, leading the league in reception yardage and average gain and ranking second in TD's. RB Lydell Mitchell placed second in AFC rushing and third in receptions. The Colts led the league in total offense, but a vulnerable defense was their undoing in the playoffs.

New England Patriots — The one-year rise from a 3-11 record to 11-3 and a "Wild Card" berth in the playoffs marked the Pats as the 1976 Cinderella team and Chuck Fairbanks as the Coach of the Year. Major reasons for the team's meteoric improvement were Steve Grogan, who proved himself an NFL-caliber QB in his first full season as a starter, and CB Mike Haynes, who was second in the AFC in punt return average and interceptions as Defensive Rookie of the Year. Led by RB's Sam Cunningham, Andy Johnson and Don Calhoun, the Pats ranked first in the league in yards per rush and second in scoring. Their 50 takeaways also were tops. After dropping their opener to Baltimore, the Pats beat overwhelming favorites Miami, Pittsburgh and Oakland in succession. Following mid-season upsets by Detroit and Miami, they won their last six games to reach the playoffs.

Miami Dolphins — After a 10-4 season in '75, Miami slipped to 6-8, Don Shula's first losing season as a head coach. A crippling series of injuries rocked the team, forcing 22 players to miss a total of 144 games. After a 6-0 preseason, Miami beat only one team above .500—a 10-3 upset of New England. The defense ranked only 26th in yards yielded, leaving too heavy a load for the offense. Rookie Duriel Harris led the NFL with a 32.9 kickoff return average.

New York Jets — Lou Holtz left North Carolina State to become the Jets' fourth head coach in four years, but his optimism turned sour and he unexpectedly resigned before the final game. Holtz inherited a sticky QB situation in which he had to choose between 33-year-old Joe Namath and rookie Richard Todd, who started six games and was the QB of record in the wins over Buffalo. Rookie free agent Clark Gaines became a starting RB in the seventh game and recorded four 100-yard games, outgaining all other NFL rookie runners and leading the club in receptions.

Buffalo Bills — O.J. Simpson's trade demands began a problem-filled year for the Bills. Simpson finally was coaxed back into the fold with a $2½ million contract over three years, but the team never recovered from the dispute. Added to the Bills' woes were the off-season departures of WR's Ahmad Rashad and J.D. Hill and defensive linemen Earl Edwards, Walt Patulski and Pat Toomay. RB Jim Braxton injured his knee in the opener and was lost for the season, as was QB Joe Ferguson, who suffered a back injury in the seventh game. A disillusioned Lou Saban resigned as head coach after five games with five years still remaining on a 10-year contract, and offensive line coach Jim Ringo replaced him. Things got even worse for Ringo. The Bills lost their last 10 games, nine under Ringo. Despite his slow start, Simpson led the NFL in rushing, but QB Gary Marangi finished last in AFC passing and the defense wasn't much better.

CENTRAL DIVISION

Pittsburgh Steelers — The two-time defending Super Bowl champs found themselves in a deep hole after losing four of their first five games, but they regrouped and won their last nine games to grab the division title for the third year in a row. The manner in which the Steelers won those last nine was awe-inspiring, as they yielded only 28 points or an average of 3.1 per game. After going 19 games without a shutout, the Steel Curtain recorded five in the last eight games. Led by All-Pro MLB Jack Lambert, the defense had a string of 15 consecutive scoreless quarters and 22 periods in a row without allowing a TD. Injuries in the fifth and 10th games sidelined QB Terry Bradshaw for two games each, but rookie Mike Kruczek filled in remarkably well, starting six games during the winning streak, including both wins over Cincinnati. RB's Franco Harris and Rocky Bleier both rushed for more than 1,000 yards behind a talented offensive line.

Cincinnati Bengals — Leading the division by two games over Pittsburgh with only three to play, the Bengals lost to the Steelers and Raiders back-to-back and watched their playoff chances go down the drain. Despite a 10-4 record, their two losses to Pittsburgh were the deciding factor. Their fine defensive showing was led by DE Coy Bacon, who recorded a league-high 26 sacks after an off-season trade from San Diego for WR Charlie Joiner. CB Ken Riley led the AFC in interceptions, and SS Tom Casanova, MLB Jim LeClair and CB Lemar Parrish were named All-Pro on defense. Offensively, QB Ken Anderson played below his league-leading pace of the previous two years but WR Isaac Curtis and TE Bob Trumpy combined for 13 TD catches.

Cleveland Browns — Forrest Gregg guided the team to a surprising 9-5 record after a 3-11 mark in his first year. Although their schedule was relatively easy, the Browns nevertheless played well. Behind a sound offensive line which allowed only 19 sacks (second in NFL), Brian Sipe developed into a respected QB. RB Greg Pruitt reached 1,000 yards for the second year in a row despite recurring ankle sprains. All-Pro DT Jerry Sherk (12 sacks) led a defense which ranked fourth in the NFL against the run. The acquisitions of LB Gerald Irons and CB Ron Bolton solidified the defense, and FS Thom Darden rebounded from knee surgery to lead the club in interceptions. After a poor 1-3 start, the Browns won eight of their next nine games before losing the finale.

Houston Oilers — Injuries and a lack of depth precipitated a fall from a 10-4 record in '75 to 5-9 in '76. After roaring to a 4-1 start, Houston lost eight of its last nine games. It lost four games by four points or less, and two of those defeats prevented it from standing 6-0 after six weeks. The running attack was far below par, and disgruntled QB Dan Pastorini asked to be traded at midseason but was injured the next week. Vet John Hadl played well as backup QB, and WR Ken Burrough had an excellent year. Despite injuries to key players, the 3-4 defense ranked high, sparked by OLB Robert Brazile (named All-Pro in his second year), MG Curley Culp and DE Elvin Bethea (14½ sacks).

WESTERN DIVISION

Oakland Raiders — Winning its fifth division title in a row, Oakland had the best record (13-1) in the NFL. Aside from a one-sided loss at New England, the defense was able to overcome a rash of injuries which sidelined three starters (Tony Cline, Horace Jones and Art Thoms) from the four-man front. Coach John Madden switched to a 3-4 alignment which gave up fewer points than in '75. Free agent John Matuszak was signed after the opener and became a starter at DE. However, the offense was primarily responsible for the team's success. QB Ken Stabler had an outstanding season, his 103.7 passer rating the sixth best of all-time. WR Cliff Branch's fine receiving stats were among the NFL's best, and RB Mark van Eeghen became only the third Raider ever to rush for 1,000 yards in a season, behind the blocking of LT Art Shell and LG Gene Upshaw.

Denver Broncos — Denver enjoyed the best season in its 17-year history but a crushing defeat at New England ended its playoff bid. Coach John Ralston, who had directed the team to its first three winning seasons during his five-year tenure, resigned under fire after the season. His successor was Red Miller, the offensive coordinator of the only team which scored more than 26 points against Denver all year. Denver ranked second in the AFC in points allowed and in rushing defense, led by LB's Tom Jackson and Randy Gradishar. The offense was less impressive, although RB Otis Armstrong gained 1,000 yards for the second time in his four-year career. Steve Ramsey held the QB job before falling into disfavor due to a poor performance in the Patriot game. Rick Upchurch averaged a league-high 13.7 yards per punt return with four TD's.

San Diego Chargers — After jumping off to a 4-2 start, the team lost six of its last eight games and finished 6-8, still a big improvement upon the 2-12 mark in '75. The defense ranked only 22nd overall, due largely to a weak pass defense. Guided by an offensive coordinator Bill Walsh, QB Dan Fouts had his best year, ranking 13th in NFL passing with more attempts than any other AFC QB. But he had only one accomplished WR in Charlie Joiner, who topped 1,000 yards in his first year as a Charger. The ground game ranked seventh in yardage per carry, with sophomore Rickey Young averaging 5.0.

Kansas City Chiefs — Four of K.C.'s five wins were against teams which finished with better records, including playoff-bound Washington. The offense ranked second in NFL passing yardage, as QB Mike Livingston finally cast aside the shadow of ex-teammate Len Dawson after eight years. Livingston had rapidly improving receivers in Walter White, Henry Marshall and Larry Brunson, and veteran RB MacArthur Lane led the NFL in receptions. The inexperienced defense was a different story, ranking 27th out of 28 teams overall.

Tampa Bay Buccaneers — The expansion team finished its first year without a win while Coach John McKay built for the future. It averaged only 8.9 points and was blanked five times, while giving up 29.4 points a game. The Bucs put a league-high 17 players on injured reserve, including six defensive starters. The play of veteran QB Steve Spurrier was so unimpressive that he was waived after the season ended. WR Morris Owens was the Bucs' most explosive offensive weapon, catching six TD passes.

FINAL TEAM STATISTICS

OFFENSE

	BALT.	BUFF.	CIN.	CLEV.	DENV.	HOUS.	K.C.	MIAMI	N.ENG.	N.Y.	OAK.	PITT.	S.D.	T.B.
FIRST DOWNS:														
Total	301	250	238	260	239	199	275	267	260	220	303	271	256	191
by Rushing	133	135	114	119	106	71	103	122	150	104	137	163	111	71
by Passing	144	102	110	112	114	110	152	125	95	93	146	94	127	93
by Penalty	24	13	14	29	19	18	20	20	15	23	20	14	18	27
RUSHING:														
Number	565	548	481	533	500	416	498	491	591	438	557	653	473	433
Yards	2303	2566	2109	2295	1932	1498	1873	2118	2948	1924	2285	2971	2040	1503
Average Yards	4.1	4.7	4.4	4.3	3.9	3.6	3.8	4.3	5.0	4.4	4.1	4.5	4.3	3.5
Touchdowns	26	11	15	9	14	6	18	15	24	10	14	33	13	5
PASSING:														
Attempts	361	383	360	373	353	423	419	346	309	393	361	277	388	376
Completions	215	156	187	209	168	227	229	193	146	180	232	143	223	181
Completion Pct.	59.6	40.7	51.9	56.0	47.6	53.7	54.7	55.8	47.2	45.8	64.3	51.6	57.5	48.1
Passing Yards	3221	2084	2443	2399	2510	2429	3303	2604	1910	1989	3195	1935	2687	1926
Avg. Yards per Att.	8.9	5.4	6.8	6.4	7.1	5.7	7.9	7.5	6.2	5.1	8.9	7.0	6.9	5.1
Avg. Yds per Comp.	15.0	13.4	13.1	11.5	14.9	10.7	14.4	13.5	13.1	11.1	13.8	13.5	12.1	10.6
Times Tackled	30	33	37	19	48	39	42	37	19	45	28	27	46	50
Yds Lost Tackled	288	246	252	152	306	357	374	336	164	383	290	269	271	423
Net Yards	2933	1838	2191	2247	2204	2072	2929	2268	1746	1606	1905	1666	2416	1503
Touchdowns	24	16	21	21	15	17	15	15	18	7	33	10	17	9
Interceptions	10	17	15	15	22	19	17	15	20	28	18	12	18	20
Pct. Intercepted	2.8	4.4	4.2	4.0	6.2	4.5	4.1	4.3	6.5	7.1	5.0	4.3	4.6	5.3
PUNTS:														
Number	59	87	76	69	84	100	68	62	67	81	67	76	82	92
Average Distance	39.7	42.3	39.5	37.4	35.1	35.3	41.1	38.2	40.1	39.7	41.6	39.2	38.7	39.3
PUNT RETURNS:														
Number	40	33	54	49	51	48	34	35	48	40	50	71	45	43
Yards	315	220	343	369	640	504	429	415	628	289	553	636	490	366
Average Yards	7.9	6.7	6.4	7.5	12.5	10.5	12.6	11.9	13.1	7.2	11.1	9.0	10.9	8.5
Touchdowns	0	1	0	0	4	1	0	1	2	1	0	0	0	0
KICKOFF RETURNS:														
Number	52	75	49	54	46	58	65	55	46	73	46	41	52	70
Yards	1072	1594	1046	1182	1075	1229	1538	1347	1087	1597	1025	855	1076	1488
Average Yards	20.6	21.3	21.3	21.9	23.4	21.2	23.7	24.5	23.6	21.9	22.3	20.9	20.7	21.3
Touchdowns	0	0	1	0	0	0	0	0	0	0	0	0	0	0
INTERCEPTION RET:														
Number	15	19	26	21	24	11	23	11	23	11	16	22	20	9
Yards	211	293	330	234	452	176	161	144	505	146	128	262	299	99
Average Yards	14.1	15.4	12.7	11.1	18.8	16.0	7.0	13.1	22.0	13.3	8.0	11.9	15.0	11.0
Touchdowns	0	1	3	1	4	0	0	0	3	0	0	0	1	0
PENALTIES:														
Number	92	91	79	107	105	99	97	70	102	71	107	111	78	109
Yards	786	797	700	1037	986	776	789	582	914	627	957	836	579	875
FUMBLES:														
Number	25	45	38	45	23	25	32	14	28	44	21	40	28	30
Number Lost	18	26	20	22	12	14	16	8	16	25	11	19	13	17
POINTS:														
Total	417	245	335	267	315	222	290	263	376	169	350	342	248	125
PAT Attempts	51	30	42	32	39	25	33	31	48	20	47	43	32	15
PAT Made	49	26	39	28	36	24	27	29	43	16	42	40	26	11
FG Attempts	27	24	27	28	21	27	38	23	25	16	19	26	20	17
FG Made	20	13	14	15	15	16	21	16	15	11	8	14	10	8
Percent FG Made	74.1	54.2	51.9	53.6	71.4	59.3	55.3	69.6	60.0	68.8	42.1	53.8	50.0	47.1
Safeties	1	0	1	1	0	0	1	0	0	0	1	1	0	0

DEFENSE

	BALT.	BUFF.	CIN.	CLEV.	DENV.	HOUS.	K.C.	MIAMI	N.ENG.	N.Y.	OAK.	PITT.	S.D.	T.B.
FIRST DOWNS:														
Total	229	262	234	244	222	226	309	268	258	277	261	182	259	284
by Rushing	83	128	116	109	90	117	161	125	102	135	98	69	113	136
by Passing	126	110	103	111	104	90	132	131	134	127	138	96	132	124
by Penalty	20	24	15	24	28	19	16	12	22	15	25	17	14	24
RUSHING:														
Number	438	533	520	445	496	540	555	525	462	582	478	452	516	588
Yards	1844	2465	1912	1761	1709	2072	2861	2411	1847	2592	1903	1457	2048	2560
Average Yards	4.2	4.6	3.7	4.0	3.4	3.8	5.2	4.6	4.0	4.5	4.0	3.2	4.0	4.4
Touchdowns	11	19	11	15	14	13	24	14	12	14	17	5	10	23
PASSING:														
Attempts	372	337	364	392	391	345	375	347	437	374	389	373	386	321
Completions	192	163	177	225	214	173	215	195	229	204	197	158	219	178
Completion Pct.	51.6	48.4	48.6	57.4	54.7	50.1	57.3	56.2	52.4	54.5	50.6	42.4	56.7	55.5
Passing Yards	2804	2475	2202	2353	2265	2259	2684	2863	2604	2468	2846	2179	2822	2142
Avg. Yards per Att.	7.5	7.3	6.0	6.0	5.8	6.5	7.2	8.3	6.0	6.6	7.3	5.8	7.3	7.5
Avg. Yds per Comp.	14.6	15.2	12.4	10.5	10.6	13.1	12.5	14.7	11.4	12.1	14.5	13.8	12.9	13.6
Times Tackled	56	28	46	32	32	50	22	20	47	16	46	41	23	24
Yds Lost Tackled	461	210	444	321	240	344	188	193	429	144	370	313	194	171
Net Yards	2343	2265	1758	2032	2025	1915	2496	2670	2175	2324	2476	1866	2628	2241
Touchdowns	16	18	13	18	8	17	25	20	16	25	13	9	21	19
Interceptions	15	19	26	21	24	11	23	11	23	11	16	22	20	9
Pct. Intercepted	4.0	5.6	7.1	5.4	6.1	3.2	6.1	3.2	5.3	2.9	4.1	5.9	5.2	2.8
PUNTS:														
Number	79	72	86	71	91	96	64	63	75	66	87	94	66	65
Average Distance	36.9	38.5	38.2	37.4	37.3	38.7	39.1	41.2	38.8	40.5	38.9	37.5	41.2	39.3
PUNT RETURNS:														
Number	33	52	41	45	43	60	39	34	37	55	38	36	45	71
Yards	231	878	323	517	372	659	376	272	288	458	264	206	601	754
Average Yards	7.0	16.9	7.9	11.5	8.7	11.0	9.6	8.0	7.8	8.3	6.9	5.7	13.4	10.6
Touchdowns	0	2	1	2	1	0	1	0	0	1	0	0	1	1
KICKOFF RETURNS:														
Number	77	48	66	57	50	53	55	57	71	39	61	61	49	35
Yards	1716	1204	1616	1347	1208	1125	1263	1246	1569	899	1123	1284	1072	717
Average Yards	22.3	25.1	24.5	23.6	24.2	21.2	23.0	21.9	22.1	23.1	18.4	21.0	21.9	20.5
Touchdowns	0	0	0	1	0	0	0	0	0	0	0	0	0	0
INTERCEPTION RET:														
Number	10	17	15	15	22	19	17	15	20	28	18	12	18	20
Yards	146	246	102	123	260	197	243	128	380	430	185	106	185	490
Average Yards	14.6	14.5	6.8	8.2	11.8	10.4	14.3	8.5	19.0	15.4	10.3	8.8	10.3	24.5
Touchdowns	1	0	0	0	1	0	1	0	0	3	0	0	1	4
PENALTIES:														
Number	89	92	90	89	88	107	88	94	83	87	96	80	92	114
Yards	770	704	768	711	715	963	762	716	715	796	918	630	823	935
FUMBLES:														
Number	32	37	34	24	23	33	35	31	37	36	26	42	24	33
Number Lost	21	23	15	11	13	17	20	18	27	21	9	24	11	19
POINTS:														
Total	246	363	210	287	206	273	376	264	236	383	237	138	285	412
PAT Attempts	29	41	25	37	25	31	51	34	29	45	31	14	34	50
PAT Made	27	39	24	32	20	29	43	30	26	42	27	12	30	48
FG Attempts	20	30	22	19	28	29	18	21	17	29	17	24	34	31
FG Made	15	26	12	11	12	18	9	10	12	23	8	14	17	20
Percent FG Made	75.0	86.7	54.5	57.9	42.9	62.1	50.0	47.6	70.6	79.3	47.1	58.3	50.0	64.5
Safeties	0	0	0	0	0	2	0	0	0	1	0	0	0	2

CONFERENCE PLAYOFFS

December 18, at Oakland (Attendance 53,045)

SCORING

OAKLAND	3	7	0	14–24
NEW ENGLAND	7	0	14	0–21

First Quarter
- N.E. — A. Johnson, 1 yard rush PAT–Smith (kick)
- Oak. — Mann, 40 yard field goal

Second Quarter
- Oak. — Biletnikoff, 31 yard pass from Stabler PAT–Mann (kick)

Third Quarter
- N.E. — Francis, 26 yard pass from Grogan PAT–Smith (kick)
- N.E. — J. Phillips, 3 yard rush PAT–Smith (kick)

Fourth Quarter
- Oak. — van Eeghen, 1 yard rush PAT–Mann (kick)
- Oak. — Stabler, 1 yard rush PAT–Mann (kick)

TEAM STATISTICS

Oak.		N.E.
20	First Downs-Total	23
5	First Downs-Rushing	10
13	First Downs-Passing	6
2	First Downs-Penalty	7
1	Fumbles-Number	1
1	Fumbles-Lost Ball	1
11	Penalties-Number	10
93	Yards Penalized	83
0	Missed Field Goals	1
70	Offensive Plays	73
302	Net Yards	331
4.3	Average Gain	4.5
1	Giveaways	3
3	Takeaways	1
+2	Difference	−2

INDIVIDUAL STATISTICS

OAKLAND	No	Yds	Avg.	NEW ENGLAND	No	Yds	Avg.
RUSHING							
van Eeghen	11	39	3.5	Cun'ham	20	68	3.4
C. Davis	7	29	4.1	Grogan	7	35	5.0
Banaszak	4	28	7.0	A. Johnson	14	32	2.0
Garrett	1	4	4.0	Calhoun	5	17	3.4
Stabler	1	1	1.0	J. Phillips	3	12	4.0
	24	101	4.2		49	164	3.3
RECEIVING							
Biletnikoff	9	137	15.2	Francis	4	96	24.0
Casper	4	47	11.8	Stingley	2	36	18.0
Branch	3	32	10.7	Cun'ham	2	14	7.0
van Eeghen	1	8	8.0	A. Johnson	2	13	6.5
C. Davis	1	5	5.0	Briscoe	1	7	7.0
Garrett	1	4	4.0	Chandler	1	1	1.0
	19	233	12.3		12	167	13.9
PUNTING							
Guy	5		37.8	Patrick	3		44.0
PUNT RETURNS							
Colzie	3	53	17.7	Haynes	1	13	13.0
KICKOFF RETURNS							
Garrett	4	119	29.8	J. Phillips	4	67	16.8
				Webster	1	0	0.0
					5	67	13.4
INTERCEPTION RETURNS							
Thomas	1	18	18.0	none			
Johnson	1	0	0.0				
	2	18	9.0				

PASSING

OAKLAND	Att.	Comp.	Comp. Pct.	Yds.	Int.	Yds/ Att.	Yds/ Comp.	Yards Lost Tackled
Stabler	32	19	59.4	233	0	7.3	12.3	4–32
NEW ENGLAND								
Grogan	23	12	52.2	167	1	7.3	13.9	
Francis	1	0	0.0	0	1	0.0	0.0	
	24	12	50.0	167	2	7.0	13.9	0–0

December 19, at Baltimore (Attendance 60,020)

SCORING

BALTIMORE	7	0	0	7–14
PITTSBURGH	9	17	0	14–40

First Quarter
- Pitt. — Lewis, 76 yard pass from Bradshaw PAT–No Good
- Pitt. — Gerela, 45 yard field goal
- Balt. — Carr, 17 yard pass from Jones PAT–Linhart (kick)

Second Quarter
- Pitt. — Harrison, 1 yard rush PAT–Gerela (kick)
- Pitt. — Swann, 29 yard pass from Bradshaw PAT–Gerela (kick)
- Pitt. — Gerela, 25 yard field goal

Fourth Quarter
- Pitt. — Swan, 11 yard pass from Bradshaw PAT–Gerela (kick)
- Balt. — Leaks, 1 yard rush PAT–Linhart (kick)
- Pitt. — Harrison, 10 yard rush PAT–Gerela (kick)

TEAM STATISTICS

BALT.		PITT.
16	First Downs-Total	29
4	First Downs-Rushing	12
8	First Downs-Passing	15
4	First Downs-Penalty	2
0	Fumbles-Number	2
0	Fumbles-Lost Ball	2
7	Penalties-Number	12
59	Yards Penalized	88
0	Missed Field Goals	0
53	Offensive Plays	65
170	Net Yards	526
3.2	Average Gain	8.1
2	Giveaways	2
2	Takeaways	2
0	Difference	0

INDIVIDUAL STATISTICS

BALTIMORE	No.	Yds	Avg.	PITTSBURGH	No.	Yds	Avg.
Mitchell	16	55	3.4	Harris	18	132	7.3
Leaks	4	12	3.0	Fugua	11	54	4.9
Jones	2	3	1.5	Harrison	10	40	4.0
McCauley	1	1	1.0	Bleier	1	−1	−1.0
	23	71	3.1		40	225	5.6
RECEIVING							
Mitchell	5	42	8.4	Swann	5	77	15.4
Chester	3	42	14.0	Harrison	4	37	9.3
Carr	2	35	17.5	Harris	3	24	8.0
Daughty	1	25	25.0	Lewis	2	103	51.5
	11	144	13.1	Fugua	2	34	17.0
				Bell	2	25	12.5
				Stallworth	1	8	8.0
					19	308	16.2
PUNTING							
D. Lee	4		40.5	Walden	1		33.0
PUNT RETURNS							
Stevens	1	11	11.0	Swann	3	12	4.0
KICKOFF RETURNS							
Stevens	3	66	22.0	Bell	1	60	60.0
H. Lee	3	39	13.0	Pough	1	19	19.0
Laird	1	3	3.0		2	79	39.5
	7	108	15.4				
INTERCEPTION RETURNS							
none				Edwards	1	26	26.0
				Wagner	1	12	12.0
					2	38	19.0

PASSING

BALTIMORE	Att.	Comp.	Comp. Pct.	Yds.	Int.	Yds/ Att.	Yds/ Comp.	Yards Lost Tackled
Jones	25	11	44.0	144	2	5.8	13.1	5–45
PITTSBURGH								
Bradshaw	18	14	77.7	264	0	14.7	18.9	1–1
Kruczek	6	5	83.3	44	0	7.3	8.8	
	24	19	79.2	308	0	12.8	16.2	1–1

1976 A.F.C. — Eastern Division

BALTIMORE COLTS 11-3 Ted Marchibroda

Scores of Each Game			Use Name	Pos.	Hgt	Wgt	Age	Int	Pts	Use Name	Pos.	Hgt	Wgt	Age	Int	Pts	Use Name	Pos.	Hgt	Wgt	Age	Int	Pts
27	New England	13	George Kunz	OT	6'5"	261	29			Jim Cheyunski	LB	6'2"	220	30			Bert Jones	QB	6'3"	212	24		12
28	CINCINNATI	27	David Taylor	OT	6'4"	264	26			Dan Dickel	LB	6'3"	230	24			Mike Kirkland	QB	6'1"	195	22		
27	Dallas	30	Elmer Collett	OG	6'4"	246	31			Derrel Luce	LB	6'3"	227	23	2	6	Bill Troup	QB	6'5"	215	25		6
42	TAMPA BAY	17	Ken Huff	OG	6'4"	257	23			Sanders Shiver	LB	6'2"	222	21			Lydell Mitchell	HB	5'11"	195	27		48
28	MIAMI	14	Robert Pratt	OG	6'4"	248	25			Ed Simonini	LB	6'	220	22			Howard Stevens	HB	5'5"	165	26		6
31	Buffalo	13	Bob Van Duyne	OG	6'5"	249	24			Stan White	LB	6'1"	223	26	3		Roosevelt Leaks	FB	5'10"	225	23		42
20	N.Y. Jets	0	Forrest Blue	C	6'5"	260	30			Tim Baylor	DB	6'6"	191	22			Ron Lee	FB	6'4"	222	22		6
38	HOUSTON	14	Ken Mendenhall	C	6'3"	250	28			Randy Hall	DB	6'3"	194	24			Don McCauley	FB-HB	6'1"	215	27		66
37	San Deigo	21	Fred Cook	DE	6'3"	246	24	1		Bruce Laird	DB	6'	198	26			Roger Carr	WR	6'3"	196	24		66
14	NEW ENGLAND	21	John Dutton	DE	6'7"	266	25			Lloyd Mumphord	DB	5'11"	178	29	1		Glenn Doughty	WR	6'2"	202	25		30
17	Miami	16	Ron Fernandes	DE	6'4"	239	24		2	Nelson Munsey	DB	6'1"	191	28	1		Freddie Scott	WR	6'2"	170	24		
33	N.Y. JETS	16	Mike Barnes	DT	6'6"	256	25			Ray Oldham	DB	6'	192	25	2		Ricky Thompson	WR	6'	170	22		
17	St. Louis	24	Joe Ehrmann	DT	6'5"	254	27			Jackie Wallace	DB	6'3"	198	25	5		Ray Chester	TE	6'3"	236	28		18
58	BUFFALO	20	Ken Novak	DT	6'7"	275	22										Jimmie Kennedy	TE	6'3"	230	24		
										Marshall Johnson – Knee Injury							David Lee	K	6'4"	224	32		
										Tom McLeod – Foot Injury							Toni Linhart	K	6'	179	34		109
										Doug Nettles – Shoulder Injury													

NEW ENGLAND PATRIOTS 11-3 Chuck Fairbanks

Scores of Each Game			Use Name	Pos.	Hgt	Wgt	Age	Int	Pts	Use Name	Pos.	Hgt	Wgt	Age	Int	Pts	Use Name	Pos.	Hgt	Wgt	Age	Int	Pts
13	BALTIMORE	27	Leon Gray	OT	6'3"	256	24			Pete Barnes	LB	6'3"	240	31			Steve Grogan	QB	6'4"	200	23		78
30	MIAMI	14	Bob McKay	OT	6'5"	265	28			Sam Hunt	LB	6'1"	240	25	2	6	Tom Owen	QB	6'1"	194	23		
30	Pittsburgh	27	Tom Neville	OT	6'4"	253	33			Steve King	LB	6'4"	225	25			Don Calhoun	HB	6'	198	24		6
48	OAKLAND	17	Sam Adams	OG	6'3"	252	27			Steve Nelson	LB	6'2"	230	25	2		Ike Forte	HB	6'	196	22		12
10	Detroit	30	John Hannah	OG	6'2"	265	25			Jim Romaniszyn	LB	6'2"	220	24			Andy Johnson	HB	6'	204	23		60
41	N.Y. JETS	7	Fred Sturt	OG	6'4"	255	25			Donnie Thomas	LB	6'2"	245	23			Jess Phillips	HB-FB	6'1"	208	29		6
26	Buffalo	22	Pete Brock	C-TE	6'5"	253	22		6	George Webster	LB	6'4"	230	30			Sam Cunningham	FB	6'3"	224	26		18
3	Miami	10	Bill Lenkaitis	C	6'3"	250	30			Steve Zabel	LB	6'4"	235	28		1	Marlin Briscoe	WR	5'10"	180	30		6
20	BUFFALO	10	Julius Adams	DE	6'3"	260	28			Doug Beaudoin	DB	6'1"	200	22			Steve Burks	WR	6'5"	211	23		
21	Baltimore	14	Mel Lunsford	DE	6'3"	250	26			Joe Blahak (from TB)	DB	5'9"	188	26			Darryl Stingley	WR	6'	195	24		24
38	N.Y. Jets	24	Tony McGee	DE	6'4"	245	27			Dick Conn	DB	6'	180	25			Randy Vataha	WR-DB	5'10"	170	27		6
38	DENVER	14	Richard Bishop	NT	6'1"	275	26			Tim Fox	DB	5'11"	186	22	3		Al Chandler	TE	6'2"	229	25		18
27	NEW ORLEANS	6	Ray Hamilton	NT	6'1"	245	25			Willie Germany	DB	6'	192	27			Russ Francis	TE	6'6"	240	23		18
31	Tampa Bay	14	Art Moore	NT	6'5"	253	25			Mike Haynes	DB	6'2"	189	23	8	12	Mike Patrick	K	6'	213	23		
			Dave Tipton	NT	6'1"	250	22			Bob Howard	DB	6'1"	177	31	3		John Smith	K	6'	185	26		87
										Prentice McCray	DB	6'1"	187	25	5	12							
			Steve Corbett – Neck Injury							Deac Sanders	DB	6'1"	178	26									
			Pete Kusick – Knee Injury																				
			Craig Hanneman – Injury							Rod Shoate – Knee Injury													
			Shelby Jordan – Declared Ineligible																				

MIAMI DOLPHINS 6-8 Don Shula

Scores of Each Game			Use Name	Pos.	Hgt	Wgt	Age	Int	Pts	Use Name	Pos.	Hgt	Wgt	Age	Int	Pts	Use Name	Pos.	Hgt	Wgt	Age	Int	Pts
30	Buffalo	21	Darryl Carlton	OT	6'6"	260	23			Nick Buoniconti	LB	5'11"	210	35			Bob Griese	QB	6'1"	190	31		
14	New England	30	Tom Drougas	OT	6'4"	255	26			Rusty Chambers (From N.O.)	LB	6'1"	215	22			Earl Morrall	QB	6'1"	210	42		
16	N.Y. JETS	0	Wayne Moore	OT	6'6"	265	31			Mike Dennery	LB	6'	225	26			Don Strock	QB	6'5"	218	25		6
28	LOS ANGELES	31	Bob Kuechenberg	OG	6'3"	252	28			Larry Gordon	LB	6'4"	230	23			Gary Davis	HB	5'10"	202	21		6
14	Baltimore	28	Larry Little	OG	6'1"	265	30			Bob Matheson	LB	6'4"	235	31	2		Clayton Heath (From BUF.)	HB	5'11"	195	25		
17	KANSAS CITY	*20	Mel Mitchell	OG	6'3"	260	23			Andy Selfridge	LB	6'4"	220	27			Benny Malone	HB	5'10"	193	24		24
23	Tampa Bay	20	Ed Newman	OG	6'2"	245	25			Steve Towle	LB	6'2"	233	22			Norm Bulaich	FB-HB	6'1"	218	29		24
10	NEW ENGLAND	3	Jim Langer	C	6'2"	253	28			Dick Anderson	DB	6'2"	196	30	1		Don Nottingham	FB	5'10"	210	27		18
27	N.Y. Jets	7	John Andrews	DE	6'6"	251	24			Charlie Babb	DB	6'	190	26	2		Stan Winfrey	FB	5'11"	223	23		12
3	Pittsburgh	14	Vern Den Herder	DE	6'6"	252	27			Ted Bachman (from SEA)	DB	6'	190	24			Duriel Harris	WR	5'11"	175	21		6
16	BALTIMORE	17	Wally Pesuit (from ATL)	DE	6'4"	260	22			Ken Ellis (from HOU)	DB	5'10"	190	28	2		Ike Hill	WR	5'10"	180	29		
13	Cleveland	17	Don Reese	DE-DT	6'6"	255	24			Tim Foley	DB	6'	194	28			Nat Moore	WR	5'9"	180	24		24
45	BUFFALO	27	Bill Stanfill	DE	6'5"	252	29			Barry Hill	DB	6'3"	185	23			Freddie Solomon	WR	5'11"	181	23		24
7	MINNESOTA	29	Randy Crowder	DT	6'2"	236	24			Mike Holmes (from BUF.)	DB-WR	6'2"	198	25			Howard Twilley	WR	5'10"	185	32		6
			Bob Heinz	DT	6'6"	265	29			Curtis Johnson	DB	6'2"	196	28	1		Jim Mandich	TE	6'3"	224	28		24
										Bryant Salter (to BAL)	DB	6'4"	196	26	1		Loaird McCreary	TE	6'5"	227	23		
			Manny Fernandez – Knee Injury							Jeris White	DB	5'11"	180	23	2		Larry Seiple	TE	6'	214	31		6
			Mike Kolen – Knee Injury														Andre Tillman	TE	6'5"	230	23		6
			Ernest Rhone – Knee Injury														Garo Yepremian	K	5'8"	175	32		77

NEW YORK JETS 3-11 Lou Holtz

Scores of Each Game			Use Name	Pos.	Hgt	Wgt	Age	Int	Pts	Use Name	Pos.	Hgt	Wgt	Age	Int	Pts	Use Name	Pos.	Hgt	Wgt	Age	Int	Pts
17	Cleveland	38	Winston Hill	OT	6'4"	272	34			Greg Buttle	LB	6'3"	235	22	2	6	Steve Joachim	QB	6'3"	215	24		
3	Denver	46	Al Krevis	OT	6'6"	263	24			John Ebersole	LB	6'3"	235	27	1		Joe Namath	QB	6'2"	200	33		
0	Miami	16	John Roman	OT	6'4"	248	24			Mike Hennigan	LB	6'2"	225	24			Richard Todd	QB	6'2"	210	22		6
6	San Francisco	17	Robert Woods	OT	6'3"	259	26			Larry Keller	LB	6'2"	220	22	1		Clark Gaines	HB	6'1"	192	22		30
17	BUFFALO	14	Gary Puetz	OG-OT	6'4"	267	24			Bob Martin	LB	6'1"	217	22	2		Louie Giammona	HB	5'9"	180	23		6
7	New England	41	Randy Rasmussen	OG	6'2"	255	31			Steve Poole	LB	6'1"	232	22		6	Bob Gresham	HB	5'11"	200	28		
0	BALTIMORE	20	Darrell Austin	C-OG	6'4"	252	24			James Rosecrans	LB	6'1"	230	23			Jazz Jackson	HB	5'8"	174	24		
19	Buffalo	14	Joe Fields	C-OG	6'2"	245	22			Carl Russ	LB	6'2"	227	23			Steve Rogers	HB	6'2"	205	23		
7	MIAMI	27	Richard Neal	DE	6'3"	263	28			Harry Howard	DB	6'	189	26			Allen Carter (from NE)	FB	5'11"	208	23		
34	TAMPA BAY	0	Billy Newsome	DE	6'4"	268	28			Tommy Marvaso	DB	6'1"	190	22			Steve Davis	FB-HB	6'1"	210	26		18
24	NEW ENGLAND	38	Lawrence Pillers	DE	6'3"	250	23			Burgess Owens	DB	6'2"	200	25			Ed Marinaro	FB	6'2"	219	26		12
16	Baltimore	33	Carl Barzilauskas	DT	6'6"	265	25			Rich Sowells	DB	6'	181	27	2		Jerome Barkum	WR	6'3"	212	26		6
16	WASHINGTON	37	Larry Faulk	DT-DE	6'3"	249	23			Shafer Suggs	DB	6'1"	194	23	1		Don Buckey	WR	5'11"	180	22		
3	CINCINNATI	42	Ed Galigher	DT	6'4"	253	25			Ed Taylor	DB	6'	172	23	2		Keith Denson	WR	5'8"	165	24		
										Phil Wise	DB	6'	202	27			Clint Haserlig	WR	6'	189	24		
			Mark Lomas – Knee Injury														David Knight	WR	6'1"	175	25		12
			Wayne Mulligan – Knee Injury							Don Coleman – Knee Injury							Lou Piccone	WR	5'9"	184	27		6
																	Howard Satterwhite	WR	5'11"	185	23		
																	Rich Caster	TE-WR	6'5"	224	27		6
																	Richard Osborne (from PHI.)	TE	6'3"	230	22		6
																	Duane Carrell	K	5'10"	185	26		
																	Pat Leahy	K	6'	200	25		49

BUFFALO BILLS 2-12 Lou Saban (2-3) Jim Ringo (0-9)

Scores of Each Game			Use Name	Pos.	Hgt	Wgt	Age	Int	Pts	Use Name	Pos.	Hgt	Wgt	Age	Int	Pts	Use Name	Pos.	Hgt	Wgt	Age	Int	Pts
21	Miami	30	Joe Devlin	OT	6'5"	258	22			Bo Cornell	LB	6'1"	222	27			Joe Ferguson	QB	6'1"	184	26		
3	HOUSTON	13	Dave Foley	OT	6'5"	247	28			Dan Jilek	LB	6'2"	212	22	2		Gary Marangi	QB	6'1"	203	24		12
14	Tampa Bay	9	Donnie Green	OT	6'7"	252	28			Merv Krakau	LB	6'2"	233	25	1		Sam Wyche (from STL)	QB	6'4"	220	30		
50	KANSAS CITY	17	Bill Adams	OG-OT	6'2"	246	26			Bob Nelson	LB	6'4"	232	23			Roland Hooks	HB	6'	197	23		
14	N.Y. Jets	17	Joe DeLamielleure	OG	6'3"	248	25			Tom Ruud	LB	6'2"	223	23			Darnell Powell	HB	6'	197	22		
13	BALTIMORE	31	Reggie McKenzie	OG	6'4"	242	26			John Skorupan	LB	6'2"	221	25	1		Andy Reid	HB	6'	195	22		
22	NEW ENGLAND	26	Mike Montler	C	6'4"	245	32			Tim Anderson	DB	6'	194	27			O.J. Simpson	HB	6'2"	212	29		54
14	N.Y. JETS	19	Willie Parker	C-OG	6'3"	245	27			Cliff Brooks (from PHI & NYJ)	DB	6'1"	190	27			Vic Washington	HB	5'10"	195	30		
10	New England	20	Bob Patton	C	6'1"	245	22			Mario Clark	DB	6'2"	190	22	2		Jim Braxton	FB	6'2"	242	27		
10	Dallas	17	Mark Johnson	DE	6'2"	240	23			Steve Freeman	DB	5'11"	185	23			Jeff Kinney (from K.C.)	FB-HB	6'2"	215	26		6
13	SAN DIEGO	34	Ken Jones	DE	6'5"	252	23			Van Green (from CLE)	DB	6'1"	192	25			Eddie Ray	FB	6'1"	240	29		
14	Detroit	27	Jeff Lloyd	DE	6'6"	255	22			Tony Greene	DB	5'10"	170	27	5	6	Bob Chandler	WR	6'	180	27		60
27	Miami	45	Marty Smith	DE	6'3"	250	22			Dwight Harrison	DB	6'1"	186	27	1		Emmett Edwards (from HOU)	WR	6'1"	190	24		
20	Baltimore	58	Sherman White	DE	6'5"	245	27	1		Doug Jones	DB	6'2"	205	26	3		Robert Gaddis	WR	5'11"	178	24		
			Mike Kadish	DT	6'5"	270	26			Keith Moody	DB	5'10"	171	23	3	6	John Holland	WR	6'	190	24		18
			Ben Williams	DT	6'3"	258	22										Fred Coleman	TE	6'4"	240	23		
			Jeff Yeates (to ATL)	DT	6'3"	248	25			Ron Holliday – Knee Injury							Reuben Gant	TE-WR	6'4"	225	24		18
										Robert James – Knee Injury							Paul Seymour	TE	6'5"	245	26		
																	Marv Bateman	K	6'4"	214	26		
																	George Jakowenko	K	5'9"	180	28		57

*—Overtime

BALTIMORE COLTS

RUSHING

Last Name	No.	Yds	Avg	TD
Mitchell	289	1200	4.2	5
Leaks	118	445	3.8	7
McCauley	69	227	3.3	9
R. Lee	41	220	5.4	1
Jones	38	214	5.6	2
Doughty	2	7	2.3	0
Stevens	1	3	3.0	1
Troup	5	−1	0.2	1
D. Lee	1	−12	−12.0	0

RECEIVING

Last Name	No.	Yds	Avg	TD
Mitchell	60	555	9	3
Carr	43	1112	26	11
Doughty	40	628	16	5
McCauley	34	347	10	2
Chester	24	467	19	3
Leaks	8	43	5	0
Scott	3	35	12	0
Kennedy	1	32	32	0
Thompson	1	11	11	0
R. Lee	1	−9	−9	0

PUNT RETURNS

Last Name	No.	Yds	Avg	TD
Stevens	39	315	8	0
R. Lee	1	0	0	0

KICKOFF RETURNS

Last Name	No.	Yds	Avg	TD
Stevens	30	710	24	0
Laird	7	143	20	0
Kennedy	4	64	16	0
Wallace	3	61	20	0
R. Lee	3	24	8	0
Pratt	1	21	21	0
Scott	1	20	20	0
McCauley	1	17	17	0
Novak	1	12	12	0
Huff	1	0	0	0

PASSING – PUNTING – KICKING

PASSING	Att	Comp	%	Yds	Yd/Att	TD	Int–%	RK
Jones	343	207	60	3104	9.0	24	9– 3	2
Troup	18	8	44	117	6.5	0	1– 6	

PUNTING	No	Avg
D. Lee	59	39.7

KICKING	XP	Att	%	FG	Att	%
Linhart	49	50	98	20	27	74

NEW ENGLAND PATRIOTS

RUSHING

Last Name	No.	Yds	Avg	TD
Cunningham	172	824	4.8	3
Calhoun	129	721	5.6	1
Johnson	169	699	4.1	6
Grogan	60	397	6.6	12
Phillips	24	164	6.8	1
Forte	25	100	4.0	1
Stingley	8	45	5.6	0
Francis	2	12	6.0	0
Burks	1	2	2.0	0
Patrick	1	−16	−16.0	0

RECEIVING

Last Name	No.	Yds	Avg	TD
Johnson	29	343	12	4
Cunningham	27	299	11	0
Francis	26	367	14	3
Stingley	17	370	22	4
Calhoun	12	56	5	0
Vataha	11	192	17	1
Briscoe	10	136	14	1
Chandler	5	49	10	3
Forte	3	9	3	1
Burks	2	27	14	0
Phillips	1	18	18	0
Brock	1	6	6	1

PUNT RETURNS

Last Name	No.	Yds	Avg	TD
Haynes	45	608	14	2
Beaudoin	2	18	9	0
Stingley	1	2	2	0

KICKOFF RETURNS

Last Name	No.	Yds	Avg	TD
Phillips	14	397	28	0
Calhoun	9	183	20	0
Beaudoin	6	134	22	0
Forte	3	62	21	0
Conn	2	29	15	0
McKay	1	23	23	0

PASSING – PUNTING – KICKING

PASSING	Att	Comp	%	Yds	Yd/Att	TD	Int–%	RK
Grogan	302	145	48	1903	6.3	18	20– 7	12
Owen	5	1	20	7	1.4	0	0– 0	
Johnson	2	0	0	0	0.0	0	0– 0	

PUNTING	No	Avg
Patrick	67	40.1

KICKING	XP	Att	%	FG	Att	%
Smith	42	46	91	15	25	60
Zabel	1	1	100			

MIAMI DOLPHINS

RUSHING

Last Name	No.	Yds	Avg	TD
Malone	186	797	4.3	4
Bulaich	122	540	4.4	4
Winfrey	52	205	3.9	1
Nottingham	63	185	2.9	3
Davis	31	160	5.2	1
Griese	23	108	4.7	0
Solomon	4	60	15.0	1
N. Moore	4	36	9.0	0
Seiple	3	14	4.7	0
Strock	2	13	6.5	1
Heath	1	0	0.0	0

RECEIVING

Last Name	No.	Yds	Avg	TD
N. Moore	33	625	19	4
Bulaich	28	151	5	0
Solomon	27	453	17	2
Harris	22	372	17	1
Mandich	22	260	12	4
Twilley	14	214	15	1
Tillman	13	130	10	1
Seiple	10	138	14	1
Malone	9	103	11	0
Winfrey	6	55	9	1
Nottingham	4	33	8	0
McCreary	2	51	26	0
Davis	2	8	4	0
Holmes	1	11	11	0

PUNT RETURNS

Last Name	No.	Yds	Avg	TD
Solomon	13	205	16	1
Harris	9	79	9	0
N. Moore	8	72	9	0
Babb	3	38	13	0
Anderson	2	21	11	0

KICKOFF RETURNS

Last Name	No.	Yds	Avg	TD
Davis	26	617	24	0
Harris	17	559	33	0
Nottingham	6	107	18	0
Holmes	4	90	23	0
N. Moore	2	28	14	0
Winfrey	2	24	12	0
Solomon	1	12	12	0
Tillman	1	0	0	0

PASSING – PUNTING – KICKING

PASSING	Att	Comp	%	Yds	Yd/Att	TD	Int–%	RK
Griese	272	162	60	2097	7.7	11	12– 4	4
Strock	47	21	45	359	7.6	3	2– 4	
Morrall	26	10	39	148	5.7	1	1– 4	
Solomon	1	0	0	0	0.0	0	0– 0	

PUNTING	No	Avg
Seiple	62	38.2

KICKING	XP	Att	%	FG	Att	%
Yepremian	29	31	94	16	23	70

NEW YORK JETS

RUSHING

Last Name	No.	Yds	Avg	TD
Gaines	157	724	4.6	3
Davis	94	418	4.4	3
Marinaro	77	312	4.1	2
Giammona	39	158	3.8	1
Todd	28	107	3.8	1
Gresham	30	92	3.1	0
Caster	6	73	12.2	0
Buttle	1	26	26.0	0
Piccone	1	11	11.0	0
Jackson	1	6	6.0	0
Namath	2	5	2.5	0
Carrell	2	0	0.0	0

RECEIVING

Last Name	No.	Yds	Avg	TD
Gaines	41	400	10	2
Caster	31	391	13	1
Marinaro	21	168	8	0
Knight	20	403	20	2
Giammona	15	145	10	0
Piccone	12	147	12	0
Gresham	11	66	6	0
Davis	8	57	7	0
Satterwhite	7	110	16	0
Barkum	5	54	11	1
Buckey	5	36	7	0
Osborne	2	9	5	1
Jackson	2	3	2	0

PUNT RETURNS

Last Name	No.	Yds	Avg	TD
Piccone	21	173	8	1
Giammona	12	117	10	0
Jackson	6	−1	0	0
Marvaso	1	0	0	0

KICKOFF RETURNS

Last Name	No.	Yds	Avg	TD
Piccone	31	699	23	0
Giammona	23	527	23	0
Jackson	10	207	21	0
Denson	6	129	22	0
Hennigan	1	22	22	0
Osborne	1	8	8	0
Gaines	1	5	5	0

PASSING – PUNTING – KICKING

PASSING	Att	Comp	%	Yds	Yd/Att	TD	Int–%	RK
Namath	230	114	50	1090	4.7	4	16– 7	14
Todd	162	65	40	870	5.4	3	12– 7	15
Gresham	1	1	100	29	29.0	0	0– 0	

PUNTING	No	Avg.
Carrell	81	39.7

KICKING	XP	Att	%	FG	Att	%
Leahy	16	20	80	11	16	69

BUFFALO BILLS

RUSHING

Last Name	No.	Yds	Avg	TD
Simpson	290	1503	5.2	8
Kinney	118	482	4.1	1
Marangi	39	230	5.9	2
Hooks	25	116	4.6	0
Ferguson	18	81	4.5	0
Washington	22	65	3.0	0
Ray	24	56	2.3	0
Powell	11	40	3.6	0
Braxton	1	0	0.0	0
Chandler	1	0	0.0	0
Edwards	1	0	0.0	0

RECEIVING

Last Name	No.	Yds	Avg	TD
Chandler	61	824	14	10
Simpson	22	259	12	1
Seymour	16	169	11	0
Holland	15	299	20	2
Kinney	14	78	6	0
Gant	12	263	22	3
Hooks	6	72	12	0
Washington	3	29	10	0
Ray	3	26	9	0
Edwards	2	53	27	0
Montler	1	6	6	0
Powell	1	6	6	0

PUNT RETURNS

Last Name	No.	Yds	Avg	TD
Moody	16	166	10	1
Hooks	11	45	4	0
Holland	4	11	3	0
Gaddis	1	6	6	0

KICKOFF RETURNS

Last Name	No.	Yds	Avg	TD
Moody	26	605	23	0
Hooks	23	521	23	0
Ruud	6	68	11	0
Powell	4	101	25	0
Holland	4	62	16	0
Washington	3	63	21	0
Cornell	2	32	16	0
Gaddis	1	16	16	0

PASSING – PUNTING – KICKING

PASSING	Att	Comp	%	Yds	Yd/Att	TD	Int–%	RK
Ferguson	151	74	49	1086	7.2	9	1– 1	3
Marangi	232	82	35	998	4.3	7	16– 7	16
Wyche	1	1	100	5	5.0	0	0– 0	

PUNTING	No	Avg
Bateman	86	42.8

KICKING	XP	Att	%	FG	Att	%
Jakowenko	21	24	88	12	17	71

PITTSBURGH STEELERS 10-4 Chuck Noll

Scores of Each Game		
28	Oakland	31
31	CLEVELAND	14
27	NEW ENGLAND	30
6	Minnesota	17
16	Cleveland	18
23	CINCINNATI	6
27	N.Y. Giants	0
23	SAN DIEGO	0
45	Kansas City	0
14	MIAMI	3
32	HOUSTON	16
7	Cincinnati	3
42	TAMPA BAY	0
21	Houston	0

Use Name	Pos.	Hgt	Wgt	Age	Int	Pts
Gordon Gravelle	OT	6'5"	250	27		
Jon Kolb	OT	6'2"	262	29		
Jim Clack	OG	6'3"	250	28		
Sam Davis	OG	6'1"	255	32		
Gerry Mullins	OG-OT	6'3"	244	27		
Ray Mansfield	C	6'3"	260	35		
Ray Pinney	C-OT	6'4"	240	22		
Mike Webster	C	6'1"	250	24		
John Banaszak	DE	6'3"	244	26		
L.C. Greenwood	DE	6'5"	250	29		
Dwight White	DE	6'4"	255	27		
Gary Dunn	DT	6'3"	240	23		
Steve Furness	DT-DE	6'4"	255	25		
Joe Greene	DT	6'4"	275	29		
Ernie Holmes	DT	6'3"	260	28		
Jack Ham	LB	6'3"	225	27	2	
Marv Kellum	LB	6'2"	225	24		
Jack Lambert	LB	6'4"	220	24	2	
Andy Russell	LB	6'3"	225	34	1	
Loren Toews	LB	6'3"	222	24		2
Jim Allen	DB	6'2"	194	24		
Mel Blount	DB	6'3"	205	28	6	
Glen Edwards	DB	6'	185	29	6	
Donnie Shell	DB	5'11"	190	24	1	
J.T. Thomas	DB	6'2"	196	25	2	
Mike Wagner	DB	6'1"	200	27	2	
Terry Bradshaw	QB	6'3"	200	27		18
Neil Graff (from SEA)	QB	6'3"	200	26		
Mike Kruczek	QB	6'1"	196	23		12
Rocky Bleier	HB	5'11"	210	30		30
Jack Deloplaine	HB	5'10"	205	22		12
John Fuqua	HB	5'11"	200	29		6
Franco Harris	FB	6'2"	225	26		84
Reggie Harrison	FB	5'11"	220	26		24
Theo Bell	WR	5'11"	180	22		6
Frank Lewis	WR	6'1"	196	29		12
Ernest Pough	WR	6'1"	174	24		6
John Stallworth	WR	6'2"	183	24		18
Lynn Swann	WR	6'	180	24		18
Larry Brown	TE	6'4"	229	27		
Bennie Cunningham	TE	6'4"	255	21		6
Randy Grossman	TE	6'1"	215	22		6
Roy Gerela	K	5'10"	185	28		82
Bobby Walden	K	6'	190	38		

Mike Collier – Knee Injury
Reggie Garrett – Back Injury

CINCINNATI BENGALS 10-4 Bill Johnson

Scores of Each Game		
17	DENVER	7
27	Baltimore	28
28	GREEN BAY	7
45	Cleveland	24
21	TAMPA BAY	0
6	Pittsburgh	23
27	Houston	7
21	CLEVELAND	6
20	LOS ANGELES	12
31	HOUSTON	27
27	Kansas City	24
3	PITTSBURGH	7
20	Oakland	35
42	N.Y. Jets	3

Use Name	Pos.	Hgt	Wgt	Age	Int	Pts
Vern Holland	OT	6'5"	272	28		
Ron Hunt	OT	6'6"	274	21		
Rufus Mayes	OT	6'5"	268	28		
Glenn Bujnoch	OG	6'5"	260	22		
Greg Fairchild	OG-OT	6'4"	258	22		
Dave Lapham	OG	6'4"	258	24		
John Shinners	OG	6'2"	259	29		
Bob Johnson	C	6'5"	255	30		
Coy Bacon	DE	6'4"	270	34		2
Gary Burley	DE	6'3"	262	23		
Ken Johnson	DE	6'5"	262	29		
Bob Brown	DT	6'5"	280	36		
Ron Carpenter	DT	6'4"	265	28		
Bill Kollar	DT	6'4"	256	23		
Glenn Cameron	LB	6'2"	230	23		
Chris Devlin	LB	6'3"	228	22	1	
Bo Harris	LB	6'3"	228	23	2	
Jim LeClair	LB	6'2"	237	25	1	
Ron Pritchard	LB	6'1"	226	29	1	
Reggie Williams	LB	6'1"	230	21	1	
Tommy Casanova	DB	6'2"	194	26	5	18
Marvin Cobb	DB	6'	191	23	3	
Bernard Jackson	DB	6'	179	26	1	
Melvin Morgan	DB	6'	175	23		6
Lemar Parrish	DB	5'11"	180	28	2	
Scott Perry	DB	6'	185	22		
Ken Riley	DB	6'	183	29	9	6
Ken Anderson	QB	6'1"	210	27		6
John Reaves	QB	6'3"	202	26		
Tony Davis	HB	5'10"	210	23		6
Lenvil Elliott	HB	6'	207	24		18
Archie Griffin	HB	5'9"	191	22		18
Willie Shelby	HB	5'10"	190	23		6
Booby Clark	FB	6'2"	245	25		48
Stan Fritts	FB-HB	6'1"	215	23		18
Billy Brooks	WR	6'3"	215	23		
Isaac Curtis	WR	6'	195	25		36
John McDaniel	WR	6'1"	194	24		6
Pat McInally	WR	6'6"	200	23		
Chip Myers	WR	6'4"	208	31		6
Bruce Coslet	TE	6'3"	225	30		12
Bob Trumpy	TE	6'6"	231	31		42
Chris Bahr	K	5'9"	170	23		81

CLEVELAND BROWNS 9-5 Forrest Gregg

Scores of Each Game		
38	N.Y. JETS	17
14	Pittsburgh	31
13	Denver	44
24	CINCINNATI	45
18	PITTSBURGH	16
20	Atlanta	17
21	SAN DIEGO	17
6	Cincinnati	21
21	Houston	7
24	PHILADELPHIA	3
24	Tampa Bay	7
17	MIAMI	13
13	HOUSTON	10
14	Kansas City	39

Use Name	Pos.	Hgt	Wgt	Age	Int	Pts
Barry Darrow	OT	6'7"	260	26		
Doug Dieken	OT	6'5"	252	27		
Henry Sheppard	OT-OG	6'6"	246	23		
Pete Adams	OG	6'4"	260	25		
Al Dennis	OG	6'4"	250	25		
Robert Jackson	OG	6'5"	245	23		
Tom DeLeone	C	6'2"	248	26		
Gerry Sullivan	C-OT	6'4"	250	24		
Earl Edwards	DE-DT	6'6"	256	30		
Joe Jones	DE	6'6"	250	28		6
Mack Mitchell	DE	6'7"	245	24		
Mike St. Clair	DE	6'5"	245	22		
Walter Johnson	DT	6'3"	265	33		
Jerry Sherk	DT	6'4"	250	28	1	
Dick Ambrose	LB	6'	235	23		
Bob Babich	LB	6'2"	231	29	2	
John Garlington	LB	6'1"	221	30		
Dave Graf	LB	6'2"	215	23		
Charlie Hall	LB	6'3"	230	27	1	
Gerald Irons	LB	6'2"	230	29	1	
Ron Bolton	DB	6'2"	170	26	3	6
Terry Brown	DB	6'1"	205	29	1	
Neil Craig	DB	6'1"	190	28	1	
Bill Craven	DB	5'11"	190	24		
Thom Darden	DB	6'2"	193	26	7	
Tony Peters	DB	6'1"	192	23		
Clarence Scott	DB	6'	180	27	4	
Dave Mays	QB	6'1"	204	27		
Mike Phipps	QB	6'2"	205	28		
Brian Sipe	QB	6'1"	190	27		1
Brian Duncan	HB	6'	201	24		6
Cleo Miller	HB-FB	5'11"	202	23		24
Larry Poole	HB	6'	195	24		6
Greg Pruitt	HB	5'10"	190	25		30
Mike Pruitt	FB	6'	214	22		
Ricky Feacher (from NE)	WR	5'10"	174	22		
Steve Holden	WR	6'	194	25		6
Dave Logan	WR	6'4"	226	22		
Willie Miller	WR	5'9"	172	29		
Reggie Rucker	WR	6'2"	190	28		48
Paul Warfield	WR	6'	188	33		36
Gary Parris	TE	6'2"	226	26		
Oscar Roan	TE	6'6"	214	24		24
Don Cockroft	K	6'1"	195	31		72

Chuck Hutchinson – Knee Injury
Billy LeFear – Injury

HOUSTON OILERS 5-9 Bum Phillips

Scores of Each Game		
20	TAMPA BAY	0
13	Buffalo	3
13	OAKLAND	14
31	New Orleans	26
17	DENVER	3
27	San Diego	30
7	CINCINNATI	27
14	Baltimore	38
7	CLEVELAND	21
27	Cincinnati	31
16	Pittsburgh	32
20	ATLANTA	14
10	Cleveland	13
0	PITTSBURGH	21

Use Name	Pos.	Hgt	Wgt	Age	Int	Pts
Elbert Drungo	OT	6'5"	265	33		
Kevin Hunt	OT	6'5"	260	27		
Greg Sampson	OT	6'6"	270	25		
Bobby Simon	OT-OG	6'3	252	23		
Ed Fisher	OG	6'3"	250	27		
Dennis Havig	OG	6'2"	256	27		
Conway Hayman	OG	6'3"	262	27		
Ron Lou	C	6'2"	242	25		
Carl Mauck	C	6'3"	250	29		
Elvin Bethea	DE	6'3	255	30		
Albert Burton	DE	6'5"	270	24		
Joe Owens	DE	6'2"	245	29		
Bubba Smith	DE	6'7"	265	31		
Tody Smith (to BUF)	DE	6'5"	250	27		
Curley Culp	NT	6'1"	265	30		
John Little	NT	6'3"	250	29		
Duane Benson	LB	6'2"	225	31		
Gregg Bingham	LB	6'1"	230	25	2	
Robert Brazile	LB	6'4"	238	23	1	
Steve Kiner	LB	6'	225	29		
Tim Rossovich	LB	6'4"	240	30		
Ted Thompson	LB	6'1"	220	23		
Ted Washington	LB	6'1"	245	28		
Willie Alexander	DB	6'2"	195	26		
Bob Atkins	DB	6'3"	210	30		
Zeke Moore	DB	6'2"	195	32	1	
Mike Reinfeldt (from OAK.)	DB	6'2"	178	23	1	
Greg Stemrick	DB	5'11"	185	24	1	
Mike Weger	DB	6'2"	200	30		
C.L. Whittington	DB	6'1"	200	24	5	6
Sam Williams	DB	6'2"	192	24		
James Foote	QB	6'2"	210	24		
John Hadl	QB	6'2"	215	36		
Dan Pastorini	QB	6'2"	205	27		
Ronnie Coleman	HB	5'10"	198	25		36
Al Johnson	HB	6'	200	26		
Altie Taylor	HB	5'10"	200	28		
Joe Dawkins	FB	5'11"	220	28		6
Don Hardeman	FB	6'2"	235	24		6
Fred Willis	FB	6'	205	28		18
Mel Baker	WR	6'	182	26		
Mike Barber	WR-TE	6'3"	235	23		
Jim Beirne	WR	6'2"	208	29		
Ken Burrough	WR	6'4"	210	28		42
Billy Johnson	WR	5'9"	170	24		24
Earl Thomas	WR	6'3"	215	27		
Mack Alston	TE	6'2"	230	29		6
Alvis Darby (from SEA)	TE	6'5"	216	21		
John Sawyer	TE	6'2"	230	23		6
Skip Butler	K	6'2"	200	28		72
Leroy Clark	K	5'11"	200	26		

Willie Frazier – Knee Injury
Willie Rogers – Injury

PITTSBURGH STEELERS

RUSHING

Last Name	No.	Yds	Avg	TD
Harris	289	1128	3.9	14
Bleier	220	1036	4.7	5
Harrison	54	235	4.4	4
Bradshaw	31	219	7.1	3
Kruczek	18	106	5.9	2
Deloplaine	17	91	5.4	2
Fugua	15	63	4.2	1
Stallworth	0	47	–	1
Lewis	2	24	12.0	1
Pough	2	8	4.0	0
Walden	3	7	2.3	0
Bell	1	5	5.0	0
Swann	1	2	2.0	0

RECEIVING

Last Name	No.	Yds	Avg	TD
Swann	28	516	18	3
Bleier	24	294	12	0
Harris	23	151	7	0
Lewis	17	306	18	1
Grossman	15	181	12	1
Stallworth	9	111	12	2
Pough	8	161	20	1
Brown	7	97	14	0
Cunningham	5	49	10	1
Bell	3	43	14	1
Harrison	2	19	10	0
Fugua	1	4	4	0
Deloplaine	1	3	3	0

PUNT RETURNS

Last Name	No.	Yds	Avg	TD
Bell	39	390	10	0
Deloplaine	17	150	9	0
Fugua	11	77	7	0
Swann	3	11	4	0
Edwards	1	8	8	0

KICKOFF RETURNS

Last Name	No.	Yds	Avg	TD
Pough	18	369	21	0
Deloplaine	17	385	23	0
Fugua	4	75	19	0
Harrison	1	26	26	0
Clack	1	0	0	0

PASSING – PUNTING – KICKING

PASSING	Att	Comp	%	Yds	Yd/Att	TD	Int–%	RK
Bradshaw	192	92	48	1177	6.1	10	9– 5	10
Kruczek	85	51	60	758	8.9	0	3– 4	

PUNTING	No	Avg
Walden	76	39.2

KICKING	XP	Att	%	FG	Att	%
Gerella	40	43	93	14	26	54

CINCINNATI BENGALS

RUSHING

Last Name	No.	Yds	Avg	TD
Clark	151	671	4.4	7
Griffin	138	625	4.5	3
Elliott	69	276	4.0	0
Fritts	47	200	4.3	3
Davis	36	178	4.9	1
Anderson	31	134	4.3	1
Curtis	3	29	9.7	0
Shelby	5	9	1.8	0
Brooks	1	−13	−13.0	0

RECEIVING

Last Name	No.	Yds	Avg	TD
Curtis	41	766	19	6
Clark	23	158	7	1
Elliott	22	188	9	3
Trumpy	21	323	15	7
Myers	17	267	16	1
Brooks	16	191	12	0
Griffin	16	138	9	0
McDaniel	12	232	19	1
Fritts	9	75	8	0
Coslet	5	73	15	0
Davis	4	29	7	0
Shelby	1	3	3	0

PUNT RETURNS

Last Name	No.	Yds	Avg	TD
Shelby	21	162	8	0
Parrish	20	122	6	0
Casanova	10	45	5	0
Cobb	3	14	5	0

KICKOFF RETURNS

Last Name	No.	Yds	Avg	TD
Shelby	30	761	25	1
Elliott	5	98	20	0
Davis	4	21	5	0
Parrish	3	62	21	0
Griffin	3	56	19	0
Hunt	2	24	12	0
Morgan	1	14	14	0
Fritts	1	10	10	0

PASSING – PUNTING – KICKING

PASSING	Att	Comp	%	Yds	Yd/Att	TD	Int–%	RK
Anderson	338	179	53	2367	7.0	19	14– 4	7
Reaves	22	8	36	76	3.5	2	1– 5	

PUNTING	No	Avg
McInally	76	39.5

KICKING	XP	Att	%	FG	Att	%
Bahr	39	42	93	14	27	52

CLEVELAND BROWNS

RUSHING

Last Name	No.	Yds	Avg	TD
G. Pruitt	209	1000	4.8	4
C. Miller	153	613	4.0	4
Poole	78	356	4.6	1
M. Pruitt	52	138	2.7	0
Sipe	18	71	3.9	0
Duncan	11	44	4.0	0
Rucker	2	30	15.0	0
Phipps	4	26	6.5	0
Mays	5	14	2.8	0
Warfield	1	3	3.0	0

RECEIVING

Last Name	No.	Yds	Avg	TD
Rucker	49	676	14	8
G. Pruitt	45	341	8	1
Warfield	38	613	16	6
C. Miller	16	145	9	0
Roan	15	174	12	4
Poole	14	70	5	0
Holden	8	128	16	1
M. Pruitt	8	26	3	0
Duncan	6	49	8	1
Logan	5	104	21	0
Parris	5	73	15	0
Feacher	2	38	19	0

PUNT RETURNS

Last Name	No.	Yds	Avg	TD
Holden	31	205	7	0
Feacher	13	142	11	0
W. Miller	5	22	4	0

KICKOFF RETURNS

Last Name	No.	Yds	Avg	TD
Feacher	24	551	23	0
Holden	19	461	24	0
Duncan	6	145	24	0
M. Pruitt	6	106	18	0
Poole	3	62	21	0
G. Pruitt	1	27	27	0
C. Miller	1	23	23	0
Ambrose	1	16	16	0
Jackson	1	16	16	0
Graf	1	15	15	0
W. Miller	1	0	0	0

PASSING – PUNTING – KICKING

PASSING	Att	Comp	%	Yds	Yd/Att	TD	Int–%	RK
Sipe	312	178	57	2113	6.8	17	14– 4	6
Phipps	37	20	54	146	3.9	3	0– 0	
Mays	20	9	45	101	5.1	0	1– 5	
G. Pruitt	3	2	67	39	13.0	1	0– 0	
Cockroft	1	0	0	0	0.0	0	0 0	

PUNTING	No	Avg
Cockroft	64	38.9
Mays	2	45.5

KICKING	XP	Att	%	FG	Att	%
Cockroft	27	30	90	15	28	54
Sipe	1	1	100			

HOUSTON OILERS

RUSHING

Last Name	No.	Yds	Avg	TD
Coleman	171	684	4.0	2
Willis	148	542	3.7	2
Hardeman	32	114	3.6	1
Dawkins	31	61	2.0	1
Pastorini	11	45	4.1	0
Burrough	3	22	7.3	0
Taylor	5	11	2.2	0
Hadl	7	11	1.6	0
B. Johnson	6	6	1.0	0
Baker	1	2	2.0	0
Butler	1	0	0.0	0

RECEIVING

Last Name	No.	Yds	Avg	TD
Burrough	51	932	18	7
B. Johnson	47	495	11	4
Coleman	40	247	6	3
Willis	32	266	8	1
Alston	19	174	9	1
Sawyer	18	208	12	1
Hardeman	7	25	4	0
Thomas	4	15	4	0
Baker	3	32	11	0
Dawkins	3	21	7	0
Taylor	2	15	8	0
Stemrick	1	10	10	0

PUNT RETURNS

Last Name	No.	Yds	Avg	TD
B. Johnson	38	403	11	0
Coleman	7	91	13	1
Whittington	3	10	3	0

KICKOFF RETURNS

Last Name	No.	Yds	Avg	TD
B. Johnson	26	579	22	0
Taylor	15	302	20	0
A. Johnson	8	150	19	0
Hardeman	7	171	24	0
Baker	1	15	15	0
Beirne	1	12	12	0

PASSING – PUNTING – KICKING

PASSING	Att	Comp	%	Yds	Yd/Att	TD	Int–%	RK
Pastorini	309	167	54	1795	5.8	10	10– 3	9
Hadl	113	60	53	634	5.6	7	8– 7	
Coleman	1	0	0	0	0.0	0	1–100	

PUNTING	No	Avg
Pastorini	70	36.7
Butler	11	33.6
Clark	10	33.5
Sawyer	1	32.0

KICKING	XP	Att	%	FG	Att	%
Butler	24	24	100	16	27	59

OAKLAND RAIDERS 13-1 John Madden

Scores of Each Game		
31	PITTSBURGH	28
24	Kansas City	21
14	Houston	13
17	New England	48
27	San Diego	17
17	Denver	10
18	GREEN BAY	14
19	DENVER	6
28	Chicago	27
21	KANSAS CITY	10
26	Philadelphia	7
49	TAMPA BAY	16
35	CINCINNATI	20
24	SAN DIEGO	0

Use Name	Pos.	Hgt	Wgt	Age	Int	Pts.
Henry Lawrence	OT	6'4"	273	24		
Art Shell	OT	6'5"	265	29		
John Vella	OT	6'4"	260	26		
George Buehler	OG	6'2"	270	29		
Dan Medlin	OG	6'4"	252	26		
Gene Upshaw	OG	6'5"	255	31		
Dave Dalby	C	6'2"	250	25		
Steve Sylvester	C	6'4"	262	23		
John Matuszak	DE	6'8"	275	25		
Herb McMath	DE	6'4"	245	21		
Charles Philyaw	DE	6'9"	270	22		
Dave Rowe	DT	6'6"	271	31		
Otis Sistrunk	DT	6'4"	273	28		

Horace Jones – Knee Injury
Kelvin Korver – Knee Injury
Art Thoms – Knee Injury

Use Name	Pos.	Hgt	Wgt	Age	Int	Pts
Rodrigo Barnes	LB	6'1"	215	26		
Greg Blankenship (to PIT)	LB	6'1"	212	22		
Rik Bonness	LB	6'3"	220	22		
Willie Hall	LB	6'2"	225	26	2	
Ted Hendricks	LB	6'7"	220	28	1	2
Monte Johnson	LB	6'4"	240	24	4	
Floyd Rice	LB	6'3"	223	27		
Phil Villapiano	LB	6'1"	225	27	1	
Butch Atkinson	DB	6'	185	29		
Willie Brown	DB	6'1"	210	35	3	
Neal Colzie	DB	6'2"	205	23		
Charlie Phillips	DB	6'2"	215	23	1	
Jack Tatum	DB	5'10"	206	27	2	
Skip Thomas	DB	6'1"	205	26	2	

Marv Hubbard – Shoulder Injury
Frank Tate – Injury

Use Name	Pos.	Hgt	Wgt	Age	Int	Pts
David Humm	QB	6'2"	184	24		
Mike Rae	QB	6'	190	25		6
Ken Stabler	QB	6'3"	215	30		6
Pete Banaszak	HB-FB	5'11"	210	32		30
Clarence Davis	HB	5'10"	195	27		18
Carl Garrett	HB	5'11"	205	29		6
Hubert Ginn	HB	5'11"	185	29		
Rick Jennings	HB	5'9"	180	23		
Manfred Moore (from TB)	HB	6'	199	25		
Terry Kunz	FB	6'1"	215	23		
Mark van Eeghen	FB	6'2"	225	24		18
Fred Biletnikoff	WR	6'1"	190	35		42
Morris Bradshaw	WR	6'	195	23		6
Cliff Branch	WR	5'11"	170	28		72
Mike Siani	WR	6'2"	195	26		12
Warren Bankston	TE	6'4"	235	29		6
Dave Casper	TE	6'4"	228	24		60
Ted Kwalick	TE	6'4"	225	29		
Ray Guy	K	6'3"	195	26		
Errol Mann (from DET)	K	6'	205	35		59
Fred Steinford	K	5'11"	180	22		28

DENVER BRONCOS 9-5 John Ralston

Scores of Each Game		
7	Cincinnati	17
46	N.Y. JETS	3
44	CLEVELAND	13
26	SAN DIEGO	0
3	Houston	17
10	OAKLAND	17
35	Kansas City	26
6	Oakland	19
48	TAMPA BAY	13
17	San Diego	0
14	N.Y. GIANTS	13
14	New England	38
17	KANSAS CITY	16
28	Chicago	14

Use Name	Pos.	Hgt	Wgt	Age	Int	Pts.
Bill Bain	OT	6'4"	270	24		
Glenn Hyde	OT	6'3"	250	25		
Claudie Minor	OT	6'4"	280	25		
Scott Parrish	OT	6'6"	270	23		
Tom Glassic	OG	6'3"	254	22		
Harvey Goodman	OG	6'4"	260	23		
Tommy Lyons	OG	6'2"	230	28		
Bobby Maples	C	6'3"	250	33		
Phil Olsen	C	6'5"	260	28		
Barney Chavous	DE	6'3"	252	25		
Paul Smith	DE	6'3"	256	31		
Jim White (from SEA)	DE	6'3"	260	27		
Lyle Alzado	DT	6'3"	252	27		
Rubin Carter	DT	6'	256	23		
John Grant	DT	6'3"	235	26		
Wayne Hammond	DT	6'5"	255	23		
Martin Imhof	DT	6'6"	255	26		
Randy Moore	DT	6'2"	241	22		

Use Name	Pos.	Hgt	Wgt	Age	Int	Pts
Rick Baska	LB	6'3"	225	24		
Larry Evans	LB	6'2"	216	23		
Randy Gradishar	LB	6'3"	233	24	3	6
Tom Jackson	LB	5'11"	220	25	7	6
Joe Rizzo	LB	6'1"	220	25	1	
Bob Swenson	LB	6'3"	220	23	2	
Godwin Turk	LB	6'2"	230	25		
Steve Foley	DB	6'2"	181	22	4	
Billy Hardee	DB	6'	185	22		
Calvin Jones	DB	5'7"	169	25	2	6
Chris Pane	DB	5'11"	181	23		
Randy Poltl	DB	6'3"	190	24	1	6
John Rowser	DB	6'1"	190	32	4	12
Bill Thompson	DB	6'1"	200	29		
Louis Wright	DB	6'2"	195	23		

Paul Howard – Injury
Carl Schaukowitz – Injury

Use Name	Pos.	Hgt	Wgt	Age	Int	Pts
Craig Penrose	QB	6'3"	222	23		
Steve Ramsey	QB	6'2"	210	28		
Norris Weese	QB	6'1"	195	25		
Otis Armstrong	HB	5'10"	196	25		36
Jim Kiick	HB	5'11"	215	30		12
Mike Franckowiak	FB	6'3"	220	23		
Jon Keyworth	FB	6'3"	230	25		24
Lonnie Perrin	FB	6'1"	222	24		12
Jack Dolbin	WR	5'10"	180	27		6
Haven Moses	WR	6'3"	208	30		42
John Schultz	WR	5'10"	182	23		
Rick Upchurch	WR	5'10"	170	24		36
Billy Van Heusen	WR	6'1"	200	30		
Boyd Brown	TE	6'4"	216	24		
Riley Odoms	TE	6'4"	230	26		30
Jim Turner	K	6'2"	205	35		81

Fran Lynch – Knee Injury
Charlie Smith – Knee Injury

SAN DIEGO CHARGERS 6-8 Tommy Prothro

Scores of Each Game		
30	Kansas City	16
23	Tampa Bay	0
43	ST. LOUIS	24
0	Denver	26
17	OAKLAND	27
30	HOUSTON	27
17	Cleveland	21
0	Pittsburgh	23
21	BALTIMORE	37
0	DENVER	17
34	Buffalo	13
20	KANSAS CITY	23
13	SAN FRANCISCO	*7
0	Oakland	24

Use Name	Pos.	Hgt	Wgt	Age	Int	Pts.
Billy Shields	OT	6'7"	272	23		
Ron Singleton	OT	6'7"	245	24		
Russ Washington	OT	6'6"	290	29		
Charles Aiu	OG	6'2"	248	22		
Don Macek	OG	6'3"	253	22		
Ralph Perretta	OG-C	6'2"	252	23		
Doug Wilkerson	OG	6'2"	262	29		
Ed Flanagan	C	6'3"	245	32		
Fred Dean	DE	6'3"	226	24		
Leroy Jones	DE	6'8"	245	25	1	
John Lee	DE	6'2"	247	23		
Charles DeJurnett	DT	6'4"	270	24		
Gary Johnson	DT	6'2"	262	24		
Louie Kelcher	DT	6'5"	282	23		

Booker Brown – Illness
John Teerlinck – Knee Injury

Use Name	Pos.	Hgt	Wgt	Age	Int	Pts
Don Goode	LB	6'2"	230	25	6	
Tom Graham	LB	6'2"	235	26	3	
Bob Horn	LB	6'3"	235	22	1	
Woodrow Lowe	LB	6'	227	22	1	
Rick Middleton	LB	6'2"	234	24		
Ray Preston	LB	6'	223	22		
Danny Colbert	DB	5'11"	182	25		
Chris Fletcher	DB	5'11"	189	27		
Mike Fuller	DB	5'9"	195	23	1	1
Tom Hayes	DB	6'1"	198	30	2	6
Hal Stringert	DB	5'11"	185	24	1	
Jim Tolbert	DB	6'3"	210	32		
Mike Williams	DB	5'10"	181	22		

Use Name	Pos.	Hgt	Wgt	Age	Int	Pts
Dan Fouts	QB	6'3"	204	25		
Neal Jeffrey	QB	6'1"	180	23		
Clint Longley	QB	6'1"	195	24		
Mercury Morris	HB	5'10"	192	29		12
Joe Washington	HB	5'10"	184	22		
Rickey Young	HB	6'2"	193	22		30
Bo Matthews	FB	6'4"	230	24		24
Sam Scarber	FB	6'2"	232	28		12
Don Woods	FB-HB	6'1"	210	25		24
Eddie Bell	WR	5'10"	160	28		
Larry Dorsey	WR	6'1"	195	23		
Walt Garrison	WR	6'1"	190	32		6
Charlie Joiner	WR	5'11"	180	28		42
Dwight McDonald	WR	6'2"	187	25		24
Artie Owens	WR	5'10"	170	23		6
Chuck Bradley	TE	6'6"	255	25		
Pat Curran	TE	6'3"	238	30		6
Larry Mialik	TE	6'2"	226	26		
Jeff West	TE	6'3"	220	23		
Toni Fritsch	K	5'7"	195	31		29
Mitch Hoopes (to HOU)	K	6'1"	210	23		
Ray Wersching	K	5'11"	222	26		26

KANSAS CITY CHIEFS 5-9 Paul Wiggin

Scores of Each Game		
16	SAN DIEGO	30
21	OAKLAND	24
17	NEW ORLEANS	27
17	Buffalo	50
33	Washington	30
20	Miami	*17
26	DENVER	35
28	Tampa Bay	19
0	PITTSBURGH	45
10	Oakland	21
24	CINCINNATI	27
23	San Diego	20
16	Denver	17
39	CLEVELAND	14

Use Name	Pos.	Hgt	Wgt	Age	Int	Pts.
Charlie Getty	OT	6'4"	260	24		
Matt Herkenhoff	OT	6'4"	255	25		
Jim Nicholson	OT	6'6"	261	26		
Ed Budde	OG	6'5"	265	35		
Tom Condon	OG	6'3"	240	23		
Rod Walters	OG	6'3"	258	22		
Charlie Ane	C	6'1"	233	24		
Orrin Olsen	C	6'1"	245	23		
Jack Rudnay	C	6'3"	240	28		
Larry Estes	DE-DT	6'6"	250	29		
John Lohmeyer	DE	6'4"	229	25		2
Whitney Paul	DE	6'3"	220	22		
Jim Wolf	DE	6'3"	250	24		
Wilbur Young	DE	6'6"	285	27		
Willie Lee	DT	6'5"	249	26		
Bob Maddox	DT	6'5"	248	27		
Keith Simons	DT	6'3"	254	22		

Use Name	Pos.	Hgt	Wgt	Age	Int	Pts
Billy Andrews	LB	6'	220	31	1	
Jimbo Elrod	LB	6'	209	22	1	
Willie Lanier	LB	6'1"	245	31	3	
Jim Lynch	LB	6'1"	225	31	2	
Dave Rozumek	LB	6'2"	215	22		
Clyde Werner	LB	6'4"	230	28		
Gary Barbaro	DB	6'4"	198	22	3	
Tim Collier	DB	6'	166	22	2	
Tim Gray	DB	6'1"	200	23	4	
Kerry Reardon	DB	5'11"	180	27	5	
Steve Taylor	DB	6'3"	204	22		
Emmitt Thomas	DB	6'2"	192	33	2	

Ken Avery – Injury
Randy Beisler – Injury
Roger Bernhardt – Injury

Use Name	Pos.	Hgt	Wgt	Age	Int	Pts
Tony Adams	QB	6'	198	26		
Mike Livingston	QB	6'3"	212	30		12
Mike Nott	QB	6'3"	203	24		
Woody Green	HB	6'1"	205	25		6
Ed Podolak	HB	6'1"	205	29		30
Tommy Reamon	HB	5'10"	192	24		30
Glynn Harrison	FB	5'11"	190	22		
MacArthur Lane	FB	6'	220	34		36
Pat McNeil	FB	5'9"	208	22		
Larry Brunson	WR	5'11"	180	27		6
Reggie Craig	WR	6'	187	23		
Henry Marshall	WR	6'2"	205	22		18
Barry Pearson	WR	5'11"	185	26		
Lawrence Williams	WR	5'10"	175	22		
Bill Masters	TE	6'5"	240	32		18
Walter White	TE	6'3"	218	25		42
Jan Stenerud	K	6'2"	187	33		90
Jerrel Wilson	K	6'4"	222	34		

TAMPA BAY BUCCANEERS 0-14 John McKay

Scores of Each Game		
0	Houston	20
0	SAN DIEGO	23
9	BUFFALO	14
17	Baltimore	42
0	Cincinnati	21
10	SEATTLE	13
20	MIAMI	23
19	KANSAS CITY	28
13	Denver	48
0	N.Y. Jets	34
7	CLEVELAND	24
16	Oakland	49
0	Pittsburgh	42
14	NEW ENGLAND	31

Use Name	Pos.	Hgt	Wgt	Age	Int	Pts.
Mike Current	OT	6'4"	270	30		
Dave Reavis	OT	6'5"	250	26		
Steve Wilson	OT	6'3"	268	22		
Randy Young	OT	6'5"	250	22		
Steve Young	OT	6'8"	272	23		
Tom Alward	OG	6'4"	255	23		
Howard Fest	OG	6'6"	263	30		
Everett Little	OG	6'4"	265	22		
Dan Ryczek	C	6'3"	250	27		
Ed McAlaney (from ATL)	DE	6'2"	235	22		
Council Rudolph	DE	6'3"	255	26		
Lee Roy Selmon	DE	6'3"	263	21		
Pat Toomay	DE	6'5"	244	31		
Larry Jameson	DT	6'7"	270	23		
Maulty Moore	DT	6'5"	265	30		
Dave Pear	DT	6'2"	248	23		
Dewey Selmon	DT	6'1"	254	22		

Charlie Evans – Knee Injury
Kent Gaydos – Injury

Use Name	Pos.	Hgt	Wgt	Age	Int	Pts
Larry Ball	LB	6'6"	235	26	1	
Bert Cooper	LB	6'1"	242	24		
Jimmy Gunn	LB	6'1"	231	27		
Charlie Hunt	LB	6'3"	218	25		
Mike Lemon	LB	6'2"	220	25		
Cal Peterson	LB	6'3"	213	23	1	
Jim Peterson	LB	6'5"	226	26		
Steve Reese	LB	6'2"	223	24		
Glenn Robinson	LB-DE	6'6"	245	24		
Jimmy Sims	LB	6'	195	25		
Richard Wood	LB	6'2"	215	23		
Mark Cotney	DB	6'	207	24	3	
Ricky Davis	DB	6'	178	23		
Earl Douthit	DB	6'2"	188	23		
Curtis Jordan	DB	6'2"	182	22	2	
Don Martin	DB	5'11"	185	26		
Frank Oliver	DB	6'	198	24		
Reggie Pierson (from DET.)	DB	5'11"	185	23		
Danny Reece	DB	5'11"	187	21		6
Ken Stone	DB	6'1"	180	25	2	
Mike Washington	DB	6'3"	190	23		
Roscoe Word (from NYJ & BUF)	DB	5'11"	169	24		

Use Name	Pos.	Hgt	Wgt	Age	Int	Pts
Parnell Dickinson	QB	6'2"	185	23		
Terry Hanratty	QB	6'1"	205	28		
Larry Lawrence	QB	6'1"	208	27		
Steve Spurrier	QB	6'2"	205	31		
Louis Carter	HB	5'11"	209	23		6
Charlie Davis	HB	5'11"	200	24		6
Harold Hart	HB	6'	208	23		
Essex Johnson	HB	5'9"	200	29		12
Jimmy DuBose	FB	5'11"	217	21		
Vince Kendrick	FB	6'	239	24		
Rod McNeill (from NO)	FB	6'2"	215	25		
Ed Williams	FB	6'2"	245	26		12
Freddie Douglass	WR	5'9"	185	22		
Isaac Hagins	WR	5'9"	179	22		
Curtis Leak	WR	5'11"	180	22		
Lee McGriff	WR	5'9"	163	22		
John McKay	WR	5'11"	175	23		6
Morris Owens (from MIA)	WR	6'	190	23		36
Barry Smith	WR	6'1"	195	25		
Bob Moore	TE	6'3"	229	27		
Jack Novak	TE	6'4"	242	23		6
Fred Pagac	TE	6'	220	24		
Dave Green	K	5'11"	208	26		35
Mirro Roder	K	6'1"	218	32		

*—Overtime

OAKLAND RAIDERS

RUSHING

Last Name	No.	Yds.	Avg	TD
van Eeghen	233	1012	4.3	3
Davis	114	516	4.5	3
Banaszak	114	370	3.2	5
Garrett	48	220	4.6	1
Ginn	10	53	5.3	0
Rae	10	37	3.7	1
Kunz	4	33	8.3	0
Jennings	10	22	2.2	0
Branch	3	12	4.0	0
Casper	1	5	5.0	0
Bradshaw	1	4	4.0	0
Moore	7	4	0.6	0
Bankston	1	3	3.0	0
Guy	1	0	0.0	0
Stabler	7	−2	−0.3	1

RECEIVING

Last Name	No.	Yds	Avg	TD
Casper	53	691	13	10
Branch	46	1111	24	12
Biletnikoff	43	551	13	7
Davis	21	191	7	0
van Eeghen	17	173	10	0
Banaszak	15	74	5	0
Siani	11	173	16	2
Garrett	9	108	12	0
Bankston	5	73	15	1
Moore	5	46	9	0
Kwalick	4	15	4	0
Bradshaw	1	25	25	1
Jennings	1	10	10	0

PUNT RETURNS

Last Name	No.	Yds	Avg	TD
Colzie	41	448	11	0
Moore	20	184	9	0
Phillips	2	7	4	0
Jennings	1	20	20	0

KICKOFF RETURNS

Last Name	No.	Yds	Avg	TD
Garrett	18	388	22	0
Jennings	16	417	26	0
Moore	8	162	20	0
Colzie	6	115	19	0
Bankston	2	27	14	0
Banaszak	2	23	12	0
Ginn	1	27	27	0

PASSING – PUNTING – KICKING

PASSING	Att	Comp	%	Yds	Yd/Att	TD	Int–%	RK
Stabler	291	194	67	2737	9.4	27	17– 6	1
Rae	65	35	54	417	6.4	6	1– 2	
Humm	5	3	60	41	8.2	0	0– 0	

PUNTING	No	Avg
Guy	67	41.6

KICKING	XP	Att	%	FG	Att	%
Mann	35	37	95	8	21	38
Steinfort	16	19	84	4	8	50
Guy	0	1	0			

DENVER BRONCOS

RUSHING

Last Name	No.	Yds.	Avg	TD
Armstrong	247	1008	4.1	5
Keyworth	122	349	2.9	3
Weese	23	142	6.2	0
Perrin	37	118	3.2	2
Kiick	31	114	3.7	1
Upchurch	6	71	11.8	1
Ramsey	13	51	3.9	0
Odoms	3	36	12.0	2
Franckowiak	12	25	2.1	0
Van Heusen	1	20	20.0	0
Dolbin	2	5	2.5	0
Penrose	2	−3	−1.5	0
Moses	1	−4	−4.0	0

RECEIVING

Last Name	No.	Yds	Avg	TD
Armstrong	39	457	12	1
Odoms	30	477	16	3
Moses	25	498	20	7
Keyworth	22	201	9	1
Dolbin	19	354	19	1
Upchurch	12	340	28	1
Kiick	10	78	8	1
Franckowiak	4	42	11	0
Perrin	4	35	9	0
Schultz	2	29	15	0
Lyons	1	−1	−1	0

PUNT RETURNS

Last Name	No.	Yds	Avg	TD
Upchurch	39	536	14	4
Thompson	6	60	10	0
Foley	5	42	8	0
Schultz	1	2	2	0

KICKOFF RETURNS

Last Name	No.	Yds	Avg	TD
Upchurch	22	514	23	0
Perrin	14	391	28	0
Schultz	3	82	27	0
B. Brown	3	41	14	0
Franckowiak	2	22	11	0
Hyde	1	17	17	0
Goodman	1	8	8	0

PASSING – PUNTING – KICKING

PASSING	Att	Comp	%	Yds	Yd/Att	TD	Int–%	RK
Ramsey	270	128	47	1931	7.2	11	13– 5	11
Weese	47	24	51	314	6.7	1	6– 13	
Penrose	36	16	44	265	7.4	3	3– 8	

PUNTING	No	Avg
Weese	52	35.6
Van Heusen	31	35.3

KICKING	XP	Att	%	FG	Att	%
Turner	36	39	92	15	21	71

SAN DIEGO CHARGERS

RUSHING

Last Name	No.	Yds.	Avg	TD
Young	162	802	5.0	4
Woods	126	450	3.6	3
Morris	50	256	5.1	2
Scarber	61	236	3.9	1
Matthews	46	199	4.3	3
Fouts	18	65	3.6	0
Longley	4	22	5.5	0
Curran	1	12	12.0	0
Hoopes	2	10	5.0	0
Jeffrey	1	0	0.0	0
West	1	0	0.0	0
Dorsey	1	−12	−12.0	0

RECEIVING

Last Name	No.	Yds	Avg	TD
Joiner	50	1056	21	7
Young	47	441	9	1
Woods	34	224	7	1
Curran	33	349	11	1
Scarber	14	96	7	1
Matthews	12	81	7	0
McDonald	11	161	15	4
Dorsey	8	108	14	0
Morris	8	52	7	0
Owens	3	54	18	1
Garrison	2	58	29	1
Bradley	1	7	7	0

PUNT RETURNS

Last Name	No.	Yds	Avg	TD
Fuller	33	436	13	0
Bell	7	31	4	0
Williams	5	23	5	0

KICKOFF RETURNS

Last Name	No.	Yds	Avg	TD
Owens	25	551	22	0
Fuller	20	420	21	0
Perretta	2	24	12	0
Middleton	1	21	21	0
Matthews	1	19	19	0
Bell	1	18	18	0
Preston	1	16	16	0
Horn	1	7	7	0

PASSING – PUNTING – KICKING

PASSING	Att	Comp	%	Yds	Yd/Att	TD	Int–%	RK
Fouts	359	208	58	2535	7.1	14	15– 4	8
Longley	24	12	50	130	5.4	2	3– 13	
Jeffrey	2	2	100	11	5.5	0	0– 0	
Woods	2	1	50	11	5.5	1	0– 0	
Joiner	1	0	0	0	0.0	0	0– 0	

PUNTING	No	Avg
Hoopes	49	37.7
West	38	40.7

KICKING	XP	Att	%	FG	Att	%
Fritsch	11	14	79	6	12	50
Wersching	14	16	88	4	8	50
Fuller	1	1	100			

KANSAS CITY CHIEFS

RUSHING

Last Name	No.	Yds.	Avg	TD
Lane	162	542	3.3	5
Podolak	88	371	4.2	5
Green	73	322	4.4	1
Reamon	103	314	3.0	4
Marshall	5	101	20.2	1
Livingston	31	89	2.9	2
Adams	5	46	9.2	0
Harrison	16	41	2.6	0
McNeil	8	26	3.3	0
White	2	15	7.5	0
Stenerud	1	0	0.0	0
Brunson	3	−1	−0.3	0

RECEIVING

Last Name	No.	Yds	Avg	TD
Lane	66	686	10	1
White	47	808	17	7
Brunson	33	656	20	1
Marshall	28	443	16	2
Masters	18	269	15	3
Podolak	13	156	12	0
Reamon	10	136	14	1
Green	9	100	11	0
McNeil	2	33	17	0
Harrison	1	12	12	0
Williams	1	9	9	0
Getty	1	−5	−5	0

PUNT RETURNS

Last Name	No.	Yds	Avg	TD
Brunson	31	387	12	0
Andrews	1	38	38	0
Reardon	1	4	4	0
Reamon	1	0	0	0

KICKOFF RETURNS

Last Name	No.	Yds	Avg	TD
Williams	25	688	28	0
Reamon	19	424	22	0
Harrison	13	278	21	0
Green	3	82	27	0
Craig	2	45	23	0
McNeil	2	21	11	0
Marshall	1	0	0	0

PASSING – PUNTING – KICKING

PASSING	Att	Comp	%	Yds	Yd/Att	TD	Int–%	RK
Livingston	338	189	56	2682	7.9	12	13– 4	5
Adams	71	36	51	575	8.1	3	4– 6	
Nott	10	4	40	46	4.6	0	0– 0	

PUNTING	No	Avg
Wilson	65	42.0
Nott	1	35.0
Stenerud	1	28.0

KICKING	XP	Att	%	FG	Att	%
Stenerud	27	33	82	21	38	55

TAMPA BAY BUCCANEERS

RUSHING

Last Name	No.	Yds.	Avg	TD
Carter	171	521	3.0	1
Williams	87	324	3.7	2
Johnson	47	166	3.5	1
McNeill	27	135	5.0	0
C. Davis	41	107	2.6	1
Dickinson	13	103	7.9	0
DuBose	20	62	3.1	0
Spurrier	12	48	4.0	0
B. Moore	2	23	11.5	0
Pagac	1	4	4.0	0
Kendrick	1	3	3.0	0
Owens	2	2	1.0	0
Hanratty	1	1	1.0	0
Green	1	0	0.0	0

RECEIVING

Last Name	No.	Yds	Avg	TD
Owens	30	390	13	6
Johnson	25	201	8	1
B. Moore	24	289	12	0
Williams	23	166	7	0
McKay	20	302	15	1
Carter	20	135	7	0
Novak	8	130	16	1
McNeill	7	33	5	0
DuBose	5	26	5	0
Smith	4	88	22	0
Douglass	3	58	19	0
C. Davis	3	32	11	0
Pagac	2	15	8	0
Green	1	9	9	0
Ryczek	1	6	6	0

PUNT RETURNS

Last Name	No.	Yds	Avg	TD
Reece	20	143	7	0
Douglass	4	78	20	0
Cotney	3	26	9	0
Stone	1	11	11	0
Hagins	1	2	2	0
Word	1	−8	−8	0

KICKOFF RETURNS

Last Name	No.	Yds	Avg	TD
McNeil	17	384	23	0
Carter	15	300	20	0
Johnson	13	287	22	0
Douglass	7	167	24	0
C. Davis	4	73	18	0
Word	2	36	18	0
Hagins	2	35	18	0
DuBose	1	34	34	0
Reece	1	30	30	0
Cooper	1	22	22	0
Pagac	1	20	20	0
Lemon	1	2	2	0

PASSING – PUNTING – KICKING

PASSING	Att	Comp	%	Yds	Yd/Att	TD	Int–%	RK
Spurrier	311	156	50	1628	5.2	7	12– 4	13
Dickinson	39	15	38	210	5.4	1	5– 13	
Hanratty	14	6	43	32	2.3	0	1– 7	
Carter	5	2	40	24	4.8	1	0– 0	
Lawrence	5	0	0	0	0.0	0	2– 40	
McGriff	1	1	100	39	39.0	0	0– 0	
R. Davis	1	1	100	−7	−7.0	0	0– 0	

PUNTING	No	Avg
Green	92	39.3

KICKING	XP	Att	%	FG	Att	%
Green	11	14	79	8	14	57
Roder				0	3	0

NFC CHAMPIONSHIP GAME

December 26, 1976 at Bloomington, Minn.
(Attendance 47,191)

SCORING

MINNESOTA	7	3	7	7–24
LOS ANGELES	0	0	13	0–13

First Quarter
Minn. — Bryant, 90 yard blocked field goal return
PAT – Cox (kick)

Second Quarter
Minn. — Cox, 25 yard field goal

Third Quarter
Minn. — Foreman, 1 yard rush
PAT – Cox (kick
L.A. — McCutcheon, 10 yard rush
PAT – Kick no good
L.A. — H. Jackson, 5 yard pass from Haden
PAT – Dempsey (kick)

Fourth Quarter
Minn. — Johnson, 12 yard rush
PAT – Cox (kick)

TEAM STATISTICS

MINN.		L.A.
13	First Downs–Total	21
6	First Downs–Rushing	14
7	First Downs–Passing	7
0	First Downs–Penalty	0
1	Fumbles–Number	4
1	Fumbles–Lost Ball	2
4	Penalty–Number	3
32	Yards Penalized	33
0	Missed Field Goals	1
60	Offensive Plays	71
267	Net Yards	336
4.5	Average Gain	4.7
2	Giveaways	4
4	Takeaways	2
+2	Difference	-2

Minnesota never looked better while bombing Washington 35-20 in an NFC semi-final playoff bout that featured two TD's apiece by RB Chuck Foreman and WR Sammy White. Los Angeles, meanwhile, just barely got by Dallas 14-12 when the Pokes failed to take advantage of a blocked punt that put the ball on L.A.'s 17-yard line with 1:59 remaining. On this frosty Sunday in Bloomington, however, the Vikes, behind sore-kneed QB Fran Tarkenton, were no match for the Rams statistically except where it counted most—on the specialty teams. The end result was a 24-13 victory for Minnesota, enabling it to make its third visit to the Super Bowl in four years.

The game's biggest play occurred early in the first quarter after the Vikings' defense put the clamps on a strong Ram drive spearheaded by the running of Lawrence McCutcheon and John Cappelletti. With the ball spotted just inches short of Minnesota's goal-line on fourth down, Ram Head Coach Chuck Knox decided to play it safe with a field goal attempt by Tom Dempsey. Earlier in the year in a 10-10 overtime tie against the same Vikings, the Rams twice failed to score from one yard out after deciding not to kick field goals. Nate Allen, who had blocked Dempsey's overtime FG attempt in that earlier game, cleanly deflected the ball after charging in from the right side, and after it took a lucky bounce in the opposite direction, Bobby Bryant picked it up and scampered 90 yards for a TD with the closest Ram 15 yards behind.

Minnesota's Matt Blair followed suit with a second-quarter block of Rusty Jackson's punt after the latter dropped the snap, and it was soon 10-0 after Fred Cox's 25-yard field goal. The Rams' special team miseries continued when Dempsey failed to convert the extra point following their first TD of the game, and when they scored again late in the third quarter, after RE Fred Dryer blindsided Tarkenton and LE Jack Youngblood recovered the subsequent fumble to set up WR Harold Jackson's TD catch, their four-point deficit (17-13) meant the Rams would have to come up with more than a field goal to overtake the Vikes.

With Pat Haden at the controls, L. A. got as far as the Viking 39 with three minutes to go before failing to convert four aerial attempts, the last one intercepted by Bryant. Tarkenton connected with Foreman on a 57-yard safety-valve pass on third down to set up Sammy Johnson's clinching 12-yard TD. Foreman accounted for 119 yards on two plays, almost half of the Vikings' total offense. His brilliant 62-yard run set up Minnesota's second TD to put it ahead 17-0 in the third quarter.

Beside Tarkenton's injury, MLB Jeff Siemon didn't start but played the last three quarters with his legs heavily taped while WR White sat out most of the game with a fever. But that wasn't enough to keep the Rams from losing their third straight NFC Championship game.

INDIVIDUAL STATISTICS

MINNESOTA	No	Yds	Avg.	LOS ANGELES	No	Yds	Avg.
RUSHING							
Foreman	15	118	7.9	McCutcheon	26	128	4.9
Miller	10	28	2.8	Cappelletti	16	59	3.7
Johnson	2	12	6.0	Haden	3	3	1.0
McClanahan	1	2	2.0	Jessie	1	3	3.0
Tarkenton	1	-2	-2.0		46	193	4.2
	29	158	5.4				
RECEIVING							
Foreman	5	81	16.2	H Jackson	4	70	17.5
Rashad	3	28	9.3	Jessie	2	60	30.0
Miller	3	24	8.0	McCutcheon	2	18	9.0
Grim	1	10	10.0	Cappelletti	1	13	13.0
	12	143	11.9		9	161	17.9
PUNTING							
Clabo	8		35.1	R. Jackson	7		29.4
PUNT RETURNS							
Willis	3	20	6.7	C. Bryant	4	31	7.8
				Bertelsen	3	19	6.3
					7	50	7.1
KICKOFF RETURNS							
Willis	3	69	23.0	Geredine	3	50	16.7
				C. Bryant	1	21	21.0
				Scribner	1	8	8.0
					5	79	15.8
INTERCEPTION RETURNS							
B. Bryant	2	17	8.5	M. Jackson	1	0	0.0

PASSING

MINNESOTA	Att.	Comp	Comp. Pct.	Yds.	Int.	Yds/ Att.	Yds/ Comp.	Yards Lost Tackled
Tarkenton	27	12	44.4	143	1	5.3	11.9	4–34
LOS ANGELES								
Haden	22	9	40.9	161	2	7.3	17.9	3–18

AFC CHAMPIONSHIP GAME

December 26, 1976 at Oakland
(Attendance 53,739)

SCORING

OAKLAND	3	14	7	0–24
PITTSBURGH	0	7	0	0– 7

First Quarter
Oak. — Mann, 39 yard field goal

Second Quarter
Oak. — C. Davis, 1 yard rush
PAT – Mann (kick)
Pitt. — Harrison, 3 yard rush
PAT – Mansfield (kick)
Oak. — Bankston, 4 yard pass from Stabler
PAT – Mann (kick)

Third Quarter
Oak. — Banaszak, 5 yard pass from Stabler
PAT – Mann (kick)

TEAM STATISTICS

OAK.		PITT.
15	First Downs–Total	13
7	First Downs–Rushing	3
7	First Downs–Passing	8
1	First Downs–Penalty	2
2	Fumbles–Number	1
0	Fumbles –Lost Ball	0
7	Penalty–Number	5
34	Yards Penalized	29
0	Missed Field Goals	0
69	Offensive Plays	59
220	Net Yards	237
3.2	Average Gain	4.0
0	Giveaways	1
1	Takeaways	0
+1	Difference	-1

Pittsburgh had a surprisingly easy time with Baltimore in the AFC semi-final, but its 40-14 victory proved costly as running backs Franco Harris and Rocky Bleier suffered rib and toe injuries, respectively, that kept them from playing Oakland in the AFC Championship Game. The Raiders' semi-final opponent, New England, was just one controversial penalty away from upsetting Oakland. Raider QB Ken Stabler engineered two late TD drives to edge the Pats 24-21, the last drive staying alive when New England NT Ray Hamilton was called for roughing Stabler on fourth down with 57 seconds remaining. Without Harris and Bleier, the Steelers were easy pickings for the Raiders as Oakland won 24-7 to end a string of six straight AFC title losses.

Forced into installing a one-back offense featuring Reggie Harrison, Steeler Head Coach Chuck Noll tried to help his confused QB Terry Bradshaw by calling all the Steelers' plays from the sidelines. Pittsburgh didn't get a first down until midway through the second quarter, at which time Oakland already led 10-0. The Raiders' rushers had a comparatively easy time, allowing Stabler to play-pass for Oakland's last two touchdowns. Willie Hall, the linebacker Raider Head Coach John Madden inserted into the starting lineup after converting to a 3-4 defense earlier in the year, set up Oakland's first TD with a brilliant 25-yard interception return to the Steelers' one-yard line. He also knocked down a pass, forced a fumble and made five unassisted tackles along with numerous assists.

Pittsburgh got on the scoreboard after an impressive second-quarter drive kept alive with the sharp third-down passing of Bradshaw but Stabler bounced right back with a demoralizing four-yard TD score to TE Warren Bankston 19 seconds before halftime. Stabler's longest pass of the day, 28 yards to WR Cliff Branch, was completed after he detected a safety blitz which earlier had thrown him for a 17-yard loss. The completion led to the second half's only score, a five-yard toss over the middle to RB Pete Banaszak on another adjusted pattern. On the play, Steeler LB Jack Ham got to Stabler, knocking a cap off Stabler's front tooth and delivering a big welt on his back that sent him to the sidelines. It didn't make much difference for the frustrated Steelers, however. Stabler's replacement, Mike Rae, ran out the clock as the Raiders relied on defense in the final period, and with no ground game to speak of, Bradshaw resorted to desperation passes in a futile attempt to get back in the game.

INDIVIDUAL STATISTICS

OAKLAND	No	Yds	Avg.	PITTSBURGH	No	Yds	Avg.
RUSHING							
van Eeghen	22	66	3.0	Harrison	11	44	4.0
C. Davis	11	54	4.9	Fuqua	8	24	3.0
Banaszak	15	46	3.1	Bradshaw	1	4	4.0
Garrett	2	4	2.0	Cunningham	1	0	0.0
Casper	1	-13.0	-13.0		21	72	3.4
	51	157	3.1				
RECEIVING							
Branch	3	46	15.3	Cunningham	4	36	9.0
Bankston	2	11	5.5	Swann	3	58	19.3
C. Davis	2	7	3.5	Fuqua	2	11	5.5
van Eeghen	1	14	14.0	Harrison	2	10	5.0
Banaszak	1	5	5.0	Brown	1	32	32.0
Casper	1	5	5.0	Stallworth	1	18	18.0
	10	88	8.8	Lewis	1	11	11.0
					14	176	12.6
PUNTING							
Guy	7		44.0	Walden	7		37.3
PUNT RETURNS							
Colzie	2	19	8.5	Bell	2	14	7.0
				Swann	1	4	4.0
					3	18	6.0
KICKOFF RETURNS							
Garrett	2	35	17.5	Pough	3	65	21.7
				Bell	1	16	16.0
				Blount	1	16	16.0
					5	97	19.4
INTERCEPTION RETURNS							
Hall	1	25	25.0	none			

PASSING

OAKLAND	Att.	Comp.	Comp Pct.	Yds.	Int.	Yds/ Att.	Yds/ Comp.	Yards Lost Tackled
Stabler	16	10	62.5	88	0	5.5	8.8	2–25
PITTSBURGH								
Bradshaw	35	14	40.0	176	1	5.0	12.6	3–11

SUPER BOWL XI
January 9, at Pasadena
(Attendance 100,421)

All the Silver

When the Oakland Raiders knocked off the defending NFL champion Pittsburgh Steelers, 24-7, to win the AFC, it seemed that coach John Madden and his Raiders would finally have their day in the sun. For all their frustration, the Raiders had won the Western Division title seven of eight times, but not since 1967, when they were humbled by Green Bay, have they appeared in the Super Bowl. Now al! that remained in their way was Fran Tarkenton and the Minneota Vikings, three-time losers of the game's most valuable prize.

As things turned out, Minnesota proved hardly an opposition for the devastating Raiders as they rang up 266 yards on the ground and 163 yards in the air. Although the first quarter went scoreless, the Raiders were on top 16-0 at the half behind a field goal, a Ken Stabler pass, and Pete Banaszak's one-yard run. Errol Mann added another field goal in the third quarter and Tarkenton finally put Minnesota on the board to make the score 19-7 as the quarter ran out.

Whatever hopes the Vikings had for a comeback were soon dispelled as Banaszak again crossed the goal line 7:21 into the fourth quarter. A few minutes later Willie Brown intercepted a Tarkenton pass and ran the ball back 75 yards for a touchdown to make the score 32-7. With Bob Lee in the game for Tarkenton, the Vikings again got on the scoreboard, but it was simply a case of too little, too late.

Although Banaszak had scored two touchdowns and Clarence Davis rushed for a career-high 137 yards, the game's most valuable player honors went to Fred Biletnikoff, who caught four passes for 79 yards and set up three scores. The secret to the Raiders overwhelming victory was their ability to exploit the weak left side of the Vikings' line and to keep premier runner Chuck Foreman in check with only 44 yards in 17 attempts.

For the black and silver clad Raiders their dreams had finally become a reality. For the Vikings, the reality seemed more like a nightmare.

LINEUPS

OAKLAND		MINNESOTA
	OFFENSE	
Branch	WR	Rashad
Shell	LT	Riley
Upshaw	LG	Goodrum
Dalby	C	Tinglehoff
Buehler	RG	E. White
Vella	RT	Yary
Casper	TE	Voigt
Biletnikoff	WR	S. White
Stabler	QB	Tarkenton
Davis	RB	Foreman
van Eeghen	RB	McClanahan
	DEFENSE	
Matuzek	LE	Eller
Rowe	LT	Sutherland
Sistrunk	RT	Page
M. Johnson	RE	Marshall
Villapiano	LLB	Blair
Willie Hall	MLB	Siemon
Hendricks	RLB	Hilgenberg
Thomas	LCB	N. Wright
Brown	RCB	Bryant
Tatum	FS	Krause
Atkinson	SS	J. Wright

SUBSTITUTES

OAKLAND

OFFENSE	
Banaszak	Medlin
Bankston	Moore
Bradshaw	Rae
Garrett	Siani
Humm	Sylvester
Lawrence	

DEFENSE	
Barnes	McMath
Bonness	Phillips
Colzie	Philyaw
Ginn	Rice

KICKERS	
Guy	Mann

MINNESOTA

OFFENSE	
Berry	Hamilton
Bueton	S. Johnson
Craig	Lee
Dumler	Miller
Grim	Willis
Groce	

DEFENSE	
Allen	McNeil
Beamon	Mullaney
Windlan Hall	J. White
Martin	Winston

KICKERS	
Clabo	Cox

SCORING

OAKLAND	0	16	3	13	–32
MINNESOTA	0	0	7	7	–14

Second Quarter		
Oak.	Mann, 24 yard field goal	0:48
Oak.	Casper, 1 yard pass from Stabler PAT—Mann (kick)	7:50
Oak.	Banaszak, 1 yard rush PAT – Kick (no good)	11:27
Third Quarter		
Oak.	Mann, 40 yard field goal	9:44
Minn.	S. White, 8 yard pass from Tarkenton PAT—Cox (kick)	14:13
Fourth Quarter		
Oak.	Banaszak, 2 yard rush PAT – Mann (kick)	7:21
Oak.	Brown, 75 yard interception return PAT—Kick (no good)	9:17
Minn.	Voigt, 13 yard pass from Lee PAT – Cox (kick)	14:35

TEAM STATISTICS

OAK.		MINN.
21	First Downs—Total	20
13	First Downs—Rushing	2
8	First Downs—Passing	15
0	First Downs—Penalty	3
0	Fumbles—Number	1
0	Fumbles—Lost Ball	1
4	Penalties—Number	2
30	Yards Penalized	25
1	Missed Field Goals	0
73	Offensive Plays	71
429	Net Yards	353
5.9	Average Gain	5.0
3	Takeaways	0
0	Giveaways	3
+3	Difference	-3

INDIVIDUAL STATISTICS

OAKLAND	No	Yds	Avg.	MINNESOTA	No	Yds	Avg.
RUSHING							
Davis	16	137	8.6	Foreman	17	44	2.6
van Eeghen	18	73	4.1	S. Johnson	2	9	4.5
Garrett	4	19	4.8	S. White	1	7	7.0
Banaszak	10	19	1.9	Lee	1	4	4.0
Ginn	2	9	4.5	Miller	2	4	2.0
Rae	2	9	4.5	McClanahan	3	3	1.0
	52	266	5.1		26	71	2.7
RECEIVING							
Biletnikoff	4	79	19.8	S. White	5	77	15.4
Casper	4	70	17.5	Foreman	5	62	12.4
Branch	3	20	6.7	Voigt	4	49	12.3
Garrett	1	11	11.0	Miller	4	19	4.8
	12	180	15.0	Rashad	3	53	17.7
				S. Johnson	3	26	8.7
					24	286	11.9
PUNTING							
Guy	4		40.5	Clabo	7		37.9
PUNT RETURNS							
Colzie	4	43	10.8	Willis	3	14	4.7
KICKOFF RETURNS							
Garrett	2	47	23.5	S. White	4	79	19.8
Siani	1	0	0.0	Willis	3	57	19.0
	3	47	15.7		7	136	19.4
INTERCEPTION RETURNS							
Brown	1	75	75.0	none			
Willie Hall	1	16	16.0				
	2	91	45.5				

PASSING

OAKLAND	Att.	Comp	Comp Pct.	Yds.	Int.	Yds/ Att.	Yds/ Comp.	Yards Lost Tackled
Stabler	19	12	63.2	180	0	9.5	15.0	2–17
MINNESOTA								
Tarkenton	35	17	48.6	205	2	5.9	12.1	1–4
Lee	9	7	77.8	81	0	9.0	11.6	
	44	24	54.5	286	2	6.5	11.9	1–4

1977 N.F.C. Freeing the Laborers

After lots of strident rhetoric and long negotiations, the NFL Players' Association and the league management reached a new labor agreement. Forged by union director Ed Garvey and management negotiator Sargent Karch, the new pact structured the rights of players for the next five years. For the fans, the highlight of the agreement was the preservation of the college draft and the modification of the free agent system. The new system provided for a specific set of draft choices which the signing team would give to the team losing the free agent, depending on the player's salary. Such a system gave football players much less freedom than their baseball counterparts enjoyed.

EASTERN DIVISION

Dallas Cowboys—By trading for Seattle's first round draft pick, the Cowboys added halfback Tony Dorsett to their arsenal. Tom Landry brought the rookie from Pitt along slowly, but by midseason, Dorsett had given the Dallas offense a new dimension. The new running threat balanced the potent passing attack, with Roger Staubach throwing and Drew Pearson the ace receiver. The Cowboys used the firepower to win their first eight games and last four games in repeating as Eastern champs. Although Lee Roy Jordan retired, the defense prospered with star performances by Harvey Martin, Tom Henderson, Charlie Waters, and Cliff Harris. Landry further strengthened the defense by making a starting tackle of Randy White.

Washington Redskins—A 20-17 loss to the Giants was George Allen's first opening day loss in 12 years as an NFL head coach. The Redskin offense couldn't quite get into gear for two months, with the team record at 4-4 in November. The attack suffered from Roy Jefferson's retirement and John Riggins' knee injury in October. Allen's famed defense kept its edge despite its age and led the Skins to a late-season rush. With Joe Theismann starting most of the games at quarterback, Washington won five of their last six games. The only loss in that stretch was a 14-7 defeat by Dallas on Thanksgiving Day. That setback kept the Redskins out of the playoffs and contributed to Allen's departure.

St. Louis Cardinals—The grade A Cardinal offense stalled in the early going, resulting in three losses in the first four games. Once Don Coryell got his attack moving, the Cards ran off six straight victories to jump into the playoff race. Although speedsters Terry Metcalf and Mel Gray won most of the headlines, the heart of the offense was the front line which featured Dan Dierdorf, Conrad Dobler, and Tom Banks. Injuries in the secondary further exposed the team's Achilles heel. Although Roger Wehrli starred at cornerback, the Dolphins massacred the Cards 55-14 on Thanksgiving. The Cardinals then skidded to three more losses, culminating in an embarrassing defeat by Tampa Bay.

Philadelphia Eagles—In his second year in charge, Dick Vermeil found a quarterback around whom to build. A trade with the Rams brought Ron Jaworski and his rifle arm to Philadelphia. Although still short on talented bodies, Vermeil fashioned a team which battled the Eastern powers without flinching. Although they lost all six games to the Cowboys, Redskins, and Cardinals, the Eagles dropped five of those by six points or less. With Bill Bergey at its heart, the new 3-4 defense improved with time, winding up the year with a 27-0 thrashing of the Giants.

New York Giants—After sending Craig Morton to Denver in the off-season, the Giants cast around for a quarterback. Jerry Golsteyn began the season with an opening day 20-17 upset of the Redskins, but he played himself onto the bench before the end of September. CFL exile Joe Pisarcik ran the offense for most of the schedule, throwing erratically behind porous pass protection. With a 3-3 record in October, a 28-0 beating by the Cardinals on Monday night began a steep slide. The Giants lost six of their final eight games, dispelling the gloom only to beat Tampa Bay 10-0 and to wreak vengence on the Cards 27-7.

CENTRAL DIVISION

Minnesota Vikings—The Vikings hit a reef when Fran Tarkenton broke a leg in a victory over the Bengals. Although in first place with a 6-3 record, the Vikes had to navigate the rest of the way without their leader. Veteran back-up Bob Lee engineered a split of the next two games. The Vikings fell behind the 49ers 24-0 in the third quarter, but rallied to a 28-27 victory behind the three touchdown passes of relief quarterback Tommy Kramer. One week later, Kramer started his first game but looked unsteady in a 35-13 loss. Going into the final weekend, the Vikings needed a victory to stay ahead of the hard-charging Chicago Bears. Traveling to Detroit, Lee started at QB as the Vikings won 30-21 and captured first place on the tiebreaker.

Chicago Bears—Walter Payton chased O.J. Simpson's single-season rushing record and carried the Bears into the playoff battle. Despite Payton's extraordinary season, the Bears stood at 3-5 after a 47-0 humiliation in Houston. From that point on, the Bears did not lose. Running behind the blocking of Revie Sorey, Payton set a single game record of 275 yards in a 10-7 victory over the Vikings. On the final Sunday, the Bears traveled to New Jersey in need of a victory to win a wild card spot. The icy field killed any chance Payton had for the rushing record, but the Bears struggled for the team goal. With the clock running low in the overtime period, Bob Thomas booted a field goal for a 12-9 victory which sent the Bears into the playoffs.

Detroit Lions—The Lions knew the heights and depths of NFL life. They looked miserable in a 37-0 loss at Dallas, then whipped the Chargers 20-0 in Detroit one week later. A balky offense frequently stalled as enemy pass rushers tormented Greg Landry. Injuries to runners Dexter Bussey and Lawrence Gaines further ruined the attack. The Lions put together a good record at home, but won only once on the road. A decisive 31-14 loss to the Bears on Thanksgiving Day effectively finished any playoff hopes, and the final game of the season ended Tommy Hudspeth's reign as head coach.

Green Bay Packers—Boos cascaded around Lambeau Field as the Packers put on a pitiful offensive show. In one mid-season stretch, the Packers lost to the Bears 26-0, were beaten by lowly Kansas City 20-10, and fell to the Rams 24-6. To make matters worse, quarterback Lynn Dickey suffered a broken leg on the last offensive play of the Rams game. Head coach Bart Starr turned to rookie David Whitehurst, and the youngster led his mates to two victories in the final three games.

Tampa Bay Buccaneers—After losing to the Seahawks in mid-season, the Bucs had a ticket for a second winless campaign. Head coach John McKay fielded a punchless offense which was shut out six times despite the addition of Ricky Bell and Anthony Davis, college stars under McKay at Southern California. Although still vulnerable to the pass, the new 3-4 defense shut down enemy rushers with strong work by Lee Roy Selmon and Dave Pear. With the loss string at 26 games, the Bucs traveled to New Orleans and stunned the Saints 33-14. The defense led the way with six interceptions. One week later, the Bucs treated their hometown fans to a 17-7 upset of the Cardinals to close out their second season.

WESTERN DIVISION

Los Angeles Rams—Joe Namath brought his flamboyant style and aching knees to Los Angeles, but his time in the spotlight was short. After a tough Monday night loss to the Bears, he spent the rest of the year on the bench. Pat Haden took over at quarterback and guided the Rams to eight wins in his ten starts. The mobile young quarterback had a star runner in Lawrence McCutcheon, a star receiver in Harold Jackson, and a solid front line featuring guard Tom Mack. The defense lost Merlin Olsen to retirement but lost none of its strength, with Jack Youngblood, Isiah Robertson, and Monte Jackson named to All-Pro teams. Chuck Knox led his charges to a repeat Western title in his final season in Los Angeles.

Atlanta Falcons—New coach Leeman Bennett inspired the Atlanta defense to a record-breaking season. The Falcons allowed 129 points, a new low mark for the 14-game schedule. With Claude Humphrey starring up front and Rolland Lawrence in the secondary, the defense kept the Falcons in the playoff chase despite a sluggish offense. A pre-season knee injury kept quarterback Steve Bartkowski out of action for the first six games, but the Falcons still won four of those contests. Mid-season losses to the 49ers and Saints braked the momentum and began an easy glide back into the pack.

San Francisco 49ers—With a new owner in Edward DeBartolo, a new general manager in Joe Thomas, and a new coach in Ken Meyer, the 49ers looked terrible in the early going. Five straight losses out of the starting gate killed any playoff hopes, but a mid-season burst of four victories rekindled hopes of next year. A late relapse of losing dampened those hopes and cost Meyer his job as coach. Particularly discouraging was the 28-27 game with the Vikings, in which the 49ers had led 24-0.

New Orleans Saints—Head coach Hank Stram had a long-term building program in mind, but the miserable short-term results cost him his job after only two years. Archie Manning recovered enough shoulder strength to withstand waves of pass rushers pouring in on him. The defense had problems keeping the opponents out of the end zone. Richie Szaro provided several thrills with his place kicks. He booted a field goal which hit the right upright and bounced through at the gun for a 27-26 upset of the Rams. Two weeks later, he hit the left upright but saw the ball bounce back in a 10-7 overtime loss to the 49ers.

FINAL TEAM STATISTICS

OFFENSE

	ATL.	CHI.	DALL.	DET.	G.B.	L.A.	MINN.	N.O.	NY G	PHIL.	ST. L.	S.F.	T.B.	WASH.
FIRST DOWNS:														
Total	198	247	272	218	195	270	245	223	201	211	247	219	168	227
by Rushing	102	141	118	94	81	139	110	115	105	98	114	126	84	79
by Passing	80	94	136	103	91	112	126	96	73	100	117	81	69	134
by Penalty	16	12	18	21	23	19	9	12	23	13	16	12	15	24
RUSHING:														
Number	582	599	564	479	469	621	510	484	548	484	507	564	465	502
Yards	1890	2811	2369	1706	1464	2575	1821	2024	1897	1722	2042	2086	1424	1752
Average Yards	3.2	4.7	4.2	3.6	3.1	4.1	3.6	4.2	3.5	3.6	4.0	3.7	3.1	3.5
Touchdowns	9	18	21	11	5	19	9	14	11	10	19	16	4	4
PASSING:														
Attempts	297	305	372	384	327	339	388	321	311	349	366	277	321	383
Completions	140	161	215	191	164	182	228	166	134	167	195	136	131	183
Completion Pct.	47.1	52.8	57.8	49.7	50.2	53.7	58.8	51.7	43.1	47.9	53.3	49.1	40.8	47.8
Passing Yards	1740	2070	2689	1959	2013	2253	2692	1933	1762	2198	2608	1797	1714	2284
Avg. Yds per Att.	5.9	6.8	7.2	5.1	6.2	6.6	6.9	6.0	5.7	6.3	7.1	6.5	5.3	6.0
Avg. Yds per Comp.	12.4	12.9	12.5	10.3	12.3	12.4	11.8	11.6	13.1	13.2	13.4	13.2	13.1	12.5
Times Tackled	40	26	33	54	32	25	35	46	46	47	15	36	48	52
Yds Lost Tackled	384	226	246	441	265	237	324	360	375	342	109	289	445	421
Net Yards	1356	1844	2443	1518	1748	2016	2368	1573	1387	1856	2499	1508	1269	1863
Touchdowns	8	11	18	7	6	16	19	13	6	18	14	9	3	15
Interceptions	16	18	10	16	21	11	22	21	22	21	21	17	30	16
Pct. Intercepted	5.4	5.9	2.7	4.2	6.4	3.2	5.7	6.5	7.1	6.0	5.7	6.1	9.3	4.2
PUNTS:														
Number	106	82	83	101	86	73	83	87	100	95	72	80	99	91
Average	41.2	39.4	38.7	36.2	39.4	35.2	39.8	41.0	39.9	36.5	36.2	35.0	39.9	38.5
PUNT RETURNS:														
Number	59	47	61	42	38	51	58	37	46	50	40	48	48	57
Yards	402	471	545	345	321	360	346	281	446	518	300	292	359	452
Average Yards	6.8	10.0	8.9	8.2	8.4	7.1	6.0	7.6	9.7	10.4	7.5	6.1	7.5	7.9
Touchdowns	0	1	0	1	1	0	0	0	1	0	0	0	0	0
KICKOFF RETURNS:														
Number	34	57	44	58	51	33	45	63	54	45	59	49	43	47
Yards	621	1273	1071	1239	947	705.3	834	1355	1036	1110	1271	1174	914	1087
Average Yards	18.3	22.3	24.3	21.4	18.6	21.4	18.5	21.5	19.2	24.7	21.5	24.0	21.3	[illegible]
Touchdowns	0	1	0	1	1	0	0	1	0	1	0	1	0	0
INTERCEPTION RET:														
Number	26	18	21	19	13	25	16	10	12	21	19	8	23	21
Yards	462	138	229	319	89	472	109	83	179	300	267	133	368	188
Average Yards	17.8	7.7	10.9	16.8	6.8	18.9	6.8	8.3	14.9	14.3	14.1	16.6	16.0	9.0
Touchdowns	2	0	1	1	1	1	0	1	2	0	1	0	3	0
PENALTIES:														
Number	101	97	106	86	82	89	75	86	91	78	95	99	88	94
Yards	898	852	865	692	690	869	556	794	880	642	837	830	717	802
FUMBLES:														
Number	28	36	26	26	24	32	36	20	27	31	31	27	30	26
Number Lost	9	17	14	14	9	17	24	11	12	17	16	8	16	14
POINTS:														
Total	179	255	345	183	134	302	231	232	181	220	272	220	103	196
PAT Attempts	20	31	42	23	14	36	30	31	20	29	36	27	11	19
PAT Made	20	27	39	19	11	32	25	29	19	25	35	25	10	19
FG Attempts	30	27	29	19	21	30	17	12	23	15	16	19	17	37
FG Made	13	14	18	8	13	18	8	5	14	7	7	11	9	21
Percent FG Made	43.3	51.9	62.1	42.1	61.9	60.0	47.1	41.7	60.9	46.7	43.8	57.9	52.9	56.8
Safeties	0	0	0	1	0	0	1	1	0	0	0	0	0	0

DEFENSE

	ATL.	CHI.	DALL.	DET.	G.B.	L.A.	MINN.	N.O.	NY G	PHIL.	ST. L.	S.F.	T.B.	WASH.
FIRST DOWNS:														
Total	192	241	205	206	259	203	212	272	224	216	258	221	240	234
by Rushing	100	124	88	93	139	90	119	153	94	95	122	108	123	112
by Passing	76	106	94	103	105	94	80	103	109	106	120	93	106	102
by Penalty	16	11	23	10	15	19	13	16	21	15	16	20	11	20
RUSHING:														
Number	504	541	457	521	583	462	548	623	519	523	513	551	581	537
Yards	1858	2157	1651	1905	2317	1698	2222	2729	1777	1917	2235	1869	2031	2039
Average Yards	3.7	4.0	3.6	3.7	4.0	3.7	4.1	4.4	3.4	3.7	4.4	3.4	3.5	3.8
Touchdowns	5	14	9	13	16	7	11	21	16	10	11	16	13	8
PASSING:														
Attempts	320	377	371	302	319	370	312	290	328	358	376	270	337	380
Completions	141	182	154	161	186	180	149	154	185	183	198	139	190	167
Completion Pct.	44.1	48.3	41.5	53.3	58.3	48.6	47.8	53.1	56.4	51.1	52.7	51.5	56.4	43.9
Passing Yards	1775	2334	1991	2123	2042	2236	1835	2127	2399	2192	2476	1948	2141	2430
Avg. Yds per Att.	5.5	6.2	5.4	7.0	6.4	6.0	5.9	7.3	7.3	6.1	6.6	7.2	6.4	6.4
Avg. Yds per Comp.	12.6	12.8	12.9	13.2	11.0	12.4	12.3	13.8	13.0	12.0	12.5	14.0	11.3	14.6
Times Tackled	42	27	53	32	37	36	30	27	38	47	25	42	30	44
Yds Lost Tackled	391	207	429	256	323	359	254	234	303	316	209	360	246	359
Net Yards	1384	2127	1562	1867	1719	1877	1581	1893	2096	1876	2267	1588	1895	2071
Touchdowns	9	7	14	14	10	11	15	15	12	14	22	14	10	12
Interceptions	26	18	21	19	13	25	16	10	12	21	19	8	23	21
Pct. Intercepted	8.1	4.8	5.7	6.3	4.1	6.8	5.1	3.4	3.7	5.9	5.1	3.0	6.8	5.5
PUNTS:														
Number	101	93	103	87	76	89	92	75	88	91	72	86	84	95
Average	36.3	39.1	37.1	39.5	36.5	38.7	38.2	38.8	38.9	38.7	39.5	37.5	39.9	36.6
PUNT RETURNS:														
Number	58	42	36	62	53	29	42	51	67	45	33	47	71	50
Yards	519	216	280	535	311	116	507	604	680	244	157	444	469	228
Average Yards	8.9	5.1	7.8	8.6	5.9	4.0	12.1	11.8	10.1	5.4	4.8	9.4	6.6	4.6
Touchdowns	0	0	1	1	0	0	1	2	0	0	0	0	0	0
KICKOFF RETURNS:														
Number	43	52	71	33	39	53	48	45	35	46	55	48	33	54
Yards	1021	1010	1614	741	786	1156	999	1075	895	940	1104	1025	699	1033
Average Yards	23.7	19.4	22.7	22.5	20.2	21.8	20.8	23.9	25.6	20.4	20.1	21.4	21.2	19.1
Touchdowns	1	1	0	0	0	0	2	0	1	0	0	1	0	0
INTERCEPTION RET:														
Number	16	18	10	16	21	11	22	21	22	21	21	17	30	16
Yards	195	171	184	207	349	136	187	392	330	256	183	298	429	296
Average Yards	12.2	9.5	18.4	12.9	16.6	12.4	8.5	18.7	15.0	12.2	8.7	17.5	14.3	18.5
Touchdowns	0	1	0	1	1	0	0	4	2	0	1	1	3	1
PENALTIES:														
Number	99	83	78	88	101	94	82	104	106	84	82	96	87	100
Yards	860	731	731	770	799	825	688	972	886	698	817	820	714	857
FUMBLES:														
Number	35	27	22	32	27	26	23	29	47	24	19	21	34	28
Number Lost	22	13	10	16	11	16	13	15	20	13	12	10	18	12
POINTS:														
Total	129	253	212	252	219	146	227	336	265	207	287	260	223	189
PAT Attempts	15	27	26	31	27	18	30	42	33	25	34	32	26	21
PAT Made	12	26	26	28	22	17	26	39	31	24	32	29	23	21
FG Attempts	16	29	15	24	23	18	17	24	22	26	26	22	27	29
FG Made	9	21	10	12	11	7	7	15	12	11	17	13	14	14
Percent FG Made	56.3	72.4	66.7	50.0	47.8	38.9	41.2	62.5	54.5	42.3	65.4	59.1	51.9	48.3
Safeties	0	1	0	1	1	0	0	0	0	0	0	0	1	0

CONFERENCE PLAYOFFS

December 26, at Irving, Texas (Attendance 62,920)

SCORING

DALLAS	7	10	17	3	– 37
CHICAGO	0	0	0	7	– 7

First Quarter
- Dall. Dennison, 2 yard rush PAT – Herrara (kick)

Second Quarter
- Dall. DuPree, 26 yard pass from Staubach PAT – Herrera (kick)
- Dall. Herrera, 21 yard field goal

Third Quarter
- Dall. Dorsett, 22 yard rush PAT – Herrera (kick)
- Dall. Herrera, 31 yard field goal
- Dall. Dorsett, 7 yard rush PAT – Herrera (kick)

Fourth Quarter
- Dall. Herrera, 27 yard field goal
- Chi. Schubert, 34 yard pass from Avellini PAT – Thomas (kick)

TEAM STATISTICS

DALLAS		CHICAGO
20	First Downs – Total	15
13	First Downs – Rushing	4
7	First Downs – Passing	9
0	First Downs – Penalty	2
2	Fumbles – Number	3
2	Fumbles – Lost Ball	3
3	Penalties – Number	4
35	Yards Penalized	43
0	Missed Field Goals	0
64	Offensive Plays	55
367	Net Yards	224
5.7	Average Gain	4.0
3	Giveaways	7
7	Takeaways	3
+4	Difference	-4

INDIVIDUAL STATISTICS

DALLAS	No	Yds	Avg.	CHICAGO	No	Yds	Avg.
RUSHING							
Dorsett	17	85	5.0	Payton	19	60	3.2
Newhouse	16	80	5.0	Harper	5	11	2.2
Dennison	8	40	5.0	Earl	2	6	3.0
Staubach	4	25	6.3	Avellini	1	4	4.0
Brinson	3	3	1.0		27	81	3.0
	48	233	4.8				
RECEIVING							
D. Pearson	2	38	19.0	Schubert	5	69	13.8
Dorsett	2	37	18.5	Payton	3	33	11.0
DuPree	1	28	28.0	Scott	3	29	9.7
Newhouse	1	13	13.0	Latta	2	25	12.5
Richards	1	12	12.0	Earl	1	15	15.0
Brinson	1	6	6.0	Harper	1	6	6.0
	8	134	16.8		15	177	11.8
PUNTING							
D. White	3		37.0	Parsons	6		43.4
PUNT RETURNS							
Johnson	3	26	8.7	Schubert	1	7	7.0
Hill	1	12	12.0				
	4	38	9.5				
KICKOFF RETURNS							
Brinson	1	28	28.0	Waltersch'd	4	98	24.5
Johnson	1	16	16.0	Payton	3	57	19.0
	2	44	22.0	Musso	1	7	7.0
					8	162	20.3
INTERCEPTION RETURNS							
Waters	3	53	17.7	Livers	1	8	8.0
Lewis	1	23	23.0				
	4	76	19.0				

PASSING

DALLAS	Att.	Comp.	Comp. Pct.	Yds.	Int.	Yds/ Att.	Yds/ Comp.	Yards Lost Tackled
Staubach	13	8	61.5	134	1	10.3	16.8	2– 2
CHICAGO								
Avellini	25	15	60.0	177	4	7.1	11.8	3–34

December 26, at Los Angeles (Attendance 62,538)

SCORING

LOS ANGELES	0	0	0	7	– 7
MINNESOTA	7	0	0	7	– 14

First Quarter
- Minn. Foreman, 5 yard rush PAT – Cox (kick)

Fourth Quarter
- Minn. Johnson, 1 yard rush PAT – Cox (kick)
- L.A. H. Jackson, 1 yard pass from Haden PAT – Septien (kick)

TEAM STATISTICS

L.A.		MINN.
14	First Downs – Total	14
7	First Downs – Rushing	9
6	First Downs – Passing	4
1	First Downs – Penalty	1
1	Fumbles – Number	1
0	Fumbles – Lost Ball	0
2	Penalties – Number	7
15	Yards Penalized	50
1	Missed Field Goals	0
62	Offensive Plays	60
267	Net Yards	189
4.3	Average Gain	3.2
3	Giveaways	0
0	Takeaways	3
-3	Difference	+3

INDIVIDUAL STATISTICS

LOS ANGELES	No	Yds	Avg.	MINNESOTA	No	Yds	Avg.
RUSHING							
McCutcheon	16	102	6.4	Foreman	31	101	3.3
Haden	3	27	9.0	Miller	12	52	4.3
Cappelletti	7	11	1.6	Johnson	3	1	0.3
Phillips	1	9	9.0	Lee	3	-10	-3.3
Nelson	1	0	0.0		49	144	2.9
Tyler	1	0	0.0				
	29	149	5.1				
RECEIVING							
Nelson	5	85	17.0	Rashad	2	37	18.5
H. Jackson	3	21	7.0	Miller	2	14	7.0
McCutcheon	2	15	7.5	Foreman	1	6	6.0
Phillips	2	0	0.0		5	57	11.4
Waddy	1	5	5.0				
Cappelletti	1	4	4.0				
	14	130	9.3				
PUNTING							
Walker	5		37.6	Clabo	5		40.8
PUNT RETURNS							
Waddy	3	17	5.7	Moore	2	30	15.0
Bryant	1	19	19.0				
Scales	1	2	2.0				
	5	38	7.6				
KICKOFF RETURNS							
Tyler	2	43	21.5	Moore	1	15	15.0
INTERCEPTION RETURNS							
none				Krause	1	14	14.0
				J. Wright	1	3	3.0
				Allen	1	0	0.0
					3	17	5.7

PASSING

LOS ANGELES	Att.	Comp.	Comp. Pct.	Yds.	Int.	Yds/ Att.	Yds/ Comp.	Yards Lost Tackled
Haden	32	14	43.8	130	3	4.1	9.3	1–12
MINNESOTA								
Lee	10	5	50.0	57	0	5.7	11.8	1–12

DALLAS COWBOYS 12-2 Tom Landry

Scores of Each Game			
16	Minnesota	10	
41	N.Y. GIANTS	21	
23	TAMPA BAY	7	
30	St. Louis	24	
34	WASHINGTON	16	
16	Philadelphia	10	
37	DETROIT	0	
24	N.Y. Giants	10	
17	ST. LOUIS	24	
13	Pittsburgh	28	
14	Washington	7	
24	PHILADELPHIA	14	
42	San Francisco	35	
14	DENVER	6	

Use Name	Pos.	Hgt	Wgt	Age	Int	Pts
Pat Donovan	OT	6'4"	255	24		
Andy Frederick	OT	6'6"	241	22		
Ralph Neely	OT	6'5"	255	33		
Rayfield Wright	OT	6'7"	260	32		
Jim Cooper	OG-C	6'5"	252	21		
Burton Lawless	OG	6'4"	250	23		
Tom Rafferty	OG-C	6'3"	250	23		
Herbert Scott	OG	6'2"	250	24		
John Fitzgerald	C	6'5"	260	29		
Too Tall Jones	DE	6'9"	265	26		
Harvey Martin	DE	6'5"	252	26		
David Stalls	DE	6'4"	236	21		
Larry Cole	DT-DE	6'4"	260	30		
Bill Gregory	DT	6'5"	260	27		
Jethro Pugh	DT	6'6"	250	33		
Randy White	DT	6'4"	245	24		
Bob Breunig	LB	6'2"	227	24	1	
Guy Brown	LB	6'4"	215	22		
Mike Hegman	LB	6'1"	225	24	1	
Tom Henderson	LB	6'2"	220	24	3	6
Bruce Huther	LB	6'1"	217	23		
D.D. Lewis	LB	6'2"	215	31	1	
Benny Barnes	DB	6'1"	195	26		
Cliff Harris	DB	6'	192	28	5	
Randy Hughes	DB	6'4"	208	24	2	
Aaron Kyle	DB	5'11"	185	23	1	
Mel Renfro	DB	6'	192	35	2	
Mark Washington	DB	5'10"	187	29	2	
Charlie Waters	DB	6'1"	198	28	3	6
Glenn Carano	QB	6'3"	195	21		
Roger Staubach	QB	6'2"	202	35		18
Danny White	QB	6'2"	192	25		
Doug Dennison	HB	6'1"	204	25		6
Tony Dorsett	HB	5'11"	192	23		78
Preston Pearson	HB	6'1"	206	32		30
Larry Brinson	FB	6'	214	23		6
Scott Laidlaw	FB	6'	205	24		6
Robert Newhouse	FB	5'10"	205	27		24
Tony Hill	WR	6'2"	196	21		
Butch Johnson	WR	6'1"	191	23		6
Drew Pearson	WR	6'	183	26		12
Golden Richards	WR	6'	180	26		18
Billy Joe DuPree	TE	6'4"	226	27		18
Jay Saldi	TE	6'3"	224	22		18
Efren Herrera	K	5'9"	190	26		93

Jim Eidson – Injury
Greg Schaum – Knee Injury
Charley Young – Knee Injury
Percy Howard – Injury

WASHINGTON REDSKINS 9-5 George Allen

Scores of Each Game			
17	N.Y. Giants	20	
10	ATLANTA	6	
24	ST. LOUIS	14	
10	Tampa Bay	0	
16	Dallas	34	
6	N.Y. GIANTS	17	
23	PHILADELPHIA	17	
3	Baltimore	10	
17	Philadelphia	14	
10	GREEN BAY	9	
7	DALLAS	14	
10	Buffalo	0	
26	St. Louis	20	
17	LOS ANGELES	14	

Use Name	Pos.	Hgt	Wgt	Age	Int	Pts
George Starke	OT	6'5"	249	29		
Tim Stokes	OT	6'5"	252	27		
Tony Hermeling	•OG	6'5"	255	31		
Dan Nugent	OG	6'3"	250	24		
Ron Saul	OG	6'2"	254	29		
Ted Fritsch	C	6'2"	242	27		
Len Hauss	C	6'2"	235	35		
Bob Kuziel	C-OT	6'5"	255	27		
Dallas Hickman	DE	6'6"	235	25		
Dennis Johnson	DE	6'4"	260	25		
Karl Lorch	DE	6'3"	253	27		
Ron McDole	DE	6'3"	265	37	2	
Bill Wynn	DE	6'4"	245	28		
Bill Brundige	DT	6'5"	270	28		
Dave Butz	DT	6'7"	285	27		
Diron Talbert	DT	6'5"	255	33		
Mike Curtis	LB	6'2"	232	34	1	
Brad Dusek	LB	6'2"	214	26	1	
Chris Hanburger	LB	6'2"	218	36		
Joe Harris	LB	6'1"	225	24		
Harold McLinton	LB	6'2"	235	30		
Stu O'Dell	LB	6'1"	220	25		
Rusty Tillman	LB	6'2"	230	31		
Pete Wysocki	LB	6'2"	225	28		
Eddie Brown	DB	5'11"	190	25	1	
Pat Fischer	DB	5'10"	170	37		
Windlan Hall (from MIN)	DB	5'11"	175	27		
Ken Houston	DB	6'3"	198	32	5	
Joe Lavender	DB	6'4"	190	28	4	
Mark Murphy	DB	6'4"	210	22		
Brig Owens	DB	5'11"	190	34		
Jake Scott	DB	6'	188	32	3	
Gerard Williams	DB	6'1"	184	25	4	
Billy Kilmer	QB	6'	204	37		
Joe Theismann	QB	6'	184	27		6
Bob Brunet	HB	6'1"	205	31		
Clarence Harmon	HB	5'11"	190	21		6
Mike Thomas	HB	5'11"	190	24		30
Calvin Hill	FB	6'3"	227	30		6
Eddie Moss	FB	6'	215	28		
John Riggins	FB	6'2"	230	28		12
Danny Buggs	WR	6'2"	185	24		6
Frank Grant	WR	5'11"	181	27		18
Larry Jones	WR	5'10"	170	26		
Howard Satterwhite (to BAL)	WR	5'11"	185	24		
Charley Taylor	WR	6'3"	210	35		
Jean Fugett	TE	6'3"	226	25		30
Jerry Smith	TE	6'2"	208	34		
Mike Bragg	K	5'11"	186	30		
Mark Moseley	K	5'11"	205	29		82

Brian Fryer – Injury

ST. LOUIS CARDINALS 7-7 Don Coryell

Scores of Each Game			
0	Denver	7	
16	CHICAGO	13	
14	Washington	24	
24	DALLAS	30	
21	Philadelphia	17	
49	NEW ORLEANS	31	
28	N.Y. GIANTS	0	
27	Minnesota	7	
24	Dallas	17	
21	PHILADELPHIA	16	
14	MIAMI	55	
7	N.Y. Giants	27	
20	WASHINGTON	26	
7	Tampa Bay	17	

Use Name	Pos.	Hgt	Wgt	Age	Int	Pts
Dan Dierdorf	OT	6'4"	288	28		
Roger Finnie	OT	6'3"	248	31		
Brad Oates	OT	6'6"	274	23		
Dan Audick	OG	6'3"	244	22		
Conrad Dobler	OG	6'3"	253	26		6
Keith Wortman	OG-OT-C	6'2"	262	27		
Bob Young	OG	6'2"	279	34		
Tom Banks	C	6'1"	244	29		
Tom Brahaney	C	6'2"	246	25		
Bob Bell	DE	6'4"	257	29		
Ron Yankowski	DE	6'5"	258	30		
John Zook	DE	6'5"	254	29		
Charlie Davis	DT	6'1"	268	25		6
Mike Dawson	DT	6'4"	274	23		
Walt Patulski	DT	6'6"	267	27		
Kurt Allerman	LB	6'3"	222	22		
Mark Arneson	LB	6'2"	224	27	2	
Tim Black	LB	6'2"	215	22		
Tim Kearney	LB	6'2"	225	26		
Marv Kellum	LB	6'2"	225	25	1	
Steve Neils	LB	6'2"	218	26		
Eric Williams	LB	6'2"	217	22		
Carl Allen	DB	6'	185	21	1	
Bill Bradley	DB	5'11"	190	30		
Rondy Colbert	DB	5'9"	165	23		
Robert Giblin	DB	6'2"	210	24		
Lee Nelson	DB	5'10"	183	23	4	
Ken Reaves	DB	6'3"	208	32	2	
Mike Sensibaugh	DB	5'11"	190	28	3	6
Jeff Severson	DB	6'1"	185	27	1	
Perry Smith	DB	6'1"	198	26		
Roger Wehrli	DB	6'1"	193	29	5	
Billy Donckers	QB	6'1"	207	26		
Jim Hart	QB	6'2"	210	33		
Steve Pisarkiewicz	QB	6'2"	205	23		
Steve Jones	HB	6'	198	26		18
Jerry Latin	HB	5'10"	186	24		12
Terry Metcalf	HB	5'10"	185	25		36
Wayne Morris	FB	6'	208	23		54
Jim Otis	FB	6'	226	29		12
Mel Gray	WR	5'9"	178	28		30
Ike Harris	WR	6'3"	205	24		18
Ken Stone	WR-DB	6'1"	180	26		
Pat Tilley	WR	5'10"	171	24		
J.V. Cain	TE	6'4"	221	26		12
Jackie Smith	TE	6'4"	226	37		6
Jim Bakken	K	6'	198	36		56
Duane Carrell (from NYJ)	K	5'10"	178	27		
Terry Joyce	K	6'6"	227	23		

Ray White – Knee Injury

PHILADELPHIA EAGLES 5-9 Dick Vermeil

Scores of Each Game			
13	TAMPA BAY	3	
0	Los Angeles	20	
13	Detroit	17	
28	N.Y. Giants	10	
17	ST. LOUIS	21	
10	DALLAS	16	
17	Washington	23	
28	NEW ORLEANS	7	
14	WASHINGTON	17	
16	St. Louis	21	
6	New England	14	
14	Dallas	24	
17	N.Y. GIANTS	14	
27	N.Y. JETS	0	

Use Name	Pos.	Hgt	Wgt	Age	Int	Pts
Ed George	OT	6'4"	270	31		
Donnie Green	OT	6'7"	261	29		
Dennis Nelson	OT	6'5"	260	31		
Stan Walters	OT	6'6"	270	29		
Wade Key	OG	6'4"	245	30		
Tom Luken	OG	6'3"	253	27		
Jerry Sisemore	OG	6'4"	260	26		
Dennis Franks	C	6'1"	236	24		
Guy Morriss	C	6'4"	255	26		
Lem Burnham	DE	6'4"	228	30		
Carl Hairston	DE	6'3"	245	24		
Manny Sistrunk	DE	6'5"	276	30		
Art Thoms	DE-NT	6'5"	250	30		
Johnny Jackson	NT	6'2"	250	24		
Charles Johnson	NT	6'3"	262	25		
Pete Lazetich	NT	6'3"	245	27		
Bill Bergey	LB	6'2"	245	32	2	
John Bunting	LB	6'1"	220	27		
Tom Ehlers	LB	6'2"	218	25		
Frank LeMaster	LB	6'2"	231	25		
Drew Mahalic	LB	6'4"	225	24		
James Reed	LB	6'2"	230	22		
Terry Tautolo	LB	6'2"	235	23		
Herman Edwards	DB	6'	194	23	6	
Eric Johnson	DB	6'1"	192	25		
Randy Logan	DB	6'1"	195	26	5	
Larry Marshall	DB	5'10"	195	27		
Mark Mitchell	DB	6'1"	180	22		
John Outlaw	DB	5'10"	180	31	2	
Deac Sanders	DB	6'1"	178	27	6	
Roman Gabriel	QB	6'4"	225	37		
Ron Jaworski	QB	6'2"	195	26		30
John Walton	QB	6'2"	210	29		
Herb Lusk	HB	6'	190	24		18
Wilbert Montgomery	HB	5'10"	195	22		18
Tom Sullivan	HB	6'	190	27		12
James Betterson	FB	6'	210	23		6
Cleveland Franklin	FB	6'2"	216	22		
Mike Hogan	FB	6'2"	215	22		6
Harold Carmichael	WR	6'7"	225	27		42
Wally Henry	WR	5'8"	170	22		
Vince Papale	WR	6'2"	195	31		
Larry Sievers	WR	6'4"	204	23		
Charlie Smith	WR	6'1"	185	27		24
Keith Krepfle	TE	6'3"	225	25		18
Richard Osborne	TE	6'3"	230	23		
Ove Johannson	K	5'10"	175	29		4
Spike Jones	K	6'2"	195	30		
Nick Mike-Mayer (from ATL)	K	5'8"	187	27		44
Horst Muhlmann	K	6'1"	211	37		26

NEW YORK GIANTS 5-9 John McVay

Scores of Each Game			
20	WASHINGTON	17	
21	Dallas	41	
3	Atlanta	17	
10	PHILADELPHIA	28	
20	SAN FRANCISCO	17	
17	Washington	6	
0	St. Louis	28	
10	DALLAS	24	
10	Tampa Bay	0	
7	CLEVELAND	21	
13	Cincinnati	30	
27	ST. LOUIS	7	
14	Philadelphia	17	
9	CHICAGO	*12	

Use Name	Pos.	Hgt	Wgt	Age	Int	Pts
Mike Gibbons	OT	6'4"	262	26		
Gordon Gravelle	OT	6'5"	252	28		
Ron Mikolajczyk	OG	6'3"	275	27		
Tom Mullen	OT	6'3"	250	25		
Brad Benson	OG	6'3"	255	21		
Bill Ellenbogen	OG-OT	6'5"	255	26		
John Hicks	OG	6'2"	258	26		
Doug Van Horn	OG-OT	6'2"	243	33		
Karl Chandler	C	6'5"	250	25		
Ralph Hill	C	6'1"	245	27		
Jack Gregory	DE	6'6"	250	32		
Gary Jeter	DE	6'4"	250	22		
George Martin	DE	6'4"	245	24	1	6
Troy Archer	DT	6'4"	250	22		
John Mendenhall	DT	6'1"	255	28		
Jim Pietrzak	DT	6'5"	260	24		
J.T. Turner	DT	6'3"	250	24		
Harry Carson	LB	6'2"	235	23		
Brian Kelley	LB	6'3"	222	26	1	
Dan Lloyd	LB	6'2"	225	23		
Frank Marion	LB	6'3"	230	26		
Andy Selfridge	LB	6'4"	220	28		
Brad Van Pelt	LB	6'5"	235	26	2	
Bill Bryant	DB	5'11"	195	26	3	6
Ernie Jones	DB	6'3"	180	24	1	
Larry Mallory	DB	5'11"	185	25	1	
Clyde Powers	DB	6'1"	195	26	1	
Beasley Reece	DB	6'1"	186	23		
Ray Rhodes	DB	5'11"	185	26	2	
Jim Stienke	DB	5'11"	182	26		
Randy Dean	QB	6'3"	195	22		
Jerry Golsteyn	QB	6'4"	210	23		
Joe Pisarcik	QB	6'4"	220	25		12
Gordon Bell	HB	5'9"	180	23		
Bob Hammond	HB	5'10"	170	25		24
Harold Hart	HB	6'	211	24		
Doug Kotar	HB	5'11"	203	26		12
Larry Csonka	FB	6'3"	233	30		6
Willie Spencer	FB	6'3"	235	24		18
Larry Watkins	FB	6'2"	230	30		
Ed Marshall	WR	6'5"	200	29		
Emery Moorehead	WR	6'2"	210	23		6
Johnny Perkins	WR	6'2"	205	24		
Jim Robinson	WR	5'9"	170	24		18
Boyd Brown	TE	6'4"	216	25		
Al Dixon	TE	6'5"	220	23		
Gary Shirk	TE	6'1"	220	27		12
Joe Danelo	K	5'9"	166	23		61
Dave Jennings	K	6'4"	203	25		

Dave Gallagher – Voluntary Retirement
Dick Leavitt – Knee Injury
Marsh White – Wrist Injury

*—Overtime

DALLAS COWBOYS

RUSHING

Last Name	No	Yds	Avg	TD
Dorsett	208	1007	4.8	12
Newhouse	180	721	4.0	3
P. Pearson	89	341	3.8	1
Staubach	51	171	3.4	3
Dennison	12	60	5.0	1
Brinson	8	28	3.5	1
D. Pearson	2	22	11.0	0
Laidlaw	9	15	1.7	0
DuPree	3	9	3.0	0
D. White	1	−2	−2.0	0
Johnson	1	−3	−3.0	0

RECEIVING

Last Name	No	Yds	Avg	TD
D. Pearson	48	870	18	2
P. Pearson	46	535	12	4
Dorsett	29	273	9	1
DuPree	28	347	12	3
Richards	17	225	13	3
Newhouse	16	106	7	1
Johnson	12	136	11	1
Saldi	11	108	10	2
Laidlaw	5	60	12	1
Hill	2	21	11	0
Dennison	1	9	9	0

PUNT RETURNS

Last Name	No	Yds	Avg	TD
Johnson	50	423	8	0
Hill	10	124	12	0
Harris	1	−2	−2	0

KICKOFF RETURNS

Last Name	No	Yds	Avg	TD
Johnson	22	536	24	0
Brinson	17	409	24	0
Hill	3	64	21	0
Dennison	1	30	30	0
DuPree	0	24	–	0
Henderson	1	8	8	0

PASSING – PUNTING – KICKING Statistics

PASSING	Att	Comp	%	Yds	Yd/Att	TD	Int–%	RK
Staubach	361	210	58	2620	7.3	18	9– 2	1
D. White	10	4	40	35	3.5	0	1– 10	
Dorsett	1	1	100	34	34.0	0	0– 0	

PUNTING	No	Avg
D. White	80	39.6
Herrera	2	22.0

KICKING	XP	Att	%	FG	Att	%
Herrera	39	41	95	18	29	62

WASHINGTON REDSKINS

RUSHING

Last Name	No	Yds	Avg	TD
Thomas	228	806	3.5	3
Harmon	94	310	3.3	0
Hill	69	257	3.7	0
Riggins	68	203	3.0	0
Theismann	29	149	5.1	1
Kilmer	10	20	2.0	0
Brunet	3	6	2.0	0
Jones	1	1	1.0	0

RECEIVING

Last Name	No	Yds	Avg	TD
Fuggett	36	631	17	5
Grant	34	480	14	3
Thomas	28	245	9	2
Buggs	26	341	13	1
Hill	18	154	9	1
Taylor	14	158	11	0
Harmon	14	119	9	1
Riggins	7	95	14	2
Jones	5	55	11	0
Smith	1	6	6	0

PUNT RETURNS

Last Name	No	Yds	Avg	TD
Brown	57	452	8	0

KICKOFF RETURNS

Last Name	No	Yds	Avg	TD
Brown	34	852	25	0
Murphy	3	44	15	0
Tillman	3	39	13	0
Jones	2	42	21	0
Brunet	2	40	20	0
Moss	2	35	18	0
Harmon	1	18	18	0
Buggs	0	17	–	0

PASSING – PUNTING – KICKING Statistics

PASSING	Att	Comp	%	Yds	Yd/Att	TD	Int–%	RK
Kilmer	201	99	49	1187	5.9	8	7– 4	6
Thiesmann	182	84	46	1097	6.0	7	9– 5	11

PUNTING	No	Avg.
Bragg	91	38.5

KICKING	XP	Att	%	FG	Att	%
Moseley	19	19	100	21	37	57

ST. LOUIS CARDINALS

RUSHING

Last Name	No	Yds	Avg	TD
Metcalf	149	739	5.0	4
Morris	165	661	4.0	8
Otis	99	334	3.4	2
Latin	56	208	3.7	2
Jones	24	77	3.2	3
Wehrli	1	19	19.0	0
Hart	11	18	1.6	0
Gray	1	−1	−1.0	0
Joyce	1	−13	−13.0	0
Carrell	2	−15	−7.5	0

RECEIVING

Last Name	No	Yds	Avg	TD
Harris	40	547	14	3
Gray	38	782	21	5
Metcalf	34	403	12	2
Cain	25	328	13	2
Morris	24	222	9	1
Jones	12	66	6	0
Latin	9	89	10	0
Tilley	5	64	13	0
J. Smith	5	49	10	1
Otis	2	18	9	0
Stone	1	40	40	0

PUNT RETURNS

Last Name	No	Yds	Avg	TD
Metcalf	14	108	8	0
Tilley	13	111	9	0
Bradley	11	77	7	0
Nelson	1	4	4	0
Severson	1	0	0	0

KICKOFF RETURNS

Last Name	No	Yds	Avg	TD
Metcalf	32	772	24	0
Jones	8	132	17	0
Bradley	7	75	19	0
Latin	3	79	26	0
Nelson	3	68	23	0
Allerman	2	39	20	0
Morris	2	39	20	0
Otis	1	16	16	0
Wortman	1	15	15	0
Oates	1	11	11	0
J. Smith	1	15	15	0
P. Smith	1	10	10	0

PASSING – PUNTING – KICKING Statistics

PASSING	Att	Comp	%	Yds	Yd/Att	TD	Int–%	RK
Hart	355	186	52	2542	7.2	13	20 6	7
Donckers	5	5	100	38	7.6	0	0– 0	
Metcalf	5	3	60	27	5.4	1	1– 20	
Joyce	1	1	100	1	1.0	0	0– 0	

PUNTING	No	Avg.
Carrell	63	36.7
Joyce	22	38.7

KICKING	XP	Att	%	FG	Att	%
Bakken	35	36	97	7	16	44

PHILADELPHIA EAGLES

RUSHING

Last Name	No	Yds	Avg	TD
Hogan	155	546	3.5	0
Sullivan	125	303	2.0	0
Betterson	62	233	3.8	1
Lusk	52	229	4.4	2
Montgomery	45	183	4.1	2
Jaworski	40	127	3.2	5
Lemaster	1	30	30.0	0
Smith	2	13	6.5	0
Franklin	1	0	0.0	0
Henry	1	−2	−2.0	0

RECEIVING

Last Name	No	Yds	Avg	TD
Carmichael	46	665	15	7
Smith	33	464	14	4
Krepfle	27	530	20	3
Sullivan	26	223	9	2
Hogan	19	118	6	1
Lusk	5	102	20	1
Betterson	4	41	10	0
Montgomery	3	18	6	0
Henry	2	16	8	0
Papale	1	15	15	0
Osborne	1	6	6	0

PUNT RETURNS

Last Name	No	Yds	Avg	TD
Marshall	46	489	11	0
Henry	2	25	13	0
Mitchell	2	4	2	0

KICKOFF RETURNS

Last Name	No	Yds	Avg	TD
Montgomery	23	619	27	1
Marshall	20	455	23	0
Lusk	1	23	23	0
Betterson	1	13	13	0

PASSING – PUNTING – KICKING Statistics

PASSING	Att	Comp	%	Yds	Yd/Att	TD	Int–%	RK
Jaworski	346	166	48	2183	6.3	18	21– 6	10
Gabriel	3	1	33	15	5.0	0	0– 0	

PUNTING	No.	Avg.
Jones	93.	37.2
Mike-Mayer	1	23.0

KICKING	XP	Att	%	FG	Att	%
Muhlmann	17	19	88	3	8	38
Mike-Mayer	14	14	100	10	22	45
Johansson	1	3	33	1	4	25

NEW YORK GIANTS

RUSHING

Last Name	No	Yds	Avg	TD
Hammond	154	577	3.7	3
Kotar	132	480	3.6	2
Csonka	134	464	3.5	1
Spencer	62	184	3.0	3
Watkins	19	71	3.7	0
Bell	16	63	3.9	0
Pisarcik	27	57	2.1	2
Moorehead	1	5	5.0	0
Golsteyn	3	−4	−1.3	0

RECEIVING

Last Name	No	Yds	Avg	TD
Robinson	22	422	19	3
Perkins	20	279	14	0
Hammond	19	136	7	0
Shirk	16	280	18	2
Kotar	15	73	5	0
Moorehead	12	143	12	1
Marshall	7	178	25	0
Dixon	6	78	13	0
Bell	4	33	8	0
Spencer	4	20	5	0
Csonka	2	20	10	0
Watkins	1	9	9	0

PUNT RETURNS

Last Name	No	Yds	Avg	TD
Hammond	32	334	10	1
Robinson	7	87	12	0
Steinke	5	30	6	0
Bell	1	0	0	0
Reece	1	−5	−5	0

KICKOFF RETURNS

Last Name	No	Yds	Avg	TD
Hammond	19	419	22	0
Bell	12	235	20	0
Reece	7	159	23	0
Moorehead	4	65	16	0
Spencer	3	44	15	0
Shirk	3	38	13	0
Kotar	2	36	18	0
Kelley	1	20	20	0
Hill	1	11	11	0
Selfridge	1	9	9	0
Mallory	1	0	0	0

PASSING – PUNTING – KICKING Statistics

PASSING	Att	Comp	%	Yds	Yd/Att	TD	Int–%	RK
Pisarcik	241	103	43	1346	5.6	4	14– 6	13
Golsteyn	70	31	44	416	5.9	2	8– 11	

PUNTING	No	Avg.
Jennings	100	39.9

KICKING	XP	Att	%	FG	Att	%
Danelo	19	20	95	14	23	61

MINNESOTA VIKINGS 9-5 Bud Grant

Scores of Each Game		
10	DALLAS	16
9	Tampa Bay	3
19	GREEN BAY	7
14	DETROIT	7
22	CHICAGO	16
3	Los Angeles	35
14	Atlanta	7
7	ST. LOUIS	27
42	CINCINNATI	10
7	Chicago	10
13	Green Bay	6
28	SAN FRANCISCO	27
13	Oakland	35
30	Detroit	21

Use Name	Pos.	Hgt	Wgt	Age	Int	Pts
Bart Buetow	OT	6'5"	250	26		
Steve Riley	OT	6'6"	258	24		
Ron Yary	OT	6'6"	255	31		
Charlie Goodrum	OG	6'3"	256	27		
Wes Hamilton	OG	6'3"	255	24		
Dennis Swilley	OG-OT	6'3	241	22		
Ed White	OG-OT	6'2"	270	30		
Doug Dumler	C	6'3"	242	26		
Mick Tinglehoff	C	6'1"	240	37		
Carl Eller	DE	6'6"	247	35		2
Joey Jackson	DE-DT	6'4"	262	28		
Jim Marshall	DE	6'3"	240	39		
Mark Mullaney	DE	6'6"	242	24		
Alan Page	DT	6'5"	245	32		
Doug Sutherland	DT	6'3"	250	29		
James White	DT	6'3"	263	23		

Use Name	Pos.	Hgt	Wgt	Age	Int	Pts
Matt Blair	LB	6'5"	229	26	1	6
Wally Hilgenberg	LB	6'3"	229	34		
Fred McNeill	LB	6'2"	229	25	1	
Jeff Siemon	LB	6'2"	237	27	1	
Scott Studwell	LB	6'2"	224	23	1	
Nate Allen	DB	5'10"	174	29	1	
Joe Blahak	DB	5'9"	185	27		
Bobby Bryant	DB	6'	170	33	4	
Tom Hannon	DB	5'11"	193	22		
Paul Krause	DB	6'3"	205	35	2	
Phil Wise	DB	6'	193	28	1	
Jeff Wright	DB	5'11"	190	28	1	
Nate Wright	DB	5'11"	180	29	3	6

Use Name	Pos.	Hgt	Wgt	Age	Int	Pts
Tommy Kramer	QB	6'1"	199	22		
Bob Lee	QB	6'2"	195	31		
Fran Tarkenton	QB	6'1"	185	37		
Chuck Foreman	HB	6'2"	207	26		54
Sammy Johnson	HB-FB	6'	226	24		12
Manfred Moore	HB	6'	200	26		
Mark Kellar	FB	6'	225	25		
Brent McClanahan	FB	5'10"	202	26		18
Robert Miller	FB	5'11"	204	24		
Bob Grim	WR	6'	188	32		
Ahmad Rashad	WR	6'2"	200	27		12
Sammy White	WR	5'11"	189	23		54
Steve Craig	TE	6'3"	231	26		
Bob Tucker (from NYG)	TE	6'3"	230	32		12
Stu Voigt	TE	6'1"	225	29		6
Neil Clabo	K	6'2"	200	24		
Fred Cox	K	5'10"	200	38		49

CHICAGO BEARS 9-5 Jack Pardee

Scores of Each Game		
30	DETROIT	20
13	St. Louis	16
24	NEW ORLEANS	42
24	LOS ANGELES	23
16	Minnesota	22
10	ATLANTA	16
26	Green Bay	0
0	Houston	47
28	KANSAS CITY	27
10	MINNESOTA	7
31	Detroit	14
10	Tampa Bay	0
21	GREEN BAY	10
12	N.Y. Giants	*9

Use Name	Pos.	Hgt	Wgt	Age	Int	Pts
Ted Albrecht	OT-OG	6'4"	253	22		
Dan Jiggetts	OT	6'4"	276	23		
Dennis Lick	OT	6'3"	268	23		
Jeff Sevy	OT-DT-DE	6'5"	261	26		
Fred Dean	OG	6'3"	253	22		
Noah Jackson	OG	6'2"	273	26		
Revie Sorey	OG	6'2"	259	23		
Dan Neal	C-OG	6'4"	248	28		
Dan Peiffer	C	6'3"	251	26		
Mike Hartenstine	DE	6'3"	257	24		
Jerry Meyers	DE-DT	6'4"	245	23		
Billy Newsome	DE	6'4"	250	29		
Wally Chambers	DT-DE	6'6"	259	26		
Jim Osborne	DT	6'3"	251	27		
Don Rydalch	DT	6'4"	257	25		
Roger Stilwell	DT-DE	6'6"	258	25		

Use Name	Pos.	Hgt	Wgt	Age	Int	Pts
Waymond Bryant	LB	6'3"	239	25		
Doug Buffone	LB	6'1"	227	33	1	
Gary Campbell	LB	6'1"	218	25		
Tom Hicks	LB	6'4"	225	24	1	
Jerry Muckensturm	LB	6'4"	226	23		
Don Rives	LB	6'2"	231	26		
Mel Rogers	LB	6'2"	230	30		
Craig Clemons	DB	5'11"	191	28		
Allan Ellis	DB	5'10"	175	26	6	
Gary Fencik	DB	6'1"	192	23	4	
Virgil Livers	DB	5'9"	178	25	2	
Doug Plank	DB	6'	201	24	4	
Terry Schmidt	DB	6'	176	25		
Mike Spivey	DB	6'	194	23		
Len Walterscheid	DB	5'11"	190	22		

Lionel Antoine – Knee Injury
Larry Schreiber – Injury

Use Name	Pos.	Hgt	Wgt	Age	Int	Pts
Bob Avellini	QB	6'2"	206	24		6
Vince Evans	QB	6'2"	216	22		
Mike Phipps	QB	6'2"	211	29		
Art Best	HB	6'1"	205	24		
Johnny Musso	HB-FB	5'11"	196	27		12
Walter Payton	HB	5'11"	205	23		96
Robin Earl	FB	6'5"	247	22		6
Roland Harper	FB	6'	209	24		
Brian Baschnagel	WR	6'	193	23		6
Bo Rather	WR	6'1"	189	26		12
Steve Rivera (from SF)	WR	5'11"	183	23		
Steve Schubert	WR	5'10"	188	26		6
James Scott	WR	6'1"	191	25		18
Chuck Bradley (from SD)	TE	6'6"	239	26		
Greg Latta	TE	6'3"	230	24		24
Bob Parsons	TE	6'4"	232	27		
Bob Thomas	K	5'10"	174	25		69

DETROIT LIONS 6-8 Tommy Hudspeth

Scores of Each Game		
20	Chicago	30
23	NEW ORLEANS	19
17	PHILADELPHIA	13
7	Minnesota	14
10	GREEN BAY	6
7	San Francisco	28
0	Dallas	37
20	SAN DIEGO	0
6	Atlanta	17
16	TAMPA BAY	7
14	CHICAGO	31
9	Green Bay	10
13	Baltimore	10
21	MINNESOTA	30

Use Name	Pos.	Hgt	Wgt	Age	Int	Pts
Rocky Freitas	OT	6'6"	275	31		
Craig Hertwig	OT	6'8"	270	25		
Dave Simonsen	OT	6'6"	248	25		
Jim Yarbrough	OT	6'6"	270	30		
Gary Anderson	OG	6'3"	250	21		
Lynn Boden	OG	6'5"	270	24		
Russ Bolinger	OG-OT	6'5"	255	22		
Mark Markovich	OG-C	6'5"	255	24		
Mel Mitchell	OG-C	6'3"	260	24		
Jon Morris	C	6'4"	250	34		
Jim Mitchell	DE	6'3"	250	28		
Ernie Price	DE	6'4"	245	26		
Ken Sanders	DE	6'5"	245	27		
John Woodcock	DE	6'3"	240	23		
Doug English	DT	6'5"	255	24		2
Larry Hand	DT	6'4"	245	37		
Herb Orvis	DT	6'5"	255	30		

Use Name	Pos.	Hgt	Wgt	Age	Int	Pts
Tony Daykin	LB	6'1"	215	22		
Jim Laslavic	LB	6'2"	240	25	1	
Mike McGraw	LB	6'2"	225	23		
Paul Naumoff	LB	6'1"	215	32		
Ed O'Neil	LB	6'3"	235	24		6
Garth Ten Napel	LB	6'1"	215	23		
Charlie Weaver	LB	6'2"	225	28	1	
Len Barney	DB	6'	190	31	3	
James Hunter	DB	6'3"	195	23	6	
Dick Jauron	DB	6'	190	26	3	
Levi Johnson	DB	6'3"	200	26	2	
Reggie Pinkney	DB	5'11"	190	22	2	6
Randy Rich (to DEN)	DB	5'10"	175	23		
Charlie West	DB	6'1"	195	31	1	
Walt Williams	DB	6'	185	23		

Lawrence Gaines – Knee Injury
Ken Long – Injury
Benny Ricardo – Shoulder Injury

Use Name	Pos.	Hgt	Wgt	Age	Int	Pts
Gary Danielson	QB	6'2"	195	25		
Greg Landry	QB	6'4"	205	30		
Joe Reed	QB	6'1"	195	29		
Andy Bolton	HB	6'1"	205	23		
Dexter Bussey	HB	6'1"	210	25		30
Rick Kane	HB	5'11"	200	22		24
Eddie Payton (from CLE)	HB	5'8"	175	26		12
Glenn Capriola	FB	5'11"	219	22		
Marv Hubbard	FB	6'1"	235	31		6
Horace King	FB	5'10"	210	24		6
Luther Blue	WR	5'11"	190	21		6
J.D. Hill	WR	6'1"	185	28		6
Ray Jarvis	WR	5'11"	190	28		6
Leonard Thompson	WR-HB	5'10"	190	25		12
David Hill	TE	6'2"	220	23		12
Bill Larson (from WAS)	TE	6'4	225	23		
Charlie Sanders	TE	6'4"	230	31		6
Mitch Hoopes	K	6'1"	204	24		
Steve Mike-Mayer	K	6'	180	29		43
Wilbur Summers	K	6'4"	220	23		

GREEN BAY PACKERS 4-10 Bart Starr

Scores of Each Game		
24	New Orleans	20
10	HOUSTON	16
7	Minnesota	19
7	CINCINNATI	17
6	Detroit	10
13	Tampa Bay	0
0	CHICAGO	26
10	Kansas City	20
6	LOS ANGELES	24
9	Washington	10
6	MINNESOTA	13
10	DETROIT	9
10	Chicago	21
16	SAN FRANCISCO	14

Use Name	Pos.	Hgt	Wgt	Age	Int	Pts
Dick Himes	OT	6'4"	260	31		
Steve Knutson	OT-OG	6'3"	254	25		
Greg Koch	OT	6'4"	265	22		
Mark Koncar	OT	6'5"	268	24		
Dennis Havig	OG	6'2"	251	28		
Melvin Jackson	OG	6'1"	267	23		
Bob Kowalkowski	OG	6'3"	245	33		
Rick Scribner	OG	6'4"	257	21		
Darrel Gofourth	C	6'3"	260	22		
Larry McCarren	C	6'3"	248	25		
Bob Barber	DE-DT	6'3"	240	25		
Mike Butler	DE	6'5"	265	23		
Ezra Johnson	DE	6'4"	240	21		
Clarence Williams	DE-DT	6'5"	255	30		
Herb McMath	DT	6'4"	250	22		
Dave Pureifory	DT	6'1"	255	28		
Dave Roller	DT	6'2"	270	27		

Use Name	Pos.	Hgt	Wgt	Age	Int	Pts
Fred Carr	LB	6'5"	240	31	1	
Jim Carter	LB	6'3"	245	28		
Jim Cheyunski	LB	6'2"	220	31		
Jim Gueno	LB	6'2"	220	23		
Don Hansen	LB	6'3"	228	33		
Blane Smith	LB	6'3"	238	23		
Tom Toner	LB	6'3"	235	27	1	
Gary Weaver	LB	6'1"	225	28		
Willie Buchanon	DB	6'	190	26	2	6
Johnnie Gray	DB	5'11"	185	23	1	
Steve Luke	DB	6'2"	205	23	4	
Mike McCoy	DB	5'11"	183	24	4	
Tim Moresco	DB	5'11"	176	22		
Terry Randolph	DB	6'	184	22		
Steve Wagner	DB	6'2"	208	23		

Use Name	Pos.	Hgt	Wgt	Age	Int	Pts
Lynn Dickey	QB	6'4"	220	27		
Brian Dowling	QB	6'2"	210	30		
David Whitehurst	QB	6'2"	204	22		6
Will Harrell	HB	5'9"	182	24		12
Terdell Middleton	HB	6'	195	22		6
Nate Simpson	HB	5'10"	176	22		
Jim Culbreath	FB	6'	209	24		
Barty Smith	FB	6'4"	240	25		18
Eric Torkelson	FB	6'2"	194	25		6
Keith Hartwig (from MIN)	WR	6'	186	23		
Steve Odom	WR	5'8"	174	24		18
Ken Payne (to PHI)	WR	6'1"	185	26		6
Ollie Smith	WR	6'2"	200	28		
Aundra Thompson	WR-HB	6'	186	24		
Randy Vataha	WR	5'10"	170	28		
Bert Askon	TE	6'3"	225	31		
Rich McGeorge	TE	6'4"	230	28		6
David Beverly	K	6'2"	180	27		
Chester Marcol	K	6'	190	27		50

TAMPA BAY BUCCANEERS 2-12 John McKay

Scores of Each Game		
3	Philadelphia	13
3	MINNESOTA	9
7	Dallas	23
0	WASHINGTON	10
23	Seattle	30
0	GREEN BAY	13
10	San Francisco	20
0	Los Angeles	31
0	N.Y. GIANTS	10
7	Detroit	16
0	ATLANTA	17
0	CHICAGO	10
33	New Orleans	14
17	ST. LOUIS	7

Use Name	Pos.	Hgt	Wgt	Age	Int	Pts
Darryl Carlton	OT	6'6"	270	24		
Blanchard Carter	OT	6'4"	250	22		
Dave Reavis	OT-OG	6'5"	250	27		
Randy Johnson	OG	6'2"	255	24		
Dan Medlin	OG	6'4"	255	27		
Steve Wilson	OG-C	6'3"	265	23		
Jeff Winans	OG-OT	6'5"	265	25		
Dan Ryczek	C	6'3"	250	28		
Charley Hannah	DE	6'5"	250	22		
Glenn Robinson	DE	6'6"	245	25		
Council Rudolph	DE	6'3"	255	27		
Lee Roy Selmon	DE	6'3"	260	22		
Greg Johnson (from BAL & CHI)	DT NT-DE	6'4"	240	23	1	6
Bill Kollar	NT	6'4"	256	24		
Dave Pear	NT	6'2"	250	24		

Howard Fest – Injury
Tody Smith – Injury

Use Name	Pos.	Hgt	Wgt	Age	Int	Pts
Rik Bonness	LB	6'3"	220	23		
Paul Harris	LB	6'3"	225	22		
Cecil Johnson	LB	6'2"	220	22	1	
Mike Lemon	LB	6'2"	220	26		
Dave Lewis	LB	6'4"	2[illegible]0	22	2	
Dewey Selmon	LB	6'1"	250	23	2	
Richard Wood	LB	6'2"	215	24	4	12
Cedric Brown	DB	6'1"	190	23	2	
Mark Cotney	DB	6'	205	25	1	
Curtis Jordan	DB	6'2"	185	23	1	
Reggie Pierson	DB	5'11"	185	24		
Danny Reece	DB	5'11"	190	22		
Mike Washington	DB	6'3"	190	24	5	6
Jeris White	DB	5'11"	180	24	4	

Mike Boryla – Knee Injury

Use Name	Pos.	Hgt	Wgt	Age	Int	Pts
Jeb Blount	QB	6'3"	200	23		
Parnell Dickinson	QB	6'2"	185	24		
Randy Hedberg	QB	6'3"	200	22		
Gary Huff	QB	6'1"	195	26		
Louis Carter	HB	5'11"	209	24		12
Anthony Davis	HB	5'10"	190	24		6
Jack Wender	HB	6'	210	23		
Ricky Bell	FB	6'2"	220	21		6
Jimmy DuBose	FB	5'11"	215	22		
Ed Williams	FB	6'2"	245	27		
Isaac Hagins	WR	5'9"	180	23		
John McKay	WR	5'11"	185	24		
Larry Mucker	WR	5'11"	190	22		
Morris Owens	WR	6'	190	24		18
George Ragsdale	WR-HB	5'11"	185	23		
Gary Butler	TE	6'3"	235	26		
Bob Moore	TE	6'3"	225	28		
Dana Nafziger	TE	6'1"	220	23		
Jack Novak	TE	6'4"	240	24		
Charles Waddell	TE	6'5"	235	24		
Dave Green	K	5'11"	205	27		17
Allan Leavitt	K	5'11"	176	21		20
Larry Swider	K	6'2"	193	22		

*—Overtime

MINNESOTA VIKINGS

RUSHING

Last Name	No.	Yds	Avg	TD
Foreman	270	1112	4.1	6
McClanahan	95	324	3.4	1
Johnson	55	217	3.9	2
Miller	46	152	3.3	0
Kellar	7	15	2.1	0
Tarkenton	15	6	0.4	0
Kramer	10	3	0.3	0
Lee	12	−8	−0.7	0

RECEIVING

Last Name	No.	Yds	Avg	TD
Rashad	51	681	13	2
S. White	41	760	19	9
Foreman	38	308	8	3
McClanahan	34	276	8	2
Miller	27	246	9	0
Voigt	20	212	11	1
Tucker	15	200	13	2
Johnson	4	21	5	0
Grim	3	65	22	0
Craig	1	14	14	0

PUNT RETURNS

Last Name	No.	Yds	Avg	TD
Moore	47	277	6	0
Grim	11	69	6	0

KICKOFF RETURNS

Last Name	No.	Yds	Avg	TD
Moore	24	524	22	0
S. White	7	113	16	0
Miller	5	66	13	0
McClanahan	4	90	23	0
Kellar	3	37	12	0
Grim	1	4	4	0
Swilley	1	0	0	0

PASSING – PUNTING – KICKING

PASSING	Att	Comp	%	Yds	Yd/Att	TD	Int– %	RK
Tarkenton	258	155	60	1734	6.7	9	14– 5	3
Lee	72	42	58	522	7.3	4	4– 6	
Kramer	57	30	53	425	7.5	5	4– 7	
Krause	1	1	100	11	11.0	1	0– 0	

PUNTING	No	Avg
Clabo	83	39.8

KICKING	XP	Att	%	FG	Att	%
Cox	25	29	86	8	17	47

CHICAGO BEARS

RUSHING

Last Name	No.	Yds	Avg	TD
Payton	339	1852	5.5	14
Harper	120	457	3.8	0
Earl	56	233	4.2	1
Musso	37	132	3.6	2
Avellini	37	109	2.9	1
Best	6	20	3.3	0
Rather	2	8	4.0	0
Baschnagel	1	0	0.0	0
Evans	1	0	0.0	0

RECEIVING

Last Name	No.	Yds	Avg	TD
Scott	50	809	16	3
Payton	27	269	10	2
Latta	26	335	13	4
Harper	19	142	8	0
Rather	17	294	17	2
Schubert	8	119	15	0
Earl	6	32	5	0
Baschnagel	4	50	13	0
Musso	3	13	4	0
Rivera	1	7	7	0

PUNT RETURNS

Last Name	No.	Yds	Avg	TD
Schubert	31	291	9	1
Walterscheid	6	59	10	0
Livers	6	46	8	0
Baschnagel	3	54	18	0
Rivera	3	7	2	0
Plank	1	21	21	0

KICKOFF RETURNS

Last Name	No.	Yds	Avg	TD
Baschnagel	23	557	24	1
Evans	13	253	19	0
Best	6	127	21	0
Musso	5	100	20	0
Walterscheid	3	59	20	0
Harper	3	44	15	0
Payton	2	95	48	0
Earl	2	38	19	0

PASSING – PUNTING – KICKING

PASSING	Att	Comp	%	Yds	Yd/Att	TD	Int– %	RK
Avellini	293	154	53	2004	6.8	11	18– 6	9
Phipps	5	3	60	5	1.0	0	0– 0	
Parsons	4	4	100	61	15.3	0	0– 0	
Harper	2	0	0	0	0.0	0	0– 0	
Baschnagel	1	0	0	0	0.0	0	0– 0	

PUNTING	No	Avg
Parsons	80	40.4

KICKING	XP	Att	%	FG	Att	%
Thomas	27	30	90	14	27	52

DETROIT LIONS

RUSHING

Last Name	No.	Yds	Avg	TD
King	155	521	3.4	1
Kane	124	421	3.4	4
Bussey	85	338	4.0	4
Hubbard	38	150	3.9	1
Landry	25	99	4.0	0
Thompson	31	91	2.9	1
Danielson	7	62	8.9	0
Payton	4	13	3.3	0
D. Hill	4	10	2.5	0
Bolton	3	4	1.3	0
Reed	1	3	3.0	0
Summers	1	0	0.0	0
Blue	1	−6	−6.0	0

RECEIVING

Last Name	No.	Yds	Avg	TD
King	40	238	6	0
D. Hill	32	465	14	2
Jarvis	28	353	13	1
J.D. Hill	24	247	10	1
Kane	18	186	10	0
C. Sanders	14	170	12	1
Bussey	11	116	11	1
Blue	8	90	11	1
Thompson	7	42	6	0
Hubbard	6	36	6	0
Payton	2	10	5	0
Bolton	1	6	6	0

PUNT RETURNS

Last Name	No.	Yds	Avg	TD
Payton	30	290	10	1
Jauron	11	41	4	0
Rich	2	18	9	0
Kane	1	13	13	0
Blue	1	0	0	0

KICKOFF RETURNS

Last Name	No.	Yds	Avg	TD
Payton	22	548	25	1
Kane	16	376	24	0
Bolton	6	86	14	0
Thompson	5	84	17	0
Rich	5	73	15	0
Hunter	4	95	24	0
Blue	1	24	24	0
Hubbard	1	18	18	0
Boden	1	14	14	0
Woodcock	1	12	12	0

PASSING – PUNTING – KICKING

PASSING	Att	Comp	%	Yds	Yd/Att	TD	Int– %	RK
Landry	240	135	56	1359	5.7	6	7– 3	4
Danielson	100	42	42	445	4.5	1	5– 5	
Reed	40	13	33	150	3.8	0	4– 10	
Summers	1	1	100	5	5.0	0	0– 0	
Thompson	1	0	0	0	0.0	0	0– 0	
D. Hill	1	0	0	0	0.0	0	0– 0	
Payton	1	0	0	0	0.0	0	0– 0	

PUNTING	No	Avg
Summers	93	36.8
Hoopes	6	39.2

KICKING	XP	Att	%	FG	Att	%
Mike-Mayer	19	21	90	8	19	42

GREEN BAY PACKERS

RUSHING

Last Name	No.	Yds	Avg	TD
Ba. Smith	166	554	3.3	2
Torkelson	103	309	3.0	1
Simpson	60	204	3.4	0
Harrell	60	140	2.3	1
Middleton	35	97	2.8	0
Whitehurst	14	55	3.9	1
Culbreath	12	53	4.4	0
Dickey	5	24	4.8	0
Odom	1	6	6.0	0
Beverly	2	−3	−1.5	0

RECEIVING

Last Name	No.	Yds	Avg	TD
Ba. Smith	37	340	9	1
Odom	27	549	20	3
O. Smith	22	357	16	0
Harrell	19	194	10	0
McGeorge	17	142	8	1
Torkelson	11	107	10	0
Vataha	10	109	11	0
Payne	7	99	14	1
Simpson	5	19	4	0
Askon	2	51	26	0
Thompson	2	12	6	0
Culbreath	2	6	3	0
Middleton	1	27	27	0

PUNT RETURNS

Last Name	No.	Yds	Avg	TD
Harrell	28	253	9	1
Gray	10	68	7	0

KICKOFF RETURNS

Last Name	No.	Yds	Avg	TD
Odom	23	468	20	0
Wagner	6	62	10	0
Culbreath	5	82	16	0
Middleton	4	141	35	1
Thompson	4	82	21	0
Harrell	3	48	16	0
Torkelson	2	36	18	0
Moresco	1	15	15	0
Gofourth	1	13	13	0
Gueno	1	0	0	0
Simpson	1	0	0	0

PASSING – PUNTING – KICKING

PASSING	Att	Comp	%	Yds	Yd/Att	TD	Int– %	RK
Dickey	220	113	51	1346	6.1	5	14– 6	12
Whitehurst	105	50	48	634	6.0	1	7– 7	
Harrell	1	1	100	33	33.0	0	0– 0	
Dowling	1	0	0	0	0.0	0	0– 0	

PUNTING	No	Avg
Beverly	85	39.9

KICKING	XP	Att	%	FG	Att	%
Marcol	11	14	79	13	21	62

TAMPA BAY BUCCANEERS

RUSHING

Last Name	No.	Yds	Avg	TD
Bell	148	436	2.9	1
Davis	95	297	3.1	1
DuBose	71	284	4.0	0
Williams	63	198	3.1	0
L. Carter	59	117	2.0	2
Hedberg	9	35	3.9	0
Blount	5	26	5.2	0
Ragsdale	3	21	7.0	0
Huff	8	10	1.3	0
Hagins	1	2	2.0	0
Green	1	0	0.0	0
Owens	2	−2	−1.0	0

RECEIVING

Last Name	No.	Yds	Avg	TD
Owens	34	655	19	3
Hagins	15	196	13	0
McKay	12	164	14	0
DuBose	11	89	8	0
Bell	11	88	8	0
Williams	10	67	7	0
L. Carter	10	65	7	0
Nafziger	9	119	13	0
Davis	8	91	11	0
Mucker	4	59	15	0
Reece	2	59	30	0
Novak	2	24	12	0
Ragsdale	2	17	9	0
Butler	1	21	21	0

PUNT RETURNS

Last Name	No.	Yds	Avg	TD
Reece	31	274	9	0
Hagins	17	85	5	0

KICKOFF RETURNS

Last Name	No.	Yds	Avg	TD
Hagins	21	493	23	0
Davis	15	277	18	0
Reece	3	72	24	0
Ragsdale	3	68	23	0
Nafziger	1	4	4	0

PASSING – PUNTING – KICKING

PASSING	Att	Comp	%	Yds	Yd/Att	TD	Int– %	RK
Huff	138	67	49	889	6.4	3	13– 9	
Hedberg	90	25	28	244	2.7	0	10– 11	
Blount	89	37	42	522	5.9	0	7– 8	
Green	2	2	100	59	29.5	0	0– 0	
L. Carter	2	0	0	0	0.0	0	0– 0	

PUNTING	No	Avg
Green	98	40.3

KICKING	XP	Att	%	FG	Att	%
Leavitt	5	5	100	5	10	50
Green	5	6	83	4	7	71

LOS ANGELES RAMS 10-4 Chuck Knox

Scores of Each Game		
6	Atlanta	17
20	PHILADELPHIA	0
34	SAN FRANCISCO	14
23	Chicago	24
14	NEW ORLEANS	7
35	MINNESOTA	3
26	New Orleans	27
31	TAMPA BAY	0
24	Green Bay	6
23	San Francisco	10
9	Cleveland	0
20	OAKLAND	14
23	ATLANTA	7
14	Washington	17

Use Name	Pos.	Hgt	Wgt	Age	Int	Pts
Doug France	OT	6'5"	272	24		
Winston Hill	OT	6'4"	272	35		
Jeff Williams	OT	6'4"	256	22		
John Williams	OT	6'3"	265	31		
Dennis Harrah	OG	6'5"	257	24		
Greg Horton	OG	6'4"	245	26		
Tom Mack	OG	6'3"	250	33		
Jackie Slater	OG	6'4"	270	23		
Rick Nuzum	C	6'4"	238	25		
Rich Saul	C	6'3"	250	29		
Al Cowlings	DE-DT	6'5"	245	30		
Fred Dryer	DE	6'6"	240	31		
Jack Youngblood	DE	6'4"	242	27		
Larry Brooks	DT	6'3"	255	27		
Mike Fanning	DT	6'6"	260	24		
Cody Jones	DT-DE	6'5"	240	26		
Bob Brudzinski	LB	6'4"	230	22	2	
Carl Ekern	LB	6'3"	220	23		
Kevin McLain	LB	6'2"	227	22		
Bob Pifferini	LB	6'2"	226	27		
Jack Reynolds	LB	6'1"	232	29		
Isiah Robertson	LB	6'3"	225	28	1	
Jim Youngblood	LB	6'3"	239	27	2	6
Nolan Cromwell	DB	6'1"	196	22		
Dave Elmendorf	DB	6'1"	195	28	2	
Monte Jackson	DB	5'11"	189	24	5	
Rod Perry	DB	5'9"	170	23	1	
Bill Simpson	DB	6'1"	180	25	6	
Pat Thomas	DB	5'9"	180	23	5	
Jackie Wallace	DB	6'3"	198	26	1	
Vince Ferragamo	QB	6'3"	208	23		
Pat Haden	QB	5'11"	182	24		12
Joe Namath	QB	6'2"	200	34		
Sonny Collins	HB	6'1"	195	24		
Lawrence McCutcheon	HB	6'1"	205	27		54
Wendell Tyler	HB	5'10"	188	22		18
Cullen Bryant	FB	6'1"	235	26		
John Cappelletti	FB-HB	6'1"	217	25		36
Jim Jodat	FB	5'11"	210	23		12
Rod Phillips	FB	6'	220	24		6
Harold Jackson	WR	5'10"	175	31		36
Ron Jessie	WR	6'	185	29		
Freeman Johns	WR	6'1"	175	23		
Dwight Scales	WR	6'2"	170	24		6
Billy Waddy	WR	5'11"	185	23		6
Terry Nelson	TE	6'2"	230	26		18
Charlie Young	TE	6'4"	235	26		6
Raphael Septien	K	5'9"	171	23		86
Glenn Walker	K	6'1"	210	25		

Willie Miller – Elbow Injury
Rob Scribner – Thigh Injury

ATLANTA FALCONS 7-7 Leeman Bennett

Scores of Each Game		
17	LOS ANGELES	6
6	Washington	10
17	N.Y. GIANTS	3
7	San Francisco	0
0	Buffalo	3
16	Chicago	10
7	MINNESOTA	14
3	SAN FRANCISCO	10
17	DETROIT	6
20	New Orleans	21
17	Tampa Bay	0
10	NEW ENGLAND	16
7	Los Angeles	23
35	NEW ORLEANS	7

Use Name	Pos.	Hgt	Wgt	Age	Int	Pts
Bob Adams	OT	6'2"	218	31		
Warren Bryant	OT	6'6"	270	21		
Phil McKinnely	OT-TE	6'4"	248	24		
Greg Kindle	OG	6'4"	265	26		
Dave Scott	OG	6'4"	285	23		
R.C. Thielemann	OG-C	6'4"	247	22		
Paul Ryczek	C	6'2"	230	25		
Jeff Van Note	OG-C	6'2"	247	31		
Edgar Fields	DE	6'2"	255	23		
Claude Humphrey	DE	6'5"	265	33		
Jeff Merrow (to OAK)	DE-LB	6'4"	230	24		
Jeff Yeates	DE-OG	6'3"	248	26		
Jim Bailey	DT	6'5"	260	29		
Wilson Faumuina	DT	6'5"	275	23		
Bob Jordan	DT	6'6"	255	22		
Mike Lewis	DT	6'3"	261	28		
Mike Tilleman	DT	6'5"	278	32		
Greg Brezina	LB	6'1"	221	31		
Rick Kay (from LA)	LB	6'4"	235	27		
Fulton Kuykendall	LB	6'5"	225	24		
Ron McCartney	LB	6'1"	220	23		
Dewey McClain	LB	6'2"	220	24	4	6
Ralph Ortega	LB	6'1"	222	22	2	6
Robert Pennywell	LB	6'2"	218	22		
Andy Spiva	DB	6'2"	202	28	5	
Ray Brown	DB	5'9"	180	26	3	6
Rick Byas	DB	6'	192	27	4	
Ray Easterling	DB	5'10"	179	26	7	
Rolland Lawrence	DB	6'	185	24		
Tom Moriarty	DB	5'11"	193	23		
Frank Reed						
Steve Bartkowski	QB	6'4"	213	24		
Scott Hunter	QB	6'2"	205	29		6
June Jones	QB	6'4"	200	24		
Kim McQuilken	QB	6'2"	203	26		
Mike Esposito	HB-DB	6'	183	24	1	
Secedrick McIntyre	HB	5'10"	190	23		6
Haskel Stanback	HB	6'	210	25		36
Monroe Eley	FB	6'2"	210	28		6
Billy Ray Pritchett	FB	6'3"	230	26		
Woody Thompson	FB	6'1"	228	25		6
Karl Farmer	WR	5'11"	165	23		
Wallace Francis	WR	5'11"	190	25		6
Al Jenkins	WR	5'10"	172	25		24
Billy Ryckman	WR	5'11"	172	22		6
Grey McCrary	TE	6'3"	230	25		6
Jim Mitchell	TE	6'2"	236	29		
John James	K	6'3"	200	28		
Fred Steinfort	K	5'11"	180	23		3[illegible]

Len Gotschalk – Knee Injury
Bubba Bean – Knee Injury

SAN FRANCISCO FORTY-NINERS 5-9 Ken Meyer

Scores of Each Game		
0	Pittsburgh	27
15	MIAMI	19
14	Los Angeles	34
0	ATLANTA	7
17	N.Y. Giants	20
28	DETROIT	7
20	TAMPA BAY	10
10	Atlanta	3
10	New Orleans	7
10	LOS ANGELES	23
20	NEW ORLEANS	17
27	Minnesota	28
35	DALLAS	42
14	Green Bay	16

Use Name	Pos.	Hgt	Wgt	Age	Int	Pts
John Ayers	OT-OG	6'5"	247	24		
Cas Banaszak	OT	6'3"	252	31		
Jean Barrett	OT-C	6'6"	250	26		
Keith Fahnhorst	OT	6'6"	263	25		
Ron Singleton	OT	6'7"	245	25		
Steve Lawson	OG	6'3"	257	28		
Johnny Miller	OG	6'1"	247	23		
Woody Peoples	OG	6'2"	250	34		
Randy Cross	C	6'3"	250	23		
Tony Cline	DE	6'2"	237	29		
Cedric Hardman	DE	6'3"	244	28		
Tommy Hart	DE	6'3"	246	32		
Bill Cooke	DT-DE	6'5"	243	26		
Cleveland Elam	DT	6'4"	251	25		
Ed Galigher	DT	6'4"	247	26		
Jimmy Webb	DT	6'5"	245	25		
Mike Baldassin	LB	6'1"	218	22		6
Ed Bradley	LB	6'2"	225	27		
Bruce Elia	LB	6'1"	220	24		
Willie Harper	LB	6'2"	205	27	1	
Dale Mitchell	LB	6'3"	225	24		
Howard Stidham	LB	6'2"	214	22		
Skip Vanderbundt	LB	6'3"	225	30	1	
Dave Washington	LB	6'5"	230	28	2	
Stan Black	DB	6'	196	21		
Mike Burns	DB	6'	181	23		
Tony Leonard	DB	5'11"	165	24	1	
Eddie Lewis	DB	6'	174	23		
Al Matthews	DB	5'11"	190	29		
Ralph McGill	DB	5'11"	180	27	1	
Mel Phillips	DB	6'	185	35	2	
Bruce Taylor	DB	6'	178	29		
Scott Bull	QB	6'5"	215	24		
Steve DeBerg	QB	6'2"	205	23		
Jim Plunkett	QB	6'3"	207	29		6
Paul Hofer	HB	6'	193	25		
Dave Williams	HB-FB	6'2"	200	23		6
Del Williams	HB	6'	195	26		54
Bob Ferrell	FB	6'	219	24		6
Wilbur Jackson	FB	6'1"	213	25		42
Kenny Harrison	WR	6'	164	23		6
Jim Lash	WR	6'2"	200	25		
Willie McGee	WR	5'11"	178	27		
Gene Washington	WR	6'1"	180	30		30
Tom Mitchell	TE	6'2"	225	33		
Jim Obradovich	TE	6'2"	227	24		
Paul Seal	TE	6'4"	223	25		6
Ray Wersching	K	5'11"	210	27		53
Tom Wittum	K	6'1"	198	27		5

Bruce Rhodes – Injury

NEW ORLEANS SAINTS 3-11 Hank Stram

Scores of Each Game		
20	GREEN BAY	24
19	Detroit	23
42	Chicago	24
0	SAN DIEGO	14
7	Los Angeles	14
31	St. Louis	49
27	LOS ANGELES	26
7	Philadelphia	28
7	SAN FRANCISCO	10
21	ATLANTA	20
17	San Francisco	20
13	N.Y. JETS	16
14	TAMPA BAY	33
7	Atlanta	35

Use Name	Pos.	Hgt	Wgt	Age	Int	Pts
Dave Hubbard	OT	6'7"	270	21		
Dave Lafary	OT	6'7"	280	22		
Marv Montgomery	OT	6'6"	255	29		
Don Morrison	OT	6'5"	250	27		
Mike Watson	OT	6'6"	272	21		
Robert Woods (from NYJ)	OT-OG	6'3"	259	27		
Kurt Schumacher	OG	6'3"	246	24		
Terry Stieve	OG	6'2"	242	23		
Emanuel Zanders	OG	6'1"	248	26		
Lee Gross	C	6'3"	235	24		
John Hill	C	6'2"	246	27		
John Watson	C-OG	6'4"	244	28		
Joe Campbell	DE	6'6"	254	22		
Elois Grooms	DE	6'4"	250	24		6
Bob Pollard	DE-DT	6'3"	236	28		6
Oakley Dalton	DT	6'6"	285	25		
Mike Fultz	DT	6'5"	278	23		
Derland Moore	DT	6'4"	253	25		
Elex Price	DT	6'3"	265	27		
Ken Bordelon	LB	6'4"	226	23		
Joe Federspiel	LB	6'1"	230	27		
Pat Hughes	LB	6'2"	225	30	1	
Rick Kingrea	LB	6'1"	222	28		
Jim Merlo	LB	6'1"	220	25	1	6
Greg Westbrooks	LB	6'2"	217	24		
Wade Bosarge	DB	5'10"	175	21		
Craig Cassady	DB	5'11"	175	23		
Clarence Chapman	DB	5'10"	185	23	1	6
Chuck Crist	DB	6'2"	205	26	4	
Ernie Jackson	DB	5'10"	176	27	1	
Jim Marsalis	DB	5'11"	190	31	1	
Tom Myers	DB	5'11"	180	26	1	6
Jimmy Stewart	DB	5'11"	190	22		
Bobby Douglass	QB	6'3"	228	30		
Archie Manning	QB	6'3"	200	28		30
Bobby Scott	QB	6'1"	197	28		
Greg Boykin	HB	6'	225	23		
Chuck Muncie	HB-FB	6'3"	220	24		42
Mike Strachan	HB	6'	200	24		
Tony Galbreath	FB	6'	230	23		18
Kim Jones	FB	6'4"	243	25		
Larry Burton	WR	6'1"	193	25		
John Gilliam (from CHI)	WR	6'1"	187	32		6
Don Herrmann	WR	6'2"	193	30		
Richard Mauti	WR	6'	190	23		
Joel Parker	WR	6'5"	215	25		
Leonard Willis (to BUF)	WR	5'10"	180	24		
Henry Childs	TE	6'2"	220	26		54
Jim Thaxton	TE-WR	6'2"	242	28		6
Tom Blanchard	K	6'	180	29		
Richie Szaro	K	5'11"	204	29		44

Mo Spencer – Neck Injury

Tinker Owens – Knee Injury

LOS ANGELES RAMS

RUSHING

Last Name	No.	Yds.	Avg	TD
McCutcheon	294	1238	4.2	7
Cappelletti	178	598	3.4	5
Tyler	61	317	5.2	3
Phillips	37	183	4.9	1
Haden	29	106	3.7	2
Bryant	6	42	7.0	0
Waddy	2	34	17.0	0
Nelson	3	31	10.3	0
Jodat	5	15	3.0	1
H. Jackson	1	6	6.0	0
Namath	4	5	1.3	0
Ferragamo	1	0	0.0	0

RECEIVING

Last Name	No.	Yds	Avg	TD
H. Jackson	48	666	14	6
Nelson	31	401	13	3
Cappelletti	28	228	8	1
McCutcheon	25	274	11	2
Waddy	23	355	15	1
Jessie	9	139	15	0
Scales	5	104	21	1
Young	5	35	7	1
Bryant	4	28	7	0
Wallace	1	13	13	0
Phillips	1	5	5	0
Tyler	1	3	3	0
Jodat	1	2	2	1

PUNT RETURNS

Last Name	No.	Yds	Avg	TD
Waddy	31	219	7	0
Bryant	20	141	7	0

KICKOFF RETURNS

Last Name	No.	Yds	Avg	TD
Tyler	24	523	22	0
Jodat	6	129	22	0
Bryant	2	35	18	0
Phillips	1	10	10	0
Ekern	1	8	8	0

PASSING – PUNTING – KICKING

PASSING	Att	Comp	%	Yds	Yd/Att	TD	Int–	%	RK
Haden	215	122	56	1551	7.2	11	6–	3	2
Namath	107	50	47	606	5.7	3	5–	5	
Ferragamo	15	9	60	83	5.5	2	0–	0	
Walker	1	1	100	13	13.0	0	0–	0	

PUNTING	No	Avg
Walker	73	35.2

KICKING	XP	Att	%	FG	Att	%
Septien	32	35	91	18	30	60

ATLANTA FALCONS

RUSHING

Last Name	No.	Yds.	Avg	TD
Stanback	247	873	3.5	6
Thompson	132	478	3.6	1
Eley	97	273	2.8	1
Esposito	34	101	3.0	0
Hunter	28	70	2.5	1
McIntyre	13	65	5.0	0
Bartkowski	18	13	0.7	0
Jenkins	2	7	3.5	0
Pritchett	3	7	2.3	0
Francis	4	6	1.5	0
Farmer	1	4	4.0	0
McQuilken	2	–1	–0.5	0
Mitchell	1	–6	–6.0	0

RECEIVING

Last Name	No.	Yds	Avg	TD
Jenkins	39	677	17	4
Stanback	30	261	9	0
Francis	26	390	15	1
Mitchell	17	178	10	0
Thompson	12	56	5	0
Eley	9	60	7	0
McCrary	2	48	24	1
Farmer	2	39	20	0
McIntyre	1	27	27	1
Ryckman	1	5	5	0
Esposito	1	–1	–1	0

PUNT RETURNS

Last Name	No.	Yds	Avg	TD
Lawrence	51	352	7	0
Ryckman	7	40	6	0
Byas	1	10	10	0

KICKOFF RETURNS

Last Name	No.	Yds	Avg	TD
Farmer	21	419	20	0
Moriarty	8	136	17	0
Francis	1	22	22	0
Eley	1	16	16	0
McIntyre	1	15	15	0
Lawrence	1	13	13	0
Ryckman	1	0	0	0

PASSING – PUNTING – KICKING

PASSING	Att	Comp	%	Yds	Yd/Att	TD	Int–	%	RK
Hunter	151	70	46	898	6.0	2	3–	2	
Bartkowski	136	64	47	796	5.9	5	13–	10	
McQuilkin	7	5	71	47	6.7	1	0–	0	
Jones	1	1	100	–1	–1.0	0	0–	0	
Esposito	1	0	0	0	0.0	0	0–	0	
James	1	0	0	0	0.0	0	0–	0	

PUNTING	No	Avg
James	105	41.4

KICKING	XP	Att	%	FG	Att	%
Steinfort	13	13	100	6	11	55

SAN FRANCISCO FORTY-NINERS

RUSHING

Last Name	No.	Yds.	Avg	TD
Del Williams	268	931	3.5	7
Jackson	179	780	4.4	7
Ferrell	41	160	3.9	1
Hofer	34	106	3.1	0
Plunkett	28	71	2.5	1
Bull	5	20	4.0	0
Harrison	6	15	2.5	0
Da. Williams	2	6	3.0	0
McGee	1	–3	–3.0	0

RECEIVING

Last Name	No.	Yds	Avg	TD
G. Washington	32	638	20	5
Jackson	22	169	8	0
Del Williams	20	179	9	2
T. Mitchell	19	226	12	0
Harrison	15	217	14	1
Seal	13	230	18	1
Hofer	5	46	9	0
Lash	3	22	7	0
McGee	2	27	14	0
O'Bradovich	2	16	8	0
Ferrell	2	12	6	0
Cline	1	15	15	0

PUNT RETURNS

Last Name	No.	Yds	Avg	TD
Leonard	22	154	7	0
Black	13	38	3	0
Da. Williams	1	60	60	0
Elia	1	1	1	0
Baldassin	1	0	0	0

KICKOFF RETURNS

Last Name	No.	Yds	Avg	TD
Hofer	36	871	24	0
Da. Williams	4	122	31	1
Ferrell	3	35	12	0
Leonard	1	68	68	0
O'Bradovich	1	9	9	0
Del Williams	1	9	9	0

PASSING – PUNTING – KICKING

PASSING	Att	Comp	%	Yds	Yd/Att	TD	Int–	%	RK
Plunkett	248	128	52	1693	6.8	9	14–	6	8
Bull	24	7	29	89	3.7	0	2–	8	
Wittum	3	1	33	15	5.0	0	0–	0	
Harrison	1	0	0	0	0.0	0	0–	0	
Del Williams	1	0	0	0	0.0	0	1–	100	

PUNTING	No	Avg
Wittum	77	36.4

KICKING	XP	Att	%	FG	Att	%
Wersching	23	23	100	10	17	59
Wittum	2	4	50	1	2	50

NEW ORLEANS SAINTS

RUSHING

Last Name	No.	Yds.	Avg	TD
Muncie	201	811	4.0	6
Galbreath	168	644	3.8	3
Strachan	55	271	4.9	0
Manning	39	270	6.9	5
Douglass	2	23	11.5	0
Jones	8	23	2.9	0
Scott	4	11	2.8	0
Thaxton	1	–3	–3.0	0
Boykin	5	–9	–1.8	0
Herrmann	1	–17	–17.0	0

RECEIVING

Last Name	No.	Yds	Avg	TD
Galbreath	41	265	7	0
Childs	33	518	16	9
Herrmann	32	408	13	0
Muncie	21	248	12	1
Thaxton	14	211	15	1
Gilliam	11	133	12	1
Mauti	4	71	18	0
Strachan	3	26	9	0
Boykin	3	21	7	0
Burton	1	13	13	0
Jones	1	9	9	0
Parker	1	7	7	0
Grooms	1	3	3	1

PUNT RETURNS

Last Name	No.	Yds	Avg	TD
Mauti	37	281	8	0

KICKOFF RETURNS

Last Name	No.	Yds	Avg	TD
Mauti	27	609	23	0
Chapman	15	385	26	1
Willis	8	148	19	0
Boykin	5	76	15	0
Campbell	2	33	17	0
Jones	2	23	12	0
Kingrea	2	21	11	0
Stewart	1	33	33	0
Muncie	1	19	19	0
Thaxton	0	8	–	0

PASSING – PUNTING – KICKING

PASSING	Att	Comp	%	Yds	Yd/Att	TD	Int–	%	RK
Manning	205	113	55	1284	6.3	8	9–	4	5
Scott	82	36	44	516	6.3	3	8–	10	
Douglass	31	16	52	130	4.2	1	3–	10	
Blanchard	3	1	33	3	1.0	1	1–	38	

PUNTING	No	Avg
Blanchard	82	42.4
Scott	3	31.7

KICKING	XP	Att	%	FG	Att	%
Szaro	29	31	94	5	12	42

1977 A.F.C. Seeing is Believing

Perhaps the most controversial team of the year was the Zebras. Game officials came under unusually harsh criticism for a number of close calls at key moments of games. The Oilers claimed that poor officiating cost them two games, while Joe Greene of Pittsburgh was furious enough to threaten physical violence after officials penalized the Steelers 17 times in a game against the Colts. In the important Patriots-Colts game and in the Raiders-Broncos battle for the A.F.C. crown, quick whistles on apparent fumbles whipped up the winds of protest. Regardless of the criticisms, no one impugned the integrity of the officials, who did their best to police a lot of action.

EASTERN DIVISION

Baltimore Colts—A late-season losing streak put their title in jeopardy, but the Colts repeated as Eastern champs. The explosive Baltimore offense led the team to nine victories in the first ten games. The arm of Bert Jones, the versatility of Lydell Mitchell, and the blocking of George Kunz paved the way for impressive triumphs over the Dolphins and Steelers. The defense also had stars in pass rusher John Dutton and ball hawk Lyle Blackwood, a pick-up from Seattle. Ahead of the pack by two games, the Colts suddenly lost to the Broncos, Dolphins, and Lions to enter the final weekend tied for first with Miami. Before a supportive hometown crowd, the Colts beat the Patriots 30-24 to earn first place on the tiebreaker formula.

Miami Dolphins—Given a taste of losing last season, Don Shula whipped his Dolphins back into the playoff race. Shula rebuilt his defense, partly out of necessity. Nick Buoniconti retired to be a full-time lawyer, while Don Reese and Randy Crowder were kept busy with federal drug charges. Into the breach stepped rookies A.J. Duhe, Bob Baumhower, and Kim Bokamper, all impressive starters. The offense still churned out points behind the sterling efforts of Bob Griese, Nat Moore, Larry Little, and Jim Langer. An impressive 55-14 victory over the Cardinals on Thanksgiving Day cost the Dolphins the services of Vern Den Herder and Charlie Babb, both injured for the rest of the year. One week later, they whipped the front-running Colts 17-6 on Monday night, but a loss to the Patriots ultimately cost the Dolphins a trip to the playoffs.

New England Patriots—The holdout of star linemen Leon Gray and John Hannah took away the team's peace of mind. Although Gray and Hannah returned to the field after sitting out three games, the talented Patriots sauntered through the first nine games without much fire. Their 5-4 record included a solid victory over the unbeaten Colts and losses to the lowly Jets and Bills. Recognizing their under-achievement, the Pats went on a tear in search of a wild card spot. Four straight victories brought them into a showdown with the Colts on the final Sunday. Leading 21-3 in the third quarter, the Pats left the field in anguish as the Colts rallied for a 30-24 decision.

Buffalo Bills—Head coach Jim Ringo took a long time winning his first game. The loser of nine straight after taking over last season, Ringo watched his team drop the first four games this year before upsetting the Falcons 3-0. Ringo was stuck with offensive and defensive units that made errors at key times, reaching new depths in a 56-17 humiliation in Seattle. The Bills lost their offensive meal ticket in that game when O.J. Simpson suffered a knee injury which required surgery. One week later, the Bills upset the Patriots 24-14, as reserve halfback Roland Hooks ran for 155 yards behind the blocking of Joe DeLamielleure and the rest of the Electric Company front line.

New York Jets—With Joe Namath gone, the Jets searched for a new identity. Rookie coach Walt Michaels brought in a host of useful rookie players, with Marvin Powell, Wesley Walker, Dan Alexander, and Scott Dierking playing on offense, Joe Klecko on defense, and Bruce Harper on the specialty squads. All these newcomers underwent a serious dose of losing in their New York debuts. The Jets began their year with a 20-0 loss to the Oilers and ended it with a 27-0 trouncing by the Eagles. Between those bookends, the Jets lost a lot of close decisions and won upset victories over the Patriots and Steelers.

CENTRAL DIVISION

Pittsburgh Steelers—No longer the awesome titans of 1974-75, the Steelers still battled their way to a Central Division title. Losses to the Raiders, Oilers, Colts, and Broncos left the Steelers at 4-4 and questioned their ability to beat the big boys. With no one taking charge in the Central, however, the Steelers took the lead with four straight triumphs. On December 11, Chuck Noll's men ran into an ambush in Cincinnati. In two degree weather, the Steelers and Bengals struggled in the cold to a 17-10 Cincinnati decision. The only playoff hope for the Steelers was to win their final game and hope that the Bengals lost their finale. The Steelers did beat San Diego, and the Bengals did their part by losing to the Oilers.

Cincinnati Bengals—The Bengals swung like a pendulum in the early going. They lost to the Browns 13-3 on opening day, beat Seattle 42-20 a week later, and then dropped a 24-3 decision to the Chargers. Inconsistent in the early fall, they started winning in November. In a gritty contest in two degree weather, the Bengals whipped the Steelers 17-10 on December 11. That victory ensured the Bengals of first place on a tiebreaker formula should they beat the Oilers in their final game. Unfortunately, quarterback Ken Anderson spent a miserable afternoon in the Astrodome, throwing incompletions and dodging Houston pass rushers with limited success. With a heartbreaking 21-16 loss, the Bengals dropped the trophy they had fought for in the cold.

Houston Oilers—Although out of the playoff race, the Oilers charged down the stretch as one of the NFL's toughest clubs. Bum Phillips was reaping the results of his careful molding process. The Oilers jumped out to three victories in their first four games, including a 27-10 decision over the Steelers. A mid-season cold spell, however, whipped away any fantasies of post-season glory. A 47-0 feast at the expense of the Bears started the Houston hot streak. The Oilers ended the year by knocking the Bengals out of the playoffs with a 21-16 decision.

Cleveland Browns—The Browns couldn't sustain their jackrabbit start and fell far off the pace by the end of the race. At the halfway point, they led the Central field with a 5-2 record, capped by a 44-7 massacre of Kansas City. Things turned bad from that point on, but the Browns still clung to first place for almost another month. They dropped back-to-back games with the Bengals and Steelers, losing quarterback Brian Sipe in the Pittsburgh gave with a separated shoulder. Although reserve QB Dave Mays led the Browns to a 21-7 victory over the Jets in his first start, four losses at the end of the schedule sent the Browns reeling into last place. Head coach Forrest Gregg lost his job one week from the end, falling just shy of three years on the job.

WESTERN DIVISION

Denver Broncos—With Red Miller's arrival came the birth of the Orange Crush defense and an epidemic of Broncomania. The new head coach combined a stingy defense with a conservative error-free offense to take Denver to the playoffs for the first time ever. The defense captured the imagination of the city and gave enemy offenses a nasty time. The 3-4 unit got All-Pro caliber play from Lyle Alzado, Rubin Carter, Randy Gradishar, Tom Jackson, Louie Wright, and Bill Thompson. The offense had little flair but did have an inspirational leader in quarterback Craig Morton, who came to Denver in a minor trade and thrived in Miller's system. Victories over the Raiders, Steelers, and Colts convinced all observers that these upstarts were for real.

Oakland Raiders—The defending Super Bowl champs lost only three games but had to settle for a wild card playoff berth behind the phenomenal Broncos. The Raiders split their two meetings with Denver only to fall to second place with losses to the Chargers and Rams. The Oakland offense counted heavily on Mark van Eeghen, who ran for over 1,200 yards behind the blocking of Gene Upshaw, Art Shell, and Dave Casper. Although still formidable, the defense lost an edge when Phil Villipiano went out with a knee injury after only two games.

San Diego Chargers—After a 24-0 loss to the Raiders on opening day, the Chargers won three games in which they allowed a total of 10 points. An excellent young line led by Louie Kelcher laid the groundwork for the defensive resurgence. The offense had less success, as Dan Fouts stayed at home in a salary dispute. James Harris played quarterback most of the season, but both he and back-up Bill Munson were knocked out with injuries in a loss to the Broncos. Little-used Cliff Olander started the next game and engineered a stunning 12-7 upset of the champion Raiders. Fouts then settled his problems with management and led the Chargers to two victories in the remaining four games.

Seattle Seahawks—The Seahawks compiled the best second-year record of any modern NFL expansion team. A crew of young offensive linemen gave Sherman Smith enough room to run impressively, and Jim Zorn got enough time to connect frequently with Steve Largent. Head coach Jack Patera still had lots of work left on his defensive unit, but they did rise to the occasion several times. The Seahawks thrashed Buffalo 56-17 at home, and they whipped the Jets 17-0 on the road. Victories over Kansas City and Cleveland ensured an escape from the Western basement.

Kansas City Chiefs—Only last year, team owner Lamar Hunt had given head coach Paul Wiggin a new three-year contract at a healthy raise. Seven games into this season, Hunt fired Wiggin. The Chiefs got off to a miserable start, dropping their first five games with a pushover defense. A 44-7 loss to the Browns finally sent Wiggin into exile. Tom Bettis took over as interim head coach and inspired his charges to a 20-10 victory over the Packers in his first game. The Chiefs lost the next six, however, including a 34-31 decision to Seattle which wrapped up last place.

FINAL TEAM STATISTICS

OFFENSE

	BALT.	BUFF.	CIN.	CLEV.	DENV.	HOU.	K.C.	MIA.	N.E.	NY J	OAK.	PIT.	S.D.	SEA.
FIRST DOWNS:														
Total	269	246	248	271	223	228	228	267	247	195	**305**	266	235	251
by Rushing	111	93	110	119	101	112	95	143	132	83	**156**	122	93	116
by Passing	136	**141**	112	119	107	91	101	107	101	96	125	124	121	116
by Penalty	22	12	26	**33**	15	25	23	17	14	16	24	20	21	19
RUSHING:														
Number	566	450	488	510	523	509	456	519	603	437	**681**	581	488	461
Yards	2123	1861	1861	2200	2043	1989	1843	2366	2303	1618	**2627**	2258	1761	1964
Average Yards	3.8	4.1	3.8	4.3	3.9	3.9	4.0	**4.6**	3.8	3.7	3.9	3.9	3.6	4.3
Touchdowns	17	3	10	9	16	15	13	18	13	6	**20**	**20**	10	12
PASSING:														
Attempts	395	**458**	385	377	313	347	374	311	305	360	324	341	369	387
Completions	**224**	221	192	208	163	181	190	182	160	170	184	173	206	175
Completion Pct.	56.7	48.3	49.9	55.2	52.1	52.2	50.8	**58.5**	52.5	47.2	56.8	50.7	55.8	45.2
Passing Yards	2686	**2803**	2550	2374	2265	2107	2514	2264	2162	2286	2338	2632	2442	2459
Avg. Yds Per Att.	6.8	6.1	6.6	6.3	7.2	6.1	6.7	7.3	7.1	6.4	7.2	**7.7**	6.6	6.4
Avg. Yds Per Comp.	12.0	12.7	13.3	11.4	13.9	11.6	13.2	12.4	13.5	13.4	12.7	**15.2**	11.9	14.1
Times Tackled	26	36	31	24	50	23	48	36	**14**	35	25	27	24	21
Yds Lost Tackled	221	273	217	199	402	232	421	303	155	284	229	245	198	**131**
Net Yards	2465	**2530**	2333	2175	1863	1875	2093	1961	2007	2002	2109	2387	2244	2328
Touchdowns	17	12	12	19	15	14	11	**22**	17	14	21	17	11	**23**
Interceptions	**12**	24	16	31	**12**	21	26	14	21	26	24	21	20	32
Pct. Intercepted	**3.0**	5.2	4.2	8.2	3.8	6.1	7.0	4.5	6.9	7.2	7.4	6.2	5.4	8.3
PUNTS:														
Number	84	83	70	62	**91**	79	89	58	68	76	59	73	73	64
Average	37.4	38.9	41.3	39.0	39.2	38.4	39.4	36.9	34.6	37.6	**43.3**	36.3	37.1	38.0
PUNT RETURNS:														
Number	42	32	41	38	**58**	36	36	40	43	38	37	46	46	32
Yards	323	380	328	322	**712**	539	236	315	429	540	373	389	521	217
Average Yards	7.7	11.9	8.0	8.5	12.3	**15.0**	6.6	7.9	10.0	12.6	10.1	8.5	11.3	6.8
Touchdowns	0	**2**	0	0	1	**2**	0	0	0	0	0	0	1	0
KICKOFF RETURNS:														
Number	48	60	46	53	34	46	63	38	39	61	49	45	39	**71**
Yards	912	1238	886	1075	732	1056	1284	1011	1051	1374	909	995	734	**1502**
Average Yards	19.0	20.6	19.7	20.3	21.5	23.0	20.4	26.6	**26.9**	22.5	18.6	22.1	18.8	21.2
Touchdowns	0	0	0	0	0	1	0	1	**3**	0	0	0	0	0
INTERCEPTION RET:														
Number	30	21	16	23	25	26	21	15	19	11	26	**31**	21	25
Yards	434	329	238	430	**491**	429	348	124	194	153	352	374	317	356
Average Yards	14.5	15.7	14.9	18.7	**19.6**	16.5	16.6	8.3	10.2	13.9	13.5	12.1	15.1	14.2
Touchdowns	0	1	2	**3**	2	1	2	0	0	1	0	0	2	1
PENALTIES:														
Number	77	87	89	**125**	91	106	82	59	112	62	89	122	97	76
Yards	620	866	859	**1046**	883	835	706	432	931	508	747	973	813	656
FUMBLES:														
Number	24	36	37	34	28	30	33	**22**	28	24	**22**	41	29	27
Number Lost	14	20	16	22	15	17	21	13	15	14	16	28	**11**	14
POINTS:														
Total	295	160	238	269	274	299	225	313	278	191	**351**	283	222	282
PAT Attempts	35	19	26	31	34	36	29	41	33	21	**42**	37	25	37
PAT Made	32	17	25	30	31	29	27	37	33	18	**39**	34	21	33
FG Attempts	26	17	27	23	19	25	18	22	21	25	**28**	14	23	18
FG Made	17	9	19	17	13	16	8	10	15	15	**20**	9	17	9
Percent FG Made	65.4	52.9	70.4	**73.9**	68.4	64.0	44.4	45.5	71.4	60.0	71.4	64.3	**73.9**	50.0
Safeties	1	1	0	1	0	**3**	0	0	1	1	0	0	0	0

DEFENSE

	BALT.	BUFF.	CIN.	CLEV.	DENV.	HOU.	K.C.	MIA.	N.E.	NY J	OAK.	PIT.	S.D.	SEA.
FIRST DOWNS:														
Total	210	260	253	261	217	247	304	227	215	283	**204**	228	228	295
by Rushing	78	134	113	113	**77**	103	169	101	86	137	86	80	102	152
by Passing	116	**98**	113	116	234	124	113	117	111	131	105	112	105	125
by Penalty	16	28	27	32	17	20	22	**9**	18	15	13	36	21	18
RUSHING:														
Number	423	589	525	524	470	522	632	467	452	575	**408**	493	508	596
Yards	798	2405	1897	2098	**1531**	1815	2971	1749	1605	2245	1754	1723	1927	2485
Average Yards	4.3	4.1	3.6	4.0	**3.3**	3.5	4.7	3.7	3.6	3.9	4.3	3.5	3.8	4.2
Touchdowns	11	21	15	14	**5**	11	23	12	8	14	7	9	11	21
PASSING:														
Attempts	382	**316**	351	340	426	379	333	414	356	377	367	357	380	349
Completions	181	**155**	196	184	235	192	175	226	188	215	177	157	172	199
Completion Pct.	47.4	49.1	55.8	54.1	55.2	50.7	52.7	54.6	52.8	57.0	48.2	**40.0**	45.3	57.0
Passing Yards	2549	2213	2453	2298	2556	2431	2244	2393	2504	2587	2503	2254	**2088**	2464
Avg. Yds Per Att.	6.7	7.0	7.0	6.8	6.0	6.4	6.7	5.8	7.0	6.9	6.8	6.3	**5.5**	7.1
Avg. Yds Per Comp.	14.1	14.3	12.5	12.5	10.9	12.7	12.8	**10.6**	13.3	12.0	14.1	14.4	12.1	12.4
Times Tackled	47	17	25	31	35	32	25	20	**58**	26	35	32	44	18
Yds Lost Tackled	359	165	226	281	312	289	222	160	**471**	184	281	285	363	131
Net Yards	2190	2048	2227	2017	2244	2142	2022	2233	2033	2403	2222	1969	**1725**	2333
Touchdowns	**10**	17	14	15	11	12	15	**10**	16	23	17	16	14	19
Interceptions	30	21	16	23	25	26	21	15	19	11	26	**31**	21	25
Pct. Intercepted	7.9	6.7	4.6	6.8	5.9	6.9	6.3	3.6	5.3	2.9	7.1	**8.7**	5.5	7.2
PUNTS:														
Number	81	73	75	70	**95**	77	63	67	78	73	74	79	76	54
Average	36.2	36.2	37.6	37.7	40.7	40.8	41.0	38.5	39.1	38.2	37.6	40.3	40.6	**36.0**
PUNT RETURNS:														
Number	44	42	38	31	55	46	50	**29**	33	46	31	34	40	42
Yards	481	604	260	558	397	340	703	267	270	448	**217**	380	378	389
Average Yards	10.9	14.4	**6.8**	18.0	7.2	7.4	14.1	9.2	8.2	9.7	7.0	11.2	9.5	9.3
Touchdowns	1	**0**	**0**	3	**0**	**0**	**0**	**0**	**0**	**0**	**0**	1	**0**	**0**
KICKOFF RETURNS:														
Number	60	**40**	48	50	50	63	44	59	52	45	63	48	47	50
Yards	1514	**814**	1029	986	1084	1331	958	1281	1086	946	997	1080	952	1240
Average Yards	25.2	20.3	21.4	19.7	21.7	21.1	21.8	21.7	20.9	21.0	**15.8**	22.5	20.3	24.8
Touchdowns	2	1	**0**	**0**	**0**	**0**	1	**0**	**0**	1	**0**	**0**	**0**	**0**
INTERCEPTION RET:														
Number	**12**	24	16	31	**12**	21	26	14	21	26	24	21	20	32
Yards	298	326	192	351	172	253	390	238	279	420	373	299	**109**	592
Average Yards	24.8	13.6	12.0	11.3	14.3	12.0	15.0	17.0	13.3	16.2	15.5	14.2	**5.5**	18.5
Touchdowns	1	**0**	**0**	**0**	**0**	1	3	**0**	2	**0**	2	1	**0**	3
PENALTIES:														
Number	78	71	103	**117**	97	97	105	82	71	89	82	82	87	96
Yards	618	638	768	**979**	718	791	929	644	610	788	717	784	831	794
FUMBLES:														
Number	27	21	34	32	28	**39**	**39**	37	20	37	31	28	28	20
Number Lost	17	12	23	16	14	**28**	23	18	10	17	21	13	10	11
POINTS:														
Total	221	313	235	267	**148**	230	349	197	217	300	230	243	205	373
PAT Attempts	27	39	29	32	**18**	26	42	23	26	39	29	29	26	43
PAT Made	24	37	26	27	**16**	24	37	21	22	34	23	27	25	42
FG Attempts	21	21	18	22	22	22	28	20	21	21	19	21	**13**	31
FG Made	11	14	11	16	**8**	16	20	12	13	10	11	14	**8**	23
Percent FG Made	52.4	66.7	61.7	72.7	**36.4**	72.7	71.4	60.0	61.9	47.6	57.9	66.7	61.5	74.2
Safeties	1	**0**	1	**0**	**0**	1	**0**	1	**0**	1	**0**	**0**	**0**	2

CONFERENCE PLAYOFFS

December 24, at Baltimore (Attendance 60,753)

SCORING

BALT.	0	10	7	14	0	0	– 31
OAK.	7	0	14	10	0	6	– 37

First Quarter
- Oak. Davis, 30 yard rush PAT – Mann (kick)

Second Quarter
- Balt. Laird, 61 yard interception return PAT – Linhart (kick)
- Balt. Linhart, 35 yard field goal

Third Quarter
- Oak. Casper, 8 yard pass from Stabler PAT – Mann (kick)
- Balt. Johnson, 87 yard kickoff return PAT – Linhart (kick)
- Oak. Casper, 10 yard pass from Stabler PAT – Mann (kick)

Fourth Quarter
- Balt. R. Lee, 1 yard rush PAT – Linhart (kick)
- Oak. Banazak, 1 yard rush PAT – Mann (kick)
- Balt. R. Lee, 13 yard rush PAT – Linhart (kick)
- Oak. Mann, 22 yard field goal

Second Overtime
- Oak. Casper, 10 yard pass from Stabler PAT – none attempted

TEAM STATISTICS

BALT.		OAK.
22	First Downs – Total	28
10	First Downs – Rushing	8
8	First Downs – Passing	17
4	First Downs – Penalty	3
1	Fumbles – Number	4
0	Fumbles – Lost Ball	2
8	Penalties – Number	7
82	Yards Penalized	65
0	Missed Field Goals	1
82	Offensive Plays	89
301	Net Yards	491
3.7	Average Gain	5.5
0	Giveaways	4
4	Takeaways	0
14	Difference	-4

INDIVIDUAL STATISTICS

BALTIMORE	No	Yds	Avg.	OAKLAND	No	Yds	Avg.
RUSHING							
Mitchell	23	67	2.9	v. Eeghen	19	76	4.0
R. Lee	11	46	4.2	Davis	16	48	3.0
Leaks	8	35	4.4	Banaszak	11	37	3.4
Jones	6	30	5.0	Garrett	1	6	6.0
McCauley	2	9	4.5		47	167	3.6
	50	187	3.7				
RECEIVING							
Mitchell	3	39	13.0	Biletnikoff	7	88	12.6
Scott	2	45	22.5	Branch	6	113	18.8
R. Lee	2	22	11.0	Casper	4	70	17.5
McCauley	2	11	5.5	v. Eeghen	2	39	19.5
Chester	1	30	30.0	Davis	2	35	17.5
Doughty	1	20	20.0		21	345	16.4
Pratt	1	-3	-3.0				
	12	164	13.7				
PUNTING							
D. Lee	12		36.5	Guy	8		46.8
PUNT RETURNS							
Blackwood	2	6	3.0	Colzie	5	42	8.4
Johnson	1	16	16.0	Bradshaw	1	0	0.0
	3	22	7.3		6	42	7.0
KICKOFF RETURNS							
Johnson	3	134	44.7	Garrett	5	169	33.8
McCauley	1	25	25.0	Davis	1	17	17.0
Blackwood	1	17	17.0		6	186	31.0
Nettles	1	17	17.0				
	6	193	32.2				
INTERCEPTION RETURNS							
Laird	2	61	30.5	none			

PASSING

BALTIMORE	Att	Comp	Comp. Pct.	Yds	Int	Yds/ Att.	Yds/ Comp	Yards Lost Tackled
Jones	26	12	46.2	164	0	6.3	13.7	6-50
OAKLAND								
Stabler	40	21	52.5	345	2	8.6	16.4	2-21

December 24, at Denver (Attendance 75,011)

SCORING

DENVER	7	7	7	13	– 34
PITTSBURGH	0	14	0	7	– 21

First Quarter
- Denv. Lytle, 7 yard rush PAT – Turner (kick)

Second Quarter
- Pitt. Bradshaw, 1 yard rush PAT – Gerela (kick)
- Denv. Armstong, 10 yard rush PAT – Turner (kick)
- Pitt. Harris, 1 yard rush PAT – Gerela (kick)

Third Quarter
- Denv. Odoms, 30 yard pass from Morton PAT – Turner (kick)

Fourth Quarter
- Pitt. Brown, 1 yard pass from Bradshaw PAT – Gerela (kick)
- Denv. Turner, 44 yard field goal
- Denv. Turner, 25 yard field goal
- Denv. Dolbin, 34 yard pass from Morton PAT – Turner (kick)

TEAM STATISTICS

DENVER		PITTS.
15	First Downs – Total	18
5	First Downs – Rushing	10
9	First Downs – Passing	8
1	First Downs – Penalty	0
3	Fumbles – Number	2
1	Fumbles – Lost Ball	1
3	Penalties – Number	10
20	Yards Penalized	67
0	Missed Field Goals	0
61	Offensive Plays	76
258	Net Yards	307
4.2	Average Gain	4.0
0	Giveaways	3
3	Takeaways	0
+3	Difference	-3

INDIVIDUAL STATISTICS

DENVER	No	Yds	Avg.	PITTSBURGH	No	Yds	Avg.
RUSHING							
Armstrong	11	44	4.0	Harris	28	92	3.3
Lytle	12	26	2.2	Bradshaw	4	21	5.3
Keyworth	5	20	4.0	Bleier	7	14	2.0
Jensen	4	13	3.3		39	127	3.3
Morton	5	0	0.0				
	37	103	2.8				
RECEIVING							
Odoms	5	43	8.6	Stallworth	4	80	20.0
Moses	2	45	22.5	Harris	4	20	5.0
Jensen	2	33	16.5	Cunningham	3	42	14.0
Dolbin	1	34	34.0	Maxson	3	11	3.7
Armstrong	1	9	9.0	Bleier	2	10	5.0
	11	164	14.9	Grossman	1	7	7.0
				Swann	1	6	6.0
				Brown	1	1	1.0
					19	177	9.3
PUNTING							
Dilts	5		37.6	Engles	5		40.8
PUNT RETURNS							
Thompson	2	5	2.5	Smith	4	31	7.8
Schultz	1	4	4.0				
Upchurch	1	3	3.0				
	4	12	3.0				
KICKOFF RETURNS							
Upchurch	3	48	19.3	Smith	4	80	20.0
Schultz	1	27	27.0	Maxson	1	24	24.0
	4	85	21.3		5	104	20.8
INTERCEPTION RETURNS							
T. Jackson	2	49	24.5	none			
B. Jackson	1	15	15.0				
	3	64	31.3				

PASSING

DENVER	Att	Comp	Comp. Pct.	Yds	Int	Yds/ Att.	Yds/ Comp	Yards Lost Tackled
Morton	23	11	47.8	164	0	7.1	14.9	1-9
PITTSBURGH								
Bradshaw	37	19	51.4	177	3	4.8	9.3	0

BALTIMORE COLTS 10-4 Ted Marchibroda

Scores of Each Game		
29	Seattle	14
20	N.Y. Jets	12
17	BUFFALO	14
45	MIAMI	28
17	Kansas City	6
3	New England	17
31	PITTSBURGH	21
10	WASHINGTON	3
31	Buffalo	13
33	N.Y. JETS	12
13	Denver	27
6	Miami	17
10	DETROIT	13
30	NEW ENGLAND	24

Use Name	Pos.	Hgt	Wgt	Age	Int	Pts
Wade Griffin	OT	6'5"	231	23		
George Kunz	OT	6'5"	262	30		
David Taylor	OT	6'4"	264	27		
Elmer Collett	OG	6'4"	241	32		
Ken Huff	OG	6'4"	262	24		
Robert Pratt	OG	6'4"	248	26		6
Bob Van Duyne	OG-OT	6'5"	244	25		
Forrest Blue	C	6'5"	260	31		
Ken Mendenhall	C	6'3"	250	29		
Fred Cook	DE	6'3"	243	25		
John Dutton	DE	6'7"	266	26		
Ron Fernandes	DE	6'4"	255	25		
Mike Barnes	DT	6'6"	256	26		
Joe Ehrmann	DT	6'5"	264	28		
Ken Novak	DT	6'7"	264	23		

Use Name	Pos.	Hgt	Wgt	Age	Int	Pts
Dan Dickel	LB	6'3"	230	25		
Derrel Luce	LB	6'3"	227	24		
Tom McCleod	LB	6'3"	224	26	2	
Sanders Shiver	LB	6'2"	222	22		
Ed Simonini	LB	6'	210	23	1	
Stan White	LB	6'1"	223	27	7	
Tim Baylor	DB	6'6"	191	23		
Lyle Blackwood	DB	6'	190	26	10	
Bruce Laird	DB	6'	198	27	3	
Lloyd Mumphord	DB	5'11"	178	30		
Nelson Munsey	DB	6'1"	186	29	3	
Doug Nettles	DB	6'	178	26	1	2
Ray Oldham	DB	6'	192	26		
Norm Thompson	DB	6'1"	180	29	3	

Delles Howell – Injury

Use Name	Pos.	Hgt	Wgt	Age	Int	Pts
Bert Jones	QB	6'3"	212	25		12
Mike Kirkland	QB	6'1"	195	23		
Bill Troup	QB	6'5"	215	26		
Don McCauley	HB-FB	6'1"	215	28		48
Lydell Mitchell	HB	5'11"	198	28		42
Howard Stevens	HB	5'5"	165	27		
Roosevelt Leaks	FB	5'10"	225	24		24
Ron Lee	FB	6'4"	228	23		18
Roger Carr	WR	6'3"	196	25		6
Glenn Doughty	WR	6'1"	205	26		24
Perry Griggs	WR	5'10"	182	23		
Marshall Johnson	WR	6'1"	190	24		
Freddie Scott	WR	6'2"	175	25		12
Ricky Thompson	WR	6'	176	23		
Mack Alston	TE	6'2"	230	30		
Ray Chester	TE	6'3"	236	29		18
Jimmie Kennedy	TE	6'3"	230	25		
David Lee	K	6'4"	216	33		
Toni Linhart	K	6'	179	35		83

MIAMI DOLPHINS 10-4 Don Shula

Scores of Each Game		
13	Buffalo	0
19	San Francisco	15
27	HOUSTON	7
28	Baltimore	45
21	N.Y. JETS	17
31	SEATTLE	13
13	SAN DIEGO	14
14	N.Y. Jets	10
17	NEW ENGLAND	5
17	Cincinnati	23
55	St. Louis	14
17	BALTIMORE	6
10	New England	14
31	BUFFALO	14

Use Name	Pos.	Hgt	Wgt	Age	Int	Pts
Mike Current	OT	6'4"	270	31		
Wayne Moore	OT	6'6"	265	32		
Steve Young	OT	6'8"	270	24		
Bob Kuechenberg	OG-C	6'3"	255	29		
Larry Little	OG-OT	6'1"	265	31		
Ed Newman	OG	6'2"	245	26		
Wally Pesuit	OG-OT	6'4"	250	23		
Jim Langer	C	6'2"	253	29		
John Alexander	DE	6'2"	250	21		
Vern Den Herder	DE	6'6"	252	28		
A.J. Duhe	DE	6'4"	247	21		
Rick Dvorak (from NYG)	DE	6'4"	245	25		
Carl Barisich	NT	6'4"	255	26		
Bob Baumhower	NT	6'5"	258	22		
Bob Heinz	NT-DE	6'6"	260	30		
Bill Windauer	NT	6'3"	250	27		

Manny Fernandez – Knee Injury
Bill Stanfill – Injury

Use Name	Pos.	Hgt	Wgt	Age	Int	Pts
Larry Ball	LB	6'6"	235	27		
Kim Bokamper	LB	6'6"	245	22		
Rusty Chambers	LB	6'1"	220	23		
Larry Gordon	LB	6'4"	230	24	1	
Mike Kolen	LB	6'2"	222	29		
Bob Matheson	LB	6'4"	235	32	1	
Earnest Rhone	LB	6'2"	212	24		
Guy Roberts	LB	6'1"	220	27		
Steve Towle	LB	6'2"	233	23		
Dick Anderson	DB	6'2"	196	31		
Charlie Babb	DB	6'	190	27	1	
Charles Cornelius	DB	5'9"	176	25		
Tim Foley	DB	6'	194	29	3	
Curtis Johnson	DB	6'2"	196	29	4	
Vern Roberson	DB	6'1"	195	25	1	
Norris Thomas	DB	5'11"	170	23	3	
Rick Volk	DB	6'3"	195	32	1	

Use Name	Pos.	Hgt	Wgt	Age	Int	Pts
Bob Griese	QB	6'1"	190	32		
Don Strock	QB	6'5"	218	26		
Gary Davis	HB	5'10"	202	22		18
Benny Malone	HB	5'10"	193	25		30
Nat Moore	HB-WR	5'9"	180	25		78
Norm Bulaich	FB	6'1"	218	30		24
Leroy Harris	FB	5'9"	220	23		24
Don Nottingham	FB	5'10"	210	28		12
Stan Winfrey (from TB) (to BUF)	FB	5'11"	223	24		
Terry Anderson	WR	5'9"	182	22		
Duriel Harris	WR	5'11"	175	22		30
Freddie Solomon	WR	5'11"	181	24		12
Jim Mandich	TE-WR	6'3"	214	29		
Loaird McCreary	TE-WR	6'5"	227	24		6
Larry Seiple	TE-WR	6'	214	32		
Andre Tillman	TE	6'5"	230	24		12
Mike Michel	K	5'10"	177	23		
Garo Yepremian	K	5'8"	175	33		67

NEW ENGLAND PATRIOTS 9-5 Chuck Fairbanks

Scores of Each Game		
21	KANSAS CITY	17
27	Cleveland	30
27	N.Y. Jets	30
31	SEATTLE	0
24	San Diego	20
17	BALTIMORE	3
24	N.Y. JETS	13
14	BUFFALO	24
5	Miami	17
20	Buffalo	7
14	PHILADELPHIA	6
16	Atlanta	10
14	MIAMI	10
24	Baltimore	30

Use Name	Pos.	Hgt	Wgt	Age	Int	Pts
Leon Gray	OT	6'3"	255	25		
Shelby Jordan	OT	6'7"	260	25		
Bob McKay	OT	6'5"	265	29		
Tom Neville	OT	6'4"	255	34		
Sam Adams	OG	6'3"	255	28		
Pete Brock	OG-C	6'5"	260	23		
John Hannah	OG	6'2"	265	26		
Fred Sturt	OG	6'4"	255	26		
Bob Hyland	C	6'5"	255	32		
Bill Lenkaitis	C	6'3"	252	31		
Julius Adams	DE	6'3"	260	29		
Greg Boyd	DE	6'6"	270	24		
Mel Lunsford	DE	6'3"	260	27		
Tony McGee	DE	6'4"	250	28		
Richard Bishop	NT	6'1"	260	27		
Ray Hamilton	NT	6'1"	250	26		
Art Moore	NT	6'5"	260	26		

Use Name	Pos.	Hgt	Wgt	Age	Int	Pts
Pete Barnes	LB	6'3"	240	32	1	
Ray Costict	LB	6'	214	22		
Sam Hunt	LB	6'1"	250	26	2	
Steve King	LB	6'4"	228	26		
Steve Nelson	LB	6'2"	228	26		
Rod Shoate	LB	6'1"	215	24		
Steve Zabel	LB	6'4"	228	29		
Doug Beaudoin	DB	6'1"	195	23		
Raymond Clayborn	DB	6'1"	181	22		20
Dick Conn	DB	6'	185	26		
Tim Fox	DB	5'11"	190	23	3	
Mike Haynes	DB	6'2"	195	24	5	
Bob Howard	DB	6'1"	175	32	4	
Prentice McCray	DB	6'1"	190	24	4	

Pete Cusick – Knee Injury
Andy Johnson – Knee Injury
Jim Romaniszyn – Injury

Use Name	Pos.	Hgt	Wgt	Age	Int	Pts
Steve Grogan	QB	6'4"	205	24		6
Tom Owen	QB	6'1"	200	24		
Don Calhoun	HB-FB	6'	215	25		24
Ike Forte	HB	6'	202	23		12
Horace Ivory	HB	6'	197	23		
Sam Cunningham	FB	6'3"	230	27		30
Jess Phillips	FB	6'1"	208	30		6
Steve Burks	WR	6'5"	210	24		
Stanley Morgan	WR	5'11"	180	22		18
Darryl Stingley	WR	6'	193	25		36
Don Westbrook	WR	5'10"	188	24		
Al Chandler	TE	6'2"	228	26		
Russ Francis	TE	6'6"	240	24		24
Don Hasselbeck	TE	6'7"	245	23		24
Mike Patrick	K	6'	195	24		
John Smith	K	6'	190	27		78

BUFFALO BILLS 3-11 Jim Ringo

Scores of Each Game		
0	MIAMI	13
6	Denver	26
14	Baltimore	17
19	N.Y. JETS	24
3	ATLANTA	0
16	CLEVELAND	27
17	Seattle	56
24	New England	14
13	BALTIMORE	31
7	NEW ENGLAND	20
20	Oakland	14
0	WASHINGTON	10
14	N.Y. Jets	10
14	Miami	31

Use Name	Pos.	Hgt	Wgt	Age	Int	Pts
Joe Devlin	OT	6 5	258	23		
Dave Foley	OT	6'5"	247	29		
Ken Jones	OT	6'5"	252	24		
Bill Adams	OG	6'2"	246	27		
Joe DeLamielleure	OG	6'3"	248	26		
Reggie McKenzie	OG	6'4"	242	27		
Willie Parker	C	6'3"	245	28		
Connie Zelencik	C-OG	6'4"	245	22		
Phil Dokes	DE	6 5	258	21		
Greg Morton	DE	6'1"	230	23		
Sherman White	DE	6'5"	250	28		
Ben Williams	DE	6 3	258	23		
Bill Dunstan	DT	6'4"	250	28		
Mike Kadish	DT	6'5"	270	27		
John Little	DT	6'3"	250	30		

Use Name	Pos.	Hgt	Wgt	Age	Int	Pts
Greg Collins	LB	6'3"	227	24		
Bo Cornell	LB	6'1"	222	28		6
Dan Jilek	LB	6'2"	219	23		
Merv Krakau	LB	6'2"	248	26		
Bob Nelson	LB	6'4"	232	24		
Shane Nelson	LB	6'1"	222	22		
Tom Ruud	LB	6'2"	223	24		
John Skorupan	LB	6'2"	221	26		
Mario Clark	DB	6'2"	190	23	7	
Steve Freeman	DB	5'11"	185	24	1	
Tony Greene	DB	5'10"	170	28	9	2
Dwight Harrison	DB	6'1"	186	28	2	
Doug Jones	DB	6'2"	205	27	2	6
Keith Moody	DB	5'10"	171	24		6
Charles Romes	DB	6'1"	191	23		

Use Name	Pos.	Hgt	Wgt	Age	Int	Pts
Fred Besana	QB	6'4"	200	23		
Joe Ferguson	QB	6'1"	184	27		12
Ken Johnson	QB	6'2"	205	26		
Curtis Brown	HB	5'10"	203	22		6
Mike Collier	HB	5'11"	200	23		
Reuben Gibson	HB	6'	196	22		
Roland Hooks	HB	6'	197	24		
O.J. Simpson	HB	6'2"	212	30		
Jim Braxton	FB	6'2"	240	28		12
Mike Franckowiak	FB	6'3"	218	24		
Mel Baker	WR	6'	190	27		
Bob Chandler	WR	6'	180	28		24
Reggie Craig (from CLE)	WR	6'	190	24		
John Holland	WR	6'	190	25		
John Kimbrough	WR	5'10"	165	23		18
Lou Piccone	WR	5'9"	184	28		12
Reuben Gant	TE	6'4"	225	25		12
Paul Seymour	TE	6'5"	245	27		
Marv Bateman	K	6'4"	215	27		
Carson Long	K	5'10"	210	22		34
Neil O'Donoghue	K	6'6"	204	24		10

NEW YORK JETS 3-11 Walt Michaels

Scores of Each Game		
0	Houston	20
12	BALTIMORE	20
30	NEW ENGLAND	27
24	Buffalo	19
17	Miami	21
27	OAKLAND	28
13	New England	24
10	MIAMI	14
0	SEATTLE	17
12	Baltimore	33
20	PITTSBURGH	23
16	New Orleans	13
10	BUFFALO	14
0	Philadelphia	27

Use Name	Pos.	Hgt	Wgt	Age	Int	Pts
Jeff Bleamer	OT-OG	6'4"	253	24		
Ken Helms	OT-C	6'4"	265	22		
Marvin Powell	OT	6'5"	264	22		
Gary Puetz	OT-OG	6'4"	265	25		
Dan Alexander	OG	6'4"	245	22		
Darrell Austin	OG-C	6'4"	252	25		
Randy Rasmussen	OG	6'2"	255	32		
John Roman	OG-OT	6'4"	251	25		
Joe Fields	C-OG	6'2"	245	23		
Al Burton	DE	6'5"	265	25		
John Hennessy	DE	6'3"	246	22		
Richard Neal	DE	6'3"	256	29		
Lawrence Pillers	DE	6'3"	257	24		
Carl Barzilauskas	DT	6'6"	270	26		
Joe Klecko	DT	6'3"	256	23		
Tank Marshall	DT	6'4"	245	22		
Abdul Salaam	DT	6'3"	260	24		

Use Name	Pos.	Hgt	Wgt	Age	Int	Pts
Greg Buttle	LB	6'3"	229	23	2	6
John Ebersole	LB	6'3"	235	28	1	
Mike Hennigan	LB	6'2"	215	25		
Jim Jerome	LB	6'4"	225	23		
Larry Keller	LB	6'2"	225	23	1	
Bob Martin	LB	6'1"	223	23	1	
Al Palewicz	LB	6'1"	217	27		
Carl Russ	LB	6'2"	227	24		
Billy Hardee	DB	6'	185	23	1	
Ron Mabra	DB	5'10"	164	26		
Tommy Marvaso	DB	6'1"	191	23		
Burgess Owens	DB	6'2"	195	26	3	
Artimus Parker	DB	6'3"	200	25	1	
Ken Schroy	DB	6'3"	191	24		
Shafer Suggs	DB	6'1"	200	24		
Ed Taylor	DB	6'	176	24	1	
Maurice Tyler	DB	6'	190	27		

Don Coleman – Knee Injury

Use Name	Pos.	Hgt	Wgt	Age	Int	Pts
Marty Domres	QB	6'4"	220	30		
Matt Robinson	QB	6'2"	196	22		
Richard Todd	QB	6'2"	205	23		12
Bruce Harper	HB-WR	5'8"	174	22		6
Kevin Long	HB	6'1"	205	22		
Charlie White	HB-FB	6'	222	24		12
Scott Dierking	FB	5'10"	215	22		6
Clark Gaines	FB-HB	6'1"	201	23		24
Tom Newton	FB	6'	205	23		
Rich Caster	WR	6'5"	230	28		6
Shelton Diggs	WR	6'1"	190	22		
David Knight	WR	6'1"	170	26		
Wesley Walker	WR	6'	172	22		18
Jerome Barkum	TE	6'3"	217	27		36
Bob Raba	TE	6'1"	222	22		
Pat Leahy	K	6'	190	26		63
Chuck Ramsey	K	6'2"	195	25		

Louie Giammona – Knee Injury

BALTIMORE COLTS

RUSHING

Last Name	No.	Yds	Avg	TD
Mitchell	301	1159	3.9	3
R. Lee	84	346	4.1	3
Leaks	59	237	4.0	3
McCauley	83	234	2.8	6
Jones	28	146	5.2	2
Doughty	2	11	5.5	0
D. Lee	2	−2	−1.0	0
Troup	7	−8	−1.1	0

RECEIVING

Last Name	No.	Yds	Avg	TD
Mitchell	71	620	9	4
McCauley	51	495	10	2
Chester	31	556	18	3
Doughty	28	435	16	4
Scott	18	267	15	2
Carr	11	199	18	1
R. Lee	10	60	6	0
Leaks	3	39	13	1
R. Thompson	1	15	15	0

PUNT RETURNS

Last Name	No.	Yds	Avg	TD
Stevens	34	301	9	0
Blackwood	7	22	3	0
Oldham	1	0	0	0

KICKOFF RETURNS

Last Name	No.	Yds	Avg	TD
Laird	24	541	23	0
Stevens	11	216	20	0
McCauley	5	67	13	0
Blackwood	1	24	24	0
Huff	1	15	15	0
Johnson	1	15	15	0
Griggs	1	12	12	0
Kennedy	1	9	9	0
Shiver	1	7	7	0
Griffin	1	6	6	0
Doughty	1	0	0	0

PASSING – PUNTING – KICKING

PASSING	Att	Comp	%	Yds	Yd/Att	TD	Int–	%	RK
Jones	393	**224**	57	2686	6.8	17	11–	3	3
Troup	2	0	0	0	0.0	0	1–	50	

PUNTING	No	Avg
D. Lee	82	38.3

KICKING	XP	Att	%	FG	Att	%
Linhart	32	35	91	17	26	65

MIAMI DOLPHINS

RUSHING

Last Name	No.	Yds	Avg	TD
Malone	129	615	**4.8**	5
Davis	126	533	4.2	2
L. Harris	91	417	4.6	4
Bulaich	91	416	4.6	4
Nottingham	44	214	4.9	2
N. Moore	14	89	6.4	1
Solomon	6	43	7.2	0
Griese	16	30	1.9	0
T. Anderson	1	11	11.0	0
Michel	1	−2	−2.0	0

RECEIVING

Last Name	No.	Yds	Avg	TD
N. Moore	52	765	15	**12**
D. Harris	34	601	18	5
Bulaich	25	180	7	0
Tillman	17	169	10	2
Davis	14	151	11	1
Solomon	12	181	15	1
Nottingham	8	58	7	0
L. Harris	7	29	4	0
Mandich	6	63	11	0
Malone	4	58	15	0
McCreary	2	10	5	1
Seiple	1	−1	−1	0

PUNT RETURNS

Last Name	No.	Yds	Avg	TD
Solomon	32	285	9	0
D. Anderson	4	3	1	0
Babb	2	10	5	0
Davis	1	11	17	0
T. Anderson	1	6	6	0

KICKOFF RETURNS

Last Name	No.	Yds	Avg	TD
Davis	14	414	30	0
Solomon	10	273	27	1
T. Anderson	7	167	24	0
D. Harris	4	91	23	0
Nottingham	2	36	18	0
McCreary	1	30	30	0

PASSING – PUNTING – KICKING

PASSING	Att	Comp	%	Yds	Yd/Att	TD	Int–	%	RK
Griese	307	180	**59**	2252	7.3	**22**	13–	4	1
Strock	4	2	50	12	3.0	0	1–	25	

PUNTING	No	Avg
Michel	35	38.2
Seiple	22	36.4

KICKING	XP	Att	%	FG	Att	%
Yepremian	37	40	93	10	22	45
Michel	0	1	0			

NEW ENGLAND PATRIOTS

RUSHING

Last Name	No.	Yds	Avg	TD
Cunningham	270	1015	3.8	4
Calhoun	198	727	3.7	4
Grogan	61	324	5.3	1
Forte	62	157	2.5	2
Stingley	3	33	11.0	1
Phillips	5	27	5.4	1
Morgan	1	10	10.0	0
Ivory	3	10	3.3	0

RECEIVING

Last Name	No.	Yds	Avg	TD
Cunningham	42	370	9	1
Stingley	39	657	17	5
Morgan	21	443	21	3
Francis	16	229	14	4
Calhoun	13	152	12	0
Hasselbeck	9	76	8	4
Forte	8	88	11	0
Chandler	7	68	10	0
Burks	5	79	16	0

PUNT RETURNS

Last Name	No.	Yds	Avg	TD
Haynes	24	200	8	0
Morgan	16	- 220	14	0
Forte	2	9	5	0
Beaudoin	1	0	0	0

KICKOFF RETURNS

Last Name	No.	Yds	Avg	TD
Clayborn	28	869	**31**	**3**
Phillips	6	93	16	0
Beaudoin	4	73	18	0
McKay	1	16	16	0

PASSING – PUNTING – KICKING

PASSING	Att	Comp	%	Yds	Yd/Att	TD	Int–	%	RK
Grogan	305	160	52	2162	7.1	17	21–	7	7

PUNTING	No	Avg
Patrick	65	36.2

KICKING	XP	Att	%	FG	Att	%
Smith	33	33	**100**	15	21	71

BUFFALO BILLS

RUSHING

Last Name	No.	Yds	Avg	TD
Simpson	126	557	4.4	0
Hooks	128	497	3.9	0
Braxton	113	372	3.3	1
Ferguson	41	279	6.8	2
Collier	31	116	3.7	0
Brown	8	34	4.3	0
Piccone	1	6	6.0	0
Franckowiak	1	0	0.0	0
Bateman	1	0	0.0	0

RECEIVING

Last Name	No.	Yds	Avg	TD
Chandler	60	745	12	4
Braxton	43	461	11	1
Gant	41	646	16	2
Piccone	17	240	14	2
Hooks	16	195	12	0
Simpson	16	138	9	0
Kimbrough	10	207	21	2
Holland	8	107	13	0
Brown	5	20	4	1
Collier	3	23	8	0
Seymour	2	21	11	0
Craig	1	5	5	0

PUNT RETURNS

Last Name	No.	Yds	Avg	TD
Moody	15	196	13	1
Kimbrough	16	184	12	1
Craig	1	0	0	0
Willis	1	0	0	0

KICKOFF RETURNS

Last Name	No.	Yds	Avg	TD
Moody	30	636	21	0
Kimbrough	15	346	23	0
Piccone	4	89	22	0
Collier	4	55	14	0
Brown	3	66	22	0
Romes	1	18	18	0
B. Nelson	1	10	10	0
Dunstan	1	9	9	0
Franckowiak	1	9	9	0

PASSING – PUNTING – KICKING

PASSING	Att	Comp	%	Yds	Yd/Att	TD	Int–	%	RK
Ferguson	**457**	221	48	**2803**	6.1	12	24–	5	13
Simpson	1	0	0	0	0.0	0	0–	0	

PUNTING	No	Avg
Bateman	81	39.9

KICKING	XP	Att	%	FG	Att	%
Long	13	14	93	7	11	64
O'Donoghue	4	5	80	2	6	33
Klaban				0	2	0

NEW YORK JETS

RUSHING

Last Name	No.	Yds	Avg	TD
Gaines	158	595	3.8	3
Dierking	79	315	4.0	0
Harper	44	198	4.5	0
Long	56	170	3.0	0
White	50	151	3.0	1
Todd	24	46	1.9	2
Robinson	5	45	9.0	0
Newton	8	39	4.9	0
Keller	1	25	25.0	0
Walker	3	25	8.3	0
Domres	4	23	5.8	0
Diggs	1	16	16.0	0
Caster	2	−15	−7.5	0

RECEIVING

Last Name	No.	Yds	Avg	TD
Gaines	55	469	9	1
Walker	35	740	**21**	3
Barkum	26	450	17	6
Harper	21	209	10	1
Caster	10	205	21	1
Knight	7	129	18	0
Newton	5	33	7	0
Long	5	17	3	0
Dierking	4	29	7	1
White	2	5	3	1

PUNT RETURNS

Last Name	No.	Yds	Avg	TD
Harper	34	425	13	0
Schroy	3	38	13	0
Hardee	1	17	17	0

KICKOFF RETURNS

Last Name	No.	Yds	Avg	TD
Harper	**42**	**1035**	25	0
Hardee	7	148	21	0
Dierking	6	91	15	0
Raba	4	64	16	0
Marvaso	2	36	18	0

PASSING – PUNTING – KICKING

PASSING	Att	Comp	%	Yds	Yd/Att	TD	Int–	%	RK
Todd	265	133	50	1863	7.0	11	17–	6	10
Robinson	54	20	37	310	5.7	2	8–	15	
Domres	40	17	43	113	2.8	1	1–	3	
Harper	1	0	0	0	0.0	0	0–	0	

PUNTING	No	Avg
Ramsey	62	37.1

KICKING	XP	Att	%	FG	Att	%
Leahy	18	21	86	15	25	60

PITTSBURGH STEELERS 9-5 Chuck Noll

Scores of Each Game		
27	SAN FRANCISCO	0
7	OAKLAND	16
28	Cleveland	14
10	Houston	27
20	CINCINNATI	14
27	HOUSTON	10
21	Baltimore	31
7	Denver	21
35	CLEVELAND	31
28	DALLAS	13
23	N.Y. Jets	20
30	SEATTLE	20
10	Cincinnati	17
10	San Diego	9

Use Name	Pos.	Hgt	Wgt	Age	Int	Pts
Larry Brown	OT-TE	6'4"	245	28		
Jon Kolb	OT	6'2"	262	30		
Jim Clack	OG-C	6'3"	250	29		
Sam Davis	OG	6'1"	255	33		
Gerry Mullins	OG-OT	6'3"	244	28		
Ted Peterson	C-OT-OG	6'5"	244	22		
Ray Pinney	C-OT	6'4"	240	23		
Mike Webster	C	6'1"	250	25		
John Banaszak	DE	6'3"	244	27		
L.C. Greenwood	DE	6'5"	250	30		
Dwight White	DE	6'4"	255	28	2	
Steve Furness	DT-DE	6'4"	255	26		
Joe Greene	DT	6'4"	264	30		
Ernie Holmes	DT	6'3"	260	29		
Robin Cole	LB-DE	6'2"	220	21		
Brad Cousino	LB	6'	215	24		
Jack Ham	LB	6'3"	225	28	4	
Dave LaCrosse	LB	6'3"	210	21		
Jack Lambert	LB	6'4"	220	25	1	
Loren Toews	LB	6'3"	222	25		2
Dennis Winston	LB	6'	228	21	2	
Jim Allen	DB	6'2"	194	25	5	
Mel Blount	DB	6'3"	205	29	6	
Tony Dungy	DB-QB	6'	188	21	3	
Glen Edwards	DB	6'	185	30	3	
Brent Sexton	DB	6'1"	190	24		
Donnie Shell	DB	5'11"	190	25	3	
J.T. Thomas	DB	6'2"	196	26	2	
Mike Wagner	DB	6'1"	200	28		
Terry Bradshaw	QB	6'3"	215	28		18
Neil Graff	QB	6'3"	205	27		
Mike Kruczek	QB	6 1	201	24		
Cliff Stoudt	QB	6'4"	218	22		
Rocky Bleier	HB	5'11"	210	31		24
Jack Deloplaine	HB	5'10"	205	23		
Alvin Mason	HB	5'11"	201	25		
Laverne Smith	HB	5'10"	193	22		
Franco Harris	FB	6'2"	225	27		66
Reggie Harrison	FB	5'11"	220	27		
Sidney Thornton	FB	5'11"	230	22		12
Frank Lewis	WR	6'1"	196	30		6
Ernest Pough	WR	6'1"	174	25		
Jim Smith	WR	6'2"	205	22		
John Stallworth	WR	6'2"	183	25		42
Lynn Swann	WR	6	180	25		42
Bennie Cunningham	TE	6'4"	247	22		12
Randy Grossman	TE	6'1"	225	23		
Rick Engles (from SEA)	K	5'11"	180	23		
Roy Gerela	K	5'10"	185	29		61
Bobby Walden	K	6'	197	39		

Gary Dunn – Knee Injury

Thao Bell – Leg Injury
John Fuqua – Broken Finger

CINCINNATI BENGALS 8-6 Bill Johnson

Scores of Each Game		
3	CLEVELAND	13
43	SEATTLE	20
3	San Diego	24
17	Green Bay	7
14	Pittsburgh	20
13	DENVER	24
13	HOUSTON	10
10	Cleveland	7
10	Minnesota	42
23	MIAMI	17
30	N.Y. GIANTS	13
27	Kansas City	7
17	PITTSBURGH	10
16	Houston	21

Use Name	Pos.	Hgt	Wgt	Age	Int	Pts
Vern Holland	OT	6'5"	265	29		
Ron Hunt	OT	6'6"	255	22		
Rufus Mayes	OT	6'5"	256	29		
Glenn Bujnoch	OG	6'5"	251	23		6
Greg Fairchild	OG-C	6'4"	257	23		
Dave Lapham	OG-OT-C	6'4"	259	25		
John Shinners	OG	6'2"	259	30		
Bob Johnson	C	6'5"	256	31		
Ken Johnson	DE	6'5"	258	30		
Coy Bacon	DE	6'4"	265	35		
Gary Burley	DE	6'3"	265	24		
Ron Carpenter	DT	6'4"	265	29		
Eddie Edwards	DT	6 5"	256	23		
Walter Johnson	DT	6'3"	265	34		
Wilson Whitley	DT	6'3"	264	22		
Glenn Cameron	LB	6'2"	217	24		
Bo Harris	LB	6'3"	221	24	2	
Jim LeClair	LB	6'2"	238	26	2	
Ray Phillips	LB	6'4"	221	23		
Ron Pritchard	LB	6'1"	208	30		
Reggie Williams	LB	6'1"	228	22	3	12
Jerry Anderson	DB	5'11"	198	23		
Tommy Casanova	DB	6'2"	196	27	1	
Marvin Cobb	DB	6'	191	24	2	
Melvin Morgan	DB	6'	186	24	1	
Lemar Parrish	DB	5'11"	183	29	3	6
Scott Perry	DB	6'	182	23		
Ken Riley	DB	6'	185	30	2	
Ken Anderson	QB	6'1"	212	28		12
John Reeves	QB	6'3"	210	27		
Mike Wells	QB	6'5"	225	26		
Lenvil Elliott	HB	6'	208	25		6
Archie Griffin	HB	5'9"	193	23		
Willie Shelby	HB	5'11"	198	24		6
Booby Clark	FB	6'2"	242	26		6
Tony Davis	FB	5'10"	210	24		12
Pete Johnson	FB	6'	240	23		24
Billy Brooks	WR	6 3	202	24		24
Isaac Curtis	WR	6'	192	26		12
Steve Holden (from CLE)	WR	6'	200	26		
John McDaniel	WR	6'1"	197	25		
Pat McInally	WR	6'6"	210	24		18
Mike Cobb	TE	6'5"	248	21		
Jim Corbett	TE	6 4	214	22		6
Bob Trumpy	TE	6'6"	228	32		6
Rick Walker	TE	6'3"	237	22		
Chris Bahr	K	5'9"	168	24		82

Chris Devlin – Leg Injury

HOUSTON OILERS 8-6 Bum Phillips

Scores of Each Game		
20	N.Y. JETS	0
16	Green Bay	10
7	Miami	27
27	PITTSBURGH	10
23	CLEVELAND	24
27	Pittsburgh	10
10	Cincinnati	13
47	CHICAGO	0
29	Oakland	34
22	Seattle	10
34	KANSAS CITY	20
14	DENVER	24
19	Cleveland	15
21	CINCINNATI	16

Use Name	Pos.	Hgt	Wgt	Age	Int	Pts
Conway Hayman	OT	6'3"	260	28		
Kevin Hunt	OT-OG	6'5"	260	28		
Greg Sampson	OT	6'6"	270	26		
Morris Towns	OT	6'4"	275	23		
Elbert Drungo	OG	6'5"	265	34		
Ed Fisher	OG-C	6'3"	250	28		
George Reihner	OG	6'4"	263	22		
David Carter	C	6'2"	225	24		
Carl Mauck	C	6'3"	250	30		
Steve Baumgartner (from NO)	DE-DT	6'7"	255	26		
Elvin Bethea	DE	6'3"	255	31		
Andy Dorris (from SEA)	DE	6'4"	240	26		
Ernest Kirk	DE	6'2"	265	25	1	
James Young	DE	6'2"	260	27		4
Curly Culp	NT	6'1"	265	31	1	
Ken Kennard	NT-DE	6'2"	245	22		2
Gregg Bingham	LB	6'1"	230	26	2	6
Robert Brazile	LB	6'4"	238	24	3	
Steve Kiner	LB	6'	225	30	1	
Art Stringer	LB	6'1"	223	23	1	
Ted Thompson	LB	6'1"	220	24		
Ted Washington	LB	6'1"	245	29	3	
Willie Alexander	DB	6'2"	195	27	3	6
Bill Currier	DB	6'	190	22	2	
Al Johnson	DB	6'	200	27		
Kurt Knoff	DB	6 2"	188	23		
Zeke Moore	DB	6'2"	195	33	3	6
Mike Reinfeldt	DB	6'2"	195	24	5	
Rich Sowells	DB	6'	180	28		
Greg Stemrick	DB	5'11"	185	25	1	6
Mike Weger	DB	6'2"	200	31		
Tom Dunivan	QB	6'3"	210	23		
John Hadl	QB	6'2"	215	37		6
Dan Pastorini	QB	6'3"	205	28		12
Ronnie Coleman	HB	5'10"	198	26		36
Mike Voight	HB	6'	214	23		
Rob Carpenter	FB	6'1"	214	22		6
Don Hardeman	FB	6'2"	235	25		18
Tim Wilson	FB	6'3"	220	23		18
Warren Anderson	WR	6'2"	195	22		
Ken Burrough	WR	6'4"	210	29		48
Eddie Foster	WR	5'10"	185	23		
Gary Garrison	WR	6'1"	194	33		
Billy Johnson	WR	5'9"	170	25		42
Mike Barber	TE	6'3"	235	24		6
Jimmie Giles	TE	6'3"	225	22		
Skip Butler	K	6'2"	200	29		2
Tom Dempsey	K	6'1"	260	36		20
Toni Fritsch	K	5'7"	189	32		55
Cliff Parsley	K	6'1"	211	22		

C.L. Whittington – Injury
Fred Willis – Injury

CLEVELAND BROWNS 6-8 Forrest Gregg (6-7), Dick Modzelewski (0-1)

Scores of Each Game		
13	Cincinnati	3
30	NEW ENGLAND	27
14	PITTSBURGH	28
10	OAKLAND	26
24	Houston	23
27	Buffalo	16
44	KANSAS CITY	7
7	CINCINNATI	10
7	Pittsburgh	10
21	N.Y. Giants	7
0	LOS ANGELES	9
14	San Diego	37
15	HOUSTON	19
19	Seattle	20

Use Name	Pos.	Hgt	Wgt	Age	Int	Pts
Barry Darrow	OT	6'7"	260	27		
Doug Dieken	OT	6'5"	252	28		
Bob Lingenfelter	OT	6'7"	277	23		
Al Dennis	OG	6'4"	250	26		
Robert Jackson	OG	6'5"	250	24		
Henry Sheppard	OG	6'6"	246	24		
Tom DeLeone	C	6'2"	248	27		
Gerry Sullivan	C	6'4"	250	25		
Joe Jones	DE	6'6"	250	29		
Mack Mitchell	DE	6'7"	245	25		
Mike St. Clair	DE	6'5"	245	23		
Earl Edwards	DT	6'6"	256	31		
Steve Okoniewski (from STL)	DT	6'3"	255	28		
Jerry Sherk	DT	6'4"	250	29		2
Mickey Sims	DT	6'5"	282	22		
Dick Ambrose	LB	6'	235	24		
Bob Babich	LB	6'2"	231	30		
John Garlington	LB	6'1"	221	31		
Dave Graf	LB	6'2"	215	24		
Charlie Hall	LB	6'3"	235	28	1	
Gerald Irons	LB	6'2"	230	30	3	6
Mark Johnson	LB	6'2"	236	24		
Ron Bolton	DB	6'2"	170	27	3	
Thom Darden	DB	6'2"	193	27	6	6
Oliver Davis	DB	6'1"	200	23	3	
Ken Ellis	DB	5'10"	195	29		
Ricky Jones	DB	6'1"	195	22	1	
Tony Peters	DB	6'1"	192	24	2	
Clarence Scott	DB	6'	180	28	3	6
Roland Woolsey	DB	6'1"	182	24	1	
Terry Luck	QB	6'3"	205	23		6
Gary Marangi	QB	6'1"	203	25		
Dave Mays	QB	6'1"	204	28		
Brian Sipe	QB	6'1"	190	28		
Larry Poole	HB	6'	195	25		24
Greg Pruitt	HB	5'10"	190	26		24
Brian Duncan	FB-HB	6'	201	25		6
Cleo Miller	FB	5'11"	202	24		30
Mike Pruitt	FB	6'	214	23		6
Ricky Feacher	WR	5'10"	174	23		
Dave Logan	WR	6'4"	226	23		6
Reggie Rucker	WR	6'2"	190	29		12
Paul Warfield	WR	6'	188	34		12
Lawrence Williams (from KC)	WR	5'10"	173	23		6
Gary Parris	TE	6'2"	226	27		30
Oscar Roan	TE	6'6"	214	25		12
Don Cockroft	K	6'1"	195	32		81
Greg Coleman	K	6'	178	22		

Pete Adams – Injury

Bill Craven – Injury

PITTSBURGH STEELERS

RUSHING

Last Name	No.	Yds	Avg	TD
Harris	300	1162	3.9	11
Bleier	135	465	3.4	4
Harrison	36	175	4.9	0
Bradshaw	31	171	5.5	3
Thornton	27	103	3.8	2
Maxson	18	56	3.1	0
L. Smith	14	55	3.9	0
Stallworth	6	47	7.8	0
Dungy	3	8	2.7	0
Deloplaine	2	7	3.5	0
Swann	2	6	3.0	0
Graff	5	3	0.6	0
Kruczek	1	0	0.0	0
Walden	1	0	0.0	0

RECEIVING

Last Name	No.	Yds	Avg	TD
Swann	50	789	16	7
Stallworth	44	784	18	7
Cunningham	20	347	17	2
Bleier	18	161	9	0
Lewis	11	263	24	1
Harris	11	62	6	0
Maxson	5	70	14	0
Grossman	5	57	11	0
J. Smith	4	80	20	0
Harrison	3	11	4	0
Thornton	1	5	5	0
Pough	1	3	3	0

PUNT RETURNS

Last Name	No.	Yds	Avg	TD
J. Smith	36	294	8	0
Swann	9	88	10	0
Deloplaine	1	7	7	0

KICKOFF RETURNS

Last Name	No.	Yds	Avg	TD
J. Smith	16	381	24	0
L. Smith	16	365	23	0
Pough	7	111	16	0
Maxson	5	120	24	0
Deloplaine	1	18	18	0

PASSING – PUNTING – KICKING Statistics

PASSING	Att	Comp	%	Yds	Yd/Att	TD	Int–	%	RK
Bradshaw	314	162	52	2523	8.0	17	19–	6	5
Graff	12	6	50	47	3.9	0	0–	0	
Dungy	8	3	38	43	5.4	0	2–	25	
Kruczek	7	2	29	19	2.7	0	0–	0	

PUNTING	No	Avg
Walden	67	37.0
Engles	9	34.0

KICKING	XP	Att	%	FG	Att	%
Gerela	34	37	92	9	14	64

CINCINNATI BENGALS

RUSHING

Last Name	No.	Yds	Avg	TD
P. Johnson	153	585	3.8	4
Griffin	137	549	4.0	0
Elliott	65	269	4.1	0
Clark	68	226	3.3	1
K. Anderson	26	128	4.9	2
Davis	27	81	3.0	2
Casanova	1	20	20.0	0
Bujnoch	1	4	4.0	1
McInally	1	4	4.0	0
Ma. Cobb	1	0	0.0	0
Reaves	5	0	0.0	0
Corbett	1	−1	−1.0	0
Brooks	2	−4	−2.0	0

RECEIVING

Last Name	No.	Yds	Avg	TD
Brooks	39	772	20	4
Elliott	29	238	8	1
Griffin	28	240	9	0
Curtis	20	338	17	2
Trumpy	18	251	14	1
McInally	17	258	15	3
McDaniel	12	148	12	0
Davis	9	83	9	0
Corbett	7	127	18	1
Clark	7	33	5	0
P. Johnson	5	49	10	0
Walker	1	13	13	0

PUNT RETURNS

Last Name	No.	Yds	Avg	TD
Davis	19	220	12	0
Shelby	11	54	5	0
Parrish	4	30	8	0
Holden	3	14	5	0
Casanova	1	6	6	0
Ma. Cobb	1	4	4	0
Williams	1	0	0	0
J. Anderson	1	0	0	0

KICKOFF RETURNS

Last Name	No.	Yds	Avg	TD
Shelby	19	403	21	0
Griffin	9	192	21	0
J. Anderson	8	129	16	0
Davis	3	42	14	0
Holden	2	42	21	0
Elliott	1	23	23	0
Parrish	1	23	23	0
Ma. Cobb	1	15	15	0
P. Johnson	1	11	11	0
Fairchild	1	6	6	0

PASSING – PUNTING – KICKING Statistics

PASSING	Att	Comp	%	Yds	Yd/Att	TD	Int–	%	RK
K. Anderson	323	166	51	2145	6.6	11	11–	3	6
Reeves	59	24	41	383	6.5	0	5–	9	
Griffin	1	1	100	18	18.0	1	0–	0	
McInally	1	1	100	4	4.0	0	0–	0	
Ma. Cobb	1	0	0	0	0.0	0	0–	0	

PUNTING	No	Avg
McInally	67	41.8
Bahr	2	44.0

KICKING	XP	Att	%	FG	Att	%
Bahr	25	26	97	19	27	70

HOUSTON OILERS

RUSHING

Last Name	No.	Yds	Avg	TD
Coleman	185	660	3.6	5
Carpenter	144	652	4.5	1
Wilson	99	343	3.5	3
Hardeman	42	162	3.9	2
B. Johnson	6	102	17.0	1
Pastorini	18	39	2.2	2
Voight	7	20	2.9	0
Burrough	4	10	2.5	0
Hadl	3	11	3.7	1
Giles	1	−10	−10.0	0

RECEIVING

Last Name	No.	Yds	Avg	TD
Burrough	43	816	19	8
Carpenter	23	156	7	0
Coleman	22	115	5	1
B. Johnson	20	412	21	3
Wilson	20	107	5	0
Giles	17	147	9	0
Foster	15	208	14	0
Hardeman	11	47	4	1
Barber	9	94	10	1
Garrison	1	5	5	0

PUNT RETURNS

Last Name	No.	Yds	Avg	TD
B. Johnson	35	539	15	2
Stemrick	1	0	0	0

KICKOFF RETURNS

Last Name	No.	Yds	Avg	TD
B. Johnson	25	630	25	1
Anderson	8	182	23	0
Voight	8	156	20	0
Wilson	2	33	17	0
Foster	1	31	31	0
Stringer	1	15	15	0
Thompson	1	9	9	0

PASSING – PUNTING – KICKING Statistics

PASSING	Att	Comp	%	Yds	Yd/Att	TD	Int–	%	RK
Pastorini	319	169	53	1987	6.2	13	18–	6	8
Hadl	24	11	46	76	3.2	0	3–	13	
Coleman	3	1	33	44	14.7	1	0–	0	
Burrough	1	0	0	0	0.0	0	0–	0	

PUNTING	No	Avg
Parsley	77	39.4

KICKING	XP	Att	%	FG	Att	%
Fritsch	19	20	95	12	16	75
Dempsey	8	11	73	4	6	67
Butler	2	3	67	0	3	0
Pastorini	0	1	0			

CLEVELAND BROWNS

RUSHING

Last Name	No.	Yds	Avg	TD
G. Pruitt	236	1086	4.6	3
Miller	163	756	4.6	4
M. Pruitt	47	205	4.4	1
Poole	38	118	3.1	1
Williams	2	30	15.0	1
Duncan	5	16	3.2	0
Sipe	10	14	1.4	0
Rucker	2	6	3.0	0
Warfield	1	2	2.0	0
Mays	4	2	0.5	0
Luck	3	−2	−0.7	0
Coleman	1	−3	−3.0	0

RECEIVING

Last Name	No.	Yds	Avg	TD
Miller	41	291	7	1
G. Pruitt	37	471	13	1
Rucker	36	565	16	2
Parris	21	213	10	5
Logan	19	284	15	1
Warfield	18	251	14	2
Poole	17	137	8	3
Roan	13	136	11	2
Williams	7	94	13	0
M. Pruitt	3	12	4	0
Duncan	1	5	5	1
Luck	1	4	4	1

PUNT RETURNS

Last Name	No.	Yds	Avg	TD
Woolsey	32	290	9	0
Feacher	2	15	8	0

KICKOFF RETURNS

Last Name	No.	Yds	Avg	TD
Williams	25	518	21	0
Duncan	15	298	20	0
Feacher	11	219	20	0
M. Pruitt	6	131	22	0
Ellis	5	80	16	0
Jackson	1	21	21	0
Ambrose	1	20	20	0
Babich	1	14	14	0
Woolsey	1	2	2	0

PASSING – PUNTING – KICKING Statistics

PASSING	Att	Comp	%	Yds	Yd/Att	TD	Int–	%	RK
Sipe	195	112	57	1233	6.3	9	14–	7	9
Mays	121	67	55	797	6.6	6	10–	8	
Luck	50	25	50	316	6.3	1	7–	14	
G. Pruitt	9	4	44	28	3.1	3	0–	0	
Logan	2	0	0	0	0.0	0	0–	0	

PUNTING	No.	Avg
Coleman	61	39.2
Cockroft	1	30.0

KICKING	XP	Att	%	FG	Att	%
Cockroft	30	31	97	17	23	74

DENVER BRONCOS 12-2 Red Miller

Scores of Each Game		
7	ST. LOUIS	0
26	BUFFALO	6
24	Seattle	13
23	KANSAS CITY	7
30	Oakland	7
24	Cincinnati	13
14	OAKLAND	24
21	PITTSBURGH	7
17	San Diego	14
14	Kansas City	7
27	BALTIMORE	13
24	Houston	14
17	SAN DIEGO	9
6	Dallas	14

Use Name	Pos.	Hgt	Wgt	Age	Int	Pts
Henry Allison (from STL)	OT-OG	6'3"	263	30		
Glenn Hyde	OT	6'3"	255	26		
Andy Maurer	OT	6'3"	265	28		
Claudie Minor	OT	6'4"	280	26		
Bill Bryan	OG	6'2"	246	22		
Tom Glassic	OG	6'3"	248	23		
Paul Howard	OG	6'3"	260	26		
Steve Schindler	OG	6'3"	252	23		
Bobby Maples	C	6'3"	250	34		
Mike Montler	C	6'4"	250	33		
Lyle Alzado	DE	6'3"	250	28		
Barney Chevous	DE	6'3"	250	26		
Brison Manor	DE	6'4"	247	25		
Paul Smith	DE	6'3"	250	32	1	
Rubin Carter	NT	6'	254	24		
John Grant	NT	6'3"	246	27		

Bill Bain – Knee Injury
Randy Moore – Injury

Use Name	Pos.	Hgt	Wgt	Age	Int	Pts
Rick Baska	LB	6'3"	224	25		
Larry Evans	LB	6'2"	218	24	1	
Randy Gradishar	LB	6'3"	231	25	3	
Tom Jackson	LB	5'11"	224	26	4	6
Rob Nairne	LB	6'4"	220	23		
Joe Rizzo	LB	6'1"	220	23	3	
Bob Swenson	LB	6'3"	223	24	1	
Goodwin Turk	LB	6'2"	230	26		
Steve Foley	DB	6'2"	190	23	3	
Bernard Jackson	DB	6'	181	27	1	
Chris Pane	DB	5'11"	185	24		
Randy Poltl	DB	6'3"	188	25		
Larry Riley	DB	5'10"	189	22		
Bill Thompson	DB	6'1"	200	30	5	
Louis Wright	DB	6'2"	195	24	3	6

Use Name	Pos.	Hgt	Wgt	Age	Int	Pts
Craig Morton	QB	6'4"	214	34		24
Craig Penrose	QB	6'3"	205	24		
Norris Weese	QB	6'1"	193	26		6
Otis Armstrong	HB	5'10"	197	26		24
Jim Kiick (to WAS)	HB	5'11"	215	31		
Rob Lytle	HB	6'1"	198	22		12
Jim Jensen	FB-TE	6'3"	240	23		6
Jon Keyworth	FB	6'3"	234	26		6
Lonnie Perrin	FB	6'1"	224	25		24
Jack Dolbin	WR	5'10"	183	28		18
Haven Moses	WR	6'3"	200	31		24
John Schultz	WR	5'10"	183	24		
Rick Upchurch	WR	5'10"	180	25		24
Ron Egloff	TE	6'5"	227	21		
Riley Odoms	TE	6'4"	232	27		18
Buck Dilts	K	5'9"	190	23		
Jim Turner	K	6'2"	212	36		76

OAKLAND RAIDERS 11-3 John Madden

Scores of Each Game		
24	SAN DIEGO	0
16	Pittsburgh	7
37	Kansas City	28
26	Cleveland	10
7	DENVER	30
28	N.Y. Jets	27
24	Denver	14
44	SEATTLE	7
34	HOUSTON	29
7	San Diego	12
34	BUFFALO	13
14	Los Angeles	20
35	MINNESOTA	13
21	KANSAS CITY	20

Use Name	Pos.	Hgt	Wgt	Age	Int	Pts
Henry Lawrence	OT-OG	6'4"	270	25		
Art Shell	OT	6'5"	275	30		
John Vella	OT	6'4"	260	27		
George Buehler	OG	6'2"	270	30		
Everett Little	OG	6'4"	265	23		
Mickey Marvin	OG	6'4"	270	21		
Gene Upshaw	OG	6'5"	255	32		
Dave Dalby	C	6'2"	250	26		
Steve Sylvester	C-OT-OG	6'4"	260	24		
John Matuszak	DE	6'8"	270	26		
Charles Philyaw	DE	6'9"	270	23		
Otis Sistrunk	DE	6'4"	270	29	1	
Pat Toomay	DE	6'5"	245	32		
Mike McCoy	NT	6'5"	275	28		
Dave Rowe	NT	6'6"	270	32		

Kelvin Korver – Knee Injury

Use Name	Pos.	Hgt	Wgt	Age	Int	Pts
Jeff Barnes	LB	6'2"	215	22		
Willie Hall	LB	6'2"	225	27	1	6
Ted Hendricks	LB	6'7"	220	29		2
Monte Johnson	LB	6'4"	240	25	2	
Rod Martin	LB	6'2"	215	23		
Randy McClanahan	LB	6'5"	225	22		
Floyd Rice	LB	6'3"	225	28	2	
Phil Villapiano	LB	6'1"	225	28	3	
Butch Atkinson	DB	6'	185	30	2	
Willie Brown	DB	6'1"	210	36	4	
Neal Colzie	DB	6'2"	205	24	3	
Lester Hayes	DB	6'	208	22	1	
Steve Jackson	DB	6'1"	192	22	1	
Charlie Phillips	DB	6'2"	215	24	2	
Jack Tatum	DB	5'10"	205	28	6	
Skip Thomas	DB	6'	205	27	1	
Jimmie Warren	DB	5'11"	175	38		

Terry Kunz – Injury

Use Name	Pos.	Hgt	Wgt	Age	Int	Pts
David Humm	QB	6'2"	185	25		
Mike Rae	QB	6'	190	26		6
Ken Stabler	QB	6'3"	215	31		
Clarence Davis	HB	5'10"	195	28		30
Carl Garrett	HB	5'11"	205	30		18
Hubert Ginn	HB	5'11"	185	30		
Pete Banaszak	FB-HB	5'11"	210	33		30
Terry Robiskie	FB	6'1"	210	22		6
Mark van Eeghen	FB	6'2"	225	25		42
Fred Biletnikoff	WR	6'1"	190	34		30
Morris Bradshaw	WR	6'	196	24		
Cliff Branch	WR	5'11"	170	29		36
Rick Jennings (from TB, SF)	WR-HB	5'9"	180	24		
Mike Siani	WR	6'2"	195	27		12
Warren Bankston	TE	6'4"	235	30		
Dave Casper	TE	6'4"	230	25		36
Ted Kwalick	TE	6'4"	225	30		
Ray Guy	K	6'3"	195	27		
Errol Mann	K	6'	205	36		99

SAN DIEGO CHARGERS 7-7 Tommy Prothro

Scores of Each Game		
0	Oakland	24
23	Kansas City	7
24	CINCINNATI	3
14	New Orleans	0
20	NEW ENGLAND	24
16	KANSAS CITY	21
14	Miami	13
0	Detroit	20
14	DENVER	17
12	OAKLAND	7
30	Seattle	28
37	CLEVELAND	14
9	Denver	17
9	PITTSBURGH	10

Use Name	Pos.	Hgt	Wgt	Age	Int	Pts
Booker Brown	OT	6'2"	257	24		
Billy Shields	OT	6'7"	254	24		
Russ Washington	OT	6'6"	290	30		
Charles Aiu	OG	6'2"	254	23		
Don Macek	OG-C	6'3"	253	23		
Doug Wilkerson	OG	6'2"	257	30		
Ralph Perretta	C	6'2"	250	24		
Bob Rush	C	6'5"	258	21		
Fred Dean	DE	6'3"	226	25	1	12
Leroy Jones	DE	6'8"	274	26	1	6
John Lee	DE	6'2"	253	24		
Charles DeJurnett	DT-DE	6'4"	270	25		
Gary Johnson	DT	6'2"	254	25		
Louie Kelcher	DT	6'5"	282	24		

Use Name	Pos.	Hgt	Wgt	Age	Int	Pts
Don Goode	LB	6'2"	231	26		
Tom Graham	LB	6'2"	235	27		
Bob Horn	LB	6'3"	237	23	1	
Woodrow Lowe	LB	6'	227	23	1	
Rick Middleton	LB	6'2"	228	25		
Ray Preston	LB	6'	215	23		
Jerome Dove	DB	6'2"	186	23	1	
Clarence Duren	DB	6'1"	190	26	4	
Mike Fuller	DB	5'9"	188	24	5	12
Pete Shaw	DB	5'10"	184	23		
Hal Stringert	DB	5'11"	185	25	4	
Mike Williams	DB	5'10"	180	23	3	

Danny Colbert – Injury

Use Name	Pos.	Hgt	Wgt	Age	Int	Pts
Dan Fouts	QB	6'3"	204	26		
James Harris	QB	6'3"	217	30		12
Neal Jeffrey	QB	6'1"	180	24		
Bill Munson	QB	6'2"	205	36		
Cliff Olander	QB	6'5"	196	22		
Hank Bauer	HB	5'10"	195	23		6
Joe Washington	HB	5'10"	182	23		
Rickey Young	HB	6'2"	198	23		24
Larry Barnes	FB-HB	5'11"	220	23		
Bo Matthews	FB	6'4"	230	25		
Clarence Williams	FB	5'9"	198	22		12
Don Woods	FB	6'1"	209	26		12
Larry Dorsey	WR	6'1"	195	24		12
Charlie Joiner	WR	5'11"	188	29		36
Dwight McDonald	WR	6'2"	187	26		
Artie Owens	WR	5'10"	174	24		
Johnnie Rodgers	WR	5'10"	180	26		
Pat Curran	TE	6'3"	238	31		
Bob Klein	TE	6'5"	245	30		6
Jeff West	TE	6'3"	211	24		
Rolf Benirschke	K	6'	165	22		72

SEATTLE SEAHAWKS 5-9 Jack Patera

Scores of Each Game		
14	BALTIMORE	29
20	Cincinnati	42
13	DENVER	24
0	New England	31
30	TAMPA BAY	23
13	Miami	31
56	BUFFALO	17
7	Oakland	44
17	N.Y. Jets	0
10	HOUSTON	22
28	SAN DIEGO	30
20	Pittsburgh	30
34	Kansas City	31
20	CLEVELAND	19

Use Name	Pos.	Hgt	Wgt	Age	Int	Pts
Steve August	OT	6'5"	254	22		
Nick Bebout	OT	6'5"	260	26		
Norm Evans	OT	6'5"	250	34		
Ron Coder	OG	6'4"	250	23		
Gordon Jolley	OG-OT	6'5"	245	28		
Tom Lynch	OG	6'5"	260	22		
Bob Newton	OG	6'4"	260	28		
Art Kuehn	C	6'3"	255	24		
Geoff Reece	C	6'4"	247	25		
John Yarno	C	6'5"	251	22		
Dennis Boyd	DE-DT	6'6"	255	21		
Richard Harris	DE	6'4"	258	29		
Horace Jones	DE	6'3"	255	28		
Alden Roche	DE	6'4"	255	32		
Ron East	DT	6'4"	248	34		
Bob Lurtsema	DT-DE	6'6"	250	35		
Steve Niehaus	DT-DE	6'4"	270	22		
Bill Sandifer	DT	6'6"	262	25		

Use Name	Pos.	Hgt	Wgt	Age	Int	Pts
Terry Beeson	LB	6'3"	240	21		
Pete Cronan	LB	6'2"	238	22		
Ken Geddes	LB	6'3"	235	29	3	
Sammy Green	LB	6'2"	230	22	1	
Mike Jones	LB	6'2"	214	23		
Amos Martin	LB	6'3"	228	28		
Charles McShane	LB	6'3"	230	23		
Autry Beamon	DB	6'1"	190	23	6	6
Dave Brown	DB	6'1"	190	24	4	6
Don Dufek	DB	6'	195	23	2	
Doug Long	DB	6'2"	189	22		
Eddie McMillan	DB	6'	190	25	4	
Walter Packer	DB	5'10"	174	21		
Steve Preece	DB	6'1"	195	30	4	
Cornell Webster	DB	6'	180	22	1	

Randy Coffield – Injury

Use Name	Pos.	Hgt	Wgt	Age	Int	Pts
Sam Adkins	QB	6'2"	214	22		
Steve Myer	QB	6'2"	188	23		
Jim Zorn	QB	6'2"	200	24		6
Al Hunter	HB	5'11"	195	22		6
David Sims	HB	6'3"	216	21		48
Sherman Smith	HB-FB	6'4"	216	22		36
Tony Benjamin	FB	6'3"	225	21		
Ed Marinaro	FB-HB	6'2"	207	27		
Don Testerman	FB	6'2"	235	24		30
Duke Fergerson	WR	6'1"	193	23		12
Steve Largent	WR	5'11"	184	22		60
Sam McCullum	WR	6'2"	203	24		6
Steve Raible	WR	6'2"	195	23		
Ron Howard	TE	6'4"	240	26		6
Fred Rayhle	TE	6'5"	216	23		
John Sawyer	TE	6'2"	230	24		
John Leypoldt	K	6'2"	230	31		60
Herman Weaver	K	6'4"	210	28		

KANSAS CITY CHIEFS 2-12 Paul Wiggin (1-6), Tom Bettis (1-6)

Scores of Each Game		
17	New England	21
7	SAN DIEGO	23
28	OAKLAND	37
7	Denver	23
6	BALTIMORE	17
21	San Diego	16
7	Cleveland	44
20	GREEN BAY	10
27	Chicago	28
7	DENVER	14
2	Houston	34
7	CINCINNATI	27
31	SEATTLE	34
20	Oakland	21

Use Name	Pos.	Hgt	Wgt	Age	Int	Pts
Matt Herkenhoff	OT	6'4"	255	26		
Jim Nicholson	OT	6'6"	275	27		
Tom Wickert (from DET)	OT-OG	6'4"	248	25		
Tom Condon	OG	6'3"	240	24		
Charlie Getty	OG-OT	6'4"	260	25		
Darius Helton	OG	6'2"	260	22		
Bob Simmons	OG-OT	6'4"	260	23		
Charlie Ane	C	6'1"	233	25		
Jack Rudnay	C	6'3"	240	29		
Larry Estes	DE	6'6"	250	30		
John Lohmeyer	DE-DT	6'4"	229	26		2
Whitney Paul	DE	6'3"	220	23	1	
Wilbur Young	DE	6'6"	290	28		
Cliff Frazier	DT	6'4"	265	22		
Willie Lee	DT	6'5"	249	27		6
Keith Simons	DT	6'3"	254	23		

Rod Walters – Injury

Use Name	Pos.	Hgt	Wgt	Age	Int	Pts
Billy Andrews	LB	6'	220	32		
Ray Burks	LB	6'3"	217	22		
Jimbo Elrod	LB	6'	223	23		
Tom Howard	LB	6'2"	208	23	1	
Willie Lanier	LB	6'1"	245	32		
Jim Lynch	LB	6'1"	225	32	3	
Otis Rodgers	LB	6'3"	230	23		
Dave Rozumek	LB	6'2"	212	23		
Gary Barbaro	DB	6'4"	198	23	8	6
Tim Collier	DB	6'	166	23	2	6
Ricky Davis	DB	6'1"	180	24		
Chris Golub	DB	6'2"	196	22		
Tim Gray	DB	6'1"	200	24	2	12
Gary Green	DB	5'11"	184	21	3	
Emitt Thomas	DB	6'2"	192	34	1	
Ricky Wesson	DB	5'9"	163	22		

Use Name	Pos.	Hgt	Wgt	Age	Int	Pts
Tony Adams	QB	6'	198	27		
Mike Livingston	QB	6'3"	211	31		6
Mark Vitali	QB	6'5"	209	22		
Ted McKnight	HB	6'1"	203	23		
Arnold Morgado	HB	6'	210	24		
Ed Podolak	HB	6'1"	205	30		30
Tony Reed	HB	5'11"	197	22		12
Mark Bailey	FB	6'3"	237	22		18
John Brockington (from GB)	FB	6'1"	225	28		12
MacArthur Lane	FB	6'	220	35		6
Pat McNeil	FB	5'9"	208	23		
Larry Brunson	WR	5'11"	180	28		
Gerald Butler	WR	6'4"	205	23		
Henry Marshall	WR	6'2"	205	23		24
Charlie Wade	WR	5'10"	163	27		
Edwin Bechman	TE	6'4"	223	22		
Tony Samuels	TE	6'4"	229	22		
Walter White	TE	6'3"	218	26		30
Jan Stenerud	K	6'2"	187	34		51
Jerrel Wilson	K	6'4"	222	35		

Woody Green – Knee Injury

DENVER BRONCOS

RUSHING

Last Name	No.	Yds	Avg	TD
Armstrong	130	489	3.8	4
Perrin	110	456	4.1	3
Lytle	104	408	3.9	1
Keyworth	83	311	3.7	1
Jensen	40	143	3.6	1
Morton	31	125	4.0	4
Weese	11	56	5.1	1
Penrose	4	24	6.0	0
Upchurch	1	19	19.0	1
Dolbin	2	12	6.0	0
Kiick	1	1	1.0	0
Dilts	1	0	0.0	0
Moses	5	−1	−0.2	0

RECEIVING

Last Name	No.	Yds	Avg	TD
Odoms	37	429	12	3
Moses	27	539	20	4
Dolbin	26	443	17	3
Armstrong	18	128	7	0
Lytle	17	198	12	1
Upchurch	12	245	20	2
Keyworth	11	48	4	0
Perrin	6	106	18	1
Jensen	4	63	16	0
Egloff	2	27	14	0
Kiick	2	14	7	0
Turner	1	25	25	1

PUNT RETURNS

Last Name	No.	Yds	Avg	TD
Upchurch	51	653	13	1
Pane	6	48	8	0
Schultz	1	11	11	0

KICKOFF RETURNS

Last Name	No.	Yds	Avg	TD
Upchurch	20	456	23	0
Schultz	6	135	23	0
Perrin	3	72	24	0
Pane	1	16	16	0
Keyworth	1	15	15	0
Hyde	1	15	15	0
Grant	1	8	8	0
Nairne	1	1	1	0
Dolbin	0	14	–	0

PASSING – PUNTING – KICKING

PASSING	Att	Comp	%	Yds	Yd/Att	TD	Int– %	RK
Morton	254	131	42	1929	7.6	14	8– 3	2
Penrose	39	21	54	217	5.6	0	4– 10	
Weese	20	11	55	119	6.0	1	0– 0	

PUNTING	No	Avg
Dilts	90	39.2
Weese	1	38.0

KICKING	XP	Att	%	FG	Att	%
Turner	31	34	91	13	19	68

OAKLAND RAIDERS

RUSHING

Last Name	No.	Yds	Avg	TD
van Eeghen	324	1273	3.9	7
Davis	194	787	4.1	5
Banaszak	67	214	3.2	5
Garrett	53	175	3.3	1
Robiskie	22	100	4.5	1
Rae	13	75	5.8	1
Ginn	5	6	1.2	0
Stabler	3	−3	−3.0	0

RECEIVING

Last Name	No.	Yds	Avg	TD
Casper	48	584	12	6
Branch	33	540	16	6
Biletnikoff	33	446	14	5
Siani	24	344	14	2
Davis	16	124	8	0
van Eeghen	15	135	9	0
Garrett	8	61	8	2
Bradshaw	5	90	18	0
Banaszak	2	14	7	0

PUNT RETURNS

Last Name	No.	Yds	Avg	TD
Colzie	32	334	10	0
Jennings	12	71	6	0

KICKOFF RETURNS

Last Name	No.	Yds	Avg	TD
Garrett	21	420	20	0
Jennings	7	153	22	0
Banaszak	7	119	17	0
Robiskie	6	83	14	0
Ginn	3	74	25	0
Davis	3	63	21	0
Hayes	3	57	19	0
Bankston	1	0	0	0
McCoy	1	0	0	0

PASSING – PUNTING – KICKING

PASSING	Att	Comp	%	Yds	Yd/Att	TD	Int– %	RK
Stabler	294	169	58	2176	7.4	20	20– 7	4
Rae	30	15	50	162	5.4	1	4– 13	

PUNTING	No	Avg
Guy	59	43.3

KICKING	XP	Att	%	FG	Att	%
Mann	39	42	93	20	29	71

SAN DIEGO CHARGERS

RUSHING

Last Name	No.	Yds	Avg	TD
Young	157	543	3.5	4
Woods	118	405	3.4	1
J. Washington	62	217	3.5	0
C. Williams	50	215	4.3	2
Matthews	43	193	4.5	0
Barnes	24	70	2.9	0
Rodgers	3	44	14.7	0
Olander	7	30	4.3	0
Harris	10	13	1.3	2
Fouts	6	13	2.2	0
Fuller	1	7	7.0	1
Bauer	4	4	1.0	0
Owens	1	3	3.0	0
Curran	1	2	2.0	0
Munson	1	2	2.0	0

RECEIVING

Last Name	No.	Yds	Avg	TD
Young	48	423	9	0
Joiner	35	542	15	6
J. Washington	31	244	8	0
Klein	20	244	12	1
Woods	18	218	12	1
McDonald	13	174	13	0
Rodgers	12	187	16	0
Dorsey	10	198	20	2
Curran	10	123	12	0
Matthews	3	41	14	0
C. Williams	3	20	7	0
Bauer	1	15	15	1
Barnes	1	10	10	0
West	1	3	3	0

PUNT RETURNS

Last Name	No.	Yds	Avg	TD
Fuller	28	360	13	1
Rodgers	15	158	11	0
Dove	1	3	3	0
M. Williams	1	0	0	0
C. Williams	1	0	0	0

KICKOFF RETURNS

Last Name	No.	Yds	Avg	TD
C. Williams	24	481	20	0
Owens	8	132	17	0
Rodgers	4	66	17	0
Woods	1	27	27	0
Middleton	1	20	20	0
Joiner	1	8	8	0

PASSING – PUNTING – KICKING

PASSING	Att	Comp	%	Yds	Yd/Att	TD	Int– %	RK
Harris	211	109	52	1240	5.9	5	11– 5	12
Fouts	109	169	63	869	8.0	4	6– 6	
Munson	31	20	65	225	7.3	1	1– 3	
Olander	16	7	44	76	4.8	0	2– 13	
J. Washington	1	1	100	32	32.0	1	0– 0	
Woods	1	0	0	0	0.0	0	0– 0	

PUNTING	No	Avg
West	72	37.6

KICKING	XP	Att	%	FG	Att	%
Benirschke	21	24	88	17	23	74

SEATTLE SEAHAWKS

RUSHING

Last Name	No.	Yds	Avg	TD
Smith	163	763	4.7	4
Testerman	119	459	3.9	1
Sims	99	369	3.7	5
Hunter	32	179	5.6	1
Zorn	25	141	5.6	1
Benjamin	13	48	3.7	0
Adkins	3	6	2.0	0
Myer	6	1	0.2	0
Weaver	1	−2	−2.0	0

RECEIVING

Last Name	No.	Yds	Avg	TD
Largent	33	643	19	10
Testerman	31	219	7	4
Smith	30	419	14	2
Fergersen	19	374	20	2
Howard	17	177	10	1
Sims	12	176	15	3
Sawyer	10	105	11	0
McCullum	9	198	22	1
Raible	5	79	16	0
Hunter	5	42	8	0
Benjamin	4	27	7	0

PUNT RETURNS

Last Name	No.	Yds	Avg	TD
Packer	20	131	7	0
Ferguson	8	54	7	0
Largent	4	32	8	0

KICKOFF RETURNS

Last Name	No.	Yds	Avg	TD
Hunter	36	820	23	0
Packer	13	280	22	0
Fergerson	11	240	22	0
Sims	4	52	13	0
Smith	3	56	19	0
Raible	2	19	10	0
Dufek	1	21	21	0
Testerman	1	14	14	0

PASSING – PUNTING – KICKING

PASSING	Att	Comp	%	Yds	Yd/Att	TD	Int– %	RK
Zorn	251	104	41	1687	6.7	16	19– 8	14
Myer	130	70	54	729	5.6	6	12– 9	
Sims	4	1	25	43	10.8	1	1– 25	
Preece	1	0	0	0	0.0	0	0– 0	
Smith	1	0	0	0	0.0	0	0– 0	

PUNTING	No	Avg
Weaver	58	39.5

KICKING	XP	Att	%	FG	Att	%
Leypoldt	33	37	89	9	18	50

KANSAS CITY CHIEFS

RUSHING

Last Name	No.	Yds	Avg	TD
Podolak	133	550	4.1	5
Reed	126	505	4.0	2
Bailey	66	266	4.0	2
Brockington	65	186	2.9	1
Lane	25	79	3.2	1
Livingston	19	78	4.1	1
McNight	11	74	6.7	0
Burks	1	51	51.0	0
Adams	5	21	4.2	0
Morgado	3	12	4.0	0
Marshall	7	11	1.6	0
Brunson	2	8	4.0	0
White	2	−3	−1.5	0

RECEIVING

Last Name	No.	Yds	Avg	TD
White	48	674	14	5
Podolak	32	313	10	0
Marshall	23	445	19	4
Brockington	21	223	11	1
Brunson	20	295	15	0
Bailey	17	206	12	1
Reed	12	125	10	0
Samuels	5	65	13	0
Lane	3	40	13	0
Morgado	2	21	11	0
McKnight	1	11	11	0
Beckman	1	3	3	0

PUNT RETURNS

Last Name	No.	Yds	Avg	TD
Green	14	115	8	0
Brunson	20	108	5	0
Podolak	2	13	7	0

KICKOFF RETURNS

Last Name	No.	Yds	Avg	TD
McNight	12	305	25	0
Reed	11	239	22	0
Brunson	11	216	20	0
Wesson	7	129	18	0
Bailey	3	46	15	0
Getty	1	15	15	0
Burks	1	15	15	0

PASSING – PUNTING – KICKING

PASSING	Att	Comp	%	Yds	Yd/Att	TD	Int– %	RK
Livingston	282	143	51	1823	6.5	9	15– 5	11
Adams	92	47	51	691	7.5	2	11– 12	

PUNTING	No	Avg
Wilson	88	39.9

KICKING	XP	Att	%	FG	Att	%
Stenerud	27	28	96	8	18	44

1977 Championship Games

NFC CHAMPIONSHIP GAME

January 1, at Irving, Tex.
(Attendance: 61,968)

SCORING

DALLAS	6	10	0	7–23
MINNESOTA	0	6	0	0– 6

First Quarter
- Dallas — Richards, 32 yard pass from Staubach; PAT – Kick (no good)

Second Quarter
- Dallas — Newhouse, 5 yard rush; PAT – Herrera (Kick)
- Minn. — Cox, 12 yard field goal
- Minn. — Cox, 37 yard field goal
- Dallas — Herrera, 21 yard field goal

Fourth Quarter
- Dallas — Dorsett, 11 yard rush; PAT – Herrera (Kick)

TEAM STATISTICS

DALLAS		MINN.
16	First Downs–Total	12
7	First Downs–Rushing	4
7	First Downs–Passing	6
2	First Downs–Penalty	2
1	Fumbles–Number	5
1	Fumbles–Lost Ball	3
5	Penalty–Number	5
84	Yards Penalized	32
0	Missed Field Goals	0
66	Offensive Plays	63
328	Net Yards	214
4.8	Average Gain	3.4
2	Giveaways	4
4	Takeaways	2
+2	Difference	-2

As expected, Dallas had no trouble at all with a young, inexperienced Chicago Bear team that turned the ball over seven times in the Pokes' 37-7 NFC semi-final victory in Irving. But it was a different story in Los Angeles that same day as Minnesota took advantage of a sloppy, mud-infested field to upset the playoff-jinxed Rams 14-7. The Cowboys proceeded to start the new year off on the right foot with a convincing 23-6 victory over the Vikes to put themselves in the Super Bowl.

The Vikings were no match for a Dallas defense led by linemen Harvey Martin, and Ed Jones and OLB Tom Henderson. After holding the Bears' Walter payton to only 60 rushing yards the week before, the Cowboys' "flex" limited Chuck Foreman to just 59. Two minutes into the first quarter, Martin tackled RB Robert Miller hard enough to cause a fumble which the big end recovered on Minnesota's 39-yard line to set up the Cowboys' first score. Robert Newhouse, who enjoyed his second-straight 80-yard playoff game, powered his way to the 32-yard line and the QB Roger Staubach took over, faking a quick screen and throwing long to WR Golden Richards in the endzone. Minnesota's Carl Eller blocked the extra point, but on the Cowboys' next TD drive, the Vikes' usually reliable specialty teams failed to stop punter Danny White's fake and subsequent 14-yard run for a first down. A defensive holding call on FS Paul Krauses moved the ball deeper into Viking territory and Newhouse responded with a five-yard TD romp to make it 13-0.

Martin recovered two fumbles while his opposite number, Jones, was an imposing force against the run. Also helping out defensively was a strong secondary effort that kept the Vikes' top receiver, Ahmad Rashad, under wraps all day with double-team coverage.

INDIVIDUAL STATISTICS

DALLAS	No	Yds	Avg.	MINNESOTA	No	Yds	Avg.
RUSHING							
Newhouse	15	81	5.4	Foreman	21	59	2.8
Dorsett	19	71	3.7	Miller	8	5	0.6
D. White	1	14	14.0	S. Johnson	1	2	2.0
Staubach	4	4	1.0		30	66	2.2
	39	170	4.3				
RECEIVING							
D. Pearson	4	62	15.5	Foreman	5	36	7.2
P. Pearson	3	48	16.0	S. White	3	46	15.3
Richards	2	34	17.0	Rashad	3	18	6.0
Newhouse	2	5	2.5	Miller	2	39	19.5
DuPree	1	16	16.0	Voigt	1	19	19.0
	12	165	13.8		14	158	11.3
PUNTING							
D. White	8		36.6	Clabo	8		34.7
PUNT RETURNS							
Hill	3	44	14.7	Moore	3	2	0.7
B. Johnson	2	13	6.5				
	5	57	11.4				
KICKOFF RETURNS							
Brinson	3	36	12.0	Moore	3	74	24.7
				S. White	1	37	37.0
				Kellar	1	11	11.0
					5	122	24.4
INTERCEPTION RETURNS							
Henderson	1	1	1.0	N. Wright	1	0	0.0

PASSING

DALLAS	Att.	Comp.	Comp. Pct.	Yds.	Int.	Yds/ Att.	Yds/ Comp.	Yards Lost Tackled
Staubach	23	12	52.2	165	1	7.2	13.8	2–7
MINNESOTA								
Lee	31	14	45.2	158	1	5.1	11.3	2–10

AFC CHAMPIONSHIP GAME

January 1, at Denver
(Attendance: 75,004)

SCORING

DENVER	7	0	7	6–20
OAKLAND	3	0	0	14–17

First Quarter
- Oak. — Mann, 20 yard field goal
- Den. — Moses, 74 yard pass from Morton; PAT–Turner (kick)

Third Quarter
- Den. — Keyworth, 1 yard rush; PAT–Turner (kick)

Fourth Quarter
- Oak. — Casper, 7 yard pass from Stabler; PAT–Mann (kick)
- Den. — Moses, 12 yard pass from Morton; PAT–No kick–pass failed
- Oak. — Casper, 17 yard pass from Stabler; PAT–Mann (kick)

TEAM STATISTICS

DENVER		OAKLAND
16	First Downs–Total	20
6	First Downs–Rushing	6
8	First Downs–Passing	11
2	First Downs–Penalty	3
2	Fumbles–Number	0
0	Fumbles–Lost Ball	0
8	Penalty–Number	2
46	Yards Penalized	6
3	Missed Field Goals	1
58	Offensive Plays	72
308	Net Yards	298
5.3	Average Gain	4.1
1	Giveaways	1
1	Takeaways	1
0	Difference	0

The defending Super Bowl champion Raiders just barely made it to AFC title game with a 37-31 overtime victory at Baltimore in one of the most exciting contests of all-time. The leader changed hands six times and Raider Errol Mann tied the score for the last time when he booted a 22-yard field goal with 26 seconds left in regulation following a clutch 42-yard reception by TE Dave Casper. Casper later scored the game winner on a 10-yard Ken Stabler pass 43 seconds into the second overtime, ending the third longest game in NFL history.

Meanwhile, Denver got past its first hurdle with a 34-21 win over Pittsburgh, after breaking open a 21-21 tie with 13 unanswered points in the fourth quarter. Just as it had done all season, the Broncos' Orange Crush defense provided good field position by forcing four turnovers, including two interceptions by All-Pro OLB Tom Jackson.

Because Oakland had more experience and the Cinderella Broncos were still somewhat of an unknown quantity in many observers' eyes, the Raiders were rated as slight favorites over the team which had beaten them to the AFC West crown. As Oakland repeatedly tried to run to the outside and failed because of the superb lateral movement of the Bronco defense, the momentum swung toward Denver. Although Oakland had taken an early lead on Mann's 20-yard field goal, QB Craig Morton struck two plays later on a 74-yard TD bomb to WR Haven Moses.

After leading 7-3 at halftime, Denver was driving for another score midway through the third quarter when perhaps the most controversial play of the season occurred. With first-and-goal at the Raider two, Rob Lytle took a handoff and vaulted over the left side of his offensive line. He was met head-on by safety Jack Tatum, who jarred the ball loose while Lytle was in mid-air. Raider MG Mike McCoy picked up the loose ball and began to run, but the play was whistled dead. The officials, apparently screened from the fumble, ruled that Denver should keep the ball. Jon Keyworth scored from the one on the next play, and Denver had a 14-3 lead.

Whether that disputed "non-fumble" would have changed the outcome of the game will be debated for years, but it certainly put Oakland at a big disadvantage. The Raiders closed the gap on Stabler's seven-yard TD pass to Casper, but the Morton-Moses duo clicked again on a 12-yard scoring pass. Oakland once again trimmed the deficit to three on a 17-yard pass to the reliable Casper with 3:16 remaining, but Denver ran out the cloke using Lonnie Perrin and Otis Armstrong.

INDIVIDUAL STATISTICS

DENVER	No	Yds	Avg.	OAKLAND	No	Yds	Avg.
RUSHING							
Perrin	11	42	3.8	van Eeghen	20	71	3.6
Lytle	7	26	3.7	Banaszak	7	22	3.1
Keyworth	8	19	2.4	Davis	9	1	0.1
Armstrong	7	16	2.3		36	94	2.6
Jensen	1	2	2.0				
Morton	2	–4	–2.0				
Moses	1	–10	–10.0				
	37	91	2.5				
RECEIVING							
Moses	5	168	33.6	Casper	5	71	14.2
Perrin	2	20	10.0	Biletnikoff	4	38	9.5
Jensen	1	20	20.0	Branch	3	59	19.7
Odoms	1	13	13.0	van Eeghen	2	8	4.0
Keyworth	1	3	3.0	Bradshaw	1	25	25.0
	10	224	22.4	Siani	1	12	12.0
				Banaszak	1	2	2.0
					17	215	12.6
PUNTING							
Dilts	4		40.8	Guy	5		36.0
PUNT RETURNS							
Upchurch	2	12	6.0	Garrett	2	5	2.5
KICKOFF RETURNS							
Upchurch	2	33	16.5	Garrett	3	111	37.0
Schultz	1	20	20.0	Davis	1	25	25.0
Lytle	1	14	14.0		4	136	36.0
	4	67	16.8				
INTERCEPTION RETURNS							
Swenson	1	14	14.0	Rice	1	11	11.0

PASSING

DENVER	Att.	Comp.	Comp. Pct.	Yds.	Int.	Yds/ Att.	Yds/ Comp	Yards Lost Tackled
Morton	20	10	50.0	224	1	11.2	22.4	1–7
OAKLAND								
Stabler	35	17	48.6	215	1	6.1	12.6	1–11

SUPER BOWL XII

January 15, at New Orleans
(Attendance 75,804)

Orange Crushed

Orange was undoubtedly the NFL's most popular color during the 77' season, but after the Dallas Cowboys swept past the Denver Broncos 27-10 in the first Super Bowl played indoors, the game's most vivid scenes had been painted in a solid shade of black and blue.

Most responsible for this setting were the imposing members of the Cowboys' defensive line—safety Randy Hughes notwithstanding—as they ripped away at the left side of Denver's offensive line and pressured quarterback Craig Morton into a miserable performance.

Morton, the NFL's Comeback Player of the Year, completed as many passes to the Cowboys as his own teammates, unintentionally entering his name into the less-distinguished portion of the Super Bowl record book.

In addition to his four interceptions, the game featured the most Super Bowl penalties ever by both teams (20 for 154 yards) as well as most fumbles, both teams (10).

Thanks, however, to the Pokes' inability to capitalize on more than a few scoring opportunities in the first half, as well as Bronco Head Coach Red Miller's decision to replace Morton with Norris Weese with 6:40 left in the third quarter, the game was kept from becoming a Super Bore.

Four plays after Hughes snatched a Morton pass on the Denver 29, Tony Dorsett's three-yard sprint off left tackle put the Cowboys on the scoreboard first with 10:31 gone in the first quarter.

Efren Herrera's 35-yard three-pointer following another interception finished up the first-period scoring, and he also provided the second quarter's only score with a 43-yarder after blowing three straight field goal attempts.

Jim Turner's 47-yarder that barely made it over the cross-bar gave the Broncos their first score early in the third quarter, but the Cowboys extended their lead to 20-3 after a stunning 45-yard TD reception by Butch Johnson as he dove across the goal line to snare QB Roger Staubach's pass.

With Weese adding much-needed mobility to the Denver attack, the Broncs scored their first TD of the game on Rob Lytle's one-yard plunge, one play after ex-Cowboy Jim Jensen galloped 16 yards with a Weese pitchout.

But the game's second exceptional TD reception—Golden Richards' 29-yard, over-the-head catch of Robert Newhouse's option pass while rolling left—made sure the Cinderella Broncos would turn back into a normal old orange pumpkin, at least until next year.

For the first time in Super Bowl history, co-winners were selected as MVP's—White (five tackles, one assist) and DE Harvey Martin (two tackles, two sacks, one deflection).

And while Staubach called a clever game, emphasizing a counteraction passing attack away from Denver's pursuit toward the middle, Dallas' Doomsday defense—and all those black and blue marks—really told the story.

LINEUPS

DALLAS		DENVER
	OFFENSE	
Richards	WR	Dolbin
Neely	LT	Maurer
Scott	LG	Glassic
Fitzgerald	C	Montler
Rafferty	RG	Howard
Donovan	RT	Minor
DuPree	TE	Odoms
D. Pearson	WR	Moses
Staubach	QB	Morton
Dorsett	RB	Armstrong
Newhouse	RB	Keyworth
	DEFENSE	
Jones	LE	Chavous
Pugh	LT-NT	Carter
R. White	RT-RE	Alzado
Martin	RE-LLB	Swenson
Henderson	LLB-LLB	Rizzo
Bruenig	MLB-RLB	Gradishar
Lewis	RLB-RLB	Jackson
Barnes	LCB	L. Wright
Kyle	RCB	Foley
Waters	SS	Thompson
Harris	FS-WS	Jackson

SUBSTITUTES

DALLAS	**OFFENSE**	
Brinson	Hill	P. Pearson
Carano	Johnson	Saldi
Cooper	Laidlaw	D. White
Dennison	Lawless	R. Wright
Frederick		
	DEFENSE	
Brown	Hegman	Renfro
Cole	Hughes	Stalls
Gregory	Huther	Washington
	KICKER	
	Herrera	
DENVER	**OFFENSE**	
Allison	Lytle	Schindler
Egloff	Maples	Schultz
Hyde	Penrose	Upchurch
Jensen	Perrin	Weese
	DEFENSE	
Evans	Nairne	Riley
Grant	Poltl	Smith
Jackson	Rich	Turk
Manor		
	KICKERS	
Dilts		Turner

SCORING

DALLAS	10	3	7	7–27
DENVER	0	0	10	0–10

First Quarter

Dallas — Dorsett, 3 yard rush — 10:31
PAT – Herrera (kick)

Dallas — Herrera, 35 yard field goal — 13:29

Second Quarter

Dallas — Herrera, 43 yard field goal — 3:44

Third Quarter

Denver — Turner, 47 yard field goal — 2:28

Dallas — Johnson, 45 yard pass from Staubach — 8:01
PAT – Herrera (kick)

Denver — Lytle, 1 yard rush — 9:21
PAT – Turner (kick)

Fourth Quarter

Dallas — Richards, 29 yard pass from Newhouse — 7:56
PAT – Herrera (kick)

TEAM STATISTICS

DALLAS		DENVER
17	First Downs–Total	11
8	First Downs–Rushing	8
8	First Downs–Passing	1
1	First Downs–Penalty	2
6	Fumbles–Number	4
2	Fumbles–Lost Ball	4
12	Penalties–Number	8
94	Yards Penalized	60
3	Missed Field Goals	0
71	Offensive Plays	58
325	Net Yards	156
4.6	Average Gain	2.7
2	Giveaways	8
8	Takeaways	2
+6	Differnece	-6

INDIVIDUAL STATISTICS

DALLAS	No	Yds	Avg.	DENVER	No	Yds	Avg.
RUSHING							
Dorsett	15	66	4.4	Lytle	10	35	3.5
Newhouse	14	55	3.9	Armstrong	7	27	3.9
D. White	1	13	13.0	Weese	3	26	8.7
P. Pearson	3	11	3.7	Jensen	1	16	16.0
Staubach	3	6	2.6	Keyworth	5	9	1.8
Laidlaw	1	1	1.0	Perrin	3	8	2.7
Johnson	1	-9	-9.0		29	121	4.2
	38	143	3.8				
RECEIVING							
P. Pearson	5	37	7.4	Dolbin	2	24	12.0
DuPree	4	66	16.5	Odoms	2	9	4.5
Newhouse	3	-1	-0.3	Moses	1	21	21.0
Johnson	2	53	26.5	Upchurch	1	9	9.0
Richards	2	38	19.0	Jensen	1	5	5.0
Dorsett	2	11	5.5	Perrin	1	-7	-7.0
D. Pearson	1	13	13.0		8	61	7.6
	19	217	11.4				
PUNTING							
D. White	5		41.6	Dilts	4		38.2
PUNT RETURNS							
Hill	1	0	0.0	Upchurch	3	22	7.3
				Schultz	1	0	0.0
					4	2	5.5
KICKOFF RETURNS							
Johnson	2	29	14.5	Upchurch	3	94	31.3
Brinson	1	22	22.0	Schultz	2	62	31.0
	3	51	17.0	Jensen	1	17	17.0
					6	173	28.8
INTERCEPTION RETURNS							
Washington	1	27	27.0	none			
Kyle	1	19	19.0				
Barnes	1	0	0.0				
Hughes	1	0	0.0				
	4	46	11.5				

PASSING

	Att.	Comp	Comp Pct.	Yds	Int.	Yds/ Att.	Yds/ Comp.	Yards Lost Tackled
DALLAS								
Staubach	25	17	68.0	183	0	7.5	10.8	
D. White	2	1	50.0	5	0	2.5	5.0	
Newhouse	1	1	100.0	29	0	29.0	29.0	
	28	19	67.9	217	0	7.8	11.4	5–35
DENVER								
Morton	15	4	26.7	39	4	2.6	9.8	2–20
Weese	10	4	40.0	22	0	2.2	5.5	2– 6
	25	8	32.0	61	4	2.4	7.6	4–26

1978 N.F.C. Flying High

The rebirth of the forward pass took another step forward with a change in the rule about "chucking." Previously, receivers were fair game for shots from defenders all the way downfield until the pass was released. With this year's rule change, defenders could hit receivers only within five yards of the line of scrimmage. Slender speedsters had only to find their way five yards downfield and then could run pass patterns without a physical beating. Together with a liberalized rule on pass blocking, this change aimed to restore the aerial circus which had flourished before zone defenses had grounded pro offenses.

EASTERN DIVISION

Dallas Cowboys—The pre-season pundits said that Dallas would win easily. They were half right. The Cowboys repeated as Eastern champs, but only after a two-month trance almost cost them their crown. Coach Tom Landry lost old pros Ralph Neely and Mel Renfro to retirement, but he still enjoyed an embarassment of riches. Roger Staubach piloted a versatile offense which featured Tony Dorsett's running, a fine corps of receivers, and a superb line starring Billy Joe DuPree and Herbert Scott. The Doomsday Defense shone from front to back, with Randy White, Cliff Harris, and Charlie Waters only the brightest of the stars. Nevertheless, the defending Super Bowl champs sleepwalked into November. By the fifth week of the season, they trailed the Redskins by two games. Back to back losses to the Vikings and Dolphins in October dropped the record to 6-4 and put a playoff berth in doubt. Suddenly, they awoke and again played inspired football. With the Redskins faltering, Dallas and Washington met on Thanksgiving Day with first place at stake. It was no contest, with the Cowboys asserting 37-10 dominance. With victories in their last six games, the Cowboys were hitting their stride as they entered the playoffs.

Philadelphia Eagles—The eagles found the key to the playoffs sitting on their bench. Wilbert Montgomery had returned kicks as a rookie last year, but rarely lined up with the offensive unit. Coach Dick Vermeil made Montgomery his starting halfback and was rewarded with the Eagles' best running threat in years. With the ground game established, quarterback Ron Jaworski could pass more selectively and more effectively. Harold Carmichael gained the most yardage of any N.F.C. receiver while running his record pass receiving string to 96 games. Linebacker Bill Bergey led the strong 3-4 defense which sparked the Eagles' resurgence in recent years under Vermeil. The season began with disappointing losses to the Rams and Redskins, but then three straight triumphs boosted the Eagles into contention. Several close calls went the Eagles' way in their quest. A last-minute fumble gave them a victory over the Giants on November 19 when defeat was all but sealed. They went into their final game with a two game losing streak and with any hope of a playoff spot depending on both the Vikings and Packers losing. The Vikings and Packers both lost, the Eagles whipped the Giants 20-3, and Philadelphia was in the playoffs for the first time since 1960.

Washington Redskins—The Jack Pardee era burst onto the Washington scene with a quick blast of glory. Pardee took charge of a squad weakened by retirements of Pat Fischer, Len Hauss, Jerry Smith, Charley Taylor, and Brig Owens, and had no high draft choices with which to rebuild. Pardee obtained Lemar Parrish and Coy Bacon from the Bengals to shore up the defense and made Joe Theismann the first-string quarterback. The results were immediate, six victories at the start of the season, including a Monday night decision over Dallas. With visions of a Super Bowl already dancing, the dream began to crumble. The veteran defense started showing its age, and the offense lost its knack at scoring points. By mid-season, Pardee tried old-timer Billy Kilmer at quarterback, and some reports of grumbling by the players turned up. Their shot at first place was in their own hands on Thanksgiving, but the Redskins were no match for the Cowboys. Mired in a losing streak, the last chance at a wild card berth went up in smoke with a final-game loss to the Bears 14-10.

St. Louis Cardinals—When the Cardinals hired 62-year-old Bud Wilkinson as head coach, fans worried. They did not want to see a legend from the past dragged down by the sullen realities of a new age. Wilkinson had last coached in 1963, when he ended his fabulously successful career at the University of Oklahoma. The fear came true for two months, as the once-powerful Cardinals lost their first eight games. Sometimes overlooked was the absence of many of St. Louis' past offensive weapons. Terry Metcalf jumped to the Canadian Football League, J.V. Cain ripped an Achilles tendon, and Ike Harris and Conrad Dobler were traded to the Saints. Injuries further decimated both offense and defense. With critics shaking their heads and the injured reserve list bulging, Wilkinson engineered a surgence of the Cardinals, leading them to victory in six of their final eight contests. Wilkinson had a lackluster crew of runners, but his offensive line, featuring Dan Dierdorf, Bob Young, and Tom Banks, kept quarterback Jim Hart well protected.

New York Giants—Defensive tackle John Mendenhall said over the summer, "I'm looking forward to the season to see what disappointments it will bring." The season would start out pleasantly for the Giants, but would result in a chokingly bitter disappointment. The Giants ran out to a 3-1 start, their best beginning in ten years. Halfway into the schedule, their good defense had them in playoff contention despite an unimaginative offense. On November 19, they brought a three game losing streak into their battle with the Eagles in Giants' stadium. With under a minute left, the Giants led 17-12, they had possession of the ball, and the Eagles had no more time outs. Instead of falling down with the ball, quarterback Joe Pisarcik attempted to run the clock out with a handoff to Larry Csonka. With the horror of a nightmare, the handoff was botched, the ball bounced free, and Eagle cornerback Herman Edwards scooped it up and dashed 26 yards for a touchdown. The Giants lost 19-17 and suffered a firestorm of press and fan criticism. Assistant coach Bob Gibson, who had called for the play, was fired, the first scapegoat tossed to the fans. Gibson's scalp was not enough, as more than a decade of frustration found its focus in that one loss. The Giants wound up losing seven of their last eight games, and both head coach John McVay and general manager Andy Robustelli followed Gibson into unemployment.

CENTRAL DIVISION

Minnesota Vikings—Bud Grant surveyed his aging squad and devised a formula to keep the Vikings in the running in the NFL's weakest division. Even with All-Pro Matt Blair at linebacker, the defense lacked the fury of the past, so Grant traded Alan Page to Chicago and used Carl Eller and Paul Krause less. Younger men thus got their chance on the Minnesota defense. The offense had lost its ability to run the ball, so Grant turned Fran Tarkenton's passing arm loose. The 38-year-old quarterback showered passes on stellar wide receivers Sammy White and Ahmad Rashad and on backs Rickey Young and Chuck Foreman. The Vikes got off to a 3-4 start which dropped them three games out of first place, but consecutive victories over Green Bay and Dallas shot them back into contention. Climbing back into a first place tie with the Packers, they traveled to Green Bay on November 26 and battled to a 10-10 deadlock. Still tied for first place, both clubs lost their final two games, so the divisional title went to the Vikings because of their victory over the Packers during the season. The title, the cheapest in the league, nevertheless tasted sweet to Tarkenton and Mick Tingelhoff, two veterans in their final season.

Green Bay Packers—"The Pack is back," blared Green Bay supporters as Bart Starr's charges built up a three game lead in the Central Division with a 6-1 start. A mean front four of Ezra Johnson, Mike Butler, Carl Barzilauskas, and Dave Roller led an improving defense which also featured Willie Buchanon at cornerback. Two new weapons spearheaded the offense. Rookie James Lofton burned defenses with his speed at wide receiver, giving young quarterback David Whitehurst a long-distance target. Second-year halfback Terdell Middleton won a starting job and blended quickness and power. A loss in Minnesota on October 22 tempered the euphoria in Green Bay, and a 42-14 trouncing by the Cowboys in Milwaukee on November 12 visibly shook their confidence. With their offense stalled, the Packers blew several opportunities to win a playoff spot. They could manage only a 10-10 tie with the Vikings on November 26, they lost to the Bears 10-0 on December 10, and they killed off their final hopes with a 31-14 defeat at the hands of the Rams on the final day of the season.

Detroit Lions—New head coach Monte Clark kept a lot of rookies on his squad, but nevertheless had to be disappointed at a 1-6 start. Quarterback Greg Landry was sacked with alarming regularity in the early games, a victim of immobile, battle-scarred knees. Unable to improve the pass blocking, Clark turned to Gary Danielson, an inexperienced quarterback with good legs. From the sixth game on, Danielson started at QB, and he showed steady progress as time passed. With the ex-WFLer passing and with Dexter Bussey running with authority, the Lions won six of their last nine games, including impressive triumphs over the Broncos and Vikings. On defense, rookie end Al Baker made the Silver Rush one of the league's best pass rushing outfits.

Chicago Bears—Under new coach Neill Armstrong, the Bears looked like a playoff team at the start of the year, a playoff team at the end of the year, and a doormat in the middle. As a result, the Bears did not make the playoffs. Bolstered by end Tommy Hart from San Francisco, the Bear defense mauled the Cardinals, 49ers, and Lions in three season-opening victories. The peerless Walter Payton ran with abandon and made up the bulk of the offense, with help from fullback Roland Harper. After the strong start, the Bears lost eight straight games. Opponents keyed on Payton and found no threat in Bob Avellini's passing. After a two-month dry spell, the Bears again remembered how to win, closing the year by dashing the playoff hopes of the Packers and Redskins.

FINAL TEAM STATISTICS

OFFENSE

	ATL.	CHI.	DALL.	DET.	G.B.	L.A.	MINN.	N.O.	NYG.	PHIL.	ST.L.	S.F.	T.B.	WASH.
FIRST DOWNS:														
Total	253	262	**342**	269	226	301	308	295	246	271	281	257	238	261
by Rushing	90	136	**146**	105	105	128	102	119	125	143	103	117	111	99
by Passing	133	99	167	141	101	148	**176**	154	101	112	158	106	101	134
by Penalty	30	27	29	23	20	25	30	22	20	16	20	**34**	26	28
RUSHING:														
Number	533	**634**	625	525	550	609	505	512	580	587	554	585	549	537
Yards	1660	2526	**2783**	2163	2023	2308	1536	1845	2304	2456	1954	2091	2098	2082
Average Yards	3.1	4.0	**4.5**	4.1	3.7	3.8	3.0	3.6	4.0	4.2	3.5	3.6	3.8	3.9
Touchdowns	13	19	**22**	12	16	12	10	17	12	16	14	14	16	10
PASSING:														
Attempts	449	352	449	429	357	466	**592**	479	382	401	508	435	361	438
Completions	221	186	251	247	180	236	**352**	294	176	207	252	190	151	212
Completion Pct.	49.2	52.8	55.9	57.6	50.4	50.6	59.5	**61.4**	46.1	51.6	49.6	43.7	41.8	48.4
Passing Yards	2883	2221	3405	2746	2358	3109	**3528**	3452	2428	2485	3357	2306	2171	2978
Avg.Yds per Att.	4.8	5.0	**6.6**	4.8	5.3	5.8	5.2	6.1	5.1	5.0	6.0	4.1	4.1	5.3
Avg. Yds per Comp.	13.1	11.9	13.6	11.1	13.1	13.2	10.0	11.7	13.8	12.0	13.3	12.1	**14.4**	14.1
Times Tackled	56	34	33	47	37	34	30	37	38	41	**22**	42	52	46
Yds Lost Tackled	481	288	229	444	274	235	285	301	283	288	**186**	350	468	413
Net Yards	2402	1933	3176	2302	2084	2874	**3243**	3153	2145	2197	3171	1956	1703	2565
Touchdowns	11	7	**25**	19	11	13	**25**	17	13	16	16	9	12	17
Interceptions	23	28	17	18	18	22	34	**16**	27	**16**	21	36	18	21
Pct. Intercepted	5.1	8.0	3.8	4.2	5.0	4.7	5.7	**3.3**	7.1	4.0	4.1	8.3	5.0	4.8
PUNTS:														
Number	**110**	96	77	87	106	85	85	86	95	92	102	97	102	104
Average	38.4	37.0	39.9	42.0	35.5	36.1	36.4	41.1	**42.1**	36.8	37.4	36.9	40.1	39.0
PUNT RETURNS:														
Number	42	41	63	47	46	**67**	49	36	48	48	51	47	62	54
Yards	345	286	502	430	393	**711**	239	242	274	416	395	323	512	527
Average Yards	8.2	7.0	8.0	9.1	8.5	**10.6**	4.9	6.7	5.7	8.7	7.7	6.9	8.3	9.8
Touchdowns	0	**1**	0	0	0	0	0	0	0	**1**	**1**	0	0	**1**
KICKOFF RET.:														
Number	59	61	47	51	52	52	55	65	60	54	55	**73**	56	58
Yards	1332	1358	896	1129	1085	1055	1057	1384	1081	1134	1148	**1421**	1095	1352
Average Yards	22.6	22.3	19.1	22.1	20.9	20.3	19.2	21.3	18.0	21.0	20.9	19.5	19.6	**23.3**
Touchdowns	**1**	0	0	0	**1**	0	0	0	0	0	0	**1**	0	**1**
INTERCEPT RET.:														
Number	12	17	23	22	27	28	22	21	21	20	26	18	**29**	22
Yards	159	216	316	292	344	427	192	319	**438**	271	249	283	312	109
Average Yards	13.3	12.7	13.7	13.3	12.7	15.3	8.7	15.2	**20.9**	9.7	9.6	15.7	10.8	8.6
Touchdowns	0	1	0	1	2	**5**	0	1	1	2	0	1	0	0
PENALTIES:														
Number	130	101	96	125	99	133	113	112	101	**94**	106	115	100	116
Yards	1083	958	816	1003	**776**	1169	817	1044	1016	805	890	930	860	978
FUMBLES:														
Number	41	**22**	36	35	35	39	34	32	23	39	28	56	35	31
Number Lost	18	**8**	18	15	24	22	17	15	12	22	14	27	20	16
POINTS:														
Total	240	253	**384**	290	249	316	294	281	264	270	248	219	241	273
PAT Attempts	27	29	**48**	33	31	33	37	35	29	36	31	25	29	31
PAT Made	26	26	**46**	32	30	31	36	33	27	30	27	24	25	30
FG Attempts	26	22	26	28	19	**43**	19	25	29	17	22	23	24	30
FG Made	16	17	16	20	11	**29**	12	12	21	8	11	15	14	19
Percent FG Made	61.5	**77.3**	61.5	71.4	57.9	67.4	63.2	48.0	72.4	47.1	50.0	65.2	58.3	63.3
Safeties	**2**	1	1	0	0	0	0	1	0	0	1	0	0	0

DEFENSE

	ATL.	CHI.	DALL.	DET.	G.B.	L.A.	MINN.	N.O.	NYG.	PHIL.	ST.L.	S.F.	T.B.	WASH.
FIRST DOWNS:														
Total	267	282	232	276	302	**229**	278	286	316	248	286	298	256	283
by Rushing	117	128	**83**	115	137	89	120	129	155	92	131	128	109	131
by Passing	**113**	134	128	125	143	**113**	137	130	127	136	131	133	131	133
by Penalty	37	20	21	36	22	27	21	27	34	20	24	37	**16**	19
RUSHING:														
Number	578	568	**477**	565	620	505	559	579	640	505	588	649	595	625
Yards	2067	2174	**1721**	2184	2439	1845	2116	2420	2656	1862	2396	2365	2049	2536
Average Yards	3.6	3.8	3.6	3.9	3.9	3.7	3.8	4.2	4.2	3.7	4.1	3.6	**3.4**	4.1
Touchdowns	21	15	13	18	19	11	20	**9**	25	11	15	17	12	15
PASSING:														
Attempts	444	436	432	**350**	463	399	442	418	443	443	428	413	419	409
Completions	215	239	202	191	254	**188**	240	215	210	228	212	219	241	197
Completion Pct.	48.4	54.8	**46.8**	54.6	54.9	47.1	54.3	51.4	47.4	51.5	49.5	53.0	57.5	48.2
Passing Yards	2789	2857	2730	2781	2910	**2449**	2917	2700	2637	2986	2641	2948	2535	2701
Avg.Yds per Att.	4.8	5.3	4.7	5.7	4.9	**4.5**	5.7	5.5	5.1	5.9	5.1	5.9	5.0	5.4
Avg. Yds per Comp.	13.0	12.0	13.5	14.6	11.5	13.0	12.2	12.6	12.6	13.1	12.5	13.5	**10.5**	13.7
Times Tackled	47	40	**58**	55	48	47	33	33	29	29	37	35	33	35
Yds Lost Tackled	425	351	442	**482**	386	401	227	236	251	213	290	289	256	323
Net Yards	2364	2506	2288	2299	2524	**2048**	2690	2464	2386	2773	2351	2659	2279	2378
Touchdowns	11	16	11	19	16	15	15	21	**10**	17	19	20	13	11
Interceptions	12	17	23	22	27	28	22	21	21	28	26	18	**29**	22
Pct. Intercepted	2.7	3.9	5.3	6.3	5.8	**7.0**	5.0	5.0	4.7	6.3	6.1	4.4	6.9	5.4
PUNTS:														
Number	**108**	96	**108**	87	90	104	92	71	90	83	94	87	97	105
Average	36.6	**35.8**	39.4	40.2	37.9	38.0	36.2	40.2	37.1	39.1	38.9	40.2	40.4	37.0
PUNT RETURNS:														
Number	54	45	**40**	. 54	51	38	52	59	61	47	59	46	62	48
Yards	305	295	311	467	286	**223**	541	539	624	354	575	356	447	328
Average Yards	5.6	6.6	7.8	8.6	**5.6**	5.9	10.4	9.1	10.2	7.5	9.7	7.7	7.2	6.8
Touchdowns	0	0	0	0	0	1	0	0	0	1	0	0	0	2
KICKOFF RET.:														
Number	49	52	73	69	52	64	61	53	55	56	51	**47**	49	55
Yards	1141	1146	1709	1424	1015	1335	1297	1035	1197	1154	1142	**928**	1146	965
Average Yards	23.3	22.0	23.4	20.6	19.5	20.9	21.3	19.5	21.8	20.6	22.4	19.7	23.4	**17.5**
Touchdowns	0	0	0	0	0	1	0	0	0	0	2	0	0	0
INTERCEPT RET.:														
Number	23	28	17	18	18	22	34	**16**	27	**16**	21	36	18	21
Yards	262	312	176	**75**	262	269	424	198	376	131	303	608	235	480
Average Yards	11.0	11.1	10.4	**4.2**	14.6	12.2	12.5	12.4	13.9	8.1	14.4	16.9	13.1	22.9
Touchdowns	2	1	1	0	1	0	2	1	2	0	1	1	1	1
PENALTIES:														
Number	116	101	95	**128**	116	100	110	110	113	104	96	154	101	91
Yards	1010	801	783	1043	949	755	1013	929	862	884	809	1301	963	830
FUMBLES:														
Number	46	32	27	41	40	33	35	37	36	40	34	**50**	32	20
Number Lost	25	16	13	19	20	15	21	20	18	20	16	**27**	14	10
POINTS:														
Total	290	274	**208**	300	269	245	306	298	298	250	296	350	259	283
PAT Attempts	36	32	**25**	39	36	28	39	33	38	30	37	40	27	30
PAT Made	35	28	**23**	38	36	26	33	32	32	28	35	39	**23**	29
FG Attempts	23	19	22	**13**	18	26	19	33	26	26	18	38	32	34
FG Made	13	16	11	8	**5**	17	13	22	12	14	13	23	24	24
Percent FG Made	56.5	84.2	50.0	61.5	**27.8**	65.4	68.4	66.7	46.2	53.8	72.2	60.5	75.0	70.6
Safeties	0	0	1	2	1	0	0	1	1	0	0	1	1	1

Tampa Bay Buccaneers—The Bucs finished last once again, but this season bore no resemblence to the past two joke-filled campaigns. The Bucs won five games, stayed in playoff contention into November, and genuinely worried opponents for the first time. John McKay's building program yielded its first harvest, a tenacious defense which burst into prominence with surprising suddenness. Lee Roy Selmon blossomed into an All-Pro end, and the tough 3-4 defense led the way to impressive victories over the Vikings and Falcons. The offense had not yet risen to the excellence of the defense, but rookie quarterback Doug Williams held out hope for the future. With a 4-4 record at mid-season, the Bucs succumbed to a rash of injuries and their inexperience, losing seven of their final eight. Nevertheless, the progress was startling.

WESTERN DIVISION

Los Angeles Rams—Because Chuck Knox hadn't gotten the team into the Super Bowl, the Rams hired George Allen as head coach. All Allen got the Rams into was turmoil, as owner Carroll Rosenbloom fired Allen two games into the pre-season schedule. During his short tenure, four players left camp in salary disputes, massive discontent brewed among the players in camp, and Rosenbloom was upset by Allen's alleged over-reaching for authority. Assistant coach Ray Malavasi took over as head coach and tried to soothe everyone's feelings. Despite the commotion and Lawrence McCutcheon's lingering thigh injury, the talent-deep Rams bolted out of the gate with seven straight victories and coasted home to their sixth Western title in a row. The defensive unit ranked with the N.F.L.'s best, with All-Pro performances from linemen Jack Youngblood and Larry Brooks, linebacker Jim Youngblood, and small cornerbacks Pat Thomas and Rod Perry. The offense suffered only from comparison with the sterling defense. Quarterback Pat Haden had a robust platoon of backs and ends, and he operated behind a top-notch line featuring Doug France, Dennis Harrah, and Tom Mack. The accurate toe of rookie placekicker Frank Corral topped the offense nicely.

Atlanta Falcons—Leeman Bennett took his overachieving Falcons into the playoffs for the first time in their history. The defense used a lot of blitzing and came up with big plays that kept the Falcons in several close games. The offense began the year with a new quarterback in June Jones, who unseated Steve Bartkowski in the pre-season. After three games, however, Bartkowski reclaimed his job. Thus inspired, Bartkowski guided the Falcons to a series of last-minute victories. On November 12, a 57-yard bomb from Barkowski to Alfred Jackson with ten seconds left gave the Falcons a 20-17 triumph over the Saints. Two weeks later, the Falcons again beat the Saints 20-17 on a touchdown pass with five seconds left. Two weeks after that, Tim Mazzetti booted a field goal at the gun to beat Washington by another 20-17 score.

New Orleans Saints—An opening day victory over the Vikings began Dick Nolan's regime on an up note. Although injuries thinned out an already sparse squad, the Saints nevertheless rose to a 5-4 mark before slumping at the back of the schedule. Guards Conrad Dobler and Emanuel Zanders both went out with injuries in September, and the running attack could never get rolling behind the patched line. Quarterback Archie Manning, however, got enough blocking to unleash a consistently dangerous passing attack. Although rookie Wes Chandler took a while to get comfortable at wide receiver, ex-Cardinal Ike Harris prospered right away. The highlight of the year was a 10-3 upset over the unbeaten Rams on October 22.

San Francisco 49ers—General manager Joe Thomas overhauled the 49ers by hiring a new head coach in Pete McCulley, sending a bundle of draft choices to Buffalo for O.J. Simpson, and trading off Del Williams, Tommy Hart, and Woody Peoples. During the pre-season, changes continued. Wilbur Jackson, Jean Barrett, and Willie Harper went out with knee injuries, and coach McCulley shockingly cut quarterback Jim Plunkett and receiver Gene Washington. The 49ers thus entered the season with a large cache of rookies. O.J. unfortunately was coming off a knee operation and had passed his peak as a runner. Thomas showed signs of panic when, with an 1-8 record, McCulley was canned and replaced by assistant Fred O'Conner. In O'Conner's first game at the helm, Simpson hurt his shoulder and went to the sidelines for the year. With the worst offense and defense in the league, the 49ers saw growing numbers of empty seats at each game. In the season finale, quarterbacks Steve DeBerg and Scott Bull both were injured, forcing O'Connor to use defensive back Bruce Threadgill and receiver Freddie Solomon as QB against the Lions. With the 2-14 record finally set, owner Eddie DeBartolo pushed the rebuilding program ahead by firing Thomas.

DALLAS COWBOYS 12-4-0 Tom Landry

Scores of Each Game		
38	BALTIMORE	0
34	N.Y. Giants	24
14	Los Angeles	27
21	ST. LOUIS	12
5	Washington	9
24	N.Y. GIANTS	3
24	St. Louis	*21
14	PHILADELPHIA	7
10	MINNESOTA	21
16	Miami	23
42	Green Bay	14
27	NEW ORLEANS	7
37	WASHINGTON	10
17	NEW ENGLAND	10
31	Philadelphia	13
30	N.Y. Jets	7

Use Name	Pos.	Hgt.	Wgt.	Age	Int.	Pts.
Pat Donovan	OT	6'4"	255	25		
Andy Frederick	OT	6'6"	245	23		
Rayfield Wright	OT	6'7"	260	33		
Burton Lawless	OG	6'4"	250	24		
Tom Rafferty	OG	6'3"	250	24		
Tom Randall	OG	6'5"	245	22		
Herbert Scott	OG	6'2"	250	25		
Jim Cooper	C-OG	6'5"	252	22		
John Fitzgerald	C	6'5"	260	30		
Too Tall Jones	DE	6'9"	265	27		
Harvey Martin	DE	6'5"	252	27	1	
Larry Bethea	DE	6'5"	254	22		
Larry Cole	DT-DE	6'4"	260	31	1	
Jethro Pugh	DT	6'6"	250	34		
David Stalls	DT-DE	6'4"	236	22		
Randy White	DT	6'4"	245	25		
Bob Breunig	LB	6'2"	227	25	1	
Guy Brown	LB	6'4"	215	23		
Mike Hegman	LB	6'1"	225	25		
Tom Henderson	LB	6'2"	220	25		
Bruce Huther	LB	6'1"	217	24		
D.D. Lewis	LB	6'2"	215	32		
Benny Barnes	DB	6'1"	195	27	5	
Cliff Harris	DB	6'	192	29	4	
Randy Hughes	DB	6'4"	208	25	2	
Aaron Kyle	DB	5'11"	185	24	3	
Dennis Thurman	DB	5'11"	170	22	2	
Mark Washington	DB	5'11"	187	30		
Charlie Waters	DB	6'1"	198	29	4	
Glenn Carano	QB	6'3"	195	22		
Roger Staubach	QB	6'2"	202	36		6
Danny White	QB	6'2"	192	26		
Alois Blackwell	HB	5'10"	195	23		
Doug Dennison	HB	6'1"	204	26		6
Tony Dorsett	HB	5'11"	192	24		60
Preston Pearson	HB	6'1"	206	33		
Larry Brinson	FB	6'	214	24		12
Scott Laidlaw	FB	6'	205	25		24
Robert Newhouse	FB	5'10"	205	28		60
Tony Hill	WR	6'2"	196	22		36
Butch Johnson	WR	6'1"	191	24		
Drew Pearson	WR	6'	183	27		18
Robert Steele	WR	6'4"	196	22		
Billy Joe DuPree	TE	6'4"	226	28		54
Jay Saldi	TE	6'3"	224	23		12
Jackie Smith	TE	6'4"	232	38		
Rafael Septien	K	5'9"	171	24		94

PHILADELPHIA EAGLES 9-7-0 Dick Vermeil

Scores of Each Game		
14	LOS ANGELES	16
30	Washington	35
24	New Orleans	17
17	MIAMI	3
17	Baltimore	14
14	New England	24
17	WASHINGTON	10
7	Dallas	14
10	ST. LOUIS	16
10	GREEN BAY	3
17	N.Y. JETS	9
19	N.Y. Giants	17
14	St. Louis	10
27	Minnesota	28
13	DALLAS	31
20	N.Y. GIANTS	3

Use Name	Pos.	Hgt.	Wgt.	Age	Int.	Pts.
Ed George	OT	6'4"	270	32		
Jerry Sisemore	OT	6'4"	260	27		
Stan Walters	OT	6'6"	270	30		
Wade Key	OG	6'4"	245	31		
Tom Luken	OG	6'3"	253	28		
Woody Peoples	OG	6'2"	250	35		
Dennis Franks	C	6'1"	245	25		
Guy Morriss	C	6'4"	255	27		
Len Burnham	DE	6'4"	240	31		
Carl Hairston	DE	6'3"	245	25		
Dennis Harrison	DE	6'8"	275	22	1	
Manny Sistrunk	DE	6'5"	275	31		
Ken Clarke	NT	6'2"	255	22		
Charles Johnson	NT	6'3"	262	26		
Bill Bergey	LB	6'2"	245	33	4	
John Bunting	LB	6'1"	220	28	1	
Frank LeMaster	LB	6'2"	231	26	3	6
Drew Mahalic	LB	6'4"	225	25	1	
Mike Osborn	LB	6'5"	235	22		
Ray Phillips (from CIN)	LB	6'3"	221	24		
Terry Tautolo	LB	6'2"	235	24		
Reggie Wilkes	LB	6'4"	230	22		
Herman Edwards	DB	6'	194	24	7	6
Bob Howard	DB	6'1"	175	33	3	
Eric Johnson	DB	6'1"	192	26		
Randy Logan	DB	6'1"	195	27	2	
John Outlaw	DB	5'10"	180	32		
Deac Sanders	DB	6'1"	175	28	5	6
John Sciarra	DB-QB	5'11"	185	24	1	12
Charles Williams	DB	6'1"	180	24		
Ron Jaworski	QB	6'2"	195	27		
John Walton	QB	6'2"	210	30		
Billy Campfield	HB	5'11"	185	22		
Louie Giammona	HB	5'9"	180	25		
Herb Lusk	HB	6'	190	25		18
Wilbert Montgomery	HB	5'10"	195	23		60
Larry Barnes (from SD, STL)	FB	5'11"	220	24		6
James Betterson	FB	6'	210	24		
Cleveland Franklin	FB	6'2"	216	23		
Mike Hogan	FB	6'2"	215	23		30
Harold Carmichael	WR	6'7"	225	28		48
Wally Henry	WR	5'8"	170	23		6
Oren Middlebrook	WR	6'2"	185	23		
Vince Papale	WR	6'2"	195	32		
Ken Payne	WR	6'1"	185	27		6
Charlie Smith	WR	6'1"	185	28		12
Keith Krepfle	TE	6'3"	225	26		18
Bill Larson	TE	6'4"	220	24		
Richard Osborne	TE	6'3"	230	24		
Rick Engles	K	5'11"	180	24		
Mitch Hoopes	K	6'1"	204	25		
Mike Michel	K	5'10"	177	24		9
Nick Mike-Mayer	K	5'8"	187	28		45

WASHINGTON REDSKINS 8-8-0 Jack Pardee

Scores of Each Game		
16	New England	14
35	PHILADELPHIA	30
28	St. Louis	10
23	N.Y. JETS	3
9	DALLAS	5
21	Detroit	19
10	Philadelphia	17
6	N.Y. Giants	17
38	SAN FRANCISCO	20
17	Baltimore	21
16	N.Y. GIANTS	*13
17	ST. LOUIS	27
10	Dallas	37
0	MIAMI	16
17	Atlanta	20
10	CHICAGO	14

Use Name	Pos.	Hgt.	Wgt.	Age	Int.	Pts.
Jim Harlan	OT	6'4"	250	24		
Terry Hermeling	OT	6'5"	255	32		
George Starke	OT	6'5"	250	30		
Jeff Williams	OT	6'4"	255	23		
Fred Dean	OG	6'3"	253	23		
Dan Nugent	OG	6'3"	250	25		
Ron Saul	OG	6'3"	254	30		
Ted Fritsch	C	6'2"	242	28		
Bob Kuziel	C	6'5"	255	28		
Coy Bacon	DE	6'4"	265	36		
Karl Lorch	DE	6'3"	258	28		
Ron McDole	DE	6'3"	265	38	1	
Perry Brooks	DT	6'3"	260	23		
Dave Butz	DT	6'7"	285	28	1	
Bob Heinz	DT	6'6"	260	31		
Diron Talbert	DT	6'5"	255	34		
Mike Curtis	LB	6'2"	232	35	1	
Brad Dusek	LB	6'2"	214	27	1	6
Chris Hanburger	LB	6'2"	218	37		
Dallas Hickman	LB-DE	6'6"	235	26		
Don Hover	LB	6'2"	222	23		
Harold McClinton	LB	6'2"	235	31		
Pete Wysocki	LB	6'2"	225	29		
Don Harris	DB	6'2"	185	24		
Ken Houston	DB	6'3"	198	33	2	
Joe Lavender	DB	6'4"	190	29	1	
Mark Murphy	DB	6'4"	210	23		
Lemar Parrish	DB	5'11"	183	30	4	
Jake Scott	DB	6'	188	33	7	
Gerard Williams	DB	6'1"	184	26	4	6
Bill Brundige-Knee Injury						
Billy Kilmer	QB	6'	204	38		
Kim McQuilken	QB	6'2"	203	27		
Joe Theismann	QB	6'	190	28		6
Ike Forte	HB	6'	196	24		
Tony Green	HB	5'9"	185	21		18
Clarence Harmon	HB-FB	5'11"	190	22		6
Benny Malone (from MIA)	HB	5'10"	193	26		6
Mike Thomas	HB	5'11"	190	25		30
John Riggins	FB	6'2"	230	29		30
Terry Anderson (from MIA)	WR	5'9"	182	23		
Danny Buggs	WR	6'2"	185	25		12
John McDaniel	WR	6'1"	197	26		24
J.T. Smith (to KC)	WR	6'2"	185	22		
Ricky Thompson	WR	6'	176	24		6
Jean Fugett	TE	6'4"	230	26		42
Reggie Haynes	TE	6'2"	229	23		
Mike Bragg	K	5'11"	186	31		
Mark Moseley	K	5'11"	205	30		87

ST. LOUIS CARDINALS 6-10-0 Bud Wilkinson

Scores of Each Game		
10	Chicago	17
6	NEW ENGLAND	16
10	WASHINGTON	28
12	Dallas	21
10	Miami	24
17	BALTIMORE	30
21	DALLAS	*24
10	N.Y. Jets	23
16	Philadelphia	10
20	N.Y. GIANTS	10
16	San Francisco	10
27	Washington	17
10	PHILADELPHIA	14
21	DETROIT	14
0	N.Y. Giants	17
42	ATLANTA	21

Use Name	Pos.	Hgt.	Wgt.	Age	Int.	Pts.
Dan Dierdorf	OT	6'4"	288	29		
Roger Finnie	OT	6'3"	248	32		
Keith Wortman	OT-OG	6'2"	262	28		
George Collins	OG	6'2"	248	22		
Tom Mullen	OG	6'3"	250	26		
Terry Stieve	OG	6'2"	245	24		
Bob Young	OG-C	6'2"	279	35		
Tom Banks	C-OG	6'1"	245	30		
Tom Brahaney	C	6'2"	246	26		
Bob Bell	DE	6'4"	257	30		
Bob Pollard	DE	6'3"	251	29		
Ron Yankowski	DE	6'5"	258	31		
John Zook	DE	6'5"	254	30		
Charlie Davis	NT	6'1"	268	26		
Mike Dawson	NT	6'4"	274	24		
Keith Simons	NT	6'3"	254	24		
Kurt Allerman	LB	6'3"	222	23		
Mark Arneson	LB	6'2"	224	28		
John Barefield	LB	6'2"	224	23		
Randy Gill (to TB)	LB	6'2"	230	22		
Tim Kearney	LB	6'2"	221	27	1	
Steve Neils	LB	6'2"	218	27	1	
Curtis Townsend	LB	6'1"	229	23		
Greg Westbrooks (to OAK)	LB	6'3"	217	25		
Eric Williams	LB	6'2"	217	23	1	
Carl Allen	DB	6'	186	22	6	
Doug Greene	DB	6'2"	205	23		
Ken Greene	DB	6'2	203	22		
Lee Nelson	DB	5'10"	185	24	1	
Mike Sensibaugh	DB	5'11"	190	29	3	6
Perry Smith	DB	6'	190	27	3	
Ken Stone	DB	6'1"	180	27	9	
Roger Wehrli	DB	6'	193	30	4	
Roland Woolsey	DB	6'1"	182	25		
J.V. Cain-Achilles Injury						
Robert Giblin-Injury						
Jim Hart	QB	6'2"	210	34		12
Mark Manges	QB	6'2"	210	22		
Steve Pisarkiewicz	QB	6'2"	205	24		
Gordon Bell	HB	5'9"	180	24		
Ted Farmer	HB	5'11"	175	24		
Will Harrell	HB	5'9"	182	25		6
Steve Jones	HB	6'	198	27		12
Wayne Morris	HB-FB	6'	208	24		12
Willie Shelby	HB	5'11"	198	25		
Jim Otis	FB	6'	226	30		48
Warren Anderson	WR	6'2"	195	23		
Jim Childs	WR	6'2"	194	22		6
Mel Gray	WR	5'9"	173	29		12
Tommy Southard (to HOU)	WR	6'	185	23		
Dave Stief	WR	6'3	195	22		24
Pat Tilley	WR	5'10	171	25		18
Al Chandler (from NE)	TE	6'2"	229	27		24
Eason Ramson	TE	6'2	220	22		6
Jim Thaxton	TE	6'3	242	29		6
Jim Bakken	K	6'	198	37		60
Steve Little	K	6'	180	22		
Mike Wood (from MIN)	K	5'11"	199	23		

NEW YORK GIANTS 6-10-0 John McVay

Scores of Each Game		
19	Tampa Bay	13
24	DALLAS	34
26	KANSAS CITY	10
27	SAN FRANCISCO	10
20	Atlanta	23
3	Dallas	24
17	TAMPA BAY	14
17	WASHINGTON	6
17	New Orleans	28
10	St. Louis	20
13	Washington	*16
17	PHILADELPHIA	19
17	Buffalo	41
17	LOS ANGELES	20
17	ST. LOUIS	0
3	Philadelphia	20

Use Name	Pos.	Hgt.	Wgt.	Age	Int.	Pts.
Bill Bain (from DEN)	OT	6'4"	270	26		
Brad Benson	OT-OG-C	6'3"	258	22		
Gordon Gravelle	OT	6'5"	252	29		
Gordon King	OT	6'6"	275	22		
Ron Mikolajczyk	OT	6'3"	275	28		
Jim Pietrzak	OT-C	6'5"	260	25		
J.T. Turner	OG	6'3"	250	25		
Doug Van Horn	OG	6'2"	245	34		
Jim Clack	C	6'3"	250	30		
Leo Tierney (from CLE)	C	6'3"	248	24		
Jack Gregory	DE	6'6"	250	33		6
George Martin	DE	6'4"	245	25		6
Troy Archer	DT	6'4"	250	23		
Larry Gillard	DT	6'4"	270	23		
Gary Jeter	DT-DE	6'4"	260	23		
Jim Krahl	DT	6'5"	252	22		
John Mendenhall	DT	6'1"	255	29		
Harry Carson	LB	6'2	235	24	3	
Randy Coffield	LB	6'3	215	24		
Brian Kelley	LB	6'3"	222	27	1	
Dan Lloyd	LB	6'2	225	24		
Frank Marion	LB	6'3	228	27		
John Skorupan	LB	6'3"	225	27		
Brad Van Pelt	LB	6'5"	235	27	3	
Bill Bryant (to PHI)	DB	5'11"	195	27		
Terry Jackson	DB	5'10"	197	22	7	6
Ernie Jones	DB	6'3"	180	25	3	
Larry Mallory	DB	5'11"	185	26		
Odis McKinney	DB	6'2"	187	21	1	
Beasley Reese	DB	6'1"	193	24		
Ray Rhodes	DB	5'11"	185	27	3	
Maurice Tyler	DB	6'	190	28		6
Fred Besana	QB	6'4"	205	24		
Randy Dean	QB	6'3"	195	23		
Jerry Golsteyn	QB	6'4"	210	24		
Joe Pisarcik	QB	6'4"	220	26		6
Bob Hammond	HB	5'10"	170	26		18
Doug Kotar	HB	5'11"	205	27		12
Billy Taylor	HB	6'	215	22		
Larry Csonka	FB	6'3"	235	31		36
Dan Doornink	FB	6'3"	210	22		6
Willie Spencer	FB	6'4"	235	25		12
Emery Moorehead	WR	6'2"	210	24		
Johnny Perkins	WR	6'2"	205	24		18
Ernest Pugh	WR	6'1	174	26		
Jim Robinson	WR	5'9	170	25		12
James Thompson	WR	6'	178	25		
Al Dixon	TE	6'5"	220	24		18
Gary Shirk	TE	6'1"	220	28		12
Joe Danelo	K	5'9"	166	24		90
Dave Jennings	K	6'4"	205	26		

*—Overtime

DALLAS COWBOYS

RUSHING

Last Name	No.	Yds.	Avg.	TD
Dorsett	290	1325	4.6	7
Newhouse	140	584	4.2	8
Laidlaw	75	312	4.2	3
Staubach	42	182	4.3	1
P. Pearson	25	104	4.2	0
Brinson	18	96	5.3	2
Dennison	14	75	5.4	1
Blackwell	9	37	4.1	0
D. Pearson	3	29	9.7	0
Hill	3	17	5.7	0
DuPree	1	15	15.0	0
D. White	5	7	1.4	0

RECEIVING

Last Name	No.	Yds.	Avg.	TD
P. Pearson	47	526	11	0
Hill	46	823	18	6
D. Pearson	44	714	16	3
Dorsett	37	378	10	2
DuPree	34	509	15	9
Newhouse	20	176	9	2
Johnson	12	155	13	0
Laidlaw	6	108	18	1
Saldi	3	8	3	2
Dennison	1	6	6	0

PUNT RETURNS

Last Name	No.	Yds.	Avg.	TD
Johnson	51	401	8	0
Hill	11	101	9	0
Thurman	1	0	0	0

KICKOFF RETURNS

Last Name	No.	Yds.	Avg.	TD
Johnson	29	603	21	0
Brinson	6	93	16	0
Blackwell	3	70	23	0
Dennison	3	63	21	0
Thurman	3	42	14	0
R. White	1	15	15	0
Lawless	1	10	10	0
Saldi	1	0	0	0

PASSING - PUNTING - KICKING

PASSING	Att.	Comp.	%	Yds.	Yd./Att.	TD	Int.-%	RK
Staubach	413	231	56	3190	**7.7**	**25**	16- 4	**1**
D. White	34	20	59	215	6.3	0	1- 3	
Dorsett	1	0	0	0	0.0	0	0- 0	
Hill	1	0	0	0	0.0	0	0- 0	

PUNTING	No.	Avg.
D. White	76	40.5

KICKING	XP	Att.	%	FG	Att.	%
Septien	**46**	**47**	98	16	26	62

PHILADELPHIA EAGLES

RUSHING

Last Name	No.	Yds.	Avg.	TD
Montgomery	259	1220	**4.7**	9
Hogan	145	607	4.2	4
Campfield	61	247	4.0	0
Franklin	60	167	2.8	0
Jaworski	30	79	2.6	0
Betterson	11	32	2.9	0
LeMaster	2	29	14.5	0
Carmichael	1	21	21.0	0
Payne	1	17	17.0	0
Engles	1	16	16.0	0
Barnes	4	12	3.0	1
Sciarra	8	11	1.4	2
Giammona	4	6	1.5	0
Michel	1	0	0.0	0
Walton	2	0	0.0	0

RECEIVING

Last Name	No.	Yds.	Avg.	TD
Carmicheal	55	**1072**	20	8
Montgomery	34	195	8	1
Hogan	31	164	5	1
Krepfle	26	374	14	3
Campfield	15	101	7	0
Payne	13	238	18	1
Osborne	13	195	11	0
Smith	11	142	13	2
Franklin	7	46	7	0
Barnes	2	13	7	0
Betterson	2	8	4	0

PUNT RETURNS

Last Name	No.	Yds.	Avg.	TD
Sciarra	37	251	7	0
Henry	11	165	15	1
Giammona	0	1	—	0

KICKOFF RETURNS

Last Name	No.	Yds.	Avg.	TD
Campfield	18	368	20	0
Giammona	12	245	20	0
Betterson	7	185	26	0
Montgomery	6	154	26	0
Lusk	3	61	20	0
Henry	3	54	18	0
Tautolo	3	45	15	0
Barnes	2	22	11	0

PASSING - PUNTING - KICKING

PASSING	Att.	Comp.	%	Yds.	Yd./Att.	TD	Int.-%	RK
Jaworski	398	206	52	2487	6.3	16	16- 4	5
Engles	1	1	100	-2	-2.0	0	0- 0	
Sciarra	1	0	0	0	0.0	0	0- 0	
Walton	1	0	0	0	0.0	0	0- 0	

PUNTING	No.	Avg.
Michel	58	35.8
Engles	33	39.6

KICKING	XP	Att.	%	FG	Att.	%
Mike-Mayer	21	22	95	8	17	47
Michel	9	12	75			

WASHINGTON REDSKINS

RUSHING

Last Name	No.	Yds.	Avg.	TD
Riggins	248	1014	4.1	5
Thomas	161	533	3.3	3
Theismann	37	177	4.8	1
Harmon	34	141	4.1	0
Malone	33	110	3.3	1
Green	22	82	3.7	1
McDaniel	2	25	12.5	0
Haynes	1	13	13.0	0
Forte	4	4	1.0	0
Kilmer	1	1	1.0	0

RECEIVING

Last Name	No.	Yds.	Avg.	TD
Buggs	36	575	16	2
Thomas	35	387	11	2
McDaniel	34	577	17	4
Riggins	31	299	10	0
Fugett	25	367	15	7
Thompson	23	350	15	1
Harmon	11	112	10	1
Green	4	89	22	0
Malone	3	29	10	0
Haynes	2	32	16	0
Anderson	1	56	56	0
Murphy	1	13	13	0

PUNT RETURNS

Last Name	No.	Yds.	Avg.	TD
Green	42	443	10	1
Anderson	5	47	9	0
Smith	4	33	8	0
Harmon	1	5	5	0
Parrish	1	4	4	0
Forte	1	-5	-5	0

KICKOFF RETURNS

Last Name	No.	Yds.	Avg.	TD
Green	34	870	26	1
Forte	11	243	22	0
Anderson	10	227	23	0
Harris	6	99	17	0
Harmon	3	52	17	0
Smith	1	18	18	0

PASSING - PUNTING - KICKING

PASSING	Att.	Comp.	%	Yds.	Yd./Att.	TD	Int.-%	RK
Theismann	390	187	48	2593	6.7	13	18- 5	8
Kilmer	46	23	50	316	6.9	4	3- 7	
Bragg	2	2	100	69	34.5	0	0- 0	

PUNTING	No.	Avg.
Bragg	103	39.4

KICKING	XP	Att.	%	FG	Att.	%
Moseley	30	31	97	19	30	63

ST. LOUIS CARDINALS

RUSHING

Last Name	No.	Yds.	Avg.	TD
Otis	197	664	3.4	8
Morris	174	631	3.6	1
Jones	105	392	3.7	2
Harrell	35	134	3.8	0
Gray	5	51	10.2	1
Tilley	1	32	32.0	0
Bell	7	23	3.3	0
Hart	11	11	1.0	2
Ramson	2	8	4.0	0
Shelby	2	5	2.5	0
Farmer	1	4	4.0	0
Little	1	0	0.0	0
Wehrli	1	0	0.0	0
Pisarkiewicz	5	-1	-0.2	0
Stief	1	-8	-8.0	0

RECEIVING

Last Name	No.	Yds.	Avg.	TD
Tilley	62	900	15	3
Gray	44	871	20	1
Morris	33	298	9	1
Jones	27	217	8	0
Stief	24	477	20	4
Ramson	23	238	10	1
Chandler	16	190	12	4
Otis	8	38	5	0
Childs	4	50	13	1
Thaxton	3	31	10	1
Bell	3	28	9	0
Harrell	3	5	2	0
Shelby	1	11	11	0

PUNT RETURNS

Last Name	No.	Yds.	Avg.	TD
Harrell	21	196	9	1
Bell	8	177	22	0
Shelby	9	211	23	0
Tilley	2	8	4	0
Southard	2	-2	-1	0
Woolsey	1	4	4	0
Smith	1	0	0	0

KICKOFF RETURNS

Last Name	No.	Yds.	Avg.	TD
Harrell	19	389	21	0
Shelby	9	211	23	0
Bell	8	177	22	0
Childs	4	77	19	0
Morris	3	66	22	0
Nelson	3	58	19	0
Southard	2	47	24	0
Woolsey	1	25	25	0
Townsend	1	13	13	0
Westbrooks	1	12	12	0
Stone	1	3	3	0

PASSING - PUNTING - KICKING

PASSING	Att.	Comp.	%	Yds.	Yd./Att.	TD	Int.-%	RK
Hart	477	240	50	3121	6.5	16	18- 4	6
Pisarkiewicz	29	10	35	164	5.7	0	3- 10	
Stief	1	1	100	43	43.0	0	0- 0	
Wood	1	1	100	29	29.0	0	0- 0	

PUNTING	No.	Avg.
Little	46	38.0
Wood	82	36.8
Bakken	4	36.8

KICKING	XP	Att.	%	FG	Att.	%
Bakken	27	30	90	11	22	50

NEW YORK GIANTS

RUSHING

Last Name	No.	Yds.	Avg.	TD
Kotar	149	625	4.2	1
Hammond	131	554	4.2	0
Csonka	91	311	3.4	6
Doornink	60	306	5.1	1
Taylor	73	250	3.4	0
Dean	14	94	6.7	0
Pisarcik	17	68	4.0	1
Spencer	38	61	1.6	2
Pough	3	33	11.0	0
Perkins	1	3	3.0	0
Kelley	1	2	2.0	0
Jennings	1	0	0.0	0
Goldsteyn	1	-3	-3.0	0

RECEIVING

Last Name	No.	Yds.	Avg.	TD
Robinson	32	620	19	2
Perkins	32	514	16	3
Kotar	22	225	10	1
Hammond	20	173	9	2
Dixon	18	376	21	3
Doornink	12	66	6	0
Shirk	10	127	13	2
Taylor	9	70	8	0
Thompson	7	113	16	0
Csonka	7	73	10	0
Moorehead	3	45	15	0
Spencer	2	25	13	0
Pough	1	2	2	0
Kelley	1	-1	-1	0

PUNT RETURNS

Last Name	No.	Yds.	Avg.	TD
Hammond	22	157	7	0
Robinson	19	106	6	0
Jackson	4	1	0	0
Thompson	2	4	2	0
Tyler	1	6	6	0

KICKOFF RETURNS

Last Name	No.	Yds.	Avg.	TD
Pough	15	313	21	0
Hammond	15	290	19	0
Taylor	11	192	17	0
Shirk	5	63	13	0
Skorupan	4	52	13	0
Kotar	3	51	17	0
Moorehead	2	52	26	0
Reece	2	40	20	0
Spencer	1	14	14	0
Marion	1	12	12	0
Tyler	1	2	2	0

PASSING - PUNTING - KICKING

PASSING	Att.	Comp.	%	Yds.	Yd./Att.	TD	Int.-%	RK
Pisarcik	301	143	48	2096	7.0	12	23- 8	13
Dean	39	19	49	188	4.8	1	3- 8	
Goldsteyn	40	12	30	110	2.8	0	1- 3	
Mallory	1	1	100	35	35.0	0	0- 0	
Jennings	1	1	100	-1	-1.0	0	0- 0	

PUNTING	No.	Avg.
Jennings	95	42.1

KICKING	XP	Att.	%	FG	Att.	%
Danelo	27	29	93	21	29	72

MINNESOTA VIKINGS 8-7-1 Bud Grant

Scores of Each Game		
24	New Orleans	31
12	DENVER	*9
10	TAMPA BAY	16
24	Chicago	20
24	Tampa Bay	7
28	Seattle	29
17	LOS ANGELES	34
21	GREEN BAY	7
21	Dallas	10
17	DETROIT	7
17	CHICAGO	14
7	SAN DIEGO	13
10	Green Bay	*10
28	PHILADELPHIA	27
14	Detroit	45
20	Oakland	27

Use Name	Pos.	Hgt.	Wgt.	Age	Int.	Pts.
Frank Myers	OT	6'5"	255	22		
Steve Riley	OT	6'6"	258	25		
Ron Yary	OT	6'6"	255	32		
Charlie Goodrum	OG	6'3"	256	28		
Wes Hamilton	OG	6'3"	255	25		
Bob Lingenfelter	OG-OT	6'7"	277	24		
Dennis Swilley	OG	6'3"	241	23		
Jim Hough	C	6'2"	267	22		
Mick Tingelhoff	C	6'1"	240	38		
Carl Eller	DE	6'6"	247	36		
Randy Holloway	DE	6'5"	245	23		
Jim Marshall	DE	6'3"	240	40		
Mark Mullaney	DE	6'6"	242	25		
Lyman Smith	DT	6'5"	250	21		
Doug Sutherland	DT	6'3"	250	30		
James White	DT	6'3"	263	24		
Matt Blair	LB	6'5"	229	26	3	6
Wally Hilgenberg	LB	6'3"	229	35		
Fred McNeill	LB	6'2"	229	26	2	6
Jeff Siemon	LB	6'2"	237	28		
Scott Studwell	LB	6'2"	224	24		
Nate Allen	DB	5'11"	174	30		
Bobby Bryant	DB	6'1"	170	34	7	
Tom Hannon	DB	5'11"	193	23	2	
Paul Krause	DB	6'3"	205	36		
Nelson Munsey	DB	6'1"	186	30		
John Turner	DB	6'	199	22	1	
Phil Wise	DB	6'	193	29	2	
Nate Wright	DB	5'11"	180	31	5	
Tommy Kramer	QB	6'1"	199	23		
Bob Lee	QB	6'2"	195	32		
Fran Tarkenton	QB	6'1"	185	38		6
Brent McClanahan	HB	5'10"	202	27		
Robert Miller	HB	5'11"	204	25		18
Rickey Young	HB	6'2"	198	24		36
Chuck Foreman	FB-HB	6'2"	207	27		42
Sammy Johnson	FB	6'1"	226	25		
Mark Kellar	FB	6'	225	26		
Kevin Miller	WR	5'10"	180	23		6
Ahmad Rashad	WR	6'2"	200	28		48
Harry Washington	WR	6'	180	22		
Sammy White	WR	5'11"	189	24		54
Steve Craig	TE	6'3"	231	27		
Bob Tucker	TE	6'3"	230	33		
Stu Voigt	TE	6'1"	225	30		
Greg Coleman	K	6'	178	23		
Rick Danmeier	K	6'	183	26		72

GREEN BAY PACKERS 8-7-1 Bart Starr

Scores of Each Game		
13	Detroit	7
28	NEW ORLEANS	17
3	OAKLAND	28
24	San Diego	3
35	DETROIT	14
24	CHICAGO	14
45	SEATTLE	28
7	Minnesota	21
9	TAMPA BAY	7
3	Philadelphia	10
14	DALLAS	42
3	Denver	16
10	MINNESOTA	*10
17	Tampa Bay	7
0	Chicago	14
14	Los Angeles	31

Use Name	Pos.	Hgt.	Wgt.	Age	Int.	Pts.
Greg Koch	OT	6'4"	265	23		
Gerald Skinner	OT	6'4"	260	23		
Tim Stokes	OT	6'5"	252	28		
Derrel Gofourth	OG	6'3'	260	23		
Leotis Harris	OG	6'1"	267	23		
Melvin Jackson	OG	6'1"	267	24		
Randy Pass	OG-C	6'3"	247	23		
Larry McCarren	C	6'3"	248	26		
Rich Nuzum	C	6'4"	238	26		
Bob Barber	DE	6'3"	240	26		
Mike Butler	DE	6'5"	265	24		
Ezra Johnson	DE	6'4"	240	22		
Carl Barzilauskas	DT	6'6"	265	27	1	
Terry Jones	DT	6'2"	259	21		
Dave Roller	DT	6'2"	270	28		
John Anderson	LB	6'3"	221	22	5	
Jim Carter	LB	6'3"	245	29		
Frank Chesley	LB	6'3"	219	23		
Mike Douglass	LB	6'	224	23		
Jim Gueno	LB	6'2"	220	24		
Mike Hunt	LB	6'2"	240	21	1	
Danny Johnson	LB	6'1"	216	23		
Paul Rudzinski	LB	6'1"	220	22		
Gary Weaver	LB	6'1"	225	29		
Willie Buchanon	DB	6'	190	27	9	6
Johnnie Gray	DB	5'11"	185	24	3	
Estus Hood	DB	5'11"	180	22	3	
Steve Luke	DB	6'2"	205	24	2	6
Mike McCoy	DB	5'11"	183	25	3	
Howard Sampson	DB	5'10"	185	22		
Steve Wagner	DB	6'2"	208	24		
Bobby Douglass	QB	6'3"	228	31		
Neil Graff	QB	6'3"	205	28		
Dennis Sproul	QB	6'2"	210	22		
David Whitehurst	QB	6'2"	204	23		6
Terdell Middleton	HB	6'	195	23		72
Nate Simpson	HB	5'11"	190	23		
Eric Torkelson	HB	6'2"	194	26		
Jim Culbreath	FB	6'	210	25		
Reggie Harrison	FB	5'11"	220	28		
Walt Landers	FB	6'	214	25		6
Barty Smith	FB	6'4"	240	26		24
James Lofton	WR	6'3"	187	22		36
Steve Odom	WR	5'8"	174	25		12
Willie Taylor	WR	6'1"	179	22		
Aundra Thompson	WR	6'	186	25		12
Walter Tullis	WR	6'	170	25		
Paul Coffman	TE	6'3"	218	22		
Rich McGeorge	TE	6'4"	230	29		6
David Beverly	K	6'2"	180	28		
Chester Marcol	K	6'	190	28		63

Lynn Dickey – Leg Injury
Mark Koncar – Leg Injury

DETROIT LIONS 7-9-0 Monte Clark

Scores of Each Game		
7	GREEN BAY	13
15	Tampa Bay	7
0	CHICAGO	19
16	Seattle	28
14	Green Bay	35
19	WASHINGTON	21
0	Atlanta	14
31	SAN DIEGO	14
21	Chicago	17
7	Minnesota	17
34	TAMPA BAY	23
17	Oakland	29
17	DENVER	14
14	St. Louis	21
45	MINNESOTA	14
33	SAN FRANCISCO	14

Use Name	Pos.	Hgt.	Wgt.	Age	Int.	Pts.
Karl Baldischwiler	OT	6'5"	265	22		
Bill Fifer (to NO)	OT	6'4"	250	22		
Donnie Green	OT	6'7"	261	30		
Brad Oates	OT	6'6'	274	24		
Lynn Boden	OG	6'5"	260	25		
Homer Elias	OG	6'3"	255	23		
Amos Fowler	OG	6'3"	250	22		
Donnie Hickman (from WAS)	OG	6'2"	260	23		
Willie Brock	C	6'3"	246	22		
Karl Chandler	C-OG	6'5"	250	26		
Mike Montler	C	6'4"	250	34		
Larry Tearry	C	6'3"	260	22		
Al Baker	DE	6'6"	260	21		
Dave Pureifory (from CIN)	DE	6'1"	255	29		
Ken Sanders	DE	6'5"	245	28		
Bill Cooke (from SEA)	DT	6'5"	250	27		
Doug English	DT	6'5"	255	25		
Dave Gallagher	DT	6'4"	256	26		
Dan Gray	DT	6'6"	240	22		
John Woodcock	DT	6'3"	240	24		
Tony Daykin	LB	6'1"	215	23		
Dan Dickel	LB	6'3"	230	26		
Paul Naumoff	LB	6'1"	215	33	1	
Ed O'Neil	LB	6'3"	235	25	4	
Dave Washington	LB	6'6"	230	29		
Charlie Weaver	LB	6'2"	225	29	3	
Jim Allen	DB	6'2"	195	26	5	6
Luther Bradley	DB	6'2"	195	23	3	6
Mike Burns	DB	6'	180	24	1	
James Hunter	DB	6'3"	195	24	2	
Reggie Pinkney	DB	5'11"	190	23	1	
Bruce Rhodes	DB	6'	190	24	1	
Tony Sumler	DB	5'10"	185	22		
Walt Williams	DB	6'	185	24	1	
Gary Danielson	QB	6'2"	195	26		
Greg Landry	QB	6'4"	205	31		
Joe Reed	QB	6'1"	195	30		
Andy Bolton	HB	6'1"	205	24		
Dexter Bussey	HB	6'1"	210	26		36
Ken Callicutt	HB	6'	190	23		
Rick Kane	HB	5'11"	200	23		12
Lawrence Gaines	FB	6'1"	240	24		6
Horace King	FB	5'10"	210	25		36
Luther Blue	WR	5'11"	190	22		12
Ray Jarvis	WR	6'1"	190	29		
Willie McGee	WR	5'11"	178	28		
Freddie Scott	WR	6'2"	175	26		12
Jessie Thompson	WR	6'1"	185	22		24
Leonard Thompson	WR	5'10"	190	26		24
William Gay	TE	6'5"	225	23		
David Hill	TE	6'2"	220	24		24
Benny Ricardo	K	5'10"	175	24		92
Tom Skladany	K	6	180	23		

Russ Bolinger – Knee Injury
Levi Johnson – Achilles Injury
Mark Markovich – Knee Injury
Jim Yarbrough – Achilles Injury
J.D. Hill – Achilles Injury
Gene Washington – Achilles Injury

CHICAGO BEARS 7-8-0 Neill Armstrong

Scores of Each Game		
17	ST. LOUIS	10
16	San Francisco	13
19	Detroit	0
20	MINNESOTA	24
19	OAKLAND	*25
14	Green Bay	24
7	Denver	16
19	Tampa Bay	33
17	DETROIT	21
29	SEATTLE	31
14	Minnesota	17
13	ATLANTA	7
14	TAMPA BAY	3
7	San Diego	40
14	GREEN BAY	0
14	Washington	10

Use Name	Pos.	Hgt.	Wgt.	Age	Int.	Pts.
Ted Albrecht	OT	6'4"	255	23		
Lionel Antoine	OT	6'6"	267	28		
Dan Jiggetts	OT	6'4"	276	24		
Dennis Lick	OT	6'3"	268	24		
Noah Jackson	OG	6'2"	273	27		
Jeff Sevy	OG	6'5"	261	27		
Revie Sorey	OG	6'2"	259	24		
Jon Morris	C	6'4"	250	35		
Dan Neal	C	6'4"	248	29		
Tommy Hart	DE	6'4"	246	33		
Mike Hartenstine	DE	6'3"	257	25		
Jerry Meyers	DT	6'4"	245	24		
Jim Osborne	DT	6'3"	251	28		
Alan Page (from MIN)	DT	6'4"	245	33		
Ron Rydalch	DT	6'4"	257	26		
Brad Shearer	DT	6'3"	254	23		
Doug Buffone	LB	6'1"	227	34	3	
Gary Campbell	LB	6'1"	218	26		
Chris Devlin (from CIN)	LB	6'2"	228	24		
Bruce Herron	LB	6'2"	220	24		
Tom Hicks	LB	6'4"	225	25		
Jerry Muckensturm	LB	6'4"	226	24		
Don Rives	LB	6'2"	231	27	2	
Gary Fencik	DB	6'1"	192	24	4	
Wentford Gaines (from PIT)	DB	6'	185	25	1	
Virgil Livers	DB	5'9"	178	26	3	6
Doug Plank	DB	6'	201	25	1	
Terry Schmidt	DB	6'	176	26	2	
Mike Spivey	DB	6'	194	24		6
Len Walterscheid	DB	5'11"	185	23	1	
Bob Avellini	QB	6 2	206	25		12
Vince Evans	QB	6 2	216	23		
Mike Phipps	QB	6 3	211	30		
Art Best	HB	6 1	205	25		
Walter Payton	HB	5 11	205	24		66
Robin Earl	FB	6 5	245	23		
Roland Harper	FB	6	209	25		48
Mike Morgan	FB	5 11	218	22		
John Skibinski	FB	6	218	23		
Brian Baschnagel	WR	6	184	24		
Bo Rather (to MIA)	WR	6 1	189	27		
Golden Richards (from DAL)	WR	6	180	27		
Steve Schubert	WR	5 10	188	27		6
James Scott	WR	6 1	191	26		30
Mike Cobb	TE	6 5	248	22		
Greg Latta	TE	6 3	230	25		
Bob Parsons	TE	6'4"	232	28		
Bob Thomas	K	5 10	174	26		77

Johnny Musso – Knee Injury
Steve Rivera – Injury

Waymond Bryant – Shoulder Injury
Allan Ellis – Knee Injury
Walt Patulski – Back Injury

TAMPA BAY BUCCANEERS 5-11-0 John McKay

Scores of Each Game		
13	N.Y. GIANTS	19
7	DETROIT	15
16	Minnesota	10
14	ATLANTA	9
7	MINNESOTA	24
30	Kansas City	13
14	N.Y. Giants	17
33	CHICAGO	19
7	Green Bay	9
23	Los Angeles	26
23	Detroit	34
31	BUFFALO	10
3	Chicago	14
7	GREEN BAY	17
3	San Francisco	6
10	NEW ORLEANS	17

Use Name	Pos.	Hgt.	Wgt.	Age	Int.	Pts.
Darryl Carlton	OT	6'6"	270	25		
Rocky Freitas	OT	6'6"	275	32		
Dave Reavis	OT	6'5"	250	28		
Greg Horton (from LA)	OG	6'4"	245	27		
Randy Johnson	OG	6'2"	255	25		
Dan Medlin	OG	6'4"	255	28		
Brett Moritz	OG	6'5"	250	23		
Gary Puetz (from NYJ)	OG-OT	6'4"	265	26		
Kurt Schumacher	OG	6'3"	255	25		
Jeff Winans	OG-OT	6'5"	265	26		
Steve Wilson	C	6'3"	265	24		
Wally Chambers	DE	6'6"	250	27	1	
Charley Hannah	DE	6'5"	250	23		
Bill Kollar	DE-NT	6'4"	256	25		
Lee Roy Selmon	DE	6'3"	260	23		
Randy Crowder	NT-DE	6'2"	245	26		
Dave Pear	NT	6'2	250	25		
Rik Bonness	LB	6 3	220	24		
Aaron Brown	LB	6 2	235	22	1	
Paul Harris (from MINN)	LB	6 3	215	23		
Earl Inmon	LB	6 1	215	24		
Cecil Johnson	LB	6 2	220	23	2	
Dave Lewis	LB	6 4	230	23	3	
Dana Nafziger	LB	6 1	220	24		
Dewey Selmon	LB	6 1	250	24	1	
Richard Wood	LB	6 2	215	25		
Jerry Anderson	DB	5 11	195	24		
Cedric Brown	DB	6 1	190	24	6	
Billy Cesare	DB	5 11	190	23		
Mark Cotney	DB	6	205	26	2	
Curtis Jordan	DB	6 2	185	24	3	
Danny Reece	DB	5 11	190	23	1	
Mike Washington	DB	6 3	190	25	5	6
Jeris White	DB	5 11	180	25	5	
Mike Boryla	QB	6 3	200	27		
Gary Huff	QB	6 1	195	27		
Mike Rae (from OAK)	QB	6	190	27		
Doug Williams	QB	6 4	215	23		6
Ricky Bell	HB	6 2	220	23		36
Louis Carter	HB	5 11	210	25		6
Dave Farmer	HB	6	205	24		
George Ragsdale	HB	5 11	185	24		12
Charlie White	HB	6	222	25		
Johnny Davis	FB	6 1	235	22		18
Jimmy DuBose	FB	5 11	215	23		24
Karl Farmer	WR	5 11	165	24		
Larry Franklin	WR	6 1	185	23		
Frank Grant (from WAS)	WR	5 11	181	28		
Isaac Hagins	WR	5 9	180	24		
John McKay	WR	5 11	185	25		6
Larry Mucher	WR	5 11	190	23		
Morris Owens	WR	6	190	25		30
Alvis Darby	TE	6 5	225	23		
Jimmie Giles	TE	6 3	225	23		12
Jim Obradovich	TE	6 2	227	28		18
Dave Green	K	5 11	205	28		3
Neil O'Donoghue	K	6 6	205	25		64

Booker Brown – Knee Injury
Randy Hedberg – Elbow Injury

*—Overtime

MINNESOTA VIKINGS

RUSHING

Last Name	No.	Yds.	Avg.	TD
Foreman	237	749	3.2	5
Young	134	417	3.1	1
R. Miller	70	213	3.0	3
Johnson	11	41	3.7	0
Kellar	11	34	3.1	0
S. White	5	30	6.0	0
McClanahan	10	26	2.6	0
Coleman	2	22	11.0	0
Kramer	1	10	10.0	0
Tarkenton	24	−6	−0.3	1

RECEIVING

Last Name	No.	Yds.	Avg.	TD
Young	88	704	8	5
Rashad	66	769	12	8
Foreman	61	396	7	2
S. White	53	741	14	9
Tucker	47	540	12	0
R. Miller	22	230	11	0
Voigt	4	52	13	0
Craig	4	31	8	0
Kellar	3	−5	−2	0
McClanahan	2	11	6	0
K. Miller	1	35	35	1
Washington	1	24	24	0

PUNT RETURNS

Last Name	No.	Yds.	Avg.	TD
K. Miller	48	239	5	0
S. White	1	0	0	0

KICKOFF RETURNS

Last Name	No.	Yds.	Avg.	TD
K. Miller	40	854	21	0
Washington	4	71	18	0
S. White	3	50	17	0
McClanahen	3	38	13	0
R. Miller	2	23	12	0
Kellar	1	13	13	0
Young	1	8	8	0
Craig	1	0	0	0

PASSING - PUNTING - KICKING

PASSING	Att.	Comp.	%	Yds.	Yd./Att.	TD	Int.–%	RK
Tarkenton	572	345	60	3468	6.1	25	32– 6	4
Kramer	16	5	31	50	3.1	0	1– 6	
Lee	4	2	50	10	2.5	0	1– 25	

PUNTING	No.	Avg.
Coleman	51	39.0

KICKING	XP	Att.	%	FG	Att.	%
Danmeier	36	37	97	12	19	63

GREEN BAY PACKERS

RUSHING

Last Name	No.	Yds.	Avg.	TD
Middleton	284	1116	3.9	11
Smith	154	567	3.7	4
Culbreath	30	92	3.1	0
Whitehurst	28	67	2.4	1
Simpson	27	58	2.1	0
Landers	7	40	5.7	0
B. Douglass	4	27	6.8	0
Thompson	4	25	6.3	0
Torkelson	6	18	3.0	0
Lofton	3	13	4.3	0
Beverly	1	0	0.0	0
Sproul	2	0	0.0	0

RECEIVING

Last Name	No.	Yds.	Avg.	TD
Lofton	46	818	18	6
Smith	37	256	7	0
Middleton	34	332	10	1
Thompson	26	527	20	2
McGeorge	23	247	11	1
Culbreath	7	78	11	0
Odom	4	60	15	1
Torkelson	2	36	18	0
Simpson	1	4	4	0

PUNT RETURNS

Last Name	No.	Yds.	Avg.	TD
Odom	33	298	9	0
Gray	11	95	9	0
Sampson	1	0	0	0
Tullis	1	0	0	0

KICKOFF RETURNS

Last Name	No.	Yds.	Avg.	TD
Odom	25	677	27	1
Thompson	6	124	21	0
Wagner	6	84	14	0
Culbreath	4	58	15	0
Hood	3	74	25	0
Sampson	1	23	23	0
Middleton	1	22	22	0
E. Johnson	1	14	14	0
Gueno	1	9	9	0
Landers	1	0	0	0
Lofton	1	0	0	0
McGeorge	1	0	0	0
Smith	1	0	0	0

PASSING - PUNTING - KICKING

PASSING	Att.	Comp.	%	Yds.	Yd./Att.	TD	Int.–%	RK
Whitehurst	328	168	51	2093	6.4	10	17– 5	10
Sproul	13	5	39	87	6.7	0	0– 0	
B. Douglass	12	5	42	90	7.5	1	1– 8	
Beverly	2	2	100	88	44.0	0	0– 0	
Lofton	2	0	0	0	0.0	0	0– 0	

PUNTING	No.	Avg.
Beverly	106	35.5

KICKING	XP	Att.	%	FG	Att.	%
Marcol	30	30	100	11	19	58

DETROIT LIONS

RUSHING

Last Name	No.	Yds.	Avg.	TD
Bussey	225	924	4.1	5
King	155	660	4.3	4
Gaines	54	178	3.3	1
Kane	44	153	3.5	2
Danielson	22	93	4.2	0
Scott	4	53	13.3	0
Landry	5	29	5.8	0
O'Neil	1	25	25.0	0
Hill	3	12	4.0	0
Blue	5	9	1.8	0
Daykin	1	8	8.0	0
L. Thompson	1	7	7.0	0
J. Thompson	2	7	3.5	0
Bolton	2	5	2.5	0
Reed	1	0	0.0	0

RECEIVING

Last Name	No.	Yds.	Avg.	TD
Hill	53	633	12	4
King	48	390	8	2
Scott	37	564	15	2
Blue	31	350	11	2
Bussey	31	275	9	1
J. Thompson	18	175	10	4
Kane	16	161	10	0
L. Thompson	10	167	17	4
Gaines	2	16	8	0
Jarvis	1	9	9	0

PUNT RETURNS

Last Name	No.	Yds.	Avg.	TD
J. Thompson	16	161	10	0
Scott	8	55	7	0
Blue	7	59	8	0
L. Thompson	3	19	6	0
Hunter	2	21	11	0
Williams	1	1	1	0

KICKOFF RETURNS

Last Name	No.	Yds.	Avg.	TD
J. Thompson	14	346	25	0
L. Thompson	8	207	26	0
Kane	8	156	20	0
Blue	7	170	24	0
Scott	3	72	24	0
Callicutt	2	12	6	0
Hunter	1	21	21	0
McGee	1	0	0	0

PASSING - PUNTING - KICKING

PASSING	Att.	Comp.	%	Yds.	Yd./Att.	TD	Int.–%	RK
Danielson	351	199	57	2294	6.5	18	17– 5	3
Landry	77	48	62	452	5.9	1	1– 1	
Skladany	1	0	0	0	0.0	0	0– 0	

PUNTING	No.	Avg.
Skladany	86	42.5

KICKING	XP	Att.	%	FG	Att.	%
Ricardo	32	33	97	20	28	71

CHICAGO BEARS

RUSHING

Last Name	No.	Yds.	Avg.	TD
Payton	333	1359	4.2	11
Harper	240	992	4.1	6
Avellini	34	54	1.6	2
Phipps	13	34	2.6	0
Evans	6	23	3.8	0
Earl	3	17	5.7	0
Best	2	11	5.5	0
Parsons	1	0	0.0	0
Baschnagel	2	0	0.0	0

RECEIVING

Last Name	No.	Yds.	Avg.	TD
Payton	50	480	10	0
Harper	43	340	8	2
Scott	42	759	18	5
Richards	28	381	14	0
Latta	15	159	11	0
Schubert	4	51	13	0
Rather	2	55	28	0
Baschnagel	2	29	15	0
Cobb	1	7	7	0
Earl	1	1	1	0

PUNT RETURNS

Last Name	No.	Yds.	Avg.	TD
Schubert	27	229	9	1
Livers	10	31	3	0
Walterscheid	3	24	8	0
Baschnagel	1	2	2	0

KICKOFF RETURNS

Last Name	No.	Yds.	Avg.	TD
Baschnagel	20	455	23	0
Walterscheid	11	335	31	0
Gaines	10	240	24	0
Morgan	5	110	22	0
Schubert	4	80	20	0
Earl	3	48	16	0
Skibinski	3	36	12	0
Spivey	2	34	17	0
Latta	2	14	7	0
Muckensturm	1	6	6	0

PASSING - PUNTING - KICKING

PASSING	Att.	Comp.	%	Yds.	Yd./Att.	TD	Int.–%	RK
Avellini	264	141	53	1718	6.5	5	16– 6	11
Phipps	83	44	53	465	5.6	2	10– 12	
Evans	3	1	33	38	12.7	0	1– 33	
Harper	1	0	0	0	0.0	0	0– 0	
Parsons	1	0	0	0	0.0	0	0– 0	

PUNTING	No.	Avg.
Parsons	96	37.0

KICKING	XP	Att.	%	FG	Att.	%
Thomas	26	28	93	17	22	77

TAMPA BAY BUCCANEERS

RUSHING

Last Name	No.	Yds.	Avg.	TD
Bell	185	679	3.7	6
Davis	97	370	3.8	3
DuBose	93	358	3.8	4
Carter	81	275	3.4	1
Rae	20	186	9.3	0
Ragsdale	25	121	4.8	1
C. White	11	42	3.8	0
Mucker	5	35	7.0	0
Williams	27	23	0.9	1
Huff	3	10	3.3	0
Green	1	0	0.0	0
Giles	1	−1	−1.0	0

RECEIVING

Last Name	No.	Yds.	Avg.	TD
Owens	32	640	20	5
Giles	23	324	14	2
Carter	19	139	7	0
Bell	15	122	8	0
O'Bradovich	14	219	16	3
Grant	14	204	15	0
Mucker	13	271	21	0
McKay	9	166	18	1
Hagins	6	65	11	0
Davis	5	13	3	0
Ragsdale	3	41	14	1
C. White	2	31	16	0
Reece	1	25	25	0
DuBose	1	3	3	0

PUNT RETURNS

Last Name	No.	Yds.	Avg.	TD
Reece	44	393	9	0
Mucker	7	49	7	0
Cotney	5	38	8	0
Hagins	4	23	6	0
C. Brown	2	9	5	0

KICKOFF RETURNS

Last Name	No.	Yds.	Avg.	TD
Ragsdale	24	555	23	0
Reece	11	240	22	0
Carter	6	97	16	0
Giles	5	60	12	0
Hagins	4	69	17	0
O'Bradovich	3	48	16	0
Mucker	2	9	5	0

PASSING - PUNTING - KICKING

PASSING	Att.	Comp.	%	Yds.	Yd./Att.	TD	Int.–%	RK
Williams	194	73	38	1170	6.0	7	8– 4	12
Rae	118	57	48	705	6.0	4	7– 6	
Huff	36	15	42	169	4.7	1	3– 8	
Carter	5	2	40	87	17.4	0	0– 0	
Boryla	5	2	40	15	3.0	0	0– 0	
Green	3	2	67	25	8.3	0	0– 0	

PUNTING	No.	Avg.
Green	100	40.9

KICKING	XP	Att.	%	FG	Att.	%
O'Donohue	25	29	86	13	23	57

LOS ANGELES RAMS 12-4-0 Ray Malavasi

Scores of Each Game			Use Name	Pos.	Hgt.	Wgt.	Age	Int.	Pts.	Use Name	Pos.	Hgt.	Wgt.	Age	Int.	Pts.	Use Name	Pos.	Hgt.	Wgt.	Age	Int.	Pts.
16	Philadelphia	14	Doug France	OT	6'5"	272	25			Bob Brudzinski	LB	6'4"	231	23	1	6	Vince Ferragamo	QB	6'3"	208	24		
10	ATLANTA	0	Jackie Slater	OT-OG	6'4"	270	24			Carl Ekern	LB	6'3"	220	24			Pat Haden	QB	5'11"	182	25		
27	DALLAS	14	John Williams	OT	6'3"	265	32			Kevin McLain	LB	6'2"	227	23			John Cappelletti	HB	6'1"	220	26		24
10	Houston	6	Ed Fulton	OG	6'3"	250	23			Jack Reynolds	LB	6'1"	232	30			Jerry Latin (from ST.L)	HB	5'10"	186	25		
26	New Orleans	20	Dennis Harrah	OG	6'5"	257	25			Isiah Robertson	LB	6'3"	225	29		6	Larry Marshall (from KC)	HB	5'10"	195	28		
27	SAN FRANCISCO	10	Tom Mack	OG	6'3"	250	34			Jim Youngblood	LB	6'3"	239	28	2		Lawrence McCutcheon	HB	6'1"	205	28		12
34	Minnesota	17	Dan Ryczek	C	6'3"	250	29			Eddie Brown	DB	5'11"	190	26			Wendell Tyler	HB	5'10"	188	23		
3	NEW ORLEANS	10	Rich Saul	C	6'3"	250	30			Nolan Cromwell	DB	6'1"	197	23	1	12	Cullen Bryant	FB	6'1"	234	27		42
7	Atlanta	15	Doug Smith	C-OG	6'3"	250	21			Dave Elmendorf	DB	6'1"	195	29	3		Jim Jodat	FB	5'11"	210	24		
26	TAMPA BAY	23	Reggie Doss	DE	6'4"	267	21			Dwayne O'Steen	DB	6'1"	190	23			Rod Phillips	FB	6'	220	25		
10	PITTSBURGH	7	Fred Dryer	DE	6'6"	240	32			Rod Perry	DB	5'9"	170	24	8	18	Preston Dennard	WR	6'1"	185	22		
31	San Francisco	28	Jack Youngblood	DE	6'4"	242	28			Bill Simpson	DB	6'1"	180	26	5		Ron Jessie	WR	6'	185	30		24
19	Cleveland	30	Larry Brooks	DT	6'3"	255	28			Pat Thomas	DB	5'9"	180	24	8	6	Willie Miller	WR	5'9"	172	31		30
20	N.Y. Giants	17	Mike Fanning	DT	6'6"	260	25			Jackie Wallace	DB	6'3"	198	27			Dwight Scales	WR	6'2"	170	25		6
19	CINCINNATI	20	Cody Jones	DT	6'5"	240	27										Ron Smith	WR	6'	185	21		
31	GREEN BAY	14															Billy Waddy	WR	5'11"	185	24		6
																	Terry Nelson	TE	6'2"	230	27		6
																	Charlie Young	TE	6'4"	235	27		
																	Frank Corral	K	6'2"	220	23		118
																	Glenn Walker	K	6'1"	210	26		

ATLANTA FALCONS 9-7-0 Leeman Bennett

Scores of Each Game			Use Name	Pos.	Hgt.	Wgt.	Age	Int.	Pts.	Use Name	Pos.	Hgt.	Wgt.	Age	Int.	Pts.	Use Name	Pos.	Hgt.	Wgt.	Age	Int.	Pts.
20	HOUSTON	14	Warren Bryant	OT	6'6"	270	22			Greg Brezina	LB	6'1"	221	32			Steve Bartkowski	QB	6'4"	213	25		12
0	Los Angeles	10	Mike Kenn	OT	6'6"	257	22			Ron McCartney	LB	6'1"	220	24			Scott Hunter	QB	6'2"	205	30		
16	CLEVELAND	24	Phil McKinnely	OT-OG	6'4"	248	24			Dewey McClain	LB	6'3"	236	24			June Jones	QB	6'4"	200	25		
9	Tampa Bay	14	Marv Montgomery	OT	6'6"	255	30			Fulton Kuykendall	LB	6'5"	225	25			Bubba Bean	HB-FB	5'11"	195	24		24
23	N.Y. GIANTS	20	Dave Scott	OG	6'4"	285	24			Ralph Ortega	LB	6'2"	220	25			Mike Esposito	HB	6'"	183	25		
7	Pittsburgh	31	R.C. Thielemann	OG	6'4"	247	23			Robert Pennywell	LB	6'1"	222	23			Ricky Patton	HB	5'11"	185	24		12
14	DETROIT	0	Paul Ryczek	C	6'2"	230	26			Steve Stewart	LB	6'2"	217	22			Ray Strong	HB	5'9"	184	22		12
20	San Francisco	17	Jeff Van Note	C	6'2"	247	32			Garth Ten Napel	LB	6'1"	215	24			George Franklin	FB	6'3"	226	24		
15	LOS ANGELES	7	Edgar Fields	DE-DT	6'2"	255	24			Rick Byas	DB	5'9"	180	27	2	6	Haskel Stanback	FB	6'	210	26		30
21	SAN FRANCISCO	10	Claude Humphrey	DE	6'5"	265	34			Ray Easterling	DB	6'	192	28	1		Wallace Francis	WR	5'11"	190	26		18
20	New Orleans	17	Jeff Merrow	DE	6'4"	230	25			Bob Glazebrook	DB	6'1"	200	22			Alfred Jackson	WR	5'11"	176	23		12
7	Chicago	13	Jeff Yeates	DE	6'3"	248	27			Rolland Lawrence	DB	5'10"	179	27	6		Al Jenkins	WR	5'10"	172	26		
20	NEW ORLEANS	17	Jim Bailey	DT	6'5"	260	30			Ernie Jackson	DB	5'10"	176	28			Dennis Pearson	WR	5'11"	177	23		6
7	Cincinnati	37	Wilson Faumuina	DT	6'5"	275	24	1		Tom Moriarty	DB	6'	185	25		6	Billy Ryckman	WR	5'11"	172	23		12
20	WASHINGTON	17	Mike Lewis	DT	6'3"	261	29			Tom Pridemore	DB	5'10"	186	22	1		Lewis Gilbert	TE	6'4"	225	22		
21	St. Louis	42								Frank Reed	DB	5'11"	193	24	1		Jim Mitchell	TE	6'2"	236	30		12
										Jim Stienke	DB	5'11"	182	27			Ken Moore	TE	6'4"	232	24		
																	James Wright	TE	6'3"	240	22		
										Brent Adams-Knee Injury							John James	K	6'3"	200	29		
										Andy Spiva-Knee Injury							Tim Mazzetti	K	6'1"	175	22		57
																	Fred Steinfort	K	5'11"	180	24		17

NEW ORLEANS SAINTS 7-9-0 Dick Nolan

Scores of Each Game			Use Name	Pos.	Hgt.	Wgt.	Age	Int.	Pts.	Use Name	Pos.	Hgt.	Wgt.	Age	Int.	Pts.	Use Name	Pos.	Hgt.	Wgt.	Age	Int.	Pts.
31	MINNESOTA	24	Kevin Hunt	OT	6'5"	260	29			Ron Crosby	LB	6'3"	225	23			Ed Burns	QB	6'3"	210	23		
17	Green Bay	28	Mark Meseroll	OT	6'5"	270	23			Joe Federspiel	LB	6'1"	230	28	2		Archie Manning	QB	6'3"	200	29		6
17	PHILADELPHIA	24	J.T. Taylor	OT	6'4"	265	22			Pat Hughes	LB	6'2"	225	31	2		Bobby Scott	QB	6'1"	197	29		
20	Cincinnati	18	John Watson	OT	6'4"	244	29			Rick Kingrea	LB	6'1"	222	29			Chuck Muncie	HB	6'3"	220	25		42
20	LOS ANGELES	26	Robert Woods	OT	6'4"	259	28			Jim Merlo	LB	6'1"	220	26			Mike Strachan	HB	6'	200	25		24
16	CLEVELAND	24	Gary Anderson (from DET)	OG	6'3"	250	22			Rusty Rebowe	LB	5'10"	213	22			James Van Wagner	HB	6'	202	23		
14	San Francisco	7	Conrad Dobler	OG	6'3"	255	27			Floyd Rice	LB	6'3"	225	29			Tony Galbreath	FB	6'	230	24		42
10	Los Angeles	3	Dave Lafary	OG	6'7"	280	23			Skip Vanderbundt	LB	6'3"	225	31			Jack Holmes	FB	5'11"	210	23		
28	N.Y. GIANTS	17	Fred Sturt (from NE)	OG	6'4"	255	27			Ray Brown	DB	6'2"	202	29	4		Kim Jones	FB	6'4"	235	26		
14	Pittsburgh	20	Emanuel Sanders	OG	6'1"	248	27			Clarence Chapman	DB	5'10"	185	24	2		Wes Chandler	WR	5'11"	186	22		12
17	ATLANTA	20	John Hill	C	6'2"	246	28			Eric Felton	DB	6'"	200	22	1		Ike Harris	WR	6'3"	205	25		24
7	Dallas	27	Joe Campbell	DE	6'6"	254	23			Ralph McGill	DB	5'11"	180	28			Rich Mauti	WR	6'	190	24		12
17	Atlanta	20	Elois Grooms	DE	6'4"	250	25			Tom Myers	DB	5'11"	180	27	6	6	Tinker Owens	WR	5'11"	170	23		12
24	SAN FRANCISCO	13	Richard Neal	DE	6'3"	263	30			Don Schwartz	DB	6'1"	191	22			Henry Childs	TE	6'2"	220	27		24
12	HOUSTON	17	Don Reese	DE	6'6"	250	26			Mo Spencer	DB	6'	176	26	4		Larry Hardy	TE	6'3"	230	22		6
17	Tampa Bay	10	Barry Bennett	DT	6'4"	257	22										Brooks Williams	TE	6'4"	226	23		
			Mike Fultz	DT	6'5"	278	24			Ken Bordelon-Knee Injury							Tom Blanchard	K	6'	180	30		
			Derland Moore	DT	6'4"	253	26			Jimmy Stewart-Knee Injury							Tom Jurich	K	5'10"	185	22		2
			Elex Price	DT	6'3"	265	28			Mike Watson-Knee Injury							John Leypoldt (from SEA)	K	6'2"	230	32		10
																	Steve Mike-Mayer	K	6'"	180	30		36
																	Richie Szaro	K	5'11"	204	30		21

SAN FRANCISCO FORTY-NINERS 2-14-0 Pete McCulley, Fred O'Connor

Scores of Each Game			Use Name	Pos.	Hgt.	Wgt.	Age	Int.	Pts.	Use Name	Pos.	Hgt.	Wgt.	Age	Int.	Pts.	Use Name	Pos.	Hgt.	Wgt.	Age	Int.	Pts.
7	Cleveland	24	John Ayers	OT-OG	6'5"	247	25			Mike Baldassin	LB	6'1"	218	23			Scott Bull	QB	6'5	211	25		6
13	CHICAGO	16	Keith Fahnhorst	OT	6'6"	263	26			Ed Bradley	LB	6'2"	225	28			Steve DeBerg	QB	6'2	205	24		6
19	Houston	20	Ron Singleton	OT	6'7"	275	26			Dan Bunz	LB	6'4"	230	22	1		Paul Hofer	HB	6'	193	26		42
10	N.Y. Giants	27	Walt Downing	OG	6'3"	254	22			Bruce Elia	LB	6'1"	220	25			O.J. Simpson	HB	6'2"	212	31		18
28	CINCINNATI	12	Ernie Hughes	OG	6'3"	250	23			Joe Harris	LB	6'1"	225	25			Elliott Walker	HB	5'11"	193	21		
10	Los Angeles	27	Steve Knutson	OG-OT	6'3"	254	26			Dean Moore	LB	6'2"	210	23			Dave Williams	HB	6'2"	200	24		6
7	NEW ORLEANS	14	Randy Cross	C	6'3"	250	24			Mark Nichols	LB	6'3"	225	21	1		Greg Boykin	FB	6'	225	24		12
17	ATLANTA	20	Kyle Davis	C	6'2"	240	25			Chuck Crist	DB	6'2"	205	27	6		Earl Carr	FB	6'	224	23		
20	Washington	38	Fred Quillan	C	6'5"	240	22			Bob Jury	DB	6'1"	188	22			Bob Ferrell	FB	6'	219	25		6
10	Atlanta	21	Cedrick Hardman	DE	6'4"	244	29			Anthony Leonard (to DET)	DB	5'11"	165	25	4	6	Elmo Boyd (to GB)	WR	6'	188	24		6
10	ST. LOUIS	16	Willie McCray	DE	6'5"	234	25			Eddie Lewis	DB	6'	174	24	3		Kenny Harrison	WR	6'	164	24		6
28	LOS ANGELES	31	Archie Reese	DE	6'3"	263	22			Wonder Monds	DB	6'3"	215	26			Larry Jones	WR	5'10"	170	27		
7	PITTSBURGH	24	Cleveland Elam	DT-DE	6'4"	251	26			Ricky Odom (from KC)	DB	6'	183	21	2		Terry LeCount	WR	5'11"	172	22		
13	New Orleans	24	Ed Galigher	DT	6'4"	247	27			Vern Roberson	DB	6'1"	195	26	1		Mike Shumann	WR	6'"	175	22		
6	TAMPA BAY	3	Jimmy Webb	DT	6'5"	245	26			Bruce Threadgill	DB-QB	6'	190	22			Freddie Solomon	WR-QB	5'11"	181	25		18
14	Detroit	33															Jack Steptoe	WR	6'1"	175	22		6
										Jean Barrett-Foot Injury							Lon Boyett	TE	6'6"	240	24		
										Willie Harper-Knee Injury							Rick DeSimone	TE	6'3"	213	22		
										Wilbur Jackson — Knee Injury							Ken McAfee	TE	6'5"	250	22		6
										Johnny Miller-Elbow Injury							Paul Seal	TE	6'4"	223	26		12
																	Mike Connell	K	6'1"	200	22		
																	Ray Wersching	K	5'11"	210	28		69

LOS ANGELES RAMS

RUSHING

Last Name	No.	Yds.	Avg.	TD
Bryant	178	658	3.7	7
Cappelletti	174	604	3.5	3
McCutcheon	118	420	3.6	0
Haden	33	206	6.2	0
Jodat	26	100	3.8	0
Phillips	28	81	2.9	0
Latin	24	72	3.0	0
Nelson	6	67	11.2	1
Tyler	14	45	3.2	0
Waddy	5	31	6.2	0
Cromwell	1	16	16.0	1
Ferragamo	2	10	5.0	0
Young	2	6	3.0	0
Miller	1	−7	−7.0	0

RECEIVING

Last Name	No.	Yds.	Avg.	TD
Miller	50	767	15	5
Jessie	49	752	15	4
Cappelletti	41	382	9	1
Nelson	23	344	15	0
Young	18	213	12	0
Waddy	14	258	18	1
McCutcheon	12	76	6	2
Bryant	8	76	10	0
Phillips	7	48	7	0
Scales	5	105	21	0
Dennard	3	35	12	0
Jodat	3	21	7	0
Tyler	2	17	9	0
R. Smith	1	15	15	0
Latin	1	3	3	0

PUNT RETURNS

Last Name	No.	Yds.	Avg.	TD
Wallace	**52**	**618**	**12**	0
Waddy	10	45	5	0
Marshall	6	51	9	0
Bryant	3	27	9	0
Brown	1	13	13	0
Cromwell	1	8	8	0

KICKOFF RETURNS

Last Name	No.	Yds.	Avg.	TD
Latin	24	515	22	0
Jodat	22	447	20	0
Marshall	9	223	25	0
Phillips	3	52	17	0
Tyler	2	31	16	0
D. Smith	1	8	8	0

PASSING – PUNTING – KICKING

PASSING	Att.	Comp.	%	Yds.	Yd./Att.	TD	Int.–%	RK
Haden	444	229	52	2995	6.8	13	19– 4	7
Ferragamo	20	7	35	114	5.7	0	2– 10	
McCutcheon	1	0	0	0	0.0	0	0– 0	
Walker	1	0	0	0	0.0	0	0– 0	

PUNTING	No.	Avg.
Walker	83	37.0

KICKING	XP	Att.	%	FG	Att.	%
Corral	31	33	94	**29**	**43**	67

ATLANTA FALCONS

RUSHING

Last Name	No.	Yds.	Avg.	TD
Bean	193	707	3.7	3
Stanback	188	588	3.1	5
Patton	68	206	3.0	1
Strong	30	99	3.3	2
Bartkowski	33	60	1.8	2
Esposito	7	21	3.0	0
Pearson	1	1	1.0	0
Jones	10	−3	−0.3	0
Franklin	1	−8	−8.0	0
Francis	2	-11	-5.5	0

RECEIVING

Last Name	No.	Yds.	Avg.	TD
Francis	45	695	15	3
Ryckman	45	679	15	2
Mitchell	32	366	11	2
Bean	31	209	7	1
A. Jackson	26	526	20	2
Stanback	12	108	9	0
Patton	10	90	9	1
Strong	7	56	8	0
Pearson	5	71	14	0
Esposito	3	10	3	0
Jenkins	2	28	14	0
Wright	2	26	13	0
Franklin	1	19	19	0

PUNT RETURNS

Last Name	No.	Yds.	Avg.	TD
Ryckman	28	227	8	0
A. Jackson	11	89	8	0
Byas	2	12	6	0
Lawrence	1	17	17	0

KICKOFF RETURNS

Last Name	No.	Yds.	Avg.	TD
Pearson	25	662	27	1
Franklin	11	258	24	0
A. Jackson	11	225	21	0
Pridemore	4	71	18	0
Strong	3	50	17	0
Wright	2	31	16	0
Fields	2	21	11	0
Mitchell	1	14	14	0

PASSING – PUNTING – KICKING

PASSING	Att.	Comp.	%	Yds.	Yd./Att.	TD	Int.–%	RK
Bartkowski	369	187	51	2489	6.8	10	18– 5	9
Jones	79	34	43	394	5.0	1	4– 5	
Bean	1	0	0	0	0.0	0	0– 0	

PUNTING	No.	Avg.
James	**109**	38.8

KICKING	XP	Att.	%	FG	Att.	%
Mazzetti	18	18	100	13	16	**81**
Steinfort	8	9	89	3	10	30

NEW ORLEANS SAINTS

RUSHING

Last Name	No.	Yds.	Avg.	TD
Galbreath	186	635	3.4	5
Muncie	160	557	3.5	7
Strachan	108	388	3.6	4
Manning	38	202	5.3	1
Jones	9	31	3.4	0
Harris	2	22	11.0	0
Chandler	2	10	5.0	0
Holmes	2	4	2.0	0
Scott	1	0	0.0	0
Blanchard	2	0	0.0	0
Childs	2	−4	−2.0	0

RECEIVING

Last Name	No.	Yds.	Avg.	TD
Galbreath	74	582	8	2
Childs	53	869	16	4
Harris	40	590	15	4
Owens	40	446	11	2
Chandler	35	472	14	2
Muncie	26	233	9	0
Strachan	10	51	5	0
Mauti	8	69	9	2
Hardy	5	131	26	1
Jones	2	10	5	0
Van Wagner	1	−1	−1	0

PUNT RETURNS

Last Name	No.	Yds.	Avg.	TD
Chandler	34	233	7	0
McGill	1	5	5	0
Schwartz	1	4	4	0

KICKOFF RETURNS

Last Name	No.	Yds.	Avg.	TD
Chandler	32	760	24	0
Mauti	17	388	23	0
Chapman	9	149	17	0
Schwartz	3	51	17	0
Hardy	2	3	2	0
Holmes	1	18	18	0
Rice	1	15	15	0

PASSING – PUNTING – KICKING

PASSING	Att.	Comp.	%	Yds.	Yd./Att.	TD	Int.–%	RK
Manning	471	291	62	3416	7.3	17	16– **3**	2
Scott	5	3	60	36	7.2	0	0– 0	
Harris	1	0	0	0	0.0	0	0– 0	
Muncie	1	0	0	0	0.0	0	0– 0	
Strachan	1	0	0	0	0.0	0	0– 0	

PUNTING	No.	Avg.
Blanchard	84	42.0

KICKING	XP	Att.	%	FG	Att.	%
Mike-Mayer	18	18	100	6	13	46
Szaro	9	9	100	4	6	67
Leypoldt	4	5	80	2	3	67
Jurich	2	2	100	0	3	0

SAN FRANCISCO FORTY-NINERS

RUSHING

Last Name	No.	Yds.	Avg.	TD
Simpson	161	593	3.7	1
Ferrell	125	471	3.8	1
Hofer	121	465	3.8	7
Boykin	102	361	3.5	2
Bull	29	100	3.4	1
Solomon	14	70	5.0	1
DeBerg	15	20	1.3	1
Williams	15	18	1.2	0
Carr	1	2	2.0	0
Elia	1	0	0.0	0
Jones	1	−9	−9.0	0

RECEIVING

Last Name	No.	Yds.	Avg.	TD
Solomon	31	458	15	2
MacAfee	22	205	9	1
Seal	21	370	18	2
Simpson	21	172	8	2
Boykin	19	112	6	0
Harrison	16	320	20	0
Ferrell	16	123	8	0
Hofer	12	170	14	0
LeCount	10	131	13	0
Williams	10	63	6	0
Boyd	9	115	13	1
Steptoe	2	46	23	1
Jones	1	21	21	0

PUNT RETURNS

Last Name	No.	Yds.	Avg.	TD
Leonard	18	140	8	0
Steptoe	11	129	12	0
Jones	10	86	9	0
Solomon	9	35	4	0
Shumann	8	40	5	0
Roberson	1	7	7	0

KICKOFF RETURNS

Last Name	No.	Yds.	Avg.	TD
Williams	34	745	22	1
Hofer	18	386	21	0
LeCount	5	91	18	0
Hughes	4	53	13	0
Nichols	3	39	13	0
Boykin	3	37	12	0
Walker	2	25	13	0
Downing	2	13	7	0
Ferrell	1	24	24	0
Quillan	1	8	8	0

PASSING – PUNTING – KICKING

PASSING	Att.	Comp.	%	Yds.	Yd./Att.	TD	Int.–%	RK
DeBerg	302	137	45	1570	5.2	8	22– 7	14
Bull	121	48	40	651	5.4	1	11– 9	
Solomon	10	5	50	85	8.5	0	1– 10	
Threadgill	2	0	0	0	0.0	0	2–100	

PUNTING	No.	Avg.
Connell	96	37.3

KICKING	XP	Att.	%	FG	Att.	%
Wersching	24	25	96	15	23	65

1978 A.F.C. Rozelle's Second Wild Card

Pete Rozelle engineered changes in the league schedule and playoffs which would answer some critics and also equalize competition among the teams. Some fans had complained that teams had lumped several pre-season games in with regular season games in season ticket plans. Rozelle responded by increasing the regular schedule from 14 to 16 games. Despite the extra two games, the N.F.L. record book was not rewritten en masse, as some had feared. In addition to expanding the schedule, the league arranged for the weaker teams to face a larger proportion of losing teams and for the stronger teams to face a steady diet of tough opponents. Although some critics claimed that this plan rewarded failure and penalized success, rebuilding clubs found their road to the playoffs shortened by this arrangement. Rozelle also created a second "wild card" playoff berth in each division, thus keeping a fistful of teams in playoff contention well into December.

A secondary aspect of the increased schedule was the booking of several Thursday and Sunday night games. Fans were treated to extra editions of ABC'S "Monday Night Football" on these other nights of the week.

EASTERN DIVISION

New England Patriots—The talented Patriots had always found a way to sabotage their Super Bowl plans. This year, they had to go to extreme lengths to accomplish it. When receiver Darryl Stingley was paralyzed in a pre-season game, the Pats sublimated their grief, obtained Harold Jackson from the Rams, and headed into the season undaunted. When Julius Adams was injured in the opening game, the team kept its spirit. The Pats won eight of their first ten games with a wide array of weapons. Although quarterback Steve Grogan was an erratic passer, he frequently hit tight end Russ Francis and wide receiver Stanley Morgan. The New England running game gained the most yardage in the league, with All-Pro lineman Leon Gray and John Hannah clearing the way for a large corps of powerful runners. The defense worked well together and enjoyed an All-Pro performance by Mike Haynes. Even the traditional Patriot late-season slump couldn't knock the Patriots out of the playoffs. What finally did break their momentum were the events of December 18, the final day of the season. Coach Chuck Fairbanks chose the afternoon of his team's Monday night game in Miami to inform them that he would be leaving the Pats after the season and joining the University of Colorado. Owner Billy Sullivan blew his top and, in a melodramatic scene worthy of daytime television, ordered Fairbanks out of the New England dressing room before the game. The Pats took a 23-3 beating that night and headed into the playoffs with their spirits dragging.

Miami Dolphins—The big winner of the O.J. Simpson trade was the Dolphins. When the 49ers obtained O.J. from the Bills, they sent incumbent halfback Del Williams to Miami. Instead of running behind the patchwork 49er line, Williams flourished behind the blocking of stars Bob Kuechenberg, Jim Langer, and Larry Little. The strong ground attack kept the Dolphins afloat even when Bob Griese missed the first five games with a knee injury. Although not as strong as the Miami teams of the early 1970's, this club won its last three games to earn a wild-card playoff berth.

New York Jets—A new Mad Bomber delighted New York rather than terrorized it. When quarterback Richard Todd broke a collarbone in the Jets' fourth game, seldom-used reserve Matt Robinson stepped into the lineup and excited fans with his willingness to throw the long pass. In Wesley Walker, he had one of the NFL's premier deep receivers. With runners Kevin Long and Scott Dierking blossoming behind a maturing line, the New York offense carried the surprising Jets into playoff contention. The new 3-4 defense was not yet of playoff caliber, but the special teams showcased stars in kicker Pat Leahy and returner Bruce Harper. The Jets were knocked out of the post-season picture only on December 10, when they staged a 24-point forth quarter to tie the game but lost to the Browns 37-34 in overtime.

Buffalo Bills—After their dismal 1977 campaign, the Bills started fresh in 1978. Chuck Knox took over as head coach with a track record of success with the Rams. Longtime meal ticket O.J. Simpson returned to his native West Coast, bringing to Buffalo a package of draft choices from San Francisco. Knox fielded a young defense with prominent rookie starters in Dee Hardison and Lucius Sanford. On offense, he gave QB Joe Ferguson a new target by obtaining veteran Frank Lewis from the Steelers. Rookie halfback Terry Miller stepped into O.J.'s shoes and, after a slow start, learned to use the blocking of linemen like Joe DeLamielluire to good advantage. On November 26, Miller ran for 208 yards in a victory over the Giants, and he capped his freshman year with 123 rushing yards against the Colts to put himself over the 1,000-yard mark.

Baltimore Colts—After three straight Eastern Division titles, the fall was far and the thud loud. Even before the season started, the Colt offense lost its key moving parts. Tight end Raymond Chester and wide receiver Freddie Scott were traded off during the summer, and after a bitter salary holdout, running back Lydell Mitchell was swapped to San Diego for Joe Washington. Worst of all, quarterback Bert Jones suffered a separated shoulder in a pre-season game. The season began in humiliating fashion, with losses to Dallas 38-0 and to Miami 42-0. When Jones came back for the seventh game, he promptly reinjured his shoulder. Three weeks later, he returned to engineer an upset over the Redskins. One week later, he led the Colts to a victory over Seattle but again was injured and went off for the year. Without him, the Colts lost their last five games. With the worst offense and defense in the A.F.C., the Colts were fortunate to win five games.

CENTRAL DIVISION

Pittsburgh Steelers—The Steelers lost one game to the Oilers, they lost one game to the Rams, and they spent the rest of the season demonstrating football excellence to the NFL. The Steel Curtain defense allowed the fewest points in the league. If Joe Greene was dropping off a bit because of age, L.C. Greenwood, Jam Ham, Jack Lambert, and Mel Blount still played peerless defense. The offense began with a sturdy line and had burly Franco Harris for its overland routes. QB Terry Bradshaw silenced his critics from the past by leading the NFL in touchdown passes, aided in this feat by superb wide receivers Lynn Swann and John Stallworth. The dynastic mentality of the Steelers kept them on top even while trading off Jim Clack, Ernie Holmes, Glen Edwards, and Frank Lewis and losing Bobby Walden to retirement and J.T. Thomas to a blood disorder. With the best record in the league, the Steelers charged into the playoffs with a 21-17 victory over Denver, their upcoming opponents, an encouraging tuneup.

Houston Oilers—The Oilers sent several draft picks and tight end Jimmie Giles to Tampa Bay for the Bucs' number one position in the college draft. Houston got a bargain, as they used the pick to acquire Earl Campbell, a 225-pound running back from the University of Texas. Often compared to Jimmy Brown as a package of speed and power, Campbell led the NFL in rushing and helped the Oilers into the playoffs for the first time in nine years. To go with his ball-control offense, coach Bum Phillips had his 3-4 defense in good shape, led by Elvin Bethea, Curly Culp, and Robert Brazile. A bread-and-butter team with little flash, the Oilers played 13 games decided by seven points or less. The most satisfying of their ten victories was a 24-17 triumph over the Steelers on Monday night, October 23. A loss to the Steelers on December 3 disappointed the Oilers, but a potential rematch in the playoffs loomed on the horizon.

Cleveland Browns—The first 240 minutes of Sam Rutigliano's tenure as head coach were glorious. The Browns won their first three games and battled the Steelers to a deadlock after four quarters on September 24. The Steelers won that game 15-9 on a razzle-dazzle pass play, and the Browns proceeded into a slump which dropped them back into the pack. Rutigliano took pride in his offense, with Brian Sipe finding Reggie Rucker and tight end Ozzie Newsome frequently with passes. Greg Pruitt ran for over 900 yards despite missing four games with a calf injury. The defense showcased an All-Pro safetyman in Thom Darden, but the pass rush fell shy of playoff quality.

Cincinnati Bengals—An 0-5 start prompted GM Paul Brown to fire his hand-picked coaching successor, Bill Johnson. Some critics claimed that Johnson suffered from excessive meddling by the front office, but a more telling problem was quarterback Ken Anderson's absence for the first four games with a broken finger. Under new coach Homer Rice, the Bengals lost their first three games but then began to show improvement. The Bengals ambushed Houston 28-13 on October 29 to break into the winning column. Rice's big change was scrapping the 3-4 defense which Johnson had installed at the start of the season. The new front four of Gary Burley, Wilson Whitley, Eddie Edwards, and rookie Ross Browner pressured quarterbacks into distraction over the last leg of the season. The Bengals salvaged their pride with a closing rush, beating the Falcons, Rams, and cross-state rival Browns in their final three games. Old faces disappeared from the Bengal roster, as Tommy Casanova retired into the medical profession and Bob Trumpy retired into the broadcast booth.

FINAL TEAM STATISTICS

OFFENSE

	BALT.	BUFF.	CIN.	CLEV.	DENV.	HOU.	K.C.	MIA.	N.E.	N.Y. J	OAK.	PIT.	S.D.	SEA.
FIRST DOWNS:														
Total	249	274	271	293	294	276	287	270	322	277	309	316	315	**345**
by Rushing	95	132	105	133	129	135	160	119	**181**	131	116	133	116	150
by Passing	124	113	141	130	137	119	98	135	125	128	164	149	**171**	156
by Penalty	30	29	25	30	28	22	29	16	16	18	29	34	28	**39**
RUSHING:														
Number	532	556	526	559	601	603	663	548	**671**	562	577	641	590	561
Yards	2044	2381	2131	2488	2451	2476	2986	2366	**3165**	2250	2186	2297	2096	2394
Average Yards	3.8	4.3	4.1	4.5	4.1	4.1	4.5	4.3	**4.7**	4.0	3.8	3.6	3.6	4.3
Touchdowns	9	15	10	17	15	19	19	18	**30**	21	18	16	16	28
PASSING:														
Attempts	383	388	470	442	391	373	370	379	390	388	433	380	**477**	467
Completions	202	203	250	236	217	201	204	226	196	193	251	212	**271**	261
Completion Pct.	52.7	52.3	53.2	53.4	55.5	53.9	55.1	**59.6**	50.3	49.7	58.0	55.8	56.8	55.9
Passing Yards	2543	2503	3039	3137	2710	2473	2032	2707	3006	2957	3095	2961	**3566**	3401
Avg. Yds per Att.	4.8	5.4	5.4	6.0	5.4	6.0	4.7	6.1	**6.8**	6.1	5.8	6.7	6.6	6.1
Avg. Yds per Comp.	12.6	12.3	12.2	13.3	12.5	12.3	10.0	12.0	**15.3**	15.3	12.3	14.0	13.2	13.0
Times Tackled	49	30	38	35	48	**17**	21	27	24	43	39	25	32	44
Yds Lost Tackled	480	254	298	278	332	**135**	198	238	206	350	368	262	191	284
Net Yards	2063	2249	2741	2859	2378	2338	1834	2469	2800	2607	2727	2699	**3375**	3117
Touchdowns	17	21	14	22	17	16	7	24	15	19	16	**28**	26	15
Interceptions	30	17	30	21	17	17	**16**	18	25	28	31	22	30	22
Pic. Intercepted	7.8	4.4	6.4	4.8	4.3	4.6	**4.3**	4.7	6.4	7.2	7.2	5.8	6.3	4.7
PUNTS:														
Number	94	89	95	79	**96**	92	80	81	61	74	83	66	75	69
Average	37.4	37.9	**42.4**	39.1	36.4	38.5	40.6	40.3	35.0	40.1	41.7	40.0	36.3	36.4
PUNT RETURNS:														
Number	35	40	**59**	39	51	46	45	41	47	33	47	58	57	40
Yards	219	375	264	317	582	416	488	341	520	413	310	451	**590**	342
Average Yards	6.3	9.4	4.5	8.1	11.4	9.0	10.8	8.3	11.1	**12.5**	6.6	7.8	10.4	8.6
Touchdowns	0	**1**	0	0	**1**	0	0	0	0	**1**	0	0	0	0
KICK OFF RET.:														
Number	**74**	66	58	72	42	58	61	53	55	67	60	44	58	67
Yards	1648	1316	1164	**1697**	952	1304	1456	1132	1172	1509	1233	1043	1252	1510
Average Yards	22.3	19.9	20.1	23.6	22.7	22.5	**23.9**	21.4	21.3	22.5	20.6	23.7	21.6	22.5
Touchdowns	**1**	**1**	0	0	0	0	0	0	0	0	0	**1**	0	0
INTERCEPT. RET.:														
Number	17	14	20	27	31	17	21	**32**	22	23	28	27	22	22
Yards	249	290	319	353	307	199	274	**458**	358	389	407	289	191	193
Average Yards	14.6	**20.7**	10.0	10.1	9.9	11.7	13.0	14.3	16.3	16.9	14.5	10.7	8.7	8.8
Touchdowns	2	1	**3**	1	1	0	0	2	1	1	1	0	2	1
PENALTIES:														
Number	90	120	110	128	132	102	110	**74**	92	102	108	109	98	94
Yards	771	1103	956	1170	1092	833	1048	**603**	852	854	948	948	748	789
FUMBLES:														
Number	38	34	36	50	28	35	32	24	35	**22**	27	35	37	36
Number Lost	17	17	19	29	17	21	18	12	21	**9**	12	17	21	19
POINTS:														
Total	239	302	252	334	282	283	243	**372**	358	359	311	356	355	345
PAT Attempts	31	39	29	40	35	35	26	45	**46**	42	39	45	43	44
PAT Made	27	36	26	37	31	31	25	41	42	41	33	**44**	37	40
FG Attempts	17	13	**30**	28	22	18	**30**	23	24	**30**	20	26	22	21
FG Made	8	10	16	19	11	14	20	19	12	**22**	12	12	18	13
Percent FG Made	47.1	76.9	53.3	67.9	50.0	77.8	66.7	**82.6**	50.0	73.3	60.0	46.2	81.8	61.9
Safeties	1	1	**2**	0	1	0	1	**2**	**2**	0	1	0	0	1

DEFENSE

	BALT.	BUFF.	CIN.	CLEV.	DENV.	HOU.	K.C.	MIA.	N.E.	N.Y. J	OAK.	PIT.	S.D.	SEA.
FIRST DOWNS:														
Total	291	305	269	329	**251**	292	284	298	258	324	299	265	273	331
by Rushing	153	171	121	116	106	120	138	120	**100**	157	125	106	114	153
by Passing	119	**104**	118	175	120	144	122	156	143	146	140	119	141	160
by Penalty	19	30	30	38	25	28	24	22	**15**	21	34	40	18	18
RUSHING:														
Number	662	677	607	563	549	556	602	543	511	600	583	513	**510**	551
Yards	3010	3228	2396	2149	1979	2072	2384	2261	1852	2701	2183	**1774**	2208	2513
Average Yards	4.5	4.8	3.9	3.8	3.6	3.7	4.0	4.2	3.6	4.5	3.7	**3.5**	4.3	4.6
Touchdowns	21	23	16	19	12	14	21	15	14	20	15	**11**	12	20
PASSING:														
Attempts	357	**317**	396	489	438	428	365	437	425	447	448	442	441	460
Completions	191	**167**	193	265	246	240	219	256	235	260	234	221	237	263
Completion Pct.	53.5	52.7	**48.7**	54.2	56.2	56.1	60.0	58.6	55.3	58.2	52.2	50.0	53.7	57.2
Passing Yards	3125	**2156**	2520	3435	2712	3125	2820	3251	3059	3052	2916	2755	2825	3225
Avg. Yds per Att.	7.5	5.8	5.2	6.2	5.3	6.1	6.6	6.1	6.0	6.0	5.7	4.9	**4.8**	6.2
Avg. Yds per Comp.	16.4	12.9	13.1	13.0	**11.0**	13.0	12.9	12.7	13.0	11.7	12.5	12.5	11.9	12.3
Times Tackled	30	22	33	31	30	37	29	41	35	22	29	44	**54**	25
Yds Lost Tackled	224	196	284	232	242	283	238	343	296	229	205	361	**974**	220
Net Yards	2901	**1960**	2236	3203	2470	2842	2582	2908	2763	2823	2711	2394	2351	3005
Touchdowns	29	20	14	20	**9**	17	17	15	21	21	17	10	23	21
Interceptions	17	14	20	27	31	17	21	**32**	22	23	28	27	22	22
Pic. Intercepted	4.8	4.4	5.1	5.5	7.1	4.0	5.8	**7.3**	5.8	5.1	6.3	6.1	5.0	4.8
PUNTS:														
Number	80	71	**108**	82	88	81	76	74	78	70	90	82	99	67
Average	**35.7**	36.5	41.6	38.4	39.9	42.7	39.9	37.0	39.5	37.4	39.5	39.4	38.5	37.4
PUNT RETURNS:														
Number	53	48	58	41	48	53	50	42	**29**	52	38	38	37	36
Yards	400	492	564	366	**226**	517	538	303	272	609	309	239	356	371
Average Yards	8.7	9.2	9.7	8.9	**4.7**	9.8	10.8	7.2	9.4	11.7	8.1	6.3	9.6	10.3
Touchdowns	0	1	0	0	0	1	0	0	0	0	0	0	1	0
KICK OFF RET.:														
Number	52	58	49	72	52	61	54	70	69	64	**51**	60	69	66
Yards	1271	1191	1105	1469	1223	1360	1087	1469	1576	1417	**992**	1336	1457	1328
Average Yards	24.4	20.5	22.6	20.4	23.5	22.3	20.1	21.0	22.8	22.1	**19.5**	22.3	21.1	20.1
Touchdowns	1	0	0	1	0	0	0	0	1	0	0	0	0	1
INTERCEPT. RET.:														
Number	30	17	30	21	17	17	**16**	18	25	28	31	22	30	22
Yards	529	219	211	343	195	**174**	209	224	252	470	374	212	470	300
Average Yards	17.6	12.9	**7.0**	16.3	11.5	10.2	10.1	12.4	10.1	16.8	12.1	9.6	15.7	13.6
Touchdowns	3	1	2	2	0	0	1	0	1	2	1	0	2	1
PENALTIES:														
Number	114	98	123	131	114	99	99	99	81	98	93	109	99	**125**
Yards	1006	941	1074	**1110**	894	940	921	865	683	855	793	987	862	997
FUMBLES:														
Number	36	27	36	35	27	28	30	**37**	34	34	29	33	32	34
Number Lost	20	16	17	18	13	17	14	**21**	**21**	17	15	**21**	16	17
POINTS:														
Total	421	354	284	356	198	298	327	254	286	364	283	**195**	309	358
PAT Attempts	54	46	34	41	**21**	34	40	30	38	45	35	22	40	43
PAT Made	53	43	30	36	**21**	33	33	28	31	40	31	**21**	36	41
FG Attempts	24	21	23	29	27	32	18	21	**19**	24	17	26	22	27
FG Made	14	11	16	22	17	19	14	14	**9**	18	14	14	11	19
Percent FG Made	58.3	52.4	69.9	75.9	63.0	59.4	77.8	66.7	**47.4**	75.0	82.4	53.8	50.0	70.4
Safeties	1	1	1	1	0	2	0	2	0	0	0	0	0	1

WESTERN DIVISION

Denver Broncos—The Orange Crush defense still came down hard enough on enemy offenses to boost the Broncos into first place. The fine-tuned unit, featuring Lyle Alzado, Randy Gradishar, Tom Jackson, Louis Wright, and Bill Thompson, allowed on average fewer than 13 points per game. The Denver offense had to work hard to score much more than that for the Broncos. Craig Morton's performance fell off from the heights of 1977, sharing some time at quarterback with Norris Weese and Craig Penrose. Nevertheless, with Riley Odoms and Haven Moses available as receivers and with six running backs getting substantial playing time, the Broncos went 7-1 in the Division and finished 10-6. The most explosive weapon for the Broncos was Rick Upchurch, who ran back kickoffs and punts with productive abandon. As the regular season ended, the most impressive statistic about the Broncos was that they had never lost two games in a row under the two-year reign of head coach Red Miller.

Oakland Raiders—Little cracks in the championship veneer of the Raiders led to their missing the playoffs for the first time in seven years. They lost both meetings with the Broncos, their main rival in the Division. With a playoff spot on the line, they went into a three game losing spin in November and December. The first of those losses was a 17-16 decision to Seattle in which an extra point was missed. The aging offensive line allowed more frequent sacks of QB Ken Stabler, and Stabler's aging arm went long less successfully and threw the most interceptions in the A.F.C. This list of horrors must not obscure the fact that the Raiders were still a winning team, although not a playoff team. Dave Casper excelled at tight end, Mark van Eeghen ran for over 1,000 yards, and rookie Art Whittington prospered at halfback after Clarence Davis and Terry Robiskie both went out with injuries. At the season's end, head coach John Madden resigned for health reasons, although sceptics looked to see if Dr. Al Davis had signed the prescription.

San Diego Chargers—Loaded with talent, the Chargers stumbled out to a 1-3 start, at which point head coach Tommy Prothro quit. Don Coryell, one-time coach at San Diego State and recently deposed choreographer of the St. Louis Cardinals offensive ballet, replaced Prothro. The team did not turn around immediately, but over the second half of the schedule, it roared to a 7-1 record and was considered the best team not to make the playoffs. As in St. Louis, Coryell cranked up an all-out passing attack. Dan Fouts had long distance targets in Charlie Joiner and rookie John Jefferson, and he could dump short passes to halfback Lydell Mitchell, a pre-season acquisition from the Colts. The pass rush by defensive linemen Fred Dean, Louie Kelcher, Gary Johnson, and Leroy Jones disrupted enemy passing attacks regularly. The Chargers left their calling card by ending the season with a 45-24 thrashing of the playoff-bound Oilers in Houston.

Seattle Seahawks—Finishing with a rush, the Seahawks amassed a winning record in their third year of operation. Coach Jack Patera didn't have a complete team of talented players, but he had enough pieces to make the Seahawks an exciting show. Quarterback Jim Zorn flung left-handed passes with a passion, making Steve Largent the A.F.C.'s leading receiver and leading his mates to several upsets. They beat the Vikings 29-28 on October 8 with an Efren Herrera field goal as time ran out. Two weeks later, they throttled the Raiders 27-7. Over the last five weeks, the Seahawks won four times, including another victory over the Raiders which severely wounded their playoff hopes. Relatively unnoticed in the aerial blitz was halfback David Sims' 15 touchdowns, the most in the league.

Kansas City Chiefs—After compiling the worst record in the N.F.L. in 1977, the Chiefs brought in Marv Levy to take charge of the rebuilding. Veteran players Ed Podolak, Willie Lanier, Jim Lynch, and Jerrell Wilson departed, taking with them past memories of Chief glory. Levy first restructured the defense, putting in a 3-4 system and installing high draft choices Art Still, Sylvester Hicks, and Gary Spani as starters. To help his young defense, Levy planned a ball-control offense which would run the ball endlessly. The wing-T formation he ordered used three running backs and only one wide receiver, and the Chiefs indeed lived and died with the run. A victory on opening day raised hopes prematurely, as six straight defeats followed. By late season, the Chiefs were ready for some moments of glory, whipping the Chargers 23-0 and beating Buffalo 14-10 the next week.

NEW ENGLAND PATRIOTS 11-5-0 Chuck Fairbanks, Ron Erhardt

Scores of Each Game		
14	WASHINGTON	16
16	St. Louis	6
27	BALTIMORE	34
21	Oakland	14
28	SAN DIEGO	23
24	PHILADELPHIA	14
10	Cincinnati	7
33	MIAMI	24
55	N.Y. JETS	21
14	Buffalo	10
23	HOUSTON	26
19	N.Y. Jets	17
35	Baltimore	14
10	Dallas	17
26	BUFFALO	24
3	Miami	23

Use Name	Pos.	Hgt.	Wgt.	Age	Int.	Pts.
Leon Gray	OT	6'3"	256	26		
Shelby Jordan	OT	6'7"	260	26		
Bob McKay	OT	6'5"	265	30		
Dwight Wheeler	OT	6'3"	255	23		
Sam Adams	OG	6'3"	260	29		
Bob Cryder	OG	6'4"	265	21		
Terry Falcon	OG	6'3"	260	23		
John Hannah	OG	6'2"	265	27		
Pete Brock	C	6'5"	260	24		
Bill Lenkaitis	C	6'3"	250	32		
Julius Adams	DE	6'3"	260	30		
Richard Bishop	DE-NT	6'1"	260	28		
Greg Boyd	DE	6'6"	265	25		
Mel Lunsford	DE	6'3"	250	28		
Tony McGee	DE	6'4"	245	29		
Greg Schaum	DE	6'4"	245	24		
Ray Hamilton	NT	6'1"	245	27		
Ernie Holmes	NT	6'3"	260	30		

Use Name	Pos.	Hgt.	Wgt.	Age	Int.	Pts.
Ray Costict	LB	6'	218	23		
Mike Hawkins	LB	6'2"	232	22		
Sam Hunt	LB	6'1"	240	27		
Steve King	LB	6'4"	230	27		
Merv Krakau (from BUF)	LB	6'2"	230	27		
Steve Nelson	LB	6'2"	230	27	5	
Rod Shoate	LB	6'1"	211	25		
Steve Zabel	LB	6'4"	235	30	1	
Doug Beaudoin	DB	6'1"	190	24	3	
Sidney Brown	DB	6'	186	22		
Raymond Clayborn	DB	6'1"	190	23	4	
Dick Conn	DB	6'	180	27	1	
Tim Fox	DB	5'11"	186	24	2	
Mike Haynes	DB	6'2"	189	25	6	6
Prentice McCray	DB	6'1"	187	27		

Pete Cusick – Knee Injury
Jim Romaniszyn – Injury
Darryl Stingley – Spinal Injury

Use Name	Pos.	Hgt.	Wgt.	Age	Int.	Pts.
Matt Cavanaugh	QB	6'1"	210	21		
Steve Grogan	QB	6'4"	200	25		30
Tom Owen	QB	6'1"	194	25		
Horace Ivory	HB	6'	198	24		66
Andy Johnson	HB	6'	204	25		18
James McAlister	HB	6'1"	205	26		12
Don Calhoun	FB-HB	6'	212	26		6
Sam Cunningham	FB	6'3"	230	28		48
Mosi Tatupu	FB	6'	229	23		
Harold Jackson	WR	5'10"	175	32		36
Stanley Morgan	WR	5'11"	176	23		30
Carlos Pennywell	WR	6'2"	180	22		
Don Westbrook	WR	5'10"	184	25		
Russ Francis	TE	6'6"	240	25		24
Don Hasselbeck	TE	6'7"	242	24		
Nick Lowery	K	6'4"	190	22		7
Mike Patrick	K	6'	213	25		
David Posey	K	5'10"	167	22		62
John Smith	K	6'	185	28		9
Jerrel Wilson	K	6'4"	222	36		

MIAMI DOLPHINS 11-5-0 Don Shula

Scores of Each Game		
20	N.Y. Jets	33
42	Baltimore	0
31	BUFFALO	24
3	Philadelphia	17
24	ST. LOUIS	10
21	CINCINNATI	0
28	San Diego	21
24	New England	33
26	BALTIMORE	8
23	DALLAS	16
25	Buffalo	24
30	Houston	35
13	N.Y. JETS	24
16	Washington	0
23	OAKLAND	6
23	NEW ENGLAND	3

Use Name	Pos.	Hgt.	Wgt.	Age	Int.	Pts.
Mike Current	OT	6'4"	270	32		
Eric Laasko	OT-OG	6'4"	265	21		
Wayne Moore	OT	6'6"	265	33		
Bob Kuechenberg	OG-OT	6'3"	255	30		
Larry Little	OG-OT	6'1"	265	32		
Mel Mitchell	OG-OT-C	6'2"	260	25		
Ed Newman	OG	6'2"	245	27		
Wally Pesuit	OG-C	6'4"	250	24		
Jim Langer	C	6'2"	253	30		
John Alexander	DE	6'2"	250	22		
Doug Betters	DE	6'7"	250	22		
Vern Den Herder	DE	6'6"	252	29		6
A.J. Duhe	DE	6'4"	247	22		
Bob Simpson	DE	6'5"	235	24		
Carl Barisich	NT	6'4"	255	27		
Bob Baumhower	NT	6'5"	258	23	1	

Use Name	Pos.	Hgt.	Wgt.	Age	Int.	Pts.
Larry Ball	LB	6'6"	235	28		
Kim Bokamper	LB	6'6"	245	23	1	
Rusty Chambers	LB	6'1"	220	24	1	
Sean Clancy	LB	6'4"	218	21		
Larry Gordon	LB	6'4"	230	25	3	
Bob Matheson	LB	6'4"	235	33		
Earnest Rhone	LB	6'2"	212	25	2	
Steve Towle	LB	6'2"	233	24	1	
Charlie Babb	DB	6'	190	28	3	6
Charles Cornelius	DB	5'9"	178	26	1	
Tim Foley	DB	6'	194	30	6	
Curtis Johnson	DB	6'2"	196	30	3	
Gerald Small	DB	5'11"	187	22	4	6
Norris Thomas	DB	5'11"	175	24	2	6
Rich Volk	DB	6'3"	195	33	4	

Don Nottingham – Shoulder Injury
Steve Young – Ankle Injury

Use Name	Pos.	Hgt.	Wgt.	Age	Int.	Pts.
Guy Benjamin	QB	6'4"	210	23		
Bob Griese	QB	6'1"	190	33		
Don Strock	QB	6'5"	220	27		
Gary Davis	HB	5'10"	202	23		18
Del Williams	HB	6'	195	27		48
Jim Braxton	FB	6'2"	240	29		12
Norm Bulaich	FB	6'1"	212	31		12
Leroy Harris	FB	5'9"	220	24		12
Jimmy Cefalo	WR	5'11"	190	21		18
Duriel Harris	WR	5'11"	175	23		18
Nat Moore	WR	5'9"	180	26		60
Bruce Hardy	TE	6'5"	235	22		12
Loaird McCreary	TE	6'5"	227	25		12
Andre Tillman	TE	6'5"	230	25		18
George Roberts	K	6'	172	23		
Garo Yepremian	K	5'8"	175	34		98

NEW YORK JETS 8-8-0 Walt Michaels

Scores of Each Game		
33	MIAMI	20
21	Buffalo	20
17	SEATTLE	24
3	Washington	23
17	PITTSBURGH	28
45	BUFFALO	14
33	Baltimore	10
23	ST. LOUIS	10
21	New England	55
31	Denver	28
9	Philadelphia	17
17	NEW ENGLAND	19
24	Miami	13
24	BALTIMORE	16
34	Cleveland	*37
7	DALLAS	30

Use Name	Pos.	Hgt.	Wgt.	Age	Int.	Pts.
Marvin Powell	OT	6'5"	264	23		
John Roman	OT	6'4"	251	26		
Chris Ward	OT	6'3"	269	22		
Dan Alexander	OG	6'4"	245	23		
Darrell Austin	OG-C	6'4"	252	26		
Randy Rasmussen	OG	6'2"	255	33		
Stan Waldemore	OG-OT	6'4"	257	23		
Joe Fields	C	6'2"	245	24		
Joe Klecko	DE	6'3"	256	24		
Lawrence Pillers	DE	6'3"	257	25		
Gregg Robinson	DE-NT	6'6"	255	22		
Joe Moreino	NT-DE	6'6"	246	23		
Joe Pellegrini	NT	6'2"	270	22		
Abdul Salaam	NT	6'3"	260	25		

Use Name	Pos.	Hgt.	Wgt.	Age	Int.	Pts.
Greg Buttle	LB	6'3"	229	24	2	
John Hennessy	LB-DE	6'3"	246	23		
Mike Hennigan	LB	6'2"	215	26	3	
Larry Keller	LB	6'2"	225	24	1	
Bob Martin	LB	6'1"	223	24	2	
Mark Merrill	LB	6'4"	237	23		
Mike Mock	LB	6'1"	225	23		
Blake Whitlach	LB	6'1"	233	22		
Reggie Grant	DB	5'9"	185	22		
Bobby Jackson	DB	5'9"	175	21	5	
Tim Moresco	DB	5'11"	176	23		
Burgess Owens	DB	6'2"	195	27	5	6
Larry Riley	DB	5'10"	195	23		
Ken Schroy	DB	6'2"	191	25		
Shafer Suggs	DB	6'1"	200	25	3	
Ed Taylor	DB	6'	176	25	2	

Use Name	Pos.	Hgt.	Wgt.	Age	Int.	Pts.
Matt Robinson	QB	6'2"	196	23		
Pat Ryan	QB	6'3"	205	22		
Richard Todd	QB	6'2"	205	24		
Bruce Harper	HB	5'8"	174	23		30
Kevin Long	HB	6'1"	205	23		60
Darnell Powell	HB	5'11"	200	24		6
Scott Dierking	FB	5'10"	215	23		24
Jim Earley	FB	6'1"	230	22		
Clark Gaines	FB	6'1"	201	24		12
Tom Newton	FB	6'	205	24		12
Kevin Bell	WR	5'10"	180	23		
Derrick Gaffney	WR	6'1"	175	23		18
Bobby Jones	WR	5'11"	180	23		
Bruce Stephens	WR	5'9"	170	21		
Wesley Walker	WR	6'	172	23		48
Jerome Barkum	TE	6'3"	217	28		18
Mark Iwanowski	TE	6'4"	230	22		
Bob Raba	TE	6'1"	222	23		
Mickey Shuler	TE	6'3"	229	22		18
Pat Leahy	K	6'	190	27		**107**
Chuck Ramsey	K	6'2"	195	26		

BUFFALO BILLS 5-11-0 Chuck Knox

Scores of Each Game		
17	PITTSBURGH	28
20	N.Y. JETS	21
24	Miami	31
24	BALTIMORE	17
28	KANSAS CITY	13
14	N.Y. Jets	45
10	Houston	17
5	CINCINNATI	0
20	Cleveland	41
10	NEW ENGLAND	14
24	MIAMI	25
10	Tampa Bay	31
41	N.Y. GIANTS	17
10	Kansas City	14
24	New England	26
21	Baltimore	14

Use Name	Pos.	Hgt.	Wgt.	Age	Int.	Pts.
Joe Devlin	OT	6'5"	250	24		
Elbert Drungo	OT	6'5"	265	35		
Craig Hertwig	OT	6'8"	270	26		
Ken Jones	OT	6'5"	250	25		
Bill Adams	OG	6'2"	246	28		
Joe DeLamielleure	OG	6'3"	245	27		
Reggie McKenzie	OG	6'4"	242	28		
Will Grant	C	6'3"	248	24		
Willie Parker	C	6'3"	245	29		
Scott Hutchinson	DE	6'4"	243	22		
Sherman White	DE	6'5"	250	29		
Ben Williams	DE	6'3"	245	24		
Phil Dokes	DT	6'5"	255	22		
Dee Hardison	DT	6'4"	269	22		
Mekeli Ieremia	DT	6'2"	244	24		
Dennis Johnson	DT	6'4"	265	26		
Mike Kadish	DT	6'5"	270	28		

Use Name	Pos.	Hgt.	Wgt.	Age	Int.	Pts.
Doug Becker (from CHI)	LB	6'	222	22		
Mario Celotto	LB	6'3"	234	22		
Tom Ehlers	LB	6'2"	218	26		
Tom Graham	LB	6'2"	235	28		
Dan Jilek	LB	6'2"	225	24		
Randy McClanahan	LB	6'5"	225	23		
Shane Nelson	LB	6'1"	225	23	3	
Lucius Sanford	LB	6'2"	216	22	1	
Mario Clark	DB	6'2"	195	24	5	
Steve Freeman	DB	5'11"	185	25		
Tony Greene	DB	5'10"	175	29	3	
Doug Jones	DB	6'2"	205	28		
Eddie McMillan	DB	6'	190	26		
Keith Moody	DB	5'10"	170	25		6
Charles Romes	DB	6'1"	190	24	2	6
Marvin Switzer	DB	6'	192	23		

Mike Collier – Foot Injury
John Holland – Knee Injury
Phil Olsen – Knee Injury
Connie Zelencik – Injury

Use Name	Pos.	Hgt.	Wgt.	Age	Int.	Pts.
Joe Ferguson	QB	6'1"	195	28		
Dave Mays	QB	6'1"	204	29		
Bill Munson	QB	6'2"	205	37		
Roland Hooks	HB	6'	195	25		18
Terry Miller	HB	5'10"	196	22		42
Steve Powell	HB	5'11"	186	22		12
Curtis Brown	FB	5'10"	203	23		30
Dennis Johnson	FB	6'3"	220	22		12
Bob Chandler	WR	6'	180	29		30
Mike Levenseller (to TB)	WR	6'1"	180	22		
Frank Lewis	WR	6'1"	196	31		42
Lou Piccone	WR	5'9"	175	29		14
Larry Walton	WR	6'	180	30		6
Leonard Willis	WR	5'11"	185	25		
Mike Franckowiak	TE	6'3"	225	25		
Reuben Gant	TE	6'4"	225	26		30
Tom Dempsey	K	6'1"	260	31		66
Rusty Jackson	K	6'2"	195	27		

BALTIMORE COLTS 5-11-0 Ted Marchibroda

Scores of Each Game		
0	Dallas	38
0	MIAMI	42
34	New England	27
17	Buffalo	24
14	PHILADELPHIA	17
30	St. Louis	17
10	N.Y. JETS	33
7	DENVER	6
8	Miami	26
21	WASHINGTON	17
17	Seattle	14
24	CLEVELAND	45
14	NEW ENGLAND	35
16	N.Y. Jets	24
13	Pittsburgh	35
14	BUFFALO	21

Use Name	Pos.	Hgt.	Wgt.	Age	Int.	Pts.
Wade Griffin	OT	6'5"	231	24		
George Kunz	OT	6'5"	262	31		
Don Morrison	OT	6'5"	250	28		
Bob Van Duyne	OT	6'5"	244	26		
Ron Baker	OG	6'4"	247	23		
Ken Huff	OG	6'4"	262	25		
Robert Pratt	OG	6'4"	248	27		
Forrest Blue	C	6'5"	260	32		
Ken Mendenhall	C	6'3"	250	30		
Geoff Reece	C	6'4"	247	26		
Fred Cook	DE	6'3"	243	26		
John Dutton	DE	6'7"	266	27		
Mike Ozdowski	DE	6'5"	243	22		
Mike Barnes	DT	6'6"	256	27		
Joe Ehrmann	DT	6'5"	254	29		
Greg Marshall	DT	6'3"	257	21		
Herb Orvis	DT	6'5"	255	31		
Dave Rowe (from OAK)	DT	6'7"	270	33		

Use Name	Pos.	Hgt.	Wgt.	Age	Int.	Pts.
Derrel Luce	LB	6'3"	227	25	1	6
Tom MacLeod	LB	6'3"	224	27		
Stu O'Dell	LB	6'1"	220	26		
Calvin O'Neal	LB	6'1"	235	23		
Sanders Shiver	LB	6'2"	222	23		
Ed Simonini	LB	6'	210	24	2	
Stan White	LB	6'1"	223	28	1	
Mike Woods	LB	6'2"	227	23		
Tim Baylor	DB	6'6"	201	24		
Lyle Blackwood	DB	6'	190	27	4	12
Dwight Harrison	DB	6'1"	185	29		
Bruce Laird	DB	6'	198	28		
Lloyd Mumphord	DB	5'11"	178	31	2	
Doug Nettles	DB	6'	178	27	1	
Norm Thompson	DB	6'1"	180	30	6	

Ron Fernandes – Knee Injury
David Taylor – Ankle Injury

Use Name	Pos.	Hgt.	Wgt.	Age	Int.	Pts.
Bert Jones	QB	6'3"	212	26		
Mike Kirkland	QB	6'1"	195	24		
Bill Troup	QB	6'5"	215	27		6
Don McCauley	HB-FB	6'1"	215	29		30
Joe Washington	HB	5'10"	182	24		12
Don Hardeman	FB	6'2"	235	26		
Roosevelt Leaks	FB	5'10"	225	25		24
Ron Lee	FB	6'4"	228	24		12
Randy Burke	WR	6'1"	186	23		
Gerald Butler	WR	6'4"	212	24		
Roger Carr	WR	6'3"	200	26		36
Glenn Doughty	WR	6'1"	205	27		18
Marshall Johnson	WR	6'1"	196	25		
Mike Siani	WR	6'2"	195	28		6
Mack Alston	TE	6'2"	238	31		12
Reese McCall	TE	6'7"	232	22		12
David Lee	K	6'4"	216	34		
Toni Linhart	K	5'11"	179	36		51

*—Overtime

NEW ENGLAND PATRIOTS

RUSHING

Last Name	No.	Yds.	Avg.	TD
Cunningham	199	768	3.9	8
Ivory	141	693	4.9	11
Johnson	147	675	4.6	3
Grogan	81	539	6.7	5
Calhoun	76	391	5.1	1
McAlister	19	77	4.1	2
Morgan	2	11	5.5	0
Jackson	1	7	7.0	0
Tatupu	3	6	2.0	0
Wilson	1	0	0.0	0
Westbrook	1	−2	−2.0	0

RECEIVING

Last Name	No.	Yds.	Avg.	TD
Francis	39	543	14	4
Jackson	37	743	20	6
Morgan	34	820	24	5
Cunningham	31	297	10	0
Johnson	26	267	10	0
Ivory	14	122	9	0
Hasselbeck	7	107	15	0
Westbrook	3	38	13	0
Calhoun	3	29	10	0
Pennywell	1	28	28	0
McAlister	1	12	12	0

PUNT RETURNS

Last Name	No.	Yds.	Avg.	TD
Morgan	32	335	11	0
Haynes	14	183	13	0
Cohn	1	2	2	0

KICKOFF RETURNS

Last Name	No.	Yds.	Avg.	TD
Clayborn	27	636	24	0
McAlister	10	186	19	0
Ivory	7	165	24	0
Westbrook	7	125	18	0
Cohn	1	26	26	0
Morgan	1	17	17	0
Tatupu	1	17	17	0
Wheeler	1	0	0	0

PASSING - PUNTING - KICKING

PASSING	Att.	Comp.	%	Yds.	Yd./Att.	TD	Int.-%	RK
Grogan	362	181	50	2824	7.8	15	23- 6	10
Owen	26	15	58	182	7.0	0	2- 8	
Johnson	2	0	0	0	0.0	0	0- 0	

PUNTING	No.	Avg.
Wilson	54	35.6
Patrick	7	30.9

KICKING	XP	Att.	%	FG	Att.	%
Posey	29	31	94	11	22	50
Smith	6	7	86	1	1	100
Lowery	7	7	100	0	1	0

MIAMI DOLPHINS

RUSHING

Last Name	No.	Yds.	Avg.	TD
Wiliams	272	1258	4.6	8
L. Harris	123	512	4.2	2
Davis	62	313	5.0	3
Bulaich	40	196	4.9	2
Braxton	50	121	2.4	2
Strock	10	23	2.3	0
Griese	9	10	1.1	0
Benjamin	1	−2	−2.0	0
N. Moore	4	−3	−0.8	0
Roberts	1	−7	−7.0	0

RECEIVING

Last Name	No.	Yds.	Avg.	TD
N. Moore	48	645	13	10
D. Harris	45	645	15	3
Tillman	31	398	13	3
L. Harris	25	211	8	0
Davis	24	218	9	0
Williams	18	192	11	0
Bulaich	16	92	6	0
Braxton	9	85	9	0
Cefalo	6	145	24	3
Hardy	4	32	8	2
McCreary	3	27	9	2
Den Herder	1	7	7	1

PUNT RETURNS

Last Name	No.	Yds.	Avg.	TD
Cefalo	28	232	8	0
Babb	9	57	6	0
Davis	2	36	18	0
N. Moore	1	11	11	0
Cornelius	1	5	5	0

KICKOFF RETURNS

Last Name	No.	Yds.	Avg.	TD
D. Harris	29	657	23	0
Davis	13	251	19	0
Cefalo	2	40	20	0
Hardy	2	27	14	0

PASSING - PUNTING - KICKING

PASSING	Att.	Comp.	%	Yds.	Yd./Att.	TD	Int.-%	RK
Griese	235	148	63	1791	7.6	11	11- 5	3
Strock	135	72	53	825	6.1	12	6- 4	
Benjamin	8	6	75	91	11.4	1	1- 13	
Williams	1	0	0	0	0.0	0	0- 0	

PUNTING	No.	Avg.
Roberts	81	40.3

KICKING	XP	Att.	%	FG	Att.	%
Yepremian	41	45	91	19	23	83

NEW YORK JETS

RUSHING

Last Name	No.	Yds.	Avg.	TD
Long	214	954	4.5	10
Dierking	170	681	4.0	4
Harper	58	303	5.2	2
Gaines	44	154	3.5	2
D. Powell	20	77	3.9	1
Newton	11	45	4.1	2
M. Robinson	28	23	0.8	0
Todd	14	18	1.3	0
Gaffney	2	−2	−1.0	0
Walner	1	−3	−3.0	0

RECEIVING

Last Name	No.	Yds.	Avg.	TD
Walker	48	1169	24	8
Gaffney	38	691	18	3
Barkum	28	391	14	3
Long	26	204	8	0
Dierking	19	152	8	0
Harper	13	196	15	2
Shuler	11	67	6	3
Newton	5	48	10	0
Gaines	3	23	8	0
Jones	1	18	18	0
Roman	1	−2	−2	0

PUNT RETURNS

Last Name	No.	Yds.	Avg.	TD
Harper	30	378	13	1
Schroy	3	35	12	0

KICKOFF RETURNS

Last Name	No.	Yds.	Avg.	TD
Harper	55	1280	23	0
D. Powell	3	50	17	0
Stephens	3	42	14	0
Gaines	3	33	11	0
Bell	2	66	33	0
Shuler	1	12	12	0
Schroy	0	26	—	0

PASSING - PUNTING - KICKING

PASSING	Att.	Comp.	%	Yds.	Yd./Att.	TD	Int.-%	RK
M. Robinson	266	124	47	2002	7.5	13	16- 6	9
Todd	107	60	56	849	7.9	6	10- 9	
Ryan	14	9	64	106	7.6	0	2- 14	
Dierking	1	0	0	0	0.0	0	0- 0	

PUNTING	No.	Avg.
Ramsey	74	40.1

KICKING	XP	Att.	%	FG	Att.	%
Leahy	41	42	98	22	30	73

BUFFALO BILLS

RUSHING

Last Name	No.	Yds.	Avg.	TD
Miller	238	1060	4.5	7
Brown	128	591	4.6	4
Hooks	76	358	4.7	2
Johnson	55	222	4.0	2
Ferguson	27	76	2.8	0
Gant	1	14	14.0	0
Jackson	1	−13	−13.0	0

RECEIVING

Last Name	No.	Yds.	Avg.	TD
Chandler	44	581	13	5
Lewis	41	735	18	7
Gant	34	408	12	5
Miller	22	246	11	0
Brown	18	130	7	0
Hooks	15	110	7	1
Johnson	10	83	8	0
Piccone	7	71	10	2
Walton	4	66	17	1
Willis	2	41	21	0
Ferguson	1	−6	−6	0

PUNT RETURNS

Last Name	No.	Yds.	Avg.	TD
Moody	19	240	13	1
Piccone	14	88	6	0
Levenseller	3	35	12	0
Hooks	3	12	4	0
Brown	1	0	0	0

KICKOFF RETURNS

Last Name	No.	Yds.	Avg.	TD
Brown	17	428	25	1
Moody	18	371	21	0
Johnson	10	204	20	0
Hooks	7	124	18	0
Frankowiak	5	60	12	0
Powell	3	53	18	0
Piccone	3	51	17	0
Miller	1	17	17	0
Hutchinson	1	8	8	0
Willis	1	0	0	0

PASSING - PUNTING - KICKING

PASSING	Att.	Comp.	%	Yds.	Yd./Att.	TD	Int.-%	RK
Ferguson	330	175	53	2136	6.5	16	15- 5	7
Munson	43	24	56	328	7.6	4	2- 5	
Mays	15	4	27	39	2.6	1	0- 0	

PUNTING	No.	Avg.
Jackson	87	38.8

KICKING	XP	Att.	%	FG	Att.	%
Dempsey	36	38	95	10	13	77

BALTIMORE COLTS

RUSHING

Last Name	No.	Yds.	Avg.	TD
Washington	240	956	4.0	0
R. Lee	81	374	4.6	1
Leaks	83	266	3.2	2
Hardeman	48	244	5.1	0
McCauley	44	107	2.4	5
Jones	9	38	4.2	0
Kirkland	8	35	4.4	0
Troup	18	25	1.4	1
Doughty	1	−1	−1.0	0

RECEIVING

Last Name	No.	Yds.	Avg.	TD
Washington	45	377	8	1
McCauley	34	296	9	0
Carr	30	629	21	6
Doughty	25	390	16	3
Alston	18	210	12	2
R. Lee	13	109	8	1
McCall	11	160	15	1
Hardeman	10	88	9	0
Leaks	9	111	12	2
Siani	6	151	25	1
Johnson	1	22	22	0

PUNT RETURNS

Last Name	No.	Yds.	Avg.	TD
Johnson	25	143	6	0
Washington	7	37	5	0
McCall	1	37	37	0
Blackwood	1	2	2	0
Burke	1	0	0	0

KICKOFF RETURNS

Last Name	No.	Yds.	Avg.	TD
Washington	19	499	26	1
Johnson	41	927	23	0
McCauley	7	150	21	0
Hardeman	3	36	12	0
Blackwood	1	18	18	0
Morrison	1	6	6	0
Burke	1	2	2	0
Van Duyne	1	0	0	0
O'Dell	0	10	—	0

PASSING - PUNTING - KICKING

PASSING	Att.	Comp.	%	Yds.	Yd./Att.	TD	Int.-%	RK
Troup	296	154	52	1882	6.4	10	21- 7	14
Jones	42	27	64	370	8.8	4	1- 2	
Kirkland	41	19	46	211	5.2	1	8- 20	
Washington	4	2	50	80	20.0	2	0- 0	

PUNTING	No.	Avg.
D. Lee	92	38.2

KICKING	XP	Att.	%	FG	Att.	%
Linhart	27	31	87	8	17	47

PITTSBURGH STEELERS 14-2-0 Chuck Noll

Scores of Each Game		
28	Buffalo	17
21	SEATTLE	10
28	Cincinnati	3
15	CLEVELAND	*9
28	N.Y. Jets	17
31	ATLANTA	7
34	Cleveland	14
17	HOUSTON	24
27	KANSAS CITY	24
20	NEW ORLEANS	14
7	Los Angeles	10
7	CINCINNATI	6
24	San Francisco	7
13	Houston	3
35	BALTIMORE	13
21	Denver	17

Use Name	Pos.	Hgt.	Wgt.	Age	Int.	Pts.
Larry Brown	OT	6'4"	245	29		
Jon Kolb	OT	6'2"	262	31		
Ray Pinney	OT	6'4"	240	24		
Steve Courson	OG	6'1"	260	22		
Sam Davis	OG	6'1"	255	34		
Gerry Mullins	OG	6'3"	244	29		
Ted Petersen	C-OT	6'5"	244	23		
Mike Webster	C	6'1"	250	26		
Fred Anderson	DE-DT	6'4"	235	23		
L.C. Greenwood	DE	6'5"	250	31		
Dwight White	DE	6'4"	255	29		
John Banaszak	DT-DE	6'3"	244	28		
Tom Beasley	DT	6'5"	253	24		
Gary Dunn	DT	6'3"	247	25		
Steve Furness	DT-DE	6'4"	255	27		
Joe Greene	DT	6'4"	264	31		
Robin Cole	LB	6'2"	220	22		
Jack Ham	LB	6'3"	225	29	3	
Jack Lambert	LB	6'4"	220	26	4	
Loren Toews	LB	6'3"	222	26	1	
Dennis Winston	LB	6'	228	22		
Larry Anderson	DB	5'11"	177	21		6
Mel Blount	DB	6'3"	205	30	4	
Tony Dungy	DB	6'	188	22	6	
Ron Johnson	DB	5'10"	200	22	4	
Ray Oldham (from BAL)	DB	6'	192	27		
Donnie Shell	DB	5'11"	190	26	3	6
Nat Terry (to DET)	DB	5'11"	165	22		
Mike Wagner	DB	6'1"	200	29	2	
Terry Bradshaw	QB	6'3"	215	29		6
Mike Kruczek	QB	6'1"	205	25		
Cliff Stoudt	QB	6'4"	218	23		
Rocky Bleier	HB	5'11"	210	32		36
Jack Deloplaine (from WAS)	HB	5'10"	205	24		
Alvin Maxson (to TB, HOU, NYG)	HB	5'11"	205	26		
Rick Moser	HB	6'	210	21		
Sidney Thornton	HB-FB	5'11"	230	23		18
Franco Harris	FB	6'2"	225	28		48
Theo Bell	WR	5'11"	180	24		6
Randy Reutershan	WR	5'10"	182	23		
Jim Smith	WR	6'2"	205	23		12
John Stallworth	WR	6'2"	183	26		54
Lynn Swann	WR	6'	180	26		66
Bennie Cunningham	TE	6'4"	247	23		12
Randy Grossman	TE	6'1"	215	24		6
Jim Mandich	TE	6'3"	214	30		
Craig Colquitt	K	6'2"	182	24		
Roy Gerela	K	5'10"	185	30		80

Laverne Smith-Leg Injury
J.T. Thomas-Illness

HOUSTON OILERS 10-6-0 Bum Phillips

Scores of Each Game		
14	Atlanta	20
20	Kansas City	17
20	SAN FRANCISCO	19
6	LOS ANGELES	10
16	Cleveland	13
17	Oakland	21
17	BUFFALO	10
24	Pittsburgh	17
13	Cincinnati	28
14	CLEVELAND	10
26	New England	23
35	MIAMI	30
17	CINCINNATI	10
3	PITTSBURGH	13
17	New Orleans	12
24	SAN DIEGO	45

Use Name	Pos.	Hgt.	Wgt.	Age	Int.	Pts.
Larry Harris	OT	6'3"	274	24		
Conway Hayman	OT-OG	6'3"	260	29		
Greg Sampson	OT	6'6"	270	27		
Morris Towns	OT	6'4"	275	24		
Ed Fisher	OG	6'3"	250	29		
George Reihner	OG	6'4"	263	23		
John Schuhmacher	OG	6'3"	275	22		
David Carter	C	6'2"	225	25		
Carl Mauck	C	6'4"	250	31		
Steve Baumgartner	DE-LB	6'7"	275	27		
Elvin Bethea	DE	6'3"	255	32		
Jimmy Dean	DE	6'4"	252	23		
Andy Dorris	DE	6'4"	240	27		
James Young	DE	6'2"	260	27		
Curley Culp	NT	6'1"	265	32		
Ken Kennard	NT	6'2"	245	23		
Gregg Bingham	LB	6'1"	230	27		
Robert Brazile	LB	6'4"	238	25	1	
Steve Kiner	LB	6'	225	31	1	
Art Stringer	LB	6'1"	223	24	1	
Ted Thompson	LB	6'1"	220	25		
Ted Washington	LB	6'1"	245	30		
Willie Alexander	DB	6'3"	195	28	5	
Bill Currier	DB	6'	190	23	1	
Al Johnson	DB	6'	200	28		
Kurt Knoff	DB	6'2"	188	24	1	
Mike Reinfeldt	DB	6'2"	195	25	1	
Greg Stemrick	DB	5'11"	185	26	3	
C.L. Whittington	DB	6'1"	200	26	1	
J.C. Wilson	DB	6'	177	22	2	
Tom Dunivan	QB	6'3"	210	24		
Gifford Nielsen	QB	6'4"	205	23		
Dan Pastorini	QB	6'3"	205	29		
Earl Campbell	HB-FB	5'11"	224	23		78
Ronnie Coleman	HB	5'10"	198	27		12
Anthony Davis (to LA)	HB	5'10"	190	25		
Brian Duncan	HB	6'	201	26		
Larry Poole	HB	6'	195	26		
Robert Turner	HB	5'11"	200	24		
Rob Carpenter	FB	6'1"	214	23		30
Tim Wilson	FB	6'3"	220	24		26
Ken Burrough	WR	6'4"	210	30		12
Rich Caster	WR	6'5"	230	29		30
Johnnie Dirden	WR	6'	190	26		
Billy Johnson	WR	5'9"	170	26		
Guido Merkens	WR-DB	6'1"	200	23		
Mike Renfro	WR	6'	184	23		12
Robert Woods	WR	5'7"	170	23		12
Mike Barber	TE	6'3"	235	25		18
Conrad Rucker	TE	6'3"	260	23		
Toni Fritsch	K	5'7"	195	33		73
Cliff Parsley	K	6'1	211	23		

Eddie Foster – Knee Injury
Mike Voight – Injury

CLEVELAND BROWNS 8-8-0 Sam Rutigliano

Scores of Each Game		
24	SAN FRANCISCO	7
13	CINCINNATI	*10
24	Atlanta	16
9	Pittsburgh	*15
13	HOUSTON	16
24	New Orleans	16
14	PITTSBURGH	34
3	Kansas City	17
41	BUFFALO	20
10	Houston	14
7	DENVER	19
45	Baltimore	24
30	LOS ANGELES	19
24	Seattle	47
37	N.Y. JETS	*34
16	Cincinnati	48

Use Name	Pos.	Hgt.	Wgt.	Age	Int.	Pts.
Leo Biedermann	OT	6'7"	254	22		
Barry Darrow	OT	6'7"	260	28		
Doug Dieken	OT	6'5"	252	29		
George Buehler (from OAK)	OG	6'2"	270	31		
Greg Fairchild	OG	6'4"	257	24		
Robert Jackson	OG	6'5"	250	25		
Henry Sheppard	OG	6'6"	246	25		
Tom DeLeone	C	6'2"	248	28		
Gerry Sullivan	C-OT	6'4"	250	26		
Joe Jones	DE	6'6"	250	30		
Mack Mitchell	DE	6'7"	245	26		
Mike St. Clair	DE	6'5"	245	24		
Earl Edwards	DT	6'6"	256	32		
Ken Novak	DT	6'7"	264	24		
Jerry Sherk	DT	6'4"	250	30		
Mickey Sims	DT	6'5"	282	23		
Jesse Turnbow	DT	6'7"	272	21		
Dick Ambrose	LB	6'	235	25	2	
Bob Babich	LB	6'2"	231	31		
Dave Graf	LB	6'2"	215	25		
Charlie Hall	LB	6'3"	235	29	1	
Gerald Irons	LB	6'2"	230	31	2	
Robert Jackson	LB	6'1"	230	24		
Clay Matthews	LB	6'2"	230	22	1	
Ron Bolton	DB	6'2"	170	28		
Thom Darden	DB	6'2"	193	28	10	
Oliver Davis	DB	6'1"	200	24	6	6
Ricky Jones	DB	6'1"	195	23		
Tom London	DB	6'1"	197	24		
Tony Peters	DB	6'1"	192	25	2	
Randy Rich (from OAK)	DB	5'10"	181	24		
Clarence Scott	DB	6'	180	29	3	
Johnny Evans	QB	6'1"	197	22		
Mark Miller	QB	6'2"	176	22		6
Brian Sipe	QB	6'1"	190	29		18
Larry Collins	HB	5'11"	189	23		6
Cleo Miller	HB-FB	5'11	202	26		6
Greg Pruitt	HB	5'10"	190	27		30
Tom Sullivan	HB	6'	190	28		
Calvin Hill	FB-HB	6'3"	227	31		42
Mike Pruitt	FB	6'	214	24		30
Ricky Feacher	WR	5'10"	174	24		
Dave Logan	WR	6'4"	226	24		24
Reggie Rucker	WR	6'2	190	30		48
Keith Wright	WR	5'10"	172	22		
Ozzie Newsome	TE	6'2"	225	22		24
Gary Parris	TE	6'2	226	28		
Oscar Roan	TE	6'6"	214	26		
Don Cockroft	K	6'1	195	33		94

CINCINNATI BENGALS 4-12-0 Bill Johnson, Homer Rice

Scores of Each Game		
23	KANSAS CITY	24
10	Cleveland	*13
3	PITTSBURGH	28
18	NEW ORLEANS	20
12	San Francisco	28
0	Miami	21
3	NEW ENGLAND	10
0	Buffalo	5
28	HOUSTON	13
13	San Diego	22
21	OAKLAND	34
6	Pittsburgh	7
10	Houston	17
37	ATLANTA	7
20	Los Angeles	19
48	CLEVELAND	16

Use Name	Pos.	Hgt.	Wgt.	Age	Int.	Pts.
Vern Holland	OT	6'5"	265	30		
Ron Hunt	OT	6'6"	255	23		
Rufus Mayes	OT	6'5"	256	30		
Mike Wilson	OT	6'5"	280	23		
Glenn Bujnoch	OG	6'5"	251	24		
Mark Donahue	OG	6'3"	261	22		
Dave Lapham	OG	6'4"	259	26		
Blair Bush	C	6'3"	254	21		
Bob Johnson	C	6'5"	256	32		
Ross Browner	DE	6'3"	262	24		
Gary Burley	DE	6'3"	265	25		
Eddie Edwards	DT-DE	6'5"	256	24	1	
Ted Vincent	DT	6'4"	262	22		
Wilson Whitley	DT	6'3"	264	23		
Glenn Cameron	LB	6'2"	217	25		
Tom DePaso	LB	6'2"	222	22		
Tom Dinkel	LB	6'3"	246	22	1	
Bo Harris	LB	6'3"	221	25		
Jim LeClair	LB	6'2"	238	27	1	
Tom Ruud	LB	6'2	230	25		
Rod Shumon	LB	6'1"	225	22	1	
Reggie Williams	LB	6'1	228	23	1	
Louis Breeden	DB	5'11	185	24	3	
Marvin Cobb	DB	6	191	25	1	
Ray Griffin	DB	5'10	186	22		
Dick Jauron	DB	6	190	27	4	6
Melvin Morgan	DB	6	186	25	1	
Scott Perry	DB	6	182	24	3	18
Ken Riley	DB	6	185	31	3	
Ken Anderson	QB	6'1	210	29		6
Rob Hertel	QB	6'2	192	23		
John Reaves	QB	6'3	210	28		
Lenvil Elliott	HB	6	208	26		
Archie Griffin	HB	5'9	193	24		18
Deacon Turner	HB	5'11	212	23		
Booby Clark	FB	6'2	245	27		
Tony Davis	FB	5'10	210	25		12
Pete Johnson	FB	6	240	24		42
Billy Brooks	WR	6'3	202	25		12
Isaac Curtis	WR	6	192	27		18
Dennis Law	WR	6'1	182	23		
Pat Mcinally	WR	6'6	210	25		
Don Bass	TE	6'2	218	23		30
Jim Corbett	TE	6'3	221	23		
Rich Walker	TE	6'3	237	23		12
Chris Bahr	K	5'9	170	25		74

*—Overtime

PITTSBURGH STEELERS

RUSHING

Last Name	No.	Yds.	Avg.	TD
Harris	310	1082	3.5	8
Bleier	165	633	3.8	5
Thornton	71	264	3.7	2
Moser	42	153	3.6	0
Bradshaw	32	93	2.9	1
Deloplaine	11	49	4.5	0
Maxson	4	9	2.3	0
Swann	1	7	7.0	0
Kruczek	5	7	1.4	0

RECEIVING

Last Name	No.	Yds.	Avg.	TD
Swann	61	880	14	11
Stallworth	41	798	20	9
Grossman	37	448	12	1
Harris	22	144	7	0
Bleier	17	168	10	1
Cunningham	16	321	20	2
Smith	6	83	14	2
Bell	6	53	9	1
Thornton	5	66	13	1
Moser	1	−1	−1	0
Bradshaw	0	1	—	0

PUNT RETURNS

Last Name	No.	Yds.	Avg.	TD
Reutershan	20	148	7	0
Bell	21	152	7	0
Smith	9	65	7	0
Terry	7	80	11	0
Shell	1	6	6	0

KICKOFF RETURNS

Last Name	No.	Yds.	Avg.	TD
L. Anderson	37	930	25	1
Terry	7	145	21	0
Maxson	3	50	17	0
Thornton	1	37	37	0
Deloplaine	1	19	19	0
Smith	1	16	16	0
Moser	1	8	8	0
Mullins	1	0	0	0

PASSING - PUNTING - KICKING

PASSING	Att.	Comp.	%	Yds.	Yd./Att.	TD	Int.–%	RK
Bradshaw	368	207	56	2915	7.9	28	20– 5	1
Kruczek	11	5	46	46	4.2	0	2– 18	
Harris	1	0	0	0	0.0	0	0– 0	

PUNTING	No.	Avg.
Colquitt	66	40.0

KICKING	XP	Att.	%	FG	Att.	%
Gerela	44	45	98	12	26	46

HOUSTON OILERS

RUSHING

Last Name	No.	Yds.	Avg.	TD
Campbell	302	1450	4.8	13
T. Wilson	126	431	3.4	0
Carpenter	82	348	4.2	5
Coleman	61	188	3.1	1
Caster	5	32	6.4	0
Barber	2	14	7.0	0
Pastorini	18	11	0.6	0
Renfro	1	9	9.0	0
Davis	3	7	2.3	0
Woods	2	4	2.0	0
Duncan	1	0	0.0	0
Burrough	3	−11	−3.7	0

RECEIVING

Last Name	No.	Yds.	Avg.	TD
Burrough	47	624	13	2
Barber	32	513	16	3
Renfro	26	339	13	2
Caster	20	316	16	5
Coleman	19	246	13	1
Carpenter	17	150	9	0
T. Wilson	15	91	6	1
Campbell	12	48	4	0
Woods	6	96	16	2
Rucker	2	38	19	0
Duncan	2	0	0	0
B. Johnson	1	10	10	0
Merkens	1	6	6	0
Sampson	1	−4	−4	0

PUNT RETURNS

Last Name	No.	Yds.	Avg.	TD
Coleman	16	142	9	0
Merkens	13	132	10	0
Woods	9	82	9	0
B. Johnson	8	60	8	0
Thompson	0	2	—	0

KICKOFF RETURNS

Last Name	No.	Yds.	Avg.	TD
Dirden	32	780	24	0
Poole	4	107	27	0
Davis	4	98	25	0
B. Johnson	4	73	18	0
Turner	4	69	17	0
Woods	3	59	20	0
Coleman	2	40	20	0
Duncan	2	38	19	0
T. Wilson	2	29	15	0
Carpenter	1	11	11	0

PASSING - PUNTING - KICKING

PASSING	Att.	Comp.	%	Yds.	Yd./Att.	TD	Int.–%	RK
Pastorini	368	199	54	2473	6.7	16	17– 5	8
Nielsen	4	2	50	0	0.0	0	0– 0	
Burrough	1	0	0	0	0.0	0	0– 0	

PUNTING	No.	Avg.
Parsley	91	38.9

KICKING	XP	Att.	%	FG	Att.	%
Fritsch	31	32	97	14	18	78

CLEVELAND BROWNS

RUSHING

Last Name	No.	Yds.	Avg.	TD
G. Pruitt	176	960	5.5	3
M. Pruitt	135	560	4.1	5
C. Miller	89	336	3.8	1
Hill	00	209	0.0	1
Newsome	13	96	7.4	2
Sipe	28	87	3.1	3
Collins	22	64	2.9	1
M. Miller	7	63	9.0	1
Rucker	2	14	7.0	0
Evans	2	12	6.0	0
T. Sullivan	5	7	1.4	0

RECEIVING

Last Name	No.	Yds.	Avg.	TD
Rucker	43	893	21	8
Newsome	38	589	16	2
G. Pruitt	38	292	8	2
Logan	37	585	16	4
Hill	25	334	13	6
C. Miller	20	152	8	0
M. Pruitt	20	112	6	0
Wright	8	76	10	0
Feacher	4	76	19	0
T. Sullivan	1	20	20	0
Collins	1	4	4	0
Parris	1	4	4	0

PUNT RETURNS

Last Name	No.	Yds.	Avg.	TD
Wright	37	288	7	0
Newsome	2	29	15	0

KICKOFF RETURNS

Last Name	No.	Yds.	Avg.	TD
Wright	30	789	26	0
Collins	32	709	22	0
T. Sullivan	4	90	23	0
Rich	2	43	22	0
G. Pruitt	1	31	31	0
B. Jackson	1	19	19	0
C. Miller	1	15	15	0
Rucker	1	1	1	0

PASSING - PUNTING - KICKING

PASSING	Att.	Comp.	%	Yds.	Yd./Att.	TD	Int.–%	RK
Sipe	399	222	56	2906	7.3	21	15– 4	4
M. Miller	39	13	33	212	5.4	1	4– 10	
Evans	1	1	100	19	19.0	0	0– 0	
G. Pruitt	3	0	0	0	0.0	0	2– 67	

PUNTING	No.	Avg.
Evans	79	39.1

KICKING	XP	Att.	%	FG	Att.	%
Cochroft	37	40	93	19	28	68

CINCINNATI BENGALS

RUSHING

Last Name	No.	Yds.	Avg.	TD
P. Johnson	180	762	4.2	7
A. Griffin	132	484	3.7	0
Turner	84	333	4.0	0
Clark	40	187	4.7	0
Anderson	29	167	5.8	1
Elliott	29	75	2.6	0
Davis	21	57	2.7	2
Reaves	6	50	8.3	0
Dinkel	1	20	20.0	0
Curtis	1	1	1.0	0
Hertel	1	0	0.0	0
Law	1	−1	−1.0	0
Bass	1	−4	−4.0	0

RECEIVING

Last Name	No.	Yds.	Avg.	TD
Curtis	47	737	16	3
A. Griffin	35	284	8	3
P. Johnson	31	236	8	0
Brooks	30	506	17	2
Bass	27	447	17	4
McInally	15	189	13	0
Corbett	12	187	16	0
Walker	12	126	11	2
Elliott	12	100	8	0
Clark	11	73	7	0
Turner	11	50	5	0
Law	5	81	16	0
Davis	2	23	11	0

PUNT RETURNS

Last Name	No.	Yds.	Avg.	TD
Davis	22	130	6	0
Law	25	106	4	0
Breeden	6	−12	−2	0
Jauron	3	32	11	0
Bass	3	8	3	0

KICKOFF RETURNS

Last Name	No.	Yds.	Avg.	TD
R. Griffin	37	787	21	0
Bass	7	138	20	0
A. Griffin	4	94	24	0
Davis	3	51	17	0
Law	2	30	15	0
Turner	1	24	24	0
Corbett	1	15	15	0
Breeden	1	12	12	0
Clark	1	11	11	0
Vincent	1	2	2	0

PASSING - PUNTING - KICKING

PASSING	Att.	Comp.	%	Yds.	Yd./Att.	TD	Int.–%	RK
Anderson	319	173	54	2219	7.0	10	22– 7	12
Reaves	144	74	51	790	5.5	3	8– 6	
A. Griffin	3	2	67	21	7.0	1	0– 0	
Hertel	4	1	25	9	2.3	0	0– 0	

PUNTING	No.	Avg.
McInally	91	43.1
Bahr	4	27.0

KICKING	XP	Att.	%	FG	Att.	%
Bahr	26	29	90	16	30	53

DENVER BRONCOS 10-6-0 Red Miller

Scores of Each Game		
14	OAKLAND	6
9	Minnesota	*12
27	SAN DIEGO	14
23	Kansas City	*17
28	SEATTLE	7
0	San Diego	23
16	CHICAGO	7
6	Baltimore	7
20	Seattle	*17
28	N.Y. JETS	31
19	Cleveland	7
16	GREEN BAY	3
14	Detroit	17
21	Oakland	6
24	KANSAS CITY	3
17	PITTSBURGH	21

Use Name	Pos.	Hgt.	Wgt.	Age	Int.	Pts.
Glenn Hyde	OT	6 3	250	27		
Claudie Minor	OT	6 4	280	27		
Tom Neville	OT	6 4	253	35		
Tom Glassic	OG	6 3	254	24		
Paul Howard	OG	6 3	260	27		
Steve Schindler	OG	6 3	260	24		
Bill Bryan	C	6 2	244	23		
Bobby Maples	C	6 3	250	35		
Lyle Alzado	DE	6 3	250	29		
Barney Chavous	DE	6 3	252	27		
Brison Manor	DE	6 4	248	26		
Paul Smith	DE	6 3	256	33		
Rubin Carter	NT	6	256	25		
John Grant	NT	6 3	246	28		
Don Latimer	NT	6 3	265	23		
Larry Evans	LB	6 2	216	25		
Randy Gradishar	LB	6 3	233	26	4	6
Tom Jackson	LB	5 11	220	27	3	6
Rob Nairne	LB	6 4	220	24		
Joe Rizzo	LB	6 1	220	27	3	
Bob Swenson	LB	6 3	220	25	1	
Godwin Turk	LB	6 3	230	27	2	
Steve Foley	DB	6 2	185	24	6	
Maurice Harvey	DB	5 10	190	22		
Bernard Jackson	DB	6	178	28	6	
Chris Pane	DB	5 11	180	25		
Bill Thompson	DB	6 1	200	31	4	6
Charlie West	DB	6 1	190	32		
Louis Wright	DB	6 2	195	25	2	
Craig Morton	QB	6'4"	210	35		
Craig Penrose	QB	6'3"	205	25		
Norris Weese	QB	6'1"	195	27		6
Otis Armstrong	HB	5'10"	196	27		12
Rob Lytle	HB	6'1"	195	23		12
Dave Preston	HB	5'10"	195	23		12
Larry Canada	FB	6'2"	235	23		18
Jon Keyworth	FB	6'3"	230	27		24
Lonnie Perrin	FB	6'1"	222	26		30
Jack Dolbin	WR	5'10"	183	29		
Vince Kinney	WR	6'2"	190	22		
Haven Moses	WR	6'3"	200	32		30
John Schultz	WR	5'10"	182	25		
Rick Upchurch	WR	5'10"	170	26		12
Ron Egloff	TE	6'5"	238	22		6
Bob Moore	TE	6'3"	225	29		
Riley Odoms	TE	6'4"	230	28		36
Bucky Dilts	K	5'9"	183	24		
Jim Turner	K	6'2"	205	37		64

Jim Jensen-Knee Injury

OAKLAND RAIDERS 9-7-0 John Madden

Scores of Each Game		
6	Denver	14
21	San Diego	20
28	Green Bay	3
14	NEW ENGLAND	21
25	Chicago	*19
21	HOUSTON	17
28	KANSAS CITY	6
7	Seattle	27
23	SAN DIEGO	27
20	Kansas City	10
34	Cincinnati	21
29	DETROIT	17
16	SEATTLE	17
6	DENVER	21
6	Miami	23
27	MINNESOTA	20

Use Name	Pos.	Hgt.	Wgt.	Age	Int.	Pts.
Henry Lawrence	OT	6'4"	270	26		
Lindsey Mason	OT	6'5"	260	23		
Art Shell	OT	6'5"	275	31		
Mickey Marvin	OG	6'4"	270	22		
Gene Upshaw	OG	6'5"	255	33		
Dave Dalby	C	6'2"	250	27		
Steve Sylvester	C-OG-OT	6'4"	260	25		
Dave Browning	DE	6'5"	245	22		
John Matuszak	DE	6'8"	275	27		
Charles Philyaw	DE-NT	6'9"	275	24		
Pat Toomay	DE	6'5"	245	33		
Mike McCoy	NT	6'5"	275	29		
Otis Sistrunk	NT-DE	6'4"	270	30		
Jeff Barnes	LB	6'2"	215	23		
Willie Hall	LB	6'2"	225	28	2	
Ted Hendricks	LB	6'7"	220	30	3	
John Huddleston	LB	6'3"	230	24		
Monte Johnson	LB	6'4"	240	26	1	
Rod Martin	LB	6'2"	205	24		
Phil Villapiano	LB	6'2"	225	29	2	
Robert Watts	LB	6'3"	218	24		
Willie Brown	DB	6'1"	210	37	1	
Neal Colzie	DB	6'2"	205	25	3	6
Mike Davis	DB	6'2"	200	22	1	
Lester Hayes	DB	6'	208	23	4	
Monte Jackson	DB	5'11"	189	25	2	
Charlie Phillips	DB	6'2"	215	25	6	18
Jack Tatum	DB	5'10"	205	29	3	
David Humm	QB	6'2"	185	26		
Jim Plunkett	QB	6'3"	207	30		
Ken Stabler	QB	6'3"	215	32		
Pete Banaszak	HB	5'11"	210	34		
Clarence Davis	HB	5'10"	195	29		
Harold Hart	HB	6'	205	25		
Art Whittington	HB	5'11"	180	22		42
Terry Robiskie	FB-HB	6'1"	210	23		12
Booker Russell	FB	6'2"	230	22		
Mark van Eeghen	FB	6'2"	225	26		60
Fred Biletnikoff	WR	6'1"	190	35		12
Morris Bradshaw	WR	6'	195	25		12
Cliff Branch	WR	5'11"	170	30		6
Larry Brunson	WR	5'11"	180	29		
Joe Stewart	WR	5'11"	180	22		
Warren Bankston	TE	6'4"	235	31		
Dave Casper	TE	6'4"	230	26		60
Ray Chester	TE	6'3"	235	30		12
Derrick Ramsey	TE	6'4"	220	21		
Jim Breech	K	5'6"	165	22		
Ray Guy	K	6'3"	195	28		
Errol Mann	K	6'	205	37		69

Bob Nelson-Injury
Sam Scarber-Injury
John Vella-Chest Injury

SAN DIEGO CHARGERS 9-7-0 Tommy Prothro, Don Coryell

Scores of Each Game		
24	Seattle	20
20	OAKLAND	21
14	Denver	27
3	GREEN BAY	24
23	New England	28
23	DENVER	0
21	MIAMI	28
14	Detroit	31
27	Oakland	23
22	CINCINNATI	13
29	KANSAS CITY	*23
13	Minnesota	7
0	Kansas City	23
40	CHICAGO	7
37	SEATTLE	10
45	Houston	24

Use Name	Pos.	Hgt.	Wgt.	Age	Int.	Pts.
Milton Hardaway	OT	6'9"	309	23		
Billy Shields	OT	6'7"	254	25		
Russ Washington	OT	6'6"	290	31		
Charles Aiu (to SEA)	OG	6'2"	250	24		
Dan Audick	OG	6'3"	255	23		
Ed White	OG	6'2"	270	31		
Doug Wilkerson	OG	6'2"	257	31		
Don Macek	C-OG	6'3"	253	24		
Ralph Perretta	C	6'2"	250	25		
Mark Slater	C	6'1"	252	23		
Fred Dean	DE	6'3"	228	26		
Leroy Jones	DE	6'8"	265	27		
John Lee	DE	6'2"	253	25		
Wilbur Young	DE	6'6"	290	29		
Charles DeJurnett	DT	6'4"	270	26		
Gary Johnson	DT	6'2"	254	26	1	6
Louie Kelcher	DT	6'5"	282	25	1	
Don Goode	LB	6'2"	225	27	1	
Bob Horn	LB	6'3"	237	24	1	
Jim Laslavic	LB	6'2"	240	26		
Woodrow Lowe	LB	6'	227	24	1	
Rick Middleton	LB	6'2"	228	26	1	
Ray Preston	LB	6'	215	24		
Jerome Dove	DB	6'	186	24	1	
Glen Edwards	DB	6'	185	31	3	
Mike Fuller	DB	5'9"	188	25	4	6
Keith King	DB	6'4"	226	23	1	
Pete Shaw	DB	5'10"	184	24	2	
Hal Stringert	DB	5'11"	185	26	2	
Mike Williams	DB	5'10"	180	24	3	
Dan Fouts	QB	6'3"	204	27		12
James Harris	QB	6'3"	217	31		
Cliff Olander	QB	6'5"	196	23		
Hank Bauer	HB	5'10"	204	24		54
Lydell Mitchell	HB	5'11"	198	29		30
Clarence Williams	HB	5'9"	198	23		
Ricky Anderson	FB	6'1"	211	25		
Bo Matthews	FB	6'4"	230	26		
Don Woods	FB	6'1"	209	27		18
Larry Burton	WR	6'1"	193	26		18
John Jefferson	WR	6'1"	190	22		78
Charlie Joiner	WR	5'11"	188	30		6
Dwight McDonald	WR	6'2"	187	27		6
Artie Owens	WR	5'10	174	25		
Johnny Rodgers	WR	5'10"	180	27		
Pat Curran	TE	6'3"	235	32		12
Bob Klein	TE	6'5"	245	31		12
Greg McCrary (from WAS)	TE	6'3"	230	26		6
Jeff West	TE	6'3"	211	25		
Rolf Benirshke	K	6'	170	23		91

Bob Rush-Knee Injury

SEATTLE SEAHAWKS 9-7-0 Jack Patera

Scores of Each Game		
10	SAN DIEGO	24
10	Pittsburgh	21
24	N.Y. Jets	17
28	DETROIT	16
7	Denver	28
29	MINNESOTA	28
28	Green Bay	45
27	OAKLAND	7
17	DENVER	*20
31	Chicago	29
14	BALTIMORE	17
13	Kansas City	10
17	Oakland	16
47	CLEVELAND	24
10	San Diego	37
23	KANSAS CITY	19

Use Name	Pos.	Hgt.	Wgt.	Age	Int.	Pts.
Steve August	OT	6'5"	254	23		
Nick Bebout	OT	6'5"	260	27		
Louis Bullard	OT	6'6"	265	22		
Norm Evans	OT	6'5"	250	35		
Ron Coder	OG	6'4"	250	24		
Tom Lynch	OG	6'5"	260	23		
Bob Newton	OG	6'4"	260	29		
Art Kuehn	C	6'3"	255	25		
John Yarno	C	6'5"	251	23		
Bill Gregory	DE	6'5"	260	28		
Dave Kraayeveld	DE-DT	6'5"	255	22		
Ernie Price (from DET)	DE	6'4"	245	27		
Alden Roche	DE	6'4"	255	33		
Dennis Boyd	DT	6'6"	255	22		
Steve Niehaus	DT	6'4"	255	23		
Bill Sandifer	DT-DE	6'6"	260	26		
Terry Beeson	LB	6'3"	240	22		
Keith Butler	LB	6'4"	225	22		
Pete Cronan	LB	6'2"	238	23	2	
Ken Geddes	LB	6'3"	235	30		
Sammy Green	LB	6'2"	230	23	1	
Charles McShane	LB	6'3"	230	24		
Autry Beamon	DB	6'1"	190	24	4	
Dave Brown	DB	6'1"	190	25	3	
John Harris	DB	6'2"	200	22	4	
Kerry Justin	DB	5'11"	175	23		
Doug Long	DB	6'	189	23		
Keith Simpson	DB	6'1"	195	22	2	6
Cornell Webster	DB	6'	180	23	5	
Sam Adkins	QB	6'2"	214	23		
Steve Myer	QB	6'2"	188	24		
Jim Zorn	QB	6'2"	200	25		36
Rufus Crawford	HB	5'10"	180	23		
Al Hunter	HB	5'11"	195	23		12
David Sims	HB	6'3"	216	22		90
Tony Benjamin	FB	6'3"	225	22		
Sherman Smith	FB	6'4"	225	23		42
Don Testerman	FB	6'2"	230	25		
Duke Fergerson	WR	6'1"	193	24		
Steve Largent	WR	5'11"	184	23		48
Sam McCullum	WR	6'2"	203	25		18
Steve Raible	WR	6'2"	195	24		6
Ron Howard	TE	6'4"	240	27		6
Brian Peets	TE	6'4"	225	22		
John Sawyer	TE	6'2"	230	25		
Efren Herrera	K	5'9"	190	27		79
Herman Weaver	K	6'4"	210	29		

Don Dufek-Knee Injury

KANSAS CITY CHIEFS 4-12-0 Marv Levy

Scores of Each Game		
24	Cincinnati	3
17	HOUSTON	20
10	N.Y. Giants	26
17	DENVER	*23
13	Buffalo	28
13	TAMPA BAY	30
6	Oakland	28
17	CLEVELAND	3
24	Pittsburgh	27
10	OAKLAND	20
23	San Diego	*29
10	SEATTLE	13
23	SAN DIEGO	0
14	BUFFALO	10
3	Denver	24
19	Seattle	23

Use Name	Pos.	Hgt.	Wgt.	Age	Int.	Pts.
Larry Brown	OT	6'5"	260	23		
Charlie Getty	OT-OG	6'4"	260	26		
Matt Herkenhoff	OT	6'4"	255	27		
Jim Nicholson	OT	6'6"	275	28		
Tom Condon	OG	6'3"	240	25		
Bob Simmons	OG	6'4"	260	24		
Rod Walters	OG-OT	6'3"	258	24		
Charlie Ane	C	6'1"	233	26		
Jack Rudnay	C	6'3"	240	30		
Sylvester Hicks	DE	6'4"	248	23		
Dave Lindstrom	DE	6'6"	249	23		
Art Still	DE	6'7"	252	22		
Stan Johnson	NT	6'4"	275	23		
Jeff Lloyd	NT	6'6"	255	24		
Don Parrish	NT	6'2"	255	23		
Jimbo Elrod	LB	6'	223	24		
Tom Howard	LB	6'2"	208	24	1	
Charles Jackson	LB	6'2"	236	23		
Whitney Paul	LB	6'3"	220	24	3	
Dave Rozumek	LB	6'1"	212	24	2	
Clarence Sanders	LB	6'4"	228	25		
Gary Spani	LB	6'2"	230	22		
Gary Barbaro	DB	6'4"	198	24	3	
Ted Burgmeier	DB	5'10"	185	22		
Tim Collier	DB	6'	166	24	3	
Tim Gray	DB	6'1"	200	25	6	
Gary Green	DB	5'11"	184	22	1	
Ray Milo	DB	5'11"	178	24		
Clyde Powers	DB	6'1"	195	27		
Emmitt Thomas	DB	6'2"	192	35	2	
Tony Adams	QB	6'	198	28		
Mike Livingston	QB	6'3"	210	32		6
Dennis Shaw	QB	6'2"	215	31		
Horace Belton	HB	5'9"	200	23		
Ted McKnight	HB	6'1"	203	24		42
Eddie Payton	HB	5'8"	175	27		
Tony Reed	HB	5'11"	197	23		36
Mark Bailey	FB	6'3"	237	23		
MacArthur Lane	FB-HB	6'	220	36		
Arnold Morgado	FB	6'	210	25		42
Larry Dorsey	WR	6'1"	195	25		12
Bill Kollar	WR	5'11"	187	22		
Henry Marshall	WR	6'2"	205	24		12
Jerrold McRae	WR	6'1"	201	23		
Ed Beckman	TE	6'4"	223	23		
Andre Samuels	TE	6'4"	229	25		
Walter White	TE	6'3"	218	27		6
Zenon Andrusyshyn	K	6'2"	210	31		
Jan Stenerud	K	6'2"	187	35		85

Ricky Davis-Shoulder Injury
Darius Helton-Shoulder Injury
Willie Lee-Knee Injury

*—Overtime

DENVER BRONCOS

RUSHING

Last Name	No.	Yds.	Avg.	TD
Perrin	108	455	4.2	4
Keyworth	112	444	4.0	3
Armstrong	112	381	3.4	1
Canada	79	365	4.6	3
Lytle	81	341	4.2	2
Preston	66	296	4.5	1
Morton	17	71	4.2	1
Weese	17	48	2.8	1
Upchurch	5	31	6.2	0
Foley	1	14	14.0	0
Odoms	2	5	5.0	0
Penrose	1	0	0.0	0

RECEIVING

Last Name	No.	Yds.	Avg.	TD
Odoms	54	829	15	6
Moses	37	744	20	5
Dolbin	24	284	12	0
Preston	24	199	8	1
Keyworth	21	166	8	1
Upchurch	17	210	12	1
Armstrong	12	98	8	1
Perrin	10	54	5	1
Canada	6	37	6	0
Lytle	6	37	6	0
Egloff	4	33	8	1
Kinney	1	23	23	0
Turner	1	−4	−4	0

PUNT RETURNS

Last Name	No.	Yds.	Avg.	TD
Upchurch	36	493	14	1
Preston	10	68	7	0
West	3	20	7	0
Thompson	1	3	3	0
Pane	1	−2	−2	0

KICKOFF RETURNS

Last Name	No.	Yds.	Avg.	TD
Perrin	12	256	21	0
B. Jackson	9	209	23	0
Upchurch	8	222	28	0
Preston	7	154	22	0
Keyworth	2	24	12	0
Pane	1	29	29	0
West	1	24	24	0
Schultz	1	20	20	0
Turk	1	14	14	0

PASSING – PUNTING – KICKING

PASSING	Att.	Comp.	%	Yds.	Yd./Att.	TD	Int.–%	RK
Morton	267	146	55	1802	6.8	11	8– 3	5
Weese	87	55	63	723	8.3	4	5– 6	
Penrose	37	16	43	185	5.0	2	4– 11	

PUNTING	No.	Avg.
Dilts	96	36.4

KICKING	XP	Att.	%	FG	Att.	%
Turner	31	35	89	11	22	50

OAKLAND RAIDERS

RUSHING

Last Name	No.	Yds.	Avg.	TD
van Eeghen	270	1080	4.0	9
Whittington	172	661	3.8	7
Robiskie	49	189	3.9	2
Banaszak	43	137	3.2	0
Russell	11	65	5.9	0
Hart	7	44	6.3	0
Bradshaw	1	5	5.0	0
Casper	1	5	5.0	0
C. Davis	14	4	0.3	0
Stabler	4	0	0.0	0
Humm	5	−4	−0.8	0

RECEIVING

Last Name	No.	Yds.	Avg.	TD
Casper	62	852	14	9
Branch	49	709	15	1
Bradshaw	40	552	14	2
van Eeghen	27	291	11	0
Whittington	23	106	5	0
Biletnikoff	20	285	14	2
Chester	13	146	11	2
Banaszak	7	78	11	0
Robiskie	5	51	10	0
C. Davis	4	24	6	0
Hart	1	1	1	0

PUNT RETURNS

Last Name	No.	Yds.	Avg.	TD
Colzie	47	310	7	0

KICKOFF RETURNS

Last Name	No.	Yds.	Avg.	TD
Whittington	23	473	21	0
Hart	11	252	23	0
Ramsey	7	125	18	0
Brunson	6	154	26	0
Stewart	4	120	30	0
Robiskie	3	58	19	0
Chester	2	27	14	0
Russell	2	−3	−2	0
Colzie	1	15	15	0
Mason	1	12	12	0

PASSING – PUNTING – KICKING

PASSING	Att.	Comp.	%	Yds.	Yd./Att.	TD	Int.–%	RK
Stabler	406	237	58	2944	7.3	16	30– 7	11
Humm	26	14	54	151	5.8	0	1– 4	
Casper	1	0	0	0	0.0	0	0– 0	

PUNTING	No.	Avg.
Guy	81	42.7

KICKING	XP	Att.	%	FG	Att.	%
Mann	33	38	87	12	20	60

SAN DIEGO CHARGERS

RUSHING

Last Name	No.	Yds.	Avg.	TD
Mitchell	214	820	3.8	3
Woods	151	514	3.4	3
Bauer	85	304	3.6	8
Matthews	71	286	4.0	0
C. Williams	27	76	2.8	0
Fouts	20	43	2.2	2
McCrary	2	18	9.0	0
Anderson	3	11	3.7	0
Jefferson	1	7	7.0	0
Harris	10	7	0.7	0
Rodgers	1	5	5.0	0
West	1	0	0.0	0
Olander	1	−3	−3.0	0

RECEIVING

Last Name	No.	Yds.	Avg.	TD
Mitchell	57	500	9	2
Jefferson	56	1001	18	13
Klein	34	413	12	2
Woods	34	295	9	0
Joiner	33	607	18	1
Matthews	11	78	7	0
Bauer	10	78	8	1
Owens	9	188	21	0
Curran	9	92	10	2
Burton	5	127	25	3
Rodgers	5	47	9	0
McDonald	3	84	28	1
McCrary	1	29	29	0
C. Williams	1	17	17	0
Anderson	1	−3	−3	0

PUNT RETURNS

Last Name	No.	Yds.	Avg.	TD
Fuller	39	436	11	0
Rodgers	11	88	8	0
Shaw	4	46	12	0
Owens	1	20	20	0
Goode	1	0	0	0
M. Williams	1	0	0	0

KICKOFF RETURNS

Last Name	No.	Yds.	Avg.	TD
Owens	20	524	26	0
Rodgers	11	287	26	0
C. Williams	6	143	24	0
Anderson	6	83	14	0
Fuller	5	109	22	0
Woods	2	37	19	0
Horn	2	27	14	0
Preston	1	15	15	0
Klein	1	13	13	0
Macek	1	6	6	0
Middleton	1	5	5	0
Slater	1	3	3	0
Stringert	1	0	0	0

PASSING – PUNTING – KICKING

PASSING	Att.	Comp.	%	Yds.	Yd./Att.	TD	Int.–%	RK
Fouts	381	224	59	2999	7.9	24	20– 5	2
Harris	88	42	48	518	5.9	2	9– 10	
Olander	8	5	63	49	6.1	0	1– 13	

PUNTING	No.	Avg.
West	73	37.3

KICKING	XP	Att.	%	FG	Att.	%
Benirshke	37	43	86	18	22	82

SEATTLE SEAHAWKS

RUSHING

Last Name	No.	Yds.	Avg.	TD
Smith	165	805	4.9	6
Sims	174	752	4.3	14
Hunter	105	348	3.3	2
Zorn	59	290	4.9	6
Testerman	43	155	3.6	0
Crawford	8	19	2.4	0
Raible	2	13	6.5	0
Myer	2	10	5.0	0
Benjamin	1	7	7.0	0
Weaver	2	−5	−2.5	0

RECEIVING

Last Name	No.	Yds.	Avg.	TD
Largent	71	1168	17	8
McCullum	37	525	14	3
Sims	30	195	7	1
Smith	28	366	13	1
Raible	22	316	14	1
Howard	18	251	14	1
Testerman	17	143	8	0
Hunter	12	172	14	0
Fergerson	11	116	11	0
Sawyer	9	101	11	0
Crawford	4	25	6	0
Peets	1	14	14	0
Benjamin	1	9	9	0

PUNT RETURNS

Last Name	No.	Yds.	Avg.	TD
Crawford	34	284	8	0
Harris	5	58	12	0
Geddes	1	0	0	0

KICKOFF RETURNS

Last Name	No.	Yds.	Avg.	TD
Hunter	16	385	24	0
Crawford	35	829	24	0
Fergerson	10	236	24	0
Long	4	35	9	0
Testerman	1	19	19	0
Boyd	1	6	6	0

PASSING – PUNTING – KICKING

PASSING	Att.	Comp.	%	Yds.	Yd./Att.	TD	Int.–%	RK
Zorn	443	248	56	3283	7.4	15	20– 5	6
Myer	22	11	50	94	4.3	0	2– 9	
Sims	1	1	100	15	15.0	0	0– 0	
Weaver	1	1	100	9	9.0	0	0– 0	

PUNTING	No.	Avg.
Weaver	66	37.0
Herrera	3	24.3

KICKING	XP	Att.	%	FG	Att.	%
Herrera	40	44	91	13	21	62

KANSAS CITY CHIEFS

RUSHING

Last Name	No.	Yds.	Avg.	TD
Reed	206	1053	5.1	5
McKnight	104	627	6.0	6
Morgado	160	593	3.7	7
Bailey	83	298	3.6	0
Lane	52	277	5.3	0
Belton	24	79	3.3	0
Livingston	23	49	2.1	1
Adams	9	15	1.7	0
Andrusyshyn	1	0	0.0	0
Marshall	1	−5	−5.0	0

RECEIVING

Last Name	No.	Yds.	Avg.	TD
Reed	48	483	10	1
White	42	340	8	1
Lane	36	279	8	0
Marshall	26	433	17	2
McKnight	14	83	6	1
Belton	11	88	8	0
Dorsey	9	169	19	2
Morgado	7	47	7	0
Samuels	6	97	16	0
Bailey	5	13	3	0

PUNT RETURNS

Last Name	No.	Yds.	Avg.	TD
Payton	32	364	11	0
Marshall	6	51	9	0
Burgmeier	4	59	15	0
Green	1	6	6	0
Sanders	1	5	5	0
Dorsey	1	3	3	0

KICKOFF RETURNS

Last Name	No.	Yds.	Avg.	TD
Payton	30	775	26	0
Belton	9	227	25	0
Morgado	5	100	20	0
Beckman	3	74	25	0
McKnight	3	65	22	0
Sanders	2	15	8	0
Green	1	27	27	0
Paul	1	0	0	0

PASSING – PUNTING – KICKING

PASSING	Att.	Comp.	%	Yds.	Yd./Att.	TD	Int.–%	RK
Livingston	290	159	55	1573	5.4	5	13– 5	13
Adams	79	44	56	415	5.3	2	3– 4	
White	1	1	100	44	44.0	0	0– 0	

PUNTING	No.	Avg.
Andrusyshym	79	41.1

KICKING	XP	Att.	%	FG	Att.	%
Stenerud	25	26	96	20	30	67

1978 N.F.C. PLAYOFFS

December 24 at Atlanta (Attendance 49,447)

SCORING

PHIL.	**6**	**0**	**7**	**0–13**
ATL.	**0**	**0**	**0**	**14–14**

First Quarter

Phil.	Carmichael 13 yard pass from Jaworski PAT – kick failed (Michel)

Third Quarter

Phil.	Montgomery 1 yard rush PAT – Michel (kick)

Fourth Quarter

Atl.	Mitchell 19 yard pass from Bartkowski PAT – Mazzetti (kick)
Atl.	Francis 37 yard pass from Bartkowski PAT – Mazzetti (kick)

TEAM STATISTICS

PHIL.		ATL.
15	First Downs	14
32–53	Rushes–Yards	27–75
164	Passing Yards	223
95	Return Yards	14
19–35–0	Passing	18–32–2
9–33.7	Punting	7–33.1
3–2	Fumbles–Lost	3–3
5–60	Penalties–Yards	6–63
2	Giveaways	5
5	Takeaways	2
–3	Difference	–3

INDIVIDUAL STATISTICS

RUSHING

PHILADELPHIA	No.	Yds.	Avg.	ATLANTA	No.	Yds.	Avg.
Hogan	14	37	2.2	Stanback	16	58	3.3
Montgomery	16	19	1.2	Bean	9	14	1.6
Jaworski	1	3	3.0	Bartkowski	2	3	1.5
Campfield	1	0	0.0				

RECEIVING

PHILADELPHIA	No.	Yds.	Avg.	ATLANTA	No.	Yds.	Avg.
Smith	7	108	15.4	Francis	6	135	22.5
Carmichael	5	45	9.0	Bean	4	44	11.0
Osborne	3	15	5.0	Mitchell	3	35	11.7
Middlebrook	1	11	11.0	Stanback	2	7	3.5
Payne	1	10	10.0	Pearson	1	13	13.0
Hogan	1	6	6.0	Ryckman	1	5	5.0
Montgomery	1	–5	–5.0	Jackson	1	4	4.0

PASSING

	Att.	Comp.	Comp. Pct.	Yds.	Int.	Yds./Att.	Yds./Comp.
PHILADELPHIA							
Jaworski	35	19	54.3	190	0	5.4	10.0
ATLANTA							
Bartkowski	32	18	56.3	243	2	7.6	13.5

December 30 at Dallas (Attendance (69,338)

SCORING

ATL.	**7**	**13**	**0**	**0–20**
DAL.	**10**	**3**	**7**	**7–27**

First Quarter

Dal.	Septien 34 yard field goal
Atl.	Bean 14 yard rush PAT – Mazzetti (kick)
Dal.	Laidlaw 12 yard rush PAT – Septien (kick)

Second Quarter

Atl.	Mazzetti 42 yard field goal
Dal.	Septien 48 yard field goal
Atl.	Francis 17 yard pass from Bartkowski PAT – Mazzetti (kick)
Atl.	Mazzetti 22 yard field goal

Third Quarter

Dal.	Smith 2 yard pass from White PAT – Septien (kick)

Fourth Quarter

Dal.	Laidlaw 1 yard rush PAT – Septien (kick)

TEAM STATISTICS

ATL		DAL.
16	First Downs	26
36–164	Rushes–Yards	37–148
52	Passing Yards	221
0	Return Yards	69
8–23–3	Passing	17–37–1
6–37.5	Punting	3–36.0
0–0	Fumbles–Lost	6–3
7–69	Penalties–Yards	7–65
3	Giveaways	4
4	Takeaways	3
–1	Difference	–1

INDIVIDUAL STATISTICS

RUSHING

ATLANTA	No.	Yds.	Avg.	DALLAS	No.	Yds.	Avg.
Bean	17	72	4.2	Laidlaw	17	66	3.9
Stanbach	9	62	6.9	Dorsett	14	65	4.6
Franklin	8	24	3.0	DuPree	1	20	20.0
Esposito	2	6	3.0	Staubach	1	3	3.0
				P. Pearson	1	–2	–2.0
				White	3	–4	–1.3

RECEIVING

ATLANTA	No.	Yds.	Avg.	DALLAS	No.	Yds.	Avg.
Francis	6	66	11.0	D. Pearson	4	75	18.8
Ryckman	1	22	22.0	DuPree	5	59	11.8
Esposito	1	7	7.0	Smith	3	38	12.7
				Hill	3	36	12.0
				Laidlaw	1	15	15.0
				Dorsett	1	9	9.0

PASSING

	Att.	Comp.	Comp. Pct.	Yds.	Int.	Yds./Att.	Yds./Comp.
ATLANTA							
Bartkowski	23	8	34.8	95	3	4.1	11.9
DALLAS							
Staubach	17	7	41.2	105	0	6.2	15.0
White	20	10	50.0	127	1	6.4	12.7

December 31 at Los Angeles (Attendance 69,631)

SCORING

MIN.	**3**	**7**	**0**	**0–10**
L.A.	**0**	**10**	**14**	**10–34**

First Quarter

Min.	Danmeier 42 yard field goal

Second Quarter

L.A.	Miller 9 yard pass from Haden PAT – Corral (kick)
L.A.	Corral 43 yard field goal
Min.	Rashad 1 yard pass from Tarkenton PAT – Danmeier (kick)

Third Quarter

L.A.	Bryant 3 yard rush PAT – Corral (kick)
L.A.	Jessie 27 yard pass from Haden PAT – Corral (kick)

Fourth Quarter

L.A.	Corral 28 yard field goal
L.A.	Jodat 3 yard rush PAT – Corral (kick)

TEAM STATISTICS

MINN.		L.A.
12	First Downs	25
16–36	Rushes–Yards	48–200
208	Passing yards	209
10	Return Yards	99
18–38–2	Passing	15–29–1
6–41.3	Punting	4–31.0
2–0	Fumbles–Lost	1–0
2–12	Penalties–Yards	4–35
2	Giveaways	1
1	Takeaways	2
–1	Difference	–1

INDIVIDUAL STATISTICS

RUSHING

MINNESOTA	No.	Yds.	Avg.	LOS ANGELES	No.	Yds.	Avg.
Foreman	13	31	2.4	Bryant	27	100	3.7
Kellar	2	7	3.5	Cappelletti	10	44	4.4
Tarkenton	1	–2	–2.0	Davis	4	17	4.3
				Haden	2	15	7.5
				Phillips	2	10	5.0
				Waddy	1	9	9.0
				Jodat	1	3	3.0
				Nelson	1	2	2.0

RECEIVING

MINNESOTA	No.	Yds.	Avg.	LOS ANGELES	No.	Yds.	Avg.
Rashad	7	84	12.0	Jessie	6	108	18.0
Young	4	49	12.3	Young	2	30	15.0
Tucker	4	48	12.0	Miller	2	29	14.5
Foreman	3	38	12.7	Nelson	1	13	13.0
				Bryant	2	13	6.5
				Waddy	1	10	10.0
				Cappelletti	1	6	6.0

PASSING

	Att.	Comp.	Comp. Pct.	Yds.	Int.	Yds./Att.	Yds./Comp.
MINNESOTA							
Tarkenton	37	18	48.6	219	2	5.9	12.2
LOS ANGELES							
Haden	29	15	51.7	209	1	7.2	13.9

1978 A.F.C. PLAYOFFS

December 24 at Miami (Attendance 70,036)

SCORING

HOU.	7	0	0	10–17
MIA.	7	0	0	2–9

First Quarter
- Mia. Tillman 13 yard pass from Griese
  - PAT-Yepremian (kick)
- Hou. Wilson 12 yard pass from Pastorini
  - PAT-Fritsch (kick)

Fourth Quarter
- Hou. Fritsch 35 yard field goal
- Hou. Campbell 1 yard rush
  - PAT-Fritsch (kick)
- Mia. Safety–Pastorini ran out of end zone

TEAM STATISTICS

HOU.		MIA.
23	First Downs	14
45–165	Rushes–Yards	25–91
290	Passing Yards	118
15	Return Yards	24
20–30–0	Passing	12–30–3
5–44.0	Punting	5–48.6
3–1	Fumbles–Lost	2–2
5–37	Penalties–Yards	1–5
1	Giveaways	5
5	Takeaways	1
+4	Difference	−4

INDIVIDUAL STATISTICS

RUSHING

HOUSTON	No.	Yds.	Avg.	MIAMI	No.	Yds.	Avg.
Campbell	26	84	3.0	L. Harris	9	43	4.8
Wilson	14	76	5.4	Williams	13	41	3.2
Poole	1	12	12.0	Moore	1	7	7.0
Coleman	1	2	2.0	Bulaich	2	0	0.0
Pastorini	3	−9	−3.0				

RECEIVING

HOUSTON	No.	Yds.	Avg.	MIAMI	No.	Yds.	Avg.
Burrough	6	103	17.2	D. Harris	4	42	10.5
Wilson	5	40	8.0	Moore	2	28	14.0
Barber	4	112	28.0	Tillman	2	24	12.0
Woods	2	22	11.0	Bulaich	2	14	7.0
Campbell	1	13	13.0	L. Harris	1	21	21.0
Caster	1	11	11.0	Williams	1	8	8.0
Coleman	1	5	5.0				

PASSING

HOUSTON	Att.	Comp.	Comp. Pct.	Yds.	Int.	Yds./ Att.	Yds./ Comp.
Pastorini	29	20	68.9	306	0	10.6	15.3
Barber	1	0	0.0	0	0	0.0	0.0
MIAMI							
Griese	28	11	39.3	114	2	4.1	10.4
Strock	2	1	50.0	23	1	16.5	23.0

December 30 at Pittsburgh (Attendance 48,921)

SCORING

DEN.	3	7	0	0–10
PIT.	6	13	0	14–33

First Quarter
- Den. Turner 37 yard field goal
- Pit. Harris 1 yard rush
  - PAT – Kick failed

Second Quarter
- Pit. Harris 18 yard rush
  - PAT – Gerela (kick)
- Pit. Gerela 24 yard field goal
- Den. Preston 3 yard rush
  - PAT – Turner (kick)
- Pit. Gerela 27 yard field goal

Fourth Quarter
- Pit. Stallworth 45 yard pass from Bradshaw
  - PAT – Gerela (kick)
- Pit. Swann 38 yard pass from Bradshaw
  - PAT – Gerela (kick)

TEAM STATISTICS

DEN.		PIT.
15	First Downs	24
27–87	Rushes–Yards	40–153
131	Passing Yards	272
110	Return Yards	93
12–22–0	Passing	16–29–1
6 34.0	Punting	2–00.0
2–2	Fumbles–Lost	4–1
8–104	Penalties–Yards	11–88
2	Giveaways	2
2	Takeaways	2
0	Difference	0

INDIVIDUAL STATISTICS

RUSHING

DENVER	No.	Yds.	Avg.	PITTSBURGH	No.	Yds.	Avg.
Weese	4	43	10.8	Harris	24	105	4.4
Preston	4	14	3.5	Bleier	8	26	3.3
Keyworth	6	12	2.0	Moser	2	6	3.0
Lytle	5	6	1.2	J. Smith	1	4	4.0
Perrin	6	6	1.0	Deloplaine	1	4	4.0
Armstrong	1	3	3.0	Bradshaw	2	4	2.0
Canada	1	3	3.0	Thornton	2	4	2.0

RECEIVING

DENVER	No.	Yds.	Avg.	PITTSBURGH	No.	Yds.	Avg.
Dolbin	4	77	19.3	Stallworth	10	156	15.6
Moses	2	33	16.5	Grossman	4	64	16.0
Preston	2	19	9.5	Swann	2	52	26.0
Perrin	2	16	8.0				
Odoms	1	24	24.0				
Lytle	1	−1	−1.0				

PASSING

DENVER	Att.	Comp.	Comp. Pct.	Yds.	Int.	Yds./ Att.	Yds./ Comp.
Morton	5	3	60.0	34	0	6.8	11.3
Weese	16	8	50.0	118	0	7.4	14.8
PITTSBURGH							
Bradshaw	29	16	55.2	272	1	9.4	17.0

December 31 at Foxboro, Mass. (Attendance 60,881)

SCORING

HOU.	0	21	3	7–31
N.E.	0	0	7	7–14

Second Quarter
- Hou. Burrough 71 yard pass from Pastorini
  - PAT – Fritsch (kick)
- Hou. Barber 19 yard pass from Pastorini
  - PAT – Fritsch (kick)
- Hou. Barber 13 yard pass from Pastorini
  - PAT – Fritsch (kick)

Third Quarter
- Hou. Fritsch 30 yard field goal
- N.E. Jackson 24 yard pass from Johnson
  - PAT – Posey (kick)

Fourth Quarter
- N.E. Francis 24 yard pass from Owen
  - PAT – Posey (kick)
- Hou. Campbell 2 yard rush
  - PAT – Fritsch (kick)

TEAM STATISTICS

HOU.		N.E.
21	First Downs	15
54–174	Rushes–Yards	20–83
170	Passing Yards	180
105	Return Yards	142
12–15–1	Passing	16–35–3
5–34.8	Punting	4–43.3
1-0	Fumbles-Lost	2-0
2-25	Penalties-Yards	8-92
1	Giveaways	3
3	Takeaways	1
+2	Difference	−2

INDIVIDUAL STATISTICS

RUSHING

HOUSTON	No.	Yds.	Avg.	NEW ENGLAND	No.	Yds.	Avg.
Campbell	27	118	4.4	Cunningham	10	42	4.2
T. Wilson	14	26	1.9	Grogan	1	16	16.0
Coleman	7	19	2.7	Johnson	6	14	2.3
Duncan	2	7	3.5	Ivory	3	11	3.7
Poole	3	7	2.3				
Nielson	1	−3	−3.0				

RECEIVING

HOUSTON	No.	Yds.	Avg.	NEW ENGLAND	No.	Yds.	Avg.
Barber	5	83	16.6	Francis	8	101	12.6
Burrough	3	91	30.3	Cunningham	3	28	9.3
Caster	2	12	6.0	Morgan	2	37	18.5
Campbell	1	10	10.0	Johnson	2	16	8.0
Woods	1	4	4.0	Jackson	1	24	24.0

PASSING

HOUSTON	Att.	Comp.	Comp. Pct.	Yds.	Int.	Yds./ Att.	Yds./ Comp.
Pastorini	15	12	80.0	200	1	13.3	16.7
NEW ENGLAND							
Grogan	12	3	25.0	38	2	3.2	12.7
Owen	22	12	54.5	144	1	6.5	12.0
Johnson	1	1	100.0	24	0	24.0	24.0

1978 Championship Games

NFC CHAMPIONSHIP GAME

January 7, 1979 at Los Angeles
(Attendance 71,086)

SCORING

DALLAS	0	0	7	21–28
LOS ANGELES	0	0	0	0– 0

Third Quarter
- Dal. Dorsett 5 yard rush PAT – Septien (kick)

Fourth Quarter
- Dal. Laidlaw 4 yard pass from Staubach PAT – Septien (kick)
- Dal. DuPree 11 yard pass from Staubach PAT – Septien (kick)
- Dal. Henderson 68 yard interception return PAT – Septien (kick)

TEAM STATISTICS

DALL.		L. A.
16	First Downs	15
33–126	Rushes–Yards	31–81
109	Passing Yards	96
163	Return Yards	22
13–25–2	Passing	14–35–5
8–35.0	Punting	5–39.0
2–1	Fumbles–Lost	3–2
10–85	Penalties–Yards	5–40
3	Giveaways	7
7	Takeaways	3
+4	Difference	–4

Three times in the past four years, Chuck Knox had led the Rams into the NFC title game only to be turned back from the gates of the Super Bowl. This year, Knox was gone and the Rams again went down to defeat in the next-to-last weekend of the season.

The sterling Los Angeles defense did its part in the first half, shutting out the Dallas offense. The Ram attack, however, failed to score any points against the Doomsday Defense of Dallas. At halftime, neither team had scored, and observers waited to see who would first cash in on their opponent's mistakes.

The Cowboys cashed in. Midway through the third period, Ram quarterback Pat Haden shot a pass at tight end Terry Nelson, only to have Dallas safety Charlie Waters pick it off. Waters presented Roger Staubach & Co. with the ball on the Los Angeles 10-yard line, and Tony Dorsett shortly broke into the end zone with the first points of the day.

The Rams responded with their biggest offensive threat of the day. They reached the Dallas 13-yard line but lost the ball on a failed fourth-and-one power play. Later in the period, Charlie Waters intercepted another Haden pass, giving Dallas possession 20 yards from the end zone. Just shy of a minute into the fourth quarter, Staubach hit Scott Laidlaw with a short touchdown pass to run the lead to a formidable 14-0

The Rams tried futilely to come back under sub QB Vince Ferragamo, who came in when Haden broke his right thumb in the third quarter. The Cowboys held the Rams off and posted two more touchdowns in the final three minutes. Staubach hit Billy Joe DuPree with a short scoring pass, and Thomas Henderson intercepted a Ferragamo pass and bolted 68 yards to score.

INDIVIDUAL STATISTICS

RUSHING

DALLAS	No.	Yds.	Avg.	LOS ANGELES	No.	Yds.	Avg.
Dorsett	17	101	5.9	Bryant	20	52	2.6
Laidlaw	10	20	2.0	Haden	2	20	10.0
Staubach	3	7	2.3	Cappelletti	3	19	6.3
Newhouse	1	4	4.0	Phillips	3	2	0.7
DuPree	1	3	3.0	Jodat	2	–5	–2.5
Smith	1	–9	–9.0	Waddy	1	–7	–7.0
	33	126	3.8		31	81	2.6

RECEIVING

DALLAS	No.	Yds.	Avg.	LOS ANGELES	No.	Yds.	Avg.
DuPree	3	48	16.0	Jessie	4	42	10.5
Johnson	2	19	9.5	Miller	3	96	32.0
D. Pearson	2	19	9.5	Waddy	2	23	11.5
Dorsett	2	15	7.5	Bryant	2	2	1.0
P. Pearson	2	12	6.0	Scales	1	18	18.0
Hill	1	9	9.0	Cappelletti	1	15	15.0
Laidlaw	1	4	4.0	Nelson	1	10	10.0
	13	126	9.7		14	206	13.9

PUNTING

DALLAS	No.	Yds.	Avg.	LOS ANGELES	No.	Yds.	Avg.
D. White	8		35.0	Walker	5		39.0

PUNT RETURNS

DALLAS	No.	Yds.	Avg.	LOS ANGELES	No.	Yds.	Avg.
Johnson	4	40	10.0	Wallace	2	22	11.0

KICKOFF RETURNS

DALLAS	No.	Yds.	Avg.	LOS ANGELES	No.	Yds.	Avg.
none				Jodat	3	59	19.7
				Marshall	2	47	23.5
					5	106	21.2

INTERCEPTION RETURNS

DALLAS	No.	Yds.	Avg.	LOS ANGELES	No.	Yds.	Avg.
Waters	2	49	24.5	Thomas	1	0	0.0
Henderson	1	68	68.0	Cromwell	1	0	0.0
Harris	1	5	5.0		2	0	0.0
Hughes	1	1	1.0				
	5	123	24.6				

PASSING

	Att.	Comp.	Comp. Pct.	Yds.	Int.	Yds./ Att.	Yds./ Comp.
DALLAS							
Staubach	25	13	52.0	126	2	5.0	9.7
LOS ANGELES							
Haden	19	7	36.8	76	3	4.0	10.0
Ferragamo	16	7	43.8	130	2	8.1	18.6

AFC CHAMPIONSHIP GAME

January 7, 1979 at Pittsburgh
(Attendance 50,725)

SCORING

HOUSTON	0	3	2	0– 5
PITTSBURGH	14	17	3	0–34

First Quarter
- Pit. Harris 7 yard rush PAT – Gerela (kick)
- Pit. Bleier 15 yard rush PAT – Gerela (kick)

Second Quarter
- Hou. Fritsch 19 yard field goal
- Pit. Swann 29 yard pass from Bradshaw PAT – Gerela (kick)
- Pit. Stallworth 17 yard pass from Bradshaw PAT – Gerela (kick)
- Pit. Gerela 37 yard field goal

Third Quarter
- Pit. Gerela 22 yard field goal
- Hou. Safety–Bleier tackled in end zone

TEAM STATISTICS

HOU.		PITT.
10	First Downs	21
26–72	Rushes–Yards	47–179
70	Passing Yards	200
179	Return Yards	217
12–26–5	Passing	11–19–2
6–39.5	Punting	1–53.0
6–4	Fumbles–Lost	6–3
5–48	Penalties–Yards	4–32
9	Giveaways	5
5	Takeaways	9
–4	Difference	+4

The setting was Three Rivers Stadium in Pittsburgh in a cold, steady rain. The principles were the time-tested Steelers and the upstart Houston Oilers. The result was a romp.

The Oilers had come this far on Earl Campbell's running, Dan Pastorini's passing, and a tough defense. The slippery footing negated Campbell, the Steel Curtain stifled Pastorini, and the Pittsburgh offense broke the Oiler defense.

The Steelers acclimated themselves to the weather right from the start. Twice in the first quarter, they drove for touchdowns, with Franco Harris and Rocky Bleier scoring the points.

Until late in the second quarter, the only points of the period were a Houston field goal. Then, within the last 48 seconds, the Steelers scored 17 points. Terry Bradshaw hit Lynn Swann with a 29-yard touchdown pass to run the score to 21-3. Oiler returner Johnnie Dirden fumbled the ensuing kickoff, Rick Moser recovered for Pittsburgh, and Bradshaw immediately threw to John Stallworth for another score. After the kickoff, Ronnie Coleman fumbled on the first play from scrimmage, giving the Steelers a chance to add three more points before time expired.

The shell-shocked Oilers returned for the second half with an insurmountable deficit. With the weather and playing field continuing to deteriorate, the only points of the second half were a Pittsburgh field goal and a safety by the Houston defense.

The confrontation between Earl Campbell and Franco Harris was defused by the rain, with Campbell running for 62 yards and Harris 51. In every team category, however, including the score, the Steelers were far superior.

INDIVIDUAL STATISTICS

RUSHING

HOUSTON	No.	Yds.	Avg.	PITTSBURGH	No.	Yds.	Avg.
Campbell	22	62	2.8	Harris	20	51	2.6
Woods	1	9	9.0	Bleier	10	45	4.5
T. Wilson	2	6	3.0	Bradshaw	7	29	4.1
Coleman	1	–5	–5.0	Deloplaine	3	28	9.3
	26	72	2.8	Thornton	3	22	7.3
				Moser	3	7	2.3
				Kruczek	1	–3	–3.0
					47	179	3.8

RECEIVING

HOUSTON	No.	Yds.	Avg.	PITTSBURGH	No.	Yds.	Avg.
Caster	5	44	8.8	Swann	4	98	24.5
T. Wilson	5	33	6.6	Bleier	4	42	10.5
Coleman	1	15	15.0	Grossman	2	43	21.5
Campbell	1	4	4.0	Stallworth	1	17	17.0
	12	96	8.0		11	200	18.2

PUNTING

HOUSTON	No.	Yds.	Avg.	PITTSBURGH	No.	Yds.	Avg.
Parsley	6		39.5	Colquitt	1		53.0

PUNT RETURNS

HOUSTON	No.	Yds.	Avg.	PITTSBURGH	No.	Yds.	Avg.
none				Bell	6	91	15.1

KICKOFF RETURNS

HOUSTON	No.	Yds.	Avg.	PITTSBURGH	No.	Yds.	Avg.
Dirden	3	72	26.0	Deloplaine	1	21	21.0
Merkens	2	57	28.5	L. Anderson	1	15	15.0
Woods	2	33	16.5		2	36	18.0
Duncan	1	17	17.0				
	8	179	22.4				

INTERCEPTION RETURNS

HOUSTON	No.	Yds.	Avg.	PITTSBURGH	No.	Yds.	Avg.
Alexander	1	0	0.0	Toews	1	35	35.0
Stemrick	1	0	0.0	Johnson	1	34	34.0
	2	0	0.0	Blount	1	16	16.0
				Shell	1	5	5.0
				Ham	1	0	0.0
					5	90	18.0

PASSING

	Att.	Comp.	Comp. Pct.	Yds.	Int.	Yds./ Att.	Yds./ Comp.
HOUSTON							
Pastorini	26	15	57.7	96	5	3.7	6.4
PITTSBURGH							
Bradshaw	19	11	57.8	200	2	10.5	18.2

January 21, 1979 at Miami

Steeling the Rubber Match

Champions clashed, both two-time Super Bowl winners and both symbols of excellence. If the Cowboys were perceived as slightly flashier, the Steelers were perceived as slightly more physical. Three years ago, the Steelers had beaten the Cowboys for the crown. Now the Cowboys were the defending champs.

The Cowboys looked like champs in their opening drive until they fumbled on a razzle-dazzle play in Pittsburgh territory. Six plays later, Terry Bradshaw threw to John Stallworth for a 7-0 Steeler lead. Later in the period, Harvey Martin caused Bradshaw to fumble, and three plays later, Roger Staubach evened the score with a pass to Tony Hill.

Dallas went ahead early in the second quarter when Mike Hegman picked up Bradshaw's fumble and raced 37 yards to score. Two minutes later, John Stallworth broke Aaron Kyle's tackle on a short pass and ran for a 75-yard TD. Just before the halftime break, the Steelers went ahead on a Bradshaw-to-Bleier pass.

The Cowboys drove into Steeler territory in the third quarter, but when Jackie Smith dropped a pass while open in the end zone, they had to settle for three points.

The Steelers increased their four-point lead in the final quarter. A pass interference call against Benny Barnes moved the Steelers deep into Dallas territory, and then the classy Pittsburgh front line opened the way for Franco Harris to rumble 22 yards to score. On the following kickoff, Randy White fumbled a short kick. Bradshaw threw to Swann in the end zone on the next play to run the score to 35-17 with about six minutes left. Although Staubach rallied the Cowboys to two touchdowns in the final minutes, the Steelers, led by MVP Bradshaw, had secured their third Super Bowl title.

LINEUPS

PITTSBURGH		DALLAS
	OFFENSE	
Stallworth	WR	Hill
Kolb	LT	Donovan
Davis	LG	Scott
Webster	C	Fitzgerald
Mullins	RG	Rafferty
Pinney	RT	Wright
Grossman	TE	DuPree
Swann	WR	D. Pearson
Bradshaw	QB	Staubach
Bleier	RB	Newhouse
Harris	RB	Dorsett
	DEFENSE	
Greenwood	LE	Jones
Greene	LT	Cole
Furness	RT	R. White
Banaszak	RE	Martin
Ham	LLB	Henderson
Lambert	MLB	Breunig
Toews	RLB	Lewis
Johnson	LCB	Barnes
Blount	RCB	Kyle
Shell	SS	Waters
Wagner	FS	Harris

SUBSTITUTES

PITTSBURGH

OFFENSE	
Bell	Mandich
Brown	Moser
Courson	Peterson
Cunningham	Smith
Deloplaine	Stoudt
Kruczek	Thornton
DEFENSE	
F. Anderson	Dunn
L. Anderson	Oldham
Beasley	White
Cole	Winston
Dungy	
KICKERS	
Colquitt	Gerela

DALLAS

OFFENSE	
Blackwell	Lawless
Brinson	P. Pearson
Carano	Randall
Cooper	Smith
Frederick	Steele
Johnson	D. White
Laidlaw	
DEFENSE	
Bethea	Pugh
Brown	Stalls
Hegman	Thurman
Hughes	Washington
Huther	
KICKERS	
Septien	

SCORING

PITTSBURGH	**7**	**14**	**0**	**14–35**
DALLAS	**7**	**7**	**3**	**14–31**

First Quarter

Pit.	Stallworth 28 yard pass from Bradshaw PAT – Gerela (kick)
Dal.	Hill 39 yard pass from Staubach PAT – Septien (kick)

Second Quarter

Dal.	Hegman 37 yard fumble return PAT – Septien (kick)
Pit.	Stallworth 75 yard pass from Bradshaw PAT – Gerela (kick)
Pit.	Bleier 7 yard pass from Bradshaw PAT – Gerela (kick)

Third Quarter

Dal.	Septien 27 yard field goal

Fourth Quarter

Pit.	Harris 22 yard rush PAT – Gerela (kick)
Pit.	Swann 18 yard pass from Bradshaw PAT – Gerela (kick)
Dal.	DuPree 7 yard pass from Staubach PAT – Septien (kick)
Dal.	Johnson 4 yard pass from Staubach PAT – Septien (kick)

TEAM STATISTICS

PIT.		DAL.
19	First Downs–Total	20
2	First Downs–Rushing	6
15	First Downs–Passing	13
2	First Downs–Penalty	1
2	Fumbles–Number	3
2	Fumbles Lost	2
5	Penalties–Number	9
35	Yards Penalized	89
1	Missed Field Goals	0
58	Offensive Plays	67
357	Net Yards	330
6.2	Average Gain	4.9
3	Giveaways	3
3	Takeaways	3
0	Difference	0

INDIVIDUAL STATISTICS

PITTSBURGH	No.	Yds.	Avg.	DALLAS	No.	Yds.	Avg.
RUSHING							
Harris	20	68	3.4	Dorsett	16	96	6.0
Bleier	2	3	1.5	Staubach	4	37	9.3
Bradshaw	2	–5	–2.5	Laidlaw	3	12	4.0
	24	66	2.8	P. Pearson	1	6	6.0
				Newhouse	8	3	0.4
					32	154	4.8
RECEIVING							
Swann	7	124	17.7	Dorsett	5	44	8.8
Stallworth	3	115	38.3	D. Pearson	4	73	18.3
Grossman	3	29	9.7	Hill	2	49	24.5
Bell	2	21	10.5	Johnson	2	30	15.0
Harris	1	22	22.0	DuPree	2	17	8.5
Bleier	1	7	7.0	P. Pearson	2	15	7.5
	17	318	18.7		17	228	13.4
PUNTING							
Colquitt	3		43.0	D. White	5		39.6
PUNT RETURNS							
Bell	4	27	6.3	Johnson	2	33	16.5
KICKOFF RETURNS							
L. Anderson	3	45	15.0	Johnson	3	63	21.0
				Brinson	2	41	20.5
				R. White	1	0	0.0
					6	104	17.3
INTERCEPTION RETURNS							
Blount	1	13	13.0	Lewis	1	21	21.0

PASSING

	Att.	Comp.	Comp. Pct.	Yds.	Int.	Yds./ Att.	Yds./ Comp.	Yards Lost Tackled
PITTSBURGH								
Bradshaw	30	17	56.7	318	1	10.6	18.7	4—27
DALLAS								
Staubach	30	17	56.7	228	1	7.6	13.4	5—52

1979 N.F.C. . . . Never to Lose Their Crowns

Many seasons ago, A.E. Housman wrote a poem mourning an athlete who died young. Those feelings were stirred with unusual frequency in 1979. In April, a car accident killed Atlanta linebacker Andy Spiva and seriously injured teammate Garth Ten Napel. In June, Giants defensive tackle Troy Archer lost his life in a car accident in New Jersey, not far from Giants Stadium. One month later, St. Louis tight end J.V. Cain keeled over on the training field and died from heart failure.

Two other NFL players almost fell to the Grim Reaper this year. Chicago quarterback Vince Evans contracted a staph infection in early October and was critically ill for several days. San Diego kicker Rolf Benirschke had been steadily losing weight until he collapsed after a game in late September. He was hospitalized with Crohn's disease, an intestinal disorder, and only extensive surgery saved his life. Although neither returned to action this year, both would recover and play again.

EASTERN DIVISION

Dallas Cowboys—Holes in the Cowboy defense raised hopes in Philadelphia and Washington. Jethro Pugh had retired, Too Tall Jones decided to quit football for a boxing career, and Charlie Waters tore up a knee in the pre-season. The Dallas defenders rallied around Randy White and Bob Breunig, however, and the Cowboys shot out to a 7-1 record. Roger Staubach piloted the offense to its usual high production. Suddenly, as November began, the Cowboys fell into a dive. They lost four out of five games, including meetings with the Eagles and Redskins. After the loss to the Redskins, coach Tom Landry cut linebacker Thomas Henderson for a supposedly lackadaisical attitude. With the troops in disorder, the Cowboys regrouped for a stretch run. They beat the Giants and the Eagles, and faced the Redskins on the final Sunday of the season with a playoff berth at issue. Washington led 34-21 with just under seven minutes left when Staubach went to work. He threw a touchdown pass to Ron Springs with three minutes left, and after the defense held the Redskins, he hit Tony Hill with a scoring pass 39 seconds from the end. Rafael Septien's kick made the score 35-34 and put the Cowboys into the playoffs, the final showcase for the retiring Staubach.

Philadelphia Eagles—The Eagles showed their maturity when Bill Bergey injured a knee in the third game of the season. With their leader out for the year, the young defense stayed tough and kept the Eagles in playoff contention. Middle guard Charles Johnson stepped into the leadership gap with inspired play. The offense did its share with star performances from Ron Jaworski, Wilbert Montgomery, Harold Carmichael, Keith Krepfle, and Stan Walters. Despite a three-game losing streak in mid-season, the Eagles beat Dallas on Monday night television and clinched a playoff berth with a 44-7 trouncing of the Lions on December 2. One week later, they lost a rematch with the Cowboys, costing Dick Vermeil & Co. a clear shot at first place in the East. Despite a closing victory over Houston, the Eagles had to settle for one of the NFC wild-card slots.

Washington Redskins—Jack Pardee's rebuilding program was supposed to get results only after a few years, but the refurbished defense kept the Redskins in the playoff race. Three young linebackers played behind a good pass-rushing line and in front of a hawkish secondary featuring Lemar Parrish and Ken Houston. The offense relied on a strong ground game and the accurate toe of Mark Moseley. The Skins beat both the Cowboys and Eagles during the year and traveled to Texas Stadium on December 16 to end the season. With a playoff berth at stake, the Redskins took a 17-0 lead over the Cowboys in the first half, but fell behind 21-17 in the third quarter. Fighting the tide of momentum, the Skins surged ahead 34-21 in the fourth quarter. With the taste of playoffs on their lips, the Redskins were thrown out of the banquet. The Cowboys rallied for two touchdowns in the final four minutes to win the game 35-34. A 42-6 Chicago Bear victory earlier in the day meant that the Skins were nosed out of the playoffs by the Bears on a point-differential tie-breaker.

New York Giants—Coach Ray Perkins inspired hope in the fans, but by early October, they had almost lost the faith. Five losses at the start of the year promised continued futility, but then the Giants began to win. Rookie quarterback Phil Simms stepped into the starting lineup in game six and led the way to an upset victory over unbeaten Tampa Bay. The defense featured linebackers Brad Van Pelt and Harry Carson, while the offense breathed new life with the arrival of Simms and fellow rookie Earnest Gray as a deep passing threat. Unheralded Billy Taylor replaced Larry Csonka and ran the ball as well as the departed star had done. A 14-6 victory over the Redskins on November 25 was the high-water point of the season, as the Giants failed to win any of their three final games.

St. Louis Cardinals—A new star come on stage in St. Louis as an old legend exited. Rookie halfback Ottis Anderson ran for 193 yards on opening day against Dallas, and he kept running through NFL defenses for a season total of 1,605 yards. His way was cleared by a line which lost Dan Dierdorf for most of the year with a knee injury, but which still showcased the skills of veterans Tom Banks and Bob Young. Despite the reborn running attack, the Cards lost close games regularly because of defensive breakdowns. Veteran cornerback Roger Wehrli turned in his usual All-Pro performance, but his young mates had much to learn about the pro game. Coach Bud Wilkinson had a strained relationship with team president Bill Bidwill, and when the two quarreled over who should play quarterback in the final three games, Wilkinson was canned. Larry Wilson took over as interim coach, used Steve Pisarkiewicz at QB at Bidwill desired, and led the Cards to two victories. The finale, however, was a 42-6 embarrassment in Chicago.

CENTRAL DIVISION

Tampa Bay Buccaneers—Not long ago, they were the butts of tactless jokes. This year, the Buccaneers stepped into Cinderella's slippers. With Lee Roy Selmon and David Lewis leading a ferocious defense, the Bucs won the first five games of their favorable schedule. While the other Central Division teams stumbled, the Buccaneers took a commanding lead by mid-season. The offense relied on Ricky Bell's running but did not measure up to the defense. Needing one victory to clinch a playoff berth, the Bucs lost three games in a row to the Bears, 49ers, and Chiefs, scoring a total of 10 points in three weeks. The playoff spot which seemed so secure a month earlier was on the line as the Buccaneers hosted the Chiefs in the final Sunday of the schedule. The Tampa Bay defense crushed any thoughts of choking and instead dominated the Kansas City offense. The Bucs could score only on Neil O'Donoghue's fourth-period field goal, but the defense made it stand up for a 3-0 triumph and a ticket to the playoffs.

Chicago Bears—The Bears shuffled quarterbacks, lost fullback Roland Harper with a bad knee, and had their receiver corps decimated by injuries. They also had the peerless Walter Payton and a hard-nosed defense, and they parlayed these assets into a wild-card playoff berth. Once November began, the Bears hit their stride. The offense depended on Payton to control the ball, while safetyman Gary Fencik led the defense to a series of good outings. Although the Lions embarrassed them 20-0 on Thanksgiving Day, the Bears kept driving. By beating Tampa Bay and Green Bay, they went into the final weekend with a slight chance of making the playoffs. Washington had to lose to Dallas, and the Bears had to beat St. Louis and run up a big score to have a better point differential for the season than the Redskins. On the morning of the game, the players learned that team president George Halas, Jr. had died in his sleep. Inspired by many things, the Bears destroyed the Cardinals 42-6, and when Dallas beat the Redskins 35-34, the Bears were in the playoffs.

Minnesota Vikings—The exodus of familiar faces continued, with Fran Tarkenton, Mick Tingelhoff, and Carl Eller no longer around. Coach Bud Grant had kept the Vikings in contention through the recent rebuilding years, but he couldn't prevent a losing season this year, the first since 1967. To add to the changes, Chuck Foreman was eased out of the lineup by rookie Ted Brown. Tommy Kramer settled in admirably at quarterback and found inviting targets in Ahmad Rashad and Sammy White. The ground game, however, was weak enough to hamstring the attack's efficiency. Although Matt Blair was at his peak at linebacker, the defense did not hold a candle to the Viking squads of the early 1970's. More Viking stand-bys bid farewell at the end of season, with Jim Marshall taking a 282-consecutive-game record into retirement along with Wally Hilgenberg and Paul Krause.

Green Bay Packers—As Bart Starr heard increasing calls for his firing, none of his efforts could prevent a Packer disintegration in the second half of the schedule. The offense suffered from an anemic running attack. Rookie fullback Eddie Lee Ivery starred in the pre-season, but he injured his knee two minutes into the opening game and went out for the year. Veteran fullback Barty Smith stepped in, but a knee injury sent him to the sidelines in October. Halfback Terdell Middleton could not repeat his sterling performance of last year because of an assortment of nagging injuries. The defense suffered from the trade of Willie Buchanon to San Diego and the knee injury which ended Carl Barzilauskas' career in October. With seven losses in the final nine games, the campaign ended with the Packers in retreat and with their leadership in question.

Detroit Lions—The pre-season polls fingered the Lions as favorites to win the Central Division title. Unfortunately, quarterback Gary Danielson suffered a severe knee injury in the final pre-season game,

FINAL TEAM STATISTICS

OFFENSE	ATL.	CHI.	DALL.	DET.	G.B.	L.A.	MINN.	N.O.	N.Y.	PHIL.	ST.L.	S.F.	T.B.	WASH.
FIRST DOWNS:														
Total	303	262	**339**	227	279	299	311	315	223	292	305	336	267	298
by Rushing	126	140	122	85	121	134	112	**160**	82	122	145	120	107	126
by Passing	150	98	195	131	133	138	168	135	111	150	136	**200**	137	144
by Penalty	27	24	22	11	25	27	**31**	20	30	20	24	16	23	28
RUSHING:														
Number	500	**627**	578	441	483	592	487	551	498	567	566	480	609	609
Yards	2200	2486	2375	1677	1861	2460	1764	2476	1820	2421	**2582**	1932	2437	2328
Average Yards	4.4	4.0	4.1	3.8	3.9	4.2	3.6	4.5	3.7	4.3	**4.6**	4.0	4.0	3.8
Touchdowns	15	17	15	11	14	16	9	**28**	12	17	24	17	13	17
PASSING:														
Attempts	479	373	503	452	444	456	566	428	401	410	492	**602**	434	401
Completions	251	195	287	218	240	242	315	257	190	209	248	**361**	183	235
Completion Pct	52.4	52.3	57.1	48.2	54.1	53.1	55.7	**60.0**	47.4	51.0	50.4	60.0	42.2	58.6
Passing Yards	3127	2429	**3883**	2775	3057	3032	3397	3291	2419	2882	2870	3760	2700	2839
Avg. Yds. per Att.	5.1	5.3	6.6	4.6	5.5	5.4	5.2	**7.1**	4.3	5.9	4.9	5.9	5.9	5.9
Avg. Yds per Comp.	12.5	12.5	13.5	12.7	12.7	12.5	10.8	12.8	12.7	13.8	11.6	10.4	**14.8**	12.1
Times Tackled	54	31	41	51	47	39	37	17	59	34	39	17	**12**	34
Yds Lost Tackled	398	278	290	439	376	359	258	140	465	272	268	119	**88**	263
Net Yards	2729	2151	3593	2336	2681	2673	3139	3151	1954	2610	2602	**3641**	2612	2576
Touchdowns	19	16	**29**	14	15	19	23	16	15	21	12	18	19	20
Interceptions	23	16	**13**	27	22	29	24	22	22	**13**	24	21	26	15
Pct. Intercepted	4.8	4.3	**2.6**	6.0	5.0	6.4	4.2	5.1	5.5	3.2	4.9	3.5	6.0	3.7
PUNTS:														
Number	84	93	76	98	69	95	91	69	**104**	76	81	72	95	78
Average	39.2	37.5	41.7	40.1	40.4	39.3	39.0	39.5	**42.7**	38.9	37.8	36.5	38.7	38.4
PUNT RETURNS:														
Number	26	39	51	45	28	58	57	30	28	57	48	44	**71**	33
Yards	188	334	334	372	141	330	266	231	109	**544**	368	314	438	271
Average Yards	7.2	8.6	6.5	8.3	5.0	5.7	5.1	7.7	3.9	**9.5**	7.7	7.1	6.2	8.2
Touchdowns	0	**1**	0	0	0	0	0	0	0	0	0	0	0	0
KICKOFF RET.:														
Number	73	51	68	**78**	61	66	61	66	67	56	71	75	51	55
Yards	1370	1054	1316	1569	1295	1292	1380	1319	1255	1261	**1609**	1538	959	1145
Average Yards	18.8	20.7	19.4	20.1	21.2	19.6	22.6	20.0	18.7	22.5	**22.7**	20.5	18.8	20.8
Touchdowns	0	1	0	0	1	0	0	0	0	**1**	**1**	1	0	0
INTERCEPT. RET.:														
Number	15	29	**13**	14	18	25	22	26	21	22	18	15	14	26
Yards	224	402	193	**73**	243	355	351	351	165	266	288	171	238	250
Average Yards	14.9	13.9	14.8	**5.2**	13.5	14.2	16.0	13.5	7.9	12.1	16.0	11.4	17.0	9.6
Touchdowns	2	2	0	1	0	2	0	2	1	0	1	0	1	1
PENALTIES:														
Number	107	100	100	110	93	98	96	93	122	90	107	95	102	**86**
Yards	1026	816	845	897	681	743	787	812	1047	**680**	954	853	905	749
FUMBLES:														
Number	31	**21**	34	37	37	38	40	24	34	38	42	37	25	**21**
Number Lost	20	13	21	19	22	20	17	14	18	16	21	18	15	**10**
POINTS:														
Total	300	306	**371**	219	246	323	259	370	237	339	307	308	273	348
PAT Attempts	37	37	45	27	31	40	31	**46**	30	39	40	36	35	39
PAT Made	31	34	40	25	24	36	28	**44**	28	36	31	32	30	39
FG Attempts	25	27	29	18	20	25	22	21	20	31	26	24	19	**33**
FG Made	13	16	19	10	12	13	13	16	9	23	12	20	11	**25**
Percent FG Made	52.0	59.3	65.5	55.6	60.0	52.0	59.1	76.2	45.0	74.2	46.2	**83.3**	57.9	75.8
Safeties	1	1	**2**	1	0	1	0	1	1	0	0	0	0	0

DEFENSE	ATL.	CHI.	DALL.	DET.	G.B.	L.A.	MINN.	N.O.	N.Y.	PHIL.	ST.L.	S.F.	T.B.	WASH.
FIRST DOWNS:														
Total	311	272	259	311	327	266	297	334	322	274	302	326	**247**	320
by Rushing	109	**100**	105	142	162	115	148	147	130	128	125	136	116	126
by Passing	177	148	134	128	146	133	133	168	159	125	149	160	**111**	165
by Penalty	25	24	20	41	19	18	**16**	19	33	21	28	30	20	29
RUSHING:														
Number	555	519	**500**	638	639	548	583	521	618	515	567	544	539	541
Yards	2163	1978	2115	2515	2885	1997	2526	2469	2452	2271	2204	2213	**1873**	2154
Average Yards	3.9	3.8	4.2	3.9	4.5	3.6	4.3	4.7	4.0	4.4	3.9	4.1	**3.5**	4.0
Touchdowns	29	**9**	15	22	14	13	24	22	14	16	18	24	13	21
PASSING:														
Attempts	487	458	435	**402**	440	454	424	488	463	459	478	441	436	470
Completions	268	222	**207**	220	249	220	229	265	253	243	258	262	250	234
Completion Pct	55.0	48.5	**47.6**	54.7	56.6	48.5	54.0	54.3	54.6	52.9	54.0	59.4	57.3	49.8
Passing Yards	3799	2908	2833	2787	3041	3007	2965	3457	3154	2798	3067	3407	**2405**	3339
Avg. Yds. per Att.	7.0	5.0	5.2	5.5	5.8	5.1	5.9	5.7	5.9	4.9	5.7	6.8	**4.4**	5.8
Avg. Yds per Comp.	14.2	13.1	13.7	12.7	12.2	13.7	13.0	13.1	12.5	11.6	11.9	13.0	**9.6**	14.3
Times Tackled	29	47	43	45	35	**52**	30	46	32	45	28	29	40	47
Yds Lost Tackled	203	380	362	345	279	**451**	268	391	228	324	194	227	329	347
Net Yards	3596	2528	2471	2442	2762	2556	2697	3066	2926	2474	2873	3180	**2076**	2992
Touchdowns	17	21	21	15	21	24	**14**	24	22	18	22	25	**14**	18
Interceptions	15	**29**	13	14	18	25	22	26	21	22	18	15	14	26
Pct. Intercepted	3.1	**6.3**	3.0	3.5	4.1	5.5	5.2	5.3	4.5	4.8	3.8	3.4	3.2	5.5
PUNTS:														
Number	73	90	96	83	64	**108**	93	71	80	85	90	74	104	70
Average	37.3	37.8	40.8	40.0	39.3	40.3	34.7	38.4	**36.7**	39.9	39.2	[illegible]	41.1	40.7
PUNT RETURNS:														
Number	41	54	34	57	43	59	48	32	60	34	45	37	47	**29**
Yards	259	404	252	440	305	405	354	223	447	200	378	262	270	**135**
Average Yards	6.3	7.5	7.4	7.7	7.1	6.9	7.4	7.0	7.5	5.9	8.4	7.1	5.7	**4.7**
Touchdowns	0	0	0	1	0	0	0	0	0	0	0	0	0	0
KICKOFF RET.:														
Number	61	59	68	51	50	58	59	76	**44**	69	57	68	55	76
Yards	1312	1252	1578	987	999	1303	1070	1523	**900**	1265	1332	1367	1254	1280
Average Yards	21.5	21.2	23.2	19.4	20.0	22.5	18.1	20.0	20.5	18.3	23.4	20.1	22.8	**16.8**
Touchdowns	0	0	1	1	0	0	0	0	0	0	1	0	0	0
INTERCEPT. RET.:														
Number	23	16	13	27	22	**29**	24	22	22	13	24	21	26	15
Yards	362	240	114	396	247	387	308	199	**449**	132	301	355	324	82
Average Yards	15.7	15.0	8.8	14.7	11.2	13.3	12.8	9.0	**20.4**	10.2	12.5	16.9	12.5	5.5
Touchdowns	**2**	0	1	**2**	**2**	0	**2**	1	1	0	1	**2**	1	**0**
PENALTIES:														
Number	98	104	70	118	106	105	93	98	105	86	92	**119**	100	76
Yards	815	864	704	972	912	**993**	786	871	800	681	744	858	870	617
FUMBLES:														
Number	35	25	20	30	30	38	23	32	36	20	40	33	**45**	34
Number Lost	21	14	10	12	14	16	11	16	17	11	19	19	**24**	21
POINTS:														
Total	388	249	313	365	316	309	337	360	323	282	358	416	**237**	295
PAT Attempts	47	**31**	38	42	36	38	42	46	39	34	43	54	28	39
PAT Made	44	**27**	34	41	32	35	32	45	35	33	41	46	25	37
FG Attempts	29	20	27	36	33	21	24	**17**	35	23	31	**17**	24	**17**
FG Made	20	12	17	24	20	14	15	11	18	15	19	14	14	**8**
Percent FG Made	69.0	60.0	63.0	66.7	60.6	66.7	62.5	64.7	51.4	65.2	61.3	82.4	58.3	**47.1**
Safeties	1	0	0	0	1	2	1	0	0	0	1	2	1	0

leaving coach Monte Clark without a seasoned QB. Although Danielson's loss was expected to hurt the offense, the entire team sagged from the blow and seemed to lose its will. Clark shuffled his defensive lineup, but no combination could prevent a demoralizing eight-game losing skid which began on the last day of September and ended with an upset 20-0 thrashing of the Bears on Thanksgiving Day. What the Lions had most of all to be thankful for was their number-one position in the upcoming college draft.

WESTERN DIVISION

Los Angeles Rams—With a roster deep in talent, the Rams nevertheless had to scramble in the weak Western Division. Before the season started, guard Tom Mack had retired and halfback John Cappelletti went to the sidelines with a groin injury. As the season progressed, injuries struck at the Los Angeles wide receivers and cornerbacks. Despite good offensive and defensive lines featuring Jack Youngblood, Larry Brooks, Dennis Harrah, and Rich Saul, the Rams had a tepid 5-6 record in mid-November. To make matters worse, quarterback Pat Haden had broken a finger, leaving the QB job to inexperienced Vince Ferragamo. Taking over for the final four games, Ferragamo led the Rams to three victories and a playoff spot. Although Ferragamo showed a talent for throwing the long ball, the Ram offense relied on the running of Wendell Tyler and Cullen Bryant. The defense feasted on enemy quarterbacks all season and hoped to continue that diet in the playoffs.

New Orleans Saints—For the pro football fans of New Orleans, it was heady stuff. The Saints were battling for first place in the West well into December. Coach Dick Nolan had put together a first-rate offense. The line enjoyed the return of guards Emanuel Zanders and Conrad Dobler from injuries, and quarterback Archie Manning had a pair of dangerous receivers in Wes Chandler and Ike Harris. On the ground, Chuck Muncie carried the ball with speed, power, and heart. Nolan even added Garo Yepremian as place kicker after the Dolphins cut him loose. The defense, unfortunately, did not measure up despite Tommy Myers' brilliant season. With high-scoring games the rule, the Saints compiled a 7-6 record as of the start of December and were tied with the Rams for first place. On December 3, the Saints hosted Oakland and bolted to a 28-7 lead in the second quarter. Six minutes into the third quarter, the Saints led 35-14, but the defense could not stand its ground. The Raiders ran off 28 unanswered points and won the game 42-35. A 35-0 loss to San Diego one week later ended the playoff dreams, but the Saints kept their spirit and beat the Rams 29-14 to end the season at .500, the first Saint squad ever to do it.

Atlanta Falcons—One year ago, the Falcons won the close games and made it into the playoffs. This year, they lost the close games and finished with a losing record. Coach Leeman Bennett had reason to expect improvement from his team this season. Rookie fullback William Andrews ran for over 100 yards in his first two games and gave the attack a new threat. Alfred Jenkins came back from an injury to start at wide receiver. On defense, however, the Falcons could not stop enemy passing attacks. After two victories to open the schedule, the Falcons lost six of their next seven matches. Four of those losses were by a margin of five points or less, and another was a 50-19 trouncing by the Raiders. On November 11, they sleepwalked through a 24-3 debacle in New Jersey. Although they beat the streaking San Diego Chargers late in the year, the Falcons chalked up the season as a major disappointment.

San Francisco 49ers—The 49ers hired Bill Walsh away from Stanford University to rebuild the team as head coach and general manager. Walsh spent the year rummaging through the rubble he inherited and through the waiver list for serviceable football players. While doing this, the 49ers lost their first seven games and won only twice all season. The defense was manned by a horde of new faces, and errors of inexperience led to many enemy scores. On offense, Walsh emphasized the pass and turned young quarterback Steve DeBerg loose. DeBerg set new NFL records for passing attempts and completions in a season. For O. J. Simpson, the premier runner of the 1970's, it was a last hurrah. He lost his starting job to Paul Hofer in mid-season, and by announcing his plan to retire at the end of the season, he was able to make token appearances over the last leg of the schedule and reap a harvest of cheers and affection from appreciative fans.

DALLAS COWBOYS 11-5-0 Tom Landry

Scores of Each Game		
22	St. Louis	21
21	San Francisco	13
24	CHICAGO	20
7	Cleveland	26
38	CINCINNATI	13
36	Minnesota	20
30	LOS ANGELES	6
22	ST. LOUIS	13
3	Pittsburgh	14
16	N.Y. Giants	14
21	PHILADELPHIA	31
20	Washington	34
24	HOUSTON	30
28	N.Y. GIANTS	7
24	Philadelphia	17
35	WASHINGTON	34

Use Name	Pos.	Hgt.	Wgt.	Age	Int.	Pts.
Jim Cooper	OT	6'5"	260	23		
Pat Donovan	OT	6'4"	250	26		
Andy Frederick	OT	6'6"	255	24		
Rayfield Wright	OT	6'7"	260	34		
Burton Lawless	OG	6'4"	255	25		
Tom Rafferty	OG	6'3"	250	25		
Herbert Scott	OG	6'2"	252	26		
John Fitzgerald	C	6'5"	260	31		
Robert Shaw	C-OG	6'4"	245	22		
Larry Cole	DE-DT	6'4"	252	32		
John Dutton	DE	6'7"	265	28		
Harvey Martin	DE	6'5"	250	28		2
Bruce Thornton	DE-DT	6'5"	265	21	1	
Larry Bethea	DT	6'5"	254	23		
David Stalls	DT	6'4"	245	23		
Randy White	DT	6'4"	250	26		

Use Name	Pos.	Hgt.	Wgt.	Age	Int.	Pts.
Bob Breunig	LB	6'2"	225	26		
Guy Brown	LB	6'4"	228	24		
Mike Hegman	LB	6'1"	225	26		
Tom Henderson	LB	6'2"	220	26		
Bruce Huther	LB	6'1"	220	25		
D.D. Lewis	LB	6'2"	215	33	2	
Benny Barnes	DB	6'1"	195	28	2	6
Cliff Harris	DB	6'	192	30	2	
Randy Hughes	DB	6'4"	207	26	2	
Aaron Kyle	DB	5'11"	185	25	2	
Wade Manning	DB	5'11"	190	24		
Aaron Mitchell	DB	6'1"	196	22	1	
Dennis Thurman	DB	5'11"	170	23	1	

Too Tall Jones – Voluntarily Retired
Charlie Waters – Knee Injury

Use Name	Pos.	Hgt.	Wgt.	Age	Int.	Pts.
Glenn Carano	QB	6'3"	202	23		
Roger Staubach	QB	6'2"	202	37		
Danny White	QB	6'2"	192	27		
Alois Blackwell	HB	5'10"	195	24		
Tony Dorsett	HB	5'11"	190	25		42
Preston Pearson	HB	6'1"	206	34		12
Ron Springs	HB	6'1"	200	22		18
Larry Brinson	FB	6'	214	25		
Scott Laidlaw	FB	6'	205	26		18
Robert Newhouse	FB	5'10"	215	29		24
Tony Hill	WR	6'2"	198	23		60
Butch Johnson	WR	6'1"	192	25		6
Drew Pearson	WR	6'	183	28		48
Steve Wilson	WR	5'10"	192	22		
Doug Cosbie	TE	6'6"	230	23		
Billy Joe DuPree	TE	6'4"	229	29		30
Jay Saldi	TE	6'3"	227	24		6
Rafael Septien	K	5'9"	171	25		97

PHILADELPHIA EAGES 11-5-0 Dick Vermeil

Scores of Each Game		
23	N.Y. GIANTS	17
10	ATLANTA	14
26	New Orleans	14
17	N.Y. Giants	13
17	PITTSBURGH	14
28	WASHINGTON	17
24	St. Louis	20
7	Washington	17
13	Cincinnati	37
19	CLEVELAND	24
31	Dallas	21
16	ST. LOUIS	13
21	Green Bay	10
44	DETROIT	7
17	DALLAS	24
26	Houston	20

Use Name	Pos.	Hgt.	Wgt.	Age	Int.	Pts.
Rufus Mayes	OT	6'5"	256	31		
Jerry Sisemore	OT	6'4"	260	28		
Stan Walters	OT	6'6"	270	31		
Wade Key	OG	6'4"	245	32		
Woody Peoples	OG	6'2"	252	36		
Petey Perot	OG	6'2"	261	22		
Guy Morriss	C	6'4"	255	28		
Mark Slater	C	6'1"	257	24		
Lem Burnham	DE	6'4"	240	32		
Carl Hairston	DE	6'3"	260	26		
Dennis Harrison	DE	6'8"	275	23		
Claude Humphrey	DE	6'5"	265	35		
Manny Sistrunk	DE	6'5"	275	32		
Ken Clarke	**NT**	6'2"	255	23		
Charles Johnson	**NT**	6'3"	262	27		

Vince Papale – Shoulder Injury

Use Name	Pos.	Hgt.	Wgt.	Age	Int.	Pts.
Bill Bergey	LB	6'2"	245	34	1	
John Bunting	LB	6'1"	220	29	2	
Al Chesley	LB	6'3"	240	22	2	
Frank LeMaster	LB	6'2"	231	27		
Ray Phillips	LB	6'4"	217	25		
Jerry Robinson	LB	6'2"	216	22		
Terry Tautolo	LB	6'2"	235	25		
Reggie Wilkes	LB	6'4"	235	23	2	
Richard Blackmore	DB	5'10"	174	23		
Herman Edwards	DB	6'	194	25	3	
Bob Howard	DB	6'1"	175	34	3	
Al Latimer	DB	5'11"	172	21		
Randy Logan	DB	6'1"	195	28	3	
Henry Monroe	DB	5'11"	180	22		
Deac Sanders	DB	6'1"	175	29		
John Sciarra	DB	5'11"	185	25	2	
Brenard Wilson	DB	6'	170	24	4	

Use Name	Pos.	Hgt.	Wgt.	Age	Int.	Pts.
Ron Jaworski	QB	6'2"	195	28		12
John Walton	QB	6'2"	210	31		
Billy Campfield	HB	5'11"	205	23		24
Louie Giammona	HB	5'9"	180	26		
Wilbert Montgomery	HB	5'10"	195	24		84
Larry Barnes	FB	5'11"	220	25		6
Earl Carr	FB	6'	224	24		
Leroy Harris	FB	5'9"	230	25		12
Harold Carmichael	WR	6'7"	225	29		66
Scott Fitzkee	WR	6'	187	22		6
Wally Henry	WR	5'8"	170	24		
Jerrold McRae	LWR	6'	187	24		
Charlie Smith	WR	6'1"	185	29		6
Keith Krepfle	TE	6'3"	225	27		18
John Spagnola	TE	6'4"	240	22		
Tony Franklin	K	5'8"	182	22		105
Max Runager	K	6'1"	189	23		

WASHINGTON REDSKINS 10-6-0 Jack Pardee

Scores of Each Game		
27	HOUSTON	29
27	Detroit	24
27	N.Y. GIANTS	0
17	St. Louis	7
16	Atlanta	7
17	Philadelphia	28
13	Cleveland	9
17	PHILADELPHIA	7
10	NEW ORLEANS	14
7	Pittsburgh	38
30	ST. LOUIS	28
34	DALLAS	20
6	N.Y. Giants	14
38	GREEN BAY	21
28	CINCINNATI	14
34	Dallas	35

Use Name	Pos.	Hgt.	Wgt.	Age	Int.	Pts.
Terry Hermeling	OT	6'5"	255	33		
George Starke	OT	6'5"	250	31		
Fred Dean	OG	6'3"	253	24		
Greg Dubinetz	OG	6'4"	260	25		
Ron Saul	OG	6'2"	254	31		
Jeff Williams	OG-OT	6'4"	260	24		
Ted Fritsch	C-OG	6'2"	247	29		
Bob Kuziel	C	6'5"	255	29		
Coy Bacon	DE	6'4"	265	37		
Joe Jones	DE	6'6"	250	31		
Karl Lorch	DE	6'3"	258	29	1	6
Paul Smith	DE	6'3"	255	34		
Perry Brooks	DT	6'3"	260	24		
Dave Butz	DT	6'7"	285	29		
Diron Talbert	DT	6'5"	255	35		

Use Name	Pos.	Hgt.	Wgt.	Age	Int.	Pts.
Monte Coleman	LB	6'2"	220	21	1	
Brad Dusek	LB	6'2"	227	28	1	
Dallas Hickman	LB-DE	6'6"	236	27		
Don Hover	LB	6'2"	227	24		6
Rich Milot	LB	6'4"	225	22		
Neal Olkewicz	LB	6'	218	22	1	
Pete Wysocki	LB	6'2"	224	30	1	
Don Harris	DB	6'2"	185	25		
Ken Houston	DB	6'3"	198	34	1	
Joe Lavender	DB	6'4"	190	30	6	
Mark Murphy	DB	6'4"	210	24	3	
Lemar Parrish	DB	5'11"	177	31	**9**	
Tony Peters	DB	6'1"	185	26	1	
Ray Waddy	DB	5'11"	175	23	1	

Gary Anderson – Ankle Injury
Dan Nugent – Back Injury
Dan Testerman – Knee Injury

Use Name	Pos.	Hgt.	Wgt.	Age	Int.	Pts.
Kim McQuilken	QB	6'2"	203	28		
Fred Martensen	QB	6'2"	195	25		
Joe Theismann	QB	6'	195	29		24
Ike Forte	HB	6'	211	25		6
Bob Hammond (from NYG)	HB	5'10"	170	27		
Buddy Hardeman	HB	6'	190	24		6
Clarence Harmon	HB-FB	5'11"	213	23		30
Benny Malone	HB	5'10"	193	27		24
John Riggins	FB	6'2"	230	30		72
Danny Buggs	WR	6'2"	185	26		6
Chris DeFrance	WR	6'1"	205	22		
Dennis Law	WR	6'1"	175	24		
John McDaniel	WR	6'1"	197	27		12
Ricky Thompson	WR	6'	177	25		24
Phil DuBois	TE	6'2"	220	22		
Jean Fugett	TE	6'3"	230	27		18
Grady Richardson	TE	6'4"	225	27		
Don Warren	TE	6'4"	229	23		
Mike Bragg	K	5'11"	186	32		
Mark Moseley	K	5'11"	205	31		**114**

NEW YORK GIANTS 6-10-0 Ray Perkins

Scores of Each Game		
17	Philadelphia	23
14	ST. LOUIS	27
0	Washington	27
13	PHILADELPHIA	17
14	New Orleans	24
17	TAMPA BAY	14
32	SAN FRANCISCO	16
21	Kansas City	17
20	Los Angeles	14
14	DALLAS	16
24	ATLANTA	3
3	Tampa Bay	31
14	WASHINGTON	6
7	Dallas	28
20	St. Louis	29
7	BALTIMORE	31

Use Name	Pos.	Hgt.	Wgt.	Age	Int.	Pts.
Brad Benson	OT	6'3"	258	23		
Gus Coppens	OT	6'5"	270	24		
Gordon King	OT	6'6"	275	23		
Ron Mikolajczyk	OT	6'3"	275	29		
Tom Neville	OT	6'4"	250	36		
Dan Fowler	OG	6'5"	260	23		
Roy Simmons	OG	6'3"	264	22		
J.T. Turner	OG	6'3"	250	26		
Doug Van Horn	OG	6'2"	245	35		
Jim Clack	C	6'3"	250	31		
Keith Eck	C-OG	6'5"	255	23		
Gary Jeter	DE	6'4"	260	24		
George Martin	DE	6'4"	245	26		
Mike McCoy	DT	6'5"	275	30		
John Mendenhall	DT	6'1"	255	30		
Calvin Miller	DT-DE	6'2"	250	25		
Phil Tabor	DT	6'4"	255	22		
Jeff Weston	DT	6'5"	250	22		

Use Name	Pos.	Hgt.	Wgt.	Age	Int.	Pts.
Harry Carson	LB	6'2"	235	25	3	6
Randy Coffield	LB	6'3"	215	25		
Brian Kelley	LB	6'3"	222	28	3	
Dan Lloyd	LB	6'2"	225	25	2	
Frank Marion	LB	6'3"	228	28		
John Skorupan	LB	6'2"	225	28		2
Brad Van Pelt	LB	6'5"	235	28		
Alan Caldwell	DB	6'	176	23	2	
Terry Jackson	DB	5'10"	197	23	3	6
Ernie Jones	DB	6'3"	180	26	2	6
Odis McKinney	DB	6'2"	187	22	1	
Ray Oldham	DB	6'	192	28	2	
Beasley Reece	DB	6'1"	195	25	1	
Ray Rhodes	DB	5'11"	185	28	2	

Larry Gillard – Knee Injury
Troy Archer – Died in Auto Accident in June

Use Name	Pos.	Hgt.	Wgt.	Age	Int.	Pts.
Randy Dean	QB	6'3"	195	24		6
Joe Pisarcik	QB	6'4"	220	27		
Dave Rader	QB	6'3"	211	22		
Phil Simms	QB	6'3"	216	23		6
Doug Kotar	HB	5'11"	205	28		18
Emery Moorehead	HB-FB	6'2"	210	25		
George Franklin	FB	6'3"	225	25		
Eddie Hicks	FB	6'2"	210	24		
Ken Johnson	FB	6'2"	220	22		6
Billy Taylor	FB-HB	6'	215	23		66
Earnest Gray	WR	6'3"	195	22		24
Johnny Perkins	WR	6'2"	205	26		24
Jim Robinson	WR	5'9"	170	26		
Dwight Scales	WR	6'2"	182	26		
Gene Washington	WR	5'9"	170	26		
Al Dixon (to KC)	TE	6'5"	220	25		
Cleveland Jackson	TE	6'4"	230	22		
Loaird McCreary	TE	6'5"	227	26		
Tom Mullady	TE	6'3"	232	22		
Gary Shirk	TE	6'1"	220	29		12
Joe Danelo	K	5'9"	166	25		55
Dave Jennings	K	6'4"	205	27		

ST. LOUIS CARDINALS 5-11-0 Bud Wilkinson, Larry Wilson

Scores of Each Game		
21	DALLAS	22
27	N.Y. Giants	14
21	PITTSBURGH	24
7	WASHINGTON	17
0	Los Angeles	21
24	Houston	17
20	PHILADELPHIA	24
13	Dallas	22
20	CLEVELAND	38
37	MINNESOTA	7
28	Washington	30
13	Philadelphia	16
28	Cincinnati	34
13	SAN FRANCISCO	10
29	N.Y. GIANTS	20
6	Chicago	42

Use Name	Pos.	Hgt.	Wgt.	Age	Int.	Pts.
Joe Bostic	OT	6'3"	265	22		
Dan Dierdorf	OT	6'4"	288	30		
Brad Oates	OT	6'6"	275	25		
Keith Wortman	OT	6'2"	275	29		
George Collins	OG	6'2"	248	23		
Terry Stieve	OG	6'2"	263	25		
Bob Young	OG	6'2"	279	36		
Tom Banks	C-OG	6'1"	245	31		
Tom Brahaney	C	6'2"	246	27		
Chuck Brown	C-OG	6'1"	235	22		
Mike Dawson	DE	6'4"	274	25		
Bob Pollard	DE	6'3"	251	30		
Jim Ramey	DE	6'4"	247	22		
Bob Rozier	DE	6'3"	240	24		
Ron Yankowski	DE	6'5"	258	32		
John Zook	DE	6'5"	254	31		
Charlie Davis	NT	6'1"	275	27		
Keith Simons	NT	6'3"	254	25		

Use Name	Pos.	Hgt.	Wgt.	Age	Int.	Pts.
Kurt Allerman	LB	6'3"	222	24		
Mark Arneson	LB	6'2"	224	29		6
John Barefield	LB	6'2"	224	24		
Sean Clancy	LB	6'4"	218	22		
Calvin Favron	LB	6'1"	225	22		
Chris Garlich	LB	6'1"	220	22		
Tim Kearney	LB	6'2"	221	28		
Steve Neils	LB	6'2"	218	28		6
Eric Williams	LB	6'2"	225	24	1	
Carl Allen	DB	6'	186	23	5	
Roy Green	DB	5'11"	190	22		6
Ken Greene	DB	6'3"	203	23	3	
Steve Henry	DB	6'2"	190	22		
Lee Nelson	DB	5'10"	185	25		
Perry Smith	DB	6'1"	190	28	1	
Ken Stone	DB	6'1"	180	28	6	
Roger Wehrli	DB	6'1"	193	31	2	6

J.V. Cain – Died of Heart Failure in July

Use Name	Pos.	Hgt.	Wgt.	Age	Int.	Pts.
Jim Hart	QB	6'2"	210	35		
Mike Loyd	QB	6'2"	216	23		
Steve Pisarkiewicz	QB	6'2"	205	25		
Ottis Anderson	HB	6'2"	210	22		60
Will Harrell	HB	5'9"	182	26		
Robert Hawkins	HB	6'	195	22		
Thomas Lott	HB	5'11"	205	22		
Randy Love	HB	6'1"	205	22		
Theotis Brown	FB	6'2"	225	22		42
Wayne Morris	FB	6'	208	25		54
Rod Phillips	FB	6'	220	26		6
Jim Childs	WR	6'2"	194	23		
Mel Gray	WR	5'9"	173	30		6
Dave Stief	WR	6'3"	195	23		
Pat Tilley	WR	5'10"	171	26		36
Al Chandler (to NE)	TE	6'2"	229	28		12
Bill Murrell	TE	6'3"	220	23		
Richard Osborne	TE	6'3"	230	25		
Gary Parris	TE	6'2"	226	29		1
Steve Little	K	6'	180	23		54

DALLAS COWBOYS

RUSHING

Last Name	No.	Yds.	Avg.	TD
Dorsett	250	1107	4.4	6
Newhouse	124	449	3.6	3
Springs	67	248	3.7	2
Laidlaw	69	236	3.4	3
Staubach	37	172	4.6	0
Brinson	14	48	3.4	0
D. Pearson	3	27	9.0	0
D. White	1	25	25.0	0
DuPree	2	19	9.5	0
Hill	2	18	9.0	0
P. Pearson	7	14	2.0	1
Johnson	1	13	13.0	0
Saldi	1	−1	−1.0	0

RECEIVING

Last Name	No.	Yds.	Avg.	TD
Hill	60	1062	18	10
D. Pearson	55	1026	19	8
Dorsett	45	375	8	1
DuPree	29	324	11	5
P. Pearson	26	333	13	1
Springs	25	251	10	1
Laidlaw	12	59	5	0
Newhouse	7	55	8	1
Johnson	6	105	18	1
Cosbie	5	36	7	0
Wilson	3	76	25	0

PUNT RETURNS

Last Name	No.	Yds.	Avg.	TD
Wilson	35	236	7	0
Manning	10	55	6	0
Hill	6	43	7	0

KICKOFF RETURNS

Last Name	No.	Yds.	Avg.	TD
Springs	38	780	21	0
Wilson	19	328	17	0
Manning	7	145	21	0
Brinson	2	23	12	0
Hill	1	32	32	0
Huther	1	8	8	0

PASSING - PUNTING - KICKING

PASSING	Att.	Comp.	%	Yds.	Yd./Att.	TD	Int.-%	RK
Staubach	461	267	58	3586	7.8	27	11- 2	1
D. White	39	19	49	267	6.9	1	2- 5	
Springs	3	1	33	30	10.0	1	0- 0	

PUNTING	No.	Avg.
D. White	76	41.7

KICKING	XP	Att.	%	FG	Att.	%
Septien	40	44	90	19	29	66

PHILADELPHIA EAGLES

RUSHING

Last Name	No.	Yds.	Avg.	TD
Montgomery	338	1512	4.5	9
Harris	107	504	4.7	2
Campfield	30	165	5.5	3
Jaworski	43	119	2.8	2
Barnes	25	74	3.0	1
Giammona	15	38	2.5	0
LeMaster	1	15	15.0	0
Carmichael	1	0	0.0	0
Carr	1	−1	−1.0	0
Walton	6	−5	−0.8	0

RECEIVING

Last Name	No.	Yds.	Avg.	TD
Carmichael	52	872	17	11
Krepfle	41	760	19	3
Montgomery	41	494	12	5
Smith	24	399	17	1
Harris	22	107	5	0
Campfield	16	115	7	0
Fitzkee	8	105	13	1
Spagnola	2	24	12	0
Barnes	1	6	6	0
Carr	1	2	2	0
McRae	1	−2	−2	0

PUNT RETURNS

Last Name	No.	Yds.	Avg.	TD
Sciarra	16	182	11	0
Henry	35	320	9	0
Giammona	5	42	8	0
Blackmore	1	0	0	0

KICKOFF RETURNS

Last Name	No.	Yds.	Avg.	TD
Henry	28	668	24	0
Giammona	15	294	20	0
Campfield	7	251	36	1
Wilson	2	0	0	0
Barnes	1	23	23	0
Latimer	1	18	18	0
Montgomery	1	6	6	0
Smith	1	1	1	0

PASSING - PUNTING - KICKING

PASSING	Att.	Comp.	%	Yds.	Yd./Att.	TD	Int.-%	RK
Jaworski	374	190	51	2669	7.1	18	12- 3	3
Walton	36	19	53	213	5.9	3	1- 3	

PUNTING	No.	Avg.
Runager	74	39.6
Franklin	1	32.0

KICKING	XP	Att.	%	FG	Att.	%
Franklin	39	36	92	23	31	74

WASHINGTON REDSKINS

RUSHING

Last Name	No.	Yds.	Avg.	TD
Riggins	260	1153	4.4	9
Malone	176	472	2.7	3
Harmon	65	267	4.1	0
Theismann	46	181	3.9	4
Forte	25	125	5.0	1
Hardeman	31	124	4.0	0
Hammond	2	5	2.5	0
McQuilken	2	−3	−1.5	0

RECEIVING

Last Name	No.	Yds.	Avg.	TD
Buggs	46	631	14	1
Harmon	32	434	14	5
Riggins	28	163	6	3
Warren	26	303	12	0
McDaniel	25	357	14	2
Thompson	22	368	17	4
Hardeman	21	197	9	1
Malone	13	137	11	1
Fugett	10	128	13	3
Forte	10	105	11	0
Hammond	2	16	8	0

PUNT RETURNS

Last Name	No.	Yds.	Avg.	TD
Hardeman	24	207	9	0
Hammond	13	75	6	0
Harmon	1	10	10	0
Peters	1	0	0	0

KICKOFF RETURNS

Last Name	No.	Yds.	Avg.	TD
Hammond	25	544	22	0
Hardeman	19	404	21	0
Forte	8	211	26	0
Harris	6	80	13	0
Harmon	5	63	13	0

PASSING - PUNTING - KICKING

PASSING	Att.	Comp.	%	Yds.	Yd./Att.	TD	Int.-%	RK
Theismann	395	233	59	2797	7.1	20	13- 3	2
Hardeman	2	1	50	30	15.0	0	1- 50	
McQuilken	4	1	25	12	3.0	0	1- 25	

PUNTING	No.	Avg.
Bragg	78	38.4

KICKING	XP	Att.	%	FG	Att.	%
Moseley	39	39	100	25	33	76

NEW YORK GIANTS

RUSHING

Last Name	No.	Yds.	Avg.	TD
Taylor	198	700	3.5	7
Kotar	160	616	3.9	3
Johnson	62	168	2.7	0
Simms	29	166	5.7	1
Moorehead	36	95	2.6	0
Dean	8	56	7.0	1
Jennings	2	11	5.5	0
Pisarcik	1	6	6.0	0
Gray	2	2	1.0	0

RECEIVING

Last Name	No.	Yds.	Avg.	TD
Shirk	31	471	15	2
Gray	28	537	19	4
Taylor	28	253	9	4
Kotar	25	230	9	0
Perkins	20	337	17	4
Johnson	16	108	7	1
Scales	14	222	16	0
Robinson	13	146	11	0
Moorehead	9	62	7	0
Dixon	2	18	9	0
Van Pelt	1	20	20	0
C. Jackson	1	7	7	0
McCreary	1	7	7	0
Danelo	1	1	1	0

PUNT RETURNS

Last Name	No.	Yds.	Avg.	TD
Robinson	6	29	5	0
Scales	2	3	2	0
Reece	1	8	8	0
T. Jackson	1	5	5	0

KICKOFF RETURNS

Last Name	No.	Yds.	Avg.	TD
Robinson	7	140	20	0
Taylor	6	131	22	0
Reece	6	81	14	0
Hicks	3	51	17	0
Kotar	2	39	20	0
Moorehead	1	16	16	0
Marion	1	14	14	0
Coffield	1	12	12	0
Gray	1	0	0	0
Lloyd	1	0	0	0

PASSING - PUNTING - KICKING

PASSING	Att.	Comp.	%	Yds.	Yd./Att.	TD	Int.-%	RK
Simms	265	134	51	1743	6.6	13	14- 5	10
Pisarcik	108	43	40	537	5.0	2	6- 6	
Dean	26	11	42	91	3.5	0	2- 8	
Jennings	2	2	100	48	24.0	0	0- 0	

PUNTING	No.	Avg.
Jennings	104	42.7

KICKING	XP	Att.	%	FG	Att.	%
Danelo	28	29	97	9	20	45

ST. LOUIS CARDINALS

RUSHING

Last Name	No.	Yds.	Avg.	TD
Anderson	331	1605	4.8	8
Morris	106	387	3.7	8
T. Brown	73	318	4.4	7
Harrell	19	100	5.3	0
Phillips	3	50	16.7	1
Lott	11	50	4.5	0
Gray	4	41	10.3	0
Pisarkiewicz	11	20	1.8	0
Hart	6	11	1.8	0
Little	2	0	0.0	0

RECEIVING

Last Name	No.	Yds.	Avg.	TD
Tilley	57	938	17	6
Anderson	41	308	8	2
Morris	35	237	7	1
Gray	25	447	18	1
T. Brown	25	191	8	0
Stief	22	324	15	0
Parris	14	174	12	0
Childs	8	93	12	0
Osborne	7	37	5	0
Chandler	6	51	9	2
Harrell	3	33	11	0
Murrell	2	20	10	0
Lott	2	8	4	0
Green	1	15	15	0
Hart	1	−4	−4	0

PUNT RETURNS

Last Name	No.	Yds.	Avg.	TD
Harrell	32	205	6	0
Green	8	42	5	0
Nelson	4	88	22	0
Lott	4	33	8	0

KICKOFF RETURNS

Last Name	No.	Yds.	Avg.	TD
Green	41	1005	25	1
Harrell	22	497	23	0
Barefield	3	62	21	0
Allerman	2	16	8	0
Lott	1	19	19	0
Favron	1	10	10	0
Garlich	1	0	0	0

PASSING - PUNTING - KICKING

PASSING	Att.	Comp.	%	Yds.	Yd./Att.	TD	Int.-%	RK
Hart	378	194	51	2218	5.9	9	20- 5	12
Pisarkiewicz	109	52	48	621	5.7	3	4- 4	
Little	3	2	67	31	10.3	0	0- 0	
Anderson	1	0	0	0	0.0	0	0- 0	
Harrell	1	0	0	0	0.0	0	0- 0	

PUNTING	No.	Avg.
Little	79	38.7

KICKING	XP	Att.	%	FG	Att.	%
Little	24	32	75	10	19	53

TAMPA BAY BUCCANEERS 10-6-0 John McKay

Scores of Each Game		
31	DETROIT	16
29	Baltimore	*26
21	Green Bay	10
21	LOS ANGELES	6
17	Chicago	13
14	N.Y. Giants	17
14	NEW ORLEANS	42
21	GREEN BAY	3
12	Minnesota	10
14	Atlanta	17
16	Detroit	14
31	N.Y. GIANTS	3
22	MINNESOTA	23
0	CHICAGO	14
7	San Francisco	23
3	KANSAS CITY	0

Use Name	Pos.	Hgt.	Wgt.	Age	Int.	Pts.
Darryl Carlton	OT	6 6	285	26		
Charley Hannan	OT	6'5"	255	24		
Dave Reavis	OT	6 5	265	29		
Darrell Austin	OG-C	6 4	250	27		
Greg Horton	OG	6 4	250	28		
Greg Roberts	OG	6 3	255	22		
George Yarno	OG	6 2	255	22		
Steve Wilson	C	6 3	270	25		
Wally Chambers	DE	6 6	250	28		
Bill Kollar	DE-NT	6 4	250	26		
Reggie Lewis	DE-NT	6 3	260	23		
Gene Sanders	DE-NT	6 3	270	22		
Lee Roy Selmon	DE	6 3	255	24		6
Randy Crowder	NT	6 2	250	27		
David Logan	NT-DE	6 2	250	22		
Rik Bonness	LB	6 3	215	25		
Aaron Brown	LB	6 2	235	23		
Cecil Johnson	LB	6 2	230	24		
Dave Lewis	LB	6 4	240	24	2	6
Dana Nafziger	LB	6 1	225	25		
Dewey Selmon	LB	6 1	245	25		
Richard Wood	LB	6 2	225	26	2	
Cedric Brown	DB	6 1	205	25	3	
Billy Cesare	DB	5 11	190	24		
Mark Cotney	DB	6	205	27	1	
Curtis Jordan	DB	6 2	210	25		
Danny Reece	DB	5 11	190	24		
Mike Washington	DB	6 3	205	26	3	6
Jeris White	DB	5 11	185	26	3	
Chuck Fusina	QB	6 1	200	22		
Mike Rae	QB	6	195	28		
Doug Williams	QB	6 4	215	24		12
Rick Berns	HB	6 2	200	23		
Jerry Eckwood	HB	6	195	24		12
George Ragsdale	HB	5 11	185	25		
Ricky Bell	FB-HB	6 2	220	24		54
Johnny Davis	FB	6 1	235	23		12
Tony Davis	FB	5 10	215	26		
Isaac Hagins	WR	5 9	180	25		18
Gordon Jones	WR	6	190	22		6
Larry Mucker	WR	5 11	195	24		30
Morris Owens	WR	6	200	26		
Jimmie Giles	TE	6 3	240	24		42
Jim Obradovich	TE	6 2	230	26		6
Tom Blanchard	K	6	180	31		
Neil O'Donoghue	K	6 6	205	26		63

Jerry Anderson – Injury
Randy Johnson – Injury
Dave Green – Achilles Injury

Jimmy DuBose – Knee Injury

CHICAGO BEARS 10-6-0 Neill Armstrong

Scores of Each Game		
6	GREEN BAY	3
26	MINNESOTA	7
20	Dallas	24
16	Miami	31
13	TAMPA BAY	17
7	Buffalo	0
7	NEW ENGLAND	27
27	Minnesota	30
28	San Francisco	27
35	DETROIT	7
27	LOS ANGELES	23
23	N.Y. JETS	13
0	Detroit	20
14	Tampa Bay	0
15	Green Bay	14
42	ST. LOUIS	6

Use Name	Pos.	Hgt.	Wgt.	Age	Int.	Pts.
Ted Albrecht	OT	6'4"	250	24		
Dan Jiggetts	OT	6'4"	269	25		
Dennis Lick	OT	6'3"	265	25		
Lynn Boden	OG	6'5"	260	26		
Noah Jackson	OG	6'2"	270	28		
Revie Sorey	OG	6'2"	263	25		
Tony Ardizzone	C	6'3"	241	22		
Dan Neal	C	6'4"	251	30		
Dan Hampton	DE	6'5"	252	21		
Al Harris	DE	6'5"	236	22		
Tommy Hart	DE	6'4"	246	34		
Mike Hartenstine	DE	6'3"	240	26		
Jerry Meyers	DT	6'4"	257	25		
Jim Osborne	DT	6'3"	246	29		
Alan Page	DT	6'5"	228	34		
Ron Rydalch	DT	6'4"	256	27		
Doug Buffone	LB	6 1	217	35	2	
Gary Campbell	LB	6 1	221	27	1	
Bruce Herron	LB	6 2	219	25		
Tom Hicks	LB	6 4	235	26	3	6
Lee Kunz	LB	6 2	221	22		
Mark Merrill (from NYJ)	LB	6 4	237	24		
Jerry Muckensturm	LB	6 4	219	25	1	
Allan Ellis	DB	5 10	174	28	3	
Gary Fencik	DB	6 1	192	25	6	
Wentford Gaines	DB	6	186	26	1	
Virgil Livers	DB	5'9"	184	27	2	
Doug Plank	DB	6'	197	26	3	
Terry Schmidt	DB	6'	179	27	6	6
Mike Spivey	DB	6'	195	25		
Len Walterscheid	DB	5'11"	189	24	1	
Bob Avellini	QB	6 2	209	26		
Vince Evans	QB	6 2	210	24		6
Mike Phipps	QB	6 3	203	31		
Jack Deloplaine (to PIT)	HB	5 10	205	25		
Willie McClendon	HB	6 1	205	21		6
Walter Payton	HB	5 11	204	25		96
Robin Earl	FB	6 5	240	24		
Lonnie Perrin (from WAS)	FB	6 1	222	27		
John Skibinski	FB	6	224	24		
Dave Williams	FB	6 2	215	25		36
Brian Baschnagel	WR	6	180	25		12
Kris Haines (from WAS)	WR	5 11	183	22		
Golden Richards	WR	6	180	28		6
Steve Schubert	WR	5 10	186	28		6
James Scott	WR	6 1	191	27		18
Harry Washington	WR	6	180	23		
Rickey Watts	WR	6 1	204	22		24
Mike Cobb	TE	6 5	240	23		
Greg Latta	TE	6 3	235	26		
Bob Parsons	TE	6'4"	225	29		
Bob Thomas	K	5 10	175	27		82

Lionel Antoine – Knee Injury
Roland Harper – Knee Injury
Brad Shearer – Knee Injury

MINNESOTA VIKINGS 7-9-0 Bud Grant

Scores of Each Game		
28	SAN FRANCISCO	22
7	Chicago	26
12	MIAMI	27
27	GREEN BAY	*21
13	Detroit	10
20	DALLAS	36
7	N.Y. Jets	14
30	CHICAGO	27
10	TAMPA BAY	12
7	St. Louis	37
7	Green Bay	19
14	DETROIT	7
23	Tampa Bay	22
21	Los Angeles	*27
10	BUFFALO	3
23	New England	27

Use Name	Pos.	Hgt.	Wgt.	Age	Int.	Pts.
Frank Myers	OT	6'5"	255	23		
Steve Riley	OT	6'6"	258	26		
Ron Yary	OT	6'6"	255	33		
Charlie Goodrum	OG	6'3"	256	29		
Wes Hamilton	OG	6'3"	255	26		
Jim Hough	OG-C	6'2"	267	23		
Dave Huffman	C-OG	6'6"	255	22		
Dennis Swilley	C	6'3"	241	24		
Randy Holloway	DE	6'5"	245	24		
Jim Marshall	DE	6'3"	240	41		
Mark Mullaney	DE	6'6"	242	26		
Steve Niehaus	DT	6'4"	255	24		
Dave Roller	DT	6'2"	270	29		
Doug Sutherland	DT	6'3"	250	31		
James White	DT	6'3"	263	25		
Matt Blair	LB	6'5"	229	27	3	
Wally Hilgenberg	LB	6'3"	229	36		
Derrel Luce	LB	6'3"	227	26		
Fred McNeill	LB	6'2"	229	27		
Jeff Siemon	LB	6'2"	237	29		
Scott Studwell	LB	6'2"	224	25	1	
Nate Allen (to DET.)	DB	5'10"	174	31	1	
Tim Baylor	DB	6'6"	190	25		
Bobby Bryant	DB	6'	170	35	2	
Tom Hannon	DB	5'11"	193	24	4	
Kurt Knoff	DB	6'2"	188	25	2	
Paul Krause	DB	6'3"	205	37	3	
Keith Nord	DB	6'	197	22		
John Turner	DB	6'	199	23	2	
Phil Wise	DB	6'	193	30		
Nate Wright	DB	5'11"	180	31	4	
Steve Dils	QB	6 1	190	23		
Tommy Kramer	QB	6 1	199	24		6
John Reaves	QB	6 3	210	29		
Jimmy Edwards	HB	5 9	185	26		
Brent McClanahan	HB	5 10	202	28		
Robert Miller	HB	5 11	204	26		12
Rickey Young	HB	6 2	195	25		42
Ted Brown	FB-HB	5 10	198	22		6
Chuck Foreman	FB	6 2	207	28		12
Doug Cunningham	WR	6 2	195	23		
Terry LeCount (from SF)	WR	5 10	172	23		12
Kevin Miller	WR	5 10	180	24		
Ahmad Rashad	WR	6 2	200	29		54
Robert Steele	WR	6 4	196	23		
Sammy White	WR	5 11	189	25		24
Bob Tucker	TE	6 3	230	34		12
Stu Voigt	TE	6 1	225	31		12
Greg Coleman	K	6	178	24		
Rick Danmeier	K	6	183	27		67

Ken Novak – Injury
Lyman Smith – Injury

GREEN BAY PACKERS 5-11-0 Bart Starr

Scores of Each Game		
3	Chicago	6
28	NEW ORLEANS	19
10	TAMPA BAY	21
21	Minnesota	*27
27	NEW ENGLAND	14
7	Atlanta	25
24	DETROIT	16
3	Tampa Bay	21
7	Miami	27
22	N.Y. JETS	27
19	MINNESOTA	7
12	Buffalo	19
10	PHILADELPHIA	21
21	Washington	38
14	CHICAGO	15
18	Detroit	13

Use Name	Pos.	Hgt.	Wgt.	Age	Int.	Pts.
Greg Koch	OT	6'4"	265	24		
Mark Koncar	OT	6'5"	268	26		
Tim Stokes	OT	6'5"	252	29		
Steve Young	OT	6'8"	270	26		
Derrel Gofourth	OG	6'3"	260	24		
Leotis Harris	OG	6'1"	267	24		
Melvin Jackson	OG	6'1"	267	25		
Larry McCarren	C	6'3"	248	27		
Mike Wellman	C	6'3"	253	23		
Bob Barber	DE	6'3"	240	27		
Mike Butler	DE	6'5"	265	25		6
Ezra Johnson	DE	6'4"	240	23		
Carl Barzilauskas	DT	6'6"	265	28		
Earl Edwards	DT	6'6"	260	33		
Charles Johnson	DT	6'1"	262	22	1	
Terry Jones	DT	6'2"	259	22		
Casey Merrill	DT-DE	6'4"	255	22		
John Anderson	LB	6'3"	230	23		4
Mike Douglass	LB	6'	224	24	3	
Jim Gueno	LB	6'2"	220	25		
Mike Hunt	LB	6'2"	240	22	1	
Joe McLaughlin	LB	6'1"	235	22		
Paul Rudzinski	LB	6'1"	220	23		
Davie Simmons	LB	6'4"	218	22		
Steve Stewart	LB	6'2"	220	23		
Gary Weaver	LB	6'1"	225	30		
Rich Wingo	LB	6'1"	230	23	2	
Johnnie Gray	DB	5'11"	185	25	5	
Estus Hood	DB	5'11"	180	23	2	
Steve Luke	DB	6'2"	205	25	1	
Mike McCoy	DB	5'11"	183	26	3	
Howard Sampson	DB	5'10"	185	23		
Wylie Turner	DB	5'10"	182	22		
Steve Wagner	DB	6'2"	208	25		
Lynn Dickey	QB	6 4	220	29		
David Whitehurst	QB	6 2	204	24		24
Ricky Patton (from ATL)	HB	5 11	189	25		
Nate Simpson	HB-FB	5 11	201	24		6
Terdell Middleton	HB	6	195	24		18
Steve Atkins	FB-HB	6	216	23		6
Jim Culbreath	FB	6	210	26		
Eddie Lee Ivery	FB	6 1	210	22		
Sammy Johnson (from PHI)	FB	6 1	226	26		
Walt Landers	FB	6	214	26		6
Barty Smith	FB	6 4	240	27		24
Eric Torkelson	FB	6 2	194	27		18
Ron Cassidy	WR	6	185	22		
Bobby Kimball	WR	6 1	190	22		
James Lofton	WR	6 3	187	23		24
Steve Odom (to NYG)	WR	5 8	174	26		
Aundra Thompson	WR	6	186	26		24
Walter Tullis	WR	6	170	26		6
Paul Coffman	TE	6 3	218	23		24
John Thompson	TE	6 3	228	22		
David Beverly	K	6 2	180	29		
Tom Birney	K	6 4	220	23		28
Chester Marcol	K	6	190	29		28

Rick Nuzum – Calf Injury

DETROIT LIONS 2-14-0 Monte Clark

Scores of Each Game		
16	Tampa Bay	31
24	WASHINGTON	27
10	N.Y. Jets	31
24	ATLANTA	23
10	MINNESOTA	13
17	New England	24
16	Green Bay	24
7	New Orleans	17
17	BUFFALO	20
7	Chicago	35
14	TAMPA BAY	16
7	Minnesota	14
20	CHICAGO	0
7	Philadelphia	44
10	MIAMI	28
13	GREEN BAY	18

Use Name	Pos.	Hgt.	Wgt.	Age	Int.	Pts.
Karl Baldischwiler	OT	6'5"	265	23		
Keith Dorney	OT	6'5"	265	21		
Don Morrison	OT-C	6'5"	259	29		
Russ Bolinger	OG	6'5"	250	24		
Homer Elias	OG	6'3"	255	24		
Amos Fowler	OG	6'3"	250	23		
Wally Pesuit	OG-C	6'4"	250	24		
Karl Chandler	C	6'5"	250	27		
Dennis Franks	C	6'1"	245	26		
Larry Tearry	C	6'3"	260	23		
Al Baker	DE	6'6"	260	22		
William Gay	DE	6'5"	225	24		6
Dave Pureifory	DE	6'1"	255	30		
Ken Sanders	DE	6'5"	245	29		
Cleveland Elam	DT	6'4"	251	27		
Doug English	DT	6'5"	260	26		2
Dave Gallagher	DT	6'4"	255	27		
Jon Brooks	LB	6'2"	215	22		
Garry Cobb	LB	6'2"	210	22		
Eddie Cole	LB	6'2"	235	22		
Ken Fantetti	LB	6'2"	230	22		
James Harrell	LB	6'1"	215	22		
Ed O'Neil	LB	6'3"	235	26		
Dave Washington	LB	6'5"	230	30		
Charlie Weaver	LB	6'2"	225	30	1	
Jim Allen	DB	6'2"	195	27	4	
Luther Bradley	DB	6'2"	195	24	4	
Ken Ellis (to LA)	DB	5'10"	180	31		
James Hunter	DB	6'3"	195	25	3	
Ernie Jackson	DB	5'10"	175	29		
Doug Jones	DB	6'2"	205	29		
Tony Leonard	DB	5'11"	175	26		
Eddie Lewis (from SF)	DB	6'	174	25		
Dave Parkin	DB	6'	190	23		
Don Patterson	DB	5'11"	175	21		
Jimmy Stewart	DB	5'11"	190	24		
Walt Williams	DB	6'	185	25	2	6
Jerry Golsteyn (to BAL)	QB	6 4	210	25		
Scott Hunter	QB	6 2	205	31		6
Jeff Komlo	QB	6 2	205	23		12
Joe Reed	QB	6 1	190	31		
Dexter Bussey	HB	6 1	210	27		6
Ken Callicutt	HB	6	190	24		
Rick Kane	HB	5 11	200	24		30
Lawrence Gaines	FB	6 1	230	25		
Horace King	FB	5 10	205	26		6
Bo Robinson	FB	6 2	225	23		12
John Arnold	WR	5 10	175	23		
Luther Blue	WR	5 11	180	23		6
Freddie Scott	WR	6 2	180	27		30
Leonard Thompson	WR	5 10	190	27		12
Gene Washington	WR	6 1	180	31		6
Robert Woods	WR	5 7	170	24		
David Hill	TE	6 2	230	25		18
Ulysses Norris	TE	6 4	225	22		6
Benny Ricardo	K	5 10	170	25		55
Larry Swider	K	6 2	195	24		
Tom Skladany	K	6	195	24		

Gary Danielson – Knee Injury
Dan Gray – Injury
Mark Markovich – Injury
Jesse Thompson – Illness

John Woodcock – Back Injury

*Overtime

TAMPA BAY BUCCANEERS

RUSHING

Last Name	No.	Yds.	Avg.	TD
Bell	283	1263	4.5	7
Eckwood	194	690	3.6	2
J. Davis	59	221	3.7	2
Williams	35	119	3.4	2
Berns	23	102	4.4	0
Mucker	4	16	4.0	0
Jones	1	12	12.0	0
Giles	2	7	3.5	0
Ragsdale	6	5	0.8	0
Rae	1	2	2.0	0
Blanchard	1	0	0.0	0

RECEIVING

Last Name	No.	Yds.	Avg.	TD
Giles	40	579	15	7
Hagins	39	692	18	3
Bell	25	248	10	2
Eckwood	22	268	12	0
Owens	20	377	19	0
Mucker	14	268	19	5
Obradovich	6	63	11	1
J. Davis	5	57	11	0
Berns	5	40	8	0
Jones	4	80	20	1
Ragsdale	3	28	9	0

PUNT RETURNS

Last Name	No.	Yds.	Avg.	TD
Reece	70	431	6	0
T. Davis	1	7	7	0

KICKOFF RETURNS

Last Name	No.	Yds.	Avg.	TD
Ragsdale	34	675	20	0
Hagins	9	196	22	0
T. Davis	4	33	8	0
Nafziger	2	36	18	0
Reece	1	13	13	0
Berns	1	6	6	0

PASSING - PUNTING - KICKING

PASSING	Att.	Comp.	%	Yds.	Yd./Att.	TD	Int.–%	RK
Williams	397	166	42	2448	6.2	18	24– 6	13
Rae	36	17	47	252	7.0	1	2– 6	
Eckwood	1	0	0	0	0.0	0	0– 0	

PUNTING	No.	Avg.
Blanchard	93	39.6

KICKING	XP	Att.	%	FG	Att.	%
O'Donoghue	30	35	86	11	19	58

CHICAGO BEARS

RUSHING

Last Name	No.	Yds.	Avg.	TD
Payton	369	1610	4.4	14
Williams	127	401	3.2	1
McClendon	37	160	4.3	1
Earl	35	132	3.8	0
Evans	12	72	6.0	1
Phipps	27	51	1.9	0
Deloplaine	7	18	2.6	0
Perrin	7	18	2.6	0
Buffone	1	14	14.0	0
Avellini	3	10	3.3	0
Skibinski	3	10	3.3	0
Watts	1	−6	−6.0	0

RECEIVING

Last Name	No.	Yds.	Avg.	TD
Williams	42	354	8	5
Payton	31	313	10	2
Baschnagel	30	452	15	2
Watts	24	421	18	3
Scott	21	382	18	3
Latta	15	131	9	0
Earl	8	56	7	0
Cobb	6	91	15	0
McClendon	6	27	5	0
Richards	5	107	21	1
Schubert	2	29	15	0
Deloplaine	2	13	7	0
Perrin	1	27	27	0
Buffone	1	22	22	0
Skibinski	1	4	4	0

PUNT RETURNS

Last Name	No.	Yds.	Avg.	TD
Schubert	25	238	10	1
Walterscheid	14	96	7	0

KICKOFF RETURNS

Last Name	No.	Yds.	Avg.	TD
Walterscheid	19	427	23	0
Watts	14	289	21	1
Baschnagel	12	260	22	0
Perrin	4	86	22	0
Schubert	2	45	23	0
McClendon	1	12	12	0
Latta	1	8	8	0
Herron	1	0	0	0

PASSING - PUNTING - KICKING

PASSING	Att.	Comp.	%	Yds.	Yd./Att.	TD	Int.–%	RK
Phipps	255	134	53	1535	6.0	9	8– 3	7
Evans	63	32	51	508	8.1	4	5– 8	
Avellini	51	27	53	310	6.1	2	3– 6	
Payton	1	1	100	54	54.0	1	0– 0	
Parsons	2	1	50	22	11.0	0	0– 0	
Baschnagel	1	0	0	0	0.0	0	0– 0	

PUNTING	No.	Avg.
Parsons	92	37.9

KICKING	XP	Att.	%	FG	Att.	%
Thomas	34	37	92	16	27	59

MINNESOTA VIKINGS

RUSHING

Last Name	No.	Yds.	Avg.	TD
Young	188	708	3.8	3
Brown	130	551	4.2	1
Foreman	87	223	2.6	2
Kramer	32	138	4.3	1
R. Miller	35	109	3.1	2
McClanahan	14	29	2.1	0
S. White	1	6	6.0	0

RECEIVING

Last Name	No.	Yds.	Avg.	TD
Rashad	80	1156	15	9
Young	72	519	7	4
S. White	42	715	17	4
Brown	31	197	6	0
Tucker	24	223	9	2
Foreman	19	147	8	0
Voigt	15	139	9	2
McClanahan	10	57	6	0
R. Miller	9	60	7	0
LeCount	6	119	20	2
Cunningham	5	50	10	0
Steele	1	10	10	0
Edwards	1	2	2	0
Kramer	0	3	–	0

PUNT RETURNS

Last Name	No.	Yds.	Avg.	TD
Edwards	33	186	6	0
K. Miller	18	85	5	0
Nord	3	11	4	0
Bryant	1	7	7	0
Turner	1	0	0	0
Allen	1	−1	−1	0

KICKOFF RETURNS

Last Name	No.	Yds.	Avg.	TD
Edwards	44	1103	25	0
Brown	8	186	23	0
McClanahan	3	53	18	0
R. Miller	3	38	13	0
Steele	1	0	0	0
Studwell	1	0	0	0
Voigt	1	0	0	0

PASSING - PUNTING - KICKING

PASSING	Att.	Comp.	%	Yds.	Yd./Att.	TD	Int.–%	RK
Kramer	566	315	56	3397	6.0	23	24– 4	6

PUNTING	No.	Avg.
Coleman	90	39.5

KICKING	XP	Att.	%	FG	Att.	%
Danmeier	28	30	93	13	22	59

GREEN BAY PACKERS

RUSHING

Last Name	No.	Yds.	Avg.	TD
Middleton	131	495	3.8	2
Torkelson	98	401	4.1	3
Atkins	42	239	5.7	1
Simpson	66	235	3.6	1
Smith	57	201	3.5	3
Patton	40	135	3.4	0
Whitehurst	18	73	4.1	4
Landers	17	41	2.4	0
Ivery	3	24	8.0	0
Wagner	1	16	16.0	0
Dickey	5	13	2.6	0
Culbreath	5	8	1.6	0
Lofton	1	−1	−1.0	0
A. Thompson	2	−18	−9.0	0

RECEIVING

Last Name	No.	Yds.	Avg.	TD
Coffman	56	711	13	4
Lofton	54	968	18	4
A. Thompson	25	395	16	3
Smith	19	155	8	1
Torkelson	19	139	7	0
Middleton	18	155	9	1
Simpson	11	46	4	0
Tullis	10	173	17	1
Atkins	10	89	9	0
Cassidy	6	102	17	0
Patton	6	41	7	0
Landers	5	60	12	1
Gueno	1	23	23	0

PUNT RETURNS

Last Name	No.	Yds.	Avg.	TD
Odom	24	106	4	0
Gray	13	61	5	0

KICKOFF RETURNS

Last Name	No.	Yds.	Avg.	TD
Odom	44	949	22	0
A. Thompson	15	346	23	1
McCoy	11	248	23	0
Sampson	4	61	15	0
Wellman	1	10	10	0
Wagner	1	8	8	0

PASSING - PUNTING - KICKING

PASSING	Att.	Comp.	%	Yds.	Yd./Att.	TD	Int.–%	RK
Whitehurst	322	179	56	2247	7.0	10	18– 6	11
Dickey	119	60	50	787	6.6	5	4– 3	
Beverly	2	1	50	23	11.5	0	0– 0	
Lofton	1	0	0	0	0.0	0	0– 0	

PUNTING	No.	Avg.
Beverly	69	40.4

KICKING	XP	Att.	%	FG	Att.	%
Birney	7	10	70	7	9	78
Marcol	16	18	89	4	10	40
Anderson	1	2	50	1	1	100

DETROIT LIONS

RUSHING

Last Name	No.	Yds.	Avg.	TD
Bussey	144	625	4.3	1
Kane	94	332	3.5	4
Robinson	87	302	3.5	2
King	39	160	4.1	1
Komlo	30	107	3.6	2
Gaines	23	55	2.4	0
G. Washington	1	24	24.0	0
Thompson	5	24	4.8	0
Scott	6	21	3.5	0
Hill	1	15	15.0	0
Reed	2	11	5.5	0
Callicut	3	6	2.0	0
S. Hunter	2	3	1.5	1
Golsteyn	1	0	0.0	0
O'Neil	1	0	0.0	0
Swider	1	0	0.0	0
Blue	1	−8	−8.0	0

RECEIVING

Last Name	No.	Yds.	Avg.	TD
Scott	62	929	15	5
Hill	47	569	12	3
Thompson	24	451	19	2
King	18	150	8	0
Bussey	15	102	7	0
G. Washington	14	192	14	1
Robinson	14	118	8	0
Kane	9	104	12	1
Blue	8	102	13	1
Norris	4	43	11	1
Callicut	2	16	8	0
Bolinger	1	−1	−1	0

PUNT RETURNS

Last Name	No.	Yds.	Avg.	TD
Arnold	19	164	9	0
Thompson	9	117	13	0
Ellis	8	43	5	0
Callicut	4	25	6	0
Woods	2	12	6	0
Leonard	1	7	7	0
Pesuit	1	5	5	0
Lewis	1	−1	−1	0

KICKOFF RETURNS

Last Name	No.	Yds.	Avg.	TD
Arnold	23	539	23	0
Callicut	24	406	17	0
Kane	13	281	22	0
Thompson	6	151	25	0
Leonard	3	70	23	0
King	2	36	18	0
Woods	2	34	17	0
Fanetti	2	18	9	0
Blue	1	26	26	0
Robinson	1	8	8	0
Gay	1	0	0	0

PASSING - PUNTING - KICKING

PASSING	Att.	Comp.	%	Yds.	Yd./Att.	TD	Int.–%	RK
Komlo	368	183	50	2238	6.1	11	23– 6	14
S. Hunter	41	18	44	321	7.8	1	1– 2	
Reed	32	14	44	164	5.1	2	1– 3	
Golsteyn	9	2	22	16	1.8	0	2– 22	
Swider	1	1	100	36	36.0	0	0– 0	
Skladany	1	0	0	0	0.0	0	0– 0	

PUNTING	No.	Avg.
Swider	88	40.0
Skladany	10	40.6

KICKING	XP	Att.	%	FG	Att.	%
Ricardo	25	26	96	10	18	56

LOS ANGELES RAMS 9-7-0 Ray Malavasi

Scores of Each Game		
17	OAKLAND	24
13	Denver	9
27	SAN FRANCISCO	24
6	Tampa Bay	21
21	ST. LOUIS	0
35	New Orleans	17
6	Dallas	30
16	SAN DIEGO	40
14	N.Y. GIANTS	20
24	Seattle	0
23	Chicago	27
20	ATLANTA	14
26	San Francisco	20
27	MINNESOTA	*21
34	Atlanta	13
14	NEW ORLEANS	29

Use Name	Pos.	Hgt.	Wgt.	Age	Int.	Pts.
Doug France	OT	6'5"	288	26		
Gordon Gravelle (from NYG)	OT	6'5"	252	30		
Jackie Slater	OT	6'4"	269	25		
John Williams	OT-OG	6'3"	256	33		
Brent Adams	OG-OT	6'5"	256	27		
Bill Bain	OG	6'4"	270	27		
Dennis Harrah	OG	6'5"	251	26		
Kent Hill	OG	6'5"	260	22		
Dan Ryczek	C	6'3"	245	30		
Rich Saul	C	6'3"	243	31		
Doug Smith	C-OG	6'3"	250	22		
Reggie Doss	DE	6'4"	267	22		
Fred Dryer	DE	6'6"	230	33		
Jerry Wilkinson	DE	6'9"	255	23		
Jack Youngblood	DE	6'4"	243	29		
Larry Brooks	DT	6'3"	255	29		
Bill Dunstan	DT	6'4"	250	30		
Mike Fanning	DT	6'6"	248	26		
George Andrews	LB	6'3"	226	23		
Bob Brudzinski	LB	6'4"	231	24	1	
Joe Harris (from MIN)	LB	6'1"	225	26		6
Kevin McLain	LB	6'2"	227	24		
Jack Reynolds	LB	6'1"	231	31		6
Greg Westbrooks (from OAK)	LB	6'3"	215	26		
Jim Youngblood	LB	6'3"	231	29	5	12
Eddie Brown	DB	5'11"	190	27	3	
Nolan Cromwell	DB	6'1"	197	24	5	6
Dave Elmendorf	DB	6'1"	196	30	3	
Sid Justin	DB	5'10"	170	25	1	6
Ricky Odom	DB	6'	183	22		
Dwayne O'Steen	DB	6'1"	190	24	4	
Rod Perry	DB	5'9"	177	25	8	18
Jeff Severson	DB	6'1"	185	29		
Ivory Sully	DB	6'	193	22		
Pat Thomas	DB	5'9"	184	25	3	
Jackie Wallare	DB	6'3"	196	28		
Vince Ferragamo	QB	6'3"	207	25		
Pat Haden	QB	5'11"	180	26		
Bob Lee	QB	6'2"	195	33		
Jeff Rutledge	QB	6'1"	[illegible]00	22		
Eddie Hill	HB	6'2"	197	22		12
Lawrence McCutcheon	HB	6'1"	205	29		
Wendell Tyler	HB	5'10"	188	24		60
Cullen Bryant	FB	6'1"	234	28		30
Jim Jodat	FB	5'11"	207	25		6
Elvis Peacock	FB	6'1"	220	22		
Preston Dennard	WR	6'1"	185	23		24
Drew Hill	WR	5'9"	170	22		6
Ron Jessie	WR	6'	181	31		12
Willie Miller	WR	5'9"	172	32		6
Ron Smith	WR	6'	185	22		6
Billy Waddy	WR	5'11"	180	25		18
Terry Nelson	TE	6'2"	241	28		18
Charlie Young	TE	6'4"	234	28		12
Ken Clark	K	6'2"	197	31		
Frank Corral	K	6'2"	220	24		75

John Cappelletti – Groin Injury
Anthony Davis – Broken Rib
Carl Ekern – Knee Injury
Cody Jones – Achilles Injury

NEW ORLEANS SAINTS 8-8-0 Dick Nolan

Scores of Each Game		
34	ATLANTA	*40
19	Green Bay	28
14	PHILADELPHIA	26
30	San Francisco	21
24	N.Y. GIANTS	14
17	LOS ANGELES	35
42	Tampa Bay	14
17	DETROIT	7
14	Washington	10
3	Denver	10
31	SAN FRANCISCO	20
24	Seattle	38
37	Atlanta	6
35	OAKLAND	42
0	SAN DIEGO	35
29	Los Angeles	14

Use Name	Pos.	Hgt.	Wgt.	Age	Int.	Pts.
Roger Finnie	OT	6'3"	250	33		
J.T. Taylor	OT	6'4"	265	23		
John Watson	OT	6'4"	244	30		
Robert Woods	OT	6'3"	259	29		
Conrad Dobler	OG	6'3"	255	28		
Dave Lafary	OG	6'7"	280	24		
Fred Sturt	OG	6'4"	255	28		
Emanuel Zanders	OG	6'1"	248	28		
John Hill	C	6'2"	246	29		
Jim Pietrzak (from NYG)	C-OT	6'5"	260	26		
Joe Campbell	DE	6'6"	254	24		
Elois Grooms	DE	6'4"	250	26	1	2
Don Reese	DE	6'6"	250	27		
Barry Bennett	DT	6'4"	257	23		
Mike Fultz	DT	6'5"	278	25		
Derland Moore	DT	6'4"	253	27		
Elex Price	DT	6'3"	265	29		
Ken Bordelon	LB	6'4"	226	25	2	6
Joe Federspiel	LB	6'1"	230	29	1	
Pat Hughes	LB	6'2"	225	32	4	
Jim Kovach	LB	6'2"	225	23		
Reggie Mathis	LB	6'2"	220	23		
Jim Merlo	LB	6'1"	220	27		
Ray Brown	DB	6'2"	202	30	1	
Clarence Chapman	CB	5'10"	185	25	2	
Eric Felton	DB	6'	200	23	4	
David Gray	DB	6'	190	24	1	
Ralph McGill	DB	5'11"	178	29	1	
Tom Myers	DB	5'11"	180	28	7	6
Ricky Ray	DB	5'11"	180	22		
Don Schwartz	DB	6'1"	191	23	2	
Ed Burns	QB	6'3"	210	24		
Archie Manning	QB	6'3"	200	30		12
Bobby Scott	QB	6'1"	197	30		
Chuck Muncie	HB-FB	6'3"	233	26		66
Mike Strachan	HB	6'	200	26		36
Wayne Wilson	HB	6'3"	208	21		
Tony Galbreath	FB	6'	230	25		67
Jack Holmes	FB	5'11"	210	26		
Kim Jones	FB	6'4"	235	27		
Wes Chandler	WR	5'11"	186	23		36
Ike Harris	WR	6'3"	210	26		12
Rich Mauti	WR	6'	190	25		
Tinker Owens	WR	5'11"	170	24		6
Henry Childs	TE	6'2"	220	28		30
Larry Hardy	TE	6'3"	230	23		6
Brooks Williams	TE	6'4"	226	24		
Russell Erxleben	K	6'4"	219	22		10
Rick Partridge	K	6'1"	175	22		
Garo Yepremian	K	5'8"	175	35		75

Mike Watson – Injury

ATLANTA FALCONS 6-10-0 Leeman Bennett

Scores of Each Game		
40	New Orleans	*34
14	Philadelphia	10
17	DENVER	*20
23	Detroit	24
7	WASHINGTON	16
25	GREEN BAY	7
19	Oakland	50
15	San Francisco	20
28	SEATTLE	31
17	TAMPA BAY	14
3	N.Y. Giants	24
14	Los Angeles	20
6	NEW ORLEANS	37
28	San Diego	26
13	LOS ANGELES	34
31	SAN FRANCISCO	21

Use Name	Pos.	Hgt.	Wgt.	Age	Int.	Pts.
Warren Bryant	OT	6'6"	270	23		
Mike Kenn	OT	6'6"	257	23		
Phil McKinnely	OT	6'4"	248	25		
Pat Howell	OG	6'5"	253	22		
Dave Scott	OG	6'4"	285	25		
R.C. Thielemann	OG	6'4"	247	24		
Chuck Correal	C	6'3"	247	23		
Paul Ryczek	C	6'2"	230	27		
Jeff Van Note	C	6'2"	247	33		
Jeff Merrow	DE	6'4"	230	26		
Don Smith	DE	6'5"	248	22		
Jeff Yeates	DE-DT	6'3"	248	28		
Wilson Faumuina	DT	6'5"	275	25		
Edgar Fields	DT-DE	6'2"	255	25		
Mike Lewis	DT	6'3"	261	30		2
Mike Zele	DT	6'3"	236	23		
Greg Brezina	LB	6'1"	221	33		
Brian Cabral	LB	6'	209	23		
Tony Daykin	LB	6'1"	215	24		
Fulton Kuykendall	LB	6'5"	225	26		
Ron McCartney	LB	6'1"	220	25		
Dewey McClain	LB	6'3"	236	25		
Robert Pennywell	LB	6'1"	222	24	1	6
Joel Williams	LB	6'1"	215	22		
Rick Byas	DB	5'9"	180	28	1	6
Ray Easterling	DB	6'	192	29	2	
Bob Glazebrook	DB	6'1"	200	23		
Jerome King	DB	5'10"	173	24		
Rolland Lawrence	DB	5'10"	179	28	6	6
Tom Moriarty	DB	6'	185	26		
Tom Pridemore	DB	5'10"	186	23	2	
Frank Reed	DB	5'11"	193	25	2	
Steve Bartkowski	QB	6'4"	213	26		12
Larry Fortner	QB	6'4"	212	23		
June Jones	QB	6'4"	200	26		
Mike Moroski	QB	6'4"	200	21		6
Bubba Bean	HB	5'11"	195	25		6
Lynn Cain	HB	6'1"	205	23		24
Haskel Stanback	HB-FB	6'	210	27		30
Ray Strong	HB	5'9"	184	23		
William Andrews	FB	6'	200	23		30
James Mayberry	FB	5'11"	210	21	1	12
Wallace Francis	WR	5'11"	190	27		48
Alfred Jackson	WR	5'11"	176	24		
Al Jenkins	WR	5'10"	172	27		18
Dennis Pearson	WR	5'11"	177	24		
Billy Ryckman	WR	5'11"	172	24		12
Russ Mikeska	TE	6'3"	225	23		
Jim Mitchell	TE	6'2"	236	31		12
John James	K	6'3"	200	30		
Tim Mazzetti	K	6'1"	175	23		70

Mike Esposito – Shoulder Injury
Lewis Gilbert – Knee Injury
James Wright – Knee Injury
Garth Ten Napel – Injured in Auto Accident in April
Andy Spiva – Died in Auto Accident in April

SAN FRANCISCO FORTY-NINERS 2-14-0 Bill Walsh

Scores of Each Game		
22	Minnesota	28
13	DALLAS	21
24	Los Angeles	27
21	NEW ORLEANS	30
9	San Diego	31
24	SEATTLE	35
16	N.Y. Giants	32
20	ATLANTA	15
27	CHICAGO	28
10	Oakland	23
20	New Orleans	31
28	DENVER	38
20	LOS ANGELES	26
10	St. Louis	13
23	TAMPA BAY	7
21	Atlanta	31

Use Name	Pos.	Hgt.	Wgt.	Age	Int.	Pts.
Jean Barrett	OT	6'6"	250	28		
Keith Fahnhorst	OT	6'6"	263	27		
Ron Singleton	OT	6'7"	267	27		
John Ayers	OG	6'5"	247	26		
Randy Cross	OG	6'3"	255	25		
Walt Downing	OG-C	6'3"	254	23		
Fred Quillan	C	6'5"	254	23		
Dwaine Board	DE	6'5"	245	22		
Al Cowlings	DE	6'5"	222	32		
Cedrick Hardman	DE	6'3"	244	30		
Archie Reese	DE	6'3"	262	23		
Ed Galigher	DT	6'4"	255	28		
Ruben Vaughn	DT	6'2"	264	23		
Ted Vincent	DT	6'4"	265	23		
Jimmy Webb	DT	6'5"	245	27		
Dan Bunz	LB	6'4"	230	23	1	
Gordy Ceresino	LB	6'	224	21		
Willie Harper	LB	6'2"	215	29		
Scott Hilton	LB	6'4"	225	25		
Bob Martin (from NYJ)	LB	6'1"	214	25		
Jeff McIntyre	LB	6'3"	232	23		
Dave Morton	LB	6'2"	224	24		
Bob Nelson	LB	6'4"	230	26		
Thomas Seabron	LB	6'3"	215	22		
Ron Shumon	LB	6'1"	234	23		
John Bristor	DB	6'	188	23		
Charles Cornelius	DB	5'9"	178	27	3	
Tony Dungy	DB	6'	190	23		
Tim Gray	DB	6'1"	200	26	1	
Dwight Hicks	DB	6'1"	189	23	5	
Charles Johnson	DB	5'10"	180	23		
Eric Johnson	DB	6'1"	192	27		
Melvin Morgan	DB	6'	180	26	1	
Gerard Williams	DB	6'1"	184	27	4	
Steve DeBerg	QB	6'2"	205	25		
Joe Montana	QB	6'2"	200	23		
Lenvil Elliott	HB-FB	6'	210	27		18
Phil Francis	HB-FB	6'1"	215	22		6
Paul Hofer	HB	6'	195	27		54
O.J. Simpson	HB	6'2"	212	32		18
Bob Ferrell	FB	6'	213	26		
Mike Hogan	FB	6'2"	215	24		
Wilbur Jackson	FB	6'1"	219	27		12
Dwight Clark	WR	6'3"	205	22		
James Owens	WR-HB-DB	5'11"	188	24		6
Mike Shumann	WR	6'	175	23		24
Freddie Solomon	WR	5'11"	188	26		48
Bob Bruer	TE	6'5"	235	26		6
Ken MacAfee	TE	6'5"	245	23		24
Eason Ramson	TE	6'2"	234	23		
Paul Seal	TE	6'4"	227	27		
Dan Melville	K	6'	185	23		
Ray Wersching	K	5'11"	210	29		92

Mike Baldassin – Injury
Lon Boyett – Injury
Ed Bradley – Broken Ankle
Scott Bull – Knee Injury
Ernie Hughes – Knee Injury
Bob Jury – Shoulder Injury

Steve Knutson – Knee Injury
Johnny Miller – Knee Injury

* – Overtime

LOS ANGELES RAMS

RUSHING

Last Name	No.	Yds.	Avg.	TD
Tyler	218	1109	5.1	9
Bryant	177	619	3.5	5
McCutcheon	73	243	3.3	0
Peacock	52	224	4.3	0
E. Hill	29	114	3.9	1
Haden	16	97	6.1	0
Dennard	4	32	8.0	0
Rutledge	5	27	5.4	0
Jodat	6	6	1.0	0
Cromwell	1	5	5.0	1
Miller	1	4	4.0	0
Clark	1	3	3.0	0
Ferragamo	3	–2	–0.7	0
Lee	4	–5	–1.3	0
Nelson	2	–16	–8.0	0

RECEIVING

Last Name	No.	Yds.	Avg.	TD
Dennard	43	766	18	4
Tyler	32	308	10	1
Bryant	31	227	7	0
Nelson	25	293	12	3
Peacock	21	261	12	0
McCutcheon	19	101	5	0
R. Smith	16	300	19	1
Waddy	14	220	16	3
Young	13	144	11	2
Jessie	11	169	15	2
Miller	8	111	14	1
D. Hill	4	94	24	1
E. Hill	4	36	9	1
Andrews	1	2	2	0

PUNT RETURNS

Last Name	No.	Yds.	Avg.	TD
Brown	56	332	6	0
D. Hill	1	0	0	0
Justin	1	–2	–2	0

KICKOFF RETURNS

Last Name	No.	Yds.	Avg.	TD
D. Hill	40	803	20	0
E. Hill	15	305	20	0
Brown	5	103	21	0
Peacock	3	46	15	0
Jodat	2	19	10	0
Tyler	1	16	16	0

PASSING – PUNTING – KICKING

PASSING	Att.	Comp.	%	Yds.	Yd./Att.	TD	Int.–%	RK
Haden	290	163	56	1854	6.4	11	14– 5	8
Lee	22	11	50	243	11.1	2	1– 5	
Ferragamo	110	53	48	778	7.1	5	10– 9	
Rutledge	32	13	41	125	3.9	1	4– 13	
Clark	2	2	100	32	16.0	0	0– 0	

PUNTING	No.	Avg.
Clark	93	40.1

KICKING	XP	Att.	%	FG	Att.	%
Corral	36	39	92	13	25	52

NEW ORLEANS SAINTS

RUSHING

Last Name	No.	Yds.	Avg.	TD
Muncie	238	1198	5.0	11
Galbreath	189	708	3.7	9
Strachan	62	276	4.5	6
Manning	35	186	5.3	2
Holmes	17	68	4.0	0
Wilson	5	26	5.2	0
Harris	2	9	4.5	0
Jones	3	5	1.7	0

RECEIVING

Last Name	No.	Yds.	Avg.	TD
Chandler	65	1069	16	6
Galbreath	58	484	8	1
Childs	51	846	17	5
Muncie	40	308	8	0
Harris	25	395	16	2
Owens	7	72	10	1
Holmes	3	19	6	0
Strachan	3	9	3	0
Mauti	2	64	32	0
Williams	2	22	11	0
Hardy	1	3	3	1

PUNT RETURNS

Last Name	No.	Yds.	Avg.	TD
Mauti	27	218	8	0
Chandler	3	13	4	0

KICKOFF RETURNS

Last Name	No.	Yds.	Avg.	TD
Mauti	36	801	22	0
Wilson	11	230	21	0
Holmes	8	120	15	0
Chandler	7	136	19	0
Williams	2	12	6	0
Kovach	1	10	10	0
Owens	1	10	10	0

PASSING – PUNTING – KICKING

PASSING	Att.	Comp.	%	Yds.	Yd./Att.	TD	Int.–%	RK
Manning	420	252	60	3169	7.6	15	20– 5	4
Scott	2	2	100	12	6.0	0	0– 0	
Galbreath	3	2	67	70	23.3	0	1– 33	
Muncie	2	1	50	40	20.0	1	0– 0	
Erxleben	1	0	0	0	0.0	0	1–100	

PUNTING	No.	Avg.
Partridge	57	40.9
Chandler	8	31.0
Erxleben	4	37.0

KICKING	XP	Att.	%	FG	Att.	%
Yepremian	39	40	98	12	16	75
Galbreath	1	2	50	2	3	67
Erxleben	4	4	100	2	2	100

ATLANTA FALCONS

RUSHING

Last Name	No.	Yds.	Avg.	TD
Andrews	239	1023	4.3	3
Bean	88	393	4.5	1
Cain	63	295	4.7	2
Stanback	36	202	5.6	5
Mayberry	45	193	4.3	1
Bartkowski	14	36	2.6	2
Moroski	3	31	10.3	1
Jones	6	19	3.2	0
Strong	2	7	3.5	0
James	1	0	0.0	0

RECEIVING

Last Name	No.	Yds.	Avg.	TD
Francis	74	1013	14	8
Jenkins	50	858	17	3
Andrews	39	309	8	2
Mitchell	16	118	7	2
Cain	15	181	12	2
Stanback	13	89	7	0
Bean	12	137	11	0
Jackson	11	156	14	0
Pearson	7	119	17	0
Mayberry	7	48	7	0
Ryckman	4	59	15	2
Glazebrook	1	20	20	0
Mikeska	1	14	14	0
Strong	1	6	6	0

PUNT RETURNS

Last Name	No.	Yds.	Avg.	TD
Pearson	12	115	10	0
Ryckman	12	72	6	0
McClain	1	2	2	0
Glazebrook	1	–1	–1	0

KICKOFF RETURNS

Last Name	No.	Yds.	Avg.	TD
Pearson	30	570	19	0
Strong	15	343	23	0
Pridemore	9	111	12	0
Cain	7	149	21	0
Stanback	6	109	18	0
Mayberry	4	49	12	0
Jackson	1	20	20	0
Byas	1	19	19	0

PASSING – PUNTING – KICKING

PASSING	Att.	Comp.	%	Yds.	Yd./Att.	TD	Int.–%	RK
Bartkowski	380	204	54	2505	6.6	17	20– 5	9
Moroski	15	8	53	97	6.5	0	0– 0	
Jones	83	38	46	505	6.1	2	3– 4	
James	1	1	100	20	20.0	0	0– 0	

PUNTING	No.	Avg.
James	83	39.7

KICKING	XP	Att.	%	FG	Att.	%
Mazzetti	31	37	84	13	25	52

SAN FRANCISCO FORTY-NINERS

RUSHING

Last Name	No.	Yds.	Avg.	TD
Hofer	123	615	5.0	7
Simpson	120	460	3.8	3
Jackson	114	375	3.3	2
Elliott	33	135	4.1	3
Francis	31	118	3.8	1
Solomon	6	85	14.2	1
Owens	7	33	4.7	0
Ferrell	8	33	4.1	0
Hogan	9	31	3.4	0
Montana	3	22	7.3	0
Shumann	1	19	19.0	0
DeBerg	17	10	0.6	0
Melville	3	0	0.0	0
Bruer	5	–4	–0.8	0

RECEIVING

Last Name	No.	Yds.	Avg.	TD
Hofer	58	662	11	2
Solomon	57	807	14	7
Jackson	53	422	8	0
Shumann	39	452	12	4
Francis	32	198	6	0
Bruer	26	254	10	1
MacAfee	24	266	11	4
Elliott	23	197	9	0
Clark	18	232	13	0
Owens	10	121	12	0
Hogan	9	65	7	0
Simpson	7	46	7	0
Seal	3	34	11	0
Ferrell	2	4	2	0

PUNT RETURNS

Last Name	No.	Yds.	Avg.	TD
Solomon	23	142	6	0
Hicks	13	120	9	0
Dungy	8	52	7	0

KICKOFF RETURNS

Last Name	No.	Yds.	Avg.	TD
Owens	41	1002	24	1
Elliott	9	170	19	0
Hofer	8	124	16	0
Francis	7	103	15	0
Ferrell	6	78	13	0
Hicks	2	36	18	0
Bruer	1	20	20	0
Barrett	1	5	5	0

PASSING – PUNTING – KICKING

PASSING	Att.	Comp.	%	Yds.	Yd./Att.	TD	Int.–%	RK
DeBerg	**578**	**347**	**60**	**3652**	6.3	17	21– 4	5
Montana	23	13	57	96	4.2	1	0– 0	
Solomon	1	1	100	12	12.0	0	0– 0	

PUNTING	No.	Avg.
Melville	71	37.0

KICKING	XP	Att.	%	FG	Att.	%
Wersching	32	35	91	20	24	**83**

1979 A.F.C. The Shouting Above

Discord rang in the halls of several N.F.L. teams. In New England, the Patriots sued Chuck Fairbanks to prevent him from leaving to coach the University of Oklahoma team. The court battle languished into the warm weather, when the Patriots gave up the fight and named Ron Erhardt their new head coach.

In New Jersey, the Giants were ripped by a feud within the Mara family. After the 1978 management was cleared out, Wellington and Tim Mara couldn't agree on new leadership. After some unseemly squabbling and intervention by Pete Rozelle, they made George Young, an assistant to Don Shula in Miami, the new general manager.

In Los Angeles, the headlines came in rapid succession. Early in the year, owner Carroll Rosenbloom sought and received permission from his fellow owners to move the Rams from the Los Angeles Coliseum to Anaheim Stadium in 1980. Although the geographical distance was not far, the citizens and leaders of Los Angeles raised the hue and cry against their "betrayal." In the spring, Rosenbloom drowned accidentally at his Florida home. Majority ownership went to his widow, Georgia, while his son Steve, a team executive, held a minority interest. The two Rosenblooms struggled bitterly for power, with Georgia finally firing Steve. Cast out by his stepmother, Steve found refuge as a high executive with the New Orleans Saints.

EASTERN DIVISION

Miami Dolphins—Two heroes from the glorious past boosted the Dolphins back into first place in the East. Larry Csonka returned to Miami as a free agent after a four-year exile in the W.F.L. and in New Jersey with the Giants. Csonka's running power and a tough defense shot the Dolphins out to a fast start in the playoff race. Young nose tackle Bob Baumhower led the defense with an All-Star performance. A hamstring injury bothered quarterback Bob Griese at the start of the year, and when the offense faltered in mid-season, coach Don Shula turned to Don Strock to run the attack. On November 25, Shula brought Griese off the bench in the second quarter against the Colts. The veteran led the Dolphins to a 28-24 victory. Four days later, the Patriots came to Miami for a first-place showdown. Strock started the game but didn't generate much offense. Griese came into the fray in the second half, directing the offense to 26 points and a 39-24 triumph. The Dolphins then sewed up first place with an easy game against the Lions.

New England Patriots—As usual, the Patriots had mountains of talent ready to erupt into a championship. As usual, the Patriots sputtered far short of their goal. The offense had a great passing attack and a stable of good runners. The offensive line suffered from the trade of Leon Gray to the Oilers, but still enjoyed the talents of John Hannah. The defense combined a strong pass rush with a swarm of young blue-chip secondary men such as Mike Haynes. New coach Ron Erhardt had the Pats in first place in mid-November with an 8-4 record. On November 25, the Bills rocked the Patriots with a 16-13 overtime upset, dropping New England into a first-place tie with Miami. Against the Dolphins on the following Thursday night, the Pats blew a first half lead and dropped a 39-24 decision. With signs of choking in full view, the Patriots went to Shea Stadium in New York on December 9. The Pats had demolished the Jets 56-3 in September, but the Jets had the last laugh. They edged the Patriots 27-26 to kill any New England hopes for a playoff berth.

New York Jets—Despite last year's strong finish, coach Walt Michaels made basic changes in both his offensive and defensive units. Michaels reinstalled the 4-3 defense and manned it with a large class of promising rookies. Marty Lyons, Stan Blinka, Mike McKibben, and Johnny Lynn started for most of the campaign, while Mark Gastineau and Donald Dykes also saw considerable action. Unfortunately, the young defense was easy meat at first for enemy passers, allowing 56 points to the Patriots and 46 to the Bills in September. On the offense, Matt Robinson won the quarterback job in the pre-season, but jammed his thumb before the opening game. Richard Todd stepped in the second week as QB, and despite barrages of boos, stayed at the helm the rest of the season. With star receiver Wesley Walker out much of the time with injuries, the Jet attack concentrated on the ground. Marvin Powell and his line mates cleared the way for the unheralded Jet backs to lead the NFL in rushing yardage. With the offense taking charge, the Jets won their last three games to finish at .500 for the second straight year.

Buffalo Bills—The Bills lost the big fish, but reeled in several other prizes. They used their number-one position in the college draft to pick Ohio State linebacker Tom Cousineau, but the young star chose instead to play with Montreal in the Canadian Football League. Nevertheless, the Bills unveiled two other freshman gems in receiver Jerry Butler and linebacker Jim Haslett. Butler helped the offense to a blistering start, scoring 51 points against the Bengals and 46 points against the Jets in September. The aerial circus of Joe Ferguson, Frank Lewis, and Butler masked a weak running attack in the early going. Once defenses realized that Terry Miller and the other runners could be lightly covered, the Buffalo offense cooled off rapidly. The new 3-4 defense kept the Bills close to the top, only one game out of first place as December began. Three straight losses at the end of the schedule, however, finished any playoff ambitions.

Baltimore Colts—The Colts put on a better show off the field than on it. Owner Bob Irsay repeatedly threatened to move the Colts to another city because the state would not improve Municipal Stadium. He accused quarterback Bert Jones of malingering on the sidelines with a sore shoulder. He frequently threatened to fire coach Ted Marchibroda. When Toni Linhart missed three field goals on September 16, Irsay rewarded his efforts with a $10,000 raise, while Marchibroda put him on waivers the next day. On the field, as Bert Jones went, so went the Colts. Jones hurt his shoulder in an opening day loss to Kansas City, sitting out the next six games. With Greg Landry at QB, the Colts dropped five of those six games. Jones then returned to the field and led the Colts to consecutive victories over the Bills, Patriots, and Bengals. Jones reinjured his shoulder in the Bengals game and went out for the year. Landry came back and guided the team to five losses in the remaining six games.

CENTRAL DIVISION

Pittsburgh Steelers—With four victories to open the season, the Steelers reasserted their dominance in the A.F.C. Occasional lapses, however, demonstrated their humanity and made them struggle to hold off challengers to their perch. Losses to the Eagles, Bengals, and Chargers dropped them into a first-place tie with Houston at 9-3. On November 25, they hosted the rising Cleveland Browns and went into overtime to take a 33-30 decision. One week later, they beat Cincinnati while the Oilers were losing. The Steelers thus took a one-game lead into the Astrodome for a Monday night confrontation on December 10. The physical Oilers outmuscled the Steelers and won the game 20-17, creating another tie going into the final weekend. The veteran Steelers geared up for the visiting Buffalo Bills. With habitual winners named Greene, Bradshaw, Harris, Swann, Stallworth, Greenwood, Lambert, Shell, and Webster on the job, the Steelers throttled Buffalo 28-0 to retain first place for another year.

Houston Oilers—Bum Phillips and his troops kept banging at the throne room door, but the Steelers wouldn't open up. Earl Campbell charged his way to a second rushing title in two years, leading an offense which suffered because of Dan Pastorini's bad shoulder. Leon Gray beefed up the blocking after arriving in a trade with New England. Age chipped away at the front line of the defense, but Robert Brazile and Mike Reinfeldt kept the back lines in top order. An early confrontation with the Steelers ended in a disappointing 38-7 loss, but the Oilers stayed on the heels of their quarry. They climbed into a first-place tie with the Steelers in November but dropped off the pace by losing to the Browns 14-7 on December 2. One week later, they launched a savage pass rush to beat the Steelers 20-17. To take first place on the final weekend, the Oilers had to beat the Eagles while the Steelers lost to the Bills. Instead, Pittsburgh won, Houston lost, and the Oilers again went into the playoffs as a wild-card team.

Cleveland Browns—The Browns began the season with a 25-22 overtime victory over the Jets, with Don Cockroft kicking field goals with four seconds left in regulation time and with 15 seconds left in overtime. They then beat the Chiefs 27-24 on a touchdown pass with 57 seconds left on the clock. One week later, Cockroft booted a field goal with under two minutes left for a 13-10 triumph over the Colts. On September 24, the Browns blew out the Cowboys 26-7 on Monday night television. During that moment of victory, halfback Greg Pruitt injured a knee, and he never fully recovered. With their offensive ace sidelined, the Browns doggedly stayed in the race. Brian Sipe, Mike Pruitt, and Ozzie Newsome developed into top offensive weapons. The Browns bolstered the defense by obtaining end Lyle Alzado from Denver, but veteran tackle Jerry Sherk offset the gain by missing a lot of time with injuries. Thom Darden led a solid secondary. An overtime loss to the Steelers on Novemer 25 severely hurt the Browns' playoff hopes. Although they rallied to beat Houston on December 2, the Raiders and Bengals beat the Browns in the final two games to seal their fate.

Cincinnati Bengals—Head coach Homer Rice led the Bengals to a strong finish last year, but he couldn't prevent a miserable beginning this year. The Bengals dropped their first six games before rising up to upset the Steelers 34-10. Although several of their losses were by close scores, the final standings would show only four victories for Cincinnati. The Bengal defense made enemy offenses healthy, with

FINAL TEAM STATISTICS

OFFENSE

	BALT.	BUFF.	CIN.	CLEV.	DENV.	HOU.	K.C.	MIA.	N.E.	N.Y. J.	OAK.	PIT.	S.D.	SEA.
FIRST DOWNS:														
Total	291	252	289	**350**	306	268	241	297	318	299	321	337	330	315
by Rushing	97	83	138	125	130	149	122	126	132	**153**	102	141	114	121
by Passing	158	147	131	189	149	100	91	140	159	126	191	179	**192**	171
by Penalty	**36**	22	20	**36**	27	19	28	31	27	20	28	17	24	23
RUSHING:														
Number	515	474	560	504	525	616	569	561	604	**634**	491	561	481	500
Yards	1674	1621	2329	2281	2036	2571	2316	2187	2252	**2646**	1763	2603	1668	1967
Average Yards	3.3	3.4	4.2	4.5	3.9	4.2	4.1	3.9	3.7	4.2	3.6	**4.6**	3.5	3.9
Touchdowns	12	11	23	16	13	24	18	19	16	23	13	**25**	**25**	24
PASSING:														
Attempts	**550**	465	426	545	476	386	361	416	475	369	513	492	541	523
Completions	313	241	228	289	260	195	190	235	237	190	311	272	**338**	292
Completion Pct.	56.9	51.8	53.5	53.0	54.6	50.5	52.6	56.5	49.9	51.5	60.6	55.3	**62.5**	55.8
Passing Yards	3575	3603	2821	3838	3433	2494	1953	3018	3600	2864	3704	3877	**4138**	3791
Avg. Yds per Att.	5.3	6.3	4.7	5.9	6.0	5.4	4.1	6.2	6.1	6.5	6.2	**7.0**	6.8	6.6
Avg. Yds per Comp.	11.4	15.0	12.4	13.3	13.2	12.8	10.3	12.8	**15.2**	15.1	11.9	14.3	12.2	13.0
Times Tackled	52	43	63	43	43	32	42	29	49	32	36	27	31	**23**
Yds Lost Tackled	403	387	511	347	327	238	293	255	382	266	293	222	223	**201**
Net Yards	3172	3216	2310	3491	3106	2256	1660	2763	3218	2598	3411	3655	**3915**	3590
Touchdowns	18	14	17	28	18	17	7	20	**30**	16	27	26	24	20
Interceptions	19	**15**	**15**	27	23	21	18	22	23	25	23	26	25	18
Pct. Intercepted	3.5	**3.2**	3.5	5.0	4.8	5.4	5.0	5.3	4.8	6.8	4.5	5.3	4.6	3.4
PUNTS:														
Number	**101**	96	91	71	89	93	90	71	84	73	70	68	75	70
Average	36.2	38.2	40.4	40.1	39.9	40.6	**43.1**	39.5	36.2	40.8	42.0	40.2	36.5	38.4
PUNT RETURNS:														
Number	49	38	42	41	43	38	58	34	37	36	35	**63**	52	34
Yards	391	318	316	345	401	221	**612**	337	311	314	179	523	488	281
Average Yards	8.0	8.4	7.5	8.4	9.3	5.8	**10.6**	9.9	8.4	8.7	5.1	8.3	9.4	8.3
Touchdowns	1	0	0	0	0	0	**2**	1	1	0	0	0	0	0
KICKOFF RET.:														
Number	70	59	**81**	75	50	67	51	51	66	76	65	51	50	70
Yards	1402	1131	1560	1531	966	1234	1004	1148	1239	**1561**	1475	987	1066	1444
Average Yards	20.0	19.2	19.3	20.4	19.3	18.4	19.7	22.5	18.8	20.5	**22.7**	19.4	21.3	20.6
Touchdowns	0	0	0	0	0	0	0	0	0	0	**1**	0	0	0
INTERCEPT RET.:														
Number	23	24	20	16	19	**34**	23	23	20	21	24	27	28	17
Yards	382	370	260	278	189	**618**	437	285	352	239	313	200	562	284
Average Yards	16.6	15.4	13.0	17.4	9.9	18.2	19.0	12.4	17.6	11.4	13.0	7.4	**20.1**	16.7
Touchdowns	1	2	1	1	0	1	1	0	1	2	**3**	1	2	1
PENALTIES:														
Number	137	104	88	83	116	109	108	**79**	99	109	119	108	108	104
Yards	12.39	887	744	709	996	947	971	**651**	864	876	1024	866	908	903
FUMBLES:														
Number	36	32	**24**	29	34	31	31	27	29	26	34	47	31	31
Number Lost	21	19	14	17	17	11	18	15	16	13	15	26	**10**	18
POINTS:														
Total	271	268	337	359	289	362	238	341	411	337	365	**416**	411	378
PAT Attempts	33	30	43	44	34	43	29	40	49	42	45	**52**	**52**	46
PAT Made	31	25	40	38	32	41	28	36	46	35	41	**50**	47	43
FG Attempts	28	**33**	23	29	21	25	23	29	**33**	30	27	30	26	23
FG Made	14	21	13	17	13	21	12	21	**23**	16	18	18	16	19
Percent FG Made	50.0	63.6	56.5	58.6	61.9	**84.0**	52.2	72.4	69.7	53.3	66.7	60.0	61.5	82.6
Safeties	0	0	0	0	1	0	0	1	1	1	0	0	**2**	1

DEFENSE

	BALT.	BUFF.	CIN.	CLEV.	DENV.	HOU.	K.C.	MIA.	N.E.	N.Y. J.	OAK.	PIT.	S.D.	SEA.
FIRST DOWNS:														
Total	265	273	334	307	273	304	297	**238**	283	331	319	260	268	350
by Rushing	106	137	133	136	100	125	102	**87**	118	107	137	95	117	146
by Passing	130	**117**	175	158	146	158	169	135	139	198	150	135	132	171
by Penalty	29	19	26	**13**	27	21	26	16	26	26	32	30	19	33
RUSHING:														
Number	559	617	528	577	502	522	522	484	495	502	534	506	**475**	533
Yards	2306	2481	2219	2604	**1693**	2225	1847	1702	1770	1706	2374	1709	1907	2375
Average Yards	4.1	4.0	4.2	4.5	**3.4**	4.3	3.5	3.5	3.6	3.4	4.4	3.4	4.0	4.5
Touchdowns	15	18	22	25	16	19	**8**	9	22	13	17	9	19	23
PASSING:														
Attempts	411	**382**	492	468	512	465	528	418	467	570	471	480	472	508
Completions	203	**193**	275	271	296	242	296	230	246	339	247	226	261	317
Completion Pct.	49.4	50.5	55.9	57.9	57.8	52.0	56.1	55.0	52.7	59.5	52.4	**47.1**	55.3	62.4
Passing Yards	3080	**2713**	3908	3289	3321	3186	3404	3051	3065	4288	3366	2912	2881	3739
Avg. Yds per Att.	6.2	6.3	7.1	6.1	6.0	5.4	5.5	6.0	4.9	7.0	6.2	**4.8**	5.0	6.4
Avg. Yds per Comp.	15.2	14.1	14.2	12.1	11.2	13.2	11.5	13.3	12.5	12.7	13.6	12.9	**11.0**	11.8
Times Tackled	39	23	32	31	19	51	38	36	**57**	22	33	49	42	37
Yds Lost Tackled	312	183	216	243	162	421	280	314	**512**	173	254	351	332	280
Net Yards	2768	**2530**	3692	3046	3159	2765	3124	2737	2553	4115	3112	2561	2549	3459
Touchdowns	23	14	27	14	**11**	18	22	17	13	31	21	19	**11**	21
Interceptions	23	24	20	16	19	**34**	23	23	20	21	24	27	28	17
Pct. Intercepted	5.6	6.3	4.1	3.4	3.7	**7.3**	4.4	5.5	4.3	3.7	5.1	5.6	5.9	3.3
PUNTS:														
Number	95	92	71	80	88	73	88	77	94	69	63	**100**	83	69
Average	40.0	38.2	39.6	41.4	42.1	41.0	38.8	37.9	38.7	**36.6**	37.7	40.0	40.7	37.9
PUNT RETURNS:														
Number	43	61	48	45	52	64	49	**25**	28	33	40	31	34	42
Yards	296	555	325	375	480	726	315	**131**	317	260	416	276	204	289
Average Yards	6.9	9.1	6.8	8.3	9.2	11.3	6.4	**5.2**	11.3	7.9	10.4	8.9	6.0	6.9
Touchdowns	1	1	0	0	0	1	0	0	1	0	1	0	0	0
KICKOFF RET.:														
Number	57	54	63	70	57	69	**51**	69	80	70	67	81	72	70
Yards	1065	1142	1258	1324	1173	1310	**1017**	1518	1621	1529	1290	1668	1535	1238
Average Yards	18.7	21.1	20.0	18.9	20.6	19.0	19.9	22.0	20.3	21.8	19.3	20.6	21.3	**17.7**
Touchdowns	0	0	0	0	1	0	0	0	0	1	0	0	1	0
INTERCEPT RET.:														
Number	19	**15**	**15**	27	23	21	18	22	23	25	23	26	25	18
Yards	321	**161**	305	315	291	290	209	382	417	414	473	401	279	105
Average Yards	16.9	10.7	20.3	11.7	12.7	13.8	11.6	17.4	18.1	16.6	20.6	15.4	11.2	**10.3**
Touchdowns	1	**0**	2	1	1	1	**0**	3	**0**	**0**	3	1	1	1
PENALTIES:														
Number	112	106	101	**118**	**118**	103	**118**	107	102	98	106	94	100	117
Yards	1014	788	871	1018	1033	920	1018	834	902	888	1018	732	812	**1045**
FUMBLES:														
Number	25	31	**39**	38	30	29	34	29	35	34	35	32	30	**39**
Number Lost	16	17	**24**	16	18	16	14	15	23	19	22	15	18	16
POINTS:														
Total	351	279	421	352	262	331	262	257	326	383	337	262	**246**	372
PAT Attempts	42	34	52	42	31	40	32	**30**	39	46	43	31	32	46
PAT Made	37	27	49	34	31	37	31	**26**	36	39	39	28	28	42
FG Attempts	28	31	27	35	26	28	21	26	26	29	22	26	**12**	29
FG Made	20	16	20	22	15	18	13	15	18	22	12	16	**8**	18
Percent FG Made	71.4	**51.6**	74.1	62.9	57.7	64.3	61.9	57.7	69.2	75.9	54.5	61.5	66.7	62.1
Safeties	1	0	0	0	0	0	0	0	1	1	2	0	1	0

their pass defense particularly heartening to quarterbacks. On offense, Ken Anderson directed one of the worst passing attacks in the NFL. The Bengals had cause for hope in rookies Jack Thompson, Charles Alexander, and Dan Ross, but for Rice, it was exit, stage left.

WESTERN DIVISION

San Diego Chargers—Air Coryell began regular service this year. Known for his exciting offenses in St. Louis, coach Don Coryell gave quarterback Dan Fouts a mandate to throw the ball endlessly. At the end of the season, Fouts had a new NFL record for passing yardage in a season, and the Chargers had captured first place in the West. Fouts had two superb targets in fleet receivers Charlie Joiner and John Jefferson. Rookie tight end Kellen Winslow provided a third receiving threat until he broke a leg in October. Coryell made some adjustments on his defensive unit. He obtained cornerback Willie Buchanon from the Packers to shore up the secondary, and when tackle Louie Kelcher injured a knee in pre-season, Coryell inserted veteran Wilbur Young into the starting lineup. Young played the best ball of his career and combined with Fred Dean as a ferocious pass rushing duo. A stretch run of six victories in seven weeks, including victories over Pittsburgh and Denver, wrapped up the trip to the playoffs.

Denver Broncos—The Orange Crush wasn't the same after Lyle Alzado was shipped to Cleveland because of a salary dispute. Although the defense featured stars like Randy Gradishar, Louie Wright, and Bill Thompson, it could not pressure passers as it had in the past. Nevertheless, the Broncos had bigger problems on offense. Coach Red Miller made Norris Weese his starting quarterback, but after six weeks of sporadic offense, Miller reinstalled Craig Morton as his starter. Despite their weaknesses, the Broncos held a share of first place until December 8, when the Seahawks beat them 28-23. On the final weekend, the Broncos journeyed to San Diego and were whipped 17-7. Only a loss by Oakland during the weekend salvaged a wild-card berth for the Bronks, who lost two games in a row for the first time ever under coach Miller.

Oakland Raiders—Tom Flores had a tough act to follow, and he stumbled on his entrance. Despite missing out on the playoffs last season, the John Madden years harvested glory and excellence. With Flores the new head coach, the Raiders lost three of their first four games. The veteran Oakland defense then strung together several outstanding performances and put the Raiders back into the playoff chase. Flores tinkered with his offense, installing a double tight end offense in mid-season. With two stars in Dave Casper and Ray Chester, the new arrangement controlled the ball for long stretches of time. Any playoff hopes looked dead when the Raiders lost to the Chiefs 24-21 on November 18, dropping them to 6-6. Valiantly, the Raiders then beat Denver, New Orleans, and Cleveland to put themselves in a long shot position to win a wild-card berth on the final weekend. It wasn't to be, as the Seahawks ended the dream with a 29-24 upset.

Seattle Seahawks—The Seahawks carted a three-ring circus around the league, combining high-wire thrills with clownish pratfalls. Preseason experts labeled the young Seattle squad as playoff contenders, but a 1-4 start showed that they were not yet ready for such heady circles. To go with a porous defense, coach Jack Patera fielded a daring offense which flirted with greatness. The Seahawks frequently delighted their fans by going for the yardage on fourth down, and fake field goals stood the fans up several times during the season. On October 29, the Seahawks beat the Falcons 31-28 by using a quarterback draw on fourth-and-five, an onside kick, and a 20 yard pass play to kicker Efren Herrera on a fake field goal. Six days later, the Rams held the Seahawks to a total offense of minus seven yards in a 24-0 smothering. Seattle played with enough consistency to win five of its last six games. On December 8, the Seahawks beat Denver 28-23 to knock the Broncos out of first place. Eight days later, Jim Zorn threw for 314 yards in a 29-24 victory which ended Oakland's playoff hopes and gave the Seahawks their second winning season.

Kansas City Chiefs—Mary Levy's rebuilding plan showed results, as the Chiefs won four of their first six games and held on to finish at a respectable 7-9. The miserable defense which Levy had inherited had improved rapidly, as shown by a 14-0 opening victory over the Colts and five other games in which the enemy scored under 10 points. The offense had less to show for its efforts, but rookie quarterback Steve Fuller held out promise for the future. On the special teams, rookie Bob Grupp led the N.F.L. in punting, and J.T. Smith broke two punt returns open for touchdowns.

MIAMI DOLPHINS 10-6-0 Don Shula

Scores of Each Game		
9	Buffalo	7
19	SEATTLE	10
27	Minnesota	12
31	CHICAGO	16
27	N.Y. Jets	33
3	Oakland	13
17	BUFFALO	7
13	New England	28
27	GREEN BAY	7
6	HOUSTON	9
19	BALTIMORE	0
24	Cleveland	*30
28	Baltimore	24
39	NEW ENGLAND	24
28	Detroit	10
24	N.Y. JETS	27

Use Name	Pos.	Hgt.	Wgt.	Age	Int.	Pts.
Mike Current	OT	6'4"	270	33		
Jon Giesler	OT	6'5"	255	22		
Cleveland Green	OT	6'3"	265	21		
Bob Kuechenberg	OT-OG	6'3"	255	31		
Eric Laasko	OG-OT	6'4"	265	22		
Larry Little	OG-OT	6'1"	265	33		
Ed Newman	OG	6'2"	245	28		
Jeff Toews	OG-C	6'3"	255	21		
Mark Dennard	C	6'1"	250	23		
Jim Langer	C	6'2"	257	31		
Doug Betters	DE	6'7"	250	23		
Vern Den Herder	DE-NT	6'6"	252	30		
A.J. Duhe	DE	6'4"	247	23		
Carl Barisich	NT	6'4"	255	28		
Bob Baumhower	NT	6'5"	258	24		

Use Name	Pos.	Hgt.	Wgt.	Age	Int.	Pts.
Kim Bokamper	LB	6'6"	245	24	1	
Rusty Chambers	LB	6'1"	220	25	1	
Larry Gordon	LB	6'4"	230	26	2	
Mel Land	LB	6'3"	243	23		
Bob Matheson	LB	6'4"	235	34	1	
Ralph Ortega	LB	6'2"	220	26		
Earnest Rhone	LB	6'2"	226	26	2	
Steve Towle	LB	6'2"	233	25	1	
Charlie Babb	DB	6'	190	29	1	
Doug Bessillieu	DB	6'1"	199	23		
Glenn Blackwood	DB	6'	183	22		
Neal Colzie	DB	6'2"	190	26	5	
Tim Foley	DB	6'	194	31	2	
Mike Kozlowski	DB	6'	187	23		
Gerald Small	DB	5'11"	187	23	5	
Ed Taylor (from NYJ)	DB	6'	175	26		
Norris Thomas	DB	5'11"	175	25	2	

Bo Rather – Injury
Andre Tillman – Broken Leg

Use Name	Pos.	Hgt.	Wgt.	Age	Int.	Pts.
Guy Benjamin	QB	6'4"	210	24		
Bob Griese	QB	6'1"	190	34		
Don Strock	QB	6'5"	220	28		
Gary Davis	HB	5'10"	202	24		6
Tony Nathan	HB-FB	6'	201	22		18
Del Williams	HB	6'	195	28		24
Norm Bulaich	FB-HB	6'1"	212	32		18
Larry Csonka	FB	6'3"	235	32		78
Steve Howell	FB-TE	6'2"	222	22		
Bob Torrey (from NYG)	FB	6'4"	230	22		6
Jimmy Cefalo	WR	5'11"	190	22		18
Duriel Harris	WR	5'11"	180	24		18
Nat Moore	WR	5'9"	180	27		36
Bruce Hardy	TE-QB	6'5"	235	23		18
Ronnie Lee	TE	6'3"	242	22		
George Roberts	K	6'	172	24		
Uwe von Schamann	K	6'	200	23		99

NEW ENGLAND PATRIOTS 9-7-0 Ron Erhardt

Scores of Each Game		
13	PITTSBURGH	*16
56	N.Y. JETS	3
20	Cincinnati	14
27	SAN DIEGO	21
14	Green Bay	27
24	DETROIT	17
27	Chicago	7
28	MIAMI	13
26	Baltimore	31
26	Buffalo	6
10	Denver	45
50	BALTIMORE	21
13	BUFFALO	*16
24	Miami	39
26	N.Y. Jets	27
27	MINNESOTA	23

Use Name	Pos.	Hgt.	Wgt.	Age	Int.	Pts.
Shelby Jordan	OT	6'7"	260	27		
Gary Puetz (from PHI)	OT-OG	6'4"	265	27		
Dwight Wheeler	OT	6'3"	255	24		
Sam Adams	OG	6'3"	260	30		
Bob Cryder	OG	6'4"	265	22		
Terry Falcon	OG	6'3"	260	24		
John Hannah	OG	6'2"	265	28		
Pete Brock	C-OT-OG-TE	6'5"	260	25		
Bill Lenkaitis	C	6'3"	255	33		
Julius Adams	DE	6'3"	263	31		
Richard Bishop	DE-NT	6'1"	260	29		
Mark Buben	DE-NT	6'3"	260	22		
Mel Lunsford	DE-NT	6'3"	260	29		
Tony McGee	DE	6'4"	250	30		
Ray Hamilton	NT	6'1"	245	28		

Use Name	Pos.	Hgt.	Wgt.	Age	Int.	Pts.
Ray Costict	LB	6'	218	24	1	
Bob Golic	LB	6'2	240	21		
Mike Hawkins	LB	6'2"	232	23	2	6
Sam Hunt	LB	6'1"	253	28		
Steve Kiner	LB	6'4"	230	28		
Bill Matthews	LB	6'2"	235	23		
Steve Nelson	LB	6'2"	230	28	1	
Rod Shoate	LB	6'1"	215	26	1	
John Zamberlin	LB	6'2"	232	23		
Doug Beaudoin	DB	6'1"	190	25	1	
Raymond Clayborn	DB	6'1"	190	24	5	
Dick Conn	DB	6'	180	28		
Tim Fox	DB	5'11"	190	25	2	
Mike Haynes	DB	6'2"	195	26	3	
Prentice McCray	DB	6'1"	190	28	3	
Rick Sanford	DB	6'1"	192	22	1	6
Mark Washington	DB	5'10"	187	31		

Sidney Brown–Injury

Use Name	Pos.	Hgt.	Wgt.	Age	Int.	Pts.
Matt Cavanaugh	QB	6'1"	210	22		
Steve Grogan	QB	6'4"	208	26		12
Tom Owen	QB	6'1"	194	26		
Horace Ivory	HB	6'	198	25		18
Allan Clark	HB	5'10"	186	22		12
Andy Johnson	HB	6'	204	26		6
Don Calhoun	FB-HB	6'	212	27		36
Sam Cunningham	FB	6'3"	230	29		30
Mosi Tatupu	FB	6'	229	24		
Harold Jackson	WR	5'10"	175	33		42
Ray Jarvis	WR	5'11"	190	30		6
Stanley Morgan	WR	5'11"	180	24		18
Carlos Pennywell	WR	6'2"	180	23		6
Don Westbrook	WR	5'10"	184	26		6
Russ Francis	TE	6'6"	242	26		30
Don Hasselbeck	TE	6'7"	245	25		
Eddie Hare	K	6'4"	209	22		
John Smith	K	6'	185	29		115

NEW YORK JETS 8-8-0 Walt Michaels

Scores of Each Game		
22	CLEVELAND	*25
3	New England	56
31	DETROIT	10
31	Buffalo	46
33	MIAMI	27
8	Baltimore	10
14	MINNESOTA	7
28	OAKLAND	19
24	Houston	*27
27	Green Bay	22
12	BUFFALO	14
13	Chicago	23
7	Seattle	30
30	BALTIMORE	17
27	NEW ENGLAND	26
27	Miami	24

Use Name	Pos.	Hgt.	Wgt.	Age	Int.	Pts.
Marvin Powell	OT	6'5"	268	24		
John Roman	OT	6'4"	251	27		
Chris Ward	OT	6'3"	270	23		
Dan Alexander	OG	6'4"	255	24		
Eric Cunningham	OG	6'3"	257	22		
Randy Rasmussen	OG	6'2"	255	34		
Stan Waldemore	OG-OT-C	6'4"	257	24		
Joe Fields	C	6'2"	253	25		
Ed McGlasson	C	6'4"	248	23		
Mark Gastineau	DE	6'5"	257	22		
Marty Lyons	DE	6'5"	245	22		
Lawrence Pillers	DE	6'3"	260	26		
Joe Klecko	DT	6'3"	262	25		
Joe Pellegrini	DT	6'2"	266	23		
Abdul Salaam	DT	6'3"	260	26		
Bob Winkel	DT-DE	6'4"	246	23		

Use Name	Pos.	Hgt.	Wgt.	Age	Int.	Pts.
Stan Blinka	LB	6'2"	230	22	2	
Greg Buttle	LB	6'3"	232	25	2	
Ron Crosby	LB	6'3"	225	24		
John Hennessy	LB-DE	6'3"	236	24		
Mike McKibben	LB	6'3"	228	22	1	
John Sullivan	LB	6'1"	221	22		
Donald Dykes	DB	5'11"	188	24		
Bobby Jackson	DB	5'9"	175	22	4	6
Johnny Lynn	DB	6'	190	22	2	6
Tim Moresco	DB	5'11"	180	24		2
Burgess Owens	DB	6'2"	200	28	6	
Ken Schroy	DB	6'2"	196	26	1	
Shafer Suggs	DB	6'1"	204	26	3	6

Larry Keller – Knee Injury
Mike Hennigan – Knee Injury
Mike Mock – Injury
Darnell Powell – Injury

Use Name	Pos.	Hgt.	Wgt.	Age	Int.	Pts.
Pat Ryan	QB	6'3"	205	23		
Matt Robinson	QB	6'2"	198	24		6
Richard Todd	QB	6'2"	203	25		30
Woody Bennett	HB	6'2"	217	24		6
Scott Dierking	HB-FB	5'10"	215	24		18
Bruce Harper	HB	5'8"	177	24		12
Clark Gaines	FB-HB	6'1"	209	25		
Kevin Long	FB-HB	6'1"	214	24		42
Tom Newton	FB	6'	213	25		36
Paul Darby	WR	5'10"	192	22		
Roger Farmer	WR	6'3"	195	23		
Derrick Gaffney	WR	6'1"	180	24		6
Bobby Jones	WR	5'11"	180	24		6
Wesley Walker	WR	6'	175	24		30
Jerome Barkum	TE	6'3"	225	29		24
Bob Raba	TE	6'1"	225	24		
Mickey Shuler	TE	6'3"	229	23		18
Dave Jacobs	K	5'7"	151	22		25
Pat Leahy	K	6'	195	28		36
Toni Linhart	K	6'	179	37		32
Chuck Ramsey	K	6'2"	189	27		
Richie Szaro	K	5'11"	204	31		2

BUFFALO BILLS 7-9-0 Chuck Knox

Scores of Each Game		
7	MIAMI	9
51	CINCINNATI	24
19	San Diego	27
46	N.Y. JETS	31
31	Baltimore	13
0	CHICAGO	7
7	Miami	17
13	BALTIMOR	14
20	Detroit	17
6	NEW ENGLAND	26
14	N.Y. Jets	12
19	GREEN BAY	12
16	New England	*13
16	DENVER	19
3	Minnesota	10
0	Pittsburgh	28

Use Name	Pos.	Hgt.	Wgt.	Age	Int.	Pts.
Jon Borchardt	OT	6'5"	255	22		
Joe Devlin	OT	6'5"	250	25		
Ken Jones	OT	6'5"	250	26		
Joe DeLamielleure	OG	6'3"	245	28		
Ed Fulton	OG	6'3"	250	24		
Reggie McKenzie	OG	6'4"	242	29		
Will Grant	C	6'3"	248	25		
Willie Parker	C	6'3"	245	30		
Tim Vogler	C-OG	6'3"	245	22		
Dee Hardison	DE-NT	6'4"	269	23		
Scott Hutchinson	DE	6'4"	243	23		
Ken Johnson	DE	6'5"	253	24		
Sherman White	DE	6'5"	250	30		
Ben Williams	DE-NT	6'3"	245	25		
Mike Kadish	NT	6'5"	270	29		
Fred Smerlas	NT	6'3"	270	22		6

Use Name	Pos.	Hgt.	Wgt.	Age	Int.	Pts.
Jim Haslett	LB	6'3"	232	23	2	
Tom Higgins	LB	6'1"	235	25		
Dan Jilek	LB	6'2"	225	25		
Chris Keating	LB	6'2"	223	21		
Shane Nelson	LB	6'1"	225	24	1	
Isiah Robertson	LB	6'3"	225	30	2	6
Lucius Sanford	LB	6'2"	216	23	2	6
Mario Clark	DB	6'2"	195	25	5	
Steve Freeman	DB	5'11"	185	26	3	6
Doug Greene	DB	6'2"	205	23	1	
Tony Greene	DB	5'10"	175	30	1	
Keith Moody	DB	5'10"	170	26		
Jeff Nixon	DB	6'3"	190	22	6	
Charles Romes	DB	6'1"	190	25	1	6

Phil Dokes – Shoulder Injury
Tom Ehlers – Pinched Nerve
Mekeli Ieremia – Knee Injury
Connie Zelencik – Knee Injury
Phil Olsen – Knee Injury

Use Name	Pos.	Hgt.	Wgt.	Age	Int.	Pts.
Joe Ferguson	QB	6'1"	195	29		6
Dan Manucci	QB	6'2"	194	21		
Bill Munson	QB	6'2"	205	38		
Roland Hooks	HB-FB	6'	195	26		36
Terry Miller	HB	5'10"	196	23		6
Steve Powell	HB	5'11"	186	23		
Curtis Brown	FB	5'10"	203	24		24
Mike Collier	FB	5'11"	200	25		12
Dennis Johnson	FB	6'3"	220	23		
Jerry Butler	WR	6'	178	21		24
Bob Chandler	WR	6'	180	30		
Dan Fulton	WR	6'2"	180	22		
Frank Lewis	WR	6'1"	196	32		12
Lou Piccone	WR	5'9"	175	30		12
Leonard Willis	WR	5'11"	185	26		
Reuben Gant	TE	6'4"	225	27		12
Ron Howard	TE	6'4"	230	28		
Joe Shipp	TE	6'4"	225	24		6
Tom Dempsey	K	6'1"	249	32		11
Rusty Jackson	K	6'2"	195	28		
Nick Mike-Mayer	K	5'8"	185	29		17

BALTIMORE COLTS 5-11-0 Ted Marchibroda

Scores of Each Game		
0	Kansas City	14
26	TAMPA BAY	*29
10	Cleveland	13
13	Pittsburgh	17
13	BUFFALO	31
10	N.Y. JETS	8
16	HOUSTON	28
14	Buffalo	13
31	NEW ENGLAND	26
38	CINCINNATI	28
0	Miami	19
21	New England	50
24	MIAMI	28
17	N.Y. Jets	30
7	KANSAS CITY	10
31	N.Y. Giants	7

Use Name	Pos.	Hgt.	Wgt.	Age	Int.	Pts.
Wade Griffin	OT	6'5"	231	25		
Jeff Hart	OT	6'5"	263	25		
David Taylor	OT	6'4"	263	29		
Ron Baker	OG	6'4"	251	24		
Ken Huff	OG	6'4"	252	26		
Robert Pratt	OG	6'4"	246	28		
Bob Van Duyne	OG	6'5"	238	27		
Lee Gross	C	6'3"	235	26		
Ken Mendenhall	C	6'3"	248	31		
Fred Cook	DE	6'3"	243	27		
Ron Fernandes	DE	6'4"	258	27		
Greg Fields	DE	6'7"	256	24		
Mike Ozdowski	DE	6'5"	236	23		
Mike Barnes	DT	6'6"	256	28		
Joe Ehrmann	DT	6'5"	259	30		
Jim Krahl	DT	6'5"	252	23		
Herb Orvis	DT	6'5"	245	32		

Use Name	Pos.	Hgt.	Wgt.	Age	Int.	Pts.
Barry Krauss	LB	6'3"	238	22		
Sanders Shiver	LB	6'2"	228	24	4	
Ed Simonini	LB	6'	214	25		
Stan White	LB	6'1"	225	29	1	
Mike Woods	LB	6'2"	231	24		
Steve Zabel	LB	6'4"	228	31		
Lyle Blackwood	DB	6'	189	28	4	
Larry Braziel	DB	6'	192	24	4	12
Nesby Glasgow	DB	5'10"	182	22	1	6
Dwight Harrison	DB	6'1"	186	30	2	
Bruce Laird	DB	6'	197	29	3	
Doug Nettles	DB	6'	184	28	2	
Reggie Pinkney	DB	5'11"	186	24		
Norm Thompson	DB	6'1"	180	31	2	

Stu O'Dell – Injury
Dave Rowe – Arm Injury
Ron Lee – Back Injury
George Kunz – Voluntarily Retired

Use Name	Pos.	Hgt.	Wgt.	Age	Int.	Pts.
Bert Jones	QB	6'3"	201	27		6
Greg Landry	QB	6'4"	210	32		
Don McCauley	HB-FB	6'1"	208	30		36
Joe Washington	HB	5'10"	182	25		42
Cleveland Franklin	FB	6'2"	216	24		
Ben Garry	FB	6'	209	23		
Don Hardeman	FB	6'2"	235	27		24
Roosevelt Leaks	FB	5'10"	226	26		6
Randy Burke	WR	6'2"	186	24		
Roger Carr	WR	6'3"	198	27		6
Brian DeRoo	WR	6'3"	190	23		6
Glenn Doughty	WR	6'1"	204	28		12
Mike Siani	WR	6'2"	199	29		12
Mack Alston	TE	6'2"	232	32		6
Reese McCall	TE	6'7"	238	23		24
Bucky Dilts	K	5'9"	183	25		
Steve Mike-Mayer	K	6'	180	31		61

*—Overtime

MIAMI DOLPHINS

RUSHING Last Name	No.	Yds.	Avg.	TD
Csonka	220	837	3.8	12
Williams	184	703	3.8	3
Davis	98	383	3.9	1
Nathan	16	68	4.3	0
Torrey	13	61	4.7	1
Bulaich	9	37	4.1	2
Griese	11	30	2.7	0
Moore	3	22	7.3	0
Harris	1	20	20.0	0
Strock	3	18	6.0	0
Howell	3	8	2.7	0

RECEIVING Last Name	No.	Yds.	Avg.	TD
Moore	48	840	18	6
Harris	42	798	19	3
Davis	34	215	6	0
Hardy	30	386	13	3
Williams	21	175	8	1
Nathan	17	213	13	2
Csonka	16	75	5	1
Cefalo	12	223	19	3
Bulaich	8	53	7	1
Howell	3	23	8	0
Lee	2	14	7	0
Torrey	2	3	2	0

PUNT RETURNS Last Name	No.	Yds.	Avg.	TD
Nathan	28	306	11	1
Kozlowski	3	21	7	0
Cefalo	2	10	5	0
Babb	1	0	0	0

KICKOFF RETURNS Last Name	No.	Yds.	Avg.	TD
Nathan	45	1016	23	0
Kozlowski	4	85	21	0
Davis	2	27	14	0
Bessillieu	0	20	—	0

PASSING	Att.	Comp.	%	Yds.	Yd./Att.	TD	Int.–%	RK
Griese	310	176	57	2160	7.0	14	16– 5	10
Strock	100	56	56	830	8.3	6	6– 6	
Benjamin	4	3	75	28	7.0	0	0– 0	
Hardy	1	0	0	0	0.0	0	0– 0	
Williams	1	0	0	0	0.0	0	0– 0	

PUNTING	No.	Avg.
Roberts	69	40.2
von Schamann	1	31.0

KICKING	XP	Att.	%	FG	Att.	%
von Schamann	36	40	90	21	29	72

NEW ENGLAND PATRIOTS

RUSHING Last Name	No.	Yds.	Avg.	TD
Cunningham	159	563	3.5	5
Ivory	143	522	3.7	1
Calhoun	137	456	3.3	5
Grogan	64	368	5.8	2
Johnson	43	132	3.1	1
Clark	19	84	4.4	2
Tatupu	23	71	3.1	0
Morgan	7	39	5.6	0
Jacison	3	12	4.0	0
Westbrook	2	8	4.0	0
Hare	1	0	0.0	0
Owen	2	−1	−0.5	0
Cavanaugh	1	−2	−2.0	0

RECEIVING Last Name	No.	Yds.	Avg.	TD
Jackson	45	1013	23	7
Morgan	44	1002	23	12
Francis	39	557	14	5
Cunningham	29	236	8	0
Ivory	23	216	9	2
Calhoun	15	66	4	1
Hasselbeck	13	158	12	0
Westbrook	9	173	19	1
Johnson	9	68	8	0
Pennywell	4	35	9	1
Clark	2	35	18	0
Jarvis	2	30	15	0
Tatupu	2	9	5	0

PUNT RETURNS Last Name	No.	Yds.	Avg.	TD
Morgan	29	289	10	1
Haynes	5	16	3	0
Westbrook	2	5	3	0
Sanford	1	1	1	0

KICKOFF RETURNS Last Name	No.	Yds.	Avg.	TD
Clark	37	816	22	0
Westbrook	11	151	14	0
Sanford	10	179	18	0
Tatupu	3	15	5	0
Clayborn	2	33	17	0
Washington	1	18	18	0
Ivory	1	15	15	0
Morgan	1	12	12	0

PASSING	Att.	Comp.	%	Yds.	Yd./Att.	TD	Int.–%	RK
Grogan	423	206	49	3286	7.8	28	20– 5	5
Owen	47	27	57	248	5.3	2	3– 6	
Westbrook	2	2	100	52	26.0	0	0– 0	
Cavanaugh	1	1	100	10	10.0	0	0– 0	
Hare	1	1	100	4	4.0	0	0– 0	
Jackson	1	0	0	0	0.0	0	0– 0	

PUNTING	No.	Avg.
Hare	83	36.6

KICKING	XP	Att.	%	FG	Att.	%
Smith	46	49	94	23	33	70

NEW YORK JETS

RUSHING Last Name	No.	Yds.	Avg.	TD
Gaines	186	905	4.9	0
Dierking	186	767	4.1	3
Long	116	442	3.8	7
Harper	65	282	4.3	0
Newton	37	145	3.9	6
Todd	36	93	2.6	5
Jones	1	4	4.0	0
Bennett	2	4	2.0	1
Robinson	3	4	1.3	1
Ramsey	2	0	0.0	0

RECEIVING Last Name	No.	Yds.	Avg.	TD
Gaffney	32	534	17	1
Gaines	29	219	8	0
Barkum	27	401	15	4
Walker	23	569	25	5
Jones	19	379	20	1
Harper	17	250	15	2
Shuler	16	225	14	3
Dierking	10	121	12	0
Long	10	115	12	0
Newton	4	33	8	0
Raba	2	9	5	0
Bennett	1	9	9	0

PUNT RETURNS Last Name	No.	Yds.	Avg.	TD
Harper	33	290	9	0
Schroy	2	24	12	0
Darby	1	0	0	0

KICKOFF RETURNS Last Name	No.	Yds.	Avg.	TD
Harper	55	1158	21	0
Jones	7	140	20	0
Schroy	6	179	30	0
Gaines	2	29	15	0
Hennessy	2	15	8	0
Raba	1	18	18	0
Shuler	1	15	15	0
Bennett	1	7	7	0
Newton	1	0	0	0

PASSING	Att.	Comp.	%	Yds.	Yd./Att.	TD	Int.–%	RK
Todd	334	171	51	2660	8.0	16	22– 7	12
Robinson	31	17	55	191	6.2	0	2– 7	
Ryan	4	2	50	13	3.3	0	1– 25	

PUNTING	No.	Avg.
Ramsey	73	40.8

KICKING	XP	Att.	%	FG	Att.	%
Leahy	12	15	80	8	13	62
Linhart	14	18	78	6	14	43
Jacobs	10	11	91	5	9	56
Szaro	2	2	100	0	2	0

BUFFALO BILLS

RUSHING Last Name	No.	Yds.	Avg.	TD
Brown	172	574	3.3	1
Miller	139	484	3.5	1
Hooks	89	320	3.6	6
Collier	34	130	3.8	2
Ferguson	22	68	3.1	1
Powell	10	29	2.9	0
Butler	2	13	6.5	0
D. Johnson	3	5	1.7	0
Mike-Myer	1	4	4.0	0
Lewis	2	−6	−3.0	0

RECEIVING Last Name	No.	Yds.	Avg.	TD
Lewis	54	1082	20	2
Butler	48	834	17	4
Brown	39	401	10	3
Piccone	33	556	17	2
Hooks	26	254	10	0
Gant	19	245	13	2
Miller	10	111	11	0
Collier	7	43	6	0
Shipp	3	43	14	1
Fulton	2	34	17	0

PUNT RETURNS Last Name	No.	Yds.	Avg.	TD
Moody	38	318	8	0

KICKOFF RETURNS Last Name	No.	Yds.	Avg.	TD
Moody	27	556	21	0
Miller	8	160	20	0
Collier	7	129	18	0
Powell	6	97	16	0
Willis	4	92	23	0
Brown	3	42	14	0
Piccone	3	41	14	0
Keating	1	14	14	0

PASSING	Att.	Comp.	%	Yds.	Yd./Att.	TD	Int.–%	RK
Ferguson	458	238	52	3572	7.8	14	15– 3	8
Munson	7	3	43	31	4.4	0	0– 0	

PUNTING	No.	Avg.
Jackson	96	38.2

KICKING	XP	Att.	%	FG	Att.	%
Mike-Mayer	17	18	94	20	29	69
Dempsey	8	11	73	1	4	25

BALTIMORE COLTS

RUSHING Last Name	No.	Yds.	Avg.	TD
Washington	242	884	3.7	4
Hardeman	109	292	2.7	3
McCauley	59	168	2.8	3
Leaks	49	145	3.0	1
Landry	31	115	3.7	0
Garry	13	41	3.2	0
Jones	10	40	4.0	1
White	1	3	3.0	0
Dilts	1	−14	−14.0	0

RECEIVING Last Name	No.	Yds.	Avg.	TD
Washington	82	750	9	3
McCauley	55	575	11	3
McCall	37	536	15	4
Doughty	35	510	15	2
Carr	27	400	15	1
Hardeman	25	115	5	1
Siani	15	214	14	2
Leaks	14	119	9	0
Alston	10	114	11	1
Burke	6	151	25	0
DeRoo	4	82	21	1
Garry	3	9	3	0

PUNT RETURNS Last Name	No.	Yds.	Avg.	TD
Glasgow	44	352	8	1
Blackwood	4	−1	0	0
Thompson	1	40	40	0

KICKOFF RETURNS Last Name	No.	Yds.	Avg.	TD
Glasgow	50	1126	23	0
Garry	8	135	17	0
Blackwood	3	41	14	0
Laird	3	34	11	0
McCauley	2	29	15	0
Hart	1	16	16	0
Van Duyne	1	12	12	0
Griffin	1	8	8	0
Washington	1	1	1	0

PASSING	Att.	Comp.	%	Yds.	Yd./Att.	TD	Int.–%	RK
Landry	457	270	59	2932	6.4	15	15– 3	7
Jones	92	43	47	643	7.0	3	3– 3	
Washington	1	0	0	0	0.0	0	1–100	

PUNTING	No.	Avg.
Dilts	99	36.9

KICKING	XP	Att.	%	FG	Att.	%
Mike-Mayer	28	29	97	11	20	55

PITTSBURGH STEELERS 12-4-0 Chuck Noll

Scores of Each Game		
16	New England	*13
38	HOUSTON	7
24	St. Louis	21
17	BALTIMORE	13
14	Philadelphia	17
51	Cleveland	35
10	Cincinnati	34
42	DENVER	7
14	DALLAS	3
38	WASHINGTON	7
30	Kansas City	3
7	San Diego	35
33	CLEVELAND	*30
37	CINCINNATI	17
17	Houston	20
28	BUFFALO	0

Use Name	Pos.	Hgt.	Wgt.	Age	Int.	Pts.
Larry Brown	OT-TE	6'4"	245	30		6
Jon Kolb	OT	6'2"	262	32		
Ted Petersen	OT-C	6'5"	244	24		
Sam Davis	OG	6'1"	255	35		
Gerry Mullins	OG	6'3"	244	30		
Steve Courson	OG	6'1"	260	23		
Thom Dornbrook	C-OG	6'2"	240	22		
Mike Webster	C	6'1"	250	27		
John Banaszak	DE-DT	6'3"	244	29	1	
L. C. Greenwood	DE	6'5"	250	32		
Dwight White	DE	6'4"	255	30		
Tom Beasley	DT	6'5"	253	25		
Gary Dunn	DT-DE	6'3"	247	6		
Steve Furness	DT-DE	6'4"	255	28		
Joe Greene	DT	6'4"	260	32		
Robin Cole	LB	6'2"	220	23		
Tom Graves	LB	6'3"	228	23		
Jack Ham	LB	6'3"	225	30	2	
Jack Lambert	LB	6'4"	220	27	6	
Loren Toews	LB	6'3"	222	27		
Zack Valentine	LB	6'2"	220	22		
Dennis Winston	LB	6'	228	23	3	6
Larry Anderson	DB	5'11"	177	22	1	
Mel Blount	DB	6'3"	205	31	3	
Ron Johnson	DB	5'10"	200	23	1	
Donnie Shell	DB	5'11"	190	27	5	
J.T. Thomas	DB	6'2"	196	28		
Mike Wagner	DB	6'1"	200	30	4	
Dwayne Woodruff	DB	5'11"	189	22	1	
Terry Bradshaw	QB	6'3"	215	30		
Mike Kruczek	QB	6'1"	205	26		
Cliff Stoudt	QB	6'4"	218	24		
Anthony Anderson	HB	6'	197	22		6
Rocky Bleier	HB	5'11"	210	33		24
Rick Moser	HB	6'	210	22		6
Sidney Thornton	HB-FB	5'11"	230	24		60
Franco Harris	FB	6'2"	225	29		72
Greg Hawthorne	FB	6'2"	225	22		6
Theo Bell	WR	5'11"	180	25		
Jim Smith	WR	6'2"	205	24		12
John Stallworth	WR	6'2"	183	27		48
Lynn Swann	WR	6'	180	27		36
Bennie Cunningham	TE	6'4"	247	24		24
Randy Grossman	TE	6'1"	215	25		6
Matt Bahr	K	5'10"	165	23		104
Craig Colquitt	K	6'2"	182	25		

Fred Anderson – Broken Hand
Ray Pinney – Stomach Injury

HOUSTON OILERS 11-5-0 Bum Phillips

Scores of Each Game		
29	Washington	27
7	Pittsburgh	38
20	KANSAS CITY	6
30	Cincinnati	*27
31	CLEVELAND	10
17	ST. LOUIS	24
28	Baltimore	16
14	Seattle	34
27	N.Y. JETS	*24
9	Miami	6
31	OAKLAND	17
42	CINCINNATI	21
30	Dallas	24
7	Cleveland	14
20	PITTSBURGH	17
20	PHILADELPHIA	26

Use Name	Pos.	Hgt.	Wgt.	Age	Int.	Pts.
Leon Gray	OT	6'3"	260	27		
Wesley Phillips	OT	6'5"	275	25		
Morris Towns	OT	6'4"	275	25		
Ed Fisher	OG	6'3"	250	30		
Conway Hayman	OG-OT	6'3"	270	30		
Tom Randall	OG	6'5"	245	23		
George Reihner	OG	6'4"	263	24		
David Carter	C	6'2"	225	26		
Carl Mauck	C	6'3"	250	32		
Jesse Baker	DE	6'5"	265	22		6
Elvin Bethea	DE	6'3"	255	33		
Andy Dorris	DE	6'4"	240	28		
James Young	DE	6'2"	260	29		
Curley Culp	NT	6'1"	265	33		
Ken Kennard	NT	6'2"	245	24		
Mike Stensrud	NT	6'5"	270	23		
Steve Baumgartner	LB	6'7"	245	28		
Gregg Bingham	LB	6'1"	230	28	3	
Robert Brazile	LB	6'4"	238	26	2	
Jimbo Elrod	LB	6'	223	25		
Daryl Hunt	LB	6'3"	220	22		
Mike Murphy	LB	6'2"	222	22		
Art Stringer	LB	6'1"	223	25	2	
Ted Thompson	LB	6'1"	220	26		
Ted Washington	LB	6'1"	245	31		
Willie Alexander	DB	6'2"	195	29	2	
Bill Currier	DB	6'	195	24		
Carter Hartwig	DB	6'	185	23	2	
Charles Jefferson	DB	6'	178	22		
Vernon Perry	DB	6'2"	211	25	3	
Mike Reinfeldt	DB	6'2"	195	26	**12**	
Greg Stemrick	DB	5'11"	185	27	2	
J.C. Wilson	DB	6'	177	23	6	6
Gifford Nielsen	QB	6'4"	205	24		
Dan Pastorini	QB	6'3"	205	30		
Earl Campbell	HB	5'11"	224	24		114
Ronnie Coleman	HB	5'10"	198	28		6
Kenny King	HB	5'11"	203	22		
Rob Carpenter	FB-HB	6'1"	214	24		24
Booby Clark	FB	6'2"	245	28		
Tim Wilson	FB	6'2"	220	25		18
Ken Burrough	WR	6'4"	210	31		36
Rich Caster	WR	6'5"	230	30		6
Richard Ellender	WR	5'11"	171	22		
Eddie Foster	WR	5'10"	185	25		
Jeff Groth **(from MIA)**	WR	5'10"	172	22		
Billy Johnson	WR	5'9"	170	27		6
Guido Merkens	WR-QB	6'1"	200	24		6
Mike Renfro	WR	6'	184	24		12
Mike Barber	TE	6'3"	235	26		18
Conrad Rucker	TE	6'3"	260	24		
Toni Fritsch	K	5'7"	195	34		104
Cliff Parsley	K	6'1"	211	24		

Greg Sampson – Illness
John Schumacher – Back Injury
C.L. Whittington – Injury

CLEVELAND BROWNS 9-7-0 Sam Rutigliano

Scores of Each Game		
25	N.Y. Jets	*22
27	Kansas City	24
13	BALTIMORE	10
26	DALLAS	7
10	Houston	31
35	PITTSBURGH	51
9	WASHINGTON	13
28	CINCINNATI	27
38	St. Louis	20
24	Philadelphia	19
24	SEATTLE	29
30	MIAMI	*24
30	Pittsburgh	*33
14	HOUSTON	7
14	Oakland	19
12	Cincinnati	16

Use Name	Pos.	Hgt.	Wgt.	Age	Int.	Pts.
Doug Dieken	OT	6'5"	252	30		
Matt Miller	OT	6'6"	270	23		
Henry Sheppard	OT	6'6"	263	26		
George Buehler	OG	6'2"	270	32		
Robert Jackson	OG	6'5"	260	26		
Cody Risien	OG	6'7"	255	22		
Tom DeLeone	C	6'2"	248	29		
Gerry Sullivan	C-OT	6'4"	250	27		
Lyle Alzado	DE	6'3"	250	30		
Jack Gregory	DE	6'6"	255	34		
Mike St. Clair	DE	6'5"	253	25		
Henry Bradley	DT	6'2"	265	25		
Rich Dimler	DT	6'6"	260	23		
Jerry Sherk	DT	6'4"	250	31		
Mickey Sims	DT	6'5"	270	24		
Dick Ambrose	LB	6'	235	26	1	
Dave Graf	LB	6'2"	221	26		
Charlie Hall	LB	6'3"	235	30	2	
Gerald Irons	LB	6'2"	230	32		
Robert Jackson	LB	6'1"	230	25		
Clay Matthews	LB	6'2"	230	23	1	
Ron Bolton	DB	6'2"	170	29	3	
Clinton Burrell	DB	6'2"	192	22		
Thom Darden	DB	6'2"	193	29	5	6
Oliver Davis	DB	6'1"	205	25	1	
Lawrence Johnson	DB	5'11"	204	21		
Ricky Jones	DB	6'1"	215	24		
Randy Rich	DB	5'10"	181	25		
Clarence Scott	DB	6'	190	30	3	
Johnny Evans	QB	6'1"	197	23		
Mark Miller	QB	6'2"	176	23		
Brian Sipe	QB	6'1"	195	30		12
Doug Dennison	HB	6'1"	205	27		
Dino Hall	HB	5'7"	165	23		6
Calvin Hill	HB-FB	6'3"	227	32		18
Cleo Miller	HB-FB	5'11"	214	26		6
Pat Moriarty	HB	6'	195	24		12
Greg Pruitt	HB	5'10"	190	28		6
Mike Pruitt	FB	6'	225	25		66
Willis Adams	WR	6'2"	194	23		
Ricky Feacher	WR	5'10"	174	25		6
Dave Logan	WR	6'4"	216	25		42
Reggie Rucker	WR	6'2"	190	31		36
John Smith	WR	6'	175	23		
Keith Wright	WR	5'10"	175	23		
Ozzie Newsome	TE	6'2"	232	23		54
Curtis Weathers	TE	6'5"	220	22		
Don Cockroft	K	6'1"	195	34		89

Rickey Anderson – Knee Injury
Larry Collins – Knee Injury

CINCINNATI BENGALS 4-12-0 Homer Rice

Scores of Each Game		
0	Denver	10
24	Buffalo	51
14	NEW ENGLAND	20
27	HOUSTON	*30
13	Dallas	38
7	KANSAS CITY	10
34	PITTSBURGH	10
27	Cleveland	28
37	PHILADELPHIA	13
28	Baltimore	38
24	SAN DIEGO	26
21	Houston	42
34	ST. LOUIS	28
17	Pittsburgh	37
14	Washington	28
16	CLEVELAND	12

Use Name	Pos.	Hgt.	Wgt.	Age	Int.	Pts.
Vern Holland	OT	6'5"	267	31		
Max Montoya	OT	6'5"	278	23		
Mike Wilson	OT	6'5"	280	24		
Glenn Bujnoch	OG	6'5"	255	25		
Barney Cotton	OG	6'5"	261	22		
Mark Donahue	OG	6'3"	251	23		
Dave Lapham	OG-C	6'4"	258	27		
Blair Bush	C	6'3"	252	22		
Bob Johnson	C	6'5"	223	33		
Ross Browner	DE	6'3"	261	25		
Gary Burley	DE	6'3"	269	26		
Mack Mitchell	DE	6'7"	253	27		
Eddie Edwards	DT	6'5"	256	25		
Mike White	DT	6'5"	266	22		
Wilson Whitley	DT	6'3"	265	24	1	
Glenn Cameron	LB	6'2"	230	26		
Tom DePaso	LB	6'2"	223	23		
Tom Dinkel	LB	6'3"	246	23		
Bo Harris	LB	6'3"	226	26		
Howie Kurnick	LB	6'2"	219	22		6
Jim LeClair	LB	6'2"	234	28	1	6
Tom Ruud	LB	6'2"	226	26		
Reggie Williams	LB	6'1"	228	24	2	
Louis Breeden	DB	5'11"	187	25		
Jim Browner	DB	6'1"	209	23	1	
Scott Bork	DB	6'2"	193	23		
Marvin Cobb	DB	6'	188	26	3	
Ray Griffin	DB	5'10"	183	23	4	6
Dick Jauron	DB	6'	184	28	6	
Vaughn Lusby	DB	5'10"	178	23		
Scott Perry	DB	6'	180	25	1	
Ken Riley	DB	6'	183	32	1	
Ken Anderson	QB	6'1"	208	30		12
Jack Thompson	QB	6'3"	217	23		30
Charles Alexander	HB-FB	6'1"	221	22		6
Archie Griffin	HB	5'9"	184	25		12
Nathan Poole	HB	5'9"	210	22		
Deacon Turner	HB	5'11"	210	24		6
Pete Johnson	FB	6'	259	25		90
Don Bass	WR-TE	6'2"	218	24		18
Billy Brooks	WR	6'3"	202	26		6
Isaac Curtis	WR	6'	192	28		48
Steve Kreider	WR	6'3"	192	21		
Mike Levenseller	WR	6'1"	180	23		
Pat McInally	WR	6'6"	209	26		
Jim Corbett	TE	6'4"	217	24		
Dan Ross	TE	6'4"	238	22		6
Rick Walker	TE	6'3"	235	24		6
Chris Bahr	K	5'9"	172	26		79

*—Overtime

PITTSBURGH STEELERS

RUSHING

Last Name	No.	Yds.	Avg.	TD
Harris	267	1186	4.4	11
Thornton	118	585	**5.0**	6
Bleier	92	434	4.7	4
Hawthorne	28	123	4.4	1
A. Anderson	18	118	6.6	1
Bradshaw	21	83	4.0	0
Moser	11	33	3.0	1
Kruczek	4	20	5.0	0
Smith	1	12	12.0	0
Swann	1	9	9.0	0

RECEIVING

Last Name	No.	Yds.	Avg.	TD
Stallworth	70	1183	17	8
Swann	41	808	20	5
Cunningham	36	512	14	4
Harris	36	291	8	1
Bleier	31	277	9	0
Smith	17	243	14	2
Thornton	16	231	14	4
Grossman	12	217	18	1
Hawthorne	8	47	6	0
Bell	3	61	20	0
Moser	1	6	6	0
Brown	1	1	1	1

PUNT RETURNS

Last Name	No.	Yds.	Avg.	TD
Smith	16	146	9	0
Bell	45	378	8	0
Dornbrook	1	0	0	0
Swann	1	−1	−1	0

KICKOFF RETURNS

Last Name	No.	Yds.	Avg.	TD
L. Anderson	34	732	22	0
A. Anderson	13	200	15	0
Hawthorne	2	46	23	0
Moser	1	6	6	0
Cole	1	3	3	0

PASSING - PUNTING - KICKING

PASSING	Att.	Comp.	%	Yds.	Yd./Att.	TD	Int.–%	RK
Bradshaw	472	259	55	3724	7.9	26	25– 5	6
Kruczek	20	13	65	153	7.7	0	1– 5	

PUNTING	No.	Avg.
Colquitt	68	40.2

KICKING	XP	Att.	%	FG	Att.	%
Bahr	50	52	96	18	30	60

HOUSTON OILERS

RUSHING

Last Name	No.	Yds.	Avg.	TD
Campbell	**368**	**1697**	4.6	**19**
Carpenter	92	355	3.9	3
T. Wilson	84	319	3.8	2
Coleman	21	81	3.9	0
Clark	22	51	2.3	0
Caster	4	25	6.3	0
Pastorini	15	23	1.5	0
King	3	9	3.0	0
Nielsen	5	7	1.4	0
Barber	2	4	2.0	0

RECEIVING

Last Name	No.	Yds.	Avg.	TD
Burrough	40	752	19	6
T. Wilson	29	208	7	1
Barber	27	377	14	3
Caster	18	239	13	1
Renfro	16	323	20	2
Carpenter	16	116	7	1
Campbell	16	94	6	0
Coleman	12	114	10	1
Johnson	6	108	18	1
Clark	6	58	10	0
Rucker	4	40	10	0
Merkens	3	44	15	0
Ellender	1	15	15	1
Groth	1	6	6	0

PUNT RETURNS

Last Name	No.	Yds.	Avg.	TD
Ellender	31	203	7	0
Johnson	4	17	4	0
Merkens	2	6	3	0
Coleman	1	−5	−5	0

KICKOFF RETURNS

Last Name	No.	Yds.	Avg.	TD
Ellender	24	514	21	0
Coleman	16	321	20	0
Hartwig	13	328	18	0
Johnson	4	37	9	0
Carpenter	2	34	17	0
T. Wilson	2	30	15	0
Merkens	2	22	11	0
Groth	1	21	21	0
King	1	17	17	0
Caster	1	0	0	0
Stemrick	1	0	0	0

PASSING - PUNTING - KICKING

PASSING	Att.	Comp.	%	Yds.	Yd./Att.	TD	Int.–%	RK
Pastorini	324	163	50	2090	6.5	14	18– 6	13
Nielsen	61	32	53	404	6.6	3	3– 5	
Burrough	1	0	0	0	0.0	0	0– 0	

PUNTING	No.	Avg.
Parsley	93	40.6

KICKING	XP	Att.	%	FG	Att.	%
Fritsch	41	43	95	21	25	**84**

CLEVELAND BROWNS

RUSHING

Last Name	No.	Yds.	Avg.	TD
M. Pruitt	264	1294	4.9	9
G. Pruitt	62	233	3.8	0
C. Miller	39	213	5.5	1
Hill	53	193	3.6	1
Sipe	45	178	4.0	2
D. Hall	22	152	6.9	1
Moriarty	14	11	0.8	2
Newsome	1	6	6.0	0
Adams	2	4	2.0	0
Feacher	1	−1	−1.0	0
Mark Miller	1	−2	−2.0	0

RECEIVING

Last Name	No.	Yds.	Avg.	TD
Logan	59	982	17	7
Newsome	55	781	14	9
Rucker	43	749	17	6
M. Pruitt	41	372	9	2
Hill	38	381	10	2
C. Miller	26	251	10	0
G. Pruitt	14	155	11	1
Feacher	7	103	15	1
D Hall	2	14	7	0
Moriarty	1	17	17	0
Weathers	1	14	14	0
Wright	1	13	13	0
Adams	1	6	6	0

PUNT RETURNS

Last Name	No.	Yds.	Avg.	TD
D. Hall	29	295	10	0
Wright	12	50	4	0

KICKOFF RETURNS

Last Name	No.	Yds.	Avg.	TD
D. Hall	50	1014	20	0
Wright	15	402	27	0
Feacher	2	51	26	0
Rich	2	10	5	0
G. Pruitt	1	22	22	0
B. Jackson	1	18	18	0
C. Miller	1	14	14	0
Matt Miller	1	0	0	0
Moriarty	1	0	0	0
Weathers	1	0	0	0

PASSING - PUNTING - KICKING

PASSING	Att.	Comp.	%	Yds.	Yd./Att.	TD	Int.–%	RK
Sipe	535	286	54	3793	7.1	**28**	26– 5	9
Mark Miller	8	2	25	31	3.9	0	1– 13	
Evans	2	1	50	14	7.0	0	0– 0	

PUNTING	No.	Avg.
Evans	69	41.2

KICKING	XP	Att.	%	FG	Att.	%
Cockroft	38	43	88	17	29	59

CINCINNATI BENGALS

RUSHING

Last Name	No.	Yds.	Avg.	TD
P. Johnson	243	865	3.6	14
A. Griffin	140	688	4.9	0
Alexander	88	286	3.3	1
Anderson	28	235	8.4	2
Thompson	21	116	5.5	5
Turner	28	86	3.1	1
Bass	4	35	8.8	0
McInally	1	18	18.0	0
Dinkel	2	14	7.0	0
Kreider	2	0	0.0	0
Poole	1	−3	−3.0	0
Curtis	2	−11	−5.5	0

RECEIVING

Last Name	No.	Yds.	Avg.	TD
Bass	58	724	13	3
A. Griffin	43	417	10	2
Ross	41	516	13	1
Curtis	32	605	19	8
P. Johnson	24	154	6	1
Alexander	11	91	8	0
Brooks	8	214	27	1
Corbett	3	34	11	0
Kreider	3	20	7	0
Turner	2	18	9	0
McInally	1	24	24	0
Walker	1	14	14	1
Poole	1	−10	−10	0

PUNT RETURNS

Last Name	No.	Yds.	Avg.	TD
Lusby	32	260	8	0
Levenseller	8	46	6	0
Jauron	1	10	10	0
Burk	1	0	0	0

KICKOFF RETURNS

Last Name	No.	Yds.	Avg.	TD
Turner	**55**	1149	21	0
Poole	7	128	18	0
Lusby	6	92	15	0
J. Browner	6	87	15	0
Kurnick	4	60	15	0
R. Browner	2	29	15	0
R. Griffin	1	15	15	0

PASSING - PUNTING - KICKING

PASSING	Att.	Comp.	%	Yds.	Yd./Att.	TD	Int.–%	RK
Anderson	339	189	56	2340	6.9	16	**10– 3**	3
Thompson	87	39	45	481	5.5	1	5– 6	

PUNTING	No.	Avg.
McInally	89	41.3

KICKING	XP	Att.	%	FG	Att.	%
Bahr	40	42	95	13	23	57

SAN DIEGO CHARGERS 12-4-0 Don Coryell

Scores of Each Game		
33	Seattle	16
30	OAKLAND	10
27	BUFFALO	19
21	New England	27
31	SAN FRANCISCO	9
0	Denver	7
20	SEATTLE	10
40	Los Angeles	16
22	Oakland	45
20	Kansas City	14
26	Cincinnati	24
35	PITTSBURGH	7
28	KANSAS CITY	7
26	ATLANTA	28
35	New Orleans	0
17	DENVER	7

Use Name	Pos.	Hgt.	Wgt.	Age	Int.	Pts.
Dan Audick	OT-OG	6'3	253	24		
Billy Shields	OT	6'7	275	26		
Russ Washington	OT	6'6	288	32		
Don Macek	OG-C	6'3	253	25		
Ed White	OG	6'2	271	32		
Doug Wilkerson	OG	6'2	263	32		
Ralph Perretta	C	6'2	251	26		
Bob Rush	C	6'5	264	23		
Fred Dean	DE	6'3	230	27		
Leroy Jones	DE	6'8	260	28		
John Lee	DE	6'2	259	26		
Charles DeJurnett	DT	6'4	260	27		
Gary Johnson	DT	6'2	252	27		
Louie Kelcher	DT	6'5	282	26		
Wilbur Young	DT	6'6	290	30		8
Don Goode	LB	6'2	231	28	1	
Bob Horn	LB	6'3	230	25	2	
Keith King	LB	6'4"	230	24		
Woodrow Lowe	LB	6'	227	25	5	12
Ray Preston	LB	6'	218	25	5	
Cliff Thrift	LB	6'2	232	23		
Willie Buchanon	DB	6'	195	28		
Jerome Dove	DB	6'2"	193	25		
Frank Duncan	DB	6'1	188	22		
Glenn Edwards	DB	6'	183	32	4	
Mike Fuller	DB	5'9"	182	26	4	
Pete Shaw	DB	5'10	178	25	3	
Hal Stringert	DB	5'11	187	27		
Mike Williams	DB	5'10	179	25	4	
Dan Fouts	QB	6'3	210	28		12
James Harris	QB	6'3	221	32		
Cliff Olander	QB	6'5"	187	24		1
Hank Bauer	HB	5'10"	200	25		48
Lydell Mitchell	HB	5'11"	198	30		6
Artie Owens	HB	5'10"	182	26		12
Mike Thomas	HB	5'11"	190	26		6
Bo Mathews	FB	6'4"	222	27		6
Clarence Williams	FB-HB	5'9"	195	24		72
Don Woods	FB	6'1"	208	28		
Larry Burton	WR	6'1"	195	27		
John Floyd	WR	6'1"	195	22		6
John Jefferson	WR	6'1"	198	23		60
Charlie Joiner	WR	5'11"	183	31		24
Bob Klein	TE	6'5"	237	32		30
Greg McCrary	TE	6'3"	235	27		2
Jeff West	TE	6'3"	210	26		
Kellen Winslow	TE-WR	6'5"	252	21		12
Rolf Benirschke	K	6'	171	24		24
Roy Gerela	K	5'10"	185	31		9
Mike Wood (from St.L)	K	5'11"	199	24		73

Pat Curran – Injury
Milton Hardaway – Knee Injury
Jim Laslavic – Knee Injury
Dwight McDonald – Injury

DENVER BRONCOS 10-6-0 Red Miller

Scores of Each Game		
10	CINCINNATI	0
9	LOS ANGELES	13
20	Atlanta	*17
37	SEATTLE	34
3	Oakland	27
7	SAN DIEGO	0
24	Kansas City	10
7	Pittsburgh	42
20	KANSAS CITY	3
10	NEW ORLEANS	3
45	NEW ENGLAND	10
38	San Francisco	28
10	OAKLAND	14
19	Buffalo	16
23	Seattle	28
7	San Diego	17

Use Name	Pos.	Hgt.	Wgt.	Age	Int.	Pts.
Kelvin Clark	OT	6'3"	245	23		
Claudie Minor	OT	6'4"	280	28		
Dave Studdard	OT-TE	6'4"	255	23		6
Tom Glassic	OG	6'3"	254	25		
Paul Howard	OG	6'3"	260	28		
Glenn Hyde	OG-OT	6'3"	252	28		
Ken Brown	C	6'1"	245	25		
Bill Bryan	C	6'2"	244	24		
Barney Chavous	DE	6'3"	252	28		
John Grant	DE	6'3"	246	29		
Brison Manor	DE	6'4"	248	27		
Bruce Radford	DE	6'5"	252	23		
Rubin Carter	NT	6'	253	26		6
Kit Lathrop (to GB)	NT	6'5"	253	23		
Don Latimer	NT	6'3"	265	24		
Larry Evans	LB	6'2"	214	26		
Randy Gradishar	LB	6'3"	231	27		
Tom Jackson	LB	5'11"	220	28	1	
Rob Nairne	LB	6'4"	220	25		6
Joe Rizzo	LB	6'1"	220	28	2	
Jim Ryan	LB	6'1"	212	22		
Bob Swenson	LB	6'3"	222	26	3	6
Butch Atkinson	DB	6'	185	32		
Steve Foley	DB	6'2"	190	25	6	
Bernard Jackson	DB	6'	180	29		
Chris Pane	DB	5'11"	188	26		
Bill Thompson	DB	6'1"	200	32	4	6
Charlie West	DB	6'1"	195	33	1	
Louis Wright	DB	6'2"	200	26	2	6
Craig Morton	QB	6'4"	211	36		6
Craig Penrose	QB	6'3"	211	26		
Norris Weese	QB	6'1"	195	28		18
Otis Armstrong	HB	5'10"	196	28		18
Zachary Dixon (to NYG)	HB	6'	200	23		
Rob Lytle	HB	6'1"	195	24		24
Dave Preston	HB	5'10"	195	24		12
Larry Canada	FB	6'2"	238	24		
Jim Jensen	FB	6'3"	230	25		12
Jon Keyworth	FB	6'3"	230	28		6
Jack Dolbin	WR	5'10"	180	30		
Vince Kinney	WR	6'2"	190	23		
Haven Moses	WR	6'2"	200	33		36
Rick Upchurch	WR	5'10"	170	27		42
Steve Watson	WR	6'4"	192	22		
Ron Egloff	TE	6'5"	238	23		
Riley Odoms	TE	6'4"	230	29		6
Luke Prestridge	K	6'4"	235	22		
Fred Steinfort	K	5'11"	180	25		
Jim Turner	K	6'2"	205	38		71

Maurice Harvey – Knee Injury
James Wright — Knee Injury

OAKLAND RAIDERS 9-7-0 Tom Flores

Scores of Each Game		
24	Los Angeles	17
10	San Diego	30
10	Seattle	27
7	Kansas City	35
27	DENVER	3
13	MIAMI	3
50	ATLANTA	19
19	N.Y. Jets	28
45	SAN DIEGO	22
23	SAN FRANCISCO	10
17	Houston	31
21	KANSAS CITY	24
14	Denver	10
42	New Orleans	35
19	CLEVELAND	14
24	SEATTLE	29

Use Name	Pos.	Hgt.	Wgt.	Age	Int.	Pts.
Bruce Davis	OT	6'6"	280	23		
Henry Lawrence	OT	6'4"	270	27		
Art Shell	OT	6'5"	275	32		
John Vella	OT	6'4"	260	29		
Mickey Marvin	OG	6'4"	270	23		
Dan Medlin	OG	6'4"	250	29		
Steve Sylvester	OG-OT-C	6'4"	260	26		
Gene Upshaw	OG	6'5"	255	34		
Dave Dalby	C	6'2"	250	28		
Joe Bell	DE	6'3"	250	23		
Dave Browning	DE	6'5"	245	23		
Willie Jones	DE	6'4"	240	21		
John Matuszak	DE	6'8"	275	28		
Charles Philyaw	DE-NT	6'9"	290	25		
Pat Toomay	DE	6'5"	245	34		
Reggie Kinlaw	NT	6'2"	240	22		
Dave Pear	NT	6'2"	250	26		
Jeff Barnes	LB	6'2"	215	24	1	
Ted Hendricks	LB	6'7"	220	31	1	6
John Huddleston	LB	6'3"	230	25		
Monte Johnson	LB	6'4"	240	27	1	6
Rod Martin	LB	6'2"	210	25		
Phil Villapiano	LB	6'2"	225	30		
Rufus Bess	DB	5'9"	180	22	1	
Mike Davis	DB	6'2"	200	23	2	
Lester Hayes	DB	6'	195	24	7	12
Monte Jackson	DB	5'11"	190	26	2	
Charlie Phillips	DB	6'2"	215	26	4	
Jack Tatum	DB	5'10"	205	30	2	
Henry Williams	DB	5'10"	180	22	3	
David Humm	QB	6'2"	190	27		
Jim Plunkett	QB	6'3"	205	31		
Ken Stabler	QB	6'3"	210	33		
Clarence Hawkins	HB	6'	205	23		6
Derrick Jensen	HB-FB	6'1"	225	23		6
Ira Matthews	HB	5'8"	175	22		6
Terry Robiskie	HB-FB	6'1"	210	24		
Art Whittington	HB	5'11"	185	23		12
Todd Christensen (from NYG)	FB	6'3"	230	23		
Booker Russell	FB	6'2"	230	23		24
Mark van Eeghen	FB	6'2"	225	27		54
Morris Bradshaw	WR	6'	195	26		
Cliff Branch	WR	5'11"	170	31		36
Larry Brunson	WR	5'11"	180	30		6
Rich Martini	WR	6'2"	185	23		12
Joe Stewart	WR	5'11"	180	23		
Dave Casper	TE	6'4"	230	27		18
Ray Chester	TE	6'3"	235	31		48
Derrick Ramsey	TE	6'4"	220	22		18
Jim Breech	K	5'6"	155	23		95
Ray Guy	K	6'3"	190	29		

Lindsey Mason – Knee Injury
Otis Sistrunk – Injury

SEATTLE SEAHAWKS 9-7-0 Jack Patera

Scores of Each Game		
16	SAN DIEGO	33
10	Miami	19
27	OAKLAND	10
34	Denver	37
6	KANSAS CITY	24
35	San Francisco	24
10	San Diego	20
34	HOUSTON	14
31	Atlanta	28
0	LOS ANGELES	24
29	Cleveland	24
38	NEW ORLEANS	24
30	N.Y. JETS	7
21	Kansas City	37
28	DENVER	23
29	Oakland	24

Use Name	Pos.	Hgt.	Wgt.	Age	Int.	Pts.
Steve August	OT	6'5"	254	24		
Nick Bebout	OT	6'5"	260	28		
Louis Bullard	OT	6'6"	265	23		
Bill Fifer	OT	6'4"	250	23		
Jeff Sevy	OT	6'5"	260	28		
Ron Coder	OG-OT	6'4"	250	25		
Tom Lynch	OG	6'5"	260	24		
Bob Newton	OG	6'4"	260	30		
Art Kuehn	C	6'3"	255	26		
John Yarno	C	6'5"	251	24		
Mark Bell	DE	6'4"	240	22		
Dennis Boyd	DE	6'6"	255	23		
Carl Eller	DE	6'6"	247	37		
Bill Gregory	DE	6'5"	260	29		
Ernie Price (to CLE)	DE	6'4"	245	28		
Bill Cooke	DT	6'5"	250	28		
Robert Hardy	DT	6'2"	250	23		
Manu Tuiasosopo	DT	6'3"	252	22		
Terry Beeson	LB	6'3"	240	23	1	
Keith Butler	LB	6'4"	225	23	1	
Pete Cronan	LB	6'2"	238	24		
Sammy Green	LB	6'2"	230	24	1	6
Michael Jackson	LB	6'1"	220	22		
Charles McShane	LB	6'3"	230	25		
Joe Norman	LB	6'1"	220	22		
Larry Polowski	LB	6'3"	235	21		
Autry Beamon	DB	6'1"	190	25	1	
Dave Brown	DB	6'1"	190	26	5	
Don Dufek	DB	6'	195	25		
John Harris	DB	6'2"	200	23	2	
Kerry Justin	DB	5'11"	175	24	1	
Mike O'Brien	DB	6'1"	195	23		
Keith Simpson	DB	6'1"	195	23	4	
Cornell Webster	DB	6'	180	24	1	6
Sam Adkins	QB	6'2"	214	24		
Steve Myer	QB	6'2"	200	25		
Jim Zorn	QB	6'2"	200	26		12
Tony Green (from NYG)	HB	5'9"	185	22		
Al Hunter	HB	5'11"	195	24		6
Jeff Moore	HB	6'	195	23		12
David Sims	HB	6'3"	216	23		
Sherman Smith	HB-FB	6'4"	225	24		90
Tony Benjamin	FB	6'3"	225	23		
Dan Doornink	FB	6'3"	210	23		54
Duke Fergerson	WR	6'1"	185	25		
Jessie Green	WR	6'3"	194	25		
Steve Largent	WR	5'11"	184	24		54
Sam McCullum	WR	6'2"	203	26		24
Steve Raible	WR	6'2"	195	25		6
Mark Bell	TE	6'4"	235	22		
Brian Peets	TE	6'4"	225	23		6
Efren Herrera	K	5'9"	190	28		100
Herman Weaver	K	6'4"	210	30		

Bill Sandifer – Knee Injury
John Sawyer – Hamstring Injury

KANSAS CITY CHIEFS 7-9-0 Marv Levy

Scores of Each Game		
14	BALTIMORE	0
24	CLEVELAND	27
6	Houston	20
35	OAKLAND	7
24	Seattle	6
10	Cincinnati	7
10	DENVER	24
17	N.Y. GIANTS	21
3	Denver	20
14	SAN DIEGO	20
3	PITTSBURGH	30
24	Oakland	21
7	San Diego	28
37	SEATTLE	21
10	Baltimore	7
0	Tampa Bay	3

Use Name	Pos.	Hgt.	Wgt.	Age	Int.	Pts.
Larry Brown	OT	6'5"	264	24		
Charlie Getty	OT	6'4"	269	27		
Matt Herkenhoff	OT	6'4"	255	28		
Jim Nicholson	OT	6'6"	275	29		
John Choma	OG	6'5"	241	24		
Tom Condon	OG	6'3"	254	26		
Bob Simmons	OG	6'4"	260	25		
Rod Walters	OG-OT	6'3"	258	25		
Charlie Ane	C	6'1"	237	27		
Jack Rudnay	C	6'3"	240	31		
Curtis Anderson	DE	6'6"	250	22		
Mike Bell	DE	6'4"	255	22		
Sylvester Hicks	DE	6'4"	252	24		
Dave Linstrom	DE	6'6"	257	24		
Art Still	DE	6'7"	252	23		
Ken Kremer	NT-DE	6'4"	250	22		
Don Parrish	NT	6'2"	255	24		
Jerry Blanton	LB	6'1"	225	23		
Tom Howard	LB	6'2"	208	25	1	
Charles Jackson	LB	6'2"	236	24		
Frank Manumaleuga	LB	6'2"	245	23	1	
Whitney Paul	LB	6'3"	220	25	1	
Cal Peterson	LB	6'3"	220	26		
Dave Rozumek	LB	6'1"	222	25		
Gary Spani	LB	6'2"	230	23		
Gary Barbaro	DB	6'4"	204	25	7	6
M.L. Carter	DB	5'9"	173	23	3	
Herb Christopher	DB	5'10"	190	25	2	
Tim Collier	DB	6'	174	25	2	
Gary Green	DB	5'11"	184	23	5	
Gerald Jackson	DB	6'1"	195	23	1	
Horace Perkins	DB	5'11"	180	25		
Jerry Reece	DB	6'3"	192	24		
Steve Fuller	QB	6'4"	198	22		6
Bill Kenney	QB	6'4"	210	24		
Mike Livingston	QB	6'3"	210	33		
Horace Belton	HB	5'8"	200	24		6
Ben Cowins	HB	6'	192	23		
Earl Gant	HB	6'	207	22		6
Tony Reed	HB	5'11"	197	24		6
Wilbert Haslip	FB	5'11"	212	22		
Ted McKnight	FB-HB	6'1"	205	25		48
Arnold Morgado	FB-HB	6'	210	26		24
Mike Williams	FB	6'3"	222	21		18
Johnnie Dirden	WR	6'	190	27		
Steve Gaunty	WR	5'10"	175	20		6
Henry Marshall	WR	6'2"	205	25		12
Stan Rome	WR	6'5"	205	23		
J.T. Smith	WR	6'2"	185	23		30
Ed Beckman	TE	6'4"	226	24		
Tony Samuels	TE	6'4"	229	24		6
Walter White	TE	6'3"	218	28		
Bob Grupp	K	5'11"	193	24		
Jan Stenerud	K	6'2"	187	36		64

Bill Kellar – Shoulder Injury
Clyde Powers – Knee Injury
Mark Bailey – Voluntarily Retired

* – Overtime

SAN DIEGO CHARGERS

RUSHING

Last Name	No.	Yds.	Avg.	TD
C. Williams	200	752	3.8	12
Thomas	91	353	3.9	1
Mitchell	63	211	3.3	0
Owens	40	151	3.8	1
Matthews	30	112	3.7	1
Fouts	26	49	1.9	2
Bauer	22	28	1.3	8
Harris	6	26	4.3	0
Fuller	1	0	0.0	0
West	1	−2	−2.0	0
Joiner	1	−12	−12.0	0

RECEIVING

Last Name	No.	Yds.	Avg.	TD
Joiner	72	1008	14	4
Jefferson	61	1090	18	10
C. Williams	51	352	7	0
Klein	37	424	12	5
Thomas	32	388	12	0
Winslow	25	255	10	2
Mitchell	19	159	8	1
Owens	15	176	12	1
Floyd	10	152	15	1
Matthews	7	40	6	0
McCrary	5	32	6	0
Burton	4	62	16	0

PUNT RETURNS

Last Name	No.	Yds.	Avg.	TD
Fuller	46	448	10	0
M. Williams	3	19	6	0
Shaw	2	21	11	0
Goode	1	0	0	0

KICKOFF RETURNS

Last Name	No.	Yds.	Avg.	TD
Owens	35	791	23	0
Fuller	6	115	19	0
Bauer	4	92	23	0
C. Williams	1	19	19	0
Mitchell	1	15	15	0
Thrift	1	11	11	0
Parretta	1	9	9	0
Matthews	1	4	4	0
Woods	0	10	—	0

PASSING - PUNTING - KICKING

PASSING	Att.	Comp.	%	Yds.	Yd./Att.	TD	Int.–%	RK
Fouts	530	**332**	**63**	**4082**	7.7	24	24– 5	1
Harris	9	5	56	38	4.2	0	1– 11	
Thomas	1	1	100	18	18.0	0	0– 0	
Fuller	1	0	0	0	0.0	0	0– 0	

PUNTING	No.	Avg.
West	75	36.5

KICKING	XP	Att.	%	FG	Att.	%
Wood	34	37	92	13	21	62
Benirschke	12	13	92	4	4	100

DENVER BRONCOS

RUSHING

Last Name	No.	Yds.	Avg.	TD
Armstrong	108	453	4.2	2
Jensen	106	400	3.8	1
Lytle	102	371	3.6	4
Keyworth	81	323	4.0	1
Preston	43	169	3.9	1
Canada	36	143	4.0	0
Weese	18	116	6.4	3
Prestridge	1	29	29.0	0
Upchurch	3	17	5.7	0
Morton	23	13	0.6	1
Dixon	3	9	3.0	0
Odoms	1	−7	−7.0	0

RECEIVING

Last Name	No.	Yds.	Avg.	TD
Upchurch	64	937	15	7
Moses	54	943	18	6
Odoms	40	638	16	1
Jensen	19	144	8	1
Preston	19	137	7	1
Keyworth	18	132	7	0
Armstrong	14	138	10	1
Lytle	13	93	7	0
Watson	6	83	14	0
Egloff	5	70	14	0
Dolbin	3	74	25	0
Canada	3	36	12	0
Turner	1	6	6	0
Studdard	1	0	0	1

PUNT RETURNS

Last Name	No.	Yds.	Avg.	TD
Upchurch	30	304	10	0
Preston	7	78	11	0
Pane	5	20	4	0
West	1	−1	−1	0

KICKOFF RETURNS

Last Name	No.	Yds.	Avg.	TD
Pane	18	354	20	0
Preston	13	336	26	0
Upchurch	5	79	16	0
B. Jackson	4	53	13	0
Dixon	3	53	18	0
Canada	3	31	10	0
Grant	1	25	25	0
Armstrong	1	21	21	0
Kinney	1	14	14	0
Egloff	1	0	0	0

PASSING - PUNTING - KICKING

PASSING	Att.	Comp.	%	Yds.	Yd./Att.	TD	Int.–%	RK
Morton	370	204	55	2626	7.1	16	19– 5	11
Weese	97	53	55	731	7.5	1	3– 3	
Penrose	5	2	40	44	8.8	0	1– 20	
Keyworth	1	1	100	32	32.0	1	0– 0	
Preston	1	0	0	0	0.0	0	0– 0	
Prestridge	1	0	0	0	0.0	0	0– 0	
Upchurch	1	0	0	0	0.0	0	0– 0	

PUNTING	No.	Avg.
Prestridge	89	39.9

KICKING	XP	Att.	%	FG	Att.	%
Turner	32	34	94	13	21	62

OAKLAND RAIDERS

RUSHING

Last Name	No.	Yds.	Avg.	TD
van Eeghen	223	818	3.7	7
Whittington	109	397	3.6	2
Jensen	73	251	3.4	0
Russell	33	190	5.8	4
Hawkins	21	72	3.4	0
Plunkett	3	18	6.0	0
Robiskie	10	14	1.4	0
Branch	1	4	4.0	0
Matthews	2	3	1.5	0
Stabler	16	−4	−0.3	0

RECEIVING

Last Name	No.	Yds.	Avg.	TD
Branch	59	844	14	6
Chester	58	712	12	8
Casper	57	771	14	3
van Eeghen	51	474	9	2
Martini	24	259	11	2
Whittington	19	240	13	0
Ramsey	13	161	12	3
Jensen	7	23	3	1
Russell	6	79	13	0
Brunson	5	49	10	1
Robiskie	5	36	7	0
Bradshaw	3	28	9	0
Hawkins	2	24	12	1
Stewart	1	3	3	0
Dalby	1	1	1	0

PUNT RETURNS

Last Name	No.	Yds.	Avg.	TD
Matthews	32	165	5	0
Brunson	2	8	4	0
M. Davis	1	6	6	0

KICKOFF RETURNS

Last Name	No.	Yds.	Avg.	TD
Brunson	17	441	**26**	0
Matthews	35	873	25	**1**
Whittington	5	46	9	0
Russell	3	21	7	0
Stewart	2	63	32	0
Hawkins	1	25	25	0
Robiskie	1	6	6	0
Jensen	1	0	0	0

PASSING - PUNTING - KICKING

PASSING	Att.	Comp.	%	Yds.	Yd./Att.	TD	Int.–%	RK
Stabler	498	304	61	3615	7.3	26	22– 4	2
Plunkett	15	7	47	89	5.9	1	1– 7	

PUNTING	No.	Avg.
Guy	69	42.6

KICKING	XP	Att.	%	FG	Att.	%
Breech	41	45	91	18	27	67

SEATTLE SEAHAWKS

RUSHING

Last Name	No.	Yds.	Avg.	TD
Smith	194	775	4.0	11
Doornink	152	500	3.3	8
Zorn	46	279	6.1	2
Hunter	34	174	5.1	1
Moore	44	168	3.8	2
Sims	20	53	2.7	0
Benjamin	5	13	2.6	0
Adkins	2	11	5.5	0
Myer	1	0	0.0	0
Weaver	2	−6	−3.0	0

RECEIVING

Last Name	No.	Yds.	Avg.	TD
Largent	66	**1237**	19	9
Doornink	54	432	8	1
Smith	48	499	10	4
McCullum	46	739	16	4
Peets	25	293	12	1
Raible	20	252	13	1
Moore	14	128	9	0
Hunter	7	77	11	0
Sims	4	28	7	0
Bell	2	20	10	0
Fergerson	2	12	6	0
Webster	1	39	39	0
Herrera	1	20	20	0
J. Green	1	9	9	0
Benjamin	1	6	6	0

PUNT RETURNS

Last Name	No.	Yds.	Avg.	TD
T. Green	19	138	7	0
Moore	10	90	9	0
Harris	8	70	9	0

KICKOFF RETURNS

Last Name	No.	Yds.	Avg.	TD
Moore	31	641	21	0
T. Green	32	651	20	0
Hunter	15	299	20	0
Benjamin	2	33	17	0
Harris	1	21	21	0
Doornink	1	13	13	0

PASSING - PUNTING - KICKING

PASSING	Att.	Comp.	%	Yds.	Yd./Att.	TD	Int.–%	RK
Zorn	505	285	56	3661	7.3	20	18– 4	4
Weaver	4	3	75	73	18.3	0	0– 0	
Myer	8	2	25	28	3.5	0	0– 0	
Smith	1	1	100	11	11.0	0	0– 0	
Sims	2	1	50	18	9.0	0	0– 0	
Adkins	3	0	0	0	0.0	0	0– 0	

PUNTING	No.	Avg.
Weaver	66	40.2
Herrera	1	36.0

KICKING	XP	Att.	%	FG	Att.	%
Herrera	43	46	93	19	23	83

KANSAS CITY CHIEFS

RUSHING

Last Name	No.	Yds.	Avg.	TD
McKnight	153	755	4.9	8
Reed	113	446	3.9	1
Fuller	50	264	5.3	1
Williams	69	261	3.8	1
Morgado	75	231	3.1	4
Gant	56	196	3.5	1
Belton	44	134	3.0	1
Marshall	2	34	17.0	1
Livingston	3	2	0.7	0
Haslip	2	1	0.5	0
Manumaleuga	1	−3	−3.0	0
Rome	1	−5	−5.0	0

RECEIVING

Last Name	No.	Yds.	Avg.	TD
McKnight	38	226	6	0
Reed	34	352	10	0
Smith	33	444	14	3
Marshall	21	332	16	1
Williams	16	129	8	2
Gant	15	101	7	0
Samuels	14	147	11	0
Gaunty	5	87	17	1
Morgado	5	55	11	0
Belton	4	44	11	0
White	3	15	5	0
Beckman	2	21	11	0

PUNT RETURNS

Last Name	No.	Yds.	Avg.	TD
Smith	**58**	**612**	11	**2**

KICKOFF RETURNS

Last Name	No.	Yds.	Avg.	TD
Belton	22	463	21	0
Gaunty	12	271	23	0
Dirden	7	154	22	0
Gant	4	75	19	0
McKnight	2	34	17	0
Haslip	1	7	7	0
Collier	1	0	0	0
Morgado	1	0	0	0
Peterson	1	0	0	0

PASSING - PUNTING - KICKING

PASSING	Att.	Comp.	%	Yds.	Yd./Att.	TD	Int.–%	RK
Fuller	270	146	54	1484	5.5	6	14– 5	14
Livingston	90	44	49	469	5.2	1	4– 4	
Grupp	1	0	0	0	0.0	0	0– 0	

PUNTING	No.	Avg.
Grupp	89	**43.6**

KICKING	XP	Att.	%	FG	Att.	%
Stenerud	28	29	97	12	23	52

1979 N.F.C. PLAYOFFS

December 23 at Philadelphia (Attendance 69, 397)

SCORING

CHICAGO	7	10	0	0–17
PHILADELPHIA	7	3	7	10–27

First Quarter
- Phi. Carmichael, 17 yard pass from Jaworski. PAT – Franklin (kick)
- Chi. Payton, 2 yard rush PAT – Thomas (kick)

Second Quarter
- Phi. Franklin, 29 yard field goal
- Chi. Payton, 1 yard rush PAT – Thomas (kick)
- Chi. Thomas, 30 yard field goal

Third Quarter
- Phi. Carmichael, 29 yard pass from Jaworski PAT – Franklin (kick)

Fourth Quarter
- Phi. Campfield, 63 yard pass from Jaworski PAT – Franklin (kick)
- Phi. Franklin, 34 yard field goal

TEAM STATISTICS

CHI.		PHI.
15	First Downs–Total	18
7	First Downs–Rushing	8
7	First Downs–Passing	8
1	First Downs–Penalty	2
1	Fumbles–Number	4
1	Fumbles–Lost Ball	2
4	Penalties–Number	4
35	Yards Penalized	46
1	Missed Field Goals	0
60	Offensive Plays	63
241	Net Yards	315
4.0	Average Gain	5.0
3	Giveaways	3
3	Takeaways	3
0	Difference	0

INDIVIDUAL STATISTICS

RUSHING

CHICAGO	No.	Yds.	Avg.	PHILADELPHIA	No.	Yds.	Avg.
Payton	16	67	4.2	Montgomery	26	87	3.3
Williams	10	23	2.3	Harris	8	33	4.1
McClendon	2	6	3.0	Jaworski	3	19	6.3
Phipps	1	3	3.0		37	139	3.8
	29	99	3.4				

RECEIVING

CHICAGO	No.	Yds.	Avg.	PHILADELPHIA	No.	Yds.	Avg.
Payton	3	52	17.3	Carmichael	6	111	18.5
Watts	3	42	14.0	Campfield	2	70	35.0
Baschnagel	3	38	12.7	Montgomery	2	0	0.0
Latta	2	6	3.0	Harris	1	15	15.0
Williams	2	4	2.0	Smith	1	8	8.0
	13	142	10.9		12	204	17.0

PUNTING

CHICAGO	No.	Yds.	Avg.	PHILADELPHIA	No.	Yds.	Avg.
Parsons	6		39.0	Runager	4		40.5

PUNT RETURNS

CHICAGO	No.	Yds.	Avg.	PHILADELPHIA	No.	Yds.	Avg.
none				Henry	4	51	12.8

KICKOFF RETURNS

CHICAGO	No.	Yds.	Avg.	PHILADELPHIA	No.	Yds.	Avg.
Walterscheid	3	66	22.0	Henry	3	76	25.3
Watts	2	31	15.5				
Baschnagel	1	27	27.0				
	6	124	20.7				

INTERCEPTION RETURNS

CHICAGO	No.	Yds.	Avg.	PHILADELPHIA	No.	Yds.	Avg.
Ellis	1	25	25.0	Edwards	1	5	5.0
				Howard	1	0	0.0
					2	5	2.5

PASSING

	Att.	Comp.	Comp. Pct.	Yds.	Int.	Yds. Att.	Yds. Comp.
CHICAGO							
Phipps	30	13	43.3	142	2	4.6	10.9
PHILADELPHIA							
Jaworski	23	12	52.2	204	1	8.9	17.0

December 29 at Tampa (Attendance 71,402)

SCORING

PHILADELPHIA	0	7	3	7–17
TAMPA BAY	7	10	0	7–24

First Quarter
- T.B. Bell, 3 yard rush PAT–O'Donoghue (kick)

Second Quarter
- T.B. O'Donoghue, 40 yard field goal
- T.B. Bell, 1 yard rush PAT–O'Donoghue (kick)
- Phi. Smith, 11 yard pass from Jaworski PAT–Franklin (kick)

Third Quarter
- Phi. Franklin, 43 yard field goal

Fourth Quarter
- T.B. Giles, 9 yard pass from Williams PAT–O'Donoghue (kick)
- Phi. Carmichael, 37 yard pass from Jaworski PAT–Franklin (kick)

TEAM STATISTICS

PHI.		T.B.
15	First Downs–Total	17
4	First Downs–Rushing	12
9	First Downs–Passing	4
2	First Downs–Penalty	1
2	Fumbles–Number	0
1	Fumbles–Lost Ball	0
8	Penalties–Number	9
62	Yards Penalized	105
1	Missed Field Goals	0
58	Offensive Plays	70
227	Net Yards	318
3.9	Average Gain	4.5
1	Giveaways	1
1	Takeaways	1
0	Difference	0

INDIVIDUAL STATISTICS

RUSHING

PHILADELPHIA	No.	Yds.	Avg.	TAMPA BAY	No.	Yds.	Avg.
Montgomery	13	35	2.7	Bell	38	142	3.7
Harris	4	13	3.3	Eckwood	8	19	2.4
Jaworski	1	0	0.0	Williams	6	19	3.2
	18	48	2.7	J. Davis	3	6	2.0
					55	186	3.4

RECEIVING

PHILADELPHIA	No.	Yds.	Avg.	TAMPA BAY	No.	Yds.	Avg.
Montgomery	4	35	8.8	Giles	3	43	14.3
Carmichael	3	92	30.7	Hagins	2	34	17.0
Smith	3	49	16.3	Mucker	1	34	34.0
Krepfle	3	23	7.7	Owens	1	21	21.0
Harris	1	2	2.0		7	132	17.1
Campfield	1	-2	-2.0				
	15	199	13.3				

PUNTING

PHILADELPHIA	No.	Yds.	Avg.	TAMPA BAY	No.	Yds.	Avg.
Runager	5		44.2	Blanchard	5		42.6

PUNT RETURNS

PHILADELPHIA	No.	Yds.	Avg.	TAMPA BAY	No.	Yds.	Avg.
Henry	4	48	12.0	Reece	3	33	11.0

KICKOFF RETURNS

PHILADELPHIA	No.	Yds.	Avg.	TAMPA BAY	No.	Yds.	Avg.
Henry	3	72	24.0	Hagins	3	59	19.7
Giammona	1	15	15.0	T. Davis	1	0	0.0
	4	87	21.8		4	59	14.8

INTERCEPTION RETURNS

PHILADELPHIA	No.	Yds.	Avg.	TAMPA BAY	No.	Yds.	Avg.
Robinson	1	37	37.0	none			

PASSING

	Att.	Comp.	Comp. Pct.	Yds.	Int.	Yds. Att.	Yds. Comp.
PHILADEL-PHIA							
Jaworski	38	15	39.5	199	0	5.2	13.3
TAMPA BAY							
Williams	15	7	46.7	132	1	8.8	17.1

December 30 at Irving, Tex. (Attendance 64,792)

SCORING

LOS ANGELES	0	14	0	7–21
DALLAS	2	3	7	7–19

First Quarter
- Dal. Safety, Ferragamo tackled in end zone

Second Quarter
- L.A. Tyler, 20 yard pass from Ferragamo PAT – Corral (kick)
- Dal. Septien, 33 yard field goal
- L.A. R. Smith, 43 yard pass from Ferragamo PAT – Corral (kick)

Third Quarter
- Dal. Springs, 1 yard rush PAT – Septien (kick)

Fourth Quarter
- Dal. Saldi, 2 yard pass from Staubach PAT – Septien (kick)
- L.A. Waddy, 50 yard pass from Ferragamo PAT – Corral (kick)

TEAM STATISTICS

L.A.		DAL.
16	First Downs–Total	17
8	First Downs–Rushing	8
7	First Downs–Passing	8
1	First Downs–Penalty	1
0	Fumbles–Number	0
0	Fumbles–Lost Ball	0
6	Penalties–Number	6
44	Yards Penalized	55
1	Missed Field Goals	0
61	Offensive Plays	64
361	Net Yards	306
5.9	Average Gain	4.8
2	Giveaways	1
1	Takeaways	2
–1	Difference	–1

INDIVIDUAL STATISTICS

RUSHING

LOS ANGELES	No.	Yds.	Avg.	DALLAS	No.	Yds.	Avg.
Tyler	19	82	4.3	Dorsett	19	87	4.6
Bryant	17	67	3.9	DuPree	1	27	27.0
Cromwell	1	7	7.0	Newhouse	7	21	3.0
Waddy	1	3	3.0	Springs	5	20	4.0
Ferragamo	1	0	0.0	Staubach	1	3	3.0
	39	159	4.1	P. Pearson	1	-2	-2.0
					34	156	4.6

RECEIVING

LOS ANGELES	No.	Yds.	Avg.	DALLAS	No.	Yds.	Avg.
Waddy	3	97	32.3	D. Pearson	4	87	21.8
R. Smith	2	55	27.5	DuPree	2	26	13.0
Tyler	2	40	20.0	Saldi	2	17	8.5
Dennard	1	15	15.0	P. Pearson	2	15	7.5
Bryant	1	3	3.0	Johnson	1	3	3.0
	9	210	23.3	Springs	1	2	2.0
				Hill	1	0	0.0
					13	150	11.5

PUNTING

LOS ANGELES	No.	Yds.	Avg.	DALLAS	No.	Yds.	Avg.
Clark	5		41.4	D. White	8		36.8

PUNT RETURNS

LOS ANGELES	No.	Yds.	Avg.	DALLAS	No.	Yds.	Avg.
E. Brown	3	17	5.7	Wilson	1	8	8.0
				Manning	1	2	2.0
					2	10	5.0

KICKOFF RETURNS

LOS ANGELES	No.	Yds.	Avg.	DALLAS	No.	Yds.	Avg.
E. Hill	3	64	21.3	Springs	3	61	20.3
Jodat	1	12	12.0	Wilson	1	18	18.0
	4	76	19.0		4	79	19.8

INTERCEPTION RETURNS

LOS ANGELES	No.	Yds.	Avg.	DALLAS	No.	Yds.	Avg.
E. Brown	1	21	21.0	Harris	1	22	22.0
				Thurman	1	18	18.0
					2	40	20.0

PASSING

	Att	Comp.	Comp. Pct.	Yds	Int.	Yds. Att.	Yds. Comp.
LOS ANGELES							
Ferragamo	21	9	42.9	210	2	10.0	23.3
DALLAS							
Staubach	28	13	46.4	150	1	5.4	11.5
Springs	1	0	0.0	0	0	0.0	0.0

1979 A.F.C. PLAYOFFS

December 23 at Houston (Attendance 48,776)

SCORING

DENVER	7	0	0	0–7
HOUSTON	3	7	0	3–13

First Quarter
Hou. Fritsch, 31 yard field goal
Denv. Preston, 7 yard pass from Morton
PAT – Turner (kick)

Second Quarter
Hou. Campbell, 3 yard rush
PAT – Fritsch (kick)

Fourth Quarter
Hou. Fritsh, 20 yard field goal

TEAM STATISTICS

DENV.		HOU.
17	First Downs–Total	15
7	First Downs–Rushing	8
9	First Downs–Passing	6
1	First Downs–Penalty	1
1	Fumbles–Number	0
0	Fumbles–Lost Ball	0
7	Penalties–Number	2
70	Yards Penalized	19
1	Missed Field Goals	0
65	Offensive Plays	65
216	Net Yards	282
3.3	Average Gain	4.3
1	Giveaways	2
2	Takeaways	1
–1	Difference	–1

INDIVIDUAL STATISTICS

RUSHING

DENVER	No.	Yds.	Avg.	HOUSTON	No.	Yds.	Avg.
Armstrong	12	51	4.3	Carpenter	16	59	3.7
Canada	4	29	7.3	Campbell	16	50	3.1
Preston	9	24	2.7	T. Wilson	8	21	2.6
Jensen	4	5	1.3	Coleman	2	5	2.5
Upchurch	1	3	3.0		42	135	3.2
Morton	2	0	0.0				
	32	112	3.5				

RECEIVING

DENVER	No.	Yds.	Avg.	HOUSTON	No.	Yds.	Avg.
Preston	4	40	10.0	T. Wilson	4	53	13.3
Moses	3	47	15.7	Carpenter	3	26	8.7
Armstrong	2	22	11.0	Coleman	1	41	41.0
Odom	2	3	1.5	Barber	1	31	31.0
Egloff	1	17	17.0	Campbell	1	7	7.0
Jensen	1	11	11.0		10	158	15.8
Canada	1	4	4.0				
	14	144	10.3				

PUNTING

DENVER	No.	Avg.	HOUSTON	No.	Avg.
Prestridge	6	44.4	Parsley	5	43.2

PUNT RETURNS

DENVER	No.	Yds.	Avg.	HOUSTON	No.	Yds.	Avg.
Upchurch	2	25	12.5	Ellender	5	42	8.4

KICKOFF RETURNS

DENVER	No.	Yds.	Avg.	HOUSTON	No.	Yds.	Avg.
Preston	3	56	18.7	Hartwig	1	26	26.0
Upchurch	1	27	27.0				
	4	83	20.7				

INTERCEPTION RETURNS

DENVER	No.	Yds.	Avg.	HOUSTON	No.	Yds.	Avg.
Thompson	1	12	12.0	Bingham	1	15	15.0
Swenson	1	0	0.0				
	2	12	6.0				

PASSING

DENVER	Att.	Comp.	Comp. Pct.	Yds.	Int.	Yds. Att.	Yds. Comp.
Morton	27	14	51.9	144	1	5.3	10.3
HOUSTON							
Pastorini	18	8	44.4	149	1	8.3	18.7
Nielsen	4	2	50.0	9	1	2.3	4.5
	22	10	45.5	158	2	7.2	15.8

December 29 at San Diego (Attendance 51,192)

SCORING

HOUSTON	0	10	7	0–17
SAN DIEGO	7	0	7	0–14

First Quarter
S.D. C. Williams, 1 yard rush
PAT – Wood (kick)

Second Quarter
Hou. Fritsch, 26 yard field goal
Hou. Clark, 1 yard rush
PAT – Fritsch (kick)

Third Quarter
S.D. Mitchell, 8 yard rush
PAT – Wood (kick)
Hou. Renfro, 47 yard pass from Nielsen
PAT – Fritsch (kick)

TEAM STATISTICS

HOU.		S.D.
15	First Downs–Total	25
9	First Downs–Rushing	6
5	First Downs–Passing	17
1	First Downs–Penalty	2
0	Fumbles–Number	0
0	Fumbles–Lost Ball	0
5	Penalties–Number	6
45	Yards Penalized	30
0	Missed Field Goals	1
59	Offensive Plays	68
259	Net Yards	380
4.4	Average Gain	5.6
1	Giveaways	5
5	Takeaways	1
–4	Difference	–4

INDIVIDUAL STATISTICS

RUSHING

HOUSTON	No.	Yds.	Avg.	SAN DIEGO	No.	Yds.	Avg.
Carpenter	18	67	3.7	Mitchell	8	33	4.1
T. Wilson	11	39	3.5	Williams	11	30	2.7
Clark	9	30	3.3		19	63	3.3
Nielsen	2	12	6.0				
	40	148	3.7				

RECEIVING

HOUSTON	No.	Yds.	Avg.	SAN DIEGO	No.	Yds.	Avg.
Carpenter	4	23	5.8	Klein	5	41	8.2
T. Wilson	3	16	5.3	Joiner	4	81	20.3
Renfro	1	47	47.0	Jefferson	4	70	17.5
Coleman	1	13	13.0	Williams	4	30	7.5
Barber	1	12	12.0	Mitchell	4	26	6.5
	10	111	11.1	Floyd	3	51	17.0
				McCrary	1	34	34.0
					25	333	13.3

PUNTING

HOUSTON	No.	Avg.	SAN DIEGO	No.	Avg.
Parlsey	6	40.7	West	2	32.0

PUNT RETURNS

HOUSTON	No.	Yds.	Avg.	SAN DIEGO	No.	Yds.	Avg.
Ellender	1	25	25.0	Fuller	3	29	9.7

KICKOFF RETURNS

HOUSTON	No.	Yds.	Avg.	SAN DIEGO	No.	Yds.	Avg.
Hartwig	2	37	18.5	Owens	3	60	20.0
Ellender	1	16	16.0	Bauer	1	24	24.0
	3	53	17.7		4	84	21.0

INTERCEPTION RETURNS

HOUSTON	No.	Yds.	Avg.	SAN DIEGO	No.	Yds.	Avg.
Perry	4	0	0.0	M. Williams	1	0	0.0
J.C. Wilson	1	3	3.0				
Reinfeldt	0	8	—				
	5	11	2.2				

PASSING

HOUSTON	Att.	Comp.	Comp. Pct.	Yds.	Int.	Yds. Att.	Yds. Comp.
Nielsen	19	10	52.6	111	1	5.8	11.1
SAN DIEGO							
Fouts	47	25	53.2	333	5	7.1	13.3

December 30 at Pittsburgh (Attendance 50,214)

SCORING

MIAMI	0	0	7	7–14
PITTSBURGH	20	0	7	7–34

First Quarter
Pit. Thornton, 1 yard rush
PAT – Bahr (kick)
Pit. Stallworth, 17 yard pass from Bradshaw
PAT – kick failed
Pit. Swann, 20 yard pass from Bradshaw
PAT–Bahr (kick)

Third Quarter
Mia. Harris, 7 yard pass from Griese
PAT–von Schamann (kick)
Pit. Bleier, 1 yard rush
PAT–Bahr (kick)

Fourth Quarter
Pit. Harris, 5 yard rush
PAT–Bahr (kick)
Mia. Csonka, 1 yard rush
PAT–von Schamann (kick)

TEAM STATISTICS

MIA.		PIT.
16	First Downs–Total	27
2	First Downs–Rushing	14
11	First Downs–Passing	12
3	First Downs–Penalty	1
0	Fumbles–Number	3
0	Fumbles–Lost Ball	3
4	Penalties–Number	8
35	Yards Penalized	41
0	Missed Field Goals	0
65	Offensive Plays	72
249	Net Yards	379
3.8	Average Gain	5.3
2	Giveaways	3
3	Takeaways	2
–1	Difference	–1

INDIVIDUAL STATISTICS

RUSHING

MIAMI	No.	Yds.	Avg.	PITTSBURGH	No.	Yds.	Avg.
Csonka	10	20	2.0	Harris	21	83	4.0
Davis	2	12	6.0	Thornton	12	52	4.3
Williams	8	1	0.1	Hawthrone	2	15	7.5
Griese	1	1	1.0	Bleier	4	13	3.3
Roberts	1	–9	–9.0	A. Anderson	1	–4	–4.0
	22	25	1.1		40	159	4.0

RECEIVING

MIAMI	No.	Yds.	Avg.	PITTSBURGH	No.	Yds.	Avg.
Williams	6	26	4.3	Stallworth	6	86	14.3
Moore	5	93	18.6	Harris	5	32	6.4
Harris	3	61	20.3	Smith	4	41	10.3
Nathan	3	27	9.0	Swann	3	37	12.3
Davis	2	24	12.0	Thornton	3	34	11.3
Hardy	2	12	6.0		21	230	10.5
Torrey	1	0	0.0				
	22	243	11.5				

PUNTING

MIAMI	No.	Avg.	PITTSBURGH	No.	Avg.
Roberts	4	36.3	Colquitt	2	29.5

PUNT RETURNS

MIAMI	No.	Yds.	Avg.	PITTSBURGH	No.	Yds.	Avg.
none				Bell	3	31	10.3
				Woodruff	1	0	0.0
					4	31	7.8

KICKOFF RETURNS

MIAMI	No.	Yds.	Avg.	PITTSBURGH	No.	Yds.	Avg.
Nathan	4	73	18.3	L. Anderson	1	26	26.0
Davis	2	14	7.0	Hawthorne	1	20	20.0
	6	87	14.5		2	46	23.0

INTERCEPTION RETURNS

MIAMI	No.	Yds.	Avg.	PITTSBURGH	No.	Yds.	Avg.
none				Winston	1	3	3.0
				Woodruff	1	0	0.0
					2	3	1.5

PASSING

MIAMI	Att.	Comp.	Comp. Pct.	Yds.	Int.	Yds. Att.	Yds. Comp.
Griese	26	14	53.8	118	1	4.5	8.4
Strock	14	8	57.1	125	1	8.9	17.4
	40	22	55.0	243	2	6.1	11.5
PITTSBURGH							
Bradshaw	31	21	67.7	230	0	7.4	10.5

1979 CHAMPIONSHIP GAMES

NFC CHAMPIONSHIP GAME

January 6, 1980 at Tampa
(Attendance 72,033)

SCORING

LOS ANGELES	0	6	0	3– 9
TAMPA BAY	0	0	0	0– 0

Second Quarter
- L.A. — Corral, 19 yard field goal
- L.A. — Corral, 21 yard field goal

Fourth Quarter
- L.A. — Corral, 23 yard field goal

TEAM STATISTICS

L.A.		T.B.
23	First Downs–Total	7
13	First Downs–Rushing	4
8	First Downs–Passing	3
2	First Downs–Penalty	0
1	Fumbles–Number	1
1	Fumbles–Lost Ball	0
3	Penalties–Number	4
20	Yards Penalized	45
1	Missed Field Goals	0
77	Offensive Plays	54
369	Net Yards	177
4.8	Average Gain	3.3
1	Giveaways	1
1	Takeaways	1
0	Difference	0

Under the sun in Tampa, the Buccaneers took the field with the best wishes of most of America. The Bucs were the Horatio Alger of the N.F.L., rising from their abject station two years ago to being one victory away from the Super Bowl. The part of America that loves underdogs loved the Buccaneers.

The Los Angeles Rams planned to spoil the scenario and play out their own Cinderella fantasy. Longtime champions of the N.F.L. West, they had failed ever to make it into the Super Bowl. This year's squad squeaked into the playoffs with a 9-7 record and small prospects. In a major surprise, they beat Dallas in the first round to come into this match.

Both clubs brought formidable defenses into the game, and both lived up to their reputations. Despite the warm climate, the game was played out on the lines of trench warfare which was long the fashion in such outposts as Chicago, Green Bay, and Detroit. The Rams ran the ball as often as possible, and with their offensive line beating the Tampa Bay linemen and linebackers, Cullen Bryant and Wendell Tyler ate up yardage in small but steady mouthfuls. The Rams controlled the ball for almost 21 minutes of the first half. Despite the ground gaining, the Rams could score only on a pair of Frank Corral field goals in the second quarter. The Bucs, on the other hand, made no headway against the Los Angeles defense. Quarterback Doug Williams missed his first eight passes and could not move his team in the few opportunities he had. At halftime, Horatio Alger trailed, 6-0.

With the Bucs clearly off-key in this pressure situation, they lost their quarterback in the third period when Williams injured his arm. Sub QB Mike Rae did guide the Bucs within scoring distance once in the third quarter, but a fourth-down pass went astray. The Bucs launched no further scoring threats, and a Frank Corral field goal in the fourth quarter made the final score 9-0.

INDIVIDUAL STATISTICS

LOS ANGELES	No.	Yds.	Avg.	TAMPA BAY	No.	Yds.	Avg.
RUSHING							
Bryant	18	106	6.0	Bell	20	59	3.0
Tyler	28	86	3.1	Mucker	1	24	24.0
McCutcheon	6	26	4.3	Eckwood	2	5	2.5
Ferragamo	1	–2	–2.0	J. Davis	2	4	2.0
	53	216	4.1	Rae	1	0	0.0
					26	92	3.5
RECEIVING							
Bryant	4	39	10.8	Hagins	2	42	21.0
Dennard	3	56	18.7	Bell	2	12	6.0
Young	3	39	13.0	Mucker	1	42	42.0
Nelson	1	15	15.0		5	96	19.2
Tyler	1	14	14.0				
	12	163	13.6				
PUNTING							
Clark	5		37.2	Blanchard	8		37.1
PUNT RETURNS							
E. Brown	6	67	11.2	Reece	2	14	7.0
				Johnson	1	0	0.0
					3	14	4.7
KICKOFF RETURNS							
E. Hill	1	27	27.0	Hagins	4	106	26.5
INTERCEPTION RETURNS							
Jim Youngbl'd	1	10	10.0	none			

PASSING

	Att.	Comp.	Comp. Pct.	Yds.	Int.	Yds./Att.	Yds./Comp.
LOS ANGELES							
Ferragamo	23	12	52.2	163	0	7.1	13.6
TAMPA BAY							
Williams	13	2	15.4	12	1	0.9	6.0
Rae	13	2	15.4	42	0	3.2	21.0
Eckwood	1	1	100.0	42	0	42.0	42.0
	27	5	18.5	96	1	3.6	19.2

AFC CHAMPIONSHIP GAME

January 6, 1980 at Pittsburgh

SCORING

HOUSTON	7	3	0	3–13
PITTSBURGH	3	14	0	10–27

First Quarter
- Hou. — Perry, 75 yard interception return; PAT – Fritsch (kick)
- Pit. — Bahr, 21 yard field goal

Second Quarter
- Hou. — Fritsch, 27 yard field goal
- Pit. — Cunningham, 16 yard pass from Bradshaw; PAT – Bahr (kick)
- Pit. — Stallworth, 20 yard pass from Bradshaw; PAT – Bahr (kick)

Fourth Quarter
- Hou. — Fritsch, 23 yard field goal
- Pit. — Bahr, 39 yard field goal
- Pit. — Bleier, 4 yard rush; PAT – Bahr (kick)

TEAM STATISTICS

HOUS.		PITTS.
11	First Downs–Total	22
2	First Downs–Rushing	9
7	First Downs–Passing	13
2	First Downs–Penalty	0
4	Fumbles–Number	1
2	Fumbles–Lost Ball	1
2	Penalties–Number	5
10	Yards Penalized	34
0	Missed Field Goals	1
52	Offensive Plays	69
227	Net Yards	358
4.4	Average Gain	5.2
3	Giveaways	2
2	Takeaways	3
–1	Difference	–1

Two titans clashed head-on, with the thunderclaps drawing a huge television audience. All eyes were on a match which was expected to produce this year's Super Bowl champion. The Steelers and the Oilers had met twice already this season. The Steelers had won in Three Rivers Stadium in September by a 38-7 margin, while the Oilers triumphed 20-17 in December in the Astrodome.

The Pittsburgh defense nullified Houston's big weapon all afternoon. Earl Campbell had won his second rushing title in two pro seasons, but the Steel Curtain keyed on him and held him to 15 yards. With their ground game thwarted, the Oilers had to rely on the pass to move the ball.

The Oilers scored early in the game on a pass, but it was thrown by Pittsburgh quarterback Terry Bradshaw. On the sixth play of the game, safety Vernon Perry grabbed the pass and dashed 75 yards to the end zone. The kick made the score 7-0.

Never one to panic, Bradshaw cooly directed the Pittsburgh offense along its usual game plan. By the end of the first quarter, the Houston lead was cut to 7-3. Toni Fritsch added a field goal early in the second quarter, but Bradshaw threw touchdown passes to Bennie Cunningham and John Stallworth for a 17-10 edge at halftime.

The key play of the game occurred in the third period. With a first down six yards from a touchdown, Dan Pastorini lofted a pass deep into the right corner of the end zone. Houston receiver Mike Renfro caught the pass as he was skidding beyond the back line of the end zone. The officials ruled that he had not kept his feet within the line as he caught the ball. After a hot dispute, the Oilers failed to score on the next two plays, and Toni Fritsch kicked a field goal. With their lead intact, the Steelers added 10 points in the fourth quarter and shut the Oilers out the rest of the way for a 27-13 triumph.

INDIVIDUAL STATISTICS

HOUSTON	No.	Yds.	Avg.	PITTSBURGH	No.	Yds.	Avg.
RUSHING							
Campbell	17	15	0.9	Harris	21	85	4.0
T. Wilson	4	9	2.3	Bleier	13	52	4.0
Caster	1	0	0.0	Bradshaw	1	25	25.0
	22	24	1.1	Thornton	1	–1	–1.0
					36	161	4.5
RECEIVING							
T. Wilson	7	60	8.6	Harris	6	50	8.3
Carpenter	5	23	4.6	Swann	4	64	16.0
Renfro	3	52	17.3	Stallworth	3	52	17.3
Coleman	2	46	23.0	Bleier	3	39	13.0
Merkens	1	12	12.0	Cunningham	2	14	7.0
Campbell	1	11	11.0		18	219	12.2
Barber	1	8	8.0				
	20	212	10.6				
PUNTING							
Parsley	4		30.0	Colquitt	3		51.0
PUNT RETURNS							
Ellender	3	8	2.7	Bell	3	8	2.7
KICKOFF RETURNS							
Ellender	4	47	11.8	L. Anderson	4	82	20.5
Hartwig	1	13	13.0				
Carpenter	1	4	4.0				
	6	64	10.7				
INTERCEPTION RETURNS							
Perry	1	75	75.0	Woodruff	1	0	0.0

PASSING

	Att.	Comp.	Comp. Pct.	Yds.	Int.	Yds./Att.	Yds./Comp.
HOUSTON							
Pastorini	28	19	67.9	203	1	7.3	10.7
Nielsen	1	1	100.0	9	0	9.0	9.0
	29	20	68.9	212	1	7.3	10.6
PITTSBURGH							
Bradshaw	30	18	60.0	219	1	7.3	12.2

Super Bowl XIV Four Rings in Four Tries

According to the common wisdom, the Los Angeles Rams had snuck into this game only to be cannon fodder for the Pittsburgh Steelers. The Rams, after all, had only the sixth best record in the N.F.C. The Steelers, on the other hand, had been to the Super Bowl three times before and won each time. Although star linebacker Jack Ham was out with an ankle injury, the battle-hardened Steelers took the field at their prime.

The Steelers scored on their first possession, with Matt Bahr kicking a 41-yard field goal. The Rams then took the kickoff and drove downfield, scoring on Cullen Bryant's plunge from the one. Pittsburgh responded by scoring on the next possession to go ahead 10-7 early in the second quarter. While the Steelers could score no more in the first half, the Rams got two field goals from Frank Corral to go ahead 13-10 at halftime.

With an upset in the wind, the Steelers took charge on a 47-yard touchdown pass from Terry Bradshaw to Lynn Swann early in the third quarter. The Rams refused to recognize any shift in momentum. Vince Ferragamo threw to Billy Waddy for a 50 yard gain, and on the next play, halfback Lawrence McCutcheon threw a 24-yard scoring pass to Ron Smith. Although Corral missed the extra point, the Rams led 19-17 after three quarters.

In the fourth quarter, the Steelers played like champions. Less than three minutes into the period, John Stallworth beat the L.A. secondary and hauled in a long bomb for a 73-yard TD pass. With the score now 24-19 against them, the Rams began a drive with under nine minutes left. They drove from their own 16 yard line to the Pittsburgh 32-yard line. Ferragamo then shot a pass at Ron Smith, but Jack Lambert picked it off. Bradshaw then used a long pass to Stallworth and a pass interference call to drive the Steelers to the clinching touchdown in a 31-19 triumph.

LINEUPS

LOS ANGELES		PITTSBURGH
	OFFENSE	
Waddy	WR	Stallworth
France	LT	Kolb
K. Hill	LG	Davis
Saul	C	Webster
Harrah	RG	Mullins
Slater	RT	Brown
Nelson	TE	Cunningham
Dennard	WR	Swann
Ferragamo	QB	Bradshaw
Tyler	RB	Harris
Bryant	RB	Bleier
	DEFENSE	
Jack Youngblood	LE	Greenwood
Fanning	LT	Greene
Brooks	RT	Dunn
Dryer	RE	Banaszak
Jim Youngblood	LLB	Winston
Reynolds	MLB	Lambert
Brudzinski	RLB	Cole
Thomas	LCB	Johnson
Perry	RCB	Blount
Elmendorf	SS	Shell
Cromwell	FS	Thomas

SUBSTITUTES

LOS ANGELES

	OFFENSE	
Bain	Jodat	Ryczek
Gravelle	Lee	R. Smith
D. Hill	McCutc'n	Young
E. Hill	Rutledge	
	DEFENSE	
Andrews	Harris	Wallace
E. Brown	O'Steen	Westbrooks
Doss	Sully	Wilkinson
Ellis		
	KICKERS	
Clark		Corral

PITTSBURGH

	OFFENSE	
A. Anderson	Grossman	Petersen
Bell	Hawth'ne	Smith
Ccurson	Kruczek	Stoudt
Dornbrook	Moser	Thornton
	DEFENSE	
L. Anderson	Graves	Valentine
Beasley	Ham	White
Furness	Toews	Woodruff
	KICKERS	
Bahr		Colquitt

SCORING

LOS ANGELES	7	6	6	0–19
PITTSBURGH	3	7	7	14–31

First Quarter
- Pit. Bahr, 41 yard field goal
- L.A. Bryant, 1 yard rush
  - PAT – Corral (kick)

Second Quarter
- Pit. Harris, 1 yard rush
  - PAT – Bahr (kick)
- L.A. Corral, 31 yard field goal
- L.A. Corral, 45 yard field goal

Third Quarter
- Pit. Swann, 47 yard pass from Bradshaw
  - PAT – Bahr (kick)
- L.A. R. Smith, 24 yard pass from McCutcheon
  - PAT – kick failed

Fourth Quarter
- Pit. Stallworth, 73 yard pass from Bradshaw
  - PAT – Bahr (kick)
- Pit. Harris, 1 yard rush
  - PAT – Bahr (kick)

TEAM STATISTICS

L.A.		PITT.
16	First Downs–Total	19
6	First Downs–Rushing	8
9	First Downs–Passing	10
1	First Downs–Penalty	1
0	Fumbles–Number	0
0	Fumbles–Lost Ball	0
2	Penalties–Number	6
26	Yards Penalized	65
0	Missed Field Goals	0
59	Offensive Plays	58
301	Net Yards	393
5.1	Average Gain	6.8
1	Giveaways	3
3	Takeaways	1
+2	Difference	−2

INDIVIDUAL STATISTICS

LOS ANGELES	No.	Yds.	Avg.	PITTSBURGH	No.	Yds.	Avg.
RUSHING							
Tyler	17	60	3.5	Harris	20	46	2.3
Bryant	6	30	5.0	Bleier	10	25	2.5
McCutcheon	5	10	2.0	Bradshaw	3	9	3.0
Ferragamo	1	7	7.0	Thornton	4	4	1.0
	29	107	3.7		37	84	2.3
RECEIVING							
Waddy	3	75	25.0	Swann	5	79	15.8
Bryant	3	21	7.0	Stallworth	3	121	40.3
Tyler	3	20	6.7	Harris	3	66	22.0
Dennard	2	32	16.0	Cunningham	2	21	10.5
Nelson	2	20	10.0	Thornton	1	22	22.0
D. Hill	1	28	28.0		14	309	22.1
R. Smith	1	24	24.0				
McCutcheon	1	16	16.0				
	16	236	14.8				
PUNTING							
Clark	5		44.0	Colquitt	2		42.5
PUNT RETURNS							
E. Brown	1	4	4.0	Bell	2	17	8.5
				Smith	2	14	7.0
					4	31	7.8
KICKOFF RETURNS							
E. Hill	3	47	15.7	L. Anderson	5	162	32.4
Judat	2	32	16.0				
Andrews	1	0	0.0				
	6	79	13.2				
INTERCEPTION RETURNS							
Elmendorf	1	10	10.0	Lambert	1	16	16.0
E. Brown	1	6	6.0				
Perry	1	−1	−1.0				
Thomas	0	6	—				
	3	21	7.0				

PASSING

LOS ANGELES	Att.	Comp.	Comp. Pct.	Yds.	Int.	Yds./ Att.	Yds./ Comp.	Yards Lost Tackled
Ferragamo	25	15	60.0	212	1	8.5	14.1	
McCutcheon	1	1	100.0	24	0	24.0	24.0	
	26	16	61.5	23.6	1	12.9	14.8	4-42
PITTSBURGH								
Bradshaw	21	14	66.7	309	3	14.7	22.1	0-0

UseName(Nickname)-Positions	Team by Year	See Section	Hgt.	Wgt.	College	Int	Pts
Abramowicz, Dan WR-OE	67-73NO 73-74SF 75Buf	2	6'1"	195	Xavier-Ohio		234
Acks, Ron LB	68-71Atl 72-73NE 74-76GB		6'2"	223	Illinois	2	6
Adamle, Mike HB-FB	71-72KC 73-74NYJ 75-76Chi	23	5'9"	196	Northwestern		38
Adams, Bill OG-OT	72-78Buf		6'2"	248	Holy Cross		
Adams, Bob TE-OT	67-71Pit 72JJ 73-74NE 75Den 76-77Atl	2	6'2"	222	U. of Pacific		
Adams, Brent OT-OG	75-77Atl 78KJ 79LA		6'5"	256	Tenn-Chattanooga		
Adams, Doug LB	71-74Cin		6'	225	Ohio State	3	
Adams, Julius DE-DT	71-85,87NE		6'3"	262	Texas Southern		
Adams, Pete OG	74Cle 75KJ 76Cle 77JJ		6'4"	260	Southern Calif.		
Adams, Sam OG	72-80NE 81NO		6'3"	256	Prairie View		
Adams, Tony QB	75-78KC 87Min	12	6'	198	Utah State		
Adkins, Margene WR	70-71Dal 72NO 73NYJ 75WFL	23	5'10"	183	Henderson J.C.		
Aiu, Charles OG	76-78SD 78Sea		6'2"	251	Hawaii		
Albert, Sergio K	74StL		6'3"	195	U.S. International		
Albrecht, Ted OT-OG	77-81Chi 82KJ		6'4"	251	California		
Alexakos, Steve OG	70Den 71NYG		6'2"	260	San Diego State		
Alexander, Glenn WR	70Buf		6'3"	205	Grambling		
Alexander, John DE	77-78Mia		6'2"	250	Rutgers		
Alexander, Willie DB	71-79Hou		6'2"	194	Alcorn State	23	6
Allen, Doug LB	74-75Buf		6'2"	228	Penn State	1	
Allen, George	HC66-70LA HC71-77Was				Michigan		
Allen, Grady LB	68-72Atl		6'3"	226	Texas A&M	2	
Allen, Jackie DB	69OakA 70-71Buf 72Phi 73JJ		6'1"	187	Baylor		
Allen, Jeff DB	71StL 72JJ		5'11'	190	Iowa State		
Allen, Jim DB	74-77Pit 78-81Det		6'2"	194	U.C.L.A.	31	6
Allen, Nate DB	71-74KC 75SF 76-79Min 79Det		5'10"	172	Texas Southern	9	12
Allison, Henry OG-OT	71-72Phi 75-77StL 77Den		6'3"	257	San Diego State		
Alston, Mack TE	70-72Was 73-76Hou 77-80Bal	2	6'2"	231	Md. Eastern Shore		90
Alward, Tom OG	76TB		6'4"	255	Nebraska		
Alzado, Lyle DE-DT	71-78Den 79-81Cle 82-84Raid		6'3"	254	Yankton		2
Ambrose, Dick (Bam Bam) LB	75-83Cle 84NJ		6'	232	Virginia	5	
Amman, Dick DE-DT	72-73Bal		6'5"	242	Florida State		
Amundson, George FB-HB	73-74Hou 75Phi	2	6'3"	215	Iowa State		30
Anderson, Bobby HB-FB	70-73Den 74BN 75Was	23	6'	208	Colorado		66
Anderson, Dick DB	68-69MiaA 70-74Mia 75KJ 76-77Mia	3	6'2"	198	Colorado	34	24
Anderson, Donny HB	66-71GB 72-74StL	234	6'3"	212	Texas Tech		336
Anderson, Gary OG	77-78Det 78NO 79NJ 80Was		6'3"	253	Stanford		
	83-85USFL						
Anderson, Jerry DB	77Cin 78TB 79JJ		5'11"	196	Oklahoma		
Anderson, Ken QB	71-86Cin	12	6'1"	210	Augustana (Ill.)		120
Anderson, Preston DB	74Cle		6'1"	183	Rice		
Anderson, Ralph (Sticks) DB	71-72Pit 73NE		6'2"	180	West Texas State	6	2
Anderson, Rickey FB	78SD 79KJ		6'1"	211	S. Carolina State		
Anderson, Scott C	74-76Min		6'4"	242	Missouri		
Anderson, Terry WR	77-78Mia 78Was 80SF		5'9"	182	Bethune-Cookman		
Anderson, Tim DB	75SF 76Buf		6'	193	Ohio State		
Anderson, Warren WR	77Hou 78StL		6'2"	195	West Virginia St.		
Andrews, Al LB	70-71Buf		6'3"	216	New Mexico State	1	
Andrews, Billy LB	67-74Cle 75SD 76-77 KC		6'	223	Southeastern La.	7	6
Andrews, John TE-HB	72SD 73-74Bal		6'3"	222	Indiana		6
Andrews, John DE-DT	75-76Mia		6'6"	251	Morgan State		
Andrusyshyn, Zenon K	78KC 79-82CFL 83-85USFL	4	6'2"	210	California		
Ane, Charlie C	75-80KC 81GB		6'1"	234	Michigan State		
Anthony, Charles LB	74SD 75KJ		6'1"	230	Southern Calif.	1	
Antoine, Lionel OT	72-76Chi 77KJ 78Chi 79KJ		6'6"	262	Southern Illinois		
Archer, Troy DT-DE	76-78NYG		6'4"	250	Colorado		6
	1979 — Died in automobile accident						
Ardizzane, Tony C	79Chi		6'3"	241	Northwestern		
Armstrong, Otis HB	73-80Den	23	5'10"	196	Purdue		192
Arneson, Jim OG-C	73-74Dal 75Was		6'3"	247	Arizona		
Arneson, Mark LB	72-80StL		6'2"	222	Arizona	5	6
Arnold, Francis OG	74Den		6'3"	295	Oregon		
Arnsparger, Bill	HC74-76NYG				Miami-Ohio		
Arrington, Rick QB	70-72Phi	1	6'2"	187	Tulsa		6
Arthur, Gary TE	70-77NYJ		6'5"	254	Miami-Ohio		
Asher, Bob OT-OG	70Dal 71JJ 72-75Chi		6'5"	254	Vanderbilt		
Ashton, Josh HB-FB	72-74NE 75StL	2	6'1"	204	Tulsa		24
Askea, Mike OT	73Den		6'4"	260	Stanford		
Askson, Bert TE-DE	71Pit 73NO 74WFL 75-77GB		6'3"	223	Texas Southern		6
Atessis, Bill DE-DT	71NE		6'3"	240	Texas		
Athas, Pete DB-WR	71-74NYG 75Cle 75Min 76NO	3	5'11"	185	Tennessee	16	6
Atkins, Bob DB	68-69StL 70-76Hou		6'3"	211	Grambling	19	6
Atkins, Dave HB	73SF 75SD		6'1"	205	Texas-El Paso		6
Atkinson, Al LB	65-69NY-A 70-74 NYJ 75KJ		6'1"	229	Villanova	21	
Atkinson, Butch DB	68-69OakA 70-77Oak 79Den	3	6'	182	Morris Brown	30	42
Austin, Darrell OG-C-OT	75-78NYJ 79-80TB 81ZJ		6'4"	252	South Carolina		
Austin, Hise LB	73KC 74WFL 75GB		6'4"	191	Prairie View		
Austin, Ocie DB	70-71Pit		6'3"	200	Utah State	3	
Avellini, Bob QB	75-84Chi 84NYJ	12	6'2"	208	Maryland		30
Avery, Ken LB	67-68NYG 69CinA 70-74Cin 75KC 76JJ		6'1"	225	Southern Miss.	2	
Babb, Charlie DB	72-79Mia		6'	190	Memphis State	12	6
Babich, Bob LB	70-72SD 73-78Cle		6'2"	231	Miami-Ohio	6	6
Babinecz, John LB	72-73Dal 74JJ 75Chi		6'1"	222	Villanova	1	
Bachman, Ted DB	76Sea 76Mia		6'	190	New Mexico State		
Bacon, Coy DE-DT	68-72LA 73-75SD 76-77Cin 78-81Was		6'4"	269	Jackson State	2	10
	83USFL						
Bailey, Jim DT-DE	70-74Bal 75NYJ 76-78 Atl		6'4"	253	Kansas	1	
Bailey, Larry DT	74Atl		6'4"	238	U. of Pacific		
Bailey, Mark FB	77-78KC 80KJ	2	6'3"	237	Long Beach State		18
Bailey, Tom HB-FB	71-74Phi 75KJ	2	6'2"	211	Florida State		12
Baker, Ed QB	72Hou		6'2"	198	Lafayette		
Baker, John DE	70NYG		6'5"	260	Norfolk State		
Baker, Melvin WR	74Mia 75NO 75NE 75SD 76Hou 77Buf		6'	189	Texas Southern		12
Baker, Tony FB-HB	68-71NO 71-72Phi 73-74LA 75SD	2	5'11"	224	Iowa State		102
Baker, Wayne DT	75SF		6'6"	270	Brigham Young		
Baldassin, Mike LB	77-78SF 79JJ		6'1"	218	Washington		6
Ball, Larry LB	72-74Mia 75Det 76TB 77-78Mia		6'6"	232	Louisville	2	6
Ballou, Mike LB	70Bos		6'3"	235	U.C.L.A.		
Banaszak, John DE-DT	75-81Pit 83-85USFL		6'3"	242	Eastern Michigan	1	
Banaszak, Pete HB-FB	66-69OakA 70-78Oak	2	5'11"	206	Miami (Fla.)		312
Banaszek, Cas OT-C	68-77SF		6'3"	249	Northwestern		
Banks, Tom C-OG	71-80StL 83-84USFL		6'1"	243	Auburn		
Banks, Willie OG	68-69Was 70NYG 73NE		6'2"	240	Alcorn State		
Bankston, Warren TE-FB	69-72Pit 73-78Oak	2	6'4"	233	Tulane		30
Bannon, Bruce LB	73-74Mia		6'3"	225	Penn State		
Barber, Bob DE-DT	76-79GB 80-81CFL 83USFL		6'3"	240	Grambling		
Barefield, John LB	78-80StL 83-85USFL		6'2"	224	Texas A&I		
Barisich, Carl NT-DT	73-75Cle 76Sea 77-80Mia 81NYG		6'4"	255	Princeton		

UseName(Nickname)-Positions	Team by Year	See Section	Hgt.	Wgt.	College	Int	Pts
Barkum, Jerome TE-WR	72-83NYJ	2	6'3"	218	Jackson State		240
Barnes, Al WR	72-73Det 74WFL		6'1"	170	New Mexico State		12
Barnes, Benny DB	72-83Dal		6'1"	192	Stanford	11	16
Barnes, Bruce K	73-74NE	4	5'11"	214	U.C.L.A.		
Barnes, Joe QB	74Chi		5'11"	196	Texas Tech		
Barnes, Larry FB-HB	77-78SD 78StL 78-79Phi 80LJ	2	5'11"	220	Tennessee State		12
Barnes, Mike DT-DE	73-81Bal		6'6"	256	Miami (Fla.)		
Barnes, Pete LB	67-68Hou 69-72SD 73-75StL 76-77NE		6'3"	242	Southern U.	15	6
Barnes, Rodrigo LB	73-74Dal 74-75NE 75Mia 76Oak		6'1"	215	Rice		
Barney, Lem DB	67-77Det	34	6'1"	189	Jackson State	56	66
Barrett, Jean OT-C-OG	73-77SF 78FJ 79-80SF		6'6"	251	Tulsa		
Barry, Fred DB	70Pit		5'10"	184	Boston U.		
Barzilauskas, Carl DT	74-77NYJ 78-79GB		6'6"	271	Indiana	1	
Baska, Rick LB	76-77Den		6'3"	225	U.C.L.A.		
Bass, Mike DB	67Det 69-73Was		6'	190	Michigan	30	24
Bateman, Marv K	72-74Dal 74-77Buf	4	6'4"	213	Utah		1
Baumgartner, Steve DE-LB-DT	73-77NO 77-79Hou		6'7"	256	Purdue		
Bayless, Tom OG	70NYJ		6'3"	240	Purdue		
Baylor, Raymond DE	74SD		6'5"	263	Texas Southern		
Baylor, Tim DB	76-78Bal 79Min		6'6"	195	Morgan State		
Beamer, Tim DB	71Buf		5'11"	185	Johnson C. Smith		
Beamon, Autry DB	75-76Min 77-79Sea 80-81Cle		6'1"	190	East Texas State	13	8
Bean, Bubba HB-FB	76-79Atl 80KJ	2	5'11"	195	Texas A&M		48
Beard, Tom C	72Buf		6'6"	280	Michigan State		
Beasley, John TE	67-70Min 71JJ 72-73Min 73-74NO	2	6'3"	229	California		84
Beasley, Terry WR	72SF 73SJ 74-75SF	2	5'10"	183	Auburn		18
Beatty, Chuck DB	69-72Pit 72StL		6'2"	203	North Texas	4	6
Beauchamp, Al LB	68-69CinA 70-75Cin 76StL		6'2"	235	Southern U.	15	18
Beauchamp, Joe DB	66-69SD-A 70-75SD		6'	185	Iowa	23	18
Beaudoin, Doug DB	76-79NE 80Mia 81SD 83-85USFL		6'1"	193	Minnesota	4	
Bebout, Nick OT	73-75Atl 76-79Sea 80Min		6'5"	261	Wyoming		
Beck, Braden K	71Hou		6'2"	200	Stanford		4
Becker, Doug LB	78Chi 78Buf		6'	222	Notre Dame		
Beckman, Tom DE	72StL		6'5"	250	Michigan		
Beirne, Jim WR-TE	68-69HouA 70-73Hou 74SD 75-76Hou	2	6'2"	198	Purdue		68
Beisler, Randy OG-DE-OT	66-68Phi 69-74SF		6'4"	249	Indiana	1	
Belk, Bill DE-DT	68-74SF		6'3"	248	Md. Eastern Shore	1	12
Bell, Bill K	71-72Atl 73NE	5	6'1"	191	Kansas		154
Bell, Bob DE-DT	71-73Det 74-78StL		6'4"	252	Cincinnati		6
Bell, Carlos TE	71NO 72JJ		6'5"	238	Houston		
Bell, Eddie WR	70-75NYJ 76SD	2	5'10"	160	Idaho State		72
Bell, Gordon HB	76-77NYG 78StL	23	5'9"	180	Michigan		12
Bell, Joe DE	79Oak		6'3"	250	Norfolk State		
Bell, Kevin WR	78NYJ		5'10"	180	Lamar		
Belser, Caesar DB-LB	68-69KC-A 70-71KC 74SD		6'	211	Ark.-Pine Bluff		
Belton, Horace HB	78-80KC 81KJ	23	5'8"	200	Southeastern La.		18
Belton, Willie HB	71-72Atl 73-74StL	23	5'11"	198	Md. Eastern Shore		6
Benjamin, Tony FB	77-79Sea		6'3"	225	Duke		
Benson, Duane LB	67-69OakA 70-71Oak 72-73Atl		6'2"	217	Hamline	3	
Berger, Ron DE-DT	69BosA 70Bos 71-72NE		6'8"	278	Wayne State		
Bergey, Bill LB	69CinA 70-73Cin 74-80Phi 81KJ		6'2"	245	Arkansas State	27	
Bergey, Bruce DE	71KC 72-73CFL 74-75WFL		6'4"	240	U.C.L.A.		
Bernhardt, Roger OG	74NYJ 75KC 76JJ		6'4"	244	Kansas		
Bernich, Ken LB	75NYJ		6'2"	250	Auburn		
Berra, Tim WR	74Bal		5'11"	185	Massachusetts		
Berry, Bob QB	65-67Min 68-72Atl 73-76Min	12	5'11"	189	Oregon		24
Berry, Reggie DB	72-74SD		6'	188	Long Beach State		
Berry, Royce DE	69CinA 70-74Cin 75BW 76Chi		6'3"	247	Houston		12
Bertelsen, Jim FB-HB	72-76LA	23	5'11"	205	Texas		108
Bertuca, Tony LB	74Bal		6'2"	225	Chico State		
Besana, Fred QB	77Buf 78NYG 83-85USFL		6'4"	203	California		
Best, Art HB	77-78Chi 80NYG		6'1"	205	Kent State		
Best, Keith LB	72KC		6'3"	220	Kansas State		
Bethea, Elvin DE	68-69HouA 70-83Hou		6'3"	257	N. Carolina A&T		8
Betterson, James FB	77-78Phi	2	6'	210	North Carolina		6
Bettiga, Mike WR	74SF		6'3"	193	Humboldt State		
Beutler, Tom LB	70Cle 71Bal		6'1"	232	Toledo		
Beverly, David K	74-75Hou 75-80GB	4	6'2"	180	Auburn		
Beverly, Ed WR	73SF		5'11"	168	Arizona State		
Biedermann, Leo OT	78Cle 82CFL 83USFL		6'7"	254	California		
Biggs, Verlon DE-DT	65-69NY-A 70NYJ 71-74Was 75KJ		6'4"	267	Jackson State	1	12
Biletnikoff, Fred WR-FL	65-69OakA 70-78Oak	2	6'1"	190	Florida State		462
Billingsley, Ron DT-DE	67-69SD-A 70SD		6'8"	278	Wyoming		
Bingham, Gregg LB	73-84Hou		6'1"	229	Purdue	21	6
Birney, Tom K	79-80GB	5	6'4"	220	Michigan State		60
Bishop, Richard NT-DE-DT	76-81NE 82Mia 83LA		6'1"	263	Louisville		
Bitterlich, Don K	76Sea		5'7"	166	Temple		10
Bjorklund, Hank HB	72-74NYJ	2	6'1"	200	Princeton		
Black, Stan DB	77SF		6'	196	Mississippi State		
Black, Tim LB	77StL		6'2"	215	Baylor		
Blackwell, Alois HB	78-79Dal 80JJ		5'10"	195	Houston		
Blahak, Joe DB	73Hou 74-75Min 76TB 76NE 77Min		5'9"	187	Nebraska	3	2
Blair, Matt LB	74-85Min		6'5"	232	Iowa State	16	12
Blair, T.C. TE	74Det		6'4"	220	Tulsa		
Blanchard, Dick LB	72NE		6'3"	225	Tulsa	1	
Blanchard, Tom K	71-73NYG 74-78NO 79-81TB	4	6'	185	Oregon		
Blankenship, Greg LB	76Oak 76Pit		6'1"	212	Hayward State		
Bleamer, Jeff OT-OG	75-76Phi 77NYJ		6'4"	253	Penn State		
Bleier, Rocky HB	68Pit 69MS 70inj from MS 71-80Pit	2	5'11"	207	Notre Dame		150
Blount, Jeb QB	77TB	1	6'3"	200	Tulsa		
Blount, Mel DB	70-83Pit	3	6'3"	205	Southern U.	57	24
Blue, Forrest C-OT	68-74SF 75-78Bal		6'5"	259	Auburn		6
Blue, Luther WR	77-79Det 80Phi	2	5'11"	185	Iowa State		24
Boatwright, Ron DT	74SD		6'5"	262	Oklahoma State		
Boden, Lynn OG-OT	75-78Det 79Chi		6'5"	266	S. Dakota State		
Bolton, Andy HB	76Sea 76-78Det		6'1"	205	Fisk		
Bolton, Ron DB	72-75NE 76-82Cle		6'2"	172	Virginia State	35	6
Bonner, Glen HB	74-75SD	2	6'2"	202	Washington		24
Bonness, Rik LB	76Oak 77-80TB		6'5"	219	Nebraska		
Boone, Dave DE	74Min		6'3"	248	Eastern Michigan		
Boozer, Emerson HB	66-69NY-A 70-75NYJ	23	5'11"	203	Md. Eastern Shore		390
Bordelon, Ken LB	76-77NO 78KJ 79-82NO 83LJ		6'4"	228	Louisiana State	3	6
Boryla, Mike QB	74-76Phi 77KJ 78TB	12	6'3"	200	Stanford		12
Bosarge, Wade DB	77Mia 77NO		5'10"	175	Tulsa		
Bouggess, Lee FB	70-71Phi 72JJ 73Phi	2	6'2"	210	Louisville		48

UseName(Nickname)-Positions	TeambyYear	See Section	Hgt.	Wgt.	College	Int	Pts
Bowdell, Gordon WR	71Den		6'2"	203	Michigan		
Boyd, Elmo WR	78SF 78GB		6'	188	Eastern Kentucky		6
Boyd, Greg DB	73NO 74NE		6'2"	201	Arizona		
Boyett, Lon TE	78SF 79JJ		6'6"	240	Northridge State		
Boykin, Greg FB-HB	77NO 78SF	2	6'	225	Northwestern		12
Bradley, Bill DB	69-76Phi 77StL	34	5'11"	190	Texas	34	6
Bradley, Chuck TE	75-77SD 77Chi		6'6"	243	Oregon		
Bradley, Dave OG	69-71GB 72StL		6'4"	245	Penn State		
Bradley, Ed LB	72-75Pit 76Sea 77-78SF 79BN		6'2"	234	Wake Forest	1	
Bradshaw, Morris WR	74-81Oak 82NE 84USFL	2	6'	196	Ohio State		78
Bradshaw, Terry QB	70-83Pit	12	6'3"	215	Louisiana Tech		192
Bragg, Mike K	68-79Was 80Bal	4	5'11"	186	Richmond		10
Brahaney, Tom C	73-81StL		6'2"	245	Oklahoma		
Branch, Cliff WR	72-81Oak 82-85Raid 86LJ	2	5'11"	170	Colorado		402
Bransletter, Kent OT	73GB		6'3"	260	Houston		
Braxton, Jim FB	71-78Buf 78Mia	2	6'2"	238	West Virginia		186
Brazile, Robert LB	75-84Hou		6'4"	241	Jackson State	13	
Breunig, Bob LB	75-84Dal		6'2"	226	Arizona State	9	
Brezina, Greg LB	68-69Atl 70KJ 71-79Atl		6'2"	222	Houston	12	
Briggs, Bob DE-DT	68-69SD-A 70SD 71-73Cle 74KC		6'4"	267	Heidelberg	1	12
Brinkman, Charlie WR	72Cle		6'2"	208	Louisville		
Brinson, Larry FB	77-79Dal 80Sea 81KJ	23	6'	214	Florida		24
Briscoe, Marlin WR-QB	68DenA 69Buf-A 70-71Buf 72-74Mia 75SD 76Det 76NE	12	5'10"	178	Nebraska-Omaha		198
Brister, Willie TE	74-75NYJ		6'4"	236	Southern U.		
Bristor, John DB	79SF		6'	188	Waynesburg		
Broadnax, Jerry TE	74Hou 75WFL		6'2"	225	Southern U.		
Brock, Willie C	78Det		6'3"	246	Colorado		
Brockington, John FB	71-77GB 77KC	2	6'1"	225	Ohio State		204
Brooks, Billy WR	76-79Cin 81SD 81Hou	2	6'3"	204	Oklahoma		42
Brooks, Bobby DB	74-76NYG		6'1"	195	Bishop	5	
Brooks, Cliff DB	72-74Cle 75-76Phi 76NYJ 76Buf		6'1"	190	Tennessee State		
Brooks, Larry DT	72-82LA		6'3"	255	Virginia State		
Brooks, Lee DT	70-72Hou 73-76StL		6'5"	256	Texas	1	
Broussard, Steve K	75GB	4	6'	200	Southern Miss.		
Brown, Aaron DE	66KC-A 67JJ 68-69KC-A 70-72KC 73-74GB		6'5"	263	Minnesota	1	6
Brown, Bob TE	69-70StL 71Min 72-73NO	2	6'3"	225	Alcorn State		6
Brown, Bob DT-DE	66-73GB 74SD 75-76Cin		6'5"	268	Ark.-Pine Bluff		2
Brown, Booker OT-OG	75SD 76IL 77SD 78KJ		6'2"	257	Southern Calif.		
Brown, Boyd TE	74-76Den 77NYG		6'4"	216	Alcorn State		
Brown, Carlos QB	75-76GB	1	6'3"	210	U. of Pacific		
Brown, Charlie WR	70Det 71JJ		6'2"	195	Northern Arizona		
Brown, Chuck C-OG	79StL		6'1"	235	Houston		
Brown, Dean DB	69Cle 70Mia 71JJ		5'10"	170	Ft. Valley State	1	
Brown, Eddie DB	74-75Cle 75-77Was 78-79LA 83-84 83-84USFL	3	5'11"	187	Tennessee	6	6
Brown, Ken HB-FB	70-75Cle	23	5'10"	204	none		54
Brown, Ken C	79Den 80GB		6'1"	245	New Mexico		
Brown, Larry HB	69-76Was	2	5'11"	195	Kansas State		330
Brown, Larry TE-OT	71-84Pit	2	6'4"	246	Kansas		30
Brown, Larry OT	78-79KC		6'5"	262	Miami (Fla.)		
Brown, Otto DB	69Dal 70-73NYG		6'1"	187	Prairie View	2	6
Brown, Ray DB	71-77Atl 78-80NO	3	6'2"	203	West Texas State	38	12
Brown, Sidney DB	78NE		6'	186	Oklahoma		
Brown, Stan WR	71Cle		5'9"	184	Purdue		
Brown, Terry DB-WR	69-70StL 71JJ 72-75Min 76Cle		6'1"	206	Oklahoma State	7	12
Browne, Gordie OT	74-75NYJ		6'5"	265	Boston College		
Brumfield, Jim HB	71Pit		6'1"	195	Indiana State		
Brundige, Bill DT-DE	70-77Was 78KJ		6'5"	270	Colorado		
Brunet, Bob HB-FB	68-73Was 74FJ 75-77Was	2	6'1"	205	Louisiana Tech		24
Brunson, Larry WR	74-77KC 78-79Oak 80Den	23	5'11"	180	Colorado		36
Brunson, Mike WR	70Atl		6'1"	187	Arizona State		
Brupbacher, Ross LB	70-72Chi 74WFL 76Chi		6'3"	216	Texas A&M	12	12
Bryant, Bill (Boone) DB	76-78NYG 78Phi		5'11"	195	Grambling	3	6
Bryant, Bobby DB	68-80Min	3	6'	171	South Carolina	51	24
Bryant, Hubie WR	70Pit 71-72NE	23	5'10"	170	Minnesota		6
Bryant, Waymond LB	74-77Chi 78SJ		6'3"	235	Tennessee State	4	
Buchanon, Willie DB	72-78GB 79-82SD		6'	189	San Diego State	28	18
Buckey, Don WR	76NYJ		5'11"	180	N. Carolina State		
Buehler, George OG	69OakA 70-78Oak 78-79Cle		6'2"	264	Stanford		
Buetow, Bart (The Mad Scientist)	73NYG 76-77Min		6'5"	250	Minnesota		
Buffone, Doug LB	66-79Chi		6'1"	227	Louisville	24	6
Buggs, Danny WR	75-76NYG 76-79Was 80CFL	2	6'2"	185	West Virginia		24
Buie, Drew WR	69OakA 70-71Oak 72Cin		6'2"	180	Catawba		12
Bulaich, Norm HB-FB	70-72Bal 73-74Phi 75-79Mia	2	6'1"	217	Texas Christian		246
Bull, Scott QB	76-78 SF 79KJ	12	6'5"	212	Arkansas		18
Bunting, John LB	72-82Phi 83-85USFL		6'1"	220	North Carolina	8	
Burchfield, Don TE	71NO		6'2"	227	Ball State		
Burgmeier, Ted DB	78KC		5'10"	185	Notre Dame		
Burk, Scott DB	79Cin		6'2"	193	Oklahoma State		
Burke, Mark DB	76Phi		6'1"	175	West Virginia		
Burke, Mike K	74LA	4	5'10"	188	Miami (Fla.)		1
Burks, Randy WR	76Chi		5'11"	170	Southeastern Okla.		6
Burks, Ray LB	77KC		6'3"	217	U.C.L.A.		
Burks, Steve WR	75-77NE	2	6'5"	211	Arkansas State		
Burnham, Lem DE	77-79Phi 80KJ		6'4"	236	U.S. International		
Burns, Bob FB	72NYJ	2	6'3"	212	Georgia		6
Burns, Ed QB	78-80NO		6'3"	210	Nebraska		
Burns, Leon FB	71SD 72StL 73JJ	2	6'2"	229	Long Beach State		18
Burns, Mike DB	77SF 78Det		6'	180	Southern Calif.	1	
Burrough, Ken WR	70NO 71-81Hou 82BN	2	6'4"	210	Texas Southern		300
Burrow, Jim DB	76GB		5'11"	181	Nebraska		
Burrow, Ken WR	71-75Atl	2	6'	190	San Diego State		126
Burton, Al DE	76-77Hou 77NYJ		6'5"	267	Bethune-Cookman		
Burton, Larry WR	75-77NO 78-79SD	2	6'1"	192	Purdue		42
Bussey, Dexter HB-FB	74-84Det	2	6'1"	209	Oklahoma, Texas-Arlington		138
Butler, Bill FB	72-74NO	2	6'2"	212	Kansas State		30
Butler, Bill LB	70Den		6'4"	226	Northridge State		
Butler, Gary TE	73KC 74KJ 75-76Chi 77TB		6'3"	235	Rice		12
Butler, Gerald WR	77KC 78Bal		6'4"	209	Nicholls State		
Butler, Skip K	71NO 71NYG 72-77Hou	45	6'2"	200	Texas-Arlington		340
Buzin, Rich OT	68-70NYG 71LA 72Chi		6'4"	250	Penn State		
Byas, Rick DB	74-80Atl		5'9"	179	Wayne State	6	16
Cagle, Jim DT	74Phi		6'5"	255	Georgia		
Cahill, Bill DB	73-74Buf		5'11"	175	Washington		6
Cain, J.V. TE-WR	74-77StL 78FJ	2	6'4"	224	Colorado		54
1979 — Died of heart failure							

UseName(Nickname)-Positions	TeambyYear	See Section	Hgt.	Wgt.	College	Int	Pts
Caldwell, Alan DB	79NYG		6'	176	North Carolina	2	
Calhoun, Don FB-HB	74-75Buf 75-81NE 82Phi 84USFL	2	6'	208	Kansas State		150
Calloway, Ernie DT-DE	69-72Phi 73KJ		6'6"	244	Texas Southern		
Cambal, Dennis TE	73NYJ		6'3"	228	William & Mary		
Campbell, Carter LB-DE	70SF 71Den 72-73NYG 74-75WFL		6'3"	232	Weber State		
Campbell, Joe DE-NT	77-80NO 80-81Oak 81TB		6'6"	253	Maryland		
Campbell, Sonny HB	70-71Atl 72JJ	2	5'11"	192	Northern Arizona		12
Campbell, Tommy DB	76Phi		6'	188	Iowa State		
Canada, Larry FB	78-79Den 80KJ 81Den 83-85USFL	2	6'2"	233	Wisconsin		42
Capone, Warren LB	75Dal 76NO		6'1"	218	Louisiana State		6
Cappelletti, John HB-FB	74-78LA 79LJ 80-83SD	2	6'1"	218	Penn State		168
Cappelman, Bill QB	70Min 73Det		6'3"	210	Florida State		
Capria, Carl DB	74Det 75NYJ		6'3"	185	Purdue		
Capriola, Glenn FB	77Det		5'11"	219	Boston College		
Carlson, Dean QB	74KC		6'3"	210	Iowa State		
Carlton, Darryl OT	75-76Mia 77-79TB		6'6"	271	Tampa		
Carmichael, Harold WR	71-83Phi 84Dal		6'7"	225	Southern U.		474
Carpenter, Ron DT-DE	70-77Cin		6'4"	261	N. Carolina State		2
Carr, Earl FB	78SF 79Phi		6'	224	Florida		
Carr, Fred LB	68-77GB		6'5"	239	Texas-El Paso	8	6
Carr, Levert OT-DT-OG	69SD-A 70-71Buf 72-73Hou		6'5"	258	North Central		
Carr, Roger WR	74-81Bal 82Sea 83SD	2	6'3"	196	Louisiana Tech		186
Carrell, Duane K	74Dal 75LA 76-77NYJ 77StL	4	5'10"	184	Florida State		
Carroll, Joe LB	72-73Oak		6'1"	220	Pittsburgh		
Carroll, Ronnie OG	74Hou		6'2"	265	Sam Houston St.		
Carter, Allen FB	75-76NE 76NYJ	3	5'11"	208	Southern Calif.		6
Carter, Blanchard OT	77TB		6'4"	250	Nevada-Las Vegas		
Carter, Jim LB	70-75GB 76BA 77-78GB		6'3"	240	Minnesota	6	6
Carter, Kent LB	74NE		6'3"	235	Southern Calif.		
Carter, Louis HB	75Oak 76-78TB	2	5'11"	207	Maryland		24
Carter, Mike WR	70GB 72SD		6'1"	210	Sacramento State		
Carter, Virgil QB	68-69Chi 70-72Cin 73AJ 74WFL 75SD 75-76Chi	12	6'1"	192	Brigham Young		49
Casanova, Tommy DB	72-77Cin	3	6'2"	197	Louisiana State	17	24
Cash, Rick DE-DT	69Atl 69-70LA 71JJ 72-73NE		6'5"	260	NE Missouri St.		
Casper, Dave TE	74-80Oak 80-82Hou 83Min 84Raid	2	6'4"	232	Notre Dame		318
Cassady, Craig DB	77NO		5'11"	175	Ohio State		
Caster, Rich TE-WR	70-77NYJ 78-80Hou 81NO 81-82Was	2	6'5"	228	Jackson State		270
Ceresino, Gordy LB	79SF		6'	224	Stanford		
Chambers, Rusty LB	75-76NO 76-80Mia		6'1"	218	Tulane	2	6
1981 — Died in automobile accident							
Chambers, Wally DT-DE	73-77Chi 78 70TB		6'6"	253	Eastern Kentucky	2	
Chandler, Al TE	73-74Cin 76-78NE 78-79StL 79NE	2	6'2"	229	Oklahoma		54
Chandler, Bob WR	71-79Buf 80-81Oak 82Raid	2	6'	180	Southern Calif.		289
Chandler, Edgar LB	68-69BufA 70-72Buf 73NE		6'3"	227	Georgia	2	8
Chandler, Karl C-OG	74-77NYG 78-79Det		6'5"	250	Princeton		
Chapman, Clarence DB	76-80NO 80-81Cin 83-84USFL 85Det	3	5'10"	185	Eastern Michigan	5	6
Chapman, Gil WR	75NO	2	5'9"	180	Michigan		
Chapple, Dave K	71Buf 72-74LA 74NE	3	6'	184	Cal.-Santa Barbara		
Charles, John DB	67-69BosA 70Min 71-74Hou		6'1"	199	Purdue	16	12
Chavous, Barney DE	73-85Den		6'3"	254	S. Carolina State		8
Cheek, Richard OG	70Buf 71KJ		6'3"	266	Auburn		
Cherry, Stan LB	73Bal		6'5"	200	Morgan State		
Chesley, Frank LB	78GB		6'3"	219	Wyoming		
Chesson, Wes WR	71-73Atl 74Phi	2	6'2"	192	Duke		
Chester, Ray TE	70-72Oak 73-77Bal 78-81Oak 83USFL	2	6'3"	232	Morgan State		288
Cheyunski, Jim LB	68-69BosA 70Bos 71-72NE 73-74Buf 75-76Bal 77GB		6'2"	222	Syracuse	9	
Childs, Henry TE	74Atl 74-80NO 81LA 84GB	2	6'2"	222	Kansas City C.C.		174
Childs, Jim WR	78-79StL	2	6'2"	194	Cal. Poly.-S.L.O.		6
Chomsyzak, Steve DT-C-OT	66NY-A 66-69CinA 70-73Cin		6'5"	270	Syracuse		
Christiansen, Bob TE	72Buf		6'4"	230	U.C.L.A.		
Cindrich, Ralph LB	72NE 73-74Hou 74Den 75Hou		6'1"	229	Pittsburgh		
Cipa, Larry QB	74-75NO	1	6'3"	209	Michigan		0
Clabo, Neil K	75-77Min	4	6'2"	200	Tennessee		
Clack, Jim C-OG	71-77Pit 78-81NYG		6'3"	250	Wake Forest		
Clancy, Sean LB	78Mia 79StL		6'4"	218	Amherst		
Clark, Al DB	71Det 72-75LA 76Phi		6'	183	Eastern Michigan	3	
Clark, Booby FB	73-78Cin 79-80Hou	2	6'2"	245	Bethune-Cookman		162
Clark, Gail LB	73Chi 74NE		6'2"	226	Michigan State		
Clark, Ken K	79LA	4	6'2"	197	St. Mary's (N.S.)		
Clark, Leroy K	76Hou		5'11"	200	Prairie View		
Clark, Wayne QB	70,72-73SD 74Cin 75KC	1	6'2"	203	U.S. International		6
Clements, Vin FB	72-73NYG 74-75WFL	2	6'3"	213	Connecticut		12
Clemons, Craig DB	72-77Chi		5'11"	195	Iowa	9	6
Cline, Tony DE	75Oak 76-77SF		6'2"	239	Miami (Fla.)	3	
Clune, Don WR	74-75NYG 76Sea		6'3"	195	Pennsylvania		
Coady, Rich C-TE	70-74Chi		6'3"	240	Memphis State		
Cobb, Marvin DB	75-79Cin 80Pit 80Min		6'	189	Southern Calif.	13	6
Cobb, Mike TE	77Cin 78-81Chi 83-84USFL	2	6'5"	244	Michigan State		
Cockroft, Don K	68-80Cle	45	6'1"	193	Adams State		1080
Coder, Ron OG-OT	76-79Sea 80StL 81KJ 84-85USFL		6'4"	250	Penn State		
Coffield, Randy LB	76-77Sea 78-79NYG		6'3"	215	Florida State		
Colavito, Steve LB	75Phi		6'	225	Wake Forest		
Colbert, Danny DB	74-76SD 77JJ		5'11"	175	Tulsa	2	
Colbert, Rondy DB	75-76NYG 77StL	3	5'9"	185	Lamar		6
Cole, Eddie LB	79-80Det		6'2"	235	Mississippi		2
Cole, Larry DE-DT	68-80Dal		6'4"	252	Hawaii	4	24
Cole, Linzy WR	70Chi 71-72Hou 72Buf	3	5'11"	170	Texas Christian		
Coleman, Al DB	68Min 69CinA 70-71Cin 72-73Phi 74JJ		6'1"	185	Tennessee State	1	2
Coleman, Dennis LB	71NE		6'3"	225	Mississippi		
Coleman, Don LB	74-75NO 76-77KJ		6'2"	220	Michigan		
Coleman, Fred TE	76Buf		6'4"	240	Northeast La.		
Coleman, Ralph LB	72Dal		6'4"	216	N. Carolina A&T		
Coleman, Ronnie HB	74-81Hou	23	5'10"	197	Alabama A&M		138
Coleman, Steve DE	74Den		6'4"	252	Delaware State		
Collett, Elmer OG	67-72SF 73-77Bal		6'4"	241	San Fran. State		
Collier, Mike HB-FB	75Pit 76KJ 77Buf 78FJ 79Buf	23	5'11"	200	Morgan State		36
Collins, Greg LB	75SF 76Sea 77Buf		6'3"	229	Notre Dame		
Collins, Gerald LB	69BufA 70-71Buf		6'1"	220	Western Michigan		
Collins, Larry HB	78Cle 79KJ 80NO 83USFL	3	5'11"	190	Texas A&I		6
Collins, Sonny HB	76Atl 77LA	2	6'1"	196	Kentucky		
Colman, Wayne LB	68-69Phi 69-74NO 75BA 76NO		6'1"	227	Temple	3	
Colzie, Neal DB	75-78Oak 79Mia 80-83TB 85USFL	3	6'2"	200	Ohio State	25	12
Condon, Tom OG	74-84KC		6'3"	255	Boston College		
Conley, Steve WR	72Cin 72StL		6'2"	225	Kansas		
Conn, Dick DB	74Pit 75WFL 75-79NE		6'	183	Georgia	1	

UseName(Nickname)-Positions	Team by Year	See Section	Hgt.	Wgt.	College	Int	Pts
Conway, Dave K	71GB		6'	195	Texas		5
Cook, Fred DE	74-80Bal		6'3"	244	Southern Miss.	2	6
Cooke, Bill DT-DE-OT	75GB 76-77SF 78Sea 78Det 79-80Sea		6'5"	249	Massachusetts		
Cooney, Mark LB	74GB		6'4"	230	Colorado		
Cooper, Bert LB	76TB		6'1"	242	Florida State		
Cope, Jim LB	76Atl		6'1"	235	Ohio State		
Copeland, Jim OG-C	67-74Cle		6'2"	242	Virginia		
Coppens, Gus OT	79NYG		6'5"	270	U.C.L.A.		
Corbett, Jim TE	77-80Cin	2	6'4"	218	Pittsburgh		6
Corbett, Steve OG	75NE 76ZJ		6'4"	248	Boston College		
Cornelius, Charles DB	77-78Mia 79-80SF		5'9"	178	Bethune-Cookman	4	
Cornell, Bo LB-FB	71-72Cle 73-77Buf		6'1"	217	Washington		6
Coslet, Bruce TE	69-76Cin 90-92HCNYJ	2	6'3"	228	U. of Pacific		54
Costict, Ray LB	77-79NE 80KJ 83USFL		6'	217	Mississippi State	1	
Cotton, Craig TE	69-72Det 73Chi 74WFL 75SD	2	6'4"	222	Youngstown State		6
Cousina, Brad LB	75Cin 76NYG 77Pit		6'	218	Miami-Ohio		
Cowins, Ben HB	79KC		6'	192	Arkansas		
Cowings, Al DE-DT-LB	70-72Buf 73-74Hou 75,77LA 79SF		6'5"	247	Southern Calif.		
Cox, Fred K	63-77Min	45	5'10"	200	Pittsburgh		1365
Craig, Neal DB	71-73Cin 74Buf 75-76Cle		6'1"	189	Fisk	8	12
Craig, Reggie WR	75-76KC 77Cle 77Buf		6'	188	Arkansas		
Craig, Steve TE	74-78Min	2	6'3"	231	Northwestern		6
Crangle, Mike DE	72NO		6'4"	243	Tennessee-Martin		
Craven, Bill DB	76Cle 77JJ		5'11"	190	Harvard		
Crawford, Rufus HB	78Sea	3	5'10"	180	Virginia State		
Creech, Bob LB	71-72Phi 73NO		6'3"	226	Texas Christian		
Crennel, Carl LB	70Pit		6'1"	230	West Virginia		
Crist, Chuck DB	72-74NYG 75-77NO 78SF		6'2"	205	Penn State	20	
Criter, Ken LB	69DenA 70-74Den		5'11"	223	Wisconsin		2
Croft, Don DT	72Buf 73KJ 74-75Buf 76Det		6'3"	256	Texas-El Paso		
Croom, Sylvester C	75NO		6'	235	Alabama		
Crosby, Steve HB	74-76NYG		5'11"	205	Ft. Hays State		
Crosswhite, Leon FB	73-74Det 75FJ		6'2"	215	Oklahoma		12
Crowder, Randy DT-NT-DE	74-76Mia 78-80TB 81-82KJ 77 — Ineligible to play pro football		6'2"	242	Penn State		
Crowe, Larry HB	72Phi 75Atl		6'1"	198	Texas Southern		
Croyle, Phil LB	71-73Hou 73Buf		6'3"	220	California		
Crum, Bob DE	74StL		6'5"	240	Arizona		
Crump, Dwayne DB	73-76StL		5'11"	180	Fresno State	1	6
Crusan, Doug OT	66-69MiaA 70-74Mia		6'5"	253	Indiana		
Csonka, Larry FB	68-69MiaA 70-74Mia 75WFL 76-78NYG 79Mia	2	6'3"	238	Syracuse		408
Culbreath, Jim FB	77-79GB 80Phi 80NYG	2	6'	210	Oklahoma		6
Cullers, Willie DE	74NYG		6'5"	250	Kansas		
Culp, Curley DT-NT-OT	68-69KC-A 70-74KC 74-80Hou 80-81Det		6'1"	265	Arizona State		
Cunningham, Dick LB-OT	67-69BufA 70-72Buf 73Phi 74JJ		6'2"	238	Arkansas		
Cunningham, Doug HB	67-73SF 74Was	23	5'11"	191	Mississippi		60
Cunningham, Doug WR	79Min		6'2"	195	Rice		
Cunningham, Sam (Bam) FB	73-79NE 80HO 81-82NE	2	6'3"	226	Southern Calif.		294
Curchin, Jeff OT-OG	70-71Chi 72Buf		6'6"	256	Florida State		
Cureton, Will QB	75Cle	1	6'3"	200	East Texas State		
Curran, Pat TE	69-74LA 75-78SD 79JJ	2	6'3"	238	Lakeland		37
Current, Mike OT	67Mia 67-75Den 76TB 77-79Mia		6'4"	267	Ohio State		
Curtis, Isaac WR	73-84Cin	2	6'	192	California, San Diego State		318
Curtis, Mike LB-FB	65-75Bal 76Sea 77-78Was		6'2"	232	Duke	25	18
Curtis, Tom DB	70-71Bal		6'1"	196	Michigan		
Cusick, Pete NT	75NE 76-78KJ		6'1"	255	Ohio State		
Dalby, Dave C-OG	72-81Oak 82-85Raid		6'2"	248	U.C.L.A.		
Dalton, Oakley DT	77NO		6'6"	285	Jackson State		
Damkroger, Maury LB	74-75NE		6'2"	230	Nebraska		
Dandridge, Jerry LB	76GB		6'1"	222	Memphis State		
Danelo, Joe K	75GB 76-82NYG 83-84Buf	5	5'9"	165	Washington State		639
Daney, George OG	66-69KC-A 70-74KC		6'3"	240	Texas-El Paso		6
Darby, Alvis TE	76Sea 76Hou 78TB		6'5"	221	Florida		
Darby, Paul WR	79-80NYJ		5'10"	192	SW Texas State		6
Darden, Thom DB	72-74Cle 75KJ 76-81Cle	3	6'2"	193	Michigan	45	18
Darrow, Barry OT	74-78Cle		6'7"	260	Montana		
Davis, Anthony HB	77TB 78Hou 78LA 79JJ 83USFL	2	5'10"	190	Southern Calif.		6
Davis, Ben DB	67-73Cle 74-76Det	3	5'11"	183	Defiance	19	12
Davis, Bob QB	67-69HouA 70-72NYJ 73NO 74-75WFL	12	6'3"	205	Virginia		12
Davis, Brad FB	75-76Atl		5'10"	204	Louisiana State		
Davis, Butch DB	70Chi		5'11"	183	Missouri	1	
Davis, Charlie HB	74Cin 75KJ 76TB	2	5'11"	200	Colorado		6
Davis, Charlie DT-NT	74Pit 75-79StL 80Hou 84USFL		6'1"	269	Texas Christian		6
Davis, Clarence HB	71-78Oak	23	5'10"	191	Southern Calif.		168
Davis, Dave WR	71-72GB 73Pit 74NO 75BN	2	6'	175	Tennessee State		6
Davis, Dick HB-FB	70Den 70NO	2	5'11"	215	Nebraska		
Davis, Gary HB	76-79Mia 80-81TB 81Cle	23	5'10"	203	Cal. Poly.-S.L.O.		48
Davis, Harrison WR	74SD	2	6'4"	220	Virginia		12
Davis, Henry LB	68-69NYG 70-73Pit 74JJ		6'3"	235	Grambling	4	6
Davis, Jerry DB	75NYJ		5'11"	182	Morris Brown		
Davis, Kyle C	75Dal 76KJ 78SF		6'4"	240	Oklahoma		
Davis, Marvin LB	74Hou		6'4"	235	Southern U.		
Davis, Ricky DB	75Cin 76TB 77KC 78AJ		6'1"	180	Alabama	1	
Davis, Ron OG	73StL 74JJ		6'2"	235	Virginia State		
Davis, Sam OG-OT	67-79Pit 80-81KJ		6'1"	251	Allen		
Davis, Sonny HB-FB	71-72Phi	2	5'11"	215	Tennessee State		6
Davis, Stan WR	73Phi		5'10"	180	Memphis State		
Davis, Steve FB-HB	72-74Pit 75-76NYJ	23	6'1"	216	Delaware State		66
Davis, Tony FB-HB	76-78Cin 79-81TB 83USFL	23	5'10"	211	Nebraska		36
Davis, Vern DB	71Phi		6'4"	208	Western Michigan		
Dawkins, Joe FB-HB	70-71Hou 71-73Den 74-75NYG 76Hou	23	5'11"	221	Wisconsin		96
Dawson, Rhett WR	72Hou 73Min		6'1"	185	Florida State		6
Daykin, Tony LB	77-78Det 79-81Atl		6'1"	215	Georgia Tech		
Dean, Fred OG	77Chi 78-80Was 81BA 82Was 83-85USFL		6'3"	253	Texas Southern		
Dean, Jimmy DE	78Hou		6'4"	252	Texas A&M		
Dean, Randy QB	77-79NYG	1	6'3"	195	Northwestern		6
DeBernardi, Fred DE	74KC		6'4"	250	Texas-El Paso		
DeFrance, Chris WR	79Was		6'1"	205	Arizona State		
DeGrener, Jack FB	74NO	2	6'1	225	Texas-Arlington		
DeLamielleure, Joe OG	73-79Buf 80-84Cle 85Buf		6'3"	250	Michigan State		
DeLeone, Tom C-OG	72-73Cin 74-84Cle		6'2"	250	Ohio State		
Del Gaizo, Jim QB	72Mia 73GB 74NYG 75Mia	1	6'1"	194	Temple		
DeLisle, Jim DT	71GB		6'4"	254	Wisconsin		
Deloplaine, Jack HB	76-77Pit 78Was 78Pit 79Chi 79Pit	2	5'10"	205	Salem		12

UseName(Nickname)-Positions	Team by Year	See Section	Hgt.	Wgt.	College	Int	Pts
Demarie, John OG-OT-C	67-75Cle 76Sea		6'3"	250	Louisiana State		
Demery, Calvin WR	72Min		6'	190	Arizona State		
Demory, Bill QB	73-74NYJ	1	6'2"	195	Arizona		
Dempsey, Tom K	69-70NO 71-74Phi 75-76LA 77Hou 78-79Buf	5	6'1"	260	Palomar J.C.		729
Den Herder, Vern DE-NT	71-81Mia		6'6"	251	Central (Iowa)	1	6
Dennery, Mike LB	74-75Oak 76Mia		6'	224	Southern Miss.		2
Dennis, Al OG	73SD 76-77Cle		6'4"	250	Grambling		
Dennis, Guy OG-C	69CinA 70-72Cin 73-75Det		6'2"	254	Florida		
Dennison, Doug HB-FB	74-78Dal 79Cle 80CFL 83-84USFL	2	6'1"	202	Kutztown		114
Denson, Keith WR	76NYJ		5'8"	165	San Diego State		
Denson, Moses FB-HB	74-75Was	2	6'1"	215	Md. Eastern Shore		12
DePaso, Tom LB	78-79Cin		6'2"	223	Penn State		
DePoyster, Jerry K	68Det 71-72Oak	45	6'1"	202	Wyoming		27
DeRatt, Jimmy DB	75NO		6'	203	North Carolina		
DeSimone, Rick TE	78SF		6'3"	213	Northridge State		
Detwiler, Chuck DB	70-72SD 73StL 74-75WFL		6'	185	Utah State	1	6
Devine, Dan	HC71-74GB				Minnesota-Duluth		
Devlin, Chris LB	75-76Cin 77FJ 78Cin 78Chi		6'2"	226	Penn State	1	
Dickel, Dan LB	74-77Bal 78Det		6'3"	225	Iowa	1	
Dickey, Lynn QB	71Hou 72PJ 73-75Hou 76-77GB 78BL 79-85GB	12	6'4"	210	Kansas State		55
Dickinson, Parnell QB	76-77TB	1	6'2"	185	Miss. Valley St.		
Dicus, Chuck WR	71-72SD	2	6'	174	Arkansas		18
Didion, John C-LB	69-70Was 71-74NO		6'4"	247	Oregon State		
Dieken, Doug OT	71-84Cle		6'5"	250	Illinois		8
Dierdorf, Dan OT-OG-C	71-83StL		6'4"	281	Michigan		
Diggs, Sheldon WR	77NYJ		6'1"	190	Southern Calif.		
Dilts, Bucky K	77-78Den 79Bal	4	5'9"	185	Georgia		
Dirden, Johnnie WR	78Hou 79KC 81Pit 83-84USFL	3	6'	188	Sam Houston St.		
Dobbins, Herb OT	74Phi		6'4"	260	San Diego State		
Dobler, Conrad OG	72-77StL 78-79NO 80-81Buf		6'3"	254	Wyoming		6
Dockery, John DB	68-69NY-A 70-71NYJ 72-73Pit		6'	186	Harvard	8	
Dodd, Al WR-DB	67Chi 69-71NO 72JJ 73-74Atl	23	6'	180	Northwestern La.		24
Dokes, Phil DT-DE	77-78Buf 79SJ 83-84USFL		6'5"	257	Oklahoma State		
Dolbin, Jack WR	75-79Den	2	5'10"	181	Wake Forest		48
Domres, Marty QB	69SD-A 70-71SD 72-75Bal 76SF 77NYJ	12	6'4"	219	Columbia		60
Domres, Tom DT-DE	68-69HouA 70-71Hou 71-72Den 73JJ		6'3"	257	Wisconsin		6
Donahue, Mark OG	78-79Cin		6'3"	256	Michigan		
Donchez, Tom FB	75Chi		6'2"	216	Penn State		
Donckers, Billy QB	76-77StL		6'1"	206	San Diego State		
Donohue, Mike TE	68,70-71Atl 73-74GB	2	6'3"	228	San Francisco		12
Donovan, Pat OT	75-83Dal		6'4"	253	Stanford		
Dorris, Andy DE	73-76NO 77Sea 77-81Hou		6'4"	238	New Mexico State		
Dorsey, Larry WR	76-77SD 78KC	2	6'1"	195	Tennessee State		24
Dorsey, Nate DE	73NE		6'4"	240	Miss. Valley St.		
Doughty, Glenn WR	72-79Bal	2	6'1"	204	Michigan		144
Douglas, Jay C	73-74SD		6'6"	251	Memphis State		
Douglas, John LB	70-73NYG 74WFL		6'2"	227	Missouri	2	
Douglass, Bobby QB	69-75Chi 75SD 76-77NO 78GB	12	6'3"	224	Kansas		133
Douglass, Freddie WR	76TB		5'9"	185	Arkansas		
Douthit, Earl DB	75Chi 76TB		6'2"	188	Iowa		
Dove, Jerome DB	77-80GB		6'2"	190	Colorado State	2	
Dowling, Brian QB	72-73NE 74-75WFL 77GB	1	6'2"	207	Yale		18
Dragon, Oscar HB-FB	72SD		6'	214	Arizona State		
Drake, Bill DB-WR	73-74LA		6'1"	195	Oregon		
Dressler, Doug FB	70-72Cin 73KJ 74Chi 75NE 75KC	2	6'3"	225	Ohio State		66
Drougas, Tom OT-OG	72-73Bal 74Den 74KC 75-76Mia		6'4"	258	Oregon		
Drunga, Elbert OT-OG	69HouA 70-71Hou 72KJ 73-77Hou		6'5"	260	Tennessee State		
Druschel, Rich OT-OG	74Pit		6'2"	248	N. Carolina State		
Dryer, Fred DE	69-71NYG 72-81LA		6'6"	238	San Diego State	1	10
Dubinetz, Greg OG	79Was		6'4"	260	Yale		
DuBose, Jimmy FB	76-78TB 79KJ	2	5'11"	216	Florida		
Duhon, Bobby HB	68NYG 69KJ 70-72NYG	23	6'	194	Tulane		36
DuLac, Bill OG	74-75NE		6'4"	260	Eastern Michigan		
Dumier, Doug C	73-75NE 76-77Min		6'3"	243	Nebraska		
Dunbar, Jubilee WR	73NO 74Cle	2	6'	196	Southern U.		24
Duncan, Brian HB-FB	76-77Cle 78Hou		6'	201	S.M.U.		12
Duncan, Jim DB	69-71Bal	3	6'2"	200	Md. Eastern Shore	2	12
Duncan, Ken K	71GB		6'2"	210	Tulsa		
Dungy, Tony DB-QB	77-78Pit 79SF		6'	189	Minnesota	9	
Dunivan, Tom QB	77-78Hou		6'3"	210	Texas Tech		
Dunlap, Lenny DB	71Bal 72-74SD 75Det	3	6'1"	197	North Texas	5	
Dunn, Paul HB-FB	70Cin		6'	210	U.S. International		
Dunstan, Bill DT	73-76Phi 77Buf 79LA		6'4"	250	Utah State		6
DuPree, Billy Joe TE	73-83Dal	2	6'4"	227	Michigan State		252
Duranko, Pete DE-DT	67-69Den-A 70-71Den 71JJ		6'2"	249	Notre Dame		
Duren, Clarence DB	73-76StL 77SD		6'1"	190	California	10	
Durko, Sandy DB	70-71Cin 72JJ 73-74NE		6'1"	185	Southern Calif.	7	
Dusek, Brad LB	74-81Was		6'2"	217	Texas A&M	4	18
Dusenberry, Bill DB	70NO		6'2"	198	Johnson C. Smith		
Dvorak, Rick DE	74-77NYG 77Mia		6'4"	240	Wichita State		
Eaglin, Larry DB	73Hou		6'3"	195	S.F. Austin State		6
Earl, Robin FB-TE	77-82Chi 84-85USFL	2	6'5"	242	Washington		30
Earley, Jim FB	78NYJ		6'1"	230	Michigan State		
East, Ron DT-DE	67-70Dal 71-73SD 74WFL 75Cle 76Atl 77Sea		6'4"	244	Montana State		2
Easterling, Ray DB	72-79Atl 80JJ		6'	192	Richmond	13	
Ebersole, John LB	70-77NYJ		6'3"	234	Penn State	8	
Eck, Keith C-OG	79NYG 80IL		6'5"	255	U.C.L.A.		
Edwards, Cid FB	66-71StL 72-74SD 75Chi	2	6'2"	230	Tennessee State		114
Edwards, Earl DE-DT	69-72SF 73-75Buf 76-78Cle 79GB		6'6"	261	Wichita State		
Edwards, Emmett WR	75-76Hou 76Buf		6'1"	189	Kansas		
Edwards, Glen DB	71-77Pit 78-81SD 83USFL	3	6'	184	Florida A&M	39	18
Edwards, Jimmy HB	79Min	3	5'9"	185	Northeast La.		
Ehlers, Tom LB	75-77Phi 78Buf 79XJ		6'2"	218	Kentucky	1	
Ehrmann, Joe DT	73-80Bal 81-82Det 83-85USFL		6'5"	256	Syracuse	1	
Eidson, Jim OG-C	76Dal 77JJ		6'3"	264	Mississipi State		1
Eischeid, Mike K	66-69OakA 70-71Oak 72-74Min	4	6'	190	Upper Iowa		70
Elam, Cleveland DT-DE	75-78SF 79Det		6'4"	252	Tennessee State		6
Eley, Monroe FB	75Atl 76JJ 77Atl	2	6'2"	210	Arizona State		6
Elia, Bruce LB	75Mia 76-78SF		6'1"	220	Ohio State		
Ellenbogen, Bill OG-OT	76-77NYG		6'5"	258	Virginia Tech		
Ellender, Rich WR	79Hou	3	5'11"	171	McNeese State		
Eller, Carl DE	64-78Min 79Sea		6'6"	252	Minnesota	1	10
Elliott, John DT-DE-LB	67-69NY-A 70-73NYJ 74WFL		6'4"	244	Texas		2
Elliott, Lenvil HB-FB	73-78Cin 79-81SF	23	6'	207	N.E. Missouri St.		108
Ellis, Allan DB	73-77Chi 78KJ 79-80Chi 81SD		5'10"	179	U.C.L.A.	22	6
Ellis, Clarence DB	72-74Atl 75KJ		5'11"	191	Notre Dame	8	

Use Name (Nickname) - Positions	Team by Year	See Section	Hgt.	Wgt.	College	Int	Pts
Ellis, Ken DB	70-75GB 76Hou 76Mia 77Cle 79Det 79LA	3	5'10"	191	Southern U.	22	30
Ellison, Glenn HB-FB	71Oak		6'1"	215	Arkansas		
Ellison, Mark OG	72-73NYG		6'2"	250	Dayton		
Ellison, Willie HB-FB	67-72LA 73-79KC	23	6'1"	204	Texas Southern		180
Elmendorf, Dave DB	71-79LA	3	6'1"	195	Texas A&M	27	12
Elrod, Jimbo LB	76-78KC 79Hou		6'	220	Oklahoma	1	
Ely, Larry LB	70-71Cin 74WFL 75Chi		6'1"	230	Iowa	1	
Emerson, Vern OT	69-71StL		6'5"	260	Minnesota-Duluth		
Enderle, Dick OG	69-71Atl 72-75NYG 76SF 76GB		6'1"	250	Minnesota		
Engel, Steve HB-FB	70Cle		6'1"	218	Colorado		
Engels, Rick K	76-77Sea 77Pit 78Phi	4	5'11"	177	Tulsa		
Enyart, Bill FB	69BufA 70Buf 71Oak 72KJ	2	6'4"	236	Oregon State		24
Ernst, Mike QB	72Cin 73Den		6'1"	190	Fullerton State		
Esposito, Mike HB	76-78Atl 79SJ	2	6'	183	Boston College	1	12
Estes, Larry DE-DT	70-71NO 72Phi 74-75WFL 75-77KC		6'6"	255	Alcorn State		
Evans, Charlie FB	71-73NYG 74Was 76KJ	2	6'1"	219	Southern Calif.		78
Evans, Johnny K-QB	78-80Cle	4	6'1"	197	N. Carolina State		
Evans, Larry LB	76-82Den 83SD		6'2"	218	Mississippi	3	
Evans, Mike C	68-73Phi		6'5"	250	Boston College		
Evans, Norm OT	65Hou 66-75Mia 76-78Sea		6'5"	248	Texas Christian		6
Fagan, Julian K	70-72NO 73NYJ	4	6'3"	205	Mississippi		
Fairbanks, Chuck	HC73-78NE				Michigan State		
Fairchild, Greg OG-C-OT	76-77Cin 78Cle 78-79CFL 83-84USFL		6'4"	257	Tulsa		
Fairley, Leonard DB	74Hou		5'11"	200	Alcorn State		
Falcon, Terry OG-OT	78-79NE 80NYG 83USFL		6'3"	260	Montana		
Fanning, Mike DT-DE-NT	75-81LA 83Det 84Sea		6'6"	257	Notre Dame		2
Fanucci, Mike DE	72Was 73Hou 74GB		6'4"	236	Arizona State		
Farasopoulos, Chris DB	71-73NYJ 74NO	3	5'11"	190	Brigham Young	4	6
Farber, Hap LB	70Min 70NO		6'1"	220	Mississippi		
Farmer, Dave HB	78TB		6'	205	Southern Calif.		
Farmer, George WR	70-75Chi 75Det	2	6'4"	212	U.C.L.A.		60
Farmer, Karl WR	76-77Atl 78TB		5'11"	165	Pittsburgh		
Farmer, Roger WR	79NYJ		6'3"	195	Baker		
Farmer, Ted HB	78StL		5'11"	175	Oregon		
Farr, Mel HB	67-73Det	2	6'2"	208	U.C.L.A.		216
Faumuina, Wilson DT-DE-NT	77-81Atl		6'5"	275	San Jose State	1	
Federspiel, Joe LB	72-80NO 81Bal 83USFL		6'1"	230	Kentucky	5	
Feller, Happy K	71Phi 72-73NO	5	5'11"	185	Texas		75
Felton, Eric DB	78-79NO 80NYG 81SJ		6'	200	Texas Tech	5	
Fergerson, Duke WR	77-79Sea 80Buf	2	6'1"	189	San Diego State		12
Ferguson, Bill LB	73-74NYJ		6'3"	225	San Diego State		
Ferguson, Gene OT-DT	69SD-A 70SD 71-72Hou		6'7"	302	Norfolk State		
Fernandes, Ron DE	76-77Bal 78KJ 79Bal 80IL 83USFL		6'4"	251	Eastern Michigan		2
Fernandez, Manny DT-NT	66-69MiaA 70-75Mia 76-77KJ		6'2"	250	Utah		
Ferrell, Bob FB-HB	76-80SF	2	6'	216	U.C.L.A.		18
Fersen, Paul OT	73NO		6'5"	260	Georgia		
Fest, Cotton DT	72Cle		6'2"	255	Dayton		
Fest, Howard OG-OT-C	66-69CinA 70-75Cin 76TB 77JJ		6'6"	263	Texas		
Fields, Edgar DE-DT	77-80Atl 81Det		6'2"	255	Texas A&M		
Fifer, Bill OT	78Det 78NO 79Sea		6'4"	250	West Texas State		
Files, Jim LB	70-73NYG		6'4"	240	Oklahoma		
Fink, Mike DB	73NO		5'11"	180	Missouri		
Finnie, Roger OT-OG-DT	69NY-A 70-72NYJ 73-78StL 79NO		6'3"	247	Florida A&M		
Fisher, Ed OG-DE-C	74-82Hou 85USFL		6'3"	249	Arizona State		
Fitzgerald, John C-OG	71-80Dal 81KJ		6'5"	255	Boston College		
Flanagan, Ed C	65-74Det 75-76SD		6'3"	246	Purdue		
Fletcher, Chris DB	70-76SD	3	5'11"	186	Temple	13	6
Flowers, Richmond DB-WR	69-71Dal 71-73NYG 74-75WFL		6'	181	Tennessee	6	
Foley, Dave OT-C	70-71NYJ 72-77Buf		6'5"	252	Ohio State		
Foley, Tim DB	70-80Mia		6'	194	Purdue	22	14
Foote, James QB	74,76Hou		6'2"	210	Delaware Valley		
Ford, Charlie DB	71-73Chi 74Phi 75Buf 75NYG 76KJ		6'3"	187	Houston	15	
Ford, James HB-FB	71-72NO 73JJ	2	6'	203	Texas Southern		12
Foreman, Chuck HB-FB	73-79Min 80NE	2	6'2"	209	Miami (Fla.)		456
Forrest, Tom OG	74Chi		6'2"	255	Cincinnati		
Forsberg, Fred LB	68DenA 70-73Den 73Buf 74SD		6'1"	233	Washington	5	6
Forte, Ike HB	76-77NE 78-80Was 81NYG	23	6'	203	Arkansas		42
Fortner, Larry QB	79-80Atl		6'4"	212	Miami-Ohio		
Forzano, Rick	HC74-76Det				Kent State		
Foster, Eddie WR	77Hou 78KJ 79Hou	2	5'10"	185	Houston		
Foster, Will LB	73NE		6'2"	230	Eastern Michigan		6
Fowler, Dan OG	79NYG		6'5"	260	Kentucky		
Fowler, Wayne C	70Buf		6'3"	260	Richmond		
France, Doug OT	75-81LA 83Hou 84SJ		6'5"	270	Ohio State		
Francis, Jon HB	87LA	2	5'11"	207	Boise State		12
Francis, Wallace WR	73-74Buf 75-81Atl	23	5'11"	190	Ark.-Pine Bluff		180
Franckowiak, Mike FB-TE	75-76Den 77-78Buf		6'3"	221	Central Michigan		
Franco, Brian K	87Cle		5'8"	165	Penn State		11
Franklin, Cleveland FB	77-78Phi 79-82Bal	2	6'2"	216	Baylor		18
Franklin, Dennis WR	75-76Det		6'1"	185	Michigan		
Franklin, George FB	78Atl 79NYG		6'3"	226	Texas A&I		
Franklin, Larry WR	78TB		6'1"	185	Jackson State		
Franklin, Willie WR	72Bal		6'2"	195	Oklahoma		
Franks, Dennis C	76-78Phi 79Det		6'1"	241	Michigan		
Frazier, Cliff DT	77KC		6'4"	265	U.C.L.A.		
Freelon, Solomon OG	72-74Hou		6'2"	250	Grambling		
Freitas, Jesse QB	74-75SD	1	6'1"	198	San Diego State		
Freitas, Rocky OT	68-77Det 78TB		6'6"	271	Oregon State		
Fritsch, Ted C	72-74Atl 75KJ 76-79Was		6'2"	242	St. Norbert		
Fritsch, Toni K	71-73Dal 74KJ 75Dal 76SD 77-81Hou 82NO 84-85USFL	5	5'7"	190	none		758
Fritts, Stan HB-FB	75-76Cin	2	6'1"	215	N. Carolina State		78
Fronbose, Bill DB	74Det		6'	185	Miami (Fla.)		
Fryer, Brian WR	76Was 77JJ		6'1"	185	Alberta		
Fugett, Jean TE-WR	72-75Dal 76-79Was	2	6'3"	225	Amherst		168
Fuller, Johnny DB	68-72SF 73-75NO	3	6'	182	Lamar	8	
Fuller, Mike DB	75-80SD 81-82Cin	3	5'9"	187	Auburn	17	25
Fulton, Ed OG	78LA 79Buf 80-82CFL 84-85USFL		6'3"	250	Maryland		
Fultz, Mike DT	77-80NO 81Mia 81Bal		6'5"	278	Nebraska		
Funchess, Tom OT	68-69BosA 70Bos 71-73Hou 74Mia		6'5"	264	Jackson State		
Fuqua, John (Frenchy) HB-FB	69NYG 70-76Pit 77BG	23	5'11"	200	Morgan State		144
Furness, Steve DT-DE	72-80Pit 81Det		6'4"	255	Rhode Island		
Gaddis, Robert WR	76Buf		5'11"	178	Miss. Valley St.		
Gagnon, Dave HB	74Chi		5'10"	210	Ferris State		
Gaines, Clark FB-HB	76-80NYJ 81-82KC	2	6'1"	206	Wake Forest		84
Gaines, Lawrence FB	76Det 77KJ 78-79Det	2	6'1"	237	Wyoming		36

Use Name (Nickname) - Positions	Team by Year	See Section	Hgt.	Wgt.	College	Int	Pts
Gaines, Wentford DB	78Pit 78-80Chi		6'	185	Cincinnati	2	
Galigher, Ed DE-DT	72-76NYJ 77-79SF		6'4"	253	U.C.L.A.		
Gallagher, Allen OT	74NE		6'3"	255	Southern Calif.		
Gallagher, Dave DT-DE	74Chi 75-76NYG 77VR 78-79Det		6'4"	256	Michigan	1	
Gallagher, Frank OG	67-72Det 73Atl 73Min		6'2"	243	North Carolina		
Gallegos, Chan QB	72Oak		5'9"	175	San Jose State		
Ganas, Rusty DT	71Bal		6'4"	257	South Carolina		
Gant, Reuben TE-WR	74-80Buf	2	6'4"	226	Oklahoma State		90
Gantt, Greg K	74-75NYJ	4	5'11"	188	Alabama		11
Gantt, Jerry OT	70Buf		6'4"	266	N. Car. Central		
Gardin, Ron DB-WR	70-71Bal 73NE	3	5'11"	180	Arizona		6
Garlich, Chris LB	79StL		6'1"	220	Missouri		
Garlington, John LB	68-77Cle		6'1"	222	Louisiana State	9	
Garrett, Carl HB	69BosA 70Bos 71-72NE 73-74Chi 75NYJ 76-77Oak	23	5'11"	209	N. Mex. Highlands		210
Garrett, Len TE	71-73GB 73-75NO 75SF		6'3"	230	N. Mex. Highlands		
Garrett, Reggie WR	74-75Pit 76XJ	2	6'1"	174	Eastern Michigan		6
Garrison, Gary WR	66-69SD-A 70-76SD 77Hou	2	6'1"	194	San Diego State		348
Garrison, Walt FB-HB	66-74Dal	23	6'	204	Oklahoma State		234
Garror, Leon DB	72-73Buf		6'	180	Alcorn State	1	
Garry, Ben FB	79-80Bal		6'	215	Southern Miss.		
Gartner, Chris K	74Cle		6'	170	Indiana		
Gatewood, Tom TE-WR	72-73NYG		6'3"	215	Notre Dame		
Gault, Don QB	70Cle		6'2"	190	Hofstra		
Gaunty, Steve WR	79KC		5'10"	175	Northern Colorado		6
Gay, Blenda DE	74SD 75-76Phi died due to knife wound — Dec. 1976		6'5"	254	Fayetteville St.		6
Gaydos, Kent WR	75GB 76JJ		6'6"	228	Florida State		
Geddes, Bob LB	72Den 73-75NE		6'2"	240	U.C.L.A.	2	6
Geddes, Ken LB	71-75LA 76-78Sea		6'3"	235	Nebraska	6	
George, Ed OT	75Bal 76-78Phi		6'4"	270	Wake Forest		
George, Steve DT	74StL 75KJ 76Atl		6'6"	265	Houston		
George, Tim WR	73Cin 74Cle		6'5"	218	Whittier		
Geredine, Tom WR	73-74Atl 76LA	23	6'2"	191	NE Missouri St.		12
Gerela, Roy K	69HouA 70Hou 71-78Pit 79SD	45	5'10"	185	New Mexico State		903
Germany, Willie DB	72Atl 73Det 74WFL 75Hou 76NE		6'	192	Morgan State	2	6
Gersbach, Carl LB	70Phi 71-72Min 73-74SD 75Chi 76StL		6'1"	230	West Chester	3	
Getty, Charlie OT-OG	74-82KC 83GB		6'4"	265	Penn State		
Giammona, Louie HB	76NYJ 77KJ 78-82Phi 83USFL	23	5'9"	180	Utah State		54
Gibbons, Mike OT	76-77NYG		6'4"	262	Southwestern Okla.		
Gibbs, Donnie K	74NO		6'2"	205	Texas Christian		
Gibbs, Pat DB	72Phi		5'10"	188	Lamar		
Giblin, Robert DE	75NYG 76SJ 77StL 78JJ		6'2"	208	Houston		
Gibson, Paul DB	72GB		6'2"	195	Texas-El Paso		
Gibson, Rueben HB	77Buf		6'	196	Memphis State		
Gibson, Tom DT	71Oak		6'6"	290	Texas El-Paso		
Gill, Randy LB	78StL 78TB		6'2"	230	San Jose State		
Gillard, Larry DT	78NYG 79KJ		6'4"	270	Mississippi State		
Gillette, Walker WR	70-71SD 72-73StL 74-76NYG	2	6'5"	200	Richmond		72
Gilliam, Joe QB	72-75Pit	1	6'2"	187	Tennessee State		6
Gilliam, John WR-HB	67-68NO 69-71StL 72-75Min 76Atl 77Chi 77NO	23	6'1"	192	S. Carolina State		312
Gillingham, Gale OG-OT	66-76GB		6'3"	257	Minnesota		
Ginn, Hubert HB	70-73Mia 73Bal 74-75Mia 76-77Oak	23	5'11"	187	Florida A&M		18
Gipson, Paul HB-FB	69-70Atl 71Det 73NE	2	6'	208	Houston		24
Gladieux, Bob (Harpo) HB	69BosA 70Bos 70Buf 71-72NE	2	5'11"	191	Notre Dame		
Glass, Chip TE	69-73Cle 74NYG	2	6'4"	236	Florida State		30
Glass, Leland WR	72-73GB	2	6'	185	Oregon		6
Glassic, Tom OG	76-83Den		6'3"	254	Virginia		
Glossen, Clyde WR	70Buf		5'11"	175	Texas-El Paso		
Glover, Rich DT	73NYG 74WFL 75Phi		6'1"	242	Nebraska		
Goeddeke, George OG-OT-C	67-69DenA 70-72Den 73JJ		6'3"	250	Notre Dame		
Gofourth, Derrel OG-C	77-82GB		6'3"	260	Oklahoma State		
Golch, Dan DT-DE	69-70Det 71NO 72-73NYG 74Den		6'4"	258	California		
Golub, Chris DB	77KC		6'2"	196	Kansas		
Gonzalez, Noe HB	74NE		6'	210	SW Texas State		
Goode, Don LB	74-79SD 80-81Cle		6'2"	230	Kansas	10	
Goodman, Brian OG	73-74Hou 75Den		6'2"	250	U.C.L.A.		
Goodman, Harvey OG	76Den		6'4"	260	Colorado		
Goodman, Les HB-FB	73-74GB	2	5'11"	206	Yankton		6
Goodrum, Charlie OT-OG	73-74Min		6'3"	256	Florida A&M		
Gordon, Dick WR-OE	65-71Chi 72-73LA 73GB 74SD	23	5'11"	190	Michigan State		216
Gordon, Ira OG-OT	70-75SD		6'3"	270	Kansas State		
Gordon, John DT	72Det		6'6"	260	Hawaii		
Gordon, Larry LB	76-82Mia Died 1983 — heart attack		6'4"	230	Arizona State	8	2
Gotshalk, Len OT-OG	72-76Atl 77KJ		6'4"	255	Humboldt State		
Gradishar, Randy LB	74-83Den		6'3"	232	Ohio State	20	24
Graf, Dave LB	75-79Cle 81Was		6'2"	217	Penn State	1	
Graff, Neil QB	74-75NE 76Sea 76-77Pit 78GB	1	6'3"	202	Wisconsin		
Graham, Tom LB	72-74Den 74KC 75-77SD 78Buf		6'2"	235	Oregon	7	
Grandberry, Ken HB	74Chi	2	6'	198	Washington State		12
Grannell, Dave TE	74SD		6'4"	230	Arizona State		
Grant, Bob LB	68-70Bal 71Was		6'2"	225	Wake Forest	5	6
Grant, Bud OE-DE	51-52Phi 53CFL HC67-83, 85Min 49-51 played in N.B.A.		6'3"	199	Minnesota		
Grant, Frank WR	73-78Was 78TB	2	5'11"	181	Southern Colorado		108
Grant, John NT-DE-DT	73-79Den		6'3"	241	Southern Calif.		
Grant, Reggie DB	78NYJ		5'9"	185	Oregon		
Grant, Wes DE-DT	71Cle 71SD 72Cle 73Hou		6'3"	245	U.C.L.A.		
Gravelle, Gordon OT	72-76Pit 77-79NYG 79La		6'5"	251	Brigham Young		
Graves, Tom LB	79Pit		6'3"	228	Michigan State		
Gray, Dan DT	78Det 79JJ		6'6"	240	Rutgers		
Gray, David DB	79NO		6'	187	San Diego State	1	
Gray, Johnnie DB	75-83GB	3	5'11"	185	Fullerton State	22	6
Gray, Leon OT	73-78NE 79-81Hou 82-83NO		6'3"	257	Jackson State		
Gray, Mel WR	71-82StL 84USFL	23	5'9"	173	Missouri		276
Gray, Tim DB	75StL 76-78KC 79SF		6'1"	200	Texas A&M	13	12
Green, Arthur HB-FB	72NO		5'11"	198	Albany State (Ga.)		
Green, Dave K	73Hou 73-75Cin 76-78TB 79FJ	45	5'11"	206	Ohio U.		125
Green, Donnie OT	71-76Buf 77Phi 78Det		6'7"	266	Purdue		
Green, Jessie WR	76GB 79-80Sea		6'3"	191	Tulsa		6
Green, Joe DB	70-71NYG		5'11"	195	Bowling Green		6
Green, Sammy LB	76-79Sea 80Hou 83USFL		6'2"	230	Florida	3	6
Green, Tony HB	78Was 79NYG 79Sea	3	5'9"	185	Florida		18
Green, Van DB	73-76Cle 76Buf		6'1"	192	Shaw	3	12
Green, Woody HB	74-76KC 77KJ	2	6'1"	205	Arizona State		66
Greene, Joe (Mean Joe) DT	69-81Pit		6'4"	269	North Texas	1	
Greene, Tony DB	71-79Buf		5'10"	171	Maryland	37	14
Greenwood, L.C. DE	69-81Pit		6'5"	246	Ark.-Pine Bluff		2

UseName(Nickname)-Positions	Team by Year	See Section	Hgt.	Wgt.	College	Int	Pts
Greer, Charlie DB	66-69DenA 70-74Den	3	6'	205	Colorado	17	1
Gregory, Bill DT-DE	71-77Dal 78-80Sea		6'5"	256	Wisconsin	2	
Gregory, Jack DE	67-71Cle 72-78NYG 79Cle		6'6"	251	Tenn.-Chattanooga	1	
Gresham, Bob HB	71-72NO 73-74Hou 75-76NYJ	23	5'11"	196	West Virginia		84
Griese, Bob QB	67-69MiaA 70-80Mia	12	6'1"	190	Purdue		42
Griffin, Archie HB	76-82Cin 84USFL	2	5'9"	188	Ohio State		78
Griffin, Wade OT	77-81Bal 82ZJ		6'5"	260	Mississippi		
Griggs, Perry WR	77Bal		5'10"	182	Baylor		
Grim, Bob WR-DB	67-71Min 72-74NYG 75Chi 76-77Min	23	6'	196	Oregon State		96
Groce, Bob FB	76Min		6'2"	210	Macalester		
Gross, Lee C	75-77NO 79Bal		6'3"	237	Auburn		
Grossman, Randy TE	74-81Pit	2	6'1"	218	Temple		30
Gueno, Jim LB	76-80GB		6'2"	220	Tulane		
Gunn, Jimmy LB	70-75Chi 75NYG 76TB		6'1"	220	Southern Calif.	2	
Guthrie, Grant K	70-71Buf	5	6'	210	Florida State		71
Guy, Ray K	73-81Oak 82-86Raid	4	6'3"	195	Southern Miss.		1
Haden, Pat QB	76-81LA	12	5'11"	183	Southern Calif.		36
Hagen, Halvor OT-C-OG-DE	69-70Dal 71-72NE 73-75Buf		6'5"	252	Weber State		
Haggerty, Steve DB	75Den		5'10"	175	Nevada-Las Vegas		
Hagins, Isaac WR	76-80TB	23	5'9"	180	Southern U.		30
Hall, Charlie LB	71-80Cle		6'3"	228	Houston	13	12
Hall, Charlie DB	71-76GB		6'1"	193	Pittsburgh	2	
Hall, Randy DB	74Bal 75FJ 76Bal		6'3"	190	Idaho		
Hall, Willie LB	72-73NO 75-78Oak		6'2"	223	Southern Calif.	5	6
Hall, Windian DB	72-75SF 76-77Min 77Was		5'11"	176	Arizona State	2	12
Halverson, Dean LB	68LA 70Atl 71-72LA 73-75Phi 76JJ		6'2"	221	Washington	1	
Ham, Jack LB	71-82Pit		6'3"	224	Penn State	32	12
Hamilton, Andy WR	73-74KC 75NO	2	6'3"	190	Louisiana State		
Hamilton, Darrell OT	89Den		6'5"	298	North Carolina		
Hamilton, Ray (Sugar Bear) NT-DT-DE	73-81NE		6'1"	244	Oklahoma		6
Hamlin, Gene C	70Was 71Chi 72Det		6'3"	245	Western Michigan		
Hammond, Bob HB	76-79NYG 79-80Was	23	5'10"	171	Morgan State		48
Hammond, Gary WR-HB	73-76StL	3	5'11"	184	S.M.U.		
Hammond, Wayne DT	76Den		6'5"	255	Montana State		
Hampton, Dave HB-FB	69-71GB 72-76Atl 76Phi	23	6'	207	Wyoming		204
Hanburger, Chris LB	65-78Was		6'2"	218	North Carolina	19	30
Hancock, Mike TE	73-74Was 75JJ		6'4"	220	Idaho State		12
Hand, Larry DE-DT	65-77Det		6'5"	247	Appalachian State	5	18
Hannah, John OG	73-85NE		6'2"	265	Alabama		6
Hanneman, Craig DE-DT	72-73Pit 74-75NE 76JJ		6'3"	243	Oregon State		
Hanratty, Terry QB	69-75Pit 76TB	1	6'1"	206	Notre Dame		6
Hansen, Don LB	66-67Min 69-75Atl 76Sea 76-77GB		6'3"	227	Illinois	10	6
Hanson, Dick DT	71NYG		6'6"	280	N. Dakota State		
Hardaway, Milton OT	78SD 79KJ		6'9"	309	Oklahoma State		
Hardee, Billy DB	76Den 77NYJ 78-82CFL 84-85USFL		6'	185	Virginia Tech	1	
Hardeman, Buddy HB	78CFL 79-80Was 83USFL	2	6'	196	Iowa State		6
Hardeman, Don (Jaws) FB	75-77Hou 78-79Bal	2	6'2"	235	Texas A&I		78
Harden, Lee DB	70GB		5'11"	195	Texas El-Paso		
Hardman, Cedrick DE	70-79SF 80-81Oak 83USFL		6'3"	250	North Texas State		8
Hardy, Cliff DB	71Chi		6'	187	Michigan State		
Hardy, Ed OG	73SF 74JJ		6'4"	242	Jackson State		
Hardy, Kevin DT-DE	68SF 69DJ 70GB 71-72SD		6'5"	271	Notre Dame		
Hare, Eddie K	79NE	4	6'4"	209	Tulsa		
Hargett, Edd QB	69-72NO 73Hou 74-75WFL	1	5'11"	187	Texas A&M		6
Hargrove, Jim LB	67Min 68MS 69-70Min 71-72StL		6'3"	229	Howard Payne	1	6
Harky, Steve HB-FB	71-72NYJ	2	6'	215	Georgia Tech		
Harlan, Jim OT	78Was		6'4"	250	Howard Payne		
Harper, Roland FB-HB	75-78Chi 79KJ 80-82Chi	2	6'	208	Louisiana Tech		108
Harper, Willie LB	73-77SF 78KJ 79-83SF 84-85USFL		6'2"	214	Nebraska	3	
Harraway, Charlie FB	66-68Cle 69-73Was 74WFL	2	6'2"	221	San Jose State		162
Harrell, Rick C	73NYJ		6'3"	238	Clemson		
Harrell, Willard HB	75-77GB 78-84StL	23	5'9"	182	U. of Pacific		96
Harris, Bo LB	75-82Cin		6'3"	225	Louisiana State	7	6
Harris, Cliff DB	70-79Dal	3	6'	188	Ouachita Baptist	29	6
Harris, Don DB	78-80Was 80NYG 81CFL 83USFL		6'2"	185	Rutgers		
Harris, Franco FB-HB	72-83Pit 84Sea	2	6'2"	227	Penn State		600
Harris, Ike WR	75-77StL 78-81NO	2	6'3"	207	Iowa State		96
Harris, James QB	69BufA 70-71Buf 73-76LA 77-81SD	12	6'3"	215	Grambling		60
Harris, Jim DB	70Was 71Cin		5'11"	173	Howard Payne		
Harris, Joe LB	75-76CFL 77Was 78SF 79Min 79-81LA 82Bal 83USFL		6'1"	225	Georgia Tech	2	18
Harris, Larry OT	78Hou		6'3"	274	Oklahoma State		
Harris, Leroy FB	77-78Mia 79-80Phi 81BA 82Phi	2	5'9"	226	Arkansas State		84
Harris, Paul LB	77TB 78Min 78TB		6'3"	220	Alabama		
Harris, Richard DE-DT	71-73Phi 74-75Chi 76-77Sea	2	6'4"	258	Grambling		
Harris, Tony DB	71SF		6'2"	190	Toledo		
Harrison, Dwight DB-WR	71-72Den 72-77Buf	2	6'1"	183	Texas A&I	19	18
Harrison, Glynn FB	76KC		5'11"	190	Georgia		
Harrison, Jim FB	71-74Chi	2	6'4"	236	Missouri		42
Harrison, Kenny WR	76-78SF 80Was	2	6'	176	S.M.U.		6
Harrison, Reggie (Booby) FB	74StL 74-77Pit 78GB	2	5'11"	218	Cincinnati		48
Hart, Harold HB	74-75Oak 76JJ 77NYG 78Oak	23	6'	207	Texas Southern		42
Hart, Jeff OT	75SF 76NO 79-83Bal 84-85USFL		6'5"	266	Oregon State		
Hart, Jim QB	66-83StL 84Was	12	6'2"	206	Southern Illinois		96
Hart, Leo QB	71Atl 72Buf		6'4"	203	Duke		
Hart, Tommie DE-LB	68-77SF 78-79Chi 80NO		6'3"	244	Morris Brown	2	14
Hartle, Greg LB	74-76StL		6'2"	225	Newberry		
Hartwig, Keith WR	77Min 77GB		6'	186	Arizona		
Harvey, Claude LB	70Hou		6'4"	225	Prairie View		
Harvey, Richard DB	70Phi 71NO		6'2"	190	Jackson State		
Hasenhorl, George DT	74NYG		6'1"	260	Ohio State		
Haselrig, Clint HB-WR	74-75Buf 75Min 76NYJ		6'	191	Michigan		
Haslip, Wilbert FB	79KC 83USFL		5'11"	212	Hawaii		
Hauss, Len C	64-77Was		6'2"	234	Georgia		
Haverdick, Dave DT	70Det		6'4"	245	Morehead State		
Havig, Dennis OG	72-75Atl 76Hou 77GB		6'2"	253	Colorado		
Havrilak, Sam WR-HB-DB	69-73Bal 74NO	2	6'2"	195	Bucknell		42
Hawkins, Clarence HB	79Oak		6'	205	Florida A&M		6
Hawkins, Nate WR	75Hou		6'1"	190	Nevada-Las Vegas		
Hawkins, Robert HB	79StL		6'	195	Kentucky		
Hayden, Leo HB-FB	71Min 72-73StL		6'	211	Ohio State		6
Hayes, Billy DB	72NO		6'1"	175	San Diego State		
Hayes, Bob WR-OE	65-74Dal 75SF	23	6'	187	Florida A&M		456
Hayes, Ed DB	70Phi		6'1"	185	Morgan State	1	
Hayes, Tom DB	71-75Atl 76SD		6'1"	197	San Diego State	19	36
Hayhoe, Bill OT	69-73GB 74JJ 75BL		6'8"	258	Southern Calif.		
Hayman, Conway OG-OT	75-80Hou		6'3"	264	Delaware		
Hayman, Gary HB	74-75Buf	3	6'1"	200	Penn State		
Haynes, Reggie TE	78Was		6'2"	229	Nevada-Las Vegas		
Haywood, Al FB	75Den		5'11"	215	Bethune-Cookman		
Heater, Don HB	72StL		6'2"	205	Montana Tech		
Heath, Clayton HB	76Buf 76Mia		5'11"	195	Wake Forest		
Hedberg, Randy QB	77TB 78EJ	1	6'3"	200	Minot State		
Hefferle, Ernie	HC75NO				Duquesne		
Hefner, Larry LB	72-75GB		6'2"	226	Clemson	1	
Heinz, Bob DT-DE-NT	69MiaA 70-74Mia 75KJ 76-77Mia 78Was		6'6"	268	U. of Pacific		
Helms, Ken OT-C	77NYJ		6'4"	265	Georgia		
Helton, Darius OG	77KC 78SJ		6'2"	260	N. Carolina Central		
Hemphill, Darryl DB	82Bal 84-85USFL		6'	195	West Texas State		
Henderson, Tom (Hollywood) LB	75-79Dal 80SF 80Hou 81BQ		6'2"	221	Langston	4	14
Hendren, Jerry WR	70Den		6'2"	187	Idaho		
Hendricks, Ted (Mad Stork) LB	69-73Bal 74GB 75-81Oak 82-83Raid		6'7"	222	Miami (Fla.)	26	34
Hennessy, John LB-DE	77-78NYJ		6'3"	243	Michigan		
Hennigan, Mike LB	73-75Det 76-78NYJ 79KJ		6'2"	217	Tennessee Tech	3	
Henson, Champ FB	75Cin		6'3"	240	Ohio State		
Hepburn, Lonnie DB	71-72Bal 74Den		5'11"	182	Texas Southern	1	
Hermeling, Terry OT-OG-DE	70-73Was 74KJ 75-80Was		6'5"	255	Nevada-Reno		
Herosian, Brian DB	73Bal		6'3"	200	Connecticut		
Herrera, Efren K	74Dal 75JJ 76-77Dal 78-81Sea 82Buf 84USFL	5	5'9"	189	U.C.L.A.		604
Herrmann, Don WR	69-74NYG 75-77NO	2	6'2"	199	Waynesburg		96
Herron, Mack HB	73-75NE 75Atl	23	5'5"	174	Kansas State		96
Hertel, Rob QB	78Cin 80Phi		6'2"	195	Southern Calif.		
Hertwig, Craig OT	75-77Det 78Buf		6'8"	270	Georgia		
Hester, Ray LB	71-73NO		6'2"	215	Tulane		
Hews, Bob OT-DE	71Buf		6'5"	240	Princeton		
Hickman, Dallas DE-LB	76-80Was 81Bal 81Was		6'6"	238	California		
Hickman, Donnie OG	78Was 78Det		6'2"	260	Southern Calif.		
Hicks, Eddie FB-HB	79-80NYG		6'2"	210	East Carolina		
Hicks, John OG	74-77NYG		6'2"	258	Ohio State		
Hicks, R.W. C	75Det		6'4"	250	Humboldt State		
Hicks, Sylvester DE	78-81KC		6'4"	251	Tennessee State		
Hicks, Tom LB	76-80Chi		6'4"	233	Illinois	4	7
Higgins, Tom LB	79Buf		6'1"	235	N. Carolina State		
Highsmith, Don HB	70-72Oak 73GB 74-75WFL	2	6'	200	Michigan State		12
Hilgenberg, Wally LB-OG	64-66Det 67JJ 68-79Min		6'3"	230	Iowa	8	14
Hill, Barry DB	73-76Mia		6'3"	185	Iowa State		
Hill, Calvin HB-FB	69-74Dal 75WFL 76-77Was 78-81Cle	2	6'3"	228	Yale		390
Hill, Ike WR-DB	70-71Buf 73-74Chi 76Mia	23	5'10"	180	Catawba		30
Hill, J.D. WR	71-75Buf 76-77Det 78FJ	2	6'1"	190	Arizona State		126
Hill, Jim DB	69SD-A 70-71SD 72-74GB 75Cle		6'2"	192	Texas A&I	19	6
Hill, John C-OT	72-74NYG 75-84NO 85SF		6'2"	249	Lehigh		
Hill, Ralph C	76-77NYG		6'1"	245	Florida A&M		
Hilton, Roy DE	65-73Bal 74NYG 75Atl		6'6"	240	Jackson State	1	12
Hilton, Scott LB	79-80SF		6'4"	228	none		
Himes, Dick OT	68-77GB		6'4"	251	Ohio State		
Hinton, Eddie WR	69-72Bal 73Hou 74NE	2	6'	200	Oklahoma		72
Hoaglin, Fred C	66-72Cle 73Bal 74-75Hou 76Sea		6'4"	246	Pittsburgh		
Hoban, Mike OG	74Chi		6'2"	235	Michigan		
Hobbs, Bill LB	69-71Phi 72NO		6'	218	Texas A&M		6
Hodgins, Norm DB	74Chi 75JJ		6'1"	190	Louisiana State		
Hoey, George DB	71StL 72-73NE 74SD 75Den 75NYJ		5'10"	174	Michigan		
Hofer, Paul HB	76-81SF	23	6'	194	Mississippi		126
Hogan, Mike FB-HB	76-78Phi 79SF 80NYG 80Phi	2	6'2"	213	Tenn.-Chattanooga		48
Holden, Sam OT	71NO		6'3"	258	Grambling		
Holden, Steve WR	73-77Cle 77Cin	23	6'	195	Arizona State		24
Holland, John WR	74Min 75-77Buf 78KJ	2	6'	190	Tennessee State		24
Holland, Vern OT	71-79Cin 80Det 80NYG		6'5"	268	Tennessee State		
Hollas, Hugo DB	70-72NO 73KJ 74SF		6'1"	190	Rice	11	
Holliday, Ron WR	73SD 74-75WFL 76KJ	2	5'9"	168	Pittsburgh		1
Holloman, Gus DB	68-69DenA 70-74NYJ	4	6'3"	195	Houston		
Holloway, Glenn OG	70-73Chi 74Cle		6'3"	249	North Texas		
Hollway, Bob	HC71-72StL				Michigan		
Holman, Willie DE-DT	68-73Chi 73Was		6'4"	250	S. Carolina State		
Holmes, Ernie (Fats) DT-NT	72-77Pit 78NE		6'3"	260	Texas Southern		
Holmes, Mel OG-OT	71-73Pit		6'3"	250	N. Carolina A&T		
Holmes, Mike DB-WR	74-75SF 76Buf 76Mia 77-82CFL 83USFL	23	6'2"	195	Texas Southern	3	6
Holmes, Robert FB	68-69KC-A 70-71KC 71-72Hou 73SD 74WFL 75Hou	23	5'9"	220	Southern U.		162
Holmes, Rudy DB	74Atl		5'10"	178	Duke		
Holtz, Lou	HC76NYJ				Kent State		
Homan, Dennis WR	68-70Dal 71-72KC	2	6'1"	180	Alabama		2
Hooker, Fair WR	69-74Cle 75WFL	2	6'1"	198	Arizona State		48
Hooks, Jim FB	73-76Det	2	5'11"	225	Central St.-Ohio		
Hooks, Roland HB-FB	76-82Buf 83KJ	23	6'	196	N. Carolina State		90
Hoopes, Mitch K	75Dal 76SD 76Hou 77Det 78Phi 83USFL	4	6'1"	207	Arizona		
Hopkins, Andy HB	71Hou		5'10"	187	S.F. Austin State		
Horn, Don QB	67-70GB 71Den 72-73Cle 74SD	1	6'2"	195	San Diego State		6
Hornsby, Ron LB	71-74NYG		6'3"	231	Southeastern La.		
Horton, Greg OG-C	76-78LA 78-79TB 80LA 83-84USFL		6'4"	246	Colorado		
Horton, Larry DE-DT	72Chi		6'2"	248	Iowa		
Hoskins, Bob DT-OG	70-75SF 76IL		6'2"	246	Wichita State		
Hoss, Clark TE	72Phi		6'8"	235	Oregon State		
Houston, Bill WR	74Dal		6'3"	208	Jackson State		
Houston, Ken DB	67-69HouA 70-72Hou 73-80Was	3	6'3"	196	Prairie View	49	72
Houston, Rich WR	69-73NYG	23	6'2"	196	East Texas State		42
Hover, Don LB	78-79Was		6'2"	225	Washington State		6
Howard, Billy DE-DT	74-76Det		6'4"	252	Alcorn State		
Howard, Bob DB	67-69SD-A 70-74SD 75-77NE 78-79Phi		6'1"	181	San Diego State	37	6
Howard, Gene DB	68-70NO 71-72LA	3	6'	190	Langston	14	12
Howard, Harry DB	76NYJ		6'	189	Ohio State		
Howard, Leroy DB	71Hou		5'11"	175	Bishop		
Howard, Percy WR	75Dal 76-77JJ		6'4"	210	Austin Peay		
Howard, Ron TE	74-75Dal 76-78Sea 79Buf	2	6'4"	229	Seattle		12
Howell, Delles DB	70-72NO 73-75NYJ 77JJ		6'3"	199	Grambling	17	
Howfield, Bobby K	68-69DenA 70Den 71-74NYJ	5	5'9"	180	none		487
Hrivnak, Gary DE	73-75Chi 76JJ		6'5"	252	Purdue		
Hubbard, Dave OT	77NO		6'7"	270	Brigham Young		
Hubbard, Marv FB	69OakA 70-75Oak 76SJ 77Det	2	6'1"	224	Colgate		144
Huddleston, John LB	78-79Oak		6'3"	230	Utah		
Hudson, Bob HB	72GB 73-74Oak	3	5'11"	207	Northeast La.		
Huff, Gary QB	73-76Chi 77-78TB 80SF 85USFL	12	6'1"	197	Florida State		12
Huff, Marty LB	72SF		6'2"	234	Michigan		

UseName(Nickname)-Positions	TeambyYear	See Section	Hgt.	Wgt.	College	Int	Pts
Hufnagel, John QB	74-75Den	1	6'1"	194	Penn State		
Hughes, Dennis TE	70-71Pit	2	6'1"	220	Georgia		18
Hughes, Pat LB-C	70-76NYG 77-79NO		6'2"	231	Boston U.	15	
Hughes, Randy DB	75-80Dal 81SJ		6'4"	207	Oklahoma	9	6
Hull, Mike FB-TE	68-70Chi 71-74Was	2	6'3"	220	Southern Calif.		6
Hull, Tom LB	74SF 75GB		6'3"	230	Penn State		
Humm, David QB	75-79Oak 80Buf 81-82Bal 83-84Raid	1	6'2"	188	Nebraska		
Humphrey, Claude DE	68-78Atl 79-81Phi		6'5"	258	Tennessee State	2	10
Humphrey, Tom C	74KC		6'6"	260	Abilene Christian		
Hunt, Calvin C	71Phi 72-73Hou		6'3"	244	Baylor		
Hunt, Charlie LB	73SF 75WFL 76TB		6'2"	215	Florida State		
Hunt, Ervin DB	70GB		6'2"	190	Fresno State		
Hunt, George K	73Bal 75NYG	5	6'1"	215	Tennessee		112
Hunt, Kevin OT-OG	72GB 73NE 73-77Hou 78NO		6'5"	260	Doane		
Hunt, Mike LB	78-80GB		6'2"	240	Minnesota	2	
Hunt, Ron OT	76-78Cin		6'6"	261	Oregon		
Hunt, Sam LB	74-80NE		6'1"	248	S.F. Austin State	7	6
Hunter, Al HB	77-80Sea	23	5'11"	195	Notre Dame		24
Hunter, James DB	76-82Det		6'3"	195	Grambling	27	6
Hunter, Scott QB	71-73GB 74Buf 76-78Atl 79Det	12	6'2"	205	Alabama		78
Hutcherson, Ken LB	74Dal 75SD 76JJ		6'1"	219	Livingston		
Hutchinson, Chuck OG	70-72StL 73-75Cle 76KJ		6'3"	242	Ohio State		
Hyatt, Freddie WR	68-72StL 73NO		6'3"	203	Auburn		
Hyland, Bob C-OG-OT	67-69GB 70Chi 71-75NYG 76GB 77NE		6'5"	253	Boston College		
Hynoski, Henry FB	75Cle		6'	210	Temple		
Iremia, Mekell DT	78Buf 79-80KJ		6'2"	244	Brigham Young		
Ilgenfritz, Mark OT-OG-C	74Cle 75WFL		6'4"	250	Vanderbilt		
Imhof, Martin DE-DT	72StL 74Was 75NE 76Den		6'6"	256	San Diego State		
Inmon, Earl LB	78TB		6'1"	215	Bethune-Cookman		
Irons, Gerald LB	70-75Oak 76-79Cle		6'2"	231	Md. Eastern Shore	13	6
Isenbarger, John HB-WR	70-73SF 74WFL	2	6'3"	203	Indiana		12
Ivory, Horace HB	77-81NE 81-82Sea	23	6'	198	Oklahoma		108
Iwanowski, Mark TE	78NYJ		6'4"	230	Pennsylvania		
Jackson, Bernard DB	72-76Cin 77-80Den 80SD	3	6'	178	Washington State	17	
Jackson, Bob OG-OT-C	75-81Cle		6'5"	253	Duke		
Jackson, Ernie DB	72-77NO 78Atl 79Det		5'10"	175	Duke	15	6
Jackson, Gerald DB	79KC		6'1"	195	Mississippi State	1	
Jackson, Harold WR	68LA 69-72Phi 73-77LA 78-81NE 82Min 83Sea	2	5'10"	175	Jackson State		456
Jackson, Honor DB	72-73NE 73-74NYG		6'1"	195	Pacific	5	
Jackson, Jazz HB	74-76NYJ	2	5'8"	169	Western Kentucky		12
Jackson, Joey DE-DT	72-73NYJ 74-75WFL 77Min		6'4"	263	New Mexico State		
Jackson, Johnny NT	77Phi		6'2"	250	Southern U.		
Jackson, Larron OG-OT	71-74Den 75-76Atl		6'3"	265	Missouri		
Jackson, Melvin OG	76-80GB		6'1"	267	Southern Calif.		
Jackson, Monte DB	75-77LA 78-81Oak 82Raid 83LA		5'11"	193	San Diego State	23	24
Jackson, Noah OG	75-83Chi 84TB		6'2"	267	Tampa		
Jackson, Randy OT	67-74Chi		6'5"	247	Florida		
Jackson, Randy HB-FB	72Buf 73SF 74Phi	2	6'	220	Wichita State		6
Jackson, Rusty K	76LA 78-79Buf	4	6'2"	193	Louisiana State		
Jackson, Steve DB	77Oak		6'1"	192	Louisiana State	1	
Jackson, Tom LB	73-86Den		5'11"	221	Louisville	20	18
Jackson, Wilbur FB-HB	74-77SF 78KJ 79SF 80-82Was	2	6'1"	217	Alabama		102
Jacobsen, Larry DT-DE	72-74NYG 75BN		6'6"	260	Nebraska		
Jakowenko, George K	74Oak 76Buf	5	5'9"	175	Syracuse		57
James, John K	72-81Atl 82Det 82-84Hou	4	6'3"	198	Florida		
James, Po HB	72-75Phi	23	6'1"	202	New Mexico State		36
James, Robert DB-WR	69BufA 70-74Buf 75-76KJ		6'1"	182	Fisk	9	6
Jameson, Larry DT	76TB		6'7"	270	Indiana		
Janet, Ernie OG	72-74Chi 75GB 75Phi 76GJ		6'4"	253	Washington		
Jankowski, Bruce WR	71-72KC		5'11"	185	Ohio State		
Jaqua, Jon DB	70-72Was 73JJ		6'	190	Lewis and Clark	1	
Jarvis, Bruce C	71-74Buf		6'7"	248	Washington		
Jarvis, David QB	74KC		6'2"	212	Kansas		
Jarvis, Ray WR	71-72Atl 73Buf 74-78Det 79NE	2	6'1"	192	Norfolk State		66
Jauron, Dick DB	73-77Det 78-80Cin 81KJ	3	6'	189	Yale	25	12
Jefferson, Charles DB	79-80Hou		6'	178	McNeese State		
Jefferson, Roy WR-FL-OE	65-69Pit 70Bal 71-76Was	23	6'2"	194	Utah		318
Jeffrey, Neal QB	76-77SD		6'1"	180	Baylor		
Jenkins, Al OG-OT-DE-DT	69-70Cle 72Mia 73Hou		6'2"	250	Tulsa		
Jenkins, Alfred WR	75-83Atl	2	5'10"	170	Morris Brown		240
Jenkins, Ed HB	72Mia 73JJ 74NYG 74Buf 74NE		6'2"	210	Holy Cross		
Jenkins, Leon DB	72Det		5'11"	165	West Virginia		
Jennings, Rick HB-WR	76Oak 77TB 77SF 77Oak		5'9"	180	Maryland		
Jensen, Jim FB-TE	76Dal 77Den 78KJ 79-80Den 81-82GB	2	6'3"	232	Iowa		42
Jerome, Jim LB	77NYJ		6'4"	225	Syracuse		
Jessie, Ron WR	71-74Det 75-79LA 80-81Buf	23	6'	183	Kansas		182
Jiggetts, Dan OT-OG	76-82Chi 84USFL		6'4"	272	Harvard		
Jilek, Dan LB	76-79Buf		6'2"	220	Michigan	2	
Jiles, Dwayne LB	85-89Phi 89NYG		6'4"	242	Texas Tech		
Joachim, Steve QB	76NYJ		6'3"	215	Temple		
Johannson, Ove K	77Phi		5'10"	175	Abilene Christian		4
Johns, Freeman WR	76-77LA		6'1"	175	S.M.U.		
Johnson, Al DB-HB	72-74Hou 75NJ 76-78Hou		6'	200	Cincinnati		
Johnson, Andy HB	74-76NE 77KJ 78-81NE 83USFL	23	6'	204	Georgia		132
Johnson, Benny DB	70-73Hou 74WFL 76NO	3	5'11"	178	Johnson C. Smith	1	
Johnson, Bill K	70NYG	4	6'4"	208	Livingston		
Johnson, Bob C	68-69CinA 70-79Cin		6'5"	257	Tennessee		
Johnson, Carl OT-OG	72-73NO		6'3"	248	Nebraska		
Johnson, Cornelius OG	68-73Bal		6'2"	245	Virginia Union		
Johnson, Danny LB	78GB		6'1"	216	Tennessee State		
Johnson, Dennis DT-DE	74-77Was 78Buf		6'4"	261	Delaware	2	
Johnson, Dennis FB-TE	78-79Buf 80NYG 83-85USFL	2	6'3"	220	Mississippi State		12
Johnson, Eric DB	74-75WFL 77-78Phi 79SF 83-84USFL		6'1"	192	Washington State		
Johnson, Essex HB	66-69CinA 70-75Cin 76TB	23	5'9"	197	Grambling		186
Johnson, Greg DT-NT-DE	77Bal 77Chi 77TB		6'4"	240	Florida State	1	6
Johnson, Ken DE-DT	71-77Cin		6'5"	261	Indiana		
Johnson, Ken QB	74WFL 77Buf 78-82CFL 83-84USFL		6'2"	205	Colorado		
Johnson, Ken FB	79NYG 83USFL		6'2"	220	Miami (Fla.)		6
Johnson, Kermit HB	75-76SF	2	6'	201	U.C.L.A.		6
Johnson, Len C-OG	70NYG		6'2"	250	St. Cloud State		
Johnson, Levi DB	73-77Det 78FJ		6'3"	196	Texas A&I	21	30
Johnson, Mark DE-LB	75-76Buf 77Cle		6'2"	239	Missouri		
Johnson, Marshall WR-HB	75Bal 76KJ 77-78Bal	3	6'1"	192	Houston		12
Johnson, Monte LB	73-79Oak 80KJ		6'4"	239	Nebraska	10	6
Johnson, Randy QB	66-70Atl 71-73NYG 74WFL 75Was 76GB	12	6'3"	202	Texas A&I		60
Johnson, Randy OG	77-78TB 79JJ		6'2"	255	Georgia		
Johnson, Ron HB	69Cle 70-75NYG	2	6'1"	205	Michigan		330
Johnson, Sammy FB-HB	74-76SF 76-78Min 79Phi 79GB	2	6'	224	North Carolina		54
Johnson, Stan NT	78KC		6'4"	275	Tennessee State		
Johnson, Walter DT	65-76Cle 77Cin		6'3"	268	Los Angeles State	2	14
Joiner, Charlie WR	69HouA 70-72Hou 72-75Cin 76-86SD	2	5'11"	184	Grambling		390
Jolitz, Evan LB	74Cin		6'2"	225	Cincinnati		
Jolley, Gordon OT-OG	72-75Det 76-77Sea		6'5"	244	Utah		
Jolley, Lexis HB-FB	72-73Hou		6'	210	North Carolina		
Jones, Andrew FB	75-76NO	2	6'2"	216	Washington State		6
Jones, Bert QB	73-81Bal 82LA	12	6'3"	210	Louisiana State		84
Jones, Bob WR	73-74Cin 75-76Atl		6'1"	194	Virginia Union		
Jones, Calvin DB	73-76Den		5'7"	170	Washington	12	6
Jones, Clint HB	67-72Min 73SD 74JJ	23	6'	206	Michigan State		126
Jones, Cody DT-DE-NT	74-78LA 79FJ 80-82LA		6'5"	243	San Jose State		
Jones, Dave WR	69-71Cle		6'2"	185	Kansas State		
Jones, Doug DB	73-74KC 75KJ 76-78Buf 79Det		6'2"	204	Northridge State	6	
Jones, Ed DB	75Buf		6'	185	Rutgers	3	
Jones, Ernie DB	76Sea 77-79NYG		6'3"	180	Miami (Fla.)	6	6
Jones, Greg HB	70-71Buf	2	6'1"	200	U.C.L.A.		18
Jones, Harris OG-C	71SD 72JJ 73-74Hou		6'4"	241	Johnson C. Smith		
Jones, Horace DE	71-75Oak 76KJ 77Sea		6'3"	251	Louisville		
Jones, Jimmie DE	69NY-A 70NYJ 71-73Was		6'3"	215	Wichita State		
Jones, Jimmie HB-FB	74Det	23	5'10"	205	U.C.L.A.		6
Jones, Joe (Turkey) DE	70-71Cle 72KJ 73Cle 74-75Phi 75-78Cle 79-80Was		6'6"	249	Tennessee State		6
Jones, John QB	75NYJ	1	6'1"	180	Fisk		
Jones, June QB	77-79Atl 80NJ 81Atl	1	6'4"	200	Portland State		
Jones, Kim FB	76-79NO	2	6'4"	238	Colorado State		
Jones, Larry WR-DB	74-77Was 78SF	3	5'10"	170	NE Missouri St.		12
Jones, Leroy DE	76-83SD		6'8"	263	Norfolk State	2	6
Jones, Mike LB	77Sea		6'2"	214	Jackson State		
Jones, Ray DB	70Phi 71Mia 72SD		6'	187	Southern U.	2	
Jones, Spike K	70Hou 71-74Buf 75-77Phi	4	6'2"	191	Georgia		
Jones, Steve HB	73-74Buf 74-78StL	2	6'	199	Duke		102
Jordan, Bob DT	77Atl		6'6"	255	Memphis State		
Jordan, Jeff HB-FB	70LA 71-72Was		6'1"	215	Washington		
Joyce, Terry K-TE	76-77StL	4	6'6"	229	Missouri Southern		
Juenger, Dave WR	73Chi		6'1"	195	Ohio U.		
Jurich, Tom K	78NO		5'10"	185	Northern Arizona		2
Jury, Bob DB	78SF 79SJ		6'1"	188	Pittsburgh		
Kaczmarek, Mike LB	73Bal		6'4"	235	Southern Illinois		
Kadish, Mike DT-NT	73-81Buf		6'5"	270	Notre Dame		8
Kadziel, Ron LB	72NE		6'4"	230	Stanford		
Kalina, Dave WR	70Pit		6'3"	205	Miami (Fla.)		
Kaminski, Larry C	68-69DenA 70-73Den		6'2"	244	Purdue		
Kampa, Bob DT	73-74Buf		6'4"	249	California		
Kay, Rick LB	73LA 74KJ 75-77LA 77Atl		6'4"	235	Colorado	1	
Kearney, Jim DB	65-66Det 67-69KC-A 70-75KC 76NO		6'2"	204	Prairie View	23	30
Kearney, Tim LB	72-74Cin 75KC 76TB 76-81StL		6'2"	225	Northern Michigan	3	
Keating, Tom DT	64-65BufA 66-67OakA 68FJ 69OakA 70-72Oak 73Pit 74-75KC		6'3"	246	Michigan		
Keeton, Durwood DB	75NE		5'10"	180	Oklahoma		
Keithly, Gary QB	73, 75StL	1 4	6'3"	210	Texas-El Paso		
Kelcher, Louie DT-NT	75-83SD 84SF		6'5"	290	S.M.U.	2	
Kellar, Mark FB	76-78Min	2	6'	225	Northern Illinois		
Keller, Larry LB	76-78NYJ 79KJ		6'2"	223	Houston	3	
Keller, Mike LB	72-73Dal		6'4"	220	Michigan		
Kelley, Brian LB	73-83NYG		6'3"	222	Cal. Lutheran	15	
Kellum, Marv TE	74-76Pit 77StL		6'2"	225	Wichita State	2	
Kelly, Jim TE	74Chi		6'4"	210	Tennessee State		
Kelly, Mike TE	70-72Cin 73NO		6'4"	217	Davidson		
Kendrick, Vince FB	74Atl 75KJ 76TB	2	6'	231	Florida		6
Kennedy, Jimmie TE	75-77Bal		6'5"	231	Colorado State		6
Kern, Rex DB	71-73Bal 74Buf		5'11"	190	Ohio State	2	
Kersey, Merritt HB-K	74-75Phi	4	6'1"	205	West Chester		
Key, Wade OG-OT	70-79Phi		6'4"	245	SW Texas State		
Keyes, Leroy HB-DB	69-72Phi 73KC	2	6'3"	208	Purdue	8	18
Keyworth, Jon FB	74-80Den	2	6'3"	231	Colorado		150
Kiick, Jim HB	68-69MiaA 70-74Mia 75WFL 76-77Den 77Was	2	5'11"	215	Wyoming		198
Killan, Gene OG	74Dal		6'4"	250	Tennessee		
Kilmer, Billy QB	61-62SF 63BL 64, 66SF 67-70NO 71-78Was	12	6'	201	U.C.L.A.		132
Kimball, Bobby WR	79-80GB		6'1"	190	Oklahoma		
Kimbrough, John WR	77Buf	2	5'10"	165	St. Cloud State		18
Kindle, Greg OT-OG	74-75StL 76-77Atl		6'4"	265	Tennessee State		
Kiner, Steve LB	70Dal 71, 73NE 74-78Hou		6'	221	Tennessee	10	2
King, Horace FB-HB	75-83Det	2	5'10"	208	Georgia		84
King, Keith LB-DB	78-81SD		6'4"	229	Colorado State	4	
King, Steve LB	73-81NE		6'4"	232	Tulsa	1	
Kingrea, Rick LB	71-72Cle 73-78NO		6'1"	228	Tulane	1	
Kingsriter, Doug TE	73-75Min		6'2"	222	Minnesota		
Kinney, Jeff HB-FB	72-76KC 76Buf	2	6'2"	215	Nebraska		36
Kinney, Steve OT	73-74Chi		6'5"	257	Utah State		
Kinney, Vince WR	78-79Den 83USFL		6'2"	190	Maryland		
Kirk, Ernest DE	77Hou		6'2"	265	Howard Payne	1	
Kirkland, Mike QB	76-78Bal	1	6'1"	195	Arkansas		
Kirnsey, Roy OG-OT	71-72NYJ 73-74Phi		6'1"	235	Md. Eastern Shore		
Klein, Bob TE	69-76LA 77-79SD	2	6'5"	237	Southern Calif.		138
Knief, Gayle WR	70Bos		6'3"	205	Morningside		6
Knight, Curt K	69-73Was	5	6'1"	190	Coast Guard		475
Knight, David WR	73-77NYJ	2	6'1"	177	William & Mary		42
Knoff, Kurt DB	77-78Hou 79-82Min		6'2"	191	Kansas	10	6
Knox, Bill DB	74-76Chi		5'9"	192	Purdue	2	
Knutson, Steve OG-OT	76-77GB 78SF 79KJ		6'3"	254	Southern Calif.		
Koegel, Vic LB	75Cin		6'	215	Ohio State		
Koegel, Warren C	71Oak 72JJ 73Cin 74NYJ		6'3"	253	Penn State		
Kolb, Jon OT-C	69-81Pit		6'2"	256	Oklahoma State		
Kolen, Mike LB	70-75Mia 76KJ 77Mia		6'2"	220	Auburn	5	
Kollar, Bill DE-DT-NT	74-76Cin 77-81TB		6'4"	253	Montana State		
Koncar, Mike OT	76-77GB 78KJ 79-81GB 82Hou		6'5"	269	Colorado		
Korver, Kelvin DT	73-75Oak 76-77KJ		6'6"	267	Northwestern	1	
Kosins, Gary HB-FB	72-74Chi	2	6'1"	216	Dayton		12
Kotar, Doug HB	74-79NYG 80KJ 81NYG	23	5'11"	205	Kentucky		26
Kowalkowski, Bob OG	66-76Det 77GB		6'3"	243	Virginia		
Koy, Ted LB-TE-HB-FB	70Oak 71-74Buf	2	6'1"	211	Texas		6
Kraayeveld, Dave DE-DT	78Sea		6'5"	255	Milton, Wisconsin		

UseName(Nickname)-Positions	TeambyYear	See Section	Hgt.	Wgt.	College	Int	Pts
Krahl, Jim DT	78NYG 79-80Bal 80SF		6'5"	252	Texas Tech		
Krakau, Merv LB	73-78Buf 78NE 83USFL		6'2"	237	Iowa State	3	
Kramer, Kent TE	66SF 67NO 69-70Min 71-74Phi	2	6'5"	234	Minnesota		48
Kratzer, Don WR	73KC		6'3"	194	Missouri Valley		
Krause, Larry HB	70-71GB 72JJ 73-74GB 75SU	3	6'	208	St. Norbert		6
Krause, Paul DB-FL	64-67Was 68-79Min		6'3"	199	Iowa	81	42
Krepfle, Keith TE	75-81Phi 82Atl	2	6'3"	227	Iowa State		114
Krevis, Al OT	75Cin 76NYJ		6'5"	263	Boston College		
Krieg, Jim WR	72Den		5'9"	172	Washinton		
Kroll, Bob DB	72GB 73JJ		6'1"	195	Northern Michigan		
Kruczek, Mike QB	76-79Pit 80Was	12	6'1"	202	Boston College		12
Krueger, Rolf DE-DT	69-72StL 72-74SF		6'4"	251	Texas A&M		
Kuechenberg, Bob OG-OT-C	70-83Mia 84JJ		6'3"	253	Notre Dame		
Kunz, George OT	69-74Atl 75-78Bal 79VR 80Bal		6'5"	260	Notre Dame		
Kunz, Terry FB	76Oak 77JJ		6'1"	215	Colorado		
Kupp, Jake OG	64-65Dal 66Was 67Atl 67-75NO		6'3"	240	Washington		
Kurnick, Howie LB	79Cin 80KJ		6'2"	219	Cincinnati		6
Kuziel, Bob C-OT	72NO 74WFL 75-80Was		6'5"	255	Pittsburgh		
Kwalick, Ted TE-WR	69-74SF 75WFL 75-77Oak	2	6'4"	226	Penn State		138
Kyle, Aaron DB	76-79Dal 80-82Den		5'11"	185	Wyoming	11	2
Laaveg, Paul OG	70-75Was 76KJ		6'4"	247	Iowa		
LaCrosse, Dave LB	77Pit		6'3"	210	Wake Forest		
LaGrand, Morris FB	75KC 75NO		6'1"	220	Tampa		6
LaHood, Mike OG	69LA 70StL 71-72LA		6'3"	250	Wyoming		
Laidlaw, Scott FB	75-79Dal 80NYG	2	6'	205	Stanford		72
Laird, Bruce DB	72-81Bal 82-83SD 84-85USFL	3	6'	193	American Inter.	19	2
Lally, Bob LB	76GB		6'2"	230	Cornell		
Lamb, Ron LB	68DenA 68-69CinA 71-72Cin 72Atl	2	6'2"	227	South Carolina		
Lambert, Jack LB	74-84Pit		6'4"	220	Kent State	28	
Landers, Walt FB	78-79GB		6'	214	Clark-Ga.		12
Landry, Greg QB	68-78Det 79-81Bal 83-84USFL 84Chi	12	6'4"	207	Massachusetts		132
Lane, MacArthur HB-FB	68-71StL 72-74GB 75-78KC	2	6'	220	Utah State		222
Langer, Jim C-OG	70-79Mia 80-81Min		6'2"	251	S. Dakota State		
Lanier, Willie LB	67-69KC-A 70-77KC		6'1"	245	Morgan State	27	14
Lapham, Dave OG-OT-C	74-83Cin 84-85USFL		6'4"	259	Syracuse		
LaPorta, Phil OT	74-75NO		6'4"	256	Penn State		
Larson, Bill TE	75SF 77Was 77Det 78Phi 80Den 80-81GB		6'4"	224	Colorado State		6
Larson, Lynn OT	71Bal		6'4"	254	Kansas State		
Lash, Jim WR	73-76Min 76-77SF	2	6'2"	200	Northwestern	1	24
Laskey, Bill LB	65BufA 66-67OakA 68FJ 69OakA 70Oak 71-72Bal 73-74Den		6'2"	237	Michigan	7	
Laslavic, Jim LB	73-77Det 78SD 79KJ 80-81SD 82GB		6'2"	237	Penn State	8	
Laster, Art OT	70Buf		6'4"	280	Md. Eastern Shore		
Latimer, Don NT	78-83Den 84USFL		6'3"	259	Miami (Fla.)	1	6
Latin, Jerry HB	75-78StL 78LA	23	5'10"	188	Northern Illinois		24
Latta, Greg TE	75-80Chi	2	6'3"	227	Morgan State		42
Lavender, Joe (Big Bird) DB	73-75Phi 76-82Was		6'4"	189	San Diego State	33	24
Law, Dennis WR	78Cin 79Was	3	6'1"	179	East Tennessee St.		
Lawless, Burton OG	75-79Dal 80Det 80Mia		6'4"	252	Florida		
Lawrence, Larry QB	74-75Oak 76TB	1	6'1"	208	Iowa		
Lawrence, Rolland DB	73-80Atl 81LJ	3	5'10"	179	Tabor	39	12
Lawson, Odell FB-HB	70Bos 71NE 73-74NO	23	6'2"	212	Langston		
Lawson, Roger HB-FB	72-73Chi	2	6'2"	215	Western Michigan		
Lawson, Steve OG	71-72Cin 73-75Min 76-77SF		6'3"	264	Kansas		
Lazetich, Pete DE-DT-NT-LB	72-74SD 76-77Phi		6'3"	241	Stanford		
Leahy, Bob QB	71Pit		6'2"	205	Emporia		
Leak, Curtis, WR	76TB		5'11"	180	Johnson C. Smith		
Leaks, Roosevelt FB	75-79Bal 80-83Buf	2	5'10"	225	Texas		192
Leavitt, Allan K	77Atl 77TB	5	5'11"	176	Georgia		20
Leavitt, Dick OT	76NYG 77KJ		6'3"	285	Bowdoin		
LeClair, Jim LB	72-83Cin 84-85USFL		6'3"	234	North Dakota	10	6
Lee, Bivian DB	71-75NO		6'3"	200	Prairie View	9	
Lee, Bob QB	69-72Min 73-74Atl 75-78Min 79-80LA	12 4	6'2"	195	U. of Pacific		18
Lee, David K	66-78Bal	4	6'4"	223	Louisiana Tech		
Lee, John DE	76-80SD 81NE 83-84USFL		6'2"	255	Nebraska		
Lee, Ken LB	71Det 72Buf		6'4"	231	Washington	6	6
Lee, Mike LB	74SD		6'	232	Nevada-Las Vegas		
Lee, Ron FB	76-78Bal 79XJ	2	6'4"	226	West Virginia		36
Lee, Willie DT	76-77KC 78KJ		6'5"	249	Bethune-Cookman		6
LeFear, Billy HB-WR	72-75Cle 76JJ	23	5'11"	197	Henderson State		
Leigh, Charlie FB-HB	68-69Cle 71-74Mia 74GB	23	5'11"	203	none		12
LeMaster, Frank LB	74-82Phi 83SJ		6'2"	232	Kentucky	10	18
Lemon, Mike LB	75NO 75Den 76-77TB		6'2"	218	Kansas		
Lenkaitis, Bill C-OG	68-69SD-A 70SD 71-81NE		6'3"	255	Penn State		
Lens, Greg DT	70-71Atl		6'5"	260	Trinity (Texas)		
Leonard, Cecil DB	69NY-A 70NYJ		5'11"	165	Tuskegee		
Leonard, Tony DB	76-78SF 78-79Det	3	5'11"	169	Virginia Union	5	12
LeVeck, Jack LB	73-74StL 75Cle		6'	224	Ohio U.		
Levenseller, Mike WR	78Buf 78TB 79-80Cin		6'1"	181	Washington State		
LeVias, Jerry WR	69HouA 70Hou 71-74SD	23	5'10"	177	S.M.U.		84
Lewis, Dave QB-K	70-73Cin	4	6'2"	216	Stanford		
Lewis, D.D. LB	68Dal 69MS 70-81Dal		6'2"	218	Mississippi State	8	6
Lewis, Eddie DB	76-79SF 79-80Det		6'	175	Kansas	3	
Lewis, Frank WR	71-77Pit 78-83Buf	2	6'1"	196	Grambling		246
Lewis, Jess LB	70Hou		6'1"	230	Oregon State		
Lewis, Mike DT-DE-NT	71-79Atl 80GB		6'3"	255	Ark.-Pine Bluff	1	4
Lewis, Rich LB	72Hou 73-74Buf 75NYJ		6'3"	217	Portland State		
Lewis, Scott DE	71Hou		6'6"	260	Grambling		
Lewis, Stan DE	75Cle		6'4"	240	Wayne State-Neb.		
Leypoldt, John K	71-76Buf 76-78Sea 78NO	5	6'2"	229	none		482
Liggett, Bob DT	70KC		6'2"	255	Nebraska		
Line, Bill DT	72Chi		6'7"	260	S.M.U.		
Lingenfelter, Bob OT-OG	77Cle 78Min		6'7"	277	Nebraska		
Linhart, Toni K	72NO 74-79Bal 79NYJ	5	6'	178	none		425
Little, Everett OG	76TB 77Oak		6'4"	265	Houston		
Little, Floyd HB	67-69Den-A 70-75Den	23	5'10"	196	Syracuse		324
Little, John DT-DE-NT	70-74NYJ 75-76Hou 77Buf		6'3"	241	Oklahoma State		
Little, Larry OG-OT-DT	67-68SD 69MiaA 70-80Mia		6'1"	266	Bethune-Cookman		
Little, Steve K	78-80StL	45	6'	180	Arkansas		80
Livers, Virgil DB	75-79Chi 80KJ 83-84USFL	3	5'9"	178	Western Kentucky	12	12
Livingston, Mike QB	68-69KC-A 70-79KC 80Min 83USFL	12	6'3"	211	S.M.U.		48
Lloyd, Dan LB	76-79NYG 80-81IL 83USFL		6'2"	225	Washington	2	
Lloyd, Jeff DE-NT	76Buf 78KC		6'6"	255	West Texas State		
Lockhart, Carl (Spider) DB	65-75NYG	3	6'2"	176	North Texas	41	18
Logan, Randy DB	73-83Phi		6'1"	195	Michigan	23	
Lohmeyer, John DE-DT	73KC 74JJ 75-77KC		6'4"	230	Kansas State		10
Lomas, Mark DE-DT	70-74NYJ 75FJ 76KJ		6'4"	241	Northern Arizona		
London, Tom DB	78Cle		6'1"	197	N. Carolina State		

UseName(Nickname)-Positions	TeambyYear	See Section	Hgt.	Wgt.	College	Int	Pts
Long, Carson K	77Buf	5	5'10"	210	Pittsburgh		34
Long, Doug LB	77-78Sea		6'	189	Whitworth		
Long, Ken OG	76Det 77JJ		6'3"	265	Purdue		
Long, Kevin FB-HB	77-81NYJ 83-84USFL	2	6'1"	212	South Carolina		168
Long, Mel LB	72-74Cle		6'	228	Toledo		
Longley, Clint QB	74-75Dal 76SD	1	6'1"	194	Abilene Christian		
Longo, Tom DB	69-70NYG 71StL		6'1"	199	Notre Dame		
Lorch, Karl DE-DT	76-81Was 83-85USFL		6'3"	258	Southern Calif.	1	6
Lott, Thomas HB	79StL 83USFL		5'11"	205	Oklahoma		
Lou, Ron C	73Hou 74JJ 75Phi 76Hou		6'2"	240	Arizona State		
Love, Walt WR	73NYG		5'9"	180	Westminister (Pa.)		
Luce, Derrel LB	75-78Bal 79-80Min 80Det		6'3"	226	Baylor	3	12
Luck, Terry QB	77Cle	1	6'3"	205	Nebraska		6
Lueck, Bill OG	68-74GB 75Phi		6'3"	239	Arizona		
Luke, Steve DB	75-80GB		6'2"	205	Ohio State	10	6
Luken, Tom OG	72-75Phi 76KJ 77-78Phi		6'3"	253	Purdue		
Lumpkin, Ron DB	73NYG		6'2"	200	Arizona State		
Lunsford, Mel DE-DT-NT	73-80NE 83USFL		6'3"	256	Central St-Ohio		
Lurtsema, Bob DE-DT	67-71NYG 72-76Min 76-77Sea		6'6"	250	Western Michigan	1	
Lusby, Vaughn DB	79Cin 80Chi	3	5'10"	180	Arkansas		
Lusk, Herb HB	76-78Phi	2	6'	190	Long Beach State		18
Lyle, Garry DB-HB	68-74Chi		6'2"	197	George Washington	12	
Lyman, Jeff LB	72Buf		6'2"	230	Brigham Young		
Lynch, Fran HB-FB	67-69DenA 70-75Den 76KJ	2	6'1"	203	Hofstra		86
Lynch, Jim LB	67-69KC-A 70-77KC		6'1"	232	Notre Dame	17	6
Lyons, Dicky DB	70NO		6'	190	Kentucky	1	
Lyons, Tommy OG-C	71-76Den		6'2"	229	Georgia		
Mabra, Ron DB	75-76Atl 77NYJ		5'10"	166	Howard		
MacAfee, Ken TE	78-79SF	2	6'5"	248	Notre Dame		30
Mack, Tom OG	66-78LA		6'3"	249	Michigan		
MacLeod, Tom LB	73GB 74-75Bal 76FJ 77-78Bal		6'3"	225	Minnesota	5	
Madden, John	HC69OakA HC70-78Oak				Cal. Poly.-S.L.O.		
Maddox, Bob DE-DT	74Cin 75-77KC		6'5"	237	Frostburg State		6
Mahalic, Drew LB	75SD 76-78Phi		6'4"	226	Notre Dame	2	
Maitland, Jack HB	70Bal 71-72NE	2	6'1"	210	Williams		18
Majors, Bobby DB	72Cle		6'1"	193	Tennessee		
Malavasi, Ray	HC66DenA HC 78-82LA				Army, Mississippi State		
Malinchak, Bill WR-OE	66-69Det 70-74, 76Was	2	6'1"	198	Indiana		32
Mallory, Irvin DB	71NE		6'1"	196	Virginia Union		
Mallory, Larry DB	76-78NYG		5'11"	185	Tennessee State	2	
Malone, Art FB-HB	70-74Atl 75-76Phi	2	5'11"	213	Arizona State		150
Malone, Benny HB	74-78Mia 78-79Was	2	5'10"	193	Arizona State		120
Manders, Dave C	64-66Dal 67JJ 68-74Dal		6'2"	247	Michigan State		
Mandich, Jim TE-WR	70-77Mia 78Pit	2	6'3"	222	Michigan		138
Manges, Mark QB	78StL		6'2"	210	Maryland		
Mann, Errol K	68GB 69-76Det 76-78Oak	5	6'	202	North Dakota		846
Manning, Archie QB	71-75NO 76SJ 77-82NO 82-83Hou 83-84Min	12	6'3"	205	Mississippi		108
Manning, Rosie DT	72-75Atl 75Phi		6'5"	257	Northeastern Okla.		
Mansfield, Ray C-DT	63Phi 64-76Pit		6'3"	252	Washington		
Maples, Bobby C-LB	65-69HouA 70Hou 71Pit 72-78Den		6'3"	247	Baylor	1	
Marangi, Gary QB	74-76Buf 77Cle	12	6'1"	201	Boston College		12
Marcol, Chester K	72-80GB 80Hou	5	6'	190	Hillsdale		525
Marinaro, Ed HB-FB	72-75Min 76NYJ 77Sea	2	6'2"	212	Cornell		78
Markovich, Mark C-OG	74-75SD 76-77Det 78KJ 79JJ		6'5"	256	Penn State		
Marsalis, Jim DB	69KC-A 70-75KC 77NO		5'11"	193	Tennessee State	15	
Marshall, Al WR	74NE 75KJ		6'2"	190	Boise State		6
Marshall, Ed WR	71Cin 74-75WFL 76NYJ 76-77NYG	2	6'5"	199	Cameron		18
Marshall, Greg DT	78Bal		6'3"	257	Oregon State		
Marshall, Larry DB-HB	72-73KC 74Min 74-77Phi 78KC 78LA	3	5'10"	195	Md. Eastern Shore		
Marshall, Randy DE	70-71Atl		6'5"	237	Linfield		6
Marshall, Tank DT	77NYJ		6'4"	245	Texas A&M		
Martin, Amos LB	72-76Min 77Sea		6'3"	228	Louisville	3	6
Martin, Bob LB	76-79NYJ 79SF		6'1"	219	Nebraska	5	
Martin, Dee DB	71NO 72KJ		6'1"	190	Kentucky State	3	
Martin, Don DB	73NE 75KC 76TB		5'11"	186	Yale		
Martin, Harvey DE	73-83Dal		6'5"	254	East Texas State	2	4
Marvaso, Tommy DB	76-77NYJ		6'1"	191	Cincinnati		
Marx, Greg DE	73Atl		6'4"	260	Notre Dame		
Maslowski, Matt WR	71LA		6'3"	210	Cal.-San Diego		6
Mason, Dave DB	73NE 74GB		6'	198	Nebraska		
Mass, Wayne OT	68-70Chi 71Mia 72Phi		6'4"	243	Clemson		
Massey, Jim DB	74-75NE		5'11"	198	Linfield		
Masters, Bill TE	67-69BufA 70-74Den 75-76KC	2	6'5"	236	Louisiana State		90
Matheson, Bob LB-DE	67-70Cle 71-79Mia		6'4"	238	Duke	12	
Matlock, John C-OT	67NY-A 68CinA 70-71Atl 72Buf		6'4"	250	Miami (Fla.)		
Matson, Pat OG	66-67DenA 68-69CinA 70-74Cin 75GB		6'1"	246	Oregon		
Matthews, Al DB	70-75GB 76Sea 77SF		5'11"	190	Texas A&I	13	12
Matthews, Bo FB	74-79SD 80-81NYG 81Mia 83-84USFL	2	6'4"	227	Colorado		72
Matthews, Henry HB	72NE 73NO		6'3"	203	Michigan State		
Matuszak, John (Tooz) DE-DT	73-74Hou 74WFL 75KC 76-81Oak 82JJ		6'8"	278	Missouri, Tampa		6
Mauck, Carl C	69Bal 70Mia 71-74SD 75-81Hou		6'3"	245	Southern Illinois		6
Maurer, Andy OG-OT	70-73Atl 74NO 74-75Min 76SF 77Den		6'3"	265	Oregon		
Maxson, Alvin HB	74-76NO 77-78Pit 78TB 78Hou 78NYG	23	5'11"	203	S.M.U.		42
Maxwell, Bruce HB-FB	70Det		6'1"	220	Arkansas		
Maxwell, Tommy DB	69-70Bal 71-73Oak 74Hou		6'2"	195	Texas A&M	5	
May, Art DE	71NE		6'3"	245	Tuskegee		
May, Ray LB	67-69Pit 70-73Bal 73-75Den		6'1"	230	Southern Calif.	13	6
Mayes, Rufus OT-OG	69Chi 70-78Cin 79Phi		6'5"	259	Ohio State		
Mayo, Ron TE	73Hou 74Bal		6'3"	223	Morgan State		
Mays, Dave QB	76-77Cle 78Buf	1	6'1"	204	Texas Southern		
Mazur, John	HC70Bos HC71-72NE				Notre Dame		
Mazzetti, Tim K	78-80Atl 83-85USFL	5	6'1"	175	Pennsylvania		230
McAleney, Ed DE	76Atl 76TB		6'2"	235	Massachusetts		
McAlister, James HB	75-76Phi 78NE	23	6'1"	205	U.C.L.A.		30
McBath, Mike DE-OT-DT	68-69BufA 70-72Buf		6'4"	248	Penn State		
McBride, Ron HB	73GB		6'	200	Missouri		
McCaffrey, Mike LB	70Buf		6'3"	235	California		
McCaffrey, Robert C	75GB		6'2"	245	Southern Calif.		
McCall, Bob HB	73NE		6'	205	Arizona		
McCann, Jim K	71-72SF 73NYG 75KC	4	6'2"	165	Arizona State		
McCarren, Larry C	73-84GB		6'3"	246	Illinois		
McCartney, Ron LB	77-79Atl		6'1"	220	Tennessee		
McCauley, Don HB-FB	71-81Bal	23	6'1"	211	North Carolina		348
McClain, Cliff HB-FB	70-73NYJ	2	6'	217	S. Carolina State		12
McClain, Dewey LB	76-80Atl 83-84USFL		6'3"	236	EC Oklahoma	1	

UseName(Nickname)-Positions	Team by Year	See Section	Hgt.	Wgt.	College	Int	Pts
McClanahan, Brent HB-FB	73-79Min	23	5'10"	202	Arizona State		60
McClanahan, Randy LB	77Oak 78Buf 80-81Oak		6'5"	225	Southwestern La.	1	
McClard, Bill K	72SD 73-75NO	5	5'10"	202	Arkansas		109
McCollum, Bubba DT	74Hou		6'	250	Kentucky		
McConnell, Brian LB	73Hou		6'4"	207	Michigan State		
McCormack, Mike OT-OG-DT	51NYY 52-53MS 54-62Cle HC73-75Phi HC80-81Bal HC82Sea		6'4"	246	Kansas		
McCoy, Mike DT-NT	70-75GB 77-78Oak 79-80NYG 80Det		6'5"	278	Notre Dame	1	6
McCrary, Greg TE	75Atl 76LJ 77Atl 78Was 78-80SD 81Was	2	6'3"	233	Clark Atlanta		26
McCray, Prentice DB	74-80NE 80Det		6'1"	188	Arizona State	15	12
McCray, Willie DE	78SF		6'5"	234	Alabama, Troy State		
McCreary, Loaird TE-WR	76-78Mia 79NYG 84USFL		6'5"	227	Tennessee State		18
McCrumbly, John LB	75Buf		6'1"	245	Texas A&M		
McCulley, Pete	HC78SF				Louisiana Tech		
McCullouch, Earl WR	68-73Det 74NO 75WFL	2	5'11"	175	Southern Calif.		114
McCullum, Sam WR	74-75Min 76-81Sea 82-83Min	2	6'2"	198	Montana State		156
McCurry, Dave DB	74NE		6'1"	187	Iowa State		
McCutcheon, Lawrence HB-FB	72-79LA 80Den 80Sea 81Buf	2	6'1"	205	Colorado State		234
McDaniel, John WR	74-77Cin 78-80Was	2	6'1"	196	Lincoln (Mo.)		42
McDonald, Dwight WR	75-78SD 79JJ	2	6'2"	187	San Diego State		48
McDonald, Mike LB	76StL		6'2"	215	Catawba		
McFarland, Jim TE	70-74StL 75Mia		6'5"	225	Nebraska		18
McGee, Molly HB	74Atl		5'10"	184	Rhode Island		
McGee, Tony DE-DT	71-73Chi 74-81NE 82-84Was		6'4"	248	Wyoming, Bishop		
McGee, Willie WR	73SD 74-75LA 76-77SF 78Det	23	5'11"	179	Alcorn State		24
McGeorge, Rich TE	70-78GB	2	6'4"	232	Elon		78
McGill, Mike LB	68-70Min 71-72StL		6'2"	236	Notre Dame	3	6
McGill, Ralph DB	72-77SF 78-79NO	3	5'11"	181	Tulsa	8	12
McGraw, Mike LB	76StL 77Det		6'2"	225	Wyoming		
McGriff, Lee WR	76TB		5'9"	163	Florida		
McIntyre, Secedrick HB	77Atl		5'10"	190	Auburn		6
McKay, Bob OT-OG	70-75Cle 76-78NE		6'5"	262	Texas		
McKay, John (J.K.) WR	76-78TN	2	5'11"	182	Southern Calif.		12
McKay, John	HC76-84TB				Oregon		
McKenzie, Reggie OG	72-82Buf 83-84Sea		6'4"	252	Michigan		
McKinley, Bill DE-LB	71Buf 72JJ		6'1"	240	Arizona		
McKinnely, Phil OT-TE-OG	76-80Atl 81LA 82Chi 84-85USFL		6'4"	248	U.C.L.A.		
McKinney, Bill LB	72Chi		6'1"	226	West Texas State		
McKinney, Royce DB	75Buf		6'1"	190	Kentucky State		
McKinnis, Hugh FB	73-75Cle 76Sea	2	6'	220	Arizona State		60
McKnight, Ted HB-FB	77-81KC 82Buf	2	6'1"	209	Minnesota-Duluth		138
McKoy, Bill LB	70-72Den 74SF		6'3"	233	Purdue		
McLain, Kevin LB	76-79LA 83-84USFL		6'2"	230	Colorado State		
McLinton, Harold LB	69-78Was		6'2"	235	Southern U.	3	6
McMakin, John TE	72-74Pit 75Det 76Sea	2	6'3"	229	Clemson		24
McMath, Herb DT-DE	76Oak 77GB		6'4"	248	Morningside		
McMillan, Eddie LB	73-75LA 76-77Sea 78Buf		6'	189	Florida State	12	
McNeill, Fred LB	74-85Min		6'2"	229	U.C.L.A.	7	6
McNeil, Pat FB	76-77KC		5'9"	208	Baylor		
McNeill, Rod FB	74-76NO 76TB	23	6'2"	218	Southern Calif.		30
McNeill, Tom K	67-69NO 70Min 71-73Phi	4	6'1"	195	S.F. Austin State		
McQuay, Leon HB	74NYG 75NE 76NO	23	5'9"	197	Tampa		6
McQuilken, Kim QB	74-77Atl 78-80Was 83USFL	1	6'2"	203	Lehigh		
McRae, Jerrold WR	78KC 79Phi		6'	194	Tennessee State		
McShane, Charles LB	77-79Sea		6'3"	230	Cal. Lutheran		
McVay, John	HC76-78NYG				Miami-Ohio		
McVea, Warren HB-WR	68CinA 69KC-A 70-71KC 72KJ 73KC	23	5'10"	182	Houston		78
Means, Dave DE	74-75Buf		6'4"	235	SW Missouri St.		
Medlin, Dan OG	74-76Oak 77-78TB 79Oak		6'3"	254	N. Carolina State		
Melville, Dan K	79SF	4	6'	185	California		
Mendenhall, John DT	72-79NYG 80Det		6'1"	255	Grambling	1	
Mendenhall, Ken C	71-80Bal		6'3"	242	Oklahoma		
Mendenhall, Terry LB	71-72Oak		6'1"	210	San Diego State		
Merlo, Jim LB	73-74NO 75JJ 76-79NO		6'1"	221	Stanford	8	18
Merrow, Jeff DE-DT-LB	75-77Atl 77Oak 78-83Atl		6'4"	236	West Virginia		
Meseroll, Mark OT	78NO 80JJ		6'5"	270	Florida State		
Metcalf, Terry HB-WR	73-77StL 78-80CFL 81Was	23	5'10"	185	Long Beach State		216
Meyer, Dennis DB	73Pit		5'11"	186	Arkansas State		
Meyer, Ken	HC77SF				Denison		
Meyers, Jerry DE-DT	76-79Chi 80KC		6'4"	249	Northern Illinois		
Mialik, Larry TE	72-74Atl 76SD		6'2"	226	Wisconsin		
Michaels, Walt LB	51GB 52-61Cle 63NYG HC77-82NYJ		6'	231	Washington & Lee		
Michel, Mike K	77Mia 78Phi	45	5'10"	177	Stanford		9
Middlebrook, Oren WR	78Phi		6'2"	185	Arkansas State		
Middleton, Rick LB	74-75NO 76-78SD		6'2"	229	Ohio State	2	
Mike-Mayer, Nick K	73-77Atl 77-78Phi 79-82Buf	5	5'8"	186	Temple		571
Mike-Mayer, Steve K	75-76SF 77Det 78NO 79-80Bal	5	6'	180	Maryland		362
Mikolajczyk, Ron OT-OG	72-73CFL 74-75WFL 76-79NYG 83-84USFL		6'3"	275	Tampa		
Milan, Don QB	75GB 76BW	1	6'3"	196	Cal. Poly.-S.L.O.		
Mildren, Jack DB	72-73Bal 74NE		6'1"	200	Oklahoma	3	
Miller, Calvin NT-DT-DE	79NYG 80Atl		6'2"	260	Oklahoma State		
Miller, Cleo HB-FB	74-75KC 75-82Cle 83-84USFL	23	5'11"	207	Ark.-Pine Bluff		102
Miller, Jim OG	71-72,74Atl		6'3"	240	Iowa		
Miller, Johnny OG	77SF 78EJ 79KJ		6'1"	247	Livingstone		
Miller, Kevin WR	78-80Min 83USFL	3	5'10"	181	Louisville		6
Miller, Mark QB	78-79Cle 80GB 83USFL	1	6'2"	176	Bowling Green		6
Miller, Red	HC77-80Den				Western Illinois		
Miller, Robert HB-FB	75-80Min	2	5'11"	204	Kansas		48
Miller, Terry LB	71-74StL		6'2"	224	Illinois		
Miller, Willie WR	75-76Cle 77EJ 78-82LA	2	5'9"	172	Colorado State		96
Milo, Ray DB	78KC		5'11"	178	New Mexico State		
Minor, Claudie OT	74-82Den		6'4"	279	San Diego State		
Mitchell, Dale LB	76-77SF		6'3"	224	Southern Calif.		
Mitchell, Jim TE	69-79Atl	2	6'2"	234	Prairie View		186
Mitchell, Jim DE-DT	70-77Det		6'3"	247	Virginia State	1	2
Mitchell, Ken LB	73-74Atl		6'1"	224	Nevada-Las Vegas		
Mitchell, Leroy DB	67-68BosA 69BO 70Hou 71-73Den		6'2"	192	Texas Southern	19	6
Mitchell, Lydell HB	72-77Bal 78-79SD 80LA	2	5'11"	199	Penn State		282
Mitchell, Mack DE	75-78Cle 79Cin 84USFL		6'7"	246	Houston		2
Mitchell, Mark DB	77Phi		6'1"	180	Tulane		
Mitchell, Mel OG-C-OT	76-77Mia 77Det 78Min 80Min		6'3"	260	Tennessee State		
Mitchell, Tom TE-WR	66OakA 68-73Bal 74-77SF	2	6'2"	219	Bucknell		144
Mock, Mike LB	78NYJ 79JJ		6'1"	225	Texas Tech		
Monds, Wonder DB	78SF		6'3"	215	Nebraska		
Monroe, Henry DB	79Phi		5'11"	180	Mississippi		
Montgomery, Marv OT	71-76Den 76-77NO 78Atl		6'6"	255	Southern Calif.	1	
Montgomery, Mike HB-WR	71SD 72-73Dal 74Hou	2	6'2"	208	Kansas State		60

UseName(Nickname)-Positions	Team by Year	See Section	Hgt.	Wgt.	College	Int	Pts
Montgomery, Randy DB	71-73Den 74Chi	3	5'11"	183	Weber State	2	6
Montgomery, Ross FB	69-70Chi	2	6'3"	220	Texas Christian		
Montler, Mike C-OT-OG	69BosA 70Bos 71-72NE 73-76Buf 77Den 78Det		6'4"	256	Colorado		
Moody, Keith DB	76-79Buf 80Oak 83USFL	3	5'10"	171	Syracuse	3	18
Mooers, Doug DT-DE	71-72NO		6'6"	265	Whittier		
Mooney, Ed LB	68-71Det 72JJ 73Bal		6'2"	231	Texas Tech		
Moore, Art NT-DT	73-74NE 75KJ 76-77NE		6'5"	255	Tulsa		
Moore, Bob TE	71-75Oak 76-77TB 78Den	2	6'3"	222	Stanford		42
Moore, Dean LB	78SF 83-84USFL		6'2"	210	Iowa		
Moore, Derland DT-NT-DE	73-86NO 86NYJ		6'4"	260	Oklahoma	1	
Moore, Jerry DB	71-72Chi 73-74NO		6'3"	208	Arkansas	2	
Moore, Joe HB	71Chi 72JJ 73Chi	2	6'1"	205	Missouri		
Moore, Ken TE	78Atl		6'4"	232	Northern Illinois		
Moore, Manfred HB	74-75SF 76TB 76Oak 77Min	3	6'	197	Southern Calif.		12
Moore, Maulty DT	72-74Mia 75Cin 76TB		6'5"	265	Bethune-Cookman		
Moore, Randy DT	76Den 77JJ		6'2"	241	Arizona		
Moore, Reynaud DB	71NO		6'2"	190	U.C.L.A.		
Moore, (Solomon) Wayne OT	70-78Mia		6'6"	265	Lamar		
Moore, Zeke DB	67-69HouA 70-77Hou	3	6'2"	195	Lincoln (Mo.)	24	24
Mooring, John OT-C	71-73NYJ 74NO		6'6"	255	Tampa		
Moorman, Mo OG-OT	68-69KC-A 70-73KC		6'5"	252	Texas A&M		
Moreino, Joe NT-DE	78NYJ		6'6"	246	Idaho State		
Moresco, Tim DB	77GB 78-80NYJ		5'11"	178	Syracuse		2
Morgado, Arnold FB-HB	77-80KC	2	6'	209	Hawaii		96
Morgan, Dennis HB	74Dal 75Phi	3	5'11"	198	Western Illinois		6
Morgan, Melvin DB	76-78Cin 79-80SF		6'	183	Miss. Valley St.	3	6
Morgan, Mike FB	78Chi		5'11"	218	Wisconsin		
Moriarty, Pat HB	79Cle		6'	195	Georgia Tech		12
Moriarty, Tom DB	77-79Atl 80Pit 81Atl 83-84USFL		6'	183	Bowling Green		6
Morin, Milt TE	66-75Cle	2	6'4"	243	Massachusetts		96
Moritz, Brett OG	78TB		6'5"	250	Army, Nebraska		
Morris, Chris OT	72-73Cle 75NO		6'3"	250	Indiana		
Morris, Donny Joe HB	74KC		5'11"	195	North Texas		
Morris, Jon C	64-69BosA 70Bos 71-74NE 75-77Det 78Chi		6'4"	247	Holy Cross		
Morris, (Eugene) Mercury HB	69MiaA 70-75Mia 76SD	23	5'10"	190	West Texas State		210
Morrison, Dennis QB	74SF	1	6'3"	211	Kansas State		
Morrison, Don OT-C	71-77NO 78Bal 79Det		6'5"	255	Texas-Arlington		
Morrison, Reece HB	68-72Cle 72-73Cin 74JJ	23	6'	206	SW Texas State		24
Mortenson, Fred QB	79Was 83-85USFL		6'2"	195	Arizona State		
Morton, Craig QB	65-74Dal 74-76NYG 77-82Den	12	6'4"	213	California		72
Morton, Dave LB	79SF		6'2"	224	U.C.L.A.		
Morton, Greg DE	77Buf		6'1"	230	Michigan		
Moseley, Mark K	70Phi 71-72Hou 74-86Was 86Cle	5	5'11"	200	Texas A&M, S.F. Austin State		1382
Mosely, Wayne HB	74Buf		6'	190	Alabama A&M		
Moses, Haven WR	68-69BufA 70-72Buf 72-81Den	2	6'3"	204	San Diego State		342
Mosier, John TE	71Den 72Bal 73NE		6'3"	220	Kansas		
Moss, Eddie FB-HB	73-76StL 77Was		6'	215	SE Missouri St.		6
Moss, Roland TE-FB	69Bal 70SD 70Buf 71NE	2	6'3"	215	Toledo		12
Muckensturm, Jerry LB	76-80Chi 81SJ 82-83Chi		6'4"	223	Arkansas State	3	
Mucker, Larry WR	77-80TB	2	5'11"	191	Arizona State		30
Muhlmann, Horst K	69CinA 70-74Cin 75-77Phi	5	6'1"	215	none		707
Mul-Key, Herb HB	72-74Was	23	6'	190	none		12
Mullen, Tom OG-OT	74-77NYG 78StL		6'3"	248	SW Missouri St.		
Mulligan, Wayne C	69-73StL 74-75NYJ 76JJ		6'2"	246	Clemson		
Mullins, Gerry OG-OT	71-79Pit		6'3"	242	Southern Calif.		18
Mumphord, Lloyd DB	69MiaA 70-74Mia 75-78Bal		5'11"	179	Texas Southern	21	18
Munsey, Nelson DB	72-77Bal 78Min		6'1"	188	Wyoming	7	12
Munson, Bill QB	64-67LA 68-75Det 76Sea 77SD 78-79Buf	12	6'2"	203	Utah State		18
Murdock, Guy C	72Hou		6'2"	245	Michigan		
Murphy, Mike LB	79Hou 83-84USFL		6'2"	222	SW Missouri St.		
Murrell, Bill TE	79StL		6'3"	220	Winston-Salem St.		
Musso, Johnny (Italian Stallion) HB-FB	75-77Chi 78KJ	2	5'11"	201	Alabama		38
Myer, Steve QB	76-79Sea 80XJ	1	6'2"	191	New Mexico		
Myers, Chip WR-FL	67SF 69CinA 70-76Cin	2	6'4"	203	Northwestern Okla.		72
Myers, Frank OT	78-79Min		6'5"	255	Texas A&M		
Myers, Tom DB	72-82NO 84-85USFL		5'11"	181	Syracuse	36	30
Myrtle, Chip LB-TE	67-69DenA 70-72Den 73JJ 74SD		6'4"	224	Maryland	4	2
Nafziger, Dana LB-TE	77-79TB 80KJ 81-82TB		6'1"	222	Cal. Poly.-S.L.O.		
Namath, Joe QB	65-69NY-A 70-76NYJ 77LA	12	6'2"	198	Alabama		48
Naponic, Bob QB	70Hou		6'	190	Illinois		
Naumoff, Paul LB	67-78Det		6'1"	216	Tennessee	6	
Neal, Dan C-OG	73-74Bal 75-83Chi		6'4"	250	Kentucky		
Neal, Lewis WR	73-74Atl	2	6'4"	215	Prairie View		6
Neal, Richard DE-DT	69-72NO 73-77NYJ 78NO		6'3"	258	Southern U.		6
Neely, Ralph OT	65-77Dal		6'5"	261	Oklahoma		
Neils, Steve LB	74-80StL		6'2"	217	Minnesota	1	6
Nelson, Bill DT	71-75LA		6'7"	270	Oregon State		
Nelson, Dennis OT	70-74Bal 76-77Phi		6'5"	260	Illinois State		
Nelson, Ralph HB	75Was 76Sea	2	6'2"	195	none		12
Nelson, Shane LB	77-82Buf		6'1"	226	Baylor	4	
Nelson, Terry TE	74-80LA	2	6'2"	233	Ark.-Pine Bluff		42
Nettles, Doug DB	74-79Bal 80NYG		6'	179	Vanderbilt	5	2
Neville, Tom OT	65-69BosA 70Bos 71-74NE 75BL 76-77NE 78Den 79NYG		6'4"	252	Mississippi State		
Newhouse, Robert FB-HB	72-83Dal	2	5'10"	209	Houston		216
Newland, Bob WR	71-74NO 75JJ	2	6'2"	190	Oregon		48
Newman, Ed OG	73-84Mia		6'2"	249	Fla. Atlantic, Duke		
Newsome, Billy DE	70-72Bal 73-74NO 75-76NYG 77Chi		6'4"	251	Grambling	3	6
Newton, Bob OG-OT	71-75Chi 76-81Sea 83-84USFL		6'4"	257	Nebraska		
Nichols, Mark LB	78SF		6'3"	225	Colorado State	1	
Nichols, Robbie LB	70-71Bal		6'3"	220	Tulsa		
Nicholson, Jim OT	74-79KC 80KJ 81SF		6'6"	269	Michigan State		
Niehaus, Steve DT-DE	76-78Sea 79Min		6'4"	263	Notre Dame		
Niland, John OG	66-74Dal 75Phi 76KJ		6'4"	247	Iowa		6
Nix, Kent QB	67-69Pit 70-71Chi 72Hou	12	6'1"	195	Texas Christian		12
Nobis, Tommy LB	66-76Atl		6'2"	237	Texas	12	12
Nock, George HB	69NY-A 70-71NYJ 72Was	2	5'10"	200	Morgan State		66
Nordquist, Mark OG-C	68-74Phi 75-76Chi 76SF		6'4"	245	Pacific		
Nott, Mike QB	76KC		6'3"	203	Santa Clara		
Nottingham, Don FB	71-73Bal 73-77Mia 78SJ	2	5'10"	210	Kent State		210
Novak, Gary DT	71SD		6'5"	247	Michigan State		
Novak, Jack TE	75Cin 76-77TB	2	6'4"	241	Wisconsin		6
Novak, Ken DT	76-77Bal 78Cle 79JJ		6'7"	268	Purdue		
Nugent, Dan OG	76-78Was 79XJ 80Was		6'3"	250	Auburn		
Nunamaker, Julian DE-DT	69BufA 70Buf 71JJ		6'3"	251	Tennessee-Martin		
Nunley, Frank (Fudgehammer) LB	67-76SF		6'2"	230	Michigan		14

UseName(Nickname)-Positions	TeambyYear	See Section	Hgt.	Wgt.	College	Int	Pts
Nuzum, Rick C	77LA 78GB 79LJ		6'4"	238	Kentucky		
Nye, Blaine OG	68-76Dal		6'4"	252	Stanford		
Nystrom, Lee OT	74GB		6'5"	260	Macalester		
Nyvall, Vic HB	70NO		5'10"	185	Northwestern La.		
Oates, Brad OT-OG	76-77StL 78Det 79-80StL		6'6"	274	Duke, Brigham Young		
Obradovich, Jim TE	75NYG 76-77SF 78-83TB	2	6'2"	227	Southern Calif.		42
O'Brien, Jim WR-K	70-72Bal 73Det	2 5	6'	195	Cincinnati		301
O'Brien, Mike DB	79Sea 83USFL		6'1"	195	California		
O'Connor, Fred	HC78SF				East Stroudsburg		
O'Dell, Stu LB	74Was 75SJ 76-77Was 78Bal 79JJ		6'1"	220	Indiana		
Odom, Ricky DB	78KC 78SF 79LA		6'	183	Southern Calif.	2	
Odom, Steve WR	74-79GB 79NYG	23	5'8"	173	Utah		90
Odoms, Riley TE	72-83Den	2	6'4"	231	Houston		264
Ogle, Rick LB	71StL 72Det		6'3"	230	Colorado		
Okoniewski, Steve DT-DE	72-73Buf 74-75GB		6'3"	257	Montana		
Olander, Cliff QB	77-79SD 80-81NYG		6'5"	191	New Mexico State		1
Oldham, Ray DB	73-78Bal 78Pit 79NYG 80-82Det		6'	193	Middle Tenn. St.	14	12
Olds, Bill FB	73-75Bal 76Sea 76Phi	2	6'1"	224	Nebraska		60
Olerich, Dave LB-TE	67-68SF 69-70StL 71Hou 72-73SF		6'1"	221	San Francisco		
Oliver, Frank DB	75Buf 76TB		6'	194	Kentucky State		
Oliver, Greg HB	73-74Phi		6'	192	Trinity (Texas)		
Olsen, Orrin C	76KC		6'1"	245	Brigham Young		
Olsen, Phil DT-C	71-74LA 75-76Den 78KJ		6'5"	263	Utah State		
O'Malley, Jim LB	73-75Den		6'1"	230	Notre Dame	1	
O'Neal, Calvin LB	78Bal		6'1"	235	Michigan		
O'Neal, Steve WR-K	69NY-A 70-72NYJ 73NO	4	6'3"	185	Texas A&M		
O'Neil, Ed LB	74-79Det 80GB		6'3"	236	Penn State	5	18
Onkontz, Dennis LB	70NYJ		6'1"	220	Penn State		
Opperman, Jim LB	75Phi		6'3"	220	Colorado State		
Orduna, Joe HB-FB	72-73NYG 74Bal	2	6'	195	Nebraska		24
Oriard, Mike C-OG	70-73KC		6'4"	223	Notre Dame		
Ortega, Ralph LB	75-78Atl 79-80Mia		6'2"	200	Florida	5	6
Orvis, Herb DT-DE	72-77Det 78-81Bal		6'5"	248	Colorado		
Osborn, Dave HB	65-75Min 76GB	2	6'	206	North Dakota		216
Osborn, Mike LB	78Phi		6'5"	235	Kansas State		
Osborne, Jim DT	72-84Chi		6'3"	251	Southern U.		2
Osborne, Richard TE	76Phi 76NYJ 77-78Phi 79StL	2	6'3"	230	Texas A&M		6
Osley, Willie DB	74KC		6'	195	Illinois		
Otis, Jim FB	70NO 71-72KC 73-78StL	2	6'	223	Ohio State		132
Outlaw, John DB	69BosA 70Bos 71-72NE 73, 75-78Phi		5'10"	180	Jackson State	14	12
Overmeyer, Bill LB	72Phi		6'3"	220	Ashland		
Owen, Tom QB	74-75SF 76-81NE 82Was 83NYG	1	6'1"	195	Wichita State		6
Owens, Artie WR-HB	76-79SD 80Buf 80NO 83USFL	23	5'10"	176	West Virginia		18
Owens, Brig DB	66-77Was		5'11"	190	Cincinnati	36	32
Owens, Burgess DB	73-79NYJ 80-81Oak 82Raid		6'2"	199	Miami (Fla.)	30	36
Owens, Joe DE	70SD 71-75NO 76Hou		6'2"	244	Alcorn State	1	4
Owens, Marv WR	73StL 74NYJ		5'11"	205	San Diego State		
Owens, Morris WR	75-76Mia 76-79TB	2	6'	192	Arizona State		84
Owens, Steve FB	70-74Det 75KJ	2	6'2"	217	Oklahoma		132
Owens, Terry OT	66-69SD-A 70-75SD		6'6"	263	Jacksonville St.		
Owens, Tinker WR	76NO 77KJ 78-80NO 81KJ	2	5'11"	170	Oklahoma		24
Ozdowski, Mike DE	78-81Bal		6'5"	242	Virginia		
Packer, Walter DB	77Sea		5'10"	174	Mississippi State		
Pagac, Fred TE	74Chi 75WFL 76TB		6'	220	Ohio State		
Page, Alan DT	67-78Min 78-81Chi		6'5"	244	Notre Dame	2	24
Palewicz, Al LB	73-75KC 77 NYJ		6'1"	215	Miami (Fla.)		
Palmer, Dick LB	70Mia 71JJ 72Buf 72-73NO 74 Atl		6'2"	229	Kentucky		
Palmer, Gary OT-DT	75KC		6'4"	255	Kansas		
Palmer, Scott DT	71NYJ 72StL		6'3"	243	Texas		
Pane, Chris DB	76-79Den		5'11"	184	New Mexico		
Papale, Vince WR	76-78Phi 79SJ		6'2"	195	St. Joseph's-Pa.		
Parish, Don LB	70-71StL 71LA 72Den		6'1"	220	Stanford	1	6
Parker, Artimus DB	74-76Phi		6'3"	208	Southern Calif.	5	
Parker, Joel WR	74-75NO 76JJ 77NO	2	6'5"	213	Forida		36
Parker, Kenny DB	70NYG		6'1"	190	Fordham		
Parker, Willie C	73-79Buf 80Det		6'3"	245	North Texas		
Parker, Dave DB	79Det		6'	190	Utah State		
Parks, Billy WR	71Sd 72Dal 73-75Hou	2	6'1"	187	Long Beach State		42
Parris, Gary TE	73-74SD 75-78Cle 79-80StL	2	6'2"	226	Florida State		31
Parrish, Lemar DB	70-77Cin 78-81Was 82Buf	3	5'11"	180	Lincoln (Mo.)	47	78
Parrish, Scott OT	76Den		6'6"	270	Utah State		
Parsley, Cliff K	77-82Hou	4	6'1"	213	Oklahoma State		
Parson, Ray OT	71Det		6'4"	250	Minnesota		
Parsons, Bob K-TE	72-83Chi 84-85USFL	4	6'5"	230	Penn State		
Partee, Dennis K	68-69SD-A 70-75SD	45	6'2"	218	S.M.U.		380
Pass, Randy OG-C	78GB		6'3"	247	Georgia Tech		
Pastorini, Dan QB	71-79Hou 80Oak 81LA 82-83Phi	12 4	6'3"	208	Santa Clara		48
Pastrana, Al QB	69DenA 70Den	1	6'1"	190	Maryland		6
Pate, Lloyd HB	70Buf	2	6'1"	205	Cincinnati		6
Patera, Jack LB-OG	55-57Bal 58-59ChiC 60-61Dal HC76-82Sea		6'1"	234	Oregon		
Patrick, Frank QB	70-72GB		6'7"	225	Nebraska		
Patrick, Mike K	75-78NE	4	6'	209	Mississippi State		
Patrick, Wayne FB	68-69BufA 70-72Buf 73KJ	2	6'2"	241	Louisville		36
Patterson, Don DB	79Det 80NYG		5'11"	175	Georgia Tech		
Patton, Bob C	76Buf		6'1"	245	Delaware		
Patton, Jerry DT	71Min 72-73Buf 74Pit 75NE		6'3"	261	Nebraska	1	
Patulski, Walt DE	72-75Buf 76KJ 77StL 78XJ		6'6"	260	Notre Dame		
Paul, Harold OT	74Oak		6'5"	245	Oklahoma		
Payne, Ken WR	74-77GB 77-78Phi	2	6'1"	185	Langston		36
Pear, Dave NT-DT	75Bal 76-78TB 79-80Oak		6'2"	248	Washington		
Pearson, Barry WR	72-73Pit 74-76KC	2	5'11"	185	Northwestern		42
Pearson, Dennis WR	78-79Atl 80KJ	3	5'11"	177	San Deigo State		6
Pearson, Drew WR	73-83Dal	2	6'	184	Tulsa		300
Pearson, Preston HB-DB	67-69Bal 70-74Pit 75-80Dal	23	6'1"	200	Illinois		198
Peay, Francis OT	66-67NYG 68-72GB 73-74KC		6'5"	250	Missouri		
Peets, Brian TE	76-79Sea 80BL 81SF	2	6'4"	225	U. of Pacific		6
Peiffer, Dan C	75-77Chi 80Was 81KJ		6'3"	252	SE Missouri St.		
Pellegrini, Joe DT-NT	78-79NYJ		6'2"	268	Idaho		
Pena, Bubba OG	72Cle 73KJ		6'2"	250	Massachusetts		
Penchion, Bobby OG-C	72-73Buf 74-75SF 76Sea		6'5"	256	Alcorn State		
Pennywell, Carlos WR	78-81NE	2	6'2"	180	Grambling		18
Pennywell, Robert LB	77-80Atl 83-85USFL		6'1"	222	Grambling	3	12
Penrose, Craig QB	76-79Den 80NYJ 83-84USFL	1	6'3"	211	San Diego State		
Peoples, Woody OG	68-75SF 76XJ 77SF 78-80Phi		6'2"	251	Grambling		
Peppler, Pat	HC76Atl				Michigan State		
Percival, Mac K	67-73Chi 74Dal	5	6'4"	219	Texas Tech		466
Pergine, John LB	69-72LA 73-75Was		6'1"	225	Notre Dame		6
Perkins, Horace DB	79KC		5'11"	180	Colorado		
Perko, Tom LB	76GB		6'3"	233	Pittsburgh		
Perretta, Ralph C-OG	75-79SD 80NYG 80SD		6'2"	251	Purdue		
Perrin, Lonnie FB	76-78Den 79Was 79Chi	23	6'1"	222	Illinois		66
Perry, Rod DB	75-82LA 83-84Cle		5'9"	178	Colorado	30	24
Perry, Scott DB	76-79Cin 80SF 80SD		6'	182	Williams	4	18
Person, Ara TE	72StL		6'2"	220	Morgan State		
Pesuit, Wally OG-C-DE-OT	76Atl 76-78Mia 79-80Det 83-84USFL		6'4"	252	Kentucky		
Peters, Tony DB	75-77Cle 79-82Was 83SL 84Was		6'1"	187	Oklahoma	14	
Petersen, Bill LB-TE	68-69CinA 70-72Cin 75KC		6'3"	228	San Jose State	5	
Peterson, Bill	HC72-73Hou				Ohio Northern		
Peterson, Cal LB	74-75Dal 76TB 79-81KC 82Raid		6'3"	220	U.C.L.A.	2	
Peterson, Jim LB	74-75LA 76TB		6'5"	235	San Diego State		
Pettigrew, Gary DT-DE	66-73Phi 74NYG		6'4"	252	Stanford		
Pharr, Tommy DB	70Buf		5'10"	187	Mississippi State		
Phillips, Charlie DB	75-79Oak 80KJ		6'2"	215	Southern Calif.	19	18
Phillips, Jess HB-FB-DB	68-69CinA 70-72Cin 73-74NO 75Oak 76-77NE	23	6'1"	208	Michigan	3	90
Phillips, Mel DB	66-77SF		6'	191	N. Carolina A&T	12	6
Phillips, Ray LB	77-78Cin 78-81Phi 83-84USFL		6'4"	224	Nebraska	1	
Phillips, Rod FB-TE	75-78LA 79-80StL	2	6'	220	Jackson State		18
Phillips, Wesley OT	79Hou 79-80CFL 83USFL		6'5"	275	Lenoir Rhyne		
Philyaw, Charles (King Kong) DE-NT	76-79Oak 83-84USFL		6'9"	276	Texas Southern		
Phipps, Mike QB	70-76Cle 77-81Chi	12	6'3"	208	Purdue		78
Picard, Bob WR	73-76Phi 76Det		6'1"	196	Eastern Washington		
Piccone, Lou WR	74-76NYJ 77-82Buf	23	5'9"	177	W. Liberty State		44
Pickard, Bob WR	74Det		6'	190	Xavier-Ohio		6
Pierce, Danny HB-FB	70Was		6'3"	215	Memphis State		
Pierson, Reggie DB	76Det 76-77TB		5'11"	185	Oklahoma State		
Pietrzak, Jim C-DT-OT	74-75NYG 76NYJ 77-79NYG 79-84NO 87KC		6'5"	260	Eastern Michigan		
Pifferini, Bob LB	72-75Chi 77LA		6'2"	226	U.C.L.A.		
Pinder, Cyril HB-LB	68-70Phi 71-72Chi 73Dal 74-75WFL	2	6'2"	218	Illinois		42
Pinkney, Reggie DB	77-78Det 79-81Bal		5'11"	188	East Carolina	4	6
Piper, Scott WR	76Atl		6'1"	179	Arizona		
Pisarkiewicz, Steve QB	77-79StL 80GB 82CFL 83,85USFL	1	6'2"	205	Missouri		
Pittman, Charlie HB	70StL 71Bal		6'1"	200	Penn State		
Pitts, Frank WR-DE-FL	65-69KC-A 70KC 71-73Cle 74Oak 75Atl	2	6'2"	198	Southern U.		174
Pitts, John DB	67-69BufA 70-72Buf 73-74Den 75Cle		6'4"	218	Arizona State	10	
Plank, Doug DB	75-82Chi 84USFL		6'	200	Ohio State	15	2
Plummer, Tony DB	70StL 71-73Atl 74LA		5'11"	189	U. of Pacific	1	6
Plunkett, Jim QB	71-75NE 76-77SF 78-81Oak 82-86Raid 87SJ	12	6'3"	215	Stanford		84
Podolak, Ed HB	69KC-A 70-77KC	23	6'1"	204	Iowa		240
Pollard, Bob DT-DE	71-77NO 78-81StL		6'3"	248	Weber State		6
Poll, Randy DB	74Min 75-77Den		6'3"	190	Stanford	1	6
Polowski, Larry LB	79Sea		6'3"	235	Boise State		
Poole, Larry HB	75-77Cle 78Hou	2	6'	195	Kent State		30
Poole, Steve LB	76NYJ		6'1"	232	Tennessee		6
Pope, Ken DB	74NE		5'11"	200	Oklahoma		
Porter, Jack C	71SD		6'4"	255	Oklahoma		
Porter, Lewis WR	70KC		5'11"	178	Southern U.		
Porter, Ron LB	67-69Bal 69-72Phi 73Min 74WFL		6'3"	232	Idaho	3	
Posey, David K	78NE	5	5'10"	167	Florida		52
Potts, Charlie DB	72Det		6'3"	210	Purdue		
Pough, Ernest WR	76-77Pit 78NYG	23	6'1"	174	Texas Southern		6
Powell, Darnell HB	77Buf 78NYJ 79JJ	2	5'11"	199	Tenn.-Chattanooga		6
Powell, Jesse LB	69MiaA 70-73Mia		6'1"	214	West Texas State		
Powell, Steve HB	78-79Buf		5'11"	186	NE Missouri St.		
Powers, Clyde DB	74-77NYG 78KC 79KJ		6'1"	195	Oklahoma	5	
Pratt, Robert OG	74-81Bal 83-85Sea		6'4"	249	North Carolina		6
Preece, Steve DB	69NO 70-72Phi 72Den 73-76LA 77Sea		6'1"	195	Oregon State	14	18
Price, Elex DT	73-80NO		6'3"	262	Alcorn State	1	12
Price, Ernie DE-DT	73-78Det 78-79Sea 79Cle 83-84USFL		6'4"	248	Texas A&I		2
Pringle, Alan K	75Det		6'	195	Rice		
Pritchard, Ron LB	69HouA 70-72Hou 72-77Cin		6'1"	231	Arizona State	3	2
Pritchett, Billy Ray FB	75Cle 76-77Atl	2	6'3"	231	West Texas State		6
Profit, Joe HB	71-73Atl 73NO	2	6'	210	Northeast La.		18
Prothro, Tommy	HC71-72LA HC74-78SD				Duke		
Protz, Jack LB	70SD		6'1"	218	Syracuse		
Prout, Bob DB	74Oak 75NYJ		6'1"	187	Knox	1	
Provost, Ted DB	70Min 71StL		6'2"	195	Ohio State		
Pruett, Perry DB	71NE		6'1"	190	North Texas		
Pruitt, Greg HB	73-81Cle 82-84Raid	23	5'10"	190	Oklahoma		282
Puetz, Gary OG-OT	73-78NYJ 78TB 79Phi 79-81NE 82Was		6'4"	263	Valparaiso		
Pugh, Jethro DT-DE	65-78Dal		6'6"	256	Elizabeth City St.	1	4
Pureifory, Dave DE-DT	72-77GB 78Cin 78-82Det 83-85USFL		6'1"	256	Eastern Michigan		4
Queen, Jeff FB-TE	69SD-A 70-71SD 72-73Oak 74Hou	2	6'1"	221	Morgan State		60
Raba, Rob TE	77-79NYJ 80Bal 81Was		6'1"	224	Maryland		
Rader, Dave QB	79NYG		6'3"	211	Tulsa		
Rae, Mike QB	76-78Oak 78-80TB 81Was 83-85USFL	12	6'	193	Southern Calif		12
Ragsdale, George HB-WR	77-79TB 80SJ 83-84USFL	23	5'11"	185	N. Carolina A&T		12
Raible, Steve WR	76-81Sea	2	6'2"	195	Georgia Tech		24
Raines, Mike DT-DE	74SF 75-82CFL 83-84USFL		6'5"	255	Alabama		
Ralston, John	HC72-76Den				California		
Ramsey, Steve QB	70NO 71-76Den	12	6'2"	210	North Texas		12
Randall, Tom OG	78Dal 79Hou		6'5"	245	Iowa State		
Randolph, Al DB	66-70SF 71GB 72Det 73Cin 74Buf		6'2"	199	Iowa	11	8
Randolph, Terry DB	77GB		6'	184	American Inter.		
Rashad, Ahmad WR	72-73StL 74Buf 75KJ 76-82Min 1972 — played as Bobby Moore	2	6'2"	202	Oregon		276
Rasley, Rocky OG	69-70, 72-73Det 74NO 75KC		6'3"	252	Oregon State		
Rasmussen, Randy OG	67-69NY-A 70-81NYJ		6'2"	256	Kearney State		6
Rather, Bo WR	73Mia 74-78Chi 78Mia 79JJ	2	6'1"	185	Michigan		42
Ratiff, Don DB	75Phi		6'5"	250	Maryland		
Ray, David WR-K	69-74LA	5	6'	195	Alabama		497
Ray, Eddie FB-TE	70Bos 71SD 72-74Atl 76Buf	2	6'1"	237	Louisiana State		66
Rayhle, Fred TE	77Sea		6'5"	216	Tenn.-Chattanooga		
Reamon, Tommy HB	76KC	2	5'10"	192	Missouri		30
Reardon, Kerry DB	71-76KC		5'11"	180	Iowa	14	
Reaves, John QB	72-74Phi 75-78Cin 79Min 81Hou 83-85USFL 87TB	12	6'3"	209	Florida		18
Reaves, Ken DB	66-73Atl 74NO 74-77StL		6'3"	206	Norfolk State	37	6
Reavis, Dave OT-OG	74-75Pit 76-83TB		6'5"	257	Arkansas		
Rebowe, Rusty LB	78NO		5'10"	213	Nicholls State		
Redmond, Rudy LB	69-71Atl 72Det 73JJ		6'	190	Pacific	8	6
Reece, Danny DB	76-80TB	3	5'11"	190	Southern Calif.	1	6

UseName(Nickname)-Positions	Team by Year	See Section	Hgt.	Wgt.	College	Int	Pts
Reece, Geoff C	76LA 77Sea 78Bal		6'4"	247	Washington State		
Reed, Alvin TE	67-69HouA 70-72Hou 73-75Was	2	6'5"	232	Prairie View		84
Reed, Frank DB	76-80Atl 83USFL		5'11"	193	Washington	6	6
Reed, Henry LB-DE	71-74NYG		6'3"	230	Weber State	3	
Reed, James LB	77Phi		6'2"	230	California		
Reed, Joe QB	72-74SF 75-79Det	12	6'1"	194	Mississippi State		12
Reed, Oscar HB-FB	68-74Min 75Atl	2	5'11"	222	Colorado State		66
Reed, Tony HB	77-80KC 81Den	2	5'11"	197	Colorado		60
Reese, Don DE-DT	74-76Mia 78-80NO 81SD 85USFL		6'6"	254	Jackson State		8
	1977 — Ineligible to play pro football						
Reese, Steve LB	74-75NYJ 76TB		6'2"	229	Louisville		
Reeves, Marion DB	74Phi		6'1"	195	Clemson		
Reid, Andy HB	76Buf		6'	195	Georgia		
Reid, Bill C	75SF 76KJ		6'1"	242	Stanford		
Reid, Mike DT	70-74Cin		6'3"	255	Penn State		
Reihner, George OG	77-79Hou 80KJ 82Hou		6'4"	263	Penn State		
Reilly, Kevin LB	73-74Phi 75NE		6'2"	220	Villanova	1	
Reinfeldt, Mike DB	76Oak 76-83Hou		6'2"	192	Wis.-Milwaukee	26	6
Renfro, Mel DB-HB	64-77Dal	3	6'	191	Oregon	52	36
Reppond, Mike WR	73Chi		6'	180	Arkansas		
Ressler, Glenn OG-C-OT-DT	65-74Bal		6'3"	247	Penn State		
Reutershan, Randy WR	78Pit		5'10"	182	Pittsburgh		
Reynolds, Jack (Hacksaw) LB	70-80LA 81-84SF		6'1"	232	Tennessee	6	6
Reynolds, Tom WR	72NE 73Chi 74JJ	2	6'3"	200	San Diego State		12
Rhodes, Bruce DB	76SF 77JJ 78Det		6'	189	San Fran. State	4	
Rhodes, Danny LB	74Bal		6'2"	220	Arkansas		
Rhodes, Ray DB-WR	74-79NYG 80SF	2	5'11"	185	Tulsa	8	42
Rhone, Earnest LB	75Mia 76KJ 77-84Mia		6'2"	220	Henderson State	14	
Rice, Andy DT	66-67KC-A 67HouA 68-69HouA 70-71SD		6'3"	268	Texas Southern		
	72-73Chi 74NYG						
Rice, Floyd LB-TE	71-73Hou 73-75SD 76-77Oak 78NO		6'3"	224	Alcorn State	7	6
Rice, Harold DE	71Oak		6'2"	230	Tennessee State		
Rice, Homer	HC78-79Cin				Centre		
Rich, Randy DB	77Det 77Den 78Oak 78-79Cle		5'10"	178	New Mexico		
Richards, Golden WR	73-78Dal 78-79Chi	23	6'	181	Hawaii		108
Richardson, Gloster WR	67-69KC-A 70KC 71Dal	2	6'	200	Jackson State		108
	72-74Cle						
Richardson, Grady TE	74-75WFL 79-80Was 83USFL		6'4"	225	Fullerton State		
Richardson, John DT	67-69MiaA 70-71Mia 72-73StL		6'2"	254	U.C.L.A.		
Richardson, Mike HB	69HouA 70-71Hou	2	5'11"	193	S.M.U.		20
Richardson, Pete DB	69BufA 70-71Buf		6'1"	197	Dayton	8	
Riggins, John FB	71-75NYJ 76-79Was 80HO 81-85Was	2	6'2"	232	Kansas State		696
Riley, Ken DB	69CinA 70-83Cin		6'	183	Florida A&M	65	30
Riley, Larry DB	77Den 78NYJ		5'10"	192	Salem		
Riley, Preston WR	70-72SF 73NO	2	6'	180	Memphis State		6
Riley, Steve OT	74-84Min		6'6"	258	Southern Calif.		
Rivera, Steve WR	76-77SF 77Chi 78JJ		5'11"	184	California		
Rivers, Jamie LB	68-73StL 74-75NYJ		6'2"	238	Bowling Green	4	
Rives, Don LB	73-78Chi		6'2"	225	Texas Tech	2	
Rizzo, Jack HB	73NYG		5'10"	195	Lehigh		
Rizzo, Joe LB	74-80Den		6'1"	220	King's Point	9	
Roach, Travis OG	74NYJ		6'2"	260	Texas		
Roan, Oscar TE	75-78Cle	2	6'6"	214	S.M.U.		54
Roberson, Vern DB	77Mia 78SF		6'1"	195	Grambling	2	
Roberts, Gary OG	70Atl		6'2"	242	Purdue		
Roberts, Guy LB	72-75Hou 76Atl 77Mia		6'1"	218	Maryland	5	
Roberts, Hal K	72StL	4	6'1"	180	Houston		
Roberts J.D.	HC72-74NO				Oklahoma		
Roberts, Willie DB	73Chi		6'1"	190	Houston		
Robertson, Isiah LB	71-78LA 79-82Buf		6'3"	226	Southern U.	25	24
Robinson, Craig OT	72-73NO		6'3"	250	Houston		
Robinson, Glenn DE-LB	75Bal 76-77TB		6'6"	242	Oklahoma State		
Robinson, Gregg DE-NT	78NYJ		6'6"	255	Dartmouth		
Robinson, Jim WR	76-79NYG 80SF 81LJ	23	5'9"	170	Georgia Tech		36
Robinson, Larry HB-FB	73Dal		6'4"	210	Tennessee		
Robinson, Paul HB	68-69CinA 70-72Cin 72-73Hou 74WFL	23	6'	199	Arizona		156
Robinson, Virgil HB	71-72NO	2	5'11"	195	Grambling		12
Robiskie, Terry FB-HB	77-79Oak 80-81Mia	2	6'1"	210	Louisiana State		30
Roche, Alden DE	70Den 71-76GB 77-78Sea		6'4"	255	Southern U.		
Roder, Mirro K	73-74Chi 76TB	5	6'1"	221	none		79
Rodgers, Johnny WR	77-78SD	23	5'10"	180	Nebraska		
Rodgers, Otis LB	77KC		6'3"	230	Iowa State		
Rodgers, Willie HB-FB	72Hou 73KJ 74-75Hou 76JJ	2	6'	210	Kentucky		50
Rogers, Mel LB	71SD 72SJ 73-74SD 75WFL 76LA 77Chi		6'2"	231	Florida A&M	1	
Rogers, Stan OT	75Den		6'4"	255	Maryland		
Rogers, Steve HB	75NO 76NYJ		6'2"	203	Louisiana State		
Roller, Dave DT	71NYG 74-75WFL 75-78GB 79-80Min		6'2"	270	Kentucky		
Roman, John OT-OG	76-82NYJ		6'4"	255	Idaho State		
Roman, Nick DE	70-71Cin 72-73Cle		6'3"	235	Ohio State	1	6
Romaniszyn, Jim LB	73-74Cle 76NE 77-78JJ		6'2"	219	Edinboro		
Rosecrans, James LB	76NYJ		6'1"	230	Penn State		
Ross, Louis DE	71-72Buf 74WFL 75KC 76JJ		6'6"	248	S. Carolina State		
Ross, Oliver HB-FB	73-75Den 76Sea	23	6'	210	Alabama A&M		
Rossovich, Tim LB-DE	68-71Phi 72-73SD 74-75WFL		6'4"	245	Southern Calif.	3	
Rothwell, Fred C	74Det		6'3"	240	Kansas State		
Roussel, Tom LB	68-70Was 71-72NO 73Phi		6'3"	235	Southern Miss.	2	
Rowden, Larry DB	71-72Chi		6'2"	220	Houston		
Rowe, Bob DT-DE	67-75StL 76XJ		6'4"	258	Western Michigan	2	6
Rowe, Dave DT-NT	67-70NO 71-73NE 74-75SD		6'6"	273	Penn State		
Rowser, John DB	67-69GB 70-73Pit 74-76Den		6'1"	185	Michigan	26	24
Rozier, Bob DE	79StL		6'3"	240	California		
Rozumek, Dave LB	76-79KC		6'1"	215	New Hampshire	2	
Rucker, Conrad TE	78-79Hou 80TB 80LA		6'3"	255	Southern U.		
Rucker, Reggie WR	70-71Dal 71NYG 71-74NE 75-81Cle	2	6'2"	190	Boston U.		264
Rudnay, Jack C	70-82KC		6'3"	240	Northwestern		
Rudnick, Tim DB	74Bal		5'10"	185	Notre Dame		
Rudolph, Council DE	72Hou 73-75StL 76-77TB		6'3"	255	Kentucky State	1	
Rudzinski, Paul LB	78-80GB 81XJ		6'1"	220	Michigan State	1	
Russ, Carl LB	75Atl 76-77NYJ		6'2"	227	Michigan		
Russell, Andy LB	63Pit 64-65MS 66-76Pit		6'3"	221	Missouri	18	13
Ruud, Tom LB	75-77Buf 78-79Cin		6'2"	225	Nebraska		
Ryckman, Billy WR	77-79Atl 80KJ 83USFL	23	5'11"	172	Louisiana Tech		30
Ryczek, Dan C	73-75Was 76-77TB 78-79LA 87Phi		6'3"	246	Virginia		
Ryczek, Paul C	74-79Atl 81NO		6'2"	231	Virginia		
Rydalch, Ron DT	75-80Chi		6'4"	259	Utah		
St. Clair, Mike DE	76-79Cle 80-82Cin 84-85USFL		6'5"	249	Grambling		6
Salaam, Abdul DT-DE	76-83NYJ		6'3"	262	Kent State		
	1976 — Played as Lary Faulk						
Salter, Bryant DB	71-73SD 74-75Was 76Mia 76Bal		6'4"	196	Pittsburgh	17	

UseName(Nickname)-Positions	Team by Year	See Section	Hgt.	Wgt.	College	Int	Pts
Sampson, Greg OT-DT-DE	72-78Hou 79IL		6'6"	266	Stanford		
Sampson, Howard DB	78-79GB		5'10"	185	Arkansas		
Samuels, Tony TE	76-80KC 80TB 81KJ 83USFL	2	6'4"	230	Bethune-Cookman		18
Sanders, Charlie TE	68-77Det	2	6'4"	227	Minnesota		186
Sanders, Clarence LB	78,80KC		6'4"	229	Cincinnati		
Sanders, Deac DB	74-76NE 77-79Phi		6'1"	177	South Dakota	17	12
Sanders, Ken DE	72-79Det 80-81Min		6'5"	242	Howard Payne		
Sanderson, Reggie HB	73Chi		5'10"	206	Stanford		
Sandler, Dill DT-DE	74-76SF 77-78Sea 79KJ		6'6"	268	U.C.L.A.		
Satterwhite, Howard WR	76NYJ 77Was 77Bal		5'11"	185	Sam Houston St.		
Saul, Rich C-OG-OT-LB	70-81LA		6'3"	241	Michigan State		
Saul, Ron OG	70-75Hou 76-81Was		6'2"	254	Michigan State		
Saunders, John DB	72Buf 74-75SF		6'3"	198	Toledo		
Sawyer, Ken DB	74Cin		6'	192	Syracuse		
Scales, Hurles DB	74Chi 74StL 75GB		6'1"	200	North Texas		
Scarber, Sam FB	75-76SD 78JJ	2	6'2"	232	New Mexico		24
Schaukowitz, Carl OG	75Den 76JJ		6'2"	237	Penn State		
Schaum, Greg DE	76Dal 77KJ 78NE		6'4"	246	Michigan State		
Schindler, Steve OG	77-78Den 79KJ		6'3"	256	Boston College		
Schmidt, Terry DB	74-75NO 76-84Chi		6'	178	Ball State	26	18
Schmiesing, Joe DT-DE	68-71StL 72Det 73Bal 74NYJ		6'4"	253	New Mexico State		
Schmit, Bob LB	75-76NYG		6'1"	220	Nebraska		
Schnarr, Steve FB	75Buf		6'2"	216	Otterbein		
Schnellenberger, Howard	HC73-74Bal				Kentucky		
Schnitker, Mike OG	69DenA 70-74Den		6'3"	243	Colorado		
Schoen, Tom DB	70Cle		5'11"	185	Notre Dame		
Schreiber, Larry HB-FB	71-75SF 76Chi 77JJ	2	6'	206	Tennessee Tech		85
Schubert, Steve WR	74NE 75-79Chi	23	5'10"	187	Massachusetts		24
Schultz, John WR	76-78Den		5'10"	182	Maryland		
Schumacher, Kurt OG-OT	75-77NO 78TB		6'3"	252	Ohio State		
Scoinik, Glenn WR	73Pit		6'3"	190	Indiana		
Scott, Bo FB	69 74Cle	23	6'3"	213	Ohio State		144
Scott, Bobby QB	73-82NO 83USFL	12	6'1"	198	Tennessee		6
Scott, Clarence DB	71-83Cle		6'	183	Kansas State	39	18
Scott, Clarence DB	69BosA 70Bos 71-72NE		6'2"	204	Morgan State	1	
Scott, Dave OG-OT	76-82Atl		6'4"	276	Kansas		
Scott, Freddie WR	74-77Bal 78-83Det 84USFL	2	6'2"	178	Amherst		126
Scott, Herbert OG	75-84Dal		6'2"	254	Virginia Union		
Scott, Jake DB	70-75Mia 76-78Was	3	6'	188	Georgia	49	6
Scott, James WR	76-80Chi 81CFL 82Chi	2	6'1"	190	Henderson J.C.		120
Scribner, Rick OG	77GB		6'4"	257	Idaho State		
Scribner, Rob HB	73-76LA 77LJ	23	6'	200	U.C.L.A.		24
Seabron, Thomas LB	79-80SF 80StL		6'3"	215	Michigan		
Seal, Paul TE	74-76NO 77-79SF	2	6'4"	223	Michigan		48
Seifert, Mike DE	74Cle		6'3"	245	Wisconsin		
Seiler, Paul OT-C	67NY-A 68MS 69NY-A 70JJ		6'4"	258	Notre Dame		
	71-73Oak 74-75WFL						
Seiple, Larry TE-HB-K	67-69MiaA 70-77Mia	2 4	6'	213	Kentucky		42
Seivers, Larry WR	77Phi		6'4"	204	Tennessee		
Selfridge, Andy LB	72Buf 74-75NYG 76Mia 77NYG		6'4"	220	Virginia	1	
Sellers, Ron WR	69BosA 70Bos 71NE 72Dal 73Mia	2	6'4"	196	Florida State		108
Selmon, Dewey LB-DT	76-80TB 81LJ 82SD		6'1"	246	Oklahoma	3	
Sensibaugh, Mike DB	71-75KC 76-78StL		5'11"	191	Ohio State	27	12
Severson, Jeff DB	72Was 73-74Hou 75Den 76-77StL	3	6'1"	183	Long Beach State	6	
	79LA						
Sevy, Jeff OT-OG-DT-DE	75-78Chi79-80Sea83-84USFL		6'5"	259	California		
Sexton, Brent DB	77Pit		6'1"	190	Elon		
Seymour, Jim WR	70-72Chi	2	6'4"	210	Notre Dame		30
Seymour, Paul TE	73-77Buf	2	6'5"	250	Michigan		18
Shanklin, Ron WR	70 74Pit 75-76Chi	2	6'1"	183	North Texas		144
Sharp, Rich OT	70-71Pit 72Den		6'3"	264	Washington		
Shaw, Bob WR	70NO		6'	194	Winston-Salem St.		
Shaw, Dennis QB	70-73Buf 74-75StL 76NYG 78KC	12	6'2"	213	San Diego State		
	84USFL						
Shears, Larry DB	71-72Atl		5'10"	185	Lincoln (Mo.)		
Shelby, Willie HB	76-77Cin 78StL	3	5'11"	195	Alabama	12	
Shell, Art OT	68-69OakA 70-81Oak 82Raid HC89-92Raid		6'5"	267	Md. Eastern Shore		
Sheppard, Henry OG-OT	76-81Cle		6'6"	255	S.M.U.		
Sherk, Jerry DT-DE-NT	70-81Cle		6'4"	252	Oklahoma State	3	2
Sherman, Rod WR-FL	67Oak A 68CinA 69OakA	23	6'	190	Southern Calif.		40
	70-71Oak 72Den 73LA						
Shinners, John OG	69-71NO 72Bal 73-77Cin		6'2"	255	Xavier-Ohio		
Shipp, Joe TE	79Buf		6'4"	225	Southern Calif.		6
Shipp, Ken	HC75NYJ				Middle Tenn. St.		
Shirk, Gary TE	74-75WFL 76-82NYG 84-85USFL	2	6'1"	220	Morehead State		66
Shoate, Rod LB	75NE 76KJ 77-81NE 83-84USFL		6'1"	214	Oklahoma	5	6
Shumon, Ron LB	78Cin 79SF		6'1"	230	Wichita State	1	
Shy, Don HB-FB	67-68Pit 69-70NO 70-72Chi 73StL	23	6'1"	209	San Diego State		84
Siani, Mike WR	72-77Oak 78-80Bal	2	6'2"	196	Villanova		102
Siemon, Jeff LB	72-82Min		6'2"	235	Stanford	11	
Sikich, Mike OG	71Cle		6'2"	243	Northwestern		
Simon, Bobby OT-OG	76Hou		6'3"	252	Grambling		
Simone, Mike LB	72-74Den		6'	210	Stanford		
Simonini, Ed LB	76-81Bal 82NO		6'	210	Texas A&M	3	
Simons, Keith NT-DT	76-77KC 78-79StL		6'3"	254	Minnesota		
Simonson, Dave OT	74Bal 75NYG 76Hou 76Sea 77Det		6'6"	248	Minnesota		
Simpson, Al OT-OG	75-76NYG		6'5"	255	Colorado State		
Simpson, Bill DB	74-78LA 79VR 80-82Buf		6'1"	184	Michigan State	33	2
Simpson, Bob DE	78Mia		6'5"	235	Colorado		
Simpson, Mike DB	70-73SF		5'11"	172	Houston	3	6
Simpson, Nate HB-FB	77-79GB	2	5'11"	189	Tennessee State		6
Simpson, O.J. (Juice) HB	69BufA70-77Buf78-79SF	23	6'2"	211	Southern Calif.		456
Sims, David HB	77-79Sea	2	6'3"	216	Georgia Tech		138
Sims, Jimmy LB	76TB		6'	195	Southern Calif.		
Sims, Mickey DT	77-79Cle		6'5"	278	S. Carolina State		
Singletary, Bill LB	74NYG		6'2"	230	Temple		
Singleton, Ron OT	76SD 77-80SF		6'7"	260	Grambling		
Sipe, Brian QB	74-83Cle 84-85USFL	12	6'1"	193	San Diego State		67
Sisemore, Jerry OT-OG	73-84Phi		6'4"	261	Texas		
Sistrunk, Manny DT-DE	70-75Was 76-79Phi		6'5"	269	Ark.-Pine Bluff		
Sistrunk, Otis DT-DE-NT	72-78Oak 79JJ		6'4"	265	none	3	2
Siwek, Mike DT	70StL		6'3"	260	Western Michigan		
Skinner, Gerald OT	78GB		6'4"	260	Arkansas		
Skorupan, John LB	73-77Buf 78-80NYG		6'2"	222	Penn State	2	2
Sledge, Leroy FB	71Hou		6'2"	230	Bakersfield J.C.		6
Sloan, Ronnie OT	73StL		6'5"	260	Austin Peay		
Slough, Greg LB	71-72Oak		6'3"	230	Southern Calif.		
Small, Eldridge DB	72-74NYG		6'1"	190	Texas A&I	1	
Small, John LB-DT	70-72Atl 73-74Det 75JJ		6'5"	260	The Citadel		

UseName(Nickname)-Positions	TeambyYear	See Section	Hgt.	Wgt.	College	Int	Pts
Smith, Barry WR	73-75GB 76TB	2	6'1"	190	Florida State		24
Smith, Barty FB	74-80GB	2	6'4"	240	Richmond		126
Smith, Blane LB	77GB		6'3"	238	Purdue		
Smith, Bubba DE-DT	67-71Bal 72KJ 73-74Oak 75-76Hou		6'7"	280	Michigan State		
Smith, Charlie HB	68-69Oak 70-74Oak 75SD 76KJ	23	6'1"	205	Utah		204
Smith, Charlie WR	74-81Phi 83-84USFL	2	6'1"	185	Grambling		150
Smith, Dave WR	70-72Pit 72Hou 72KC	2	6'2"	205	Indiana State		42
Smith, Donnell DE	71GB 73-74NE		6'4"	247	Southern U.		
Smith, Ed DE	73-74Den 75KJ		6'5"	241	Colorado College	1	
Smith, Jack DB	71Phi		6'4"	204	Troy State		
Smith, Jerry OG-LB	52-53SF 54-55MS 56SF 56GB HC71Den		6'1"	230	Wisconsin		
Smith, Jerry TE-WR	65-77Was	2	6'2"	209	Arizona State		360
Smith, John K	74-83NE	5	6'	186	King Alfred's (U.K.), SouthamptonU. (U.K.)		692
Smith, John WR	79Cle		6'	175	Tennessee State		
Smith, Ken TE	73Cle 74JJ		6'4"	225	New Mexico		
Smith, Larry HB	69-73LA 74Was	2	6'3"	220	Florida		96
Smith, Laverne HB	77Pit 78LJ		5'10"	193	Kansas		
Smith, Lyman DT	78Min 79JJ		6'5"	250	Duke		
Smith, Marty DE	76Buf		6'3"	250	Louisville		
Smith, Ollie WR	73-74Bal 76-77GB	2	6'2"	198	Tennessee		6
Smith, Paul DT-DE	68-69DenA 70-78Den 79-80Was		6'3"	254	New Mexico	2	6
Smith, Perry DB	73-76GB 77-79StL 80-81Den		6'1"	193	Colorado State	13	
Smith, Ron DB-FL-HB	65Chi 66-67Atl 68-69LA 70-72Chi 73SD 74Oak	23	6'1"	191	Wisconsin	13	36
Smith, Royce OG	72-73NO 74-76Atl		6'3"	250	Georgia		
Smith, Sherman HB-FB	76-82Sea 83SD	2	6'4"	223	Miami-Ohio		228
Smith, Sid C-OT	70-72KC 73JJ 74Hou		6'4"	260	Southern Calif.		
Smith, Steve OT-DE-TE	66Pit 68-70Min 71-74Phi		6'5"	246	Michigan		6
Smith, Toby DE	71-72Dal 73-76Hou 76Buf 77JJ		6'5"	248	Southern Calif.	1	
Sniadecki, Jim LB	69-73SF 74-75WFL		6'2"	224	Indiana	1	
Snider, Mel OG-OT	69-71Atl 72-74GB		6'5"	250	Michigan State		
Snow, Jack WR-DE	65-75LA	2	6'2"	195	Notre Dame		270
Snowden, Cal DE	69-70StL 71Buf 72-73SD		6'4"	247	Indiana		
Snyder, Todd WR	70-72Atl	2	6'2"	187	Ohio U.		12
Sodaski, John LB-DB	70-72Pit 73Phi		6'1"	214	Villanova	1	
Sorey, Revie OG	75-81Chi 82ZJ 83Chi		6'2"	262	Illinois		
Southard, Tommy WR	78StL 78Hou		6'	185	Furman		
Sowells, Rich DB	71-76NYJ 77Hou		6'	179	Alcorn State	10	6
Spencer, Mo DB	74-76NO 77ZJ 78NO		6'	176	N. Car. Central	5	
Spencer, Willie FB	76Min 77-78NYG	2	6'3"	235	none		30
Speyrer, Cotton WR	72-74Bal 75Mia	23	6'	175	Texas		36
Spicer, Bob LB	73NYJ		6'4"	227	Indiana		
Spills, John WR	69-71GB	2	6'3"	205	Northern Illinois		6
Spiva, Andy LB	77Atl 78KJ		6'2"	218	Tennessee		
Sprout, Dennis QB	78GB		6'2"	210	Arizona State		
Spurrier, Steve QB	67-75SF 76TB	12 4	6'2"	202	Florida		12
Stabler, Ken (Snake) QB	70-79Oak 80-81Hou 82-84NO	12	6'3"	210	Alabama		24
Staggers, Jon WR	70-71Pit 72-74GB 75Det	23	5'10"	185	Missouri		66
Staggs, Jeff LB-DE	67-69SD-A 70-71SD 73-74StL 74SD		6'2"	242	San Diego State	3	
Staley, Bill DT	68-69CinA 70-72Chi		6'3"	249	Utah State		
Stanback, Haskel HB-FB	74-79Atl	2	6'	210	Tennessee		156
Stanfill, Bill DE	69MiaA 70-76Mia 77ZJ		6'5"	251	Georgia	2	12
Starch, Ken FB	76GB		5'11"	210	Wisconsin		
Starke, George OT	73-84Was		6'5"	252	Columbia		
Staroba, Paul WR	72Cle 73GB		6'3"	204	Michigan		6
Staubach, Roger (The Dodger) QB	69-79Dal	12	6'2"	198	Navy		120
Steele, Robert WR	78Dal 79Min		6'4"	196	North Alabama		
Stegent, Larry HB	71StL 72SJ		6'1"	200	Texas A&M		
Stein, Bob LB-DE	69KC-A 70-72KC 73-74LA 75SD 75Min 76JJ		6'2"	235	Minnesota	2	
Steinfort, Fred K	76Oak 77-78Atl 79-81Den 82Buf	5	5'11"	180	Boston College		304
Stemrick, Greg DB	75-82Hou 83NO		5'11"	185	Colorado State	15	6
Stenerud, Jan K	67-69KC-A 70-79KC 80-83GB 84-85Min	5	6'2"	188	Montana State		1699
Stenger, Brian LB	69-72Pit 73NE		6'4"	226	Notre Dame	3	
Stephens, Bruce WR	78NYJ		5'9"	170	Columbia		
Steptoe, Jack WR	78SF 84USFL		6'1"	175	Utah		6
Stevens, Dick OT	70-74Phi		6'4"	241	Baylor		
Stevens, Howard WR	73-74NO 75-77Bal	23	5'5"	167	Louisville		24
Stevenson, Ricky DB	70Cle		5'11"	188	Arizona		
Stewart, Jimmy DB	77NO 78KJ 79Det 80LJ		5'11"	190	Tulsa		
Stewart, Joe WR	78-79Oak		5'11"	180	Missouri		
Stewart, Steve LB	78Atl 79GB		6'2"	219	Minnesota		
Stewart, Wayne TE	69NY-A 70-72NYJ 74SD	2	6'7"	214	California		12
Stidham, Howard LB	77SF		6'2"	214	Tennessee Tech		
Stienke, Jim DB	73Cle 74-77NYG 78Atl		5'11"	183	SW Texas State	4	6
Stillwell, Roger DT-DE	75-77Chi		6'5"	259	Stanford		
Stincic, Tom LB	69-71Dal 72NO		6'2"	229	Michigan	1	
Stingley, Darryl WR	73-77NE 78XJ 1978- Paralyzed in game	2	6'	194	Purdue		96
Stokes, Tim OT	74LA 75-77Was 78-80GB 81NYG 81-82GB		6'5"	252	Oregon		
Stolberg, Eric WR	71NE		6'2"	180	Indiana		
Stone, Ken DB-WR	72Buf 73-75Was 76TB 77-80StL		6'1"	180	Vanderbilt	27	6
Story, Bill OT	75KC		6'3"	245	Southern Illinois		
Stowe, Otto WR	71-72Mia 73Dal 74Den	2	6'2"	188	Iowa State		12
Strachan, Mike HB	75-80NO	2	6'	199	Iowa State		84
Strada, John TE	74KC		6'3"	230	William Jewell		
Strayhorn, Les HB	73-74Dal		5'10"	205	East Carolina		6
Stringer, Art LB	77-81Hou		6'1"	223	Ball State	4	
Stringert, Hal DB	75-80SD		5'11"	185	Hawaii	8	
Strong, Jim HB-FB	70SF 71-72NO	2	6'1"	204	Houston		18
Stroud, Morris TE	69KC-A 70-74KC	2	6'10"	250	Clark-Ga.		42
Strozier, Art TE	70-71SD		6'2"	220	Kansas State		
Stuckey, Henry DB	73-74Mia 75-76NYG		6'1"	180	Missouri	2	
Studdard, Vern WR	71NYJ		5'11"	175	Mississippi		
Stukes, Charlie DB	67-72Bal 73-74LA 75KJ		6'3"	212	Md. Eastern Shore	32	6
Sturt, Fred OG	74Was 76-78NE 78-81NO		6'4"	255	Bowling Green		
Suggs, Shafer DB	76-80NYJ 80Cin 81CFL 83USFL		6'1"	200	Ball State	7	6
Sullivan, Dave WR	73-74Cle		5'11"	185	Virginia		
Sullivan, Gerry C-OT-OG	74-81Cle 84-85USFL		6'4"	250	Illinois		
Sullivan, Jim DT-DE	70Atl		6'4"	240	Lincoln (Mo.)		
Sullivan, John LB	79-80NYJ		6'1"	223	Illinois		
Sullivan, Pat QB	72-75Atl	1	6'	200	Auburn		
Sullivan, Tom (Silky) HB-FB	72-77Phi 78Cle	23	6'	190	Miami (Fla.)		132
Sumler, Tony DB	78Det		5'10"	185	Wichita State		
Summerell, Carl QB	74-75NYG	1	6'4"	208	East Carolina		
Summers, Freddie DB	69-71Cle		6'1"	180	Wake Forest		
Sumers, Wilbur K	77Det	4	6'4"	220	Louisville		
Sumner, Walt DB	69-74Cle		6'1"	188	Florida State	15	6

UseName(Nickname)-Positions	TeambyYear	See Section	Hgt.	Wgt.	College	Int	Pts
Sutherland, Doug DT-OG-DE	70NO 71-80Min 81Sea		6'3"	250	Wis.-Superior		
Sutton, Mitch DT	74-75Phi		6'4"	260	Kansas		
Swann, Lynn WR	74-82Pit	23	6'	180	Southern Calif.		318
Sweeney, Steve WR	73Oak		6'3"	205	California		
Sweet, Joe WR	72-73LA 74NE 75SD	2	6'2"	196	Tennessee State		8
Swenson, Bob LB	75-79Den 80BA 81-83Den 84KJ		6'3"	222	California	11	6
Swift, Doug LB	70-75Mia		6'3"	228	Amherst	5	
Swinney, Clovis DT	70NO 71NYJ		6'3"	240	Arkansas State		
Switzer, Marvin DB	78Buf		6'	192	Kansas State		
Sykes, Al WR	71NE		6'3"	180	Florida A&M		
Sykes, John HB	72SD		5'11"	195	Morgan State		
Sylvester, Steve C-OG-OT	75-81Oak 82-83Raid		6'4"	261	Notre Dame		
Szaro, Richie K	75-78NO 79NYJ	5	5'11"	204	Harvard		193
Taffoni, Joe OT-OG	67-70Cle 72-73NYG		6'3"	251	West Virginia,		
Tagge, Jerry QB	72-74GB	12	6'2"	218	Nebraska		18
Talbert, Diron DT-DE	67-70LA 71-80Was		6'5"	252	Texas		
Tannen, Steve DB	70-74NYJ 75SJ		6'1"	194	Florida	12	6
Tanner, John LB	71SD 73-74NE		6'4"	231	Tennessee Tech		6
Tarver, John FB	72-74NE 75Phi	2	6'3"	224	Colorado		48
Tatarek, Bob DT	68-69BufA 70-72Buf 72Det		6'4"	260	Miami (Fla.)		
Tate, Frank LB	75SD 76JJ		6'3"	225	N. Car. Central		
Tate, John LB	76NYG		6'2"	230	Jackson State		
Tatum, Jack DB	71-79Oak 80Hou		5'10"	203	Ohio State	37	6
Taylor, Altie HB	69-75Det 76Hou	23	5'10"	199	Utah State		180
Taylor, Bruce DB	70-77SF	3	6'	184	Boston U.	18	12
Taylor, Charley WR-HB-OE	64-75Was 76SJ 77Was	2	6'3"	210	Arizona State		540
Taylor, Clifton HB	74,76GB	3	6'	198	Memphis State		12
Taylor, David OT	73-77Bal 78NJ 79Bal		6'4"	260	Catawba		
Taylor, Ed DB	75-79NYJ 79-81Mia 83USFL		6'	174	Memphis State	8	
Taylor, Jesse HB	72SD	3	6'	200	Cincinnati		6
Taylor, Joe DB	67-74Chi		6'2"	189	N. Carolina A&T	15	
Taylor, Mike OT	68-69Pit 69-70NO 71Was 73StL		6'4"	247	Southern Calif.		
Taylor, Mike LB	72-73NYJ 74WFL		6'1"	230	Michigan	1	
Taylor, Otis WR-FL-OE	65-69KC-A 70-75KC	2	6'2"	215	Prairie View		360
Taylor, Steve DB	76KC		6'3"	204	Kansas		
Taylor, Willie WR	78GB		6'1"	179	Pittsburgh		
Tearry, Larry C	78-79Det		6'3"	260	Wake Forest		
Teel, Jim LB	73Det		6'3"	225	Purdue		
Teerlinck, John DT	74-75SD 76KJ		6'5"	248	Western Illinois		
Ten Napel, Garth LB	76-77Det 78Atl 79AA		6'1"	213	Texas A&M		
Terry, Nat DB	78Pit 78Det		5'11"	165	Florida State		
Testerman, Don FB	76-78Sea 79KJ 80Mia	2	6'2"	231	Clemson		42
Thaxton, Jim TE-WR	73-74SD 74Cle 76-77NO 78StL	2	6'2"	241	Tennessee State	1	30
Thomas, Bill FB	72Dal 73Hou 74KC	3	6'2"	225	Boston College		
Thomas, Bob HB	71-72LA 73-74SD	2	5'10"	201	Arizona State		24
Thomas, Charlie HB	75KC		5'9"	180	Tennessee State		
Thomas, Donnie LB	76NE		6'2"	245	Indiana		
Thomas, Duane HB-FB	70-71Dal 72HO 73-74Was	2	6'1"	215	West Texas State		144
Thomas, Earl WR-TE	71-73Chi 74-75StL 76Hou	2	6'3"	219	Houston		90
Thomas, Earlie DB	70-74NYJ 75Den		6'1"	190	Colorado State	7	6
Thomas, Emmitt DB	66-69KC-A 70-78KC	3	6'2"	192	Bishop	58	30
Thomas, Ike DB-WR	71Dal 71-73GB 74-75WFL 75Buf	3	6'2"	194	Bishop	2	12
Thomas, Jimmy HB-WR	69-73SF	2	6'1"	215	Texas-Arlington		72
Thomas, Joe	HC74Bal				Ohio Northern		
Thomas, J.T. DB	73-77Pit 78IL 79-81Pit 82Den		6'2"	196	Florida State	20	12
Thomas, Lee DE	71-72SD 73Cin 75LJ		6'5"	246	Jackson State		
Thomas, Mike HB	75-78Was 79-80SD	2	5'11"	190	Nevada-Las Vegas		180
Thomas, Pat DB	76-82LA		5'9"	183	Texas A&M	26	6
Thomas, Skip (Dr. Death) DB	72-77Oak		6'1"	205	Southern Calif.	17	6
Thomas, Speedy WR	69CinA 70-72Cin 73-74NO	2	6'1"	174	Utah		54
Thomas, Spencer DB	75Was		6'2"	185	Washburn		
Thompson, Billy DB	69DenA 70-81Den	3	6'1"	200	Md. Eastern Shore	40	42
Thompson, Bobby HB	75-76Det	23	5'11"	195	Oklahoma		6
Thompson, Dave OT-C-OG	71-73Det 74-75NO		6'4"	271	Clemson		
Thompson, James WR	78NYG		6'	178	Memphis State		
Thompson, Jesse WR	78Det 79IL 80Det 81FJ	2	6'1"	185	California		24
Thompson, Norm DB	71-76StL 77-79Bal		6'1"	179	Utah	33	24
Thompson, Ricky WR	76-77Bal 78-81Was 82StL	2	6'	176	Baylor		84
Thompson (born Symonds), Rocky HB	71-73NYG	23	5'11"	200	West Texas State		18
Thompson, Steve DT-DE	68-69NY-A 70NYJ 71VR 72-73NYJ 74WFL		6'5"	244	Washington		
Thompson, Ted LB	75-84Hou		6'1"	220	S.M.U.		4
Thompson, Tommy HB	74SD		6'1"	205	Southern Illinois		
Thompson, Woody FB	75-77Atl	2	6'1"	228	Miami (Fla.)		6
Thoms, Art DT-DE-NT	69OakA 70-75Oak 76KJ 77Phi		6'5"	251	Syracuse	2	6
Thornbladh, Bob LB	74KC		6'1"	220	Michigan		
Threadgill, Bruce DB-QB	78SF 79-82CFL 84-85USFL		6'	190	Mississippi State		
Thrower, Jim DB	70-72Phi 73-74Det 75KJ		6'2"	194	East Texas State		
Tierney, Leo C	78Cle 78NYG		6'3"	248	Georgia Tech		
Tilleman, Mike DT	66Min 67-70NO 71-72Hou 73-76Atl		6'5"	275	Montana		
Tillman, Andre TE	75-78Mia 79BL	2	6'5"	230	Texas Tech		36
Tillman, Faddie DE-DT	72NO		6'5"	230	Boise State		
Tillman, Rusty LB	70-77Was		6'2"	230	Northern Arizona		
Tinker, Gerald WR	74-75Atl 75GB 76KJ	3	5'9"	173	Kent State		18
Tipton, Dave DE-DT	71-73NYG 74-75SD 75NE 76Sea		6'6"	242	Stanford		
Tipton, Dave NT-DT	75NE 75SD 76NE 77CFL 83-85USFL		6'1"	253	Western Illinois		
Tolbert, Jim DB	66-69SD-A 70-71SD 72Hou 73-75StL 76SD		6'3"	207	Lincoln (Mo.)	10	
Tom, Mel DE	67-73Phi 73-75Chi		6'4"	247	Hawaii, San Jose St.		2
Toner, Tom LB	73GB 74BC 75-77GB		6'3"	233	Idaho State	4	2
Toomay, Pat DE	70-74Dal 75Buf 76TB 77-79Oak		6'4"	245	Vanderbilt	2	6
Torkelson, Eric HB-FB	74-79GB 80LJ 81GB	2	6'2"	196	Connecticut		54
Torrey, Bob FB	79NYG 79Mia 80Phi		6'4"	231	Penn State		6
Towle, Steve LB	75-80Mia 81LJ		6'2"	233	Kansas	3	
Townsend, Curtis DB	78StL		6'1"	229	Arkansas		
Troup, Bill QB	74Bal 75Phi 76-79Bal 80GB	12	6'5"	218	South Carolina		12
Trumpy, Bob TE-WR	68-69CinA 70-77Cin	2	6'6"	226	Illinois, Utah		210
Tucker, Bob TE	70-77NYG 77-80Min	2	6'3"	230	Bloomsburg		168
Tullis, Walter WR	78-79GB 83USFL	2	6'	170	Delaware State		6
Turk, Goodwin LB	75NYJ 76-78Den		6'3"	230	Southern U.	4	
Turnbow, Jesse DT	78Cle		6'7"	272	Tenessee		
Turner, Cecil WR	68-73Chi	23	5'10"	172	Cal. Poly.-S.L.O.		36
Turner, Clem FB	69CinA 70-72Den	2	6'1"	238	Cincinnati		18
Turner, Deacon HB	78-80Cin	23	5'11"	211	San Diego State		12
Turner, Jim K	64-69NY-A 70NYJ 71-79Den	5	6'2"	206	Utah State		1439
Turner, Robert HB	78Hou		5'11"	200	Oklahoma State		
Turner, Rocky WR-DB	72-73NYJ		6'	195	Tenn.-Chattanooga		

UseName(Nickname)-Positions	Team by Year	See Section	Hgt.	Wgt.	College	Int	Pts
Turner, Wylie DB	79-80GB		5'10"	182	Angelo State	2	
Twilley, Howard WR	66-69MiaA 70-76Mia	2	5'10"	183	Tulsa		138
Tyler, Maurice DB	72Buf 73-74Den 75SD 76Det 77NYJ 78NYG 80CFL 83-84USFL		6'	189	Morgan State	5	6
Upchurch, Rick WR	75-83Den	23	5'10"	175	Minnesota		210
Uperesa, Tuufuli OG	71Phi		6'3"	255	Montana		
Upshaw, Gene OG-OT	67-69OakA 70-81Oak		6'5"	255	Texas A&I		
Upshaw, Marv DE-DT	68-69Cle 70-75KC 76StL		6'3"	253	Trinity (Texas)	2	6
Vactor, Ted DB	69-73Was 74JJ 75Chi	3	6'	185	Nebraska	2	6
Vanderbundt, Skip LB	69-77SF 78NO		6'3"	227	Oregon State	14	18
Van Duyne, Bob OG-OT	74-80Bal 81-82CFL 83-84USFL		6'5"	243	Idaho		
Van Dyke, Bruce OG	66Phi 67-73Pit 74-76GB		6'2"	248	Missouri		
van Eeghen, Mark FB-HB	74-81Oak 82-83NE	2	6'2"	223	Colgate		252
Van Galder, Tim QB	72StL	1	6'1"	190	Iowa State		
Van Heusen, Bill WR-K	68-69DenA 70-76Den	2 4	6'1"	200	Maryland		72
Van Horn, Doug OG-OT	66Det 68-79NYG		6'2"	245	Ohio State		
Van Note, Jeff C-OG-LB	69-86Atl		6'2"	248	Kentucky		
Vanoy, Vern DT	71NYG 72GB		6'3"	270	Kansas		
Van Pelt, Brad LB	73-83NYG 84-85Raid 86Cle		6'5"	235	Michigan State	20	
Van Valkenberg, Pete HB	73Buf 74GB 74Chi		6'2"	194	Brigham Young		
Van Wagner, James HB	78NO		6'	202	Michigan Tech		
Varty, Mike LB	74Was 75Bal		6'1"	223	Northwestern		
Vataha, Randy WR	71-76NE 77GB	2	5'10"	173	Stanford		138
Vella, John OT	72-77Oak 78Chest Injury 79Oak 80Min		6'4"	258	Southern Calif.		
Vermeil, Dick	HC76-82Phi				San Jose State		
Verteteuille, Brian OT	74SD		6'3"	252	Idaho State		
Villapiano, Phil LB	71-79Oak 80-83Buf		6'1"	222	Bowling Green	11	8
Vincent, Ted DT	78Cin 79-80SF		6'4"	264	Wichita State		
Vinyard, Kenny K	70Atl	5	5'10"	190	Texas Tech		50
Vitali, Mark QB	77KC		6'5"	209	Purdue		
Voight, Mike HB	77Hou 78JJ		6'	214	North Carolina		
Voigt, Stu TE	70-80Min	2	6'1"	223	Wisconsin		108
Volk, Rick DB	67-75Bal 76NYG 77-78Mia	3	6'3"	195	Michigan	38	6
Waddell, Charles TE	77TB		6'5"	235	North Carolina		
Wade, Charlie WR	74Chi 75GB 77KC	2	5'10"	163	Tennessee State		6
Wafer, Carl DT	74NYG		6'3"	250	Tennessee State		
Wages, Harmon FB-HB	69-71Atl 72KJ 73Atl	2	6'1"	214	Florida		60
Wagner, Mike DB	71-80Pit		6'1"	200	Western Illinois	36	6
Wagner, Steve DB	76-79GB 80Phi 81SJ		6'2"	206	Wisconsin		
Walden, Bobby K	64-67Min 68-77Pit	4	6'	192	Georgia		
Walik, Billy WR	70-72Phi	3	5'11"	180	Villanova		6
Walker, Chuck DT-DE	64-72StL 72-75Atl		6'2"	249	Duke	1	
Walker, Cleo LB-C	70GB 71Atl		6'3"	220	Louisville		
Walker, Donnie DB	73-74Buf 75NYJ	3	6'1"	182	Central St.-Ohio	1	
Walker, Elliott HB	78SF		5'11"	193	Pittsburgh		
Walker, Glen K	77-78LA 83USFL	4	6'1"	210	Southern Calif.		
Walker, Louie LB	74Dal		6'1"	216	Colorado State		
Walker, Mike K	73NE	5	6'	190	none		21
Walker, Mike DE	71NO		6'4"	235	Tulane		
Walker, Randy K	74GB 75JJ	4	5'10"	177	Northwestern La.		
Wallace, Bob TE-WR	68-72Chi	2	6'3"	213	Texas-El Paso		54
Wallace, Jackie DB	74Min 75-76Bal 77-79LA	3	6'3"	197	Arizona	10	12
Wallace, Rodney OG-OT	71-73Dal 74JJ		6'5"	255	New Mexico		
Wallace, Roger WR	76NYG		5'11"	180	Bowling Green		
Walsh, Ward HB	71-72Hou 72GB	2	6'	213	Colorado		12
Walters, Rod OG-OT	76KC 77JJ 78-80KC 80Mia 80Det 84-85USFL		6'3"	258	Iowa		
Walters, Stan OT	72-74Cin 75-83Phi		6'6"	271	Syracuse		
Walton, Bruce OT-OG-C	73-75Dal		6'6"	261	U.C.L.A.		
Walton, Chuck OG	67-74Det		6'3"	253	Iowa State		
Walton, John QB	75WFL 76-79Phi 83-85USFL	1	6'2"	210	Elizabeth City St.		
Walton, Larry WR	69-74Det 75KJ 76Det 78Buf	2	6'	181	Arizona State		168
Walton, Wayne OT-OG	71NYG 73-74KC		6'5"	252	Abilene Christian		
Ward, John OG-C-DE	70-73Min 74LJ 75Min 76TB 76Chi		6'4"	258	Oklahoma State		
Warfield, Paul WR	64-69Cle 70-74Mia 75WFL 76-77Cle	2	6'	188	Ohio State		516
Washington, Dave LB-TE	70-71Den 72-74Buf 75-77SF		6'5"	224	Alcorn State	6	20
Washington, Eric DB	72-73StL		6'2"	190	Texas-El Paso		
Washington, Gene WR	67-72Min 73Den	2	6'3"	212	Michigan State		156
Washington, Gene WR	69-77SF 78FJ 79Det	2	6'1"	185	Stanford		360
Washington, Gene WR	79NYG		5'9"	170	Georgia		
Washington, Harry WR	78Min 79Chi		6'	180	Colorado State		
Washington, Joe HB	73Atl		5'9"	180	Illinois State		
Washington, Mark DB	70-78Dal 79NE		5'10"	187	Morgan State	13	8
Washington, Russ OT	68-69SD-A 70-82SD		6'7"	290	Missouri		
Washington, Ted LB	73-82Hou		6'1"	244	Miss. Valley St.		
Washington, Vic HB-DB-WR	71-73SF 74Hou 75-76Buf	23	5'10"	196	Wyoming		132
Waters, Charlie DB	70-78Dal 79KJ 80-81Dal		6'1"	195	Clemson	41	18
Watkins, Larry FB-HB	69Det 70-72Phi 73-74Buf 75-77NYG	2	6'2"	226	Alcorn State		78
Watson, Allen K	70Pit	5	5'10"	165	Newport-Wales		22
Watson, John OT-OG-C	71-76SF 77-79NO		6'4"	246	Oklahoma		
Watson, Mike OT	77NO 78KJ 79JJ		6'6"	272	Miami-Ohio		
Watson, Pete TE	72Cin		6'1"	210	Tufts		
Watts, Robert LB	78Oak		6'3"	218	Boston College		
Weatherly, Jim C	76Atl		6'3"	245	none		
Weathers, Carl LB	70-71Oak		6'2"	220	San Diego State		
Weatherspoon, Cephus WR	72NO		6'1"	182	Fort Lewis		
Weaver, Charlie LB	71-80Det 81Was		6'2"	223	Southern Calif.	15	
Weaver, Gary LB	73-74Oak 75-79GB		6'1"	225	Fresno State		
Weaver, Herman K	70-76Det 77-80Sea 83USFL	4	6'4"	210	Tennessee		
Webb, Jimmy DT-DE	75-80SF 81SD		6'5"	246	Mississippi State		
Webster, Cornell DB	77-80Sea		6'	180	Tulsa	8	6
Webster, George LB	67-69Hou 70-72Hou 72-73Pit 74-76NE		6'4"	225	Michigan State	5	
Webster, Tim K	71GB	5	6'	195	Arkansas		26
Weese, Norris QK	76-79Den	12 4	6'1"	195	Mississippi		30
Weger, Mike DB	67-73Det 74JJ 75Det 76-77Hou		6'2"	197	Bowling Green	17	12
Wehrli, Roger DB	69-82StL	3	6'1"	193	Missouri	40	19
Welch, Claxton HB-FB	69-71Dal 73NE	2	5'11"	202	Oregon		12
Wellman, Mike C	79-80GB		6'3"	253	Kansas		
Wells, Mike QB	75-76NYG 77Cin		6'5"	225	Illinois		
Wells, Terry HB	74Hou 75GB	2	5'11"	195	Southern Miss.		
Wender, Jack HB	77TB		6'	210	Fresno State		
Werner, Clyde LB	70KC 71KJ 72-74KC 75FJ 76KC		6'4"	227	Washington	2	
Wesson, Ricky DB	77KC		5'9"	163	S.M.U.		
West, Bill DB	72Den		5'10"	185	Tennessee State		
West, Bob WR	72-73KC 74SF	2	6'4"	218	San Diego State		18
West, Charlie DB	68-73Min 74-77Det 78-79Den	3	6'1"	194	Texas-El Paso	15	6
Westbrook, Don WR	77-81NE	2	5'10"	185	Nebraska		18

UseName(Nickname)-Positions	Team by Year	See Section	Hgt.	Wgt.	College	Int	Pts
Westbrooks, Greg LB	75-77NO 78StL 78-79Oak 79LA		6'2"	217	Colorado	1	
Wheeler, Wayne WR	74Chi		6'2"	180	Alabama		6
Whitaker, Creston WR	72NO		6'2"	187	North Texas		
White, Charlie HB-FB	77NYJ 78TB	2	6'	222	Bethune-Cookman		12
White, Daryl OG	74Det		6'3"	250	Nebraska		
White, Dwight DE	71-80Pit		6'4"	253	East Texas State	4	4
White, Ed OG-OT	69-77Min 78-85SD		6'2"	270	California		
White, James (Duck) DT-NT	76-83Min		6'3"	265	Oklahoma State	1	
White, Jan TE	71-72Buf	2	6'2"	216	Ohio State		12
White, Jeff K	73NE	5	5'11"	170	Texas-El Paso		63
White, Jeris DB	74-76Mia 77-79TB 80-82Was		5'11"	183	Hawaii	19	
White, Jim DE	72NE 74-75Hou 76Sea 76Den		6'3"	257	Colorado State		
White, Lee FB	68-69NY-A 70NYJ 72LA 72SD	2	6'4"	238	Weber State		6
White, Marsh FB	75-76NYG 77BN	2	6'2"	220	Arkansas		12
White, Paul HB	70-71StL		6'	200	Texas-El Paso		
White, Ray LB	71-72SD 73JJ 75-76StL 77KJ		6'1"	227	Syracuse	2	2
White, Sherman DE	72-75Cin 76-83Buf		6'5"	251	California	2	2
White, Stan LB	72-79Bal 80-82Det 83-84USFL		6'1"	224	Ohio State	34	12
White, Walter TE	75-79KC	2	6'3"	216	Maryland		96
Whitlach, Blake LB	78NYJ		6'1"	233	Louisiana State		
Whittington, C.L. DB	74-76Hou 77JJ 78Hou 79JJ		6'1"	200	Prairie View	7	6
Wickert, Tom OT-OG	74Mia 75-76NO 77Det 77KC		6'4"	248	Washington State		
Wicks, Bob WR	72StL 74NO		6'3"	200	Utah State		
Widby, Ron K	68-71Dal 72-73BB 74KJ 1967-68 — Played in A.B.A.	4	6'4"	212	Tennessee		
Wilkerson, Doug OG	70Hou 71-84SD		6'2"	256	N. Car. Central		
Wilkinson, Bud	HC78-79StL				Minnesota		
Williams, Charles DB	78Phi		6'1"	180	Jackson State		
Williams, Clarence (Sweeney) DE	70-77GB		6'5"	255	Prairie View	1	6
Williams, Clarence HB-FB	77-81SD	23	5'9"	194	South Carolina		114
Williams, Dave WR-FL	67-71StL 72-73SD 73Pit	2	6'2"	205	Washington		150
Williams, Dave FB-HB	77-78SF 79-81Chi	23	6'2"	210	Colorado		66
Williams, Delvin HB	74-77SF 78-80Mia 81GB	2	6'	197	Kansas		234
Williams, Donnie WR	70LA		6'3"	210	Prairie View		
Williams, Ed FB	74-75Cin 76-77TB	2	6'2"	245	Langston		54
Williams, Gerard DB	76-78Was 79SF 80StL 80SF		6'1"	184	Langston	13	6
Williams, Jeff OG-OT	77LA 78-80Was 81SD 82Chi		6'4"	258	Rhode Island		
Williams, Joe HB	71Dal 72NO	2	6'	194	Wyoming		6
Williams, John OT-OG-DE	68-71Bal 72-79LA		6'3"	257	Minnesota		
Williams, Lawrence WR	76-77KC 77Cle	3	5'10"	174	Texas Tech		6
Williams, Mike DB	75-82SD 83LA		5'10"	181	Louisiana State	24	
Williams, Perry FB	69-73GB 74Chi	2	6'2"	220	Purdue		12
Williams, Richard WR	72NO		5'11"	170	Abilene Christian		
Williams, Roger DB-WR	71-72LA		5'10"	180	Grambling		
Williams, Sam DB	74-75SD 76Hou		6'2"	190	California	2	
Williams, Steve DE	74Bal		6'6"	260	Western Carolina		
Williams, Tom DT	70-71SD		6'4"	250	Cal.-Davis		
Willingham, Larry DB	71-72StL		6'1"	190	Auburn		
Willis, Fred FB	71-72Cin 72-76Hou 77JJ	2	6'	209	Boston College		138
Willis, Larry DB	73Was		5'11"	170	Texas-El Paso		
Willis, Leonard WR	76Min 77NO 77-79Buf 83-85USFL	3	5'11"	183	Ohio State		
Wilson, Joe HB-FB	73Cin 74NE 75NJ	2	5'10"	210	Holy Cross		
Wilson, Mike OG-OT	69CinA 70Cin 71Buf 75KC		6'1"	243	Dayton		
Wilson, Nemiah DB	65-67DenA 68-69OakA 70-74Oak 75Chi		6'	166	Grambling	27	24
Winans, Jeff DE-OG-OT-DT	73-75Buf 76Oak 76NO 77-78TB 80JJ		6'5"	263	Southern Calif.		
Windauer, Bill DT-NT	73-74Bal 75Mia 75BYG 76Atl 77Mia		6'3"	248	Iowa		
Windsor, Bob TE	67-71SF 72-75NE	2	6'4"	227	Kentucky		90
Winfield, Vern OG	72-73Phi		6'2"	248	Minnesota		
Winfrey, Carl LB	71Min 72Pit		6'	230	Wisconsin		
Winfrey, Stan FB	75-76Mia 77TB 79Mia 79Buf	2	5'11"	223	Arkansas State		12
Winkel, Bob DT-DE	79-80NYJ		6'4"	251	Kentucky		
Winslow, Doug WR	73NO 74-75WFL 76Was		5'11"	181	Drake		
Winther, Wimpy C	71GB 72NO		6'3"	260	Mississippi		
Wirgowski, Dennis DE-DT	70Bos 71-72NE 73Phi		6'5"	253	Purdue	1	
Wise, Phil DB	71-76NYJ 77-79Min		6'	192	Nebraska-Omaha	6	6
Withrow, Phil C	70SD 71-73GB 74StL		6'	240	Kentucky		
Wittum, Tom K	73-77SF	4	6'1"	191	Northern Illinois		5
Wocjik, Greg DT	71LA 72-73SD 74WFL 75SD		6'6"	268	Southern Calif.		
Wolf, Jim DE	74Pit 76KC		6'3"	240	Prairie View		
Woodall, Al QB	69NY-A 70-71NYJ 72JJ 73-74NYJ 75KJ	12	6'5"	202	Duke		
Woodcock, John DE-DT-LB	76-78Det 79XJ 80Det 81-82SD		6'3"	246	New Mexico, Hawaii		
Woods, Don HB-FB	74-80SD 80SF	2	6'1"	209	New Mexico		126
Woods, Larry DT	71-72Det 73Mia 74-75NYJ 76Sea		6'6"	265	Tennessee State		
Woods, Mike LB	78-81Bal		6'2"	233	Cincinnati	1	
Woods, Robert OT-OG	73-77NYJ 77-80NO 81Was 83-85USFL		6'3"	258	Tennessee State		
Woods, Robert WR	78Hou 79Det		5'7"	170	Grambling		12
Woolsey, Roland DB	75Dal 76Sea 77Cle 78StL	3	6'1"	182	Boise State	5	
Word, Roscoe DB	74-76NYJ 76Buf 76TB	3	5'11"	170	Jackson State	3	
Wortman, Keith OT-OG	72-75GB 76-81StL		6'2"	259	Nebraska		
Wright, Elmo WR	71-74KC 75Hou 75NE	2	6'	190	Houston		42
Wright, George DT	70-71Bal 72Cle		6'3"	262	Sam Houston St.		
Wright, Jeff DB	71-77Min		5'11"	190	Minnesota	11	
Wright, Keith WR	78-80Cle	23	5'10"	174	Memphis State		18
Wright, Nate DB	69Atl 69-70StL 71-80Min		5'11"	180	San Diego State	35	6
Wright, Rayfield OT-TE	67-79Dal		6'7"	254	Ft. Valley State		6
Wyatt, Alvin DB	70Oak 71-72Buf 73Hou 74-75WFL	3	5'10"	183	Bethune-Cookman	5	18
Wyatt, Doug DB	70-72NO 73-74Det		6'1"	195	Tulsa	8	12
Wyche, Sam QB	68-69CinA 70Cin 71-72Was 74Det 76StL 76Buf HC84-91Cin 92TB	12	6'4"	214	Furman		18
Wycinski, Craig OG	72Cle		6'3"	243	Michigan		
Wynn, Will DB	73-76Phi 77Was		6'4"	244	Tennessee State		12
Wysocki, Pete LB	75-80Was		6'2"	225	Western Michigan	1	
Yanchar, Bill DT	70Cle		6'3"	250	Purdue		
Yankowski, Ron DE	71-80StL		6'5"	244	Kansas State		6
Yarbrough, Jim OT	69-77Det 78FJ		6'6"	261	Florida		
Yary, Ron OT	68-81Min 82LA		6'6"	256	Southern Calif.		
Yeates, Jeff DE-DT-OG	74-76Buf 76-84Atl		6'3"	249	Boston College	1	
Yepremian, Garo K	66-67Det 70-78Mia 79NO 80-81TB	5	5'8"	172	none		1074
Young, Adrian LB	68-72Phi 72Det 73Chi		6'1"	230	Southern Calif.		
Young, Al WR	71-72Pit 73IL		6'1"	195	S. Carolina State		
Young, Bob OG-DT	66-69DenA 70Den 71Hou 72-79StL 80Hou 81NO		6'2"	269	Texas, Howard Payne, SW Texas State		
Young, Charley HB	74-76Dal 77KJ	2	6'1"	213	N. Carolina State		24
Young, Charle TE	73-76Phi 77-79LA 80-82SF 83-85Sea	2	6'4"	235	Southern Calif.		168
Young, James DE	77-79Hou		6'2"	260	Texas Southern		4
Young, Randy OT	76TB		6'5"	250	Iowa State		
Young, Rickey HB	75-77SD 78-83Min	2	6'2"	196	Jackson State		234

UseName(Nickname)-Positions	TeambyYear	See Section	Hgt.	Wgt.	College	Int	Pts
Young, Steve OT	76TB 77Mia 78NJ 79GB		6'8"	271	Colorado		
Young, Wilbur DE-DT	71-77KC 78-80SD 81Was 81-82SD 84-85USFL		6'6"	289	William Penn	1	14
Young, Willie (Sugar Bear) OT	66-75NYG		6'	259	Grambling		
Young, Willie OT	71-72Buf 73Mia		6'4"	270	Alcorn State		
Youngblood, Jack DE	71-84LA		6'4"	247	Florida		4
Youngblood, Jim LB	73-84LA		6'3"	235	Tennessee Tech	14	30
Zabel, Steve LB-TE	70-74Phi 75-78NE 79Bal	2	6'4"	233	Oklahoma	6	19
Zanders, Emanuel OG	74-80NO 81Chi		6'1"	251	Jackson State		

UseName(Nickname)-Positions	TeambyYear	See Section	Hgt.	Wgt.	College	Int	Pts
Zapalas, Bill LB-DE	71-73NYJ		6'4"	225	Texas		
Zaunbrechner, Godfrey C	71-73Min		6'4"	238	Louisiana State		
Zelencik, Connie C-OG	77Buf 78JJ 79KJ		6'4"	245	Purdue		
Zeno, Coleman WR	71NYG		6'4"	210	Grambling		
Zimmerman, Don WR	73-76Phi 76GB	2	6'3"	195	Northeast La.		30
Zotko, Mickey HB	71-74Det 74NYG	3	6'3"	195	Auburn		1
Zook, John DE	69-75Atl 76-79StL		6'5"	248	Kansas	4	8

Lifetime Statistics- 1970- 1979 Players Section 1 — PASSING
(All men with 25 or more passing attempts)

Name	Years	Att.	Comp.	Comp. Pct.	Yards	Yds./ Att.	TD	Int.	Pct. Int.
Tony Adams	75-78,87	408	212	52.0	2733	6.7	12	27	6.6
Ken Anderson	71-84	4475	2654	59.3	32838	7.3	197	160	3.6
Rick Arrington	70-72	204	97	47.5	950	4.7	3	9	4.4
Bob Avellini	75-84	1110	560	50.5	7111	6.4	33	69	6.2
Bob Berry	65-76	1173	661	56.4	9197	7.8	64	64	5.5
Jeb Blount	77	89	37	41.6	522	5.9	0	7	7.9
Mike Boryla	74-76,78	519	272	52.4	2838	5.5	20	29	5.6
Terry Bradshaw	70-83	3901	2105	54.0	27989	7.2	212	210	5.4
Marlin Briscoe	68-76	233	97	41.6	1697	7.3	14	14	6.0
Carlos Brown	75-76	78	29	37.2	396	5.1	3	6	7.7
Scott Bull	76-78	193	76	39.4	992	5.1	3	17	8.8
Virgil Carter	68-72,75-76	785	425	54.1	5063	6.4	29	31	3.9
Larry Cipa	74-75	92	34	37.0	424	4.6	1	3	3.3
Wayne Clark	70,72-75	120	52	43.3	745	6.2	0	14	11.7
Will Cureton	75	32	10	31.3	95	3.0	1	1	3.1
Bob Davis	67-73	324	137	42.3	1553	4.8	14	23	7.1
Randy Dean	77-79	65	30	46.2	279	4.3	1	5	7.7
Jim Del Gaizo	72-75	103	44	32.7	648	6.3	4	10	9.7
Bill Demory	73-74	39	12	30.8	159	4.1	2	8	20.5
Lynn Dickey	71-77,79-85	3125	1747	55.9	23322	7.5	141	179	5.7
Parnell Dickinson	76-77	39	15	38.5	210	5.4	1	5	12.8
Marty Domres	69-77	809	399	49.3	4904	6.1	27	50	6.2
Bobby Douglass	69-78	1178	507	43.0	6493	5.5	36	64	5.4
Brian Dowling	72-73,77	55	29	52.7	383	7.0	2	1	1.8
Jesse Freitas	74-75	219	98	44.7	1244	5.7	8	13	5.9
Joe Gilliam	72-75,83	331	147	44.4	2103	6.4	9	17	5.1
Neil Graff	74-78	48	25	52.1	288	6.0	2	3	6.3
Bob Griese	67-80	3429	1926	56.2	25092	7.3	192	172	5.0
Pat Haden	76-81	1363	731	53.6	9296	6.8	52	60	4.4
Terry Hanratty	69-76	431	165	38.3	2510	5.8	24	35	8.1
Edd Hargett	69-73	437	205	46.9	2727	6.2	11	10	2.3
James Harris	69-71,73-81	1149	607	52.8	8136	7.1	45	59	5.1
Jim Hart	66-84	5076	2593	51.1	34665	6.8	209	247	4.9
Randy Hedberg	77	90	25	27.8	244	2.7	0	10	11.1
Don Horn	67-74	465	232	49.9	3369	7.2	20	36	7.7
Gary Huff	73-78,80	788	392	49.7	4329	5.5	16	50	6.3
John Hufnagel	74-75	61	22	36.1	357	5.9	1	9	14.8
David Humm	75-84	137	63	46.0	753	5.5	3	8	5.8
Scott Hunter	71-74,76-79	748	335	44.8	4756	6.4	23	38	5.1
Randy Johnson	66-73,75-76	1286	647	50.3	8329	6.5	51	90	7.0
Bert Jones	73-82	2551	1430	56.1	18190	7.1	124	101	4.0
John Jones	75	57	16	28.1	181	3.2	1	5	8.8
June Jones	77-79,81	166	75	45.2	923	5.6	3	7	4.2
Gary Keithley	73,75	73	32	43.8	369	5.1	1	5	6.8
Billy Kilmer	61-78	2984	1585	53.1	20495	6.9	152	146	4.9
Mike Kirkland	76-78	41	19	46.3	211	5.2	1	8	19.5
Mike Kruczek	76-80	154	93	60.4	1185	7.7	0	8	5.2
Greg Landry	68-81,84	2300	1276	55.5	16052	7.0	98	103	4.5
Larry Lawrence	74-76	31	9	29.0	79	2.5	0	4	12.9
Bob Lee	69-80	730	368	50.4	5034	6.9	30	40	5.5
Mike Livingston	68-80	1751	912	52.1	11295	6.5	56	83	4.7
Clint Longley	74-76	68	31	45.6	441	6.5	5	4	5.9
Mike Loyd	79-80	28	5	17.9	49	1.8	0	1	3.6
Terry Luck	77	50	25	50.0	316	6.3	1	7	14.0
Archie Manning	71-75,77-84	3642	2011	55.2	23911	6.6	125	173	4.8
Gary Marangi	74-77	283	104	36.7	1373	4.9	12	21	7.4
Dave Mays	76-78	156	80	51.3	937	6.0	7	11	7.1
Kim McQuilkin	74-80	272	108	39.7	1135	4.1	4	29	10.7
Don Milan	75-76	32	15	48.9	181	5.7	1	1	3.1
Mark Miller	78-80	47	15	31.9	243	5.2	1	5	10.6
Dennis Morrison	74	51	21	41.2	227	4.5	1	5	9.8
Craig Morton	65-82	3786	2053	54.2	27908	7.4	183	187	4.9
Bill Munson	64-79	1982	1070	54.0	12896	6.5	84	80	4.0
Steve Myer	76-79	160	83	51.9	851	5.3	6	14	8.8
Joe Namath	65-77	3762	1886	50.1	27663	7.4	173	220	5.8
Kent Nix	67-72	652	301	46.2	3644	5.6	23	49	7.5
Tom Owen	74-81	349	170	48.7	2300	6.6	14	26	7.5
Dan Pastorini	71-83	3055	1556	50.9	18515	6.1	103	161	5.3
Al Pastrana	69-70	75	29	38.7	420	5.6	1	9	12.0
Craig Penrose	76-80	117	55	47.0	711	6.1	5	12	10.3
Mike Phipps	70-81	1799	886	49.3	10506	5.8	55	108	8.2
Steve Pisarkiewicz	77-80	143	64	44.8	804	5.6	3	7	4.9
Jim Plunkett	71-86	3701	1943	52.5	25882	7.0	164	198	5.3
Mike Rae	76-81	249	124	49.8	1536	6.2	12	14	5.6
Steve Ramsey	70-76	921	456	49.5	6437	7.0	35	58	6.3
John Reaves	72-79,81,87	616	286	46.4	3617	5.9	17	34	5.5
Joe Reed	72-79	513	225	46.8	2825	5.5	18	31	6.0
Bobby Scott	73-81	500	237	47.4	2781	5.6	15	28	5.6
Dennis Shaw	70-76,78	924	489	52.9	6347	6.9	35	68	7.4
Brian Sipe	74-83	3439	1944	56.5	23713	6.9	154	159	4.6
Steve Spurrier	67-76	1151	597	51.9	6878	6.0	40	60	5.3
Ken Stabler	70-84	3793	2270	59.8	27938	7.4	194	222	5.9
Roger Staubach	69-79	2958	1685	57.0	22700	7.7	153	109	3.7
Pat Sullivan	72-75	220	93	42.3	1155	5.3	5	16	7.3
Carl Summerell	74-75	29	13	44.8	157	5.4	0	5	17.2
Jerry Tagge	72-74	281	136	48.4	1583	5.6	3	17	6.0
Bill Troup	74-80	328	166	50.6	2047	6.2	10	26	7.9
Tim Van Galder	72	79	40	50.6	434	5.5	1	7	8.9
John Walton	76-79	65	31	47.7	338	5.2	3	3	4.6
Norris Weese	76-79	251	143	57.0	1887	7.5	7	14	5.6
Al Woodall	69-71,73-74	503	246	48.9	2970	5.9	18	23	4.6
Sam Wyche	68-72,74,76	222	116	52.7	1748	7.9	12	9	4.6

Name	Years	RUSHING Att.	Yards	Avg.	TD	RECEIVING Rec.	Yards	Avg.	TD
Dan Abramowicz	67-75	6	95	15.8	0	369	5686	15.4	39
Mike Adamle	71-76	308	1149	3.7	4	53	368	6.9	2
Bob Adams	69-71, 73-77	2	7	3.5	0	61	732	12.0	0
Tony Adams	75-78,87	38	155	4.1	0	1	-7	-7.0	0
Margene Adkins	70-73					19	258	13.6	0
Mack Alston	70-80	2	10	5.0	0	108	1247	11.5	15
George Amundson	73-75	74	194	2.6	4	25	212	8.5	1
Bobby Anderson	70-73,75	314	1282	4.1	9	84	861	10.3	2
Donny Anderson	66-74	1197	4696	3.9	41	209	2548	12.2	14
Ken Anderson	71-86	397	2220	5.6	20				
Otis Armstrong	73-80	1023	4453	4.4	25	131	1302	9.9	7
Josh Ashton	72-75	257	894	3.9	3	33	320	9.7	1
Bob Avellini	75-84	104	225	2.2	5				
Mark Bailey	77-78	149	564	3.8	2	22	219	10.0	1
Tom Bailey	71-75	42	186	3.9	15	28	194	6.9	1
Tony Baker	68-75	536	2087	3.9	15	82	685	8.4	2
Pete Banaszak	66-78	964	3772	3.9	47	121	1022	8.4	5
Warren Bankston	69-78	167	684	4.1	3	38	283	7.4	2
Jerome Barkum	72-83	3	-3	-1.0	0	326	4789	14.7	40
Larry Barnes	77-79	53	156	2.9	2	4	29	7.3	0
Bubba Bean	76, 78-79	405	1528	3.8	6	59	494	8.4	2
John Beasley	67-70, 72-74					151	1607	10.6	13
Terry Beasley	72, 74-75	2	2	1.0	0	38	570	15.0	3
Jim Beirne	68-76	1	3	3.0	0	142	2011	14.2	11
Eddie Bell	70-76	3	-12	-4.0	0	118	1774	15.0	12
Gordon Bell	76-78	90	319	3.5	2	32	259	8.1	0
Horace Belton	79-80	136	486	3.6	3	20	226	11.3	0
Willie Belton	71-74	78	306	3.9	1	4	21	5.3	0
Bob Berry	65-76	109	409	3.8	4				
Jim Bertelsen	72-76	614	2466	4.0	16	88	1014	11.5	2
James Betterson	77-78	73	265	3.6	1	6	49	8.2	0
Fred Biletnikoff	65-78					589	8974	15.2	76
Hank Bjorklund	72-74	60	171	2.9	0	8	84	10.5	0
Rocky Bleier	68-69, 71-80	928	3865	4.2	23	136	1294	9.5	2
Luther Blue	77-80	7	-5	-0.7	0	47	542	11.5	4
Glen Bonner	74-75	94	319	3.4	3	13	109	8.4	1
Emerson Boozer	66-75	1291	5135	4.0	52	139	1488	10.7	12
Mike Boryla	74-76, 78	43	224	5.2	2				
Lee Bouggess	70-71, 73	271	697	2.6	5	78	589	7.6	3
Greg Boykin	77-78	107	352	3.3	2	22	133	6.0	0
Morris Bradshaw	74-82	2	-1	-0.5	0	90	1416	15.7	12
Terry Bradshaw	70-83	444	2257	5.1	32	0	1	—	0
Cliff Branch	72-84	11	70	6.4	0	501	8685	17.3	67
Jim Braxton	71-78	741	2890	3.9	25	144	1473	10.2	6
Larry Brinson	77-80	56	229	4.1	4	1	9	9.0	0
Marlin Briscoe	68-76	49	336	3.9	3	224	3537	15.8	30
John Brockington	71-77	1347	5185	3.8	30	157	1297	8.3	4
Billy Brooks	76-81	3	-17	-5.7	0	96	1720	17.9	7
Bob Brown	69-73	1	8	8.0	0	28	448	16.0	1
Ken Brown	70-75	346	1193	3.4	7	58	468	8.1	2
Larry Brown	69-76	1530	5875	3.8	35	238	2485	10.4	20
Larry Brown	71-81					48	636	13.3	5
Bob Brunet	68-77	131	406	3.1	3	24	200	8.3	1
Larry Brunson	74-80	12	63	5.3	0	104	1787	17.2	6
Hubie Bryant	70-72	7	26	3.7	0	22	366	16.6	1
Danny Buggs	75-79	1	0	0.0	0	110	1572	14.3	4
Norm Bulaich	70-79	814	3362	4.1	30	224	1766	7.9	11
Scott Bull	76-78	49	186	3.8	3				
Steve Burke	75-77	1	2	2.0	0	13	264	20.3	0
Bob Burns	74	40	158	4.0	0	11	83	7.5	1
Leon Burns	71-72	87	292	3.4	3	9	44	4.9	0
Ken Burrough	70-81	17	63	3.7	1	421	7102	16.9	49
Ken Burrow	71-75	6	25	4.2	0	152	2668	17.6	21
Larry Burton	75-79	5	4	0.8	0	44	804	18.3	7
Dexter Bussey	74-84	1203	5105	4.2	18	193	1616	8.4	5
Bill Butler	72-74	162	655	4.0	1	46	354	7.7	4
J.V. Cain	74-77					76	1014	13.3	9
Don Calhoun	74-83	860	3559	4.1	23	84	624	7.4	2
Sonny Campbell	70-71	57	195	3.4	2	10	132	13.2	0
Larry Canada	78-81	148	621	4.2	6	12	110	9.2	1
John Cappelletti	74-83	824	2751	3.3	24	135	1233	9.1	4
Harold Carmichael	71-84	9	64	7.1	0	589	8985	15.2	79
Roger Carr	74-83	1	-8	-8.0	0	271	5071	18.7	31
Louis Carter	75-78	322	940	2.9	4	51	378	7.4	0
Virgil Carter	68-72,75-76	109	640	5.9	8				
Dave Casper	74-84	6	27	4.5	0	378	5216	13.8	52
Rich Caster	70-82	23	119	5.2	0	322	5515	17.1	45
Al Chandler	73-74,76-79					35	367	10.5	9
Bob Chandler	71-81	11	18	1.6	0	370	5243	14.2	48
Wes Chesson	71-74	1	-4	-4.0	0	40	598	15.0	2
Ray Chester	70-81	5	9	1.8	0	364	5013	13.8	48
Henry Childs	74-81	4	12	3.0	1	223	3401	15.3	28
Jim Childs	78-79					12	143	11.9	1
Booby Clark	73-80	802	3032	3.8	25	157	1197	7.6	2
Vin Clements	72-73	103	435	4.2	1	24	247	10.3	1
Mike Cobb	77-81					11	134	12.2	0
Ronnie Coleman	74-81	770	2769	3.6	16	150	1239	8.3	6
Mike Collier	75, 77, 79	86	370	4.3	5	11	73	6.6	0
Sonny Collins	76-77	91	319	3.5	0	4	37	9.3	0
Jim Corbett	77-80	1	-1	-1.0	0	25	376	15.0	1
Bruce Coslet	69-76	1	1	1.0	0	61	878	14.4	9
Craig Cotton	69-73, 75					28	409	14.6	1
Steve Craig	74-78					18	172	9.6	1
Larry Csonka	68-74, 76-79	1891	8081	4.3	64	106	820	7.7	4
Jim Culbreath	77-80	48	156	3.3	0	9	84	9.3	0
Doug Cunningham	67-74	406	1515	3.7	10	137	1171	8.5	0
Sam Cunningham	73-82	1385	5453	3.9	43	210	1905	9.1	6
Pat Curran	69-78	30	127	4.2	0	106	1266	11.9	5
Isaac Curtis	73-84	25	56	2.2	0	416	7101	17.1	53
Anthony Davis	77-78	98	304	3.1	1	8	91	11.4	0
Bob Davis	67-73	52	332	6.4	2				
Charlie Davis	74-76	113	482	4.3	1	22	203	9.2	0
Clarence Davis	71-78	804	3640	4.5	26	99	865	8.7	2
Dave Davis	71-74	2	0	0.0	0	11	192	17.5	1
Dick Davis	70	27	94	3.5	0	4	29	7.3	0

Name	Years	RUSHING Att.	Yards	Avg.	TD	RECEIVING Rec.	Yards	Avg.	TD
Gary Davis	76-81	324	1410	4.4	7	83	671	8.1	1
Harrison Davis	74	2	-7	-7.0	0	18	432	24.0	2
Sonny Davis	71-72	47	163	3.5	1	11	46	4.2	0
Steve Davis	72-76	322	1305	4.1	9	33	301	9.1	2
Tony Davis	76-81	91	345	3.8	5	27	250	9.3	1
Joe Dawkins	70-76	698	2661	3.8	13	145	1316	9.1	3
Jack DeGrener	74	33	110	3.3	0	4	13	3.3	0
Jack Deloplaine	76-79	37	165	4.5	2	3	16	5.3	0
Doug Dennison	74-79	306	1112	3.6	19	14	110	7.9	0
Moses Denson	74-75	159	586	3.7	0	39	255	6.5	2
Lynn Dickey	71-77,79-85	140	121	0.9	9				
Chuck Dicus	71-72	2	-13	-6.5	0	24	316	13.2	3
Al Dodd	67,69-71,73-74	9	50	5.6	0	111	1803	16.2	3
Jack Dolbin	75-79	9	89	9.9	0	94	1579	16.8	7
Marty Domres	69-77	130	679	5.2	10				
Mike Donohue	70-71,73-74					10	106	10.6	2
Larry Dorsey	76-78	1	-12	-12.0	0	27	475	17.6	4
Glenn Doughty	72-79	26	202	7.8	0	219	3547	16.2	24
Bobby Douglass	69-78	410	2654	6.5	22	1	-2	-2.0	0
Doug Dressler	70-72,74-75	278	1125	4.0	9	90	695	7.7	2
Jimmy DuBose	76-79	184	704	3.8	4	17	118	6.9	0
Bobby Duhon	68,70-72	221	840	3.8	4	68	717	10.5	1
Jubilee Dunbar	73-74	3	3	1.0	0	29	521	18.0	4
Billy Joe DuPree	73-83	26	178	6.9	1	267	3565	13.4	41
Cid Edwards	68-75	698	3006	4.3	15	144	1491	10.4	4
Monroe Eley	75-77	98	276	2.8	1	9	60	6.7	0
Lenvil Elliot	73-81	440	1900	4.3	8	159	1484	9.3	10
Willie Ellison	67-74	801	3426	4.3	24	104	888	8.5	6
Bill Enyart	69-71	105	387	3.7	1	54	421	7.8	3
Mike Esposito	76-78	101	439	4.3	2	21	97	4.6	0
Charlie Evans	71-74	205	644	3.1	12	54	470	8.7	1
George Farmer	70-75	4	6	1.5	0	119	1995	16.8	10
Mel Farr	67-73	739	3072	4.2	26	146	1374	9.4	10
Duke Fergerson	77-80					35	543	15.5	2
Bob Ferrell	76-80	183	692	3.8	3	21	148	7.0	0
James Ford	71-72	104	407	3.9	2	8	63	7.9	0
Chuck Foreman	73-80	1556	5950	3.8	53	350	3156	9.0	23
Ike Forte	76-81	165	511	3.1	5	39	387	9.9	2
Eddie Foster	77,79					15	208	13.9	0
Wallace Francis	73-81	10	27	2.7	1	244	3695	15.1	27
Cleveland Franklin	77-82	208	635	3.1	3	36	258	7.2	0
Stan Fritts	75-76	141	575	4.1	11	15	138	9.2	2
Jean Fugett	72-79	7	38	5.4	0	156	2270	14.6	28
Frenchy Fuqua	69-76	719	3031	4.2	21	135	1247	9.2	3
Clark Gaines	76-82	582	2552	4.4	8	166	1438	8.7	6
Lawrence Gaines	76,78-79	232	892	3.8	5	25	146	5.8	1
Reuben Gant	74-80	1	14	14.0	0	127	1850	14.6	15
Carl Garrett	69-77	1031	4197	4.1	28	182	1931	10.6	7
Reggie Garrett	74-75					13	178	13.7	1
Gary Garrison	66-77	12	29	2.4	0	405	7538	18.6	58
Walt Garrison	66-74	899	3886	4.3	30	182	1794	9.9	9
Tom Geredine	73-74,76	2	5	2.5	0	17	323	19.0	2
Louie Giammona	76,78-82	201	682	3.4	7	46	444	9.7	2
Walker Gillette	70-76	1	-4	-4.0	0	153	2291	15.0	12
John Gilliam	67-77	35	293	8.4	2	382	7056	18.5	48
Hubert Ginn	70-77	132	521	3.9	3	9	49	5.4	0
Paul Gipson	69-71,73	123	491	4.0	1	21	240	11.4	3
Bob Gladieux	69-72	65	239	3.7	0	25	252	10.1	0
Chip Glass	69-74					34	642	18.9	5
Leland Glass	72-73	2	13	6.5	0	26	380	14.6	1
Les Goodman	73-74	38	189	5.0	1	7	38	5.4	0
Dick Gordon	65-74	15	90	6.0	0	243	3594	14.8	36
Ken Grandberry	74	144	475	3.3	2	30	212	7.1	0
Frank Grant	73-78	5	27	5.4	0	149	2486	16.7	18
Mel Gray	71-82	15	154	10.3	1	351	6644	18.9	45
Woody Green	74-76	375	1442	3.8	9	58	562	9.7	2
Bob Gresham	71-76	410	1360	3.3	12	90	728	8.1	1
Bob Griese	67-80	261	994	3.8	7				
Archie Griffin	76-82	691	2808	4.1	7	192	1607	8.4	6
Bob Grim	67-77	8	137	17.1	0	194	2914	15.0	16
Randy Grossman	74-81					119	1514	12.7	5
Pat Haden	76-81	124	609	4.9	6				
Isaac Hagins	76-80	4	26	6.5	0	83	1317	14.7	5
Andy Hamilton	73-75					16	270	16.9	0
Bob Hammond	76-80	332	1401	4.2	3	65	528	8.1	3
Dave Hampton	69-76	1148	4536	4.0	25	119	1156	9.7	6
Buddy Hardeman	79-80	71	256	3.6	0	37	375	10.1	1
Don Hardeman	75-79	397	1460	3.7	11	58	285	4.9	2
Steve Harky	71-72	65	191	2.9	0	14	142	10.1	0
Roland Harper	75-78,80-82	757	3044	4.0	15	128	1013	7.9	3
Charlie Harraway	66-73	822	3019	3.7	20	158	1304	8.3	7
Willard Harrell	75-84	429	1391	3.2	10	127	1135	8.9	4
Franco Harris	72-84	2949	12120	4.1	91	307	2287	7.4	9
Ike Harris	73-81	4	31	17.6	0	211	3305	15.7	16
James Harris	69-71,73-81	121	367	3.0	10				
Leroy Harris	77-82	442	1813	4.1	13	72	571	7.9	1
Dwight Harrison	71-77	6	45	7.5	0	20	281	14.1	2
Jim Harrison	71-74	272	1009	3.7	3	31	248	8.0	3
Kenny Harrison	76-78,80	8	4	0.5	0	42	668	15.9	1
Reggie Harrison	74-78	134	631	4.7	8	7	36	5.1	0
Harold Hart	74-75,77-78	114	485	4.3	5	8	32	4.0	0
Jim Hart	66-84	159	207	1.3	16	1	-4	-4.0	0
Sam Havrilak	69-74	73	289	4.0	3	51	761	14.9	4
Bob Hayes	65-75	24	68	2.8	2	371	7414	20.0	71
Don Herriman	69-77	4	-8	-2.0	0	234	3039	13.0	16
Mack Herron	73-75	354	1298	3.7	9	61	789	12.9	6
Don Highsmith	70-73	94	327	3.5	2	12	143	11.9	0
Calvin Hill	69-74,76-81	1452	6083	4.2	42	271	2861	10.6	23
Ike Hill	70-74,76	3	-14	-4.7	0	22	283	12.9	2
J.D. Hill	71-77	3	14	4.7	0	185	2880	15.6	21
Eddie Hinton	69-74	12	110	9.2	2	111	1822	16.4	10
Paul Hofer	76-81	416	1746	4.2	16	147	1634	11.1	5
Mike Hogan	76-80	466	1835	3.9	6	79	482	6.1	2
Steve Holden	73-77	3	2	0.7	0	62	927	15.0	4
John Holland	74-77					35	634	18.1	3

Lifetime Statistics- 1970- 1979 Players Section 2 - RUSHING and RECEIVING
(All men with 25 or more rushing attempts or 10 or more receptions)

		RUSHING				RECEIVING			
Name	Years	Att.	Yards	Avg.	TD	Rec.	Yards	Avg.	TD
Ron Holiday	73	6	70	11.7	0	14	182	13.0	0
Mike Holmes	74-76	1	-4	-4.0	0	17	231	13.6	1
Robert Holmes	68-73, 75	639	2510	3.9	23	113	982	8.7	4
Dennis Homan	68-72	2	-3	-1.5	0	37	619	16.7	2
Fair Hooker	69-74					129	1845	14.3	8
Jim Hooks	73-76	67	245	3.7	0	11	64	5.8	0
Roland Hooks	76-82	399	1684	4.2	12	96	950	9.9	3
Rich Houston	69-73	3	13	4.3	0	65	1121	17.2	7
Ron Howard	74-79	1	2	2.0	0	72	850	11.8	2
Marv Hubbard	69-75,77	951	4544	4.8	23	85	628	7.4	1
Gary Huff	73-78,80	50	86	1.7	2				
Dennis Hughes	70-71	1	-4	-4.0	0	24	332	13.8	3
Mike Hull	68-74	77	207	2.7	1	29	127	4.4	0
Al Hunter	77-80	180	715	4.0	4	27	331	12.3	0
Scott Hunter	71-74,76-79	95	204	2.1	13				
John Isenbarger	70-73	27	80	3.0	0	21	291	13.9	2
Horace Ivory	77-82	351	1425	4.1	15	54	471	8.7	2
Harold Jackson	68-83	33	181	5.5	0	579	10372	17.9	76
Jazz Jackson	74-76	27	91	3.4	0	9	101	11.2	1
Randy Jackson	72-74	30	73	2.3	0	15	58	3.9	1
Wilbur Jackson	74-82	971	3852	4.0	13	184	1592	8.7	4
Po James	72-75	328	1215	3.7	4	102	747	7.3	2
Ray Jarvis	71-79	2	13	6.5	0	104	1832	17.6	11
Roy Jefferson	65-76	25	188	7.5	0	451	7539	16.7	52
Alfred Jenkins	75-83	2	7	3.5	0	359	6258	17.4	40
Jim Jensen	76-77,79-82	283	1126	4.0	4	80	651	8.1	3
Ron Jessie	71-81	19	91	4.8	2	265	4278	16.1	26
Andy Johnson	74-76,78-81	491	2017	4.1	13	161	1807	11.2	9
Dennis Johnson	78-80	58	227	3.9	2	10	83	8.3	0
Essex Johnson	68-76	722	3236	4.5	19	146	1742	11.9	12
Kermit Johnson	75-76	36	124	3.4	1	1	11	11.0	0
Randy Johnson	66-73,75-76	114	573	5.0	10				
Ron Johnson	69-75	1203	4307	3.6	40	213	1977	9.3	15
Sammy Johnson	74-79	206	830	4.0	9	45	378	8.4	0
Charlie Joiner	69-86	8	22	2.8	0	750	12146	16.2	65
Andrew Jones	75-76	43	110	2.6	1	10	52	5.2	0
Bert Jones	73-82	247	1429	5.8	14				
Clint Jones	67-73	602	2178	3.6	20	38	431	11.3	0
Greg Jones	70-71	47	166	3.5	1	24	202	8.4	1
Jimmie Jones	74	32	147	4.6	1	4	35	8.8	0
Kim Jones	76-79	26	80	3.1	0	4	33	8.3	0
Steve Jones	73-78	300	1204	4.0	15	87	629	7.2	2
Mark Kellar	76-78	25	74	3.0	0	5	17	3.4	0
Vince Kendrick	74, 76	18	74	4.1	0	12	86	7.2	1
Leroy Keyes	69-73	125	369	3.0	3	30	270	9.0	0
Jon Keyworth	74-80	699	2653	3.4	22	141	1057	7.5	3
Jim Kiick	68-74, 76-77	1029	3759	3.7	29	233	2302	9.9	4
Billy Kilmer	61-78	362	1509	4.2	21				
John Kimbrough	77					10	207	20.7	2
Horace King	75-83	549	2081	3.8	9	197	1573	8.0	5
Jeff Kinney	72-76	353	1285	3.6	5	68	502	7.4	1
Bob Klein	69-79	4	14	3.5	0	219	2687	12.3	23
David Knight	73-77					73	1189	16.3	7
Gary Kosins	72-74	35	100	2.9	1	7	26	3.7	1
Doug Kotar	74-79,81	900	3380	3.8	20	126	1022	8.1	1
Ted Koy	70-74	1	9	9.0	0	11	142	12.9	1
Kent Kramer	66-67,69-74					45	586	12.8	8
Keith Krepfle	75-83	1	2	2.0	0	152	2425	16.0	19
Mike Kruczek	76-80	37	138	3.7	2				
Ted Kwalick	69-77	19	175	9.2	0	168	2570	15.3	23
Scott Laidlaw	75-80	255	1007	3.9	9	74	668	9.0	3
Ron Lamb	68-69,71-72	49	128	2.6	0	8	97	12.1	0
Greg Landry	68-81,84	430	2655	6.2	21				
MacArthur Lane	68-78	1206	4656	3.9	30	287	2786	9.7	7
Jim Lash	73-77	3	5	1.7	0	91	1464	16.1	3
Jerry Latin	75-78	130	560	4.3	4	16	152	9.5	0
Greg Latta	75-80	2	-8	-4.0	0	90	1081	12.0	7
Odell Lawson	70-71,73-74	70	130	1.9	0	13	108	8.3	0
Roger Lawson	72-73	57	176	3.1	1	17	180	10.6	0
Roosevelt Leaks	75-83	663	2406	3.6	28	71	590	8.3	4
Bob Lee	69-80	92	197	2.1	3				
Ron Lee	76-78	206	940	4.6	5	24	160	6.7	1
Billy LeFear	72-75	35	143	4.1	0	10	73	7.3	0
Charlie Leigh	68-69,71-74	72	372	5.2	2	9	-4	-0.4	0
Jerry LeVias	69-74	19	161	8.5	0	144	2139	14.9	14
Frank Lewis	71-83	12	146	12.1	1	397	6724	16.9	40
Floyd Little	67-75	1641	6323	3.9	43	215	2417	11.2	9
Mike Livingston	68-80	156	682	4.4	7				
Kevin Long	77-81	564	2190	3.9	25	74	539	7.3	3
Herb Lusk	76-78	113	483	4.3	2	18	221	12.3	1
Fran Lynch	67-75	304	1258	4.1	12	35	357	10.2	2
Ken MacAfee	78-79					46	471	10.2	5
Jack Maitland	70-72	100	267	2.7	2	14	106	7.6	1
Bill Malinchak	66-74,76					35	508	14.5	4
Art Malone	70-76	635	2457	3.9	19	161	1465	9.1	6
Benny Malone	74-79	706	2693	3.8	19	33	400	12.1	1
Jim Mandich	70-78					121	1406	11.6	23
Archie Manning	71-75,77-84	346	2197	6.4	18	1	-7	-7.0	0
Gary Marangi	74-77	50	328	6.6	2				
Ed Marinaro	72-77	383	1319	3.4	4	146	1176	8.1	7
Ed Marshall	71, 76-77					17	362	21.3	3
Bill Masters	67-76	18	114	6.3	0	169	2268	13.4	15
Bo Matthews	74-81	424	1566	3.7	11	75	488	6.5	0
Alvin Maxson	74-78	360	1270	3.5	6	95	619	6.5	1
James McAlister	75-76,78	190	677	3.6	3	30	218	7.3	2
Don McCauley	71-81	770	2627	3.4	40	333	3026	9.1	17
Cliff McClain	70-73	79	445	5.6	2	13	151	11.6	0
Brent McClanahan	73-79	367	1207	3.3	6	107	772	7.2	4
Greg McCrary	75,77-81	2	18	9.0	0	22	228	10.4	3
Earl McCullough	68-74	8	29	3.6	0	124	2319	18.7	19
Sam McCullum	74-83					274	4017	14.7	26
Lawrence McCutcheon	72-81	1521	6578	4.3	26	198	1799	9.1	13
John McDaniel	74-80	4	28	7.0	0	89	1547	17.4	7
Dwight McDonald	75-78					46	717	15.6	8
Willie McGee	73-78	4	9	2.3	0	24	446	18.6	4
Rich McGeorge	70-78	1	3	3.0	0	175	2370	13.5	13

		RUSHING				RECEIVING			
Name	Years	Att.	Yards	Avg.	TD	Rec.	Yards	Avg.	TD
Pat McInally	76-81	4	-5	-1.3	0	57	808	14.2	5
John McKay	76-78					41	632	7.2	2
Hugh McKinnis	73-76	269	960	3.6	10	65	572	8.8	0
Ted McKnight	77-82	528	2344	4.4	22	99	717	7.2	1
John McMakin	72-76	1	0	0.0	0	45	673	15.0	4
Rod McNeill	74-76	110	428	3.9	3	30	235	7.8	2
Leon McQuay	74-76	88	287	3.3	1	9	86	9.6	0
Warren McVea	68-71,73	248	1186	4.8	11	38	358	9.4	2
Terry Metcalf	73-77,81	766	3498	4.6	24	245	2457	10.0	9
Cleo Miller	74-82	593	2491	4.2	16	140	1175	8.4	1
Robert Miller	75-80	275	951	3.5	7	95	771	8.1	1
Willie Miller	75-76,78-82	5	-2	-0.4	0	112	1786	15.9	15
Jim Mitchell	69-79	26	187	7.2	1	305	4358	14.3	28
Lydell Mitchell	72-80	1675	6534	3.9	27	376	3203	8.5	17
Tom Mitchell	66,68-77	3	14	4.7	0	239	3181	13.3	24
Mike Montgomery	71-74	96	291	3.1	2	59	835	14.2	7
Ross Montgomery	69-70	77	281	3.6	0	16	83	5.2	0
Bob Moore	71-78	2	23	11.5	0	115	1270	11.0	7
Joe Moore	71,73	87	281	3.2	0	8	39	7.8	0
Arnold Morgado	77-80	284	956	3.4	15	19	150	7.9	1
Milt Morin	66-75	5	41	8.2	0	271	4208	15.5	16
Mercury Morris	69-76	804	4133	5.1	31	54	543	10.1	1
Reece Morrison	68-73	160	526	3.3	2	14	210	15.0	2
Craig Morton	65-81	215	627	2.9	12				
Haven Moses	68-81	18	43	2.4	1	448	8091	18.1	56
Roland Moss	69-71					11	155	14.1	1
Larry Mucker	77-80	9	51	5.7	0	33	635	19.2	5
Herb Mul-Key	72-74	42	178	4.2	1	4	66	16.5	0
Bill Munson	64-79	130	548	4.2	3	1	-6	-6.0	0
Johnny Musso	75-77	100	365	3.7	6	7	39	5.6	0
Chip Myers	67,69-76					220	3092	14.1	12
Joe Namath	65-77	71	140	2.0	7				
Lewis Neal	73-74	1	-1	-1.0	0	13	230	17.7	10
Ralph Nelson	75-76	83	312	3.8	1	17	154	9.1	1
Terry Nelson	74-80	12	85	7.1	1	87	1113	12.8	6
Robert Newhouse	72-83	1160	4784	4.1	31	120	956	8.0	5
Bob Newland	71-74	1	6	6.0	0	124	1877	15.1	0
Kent Nix	67-72	43	145	3.4	2				
George Nock	69-72	192	556	2.9	8	24	190	7.9	3
Don Nottingham	71-78	611	2496	4.1	34	67	502	7.5	0
Jack Novak	75-77					12	188	15.7	1
Jim Obradovich	75-83					56	661	11.8	7
Jim O'Brien	70-73	3	9	3.0	0	14	305	21.8	2
Steve Odom	74-79	16	205	12.8	1	84	1613	19.2	11
Riley Odoms	72-83	25	211	8.4	2	396	5755	14.5	41
Bill Olds	73-76	287	985	3.4	6	62	372	6.0	4
Joe Orduna	72-74	74	236	3.2	3	11	58	5.3	1
Dave Osborn	65-76	1179	4336	3.7	29	173	1412	8.2	7
Richard Osborne	76-79					23	197	8.6	1
Jim Otis	70-78	1160	4350	3.8	19	90	549	6.1	3
Artie Owens	76-80	41	154	3.8	1	27	418	15.5	2
Morris Owens	75-79	4	0	0.0	0	116	2062	17.8	14
Steve Owens	70-74	635	2451	3.9	20	99	861	8.7	2
Tinker Owens	76-80					60	785	13.1	4
Joel Parker	74-77	2	2	1.0	0	51	585	11.5	6
Billy Parks	71-75	5	77	15.4	0	123	1826	14.8	7
Gary Parris	73-80					45	512	11.4	5
Bob Parsons	72-81	8	2	0.3	0	19	231	12.2	4
Dan Pastorini	71-83	216	685	3.2	8				
Lloyd Pate	70	46	162	3.1	1	19	103	5.4	0
Wayne Patrick	68-72	264	1084	4.1	5	96	745	7.8	1
Ken Payne	74-78	2	15	7.5	0	116	1633	14.1	6
Barry Pearson	72-76	1	1	1.0	0	86	1212	14.1	7
Dennis Pearson	78-80	1	1	1.0	0	12	190	15.8	0
Drew Pearson	73-83	21	189	9.0	0	489	7822	16.0	48
Preston Pearson	67-80	941	3609	3.8	13	254	3095	12.2	17
Brian Peets	78-81					27	312	11.6	1
Carlos Pennywell	78-81	1	3	3.0	0	12	143	11.9	3
Lonnie Perrin	76-79	262	1047	4.0	9	21	222	10.6	2
Jess Phillips	68-77	888	3568	4.0	13	114	694	6.1	2
Rod Phillips	75-80	121	595	4.9	3	14	86	6.1	0
Mike Phipps	70-81	254	1278	5.0	13				
Lou Piccone	74-82	2	17	8.5	0	100	1380	13.8	6
Cyril Pinder	68-73	428	1709	4.0	7	67	556	8.3	0
Frank Pitts	68-75	28	257	9.2	1	175	2897	16.6	27
Jim Plunkett	71-86	323	1337	4.1	14				
Ed Podolak	69-77	1157	4451	3.8	34	288	2456	8.5	6
Larry Poole	75-78	133	588	4.4	2	32	212	6.6	3
Ernest Pough	76-78	5	41	8.3	0	10	166	16.6	1
Darnell Powell	76,78-79	31	117	3.8	1	1	6	6.0	0
Billy Ray Pritchett	75-77	92	290	3.2	1	17	110	6.5	0
Joe Profit	71-73	133	471	3.5	3	14	130	9.3	0
Greg Pruitt	73-84	1196	5672	4.7	27	328	3069	9.4	18
Jeff Queen	69-74	178	596	3.3	5	54	658	12.2	5
Mike Rae	76-81	44	300	6.8	2				
George Ragsdale	77-80	34	147	4.3	1	8	86	10.8	1
Steve Raible	76-81	3	15	5.0	0	68	1017	15.0	3
Steve Ramsey	70-76	33	108	3.3	2				
Ahmad Rashad	72-74,76-82	10	52	5.2	0	495	6831	13.8	44
Bo Rather	73-78	9	46	5.1	0	92	1467	15.9	7
Eddie Ray	70-74,76	181	691	3.8	9	33	275	8.3	2
Tommy Reamon	76	103	314	3.0	4	10	136	13.6	1
John Reaves	72-79,81	44	195	4.4	3				
Alvin Reed	67-75	1	0	0.0	0	214	2983	13.9	14
Joe Reed	72-79	84	484	5.8	2				
Oscar Reed	68-75	504	2008	4.0	8	94	677	7.2	3
Tony Reed	77-81	581	2340	4.0	8	172	1699	9.9	2
Tom Reynolds	72-73					15	279	18.6	2
Ray Rhodes	74-80	6	0	0.0	0	51	980	19.2	7
Golden Richards	73-79	5	15	3.0	0	122	2136	17.5	17
Gloster Richardson	67-74	5	-8	-1.8	0	92	1976	21.5	18
Mike Richardson	69-71	125	452	3.6	2	38	398	10.5	1
John Riggins	71-79,81-85	2916	11352	3.9	104	250	2090	8.4	12
Preston Riley	70-72					21	331	15.8	1
Oscar Roan	75-78					69	773	11.2	9

		RUSHING				RECEIVING			
Name	**Years**	**Att.**	**Yards**	**Avg.**	**TD**	**Rec.**	**Yards**	**Avg.**	**TD**
Jim Robinson	76-80					85	1437	16.9	6
Paul Robinson	68-73	737	2947	4.0	24	90	612	6.8	2
Virgil Robinson	71-72	34	97	2.9	1	12	53	4.4	1
Terry Robiskie	77-81	159	549	3.5	5	23	147	6.4	0
Johnny Rodgers	77-78	4	49	12.3	0	17	234	13.8	0
Willie Rodgers	72-75	211	672	3.2	8	30	214	7.1	0
Oliver Ross	73-76	63	173	2.7	0	10	104	10.4	0
Reggie Rucker	70-81	12	68	5.7	0	447	7065	15.8	44
Billy Ryckman	77-80					50	743	14.9	4
Tony Samuels	77-81					33	419	12.7	2
Sam Scarber	75-76,78	76	304	4.0	2	26	164	6.3	2
Larry Schreiber	71-76	506	1794	3.5	10	117	982	8.4	4
Steve Schubert	74-79					24	362	15.1	1
Bo Scott	69-74	554	2124	3.8	18	112	826	7.4	7
Bobby Scott	73-81	30	74	2.5	1				
Freddie Scott	74-83	25	191	7.6	1	262	4270	16.3	20
James Scott	76-82	2	-4	-2.0	0	177	3202	18.1	20
Rob Scribner	73-76	73	361	4.9	3	6	75	12.5	1
Paul Seal	74-79	5	10	2.0	1	106	1586	6.1	7
Larry Seiple	67-77	15	145	9.7	0	73	934	12.8	7
Ron Sellers	69-73					112	2184	19.5	18
Jim Seymour	70-72	1	-9	-9.0	0	21	385	18.3	5
Paul Seymour	73-77					62	818	13.2	3
Ron Shanklin	70-76	5	2	0.4	0	168	3079	18.3	24
Dennis Shaw	70-76, 78	95	420	4.4	0				
Rod Sherman	67-73	4	20	5.0	0	105	1576	15.0	5
Gary Shirk	76-82					130	1640	12.6	11
Don Shy	67-73	457	1577	3.5	10	76	835	11.0	3
Mike Siani	72-80					158	2618	16.6	17
Nate Simpson	77-79	153	497	3.2	1	17	69	4.1	0
O.J. Simpson	69-79	2404	11236	4.7	61	203	2142	10.5	14
David Sims	77-79	293	1174	4.0	19	46	399	8.7	4
Brian Sipe	74-83	223	762	3.4	11				
Barry Smith	73-76	10	24	2.4	0	46	692	15.0	4
Barty Smith	74-80	544	1942	3.6	18	120	979	8.2	3
Charlie Smith	68-75	858	3351	3.9	24	141	1596	11.3	10
Charlie Smith	74-81	27	161	6.0	1	218	3349	15.4	24
Dave Smith	70-73	2	-4	-2.0	0	109	1457	13.4	7
Jerry Smith	65-77	8	56	7.0	0	421	5496	13.1	60
Larry Smith	69-74	528	2027	3.3	11	149	1176	7.9	5
Ollie Smith	73-74, 76-77	1	-3	-3.0	0	44	772	17.5	1
Ron Smith	65-74	8	42	5.3	0	11	227	20.6	0
Sherman Smith	76-83	834	3520	4.2	28	217	2393	11.0	10
Jack Snow	65-75	2	3	1.5	0	340	6012	17.7	45
Todd Snyder	70-72					24	330	13.8	2
Willie Spencer	76-78	104	247	2.4	5	6	45	7.5	0
Cotton Spreyer	72-75	1	1	1.0	0	34	535	15.7	5
John Spilis	69-71					27	446	16.5	1
Steve Spurrier	67-76	61	258	4.2	2				
Ken Stabler	70-84	118	93	0.8	4				
Jon Staggers	70-75	8	56	7.0	1	93	1370	14.7	7
Haskel Stanback	74-79	728	2662	3.7	25	98	786	8.0	1
Roger Staubach	69-79	410	2264	5.4	20	1	-13	-13.0	0
Howard Stevens	73-77	89	376	4.2	4	17	120	7.1	0
Wayne Stewart	74					19	283	14.9	1
Darryl Stingley	73-77	28	244	8.7	2	110	1883	17.1	14
Otto Stowe	71-74	4	29	7.3	0	43	742	17.3	10
Steve Strachan	85-88	52	174	3.3	0	7	61	8.7	0
Jim Strong	70-72	134	527	3.9	3	30	201	6.7	0
Morris Stroud	69-74					54	977	18.1	7
Tom Sullivan	72-78	876	3142	3.6	17	162	1286	7.9	5
Lynn Swann	74-82	11	72	6.5	0	336	5462	16.3	51
Joe Sweet	72-75	1	1	1.0	0	10	173	17.3	1
Jerry Tagge	72-74	41	117	2.9	3				
John Tarver	72-75	162	562	3.5	7	34	214	6.3	1
Altie Taylor	69-76	1170	4308	3.7	24	175	1538	8.8	6
Charley Taylor	64-75, 77	442	1488	3.4	11	649	9110	14.0	79
Otis Taylor	65-75	30	161	5.4	3	410	7306	17.8	57
Don Testerman	76-78, 80	230	865	3.8	2	73	604	8.3	5

		RUSHING				RECEIVING			
Name	**Years**	**Att.**	**Yards**	**Avg.**	**TD**	**Rec.**	**Yards**	**Avg.**	**TD**
Jim Thaxton	73-74, 76-78	2	-13	-6.5	0	35	544	15.5	5
Bob Thomas	71-74	120	537	4.5	3	19	155	8.2	1
Duane Thomas	70-71, 73-74	453	2038	4.5	21	38	297	7.8	3
Earl Thomas	71-76	6	18	3.0	0	106	1651	15.6	14
Jimmy Thomas	69-73	165	824	5.0	4	67	923	13.8	8
Mike Thomas	75-80	1087	4196	3.9	19	192	2011	10.5	11
Speedy Thomas	69-72, 74	8	22	2.8	1	19	122	6.4	0
Bobby Thompson	75-76	64	310	4.8	1	29	230	7.9	0
Jesse Thompson	78,80	3	3	1.0	0	29	312	10.8	4
Ricky Thompson	76-81					97	1480	15.3	14
Rocky Thompson	71-73	68	217	3.2	1	16	85	5.3	0
Woody Thompson	75-77	242	877	3.6	1	42	259	6.2	0
Andre Tillman	75-78					66	757	11.5	6
Eric Torkelson	74-81	351	1307	3.7	8	59	469	7.9	0
Bill Troup	74-78,80	30	16	0.5	2				
Bob Trumpy	68-77	1	-1	-1.0	0	298	4600	15.4	35
Bob Tucker	70-80	6	6	1.0	1	422	5421	12.8	27
Walter Tullis	78-79					10	173	17.3	1
Cecil Turner	68-73	8	13	1.6	0	21	364	17.3	2
Clem Turner	69-72	74	270	3.6	2	21	114	5.4	1
Deacon Turner	78-80	142	549	3.9	1	25	141	5.6	1
Howard Twilley	66-76					212	3064	14.5	23
Rick Upchurch	75-84	49	349	7.1	3	267	4369	16.4	24
Mark van Eeghen	74-83	1652	6651	4.0	37	174	1583	9.1	4
Bill Van Heusen	68-76	13	171	13.2	1	82	1684	20.5	11
Randy Vataha	71-77	6	-2	-0.3	0	188	3164	16.8	23
Stu Voigt	70-80	2	3	1.5	1	177	1919	10.8	17
Charlie Wade	74-75,77	1	-15	-15.0	0	39	683	17.5	1
Harmon Wages	68-71,73	332	1321	4.0	5	85	765	9.0	5
Bob Wallace	68-72	8	45	5.6	0	109	1403	12.9	9
Ward Walsh	71-72	46	165	3.6	0	10	58	5.8	1
Larry Walton	69-74,76,78	12	101	8.4	1	172	2682	15.6	27
Paul Warfield	64-74,76-77	22	204	9.6	0	427	8565	20.1	85
Gene Washington	67-73					182	3237	17.8	26
Gene Washington	69-77,79	6	23	3.8	0	385	6856	17.8	60
Vic Washington	71-76	588	2208	3.8	16	130	1090	8.4	5
Larry Watkins	69-77	448	1711	3.8	12	51	284	5.6	1
Norris Weese	76-79	69	362	5.2	5				
Claxton Welch	69-71,73	26	83	3.2	2	7	21	3.0	0
Terry Wells	74-75	33	139	4.2	0	7	20	2.9	0
Bob West	72-74	2	2	1.0	0	13	230	17.7	2
Don Westbrook	77-81	3	6	2.0	0	23	393	17.1	3
Charlie White	77-78	61	193	3.2	1	4	36	9.0	1
Jan White	71-72					25	276	11.1	2
Lee White	68-72	123	389	3.2	0	16	143	8.9	1
Marsh White	75-76	86	313	3.6	2	5	22	4.4	0
Walter White	75-79	4	12	3.0	0	163	2396	14.7	16
Clarence Williams	77-81	394	1327	3.4	17	93	727	7.8	2
Dave Williams	67-73	6	69	11.5	0	183	2768	15.1	25
Dave Williams	77-81	172	501	2.9	1	92	675	7.3	7
Delvin Williams	74-81	1312	5598	4.3	33	152	1415	9.3	6
Ed Williams	74-77	243	896	3.7	7	56	427	7.6	2
Joe Williams	71-72	52	139	2.7	1	19	175	9.2	0
Perry Williams	69-74	177	547	3.1	1	37	285	7.7	0
Fred Willis	71-76	780	2831	3.6	18	203	1380	6.8	5
Joe Wilson	73-75	25	96	3.8	0	3	38	12.7	0
Bob Windsor	67-75	9	57	6.3	0	185	2307	12.5	14
Stan Winfrey	75-77	55	225	4.1	1	6	55	9.2	1
Al Woodall	69-71,73-74	60	214	3.6	0				
Don Woods	74-80	763	3087	4.0	16	145	1358	9.4	5
Elmo Wright	71-75	10	69	6.9	0	70	1116	15.9	6
Keith Wright	78-80					12	151	12.6	3
Sam Wyche	68-72,74,76	45	303	6.7	3	1	5	5.0	0
Charley Young	74-76	131	638	4.9	2	40	391	9.8	2
Charle Young	73-85	16	80	5.0	1	418	5106	12.2	27
Rickey Young	75-83	1011	3666	3.6	23	408	3285	8.1	16
Steve Zabel	70-79	1	-5	-5.0	0	10	123	12.3	3
Don Zimmerman	73-76	1	3	3.0	0	53	601	11.3	5

(All men with 25 or more punt returns or 25 or more kickoff returns)

		PUNT RETURNS				KICKOFF RETURNS			
Name	Years	No.	Yards	Avg.	TD	No.	Yards	Avg.	TD
Mike Adamle	71-76	1	2	2.0	0	34	636	18.7	0
Margene Adkins	70-73	15	49	3.3	0	81	1784	22.0	0
Bobby Anderson	70-75					30	720	24.0	0
Dick Anderson	68-77	40	272	6.8	0	7	114	16.3	0
Donny Anderson	66-74	15	222	14.8	1	34	759	22.3	0
Otis Armstrong	73-80					37	879	23.8	0
John Arnold	79-80	47	368	7.6	0	32	684	21.4	0
Pete Athas	71-76	92	818	8.9	0	8	163	20.4	0
Butch Atkinson	68-77,79	148	1247	8.4	3	76	1893	24.9	0
Gordon Bell	76-78	16	102	6.4	0	38	764	20.1	0
Horace Belton	78-80					37	800	21.6	0
Willie Belton	71-74	52	283	5.4	0	57	1341	23.5	0
Jim Bertelsen	72-76	74	810	10.9	0	6	120	20.0	0
Mel Blount	70-82	1	52	52.0	0	36	911	25.3	0
Emerson Boozer	66-75					37	872	23.6	1
Bill Bradley	69-77	122	953	7.8	0	27	564	20.9	0
Larry Brinson	77-80					25	525	21.0	0
Eddie Brown	74-79	172	1511	8.8	1	81	1957	24.2	0
Ken Brown	70-75					44	973	22.1	0
Ray Brown	71-80	60	539	9.0	0				
Larry Brunson	74-80	75	630	8.4	0	87	2022	23.2	0
Cullen Bryant	73-84	71	707	10.0	0	69	1813	26.3	3
Bobby Bryant	68-80	69	404	5.9	0	22	437	19.9	0
Hubie Bryant	73-75	19	218	11.5	0	48	1266	26.4	2
Allen Carter	75-76					33	898	27.2	1
Tommy Casanova	72-77	91	784	8.7	1	2	82	41.0	0
Clarence Chapman	76-81,85					35	768	21.9	1
Gill Chapman	75	17	207	12.2	0	28	614	21.9	0
Rondy Colbert	75-77	40	310	7.8	1	19	450	23.7	0
Linzy Cole	70-72	35	225	6.4	0	50	1290	25.8	0
Ronnie Coleman	74-81	25	228	9.1	1	29	601	20.7	0
Mike Collier	75,77-79					33	707	21.4	1
Larry Collins	78,80					32	709	22.2	0
Neal Colzie	75-83	170	1759	10.3	0	7	130	18.6	0
Rufus Crawford	78	34	284	8.4	0	35	829	23.7	0
Doug Cunningham	67-74	30	272	9.1	0	68	1613	23.7	0
Thom Darden	72-81	45	285	6.3	0	1	-1	-1.0	0
Ben Davis	67-68,70-76	27	240	8.9	1	35	860	24.6	0
Clarence Davis	71-78					79	2140	27.1	0
Gary Davis	76-81	3	47	15.7	0	104	2341	22.5	0
Steve Davis	72-76					54	1363	25.2	0
Tony Davis	76-81	42	357	8.5	0	21	256	12.2	0
Joe Dawkins	70-76	1	0	0.0	0	32	799	25.0	0
Johnnie Dirden	78-81					42	979	22.3	0
Al Dodd	67,69-71,73-74	80	744	9.3	0	38	776	20.4	0
Bobby Duhon	68,70-72	40	286	7.2	1	40	716	17.9	0
Lenny Dunlap	71-75	27	291	10.8	0	15	337	22.5	0
Glen Edwards	71-81	104	959	9.2	0	13	257	19.8	0
Jimmy Edwards	79	33	186	5.6	0	44	1103	25.1	0
Richard Ellender	79	31	203	6.5	0	24	514	21.4	0
Lenvil Elliott	73-81					47	877	18.7	0
Ken Ellis	70-77,79	71	469	6.6	1	41	882	21.5	0
Willie Ellison	67-74					42	1011	24.1	0
Dave Elmendorf	71-79	57	502	8.8	0	2	23	11.5	0
Chris Farasopoulos	71-74	53	481	9.1	1	51	1172	23.0	0
Chris Fletcher	70-76	28	205	7.3	0	28	599	21.4	0
Ike Forte	76-81	3	4	1.3	0	26	630	24.2	0
Wallace Francis	73-81					84	2077	24.0	2
Johnny Fuller	68-75	25	114	4.6	0	10	186	18.6	0
Mike Fuller	75-82	252	2660	10.6	2	79	1701	21.5	0
Frenchy Fuqua	69-76	12	77	6.4	0	26	496	19.1	0
Ron Gardin	70-71,73	34	419	12.3	1	25	586	23.4	0
Carl Garrett	69-77	43	487	11.3	0	154	3704	24.1	0
Walt Garrison	66-74					41	813	19.8	0
Tom Geredine	73-74,76					27	611	22.6	0
Louie Giammona	76,78-81	18	167	9.3	0	58	1167	20.1	0
John Gillam	67-77	23	94	4.1	0	74	1884	25.5	2
Hubert Ginn	70-77	1	4	4.0	0	50	1105	22.1	0
Dick Gordon	65-74	31	148	4.8	0	79	1925	24.4	0
Johnnie Gray	75-83	85	656	7.7	0	21	317	15.1	0
Mel Gray	71-81	9	49	5.4	0	51	1191	23.4	0
Tony Green	71-79	61	581	9.5	1	66	1521	23.0	1
Charlie Greer	68-74	55	426	7.7	1	2	41	20.5	0
Bob Gresham	71-76					46	1116	24.3	1
Bob Grim	67-77	59	282	4.8	0	26	549	21.1	0
Isaac Hagins	76-80	22	110	5.0	0	40	875	21.9	0
Bob Hammond	76-80	67	566	8.4	1	61	1297	21.3	0
Gary Hammond	73-76	40	291	7.3	0	38	872	22.9	0
Dave Hampton	69-76					113	2923	25.9	3
Willard Harrell	75-84	123	854	6.9	2	97	1921	19.8	0
Cliff Harris	70-79	66	418	6.3	0	63	1622	25.7	0
Harold Hart	74-78					46	1236	26.9	1
Bob Hayes	64-75	104	1158	11.1	3	23	581	25.3	0
Gary Hayman	74-75	27	229	8.5	0	8	179	22.4	0
Mack Herron	73-75	84	982	11.7	0	82	1985	24.2	1
Ike Hill	70-71,73-74,76	102	622	6.1	2	21	445	21.2	0
Paul Hofer	76-81					68	1474	21.7	0
Steve Holden	73-77	36	238	6.6	0	29	675	23.3	0
Mike Holmes	74-76	9	45	5.0	0	31	761	24.5	0
Robert Holmes	68-73,75					35	928	26.5	0
Roland Hooks	76-82	43	302	7.0	0	48	969	20.2	0
Ken Houston	67-80	51	333	6.5	0	3	80	26.7	0
Rich Houston	69-73					35	800	22.9	0
Gene Howard	68-72	22	129	5.9	0	41	975	23.8	0
Bob Hudson	72-74	1	0	0.0	0	25	597	23.9	0
Al Hunter	77-80					78	1717	22.0	0
Horace Ivory	77-82					70	1696	24.2	1
Bernard Jackson	72-80					118	2709	23.0	0
Po James	72-75					41	962	23.5	0
Dick Jauron	73-80	44	447	10.2	0	19	426	22.4	0
Roy Jefferson	65-76	58	436	7.5	1	5	91	18.2	0
Ron Jessie	71-81					47	1237	26.3	2
Andy Johnson	74-76,78-81	6	60	10.0	0	28	544	19.4	0
Benny Johnson	70-73,76					28	550	19.6	0
Essex Johnson	68-76	51	303	5.9	0	49	1036	21.1	0
Marchall Johnson	75,77-78	25	147	5.9	0	49	1076	22.0	0

		PUNT RETURNS				KICKOFF RETURNS			
Name	Years	No.	Yards	Avg.	TD	No.	Yards	Avg.	TD
Clint Jones	67-73					99	2426	24.5	1
Jimmie Jones	74					38	927	24.4	0
Larry Jones	74-78	72	562	7.8	1	73	1816	24.9	1
Doug Kotar	74-79,81	4	19	4.8	0	42	920	21.9	0
Larry Krause	70-71,73-74					35	864	24.7	1
Bruce Laird	72-83	61	405	6.6	0	152	3728	24.5	0
Jerry Latin	75-78					43	951	22.1	0
Dennis Law	78-79	25	106	4.2	0	2	30	15.0	0
Rolland Lawrence	73-80	109	734	6.7	0	29	685	23.6	0
Odell Lawson	70-71,73-74	1	0	0.0	0	28	613	21.9	0
Billy LeFear	72-75	10	56	5.6	0	60	1461	24.4	0
Charlie Leigh	68-69,71-74	50	368	7.4	0	46	1082	23.5	0
Tony Leonard	76-79	76	594	7.8	1	30	691	23.0	0
Jerry LeVais	69-74	88	687	7.8	0	94	2213	23.5	0
Floyd Little	67-75	81	893	11.0	2	104	2523	24.3	0
Virgil Livers	75-79	86	738	8.6	0	27	543	20.1	0
Spider Lockhart	65-75	64	328	5.1	0	1	19	19.0	0
Larry Marshall	72-78	162	1466	9.0	0	138	3396	24.6	0
Alvin Maxson	74-78					25	464	18.6	0
James McAlister	75-76,78					31	636	20.5	0
Don McCauley	71-81					45	967	22.5	1
Brent McClanahan	73-79					66	1500	22.7	0
Ralph McGill	72-79	106	969	9.1	1	27	566	21.0	0
Rod McNeill	74-76	1	0	0.0	0	27	660	24.4	0
Leon McQuay	74-76	9	86	9.6	0	48	1092	22.8	0
Warren McVea	68-71,73					47	1008	21.4	0
Terry Metcalf	73-77,81	84	936	11.4	1	120	3087	25.7	2
Cleo Miller	74-82					34	660	19.4	0
Kevin Miller	78-80	66	324	4.9	0	40	854	21.4	0
Randy Montgomery	71-74					33	836	25.3	1
Keith Moody	76-80	88	920	10.5	3	109	2318	21.3	0
Manfred Moore	74-77	88	770	8.8	1	76	1734	22.8	0
Zeke Moore	67-77	8	93	11.6	0	64	1618	25.3	1
Dennis Morgan	74-75	27	347	12.9	1	42	993	23.6	0
Mercury Morris	69-76	27	171	6.3	0	111	2947	26.5	3
Reece Morrison	68-73	26	182	7.0	0	32	727	22.7	0
Herb Mul-Key	72-74	24	243	10.1	0	54	1505	27.4	1
Steve Odom	74-79	73	595	8.2	1	194	4251	21.9	2
Artie Owens	76-80	1	20	20.0	0	96	2155	22.4	0
Lemar Parrish	70-82	131	1205	9.2	4	61	1504	24.7	1
Dennis Pearson	78-80	12	115	9.6	0	55	1232	22.4	1
Preston Pearson	67-80	7	40	5.7	0	114	2801	24.6	2
Lonnie Perrin	76-79					33	805	24.4	0
Jess Phillips	68-77	2	16	8.0	0	45	1048	23.3	0
Lou Piccone	74-82	73	482	6.6	1	111	2559	23.1	0
Ed Podolak	69-77	86	739	8.6	0	34	697	20.5	0
Ernest Pough	76-78					40	793	19.8	0
Greg Pruitt	73-84	194	2007	10.3	1	106	2514	23.7	1
George Ragsdale	77-79					61	1298	21.2	0
Danny Reece	76-80	222	1554	7.0	0	23	483	21.0	0
Mel Renfro	64-77	109	842	7.7	1	85	2246	26.4	2
Golden Richards	73-79	62	501	8.1	1	3	44	14.7	0
Jim Robinson	76-80	59	364	6.2	0	27	584	21.6	0
Paul Robinson	68-73	2	1	0.5	0	40	924	23.1	0
Johnny Rodgers	77-78	26	246	9.5	0	15	353	23.5	0
Oliver Ross	73-76					38	792	20.8	0
Billy Ryckman	77-80	47	339	7.2	0	1	0	0.0	0
Steve Schubert	74-79	103	866	8.4	3	21	586	18.4	0
Bo Scott	69-74					25	722	20.9	0
Jake Scott	70-78	130	1357	10.4	1	6	137	22.8	0
Rob Scribner	73-76	45	361	8.0	0	16	392	24.5	0
Jeff Severson	72-79	28	212	7.6	0	9	148	16.4	0
Willie Shelby	76-78	42	304	7.2	0	58	1375	23.7	1
Rod Sherman	67-73	27	212	7.9	0	8	145	18.1	0
Don Shy	67-73	29	202	7.0	0	26	618	23.8	0
O.J. Simpson	69-79					33	990	30.0	1
Charlie Smith	68-75					30	659	22.0	0
Ron Smith	65-74	235	1788	7.6	2	275	6922	25.2	3
Cotton Speyrer	72-75	8	54	6.8	0	39	1035	26.5	1
Jon Staggers	70-75	94	792	8.4	3	35	854	24.4	0
Howard Stevens	73-77	163	1559	9.6	0	103	2336	22.7	0
Tom Sullivan	72-78					27	592	21.9	0
Lynn Swann	74-82	61	739	12.1	1	3	11	3.7	0
Altie Taylor	69-76					27	597	22.1	0
Bruce Taylor	70-77	142	1323	9.3	0	12	190	15.8	0
Clifton Taylor	74,76					30	626	20.9	0
Jesse Taylor	72	1	0	0.0	0	31	676	21.8	0
Bill Thomas	72-74					27	621	23.0	0
Emmitt Thomas	66-78	11	64	5.8	0	29	673	23.2	0
Ike Thomas	71-75					51	1394	27.3	0
Billy Thompson	69-81	157	1814	11.6	0	46	1156	25.1	0
Bobby Thompson	75-76					44	996	22.6	0
Rocky Thompson	71-73					65	1768	27.2	2
Gerald Tinker	74-75	20	218	10.9	1	42	1011	24.1	0
Cecil Turner	68-73	27	114	4.2	0	108	2616	24.2	4
Deacon Turner	78-80					65	1346	20.7	0
Rick Upchurch	75-83	248	3008	12.3	8	95	2355	24.8	0
Ted Vactor	69-75	42	290	6.9	0	30	746	24.9	0
Rick Volk	67-78	84	548	6.5	0	2	16	8.0	0
Billy Walik	70-72	28	130	4.6	0	67	1640	24.5	0
Donnie Walker	73-75	68	594	8.7	0	1	20	20.0	0
Jackie Wallace	74-79	83	852	10.3	0	6	92	15.3	0
Vic Washington	71-76					129	3341	25.9	1
Roger Wehrli	69-81	42	310	7.4	0	5	38	7.6	0
Charlie West	68-79	158	1099	7.0	1	85	2127	25.0	0
Clarence Williams	77-81	1	0	0.0	0	35	690	19.7	0
Dave Williams	77-81	1	60	60.0	0	88	2019	22.9	3
Lawrence Williams	76-77					50	1206	24.1	0
Leonard Willis	76-79	30	207	6.9	0	37	792	21.4	0
Roland Woolsey	75-78	39	324	8.3	0	14	274	19.6	0
Roscoe Word	74-76	39	293	7.5	0	7	127	18.1	0
Keith Wright	78-80	78	467	6.0	0	70	1767	25.2	0
Alvin Wyatt	70-73	59	504	8.5	2	60	1480	24.7	0
Mickey Zofko	71-74					30	656	21.9	0

Lifetime Statistics - 1970- 1979 Section 4 - PUNTING
(All men with 25 or more punts)

Name	Years	No.	Avg.
Donny Anderson	66-74	387	39.6
Zenon Andrusyshyn	78	79	41.1
Bruce Barnes	73-74	100	37.4
Lem Barney	67-77	113	35.5
Marv Bateman	72-77	401	40.9
David Beverly	74-80	586	38.1
Tom Blanchard	71-81	819	41.3
Bill Bradley	69-77	213	39.0
Mike Bragg	68-80	978	39.8
Steve Broussard	75	29	31.8
Mike Burke	74	46	37.0
Skip Butler	71-77	50	36.4
Duane Carrell	74-77	257	38.9
Dave Chapple	71-74	162	40.2
Neil Clabo	75-77	225	39.9
Ken Clark	79	93	40.1
Don Cockroft	68-80	651	40.3
Fred Cox	63-77	70	38.7
Jerry DePoyster	68,71-72	106	38.2
Bucky Dilts	77-79	285	37.5
Mike Eischeid	66-74	564	41.3
Rick Engels	76-78	122	38.4
Johnny Evans	78-80	214	39.5
Julian Fagan	70-73	299	40.5
Greg Gantt	74-75	134	36.2
Roy Gerela			
Dave Green	73-78	424	40.1
Ray Guy	73-86	1052	42.3
Eddie Hare	79	83	36.6
Gus Holloman	68-74	47	38.7
Mitch Hoopes	75-78	123	38.7
Rusty Jackson	76,78-79	260	38.7
John James	72-84	1083	40.6
Bill Johnson	70	43	39.5
Spike Jones	70-77	592	39.1
Terry Joyce	76-77	86	37.0
Gary Keithly	73, 75	66	37.5
Merrit Kersey	74-75	97	32.5
Bob Lee	69-80	156	39.7
David Lee	66-78	838	40.6
David Lewis	70-73	285	43.7
Steve Little	78-80	125	38.5
Jim McCann	71-73,75	139	37.6
Tom McNeill	69-73	317	41.1
Dan Melville	79	71	37.0
Mike Michel	77-78	93	36.7
Steve O'Neal	69-73	337	40.7
Cliff Parsley	77-81	407	39.8
Bob Parsons	72-83	884	38.6
Dennis Partee	68-75	519	41.3
Dan Pastorini	71-81	316	39.7
Mike Patrick	75-78	222	38.2
Hal Roberts	74	81	38.7
Larry Seiple	67-77	633	40.0
Steve Spurrier	67-76	230	38.3
Wilbur Sumers	77	93	36.8
Bill Van Heusen	68-76	574	41.7
Bobby Walden	64-77	974	41.6
Glenn Walker	77-78	156	36.1
Randy Walker	74	69	38.4
Herman Weaver	70-80	635	40.3
Norris Weese	76-79	53	35.7
Tom Wittum	73-77	303	41.9

Lifetime Statistics - 1970-1979 Section 5 - KICKING
(All men with 10 or more PAT or field goal attempts)

Name	Years	PAT	PAT Att.	PAT Pct.	FG	FG Att.	FG Pct.
Bill Bell	71-73	64	69	93	30	55	55
Tom Birney	79-80	21	28	75	13	21	62
Skip Butler	71-77	127	133	95	71	132	54
Don Cockroft	68-80	432	457	95	216	328	66
Fred Cox	63-77	519	539	96	282	455	62
Joe Danelo	75-84	240	250	96	133	228	58
Tom Dempsey	69-79	252	282	89	159	258	62
Jerry DePoyster	68, 71-72	18	20	90	3	15	20
Happy Feller	71-73	27	28	96	16	43	37
Toni Fritsch	71-73, 75-82	287	300	96	157	231	68
Roy Gerela	69-79	351	365	96	184	306	60
Dave Green	73-78	56	65	86	23	43	54
Grant Guthrie	70-71	32	34	94	13	29	45
Efren Herrera	74,76-82	256	268	96	116	171	69
Bobby Howfield	68-74	193	201	96	98	166	59
George Hunt	73, 75	46	53	87	22	39	56
George Jakowenko	74, 76	21	24	88	12	17	71
Curt Knight	69-73	172	175	98	101	175	58
Allan Leavitt	77	5	5	100	5	10	50
John Leypoldt	71-78	203	222	91	93	154	60
Toni Linhart	72,74-79	200	213	94	75	127	59
Steve Little	78-80	41	51	80	13	27	48
Carson Long	77	13	14	93	7	11	64
Errol Mann	68-78	315	333	95	177	276	64
Chester Marcol	72-80	156	167	93	121	196	62
Tim Mazzetti	78-80	95	104	91	45	68	66
Bill McClard	72-75	31	32	97	26	51	51
Mike Michel	77-78	9	13	69			
Nick Mike-Mayer	73-82	226	234	97	115	204	56
Steve Mike-Mayer	75-80	161	175	92	67	131	51
Mark Moseley	70-86	482	511	94	300	457	66
Horst Muhlmann	69-77	245	257	95	154	239	64
Jim O'Brien	70-73	109	112	97	60	108	56
Dennis Partee	68-75	165	175	94	71	121	59
Mac Percival	67-74	163	167	98	101	190	53
David Posey	78	29	31	94	11	22	50
David Ray	69-74	167	175	95	110	178	62
Mirro Roder	73-74,76	28	29	97	17	32	53
John Smith	74-83	308	326	95	128	191	67
Fred Steinfort	76-81,83	122	129	95	63	114	55
Jan Stenerud	67-85	580	601	97	373	558	67
Rich Szaro	75-79	82	88	93	37	59	63
Jim Turner	64-79	521	544	96	304	488	62
Kenny Vinyard	70	23	26	88	9	25	36
Mike Walker	72	15	15	100	2	8	25
Allen Watson	70	7	8	88	5	10	50
Tim Webster	71	8	8	100	6	11	55
Jeff White	73	21	25	84	14	25	56
Garo Yepremian	66-67, 70-81	444	464	96	210	313	67

1980—1993

1980-1993
NEW CHALLENGES, NEW TRIUMPHS

By winning the final two Super Bowls of the 1980s to add to their Super Bowl victories after the 1981 and 1984 seasons, the San Francisco 49ers ascended to the title of "Team of the '80s." Led by quarterback Joe Montana and wide receiver Jerry Rice, the 49ers' offense kept them a step in front of the competition. Nevertheless, most observers ranked San Francisco behind the Steelers' 1970s dynasty and the Lombardi-led Packers of the 1960s. The earlier powerhouses were usually given the edge in defense and because their superiority over their contemporaries was greater. A computer simulation by NFL Films during the 1989 season even awarded the "greatest team" ever mantle to the 1978 Steelers over the 1988 49ers.

The Washington Redskins and Chicago Bears were consistently strong through the 1980s and the New York Giants, Denver Broncos and several other clubs had their moments. The influence of the draft and the possibility of new free-agent rules seem likely to continue the diversity of strength throughout the league for some time to come.

Experiments

In 1986, the NFL tried a novel experiment with television instant replay, first attempted by the USFL, to allow officials in the booth to overrule on-field officials. As suspected, the replays proved the field officials were usually right, some replays were inconclusive and the process slowed the already long games. Nevertheless, the process was approved by most fans. Somewhat grudgingly, the NFL owners have extended instant replay each year since then.

To speed up games, which were averaging over three hours, halftimes were cut to 13 minutes once teams reached their locker-rooms and rules concerning timeouts and the 30-second clock were tightened before the 1990 season. Several teams, particularly Cincinnati and Buffalo, experimented with no-huddle offenses to keep opponents from changing defensive personnel, and this also tended to speed up games. On the other hand, the tendency for more passing lengthened the elapsed time because of the frequent clock stoppages.

The Three-Dollar League

Eight years after the WFL debacle, the NFL faced a new and more serious challenge. The United States Football League began operations in the spring of 1983 with twelve franchises: Arizona Wranglers, Birmingham Stallions, Boston Breakers, Chicago Blitz, Denver Gold, Los Angeles Express, Michigan Panthers, New Jersey Generals, Oakland Raiders, Philadelphia Stars, Tampa Bay Bandits and Washington Federals. The new league avoided direct confrontation at the gate with the NFL by playing its games from March to July, but it went head-to-head with the established league in attempting you sign "name" college stars. It was successful there, in that it signed Heisman Trophy winners Herschel Walker, Mike Rozier and Doug Flutie in each of its three seasons. Aside for the loss of a few talented athletes, the NFL's major difficulty was that the presence of an alternative league sent player salaries skyrocketing.

Aided by a modest TV contract with cable network ESPN, the USFL pronounced its first season a success and added six new teams in '84: Houston Gamblers, Jacksonville Bulls, Memphis Showboats, Oklahoma Outlaws, Pittsburgh Maulers and San Antonio Gunslingers. The Breakers franchise shifted to New Orleans. In the league's third season, the Breakers moved to Portland, the Stars to Baltimore, and the Federals to Orlando. Michigan combined with Oakland, and Pittsburgh, Oklahoma and Chicago quit altogether.

After three years, the USFL had begun to resemble the WFL in its hordes of unheralded players, its small presence in the media, its frequent franchise shifts, and its large financial losses.

Then, against the wishes of some of its owners, the USFL voted to play its fourth season in the fall of 1986 — opposite the NFL. That season, however, was never played. It soon became obvious that the USFL's hopes rested on a $1.69 billion suit, charging the NFL with excersing monopolistic practices to keep the USFL from gaining a lucrative TV contract. In July 1986, a federal jury in New York found the NFL was indeed a monopoly, but that the USFL's problems were of its own making. The damage award of $1 (trebled to $3) meant that the USFL — with $150 million is debts — was finished, although it was not until early 1988 when the USFL lost its last appeal that the final coffin nail was hammered home.

TV Holds Sway

A five-year contract with the three television networks signed in 1981 provided a $656 million package for broadcast rights. Under this pact, each team received about $5 million annually in TV revenue. Expanded playoffs and parity-minded scheduling sought to put the best show possible on the field and on television.

Nevertheless, pro football's TV ratings fell. Some argued over-exposure; others blamed a general decline in network viewing caused by cable TV. In March 1987, Rozelle announces a new three-year, $1.428 billion TV contract that included CBS, NBC, ABC and, for the first time, ESPN. The $476 million annual yield, though down 3.4 percent from 1986, kept most teams in the black.

For the 1990 season, the NFL again expanded its TV base. This was done in part by adding TNT, a new cable network to its cable coverage. Under the contract, TNT broadcast Sunday night games through the first half of the season and ESPN televised them during the second half. CBS and NBC were pacified for slipping ratings by extending the regular season to 17 weeks, with each team receiving a bye during the season. And ABC, whose Monday Night Football remained a prime-time staple, was rewarded with a playoff game by adding a third wild-card teams to the postseason. Through its various contracts the NFL stood to reap $3.6 billion.

Player Movement

The 1977 agreement with the NFLPA governed the game for five years, but Rozelle and the owners again faced Ed Garvey and a list of demands as the 1982 expiration approached. The players offered some radical proposals for a new labor contract. Of the many features, the most prominant was that the players receive their salaries out of a pool made up of 55 percent of the team's gross receipts from tickets and television. Out of this pool, the salary share of each player would be set by a formula based on years in the league and incentive clauses. The players also wanted a less restrictive free-agent arrangement. The owners flatly rejected setting aside any fixed portion of their receipts for the players, and once again, hard negotiations proceeded under careful threats of a strike.

The players made good on the threats, walking off of the field two weeks into the 1982 season. For 57 days, negotiations dragged on. America spent its first October without NFL football since 1919. The parties reached a new arrangement on November 16, leaving pro football structurally unchanged. Although there would be more money for the players, none of the novel proposals of the union were adopted. Play resumed less than a week later amid fears of fan resentment. Attendance was down in some cities, but, by the time the Super Bowl rolled around, the fan backlash had played itself out.

In 1987, new contract negotiations brought new exasperation to fans because of a 24-day players' strike in what many called a "season of unreason." After the season's first two games, the players walked out with a variety of demands. In 1982, it was the players who had stopped the season, but this time the owners were prepared. After only one week off, games were continued with what the owners called "replacement players" and what the NFLPA termed "scabs." For three weeks, the replacements performed to the constant carping of fans, media, union players and some NFL coaches. Attendance dropped and much of the play was ragged but the games counted in the standings. Union players soon began crossing the picket lines. Finally, the union gave in — a crushing defeat — vowing to pursue their goals in the courts.The fans came back almost immediately, and by the end of the season attendance was back to normal. But wounds had been opened between players and management that will take years to heal.

In 1989, as part of its strategy to win free agency for players through antitrust action in the courts, the NFLPA decertified itself as the sole bargaining agent for the players. In the meantime, the NFL came up with a limited free-agent plan — the so-called Plan B. Under this system, teams can protect about two-thirds of their rosters while opening the remaining one-third to free agency by leaving them unprotected until April 1 of every year. Although Plan B has benefitted marginal players and some in the higher-age brackets, only a few of those signing with new teams have made an impact on the championship races.

Despite a great deal of discussion, suggestions such as salary caps (particularly for first-year players) have yet to be implemented. In addition to the high cost of signing college seniors, the NFL was forced to drop is rule against signing underclassmen, a policy that had been in effect since the 1920s. Rather than face still another court fight — one it would surely lose — the league agreed to make underclassmen who announced their intention to turn professional eligible for the draft. The success of such players as Detroit's Barry Sanders proved that some college juniors were ready to compete in the NFL.

Trouble in the ranks

At the start of the 1980s, Rozelle also found himself locked in combat with one of the NFL management lodge brothers. Al Davis, the principle owner of the Oakland Raiders, took the NFL to court in a lawsuit that could change the face of pro football as much as the demands of the NFL Players Association. The chain reaction began with the decision of the Los Angeles Rams to move to Anaheim, a suburban city that was still within metropolitan Los Angeles, for the 1980 season. Davis, meanwhile, was having trouble negotiating a contract with the Oakland Stadium authorities. Davis claimed that the abandoned Los Angeles Coliseum had made a better offer than the Oakland officials, so he announced his decision to move the Raiders to Los Angeles for the 1981 season. Possibly the biggest lure for Davis was the prospect of major profits in Los Angeles through pay television.

Davis quickly found out that his decision could not so easily be carried out. An NFL bylaw provided that a franchise could not move unless 21 of the 28 owners gave their approval. The owners turned thumbs down on the proposal, citing the proximity of Anaheim to Los Angeles. A furious and frustrated Davis then turned to the courts. Joined by the Los Angeles Coliseum, the Raiders sued the NFL in federal court, claiming that the league bylaws on moving franchises violated U.S. antitrust laws. While waiting for the trial to come up on the court calendar, Davis relished the Super Bowl XV triumph of his Raiders and the presentation of the trophy by Rozelle, now his bitter personal enemy.

The first trial ended in a hung jury in 1981, but the court delay had forced the Raiders to stay in Oakland for that season. When the case was retried in the spring of 1982, the jury found that the NFL rule did violate the law and that Davis was entitled to move his team to Los Angeles. With league control thus weakened, the Baltimore Colts moved to Indianapolis for the 1984 season without seeking league approval. After the 1987 season, St. Louis Cardinals owner Bill Bidwell received league approval to move his franchise to Phoenix.

Comings and Goings

Regardless of labor and internal problems, an NFL franchise was still a prestige purchase. Real-estate developer Alex Spanos became the majority owner of the San Diego Chargers in the 1984 for $40 million, car dealer Norman Braman paid $65 million for the Philadelphia Eagles in 1985, the New England Patriots were sold to Remington manufacturer Victor Kiam in 1987 for $90 million, and the Seattle Seahawks went for $80 million to real estate executive Ken Behring in 1988.

The most publicized sale was that of the Dallas Cowboys to oilman Jerry Jones for $140 million. Jones purchased the team from H.R. "Bum" Bright who had headed an 11-person limited partnership that had bought the Cowboys from their original owner, Clint Murchison Jr., in 1984 for $80 million. Under Bright, the Cowboys had become a losing team on the field. Jones startled the football world by ousting team president Tex Schramm and coach Tom Landry, the two men who had guided the Cowboys since the team's entrance into the NFL. As his new head coach, Jones hired Jimmy Johnson, his Arkansas roommate when both played for the Razorbacks about the time the Cowboys were being born. After a disastrous 1-15 first season, Johnson, formerly a highly successfully college coach at Miami (Fla.), bought the Cowboys to a .500 season in 1990.

The Chicago Bears also underwent an ownership change when George Halas died in 1983. Pro football's winningest coach and the man who created the Bears in 1922 and is a charter member of the Pro Football Hall of Fame, Halas was arguably the most important contributor to the NFL's ultimate success. Control of the team passed to his son-in-law Edward McCaskey and grandson Michael McCaskey.

Tomorrow the World

Although the NFL drags its feet, expansion by at least two more teams seems inevitable. There have been many suggestions that when the league finally takes in new franchises, it should also realign along more logical divisions (for example, move Phoenix out of the Eastern Division and Atlanta out of the West. Another complaint, specifically from television executives, is that the NFC has most of the country's largest markets. Unfortunately, any realignment suggestions run into arguments about ancient (and lucrative) rivalries.

However, while true expansion waited, in 1989 the league established the World League of American Football (WLAF) with teams in both Europe and North America that began play in March 1991. Schramm was named president, but he was later succeeded by Mike Lynn, the Vikings' general manager.

It was hoped that the new league would function as a farm system for the NFL, open new markets and eventually serve as a base for international expansion.

Goodbye, Pete; Hello, Paul

Early in 1989, Pete Rozelle announced his intention to retire as commissioner after 29 years. "We must replace the irreplaceable man," Giants owner Wellington Mara commented. The favorite to succeed Rozelle was Saints general manager Jim Finks, but he was unable to muster enough votes. The owners split into two camps, the "Old Guard" who favored Finks and the "Young Turks" who wanted a younger, more market-conscious commissioner. Finally, in October 1989, the owners were able to agree on league counsel Paul Tagliabue as the new commissioner. His first, and perhaps most important, job was to negotiate the new TV contracts with the networks and cable companies. That he was once again able to increase revenue got his term in office off to a rousing start.

However, Tagliabue said from the start that a new collective bargaining agreement with the players would be his No. 1 priority. In the next three years, more than 20 suits were filed by the owners and players, although the games continued to be played and players continued to be paid according to terms of the expired 1982 agreement.

In September 1992, Judge David Doty from the Federal District Court in Minneapolis declared the NFL's Plan B form of free agency illegal. In another decision, Doty proclaimed four players, including Philadelphia's Keith Jackson, the best tight end in the league, as immediate free agents. Throughout the 1992 season, the two sides worked on reaching a new agreement. Just when things looked like they were going to fall apart, Doty gave the two sides 24 hours to reach a settlement, or else he would do it himself. They did.

A New Era

First was an end to all the litigation and lawsuits. Players were awarded free agency after five years in the league, assuming their contracts had expired, with a restricted form of free agency for three- and four-year veterans. And the draft was cut to eight rounds, allowing more players free agency in another form.

The owners won, too. They gained a salary cap aimed at controlling their costs and giving them financial stability.

As the 1993 offseason got underway, Reggie White led nearly 400 players into the new era of free agency. Some of the biggest names to change teams included Ronnie Lott, Jeff Hostetler and Jim McMahon.

The new agreement will last until 1999, meaning strikes would not be a threat until the end of the century.

The 1993 season ended much as it began — with a Dallas Super Bowl victory over Buffalo. On the field it was the Year of the Kicker, with field goals sailing through uprights at a record pace and percentage.

Miami's Don Shula surpassed the legendary George Halas as the NFL's all-time winningest head coach. Shula ended the season with 327 lifetime victories.

When the year began, Tagliabue said his three goals were peace with the players, a new television contract and expansion. The commissioner went 3 for 3, hitting home runs on all three issues.

Free agency worked well, with 120 players switching teams while salaries rose 51 percent over 1992 to an average of $737,850 per player. Old faces in new places added badly needed life to the NFL.

The story of the new TV contract was that CBS got outfoxed by upstart Fox Network. Fox paid a whopping $1.58 billion for the rights to televise NFC games, and CBS, which had televised NFL games since 1956, was left out in the cold. The overall TV contract was $4.35 billion, which also upped the salary cap for future years.

The NFL also announced two new expansion teams that would begin play in 1995 — the Carolina Panthers and Jacksonville Jaguars. The Carolina franchise wasn't much of a surprise because the market is hot and the ownership group headed by former Colt receiver Jerry Richardson was rock-solid. But when Jacksonville became the 30th franchise a month later, on November 30, eyebrows were raised because St. Louis and Baltimore were shut out. Shoe magnate Wayne Weaver was the one who persuaded NFL owners that the growing Southeast was a better choice than the former NFL locales.

1980 N.F.C. Freedom Fever

The free agent system in the NFL gave the players much less freedom than their baseball counterparts. As a result, several players staged long holdouts in attempts to win salary increases from their teams. The Rams had a rash of discontent after they announced a big-money contract for rookie Johnnie Johnson. Four veteran players, making no more money than the rookie, stayed away from camp for over a month while insisting upon renegotiation of their contracts. The Rams stood firm, and Jim Youngblood, Jack Youngblood, and Larry Brooks all returned in time for the opening game. Dennis Harrah came back for the second game.

The New England Patriots had a similar situation on their hands. Sam Cunningham, Mike Haynes, Richard Bishop, and Tom Owens all boycotted training camp while negotiating contracts. Haynes and Bishop didn't report until late September, Owen didn't suit up until early November, and Cunningham held out for the entire season.

Other noteworthy holdouts included John Riggins of the Redskins, who sat out all of 1980, and Fred Dean of the San Diego Chargers, who held out two weeks into the season.

EASTERN DIVISION

Philadelphia Eagles—With an unusual comeback in their final game, the Eagles won first place in the East. They soared to an 11-1 record in late November, combining offensive and defensive excellence. The leak-proof defense blended experience and youth. Bill Bergey returned from a knee injury to play with gusto, while Charles Johnson, Carl Hairston, Randy Logan, and Jerry Robinson all ripened into star defenders. The offense suffered from Wilbert Montgomery's visits to sick bay, but Ron Jaworski stepped up the air attack to compensate. With a playoff bid locked up, the Eagles went into a skid which put first place in jeopardy. If they lost by 25 points or more to Dallas on Demcember 21, the Cowboys would finish in first place under tie-breaker rules. Early in the fourth period, the Cowboys took a 35-10 lead and threatened to pour it on. The Eagles bore down and closed the gap to 35-27 by the end. Harold Carmichael was shaken up in the second quarter of the game and did not catch a pass, ending his receiving streak at 127 games.

Dallas Cowboys—When Tom Landry predicted an 8-8 finish for his Cowboys, he may have been shucking his opposition. Roger Staubach had retired, leaving the fine-tuned offense in the hands of apprentice Danny White. Novices also manned three of the four secondary positions, adding to Landry's anxiety. Everything worked out fine for the master coach. White kept the offense moving, even showing a talent for running the two-minute drill. Star blockers Herbert Scott and Pat Donovan helped White and runner Tony Dorsett do their job. The young secondary made mistakes, but it held together under the leadership of tackle Randy White and linebacker Bob Breunig. Too Tall Jones returned from his boxing sojourn to beef up the defensive line. The Broncos darkened Landry's mood by blasting the Cowboys 41-20 on September 14, but Cowboy class asserted itself over the long haul. Five victories in the last six games fell just shy of taking first place, but did earn a wild-card ticket into the playoffs.

Washington Redskins—When John Riggins left camp in a salary dispute, he took much of the Redskin offense with him. Without the big fullback, the Skins could not control the ball as they had in recent years. Even with rookie Art Monk juicing up the receiving, the attack moved only in spurts. A long slump by kicker Mark Moseley only worsened the problem. A 1-5 start sparked rumors of coach Jack Pardee's impending demise. A 23-0 pasting of St. Louis on October 19 raised some hopes, but an embarrassing 24-0 loss to the Eagles on November 16 deflated the team's spirit. Brightening the dark days was the Washington secondary, which led the NFC in interceptions. Pardee rallied his team for a late spurt. They beat the Chargers 40-17 on December 7, then ended the year with victories over the Giants and Cardinals. The spurt, however, did not save Pardee's job.

St. Louis Cardinals—Jim Hanifan had helped Don Coryell build a contender in St. Louis in the mid-1970's, and now he returned to run another renewal program. The Cards lost their first three games, but then whipped the Eagles and Saints to encourage their new coach. For the rest of the year, however, the club won only three times. A weak defense dragged the team down, with a feeble pass rush the main culprit. On offense, Hanifan had a blue chip in Ottis Anderson, a devastating runner for the second straight year. He ran for 1,352 yards behind a patched-up forward line. Veterans Bob Young and Tom Banks were sent packing, while injuries claimed Keith Wortman and Terry Stieve. Dan Dierdorf did return from a knee injury to lay a foundation for the new offensive line. Tragedy touched the Cardinals when kicker Steve Little was crippled in a car accident in October, only a few days after being cut from the team.

New York Giants—A 41-35 triumph over the Cardinals on opening day had New York fans celebrating the return of good times. That optimism wilted in the heat of an eight-game losing streak in which the Giants played spiritless football. The secondary was manned by young players who made mistakes in bunches, while the offense looked as if it had punched itself out in the first round. The Giants did end the string with a lively 38-35 victory over the Cowboys, but such savory moments were few. Injuries did contribute to the team's poor showing. Doug Kotar missed the entire season and was joined by Billy Taylor for part of the season. The strong linebacking corps was depleted by Dan Lloyd's bout with cancer and by early-season knee injuries to Brian Kelley and Harry Carson. No one could claim, however, that injuries were the only cause.

CENTRAL DIVISION

Minnesota Vikings—Bud Grant recaptured past Viking glory by taking this young squad to the playoffs. Over the first half of the season, the Vikes played like a retooling also-ran. In building a 3-5 record, the running game reaped a sparse harvest, and quarterback Tommy Kramer threw a bushel of interceptions. On the back half of the schedule, the Vikings played sound fundamental football and battled back into the playoff race. They trounced front-running Detroit 34-0 on November 9, and moved into a first-place tie one week later. By beating the Buccaneers 21-10 on December 7, the Vikes moved into first place alone. One week later, they sewed up a playoff spot with a miraculous pass play. Trailing the Browns 23-22 with five seconds left on the clock, Kramer heaved the ball from midfield toward the end zone. The ball was tipped into the air and grabbed by Ahmad Rashad, who stepped over the goal line. Even with a loss on the final weekend, the Vikings took first place over the Lions on tiebreaking rules.

Detroit Lions—Everything was just right for winning a playoff berth. The Lions had a stunning new runner in rookie Billy Sims, they had quarterback Gary Danielson back in good health, they had an easy schedule, and they were part of the N.F.L.'s weakest division. The plan worked for four weeks. After a 43-28 trouncing by the Falcons on October 5, the Lions struggled to hold onto first place. Four mid-season losses in five games dropped them into a dogfight with the Vikings for the top spot. Two late losses scratched the Lions from the playoff picture. On Thanksgiving Day, they led the Bears 17-3 entering the fourth quarter, only to have the Bears knot the score with a touchdown and conversion as the clock ran out. When the Bears won the coin toss for overtime, Chicago's Dave Williams took the kickoff and ran 95 yards to end the game. Ten days later, Roy Green of St. Louis ran a punt back for a touchdown late in the final quarter to beat the Lions 24-23. Detroit came back to win its final two games, but the Vikings had already sewn up first place.

Chicago Bears—The Bears had everything except a passing attack. Their solid defense featured all-star performances by Dan Hampton, veteran Alan Page, and Gary Fencik. Walter Payton carried the freight on the ground in peerless fashion, assisted by fullback Roland Harper, who rebounded from knee surgery. Because the Bears could not throw the ball, they did not repeat as a playoff team. Mike Phipps had driven the Bears to the playoffs last year with a conservative and error-free job at quarterback. In this year's early games, Phipps had problems moving the offense and suffered a plague of interceptions. Vince Evans took over as a starter on October 19 and juiced up the attack with his bazooka arm and strong running. After a shakey mid-season, the Bears won three of their last four games, including an overtime victory over the Lions on Thanksgiving Day and a 61-7 drubbing of the Packers ten days later.

Tampa Bay Buccaneers—The clock struck twelve for John McKay's Cinderella team. The Bucs fell out of the playoffs by posting a 1-6-1 record against other Central Division teams and by losing six of their last seven games. The offense suffered from Ricky Bell's injury-spoiled year, but the fate of the Bucs fell with the quality of the defense. The front line suffered the end of Wally Chambers' career and an early knee injury to Randy Crowder. McKay, however, put much of the blame on the heralded linebacking corps which did not play up to its clippings. Lee Roy Selmon continued to grow in skill and stature, but the rest of the defensive unit could not follow suit. The Bucs often made costly mistakes, twice killing last minute drives in close games with mental errors.

Green Bay Packers—The high point came on opening day, when kicker Chester Marcol grabbed his blocked field goal and scooted to a touchdown for a 12-6 overtime victory over Chicago. Three losses followed, including a 51-21 beating by the Rams. Rumors flourished that Bart Starr was about to go as coach and general manager, but he held onto his jobs for the course of the season. Starr didn't get much

FINAL TEAM STATISTICS

OFFENSE

	ATL.	CHI.	DALL.	DET.	G.B.	L.A.	MINN.	N.O.	NYG	PHIL.	ST. L.	S.F.	T.B.	WASH.
FIRST DOWNS:														
Total	336	286	337	308	307	316	324	285	261	326	281	298	281	279
by Rushing	145	139	143	143	119	144	100	80	100	118	123	105	102	109
by Passing	166	121	171	143	164	157	191	183	136	186	137	171	154	148
by Penalty	25	26	23	22	24	15	33	22	25	22	21	22	25	22
RUSHING:														
Number	559	579	595	572	493	615	433	348	483	527	519	415	477	517
Yards	2405	2440	2378	2599	1806	2799	1642	1362	1730	1995	2183	1743	1839	2016
Average Yards	4.3	4.2	4.0	4.5	3.7	4.6	3.8	3.9	3.6	3.8	4.2	4.2	3.9	3.9
Touchdowns	15	22	26	21	13	17	14	9	10	19	19	10	9	12
PASSING:														
Attempts	467	404	449	423	511	451	574	566	514	477	470	597	530	486
Completions	259	209	265	248	289	261	331	334	245	275	239	363	256	284
Completion Pct.	55.5	51.7	59.0	58.6	56.6	57.9	57.7	59.0	47.7	57.7	50.9	60.8	48.3	58.4
Passing Yards	3568	2669	3356	3287	3651	3441	3934	4010	2931	3771	3063	3799	3414	3171
Avg. Yds. per Att.	6.5	5.5	6.5	6.3	5.9	6.7	6.0	6.0	4.7	6.9	5.2	5.7	5.8	5.4
Avg Yds per Comp.	13.8	12.8	12.7	13.3	12.6	13.2	11.9	12.0	12.0	13.7	12.8	10.5	13.3	11.2
Times Tackled	35	33	31	45	43	29	41	46	47	32	50	30	24	36
Yds Lost Tackled	324	274	252	346	360	234	246	362	322	247	387	222	194	333
Net Yards	3244	2395	3104	2941	3291	3207	3688	3648	2609	3524	2676	3577	3220	2838
Touchdowns	31	13	30	13	15	31	22	26	19	28	16	27	20	17
Interceptions	17	25	25	12	29	23	23	22	25	12	24	26	17	18
Pct. Intercepted	3.6	6.2	5.6	2.8	5.7	5.1	4.0	3.9	4.9	2.5	5.1	4.4	3.2	3.7
PUNTS:														
Number	79	79	71	73	87	77	81	89	94	76	100	77	89	85
Average	39.1	40.6	40.9	41.6	38.2	39.0	38.8	39.3	44.8	38.8	41.1	40.9	41.8	39.2
PUNT RETURNS:														
Number	53	41	55	56	37	47	34	22	37	83	50	45	57	48
Yards	536	277	556	463	297	315	251	176	302	560	399	409	313	487
Average Yards	10.1	6.8	10.1	8.3	8.0	6.7	7.4	8.0	8.2	8.9	8.0	9.1	5.5	10.1
Touchdowns	0	0	0	0	0	0	0	0	0	0	1	2	0	0
KICKOFF RET.:														
Number	53	56	58	57	73	53	63	88	71	53	65	75	67	57
Yards	958	1153	1259	1169	1415	979	1386	1973	1319	955	1297	1385	1294	1204
Average Yards	18.1	20.6	21.7	20.5	19.4	18.5	22.0	22.4	18.6	18.0	20.0	18.5	19.3	21.1
Touchdowns	0	1	0	1	0	1	1	0	0	0	0	1	0	0
INTERCEPT RET.:														
Number	26	17	27	23	13	25	24	12	18	25	20	17	15	33
Yards	313	162	523	168	92	546	296	196	113	170	327	186	179	319
Average Yards	12.0	9.5	19.4	7.3	7.1	21.8	12.3	16.3	6.3	6.8	16.4	10.9	11.9	9.7
Touchdowns	0	1	3	1	0	4	2	0	0	0	1	0	1	1
PENALTIES:														
Number	91	100	109	104	84	118	90	98	98	96	103	109	90	114
Yards	861	842	908	844	697	973	717	837	962	809	922	933	840	1008
FUMBLES:														
Number	32	23	26	40	36	29	15	28	33	29	24	39	28	35
Number Lost	9	14	14	19	12	13	3	13	18	16	13	14	21	18
POINTS:														
Total	405	304	454	334	231	424	317	291	249	384	299	320	271	261
PAT Attempts	49	37	60	36	28	54	39	37	29	48	37	40	32	30
PAT Made	46	35	59	35	24	52	33	33	27	48	35	33	31	27
FG Attempts	27	18	17	42	20	30	26	22	24	31	23	19	23	33
FG Made	19	13	11	27	11	16	16	12	16	16	14	15	16	18
Percent FG Made	70.4	72.2	64.7	64.3	55.0	53.3	61.5	54.5	66.7	51.6	60.9	78.9	69.6	54.5
Safeties	1	1	1	1	0	0	1	0	0	0	0	1	0	0

DEFENSE

	ATL.	CHI.	DALL.	DET.	G.B.	L.A.	MINN.	N.O.	NYG	PHIL.	ST. L.	S.F.	T.B.	WASH.
FIRST DOWNS:														
Total	298	285	286	265	316	281	330	360	336	270	311	341	313	298
by Rushing	100	111	98	100	136	112	135	178	156	87	115	137	126	144
by Passing	175	149	160	143	166	141	170	155	160	157	176	185	168	127
by Penalty	23	25	28	22	14	28	25	27	20	26	20	19	19	27
RUSHING:														
Number	441	506	469	449	565	445	531	630	584	445	547	556	548	585
Yards	1670	2015	2069	1599	2399	1945	2456	3106	2507	1618	2059	2218	2101	2524
Average Yards	3.8	4.0	4.4	3.6	4.2	4.4	4.6	4.9	4.3	3.6	3.8	4.0	3.8	4.3
Touchdowns	8	10	15	9	19	13	15	28	31	8	17	20	20	16
PASSING:														
Attempts	564	451	484	462	460	510	499	445	448	543	531	495	516	392
Completions	333	238	231	256	259	245	283	255	255	265	287	327	328	187
Completion Pct.	59.0	52.8	47.7	55.4	56.3	48.0	56.7	57.3	56.9	48.8	54.0	66.1	63.6	47.7
Passing Yards	3990	3271	3568	3234	3617	3097	3644	3341	3469	3180	3616	3958	3477	2504
Avg. Yds. per Att.	5.9	5.8	6.1	5.8	6.9	4.6	6.4	6.6	6.8	4.8	5.8	7.1	6.1	5.0
Avg Yds per Comp.	12.0	13.7	15.5	12.6	14.0	12.6	12.9	13.1	13.6	12.0	12.6	12.1	10.6	13.4
Times Tackled	46	46	43	44	34	56	30	27	28	44	38	31	24	43
Yds Lost Tackled	396	379	358	300	234	496	244	229	224	355	291	207	173	333
Net Yards	3594	2892	3210	2934	3383	2601	3400	3112	3245	2825	3325	3571	3304	2171
Touchdowns	24	20	21	14	19	23	24	31	22	16	23	29	17	17
Interceptions	26	17	27	23	13	25	24	12	18	25	20	17	15	33
Pct. Intercepted	4.6	3.8	5.6	5.0	2.8	4.9	4.8	2.7	4.0	4.6	3.7	3.4	2.9	8.4
PUNTS:														
Number	85	82	76	93	83	90	71	64	70	89	89	67	89	84
Average	41.3	39.0	43.5	41.6	39.1	42.1	39.3	38.5	40.3	41.3	40.1	38.2	42.0	40.7
PUNT RETURNS:														
Number	36	46	32	38	50	42	42	48	58	35	62	48	54	52
Yards	240	415	215	300	342	353	259	490	506	224	645	530	529	351
Average Yards	6.7	9.0	6.7	7.9	6.8	8.4	6.2	10.2	8.7	6.4	10.4	11.0	9.8	6.8
Touchdowns	0	0	0	1	0	0	0	1	0	0	1	0	1	0
KICKOFF RET.:														
Number	73	58	73	64	52	78	62	58	52	70	57	58	62	60
Yards	1579	1251	1568	1289	902	1553	1048	1159	1047	1307	1142	1203	1417	1102
Average Yards	21.6	21.6	21.5	20.1	17.3	19.9	16.9	20.0	20.1	18.7	20.0	20.7	22.9	18.4
Touchdowns	0	0	0	3	0	0	0	0	1	0	0	0	1	1
INTERCEPT RET.:														
Number	17	25	25	12	29	23	23	22	25	12	24	26	17	18
Yards	143	161	179	173	483	307	187	217	376	220	246	319	185	219
Average Yards	8.4	6.4	7.2	14.4	16.7	13.3	8.1	9.9	15.0	18.3	10.3	12.3	10.9	12.2
Touchdowns	0	1	1	1	4	1	1	0	1	1	1	2	0	1
PENALTIES:														
Number	101	129	106	98	109	83	111	79	108	87	101	92	117	90
Yards	919	1109	989	815	872	778	914	690	862	789	919	826	1077	766
FUMBLES:														
Number	33	32	33	20	27	30	33	27	48	27	27	34	32	25
Number Lost	16	14	20	11	14	17	14	12	23	10	14	17	13	12
POINTS:														
Total	272	264	311	272	371	289	308	487	425	222	350	415	341	293
PAT Attempts	32	31	38	31	43	38	40	60	55	26	42	52	40	36
PAT Made	30	30	38	30	36	34	32	56	51	24	41	50	39	36
FG Attempts	25	27	28	21	27	20	20	31	24	26	33	26	33	17
FG Made	16	14	15	16	25	9	12	23	14	14	17	17	20	13
Percent FG Made	64.0	51.9	53.6	76.2	92.6	45.0	60.0	74.2	58.3	53.8	51.5	65.4	60.6	76.5
Safeties	1	0	0	1	1	0	0	1	1	0	0	1	1	1

help from his two first-round draft picks. Defensive tackle Bruce Clark played in Canada, while linebacker George Cumby went out with a knee injury in early November. Injuries also took key young veterans Mark Koncar and Rich Wingo out of the lineup for practically the entire year. The Packers had one of the NFL's brightest stars in receiver James Lofton, but the rest of the squad had a dreary overtone. The Packers slunk away with four straight losses at the end of the year, including a 61-7 humiliation at the hands of the Bears.

WESTERN DIVISION

Atlanta Falcons—After a slow start, the Falcons whipped unbeaten San Francisco and Detroit and then roared into the playoffs with a strong defense and versatile offense. Steve Bartkowski blossomed into a dangerous offensive leader, showering passes on rookie tight end Junior Miller and veteran wide receivers Al Jenkins and Wallace Francis. William Andrews and Lynn Cain combined for over 2,000 yards on the ground, moving behind a strong line that featured Mike Kenn and Jeff Van Note. The defense revived with the spirited play of rookie linebackers Buddy Curry and Al Richardson. With coach Leeman Bennett keeping all the ingredients in balance, the Falcons began a winning streak in mid-October that ended only with an overtime loss to the Rams on the final day of the season. Even with that loss, the Falcons had the first Divisional championship in their history.

Los Angeles Rams—For the first time since 1972, the Rams finished out of first place in the West. They did, however, win a wildcard playoff berth with five victories in their last six games. On opening day, the Rams debuted in Anaheim by losing to the Lions 41-20. In that game, quarterback Pat Haden broke his right thumb and gave way to Vince Ferragamo. A hero in last year's playoffs, Ferragamo had lost the QB job to Haden in pre-season but made good on this second chance. As usual, the Ram defense made life miserable for enemy passers, with Jack Youngblood leading the pass rush and with Pat Thomas and Nolan Cromwell prowling the secondary. The offensive line propped the attack up, with Doug France, Kent Hill, and Rich Saul the standouts on a top unit. Injuries struck the running back corps. Star runner Wendell Tyler was injured in a summer car accident, returned only in mid-season, and quickly went off for the year with an elbow injury. Elvis Peacock played halfback for most of the year until injuring a knee late in the campaign. Coach Ray Malavasi simply delved into his reserves and came up with two fine rookie runners in Jewerl Thomas and Mike Guman.

San Francisco '49ers—After winning only two games last year, the 49ers bolted out to three straight victories at the start of the season. The realities of rebuilding then set in, but the 49ers did string together three more successes later in the fall. Bill Walsh tried lots of new faces on defense, with the Rams and Cowboys running up big scores in October. On offense, the 49ers threw the ball a lot. Steve DeBerg did the passing during the early win streak, but by the end of the year, Joe Montana had captured the starting QB job with his mobility and intelligent play. Second-year receiver Dwight Clark won a starting job with sure hands and quick moves, while rookie fullback Earl Cooper ran for power and hauled in lots of passes. Halfback Paul Hofer was off to an excellent year when a knee injury felled him in October.

New Orleans Saints—The promise of 1979 was choked by the brutal failure of 1980. The Saints began losing on opening day and pursued it with a vengence. With an atrocious defense and widespread griping, the Saints quickly settled into a listless, defeatist style of football. Head coach Dick Nolan traded runner Chuck Muncie to San Diego after some personal friction, but that move only reduced the New Orleans running game to puny proportions. With their team self-destructing every Sunday, fans rechristened the team the Aints and took to wearing paper bags over their heads at games. The Saints reached their nadir on November 24, when they walked through a 27-7 beating at the hands of the Rams on Monday night television. Nolan was fired after that game, and Dick Stanfel took over for the balance of the season. On December 7, the Saints took a 35-7 halftime lead over the 49ers, but wound up losing 38-35 in overtime. With a perfect record closing in on them, the Saints escaped history by beating the Jets 21-20 on December 14. A fall-from-ahead loss to the Patriots one week later closed out a memorable year.

PHILADELPHIA EAGLES 12-4-0 Dick Vermeil

Scores of Each Game		
27	DENVER	6
42	Minnesota	7
35	N.Y. GIANTS	3
14	St. Louis	24
24	WASHINGTON	14
31	N.Y. Giants	16
17	DALLAS	10
17	CHICAGO	14
27	Seattle	20
34	New Orleans	21
24	Washington	0
10	OAKLAND	7
21	San Diego	22
17	ATLANTA	20
17	ST. LOUIS	3
27	Dallas	35

Use Name	Pos.	Hgt.	Wgt.	Age	Int.	Pts.
Steve Kenney	OT	6'4"	262	24		
Jerry Sisemore	OT	6'4"	265	29		
Stan Walters	OT	6'6"	275	32		
Ron Baker	OG	6'4"	250	25		
Woody Peoples	OG	6'2"	260	37		
Petey Perot	OG	6'2"	261	23		
Guy Morriss	C	6'4"	255	29		
Mark Slater	C	6'1"	257	25		
Thomas Brown	DE	6'4"	240	23		
Carl Hairston	DE	6'3"	260	27	1	
Dennis Harrison	DE	6'8"	275	24		
Claude Humphrey	DE	6'5"	258	36		
Ken Clarke	NT	6'2"	260	24		
Charles Johnson	NT	6'3"	262	28	3	

Use Name	Pos.	Hgt.	Wgt.	Age	Int.	Pts.
Bill Bergey	LB	6'2"	245	35	1	
John Bunting	LB	6'1"	220	30		
Al Chesley	LB	6'3"	240	23		
Frank LeMaster	LB	6'2"	238	28	1	
Ray Phillips	LB	6'4"	230	26		
Jerry Robinson	LB	6'2"	218	23	2	6
Reggie Wilkes	LB	6'4"	230	24	1	
Richard Blackmore	DB	5'10"	174	24	2	
Herman Edwards	DB	6'	190	26	3	
Zac Henderson	DB	6'1"	190	25		
Randy Logan	DB	6'1"	195	29	1	
John Sciarra	DB	5'11"	185	26		
Steve Wagner	DB	6'2"	208	26		
Brenard Wilson	DB	6'	175	25	6	
Roynell Young	DB	6'1"	181	22	4	

Larry Barnes – Thigh Injury
Lem Burnham – Knee Injury

Use Name	Pos.	Hgt.	Wgt.	Age	Int.	Pts.
Rob Hertel	QB	6'2"	198	25		
Ron Jaworski	QB	6'2"	196	29		6
Joe Pisarcik	QB	6'4"	220	28		
Billy Campfield	HB	5'11"	205	24		18
Zachary Dixon (to BAL)	HB	6'	200	24		
Louie Giammona	HB	5'9"	180	27		30
Wilbert Montgomery	HB	5'10"	195	25		60
Jim Culbreath (to NYG)	FB	6'	210	27		
Perry Harrington	FB-HB	5'11"	210	22		6
Leroy Harris	FB	5'9"	230	26		24
Bob Torrey	FB	6'4"	232	23		
Luther Blue	WR	5'11"	180	24		
Harold Carmichael	WR	6'7"	225	30		54
Scott Fitzkee	WR	6'	187	23		12
Wally Henry	WR	5'8"	180	25		
Rodney Parker	WR	6'1"	190	27		6
Charlie Smith	WR	6'1"	185	30		18
Ken Dunek	TE	6'6"	235	23		
Lewis Gilbert (to SF)	TE	6'4"	225	24		
Keith Krepfle	TE	6'3"	230	28		24
John Spagnola	TE	6'4"	240	23		18
Tony Franklin	K	5'8"	182	23		96
Max Runager	K	6'1"	189	24		

DALLAS COWBOYS 12-4-0 Tom Landry

Scores of Each Game		
17	Washington	3
20	Denver	41
28	TAMPA BAY	17
28	Green Bay	7
24	N.Y. GIANTS	3
59	SAN FRANCISCO	14
10	Philadelphia	17
42	SAN DIEGO	31
27	St. Louis	24
35	N.Y. Giants	38
31	ST. LOUIS	21
14	WASHINGTON	10
51	SEATTLE	7
19	Oakland	13
14	Los Angeles	38
35	PHILADELPHIA	27

Use Name	Pos.	Hgt.	Wgt.	Age	Int.	Pts.
Jim Cooper	OT	6'5"	260	24		
Pat Donovan	OT	6'4"	250	27		
Andy Frederick	OT	6'6"	255	25		
Kurt Petersen	OG	6'4"	251	23		
Tom Rafferty	OG	6'3"	250	26		
Herbert Scott	OG	6'2"	252	27		
Norm Wells	OG	6'5"	261	22		
John Fitzgerald	C	6'5"	260	32		
Robert Shaw	C	6'4"	245	23		
Too Tall Jones	DE	6'9"	260	29		
Harvey Martin	DE	6'5"	250	29		
Bruce Thornton	DE-DT	6'5"	265	22		
Larry Bethea	DT	6'5"	254	24		
Larry Cole	DT	6'4"	252	33	1	6
John Dutton	DT	6'7"	265	29	1	6
Randy White	DT	6'4"	250	27		

Use Name	Pos.	Hgt.	Wgt.	Age	Int.	Pts.
Bob Breunig	LB	6'2"	225	27	3	
Guy Brown	LB	6'4"	228	25		
Anthony Dickerson	LB	6'2"	214	23	2	
Mike Hegman	LB	6'1"	225	27	2	6
Bruce Huther	LB	6'1"	220	26		
D.D. Lewis	LB	6'2"	215	34		
Bill Roe	LB	6'3"	230	22		
Benny Barnes	DB	6'1"	195	29	1	
Dextor Clinkscale	DB	5'11"	189	22		
Randy Hughes	DB	6'4"	207	27		
Eric Hurt	DB	5'11"	171	23		
Wade Manning	DB	5'11"	190	25		
Aaron Mitchell	DB	6'1"	196	23	3	
Roland Solomon (to BUFF)	DB	6'	196	24		
Dennis Thurman	DB	5'11"	170	24	5	6
Charlie Waters	DB	6'1"	200	31	5	
Steve Wilson	DB	5'10"	192	23	4	

Use Name	Pos.	Hgt.	Wgt.	Age	Int.	Pts.
Glenn Carano	QB	6'3"	202	24		
Gary Hogeboom	QB	6'4"	201	22		
Danny White	QB	6'2"	192	28		6
Tony Dorsett	HB	5'11"	190	26		66
James Jones	HB-FB	5'10"	201	21		
Preston Pearson	HB	6'1"	196	35		12
Robert Newhouse	FB	5'10"	215	30		36
Timmy Newsome	FB	6'1"	227	22		12
Ron Springs	FB	6'1"	200	23		42
Tony Hill	WR	6'2"	198	24		48
Butch Johnson	WR	6'1"	192	26		24
Drew Pearson	WR	6'	183	29		36
Doug Cosbie	TE	6'6"	230	24		6
Billy Joe DuPree	TE	6'4"	229	30		42
Jay Saldi	TE-WR	6'3"	227	25		6
Rafael Septien	K	5'9"	171	26		92

WASHINGTON REDSKINS 6-10-0 Jack Pardee

Scores of Each Game		
3	DALLAS	17
23	N.Y. Giants	21
21	Oakland	24
0	SEATTLE	14
14	Philadelphia	24
17	Denver	20
23	ST. LOUIS	0
22	NEW ORLEANS	14
14	MINNESOTA	39
21	Chicago	35
0	PHILADELPHIA	24
10	Dallas	14
6	Atlanta	10
40	SAN DIEGO	17
16	N.Y. GIANTS	13
31	St. Louis	7

Use Name	Pos.	Hgt.	Wgt.	Age	Int.	Pts.
Terry Hermeling	OT	6'5"	255	34		
Jerry Scanlan	OT	6'5"	270	23		
George Starke	OT	6'5"	250	32		
Gary Anderson	OG	6'3"	259	24		
Fred Dean	OG	6'3"	253	25		
Dan Nugent	OG	6'3"	250	27		
Ron Saul	OG	6'2"	254	32		
Jeff Williams	OG-OT	6'4"	255	25		
Jeff Bostic	C	6'2"	246	21		
Bob Kuziel	C	6'5"	255	30		
Dan Peiffer	C	6'3"	251	29		
Coy Bacon	DE	6'4"	265	38		
Dallas Hickman	DE-LB	6'6"	242	28		
Joe Jones	DE	6'6"	250	32		
Karl Lorch	DE	6'3"	258	30		
Perry Brooks	DT	6'3"	260	25		
Dave Butz	DT	6'7"	285	30		
Paul Smith	DT	6'3"	255	35	1	
Diron Talbert	DT	6'5"	255	36		

Use Name	Pos.	Hgt.	Wgt.	Age	Int.	Pts.
Monte Coleman	LB	6'2"	230	22	3	
Brad Dusek	LB	6'2"	223	29		
Rich Milot	LB	6'4"	230	23	4	
Neal Olkewicz	LB	6'	227	23		
Pete Wysocki	LB	6'2"	224	31		
Ken Houston	DB	6'3"	202	35		
Joe Lavender	DB	6'4"	185	31	6	6
Mark Murphy	DB	6'4"	210	25	6	
Mike Nelms	DB	6'1"	185	25		
Lemar Parrish	DB	5'11"	170	32	7	
Tony Peters	DB	6'1"	177	27	4	
Ray Waddy	DB	5'11"	175	24		
Jeris White	DB	5'11"	188	27	2	

John Riggins – Holdout

Use Name	Pos.	Hgt.	Wgt.	Age	Int.	Pts.
Mike Kruczek	QB	6'1"	205	27		
Kim McQuilken	QB	6'2"	203	29		
Joe Theismann	QB	6'	195	30		18
Rickey Claitt	HB-FB	5'10"	206	23		12
Ike Forte	HB	6'	202	26		12
Bob Hammond	HB	5'10"	170	28		6
Buddy Hardeman	HB	6'	202	25		
Clarence Harmon	HB-FB	5'11"	209	24		48
Wilbur Jackson	FB	6'1"	219	28		24
Kenny Harrison	WR	6'	170	26		
John McDaniel	WR	6'1"	198	28		
Zion McKinney	WR	6'	200	22		
Art Monk	WR	6'3"	209	22		18
Ricky Thompson	WR	6'	177	26		30
Phil DuBois	TE	6'2"	221	23		
Grady Richardson	TE	6'4"	225	28		
Rick Walker	TE	6'3"	235	25		6
Don Warren	TE	6'4"	236	24		
Mike Connell	K	6'1"	200	24		
Mark Moseley	K	5'11"	205	32		81

ST. LOUIS CARDINALS 5-11-0 Jim Hanifan

Scores of Each Game		
35	N.Y. GIANTS	41
21	San Francisco	*24
7	Detroit	20
24	PHILADELPHIA	14
40	New Orleans	7
13	LOS ANGELES	21
0	Washington	23
17	Baltimore	10
24	DALLAS	27
27	ATLANTA	*33
21	Dallas	31
13	KANSAS CITY	21
23	N.Y. Giants	7
24	DETROIT	23
3	Philadelphia	17
7	WASHINGTON	31

Use Name	Pos.	Hgt.	Wgt.	Age	Int.	Pts.
George Collins	OT-OG	6'2"	260	24		
Dan Dierdorf	OT	6'4"	288	31		
Mark Goodspeed	OT	6'5"	270	23		
Brad Oates (to KC)	OT	6'6"	275	26		
Keith Wortman	OT	6'2"	275	30		
Tom Banks	OG-C	6'1"	245	32		
Joe Bostic	OG-OT	6'3"	265	23		
Ron Coder	OG	6'4"	250	26		
Barney Cotton	OG	6'5"	265	23		
Tom Brahaney	C	6'2"	246	28		
Randy Clark	C-OG-OT	6'3"	254	23		
Curtis Greer	DE	6'4"	252	22		
Stafford Mays	DE	6'2"	242	22		
Bob Pollard	DE	6'3"	252	31		
Ron Yankowski	DE	6'5"	258	33		
Bill Acker	NT	6'2"	255	24		
Rush Brown	NT	6'2"	257	26	1	
Mike Dawson	NT	6'4"	275	26		
Oudious Lee	NT	6'1"	253	24		

Use Name	Pos.	Hgt.	Wgt.	Age	Int.	Pts.
Mark Arneson	LB	6'2"	224	30		
Charlie Baker	LB	6'2"	217	22		
John Barefield	LB	6'2"	224	25		
Kirby Criswell	LB	6'5"	238	23		
Calvin Favron	LB	6'1"	225	23		
Tim Kearney	LB	6'2"	221	29	1	
Jeff McIntyre	LB	6'3"	232	24		
Steve Neils	LB	6'2"	218	29		
Eric Williams	LB	6'2"	225	25	2	
Carl Allen	DB	6'	186	24	3	6
Tim Collier	DB	6'	174	26	2	
Roy Green	DB	5'11"	190	23	1	6
Ken Greene	DB	6'3"	203	24	4	
Lee Nelson	DB	5'10"	185	26		
Ken Stone	DB	6'1"	180	29	5	
Roger Wehrli	DB	6'1"	193	32	1	

Terry Stieve – Knee Injury

Use Name	Pos.	Hgt.	Wgt.	Age	Int.	Pts.
Jim Hart	QB	6'2"	210	36		
Rusty Lisch	QB	6'3"	213	23		
Mike Loyd	QB	6'2"	216	24		
Ottis Anderson	HB	6'2"	215	23		54
Will Harrell	HB	5'9"	182	27		18
Randy Love	HB	6'1"	205	23		
Theotis Brown	FB	6'2"	225	23		12
Wayne Morris	FB	6'	208	26		42
Rod Phillips	FB	6'	221	27		
Mark Bell	WR	5'9"	175	23		
Mel Gray	WR	5'9"	173	31		18
Jeff Lee	WR	6'2"	195	25		
Dave Stief	WR	6'3"	195	24		
Pat Tilley	WR	5'10"	171	27		36
Chris Combs	TE	6'4"	239	22		6
Doug Marsh	TE	6'3"	236	22		24
Gary Parris	TE	6'2"	226	30		
Steve Little	K	6'	180	24		26
Neil O'Donoghue	K	6'6"	210	27		51
Larry Swider	K	6'2"	195	25		

NEW YORK GIANTS 4-12-0 Ray Perkins

Scores of Each Game		
41	St. Louis	35
21	WASHINGTON	23
3	Philadelphia	35
7	LOS ANGELES	28
3	Dallas	24
16	PHILADELPHIA	31
7	San Diego	44
9	DENVER	14
13	Tampa Bay	30
38	DALLAS	35
27	GREEN BAY	21
0	San Francisco	12
7	ST. LOUIS	23
27	Seattle	21
13	Washington	16
17	OAKLAND	33

Use Name	Pos.	Hgt.	Wgt.	Age	Int.	Pts.
Brad Benson	OT	6'3"	258	24		
Vern Holland (from DET)	OT	6'5"	267	32		
Gordon King	OT	6'6"	275	24		
Jeff Weston	OT	6'5"	255	23		
Terry Falcon	OG-OT	6'3"	260	25		
Roy Simmons	OG	6'3"	264	23		
John Sinnott	OG-OT	6'4"	275	22		
J.T. Turner	OG	6'3"	255	27		
Jim Clack	C	6'3"	250	32		
Kelly Saalfeld	C	6'3"	246	24		
Steve Tobin	C	6'4"	258	23		
Gary Jeter	DE	6'4"	260	25		
Chris Linnin	DE	6'4"	255	23		
Dale Markham	DE	6'8"	280	23		
George Martin	DE-TE	6'4"	245	27		6
Myron Lapka	NT-DE	6'4"	255	24		
Curtis McGriff	NT	6'5"	270	22		
George Small	NT	6'2"	260	23		
Phil Tabor	NT	6'4"	255	23		

Keith Eck – Illness
Doug Kotar – Knee Injury
Dan Lloyd – Illness

Use Name	Pos.	Hgt.	Wgt.	Age	Int.	Pts.
Ben Apuna	LB	6'1"	222	23		
Phil Cancik	LB	6'1"	225	23		
Harry Carson	LB	6'2"	240	26		
Brian Kelley	LB	6'3"	222	29		
Frank Marion	LB	6'3"	228	29	1	
Joe McLaughlin	LB	6'1"	235	23		
John Skorupan	LB	6'2"	225	29		
Kevin Turner	LB	6'2"	225	25		
Brad Van Pelt	LB	6'5"	235	29	3	
Whip Walton	LB	6'2"	225	25		
Mike Whittington	LB	6'2"	220	22		
Kervin Wyatt	LB	6'2"	235	22		
Tony Blount	DB	6'1"	195	21		
Mike Dennis	DB	5'10"	190	21	5	
Eric Felton	DB	6'	200	24		
Don Harris	DB	6'2"	185	26		
Mark Haynes	DB	5'11"	185	21	1	
Bud Hebert	DB	6'	190	23	1	
Steve Henry	DB	6'2"	190	23	1	
Terry Jackson	DB	5'10"	197	24	1	
Doug Nettles	DB	6'	180	29		
Don Patterson	DB	5'11"	175	22		
Beasley Reece	DB	6'1"	195	26	3	
Gary Woolford	DB	6'	182	26	2	

Use Name	Pos.	Hgt.	Wgt.	Age	Int.	Pts.
Scott Brunner	QB	6'5"	200	23		
Cliff Olander	QB	6'5"	187	25		
Phil Simms	QB	6'3"	216	24		6
Art Best	HB	6'1"	205	27		
Alvin Garrett	HB-WR	5'7"	178	23		6
Larry Heater	HB	5'11"	205	22		18
Billy Taylor	HB-FB	6'	215	24		24
Eddie Hicks	FB-HB	6'2"	210	25		
Mike Hogan (to PHIL)	FB	6'2"	215	25		12
Scott Laidlaw	FB	6'	205	27		
Bo Matthews	FB	6'4"	222	28		
Leon Perry	FB	5'11"	225	23		12
Nate Rivers	FB	6'3"	215	25		
Mike Friede (from DET)	WR	6'3"	200	22		
Earnest Gray	WR	6'3"	195	23		60
Nate Johnson	WR	5'11"	192	23		
Johnny Perkins	WR	6'2"	205	27		18
Danny Pittman	WR	6'2"	205	22		
Dennis Johnson	TE	6'3"	220	24		
Tom Mullady	TE	6'3"	232	23		12
Gary Shirk	TE	6'1"	220	30		6
Joe Danelo	K	5'9"	166	26		75
Dave Jennings	K	6'4"	205	28		

*—Overtime

PHILADELPHIA EAGLES

RUSHING

Last Name	No.	Yds.	Avg.	TD
Montgomery	193	778	4.0	8
Giammona	97	361	3.7	4
Harris	104	341	3.3	3
Harrington	32	166	5.2	1
Campfield	44	120	2.7	1
Jaworski	27	95	3.5	1
Smith	5	33	6.6	0
LeMaster	2	21	10.5	0
Fitzkee	1	15	15.0	0
Sciarra	3	11	3.7	0
Dixon	2	8	4.0	0
Culbreath	1	3	3.0	0
Krepfle	1	2	2.0	0
Pisarcik	3	−3	−1.0	0

RECEIVING

Last Name	No.	Yds.	Avg.	TD
Montgomery	50	407	8	2
Carmichael	48	815	17	9
Smith	47	825	18	3
Krepfle	30	450	15	4
Campfield	26	275	11	2
Spagnola	18	193	11	3
Giammona	17	178	11	1
Harris	15	207	14	1
Parker	9	148	16	1
Fitzkee	6	169	28	2
Henry	4	68	17	0
Harrington	3	24	8	0
Gilbert	1	7	7	0
Dixon	1	5	5	0

PUNT RETURNS

Last Name	No.	Yds.	Avg.	TD
Sciarra	36	330	9	0
Henry	26	222	9	0
Giammona	1	8	8	0

KICKOFF RETURNS

Last Name	No.	Yds.	Avg.	TD
Campfield	26	540	21	0
Henry	7	154	22	0
Giammona	7	82	12	0
Harrington	6	104	17	0
Dixon	2	30	15	0
Montgomery	1	23	23	0
Blue	1	16	16	0
Baker	1	6	6	0
Clarke	1	0	0	0
Spagnola	1	0	0	0

PASSING - PUNTING - KICKING

PASSING	Att.	Comp.	%	Yds.	Yd./Att.	TD	Int.-%	RK
Jaworski	451	257	57	3529	7.8	27	12- 3	1
Pisarcik	22	15	68	187	8.5	0	0- 0	
Giammona	3	3	100	55	18.3	1	0- 0	
Montgomery	1	0	0	0	0.0	0	0- 0	

PUNTING	No.	Avg.
Runager	75	39.3

KICKING	XP	Att.	%	FG	Att.	%
Franklin	48	48	100	16	31	52

DALLAS COWBOYS

RUSHING

Last Name	No.	Yds.	Avg.	TD
Dorsett	278	1185	4.3	11
Newhouse	118	451	3.8	6
Springs	89	326	3.7	6
J. Jones	41	135	3.3	0
D. White	27	114	4.2	1
Newsome	25	79	3.2	2
D. Pearson	2	30	15.0	0
Hill	4	27	6.8	0
DuPree	4	19	4.8	0
P. Pearson	3	6	2.0	0
Carano	4	6	1.5	0

RECEIVING

Last Name	No.	Yds.	Avg.	TD
Hill	60	1055	18	8
D. Pearson	43	568	13	6
Dorsett	34	263	8	0
DuPree	29	312	11	7
Saldi	25	311	12	1
P. Pearson	20	213	11	2
Johnson	19	263	14	4
Springs	15	212	14	1
Newhouse	8	75	9	0
J. Jones	5	39	8	0
Newsome	4	43	11	0
Cosbie	2	11	6	1
D. White	1	−9	−9	0

PUNT RETURNS

Last Name	No.	Yds.	Avg.	TD
J. Jones	54	**548**	10	0
Solomon	1	8	8	0

KICKOFF RETURNS

Last Name	No.	Yds.	Avg.	TD
J. Jones	32	720	23	0
Newsome	12	293	24	0
Wilson	7	139	20	0
Hurt	4	71	18	0
Saldi	1	23	23	0
Cosbie	1	13	13	0
Waters	1	0	0	0

PASSING - PUNTING - KICKING

PASSING	Att.	Comp.	%	Yds.	Yd./Att.	TD	Int.-%	RK
D. White	436	260	60	3287	7.5	28	25- 6	7
Carano	12	5	42	69	5.8	2	0- 0	
Dorsett	1	0	0	0	0.0	0	0- 0	

PUNTING	No.	Avg.
D. White	71	40.9

KICKING	XP	Att.	%	FG	Att.	%
Septien	**59**	**60**	98	11	17	65

WASHINGTON REDSKINS

RUSHING

Last Name	No.	Yds.	Avg.	TD
Jackson	176	708	4.0	3
Harmon	128	484	3.8	4
Hammond	45	265	5.9	0
Claitt	57	215	3.8	1
Theismann	29	175	6.0	3
Hardeman	40	132	3.3	0
Forte	30	51	1.7	1
Kruczek	9	5	0.6	0
Walker	1	−8	−8.0	0
Harrison	2	−11	−5.5	0

RECEIVING

Last Name	No.	Yds.	Avg.	TD
Monk	58	797	14	3
Harmon	54	534	10	4
Warren	31	323	10	0
Jackson	27	279	10	1
Hammond	24	203	9	1
Thompson	22	313	14	5
Hardeman	16	178	11	0
Forte	15	174	12	1
McDaniel	14	154	11	0
Walker	10	88	9	1
Harrison	8	66	8	0
Claitt	3	34	11	1
DuBois	1	16	16	0
Coleman	1	12	12	0

PUNT RETURNS

Last Name	No.	Yds.	Avg.	TD
Nelms	48	487	10	0

KICKOFF RETURNS

Last Name	No.	Yds.	Avg.	TD
Nelms	38	810	21	0
Jackson	8	204	26	0
Forte	4	114	29	0
McKinney	2	48	24	0
Claitt	2	18	9	0
Monk	1	10	10	0
Anderson	1	0	0	0
Thompson	1	0	0	0

PASSING - PUNTING - KICKING

PASSING	Att.	Comp.	%	Yds.	Yd./Att.	TD	Int.-%	RK
Theisman	454	262	58	2962	6.5	17	16- 4	8
Kruczek	31	22	71	209	6.7	0	2- 7	
Hardeman	1	0	0	0	0.0	0	0- 0	

PUNTING	No.	Avg.
Connell	85	39.2

KICKING	XP	Att.	%	FG	Att.	%
Moseley	27	30	90	18	33	55

ST. LOUIS CARDINALS

RUSHING

Last Name	No.	Yds.	Avg.	TD
Anderson	301	1352	4.5	9
Morris	117	456	3.9	6
T. Brown	40	186	4.7	1
Harrell	42	170	4.0	3
Hart	9	11	1.2	0
Phillips	2	6	3.0	0
Love	1	3	3.0	0
Loyd	6	2	0.3	0
Gray	1	−3	−3.0	0

RECEIVING

Last Name	No.	Yds.	Avg.	TD
Tilley	68	966	14	6
Gray	40	709	18	3
Anderson	36	308	9	0
Marsh	22	269	12	4
T. Brown	21	290	14	1
Stief	16	165	10	0
Morris	15	110	7	1
Harrell	9	52	6	0
Bell	8	123	15	0
Combs	2	52	26	1
J. Lee	2	19	10	0

PUNT RETURNS

Last Name	No.	Yds.	Avg.	TD
Green	16	168	11	1
Bell	21	195	9	0
Harrell	11	31	3	0
Nelson	1	5	5	0
Allen	1	0	0	0

KICKOFF RETURNS

Last Name	No.	Yds.	Avg.	TD
Green	32	745	23	0
Harrell	19	348	18	0
Love	3	46	15	0
Stone	3	34	11	0
Phillips	2	28	14	0
T. Brown	2	26	13	0
Clark	2	14	7	0
Nelson	1	29	29	0
Collins	1	0	0	0
Baker	0	27	—	0

PASSING - PUNTING - KICKING

PASSING	Att.	Comp.	%	Yds.	Yd./Att.	TD	Int.-%	RK
Hart	425	228	54	2946	6.9	16	20- 5	12
Loyd	28	5	18	49	1.8	0	1- 4	
Lisch	17	6	35	68	4.0	0	3- 18	

PUNTING	No.	Avg.
Swider	**99**	41.5

KICKING	XP	Att.	%	FG	Att.	%
O'Donoghue	18	18	**100**	11	15	73
Little	17	19	89	3	8	38

NEW YORK GIANTS

RUSHING

Last Name	No.	Yds.	Avg.	TD
Taylor	147	580	3.9	4
Heater	111	360	3.2	3
Perry	59	272	4.6	1
Simms	36	190	5.3	1
Matthews	64	180	2.8	0
Hogan	34	90	2.6	2
Hicks	19	50	2.6	0
Garrett	9	31	3.4	0
Brunner	10	18	1.8	0
Laidlaw	5	10	2.0	0
Pittman	1	−7	−7.0	0

RECEIVING

Last Name	No.	Yds.	Avg.	TD
Gray	52	777	15	**10**
Taylor	33	253	8	0
Mullady	28	391	14	2
Pittman	25	308	12	0
Friede	22	371	17	0
Shirk	21	211	10	1
Matthews	19	86	5	0
Perkins	14	193	14	3
Heater	10	139	14	0
Perry	8	84	11	1
Garrett	5	69	14	1
Hogan	5	46	9	0
Laidlaw	2	16	8	0
Hicks	1	4	4	0
Martin	1	4	4	1

PUNT RETURNS

Last Name	No.	Yds.	Avg.	TD
Garrett	35	287	8	0
Reece	2	15	8	0

KICKOFF RETURNS

Last Name	No.	Yds.	Avg.	TD
Reece	24	471	20	0
Garrett	28	527	19	0
Heater	5	103	21	0
N. Johnson	5	89	18	0
Pittman	2	41	21	0
Haynes	2	40	20	0
McLaughlin	2	27	14	0
Laidlaw	1	18	18	0
Lapka	1	3	3	0
Wyatt	1	0	0	0

PASSING - PUNTING - KICKING

PASSING	Att.	Comp.	%	Yds.	Yd./Att.	TD	Int.-%	RK
Simms	402	193	48	2321	5.8	15	19- 5	15
Brunner	112	52	46	610	5.5	4	6- 5	

PUNTING	No.	Avg.
Jennings	94	**44.8**

KICKING	XP	Att.	%	FG	Att.	%
Danelo	27	28	96	16	24	67

MINNESOTA VIKINGS 9-7-0 Bud Grant

Scores of Each Game		
24	ATLANTA	23
7	PHILADELPHIA	42
34	Chicago	14
7	Detroit	27
17	PITTSBURGH	23
13	CHICAGO	7
0	Cincinnati	14
3	Green Bay	16
39	Washington	14
34	DETROIT	0
38	TAMPA BAY	30
13	GREEN BAY	25
23	New Orleans	20
21	Tampa Bay	10
28	CLEVELAND	23
16	Houston	20

Use Name	Pos.	Hgt.	Wgt.	Age	Int.	Pts.
Nick Bebout	OT	6'5"	260	29		
Dave Huffman	OT-OG-C	6'6"	258	23		
Steve Riley	OT	6'6"	258	27		
John Vella	OT	6'4"	260	30		
Ron Yary	OT	6'6"	255	34		
Brent Boyd	OG	6'3"	260	23		
Wes Hamilton	OG	6'3"	266	27		
Jim Hough	OG-C	6'2"	270	24		
Mel Mitchell	OG	6'3"	260	27		
Jim Langer	C	6'2"	253	32		
Dennis Swilley	C	6'3"	241	25		
Randy Holloway	DE	6'5"	252	25		2
Doug Martin	DE	6'3"	258	23		
Mark Mullaney	DE	6'6"	242	27		
Ken Sanders	DE	6'5"	245	30		
Dave Roller	DT	6'2"	270	30		
Doug Sutherland	DT	6'3"	250	32		
James White	DT	6'3"	263	26		
Matt Blair	LB	6'5"	237	29	3	
Dennis Johnson	LB	6'3"	231	22		
Henry Johnson	LB	6'1"	235	22		
Fred McNeill	LB	6'2"	226	28		
Jeff Siemon	LB	6'2"	237	30		
Scott Studwell	LB	6'2"	224	26	1	
Larry Brune	DB	6'2"	202	27	2	
Bobby Bryant	DB	6'	177	36	3	
Tom Hannon	DB	5'11"	190	25	4	6
Kurt Knoff	DB	6'2"	202	26	3	6
Keith Nord	DB	6'	193	23		6
Willie Teal	DB	5'10"	195	23		
John Turner	DB	6'	199	24	6	
Nate Wright	DB	5'11"	180	32	2	
Steve Dils	QB	6'1"	192	24		
Tommy Kramer	QB	6'1"	204	25		6
Mike Livingston	QB	6'3"	215	34		
Robert Miller	HB	5'11"	204	27		6
Eddie Payton	HB	5'8"	175	29		
Rickey Young	HB	6'2"	195	26		30
Ted Brown	FB	5'10"	200	23		60
Doug Paschal	FB	6'2"	219	22		6
Terry LeCount	WR	5'10"	187	24		
Kevin Miller	WR	5'10"	184	25		
Ahmad Rashad	WR	6'2"	200	30		30
Sammy White	WR	5'11"	189	26		30
Bob Bruer (from SF)	TE	6'5"	235	27		
Joe Senser	TE	6'4"	238	24		42
Bob Tucker	TE	6'3"	230	35		6
Stu Voigt	TE	6'1"	225	32		
Greg Coleman	K	6'	184	25		
Rick Danmeier	K	6'	204	28		81

DETROIT LIONS 9-7-0 Monte Clark

Scores of Each Game		
41	Los Angeles	20
29	Green Bay	7
20	ST. LOUIS	7
27	MINNESOTA	7
28	Atlanta	43
24	NEW ORLEANS	13
7	Chicago	24
17	Kansas City	20
17	SAN FRANCISCO	13
0	Minnesota	34
9	BALTIMORE	10
24	Tampa Bay	10
17	CHICAGO	*23
23	St. Louis	24
27	TAMPA BAY	14
24	GREEN BAY	3

Use Name	Pos.	Hgt.	Wgt.	Age	Int.	Pts.
Karl Baldischwiler	OT	6'5"	260	24		
Chris Dieterich	OT-OG	6'3"	255	22		
Keith Dorney	OT	6'5"	260	22		
Mike Whited	OT	6'4"	250	22		
Russ Bolinger	OG	6'5"	255	25		
Homer Elias	OG-OT	6'3"	255	25		
Tommie Ginn	OG-C	6'3"	250	22		
Burton Lawless	OG	6'4"	255	26		
Amos Fowler	C	6'3"	250	24		
Willie Parker	C	6'3"	245	31		
Wally Pesuit	C	6'4"	250	26		
Tom Turnure	C	6'4"	250	23		
Al Baker	DE	6'6"	245	23	1	
Dave Pureifory	DE	6'1"	255	31		
William Gay	DT-DE	6'5"	250	25		
Mike McCoy (from NYG)	DT	6'5"	275	31		
John Mendenhall	DT	6'1"	255	31		
Tom Tuinei	DT	6'4"	250	22		
John Woodcock	DT	6'3"	250	26		
Garry Cobb	LB	6'2"	225	23		
Eddie Cole	LB	6'2"	235	23		2
Ken Fantetti	LB	6'2"	230	23	1	
James Harrell	LB	6'1"	220	23		
Derrel Luce (from MIN)	LB	6'3"	225	27		
Davie Simmons	LB	6'4"	218	23		
Charlie Weaver	LB	6'2"	225	31	1	
Stan White	LB	6'1"	225	30	2	
Jim Allen	DB	6'2"	190	28	6	
Luther Bradley	DB	6'2"	190	25	1	
James Hunter	DB	6'3"	195	26	6	
Eddie Lewis	DB	6'	175	26		
Prentice McCray (from NE)	DB	6'1"	190	29		
Ray Oldham	DB	6'	190	29	3	6
Wayne Smith	DB	6'	170	23	1	
Walt Williams	DB	6'	185	26	1	
Gary Danielson	QB	6'2"	195	28		12
Eric Hipple	QB	6'2"	200	22		
Jeff Komlo	QB	6'2"	200	24		
Ken Callicutt	HB	6'	195	25		
Rick Kane	HB	5'11"	200	25		
Billy Sims	HB	6'	210	24		96
Dexter Bussey	FB	6'1"	210	28		18
Horace King	FB	5'10"	205	27		12
Bo Robinson	FB	6'2"	225	24		
John Arnold	WR	5'10"	175	24		
Freddie Scott	WR	6'2"	180	28		30
Jesse Thompson	WR	6'1"	185	24		
Leonard Thompson	WR	5'10"	190	28		18
Ray Williams	WR	5'9"	170	21		18
David Hill	TE	6'2"	230	26		6
Ulysses Norris	TE	6'4"	230	23		
Eddie Murray	K	5'10"	165	24		116
Tom Skladany	K	6'	195	25		

Doug English – Voluntarily Retired

CHICAGO BEARS 7-9-0 Neill Armstrong

Scores of Each Game		
6	Green Bay	*12
22	NEW ORLI ANS	3
14	MINNESOTA	34
3	Pittsburgh	38
23	TAMPA BAY	0
7	Minnesota	13
24	DETROIT	7
14	Philadelphia	17
21	Cleveland	27
35	WASHINGTON	21
6	HOUSTON	10
17	Atlanta	28
23	Detroit	*17
61	GREEN BAY	7
14	CINCINNATI	*17
14	Tampa Bay	13

Use Name	Pos.	Hgt.	Wgt.	Age	Int.	Pts.
Ted Albrecht	OT	6'4"	250	25		
Dan Jiggetts	OT	6'4"	270	26		
Dennis Lick	OT	6'3"	265	26		
Noah Jackson	OG	6'2"	265	29		
Rocco Moore	OG-OT	6'5"	276	25		
Revie Sorey	OG	6'2"	260	26		
Dan Neal	C	6'4"	255	31		
Paul Tabor	C-OG	6'4"	241	23		
Dan Hampton	DE	6'5"	255	22		
Al Harris	DE	6'5"	240	23		
Mike Hartenstine	DE	6'3"	243	27		
Jim Osborne	DT	6'3"	245	30		
Alan Page	DT	6'5"	225	35	1	8
Ron Rydalch	DT	6'4"	260	28		
Brad Shearer	DT	6'3"	247	25		
Gary Campbell	LB	6'1"	220	28	3	
Bruce Herron	LB	6'2"	220	26		
Tom Hicks	LB	6'4"	235	27	1	
Lee Kunz	LB	6'2"	225	23		
Jerry Muckensturm	LB	6'4"	220	26	2	
Otis Wilson	LB	6'2"	222	22	2	
Dave Becker	DB	6'2"	190	23		
Allan Ellis	DB	5'10"	177	29	1	
Gary Fencik	DB	6'1"	197	26	1	
Wentford Gaines	DB	6'	185	27		
Jonathan Hoke	DB	5'11"	175	23		
Vaughn Lusby	DB	5'10"	181	24		
Doug Plank	DB	6'	202	27	1	
Terry Schmidt	DB	6'	177	28	1	
Mike Ulmer	DB	6'	190	25		
Len Walterscheid	DB	5'11"	190	25	4	6
Bob Avellini	QB	6'2"	210	27		
Vince Evans	QB	6'2"	212	25		48
Mike Phipps	QB	6'3"	209	32		12
Willie McClendon	HB	6'1"	205	22		6
Walter Payton	HB	5'11"	202	26		42
Roland Harper	FB	6'	210	27		30
John Skibinski	FB	6'	222	25		
Matt Suhey	FB	5'11"	212	22		
Dave Williams	FB	6'2"	217	26		6
Brian Baschnagel	WR	6'	184	26		12
Kris Haines	WR	5'11"	180	23		
James Scott	WR	6'1"	190	28		18
Rickey Watts	WR	6'1"	203	23		12
Mike Cobb	TE	6'5"	243	24		
Robin Earl	TE	6'5"	240	25		18
Robert Fisher	TE	6'3"	240	22		12
Greg Latta	TE	6'3"	225	27		
Bob Parsons	TE	6'4"	225	30		
Bob Thomas	K	5'10"	175	28		74

Virgil Livers – Knee Injury

TAMPA BAY BUCCHANEERS 5-10-1 John McKay

Scores of Each Game		
17	Cincinnati	12
10	LOS ANGELES	9
17	Dallas	28
27	CLEVELAND	34
0	Chicago	23
14	GREEN BAY	*14
14	Houston	20
24	San Francisco	23
30	N.Y. GIANTS	13
21	PITTSBURGH	24
30	Minnesota	38
10	DETROIT	24
20	Green Bay	17
10	MINNESOTA	21
14	Detroit	27
13	CHICAGO	14

Use Name	Pos.	Hgt.	Wgt.	Age	Int.	Pts.
Darrell Austin	OT-OG	6'4"	255	28		
Charley Hannah	OT	6'5"	260	25		
Dave Reavis	OT	6'5"	260	30		
Greg Roberts	OG	6'3"	260	23		
Gene Sanders	OG	6'3"	260	23		
Ray Snell	OG	6'3"	255	22		
George Yarno	OG	6'2"	255	23		
Jim Leonard	C	6'3"	250	22		
Steve Wilson	C	6'3"	265	26		
Bill Kollar	DE-NT	6'4"	250	27		
Reggie Lewis	DE	6'3"	255	24		
Lee Roy Selmon	DE	6'3"	250	25		
David Stalls	DE	6'4"	255	24		
Randy Crowder	NT	6'2"	250	28		
David Logan	NT	6'2"	250	23		6
Bruce Radford	NT-DE	6'5"	260	24		
Rik Bonness	LB	6'3"	220	26		
Scot Brantley	LB	6'1"	230	22	1	
Aaron Brown	LB	6'2"	235	24		
Andy Hawkins	LB	6'2"	215	22		
Cecil Johnson	LB	6'2"	230	25		
Dave Lewis	LB	6'4"	245	25	1	
Dewey Selmon	LB	6'1"	240	26		
Richard Wood	LB	6'2"	230	27	3	6
Cedric Brown	DB	6'1"	205	26	1	6
Neal Colzie	DB	6'2"	195	27	1	
Mark Cotney	DB	6'	205	28	3	
Curtis Jordan	DB	6'2"	205	26		
Danny Reece	DB	5'11"	195	25		
Norris Thomas	DB	5'11"	185	26	1	
Mike Washington	DB	6'3"	200	27	4	
Chuck Fusina	QB	6'1"	195	23		
Mike Rae	QB	6'	200	29		
Doug Williams	QB	6'4"	215	25		24
Rick Berns	HB	6'2"	205	24		
Gary Davis	HB	5'10"	200	25		
Jerry Eckwood	HB	6'	200	25		18
Ricky Bell	FB-HB	6'2"	215	25		18
Johnny Davis	FB	6'1"	235	24		6
Tony Davis	FB	5'10"	210	27		6
Isaac Hagins	WR	5'9"	180	26		12
Kevin House	WR	6'1"	175	22		30
Gordon Jones	WR	6'	190	23		30
Larry Mucker	WR	5'11"	190	25		
Mike Shumann	WR	6'	175	24		6
Jimmie Giles	TE	6'3"	245	25		24
Jim Obradovich	TE	6'2"	230	27		
Tom Blanchard	K	6'	185	32		
Garo Yepremian	K	5'8"	175	36		79

Dana Nafziger – Knee Injury
George Ragsdale – Shoulder Injury

GREEN BAY PACKERS 5-10-1 Bart Starr

Scores of Each Game		
12	CHICAGO	*6
7	DETROIT	29
21	Los Angeles	51
7	DALLAS	28
14	CINCINNATI	9
14	Tampa Bay	*14
21	Cleveland	26
16	MINNESOTA	3
20	Pittsburgh	22
23	SAN FRANCISCO	16
21	N.Y. Giants	27
25	Minnesota	13
17	TAMPA BAY	20
7	Chicago	61
3	HOUSTON	22
3	Detroit	24

Use Name	Pos.	Hgt.	Wgt.	Age	Int.	Pts.
Buddy Aydelette	OT	6'4"	250	24		
Greg Koch	OT	6'4"	265	25		
Mark Koncar	OT	6'5"	268	27		
Tim Stones	OT	6'5"	252	30		
Karl Swanke	OT-C	6'6"	251	22		
Derrell Gofourth	OG	6'3"	260	25		
Leotis Harris	OG	6'1"	267	25		
Melvin Jackson	OG	6'1"	267	26		
Syd Kitson	OG	6'4"	252	21		
Ken Brown	C	6'1"	245	26		
Larry McCarren	C	6'3"	248	28		
Mike Wellman	C	6'3"	253	24		
Mike Butler	DE	6'5"	265	26		
Ezra Johnson	DE	6'4"	240	24		
Kit Lathrop	DE	6'5"	253	24		
Casey Merrill	DE	6'4"	255	23		
Rich Dimler	NT	6'6"	260	24		
Charles Johnson	NT	6'1"	262	23		
Terry Jones	NT	6'2"	259	23		
Mike Lewis	NT	6'3"	260	31		
Kurt Allerman	LB	6'3"	222	25		
John Anderson	LB	6'3"	221	24		
Bruce Beekley	LB	6'2"	225	23		
Brian Cabral	LB	6'	224	24		
George Cumby	LB	6'	215	24		
Mike Douglass	LB	6'	224	25		
Jim Gueno	LB	6'2"	220	26		
Mike Hunt	LB	6'2"	240	23		
Ed O'Neil	LB	6'3"	235	27		
Paul Rudzinski	LB	6'1"	220	24	1	
Johnnie Gray	DB	5'11"	185	26	5	
Estus Hood	DB	5'11"	180	24	1	
Mike Jolly	DB	6'3"	185	22	2	
Mark Lee	DB	5'11"	187	22		
Steve Luke	DB	6'2"	205	26	1	
Mike McCoy	DB	5'11"	183	27	1	
Mark Murphy	DB	6'2"	199	22		
Wylie Turner	DB	5'10"	182	23	2	
Lynn Dickey	QB	6'4"	220	30		6
Mark Miller	QB	6'2"	176	24		
Steve Pisarkiewicz	QB	6'2"	205	26		
Bill Troup	QB	6'5"	220	29		
David Whitehurst	QB	6'2"	204	25		
Harlan Huckleby	HB	6'1"	199	22		6
Eddie Lee Ivery	HB-FB	6'1"	210	23		24
Terdell Middleton	HB	6'	195	25		12
Vickey Ray Anderson	FB	6'	205	24		
Steve Atkins	FB	6'	216	24		12
Gerry Ellis	FB	5'11"	215	22		48
Barty Smith	FB	6'4"	240	28		
Ron Cassidy	WR	6'	185	23		
Bobby Kimball	WR	6'1"	190	23		
James Lofton	WR-DB	6'3"	187	24		24
Fred Nixon	WR	5'11"	191	21		
Aundra Thompson	WR	6'	186	27		12
Paul Coffman	TE	6'3"	218	24		18
Bill Larson (from DEN)	TE	6'4"	225	26		6
John Thompson	TE	6'3"	228	23		
David Beverly	K	6'2"	180	30		
Tom Birney	K	6'4"	220	24		32
Chester Marcol (to HOU)	K	6'	190	30		23
Jan Stenerud	K	6'2"	190	37		12

Eric Torkelson – Leg Injury
Rich Wingo – Back Injury

*—Overtime

MINNESOTA VIKINGS

RUSHING

Last Name	No.	Yds.	Avg.	TD
Brown	219	912	4.2	8
Young	130	351	2.7	3
Kramer	31	115	3.7	1
R. Miller	27	98	3.6	1
S. White	4	65	16.3	0
Paschal	15	53	3.5	1
Dils	3	26	8.7	0
Payton	2	15	7.5	0
Rashad	1	8	8.0	0
Senser	1	−1	−1.0	0

RECEIVING

Last Name	No.	Yds.	Avg.	TD
Rashad	69	1095	16	5
Young	64	499	8	2
Brown	62	623	10	2
S. White	53	887	17	5
Senser	42	447	11	7
Tucker	15	173	12	1
LeCount	13	168	13	0
R. Miller	10	19	2	0
Paschal	2	18	9	0
Yary	1	5	5	0

PUNT RETURNS

Last Name	No.	Yds.	Avg.	TD
Payton	34	251	7	0

KICKOFF RETURNS

Last Name	No.	Yds.	Avg.	TD
Payton	**53**	**1184**	22	0
Paschal	4	66	17	0
Bruer	2	20	10	0
Nord	1	70	70	1
R. Miller	1	23	23	0
Boyd	1	20	20	0
Yary	1	3	3	0

PASSING - PUNTING - KICKING

PASSING	Att.	Comp.	%	Yds.	Yd./Att.	TD	Int.–%		RK
Kramer	**522**	299	57	3582	6.9	19	23–	4	9
Dils	51	32	63	352	6.9	3	0–	0	
Senser	1	0	0	0	0.0	0	0–	0	

PUNTING	No.	Avg.
Coleman	81	38.8

KICKING	XP	Att.	%	FG	Att.	%
Danmeier	33	38	87	16	26	62

DETROIT LIONS

RUSHING

Last Name	No.	Yds.	Avg.	TD
Sims	313	1303	4.2	**13**
Bussey	145	720	**5.0**	3
Danielson	48	232	4.8	2
Kane	31	125	4.0	0
Scott	5	86	17.2	1
L. Thompson	6	61	10.2	0
King	18	57	3.2	1
R. Williams	2	17	8.5	1
Robinson	3	2	0.7	0
J. Thompson	1	−4	−4.0	0

RECEIVING

Last Name	No.	Yds.	Avg.	TD
Scott	53	834	16	4
Sims	51	621	12	3
Hill	39	424	11	1
Bussey	39	364	9	0
L. Thompson	19	511	27	3
King	19	184	10	1
J. Thompson	11	137	13	0
R. Williams	10	146	15	1
Kane	5	26	5	0
Callicutt	1	19	19	0

PUNT RETURNS

Last Name	No.	Yds.	Avg.	TD
R. Williams	27	259	10	0
Arnold	28	204	7	0
Callicutt	1	0	0	0

KICKOFF RETURNS

Last Name	No.	Yds.	Avg.	TD
Kane	23	495	22	0
Callicutt	16	301	19	0
R. Williams	9	228	25	1
Arnold	9	145	16	0

PASSING - PUNTING - KICKING

PASSING	Att.	Comp.	%	Yds.	Yd./Att.	TD	Int.–%		RK
Danielson	417	244	59	3223	7.7	13	11–	**3**	5
Komlo	4	2	50	26	6.5	0	1–	25	
Skladany	2	2	100	38	19.0	0	0–	0	

PUNTING	No.	Avg.
Skladany	72	42.2

KICKING	XP	Att.	%	FG	Att.	%
Murray	35	36	97	**27**	**42**	64

CHICAGO BEARS

RUSHING

Last Name	No.	Yds.	Avg.	TD
Payton	**317**	**1460**	4.6	6
Harper	113	404	3.6	5
Evans	60	306	5.1	8
McClendon	10	88	8.8	1
Williams	26	57	2.2	0
Skibinski	13	54	4.2	0
Suhey	22	45	2.0	0
Phipps	15	38	2.5	2
Parsons	2	4	2.0	0
Watts	1	−16	−16.0	0

RECEIVING

Last Name	No.	Yds.	Avg.	TD
Payton	46	367	8	1
Scott	36	696	**19**	3
Baschnagel	28	396	14	2
Watts	22	444	20	2
Williams	22	132	6	0
Earl	18	223	12	3
Fisher	12	203	17	2
Suhey	7	60	9	0
Harper	7	31	4	0
Skibinski	5	18	4	0
Haines	4	83	21	0
Cobb	2	16	8	0

PUNT RETURNS

Last Name	No.	Yds.	Avg.	TD
Walterscheid	33	239	7	0
Lusby	4	14	4	0
Watts	2	20	10	0
Suhey	1	4	4	0
Plank	1	0	0	0

KICKOFF RETURNS

Last Name	No.	Yds.	Avg.	TD
Williams	27	666	25	1
Suhey	19	406	21	0
Fisher	3	32	11	0
Walterscheid	1	12	12	0
Watts	1	12	12	0
Earl	1	11	11	0
McClendon	1	11	11	0
Herron	1	5	5	0
Haines	1	0	0	0
Ulmer	1	−2	−2	0

PASSING - PUNTING - KICKING

PASSING	Att.	Comp.	%	Yds.	Yd./Att.	TD	Int.–%		RK
Evans	278	148	53	2039	7.3	11	16–	6	14
Phipps	122	61	50	630	5.2	2	9–	7	
Parsons	1	0	0	0	0.0	0	0–	0	
Payton	3	0	0	0	0.0	0	0–	0	

PUNTING	No.	Avg.
Parsons	79	40.6

KICKING	XP	Att.	%	FG	Att.	%
Thomas	35	37	95	13	18	72

TAMPA BAY BUCCANEERS

RUSHING

Last Name	No.	Yds.	Avg.	TD
Bell	174	599	3.4	2
Eckwood	149	504	3.4	2
Williams	58	370	6.4	4
Berns	39	131	3.4	0
J. Davis	39	130	3.3	1
House	1	32	32.0	0
Hagins	3	24	8.0	0
T. Davis	5	24	4.8	0
G. Davis	7	21	3.0	0
Fusina	1	14	14.0	0
Jones	1	−10	−10.0	0

RECEIVING

Last Name	No.	Yds.	Avg.	TD
Jones	48	669	14	5
Eckwood	47	475	10	1
Bell	38	292	8	1
Giles	33	602	18	4
House	24	531	22	5
Hagins	23	364	16	2
T. Davis	12	115	10	1
Obradovich	11	152	14	0
G. Davis	9	79	9	0
Schumann	4	75	19	1
J. Davis	4	17	4	0
Mucker	2	37	19	0
Berns	1	6	6	0

PUNT RETURNS

Last Name	No.	Yds.	Avg.	TD
Reece	**57**	313	6	0

KICKOFF RETURNS

Last Name	No.	Yds.	Avg.	TD
G. Davis	44	951	22	0
Reece	7	128	18	0
Obradovich	5	46	9	0
Hagins	4	82	21	0
T. Davis	4	58	15	0
Berns	1	19	19	0
Jordan	1	0	0	0

PASSING - PUNTING - KICKING

PASSING	Att.	Comp.	%	Yds.	Yd./Att.	TD	Int.–%		RK
Williams	521	254	49	3396	6.5	20	16–	3	11
Fusina	4	2	50	18	4.5	0	1	25	
Eckwood	4	0	0	0	0.0	0	0–	0	
Hannah	1	0	0	0	0.0	0	0–	0	

PUNTING	No.	Avg.
Blanchard	88	42.3

KICKING	XP	Att.	%	FG	Att.	%
Yepremian	31	32	97	16	23	70

GREEN BAY PACKERS

RUSHING

Last Name	No.	Yds.	Avg.	TD
Ivery	202	831	4.1	3
Ellis	126	545	4.3	5
Atkins	67	216	3.2	1
Middleton	56	155	2.8	2
Beverly	6	21	3.5	0
Huckleby	6	11	1.8	1
Dickey	19	11	0.6	1
V. Anderson	4	5	1.3	0
A. Thompson	5	5	1.0	0
Coffman	1	3	3.0	0
Smith	1	3	3.0	0

RECEIVING

Last Name	No.	Yds.	Avg.	TD
Lofton	71	**1226**	17	4
Ivery	50	481	10	1
Ellis	48	496	10	3
Coffman	42	496	12	3
A. Thompson	40	609	15	2
Middleton	13	59	5	0
Atkins	7	49	7	1
Cassidy	5	109	22	0
Larson	5	44	9	1
Nixon	4	78	20	0
Huckleby	3	11	4	0
V. Anderson	2	2	1	0

PUNT RETURNS

Last Name	No.	Yds.	Avg.	TD
Cassidy	17	139	8	0
Nixon	11	85	8	0
Lee	5	32	6	0
Gray	4	41	10	0

KICKOFF RETURNS

Last Name	No.	Yds.	Avg.	TD
Lee	30	589	20	0
A. Thompson	15	283	19	0
McCoy	14	261	19	0
Nixon	6	160	27	0
Gray	5	63	13	0
Huckleby	3	59	20	0

PASSING - PUNTING - KICKING

PASSING	Att.	Comp.	%	Yds.	Yd./Att.	TD	Int.–%		RK
Dickey	478	278	58	3529	7.4	15	25–	5	10
Whitehurst	15	5	33	55	3.7	0	1–	7	
Troup	12	4	33	48	4.0	0	3–	25	
Pisarkiewicz	5	2	40	19	3.8	0	0–	0	
Beverly	1	0	0	0	0.0	0	0–	0	

PUNTING	No.	Avg.
Beverly	86	38.3
Marcol	1	33.0

KICKING	XP	Att.	%	FG	Att.	%
Birney	14	18	78	6	12	50
Marcol	8	10	80	3	4	75
Stenerud	3	3	100	3	5	60

ATLANTA FALCONS 12-4-0 Leeman Bennett

Scores of Each Game		
23	Minnesota	24
37	New England	21
17	MIAMI	20
20	San Francisco	17
43	DETROIT	28
7	N.Y. JETS	14
41	New Orleans	14
13	LOS ANGELES	10
30	Buffalo	14
33	St. Louis	*27
31	NEW ORLEANS	13
28	CHICAGO	17
10	WASHINGTON	6
20	Philadelphia	17
35	SAN FRANCISCO	10
17	Los Angeles	*20

Use Name	Pos.	Hgt.	Wgt.	Age	Int.	Pts.
Warren Bryant	OT	6'6"	270	24		
Mike Kenn	OT	6'6"	257	24		
Phil McKinnely	OT	6'4"	248	26		
Chuck Herman	OG	6'3"	250	21		
Pat Howell	OG	6'5"	253	23		
Dave Scott	OG	6'4"	265	26		
R.C. Thielemann	OG	6'4"	247	25		
Chuck Correal	C	6'3"	247	24		
Jeff Van Note	C	6'2"	247	34		
Edgar Fields	DE	6'2"	255	26		
Jeff Merrow	DE	6'4"	230	27		
Matthew Teague	DE	6'5"	240	21		
Jeff Yeates	DE	6'3"	248	29	1	
Wilson Faumuina	NT	6'5"	275	26		
Calvin Miller	NT	6'2"	270	26		
Don Smith	NT-DE	6'5"	248	23		
Mike Zele	NT	6'3"	236	24		

Bubba Bean – Knee Injury
Ray Easterling – Injury
June Jones — Ankle Injury

Use Name	Pos.	Hgt.	Wgt.	Age	Int.	Pts.
Jon Brooks (to LA)	LB	6'2"	215	23		
Buddy Curry	LB	6'3"	221	22	3	6
Tony Daykin	LB	6'1"	215	25		
Fulton Kuykendall	LB	6'5"	225	27		
Jim Laughlin	LB	6'	212	22	1	
Dewey McClain	LB	6'3"	236	26		
Robert Pennywell	LB	6'1"	222	25		
Al Richardson	LB	6'2"	206	22	7	6
Stan Sytsma	LB	6'2"	220	24		
Joel Williams	LB	6'1"	215	23	2	8
Rick Byas	DB	5'9"	180	29		
Bob Glazebrook	DB	6'1"	200	24	2	
Kenny Johnson	DB	5'10"	176	22	4	
Earl Jones	DB	6'	178	23	1	
Jerome King (to NYG)	DB	5'10"	173	25		
Rolland Lawrence	DB	5'10"	179	29	3	
Tom Pridemore	DB	5'10"	186	24	2	
Frank Reed	DB	5'11"	193	26		6

Dennis Pearson – Knee Injury
Billy Ryckman – Knee Injury

Use Name	Pos.	Hgt.	Wgt.	Age	Int.	Pts.
Steve Bartkowski	QB	6'4"	213	27		12
Larry Fortner	QB	6'4"	212	24		
Mike Moroski	QB	6'4"	200	22		
Anthony Anderson	HB	6'	197	23		
Lynn Cain	HB	6'1"	205	24		54
Ray Strong	HB	5'9"	184	24		6
William Andrews	FB	6'	200	24		30
Quinn Jones	FB	6'1"	215	24		
James Mayberry	FB	5'11"	210	22		
Wallace Francis	WR	5'11"	190	28		42
Alfred Jackson	WR	5'11"	176	25		42
Alfred Jenkins	WR	5'10"	172	28		36
Mike Smith	WR	5'10"	194	22		
Reggie Smith	WR	5'4"	168	24		
Russ Mikeska	TE	6'3"	225	24		
Junior Miller	TE	6'4"	235	22		54
John James	K	6'3"	200	31		
Tim Mazzetti	K	6'1"	175	24		103

LOS ANGELES RAMS 11-5-0 Ray Malavasi

Scores of Each Game		
20	DETROIT	41
9	Tampa Bay	10
51	GREEN BAY	21
28	N.Y. Giants	7
48	SAN FRANCISCO	26
21	St. Louis	13
31	San Francisco	17
10	Atlanta	13
45	NEW ORLEANS	31
14	MIAMI	35
17	New England	14
27	New Orleans	7
38	N.Y. JETS	13
7	Buffalo	*10
38	DALLAS	14
20	ATLANTA	*17

Use Name	Pos.	Hgt.	Wgt.	Age	Int.	Pts.
Doug France	OT	6'5"	270	27		
Irv Pankey	OT	6'4"	269	22		
Jackie Slater	OT	6'4"	271	26		
Bill Bain	OG	6'4"	277	28		
Dennis Harrah	OG-C	6'5"	255	27		
Kent Hill	OG	6'5"	260	23		
Greg Horton	OG-C	6'4"	248	29		
Ed McGlasson	OG-C	6'4"	248	24		
Doug Smith	OG-C	6'3"	255	23		
Rich Saul	C	6'3"	245	32		
Reggie Doss	DE	6'4"	267	23		
Fred Dryer	DE	6'6"	231	34		
Jack Youngblood	DE	6'4"	244	30		
Larry Brooks	DT	6'3"	253	30		
Mike Fanning	DT	6'6"	252	27		
Cody Jones	DT	6'5"	244	29		
Phil Murphy	DT	6'5"	280	22		

Use Name	Pos.	Hgt.	Wgt.	Age	Int.	Pts.
George Andrews	LB	6'3"	223	24		
Bob Brudzinski	LB	6'4"	229	25		
Carl Ekern	LB	6'3"	223	26		
Joe Harris	LB	6'1"	224	27		
Jack Reynolds	LB	6'1"	227	32	1	
Greg Westbrooks (from OAK)	LB	6'3"	220	27		
Jim Youngblood	LB	6'3"	231	30	1	6
Nolan Cromwell	DB	6'1"	198	25	8	7
Jeff Delaney	DB	6'	195	23	2	
LeRoy Irvin	DB	5'11"	180	22	2	
Johnnie Johnson	DB	6'1"	185	23	3	6
Rod Perry	DB	5'9"	182	26	5	6
Lucious Smith	DB	5'10"	190	23		
Ivory Sully	DB	6'	193	23		
Pat Thomas	DB	5'9"	182	26	3	

Use Name	Pos.	Hgt.	Wgt.	Age	Int.	Pts.
Vince Ferragamo	QB	6'3"	212	26		6
Pat Haden	QB	5'11"	185	27		
Bob Lee	QB	6'2"	190	34		
Jeff Rutledge	QB	6'1"	202	23		
Mike Guman	HB-FB	6'2"	210	22		24
Eddie Hill	HB	6'2"	197	23		
Lydell Mitchell	HB	5'11"	198	31		
Elvis Peacock	HB-FB	6'1"	208	23		54
Jewerl Thomas	HB-FB	5'10"	223	22		18
Wendell Tyler	HB	5'10"	195	25		
Cullen Bryant	FB	6'1"	236	29		36
Preston Dennard	WR	6'1"	183	24		36
Drew Hill	WR	5'9"	170	23		18
Willie Miller	WR	5'9"	172	33		48
Jeff Moore	WR	6'1"	200	23		6
Billy Waddy	WR	5'11"	188	26		30
Walt Arnold	TE	6'3"	225	22		6
Victor Hicks	TE	6'3"	250	23		18
Terry Nelson	TE	6'2"	240	29		
Conrad Rucker (from TB)	TE	6'3"	245	25		
Frank Corral	K	6'2"	228	25		99

SAN FRANCISCO FORTY-NINERS 6-10-0 Bill Walsh

Scores of Each Game		
26	New Orleans	23
24	ST. LOUIS	*21
37	N.Y. Jets	27
17	ATLANTA	20
26	Los Angeles	48
14	Dallas	59
17	LOS ANGELES	31
23	TAMPA BAY	24
13	Detroit	17
16	Green Bay	23
13	Miami	17
12	N.Y. GIANTS	0
21	NEW ENGLAND	17
38	NEW ORLEANS	*35
10	Atlanta	35
13	BUFFALO	18

Use Name	Pos.	Hgt.	Wgt.	Age	Int.	Pts.
Jean Barrett	OT	6'6"	250	29		
Ken Bungarda	OT	6'6"	270	23		
Keith Fahnhorst	OT	6'6"	263	28		
Ron Singleton	OT	6'7"	267	28		
John Ayers	OG	6'5"	255	27		
Randy Cross	OG	6'3"	255	26		
Walt Downing	OG-C	6'3"	254	24		
Ernie Hughes	OG	6'3"	255	25		
Fred Quillan	C	6'5"	260	24		
Dwaine Board	DE	6'5"	245	23		
Mel Land	DE	6'3"	242	24		
Lawrence Pillers (from NYJ)	DE-DT	6'3"	260	27		
Jim Stuckey	DE	6'4"	251	22		2
Jimmy Webb	DE	6'5"	245	28		
Mike Calhoun (from TB)	DT-DE	6'4"	260	23		
Jim Krahl (from BAL)	DT	6'5"	252	24		
Archie Reese	DT	6'3"	262	24		
Ken Times	DT	6'2"	246	24		
Ted Vincent	DT	6'4"	265	24		
George Visger	DT	6'4"	250	21		

Use Name	Pos.	Hgt.	Wgt.	Age	Int.	Pts.
Dan Bunz	LB	6'4"	225	24		
Willie Harper	LB	6'2"	215	30		
Scott Hilton	LB	6'4"	230	26		
Bobby Leopold	LB	6'1"	215	22	2	
Craig Puki	LB	6'1"	231	23	1	
Thomas Seabron (TO STL)	LB	6'3"	215	23		
Terry Tautolo	LB	6'2"	235	26	1	
Keena Turner	LB	6'2"	219	21	2	
Ricky Churchman	DB	6'1"	193	22	4	
Charles Cornelius	DB	5'9"	178	28		
Dwight Hicks	DB	6'1"	189	24	4	
Charles Johnson	DB	5'10"	180	24	1	
Al Latimer	DB	5'11"	172	22		
Melvin Morgan	DB	6'	186	27		
Scott Perry (to SD)	DB	6'	180	26		
Ray Rhodes	DB	5'11"	185	29	1	
Gerard Williams (from STL)	DB	6'1"	184	28	1	
Herb Williams	DB	6'	198	22		

Use Name	Pos.	Hgt.	Wgt.	Age	Int.	Pts.
Steve DeBerg	QB	6'2"	205	26		
Gary Huff	QB	6'1"	200	29		
Joe Montana	QB	6'2"	200	24		12
Lenvil Elliott	HB	6'	210	28		18
Paul Hofer	HB	6'	195	28		18
Ricky Patton	HB	5'11"	192	26		
Don Woods (from SD)	HB-FB	6'1"	204	29		
Jerry Aldridge	FB	6'2"	220	24		
Earl Cooper	FB	6'2"	227	22		54
Bob Ferrell	FB	6'	219	27		
Phil Francis	FB	6'1"	215	23		
Terry Anderson	WR	5'9"	182	25		
Dwight Clark	WR	6'3"	205	23		48
James Owens	WR	5'11"	188	25		6
Jim Robinson	WR	5'9"	170	27		
Freddie Solomon	WR	5'11"	188	27		60
Eason Ramson	TE	6'2"	234	24		12
Charlie Young	TE	6'4"	234	29		12
Jim Miller	K	5'11"	183	23		
Ray Wersching	K	5'11"	210	30		78

NEW ORLEANS SAINTS 1-15-0 Dick Nolan, Dick Stanfel

Scores of Each Game		
23	SAN FRANCISCO	26
3	Chicago	22
26	BUFFALO	35
16	Miami	21
7	ST. LOUIS	40
13	Detroit	24
14	ATLANTA	41
14	Washington	22
31	Los Angeles	45
21	PHILADELPHIA	34
13	Atlanta	31
7	LOS ANGELES	27
20	MINNESOTA	23
35	San Francisco	*38
21	N.Y. Jets	20
27	NEW ENGLAND	38

Use Name	Pos.	Hgt.	Wgt.	Age	Int.	Pts.
Stan Brock	OT	6'6"	275	22		
Dave Lafary	OT-OG	6'7"	280	25		
J.T. Taylor	OT	6'4"	265	24		
Larry Coombs	OG-C	6'4"	260	23		
Fred Sturt	OG	6'4"	255	29		
Robert Woods	OG-OT	6'3"	259	30		
Emanuel Zanders	OG	6'1"	248	29		
John Hill	C	6'2"	246	30		
Jim Pietrzak	C	6'5"	260	27		
Elois Grooms	DE	6'4"	250	27	1	
Tommy Hart	DE	6'4"	246	35		
Steve Parker	DE	6'6"	265	23		
Don Reese	DE	6'6"	250	28		6
Barry Bennett	DT	6'4"	257	24		
Mike Fultz	DT	6'5"	278	26		
Derland Moore	DT	6'4"	253	28		
Elex Price	DT	6'3"	265	30		6

Use Name	Pos.	Hgt.	Wgt.	Age	Int.	Pts.
Ken Bordelon	LB	6'4"	226	26		
Chuck Evans	LB	6'3"	235	23		
Joe Federspiel	LB	6'1"	230	30		
Stan Holloway	LB	6'2"	218	22		
Jim Kovach	LB	6'2"	225	24	1	
Reggie Mathis	LB	6'2"	220	24	1	
Dave Washington	LB	6'5"	225	31		
Ray Brown	DB	6'2"	202	31	2	
Clarence Chapman (to CIN)	DB	5'10"	185	26		
James Marshall	DB	6'	187	27	2	
Tom Myers	DB	5'11"	180	29	5	
Ricky Ray	DB	5'11"	180	23		
Don Schwartz	DB	6'1"	191	24		
Dave Waymer	DB	6'1"	195	22		

Use Name	Pos.	Hgt.	Wgt.	Age	Int.	Pts.
Guy Benjamin	QB	6'4"	210	25		
Ed Burns	QB	6'3"	210	25		
Archie Manning	QB	6'3"	200	31		
Bobby Scott	QB	6'1"	197	31		
Larry Collins	HB	5'11"	190	25		
Jack Holmes	HB-FB	5'11"	210	27		18
Jimmy Rogers	HB	5'10"	190	25		18
Mike Strachan	HB	6'	198	27		
Tony Galbreath	FB	6'	230	26		30
Wayne Wilson	FB	6'3"	208	22		12
Gordon Banks	WR	5'9"	175	22		
Wes Chandler	WR	5'11"	186	24		36
Tom Donovan	WR	5'11"	179	23		
Ike Harris	WR	6'3"	210	27		36
Rich Mauti	WR	6'	190	26		
Tinker Owens	WR	5'11"	170	25		
Henry Childs	TE	6'2"	220	29		36
Larry Hardy	TE	6'3"	230	24		
Brooks Williams	TE	6'4"	226	25		12
Russell Erxleben	K	6'4"	219	23		8
Benny Ricardo	K	5'10"	170	26		61

*—Overtime

ATLANTA FALCONS

RUSHING

Last Name	No.	Yds.	Avg.	TD
Andrews	265	1308	4.9	4
Cain	235	914	3.9	8
Mayberry	18	88	4.9	0
Strong	6	42	7.0	1
Bartkowski	25	35	1.4	2
James	1	13	13.0	0
Anderson	6	5	0.8	0
Francis	1	2	2.0	0
J. Miller	2	−2	−1.0	0

RECEIVING

Last Name	No.	Yds.	Avg.	TD
Jenkins	57	1026	18	6
Francis	54	862	16	7
Andrews	51	456	9	1
J. Miller	46	584	13	9
Cain	24	223	9	1
Jackson	23	412	18	7
Mayberry	3	1	0	0
Mikeska	1	4	4	0

PUNT RETURNS

Last Name	No.	Yds.	Avg.	TD
Johnson	23	281	12	0
R. Smith	27	262	10	0
Lawrence	3	−7	−2	0

KICKOFF RETURNS

Last Name	No.	Yds.	Avg.	TD
R. Smith	25	512	21	0
Strong	10	168	17	0
Anderson	7	97	14	0
Jackson	3	70	23	0
M. Smith	3	58	19	0
Pridemore	3	39	13	0
Fields	1	11	11	0
Daykin	1	3	3	0

PASSING – PUNTING – KICKING

PASSING	Att.	Comp.	%	Yds.	Yd./Att.	TD	Int.–%	RK
Bartkowski	463	257	56	3544	7.7	31	16– 4	3
James	1	0	0	0	0.0	0	1–100	
Moroski	3	2	67	24	8.0	0	0– 0	

PUNTING	No.	Avg.
James	79	39.1

KICKING	XP	Att.	%	FG	Att.	%
Mazzetti	46	49	94	19	27	70

LOS ANGELES RAMS

RUSHING

Last Name	No.	Yds.	Avg.	TD
Bryant	183	807	4.4	3
Peacock	164	777	4.7	7
J. Thomas	65	427	6.6	2
Guman	100	410	4.1	4
Tyler	30	157	5.2	0
E. Hill	39	120	3.1	0
Ferragamo	15	34	2.3	1
Dennard	2	20	10.0	0
Hicks	1	19	19.0	0
Mitchell	7	16	2.3	0
Haden	3	12	4.0	0
D. Hill	1	4	4.0	0
Cromwell	2	0	0.0	0
Lee	1	−1	−1.0	0
Waddy	1	−1	−1.0	0
Miller	1	−2	−2.0	0

RECEIVING

Last Name	No.	Yds.	Avg.	TD
Bryant	53	386	7	3
Waddy	38	670	18	5
Dennard	36	596	17	6
Peacock	25	213	9	2
Hicks	23	318	14	3
Miller	22	358	16	8
D. Hill	19	416	22	2
Guman	14	131	9	0
Moore	10	168	17	1
Arnold	5	75	15	1
J. Thomas	5	30	6	0
E. Hill	4	29	7	0
Nelson	3	22	7	0
Mitchell	2	21	11	0
Tyler	2	8	4	0

PUNT RETURNS

Last Name	No.	Yds.	Avg.	TD
Irvin	42	296	7	0
Waddy	2	10	5	0
Guman	2	6	3	0
J. Johnson	1	3	3	0

KICKOFF RETURNS

Last Name	No.	Yds.	Avg.	TD
D. Hill	43	880	21	1
Sully	4	36	9	0
Guman	2	25	13	0
J. Thomas	2	21	11	0
P. Thomas	1	12	12	0
Irvin	1	5	5	0

PASSING – PUNTING – KICKING

PASSING	Att.	Comp.	%	Yds.	Yd./Att.	TD	Int.–%	RK
Ferragamo	404	240	59	3199	7.9	30	19– 5	2
Haden	41	19	46	185	4.5	0	4– 10	
Cromwell	1	0	0	0	0.0	0	0– 0	
Guman	1	1	100	31	31.0	1	0– 0	
Rutledge	4	1	25	26	6.5	0	0– 0	

PUNTING	No.	Avg.
Corral	76	39.5

KICKING	XP	Att.	%	FG	Att.	%
Corral	51	52	98	16	30	53

SAN FRANCISCO FORTY-NINERS

RUSHING

Last Name	No.	Yds.	Avg.	TD
Cooper	171	720	4.2	5
Elliott	76	341	4.5	2
Hofer	60	293	4.9	1
Woods	54	239	4.4	0
Montana	32	77	2.4	2
Solomon	8	56	7.0	0
Francis	7	36	5.1	0
DeBerg	6	4	0.7	0
Patton	1	1	1.0	0
Ramson	2	−2	−1.0	0
Miller	2	−12	−6.0	0

RECEIVING

Last Name	No.	Yds.	Avg.	TD
Cooper	83	567	7	4
Clark	82	991	12	8
Solomon	48	658	14	8
Hofer	41	467	11	2
Young	29	325	11	2
Elliott	27	285	11	1
Ramson	21	179	9	2
Woods	20	171	9	0
Owens	9	133	15	0
Francis	3	23	8	0

PUNT RETURNS

Last Name	No.	Yds.	Avg.	TD
Solomon	27	298	11	2
Hicks	12	58	5	0
Robinson	3	36	12	0
Churchman	2	16	8	0
Ferrell	1	1	1	0

KICKOFF RETURNS

Last Name	No.	Yds.	Avg.	TD
Owens	31	726	23	1
Elliott	18	321	18	0
Anderson	6	104	17	0
Francis	5	60	12	0
Solomon	4	61	15	0
Patton	4	43	11	0
Johnson	2	10	5	0
Ramson	1	18	18	0
Tautolo	1	16	16	0
Young	1	14	14	0
Hughes	1	10	10	0
Hofer	1	2	2	0

PASSING – PUNTING – KICKING

PASSING	Att.	Comp.	%	Yds.	Yd./Att.	TD	Int.–%	RK
Montana	273	176	65	1795	6.6	15	9– 3	4
DeBerg	321	186	58	1998	6.2	12	17– 5	13
Solomon	1	0	0	0	0.0	0	0– 0	
Woods	2	1	50	6	3.0	0	0– 0	

PUNTING	No.	Avg.
Miller	77	40.9

KICKING	XP	Att.	%	FG	Att.	%
Wersching	33	39	85	15	19	79

NEW ORLEANS SAINTS

RUSHING

Last Name	No.	Yds.	Avg.	TD
Rogers	80	366	4.6	1
Galbreath	81	308	3.8	3
Wilson	63	188	3.0	1
Manning	23	166	7.2	0
Holmes	38	119	3.1	2
Strachan	20	41	2.1	0
Chandler	1	9	9.0	0
Mauti	1	2	2.0	0
Banks	1	−5	−5.0	0

RECEIVING

Last Name	No.	Yds.	Avg.	TD
Chandler	65	975	15	6
Galbreath	57	470	8	2
Harris	37	692	19	6
Childs	34	463	14	6
Wilson	31	241	8	1
Holmes	29	226	8	1
Rogers	27	267	10	2
Williams	26	351	14	2
Hardy	13	197	15	0
Strachan	5	60	12	0
T. Owens	1	26	26	0
Mauti	1	10	10	0
Banks	1	7	7	0

PUNT RETURNS

Last Name	No.	Yds.	Avg.	TD
Mauti	11	111	10	0
Chandler	8	36	5	0
Waymer	3	29	10	0

KICKOFF RETURNS

Last Name	No.	Yds.	Avg.	TD
Mauti	31	798	26	0
Rogers	41	930	23	0
Wilson	9	159	18	0
Galbreath	6	86	14	0
Holloway	1	0	0	0

PASSING – PUNTING – KICKING

PASSING	Att.	Comp.	%	Yds.	Yd./Att.	TD	Int.–%	RK
Manning	509	309	61	3716	7.3	23	20– 4	6
Scott	33	16	49	200	6.1	2	1– 3	
Benjamin	17	7	41	28	1.7	0	1– 6	
Chandler	1	1	100	43	43.0	0	0– 0	
Erxleben	1	0	0	0	0.0	0	0– 0	
Galbreath	2	0	0	0	0.0	0	0– 0	
Holmes	3	1	33	23	7.7	1	0– 0	

PUNTING	No.	Avg.
Erxleben	89	39.3

KICKING	XP	Att.	%	FG	Att.	%
Ricardo	31	34	91	10	17	59
Erxleben	2	2	100	2	5	40

1980 A.F.C. Home Sweet Home

The newest pro football lawsuit began when Al Davis decided to move the Raiders from Oakland to the Los Angeles Coliseum for this season. Davis claimed he could not reach a new stadium contract in Oakland, but he was apparently lured by the possibilities of pay television in Los Angeles. Commissioner Pete Rozelle pointed to the NFL rule requiring 21 of the team owners to approve any shift of a franchise. The owners turned thumbs down on the move, and Davis filed a lawsuit in which he claimed that this rule was illegal because it violated antitrust laws. With the case mired in the courts, Davis resigned himself to a 1980 season in Oakland. Raider fans showed their protest by staying outside the stadium in thousands for the first five minutes of a Monday night game on December 1. Bitter words and charges flew back and forth between Davis and Rozelle, making their possible meeting at a Super Bowl trophy award presentation a much-anticipated event.

EASTERN DIVISION

Buffalo Bills—Chuck Knox worked his magic to take the Bills to the playoffs for the first time since 1974. The first-place finish coincided with the arrival of Joe Cribbs, a sleek rookie runner. The improved running attack plus occasional use of the shotgun formation juiced up the Buffalo offense. The defense shut enemy attacks down with a precision secondary and outstanding play by nose tackle Fred Smerlas. The Bills started quick with five straight victories, the fifth being a 26-24 upset of the unbeaten Chargers in San Diego. After a mid-season slump, the Bills regained their stride just as the rival Patriots were breaking down. Five victories in the final seven games included a 28-13 decision over the Steelers, a 10-7 overtime triumph over the Rams, and an 18-13 beating of the 49ers which sewed up first place on the final Sunday.

New England Patriots—All they didn't have was heart. Despite some hold-out problems, the Patriots had a full arsenal of weapons and were in the thick of the playoff chase in early November. In first place with a 7-2 record, the Pats fell on their faces as the weather grew colder. They lost close games to the Oilers and Rams to fall one game off the pace in the East. The Pats regrouped and reignited their potent offense in a 47-21 trouncing of the Colts. With hope that the swoon was over, the Pats went to San Francisco to face the 4-8 49ers. With the chips on the table, the Patriots folded, dropping an error-filled 21-17 decision. Still only one game behind Buffalo, the Patriots flew to Miami for a Monday night game. The Patriots played very conservative football and lost the game in overtime. Although the Pats revived to beat first-place Buffalo and the Saints, the comeback came too late. The only harvest of the season was all-star attention for John Hannah, Stanley Morgan, Steve Nelson, and Mike Haynes, and a shaky hold on his job for head coach Ron Erhardt.

Miami Dolphins—Two old heroes faded into history, taking with them Miami's playoff hopes for this year. Larry Csonka demanded renegotiation of his contract after his 1979 performance, but the Dolphins instead cut him loose. Without him, the Dolphins lacked a pile-driving short-yardage runner. The other legend, quarterback Bob Griese, had an ailing right shoulder which grew steadily worse. In three come-from-behind victories in September, Griese twice came off the bench to engineer fourth quarter rallies. After a 30-17 loss to the Colts on October 5, Griese went to the sidelines for good. The offense stumbled for a while, but by the later stages of the campaign, rookie David Woodley had brought a youthful verve to the QB position. Despite a rebuilt secondary, the Miami defense continued at a high level, leading the team to impressive victories over the Bills and Patriots. But with the mid-season changes and an intangible lack of enthusiasm, the Dolphins missed out on the playoffs with a break-even record.

Baltimore Colts—With Bert Jones back in good health, the Colts made a run at the playoffs. After two injury-spoiled seasons, Jones directed an offense which had rookie help in halfback Curtis Dickey and wide receiver Ray Butler. With a 4-2 record, the Colts stood only one game out of first place in October. The defense, however, sabotaged any Baltimore playoff hopes with weak play. Bruce Laird led a competent secondary, but the front four played inconsistently. The Colts dropped four of their final five games, but the single victory was a 28-24 upset over the first-place Bills. Head coach Mike McCormack debuted in Baltimore with a squad that won only two games at home all season. Baltimore fans responded with the lowest attendance in the NFL, capped by a paultry 16,941 fans on hand for the Colts' final game.

New York Jets—High hopes ran unchecked through the pre-season. The Jets had resolved their quarterback question by sending Matt Robinson to Denver and making Richard Todd the offensive leader. The league-leading running game returned intact, and the passing attack had a new explosive weapon in rookie Johnny Lam Jones, a world-class runner. Although the defense looked like the weak link on the team, it had played well enough during the later stages of last year to fuel optimism. By early October, the Jets were 0-5 and the biggest disappointment of the year. On offense, Jones dropped an alarming number of passes, Wesley Walker, Clark Gaines, and Randy Rasmusson, went out in mid-season with injuries, and Todd played with uncertainty. The defense earned even more jeers, with the inexperienced secondary an easy mark for enemy sharpshooters. The high hopes fell to a masochistic low on December 14, as a New York audience watched the Jets lose to the winless Saints.

CENTRAL DIVISION

Cleveland Browns—The Kardiac Kids, they were called, and the Browns indeed raised pulses with a series of games that were in contention into the final minute. Thanks to Brian Sipe, the Browns won enough of them to dethrone the Steelers as Central Division champions. Sipe repeatedly completed clutch passes while keeping his interception total low. The Cleveland passing attack thrived despite an unbalanced running game. Mike Pruitt provided muscle at fullback, but neither injury-scarred Greg Pruitt nor Heisman Trophy rookie Charles White was much of a running threat at halfback. Head Coach Sam Rutigliano had in recent years brought in leaders for each of his lines, guard Joe DeLamiellure from Buffalo and defensive end Lyle Alzado from Denver. Rutigliano switched to the 3-4 defense this season, but Jerry Sherk's knee injury in the first game hurt the pass rush badly. The key victory of the year was a 17-14 triumph over the Oilers on November 30. Although the Browns and Oilers finished with identical 11-5 records, the Browns captured first place on tie-breaking calculations.

Houston Oilers—After the Steelers had ousted the Oilers from the playoffs last season, Bum Phillips promised to "kick in" the door to the AFC title. Although the Steelers failed to make the playoffs this year, the Browns cut in line ahead of the Oilers and entered the throne room. Phillips had spared no cost in beefing up his squad for this campaign. He swapped quarterback Dan Pastorini to Oakland for crafty Ken Stabler, obtained veteran guard Bob Young from the Cardinals, and sent a package of draft choices to the Raiders in October for tight end Dave Casper. With receiver Ken Burrough injured for much of the year and with Stabler's arm on the wane, the Houston offense used double tight ends and relied more than ever on the running of Earl Campbell. Enemy defenses knew that the Oilers would rely on straight-ahead muscle football. A frustrating 31-17 loss to the Steelers on opening day ushered the Oilers to a slow start, but a revival in mid-October put them back into the race. Their fate was sealed by losses to the Jets and Browns in November, but the Oilers had the satisfaction of knocking the Steelers out of the playoffs with a 6-0 beating on Thursday night, December 4. When the dust cleared at the end of the schedule, the Oilers again had to settle for a wild-card ticket to the playoffs.

Pittsburgh Steelers—After a 4-1 start, age and injuries brought the Steelers down from their pedestal of excellence. Sam Adams sat out the entire year while John Stallworth went out after two games. Jon Kolb and Steve Courson missed half the schedule, Franco Harris and Lynn Swann each lost three games to injuries, and Terry Bradshaw and Jack Lambert each spent some time in sick bay. Chuck Noll deployed his deep bench, but the casualty list was too long to overcome. Although Lambert and Donnie Shell kept their play at an all-star level, the duo of L.C. Greenwood and Joe Greene slowed down noticeably. With Terry Bradshaw passing effectively, the Steelers climbed back into the race with a mid-season winning streak, but a loss to Buffalo on November 23 spelled the beginning of the end. The true back-breaker was a 6-0 struggle which the Steelers lost to the Oilers on December 4. Instead of a fifth Super Bowl appearance, the Steelers got to go home for Christmas.

Cincinnati Bengals—General manager Paul Browns hired Forrest Gregg to be head coach with the style of a first sergeant. Gregg made the tail-ender Bengals competitive in the early going. They lost two close games, then upset the champion Steelers 30-28. After two more close losses, they traveled to Pittsburgh and again whipped the Steelers. After beating the Vikings a week later, the Bengals fell off into a five-week slump. Gregg got his best results with the defense, which played well in the newly installed 3-4 setup. The offense had tougher going. Pete Johnson provided ball control running, but numerous injuries plagued quarterback Ken Anderson. After the dry spell, the Bengals won three of their last four games to raise hopes that they may someday climb out of the basement in the strong Central Division.

FINAL TEAM STATISTICS

OFFENSE	BALT.	BUFF.	CIN.	CLEV.	DENV.	HOU.	K.C.	MIA.	N.E.	NY J	OAK.	PIT.	S.D.	SEA.
FIRST DOWNS:														
Total	327	317	283	336	286	329	270	284	319	289	281	308	**372**	302
by Rushing	128	134	111	102	107	**155**	130	107	139	124	108	111	106	114
by Passing	174	157	147	207	158	152	122	149	154	146	149	177	**244**	166
by Penalty	25	26	25	27	21	22	18	**28**	26	19	24	20	22	22
RUSHING:														
Number	527	**603**	513	436	480	573	552	492	588	470	541	512	509	456
Yards	2078	2222	2069	1673	1865	**2635**	1873	1876	2240	1873	2146	1986	1879	1783
Average Yards	3.9	3.7	4.0	3.8	3.9	**4.6**	3.4	3.8	3.8	4.0	4.0	3.9	3.7	3.9
Touchdowns	**20**	17	9	15	16	18	15	9	19	17	14	15	18	13
PASSING:														
Attempts	493	461	510	554	467	463	401	492	413	481	456	484	**594**	517
Completions	272	262	281	337	262	296	237	267	240	265	235	250	**350**	287
Completion Pct.	55.2	56.8	55.1	60.8	56.1	**63.9**	59.1	54.3	58.1	55.1	51.5	51.7	58.9	55.5
Passing Yards	3409	2936	3102	4132	3107	3271	2869	2953	3395	3335	3294	3832	**4741**	3494
Avg. Yds per Att.	5.9	5.7	5.2	6.8	5.4	6.1	5.3	5.1	**7.3**	5.8	5.8	6.9	7.2	5.5
Avg Yds per Comp.	12.5	11.2	11.0	12.3	11.9	11.1	12.1	11.1	14.2	12.6	14.0	**15.3**	13.6	12.2
Times Tackled	36	**20**	37	23	44	27	57	31	25	42	47	37	32	51
Yds Lost Tackled	281	**186**	287	217	330	264	421	265	200	326	395	264	210	398
Net Yards	3128	2750	2815	3915	2777	3007	2448	2688	3195	3009	2899	3568	**4531**	3096
Touchdowns	25	20	17	**30**	14	15	15	21	27	17	23	26	**30**	18
Interceptions	24	19	25	**14**	25	28	**14**	26	27	30	24	24	26	23
Pct. Intercepted	4.9	4.1	4.9	**2.5**	5.4	6.0	3.5	5.3	6.5	6.2	5.3	5.0	4.4	4.4
PUNTS:														
Number	84	74	**87**	66	70	67	85	79	63	74	71	66	61	70
Average	38.1	38.2	39.7	38.3	**43.9**	40.7	39.0	41.5	38.0	41.8	43.6	40.2	38.5	40.4
PUNT RETURNS:														
Number	26	39	39	35	42	48	40	32	**60**	33	49	45	41	41
Yards	188	259	252	170	408	384	**581**	213	513	269	421	391	335	349
Average Yards	7.2	6.6	6.5	4.9	9.7	8.0	**14.5**	6.7	8.6	8.2	8.6	8.7	8.2	8.5
Touchdowns	0	0	0	0	0	0	**2**	0	1	0	0	0	0	1
KICKOFF RET.:														
Number	67	47	68	63	62	53	62	61	56	**74**	62	65	62	73
Yards	1383	827	1199	1308	1290	981	1249	1234	1281	**1491**	1180	1350	1135	1489
Average Yards	20.6	17.6	17.6	20.8	20.8	18.5	20.1	20.2	**22.9**	20.1	19.0	20.8	18.3	20.4
Touchdowns	0	0	0	0	0	0	0	0	1	0	**2**	0	0	0
INTERCEPT RET.:														
Number	17	24	20	22	16	26	28	28	24	23	**35**	26	20	23
Yards	310	334	255	266	343	313	364	198	288	293	**501**	260	270	95
Average Yards	18.2	13.9	12.8	12.1	**21.4**	12.0	13.0	7.1	12.0	12.7	14.3	10.0	13.5	4.1
Touchdowns	1	**2**	**2**	0	**2**	0	**2**	0	1	**2**	**2**	0	**2**	0
PENALTIES:														
Number	104	90	118	117	93	101	**74**	**74**	79	103	98	111	109	109
Yards	914	731	949	1042	899	838	591	**567**	696	767	929	933	912	901
FUMBLES:														
Number	23	36	22	24	25	33	42	33	**19**	27	38	38	40	38
Number Lost	13	22	**8**	14	12	19	16	16	9	11	20	18	22	15
POINTS:														
Total	355	320	244	357	310	295	319	266	**441**	302	364	352	418	291
Pat Attempts	46	40	28	45	33	34	37	32	52	37	44	42	50	33
Pat Made	43	37	27	39	32	31	37	32	**51**	36	41	39	46	33
FG Attempts	23	23	29	26	34	25	26	23	34	22	**37**	28	36	31
FG Made	12	13	15	16	**26**	20	20	14	**26**	14	19	19	24	20
Percent FG Made	52.2	56.5	51.7	61.5	76.5	**80.0**	76.9	60.9	76.5	63.6	51.4	67.9	66.7	64.5
Safeties	0	**2**	**2**	0	1	0	0	0	0	1	1	**2**	0	0

DEFENSE	BALT.	BUFF.	CIN.	CLEV.	DENV.	HOU.	K.C.	MIA.	N.E.	NY J	OAK.	PIT.	S.D.	SEA.
FIRST DOWNS:														
Total	338	**251**	286	340	303	259	328	309	270	348	319	302	284	301
by Rushing	140	109	111	105	125	**94**	136	107	118	127	108	101	101	129
by Passing	164	**120**	154	197	158	147	179	185	141	198	181	171	156	147
by Penalty	34	22	21	38	20	18	13	17	**11**	23	30	30	27	25
RUSHING:														
Number	574	486	469	485	554	**444**	536	530	482	508	501	486	478	550
Yards	2210	1819	**1680**	1761	2120	1811	2206	2018	1876	1951	1726	1762	1842	2067
Average Yards	3.9	3.7	3.6	3.6	3.8	4.1	4.1	3.8	3.9	3.8	**3.4**	3.6	3.9	3.8
Touchdowns	20	14	13	12	10	**8**	17	13	12	20	19	9	18	17
PASSING:														
Attempts	476	**433**	491	536	448	454	523	505	458	544	524	532	519	462
Completions	260	**240**	284	336	270	246	278	290	266	337	296	280	300	267
Completion Pct.	54.6	55.4	57.8	62.7	60.3	54.2	53.2	57.4	58.1	61.9	56.5	**52.6**	57.8	57.8
Passing Yards	3576	**2561**	3246	4089	3449	3053	3393	3439	3232	3899	3731	3517	3324	3280
Avg. Yds per Att.	6.6	**4.9**	5.9	6.8	6.4	5.7	5.6	6.0	5.8	6.4	5.7	6.1	4.9	6.4
Avg Yds per Comp.	13.8	**10.7**	12.1	12.2	12.8	12.4	12.2	11.9	12.2	11.6	12.6	12.6	11.1	12.3
Times Tackled	30	33	35	32	39	34	37	27	44	28	54	18	**60**	26
Yds Lost Tackled	240	279	302	224	324	252	284	233	346	235	419	145	**475**	170
Net Yards	3336	**2282**	3124	3865	3125	2801	3109	3206	2886	2664	3312	3372	2849	3101
Touchdowns	21	**15**	22	23	20	16	25	21	28	27	17	25	18	28
Interceptions	17	24	20	22	16	26	28	28	24	23	**35**	26	20	23
Pct. Intercepted	3.6	5.5	4.1	4.1	3.6	5.7	5.4	5.5	5.2	4.2	**6.7**	4.9	3.9	5.0
PUNTS:														
Number	72	82	72	63	70	78	66	72	**92**	63	87	73	86	66
Average	39.7	39.3	38.5	37.4	41.6	40.9	42.2	**37.3**	41.0	39.9	38.9	40.7	40.4	40.2
PUNT RETURNS:														
Number	49	34	46	38	52	40	44	42	**28**	46	34	34	43	42
Yards	357	**204**	478	245	443	394	289	339	237	369	268	217	359	476
Average Yards	7.3	**6.0**	10.4	6.4	8.5	9.9	6.6	8.1	8.5	8.0	7.9	6.4	8.3	11.3
Touchdowns	1	0	0	0	1	0	0	0	0	1	0	0	0	0
KICKOFF RET.:														
Number	54	**52**	57	71	55	68	61	53	89	54	66	68	75	64
Yards	1062	1051	1180	**1018**	1187	1265	1253	1210	1649	1207	1315	1339	1617	1223
Average Yards	19.7	20.2	20.7	**14.3**	21.6	18.6	20.5	22.8	18.5	22.4	19.9	19.7	21.6	19.1
Touchdowns	1	0	1	0	0	0	0	0	0	0	0	0	0	0
INTERCEPT RET.:														
Number	24	19	25	**14**	25	28	**14**	26	27	30	24	24	26	23
Yards	378	193	351	270	388	424	**130**	386	369	408	153	226	419	170
Average Yards	15.8	10.2	14.0	19.3	15.5	15.1	9.3	14.8	13.7	13.6	**6.4**	9.4	16.1	7.4
Touchdowns	1	1	**0**	2	2	2	**0**	1	**0**	1	**0**	2	1	2
PENALTIES:														
Number	98	97	106	96	101	101	82	**108**	92	90	102	93	104	103
Yards	775	805	809	766	850	763	617	**923**	833	872	922	806	880	876
FUMBLES:														
Number	32	37	**44**	23	26	22	26	31	31	26	34	23	39	33
Number Lost	17	20	**22**	10	12	13	15	17	10	9	17	14	18	11
POINTS:														
Total	387	260	312	310	323	**251**	336	305	325	395	306	313	237	408
Pat Attempts	47	31	38	37	34	**27**	42	36	40	51	37	37	40	47
Pat Made	45	29	36	32	32	**26**	39	33	39	50	36	34	39	43
FG Attempts	30	**20**	27	29	40	29	30	25	**20**	24	24	29	34	33
FG Made	20	15	16	18	29	21	15	18	14	**13**	14	19	16	25
Percent FG Made	66.7	75.0	59.3	62.1	72.5	72.4	50.0	72.0	70.0	54.2	58.3	65.5	**47.1**	75.8
Safeties	0	0	0	1	0	0	0	1	2	0	0	0	0	3

WESTERN DIVISION

San Diego Chargers—After four weeks of play, the Chargers had beaten each of the other Western teams. A letdown followed, with the Chargers losing four of their next six games, but Don Coryell rallied his club to a second straight divisional title. The soul of the Chargers was its all out passing attack. Don Fouts threw the ball often and accurately, making Kellen Winslow, John Jefferson, and Charlie Joiner all 1,000-yard receivers. To balance the attack, the Chargers obtained runner Chuck Muncie from the Saints in late September. The offensive line kept the offense moving despite losing Russ Washington to a knee injury in mid-October. The defense launched a great pass rush, with Fred Dean, Gary Johnson, Louie Kelcher, and Leroy Jones applying the pressure. To get into the playoffs, the Chargers won five of their last six games, culminating in a 26-17 victory over the Steelers on the final Monday night of the schedule.

Oakland Raiders—The Raiders brought lots of new faces into training camp, most notably quarterback Dan Pastorini. Lightly regarded because of the wholesale changes, the Raiders lived up to these predictions by dropping three of their first five games. To make matters worse, Pastorini went out for the year with a broken leg suffered in the third loss. Into the lineup came Jim Plunkett, whose career had floundered badly in recent years. Playing error-free ball, Plunkett sparked the Raiders into a six-game winning streak which shot them back into the Western race. Plunkett was the glamour boy of the resurgence, but the Oakland defense was its heart. Game after game, the defense would come up with a clutch big play to stymie enemy drives. Leading this crew of pirates was linebacker Ted Hendricks and sticky-fingered back Lester Hayes. Over the last month of the campaign, the Raiders and Chargers battled for the lead. The Raiders wrapped up a playoff berth with a final victory over the Giants, but settled for a wild-card spot when the Chargers beat Pittsburgh and took first place on the tiebreaker rules.

Kansas City Chiefs—With their offensive line chewed up by injuries, the Chiefs lost their first four games of the season. After the blockers healed, however, the Chiefs won eight of twelve games to forge ahead out of the Western basement. Head coach Marv Levy had built a fine defense, with all-stars in end Art Still, cornerback Gary Green, and safety Gary Barbaro. Oakland and Houston both lost matches with the rising Chiefs. The offense was slowly becoming more versatile, with reserve quarterback Bill Kenney doing well in the last three games while Steve Fuller was hurt. J.T. Smith kept up his fine punt returning, while young Nick Lowery wrested the kicking job away from old-timer Jan Stenerud.

Denver Broncos—For the second year in a row, coach Red Miller turned the Denver offense over to a young quarterback. Matt Robinson came from the Jets with a reputation as a dangerous passer, but he started the season as if overwhelmed by doubt. Although the Broncos beat Dallas 41-20 on September 14, they had a 1-3 record at the end of the month. In the next two games, veteran Craig Morton came off the bench to take the Broncos to victory. From that point on, Morton started and Robinson worked mostly as a kick holder. By late November, the Broncos were 7-5 and trailed the Chargers and Raiders by only one game. With their fate in their own hands, they dropped the ball. They lost to Oakland 9-3 on Monday night, December 1. One week later, they were beaten by the Chiefs 31-14, and they followed that by losing again to the Raiders 24-21. The defense held together around linebacker Randy Gradishar after the loss of Bob Swenson and Joe Rizzo to injuries. Otis Armstrong was forced to retire in mid-season by a spinal condition, and coach Miller would not return when new owners bought the club during the off-season.

Seattle Seahawks—The Seahawks angered their fans by losing all of their eight home games. Although they broke even on the road, the 4-12 season was a bitter disappointment after two promising .500 years. The collapse cursed all sectors of the team. The offense gained little yardage on the ground after Sherman Smith ripped up a knee in the third game of the season. The offensive line also fell down on its pass protection, subjecting quarterback Jim Zorn to steady pressure from opposing linemen. While dodging tacklers, Zorn delivered the ball to Steve Largent with accustomed frequency. The defense played poorly despite good work by linebacker Michael Jackson and rookie end Jacob Green. Although they started the year well enough, the Seahawks ended it with a demoralizing nine-game losing streak, including a 51-7 beating by the Cowboys.

BUFFALO BILLS 11-5-0 Chuck Knox

Scores of Each Game		
17	MIAMI	7
20	N.Y. JETS	10
35	New Orleans	26
24	OAKLAND	7
26	San Diego	24
12	BALTIMORE	17
14	Miami	17
31	NEW ENGLAND	13
14	ATLANTA	30
31	N.Y. Jets	24
14	Cincinnati	0
28	PITTSBURGH	13
24	Baltimore	28
10	LOS ANGELES	*7
2	New England	24
18	San Francisco	13

Use Name	Pos.	Hgt.	Wgt.	Age	Int.	Pts.
Joe Devlin	OT	6'5"	250	26		
Dee Hardison	OT	6'4"	269	24		
Ken Jones	OT	6'5"	250	27		
Jon Borchardt	OG-OT	6'5"	255	23		
Conrad Dobler	OG	6'3"	255	29		
Ed Fulton	OG	6'3"	250	25		
Reggie McKenzie	OG	6'4"	242	30		
Will Grant	C	6'3"	248	26		
Jim Ritcher	C	6'3"	251	22		
Tim Vogler	C	6'3"	245	23		
Scott Hutchinson	DE	6'4"	243	24		
Darrell Irvin	DE	6'4"	255	23		
Ken Johnson	DE	6'5"	253	25		2
Sherman White	DE	6'5"	250	31	1	
Ben Williams	DE	6'3"	245	26		
Mike Kadish	NT	6'5"	270	30		
Fred Smerlas	NT	6'3"	270	23		
Jim Haslett	LB	6'3"	232	24	2	
Chris Keating	LB	6'2"	223	22		
Shane Nelson	LB	6'1"	225	25		
Ervin Parker	LB	6'4"	225	22		
Isiah Robertson	LB	6'3"	225	31	2	
Lucius Sanford	LB	6'2"	216	24		6
Phil Villapiano	LB	6'2"	225	31		
Rufus Bess	DB	5'9"	180	23		
Larry Carter	DB	5'11"	185	23		
Mario Clark	DB	6'2"	195	26	1	
Steve Freeman	DB	5'11"	185	27	7	6
Doug Greene	DB	6'2"	205	24		
Rod Kush	DB	6'	188	23		
Jeff Nixon	DB	6'3"	190	23	5	6
Charles Romes	DB	6'1"	190	26	2	
Bill Simpson	DB	6'1"	191	28	4	2
Joe Ferguson	QB	6'1"	195	30		
David Humm	QB	6'2"	190	28		
Dan Manucci	QB	6'2"	194	22		
Joe Cribbs	HB	5'11"	190	22		72
Roland Hooks	HB	6'	195	27		6
Terry Miller	HB	5'10"	196	24		
Curtis Brown	FB	5'10'	203	25		18
Roosevelt Leaks	FB	5'10"	225	27		18
Jerry Butler	WR	6'	178	22		36
Duke Fergerson	WR	6'1"	185	26		
Ron Jessie	WR	6'	181	32		6
Mike Kirtman	WR	6'1"	180	24		
Frank Lewis	WR	6'1"	196	33		36
Artie Owens (to NO)	WR	5'10"	182	27		
Lou Piccone	WR	5'9"	175	31		
Mark Brammer	TE	6'3"	238	22		24
Reuben Gant	TE	6'4"	225	28		6
Greg Cater	K	6'	191	23		
Nick Mike-Mayer	K	5'8"	185	30		76

Mikeli Ieremia – Knee Injury

NEW ENGLAND PATRIOTS 10-6-0 Ron Erhardt

Scores of Each Game		
34	CLEVELAND	17
21	ATLANTA	37
37	Seattle	31
23	DENVER	14
21	N.Y. Jets	11
34	MIAMI	0
37	Baltimore	21
13	Buffalo	31
34	N.Y. JETS	21
34	Houston	38
14	LOS ANGELES	17
47	BALTIMORE	21
17	San Francisco	21
13	Miami	*16
24	BUFFALO	2
38	New Orleans	27

Use Name	Pos.	Hgt.	Wgt.	Age	Int.	Pts.
Shelby Jordan	OT	6'7"	260	28		
Gary Puetz	OT	6'4"	265	28		
Dwight Wheeler	OT	6'3"	255	25		
Sam Adams	OG	6'3"	260	31		
Bob Cryder	OG	6'4"	265	23		
John Hannah	OG	6'2"	265	29		
Pete Brock	C-OT	6'5"	260	26		
Bill Lenkaitis	C	6'3"	255	34		
Julius Adams	DE	6'3"	263	32		
Mel Lunsford	DE	6'3"	260	30		
Doug McDougald	DE	6'5"	271	23		
Tony McGee	DE	6'4"	250	31		
Richard Bishop	NT-DE	6'1"	260	30		
Ray Hamilton	NT	6'1"	245	29		
Steve McMichael	NT	6'2"	245	22		
Bob Golic	LB	6'2"	240	22		
Mike Hawkins	LB	6'2"	232	24	2	
Sam Hunt	LB	6'1"	270	29		
Steve King	LB	6'4"	230	29		
Bill Matthews	LB	6'2"	235	24	1	
Larry McGrew	LB	6'4"	231	23		
Steve Nelson	LB	6'2"	230	29	3	
Rod Shoate	LB	6'1"	215	27	3	6
John Zamberlin	LB	6'2"	232	24		
Raymond Clayborn	DB	6'1"	190	25	5	
Bill Currier	DB	6'	195	25		
Tim Fox	DB	5'11"	190	26	4	
Mike Haynes	DB	6'2"	195	27	1	6
Roland James	DB	6'2"	189	22	4	6
Rick Sanford	DB	6'1"	192	23	1	6
Matt Cavanaugh	QB	6'1"	210	23		
Steve Grogan	QB	6'4"	208	27		6
Tom Owen	QB	6'1"	194	27		
Allan Clark	HB	5'10"	186	23		12
Vagas Ferguson	HB	6'1"	194	23		12
Horace Ivory	HB	6'	198	26		18
Andy Johnson	HB	6'	204	27		18
Don Calhoun	FB	6'	212	28		54
Chuck Foreman	FB	6'2"	212	29		6
Mosi Tatupu	FB	6'	229	25		18
Preston Brown	WR	5'10"	184	22		
Harold Jackson	WR	5'10"	175	34		30
Stanley Morgan	WR	5'11"	180	25		36
Carlos Pennywell	WR	6'2"	180	24		6
Don Westbrook	WR	5'10"	185	27		
Russ Francis	TE	6'6"	242	27		48
Don Hasselbeck	TE	6'7"	245	26		24
Mike Hubach	K	5'10"	185	22		
John Smith	K	6'	185	30		**129**

Mark Buben – Injury
Ray Costict – Knee Injury
Steve Schindler – Knee Injury
Jimmy Stewart – Hamstring Injury
Sam Cunningham – Holdout

MIAMI DOLPHINS 8-8-0 Don Shula

Scores of Each Game		
7	Buffalo	17
17	CINCINNATI	16
20	Atlanta	17
21	NEW ORLEANS	16
17	BALTIMORE	30
0	New England	34
17	BUFFALO	14
14	N.Y. Jets	17
10	Oakland	16
35	Los Angeles	14
17	SAN FRANCISCO	13
24	SAN DIEGO	*27
10	Pittsburgh	23
16	NEW ENGLAND	*13
24	Baltimore	14
17	N.Y. JETS	24

Use Name	Pos.	Hgt.	Wgt.	Age	Int.	Pts.
Jon Giesler	OT	6'5"	260	33		
Cleveland Green	OT	6'3"	265	22		
Eric Laasko	OT	6'4'	265	23		
Thom Dornbrook	OG-C	6'2"	240	23		
Bob Kuechenberg	OG-OT	6'3"	255	32		
Larry Little	OG-OT	6'1"	260	34		
Ed Newman	OG	6'2"	255	29		
Jeff Toews	OG	6'3"	255	22		
Mark Dennard	C	6'1"	252	24		
Dwight Stephenson	C	6'2"	255	22		
Bill Barnett	DE-NT	6'4"	255	24		
Doug Betters	DE	6'7"	260	24		
Vern Den Herder	DE	6'6"	252	31		
Carl Barisich	NT	6'4"	255	29		
Bob Baumhower	NT	6'5"	260	25		
Kim Bokamper	LB	6'6"	247	25	1	
Rusty Chambers	LB	6'1"	220	26		
A. J. Duhe	LB-DE	6'4"	252	24		
Larry Gordon	LB	6'4"	230	27	1	
Ralph Ortega	LB	6'2"	225	27	1	
Earnest Rhone	LB	6'2"	224	27	3	
Steve Shull	LB	6'1"	218	22		
Steve Towle	LB	6'2"	230	26		
Jeff Allen	DB	5'11"	185	22		
Doug Beaudoin	DB	6'1"	190	26		
Don Bessillieu	DB	6'1"	200	24	4	6
Glenn Blackwood	DB	6'	183	23	3	
Billy Cesare	DB	5'11"	195	25		
Tim Foley	DB	6'	198	32		
Don McNeal	DB	5'11"	192	22	5	
Gerald Small	DB	5'11"	192	24	7	
Ed Taylor	DB	6'	175	27	3	
Bob Griese	QB	6'1"	190	35		
Don Strock	QB	6'5"	220	29		
David Woodley	QB	6'2"	196	21		18
Pete Woods	QB	6'3"	214	24		
Nick Giaquinto	HB	5'11"	204	25		12
Rick Moser	HB	6'	210	23		
Tony Nathan	HB	6'	206	23		36
Del Williams	HB	6'	200	29		12
Woody Bennett (from NYJ)	FB	6'2"	222	25		6
Steve Howell	FB	6'2"	230	23		6
Terry Robiskie	FB	6'1"	210	25		12
Don Testerman	FB	6'2"	230	27		
Elmer Bailey	WR	6'	195	22		
Jimmy Cefalo	WR	5'11"	188	23		6
Duriel Harris	WR	5'11"	184	25		12
Nat Moore	WR	5'9"	188	28		42
Bruce Hardy	TE	6'5"	230	24		12
Ronnie Lee	TE	6'3"	235	23		12
Joe Rose	TE	6'3"	225	23		
George Roberts	K	6'	184	25		
Uwe von Schamann	K	6'	188	24		74

Mike Kozlowski–Ankle Injury

BALTIMORE COLTS 7-9-0 Mike McCormack

Scores of Each Game		
17	N.Y. Jets	14
17	PITTSBURGH	20
16	Houston	21
35	N.Y. JETS	21
30	Miami	17
17	Buffalo	12
21	NEW ENGLAND	37
10	ST. LOUIS	17
31	Kansas City	24
27	CLEVELAND	28
10	Detroit	9
21	New England	47
28	BUFFALO	24
33	Cincinnati	34
14	MIAMI	24
28	KANSAS CITY	38

Use Name	Pos.	Hgt.	Wgt.	Age	Int.	Pts.
Wade Griffin	OT	6'5"	245	26		
Jeff Hart	OT	6'5"	265	26		
George Kunz	OT	6'5"	275	33		
Chris Foote	OG-C	6'3"	250	23		
Ken Huff	OG	6'4"	258	27		
Robert Pratt	OG	6'4"	243	29		
Bob Van Duyne	OG	6'5'	247	28		
Ray Donaldson	C-OG	6'3"	252	22		
Ken Mendenhall	C	6'3"	238	32		
Fred Cook	DE	6'3"	252	28		
Greg Fields	DE	6'7"	262	25		
Mike Ozdowski	DE	6'5"	247	24		
Mike Barnes	DT	6'6"	251	29		
Joe Ehrmann	DT	6'5"	252	31	1	
Gary Don Johnson	DT	6'4"	263	24		
Herb Orvis	DT	6'5"	255	33		
Steve Heimkreiter	LB	6'2"	226	23		
Ricky Jones	LB	6'1"	215	25		
Barry Krauss	LB	6'3"	238	23		
Sanders Shiver	LB	6'2"	228	25	1	6
Ed Simonini	LB	6'	206	26		
Ed Smith	LB	6'2"	217	23		
Mike Woods	LB	6'2"	237	25	1	
Kim Anderson	DB	5'11"	182	23	2	
Lyle Blackwood	DB	6'	188	29	1	
Larry Braziel	DB	6'	195	25	2	
Nesby Glasgow	DB	5'10"	185	23	4	
Derrick Hatchett	DB	5'11"	180	22		
Bruce Laird	DB	6'	194	30	5	
Reggie Pinkney	DB	5'11"	187	25		
Bert Jones	QB	6'3"	209	28		12
Greg Landry	QB	6'4"	210	33		6
Curtis Dickey	HB-FB	6'1"	201	23		78
Don McCauley	HB-FB	6'1"	211	31		30
Joe Washington	HB	5'10"	179	26		24
Cleveland Franklin	FB	6'2"	212	25		12
Ben Garry	FB	6'	223	24		
Marvin Sims	FB	6'4"	237	23		12
Randy Burke	WR	6'2"	190	25		18
Ray Butler	WR	6'3"	190	23		12
Roger Carr	WR	6'3"	193	28		30
Brian DeRoo	WR	6'3"	190	24		
Mike Siani	WR	6'2"	199	30		6
Mack Alston	TE	6'2"	232	33		
Ron LaPointe	TE	6'2"	235	23		
Reese McCall	TE	6'7"	235	24		30
Bob Raba	TE	6'1"	225	25		
Mike Bragg	K	5'11"	186	33		
Steve Mike-Mayer	K	6'	180	32		79

Mark Bailey – Knee Injury
Ron Fernandes – Illness

NEW YORK JETS 4-12-0 Walt Michaels

Scores of Each Game		
14	BALTIMORE	17
10	Buffalo	20
27	SAN FRANCISCO	37
21	Baltimore	35
11	NEW ENGLAND	21
14	Atlanta	7
17	SEATTLE	27
17	MIAMI	14
21	New England	34
24	BUFFALO	31
24	Denver	31
31	HOUSTON	*28
13	Los Angeles	38
14	Cleveland	17
20	NEW ORLEANS	21
24	Miami	17

Use Name	Pos.	Hgt.	Wgt.	Age	Int.	Pts.
Marvin Powell	OT	6'5"	268	25		
John Roman	OT	6'4"	260	28		
Chris Ward	OT	6'3"	270	24		
Dan Alexander	OG	6'4"	255	25		
Guy Bingham	OG-C	6'3"	255	22		
Eric Cunningham (from STL)	OG	6'3"	257	23		
Randy Rasmussen	OG	6'2"	255	35		
Stan Waldemore	OG-C-OT	6'4"	250	25		
Joe Fields	C	6'2"	253	26		
Mark Gastineau	DE	6'5"	280	23		
Chris Godfrey	DE-DT	6'3"	250	22		
Joe Klecko	DE	6'3"	265	26		
Wes Roberts	DE	6'6"	253	23		
Marty Lyons	DT	6'5"	260	23		
Abdul Salaam	DT	6'3"	265	27		
Bob Winkel	DT	6'4"	255	24		
Stan Blinka	LB	6'2"	230	23		
Greg Buttle	LB	6'3"	232	26	1	
Ron Crosby	LB	6'3"	220	25	2	
Mike McKibben	LB	6'3"	228	23		
Lance Mehl	LB	6'3"	230	22		
John Sullivan	LB	6'1"	225	23		
Steve Carpenter	DB	6'2"	195	22		
Donald Dykes	DB	5'11"	180	25	5	
Jerry Holmes	DB	6'2"	175	22		
Bobby Jackson	DB	5'9"	175	23	1	
Jesse Johnson	DB	6'3"	185	23		
Saladin Martin	DB	6'	179	24		
Tim Moresco	DB	5'11"	180	25		
Darrol Ray	DB	6'1"	200	22	6	12
Ken Schroy	DB	6'2"	196	27	8	6
Craig Penrose	QB	6'3"	212	27		
Pat Ryan	QB	6'3"	205	24		
Richard Todd	QB	6'2"	203	26		30
Bobby Batton	HB	5'11"	185	23		
Scott Dierking	HB	5'10"	215	25		42
Bruce Harper	HB	5'8"	177	25		18
Kenny Lewis	HB	6'	190	22		
Clark Gaines	FB	6'1"	215	26		18
Kevin Long	FB	6'1"	218	25		36
Tom Newton	FB	6'	213	26		
Gerald Carter (to TB)	WR	6'1"	185	23		
Paul Darby	WR	5'10"	192	23		6
Derrick Gaffney	WR	6'1"	180	25		12
Bobby Jones	WR	5'11"	180	25		
Johnny "Lam" Jones	WR	5'11"	180	22		18
Wesley Walker	WR	6'	175	25		6
Jerome Barkum	TE	6'3"	225	30		6
Mickey Shuler	TE	6'3"	235	24		12
Pat Leahy	K	6'	195	29		78
Chuck Ramsey	K	6'2"	189	28		

Johnny Lynn–Knee Injury

*—Overtime

BUFFALO BILLS

RUSHING

Last Name	No.	Yds.	Avg.	TD
Cribbs	306	1185	3.9	11
Brown	153	559	3.7	3
Leaks	67	219	3.3	2
Hooks	25	118	4.7	1
Ferguson	31	65	2.1	0
Miller	12	35	2.9	0
Manucci	3	29	9.7	0
Butler	1	18	18.0	0
Brammer	1	8	8.0	0
Humm	1	5	5.0	0
Jessie	1	−9	−9.0	0
Cater	2	−10	−5.0	0

RECEIVING

Last Name	No.	Yds.	Avg.	TD
Butler	57	832	15	6
Cribbs	52	415	8	1
Lewis	40	648	16	6
Brown	27	137	5	0
Brammer	26	283	11	4
Hooks	23	179	8	0
Gant	12	181	15	1
Leaks	8	57	7	1
Piccone	7	82	12	0
Jessie	4	56	14	1
Fergerson	3	41	14	0
Miller	3	25	8	0

PUNT RETURNS

Last Name	No.	Yds.	Avg.	TD
Cribbs	29	154	5	0
Hooks	8	90	11	0
Piccone	2	15	8	0

KICKOFF RETURNS

Last Name	No.	Yds.	Avg.	TD
Miller	16	303	19	0
Brown	10	181	18	0
Owens	8	157	20	0
Hooks	7	109	16	0
Keating	3	38	13	0
Cribbs	2	39	20	0
Vogler	1	0	0	0

PASSING - PUNTING - KICKING

PASSING	Att.	Comp.	%	Yds.	Yd./Att.	TD	Int.-%	RK
Ferguson	439	251	57	2805	6.4	20	18– 4	7
Humm	14	9	29	39	2.8	0	1– 7	
Cater	1	1	100	15	15.0	0	0– 0	
Cribbs	1	1	100	13	13.0	0	0– 0	
Manucci	6	5	83	64	10.7	0	0– 0	

PUNTING	No.	Avg.
Cater	73	38.7

KICKING	XP	Att.	%	FG	Att.	%
Mike-Mayer	37	39	95	13	23	57

NEW ENGLAND PATRIOTS

RUSHING

Last Name	No.	Yds.	Avg.	TD
Ferguson	211	818	3.9	2
Calhoun	200	787	3.9	9
Grogan	30	112	3.7	1
Ivory	42	111	2.6	2
Cavanaugh	19	97	5.1	0
Tatupu	33	97	2.9	3
Foreman	23	63	2.7	1
Clark	9	56	6.2	1
Jackson	5	37	7.4	0
Morgan	4	36	9.0	0
Johnson	11	26	2.4	0
Hubach	1	0	0.0	0

RECEIVING

Last Name	No.	Yds.	Avg.	TD
Morgan	45	991	**22**	6
Francis	41	664	16	8
Jackson	35	737	21	5
Calhoun	27	129	5	0
Johnson	24	259	11	3
Ferguson	22	173	8	0
Foreman	14	99	7	0
Ivory	12	95	8	0
Hasselbeck	8	130	16	4
Westbrook	4	60	15	0
Pennywell	4	31	8	1
Tatupu	4	27	7	0

PUNT RETURNS

Last Name	No.	Yds.	Avg.	TD
James	33	331	10	1
Haynes	17	140	8	0
Brown	10	42	4	0

KICKOFF RETURNS

Last Name	No.	Yds.	Avg.	TD
Ivory	36	992	**28**	1
Brown	9	156	17	0
Currier	6	98	16	0
Clark	3	21	7	0
Westbrook	1	14	14	0
Pennywell	1	0	0	0

PASSING - PUNTING - KICKING

PASSING	Att.	Comp.	%	Yds.	Yd./Att.	TD	Int.-%	RK
Grogan	306	175	57	2475	**8.1**	18	22– 7	8
Cavanaugh	105	63	60	885	8.4	9	5– 5	
Jackson	2	2	100	35	175	0	0– 0	

PUNTING	No.	Avg.
Hubach	63	38.0

KICKING	XP	Att.	%	FG	Att.	%
Smith	**51**	**51**	**100**	**26**	34	77

MIAMI DOLPHINS

RUSHING

Last Name	No.	Yds.	Avg.	TD
Williams	187	671	3.6	2
Nathan	60	327	5.5	1
Robiskie	78	250	3.2	2
Woodley	55	214	3.9	3
Howell	60	206	3.4	1
Bennett	46	200	4.3	0
Giaquinto	5	16	3.2	0
Testerman	1	5	5.0	0
Moore	1	3	3.0	0
Griese	1	0	0.0	0
Strock	1	−3	−3.0	0

RECEIVING

Last Name	No.	Yds.	Avg.	TD
Nathan	57	588	10	5
Moore	47	564	12	7
Harris	33	583	18	2
Williams	31	207	7	0
Giaquinto	24	192	8	1
Hardy	19	159	8	2
Rose	13	149	12	0
Robiskie	13	60	5	0
Cefalo	11	199	18	1
Lee	7	83	12	2
Howell	5	38	8	0
Bailey	4	105	26	0
Bennett	3	26	9	1

PUNT RETURNS

Last Name	No.	Yds.	Avg.	TD
Nathan	23	178	8	0
Giaquinto	7	35	5	0
Blackwood	1	0	0	0
Bessillieu	1	0	0	0

KICKOFF RETURNS

Last Name	No.	Yds.	Avg.	TD
Bessillieu	40	890	22	0
Giaquinto	9	146	16	0
Bennett	6	88	15	0
Nathan	5	102	20	0
Harris	5	89	18	0
Barnett	1	7	7	0
Allen	1	0	0	0

PASSING - PUNTING - KICKING

PASSING	Att.	Comp.	%	Yds.	Yd./Att.	TD	Int.-%	RK
Woodley	327	176	54	1850	5.7	14	17– 5	13
Griese	100	61	61	790	7.9	6	4– 4	
Strock	62	30	48	313	5.1	1	5– 8	
Moore	1	0	0	0	0.0	0	0– 0	
Nathan	1	0	0	0	0.0	0	0– 0	
Williams	1	0	0	0	0.0	0	0– 0	

PUNTING	No.	Avg.
Roberts	77	42.6

KICKING	XP	Att.	%	FG	Att.	%
von Schamann	32	32	**100**	14	23	61

BALTIMORE COLTS

RUSHING

Last Name	No.	Yds.	Avg.	TD
Dickey	176	800	4.5	11
Washington	144	502	3.5	1
Franklin	83	264	3.2	2
Sims	54	186	3.4	2
B. Jones	27	175	6.5	2
McCauley	35	133	3.8	1
Landry	7	26	3.7	1
Carr	1	−8	−8.0	0

RECEIVING

Last Name	No.	Yds.	Avg.	TD
Carr	61	924	15	5
Washington	51	494	10	3
Butler	34	574	17	2
McCauley	34	313	9	4
Dickey	25	204	8	2
McCall	18	322	18	5
Burke	14	185	13	3
Franklin	14	112	8	0
Siani	9	174	19	1
Sims	9	64	7	0
DeRoo	2	34	17	0
Garry	1	9	9	0

PUNT RETURNS

Last Name	No.	Yds.	Avg.	TD
Glasgow	23	187	8	0
Anderson	3	1	0	0

KICKOFF RETURNS

Last Name	No.	Yds.	Avg.	TD
Glasgow	33	743	23	0
Anderson	20	386	19	0
Dickey	4	86	22	0
Garry	3	55	18	0
Blackwood	2	41	21	0
LaPointe	1	18	18	0
McCauley	1	18	18	0
Hart	1	17	17	0
Sims	1	10	10	0
Foote	1	9	9	0

PASSING - PUNTING - KICKING

PASSING	Att.	Comp.	%	Yds.	Yd./Att.	TD	Int.-%	RK
B. Jones	446	248	56	3134	7.0	23	21– 5	5
Landry	47	24	51	275	5.9	2	3– 6	

PUNTING	No.	Avg.
Bragg	82	39.1

KICKING	XP	Att.	%	FG	Att.	%
Mike-Mayer	43	46	93	12	23	57

NEW YORK JETS

RUSHING

Last Name	No.	Yds.	Avg.	TD
Dierking	156	567	3.6	6
Long	115	355	3.1	6
Todd	49	330	6.7	5
Newton	59	299	5.1	0
Gaines	36	174	4.8	0
Harper	45	126	2.8	0
Darby	1	15	15.0	0
J. Jones	2	5	2.5	0
Batton	3	4	1.3	0
Ramsey	1	−15	−15.0	0

RECEIVING

Last Name	No.	Yds.	Avg.	TD
Harper	50	634	13	3
Gaines	36	310	9	3
J. Jones	25	482	19	3
Gaffney	24	397	17	2
Shuler	22	226	10	2
Newton	20	144	7	0
Long	20	137	7	0
Dierking	19	138	7	1
Walker	18	376	21	1
B. Jones	14	193	14	0
Barkum	13	244	19	1
Darby	3	48	16	1
Lewis	1	6	6	0

PUNT RETURNS

Last Name	No.	Yds.	Avg.	TD
Harper	28	242	9	0
Schroy	4	27	7	0
B. Jones	1	0	0	0

KICKOFF RETURNS

Last Name	No.	Yds.	Avg.	TD
Harper	**49**	**1070**	22	0
Darby	7	139	20	0
J. Jones	4	67	17	0
B. Jones	2	50	25	0
Shuler	2	25	13	0
Bingham	1	19	19	0
Schroy	1	17	17	0
Carter	1	12	12	0
Winkel	1	4	4	0

PASSING - PUNTING - KICKING

PASSING	Att.	Comp.	%	Yds.	Yd./Att.	TD	Int.-%	RK
Todd	479	264	55	3329	7.0	17	30– 6	14
Ramsey	2	1	50	6	3.0	0	0– 0	

PUNTING	No.	Avg.
Ramsey	73	42.4

KICKING	XP	Att.	%	FG	Att.	%
Leahy	36	36	100	14	22	64

CLEVELAND BROWNS 11-5-0 Sam Rutigliano

Scores of Each Game		
17	New England	34
7	HOUSTON	16
20	KANSAS CITY	13
34	Tampa Bay	27
16	DENVER	19
27	Seattle	3
26	GREEN BAY	21
27	PITTSBURGH	26
27	CHICAGO	21
28	Baltimore	27
13	Pittsburgh	16
31	CINCINNATI	7
17	Houston	14
17	N.Y. JETS	14
23	Minnesota	28
27	Cincinnati	24

Use Name	Pos.	Hgt.	Wgt.	Age	Int.	Pts.
Doug Dieken	OT	6'5"	252	31		
Joel Patten	OT	6'6"	240	22		
Cody Risien	OT	6'7"	255	23		
Joe DeLamielleure	OG	6'3"	245	29		
Robert Jackson	OG	6'5"	260	27		
Henry Sheppard	OG-OT	6'6"	263	27		
Tom DeLeone	C	6'2"	248	30		
Gerry Sullivan	C-OT	6'4"	250	28		
Lyle Alzado	DE	6'3"	250	31		
Cleveland Crosby	DE	6'4"	252	24		
Elvis Franks	DE	6'4"	238	23		
Marshall Harris	DE	6'6"	261	24		
Jerry Sherk	DE	6'4"	250	32		
Jerry Wilkinson (to SF)	DE	6'9"	260	24		
Henry Bradley	NT	6'2"	260	26		
Ron Crews	NT-DE	6'3"	256	23		

Use Name	Pos.	Hgt.	Wgt.	Age	Int.	Pts.
Dick Ambrose	LB	6'	228	27		
Bill Cowher	LB	6'3"	225	23		
Don Goode	LB	6'2"	231	29		
Charlie Hall	LB	6'3"	235	31	2	
Robert Jackson	LB	6'1"	230	26	2	
Clay Matthews	LB	6'2"	230	24	1	
John Mohring (from DET)	LB	6'3"	240	24		
Cliff Odom	LB	6'2"	220	22		
Autry Beamon	DB	6'1"	190	26		
Ron Bolton	DB	6'2"	170	30	6	
Clinton Burrell	DB	6'2"	192	23	5	
Thom Darden	DB	6'2"	193	30	2	
Oliver Davis	DB	6'1"	205	26	1	
Judson Flint	DB	6'	201	23		
Lawrence Johnson	DB	5'11"	204	22	1	
Clarence Scott	DB	6'	190	31	2	

Matt Miller – Knee Injury

Use Name	Pos.	Hgt.	Wgt.	Age	Int.	Pts.
Johnny Evans	QB	6'1"	197	24		
Paul McDonald	QB	6'2"	185	22		
Brian Sipe	QB	6'1"	195	31		6
Dino Hall	HB	5'7"	165	24		
Calvin Hill	HB	6'3"	227	33		36
Greg Pruitt	HB	5'10"	190	29		30
Charles White	HB	5'10"	183	22		36
Cleo Miller	FB-HB	5'11"	214	27		18
Mike Pruitt	FB	6'	225	26		36
Willis Adams	WR	6'2"	194	24		
Ricky Feacher	WR	5'10"	174	26		24
Dave Logan	WR	6'4"	216	26		24
Reggie Rucker	WR	6'2"	190	32		24
Keith Wright	WR	5'10"	175	24		18
Ozzie Newsome	TE	6'2"	232	24		18
McDonald Oden	TE	6'4"	228	22		
Curtis Weathers	TE	6'5"	220	23		
Don Cockroft	K	6'1"	195	35		87

HOUSTON OILERS 11-5-0 Bum Phillips

Scores of Each Game		
17	Pittsburgh	31
16	Cleveland	7
21	BALTIMORE	16
13	Cincinnati	10
7	SEATTLE	26
20	Kansas City	21
20	TAMPA BAY	14
23	CINCINNATI	3
20	Denver	16
38	NEW ENGLAND	34
10	Chicago	6
28	N.Y. Jets	*31
14	CLEVELAND	17
6	PITTSBURGH	0
22	Green Bay	3
20	MINNESOTA	16

Use Name	Pos.	Hgt.	Wgt.	Age	Int.	Pts.
Angelo Fields	OT	6'6"	330	22		
Leon Gray	OT	6'3"	260	28		
Conway Hayman	OT	6'3"	270	31		
Morris Towns	OT-OG	6'4"	275	26		
David Carter	OG-C	6'2"	245	27		
Ed Fisher	OG	6'3"	250	31		
Bob Young	OG	6'2"	279	37		
Greg Davidson	C	6'2"	250	22		
Carl Mauck	C	6'3"	250	33		
Jesse Baker	DE	6'5"	265	23		
Elvin Bethea	DE	6'3"	255	34		
Andy Dorris	DE	6'4"	240	29		
Mike Stensrud	DE-NT	6'5"	280	24		
Curley Culp (to DET)	NT-DT	6'1"	265	34		
Charlie Davis	NT	6'1"	275	28		
Ken Kennard	NT	6'2"	245	25		

Use Name	Pos.	Hgt.	Wgt.	Age	Int.	Pts.
Gregg Bingham	LB	6'1"	230	29		
Robert Brazile	LB	6'4"	238	27	2	
John Corker	LB	6'5"	240	21		6
Sammy Green	LB	6'2"	230	25		
Tom Henderson (from SF)	LB	6'2"	220	27	1	
Daryl Hunt	LB	6'3"	220	23		
Art Stringer	LB	6'1"	223	26		
Ted Thompson	LB	6'1"	220	27		4
Ted Washington	LB	6'1"	245	32		
Carter Hartwig	DB	6'	205	24	1	
Charles Jefferson	DB	6'	178	23		
Vernon Perry	DB	6'2"	211	26	5	
Mike Reinfeldt	DB	6'2"	195	27	4	
Greg Stemrick	DB	5'11"	185	28	4	
Jack Tatum	DB	5'10"	205	31	7	
J.C. Wilson	DB	6'	177	24	2	

George Reihner – Knee Injury
John Schumacher – Back Injury

Use Name	Pos.	Hgt.	Wgt.	Age	Int.	Pts.
Craig Bradshaw	QB	6'5"	215	23		
Gifford Nielsen	QB	6'4"	205	25		
Ken Stabler	QB	6'3"	210	34		
Earl Campbell	HB	5'11"	224	25		78
Ronnie Coleman	HB	5'10"	198	29		6
Adger Armstrong	FB	6'	210	23		
Rob Carpenter	FB-HB	6'1"	230	25		18
Booby Clark	FB	6'2"	245	29		
Tim Wilson	FB	6'3"	220	26		12
Ken Burrough	WR	6'4"	210	32		
Jeff Groth	WR	5'10"	172	23		
Billy Johnson	WR	5'9"	170	28		12
Guido Merkens (to NO)	WR-DB	6'1"	200	25		
Mike Renfro	WR	6'	184	25		6
Carl Roaches	WR	5'8"	165	26		
Tim Smith	WR	6'2"	192	23		
Mike Barber	TE	6'3"	225	27		30
Dave Casper (from OAK)	TE	6'4"	230	28		24
Rich Caster	TE	6'5"	230	31		18
Toni Fritsch	K	5'7"	180	35		83
Cliff Parsley	K	6'1"	211	25		

PITTSBURGH STEELERS 9-7-0 Chuck Noll

Scores of Each Game		
31	HOUSTON	17
20	Baltimore	17
28	Cincinnati	30
38	CHICAGO	3
23	Minnesota	17
16	CINCINNATI	17
34	OAKLAND	45
26	Cleveland	27
22	GREEN BAY	20
24	Tampa Bay	21
16	CLEVELAND	13
13	Buffalo	28
23	MIAMI	10
0	Houston	6
21	KANSAS CITY	16
17	San Diego	26

Use Name	Pos.	Hgt.	Wgt.	Age	Int.	Pts.
Larry Brown	OT	6'4"	265	31		
Jon Kolb	OT	6'2"	262	33		
Ted Petersen	OT	6'5"	244	25		
Steve Courson	OG	6'1"	260	24		
Tunch Ilkin	OG-OT	6'3"	253	22		
Tyrone McGriff	OG	6'	273	22		
Ray Pinney	OG-OT-C	6'4"	250	26		
Craig Wolfley	OG	6'1"	258	22		
Mike Webster	C	6'1"	255	28		
John Banaszak	DE	6'3"	244	30		
Tom Beasley	DE-DT	6'5"	253	26		
L.C. Greenwood	DE	6'5"	250	33		
Dwight White	DE	6'4"	255	31		
Gary Dunn	DT-DE	6'3"	247	27		
Steve Furness	DT	6'4"	255	29		
Joe Greene	DT	6'4"	260	33		

Use Name	Pos.	Hgt.	Wgt.	Age	Int.	Pts.
Robin Cole	LB	6'2"	220	24	1	
Jack Ham	LB	6'3"	225	31	2	
Jack Lambert	LB	6'4"	220	28	2	
Loren Toews	LB	6'3"	222	28		2
Zack Valentine	LB	6'2"	225	23		
Dennis Winston	LB	6'	228	24		6
Larry Anderson	DB	5'11"	177	23		
Mel Blount	DB	6'3"	205	32	4	
Marvin Cobb (to MINN)	DB	6'	188	27		
Ron Johnson	DB	5'10"	200	24	1	
Tom Moriarty	DB	6'	180	27		
Donnie Shell	DB	5'11"	190	28	7	
J.T. Thomas	DB	6'2"	196	29	2	
Mike Wagner	DB	6'1"	190	31	6	
Dwayne Woodruff	DB	5'11"	189	23	1	

Sam Davis – Knee Injury

Use Name	Pos.	Hgt.	Wgt.	Age	Int.	Pts.
Terry Bradshaw	QB	6'3"	215	31		12
Mark Malone	QB	6'4"	223	21		
Cliff Stoudt	QB	6'4"	218	25		
Rocky Bleier	HB	5'11"	210	34		12
Greg Hawthorne	HB-FB	6'2"	225	23		24
Frank Pollard	HB	5'10"	210	23		
Sidney Thornton	HB-FB	5'11"	230	25		24
Russell Davis	FB	6'1"	215	24		6
Franco Harris	FB	6'2"	225	30		36
Theo Bell	WR	5'11"	180	26		12
Jim Smith	WR	6'2"	205	25		54
John Stallworth	WR	6'2"	183	28		6
Lynn Swann	WR	6'	180	28		42
Calvin Sweeney	WR	6'2"	180	25		6
Bennie Cunningham	TE	6'4"	247	25		12
Randy Grossman	TE	6'1"	215	26		
Matt Bahr	K	5'10"	165	24		96
Craig Colquitt	K	6'2"	182	26		

CINCINNATI BENGALS 6-10-0 Forrest Gregg

Scores of Each Game		
12	TAMPA BAY	17
16	Miami	17
30	PITTSBURGH	28
10	HOUSTON	13
9	Green Bay	14
17	Pittsburgh	16
14	MINNESOTA	0
3	Houston	23
14	SAN DIEGO	31
17	Oakland	28
0	BUFFALO	14
7	Cleveland	31
20	Kansas City	6
34	BALTIMORE	33
17	Chicago	*14
24	CLEVELAND	27

*—Overtime

Use Name	Pos.	Hgt.	Wgt.	Age	Int.	Pts.
Anthony Munoz	OT	6'6"	278	22		
Mike Wilson	OT	6'5"	271	25		
Glenn Bujnoch	OG	6'5"	258	26		
Bill Glass	OG	6'4"	261	22		
Dave Lapham	OG-OT	6'4"	262	28		
Max Montoya	OG	6'5"	275	24		
Blair Bush	C	6'3"	250	23		
Blake Moore	C	6'5"	260	22		
Ross Browner	DE	6'3"	261	26		
Gary Burley	DE	6'3"	270	27		
Eddie Edwards	DE	6'5"	261	26		
Mike St. Clair	DE	6'5"	250	26		
Mike White	DE-NT	6'5"	267	23		
Rod Horn	NT	6'4"	268	23		
Wilson Whitley	NT	6'3"	265	25		

Use Name	Pos.	Hgt.	Wgt.	Age	Int.	Pts.
Glenn Cameron	LB	6'2"	228	27	3	
Tom Dinkel	LB	6'3"	235	24		
Bo Harris	LB	6'3"	226	27		
Jim LeClair	LB	6'2"	234	29		
Andrew Melontree	LB	6'4"	228	22		
Rick Razzano	LB	5'11"	227	24		
Ron Simpkins	LB	6'1"	235	22		
Reggie Williams	LB	6'1"	228	25	2	2
Louis Breeden	DB	5'11"	185	26	7	
Greg Bright	DB	6'	208	23	1	
Jim Browner	DB	6'1"	207	24		
Ray Griffin	DB	5'10"	186	24	2	12
Jo Jo Heath	DB	5'10"	182	23		
Bryan Hicks	DB	6'	192	23	1	
Dick Jauron	DB	6'	190	29	[illegible]	
Ken Riley	DB	6'	183	33	3	
Shafer Suggs (from NYJ)	DB	6'1"	204	27		

Howie Kurnick – Knee Injury

Use Name	Pos.	Hgt.	Wgt.	Age	Int.	Pts.
Ken Anderson	QB	6'1"	208	31		
Turk Schonert	QB	6'1"	185	23		
Jack Thompson	QB	6'3"	217	24		6
Charles Alexander	HB-FB	6'1"	226	23		12
Archie Griffin	HB	5'9"	184	26		
Deacon Turner	HB	5'11"	210	25		6
Pete Johnson	FB	6'	249	26		42
Nathan Poole	FB	5'9"	205	23		
Alton Alexis	WR	6'	184	22		
Don Bass	WR	6'2"	220	25		36
Isaac Curtis	WR	6'	192	29		18
Steve Kreider	WR	6'3"	192	22		
Mike Levenseller	WR	6'1"	184	24		
Pat McInally	WR	6'6"	212	27		12
Cle Montgomery	WR	5'8"	183	24		
Jim Corbett	TE	6'4"	220	25		
M. L. Harris	TE	6'5"	238	26		
Dan Ross	TE	6'4"	235	23		24
Jim Breech	K	5'6"	155	24		23
Ian Sunter	K	6'1"	215	28		48
Sandro Vitiello	K	6'2"	197	22		1

CLEVELAND BROWNS

RUSHING

Last Name	No.	Yds.	Avg.	TD
M. Pruitt	249	1034	4.2	6
White	86	279	3.2	5
Miller	28	139	5.0	3
G. Pruitt	40	117	2.9	0
Sipe	20	55	2.8	1
D. Hall	2	26	13.0	0
Newsome	2	13	6.5	0
Hill	1	11	11.0	0
Adams	2	7	3.5	0
McDonald	3	−2	−0.7	0
Evans	3	−6	−2.0	0

RECEIVING

Last Name	No.	Yds.	Avg.	TD
M. Pruitt	63	471	8	0
Rucker	52	768	15	4
Logan	51	822	16	4
Newsome	51	594	12	3
G. Pruitt	50	444	9	5
Hill	27	383	14	6
White	17	153	9	1
Feacher	10	244	24	4
Adams	8	165	21	0
Wright	3	62	21	3
Oden	3	18	6	0
Miller	2	8	4	0

PUNT RETURNS

Last Name	No.	Yds.	Avg.	TD
Wright	29	129	4	0
D. Hall	6	41	7	0

KICKOFF RETURNS

Last Name	No.	Yds.	Avg.	TD
Wright	25	576	23	0
D. Hall	32	691	22	0
Miller	2	22	11	0
White	1	20	20	0
Flint	1	0	0	0
B. Jackson	1	0	0	0
Darden	1	−1	−1	0

PASSING - PUNTING - KICKING

PASSING	Att.	Comp.	%	Yds.	Yd./Att.	TD	Int.–%	RK
Sipe	554	337	61	4132	7.5	30	14– 3	1

PUNTING	No.	Avg.
Evans	66	38.3

KICKING	XP	Att.	%	FG	Att.	%
Cockroft	39	44	89	16	26	62

HOUSTON OILERS

RUSHING

Last Name	No.	Yds.	Avg.	TD
Campbell	**373**	**1934**	**5.2**	**13**
Carpenter	97	359	3.7	3
T. Wilson	66	257	3.9	1
Coleman	14	82	5.9	1
Renfro	1	12	12.0	0
Casper	2	8	4.0	0
Clark	1	3	3.0	0
Barber	1	1	1.0	0
Johnson	2	1	0.5	0
Nielsen	1	0	0.0	0
Stabler	15	−22	−1.5	0

RECEIVING

Last Name	No.	Yds.	Avg.	TD
Barber	59	712	12	5
Casper	56	796	14	4
Carpenter	43	346	8	0
Renfro	35	459	13	1
Johnson	31	343	11	2
T. Wilson	30	170	6	1
Caster	27	341	13	3
Coleman	16	168	11	0
Campbell	11	47	4	0
Burrough	4	91	23	0
Groth	4	47	12	0
Smith	2	21	11	0

PUNT RETURNS

Last Name	No.	Yds.	Avg.	TD
Roaches	47	384	8	0
Groth	1	0	0	0

KICKOFF RETURNS

Last Name	No.	Yds.	Avg.	TD
Roaches	37	746	20	0
Growth	12	216	18	0
Barber	1	12	12	0
Carpenter	1	7	7	0
Bingham	1	0	0	0
Smith	1	0	0	0

PASSING - PUNTING - KICKING

PASSING	Att.	Comp.	%	Yds.	Yd./Att.	TD	Int.–%	RK
Stabler	457	293	**64**	3202	7.0	13	28– 6	11
Campbell	2	1	50	57	28.5	1	0– 0	
Nielsen	4	2	50	12	3.0	1	0– 0	

PUNTING	No.	Avg.
Parsley	67	40.7

KICKING	XP	Att.	%	FG	Att.	%
Fritsch	26	27	96	19	24	**79**
Thompson	4	4	100			

PITTSBURGH STEELERS

RUSHING

Last Name	No.	Yds.	Avg.	TD
Harris	208	789	3.8	4
Bleier	78	340	4.4	1
Thornton	78	325	4.2	3
Hawthorne	63	226	3.6	4
Davis	33	132	4.0	1
Bradshaw	36	111	3.1	2
Stoudt	9	35	3.9	0
Colquitt	1	17	17.0	0
Pollard	4	16	4.0	0
Smith	1	−1	−1.0	0
Swann	1	−4	−4.0	0

RECEIVING

Last Name	No.	Yds.	Avg.	TD
Swann	44	710	16	7
Smith	37	711	19	9
Harris	30	196	7	2
Bell	29	748	26	2
Grossman	23	293	13	0
Bleier	21	174	8	1
Cunningham	18	232	13	2
Thornton	15	131	9	1
Sweeney	12	282	24	1
Hawthorne	12	158	13	0
Stallworth	9	197	22	1

PUNT RETURNS

Last Name	No.	Yds.	Avg.	TD
Bell	34	339	10	0
Smith	7	28	4	0
Cobb	3	19	6	0
Pollard	1	5	5	0

KICKOFF RETURNS

Last Name	No.	Yds.	Avg.	TD
Pollard	22	494	23	0
Anderson	14	379	27	0
Hawthorne	9	169	19	0
Davis	9	160	18	0
Bell	3	50	17	0
Sweeney	3	42	14	0
Cobb	1	19	19	0
Thornton	1	15	15	0
Winston	1	13	13	0
Blount	1	9	9	0
Valentine	1	0	0	0

PASSING - PUNTING - KICKING

PASSING	Att.	Comp.	%	Yds.	Yd./Att.	TD	Int.–%	RK
Bradshaw	424	218	51	3339	7.9	24	22– 5	6
Stoudt	60	32	53	493	8.2	2	2– 3	

PUNTING	No.	Avg.
Colquitt	61	40.7
Bradshaw	5	34.6

KICKING	XP	Att.	%	FG	Att.	%
Bahr	39	42	93	19	28	68

CINCINNATI BENGALS

RUSHING

Last Name	No.	Yds.	Avg.	TD
Johnson	186	747	4.0	6
Alexander	169	702	4.2	2
A. Griffin	85	260	3.1	0
Turner	30	130	4.3	0
Anderson	16	122	7.6	0
Thompson	18	84	4.7	1
Montgomery	1	12	12.0	0
Levenseller	1	6	6.0	0
Poole	5	6	1.2	0
M. Harris	1	0	0.0	0
McInally	1	0	0.0	0

RECEIVING

Last Name	No.	Yds.	Avg.	TD
Ross	56	724	13	4
Curtis	43	610	14	3
Alexander	36	192	5	0
Bass	32	409	13	6
A. Griffin	28	196	7	0
Johnson	21	172	8	1
McInally	18	269	15	2
Kreider	17	272	16	0
Turner	12	73	6	1
M. Harris	10	137	14	0
Corbett	3	28	9	0
Levenseller	2	30	15	0
Poole	2	−4	−2	0
Munoz	1	−6	−6	0

PUNT RETURNS

Last Name	No.	Yds.	Avg.	TD
Montgomery	31	223	7	0
Heath	6	29	5	0
Bright	1	0	0	0
Williams	1	0	0	0

KICKOFF RETURNS

Last Name	No.	Yds.	Avg.	TD
Montgomery	44	843	19	0
Turner	9	173	19	0
Hicks	5	87	17	0
Heath	3	51	17	0
Simpkins	3	8	3	0
J. Browner	2	10	5	0
Kreider	1	19	19	0
Poole	1	8	8	0

PASSING - PUNTING - KICKING

PASSING	Att.	Comp.	%	Yds.	Yd./Att.	TD	Int.–%	RK
Anderson	275	166	60	1778	6.5	6	13– 5	12
Thompson	234	115	49	1324	5.7	11	**12–** 5	15
Kreider	1	0	0	0	0.0	0	0– 0	

PUNTING	No.	Avg.
McInally	83	40.8

KICKING	XP	Att.	%	FG	Att.	%
Sunter	15	15	**100**	11	20	55
Breech	11	12	92	4	7	57
Vitiello	1	1	100	0	2	0

SAN DIEGO CHARGERS 11-5-0 Don Coryell

Scores of Each Game		
34	Seattle	13
30	OAKLAND	*24
30	Denver	13
24	Kansas City	7
24	BUFFALO	26
24	Oakland	38
44	N.Y. GIANTS	7
31	Dallas	42
31	Cincinnati	14
13	DENVER	20
20	KANSAS CITY	7
27	Miami	*24
22	PHILADELPHIA	21
17	Washington	40
21	SEATTLE	14
26	PITTSBURGH	17

Use Name	Pos.	Hgt.	Wgt.	Age	Int.	Pts.
Dan Audick	OT-OG	6'3"	253	25		
Chuck Loewen	OT-OG	6'3"	259	23		
Billy Shields	OT	6'7"	275	27		
Russ Washington	OT	6'6"	284	33		
Ralph Perretta (from NYG)	OG-C	6'2"	251	27		
Ed White	OG	6'2"	271	33		
Doug Wilkerson	OG	6'2"	262	33		
Don Macek	C	6'3"	253	26		
Bob Rush	C-OT	6'5"	264	24		
Fred Dean	DE	6'3"	230	28		
Leroy Jones	DE	6'8"	260	29		
John Lee	DE	6'2"	259	27		
Wilbur Young	DE-DT	6'6"	290	31		
Charles DeJurnett	DT	6'4"	260	28		
Gary Johnson	DT	6'2"	252	28		
Louie Kelcher	DT	6'5"	282	27	1	
Bob Horn	LB	6'3"	230	26		
Keith King	LB	6'4"	230	25	2	
Jim Laslavic	LB	6'2"	236	28		
Woodrow Lowe	LB	6'	227	26	3	6
Carl McGee	LB	6'3"	228	24		
Ray Preston	LB	6'	218	26		
Cliff Thrift	LB	6'2"	232	24	1	
Willie Buchanon	DB	6'	185	29	2	
Jerome Dove	DB	6'2"	193	26		
Frank Duncan	DB	6'1"	188	23		
Glen Edwards	DB	6	183	33	5	6
Mike Fuller	DB	5'9"	182	27		
Pete Shaw	DB	5'10"	178	26	4	
Hal Stringert	DB	5'11"	187	28	1	
Mike Williams	DB	5'10"	179	26	1	
Dan Fouts	QB	6'3	210	29		12
James Harris	QB	6'3"	221	33		
Ed Luther	QB	6'3"	206	23		
Hank Bauer	HB	5'10"	200	26		6
Mike Thomas	HB	5'11"	190	27		18
Clarence Williams	HB	5'9"	195	25		24
John Cappelletti	FB	6'1"	225	28		30
LaRue Harrington	FB	6'	210	23		
Chuck Muncie (from NO)	FB-HB	6'3"	233	27		36
Booker Russell	FB	6'2"	235	24		
John Floyd	WR	6'1"	195	23		6
John Jefferson	WR	6'1"	198	24		78
Charlie Joiner	WR	5'11"	183	32		24
Ron Smith	WR	6'	185	23		
Greg McCrary	TE	6'3"	235	28		12
Kellen Winslow	TE	6'5"	252	22		54
Rolf Benirschke	K	6'	175	25		118
Rick Partridge	K	6'1	175	23		
Mike Wood	K	5'11"	199	25		

Jim Nicholson – Knee Injury

OAKLAND RAIDERS 11-5-0 Tom Flores

Scores of Each Game		
27	Kansas City	14
24	San Diego	*30
24	WASHINGTON	21
7	Buffalo	24
17	KANSAS CITY	31
38	SAN DIEGO	24
45	Pittsburgh	34
33	SEATTLE	14
16	MIAMI	10
28	CINCINNATI	17
19	Seattle	17
7	Philadelphia	10
9	DENVER	3
13	DALLAS	19
24	Denver	21
33	N.Y. Giants	17

Use Name	Pos.	Hgt.	Wgt.	Age	Int.	Pts.
Bruce Davis	OT-OG	6'6"	280	24		
Henry Lawrence	OT	6'4"	270	28		
Lindsey Mason	OT	6'5"	265	25		
Art Shell	OT	6'5"	280	33		
Mickey Marvin	OG	6'4"	270	24		
Steve Sylvester	OG-C-OT	6'4"	260	27		
Gene Upshaw	OG	6'5"	255	35		
Dave Dalby	C	6'2"	250	29		
Dave Browning	DE	6'5"	245	24		
Joe Campbell (from NO)	DE-MG	6'6"	254	25		
Cedrick Hardman	DE	6'3"	245	31		
Willie Jones	DE	6'4"	245	22		6
John Matuszak	DE	6'8"	280	29		
Reggie Kinlaw	NT	6'2"	240	23		
Alva Liles (to DET)	NT-DT	6'3"	255	24		
Dave Pear	NT	6'2"	250	27		
Jeff Barnes	LB	6'2"	215	25		
Mario Celotto	LB	6'3"	225	24		
Ted Hendricks	LB	6'7"	225	32	3	2
Rod Martin	LB	6'2"	210	26	2	6
Randy McClanahan	LB	6'5"	225	25	1	
Matt Millen	LB	6'2"	260	22	2	
Bob Nelson	LB	6'4"	230	27	1	
Mike Davis	DB	6'2"	200	24	3	
Dwight Harrison	DB	6'1"	180	31		
Lester Hayes	DB	6'	195	25	**13**	6
Monte Jackson	DB	5'11"	200	27	1	
Odis McKinney	DB	6'2"	190	23	3	
Keith Moody	DB	5'10"	175	27		
Dwayne O'Steen	DB	6'1"	195	25	3	
Burgess Owens	DB	6'2"	200	29	3	6
Mike Spivey (to NO)	DB	6'	200	26		
Kyle Grossart	QB	6'4	210	25		
Dan Pastorini	QB	6'3	205	31		
Jim Plunkett	QB	6'3"	205	32		12
Marc Wilson	QB	6'6"	205	23		
I.M. Hipp	HB	5'10	200	24		
Kenny King	HB	5'11"	205	23		24
Ira Matthews	HB-WR	5'8	175	23		
Art Whittington	HB	5'11"	180	24		24
Todd Christensen	FB-TE	6'3	230	24		6
Derrick Jensen	FB	6'1	225	24		6
Mark van Eeghen	FB	6'2"	225	28		30
Morris Bradshaw	WR	6	195	27		6
Cliff Branch	WR	5'11	170	32		42
Bob Chandler	WR	6'	180	31		60
Rich Martini	WR	6'2"	185	24		
Ray Chester	TE	6'3	235	32		24
Derrick Ramsey	TE	6'5"	225	23		
Chris Bahr	K	5'9"	175	27		98
Ray Guy	K	6'3"	190	30		

Mark Meseroll – Injury
Jeff Winans – Injury
Monte Johnson – Knee Injury
Charlie Phillips – Knee Injury

KANSAS CITY CHIEFS 8-8-0 Marv Levy

Scores of Each Game		
14	OAKLAND	27
16	SEATTLE	17
13	Cleveland	20
7	SAN DIEGO	24
31	Oakland	17
21	HOUSTON	20
23	Denver	17
20	DETROIT	17
24	BALTIMORE	31
31	Seattle	30
7	San Diego	20
21	St. Louis	13
6	CINCINNATI	20
31	DENVER	14
16	Pittsburgh	21
38	Baltimore	28

Use Name	Pos.	Hgt.	Wgt.	Age	Int.	Pts.
Charlie Getty	OT	6'4"	269	28		
Matt Herkenhoff	OT	6'4"	270	29		
Jim Rourke	OT-OG-C	6'5"	264	23		
Franky Smith	OT	6'6"	279	26		
Brad Budde	OG	6'4"	255	22		
Tom Condon	OG	6'3"	254	27		
Bob Simmons	OG-OT	6'4"	260	26		
Rod Walters (to MIA, DET)	OG	6'3"	258	26		
Charlie Ane	C	6'1"	237	28		
Jack Rudnay	C	6'3"	242	32		
Mike Bell	DE	6'4"	255	23		
Sylvester Hicks	DE	6'4"	252	25		
Dave Lindstrom	DE	6'6"	257	25		
Jerry Meyers	DE	6'4"	253	26		
Art Still	DE	6'7"	252	24		
Ken Kremer	NT-DE	6'4"	250	23		
Dino Mangiero	NT	6'2"	265	21	1	
Don Parrish	NT	6'2"	259	25		
Jerry Blanton	LB	6'1"	225	24		
Tom Howard	LB	6'2"	208	26		6
Charles Jackson	LB	6'2"	220	25		
Kelly Kirchbaum	LB	6'2"	240	23		
Frank Manumaleuga	LB	6'2"	245	24	3	6
Whitney Paul	LB	6'3"	220	26	1	6
Cal Peterson	LB	6'3"	220	27		
Clarence Sanders	LB	6'4"	230	27		
Gary Spani	LB	6'2"	230	24	1	12
Gary Barbaro	DB	6'4"	204	26	10	
M.L. Carter	DB	5'9"	173	24		
Herb Christopher	DB	5'10"	190	26	2	
Paul Dombroski	DB	6'	185	24	1	
Gary Green	DB	5'11"	184	24	2	
Eric Harris	DB	6'3"	191	25	7	
Jerry Reese	DB	6'3"	192	25		
Donovan Rose	DB	6'1"	180	23		
Tom Clements	QB	6'	183	27		
Steve Fuller	QB	6'4"	198	23		24
Bill Kenney	QB	6'4"	210	25		
Horace Belton	HB	5'8"	200	25		12
Earl Gant	HB	6	207	23		
Tony Reed	HB	5'11"	197	25		6
Ken Talton	HB	6'	205	24		
Jim Hadnot	FB	6'2"	244	23		12
Ted McKnight	FB-HB	6'1"	216	26		18
Arnold Morgado	FB-HB	6'	205	27		30
Carlos Carson	WR	5'10"	172	21		
Bubba Garcia	WR	5'11"	185	22		6
Henry Marshall	WR	6'2"	214	26		36
Stan Rome	WR	6'5"	205	24		
J.T. Smith	WR	6'2"	185	24		24
Ed Beckman	TE	6'4"	226	25		
Al Dixon	TE	6'5"	220	26		6
Tony Samuels (to TB)	TE	6'4"	233	25		12
Mike Williams	TE	6'3"	222	22		6
Bob Grupp	K	5'11"	193	25		
Nick Lowery	K	6'4"	190	24		97

Alois Blackwell – Injured

DENVER BRONCOS 8-8-0 Red Miller

Scores of Each Game		
6	Philadelphia	27
41	DALLAS	20
13	SAN DIEGO	30
14	New England	23
19	Cleveland	16
20	WASHINGTON	17
17	KANSAS CITY	23
14	N.Y. Giants	9
16	HOUSTON	20
20	San Diego	13
31	N.Y. JETS	24
36	SEATTLE	20
3	Oakland	9
14	Kansas City	31
21	OAKLAND	24
25	Seattle	17

Use Name	Pos.	Hgt.	Wgt.	Age	Int.	Pts.
Kelvin Clark	OT	6'3"	245	24		
Claudie Minor	OT	6'4"	275	29		
Dave Studdard	OT	6'4"	255	24		
Tom Glassic	OG	6'3"	250	26		
Paul Howard	OG	6'3"	260	29		
Glenn Hyde	OG	6'3"	252	29		
Arland Thompson	OG	6'3"	265	22		
Keith Bishop	C-OG	6'3"	260	23		
Bill Bryan	C	6'2"	244	25		
Greg Boyd	DE	6'6"	280	27		
Barney Chavous	DE	6'3"	245	29		
Rulon Jones	DE	6'6"	260	22		2
Brison Manor	DE	6'4"	248	28		
Rubin Carter	NT	6'	253	27		
Don Latimer	NT	6'3"	253	25	1	6
Laval Short	NT	6'3"	250	21		
Greg Bracelin	LB	6'1"	218	23		
Larry Evans	LB	6'2"	220	27	1	
Randy Gradishar	LB	6'3"	231	28	2	6
Tom Jackson	LB	5'11"	228	29		
Rob Nairne	LB	6'4"	220	26	1	
Joe Rizzo	LB	6'1"	220	29		
Jim Ryan	LB	6'1"	212	23	1	
Art Smith	LB	6'1"	222	24		
Steve Foley	DB	6'2"	190	26	4	
Mike Harden	DB	6'	188	22		
Maurice Harvey	DB	5'10"	190	24	1	
Bernard Jackson (to SD)	DB	6'	180	30	1	
Aaron Kyle	DB	5'11"	185	26		
Perry Smith	DB	6'1"	190	29	2	
Bill Thompson	DB	6'1"	197	33	2	6
Louis Wright	DB	6'2"	200	27		
Jeff Knapple	QB	6'2"	200	24		
Craig Morton	QB	6'4"	211	37		6
Matt Robinson	QB	6'2"	196	25		18
Otis Armstrong	HB	5'10"	196	29		24
Rob Lytle	HB-FB	6'1"	195	25		6
Ben Norman	HB	6'	212	25		
Dave Preston	HB	5'10"	195	25		24
Jim Jensen	FB	6'3"	230	26		18
Jon Keyworth	FB	6'3"	230	29		6
Larry Brunson	WR	5'11"	180	31		
Emery Moorehead	WR	6'2"	210	26		
Haven Moses	WR	6'3"	201	34		24
Rick Upchurch	WR	5'10"	176	28		18
Steve Watson	WR	6'4"	192	23		
Ron Egloff	TE	6'5"	227	24		
Riley Odoms	TE	6'4"	230	30		36
James Wright	TE	6'3"	240	24		
Luke Prestridge	K	6'4"	235	23		
Fred Steinfort	K	5'11"	180	26		110

Larry Canada – Knee Injury
Bob Swenson – Broken Arm

SEATTLE SEAHAWKS 4-12-0 Jack Patera

Scores of Each Game		
13	SAN DIEGO	34
17	Kansas City	16
31	NEW ENGLAND	37
14	Washington	0
26	Houston	7
3	CLEVELAND	27
27	N.Y. Jets	17
14	Oakland	33
20	PHILADELPHIA	27
30	KANSAS CITY	31
17	OAKLAND	19
20	Denver	36
7	Dallas	51
21	N.Y. GIANTS	27
14	San Diego	21
17	DENVER	25

Use Name	Pos.	Hgt.	Wgt.	Age	Int.	Pts.
Steve August	OT	6'5"	254	25		
Louis Bullard	OT	6'6"	265	24		
Ron Essink	OT-TE	6'6"	246	22		6
Andre Hines	OT	6'6"	275	22		
Tom Lynch	OG	6'5"	260	25		
Bob Newton	OG	6'4"	260	31		
Jeff Sevy	OG	6'5"	260	29		
Art Kuehn	C	6'3"	255	27		
John Yarno	C	6'5"	251	25		
Fred Anderson	DE	6'4"	235	25		
Mark Bell	DE	6'4"	240	23		
Terry Dion	DE	6'6"	254	22		
Jacob Green	DE	6'3"	247	23		
Bill Gregory	DE	6'5"	260	30		
Bill Cooke	DT	6'5"	250	29		
Robert Hardy	DT	6'2"	250	24		
Manu Tuiasosopo	DT	6'3"	252	23		
Terry Beeson	LB	6'3"	240	24		
Keith Butler	LB	6'4"	225	24	2	
Michael Jackson	LB	6'1"	220	23	2	
Joe Norman	LB	6'1"	220	23	1	
Terry Rennaker	LB	6'6"	225	22		
Tim Walker	LB	6'1"	230	22		
Dave Brown	DB	6'1"	190	27	6	
Don Dufek	DB	6'	195	26		
John Harris	DB	6'2"	200	24	6	
Kerry Justin	DB	5'11"	175	25	1	
Will Lewis	DB	5'9"	185	22		6
Vic Minor	DB	6'	198	21	1	
Keith Simpson	DB	6'1"	195	24	3	
Cornell Webster	DB	6'	180	25	1	
Sam Adkins	QB	6'2"	214	25		
Dave Krieg	QB	6'1"	185	21		
Jim Zorn	QB	6'2"	200	27		6
Dan Doornink	HB-FB	6'3"	210	24		30
Al Hunter	HB	5'11"	195	25		
Lawrence McCutcheon (from DEN)	HB-FB	6'1"	205	30		24
Jeff Moore	HB	6'	195	24		
Sherman Smith	HB	6'4"	225	25		6
Larry Brinson	FB	6'	214	26		6
Jim Jodat	FB	5'11"	213	26		36
Jim Walsh	FB	5'11"	220	23		
Jessie Green	WR	6'3"	194	26		6
Steve Largent	WR	5'11"	184	25		36
Sam McCullum	WR	6'2"	190	27		36
Steve Raible	WR	6'2"	195	26		
Mark Bell	TE	6'4"	235	23		
John Sawyer	TE	6'2"	230	27		
Effren Herrera	K	5'9"	190	29		93
Herman Weaver	K	6'4"	210	31		

Dennis Boyd – Broken Arm
Pete Cronan – Neck Injury
Steve Myer – Back Injury
Brian Peets – Broken Leg

*—Overtime

SAN DIEGO CHARGERS

RUSHING

Last Name	No.	Yds.	Avg.	TD
Muncie	175	827	4.7	6
Thomas	118	484	4.1	3
Cappelletti	101	364	3.6	5
C. Williams	97	258	2.7	3
Russell	8	41	5.1	0
Bauer	10	34	3.4	1
Jefferson	1	16	16.0	0
Fouts	23	15	0.7	2
Luther	3	5	1.7	0
Fuller	2	0	0.0	0
Partridge	3	0	0.0	0
Harrington	4	−7	−1.8	0

RECEIVING

Last Name	No.	Yds.	Avg.	TD
Winslow	**89**	1290	15	9
Jefferson	82	**1340**	16	**13**
Joiner	71	1132	16	4
Muncie	31	259	8	0
Thomas	29	218	8	0
C. Williams	26	230	9	1
Cappelletti	13	112	9	0
McCrary	11	106	10	2
Smith	4	48	12	0
Floyd	1	31	31	1

PUNT RETURNS

Last Name	No.	Yds.	Avg.	TD
Fuller	30	298	10	0
Shaw	5	20	4	0
Edwards	4	17	4	0
Floyd	1	0	0	0
Horn	1	0	0	0

KICKOFF RETURNS

Last Name	No.	Yds.	Avg.	TD
Muncie	16	344	22	0
Fuller	15	289	19	0
Smith	10	186	19	0
Duncan	5	85	17	0
Bauer	2	37	19	0
Laslavac	2	26	13	0
Russell	1	19	19	0
Cappelletti	1	0	0	0
Jefferson	1	0	0	0

PASSING - PUNTING - KICKING

PASSING	Att.	Comp.	%	Yds.	Yd./Att.	TD	Int.–%	RK
Fouts	**589**	**348**	59	**4715**	8.0	**30**	24– 4	2
Luther	3	2	67	26	8.7	0	1– 33	
Thomas	2	0	0	0	0.0	0	1– 50	

PUNTING	No.	Avg.
Partridge	60	39.1

KICKING	XP	Att.	%	FG	Att.	%
Benirschke	46	48	96	24	36	67

OAKLAND RAIDERS

RUSHING

Last Name	No.	Yds.	Avg.	TD
van Eeghen	222	838	3.8	5
King	172	761	4.4	4
Whittington	91	299	3.3	3
Plunkett	28	141	5.0	2
Guy	3	38	12.7	0
Jensen	14	30	2.1	0
Pastorini	4	24	6.0	0
Matthews	5	11	2.2	0
Wilson	1	3	3.0	0
Branch	1	1	1.0	0

RECEIVING

Last Name	No.	Yds.	Avg.	TD
Chandler	49	786	16	10
Branch	44	858	20	7
van Eeghen	29	259	9	0
Chester	28	366	13	4
King	22	145	7	0
Whittington	19	205	11	0
Jensen	7	87	12	0
Bradshaw	6	132	22	1
Ramsey	5	117	23	0
Matthews	3	33	11	0
Martini	1	36	36	0

PUNT RETURNS

Last Name	No.	Yds.	Avg.	TD
Matthews	**48**	421	9	0
McKinney	1	0	0	0

KICKOFF RETURNS

Last Name	No.	Yds.	Avg.	TD
Matthews	29	585	20	0
Whittington	21	392	19	1
Moody	8	150	19	0
Jensen	1	33	33	1
Christensen	1	10	10	0
Ramsey	1	10	10	0
Hayes	1	0	0	0

PASSING - PUNTING - KICKING

PASSING	Att.	Comp.	%	Yds.	Yd./Att.	TD	Int.–%	RK
Plunkett	320	165	52	2299	7.2	18	16– 5	9
Pastorini	130	66	51	932	7.2	5	8– 6	
Guy	1	1	100	32	32.0	0	0– 0	
Wilson	5	3	60	31	6.2	0	0– 0	

PUNTING	No.	Avg.
Guy	71	43.6

KICKING	XP	Att.	%	FG	Att.	%
Bahr	41	44	93	19	**37**	51

KANSAS CITY CHIEFS

RUSHING

Last Name	No.	Yds.	Avg.	TD
McKnight	206	693	3.4	3
Fuller	60	274	4.6	4
Belton	68	273	4.0	2
Hadnot	76	244	3.2	2
Reed	68	180	2.6	0
Morgado	47	120	2.6	4
Carson	2	41	20.5	0
Gant	9	32	3.6	0
Marshall	3	22	7.3	0
Kenney	8	8	1.0	0
Clements	2	0	0.0	0
Grupp	3	−14	−4.7	0

RECEIVING

Last Name	No.	Yds.	Avg.	TD
Marshall	47	799	17	6
J. Smith	46	655	14	2
Reed	44	422	10	1
McKnight	38	320	8	0
Hadnot	15	97	7	0
Gant	9	68	8	0
Samuels	8	110	14	2
Dixon	7	115	16	1
Belton	5	94	19	0
Carson	5	68	14	0
Morgado	5	27	5	1
Rome	3	58	19	0
Garcia	3	27	9	1
Williams	2	9	5	1

PUNT RETURNS

Last Name	No.	Yds.	Avg.	TD
J. Smith	40	**581**	**15**	**2**

KICKOFF RETURNS

Last Name	No.	Yds.	Avg.	TD
Carson	40	917	23	0
Belton	6	110	18	0
Williams	4	79	20	0
Gant	3	44	15	0
Beckman	3	38	13	0
Budde	3	28	9	0
Morgado	2	33	17	0
Samuels	1	10	10	0
Dixon	1	0	0	0

PASSING - PUNTING - KICKING

PASSING	Att.	Comp.	%	Yds.	Yd./Att.	TD	Int.–%	RK
Fuller	320	193	60	2250	7.0	10	**12**– 4	4
Kenney	69	37	54	542	7.9	5	2– 3	
Clements	12	7	58	77	6.4	0	0– 0	

PUNTING	No.	Avg.
Grupp	**84**	39.5

KICKING	XP	Att.	%	FG	Att.	%
Lowery	37	37	**100**	20	26	77

DENVER BRONCOS

RUSHING

Last Name	No.	Yds.	Avg.	TD
Jensen	101	476	4.7	2
Armstrong	106	470	4.4	3
Preston	111	385	3.5	4
Lytle	57	223	3.9	1
Keyworth	38	127	3.3	1
Upchurch	5	49	9.8	0
Robinson	21	47	2.2	3
Morton	21	29	1.4	1
Moorehead	2	7	3.5	0
Knapple	6	0	0.0	0

RECEIVING

Last Name	No.	Yds.	Avg.	TD
Jensen	49	377	8	1
Upchurch	46	605	13	3
Odoms	39	590	15	6
Moses	38	674	18	4
Preston	35	309	9	0
Lytle	18	177	10	0
Keyworth	15	87	6	0
Armstrong	7	23	3	0
Watson	6	146	24	0
Egloff	6	85	14	0
Brunson	1	15	15	0

PUNT RETURNS

Last Name	No.	Yds.	Avg.	TD
Upchurch	37	353	10	0
Harden	2	36	18	0
Brunson	2	12	6	0
Preston	1	7	7	0

KICKOFF RETURNS

Last Name	No.	Yds.	Avg.	TD
Brunson	40	923	23	0
Harden	12	214	18	0
B. Jackson	9	149	17	0
Preston	5	106	21	0
Lytle	1	19	19	0
Moorehead	1	18	18	0
Jensen	1	5	5	0
Watson	1	5	5	0
Ryan	1	0	0	0

PASSING - PUNTING - KICKING

PASSING	Att	Comp.	%	Yds.	Yd./Att.	TD	Int.–%	RK
Morton	301	183	61	2150	7.1	12	13– 4	3
Robinson	162	78	48	942	5.8	2	12– 7	
Knapple	4	1	25	15	3.8	0	0– 0	

PUNTING	No.	Avg.
Prestridge	70	**43.9**

KICKING	XP	Att.	%	FG	Att.	%
Steinfort	32	33	97	**26**	34	77

SEATTLE SEAHAWKS

RUSHING

Last Name	No.	Yds.	Avg.	TD
Jodat	155	632	4.1	5
Doornink	100	344	3.4	3
McCutcheon	52	254	4.9	3
Zorn	44	214	4.9	1
Moore	60	202	3.4	0
Smith	23	94	4.1	0
Brinson	16	57	3.6	1
Adkins	6	18	3.0	0
Hunter	9	14	1.6	0
Walsh	2	4	2.0	0
Largent	1	2	2.0	0

RECEIVING

Last Name	No.	Yds.	Avg.	TD
Largent	66	1064	16	6
McCullum	62	874	14	6
Sawyer	36	410	11	0
Doornink	31	237	8	2
Jodat	26	190	7	1
Moore	25	231	9	0
Raible	16	232	15	0
McCutcheon	9	76	8	1
Smith	6	72	12	1
Je. Green	4	47	12	0
Hunter	3	40	13	0
Bell	1	13	13	0
Brinson	1	9	9	0
Herrera	1	9	9	0
Essink	1	2	2	1

PUNT RETURNS

Last Name	No.	Yds.	Avg.	TD
Lewis	41	349	9	1

KICKOFF RETURNS

Last Name	No.	Yds.	Avg.	TD
Lewis	25	585	23	0
Webster	21	406	19	0
Je. Green	15	274	18	0
Hunter	11	213	19	0
Moore	1	11	11	0

PASSING - PUNTING - KICKING

PASSING	Att.	Comp.	%	Yds.	Yd./Att.	TD	Int.–%	RK
Zorn	488	276	57	3346	6.9	17	20– 4	10
Adkins	23	10	44	136	5.9	1	3– 13	
Krieg	2	0	0	0	0.0	0	0– 0	
McCutcheon	2	1	50	12	6.0	0	0– 0	
Weaver	2	0	0	0	0.0	0	0– 0	

PUNTING	No.	Avg.
Weaver	67	41.8
Herrera	1	29.0

KICKING	XP	Att.	%	FG	Att.	%
Herrera	33	33	**100**	20	31	65

1980 N.F.C. — PLAYOFFS

December 28 at Irving, Tex. (Attendance 64,533)

SCORING

LOS ANGELES	6	7	0	0–13
DALLAS	3	10	14	7–34

First Quarter
- Dal. Septien 28 yard field goal
- L.A. Thomas, 1 yard run
  PAT–Kick failed

Second Quarter
- Dal. Septien, 29 yard field goal
- L.A. Dennard, 21 yard pass from Ferragamo
  PAT–Corral (kick)
- Dal. Dorsett, 12 yard rush
  PAT–Septien (kick)

Third Quarter
- Dal. Dorsett, 10 yard pass from D. White
  PAT–Septien (kick)
- Dal. B. Johnson, 35 yard pass from D. White
  PAT–Septien (kick)

Fourth Quarter
- Dal. D. Pearson, 11 yard pass from D. White
  PAT–Septien (kick)

TEAM STATISTICS

L.A.		DAL.
15	First Downs-Total	29
6	First Downs-Rushing	19
7	First Downs-Passing	9
2	First Downs-Penalty	1
1	Fumbles-Number	2
0	Fumbles-Lost Ball	0
5	Penalties-Number	11
50	Yards Penalized	79
0	Missed Field Goals	0
55	Offensive Plays	71
260	Net Yards	528
4.7	Average Gain	7.4
3	Giveaways	3
3	Takeaways	3
0	Difference	0

INDIVIDUAL STATISTICS

RUSHING

LOS ANGELES	No.	Yds.	Avg.	DALLAS	No.	Yds.	Avg.
J. Thomas	14	48	3.4	Dorsett	22	160	7.3
Bryant	10	44	4.4	Springs	4	58	14.5
	24	92	3.8	Newhouse	11	46	4.2
				J. Jones	5	38	7.6
				Newsome	2	34	17.0
				D. White	2	2	1.0
					46	338	7.3

RECEIVING

LOS ANGELES	No.	Yds.	Avg.	DALLAS	No.	Yds.	Avg.
Dennard	6	117	19.5	D. Pearson	4	60	15.0
J. Thomas	3	26	8.7	Dorsett	3	28	9.3
Bryant	2	7	3.5	Saldi	2	52	26.0
Nelson	1	12	12.0	B. Johnson	1	35	35.0
Waddy	1	9	9.0	Hill	1	8	8.0
Guman	1	5	5.0	DuPree	1	7	7.0
	14	176	12.4		12	190	15.8

PUNTING

LOS ANGELES	No.		Avg.	DALLAS	No.		Avg.
Corral	6		39.3	D. White	2		44.5

PUNT RETURNS

LOS ANGELES	No.	Yds.	Avg.	DALLAS	No.	Yds.	Avg.
Irvin	1	2	2.0	J. Jones	5	81	16.2

KICKOFF RETURNS

LOS ANGELES	No.	Yds.	Avg.	DALLAS	No.	Yds.	Avg.
D. Hill	5	110	22.0	J. Jones	3	72	24.0
L. Smith	1	10	10.0				
	6	120	20.0				

INTERCEPTION RETURNS

LOS ANGELES	No.	Yds.	Avg.	DALLAS	No.	Yds.	Avg.
Cromwell	1	44	44.0	Mitchell	1	12	12.0
L. Smith	1	7	7.0	Wilson	1	8	8.0
Irvin	1	0	0.0	Clinkscale	1	2	2.0
	3	51	17.0		3	22	7.3

PASSING

	Att.	Comp.	Comp. Pct.	Yds.	Int.	Yds. Att.	Yds. Comp.
LOS ANGELES							
Ferragamo	30	14	47.3	176	3	5.9	12.4
DALLAS							
D. White	25	12	48.0	190	3	7.6	15.8

January 3, 1981 at Philadelphia (Attendance 68,434)

SCORING

MINNESOTA	7	7	2	0–16
PHILADELPHIA	0	7	14	10–31

First Quarter
- Min. S. White, 30 yard pass from Kramer
  PAT–Danmeier (kick)

Second Quarter
- Min. Brown, 1 yard rush
  PAT–Danmeier (kick)
- Phila. Carmichael, 9 yard pass from Jaworski
  PAT–Franklin (kick)

Third Quarter
- Phi. Montgomery, 8 yard rush
  PAT–Franklin (kick)
- Min. Safety, Jaworski tackled in end zone
- Phi. Montgomery, 5 yard rush
  PAT–Franklin (kick)

Fourth Quarter
- Phi. Franklin, 33 yard field goal
- Phi. Harrington, 2 yard rush
  PAT–Franklin (kick)

TEAM STATISTICS

MIN.		PHI.
14	First Downs-Total	24
3	First Downs-Rushing	12
10	First Downs-Passing	12
1	First Downs-Penalty	0
3	Fumbles-Number	1
3	Fumbles-Lost Ball	1
5	Penalties-Number	4
27	Yards Penalized	30
0	Missed Field Goals	1
55	Offensive Plays	82
215	Net Yards	305
3.9	Average Gain	3.7
8	Giveaways	3
3	Takeaways	8
−5	Difference	+5

INDIVIDUAL STATISTICS

RUSHING

MINNESOTA	No.	Yds.	Avg.	PHILADELPHIA	No.	Yds.	Avg.
Paschal	4	26	6.5	Montgomery	26	74	2.8
Brown	5	14	2.8	Harris	7	27	3.9
R. Miller	1	2	2.0	Parker	1	12	12.0
Young	2	0	0.0	Giammona	7	11	1.6
S. White	1	−6	−6.0	Harrington	1	2	2.0
	13	36	2.8		42	126	3.0

RECEIVING

MINNESOTA	No.	Yds.	Avg.	PHILADELPHIA	No.	Yds.	Avg.
Young	6	57	9.5	Carmichael	7	84	12.0
Brown	4	25	6.3	Krepfle	2	27	13.5
Senser	4	25	6.3	Montgomery	2	26	13.0
S. White	2	52	26.0	Campfield	2	21	10.5
Rashad	1	23	23.0	Fitzkee	2	19	9.5
Paschal	1	19	19.0	Harris	2	13	6.5
Bruer	1	8	8.0		17	190	11.2
	19	209	11.0				

PUNTING

MINNESOTA	No.		Avg.	PHILADELPHIA	No.		Avg.
Coleman	5		40.0	Runager	4		33.8

PUNT RETURNS

MINNESOTA	No.	Yds.	Avg.	PHILADELPHIA	No.	Yds.	Avg.
Payton	2	18	9.0	Giammona	3	21	7.0

KICKOFF RETURNS

MINNESOTA	No.	Yds.	Avg.	PHILADELPHIA	No.	Yds.	Avg.
Payton	6	102	17.0	Campfield	3	55	18.3
Huffman	1	15	15.0				
	7	117	16.7				

INTERCEPTION RETURNS

MINNESOTA	No.	Yds.	Avg.	PHILADELPHIA	No.	Yds.	Avg.
Hannon	1	0	0.0	Edwards	2	15	7.5
Turner	1	0	0.0	Young	2	0	0.0
	2	0	0.0	LeMaster	1	7	7.0
					5	22	4.4

PASSING

	Att.	Comp.	Comp. Pct.	Yds.	Int.	Yds. Att.	Yds. Comp.
MINNESOTA							
Kramer	39	19	48.7	209	5	5.4	11.0
PHILADELPHIA							
Jaworski	38	17	44.7	190	2	5.0	11.2

January 4, 1981 at Atlanta (Attendance 60,022)

SCORING

DALLAS	3	7	0	20–30
ATLANTA	10	7	7	3–27

First Quarter
- Atl. Mazzetti, 38 yard field goal
- Atl. Jenkins, 60 yard pass from Bartkowski
  PAT–Mazzetti (kick)
- Dal. Septien, 38 yard field goal

Second Quarter
- Dal. DuPree, 5 yard pass from D. White
  PAT–Septien (kick)
- Atl. Cain, 1 yard rush
  PAT–Mazzetti (kick)

Third Quarter
- Atl. Andrews, 12 yard pass from Bartkowski
  PAT–Mazzetti (kick)

Fourth Quarter
- Dal. Newhouse, 1 yard rush
  PAT–Septien (kick)
- Atl. Mazzetti, 34 yard field goal
- Dal. D. Pearson, 14 yard pass from D. White
  PAT–Septien (kick)
- Dal. D. Pearson, 23 yard pass from D. White
  PAT–pass failed

TEAM STATISTICS

DAL.		ATL.
22	First Downs-Total	18
5	First Downs-Rushing	6
16	First Downs-Passing	11
1	First Downs-Penalty	1
4	Fumbles-Number	1
1	Fumbles-Lost Ball	1
6	Penalties-Number	4
72	Yards Penalized	48
0	Missed Field Goals	0
65	Offensive Plays	64
422	Net Yards	349
6.5	Average Gain	5.5
2	Giveaways	2
2	Takeaways	2
0	Difference	0

INDIVIDUAL STATISTICS

RUSHING

DALLAS	No.	Yds.	Avg.	ATLANTA	No.	Yds.	Avg.
Dorsett	10	51	5.1	Andrews	14	43	3.1
Newhouse	6	31	5.2	Cain	13	43	3.3
P. Pearson	1	11	11.0		27	86	3.2
D. Pearson	1	9	9.0				
DuPree	1	5	5.0				
Newsome	1	4	4.0				
D. White	4	1	0.3				
	24	112	4.7				

RECEIVING

DALLAS	No.	Yds.	Avg.	ATLANTA	No.	Yds.	Avg.
D. Pearson	5	90	18.0	Francis	6	66	11.0
Dorsett	5	40	8.0	Jenkins	4	155	38.8
Hill	4	53	13.3	Miller	3	48	16.0
P. Pearson	4	51	12.8	Cain	2	20	10.0
Springs	3	39	13.0	Andrews	2	19	9.5
DuPree	3	29	9.7	Jackson	1	12	12.0
Johnson	1	20	20.0		18	320	17.8
	25	322	12.9				

PUNTING

DALLAS	No.		Avg.	ATLANTA	No.		Avg.
D. White	4		38.8	James	4		36.0

PUNT RETURNS

DALLAS	No.	Yds.	Avg.	ATLANTA	No.	Yds.	Avg.
J. Jones	2	−4	−2.0	Johnson	3	8	2.7

KICKOFF RETURNS

DALLAS	No.	Yds.	Avg.	ATLANTA	No.	Yds.	Avg.
J. Jones	3	58	19.3	M. Smith	5	108	21.6
Newsome	3	46	15.3				
	6	104	17.3				

INTERCEPTION RETURNS

DALLAS	No.	Yds.	Avg.	ATLANTA	No.	Yds.	Avg.
Wilson	1	6	6.0	Pridemore	1	22	22.0

PASSING

	Att.	Comp.	Comp. Pct.	Yds.	Int.	Yds. Att.	Yds. Comp.
DALLAS							
D. White	39	25	64.1	322	1	8.3	12.9
Springs	1	0	0.0	0	0	0.0	0.0
	40	25	62.5	322	1	8.1	12.9
ATLANTA							
Barkowski	33	18	54.5	320	1	9.7	17.8

1980 A.F.C. PLAYOFFS

December 28 at Oakland (Attendance 52,762)

SCORING

HOUSTON	7	0	0	0– 7
OAKLAND	3	7	0	17–27

First Quarter
- Oak. Bahr, 47 yard field goal
- Hou. Campbell, 1 yard rush PAT–Fritsch (kick)

Second Quarter
- Oak. Christensen, 1 yard pass from Plunkett PAT–Bahr (kick)

Fourth Quarter
- Oak. Whittington, 44 yard pass from Plunkett PAT–Bahr (kick)
- Oak. Bahr, 37 yard field goal
- Oak. Hayes, 20 yard interception return PAT–Bahr (kick)

TEAM STATISTICS

HOU.		OAK.
18	First Downs–Total	12
5	First Downs–Rushing	4
11	First Downs–Passing	7
2	First Downs–Penalty	1
1	Fumbles–Number	2
1	Fumbles–Lost Ball	0
8	Penalties–Number	14
64	Yards Penalized	91
2	Missed Field Goals	0
67	Offensive Plays	61
275	Net Yards	250
4.1	Average Gain	4.1
3	Giveaways	1
1	Takeaways	3
–2	Difference	+2

INDIVIDUAL STATISTICS

RUSHING

HOUSTON	No.	Yds.	Avg.	OAKLAND	No.	Yds.	Avg.
Campbell	27	91	3.4	King	13	55	4.2
Carpenter	5	9	1.8	Van Eeghen	14	46	3.3
T. Wilson	1	–3	–3.0	Whittingon	5	11	2.5
	33	97	2.9	Jensen	2	0	0.0
				Plunkett	1	–1	–1.0
					35	111	3.2

RECEIVING

HOUSTON	No.	Yds.	Avg.	OAKLAND	No.	Yds.	Avg.
Barber	4	83	20.8	Whittingon	2	64	32.0
Renfro	3	69	23.0	Chester	2	12	6.0
Casper	3	31	10.3	King	1	37	37.0
Carpenter	3	26	8.7	Branch	1	33	33.0
Coleman	1	23	23.0	van Eeghen	1	21	21.0
B. Johnson	1	11	11.0	Christen'n	1	1	1.0
	15	243	16.2		8	168	21.0

PUNTING

HOUSTON	No.	Yds.	Avg.	OAKLAND	No.	Yds.	Avg.
Parsley	9		44.0	Guy	9		51.1

PUNT RETURNS

HOUSTON	No.	Yds.	Avg.	OAKLAND	No.	Yds.	Avg.
Roaches	7	84	12.0	Moody	4	27	6.8
				Matthews	2	2	1.0
					6	29	4.8

KICKOFF RETURNS

HOUSTON	No.	Yds.	Avg.	OAKLAND	No.	Yds.	Avg.
Coleman	4	70	17.5	Moody	1	33	33.0
Roaches	2	48	24.0	Matthews	1	14	14.0
	6	118	19.7		2	47	23.5

INTERCEPTION RETURNS

HOUSTON	No.	Yds.	Avg.	OAKLAND	No.	Yds.	Avg.
Perry	1	0	0.0	Hayes	2	26	13.0

PASSING

HOUSTON	Att.	Comp.	Comp. Pct.	Yds.	Int.	Yds. Att.	Yds. Comp.
Stabler	26	15	57.7	243	2	9.3	16.2
Campbell	1	0	0.0	0	0	0.0	0.0
	27	15	55.6	243	2	9.0	16.2
OAKLAND							
Plunkett	23	8	34.8	168	1	7.3	21.0

January 3, 1981 at San Diego (Attendance 52,028)

SCORING

BUFFALO	0	14	0	0–14
SAN DIEGO	3	0	7	10–20

First Quarter
- S.D. Benirschke, 22 yard field goal

Second Quarter
- Buf. Leaks, 1 yard rush PAT–Mike-Mayer (kick)
- Buf. Lewis, 9 yard pass from Ferguson PAT–Mike-Mayer (kick)

Third Quarter
- S.D. Joiner, 9 yard pass from Fouts PAT–Benirschke (kick)

Fourth Quarter
- S.D. Benirschke, 22 yard field goal
- S.D. Smith, 50 yard pass from Fouts PAT–Benirschke (kick)

TEAM STATISTICS

BUF.		S.D.
17	First Downs-Total	21
6	First Downs-Rushing	6
9	First Downs-Passing	14
2	First Downs-Penalty	1
0	Fumbles-Number	3
0	Fumbles-Lost Ball	2
5	Penalties-Number	6
40	Yards Penalized	66
2	Missed Field Goals	1
66	Offensive Plays	64
244	Net Yards	397
3.7	Average Gain	6.2
3	Giveaways	3
3	Takeaways	3
0	Difference	0

INDIVIDUAL STATISTICS

RUSHING

BUFFALO	No.	Yds.	Avg.	SAN DIEGO	No.	Yds.	Avg.
Cribbs	18	53	2.9	Muncie	18	80	4.4
Manucci	2	21	10.5	Thomas	5	22	4.4
Brown	9	17	1.9	Fouts	2	–6	–3.0
Leaks	4	6	1.5		25	96	3.8
	33	97	2.9				

RECEIVING

BUFFALO	No.	Yds.	Avg.	SAN DIEGO	No.	Yds.	Avg.
Brammer	4	62	15.5	Jefferson	7	102	14.6
Cribbs	4	36	9.0	Muncie	6	53	8.8
Lewis	3	45	15.0	Joiner	4	83	20.8
Butler	2	19	9.5	McCrary	2	19	9.5
Leaks	1	17	17.0	Smith	1	50	50.0
Hooks	1	1	1.0	Winslow	1	5	5.0
	15	180	12.0	Thomas	1	2	2.0
					22	314	14.2

PUNTING

BUFFALO	No.	Yds.	Avg.	SAN DIEGO	No.	Yds.	Avg.
Cater	6		44.5	Partridge	3		37.0

PUNT RETURNS

BUFFALO	No.	Yds.	Avg.	SAN DIEGO	No.	Yds.	Avg.
Hooks	2	13	6.5	Fuller	3	29	9.7

KICKOFF RETURNS

BUFFALO	No.	Yds.	Avg.	SAN DIEGO	No.	Yds.	Avg.
Solomon	5	84	16.8	Bauer	2	39	19.5
				Duncan	1	11	11.0
					3	50	16.7

INTERCEPTION RETURNS

BUFFALO	No.	Yds.	Avg.	SAN DIEGO	No.	Yds.	Avg.
Simpson	1	0	0.0	Edwards	2	27	13.5
				Fuller	1	20	20.0
					3	47	15.7

PASSING

BUFFALO	Att.	Comp.	Comp. Pct.	Yds.	Int.	Yds. Att.	Yds. Comp.
Ferguson	29	15	51.7	180	3	6.2	12.0
Manucci	1	0	0.0	0	0	0.0	0.0
	30	15	50.0	180	3	6.0	12.0
SAN DIEGO							
Fouts	37	22	59.5	314	1	8.5	14.2

January 4, 1981 at Cleveland (Attendance 77,655)

SCORING

OAKLAND	0	7	0	7–14
CLEVELAND	0	6	6	0–12

Second Quarter
- Cle. Bolton, 42 yard interception return PAT–kick failed
- Oak. van Eeghen, 1 yard rush PAT–Bahr (kick)

Third Quarter
- Cle. Cockroft, 30 yard field goal
- Cle. Cockroft, 29 yard field goal

Fourth Quarter
- Oak. van Eeghen, 1 yard rush PAT–Bahr (kick)

TEAM STATISTICS

OAK.		CLE.
12	First Downs-Total	17
4	First Downs-Rushing	6
8	First Downs-Passing	8
0	First DownsPenalty	3
2	Fumbles-Number	6
1	Fumbles-Lost Ball	1
5	Penalties-Number	2
39	Yards Penalized	10.
0	Missed Field Goals	2
70	Offensive Plays	69
208	Net Yards	254
3.0	Average Gain	3.7
3	Giveaways	4
4	Takeaways	3
+1	Difference	–1

INDIVIDUAL STATISTICS

RUSHING

OAKLAND	No.	Yds.	Avg.	CLEVELAND	No.	Yds.	Avg.
van Eeghen	20	45	2.3	M. Pruitt	13	48	3.7
King	12	23	1.9	Hill	2	23	11.5
Plunkett	4	8	2.0	Sipe	6	13	2.2
Whittington	1	1	1.0	G. Pruitt	4	11	2.8
Jensen	1	–1	–1.0	Miller	1	1	1.0
	38	76	2.0	McDonald	1	–11	–11.0
					27	85	3.1

RECEIVING

OAKLAND	No.	Yds.	Avg.	CLEVELAND	No.	Yds.	Avg.
King	4	14	3.2	Newsome	4	51	12.8
Chester	3	64	21.3	G. Pruitt	3	54	18.0
van Eeghen	3	23	7.7	Rucker	2	38	19.0
Branch	2	23	11.5	Logan	2	36	18.0
Chandler	1	15	15.0	Hill	2	4	2.0
Whittington	1	10	10.0		13	183	14.1
	14	149	10.6				

PUNTING

OAKLAND	No.	Yds.	Avg.	CLEVELAND	No.	Yds.	Avg.
Guy	9		38.3	Evans	6		39.5

PUNT RETURNS

OAKLAND	No.	Yds.	Avg.	CLEVELAND	No.	Yds.	Avg.
Moody	1	1	1.0	D. Hall	5	57	11.4
				Wright	2	24	12.0
					7	81	11.6

KICKOFF RETURNS

OAKLAND	No.	Yds.	Avg.	CLEVELAND	No.	Yds.	Avg.
Whittington	2	44	22.0	D.Hall	2	47	23.5
Moody	1	14	14.0	White	1	28	28.0
Christensen	1	7	7.0		3	75	25.0
	4	65	16.3				

INTERCEPTION RETURNS

OAKLAND	No.	Yds.	Avg.	CLEVELAND	No.	Yds.	Avg.
Hayes	2	3	1.5	Bolton	2	42	21.0
M. Davis	1	0	0.0				
	3	3	1.0				

PASSING

OAKLAND	Att.	Comp.	Comp. Pct.	Yds.	Int.	Yds. Att.	Yds. Comp.
Plunkett	30	14	46.7	149	2	5.0	10.6
CLEVELAND							
Sipe	40	13	32.5	183	3	4.6	14.1

1980 Championship Games

NFC CHAMPIONSHIP GAME
January 11, 1981 at Philadelphia
(Attendance 70,696)

Two clubs from the Eastern Division met in Philadelphia for a place in the Super Bowl. The Eagles had captured first place and beat Minnesota to get to this game. The Cowboys had taken a longer path, beating the Rams and Falcons as a wild-card team. The two teams had split their meetings during the season, but the Cowboys had won the most recent meeting and had plenty of big game experience.

The Eagles, however, showed no jitters. On the second play after the opening kickoff, Wilbert Montgomery bolted 42 yards for a touchdown. With the temperature hovering around zero, the quick lead steeled the Eagles' confidence. With their passing game hampered by the cold, the Eagles called on Montgomery to carry the ball repeatedly. Although the Philadelphia blockers controlled the line of scrimmage, the Eagles scored no more points in the first half. The Cowboys did drive to a touchdown in the second quarter and left the field at halftime with a 7-7 tie despite being clearly outplayed.

In the third quarter, the Eagles cashed in on Cowboy mistakes. When sacked by Carl Hairston, quarterback Danny White fumbled the ball away deep in Dallas territory. Although the Cowboy defense held, Tony Franklin put the Eagles ahead 10-7 with a field goal.

After the kickoff, Dallas drove across midfield only to lose the ball on a Tony Dorsett fumble. Jerry Robinson returned the ball to the Dallas 38 yard line, and the Eagles soon scored on a run by Leroy Harris.

Ahead 17-7 at the start of the fourth quarter, the Eagles joined with the weather in making Danny White's life miserable. The Cowboys would score no more, and a Franklin field goal made the final tally 20-7. Montgomery ran for a total of 194 yards, two yards shy of the playoff record set by Steve Van Buren in 1947.

SCORING

DALLAS	**0**	**7**	**0**	**0– 7**
PHILADELPHIA	**7**	**0**	**10**	**3–20**

First Quarter
Phi. Montgomery, 42 yard rush
PAT–Franklin (kick)

Second Quarter
Dal. Dorsett, 3 yard rush
PAT–Septien (kick)

Third Quarter
Phi. Franklin, 26 yard field goal
Phi. Harris, 9 yard rush
PAT–Franklin (kick)

Fourth Quarter
Phi. Franklin, 20 yard field goal

TEAM STATISTICS

DAL		PHIL
11	First Downs-Total	19
5	First Downs-Rushing	13
6	First Downs-Passing	5
0	First Downs-Penalty	1
5	Fumbles-Number	4
3	Fumbles-Lost Ball	0
5	Penalties-Number	5
40	Yards Penalized	45
0	Missed Field Goals	1
55	Offensive Plays	71
202	Net Yards	340
3.7	Average Gain	4.8
4	Giveaways	2
2	Takeaways	4
–2	Difference	+2

INDIVIDUAL STATISTICS

DALLAS	No.	Yds.	Avg.	PHILADELPHIA	No.	Yds.	Avg.
RUSHING							
Newhouse	7	44	6.3	Montgomery	26	194	7.5
Dorsett	13	41	3.2	Harris	10	60	6.0
Johnson	1	5	5.0	Harrington	1	4	4.0
D. White	1	–4	–4.0	Campfield	1	3	3.0
	22	86	3.9	Jaworski	2	2	1.0
					40	263	6.6
RECEIVING							
Dorsett	3	27	9.0	Parker	4	31	7.8
P. Pearson	2	32	16.0	Krepfle	2	22	11.0
Johnson	2	27	13.5	Campfield	1	17	17.0
D. Pearson	2	15	7.5	Montgomery	1	14	14.0
Springs	2	–2	–1.0	Carmichael	1	7	7.0
Saldi	1	28	28.0		9	91	10.1
	12	127	10.6				
PUNTING							
D. White	7		33.7	Runager	4		34.3
PUNT RETURNS							
J. Jones	3	4	1.3	Sciarra	6	69	11.5
KICKOFF RETURNS							
J. Jones	3	70	23.3	Campfield	2	40	20.0
Wilson	1	19	19.0				
Newsome	1	15	15.0				
	5	104	20.8				
INTERCEPTION RETURNS							
Dickerson	1	0	0.0	Young	1	5	5.0
Mitchell	1	0	0.0				
	2	0	0.0				

PASSING

DALLAS	Att.	Comp.	Comp. Pct.	Yds.	Int.	Yds./ Att.	Yds./ Comp.
D. White	31	12	38.7	127	1	4.1	10.6
D. Pearson	1	0	0.0	0	0	0.0	0.0
	32	12	37.5	127	1	4.0	10.6
PHILADELPHIA							
Jaworski	29	9	31.0	91	2	3.1	10.1

AFC CHAMPIONSHIP GAME
January 11, 1981 at San Diego
(Attendance 52,428)

The best of the West met for the AFC title in balmy San Diego. The Raiders had played one week earlier in one-degree weather in Cleveland, beating the Browns 14-12 in a thrilling contest. The Chargers came off a 20-14 victory over Buffalo and were rated as solid favorites. The two combatants split their two games during the season, but did not meet after mid-October.

The Raiders took the field with a missionary's zeal. They drew first blood with an early 65-yard touchdown pass from Jim Plunkett to Ray Chester. The famous San Diego offense responded, with Charlie Joiner scoring on a 48-yard pass from Dan Fouts.

Now it was the Raiders' turn again. Plunkett capped a drive by running five yards for the score. Before the quarter ended, the Raiders scored again on a pass to Kenny King. Those rooting for the Chargers demanded that their team stop fooling around.

But the swarming Oakland defense smothered the San Diego fleet of receivers and stopped their runners dead. Plunkett directed another Oakland rally which led to a Mark van Eeghen touchdown. With the score now 28-7, the hometown fans began to panic. The Chargers stayed calm and cut the lead to 28-14 by halftime.

The Chargers dominated the first part of the third quarter. On a Rolf Benirschke field goal and a Chuck Muncie touchdown, they cut the lead to 28-24 and brought their fans alive. The Chargers, however, would get no closer. The Raiders began grinding the yards out on the ground, eating up the clock as they traveled. While holding Fouts in check, Oakland used two field goals to fortify their lead. With the Raider defense holding firm, Oakland triumphed 34-27 and earned the first wild-card trip to the Super Bowl.

SCORING

OAKLAND	**21**	**7**	**3**	**3–34**
SAN DIEGO	**7**	**7**	**10**	**3–27**

First Quarter
Oak. Chester, 65 yard pass from Plunkett
PAT–Bahr (kick)
S.D. Joiner, 48 yard pass from Fouts
PAT–Benirschke (kick)
Oak. Plunkett, 5 yard rush
PAT–Bahr (kick)
Oak. King, 21 yard pass from Plunkett
PAT–Bahr (kick)

Second Quarter
Oak. van Eeghen, 3 yard rush
PAT–Bahr (kick)
S.D. Joiner, 8 yard pass from Fouts
PAT–Benirschke (kick)

Third Quarter
S.D. Benirschke, 26 yard field goal
S.D. Muncie, 6 yard rush
PAT–Benirschke (kick)
Oak. Bahr, 27 yard field goal

Fourth Quarter
Oak. Bahr, 33 yard field goal
S.D. Benirschke, 27 yard field goal

TEAM STATISTICS

OAK		S.D.
21	First Downs-Total	26
8	First Downs-Rushing	6
12	First Downs-Passing	17
1	First Downs-Penalty	3
0	Fumbles-Number	5
0	Fumbles-Lost Ball	1
7	Penalties-Number	6
54	Yards Penalized	45
0	Missed Field Goals	0
66	Offensive Plays	71
362	Net Yards	434
5.5	Average Gain	6.1
0	Giveaways	3
3	Takeaways	0
+3	Difference	–3

INDIVIDUAL STATISTICS

OAKLAND	No.	Yds.	Avg.	SAN DIEGO	No.	Yds.	Avg.
RUSHING							
van Eeghen	20	85	4.3	Thomas	12	48	4.0
King	11	35	3.2	Muncie	9	34	3.8
Jensen	2	7	3.5	Fouts	1	2	2.0
Plunkett	4	6	1.5	Smith	1	–1	–1.0
Whittington	5	5	1.0		23	83	3.6
	42	138	3.3				
RECEIVING							
Chester	5	102	20.4	Joiner	6	130	21.7
Branch	3	78	26.0	Thomas	5	40	8.0
King	2	43	21.5	Jefferson	4	71	17.8
Chandler	2	27	13.5	Smith	3	76	25.3
Whittington	2	11	5.5	Winslow	3	42	14.0
	14	261	18.6	Muncie	2	5	2.5
					23	364	15.8
PUNTING							
Guy	4		56.0	Partridge	2		40.5
PUNT RETURNS							
Matthews	2	20	10.0	Fuller	2	41	20.5
KICKOFF RETURNS							
Whittington	4	67	16.8	Bauer	5	89	17.8
Moody	2	36	18.0	Duncan	1	10	10.0
	6	103	17.2		6	99	16.5
INTERCEPTION RETURNS							
Owens	1	25	25.0	none			
Hayes	1	16	16.0				
	2	41	20.5				

PASSING

OAKLAND	Att.	Comp.	Comp. Pct.	Yds.	Int.	Yds./ Att.	Yds./ Comp.
Plunkett	18	14	77.8	261	0	14.5	18.6
SAN DIEGO							
Fouts	45	22	48.9	336	2	7.5	15.3
Winslow	1	1	100.0	28	0	28.0	28.0
	46	23	50.0	364	2	7.9	15.8

January 25, 1981 at New Orleans
(Attendance 75,500)

Super Bowl XV Davis' Bulldog Brigade

The Raiders didn't bring a pedigree to the Super Bowl, they just brought a lot of spirit. It was the spirit of the redeemed, of those who had come back from the garbage pile to smell the roses. Lightly regarded before the season, the Raiders were stocked with many players who had been cut loose by other clubs. Jim Plunkett had been released by the 49ers, Kenny King had ridden the bench for the Oilers, and John Matuszak was unwanted before Al Davis called. Other Oakland players had made similar unorthodox journeys. Davis himself was embroiled in a nasty lawsuit over whether he could move the Raiders to Los Angeles. This crew of pirates even took the hard road in the playoffs, starting out on wild-card weekend and beating the Oilers, Browns, and Chargers. The Eagles had a less colorful story but ranked as three-point favorites because of their tough defense and quick-strike offense.

The feisty mutts dominated the game. Rod Martin picked off Ron Jaworski's first pass of the day and returned it to the Philadelphia 30-yard line. Before seven minutes had elapsed, the Raiders scored a touchdown and led 7-0. The Eagles replied with a long touchdown pass to Rodney Parker, but a penalty wiped the score out. Late in the quarter, Oakland had the ball on its own 20-yard line. Plunkett threw a pass to King near the 40-yard line, and the halfback outsprinted the napping secondary for an 80-yard touchdown. With a 14-0 lead, the confidence of the Raiders was growing as the Eagles realized that they were collectively off their best form. A Tony Franklin field goal cut the lead to 14-3 at halftime.

In need of a second-half revival, the Eagles instead sank out of the game in the third quarter. Unable to score, they fell prey to Plunkett's precision quarterbacking. A touchdown pass to Cliff Branch in the third quarter lengthened the lead to 21-3 and put the handwriting on the wall for the Eagles. Although Jaworski kept throwing and did connect with Keith Krepfle for a score in the fourth quarter, the Raiders stormed to a 27-10 victory. Plunkett won the MVP award, while Martin starred on defense with three interceptions. In the clubhouse after the game, Pete Rozelle presented the championship trophy to Al Davis in a polite ceremony which skirted the bitter feelings between the two men and which must have given Davis an extra rich taste of victory.

LINEUPS

OAKLAND		PHILADELPHIA
	OFFENSE	
Branch	WR	Carmichael
Shell	LT	Walters
Upshaw	LG	Perot
Dalby	C	Morriss
Marvin	RG	Peoples
Lawrence	RT	Sisemore
Chester	TE	Krepfle
Chandler	WR/TE	Spagnola
Plunkett	QB	Jaworski
van Eeghen	RB	Montgomery
King	RB	Harris
	DEFENSE	
Matuszak	LE	Harrison
Kinlaw	MG	Johnson
Browning	RE	Hairston
Hendricks	LLB	Bunting
Millor	ILB	Bergey
Nelson	ILB	LeMaster
Martin	RLB	Robinson
Hayes	LCB	Young
O'Steen	RCB	Edwards
M. Davis	SS	Logan
Owens	FS	Wilson

SUBSTITUTES

OAKLAND

	OFFENSE	
Bradshaw	Martini	Sylvester
Christ'sen	Mason	Whittington
B. Davis	Matthews	Wilson
Jensen	Ramsey	
	DEFENSE	
Barnes	Jackson	McKinney
Campbell	Jones	Moody
Celotto	McClan'n	Pear
Hardman		
	KICKERS	
Bahr	Guy	

PHILADELPHIA

	OFFENSE	
Baker	Henry	Pisarcik
Campfield	Hertel	Slater
Giammona	Kenney	Smith
Harrington	Parker	Torrey
	DEFENSE	
Blackmore	Clarke	Phillips
Brown	Hender'n	Sciarra
Chesley	Humphrey	Wilkes
	KICKERS	
Franklin		Runager

SCORING

OAKLAND	14	0	10	3	27
PHILADELPHIA	0	3	0	7	10

First Quarter
- Oak. Branch, 2 yard pass from Plunkett PAT–Bahr (kick)
- Oak. King, 80 yard pass from Plunkett PAT–Bahr (kick)

Second Quarter
- Phi. Franklin, 30 yard field goal

Third Quarter
- Oak. Branch, 29 yard pass from Plunkett PAT–Bahr (kick)
- Oak. Bahr, 46 yard yard field goal

Fourth Quarter
- Phi. Krepfle, 8 yard pass from Jaworski PAT–Franklin (kick)
- Oak. Bahr, 35 yard field goal

TEAM STATISTICS

OAK.		PHI.
17	First Downs–Total	19
6	First Downs–Rushing	3
10	First Downs–Passing	14
1	First Downs–Penalty	2
0	Fumbles–Number	1
0	Fumbles–Lost Ball	1
5	Penalties–Number	6
37	Yards Penalized	57
1	Missed Field Goals	1
56	Offensive Plays	64
377	Net Yards	360
6.7	Average Gain	5.6
0	Giveaways	4
4	Takeaways	0
+4	Difference	−4

INDIVIDUAL STATISTICS

OAKLAND	No.	Yds.	Avg.	PHILADELPHIA	No.	Yds.	Avg.
RUSHING							
van Eeghen	19	80	4.2	Montgomery	16	44	2.8
King	6	18	3.0	Harris	7	14	2.0
Jensen	3	12	4.0	Giammona	1	7	7.0
Plunkett	3	9	3.0	Harrington	1	4	4.0
Whittington	3	−2	−0.7	Jaworski	1	0	0.0
	34	117	3.4		26	69	2.4
RECEIVING							
Branch	5	07	13.4	Montgomery	6	91	15.2
Chandler	4	77	19.3	Carmichael	5	83	16.6
King	2	93	46.5	Krepfle	2	16	8.0
Chester	2	24	12.0	Smith	2	59	29.5
	13	261	20.1	Spagnola	1	22	22.0
				Parker	1	19	19.0
				Harris	1	1	1.0
					18	291	16.2
PUNTING							
Guy	3		42.0	Runager	3		36.7
PUNT RETURNS							
Matthews	2	1	0.5	Sciarra	2	18	9.0
				Henry	1	2	2.0
					3	20	6.7
KICKOFF RETURNS							
Matthews	2	29	14.5	Campfield	5	87	17.4
Moody	1	19	19.0	Harrington	1	0	0.0
	3	48	16.0		6	87	14.5
INTERCEPTION RETURNS							
Martin	3	44	14.7	none			

PASSING

OAKLAND	Att.	Comp.	Comp. Pct.	Yds.	Int.	Yds./Att.	Yds./Comp.	Yards Lost Tackled
Plunkett	21	13	61.9	261	0	12.4	20.1	1-1
PHILADELPHIA								
Jaworski	38	18	47.4	291	3	7.7	16.2	0-0

1981 N.F.C. From Montreal to Dallas

Waving a stack of dollars, Nelson Skalbania signed up a crew of prominent players for his newly purchased Montreal team of the Canadian Football League. He snatched three veteran players out of the NFL. Quarterback Vince Ferragamo left the Los Angeles Rams to head north, while James Scott of the Bears and Billy Johnson of the Oilers went to Montreal as Ferragamo's receivers. Skalbania also signed two college players taken in the first round of the N.F.L. draft. Defensive end Keith Gary turned down the Pittsburgh Steelers, and running back David Overstreet chose Montreal over Miami. With all this flashy talent, the Alouettes suffered through a miserable season, and by the end of the year, the club was swimming in debt and teetering on the edge of bankruptcy.

EASTERN DIVISION

Dallas Cowboys—Dallas fans worried when the 49ers whipped the Cowboys 45–14 on October 11. That loss dropped the Pokes two games behind the streaking Eagles. By the end of the season, however, Cowboy excellence had worn down the other Eastern teams like water eating away rock. Some of the excellence at Tom Landry's command were the running of Tony Dorsett, the blocking of Herbert Scott and Pat Donovan, and the pass rushing of Randy White and Too Tall Jones. Landry also plugged his leaky secondary with talented rookies Everson Walls and Michael Downs. The Cowboys reclaimed a share of first place on November 1 by beating the Eagles 17–14. While the Eagles faded over the backstretch of the schedule, the Cowboys won four of their last five games, including another victory over Philadelphia. When the standings were final, the Cowboys had taken first place and their fifteenth playoff berth in 16 years.

Philadelphia Eagles—For two months, the Eagles looked like the N.F.L.'s next dominant team. They won their first six games and perched atop the N.F.C. East with a 7–1 record as October ended. Even the loss of Bill Bergey didn't weaken the defense, as coach Dick Vermeil had rigged up a tight unit around stars Charles Johnson, Jerry Robinson, and Roynell Young. After a defeat by Dallas on November 1, the Eagles destroyed St. Louis 52–10 and Baltimore 38–13. Then, with a first place battle on their hands, the Eagles plummeted to earth. The offense showed the effects of losing fullbacks Leroy Harris and Perry Harrington to injuries and a lack of game-breaking speed. Four weeks in a row, the Eagles scored under 14 points and lost despite good defensive work. Although their early rush had sewn up a wild-card spot for them, the Eagles looked like an error-prone loser in December. A 38–0 victory over the Cardinals on the final weekend gave Vermeil hope that his team was returning to form just in time.

New York Giants—Two new faces turned the Giants around with will and desire. Lawrence Taylor joined the team from North Carolina via the first round of the college draft. A linebacker with amazing speed, his endless pursuit and jarring tackles threw enemy offenses out of their normal game plans. Joining the Giants in October was fullback Rob Carpenter, a pickup from the Oilers. Carpenter ran the ball with power and persistence, enabling the Giants to control the ball on offense. Although these two led the way, other players helped them take the Giants into the playoffs for the first time since 1963. Harry Carson came back from a knee injury to star at linebacker, and Mark Haynes rebounded from a miserable rookie year to blossom into a top cornerback. Reserve quarterback Scott Brunner also came through when needed. Phil Simms went out with a separated shoulder during a 30–27 overtime loss to the Redskins on November 15. With Brunner at the helm, the Giants won four of their final five games, including a 13-10 overtime victory against the Cowboys on the final weekend.

Washington Redskins—Hired from Don Coryell's San Diego staff, Joe Gibbs came to Washington to install a pass-oriented offense. The players took a while to get the hang of it, as they lost their first five games. With signs of panic in the media, the Skins turned around and won eight of their final eleven games. Joe Theismann enjoyed the increased passing, but the offense profited most from the return of fullback John Riggins after his holdout and the addition of halfback Joe Washington from Baltimore. Gibbs overhauled both the offensive and defensive lines, and both units improved as the season wore on. Although the Skins harbored some wild-card playoff hopes in mid-season, the early losses were too much to make up. Nevertheless, the Redskins ended the season on the upswing, beating the Eagles 15–13, the Colts 38–14, and the Rams 30–7.

St. Louis Cardinals—Although they improved two games over their 1980 record, the Cardinals still finished last with the only losing record in the N.F.C. East. A feeble pass rush and a patchy secondary prevented any further improvement. Two young faces made the Cardinals an interesting bunch despite the losing record. Roy Green began the season as a kick returner and defensive back. When injuries struck the St. Louis receiving corps, Green shifted to offense and starred as a deep threat. While working as a receiver, he also played defense as a fifth back on passing downs, raising romantic memories of two-way players. Despite Green's heroics, the Cards dropped to a 3–7 record after a 52–10 debacle with the Eagles on November 8. Coach Jim Hanifan benched veteran quarterback Jim Hart the next week and started rookie Neil Lomax. With the freshman at QB, the Cards ran off four straight victories, including impressive beatings of the Bills and Saints. Although they dropped the final two games of the year, the Cardinals hoped that they had found a passing combination for the 1980s.

CENTRAL DIVISION

Tampa Bay Buccaneers—For most of the year, the Bucs did not look like champions. Nevertheless, when none of the other NFC Central teams took control of the race, the brass ring was still there when the Bucs made their move. After a 24–7 loss to Denver on November 15, the Buccaneers fell to a 5–6 mark, two games behind the first place Vikings. Instead of fading, John McKay rallied his club for a late-season push. They beat Green Bay, New Orleans, and Atlanta to forge ahead into first place with two weeks to go. A last-minute 24–23 loss to the Chargers on December 13 threw the race into a tie, to be settled on the final Sunday between the Bucs and Lions in the Pontiac Silverdome. Doug Williams hit Kevin House with an 84-yard touchdown pass in the second quarter for a 10–7 halftime lead. In the second half, Lee Roy Selmon sacked Detroit's Eric Hipple, and David Logan returned the resulting fumble for a touchdown. The 20–17 victory on enemy turf put the Buccaneers into the playoffs for the second time in three years. The big changes from two years ago were the infrequent play of runner Ricky Bell and the sparkling rookie season of linebacker Hugh Green.

Detroit Lions—When quarterback Gary Danielson injured his wrist on September 27, visions of disaster danced before coach Monte Clark. Jeff Komlo started the next two games, but two losses dropped the Lions to a 2-4 record. Clark then turned to Eric Hipple, an untried second-year benchwarmer. In his starting debut, he led the Lions to a 48–17 victory over the Bears on a Monday night. In his first eight starts, Hipple engineered seven victories and boosted the Lions into a first-place tie. Along the way, the Lions beat Dallas 27–24 on a last-minute field goal; photographs showed that the Lions had twelve men on the field for the kick, but the win stood up in the standings. Hipple was aided greatly by the running of Billy Sims, and tackle Doug English returned from a year's retirement to shine on defense. The Lions lost to the Packers on December 6, but beat the Vikings one week later to set up a first-place showdown with the Buccaneers in the Pontiac Silverdome. The Lions had won all seven of their home games, but the Bucs broke the string and their hearts by winning the contest 20–17.

Green Bay Packers—Stripped of his general manager duties, Bart Starr kept a fingertip grip on his coaching job. The Packers beat the Bears on opening day but lost halfback Eddie Lee Ivery to knee surgery. Six defeats in the next seven games put the wolves at Starr's door, but then the Packers rescued him by going on a hot streak. With six victories over the back half of the schedule, the Packers charged into the race for a playoff spot. The offense learned how to use two standout receivers, James Lofton and John Jefferson. Obtained from San Diego after the start of the season, Jefferson gave quarterback Lynn Dickey a matched set of speedburners to fire away at. Just as important to Dickey was the improved offensive line, with center Larry McCarren shining brightest. The defense had its shaky moments but did profit by the return to health of linebackers Rich Wingo, George Cumby, and John Anderson. Down the stretch, the Packers beat the Vikings, Lions, and Saints to set up a do-or-die match with the Jets in New York on the final Sunday. A victory would wrap up a wild-card berth, but the Jets needed a victory just as badly and blew the Pack out 28–3.

Minnesota Vikings—They didn't have the best material, but Bud Grant had coaxed his Vikings into first place in mid-November. Their 7–4 record put them two games ahead of the pack in the NFC Central. The Vikes had a second-rate defense but a first-rate passing attack. Tommy Kramer unleashed the usual barrage of passes to wide receivers Ahmad Rashad and Sammy White, but he also sent a lot of footballs toward Joe Senser, the new tight end. On the way to the top, the Vikings had beaten undefeated Philadelphia and won games over Detroit and San Diego on late field goals. With Bud Grant's track record as a winner, fans were surprised to see the Vikings come apart like a cheap Coney Island shirt. That two-game lead evaporated in a five-game losing streak which ended only when the players went home for the winter. The unbalanced offense abruptly dried up, while the defense allowed Detroit to score 45 points. They key loss came at home on November 26, as the Vikes blew a 14–0 lead and were beaten 35–23 by the Packers.

Chicago Bears—For two months, the Bears played like dispirited, disinterested losers. With minor injuries hampering Walter Payton and with James Scott playing for Montreal in the C.F.L., the Chicago offense rarely scored more than 20 points. Despite another star season

FINAL TEAM STATISTICS

DEFENSE	ATL.	CHI.	DALL.	DET.	G.B.	L.A.	MINN.	N.O.	NY G	PHIL.	STL.	S.F.	T.B.	WASH.
FIRST DOWNS:														
Total	318	278	321	340	308	305	343	280	253	332	300	317	269	334
by Rushing	116	126	137	167	104	142	91	126	92	157	135	110	95	136
by Passing	176	126	158	150	174	134	217	124	140	150	141	183	159	173
by Penalty	26	26	26	23	30	29	35	30	21	25	24	24	15	25
RUSHING:														
Number	495	608	630	596	478	559	391	546	481	559	519	560	458	532
Yards	1965	2171	2711	2795	1670	2236	1512	2286	1685	2509	2213	1941	1731	2157
Average Yards	4.0	3.6	4.3	4.7	3.5	4.0	3.9	4.2	3.5	4.5	4.3	3.5	3.8	4.1
Touchdowns	15	13	15	26	11	17	8	16	11	17	20	17	13	19
PASSING:														
Attempts	563	489	439	436	514	477	709	441	506	476	477	517	473	525
Completions	311	222	241	228	286	235	382	238	251	258	253	328	239	307
Completion Pct.	55.2	45.4	54.9	52.3	55.6	49.3	53.9	54.0	49.6	54.2	53.0	63.4	50.5	58.5
Passing Yards	3986	2728	3414	3475	3576	3008	4567	2778	3009	3249	3269	3766	3565	3743
Avg. Yds per Att.	6.2	4.7	6.7	6.5	5.6	4.9	5.9	5.0	4.8	6.1	5.5	6.5	7.0	6.3
Avg. Yds per Comp.	12.8	12.3	14.2	15.2	12.5	12.8	12.0	11.7	12.0	12.6	12.9	11.5	14.9	12.2
Times Tackled	37	35	31	44	52	50	29	41	47	22	48	29	19	30
Yds Lost Tackled	287	266	245	337	387	451	234	359	368	205	405	223	136	277
Net Yards	3699	2462	3169	3138	3189	2557	4333	2419	2641	3044	2864	3543	2429	3466
Touchdowns	30	14	24	18	24	15	27	8	16	25	15	20	20	19
Interceptions	24	23	15	23	24	32	29	27	20	22	24	13	14	22
Pct. Intercepted	4.3	4.7	3.4	5.3	4.7	6.7	4.1	6.1	4.0	4.6	5.0	2.5	3.0	4.2
PUNTS:														
Number	88	114	81	64	84	89	88	66	97	64	69	93	82	73
Average	40.3	39.7	40.5	43.5	39.6	42.0	41.4	40.5	43.3	40.3	41.8	41.5	41.2	40.0
PUNT RETURNS														
Number	50	45	45	52	40	49	39	41	64	58	43	48	38	49
Yards	383	518	235	450	306	676	303	426	502	422	463	344	244	507
Average Yards	7.7	11.5	5.2	8.7	7.7	13.8	7.8	10.4	7.8	7.3	10.5	7.2	6.4	10.3
Touchdowns	0	1	0	1	1	3	0	0	0	0	1	0	0	2
KICKOFF RET.:														
Number	62	64	53	61	58	68	67	70	57	43	75	45	46	67
Yards	1419	1214	981	1164	1066	1244	1328	1523	1120	832	1625	909	912	1673
Average Yards	22.9	19.0	18.5	19.1	18.4	18.3	19.8	21.8	19.6	19.3	21.7	20.2	19.8	25.0
Touchdowns	0	0	0	0	0	0	1	0	0	0	0	1	0	0
INTERCEPT RET.:														
Number	25	18	37	24	30	17	16	17	17	26	21	27	32	24
Yards	494	345	482	286	495	237	120	214	222	266	281	448	648	249
Average Yards	19.8	19.2	13.0	11.9	16.5	13.9	7.5	12.6	13.1	10.2	13.4	16.6	20.3	10.4
Touchdowns	3	3	0	1	1	0	0	0	1	0	1	4	4	2
PENALTIES:														
Number	90	121	103	111	84	117	109	109	108	113	106	92	89	98
Yards	940	996	839	990	687	916	865	899	897	855	877	752	779	940
FUMBLES:														
Number	31	37	45	41	31	34	39	40	38	33	33	26	27	32
Number Lost	17	17	20	20	17	15	21	20	16	17	20	12	14	19
POINTS:														
Total	426	253	367	397	324	303	325	207	295	368	315	357	315	347
PAT Attempts	52	31	40	46	37	36	37	24	32	44	37	43	38	42
PAT Made	51	29	40	46	36	36	34	24	31	42	36	42	36	38
FG Attempts	33	23	35	35	24	26	25	25	38	31	32	29	28	30
FG Made	21	12	27	25	22	17	21	13	24	20	19	19	17	19
Percent FG Made	63.6	52.2	77.1	71.4	91.7	65.4	84.0	52.0	63.2	64.5	59.4	65.5	60.7	63.3
Safeties	0	1	3	0	0	0	3	0	0	1	0	0	0	0

DEFENSE	ATL.	CHI.	DALL.	DET.	G.B.	L.A.	MINN.	N.O.	NY G	PHIL.	STL.	S.F.	T.B.	WASH.
FIRST DOWNS:														
Total	303	290	286	279	326	285	299	303	291	266	328	280	320	310
by Rushing	94	120	106	93	140	125	117	127	106	102	134	113	123	133
by Passing	172	144	162	158	168	128	163	161	156	137	171	144	174	152
by Penalty	37	26	18	28	18	32	19	15	29	27	23	23	23	25
RUSHING:														
Number	459	521	468	469	546	585	540	504	553	476	509	464	551	532
Yards	1666	2146	2049	1623	2098	2397	2045	1916	1891	1751	2428	1918	2172	2161
Average Yards	3.6	4.1	4.4	3.5	3.8	4.1	3.8	3.8	3.4	3.7	4.8	4.1	3.9	4.1
Touchdowns	10	13	16	14	21	19	15	17	10	11	20	10	16	17
PASSING:														
Attempts	565	525	511	475	505	439	481	471	544	507	495	514	541	452
Completions	322	233	236	261	284	204	265	287	294	248	282	273	317	214
Completion Pct.	57.0	44.4	46.2	54.9	56.2	46.5	55.1	60.9	54.0	48.9	57.0	53.1	58.6	47.3
Passing Yards	3927	3527	3717	3596	3353	3057	3599	3578	3318	3050	3547	3135	3297	3310
Avg. Yds per Att.	6.2	5.8	6.1	6.2	5.7	5.7	6.5	6.7	5.0	4.9	6.3	5.2	5.6	6.3
Avg. Yds per Comp.	12.2	15.1	15.8	13.8	11.8	15.0	13.6	12.5	11.3	12.3	12.6	11.5	10.4	15.5
Times Tackled	29	31	42	47	36	43	33	27	44	40	32	36	23	32
Yds Lost Tackled	239	279	347	373	266	330	271	241	284	354	252	290	157	265
Net Yards	3688	3248	3370	3223	3087	2727	3328	3337	2934	2696	3295	2845	3140	3045
Touchdowns	30	23	17	22	18	17	26	26	14	12	29	16	10	21
Interceptions	25	18	37	24	30	17	16	17	17	26	21	27	32	24
Pct. Intercepted	4.4	3.4	7.2	5.1	5.9	3.9	3.3	3.6	3.1	5.1	4.2	5.3	5.9	5.3
PUNTS:														
Number	96	98	80	81	69	94	84	69	105	76	69	83	73	80
Average	42.2	40.7	41.2	42.9	39.7	41.0	40.7	44.1	39.6	40.7	41.3	41.4	41.2	41.7
PUNT RETURNS														
Number	59	66	38	39	50	52	46	36	61	34	37	57	52	50
Yards	577	594	231	299	511	481	399	282	561	246	276	664	668	388
Average Yards	9.8	9.0	6.1	7.7	10.2	9.3	8.7	7.8	9.2	7.2	7.5	11.6	12.8	7.8
Touchdowns	2	1	0	0	0	0	1	0	1	0	0	1	1	1
KICKOFF RET.:														
Number	67	44	71	70	70	60	62	50	50	60	55	67	64	69
Yards	1286	937	1508	1257	1183	1443	1260	966	959	1334	1163	1389	1332	1275
Average Yards	19.2	21.3	21.2	18.0	16.9	24.1	20.3	19.3	19.2	22.2	21.1	20.7	20.8	18.5
Touchdowns	0	0	0	0	0	2	0	0	0	0	0	0	0	0
INTERCEPT RET.:														
Number	24	23	15	23	24	32	29	27	20	22	24	13	14	22
Yards	301	385	124	274	475	361	384	479	252	357	312	297	179	391
Average Yards	12.5	16.7	8.3	11.9	19.8	11.3	13.2	17.7	12.6	16.2	13.0	22.8	12.8	17.8
Touchdowns	0	2	1	1	3	1	3	1	2	2	0	2	0	1
PENALTIES:														
Number	97	119	104	95	108	118	115	118	111	91	98	108	79	108
Yards	804	961	837	872	907	1018	991	1089	876	813	845	866	650	921
FUMBLES:														
Number	43	33	43	29	42	37	27	31	38	38	35	36	32	32
Number Lost	21	22	16	15	24	16	19	17	17	21	17	21	14	15
POINTS:														
Total	355	324	277	322	361	351	369	378	257	221	408	250	268	349
PAT Attempts	43	39	34	38	45	39	46	46	27	26	50	30	27	43
PAT Made	41	37	31	37	43	37	42	45	27	23	48	29	27	38
FG Attempts	29	29	29	22	24	33	27	25	33	28	26	23	33	24
FG Made	18	17	14	19	16	26	17	19	22	14	20	13	25	17
Percent FG Made	62.1	58.6	48.3	86.4	66.7	78.8	63.0	76.0	66.7	50.0	76.9	56.5	75.8	70.8
Safeties	1	1	0	0	0	1	0	0	1	0	0	1	2	1

from Gary Fencik, the defense also suffered periodic breakdowns. Things picked up at the end of the year. After a close loss to the Cowboys on Thanksgiving, the Bears beat the Vikings, Raiders, and Broncos to end the season on an assertive note. Also asserting himself was N.F.L. patriarch George Halas, the 86-year-old owner of the franchise from its earliest days. He took a more active role in the running of the club, taking under his scrutiny the fates of coach Neill Armstrong and general manager Jim Finks. At the conclusion of the schedule, the verdict came in; Finks stays, Armstrong goes.

WESTERN DIVISION

San Francisco '49ers—They didn't look like much on paper, but Bill Walsh led the 49ers to a surprise divisional title. Two losses in the first three games promised the usual losing season. Starting on September 27, however, the 49ers won 12 of 13 games with an open offense and swarming defense. The offense used their runners only to set up an all-out passing attack. In his first full season as a starter, quarterback Joe Montana engineered the complex offense with the coolness of a surgeon. Lanky receiver Dwight Clark broke clear for lots of passes despite his limited speed. With Randy Cross leading the way, the offensive line gave Montana plenty of time to operate. The defense blended youth with two veteran pickups. Inside linebacker Jack Reynolds came from Los Angeles to inject ferocity into the heart of the unit, while end Fred Dean left San Diego in a salary dispute to give Walsh a pass-rushing maniac. The secondary combined three rookies with third-year safety Dwight Hicks. Rather than stumbling in their inexperience, the secondary terrorized quarterbacks with daring, as Hicks and cornerback Ronnie Lott feasted on errant passes. With a 4–1 record within their division, the 49ers went to the playoffs for the first time since 1972.

Atlanta Falcons—For every step the offense took, the defense went back one. After three straight victories to open the season, the Falcons lost three straight and never again hit their stride. The offense had aces in all departments. William Andrews plugged away for his third 1,000-yard rushing season in as many tries. Working off this running threat, Steve Bartkowski ate up yardage with his passes, with Al Jenkins burning defenses regularly. Led by tackle Mike Kenn, the offensive line supported both the ground and air attacks handsomely. While the Falcons rang up scores with passing, enemy air attacks victimized the Atlanta defense. An injury to linebacker Joel Williams cut the best pass rusher out of the lineup. With a secondary high on inexperience and low on speed, the Falcons couldn't stop enemy passers. Although the Falcons stayed in the running for a wild-card berth into December, three losses at the end of the year crushed that hope.

Los Angeles Rams—Things went badly for the Rams over the summer and never improved much. Salary hassles sent linebacker Jack Reynolds to San Francisco and quarterback Vince Ferragamo to Montreal of the CFL. Pat Haden brought experience to the QB position, but he did not have Ferragamo's long distance arm. To make Haden's job impossible, the offensive line broke down after years of excellence. Doug France's shoulder injury and poor seasons by Kent Hill and Jackie Slater exposed Haden to a pass rush which gave him a set of bruised ribs. To juice up the offense, coach Ray Malavasi signed Dan Pastorini in mid-season, but the ex-Oiler quarterback had no greater success than Haden. The defense suffered from the departure of Reynolds, Bob Brudzinski, and Fred Dryer. Although Nolan Cromwell starred in the secondary and Wendell Tyler rebounded from injuries to run for over 1,000 yards, the Rams had a collective off-season and lost six of their last seven games. Their losing record was the first since 1972.

New Orleans Saints—Although the Saints didn't win too often under Bum Phillips, they didn't feel like doormats any longer. Released by the Oilers after a string of playoff seasons, Phillips began rebuilding the Saints in the image of his old Houston club. With the number one position in the college draft, he picked workhorse runner George Rogers from South Carolina. Phillips immediately structured the offense around Rogers, forced in part by an injury to receiver Ike Harris and the trade of Wes Chandler to San Diego. When injuries slowed quarterback Archie Manning, rookie Dave Wilson got some experience at running the attack. Although he had a good rookie class, Phillips still had a long way to go in building his club up to the standards he had set in Houston. An opening day loss to Atlanta by a 27–0 score dampened some spirits, but the Saints enjoyed beating the Rams twice for the first time ever. They also beat the playoff-bound 49ers and relished a 27–24 upset over the Oilers in the Astrodome, a fine homecoming for Bum.

DALLAS COWBOYS 12-4-0 Tom Landry

Scores of Each Game		
26	Washington	10
30	ST. LOUIS	17
35	New England	21
18	N.Y. GIANTS	10
17	St. Louis	20
14	San Francisco	45
29	LOS ANGELES	17
28	MIAMI	27
17	Philadelphia	14
27	BUFFALO	14
24	Detroit	27
24	WASHINGTON	10
10	CHICAGO	9
37	Baltimore	13
21	PHILADELPHIA	10
10	N.Y. Giants	*13

Use Name	Pos.	Hgt.	Wgt.	Age	Int.	Pts.
Jim Cooper	OT-C	6'5"	260	25		
Pat Donovan	OT	6'4"	250	28		
Andy Frederick	OT	6'6"	255	26		
Steve Wright	OT	6'5"	245	22		
Kurt Petersen	OG	6'4"	250	24		
Howard Richards	OG-OT	6'6"	262	22		
Herbert Scott	OG	6'2"	252	28		
Glen Titensor	OG-C	6'4"	256	23		
Tom Rafferty	C-OG	6'3"	250	27		
Robert Shaw	C	6'4"	245	24		
Too Tall Jones	DE	6'9"	270	30		
Harvey Martin	DE	6'5"	250	30		2
Don Smerek	DE	6'7"	246	23		
Bruce Thornton	DE-DT	6'5"	265	23		
Larry Bethea	DT-DE	6'5"	254	25		
John Dutton	DT	6'7"	265	30		2
Randy White	DT	6'4"	250	28		

Use Name	Pos.	Hgt.	Wgt.	Age	Int.	Pts.
Bob Breunig	LB	6'2"	225	28	2	
Guy Brown	LB	6'4"	228	26	1	
Anthony Dickerson	LB	6'2"	215	24		
Mike Hegman	LB	6'1"	225	28		
Angelo King	LB	6'1"	220	23		
D.D. Lewis	LB	6'2"	215	35	1	
Danny Spradlin	LB	6'1"	228	22		
Benny Barnes	DB	6'1"	195	30	1	6
Michael Downs	DB	6'3"	195	22	7	
Ron Fellows	DB	6'	173	22		
Dennis Thurman	DB	5'11"	170	25	9	
Everson Walls	DB	6'1"	195	21	11	
Charlie Waters	DB	6'1"	200	32	3	
Steve Wilson	DB	5'10"	192	24	2	

Dextor Clinkscale – Achilles Injury
John Fitzgerald – Knee Injury
Randy Hughes – Shoulder Injury
Bill Roe – Ankle Injury

Use Name	Pos.	Hgt.	Wgt.	Age	Int.	Pts.
Glenn Carano	QB	6'3"	202	25		
Gary Hogeboom	QB	6'4"	200	23		
Danny White	QB	6'2"	192	29		
Tony Dorsett	HB	5'11"	190	27		36
James Jones	HB	5'10"	200	22		6
Robert Newhouse	FB	5'10"	215	31		
Timmy Newsome	FB	6'1"	227	23		
Ron Springs	FB-HB	6'1"	200	24		72
Doug Donley	WR	6'	174	22		
Tony Hill	WR	6'2"	198	25		24
Butch Johnson	WR	6'1"	192	27		30
Drew Pearson	WR	6'	183	30		18
Doug Cosbie	TE	6'6"	230	25		30
Billy Joe DuPree	TE	6'4"	229	31		12
Jay Saldi	TE	6'3"	227	26		6
Rafael Septien	K	5'9"	171	27		121

PHILADELPHIA EAGLES 10-6-0 Dick Vermeil

Scores of Each Game		
24	N.Y. Giants	10
13	NEW ENGLAND	3
20	Buffalo	14
36	WASHINGTON	13
16	ATLANTA	13
31	New Orleans	14
23	Minnesota	35
20	TAMPA BAY	10
14	DALLAS	17
52	St. Louis	10
38	BALTIMORE	13
10	N.Y. GIANTS	20
10	Miami	13
13	Washington	15
10	Dallas	21
38	ST. LOUIS	0

Use Name	Pos.	Hgt.	Wgt.	Age	Int.	Pts.
Frank Giddens	OT	6'7"	300	22		
Jerry Sisemore	OT	6'4"	265	30		
Stan Walters	OT	6'6"	275	33		
Ron Baker	OG	6'4"	250	26		
Steve Kenney	OG-OT	6'4"	262	25		
Dean Miraldi	OG	6'5"	254	23		
Petey Perot	OG	6'2"	261	24		
Guy Morriss	C	6'4"	255	30		
Mark Slater	C	6'1"	257	26		
Greg Brown	DE	6'5"	235	24		6
Carl Hairston	DE	6'3"	260	28		
Dennis Harrison	DE	6'8"	275	25		
Claude Humphrey	DE	6'5"	258	37		
Leonard Mitchell	DE	6'7"	272	22		
Ken Clarke	NT	6'2"	255	25		2
Charles Johnson	NT	6'3"	262	29		1

Use Name	Pos.	Hgt.	Wgt.	Age	Int.	Pts.
John Bunting	LB	6'1"	220	31		
Al Chesley	LB	6'3"	240	24	2	
Mike Curcio	LB	6'1"	237	24		
Frank LeMaster	LB	6'2"	238	29	2	6
Ray Phillips	LB	6'4"	230	27	1	
Jerry Robinson	LB	6'2"	218	24	1	
Reggie Wilkes	LB	6'4"	230	25	2	1
Richard Blackmore	DB	5'10"	174	25	2	
Herman Edwards	DB	6'	190	27	3	
Ray Ellis	DB	6'1"	192	22		
Jo Jo Heath	DB	5'10"	182	24		
Randy Logan	DB	6'1"	195	30	2	
John Sciarra	DB	5'11"	185	27	1	
Brenard Wilson	DB	6'	175	26	5	
Roynell Young	DB	6'1"	181	23	4	

Bill Bergey – Knee Injury
Leroy Harris – Broken Arm
Steve Wagner – Shoulder Injury

Use Name	Pos.	Hgt.	Wgt.	Age	Int.	Pts.
Ron Jaworski	QB	6'2"	196	30		
Joe Pisarcik	QB	6'4"	220	29		
Steve Atkins (from G.B.)	HB	6'	216	25		
Billy Campfield	HB-FB	5'11"	205	25		24
Louie Giammona	HB	5'9"	180	28		12
Wilbert Montgomery	HB	5'10"	195	26		60
Calvin Murray	HB	5'11"	188	22		
Mickey Fitzgerald (from ATL)	FB	6'2"	235	23		
Perry Harrington	FB	5'11"	210	23		12
Hubie Oliver	FB	5'10"	212	23		6
Booker Russell	FB	6'2"	235	25		24
Harold Carmichael	WR	6'7"	225	31		36
Wally Henry	WR	5'8"	180	26		12
Alvin Hooks	WR	5'11"	170	24		
Rodney Parker	WR	6'1"	190	28		12
Charlie Smith	WR	6'1"	185	31		24
Ron Smith (from S.D.)	WR	6'	185	24		12
Steve Folsom	TE	6'4"	230	23		
Keith Krepfle	TE	6'3"	230	29		30
John Spagnola	TE	6'4"	240	24		
Tony Franklin	K	5'8"	182	24		101
Max Runager	K	6'1"	189	25		

NEW YORK GIANTS 9-7-0 Ray Perkins

Scores of Each Game		
10	PHILADELPHIA	24
17	Washington	7
20	NEW ORLEANS	7
10	Dallas	18
14	GREEN BAY	27
34	ST. LOUIS	14
32	Seattle	0
27	Atlanta	*24
7	N.Y. JETS	26
24	Green Bay	26
27	WASHINGTON	*30
20	Philadelphia	10
10	San Francisco	17
10	LOS ANGELES	7
20	St. Louis	10
13	DALLAS	*10

Use Name	Pos.	Hgt.	Wgt.	Age	Int.	Pts.
Brad Benson	OT	6'3"	258	25		
Gordon King	OT	6'6"	275	25		
Jeff Weston	OT	6'5"	250	24		
Billy Ard	OG	6'3"	250	22		
Roy Simmons	OG	6'3"	264	24		
J.T. Turner	OG	6'3"	250	28		
Jim Clack	C	6'3"	250	33		
Ernie Hughes	C	6'3"	260	26		
Ed McGlasson	C	6'4"	248	25		
Dee Hardison	DE	6'4"	269	25		
Gary Jeter	DE	6'4"	260	26		
George Martin	DE	6'4"	245	28		12
Curtis McGriff	DE	6'5"	270	23		
Phil Tabor	DE	6'4"	255	24		
Carl Barisich	NT	6'4"	255	30		
Jim Burt	NT	6'1"	255	22		
Bill Neill	NT	6'4"	255	22		

Use Name	Pos.	Hgt.	Wgt.	Age	Int.	Pts.
Harry Carson	LB	6'2"	235	27		
Byron Hunt	LB	6'4"	230	22	1	
Brian Kelley	LB	6'3"	222	30	2	
Frank Marion	LB	6'3"	228	30		
Joe McLaughlin	LB	6'1"	235	24		
Lawrence Taylor	LB	6'3"	237	22	1	
Brad Van Pelt	LB	6'5"	235	30	1	
Mike Whittington	LB	6'2"	220	23		
Bill Currier	DB	6'	195	26	3	
Mike Dennis	DB	5'10"	190	22		6
Larry Flowers	DB	6'1"	190	23	1	
Mark Haynes	DB	5'11"	185	22	1	
Terry Jackson	DB	5'10"	197	25	3	6
Beasley Reece	DB	6'1"	195	27	4	6

Eric Felton – Shoulder Injury
Larry Heater – Thumb Injury
Myron Lapka – Knee Injury
Dan Lloyd – Illness
Kervin Wyatt – Injury

Use Name	Pos.	Hgt.	Wgt.	Age	Int.	Pts.
Scott Brunner	QB	6'5"	200	24		
Cliff Olander	QB	6'5"	187	26		
Phil Simms	QB	6'3"	216	25		
Leon Bright	HB	5'9"	192	26		12
Ike Forte	HB	6'	211	27		
Alvin Garrett (to WAS)	HB-WR	5'7"	178	24		
Louis Jackson	HB	5'11"	195	23		6
Doug Kotar	HB	5'11"	205	30		6
Billy Taylor (to NYJ)	HB	6'	215	25		12
Rob Carpenter (from HOU)	FB-HB	6'1"	230	26		36
Bo Matthews (to MIA)	FB	6'4"	222	29		
Leon Perry	FB	5'11"	225	24		6
Mike Friede	WR	6'3"	205	23		6
Earnest Gray	WR	6'3"	195	24		12
John Mistler	WR	6'2"	186	22		6
Johnny Perkins	WR	6'2"	205	28		36
Danny Pittman	WR	6'2"	205	23		
Tom Mullady	TE	6'3"	232	24		6
Gary Shirk	TE	6'1"	220	31		18
Dave Young	TE	6'5"	242	22		6
Joe Danelo	K	5'9"	166	27		103
Dave Jennings	K	6'4"	205	29		

WASHINGTON REDSKINS 8-8-0 Jack Gibbs

Scores of Each Game		
10	DALLAS	26
7	N.Y. GIANTS	17
30	St. Louis	40
13	Philadelphia	36
17	SAN FRANCISCO	30
24	Chicago	7
10	Miami	13
24	NEW ENGLAND	22
42	ST. LOUIS	21
33	DETROIT	31
30	N.Y. Giants	*27
10	Dallas	24
14	Buffalo	21
15	PHILADELPHIA	13
38	BALTIMORE	14
30	Los Angeles	7

Use Name	Pos.	Hgt.	Wgt.	Age	Int.	Pts.
Mike Daum	OT	6'6"	256	22		
Joe Jacoby	OT	6'7"	282	22		
Mark May	OT	6'6"	270	21		
Jerry Scanlan	OT-OG	6'5"	270	24		
George Starke	OT	6'5"	250	33		
Robert Woods	OT-OG	6'3"	259	31		
Darryl Grant	OG-C-OT	6'1"	230	21		
Russ Grimm	OG-C	6'3"	250	22		
Melvin Jones	OG	6'2"	260	25		
Ron Saul	OG	6'2"	254	33		
Jeff Bostic	C	6'2"	246	22		
Coy Bacon	DE	6'4"	265	39		
Calvin Clark	DE	6'4"	260	22		
Mike Clark	DE	6'4"	240	22		
Dallas Hickman (from BAL)	DE-LB	6'6"	245	29		
Karl Lorch	DE-DT	6'3"	258	31		
Dexter Manley	DE	6'3"	240	22		
Mat Mendenhall	DE	6'6"	253	24		
Perry Brooks	DT	6'3"	260	26		
Dave Butz	DT	6'7"	285	31	1	
Pat Ogrin	DT	6'5"	265	23		
Wilbur Young (to S.D.)	DT	6'6"	290	32		

Use Name	Pos.	Hgt.	Wgt.	Age	Int.	Pts.
Monte Coleman	LB	6'2"	230	3	6	
Pete Cronan (from SEA)	LB	6'2"	238	26		
Brad Dusek	LB	6'2"	223	30		
Dave Graf	LB	6'2"	220	28		
Mel Kaufman	LB	6'2"	227	23	2	
Quentin Lowry	LB	6'3"	235	23		
Rich Milot	LB	6'4"	230	24		
Neal Olkewicz	LB	6'	227	24	2	6
Trent Bryant	DB	5'9"	180	22		
Cris Crissy	DB	5'11"	195	22		
Curtis Jordan	DB	6'2"	205	27		
Joe Lavender	DB	6'4"	190	32	4	
LeCharls McDaniel	DB	5'9"	183	22		
Mark Murphy	DB	6'4"	210	26	7	
Mike Nelms	DB	6'1"	185	26	1	12
Lemar Parrish	DB	5'11"	170	33	1	
Tony Peters	DB	6'1"	177	28	3	
Jeris White	DB	5'11"	188	28		

Fred Dean – Arm Injury
Dan Peiffer – Knee Injury
Ray Waddy – Leg Injury

Use Name	Pos.	Hgt.	Wgt.	Age	Int.	Pts.
Tom Flick	QB	6'3"	190	23		
Mike Rae	QB	6'	195	30		
Joe Theismann	QB	6'	195	31		12
Rickey Claitt	HB	5'10"	206	24		
Nick Giaquinto (from MIA)	HB-FB	5'11"	204	26		12
Clarence Harmon	HB-FB	5'11"	210	25		
Joe Washington	HB	5'10"	179	27		42
Wilbur Jackson	FB	6'1"	219	29		
John Riggins	FB	6'2"	230	32		78
Otis Wonsley	FB	5'10"	205	24		
Terry Metcalf	WR-HB	5'10"	183	29		
Art Monk	WR	6'3"	210	23		36
Virgil Seay	WR	5'8"	170	23		18
Ricky Thompson	WR	6'	177	27		24
Greg McCrary	TE	6'3"	235	29		
Bob Raba	TE	6'1"	225	26		
Rick Walker	TE	6'3"	236	26		6
Don Warren	TE	6'4"	236	25		6
Mike Connell	K	6'1"	200	25		
Mark Moseley	K	5'11"	205	33		95

ST. LOUIS CARDINALS 7-9-0 Jim Hanifan

Scores of Each Game		
7	MIAMI	20
17	Dallas	30
40	WASHINGTON	30
10	Tampa Bay	20
20	DALLAS	17
14	N.Y. Giants	34
20	Atlanta	41
30	MINNESOTA	17
21	Washington	42
10	PHILADELPHIA	52
24	BUFFALO	0
35	Baltimore	24
27	New England	20
30	NEW ORLEANS	3
10	N.Y. GIANTS	20
0	Philadelphia	38

Use Name	Pos.	Hgt.	Wgt.	Age	Int.	Pts.
George Collins	OT-OG	6'2"	260	25		
Dan Dierdorf	OT	6'4"	288	32		
Dale Markham	OT	6'8"	280	24		
Art Plunkett	OT	6'7"	260	22		
Keith Wortman	OT	6'2"	275	31		
Joe Bostic	OG	6'3"	265	24		
Barney Cotton	OG	6'5"	265	24		
Terry Stieve	OG	6'2"	263	27		
Tom Brahaney	C	6'2"	246	29		
Randy Clark	C-OT	6'3"	254	24		
Rush Brown	DE	6'2"	257	27		
Kirby Criswell	DE	6'5"	238	24		
Curtis Greer	DE	6'4"	252	23		
Stafford Mays	DE	6'2"	240	23		
Bob Pollard	DE	6'3"	252	32		
Bill Acker	NT	6'2"	255	25		
Mike Dawson	NT	6'4"	275	27		
Bruce Radford	NT-DE	6'5"	260	25		
Ken Times	NT	6'2"	246	25		

Use Name	Pos.	Hgt.	Wgt.	Age	Int.	Pts.
Dave Ahrens	LB	6'3"	228	22	1	6
Charlie Baker	LB	6'2"	217	23		
Calvin Favron	LB	6'1"	225	24	1	
Doak Field	LB	6'2"	226	22		
John Gillen	LB	6'3"	227	22		
E.J. Junior	LB	6'3"	235	21	1	
Tim Kearney	LB	6'2"	224	30		
Eric Williams	LB	6'2"	225	26	1	
Carl Allen	DB	6'	186	25		
Steve Carpenter	DB	6'2"	195	23		
Tim Collier	DB	6'	174	27	1	
Ken Greene	DB	6'3"	203	25	7	
Jeff Griffin	DB	6'	185	23	1	
Charles Johnson	DB	5'10"	180	25	1	
Lee Nelson	DB	5'10"	185	27		
Don Schwartz	DB	6'1"	191	25		
Roger Wehrli	DB	6'1"	194	33	4	
Herb Williams	DB	6'	198	23		

Ron Coder – Knee Injury

Use Name	Pos.	Hgt.	Wgt.	Age	Int.	Pts.
Jim Hart	QB	6'2"	210	37		
Rusty Lisch	QB	6'3"	215	24		
Neil Lomax	QB	6'3"	215	22		12
Ottis Anderson	HB-FB	6'2"	225	24		54
Will Harrell	HB	5'9"	182	28		12
Stump Mitchell	HB	5'9"	188	22		12
Randy Love	FB	6'1"	205	24		
Wayne Morris	FB	6'	208	27		30
Mark Bell	WR	5'9"	175	24		
Ralph Clayton	WR-FB	6'3"	222	22		
Mike Fisher	WR	5'11"	172	23		
John Floyd	WR	6'1"	195	24		
Mel Gray	WR	5'9"	173	32		12
Roy Green	WR-DB	5'11"	190	24	3	30
Dave Stief	WR	6'3"	195	25		6
Pat Tilley	WR	5'10"	171	28		18
Chris Combs	TE-OT	6'4"	237	23		
Greg LaFleur	TE	6'4"	237	22		12
Doug Marsh	TE	6'3"	236	23		6
Carl Birdsong	K	6'	192	22		
Neil O'Donoghue	K	6'6"	210	28		93

*—Overtime

DALLAS COWBOYS

RUSHING

Last Name	No.	Yds.	Avg.	TD
Dorsett	342	1646	4.8	4
Springs	172	625	3.6	10
J. Jones	34	183	5.4	1
D. White	38	104	2.7	0
Newsome	13	38	2.9	0
Cosbie	4	33	8.3	0
Newhouse	14	33	2.4	0
Pearson	3	31	10.3	0
DuPree	1	12	12.0	0
Carano	8	9	1.1	0
Hill	1	−3	−3.0	0

RECEIVING

Last Name	No.	Yds.	Avg.	TD
Hill	46	953	21	4
Springs	46	359	8	2
Pearson	38	614	16	3
Dorsett	32	325	10	2
Johnson	25	552	22	5
DuPree	19	214	11	2
Cosbie	17	225	13	5
Saldi	8	82	10	1
J. Jones	6	37	6	0
Donley	3	32	11	0
Newhouse	1	21	21	0

PUNT RETURNS

Last Name	No.	Yds.	Avg.	TD
J. Jones	33	188	6	0
Fellows	11	44	4	0
Donley	1	3	3	0

KICKOFF RETURNS

Last Name	No.	Yds.	Avg.	TD
J. Jones	27	517	19	0
Newsome	12	228	19	0
Fellows	8	170	21	0
Newhouse	3	34	11	0
Wilson	2	32	16	0
Cosbie	1	0	0	0

PASSING – PUNTING – KICKING

PASSING	Att.	Comp.	%	Yds.	Yd./Att.	TD	Int.–%	RK
D. White	391	223	57	3098	7.9	22	13– 3	2
Carano	45	16	36	235	5.2	1	1– 2	
Pearson	2	2	100	81	40.5	1	0– 0	
Springs	1	0	0	0	0.0	0	1–100	

PUNTING	No.	Avg.
D. White	79	40.8
Septien	2	31.0

KICKING	XP	Att.	%	FG	Att.	%
Septien	40	40	100	35	27	77

PHILADELPHIA EAGLES

RUSHING

Last Name	No.	Yds.	Avg.	TD
Montgomery	286	1402	4.9	8
Oliver	75	329	4.4	1
Harrington	34	140	4.1	2
Murray	23	134	5.8	0
Jaworski	22	128	5.8	0
Russell	38	123	3.2	4
Campfield	31	115	3.7	1
Giammona	35	98	2.8	1
Atkins	12	33	2.8	0
LeMaster	1	7	7.0	0
R. Smith	1	7	7.0	0
C. Smith	2	5	2.5	0
Carmichael	1	1	1.0	0
Pisarcik	7	1	0.1	0
Sciarra	1	0	0.0	0
Henry	1	−2	−2.0	0

RECEIVING

Last Name	No.	Yds.	Avg.	TD
Carmichael	61	1028	17	6
Montgomery	49	521	11	2
C. Smith	38	564	15	4
Campfield	36	326	9	3
Krepfle	20	210	11	5
Oliver	10	37	4	0
Henry	9	145	16	2
Harrington	9	27	3	0
Parker	8	168	21	2
R. Smith	7	168	24	2
Spagnola	6	83	14	0
Giammona	6	54	9	1
Murray	1	7	7	0
Atkins	1	2	2	0
Russell	1	−5	−5	0

PUNT RETURNS

Last Name	No.	Yds.	Avg.	TD
Henry	54	396	7	0
Sciarra	4	26	7	0

KICKOFF RETURNS

Last Name	No.	Yds.	Avg.	TD
Henry	25	533	21	0
Campfield	12	223	19	0
R. Smith	2	32	16	0
Russell	2	28	14	0
Giammona	1	19	19	0
Atkins	1	15	15	0
Murray	1	14	14	0
Clarke	1	0	0	0

PASSING – PUNTING – KICKING

PASSING	Att.	Comp.	%	Yds.	Yd./Att.	TD	Int.–%	RK
Jaworski	461	250	54	3095	6.7	23	20– 4	8
Pisarcik	15	8	53	154	10.3	2	2– 13	

PUNTING	No.	Avg.
Runager	63	40.7
Franklin	1	13.0

KICKING	XP	Att.	%	FG	Att.	%
Franklin	41	43	95	20	31	65

NEW YORK GIANTS

RUSHING

Last Name	No.	Yds.	Avg.	TD
Carpenter	208	822	4.0	5
Perry	72	257	3.6	0
Bright	51	197	3.9	2
Kotar	46	154	3.3	1
B. Taylor	38	111	2.9	2
Forte	19	74	3.9	0
L. Jackson	27	68	2.5	1
Simms	19	42	2.2	0
Brunner	14	20	1.4	0
Matthews	4	14	3.5	0
Garrett	1	2	2.0	0
Perkins	2	−1	−0.5	0

RECEIVING

Last Name	No.	Yds.	Avg.	TD
Perkins	51	858	17	6
Shirk	42	445	11	3
Carpenter	37	281	8	1
Bright	28	291	10	0
Gray	22	360	16	2
Friede	18	250	14	1
Mullady	14	136	10	1
Perry	13	140	11	1
Kotar	9	32	4	0
Mistler	8	119	15	1
B. Taylor	8	71	9	0
Young	5	49	10	1
L. Jackson	3	25	8	0
Forte	3	11	4	0
Matthews	2	13	7	0
Pittman	1	8	8	0

PUNT RETURNS

Last Name	No.	Yds.	Avg.	TD
Bright	52	410	8	0
Garrett	8	57	7	0
T. Jackson	2	22	11	0
Pittman	1	13	13	0
Reece	1	0	0	0

KICKOFF RETURNS

Last Name	No.	Yds.	Avg.	TD
Garrett	18	401	22	0
Bright	25	481	19	0
Pittman	10	194	19	0
Dennis	3	51	17	0
McLaughlin	2	9	5	0
Reece	1	24	24	0

PASSING – PUNTING – KICKING

PASSING	Att.	Comp.	%	Yds.	Yd./Att.	TD	Int.–%	RK
Simms	316	172	54	2031	6.4	11	9– 3	7
Brunner	190	79	42	978	5.2	5	11– 6	

PUNTING	No.	Avg.
Jennings	97	43.3

KICKING	XP	Att.	%	FG	Att.	%
Danelo	31	31	100	24	38	63

WASHINGTON REDSKINS

RUSHING

Last Name	No.	Yds.	Avg.	TD
Washington	210	916	4.4	4
Riggins	195	714	3.7	13
Jackson	46	183	4.0	0
Theismann	36	177	4.9	2
Giaquinto	20	104	5.2	0
Metcalf	18	60	3.3	0
Claitt	3	19	6.3	0
Wonsley	3	11	3.7	0
Walker	1	5	5.0	0
Harmon	1	4	4.0	0
Connell	1	0	0.0	0
Monk	1	−5	−5.0	0

RECEIVING

Last Name	No.	Yds.	Avg.	TD
Washington	70	558	8	3
Monk	56	894	16	6
Metcalf	48	595	12	0
Warren	29	335	12	1
Thompson	28	423	15	4
Seay	26	472	18	3
Giaquinto	12	93	8	2
Walker	11	112	10	1
Harmon	11	98	9	0
Jackson	7	51	7	0
Riggins	6	59	10	0
McCrary	3	13	4	0
Wonsley	1	5	5	0
Bostic	1	−4	−4	0

PUNT RETURNS

Last Name	No.	Yds.	Avg.	TD
Nelms	45	492	11	2
Metcalf	4	15	4	0

KICKOFF RETURNS

Last Name	No.	Yds.	Avg.	TD
Nelms	37	1099	30	0
Metcalf	14	283	20	0
Wonsley	6	124	21	0
Cronan	3	60	20	0
Seay	2	36	18	0
Jackson	2	34	17	0
Giaquinto	1	22	22	0
Grant	1	20	20	0
Claitt	1	14	14	0
Peters	1	5	5	0

PASSING – PUNTING – KICKING

PASSING	Att.	Comp.	%	Yds.	Yd./Att.	TD	Int.–%	RK
Theismann	496	293	59	3568	7.2	19	20– 4	5
Flick	27	13	48	143	5.3	0	2– 7	
Washington	2	1	50	32	16.0	0	0– 0	

PUNTING	No.	Avg.
Connell	73	40.0

KICKING	XP	Att.	%	FG	Att.	%
Moseley	38	42	90	19	30	63

ST. LOUIS CARDINALS

RUSHING

Last Name	No.	Yds.	Avg.	TD
Anderson	328	1376	4.2	9
Morris	109	417	3.8	5
Mitchell	31	175	5.6	0
Lomax	19	104	5.5	2
Green	3	60	20.0	1
Love	3	11	3.7	0
Stief	1	8	8.0	0
Harrell	5	6	1.2	1
Gray	1	4	4.0	0
Hart	3	2	0.7	0
Birdsong	1	−2	−2.0	0

RECEIVING

Last Name	No.	Yds.	Avg.	TD
Tilley	66	1040	16	3
Anderson	51	387	8	0
Green	33	708	22	4
Gray	27	310	12	2
Morris	19	165	9	0
LaFleur	14	190	14	2
Harrell	14	131	9	1
Marsh	6	80	13	1
Mitchell	6	35	6	1
Stief	5	77	15	1
Combs	5	54	11	0
Floyd	3	32	11	0

PUNT RETURNS

Last Name	No.	Yds.	Avg.	TD
Mitchell	42	445	11	1
Harrell	1	8	8	0

KICKOFF RETURNS

Last Name	No.	Yds.	Avg.	TD
Mitchell	55	1292	24	0
Green	8	135	17	0
Harrell	7	118	17	0
Love	3	46	15	0
Griffin	2	34	17	0

PASSING – PUNTING – KICKING

PASSING	Att.	Comp.	%	Yds.	Yd./Att.	TD	Int.–%	RK
Hart	241	134	56	1694	7.0	11	14– 6	11
Lomax	236	119	50	1575	6.7	4	10– 4	14

PUNTING	No.	Avg.
Birdsong	69	41.8

KICKING	XP	Att.	%	FG	Att.	%
O'Donoghue	36	37	97	19	32	59

TAMPA BAY BUCCANEERS 9-7-0 John McKay

Scores of Each Game		
21	MINNESOTA	13
10	Kansas City	19
17	Chicago	28
20	ST LOUIS	10
28	DETROIT	10
21	Green Bay	10
16	Oakland	18
10	Philadelphia	20
20	CHICAGO	10
10	Minnesota	25
7	DENVER	24
37	GREEN BAY	3
31	New Orleans	14
24	ATLANTA	23
23	SAN DIEGO	24
20	Detroit	17

Use Name	Pos.	Hgt.	Wgt.	Age	Int.	Pts.
Charley Hannah	OT	6'5"	260	26		
Dave Reavis	OT	6'5"	260	31		
Gene Sanders	OT	6'3"	260	24		
Greg Roberts	OG	6'3"	260	24		
Ray Snell	OG-OT	6'3"	255	23		
George Yarno	OG	6'2"	255	24		
Jim Leonard	OG-C	6'3"	250	23		
Steve Wilson	C	6'3"	265	27		
Joe Campbell (from OAK)	DE	6'6"	250	26		
Scott Hutchinson	DE	6'4"	245	25		
Bill Kollar	DE	6'4"	250	28		
Lee Roy Selmon	DE	6'3"	250	26		
David Stalls	DE	6'4"	250	25		
David Logan	NT	6'2"	250	24		6
Laval Short	NT	6'3"	250	22		
Brad White	NT	6'2"	250	23		

Use Name	Pos.	Hgt.	Wgt.	Age	Int.	Pts.
Scot Brantley	LB	6'1"	230	23	1	
Hugh Green	LB	6'2"	225	22	2	
Andy Hawkins	LB	6'2"	220	23		
Cecil Johnson	LB	6'2"	230	26	5	
Dave Lewis	LB	6'4"	245	26	2	
Dana Nafziger	LB	6'1"	220	27		
Richard Wood	LB	6'2"	230	28		
Cedric Brown	DB	6'1"	205	27	9	12
Billy Cesare	DB	5'11"	190	26		
Neal Colzie	DB	6'2"	195	28	6	6
John Holt	DB	5'11"	180	22	1	
Aaron Mitchell	DB	6'1"	196	24		
Norris Thomas	DB	5'11"	185	27		
Mike Washington	DB	6'3"	200	28	6	6

Darrell Austin – Neck Injury
Mark Cotney – Knee Injury
Randy Crowder – Knee Injury
Tony Samuels – Knee Injury
Dewey Selmon – Hamstring Injury

Use Name	Pos.	Hgt.	Wgt.	Age	Int.	Pts.
Mike Ford	QB	6'3"	220	22		
Chuck Fusina	QB	6'1"	195	24		
Doug Williams	QB	6'4"	215	26		24
Ricky Bell	HB-FB	6'2"	215	26		
Gary Davis (to CLE)	HB	5'10"	210	26		
Jerry Eckwood	HB-FB	6'	200	26		12
James Owens	HB	5'11"	188	26		18
Tony Davis	FB	5'10"	210	28		
James Wilder	FB	6'2"	220	23		30
Theo Bell	WR	5'11"	180	27		12
Gerald Carter	WR	6'1"	185	24		
Kevin House	WR	6'1"	175	23		54
Gordon Jones	WR	6'	190	24		6
Jimmie Giles	TE	6'3"	240	26		36
Jim Obradovich	TE	6'2"	230	28		6
Tom Blanchard	K	6'	180	33		
Bill Capece	K	5'7"	170	22		75
Larry Swider	K	6'2"	195	26		
Garo Yepremian	K	5'8"	175	37		12

DETROIT LIONS 8-8-0 Monte Clark

Scores of Each Game		
24	SAN FRANCISCO	17
23	San Diego	28
24	Minnesota	26
16	OAKLAND	0
10	Tampa Bay	28
21	Denver	27
48	CHICAGO	17
31	GREEN BAY	27
13	Los Angeles	20
31	Washington	33
27	DALLAS	24
23	Chicago	7
27	KANSAS CITY	10
17	Green Bay	31
45	MINNESOTA	7
17	TAMPA BAY	20

Use Name	Pos.	Hgt.	Wgt.	Age	Int.	Pts.
Karl Baldischwiler	OT	6'5"	265	25		
Chris Dieterich	OT	6'3"	269	23		
Keith Dorney	OT	6'5"	265	23		
Russ Bolinger	OG	6'5"	255	26		
Homer Elias	OG	6'3"	255	26		
Tommie Ginn	OG	6'3"	255	23		
Larry Lee	OG-C	6'2"	274	21		
Amos Fowler	C	6'3"	250	25		
Tom Turnure	C	6'4"	243	24		
Al Baker	DE	6'6"	250	24		
Dave Pureifory	DE	6'1"	255	32		
Curly Culp	DT	6'1"	265	35		
Joe Ehrmann	DT	6'5"	250	32		
Doug English	DT	6'5"	255	28		
Edgar Fields	DT	6'2"	255	27		
Steve Furness	DT	6'4"	255	30		
William Gay	DT-DE	6'5"	250	26		
Curtis Green	DT-DE	6'3"	256	24		

Use Name	Pos.	Hgt.	Wgt.	Age	Int.	Pts.
Garry Cobb	LB	6'2"	210	24	3	
Ken Fantetti	LB	6'2"	230	24	2	
James Harrell	LB	6'1"	215	24		
Terry Tautolo (from S.F.)	LB	6'2"	235	27		
Charlie Weaver (to WAS)	LB	6'2"	225	32		
Stan White	LB	6'1"	225	31	4	
Jim Allen	DB	6'2"	195	29	9	
Luther Bradley	DB	6'2"	195	26	1	
Jeff Delaney (to T.B.)	DB	6'	195	24		
Hector Gray	DB	6'1"	197	24	1	
Alvin Hall	DB	5'10"	193	23	1	6
James Hunter	DB	6'3"	195	27	1	
Ray Oldham	DB	6'	192	30	1	
Wayne Smith	DB	6'	170	24		

Jesse Thompson – Achilles Injury
Steve Towle – Hamstring Injury
Ray Williams – Knee Injury

Use Name	Pos.	Hgt.	Wgt.	Age	Int.	Pts.
Gary Danielson	QB	6'2	195	29		12
Eric Hipple	QB	6'2"	196	23		42
Jeff Komlo	QB	6'2"	200	25		
Ken Callicutt	HB	6'	190	26		
Rick Kane	HB-FB	5'11"	200	26		18
Billy Sims	HB	6'	212	25		90
Dexter Bussey	FB	6'1"	210	29		
Horace King	FB-HB	5'10"	210	28		6
Vince Thompson	FB	6'	230	24		6
Robbie Martin	WR	5'8"	179	22		6
Mark Nichols	WR	6'2"	213	21		6
Tracy Porter	WR	6'1"	196	22		6
Freddie Scott	WR	6'2"	175	29		30
Leonard Thompson	WR	5'10"	190	29		24
David Hill	TE	6'2"	230	27		24
Bob Niziolek	TE	6'4"	220	23		
Ulysses Norris	TE	6'4"	225	24		
Eddie Murray	K	5'10"	165	25		121
Tom Skladany	K	6'	195	26		

GREEN BAY PACKERS 8-8-0 Bart Starr

Scores of Each Game		
16	Chicago	9
17	ATLANTA	31
23	Los Angeles	35
13	MINNESOTA	30
27	N.Y. Giants	14
10	TAMPA BAY	21
3	SAN FRANCISCO	13
27	Detroit	31
34	SEATTLE	24
26	N.Y. GIANTS	24
21	CHICAGO	17
3	Tampa Bay	37
35	Minnesota	23
31	DETROIT	17
35	New Orleans	7
3	N.Y. Jets	28

Use Name	Pos.	Hgt.	Wgt.	Age	Int.	Pts.
Tim Huffman	OT-OG	6'5"	277	22		
Greg Koch	OT	6'4"	265	26		
Mark Koncar	OT	6'5"	268	28		
Tim Stokes (from NYG)	OT	6'5"	252	31		
Karl Swanke	OT-OG	6'6"	250	23		6
Derrel Gofourth	OG	6'3"	260	26		
Leotis Harris	OG	6'1"	267	26		
Syd Kitson	OG-OT	6'4"	252	22		
Arland Thompson	OG	6'3"	265	23		
Charlie Ane	C	6'1"	237	29		
Larry McCarren	C	6'3"	238	29		
Byron Braggs	DE	6'4"	290	21		
Mike Butler	DE	6'5"	265	27		
Ezra Johnson	DE	6'4"	240	25		
Casey Merrill	DE	6'4"	255	24		
Terry Jones	NT	6'2"	259	24		
Richard Turner	NT	6'2"	260	22		

Use Name	Pos.	Hgt.	Wgt.	Age	Int.	Pts.
Kurt Allerman	LB	6'3"	222	26		
John Anderson	LB	6'3"	221	25	3	
George Cumby	LB	6'1"	215	25	3	
Mike Douglass	LB	6'	224	26	3	
Cliff Lewis	LB	6'1"	226	21		
Guy Prather	LB	6'2"	230	23		
Randy Scott	LB	6'1"	220	22		
Rich Wingo	LB	6'1"	230	25	1	1
Johnnie Gray	DB	5'11"	185	27		
Maurice Harvey	DB	5'10"	190	25	6	
Estus Hood	DB	5'11"	180	25	3	6
Mark Lee	DB	5'11"	186	23	6	6
Mike McCoy	DB	5'11"	183	28	2	
Mark Murphy	DB	6'2"	199	23	3	
David Petway	DB	6'1"	207	25		
Bill Whitaker	DB	6'	182	21		

Buddy Aydelette – Knee Injury
Chris Godfrey – Knee Injury
Mike Jolly – Knee Injury
Paul Rudzinski – Back Injury

Use Name	Pos.	Hgt.	Wgt.	Age	Int.	Pts.
Rich Campbell	QB	6'4"	224	22		
Lynn Dickey	QB	6'4"	220	31		
David Whitehurst	QB	6'2"	204	26		6
Harlan Huckleby	HB	6'1"	200	23		48
Eddie Lee Ivery	HB	6'1"	210	24		6
Terdell Middleton	HB	6'	195	26		6
Del Williams	HB	6'	200	30		
Gerry Ellis	FB	5'11"	215	23		42
Jim Jensen	FB	6'3"	230	27		
Eric Torkelson	FB-HB	6'2"	210	29		
Ron Cassidy	WR	6'	185	24		
John Jefferson	WR	6'1"	198	25		24
James Lofton	WR	6'3"	187	25		48
Fred Nixon	WR	5'11"	190	22		
Paul Coffman	TE	6'3"	218	25		24
Bill Larson	TE	6'4"	225	27		
Gary Lewis	TE-WR	6'5"	234	22		
John Thompson	TE	6'3"	228	24		
Ray Stachowicz	K	5'11"	185	22		
Jan Stenerud	K	6'2"	190	38		10

MINNESOTA VIKINGS 7-9-0 Bud Grant

Scores of Each Game		
13	Tampa Bay	21
10	OAKLAND	36
26	DETROIT	24
30	Green Bay	13
24	CHICAGO	21
33	San Diego	31
35	PHILADELPHIA	23
17	St. Louis	30
17	Denver	19
25	TAMPA BAY	10
20	NEW ORLEANS	10
30	Atlanta	31
23	GREEN BAY	35
9	Chicago	10
7	Detroit	45
6	KANSAS CITY	10

Use Name	Pos.	Hgt.	Wgt.	Age	Int.	Pts.
Tim Irwin	OT	6'6"	275	24		
Steve Riley	OT	6'6"	253	28		
Ron Yary	OT	6'6"	255	35		
Brent Boyd	OG	6'3"	260	24		
Wes Hamilton	OG	6'3"	255	28		
Jim Hough	OG	6'2"	267	25		
Dave Huffman	OG	6'6"	255	24		
Jim Langer	C	6'2"	253	33		
Dennis Swilley	C	6'3"	241	26		
Neil Elshire	DE	6'6"	256	23		
Randy Holloway	DE	6'5"	245	26		6
Doug Martin	DE	6'3"	258	24		
Mark Mullaney	DE	6'6"	242	28		
Ken Sanders	DE	6'5"	245	31		
James White	NT	6'3"	263	27		
Ray Yakavonis	NT	6'4"	243	24		

Use Name	Pos.	Hgt.	Wgt.	Age	Int.	Pts.
Matt Blair	LB	6'5"	229	30	1	
Dennis Johnson	LB	6'3"	230	23		
Henry Johnson	LB	6'1"	235	23		
Fred McNeill	LB	6'2"	229	29	2	
Robin Sendlein	LB	6'3"	224	22		
Jeff Siemon	LB	6'2"	237	31		
Scott Studwell	LB	6'2"	237	27		
Tom Hannon	DB	5'11"	193	26	4	4
Kurt Knoff	DB	6'2"	188	27	3	
Keith Nord	DB	6'	197	24		
John Swain	DB	6'1"	195	21	2	
Willie Teal	DB	5'10"	195	23	4	
John Turner	DB	6'	199	25		
Walt Williams	DB	6'	185	27		2

Doug Paschal – Knee Injury

Use Name	Pos.	Hgt.	Wgt.	Age	Int.	Pts.
Steve Dils	QB	6'1"	190	25		
Tommy Kramer	QB	6'1"	199	26		
Wade Wilson	QB	6'3"	212	22		
Eddie Payton	HB	5'8"	179	30		6
Jarvis Redwine	HB	5'10"	198	24		
Rickey Young	HB	6'2"	195	27		12
Ted Brown	FB-HB	5'10"	198	24		48
Tony Galbreath	FB	6'	230	27		12
Sam Harrell	FB	6'2"	213	24		
Terry LeCount	WR	5'10"	172	25		12
Leo Lewis	WR	5'8"	170	24		
Mardye McDole	WR	5'11"	195	22		
Ahmad Rashad	WR	6'2"	200	31		42
Sammy White	WR	5'11"	189	27		18
Bob Bruer	TE	6'5"	235	28		18
Joe Senser	TE	6'4"	238	25		48
Greg Coleman	K	6'	178	26		
Rick Danmeier	K	6'	200	29		97

CHICAGO BEARS 6-10-0 Neill Armstrong

Scores of Each Game		
9	GREEN BAY	16
17	San Francisco	28
28	TAMPA BAY	17
7	LOS ANGELES	24
21	Minnesota	24
7	WASHINGTON	24
17	Detroit	48
20	SAN DIEGO	*17
10	Tampa Bay	20
16	Kansas City	*13
17	Green Bay	21
7	DETROIT	23
9	Dallas	10
10	MINNESOTA	9
23	Oakland	6
35	DENVER	24

Use Name	Pos.	Hgt.	Wgt.	Age	Int.	Pts.
Ted Albrecht	OT-OG	6'4"	250	26		
Dan Jiggetts	OT-OG	6'4"	270	27		
Dennis Lick	OT	6'3"	265	27		
Keith Van Horne	OT	6'6"	265	23		
Noah Jackson	OG	6'2"	265	30		
Revie Sorey	OG	6'2"	260	27		
Emanuel Zanders	OG	6'1"	248	30		
Jay Hilgenberg	C	6'3"	250	22		
Dan Neal	C	6'4"	255	32		
Dan Hampton	DE-DT	6'5"	255	23		
Al Harris	DE	6'5"	240	24	1	6
Mike Hartenstine	DE	6'3"	243	28		
Steve McMichael	DT	6'1"	245	23		
Jim Osborne	DT	6'2"	245	31		
Alan Page	DT	6'5"	225	36		
Brad Shearer	DT	6'3"	247	26		

Use Name	Pos.	Hgt.	Wgt.	Age	Int.	Pts.
Brian Cabral	LB	6'	224	25		
Gary Campbell	LB	6'1"	220	29		
Bruce Herron	LB	6'2"	220	27		
Lee Kunz	LB	6'2"	225	24		
Mike Singletary	LB	5'11"	230	22	1	
Otis Wilson	LB	6'2"	222	23		
Todd Bell	DB	6'1"	207	22	1	6
Gary Fencik	DB	6'1"	197	27	6	6
Jeff Fisher	DB	5'11"	188	23	2	6
Leslie Frazier	DB	6'	189	22		
Reuben Henderson	DB	6'1"	200	22	4	
Doug Plank	DB	6'	202	28		2
Terry Schmidt	DB	6'	177	29	2	
Len Walterscheid	DB	5'11"	190	26	1	

Jerry Muckensturm – Shoulder Injury
Paul Tabor – Knee Injury

Use Name	Pos.	Hgt.	Wgt.	Age	Int.	Pts.
Bob Avellini	QB	6'2"	210	28		
Vince Evans	QB	6'2"	212	26		18
Mike Phipps	QB	6'3"	209	33		
Willie McClendon	HB	6'1"	205	23		
Walter Payton	HB	5'11"	202	27		48
Roland Harper	FB	6'	210	28		6
John Skibinski	FB	6'	222	26		
Matt Suhey	FB	5'11"	212	23		18
Dave Williams	FB-HB	6'2"	217	27		12
Marcus Anderson	WR	6'	178	22		12
Brian Baschnagel	WR	6'	184	27		18
Kris Haines	WR	5'11"	180	24		
Ken Margerum	WR	5'11"	170	22		6
Emery Moorehead	WR	6'2"	210	27		
Rickey Watts	WR	6'1"	203	24		18
Mike Cobb	TE	6'5"	243	25		
Robin Earl	TE	6'5"	240	26		6
Robert Fisher	TE	6'3"	240	23		
Bob Parsons	TE	6'4"	225	31		
Hans Nielsen	K	5'11"	165	28		8
John Roveto	K	5'11"	175	23		49
Bob Thomas	K	5'10"	175	29		8

*—Overtime

TAMPA BAY BUCCANEERS

RUSHING

Last Name	No.	Yds.	Avg.	TD
Eckwood	172	651	3.8	2
Owens	91	406	4.5	3
Wilder	107	370	3.5	4
Williams	48	209	4.4	4
R. Bell	30	80	2.7	0
House	2	9	4.5	0
T. Bell	1	7	7.0	0
T. Davis	2	5	2.5	0
Fusina	3	3	1.0	0
Blanchard	1	0	0.0	0
Swider	1	−9	−9.0	0

RECEIVING

Last Name	No.	Yds.	Avg.	TD
House	56	1176	**21**	9
Wilder	48	507	11	1
Giles	45	786	18	6
Eckwood	24	213	9	0
T. Bell	21	318	15	2
Jones	20	276	14	1
Owens	12	145	12	0
R. Bell	8	92	12	0
Obradovich	4	42	11	1
Carter	1	10	10	0

PUNT RETURNS

Last Name	No.	Yds.	Avg.	TD
T. Bell	27	132	5	0
Holt	9	100	11	0
Colzie	2	12	6	0

KICKOFF RETURNS

Last Name	No.	Yds.	Avg.	TD
Owens	24	473	20	0
Holt	11	274	25	0
G. Davis	5	81	16	0
T. Davis	3	51	17	0
Wilder	1	19	19	0
Obradovich	1	14	14	0
Brantley	1	0	0	0

PASSING - PUNTING - KICKING

PASSING	Att.	Comp.	%	Yds.	Yd./Att.	TD	Int.-%	RK
Williams	471	238	51	3563	7.6	19	14– 3	6
Fusina	1	1	100	2	2.0	1	0– 0	
House	1	0	0	0	0.0	0	0– 0	

PUNTING	No.	Avg.
Swider	58	42.7
Blanchard	22	40.9

KICKING	XP	Att.	%	FG	Att.	%
Capece	30	32	93	15	24	63
Yepremian	6	6	100	2	4	50

DETROIT LIONS

RUSHING

Last Name	No.	Yds.	Avg.	TD
Sims	296	1437	4.9	**13**
Bussey	105	446	4.2	0
Kane	77	332	4.3	2
V. Thompson	35	211	6.0	1
Hipple	41	168	4.1	7
L. Thompson	10	75	7.5	1
Nichols	3	50	16.7	0
King	7	25	3.6	0
Scott	7	25	3.6	0
Danielson	9	23	2.6	2
Komlo	6	3	0.5	0

RECEIVING

Last Name	No.	Yds.	Avg.	TD
Scott	53	1022	19	5
Hill	33	462	14	4
L. Thompson	30	550	18	3
Sims	28	451	16	2
King	20	211	11	1
Kane	18	187	10	1
Bussey	18	92	5	0
Nichols	10	222	22	1
Norris	8	132	17	0
V. Thompson	4	40	10	0
Porter	3	63	21	1
Callicutt	2	24	12	0
Cobb	1	19	19	0

PUNT RETURNS

Last Name	No.	Yds.	Avg.	TD
Martin	52	450	9	1

KICKOFF RETURNS

Last Name	No.	Yds.	Avg.	TD
Hall	25	525	21	0
Martin	25	509	20	0
Nichols	4	74	19	0
King	3	33	11	0
Callicutt	2	23	12	0
Harrell	1	0	0	0
Lee	1	0	0	0

PASSING - PUNTING - KICKING

PASSING	Att.	Comp.	%	Yds.	Yd./Att.	TD	Int.-%	RK
Hipple	279	140	50	2358	**8.5**	14	15– 5	9
Danielson	96	56	58	784	8.2	3	5– 5	
Komlo	57	29	51	290	5.1	1	3– 5	
Skladany	3	3	100	43	14.3	0	0– 0	
Scott	1	0	0	0	0.0	0	0– 0	

PUNTING	No.	Avg.
Skladany	64	**43.5**

KICKING	XP	Att.	%	FG	Att.	%
Murray	46	46	**100**	25	35	71

GREEN BAY PACKERS

RUSHING

Last Name	No.	Yds.	Avg.	TD
Ellis	196	860	4.4	4
Huckleby	139	381	2.7	5
Middleton	53	181	3.4	0
Jensen	27	79	2.9	0
Ivery	14	72	5.1	1
Whitehurst	15	51	3.4	1
Jefferson	2	22	11.0	0
Dickey	19	6	0.3	0
Torkelson	1	4	4.0	0

RECEIVING

Last Name	No.	Yds.	Avg.	TD
Lofton	71	1294	18	8
Ellis	65	499	8	3
Coffman	55	687	13	4
Jefferson	39	632	16	4
Huckleby	27	221	8	3
Middleton	12	86	7	1
Jensen	5	49	10	0
Lewis	3	31	10	0
Nixon	2	27	14	0
Ivery	2	10	5	0
Cassidy	1	6	6	0
Swanke	1	2	2	1

PUNT RETURNS

Last Name	No.	Yds.	Avg.	TD
Lee	20	187	9	1
Nixon	15	118	8	0
Whitaker	2	1	1	0
Cassidy	2	0	0	0
Gray	1	0	0	0

KICKOFF RETURNS

Last Name	No.	Yds.	Avg.	TD
Lee	14	270	19	0
Nixon	12	222	19	0
McCoy	11	221	20	0
Huckleby	7	134	19	0
Middleton	6	100	17	0
Coffman	3	77	26	0
Gray	2	24	12	0
Jensen	1	15	15	0
Jefferson	1	3	3	0
Braggs	1	0	0	0

PASSING - PUNTING - KICKING

PASSING	Att.	Comp.	%	Yds.	Yd./Att.	TD	Int.-%	RK
Dickey	354	204	58	2593	7.3	17	15– 4	4
Whitehurst	128	66	52	792	6.2	7	5– 4	
Campbell	30	15	50	168	5.6	0	4– 13	
Ellis	2	1	50	23	11.5	0	0– 0	

PUNTING	No.	Avg.
Stachowicz	82	40.6

KICKING	XP	Att.	%	FG	Att.	%
Stenerud	35	36	97	22	24	**92**

MINNESOTA VIKINGS

RUSHING

Last Name	No.	Yds.	Avg.	TD
Brown	274	1063	3.9	6
Galbreath	42	198	4.7	2
Young	47	129	2.7	0
LeCount	3	51	17.0	0
Redwine	5	20	4.0	0
Lewis	1	16	16.0	0
Dils	4	14	3.5	0
Kramer	10	13	1.3	0
Harrell	1	7	7.0	0
Senser	1	2	2.0	0
Siemon	1	0	0.0	0
S. White	2	−1	−0.5	0

RECEIVING

Last Name	No.	Yds.	Avg.	TD
Brown	83	694	8	2
Senser	79	1004	13	8
S. White	66	1001	15	3
Rashad	58	884	15	7
Young	43	296	7	2
LeCount	24	425	18	2
Galbreath	18	144	8	0
Bruer	7	38	5	4
Lewis	2	58	29	0
Harrell	2	23	12	0

PUNT RETURNS

Last Name	No.	Yds.	Avg.	TD
Payton	38	303	8	0
S. White	1	0	0	0

KICKOFF RETURNS

Last Name	No.	Yds.	Avg.	TD
Payton	39	898	23	1
Nord	14	229	16	0
McDole	11	170	16	0
Galbreath	1	16	16	0
Young	1	15	15	0
Blair	1	0	0	0

PASSING - PUNTING - KICKING

PASSING	Att.	Comp.	%	Yds.	Yd./Att.	TD	Int.-%	RK
Kramer	**593**	**322**	54	**3912**	6.6	26	24– 4	10
Dils	102	54	53	607	6.0	1	2– 2	
Wilson	13	6	46	48	3.7	0	2– 15	
Brown	1	0	0	0	0.0	0	1–100	

PUNTING	No.	Avg.
Coleman	88	41.4

KICKING	XP	Att.	%	FG	Att.	%
Danmeier	34	37	92	21	25	84

CHICAGO BEARS

RUSHING

Last Name	No.	Yds.	Avg.	TD
Payton	339	1222	3.6	6
Suhey	150	521	3.5	3
Evans	43	218	5.1	3
Harper	34	106	3.1	1
McClendon	30	74	2.5	0
Williams	2	19	9.5	0
Margerum	1	11	11.0	0
Baschnagel	1	10	10.0	0
Avellini	5	2	0.4	0
Phipps	1	0	0.0	0
Neal	1	−6	−6.0	0
Parsons	1	−6	−6.0	0

RECEIVING

Last Name	No.	Yds.	Avg.	TD
Payton	41	379	9	2
Margerum	39	584	15	1
Baschnagel	34	554	16	3
Suhey	33	168	5	0
Watts	27	465	17	3
Williams	18	126	7	2
Earl	10	118	12	1
Anderson	9	243	27	2
Cobb	2	20	10	0
Harper	2	10	5	0
McClendon	2	4	2	0
Harris	1	18	18	0
Zanders	1	7	7	0

PUNT RETURNS

Last Name	No.	Yds.	Avg.	TD
J. Fisher	43	509	12	1
Walterscheid	1	6	6	0
Plank	1	3	3	0

KICKOFF RETURNS

Last Name	No.	Yds.	Avg.	TD
Williams	23	486	21	0
Moorehead	23	476	21	0
J. Fisher	7	108	15	0
Frazier	6	77	13	0
Baschnagel	2	34	17	0
R. Fisher	1	9	9	0
Anderson	1	−5	−5	0

PASSING - PUNTING - KICKING

PASSING	Att.	Comp.	%	Yds.	Yd./Att.	TD	Int.-%	RK
Evans	436	195	45	2354	5.4	11	20– 5	15
Avellini	32	15	47	185	5.8	1	3– 9	
Phipps	17	11	65	171	10.1	2	0– 0	
Baschnagel	1	1	100	18	18.0	0	0– 0	
Parsons	1	0	0	0	0.0	0	0– 0	
Payton	2	0	0	0	0.0	0	0– 0	

PUNTING	No.	Avg.
Parsons	**114**	39.7

KICKING	XP	Att.	%	FG	Att.	%
Roveto	19	20	95	10	18	56
Thomas	2	3	67	2	3	67
Nielsen	8	8	100	0	2	0

SAN FRANCISCO FORTY-NINERS 13-3-0 Bill Walsh

Scores of Each Game		
17	Detroit	24
28	CHICAGO	17
17	Atlanta	34
21	NEW ORLEANS	14
30	Washington	17
45	DALLAS	14
13	Green Bay	3
20	LOS ANGELES	17
17	Pittsburgh	14
17	ATLANTA	14
12	CLEVELAND	15
33	Los Angeles	31
17	N.Y. GIANTS	10
21	Cincinnati	3
28	HOUSTON	6
21	New Orleans	17

Use Name	Pos.	Hgt.	Wgt.	Age	Int.	Pts.
Dan Audick	OT	6'3"	253	26		
Keith Fahnhorst	OT	6'6"	263	29		
Allan Kennedy	OT	6'7"	268	23		
Jim Nicholson	OT	6'6"	275	31		
John Ayers	OG-OT	6'5"	255	28		
John Choma	OG-OT	6'5"	261	26		
Randy Cross	OG	6'3"	255	27		
Walt Downing	C-OG	6'3"	254	25		
Fred Quillan	C	6'5"	260	25		
Dwaine Board	DE	6'5"	245	24		
Fred Dean (from S.D.)	DE	6'3"	230	29		
Lawrence Pillers	DE	6'3"	260	28		
Jim Stuckey	DE	6'4"	250	23		
John Harty	NT	6'4"	253	22		
Pete Kugler	NT-DE	6'4"	255	22		
Archie Reese	NT	6'3"	262	25		
Dan Bunz	LB	6'4"	225	25		
Willie Harper	LB	6'2"	215	31		
Bobby Leopold	LB	6'1"	215	23		
Jim Looney	LB	6'	225	24		
Milt McColl	LB	6'6"	220	22	1	
Craig Puki	LB	6'1"	230	24		
Jack Reynolds	LB	6'1"	232	33	1	
Keena Turner	LB	6'2"	220	22	1	
Ricky Churchman	DB	6'1"	193	23		
Rick Gervais	DB	5'11"	190	21		
Dwight Hicks	DB	6'1"	189	25	9	12
Ronnie Lott	DB	6'	199	22	7	18
Saladin Martin	DB	6'	180	25	1	
Lynn Thomas	DB	5'11"	181	22		
Carlton Williamson	DB	6'	204	23	4	
Eric Wright	DB	6'1"	180	22	3	
Guy Benjamin	QB	6'4"	210	26		
Joe Montana	QB	6'2"	200	25		12
Lenvil Elliott	HB	6'	210	29		
Paul Hofer	HB	6'	195	29		6
Amos Lawrence	HB	5'11"	181	23		12
Ricky Patton	HB	5'11"	192	27		30
Bill Ring	HB-FB	5'10"	215	24		6
Earl Cooper	FB	6'2"	226	23		6
Johnny Davis	FB	6'1"	235	25		42
Walt Easley	FB	6'1"	226	23		6
Arrington Jones	FB	6'	225	21		
Matt Bouza	WR	6'2"	205	23		
Dwight Clark	WR	6'3"	205	24		24
Mike Shumann	WR	6'	175	25		
Freddie Solomon	WR	5'11"	188	28		48
Mike Wilson	WR	6'3"	210	22		6
Brian Peets	TE	6'4"	225	25		
Eason Ramson	TE	6'2"	235	25		
Charlie Young	TE	6'4"	235	30		30
Jim Miller	K	5'11"	185	24		
Ray Wersching	K	5'11"	222	31		81

Ken Bungarda – Knee Injury
Phil Francis – Knee Injury
George Visger – Knee Injury

ATLANTA FALCONS 7-9-0 Leeman Bennett

Scores of Each Game		
27	NEW ORLEANS	0
31	Green Bay	17
34	SAN FRANCISCO	17
17	Cleveland	28
13	Philadelphia	16
35	LOS ANGELES	37
41	ST. LOUIS	20
24	N.Y. GIANTS	*27
41	New Orleans	10
14	San Francisco	17
20	PITTSBURGH	34
31	MINNESOTA	30
31	Houston	27
23	Tampa Bay	24
16	Los Angeles	21
28	CINCINNATI	30

Use Name	Pos.	Hgt.	Wgt.	Age	Int.	Pts.
Warren Bryant	OT	6'6"	270	25		
Mike Kenn	OT	6'6"	257	25		
Eric Sanders	OT-C	6'6"	255	22		
Pat Howell	OG	6'5"	253	24		
Dave Scott	OG	6'4"	265	27		
R.C. Thielemann	OG	6'4"	247	26		
John Scully	C	6'5"	255	23		
Jeff Van Note	C	6'2"	247	35		
Wilson Faumuina	DE	6'5"	275	27		
Jeff Merrow	DE	6'4"	230	28		
Matthew Teague	DE	6'5"	240	22		
Jeff Yeates	DE	6'3"	248	30		
Don Smith	NT	6'5"	248	24		
Mike Zele	NT	6'3"	236	25		
Buddy Curry	LB	6'3"	220	23	1	6
Paul Davis	LB	6'2"	214	23		
Tony Daykin	LB	6'1"	215	26		
Fulton Kuykendall	LB	6'5"	225	28	1	6
Jim Laughlin	LB	6'	212	23		
Neal Musser	LB	6'2"	218	24	1	
Al Richardson	LB	6'2"	206	23	1	
Lyman White	LB	6'	217	22		
Joel Williams	LB	6'1"	215	24	1	6
Bobby Butler	DB	5'11"	170	22	5	
Blaine Gaison	DB	6'	185	23	1	
Bob Glazebrook	DB	6'1"	200	25	2	
Kenny Johnson	DB	5'10"	176	23	3	12
Earl Jones	DB	6'	178	24	2	
Tom Moriarty	DB	6'	180	28		
Tom Pridemore	DB	5'10"	186	25	7	6
Scott Woerner	DB	6'	195	22		
Steve Bartkowski	QB	6'4"	213	28		
June Jones	QB	6'4"	200	28		
Mike Moroski	QB	6'4"	200	23		
Lynn Cain	HB	6'1"	205	25		36
Ray Strong	HB	5'9"	184	25		
William Andrews	FB	6'	200	25		72
James Mayberry	FB-HB	5'11"	210	23		
Bo Robinson	FB	6'2"	225	25		
Wallace Francis	WR	5'11"	190	29		30
Alfred Jackson	WR	5'11"	176	26		42
Al Jenkins	WR	5'10"	172	29		78
Reggie Smith	WR	5'4"	168	25		
Russ Mikeska	TE	6'3"	225	25		
Junior Miller	TE	6'4"	243	23		18
John James	K	6'3"	200	32		
Mick Luckhurst	K	6'	180	23		114

Rolland Lawrence – Hamstring Injury

LOS ANGELES RAMS 6-10-0 Ray Malavasi

Scores of Each Game		
20	HOUSTON	27
17	New Orleans	23
35	GREEN BAY	23
24	Chicago	7
27	CLEVELAND	16
37	Atlanta	35
17	Dallas	29
17	San Francisco	20
20	DETROIT	13
13	NEW ORLEANS	21
10	Cincinnati	24
31	SAN FRANCISCO	33
0	Pittsburgh	24
7	N.Y. Giants	10
21	ATLANTA	16
7	WASHINGTON	30

Use Name	Pos.	Hgt.	Wgt.	Age	Int.	Pts.
Doug France	OT	6'5"	270	28		
Phil McKinnely	OT	6'4"	248	27		
Irv Pankey	OT	6'4"	270	23		
Jackie Slater	OT	6'4"	271	27		
Bill Bain	OG	6'4"	277	29		
Dennis Harrah	OG-C	6'5"	255	28		
Kent Hill	OG-OT	6'5"	260	24		
Doug Smith	OG-C-OT	6'3"	255	24		
Rich Saul	C	6'3"	245	33		
Bob Cobb	DE	6'4"	248	23		
Fred Dryer	DE	6'6"	231	35		
Cody Jones	DE	6'5"	244	30		
Jack Youngblood	DE	6'4"	244	31		
Larry Brooks	DT	6'3"	253	31		
Reggie Doss	DT-DE	6'4"	267	24		
Mike Fanning	DT	6'6"	252	28		
Greg Meisner	DT	6'3"	250	22		
Phil Murphy	DT	6'5"	300	23		
George Andrews	LB	6'3"	223	25		
Howard Carson	LB	6'2"	233	24		
Jim Collins	LB	6'2"	230	23		
Carl Ekern	LB	6'3"	223	27		
Joe Harris	LB	6'1"	224	28	1	6
Mel Owens	LB	6'2"	225	22		
Jim Youngblood	LB	6'3"	231	31	1	
Kirk Collins	DB	5'11"	179	23		
Nolan Cromwell	DB	6'1"	198	26	5	
LeRoy Irvin	DB	5'11"	180	23	3	18
Johnnie Johnson	DB	6'1"	185	24		
Rod Perry	DB	5'9"	182	27	3	
Lucious Smith	DB	5"10"	190	24		
Ivory Sully	DB	6'	193	24		
Pat Thomas	DB	5'9"	182	27	4	
Pat Haden	QB	5'11"	185	28		
Jeff Kemp	QB	6'	200	22		
Dan Pastorini	QB	6'3"	205	32		
Jeff Rutledge	QB	6'1"	190	24		
Jewerl Thomas	HB-FB	5'10"	235	23		
Wendell Tyler	HB	5'10"	195	26		102
Cullen Bryant	FB	6'1"	236	30		6
Mike Guman	FB-HB	6'2"	210	23		24
Jairo Penaranda	FB	5'11"	217	23		
Preston Dennard	WR	6'1"	183	25		24
Drew Hill	WR	5'9"	170	24		18
Willie Miller	WR	5'9"	172	34		
Jeff Moore	WR	6'1"	187	24		
Billy Waddy	WR	5'11"	188	27		
Walt Arnold	TE	6'3"	225	23		12
Ron Battle	TE	6'3"	220	22		
Henry Childs	TE	6'2"	231	30		6
Phil DuBois	TE	6'2"	230	24		
Lewis Gilbert	TE	6'4"	225	25		
Frank Corral	K	6'2"	228	26		87

Victor Hicks – Achilles Injury

NEW ORLEANS SAINTS 4-12-0 Bum Phillips

Scores of Each Game		
0	Atlanta	27
23	LOS ANGELES	17
7	N.Y. Giants	20
14	San Francisco	21
6	PITTSBURGH	20
14	PHILADELPHIA	31
17	Cleveland	20
17	CINCINNATI	7
10	ATLANTA	41
21	Los Angeles	13
10	Minnesota	20
27	Houston	24
14	TAMPA BAY	31
3	St. Louis	30
7	GREEN BAY	35
17	SAN FRANCISCO	21

*—Overtime

Use Name	Pos.	Hgt.	Wgt.	Age	Int.	Pts.
Stan Brock	OT	6'6"	275	23		
Dave Lafary	OT	6'7"	280	26		
J.T. Taylor	OT	6'4"	265	25		
Sam Adams	OG	6'3"	260	32		
Nat Hudson	OG	6'3"	270	23		
Fred Sturt	OG	6'4"	255	30		
Bob Young	OG	6'2"	279	38		
John Hill	C	6'2"	246	31		
Jim Pietrzak	C-OT	6'5"	260	28		
Paul Ryczek	C	6'2"	230	29		
Elois Grooms	DE	6'4"	250	28		
Derland Moore	DE	6'4"	253	29		
Frank Warren	DE	6'4"	275	21		
Jim Wilks	DE	6'4"	252	23		
Barry Bennett	NT	6'4"	257	25		
Monte Bennett	NT	6'3"	260	22		
Jerry Boyarsky	NT	6'3"	290	22		
Ken Bordelon	LB	6'4"	226	27	1	
Chuck Evans	LB	6'3"	235	24		
Rickey Jackson	LB	6'2"	230	23		
Jim Kovach	LB	6'2"	225	25	1	
Rob Nairne	LB	6'4"	227	27	1	
Scott Pelleur	LB	6'2"	210	22		
Glen Redd	LB	6'1"	225	23	1	
Russell Gary	DB	5'11"	195	22	1	
Bill Hurley	DB	5'11"	195	24		
Tom Myers	DB	5'11"	180	30	2	
Johnnie Poe	DB	6'1"	182	22	1	
Ricky Ray (to MIA)	DB	5'11"	180	24	1	
Mike Spivey	DB	6'	198	27	1	
Frank Wattelet	DB	6'	185	22	3	
Dave Waymer	DB	6'1"	195	23	4	
Archie Manning	QB	6'3"	200	32		
Bobby Scott	QB	6'1"	197	32		
Dave Wilson	QB	6'3"	195	22		
George Rogers	HB	6'2"	224	22		78
Jimmy Rogers	HB	5'10"	190	26		
Scott Stauch	HB	5'11"	204	22		
Wayne Wilson	HB-FB	6'3"	208	23		30
Jack Holmes	FB	5'11"	210	28		12
Toussaint Tyler	FB	6'2"	220	22		
Gordon Banks	WR	5'9"	178	23		
Jeff Groth	WR	5'10"	172	24		6
Ike Harris	WR	6'3"	210	28		
Rich Martini	WR	6'2"	185	25		
Guido Merkens	WR	6'1"	200	26		6
Aundra Thompson (from GB, SD)	WR	6'	186	28		
Hoby Brenner	TE	6'4"	240	22		
Rich Caster (to WAS)	TE	6'5"	230	32		
Larry Hardy	TE	6'3"	230	25		6
Brooks Williams (to CHI)	TE	6'4"	226	26		
Russell Erxleben	K	6'4"	220	24		
Benny Ricardo	K	5'10"	170	27		63

Rich Mauti – Broken Collarbone
Tinker Owens – Knee Injury

SAN FRANCISCO FORTY-NINERS

RUSHING

Last Name	No.	Yds.	Avg.	TD
Patton	152	543	3.6	4
Cooper	98	330	3.4	1
Davis	94	297	3.2	7
Easley	76	224	2.9	1
Hofer	60	193	3.2	1
Ring	22	106	4.8	0
Montana	25	95	3.8	2
Lawrence	13	48	3.7	1
Solomon	9	43	4.8	0
Clark	3	32	10.7	0
Elliott	7	29	4.1	0
Benjamin	1	1	1.0	0

RECEIVING

Last Name	No.	Yds.	Avg.	TD
Clark	**85**	1105	13	4
Solomon	59	969	16	8
Cooper	51	477	9	0
Young	37	400	11	5
Hofer	27	244	9	0
Patton	27	195	7	1
Wilson	9	125	14	1
Easley	9	62	7	0
Elliott	7	81	12	0
Ramson	4	45	11	0
Ring	3	28	9	1
Shumann	3	21	7	0
Lawrence	3	10	3	0
Davis	3	−1	0	0
Peets	1	5	5	0

PUNT RETURNS

Last Name	No.	Yds.	Avg.	TD
Hicks	19	171	9	0
Solomon	29	173	6	0

KICKOFF RETURNS

Last Name	No.	Yds.	Avg.	TD
Lawrence	17	437	26	1
Ring	10	217	22	0
Lott	7	111	16	0
Wilson	4	67	17	0
Jones	3	43	14	0
Hicks	1	22	22	0
Ramson	1	12	12	0
Davis	1	0	0	0
Patton	1	0	0	0

PASSING – PUNTING – KICKING

PASSING	Att.	Comp.	%	Yds.	Yd./Att.	TD	Int.–%		RK
Montana	488	311	**64**	3565	7.3	19	12–	**3**	1
Benjamin	26	15	58	171	6.6	1	1–	4	
Solomon	1	1	100	25	25.0	0	0–	0	
Easley	1	1	100	5	5.0	0	0–	0	
Clark	1	0	0	0	0.0	0	0–	0	

PUNTING	No.	Avg.
Miller	93	41.5 •

KICKING	XP	Att.	%	FG	Att.	%
Wersching	30	30	**100**	17	23	74

ATLANTA FALCONS

RUSHING

Last Name	No.	Yds.	Avg.	TD
Andrews	289	1301	4.5	10
Cain	156	542	3.5	4
Mayberry	18	66	3.7	0
Robinson	9	24	2.7	0
Moroski	3	17	5.7	0
Francis	1	8	8.0	1
Strong	3	6	2.0	0
Jackson	2	5	2.5	0
Daykin	1	2	2.0	0
Bartkowski	11	2	0.2	0
J. Jones	1	−1	−1.0	0
James	1	−7	−7.0	0

RECEIVING

Last Name	No.	Yds.	Avg.	TD
Andrews	81	735	9	2
Jenkins	70	**1358**	19	**13**
Cain	55	421	8	2
Jackson	37	604	16	6
Miller	32	398	12	3
Francis	30	441	15	4
Mayberry	3	4	1	0
Mikeska	2	16	8	0
Strong	1	9	9	0

PUNT RETURNS

Last Name	No.	Yds.	Avg.	TD
Woerner	33	278	8	0
R. Smith	12	99	8	0
Johnson	4	6	2	0
Pridemore	1	0	0	0

KICKOFF RETURNS

Last Name	No.	Yds.	Avg.	TD
R. Smith	47	1143	24	0
Woerner	10	210	21	0
Gaison	3	43	14	0
Mayberry	2	23	12	0

PASSING – PUNTING – KICKING

PASSING	Att.	Comp.	%	Yds.	Yd./Att.	TD	Int.–%		RK
Bartkowski	533	297	56	3829	7.2	**30**	23–	4	3
Moroski	26	12	46	132	5.1	0	1–	4	
J. Jones	3	2	67	25	8.3	0	0–	0	
James	1	0	0	0	0.0	0	0–	0	

PUNTING	No.	Avg.
James	87	40.7

KICKING	XP	Att.	%	FG	Att.	%
Luckhurst	**51**	**51**	**100**	21	33	64

LOS ANGELES RAMS

RUSHING

Last Name	No.	Yds.	Avg.	TD
Tyler	260	1074	4.1	12
Bryant	109	436	4.0	1
Guman	115	433	3.8	4
J. Thomas	34	118	3.5	0
Haden	18	104	5.8	0
Dennard	6	29	4.8	0
D. Hill	1	14	14.0	0
Kemp	2	9	4.5	0
Pastorini	7	5	0.7	0
Childs	1	0	0.0	0
Rutledge	5	−3	0.6	0

RECEIVING

Last Name	No.	Yds.	Avg.	TD
Dennard	49	821	17	4
Tyler	45	436	10	5
Waddy	31	460	15	0
Bryant	22	160	7	0
Arnold	20	212	11	2
Guman	18	130	7	0
D. Hill	16	355	22	3
Childs	12	145	12	1
Miller	10	147	15	0
Moore	7	105	15	0
J. Thomas	5	37	7	0

PUNT RETURNS

Last Name	No.	Yds.	Avg.	TD
Irvin	46	**615**	**13**	**3**
D. Hill	2	22	11	0
Johnson	1	39	39	0

KICKOFF RETURNS

Last Name	No.	Yds.	Avg.	TD
D. Hill	**60**	1170	20	0
Sully	3	31	10	0
Meisner	1	17	17	0
J. Thomas	1	15	15	0
Guman	1	10	10	0
Penaranda	1	1	1	0
Pankey	1	0	0	0

PASSING – PUNTING – KICKING

PASSING	Att.	Comp.	%	Yds.	Yd./Att.	TD	Int.–%		RK
Haden	267	138	52	1815	6.8	9	13–	5	12
Pastorini	152	64	42	719	4.7	2	14–	9	
Rutledge	50	30	60	442	8.8	3	4–	8	
Kemp	6	2	33	25	4.2	0	1–	17	
Guman	1	1	100	7	7.0	1	0–	0	
Corral	1	0	0	0	0.0	0	0–	0	

PUNTING	No.	Avg.
Corral	89	42.0

KICKING	XP	Att.	%	FG	Att.	%
Corral	36	36	**100**	17	26	65

NEW ORLEANS SAINTS

RUSHING

Last Name	No.	Yds.	Avg.	TD
G. Rogers	**378**	**1674**	4.4	**13**
Holmes	58	194	3.3	2
Tyler	36	183	5.1	0
W. Wilson	44	137	3.1	1
J. Rogers	9	37	4.1	0
Manning	2	28	14.0	0
Groth	2	27	13.5	0
Erxleben	2	10	5.0	0
Stauch	2	6	3.0	0
Thompson	1	2	2.0	0
D. Wilson	5	1	0.2	0
Merkens	2	−1	−0.5	0
Myers	2	−3	−1.5	0
Caster	1	−3	−3.0	0
Scott	3	−4	−1.3	0

RECEIVING

Last Name	No.	Yds.	Avg.	TD
Holmes	38	206	5	0
W. Wilson	31	384	12	4
Merkens	29	458	16	1
Hardy	23	275	12	1
Tyler	23	135	6	0
Groth	20	380	19	1
G. Rogers	16	126	8	0
Caster	12	185	15	0
Thompson	8	111	14	0
Williams	8	82	10	0
Martini	8	72	9	0
Brenner	7	143	20	0
Harris	2	33	17	0
Banks	2	18	9	0
J. Rogers	2	12	6	0
Stauch	1	7	7	0
Lafary	1	5	5	0

PUNT RETURNS

Last Name	No.	Yds.	Avg.	TD
Groth	37	436	12	0
Banks	2	0	0	0
Poe	1	2	2	0
Merkens	1	−12	−12	0

KICKOFF RETURNS

Last Name	No.	Yds.	Avg.	TD
W. Wilson	31	722	23	0
J. Rogers	28	621	22	0
Stauch	3	65	22	0
Groth	3	50	17	0
Thompson	2	44	22	0
Merkens	2	38	19	0
Brock	2	18	9	0
Williams	1	35	35	0
Banks	1	9	9	0

PASSING – PUNTING – KICKING

PASSING	Att.	Comp.	%	Yds.	Yd./Att.	TD	Int.–%		RK
Manning	232	134	58	1447	6.2	5	11–	5	13
D. Wilson	159	82	52	1058	6.7	1	11–	7	
Scott	46	20	44	245	5.3	1	5–	11	
Merkens	2	1	50	20	10.0	0	0–	0	
Myers	2	1	50	8	4.0	1	0–	0	

PUNTING	No.	Avg.
Erxleben	66	40.5

KICKING	XP	Att.	%	FG	Att.	%
Ricardo	24	24	**100**	13	25	52

1981 A.F.C. Raiding the Courtroom

Pete Rozelle had a hard time with both management and labor this year. The lawsuit involving the Oakland Raiders' planned move to Los Angeles went to trial in the federal court in Los Angeles. Both Rozelle and Al Davis had exchanged bitter words and charges in the media, and they now appeared as the principal actors in a long courtroom drama. When the jury sat down to decide the case, they could not reach a unanimous decision, and the judge declared a mistrial. A new trial was scheduled for the spring of 1982, when Rozelle would again argue for the need for the rule requiring permission of the other owners before a club could be moved.

While dealing with Davis's challenge to the N.F.L. by-laws, Rozelle also took part in negotiations with Ed Garvey, the executive director of the N.F.L. Players Association. The collective bargaining agreement between the players and the league would expire in July of 1982, and negotiations moved slowly under the threat of a players' strike when the contract ran out. Garvey made strong demands for the players to share in the profits of the teams, but the owners declared that they didn't want any new partners in the players.

EASTERN DIVISION

Miami Dolphins—Under Don Shula's master touch, the Dolphins made it back into the playoffs after a one-year sabbatical. They lost a prospect when first-round draft pick David Overstreet, a halfback from Oklahoma, chose to play with Montreal in the C.F.L. Shula simply fashioned the personnel at hand into a divisional champion. The gritty defensive unit gave up the fewest points in the A.F.C. despite the summer death of linebacker Rusty Chambers and the unproductive switch of Kim Bokamper from linebacker to defensive end. As usual, nose tackle Bob Baumhower stood out on an excellent unit. The offense was manned by lots of young faces, although veteran guard Ed Newman led the blocking. Second year quarterback David Woodley played well in spurts, ably assisted by relief pitcher Don Strock. Making Overstreet's absence less noticeable was halfback Tony Nathan, a kick-returning star who brought speed into the offensive backfield. In a stretch run battle with the Jets and Bills, the Dolphins ran off four straight victories at the end of the year, including a 16-6 whipping of the Bills on the final Sunday to clinch the Eastern title.

New York Jets—Three embarrassing losses at the start of the year pushed coach Walt Michaels to the brink of unemployment. The Jets saved his job with a 33-17 trouncing of the Oilers, teeing off for seven quarterback sacks. They then went to Miami and played an inspirational 28-28 tie with the unbeaten Dolphins. Just like that, the Jets began believing in themselves and began winning. Without any warning, they won 10 of their last 13 games to charge into the playoffs for the first time since 1969. A ferocious defense made quarterback hunting the team's signature. The front four became known as the New York Sack Exchange, with ends Joe Klecko and Mark Gastineau doing the greatest business in enemy backfields. Without much fanfare, safety Darrol Ray grew into a leader in the secondary. The stars on the offense were blockers like Marvin Powell and Joe Fields, whose efforts made high-yardage runners out of a corps of yeoman backs. The magic streak of success included intoxicating moments such as a revenge 33-14 beating of the Bills and a 16-15 victory over the Dolphins on a last-minute touchdown. A surprise loss to the Seahawks on December 6 put the playoffs in doubt, but victories over the Browns and Packers gave the Jets a wild-card ticket undreamed of three months earlier.

Buffalo Bills—Over the first two months of the season, the Bills didn't live up to their hopes of a dominant campaign in the AFC East. Dawdling along with a 6-5 record in mid-November, the Bills threw themselves into gear and won the next four games. They had a chance to take first place by beating Miami on the final Saturday, but the Dolphins smothered them in a 16-6 decision. Nevertheless, the Bills marched into the wild-card showdown with a solid outfit. The defense ranked with the best in the league, beginning with star nose tackle Fred Smerlas and moving through a deep platoon of talented linebackers and backs. The offense made good use of a quick front line. Joe Cribbs ran through enough holes to chalk up his second 1,000-yard season in as many years, while quaterback Joe Ferguson had enough protection to make oldster Frank Lewis one of the most productive receivers in pro football.

Baltimore Colts—With their hopes fueled by a classy rookie crop, the Colts beat New England 29-28 to earn a share of first place. After that, the script turned so sour that some fans called their team the Dolts by the end of the year. Simply put, the Colts fielded the worst defense in NFL history, allowing an unprecedented 533 points. Bert Jones threw bushels of passes to keep the Colts competitive, but the production of enemy offenses could not be matched. As the losses piled up, the mood of the team turned ugly. In November, quarterback Jones and halfback Curtis Dickey broke into bitter public feuding, showing to everyone that the Colts indeed were in a sorry state. On the final Sunday of the schedule, the Colts entertained the Patriots in a battle for the number-one pick in the upcoming college draft. The Colts lost the pick by winning the game, but the victory didn't stave off the firing of head coach Mike McCormick.

New England Patriots—After just missing the playoffs for the last several seasons, the Patriots spared everyone the suspense by collapsing right at the start of the schedule. Although they rarely lost by huge scores, the Pats lost consistently. They lost their first four games, and they lost their last nine games. Any number of reasons could be cited. Tight end Russ Francis announced his retirement at the peak of a brilliant career. Injuries kept linebacker Steve Nelson and cornerback Mike Haynes out of action for much of the campaign. The defensive line got old in a hurry and exerted little pressure on enemy passers. But no matter how many reasons could be found, the blame ultimately landed on head coach Ron Erhardt, who was canned after the season.

CENTRAL DIVISION

Cincinnati Bengals—At the start of the year, fans talked about the Bengals' new striped helmets. By the end of the year, they talked about the Bengals' fabulous rise to the top of the Central Division. Like a magical charm, the helmets turned a last-place club into champions. The magic worked slowly on quarterback Ken Andersón, who was benched in the opener and was booed lustily for most of September. For most of the year, his precision passing shredded enemy defenses and made Cincinnati the site of repeated scoring outbursts. Rookie Chris Collinsworth, a gangling and elusive receiver, assisted Anderson in reviving the Bengal air attack. Pete Johnson handled the bulk of the running chores with his massive power. On the effective front line, tackle Anthony Munoz moved into the front ranks of blockers in his second pro year. Although the 3-4 Cincinnati defense lacked any star players, it played well enough to take the Bengals to the playoffs for the first time since 1975.

Pittsburgh Steelers—Their fans had hoped that 1980 was merely a one-year's hiatus, but 1981 proved that the Steeler dynasty was over. Chuck Noll's crew put together bursts of championship football but could not sustain it. They lost their first two games of the season very unimpressively, but bounced back with four victories. By November 8, however, a loss to Seattle dropped them to the .500 level. Regrouping for a drive to the playoffs, the Steelers won three straight contests to climb into wild-card contention. On December 7, the Raiders edged the Steelers 30-27 and sent Terry Bradshaw to the sidelines with a broken hand. In the glorious past, the Steelers had gone on winning despite injuries to Bradshaw. This time, they lost their final two games to finish at 8-8. When Bradshaw was healthy and at his best, the attack still moved the football with force. The defense still fielded stars in Jack Lambert, Mel Blount, and Donnie Shell, but the front line launched a puny pass rush. Old pros Joe Greene and L. C. Greenwood slipped into senior status and played only in spots.

Houston Oilers—Ed Biles stepped into a miserable situation for a new head coach. The Oilers had canned Bum Phillips for not getting to the Super Bowl, despite a string of three playoff berths. The Oilers were styled to Phillips' particular brand of hard-nosed football, and many of the players were angry to see him replaced by the disciplinarian Biles. Just before training camp, quarterback Ken Stabler announced his retirement, only to return in time for the regular season opener when Gifford Nielsen was injured. Stabler's name then was linked to a probe of gambling which grabbed headlines. On the field, Biles tried to diversify the Houston offense. Unfortunately, with Stabler's limited passing range, Biles was forced to return to an attack which relied predominantly on Earl Campbell's power running. A mid-season stretch of six losses in seven games dropped the Oilers out of the playoff picture and pointed to the need for extensive retooling.

Cleveland Browns—The Kardiac Kids gave their fans only heartache with a general collapse this season. The Browns had won close games galore and coaxed super seasons out of a bunch of players in 1980, but they could not repeat the charm. Brian Sipe still took the Browns up the field with his passing arm, but the high yardage was converted into fewer points. The defense never put any pressure on enemy passers and suffered from successful air attacks. On opening day, the tone was set for the year by a 44-14 drubbing at the hands of the Chargers. Although the Browns recovered to reach the .500 level in mid-season, they dropped their final six games to fall into the basement of the Central Division. A final Sunday loss to the Seahawks by a 42-21 score sent the Browns home for the summer with much to think about.

WESTERN DIVISION

San Diego Chargers—The Chargers were good enough to lose both John Jefferson and Fred Dean and still repeat as divisional champions.

FINAL TEAM STATISTICS

	BALT.	BUFF.	CIN.	CLEV.	DENV.	HOU.	K.C.	MIA.	N.E.	NY J	OAK.	PIT.	S.D.	SEA.
FIRST DOWNS:														
Total	274	315	361	364	306	241	315	306	306	318	296	318	379	295
by Rushing	95	127	124	131	91	103	160	123	124	122	108	137	127	103
by Passing	158	163	210	196	181	124	132	157	166	170	166	156	224	166
by Penalty	21	25	27	37	34	14	23	26	16	26	22	25	28	26
RUSHING														
Number	441	524	493	474	515	466	610	535	499	571	493	554	481	440
Yards	1850	2125	1973	1929	1895	1734	2633	2173	2040	2341	2058	2372	2005	1594
Average Yards	4.2	4.1	4.0	4.1	3.7	3.7	4.3	4.1	4.1	4.1	4.2	4.3	4.2	3.6
Touchdowns	11	13	19	11	12	11	22	18	23	11	11	21	26	14
PASSING:														
Attempts	479	503	550	624	485	441	410	498	482	507	545	461	629	524
Completions	265	253	332	348	289	258	224	271	254	283	267	247	368	307
Completion Pct.	55.3	50.3	60.4	55.8	59.6	58.5	54.6	54.4	52.7	55.8	49.0	53.6	58.5	58.6
Passing Yards	3379	3661	4200	4339	3992	3119	2917	3385	3904	3279	3356	3457	4873	3727
Avg. Yds per Att.	5.9	6.8	6.8	6.0	6.5	5.8	5.9	6.0	6.8	5.7	4.9	6.6	7.3	6.1
Avg. Yds per Comp.	12.8	14.5	12.7	12.5	13.8	12.1	13.0	12.5	15.4	11.6	12.6	14.0	13.2	12.1
Times Tackled	37	16	35	40	61	40	37	30	45	30	53	27	19	37
Yds Lost Tackled	321	146	205	353	461	342	277	236	321	224	437	231	134	300
Net Yards	3058	3515	3995	3986	3531	2777	2640	3149	3583	3055	2919	3226	4739	3427
Touchdowns	21	25	30	21	27	21	12	18	17	26	18	25	34	21
Interceptions	23	20	12	27	21	23	22	21	34	14	28	19	18	15
Pct. Intercepted	4.8	4.0	2.2	4.3	4.3	5.2	5.4	4.2	7.1	2.8	5.1	4.1	2.9	2.9
PUNTS:														
Number	78	70	73	70	86	79	70	83	75	81	98	84	63	68
Average	39.4	39.7	44.8	41.2	40.4	39.7	38.5	40.8	39.3	40.6	43.2	43.3	40.3	39.0
PUNT RETURNS:														
Number	12	35	29	50	51	41	50	45	31	50	52	50	31	32
Yards	56	292	205	369	441	325	528	458	199	337	380	412	378	293
Average Yards	4.7	8.3	7.1	7.4	8.6	7.9	10.6	10.2	6.4	6.7	7.3	8.2	12.2	9.2
Touchdowns	0	0	0	0	0	0	0	1	0	0	1	0	0	0
KICKOFF RET.:														
Number	84	57	49	72	47	72	52	54	65	58	71	53	70	69
Yards	1651	1085	1056	1537	801	1722	1043	1228	1190	1151	1411	1096	1422	1278
Average Yards	19.7	19.0	21.6	21.3	17.0	23.9	20.1	22.7	18.3	19.8	19.9	20.7	20.3	18.5
Touchdowns	0	0	0	0	0	2	0	1	0	0	0	0	0	0
INTERCEPT RET.:														
Number	16	19	19	15	23	18	26	18	16	21	13	30	23	21
Yards	210	352	318	165	342	330	406	254	195	432	97	376	224	397
Average Yards	13.1	18.5	16.7	11.0	10.5	18.3	15.6	14.1	12.2	20.6	7.5	12.5	9.7	18.9
Touchdowns	0	0	1	0	0	0	1	0	0	2	1	1	1	3
PENALTIES:														
Number	106	114	109	109	99	93	97	71	89	112	101	97	128	106
Yards	913	1001	896	971	833	825	924	541	742	936	867	840	947	823
FUMBLES:														
Number	27	33	25	38	26	33	36	26	32	38	42	39	39	41
Number Lost	14	18	12	26	18	21	24	10	16	17	20	22	22	23
POINTS:														
Total	259	311	421	276	321	281	343	345	322	355	273	356	478	322
PAT Attempts	33	38	51	32	39	34	38	39	40	40	33	46	61	40
PAT Made	29	37	49	31	36	32	37	37	37	38	27	38	55	37
FG attempts	18	24	32	33	30	22	36	31	24	36	24	17	26	24
FG Made	10	14	22	17	17	15	26	24	15	25	14	12	19	15
Percent FG Made	55.6	58.3	68.8	51.5	56.7	68.2	72.2	77.9	62.5	69.4	58.3	70.6	73.1	62.5
Safeties	1	2	0	1	0	0	0	1	0	1	3	0	0	0

	BALT.	BUFF.	CIN.	CLEV.	DENV.	HOU.	K.C.	MIA.	N.E.	NY J	OAK.	PIT.	S.D.	SEA.
FIRST DOWNS:														
Total	406	298	324	299	268	325	316	296	328	291	316	323	365	371
by Rushing	162	113	126	119	108	138	112	124	160	112	104	114	114	175
by Passing	214	154	167	157	142	162	177	160	148	155	178	181	216	173
by Penalty	30	31	31	23	23	25	27	12	20	24	34	28	35	23
RUSHING														
Number	607	516	465	516	467	549	507	492	644	465	524	500	491	588
Yards	2665	2075	1881	2078	2005	2411	1747	2032	2950	1867	1832	1869	1825	2806
Average Yards	4.4	4.0	4.0	4.0	4.3	4.4	3.4	4.1	4.6	4.0	3.5	3.7	3.7	4.8
Touchdowns	30	7	12	14	17	16	17	10	20	19	15	10	25	20
PASSING:														
Attempts	491	474	548	469	497	502	567	509	439	505	537	544	571	502
Completions	301	267	316	275	267	295	291	297	243	275	289	302	313	294
Completion Pct.	61.3	56.3	57.7	58.6	53.7	58.8	51.3	58.3	55.4	54.5	53.8	55.5	54.8	58.6
Passing Yards	4228	3243	3757	3512	3168	3554	3821	3645	3052	3522	4011	4108	4695	3394
Avg. Yds per Att.	8.2	5.5	5.8	6.6	5.4	6.2	6.1	6.1	6.3	5.3	6.2	6.5	7.0	5.8
Avg. Yds per Comp.	14.1	12.2	11.9	12.8	11.9	12.1	13.1	12.3	12.6	12.8	13.9	13.6	15.0	11.5
Times Tackled	13	47	42	29	36	33	27	38	20	66	52	40	47	36
Yds Lost Tackled	100	373	349	223	295	239	195	314	175	518	370	325	384	260
Net Yards	4128	2870	3408	3289	2873	3315	3626	3331	2877	3004	3641	3783	4311	3134
Touchdowns	37	21	24	28	13	22	16	23	18	15	24	22	22	25
Interceptions	16	19	19	15	23	18	26	18	16	21	13	30	23	21
Pct. Intercepted	3.3	4.0	3.5	3.2	5.8	5.5	8.2	6.1	4.9	7.2	4.1	9.3	6.3	5.7
PUNTS:														
Number	48	77	81	78	88	70	80	87	74	94	101	78	72	55
Average	37.9	42.0	40.3	40.7	43.1	41.9	38.9	41.0	38.8	40.4	38.9	42.1	40.3	42.5
PUNT RETURNS:														
Number	44	34	42	30	46	47	46	45	35	31	45	34	31	33
Yards	402	220	416	253	388	360	293	286	305	149	514	358	168	153
Average Yards	9.1	6.5	9.9	8.4	8.4	7.7	6.4	6.4	8.7	4.8	11.4	10.5	5.4	4.6
Touchdowns	0	0	0	0	0	0	0	0	1	0	0	2	0	0
KICKOFF RET.:														
Number	43	61	80	45	47	59	68	60	68	63	49	52	88	67
Yards	864	1268	1612	1156	1007	1201	1296	1218	1326	1415	1068	1253	1528	1177
Average Yards	20.1	20.8	20.2	25.7	21.4	20.4	19.1	20.3	19.5	22.5	21.8	24.1	17.4	17.6
Touchdowns	0	1	1	0	0	0	0	0	0	0	1	0	0	0
INTERCEPT RET.:														
Number	23	20	12	27	21	23	22	21	34	14	28	19	18	15
Yards	281	333	143	347	405	289	247	288	570	212	339	226	377	257
Average Yards	12.2	16.7	11.9	12.9	19.3	12.6	11.2	13.6	16.8	15.1	12.1	11.9	20.9	17.1
Touchdowns	1	0	1	1	4	0	1	0	1	0	0	0	1	1
PENALTIES:														
Number	101	93	104	100	104	102	89	104	83	106	102	112	108	104
Yards	776	690	787	870	949	838	740	886	763	935	826	960	877	944
FUMBLES:														
Number	28	38	32	31	36	20	42	30	34	35	28	31	38	43
Number Lost	14	17	18	20	23	13	21	15	17	15	19	16	18	27
POINTS:														
Total	533	276	304	375	289	355	290	275	370	287	343	297	390	388
PAT Attempts	68	30	38	45	35	39	34	33	41	36	42	35	48	46
PAT Made	65	30	38	40	34	38	29	33	39	33	38	33	45	41
FG attempts	31	26	21	34	27	42	27	21	39	20	30	33	26	29
FG Made	20	22	12	21	15	27	19	14	25	12	17	18	19	23
Percent FG Made	64.5	84.6	57.1	61.8	55.6	64.3	70.4	66.7	64.1	60.0	56.7	54.5	73.1	79.3
Safeties	0	0	1	1	0	1	0	1	2	1	1	0	0	1

Bitter salary disputes prompted the trading of these two stars. Wes Chandler came from New Orleans to join Kellen Winslow and Charlie Joiner as Dan Fouts' primary targets, while Chuck Muncie handled most of the running on this explosive offense. Russ Washington recovered from his knee injury to play offensive tackle, while guard Doug Wilkerson had the best campaign of his life. The explosive attack scored 44 points on opening day and went over 40 points three more times during the year. The defense, however, broke down several times, giving up 40 or more points on three occasions. Although Louie Kelcher and Gary Johnson anchored the center of the defensive line, the absence of Dean's pass rushing was felt throughout the back ranks of the platoon. After an embarrassing 44-23 loss to Seattle on Monday night November 16, the Chargers stood two games behind the Denver Broncos. Coming down the stretch, the Chargers reeled off four victories in five games, edging the Broncos for first place on the tiebreaker calculations.

Denver Broncos—The new Denver ownership brought in Dan Reeves as the new head coach. Heir apparent to Tom Landry at Dallas, Reeves brought the Cowboy winning touch with him for most of the season. He kept the rugged Denver defense intact and was rewarded with low enemy scoring and star performances from Randy Gradishar and Bob Swenson. Reeves worked his biggest changes on the offense. He uncovered a fine small fullback in Rick Parros, and he gave back-up receiver Steve Watson a starting job with marvelous results. Craig Morton, a former teammate of Reeves, thrived under the new regime. He burned the Chargers for 42 points on September 27 and had the Broncos in first place by one game in mid-November. Suddenly, the defense cracked under the pressure of a playoff drive. The Bengals and Chargers both ran up scores of over 30 points in beating the Broncos and dropping them into a three-way tie for first. Victories in the next two games put them one game ahead of the Chargers going into the final weekend. The Broncos went to Chicago on Sunday and were stunned by a 35-24 loss. When the Chargers beat Oakland on Mondy night, the Chargers took first place on the tiebreaker and the Broncos went home for Christmas.

Kansas City Chiefs—With little attention from the national media, the Chiefs stayed in the playoff race until the late stages of the schedule. Known as a conservative offensive team, the Chiefs unveiled a flashy new weapon in rookie halfback Joe Delaney, a small speedster who ran for over 1,000 yards despite backing up Ted McKnight in the early games. A knee injury sent McKnight to the sidelines in mid-season, just as quarterback Steve Fuller was returning from a two-month layoff with his own knee injury. A bad knee also hampered star defensive end Art Still. The defense nevertheless kept the Chiefs in playoff contention, led by star backs Gary Green and Gary Barbaro. Head Coach Marv Levy had his club in a first-place tie through most of November, dropping off the pace with a Thanksgiving Day loss in Detroit. Ten days later, they traveled to Denver and were beaten 16-13. A 17-7 loss to the Dolphins at home finally sent the Kansas City playoff hopes to the deep.

Oakland Raiders—The Raiders made headlines this year not by winning the Super Bowl, but by going three full games without scoring a point. Not since the Brooklyn Dodgers of the World War II era had an NFL club been shutout three straight times. The radical decline in the Oakland offense dropped them out of the playoff picture and cost several players their starting jobs. Super Bowl hero Jim Plunkett went to the bench together with Ray Chester, Art Shell, Gene Upshaw, and Dave Dalby. Injuries also took Bob Chandler, and Mark van Eeghen out of the lineup for much of the schedule. The defense lost Mike Davis, Reggie Kinlaw, and Bob Nelson to injuries, but Ted Hendricks and Lester Hayes successfully kept enemy attacks in check. After the string of shutouts, the Raiders battled back to the .500 mark with lots of young players on the field, but two closing losses sealed a season of disappointment.

Seattle Seahawks—Even though they came in last in the West, the Seahawks shed the abject look of last year. They got off to a miserable start, dropping six of their first seven games. A lethargic 32-0 beating at the hands of the Giants on Octoger 18 humiliated the Seahawks before their hometown fans, but it also served as a turn-around point. From that week on, the Hawks won five of their remaining nine games. Theotis Brown came in a trade with St. Louis and helped the resurgence with forceful running in the league's worst ground game. One high point of the season was a 44-23 ambush of the Chargers on Monday night television on November 16. Two weeks later, they blew a 24-3 lead and lost 32-31 to Oakland, with quarterback Jim Zorn suffering a broken ankle. Unheralded Dave Krieg stepped in for Zorn and engineered a 27-23 upset over the streaking Jets. Krieg also took the Hawks to a 42-21 victory over the Browns in the season's finale, their fifth triumph of the year before the home fans.

MIAMI DOLPHINS 11-4-1 Don Shula

Scores of Each Game		
20	St. Louis	7
30	PITTSBURGH	10
16	Houston	10
31	Baltimore	28
28	N.Y. JETS	*28
21	Buffalo	31
13	WASHINGTON	10
27	Dallas	28
27	BALTIMORE	10
30	New England	*27
17	OAKLAND	33
15	N.Y. Jets	16
13	PHILADELPHIA	10
24	NEW ENGLAND	14
17	Kansas City	7
16	BUFFALO	6

Use Name	Pos.	Hgt.	Wgt.	Age	Int.	Pts.
Jon Giesler	OT	6'5	260	24		
Cleveland Green	OT	6'3	265	23		
Eric Laasko	OT-OG	6'4	265	24		
Bob Kuechenberg	OG-OT-C	6'3	255	33		
Burton Lawless	OG	6'4	255	27		
Ed Newman	OG	6'2	255	30		
Jeff Toews	OG-C	6'3	255	23		
Mark Dennard	C	6'1	252	25		
Dwight Stephenson	C-OT	6'2	255	23		
Bill Barnett	DE-NT	6'4	255	25		
Doug Betters	DE	6'7	260	25		
Kim Bokamper	DE-LB	6'6	247	26		
Vern Den Herder	DE-NT	6'6	252	32		
Ken Poole	DE	6'3	251	22		
Bob Baumhower	NT	6'5	260	26		
Bob Brudzinski	LB	6'4	230	26	2	
A.J. Duhe	LB	6'4	252	25	1	
Larry Gordon	LB	6'4	230	28		2
Steve Potter	LB	6'3	235	23		
Earnest Rhone	LB	6'2	224	28	3	
Steve Shull	LB	6'1	218	23		
Don Bessillieu	DB	6'1	200	25	1	
Glenn Blackwood	DB	6'	183	24	4	
Lyle Blackwood	DB	6'	188	30	3	
Mike Kozlowski	DB	6'	197	25	3	6
Don McNeal	DB	5'11	192	23		
Gerald Small	DB	5'11	192	25		
Ed Taylor	DB	6	175	28		
Fulton Walker	DB	5'10	193	23	1	6
Jim Jensen	QB	6'4	212	22		
Don Strock	QB	6'5	220	30		
David Woodley	QB	6'2	204	22		24
Eddie Hill	HB	6'2	210	24		12
Tony Nathan	HB-FB	6'	206	24		48
Tommy Vigorito	HB	5'10	197	21		24
Woody Bennett	FB	6'2	222	26		
Andra Franklin	FB	5'10	225	21		48
Steve Howell	FB	6'2	230	24		
Terry Robiskie	FB	6'1	210	26		
Elmer Bailey	WR	6	195	23		
Jimmy Cefalo	WR	5'11	188	24		18
Duriel Harris	WR	5'11	184	26		12
Nat Moore	WR	5'9	188	29		12
Bruce Hardy	TE	6'5	230	25		
Ronnie Lee	TE	6'3	235	24		6
Joe Rose	TE	6'3	225	24		12
Tom Orosz	K	6'1	204	21		
Uwe von Schamann	K	6'	188	25		109

Tom Henderson – Broken Neck
Rusty Chambers – Killed in auto accident in July

NEW YORK JETS 10-5-1 Walt Michaels

Scores of Each Game		
0	Buffalo	31
30	CINCINNATI	31
10	Pittsburgh	38
33	HOUSTON	17
28	Miami	*28
28	NEW ENGLAND	24
33	BUFFALO	14
3	SEATTLE	19
26	N.Y. Giants	7
41	Baltimore	14
17	New England	6
16	MIAMI	15
25	BALTIMORE	0
23	Seattle	27
14	Cleveland	13
28	GREEN BAY	3

Use Name	Pos.	Hgt.	Wgt.	Age	Int.	Pts.
Marvin Powell	OT	6'5	268	26		
John Roman	OT	6'4	260	29		
Chris Ward	OT	6'3	270	25		
Dan Alexander	OG	6'4	255	26		
Randy Rasmussen	OG	6'2	255	36		
Stan Waldemore	OG-C	6'4	269	26		
Guy Bingham	C-OG-OT	6'3	255	23		
Joe Fields	C	6'2	253	27		
Ralph DeLoach	DE	6'5	254	24		
Mark Gastineau	DE	6'5	280	24		
Joe Klecko	DE	6'3	265	27		
Kenny Neil	DE-DT	6'4	244	22		
Marty Lyons	DT	6'5	260	24		
Abdul Salaam	DT	6'3	265	28		
Ben Rudolph	DT-DE	6'5	271	24		
Stan Blinka	LB	6'2	230	24	1	
Greg Buttle	LB	6'3	232	27	2	2
Ron Crosby	LB	6'3	222	26		
Lance Mehl	LB	6'3	230	23	3	
Al Washington	LB	6'3	235	22		
Marty Wetzel	LB	6'3	235	23		
John Woodring	LB	6'2	230	22		
Donald Dykes	DB	5'11	180	26		
Jerry Holmes	DB	6'2	175	23	1	
Bobby Jackson	DB	5'9	175	24		
Jesse Johnson	DB	6'3	185	24		
Johnny Lynn	DB	6'	190	24	3	
Darrol Ray	DB	6'1	200	23	7	12
Ken Schroy	DB	6'2	196	28	2	
Kirk Springs	DB	6	192	23	2	
Kyle Grossart	QB	6'4	210	26		
Pat Ryan	QB	6'3	205	25		
Richard Todd	QB	6'2	203	27		
Scott Dierking	HB-FB	5'10	215	26		12
Bruce Harper	HB	5'8	177	26		30
Kenny Lewis	HB	6'	190	23		
Freeman McNeil	HB	5'11	225	22		18
Mike Augustyniak	FB	5'11	220	25		6
Kevin Long	FB	6'1	218	26		30
Tom Newton	FB	6'	213	27		6
Derrick Gaffney	WR	6'1	180	26		
Bobby Jones	WR	5'11	180	26		12
Johnny "Lam" Jones	WR	5'11	180	23		18
Kurt Sohn	WR	5'11	176	24		
Wesley Walker	WR	6	175	26		54
Jerome Barkum	TE	6'3	225	31		42
Mickey Shuler	TE	6'3	235	25		
Steve Stephens	TE	6'3	227	24		
Pat Leahy	K	6'	195	30		113
Chuck Ramsey	K	6'2	189	29		

Mike McKibben–Knee Injury

BUFFALO BILLS 10-6-0 Chuck Knox

Scores of Each Game		
31	N.Y. JETS	0
35	Baltimore	3
14	PHILADELPHIA	20
24	Cincinnati	*27
23	BALTIMORE	17
31	MIAMI	21
14	N.Y. Jets	33
9	DENVER	7
22	CLEVELAND	13
14	Dallas	27
0	St. Louis	24
20	NEW ENGLAND	17
21	WASHINGTON	14
28	San Diego	27
19	New England	10
6	Miami	16

Use Name	Pos.	Hgt.	Wgt.	Age	Int.	Pts.
Jon Borchardt	OT-OG	6'5	255	24		
Joe Devlin	OT	6'5	250	27		
Ken Jones	OT	6'5	250	28		
Conrad Dobler	OG	6'3	255	30		
Tom Lynch	OG	6'5	260	26		
Reggie McKenzie	OG	6'4	242	31		
Jim Ritcher	OG-C	6'3	251	23		
Will Grant	C	6'3"	248	27		
Tim Vogler	C-OG	6'3	245	24		
Darrell Irvin	DE	6'4	255	24		
Ken Johnson	DE	6'5	253	26		
Sherman White	DE	6'5	250	32		
Ben Williams	DE	6'3	245	27	1	2
Mike Kadish	NT	6'5	270	31		
Fred Smerlas	NT	6'3	270	24		
Jim Haslett	LB	6'3	237	25		
Mike Humiston	LB	6'3	238	22		
Chris Keating	LB	6'2	223	23		
Shane Nelson	LB	6'1	232	26	1	
Ervin Parker	LB	6'4	240	23		
Isiah Robertson	LB	6'3	225	32	2	
Lucius Sanford	LB	6'2	216	25		
Phil Villapiano	LB	6'2	225	32		
Rufus Bess	DB	5'9	180	24	1	
Mario Clark	DB	6'2	195	27	5	
Steve Freeman	DB	5'11	185	28		
Rod Kush	DB	6	188	24	1	
Jeff Nixon	DB	6'3	190	24		
Charles Romes	DB	6'1	190	27	4	
Bill Simpson	DB	6'1	191	29	4	
Joe Ferguson	QB	6'1	195	31		6
Matt Robinson	QB	6'2	196	26		
Joe Cribbs	HB	5'11	190	23		60
Roland Hooks	HB	6	195	28		30
Robb Riddick	HB	6	195	23		
Curtis Brown	FB	5'10	203	26		6
Roosevelt Leaks	FB	5'10	225	28		36
Lawrence McCutcheon	FB	6'1	205	31		
Jerry Butler	WR	6	178	23		48
Byron Franklin	WR	6'1	179	22		
Ron Jessie	WR	6	181	33		
Frank Lewis	WR	6'1	196	34		24
Lou Piccone	WR	5'9	175	32		
Steve Alvers	TE-C	6'4	240	24		
Buster Barnett	TE	6'5	225	22		6
Mark Brammer	TE	6'3	235	23		12
Greg Cater	K	6	191	24		
Nick Mike-Mayer	K	5'8"	185	31		79

Sid Justin – Injury

BALTIMORE COLTS 2-14-0 Mike McCormack

Scores of Each Game		
29	New England	28
3	BUFFALO	35
10	Denver	28
28	MIAMI	31
17	Buffalo	23
19	CINCINNATI	41
14	SAN DIEGO	43
28	Cleveland	42
10	Miami	27
14	N.Y. JETS	41
13	Philadelphia	38
24	ST. LOUIS	35
0	N.Y. Jets	25
13	DALLAS	37
14	Washington	38
23	NEW ENGLAND	21

Use Name	Pos.	Hgt.	Wgt.	Age	Int.	Pts.
Tim Foley	OT	6'6"	275	23		
Wade Griffin	OT	6'5"	270	27		
Jeff Hart	OT	6'5"	272	27		
Randy Van Divier	OT	6'5"	282	23		
Ken Huff	OG	6'4"	253	28		
Jimmy Moore	OG	6'5"	268	24		
Robert Pratt	OG	6'4"	250	30		
Ray Donaldson	C	6'3"	263	23		
Chris Foote	C-OG	6'3"	247	24		
Mike Ozdowski	DE	6'5"	243	25		
Hosea Taylor	DE	6'5"	250	22		2
Donnell Thompson	DE	6'4"	252	22		
Daryl Wilkerson	DE	6'4"	255	22		
Mike Barnes	DT	6'6"	264	30		
Mike Fultz (from MIA)	DT	6'5"	278	27		
Bubba Green	DT	6'4"	278	22	1	
Herb Orvis	DT	6'5"	255	34		
Joe Federspiel	LB	6'1"	230	31		
Ricky Jones	LB	6'1"	222	26		
Barry Krauss	LB	6'3"	238	24	1	
Sanders Shiver	LB	6'2"	230	26		
Ed Simonini	LB	6'	206	27		
Ed Smith	LB	6'2"	216	24	2	
Mike Woods	LB	6'2"	237	26		
Kim Anderson	DB	5'11"	184	24	1	
Larry Braziel	DB	6'	184	26	3	
Nesby Glasgow	DB	5'10"	185	24	2	
Derrick Hatchett	DB	5'11"	186	23	2	
Steve Henry	DB	6'2"	190	24		
Bruce Laird	DB	6'	194	31	3	
Reggie Pinkney	DB	5'11"	187	26	1	
David Humm	QB	6'2"	190	29		
Bert Jones	QB	6'3"	218	29		
Greg Landry	QB	6'4"	208	34		6
Jay Venuto	QB	6'1"	195	23		
Curtis Dickey	HB	6'1"	205	24		60
Zachary Dixon	HB	6'	204	25		6
Don McCauley	HB	6'1"	211	32		12
Cleveland Franklin	FB	6'2"	220	26		6
Randy McMillan	FB	6'	226	22		24
Marvin Sims	FB	6'4"	234	24		
Randy Burke	WR	6'2"	198	26		
Ray Butler	WR	6'3"	190	24		54
Roger Carr	WR	6'3"	195	29		18
Brian DeRoo	WR	6'3"	200	25		
Dave Shula	WR	5'11"	182	22		
Kevin Williams	WR	5'8"	164	23		
Reese McCall	TE	6'7"	243	25		12
Tim Sherwin	TE	6'5"	239	23		
Mike Garrett	K	6'1"	184	24		
Mike Wood	K	5'11"	199	26		59

NEW ENGLAND PATRIOTS 2-14-0 Ron Erhardt

Scores of Each Game		
28	BALTIMORE	29
3	Philadelphia	13
21	DALLAS	35
21	Pittsburgh	*27
33	KANSAS CITY	17
24	N.Y. Jets	28
38	HOUSTON	10
22	Washington	24
17	Oakland	27
27	MIAMI	*30
6	N.Y. JETS	17
17	Buffalo	20
20	ST. LOUIS	27
14	Miami	24
10	BUFFALO	19
21	Baltimore	23

Use Name	Pos.	Hgt.	Wgt.	Age	Int.	Pts.
Brian Holloway	OT	6'7"	273	22		
Shelby Jordan	OT	6'7"	260	29		
Dwight Wheeler	OT-C	6'3"	255	26		
Bob Cryder	OG	6'4"	265	24		
John Hannah	OG	6'2"	265	30		
Gary Puetz	OG-OT	6'4"	265	29		
Pete Brock	C	6'5"	260	27		
Bill Lenkaitis	C	6'3"	255	35		
Julius Adams	DE	6'3"	263	33		
Mark Buben	DE	6'3"	260	24	1	
Steve Clark	DE	6'5"	258	21		
John Lee	DE	6'2"	259	28		
Tony McGee	DE	6'4"	250	32		
Richard Bishop	NT	6'1"	260	31		
Ray Hamilton	NT	6'1"	245	30		
Don Blackmon	LB	6'3"	235	23		
Bob Golic	LB	6'2"	240	23		
Mike Hawkins	LB	6'2"	235	25	1	
Steve King	LB	6'4"	230	30		
Bill Matthews	LB	6'2"	235	25		
Steve Nelson	LB	6'2"	230	30		
Rod Shoate	LB	6'1"	215	28	1	
John Zamberlin	LB	6'2"	230	25	1	
Raymond Clayborn	DB	6'1"	190	26	2	
Paul Dombroski	DB	6'	185	25		
Tim Fox	DB	5'11"	190	27	3	
Mike Haynes	DB	6'2"	195	28	1	
Roland James	DB	6'2"	189	23	2	
Keith Lee	DB	5'11"	192	23	1	
Rick Sanford	DB	6'1"	192	24	3	
Darrell Wilson	DB	5'11"	180	23		
Matt Cavanaugh	QB	6'1"	210	24		18
Steve Grogan	QB	6'4"	208	28		12
Tom Owen	QB	6'1"	194	28		
Tony Collins	HB	5'11"	202	22		42
Vagas Ferguson	HB	6'1"	194	24		18
Andy Johnson	HB	6'	204	28		6
Don Calhoun	FB	6'	212	29		12
Sam Cunningham	FB	6'3"	230	31		24
Mosi Tatupu	FB	6'	225	26		18
Harold Jackson	WR	5'10"	175	35		
Stanley Morgan	WR	5'11"	180	26		36
Carlos Pennywell	WR	6'2"	180	25		6
Ken Toler	WR	6'2"	195	22		
Don Westbrook	WR	5'10"	184	28		12
Lin Dawson	TE	6'3"	235	22		
Don Hasselbeck	TE	6'7"	245	27		36
Rich Camarillo	K	5'11"	189	21		
Ken Hartley	K	6'2"	200	24		
Mike Hubach	K	5'10"	185	23		
John Smith	K	6'	185	31		82

Preston Brown – Back Injury
Allan Clark – Knee Injury
Larry McGrew – Knee Injury

*—Overtime

MIAMI DOLPHINS

RUSHING

Last Name	No.	Yds.	Avg.	TD
Nathan	147	782	**5.3**	5
Franklin	201	711	3.5	7
Woodley	63	272	4.3	4
Hill	37	146	3.9	1
Vigorito	35	116	3.3	1
Bennett	28	104	3.7	0
Howell	5	21	4.2	0
Orosz	1	13	13.0	0
Moore	1	3	3.0	0
Strock	14	−26	−1.9	0

RECEIVING

Last Name	No.	Yds.	Avg.	TD
Harris	53	911	17	2
Nathan	50	452	9	3
Vigorito	33	237	7	2
Cefalo	29	631	22	3
Moore	26	452	17	2
Rose	23	316	14	2
Hardy	15	174	12	0
Lee	14	64	5	1
Hill	12	73	6	1
Bennett	4	22	6	0
Franklin	3	6	2	1
Howell	2	9	5	0

PUNT RETURNS

Last Name	No.	Yds.	Avg.	TD
Vigorito	36	379	11	1
Walker	5	50	10	0
G. Blackwood	2	8	4	0
Bessillieu	1	12	12	0
Kozlowski	1	9	9	0

KICKOFF RETURNS

Last Name	No.	Yds.	Avg.	TD
Walker	38	932	25	1
Bessillieu	7	114	16	0
Vigorito	4	84	21	0
Kozlowski	1	40	40	0
Harris	1	20	20	0
Hill	1	11	11	0
Rose	1	5	5	0

PASSING - PUNTING - KICKING

PASSING	Att.	Comp.	%	Yds.	Yd./Att.	TD	Int.-%	RK
Woodley	366	191	52	2470	6.8	12	13– 4	9
Strock	130	79	61	901	6.9	6	8– 6	
Hill	1	1	100	14	14.0	0	0– 0	
Nathan	1	0	0	0	0.0	0	0– 0	

PUNTING	No.	Avg.
Orosz	83	40.8

KICKING	XP	Att.	%	FG	Att.	%
von Schamann	37	38	97	24	31	**77**

NEW YORK JETS

RUSHING

Last Name	No.	Yds.	Avg.	TD
McNeil	137	623	4.5	2
Harper	81	393	4.9	4
Augustyniak	85	339	4.0	1
Dierking	74	328	4.4	1
Long	73	269	3.7	2
Newton	73	244	3.3	1
Todd	32	131	4.1	0
Lewis	6	18	3.0	0
J. Jones	2	0	0.0	0
Ramsey	3	0	0.0	0
Ryan	3	−5	−1.7	0

RECEIVING

Last Name	No.	Yds.	Avg.	TD
Harper	52	459	9	1
Walker	47	770	16	9
Barkum	39	495	13	7
Dierking	26	228	9	1
J. Jones	20	342	17	3
McNeil	18	171	10	1
Augustyniak	18	144	8	0
Newton	17	104	6	0
B. Jones	16	239	15	1
Gaffney	14	246	18	0
Long	13	66	5	3
Stephens	2	21	11	0
Lewis	2	14	7	0
Rudolph	1	8	8	0
Todd	1	1	1	0

PUNT RETURNS

Last Name	No.	Yds.	Avg.	TD
Harper	35	265	8	0
Sohn	13	66	5	0
Schroy	1	5	5	0
B. Jones	1	1	1	0

KICKOFF RETURNS

Last Name	No.	Yds.	Avg.	TD
Harper	23	480	21	0
Sohn	26	528	20	0
Lewis	5	108	22	0
J. Jones	1	6	6	0

PASSING - PUNTING - KICKING

PASSING	Att.	Comp.	%	Yds.	Yd./Att.	TD	Int.-%	RK
Todd	497	279	56	3231	6.5	25	13– 3	6
Ryan	10	4	40	48	4.8	1	1– 10	

PUNTING	No.	Avg.
Ramsey	81	40.6

KICKING	XP	Att.	%	FG	Att.	%
Leahy	38	39	97	25	**36**	69

BUFFALO BILLS

RUSHING

Last Name	No.	Yds.	Avg.	TD
Cribbs	257	1097	4.3	3
Leaks	91	357	3.9	6
Hooks	51	250	4.9	3
Brown	62	226	3.6	0
McCutcheon	34	138	4.1	0
Riddick	3	29	9.7	0
Ferguson	20	29	1.5	1
Brammer	2	17	8.5	0
Butler	1	1	1.0	0
Robinson	1	−2	−2.0	0
Kush	1	−6	−6.0	0
Franklin	1	−11	−11.0	0

RECEIVING

Last Name	No.	Yds.	Avg.	TD
Lewis	70	**1244**	18	4
Butler	55	842	15	8
Cribbs	40	603	15	7
Brammer	33	365	11	2
Jessie	15	200	13	0
Hooks	10	140	14	2
Leaks	7	51	7	0
Brown	7	46	7	1
Piccone	5	65	13	0
McCutcheon	5	40	8	0
Barnett	4	36	9	1
Franklin	2	29	15	0

PUNT RETURNS

Last Name	No.	Yds.	Avg.	TD
Hooks	17	142	8	0
Piccone	9	57	6	0
Franklin	5	45	9	0
Riddick	4	48	12	0

KICKOFF RETURNS

Last Name	No.	Yds.	Avg.	TD
Franklin	21	436	21	0
Riddick	14	257	18	0
Hooks	11	215	20	0
Brown	7	140	20	0
Piccone	2	31	16	0
Bess	1	6	6	0
Freeman	1	0	0	0

PASSING - PUNTING - KICKING

PASSING	Att.	Comp.	%	Yds.	Yd./Att.	TD	Int.-%	RK
Ferguson	498	252	51	3652	7.3	24	20– 4	8
Cribbs	1	1	100	9	9.0	1	0– 0	
Leaks	1	0	0	0	0.0	0	0– 0	
Mike-Mayer	1	0	0	0	0.0	0	0– 0	
Robinson	2	0	0	0	0.0	0	0– 0	

PUNTING	No.	Avg.
Cater	80	39.7

KICKING	XP	Att.	%	FG	Att.	%
Mike-Mayer	37	37	**100**	14	24	58

BALTIMORE COLTS

RUSHING

Last Name	No.	Yds.	Avg.	TD
Dickey	164	779	4.8	7
McMillan	149	597	4.0	3
Dixon	73	285	3.9	0
B. Jones	20	85	4.3	0
Franklin	21	52	2.5	1
McCauley	10	37	3.7	0
Landry	1	11	11.0	0
Garrett	2	4	2.0	0
Anderson	1	0	0.0	0

RECEIVING

Last Name	No.	Yds.	Avg.	TD
McMillan	50	466	9	1
Butler	46	832	18	9
Carr	38	584	15	3
Dickey	37	419	11	3
McCauley	36	347	10	2
McCall	21	314	15	2
Dixon	17	169	10	1
Burke	10	153	15	0
Franklin	6	39	7	0
Sherwin	2	19	10	0
DeRoo	1	38	38	0
Huff	1	−1	−1	0

PUNT RETURNS

Last Name	No.	Yds.	Avg.	TD
Shula	10	50	5	0
Anderson	2	6	3	0

KICKOFF RETURNS

Last Name	No.	Yds.	Avg.	TD
Dixon	36	737	21	0
Williams	20	399	20	0
Anderson	20	393	20	0
Shula	5	65	13	0
Glasgow	1	35	35	0
Sims	1	22	22	0
Foote	1	0	0	0

PASSING - PUNTING - KICKING

PASSING	Att.	Comp.	%	Yds.	Yd./Att.	TD	Int.-%	RK
B. Jones	426	244	57	3094	7.3	21	20– 5	7
Landry	29	14	48	195	6.7	0	1– 3	
Humm	24	7	29	90	3.8	0	2– 8	

PUNTING	No.	Avg.
Garrett	78	39.4

KICKING	XP	Att.	%	FG	Att.	%
Wood	29	33	88	10	18	56

NEW ENGLAND PATRIOTS

RUSHING

Last Name	No.	Yds.	Avg.	TD
Collins	204	873	4.3	7
Ferguson	78	340	4.4	3
Cunningham	86	269	3.1	4
Calhoun	57	205	3.6	2
Tatupu	38	201	5.3	2
Cavanaugh	17	92	5.4	3
Grogan	12	49	4.1	2
Morgan	2	21	10.5	0
Pennywell	1	3	3.0	0
Johnson	2	1	0.5	0
Jackson	2	−14	−7.0	0

RECEIVING

Last Name	No.	Yds.	Avg.	TD
Hasselbeck	46	808	18	6
Morgan	44	1029	**23**	6
Jackson	39	669	17	0
Johnson	39	429	11	1
Collins	26	232	9	0
Tatupu	12	132	11	1
Cunningham	12	92	8	0
Dawson	7	126	18	0
Westbrook	7	122	17	2
Calhoun	7	71	10	0
Toler	5	70	14	0
Ferguson	4	39	10	0
Pennywell	3	49	16	1
Grogan	2	27	14	0
Cavanaugh	1	9	9	0

PUNT RETURNS

Last Name	No.	Yds.	Avg.	TD
Morgan	15	116	8	0
James	7	56	8	0
Haynes	6	12	2	0
Collins	3	15	5	0

KICKOFF RETURNS

Last Name	No.	Yds.	Avg.	TD
Collins	39	773	20	0
Toler	9	148	16	0
Sanford	4	82	21	0
Dombroski	3	66	22	0
Johnson	3	53	18	0
Calhoun	2	38	19	0
K. Lee	2	20	10	0
Hasselbeck	1	7	7	0
Matthews	1	5	5	0
Hamilton	1	0	0	0

PASSING - PUNTING - KICKING

PASSING	Att.	Comp.	%	Yds.	Yd./Att.	TD	Int.-%	RK
Grogan	216	117	54	1859	**8.6**	7	16– 7	13
Cavanaugh	219	115	53	1633	7.5	5	13– 6	14
Owen	36	15	42	218	6.1	1	4– 11	
Johnson	9	7	78	194	21.6	4	1– 11	
Collins	1	0	0	0	0.0	0	0– 0	
Jackson	1	0	0	0	0.0	0	0– 0	

PUNTING	No.	Avg.
Camarillo	47	41.7
Hubach	19	38.2
Hartley	9	29.6

KICKING	XP	Att.	%	FG	Att.	%
Smith	37	39	95	15	24	63

1981 A.F.C. — Central Division

CINCINNATI BENGALS 12-4-0 Forrest Gregg

Scores of Each Game		
27	SEATTLE	21
31	N.Y. Jets	30
17	CLEVELAND	20
27	BUFFALO	*24
10	Houston	17
41	Baltimore	19
34	PITTSBURGH	7
7	New Orleans	17
34	HOUSTON	21
40	San Diego	17
24	LOS ANGELES	10
38	DENVER	21
41	Cleveland	21
3	SAN FRANCISCO	21
17	Pittsburgh	10
30	Atlanta	28

Use Name	Pos.	Hgt.	Wgt.	Age	Int.	Pts.
Anthony Munoz	OT	6'6"	278	23		
Mike Obrovac	OT-OG	6'6"	275	25		
Mike Wilson	OT	6'5"	271	26		
Glenn Bujnoch	OG	6'5"	265	27		
Dave Lapham	OG	6'4"	262	29		
Max Montoya	OG	6'5"	275	25		
Brad Oates (to G.B.)	OG	6'6"	275	27		
Bobby Whitten	OG	6'3"	265	22		
Blair Bush	C	6'3"	252	24		
Blake Moore	C-OT-OG	6'5"	267	23		
Ross Browner	DE	6'3"	261	27		
Gary Burley	DE	6'3"	274	28		
Eddie Edwards	DE	6'5"	256	27		
Mike St. Clair	DE	6'5"	250	27		6
Rod Horn	NT	6'4"	268	24		
Wilson Whitley	NT	6'3"	265	26		

Use Name	Pos.	Hgt.	Wgt.	Age	Int.	Pts.
Glenn Cameron	LB	6'2"	228	28	1	
Tom Dinkel	LB	6'3"	237	25		
Guy Frazier	LB	6'2"	215	22		
Bo Harris	LB	6'3"	226	28	2	
Jim LeClair	LB	6'2"	234	30	1	
Rick Razzano	LB	5'11"	227	25	1	
Jeff Schuh	LB	6'2"	228	23		
Reggie Williams	LB	6'1"	228	26	4	
Louis Breeden	DB	5'11"	185	27	4	6
Greg Bright	DB	6'	208	24		
Clarence Chapman	DB	5'10"	182	27		
Oliver Davis	DB	6'1"	205	27		
Mike Fuller	DB	5'9"	182	28	1	
Ray Griffin	DB	5'10"	186	25		
Bryan Hicks	DB	6'	192	24		
Bobby Kemp	DB	6'	186	22		
Ken Riley	DB	6'	183	34	5	
John Simmons	DB	5'11"	192	22		

Dick Jauron – Knee Injury
Ron Simpklins – Hamstring Injury

Use Name	Pos.	Hgt.	Wgt.	Age	Int.	Pts.
Ken Anderson	QB	6'1"	212	32		6
Turk Schonert	QB	6'1"	185	24		
Jack Thompson	QB	6'3"	217	25		
Charles Alexander	HB-FB	6'1"	221	24		18
Archie Griffin	HB	5'9"	184	27		24
Elvis Peacock	HB	6'1"	208	24		
Jim Hargrove	FB	6'2"	228	23		6
Pete Johnson	FB	6'	249	27		96
Don Bass	WR-TE	6'2"	220	26		
Cris Collinsworth	WR	6'5"	192	22		48
Isaac Curtis	WR	6'	192	30		12
Steve Kreider	WR	6'3"	192	23		30
Pat McInally	WR	6'6"	213	28		
David Verser	WR	6'1"	200	23		12
M.L. Harris	TE	6'5"	238	27		12
Dan Ross	TE	6'4"	235	24		30
Jim Breech	K	5'6"	157	25		115

PITTSBURGH STEELERS 8-8-0 Chuck Noll

Scores of Each Game		
33	KANSAS CITY	37
10	Miami	30
38	N.Y. JETS	10
27	NEW ENGLAND	*21
20	New Orleans	6
13	CLEVELAND	7
7	Cincinnati	34
26	HOUSTON	13
14	SAN FRANCISCO	17
21	Seattle	24
34	Atlanta	20
32	Cleveland	10
24	LOS ANGELES	0
27	Oakland	30
10	CINCINNATI	17
20	Houston	21

Use Name	Pos.	Hgt.	Wgt.	Age	Int.	Pts.
Larry Brown	OT	6'4"	265	32		
Tunch Ilkin	OT-OG-C	6'3"	253	23		
Jon Kolb	OT	6'2"	262	34		
Ted Petersen	OT	6'5"	244	26		
Ray Pinney	OT-C-OG	6'4"	240	27		6
Steve Courson	OG	6'1"	260	25		
Tyrone McGriff	OG	6'	267	23		
Craig Wolfley	OG	6'1"	258	23		
Mike Webster	C	6'1"	250	29		
John Banaszak	DE-DT	6'3"	244	31		
John Goodman	DE-DT	6'6"	250	22		
L.C. Greenwood	DE	6'5"	250	34		
Bob Kohrs	DE	6'3"	245	22		
Tom Beasley	DT-DE	6'5"	253	27		
Gary Dunn	DT	6'3"	247	28		
Joe Greene	DT	6'4"	260	34		

Use Name	Pos.	Hgt.	Wgt.	Age	Int.	Pts.
Robin Cole	LB	6'2"	220	25	1	
Jack Ham	LB	6'3"	225	32	1	
Jack Lambert	LB	6'4"	220	29	6	
David Little	LB	6'1"	220	22		
Loren Toews	LB	6'3"	222	29		
Zack Valentine	LB	6'2"	220	24		
Dennis Winston	LB	6'	228	25	1	
Larry Anderson	DB	5'11"	177	24		
Mel Blount	DB	6'3"	205	33	6	6
Ron Johnson	DB	5'10"	200	25	2	
Donnie Shell	DB	5'11"	190	29	5	
J.T. Thomas	DB	6'2"	196	30	4	
Anthony Washington	DB	6'1"	204	23	3	
Dwayne Woodruff	DB	5'11"	189	24	1	

Sam Davis – Knee Injury

Use Name	Pos.	Hgt.	Wgt.	Age	Int.	Pts.
Terry Bradshaw	QB	6'3"	215	32		12
Mark Malone	QB-WR	6'4"	223	22		18
Cliff Stoudt	QB	6'4"	218	26		
Greg Hawthorne	HB	6'2"	225	24		12
Rick Moser (from K.C.)	HB	6'	210	24		6
Frank Pollard	HB-FB	5'10"	210	24		12
Sidney Thornton	HB	5'11"	230	26		24
Russell Davis	FB	6'1"	231	25		6
Franco Harris	FB	6'2"	225	31		54
Johnnie Dirden	WR	6'	184	29		
Jim Smith	WR	6'2"	205	26		42
John Stallworth	WR	6'2"	183	29		30
Lynn Swann	WR	6'	180	29		30
Calvin Sweeney	WR	6'2"	180	26		
Bennie Cunningham	TE	6'4"	260	26		18
Randy Grossman	TE	6'1"	225	27		6
Craig Colquitt	K	6'2"	185	27		
David Trout	K	5'6"	165	23		74

HOUSTON OILERS 7-9-0 Ed Biles

Scores of Each Game		
27	Los Angeles	20
9	Cleveland	3
10	MIAMI	16
17	N.Y. Jets	33
17	CINCINNATI	10
35	SEATTLE	17
10	New England	38
13	Pittsburgh	26
21	Cincinnati	34
17	OAKLAND	16
10	Kansas City	23
24	NEW ORLEANS	27
27	ATLANTA	31
17	CLEVELAND	13
6	San Francisco	28
21	PITTSBURGH	20

Use Name	Pos.	Hgt.	Wgt.	Age	Int.	Pts.
Nick Eyre	OT	6'5"	274	22		
Angelo Fields	OT	6'6"	319	23		
Leon Gray	OT	6'3"	260	29		
Morris Towns	OT	6'4"	275	27		
David Carter	OG-C	6'2"	258	28		
Ed Fisher	OG	6'3"	250	32		
John Schuhmacher	OG	6'3"	275	25		
Greg Davidson	C	6'2"	250	23		
Carl Mauck	C	6'3"	250	34		
Jesse Baker	DE	6'5"	265	24		
Elvin Bethea	DE	6'3"	255	35		
Andy Dorris	DE	6'4"	240	30		
Mike Stensrud	DE	6'5"	280	25		
Ken Kennard	NT	6'2"	245	26		
Daryle Skaugstad	NT	6'5"	254	24		

Use Name	Pos.	Hgt.	Wgt.	Age	Int.	Pts.
Gregg Bingham	LB	6'1"	230	30	2	
Robert Brazile	LB	6'4"	238	28	2	
John Corker	LB	6'5"	240	22		
Daryl Hunt	LB	6'3"	220	24		
Avon Riley	LB	6'3"	211	22		
Art Stringer	LB	6'1"	223	27		
Ted Thompson	LB	6'1"	220	28		
Ted Washington	LB	6'1"	245	33	1	
Carter Hartwig	DB	6'	205	25	3	
Bill Kay	DB	6'1"	190	21	2	
Vernon Perry	DB	6'2"	211	27	2	
Mike Reinfeldt	DB	6'2"	195	28	2	
Greg Stemrick	DB	5'11"	185	29	3	
Willie Tullis	DB	6'	190	23		6
J.C. Wilson	DB	6'	177	25	1	

Use Name	Pos.	Hgt.	Wgt.	Age	Int.	Pts.
Gifford Nielsen	QB	6'4"	205	26		
John Reaves	QB	6'3"	205	31		
Ken Stabler	QB	6'3"	210	35		
Earl Campbell	HB-FB	5'11"	237	26		60
Ronnie Coleman	HB	5'10"	198	30		6
Rich Tomaselli	HB	6'1"	195	24		
Adger Armstrong	FB	6'	220	24		6
Tim Wilson	FB	6'3"	220	27		
Harold Bailey	WR	6'2"	197	24		
Billy Brooks (from S.D.)	WR	6'3"	202	28		
Ken Burrough	WR	6'4"	210	33		42
Mike Holston	WR	6'3"	184	23		12
Mike Renfro	WR	6'	184	26		6
Carl Roaches	WR	5'8"	165	27		6
Tim Smith	WR	6'2"	192	24		
Mike Barber	TE	6'3"	233	28		6
Dave Casper	TE	6'4"	230	29		48
Toni Fritsch	K	5'7"	180	36		77
Cliff Parsley	K	6'1"	211	26		

CLEVELAND BROWNS 5-11-0 Sam Rutigliano

Scores of Each Game		
14	SAN DIEGO	44
3	HOUSTON	9
20	Cincinnati	17
28	ATLANTA	17
16	Los Angeles	27
7	Pittsburgh	13
20	NEW ORLEANS	17
42	BALTIMORE	28
13	Buffalo	22
20	Denver	*23
15	San Francisco	12
10	PITTSBURGH	32
21	CINCINNATI	41
13	Houston	17
13	N.Y. JETS	14
21	Seattle	42

Use Name	Pos.	Hgt.	Wgt.	Age	Int.	Pts.
Doug Dieken	OT	6'5"	252	32		
Matt Miller	OT-OG	6'6"	270	25		
Cody Risien	OT	6'7"	255	24		
Joe DeLamielleure	OG	6'3"	245	30		
Robert Jackson	OG-C	6'5"	260	28		
Henry Sheppard	OG-OT	6'6"	263	28		
Chuck Correal	C	6'3"	247	25		
Tom DeLeone	C	6'2"	248	31		
Gerry Sullivan	C-OG	6'4"	250	29		
Lyle Alzado	DE	6'3"	250	32		
Thomas Brown	DE-NT	6'4"	245	24		
Elvis Franks	DE	6'4"	238	24		
Marshall Harris	DE-NT	6'6"	261	25		
Mike Robinson	DE	6'5"	260	25		
Henry Bradley	NT	6'2"	260	27		
Jerry Sherk	NT-DE	6'4"	250	33		

Use Name	Pos.	Hgt.	Wgt.	Age	Int.	Pts.
Dick Ambrose	LB	6'	228	28	1	
Don Goode	LB	6'2"	231	30	1	
Bruce Huther	LB	6'1"	230	27		
Robert Jackson	LB	6'1"	230	27		
Eddie Johnson	LB	6'1"	210	22		
Clay Matthews	LB	6'2"	230	25	2	
Curtis Weathers	LB	6'5"	220	24		
Autry Beamon	DB	6'1"	190	27		
Ron Bolton	DB	6'2"	170	31	1	
Clinton Burrell	DB	6'2"	192	24		
Thom Darden	DB	6'2"	193	31	3	
Hanford Dixon	DB	5'11"	182	22		
Judson Flint	DB	6'	201	24	2	
Lawrence Johnson	DB	5'11"	204	23		
Clarence Scott	DB	6'	190	32	4	

Joel Patten–Knee Injury

Use Name	Pos.	Hgt.	Wgt.	Age	Int.	Pts.
Paul McDonald	QB	6'2"	185	23		
Brian Sipe	QB	6'1"	195	32		6
Rick Trocano	QB-DB	6'	188	22		
Dino Hall	HB	5'7"	165	25		
Calvin Hill	HB-FB	6'3"	227	34		12
Cleo Miller	HB-FB	5'11"	214	28		12
Greg Pruitt	HB	5'10"	190	30		24
Charles White	HB	5'10"	183	23		6
Mike Pruitt	FB	6'	225	27		48
Willis Adams	WR	6'2"	194	25		
Ricky Feacher	WR	5'10"	174	27		18
Dan Fulton	WR	6'2"	186	24		
Dave Logan	WR-DB	6'4"	216	27	1	24
Cle Montgomery (to OAK)	WR	5'8"	183	25		
Reggie Rucker	WR	6'2"	190	33		6
Ozzie Newsome	TE	6'2"	232	25		36
McDonald Oden	TE	6'4"	228	23		
Matt Bahr (from S.F.)	K	5'10"	165	25		79
Steve Cox	K	6'4"	195	23		
Dave Jacobs	K	5'7"	155	24		21

CINCINNATI BENGALS

RUSHING

Last Name	No.	Yds.	Avg.	TD
Johnson	274	1077	3.9	12
Anderson	46	320	7.0	1
Alexander	98	292	3.0	2
A. Griffin	47	163	3.5	3
Hargrove	16	66	4.1	1
Schonert	7	41	5.9	0
Kreider	1	21	21.0	0
Verser	2	11	5.5	0
Bass	1	9	9.0	0
McInally	1	−27	−27.0	0

RECEIVING

Last Name	No.	Yds.	Avg.	TD
Ross	71	910	13	5
Collinsworth	67	1009	15	8
Johnson	46	320	7	4
Curtis	37	609	17	2
Kreider	37	520	14	5
Alexander	28	262	9	1
A. Griffin	20	160	8	1
M. Harris	13	181	14	2
Verser	6	161	27	2
McInally	6	68	11	0
Hargrove	1	0	0	0

PUNT RETURNS

Last Name	No.	Yds.	Avg.	TD
Fuller	23	177	8	0
Simmons	5	24	5	0
Hicks	1	4	4	0

KICKOFF RETURNS

Last Name	No.	Yds.	Avg.	TD
Verser	29	691	24	0
Chapman	8	171	21	0
A. Griffin	6	119	20	0
R. Griffin	2	31	16	0
Fuller	1	34	34	0
Simmons	1	10	10	0
Dinkel	1	0	0	0
Kemp	1	0	0	0

PASSING - PUNTING - KICKING

PASSING	Att.	Comp.	%	Yds.	Yd./Att.	TD	Int.–%	RK
Anderson	479	300	**63**	3754	7.8	29	10– **2**	**1**
Thompson	49	21	43	267	5.5	1	2– 4	
Schonert	19	10	53	166	8.7	0	0– 0	
Kreider	3	1	33	13	4.3	0	0– 0	

PUNTING	No.	Avg.
McInally	72	**45.4**

KICKING	XP	Att.	%	FG	Att.	%
Breech	49	51	96	22	32	69

PITTSBURGH STEELERS

RUSHING

Last Name	No.	Yds.	Avg.	TD
Harris	242	987	4.1	8
Pollard	123	570	4.6	2
Davis	47	270	5.7	1
Thornton	56	202	3.6	4
Bradshaw	38	162	4.3	2
Malone	16	68	4.3	2
Hawthorne	25	58	2.3	2
Stallworth	1	17	17.0	0
Smith	1	15	15.0	0
Stoudt	3	11	3.7	0
Colquitt	1	8	8.0	0
Moser	1	4	4.0	0

RECEIVING

Last Name	No.	Yds.	Avg.	TD
Stallworth	63	1098	17	5
Cunningham	41	574	14	3
Harris	37	250	7	1
Swann	34	505	15	5
Smith	29	571	20	7
Pollard	19	156	8	0
Thornton	8	78	10	0
Davis	4	34	9	0
Hawthorne	4	23	6	0
Grossman	3	19	6	1
Sweeney	2	53	27	0
Malone	1	90	90	1
Moser	1	5	5	1
Pinney	1	1	1	1

PUNT RETURNS

Last Name	No.	Yds.	Avg.	TD
Anderson	20	208	10	0
Smith	30	204	7	0

KICKOFF RETURNS

Last Name	No.	Yds.	Avg.	TD
Anderson	37	825	22	0
Hawthorne	7	138	20	0
Moser	3	76	25	0
Dirden	3	45	15	0
Davis	1	8	8	0
Malone	1	3	3	0
Thornton	1	1	1	0

PASSING - PUNTING - KICKING

PASSING	Att.	Comp.	%	Yds.	Yd./Att.	TD	Int.–%	RK
Bradshaw	370	201	54	2887	7.8	22	14– 4	4
Malone	88	45	51	553	6.3	3	5– 6	
Stoudt	3	1	33	17	5.7	0	0– 0	

PUNTING	No.	Avg.
Colquitt	84	43.3

KICKING	XP	Att.	%	FG	Att.	%
Trout	38	46	83	12	17	71

HOUSTON OILERS

RUSHING

Last Name	No.	Yds.	Avg.	TD
Campbell	**361**	**1376**	3.8	10
Armstrong	31	146	4.7	0
Coleman	21	91	4.3	1
T. Wilson	13	35	2.7	0
Reaves	6	13	2.2	0
Nielsen	6	2	0.3	0
Stabler	10	−3	−0.3	0

RECEIVING

Last Name	No.	Yds.	Avg.	TD
Burrough	40	668	17	7
Renfro	39	451	12	1
Campbell	36	156	4	0
Casper	33	572	17	8
Armstrong	29	278	10	1
Holston	27	427	16	2
Coleman	19	211	11	0
Barber	13	190	15	1
T. Wilson	5	33	7	0
Brooks	3	37	12	0
Smith	2	37	19	0

PUNT RETURNS

Last Name	No.	Yds.	Avg.	TD
Roaches	59	296	8	0
Tullis	2	29	15	0

KICKOFF RETURNS

Last Name	No.	Yds.	Avg.	TD
Roaches	28	769	**28**	1
Tullis	32	779	24	1
T. Wilson	3	41	14	0
Armstrong	3	36	12	0
Hunt	3	19	6	0
J. Wilson	2	27	14	0
Riley	1	51	51	0

PASSING - PUNTING - KICKING

PASSING	Att.	Comp.	%	Yds.	Yd./Att.	TD	Int.–%	RK
Stabler	285	165	58	1988	7.0	14	18– 6	10
Nielsen	93	60	65	709	7.6	5	3– 3	
Reaves	61	31	51	379	6.2	2	2– 3	
Parsley	2	2	100	43	21.5	0	0– 0	

PUNTING	No.	Avg.
Parsley	79	39.7

KICKING	XP	Att.	%	FG	Att.	%
Fritsch	32	34	94	15	22	68

CLEVELAND BROWNS

RUSHING

Last Name	No.	Yds.	Avg.	TD
M. Pruitt	247	1103	4.5	7
White	97	342	3.5	1
C. Miller	52	165	3.2	2
Sipe	38	153	4.0	1
G. Pruitt	31	124	4.0	0
Hill	4	23	5.8	0
Newsome	2	20	10.0	0
McDonald	2	0	0.0	0
Feacher	1	−1	−1.0	0

RECEIVING

Last Name	No.	Yds.	Avg.	TD
Newsome	69	1002	15	6
G. Pruitt	65	636	10	4
M. Pruitt	63	442	7	1
Logan	31	497	16	4
Feacher	29	654	23	3
Rucker	27	532	20	1
White	27	219	8	0
Hill	17	150	9	2
C. Miller	16	139	9	0
Fulton	2	38	19	0
Adams	1	24	24	0
Oden	1	6	6	0

PUNT RETURNS

Last Name	No.	Yds.	Avg.	TD
Hall	33	248	8	0
Montgomery	17	121	7	0

KICKOFF RETURNS

Last Name	No.	Yds.	Avg.	TD
Hall	36	813	23	0
Montgomery	17	382	23	0
White	12	243	20	0
G. Pruitt	3	82	27	0
C. Miller	3	35	12	0
Brown	2	17	9	0
E. Johnson	1	7	7	0
M. Miller	1	6	6	0

PASSING - PUNTING - KICKING

PASSING	Att.	Comp.	%	Yds.	Yd./Att.	TD	Int.–%	RK
Sipe	567	313	55	3876	6.8	17	25– 4	11
McDonald	57	35	61	463	8.1	4	2– 4	

PUNTING	No.	Avg.
Cox	68	42.4

KICKING	XP	Att.	%	FG	Att.	%
Bahr	34	34	**100**	15	26	58
Jacobs	9	10	90	4	12	33
Cox				0	1	0

SAN DIEGO CHARGERS 10-6-0 Don Corye II

Scores of Each Game		
44	Cleveland	14
28	DETROIT	23
42	Kansas City	31
24	Denver	42
24	SEATTLE	10
31	MINNESOTA	33
43	Baltimore	14
17	Chicago	*20
22	KANSAS CITY	20
17	CINCINNATI	40
23	Seattle	44
55	Oakland	21
34	DENVER	17
27	BUFFALO	28
24	Tampa Bay	23
23	OAKLAND	10

Use Name	Pos.	Hgt.	Wgt.	Age	Int.	Pts.
Sammy Claphan	OT	6'6"	267	24		
Chuck Loewen	OT-OG	6'3"	259	24		
Billy Shields	OT	6'7"	275	28		
Russ Washington	OT	6'6"	288	34		
Ed White	OG	6'2"	271	34		
Doug Wilkerson	OG	6'2"	262	34		
Jeff Williams	OG	6'4"	264	26		
Don Macek	C	6'3"	253	27		
Bob Rush	C	6'5"	264	25		
Keith Ferguson	DE	6'5"	240	22		
Leroy Jones	DE	6'8"	260	30	1	
Don Reese	DE	6'6"	262	29		
John Woodcock	DE	6'3"	250	27		
Gary Johnson	DT	6'2"	252	29	1	6
Louie Kelcher	DT	6'5"	282	28		
Jimmy Webb	DT	6'5"	245	29		

Use Name	Pos.	Hgt.	Wgt.	Age	Int.	Pts.
Carlos Bradley	LB	6'	221	21		
Bob Horn	LB	6'3"	230	27	1	
Keith King	LB	6'4"	230	26	1	
Jim Laslavic	LB	6'2"	236	29		
Woodrow Lowe	LB	6'	227	27	3	
Ray Preston	LB	6'	218	27		
Cliff Thrift	LB	6'2"	232	25		
Doug Beaudoin	DB	6'1"	190	27		
Willie Buchanon	DB	6'	185	30	5	
Frank Duncan	DB	6'1"	188	24	1	
Glen Edwards	DB	6'	183	34	2	
Allan Ellis	DB	5'10"	177	30		
Bob Gregor	DB	6'2"	187	24	2	
Wyatt Henderson	DB	5'10"	180	24		
Irvin Phillips	DB	6'1"	192	21		
Pete Shaw	DB	5'10"	178	27	3	
Mike Williams	DB	5'10"	179	27	3	

Charles DeJurnett – Achilles Injury

Use Name	Pos.	Hgt.	Wgt.	Age	Int.	Pts.
Dan Fouts	QB	6'3"	210	30		
James Harris	QB	6'3"	221	34		
Ed Luther	QB	6'3"	206	24		
Hank Bauer	HB-FB	5'10"	200	27		6
James Brooks	HB	5'9"	180	22		36
Clarence Williams	HB	5'9"	195	26		6
John Cappelletti	FB	6'1"	220	29		30
Chuck Muncie	FB-HB	6'3"	233	28		114
Wes Chandler (from N.O.)	WR	5'11"	186	25		36
Scott Fitzkee	WR	6'	187	24		
Charlie Joiner	WR	5'11"	183	33		42
Dwight Scales	WR	6'2"	185	28		6
Pete Holohan	TE	6'4"	226	22		
Eric Sievers	TE	6'4"	234	22		18
Kellen Winslow	TE	6'5"	252	23		60
Rolf Benirschke	K	6'	175	26		112
George Roberts	K	6'	186	26		

DENVER BRONCOS 10-6-0 Dan Reeves

Scores of Each Game		
9	OAKLAND	7
10	Seattle	13
28	BALTIMORE	10
42	SAN DIEGO	24
17	Oakland	0
27	DETROIT	21
14	Kansas City	28
7	Buffalo	9
19	MINNESOTA	17
23	CLEVELAND	*20
24	Tampa Bay	7
21	Cincinnati	38
17	San Diego	34
16	KANSAS CITY	13
23	SEATTLE	13
24	Chicago	35

Use Name	Pos.	Hgt.	Wgt.	Age	Int.	Pts.
Kelvin Clark	OT	6'3"	245	25		
Ken Lanier	OT	6'3"	269	22		
Claudie Minor	OT	6'4"	275	30		
Dave Studdard	OT-OG	6'4"	255	25		
Tom Glassic	OG	6'3"	250	27		
Paul Howard	OG	6'3"	260	30		
Glenn Hyde	OG-C	6'3"	252	30		
Bill Bryan	C	6'2"	244	26		
Greg Boyd	DE	6'6"	280	28		
Barney Chavous	DE	6'3"	245	30		
Rulon Jones	DE	6'6"	260	23		
Brison Manor	DE	6'4"	248	29	1	
Rubin Carter	NT	6'	253	28		
Don Latimer	NT	6'3"	253	26		

Use Name	Pos.	Hgt.	Wgt.	Age	Int.	Pts.
Steve Busick	LB	6'4"	227	22		
Larry Evans	LB	6'2"	220	28	1	
Randy Gradishar	LB	6'3"	231	29	4	
Tom Jackson	LB	5'11"	228	30		
Mark Merrill	LB	6'4"	240	26		
Jim Ryan	LB	6'1"	212	24		
Bob Swenson	LB	6'3"	225	28	3	
Steve Foley	DB	6'2"	190	27	5	
Mike Harden	DB	6'	188	23	2	
Aaron Kyle	DB	5'11"	185	27	2	
Dennis Smith	DB	6'3"	200	22	1	
Perry Smith	DB	6'1"	190	30		
Roland Solomon	DB	6'	189	25		
Bill Thompson	DB	6'1"	197	34	4	
Steve Trimble	DB	5'10"	181	23		
Louis Wright	DB	6'2"	200	28		

Keith Bishop – Foot Injury
Jim Robinson – Hamstring Injury

Use Name	Pos.	Hgt.	Wgt.	Age	Int.	Pts.
Steve DeBerg	QB	6'2"	205	27		
Mark Herrmann	QB	6'4"	184	22		
Craig Morton	QB	6'4"	211	38		
Rob Lytle	HB	6'1"	195	26		30
Dave Preston	HB	5'10"	195	26		18
Tony Reed	HB	5'11"	197	26		
Larry Canada	FB	6'2"	226	26		24
Rick Parros	FB	5'11"	200	23		18
Wade Manning	WR	5'11"	190	26		
Haven Moses	WR	6'3"	201	35		6
Rick Upchurch	WR	5'10"	176	29		18
Steve Watson	WR	6'4"	192	24		78
Ron Egloff	TE	6'5"	227	25		6
Riley Odoms	TE	6'4"	230	31		30
James Wright	TE	6'3"	240	25		6
Luke Prestridge	K	6'4"	235	24		
Fred Steinfort	K	5'11"	180	27		87

KANSAS CITY CHIEFS 9-7-0 Marv Levy

Scores of Each Game		
37	Pittsburgh	33
19	TAMPA BAY	10
31	SAN DIEGO	42
20	Seattle	14
17	New England	33
27	OAKLAND	0
28	DENVER	14
28	Oakland	17
20	San Diego	22
13	CHICAGO	*16
23	HOUSTON	10
40	SEATTLE	13
10	Detroit	27
13	Denver	16
7	MIAMI	17
10	Minnesota	6

Use Name	Pos.	Hgt.	Wgt.	Age	Int.	Pts.
Charlie Getty	OT	6'4"	269	29		
Matt Herkenhoff	OT	6'4"	270	30		
Roger Taylor	OT	6'6"	271	23		
Brad Budde	OG	6'4"	255	23		
Tom Condon	OG	6'3"	272	28		
Jim Rourke	OG-OT-C	6'5"	265	24		
Bob Simmons	OG	6'4"	260	27		
Jack Rudnay	C	6'3"	242	33		
Todd Thomas	C	6'5"	262	21		
Mike Bell	DE	6'4"	255	24		
Frank Case	DE	6'4"	243	23		
Sylvester Hicks	DE	6'4"	252	26		
Dave Lindstrom	DE	6'6"	257	26		
Art Still	DE	6'7"	252	25		
Ken Kremer	NT	6'4"	250	24		
Dino Mangiero	NT-DE	6'2"	265	22		
Don Parrish	NT	6'2"	259	26		

Use Name	Pos.	Hgt.	Wgt.	Age	Int.	Pts.
Jerry Blanton	LB	6'1"	225	25		
Phil Cancik	LB	6'1"	230	24		
Tom Howard	LB	6'2"	215	27		6
Charles Jackson	LB	6'2"	220	26		
Dave Klug	LB	6'4"	230	23		
Frank Manumaleuga	LB	6'2"	245	25	2	
John Olenchalk	LB	6'	228	25		
Whitney Paul	LB	6'3"	220	27	2	6
Cal Peterson	LB	6'3"	220	28		
Gary Spani	LB	6'2"	230	25		6
Gary Barbaro	DB	6'4"	204	27	5	
Lloyd Burruss	DB	6'	201	23	4	6
M.L. Carter	DB	5'9"	173	25		
Deron Cherry	DB	5'11"	185	21	1	
Herb Christopher	DB	5'10"	202	27		
Gary Green	DB	5'11"	184	25	5	
Eric Harris	DB	6'3"	191	26	7	

Horace Belton – Knee Injury

Use Name	Pos.	Hgt.	Wgt.	Age	Int.	Pts.
Steve Fuller	QB	6'4"	198	24		
Bob Gagliano	QB	6'3"	193	22		
Bill Kenney	QB	6'4"	210	26		6
Curtis Bledsoe	HB-FB	5'11"	215	24		
Joe Delaney	HB	5'10"	184	22		18
Clark Gaines	HB	6'1"	209	27		
Ted McKnight	HB	6'1"	216	27		30
Jim Hadnot	FB	6'2"	244	24		18
Billy Jackson	FB-HB	5'10"	223	21		66
Mike Williams	FB	6'3"	222	23		
Carlos Carson	WR	5'10"	172	22		6
Bubba Garcia	WR	5'11"	185	23		
Henry Marshall	WR	6'2"	214	27		24
James Murphy (from ATL)	WR	5'10"	177	21		
Stan Rome	WR	6'5"	218	25		6
J.T. Smith	WR	6'2"	185	25		12
Ed Beckman	TE	6'4"	226	26		
Al Dixon	TE	6'5"	235	27		12
Marvin Harvey	TE-WR	6'2"	220	21		
Willie Scott	TE	6'4"	245	22		6
Jeff Gossett	K	6'2"	195	24		
Bob Grupp	K	5'11"	193	26		
Nick Lowery	K	6'4"	190	25		115

OAKLAND RAIDERS 7-9-0 Tom Flores

Scores of Each Game		
7	Denver	9
36	Minnesota	10
20	SEATTLE	10
0	Detroit	16
0	DENVER	17
0	Kansas City	27
18	TAMPA BAY	16
17	KANSAS CITY	28
27	NEW ENGLAND	17
16	Houston	17
33	Miami	17
21	SAN DIEGO	55
32	Seattle	31
30	PITTSBURGH	27
6	CHICAGO	23
10	San Diego	23

Use Name	Pos.	Hgt.	Wgt.	Age	Int.	Pts.
Henry Lawrence	OT	6'4"	270	29		
Lindsey Mason	OT	6'5"	270	26		
Art Shell	OT	6'5"	285	34		
Bruce Davis	OG-OT	6'6"	280	25		
Curt Marsh	OG	6'5"	275	22		
Mickey Marvin	OG	6'4"	275	25		
Gene Upshaw	OG	6'5"	255	36		
Dave Dalby	C	6'2"	250	30		
Steve Sylvester	C-OG	6'4"	260	28		
Dave Browning	DE	6'5"	245	25	1	
Cedrick Hardman	DE	6'3"	245	32		6
Willie Jones	DE	6'4"	245	23		6
John Matuszak	DE	6'8"	285	30		
Reggie Kinlaw	NT	6'2"	240	24		
Howie Long	NT-DE	6'5"	265	21		
Johnny Robinson	NT	6'2"	260	22		2

Use Name	Pos.	Hgt.	Wgt.	Age	Int.	Pts.
Jeff Barnes	LB	6'2"	220	26		
Greg Bracelin	LB	6'1"	218	24		
Mario Celotto (to BAL, LA)	LB	6'3"	225	25		
Ted Hendricks	LB	6'7"	225	33		
Rod Martin	LB	6'2"	215	27	1	
Randy McClanahan	LB	6'5"	225	26		
Matt Millen	LB	6'2"	255	23		
Greg Westbrooks	LB	6'3"	220	28		
Mike Davis	DB	6'2"	200	25	1	
Lester Hayes	DB	6'	200	26	3	
Kenny Hill	DB	6'	185	23		
Monte Jackson	DB	5'11"	200	28		
Odis McKinney	DB	6'2"	185	24	3	
Dwayne O'Steen	DB	6'1"	195	26	1	
Burgess Owens	DB	6'2"	200	30	2	6
Ted Watts	DB	6'	190	23	1	6

Bob Nelson – Shoulder Injury

Use Name	Pos.	Hgt.	Wgt.	Age	Int.	Pts.
Jim Plunkett	QB	6'3"	210	33		6
Marc Wilson	QB	6'6"	210	24		12
Kenny King	HB-FB	5'11"	205	24		
Art Whittington	HB	5'11"	180	25		18
Chester Willis	HB	5'11"	195	23		6
Frank Hawkins	FB	5'9"	210	22		
Derrick Jensen	FB	6'1"	225	25		24
Mark van Eeghen	FB	6'2"	225	29		12
Malcolm Barnwell	WR	5'11"	180	23		6
Morris Bradshaw	WR	6'	195	28		18
Cliff Branch	WR	5'11"	170	33		6
Bob Chandler	WR	6'	180	32		24
Ira Matthews	WR	5'8"	175	24		
Ray Chester	TE	6'3"	235	33		6
Todd Christensen	TE-FB-C	6'3"	230	25		14
Derrick Ramsey	TE	6'5"	230	24		24
Chris Bahr	K	5'9"	175	28		69
Ray Guy	K	6'3"	200	31		

SEATTLE SEAHAWKS 6-10-0 Jack Patera

Scores of Each Game		
21	Cincinnati	27
13	DENVER	10
10	Oakland	20
14	KANSAS CITY	20
10	San Diego	24
17	Houston	35
0	N.Y. GIANTS	32
19	N.Y. Jets	3
24	Green Bay	34
24	PITTSBURGH	21
44	SAN DIEGO	23
13	Kansas City	40
31	OAKLAND	32
27	N.Y. JETS	23
13	Denver	23
42	CLEVELAND	21

*—Overtime

Use Name	Pos.	Hgt.	Wgt.	Age	Int.	Pts.
Steve August	OT	6'5"	254	26		
Dennis Boyd	OT-C	6'6"	255	25		6
Ron Essink	OT	6'6"	246	23		
Edwin Bailey	OG	6'4"	265	22		
Bill Dugan	OG	6'4"	271	22		
Bob Newton	OG	6'4"	260	32		
Art Kuehn	C	6'3"	255	28		
John Yarno	C	6'5"	251	26		
Fred Anderson	DE	6'4"	235	26		
Jacob Green	DE	6'3"	247	24		
Mike White	DE-DT	6'5"	266	24		
Robert Hardy	DT	6'2"	250	25		
Doug Sutherland	DT	6'3"	250	33		
Manu Tuiasosopo	DT-DE	6'3"	252	24		

Use Name	Pos.	Hgt.	Wgt.	Age	Int.	Pts.
Terry Beeson	LB	6'3"	240	21		
Keith Butler	LB	6'4"	225	25	2	
Brian Flones	LB	6'1"	228	22		
Greg Gaines	LB	6'3"	202	22		
Michael Jackson	LB	6'1"	220	24	2	
Joe Norman	LB	6'1"	220	24		
Rodell Thomas (from MIA)	LB	6'2"	227	23		6
Kevin Turner **(from WAS)**	LB	6'2"	225	23		
Dave Brown	DB	6'1"	190	28	2	
Don Dufek	DB	6'	195	27		
Kenny Easley	DB	6'3"	206	22	3	6
John Harris	DB	6'2"	200	25	10	12
Greggory Johnson	DB	6'1"	188	22		6
Kerry Justin	DB	5'11"	175	26		
Will Lewis	DB	5'9"	185	23		
Vic Minor	DB	6'	198	22		
Keith Simpson	DB	6'1"	195	25	2	

Larry Brinson – Knee Injury
Mark Bell – Knee Injury

Use Name	Pos.	Hgt.	Wgt.	Age	Int.	Pts.
Sam Adkins	QB	6'2"	214	26		
Dave Krieg	QB	6'1"	185	22		6
Jim Zorn	QB	6'2"	200	28		6
Theotis Brown (from STL)	HB-FB	6'2"	225	24		48
Horace Ivory (from N.E.)	HB	6'	198	27		
Eric Lane	HB	6'	195	22		
Terry Miller	HB	5'10"	196	25		
Jeff Moore	HB	6'	195	25		
Sherman Smith	HB	6'4"	225	26		24
Dan Doornink	FB	6'3"	210	25		30
David Hughes	FB	6'	220	22		12
Jim Jodat	FB	5'11"	213	27		6
Paul Johns	WR	5'11"	170	22		6
Steve Largent	WR	5'11"	184	26		60
Sam McCullum	WR	6'2"	190	28		18
Mark McGrath	WR	5'11"	175	23		
Steve Raible	WR	6'2"	195	27		
John Sawyer	TE	6'2"	230	28		
Mike Tice	TE	6'7"	235	22		
Wilson Alvarez	K	6'	165	24		23
Frank Garcia	K	6'	190	24		
Efren Herrera	K	5'9"	190	30		59
Jeff West	K	6'3"	210	28		

SAN DIEGO CHARGERS

RUSHING

Last Name	No.	Yds.	Avg.	TD
Muncie	251	1144	4.6	**19**
Brooks	109	525	4.8	3
Cappelletti	68	254	3.7	4
Fouts	22	56	2.5	0
C. Williams	20	26	1.3	0
Bauer	2	7	3.5	0
Roberts	1	2	2.0	0
Chandler	5	−1	−0.2	0
Luther	3	−8	−2.7	0

RECEIVING

Last Name	No.	Yds.	Avg.	TD
Winslow	**88**	1075	12	10
Joiner	70	1188	17	7
Chandler	69	1142	17	6
Brooks	46	329	7	3
Muncie	43	362	8	0
Sievers	22	276	13	3
Scales	19	429	23	1
C. Williams	12	108	9	1
Cappelletti	10	126	13	1
Holohan	1	14	14	0
Bauer	1	4	4	0

PUNT RETURNS

Last Name	No.	Yds.	Avg.	TD
Brooks	22	290	**13**	0
Chandler	5	79	16	0
Bauer	1	7	7	0
Edwards	1	1	1	0
Shaw	1	1	1	0
Phillips	1	0	0	0

KICKOFF RETURNS

Last Name	No.	Yds.	Avg.	TD
Brooks	**40**	**949**	24	0
Chandler	8	125	16	0
Shaw	6	103	17	0
C. Williams	4	47	12	0
Gregor	3	47	16	0
Sievers	2	4	2	0
Beaudoin	1	31	31	0
Henderson	1	26	26	0
Bauer	1	14	14	0

PASSING - PUNTING - KICKING

PASSING	Att.	Comp.	%	Yds.	Yd./Att.	TD	Int.–%	RK
Fouts	**609**	**360**	59	**4802**	7.9	**33**	17– 3	3
Luther	15	7	47	68	4.5	0	1– 7	
Muncie	1	1	100	3	3.0	1	0– 0	
Chandler	2	0	0	0	0.0	0	0– 0	
Winslow	2	0	0	0	0.0	0	0– 0	

PUNTING	No.	Avg.
Roberts	62	41.0

KICKING	XP	Att.	%	FG	Att.	%
Benirschke	**55**	**61**	90	19	26	73

DENVER BRONCOS

RUSHING

Last Name	No.	Yds.	Avg.	TD
Parros	176	749	4.3	2
Preston	183	640	3.5	3
Reed	68	156	2.3	0
Canada	33	113	3.4	3
Lytle	30	106	3.5	4
Upchurch	5	56	11.2	0
DeBerg	9	40	4.4	0
Morton	8	18	2.3	0
Wright	1	11	11.0	0
Watson	2	6	3.0	0

RECEIVING

Last Name	No.	Yds.	Avg.	TD
Watson	60	**1244**	21	**13**
Preston	52	507	10	0
Odoms	38	516	14	5
Reed	34	317	9	0
Upchurch	32	550	17	3
Parros	25	216	9	1
Egloff	17	231	14	1
Moses	15	246	16	1
Lytle	6	47	8	1
Manning	3	49	16	0
Canada	3	37	12	1
J. Wright	3	22	7	1
Studdard	1	10	10	0

PUNT RETURNS

Last Name	No.	Yds.	Avg.	TD
Manning	41	378	9	0
Upchurch	9	63	7	0
Kyle	1	0	0	0

KICKOFF RETURNS

Last Name	No.	Yds.	Avg.	TD
Manning	26	514	20	0
Harden	11	178	16	0
Lytle	5	80	16	0
Canada	2	19	10	0
Egloff	1	7	7	0
Ryan	1	2	2	0
Preston	1	1	1	0

PASSING - PUNTING - KICKING

PASSING	Att.	Comp.	%	Yds.	Yd./Att.	TD	Int.–%	RK
Morton	376	225	60	3195	8.5	21	14– 4	2
DeBerg	108	64	59	797	7.4	6	6– 6	
Reed	1	0	0	0	0.0	0	1–100	

PUNTING	No.	Avg.
Prestridge	86	40.4

KICKING	XP	Att.	%	FG	Att.	%
Steinfort	36	37	97	17	30	57

KANSAS CITY CHIEFS

RUSHING

Last Name	No.	Yds.	Avg.	TD
Delaney	234	1121	4.8	3
Hadnot	140	603	4.3	3
B. Jackson	111	398	3.6	10
McKnight	54	195	3.6	5
Fuller	19	118	6.2	0
Kenny	24	89	3.7	1
Marshall	3	69	23.0	0
Bledsoe	20	65	3.3	0
Williams	2	0	0.0	0
Carson	1	−1	−1.0	0
Dixon	1	−5	−5.0	0
Grupp	1	−9	−9.0	0

RECEIVING

Last Name	No.	Yds.	Avg.	TD
Smith	63	852	14	2
Marshall	38	620	16	4
Dixon	29	356	12	2
Hadnot	23	215	9	0
Delaney	22	246	11	0
Rome	17	203	12	1
McKnight	8	77	10	0
Carson	7	179	26	1
B. Jackson	6	31	5	1
Scott	5	72	14	1
Bledsoe	3	27	9	0
Murphy	2	36	18	0
Williams	1	3	3	0

PUNT RETURNS

Last Name	No.	Yds.	Avg.	TD
Smith	**50**	**528**	11	0

KICKOFF RETURNS

Last Name	No.	Yds.	Avg.	TD
Murphy	20	457	23	0
Carson	10	227	23	0
Bledsoe	6	117	20	0
Burruss	5	91	18	0
B. Jackson	3	60	20	0
Cherry	3	52	17	0
Rourke	2	0	0	0
Delaney	1	11	11	0
Williams	1	7	7	0

PASSING - PUNTING - KICKING

PASSING	Att.	Comp.	%	Yds.	Yd./Att.	TD	Int.–%	RK
Kenny	274	147	54	1983	7.2	9	16– 6	12
Fuller	134	77	58	934	7.0	3	4– 3	
Hadnot	1	0	0	0	0.0	0	1–100	
Marshall	1	0	0	0	0.0	0	0– 0	

PUNTING	No.	Avg.
Grupp	41	38.0
Gossett	29	39.3

KICKING	XP	Att.	%	FG	Att.	%
Lowery	37	38	97	**26**	**36**	72

OAKLAND RAIDERS

RUSHING

Last Name	No.	Yds.	Avg.	TD
King	170	828	4.9	0
Jensen	117	456	3.9	4
Whittington	69	220	3.2	1
Hawkins	40	165	4.1	0
van Eeghen	39	150	3.8	2
Wilson	30	147	4.9	2
Willis	16	54	3.4	1
Plunkett	12	38	3.2	1

RECEIVING

Last Name	No.	Yds.	Avg.	TD
Ramsey	52	674	13	4
Branch	41	635	16	1
Jensen	28	271	10	0
King	27	216	8	0
Chandler	26	458	18	4
Whittington	23	213	9	2
Bradshaw	22	298	14	3
Matthews	15	92	6	0
Chester	13	93	7	1
Hawkins	10	109	11	0
Barnwell	9	190	21	1
Christensen	8	115	14	2
van Eeghen	7	60	9	0
Willis	1	24	24	0

PUNT RETURNS

Last Name	No.	Yds.	Avg.	TD
Watts	35	284	8	1
Whittington	2	4	2	0

KICKOFF RETURNS

Last Name	No.	Yds.	Avg.	TD
Whittington	25	563	23	0
Willis	15	309	21	0
Barnwell	15	265	18	0
Matthews	7	144	21	0
Christensen	4	54	14	0
Hill	1	21	21	0
Hawkins	1	7	7	0

PASSING - PUNTING - KICKING

PASSING	Att.	Comp.	%	Yds.	Yd./Att.	TD	Int.–%	RK
Wilson	366	173	47	2311	6.3	14	19– 5	15
Plunkett	179	94	53	1045	5.8	4	9– 5	

PUNTING	No.	Avg.
Guy	**96**	43.7
Bahr	2	21.5

KICKING	XP	Att.	%	FG	Att.	%
Bahr	27	33	82	14	24	58

SEATTLE SEAHAWKS

RUSHING

Last Name	No.	Yds.	Avg.	TD
J. Brown	156	583	3.7	8
Smith	83	253	3.0	3
Doornink	65	194	3.0	1
Zorn	30	140	4.7	1
Hughes	47	135	2.9	0
Jodat	31	106	3.4	1
Krieg	11	56	5.1	1
Largent	6	47	7.8	1
Ivory	9	38	4.2	0
Adkins	3	28	9.3	0
West	3	25	8.3	0
Lane	8	22	2.8	0
Moore	1	15	15.0	0
Miller	2	4	4.0	0

RECEIVING

Last Name	No.	Yds.	Avg.	TD
Largent	75	1224	16	9
McCullum	46	567	12	3
Smith	44	406	9	1
Hughes	35	263	8	2
T. Brown	29	328	11	0
Doornink	27	350	13	4
Sawyer	21	272	13	0
Johns	8	131	16	1
Lane	7	58	8	0
Tice	5	47	9	0
Jodat	4	52	13	0
McGrath	4	47	12	0
Moore	3	18	6	0
Raible	1	12	12	0
August	1	9	9	0
Boyd	1	3	3	0

PUNT RETURNS

Last Name	No.	Yds.	Avg.	TD
Johns	16	177	11	0
Lewis	15	100	7	0
Johnson	1	16	16	0

KICKOFF RETURNS

Last Name	No.	Yds.	Avg.	TD
Lewis	20	378	19	0
Ivory	16	300	19	0
Johnson	13	235	18	0
Lane	10	208	21	0
Johns	5	81	16	0
Dufek	3	45	15	0
Sawyer	1	8	8	0

PASSING - PUNTING - KICKING

PASSING	Att.	Comp.	%	Yds.	Yd./Att.	TD	Int.–%	RK
Zorn	397	236	59	2788	7.0	13	9– **2**	5
Krieg	112	64	57	843	7.5	7	5– 5	
Adkins	13	7	54	96	7.4	1	1– 8	
Largent	1	0	0	0	0.0	0	0– 0	
West	1	0	0	0	0.0	0	0– 0	

PUNTING	No.	Avg.
West	66	39.1
Garcia	2	37.0

KICKING	XP	Att.	%	FG	Att.	%
Herrera	23	25	92	12	17	74
Alvarez	14	15	93	3	7	43

1981 N.F.C. — PLAYOFFS

December 27 at Philadelphia (Attendance 71,611)

SCORING

NEW YORK	**20**	**7**	**0**	**0–27**
PHILADELPHIA	**0**	**7**	**7**	**7–21**

First Quarter
- N.Y. — Bright, 9 yard pass from Brunner; PAT–Kick failed
- N.Y. — Mistler, 10 yard pass from Brunner; PAT–Danelo (kick)
- N.Y. — Haynes, fumble recovery in end zone; PAT–Danelo (kick)

Second Quarter
- Phil. — Carmichael, 15 yard pass from Jaworski; PAT–Franklin (kick)
- N.Y. — Mullady, 22 yard pass from Brunner; PAT–Danelo (kick)

Third Quarter
- Phil. — Montgomery, 6 yard rush; PAT–Franklin (kick)

Fourth Quarter
- Phil. — Montgomery, 1 yard rush; PAT–Franklin (kick)

TEAM STATISTICS

N.Y.		PHIL.
16	First Downs-Total	19
10	First Downs-Rushing	8
6	First Downs-Passing	8
0	First Downs- Penalty	3
1	Fumbles-Number	5
0	Fumbles-Lost Ball	2
5	Penalties-Number	4
54	Yards Penalized	23
1	Missed Field Goals	0
57	Offensive Plays	56
275	Net Yards	226
4.8	Average Gain	4.0
1	Giveaways	2
2	Takeaways	1
+1	Difference	−1

INDIVIDUAL STATISTICS

RUSHING

NEW YORK	No.	Yds.	Avg.	PHILADELPHIA	No.	Yds.	Avg.
Carpenter	33	161	4.9	Montgomery	18	65	3.6
Perry	3	11	3.7	Oliver	5	12	2.4
Brunner	6	11	1.8	Campfield	1	10	10.0
	42	183	4.4	Jaworski	5	6	1.2
					29	93	3.2

RECEIVING

NEW YORK	No.	Yds.	Avg.	PHILADELPHIA	No.	Yds.	Avg.
Carpenter	4	32	8.0	Montgomery	3	32	10.7
Mullady	1	22	22.0	R. Smith	3	31	10.3
Gray	1	12	12.0	Carmichael	2	43	21.5
Perkins	1	11	11.0	C. Smith	2	19	9.5
Mistler	1	10	10.0	Krepfle	1	18	18.0
Bright	1	9	9.0	Oliver	1	7	7.0
	9	96	10.7	Russell	1	4	4.0
					13	154	11.8

PUNTING

NEW YORK	No.		Avg.	PHILADELPHIA	No.		Avg.
Jennings	4		44.8	Runager	7		42.4

PUNT RETURNS

NEW YORK	No.	Yds.	Avg.	PHILADELPHIA	No.	Yds.	Avg.
Bright	4	32	8.0	Sciarra	2	16	8.0
Reece	1	9	9.0	Henry	1	0	0.0
	5	41	8.2		3	16	5.3

KICKOFF

NEW YORK	No.	Yds.	Avg.	PHILADELPHIA	No.	Yds.	Avg.
Reece	3	64	21.3	Russell	2	24	12.0
Jackson	1	23	23.0	Henry	2	16	8.0
	4	87	21.8	Campfield	1	19	19.0
					5	59	11.8

INTERCEPTION RETURNS

NEW YORK	No.	Yds.	Avg.	PHILADELPHIA	No.	Yds.	Avg.
none				Edwards	1	1	1.0

PASSING

	Att.	Comp.	Comp. Pct.	Yds.	Int.	Yds./ Att.	Yds./ Comp.
NEW YORK							
Brunner	14	9	64.2	96	1	6.9	10.7
PHILADELPHIA							
Jaworski	24	13	54.1	154	0	6.4	11.8

January 2, 1982 at Irving, Tex. (Attendance 68,848)

SCORING

TAMPA BAY	**0**	**0**	**0**	**0– 0**
DALLAS	**0**	**10**	**21**	**7–38**

Second Quarter
- Dal. — Hill, 9 yard pass from D. White; PAT Septien (kick)
- Dal. — Septien, 32 yard field goal

Third Quarter
- Dal. — Springs, 1 yard rush; PAT–Septien (kick)
- Dal. — Dorsett, 5 yard rush; PAT–Septien (kick)
- Dal. — J. Jones, 5 yard rush; PAT–Septien (kick)

Fourth Quarter
- Dal. — Newsome, 1 yard rush; PAT–Septien (kick)

TEAM STATISTICS

T.B.		DAL.
12	First Downs-Total	26
3	First Downs-Rushing	15
7	First Downs-Passing	10
2	First Downs-Penalty	1
2	Fumbles-Number	0
0	Fumbles-Lost Ball	0
10	Penalties-Number	5
105	Yards Penalized	40
0	Missed Field Goals	0
55	Offensive Play	73
222	Net Yards	345
4.0	Average Gain	4.7
4	Giveaways	0
0	Takeaways	4
−4	Difference	+4

INDIVIDUAL STATISTICS

RUSHING

TAMPA BAY	No.	Yds.	Avg.	DALLAS	No.	Yds.	Avg.
Owens	12	40	3.3	Dorsett	16	86	5.4
Wilder	4	23	5.8	Springs	15	70	4.7
Williams	2	9	4.5	J. Jones	9	32	3.6
Eckwood	4	2	0.5	Newhouse	4	23	5.8
	22	74	3.4	Newsome	1	1	1.0
				Cosbie	1	0	0.0
					46	212	4.6

RECEIVING

TAMPA BAY	No.	Yds.	Avg.	DALLAS	No.	Yds.	Avg.
T. Bell	3	36	12.0	Dorsett	4	48	12.0
Owens	3	32	10.7	DuPree	3	22	7.3
Giles	2	98	49.0	Pearson	2	21	7.0
Wilder	1	11	11.0	Hill	2	18	9.0
House	1	10	10.0	J. Jones	2	15	7.5
	10	187	18.7	Donley	1	14	14.0
				Cosbie	1	5	5.0
					15	143	9.5

PUNTING

TAMPA BAY	No.		Avg.	DALLAS	No.		Avg.
Swider	5		38.4	D. White	4		30.0

PUNT RETURNS

TAMPA BAY	No.	Yds.	Avg.	DALLAS	No.	Yds.	Avg.
T. Bell	1	1	1.0	J. Johes	3	53	17.7

KICKOFF RETURNS

TAMPA BAY	No.	Yds.	Avg.	DALLAS	No.	Yds.	Avg.
Owens	3	92	30.7	none			
Holt	2	55	27.5				
	5	147	29.4				

INTERCEPTION RETURNS

TAMPA BAY	No.	Yds.	Avg.	DALLAS	No.	Yds.	Avg.
none				Thurman	2	50	25.0
				Downs	1	21	21.0
				T. Jones	1	0	0.0
					4	71	17.8

PASSING

	Att.	Comp.	Comp. Pct.	Yds.	Int.	Yds./ Att.	Yds./ Comp.
TAMPA BAY							
Williams	29	10	34.5	187	4	6.4	18.7
DALLAS							
D. White	26	15	57.7	143	0	5.5	9.5

January 3, 1982 at San Francisco (Attendance 58, 360)

SCORING

NEW YORK	**7**	**3**	**7**	**7–24**
SAN FRANCISCO	**7**	**17**	**9**	**14–38**

First Quarter
- S.F. — Young, 8 yard pass from Montana; PAT–Wersching (kick)
- N.Y. — Gray, 72 yard pass from Brunner; PAT–Danelo (kick)

Second Quarter
- S.F. — Wersching, 22 yard field goal
- S.F. — Solomon, 58 yard pass from Montana; PAT–Wersching (kick)
- S.F. — Patton, 25 yard rush; PAT–Wersching (kick)
- N.Y. — Danelo, 48 yard field goal

Third Quarter
- N.Y. — Perkins, 59 yard pass from Brunner; PAT–Danelo (kick)

Fourth Quarter
- S.F. — Ring, 3 yard rush; PAT–Wersching (kick)
- S.F. — Lott, 20 yard interception return; PAT–Wersching (kick)
- N.Y. — Perkins, 17 yard pass from Brunner; PAT–Danelo (kick)

TEAM STATISTICS

N.Y.		S.F.
13	First Downs-Total	24
3	First Downs-Rushing	8
9	First Downs-Passing	13
1	First Downs-Penalty	3
4	Fumbles-Number	2
2	Fumbles-Lost Ball	0
9	Penalties-Number	14
61	Yards Penalized	145
1	Missed Field Goals	1
61	Offensive Plays	68
346	Net Yards	423
5.7	Average Gain	6.2
4	Giveaways	1
1	Takeaways	4
−3	Difference	+3

INDIVIDUAL STATISTICS

RUSHING

NEW YORK	No.	Yds.	Avg.	SAN FRANCISCO	No.	Yds.	Avg.
Carpenter	17	61	3.6	Cooper	7	52	7.4
Bright	1	5	5.0	Patton	7	32	4.6
Perry	2	1	0.5	Ring	10	29	2.9
Brunner	2	−2	−1.0	Solomon	1	12	12.0
	22	65	3.0	Easley	4	9	2.3
				Clark	1	6	6.0
				Davis	1	4	4.0
				Montana	3	−9	−3.0
					34	135	4.0

RECEIVING

NEW YORK	No.	Yds.	Avg.	SAN FRANCISCO	No.	Yds.	Avg.
Perkins	1	121	17.3	Solomon	6	107	17.8
Gray	3	118	39.3	Clark	5	104	20.8
Carpenter	3	18	6.0	Patton	2	38	19.0
Young	2	15	7.5	Young	2	22	11.0
Mistler	1	18	18.0	Wilson	2	21	10.5
	16	290	18.1	Ramson	1	11	11.0
				Elliott	1	5	5.0
				Ring	1	−4	−4.0
					20	304	15.2

PUNTING

NEW YORK	No.		Avg.	SAN FRANCISCO	No.		Avg.
Jennings	9		43.8	Miller	5		41.2

PUNT RETURNS

NEW YORK	No.	Yds.	Avg.	SAN FRANCISCO	No.	Yds.	Avg.
Bright	3	18	6.0	Solomon	1	22	22.0

KICKOFF RETURNS

NEW YORK	No.	Yds.	Avg.	SAN FRANCISCO	No.	Yds.	Avg.
Bright	5	113	22.6	Lawrence	3	88	29.3
McLaughlin	1	15	15.0	Ring	1	5	5.0
Dennis	1	14	14.0	Lott	1	0	0.0
	7	142	20.3		5	93	18.6

INTERCEPTION RETURNS

NEW YORK	No.	Yds.	Avg.	SAN FRANCISCO	No.	Yds.	Avg.
Currier	1	2	2.0	Lott	2	32	16.0

PASSING

	Att.	Comp.	Comp. Pct.	Yds.	Int.	Yds./ Att.	Yds./ Comp.
NEW YORK							
Brunner	37	16	43.2	290	2	7.8	18.1
SAN FRANCISCO							
Montana	31	20	62.5	304	1	9.8	15.2

1981 A.F.C. PLAYOFFS

December 27 at New York (Attendance 57,050)

SCORING

BUFFALO	17	7	0	7–31
NEW YORK	0	10	3	14–27

First Quarter
- Buf. Romes, 26 yard fumble return PAT-Mike-Mayer (kick)
- Buf. Lewis, 50 yard pass from Ferguson PAT-Mike-Mayer (kick)
- Buf. Mike-Mayer 29 yard field goal

Second Quarter
- Buf. Lewis, 26 yard pass from Ferguson PAT-Mike-Mayer (kick)
- N.Y. Shuler, 30 yard pass from Todd PAT-Leahy (kick)
- N.Y. Leahy, 26 yard field goal

Third Quarter
- N.Y. Leahy, 19 yard field goal

Fourth Quarter
- Buf. Cribbs, 45 yard rush PAT-Mike-Mayer (kick)
- N.Y. B. Jones, 30 yard pass from Todd PAT-Leahy (kick)
- N.Y. Long, 1 yard rush PAT-Leahy (kick)

TEAM STATISTICS

BUFF.		N.Y.
15	First Downs-Total	23
4	First Downs-Rushing	3
11	First Downs-Passing	17
0	First Downs-Penalty	3
1	Fumbles-Number	3
0	Fumbles-Lost Ball	1
8	Penalties-Number	6
62	Yards Penalized	55
1	Missed Field Goals	1
58	Offensive Plays	77
321	Net Yards	419
5.5	Average Gain	5.4
4	Giveaways	5
5	Takeaways	4
+1	Difference	−1

INDIVIDUAL STATISTICS

BUFFALO	No.	Yds.	Avg.	NEW YORK	No.	Yds.	Avg.
RUSHING							
Cribbs	14	83	5.9	McNeil	12	32	2.7
Leaks	6	12	2.0	Long	8	28	3.5
Ferguson	2	-4	−2.0	odd	2	11	5.5
	22	91	4.1		22	71	3.2
RECEIVING							
Lewis	7	158	22.6	Dierking	7	52	7.4
Cribbs	4	64	16.0	Shuler	6	116	19.3
Leaks	3	23	7.7	B. Jones	4	64	16.0
Brammer	2	17	8.5	Gaffney	4	64	16.0
Butler	1	6	6.0	Walker	3	24	8.0
	17	268	15.8	Barkum	2	41	20.5
				Newton	1	12	12.0
				Harper	1	4	4.0
					28	377	13.5
PUNTING							
Cater	4		43.8	Ramsey	4		33.0
PUNT RETURNS							
Riddick	1	1	6.0	Harper	3	31	10.3
Piccone	1	5	5.0				
	2	11	5.5				
KICKOFF RETURNS							
Riddick	4	73	18.3	Harper	4	82	20.5
Brown	1	27	27.0	Sohn	1	28	28.0
	5	100	20.0		5	110	22.0
INTERCEPTION RETURNS							
Simpson	2	12	6.0	Buttle	2	40	20.0
Bess	1	49	49.0	Dykes	1	20	20.0
Villipiano	1	18	18.0	Holmes	1	0	0.0
	4	79	19.8		4	60	15.0

PASSING

	Att.	Comp.	Comp. Pct.	Yds.	Int.	Yds./Att.	Yds./Comp.
BUFFALO							
Ferguson	34	17	50.0	268	4	7.9	15.8
NEW YORK							
Todd	51	28	54.9	377	4	7.4	13.5

January 2, 1982 at Miami (Attendance 73,735)

SCORING

SAN DIEGO	24	0	7	7	3–41
MIAMI	0	17	14	7	0–38

First Quarter
- S.D. Benirschke, 32 yard field goal
- S.D. Chandler, 56 yard punt return PAT–Benirschke (kick)
- S.D. Muncie, 1 yard, rush PAT–Benirschke (kick)
- S.D. Brooks, 8 yard pass from Fouts PAT–Benirschke (kick)

Second Quarter
- Mia. von Schaman, 34 yard field goal
- Mia. Rose, 1 yard pass from Strock PAT–von Schamann (kick)
- Mia. Nathan, 40 yard pass from Strock PAT–von Schamann (kick)

Third Quarter
- Mia. Rose, 15 yard pass from Strock PAT–von Schaman (kick)
- S.D. Winslow, 25 yard pass from Fouts PAT–Bernirschke (kick)
- Mia. Hardy, 50 yard pass from Strock PAT–von Schaman (kick)

Fourth Quarter
- Mia. Nathan, 12 yard rush PAT–von Schamann (kick)
- S.D. Brooks, 9 yard pass from Fouts PAT–Benirschke (kick)

Overtime
- S.D. Benirschke, 29 yard field goal

TEAM STATISTICS

S.D.		MIAMI
33	First Downs-Total	25
10	First Downs-Rushing	3
21	First Downs-Passing	21
2	First Downs-Penalty	1
3	Fumbles-Number	2
3	Fumbles-Lost Ball	1
8	Penalties-Number	7
45	Yards Penalized	44
2	Missed Field Goals	2
85	Offensive Plays	78
564	Net Yards	466
6.6	Average Gain	6.0
4	Giveaways	3
3	Takeaways	4
-1	Difference	+1

INDIVIDUAL STATISTICS

SAN DIEGO	No.	Yds.	Avg.	MIAMI	No.	Yds.	Avg.
RUSHING							
Muncie	24	120	5.0	Nathan	14	48	3.4
Brooks	3	19	6.3	Woodley	1	10	10.0
Fouts	2	10	5.0	Hill	3	8	2.7
	29	149	5.1	Vigorito	1	6	6.0
				Franklin	9	6	0.7
					28	78	2.8
RECEIVING							
Winslow	13	166	12.8	Nathan	8	108	13.5
Joiner	7	108	15.4	Harris	6	106	17.7
Chandler	6	106	17.7	Hardy	5	89	17.8
Brooks	4	31	7.8	Rose	4	37	9.3
Muncie	2	5	2.5	Cefalo	3	62	20.7
Scales	1	17	17.0	Vigorito	2	12	6.0
	33	433	13.1	Hill	2	3	1.5
					30	417	13.9
PUNTING							
Roberts	4		40.3	Orosz	5		42.0
PUNT RETURNS							
Chandler	1	56	56.0	Vigorito	1	12	12.0
Brooks	1	8	8.0				
	2	64	32.0				
KICKOFF RETURNS							
Brooks	5	75	15.0	Vigorito	4	67	16.8
Beaudoin	1	15	15.0	Walker	1	18	18.0
	6	90	15.0	Hill	1	13	13.0
					6	98	16.3
INTERCEPTION RETURNS							
Edwards	1	35	35.0	L. Blackwood	1	8	8.0
Buchanon	1	0	0.0				
	2	35	17.5				

PASSING

	Att.	Comp.	Comp. Pct.	Yds.	Int.	Yds./Att.	Yds./Comp.
SAN DIEGO							
Fouts	53	33	62.3	33	1	8.2	13.1
Muncie	1	0	0.0	0	0	0.0	0.0
	54	33	61.1	433	1	8.0	13.1
MIAMI							
Woodley	5	2	40.0	20	1	4.0	10.0
Strock	42	28	66.7	397	1	9.5	14.2
	47	30	63.8	417	2	8 9	13.9

January 3, 1982 at Cincinnati (Attendance 55,420)

SCORING

BUFFALO	0	7	7	7–21
CINCINNATI	14	0	7	7–28

First Quarter
- Cin. Alexander, 4 yard rush PAT-Breech (kick)
- Cin. Johnson, 1 yard rush PAT-Breech (kick)

Second Quarter
- Buf. Cribbs, 1 yard rush PAT-Mike-Mayer (kick)

Third Quarter
- Buf. Cribbs, 44 yard rush PAT-Mike-Mayer (kick)
- Cin. Alexander, 20 yard rush PAT-Breech (kick)

Fourth Quarter
- Buf Butler, 21 yard pass from Ferguson PAT-Mike-Mayer
- Cin. Collinsworth, 16 yard pass from Anderson PAT-Breech (kick)

TEAM STATISTICS

BUF.		CIN.
21	First Downs-Total	22
11	First Downs-Rushing	11
8	First Downs-Passing	9
2	First Downs-Penalty	2
0	Fumbles-Number	0
0	Fumbles-Lost Ball	0
6	Penalties-Number	5
56	Yards Penalized	44
0	Missed Field Goals	1
59	Offensive Plays	58
336	Net Yards	305
5.7	Average Gain	5.3
2	Giveaways	0
0	Takeaways	2
−2	Difference	+2

INDIVIDUAL STATISTICS

BUFFALO	No.	Yds.	Avg.	CINCINNATI	No.	Yds.	Avg.
RUSHING							
Cribbs	15	90	6.0	Alexander	13	72	5.5
Hooks	9	30	3.3	Johnson	17	45	2.6
Leaks	3	12	4.0	A. Griffin	1	4	4.0
Brown	1	2	2.0	Anderson	2	4	2.0
	28	134	4.8		33	125	3.8
RECEIVING							
Butler	4	98	24.5	Ross	6	71	11.8
Lewis	3	38	12.7	Johnson	3	23	7.7
Brammer	3	23	7.7	Collinsworth	2	24	12.0
Leaks	2	16	8.0	Kreider	1	42	42.0
Hooks	2	15	7.5	Curtis	1	22	22.0
Jessie	1	12	12.0	Alexander	1	10	10.0
	15	202	13.5		14	192	13.7
PUNTING							
Cater	3		42.0	McInally	4		44.5
PUNT RETURNS							
Riddick	2	8	4.0	Fuller	1	27	27.0
KICKOFF RETURNS							
Riddick	4	68	17.0	Verser	4	94	23.5
Brown	1	14	14.0				
	5	82	16.4				
INTERCEPTION RETURNS							
none				B. Harris	1	16	16.0
				Riley	1	0	0.0
					2	16	8.0

PASSING

	Att.	Comp.	Comp. Pct.	Yds.	Int.	Yds. Att.	Yds. Comp.
BUFFALO							
Ferguson	31	15	48.4	202	2	6.5	13.5
CINCINNATI							
Anderson	21	14	66.7	192	0	9.1	13.7

1981 CHAMPIONSHIP GAMES

NFC CHAMPIONSHIP GAME

January 10, 1982 at San Francisco
(Attendance 60,525)

SCORING

DALLAS	10	7	0	10–	27
SAN FRANCISCO	7	7	7	7–	28

First Quarter
- S.F. — Solomon, 8 yard pass from Montana, PAT–Wersching (kick)
- Dal. — Septien, 44 yard field goal
- Dal. — Hill, 26 yard pass from D. White, PAT–Septien (kick)

Second Quarter
- S.F. — Clark, 20 yard pass from Montana, PAT–Wersching (kick)
- Dal. — Dorsett, 5 yard rush, PAT–Septien (kick)

Third Quarter
- S.F. — Davis, 2 yard rush, PAT–Wersching (kick)

Fourth Quarter
- Dal. — Septien, 22 yard field goal
- Dal. — Cosbie, 21 yard pass from D. White, PAT–Septien (kick)
- S.F. — Clark, 6 yard pass from Montana, PAT–Wersching (kick)

TEAM STATISTICS

DALLAS		S.F.
16	First Downs–Total	26
5	First Downs–Rushing	6
9	First Downs–Passing	17
2	First Downs–Penalty	3
4	Fumbles–Number	3
2	Fumbles–Lost Ball	3
5	Penalty–Number	7
39	Yards Penalized	106
0	Missed Field Goals	0
60	Offensive Plays	69
250	Net Yards	393
4.2	Average Gain	5.7
3	Giveaways	6
6	Takeaways	3
−3	Difference	−3

Although San Francisco had been plagued with hard rains and flooding, the playing field at Candlestick Park was in fine shape as the 49ers hosted the Dallas Cowboys. The 49ers had whipped the Cowboys 45–14 in October, but Tom Landry's crew came into this match with lots of championship experience, a commodity in short supply on the 49er roster.

But on the opening series, the 49ers showed composure and calm. They took the kickoff and drove downfield, scoring on an eight-yard pass from Joe Montana to Freddie Solomon. For the rest of the first half, the two combatants traded the lead back and forth. At the intermission, the Cowboys held a 17-14 edge.

The defensive units dominated the third quarter, with the 49er unit creating the only scoring opportunity. Bobby Leopold intercepted a pass and started a San Francisco drive which led to Johnny Davis's touchdown plunge. At the end of three quarters, the 49ers led 21–17.

Both teams rose to their fullest stature in the final period, with the young 49ers standing up to the veteran Cowboys. Raphael Septien kicked a 22-yard field goal early in the quarter to close the gap to 21-20. Midway through the period, the Cowboys launched an offensive which ended in Doug Cosbie's touchdown on a pass from Danny White. With the extra point, the Cowboys led 27–21.

With just under five minutes left on the clock, the 49ers began a do-or-die drive from their own 10-yard line. Joe Montana moved his team downfield on pinpoint passes and some hard-fought running gains, taking his team to the Dallas six-yard line. On third down, Montana rolled to the right and, eluding Larry Bethea, threw to Dwight Clark for the go-ahead touchdown. The Cowboys began moving downfield after the kickoff, but a fumble by Danny White was recovered by the 49ers, who killed off the clock and prepared for the Super Bowl.

INDIVIDUAL STATISTICS

DALLAS	No.	Yds.	Avg.	SAN FRANCISCO	No.	Yds.	Avg.
RUSHING							
Dorsett	22	91	4.1	Elliott	10	48	4.8
J. Jones	4	14	3.5	Cooper	8	35	4.4
Springs	5	10	2.0	Ring	6	27	4.5
D. Whte	1	0	C.0	Solomon	1	14	14.0
				Easley	2	6	3.0
	32	115	3.6	Davis	1	2	2.0
				Montana	3	−5	−1.7
					31	127	5.0
RECEIVING							
J. Jones	3	17	5.7	Clark	8	120	15.0
DuPree	3	15	5.0	Solomon	6	75	12.5
Springs	3	13	4.3	Young	4	45	11.3
Hill	2	43	21.5	Cooper	2	11	5.5
Pearson	1	31	31.0	Elliott	1	24	24.0
Cosbie	1	21	21.0	Shumann	1	11	11.0
Johnson	1	20	20.0				
Saldi	1	9	9.0		22	286	13.0
Donley	1	4	4.0				
	16	173	10.8				
PUNTING							
D. White	6		39.3	Miller	3		35.7
PUNT RETURNS							
J. Jones	3	13	4.3	Hicks	2	21	10.5
				Solomon	1	3	3.0
					3	24	8.0
KICKOFF RETURNS							
J. Jones	3	56	18.7	Lawrence	3	60	20.0
Newsome	2	33	16.5	Ring	3	47	15.7
	5	89	17.8		6	107	17.8
INTERCEPTION RETURNS							
Walls	2	0	0.0	Leopold	1	5	5.0
R. White	1	0	0.0				
	3	0	0.0				

PASSING

	Att.	Comp.	Comp. Pct.	Yds.	Int.	Yds./ Att.	Yds./ Comp.
DALLAS							
D. White	24	16	66.7	173	1	7.2	10.8
SAN FRANCISCO							
Montana	33	25	75.8	286	3	8.7	13.0

AFC CHAMPIONSHIP GAME

January 10, 1982 at Cincinnati
(Attendance 46,302)

SCORING

SAN DIEGO	0	7	0	0–	7
CINCINNATI	10	7	3	7–	27

First Quarter
- Cin. — Breech, 31 yard field goal
- Cin. — M. Harris, 8 yard pass from Anderson, PAT–Breech (kick)

Second Quarter
- S.D. — Winslow, 33 yard pass from Fouts, PAT–Benirschke (kick)
- Cin. — Johnson, 1 yard rush, PAT–Breech (kick)

Third Quarter
- Cin. — Breech, 38 yard field goal

Fourth Quarter
- Cin. — Bass, 3 yard pass from Anderson, PAT–Breech (kick)

TEAM STATISTICS

SAN DIEGO		CIN.
18	First Downs–Total	19
11	First Downs–Rushing	8
7	First Downs–Passing	11
0	First Downs–Penalty	0
4	Fumbles–Number	3
2	Fumbles–Lost Ball	1
2	Penalty–Number	3
15	Yards Penalized	25
2	Missed Field Goals	0
61	Offensive Plays	59
301	Net Yards	318
4.9	Average Gain	5.4
4	Giveaways	1
1	Takeaways	4
−3	Difference	−3

The weather was the story. At gametime in Cincinnati, the temperature was 11 below zero, with a stiff wind driving the wind chill factor down to 59 below. Pete Rozelle even considered postponing the game, but after collecting medical opinions, he ordered the game to start. 46,302 fanatics were in their seats, warmed internally and externally by a variety of devices.

Onto the Riverfront Stadium tundra charged the Bengals and Chargers, both expert practitioners of the forward pass. The Bengals were coming off a 28–21 victory over Buffalo, while the Chargers arrived here after downing Miami 41–38 in an overtime slugfest. In the extreme conditions prevailing on this day, predictions were impossible to make.

The Bengals got onto the scoreboard early, with Jim Breech booting a 31-yard field goal. On the following kickoff, James Brooks fumbled and the Bengals recovered on the 12-yard line. A short pass from Ken Anderson to M.L. Harris quickly made the score 10–0.

San Diego's Dan Fouts had trouble passing in the wind-swept freeze, but he did throw a 33-yard scoring strike to Kellen Winslow in the second quarter to cut the score to 10–7. Fouts led the Chargers deep into Cincinnati territory two other times, but threw interceptions to end the drives. With momentum up for grabs, the Bengals drove to another touchdown before the half to take a 17-7 lead into the clubhouse.

The San Diego attack remained stuck in the second half, while the Bengals adapted to the conditions to grind out ten more points. Breech kicked another field goal, and Anderson threw a touchdown pass to Don Bass. It was cold for both the teams on the field, and the Bengals played well enough in discomfort to earn a ticket to the Super Bowl.

INDIVIDUAL STATISTICS

SAN DIEGO	No.	Yds.	Avg.	CINCINNATI	No.	Yds.	Avg.
RUSHING							
Muncie	23	94	4.1	Johnson	21	80	3.6
Brooks	6	23	3.8	Anderson	5	39	7.8
Fouts	1	6	6.0	Alexander	9	22	2.4
Cappelletti	1	5	5.0	Collinsworth	1	2	2.0
	31	128	4.1		36	143	4.0
RECEIVING							
Chandler	6	79	13.2	Ross	5	69	13.8
Winslow	3	47	15.7	Alexander	3	25	8.3
Joiner	3	41	13.7	Collinsworth	2	28	14.0
Brooks	2	5	2.5	Curtis	2	28	14.0
Sievers	1	13	13.0	Johnson	1	14	14.0
	15	185	12.3	M. Harris	1	8	8.0
				Bass	1	3	3.0
					15	175	11.7
PUNTING							
Roberts	2		29.5	McInally	3		30.6
PUNT RETURNS							
Chandler	1	7	7.0	none			
KICKOFF RETURNS							
Brooks	4	87	21.8	Verser	1	40	40.0
Shaw	1	7	7.0				
	5	94	18.8				
INTERCEPTION RETURNS							
none				Kemp	1	24	24.0
				Breeden	1	0	0.0
					2	24	12.0

PASSING

	Att.	Comp.	Comp. Pct.	Yds.	Int.	Yds./ Att.	Yds./ Comp.
SAN DIEGO							
Fouts	28	15	53.6	185	2	6.6	12.3
CINCINNATI							
Anderson	22	14	63.6	161	0	7.3	11.5
Thompson	1	1	100.0	14	0	14.0	14.0
	23	15	65.2	175	0	7.6	11.7

Striking Gold at the Silverdome

There was no Goliath, only two Davids who had risen up to slay all the giants in their way. Both the Bengals and the 49ers had lost regularly in recent years, and they were given little pre-season hope of any playoff appearance. Coaches Bill Walsh of San Francisco and Forrest Gregg of Cincinnati led their overachievers into the first Super Bowl staged outside the Sun Belt. While the countryside was gripped by a bitter Michigan winter, the players and fans settled in for an afternoon of football in the comfortable Pontiac Silverdome.

Cincinnati kicked off and immediately grabbed a fumble by Amos Lawrence. Stunned by the sudden change of fortune, the 49ers allowed the Bengals to drive to the five-yard line. Regaining their composure, the 49ers sacked Ken Anderson for a six-yard loss, then picked off his next pass to end the threat.

Joe Montana then led his mates to a sustained drive downfield. He completed several passes while rolling out, and he also took part in a flea-flicker play which gained 14 yards. On the eleventh play of the drive, Montana dived over for a touchdown.

In the second quarter, the Bengals moved deep into Cincinnati turf only to lose the ball on Chris Collinsworth's fumble. Starting on the eight-yard line, Montana moved his team with passes and hit Earl Cooper with a scoring strike to make the score 14–0. With 15 seconds left on the first-half clock, Ray Wersching kicked a field goal for a 17–0 lead. On the kickoff, Archie Griffin fumbled and the 49ers recovered, setting Wersching up for another chip shot and a 20-0 lead.

The Bengals returned for the second half faced with the most one-sided score in Super Bowl history. They took the kickoff and relit their spirits with an 83-yard drive for a touchdown. Along the way, they delighted fans with a razzle-dazzle play to match that of the 49ers in the first half. For the rest of the third quarter, the score stayed at 20-7. Although the Bengals upped the score to 20–14 in the fourth quarter, the 49ers recaptured the momentum by stopping the Bengals on downs on the one-yard line, shutting down powerful fullback Pete Johnson on fourth down. Two more field goals by Wersching padded the San Francisco lead and paved the road to the 26–21 triumph. Of the two Cinderella teams, the 49ers had played in their usual loose style, while the Bengals looked as if the pressure was riding their backs.

LINEUPS

CINCINNATI		SAN FRANCISCO
	OFFENSE	
Collinsworth	WR	Clark
Munoz	LT	Audick
Lapham	LG	Ayers
Bush	C	Quillan
Mantoya	RG	Cross
Wilson	RT	Fahnhorst
Ross	TE	Young
Curtis	WR	Solomon
Anderson	QB	Montana
Alexander	HD	Patton
Johnson	FB	Cooper
	DEFENSE	
St. Clair	LE	Stuckey
Whitley	NT	Reese
Browner	RT	Board
B. Harris	LLB	Harper
LeClair	LLB	Reynolds
Cameron	RLB	Puki
Williams	RLB	Turner
Breeden	LCB	Lott
Riley	RCB	Wright
Kemp	SS	Williamson
Hicks	FS	Hicks

SUBSTITUTES

CINCINNATI

	OFFENSE	
Bass	Kreider	Obrovac
A. Griffin	McInally	Schonert
Hargrove	Moore	Thompson
M. Harris		Verser
	DEFENSE	
Burley	Frazier	R. Griffin
Davis	Fuller	Razzano
Dinkel	Horn	Schuh
Edwards		Simmons
	KICKER	
	Breech	

SAN FRANCISCO

	OFFENSE	
Benjamin	Easley	Ramson
Choma	Elliott	Ring
Davis	Kennedy	Schumann
Downing	Lawrence	Wilson
	DEFENSE	
Bunz	Harty	McColl
Dean	Leopold	Pillers
Gervais	Martin	Thomas
	KICKERS	
Miller		Wersching

SCORING

CINCINNATI	0	0	7	14–	21
SAN FRANCISCO	7	13	0	6–	26

First Quarter
- S.F. Montana, 1 yard rush
  PAT–Wersching (kick)

Second Quarter
- S.F. Cooper, 11 yard pass from Montana
  PAT–Wersching (kick)
- S.F. Wersching, 22 yard field goal
- S.F. Wersching, 26 yard field goal

Third Quarter
- Cin. Anderson, 5 yard rush
  PAT–Breech (kick)

Fourth Quarter
- Cin. Ross, 4 yard pass from Anderson
  PAT–Breech (kick)
- S.F. Wersching, 40 yard field goal
- S.F. Wersching, 23 yard field goal
- Cin. Ross, 3 yard pass from Anderson
  PAT–Breech (kick)

TEAM STATISTICS

CIN.		S.F.
24	First Downs–Total	20
7	First Downs–Rushing	9
13	First Downs–Passing	9
4	First Downs–Penalty	2
2	Fumbles–Number	2
2	Fumbles–Lost Ball	1
8	Penalties–Number	8
57	Yards Penalized	65
0	Missed Field Goals	0
63	Offensive Plays	63
356	Net Yards	275
5.7	Average Gain	4.4
4	Giveaways	1
1	Takeaways	4
–3	Difference	–3

INDIVIDUAL STATISTICS

CINCINNATI	No.	Yds.	Avg.	SAN FRANCISCO	No.	Yds.	Avg.
RUSHING							
Johnson	14	36	2.6	Patton	17	55	3.2
Alexander	5	17	3.4	Cooper	9	31	3.8
Anderson	4	15	3.8	Montana	6	18	3.0
A. Griffin	1	4	4.0	Ring	5	17	3.4
	24	72	3.0	Davis	2	5	2.5
				Clark	1	–2	–2.0
					40	127	3.2
RECEIVING							
Ross	11	104	9.5	Solomon	4	52	13.0
Collinsworth	5	107	21.4	Clark	4	45	11.3
Curtis	3	42	14.0	Cooper	2	15	7.5
Kreider	2	36	18.0	Wilson	1	22	22.0
Johnson	2	8	4.0	Young	1	14	14.0
Alexander	2	3	1.5	Patton	1	6	6.0
	25	300	12.0	Ring	1	3	3.0
					14	157	11.2
PUNTING							
McInally	3		43.7	Miller	4		46.3
PUNT RETURNS							
Fuller	4	35	8.8	Hicks	1	6	6.0
KICKOFF RETURNS							
Verser	5	52	10.4	Hicks	1	23	23.0
Frazier	1	0	0.0	Lawrence	1	17	17.0
A. Griffin	1	0	0.0	Clark	1	0	0.0
	7	52	7.4		3	40	13.3
INTERCEPTION RETURNS							
none				Hicks	1	27	27.0
				Wright	1	25	25.0
					2	52	26.0

PASSING

	Att.	Comp.	Comp. Pct.	Yds.	Int.	Yds./ Att.	Yds./ Comp.	Yards Lost Tackled
CINCINNATI								
Anderson	34	25	73.5	300	2	8.8	12.0	9–16
SAN FRANCISCO								
Montana	22	14	63.6	157	0	7.1	11.2	1–9

1982 N.F.C. From Strike to a Long Season

The N.F.L. Players Association presented a set of demands unseen in any other pro sport. The old labor agreement expired in July, leaving the fate of the 1982 season in the hands of hard-bitten negotiators. Ed Garvey, executive director of the union, wanted the team owners to set aside 55 percent of gross revenues from all sources as a pool for player salaries; players would receive a salary determined by a formula which considered experience and playing excellence. The union did not demand more liberal free agency as its primary objective, emphasizing instead a guaranteed piece of the pie. Jack Donlan, the negotiator for the owners, scoffed at the proposal as socialistic. Although both sides compromised as they talked, the players finally went out on strike after the second week of play.

The sudden stoppage of play left a television vacuum that was filled by Canadian Football League games, the World Series and sundry other sporting events. On the first weekend of the strike, some fans held tailgate parties outside empty ballparks, and some radio stations broadcast fantasy versions of canceled games. As the strike dragged on, however, pro football stepped down in the national consciousness. The union staged all-star games in Washington on October 17 and in Los Angeles on October 18. Very few stars played, and very few fans paid or cared. Fifty-seven days after it began, the strike ended on November 16 with an agreement that left the basic structure of the game untouched. Players would still negotiate individual contracts, but the owners agreed that total player salaries for 1983-86 would total at least $1.28 billion. In addition, minimum salaries were raised, severance pay was instituted, and a fund of $60 million was set aside as a one-time bonus for the players.

Play resumed on November 21 with a revamped playoff scheme. Regular-season play was extended through the first weekend of January. The wild-card weekend and the open weekend before the Super Bowl were eliminated. Eight teams from each conference would make the playoffs and then fight through January for the N.F.L. title. Despite grumbling by fans and low attendance in some cities, the post-strike season regenerated interest, which reached its usual frenzied peak in the Super Bowl.

EASTERN DIVISION

Washington Redskins — The Redskins made the fewest mistakes and had the most nicknames in the N.F.L. The improved offensive line was known as the Hogs, the corps of small receivers as the Smurfs, and the players who celebrated touchdowns with choreographed endzone high-fives as the Fun Bunch. Such nicknames sprang from the joy of Washington's first playoff berth since 1976. Strong finishers last year, the Skins won their first two games and continued their polished play after the strike. The offense prospered with Joe Theismann's high-percentage passing and John Riggins' relentless plowing behind the Hogs. Although Mike Nelms starred as a kick returner, the ace of the special teams was kicker Mark Moseley. He clicked on a miraculous 20-of-21 field-goal attempts, a performance so impressive that he won the league MVP award. The Skins lost only to the Cowboys and relished the prospect of a rematch in the playoffs.

Dallas Cowboys — An embarrassing 36-28 loss to the Steelers on the opening Monday night augured ill for the Cowboys. They did win their second game and then asserted their usual dominance by winning their first five games after the strike. This drive clinched a playoff spot and included a strong 24-10 victory in Washington. The defense overcame the retirements of Charlie Waters and D.D. Lewis, relying heavily on linemen Too Tall Jones, Harvey Martin and Randy White. Everson Walls capitalized on the strong pass rush to lead the N.F.C. in rushing, and Danny White ranked near the top in passing. Losses in the last two games, however, caused a little nervousness going into the playoffs.

St. Louis Cardinals — The Cards edged into the expanded playoffs for the first time since 1975 by winning two of their last three games. Although they didn't score points at a rapid rate, the Cards fielded good young talent in quarterback Neil Lomax, runner Ottis Anderson and receiver Roy Green. At the other end of the spectrum were receiver Mel Gray and cornerback Roger Wehrli, finishing their long careers in secondary roles.

New York Giants —Last year's magic faded and the Giants tumbled once again out of the playoffs. On offense, quarterback Phil Simms went out with a pre-season knee injury. Fullback Rob Carpenter joined him on the sidelines until December in a contract dispute. The defense stayed tough, showcasing stars in Lawrence Taylor, Harry Carson and Mark Haynes, and kept the Giants in the running for a playoff berth. On December 15, coach Ray Perkins announced that he would leave at the end of the season to succeed Bear Bryant at the University of Alabama. The Giants promptly dropped close games to the Redskins and Cardinals to poison their chances. They edged the Eagles in the finale but lost out on the tiebreaking formula.

Philadelphia Eagles — The Eagles had been flying high as recently as last November. They stumbled in the home stretch then, and they plunged to the depths this year by losing their first four games after the strike. The offense put points on the board regularly, but the defense lost its shape and crispness. It survived the loss of Bill Bergey last year, but the trade of Charles Johnson during training camp was too much to absorb. Johnson had expressed his unhappiness with the severe regime of Dick Vermeil, prompting his swap to Minnesota. The Eagles perhaps suffered a case of burnout, and Vermeil would quit after the season to seek a less-consuming job.

CENTRAL DIVISION

Green Bay Packers — Last year's strong finish carried over into a stirring opening game. The Rams raced to a 23-0 halftime lead, but the embarrassed Pack stormed back to win the game 35-23. One week later, they trailed the Jets 19-7 in the third quarter, yet triumphed by a 27-19 score. They played only .500 ball after the strike, but that was good enough for a playoff berth, the first in Bart Starr's eight-year reign. The team's heart was its passing attack, with Lynn Dickey throwing to James Lofton and John Jefferson. Eddie Lee Ivery made his second comeback from knee surgery to handle the heavy running duties. Despite the hot-and-cold late season, the Pack still finished with the third-best record in the N.F.C.

Minnesota Vikings — Bud Grant put last year's collapse behind him and led his Vikings back into the playoffs. He programmed his offense to pass the ball about 80 percent of the time, and Tommy Kramer's strong arm made it work. Ted Brown caught a lot of passes coming out of the backfield and was the team's only effective runner. First-round draft pick Darrin Nelson never settled in as Brown's running mate. The Vikes never put together a winning streak, but they earned their post-season appearance by avoiding losing streaks.

Tampa Bay Buccaneers — Two pre-strike losses put the Bucs in a weak position when play resumed. With three weeks remaining, they had a 2-4 record and only slight hopes of a playoff spot. John McKay again engineered a late-season drive, which earned the Bucs a place in the second season. They swept their last three games, finishing with a 26-23 overtime victory over the Bears. The offense moved primarily on Doug Williams' arm, with fullback James Wilder both the leading receiver and leading runner. The defense ranked with the N.F.L.'s best, combining mobility with hard hitting. The Bucs had stars in each defensive area; end Lee Roy Selmon rushed passers to distraction, linebacker Hugh Green swarmed the field and safety Neal Colzie policed the secondary with an iron hand.

Detroit Lions — The strike hurt the Lions more than anyone. They swept their first two games, then joined the rest of the league on the sidelines. Once play resumed, the Lions lost their edge and dropped their first three games. They regained their stride on December 12 by beating the Packers 30-10. Two more losses followed, reducing Detroit's record to 3-5. A 27-24 victory over the Packers in the finale salvaged a playoff spot despite the team's losing record. Monte Clark had stars in runner Billy Sims and defensive tackle Doug English, but he never got consistent work from either of his quarterbacks, Eric Hipple and Gary Danielson.

Chicago Bears — The Bears reached back into their glorious past by hiring Mike Ditka as their new head coach. A star on the 1963 championship team, Ditka brought a disciplined, hard-nosed attitude to the anemic Bears. Despite Ditka's changes,

FINAL TEAM STATISTICS

OFFENSE

	ATL.	CHI.	DALL.	DET.	G.B.	L.A.	MINN.	N.O.	NY G	PHIL.	STL.	S.F.	T.B.	WASH.
FIRST DOWNS:														
Total	190	153	180	160	175	163	167	173	153	157	162	183	163	165
by Rushing	79	56	70	60	59	61	52	79	47	48	71	49	52	66
by Passing	92	83	99	83	97	90	107	76	96	100	81	121	105	87
by Penalty	19	14	11	17	19	12	8	18	10	9	10	13	6	12
RUSHING:														
Number	310	276	296	283	283	251	245	331	244	211	307	219	268	315
Yards	1181	988	1313	1022	1081	1025	912	1257	842	829	1209	740	952	1140
Average Yards	3.8	3.6	4.4	3.6	3.8	4.1	3.7	3.8	3.5	3.9	3.9	3.4	3.6	3.6
Touchdowns	12	5	10	5	12	13	6	8	7	11	10	6	6	5
PASSING:														
Attempts	275	262	258	285	267	297	334	248	298	288	240	348	308	253
Completions	176	141	160	136	143	166	187	137	161	168	129	215	164	162
Completion Pct.	64.0	53.8	62.0	47.7	53.6	55.9	56.0	55.2	54.0	58.3	53.8	61.8	53.2	64.0
Passing Yards	1992	1749	2150	1754	2068	2136	2105	1571	2017	2100	1576	2668	2071	2068
Avg. Yds per Att.	5.9	5.1	6.7	4.8	6.1	6.4	5.5	5.2	6.0	5.8	4.9	6.8	6.1	6.5
Avg. Yds per Comp.	11.3	12.4	13.4	12.9	14.5	12.9	11.3	11.5	12.5	12.5	12.2	12.4	12.6	12.8
Times Tackled	25	33	25	30	32	15	22	23	17	31	32	20	11	30
Yds Lost Tackled	210	244	264	242	239	137	138	173	130	244	243	166	128	223
Net Yards	1782	1505	1886	1512	1829	1999	1967	1398	1887	1856	1333	2502	1943	1845
Touchdowns	9	10	16	12	12	11	15	8	10	12	6	17	9	13
Interceptions	11	11	14	18	15	14	12	14	9	13	6	11	11	9
Pct. Intercepted	4.0	4.2	5.4	6.3	5.6	4.7	3.6	5.6	3.0	4.5	2.5	3.2	3.6	3.6
PUNTS:														
Number	43	59	37	48	42	46	58	46	49	44	54	45	40	52
Average	39.3	41.6	41.7	40.9	40.2	42.6	41.1	43.0	42.8	40.5	43.8	37.2	40.5	37.3
PUNT RETURNS														
Number	24	24	30	26	26	22	24	21	44	22	32	30	25	38
Yards	273	142	242	275	198	242	196	144	373	108	192	332	143	295
Average Yards	11.4	5.9	8.1	10.8	7.6	11.0	8.2	6.9	8.5	4.9	6.0	11.1	5.7	7.8
Touchdowns	0	0	0	0	0	1	0	0	0	0	0	1	0	0
KICKOFF RET.:														
Number	29	34	33	36	34	45	37	26	39	39	35	36	33	30
Yards	513	622	651	750	664	869	786	577	783	768	702	742	548	649
Average Yards	17.7	18.3	19.7	20.8	19.5	19.3	21.2	22.2	20.1	19.7	20.1	20.6	16.6	21.6
Touchdowns	0	0	0	1	0	0	0	0	0	0	0	0	0	0
INTERCEPT RET.:														
Number	10	13	15	18	12	11	12	9	12	15	6	9	11	11
Yards	90	99	163	154	174	106	91	108	205	42	52	150	139	85
Average Yards	9.0	7.6	10.9	8.6	14.5	9.6	7.6	12.0	17.1	2.8	8.7	16.7	12.6	7.7
Touchdowns	0	1	1	1	0	0	1	0	1	1	0	1	0	0
PENALTIES:														
Number	77	58	42	58	42	63	62	63	47	38	56	45	38	46
Yards	655	422	304	548	343	550	496	514	369	253	528	451	297	404
FUMBLES:														
Number	14	16	29	23	20	23	12	17	19	26	17	17	28	15
Number Lost	10	8	12	8	11	10	5	10	10	10	10	10	12	7
POINTS:														
Total	183	141	226	181	226	200	187	129	164	191	135	209	158	190
PAT Attempts	22	16	28	19	27	25	23	16	18	25	16	25	15	19
PAT Made	21	16	28	19	25	23	23	15	18	23	15	23	14	16
FG Attempts	14	20	14	17	18	15	14	13	21	9	13	17	23	21
FG Made	10	9	10	16	13	9	8	6	12	6	8	12	18	20
Percent FG Made	71.4	45.0	71.4	94.1	72.2	60.0	57.1	46.2	57.1	66.7	61.5	70.6	78.3	95.2
Safeties	0	1	0	0	0	0	1	0	1	0	0	0	0	0

DEFENSE

	ATL.	CHI.	DALL.	DET.	G.B.	L.A.	MINN.	N.O.	NY G	PHIL.	STL.	S.F.	T.B.	WASH.
FIRST DOWNS:														
Total	170	166	162	162	164	193	159	151	149	177	163	170	160	151
by Rushing	66	53	56	54	58	75	53	58	55	68	58	71	72	47
by Passing	84	102	95	96	96	107	87	81	85	100	98	88	76	93
by Penalty	20	11	11	12	10	11	19	12	9	9	7	11	12	11
RUSHING:														
Number	253	261	260	271	275	307	260	255	301	299	256	303	285	247
Yards	1044	902	1011	854	932	1202	1020	974	1118	1031	995	1199	1058	946
Average Yards	4.1	3.5	3.9	3.2	3.4	3.9	3.9	3.8	3.7	3.4	3.9	4.0	3.7	3.8
Touchdowns	13	4	5	6	9	13	8	8	7	5	5	9	9	8
PASSING:														
Attempts	280	294	289	288	327	281	292	245	244	285	291	278	254	275
Completions	157	164	152	155	177	175	157	149	148	168	174	158	145	146
Completion Pct.	56.1	55.8	52.6	53.8	54.1	62.3	53.8	60.8	60.7	58.9	59.8	56.8	57.1	53.1
Passing Yards	1945	2189	2002	2098	1950	2290	2106	1864	1810	2136	2035	1949	1608	1870
Avg. Yds per Att.	6.1	6.0	5.4	5.8	5.1	7.1	5.8	5.9	5.7	6.1	5.9	6.3	5.0	5.3
Avg. Yds per Comp.	12.4	13.4	13.2	13.5	11.0	13.1	13.4	12.5	12.2	12.7	11.7	12.3	11.1	12.8
Times Tackled	18	30	32	32	20	18	30	31	31	30	23	15	25	32
Yds Lost Tackled	141	240	260	230	175	159	231	231	244	229	182	113	224	256
Net Yards	1804	1949	1742	1868	1775	2131	1875	1633	1566	1907	1853	1836	1384	1614
Touchdowns	12	14	10	11	9	16	11	11	10	14	16	14	10	8
Interceptions	10	13	15	18	12	11	12	9	12	15	6	9	11	11
Pct. Intercepted	3.6	4.4	5.2	6.3	3.7	3.9	4.1	3.7	4.9	5.3	2.1	3.2	4.3	4.0
PUNTS:														
Number	38	49	49	46	46	42	50	51	59	38	51	50	42	56
Average	41.7	41.6	42.5	39.8	41.8	38.1	41.9	41.1	41.0	36.8	41.2	42.7	43.4	40.1
PUNT RETURNS														
Number	24	34	21	26	27	31	30	29	25	31	36	20	23	30
Yards	197	314	118	237	286	401	176	239	207	316	288	224	192	106
Average Yards	8.2	9.2	5.6	9.1	10.6	12.9	5.9	8.2	8.3	10.2	8.0	11.2	8.3	3.5
Touchdowns	0	0	0	0	0	1	0	0	0	0	0	1	0	0
KICKOFF RET.:														
Number	30	30	41	38	45	36	38	20	34	39	27	40	40	42
Yards	678	537	936	755	875	844	663	388	616	885	558	857	870	726
Average Yards	22.6	17.9	22.8	19.9	19.4	23.4	17.4	19.4	18.1	22.7	20.7	21.4	21.8	17.3
Touchdowns	0	0	0	0	1	0	0	0	0	0	0	0	0	0
INTERCEPT RET.:														
Number	11	11	14	18	15	14	12	14	9	13	6	11	11	9
Yards	58	195	125	248	146	98	337	79	29	118	37	130	114	68
Average Yards	5.3	17.7	8.9	13.8	9.7	7.0	28.1	5.6	3.2	9.1	6.2	11.8	10.4	7.6
Touchdowns	0	2	1	1	0	0	3	0	0	0	0	0	1	0
PENALTIES:														
Number	60	52	52	74	72	64	48	52	54	45	54	58	38	52
Yards	549	451	431	605	629	531	399	459	417	341	420	542	325	419
FUMBLES:														
Number	24	20	20	21	26	15	22	23	19	20	14	14	15	23
Number Lost	15	7	10	8	11	7	9	13	6	12	9	4	10	13
POINTS:														
Total	199	174	145	176	169	250	198	160	160	195	170	206	178	128
PAT Attempts	26	20	17	20	19	30	24	19	18	19	21	24	21	16
PAT Made	25	18	16	20	17	28	21	19	16	19	20	23	16	14
FG Attempts	12	17	15	21	18	19	19	12	13	22	18	19	17	9
FG Made	6	12	9	12	12	14	11	9	12	20	8	13	12	6
Percent FG Made	50.0	70.6	60.0	57.1	66.7	73.7	57.9	75.0	92.3	90.9	44.4	68.4	70.6	66.7
Safeties	0	0	0	0	1	0	0	0	0	1	0	0	0	0

they dropped their pre-strike games, the second a 10-0 humbling by the Saints. They won the first game after play resumed, with rookie Jim McMahon taking over as the starting quarterback. The Chicago offense sputtered the rest of the way, but the Bears no longer had a doormat look. Walter Payton still shone as an all-purpose offensive weapon. The defense featured the pass rushing of tackle Dan Hampton.

WESTERN DIVISION

Atlanta Falcons — After a year out, the Falcons returned to the playoffs with a strong offense that covered for a weak defense. William Andrews and rookie Gerald Riggs ran well behind a big offensive line, which featured all-pros Mike Kenn, R.C. Thielemann and Jeff Van Note. The same blockers kept Steve Bartkowski healthy and gave him time to pass over run-conscious defenses. The Atlanta defense failed to mount a competent pass rush despite the return to form of Joel Williams. The Falcons made their season by winning four of their first five games after the strike. With a playoff date assured, they then looked horrible in their final two matches, losing 38-7 to Green Bay and 35-6 to New Orleans.

New Orleans Saints — It looked like the Saints were finally going to make the playoffs. Bum Phillips had built a good defense out of an unheralded group of players. His conservative offensive philosophy found perfect expression in George Rogers and Ken Stabler. Despite news that he had spent about $10,000 last year on cocaine, Rogers was the heavy-duty tank that could control the ball. Phillips signed Stabler after the Oilers cut the old quarterback loose during the summer. Given the QB job, Stabler used his guile to take the Saints to a 3-1 record at the start of December. With a post-season position within grasp, the Saints tragically dropped four straight games, including a 35-0 thumping by the Falcons on December 12. Despite the aches of frequent sackings, Stabler engineered a 35-6 vengeance over the Falcons in the season finale. The playoff berth, however, slipped away for still another year.

San Francisco 49ers — Three problem areas turned the Super Bowl champs into also-rans. The pedestrian ground attack actually lost some of its bite. The pass rush fell off considerably, with Dwaine Board hobbled by a bad knee and Fred Dean reaching quarterbacks less frequently. With the pass rush diminished, the young secondary began making the errors of inexperience. The season began with a 23-17 loss to the Raiders and a 24-21 loss at the final gun to the Broncos. After the strike, Joe Montana's passing and Dwight Clark's receiving kept the Niners competitive, but their problems kept them inconsistent. Their last shot at the playoffs died with a 21-20 loss to the Rams in the finale.

Los Angeles Rams — Opening day was a disaster, with the Rams blowing a 23-0 halftime lead and losing to the Packers 35-23. The Rams thereafter made it a regular practice to dissipate halftime leads. They fielded an absolutely porous defense, which nullified a pretty good offense. Two veteran quarterbacks joined the team, Bert Jones from the Colts and Vince Ferragamo from his one-year sojourn in Montreal. Jones began the season as the starter but went to the bench with a neck injury. Wendell Tyler, as usual, spearheaded the attack. The Rams ended a four-game losing streak by beating San Francisco in the finale, but that wasn't enough to save the job of Ray Malavasi, a Super Bowl coach only two years ago.

WASHINGTON REDSKINS 8-1-0 Joe Gibbs

Scores of Each Game		
37	Philadelphia	34
21	Tampa Bay	13
27	N.Y.Giants	17
13	PHILADELPHIA	9
10	DALLAS	24
12	St.Louis	7
15	N.Y.GIANTS	14
27	New Orleans	10
28	ST.LOUIS	0

Use Name	Pos.	Hgt	Wgt	Age	Int	Pts
Joe Jacoby	OT	6'7"	295	23		
Donald Laster	OT	6'5"	285	23		
Garry Puetz	OT	6'4"	255	30		
George Starke	OT	6'5"	260	34		
Fred Dean	OG	6'3"	255	27		
Russ Grimm	OG	6'3"	273	23		
Mark May	OG	6'6"	288	22		
Jeff Bostic	C	6'2"	245	23		
Todd Liebenstein	DE	6'6"	245	22		
Dexter Manley	DE	6'3"	253	23	1	
Tony McGee	DE	6'4"	250	33		
Mat Mandenhall	DE	6'6"	255	25		
Perry Brooks	DT	6'3"	265	27		
Dave Butz	DT	6'7"	295	32		
Darryl Grant	DT	6'1"	265	23		
Pat Ogrin	DR	6'5"	265	24		
Stuart Anderson	LB	6'1"	247	22		
Monte Coleman	LB	6'2"	235	24		
Pete Cronan	LB	6'2"	238	27		
Mel Kaufman	LB	6'2"	218	24		
Larry Kubin	LB	6'2"	234	23		
Quentin Lowry	LB	6'3"	225	24		
Rich Milot	LB	6'4"	237	25		
Neal Olkewicz	LB	6'	227	25		
Vernon Dean	DB	5'11"	178	23	3	
Curtis Jordan	DB	6'2"	205	28		6
Joe Lavender	DB	6'4"	185	33		
LeCharls McDaniel	DB	5'9"	169	23	1	
Mark Murphy	DB	6'4"	210	27	2	
Mike Nelms	DB	6'1"	185	27		
Tony Peters	DB	6'1"	190	29	1	
Jeris White	DB	5'11"	188	29	3	
Greg Williams	DB	5'11"	185	23		
Bob Holly	QB	6'2"	205	22		
Tom Owen	QB	6'1"	194	30		
Joe Theismann	QB	6'	195	32		
Nick Giaquinto	HB-FB	5'11"	204	27		
Clarence Harmon	HB-FB	5'11"	209	26		6
Wilbur Jackson	HB	6'1"	219	30		
Joe Washington	HB	5'10"	179	28		12
John Riggins	FB	6'2"	235	33		18
Otis Wonsley	FB-HB	5'10"	214	25		6
Charlie Brown	WR	5'10"	179	23		48
Alvin Garrett	WR	5'7"	178	25		
Art Monk	WR	6'3"	209	24		6
Virgil Seay	WR	5'8"	175	24		
Rich Caster	TE	6'5"	230	33		
Clint Didier	TE	6'5"	240	23		6
Rick Walker	TE	6'3"	235	27		6
Don Warren	TE	6'4"	242	26		
Mike Williams	TE	6'4"	245	23		
Jeff Hayes	K	5'11"	175	23		
Mark Moseley	K	5'11"	205	34		76

Rickey Claitt - Knee Injury
Cris Crissy - Fractured Cheeckbone

DALLAS COWBOYS 6-3-0 Tom Landry

Scores of Each Game		
28	PITTSBURGH	36
24	St.Louis	7
14	TAMPA BAY	9
31	CLEVELAND	14
24	Washington	10
37	Houston	7
21	NEW ORLEANS	7
20	PHILADELPHIA	24
27	Minnesota	31

Use Name	Pos.	Hgt	Wgt	Age	Int	Pts
Jim Cooper	OT	6'5"	263	26		
Pat Donovan	OT	6'4"	257	29		
Phil Pozderac	OT	6'9"	270	22		
Kurt Petersen	OG	6'4"	268	25		
Howard Richards	OG-OT	6'6"	258	23		
Herbert Scott	OG	6'2"	260	29		
Glen Titensor	OG-C	6'4"	260	24		
Steve Wright	OG-OT	6'6"	263	23		
Brian Baldinger	C-OG	6'4"	253	23		
Tom Rafferty	C-OG	6'3"	259	28		
Larry Bethea	DE-DT	6'5"	244	26		
Too Tall Jones	DE	6'9"	272	31	1	
Harvey Martin	DE	6'5"	260	31		
John Dutton	DT	6'7"	275	31		
Don Smerek	DT-DE	6'7"	257	24		
Randy White	DT	6'4"	268	29		
Bob Breunig	LB	6'2"	225	29	1	
Guy Brown	LB	6'4"	227	27		
Anthony Dickerson	LB	6'2"	222	25	1	
Mike Hegman	LB	6'1"	228	29		
Angelo King	LB	6'1"	230	24		
Jeff Rohrer	LB	6'3"	232	23		
Danny Spradlin	LB	6'1"	241	23		
Benny Barnes	DB	6'1"	204	31		
Dextor Clinkscale	DB	5'11"	190	24	1	
Micheal Downs	DB	6'3"	203	23	1	6
Ron Fellows	DB	6'	174	23		
Rod Hill	DB	6'	182	23		
Monty Hunter	DB	6'	202	23		
Dennis Thurman	DB	5'11"	183	26	3	6
Everson Walls	DB	6'1"	194	22	7	
Glenn Carano	QB	6'3"	204	26		
Gary Hogeboom	QB	6'4"	199	24		
Danny White	QB	6'2"	196	30		
Brad Wright	QB	6'2"	209	23		
Tony Dorsett	HB	5'11"	192	28		30
James Jones	HB	5'10"	202	23		
Robert Newhouse	FB	5'10"	219	32		6
Timmy Newsome	FB	6'1"	231	24		12
George Peoples	FB	6'	211	22		
Ron Springs	FB-HB	6'1"	210	25		24
Doug Donley	WR	6'	173	23		
Tony Hill	WR	6'2"	198	26		6
Butch Johnson	WR	6'1"	187	28		18
Drew Pearson	WR	6'	193	31		18
Doug Cosbie	TE	6'6"	232	26		24
Billy Joe DuPree	TE	6'4"	223	32		18
Jay Saldi	TE	6'3"	230	27		
Rafael Septien	K	5'10"	180	28		58

Robert Shaw - Knee Injury
Norman Wells - Knee Injury

ST. LOUIS CARDINALS 5-4-0 Jim Hanifan

Scores of Each Game		
21	New Orleans	7
7	DALLAS	24
20	SAN FRANCISCO	31
23	Atlanta	20
23	Philadelphia	20
7	WASHINGTON	12
10	Chicago	7
24	N.Y.GIANTS	21
0	Washington	28

Use Name	Pos.	Hgt	Wgt	Age	Int	Pts
Art Plunkett	OT	6'7"	270	23		
Tootie Robbins	OT	6'5"	278	24		
Luis Sharpe	OT	6'4"	260	22		
Joe Bostic	OG	6'3"	265	25		
George Collins	OG-OT	6'2"	270	26		
Terry Stieve	OG	6'2"	265	28		
Randy Clark	C	6'3"	254	25		
Dan Dierdorf	C	6'4"	290	33		
Curtis Greer	DE	6'4"	252	24		
Elois Grooms	DE	6'4"	250	29		
Stafford Mays	DE-DT	6'2"	250	24		
Rush Brown	DT	6'2"	260	28		
Mike Dawson	DT	6'4"	270	28	1	
David Galloway	DT	6'3"	277	23		
Bruce Thornton	DT-DE	6'5"	263	24		
Dave Ahrens	LB	6'3"	228	23		
Kurt Allerman	LB	6'2"	222	27		
Charlie Baker	LB	6'2"	217	24		
Calvin Favron	LB	6'1"	227	25		
John Gillen	LB	6'3"	228	23		
E.J.Junior	LB	6'3"	235	22		
Craig Puki	LB	6'1"	231	25		
Craig Shaffer	LB	6'	230	23		
Carl Allen	DB	6'	190	26	1	
Don Bessillieu	DB	6'1"	200	26		
Tim Collier (to SF)	DB	6'	176	28		
Ken Greene	DB	6'3"	205	26	1	
Jeff Griffin	DB	6'	185	24	1	
Lee Nelson	DB	5'10"	185	28	1	
Benny Perrin	DB	6'2"	178	22	1	
Dave Stief	DB	6'3"	195	26		
Roger Wehrli	DB	6'1"	194	34		6
Herb Williams	DB	6'	200	24		
Jim Hart	QB	6'2"	210	38		
Rusty Lisch	QB	6'3"	213	25		
Neil Lomax	QB	6'3"	215	23		6
Ottis Anderson	HB	6'2"	220	25		18
Will Harrell	HB	5'8"	182	29		
Stump Mitchell	HB	5'9"	188	23		6
Earl Ferrell	FB	6'	215	24		
Randy Love	FB	6'1"	205	25		
Wayne Morris	FB	6'	210	28		24
Mel Gray	WR	5'9"	175	33		
Roy Green	WR	6'	195	25		18
Mike Shumann	WR	6'	185	26		
Ken Thompson	WR	6'1"	178	23		
Ricky Thompson	WR	6'	177	28		
Pat Tilley	WR	5'10"	178	29		12
Greg LaFleur	TE	6'4"	236	23		6
Doug Marsh	TE	6'3"	240	24		
Eddie McGill	TE	6'6"	225	22		
Carl Birdsong	K	6'	192	23		
Neil O'Donoghue	K	6'6"	210	29		39

Barney Cotton - Knee Injury

NEW YORK GIANTS 4-5-0 Ray Perkins

Scores of Each Game		
14	ATLANTA	16
19	GREEN BAY	27
17	WASHINGTON	27
13	Detroit	6
17	HOUSTON	14
23	PHILADELPHIA	7
14	Washington	15
21	St.Louis	24
26	Philadelphia	24

Use Name	Pos.	Hgt	Wgt	Age	Int	Pts
Rich Baldinger	OT	6'4"	270	22		
Brad Benson	OT	6'3"	258	26		
Gordon King	OT	6'6"	275	26		
Jeff Weston	OT	6'5"	280	25		
Billy Ard	OG	6'3"	250	23		
Bruce Kimball	OG	6'2"	260	26		
John Tautolo	OG	6'3"	260	23		
J.T.Turner	OG	6'3"	250	29		
Chris Foote	C	6'3"	250	25		
Ernie Hughes	C-OG	6'3"	265	27		
Rich Umphrey	C	6'3"	255	23		
Dee Hardison	DE	6'4"	269	26		
Gary Jeter	DE	6'4"	260	27		
George Martin	DE	6'4"	245	29		
Curtis McGriff	DE	6'5"	265	24		
Phil Tabor	DE	6'4"	255	25		
Jim Burt	NT	6'1"	255	23		
Bill Neill	NT	6'4"	255	23		
Jerome Sally	NT	6'3"	260	23		
Harry Carson	LB	6'2"	235	28	1	
Byron Hunt	LB	6'5"	230	23		
Brian Kelley	LB	6'3"	222	31	3	
Frank Marion	LB	6'3"	223	31		
Joe McLaughlin	LB	6'1"	235	25		
Lawrence Taylor	LB	6'3"	237	23	1	6
Brad Van Pelt	LB	6'5"	235	31		
Mike Whittington	LB	6'2"	220	24		
Brian Carpenter	DB	5'10"	167	21		
Bill Currier	DB	6'	202	27	1	
Mike Dennis	DB	5'10"	190	23		
Larry Flowers	DB	6'1"	190	24		
Mark Haynes	DB	5'11"	198	23	1	
Terry Jackson	DB	5'10"	197	26	4	
Mike Mayock	DB	6'2"	195	24		
Beasley Reece	DB	6'1"	195	28	1	
Pete Shaw	DB	5'10"	183	28		
Scott Brunner	QB	6'5"	200	25		6
Mark Reed	QB	6'3"	195	23		
Jeff Rutledge	QB	6'1"	190	25		
Leon Bright	HB	5'9"	192	27		
Larry Heater	HB	5'11"	205	24		
Joe Morris	HB	5'7"	190	21		6
Butch Woolfolk	HB	6'1"	207	22		24
Rob Carpenter	FB	6'1"	230	27		6
Cliff Chatman	FB	6'2"	225	23		12
Leon Perry	FB	5'11"	230	25		
Floyd Eddings	WR	5'11"	177	24		
Earnest Gray	WR	6'3"	195	25		24
John Mistler	WR	6'2"	186	23		12
Johnny Perkins	WR	6'2"	205	29		12
Danny Pittman	WR	6'2"	205	24		
Steve Folson	TE	6'4"	230	24		
Tom Mullady	TE	6'3"	232	25		
Gary Shirk	TE	6'1"	220	32		
Joe Danelo	K	5'9"	166	28		54
Dave Jennings	K	6'4"	205	30		

Bill Matthews - Knee Injury
Phil Simms - Knee Injury
Roy Simmons - Retired List

PHILADELPHIA EAGLES 3-6-0 Dick Vermeil

Scores of Each Game		
34	WASHINGTON	*37
24	Cleveland	21
14	CINCINNATI	18
9	Washington	13
20	ST.LOUIS	23
7	N.Y.Giants	23
35	HOUSTON	14
24	Dallas	20
24	N.Y.GIANTS	26

Use Name	Pos.	Hgt	Wgt	Age	Int	Pts
Frank Giddens	OT	6'7"	300	23		
Jerry Sisemore	OT	6'4"	265	31		
Stan Walters	OT	6'6"	275	34		
Ron Baker	OG	6'4"	250	27		
Steve Kenney	OG	6'4"	262	26		
Dean Miraldi	OG	6'5"	254	24		
Petey Perot	OG	6'2"	261	25		
Guy Morriss	C	6'4"	255	31		
Mark Slater	C	6'2"	257	27		
Greg Brown	DE	6'5"	240	25		6
Carl Hairston	DE	6'3"	260	29		
Dennis Harrison	DE	6'8"	275	26		
Leonard Mitchell	DE	6'7"	272	23		
Harvey Armstrong	NT	6'2"	255	22		
Ken Clarke	NT	6'2"	255	26		
John Bunting	LB	6'1"	220	32	1	
Mike Curcio (from NYG)	LB	6'1"	237	25		
Anthony Griggs	LB	6'3"	220	22		
Frank LeMaster	LB	6'2"	238	30		
Jerry Robinson	LB	6'2"	218	25	3	
Zack Valentine	LB	6'2"	220	25		
Reggie Wilkes	LB	6'4"	230	26		
Richard Blackmore	DB	5'10"	174	26	1	6
Dennis DeVaughn	DB	5'10"	175	21		
Herman Edwards	DB	6'	190	28	5	
Ray Ellis	DB	6'1"	192	23		
Randy Logan	DB	6'1"	195	31		
Von Mansfield	DB	5'11"	185	22		
John Sciarra	DB	5'11"	185	28		
Brenard Wilson	DB	6'	175	27	1	
Roynell Young	DB	6'1"	181	24	4	
Ron Jaworski	QB	6'2"	196	31		
Dan Pastorini	QB	6'3"	205	33		
Joe Pisarcik	QB	6'4"	220	30		
Billy Campfield	HB	5'11"	205	26		6
Louie Giammona	HB	5'9"	180	29		6
Wilbert Montgomery	HB	5'10"	195	27		54
Calvin Murray	HB	5'11"	182	23		
Don Calhoun	FB	6'	213	29		
Perry Harrington	FB	5'11"	210	24		6
Leroy Harris	FB	5'9"	230	28		12
Harold Carmichael	WR	6'7"	225	32		24
Wally Henry	WR	5'8"	180	27		
Melvin Hoover	WR	6'	185	23		
Mike Quick	WR	6'2"	190	23		6
Ron Smith	WR	6'	185	25		6
Tony Woodruff	WR	6'	175	23		
Vyto Kab	TE	6'5"	255	22		6
Lawrence Sampleton	TE	6'5"	233	22		
John Spagnola	TE	6'4"	240	25		12
Tony Franklin	K	5'8"	182	25		41
Max Runager	K	6'1"	189	26		

Charles Johnson - Hamstring Injury

*Overtime

WASHINGTON REDSKINS

RUSHING

Last Name	No.	Yds	Avg	TD
Riggins	177	553	3.1	3
Washington	44	190	4.3	1
Harmon	38	168	4.4	1
Theismann	31	150	4.8	0
Wonsley	11	36	3.3	0
Monk	7	21	3.0	0
Walker	2	11	5.5	0
Jackson	4	6	1.5	0
Giaquinto	1	5	5.0	0

RECEIVING

Last Name	No.	Yds	Avg	TD
Monk	35	447	12.8	1
Brown	32	690	21.6	8
Warren	27	310	11.5	0
Washington	19	134	7.1	1
Walker	12	92	7.7	1
Harmon	11	86	7.8	0
Riggins	10	50	5.0	0
Seay	6	154	25.7	0
M. Williams	3	14	4.7	0
Giaquinto	2	65	32.5	0
Didier	2	10	5.0	1
Jackson	1	9	9.0	0
Garrett	1	6	6.0	0
Wonsley	1	1	1.0	1

PUNT RETURNS

Last Name	No.	Yds	Avg	TD
Nelms	32	252	7.9	0
Giaquinto	5	34	6.8	0
G. Williams	1	9	9.0	0

KICKOFF RETURNS

Last Name	No.	Yds	Avg	TD
Nelms	23	557	24.2	0
Garrett	2	35	17.5	0
Giaquinto	1	21	21.0	0
Wonsley	1	14	14.0	0
Harmon	1	13	13.0	0
Anderson	1	7	7.0	0
G. Williams	1	2	2.0	0

PASSING — PUNTING — KICKING

PASSING	Att	Comp	%	Yds	Yd/Att	TD	Int-	%	RK
Theismann	252	161	64	2033	8.06	13	9-	4	1
Washington	1	1	100	35	35.00	0	0-	0	

PUNTING	No	Avg
Hayes	51	38.0

KICKING	XP	Att	%	FG	Att	%
Moseley	16	19	84	20	21	95

DALLAS COWBOYS

RUSHING

Last Name	No.	Yds	Avg	TD
Dorsett	177	745	4.2	5
Springs	59	243	4.1	2
Newsome	15	98	6.5	1
D. White	17	91	5.4	0
Newhouse	14	79	5.6	1
T. Hill	1	22	22.0	0
Peoples	7	22	3.1	0
Johnson	1	9	9.0	0
DuPree	1	6	6.0	1
Hogeboom	3	0	0.0	0
Cosbie	1	-2	-2.0	0

RECEIVING

Last Name	No.	Yds	Avg	TD
T. Hill	35	526	15.0	1
Cosbie	30	441	14.7	4
Pearson	26	382	14.7	3
Dorsett	24	179	7.5	0
Springs	17	163	9.6	2
Johnson	12	269	22.4	3
DuPree	7	41	5.9	2
Newsome	6	118	19.7	1
Donley	2	23	11.5	0
Saldi	1	8	8.0	0

PUNT RETURNS

Last Name	No.	Yds	Avg	TD
Fellows	25	189	7.6	0
R. Hill	4	39	9.8	0
Donley	1	14	14.0	0

KICKOFF RETURNS

Last Name	No.	Yds	Avg	TD
Fellows	16	359	22.4	0
Donley	8	151	18.9	0
Newsome	5	74	14.8	0
J. Jones	2	46	23.0	0
Thurman	1	17	17.0	0
Cosbie	1	4	4.0	0

PASSING — PUNTING — KICKING

PASSING	Att	Comp	%	Yds	Yd/Att	TD	Int-	%	RK
D. White	247	156	63	2079	8.42	16	12-	5	2
Hogeboom	8	3	38	45	5.63	0	1-	13	
Pearson	2	1	50	26	13.00	0	1-	50	
Dorsett	1	0	0	0	0.00	0	0-	0	

PUNTING	No	Avg
D. White	37	41.7

KICKING	XP	Att	%	FG	Att	%
Septien	28	28	100	10	14	71

ST. LOUIS CARDINALS

RUSHING

Last Name	No.	Yds	Avg	TD
Anderson	145	587	4.0	3
Morris	84	274	3.3	4
Mitchell	39	189	4.8	1
Lomax	28	119	4.3	1
Wehrli	1	18	18.0	1
Harrell	4	14	3.5	0
Green	6	8	1.2	0

RECEIVING

Last Name	No.	Yds	Avg	TD
Tilley	36	465	14.5	2
Green	32	454	14.2	3
Anderson	14	106	7.6	0
Mitchell	11	149	13.5	0
Harrell	11	127	11.5	0
Marsh	5	83	16.6	0
LaFleur	5	67	13.4	1
Shumann	5	58	11.6	0
Gray	4	34	8.5	0
Morris	4	19	4.8	0
Lomax	1	10	10.0	0
Thompson	1	5	5.0	0

PUNT RETURNS

Last Name	No.	Yds	Avg	TD
Mitchell	27	165	6.1	0
Green	3	20	6.7	0
Ferrell	1	6	6.0	0
Harrell	1	1	1.0	0

KICKOFF RETURNS

Last Name	No.	Yds	Avg	TD
Mitchell	16	364	22.8	0
Harrell	8	150	18.8	0
Ferrell	4	88	22.0	0
Love	4	69	17.3	0
Morris	1	14	14.0	0
Griffin	1	12	12.0	0
Ahrens	1	5	5.0	0

PASSING — PUNTING — KICKING

PASSING	Att	Comp	%	Yds	Yd/Att	TD	Int-	%	RK
Lomax	205	109	53	1367	6.70	5	6-	3	12
Hart	33	19	58	199	6.00	1	0-	0	
Harrell	1	1	100	10	10.00	0	0-	0	
Green	1	0	0	0	0.00	0	0-	0	

PUNTING	No	Avg
Birdsong	54	43.8

KICKING	XP	Att	%	FG	Att	%
O'Donoghue	15	16	94	8	13	62

NEW YORK GIANTS

RUSHING

Last Name	No.	Yds	Avg	TD
Woolfolk	112	439	3.9	2
R. Carpenter	67	204	3.0	1
Chatman	22	80	3.6	2
Morris	15	48	3.2	1
Brunner	19	27	1.4	1
Perry	3	14	4.7	0
Heater	3	13	4.3	0
Eddings	2	12	6.0	0
Bright	1	5	5.0	0

RECEIVING

Last Name	No.	Yds	Avg	TD
Mullady	27	287	10.6	0
Perkins	26	430	16.5	2
Gray	25	426	17.0	4
Woolfolk	23	224	9.7	2
Mistler	18	191	10.6	2
Eddings	14	275	19.6	0
Moris	8	34	4.3	0
R. Carpenter	7	29	4.1	0
Shirk	6	54	9.0	0
Bright	2	19	9.5	0
Heater	2	15	7.5	0
Pittman	1	21	21.0	0
Chatman	1	13	13.0	0
Perry	1	-1	-1.0	0

PUNT RETURNS

Last Name	No.	Yds	Avg	TD
Bright	37	325	8.8	0
Pittman	6	40	6.7	0
Reece	1	8	8.0	0

KICKOFF RETURNS

Last Name	No.	Yds	Avg	TD
Woolfolk	20	428	21.4	0
Pittman	5	117	23.4	0
Heater	5	84	16.8	0
Bright	4	72	18.0	0
Dennis	3	68	22.7	0
McLaughlin	1	14	14.0	0
Shaw	1	0	0.0	0

PASSING — PUNTING — KICKING

PASSING	Att	Comp	%	Yds	Yd/Att	TD	Int-	%	RK
Brunner	298	161	54	2017	6.77	10	9-	3	10

PUNTING	No	Avg
Jennings	49	42.8

KICKING	XP	Att	%	FG	Att	%
Danelo	18	18	100	12	21	57

PHILADELPHIA EAGLES

RUSHING

Last Name	No.	Yds	Avg	TD
Montgomery	114	515	4.5	7
Harrington	56	231	4.1	1
Harris	17	39	2.3	2
Giammona	11	29	2.6	1
Jaworski	10	9	0.9	0
Hoover	1	5	5.0	0
Campfield	1	2	2.0	0
LeMaster	1	-2	-2.0	0

RECEIVING

Last Name	No.	Yds	Avg	TD
Carmichael	35	540	15.4	4
R. Smith	34	475	14.0	1
Spagnola	26	313	12.0	2
Montgomery	20	258	12.9	2
Campfield	14	141	10.1	1
Harrington	13	74	5.7	0
Quick	10	156	15.6	1
Giammona	8	67	8.4	0
Kab	4	35	8.8	0
Harris	3	17	5.7	0
Sampleton	1	24	24.0	0

PUNT RETURNS

Last Name	No.	Yds	Avg	TD
Henry	20	103	5.2	0
Sciarra	2	5	2.5	0
Giammona	0	0	0.0	0

KICKOFF RETURNS

Last Name	No.	Yds	Avg	TD
Henry	24	541	22.5	0
Hoover	7	113	16.1	0
Murray	3	42	14.0	0
Campfield	2	30	15.0	0
Slater	2	30	15.0	0
Montgomery	1	12	12.0	0

PASSING — PUNTING — KICKING

PASSING	Att	Comp	%	Yds	Yd/Att	TD	Int-	%	RK
Jaworski	286	167	58	2076	7.30	12	12-	4	7
Pisarcik	1	1	100	24	24.00	0	0-	0	
Giammona	1	0	0	0	0.00	0	1-	100	

PUNTING	No	Avg
Runager	44	40.5

KICKING	XP	Att	%	FG	Att	%
Franklin	23	25	92	6	9	67

1982 N.F.C. - Central Division

GREEN BAY PACKERS 5-3-1 Bart Starr

Scores of Each Game		
35	L.A.RAMS	23
27	N.Y.Giants	19
26	MINNESOTA	7
13	N.Y.Jets	15
33	BUFFALO	21
10	DETROIT	30
20	Baltimore	*20
38	Atlanta	7
24	Detroit	27

Use Name	Pos.	Hgt	Wgt	Age	Int	Pts
Greg Koch	OT	6'4"	265	27		
Tim Stokes	OT	6'5"	252	32		
Karl Swanke	OT-C	6'6"	251	24		
Derrel Gofourth	OG	6'3"	260	27		
Ron Hallstrom	OG	6'6"	286	22		
Leotis Harris	OG	6'1"	267	27		
Tim Huffman	OG	6'5"	277	23		
Larry McCarren	C	6'3"	238	30		
Larry Rubens	C	6'1"	253	23		
Byron Braggs	DE	6'4"	290	22		
Robert Brown	DE	6'2"	238	21		
Mike Butler	DE	6'5"	265	28		
Ezra Johnson	DE	6'4"	240	26		
Casey Merrill	DE	6'4"	255	25		
Terry Jones	NT	6'2"	259	25		
Richard Turner	NT	6'2"	260	23		
John Anderson	LB	6'3"	221	26	3	
George Cumby	LB	6'	215	26	1	
Mike Douglass	LB	6'	224	27	2	
Jim Laslavic	LB	6'2"	236	30		
Cliff Lewis	LB	6'1"	226	22		
Mark Merrill (from DEN)	LB	6'4"	234	27		
Guy Prather	LB	6'2"	230	24		
Randy Scott	LB	6'1"	220	23		
Rich Wingo	LB	6'1"	230	26	1	
Johnnie Gray	DB	5'11"	185	28	1	
Maurice Harvey	DB	5'10"	190	26	2	6
Estus Hood	DB	5'11"	180	26	1	
Mike Jolly	DB	6'3"	185	23		
Mark Lee	DB	5'11"	187	24	1	
Mike McCoy	DB	5'11"	183	29		
Mark Murphy	DB	6'2"	199	24		
Bill Whitaker	DB	6'	182	22		
Rich Campbell	QB	6'4"	224	23		
Lynn Dickey	QB	6'4"	220	32		
David Whitehurst	QB	6'2"	204	27		
Allan Clark (from BUF)	HB	5'10"	186	24		
Harian Huckleby	HB	6'1"	199	24		
Eddie Lee Ivery	HB	6'1"	210	25		60
Del Rodgers	HB	5'10"	197	22		18
Gerry Ellis	FB	5'11"	216	24		6
Jim Jensen	FB	6'3"	235	28		6
Mike Meade	FB	5'11"	228	22		
Phillip Epps	WR	5'10"	165	23		12
John Jefferson	WR	6'1"	196	26		
James Lofton	WR	6'3"	187	26		30
Paul Coffman	TE	6'3"	218	26		12
Gary Lewis	TE	6'5"	234	23		
John Thompson	TE	6'3"	228	25		12
Ray Stachowicz	K	5'11"	185	23		
Jan Stenerud	K	6'2"	190	39		64

Ron Cassidy - Shoulder Injury
Syd Kitson - Shoulder Injury
Fred Nixon - Knee Injury

MINNESOTA VIKINGS 5-4-0 Bud Grant

Scores of Each Game		
17	TAMPA BAY	10
22	Buffalo	23
7	Green Bay	26
35	CHICAGO	7
14	Miami	22
13	BALTIMORE	10
34	Detroit	31
14	N.Y.JETS	42
31	DALLAS	27

Use Name	Pos.	Hgt	Wgt	Age	Int	Pts
Tim Irwin	OT	6'6"	275	23		
Steve Riley	OT	6'6"	255	29		
Terry Tausch	OT	6'5"	275	23		
Brent Boyd	OG	6'3"	260	25		
Wes Hamilton	OG	6'3"	268	29		
Jim Hough	OG	6'2"	267	26		
David Huffman	OG-C	6'6"	255	25		
Curtis Rouse	OG	6'3"	290	22		
Dennis Swilley	C	6'6"	260	24		
Neil Elshire	DE	6'6"	260	24		
Randy Holloway	DE	6'5"	250	27	1	
Doug Martin	DE	6'3"	255	25	1	
Mark Mullaney	DE	6'6"	245	29		2
Charles Johnson	NT	6'3"	265	30		6
James White	NT	6'3"	270	28		
Ray Yakavonis	NT	6'4"	250	25		
Matt Blair	LB	6'5"	234	31		
Dennis Johnson	LB	6'3"	230	24		
Henry Johnson	LB	6'1"	235	24		
Fred McNeill	LB	6'2"	230	30		
Robin Sendlein	LB	6'3"	224	23		
Jeff Siemon	LB	6'2"	235	32		
Scott Studwell	LB	6'2"	225	28	1	
Rufus Bess	DB	5'9"	185	25		
Tom Hannon	DB	5'11"	190	27		
Bryan Howard	DB	6'	200	23		
Kurt Knoff	DB	6'2"	190	28	1	
Keith Nord	DB	6'	195	25		
John Swain	DB	6'1"	195	22	2	
Willie Teal	DB	5'10"	195	24	4	
John Turner	DB	6'	199	26	2	6
Steve Dils	QB	6'1"	190	26		
Tommy Kramer	QB	6'2"	200	27		18
Wade Wilson	QB	6'3"	210	23		
Ted Brown	HB-FB	5'10"	210	25		18
Darrin Nelson	HB	5'9"	180	23		
Jarvis Redwine	HB	5'10"	205	25		
Rickey Young	HB	6'2"	200	28		12
Eddie Payton	HB	5'8"	179	31		
Tony Galbreath	FB	6'	230	28		6
Sam Harrell	FB	6'2"	225	25		
Harold Jackson	WR	5'10"	175	36		
Terry LeCount	WR	5'10"	180	26		6
Leo Lewis	WR	5'8"	170	25		18
Sam McCullum	WR	6'2"	190	29		
Mardye McDole	WR	5'11"	195	23		
Ahmad Rashad	WR	6'2"	200	32		
Sammy White	WR	5'11"	190	28		30
Bob Bruer	TE	6'5"	235	28		12
Steve Jordan	TE	6'3"	230	21		
Joe Senser	TE	6'4"	235	26		6
Greg Coleman	K	6'	185	27		
Rick Danmeier	K	6'	200	30		47

TAMPA BAY BUCCANEERS 5-4-0 John McKay

Scores of Each Game		
10	Minnesota	17
13	WASHINGTON	21
9	Dallas	14
23	MIAMI	17
13	New Orleans	10
17	N.Y.Jets	32
24	BUFFALO	23
23	DETROIT	21
26	CHICAGO	*23

Use Name	Pos.	Hgt	Wgt	Age	Int	Pts
Charley Hannah	OT	6'5"	265	27		
Dave Reavis	OT	6'5"	265	32		
Gene Sanders	OT	6'3"	270	25		
Sean Farrell	OG	6'3"	260	22		
Greg Roberts	OG	6'3"	265	25		
George Yarno	OG	6'2"	260	25		
Ray Snell	OG-OT	6'4"	265	24		
Jim Leonard	C-OG	6'3"	260	24		
Steve Wilson	C	6'3"	265	22		
John Cannon	DE	6'5"	250	22		
Bob Cobb	DE	6'4"	250	24		
Booker Reese	DE	6'6"	260	22		
Lee Roy Selmon	DE	6'3"	250	27		
Dave Stalls	DE	6'5"	250	26		
David Logan	NT	6'2"	255	25		
Brad White	NT	6'2"	250	24		
Scott Brantley	LB	6'1"	230	24		
Jeff Davis	LB	6'	225	22		
Hugh Green	LB	6'2"	225	23	1	
Andy Hawkins	LB	6'2"	230	24		
Cecil Johnson	LB	6'2"	235	27		
Dana Nafziger	LB	6'1"	225	28		
Richard Wood	LB	6'2"	230	29		
Cedric Brown	DB	6'1"	200	28	3	
Neal Colzie	DB	6'2"	200	29	3	
Mark Cotney	DB	6'	200	30		
John Holt	DB	5'11"	180	23		
Thomas Morris	DB	5'11"	175	22		
Johnny Ray Smith	DB	5'9"	180	24		
Norris Thomas	DB	5'11"	185	28	1	
Mike Washington	DB	6'3"	200	29	3	
Jerry Golsteyn	QB	6'4"	200	28		
Jeff Quinn (from PIT)	QB	6'3"	205	24		
Doug Williams	QB	6'4"	220	27		12
Terdell Middleton	HB	6'	205	27		
Michael Morton	HB	5'8"	180	22		
James Owens	HB	5'11"	195	27		6
Dave Barrett	FB	6	230	22		
Melvin Carver	FB	5'11"	215	23		12
James Wilder	FB	6'3"	225	24		24
Theo Bell	WR	6'	190	28		
Gerald Carter	WR	6'1"	190	25		
Kevin House	WR	6'1"	180	24		12
Gordon Jones	WR	6'	190	25		6
Jerry Bell	TE	6'5"	230	23		
Jim Obradovich	TE	6'2"	225	19		
Jimmie Giles	TE	6'3"	245	27		18
Bill Capece	K	5'7"	170	23		68
Brian Clark	K	6'2"	190	24		
Larry Swider	K	6'2"	195	27		

Randy Crowder - Knee Injury

DETROIT LIONS 4-5-0 Monte Clarke

Scores of Each Game		
17	CHICAGO	10
19	L.A.Rams	14
17	Chicago	20
6	N.Y.GIANTS	13
13	N.Y.JETS	28
30	Green Bay	10
31	MINNESOTA	34
21	Tampa Bay	23
27	GREEN BAY	24

Use Name	Pos.	Hgt	Wgt	Age	Int	Pts
Karl Baldischwiler	OT	6'5"	260	26		
Chris Dieterich	OT	6'3"	255	24		
Keith Dorney	OT	6'5"	260	24		
Russ Bolinger	OG	6'5"	260	27		
Homer Elias	OG	6'3"	255	27		
Don Greco	OG	6'3"	255	23		
Larry Lee	OG-C	6'2"	260	22		
Amos Fowler	C	6'3"	253	26		
Tom Turnure	C	6'4"	250	25		
Al Baker	DE	6'6"	260	25		
Dave Pureifoy	DE	6'1"	255	33		
William Gay	DE-DT	6'5"	255	27	1	
Curtis Green	DE-DT	6'3"	252	25		
Joe Ehrmann	DT	6'5"	250	33		
Doug English	DT	6'5"	258	29		
Martin Moss	DT	6'4"	252	23		
Roosevelt Barnes	LB	6'2"	220	24		
Garry Cobb	LB	6'2"	227	25	2	
Steve Doig	LB	6'2"	240	22		
Ken Fantetti	LB	6'2"	227	25		
James Harrell	LB	6'1"	220	25		
Terry Tautolo	LB	6'2"	227	28		
Stan White	LB	6'1"	223	32	3	
Jimmy Williams	LB	6'3"	221	21	1	
Billy Cesare	DB	5'11"	190	27		
William Graham	DB	5'11"	191	22		
Hector Gray	DB	6'1"	190	25	1	
Alvin Hall	DB	5'10"	184	24	1	6
James Hunter	DB	6'3"	195	28	2	
Al Latimer	DB	5'11"	177	24		
Bruce McNorton	DB	5'11"	175	23		
Ray Oldham	DB	6'	192	31	1	6
Wayne Smith (to STL)	DB	6'	170	25		
Dan Wagoner	DB	5'10"	177	22		
Bobby Watkins	DB	5'10"	184	22	5	
Gary Danielson	QB	6'2"	196	30		
Eric Hipple	QB	6'2"	196	24		
Mike Machurek	QB	6'1"	205	22		
Ken Callicutt	HB	6'	190	27		
Rick Kans	HB	5'11"	200	27		
Ricky Porter	HB	5'10"	186	22		
Billy Sims	HB	6'	212	26		24
Dexter Bussey	FB	6'1"	210	30		
Horace King	FB	5'10"	205	29		6
Robbie Martin	WR	5'8"	177	23		
Mark Nichols	WR	6'2"	213	22		12
Tracy Porter	WR	6'1"	196	23		
Freddie Scott	WR	6'2"	190	30		6
Leonard Thompson	WR	5'11"	192	30		24
David Hill	TE	6'2"	228	28		24
Ulysses Norris	TE	6'4"	232	25		
Rob Rubick	TE	6'3"	228	21		6
Eddie Murray	K	5'10"	170	26		49
Tom Skladany	k	6'	195	27		

Tommie Ginn - Knee Injury
Vince Thompson - Abdominal Injury

CHICAGO BEARS 3-6-0 Mike Ditka

Scores of Each Game		
10	Detroit	17
0	New Orleans	10
20	DETROIT	17
7	Minnesota	35
26	NEW ENGLAND	13
14	Seattle	20
7	ST.LOUIS	10
34	L.A.Rams	26
23	Tampa Bay	*26

Use Name	Pos.	Hgt	Wgt	Age	Int	Pts
Jerry Doerger	OT	6'5"	270	22		
Dan Jiggetts	OT	6'4"	270	28		
Dennis Lick	OT	6'3"	265	28		
Phil McKinnely	OT	6'4"	250	28		
Keith Van Horne	OT	6'6"	265	24		
Kurt Becker	OG	6'5"	251	23		
Perry Hartnett	OG	6'5"	275	22		
Noah Jackson	OG	6'2"	265	28		
Jeff Williams	OG	6'4"	260	27		
Jay Hilgenberg	C	6'3"	250	23		
Dan Neal	C	6'4"	255	33		
Al Harris	DE	6'5"	250	25		
Mike Hartenstine	DE	6'3"	243	29		
Henry Waechter	DE	6'5"	270	23		
Dan Hampton	DT	6'5"	255	24		
Steve McMichael	DT	6'2"	245	24		
Jim Osborne	DT	6'3"	245	32		2
Brian Cabral	LB	6'	224	26		
Gary Campbell	LB	6'1"	220	30		
Al Chesley (from PHI)	LB	6'3"	240	25		
Bruce Herron	LB	6'2"	220	28		
Bruce Huther	LB	6'1"	220	28		
Jerry Muckensturm	LB	6'4"	220	28		
Dan Rains	LB	6'1"	222	26		
Mike Singletary	LB	5'11"	230	23		
Otis Wilson	LB	6'2"	222	24	2	6
Todd Bell	DB	6'1"	207	23		
Gary Fencik	DB	6'1"	197	28	2	
Jeff Fisher	DB	5'11"	188	24	3	
Leslie Frazier	DB	6'	189	23	2	
Reuben Henderson	DB	6'1"	200	23		
Doug Plank	DB	6'	202	29		
Terry Schmidt	DB	6'	177	30	4	
Len Walterscheid	DB	5'11"	190	27		
Walt Williams (from MIN)	DB	6'	185	28		
Bob Avellini	QB	6'2"	210	29		
Vince Evans	QB	6'2"	212	27		
Jim McMahon	QB	6'	187	23		6
Dennis Gentry	HB	5'8"	173	23		
Walter Payton	HB	5'11"	202	28		6
Roland Harper	FB	6'	210	29		
Willie McClendon	FB	6'1"	205	24		
Matt Suhey	FB	5'11"	217	24		18
Calvin Thomas	FB	5'11"	220	22		
Brian Baschnagel	WR	6'	184	28		12
Ken Margerum	WR	6'	170	23		18
James Scott	WR	6'1"	190	30		
Rickey Watts	WR	6'1"	203	25		
Robin Earl	TE	6'5"	240	27		
Emery Moorehead	TE	6'2"	220	28		30
Brooks Williams	TE	6'4"	226	27		
Bob Parsons	K	6'4"	225	32		
John Roveto	K	6'	180	24		22
Bob Thomas (from DET)	K	5'10"	175	30		39

Ted Albrecht - Knee Injury
Revie Sorey - Larynx Injury

* Overtime

GREEN BAY PACKERS

RUSHING

Last Name	No.	Yds	Avg	TD
Ivery	127	453	3.6	9
Ellis	62	228	3.7	1
Rodgers	46	175	3.8	1
Lofton	4	101	25.3	1
Meade	14	42	3.0	0
Jensen	9	28	3.1	0
Huckleby	4	19	4.8	0
Dickey	13	19	1.5	0
Jefferson	2	16	8.0	0
Stachowicz	2	0	0.0	0

RECEIVING

Last Name	No.	Yds	Avg	TD
Lofton	35	696	19.9	4
Jefferson	27	452	16.7	0
Coffman	23	287	12.5	2
Ellis	18	140	7.8	0
Ivery	16	186	11.6	1
Epps	10	226	22.6	2
Rodgers	3	23	7.7	0
G. Lewis	3	21	7.0	0
Jensen	3	18	6.0	1
Meade	3	-5	-1.7	0
Thompson	2	24	12.0	0

PUNT RETURNS

Last Name	No.	Yds	Avg	TD
Epps	20	150	7.5	0
Gray	6	48	8.0	0

KICKOFF RETURNS

Last Name	No.	Yds	Avg	TD
Rodgers	20	436	21.8	0
Huckleby	5	89	17.8	0
Clark	4	75	18.8	0
Gray	2	29	14.5	0
C. Lewis	1	4	4.0	0

PASSING — PUNTING — KICKING

PASSING	Att	Comp	%	Yds	Yd/Att	TD	Int-	%	RK
Dickey	218	124	57	1790	8.21	12	14-	6	9
Whitehurst	47	18	38	235	5.00	0	1-	2	
Lofton	1	1	100	43	43.00	0	0-	0	
Ivery	1	0	0	0	0.00	0	0-	0	

PUNTING	No	Avg
Stachowicz	42	40.2

KICKING	XP	Att	%	FG	Att	%
Stenerud	25	27	93	13	18	72

MINNESOTA VIKINGS

RUSHING

Last Name	No.	Yds	Avg	TD
Brown	120	515	4.3	1
Nelson	44	136	3.1	0
Galbreath	39	116	3.0	1
Kramer	21	77	3.7	3
Young	16	49	3.0	1
Coleman	1	15	15.0	0
Dils	1	5	5.0	0
Redwine	2	2	1.0	0
LeCount	1	-3	-3.0	0

RECEIVING

Last Name	No.	Yds	Avg	TD
Brown	31	207	6.7	2
S. White	29	503	17.3	5
Senser	29	261	9.0	1
Rashad	23	233	10.1	0
Galbreath	17	153	9.0	0
LeCount	14	179	12.8	1
McCullum	12	131	10.9	0
Nelson	9	100	11.1	0
Lewis	8	150	18.8	3
Bruer	8	102	12.8	2
Young	4	44	11.0	1
Jordan	3	42	14.0	0

PUNT RETURNS

Last Name	No.	Yds	Avg	TD
Payton	22	179	8.1	0
Bess	2	17	8.5	0
Hannon	0	0	0.0	0

KICKOFF RETURNS

Last Name	No.	Yds	Avg	TD
Redwine	12	286	23.8	0
Payton	12	271	22.6	0
Nelson	6	132	22.0	0
Nord	3	43	14.3	0
Harrell	2	21	10.5	0
McDole	1	26	26.0	0
Elshire	1	7	7.0	0

PASSING — PUNTING — KICKING

PASSING	Att	Comp	%	Yds	Yd/Att	TD	Int-	%	RK
Kramer	308	176	57	2037	6.61	15	12-	4	8
Dils	26	11	42	68	2.61	0	0-	0	

PUNTING	No	Avg
Coleman	58	41.1

KICKING	XP	Att	%	FG	Att	%
Danmeier	23	23	100	8	14	57

TAMPA BAY BUCCANEERS

RUSHING

Last Name	No.	Yds	Avg	TD
Wilder	83	324	3.9	3
Owens	76	238	3.1	0
Carver	70	229	3.3	1
Williams	35	158	4.5	2
Morton	2	3	1.5	0
Giles	1	1	1.0	0
House	1	-1	-1.0	0

RECEIVING

Last Name	No.	Yds	Avg	TD
Wilder	53	466	8.8	1
Giles	28	499	17.8	3
House	28	438	15.6	2
T. Bell	15	203	13.5	0
Jones	14	205	14.6	1
Carter	10	140	14.0	0
Owens	8	42	5.3	1
Carver	4	46	11.5	1
Obradovich	2	22	11.0	0
J. Bell	1	5	5.0	0
Morton	1	5	5.0	0

PUNT RETURNS

Last Name	No.	Yds	Avg	TD
Holt	16	81	5.1	0
T. Bell	9	62	6.9	0

KICKOFF RETURNS

Last Name	No.	Yds	Avg	TD
Morton	21	361	17.2	0
Carver	3	62	20.7	0
Owens	3	52	17.3	0
J.R. Smith	3	47	15.7	0
Yarno	1	14	14.0	0
Obradovich	1	12	12.0	0
Davis	1	0	0.0	0

PASSING — PUNTING — KICKING

PASSING	Att	Comp	%	Yds	Yd/Att	TD	Int-	%	RK
Williams	307	164	53	2071	6.75	9	11-	4	13
Golsteyn	1	0	0	0	0.00	0	0-	0	

PUNTING	No	Avg
Swider	39	41.5

KICKING	XP	Att	%	Fg	Att	%
Capece	14	14	100	18	23	78

DETROIT LIONS

RUSHING

Last Name	No.	Yds	Avg	TD
Sims	172	639	3.7	4
Bussey	48	136	2.8	0
Danielson	23	92	4.0	0
King	18	67	3.7	0
Hipple	10	57	5.7	0
Kane	7	17	2.4	0
L. Thompson	2	16	8.0	0
Nichols	1	3	3.0	0
Rubick	1	1	1.0	0
Scott	1	-6	-6.0	0

RECEIVING

Last Name	No.	Yds	Avg	TD
Sims	34	342	10.1	0
Hill	22	252	11.5	4
L. Thompson	17	328	19.3	4
Bussey	16	138	8.6	0
Scott	13	231	17.8	1
Porter	9	124	13.8	0
King	9	74	8.2	1
Nichols	8	146	18.3	2
Norris	3	51	17.0	0
Kane	3	25	8.3	0
Cobb	1	25	25.0	0
Martin	1	18	18.0	0

PUNT RETURNS

Last Name	No.	Yds	Avg	TD
Martin	26	275	10.6	0

KICKOFF RETURNS

Last Name	No.	Yds	Avg	TD
Hall	16	426	26.6	1
Martin	16	268	16.8	0
King	2	23	11.5	0
Kane	1	19	19.0	0
L. Lee	1	14	14.0	0

PASSING — PUNTING — KICKING

PASSING	Att	Comp	%	Yds	Yd/Att	TD	Int-	%	RK
Danielson	197	100	51	1343	6.82	10	14-	7	14
Hipple	86	36	42	411	4.78	2	4-	5	
Porter	1	0	0	0	0.00	0	0-	0	
Skladany	1	0	0	0	0.00	0	0-	0	

PUNTING	No	Avg
Skladany	36	41.2

KICKING	XP	Att	%	FG	Att	%
Murray	16	16	100	11	12	92

CHICAGO BEARS

RUSHING

Last Name	No.	Yds	Avg	TD
Payton	148	596	4.0	1
Suhey	70	206	2.9	3
McMahon	24	105	4.4	1
McClendon	17	47	2.8	0
Gentry	4	21	5.3	0
Harper	3	7	2.3	0
C. Thomas	5	4	0.8	0
Moorehead	2	3	1.5	0
Evans	2	0	0.0	0
Watts	1	-1	-1.0	0

RECEIVING

Last Name	No.	Yds	Avg	TD
Suhey	36	333	9.3	0
Payton	32	311	9.7	0
Moorehead	30	363	12.1	5
Margerum	14	207	14.8	3
Baschnagel	12	194	16.2	2
Watts	8	217	27.1	0
Earl	4	56	14.0	0
Scott	2	44	22.0	0
Gentry	1	9	9.0	0
Harper	1	8	8.0	0
McClendon	1	7	7.0	0

PUNT RETURNS

Last Name	No.	Yds	Avg	TD
Gentry	17	89	5.2	0
Fisher	7	53	7.6	0

KICKOFF RETURNS

Last Name	No.	Yds	Avg	TD
Watts	14	330	23.6	0
Gentry	9	161	17.9	0
Fisher	7	102	14.6	0
Harper	2	10	5.0	0
Bell	1	14	14.0	0
Muckensturm	1	5	5.0	0

PASSING — PUNTING — KICKING

PASSING	Att	Comp	%	Yds	Yd/Att	TD	Int-	%	RK
McMahon	210	120	57	1501	7.15	9	7-	3	4
Avellini	20	8	40	84	4.20	0	0-	0	
Evans	28	12	43	125	4.46	0	4-	14	
Payton	3	1	33	39	13.00	1	0-	0	
Baschnagel	1	0	0	0	0.00	0	0-	0	

PUNTING	No	Avg
Parsons	58	41.3
McMahon	1	59.0

KICKING	XP	Att	%	FG	Att	%
Roveto	10	10	100	4	13	31
Thomas	9	9	100	10	12	71

ATLANTA FALCONS 5-4-0 Leeman Bennett

Scores of Each Game		
16	N.Y.Giants	14
14	L.A.RAIDERS	38
34	L.A.RAMS	17
20	ST.LOUIS	23
34	Denver	27
35	NEW ORLEANS	0
17	San Francisco	7
7	GREEN BAY	38
6	New Orleans	35

Use Name	Pos.	Hgt	Wgt	Age	Int	Pts
Warren Bryant	OT	6'6"	270	26		
Mike Kenn	OT	6'6"	257	26		
Eric Sanders	OT	6'6"	255	23		
Pat Howell	OG	6'5"	253	25		
Dave Scott	OG	6'4"	265	28		
R.C. Thielemann	OG	6'4"	247	27		
John Scully	C	6'6"	255	24		
Jeff Van Note	C	6'2"	247	36		
Jeff Merrow	DE	6'4"	255	29		
Doug Rogers	DE	6'5"	255	22		
Jeff Yeates	DE	6'3"	248	31		
Mike Perko	NT	6'4"	235	25		
Don Smith	NT	6'5"	248	25		
Mike Zele	NT	6'3"	236	26		
Buddy Curry	LB	6'3"	221	24	1	
Paul Davis	LB	6'2"	215	24		
Robert Jackson	LB	6'1"	230	28		
Fulton Kuykendall	LB	6'5"	225	29	2	
Jim Laughlin	LB	6'	212	24		
Neal Musser	LB	6'2"	218	25		
Al Richardson	LB	6'2"	206	24		
Lyman White	LB	6'	217	23		
Joel Williams	LB	6'1"	215	25		
Bobby Butler	DB	5'11"	170	23	2	
Biane Galson	DB	6'	185	24	1	
Bob Glazebrook	DB	6'1"	200	26	1	6
Kenny Johnson	DB	5'10"	176	24	2	
Earl Jones	DB	6'	178	25		
Tom Pridemore	DB	5'10"	186	26	1	
Mike Spivey	DB	6'	196	28		
Steve Bartkowski	QB	6'4"	213	29		6
Jeff Komlo	QB	6'2"	200	26		
Mike Moroski	QB	6'4"	200	24		
Lynn Cain	HB	6'1"	205	26		12
Ray Strong	HB	5'9"	184	26		
William Andrews	FB	6'	200	26		42
Reggie Brown	FB	5'11"	211	22		
Gerald Riggs	FB	6'1"	230	21		30
Bo Robinson	FB	6'2"	225	26		12
Stacey Bailey	WR	6'	162	22		6
Willie Curran	WR	5'10"	175	22		
Floyd Hodge	WR	6'	195	23		
Alfred Jackson	WR	5'11"	176	27		6
Alfred Jenkins	WR	5'9"	155	30		6
Billy Johnson	WR	5'9"	170	30		
Clay Brown	TE	6'3"	225	23		
Keith Krepfle	TE	6'3"	230	30		
Russ Mikeska	TE	6'3"	225	26		
Junior Miller	TE	6'4"	235	24		6
Mick Luckhurst	K	6'	180	24		51
Dave Smigelsky	K	5'11"	180	23		
George Roberts	K	6'	186	28		

NEW ORLEANS SAINTS 4-5-0 Bum Phillips

Scores of Each Game		
7	ST.LOUIS	21
10	Chicago	0
27	KANSAS CITY	17
23	San Francisco	20
10	TAMPA BAY	13
0	Atlanta	35
7	Dallas	21
10	WASHINGTON	27
35	ATLANTA	6

Use Name	Pos.	Hgt	Wgt	Age	Int	Pts
Stan Brock	OT	6'6"	285	24		
Leon Gray	OT	6'3"	258	30		
Dave Lafary	OT	6'7"	275	27		
Chuck Slaughter	OT	6'5"	260	23		
Kelvin Clark	OG	6'3"	265	26		
Brad Edelman	OG	6'6"	255	21		
Louis Oubre	OG	6'4"	262	24		
John Hill	C	6'2"	246	32		
Jim Pietrzak	C	6'5"	260	29		
Bruce Clark	DE	6'3"	250	24		
Reggie Lewis	DE	6'2"	248	28		
Frank Warren	DE	6'4"	275	22		
Jim Wilks	DE	6'5"	252	24		
Tony Elliott	NT	6'2"	247	23		
Derland Moore	NT	6'4"	253	30		
Ken Bordelon	LB	6'4"	226	28		
Rickey Jackson	LB	6'2"	230	24	1	
Jim Kovach	LB	6'2"	225	26		
Rob Nairne	LB	6'4"	227	28	1	
Whitney Paul	LB	6'3"	220	26	1	
Scott Pelluer	LB	6'2"	215	23		
Ed Simonini	LB	6'	206	27		
Denis Winston	LB	6'	228	26	2	
Russell Gary	DB	5'11"	195	23	2	
Kevin Gray	DB	5'11"	179	24		
Bill Hurley	DB	5'11"	195	25	1	6
John Krimm	DB	6'2"	190	22		
Rodney Lewis	DB	5'11"	190	23	1	
Johnnie Poe	DB	6'1"	185	23		
Frank Wattelet	DB	6'	185	23		
Dave Waymer	DB	6'1"	195	24		
Guido Merkens	QB	6'1"	195	27		
Bobby Scott	QB	6'1"	197	33		
Ken Stabler	QB	6'3"	210	36		
George Rogers	HB	6'2"	229	23		18
Jimmy Rogers	HB	5'10"	190	27		12
Hokie Gajan	FB	5'11"	211	22		
Jack Holmes	FB	5'11"	210	29		
Marvin Lewis	FB	6'3"	208	22		
Toussaint Tyler	FB	6'2"	220	23		
Wayne Wilson	FB	6'3"	208	24		30
Kenny Duckett	WR	6'	187	22		12
Jeff Groth	WR	5'10"	172	25		6
Rich Mauti	WR	6'	190	28		
Lindsay Scott	WR	6'1"	190	21		
Aundra Thompson	WR	6'	186	29		6
Don Bass	TE	6'2"	220	26		
Hoby Brenner	TE	6'4"	240	23		
Larry Hardy	TE	6'3"	230	26		6
Morten Andersen	K	6'2"	190	22		12
Russell Erxleben	K	6'4"	219	25		1
Toni Fritsch	K	5'7"	201	37		20

Glen Redd - Knee Injury
Tom Myers - Knee Injury
Dave Wilson - Knee Injury

SAN FRANCISCO 49ERS 3-6-0 Bill Walsh

Scores of Each Game		
17	L.A.RAIDERS	23
21	Denver	24
31	St.Louis	20
20	NEW ORLEANS	23
30	L.A.RAMS	24
37	SAN DIEGO	41
7	ATLANTA	17
26	Kansas City	13
20	L.A.RAMS	21

Use Name	Pos.	Hgt	Wgt	Age	Int	Pts
Keith Fahnhorst	OT	6'6"	273	30		
Lindsey Mason	OT	6'5"	275	27		
Dan Audick	OG-OT	6'3"	253	27		
John Ayers	OG	6'5"	265	29		
Randy Cross	OG	6'3"	265	28		
John Choma	OG-C	6'6"	261	27		
Walt Downing	C-OG	6'3"	270	26		
Fred Quillan	C	6'5"	266	26		
Dwaine Board	DE	6'5"	250	25		
Mike Clark	DE	6'4"	250	23		
Fred Dean	DE	6'3"	236	30		
Jeff Stover	DE	6'5"	275	24		
Jim Stuckey	DE	6'4"	251	24		
John Harty	NT	6'4"	263	23		
Pete Kugler	NT-DE	6'4"	255	23		
Lawrence Pillers	NT-DE	6'3"	250	29		
Terry Beeson	LB	6'3"	233	26		
Dan Bunz	LB	6'4"	225	26		
Ron Ferrari	LB	6'	212	23		
Willie Harper	LB	6'2"	215	32	1	
Bob Horn	LB	6'3"	230	28	1	
Ed Judie	LB	6'2"	231	23		
Bobby Leopold	LB	6'1"	215	24		
Milt McColl	LB	6'6"	220	23		
Jack Reynolds	LB	6'1"	232	34	1	
Eric Scoggins	LB	6'2"	235	23		
Keena Turner	LB	6'2"	219	23		
Rick Gervais	DB	5'11"	190	22		
Dwight Hicks	DB	6'1"	189	26	3	
Ronnie Lott	DB	6'	199	23	2	6
Dana McLemore	DB	5'10"	183	22		6
Lynn Thomas	DB	5'11"	181	23		
Tim Washington	DB	5'9"	184	22		
Carlton Williamson	DB	6'	204	24		
Eric Wright	DB	6'1"	180	23	1	
Guy Benjamin	QB	6'4"	210	27		
Bryan Clark	QB	6'2"	196	22		
Joe Montana	QB	6'2"	200	26		6
Amos Lawrence	HB	5'11"	179	24		
Jeff Moore	HB	6'	196	26		48
Ricky Patton	HB	5'11"	192	28		
Bill Ring	HB	5'10"	215	25		6
Newton Williams	HB	5'10"	204	23		
Earl Cooper	FB	6'2"	227	24		6
Walt Easley	FB	6'1"	226	24		
Vince Williams	FB	6'	231	22		
Dwight Clark	WR	6'4"	210	25		30
Renaldo Nehemiah	WR	6'1"	177	23		6
Freddie Solomon	WR	5'11"	185	29		18
Mike Wilson	WR	6'3"	210	23		6
Russ Francis	TE	6'6"	242	29		12
Eason Ramson	TE	6'2"	234	26		
Charle Young	TE	6'4"	234	31		
Jim Miller	K	5'11"	183	25		
Ray Wersching	K	5'11"	210	32		59

Allan Kennedy - Ankle Injury

LOS ANGELES RAMS 2-7-0 Ray Malavasi

Scores of Each Game		
23	Green Bay	35
14	DETROIT	19
17	Atlanta	43
20	KANSAS CITY	14
24	SAN FRANCISCO	30
24	DENVER	27
31	L.A.Raiders	37
26	CHICAGO	34
21	San Francisco	20

Use Name	Pos.	Hgt	Wgt	Age	Int	Pts
Wally Kersten	OT	6'5"	270	22		
Irv Pankey	OT	6'4"	267	23		
Jackie Slater	OT	6'4"	271	28		
Ron Yary	OT	6'6"	255	36		
Bill Bain	OG	6'4"	285	30		
Dennis Harrah	OG	6'5"	255	29		
Kent Hill	OG	6'5"	260	25		
George Lilja	C	6'4"	250	24		
Doug Smith	C	6'3"	253	25		
Doug Bennett	DE-C	6'3"	250	22		
Reggie Doss	DE	6'4"	263	25		
Greg Meisner	DE	6'3"	253	23		
Jack Youngblood	DE	6'4"	242	32		
Larry Brooks	DT	6'3"	255	32		
Charles DeJurnett	DT	6'4"	260	30		
Mike Fanning	DT	6'6"	255	29		
Cody Jones	DT	6'5"	255	31		
Myron Lapka	DT	6'4"	260	26		
George Andrews	LB	6'3"	221	26		
Howard Carson	LB	6'2"	230	25		
Jim Collins	LB	6'2"	230	24		
Carl Ekern	LB	6'3"	222	28	1	
Mel Owens	LB	6'2"	224	23		
Mike Reilly	LB	6'4"	217	23		
Eric Williams	LB	6'2"	235	27		
Jim Youngblood	LB	6'3"	231	32		
Kirk Collins	DB	5'11"	183	24		
Nolan Cromwell	DB	6'1"	200	27	3	6
LeRoy Irvin	DB	5'11"	184	24		6
Johnnie Johnson	DB	6'1"	183	25	1	
Rod Perry	DB	5'9"	185	28	3	
Lucious Smith	DB	5'10"	190	25		
Ivory Sully	DB	6'	201	25		
Pat Thomas	DB	5'9"	190	28	3	
Vince Ferragamo	QB	6'3"	212	28		6
Bert Jones	QB	6'3"	209	30		
Jeff Kemp	QB	6'	201	23		
Robert Alexander	HB	6'	185	24		
Wendell Tyler	HB	5'10"	200	27		78
Barry Redden	HB-FB	5'10"	205	22		
Jewerl Thomas	HB-FB	5'10"	228	24		
Cullen Bryant	FB	6'1"	235	31		
Mike Guman	FB	6'2"	218	24		12
A.J. Jones	FB	6'1"	202	23		
Preston Dennard	WR	6'1"	183	26		12
George Farmer	WR	5'10"	175	23		12
Drew Hill	WR	5'9"	170	25		
Willie Miller	WR	5'9	173	34		6
Billy Waddy	WR	5'11"	190	28		
Mike Barber	TE	6'3"	237	29		6
Ron Battle	TE	6'3"	225	23		6
Kerry Locklin	TE	6'3"	217	22		
Mike Lansford	K	6'	183	24		50
John Misko	K	6'5"	207	27		

ATLANTA FALCONS

RUSHING

Last Name	No.	Yds	Avg	TD
Andrews	139	573	4.1	5
Riggs	78	299	3.8	5
Cain	54	173	3.2	1
Robinson	19	108	5.7	0
Hodge	2	11	5.5	0
Strong	4	9	2.3	0
Jackson	1	4	4.0	0
Bartkowski	13	4	0.3	1

RECEIVING

Last Name	No.	Yds	Avg	TD
Andrews	42	503	12.0	2
Jackson	26	361	13.9	1
Jenkir.s	24	347	14.5	1
Riggs	23	185	8.0	0
Miller	20	221	11.1	1
Hodge	14	160	11.4	0
Cain	13	101	7.8	1
Robinson	7	55	7.9	2
Bailey	2	24	12.0	1
Mikesla	2	19	9.5	0
B. Johnson	2	11	5.5	0
Krepfle	1	5	5.0	0

PUNT RETURNS

Last Name	No.	Yds	Avg	TD
B. Johnson	24	273	11.4	0

KICKOFF RETURNS

Last Name	No.	Yds	Avg	TD
Brown	24	466	19.4	0
Galson	2	14	7.0	0
Hodge	1	23	23.0	0
Laughlin	1	10	10.0	0
Scully	1	0	0.0	0

PASSING — PUNTING — KICKING

PASSING	Att	Comp	%	Yds	Yd/Att	TD	Int-	%	RK
Bartkowski	262	166	63	1905	7.27	8	11-	4	5
Moroski	13	10	77	87	6.69	1	0-	0	
Andrews	0	0	0	0	0.00	0	0-	0	

PUNTING	No	Avg
Smigelsy	26	38.5
Roberts	17	40.6

KICKING	XP	Att	%	FG	Att	%
Luckhurst	21	22	95	10	14	71

NEW ORLEANS SAINTS

RUSHING

Last Name	No.	Yds	Avg	TD
G. Rogers	122	535	4.4	3
W. Wilson	103	413	4.0	3
J. Rogers	60	178	3.0	2
Gajan	19	77	4.1	0
Merkens	9	30	3.3	0
Tyler	10	21	2.1	0
Holmes	2	8	4.0	0
Thompson	1	2	2.0	0
Groth	1	1	1.0	0
Stabler	3	-4	-1.3	0
L. Scott	1	-4	-4.0	0

RECEIVING

Last Name	No.	Yds	Avg	TD
Groth	30	383	12.8	1
W. Wilson	25	175	7.0	2
L. Scott	17	251	14.8	0
Brenner	16	171	10.7	0
Duckett	12	196	16.3	2
Thompson	8	138	17.3	1
Hardy	8	67	8.4	1
Mauti	4	70	17.5	0
Tyler	4	31	7.8	0
G. Rogers	4	21	5.3	0
J. Rogers	4	17	4.3	0
Gajan	3	10	3.3	0
Hurley	1	39	39.0	1
Holmes	1	2	2.0	0

PUNT RETURNS

Last Name	No.	Yds	Avg	TD
Groth	21	144	6.9	0

KICKOFF RETURNS

Last Name	No.	Yds	Avg	TD
Thompson	10	211	21.1	0
W. Wilson	7	192	27.4	0
Mauti	5	93	18.6	0
Duckett	2	39	19.5	0
J. Rogers	1	24	24.0	0
Gajan	1	18	18.0	0

PASSING — PUNTING — KICKING

PASSING	Att	Comp	%	Yds	Yd/Att	TD	Int-	%	RK
Stabler	189	117	62	1343	7.11	6	10-	5	11
Merkens	49	18	37	186	3.80	1	2-	4	
Erxleben	2	1	50	39	19.50	1	0-	0	
Holmes	1	0	0	0	0.00	0	0-	0	

PUNTING	No	Avg
Erxleben	46	43.0

KICKING	XP	Att	%	FG	Att	%
Fritsch	8	9	89	4	7	57
Andersen	6	6	100	2	5	40
Erxleben	1	1	100	0	1	0

SAN FRANCISCO 49ERS

RUSHING

Last Name	No.	Yds	Avg	TD
Moore	85	281	3.3	4
Ring	48	183	3.8	1
Montana	30	118	3.9	1
Cooper	24	77	3.2	0
V. Williams	20	68	3.4	0
Easley	5	11	2.2	0
Lawrence	5	7	1.4	0
Nehemiah	1	-1	-1.0	0
Solomon	1	-4	-4.0	0

RECEIVING

Last Name	No.	Yds	Avg	TD
D. Clark	60	913	15.2	5
Moore	37	405	10.9	4
Francis	23	278	12.1	2
Young	22	189	8.6	0
Solomon	19	323	17.0	3
Cooper	19	153	8.1	1
Ring	13	94	7.2	0
Nehemiah	8	161	20.1	1
Wilson	6	80	13.3	1
V. Williams	4	33	8.3	0
Ramson	2	27	13.5	0
Lawrence	2	12	6.0	0

PUNT RETURNS

Last Name	No.	Yds	Avg	TD
Solomon	13	122	9.4	0
Hicks	10	54	5.4	0
McLemore	7	156	22.3	1
Ring	0	0	0.0	0

KICKOFF RETURNS

Last Name	No.	Yds	Avg	TD
McLemore	16	353	22.1	0
Lawrence	9	190	21.1	0
Ring	6	145	24.2	0
Ramson	2	20	10.0	0
Ferrari	2	19	9.5	0
Moore	1	15	15.0	0

PASSING — PUNTING — KICKING

PASSING	Att	Comp	%	Yds	Yd/Att	TD	Int-	%	RK
Montana	346	213	62	2613	7.55	17	11-	3	3
Francis	1	1	100	45	45.00	0	0-	0	
Benjamin	1	1	100	10	10.00	0	0-	0	

PUNTING	No	Avg
Miller	44	38.1

KICKING	XP	Att	%	FG	Att	%
Wersching	23	25	92	12	17	71

LOS ANGELES RAMS

RUSHING

Last Name	No.	Yds	Avg	TD
Tyler	137	564	4.1	9
Guman	69	266	3.9	2
J. Thomas	16	80	5.0	0
B. Jones	11	73	6.6	0
Redden	8	24	3.0	0
Cromwell	1	17	17.0	1
Miller	1	5	5.0	0
Ferragamo	4	3	0.8	1
Alexander	1	3	3.0	0
Battle	1	1	1.0	0
Waddy	2	-11	-5.5	0

RECEIVING

Last Name	No.	Yds	Avg	TD
Tyler	38	375	9.9	4
Guman	31	310	10.0	0
Dennard	25	383	15.3	2
Barber	18	166	9.2	1
Farmer	17	344	20.2	2
Miller	15	346	23.1	1
J. Thomas	8	49	6.1	0
D. Hill	7	92	13.1	0
Redden	4	16	4.0	0
Battle	2	62	31.0	1
Alexander	1	-7	-7.0	0

PUNT RETURNS

Last Name	No.	Yds	Avg	TD
Irvin	22	242	11.0	1

KICKOFF RETURNS

Last Name	No.	Yds	Avg	TD
Redden	22	502	22.8	0
Alexander	8	139	17.4	0
Guman	8	102	12.8	0
Sully	5	84	16.8	0
D. Hill	2	42	21.0	0

PASSING — PUNTING — KICKING

PASSING	Att	Comp	%	Yds	Yd/Att	TD	Int-	%	RK
Ferragamo	209	118	57	1609	7.70	9	9-	4	6
B. Jones	87	48	55	527	6.06	2	4-	5	
Guman	1	0	0	0	0.00	0	1-	100	

PUNTING	No	Avg
Misko	45	43.6

KICKING	XP	Att	%	FG	Att	%
Lansford	23	24	96	9	15	60

Long victorious on the field, the Oakland Raiders triumphed in their lawsuit against the N.F.L. The jury listened to both sides, then decided that the league rule which required any franchise shift to be approved by 21 teams was a violation of federal antitrust law. With this rule declared void, Raider chief Al Davis was free to move his team to Los Angeles. The Raiders still practiced during the week in Oakland, but the home field on Sundays was the Los Angeles Coliseum, abandoned by the Rams in 1980. Further legal hurdles lay ahead for Davis. The league would appeal this decision, and Oakland's city fathers would seek to take control of the team through a court order of condemnation. Davis nevertheless figured to prevail in these court actions. The future of franchise shifts was impossible to predict, with teams free to move without league approval.

EASTERN DIVISION

Miami Dolphins — Without the brilliance of any superstars, the Dolphins still played on a par with the N.F.L.'s elite. On opening day, they charged into Shea Stadium and ripped the Jets 45-28 before a shocked New York audience. After the strike, the Dolphins took awhile to regain their edge. They lost to Tampa Bay and dropped a 3-0 heartbreaker in a snowstorm in New England. In the stretch run, however, the Dolphins hit their stride and won their last three games. Of these late victories, a 20-19 triumph over the Jets was the key. The Miami offense emphasized the ground attack, with Andra Franklin the top runner and Ed Newman the star blocker. The defense hounded enemy passers and became known as the Killer Bees. The head Bee was nose tackle Bob Baumhower.

New York Jets — The strike actually gave the Jets a needed breather. The Dolphins trounced them on opening day, and Joe Klecko suffered a severe knee injury one week later. The New York Sack Exchange would never again reach the same heights, but Mark Gastineau still harassed quarterbacks regularly. The defense played well enough that the scintillating Jet offense won the first four games after the strike. Richard Todd engineered an offense that had stars in slashing runner Freeman McNeil, swift receiver Wesley Walker and blockers Marvin Powell and Joe Fields. On December 18, the Jets battled the Dolphins in Miami and dropped a 20-19 squeaker. After a meaningless closing loss to the Chiefs, coach Walt Michaels and his players hoped for a third meeting with the Dolphins.

New England Patriots — New head coach Ron Meyer brought discipline and lots of changes to the Pats. After cutting many veterans, he named Matt Cavanaugh as the starting quarterback over Steve Grogan. He also had the first player chosen in the college draft, defensive end Kenneth Sims from Texas. The experiment with Cavanaugh ended in week four when Grogan re-emerged as the starter. Sims didn't set the league on fire while learning his trade. The defense as a whole, however, shone in December, shutting out the Dolphins and Seahawks back to back. Despite the changes, the star Pats were holdovers Tony Collins, Stanley Morgan and John Hannah on offense and a healthy Mike Haynes on defense. Last year, they played on a loser; this year, they went to the playoffs.

Buffalo Bills — Joe Cribbs insisted that the Bills renegotiate his contract, and he held out for the first two regular-season games when the team refused. The Bills won both pre-strike games despite Cribbs' absence. When play resumed in November, Cribbs was back in uniform to aid in the playoff drive. The solid Buffalo defense reached its peak on December 12 with a 13-0 shutout of the Steelers. Fred Smerlas anchored the unit at nose tackle, but the linebacking corps was lessened by a string of injuries. With a post-season berth within grasp, the Bills blew a tire and lost their last three games. The collapse ended a five-year regime of coach Chuck Knox, who resigned to take over in Seattle.

Baltimore Colts — New head coach Frank Kush lived up to his reputation as an iron-willed disciplinarian. His grueling training camp saw massive personnel turnover and a major change in the Colts' identity. Veteran quarterback Bert Jones had been traded during the off-season to the Rams. In his absence, rookie Mike Pagel beat fellow freshman Art Schlichter for the starting job. The revamped roster needed time to work together, and the Colts looked outclassed in two pre-strike losses. The Jets whipped them 37-0 on November 21, and the Bills won 20-0 a week later. The Colts did gain some respect with a 20-17 loss to the Bengals on December 5 and a 20-20 tie with the Packers on December 19. There would be no victories, however, for the Colts this year.

CENTRAL DIVISION

Cincinnati Bengals — No longer surprise upstarts, the Bengals stayed in the front ranks of the A.F.C. Ken Anderson passed with such precision that he set an N.F.L. single-season record with a 70.6 completion percentage. Reeling in the most passes were tall Cris Collinsworth and burly Dan Ross, a brace of all-pro receivers. When running was needed, massive fullback Pete Johnson responded with power. Anthony Munoz led the offensive line in supporting both the air and ground attacks. The Bengal defense was less impressive, getting burned by San Diego 50-34 on Monday night, December 20. Head coach Forrest Gregg aimed for a march through the playoffs for another shot at the Super Bowl ring which got away last year.

Pittsburgh Steelers — Bowing to the new pass-oriented rules, coach Chuck Noll installed a new 3-4 defense which replaced the fabled Steel Curtain in many situations. Veterans Joe Greene and L.C. Greenwood were gone, but Jack Lambert and Donnie Shell still carried the burden as they had in the 1970s. The season got off to a rousing start with victories over the Cowboys and Bengals. The Steelers hit a cold streak after the strike, getting shut out by the Seahawks and Bills in a three-week period. The past champions bore down at the end and won their last two games, winning a ticket to the playoffs for the first time since 1979.

Cleveland Browns — The Browns added two heralded linebackers in Tom Cousineau and Chip Banks. Cousineau was the first pick in the 1979 draft and returned to the United States after three seasons with Montreal of the Canadian Football League. Banks was a blue-chip rookie out of USC. Where the Browns really needed help this year was on offense. Despite the ace receiving of Ozzie Newsome, Cleveland had problems scoring. Brian Sipe couldn't spark the thrills of 1980 and lost his starting job to Paul McDonald. The left-handed McDonald started the last three games and engineered two victories, enough to inch the Browns into the expanded playoffs.

Houston Oilers — In the second year of Ed Biles' reign, the Oilers collapsed into the depths of the league. He cut quarterback Ken Stabler before the season and gave his job to Gifford Nielsen. One week into the schedule, Biles reconsidered and traded for Archie Manning of the Saints. The Oilers split the two pre-strike games, then nose-dived to seven straight losses after the break. Of the losses, a 35-7 drubbing at home by Dallas on Monday night was the most dispiriting. With the offensive line slumping, Earl Campbell endured his least productive season.

WESTERN DIVISION

Los Angeles Raiders — The Raiders celebrated their move by returning to a dominant position in the A.F.C. Al Davis and coach Tom Flores fortified the defense with Lyle Alzado, the ace lineman of the Cleveland Browns. Alzado combined with Ted Hendricks to give the defense a pair of hard-hitting leaders. Davis and Flores equipped the offense with a marvelous new

FINAL TEAM STATISTICS

OFFENSE

	BALT.	BUFF.	CIN.	CLEV.	DENV.	HOU.	K.C.	RAID.	MIA.	N.E.	NY.J.	PIT.	S.D.	SEA.
FIRST DOWNS:														
Total	152	180	207	176	170	138	163	175	165	146	193	171	233	159
by Rushing	62	83	63	64	52	52	71	65	84	74	87	69	72	51
by Passing	80	84	123	96	103	81	79	95	66	63	95	91	145	89
by Penalty	10	13	21	16	15	5	13	15	15	9	11	11	16	19
RUSHING:														
Number	293	319	269	256	257	225	269	292	333	324	304	289	267	227
Yards	1044	1371	949	873	1018	799	943	1080	1344	1347	1317	1187	1121	795
Average Yards	3.6	4.3	3.5	3.4	4.0	3.6	3.5	3.7	4.0	4.2	4.3	4.1	4.2	3.5
Touchdowns	4	9	13	7	6	5	3	15	11	3	13	7	15	4
PASSING:														
Attempts	283	273	310	334	311	287	264	267	238	187	279	275	338	326
Completions	142	149	219	174	181	153	145	154	129	93	165	141	208	176
Completion Pct.	50.2	54.6	70.6	52.1	58.2	53.3	54.9	57.7	54.2	49.7	59.1	51.3	61.5	54.0
Passing Yards	1613	1671	2501	2057	2019	1882	1864	2086	1401	1420	2107	1922	3021	2068
Avg. Yds per Att.	4.8	5.5	6.9	5.1	5.4	4.8	5.1	6.5	5.3	6.4	6.3	6.1	8.7	5.0
Avg. Yds per Comp.	11.4	11.2	11.4	11.8	11.2	12.3	12.9	13.6	10.9	15.3	12.8	13.6	14.5	11.6
Times Tackled	20	12	27	26	24	39	40	23	11	15	23	19	12	36
Yds Lost Tackled	174	115	162	212	200	308	309	211	87	134	206	139	94	269
Net Yards	1439	1556	2339	1845	1819	1574	1555	1875	1314	1286	1901	1783	2927	1799
Touchdowns	6	8	12	9	8	12	10	14	8	12	16	17	19	9
Interceptions	10	17	9	16	19	15	8	15	13	9	9	16	12	13
Pct. Intercepted	3.5	6.2	2.9	4.8	6.1	5.2	3.0	5.6	5.5	4.8	3.2	5.8	3.6	4.0
PUNTS:														
Number	46	35	31	49	45	55	38	47	35	49	36	49	23	49
Average	44.4	37.9	38.7	38.3	45.0	39.7	40.5	39.1	38.7	43.7	37.4	40.4	37.7	38.6
PUNT RETURNS														
Number	14	26	17	23	21	19	15	27	22	16	23	36	12	21
Yards	78	119	95	134	305	104	129	209	194	139	184	317	138	228
Average Yards	5.6	4.6	5.6	5.8	14.5	5.5	8.6	7.7	8.8	8.7	8.0	8.8	11.5	10.9
Touchdowns	0	0	0	0	2	0	0	0	1	0	0	0	0	0
KICKOFF RET.:														
Number	42	36	31	38	40	45	34	36	24	28	33	28	45	29
Yards	753	792	643	754	818	905	723	754	507	646	667	569	890	544
Average Yards	17.9	22.0	20.7	19.8	20.5	20.1	21.3	20.9	21.1	23.1	20.2	20.3	19.8	18.8
Touchdowns	0	0	0	0	0	0	0	0	0	1	0	0	0	0
INTERCEPT RET.:														
Number	5	13	14	17	12	3	12	18	19	12	17	17	12	13
Yards	150	122	240	102	106	47	208	356	281	176	261	127	138	160
Average Yards	30.0	9.4	17.1	6.0	8.8	15.7	17.3	19.8	14.8	14.7	15.4	7.5	11.5	12.3
Touchdowns	1	0	2	1	0	0	3	3	2	1	1	0	0	1
PENALTIES:														
Number	52	69	56	59	54	52	43	86	34	52	63	59	64	59
Yards	433	582	475	461	516	424	372	840	240	412	533	459	530	523
FUMBLES:														
Number	24	23	12	15	24	14	13	22	15	16	18	18	17	21
Number Lost	11	9	7	8	17	11	4	9	10	8	9	9	8	11
POINTS:														
Total	113	150	232	140	148	136	176	260	198	143	245	204	288	127
PAT Attempts	11	18	27	17	16	18	17	33	22	17	31	24	34	14
PAT Made	11	15	26	17	15	16	17	32	21	15	26	22	32	13
FG Attempts	18	18	18	16	13	6	24	16	20	13	17	12	22	14
FG Made	10	9	14	7	11	4	19	10	15	8	11	10	16	10
Percent FG Made	55.6	50.0	77.8	43.8	84.6	66.7	79.2	62.5	75.0	61.5	64.7	83.3	72.7	71.4
Safeties	0	0	1	0	2	0	0	0	0	1	0	1	2	0

DEFENSE

	BALT.	BUFF.	CIN.	CLEV.	DENV.	HOU.	K.C.	RAID.	MIA.	N.E.	NY.J.	PIT.	S.D.	SEA.
FIRST DOWNS:														
Total	197	151	170	189	176	187	170	206	147	185	160	174	196	167
by Rushing	87	64	61	82	53	67	69	53	77	87	54	49	65	86
by Passing	89	72	102	94	104	106	92	121	65	88	88	111	119	68
by Penalty	21	15	7	13	19	14	9	32	5	10	18	14	12	13
RUSHING:														
Number	348	268	223	306	293	298	280	234	293	315	269	236	230	337
Yards	1473	1034	850	1292	935	1225	1065	778	1285	1289	983	762	961	1461
Average Yards	4.2	3.9	3.8	4.2	3.2	4.1	3.8	3.3	4.4	4.1	3.7	3.2	4.2	4.3
Touchdowns	10	6	8	13	8	10	7	12	7	9	5	5	10	12
PASSING:														
Attempts	246	256	306	266	307	284	262	375	226	267	298	329	342	246
Completions	138	114	187	144	172	179	155	193	119	142	159	176	233	138
Completion Pct.	56.1	44.5	61.1	54.1	56.0	63.0	59.2	51.5	52.7	53.2	53.4	53.5	68.1	56.1
Passing Yards	1920	1382	2250	1967	2350	2453	1787	2617	1281	1691	1817	2385	2437	1468
Avg. Yds per Att.	7.1	4.9	6.2	6.3	6.9	7.0	6.0	5.5	4.0	5.3	5.2	5.8	6.4	5.1
Avg. Yds per Comp.	13.9	12.1	12.0	13.7	13.7	13.7	11.5	13.6	10.8	11.9	11.4	13.6	10.5	10.6
Times Tackled	11	12	22	22	16	31	15	38	29	20	20	34	19	17
Yds Lost Tackled	97	82	207	145	116	240	120	329	254	172	171	273	145	135
Net Yards	1823	1300	2043	1822	2234	2213	1667	2288	1027	1519	1646	2112	2292	1333
Touchdowns	18	8	12	9	14	18	12	11	7	9	10	12	10	4
Interceptions	5	13	14	17	12	3	12	18	19	12	17	17	13	13
Pct. Intercepted	2.0	5.1	4.6	6.4	3.9	1.1	4.6	4.8	8.4	4.5	5.7	5.2	3.8	5.3
PUNTS:														
Number	41	44	37	40	42	38	37	49	40	43	42	53	27	50
Average	39.9	39.3	40.1	38.8	39.4	43.0	39.7	38.3	40.1	39.7	42.1	38.1	44.9	40.6
PUNT RETURNS														
Number	26	10	17	30	25	35	22	17	14	26	17	28	7	19
Yards	226	30	68	216	227	293	338	71	77	191	153	182	86	69
Average Yards	8.7	3.0	4.0	7.2	9.1	8.4	15.4	4.2	5.5	7.3	9.0	6.5	12.3	3.6
Touchdowns	0	0	0	0	0	0	2	0	0	0	1	0	0	0
KICKOFF RET.:														
Number	25	34	45	23	26	26	42	43	33	32	35	36	51	24
Yards	538	604	851	424	541	564	794	851	704	614	743	821	991	361
Average Yards	21.5	17.8	18.9	18.4	20.8	21.7	18.9	19.8	21.3	19.2	21.2	22.8	19.4	15.0
Touchdowns	0	0	0	0	0	0	0	0	0	0	1	0	0	0
INTERCEPT RET.:														
Number	10	17	9	16	19	15	8	15	13	9	9	16	12	13
Yards	129	268	93	164	431	47	182	180	96	100	152	168	262	88
Average Yards	12.1	15.8	10.3	10.3	22.7	3.1	22.8	12.0	7.4	11.1	16.9	10.5	21.8	6.8
Touchdowns	0	0	1	0	3	1	1	1	0	0	3	0	3	1
PENALTIES:														
Number	59	49	64	57	63	59	60	53	57	39	43	45	70	44
Yards	466	395	551	436	571	454	486	588	461	290	345	355	612	406
FUMBLES:														
Number	11	14	19	20	17	20	23	18	17	19	20	17	19	18
Number Lost	6	8	6	11	7	14	10	11	8	11	9	8	12	9
POINTS:														
Total	236	154	177	182	226	245	184	200	131	157	166	146	221	147
PAT Attempts	28	15	20	23	25	30	22	24	15	18	20	17	24	18
PAT Made	26	14	19	21	25	30	20	23	14	17	19	17	23	17
FG Attempts	19	20	12	11	24	18	14	14	15	15	15	14	19	15
FG Made	14	16	10	7	17	11	10	11	9	10	9	9	16	6
Percent FG Made	73.7	80.0	83.3	63.6	70.8	61.1	71.4	78.6	60.0	66.7	60.0	64.3	84.2	40.0
Safeties	0	1	1	1	0	1	1	0	0	1	0	0	0	2

weapon in halfback Marcus Allen from USC. A top-notch runner and receiver, Allen rushed for 116 yards in an opening-day victory over Super Bowl champion San Francisco. Another new offensive ace was Todd Christensen, a special-teams player who unexpectantly shone at tight end. The only blemish on the season's record was a 31-17 loss to the Bengals on November 28.

San Diego Chargers — En route to a fourth straight playoff berth, the Chargers scored a lot of points and allowed a lot of points. The usual cast of characters manned the Air Coryell attack. Dan Fouts tormented opponents with passes to Wes Chandler, Charlie Joiner and Kellen Winslow while Chuck Muncie and rookie James Brooks kept defenses honest with their running. The offensive line featured veterans Russ Washington and Doug Wilkerson. The defense simply could not stop enemy passers despite all-pro work from tackle Gary Johnson and newly acquired safety Tim Fox. In three weeks in December, the Chargers beat the 49ers 41-37, Bengals 50-34 and Colts 44-26, displaying their true character on both sides of the line.

Seattle Seahawks — Turmoil ripped the Seahawks before the season started. Wide receiver Sam McCullum was cut before the opener; many suspected that his role as union representative cost him his job. The players almost called for a strike on opening day, relenting in an atmosphere of bitterness. The Seahawks lost the two pre-strike games with young Dave Krieg at quarterback. During the strike, management fired coach Jack Patera and replaced him for the remainder of the season with Mike McCormack. Morale picked up, especially when the popular Jim Zorn was restored to the starting lineup. Fueling the second-half improvement was a talented defense led by Jacob Green, Kenny Easley and Keith Simpson.

Kansas City Chiefs — Things started going badly in May, with Joe Delaney undergoing eye surgery for a detached retina. The offense suffered from his reduced availability and from the shuffling of quarterbacks Steve Fuller and Bill Kenney. Neither gave coach Marv Levy any reason to choose a full-time quarterback. After the strike, the Chiefs lost their first four games, killing their playoff hopes and public interest in the team. In the season finale, they whipped the Jets 37-13 before a paltry crowd of 11,902. That was the last game for Jack Rudnay after a long career with the Chiefs. Also departing was Levy after a five-year stint that led to no post-season appearances.

Denver Broncos — Dan Reeves suffered through a general collapse of the Broncos in his second year as coach. The defense softened under Bill Thompson's retirement, Steve Foley's opening-day broken arm and Bob Swenson's holdout for much of the season. Turnovers plagued the offense. Craig Morton began as the starting quarterback but yielded his job to younger Steve DeBerg after the strike. The poor post-strike record was a team effort, but a few individual kudos were merited. Steve Watson continued his effective receiving, rookie Gerald Willhite ran well and Rick Upchurch carried two punt returns all the way for touchdowns.

MIAMI DOLPHINS 7-2-0 Don Shula

Scores of Each Game		
45	N.Y.Jets	26
24	BALTIMORE	20
9	Buffalo	7
17	Tampa Bay	23
22	MINNESOTA	14
0	New England	3
20	N.Y.JETS	19
27	BUFFALO	10
34	Baltimore	7

Use Name	Pos.	Hgt	Wgt	Age	Int	Pts
Jon Giesler	OT	6'5"	260	25		
Cleveland Green	OT	6'3"	262	24		
Erik Laakso	OT	6'4"	265	25		
Roy Foster	OG-OT	6'4"	275	22		
Bob Kuechenberg	OG	6'3"	255	34		
Ed Newman	OG	6'2"	255	31		
Jeff Toews	OG	6'3"	255	34		
Mark Dennard	C	6'1"	252	26		
Dwight Stephenson	C	6'2"	255	24		
Bill Barnett	DE	6'4"	260	26		
Doug Betters	DE	6'7"	260	26		
Kim Bokamper	DE	6'6"	250	27	1	
Vern Den Herder	DE	6'6"	252	33		
Bob Baumhower	NT	6'5"	260	27		
Richard Bishop	NT	6'1"	265	32		
Steve Clark	NT	6'4"	255	22		
Charles Bowser	LB	6'3"	222	22		
Bob Brudzinski	LB	6'4"	230	27	1	
A.J. Duhe	LB	6'4"	248	26	1	
Larry Gordon	LB	6'4"	230	29	1	
Ron Hester	LB	6'1"	218	23		
Steve Potter	LB	6'3"	235	24		
Earnest Rhone	LB	6'2"	224	29	1	
Steve Shull	LB	6'1"	220	24		
Glenn Blackwood	DB	6'	186	25	2	6
Lyle Blackwood	DB	6'	188	31	2	
William Judson	DB	6'1"	181	23		
Mike Kozlowski	DB	6'	196	26	1	
Paul Lankford	DB	6'1"	178	24		
Don McNeal	DB	5'11"	192	24	4	6
Gerald Small	DB	5'11"	192	26	2	
Fulton Walker	DB	5'10"	193	24	3	
Jim Jensen	QB	6'4"	212	23		
Don Strock	QB	6'5"	220	31		
David Woodley	QB	6'2"	204	23		18
Eddie Hill	HB	6'2"	210	25		
Tony Nathan	HB	6'	206	25		6
Tommy Vigorito	HB	5'10"	197	22		12
Woody Bennett	FB	6'2"	222	27		
Rich Diana	FB	5'9"	220	21		
Andra Franklin	FB	5'10"	225	22		42
Jimmy Cefalo	WR	5'11"	188	25		6
Mark Duper	WR	5'9"	185	23		
Duriel Harris	WR	5'11"	176	27		6
Vince Heflin	WR	6'	185	23		
Nat Moore	WR	5'9"	186	30		6
Bruce Hardy	TE	6'5"	230	26		12
Ronnie Lee	TE	6'3"	236	25		
Joe Rose	TE	6'3"	230	25		12
Tom Orosz	K	6'1"	204	22		
Uwe von Schamann	K	6'	188	26		66

Ken Poole - Back Injury

NEW YORK JETS 6-3-0 Walt Michaels

Scores of Each Game		
28	MIAMI	45
31	New England	7
37	BALTIMORE	0
15	GREEN BAY	13
28	Detroit	13
32	TAMPA BAY	17
19	Miami	20
42	Minnesota	14
13	Kansas City	37

Use Name	Pos.	Hgt	Wgt	Age	Int	Pts
Jim Luscinski	OT-OG	6'5"	275	23		
Marvin Powell	OT	6'5"	271	27		
John Roman	OT	6'4"	265	30		
Chris Ward	OT	6'3"	267	26		
Dan Alexander	OG	6'4"	260	27		
Guy Bingham	OG-C	6'3"	255	24		
Stan Waldemore	OG-C	6'4"	269	27		
Joe Fields	C-OG	6'2"	253	28		
Joe Pellegrini	C-OG	6'4"	252	25		
Mark Gastineau	DE	6'5"	269	25		
Rusty Guilbeau	DE	6'4"	250	23		
Joe Klecko	DE	6'3"	269	28		
Kenny Neil	DE-DT	6'4"	244	23		
Barry Bennett	DT-DE	6'4"	257	26		
Marty Lyons	DT	6'5"	269	25		
Ben Rudolph	DT-DE	6'5"	270	25		
Abdul Salaam	DT	6'3"	269	29		
Stan Blinka	LB	6'2"	230	24		
Greg Buttle	LB	6'3"	232	28	1	
Bob Crable	LB	6'3"	228	22		
Ron Crosby	LB	6'3"	227	27		
Lance Mehl	LB	6'3"	235	24	2	
John Woodring	LB	6'2"	232	23		
George Floyd	DB	5'11"	190	21		
Jerry Holmes	DB	6'2"	175	24	3	
Bobby Jackson	DB	5'9"	180	25	5	12
Jesse Johnson	DB	6'3"	188	25		
Johnny Lynn	DB	6'	198	25	1	
Darrol Ray	DB	6'1"	206	24	3	
Ken Schroy	DB	6'2"	198	29	1	
Kirk Springs	DB	6'	192	24	1	
Pat Ryan	QB	6'3"	210	26		
Richard Todd	QB	6'2"	206	28		6
Scott Dierking	HB	5'10"	220	27		12
Bruce Harper	HB	5'8"	177	27		6
Freeman McNeil	HB	5'11"	216	23		42
Mike Augustyniak	FB	5'11"	226	26		24
Marion Barber	FB	6'3"	224	25		
Dwayne Crutchford	FB	6'	235	22		6
Tom Newton	FB	6'	220	28		
Derrick Gaffney	WR	6'1"	182	27		6
Bobby Jones	WR	5'11"	185	27		
Johnny "Lam" Jones	WR	5'11"	180	24		12
Kurt Sohn	WR	5'11"	176	25		
Wesley Walker	WR	6'	179	27		36
Steve Alvers	TE	6'4"	240	24		
Jerome Barkum	TE	6'4"	227	32		6
Tom Coombs	TE	6'3"	236	23		
Mickey Shuler	TE	6'3"	236	26		18
Pat Leahy	K	6'	189	31		59

NEW ENGLAND PATRIOTS 5-4-0 Ron Meyer

Scores of Each Game		
24	Baltimore	13
7	N.Y.Jets	31
7	Cleveland	10
29	HOUSTON	21
13	Chicago	26
3	MIAMI	0
16	Seattle	0
14	Pittsburgh	37
30	BUFFALO	19

Use Name	Pos.	Hgt	Wgt	Age	Int	Pts
Darryl Haley	OT	6'4"	279	21		
Brian Holloway	OT	6'7"	288	23		
Shelby Jordan	OT	6'7"	280	30		
Bob Cryder	OG	6'4"	293	25		
John Hannah	OG	6'2"	282	31		
Ron Wooten	OG	6'4"	280	23		
Pete Brock	C	6'5"	275	28		
Dwight Wheeler	C	6'3"	269	27		
Julius Adams	DE	6'3"	270	34		
George Crump	DE	6'4"	260	23		2
Kenneth Sims	DE	6'5"	279	22		
Ron Spears	DE	6'6"	255	22		
Luther Henson	NT	6'	275	23		
Dennis Owens	NT	6'1"	252	22		
Lester Williams	NT	6'2"	272	23		
Don Blackmon	LB	6'3"	245	24	2	
Tim Golden	LB	6'1"	220	22		
Brian Ingram	LB	6'4"	230	22		
Larry McGrew	LB	6'5"	233	25		
Steve Nelson	LB	6'2"	230	31		
Andre Tippett	LB	6'3"	231	22		
Clayton Weishuhn	LB	6'2"	220	22		
John Zamberlin	LB	6'2"	226	26		
Raymond Clayborn	DB	6'1"	186	27	1	
Paul Dombroski	DB	6'	185	26		
Mike Haynes	DB	6'2"	202	29	4	
Roland James	DB	6'2"	191	24	3	
Keith Lee	DB	5'11"	193	24		
Fred Marion	DB	6'2"	196	23		
Rick Sanford	DB	6'1"	192	25	2	6
Ricky Smith	DB	6'	174	22		6
Matt Cavanaugh	QB	6'2"	212	25		
Tom Flick	QB	6'3"	190	24		
Steve Grogan	QB	6'4"	210	29		6
Tony Collins	HB	5'11"	203	23		18
Larry Cowan (from MIA)	HB	5'11"	194	22		
Vagas Ferguson	HB	6'1"	213	25		
Greg Taylor	HB	5'8"	175	23		
Mosi Tatupu	FB	6'	227	27		
Mark van Eeghen	FB	6'2"	220	30		6
Robert Weathers	FB	6'2"	217	21		6
Morris Bradshaw	WR	6'1"	195	29		6
Preston Brown	WR	5'11"	187	24		6
Cedric Jones	WR	6'	184	22		
Stanley Morgan	WR	5'11"	181	27		18
Ken Tofer	WR	6'2"	191	23		12
Lin Dawson	TE	6'3"	240	23		6
Don Hasselbeck	TE	6'7"	245	27		6
Brian Williams	TE	6'5"	240	24		
Rich Camarilklo	K	5'11"	191	22		
Rex Robinson	K	5'11"	205	23		8
John Smith	K	6'	185	32		21

Steve Clark - Ankle Injury

BUFFALO BILLS 4-5-0 Chuck Knox

Scores of Each Game		
14	KANSAS CITY	9
23	MINNESOTA	22
7	MIAMI	9
20	BALTIMORE	0
21	Green Bay	33
13	PITTSBURGH	0
23	Tampa Bay	24
10	Miami	27
19	New England	30

Use Name	Pos.	Hgt	Wgt	Age	Int	Pts
Justin Cross	OT	6'6"	257	23		
Joe Devlin	OT	6'5"	250	28		
Ken Jones	OT	6'5"	250	29		
Jon Borchardt	OG	6'5"	255	25		
Tom Lynch	OG	6'5"	250	27		
Reggie McKenzie	OG	6'4"	242	32		
Jim Ritcher	OG-C	6'3"	251	24		
Will Grant	C	6'3"	248	28		
Tim Vogler	C	6'3"	245	25		
Darrell Irvin	DE	6'4"	255	25		
Ken Johnson	DE	6'5"	253	27		
Sherman White	DE	6'5"	250	33		
Ben Williams	DE	6'3"	245	28	1	
Mark Roopenian	NT	6'5"	254	24		
Fred Smerlas	NT	6'3"	270	25		
Jim Haslett	LB	6'3"	232	26		
Chris Keating	LB	6'2"	223	24	1	
Joey Lumpkin	LB	6'2"	230	22		
Eugene Marve	LB	6'2"	230	21	1	
Shane Nelson	LB	6'1"	225	27		
Ervin Parker	LB	6'4"	240	24		
Isiah Robertson	LB	6'3"	225	33	1	
Lucius Sanford	LB	6'2"	216	26		
Phil Villapiano	LB	6'2"	225	33		
Mario Clark	DB	6'2"	195	28		
Steve Freeman	DB	5'11"	185	29	3	
Rod Kush	DB	6'	188	25		
Jeff Nixon	DB	6'3"	190	25		
Lemar Parrish	DB	5'11"	170	34	1	
Charles Romes	DB	6'1"	190	28	1	
Bill Simpson	DB	6'1"	191	30	4	
Chris Williams	DB	6'	197	23		
Joe Ferguson	QB	6'1"	195	32		12
Matt Kofler	QB	6'3"	192	23		
Matt Robinson	QB	6'2"	196	27		
Joe Cribbs	HB	5'11"	190	24		18
Roland Hooks	HB	6'	195	29		
Art Whittington	HB	5'11"	185	26		
Curtis Brown	FB	5'10"	203	27		
Roosevelt Leaks	FB	5'10"	225	29		30
Ted McKnight	FB	6'1"	212	28		
Booker Moore	FB	5'11"	224	23		
Jerry Butler	WR	6'	178	24		24
Robert Holt	WR	6'1"	182	22		
Frank Lewis	WR	6'1"	196	35		12
Mike Mosley	WR	6'2"	192	24		
Lou Piccone	WR	5'9"	175	33		
Perry Tuttle	WR	6'	178	23		
Buster Barnett	TE	6'5"	225	23		
Mark Brammer	TE	6'3"	235	24		12
Greg Cater	K	6'	191	25		
Efren Herrera	K	5'9"	190	31		35
Nick Mike-Mayer	K	5'8"	185	32		7

Byron Franklin - Sciatic Nerve Injury
Robb Riddick - Knee Injury

BALTIMORE COLTS 0-8-1 Frank Kush

Scores of Each Game		
13	NEW ENGLAND	24
20	Miami	24
0	N.Y.Jets	37
0	Buffalo	20
17	CINCINNATI	20
10	Minnesota	13
20	GREEN BAY	20
26	San Diego	44
7	MIAMI	34

Use Name	Pos.	Hgt	Wgt	Age	Int	Pts
Jeff Hart	OT	6'5"	272	28		
Greg Murtha	OT	6'6"	268	25		
John Sinnott	OT	6'4"	275	24		
Terry Crouch	OG	6'2"	278	23		
Nat Hudson	OG	6'3"	265	24		
Ken Huff	OG	6'4"	259	29		
Arland Thompson	OG	6'3"	265	24		
Ben Utt	OG	6'4"	255	23		
Ray Donaldson	C	6'3"	260	24		
Glenn Hyde	C	6'3"	252	31		
Cleveland Crosby	DE	6'4"	250	26		
Steve Durham	DE	6'5"	256	23		
Fletcher Jenkins	DE-NT	6'2"	258	22		
Harry Stanback	DE	6'5"	255	24		
Donnell Thompson	DE	6'4"	254	23		
James Hunter	NT-DE	6'5"	251	24		
Leo Wisniewski	NT	6'1"	263	22		
Greg Bracelin	LB	6'1"	210	25	1	
Johnie Cooks	LB	6'4"	243	23		
Joe Harris	LB	6'1"	230	29		
Mike Humiston	LB	6'3"	238	23		
Ricky Jones	LB	6'1"	222	27		
Barry Krauss	LB	6'3"	232	25		6
Cliff Odom	LB	6'2"	225	23		
Gary Padjen	LB	6'2"	246	24		
Sanders Shiver	LB	6'2"	227	27		
Dave Simmons	LB	6'5"	219	25		
Kim Anderson	DB	5'11"	182	25		
Larry Anderson	DB	5'11"	188	25	2	
James Burroughs	DB	6'1"	192	24	1	6
Jeff Delaney	DB	6'	197	25		
Nesby Glasgow	DB	5'10"	180	25		
Derrick Hatchett	DB	5'11"	183	24	1	
Darryl Hemphill	DB	6'	195	22		
Sid Justin	DB	5'10"	170	28		
Dwayne O'Steen (to TB for playoff game)	DB	6'1"	195	27		
David Humm	QB	6'2"	190	30		
Mike Pagel	QB	6'2"	201	21		6
Art Schlichter	QB	6'2"	210	22		
Curtis Dickey	HB	6'1"	209	25		6
Zachary Dixon	HB	6'1"	204	26		6
Cleveland Franklin	FB	6'2"	216	27		
Randy McMillan	FB	6'	220	23		6
Johnnie Wright	FB	6'2"	210	23		
Elmer Bailey	WR	6'	195	24		
Matt Bouza	WR	6'3"	211	23		12
Ry Butler	WR	6'3"	195	25		12
Bernard Henry	WR	6'	185	22		
Holden Smith	WR	6'1"	191	23		
Pat Beach	TE	6'4"	243	22		6
Reese McCall	TE	6'7"	238	26		
Tim Sherwin	TE	6'6"	237	24		6
Dan Miller (from NE)	K	5'10"	172	21		27
Rohn Stark	K	6'3"	195	23		
Mike Wood	K	5'11"	199	27		24

Tim Foley - Achilles' Tendon Injury
Wade Griffin - Neck Injury
Hosea Taylor - Injury

MIAMI DOLPHINS

RUSHING

Last Name	No.	Yds	Avg	TD
Franklin	177	701	4.0	7
Nathan	66	233	3.5	1
Woodley	36	207	5.8	2
Vigorito	19	99	5.2	1
Hill	13	51	3.9	0
Diana	8	31	3.9	0
Bennett	9	15	1.7	0
Harris	1	13	13.0	0
Strock	3	-9	-3.0	0
Cowan	1	3	3.0	0

RECEIVING

Last Name	No.	Yds	Avg	TD
Vigorito	24	186	7.8	0
Harris	22	331	15.0	1
Cefalo	17	357	20.9	1
Rose	16	182	11.4	2
Nathan	16	114	7.1	0
Hardy	12	66	5.5	2
Moore	8	82	10.3	1
Hill	6	33	5.5	0
Franklin	3	9	3.0	0
Diana	2	21	10.5	0
Lee	2	6	3.0	0
Woodley	1	15	15.0	1

PUNT RETURNS

Last Name	No.	Yds	Avg	TD
Vigorito	20	192	9.6	1
G. Blackwood	2	2	1.0	0
Kozlowski	0	0	0.0	0

KICKOFF RETURNS

Last Name	No.	Yds	Avg	TD
Walker	20	433	21.7	0
Heflin	2	49	24.5	0
Diana	1	15	15.0	0
Kozlowski	1	10	10.0	0

PASSING — PUNTING — KICKING

PASSING	Att	Comp	%	Yds	Yd/Att	TD	Int-	%	RK
Woodley	179	98	55	1080	6.03	5	8-	4	10
Strock	55	30	55	306	5.56	2	5-	9	
Nathan	2	1	50	15	7.50	1	0-	0	
Hill	1	0	0	0	0.0	0	0-	0	
Jensen	1	0	0	0	0.0	0	0-	0	

PUNTING	No.	Avg.
Orosz	35	38.7

KICKING	XP	Att.	%	FG	Att	%
von Schamann	21	22	96	15	20	75

NEW YORK JETS

RUSHING

Last Name	No.	Yds	Avg	TD
McNeil	151	786	5.2	6
Augustyniak	50	178	3.6	4
Dierking	38	130	3.4	1
Harper	20	125	6.3	0
Crutchfield	22	78	3.5	1
Barber	8	24	3.0	0
J. Jones	1	2	2.0	0
Ryan	1	-1	-1.0	0
Todd	13	-5	-0.4	1

RECEIVING

Last Name	No.	Yds	Avg	TD
Walker	39	620	15.9	6
Augustyniak	24	189	7.9	0
Barkum	19	182	9.6	1
J. Jones	18	294	16.3	2
McNeil	16	187	11.7	1
Harper	14	177	12.7	1
Dierking	12	80	6.7	1
Gaffney	11	207	18.8	1
Shuler	8	132	16.5	3
B. Jones	3	32	10.7	0
Newton	1	7	7.0	0

PUNT RETURNS

Last Name	No.	Yds	Avg	TD
Harper	23	184	8.0	0

KICKOFF RETURNS

Last Name	No.	Yds	Avg	TD
Harper	18	368	20.4	0
Sohn	15	299	19.9	0

PASSING — PUNTING — KICKING

PASSING	Att	Comp	%	Yds	Yd/Att	TD	Int-	%	RK
Todd	261	153	59	1961	7.51	14	8-	3	3
Ryan	18	12	67	146	8.11	2	1-	6	

PUNTING	No.	Avg.
Ramsey	35	38.5

Kicking	XP	Att	%	FG	Att	%
Leahy	26	31	84	11	17	65

NEW ENGLAND PATRIOTS

RUSHING

Last Name	No.	Yds	Avg	TD
Collins	164	632	3.9	1
Van Eeghen	82	386	4.7	0
Tatupu	30	168	5.6	0
Weathers	24	83	3.5	1
Grogan	9	42	4.7	0
Cunningham	9	21	2.3	0
Ferguson	1	5	5.0	0
Toler	1	4	4.0	0
Cavanaugh	2	3	1.5	0
Morgan	2	3	1.5	0

RECEIVING

Last Name	No.	Yds	Avg	TD
Morgan	28	584	20.9	3
Collins	19	187	9.8	2
Hasselbeck	15	158	10.5	1
Dawson	13	160	12.3	1
Bradshaw	6	11	18.5	1
Brown	4	114	28.5	1
Weathers	3	24	8.0	0
Toler	2	63	31.5	2
Van Eeghen	2	14	7.0	1
Jones	1	5	5.0	0

PUNT RETURNS

Last Name	No.	Yds	Avg	TD
R. Smith	16	139	8.7	0

KICKOFF RETURNS

Last Name	No.	Yds	Avg	TD
R. Smith	24	567	23.6	1
Taylor	2	46	23.0	0
Dombrowski	1	19	19.0	0
Lee	1	14	14.0	0

PASSING — PUNTING — KICKING

PASSING	Att	Comp	%	Yds	Yd/Att	TD	Int-	%	RK
Grogan	122	66	54	930	7.62	7	4-	3	4
Cavanaugh	60	27	45	490	8.17	5	5-	8	
Flick	5	0	0	0	0.0	0	0-	0	

PUNTING	No	Avg
Camarillo	49	43.7

KICKING	XP	ATT	%	FG	ATT	%
J. Smith	6	7	86	5	8	63
Robinson	5	5	100	1	2	50

BUFFALO BILLS

RUSHING

Last Name	No.	Yds	Avg	TD
Cribbs	134	633	4.7	3
Leaks	97	405	4.2	5
Brown	41	187	4.6	0
Ferguson	16	46	2.9	1
Moore	16	38	2.4	0
Hooks	5	23	4.6	0
Kofler	2	21	10.5	0
Whitington	7	15	2.2	0
Holt	1	3	3.0	0

RECEIVING

Last Name	No.	Yds	Avg	TD
Lewis	28	443	15.8	2
Butler	26	336	12.9	4
Brammer	25	225	9.0	2
Cribbs	13	99	7.6	0
Leaks	13	91	7.0	0
Piccone	12	140	11.7	0
Mosley	9	96	10.7	0
Tuttle	7	107	15.3	0
Brown	6	38	6.3	0
Holt	4	45	11.3	0
Barnett	4	49	9.8	0
Moore	1	8	8.0	0
Haslett	1	4	4.0	0

PUNT RETURNS

Last Name	No.	Yds	Avg	TD
Mosley	11	61	5.5	0
Holt	10	45	4.5	0
Hooks	4	13	3.3	0
Simpson	1	0	0.0	0
Tuttle	0	0	0.0	0

KICKOFF RETURNS

Last Name	No.	Yds	Avg	TD
Mosley	18	487	27.1	0
Holt	7	156	22.3	0
Piccone	3	50	16.7	0
McKnight	3	34	11.3	0
Whittington	2	39	19.5	0
Brown	1	17	17.0	0
Keating	1	9	9.0	0
Roopenian	1	0	0.0	0

PASSING — PUNTING — KICKING

PASSING	Att	Comp	%	Yds	Yd/Att	TD	Int-	%	RK
Ferguson	264	144	55	1597	6.05	7	16-	6	16
Robinson	8	5	63	74	9.25	1	0-	0	
Cribbs	1	0	0	0	0.0	0	1-	100	

PUNTING	No	Avg
Cater	35	37.9

KICKING	XP	Att	%	FG	Att	%
Herrera	11	12	92	8	14	57
Mike-Mayer	4	5	80	1	4	25

BALTIMORE COLTS

RUSHING

Last Name	No.	Yds	Avg	TD
McMillan	101	305	3.0	1
Dixon	58	249	4.3	1
Dickey	66	232	3.5	1
Franklin	43	152	3.5	0
Pagel	19	82	4.3	1
Butler	3	10	3.3	0
Stark	1	8	8.0	0
Wright	1	3	3.0	0
Schlichter	1	3	3.0	0

RECEIVING

Last Name	No.	Yds	Avg	TD
Bouza	22	287	13.0	2
Sherwin	21	280	13.3	0
Dickey	21	228	10.9	0
Dixon	20	185	9.3	0
Butler	17	268	15.8	2
McMillan	15	90	6.0	0
Franklin	9	61	6.8	0
Henry	7	110	15.7	0
Beach	4	45	11.3	1
Smith	2	36	18.0	0
McCall	2	6	3.0	0
Wright	1	12	12.0	0
Krauss	1	5	5.0	1

PUNT RETURNS

Last Name	No.	Yds	Avg	TD
L. Anderson	8	54	6.8	0
Glasgow	4	24	6.0	0
Bouza	2	0	0.0	0

KICKOFF RETURNS

Last Name	No.	Yds	Avg	TD
L. Anderson	27	517	19.1	0
Dixon	11	197	17.9	0
Bouza	3	31	10.3	0
Franklin	1	8	8.0	0

PASSING — PUNTING — KICKING

PASSING	Att	Comp	%	Yds	Yd/Att	TD	Int-	%	RK
Pagel	221	111	50	1281	5.80	5	7-	3	11
Humm	23	13	57	130	5.70	0	1-	4	
Schlichter	37	17	46	197	5.30	0	2-	5	
Wood	1	1	100	5	5.00	1	0-	0	
Stark	1	0	0	0	0.0	0	0-	0	

PUNTING	No	Avg
Stark	46	44.4

KICKING	XP	ATT	%	FG	ATT	%
Wood	6	6	100	6	10	60
Miller	9	10	90	6	11	55

CINCINNATI BENGALS 7-2-0 Forrest Gregg

Scores of Each Game		
27	HOUSTON	6
20	Pittsburgh	*26
18	Philadelphia	14
31	L.A.RAIDERS	17
20	Baltimore	17
23	CLEVELAND	10
34	San Diego	50
24	SEATTLE	10
35	Houston	27

Use Name	Pos.	Hgt	Wgt	Age	Int	Pts
Anthony Munoz	OT	6'6"	278	24		
Mike Obrovac	OT	6'6"	275	26		
Ray Wagner	OT	6'3"	290	24		
Mike Wilson	OT	6'5"	271	27		
Glenn Bujnoch	OG	6'5"	265	28		
Dave Lapham	OG	6'4"	262	30		
Max Montoya	OG	6'5"	275	26		
Blair Bush	C	6'3"	252	25		
Blake Moore	C	6'5"	267	24		
Ross Browner	DE	6'3"	261	28	1	
Gary Burley	DE	6'3"	274	29		
Glen Collins	DE	6'6"	260	23		
Eddie Edwards	DE	6'5"	256	28		
Mike St.Clair	DE	6'5"	254	28		
Jerry Boyarsky	NT	6'3"	290	23		
Emanuel Weaver	NT	6'4"	260	22		
Wilson Whitley	NT	6'3"	265	27		

Use Name	Pos.	Hgt	Wgt	Age	Int	Pts
Glenn Cameron	LB	6'2"	228	29		
Tom Dinkel	LB	6'3"	237	26		
Guy Frazier	LB	6'2"	215	23		
Bo Harris	LB	6'3"	226	29	1	6
Jim LeClair	LB	6'2"	234	31	1	
Rick Razzano	LB	5'11"	227	26		
Jeff Schuh	LB	6'2"	228	24		
Ron Simpkins	LB	6'1"	235	24		
Reggie Williams	LB	6'1"	228	27	1	2
Louis Breeden	DB	5'11"	185	28	2	
Oliver Davis	DB	6'1"	205	28		
Mike Fuller	DB	5'9"	182	29	1	
Ray Griffin	DB	5'10"	186	26	1	
Bryan Hicks	DB	6'	192	25		
Robert Jackson	DB	5'10"	184	23		
Bobby Kemp	DB	6'	186	23	1	
Ken Riley	DB	6'	183	35	5	6
John Simmons	DB	5'11"	192	23		

Use Name	Pos.	Hgt	Wgt	Age	Int	Pts
Ken Anderson	QB	6'1"	212	33		24
Turk Schonert	QB	6'1"	185	25		
Jack Thompson	QB	6'3"	217	26		
Archie Griffin	HB	5'9"	184	28		6
Rodney Tate	HB	5'11"	190	23		
Charles Alexander	FB	6'1"	221	25		12
Pete Johnson	FB	6'	249	28		42
Cris Collinsworth	WR	6'5"	192	23		6
Isaac Curtis	WR	6'	192	31		6
Steve Kreider	WR	6'3"	192	24		7
David Verser	WR	6'1"	200	24		6
M.L.Harris	TE	6'5"	238	28		18
Rodney Holman	TE	6'3"	230	22		6
Dan Ross	TE	6'4"	235	25		18
Jim Breach	K	5'6"	161	26		67
Pat McInally	K	6'6"	212	29		

PITTSBURGH STEELERS 6-3-0 Chuck Noll

Scores of Each Game		
36	Dallas	28
26	CINCINNATI	*20
24	Houston	10
0	Seattle	16
35	KANSAS CITY	14
0	Buffalo	13
9	Cleveland	10
37	NEW ENGLAND	14
37	CLEVELAND	21

Use Name	Pos.	Hgt	Wgt	Age	Int	Pts
Larry Brown	OT	6'4"	270	33		
Tunch Ilkin	OT	6'3"	253	24		
Ted Petersen	OT	6'5"	256	27		
Ray Pinney	OT	6'4"	256	28		6
Steve Courson	OG	6'1"	260	26		
Tyrone McGriff	OG	6'	267	24		
Craig Wolfley	OG	6'1"	265	24		
Emil Boures	C-OG	6'1"	252	22		
Rick Donnalley	C-OG	6'2"	257	23		
Mike Webster	C	6'1"	255	30		
Tom Beasley	DE-NT	6'5"	248	28		
John Goodman	DE	6'6"	250	23		
Keith Willis	DE	6'1"	251	23		
Gary Dunn	NT	6'3"	260	29		
Edmund Nelson	NT-DE	6'3"	263	22		

Use Name	Pos.	Hgt	Wgt	Age	Int	Pts
Craig Bingham	LB	6'2"	211	22		
Robin Cole	LB	6'2"	220	26		
Jack Ham	LB	6'3"	220	33	1	
Bryan Hinkle	LB	6'1"	214	23		
Bob Kohrs	LB-DE	6'3"	245	23		
Jack Lambert	LB	6'4"	220	30	1	
David Little	LB	6'1"	220	23		
Mike Merriweather	LB	6'2"	215	21		
Guy Ruff	LB	6'1"	215	22		
Loren Toews	LB	6'3"	220	30	1	
Mel Blount	DB	6'3"	205	34	1	
Fred Bohannon	DB	6'	201	24		
Ernest French	DB	5'11"	195	22		
Ron Johnson	DB	5'10"	200	26	2	
Donnie Shell	DB	5'11"	190	30	5	
Anthony Washington	DB	6'1"	204	24		
Sam Washington	DB	5'8"	180	22		
Dwayne Woodruff	DB	5'11"	198	25	5	
Rick Woods	DB	6'	196	22	1	

Craig Colquitt - Achilles Tendon Injury

Use Name	Pos.	Hgt	Wgt	Age	Int	Pts
Terry Bradshaw	QB	6'3"	210	33		
Mark Malone	QB	6'4"	223	23		
Cliff Stoudt	QB	6'4"	218	27		
Walter Abercrombie	HB	5'11"	201	22		12
Greg Hawthorne	HB-WR	6'2"	225	25		18
Rick Moser (to TB)	HB	6'	210	25		
Frank Pollard	HB-FB	5'10"	210	25		12
Russell Davis	FB	6'1"	231	26		
Franco Harris	FB	6'2"	225	32		12
Sidney Thornton	FB	5'11"	230	27		6
Jim Smith	WR	6'2"	205	27		24
John Stallworth	WR	6'2"	191	30		42
Lynn Swann	WR	6'	180	30		
Calvin Sweeney	WR	6'2"	190	27		
Willie Sydnor	WR	5'11"	170	23		
Bennie Cunningham	TE	6'4"	260	27		12
John Rodgers	TE	6'2"	220	22		6
Frank Wilson	TE-FB	6'2"	233	23		
Gary Anderson	K	5'11"	156	23		52
John Goodson	K	6'3"	204	22		

CLEVELAND BROWNS 4-5-0 Sam Rutigliano

Scores of Each Game		
21	Seattle	7
21	PHILADELPHIA	24
10	NEW ENGLAND	7
14	Dallas	31
13	SAN DIEGO	30
10	Cincinnati	23
10	PITTSBURGH	9
20	Houston	14
21	Pittsburgh	37

Use Name	Pos.	Hgt	Wgt	Age	Int	Pts
Doug Dieken	OT	6'5"	252	33		
Andy Frederick	OT	6'6"	265	28		
Matt Miller	OT	6'6"	270	26		
Cody Risien	OT	6'7"	255	25		
Joe DeLamielleure	OG	6'3"	245	31		
Robert Jackson	OG	6'5"	260	29		
Mike Baab	C	6'4"	270	22		
Tom DeLeone	C	6'2"	248	32		
Keith Baldwin	DE	6'4"	245	21		
Elvis Franks	DE	6'4"	238	25		
Marshall Harris	DE	6'6"	261	26		
Mike Robinson	DE	6'5"	270	26		
Henry Bradley	NT	6'2"	260	28		
Mark Buben	NT	6'3"	260	25		
Bob Golic	NT	6'2"	248	24		

Use Name	Pos.	Hgt	Wgt	Age	Int	Pts
Dick Ambrose	LB	6'	228	29	1	
Chip Banks	LB	6'4"	233	22	1	
Tom Cousineau	LB	6'3"	225	25	1	
Bill Cowher	LB	6'3"	225	25		
Eddie Johnson	LB	6'1"	210	23		
Clay Matthews	LB	6'2"	230	26		
Scott Nicolas	LB	6'3"	226	22		
Kevin Turner	LB	6'2"	223	24		
Curtis Weathers	LB	6'5"	220	25		
Ron Bolton	DB	6'2"	170	32	1	
Larry Braziel	DB	6'	184	27		
Clinton Burrell	DB	6'2"	192	25	1	6
Hanford Dixon	DB	5'11"	182	23	4	
Judson Flint	DB	6'	201	25	1	
Bill Jackson	DB	6'1"	202	22		
Lawrence Johnson	DB	5'11"	204	24	4	
Mark Kafentzis	DB	5'10"	185	24		
Clarence Scott	DB	6'	190	33	3	

Use Name	Pos.	Hgt	Wgt	Age	Int	Pts
Paul McDonald	QB	6'2"	185	24		
Brian Sipe	QB	6'1"	195	33		
Rick Trocano	QB-DB	6'	188	23		
David Green	HB	5'10"	200	28		
Dino Hall	HB	5'7"	165	26		6
Dwight Walker	HB	5'10"	185	23		
Charles White	HB	5'10"	183	24		18
Johnny Davis	FB	6'1"	235	26		6
Cleo Miller	FB	5'11"	214	29		
Mike Pruitt	FB	6'	225	28		18
Willis Adams	WR	6'2"	194	26		
Ricky Feacher	WR	5'10"	174	28		18
Dan Fulton	WR	6'2"	186	25		
Dave Logan	WR	6'4"	216	28		12
Mike Whitwell	WR	6'	175	23		
Ozzie Newsome	TE	6'2"	232	26		18
McDonald Oden	TE	6'4"	245	25		
Matt Bahr	K	5'10"	165	26		38
Steve Cox	K	6'4"	195	24		

HOUSTON OILERS 1-8-0 Ed Biles

Scores of Each Game		
6	Cincinnati	27
23	SEATTLE	21
10	PITTSBURGH	24
21	New England	29
14	N.Y. Giants	17
7	DALLAS	35
14	Philadelphia	35
14	CLEVELAND	20
27	CINCINNATI	35

Use Name	Pos.	Hgt	Wgt	Age	Int	Pts
Mark Koncar	OT	6'5"	270	29		
John Schuhmacher	OT	6'3"	269	26		
Morris Towns	OT	6'4"	261	28		
Ralph Williams	OT	6'3"	276	24		
Ed Fisher	OG	6'3"	259	33		
Mike Munchak	OG	6'3"	263	22		
George Reihner	OG	6'4"	260	27		
David Carter	C	6'2"	262	29		
Greg Davidson	C	6'2"	254	24		
Jesse Baker	DE	6'5"	272	25		
Elvin Bethea	DE	6'3"	252	36		
Ken Kennard	DE	6'2"	258	27		
Malcolm Taylor	DE	6'6"	288	22		
Daryle Skaugstad	NT	6'5"	268	25		
Mike Stensrud	NT	6'5"	290	26		

Use Name	Pos.	Hgt	Wgt	Age	Int	Pts
Robert Abraham	LB	6'1"	217	22		
Gregg Bingham	LB	6'1"	225	31	1	
Robert Brazile	LB	6'4"	245	29	1	
John Corker	LB	6'5"	240	23		
Daryl Hunt	LB	6'3"	239	25		
Avon Riley	LB	6'3"	219	23		
Ted Thompson	LB	6'1"	229	29		
Ted Washington	LB	6'1"	248	34		
Carter Hartwig	DB	6'	205	26		
Bill Kay	DB	6'1"	190	22		
Vernon Perry	DB	6'2"	210	28	1	
Tate Randle	DB	6'	202	23		
Mike Reinfeldt	DB	6'2"	196	29		6
Greg Stemrick	DB	5'11"	185	30		
Willie Tullis	DB	6'	190	24		
J.C.Wilson	DB	6'	178	26		

Ken Burrough - Broken Ankle

Use Name	Pos.	Hgt	Wgt	Age	Int	Pts
Oliver Luck	QB	6'2"	198	22		
Archie Manning (from NO)	QB	6'3"	211	33		
Gifford Nielsen	QB	6'4"	210	27		
Gary Allen	HB	5'10"	183	22		6
Earl Campbell	HB-FB	5'11"	240	27		12
Adger Armstrong	FB	6'	225	25		
Donnie Craft	FB	6'	209	22		24
Stan Edwards	FB	6'	215	22		
Rich Thomaselli	FB	6'1"	196	25		
Harold Bailey	WR	6'2"	193	25		
Steve Bryant	WR	6'2"	194	22		
Mike Holston	WR	6'3"	192	24		6
Mike Renfro	WR	6'	184	27		18
Carl Roaches	WR	5'8"	170	28		
Tim Smith	WR	6'2"	202	25		
Walt Arnold	TE	6'3"	234	24		
Dave Casper	TE	6'4"	241	30		36
Tim Wilson	TE	6'3"	235	28		
John James (from DET)	K	6'3"	196	33		
Florian Kempf	K	5'9"	170	26		28
Cliff Parsley	K	6'1"	223	27		

* Overtime

CINCINNATI BENGALS

RUSHING

Last Name	No.	Yds	Avg	TD
Johnson	156	622	4.0	7
Alexander	64	207	3.2	1
Anderson	25	85	3.4	4
A. Griffin	12	39	3.3	1
Curtis	3	15	5.0	0
Tate	2	2	1.0	0
Verser	1	1	1.0	0
M.L. Harris	2	-3	-1.5	0
Schonert	3	-8	-2.7	0
Collinsworth	1	-11	-11.0	0

RECEIVING

Last Name	No.	Yds	Avg	TD
Collinsworth	49	700	14.3	1
Ross	47	508	10.8	3
Johnson	31	267	8.6	0
Curtis	23	320	13.9	1
A. Griffin	22	172	7.9	1
Kreider	16	230	14.4	1
Alexander	14	85	6.1	1
M.L. Harris	10	103	10.3	3
Verser	4	98	24.5	1
Holman	3	18	6.0	1

PUNT RETURNS

Last Name	No.	Yds	Avg	TD
Fuller	17	95	5.6	0

KICKOFF RETURNS

Last Name	No.	Yds	Avg	TD
Verser	16	320	20.0	0
Tate	14	314	22.4	0
Fuller	1	9	9.0	0

PASSING — PUNTING — KICKING

PASSING	Att	Comp	%	Yds	Yd/Att	TD	Int-	%	RK
Anderson	309	218	71	2495	8.07	12	9-	3	1
Schonert	1	1	100	6	6.00	0	0-	0	

PUNTING	No	Avg
McInally	31	38.7

KICKING	XP	Att	%	FG	Att	%
Breech	25	26	96	14	18	78
Kreider	1	1	100	0	0	0

PITTSBURGH STEELERS

RUSHING

Last Name	No.	Yds	Avg	TD
Harris	140	604	4.3	2
Pollard	62	238	3.8	2
Abercrombie	21	100	4.8	2
Davis	24	72	3.0	0
Hawthorne	15	68	4.5	0
Thornton	6	33	5.5	1
Stoudt	11	28	2.5	0
Swann	1	25	25.0	0
Bradshaw	8	10	1.3	0
Stallworth	1	9	9.0	0

RECEIVING

Last Name	No.	Yds	Avg	TD
Harris	31	249	8.0	0
Stallworth	27	441	16.3	7
Cunningham	21	277	13.2	2
Swann	18	265	14.7	0
Smith	17	387	22.8	4
Hawthorne	12	182	15.2	3
Pollard	6	39	6.5	0
Sweeney	5	50	10.0	0
Abercrombie	1	14	14.0	0
Davis	1	11	11.0	0
Thornton	1	4	4.0	0
Pinney	1	3	3.0	0

PUNT RETURNS

Last Name	No.	Yds	Avg	TD
Sydnor	22	172	7.8	0
Woods	13	142	10.9	0
Merriweather	1	3	3.0	0

KICKOFF RETURNS

Last Name	No.	Yds	Avg	TD
Bohannon	14	329	23.5	0
Abercrombie	7	139	19.9	0
French	2	38	19.0	0
Sydnor	2	37	18.5	0
Moser	1	18	18.0	0
Donnalley	1	8	8.0	0
Swann	1	0	0.0	0

PASSING — PUNTING — KICKING

PASSING	Att	Comp	%	Yds	Yd/Att	TD	Int-	%	RK
Bradshaw	240	127	53	1768	7.37	17	11-	5	5
Stoudt	35	14	40	154	4.40	0	5-	14	

PUNTING	No	Avg
Goodson	49	40.4

KICKING	XP	Att	%	FG	Att	%
Anderson	22	23	96	10	12	83

CLEVELAND BROWNS

RUSHING

Last Name	No.	Yds	Avg	TD
Pruitt	143	516	3.6	3
White	69	259	3.8	3
C. Miller	16	61	3.8	0
Sipe	13	44	3.4	0
Hall	2	14	7.0	0
Davis	4	3	0.8	1
Cox	2	-11	-5.5	0
McDonald	7	-13	-1.9	0

RECEIVING

Last Name	No.	Yds	Avg	TD
Newsome	49	633	12.9	3
White	34	283	8.3	0
Feacher	28	408	14.6	3
Logan	23	346	15.0	2
Pruitt	22	140	6.4	0
Walker	8	136	17.0	0
Hall	5	78	15.6	1
C. Miller	3	20	6.7	0
Fulton	1	9	9.0	0
Oden	1	4	4.0	0

PUNT RETURNS

Last Name	No.	Yds	Avg	TD
Walker	19	101	5.3	0
Hall	4	33	8.3	0

KICKOFF RETURNS

Last Name	No.	Yds	Avg	TD
Hall	22	430	19.5	0
Walker	13	295	22.7	0
Nicolas	2	16	8.0	0
Green	1	13	13.0	0

PASSING — PUNTING — KICKING

PASSING	Att	Comp	%	Yds	Yd/Att	TD	Int-	%	RK
Sipe	185	101	55	1064	5.75	4	8-	4	14
McDonald	149	73	49	993	6.66	5	8-	5	15

PUNTING	No	Avg
Cox	48	39.1

KICKING	XP	Att.	%	FG	Att	%
Bahr	17	17	100	7	15	47
Cox				0	1	0

HOUSTON OILERS

RUSHING

Last Name	No.	Yds	Avg	TD
Campbell	157	538	3.4	2
Manning	13	85	6.5	0
Edwards	15	58	3.9	0
Craft	18	42	2.3	3
Nielsen	9	37	4.1	0
Armstrong	8	15	1.9	0
Bailey	1	13	13.0	0
Casper	2	9	4.5	0
Allen	2	2	1.0	0

RECEIVING

Last Name	No.	Yds	Avg	TD
Casper	36	573	15.9	6
Bailey	26	367	14.1	0
Craft	23	230	10.0	1
Renfro	21	295	15.0	3
Campbell	18	130	7.2	0
Armstrong	12	75	6.3	0
Edwards	9	53	5.9	0
Holston	5	116	23.2	1
Allen	2	35	17.5	1
Thomaselli	1	8	8.0	0

PUNT RETURNS

Last Name	No.	Yds	Avg	TD
Roaches	19	104	5.5	0

KICKOFF RETURNS

Last Name	No.	Yds	Avg	TD
Roaches	21	441	21.0	0
Allen	15	292	19.5	0
Tullis	5	91	18.2	0
T. Wilson	2	40	20.0	0
Riley	1	27	27.0	0
Thomaselli	1	7	7.0	0
Smith	0	7	—	0

PASSING — PUNTING — KICKING

PASSING	Att	Cmp	%	Yds	Yd/Att	TD	Int-	%	RK
Manning	132	67	51	880	6.67	6	8-	6	13
Nielson	161	87	54	1005	6.24	6	8-	5	9
Campbell	1	0	0	0	0.00	0	1-	100	

PUNTING	No.	Avg.
James	43	40.5

KICKING	XP	Att	%	FG	Att	%
Kempf	16	18	89	4	6	67

LOS ANGELES RAIDERS 8-1-0 Tom Flores

Scores of Each Game		
23	San Francisco	17
38	Atlanta	14
28	SAN DIEGO	24
17	Cincinnati	31
28	SEATTLE	23
21	Kansas City	16
37	L.A.RAMS	31
27	DENVER	10
41	San Diego	34

Use Name	Pos.	Hgt	Wgt	Age	Int	Pts
Bruce Davis	OT	6'6"	280	26		
Henry Lawrence	OT	6'4"	270	30		
Ed Muransky	OT	6'7"	280	22		
Art Shell	OT	6'5"	285	35		
Curt Marsh	OG	6'5"	270	23		
Mickey Marvin	OG	6'4"	270	26		
Randy Van Divier	OG	6'5"	265	24		
Dave Dalby	C	6'2"	250	31		
Jim Romano	C	6'3"	260	22		
Steve Sylvester	C-OG	6'4"	260	29		
Lyle Alzado	DE	6'3"	250	33		
Dave Browning	DE	6'5"	245	26		
Howie Long	DE	6'5"	265	22		
Reggie Kinlaw	NT	6'2"	245	25		
Archie Reese	NT	6'3"	275	26		6
Johnny Robinson	NT	6'2"	260	23		
Ruben Vaughn	NT	6'2"	260	26		

Use Name	Pos.	Hgt	Wgt	Age	Int	Pts
Jeff Barnes	LB	6'2"	225	27		
Mike Hawkins	LB	6'2"	245	26		
Ted Hendricks	LB	6'7"	230	34		
Rod Martin	LB	6'2"	215	28	3	6
Matt Millen	LB	6'2"	255	24	3	
Bob Nelson	LB	6'4"	235	29		
Cal Peterson	LB	6'3"	225	29		
Jack Squirek	LB	6'4"	225	23		
James Davis	DB	6'	190	25	2	6
Mike Davis	DB	6'3"	205	26	1	6
Lester Hayes	DB	6'	200	27	2	
Kenny Hill	DB	6'	195	24		
Monte Jackson	DB	5'11"	195	29	1	
Vann McElroy	DB	6'2"	190	22	1	
Odis McKinney	DB	6'2"	190	25		
Burgess Owens	DB	6'2"	200	31	4	
Ted Watts	DB	6'	190	24	1	

Willie Jones - Knee Injury
John Matuszek - Injured Reserve
Gene Upshaw - Injured Reserve

Use Name	Pos.	Hgt	Wgt	Age	Int	Pts
Jim Plunkett	QB	6'3"	215	34		
Marc Wilson	QB	6'6"	205	25		
MarcusAllen	HB	6'2"	205	22		84
Rick Berns	HB	6'2"	205	26		
Kenny King	HB-FB	5'11"	205	25		12
Cle Montgomery	HB	5'8"	185	26		
Greg Pruitt	HB	5'10"	190	31		6
Chester Willis	HB	5'11"	195	24		
Frank Hawkins	FB	5'9"	210	23		18
Derrick Jensen	FB	6'1"	220	26		
Malcolm Barnwell	WR	5'11"	185	24		
Cliff Branch	WR	5'11"	170	34		24
Bob Chandler	WR	6'	180	33		
Calvin Muhammad	WR	6'	190	23		6
Todd Christensen	TE	6'3"	230	26		24
Derrick Ramsey	TE	6'5"	235	25		
Chris Bahr	K	5'10"	175	29		62
Ray Guy	K	6'3"	195	32		

SAN DIEGO CHARGERS 6-3-0 Don Coryell

Scores of Each Game		
23	Denver	3
12	Kansas City	19
24	L.A.Raiders	28
30	DENVER	20
30	Cleveland	13
41	San Francisco	37
50	CINCINNATI	34
44	BALTIMORE	26
34	L.A.RAIDERS	41

Use Name	Pos.	Hgt	Wgt	Age	Int	Pts
Sam Claphan	OT	6'6"	267	25		
Andrew Gissinger	OT	6'5"	279	23		
Billy Shields	OT	6'7"	284	29		
Russ Washington	OT	6'7"	295	35		
Chuck Loewen	OG-OT	6'3"	264	25		
Ed White	OG	6'2"	279	35		
Doug Wilkerson	OG	6'2"	258	35		
Don Macek	C-OG	6'3"	260	28		
Dennis McKnight	C-OG	6'3"	253	22		
Bob Rush	C-OT	6'5"	270	27		
Keith Ferguson	DE	6'5"	241	23		
Leroy Jones	DE	6'8"	270	31		
John Woodcock	DE	6'3"	257	28		
Richard Ackerman	DT	6'4"	254	23		
Gary Johnson	DT	6'2"	251	29		2
Louie Kelcher	DT	6'5"	310	29		
Wilbur Young	DT	6'6"	285	33		

Use Name	Pos.	Hgt	Wgt	Age	Int	Pts
Carlos Bradley	LB	6'	226	22		
Linden King	LB	6'4"	245	27		
Dave Lewis	LB	6'4"	245	27		
Woodrow Lowe	LB	6'	226	28	1	
Ray Preston	LB	6'	220	28		
Dewey Selmon	LB	6'1"	240	28		
Cliff Thrift	LB	6'2"	230	26	2	
Jeff Allen	DB	5'11"	194	24	1	
Willie Buchanon	DB	6'	185	31		
Donald Dykes	DB	5'11"	185	27		
Tim Fox	DB	5'11"	186	28	4	
Bob Gregor	DB	6'2"	190	25	1	
Bruce Laird	DB	6'	195	32		
Miles McPherson	DB	5'11"	175	22		
Mike Williams	DB	5'10"	186	28	2	
Andre Young	DB	6'	203	21	2	

Use Name	Pos.	Hgt	Wgt	Age	Int	Pts
Dan Fouts	QB	6'3"	205	31		6
Ed Luther	QB	6'3"	202	25		
James Brooks	HB	5'9"	177	23		36
Jim Jodat	HB	5'11"	208	28		
Chuck Muncie	HB	6'3"	228	29		54
Hank Bauer	FB-HB	5'10"	200	28		
Ricky Bell	FB	6'2"	216	27		
John Cappelletti	FB	6'1"	215	30		
Wes Chandler	WR	6'	183	26		54
Bobby Duckworth	WR	6'3"	197	23		
Scott Fitzkee	WR	6'	187	25		6
Charlie Joiner	WR	5'11"	180	34		
Dwight Scales	WR	6'2"	182	29		6
Pete Holohan	TE	6'4"	240	23		
Eric Sievers	TE	6'4"	235	23		6
Kellen Winslow	TE	6'5"	251	24		36
Rolf Benirschke	K	6'1"	179	27		80
Maury Buford	K	6'	185	22		

SEATTLE SEAHAWKS 4-5-0 Jack Patera, Mike McCormack

Scores of Each Game		
7	CLEVELAND	21
21	Houston	23
17	Denver	10
16	PITTSBURGH	0
23	L.A.Raiders	28
20	CHICAGO	14
0	NEW ENGLAND	16
10	Cincinnati	24
13	DENVER	11

Use Name	Pos.	Hgt	Wgt	Age	Int	Pts
Steve August	OT	6'5"	254	27		
Dennis Boyd	OT	6'6"	255	26		
Jack Campbell	OT	6'5"	277	23		
Ron Essink	OT	6'6"	254	24		
Edwin Bailey	OG-OT	6'4"	265	23		
Bill Dugan	OG	6'4"	271	23		
Robert Pratt	OG	6'4"	250	31		
Kani Kauahi	C-OG	6'2"	260	22		
Art Kuehn	C	6'3"	255	29		
John Yarno	C	6'5"	251	27		
Fred Anderson	DE	6'4"	245	27		
Mark Bell	DE	6'4"	240	25		
Jeff Bryant	DE	6'5"	260	22		
David Graham	DE	6'6"	250	23		
Jacob Green	DE	6'3"	247	25		
Robert Hardy	DT	6'2"	250	26		
Joe Nash	DT	6'2"	250	21		
Manu Tulasosopo	DT	6'3"	252	25		
Mike White	DT	6'5"	266	25		

Use Name	Pos.	Hgt	Wgt	Age	Int	Pts
Keith Butler	LB	6'4"	225	26		
Brian Flones	LB	6'1"	228	23		
Micheal Jackson	LB	6'1"	220	25	2	
Shelton Robinson	LB	6'2"	233	21		
Bruce Scholtz	LB	6'6"	240	23	1	6
Rodell Thomas	LB	6'2"	225	24		
Eugene Williams	LB	6'1"	220	22		
Dave Brown	DB	6'1"	190	29	1	
Don Dufek	DB	6'	195	28	1	
Kenny Easley	DB	6'3"	206	23	4	
John Harris	DB	6'2"	200	26	4	
Greggory Johnson	DB	6'1"	188	23		
Kerry Justin	DB	5'11"	175	27		
Ken McAlister	DB	6'5"	210	22		
Keith Simpson	DB	6'1"	195	26		

Greg Gaines - Knee Injury
Joe Norman - Knee Injury

Use Name	Pos.	Hgt	Wgt	Age	Int	Pts
Sam Adkins	QB	6'2"	214	27		
Dave Krieg	QB	6'1"	185	23		
Jim Zorn	QB	6'2"	200	29		6
Theotis Brown	HB-FB	6'2"	225	25		12
Horace Ivory	HB	6'	198	28		6
Eric Lane	HB	6'	195	23		
Sherman Smith	HB	6'4"	225	27		
Dan Doornink	FB	6'3"	210	26		
David Hughes	FB	6'	220	23		6
Roger Carr	WR	6'3"	195	30		12
Paul Johns	WR	5'11"	170	23		6
Steve Largent	WR	5'11"	184	27		18
Byron Walker	WR	6'4"	190	22		12
Pete Metzelaars	TE	6'7"	240	22		
John Sawyer	TE	6'2"	230	29		
Mike Tice	TE	6'7"	250	23		
Norm Johnson	K	6'2"	193	22		43
Jeff West	K	6'3"	220	29		

KANSAS CITY CHIEFS 3-6-0 Marv Levy

Scores of Each Game		
9	Buffalo	14
19	SAN DIEGO	12
17	New Orleans	27
14	L.A.Rams	20
14	Pittsburgh	35
16	L.A.RAIDERS	21
37	Denver	16
13	SAN FRANCISCO	26
37	N.Y.JETS	13

Use Name	Pos.	Hgt	Wgt	Age	Int	Pts
Charlie Getty	OT	6'4"	270	30		
Matt Herkenhoff	OT	6'4"	272	31		
Jim Rourke	OT-OG	6'5"	263	25		
Brad Budde	OG	6'4"	260	24		
Tom Condon	OG	6'3"	275	29		
Bob Simmons	OG	6'4"	255	28		
Al Steinfeld	C-OT	6'4"	256	23		
Jack Rudnay	C	6'3"	242	34		
Les Studdard	C	6'4"	260	23		
Mike Bell	DE	6'4"	260	25		
Dave Lindstrom	DE	6'6"	255	27		
Art Still	DE	6'7"	252	26		
Bill Acker	NT-DE	6'3"	255	25		
Dino Mangiero	NT-DE	6'2"	264	23		
Don Parrish	NT-DE	6'2"	255	27		
Ken Kremer	NT	6'4"	252	25		

Use Name	Pos.	Hgt	Wgt	Age	Int	Pts
Jerry Bianton	LB	6'1"	236	26		
Calvin Daniels	LB	6'3"	236	23		
Louis Haynes	LB	6'	227	22		
Tom Howard	LB	6'2"	215	28	2	
Charles Jackson	LB	6'2"	222	27		
Dave Klug	LB	6'4"	230	24		6
John Olenchalk	LB-C	6'	225	26		
Gary Spani	LB	6'2"	228	26		
Gary Barbaro	DB	6'4"	210	28	3	6
Trent Bryant	DB	5'10"	178	25		
Lloyd Burruss	DB	6'	202	24	1	
Deron Cherry	DB	5'11"	190	22		
Herb Christopher	DB	5'10"	198	28		
Gary Green	DB	5'11"	191	26	2	6
Eric Harris	DB	6'3"	202	27	3	6
Durwood Roquemore	DB	6'1"	180	22	1	

Use Name	Pos.	Hgt	Wgt	Age	Int	Pts
Steve Fuller	QB	6'4"	198	25		
Bob Gagliano	QB	6'3"	195	23		
Bill Kennedy	QB	6'4"	211	27		
Curtis Bledsoe	HB-FB	5'11"	215	25		
Joe Delaney	HB	5'10"	184	23		
Del Thompson	HB	6'	203	24		
Clark Gaines	FB	6'1"	214	28		
James Hadnot	FB	6'2"	245	25		
Billy Jackson	FB-HB	5'10"	215	22		18
Carlos Carson	WR	5'10"	174	23		12
Anthony Hancock	WR	6'	187	22		6
Henry Marshall	WR	6'2"	220	28		18
Stan Rome	WR	6'5"	218	26		
J.T. Smith	WR	6'2"	185	26		6
Ed Beckman	TE	6'4"	239	27		
Al Dixon	TE	6'5"	238	28		12
Willie Scott	TE	6'4"	245	23		6
Case deBruijn	K	6'1"	176	22		
Jeff Gossett	K	6'2"	197	25		
Nick Lowery	K	6'4"	189	26		74

DENVER BRONCOS 2-7-0 Dan Reeves

Scores of Each Game		
3	SAN DIEGO	23
24	SAN FRANCISCO	21
10	SEATTLE	17
20	San Diego	30
27	ATLANTA	34
27	L.A.Rams	24
16	KANSAS CITY	37
10	L.A.Raiders	27
11	Seattle	13

Use Name	Pos.	Hgt	Wgt	Age	Int	Pts
Brian Clark	OT	6'6"	260	21		
Ken Lanier	OT	6'3"	269	23		
Claudie Minor	OT	6'4"	278	31		
Dave Studdard	OT	6'4"	260	26		
Keith Uecker	OT	6'5"	260	22		
Tom Glassic	OG	6'3"	260	28		
Paul Howard	OG	6'3"	260	31		
Keith Bishop	C-OG	6'3"	260	25		
Bill Bryan	C	6'2"	258	27		
Greg Boyd	DE	6'6"	280	29		2
Barney Chavous	DE	6'3"	258	31		2
Rulon Jones	DE	6'6"	260	24		
Brison Manor	DE	6'4"	248	30		
Rubin Carter	NT	6'	256	29		
Don Latimer	NT	6'3"	253	27		

Use Name	Pos.	Hgt	Wgt	Age	Int	Pts
Steve Busick	LB	6'4"	227	23		
Darren Comeaux	LB	6'1"	227	22		
Rick Dennison	LB	6'2"	215	24		
Larry Evans	LB	6'2"	220	29		
Randy Gradishar	LB	6'3"	231	30		
Tom Jackson	LB	5'11"	220	31	1	
Jim Ryan	LB	6'1"	215	25		
Bob Swenson	LB	6'3"	225	29		
Ken Woodard	LB	6'1"	218	22		
Steve Foley	DB	6'2"	190	28		
Mike Harden	DB	6'1"	192	24	2	
Roger Jackson	DB	6'	186	23		
Aaron Kyle	DB	5'11"	185	28	2	
Dennis Smith	DB	6'3"	200	23	1	
J.T.Thomas	DB	6'2"	196	31	1	
Steve Trimble	DB	5'10"	181	24		
Steve Wilson	DB	5'10"	195	25	2	
Louis Wright	DB	6'2"	200	29	2	

Use Name	Pos.	Hgt	Wgt	Age	Int	Pts
Steve DeBerg	QB	6'2"	205	28		6
Mark Herrmann	QB	6'4"	195	23		6
Craig Morton	QB	6'4"	211	39		
Dave Preston	HB	5'10"	195	27		
Gerald Willhite	HB	5'10"	200	23		12
Sammy Winder	HB	5'11"	203	23		6
Rob Lytle	FB	6'1"	195	27		
Rick Parros	FB	5'11"	200	24		18
Nathan Poole	FB	5'9"	212	25		
Wade Manning	WR	5'11"	190	27		
Orlando McDaniel	WR	6'	180	21		
Rick Upchurch	WR	5'10"	180	30		30
Steve Watson	WR	6'4"	195	25		12
Ron Egloff	TE	6'5"	227	26		
Riley Odoms	TE	6'4"	235	32		
James Wright	TE	6'3"	240	26		6
Rich Karlis	K	6'	180	23		48
Luke Prestridge	K	6'4"	235	25		

LOS ANGELES RAIDERS

RUSHING

Last Name	No.	Yds	Avg	TD
Allen	160	697	4.4	11
King	69	264	3.8	2
Hawkins	27	54	2.0	2
Pruitt	4	22	5.5	0
Barnwell	2	18	9.0	0
Willis	6	15	2.5	0
Branch	2	10	5.0	0
Plunkett	15	6	0.4	0
Taylor	4	3	0.8	0
Guy	2	-3	-1.5	0
Christensen	1	-6	-6.0	0

RECEIVING

Last Name	No.	Yds	Avg	TD
Christensen	42	510	12.1	4
Allen	38	401	10.6	3
Branch	30	575	19.2	4
Barnwell	23	387	16.8	0
King	9	57	6.3	0
Hawkins	7	35	5.0	1
Muhammad	3	92	30.7	1
Pruitt	2	29	14.5	1

PUNT RETURNS

Last Name	No.	Yds	Avg	TD
Pruitt	27	209	7.7	0

KICKOFF RETURNS

Last Name	No.	Yds	Avg	TD
Pruitt	14	371	26.5	0
Montgomery	17	312	18.4	0
Hill	2	20	10.0	0
Jensen	1	27	27.0	0
Millen	1	13	13.0	0
Willis	1	11	11.0	0

PASSING — PUNTING — KICKING

PASSING	Att	Comp	%	Yds	Yd/Att	TD	Int-	%	RK
Plunkett	261	152	58	2035	7.80	14	15-	6	6
Allen	4	1	25	47	11.75	0	0-	0	
Wilson	2	1	50	4	2.00	0	0-	0	

PUNTING	No	Avg
Guy	47	39.1

KICKING	XP	Att	%	FG	Att	%
Bahr	32	33	97	10	16	63

SAN DIEGO CHARGERS

RUSHING

Last Name	No.	Yds	Avg	TD
Muncie	138	569	4.1	8
Brooks	87	430	4.9	6
Cappelletti	22	82	3.7	0
Chandler	5	32	6.4	0
Fouts	9	8	0.9	1
Jodat	3	7	2.3	0
Bell	2	6	3.0	0
Luther	1	-13	-13.0	0

RECEIVING

Last Name	No.	Yds	Avg	TD
Winslow	54	721	13.4	6
Chandler	49	1032	21.1	9
Joiner	36	545	15.1	0
Muncie	25	207	8.3	1
Brooks	13	66	5.1	0
Sievers	12	173	14.4	1
Cappelletti	7	48	6.9	0
Scales	6	105	17.5	1
Fitzkee	3	47	15.7	1
Duckworth	2	77	38.5	0
Jodat	1	0	0.0	0

PUNT RETURNS

Last Name	No.	Yds	Avg	TD
Brooks	12	138	11.5	0
Chandler	0	0	0.0	0

KICKOFF RETURNS

Last Name	No.	Yds	Avg	TD
Brooks	33	749	22.7	0
A. Young	4	45	11.3	0
Jodat	3	45	15.0	0
Bauer	2	24	12.0	0
Sievers	1	17	17.0	0
Bell	1	10	10.0	0
Gissinger	1	0	0.0	0

PASSING — PUNTING — KICKING

PASSING	Att	Comp	%	Yds	Yd/Att	TD	Int-	%	RK
Fouts	330	204	62	2883	8.74	17	11-	3	2
Luther	4	2	50	55	13.75	0	1-	25	
Muncie	3	2	67	83	27.67	2	0-	0	
Winslow	1	0	0	0	0.00	0	0-	0	

PUNTING	No	Avg
Buford	21	41.3

KICKING	XP	Att	%	FG	Att	%
Benirschke	32	34	94	16	22	73

SEATTLE SEAHAWKS

RUSHING

Last Name	No.	Yds	Avg	TD
Smith	63	202	3.2	0
Doornink	45	178	4.0	0
T. Brown	53	141	2.7	2
Zorn	15	113	7.5	1
Hughes	30	106	3.5	0
Ivory	13	51	3.9	1
Largent	1	8	8.0	0
Johns	1	-1	-1.0	0
Krieg	6	-3	-0.5	0

RECEIVING

Last Name	No.	Yds	Avg	TD
Largent	34	493	14.5	3
Doornink	22	176	8.0	0
Smith	19	196	10.3	0
Carr	15	265	17.7	2
Johns	15	234	15.6	1
Metzelaars	15	152	10.1	0
T. Brown	12	95	7.9	0
Hughes	11	98	8.9	1
Walker	10	156	15.6	2
Tice	9	46	5.1	0
Sawyer	8	92	11.5	0
Ivory	5	38	7.6	0
Zorn	1	27	27.0	0

PUNT RETURNS

Last Name	No.	Yds	Avg	TD
Johns	19	210	11.1	0
Easley	1	15	15.0	0
G. Johnson	1	3	3.0	0

KICKOFF RETURNS

Last Name	No.	Yds	Avg	TD
Lane	11	172	15.6	0
Ivory	10	224	22.4	0
McAlister	2	41	20.5	0
T. Brown	2	33	16.5	0
Johns	3	57	19.0	0
Hughes	1	17	17.0	0

PASSING — PUNTING — KICKING

PASSING	Att	Comp	%	Yds	Yd/Att	TD	Int-	%	RK
Zorn	245	126	51	1540	6.29	7	11-	5	12
Krieg	78	49	63	501	6.42	2	2-	3	
N. Johnson	1	1	100	27	27.00	0	0-	0	
Smith	1	0	0	0	0.00	0	0-	0	
Lane	1	0	0	0	0.00	0	0-	0	

PUNTING	No	Avg
West	48	38.2
Doornink	1	54.0

KICKING	XP	Att	%	FG	Att	%
N. Johnson	13	14	93	10	14	71

KANSAS CITY CHIEFS

RUSHING

Last Name	No.	Yds	Avg	TD
Delaney	95	380	4.0	0
B. Jackson	86	243	2.8	3
Hadnot	46	172	3.7	0
Fuller	10	56	5.6	0
Kenney	13	40	3.1	0
Marshall	3	25	8.3	0
Bledsoe	10	20	2.0	0
Thompson	4	7	1.8	0
Gaines	1	0	0.0	0
Studdard	1	0	0.0	0

RECEIVING

Last Name	No.	Yds	Avg	TD
Marshall	40	549	13.7	3
Carson	27	494	18.3	2
Dixon	18	251	13.9	2
Hadnot	14	96	6.9	0
Delaney	11	53	4.8	0
Smith	10	168	16.8	1
Scott	8	49	6.1	1
Hancock	7	116	16.6	1
B. Jackson	5	41	8.2	0
Rome	2	25	12.5	0
Gaines	2	17	8.5	0
Bledsoe	1	5	5.0	0

PUNT RETURNS

Last Name	No.	Yds	Avg	TD
Hancock	12	103	8.6	0
Smith	3	26	8.7	0

KICKOFF RETURNS

Last Name	No.	Yds	Avg	TD
Hancock	27	609	22.6	0
Thompson	2	41	20.5	0
Roquemore	2	25	12.5	0
Cherry	1	39	39.0	0
Mangiero	1	8	8.0	0
Lindstrom	1	1	1.0	0

PASSING — PUNTING — KICKING

PASSING	Att	Comp	%	Yds	Yd/Att	TD	Int-	%	RK
Kenney	169	95	56	1192	7.05	7	6-	4	7
Fuller	93	49	53	665	7.15	3	2-	2	
Gagliano	1	1	100	7	7.00	0	0-	0	
Marshall	1	0	0	0	0.00	0	0-	0	

PUNTING	No	Avg
Gossett	33	41.4
deBruijn	5	34.8

KICKING	XP	Att	%	FG	Att	%
Lowery	17	17	100	19	24	79

DENVER BRONCOS

RUSHING

Last Name	No.	Yds	Avg	TD
Willhite	70	347	5.0	2
Parros	77	277	3.6	1
Winder	67	259	3.9	1
Preston	19	81	4.3	0
Poole	7	36	5.1	0
DeBerg	8	27	3.4	1
Herrmann	3	7	2.3	1
Lytle	2	2	1.0	0
Watson	1	-4	-4.0	0
Wright	1	-4	-4.0	0
Upchurch	2	-10	-5.0	0

RECEIVING

Last Name	No.	Yds	Avg	TD
Parros	37	259	7.0	2
Watson	36	555	15.4	2
Upchurch	26	407	15.7	3
Willhite	26	227	8.7	0
Preston	14	134	9.6	0
Winder	11	83	7.5	0
Egloff	10	96	9.6	0
Wright	9	120	13.3	1
Odoms	8	82	10.3	0
Manning	3	46	15.3	0
Lytle	1	10	10.0	0

PUNT RETURNS

Last Name	No.	Yds	Avg	TD
Upchurch	15	242	16.1	2
Willhite	6	63	10.5	0

KICKOFF RETURNS

Last Name	No.	Yds	Avg	TD
Willhite	17	337	19.8	0
Manning	15	346	23.1	0
Wilson	6	123	20.5	0
Uecker	1	12	12.0	0
Poole	1	0	0.0	0

PASSING — PUNTING — KICKING

PASSING	Att	Comp	%	Yds	Yd/Att	TD	Int-	%	RK
DeBerg	223	131	59	1405	6.30	7	11-	5	8
Herrmann	60	32	53	421	7.02	1	4-	7	
Morton	26	18	69	193	7.42	0	3-	11	
Upchurch	0	0	0	0	0.00	0	0-	0	
Willhite	2	0	0	0	0.00	0	1-	50	

PUNTING	No	Avg
Prestridge	45	45.0

KICKING	XP	Att	%	FG	Att	%
Karlis	15	16	94	11	13	85

1982 N.F.C. PLAYOFFS

January 8, 1983 at Washington (Attendance 55,045)

SCORING

DETROIT	0	0	7	0- 7
WASHINGTON	10	14	7	0- 31

First Quarter

Was.	White, 77 yard interception return PAT—Moseley (kick)
Was.	Moseley, 26 yard field goal

Second Quarter

Was.	Garrett, 21 yard pass from Theismann PAT—Moseley (kick)
Was.	Garrett, 21 yard pass from Theismann PAT— Moseley (kick)

Third Quarter

Was.	Garrett, 27 yard pass from Theismann PAT—Moseley (kick)
Det.	Hill, 15 yard pass from Hipple PAT—Murray (kick)

TEAM STATISTICS

DET.		WAS.
20	First Downs- Total	18
6	First Down- Rushing	10
12	First Downs- Passing	8
2	First Downs- Penalty	0
3	Fumbles- Number	0
3	Fumbles- Lost Ball	0
5	Penalties- Number	4
29	Yards Penalized	20
1	Missed Field Goals	1
63	Offensive Plays	59
364	Net Yards	366
5.8	Average Gain	6.2
5	Giveaways	0
0	Takeaways	5
-5	Difference	+5

INDIVIDUAL STATISTICS

RUSHING

DETROIT	No.	Yds.	Avg.	WASHINGTON	No.	Yds.	Avg.
Hipple	6	47	7.8	Riggins	25	119	4.8
Bussey	5	19	3.8	Jackson	8	27	3.4
Sims	6	19	3.2	Walker	2	14	7.0
King	4	10	2.5	Washington	1	9	9.0
	21	95	4.5	Theismann	2	6	3.0
					38	175	4.6

RECEIVING

DETROIT	No.	Yds.	Avg.	WASHINGTON	No.	Yds.	Avg.
Thompson	7	150	21.4	Garrett	6	110	18.3
Sims	6	68	11.3	Brown	3	69	23.0
Porter	2	31	15.5	Walker	4	16	4.0
Hill	3	29	9.7	Washington	1	15	15.0
Scott	1	14	14.0		14	210	15.0
King	2	8	4.0				
Bussey	1	-2	-2.0				
	22	298	13.5				

PUNTING

Skladany	3		38.3	Hayes	4		31.3

PUNT RETURNS

Martin	2	13	6.5	Nelms	3	60	20.0

KICKOFF RETURNS

Hall	6	123	20.5	Nelms	2	37	18.5

INTERCEPTION RETURNS

none				White	2	77	38.5

PASSING

	Att.	Comp.	Comp. Pct.	Yds.	Int.	Yds./ Att.	Yds./ Comp.
DETROIT							
Hipple	38	22	57.9	298	2	7.8	13.5
WASHINGTON							
Theismann	19	14	73.7	210	0	11.1	15.0

January 8, 1983 at Green Bay, Wis. (Attendance 54,282)

SCORING

ST. LOUIS	3	6	0	7- 16
GREEN BAY	7	21	10	3- 41

First Quarter

St.L.	O'Donoghue, 18 yard field goal
G.B.	Jefferson, 60 yard pass from Dickey PAT—Stenerud (kick)

Second Quarter

G.B.	Lofton, 20 yard pass from Dickey PAT—Stenerud (kick)
G.B.	Ivery, 2 yard rush PAT—Stenerud (kick)
G.B.	Ivery, 4 yard pass from Dickey PAT—Stenerud (kick)
St.L.	Tilley, 5 yard pass from Lomax PAT—kick failed

Third Quarter

G.B.	Stenerud, 46 yard field goal
G.B.	Jefferson, 7 yard pass from Dickey PAT—Stenerud (kick)

Fourth Quarter

G.B.	Stenerud, 34 yard field goal
St.L.	Shumann, 18 yard pass from Lomax PAT—O'Donoghue (kick)

TEAM STATISTICS

ST.L.		G.B.
27	First Downs- Total	22
8	First Down- Rushing	7
18	First Downs- Passing	13
1	First Downs- Penalty	2
3	Fumbles- Number	1
2	Fumbles- Lost Ball	1
6	Penalties- Nuamber	5
78	Yards Penalized	35
3	Missed Field Goals	0
79	Offensive Plays	57
453	Net Yards	394
5.7	Average Gain	6.9
4	Giveaways	1
1	Takeaways	4
-3	Difference	+3

INDIVIDUAL STATISTICS

RUSHING

ST. LOUIS	No.	Yds.	Avg.	GREEN BAY	No.	Yds.	Avg.
Anderson	8	58	7.3	Ivery	13	67	5.2
Mitchell	7	21	3.0	Ellis	5	27	5.4
Morris	3	14	4.7	Rodgers	6	18	3.0
Lomax	4	9	2.3	Jensen	3	10	3.3
Green	1	4	4.0	Dickey	1	0	0.0
	23	106	4.6	Huckleby	2	-1	-1.0
				Lofton	1	-13	-13.0
					31	108	3.5

RECEIVING

ST. LOUIS	No.	Yds.	Avg.	GREEN BAY	No.	Yds.	Avg.
Green	9	113	12.6	Jefferson	6	148	24.7
Shumann	4	59	14.8	Lofton	3	52	17.3
Mitchell	4	57	14.3	Coffman	4	39	9.8
Tilley	5	55	11.0	Ellis	3	29	9.7
Thompson	3	41	13.7	Rodgers	1	10	10.0
Morris	3	32	10.7	Ivery	1	4	4.0
Marsh	2	18	9.0	Jensen	1	4	4.0
Harrell	2	10	5.0		19	286	15.1
	32	385	12.0				

PUNTING

none				Stachowicz	1		28.0

PUNT RETURNS

none				none			

KICKOFF RETURNS

Mitchell	3	105	35.0	Rodgers	2	47	23.5
Harrell	3	53	17.7	Coffman	1	12	12.0
Love	1	20	20.0		3	59	19.7
	7	178	25.4				

INTERCEPTION RETURNS

none				Murphy	1	22	22.0
				Hood	1	0	0.0
					2	22	11.0

PASSING

	Att.	Comp.	Comp. Pct.	Yds.	Int.	Yds./ Att.	Yds./ Comp.
ST. LOUIS							
Lomax	51	32	62.7	385	2	7.5	12.0
GREEN BAY							
Dickey	23	17	73.9	260	0	11.3	15.3

January 9, 1983 at Irving, Tex. (Attendance 65,042)

SCORING

TAMPA BAY	0	10	7	0- 17
DALLAS	6	7	3	14- 30

First Quarter

Dal.	Septien, 33 yard field goal
Dal.	Septien, 33 yard field goal

Second Quarter

T.B.	Green, 60 yard fumble recovery return PAT—Capece (kick)
T.B.	Capece, 32 yard field goal
Dal.	Springs, 6 yard pass from D. White PAT—Septien (kick)

Third Quarter

Dal.	Septien, 19 yard field goal
T.B.	Jones, 49 yard pass from Williams PAT—Capece (kick)

Fourth Quarter

Dal.	Hunter, 19 yard interception return PAT—Septien(kick)
Dal.	Newsome, 10 yard pass from D. White PAT—Septien (kick)

TEAM STATISTICS

T.B.		DAL.
8	First Downs- Total	29
3	First Downs- Rushing	9
4	First Downs- Passing	19
1	First Downs- Penalty	1
0	Fumbles- Number	1
0	Fumbles- Lost Ball	1
4	Penalties- Number	6
41	Yards Penalized	45
0	Missed Field Goals	0
49	Offensive Plays	92
218	Net Yards	456
4.4	Average Gain	5.0
3	Giveaways	3
3	Takeaways	3
0	Difference	0

INDIVIDUAL STATISTICS

RUSHING

TAMPA BAY	No.	Yds.	Avg.	DALLAS	No.	Yds.	Avg.
Wilder	14	93	6.6	Dorsett	26	110	4.2
Carver	7	12	1.7	Donley	1	25	25.0
	21	105	5.0	Springs	7	24	3.4
				Newhouse	5	15	3.0
				Pearson	1	4	4.0
				DuPree	1	1	1.0
				D. White	1	0	0.0
					42	179	4.3

RECEIVING

TAMPA BAY	No.	Yds.	Avg.	DALLAS	No.	Yds.	Avg.
House	4	52	13.0	Pearson	7	95	13.6
Jones	1	49	49.0	Johnson	4	76	19.0
Giles	1	7	7.0	T. Hill	4	45	11.3
Wilder	2	5	2.5	Cosbie	3	32	10.7
	8	113	14.1	Springs	3	16	5.3
				Dorsett	2	14	7.0
				Newsome	2	14	7.0
				Newhouse	1	11	11.0
				DuPree	1	9	9.0
					27	312	11.6

PUNTING

Swider	6		43.5	D. White	3		37.3

PUNT RETURNS

T. Bell	1	8	8.0	Fellows	5	57	11.4

KICKOFF RETURNS

Owens	5	110	22.0	Fellows	4	71	17.8

INTERCEPTION RETURNS

Cotney	1	50	50.0	Hunter	1	19	19.0
Holt	1	0	0.0	Clinkscale	1	11	11.0
	2	50	25.0	Thurman	1	0	0.0
					3	30	10.0

PASSING

	Att.	Comp.	Comp. Pct.	Yds.	Int.	Yds./ Att.	Yds./ Comp.
TAMPA BAY							
Williams	28	8	28.6	113	3	4.0	14.1
DALLAS							
D. White	45	27	60.0	312	2	6.9	11.6

1982 N.F.C. PLAYOFFS

January 9, 1983 at Minneapolis (Attendance 60,560)

SCORING

ATLANTA	7	0	14	3	24
MINNESOTA	3	10	3	14	30

First Quarter
- Atl. Rogers recovered blocked punt in endzone PAT—Luckhurst (kick)
- Min. Danmeier, 33 yard field goal

Second Quarter
- Min. White, 36 yard pass from Kramer PAT—Danmeier (kick)
- Min. Danmeier, 30 yard field goal

Third Quarter
- Atl. Luckhurst, 17 yard rush PAT—Luckhurst (kick)
- Atl. Glazebrook, 35 yard interception return PAT—Luckhurst (kick)
- Min. Danmeier, 39 yard field goal

Fourth Quarter
- Min. McCullum, 11 yard pass from Kramer PAT—Danmeier (kick)
- Atl. Luckhurst, 41 yard field goal
- Min. Brown, 5 yard rush PAT—Danmeier (kick)

TEAM STATISTICS

ATL.		MIN.
14	First Downs-Total	24
5	First Downs-Rushing	8
5	First Downs-Passing	12
4	First Downs-Penalty	4
1	Fumbles-Number	4
0	Fumbles-Lost Ball	0
7	Penalties-Number	10
98	Yards Penalized	84
0	Missed Field Goals	0
50	Offensive Plays	76
235	Net Yards	378
4.7	Average Gain	5.0
2	Giveaways	1
1	Takeaways	2
-1	Difference	+1

INDIVIDUAL STATISTICS

RUSHING

ATLANTA	No.	Yds.	Avg.	MINNESOTA	No.	Yds.	Avg.
Andrews	11	48	4.4	Brown	23	81	3.5
Riggs	9	38	4.2	Nelson	4	24	6.0
Cain	3	17	5.7	Kramer	8	13	1.6
Luckhurst	1	17	17.0	Galbreath	6	10	1.7
	24	120	5.0	S. White	1	-3	-3.0
					42	125	3.0

RECEIVING

ATLANTA	No.	Yds.	Avg.	MINNESOTA	No.	Yds.	Avg.
Jenkins	2	52	26.0	Senser	6	81	13.5
Hodge	2	29	14.5	S. White	2	61	30.5
Kreple	1	18	18.0	McCullum	4	51	12.8
Riggs	2	16	8.0	LeCount	2	24	12.0
Cain	1	14	14.0	Galbreath	3	14	4.7
A. Jackson	1	5	5.0	Young	2	13	6.5
	9	134	14.9	Brown	1	9	9.0
					20	253	12.7

PUNTING

Roberts	5		42.6	Coleman	4		40.0

PUNT RETURNS

B. Johnson	1	0	0.0	Bess	5	65	13.0

KICKOFF RETURNS

Brown	7	120	17.1	Redwine	3	58	19.3
				Nelson	1	30	30.0
					7	165	23.6

INTERCEPTION RETURNS

Glazebrook	1	35	35.0	Turner	2	25	12.5

PASSING

ATLANTA	Att.	Comp.	Comp. Pct.	Yds.	Int.	Yds./Att.	Yds./Comp.
Bartkowski	23	9	39.1	134	2	5.8	14.9
MINNESOTA							
Kramer	34	20	58.8	253	1	7.4	12.7

January 15, 1983 at Washington (Attendance 54,593)

SCORING

MINNESOTA	0	7	0	0	7
WASHINGTON	14	7	0	0	21

First Quarter
- Was. Warren, 3 yard pass from Theismann PAT—Moseley (kick)
- Was. Riggins, 2 yard rush PAT—Moseley (kick)

Second Quarter
- Min. T. Brown, 18 yard rush PAT—Danmeier (kick)
- Was. Garrett, 18 yard pass from Theismann PAT—Moseley (kick)

TEAM STATISTICS

MIN.		WAS.
15	First Downs-Total	23
3	First Downs-Rushing	12
11	First Downs-Passing	11
1	First Downs-Penalty	0
1	Fumbles-Number	0
0	Fumbles-Lost Ball	0
5	Penalties-Number	3
39	Yards Penalized	25
1	Missed Field Goals	2
59	Offensive Plays	67
317	Net Yards	415
5.4	Average Gain	6.2
0	Giveaways	1
1	Takeaways	0
+1	Difference	-1

INDIVIDUAL STATISTICS

RUSHING

MINNESOTA	No.	Yds.	Avg.	WASHINGTON	No.	Yds.	Avg.
Brown	14	65	4.6	Riggins	37	185	5.0
Young	1	6	6.0	Washington	1	11	11.0
Nelson	1	4	4.0	Garrett	1	4	4.0
Galbreath	1	4	4.0	Theismann	3	4	1.3
Kramer	1	0	0.0		42	204	4.9
	18	79	4.4				

RECEIVING

MINNESOTA	No.	Yds.	Avg.	WASHINGTON	No.	Yds.	Avg.
McCullum	3	63	21.0	Garrett	3	75	25.0
T. Brown	7	62	8.9	C. Brown	5	59	11.8
LeCount	3	57	19.0	Giaquinto	2	39	19.5
Senser	1	32	32.0	Warren	4	20	5.0
Jackson	1	14	14.0	Walker	2	15	7.5
S. White	1	13	13.0	Washington	1	5	5.0
Jordan	2	11	5.5		17	213	12.5
	18	252	14.0				

PUNTING

Coleman	4		39.2	Hayes	2		30.0

PUNT RETURNS

none				Nelms	1	9	9.0

KICKOFF RETURNS

Redwine	2	33	16.5	Nelms	1	22	22.0
Nelson	1	12	12.0	Jackson	1	18	18.0
	3	45	15.0		2	40	20.0

INTERCEPTION RETURNS

none				Swain	1	0	0.0

PASSING

MINNESOTA	Att.	Comp.	Comp. Pct.	Yds.	Int.	Yds./Att.	Yds./Comp.
Kramer	39	18	46.2	252	0	6.5	14.0
WASHINGTON							
Theismann	23	17	73.9	213	1	9.3	12.5

January 16, 1983 at Irving, Tex. (Attendance 63,972)

SCORING

GREEN BAY	0	7	6	13	26
DALLAS	6	14	3	14	37

First Quarter
- Dal. Septien, 50 yard field goal
- Dal. Septien, 34 yard field goal

Second Quarter
- G.B. Lofton, 6 yard pass from Dickey PAT—Stenerud (kick)
- Dal. Newsome, 2 yard rush PAT—Septien (kick)
- Dal. Thurman, 39 yard interception return PAT—Septien (kick)

Third Quarter
- G.B. Stenerud, 30 yard field goal
- G.B. Stenerud, 33 yard field goal
- Dal Septien, 24 yard field goal

Fourth Quarter
- G.B. Lofton, 71 yard rush PAT—kick failed
- Dal. Cosbie, 7 yard pass from D. White PAT—Septien (kick)
- G.B. Lee, 22 yard interception return PAT—Stenerud (kick)
- Dal. Newhouse, 1 yard rush PAT—Septien (kick)

TEAM STATISTICS

G.B.		DAL.
21	First Downs-Total	24
5	First Downs-Rushing	10
16	First Downs-Passing	13
0	First Downs-Penalty	1
4	Fumbles-Number	1
2	Fumbles-Lost Ball	1
4	Penalties-Number	5
35	Yards Penalized	30
0	Missed Field Goals	0
57	Offensive Plays	77
466	Net Yards	375
8.1	Average Gain	4.8
5	Giveaways	2
2	Takeaways	5
-3	Difference	+3

INDIVIDUAL STATISTICS

RUSHING

GREEN BAY	No.	Yds.	Avg.	DALLAS	No.	Yds.	Avg.
Lofton	1	71	71.0	Dorsett	27	99	3.7
Rodgers	4	42	10.5	Newsome	1	2	2.0
Ivery	7	24	3.4	Newhouse	7	15	2.1
Ellis	4	21	5.3	D. White	4	-7	-1.8
Dickey	1	0	0.0		39	109	2.8
	17	158	9.3				

RECEIVING

GREEN BAY	No.	Yds.	Avg.	DALLAS	No.	Yds.	Avg.
Lofton	5	109	21.8	T. Hill	7	142	20.3
Coffman	5	72	14.4	Newsome	7	70	10.0
Ellis	5	70	14.0	Cosbie	4	36	9.0
Jefferson	2	40	20.0	DuPree	2	14	7.0
Ivery	1	25	25.0	Dorsett	3	9	3.0
Epps	1	16	16.0	Pearson	1	3	3.0
	19	332	17.5		24	274	11.4

PUNTING

Stachowicz	4		42.0	D. White	4		34.8

PUNT RETURNS

Epps	1	8	8.0	R. Hill	2	18	9.0
				Fellows	1	5	5.0
					3	23	7.7

KICKOFF RETURNS

Rodgers	7	148	21.1	R. Hill	3	118	39.3
				Fellows	2	37	18.5
				Donley	1	18	18.0
					6	173	28.8

INTERCEPTION RETURNS

Lee	1	22	22.0	Thurman	3	58	19.3

PASSING

GREEN BAY	Att.	Comp.	Comp. Pct.	Yds.	Int.	Yds./Att.	Yds./Comp.
Dickey	36	19	52.8	332	3	9.2	17.5
DALLAS							
D. White	36	23	63.9	225	1	6.3	9.8
Pearson	1	1	100.0	49	0	49.0	49.0
	37	24	64.9	274	1	7.4	11.4

1982 A.F.C. PLAYOFFS

January 8, 1983 at Miami (Attendance 68,842)

SCORING

NEW ENGLAND	0	3	3	7- 13
MIAMI	0	14	7	7- 28

Second Quarter
- N.E. — J. Smith, 23 yard field goal
- Mia. — Hardy, 2 yard pass from Woodley; PAT—von Schamann (kick)
- Mia. — Franklin, 1 yard rush; PAT—von Schamann (kick)

Third Quarter
- N.E. — J. Smith, 42 yard field goal
- Mia. — Bennett, 2 yard rush; PAT—von Schamann (kick)

Fourth Quarter
- Mia. — Hardy, 2 yard pass from Woodley; PAT—von Schamann (kick)
- N.E. — Hasselbeck, 22 yard pass from Grogan; PAT—J. Smith (kick)

TEAM STATISTICS

N.E.		MIA.
14	First Downs- Total	27
6	First Down- Rushing	12
8	First Downs- Passing	14
0	First Downs- Penalty	1
1	Fumbles- Number	3
1	Fumbles- Lost	3
4	Penalties- Number	2
27	Yards Penalized	15
0	Missed Field Goals	1
52	Offensive Plays	66
237	Net Yards	448
4.6	Average Gain	6.8
3	Giveaways	3
3	Takeaways	3
0	Difference	0

INDIVIDUAL STATISTICS

RUSHING

NEW ENGLAND	No.	Yds.	Avg.	MIAMI	No.	Yds.	Avg.
van Eeghen	9	40	4.4	Franklin	26	112	4.3
Collins	7	35	5.0	Nathan	12	71	5.9
Tatupu	1	4	4.0	Woodley	1	16	16.0
Morgan	1	-2	-2.0	Bennett	5	10	2.0
	18	77	4.3	Vigorito	1	5	5.0
					45	214	4.8

RECEIVING

NEW ENGLAND	No.	Yds.	Avg.	MIAMI	No.	Yds.	Avg.
Hasselbeck	7	87	12.4	Nathan	5	68	13.6
Dawson	4	49	12.3	Rose	2	47	23.5
Collins	1	17	17.0	Vigorito	2	40	20.0
Toler	1	16	16.0	Harris	1	36	36.0
Brown	1	8	8.0	Cefalo	2	27	13.5
Johnson	1	7	7.0	Hardy	3	23	7.7
van Eeghen	1	5	5.0	Diana	1	5	5.0
	16	189	11.8		16	246	15.4

PUNTING

Camarillo	5		43.6	Orosz	1		51.0

PUNT RETURNS

none				Vigorito	4	40	10.0

KICKOFF RETURNS

R. Smith	3	54	18.0	Walker	3	73	24.3

INTERCEPTION RETURNS

none				McNeal	1	16	16.0
				Small	1	0	0.0
				Walker	0	9	—
					2	25	12.5

PASSING

NEW ENGLAND	Att.	Comp.	Comp. Pct.	Yds.	Int.	Yds./ Att.	Yds./ Comp.
Grogan	30	16	53.3	189	2	6.3	11.8
MIAMI							
Woodley	19	16	84.2	246	0	12.9	15.4

January 8, 1983 at Los Angeles (Attendance 56,555)

SCORING

CLEVELAND	0	10	0	0- 10
L.A. RAIDERS	3	10	7	7- 27

First Quarter
- Raid. — C. Bahr, 27 yard field goal

Second Quarter
- Cle. — M. Bahr, 52 yard field goal
- Raid. — Allen, 2 yard rush; PAT—C. Bahr (kick)
- Cle. — Feacher, 43 yard pass from McDonald; PAT—M. Bahr (kick)
- Raid. — C. Bahr, 37 yard field goal

Third Quarter
- Raid. — Allen, 3 yard rush; PAT—C. Bahr (kick)

Fourth Quarter
- Raid. — Hawkins, 1 yard rush; PAT—C. Bahr (kick)

TEAM STATISTICS

CLE.		RAID.
17	First Downs- Total	25
1	First Downs- Rushing	11
11	First Downs- Passing	14
5	First Downs- Penalty	0
2	Fumbles- Number	2
1	Fumbles- Lost Ball	0
4	Penalties- Number	6
35	Yards Penalized	65
0	Missed Field Goals	1
61	Offensive Plays	75
284	Net Yards	510
4.7	Average Gain	6.8
1	Giveaways	2
2	Takeaways	1
+1	Difference	-1

INDIVIDUAL STATISTICS

RUSHING

CLEVELAND	No.	Yds.	Avg.	L.A. RAIDERS	No.	Yds.	Avg.
White	9	30	3.3	Allen	17	72	4.2
Pruitt	8	19	2.4	King	7	30	4.3
McDonald	1	7	7.0	Pruitt	3	15	5.0
	18	56	3.1	F. Hawkins	4	10	2.5
				Plunkett	2	10	5.0
				Willis	3	3	1.0
					36	140	3.9

RECEIVING

CLEVELAND	No.	Yds.	Avg.	L.A. RAIDERS	No.	Yds.	Avg.
Feacher	4	124	31.0	Branch	5	121	24.2
Newsome	4	51	12.8	Christensen	6	93	15.5
Walker	4	47	11.8	Allen	6	75	12.5
Logan	1	27	27.0	Barnwell	2	38	19.0
Pruitt	3	17	5.7	Ramsey	1	25	25.0
White	2	15	7.5	Pruitt	2	14	7.0
	18	281	15.6	King	1	11	11.0
				F. Hawkins	1	9	9.0
					24	386	16.1

PUNTING

Cox	6		48.5	Guy	3		39.0

PUNT RETURNS

Walker	1	10	10.0	Pruitt	5	45	9.0

KICKOFF RETURNS

Hall	4	86	21.5	Pruitt	2	57	28.5
				Montgomery	1	26	26.0
					3	83	27.7

INTERCEPTION RETURNS

Scott	1	3	3.0	none			
Dixon	1	0	0.0				
	2	3	1.5				

PASSING

CLEVELAND	Att.	Comp.	Comp. Pct.	Yds.	Int.	Yds./ Att.	Yds./ Comp.
McDonald	37	18	48.6	281	0	7.6	15.6
L.A. RAIDERS							
Plunkett	37	24	64.9	386	2	10.4	16.1

January 9, 1983 at Cincinnati (Attendance 57,560)

SCORING

N.Y. JETS	3	17	3	21- 44
CINCINNATI	14	0	3	0- 17

First Quarter
- Cin. — Curtis, 32 yard pass from Anderson; PAT—Breech (kick)
- N.Y.J. — Leahy, 33 yard field goal
- Cin. — Ross, 2 yard pass from Anderson; PAT—Breech (kick)

Second Quarter
- N.Y.J. — Gaffney, 14 yard pass from McNeil; PAT—Leahy (kick)
- N.Y.J. — Walker, 4 yard pass from Todd; PAT—Leahy (kick)
- N.Y.J. — Leahy, 24 yard field goal

Third Quarter
- N.Y.J. — Leahy, 47 yard field goal
- Cin. — Breech, 20 yard field goal

Fourth Quarter
- N.Y.J. — McNeil, 20 yard rush; PAT—Leahy (kick)
- N.Y.J. — Ray, 98 yard interception return; PAT—Leahy (kick)
- N.Y.J. — Crutchfield, 1 yard rush; PAT—Leahy (kick)

TEAM STATISTICS

N.Y.J.		CIN.
27	First Downs- Total	23
12	First Downs- Rushing	3
13	First Downs- Passing	18
2	First Downs- Penalty	2
2	Fumbles- Number	2
1	Fumbles- Lost Ball	1
12	Penalties- Number	7
95	Yards Penalized	60
0	Missed Field Goals	1
63	Offensive Plays	61
517	Net Yards	395
8.2	Average Gain	6.5
2	Giveaways	4
4	Takeaways	2
+2	Difference	-2

INDIVIDUAL STATISTICS

RUSHING

N.Y. JETS	No.	Yds.	Avg.	CINCINNATI	No.	Yds.	Avg.
McNeil	22	211	9.6	Johnson	9	26	2.9
Dierking	3	11	3.7	A. Griffin	3	17	5.7
Newton	2	6	3.0	Alexander	7	14	2.0
Todd	3	3	1.0	Anderson	2	5	2.5
Augustyniak	2	2	1.0		21	62	3.0
Crutchfield	1	1	1.0				
Harper	1	0	0.0				
	34	234	6.9				

RECEIVING

N.Y. JETS	No.	Yds.	Avg.	CINCINNATI	No.	Yds.	Avg.
Walker	8	145	18.1	Collinsworth	7	120	17.1
Gaffney	4	50	12.5	Ross	6	89	14.8
Harper	2	35	17.5	Curtis	3	63	21.0
J. Jones	2	22	11.0	Kreider	3	41	13.7
Barkum	1	9	9.0	M. Harris	1	20	20.0
McNeil	1	9	9.0	A. Griffin	3	14	4.7
Dierking	2	9	4.5	Johnson	3	7	2.3
Augustyniak	1	4	4.0		26	354	13.6
	21	283	13.5				

PUNTING

none				McInally	2		43.0

PUNT RETURNS

Harper	1	2	2.0	none			

KICKOFF RETURNS

Sohn	3	51	17.0	Verser	7	116	16.6
Harper	1	18	18.0	Tate	1	22	22.0
	4	69	17.3		8	138	17.3

INTERCEPTION RETURNS

Ray	1	98	98.0	Riley	1	0	0.0
Lynn	2	40	20.0				
	3	138	46.0				

PASSING

N.Y. JETS	Att.	Comp.	Comp. Pct.	Yds.	Int.	Yds./ Att.	Yds./ Comp.
Todd	28	20	71.4	269	1	9.6	13.5
McNeil	1	1	100.0	14	0	14.0	14.0
	29	21	72.4	283	1	9.8	13.5
CINCINNATI							
Anderson	35	26	74.3	354	3	10.1	13.6
Schonert	1	0	0.0	0	0	0.0	0.0
	36	26	72.2	354	3	9.8	13.6

1982 A.F.C. PLAYOFFS

January 9, 1983 at Pittsburgh (Attendance 53,546)

SCORING

SAN DIEGO	3	14	0	14	– 31
PITTSBURGH	14	0	7	7	– 28

First Quarter
- Pit. Ruff recovered fumble in endzone; PAT—Anderson (kick)
- S.D. Benirschke, 25 yard field goal
- Pit. Bradshaw, 1 yard rush; PAT—Anderson (kick)

Second Quarter
- S.D. Brooks, 18 yard rush; PAT—Benirschke (kick)
- S.D. Sievers, 10 yard pass from Fouts; PAT—Benirschke (kick)

Third Quarter
- Pit. Cunningham, 2 yard pass from Bradshaw; PAT—Anderson (kick)

Fourth Quarter
- Pit. Stallworth, 14 yard pass from Bradshaw; PAT—Anderson (kick)
- S.D. Winslow, 8 yard pass from Fouts; PAT—Benirschke (kick)
- S.D. Winslow, 12 yard pass from Fouts; PAT—Benirschke (kick)

TEAM STATISTICS

S.D.		PIT.
29	First Downs-Total	26
6	First Downs-Rushing	6
19	First Downs-Passing	19
4	First Downs-Penalty	1
3	Fumbles-Number	1
2	Fumbles-Lost Ball	0
6	Penalties-Number	6
51	Yards Penalized	54
0	Missed Field Goals	0
71	Offensive Plays	62
479	Net Yards	422
6.7	Average Gain	6.8
2	Giveaways	2
2	Takeaways	2
0	Difference	0

INDIVIDUAL STATISTICS

SAN DIEGO	No.	Yds.	Avg.	PITTSBURGH	No.	Yds.	Avg.
RUSHING							
Muncie	25	126	5.0	Pollard	9	47	5.2
Brooks	3	20	6.7	Harris	10	35	3.5
Cappelletti	1	0	0.0	Bradshaw	2	12	6.0
	29	146	5.0	Hawthorne	2	3	1.5
					23	97	4.2
RECEIVING							
Chandler	9	124	13.8	Stallworth	8	116	14.5
Winslow	7	102	14.6	Harris	11	71	6.5
Joiner	5	68	13.6	Cunningham	5	55	11.0
Sievers	2	17	8.5	Smith	1	40	40.0
Muncie	1	12	6.0	Pollard	2	29	14.5
Fitzkee	1	8	8.0	Swann	1	14	14.0
Brooks	1	4	4.0		28	325	11.6
Cappelletti	1	-2	-2.0				
	27	333	12.3				
PUNTING							
Buford	1		48.0	Goodson	2		32.5
PUNT RETURNS							
none				Woods	1	12	12.0
KICKOFF RETURNS							
Brooks	3	33	11.0	Abercrombie	4	72	18.0
				Pollard	1	18	18.0
					5	90	18.0
INTERCEPTION RETURNS							
Laird	1	35	35.0	none			
Allen	1	8	8.0				
	2	43	21.5				

PASSING

	Att.	Comp.	Comp. Pct.	Yds.	Int.	Yds./ Att.	Yds./ Comp.
SAN DIEGO							
Fouts	42	27	64.3	333	0	7.9	12.3
PITTSBURGH							
Bradshaw	39	28	71.8	325	2	8.3	11.6

January 15, 1983 at Los Angeles (Attendance 90,038)

SCORING

N.Y. JETS	7	3	0	7	– 17
L.A. RAIDERS	0	0	14	0	– 14

First Quarter
- N.Y.J. Walker, 20 yard pass from Todd; PAT—Leahy (kick)

Second Quarter
- N.Y.J. Leahy, 30 yard field goal

Third Quarter
- Raid. Allen, 3 yard rush; PAT—Bahr (kick)
- Raid. Barnwell, 57 yard pass from Plunkett; PAT—Bahr (kick)

Fourth Quarter
- N.Y.J. Dierking, 1 yard rush; PAT—Leahy (kick)

TEAM STATISTICS

N.Y.J.		RAID.
21	First Downs-Total	19
8	First Downs-Rushing	7
11	First Downs-Passing	11
2	First Downs-Penalty	1
4	Fumbles-Number	2
3	Fumbles-Lost Ball	2
7	Penalties-Number	5
64	Yards Penalized	55
1	Missed Field Goals	1
62	Offensive Plays	65
391	Net Yards	339
6.3	Average Gain	5.2
5	Giveaways	5
5	Takeaways	5
0	Difference	0

INDIVIDUAL STATISTICS

N.Y. JETS	No.	Yds.	Avg.	L.A. RAIDERS	No.	Yds.	Avg.
RUSHING							
McNeil	23	105	4.6	Allen	15	36	2.4
Augustyniak	4	22	5.5	Plunkett	4	18	4.5
Todd	5	8	1.6	King	5	16	3.2
Dierking	2	4	2.0	Montgomery	1	11	11.0
	34	139	4.1	Hawkins	3	4	1.3
				Pruitt	1	4	4.0
				Barnwell	1	4	4.0
					30	93	3.1
RECEIVING							
Walker	7	169	24.1	Barnwell	2	83	41.5
J. Jones	2	52	26.0	Branch	5	82	16.4
Augustyniak	2	18	9.0	Allen	6	37	6.2
Barkum	1	11	11.0	Christensen	5	31	6.2
McNeil	1	11	11.0	Hawkins	1	15	15.0
Shuler	1	9	9.0	Ramsey	1	14	14.0
Dierking	1	7	7.0	King	1	4	4.0
	15	277	18.5		21	266	12.7
PUNTING							
Ramsey	2		31.5	Guy	4		41.3
PUNT RETURNS							
Sohn	1	4	4.0	Pruitt	1	0	0.0
				Squirek	1	0	0.0
					2	0	0.0
KICKOFF RETURNS							
none				Montgomery	2	49	24.5
INTERCEPTION RETURNS							
Mehl	2	20	10.0	Hayes	1	0	0.0
Jackson	1	10	10.0	Owens	1	0	0.0
	3	30	15.0		2	0	0.0

PASSING

	Att.	Comp.	Comp. Pct.	Yds.	Int.	Yds./ Att.	Yds./ Comp.
N.Y. JETS							
Todd	24	15	62.5	277	2	11.5	18.5
L.A. RAIDERS							
Plunkett	33	21	63.6	266	3	8.1	12.7

January 16, 1983 at Miami (Attendance 71,383)

SCORING

SAN DIEGO	0	13	0	0	– 13
MIAMI	7	20	0	7	– 34

First Quarter
- Mia. Moore, 3 yard pass from Woodley; PAT—von Schamann (kick)

Second Quarter
- Mia. Franklin, 3 yard rush; PAT—von Schamann (kick)
- Mia. Lee, 6 yard pass from Woodley; PAT—von Schamann (kick)
- Mia. von Schamann, 24 yard field goal
- S.D. Joiner, 28 yard pass from Fouts; PAT—kick failed
- Mia. von Schamann, 23 yard field goal
- S.D. Muncie, 1 yard rush; PAT—Benirschke (kick)

Fourth Quarter
- Mia. Woodley, 7 yard rush; PAT—von Schamann (kick)

TEAM STATISTICS

S.D.		MIA.
17	First Downs-Total	29
5	First Downs-Rushing	15
9	First Downs-Passing	11
3	First Downs-Penalty	3
3	Fumbles-Number	2
2	Fumbles-Lost Ball	1
7	Penalties-Number	6
62	Yards Penalized	70
0	Missed Field Goals	0
54	Offensive Plays	80
247	Net Yards	413
4.6	Average Gain	5.2
7	Giveaways	2
2	Takeaways	7
-5	Difference	+5

INDIVIDUAL STATISTICS

SAN DIEGO	No.	Yds.	Avg.	MIAMI	No.	Yds.	Avg.
RUSHING							
Muncie	11	62	5.6	Franklin	23	96	4.2
Brooks	3	9	3.0	Nathan	19	83	4.4
Cappelletti	1	5	5.0	Bennett	7	14	2.0
Fouts	2	3	1.5	Woodley	3	14	4.7
	17	79	4.6	Orosz	1	11	11.0
				Vigorito	1	2	2.0
				Jensen	2	-6	-3.0
					56	214	3.8
RECEIVING							
Muncie	6	53	8.8	Cefalo	2	69	34.5
Chandler	2	38	19.0	Nathan	8	55	6.9
Joiner	1	28	28.0	Hardy	3	45	15.0
Brooks	2	25	12.5	Vigorito	2	22	11.0
Sievers	2	21	10.5	Harris	1	15	15.0
Winslow	1	18	18.0	Lee	1	6	6.0
Holohan	1	8	8.0	Moore	1	3	3.0
	15	191	12.7		18	215	11.9
PUNTING							
Buford	4		41.2	Orosz	3		40.3
PUNT RETURNS							
Brooks	3	16	5.3	Vigorito	2	4	2.0
KICKOFF RETURNS							
Brooks	5	78	15.6	Walker	2	28	14.0
Sievers	1	15	15.0	Hill	1	12	12.0
Bauer	1	0	0.0		3	40	13.3
	7	93	13.3				
INTERCEPTION RETURNS							
Fox	1	18	18.0	McNeal	1	20	20.0
				G. Blackwood	2	19	9.5
				Small	1	16	16.0
				L. Blackwood	1	-1	-1.0
					5	54	10.8

PASSING

	Att.	Comp.	Comp. Pct.	Yds.	Int.	Yds./ Att.	Yds./ Comp.
SAN DIEGO							
Fouts	34	15	44.1	191	5	5.6	12.7
MIAMI							
Woodley	22	17	77.3	195	1	8.9	11.5
Nathan	1	1	100.0	20	0	20.0	20.0
	23	18	78.3	215	1	9.3	11.9

1982 Championship Games

NFC CHAMPIONSHIP GAME

January 22, 1983 at Washington
(Attendance 55,045)

SCORING

DALLAS	3	0	14	0-	17
WASHINGTON	7	7	7	10-	31

First Quarter
- Dal. Septien, 27 yard field goal
- Was. Brown, 19 yard pass from Theismann; PAT—Moseley (kick)

Second Quarter
- Was. Riggins, 1 yard rush; PAT—Moseley (kick)

Third Quarter
- Dal. Pearson, 6 yard pass from Hogeboom; PAT—Septien (kick)
- Was. Riggins, 4 yard rush; PAT—Moseley (kick)
- Dal. Johnson, 23 yard pass from Hogeboom; PAT—Septien (kick)

Fourth Quarter
- Was. Moseley, 29 yard field goal
- Was. Grant, 10 yard interception return; PAT—Moseley (kick)

TEAM STATISTICS

DAL.		WAS.
21	First Downs-Total	18
2	First Downs-Rushing	11
19	First Downs-Passing	5
0	First Downs-Penalty	2
2	Fumbles-Number	1
1	Fumbles-Lost Ball	0
3	Penalties-Number	3
15	Yards Penalized	25
1	Missed Field Goals	1
65	Offensive Plays	63
340	Net Yards	260
5.2	Average Gain	4.1
3	Giveaways	0
0	Takeaways	3
-3	Difference	+3

Excellent throughout a fluky season, the Redskins won both respect and a ticket to the Super Bowl. The Cowboys had their own devils to exorcise, having lost in the NFC title game the past two years.

Dallas took the opening kickoff and drove into position for a Rafael Septien field goal. The Redskins then marched 84 yards for a touchdown. From the first series, John Riggins relentlessly plowed for yardage behind the charge of the Hogs. The Cowboys hurt themselves in the second quarter when Rod Hill fumbled a punt deep in Dallas territory. The Skins recovered on the 11-yard line, and Riggins blasted into the endzone four plays later. Just before the halftime break, Dexter Manley flattened Cowboy QB Danny White and left him groggy with a concussion.

Down 14-3, the Cowboys bounced back in the third quarter behind reserve QB Gary Hogeboom. He closed the gap to 14-10 early in the period with a TD pass to Drew Pearson. Again, the Redskins came up with a big play as Mike Nelms carried a punt 76 yards to the Dallas 20-yard line. Five plays later, Riggins plunged for the score, upping the Washington lead to 10 points. Undaunted, Hogeboom capped another scoring drive with a pass to Butch Johnson.

But the fourth quarter belonged to the Redskins. Midway through the period, Mel Kaufman intercepted a Hogeboom pass, setting up a Mark Moseley field goal. Less than a minute later, Manley tipped Hogeboom's pass into the hands of Darryl Grant, who ran 10 yards to ice the victory.

INDIVIDUAL STATISTICS

RUSHING

DALLAS	No.	Yds.	Avg.	WASHINGTON	No.	Yds.	Avg.
Dorsett	15	57	3.8	Riggins	36	140	3.9
Springs	4	15	3.8	Washington	2	2	1.0
Pearson	1	-1	-1.0	Garrett	1	-2	-2.0
T. Hill	1	-6	-6.0	Theismann	1	-3	-3.0
	21	65	3.1		40	137	3.4

RECEIVING

DALLAS	No.	Yds.	Avg.	WASHINGTON	No.	Yds.	Avg.
Johnson	5	73	14.6	Garrett	4	46	11.5
T. Hill	5	59	11.8	Brown	3	54	18.0
Pearson	5	55	11.0	Warren	2	24	12.0
Newsome	3	24	8.0	Washington	1	13	13.0
Dorsett	2	29	14.5	Walker	1	9	9.0
Cosbie	2	26	13.0	Harmon	1	4	4.0
DuPree	1	9	9.0		12	150	12.5
	23	275	12.0				

PUNTING

DALLAS	No.	Yds.	Avg.	WASHINGTON	No.	Yds.	Avg.
D. White	3		31.0	Hayes	5		40.2

PUNT RETURNS

DALLAS	No.	Yds.	Avg.	WASHINGTON	No.	Yds.	Avg.
Donley	2	10	5.0	Nelms	2	14	7.0
R. Hill	1	0	0.0				
	3	10	3.3				

KICKOFF RETURNS

DALLAS	No.	Yds.	Avg.	WASHINGTON	No.	Yds.	Avg.
R. Hill	2	45	22.5	Nelms	4	128	32.0
Donley	1	22	22.0				
Fellows	1	15	15.0				
Cosbie	1	12	12.0				
	5	94	18.8				

INTERCEPTION RETURNS

DALLAS	No.	Yds.	Avg.	WASHINGTON	No.	Yds.	Avg.
none				Grant	1	10	10.0
				Kaufman	1	2	2.0
					2	12	6.0

PASSING

	Att.	Comp.	Comp Pct.	Yds.	Int.	Yds./ Att.	Yds./ Comp.
DALLAS							
D. White	15	9	60.0	113	0	7.5	12.6
Hogeboom	29	14	48.3	162	2	5.6	11.6
	44	23	52.3	275	2	6.3	12.0
WASHINGTON							
Theismann	20	12	60.0	150	0	7.5	12.5

AFC CHAMPIONSHIP GAME

January 23, 1983 at Miami
(Attendance 67,396)

SCORING

N.Y. JETS	0	0	0	0-	0
MIAMI	0	0	7	7-	14

Third Quarter
- Mia. Bennett, 7 yard rush; PAT—von Schamann (kick)

Fourth Quarter
- Mia. Duhe, 35 yard interception return; PAT—von Schamann (kick)

TEAM STATISTICS

N.Y.J.		MIA
10	First Downs- Total	13
2	First Downs- Rushing	7
6	First Downs- Passing	5
2	First Downs- Penalty	1
1	Fumbles- Number	3
0	Fumbles- Lost Ball	1
6	Penalties- Number	3
42	Yards Penalized	15
0	Missed Field Goals	0
65	Offensive Plays	66
139	Net Yards	198
2.1	Average Gain	3.0
5	Giveaways	4
4	Takeaways	5
-1	Difference	+1

For the second straight year, the weather played a prominent role in the AFC title game. Rain pounded the Orange Bowl beginning the night before the game through the afternoon, turning the uncovered field into a sloppy mudpit. The Miami management had not used a tarp because it expected the turf to drain. At game time, however, the potent New York Jet offense and Miami's Killer Bee defense faced each other in a messy quagmire.

Neither team scored in the first half. Miami QB David Woodley had little success in the muck, and his runners made no headway against the Jet front four. The New York offense was stymied by a strong pass rush, double coverage on Wesley Walker and Freeman McNeil's lack of solid footing. As the half ended, each team waited for the big break in the deadlock.

Early in the third quarter, A.J. Duhe intercepted a short Jet pass that tipped off the hands of FB Mike Augustyniak. Starting 48 yards away, the Dolphins reached the endzone in seven plays. Woody Bennett's touchdown gave Miami a 7-0 lead, which loomed large in the rain.

Bothered by the wet ball and the Dolphin pass rush, Richard Todd couldn't drive the Jets to the equalizer. Early in the final quarter, Duhe grabbed his third Todd pass of the day and dashed 35 yards for the score which broke the game open.

INDIVIDUAL STATISTICS

RUSHING

N.Y. JETS	No.	Yds.	Avg.	MIAMI	No.	Yds.	Avg.
McNeil	17	46	2.7	Woodley	8	46	5.8
Todd	4	10	2.5	Franklin	13	44	3.4
Augustyniak	2	5	2.5	Nathan	7	24	3.4
Dierking	1	1	1.0	Bennett	13	24	1.8
	24	62	2.6		41	138	3.4

RECEIVING

N.Y. JETS	No.	Yds.	Avg.	MIAMI	No.	Yds.	Avg.
Harper	4	14	3.5	Vigorito	3	29	9.7
J. Jones	3	35	11.7	Harris	2	28	14.0
Barkum	2	20	10.0	Nathan	2	4	2.0
Augustyniak	2	12	6.0	Rose	1	20	20.0
McNeil	1	9	9.0	Lee	1	6	6.0
Gaffney	1	7	7.0		9	87	9.7
Dierking	1	6	6.0				
Walker	1	0	0.0				
	15	103	6.9				

PUNTING

N.Y. JETS	No.	Yds.	Avg.	MIAMI	No.	Yds.	Avg.
Ramsey	10		35.7	Orosz	10		33.3

PUNT RETURNS

N.Y. JETS	No.	Yds.	Avg.	MIAMI	No.	Yds.	Avg.
Sohn	6	65	10.8	Vigorito	3	20	6.7

KICKOFF RETURNS

N.Y. JETS	No.	Yds.	Avg.	MIAMI	No.	Yds.	Avg.
Sohn	1	31	31.0	Walker	1	20	20.0

INTERCEPTION RETURNS

N.Y. JETS	No.	Yds.	Avg.	MIAMI	No.	Yds.	Avg.
Schroy	2	1	0.5	Duhe	3	36	12.0
Buttle	1	0	0.0	Small	1	8	8.0
	3	1	0.3	G. Blackwood	1	4	4.0
					5	48	9.6

PASSING

	Att.	Comp.	Comp. Pct.	Yds.	Int.	Yds./ Att.	Yds./ Comp.
N.Y. JETS							
Todd	37	15	40.5	103	5	2.8	6.9
MIAMI							
Woodley	21	9	42.9	87	3	4.1	9.7

SUPER BOWL XVII

January 30, 1983 at Pasadena, Calif.

(Attendance 103,667)

The Hogs Lead Riggins, the Smurfs and the Fun Bunch

Each team had the reputation of an underrated overachiever. The Redskins had not even figured to make the playoffs this season, and the Dolphins certainly ranked below some other A.F.C. teams in the eyes of acknowledged experts. The Redskins and Dolphins made liars of the experts. The Skins came into the game on a six-game winning streak, victorious in 14 of their last 15 matches. They had rolled over their three playoff foes behind a complex defense and the determined running of John Riggins. The Dolphins had just defused the potent San Diego and New York Jet offenses en route to this rematch of the Super Bowl that had crowned Miami's unbeaten 1972 season.

Washington's defensive plan was to stop the Miami ground game, thus forcing David Woodley to pass more than usual. Although the plan worked, Woodley burned the Skins in the first quarter with a 76-yard touchdown toss to Jimmy Cefalo. The Redskin offense, meanwhile, had success moving the ball against the Killer Bee defense but fell short in its first few series. The teams traded field goals in the second period, making the score 10-3 in favor of Miami. With its big offensive line leading the way, Washington drove 80 yards in 11 plays to score on a short pass from Joe Theismann to Alvin Garrett. With the score knotted at 10-10, Fulton Walker then took the kickoff and ran 98 yards to return Miami to a seven-point lead, 17-10 at the intermission.

What that score hid was Washington's dominance on offense and defense. The Skins came back onto the field, looking to prevent any more big plays and to keep the pressure on the Miami defense. As the second half progressed, the quick Killer Bee defense struggled to contain the physical charge of the Hogs and Riggins. The Dolphin offense could do nothing against the Washington defense, chalking up only two first downs and no completed passes in the entire half. Despite their increasing momentum, the Redskins scored only on a Mark Moseley field goal in the third quarter, cutting the Miami lead to 17-13.

Early in the final period, Washington began another drive. On fourth-and-inches at the Miami 43-yard line, coach Joe Gibbs decided to go for it. Riggins took the handoff, headed to his left, ran over cornerback Don McNeal, and dashed down the sideline in front of a shocked Miami bench. Moseley's kick made the score 20-17 in favor of the Skins with 10 minutes left. In those final minutes, the Miami attack couldn't move the ball behind either Woodley or relief quarterback Don Strock. Riggins kept churning out the yards, and a late touchdown pass from Theismann to Charlie Brown made the final score 27-17. The MVP award went to Riggins, who dominated the field and set a rushing record of 166 yards.

LINEUPS

MIAMI		WASHINGTON
	OFFENSE	
Harris	WR	Garrett
Giesler	LT	Jacoby
Kuechenberg	LG	Grimm
Stephenson	C	Bostic
Toews	RG	Dean
Laakso	RT	Starke
Hardy	TE	Warren
Cefalo	WR	Brown
Woodley	QB	Theismann
Nathan	RB	Riggins
Franklin	RB/TE	Walker
	DEFENSE	
Betters	LE	Mendenhall
Baumhower	NT/LT	Butz
Bokamper	RE/RT	Grant
Brudzinski	LOLB/RE	Manley
Duhe	LILB/LLB	Kaufman
Rhone	RILB/MLB	Olkewicz
Gordon	ROLB/RLB	Milot
Small	LCB	White
McNeal	RCB	Dean
G. Blackwood	SS	Peters
L. Blackwood	FS	Murphy

SUBSTITUTES

MIAMI		
	OFFENSE	
Strock	Diana	Rose
Jensen	Heflin	Foster
Hill	Moore	Green
Vigorito	Lee	Dennard
Bennett	Duper	
	DEFENSE	
Den Herder	Bowser	Kozlowski
Shull	Lankford	Bishop
Hester	Judson	Clark
Potter	Walker	
	KICKERS	
von Schamann	Orosz	
WASHINGTON		
	OFFENSE	
Giaquinto	Didier	Owen
Harmon	May	Washington
Wonsley	Laster	Puetz
Jackson	Holly	Caster
Seay		
	DEFENSE	
McGee	Coleman	McDaniel
Liebenstein	Cronan	Jordan
Brooks	Lowry	Williams
Kubin	Lavender	Nelms
	KICKERS	
Moseley	Hayes	

SCORING

MIAMI	7	10	0	0-	17
WASHINGTON	0	10	3	14-	27

First Quarter
- Mia. Cefalo, 76 yard pass from Woodley
  PAT—von Schamann (kick)

Second Quarter
- Was. Moseley, 31 yard field goal
- Mia. von Schamann, 20 yard field goal
- Was. Garrett, 4 yard pass from Theismann
  PAT—Moseley (kick)
- Mia. Walker, 98 yard kickoff return
  PAT—von Schamann (kick)

Third Quarter
- Was. Moseley, 20 yard field goal

Fourth Quarter
- Was. Riggins, 43 yard rush
  PAT—Moseley (kick)
- Was. Brown, 6 yard pass from Theismann
  PAT—Moseley (kick)

TEAM STATISTICS

MIA.		WAS.
9	First Downs- Total	24
7	First Downs- Rushing	14
2	First Downs- Passing	9
0	First Downs- Penalty	1
2	Fumbles- Number	0
1	Fumbles- Lost Ball	0
4	Penalties- Number	5
55	Yards Penalized	36
0	Missed Field Goals	0
47	Offensive Plays	78
176	Net Yards	400
3.7	Average Gain	5.1
2	Giveaways	2
2	Takeaways	2
0	Difference	0

INDIVIDUAL STATISTICS

MIAMI	No.	Yds.	Avg.	WASHINGTON	No.	Yds.	Avg.
RUSHING							
Franklin	16	49	3.1	Riggins	38	166	4.4
Nathan	7	26	3.7	Garrett	1	44	44.0
Woodley	4	16	4.0	Harmon	9	40	4.4
Vigorito	1	4	4.0	Theismann	3	20	6.7
Harris	1	1	1.0	Walker	1	6	6.0
	29	96	3.3		52	276	5.3
RECEIVING							
Cefalo	2	82	41.0	Brown	6	60	10.0
Harris	2	15	7.5	Warren	5	28	5.6
	4	97	24.3	Garrett	2	13	6.5
				Walker	1	27	27.0
				Riggins	1	15	15.0
					15	143	9.5
PUNTING							
Orosz	6		37.8	Hayes	4		42.0
PUNT RETURNS							
Vigorito	2	22	11.0	Nelms	6	52	8.7
KICKOFF RETURNS							
Walker	4	190	47.5	Nelms	2	44	22.0
L. Blackwood	2	32	16.0	Wonsley	1	13	13.0
	6	222	37.0		3	57	19.0
INTERCEPTION RETURNS							
Duhe	1	0	0.0	Murphy	1	0	0.0
L. Blackwood	1	0	0.0				
	2	0	0.0				

PASSING

MIAMI	Att.	Comp.	Comp. Pct.	Yds.	Int.	Yds./ Att.	Yds./ Comp.	Yards Lost Tackled
Woodley	14	4	28.6	97	1	6.9	24.3	1-17
Strock	3	0	0.0	0	0	0.0	0.0	0-0
	17	4	23.5	97	1	5.7	24.3	1-17
WASHINGTON								
Theismann	23	15	65.2	143	2	6.2	9.5	3-19

1983 N.F.C. Off-the-Field Problems

America saw the melancholy specter of its athletic heroes dragged down by vice. Drug abuse wasted many of the nation's youth and dragged several N.F.L. players into humiliating exposures. Commissioner Pete Rozelle handed out four-game suspensions to Ross Browner and Pete Johnson of Cincinnati, E.J. Junior of St. Louis and Greg Stemrick of New Orleans for drug use. Tony Peters of Washington was docked for the entire season after a conviction for sale of cocaine. To vary the vices, Art Schlichter of Baltimore sat out the year after revelation that he was a compulsive gambler who had bet on N.F.L. games.

EASTERN DIVISION

Washington Redskins — The Redskins proved they were true champions, not fluke victors in a strike-ripped season. They flopped on opening day by losing to the Cowboys 31-30 after leading 23-3 at the half. Shrugging off their disappointment, the Skins tore through the rest of the schedule, losing only a 48-47 shootout with the Packers on October 17. The Washington pass defense was vulnerable despite Mark Murphy's excellence; Tony Peters was suspended, Jeris White held out, Joe Lavender retired and Vernon Dean slumped. The brilliant offense, however, simply blew opponents away. If not handing off to John Riggins, Joe Theismann was unleashing a salvo of passes. Charlie Brown blossomed into a leading receiver in his second pro season. Supporting the entire structure were the Hogs, with Joe Jacoby, Russ Grimm and Jeff Bostic singled out for special praise. Two games sent Redskin fans into fits of delight. On October 2, the Skins scored 17 points in the final seven minutes to edge the Raiders 37-35. On December 11, the hated Cowboys were demolished 31-10 in a showdown for first place in the East.

Dallas Cowboys — The Cowboys had a lot of good football players in a very good system. The offense moved the ball through the air to a variety of receivers. To balance the attack, Danny White had the running skills of Tony Dorsett at his call. Of the offensive linemen, tight end Doug Cosbie developed into the star. Like the Redskins, the Cowboys could be beaten by enemy passes. Everson Walls was the leader of a shaky secondary that got some relief from the pass rushing of Randy White and Too Tall Jones. Dallas' excellence emerged in seven straight victories at the start of the schedule, including a 31-30 comeback over the Redskins. On December 11, both Washington and Dallas brought 12-2 records into Texas Stadium. Unable to run the ball, the Cowboys lost 31-10 to fall into second place. A 42-17 humbling at the hands of the 49ers then sent the Cowboys reeling into the playoffs at their lowest ebb of the year.

St. Louis Cardinals — While E.J. Junior sat out the first four games, the St. Louis defense was badly mauled in three losses. Beaten in five of their first six games, the Cards rebounded to win five of their next six. Although the defense never really jelled, it had solid newcomers in end Al Baker from Detroit and rookie cornerback Lionel Washington. The big offensive weapons were Roy Green and Ottis Anderson. Green burned the Seahawks on November 13 with four touchdowns in the first half. The late drive included a 44-14 whipping of the Chargers and a 34-24 victory over the Raiders after trailing 17-0. Any playoff hopes died in four losses to the Redskins and Cowboys, none closer than 17 points.

Philadelphia Eagles — New coach Marion Campbell revived the Eagles after their rapid fall from grace last year. Four victories in the first six games fueled hopes of a return to the playoffs after only one year away. It wasn't to be, as the Eagles lost nine of their last 10 games. Wilbert Montgomery's bad knee and Michael Haddix's poor rookie year forced the Eagles to forego the ground game for an aerial attack. Campbell unleashed a new weapon in Mike Quick, a deep receiving threat who moved into the starting lineup with flair. During their cold stretch, the Eagles lost a lot of close games, including tough matches with the Cowboys and Redskins. A 13-9 triumph over the Rams on December 4 broke the late-season gloom.

New York Giants — Bill Parcells moved up from defensive coordinator to head coach with terrible short-term results. After a 2-2 start, the Giants won only once in their final 12 games. The defense kept up its good work, hanging together around stars Lawrence Taylor, Harry Carson and Mark Haynes. The offense plagued Parcells with many turnovers and few points. The front line was a patchwork affair that undermined both the ground and air attacks. Injuries knocked Phil Simms and then Scott Brunner out of action, leaving third-stringer Jeff Rutledge as the only healthy quarterback by season's end. Earnest Gray hauled in 78 passes from all three of them to lead the N.F.C. in receptions. In a depressing season, the high points were a 27-3 victory over Green Bay on Monday night TV and a 23-0 shutout of the Eagles. The most alarming sign was the 51,589 no-shows for the December 4 game at Giants Stadium.

CENTRAL DIVISION

Detroit Lions — After blanking Tampa Bay on opening day, the Lions lost their next four games. From that point on, the Lions were one of the N.F.L.'s best teams. The Detroit defense led the way back from the depths. Doug English starred on the front line, joined by pass-rushing William Gay, the replacement for the traded Al Baker. Bruce McNorton won a job in the secondary with his aggressive ballhawking. The offense relied on the slick running of Billy Sims, who bounced back from a broken hand suffered in the third game. The Lions shocked a national audience on Thansgiving Day by destroying the Steelers 45-3. Their next time out, they smothered Minnesota 13-2 to take first place in the division. They iced the title the final weekend by beating Tampa Bay while the Packers lost to the Bears.

Green Bay Packers — The Packers were regularly becoming a cold-weather San Diego Chargers. They had a marvelous passing attack and a feeble defense, which worked against each other. The defense got off to a bad start when end Mike Butler was cut after signing a contract with the U.S.F.L. By mid-season, coach Bart Starr had placed starters Casey Merrill and Maurice Harvey on waivers. On offense, Lynn Dickey had receiving riches in James Lofton, John Jefferson and Paul Coffman. The running game suffered when Eddie Lee Ivery departed in mid-season with a drug problem. The Packers reached their extremes by beating Tampa Bay 55-14, beating Washington 48-47, and losing to Atlanta 47-41. They entered the final weekend tied for first place in the Central, but fell by the wayside with a last-minute, 23-21 defeat to the Bears. That loss ended Bart Starr's nine-year reign as head coach.

Chicago Bears — The death of George Halas snatched away the team's founder and guiding light through years of greatness. After an inept start, the 1983 Bears recaptured some of the flair of their storied ancestors. They won five of their last six games with a solid defense and ball-control offense. They whipped Tampa Bay 27-0 on November 20, then shocked San Francisco 13-3 a week later. On the final two weekends, they eliminated the Vikings and Packers from the Central Division race. The offense was, as usual, centered around Walter Payton, but new speed arrived in the person of Willie Gault, a dangerous receiver who decided to skip the 1984 Olympics to sign with the Bears. The swarming defense had developed stars in Dan Hampton, Mike Singletary and Leslie Frazier.

Minnesota Vikings — The Vikings led the Pack at mid-season with a 6-2 record. Over the back leg of the schedule, however, an onslaught of injuries sent the team into a dive. Joe Senser suffered a knee injury in the pre-season and never played a down. Tommy Kramer's season ended in week three with a knee injury and Ted Brown's in week 10 with a separated shoulder. Add injuries to Mark Mullaney and Sammy White, and the Vikes were undermanned down the stretch. A 17-16 loss to the Saints on November 27 dropped them into a first-place tie with the Lions, and a showdown in the Pontiac Silverdome one week later left the Vikings 13-2 losers and playoff also-rans. After 17 years at the helm, coach Bud Grant chose this moment to retire to other pursuits.

Tampa Bay Buccaneers — When the Bucs lost their first nine games, fans turned their criticism on coach John McKay. With Doug Williams gone to the U.S.F.L., McKay settled on Jack Thompson and Jerry Golsteyn as his new quarterbacks. Neither man had much success behind an injury-shredded line, enduring the indignity of three shutouts. The offense relied heavily on running back James Wilder. He carried the ball a record

FINAL TEAM STATISTICS

OFFENSE

	ATL.	CHI.	DALL.	DET.	G.B.	L.A.	MINN	N.O.	NY G	PHIL.	STL.	S.F.	T.B.	WASH.
FIRST DOWNS:														
Total	325	308	342	315	340	316	303	286	296	253	296	344	249	353
by Rushing	118	154	109	136	99	148	112	135	104	91	123	129	72	165
by Passing	190	136	205	156	214	150	169	136	164	150	147	199	157	173
by Penalty	17	18	28	23	27	18	22	15	28	12	26	16	20	15
RUSHING:														
Number	492	583	519	513	439	511	470	595	506	402	525	511	428	629
Yards	2224	2727	2117	2181	1807	2253	1808	2461	1794	1417	2277	2257	1353	2625
Average Yards	4.5	4.7	4.1	4.3	4.1	4.4	3.8	4.1	3.5	3.5	4.3	4.4	3.2	4.2
Touchdowns	17	14	21	18	15	20	17	19	9	5	15	17	9	30
PASSING:														
Attempts	507	447	554	503	526	489	555	425	575	486	460	528	528	463
Completions	321	255	346	263	311	286	310	243	284	252	267	339	300	278
Completion Pct.	63.3	57.0	62.5	52.3	59.1	58.5	55.9	57.2	49.4	51.9	58.0	64.2	56.8	60.0
Passing Yards	3793	3461	4156	3297	4688	3411	3514	2782	3854	3532	3309	4021	3490	3765
Avg. Yds per Att.	6.1	6.2	6.5	5.4	7.7	6.3	5.4	5.4	6.7	5.7	5.5	6.8	5.4	7.1
Avg. Yds per Comp.	11.8	13.6	12.0	12.5	15.1	11.9	11.3	11.5	13.6	14.0	12.4	11.9	11.6	13.5
Times Tackled	55	53	37	45	42	23	43	35	49	57	59	33	49	35
Yds Lost Tackled	389	358	314	342	323	190	303	305	363	415	441	224	366	251
Net Yards	3404	3103	3842	2955	4365	3221	3211	2477	3491	3117	2868	3797	3124	3514
Touchdowns	24	21	31	19	33	23	15	14	12	22	29	27	18	29
Interceptions	10	22	25	23	32	23	22	25	31	18	21	12	24	11
Pct. Intercepted	2.0	4.9	4.5	4.6	6.1	4.7	4.0	5.9	5.4	3.7	4.6	4.2	4.5	2.4
PUNTS:														
Number	71	94	83	72	70	83	91	78	85	86	85	66	96	72
Average	39.8	36.2	39.4	40.4	41.0	39.8	41.5	40.7	39.8	40.9	41.5	38.7	41.8	38.8
PUNT RETURNS														
Number	46	56	51	46	41	55	24	39	55	45	58	36	42	40
Yards	489	447	461	522	329	538	210	275	377	259	461	365	299	387
Average Yards	10.6	8.0	9.0	11.3	8.0	9.8	8.8	7.1	6.9	5.8	7.9	10.1	7.1	7.9
Touchdowns	1	1	1	1	1	1	0	0	0	0	0	1	0	0
KICKOFF RET.:														
Number	67	58	71	61	79	52	68	66	71	62	72	52	68	63
Yards	1258	953	1351	1191	1339	946	1466	1339	1333	1168	1459	958	1314	1301
Average Yards	18.8	16.4	19.0	19.5	16.9	18.2	21.6	20.3	18.8	18.8	20.3	18.4	19.3	20.7
Touchdowns	0	0	0	0	0	0	0	0	0	0	0	0	0	0
INTERCEPT RET.:														
Number	15	21	27	22	19	24	25	23	23	8	28	24	23	34
Yards	212	215	467	185	227	515	168	412	210	79	266	437	367	437
Average Yards	14.1	10.2	17.3	8.4	11.9	21.5	6.7	17.9	9.1	9.9	9.5	18.2	16.0	12.9
Touchdowns	2	2	2	0	1	3	0	3	1	0	0	5	3	1
PENALTIES:														
Number	90	107	99	118	80	96	90	91	113	79	89	89	94	90
Yards	806	869	847	988	648	748	748	802	1020	637	770	695	832	776
FUMBLES:														
Number	36	25	30	41	37	38	33	37	39	37	50	27	39	13
Number Lost	19	14	14	16	18	24	10	22	27	18	27	19	13	7
POINTS:														
Total	370	311	479	347	429	361	316	319	267	233	374	432	241	541
PAT Attempts	45	39	59	38	52	47	34	38	23	27	47	51	31	63
PAT Made	43	35	57	38	52	42	33	37	22	24	45	51	25	62
FG Attempts	22	25	27	32	26	20	33	24	42	26	28	30	24	47
FG Made	17	14	22	25	21	11	25	18	35	15	15	25	10	33
Percent FG Made	77.3	56.0	81.5	78.1	80.8	55.0	75.8	75.0	83.3	57.7	53.6	83.3	41.7	70.2
Safeties	0	0	1	3	1	2	2	0	1	1	1	0	0	1

DEFENSE

	ATL.	CHI.	DALL.	DET.	G.B.	L.A.	MINN.	N.O.	NY G	PHIL.	STL.	S.F.	T.B.	WASH.
FIRST DOWNS:														
Total	342	286	286	324	366	311	318	289	289	310	286	302	320	290
by Rushing	139	113	82	133	171	118	147	108	98	144	107	98	124	76
by Passing	187	154	181	161	187	179	150	159	167	149	161	181	172	196
by Penalty	16	19	23	30	8	14	21	22	24	17	18	23	24	18
RUSHING:														
Number	499	482	410	503	597	489	579	472	502	633	443	449	561	349
Yards	2309	2000	1499	2104	2641	1781	2584	2000	1733	2655	1838	1936	2082	1289
Average Yards	4.6	4.1	3.7	4.2	4.4	3.6	4.5	4.2	3.5	4.2	4.1	4.3	3.7	3.7
Touchdowns	20	20	12	11	28	21	16	11	10	14	23	10	19	9
PASSING:														
Attempts	493	490	558	515	518	556	478	496	493	430	519	526	490	570
Completions	313	249	299	297	300	319	263	271	283	247	290	322	300	301
Completion Pct.	63.5	50.8	53.6	57.7	57.9	57.4	55.0	54.6	57.4	57.4	55.9	61.2	61.2	52.8
Passing Yards	3734	3516	4365	3401	4033	3869	3229	3128	3584	3048	3635	3701	3624	4377
Avg. Yds per Att.	6.7	5.8	6.4	5.6	6.7	6.1	5.5	4.9	6.1	6.0	5.5	5.6	6.2	6.4
Avg. Yds per Comp.	11.9	14.1	14.6	11.5	13.4	12.1	12.3	11.5	12.7	12.3	12.5	11.5	12.1	14.5
Times Tackled	31	51	57	43	41	33	47	56	44	36	59	57	42	51
Yds Lost Tackled	217	384	437	289	271	258	326	437	323	256	468	448	309	402
Net Yards	3517	3132	3928	3112	3762	3611	2903	2691	3261	2792	3167	2253	3315	3975
Touchdowns	28	15	27	21	20	18	23	20	26	20	24	23	15	28
Interceptions	15	21	27	22	19	24	25	23	23	8	28	24	23	34
Pct. Intercepted	3.0	4.3	4.8	4.3	3.7	4.3	5.2	4.6	4.7	1.9	5.4	4.6	4.7	6.0
PUNTS:														
Number	67	99	84	79	78	83	77	83	99	80	88	74	79	66
Average	42.0	38.6	41.8	40.1	39.1	41.7	39.3	41.8	39.2	37.8	40.3	40.4	40.7	41.6
PUNT RETURNS														
Number	34	44	53	39	43	39	40	51	47	57	47	38	59	41
Yards	179	322	588	302	384	251	297	573	283	511	307	378	603	407
Average Yards	5.3	7.3	11.1	7.7	8.9	6.4	7.4	11.2	6.0	9.0	6.5	7.3	10.2	9.9
Touchdowns	0	0	1	0	1	0	0	2	0	0	0	0	1	1
KICKOFF RET.:														
Number	60	66	78	71	78	71	70	44	67	45	66	78	50	91
Yards	1212	1229	1806	1146	1429	1325	1392	938	1296	804	1300	1675	1039	1772
Average Yards	20.2	18.6	23.2	16.1	18.3	18.7	19.9	21.3	19.3	17.9	19.7	21.5	20.8	19.5
Touchdowns	0	0	0	0	0	0	0	0	0	0	1	0	0	0
INTERCEPT RET.:														
Number	10	22	25	23	32	23	22	25	31	18	21	12	24	11
Yards	94	291	358	241	337	303	308	424	436	155	385	168	316	90
Average Yards	9.4	13.2	14.3	10.5	10.5	13.2	14.0	17.0	14.1	8.6	18.3	14.0	13.2	8.2
Touchdowns	0	1	1	0	4	0	2	5	2	0	0	1	4	0
PENALTIES:														
Number	81	86	100	117	110	89	92	96	114	94	102	91	105	80
Yards	710	687	873	1062	965	804	759	814	927	755	819	793	799	710
FUMBLES:														
Number	26	37	31	33	32	38	33	33	31	30	32	39	43	46
Number Lost	15	17	21	15	12	20	23	16	13	15	20	18	18	27
POINTS:														
Total	389	301	360	286	439	344	348	337	347	322	428	293	380	332
PAT Attempts	49	36	42	33	54	42	42	39	40	34	56	35	42	39
PAT Made	44	34	42	32	50	39	40	37	39	34	54	32	40	38
FG Attempts	26	23	30	26	29	28	27	34	32	37	15	27	34	28
FG Made	17	17	22	18	19	17	18	20	22	28	12	17	28	20
Percent FG Made	65.4	73.9	73.3	69.2	65.5	60.7	66.7	58.8	68.8	75.7	80.0	63.0	82.4	71.4
Safeties	0	0	0	1	1	1	1	3	1	0	1	0	2	0

42 times against the Steelers on October 30, gained 219 yards against the Vikings on November 6, then suffered broken ribs a week later to end his season. The defense also fell off in performance, although Lee Roy Selmon and Hugh Green still were all-pros.

WESTERN DIVISION

San Francisco 49ers — The Niners proved that last year was a fluke, storming back into the playoffs with overall improvement. The intricate offense now had a welcome pair of runners in ex-Ram Wendell Tyler and rookie Roger Craig. They balanced the potent passing attack, which featured Joe Montana and Dwight Clark. The defense prospered from Fred Dean's renewed pass rushing and the return to form of Ronnie Lott and other young defensive backs. The team announced its resurgence by winning four of its first five games. A cold spell in mid-season left the Niners one game behind the Rams with three weeks left. While the Rams lost their next two games, the 49ers won twice and moved into first place. A 42-17 thrashing of the Cowboys on the final Monday night clinched the top spot and boded well for the playoffs.

Los Angeles Rams — Two additions turned the Rams around and led them into the playoffs. USC coach John Robinson moved into the pro ranks and rallied a demoralized team. Robinson had a superb siege gun in rookie Eric Dickerson, a magnificent runner who combined size with speed. The Los Angeles offense revived behind Dickerson's excellence and an improved front line. The defense shed its clownish look and prospered in a new 4-3 alignment. The new-look Rams dove into the playoff race and actually held first place at the start of December. Losses to the Eagles and Patriots dropped them out of first place and into a must-win situation in the season's finale against the Saints. The L.A. offense didn't score a point until the game was almost over, but Mike Lansford's 42-yard field goal with two seconds left gave the Rams a 26-24 victory and a ticket to the playoffs.

New Orleans Saints — It was close, but still no cigar. The Saints came within two seconds of a playoff berth before coming up empty as they had in every season of their life. One low point came on September 25 as they lost at Dallas 21-20 on a safety in the final two minutes. One week later, the Saints ambushed the Dolphins 17-7. A last-second victory at Atlanta in the next game raised New Orleans' record to 4-2. The Saints struggled on offense, with a weak passing attack negating the strong running of George Rogers and Wayne Wilson. New Orleans failed to score at all in games at San Francisco and New England. But the good young defense, featuring Rickey Jackson, Johnnie Poe and Russell Gary, kept the Saints in the running into the final weekend. Before more than 70,000 hometown fans, they took a 24-23 lead with a touchdown late in the final period, but a field goal gave the Rams a 26-24 victory and a playoff spot two seconds from the end.

Atlanta Falcons — Dan Henning's arrival as coach coincided with a tumble into last place in the West. Each platoon lost a key player, as linebacker Joel Williams was traded to the Eagles and receiver Alfred Jackson injured his shoulder only four games into the season. Jackson's injury came at the start of a four-game losing streak that made the playoffs a doubtful prospect. With the passing game diminished, the offense relied on William Andrews running behind linemen Mike Kenn and R.C. Thielemann. Two mid-season games lifted the team's spirits. On November 20, they beat the 49ers 28-24 as Billy Johnson grabbed a desperation pass at the final gun and lunged over the goalline. One week later, Kenny Johnson ran his second interception back for a touchdown to beat the Packers 47-41 in overtime. At the end, however, the Falcons petered out with two losses in the final three weeks. In the final two home games, attendance never topped 36,000.

1983 N.F.C. - Eastern Division

WASHINGTON REDSKINS 14-2-0 Joe Gibbs

Scores of Each Game		
30	DALLAS	31
23	Philadelphia	13
27	KANSAS CITY	12
27	Seattle	17
37	L.A.RAIDERS	35
38	St.Louis	14
47	Green Bay	48
38	DETROIT	17
27	San Diego	24
45	ST.LOUIS	7
33	N.Y.Giants	17
42	L.A.Rams	20
28	PHILADELPHIA	24
37	ATLANTA	21
31	Dallas	10
31	N.Y.GIANTS	22

Use Name	Pos.	Hgt	Wgt	Age	Int	Pts
Joe Jacoby	OT	6'7"	300	24		
George Starke	OT	6'5"	260	35		
Russ Grimm	OG	6'3"	290	24		
Ken Huff	OG	6'4"	265	30		
Bruce Kimball	OG	6'2"	260	27		
Mark May	OG	6'6"	288	23		
Roy Simmons	OG-OT	6'3"	264	26		
Jeff Bostic	C	6'2"	250	24		
Todd Liebenstein	DE	6'6"	255	23		
Dexter Manley	DE	6'3"	250	24	1	
Charles Mann	DE	6'6"	250	22		2
Tony McGee	DE	6'4"	249	34		
Perry Brooks	DT	6'3"	270	28		
Dave Butz	DT	6'7"	295	33		
Darryl Grant	DT	6'1"	265	23		
Stuart Anderson	LB	6'1"	224	23		
Monte Coleman	LB	6'2"	230	25		
Pete Cronan	LB	6'2"	238	28		
Mel Kaufman	LB	6'2"	220	25	2	12
Larry Kubin	LB	6'2"	234	24		
Rich Milot	LB	6'4"	237	26	2	
Neal Olkewicz	LB	6'	233	26	1	
Brian Carpenter	DB	5'10"	167	22	1	
Ken Coffey	DB	6'	190	23	4	
Vernon Dean	DB	5'11"	178	24	5	6
Darrell Green	DB	5'8"	170	22	2	
Curtis Jordan	DB	6'2"	205	29	1	
Mark Murphy	DB	6'4"	210	28	9	
Mike Nelms	DB	6'1"	185	28		
Anthony Washington	DB	6'1"	204	25	4	
Greg Williams	DB	5'11"	185	24	2	
Bob Holly	QB	6'2"	196	23		
Babe Laufenberg	QB	6'2"	195	23		
Joe Theismann	QB	6'	198	33		6
Reggie Evans	HB	5'11"	201	24		24
Joe Washington	HB	5'10"	179	29		36
Nick Giaquinto	HB-FB	5'11"	204	28		6
John Riggins	FB	6'2"	235	34		144
Otis Wonsley	FB	5'10"	214	26		
Charlie Brown	WR	5'10"	179	24		48
Alvin Garrett	WR	5'7"	185	26		6
Mark McGrath	WR	5'11"	175	25		
Art Monk	WR	6'3"	209	25		30
Virgil Seay	WR	5'8"	175	25		6
Dave Steif	WR	6'3"	195	27		
Clint Didier	TE	6'5"	240	24		30
Rick Walker	TE	6'3"	235	28		12
Don Warren	TE	6'4"	242	27		12
Mike Williams	TE	6'4"	251	24		
Jeff Hayes	K	5'11"	175	24		
Mark Moseley	K	5'11"	205	35		161

Donald Laster - Neck Injury
Mat Mendenhall - Non-Football Illness
Tony Peters - Suspended by N.F.L.

DALLAS COWBOYS 12-4-0 Tom Landry

Scores of Each Game		
31	Washington	30
34	St.Louis	17
28	N.Y.GIANTS	13
21	NEW ORLEANS	20
37	Minnesota	24
27	TAMPA BAY	*24
37	PHILADELPHIA	7
38	L.A.RAIDERS	40
38	N.Y.Giants	20
27	Philadelphia	20
23	San Diego	24
41	KANSAS CITY	21
35	ST.LOUIS	17
35	Seattle	10
10	WASHINGTON	31
17	San Francisco	42

Use Name	Pos.	Hgt	Wgt	Age	Int	Pts
Jim Cooper	OT	6'5"	263	27		
Pat Donovan	OT	6'4"	257	30		
Phil Pozderac	OT	6'9"	270	23		
Chris Schultz	OT	6'8"	265	23		
Howard Richards	OT-OG	6'6"	258	24		
Kurt Petersen	OG	6'4"	268	26		
Herbert Scott	OG	6'2"	260	30		
Brian Baldinger	OG	6'4"	253	24		
Tom Rafferty	C	6'3"	259	29		
Glen Titensor	C	6'4"	260	25		
Jim Jeffcoat	DE	6'5"	264	22		
Too Tall Jones	DE	6'9"	272	32		
Harvey Martin	DE	6'5"	260	32		
Larry Bethea	DT	6'5"	244	27		
John Dutton	DT	6'7"	275	32		
Don Smerek	DT	6'7"	257	25		
Mark Tuinei	DT	6'5"	270	23		
Randy White	DT	6'4"	263	30		
Bob Breunig	LB	6'2"	225	30	1	
Anthony Dickerson	LB	6'2"	222	26	1	2
Mike Hegman	LB	6'1"	228	30		6
Bruce Huther	LB	6'1"	220	29		
Angelo King	LB	6'1"	230	25		
Scott McLean	LB	6'4"	233	22		
Jeff Rohrer	LB	6'3"	232	24		
Michael Walter	LB	6'3"	238	22		
Bill Bates	DB	6'1"	195	22		
Dextor Clinkscale	DB	5'11"	190	25	2	6
Michael Downs	DB	6'3"	203	23	4	6
Ron Fellows	DB	6'	174	24	5	12
Rod Hill	DB	6'	182	24	2	
Dennis Thurman	DB	5'11"	183	27	6	6
Everson Walls	DB	6'1"	194	23	4	
Glenn Carano	QB	6'3"	204	27		
Gary Hogeboom	QB	6'4"	199	25		
Danny White	QB	6'2"	196	31		30
Gary Allen (from HOU)	HB	5'10"	183	23		6
Tony Dorsett	HB	5'11"	192	29		54
Chuck McSwain	HB	6'	191	22		
Robert Newhouse	FB	5'10"	219	33		
Timmy Newsome	FB	6'1"	231	25		36
Ron Springs	FB-HB	6'1"	210	26		48
Doug Donley	WR	6'	173	24		12
Tony Hill	WR	6'2"	196	27		42
Butch Johnson	WR	6'1"	187	29		18
Drew Pearson	WR	6'	193	32		30
Doug Cosbie	TE	6'6"	232	27		36
Billy Joe DuPree	TE	6'4"	223	33		6
Cleo Simmons	TE	6'2"	225	21		
Jim Miller	K	5'11"	183	26		
Rafael Septien	K	5'10"	180	29		123
John Warren	K	6'	207	22		

James Jones - Knee Injury

ST. LOUIS CARDINALS 8-7-1 Jim Hanifan

Scores of Each Game		
17	New Orleans	28
17	DALLAS	34
27	SAN FRANCISCO	42
14	Philadelphia	11
14	Kansas City	38
14	WASHINGTON	38
34	Tampa Bay	27
20	N.Y.GIANTS	*20
41	MINNESOTA	31
7	WASHINGTON	45
33	SEATTLE	28
44	SAN DIEGO	14
17	Dallas	35
10	N.Y.Giants	6
34	L.A.Raiders	24
31	PHILADELPHIA	7

Use Name	Pos.	Hgt	Wgt	Age	Int	Pts
Art Plunkett	OT	6'7"	270	24		
Tootie Robbins	OT	6'5"	278	25		
Luis Sharpe	OT	6'4"	260	23		
Dan Audick	OG-OT	6'3"	253	28		
Joe Bostic	OG	6'3"	265	26		
Terry Stieve	OG	6'2"	265	29		
Randy Clark	C	6'3"	254	26		
Dan Dierdorf	C	6'4"	290	34		
Carlos Scott	C	6'4"	300	23		
Al Baker	DE	6'6"	260	26	2	
Curtis Greer	DE	6'4"	252	25		
Elois Grooms	DE	6'4"	250	30	1	6
Stafford Mays	DE	6'2"	250	25		
Rush Brown	DT	6'2"	260	29		
Mark Duda	DT	6'3"	263	22		
David Galloway	DT	6'3"	277	24	1	2
Dave Ahrens	LB	6'3"	228	24		
Kurt Allerman	LB	6'2"	222	28		
Charlie Baker	LB	6'2"	217	25		
Paul Davis (from NYG)	LB	6'2"	235	23	3	
Bob Harris	LB	6'2"	215	22		
E.J. Junior	LB	6'3"	235	23		
Craig Shaffer	LB	6'	230	24		
Bill Whitaker	LB	6'	182	23		
Jeff Griffin	DB	6'	185	25		
Victor Heflin	DB	6'	184	23		
Monty Hunter	DB	6'	202	24		
Cedric Mack	DB	6'	190	22	3	
Lee Nelson	DB	5'10"	185	29	1	6
Chet Parlavecchio (from GB)	DB	6'2"	225	23		
Benny Perrin	DB	6'2"	178	23	4	6
George Schmitt	DB	5'11"	193	22		
Leonard Smith	DB	5'11"	190	22		
Wayne Smith	DB	6'	175	26	2	
Lionel Washington	DB	6'	184	22	8	
Jim Hart	QB	6'2"	210	38		
Rusty Lisch	QB	6'3"	213	26		
Neil Lomax	QB	6'3"	215	24		12
Ottis Anderson	HB	6'2"	220	26		36
Will Harrell	HB	5'9"	182	30		
Stump Mitchell	HB	5'9"	188	24		18
Earl Ferrell	FB	6'	215	25		6
Randy Love	FB	6'1"	205	26		18
Wayne Morris	FB	6'	210	29		12
Steve Bird	WR	5'11"	171	22		
Roy Green	WR	6'	195	26		84
Mike Shumann	WR	6'	185	27		
Ken Thompson	WR	6'1"	178	24		
Pat Tilley	WR	5'10"	178	30		30
Greg LaFleur	TE	6'4"	236	24		
Doug Marsh	TE	6'3"	240	25		48
Eddie McGill	TE	6'6"	225	23		
Jamie Williams	TE	6'4"	232	23		
Carl Birdsong	K	6'	192	24		
Neil O'Donoghue	K	6'6"	210	30		90

PHILADELPHIA EAGLES 5-11-0 Marion Campbell

Scores of Each Game		
22	San Francisco	17
13	WASHINGTON	23
13	Denver	10
11	ST.LOUIS	14
28	ATLANTA	24
17	N.Y.Giants	13
7	Dallas	37
6	CHICAGO	37
21	BALTIMORE	22
20	DALLAS	27
14	Chicago	17
0	N.Y.GIANTS	23
24	Washington	28
13	L.A.RAMS	9
17	NEW ORLEANS	*20
7	St.Louis	31

Use Name	Pos.	Hgt	Wgt	Age	Int	Pts
Jerry Sisemore	OT	6'4"	265	32		
Stan Walters	OT	6'6"	275	35		
Jim Fritzche	OT-OG	6'8"	265	22		
Dean Miraldi	OT-OG	6'5"	254	25		
Ron Baker	OG	6'4"	250	28		
Steve Kenney	OG	6'4"	262	27		
Gerry Feehery	C-OG	6'2"	268	23		
Guy Morriss	C	6'4"	255	32		
Mark Slater	C	6'2"	257	28		
Greg Brown	DE	6'5"	240	26		
Byron Darby	DE	6'4"	250	23		
Carl Hairston	DE	6'3"	260	30		
Dennis Harrison	DE	6'8"	275	27		
Leonard Mitchell	DE	6'7"	272	24		
Thomas Strauthers	DE	6'4"	255	22		
Harvey Armstrong	NT	6'2"	255	23		
Ken Clarke	NT	6'2"	255	27		
Bill Cowher	LB	6'3"	225	26		
Anthony Griggs	LB	6'3"	230	23	3	
Rich Kraynak	LB	6'1"	221	23		
Jerry Robinson	LB	6'2"	225	26		
Jody Schulz	LB	6'3"	235	23		
Reggie Wilkes	LB	6'4"	230	27		
Joel Williams	LB	6'1"	220	26		
Dennis DeVaughn	DB	5'10"	175	22		
Herman Edwards	DB	6'	190	29	1	
Ray Ellis	DB	6'1"	192	24	1	
Elbert Foules	DB	5'11"	185	22	1	
Wes Hopkins	DB	6'1"	205	21		
Randy Logan	DB	6'1"	195	32	1	
John Sciarra	DB	5'11"	185	29		
Brenard Wilson	DB	6'	175	28		
Roynell Young	DB	6'1"	181	25	1	
Ron Jaworski	QB	6'2"	196	32		6
Dan Pastorini	QB	6'3"	205	34		
Joe Pisarcik	QB	6'4"	220	31		
Wilbert Montgomery	HB	5'10"	195	28		
Major Everett	FB	5'10"	207	23		
Michael Haddix	FB	6'2"	225	21		12
Perry Harrington	FB	5'11"	210	25		6
Hubie Oliver	FB	5'10"	212	25		18
Michael Williams	FB	6'2"	217	22		
Harold Charmichael	WR	6'7"	225	33		18
Melvin Hoover	WR	6'	185	24		
Mike Quick	WR	6'2"	190	24		78
Ron Smith	WR	6'	185	26		
Tony Woodruff	WR	6'	175	24		12
Glen Young	WR	6'2"	205	22		6
Al Dixon	TE	6'5"	238	29		
Vyto Kab	TE	6'5"	240	23		6
Lawrence Sampleton	TE	6'5"	233	23		
Tony Franklin	K	5'8"	182	26		69
Max Runager	K	6'1"	189	27		
Tom Skladany	K	6'	195	28		

Petey Perot - Shoulder Injury
John Spagnola - Back Injury
Zach Valentine - Knee Injury

NEW YORK GIANTS 3-12-1 Bill Parcells

Scores of Each Game		
6	L.A.RAMS	16
16	Atlanta	*13
13	Dallas	28
27	GREEN BAY	3
34	SAN DIEGO	41
13	PHILADELPHIA	17
17	Kansas City	38
20	St.Louis	*20
20	DALLAS	38
9	Detroit	15
17	WASHINGTON	33
23	Philadelphia	0
12	L.A.Raiders	27
6	ST.LOUIS	10
12	SEATTLE	17
22	Washington	31

Use Name	Pos.	Hgt	Wgt	Age	Int	Pts
Brad Benson	OT	6'3"	258	27		
Gordon King	OT	6'6"	275	27		
Billy Ard	OT	6'3"	250	24		
Kevin Belcher	OG	6'3"	255	22		
John Tautolo	OG	6'3"	260	24		
J.T.Turner	OG	6'3"	250	30		
Chris Foote	C	6'3"	250	26		
Ernie Hughes	C	6'3"	265	28		
Rich Umphrey	C	6'3"	255	24		
Dee Hardison	DE	6'4"	269	27		
Leonard Marshall	DE	6'3"	285	21		2
George Martin	DE	6'4"	245	30		
Curtis McGriff	DE	6'5"	265	25		
Casey Merrill (from GB)	DE	6'4"	255	26		
Jim Burt	NT	6'1"	255	24		
Charles Cook	NT	6'3"	255	24		
Bill Neill	NT	6'4"	255	24		
Jerome Sally	NT	6'3"	260	24		
Harry Carson	LB	6'2"	235	29		
Andy Headen	LB	6'5"	230	23		
Byron Hunt	LB	6'5"	230	24		
Brian Kelley	LB	6'3"	222	32	1	
Frank Marion	LB	6'3"	223	32		
Joe McLaughlin	LB	6'1"	235	26		
Lawrence Taylor	LB	6'3"	237	24	2	
Brad Van Pelt	LB	6'5"	235	32	2	
Mike Whittington	LB	6'2"	220	25		
Bill Currier	DB	6'	202	28	2	6
Mike Dennis	DB	5'10"	190	24	1	
Larry Flowers	DB	6'1"	190	25	1	
Mark Haynes	DB	5'11"	198	24	3	
Terry Jackson	DB	5'10"	197	27		
Terry Kinard	DB	6'1"	190	23	3	
Mike Maycock	DB	6'2"	195	25		
LeCharls McDaniel	DB	5'9"	170	24		
Beasley Reese (to TB)	DB	6'1"	195	29	8	
Pete Shaw	DB	5'10"	183	29		
Scott Brunner	QB	6'5"	200	26		
Tom Owen	QB	6'1"	194	31		
Jeff Rutledge	QB	6'1"	190	26		
Phil Simms	QB	6'3"	216	26		
Leon Bright	HB	5'9"	192	28		
Billy Campfield	HB	5'11"	205	27		
Larry Heater	HB	5'11"	205	25		
Joe Morris	HB	5'7"	190	22		6
Rob Carpenter	FB	6'1"	230	28		36
John Tuggle	FB	6'1"	210	22		6
Butch Woolfolk	FB	6'1"	207	23		24
Floyd Eddings	WR	5'11"	177	25		
Earnest Gray	WR	6'3"	195	26		30
Keith Hugger	WR	5'11"	175	22		
Mike Miller	WR	6'	182	23		
John Mistler	WR	6'2"	186	24		
Johnny Perkins	WR	6'2"	205	30		
Danny Pittman (to STL)	WR	6'2"	205	25		6
Byron Williams	WR	6'2"	180	22		6
Zeke Mowatt	TE	6'3"	238	22		6
Tom Mullady	TE	6'3"	232	26		
Malcolm Scott	TE	6'4"	240	22		
Ali Haji-Sheikh	K	6'	172	22		127
Dave Jennings	K	6'4"	205	31		

* Overtime

WASHINGTON REDSKINS

RUSHING

Last Name	No.	Yds	Avg	TD
Riggins	375	1347	3.6	24
J. Washington	145	772	5.3	0
Theismann	37	234	6.3	1
Wonsley	25	88	3.5	0
Hayes	2	63	31.5	0
Brown	4	53	13.3	0
Giaquinto	14	53	3.8	1
Holly	4	13	3.3	0
Evans	16	11	0.7	4
Walker	2	10	5.0	0
Garrett	2	0	0.0	0
Monk	3	-19	-6.3	0

RECEIVING

Last Name	No.	Yds	Avg	TD
Brown	78	1225	15.7	8
Monk	47	748	15.9	5
J. Washington	47	454	9.7	6
Giaquinto	27	372	13.8	0
Garrett	25	332	13.3	1
Warren	20	225	11.3	2
Walker	17	168	9.9	2
Didier	9	153	17.0	4
Riggins	5	29	5.8	0
Seay	2	55	27.5	1
McGrath	1	6	6.0	0

PUNT RETURNS

Last Name	No.	Yds	Avg	TD
Nelms	38	289	7.6	0
Seay	5	57	11.4	0
Green	4	29	7.3	0
Giaquinto	2	12	6.0	0

KICKOFF RETURNS

Last Name	No.	Yds	Avg	TD
Nelms	35	802	22.9	0
Evans	10	141	14.1	0
Seay	9	218	24.2	0
Garrett	2	50	25.0	0
Wonsley	2	36	18.0	0
Cronan	1	17	17.0	0
Giaquinto	1	0	0.0	0
Sawyer	1	15	15.0	0
G. Williams	1	6	6.0	0

PASSING — PUNTING — KICKING

PASSING	Att	Cmp	%	Yds	Yd/Att	TD	Int—	%	RK
Theismann	459	276	60	3714	8.09	29	11—	2	2
Holly	1	1	100	5	5.00	0	0—	0	
Monk	1	1	100	46	46.00	0	0—	0	
Riggins	1	0	0	0	0.00	0	0—	0	
J. Washington	1	0	0	0	0.00	0	0—	0	

PUNTING	No.	Avg.
Hayes	72	38.8

KICKING	XP	Att	%	FG	Att	%
Moseley	62	63	98	33	47	70

DALLAS COWBOYS

RUSHING

Last Name	No.	Yds	Avg	TD
Dorsett	289	1321	4.6	8
Springs	149	541	3.6	7
Newsome	44	185	4.2	2
Newhouse	9	34	3.8	0
D. White	18	31	1.7	4
Pearson	2	13	6.5	0
Allen	1	5	5.0	0
T. Hill	1	2	2.0	0
Johnson	1	0	0.0	0
Hogeboom	6	-10	-1.7	0

RECEIVING

Last Name	No.	Yds	Avg	TD
Springs	73	589	8.1	1
T. Hill	49	801	16.3	7
Pearson	47	545	11.6	5
Cosbie	46	588	12.8	6
Johnson	41	561	13.7	3
Dorsett	40	287	7.2	1
Donley	18	370	20.6	2
Newsome	18	250	13.9	4
DuPree	12	142	11.8	1
D. White	1	15	15.0	1
Rafferty	1	8	8.0	0

PUNT RETURNS

Last Name	No.	Yds	Avg	TD
R. Hill	30	232	7.7	0
Fellows	10	75	7.5	0
Allen	9	153	17.0	1
Donley	1	1	1.0	0
Newhouse	1	0	0.0	0

KICKOFF RETURNS

Last Name	No.	Yds	Avg	TD
Fellows	43	855	19.9	0
R. Hill	14	243	17.4	0
Allen	8	178	22.3	0
Cosbie	2	17	8.5	0
Huther	1	0	0.0	0
McSwain	1	17	17.0	0
Newsome	1	28	28.0	0
Springs	1	13	13.0	0

PASSING — PUNTING — KICKING

PASSING	Att	Cmp	%	Yds	Yd/Att	TD	Int—	%	RK
D. White	533	334	63	3980	7.47	29	23—	4	6
Hogeboom	17	11	65	161	4.70	1	1—	6	
Springs	2	1	50	15	15.00	1	0—	0	
Dorsett	1	0	0	0	0.00	0	0—	0	
Pearson	1	0	0	0	0.00	0	1—	100	

PUNTING	No.	Avg.
Warren	39	39.8
D. White	38	40.6
Miller	5	35.6

KICKING	XP	Att	%	FG	Att	%
Septien	57	59	97	22	27	82

ST. LOUIS CARDINALS

RUSHING

Last Name	No.	Yds	Avg	TD
Anderson	296	1270	4.3	5
Mitchell	68	373	5.5	3
Morris	75	257	3.4	2
Lomax	27	127	4.7	2
Love	35	103	2.9	2
Farrell	7	53	7.6	1
Green	4	49	12.3	0
Harrell	4	13	3.3	0
Hart	5	12	2.4	0
Sharpe	1	11	11.0	0
Lisch	2	9	4.5	0
Perrin	1	0	0.0	0

RECEIVING

Last Name	No.	Yds	Avg	TD
Green	78	1227	15.7	14
Anderson	54	459	8.5	1
Tilley	44	690	15.7	5
Marsh	32	421	13.2	8
Morris	14	55	3.9	0
LaFleur	12	99	8.3	0
Shumann	11	154	14.0	0
Mitchell	7	54	7.7	0
Love	6	58	9.7	1
Harrell	3	25	8.3	0
Thompson	2	31	15.5	0
McGill	1	11	11.0	0
Ahrens	1	4	4.0	0

PUNT RETURNS

Last Name	No.	Yds	Avg	TD
Mitchell	38	337	8.9	0
Bird	14	76	5.4	0
Harrell	5	31	6.2	0
Ferrell	1	17	17.0	0

KICKOFF RETURNS

Last Name	No.	Yds	Avg	TD
Mitchell	36	778	21.6	0
Ferrell	13	257	19.8	0
Bird	9	194	21.6	0
Schmitt	4	41	10.3	0
Harrell	3	62	20.7	0
Love	3	71	23.7	0
Allerman	1	11	11.0	0
Duda	1	12	2.0	0
Green	1	14	14.0	0
L. Smith	1	19	19.0	0

PASSING — PUNTING — KICKING

PASSING	Att	Cmp	%	Yds	Yd/Att	TD	Int—	%	RK
Lomax	354	209	59	2636	7.45	24	11—	3	4
Hart	91	50	55	592	6.51	4	8—	9	
Lisch	13	6	46	66	5.08	1	2—	15	
Birdsong	1	1	100	11	11.00	0	0—	0	
Perrin	1	1	100	4	4.00	0	0—	0	

PUNTING	No.	Avg.
Birdsong	85	41.5

KICKING	XP	Att	%	FG	Att	%
O'Donoghue	45	47	96	15	28	54

PHILADELPHIA EAGLES

RUSHING

Last Name	No.	Yds	Avg	TD
Oliver	121	434	3.6	1
M. Williams	103	385	3.7	0
Haddix	91	220	2.4	0
Montgomery	29	139	4.8	0
Jaworski	25	129	5.2	1
Harrington	23	98	4.3	1
Everett	5	7	1.4	0
Runager	1	6	6.0	0
Pastorini	1	0	0.0	0
Pisarcik	3	-1	-0.3	0

RECEIVING

Last Name	No.	Yds	Avg	TD
Quick	69	1409	20.4	13
Oliver	49	421	8.6	2
Carmichael	38	515	13.6	3
Haddix	23	254	11.0	0
Kab	18	195	10.8	1
M. Williams	17	142	8.4	0
Hoover	10	221	22.1	0
Montgomery	9	53	5.9	0
Woodruff	6	70	11.7	2
Dixon	4	54	13.5	0
G. Young	3	125	41.7	1
Sampleton	2	28	14.0	0
Everett	2	18	9.0	0
Harrington	1	19	19.0	0
Smith	1	8	8.0	0

PUNT RETURNS

Last Name	No.	Yds	Avg	TD
Sciarra	22	115	5.2	0
G. Young	14	93	6.6	0
Hoover	7	44	6.3	0
Foules	1	7	7.0	0
Logan	1	0	0.0	0

KICKOFF RETURNS

Last Name	No.	Yds	Avg	TD
G. Young	26	547	21.0	0
Everett	14	275	19.6	0
Ellis	7	119	17.0	0
Harrington	4	79	19.8	0
Haddix	3	51	17.0	0
M. Williams	3	59	19.7	0
Darby	2	3	1.5	0
Fritzche	2	17	8.5	0
R. Young	1	18	18.0	0

PASSING — PUNTING — KICKING

PASSING	Att	Cmp	%	Yds	Yd/Att	TD	Int—	%	RK
Jaworski	446	235	53	3315	7.43	20	18—	4	9
Pisarcik	34	16	47	172	5.06	1	0—	0	
Pastorini	5	0	0	0	0.00	0	0—	0	
Carmichael	1	1	100	45	45.00	1	0—	0	

PUNTING	No.	Avg.
Runager	59	41.7
Skladany	27	39.3

KICKING	XP	ATT	%	FG	ATT	%
Franklin	24	27	89	15	26	58

NEW YORK GIANTS

RUSHING

Last Name	No.	Yds	Avg	TD
Woolfolk	246	857	3.5	4
Carpenter	170	624	3.7	4
Morris	35	145	4.1	0
Brunner	26	64	2.5	0
Tuggle	17	49	2.9	1
Rutledge	7	27	3.9	0
Campfield	2	21	10.5	0
Eddings	1	3	3.0	0
Bright	1	2	2.0	0
Miller	1	2	2.0	0

RECEIVING

Last Name	No.	Yds	Avg	TD
Gray	78	1139	14.6	5
Mistler	45	422	9.4	0
Woolfolk	28	368	13.1	0
Carpenter	26	258	9.9	2
Mowatt	21	280	13.3	1
B. Williams	20	346	17.3	1
Scott	17	206	12.1	0
Eddings	14	231	16.5	0
Mullady	16	184	14.2	1
Miller	7	170	24.3	0
Pittman	9	175	19.4	1
Miller	7	170	24.3	0
Tuggle	3	50	16.7	0
Bright	2	33	16.5	0
Morris	2	1	0.5	1
Campfield	1	12	12.0	0

PUNT RETURNS

Last Name	No.	Yds	Avg	TD
Shaw	29	234	8.1	0
Bright	17	117	6.9	0
Reece	9	26	2.9	0
Pittman	0	0	—	0

KICKOFF RETURNS

Last Name	No.	Yds	Avg	TD
Bright	21	475	22.6	0
Morris	14	255	18.2	0
Campfield	9	154	17.1	0
Tuggle	9	156	17.3	0
Pittman	6	107	17.8	0
Heater	5	71	14.2	0
Miller	2	31	15.5	0
Woolfolk	2	13	6.5	0
Dennis	1	54	54.0	0

PASSING — PUNTING — KICKING

PASSING	Att	Cmp	%	Yds	Yd/Att	TD	Int—	%	RK
Brunner	386	190	49	2516	6.52	9	22—	6	14
Rutledge	174	87	50	1208	6.94	3	8—	5	
Simms	13	7	54	130	10.00	0	1—	7	
Jennings	1	0	0	0	0.00	0	0—	0	
Mistler	1	0	0	0	0.00	0	0—	0	

PUNTING	No.	Avg.
Jennings	84	40.3

KICKING	XP	ATT	%	FG	Att	%
Haji-Sheikh	22	23	96	35	42	83

1983 N.F.C. - Central Division

DETROIT LIONS 9-7-0 Monte Clark

Scores of Each Game		
11	Tampa Bay	0
26	CLEVELAND	31
14	ATLANTA	30
17	Minnesota	20
10	L.A.Rams	21
38	GREEN BAY	14
31	CHICAGO	17
17	Washington	38
38	Chicago	17
15	N.Y.Giants	9
17	Houston	27
23	Green Bay	*20
45	PITTSBURGH	3
13	MINNESOTA	2
9	Cincinnati	17
23	TAMPA BAY	20

Use Name	Pos.	Hgt	Wgt	Age	Int	Pts
Chris Dietrich	OT	6'3"	255	25		
Keith Droney	OT	6'5"	265	25		
Rich Strenger	OT	6'7"	269	23		
Homer Elias	OG	6'3"	255	28		
Don Greco	OG	6'3"	255	24		
Larry Lee	OG-C	6'2"	260	23		
Amos Fowler	C	6'3"	253	27		
Steve Mott	C	6'3"	260	22		
Tom Turnure	C	6'4"	250	26		
Mike Cofer	DE	6'5"	245	23		
William Gay	DE	6'3"	255	28		
Curtis Green	DE	6'3"	252	26		
Mike Dawson	DT	6'4"	254	29		
Doug English	DT	6'5"	258	30		4
Mike Fanning	DT	6'6"	260	30		2
Martin Moss	DT	6'4"	252	24		
Roosevelt Barnes	LB	6'2"	220	25	2	
Garry Cobb	LB	6'2"	227	26	4	
August Curley	LB	6'3"	226	23		
Steve Doig	LB	6'2"	242	23		
Ken Fantetti	LB	6'2"	227	26	2	
James Harrell	LB	6'1"	220	26		
Jimmy Williams	LB	6'2"	221	22		
James Caver	DB	5'9"	175	22		
William Graham	DB	5'11"	191	23		
Hector Gray	DB	6'1"	190	26		
Alvin Hall	DB	5'10"	184	25	2	
Maurice Harvey (from GB)	DB	5'10"	187	27		
Demetrious Johnson	DB	5'11"	190	22		
Al Latimer	DB	5'11"	177	25	1	
Bruce McNorton	DB	5'11"	175	24	7	
Dan Wagoner	DB	5'10"	180	23		
Bobby Watkins	DB	5'10"	184	23	4	
Gary Danielson	QB	6'2"	196	31		
Eric Hipple	QB	6'2"	196	25		18
Mike Machurek	QB	6'1"	205	23		
Ken Jenkins	HB	5'8"	184	24		
Rick Kane	HB	5'11"	200	28		
Billy Sims	HB	6'	212	27		42
Dexter Bussey	FB	6'1"	210	31		6
James Jones	FB	6'2"	228	22		42
Horace King	FB	5'10"	205	30		
Vince Thompson	FB	6'	225	26		6
Jeff Chadwick	WR	6'3"	185	22		24
Robbie Martin	WR	5'8"	177	23		6
Mark Nichols	WR	6'2"	208	23		6
Freddie Scott	WR	6'2"	190	31		6
Leonard Thompson	WR	5'11"	192	31		24
Reese McCall	TE	6'7"	232	27		
Ulysses Norris	TE	6'4"	232	26		42
Ron Rubick	TE	6'3"	228	22		6
Mike Black	K	6'1"	197	22		
Eddie Murray	K	5'10"	170	27		113

GREEN BAY PACKERS 8-8-0 Bart Starr

Scores of Each Game		
41	Houston	*38
21	PITTSBURGH	25
27	L.A.RAMS	24
3	N.Y.Giants	27
55	TAMPA BAY	14
14	Detroit	38
48	WASHINGTON	47
17	MINNESOTA	*20
14	Cincinnati	34
35	CLEVELAND	21
29	Minnesota	21
20	DETROIT	*23
41	Atlanta	*47
31	CHICAGO	28
12	Tampa Bay	9
21	Chicago	23

Use Name	Pos.	Hgt	Wgt	Age	Int	Pts
Charlie Getty	OT	6'4"	270	31		
Ron Hallstron	OT	6'6"	283	23		
Greg Koch	OT	6'4"	276	28		
Karl Swanke	OT-C	6'6"	262	25		
Dave Drechsler	OG	6'3"	264	23		
Leotis Harris	OG	6'1"	265	28		
Tim Huffman	OG	6'5"	277	24		
Syd Kitson	OG	6'4"	264	24		
Ron Sams	OG	6'3"	269	22		
Larry McCarren	C	6'3"	251	31		
Larry Rubens	C	6'1"	250	23		
Greg Boyd	DE	6'6"	280	29		
Byron Braggs	DE	6'4"	290	23		
Robert Brown	DE	6'2"	250	22		
Ezra Johnson	DE	6'4"	259	27		
Ron Spears (from NE)	DE	6'6"	255	23		
Charles Johnson	NT	6'1"	265	26		
Terry Jones	NT	6'2"	253	26		
Daryle Skaugstad (from SF)	NT	6'5"	268	26		
Richard Turner	NT	6'2"	261	24		
John Anderson	LB	6'3"	221	27	5	6
George Cumby	LB	6'	225	27		
Mike Curcio	LB	6'1"	232	26		
Mike Douglass	LB	6'	214	28		12
Jim Laughlin	LB	6'	222	25	1	
Cliff Lewis	LB	6'1"	226	23		
Guy Prather	LB	6'2"	229	25		
Randy Scott	LB	6'1"	220	24	1	
Rich Wingo	LB	6'1"	227	27		
Johnnie Gray	DB	5'11"	202	29	2	
Estus Hood	DB	5'11"	189	27		
Mike Jolly	DB	6'3"	195	24	1	
Mark Lee	DB	5'11"	188	25	4	
Tim Lewis	DB	5'11"	191	21	5	
Mike McCoy	DB	5'11"	183	30		
Mark Murphy	DB	6'2"	201	25		
Dwayne O'Steen (from TB)	DB	6'1"	195	28		
Rich Campbell	QB	6'4"	219	23		
Lynn Dickey	QB	6'4"	210	32		18
David Whitehurst	QB	6'2"	204	28		
Harlan Huckleby	HB	6'1"	201	25		24
Eddie Lee Ivery	HB	6'1"	214	26		10
Chet Winters	HB	5'11"	204	21		
Jessie Clark	FB	6'	233	23		6
Gerry Ellis	FB	5'11"	216	25		36
Mike Meade	FB	5'11"	224	21		18
Ron Cassidy	WR	6'	180	26		
Phillip Epps	WR	5'10"	165	23		6
John Jefferson	WR	6'1"	204	27		42
James Lofton	WR	6'3"	197	27		48
Paul Coffman	TE	6'3"	225	27		66
Gary Lewis	TE	6'5"	234	24		12
Eddie Garcia	K	5'8"	178	24		
Bucky Scribner	K	6'	202	23		
Jan Stenerud	K	6'2"	190	40		115

Calvin Favron - Broken Leg
Del Rodgers - Neck Injury

CHICAGO BEARS 8-8-0 Mike Ditka

Scores of Each Game		
17	ATLANTA	20
17	TAMPA BAY	10
31	New Orleans	*34
19	Baltimore	*22
31	DENVER	14
14	MINNESOTA	23
17	Detroit	31
7	Philadelphia	6
17	DETROIT	38
14	L.A. Rams	21
17	PHILADELPHIA	38
27	Tampa Bay	0
13	SAN FRANCISCO	3
28	Green Bay	31
19	Minnesota	13
23	GREEN BAY	21

Use Name	Pos.	Hgt	Wgt	Age	Int	Pts
Jim Covert	OT	6'4"	283	23		
Andy Frederick	OT	6'6"	265	29		
John Janata	OT	6'7"	274	22		
Keith Van Horne	OT	6'6"	276	25		
Kurt Becker	OG	6'5"	270	24		
Mark Bortz	OG	6'6"	271	22		
Rob Fada	OG	6'2"	272	22		
Perry Hartnett	OG	6'5"	275	23		
Noah Jackson	OG	6'2"	265	29		
Tim Norman	OG	6'6"	270	24		
Revie Sorey	OG	6'2"	260	29		
Jay Hilgenberg	C	6'3"	255	24		
Dan Neal	C	6'4"	255	34		
Richard Dent	DE	6'5"	253	22		
Mike Hartenstine	DE	6'3"	253	30		8
Tyrone Keys	DE	6'7"	267	23		
Dan Hampton	DT	6'5"	266	25		
Steve McMichael	DT	6'2"	263	25		
Jim Osborne	DT	6'3"	259	33		
Kelvin Atkins	LB	6'3"	235	23		
Brian Cabral	LB	6'	227	27		
Gary Campbell	LB	6'1"	220	31		
Al Harris	LB	6'5"	253	26		
Jerry Muckensturn	LB	6'4"	220	29		
Dan Rains	LB	6'1"	222	27		
Dave Simmons	LB	6'4"	228	26		
Mike Singletary	LB	5'11"	228	24	1	
Otis Wilson	LB	6'2"	231	25	1	
Todd Bell	DB	6'1"	205	24		
Dave Duerson	DB	6'	205	22		
Gary Fencik	DB	6'1"	193	29	2	
Jeff Fisher	DB	5'11"	190	25		
Leslie Frazier	DB	6'	189	24	7	6
Kevin Potter	DB	5'10"	183	23		
Mike Richardson	DB	6'	188	22	5	
Terry Schmidt	DB	6'	184	31	5	6
Walt Williams	DB	6'	184	29		
Bob Avellini	QB	6'2"	209	30		
Vince Evans	QB	6'2"	212	28		6
Jim McMahon	QB	6'1"	187	24		18
Dennis Gentry	HB	5'8"	184	24		
Anthony Hutchison	HB	5'10"	186	22		6
Walter Payton	HB	5'11"	202	29		48
Matt Suhey	FB	5'11"	216	25		30
Calvin Thomas	FB	5'11"	235	23		
Brian Baschnagel	WR	6'	184	29		
Willie Gault	WR	6'	178	22		48
Ken Margerum	WR	6'	178	24		12
Dennis McKinnon	WR	6'1"	185	22		30
Rickey Watts	WR	6'1"	213	26		
Pat Dunsmore	TE	6'3"	237	23		
Emery Moorehead	TE	6'2"	225	29		18
Jay Saldi	TE	6'3"	227	26		
Bob Parsons	K	6'4"	225	33		
Ray Stachowicz	K	5'11"	192	24		
Bob Thomas	K	5'10"	177	31		77

MINNESOTA VIKINGS 8-8-0 Bud Grant

Scores of Each Game		
27	Cleveland	21
17	SAN FRANCISCO	48
19	Tampa Bay	*16
20	DETROIT	17
24	DALLAS	37
23	Chicago	14
34	HOUSTON	14
20	Green Bay	*17
31	St.Louis	41
12	TAMPA BAY	17
21	GREEN BAY	29
17	Pittsburgh	14
16	New Orleans	17
2	Detroit	13
13	CHICAGO	19
20	CINCINNATI	14

Use Name	Pos.	Hgt	Wgt	Age	Int	Pts
Tim Irwin	OT	6'6"	294	26		
Steve Riley	OT	6'6"	270	30		
Terry Tausch	OT	6'5"	269	24		
Brent Boyd	OG	6'3"	275	26		
Wes Hamilton	OG	6'3"	270	30		
Jim Hough	OG	6'2"	275	27		
Dave Huffman	OG-C	6'6"	255	26		6
Curtis Rouse	OG	6'3"	305	22		
Dennis Swilley	C	6'3"	245	28		
Neil Elshire	DE	6'6"	250	25		
Randy Holloway	DE	6'5"	255	28		
Doug Martin	DE-NT	6'3"	258	26		
Mark Mullaney	DE	6'6"	245	30		
Charles Johnson	NT	6'3"	275	31	1	6
James White	NT	6'3"	270	29	1	
Walker Lee Ashley	LB	6'	240	23		
Matt Blair	LB	6'5"	235	32	1	
Dennis Johnson	LB	6'3"	235	25		
Henry Johnson	LB	6'1"	235	25		
Fred McNeill	LB	6'2"	230	21		
Robin Sendlein	LB	6'3"	225	24		
Scott Studwell	LB	6'2"	230	29		
Rufus Bess	DB	5'9"	185	27	3	
Joey Browner	DB	6'2"	205	23	2	
Tom Hannon	DB	5'11"	195	28		
Carl Lee	DB	6'	185	22	1	
Keith Nord	DB	6'	195	26	1	
John Swain	DB	6'1"	195	23	6	
Willie Teal	DB	5'10"	195	25	3	
John Turner	DB	6'	200	27	6	
Steve Dils	QB	6'1"	195	27		
Tommy Kramer	QB	6'2"	205	28		
Wade Wilson	QB	6'3"	210	24		
Rick Bell	HB	6'	205	22		
Ted Brown	HB	5'10"	210	26		66
Darrin Nelson	HB	5'9"	185	24		6
Jarvis Redwine	HB	5'10"	205	26		
Rickey Young	HB	6'2"	200	29		12
Tony Galbreath	FB	6'	228	29		36
Mike Jones	WR	5'11"	176	23		
Terry LeCount	WR	5'10"	185	27		12
Leo Lewis	WR	5'8"	170	26		
Mardye McDole	WR	5'11"	205	24		
Sammy White	WR	5'11"	195	29		24
Sam McCullum	WR	6'2"	195	30		12
Norris Brown	TE	6'3"	220	22		
Bob Bruer	TE	6'5"	240	29		12
Dave Casper (from HOU)	TE	6'4"	241	31		
Steve Jordan	TE	6'3"	230	22		12
Mark Mularkey	TE	6'4"	245	21		
Greg Coleman	K	6'	185	28		
Benny Ricardo	K	5'10"	170	29		108

Rick Danmeier - Back Injury
Joe Senser - Knee Injury

TAMPA BAY BUCCANEERS 2-14-0 John McKay

Scores of Each Game		
0	DETROIT	11
10	Chicago	17
16	MINNESOTA	*19
17	CINCINNATI	23
14	Green Bay	55
24	Dallas	*27
27	St.Louis	34
21	NEW ORLEANS	24
12	Pittsburgh	17
17	Minnesota	12
0	Cleveland	20
0	CHICAGO	27
33	HOUSTON	24
21	San Francisco	35
9	GREEN BAY	*12
20	DETROIT	23

Use Name	Pos.	Hgt	Wgt	Age	Int	Pts
Dave Reavis	OT	6'5"	263	33		
Gene Sanders	OT	6'3"	280	26		
Kelley Thomas	OT	6'6"	270	22		
Glenn Bujnoch	OG	6'5"	265	29		
Sean Farrell	OG	6'3"	260	23		
Randy Grimes	OG-C	6'4"	265	23		
Ray Snell	OG-OT	6'4"	265	25		
George Yarno	OG	6'2"	260	26		
Jim Leonard	C-OG	6'3"	260	25		
Steve Wilson	C	6'3"	270	29		
Hasson Arbubakrr	DE	6'4"	250	22		
John Cannon	DE	6'5"	260	23		
Booker Reese	DE	6'6"	260	23		2
Lee Roy Selmon	DE	6'3"	260	28		
David Logan	NT	6'2"	250	26		6
Brad White	NT	6'2"	255	25		
Scott Branley	LB	6'1"	230	25	1	
Jeff Davis	LB	6'	230	23		
Hugh Green	LB	6'2"	225	24	2	12
Andy Hawkins	LB	6'2"	230	25		
Cecil Johnson	LB	6'2"	235	28		
Ed Judie (from SF)	LB	6'2"	235	24		
Quentin Lowry (from WAS)	LB	6'3"	235	25		
Danny Spradlin	LB	6'1"	235	24		
Robert Thompson	LB	6'3"	225	23		
Richard Wood	LB	6'2"	230	30		
Cedric Brown	DB	6'1"	200	29	4	
Jeremiah Castille	DB	5'10"	175	22	1	6
Neal Cozie	DB	6'2"	205	30		
Mark Cotney	DB	6'	205	31	2	
John Holt	DB	5'11"	175	24	3	
Sandy LaBeaux	DB	6'3"	210	22		
Thomas Morris	DB	5'11"	175	23		
Johnny Ray Smith	DB	5'9"	185	25		
Norris Thomas	DB	5'11"	180	29		
Mike Washington	DB	6'3"	200	30	2	
Jerry Goldsteyn	QB	6'4"	200	29		
Bob Hewko	QB	6'3"	195	23		
Jeff Komlo	QB	6'2"	195	27		
Jack Thompson	QB	6'3"	220	27		
Terdell Middleton	HB	6'	205	28		
Michael Morton	HB	5'8"	180	23		
James Owens	HB	5'11"	195	28		36
Adger Armstrong	FB	6'	225	26		12
Melvin Carver	FB	5'11"	215	24		6
James Wilder	FB	6'3"	220	25		36
Theo Bell	WR	6'	190	29		12
Gene Branton	WR	6'4"	210	22		
Gerald Carter	WR	6'1"	190	26		12
Kevin House	WR	6'1"	175	25		30
Andre Tyler	WR	6'	180	24		
Jerry Bell	TE	6'5"	225	24		6
Jimmie Giles	TE	6'3"	245	28		6
Jim Obradovich	TE	6'2"	225	30		6
Mark White	TE	6'3"	235	23		
Bill Capece	K	5'7"	170	24		53
Frank Garcia	K	6'	205	26		
David Warnke	K	5'11"	185	23		1

David Barrett - Knee Injury

* Overtime

DETROIT LIONS

RUSHING

Last Name	No.	Yds	Avg	TD
Sims	220	1040	4.7	7
Jones	135	475	3.5	6
Bussey	57	249	4.4	0
Hipple	41	171	4.2	3
V. Thompson	40	138	3.5	1
L. Thompson	4	72	18.0	1
Kane	4	19	4.8	0
Nichols	1	13	13.0	0
Danielson	6	8	1.3	0
King	3	6	2.0	0
Black	2	-10	-5.0	0

RECEIVING

Last Name	No.	Yds	Avg	TD
Jones	46	467	10.2	1
Sims	42	419	10	0
L. Thompson	41	752	18.3	3
Chadwick	40	617	15.4	4
Nichols	29	437	15.1	1
Norris	26	291	11.2	7
Rubick	10	81	8.1	1
King	9	76	8.4	0
Bussey	8	49	6.1	1
Scott	5	71	14.2	1
V. Thompson	4	16	4.0	0
Kane	2	15	7.5	0
McCall	1	6	6.0	0

PUNT RETURNS

Last Name	No.	Yds	Avg	TD
Jenkins	23	230	10.0	0
Martin	15	183	12.2	1
Hall	8	109	13.6	0

KICKOFF RETURNS

Last Name	No.	Yds	Avg	TD
Hall	23	492	21.4	0
Jenkins	22	459	20.9	0
Martin	8	140	17.5	0
Caver	4	71	17.8	0
Curley	1	7	7.0	0
King	1	11	11.0	0
Lee	1	11	11.0	0
Norris	1	0	0.0	0

PASSING — PUNTING — KICKING

PASSING	Att	Cmp	%	Yds	Yd/Att	TD	Int—	%	RK
Hipple	387	204	53	2577	6.66	12	18—	5	12
Danielson	113	59	52	720	6.37	7	4—	4	
Jones	2	0	0	0	0.00	0	0—	0	
Black	1	0	0	0	0.00	0	1—	100	

PUNTING	No.	Avg.
Black	71	41.0

KICKING	XP	Att	%	FG	Att	%
Murray	38	38	100	25	32	78

GREEN BAY PACKERS

RUSHING

Last Name	No.	Yds	Avg	TD
Ellis	141	696	4.9	4
Ivery	86	340	4.0	2
J. Clark	71	328	4.6	0
Meade	55	201	3.7	1
Huckleby	50	182	3.6	4
Lofton	9	36	4.0	0
G. Lewis	4	16	4.0	1
Dickey	21	12	0.6	3
Whitehurst	2	-4	-2.0	0

RECEIVING

Last Name	No.	Yds	Avg	TD
Lofton	58	1300	22.4	8
Jefferson	57	830	14.6	7
Coffman	54	814	15.1	11
Ellis	52	603	11.6	2
Epps	18	313	17.4	0
J. Calrk	18	279	15.5	1
Ivery	16	139	8.7	1
Meade	16	110	6.9	2
G. Lewis	11	204	18.5	1
Huckleby	10	87	8.7	0
Kitson	1	9	9.0	0

PUNT RETURNS

Last Name	No.	Yds	Avg	TD
Epps	36	324	9.0	1
Gray	2	9	4.5	0
Hood	1	0	0.0	0
C. Lewis	1	0	0.0	0
Lee	1	-4	-4.0	0

KICKOFF RETURNS

Last Name	No.	Yds	Avg	TD
Huckleby	41	757	18.5	0
T. Lewis	20	358	17.9	0
Gray	11	178	16.2	0
Winters	3	28	9.3	0
Dreschsler	1	1	1.0	0
Ivery	1	17	17.0	0
Kitson	1	0	0.0	0
Lee	1	0	0.0	0

PASSING — PUNTING — KICKING

PASSING	Att	Cmp	%	Yds	Yd/Att	TD	Int—	%	RK
Dickey	484	289	60	4458	9.21	32	29—	6	5
Whitehurst	35	18	51	149	4.26	0	2—	6	
Ellis	5	2	40	31	6.20	1	1—	20	
Ivery	2	2	100	50	25.00	0	0—	0	

PUNTING	No.	Avg.
Scribner	69	41.6

KICKING	XP	Att	%	FG	Att	%
Stenerud	52	52	100	21	26	81

CHICAGO BEARS

RUSHING

Last Name	No.	Yds	Avg	TD
Payton	314	1421	4.5	6
Suhey	149	681	4.6	4
McMahon	55	307	5.6	2
Evans	22	142	6.5	1
Gentry	16	65	4.1	0
Gault	4	31	7.8	0
Parsons	1	27	27.0	0
C. Thomas	8	25	3.1	0
Hutchison	6	13	2.2	1
Margerum	1	7	7.0	0
Moorehead	5	6	1.2	0
Baschnagel	2	2	1.0	0

RECEIVING

Last Name	No.	Yds	Avg	TD
Payton	53	607	11.5	2
Suhey	49	429	8.8	1
Moorehead	42	597	14.2	3
Gault	40	836	20.9	8
Margerum	21	336	16.0	2
McKinnon	20	326	16.3	4
Saldi	12	119	9.9	0
Dunsmore	8	102	12.8	0
Baschnagel	5	70	14.0	0
C. Thomas	2	13	6.5	0
Gentry	2	8	4.0	0
McMahon	1	18	18.0	1

PUNT RETURNS

Last Name	No.	Yds	Avg	TD
McKinnon	34	316	9.3	1
Fisher	13	71	5.5	0
Gault	9	60	6.7	0

KICKOFF RETURNS

Last Name	No.	Yds	Avg	TD
Hutchison	17	259	15.2	0
Gault	13	276	21.2	0
Gentry	7	130	18.6	0
Watts	5	79	15.8	0
Baschnagel	3	42	14.0	0
Duerson	3	66	22.0	0
Bell	2	18	9.0	0
Cabral	2	11	5.5	0
McKinnon	2	42	21.0	0
Rains	2	11	5.5	0
Janata	1	2	2.0	0
Richardson	1	17	17.0	0

PASSING — PUNTING — KICKING

PASSING	Att	Cmp	%	Yds	Yd/Att	TD	Int—	%	RK
McMahon	295	175	59	2184	7.40	12	13—	4	7
Evans	145	76	52	1108	7.65	5	7—	5	
Payton	6	3	50	95	15.83	3	2—	33	
Suhey	1	1	100	74	74.00	1	0—	0	

PUNTING	No.	Avg.
Parsons	79	36.9
Stachowicz	12	37.3
McMahon	1	36.0

KICKING	XP	Att	%	FG	Att	%
B. Thomas	35	38	92	14	25	56

MINNESOTA VIKINGS

RUSHING

Last Name	No.	Yds	Avg	TD
Nelson	154	642	4.2	1
T. Brown	120	476	4.0	10
Galbreath	113	474	4.2	4
Young	39	90	2.3	2
Redwine	10	48	4.8	0
LeCount	2	42	21.0	0
Dils	16	28	1.8	0
Jones	1	9	9.0	0
S. White	1	7	7.0	0
Kramer	8	3	0.4	0
Lewis	1	2	2.0	0
Manning	1	-1	-1.0	0
Wilson	3	-3	-1.0	0
Coleman	1	-9	-9.0	0

RECEIVING

Last Name	No.	Yds	Avg	TD
Nelson	51	618	12.1	0
Galbreath	45	348	7.7	2
T. Brown	41	357	8.7	1
Bruer	31	315	10.2	2
S. White	29	412	14.2	2
LeCount	21	318	15.1	2
McCullum	21	314	15.0	2
Young	21	193	9.2	0
Casper	20	251	12.6	0
Jordan	15	212	14.1	2
Lewis	12	127	10.6	0
Jones	6	95	15.8	0
McDole	3	29	9.7	0
Redwine	1	4	4.0	0

PUNT RETURNS

Last Name	No.	Yds	Avg	TD
Bess	21	158	7.5	0
Lewis	3	52	17.3	0

KICKOFF RETURNS

Last Name	No.	Yds	Avg	TD
Nelson	18	445	24.7	0
Redwine	38	838	22.1	0
Huffman	3	42	14.0	0
Young	3	27	9.0	0
Bess	2	44	22.0	0
Jones	2	31	15.5	0
Bell	1	14	14.0	0
Lewis	1	25	25.0	0

PASSING — PUNTING — KICKING

PASSING	Att	Cmp	%	Yds	Yd/Att	TD	Int—	%	RK
Dils	444	239	54	2840	6.40	11	16—	4	11
Kramer	82	55	67	550	6.71	3	4—	5	
Wilson	28	16	57	124	4.43	1	2—	7	
LeCount	1	0	0.0	0	0.00	0	0—	0	

PUNTING	No.	Avg.
Coleman	91	41.5

KICKING	XP	Att	%	FG	Att	%
Ricardo	33	34	97	25	33	76

TAMPA BAY BUCCANEERS

RUSHING

Last Name	No.	Yds	Avg	TD
Wilder	161	640	4.0	4
Carver	114	348	3.1	0
Owens	96	266	2.8	5
Armstrong	7	90	4.3	0
Morton	13	28	2.2	0
J. Thompson	26	27	1.0	0
Komlo	2	11	5.5	0
Middleton	2	4	2.0	0
Golsteyn	5	3	0.6	0
Carter	1	0	0.0	0
House	1	-4	-4.0	0

RECEIVING

Last Name	No.	Yds	Avg	TD
Wilder	57	380	6.7	2
Carter	48	694	14.5	2
House	47	769	16.4	5
Carver	32	262	8.2	1
T. Bell	25	410	16.4	2
Giles	25	349	14.0	1
J. Bell	18	200	11.1	1
Armstrong	15	173	11.5	2
Owens	15	81	5.4	1
Obradovich	9	71	7.9	1
Tyler	6	77	12.8	0
Witte	2	15	7.5	0
Morton	1	9	9.0	0

PUNT RETURNS

Last Name	No.	Yds	Avg	TD
Tyler	27	208	7.7	0
T. Bell	10	48	4.8	0
Holt	5	43	8.6	0

KICKOFF RETURNS

Last Name	No.	Yds	Avg	TD
Morton	30	689	23.0	0
Owens	20	380	19.0	0
Smith	8	136	17.0	0
Spradlin	3	35	11.7	0
Carver	2	24	12.0	0
O'Steen	2	30	15.0	0
Armstrong	1	10	10.0	0
Middleton	1	10	10.0	0
Obradovich	1	0	0.0	0

PASSING — PUNTING — KICKING

PASSING	Att	Cmp	%	Yds	Yd/Att	TD	Int—	%	RK
J. Thompson	423	249	59	2906	6.87	18	21—	5	10
Golsteyn	97	47	49	535	5.51	0	2—	2	
Komlo	8	4	50	49	6.13	0	1—	13	

PUNTING	No.	Avg.
Garcia	95	42.2

KICKING	XP	Att	%	FG	Att	%
Capece	23	26	89	10	23	44
Warnke	1	2	50	0	1	0
Yarno	1	1	100	0	0	0

SAN FRANCISCO 49ERS 10-6-0 Bill Walsh

Scores of Each Game		
17	PHILADELPHIA	22
48	Minnesota	17
42	St.Louis	27
24	ATLANTA	20
33	New England	13
7	L.A.RAMS	10
32	New Orleans	13
45	L.A.Rams	35
13	N.Y.JETS	27
17	MIAMI	20
27	NEW ORLEANS	0
24	Atlanta	28
3	Chicago	13
35	TAMPA BAY	21
23	Buffalo	10
42	DALLAS	17

Use Name	Pos.	Hgt	Wgt	Age	Int	Pts
Keith Fahnhorst	OT	6'6"	273	31		
Allan Kennedy	OT	6'7"	275	25		
Bubba Paris	OT	6'6"	295	22		
John Ayers	OG	6'5"	265	30		
Randy Cross	OG	6'3"	265	29		
Jesse Sapolu	OG	6'4"	260	22		
John Choma	OG-C	6'5"	261	28		
Walt Downing	C-OG	6'3"	270	27		
Fred Quillan	C	6'5"	266	27		
Dwaine Board	DE	6'5"	248	26		6
Fred Dean	DE	6'3"	236	31		
Jeff Stover	DE	6'5"	275	25		
Jim Stuckey	DE	6'4"	253	25		
Pete Kugler	NT-DE	6'4"	255	24		
Lawrence Pillers	NT-DE	6'3"	250	30	1	
John Harty	NT	6'4"	263	24		

Use Name	Pos.	Hgt	Wgt	Age	Int	Pts
Dan Bunz	LB	6'4"	225	27		
Riki Ellison	LB	6'2"	225	27		
Ron Ferrari	LB	6'	212	24		
Willie Harper	LB	6'2"	215	33	1	
Bob Horn	LB	6'3"	230	29		
Bobby Leopold	LB	6'1"	215	25	2	
Ken McAlister (from SEA-DB)	LB	6'5"	210	23		
Milt McColl	LB	6'6"	230	24		
Blanchard Montgomery	LB	6'2"	236	22		
Gary Moten	LB	6'1"	210	22		
Jack Reynolds	LB	6'1"	232	35		
Keena Turner	LB	6'2"	219	24		
Richard Blackmore	DB	5'10"	174	27		
Tim Collier	DB	6'	176	29	3	6
Rick Gervais	DB	5'11"	190	23		
Dwight Hicks	DB	6'1"	192	27	2	12
Tom Holmoe	DB	6'2"	180	23		
Ronnie Lott	DB	6'	199	24	4	
Dana McLemore	DB	5'10"	183	23		
Carlton Williamson	DB	6'	204	25	4	
Eric Wright	DB	6'1"	180	24	7	12

Bryan Clark - Separated Shoulder
Frank LeMaster - Dislocated Shoulder
Mike Wood - Injury

Use Name	Pos.	Hgt	Wgt	Age	Int	Pts
Guy Benjamin	QB	6'4"	210	28		
Matt Cavanaugh	QB	6'2"	212	26		
Joe Montana	QB	6'2"	195	27		12
Carl Monroe	HB	5'8"	166	23		
Jeff Moore	HB	6'	196	27		6
Bill Ring	HB	5'10"	205	26		12
Wendell Tyler	HB	5'10"	200	28		36
Earl Cooper	FB	6'2"	227	24		18
Roger Craig	FB	6'	222	23		72
Vince Williams	FB	6'	231	23		
Dwight Clark	WR	6'4"	210	26		48
Darius Durham	WR	6'2"	185	22		
Renaldo Nehemiah	WR	6'1"	183	24		6
Freddie Solomon	WR	5'11"	188	30		24
Mike Wilson	WR	6'3"	210	24		
Russ Francis	TE	6'6"	242	30		24
Eason Ramson	TE	6'2"	234	27		6
Tom Orosz	K	6'1"	204	23		
Ray Wersching	K	5'11"	210	33		126

LOS ANGELES RAMS 9-7-0 John Robinson

Scores of Each Game		
16	N.Y. Giants	6
30	NEW ORLEANS	27
24	Green Bay	27
24	N.Y. Jets	*27
21	DETROIT	10
10	San Francisco	45
27	ATLANTA	21
35	SAN FRANCISCO	45
14	Miami	30
21	CHICAGO	14
36	Atlanta	13
20	WASHINGTON	42
41	BUFFALO	17
9	Philadelphia	13
7	NEW ENGLAND	21
26	New Orleans	24

Use Name	Pos.	Hgt	Wgt	Age	Int	Pts
Bill Bain	OT	6'4"	285	31		
Gary Kowalski	OT	6'6"	275	23		
Jackie Slater	OT	6'4"	271	29		
Russ Bolinger	OG	6'5"	255	28		
Dennis Harrah	OG	6'5"	265	30		
Kent Hill	OG	6'5"	260	26		
Joe Shearin	OG	6'4"	250	23		
Doug Smith	C	6'3"	253	26		
Dour Barnett	DE	6'3"	253	26		
Reggie Doss	DE	6'4"	263	26		
Gary Jeter	DE	6'4"	260	28		
Jack Youngblood	DE	6'4"	242	33		2
Richard Bishop	NT	6'1"	265	33		
Charles DeJurnett	NT	6'4"	260	31		
Myron Lapka	NT	6'4"	260	27		
Greg Meisner	NT	6'3"	253	24		

Use Name	Pos.	Hgt	Wgt	Age	Int	Pts
George Andrews	LB	6'3"	225	27	1	
Howard Carson	LB	6'2"	230	26		
Jim Collins	LB	6'2"	230	25		
Carl Ekern	LB	6'3"	222	29	1	
Mark Jerue	LB	6'3"	229	23		
Dave Lewis	LB	6'4"	245	28		
Mel Owens	LB	6'2"	224	24		
Mike Wilcher	LB	6'3"	235	23		
Eric Williams	LB	6'2"	235	28		
Jim Youngblood	LB	6'3"	231	33		
Kirk Collins	DB	5'11"	183	25	5	
Nolan Cromwell	DB	6'1"	200	28	3	6
Eric Harris	DB	6'3"	202	28	4	
LeRoy Irvin	DB	5'11"	184	25	4	
Monte Jackson	DB	5'11"	195	30		
Johnnie Johnson	DB	6'1"	183	26	4	12
Vince Newsome	DB	6'1"	179	22		
Ivory Sully	DB	6'	200	26		
Henry Williams (to SD)	DB	5'10"	180	26		
Mike Williams	DB	5'10"	186	29		

Drew Hill - Back Injury
Irv Pankey - Torn Achilles Tendon
Mike Reilly - Suspended by N.F.L.

Use Name	Pos.	Hgt	Wgt	Age	Int	Pts
Vince Ferragamo	QB	6'3"	212	29		
Steve Fuller	QB	6'4"	198	26		
Jeff Kemp	QB	6'	201	24		
Robert Alexander	HB	6'	185	25		
Barry Redden	HB-FB	5'10"	205	23		12
Eric Dickerson	FB	6'3"	220	22		120
Mike Guman	FB	6'2"	218	25		24
A.J. Jones	FB	6'1"	202	24		
Preston Dennard	WR	6'1"	183	27		30
Henry Ellard	WR	5'11"	170	22		6
George Farmer	WR	5'10"	175	24		30
Otis Grant	WR	6'3"	197	22		6
Gordon Jones	WR	6'	190	26		
Jeff Simmons	WR	6'3"	195	23		
Mike Barber	TE	6'3"	237	30		18
David Hill	TE	6'2"	228	29		12
James McDonald	TE	6'5"	230	22		6
Mike Lansford	K	6'	183	25		27
John Misko	K	6'5"	207	28		
Chuck Nelson	K	6'	175	23		48

NEW ORLEANS SAINTS 8-8-0 Bum Phillips

Scores of Each Game		
28	ST. LOUIS	17
27	L.A. Rams	30
34	CHICAGO	*31
20	Dallas	21
17	MIAMI	7
19	Atlanta	17
13	SAN FRANCISCO	32
24	Tampa Bay	21
21	Buffalo	27
27	ATLANTA	10
0	San Francisco	27
28	N.Y. JETS	31
17	MINNESOTA	16
0	New England	7
20	Philadelphia	*17
24	L.A. RAMS	26

Use Name	Pos.	Hgt	Wgt	Age	Int	Pts
Stan Brock	OT	6'6"	285	25		
Angelo Fields	OT	6'6"	315	25		
Leon Gray	OT	6'3"	258	31		
Dave Lafary	OT	6'7"	280	28		
Kelvin Clark	OG	6'3"	265	27	6	
Brad Edelman	OG	6'6"	265	22		
Steve Korte	OG	6'2"	270	23	6	
Louis Oubre	OG	6'4"	262	25		
John Hill	C	6'2"	260	33		
Jim Pietrzak	C	6'5"	260	30		
Bruce Clark	DE	6'3"	275	25		
Reggie Lewis	DE	6'2"	260	29	1	6
Frank Warren	DE	6'4"	275	23	1	
Jim Wilks	DE	6'5"	260	25		
Tony Elliott	NT	6'2"	265	24		
Gary Lewis	NT	6'3"	260	22		
Derland Moore	NT	6'4"	270	31		

Use Name	Pos.	Hgt	Wgt	Age	Int	Pts
Rickey Jackson	LB	6'2"	230	25	1	
Jim Kovach	LB	6'2"	225	27		
Chris Martin	LB	6'2"	220	22		
Rob Nairne	LB	6'4"	227	29		
Whitney Paul	LB	6'3"	220	27	2	
Scott Pelluer	LB	6'2"	215	24		
Glen Redd	LB	6'1"	225	25		
Dennis Winston	LB	6'	230	27	3	
Russell Gary	DB	5'11"	195	24	3	
Bobby Johnson	DB	6'	191	23	2	6
Rodney Lewis	DB	5'11"	190	24		
Vernon Perry	DB	6'2"	210	29		
Johnnie Poe	DB	6'1"	185	24	7	6
Greg Stemrick	DB	5'11"	185	31	1	
Frank Wattelet	DB	6'	185	24	2	
Dave Waymer	DB	6'1"	195	25		

Ken Bordelon - Achilles Tendon Injury
John Krimm - Knee Injury

Use Name	Pos.	Hgt	Wgt	Age	Int	Pts
Guido Merkens	QB	6'1"	195	28		
Ken Stabler	QB	6'3"	210	37		
Dave Wilson	QB	6'3"	210	24		6
Cliff Austin	HB	6'	190	23		
George Rogers	HB	6'2"	229	24		30
Jimmy Rogers	HB	5'10"	190	28		
Hokie Gajan	FB	5'11"	220	23		24
Tim Wilson	FB	6'3"	235	29		
Wayne Wilson	FB	6'3"	220	25		66
Kenny Duckett	WR	6'	187	23		12
Eugene Goodlow	WR	6'2"	190	24		12
Jeff Groth	WR	5'10"	175	26		6
Rich Mauti	WR	6'	195	29		
Lindsay Scott	WR	6'1"	190	22		
Tyrone Young	WR	6'6"	190	23		18
Hoby Brenner	TE	6'4"	240	24		18
Larry Hardy	TE	6'3"	230	27		
Greg Knafelc	TE	6'4"	220	24		
John Tice	TE	6'5"	242	23		6
Morten Andersen	K	6'2"	200	23		91
Russell Erxleben	K	6'4"	221	26		

ATLANTA FALCONS 7-9-0 Dan Henning

Scores of Each Game		
20	Chicago	17
13	N.Y. GIANTS	*16
30	Detroit	14
20	San Francisco	24
24	PHILADELPHIA	28
17	NEW ORLEANS	19
21	L.A. Rams	27
27	N.Y. Jets	21
24	NEW ENGLAND	27
10	New Orleans	27
13	L.A. RAMS	36
28	SAN FRANCISCO	24
47	GREEN BAY	*41
21	Washington	37
24	Miami	31
31	BUFFALO	14

Use Name	Pos.	Hgt	Wgt	Age	Int	Pts
Warren Bryant	OT	6'6"	270	27		
Mike Kenn	OT	6'7"	255	27		
Brett Miller	OT	6'7"	275	24		
Eric Sanders	OT	6'7"	270	24		
Dan Dufour	OG	6'5"	280	22		
Ronnie Lee	OG	6'3"	260	26		
R.C. Theilemann	OG	6'4"	252	28		
John Scully	C	6'6"	255	25		
Jeff Van Note	C	6'2"	250	37		
Jeff Merrow	DE	6'4"	255	30		
Mike Pitts	DE	6'5"	260	22		
Jeff Yeates	DE	6'3"	252	32		
Dan Benish	DT	6'5"	265	21		
Andrew Provence	DT	6'3"	265	22		
Don Smith	DT	6'5"	260	26		
Mike Zele	DT	6'3"	250	27		

Use Name	Pos.	Hgt	Wgt	Age	Int	Pts
Buddy Curry	LB	6'4"	228	25		
Rich Dixon	LB	6'2"	235	24		
David Frye	LB	6'2"	213	22		
John Harper	LB	6'3"	230	23		
Fulton Kuykendall	LB	6'5"	228	30		
Dave Levenick	LB	6'3"	220	24		
John Rade	LB	6'1"	220	23		6
Al Richardson	LB	6'2"	206	25	1	
James Britt	DB	6'	185	22		
Bobby Butler	DB	5'11"	175	24	4	
Blane Gaison	DB	6'	188	25		6
Bob Glazebrook	DB	6'1"	200	27	3	
Steve Haworth	DB	5'11"	190	21		
Kenny Johnson	DB	5'10"	176	25	2	12
Earl Jones	DB	6'	175	26	1	
Tom Pridemore	DB	5'10"	186	27	4	
Tom Tutson	DB	6'1"	180	25		

Russ Mikeska - Arch Injury
Neal Musser - Elbow Injury

Use Name	Pos.	Hgt	Wgt	Age	Int	Pts
Steve Bartkowski	QB	6'4"	218	30		6
Mike Moroski	QB	6'4"	200	25		
Lynn Cain	HB	6'1"	205	27		6
Richard Williams	HB	6'	205	23		
William Andrews	FB	6'	213	27		6
Reggie Brown	FB	5'11"	211	23		
Gerald Riggs	FB	6'1"	230	22		48
Bo Robinson	FB	6'2"	235	27		
Stacey Bailey	WR	6'	160	23		36
Willie Curran	WR	5'10"	175	23		
Floyd Hodge	WR	6'	190	24		24
Alfred Jackson	WR	5'11"	185	28		18
Alfred Jenkins	WR	5'10"	155	31		6
Billy Johnson	WR	5'9"	170	31		30
Arthur Cox	TE	6'2"	245	22		6
Allama Matthews	TE	6'2"	230	22		
Junior Miller	TE	6'4"	240	25		
Ben Young	TE	6'4"	225	23		6
Ralph Giacomarro	K	6'1"	190	22		
Mick Luckhurst	K	6'	180	25		94
Dave Smigelsky	K	5'11"	180	24		

* Overtime

SAN FRANCISCO FORTY-NINERS

RUSHING

Last Name	No.	Yds	Avg	TD
Tyler	176	856	4.9	4
Craig	176	725	4.1	8
Montana	61	284	4.7	2
Ring	64	254	4.0	2
Moore	15	43	2.9	1
Orosz	2	39	19.5	0
Monroe	10	23	2.3	0
D. Clark	3	18	6.0	0
Cavanaugh	1	8	8.0	0
Ramson	1	3	3.0	0
Solomon	1	3	3.0	0
Benjamin	1	1	1.0	0

RECEIVING

Last Name	No.	Yds	Avg	TD
D. Clark	70	840	12.0	8
Craig	48	427	8.9	4
Tyler	34	285	8.4	2
Francis	33	357	10.8	4
Solomon	31	662	21.4	4
Wilson	30	433	14.4	0
Ring	23	182	7.9	0
Moore	19	206	10.8	0
Nehemiah	17	236	13.9	1
Ramson	17	125	7.4	1
Cooper	15	207	13.8	3
Monroe	2	61	30.5	0

PUNT RETURNS

Last Name	No.	Yds	Avg	TD
McLemore	30	331	10.7	1
Solomon	5	34	6.8	0

KICKOFF RETURNS

Last Name	No.	Yds	Avg	TD
McLemore	30	576	19.2	0
Monroe	8	152	19.0	0
Moore	7	117	16.7	0
Ring	4	68	17.0	0
Cooper	3	45	15.0	0

PASSING — PUNTING — KICKING

PASSING	Att	Cmp	%	Yds	Yd/Att	TD	Int—	%	RK
Montana	515	332	65	3910	7.59	26	12—	2	3
Benjamin	12	7	58	111	9.25	1	0—	0	
D. Clark	1	0	0	0	0.00	0	0—	0	

PUNTING	No.	Avg.
Orosz	65	39.3

KICKING	XP	Att	%	FG	Att	%
Wersching	51	51	100	25	30	83

LOS ANGELES RAMS

RUSHING

Last Name	No.	Yds	Avg	TD
Dickerson	390	1808	4.6	18
Redden	75	372	5.0	2
Guman	7	42	6.0	0
Alexander	7	28	4.0	0
Ferragamo	22	17	0.8	0
Ellard	3	7	2.3	0
Cromwell	1	0	0.0	0
Kemp	3	-2	-0.7	0
Farmer	1	-9	-9.0	0
Grant	2	-10	-5.0	0

RECEIVING

Last Name	No.	Yds	Avg	TD
Barber	55	657	11.9	3
Dickerson	51	404	7.9	2
Farmer	40	556	13.9	5
Guman	34	347	10.2	4
Dennard	33	465	14.1	5
Da. Hill	28	280	10.0	2
Ellard	16	268	16.8	0
Grant	12	221	18.4	1
G. Jones	11	172	15.6	0
Redden	4	30	7.5	0
Alexander	1	10	10.0	0
McDonald	1	1	1.0	1

PUNT RETURNS

Last Name	No.	Yds	Avg	TD
Ellard	16	217	13.6	1
Irvin	25	212	8.5	0
Johnson	14	109	7.8	0

KICKOFF RETURNS

Last Name	No.	Yds	Avg	TD
Redden	19	358	18.8	0
Ellard	15	314	20.9	0
Alexander	13	222	17.1	0
Guman	2	30	15.0	0
Barnett	1	0	0.0	0
Irvin	1	22	22.0	0

PASSING — PUNTING — KICKING

PASSING	Att	Cmp	%	Yds	Yd/Att	TD	Int—	%	RK
Ferragamo	464	274	59	3276	7.06	22	23—	5	8
Kemp	25	12	48	135	5.40	1	0—	0	

PUNTING	No.	Avg.
Misko	82	40.3

KICKING	XP	Att	%	FG	Att	%
Nelson	33	37	89	5	11	45
Lansford	9	9	100	6	9	67

NEW ORLEANS SAINTS

RUSHING

Last Name	No.	Yds	Avg	TD
G. Rogers	256	1144	4.5	5
W. Wilson	199	787	4.0	9
Gajan	81	415	5.1	4
J. Rogers	26	80	3.1	0
T. Wilson	8	21	2.6	0
Austin	4	16	4.0	0
Merkens	1	16	16.0	0
Groth	1	15	15.0	0
Goodlow	1	3	3.0	0
D. Wilson	5	3	0.6	1
Erxleben	2	-9	-4.5	0
Stabler	9	-14	-1.6	0
Duckett	2	-16	-8.0	0

RECEIVING

Last Name	No.	Yds	Avg	TD
Groth	49	585	11.9	1
Brenner	41	574	14.0	3
Goodlow	41	487	11.9	2
Scott	24	274	11.4	0
W. Wilson	20	178	8.9	2
Duckett	19	283	14.9	2
Gajan	17	130	7.6	0
G. Rogers	12	69	5.8	0
Young	7	85	12.1	3
Tice	7	33	4.7	1
Mauti	2	30	15.0	0
Hardy	2	29	14.5	0
Austin	2	25	12.5	0

PUNT RETURNS

Last Name	No.	Yds	Avg	TD
Groth	39	275	7.1	0

KICKOFF RETURNS

Last Name	No.	Yds	Avg	TD
Duckett	33	719	21.8	0
W. Wilson	9	239	26.6	0
Mauti	8	147	18.4	0
Austin	7	112	16.0	0
J. Rogers	7	103	14.7	0
Brock	1	15	15.0	0
Wattelet	1	4	4.0	0

PASSING — PUNTING — KICKING

PASSING	Att	Cmp	%	Yds	Yd/Att	TD	Int—	%	RK
Stabler	311	176	57	1988	6.39	9	18—	6	13
D. Wilson	112	66	59	770	6.88	5	7—	6	
Erxleben	1	1	100	24	24.00	0	0—	0	
Gajan	1	0	0	0	0.00	0	0—	0	

PUNTING	No.	Avg.
Erxleben	74	41.0
Merkens	4	36.0

KICKING	XP	Att	%	FG	Att	%
Andersen	37	38	97	18	24	75

ATLANTA FALCONS

RUSHING

Last Name	No.	Yds	Avg	TD
Andrews	331	1567	4.7	7
Riggs	100	437	4.4	8
B. Johnson	15	83	5.5	0
Cain	19	63	3.3	1
Bartkowski	16	38	2.4	1
Giacomarro	2	13	6.5	0
Moroski	2	12	6.0	0
Robinson	3	9	3.0	0
Williams	1	5	5.0	5
Miller	1	2	2.0	0
Bailey	2	-5	-2.5	0

RECEIVING

Last Name	No.	Yds	Avg	TD
B. Johnson	64	709	11.1	4
Andrews	59	609	10.3	4
Bailey	55	881	16.0	6
Jenkins	38	487	12.8	1
Hodge	25	280	11.2	4
Riggs	17	149	8.8	0
Miller	16	125	7.8	0
Jackson	13	220	16.9	3
Robinson	12	100	8.3	0
Cox	9	83	9.2	1
Young	6	74	12.3	1
Matthews	3	37	12.3	0
Cain	3	24	8.0	0
Curran	1	15	15.0	0

PUNT RETURNS

Last Name	No.	Yds	Avg	TD
B. Johnson	46	489	10.6	1

KICKOFF RETURNS

Last Name	No.	Yds	Avg	TD
K. Johnson	11	224	20.4	0
Williams	23	461	20.0	0
Riggs	17	330	19.4	0
Cain	11	200	18.2	0
Butler	1	17	17.0	0
Curran	2	26	13.0	0
Glazebrook	2	0	0.0	0

PASSING — PUNTING — KICKING

PASSING	Att	Cmp	%	Yds	Yd/Att	TD	Int—	%	RK
Bartkowski	432	274	63	3167	7.33	22	5—	1	1
Moroski	70	45	64	575	8.12	2	4—	6	
Hodge	2	1	50	28	14.00	0	1—	50	
Andrews	1	0	0	0	0.00	0	0—	0	
Giacomarro	1	1	100	23	23.00	0	0—	0	
B. Johnson	1	0	0	0	0.00	0	0—	0	

PUNTING	No.	Avg.
Giacomarro	70	40.3

KICKING	XP	Att	%	FG	Att	%
Luckhurst	43	45	96	17	22	77

1983 A.F.C. Another New League

A new competitor with a novel idea challenged the N.F.L. for a share of the pro football market. The United States Football League broke new ground by playing from March to July, hoping to cash in on the American public's insatiable appetite for football. Aside from its scheduling novelty, the U.S.F.L. looked like any other new league with big-time aspirations. Teams took the field in Boston, New Jersey, Philadelphia, Washington, Tampa Bay, Birmingham, Michigan, Chicago, Denver, Arizona, Los Angeles and Oakland, manned mostly by anonymous rookies and N.F.L. castoffs. The league did sign a group of well-known college stars, mostly in the offensive skill positions. The most famous was Heisman Trophy winner Herschel Walker, who passed up his senior year at Georgia to carry the ball for the New Jersey Generals for $5 million over three years. Although not nearly as well-paid, Kelvin Bryant ran just as well for the Philadelphia Stars and led them into the title game against the Michigan Panthers. With quarterback Bobby Hebert, receiver Anthony Carter and linebacker John Corker in the fore, the Panthers captured their first U.S.F.L. title 24-22 before 50,906 fans in Denver. Despite a TV contract with ABC, most U.S.F.L. teams lost money and played before small crowds.

EASTERN DIVISION

Miami Dolphins — The Miami offense worried coach Don Shula in the early going. Jimmy Cefalo went out with a knee injury on opening day and David Woodley had little success moving the team. On September 19, Shula sent first draft pick Dan Marino into the game in relief of Woodley. Despite Marino's two TD passes, the Dolphins lost 27-14 to the Raiders. On October 2, Marino again relieved in a 17-7 loss to the Saints. The next week, Marino started and threw three TD passes, but the Dolphins dropped to 3-3 by losing 38-35 to Buffalo in overtime. From then on, the Dolphins won nine of 10 games as Marino singed enemy defenses with his quick release. Mark Duper broke into the lineup as Marino's favorite receiver. Star linemen Ed Newman, Eric Laakso and Dwight Stephenson gave the freshman quarterback time to learn without heavy pressure. Complementing the reborn offense was the swarming Killer Bee defense. Linemen Doug Betters and Bob Baumhower starred in a unit which emphasized ensemble team play.

New England Patriots — A maddening inconsistency sentenced the Patriots to an early winter vacation. After losing their first two games, they then whipped the Jets and Steelers to even their mark. The Patriots played almost perfectly in beating Buffalo 31-0 on October 23. After beating the Dolphins 17-6 on November 13, they turned around and lost 30-0 to the Browns and 26-3 to the Jets. Victories over the Saints and Rams put the playoffs within grasp. New England squared off against the Seahawks on December 18 with one playoff berth available; Seattle won 24-6 and ended the Patriots' hopes. Despite Tony Collins' fine running and the sure blocking of John Hannah and Brian Holloway, the offense sputtered because of a weak passing game. Rookie QB Tony Eason started the final four games after an injury sidelined Steve Grogan. A broken leg kept defensive end Kenneth Sims under wraps for the first 11 games, but the defense nevertheless played well.

Buffalo Bills — The Bills went into the season with a new coach and a lame-duck star. Kay Stephenson replaced Chuck Knox at the helm and structured his offense around running back Joe Cribbs. Already signed by the U.S.F.L. for the 1984 season, Cribbs gave the Bills all-out running in his final Buffalo season. The Bills won three of their first four games and entered the stretch run at 7-4, hot in pursuit of a playoff spot. A close 27-24 loss to the Raiders was followed by a 41-17 pommeling by the Rams. After eking out a 14-9 victory at Kansas City, the Bills lost to the 49ers and Falcons to sag out of contention. While Cribbs was the offensive ace, the defense relied most heavily on nose tackle Fred Smerlas and safety Steve Freeman.

Baltimore Colts — First draft pick John Elway flatly refused to sign with the Colts anf forced a pre-season trade with Denver. Baltimore's anger faded when the Colts won their opener on a fumble return in overtime, then swept to victory in four of their first six games. A five-game losing streak would kill the surprise playoff bid, but the Colts still finished better than expected. Rookie guard Chris Hinton, part of the Elway trade, starred from day one and helped rushers Curtis Dickey and Randy McMillan to impressive seasons. Rookie linebacker Vernon Maxwell gave the offense a shot of verve. Elway faced the Colts twice. He was unimpressive in a 17-10 Denver victory on September 11, but threw for three fourth-quarter touchdowns in a 21-19 victory on December 11. In eight home games, the attendance broke 40,000 only twice, with the final two games drawing crowds of under 30,000. Team owner Robert Irsay reacted with threats to take the Colts out of Baltimore.

New York Jets — Joe Walton stepped up to the top job when Walt Michaels resigned after last year's playoffs. The tough contenders of 1982 turned into inconsistent also-rans under Walton. After beating the Chargers on opening day, the Jets played without character and fell to a 4-7 record by late November. In a long-shot bid for a playoff berth, they swept the Saints, Patriots and Colts before collapsing in the final two losses. Blame for the offensive failure could be put on an injury to Freeman McNeil and on Richard Todd's mediocre season. Darrell Ray's slump hurt the defense. Also hurting morale was the announcement that the team would move to Giants Stadium next year, leaving the crowd at Shea Stadium in a surly mood.

CENTRAL DIVISION

Pittsburgh Steelers — The old pros were getting scarce. Lynn Swann and Jack Ham had retired, John Stallworth missed 12 games with a hamstring injury, and Terry Bradshaw sat out all but 30 minutes of the season with a bad elbow. In addition, a group of veteran reserves jumped to the U.S.F.L. The mixture of new and old Steelers reeled off seven straight victories in mid-season to ensure a playoff spot. Franco Harris churned out 1,000 yards with his 33-year-old body running behind a line led by veteran Mike Webster. New faces manned the passing game with less success than the oldsters. Cliff Stoudt couldn't fill Bradshaw's shoes and became the target for jeers in Three Rivers Stadium. The defense stayed strong, with Jack Lambert in his usual leading role. The Steelers uncharacteristically stumbled late in the year, losing four of their last five games. Most embarrassing was a 45-3 loss in Detroit before a national TV audience on Thanksgiving Day.

Cleveland Browns — Splitting their first 10 games, the Browns launched a late bid for a wild-card playoff spot. They began with consecutive shutouts of Tampa Bay and New England, then trounced Baltimore 41-23. The momentum screeched to a halt, however, with losses to Denver and Houston. In the finale, Brian Sipe tossed four touchdown passes to beat the Steelers 30-17, not enough for a prized post-season bid. Sipe ended his Cleveland career with that game by signing a contract with the New Jersey Generals of the U.S.F.L. His chief offensive aide this year was fullback Mike Pruitt, while linebackers Chip Banks, Tom Cousineau and Clay Matthews formed the heart of the defense.

Cincinnati Bengals — Personnel woes savaged the team's morale from the start of training camp. The league suspended Pete Johnson and Ross Browner for the first four games for drug usage. The U.S.F.L. snatched away offensive coordinator Lindy Infante, while star receivers Cris Collinsworth and Dan Ross came to camp committed to the U.S.F.L. in the future. The Bengals lost their first three games and six of their first seven to skid completely out of the playoff picture. With Ken Anderson out for three games in mid-season, Turk Schonert quarterbacked the team to its first consecutive victories of the year. Anderson took over when healthy and engineered a 55-14 thrashing of the Oilers. The early disaster faded as the Bengals won six of their last nine games. Although the offense improved with time, the Cincinnati defense carried the team most of the year. Cornerback Ken Riley capped his long career with a terrific final season. Also leaving town would be coach Forrest Gregg, who headed north to Green Bay for 1984.

Houston Oilers — The bad times kept rolling for the Oilers. They lost their first 10 games, running their losing streak to 17 over two seasons. Ed Biles lost his job as head coach in the flood of losses and was replaced by assistant Chuck Studley. Things might have gone differently had the Oilers beaten Green Bay on opening day rather than losing in overtime. Three

OFFENSE

	BALT.	BUFF.	CIN.	CLEV.	DENV.	HOU.	K.C.	RAID.	MIA.	N.E.	NY.J.	PIT.	S.D.	SEA.
FIRST DOWNS:														
Total	272	309	327	327	292	295	314	356	314	284	313	312	361	300
by Rushing	146	100	127	113	99	120	83	143	132	130	126	156	106	131
by Passing	110	171	179	186	155	155	208	181	151	138	171	141	230	153
by Penalty	16	38	21	28	38	20	23	32	31	16	16	15	25	16
RUSHING:														
Number	601	415	542	465	471	502	387	542	568	538	474	614	423	546
Yards	2695	1736	2104	1922	1784	1998	1254	2240	2150	2605	2068	2610	1536	2119
Average Yards	4.5	4.2	3.9	4.1	3.8	4.0	3.2	4.1	3.8	4.8	4.4	4.3	3.6	3.9
Touchdowns	10	4	24	13	15	16	13	18	16	19	11	17	16	19
PASSING:														
Attempts	377	571	454	567	499	482	641	504	442	412	559	409	635	449
Completions	188	317	290	324	254	260	369	301	254	220	330	211	369	251
Completion Pct.	49.9	55.5	63.9	57.1	50.9	53.9	57.6	59.7	57.5	53.3	59.0	51.6	58.1	55.9
Passing Yards	2663	3438	3492	3932	3466	3286	4684	3910	3235	3040	3742	2754	4891	3316
Avg. Yds per Att.	5.5	5.1	6.4	6.1	5.5	6.8	6.3	6.2	6.6	7.4	5.7	5.2	7.0	6.0
Avg. Yds per Comp.	14.2	10.9	12.0	12.1	13.7	12.6	12.7	13.0	12.7	13.8	11.3	13.1	13.3	13.2
Times Tackled	47	37	40	33	55	49	46	55	23	45	43	52	28	47
Yds Lost Tackled	340	351	309	271	439	384	343	464	190	334	317	350	230	343
Net Yards	2323	3087	3183	3661	3027	2902	4341	3446	3045	2706	3425	2404	4661	2973
Touchdowns	12	30	14	27	17	16	29	31	28	16	21	15	27	25
Interceptions	22	28	18	28	22	29	19	24	11	18	28	23	33	18
Pct. Intercepted	5.8	4.9	4.0	4.9	4.4	6.0	3.0	4.8	2.5	4.4	5.0	5.6	5.2	4.0
PUNTS:														
Number	91	89	69	70	87	80	93	78	75	81	82	80	63	79
Average	45.3	39.7	40.6	40.8	41.6	39.2	39.9	42.8	42.5	44.6	39.2	41.9	43.9	39.5
PUNT RETURNS														
Number	44	44	49	42	38	20	40	58	55	44	38	51	33	34
Yards	294	241	410	310	420	159	291	666	581	399	420	421	213	366
Average Yards	6.7	5.5	8.4	7.4	11.1	8.0	7.3	11.5	10.6	9.1	11.1	8.3	6.5	10.8
Touchdowns	0	0	0	0	1	0	0	1	1	0	1	0	0	1
KICKOFF RET.:														
Number	62	64	54	63	56	83	54	61	47	57	66	59	74	71
Yards	1198	1363	1097	1290	1077	1676	929	1175	1085	1155	1375	1068	1377	1575
Average Yards	19.3	21.3	20.3	20.5	19.2	20.2	17.2	19.3	23.1	20.3	20.8	18.1	18.6	22.2
Touchdowns	0	0	0	0	0	2	0	0	0	0	0	0	0	1
INTERCEPT RET.:														
Number	20	13	23	22	27	14	30	20	26	17	22	28	16	26
Yards	314	154	369	296	355	135	482	238	345	202	342	435	153	363
Average Yards	15.7	11.8	16.0	13.5	13.1	9.6	16.1	11.9	13.3	11.9	15.5	15.5	9.6	14.0
Touchdowns	1	1	4	2	0	0	2	2	3	1	3	4	1	2
PENALTIES:														
Number	120	144	99	115	100	84	113	121	64	90	110	99	115	102
Yards	986	1094	837	991	804	784	911	992	567	815	1059	836	961	890
FUMBLES:														
Number	32	24	35	21	34	26	31	46	30	47	29	42	42	36
Number Lost	11	12	15	10	19	18	19	25	16	20	19	20	22	20
POINTS:														
Total	264	283	346	356	302	288	386	442	389	274	313	355	358	403
PAT Attempts	24	36	43	40	34	34	45	54	48	36	38	39	45	50
PAT Made	22	34	40	38	33	33	44	51	45	31	37	38	43	49
FG Attempts	35	26	23	25	25	21	30	27	27	22	24	31	24	25
FG Made	30	11	16	22	21	17	24	21	18	9	16	27	15	18
Percent FG Made	85.7	42.3	69.6	88.0	84.0	81.0	80.0	77.8	66.7	40.9	66.7	87.1	62.5	72.0
Safeties	1	0	0	0	1	0	0	2	1	0	0	1	0	0

DEFENSE

	BALT.	BUFF.	CIN.	CLEV.	DENV.	HOU.	K.C.	RAID.	MIA.	N.E.	NY.J.	PIT.	S.D.	SEA.
FIRST DOWNS:														
Total	321	332	276	309	321	332	319	285	288	326	298	278	347	351
by Rushing	123	148	96	138	119	161	136	86	122	129	126	100	137	128
by Passing	166148	156	155	185	150	158	170	147	172	151	151	187	195	
by Penalty	32	36	24	16	17	21	25	29	19	25	21	27	23	28
RUSHING:														
Number	516	566	430	528	509	576	554	436	460	549	547	509	552	511
Yards	2118	2503	1499	2065	1938	2787	2275	1586	2037	2281	2378	1833	2173	2198
Average Yards	4.1	4.4	3.5	3.9	3.8	4.8	4.1	3.6	4.4	4.2	4.3	3.6	3.9	4.3
Touchdowns	13	14	16	15	14	23	18	13	11	9	13	14	26	14
PASSING:														
Attempts	488	480	502	469	552	424	500	531	480	514	463	447	544	521
Completions	281	286	288	280	307	252	261	282	277	277	269	238	330	311
Completion Pct.	57.6	59.6	57.4	59.7	55.6	59.4	52.2	53.1	57.7	53.9	58.1	53.2	60.7	59.7
Passing Yards	3832	3553	3163	3316	3988	3095	3361	3646	3365	3565	3301	3260	4051	4182
Avg. Yds per Att.	6.7	6.5	5.2	6.1	6.2	6.3	5.8	5.4	5.7	6.0	5.7	5.8	6.6	6.8
Avg. Yds per Comp.	13.6	12.4	11.0	11.8	13.0	12.3	12.9	12.9	12.2	12.9	12.3	13.7	12.3	13.5
Times Tackled	41	32	41	32	38	31	35	57	49	39	48	50	31	43
Yds Lost Tackled	310	247	335	239	317	250	250	484	363	270	378	361	269	351
Net Yards	3522	3306	2828	3077	3671	2845	3111	3162	3002	3295	2923	2899	3782	3831
Touchdowns	31	22	17	22	18	26	21	20	19	19	22	19	28	33
Interceptions	20	13	23	22	27	14	30	20	26	17	22	28	16	26
Pct. Intercepted	4.1	2.7	4.6	4.7	4.9	3.3	6.0	3.8	5.4	3.3	4.8	6.3	2.9	5.0
PUNTS:														
Number	80	78	76	73	77	65	85	100	90	78	85	88	70	68
Average	41.6	42.9	42.3	40.5	44.2	39.5	41.2	40.6	40.8	42.0	41.1	41.1	39.7	40.5
PUNT RETURNS														
Number	55	42	41	30	55	47	54	35	32	48	47	44	35	36
Yards	642	403	310	309	524	354	559	334	229	392	367	418	299	185
Average Yards	11.7	9.6	7.6	10.3	9.5	7.5	10.4	9.5	7.2	8.2	7.8	9.5	8.5	5.1
Touchdowns	1	0	0	0	0	0	1	2	0	0	1	1	0	0
KICKOFF RET.:														
Number	61	53	68	61	46	61	75	68	54	55	50	65	70	59
Yards	1138	949	1299	1155	823	1280	1528	1227	1024	1082	1063	1507	1426	952
Average Yards	18.7	17.9	19.1	18.9	12.8	21.0	20.4	18.0	19.0	19.7	21.3	23.2	20.4	16.1
Touchdowns	0	0	0	1	3	0	0	0	0	0	0	1	0	0
INTERCEPT RET.:														
Number	22	28	18	28	22	29	19	24	11	18	28	23	33	18
Yards	117	330	298	508	281	392	323	381	203	361	372	252	377	279
Average Yards	5.3	11.8	16.6	18.1	12.8	13.5	17.0	15.9	18.5	20.1	13.3	11.0	11.4	15.5
Touchdowns	0	2	2	3	3	2	2	0	1	1	3	2	2	1
PENALTIES:														
Number	82	128	100	105	138	104	105	109	95	84	96	96	111	91
Yards	666	1296	871	940	1097	825	837	947	837	674	784	782	953	725
FUMBLES:														
Number	29	32	35	30	46	34	35	31	38	30	29	34	26	44
Number Lost	16	18	16	10	20	15	21	16	17	19	14	17	17	28
POINTS:														
Total	354	351	302	342	327	460	367	338	250	289	331	303	462	397
PAT Attempts	45	39	36	42	36	53	44	40	32	30	39	37	56	48
PAT Made	42	39	35	40	34	49	43	39	31	29	35	36	54	43
FG Attempts	23	39	22	22	33	36	26	25	15	31	28	20	29	26
FG Made	14	26	17	16	25	29	20	19	9	24	20	15	22	20
Percent FG Made	60.9	66.7	77.3	72.7	75.8	80.6	76.9	76.0	60.0	77.4	71.4	75.0	75.9	76.9
Safeties	0	0	0	1	1	0	0	1	0	1	1	0	0	3

weeks into the schedule, quarterback Archie Manning and tight end Dave Casper were traded to the Vikings for draft choices, opening the way for younger players. Gifford Nielsen started the next seven losses at quarterback, with Oliver Luck at the helm for the final six games. Luck's tenure produced six victories, aided by a good offensive line, Tim Smith's receiving and Earl Campbell's always strong rushing.

WESTERN DIVISION

Los Angeles Raiders — Coach Tom Flores had top-flight players in almost all areas. Howie Long blossomed into a major force on the defensive line, backed by intense linebackers Ted Hendricks and Rod Martin. Lester Hayes and Vann McElroy ranged far in the secondary, joined by Mike Haynes after a November trade with New England. The offensive line supported Marcus Allen's running and Todd Christensen's clutch receiving. The only serious question mark was at quarterback, where Jim Plunkett started the year. The Raiders won their four September games, but had tough sledding in October. After Plunkett played poorly in a 38-36 loss at Seattle on October 16, Flores made young Marc Wilson the starter. Wilson played well in a victory over Dallas and another loss to Seattle, but he hurt his shoulder in the second half against Kansas City. Plunkett led his mates to victory over the Chiefs and played well as a starter the rest of the year. With six victories in their final seven games, the physical Raiders went into the playoffs at a fine edge.

Seattle Seahawks — Chuck Knox brought his winning knack to Seattle. The centerpiece of his offense was rookie Curt Warner, a heavy-duty back who led the A.F.C. in rushing. To support Warner, Knox brought in Charle Young, Reggie McKenzie and Blair Bush from other N.F.L. clubs. Already in place was the passing combination of Jim Zorn and Steve Largent. The Seahawks upset the Raiders 38-36 on October 16 despite Zorn's 4-of-16 passing mark. One week later, the Seahawks generated no offense in the first half, falling behind the Steelers 24-0. Knox put Dave Krieg into the game at quarterback and, despite some rough spots, Krieg ran the offense the rest of the way. In his first start, he took Seattle to another victory over the Raiders. Down the homestretch, the Seahawks won three of their last four, clinching their first-ever playoff berth by swamping New England on the final weekend.

Denver Broncos — Billed as the next great N.F.L. quarterback, John Elway needed time to learn his trade. Dan Reeves started Elway for the first five games, often relieving him with Steve DeBerg. DeBerg then started the next five games until dislocating a shoulder. Elway and fellow rookie Gary Kubiak were thrown in and swam, winning three of the final six games to ice a wild-card spot. Despite the quarterback flux, the Broncos improved greatly over last year's squad. Receiver Steve Watson and runner Sammy Winder regularly gained yardage, while the defense was led by two veterans of the old Orange Crush — Randy Gradishar and Louis Wright.

San Diego Chargers — The wave broke for the Chargers without ever reaching the Super Bowl. The terrific passing attack still ate up yardage, but the offense was less able to run the ball. The line underwent changes, as veteran Russ Washington was unexpectedly cut and Doug Wilkerson missed the first four games with a broken arm. A new 3-4 alignment didn't rid the Chargers of their reputation as a defensive soft touch. Four rookies started on defense, with cornerback Danny Walters the most successful. After a 3-3 start, a four-game losing streak doused the team's chances, aided by Dan Fouts' mid-season shoulder injury.

Kansas City Chiefs — Joe Delaney died tragically in the summer, robbing the Chiefs of an offensive ace and a valued teammate. New coach John Mackovic gave the offense a new look by turning the passing game loose. With Steve Fuller traded away, Bill Kenney played quarterback full-time and prospered. Carlos Carson received the greatest attention in the new offensive outlook. The defense lost a leader when Gary Barbaro held out and eventually signed with the U.S.F.L. New Jersey Generals. Deron Cherry replaced Barbaro admirably and joined Gary Green as a secondary star. The inconsistent play and losing record put off the public, with only 11,377 showing up for the home finale.

MIAMI DOLPHINS 12-4-0 Don Shula

Scores of Each Game			
12	BUFFALO	0	
34	New England	24	
14	L.A.RAIDERS	27	
14	Kansas City	6	
7	NEW ORLEANS	17	
35	Buffalo	*38	
32	N.Y.JETS	14	
21	BALTIMORE	7	
30	L.A.Rams	14	
20	SAN FRANCISCO	17	
37	NEW ENGLAND	17	
38	Baltimore	0	
38	Cincinnati	14	
24	HOUSTON	17	
31	Atlanta	24	
34	N.Y.Jets	14	

Use Name	Pos.	Hgt	Wgt	Age	Int	Pts
Jon Giesler	OT	6'5"	260	26		
Cleveland Green	OT	6'3"	262	25		
Eric Laakso	OT	6'4"	265	26		
Roy Foster	OG-OT	6'4"	272	23		
Bob Kuechenberg	OG	6'3"	255	35		
Ed Newman	OG	6'2"	255	32		
Jeff Toews	OG	6'3"	255	25		
Mark Dennard	C	6'1"	252	27		
Dwight Stephenson	C	6'2"	255	25		
Bill Barnett	DE	6'4"	260	27		
Charles Benson	DE	6'3"	267	22		
Doug Betters	DE	6'7"	260	27		
Kim Bokamper	DE	6'6"	250	28	2	6
Bob Baumhower	NT	6'5"	265	28		
Mike Charles	NT	6'4"	283	20		2
Steve Clark	NT	6'4"	255	23		
Charles Bowser	LB	6'3"	232	23		
Mark Brown	LB	6'2"	218	22	1	
Bob Brudzinski	LB	6'4"	230	28		
A.J.Duhe	LB	6'4"	248	27		
Earnest Rhone	LB	6'2"	224	30	1	
Terry Tautolo	LB	6'2"	227	29		
Rodell Thomas	LB	6'2"	225	25		
Emmett Tilley	LB	5'11"	240	22		
Glenn Blackwood	DB	6'	186	26	3	
Lyle Blackwood	DB	6'	195	32	4	
William Judson	DB	6'1"	187	24		
Mike Kozlowski	DB	6'	198	27	2	12
Paul Lankford	DB	6'1"	182	25	1	
Gerald Small	DB	5'11"	192	27	5	
Robert Sowell	DB	5'11"	175	22		
Fulton Walker	DB	5'10"	196	25	1	
Jim Jensen	QB-TE	6'4"	215	24		
Dan Marino	QB	6'4"	214	21		12
Don Strock	QB	6'5"	220	32		
David Woodley	QB	6'2"	204	24		
Eddie Hill	HB	6'2"	206	26		
Tony Nathan	HB	6'	206	26		24
Tommy Vigorito	HB	5'10"	190	23		
David Overstreet	HB-FB	5'11"	206	24		18
Woody Bennett	FB	6'2"	222	28		12
Andra Franklin	FB	5'10"	228	23		48
Jimmy Cefalo	WR	5'11"	188	26		
Mark Clayton	WR	5'9"	172	22		12
Mark Duper	WR	5'9"	193	24		60
Duriel Harris	WR	5'11"	176	28		6
Vince Heflin	WR	6'	185	24		
Nat Moore	WR	5'9"	188	31		36
Bruce Hardy	TE	6'5"	232	27		
Dan Johnson	TE	6'3"	230	26		28
Joe Rose	TE	6'3"	230	26		
Reggie Roby	K	6'2"	243	22		
Uwe Von Schamann	K	6'	188	27		99

Steve Shull - Knee Injury
Larry Gordon - Died;Heart Attack
Ron Hester - Knee Injury
Don McNeal - Achilles Tendon Injury

NEW ENGLAND PATRIOTS 8-8-0 Ron Meyer

Scores of Each Game			
23	Baltimore	*29	
24	MIAMI	34	
23	N.Y.Jets	13	
28	PITTSBURGH	23	
13	San Francisco	33	
7	BALTIMORE	12	
37	San Diego	21	
31	BUFFALO	0	
13	ATLANTA	24	
21	Buffalo	7	
17	Miami	6	
0	Cleveland	30	
3	N.Y.JETS	26	
7	New Orleans	0	
21	L.A.RAMS	7	
6	SEATTLE	24	

Use Name	Pos.	Hgt	Wgt	Age	Int	Pts
Bob Cryder	OT	6'4"	282	26		
Darryl Haley	OT	6'4"	265	22		
Brian Holloway	OT	6'7"	288	24		
Steve Moore	OT	6'4"	285	22		
John Hannah	OG	6'2"	265	32		
Ron Wooten	OG	6'4"	273	24		
Pete Brock	C	6'5"	270	29		
Art Kuehn	C	6'3"	255	30		
Dwight Wheeler	C	6'3"	269	28		
Julius Adams	DE	6'3"	270	35		
Dave Browning	DE	6'5"	245	27		
George Crump	DE	6'4"	260	24		
Marshall Harris	DE	6'6"	261	27		
Doug Rogers (from ATL)	DE	6'5"	260	23		
Kenneth Sims	DE	6'5"	271	23		
Toby Williams	DE	6'3"	254	23		
Luther Henson	NT	6'	275	24		
Dennis Owens	NT	6'1"	258	23		
Lester Williams	NT	6'3"	272	24		
Don Blackman	LB	6'3"	235	25	1	
John Gillen	LB	6'3"	228	24		
Tim Golden	LB	6'1"	220	23		
Brian Ingram	LB	6'4"	235	23		
Larry McGrew	LB	6'5"	233	26	1	
Steve Nelson	LB	6'2"	230	32	1	
Johnny Rembert	LB	6'3"	234	22		
Ed Reynolds	LB	6'5"	230	21		
Andre Tippett	LB	6'3"	241	23		
Clayton Weishuhn	LB	6'2"	221	23		6
Raymond Clayborn	DB	6'1"	186	28		
Paul Dombroski	DB	6'	185	27		
Roland James	DB	6'2"	191	25	5	
Keith Lee	DB	5'11"	193	25		
Ronnie Lippett	DB	5'11"	180	22		
Fred Marion	DB	6'2"	191	24	2	
Rick Sanford	DB	6'1"	192	26	7	
Ricky Smith	DB	6'	182	23		
Tony Eason	QB	6'4"	212	23		
Steve Grogan	QB	6'4"	210	30		12
Mike Kerrigan	QB	6'3"	205	23		
Tony Collins	HB	5'11"	203	24		60
George Peoples	HB	6'	215	23		
Mosi Tatupu	FB	6'	227	28		30
Mark van Eeghen	FB	6'2"	220	31		6
Robert Weathers	FB	6'2"	222	22		6
Cedric Jones	WR	6'	184	23		6
Stanley Morgan	WR	5'11"	181	28		12
Stephen Starring	WR	5'10"	172	22		12
Clarence Weathers	WR	5'9"	170	21		18
Darryal Wilson	WR	6'	182	22		
Lin Dawson	TE	6'3"	240	24		6
Derrick Ramsey (from RAID)	TE	6'5"	235	26		
Brooks Williams	TE	6'4"	226	28		
Rich Camarillo	K	5'11"	191	23		
John Smith	K	6'	185	33		21
Fred Steinfort (from BUF)	K	5'11"	180	29		34
Joaquin Zendejas	K	5'11"	176	23		3

BUFFALO BILLS 8-8-0 Kay Stephenson

Scores of Each Game			
0	Miami	12	
10	CINCINNATI	6	
28	Baltimore	23	
30	Houston	13	
10	N.Y.Jets	34	
38	MIAMI	*35	
30	BALTIMORE	7	
0	New England	31	
27	New Orleans	21	
7	NEW ENGLAND	21	
24	N.Y.JETS	17	
24	L.A.Raiders	27	
17	L.A.RAMS	41	
14	KANSAS CITY	9	
10	San Francisco	23	
14	ATLANTA	31	

Use Name	Pos.	Hgt	Wgt	Age	Int	Pts
Darryl Caldwell	OT	6'5"	245	23		
Justin Cross	OT	6'6"	265	24		
Ken Jones	OT	6'5"	256	30		
Jon Borchardt	OG	6'5"	255	26		
Tom Lynch	OG	6'5"	250	28		
Jim Ritcher	OG-C	6'3"	251	25		
Will Grant	C	6'3"	248	29		
Tim Vogler	C	6'3"	245	26		
Scott Hutchinson	DE	6'4"	255	27		
Ken Johnson	DE	6'5"	253	28		
Scott Virkus	DE	6'5"	248	23		
Sherman White	DE	6'5"	250	34		
Ben Williams	DE	6'3"	245	29		
Bill Acker	NT	6'3"	255	26		
Mark Roopenian	NT	6'5"	254	25		
Fred Smerlas	NT	6'3"	270	26		
Jim Haslett	LB	6'3"	232	27		
Trey Junkin	LB	6'2"	221	22		
Chris Keating	LB	6'2"	223	25	2	
Joey Lumpkin	LB	6'2"	230	23		
Eugene Marve	LB	6'2"	230	23		
Mark Merrill	LB	6'4"	234	28		
Ervin Parker	LB	6'4"	240	25		
Lucius Sanford	LB	6'2"	216	27	2	
Darryl Talley	LB	6'4"	231	23		
Phil Villapiano	LB	6'2"	225	34		
Mario Clark	DB	6'2"	195	29		
Judson Flint	DB	6'	201	26		
Steve Freeman	DB	5'11"	185	30	3	
Bill Hurley (from NO)	DB	5'11"	185	26		
Mike Kennedy	DB	6'	195	24	1	6
David Kilson	DB	6'1"	200	22		6
Rod Kush	DB	6'	188	26		
Charles Romes	DB	6'1"	190	29	2	
Garry Thompson	DB	6'	180	24		
Len Walterscheid	DB	5'11"	190	28		
Chris Williams	DB	6'	197	24	3	
Joe Dufek	QB	6'4"	215	22		
Joe Ferguson	QB	6'1"	195	33		
Matt Kofler	QB	6'3"	192	24		
Joe Cribbs	HB	5'11"	190	25		60
Robb Riddick	HB	6'	195	26		
Van Williams	HB	6'	208	24		
Roosevelt Leaks	FB	5'10"	225	30		6
Booker Moore	FB	5'11"	224	24		6
Jerry Butler	WR	6'	178	25		18
Julius Dawkins	WR	6'1"	196	22		6
Byron Franklin	WR	6'1"	179	24		24
Frank Lewis	WR	6'1"	196	36		18
Mike Mosley	WR	6'2"	192	25		18
Perry Tuttle	WR	6'	178	24		18
Buster Barnett	TE	6'5"	225	24		
Mark Brammer	TE	6'3"	235	25		12
Tony Hunter	TE	6'3"	237	23		18
Greg Cater	K	6'	191	26		
Joe Danelo	K	5'9"	166	29		63

Joe Devlin - Broken Ankle
Robert Holt - Knee Injury
Roland Hooks - Knee Injury
Jeff Nixon - Knee Injury

BALTIMORE COLTS 7-9-0 Frank Kush

Scores of Each Game			
29	NEW ENGLAND	*23	
10	Denver	17	
23	BUFFALO	28	
22	Chicago	*19	
34	CINCINNATI	31	
12	New England	7	
7	Buffalo	30	
7	Miami	21	
22	PHILADELPHIA	21	
17	N.Y.JETS	14	
13	Pittsburgh	24	
0	MIAMI	37	
23	CLEVELAND	41	
6	N.Y.Jets	10	
19	DENVER	21	
20	Houston	10	

Use Name	Pos.	Hgt	Wgt	Age	Int	Pts
Sid Abramowitz	OT	6'6"	279	23		
Karl Baldischwiler	OT	6'5"	267	27		
Jeff Hart	OT	6'5"	272	29		
Lindsey Mason	OT	6'5"	275	28		
Jim Mills	OT	6'9"	271	21		
Chris Hinton	OG	6'4"	280	22		
Ben Utt	OG	6'4"	255	24		
Steve Wright	OG	6'6"	263	24		
Ray Donaldson	C	6'3"	269	25		
Grant Feasel	C	6'7"	267	23		
Mark Bell	DE	6'4"	240	26		
Steve Parker	DE	6'4"	250	23		
Hosea Taylor	DE	6'5"	260	24		
Donnell Thompson	DE	6'4"	263	24		2
Henry Waechter	DE	6'5"	270	24		
Quinton Ballard	NT	6'3"	289	22		
Earnest Barnes	NT	6'4"	260	22		
Leo Wisniewski	NT	6'1"	264	23		
Greg Bracelin	LB	6'1"	210	26	2	
Johnie Cooks	LB	6'4"	243	24	1	6
Ricky Jones	LB	6'1"	234	28		
Barry Krauss	LB	6'3"	247	26		
Vernon Maxwell	LB	6'2"	219	22	1	
Cliff Odom	LB	6'2"	233	24		
Gary Padjen	LB	6'2"	251	25		
Sanders Shiver	LB	6'2"	227	28		
Kim Anderson	DB	5'11"	189	26	2	6
Larry Anderson	DB	5'11"	192	26	1	6
James Burroughs	DB	6'1"	198	25	2	
Jeff Delaney	DB	6'	197	26	2	
Nesby Glasgow	DB	5'10"	180	26	3	
Derrick Harchett (to HOU)	DB	5'11"	183	25	4	
Mark Kafentzis	DB	5'10"	185	25		
Tate Randle (from HOU)	DB	6'	202	24	1	
Marco Tongue	DB	5'9"	174	23		
Kendall Williams	DB	5'9"	189	24	1	
Mark Herrmann	QB	6'4"	199	24		
Mike Pagel	QB	6'2"	201	22		
Mark Reed	QB	6'3"	204	24		
Jim Bob Taylor	QB	6'2"	197	23		
Curtis Dickey	HB	6'1"	214	26		42
Alvin Moore	HB	6'	194	24		6
Ricky Porter	HB	5'10"	204	23		
Newton Williams	HB-FB	5'10"	204	24		
Randy McMillan	FB	6'	220	24		36
Matt Bouza	WR	6'3"	211	24		
Ray Butler	WR	6'3"	206	26		18
Bernard Henry	WR	6'	179	23		24
Victor Oatis	WR	6'	177	24		
Tracy Porter	WR	6'1"	196	24		
Phil Smith	WR	6'3"	188	22		
Pat Beach	TE	6'4"	243	23		6
Tim Sherwin	TE	6'6"	237	25		
Dave Young	TE	6'5"	240	24		
Raul Allegre	K	5'10"	165	24		112
Rohn Stark	K	6'3"	199	24		

John Sinnott - Back Injury
Mike Humiston - Ankle Injury
Art Schlichter - Suspended by N.F.L.

NEW YORK JETS 7-9-0 Joe Walton

Scores of Each Game			
41	SAN DIEGO	29	
10	Seattle	17	
13	NEW ENGLAND	23	
27	L.A.Rams	*24	
34	BUFFALO	10	
7	CLEVELAND	10	
14	Miami	32	
21	Atlanta	27	
27	SAN FRANCISCO	13	
14	Baltimore	17	
17	Buffalo	24	
31	NEW ORLEANS	28	
26	New England	3	
10	BALTIMORE	6	
7	Pittsburgh	34	
14	MIAMI	34	

Use Name	Pos.	Hgt	Wgt	Age	Int	Pts
Reggie McElroy	OT	6'6"	270	23		
Marvin Powell	OT	6'5"	260	28		
Chris Ward	OT	6'3"	269	27		
Guy Bingham	OG-OT	6'3"	255	25		
Stan Waldemore	OG-OT	6'4"	269	28		
Dan Alexander	OG	6'4"	252	28		
Joe Pellegrini	C-OG	6'4"	252	26		
Joe Fields	C	6'2"	253	29		
George Lilja	C	6'4"	250	25		
Mark Gastineau	DE	6'5"	265	26		6
Rusty Guilbeau	DE	6'4"	260	24		
Joe Klecko	DE	6'3"	263	29		
Kenny Neil	DE-DT	6'4"	244	24		
Barry Bennett	DT-DE	6'4"	257	27		
Ben Rudolph	DT-DE	6'5"	266	26		
Marty Lyons	DT	6'5"	265	26		
Abdul Salaam	DT	6'3"	269	30		
Stan Blinka	LB	6'2"	230	25		
Greg Buttle	LB	6'3"	232	29	1	
Bob Crable	LB	6'3"	232	23	1	
Ron Crosby	LB	6'3"	227	28		
Jim Eliopulos (from STL)	LB	6'2"	229	24		
Lance Mehl	LB	6'3"	233	25	7	6
John Woodring	LB	6'2"	232	24		
Jerry Holmes	DB	6'2"	175	25	3	12
Bobby Jackson	DB	5'9"	180	26	2	
Jesse Johnson	DB	6'3"	188	26		
Johnny Lynn	DB	6'	198	26	3	6
Davlin Mullen	DB	6'1"	177	23		
Darrol Ray	DB	6'1"	198	25	3	
Ken Schroy	DB	6'2"	198	30	2	
Kirk Springs	DB	6'	192	25		6
Ken O'Brien	QB	6'4"	210	22		
Pat Ryan	QB	6'3"	210	27		1
Richard Todd	QB	6'2"	206	29		
Scott Dierking	HB	5'10"	220	28		18
Bruce Harper	HB	5'8"	177	28		18
Johnny Hector	HB	5'11"	197	22		6
Freeman McNeil	HB	5'11"	218	24		24
Mike Augustyniak	FB	5'11"	226	27		18
Marion Barber	FB	6'3"	224	23		12
Dwayne Crutchfield (to HOU)	FB	6'3"	235	23		18
Rocky Klever	FB	6'3"	225	24		
Kenny Lewis	FB	6'	196	25		
Preston Brown	WR	5'11"	187	25		
Nick Bruckner	WR	5'11"	185	22		
Derrick Gaffney	WR	6'1"	182	28		
Mike Harmon	WR	6'	185	22		
Johnny "Lam" Jones	WR	5'11"	180	25		24
Wesley Walker	WR	6'	179	28		42
Jerome Barkum	TE	6'3"	227	33		6
Tom Coombs	TE	6'3"	227	33		
Mickey Shuler	TE	6'3"	231	27		6
Pat Leahy	K	6'	189	32		84
Chuck Ramsey	K	6'2"	189	31		

George Floyd - Knee Injury
Jim Luscinski - Broken Vertebrae
Kurt Sohn - Knee Injury

* Overtime

MIAMI DOLPHINS

RUSHING

Last Name	No.	Yds	Avg	TD
Franklin	224	746	3.3	8
Nathan	151	685	4.5	3
Overstreet	85	392	4.6	1
Bennett	49	197	4.0	2
Woodley	19	78	4.1	0
Marino	28	45	1.6	2
Hill	2	12	6.0	0
Clayton	2	9	4.5	0
Hardy	1	2	2.0	0
Harris	1	0	0.0	0
Strock	6	-16	-2.7	0

RECEIVING

Last Name	No.	Yds	Avg	TD
Nathan	52	461	8.9	1
Duper	51	1003	19.7	10
Moore	39	558	14.3	6
Rose	29	345	11.9	3
Johnson	24	189	7.9	4
Hardy	22	202	9.2	0
Harris	15	260	17.3	1
Overstreet	8	55	6.9	2
Clayton	6	114	19.0	1
Bennett	6	35	5.8	0
Vigorito	1	7	7.0	0
Woodley	1	6	6.0	0

PUNT RETURNS

Last Name	No.	Yds	Avg	TD
Clayton	41	392	9.6	1
Walker	8	86	10.8	0
Kozlowski	2	12	6.0	0
G. Blackwood	1	10	10.0	0
Heflin	1	19	19.0	0
Sowell	1	0	0.0	0
Vigorito	1	62	62.0	0

KICKOFF RETURNS

Last Name	No.	Yds	Avg	TD
Walker	36	962	26.7	0
Kozlowski	4	50	12.5	0
Nathan	3	15	5.0	0
Bennett	1	6	6.0	0
Brown	1	0	0.0	0
Clayton	1	25	25.0	0
Heflin	1	27	27.0	0

PASSING — PUNTING — KICKING

PASSING	Att	Cmp	%	Yds	Yd/Att	TD	Int—	%	RK
Marino	296	173	58	2210	7.47	20	6—	2	1
Woodley	89	43	48	528	5.93	3	4—	5	
Strock	52	34	65	403	7.75	4	1—	2	
Nathan	4	3	75	46	11.50	0	0—	0	
Clayton	1	1	100	48	48.00	1	0—	0	

PUNTING	No.	Avg.
Roby	74	43.1

KICKING	XP	Att	%	FG	Att	%
von Schamann	45	48	94	18	27	67

NEW ENGLAND PATRIOTS

RUSHING

Last Name	No.	Yds	Avg	TD
Collins	219	1049	4.8	10
Tatupu	106	578	5.5	4
R. Weathers	73	418	5.7	1
van Eeghen	95	358	3.8	2
Grogan	23	108	4.7	2
Eason	19	39	2.1	0
C. Weathers	1	28	28.0	0
Kerrigan	1	14	14.0	0
Morgan	1	13	13.0	0

RECEIVING

Last Name	No.	Yds	Avg	TD
Morgan	58	863	14.9	2
Collins	27	257	9.5	0
Ramsey	24	335	14.0	6
R. Weathers	23	212	9.2	0
Jones	20	323	16.2	1
C. Weathers	19	379	19.9	3
Starring	17	389	22.9	2
van Eeghen	10	102	10.2	0
Tatupu	10	97	9.7	1
Dawson	9	84	9.3	1
B. Williams	1	0	0.0	0
Grogan	1	-8	-8.0	0

PUNT RETURNS

Last Name	No.	Yds	Avg	TD
R. Smith	38	398	10.5	0
C. Weather	4	1	0.3	0
Lee	1	0	0.0	0
Sanford	1	0	0.0	0

KICKOFF RETURNS

Last Name	No.	Yds	Avg	TD
R. Smith	42	916	21.8	0
Jones	4	63	15.8	0
Lee	4	40	10.0	0
C. Weathers	3	58	19.3	0
R. Weathers	3	68	22.7	0
Golden	1	10	10.0	0

PASSING — PUNTING — KICKING

PASSING	Att	Cmp	%	Yds	Yd/Att	TD	Int—	%	RK
Grogan	303	168	55	2411	7.96	15	12—	4	6
Eason	95	46	48	557	5.86	1	5—	5	
Kerrigan	14	6	43	72	5.14	0	1—	7	

PUNTING	No.	Avg.
Camarillo	81	44.6

KICKING	XP	Att.	%	FG	Att	%
Steinfort	17	18	94	7	21	33
J. Smith	12	15	80	3	6	50
Zendejas	3	4	75	0	1	0

BUFFALO BILLS

RUSHING

Last Name	No.	Yds	Avg	TD
Cribbs	263	1131	4.3	3
Moore	60	275	4.6	0
Leaks	58	157	2.7	1
Ferguson	20	88	4.4	0
Hunter	2	28	14.0	0
Kofler	4	25	6.3	0
Riddick	4	18	4.5	0
V. Williams	3	11	3.7	0
Franklin	1	3	3.0	0

RECEIVING

Last Name	No.	Yds	Avg	TD
Cribbs	57	524	9.2	7
Lewis	36	486	13.5	3
Hunter	36	402	11.2	3
Butler	36	385	10.7	3
Moore	34	199	5.9	1
Franklin	30	452	15.1	4
Brammer	25	215	8.6	2
Tuttle	17	261	15.4	3
Mosley	14	180	12.9	3
Dawkins	11	123	11.2	1
Barnett	10	94	9.4	0
Leaks	8	74	9.3	0
Riddick	3	43	14.3	0

PUNT RETURNS

Last Name	No.	Yds	Avg	TD
Riddick	42	241	5.7	0
Hurley	1	0	0.0	0
V. Williams	1	0	0.0	0

KICKOFF RETURNS

Last Name	No.	Yds	Avg	TD
V. Williams	22	494	22.5	0
Riddick	28	568	20.3	0
Mosley	9	236	26.2	0
B. Williams	3	56	18.7	0
Talley	2	9	4.5	0

PASSING — PUNTING — KICKING

PASSING	Att	Cmp	%	Yds	Yd/Att	TD	Int—	%	RK
Ferguson	508	281	55	2995	5.90	26	25—	5	11
Kofler	61	35	57	440	7.21	4	3—	5	
Cribbs	2	1	50	3	1.50	0	0—	0	

PUNTING	No.	Avg.
Cater	89	39.7

KICKING	XP	ATT	%	FG	ATT	%
Danelo	33	34	97	10	20	50

BALTIMORE COLTS

RUSHING

Last Name	No.	Yds	Avg	TD
Dickey	254	1122	4.4	4
McMillan	198	802	4.1	5
Pagel	54	441	8.2	0
Moore	57	205	3.6	1
N. Williams	28	77	2.8	0
Reed	2	27	13.5	0
Dixon	5	14	28	0
Stark	1	8	8.0	0
Herrmann	1	0	0.0	0
Krauss	1	-1	-1.0	0

RECEIVING

Last Name	No.	Yds	Avg	TD
Henry	30	416	13.9	4
T. Porter	28	384	13.7	0
Bouza	25	385	15.4	0
Sherwin	25	358	14.3	0
Dickey	24	483	20.1	3
McMillan	24	195	8.1	1
Butler	10	207	20.7	3
Oatis	6	93	15.5	0
Moore	6	38	6.3	0
Beach	5	56	11.2	1
N. Williams	4	46	11.5	0
Dixon	1	2	2.0	0

PUNT RETURNS

Last Name	No.	Yds	Avg	TD
L. Anderson	20	138	6.9	0
R. Porter	14	104	7.4	0
K. Williams	9	43	4.8	0
Glasgow	1	9	9.0	0

KICKOFF RETURNS

Last Name	No.	Yds	Avg	TD
K. Williams	20	490	24.5	0
R. Porter	18	340	18.9	0
L. Anderson	18	309	17.2	0
Dixon	2	23	11.5	0
Moore	2	40	20.0	0
Beach	1	0	0.0	0
Bouza	1	-4	-4.0	0

PASSING — PUNTING — KICKING

PASSING	Att	Cmp	%	Yds	Yd/Att	TD	Int—	%	RK
Pagel	328	163	50	2353	7.17	12	17—	5	13
Herrmann	36	18	50	256	7.11	0	3—	8	
Reed	10	6	60	34	3.40	0	1—	10	
J. Taylor	2	1	50	20	10.00	0	1—	50	
Stark	1	0	0	0	0.00	0	0—	0	

PUNTING	No.	Avg.
Stark	91	45.3

KICKING	XP	Att	%	FG	Att	%
Allegre	22	24	92	30	35	86

NEW YORK JETS

RUSHING

Last Name	No.	Yds	Avg	TD
McNeil	160	654	4.1	1
Crutchfield	137	571	4.2	3
Harper	51	354	6.9	1
Dierking	28	113	4.0	3
Todd	35	101	2.9	0
Hector	16	85	5.3	0
Barber	15	77	5.1	1
Augustyniak	18	50	2.8	2
Lewis	5	25	5.0	0
Ryan	4	23	5.8	0
Jones	4	10	2.5	0
Crosby	1	5	5.0	0

RECEIVING

Last Name	No.	Yds	Avg	TD
Walker	61	868	14.2	7
Harper	48	413	8.6	2
Jones	43	734	17.1	4
Dierking	33	275	8.3	0
Barkum	32	385	12.0	1
Shuler	26	272	10.5	1
McNeil	21	172	8.2	3
Crutchfield	19	133	7.0	0
Gaffney	17	243	14.3	0
Augustyniak	10	71	7.1	1
Barber	7	48	6.9	1
Lewis	6	62	10.3	0
Hector	5	61	12.2	1
Harmon	1	4	4.0	0

PUNT RETURNS

Last Name	No.	Yds	Avg	TD
Springs	23	287	12.5	1
Harmon	12	109	9.1	0
Mullen	2	13	6.5	0
Schroy	1	11	11.0	0

KICKOFF RETURNS

Last Name	No.	Yds	Avg	TD
Springs	16	364	22.8	0
Brown	29	645	22.2	0
Hector	14	274	19.6	0
Mullen	3	57	19.0	0
Barber	1	9	9.0	0
Harper	1	16	16.0	0
McElroy	1	7	7.0	0
Shuler	1	3	3.0	0

PASSING — PUNTING — KICKING

PASSING	Att	Cmp	%	Yds	Yd/Att	TD	Int—	%	RK
Todd	518	308	60	3478	6.71	18	26—	5	10
Ryan	40	21	53	259	6.25	2	2—	5	
McNeil	1	1	100	5	5.00	1	0—	0	

PUNTING	No.	Avg.
Ramsey	81	39.7

KICKING	XP	Att	%	FG	Att	%
Leahy	36	37	97	16	24	67
Ryan	1	1	100	0	0	0

1983 A.F.C. - Central Division

PITTSBURGH STEELERS 10-6-0 Chunk Noll

Scores of Each Game		
10	Denver	14
25	GREEN BAY	21
40	HOUSTON	28
23	New England	28
17	Houston	10
24	CINCINNATI	14
44	CLEVELAND	17
27	SEATTLE	21
17	Tampa Bay	12
26	San Diego	3
24	BALTIMORE	13
14	Minnesota	17
3	DETROIT	45
10	Cincinnati	23
34	N.Y.JETS	7
17	Cleveland	30

Use Name	Pos.	Hgt	Wgt	Age	Int	Pts
Larry Brown	OT	6'4"	270	34		
Tunch Ilkin	OT	6'3"	255	25		
Ted Petersen	OT	6'5"	245	28		
Steve Courson	OG	6'1"	270	27		
Blake Wingle	OG	6'2"	267	23		
Craig Wolfley	OG	6'1"	265	25		
Emil Boures	C-OG	6'1"	261	23		
Rick Donnalley	C-OG	6'2"	257	24		
Mike Webster	C	6'1"	250	31		
Tom Beasley	DE-NT	6'5"	248	29		
John Goodman	DE	6'6"	250	24		
Keith Gary	DE	6'3"	255	23		
Keith Willis	DE-NT	6'1"	255	24		
Gary Dunn	NT	6'3"	260	30		
Edmund Nelson	NT-DE	6'3"	270	23		
Gabe Rivera	NT	6'2"	293	22		
Craig Bingham	LB	6'2"	211	23		
Robin Cole	LB	6'2"	220	27		
Bryan Hinkle	LB	6'1"	220	24	1	6
Bob Kohrs	LB	6'3"	235	24		2
Jack Lambert	LB	6'4"	220	31	2	
David Little	LB	6'1"	220	31	2	
Mike Merriweather	LB	6'2"	215	22	3	6
Loren Toews	LB	6'3"	220	31		
Greg Best	DB	5'10"	185	23		6
Mel Blount	DB	6'3"	205	35	4	6
Harvey Clayton	DB	5'9"	170	22	1	6
Ron Johnson	DB	5'10"	200	27	3	6
Donnie Shell	DB	5'11"	190	31	5	
Sam Washington	DB	5'8"	180	23	1	
Eric Williams	DB	6'1"	183	23		
Dwayne Woodruff	DB	5'11"	196	26	3	
Rick Woods	DB	6'	196	23	5	6
Terry Bradshaw	QB	6'3"	210	34		
Mark Malone	QB	6'4"	223	24		
Cliff Stoudt	QB	6'4"	218	28		23
Walter Abercombie	HB	5'11"	201	23		42
Tim Harris	HB	5'9"	206	22		
Greg Hawthorne	HB	6'2"	225	26		
Henry Odom	HB	5'10"	200	24		
Frank Pollard	HB-FB	5'10"	210	26		24
Russell Davis	FB	6'1"	231	27		
Franco Harris	FB	6'2"	225	33		42
Wayne Capers	WR	6'2"	193	22		6
Gregg Garrity	WR	5'10"	171	22		6
Paul Skanel	WR	5'11"	190	22		
John Stallworth	WR	6'2"	191	31		
Calvin Sweeney	WR	6'2"	190	28		30
Bennie Cunningham	TE	6'4"	260	28		18
Craig Dunaway	TE	6'2"	233	22		
John Rodgers	TE	6'2"	220	23		
Gary Anderson	K	5'11"	156	24		119
Craig Colquitt	K	6'2"	182	29		

Ernest French - Knee Injury

CLEVELAND BROWNS 9-7-0 Sam Rutigliano

Scores of Each Game		
21	Minnesota	27
31	DETROIT	26
17	Cincinnati	7
30	SAN DIEGO	*24
9	Seattle	24
10	N.Y.Jets	7
17	Pittsburgh	44
21	CINCINNATI	28
25	Houston	*19
21	GREEN BAY	35
20	Tampa Bay	0
30	NEW ENGLAND	0
41	Baltimore	23
6	DENVER	27
27	HOUSTON	34
30	PITTSBURGH	17

Use Name	Pos.	Hgt	Wgt	Age	Int	Pts
Bill Contz	OT	6'5"	260	21		
Doug Dieken	OT	6'5"	252	34		6
Paul Farren	OT	6'5"	251	22		
Thomas Hopkins	OT	6'6"	260	23		
Cody Risien	OT	6'7"	270	26		
Joe DeLamielleure	OG	6'3"	260	32		
Robert Jackson	OG	6'5"	260	30		
Mike Baab	C	6'4"	270	23		
Tom DeLeone	C	6'2"	254	33		
Keith Baldwin	DE	6'4"	250	22		
Thomas Brown	DE	6'4"	255	26		
Reggie Camp	DE	6'4"	264	22		
Elvis Franks	DE	6'4"	265	26		
Bob Golic	NT	6'2"	260	25	1	6
Dave Puzzudi	NT	6'3"	260	22		
Dick Ambrose	LB	6'	228	30		
Chip Banks	LB	6'4"	233	23	3	6
Dale Carver	LB	6'2"	225	22		
Tom Cousineau	LB	6'3"	225	26	4	
Eddie Johnson	LB	6'1"	215	24		
Clay Matthews	LB	6'2"	230	27		
Scott Nicolas	LB	6'3"	226	23		
Curtis Weathers	LB	6'5"	230	26		
Larry Braziel	DB	6'	184	28		
Clinton Burrell	DB	6'2"	192	26	2	
Hanford Dixon	DB	5'11"	182	24	3	
Al Gross	DB	6'3"	186	22	1	
Lawrence Johnson	DB	5'11"	204	25	2	
Rod Perry	DB	5'9"	185	29	1	
Clarence Scott	DB	6'	190	34	2	
Mike Whitwell	DB	6'	175	24	3	
Paul McDonald	QB	6'2"	190	25		
Brian Sipe	QB	6'1"	195	34		
Rick Trocano	QB	6'	188	24		
Dino Hall	HB	5'7"	165	27		
Dwight Walker	HB	5'10"	185	24		6
Johnny Davis	FB	6'1"	235	27		
Vagas Ferguson (to HOU)	FB	6'1"	213	26		
Boyce Green	FB	5'11"	215	23		24
Mike Pruitt	FB	6'	225	29		72
Willis Adams	WR	6'2"	194	27		12
Ricky Belk	WR	6'	187	23		12
Ricky Feacher	WR	5'10"	180	29		18
Michael Harmon	WR	6'	208	22		
Bobby Jones	WR	5'11"	185	28		24
Dave Logan	WR	6'4"	216	29		12
Harry Holt	TE	6'4"	230	25		18
Ozzie Newsome	TE	6'2"	232	27		36
Stracka	TE	6'3"	225	23		
Matt Bahr	K	5'10"	175	27		101
Steve Cox	K	6'4"	195	25		3
Gossett	K	6'2"	197	26		

Charles White - Broken Ankle

CINCINNATI BENGALS 7-9-0 Forrest Gregg

Scores of Each Game		
10	L.A.Raiders	20
6	Buffalo	10
7	CLEVELAND	17
23	TAMPA BAY	17
31	Baltimore	34
14	Pittsburgh	24
17	DENVER	24
28	Cleveland	21
34	Green Bay	14
55	HOUSTON	14
15	KANSAS CITY	20
38	Houston	10
14	MIAMI	38
23	PITTSBURGH	10
17	Detroit	9
14	MINNESOTA	20

Use Name	Pos.	Hgt	Wgt	Age	Int	Pts
Jim Hannula	OT	6'6"	264	24		
Anthony Munoz	OT	6'6"	278	25		
Mike Wilson	OT	6'5"	271	28		
Max Montoya	OG	6'5"	275	27		
Mike Obravac	OG	6'6"	275	27		
Dave Rimington	C	6'3"	288	21		
Dave Lapham	C	6'4"	262	31		
Blake Moore	C	6'5"	267	25		
Ross Browner	DE	6'3"	261	29	1	
Gary Burley	DE	6'3"	282	30		
Gler Collins	DE	6'6"	265	24		
Edd Edwards	DE	6'5"	256	29		
Chri Lindstrom	DE	6'7"	260	23		
Jerr Boyarsky	NT	6'3"	290	24		
Tim umrie	NT	6'2"	262	23		
Glenn Cameron	LB	6'1"	228	30		
Tom Dinkel	LB	6'3"	237	27		
Guy Frazier	LB	6'2"	215	24		
Jim LeClair	LB	6'2"	234	33		
Steve Maidlow	LB	6'2"	228	25		
Rick Razzano	LB	5'11"	227	27		
Jeff Schuh	LB	6'2"	228	25		
Ron Simpkins	LB	6'1"	235	25		
Reggie Williams	LB	6'1"	228	28		6
Louis Breeden	DB	5'11"	185	29	2	
James Griffin	DB	6'2"	197	21	1	6
Ray Griffin	DB	5'10"	186	27	2	
Ray Horton	DB	5'11"	190	23	5	6
Robert Jackson	DB	5'10"	186	24	2	
Bobby Kemp	DB	6'	186	24	3	
Ken Riley	DB	6'	191	36	8	12
John Simmons	DB	5'11"	192	24		
Jimmy Turner	DB	6'	187	24		
Ken Anderson	QB	6'1"	212	34		6
Jeff Christensen	QB	6'3"	202	23		
Turk Schonert	QB	6'1"	190	26		12
Rodney Tate	HB	5'11"	190	24		
Stanley Wilson	HB-FB	5'10"	210	22		12
Charles Alexander	FB	6'1"	226	26		18
Pete Johnson	FB	6'	272	29		84
Larry Kinnebrew	FB	6'1"	252	24		18
Cris Collinsworth	WR	6'5"	192	24		30
Isaac Curtis	WR	6'	192	32		12
Steve Kreider	WR	6'3"	192	25		6
Mike Martin	WR	5'10"	186	22		
David Verser	WR	6'1"	202	25		
Andy Gibler	TE	6'4"	234	22		
M.L.Harris	TE	6'5"	238	29		12
Rodney Holman	TE	6'3"	232	23		
Dan Ross	TE	6'4"	235	26		18
Jim Breech	K	5'6"	161	27		87
Pat McInally	K	6'6"	212	30		

Bryan Hicks - Shoulder Injury
Emanuel Weaver - Knee Injury

HOUSTON OILERS 2-14-0 Ed Biles (0-6-0), Chuck Studley (2-8-0)

Scores of Each Game		
38	Green Bay	*41
6	L.A.RAIDERS	20
28	Pittsburgh	40
13	BUFFALO	30
10	PITTSBURGH	17
14	Denver	26
14	MINNESOTA	34
10	Kansas City	*13
19	CLEVELAND	*25
14	Cincinnati	55
27	Detroit	17
10	CINCINNATI	38
24	TAMPA BAY	33
17	Miami	24
34	Cleveland	27
10	BALTIMORE	20

Use Name	Pos.	Hgt	Wgt	Age	Int	Pts
Doug France	OT	6'5"	266	30		
Harvey Salem	OT	6'6"	264	22		
Morris Towns	OT	6'4"	263	29		
Bruce Matthews	OG-OT	6'4"	269	22		
Pat Howell (from ATL)	OG	6'5"	260	26		
Mike Munchak	OG	6'3"	275	23		
John Schuhmacher	OG	6'3"	269	27		
Al Steinfeld (to NYG)	OG	6'5"	256	24		
Ralph Williams	OG	6'3"	276	25		
David Carter	C	6'2"	260	24		
Les Studdard	C	6'4"	260	24		
Jesse Baker	DE	6'5"	272	26		
Elvin Bethea	DE	6'3"	272	26		
Jerome Foster	DE	6'2"	252	37		
Bob Hamm	DE	6'4"	248	24		
Ken Kennard	DE	6'2"	255	28		
Malcolm Taylor	DE	6'6"	280	23		
Brain Sochia	NT	6'3"	250	22		
Mike Stenarud	NT	6'5"	285	27		
Robert Abraham	LB	6'1"	215	23	1	
Gregg Bingham	LB	6'1"	225	32	1	
Robert Brazile	LB	6'4"	245	30		
Daryl Hunt	LB	6'3"	235	26		
Tim Joiner	LB	6'4"	224	22		
Avon Riley	LB	6'3"	225	30	1	
Ted Thomspon	LB	6'1"	219	30		
Keith Bostic	DB	6'1"	212	22	2	
Steve Brown	DB	5'11"	188	23	1	6
Carter Hartwig	DB	6'	207	27		
Greg Hill	DB	6'1"	189	22		
Bill Kay	DB	6'1"	190	23	2	
Darryl Meadows	DB	6'1"	199	22		
Vernon Perry	DB	6'2"	210	28		
Mike Reinfeldt	DB	6'2"	192	30	1	
Willie Tullis	DB	6'	193	25	5	
J.C.Wilson	DB	6'	184	27		
Oliver Luck	QB	6'2"	193	23		
Archie Manning (to MIN)	QB	6'3"	211	34		
Gifford Nielsen	QB	6'4"	210	28		
Brian Ransom	QB	6'3"	205	23		
Earl Campbell	HB-FB	5'11"	238	28		72
Curtis Brown	FB	5'10"	203	28		6
Donnie Craft	FB	6'	205	23		
Stan Edwards	FB	6'	205	23		6
Larry Moriarty	FB	6'1"	228	25		18
Steve Bryant	WR	6'2"	191	23		
Mike Holston	WR	6'3"	188	25		
Mike Renfro	WR	6'	184	28		12
Carl Roaches	WR	5'8"	170	29		6
Tim Smith	WR	6'2"	203	26		36
Herkie Walls	WR	5'8"	154	22		6
Walt Arnold	TE	6'3"	234	25		6
Chris Dressel	TE	6'4"	231	22		24
Mike McCloskey	TE	6'5"	240	22		6
John James	K	6'3"	196	34		
Florian Kempf	K	5'9"	170	27		84

* Overtime

PITTSBURGH STEELERS

RUSHING

Last Name	No.	Yds	Avg	TD
F. Harris	279	1007	3.6	5
Pollard	135	608	4.5	4
Stoudt	77	479	6.2	4
Abercrombie	112	446	4.0	4
Hawthrone	5	47	9.4	0
T. Harris	2	15	7.5	0
Odom	2	7	3.5	0
Bradshaw	1	3	3.0	0
Sweeney	1	-2	-2.0	0

RECEIVING

Last Name	No.	Yds	Avg	TD
Sweeney	39	577	14.8	5
Cunningham	35	442	12.6	3
F. Harris	34	278	8.2	2
Abercrombie	26	391	15.0	3
Hawthorne	19	300	15.8	0
Garrity	19	279	14.7	1
Pollard	16	127	7.9	0
Capers	10	185	18.5	1
Stallworth	8	100	12.5	0
Skansi	3	39	13.0	0
Rodgers	2	36	18.0	0

PUNT RETURNS

Last Name	No.	Yds	Avg	TD
Skansi	43	363	8.4	0
Woods	5	46	9.2	0
T. Harris	3	12	4.0	0

KICKOFF RETURNS

Last Name	No.	Yds	Avg	TD
Odom	39	756	19.4	0
T. Harris	18	289	16.1	0
Bingham	1	15	15.0	0
Kohrs	1	6	6.0	0
Donnalley	0	2	—	0

PASSING — PUNTING — KICKING

PASSING	Att	Cmp	%	Yds	Yd/Att	TD	Int—	%	RK
Stoudt	381	197	52	2553	6.70	12	21—	6	15
Malone	20	9	45	124	6.20	1	2—	10	
Bradshaw	8	5	63	77	9.63	2	0—	0	

PUNTING	No.	Avg.
Colquitt	80	41.9

KICKING	XP	Att	%	FG	Att	%
Anderson	38	39	97	27	31	87

CLEVELAND BROWNS

RUSHING

Last Name	No.	Yds	Avg	TD
Pruitt	293	1184	4.0	10
Green	104	497	4.8	3
Walker	19	100	5.3	0
Sipe	26	56	2.2	0
Davis	13	42	3.2	0
Jones	1	19	19.0	0
McDonald	3	17	5.7	0
Holt	3	8	2.7	0
Adams	1	2	2.0	0
Hall	1	2	2.0	0
Belk	1	-5	-5.0	0

RECEIVING

Last Name	No.	Yds	Avg	TD
Newsome	89	970	10.9	6
Logan	37	627	16.9	2
Jones	36	507	14.1	4
Pruitt	30	157	5.2	2
Holt	29	420	14.5	3
Walker	29	273	9.4	1
Green	25	167	6.7	1
Adams	20	374	18.7	2
Feacher	13	217	16.7	3
Belk	5	141	28.2	2
Davis	5	20	4.0	0
Hall	4	33	8.3	0
Dieken	1	14	14.0	1
Stracka	1	12	12.0	0

PUNT RETURNS

Last Name	No.	Yds	Avg	TD
Hall	39	284	7.3	0
Walker	3	26	8.7	0

KICKOFF RETURNS

Last Name	No.	Yds	Avg	TD
Walker	29	627	21.6	0
Green	17	350	20.6	0
Hall	11	237	21.5	0
Ferguson	2	36	18.0	0
Nicolas	2	29	14.5	0
Contz	1	3	3.0	0
Davis	1	8	8.0	0

PASSING — PUNTING — KICKING

PASSING	Att	Cmp	%	Yds	Yd/Att	TD	Int—	%	RK
Sipe	496	291	59	3566	7.19	26	23—	5	9
McDonald	68	32	47	341	5.01	1	4—	6	
Walker	3	1	33	25	8.33	0	1—	33	

PUNTING	No.	Avg.
Gossett	70	40.8

KICKING	XP	Att	%	FG	Att	%
Bahr	38	40	95	21	24	88
Cox	0	0	0	1	1	100

CINCINNATI BENGALS

RUSHING

Last Name	No.	Yds	Avg	TD
Johnson	210	763	3.6	14
Alexander	153	523	3.4	3
S. Wilson	56	267	4.8	1
Kinnebrew	39	156	4.0	3
Anderson	22	147	6.7	1
Schonert	29	117	4.0	2
Tate	25	77	3.1	0
Verser	2	31	15.5	0
Martin	2	21	10.5	0
Collinsworth	2	2	1.0	0
Kreider	1	2	2.0	0

RECEIVING

Last Name	No.	Yds	Avg	TD
Collinsworth	66	1130	17.1	5
Curtis	42	571	13.6	2
Kreider	42	554	13.2	1
Ross	42	483	11.5	3
Alexander	32	187	5.8	0
Tate	18	142	7.9	0
Johnson	15	129	8.6	0
S. Wilson	12	107	8.9	1
Harris	8	66	8.3	2
Verser	7	82	11.7	0
Martin	2	22	11.0	0
Holman	2	15	7.5	0
Kinnebrew	2	4	2.0	0

PUNT RETURNS

Last Name	No.	Yds	Avg	TD
Martin	23	227	9.9	0
Simmons	25	173	6.9	0
Horton	1	10	10.0	0

KICKOFF RETURNS

Last Name	No.	Yds	Avg	TD
Simmons	14	317	22.6	0
Tate	13	218	16.8	0
Verser	13	253	19.5	0
S. Wilson	7	161	23.0	0
Horton	5	128	25.6	0
Dinkel	1	1	1.0	0
Martin	1	19	19.0	0

PASSING — PUNTING — KICKING

PASSING	Att	Cmp	%	Yds	Yd/Att	TD	Int—	%	RK
Anderson	297	198	67	2333	7.86	12	13—	4	4
Schonert	156	92	59	1159	7.43	2	5—	3	
Kreider	1	0	0	0	0.00	0	0—	0	

PUNTING	No.	Avg.
McInally	67	41.9

KICKING	XP	Att	%	FG	Att	%
Breech	39	41	95	16	23	70
Browner	1	1	100	0	0	0

HOUSTON OILERS

RUSHING

Last Name	No.	Yds	Avg	TD
Campbell	322	1301	4.0	12
Moriarty	65	321	4.9	3
Craft	55	147	2.7	0
Luck	17	55	3.2	0
Walls	5	44	8.8	0
Nielsen	8	43	5.4	0
Edwards	16	40	2.5	0
Smith	2	16	8.0	0
Manning	2	13	6.5	0
Crutchfield	3	7	2.3	0
Dressel	1	3	3.0	0
Renfro	1	3	3.0	0
C. Brown	3	0	0.0	0
James	1	0	0.0	0

RECEIVING

Last Name	No.	Yds	Avg	TD
Smith	83	1176	14.2	6
Dressel	32	316	9.9	4
Renfro	23	316	13.7	2
Campbell	19	216	11.4	0
Bryant	16	211	13.2	0
McCloskey	16	137	8.6	1
Holston	14	205	14.6	0
Walls	12	276	23.0	1
Arnold	12	137	11.4	1
Craft	12	99	8.3	0
Edwards	9	79	8.8	1
Moriarty	4	32	8.0	0
Kempf	1	7	7.0	0

PUNT RETURNS

Last Name	No.	Yds	Avg	TD
Roaches	20	159	8.0	0

KICKOFF RETURNS

Last Name	No.	Yds	Avg	TD
S. Brown	31	795	25.6	1
Roaches	34	641	18.9	1
Walls	9	110	12.2	0
Dressel	4	40	10.0	0
Moriarty	2	25	12.5	0
Hunt	1	12	12.0	0
McCloskey	1	11	11.0	0
Tullis	1	16	16.0	0
Riley	0	26	—	0

PASSING — PUNTING — KICKING

PASSING	Att	Cmp	%	Yds	Yd/Att	TD	Int—	%	RK
Luck	217	124	57	1375	6.34	8	13—	6	14
Nielsen	175	90	51	1125	6.43	5	8—	5	
Manning	88	44	50	755	8.58	2	8—	9	
Bryant	1	1	100	24	24.00	1	0—	0	
James	1	1	100	7	7.00	0	0—	0	

PUNTING	No.	Avg.
James	79	39.7

KICKING	XP	Att	%	FG	Att	%
Kempf	33	34	97	17	21	81

LOS ANGELES RAIDERS 12-4-0 Tom Flores

Scores of Each Game		
20	CINCINNATI	10
20	Houston	6
27	Miami	14
22	DENVER	7
35	WASHINGTON	37
21	Kansas City	20
36	SEATTLE	38
40	DALLAS	38
21	Seattle	34
28	KANSAS CITY	20
22	Denver	20
27	BUFFALO	24
27	N.Y.Giants	12
42	SAN DIEGO	10
24	St. Louis	34
30	San Diego	14

Use Name	Pos.	Hgt	Wgt	Age	Int	Pts
Bruce Davis	OT	6'6"	280	27		
Shelby Jordan	OT	6'7"	285	31		
Henry Lawrence	OT	6'4"	270	31		
Don Mosebar	OT	6'6"	270	21		
Ed Muransky	OT	6'7"	275	23		
Charley Hannah	OG	6'5"	260	28		
Mickey Marvin	OG	6'4"	265	27		
Dave Dalby	C	6'2"	250	32		
Jim Romano	C	6'3"	255	30		
Steve Sylvester	C-OG	6'4"	260	30		
Lyle Alzado	DE	6'3"	260	34		2
Howie Long	DE	6'5"	270	23		
Bill Pickel	DE	6'5"	260	23		
Greg Townsend	DE	6'3"	240	21		8
Reggie Kinlaw	NT	6'2"	245	26		
Archie Reese	NT	6'3"	275	27		
Johny Robinson	NT	6'2"	255	24		
David Stalls (from TB-DE)	NT	6'5"	250	27		

Use Name	Pos.	Hgt	Wgt	Age	Int	Pts
Jeff Barnes	LB	6'2"	225	28		
Darryl Byrd	LB	6'1"	220	22		
Tony Caldwell	LB	6'1"	225	22		
Ted Hendricks	LB	6'7"	240	35		
Rod Martin	LB	6'2"	220	29	4	12
Matt Millen	LB	6'2"	250	25	1	
Bob Nelson	LB	6'4"	235	30		
Jack Squirek	LB	6'4"	225	24		
Don Bessillieu	DB	6'1"	200	27		
James Davis	DB	6'	195	26	1	
Mike Davis	DB	6'3"	205	27	1	
Lester Hayes	DB	6'	200	28	2	
Mike Haynes	DB	6'2"	190	30	1	
Kenny Hill	HB	6'	195	25		
Vann McElroy	DB	6'2"	190	23	8	
Odis McKinney	DB	6'2"	190	26	1	
Irvin Phillips	DB	6'1"	190	23		
Ted Watts	DB	6'	195	25	1	

Curt Marsh - Back Injury

Use Name	Pos.	Hgt	Wgt	Age	Int	Pts
David Humm	QB	6'2"	190	31		
Jim Plunkett	QB	6'3"	215	35		
Marc Wilson	QB	6'6"	220	26		
Marcus Allen	HB	6'2"	205	23		72
Rick Berns	HB	6'2"	215	27		
Cle Montgomery	HB	5'8"	180	27		
Greg Pruitt	HB	5'10"	190	32		18
Chester Willis	HB	5'11"	195	25		
Kenny King	HB-FB	5'11"	205	26		12
Frank Hawkins	FB	5'9"	210	24		48
Derrick Jensen	FB	6'1"	220	27		6
Malcolm Barnwell	WR	5'11"	185	25		6
Cliff Branch	WR	5'11"	170	35		30
Calvin Muhammad	WR	6'	190	24		12
Dokie Williams	WR	5'11"	180	23		18
Todd Christensen	TE	6'3"	230	27		72
Don Hasselbeck (from NE)	TE	6'7"	245	28		12
Chris Bahr	K	5'10"	175	30		114
Ray Guy	K	6'3"	190	33		

SEATTLE SEAHAWKS 9-7-0 Chuck Knox

Scores of Each Game		
13	KANSAS CITY	17
17	N.Y.JETS	10
34	San Diego	31
17	Washington	27
24	CLEVELAND	9
21	SAN DIEGO	28
38	L.A.Raiders	36
21	Pittsburgh	27
34	L.A.RAIDERS	21
27	Denver	19
28	ST.LOUIS	33
27	DENVER	38
51	Kansas City	*48
10	Dallas	35
17	N.Y.GIANTS	12
24	New England	6

Use Name	Pos.	Hgt	Wgt	Age	Int	Pts
Steve August	OT	6'5"	258	28		
Ron Essink	OT	6'6"	260	25		
Matt Hernandez	OT	6'6"	260	21		
Edwin Bailey	OG	6'4"	265	24		
Bill Dugan	OG	6'4"	271	24		
Reggie McKenzie	OG	6'4"	255	33		
Robert Pratt	OG	6'4"	250	32		
Blair Bush	C	6'3"	252	26		
Kani Kauahi	C	6'2"	260	23		
Jeff Bryant	DE	6'5"	270	23		
Sam Clancy	DE	6'6"	244	25		
Jacob Green	DE	6'3"	255	26	1	6
Darrell Irvin	DE	6'4"	270	26		
Joe Nash	NT	6'2"	250	22		
Manu Tulasosopo	NT	6'3"	252	26		

Use Name	Pos.	Hgt	Wgt	Age	Int	Pts
Jerome Boyd	LB	6'2"	225	21		
Keith Butler	LB	6'4"	225	27	1	
Greg Gaines	LB	6'3"	220	24		
Mark Hicks	LB	6'2"	225	22		
Michael Jackson	LB	6'1"	220	26		
Sam Merriman	LB	6'3"	225	22		
Joe Norman	LB	6'1"	220	26		
Shelton Robinson	LB	6'2"	233	22	1	12
Bruce Scholtz	LB	6'6"	240	24	1	
Eugene Wiliams	LB	6'1"	220	23	1	
Gary Wimmer	LB	6'2"	225	22		
Dave Brown	DB	6'1"	192	30	6	
Don Dufek	DB	6'	195	29		
Kenny Easley	DB	6'3"	205	24	7	
John Harris	DB	6'2"	200	27	2	
Greggory Johnson	DB	6'1"	188	24		
Kerry Justin	DB	5'11"	175	28	1	
Paul Moyer	DB	6'1"	201	22	1	6
Keith Simpson	DB	6'1"	195	27	4	

Brian Flones - Knee Injury
Robert Hardy - Broken Leg

Use Name	Pos.	Hgt	Wgt	Age	Int	Pts
Dave King	QB	6'1"	185	24		12
Jim Zorn	QB	6'2"	200	30		6
Zachary Dixon (from BAL)	HB	6'1"	204	26		6
Eric Lane	HB	6'	195	24		
Curt Warner	HB	5'11"	205	22		6
Cullen Bryant	FB	6'1"	236	32		
Dan Doornink	FB	6'3"	210	27		24
David Hughes	FB	6'	220	24		12
Chris Castor	WR	6'	170	23		
Harold Jackson	WR	5'10"	175	37		6
Paul Johns	WR	5'11"	170	24		30
Steve Largent	WR	5'11"	184	28		66
Byron Walker	WR	6'4"	190	23		12
Pete Metzelaars	TE	6'7"	240	23		6
Mike Tice	TE	6'7"	250	24		
Charle Young	TE	6'4"	234	32		12
Norm Johnson	K	6'2"	193	23		103
Jeff West	K	6'3"	205	30		

DENVER BRONCOS 9-7-0 Dan Reeves

Scores of Each Game		
14	PITTSBURGH	10
17	BALTIMORE	10
10	Philadelphia	13
7	L.A. Raiders	22
14	CHICAGO	31
26	HOUSTON	14
24	Cincinnati	17
14	San Diego	6
27	Kansas City	24
19	SEATTLE	27
20	L.A. RAIDERS	22
38	Seattle	27
7	SAN DIEGO	31
27	Cleveland	6
21	Baltimore	19
17	KANSAS CITY	48

Use Name	Pos.	Hgt	Wgt	Age	Int	Pts
Mark Cooper	OT	6'5"	267	23		
Shawn Hollingsworth	OT	6'2"	260	21		
Ken Lanier	OT	6'3"	269	24		
Dave Studdard	OT	6'4"	260	27		
Keith Uecker	OT	6'5"	260	23		
Tom Glassic	OG	6'3"	260	29		
Paul Howard	OG	6'3"	260	32		
Keth Bishop	C-OG	6'3"	260	26		
Bill Bryan	C	6'2"	258	28		
Walt Bowyer	DE	6'4"	245	22		
Barney Chavous	DE	6'3"	258	32		6
Rulon Jones	DE	6'6"	260	25		2
Brison Manor	DE	6'4"	248	31		
Jerry Baker	NT	6'2"	297	23		
Rubin Carter	NT	6'	256	30		
Don Latimer	NT	6'3"	265	28		
Rich Stachowski	NT	6'4"	245	22		

Use Name	Pos.	Hgt	Wgt	Age	Int	Pts
Steve Busick	LB	6'4"	227	24		
Darren Comeaux	LB	6'1"	227	23		
Rick Dennison	LB	6'2"	215	25		
Randy Gradishek	LB	6'3"	231	31	1	
Tom Jackson	LB	5'11"	220	32	1	
Karl Mecklenburg	LB	6'3"	250	23		
Jim Ryan	LB	6'1"	215	26		
Bob Swenson	LB	6'3"	225	30		
Ken Woodard	LB	6'1"	218	23		
Myron Dupree	DB	5'11"	180	21		
Steve Foley	DB	6'2"	190	29	5	
Mike Harden	DB	6'1"	192	25	4	
Roger Jackson	DB	6'	186	24	1	
Wilbur Myers	DB	5'11"	195	22		
Dennis Smith	DB	6'3"	200	24	4	
Steve Trimble	DB	5'10"	181	25		
Steve Wilson	DB	5'10"	195	26	5	
Louis Wright	DB	6'2"	200	30	6	

Use Name	Pos.	Hgt	Wgt	Age	Int	Pts
Steve DeBerg	QB	6'2"	205	29		6
John Elway	QB	6'3"	202	23		6
Gary Kubiak	QB	6'	192	22		6
Rob Lytle	HB	6'1"	195	28		
Dave Preston	HB	5'10"	195	28		12
Sammy Winder	HB	5'11"	203	24		18
Jesse Myles	HB-FB	5'10"	210	22		6
Rick Parros	FB	5'11"	200	25		18
Nathan Poole	FB	5'9"	212	26		24
Gerald Willhite	FB	5'10"	200	24		24
Clint Sampson	WR	5'11"	183	22		18
Zach Thomas	WR	6'	182	22		6
Rick Upchurch	WR	5'10"	180	31		12
Steve Watson	WR	6'4"	195	26		30
Dean Barnett	TE	6'2"	225	24		
Clay Brown	TE	6'3"	225	24		
Ron Egloff	TE	6'5"	227	27		12
Riley Odoms	TE	6'4"	235	33		
John Sawyer (from WAS)	TE	6'2"	230	30		
James Wright	TE	6'3"	240	27		
Rich Karlis	K	6'	180	24		96
Luke Prestridge	K	6'4"	235	26		

KANSAS CITY CHIEFS 6-10-0 John Mackovic

Scores of Each Game		
17	Seattle	13
14	San Diego	17
12	WASHINGTON	27
6	MIAMI	14
38	St.Louis	14
20	L.A.RAIDERS	21
38	N.Y.Giants	17
13	HOUSTON	*10
24	DENVER	27
20	L.A.Raiders	28
20	Cincinnati	15
21	DALLAS	41
48	SEATTLE	*51
9	Buffalo	14
38	SAN DIEGO	41
48	Denver	17

Use Name	Pos.	Hgt	Wgt	Age	Int	Pts
Matt Herkenhoff	OT	6'4"	272	32		
David Lutz	OT	6'6"	280	23		
Rich Baldinger (from NYG)	OT-OG	6'4"	280	23		
Ellis Gardner	OT-OG	6'4"	263	21		
Mark Kirchner (from PIT)	OT-OG	6'3"	261	23		
Jim Rourke	OT-OG	6'5"	263	26		
Brad Budde	OG	6'4"	260	25		
Tom Condon	OG	6'3"	275	30		
Bob Simmons	OG	6'4"	260	29		
Adam Lingner	C-OG	6'4"	240	22		
Bob Rush	C	6'5"	264	28		
Mike Bell	DE	6'4"	260	26		
Dave Lindstrom	DE	6'6"	255	28		
Dean Prater	DE	6'4"	245	24		
Art Still	DE	6'7"	245	27		
Dino Mangiero	NT	6'2"	264	24		
Ken Kremer	NT	6'4"	252	26		
Ray Yakavonis	NT	6'4"	250	26		

Use Name	Pos.	Hgt	Wgt	Age	Int	Pts
Jerry Blanton	LB	6'1"	236	27		
Calvin Daniels	LB	6'3"	236	24		
Louis Haynes	LB	6'	227	23		
Tom Howard	LB	6'2"	215	29		
Charles Jackson	LB	6'2"	222	28		6
Dave Klug	LB	6'4"	230	25		
Steve Potter	LB	6'3"	235	25	1	
Gary Spani	LB	6'2"	228	27		
James Walker	LB	6'1"	250	23		
John Zamberlin	LB	6'2"	226	27		
Gary Barbaro	DB	6'4"	210	29	3	6
Trent Bryant	DB	5'10"	178	26	1	
Lloyd Burruss	DB	6'	202	25	4	
Deron Cherry	DB	5'11"	190	23	7	
Gary Green	DB	5'11"	191	27	6	
Van Jakes	DB	6'	185	22		
Albert Lewis	DB	6'2"	190	22	4	
Durwood Roquemore	DB	6'1"	180	23		
Lucious Smith	DB	5'10"	190	26	3	6

Del Thompson - Injury

Use Name	Pos.	Hgt	Wgt	Age	Int	Pts
Todd Blackledge	QB	6'3"	225	22		
Bob Gagliano	QB	6'3"	195	24		
Bill Kenney	QB	6'4"	211	28		18
Billy Jackson	HB	5'10"	215	23		12
Lawrence Ricks	HB	5'9"	194	22		
Ken Thomas	HB	5'9"	211	23		6
Theotis Brown (from SEA)	FB	6'2"	225	26		60
James Hadnot	FB	6'2"	245	26		
Jewerl Thomas	FB	5'10"	228	25		
Carlos Carson	WR	5'11"	174	24		42
Anthony Hancock	WR	6'	187	23		6
Henry Marshall	WR	6'2"	220	29		36
Stephone Paige	WR	6'2"	180	21		36
J.T.Smith	WR	6'2"	185	27		
Ed Beckman	TE	6'4"	239	28		
Willie Scott	TE	6'4"	245	24		36
Ron Wetzel	TE	6'5"	242	22		
Jim Arnold	K	6'2"	212	22		
Nick Lowery	K	6'4"	189	27		116

SAN DIEGO CHARGERS 6-10-0 Don Coryell

Scores of Each Game		
29	N.Y.Jets	41
17	KANSAS CITY	14
31	SEATTLE	34
24	Cleveland	*30
41	N.Y.GIANTS	34
28	Seattle	21
21	NEW ENGLAND	37
6	DENVER	14
24	Washington	27
3	PITTSBURGH	26
24	Dallas	23
14	ST.LOUIS	44
31	Denver	7
10	L.A.Raiders	42
41	Kansas City	38
14	L.A.RAIDERS	30

Use Name	Pos.	Hgt	Wgt	Age	Int	Pts
Don Brown	OT	6'6"	262	24		
Sam Claphan	OT	6'6"	267	26		
Andrew Gissinger	OT	6'5"	279	24		
Billy Shields	OT	6'7"	284	30		
Bill Elko	OG	6'5"	277	23		
Ed White	OG	6'2"	279	36		
Doug Wilkerson	OG	6'2"	258	36		
Darrel Gofourth	OG-C	6'3"	260	28		
Don Macek	C-OG	6'3"	260	29		
Dennis McKnight	C-OG	6'3"	253	23		
Chuck Ehin	DE	6'4"	254	22		
Keith Ferguson	DE	6'5"	241	24		
Leroy Jones	DE	6'8"	270	32		
Richard Ackerman	NT	6'4"	254	22		
Gary Johnson	NT	6'2"	251	31		
Louie Kelcher	NT	6'5"	310	30		

Use Name	Pos.	Hgt	Wgt	Age	Int	Pts
Carlos Bradley	LB	6'	226	23		
Larry Evans	LB	6'2"	220	30		
Mike Green	LB	6'	226	22	1	
Linden King	LB	6'4"	245	28	1	
Woodrow Lowe	LB	6'	226	29		
Derrie Nelson	LB	6'2"	234	25		6
Ray Preston	LB	6'	220	29	1	
Billy Ray Smith	LB	6'3"	239	22		
Clif Thrift	LB	6'2"	230	27		
Gill Byrd	DB	5'11"	191	22	1	
Tim Fox	DB	5'11"	186	29	2	
Ken Greene	DB	6'3"	203	27		
Bob Gregor	DB	6'2"	203	27		
Reuben Henderson	DB	6'1"	188	24		
Bruce Laird	DB	6'	195	33		
Miles McPherson	DB	5'11"	183	23	1	
Darrell Pattillo	DB	5'10"	194	22		
Danny Walters	DB	6'1"	187	22	7	
Andre Young	DB	6'	203	22	2	6

Chuck Loewen - Back Injury

Use Name	Pos.	Hgt	Wgt	Age	Int	Pts
Dan Fouts	QB	6'3"	205	32		6
Ed Luther	QB	6'3"	210	26		
Bruce Mathison	QB	6'3"	210	24		
James Brooks	HB	5'9"	177	24		18
Earnest Jackson	HB	5'9"	208	23		
John Cappeletti	FB	6'1"	215	31		
Jim Jodat	FB	5'11"	213	29		
Chuck Muncie	FB	6'3"	228	30		78
Sherman Smith	FB	6'4"	225	28		
Roger Carr	WR	6'3"	195	31		
Wes Chandler	WR	6'	183	27		30
Bobby Duckworth	WR	6'3"	197	24		30
Hosea Fortune	WR	6'	176	24		
Charlie Joiner	WR	5'11"	180	35		18
Dwight Scales	WR	6'2"	182	30		
Pete Holohan	TE	6'4"	240	24		12
Eric Sievers	TE	6'4"	233	24		18
Kellen Winslow	TE	6'5"	251	25		48
Rolf Benirschke	K	6'	179	26		88
Maury Buford	K	6'	185	23		

* Overtime

LOS ANGELES RAIDERS

RUSHING

Last Name	No.	Yds	Avg	TD
Allen	266	1014	3.8	9
Hawkins	110	526	4.8	6
King	82	294	3.6	1
Pruitt	26	154	5.9	2
Wilson	13	122	9.4	0
Plunkett	26	78	3.0	0
Berns	6	22	3.7	0
Branch	1	20	20.0	0
Barnwell	1	12	12.0	0
Montgomery	2	7	3.5	0
Jensen	1	5	5.0	0
Willis	5	0	0.0	0
Humm	1	-1	-1.0	0
Guy	2	-13	-6.5	0

RECEIVING

Last Name	No.	Yds	Avg	TD
Christensen	92	1247	13.6	12
Allen	68	590	8.7	2
Branch	39	696	17.8	5
Barnwell	35	513	14.7	1
Hawkins	20	150	7.5	2
Williams	14	259	18.5	3
King	14	149	10.6	1
Muhammad	13	252	19.4	2
Montgomery	2	29	14.5	0
Hasselbeck	3	24	8.0	2
Pruitt	1	6	6.0	0
Jensen	1	2	2.0	1

PUNT RETURNS

Last Name	No.	Yds	Avg	TD
Pruitt	58	666	11.5	1

KICKOFF RETURNS

Last Name	No.	Yds	Avg	TD
Montgomery	21	464	22.1	0
Pruitt	31	604	19.5	0
Williams	5	88	17.6	0
Millen	2	19	9.5	0
Jensen	1	0	0.0	0
Martin	1	0	0.0	0

PASSING — PUNTING — KICKING

PASSING	Att	Cmp	%	Yds	Yd/Att	TD	Int—	%	RK
Plunkett	379	230	60	2935	7.74	20	18—	4	5
Wilson	117	67	57	864	7.38	8	6—	5	
Allen	7	4	57	111	15.86	3	0—	0	
Pruitt	1	0	0	0	0.00	0	0—	0	

PUNTING	No.	Avg.
Guy	78	42.8

KICKING	XP	ATT	%	FG	ATT	%
Bahr	51	53	96	21	27	77

SEATTLE SEAHAWKS

RUSHING

Last Name	No.	Yds	Avg	TD
Warner	335	1449	4.3	13
Hughes	83	313	3.8	1
Doornink	40	99	2.5	2
C. Bryant	27	87	3.2	0
Zorn	30	71	2.4	1
Krieg	16	55	3.4	2
Dixon	4	18	4.5	0
T. Brown	6	14	2.3	0
Johns	2	12	6.0	0
Lane	3	1	0.3	0

RECEIVING

Last Name	No.	Yds	Avg	TD
Largent	72	1074	14.9	11
Warner	42	325	7.7	1
Young	36	529	14.7	2
Johns	34	486	14.3	4
Doornink	24	328	13.7	2
Walker	12	248	20.7	2
Hughes	10	100	10.0	1
H. Jackson	8	126	15.8	1
Metzelaars	7	72	10.3	1
C. Bryant	3	8	2.7	0
Lane	2	9	4.5	0
Krieg	1	11	11.0	0

PUNT RETURNS

Last Name	No.	Yds	Avg	TD
Johns	28	316	11.3	1
G. Johnson	3	17	5.7	0
Harris	2	27	13.5	0
Easley	1	6	6.0	0

KICKOFF RETURNS

Last Name	No.	Yds	Avg	TD
Dixon	51	1171	23.0	1
Hughes	12	282	23.5	0
Lane	4	58	14.5	0
McAlister	3	59	19.7	0
Tice	2	28	14.0	0
Metzelaars	1	0	0.0	0

PASSING — PUNTING — KICKING

PASSING	Att	Cmp	%	Yds	Yd/Att	TD	Int—	%	RK
Krieg	243	147	61	2139	8.80	18	11—	5	2
Zorn	205	103	50	1166	5.69	7	7—	3	12
Largent	1	1	100	11	11.00	0	0—	0	

PUNTING	No.	Avg.
West	79	39.5

KICKING	XP	ATT	%	FG	ATT	%
N. Johnson	49	50	98	18	25	72

DENVER BRONCOS

RUSHING

Last Name	No.	Yds	Avg	TD
Winder	196	757	3.9	3
Poole	81	246	3.0	4
Preston	57	222	3.9	1
Willhite	43	188	4.4	3
Elway	28	146	5.2	1
Parros	30	96	3.2	1
Myles	8	52	6.5	0
DeBerg	13	28	2.2	1
Upchurch	6	19	3.2	0
Kubiak	4	17	4.3	1
Watson	3	17	5.7	0
Prestridge	1	7	7.0	0
J. Wright	1	-11	-11.0	0

RECEIVING

Last Name	No.	Yds	Avg	TD
Watson	59	1133	19.2	5
Upchurch	40	639	16.0	2
Winder	23	150	6.5	0
Egloff	20	205	10.3	2
Poole	20	184	9.2	0
Preston	17	137	8.1	1
Willhite	14	153	10.9	1
J. Wright	13	134	10.3	0
Thomas	12	182	15.2	0
Parros	12	126	10.5	2
Sampson	10	200	20.0	3
Myles	7	119	17.0	1
Odoms	4	62	15.5	0
Sawyer	3	42	14.0	0

PUNT RETURNS

Last Name	No.	Yds	Avg	TD
Thomas	33	368	11.2	1
Upchurch	4	52	13.0	0
L. Wright	1	0	0.0	0

KICKOFF RETURNS

Last Name	No.	Yds	Avg	TD
Thomas	28	573	20.5	0
Wilson	24	485	20.2	0
Studdard	2	8	4.0	0
Harden	1	9	9.0	0
T. Jackson	1	2	2.0	0

PASSING — PUNTING — KICKING

PASSING	Att	Cmp	%	Yds	Yd/Att	TD	Int-	%	RK
DeBerg	215	119	55	1617	7.52	9	7—	3	8
Elway	259	123	47	1663	6.42	7	14—	5	17
Kubiak	22	12	55	186	8.45	1	1—	5	
Upchurch	2	0	0	0	0	0	0—	0	
Willhite	1	0	0	0	0	0	0—	0	

PUNTING	No.	Avg.
Prestridge	87	41.6

KICKING	XP	ATT	%	FG	ATT	%
Karlis	33	34	97.1	21	25	84

KANSAS CITY CHIEFS

RUSHING

Last Name	No.	Yds	Avg	TD
B. Jackson	152	499	3.3	2
Brown	124	467	3.8	8
J. Thomas	44	115	2.6	0
Kenney	23	59	2.6	3
K. Thomas	15	55	3.7	0
Ricks	21	28	1.3	0
Carson	2	20	10.0	0
Hadnot	4	10	2.5	0
Scott	1	1	1.0	0
Blackledge	1	0	0.0	0

RECEIVING

Last Name	No.	Yds	Avg	TD
Carson	80	1351	16.9	7
Marshall	50	788	15.8	6
Brown	47	418	8.9	2
Hancock	37	584	15.8	1
B. Jackson	32	243	7.6	0
Paige	30	528	17.6	6
Scott	29	247	8.5	6
K. Thomas	28	236	8.4	1
Beckman	13	130	10.0	0
J. Thomas	10	51	5.1	0
J. Smith	7	85	12.1	0
Ricks	3	5	1.7	0
Hadnot	2	18	9.0	0
Kenney	1	0	0.0	0

PUNT RETURNS

Last Name	No.	Yds	Avg	TD
J. Smith	26	210	8.1	0
Hancock	14	81	5.8	0

KICKOFF RETURNS

Last Name	No.	Yds	Avg	TD
Hancock	29	515	17.8	0
Brown	15	301	20.1	0
Roquemore	3	36	12.0	0
Cherry	2	54	27.0	0
Carson	1	12	12.0	0
Daniels	1	0	0.0	0
Lindstrom	1	0	0.0	0
J. Smith	1	5	5.0	0
K. Thomas	1	6	6.0	0
Burruss	0	0	0.0	0

PASSING — PUNTING — KICKING

PASSING	Att	Cmp	%	Yds	Yd/Att	TD	Int—	%	RK
Kenney	603	346	57	4348	7.21	24	18—	3	7
Blackledge	34	20	59	259	7.62	3	0—	0	
J. Thomas	2	1	50	18	9.00	1	1—	50	
Brown	1	1	100	11	11.00	0	0—	0	
Carson	1	1	100	48	48.00	1	0—	0	
Marshall	0	0	0	0	0	0	0—	0	

PUNTING	No.	Avg.
Arnold	93	39.9

KICKING	XP	Att	%	FG	Att	%
Lowery	44	45	98	24	30	80

SAN DIEGO CHARGERS

RUSHING

Last Name	No.	Yds	Avg	TD
Muncie	235	886	3.8	12
Brooks	127	516	4.1	3
S. Smith	24	91	3.8	0
Jackson	11	39	3.5	0
Chandler	2	25	12.5	0
Cappelletti	1	5	5.0	0
Mathison	1	0	0.0	0
Fouts	12	-5	-0.4	1
Sievers	1	-7	-7.0	0
Luther	9	-14	-1.6	0

RECEIVING

Last Name	No.	Yds	Avg	TD
Winslow	88	1172	13.3	8
Joiner	65	960	14.8	3
Chandler	58	845	14.6	5
Muncie	42	396	9.4	1
Sievers	33	452	13.7	3
Brooks	25	215	8.6	0
Holohan	23	272	11.8	2
Duckworth	20	422	21.1	5
S. Smith	6	51	8.5	0
Jackson	5	42	8.4	0
Carr	2	36	18.0	0
Scales	2	28	14.0	0

PUNT RETURNS

Last Name	No.	Yds	Avg	TD
Brooks	18	137	7.6	0
Chandler	8	26	3.3	0
Fortune	4	16	4.0	0
Scales	2	34	17.0	0
Laird	1	0	0.0	0

KICKOFF RETURNS

Last Name	No.	Yds	Avg	TD
Brooks	32	607	19.0	0
Laird	15	342	22.8	0
Jackson	11	201	18.3	0
McPherson	5	77	15.4	0
Jodat	3	45	15.0	0
Young	3	41	13.7	0
S. Smith	2	32	16.0	0
B. Smith	1	10	10.0	0
Scales	1	16	16.0	0
Sievers	1	6	6.0	0

PASSING — PUNTING — KICKING

PASSING	Att	Cmp	%	Yds	Yd/Att	TD	Int—	%	RK
Fouts	340	215	63	2975	8.75	20	15—	4	3
Luther	287	151	53	1875	6.53	7	17—	6	16
Mathison	5	3	60	41	8.20	0	1—	20	
Buford	1	0	0	0	0.00	0	0—	0	
Holohan	1	0	0	0	0.00	0	0—	0	
S. Smith	1	0	0	0	0.00	0	0—	0	
Chandler	0	0	0	0	0.00	0	0—	0	

PUNTING	No.	Avg.
Buford	63	43.9

KICKING	XP	Att.	%	FG	Att	%
Benirschke	43	45	96	15	24	63

1983 N.F.C.—PLAYOFFS

December 26, 1983 at Irving, Tx. (Attendance 43,521)

SCORING

L.A. RAMS	7	0	7	10-	24
DALLAS	0	7	3	7-	17

First Quarter
- L.A. — Da., Hill 18 yard pass from Ferragamo; PAT-Lansford (kick)

Second Quarter
- Dal. — T. Hill, 14 yard pass from White; PAT—Septien (kick)

Third Quarter
- Dal. — Septien, 41 yard field goal
- L.A. — Dennard, 16 yard pass from Ferragamo; PAT-Lansford (kick)

Fourth Quarter
- L.A. — Farmer, 8 yard pass from Ferragamo; PAT-Lansford (kick)
- L.A. — Lansford, 20 yard field goal
- Dal. — Cosbie, 2 yard pass from White; PAT-Septien (kick)

TEAM STATISTICS

L.A.		DALL.
19	First Downs- Total	24
5	First Downs-Rushing	4
11	First Downs-Passing	20
3	First Downs- Penalty	0
0	Fumbles- Number	2
0	Fumbles- Lost Ball	1
4	Penalties- Number	6
18	Yards Penalized	40
0	Missed Field Goals	0
63	Offensive Plays	76
243	Net Yards	363
3.5	Average Gain	4.8
0	Giveaways	4
4	Takeaways	0
+4	Difference	-4

INDIVIDUAL STATISTICS

RUSHING

L.A. RAMS	No.	Yds.	Avg.	DALLAS	No.	Yds.	Avg.
Dickerson	23	99	4.3	Dorsett	17	59	3.5
Redden	3	5	1.6	Springs	2	4	2.0
Ferragamo	4	-10	-2.5	White	1	0	0.0
	30	94	3.1		20	63	3.2

RECEIVING

L.A. RAMS	No.	Yds.	Avg.	DALLAS	No.	Yds.	Avg.
Farmer	5	47	9.4	T. Hill	9	115	12.8
Dennard	4	44	11.0	Springs	6	38	6.3
Barber	2	20	10.0	Cosbie	5	62	12.4
Dickerson	2	11	5.5	Dorsett	4	12	3.0
Da. Hill	2	19	9 5	Johnson	3	20	6.7
Ellard	1	22	22.0	Pearson	2	49	24.5
	16	163	10.2	Newsome	2	25	12.5
				DuPree	1	9	9.0
					33	330	10.0

PUNTING

L.A. RAMS	No.		Avg.	DALLAS	No.		Avg.
Misko	6		37.3	D. White	5		31.4

PUNT RETURNS

L.A. RAMS	No.	Yds.	Avg.	DALLAS	No.	Yds.	Avg.
Ellard	1	7	7.0	Allen	4	16	4.0
Johnson	1	3	3.0				
	2	10	5.0				

KICKOFF RETURNS

L.A. RAMS	No.	Yds.	Avg.	DALLAS	No.	Yds.	Avg.
Guman	2	37	18.5	Fellows	4	68	17.0
Ellard	2	37	18.5	Springs	1	12	12.0
	3	46	15.3		5	80	16.0

INTERCEPTION RETURNS

L.A. RAMS	No.	Yds.	Avg.	DALLAS	No.	Yds.	Avg.
Irvin	1	94	94.0	none			
J. Collins	1	12	12.0				
Owens	1	5	5.0				
	3	111	37.0				

PASSING

L.A. RAMS	Att.	Comp.	Comp. Pct.	Yds.	Int.	Yds./ Att.	Yds./ Comp.
Ferragamo	30	15	50.0	162	0	5.4	10.8
Dickerson	1	1	100.0	1	0	1.0	1.0
	31	16	51.6	163	0	5.3	10.2
DALLAS							
White	53	32	60.3	330	3	6.2	10.3

December 31, 1983 at San Francisco (Attendance 59,979)

SCORING

DETROIT	3	6	0	14-	23
SAN FRAN.	7	7	3	7-	24

First Quarter
- Det. — Murray, 37 yard field goal
- S.F. — Craig, 1 yard rush; PAT-Wersching (kick)

Second Quarter
- S.F. — Tyler, 2 yard rush; PAT-Wersching (kick)
- Det. — Murray, 21 yard field goal
- Det. — Murray, 54 yard field goal

Third Quarter
- S.F. — Wersching, 19 yard field goal

Fourth Quarter
- Det. — Sims, 11 yard rush; PAT-Murray (kick)
- Det. — Sims, 3 yard rush; PAT-Murray (kick)
- S.F. — Solomon, 14 yard pass from Montana; PAT-Wersching (kick)

TEAM STATISTICS

DET.		S.F.
22	First Downs- Total	20
9	First Downs-Rushing	9
11	First Downs-Passing	10
2	First Downs- Penalty	1
0	Fumbles- Number	2
3	Fumbles- Lost Ball	1
7	Penalties- Number	5
63	Yards Penalized	25
2	Missed Field Goals	2
75	Offensive Plays	60
412	Net Yards	291
5.5	Average Gain	4.9
5	Giveaways	2
2	Takeaways	5
-3	Difference	+3

INDIVIDUAL STATISTICS

RUSHING

DETROIT	No.	Yds.	Avg.	SAN FRANCISCO	No.	Yds.	Avg.
Sims	20	114	5.7	Tyler	17	74	4.4
Jones	10	33	3.3	Montana	3	16	5.3
Thompson	1	24	24.0	Craig	7	13	1.9
Danielson	4	17	4.3		27	103	3.8
	35	188	5.4				

RECEIVING

DETROIT	No.	Yds.	Avg.	SAN FRANCISCO	No.	Yds.	Avg.
Thompson	6	74	12.3	Craig	7	61	8.7
Chadwick	5	58	11.6	Francis	4	75	18.8
Jones	5	44	8.8	Solomon	2	16	8.0
Sims	4	26	6.5	Tyler	2	15	7.5
Scott	3	29	9.7	Wilson	1	26	26.0
Norris	1	5	5.0	Ramson	1	4	4.0
	24	217	9.0	Moore	1	4	4.0
					18	201	11.2

PUNTING

DETROIT	No.		Avg.	SAN FRANCISCO	No.		Avg.
Black	2		36.5	Orosz	5		35.8

PUNT RETURNS

DETROIT	No.	Yds.	Avg.	SAN FRANCISCO	No.	Yds.	Avg.
Martin	4	30	7.5	none			

KICKOFF RETURNS

DETROIT	No.	Yds.	Avg.	SAN FRANCISCO	No.	Yds.	Avg.
Hall	2	45	22.5	Moore	3	48	16.0
Jenkins	2	43	21.5	McLemore	2	44	22.0
	4	88	22.0		5	92	18.4

INTERCEPTION RETURNS

DETROIT	No.	Yds.	Avg.	SAN FRANCISCO	No.	Yds.	Avg.
Watkins	1	24	24.0	Ellison	2	8	4.0
				Hicks	1	22	22.0
				Turner	1	11	11.0
				Lott	1	0	0.0
					5	41	8.2

PASSING

DETROIT	Att.	Comp.	Comp. Pct.	Yds.	Int.	Yds./ Att.	Yds./ Comp.
Danielson	38	24	63.2	236	5	6.2	9.8
SAN FRANCISCO							
Montana	31	18	58.1	201	1	6.5	11.2

January 1, 1984 at Washington, D.C. (Attendance 55,363)

SCORING

L.A. RAMS	0	7	0	0-	7
WASHINGTON	17	21	6	7-	51

First Quarter
- Wash. — Riggins, 3 yard rush return; PAT-Moseley (kick)
- Wash. — Monk, 40 yard pass from Theismann; PAT-Moseley (kick)
- Wash. — Moseley, 42 yard field goal

Second Quarter
- Wash. — Riggins, 1 yard rush; PAT-Moseley (kick)
- L.A. — Dennard, 32 yard pass from Ferragamo; PAT-Lansford (kick)
- Wash. — Monk, 21 yard pass from Theismann; PAT-Moseley (kick)
- Wash. — Riggins [illegible] rush; PAT-Moseley (kick)

Third Quarter
- Wash. — Moseley, 36 yard field goal
- Wash. — Moseley, 41 yard field goal

Fourth Quarter
- Wash. — Green, 72 yard interception return; PAT-Moseley (kick)

TEAM STATISTICS

L.A. RAMS		WASH.
12	First Downs- Total	23
2	First Downs-Rushing	10
9	First Downs-Passing	12
1	First Downs-Penalty	1
2	Fumbles-Number	2
1	Fumbles-Lost Ball	1
7	Penalties- Number	6
41	Yards Penalized	55
0	Missed Field Goals	0
62	Offensive Plays	65
204	Net Yards	445
3.3	Average Gain	6.8
4	Giveaways	1
1	Takeaways	4
-3	Difference	+3

INDIVIDUAL STATISTICS

RUSHING

L.A. RAMS	No.	Yds.	Avg.	WASHINGTON	No.	Yds.	Avg.
Jones	4	28	7.0	Riggins	25	119	4.7
Dickerson	10	16	1.6	Giaquinto	4	9	2.3
Redden	2	7	3.5	Evans	3	4	1.3
	16	51	3.2	Wonsley	2	3	1.5
				Washington	5	-2	-0.4
				Holly	1	-3	-3.0
					40	130	3.3

RECEIVING

L.A. RAMS	No.	Yds.	Avg.	WASHINGTON	No.	Yds.	Avg.
Dickerson	6	9	1.5	Brown	6	171	28.5
Guman	5	29	5.8	Monk	4	60	15.0
Barber	3	42	14.0	Warren	3	23	7.7
Ellard	3	39	13.0	Giaquinto	2	17	8.5
Dennard	2	50	25.0	Garrett	2	13	6.5
Johnson	1	17	17.0	Walker	1	14	14.0
Da. Hill	1	6	6.0	Washington	1	10	10.0
	20	175	8.8	Didier	1	7	7.0
					20	315	15.8

PUNTING

L.A. RAMS	No.		Avg.	WASHINGTON	No.		Avg.
Misko	7		33.8	Hayes	3		28.0

PUNT RETURNS

L.A. RAMS	No.	Yds.	Avg.	WASHINGTON	No.	Yds.	Avg.
Ellard	1	4	4.0	Giaquinto	3	56	18.7

KICKOFF RETURNS

L.A. RAMS	No.	Yds.	Avg.	WASHINGTON	No.	Yds.	Avg.
Ellard	7	120	17.1	Garrett	2	47	23.5
Redden	2	22	11.0				
E. Williams	1	9	9.0				
	10	151	15.1				

INTERCEPTION RETURNS

L.A. RAMS	No.	Yds.	Avg.	WASHINGTON	No.	Yds.	Avg.
none				Washington	1	0	0.0
				Coffey	1	0	0.0
				Green	1	72	72.0
					3	72	24.0

PASSING

L.A. RAMS	Att.	Comp.	Comp. Pct.	Yds.	Int.	Yds./ Att.	Yds./ Comp.
Ferragamo	43	20	46.5	175	3	4.1	8.8
WASHINGTON							
Holly	2	2	100.0	13	0	6.5	6.5
Theismann	23	18	72.0	302	0	13.1	16.8
	25	20	80.0	315	0	12.6	15.8

1983 A.F.C.—PLAYOFFS

December 24, 1983 at Seattle (Attendance 60,752)

SCORING

DENVER	7	0	0	0-	7
SEATTLE	7	3	7	14-	31

First Quarter
- Sea. — Largent 17 pass from Krieg; PAT-N. Johnson (kick)
- Den. — Myles 13 pass from DeBerg; PAT-Karlis (kick)

Second Quarter
- Sea. — N. Johnson, 37 yard field goal

Third Quarter
- Sea. — Metzelaars 5 pass from Krieg; PAT-N.Johnson (kick)

Fourth Quarter
- Sea. — Johns 18 pass from Krieg; PAT-N.Johnson (kick)
- Sea. — Hughes 2 yard rush; PAT-N. Johnson (kick)

TEAM STATISTICS

DEN.		SEA.
21	First Downs- Total	17
5	First Downs-Rushing	8
14	First Downs-Passing	9
2	First Downs- Penalty	0
1	Fumbles-Number	1
1	Fumbles-Lost Ball	0
5	Penalties-Number	3
35	Yards Penalized	34
0	Missed Field Goals	0
69	Offensive Plays	53
360	Net Yards	324
5.2	Average Gain	6.1
3	Giveaways	0
0	Takeaways	3
-3	Difference	+3

INDIVIDUAL STATISTICS

DENVER	No.	Yds.	Avg.	SEATTLE	No.	Yds.	Avg.
RUSHING							
Winder	16	59	3.9	Warner	23	99	4.3
Poole	7	25	3.6	Hughes	3	16	5.3
Elway	3	16	5.3	C. Bryant	5	15	3.0
Willhite	5	16	3.2	Krieg	3	9	3.0
Sampson	1	8	8.0	Dixon	3	4	1.3
Watson	1	1	1.0	Zorn	1	2	2.0
	33	125	3.8		38	145	3.8
RECEIVING							
Myles	7	73	10.4	Largent	4	76	19.0
Watson	4	51	12.8	Warner	3	22	7.3
Poole	4	17	4.3	Johns	2	59	29.5
Sampson	3	52	17.3	Young	2	38	19.0
Winder	2	13	6.5	Metzelaars	1	5	5.0
Thomas	1	19	19.0		12	200	16.7
Egloff	1	16	16.0				
Wilson	1	12	12.0				
Willhite	1	1	1.0				
	24	254	10.6				
PUNTING							
Prestridge	4		47.8	West	3		41.7
PUNT RETURNS							
Thomas	3	10	3.3	Johns	4	58	14.5
KICKOFF RETURNS							
Thomas	4	81	20.3	Dixon	2	43	21.5
Wilson	2	37	18.5				
	6	118	19.7				
INTERCEPTION RETURNS							
none				Justin	1	45	45.0
				G. Johnson	1	0	0.0
					2	45	22.5

PASSING

DENVER	Att.	Comp.	Comp. Pct.	Yds.	Int.	Yds./ Att.	Yds./ Comp.
DeBerg	19	14	73.7	131	1	6.9	9.4
Elway	15	10	66.7	123	1	8.2	12.3
	34	24	70.6	254	2	7.5	10.6
SEATTLE							
Krieg	13	12	92.3	200	0	15.4	16.7

December 31, 1983 at Miami (Attendance 71,032)

SCORING

SEATTLE	0	7	7	13-	27
MIAMI	0	13	0	7-	20

Second Quarter
- MIA. — D. Johnson 19 pass from Marino; PAT-kick blocked
- SEA. — C. Bryant 6 pass from Krieg; PAT-N. Johnson (kick)
- MIA. — Duper 32 pass from Marino; PAT-von Schamann (kick)

Third Quarter
- SEA. — Warner 1 yard rush; PAT—N. Johnson (kick)

Fourth Quarter
- SEA. — N. Johnson 27 yard field goal
- MIA. — Bennett, 2 yard rush; PAT—von Schamann (kick)
- SEA. — Warner 2 yard rush; PAT-N.Johnson (kick)
- SEA. — N. Johnson 37 yard field goal

TEAM STATISTICS

SEA.		MIA.
21	First Downs- Total	21
12	First Downs-Rushing	9
9	First Downs- Passing	11
0	First Downs- Penalty	1
0	Fumbles- Number	3
0	Fumbles- Lost Ball	3
2	Penalties- Number	5
15	Yards Penalized	30
1	Missed Field Goals	0
72	Offensive Plays	56
334	Net Yards	321
4.6	Average Gain	5.7
1	Giveaways	5
5	Takeaways	1
-4	Difference	-4

INDIVIDUAL STATISTICS

SEATTLE	No.	Yds.	Avg.	MIAMI	No.	Yds.	Avg.
RUSHING							
Warner	29	113	3.9	Overstreet	9	50	8.0
C. Bryant	5	22	4.4	Bennett	7	31	4.4
Hughes	4	21	5.3	Franklin	6	28	4.7
Krieg	4	-5	-1.3	Nathan	8	19	2.4
	42	151	3.6		30	128	4.3
RECEIVING							
Warner	4	25	6.3	Duper	9	117	13.0
Johns	4	60	15.0	Johnson	2	29	14.5
Largent	2	56	28.0	N. Moore	2	26	13.0
Doornink	2	26	13.0	Nathan	1	6	6.0
C. Bryant	2	12	6.0	Rose	1	15	15.0
	16	192	12.0		15	193	12.9
PUNTING							
West	4		38.0	Roby	4		35.5
PUNT RETURNS							
none				Clayton	2	32	16.0
KICKOFF RETURNS							
Dixon	2	86	43.0	Walker	6	104	17.3
Hughes	2	44	22.0				
	4	130	32.5				
INTERCEPTION RETURNS							
Harris	1	0	0.0	Small	1	18	18.0
Justin	1	0	0.0				
	2	0	0.0				

PASSING

SEATTLE	Att.	Comp.	Comp. Pct.	Yds.	Int.	Yds./ Att.	Yds./ Comp.
Krieg	28	15	53.6	192	1	6.9	12.8
Zorn	1	0	0.0	0	0	0.0	0.0
	29	15	51.7	192	1	6.6	12.8
MIAMI							
Marino	25	15	60.0	193	2	7.7	12.9
Clayton	1	0	0.0	0	0	0.0	0.0
	26	15	57.7	193	2	7.4	12.9

January 1, 1984 at Los Angeles (Attendance 90,334)

SCORING

PITTSBURGH	3	0	7	0-	10
L.A. RAIDERS	7	10	21	0-	38

First Quarter
- Pitt. — Anderson 17 yard field goal
- L.A. — Hayes 18 yard interception return; PAT-Bahr (kick)

Second Quarter
- L.A. — Allen 4 yard rush; PAT—Bahr (kick)
- L.A. — Bahr 45 yard field goal

Third Quarter
- L.A. — King 9 yard rush; PAT-Bahr (kick)
- L.A. — Allen 49 yard rush; PAT-Bahr (kick)
- Pitt. — Stallworth 58 pass from Stoudt; PAT-Anderson (kick)
- L.A. — Hawkins 2 yard rush; PAT—Bahr (kick)

TEAM STATISTICS

PITT.		L.A.
17	First Downs- Total	24
9	First Downs-Ruching	13
8	First Downs-Passing	9
0	First Downs-Penalty	2
2	Fumbles- Number	2
1	Fumbles-Lost Ball	0
4	Penalties-Number	2
30	Yards Penalized	15
0	Missed Field Goals	0
64	Offensive Plays	68
331	Net Yards	413
5.2	Average Gain	6.1
2	Giveaways	0
0	Takeaways	2
-2	Difference	+2

INDIVIDUAL STATISTICS

PITTSBURGH	No.	Yds.	Avg.	LOS ANGELES	No.	Yds.	Avg.
RUSHING							
Stoudt	9	50	5.6	Allen	13	121	9.3
Pollard	9	37	4.1	Plunkett	2	23	11.5
Abercrombie	6	36	6.0	Hawkins	10	25	2.5
F. Harris	6	33	5.5	King	0	0	0.0
Odom	1	4	4.0	Guy	1	2	2.0
T. Harris	1	2	2.0	Wilson	1	-3	-3.0
	32	162	5.1		33	191	5.8
RECEIVING							
F. Harris	4	31	7.8	Christensen	7	88	12.6
Capers	2	54	37.0	Branch	6	76	12.7
Cunningham	2	32	16.0	Allen	5	38	7.6
Sweeney	2	24	12.0	Barnwell	3	30	10.0
Stallworth	1	58	58.0		21	232	11.0
Odom	1	6	6.0				
Abercrombie	1	4	4.0				
	13	209	16.1				
PUNTING							
Colquitt	8		40.9	Guy	6		41.3
PUNT RETURNS							
Woods	3	21	7.0	Pruitt	5	47	9.4
				Montgomery	1	5	5.0
					6	52	8.7
KICKOFF RETURNS							
Odom	4	84	21.0	Montgomery	3	87	29.0
T. Harris	1	19	19.0				
	5	103	20.6				
INTERCEPTION RETURNS							
none				Hayes	1	18	18.0

PASSING

PITTSBURGH	Att.	Comp.	Comp. Pct.	Yds.	Int.	Yds./ Att.	Yds./ Comp.
Stoudt	20	10	50.0	187	1	9.4	18.7
Malone	7	3	43.0	22	0	3.1	7.3
	27	13	48.1	209	1	7.7	16.1
LOS ANGELES							
Plunkett	34	21	62.0	232	0	6.8	11.0

1983 Championship Games

NFC CHAMPIONSHIP GAME

January 8, 1984 at Washington
(Attendance 55,363)

SCORING

SAN FRANCISCO	0	0	0	21-	21
WASHINGTON	0	7	14	3-	24

Second Quarter
- Wash. — Riggins, 4 yard rush; PAT—Moseley (kick)

Third Quarter
- Wash. — Riggins, 1 yard rush; PAT—Moseley (kick)
- Wash. — Brown, 70 yard pass from Theismann; PAT—Moseley (kick)

Fourth Quarter
- S.F. — Wilson, 5 yard pass from Montana; PAT—Wersching (kick)
- S.F. — Solomon, 76 yard pass from Montana; PAT—Wersching (kick)
- S.F. — Wilson, 12 yard pass from Montana; PAT—Wersching (kick)
- Wash. — Moseley, 25 yard field goal

TEAM STATISTICS

S.F.		WASH.
19	First Downs-Total	24
3	First Downs-Rushing	11
16	First Downs-Passing	10
0	First Downs-Penalty	3
4	Fumbles-Number	2
2	Fumbles-Lost Ball	1
6	Penalties-Number	4
72	Yards Penalized	35
2	Missed Field Goals	4
64	Offensive Plays	75
425	Net Yards	410
6.6	Average Gain	5.5
3	Giveaways	2
2	Takeaways	3
-1	Difference	+1

The last two Super Bowl winners faced each other before a full house at RFK Stadium in Washington.

Both the Redskins and 49ers started slowly, killing their own scoring drives with fumbles. In the second quarter, Joe Theismann hit Clint Didier with a 46-yard pass that moved the ball within the shadows of the goalposts. John Riggins soon blasted into the endzone, and Mark Moseley's kick made the score 7-0. The Redskin defense kept Joe Montana off stride, and Washington took its 7-0 lead into the halftime break.

The Skins kept banging away in the third quarter and apparently broke the game open. Darrell Green's clothesline tackle of Freddie Solomon caused a fumble that set up Riggins' second touchdown. Two minutes later, Theismann hit Charlie Brown with a bomb for a 70-yard score.

Ahead 21-0 after three quarters, the Redskins got the scare of their lives. San Francisco got its first touchdown early in the final period, then quickly cut the lead to 21-14 on a 76-yard scoring pass from Montana to Solomon. With seven minutes left, the Niners tied the score on a TD catch by Mike Wilson.

Staggering on the ropes, the Redskins regrouped, held the 49ers the rest of the period and drove into San Francisco territory late in the game with the benefit of controversial penalty calls against Eric Wright and Ronnie Lott. Unsuccessful in four previous tries, Moseley booted a field goal with 40 seconds left for the victory.

INDIVIDUAL STATISTICS

SAN FRANCISCO	No.	Yds.	Avg.	WASHINGTON	No.	Yds.	Avg.
RUSHING							
Tyler	8	44	5.5	Riggins	36	123	3.4
Montana	5	40	8.0	Washington	6	23	3.8
Craig	3	3	1.0	Hayes	1	14	14.0
	16	87	5.4	Theismann	2	12	6.0
					45	172	3.8
RECEIVING							
Wilson	8	57	7.1	Brown	5	137	27.4
Solomon	4	106	26.5	Didier	3	61	20.3
Francis	4	48	12.0	Monk	3	35	11.7
Ramson	3	47	15.7	Washington	3	21	7.0
Nehemiah	3	46	15.3	Walker	1	11	11.0
Craig	3	15	5.0		1	7	7.0
Tyler	1	17	17.0		15	265	17.7
Cooper	1	11	11.0				
	27	347	12.9				
PUNTING							
Orosz	7		33.6	Hayes	5		40.2
PUNT RETURNS							
McLemore	2	7	3.5	Giaquinto	4	31	7.8
KICKOFF RETURNS							
McLemore	5	98	19.6	Evans	1	8	8.0
				Garrett	2	31	15.5
				Coleman	1	9	9.0
					4	48	12.0
INTERCEPTION RETURNS							
Wright	1	0	0.0	Dean	1	5	5.0

PASSING

SAN FRANCISCO	Att.	Comp.	Comp Pct.	Yds.	Int.	Yds./ Att.	Yds./ Comp.
Montana	48	27	56.3	347	1	7.2	12.9
WASHINGTON							
Theismann	26	14	53.8	229	1	8.8	16.4
Riggins	1	1	100.0	36	0	36.0	36.0
	27	15	55.6	265	1	9.8	17.7

AFC CHAMPIONSHIP GAME

January 8, 1984 at Los Angeles
(Attendance 88,734)

SCORING

SEATTLE	0	0	7	7	- 14
L.A. RAIDERS	3	17	7	3	- 30

First Quarter
- Raid. — Bahr, 20 yard field goal

Second Quarter
- Raid. — Hawkins, 1 yard rush; PAT—Bahr (kick)
- Raid. — Hawkins, 5 yard rush; PAT—Bahr (kick)
- Raid. — Bahr, 45 yard field goal

Third Quarter
- Raid. — Allen, 3 yard pass from Plunkett; PAT—Bahr (kick)
- Sea. — Doornink, 11 pass from Zorn; PAT—Bahr (kick)

Fourth Quarter
- Raid. — Bahr, 35 yard field goal
- Sea. — Young, 9 yard pass from Zorn; PAT—N. Johnson (kick)

TEAM STATISTICS

SEA.		RAID.
16	First Downs- Total	21
4	First Downs- Rushing	10
10	First Downs- Passing	11
2	First Downs- Penalty	0
1	Fumbles- Number	3
0	Fumbles- Lost Ball	2
2	Penalties- Number	7
20	Yards Penalized	53
0	Missed Field Goals	0
58	Offensive Plays	72
167	Net Yards	401
2.9	Average Gain	5.6
5	Giveaways	4
4	Takeaways	5
-1	Difference	+1

The Seahawks had beaten the Broncos and Dolphins in their first playoff action ever, enabling them to reach the AFC title game. The host Raiders, on the other hand, were seasoned veterans of post-season combat. That experience shone crystal-clear in this one-sided match.

The Raiders devoted most of their attention to stopping Curt Warner, the centerpiece of the Seattle offense. Not only was Warner shut down almost completely, but Dave Krieg also was ineffective under heavy pressure. Altogether, Seahawk quarterbacks threw five interceptions, further handicapping a lackluster attack.

While the Seahawk offense was being routed, Marcus Allen ripped the Seattle defense for big yardage. At halftime, the score was 20-0.

When Krieg threw his third interception early in the third quarter, he was yanked in favor of Jim Zorn. Although Zorn threw for two touchdowns, the second came in the final two minutes of the 30-14 Raider victory.

For the fourth time, a Chuck Knox team was knocked out of the playoffs one win shy of the Super Bowl.

INDIVIDUAL STATISTICS

SEATTLE	No.	Yds.	Avg.	L.A. RAIDERS	No.	Yds.	Avg.
RUSHING							
Warner	11	26	2.4	Allen	25	154	6.2
Dixon	3	24	8.0	Plunkett	7	26	3.7
Hughes	3	14	4.7	Hawkins	10	24	2.4
C. Bryant	1	1	1.0	Pruitt	1	4	4.0
	18	65	4.6	King	2	0	0.0
				Wilson	1	-3	-3.0
					46	205	4.5
RECEIVING							
Doornink	6	48	8.0	Allen	7	62	8.9
Johns	5	49	9.8	Barnwell	5	116	23.2
Largent	2	25	12.5	Christensen	3	14	4.7
Warner	2	10	5.0	Branch	2	22	11.0
Young	1	9	9.0		17	220	12.9
H. Jackson	1	5	5.0				
	17	146	8.6				
PUNTING							
West	5		32.0	Guy	2		34.0
PUNT RETURNS							
none				Pruitt	1	1	1.0
KICKOFF RETURNS							
Hughes	2	60	30.0	Montgomery	2	46	23.0
Dixon	3	54	18.0				
Lane	1	10	10.				
Scholtz	1	12	12.0				
	7	136	19.4				
INTERCEPTION RETURNS							
Scholtz	1	8	8.0	M. Davis	2	2	1.0
G. Johnson	1	0	0.0	Hayes	1	44	44.0
	2	8	4.0	Millen	1	13	13.0
				McElroy	1	-6	-6.0
					5	53	10.6

PASSING

SEATTLE	Att.	Comp.	Comp. Pct.	Yds.	Int.	Yds./ Att.	Yds./ Comp.
Zorn	27	14	51.9	134	2	5.0	9.6
Krieg	9	3	33.3	12	3	1.3	4.0
	36	17	47.2	146	5	4.1	8.6
L.A. RAIDERS							
Plunkett	24	17	70.8	214	2	8.9	12.6

January 22, 1984 at Tampa
(Attendance 72,920)

The Raider Defense Is Super

Both clubs brought an air of invincibility into this contest. The Redskins had won 27 of their last 30 games with a blend of crunching strength and surgical finesse. The Raiders were relentless winners, modeled over time by feisty owner Al Davis. Although the Skins had beaten the Raiders in October, neither team was a clear favorite as they lined up for the opening kickoff.

Five minutes into the game, lightning struck. Derrick Jensen broke through the Washington front wall, blocked Jeff Hayes' punt and covered the ball after it bounced into the endzone. With the clubs still feeling each other out, the Raiders had grabbed a 7-0 lead. The Redskins soon got a break when the Raiders fumbled back a punt, but they squandered the opportunity when Mark Moseley missed a 44-yard field-goal try.

As the second quarter progressed, thc Washington offense was ineffective against the Raider defense. The heralded Hogs were being beaten by the linemen and linebackers from Los Angeles. With his blockers unable to clear a path, John Riggins had slow going on the ground. Forced to the air more than usual, Joe Theismann was thwarted by a strong pass rush and the flypaper coverage of cornerbacks Lester Hayes and Mike Haynes. With the Redskins unable to move the ball, the Raiders scored early in the second period on a three-yard drive, two of which were Jim Plunkett-to-Cliff Branch passes. Midway through the period, the Redskins launched a 13-play drive which culminated in a 24-yard field goal. Although the Raiders still led 14-3, the Redskins seemed to have stemmed the flow of momentum. With 12 seconds left on the first-half clock, Washington had the ball deep in its own territory. Rather than run the clock out or go for a deep pass, the Redskins chose to throw a short sideline pass to Joe Washington. In one stunning motion, linebacker Jack Squirek cut in front of the receiver, grabbed the ball and stepped five yards into the endzone. The play gave Los Angeles a 21-3 halftime lead and a massive psychological boost.

The Redskins came out for the second half with grim determination, cranking out a touchdown with a 70-yard drive on their first possession. When the Raiders responded with their own TD drive, the game moved more firmly into their grasp. When Marcus Allen broke away for a 74-yard gallop on the final play of the third period, the Raiders had the game won.

LINEUPS

WASHINGTON		L.A. RAIDERS
	OFFENSE	
Brown	WR	Branch
Jacoby	LT	Davis
Grimm	LG	Hannah
Bostic	C	Dalby
May	RG	Marvin
Starke	RT	Lawrence
Warren	TE	Christensen
Monk	WR	Barnwell
Theismann	QB	Plunkett
Riggins	RB	Allen
Walker	RB	King
	DEFENSE	
Liebenstein	LE	Long
Butz	LT/NT	Kinlaw
Grant	RT/RE	Alzado
Manley	RE/LOLB	Hendricks
Kaufman	LLB/LILB	Millen
Olkewicz	MLB/RILB	Nelson
Milot	RLB/ROLB	Martin
Green	LCB	Hayes
Washington	RCB	Haynes
Coffey	SS	Davis
Murphy	FS	McElroy

SUBSTITUTES

WASHINGTON

	OFFENSE	
Evans	J. Williams	Holly
Giaquinto	Garrett	Laufenberg
Washington	Simons	McGrath
Wonsley	Huff	Seay
Didier	Kimball	
	DEFENSE	
Mann	Coleman	Dean
McGee	Cronan	C. Jordan
Brooks	Kubin	G. Williams
Anderson	Carpenter	
	KICKERS	
Moseley	Hayes	

L.A. RAIDERS

	OFFENSE	
Humm	Wilson	Hawkins
Pruitt	Willis	Hasselbeck
Jensen	Montgomery	Muhammad
D. Williams	S. Jordan	Mosebar
Sylvester		
	DEFENSE	
Robinson	Townsend	Pickel
Stalls	Barnes	Davis
Caldwell	Squirek	Byrd
Watts	Hill	McKinney
	KICKERS	
Bahr	Guy	

SCORING

WASHINGTON	0	3	6	0-	9
L.A. RAIDERS	7	14	14	3-	38

First Quarter
- Raid. — Jensen recovered blocked punt in endzone
  - PAT—Bahr (kick)

Second Quarter
- Raid. — Branch, 12 yard pass from Plunkett
  - PAT—Bahr (kick)
- Wash. — Moseley, 24 yard field goal
- Raid. — Squirek, 5 yard interception return
  - PAT—Bahr (kick)

Third Quarter
- Wash. — Riggins, 1 yard rush
  - PAT—Kick blocked
- Raid. — Allen, 5 yard rush
  - PAT—Bahr (kick)
- Raid. — Allen, 74 yard rush
  - PAT—Bahr (kick)

Fourth Quarter
- Raid. — Bahr, 21 yard field goal

TEAM STATISTICS

WASH.		RAID.
19	First Downs- Total	18
7	First Downs- Rushing	8
10	First Downs- Passing	9
2	First Downs- Penalty	1
1	Fumbles- Number	3
1	Fumbles- Lost Ball	2
4	Penalties- Number	7
62	Yards Penalized	56
1	Missed Field Goals	0
73	Offensive Plays	60
283	Net Yards	385
3.9	Average Gain	6.4
3	Giveaways	2
2	Takeaways	3
-1	Difference	+1

INDIVIDUAL STATISTICS

WASHINGTON	No.	Yds.	Avg.	L.A. RAIDERS	No.	Yds.	Avg
				RUSHING			
Riggins	26	64	2.5	Allen	20	191	9.6
Theismann	3	18	6.0	Pruitt	5	17	3.4
Washington	3	8	2.7	King	3	12	4.0
	32	90	2.8	Willis	1	7	7.0
				Hawkins	3	6	2.0
				Plunkett	1	-2	-2.0
					33	231	7.0
				RECEIVING			
Didier	5	65	13.0	Branch	6	94	15.7
Brown	3	93	31.0	Christensen	4	32	8.0
Washington	3	20	6.7	Hawkins	2	20	10.0
Giaquinto	2	21	10.5	Allen	2	18	9.0
Monk	1	26	26.0	King	2	8	4.0
Garrett	1	17.0	17.0		16	172	10.8
Riggins	1	1	1.0				
	16	243	15.2				
				PUNTING			
Hayes	7		37.0	Guy	7		42.7
				PUNT RETURNS			
Green	1	34	34.0	Pruitt	1	8	8.0
Giaquinto	1.	1	1.0	Watts	1	0	0.0
	2	35	17.5		2	8	4.0
				KICKOFF RETURNS			
Garrett	5	100	20.0	Pruitt	1	17	17.0
Grant	1	32	32.0				
Kimball	1	0	0.0				
	7	132	18.9				
				INTERCEPTION RETURNS			
none				Squirek	1	5	5.0
				Haynes	1	0	0.0
					2	5	2.5

PASSING

	Att.	Comp.	Comp. Pct.	Yds.	Int.	Yds./ Att.	Yds./ Comp.	Yards Lost Tackled
WASHINGTON								
Theismann	35	16	45.7	243	2	6.9	15.2	6-50
L.A. RAIDERS								
Plunkett	25	16	64.0	172	0	6.9	10.8	2-18

1984 N.F.C. 49ers Almost Perfect

The United States Football League completed its second season, something the late, lamented World Football League never did. To broaden its base, the U.S.F.L. expanded from 12 to 18 teams, moving into Pittsburgh, Jacksonville, Memphis, Houston, San Antonio and Oklahoma. The 1983 Boston Breakers moved to New Orleans, while the owners of the Chicago and Arizona teams swapped franchises. Some big-name talent joined the spring circuit. Doug Williams, Joe Cribbs, Brian Sipe, Dan Ross and Cliff Stoudt all jumped from the N.F.L. Among the rookies, Heisman Trophy winner Mike Rozier ran for Pittsburgh, while quarterback Jim Kelly starred for the Houston Gamblers. Another young passer, Steve Young of Brigham Young, signed a fabulous long-term contract with the Los Angeles Express. Without any famous newcomers, the Philadelphia Stars maintained a spring-long excellence. They compiled a 16-2 record behind runner Kelvin Bryant and quarterback Chuck Fusina, then beat George Allen's Arizona Wranglers for the title.

EASTERN DIVISION

Washington Redskins — They didn't steamroll through their schedule, but the Redskins beat injuries and a slow start to win the Eastern Division. An opening-day loss to Miami was followed by a close loss to San Francisco. With their throne creaking, the Skins fought back to win five straight games, including a 34-14 victory over the Cowboys. The midpoint of the schedule brought a relapse, two losses to the Cardinals and Giants. With a playoff berth in doubt, the Redskins traveled to Dallas on December 9. They fell behind 21-6 at halftime, then rallied in a brilliant second half to a 30-28 victory. One week later, Mark Moseley kicked a field goal with under two minutes left to beat St. Louis 29-27 and earn another divisional title. Injuries spoiled the season for Mark Murphy and Charlie Brown, while John Riggins labored with a bad back. Art Monk stayed free of injuries and set an N.F.L. record with 106 receptions.

New York Giants — In his second season, coach Bill Parcells launched a major housecleaning. The offensive line was revamped, and Phil Simms was installed at quarterback. Parcells kept the strong defense intact with Lawrence Taylor, Harry Carson and Mark Haynes still functioning at all-pro levels. Hoping for respectability, the Giants jumped out to three victories in the first four games. An early autumn slump dropped them to 4-4, but the ugly duckling then blossomed into a swan. The mid-season Giants charged into playoff territory with five wins in six weeks. They trounced the Redskins and Cowboys back to back and beat the Cardinals two weeks after that. Losses to the Cardinals and Saints leveled their record out, but the Giants still captured an unexpected wild-card spot.

St. Louis Cardinals — The Cardinals lost three September games before their defense dramatically improved. With E.J. Junior and Curtis Greer in the fore, the Cards began a four-game winning streak, including victories over the Cowboys and Redskins. St. Louis' offense spewed points from the start of the year. Ottis Anderson cranked out more than 1,100 yards on the ground, while Neil Lomax and Roy Green demoralized opposing pass defenses. Supporting the attack was a fine front line featuring Luis Sharpe. An offensive slump in November led to three straight losses and put the playoffs in question. Victories over the Eagles, Patriots and Giants set the stage for a showdown in Washingon on the final weekend. With a post-season berth at stake, the Cards led the Redskins until a late field goal put Washington ahead 29-27. With time ebbing away, the Cardinals drove downfield, only to have Neil O'Donoghue's hurried kick sail wide left at the gun.

Dallas Cowboys — The retirements of Drew Pearson, Harvey Martin, Pat Donovan, Billy Joe DuPree and Robert Newhouse had critics relishing the downfall of the Cowboys. Tom Landry made Gary Hogeboom the starting quarterback over Danny White, a further sign of change in Dallas. After a strong 4-1 start, the Cowboys suffered a spate of injuries in the offensive line. Randy White, Everson Walls and Michael Downs led the still-tough flex defense. The Cowboys had a hard time with their Eastern rivals, losing twice to both New York and Washington and once to St. Louis. Although Danny White had recaptured the quarterback job by mid-season, the offense never clicked, falling apart in a 14-3 loss to winless Buffalo. With their nine-year playoff run on the table, the Cowboys dropped a heartbreaker to the Redskins and faded away with a close loss to Miami on the final Monday night.

Philadelphia Eagles — Stuck in the N.F.C.'s toughest division, the Eagles played respectably while bringing up the rear in the East. The offense had a receiving ace in Mike Quick, but no strong running threat. After November 25, it had no first-string quarterback, as Ron Jaworski broke his leg against the Cardinals. The defense improved, with Ken Clarke and Wes Hopkins becoming major forces. The Eagles beat the Giants and Redskins along the way, but their greatest victory may have been in the decision to stay in Philadelphia despite Phoenix's strong bid to lure them away.

CENTRAL DIVISION

Chicago Bears — Last year's strong finish carried over into 1984. The Bears won their first three games, including a 27-0 trouncing of the Broncos. A November 4 victory over the Raiders raised their record to 7-3 and made a playoff berth a virtual certainty. In that game, quarterback Jim McMahon suffered a lacerated kidney that ended his season. When backup Steve Fuller separated his shoulder on December 3, the Bears had severe QB problems. Rusty Lisch couldn't move the offense, Greg Landry signed as a free agent, and Walter Payton even played shotgun quarterback for six plays against Green Bay. Payton excelled in his usual role as a runner, gaining more than 1,600 yards and passing Jim Brown as the all-time rushing leader. Regardless of developments on offense, the Bears were feared for their swarming defense. Cleverly deployed and relentlessly physical, the Chicago defense had stars in linemen Dan Hampton and Richard Dent, linebackers Mike Singletary and Otis Wilson, and safeties Todd Bell and Gary Fencik. The 10-6 record put the Bears into the playoffs for the first time since 1979.

Green Bay Packers — Forrest Gregg returned to Green Bay to recapture the glory which eluded Bart Starr in his coaching days. An opening-day victory over St. Louis gave way to seven straight losses. In the gloom of autumn, the Packers suddenly turned around and won seven of their last eight games. The secondary led the way to improved defense, with cornerback Tim Lewis reaching all-pro heights. The offense had star receivers in James Lofton and Paul Coffman, although John Jefferson suffered through a bad season. The cold-weather surge included victories over the playoff-bound Rams and Bears.

Tampa Bay Buccaneers — A playoff spot was not in the cards, but the Buccaneers stepped up from their 1983 depths. Steve DeBerg came east from Denver and revived the moribund Tampa Bay passing game. The offense had a scattering of stars in receiver Kevin House, back James Wilder and guard Sean Farrell. The defense was a bigger problem this year. Although Lee Roy Selmon and David Logan excelled in the line, Hugh Green's absence after an October car crash left a hole in the unit. A gap loomed at the top, as coach John McKay announced on November 5 that he would not return in 1985 as coach. At home for their final two games, the Bucs beat Atlanta 23-6 and demolished the Jets 41-21 to give McKay a coaching bon voyage.

Detroit Lions — The Lions had gotten off to a rotten start in 1983 and had stormed back into the playoffs. They started badly again this year and stayed bad. They lost five of their first six games, most of them by close scores. After a brief mid-season resurgence, the Lions tumbled into a spiritless home stretch. Only once did they win in their final eight games, edging Green Bay 31-28 on Thanksgiving Day. The collapse affected both offense and defense. Gary Danielson won the quarterback job in training camp, only to lose ace runner Billy Sims to a knee injury on October 21. The disappointing season cost coach Monte Clark his job after seven seasons.

Minnesota Vikings — Bud Grant had run the Vikings with a calm and easy manner. When Grant retired, the Vikes named 38-year-old Les Steckel to replace him. The youngest head coach in the league, Steckel brought a gung-ho approach to his job. The veteran Minnesota squad did not take well to this change in tone. The undertalented Vikings split their first four games, then nosedived into 11 losses in their remaining 12

FINAL TEAM STATISTICS

OFFENSE

	ATL.	CHI.	DALL.	DET.	G.B.	L.A.	MINN.	N.O.	NY G	PHIL.	STL.	S.F.	T.B.	WASH.
FIRST DOWNS:														
Total	292	297	323	306	315	258	289	298	310	280	345	356	344	339
by Rushing	123	164	93	118	120	140	111	131	97	83	129	138	114	154
by Passing	151	115	202	170	168	100	150	137	198	176	200	204	209	164
by Penalty	18	18	28	18	27	18	28	30	15	21	16	14	21	21
RUSHING:														
Number	489	674	469	446	461	541	444	523	493	381	488	534	483	588
Yards	1994	2974	1714	2017	2019	2864	1844	2171	1660	1338	2088	2465	1776	2274
Average Yards	4.1	4.4	3.7	4.5	4.4	5.3	4.2	4.2	3.4	3.5	4.3	4.6	3.7	3.9
Touchdowns	16	22	12	13	18	16	10	9	12	6	21	21	17	20
PASSING:														
Attempts	478	390	604	531	506	358	533	476	535	606	566	496	563	485
Completions	294	226	322	298	281	176	281	246	288	331	347	312	334	286
Completion Pct.	61.5	57.9	53.3	56.1	55.5	49.2	52.7	51.7	53.8	54.6	61.3	62.9	59.3	59.0
Passing Yards	3546	2695	3995	3787	3740	2382	3337	3198	4066	3823	4634	4079	3907	3417
Avg. Yds per Att.	7.4	6.9	6.6	7.1	7.4	6.7	6.3	6.7	7.6	6.3	8.2	8.2	6.9	7.1
Avg. Yds per Comp.	12.1	11.9	12.4	12.7	13.3	13.5	11.9	13.0	14.1	11.6	13.4	13.1	11.7	12.0
Times Tackled	67	36	48	61	42	32	64	45	55	60	49	27	45	48
Yds Lost Tackled	496	232	389	486	310	240	465	361	434	463	377	178	362	341
Net Yards	3050	2463	3606	3301	3430	2142	2872	2837	3632	3360	4257	3901	3545	3076
Touchdowns	14	14	19	19	30	16	18	21	22	19	28	32	22	24
Interceptions	20	15	26	22	30	17	25	28	18	17	16	10	23	13
Pct. Intercepted	4.2	3.8	4.3	4.1	5.9	4.7	4.7	5.9	3.4	2.8	2.8	2.0	4.1	2.7
PUNTS:														
Number	70	85	108	76	85	74	82	70	94	92	68	62	68	73
Average	40.8	39.2	38.2	41.6	42.3	38.7	42.4	43.1	38.3	42.2	38.1	40.9	41.9	38.8
PUNT RETURNS														
Number	41	63	54	36	48	40	31	33	55	40	47	45	34	55
Yards	264	558	446	241	351	489	217	268	368	250	399	521	207	474
Average Yards	6.4	8.9	8.3	6.7	7.3	12.2	7.0	8.1	6.7	6.3	8.5	11.6	6.1	8.6
Touchdowns	0	0	0	0	0	2	0	0	0	0	0	1	0	0
KICKOFF RET.:														
Number	70	49	63	74	67	58	86	72	61	59	74	47	68	60
Yards	1367	896	1199	1347	1362	1244	1775	1465	1117	1156	1563	1039	1354	1174
Average Yards	19.5	18.3	19.0	18.2	20.3	21.4	20.6	20.3	18.3	19.6	21.1	22.1	19.9	19.6
Touchdowns	0	0	0	0	1	1	0	0	0	1	0	0	0	0
INTERCEPT RET.:														
Number	12	21	28	14	27	17	11	13	19	20	21	25	18	21
Yards	147	290	297	87	338	399	120	213	182	287	163	345	308	401
Average Yards	12.3	13.8	10.6	6.2	12.5	23.5	10.9	16.4	9.6	14.4	7.8	13.8	17.1	18.6
Touchdowns	1	1	2	0	2	3	1	3	0	0	1	2	1	4
PENALTIES:														
Number	125	114	100	138	110	93	90	101	79	77	109	100	118	80
Yards	1011	851	947	1165	915	830	762	849	703	632	904	884	875	723
FUMBLES:														
Number	39	31	35	36	17	31	39	22	17	23	32	26	36	33
Number Lost	21	16	17	14	7	18	16	13	9	16	20	12	20	15
POINTS:														
Total	281	325	308	283	390	346	276	298	299	278	423	475	335	426
PAT Attempts	31	37	34	31	51	38	31	34	36	27	51	57	40	51
PAT Made	31	35	33	31	48	37	30	34	32	26	48	56	38	48
FG Attempts	27	28	29	27	21	33	23	27	33	37	35	35	26	31
FG Made	20	22	23	20	12	25	20	20	17	30	23	25	19	24
Percent FG Made	74.1	78.6	79.3	74.1	57.1	75.8	87.0	74.1	51.5	81.1	65.7	71.4	73.1	77.4
Safeties	2	1	1	0	0	3	0	0	0	0	0	1	0	0

DEFENSE

	ATL.	CHI.	DALL.	DET.	G.B.	L.A.	MINN.	N.O.	NYG	PHIL.	STL.	S.F.	T.B.	WASH.
FIRST DOWNS:														
Total	317	216	283	328	323	309	342	298	296	307	292	302	311	307
by Rushing	131	72	106	120	136	108	144	134	107	123	108	101	139	91
by Passing	162	122	155	177	166	179	182	142	174	171	157	173	157	194
by Penalty	24	22	22	31	21	22	16	22	15	13	27	28	15	22
RUSHING:														
Number	538	378	510	519	545	449	547	549	474	556	442	432	511	390
Yards	2153	1377	2226	1808	2145	1600	2573	2461	1818	2189	1923	1795	2233	1589
Average Yards	4.0	3.6	4.4	3.5	3.9	3.6	4.7	4.5	3.8	3.9	4.4	4.2	4.4	4.1
Touchdowns	16	10	8	17	14	15	20	13	10	12	11	10	27	13
PASSING:														
Attempts	443	435	527	466	551	566	490	422	529	492	494	546	490	575
Completions	262	198	250	288	315	346	319	239	288	262	251	298	286	318
Completion Pct.	59.1	45.5	47.4	61.8	57.2	61.1	65.1	56.6	54.4	53.3	50.8	54.6	58.4	55.3
Passing Yards	3413	3069	3200	3782	3470	3964	3954	2873	3736	3506	3574	3744	3480	4301
Avg. Yds per Att.	7.7	7.1	6.1	8.1	6.3	7.0	8.1	6.8	7.1	7.1	7.2	6.9	7.1	7.5
Avg. Yds per Comp.	13.0	15.5	12.8	13.1	11.0	11.5	12.4	12.0	13.0	13.4	14.2	12.6	12.2	13.5
Times Tackled	38	72	57	37	44	43	25	55	48	60	55	51	32	66
Yds Lost Tackled	287	583	390	271	324	298	175	420	361	456	403	363	239	529
Net Yards	3126	2486	2810	3511	3146	3666	3779	2453	3375	3050	3171	3381	3241	3772
Touchdowns	27	14	23	27	16	18	35	23	20	22	26	14	20	25
Interceptions	12	21	28	14	27	17	11	13	19	20	21	25	18	21
Pct. Intercepted	2.7	4.8	5.3	3.0	4.9	3.0	2.2	5.9	3.6	4.1	4.3	4.6	3.7	3.7
PUNTS:														
Number	60	100	99	73	89	71	68	84	92	89	81	80	68	78
Average	41.6	41.6	42.8	40.0	40.9	41.5	40.8	41.6	40.0	39.3	39.0	40.5	41.0	39.9
PUNT RETURNS														
Number	42	41	55	49	46	35	49	47	50	58	27	30	36	38
Yards	450	249	230	516	368	196	435	550	479	486	239	190	310	187
Average Yards	10.7	6.1	4.2	10.5	8.0	5.6	8.9	11.7	9.6	8.4	8.9	6.3	8.6	4.9
Touchdowns	1	0	0	1	0	0	0	1	2	0	0	0	0	0
KICKOFF RET.:														
Number	48	68	65	60	73	74	59	45	55	69	85	78	67	73
Yards	1053	1443	1310	1250	1171	1288	1281	916	1088	1298	1549	1499	1336	1404
Average Yards	21.9	21.2	20.2	20.8	16.0	17.4	21.7	20.4	19.8	18.8	18.2	19.2	19.9	19.2
Touchdowns	0	1	0	0	0	0	0	0	0	0	1	0	0	1
INTERCEPT RET.:														
Number	20	15	26	22	30	17	25	28	18	17	16	10	23	13
Yards	304	241	382	251	317	240	344	420	222	211	219	155	249	159
Average Yards	15.2	16.1	14.7	11.4	10.6	14.1	13.8	16.4	12.3	12.4	13.7	15.5	10.8	12.2
Touchdowns	2	3	4	1	2	2	2	3	1	1	0	0	0	0
PENALTIES:														
Number	93	86	95	107	145	115	113	119	93	96	75	91	136	84
Yards	820	698	868	968	1129	871	1047	1025	699	904	578	723	1078	803
FUMBLES:														
Number	36	33	35	28	33	42	35	28	24	32	20	28	27	32
Number Lost	20	13	16	11	15	22	18	10	16	11	12	13	14	22
POINTS:														
Total	382	248	308	408	309	316	484	361	301	320	345	227	380	310
PAT Attempts	48	29	36	48	34	36	59	41	35	36	39	24	46	39
PAT Made	46	26	35	48	33	32	58	41	34	36	36	24	44	37
FG Attempts	30	22	28	29	31	31	28	33	26	35	38	25	27	20
FG Made	16	16	19	24	24	22	24	24	17	22	25	19	18	13
Percent FG Made	53.3	72.7	67.9	82.8	77.4	71.0	85.7	72.7	65.4	62.9	65.8	76.0	66.7	65.0
Safeties	0	0	0	0	0	1	0	0	3	1	0	1	0	0

games. Three of those losses killed morale: a 45-17 debacle at Green Bay, 42-21 at Denver, and 51-7 at San Francisco. Within a week of the final game, Steckel became the league's youngest ex-coach, with Grant ending his retirement to regroup his battered charges.

WESTERN DIVISION

San Francisco 49ers — The Niners were brilliant in building the N.F.L.'s best record. After edging Detroit and Washington, both offense and defense hit a fine rhythm that was jarred only by the Steelers on October 14. Joe Montana engineered the multi-dimensional attack with virtuoso skill. Wendell Tyler ran for more than 1,200 yards to balance the precise San Francisco passing game. In the front line, all-pro honors were heaped on Randy Cross, Keith Fahnhorst and Fred Quillan. The 49er defense dominated opponents despite Fred Dean's absence until mid-November in a contract dispute. Keena Turner starred among the linebackers, while the entire secondary of Ronnie Lott, Eric Wright, Carlton Williamson and Dwight Hicks went to the Pro Bowl. Bill Walsh led his team into the playoffs with a nine-game winning streak at their backs.

Los Angeles Rams — The Rams loved the run and hated the pass. On offense, they had Eric Dickerson running for record yardage behind an all-star line of Kent Hill, Doug Smith, Dennis Harrah, Bill Bain and Jackie Slater. The Rams passed sparingly after Vince Ferragamo broke his hand in the third game of the year. Jeff Kemp kept the offense moving by minimizing his mistakes and relying on Dickerson. The defense had a similar bias. Led by ancient Jack Youngblood and young Jim Collins, the Rams gave up running yardage only grudgingly. Opponents gained more easily through the air, as Johnnie Johnson missed part of the season on injured reserve. Before dropping their finale in San Francisco, the Rams won five of six games to ice their second straight wild-card berth.

New Orleans Saints — Two controversial trades spurred conversation but failed to earn the Saints their first playoff spot. In the off-season, they sent a first-round draft choice to the Jets for Richard Todd, a quarterback coming off a subpar season. In October, Bum Phillips sent another first-round choice to Houston for Earl Campbell, his battering ram when he coached the Oilers. The Saints already had George Rogers and other competent backs, so the Campbell trade cut the playing time available to each back. Todd started at quarterback, prompting Ken Stabler to retire eight games into the season. The defense was the team's backbone, with Rickey Jackson and Bruce Clark starring. Losers of three of their last four games, the Saints still had never broken the .500 barrier.

Atlanta Falcons — A severe pre-season knee injury sidelined William Andrews and cast a pall on the team which never lifted. Gerald Riggs stepped in and ran for 202 yards on opening day to raise spirits a bit. On October 7, Billy Johnson tore up his knee and departed for the year, triggering a nine-game losing streak, which ended only in the season's final game. Quarterback Steve Bartkowski joined Andrews and Johnson with his own season-ending knee surgery on November 18. Although Stacey Bailey emerged as a star, this season generated little optimism in Atlanta.

WASHINGTON REDSKINS 11-5-0 Joe Gibbs

Scores of Each Game		
17	MIAMI	35
31	San Francisco	37
30	N.Y.GIANTS	14
26	New England	10
20	PHILADELPHIA	0
35	Indianapolis	7
34	DALLAS	14
24	St.Louis	26
13	N.Y.Giants	37
27	ATLANTA	14
28	DETROIT	14
10	Philadelphia	16
41	BUFFALO	14
31	Minnesota	17
30	Dallas	28
29	ST.LOUIS	27

Use Name	Pos.	Hgt	Wgt	Age	Int	Pts
Joe Jacoby	OT	6'7"	305	25		6
George Starke	OT	6'5"	260	36		
Morris Towns	OT	6'4"	263	30		
Russ Grimm	OG	6'3"	273	25		
Ken Huff	OG	6'4"	265	31		
Bruce Kimball	OG	6'2"	260	28		
Mark May	OG	6'6"	295	25		
J.T.Turner	OG	6'3"	265	31		
Rick Donnalley	C-OG	6'2"	257	25		
Jeff Bostic	C	6'2"	258	25		
Todd Liebenstein	DE	6'6"	255	24		
Dexter Manley	DE	6'3"	250	25		
Charles Mann	DE	6'6"	260	23		
Tony McGee	DE	6'4"	249	35		
Tom Beasley	DT	6'5"	248	30		
Perry Brooks	DT	6'3"	270	29		
Dave Butz	DT	6'7"	295	34		
Darryl Grant	DT	6'1"	275	24		6
Monte Coleman	LB	6'2"	230	26	1	6
Pete Cronan	LB	6'2"	238	29		
Trey Junkin (from BUF)	LB	6'2"	221	23		
Mel Kaufman	LB	6'2"	218	26		
Larry Kibin	LB	6'2"	234	25		
Rich Milot	LB	6'4"	237	27	3	
Neal Olkewicz	LB	6'	233	27		
Ken Coffey	DB	6'	190	23	1	
Vernon Dean	DB	5'11"	178	25	7	12
Darrell Green	DB	5'8"	170	24	5	6
Curtis Jordan	DB	6'2"	205	30	2	6
Mark Murphy	DB	6'4"	210	29		
Mike Nelms	DB	6'1"	202	29		
Tony Peters	DB	6'1"	190	31		
Ricky Smith (from NE)	DB	6'	182	24	1	
Anthony Washington	DB	6'1"	204	26	1	
Greg Williams	DB	5'11"	185	25		
Jim Hart	QB	6'2"	210	40		
Jay Schroeder	QB	6'4"	215	23		
Joe Theismann	QB	6'	196	34		6
Keith Griffin	HB	5'8"	185	22		
Jeff Moore	HB	6'	196	28		12
Joe Washington	HB	5'10"	179	30		6
Rick Kane	FB-HB	5'11"	200	29		
John Riggins	FB	6'2"	240	35		84
Otis Wonsley	FB	5'10"	214	27		24
Charlie Brown	WR	5'10"	179	25		18
Alvin Garrett	WR	5'7"	178	27		
Rich Mauti	WR	6'	195	30		
Mark McGrath	WR	5'11"	175	26		6
Art Monk	WR	6'3"	209	26		42
Calvin Muhammad	WR	6'	190	25		24
Virgil Seay (to ATL)	WR	5'8"	180	26		6
Clint Didier	TE	6'5"	240	25		3
Anthony Jones	TE	6'3"	248	24		
Rick Walker	TE	6'3"	235	29		6
Don Warren	TE	6'4"	242	28		
Mike Williams	TE	6'4"	251	25		
Jeff Hayes	K	5'11"	175	25		
Mark Moseley	K	5'11"	205	36		120

Babe Laufenberg - Rotor Cuff Injury

NEW YORK GIANTS 9-7-0 Bill Parcells

Scores of Each Game		
28	PHILADELPHIA	27
28	DALLAS	7
14	Washington	30
17	TAMPA BAY	14
12	L.A.Rams	33
10	SAN FRANCISCO	31
19	Atlanta	7
10	Philadelphia	24
37	WASHINGTON	13
19	Dallas	7
17	Tampa Bay	20
16	ST.LOUIS	10
28	KANSAS CITY	27
20	N.Y.Jets	10
21	St.Louis	31
3	NEW ORLEANS	10

Use Name	Pos.	Hgt	Wgt	Age	Int	Pts
Brad Benson	OT	6'3"	270	28		
Chris Godfrey	OT	6'3"	265	26		
Conrad Goode	OT	6'6"	285	22		
Karl Nelson	OT	6'6"	285	24		
Bill Roberts	OT	6'5"	280	22		
Billy Ard	OG	6'3"	270	25		
Kevin Belcher	OG	6'3"	276	23		
David Jordan	OG	6'6"	276	22		
Rich Umphrey	C	6'3"	270	25		
Dee Hardison	DE	6'4"	274	28		
Leonard Marshall	DE	6'3"	285	22		
George Martin	DE	6'4"	255	31		
Curtis McGriff	DE	6'5"	276	26		
Casey Merrill	DE	6'4"	260	27		
Jim Burt	NT	6'1"	260	25		
Jerome Sally	NT	6'3"	270	25		
Carl Banks	LB	6'4"	235	22		
Harry Carson	LB	6'2"	240	30	1	
Andy Headen	LB	6'5"	242	24	1	6
Byron Hunt	LB	6'5"	242	25	1	
Robbie Jones	LB	6'2"	230	24		
Joe McLaughlin	LB	6'1"	235	27		
Gary Reasons	LB	6'4"	235	22	2	
Lawrence Taylor	LB	6'3"	243	25	1	
Bill Currier	DB	6'	196	29	1	
Kenny Daniel	DB	5'10"	180	24		
Larry Flowers	DB	6'1"	195	26		
Mark Haynes	DB	5'11"	195	25	7	
Kenny Hill	DB	6'	195	26		
Terry Kinard	DB	6'1"	200	24	2	
Elvis Patterson	DB	5'11"	190	23		
Pete Shaw	DB	5'10"	183	30		
Perry Williams	DB	6'2"	203	23	3	
Jeff Hostetler	QB	6'3"	212	23		
Jeff Rutledge	QB	6'1"	195	27		
Phil Simms	QB	6'3"	216	27		
Frank Cephous	HB	5'10"	205	23		
Joe Morris	HB	5'7"	195	23		24
Rob Carpenter	FB	6'1"	226	29		48
Tony Galbreath	FB	6'	228	30		
Butch Woolfolk	FB	6'1"	212	24		6
Earnest Gray	WR	6'3"	191	27		12
Bobby Johnson	WR	5'11"	171	22		42
Lionel Manuel	WR	5'11"	175	22		24
Phil McConkey	WR	5'10"	170	27		6
John Mistler (to BUF)	WR	6'2"	186	25		
Byron Williams	WR	6'2"	183	23		12
Zeke Mowatt	TE	6'3"	238	23		36
Tom Mullady	TE	6'3"	235	27		
Ali Haji-Sheikh	K	6'	172	23		83
Dave Jennings	K	6'4"	200	32		

Gordon King - Broken Arm
John Tuggle - Knee Injury

DALLAS COWBOYS 9-7-0 Tom Landry

Scores of Each Game		
20	L.A.Rams	13
7	N.Y.Giants	28
23	PHILADELPHIA	17
20	GREEN BAY	6
23	Chicago	14
20	ST.LOUIS	31
14	Washington	34
30	NEW ORLEANS	*27
22	INDIANAPOLIS	3
7	N.Y.GIANTS	19
24	St.Louis	17
3	Buffalo	14
20	NEW ENGLAND	17
26	Philadelphia	10
28	WASHINGTON	30
21	Miami	28

Use Name	Pos.	Hgt	Wgt	Age	Int	Pts
Jim Cooper	OT	6'5"	267	28		
John Hunt	OT	6'4"	254	21		
Phil Pozderac	OT	6'9"	276	24		
Howard Richards	OT-OG	6'6"	258	25		
Dowe Aughtman	OG	6'2"	258	23		
Kurt Petersen	OG	6'4"	268	27		
Herbert Scott	OG	6'2"	263	31		
Brian Baldinger	OG-OT	6'4"	258	25		
Tom Rafferty	C	6'3"	254	30		
Glen Titensor	C-OG	6'4"	264	26		
Jim Jeffcoat	DE	6'5"	264	23		6
Too Tall Jones	DE	6'9"	287	33		
John Dutton	DT	6'7"	267	33		2
Don Smerek	DT	6'7"	257	26		
Mark Tuinei	DT	6'5"	274	24		
Randy White	DT	6'4"	268	31		
Bob Breunig	LB	6'2"	225	31		
Billy Cannon	LB	6'4"	231	22		
Steve DeOssie	LB	6'2"	249	21		
Anthony Dickerson	LB	6'2"	222	27	1	
Mike Hegman	LB	6'1"	231	31	3	
Eugene Lockhart	LB	6'2"	231	23	1	
Jeff Rohrer	LB	6'3"	225	25		
Jimmie Turner	LB	6'2"	220	22		
Vince Albritton	DB	6'2"	209	22		
Bill Bates	DB	6'1"	200	23	1	
Dextor Clinkscale	DB	5'11"	190	26	3	
Michael Downs	DB	6'3"	203	25	7	6
Ron Fellows	DB	6'	174	25	3	
Carl Howard	DB	6'2"	188	22		
Victor Scott	DB	6'	196	22	1	
Dennis Thurman	DB	5'11	179	28	5	6
Everson Walls	DB	6'1"	194	24	3	
Gary Hogeboom	QB	6'4"	199	26		
Steve Pelluer	QB	6'4"	208	22		
Danny White	QB	6'2"	196	32		
Gary Allen	HB	5'10"	179	24		
Tony Dorsett	HB	5'11"	185	30		42
James Jones	HB	5'10"	200	25		6
Chuck McSwain	HB	6'	191	23		
Norm Granger	FB	5'9"	221	22		
Timmy Newsome	FB	6'1"	231	26		30
Ron Springs	FB-HB	6'1"	224	27		24
Harold Carmichael	WR	6'7"	225	34		
Doug Donley	WR	6'	178	25		12
Tony Hill	WR	6'2"	198	28		30
Kirk Phillips	WR	6'1"	202	24		
Mike Renfro	WR	6'	188	29		12
Waddell Smith	WR	6'2"	180	29		
Fred Cornwell	TE	6'6"	238	23		6
Doug Cosbie	TE	6'6"	232	28		24
Brian Salonen	TE	6'3"	229	23		
Jim Miller	K	5'11"	183	27		
Rafael Septien	K	5'10"	180	30		102
John Warren	K	6'	207	23		

Chris Schultz - Knee Injury

ST. LOUIS CARDINALS 9-7-0 Jim Hanifan

Scores of Each Game		
23	Green Bay	24
37	BUFFALO	7
34	Indianapolis	33
24	New Orleans	34
28	MIAMI	36
31	Dallas	20
38	CHICAGO	21
26	WASHINGTON	24
34	Philadelphia	14
13	L.A.RAMS	16
17	DALLAS	24
10	N.Y.Giants	16
17	PHILADELPHIA	16
33	New England	10
31	N.Y.GIANTS	21
27	Washington	29

Use Name	Pos.	Hgt	Wgt	Age	Int	Pts
Art Plunkett	OT	6'7"	270	25		
Tootie Robbins	OT	6'5"	278	26		
Luis Sharpe	OT	6'4"	260	24		
Dan Audick	OG-OT	6'3"	253	29		
Ramsey Dardar	OG-OT	6'2"	264	24		
Joe Bostic	OG	6'3"	265	27		
Doug Dawson	OG	6'3"	267	22		
Terry Stieve	OG	6'2"	265	30		
Randy Clark	C	6'3"	254	27		
Carlos Scott	C	6'4"	300	24		
Al Baker	DE	6'6"	270	27		
Curtis Greer	DE	6'4"	258	26		
Elois Grooms	DE	6'4"	250	31		
Stafford Mays	DE	6'2"	250	26		
Mark Duda	DT	6'3"	263	23		
David Galloway	DT	6'3"	277	25		
Dan Ralph	DT	6'4"	260	23		
Dave Ahrens	LB	6'3"	228	25		
Kurt Allerman	LB	6'2"	232	29		
Charlie Baker	LB	6'2"	234	26		
Billy Davis	LB	6'4"	210	22		
Bob Harris	LB	6'2"	215	23		
Tom Howard	LB	6'2"	220	30	2	6
E.J.Junior	LB	6'3"	235	24	1	
Niko Noga	LB	6'1"	230	22		
Craig Shaffer	LB	6'	230	25		
Jeff Griffin	DB	6'	185	26	2	
Victor Heflin	DB	6'	184	24		
Bill Kay (to SD)	DB	6'1"	190	24		
Cedric Mack	DB-WR	6'	190	23		
Lee Nelson	DB	5'10"	185	30		
Benny Perrin	DB	6'2"	178	24	4	
Leonard Smith	DB	5'11"	190	23	2	6
Wayne Smith	DB	6'	175	27	4	
Lionel Washington	DB	6'	184	23	5	
Bill Whitaker	DB	6'	182	24		
Neil Lomax	QB	6'3"	215	25		18
Kyle Mackey	QB	6'2"	220	22		
Rick McIvor	QB	6'4"	210	23		
Ottis Anderson	HB	6'2"	220	27		48
Will Harrell	HB	5'9"	190	31		6
Stump Mitchell	HB	5'9"	188	25		66
Earl Ferrell	FB	6'	215	26		12
Perry Harrington	FB	5'11"	210	26		
Randy Love	FB	6'1"	205	27		12
Steve Bird (to SD)	WR	5'11"	171	23		
Clyde Duncan	WR	6'1"	192	23		
Roy Green	WR	6'	195	27		72
Danny Pittman	WR	6'2"	205	26		
Pat Tilley	WR	5'10"	178	31		30
Quentin Walker	WR	6'1"	200	23		
John Goode	TE	6'2"	222	21		
Greg LaFleur	TE	6'4"	236	25		
Doug Marsh	TE	6'3"	240	26		30
Carl Birdsong	K	6'	192	25		
Neil O'Donoghue	K	6'6"	210	31		117

John Walker - Eye Injury
George Schmitt - Back Injury
Alan Bowers - Ankle Injury
Rod Clark - Knee Injury
Eddie McGill - Knee Injury

PHILADELPHIA EAGLES 6-9-1 Marion Campbell

Scores of Each Game		
27	N.Y.Giants	28
19	MINNESOTA	17
17	Dallas	23
9	SAN FRANCISCO	21
0	Washington	20
27	Buffalo	17
16	INDIANAPOLIS	7
24	N.Y.GIANTS	10
14	ST.LOUIS	34
23	Detroit	*23
23	Miami	24
16	WASHINGTON	10
16	St.Louis	17
10	DALLAS	26
27	NEW ENGLAND	17
10	Atlanta	26

Use Name	Pos.	Hgt	Wgt	Age	Int	Pts
Rusty Russell	OT	6'5"	295	21		
Jerry Sisemore	OT	6'4"	265	33		
Dean Miraldi	OT-OG	6'5"	285	26		
Ron Baker	OG	6'4"	270	29		
Steve Kenney	OG	6'4"	270	28		
Petey Perot	OG	6'2"	261	27		
Gerry Feehery	C-OG	6'2"	268	24		
Dave Pacella	C-OG	6'3"	266	24		
Mark Dennard	C	6'1"	252	28		
Greg Brown	DE	6'5"	260	27		
Byron Darby	DE	6'4"	260	24		
Dennis Harrison	DE	6'8"	280	28		
Leonard Mitchell	DE	6'7"	285	25		
Thomas Strauthers	DE	6'4"	265	23		
Harvey Armstrong	NT	6'2"	265	24		
Ken Clarke	NT	6'2"	255	28		
Bill Cowher	LB	6'3"	230	27		
Anthony Griggs	LB	6'3"	220	24		
Rich Kraynak	LB	6'1"	225	24		6
Mike Reichenbach	LB	6'2"	235	22		
Jerry Robinson	LB	6'2"	225	27		
Jody Schulz	LB	6'3"	235	24		
Reggie Wilkes	LB	6'4"	235	28	1	
Joel Williams	LB	6'1"	225	27		
Evan Cooper	DB	5'11"	180	22		
Herman Edwards	DB	6'	190	30	2	
Ray Ellis	DB	6'1"	192	25	7	
Elbert Foules	DB	5'11"	185	23	4	
Wes Hopkins	DB	6'1"	210	22	5	
Lou Rash	DB	5'9"	170	24		
Andre Waters	DB	5'11"	182	22	6	
Brenard Wilson	DB	6'	180	29	1	
Roynell Young	DB	6'1"	181	26		
Jeff Christensen	QB	6'3"	202	24		
Bob Holly (to ATL)	QB	6'2"	205	24		
Ron Jaworski	QB	6'2"	196	33		6
Dean May	QB	6'5"	220	22		
Joe Pisarcik	QB	6'4"	220	32		12
Joe Hayes	HB-WR	5'9"	185	23		
Wilbert Montgomery	HB	5'10"	195	29		12
Major Everett	FB	5'10"	215	24		
Michael Haddix	FB	6'2"	225	22		6
Andre Hardy	FB	6'1"	233	22		
Hubie Oliver	FB	5'10"	212	26		
Michael Williams	FB	6'2"	225	23		
Melvin Hoover	WR	6'	185	25		12
Kenny Jackson	WR	6'	180	22		6
Mike Quick	WR	6'2"	190	25		54
Tony Woodruff	WR	6'	185	25		18
Vyto Kab	TE	6'5"	240	24		18
Lawrence Sampleton	TE	6'5"	233	24		
John Spagnola	TE	6'4"	240	27		6
Mike Horan	K	5'11"	190	25		
Paul McFadden	K	5'11"	155	22		116

Leon Evans- Knee Injury
Tom Jelesky - Knee Injury
Sam Slater - Shoulder Injury
Todd Thomas - Back Injury

* Overtime

WASHINGTON REDSKINS

RUSHING

Last Name	No.	Yds	Avg	TD
Riggins	327	1239	3.8	14
Griffin	97	408	4.2	0
Theismann	62	314	5.1	1
J. Washington	56	192	3.4	1
Kane	17	43	2.5	0
Wonsley	18	38	2.1	4
Monk	2	18	9.0	0
Hayes	2	13	6.5	0
Moore	3	13	4.3	0
Walker	1	2	2.0	0
Hart	3	-6	-2.0	0

RECEIVING

Last Name	No.	Yds	Avg	TD
Monk	106	1372	12.9	7
Muhammad	42	729	17.4	4
Didier	30	350	11.7	5
Brown	18	200	11.1	3
Warren	18	192	10.7	0
Moore	17	115	6.8	2
J. Washington	13	74	5.7	0
McGrath	10	118	11.8	1
Seay	9	111	12.3	1
Griffin	8	43	5.4	0
Riggins	7	43	6.1	0
Walker	5	52	10.4	1
Kane	1	7	7.0	0
Jones	1	6	6.0	0
Garrett	1	5	5.0	0

PUNT RETURNS

Last Name	No.	Yds	Avg	TD
Nelms	49	428	8.7	0
Green	2	13	6.5	0
Coffey	1	6	6.0	0
Mauti	1	2	2.0	0
Seay	1	-2	-2.0	0
G. Williams	1	0	0.0	0
Coleman	0	27	—	0

KICKOFF RETURNS

Last Name	No.	Yds	Avg	TD
Nelms	42	860	20.5	0
Griffin	9	164	18.2	0
Kane	3	43	14.3	0
Seay	3	53	17.7	0
J. Smith	2	38	19.0	0
Mauti	1	16	16.0	0
R. Smith	1	22	22.0	0

PASSING — PUNTING — KICKING

PASSING	Att	Cmp	%	Yds	Yd/Att	TD	Int-	%	RK
Theismann	477	283	59	3391	7.1	24	13-	3	5
Hart	7	3	43	26	3.7	0	0-	0	
J. Washington	1	0	0	0	0.0	0	0-	0	

PUNTING	No	Avg
Hayes	72	39.4

KICKING	XP	Att	%	FG	Att	%
Moseley	48	51	94	24	31	77

NEW YORK GIANTS

RUSHING

Last Name	No.	Yds	Avg	TD
Carpenter	250	795	3.2	7
Morris	133	510	3.8	4
Simms	42	162	3.9	0
Galbreath	22	97	4.4	0
Woolfolk	40	92	2.3	1
Cephous	3	2	0.7	0
Manuel	3	2	0.7	0

RECEIVING

Last Name	No.	Yds	Avg	TD
Johnson	48	795	16.6	7
Mowatt	48	698	14.5	6
Gray	38	529	13.9	2
Galbreath	37	357	9.6	0
Manuel	33	619	18.8	4
Carpenter	26	209	8.0	1
B. Williams	24	471	19.6	2
Morris	12	124	10.3	0
Woolfolk	9	53	5.9	0
McConkey	8	154	19.3	0
Mullady	2	35	17.5	0
Simms	1	13	13.0	0
Mistler	1	5	5.0	0
Belcher	1	4	4.0	0

PUNT RETURNS

Last Name	No.	Yds	Avg	TD
McConkey	46	306	6.7	0
Manuel	8	62	7.8	0
Kinnard	1	0	0.0	0

KICKOFF RETURNS

Last Name	No.	Yds	Avg	TD
McConkey	28	541	19.3	0
Woolfolk	14	232	16.6	0
Cephous	9	178	19.8	0
Morris	9	69	11.5	0
McLaughlin	2	18	9.0	0
Daniel	1	52	52.0	0
Hill	1	27	27.0	0

PASSING — PUNTING — KICKING

PASSING	Att	Cmp	%	Yds	Yd/Att	TD	Int-	%	RK
Simms	533	286	54	4044	7.6	22	18-	3	10
Galbreath	1	1	100	13	13.0	0	0-	0	
Rutledge	1	1	100	9	9.0	0	0-	0	

PUNTING	No	Avg
Jennings	90	40.0

KICKING	XP	Att	%	FG	Att	%
Haji-Sheikh	32	35	91	17	33	52

DALLAS COWBOYS

RUSHING

Last Name	No.	Yds	Avg	TD
Dorsett	302	1189	3.9	6
Newsome	66	268	4.1	5
Springs	68	197	2.9	1
D. White	6	21	3.5	0
Hogeboom	15	19	1.3	0
J. Jones	8	13	1.6	0
T. Hill	1	7	7.0	0
Donley	2	5	2.5	0
Smith	1	-5	-5.0	0

RECEIVING

Last Name	No.	Yds	Avg	TD
Cosbie	60	789	13.2	4
T. Hill	58	864	14.9	5
Dorsett	51	459	9.0	1
Springs	46	454	9.9	3
Renfro	35	583	16.7	2
Donley	32	473	14.8	2
Newsome	26	263	10.1	0
J. Jones	7	57	8.1	1
Cornwell	2	23	11.5	1
Smith	1	7	7.0	0
Carmichael	1	7	7.0	0
Phillips	1	6	6.0	0
Pozderac	1	1	1.0	0
Harris	1	9	9.0	0

PUNT RETURNS

Last Name	No.	Yds	Avg	TD
Allen	54	446	8.3	0

KICKOFF RETURNS

Last Name	No.	Yds	Avg	TD
Allen	33	666	20.2	0
McSwain	20	403	20.2	0
Fellows	6	94	15.7	0
Salonen	2	30	15.0	0
Granger	2	6	3.0	0

PASSING — PUNTING — KICKING

PASSING	Att	Cmp	%	Yds	Yd/Att	TD	Int-	%	RK
D. White	233	126	54	1580	6.8	11	11-	5	12
Hogeboom	367	195	53	2366	6.5	7	14-	3.8	14
Renfro	2	1	50	49	24.5	1	0-	0	
Springs	1	0	0	0	0.0	0	0-	0	
Dorsett	1	0	0	0	0.0	0	1-	100	

PUNTING	No	Avg
D. White	82	38.4
Warren	21	38.0
Miller	5	34.6

KICKING	XP	Att	%	FG	Att	%
Septien	33	34	97	23	29	79

ST. LOUIS CARDINALS

RUSHING

Last Name	No.	Yds	Avg	TD
Anderson	289	1174	4.1	6
Mitchell	81	434	5.4	9
Ferrell	44	203	4.6	1
Lomax	35	184	5.3	3
Love	25	90	3.6	1
Harrell	5	7	1.4	1
Harrington	3	6	2.0	0
McIvor	3	5	1.7	0
Marsh	1	-5	-5.0	0
Green	1	-10	-10.0	0

RECEIVING

Last Name	No.	Yds	Avg	TD
Green	78	1555	19.9	12
Anderson	70	611	8.7	2
Tilley	52	758	14.6	5
Marsh	39	608	15.6	5
Mitchell	26	318	12.2	2
Ferrell	26	218	8.4	1
LaFleur	17	198	11.6	0
Harrell	14	106	7.6	0
Pittman	10	145	14.5	0
Love	7	33	4.7	1
Mack	5	61	12.2	0
Goode	3	23	7.7	0

PUNT RETURNS

Last Name	No.	Yds	Avg	TD
Mitchell	38	333	8.2	0
Bird	6	60	10.0	0
Pittman	4	10	2.5	0

KICKOFF RETURNS

Last Name	No.	Yds	Avg	TD
Mitchell	35	804	23.0	0
Pittman	14	319	22.8	0
Harrell	13	231	17.8	0
Bird	11	205	18.6	0
Green	1	18	18.0	0
Love	1	1	1.0	0
Ferrell	1	0	0.0	0

PASSING — PUNTING — KICKING

PASSING	Att	Cmp	%	Yds	Yd/Att	TD	Int-	%	RK
Lomax	560	345	62	4614	8.2	28	16-	3	3
McIvor	4	0	0	0	0.0	0	0-	0	
Mitchell	1	1	100	20	20.0	0	0-	0	
Perrin	1	1	100	0	0.0	0	0-	0	

PUNTING	No	Avg
Birdsong	67	38.7

KICKING	XP	Att	%	FG	ATt	%
O'Donoghue	48	51	94	23	35	66

PHILADELPHIA EAGLES

RUSHING

Last Name	No.	Yds	Avg	TD
Montgomery	201	789	3.9	2
Oliver	72	263	3.7	0
Haddix	48	130	2.7	1
M. Williams	33	83	2.5	0
Hardy	14	41	2.9	0
Pisarcik	7	19	2.7	2
Jaworski	5	18	3.6	1
Quick	1	-5	-5.0	0

RECEIVING

Last Name	No.	Yds	Avg	TD
Spagnola	65	701	10.8	1
Quick	61	1052	17.2	9
Montgomery	60	501	8.4	0
Haddix	33	231	7.0	0
Oliver	32	142	4.4	0
Woodruff	30	484	16.1	3
Jackson	26	398	15.3	1
Kab	9	102	11.3	3
M. Williams	7	47	6.7	0
Hoover	6	143	23.8	2
Hardy	2	22	11.0	0

PUNT RETURNS

Last Name	No.	Yds	Avg	TD
Cooper	40	250	6.3	0

KICKOFF RETURNS

Last Name	No.	Yds	Avg	TD
Hayes	22	441	20.0	0
Cooper	17	299	17.6	0
Waters	13	319	24.5	1
Hardy	1	20	20.0	0
Everett	3	40	13.3	0
Ellis	2	25	12.5	0
Strauthers	1	12	12.0	0

PASSING — PUNTING — KICKING

PASSING	Att	Cmp	%	Yds	Yd/Att	TD	Int-	%	RK
Jaworski	427	234	55	2754	6.5	16	14-	3	11
Pisarcik	176	96	55	1036	5.9	3	3-	2	
Montgomery	2	0	0	0	0.0	0	0-	0	
May	1	1	100	33	33.0	0	0-	0	

PUNTING	No	Avg
Horan	92	42.2

KICKING	XP	Att	%	FG	Att	%
McFadden	26	27	96	30	37	81

CHICAGO BEARS 10-6-0 Mike Ditka

Scores of Each Game		
34	TAMPA BAY	14
27	DENVER	0
9	Green Bay	7
9	Seattle	38
14	DALLAS	23
20	NEW ORLEANS	7
21	St.Louis	38
44	Tampa Bay	9
16	MINNESOTA	7
17	L.A.RAIDERS	6
13	L.A.Rams	29
16	DETROIT	14
34	Minnesota	3
7	San Diego	20
14	GREEN BAY	20
30	Detroit	13

Use Name	Pos.	Hgt	Wgt	Age	Int	Pts
Jim Covert	OT	6'4"	283	24		
Andy Frederick	OT	6'6"	265	30		
Keith Van Horne	OT	6'6"	275	26		
Tom Andrews	OT-C	6'4"	261	22		
Kurt Becker	OG	6'5"	270	25		
Mark Bortz	OG	6'6"	271	23		
Rob Fada	OG	6'2"	265	23		
Stefan Humphries	OG	6'3"	265	22		
Jay Hilgenberg	C	6'3"	255	25		
Richard Dent	DE	6'5"	253	23		
Mike Hartenstine	DE	6'3"	258	31		
Tyrone Keys	DE	6'7"	267	24		
Dan Hampton	DT	6'5"	266	26		
Steve McMichael	DT	6'2"	260	26		
Jim Osborne	DT	6'3"	259	34		
Brian Cabral	LB	6'	224	28		
Al Harris	LB	6'5"	250	27	1	
Wilber Marshall	LB	6'1"	225	22		
Dan Rains	LB	6'1"	220	28		
Ron Rivera	LB	6'3"	244	22		
Mike Singletary	LB	6'	230	25	1	
Otis Wilson	LB	6'2"	231	26		
Todd Bell	DB	6'1"	207	25	4	6
Jack Cameron	DB	6'	182	22		
Dave Duerson	DB	6'1"	202	23	1	
Gary Fencik	DB	6'1"	197	30	5	
Jeff Fisher	DB	5'11"	195	25		
Leslie Frazier	DB	6'	189	25	5	
Shaun Gayle	DB	5'11"	191	22	1	
Kevin Potter	DB	5'10"	188	24		
Mike Richardson	DB	6'	188	23	2	
Terry Schmidt	DB	6'	185	32	1	
Steve Fuller	QB	6'4"	195	27		6
Greg Landry	QB	6'4"	210	37		6
Rusty Lisch	QB	6'3"	215	27		
Jim McMahon	QB	6'1"	187	25		12
Dennis Gentry	HB	5'8"	181	25		6
Anthony Hutchison	HB	5'10"	186	23		6
Walter Payton	HB	5'11"	202	30		66
Donald Jordan	FB	6'	210	22		
Matt Suhey	FB	5'11"	217	26		36
Calvin Thomas	FB	5'11"	235	24		6
Brad Anderson	WR	6'2"	196	23		6
Brian Baschnagel	WR	6'	193	30		
Willie Gault	WR	6'	178	23		36
Dennis McKinnon	WR	6'1"	185	23		18
Pat Dunsmore	TE	6'3"	237	24		6
Mitch Krenk	TE	6'2"	225	24		
Emery Moorehead	TE	6'2"	225	30		6
Jay Saldi	TE	6'3"	230	29		
Dave Finzer	K	6'1"	195	25		
Bob Thomas	K	5'10"	175	32		101

Ken Margerum - Knee Injury
Rickey Watts - Injury

GREEN BAY PACKERS 8-8-0 Forrest Gregg

Scores of Each Game		
24	ST.LOUIS	23
7	L.A.Raiders	28
7	CHICAGO	9
6	Dallas	20
27	Tampa Bay	*30
28	SAN DIEGO	34
14	Denver	17
24	SEATTLE	30
41	DETROIT	9
23	New Orleans	13
45	MINNESOTA	17
31	L.A.RAMS	6
28	Detroit	31
27	TAMPA BAY	14
20	Chicago	14
38	Minnesota	14

Use Name	Pos.	Hgt	Wgt	Age	Int	Pts
Ron Hallstrom	OT	6'6"	286	25		
Gary Hoffman	OT	6'7"	282	22		
Boyd Jones	OT	6'3"	265	23		
Greg Koch	OT	6'4"	276	29		
Karl Swanke	OT-C	6'6"	262	26		
Keith Uecker	OT	6'5"	270	24		
Dave Drechsler	OG	6'3"	264	24		
Tim Huffman	OG	6'5"	282	25		
Syd Kitson (to DAL)	OG	6'4"	264	25		
Mark Cannon	C	6'3"	258	22		
Larry McCarren	C	6'3"	248	32		
Blake Moore	C	6'5"	272	26		6
Robert Brown	DE	6'2"	250	23	1	6
Alphonso Carreker	DE	6'6"	260	22		
Donnie Humphrey	DE	6'3"	275	23		
Ezra Johnson	DE	6'4"	259	28		
Charles Martin	DE	6'4"'	270	25		
Terry Jones	NT	6'2"	253	27		
Bill Neill	NT	6'4"	267	25		
John Anderson	LB	6'3"	228	28	3	
George Cumby	LB	6'	224	28	1	
John Dorsey	LB	6'3"	235	24		
Mike Douglass	LB	6'	214	29		
Cliff Lewis	LB	6'1"	224	24		
Guy Prather	LB	6'2"	230	26		
Randy Scott	LB	6'1"	220	25		
Rich Wingo	LB	6'1"	230	28		
Tom Flynn	DB	6'	195	22	9	
Gary Hayes	DB	5'10"	180	27		
Estus Hood	DB	5'11"	189	28	1	
Daryll Jones	DB	6'	190	22		
Mark Lee	DB	5'11"	187	26	3	
Tim Lewis	DB	5'11"	191	22	7	6
Mike McLeod	DB	6'	180	26	1	
Mark Murphy	DB	6'2"	199	26	1	
Dwayne O'Steen	DB	6'1"	195	29		
Rich Campbell	QB	6'4"	219	25		
Lynn Dickey	QB	6'4"	210	34		18
Randy Wright	QB	6'2"	194	23		
Harlan Huckleby	HB	6'1"	199	26		
Eddie Lee Ivery	HB	6'1"	210	27		42
Del Rodgers	HB	5'10"	202	24		6
Jessie Clark	FB	6'	233	24		36
Ray Crouse	FB	5'11"	214	25		6
Gerry Ellis	FB	5'11"	225	26		36
Ron Cassidy	WR	6'	180	27		
Phillip Epps	WR	5'10"	165	24		18
John Jefferson	WR	6'1"	198	28		
James Lofton	WR	6'3"	197	28		42
Lenny Taylor	WR	5'10"	179	23		
Henry Childs	TE	6'2"	225	33		
Paul Coffman	TE	6'3"	225	28		54
Gary Lewis	TE	6'5"	234	25		
Ed West	TE	6'1"	242	23		30
Al Del Greco	K	5'10"	190	22		61
Eddie Garcia	K	5'8"	178	25		23
Bucky Scribner	K	6'	202	24		

Leotis Harris - Knee Injury
Mike McCoy - Leg Injury
Ken Walter - Ankle Injury
Scott Brunner - Knee Injury

TAMPA BAY BUCCANEERS 6-10-0 John McKay

Scores of Each Game		
14	Chicago	34
13	New Orleans	17
21	DETROIT	17
14	N.Y.Giants	17
30	GREEN BAY	*27
35	MINNESOTA	31
7	Detroit	*13
9	CHICAGO	44
20	Kansas City	24
24	Minnesota	27
20	N.Y.GIANTS	17
17	San Francisco	24
33	L.A.RAMS	34
14	Green Bay	27
23	ATLANTA	6
41	N.Y.JETS	21

Use Name	Pos.	Hgt	Wgt	Age	Int	Pts
Ron Heller	OT	6'6"	270	22		
Ken Kaplan	OT	6'4"	270	24		
Gene Sanders	OT	6'3"	285	27		
Kelly Thomas	OT	6'6"	270	23		
Glenn Bujnoch	OG	6'5"	265	30		
Steve Courson	OG	6'1"	270	28		
Sean Farrell	OG	6'3"	260	24		
Randy Grimes	OG-C	6'4"	265	24		
Noah Jackson	OG	6'2"	265	33		
Steve Wilson	C	6'3"	270	30		
Byron Braggs	DE	6'4"	290	24		
John Cannon	DE	6'5"	260	24	1	
Phil Darns	DE	6'3"	245	25		
Brison Manor (from DEN)	DE	6'4"	248	32		
Lee Roy Selmon	DE	6'3"	250	29		
David Logan	NT	6'2"	250	27	1	6
Karl Morgan	NT	6'1"	255	23		
Scott Brantley	LB	6'1"	230	25	3	
Keith Browner	LB	6'5"	240	22		
Jeff Davis	LB	6'	230	24	1	
Hugh Green	LB	6'2"	225	25		
Cecil Johnson	LB	6'2"	235	29		
Danny Spradlin	LB	6'1"	235	25		
Robert Thompson	LB	6'3"	230	24		
Chris Washington	LB	6'4"	225	22		
Richard Wood	LB	6'2"	230	31		
Fred Acorn	DB	5'10"	180	23	1	
Cedric Brown	DB	6'1"	200	30	1	
Jeremiah Castille	DB	5'10"	175	23	3	
Randy Clark	DB	6'	204	23		
Mark Cotney	DB	6'	205	32	5	
Craig Curry	DB	6'	187	23		
Maurice Harvey	DB	5'10"	187	28		
John Holt	DB	5'11"	180	25	1	
Beasley Reece	DB	6'1"	195	30	1	
Norris Thomas	DB	5'11"	180	30		
Mike Washington	DB	6'3"	200	31		
Steve DeBerg	QB	6'2"	205	30		12
Blair Kiel	QB	6'	200	22		
Jack Thompson	QB	6'3"	220	28		
Leon Bright	HB	5'9"	192	29		
Scott Dierking	HB-FB	5'11"	225	29		6
Michael Morton	HB	5'8"	180	24		
James Owens	HB	5'11"	200	29		6
Adger Armstrong	FB	6'	225	27		30
Melvin Carver	FB	5'11"	225	25		
George Peoples	FB	6'	215	24		
James Wilder	FB	6'3"	225	26		78
Theo Ball	WR	6'	195	30		
Gerald Carter	WR	6'1"	190	27		30
Dwayne Dixon	WR	6'1"	205	22		
Kevin House	WR	6'1"	185	26		30
Jerry Bell	TE	6'5"	230	25		24
Jay Carroll	TE	6'4"	230	22		6
Jimmie Giles	TE	6'3"	240	29		12
Mark Witte	TE	6'3"	235	24		
Obed Ariri	K	5'8"	170	28		95
Frank Garcia	K	6'	205	27		

Andre Tyler - Shoulder Injury
Jeff Komlo - Back Injury
Gene Branton - Hamstring Injury
Don Swafford - Back Injury
Rick Mallory - Ankle Injury

DETROIT LIONS 4-11-1 Monte Clark

Scores of Each Game		
27	SAN FRANCISCO	30
27	Atlanta	*24
17	Tampa Bay	21
28	MINNESOTA	29
24	San Diego	27
7	DENVER	28
13	TAMPA BAY	*7
16	Minnesota	14
9	Green Bay	41
23	PHILADELPHIA	23
14	Washington	28
14	Chicago	16
31	GREEN BAY	28
17	Seattle	38
3	L.A.RAIDERS	24
13	CHICAGO	30

Use Name	Pos.	Hgt	Wgt	Age	Int	Pts
Chris Dieterich	OT-OG	6'3"	260	26		
Keith Dorney	OT	6'5"	260	26		
Donald Laster	OT	6'5"	278	25		
Rich Strenger	OT	6'7"	276	24		
Homer Elias	OG	6'3"	255	29		
Don Greco	OG	6'3"	265	25		
Larry Lee	OG-C	6'2"	260	24		
Amos Fowler	C	6'3"	253	28		
David Jones	C	6'2"	260	22		
Steve Mott	C	6'3"	265	23		
Mike Cofer	DE	6'5"	245	24		
William Gay	DE	6'5"	255	29		
Curtis Green	DE	6'3"	258	27		
Steve Baack	DT-DE	6'4"	260	23		
Doug English	DT	6'5"	258	31		
Martin Moss	DT	6'4"	252	25		
Eric Williams	DT	6'4"	260	22		
Roosevelt Barnes	LB	6'2"	228	26		
Garry Cobb	LB	6'2"	227	27		
August Curley	LB	6'3"	226	24		
Kirk Dodge	LB	6'1"	231	22		
Steve Doig	LB	6'2"	245	24		
Ken Fantetti	LB	6'2"	232	27	1	
Angelo King	LB	6'1"	222	26		
Terry Tautolo	LB	6'2"	227	30		
Jimmy Williams	LB	6'3"	230	23		
William Frizzell	DB	6'2"	195	21		
William Graham	DB	5'11"	191	24	3	
Alvin Hall	DB	5'10"	184	26	2	
Demetrious Johnson	DB	5'11"	190	23		
Al Latimer	DB	5'11"	181	26		
Bruce McNorton	DB	5'11"	175	25	2	
Bobby Watkins	DB	5'10"	184	24	6	
Gardner Williams	DB	6'2"	199	22		
Gary Danielson	QB	6'2"	196	32		24
Eric Hipple	QB	6'2"	196	26		
Mike Machurek	QB	6'1"	205	24		
John Witkowski	QB	6'1"	200	22		
Ken Jenkins	HB	5'8"	184	25		6
Billy Sims	HB	6'	212	28		30
Dexter Bussey	FB	6'1"	210	32		
Dave D'Addio	FB	6'1"	230	23		
James Jones	FB	6'2"	228	23		48
Mike Meade	FB	5'11"	224	24		
Carl Bland	WR	5'11"	180	23		
Jeff Chadwick	WR	6'3"	190	23		18
Pete Mandley	WR	5'10"	191	23		
Robbie Martin	WR	5'8"	177	25		
Mark Nichols	WR	6'2"	208	24		6
Leonard Thompson	WR	5'11"	192	32		36
David Lewis	TE	6'3"	230	23		18
Reese McCall	TE	6'7"	245	28		
Rob Rubick	TE	6'3"	234	23		6
Mike Black	K	6'1"	197	23		
Eddie Murray	K	5'10"	175	28		91

MINNESOTA VIKINGS 3-13-0 Les Steckel

Scores of Each Game		
13	SAN DIEGO	42
17	Philadelphia	19
27	ATLANTA	20
29	Detroit	28
12	SEATTLE	20
31	Tampa Bay	35
20	L.A.Raiders	23
14	DETROIT	16
7	Chicago	16
27	TAMPA BAY	24
17	Green Bay	45
21	Denver	42
3	CHICAGO	34
17	WASHINGTON	31
7	San Francisco	51
14	GREEN BAY	38

Use Name	Pos.	Hgt	Wgt	Age	Int	Pts
Matt Hernandez	OT	6'6"	260	22		
Tim Irwin	OT	6'6"	285	25		
Steve Riley	OT	6'6"	260	31		
Terry Tausch	OT	6'5"	275	25		
Malcolm Carson	OG	6'2"	260	24		
Robert Cobb	OG-OT	6'2"	260	22		
Bill Dugan	OG	6'4"	271	25		
Wes Hamilton	OG	6'3"	268	31		
Jim Hough	OG	6'2"	267	28		
Curtis Rouse	OG	6'3"	305	24		
Ron Sams	OG	6'3"	255	23		
Grant Feasel (from IND)	C	6'7"	278	24		
Hasson Arbubakrr	DE	6'4"	250	23		
Neil Elshire	DE	6'6"	260	26		
Randy Holloway (to STL)	DE	6'5"	255	29		
Doug Martin	DE-NT	6'3"	258	27		
Mark Mullaney	DE	6'6"	242	31		
Ruben Vaughn	DE	6'2"	260	28		
John Haines	NT	6'6"	260	22		
Charles Johnson	NT	6'3"	275	32		
Gregory Smith	NT	6'3"	261	24		
Paul Sverchek	NT	6'3"	252	23		
Walker Lee Ashley	LB	6'	240	24		
Matt Blair	LB	6'5"	235	33		
Dennis Fowlkes	LB	6'2"	235	23		
Dennis Johnson	LB	6'3"	235	26		
Chris Martin	LB	6'2"	230	23		6
Fred McNeill	LB	6'2"	230	32	1	
Robin Sendlein	LB	6'3"	224	25		
Mark Stewart	LB	6'3"	232	24		
Scott Studwell	LB	6'2"	230	30	1	
Rufus Bess	DB	5'9"	185	28	3	
Joey Browner	DB	6'2"	205	24	1	6
Jeff Colter	DB	5'10"	171	23		
Marcellus Greene	DB	6'	185	26		
Tom Hannon	DB	5'11"	193	29	1	
Carl Lee	DB	6'	185	23	1	
John Swain	DB	6'1"	195	24	2	
Willie Teal	DB	5'10"	195	26	1	6
Dan Wagoner (from DET)	DB	5'10"	180	24		
Tommy Kramer	QB	6'2"	205	29		6
Archie Manning	QB	6'3"	211	35		
Wade Wilson	QB	6'3"	210	25		
Ted Brown	HB	5'10"	208	27		36
Darrin Nelson	HB	5'9"	185	25		24
Maurice Turner	HB-FB	5'11"	200	23		
Alfred Anderson	FB	6'1"	213	23		18
David Nelson	FB	6'2"	230	23		
Allen Rice	FB	5'10"	198	22		12
Dwight Collins	WR	6'1"	208	23		
Mike Jones	WR	5'11"	180	24		6
Terry LeCount	WR	5'10"	180	28		
Leo Lewis	WR	5'8"	170	27		24
Billy Waddy	WR	5'11"	190	30		
Sammy White	WR	5'11"	195	30		6
Don Hasselbeck	TE	6'7"	245	29		
Steve Jordan	TE	6'4"	230	23		18
Mike Mularkey	TE	6'4"	245	22		12
Joe Senser	TE	6'4"	238	28		
Greg Coleman	K	6'	178	29		
Jan Stenerud	K	6'2"	190	41		90

Brent Boyd - Knee Injury
Bob Bruer - Knee Injury
Keith Nord - Achilles Tendon Injury

* Overtime

CHICAGO BEARS

RUSHING

Last Name	No.	Yds	Avg	TD
Payton	381	1684	4.4	11
Suhey	124	424	3.4	4
McMahon	39	276	7.1	2
C. Thomas	40	186	4.4	1
Lisch	18	121	6.7	0
Fuller	15	89	5.9	1
Gentry	21	79	3.8	1
Jordan	11	70	6.4	0
Hutchison	14	39	2.8	1
McKinnon	2	12	6.0	0
Landry	2	1	0.5	1
Baschnagel	1	0	0.0	0
Finzer	2	0	0.0	0
Moorehead	1	-2	-2.0	0

RECEIVING

Last Name	No.	Yds	Avg	TD
Payton	45	368	8.2	0
Suhey	42	312	7.4	2
Gault	34	587	17.3	6
Moorehead	29	497	17.1	1
McKinnon	29	431	14.9	3
Dunsmore	9	106	11.8	1
Saldi	9	90	10.0	0
C. Thomas	9	39	4.3	0
Baschnagel	6	53	8.8	0
Gentry	4	29	7.3	0
Anderson	3	77	25.7	1
Krenk	2	31	15.5	0
McMahon	1	42	42.0	0
Cameron	1	13	13.0	0
Cabral	1	7	7.0	0
Hutchison	1	7	7.0	0
Jordan	1	6	6.0	0

PUNT RETURNS

Last Name	No.	Yds	Avg	TD
Fisher	57	492	8.6	0
McKinnon	5	62	12.4	0
Duerson	1	4	4.0	0

KICKOFF RETURNS

Last Name	No.	Yds	Avg	TD
Cameron	26	485	18.7	0
Gentry	11	209	19.0	0
Jordan	5	62	12.4	0
Duerson	4	95	23.8	0
Bell	2	33	16.5	0
Gault	1	12	12.0	0

PASSING — PUNTING — KICKING

PASSING	Att	Cmp	%	Yds	Yd/Att	TD	Int-	%	RK
McMahon	143	85	59	1146	8.0	8	2-	1	2
Lisch	85	43	51	413	4.9	0	6-	7	
Fuller	78	53	68	595	7.6	3	0-	0	
Landry	20	11	55	199	10.0	1	3-	15	
Payton	8	3	38	47	5.9	2	1-	13	
Baschnagel	2	1	50	7	3.5	0	0-	0	
Suhey	1	0	0	0	0.0	0	0-	0	

PUNTING	No	Avg
Finzer	83	40.1

KICKING	XP	Att	%	FG	Att	%
B. Thomas	35	37	95	22	28	79

GREEN BAY PACKERS

RUSHING

Last Name	No.	Yds	Avg	TD
Ellis	123	581	4.7	4
Ivery	99	552	5.6	6
Clark	87	375	4.3	4
Crouse	53	169	3.2	0
Huckleby	35	145	4.1	0
Rodgers	25	94	3.8	0
Lofton	10	82	8.2	0
Wright	8	11	1.4	0
Dickey	18	6	0.3	3
Campbell	2	2	1.0	0
West	1	2	2.0	1

RECEIVING

Last Name	No.	Yds	Avg	TD
Lofton	62	1361	22.0	7
Coffman	43	562	13.1	9
Ellis	36	312	8.7	2
Clark	29	234	8.1	2
Epps	26	435	16.7	3
Jefferson	26	339	13.0	0
Ivery	19	141	7.4	1
Crouse	9	93	10.3	1
Huckleby	8	65	8.1	0
West	6	54	9.0	4
Rodgers	5	56	11.2	0
Childs	4	32	8.0	0
G. Lewis	4	29	7.3	0
Cassidy	2	16	8.0	0
Moore	1	3	3.0	1
Taylor	1	8	8.0	0

PUNT RETURNS

Last Name	No.	Yds	Avg	TD
Epps	29	199	6.9	0
Flynn	15	128	8.5	0
Hayes	4	24	6.0	0
Murphy	0	0	—	0

KICKOFF RETURNS

Last Name	No.	Yds	Avg	TD
Rodgers	39	843	21.6	1
Epps	12	232	19.3	0
Huckleby	14	261	18.6	0
D. Jones	1	19	19.0	0
Prather	1	7	7.0	0

PASSING — PUNTING — KICKING

PASSING	Att	Cmp	%	Yds	Yd/Att	TD	Int-	%	RK
Dickey	401	237	59	3195	8.0	25	19-	5	6
Wright	62	27	44	310	5.0	2	6-	10	
Campbell	38	16	42	218	5.7	3	5-	13	
Ellis	4	1	25	17	4.3	0	0-	0	

PUNTING	No	Avg
Scribner	85	42.3

KICKING	XP	Att	%	FG	Att	%
Del Greco	34	34	100	9	12	75
Garcia	14	15	93	3	9	33

TAMPA BAY BUCCANEERS

RUSHING

Last Name	No.	Yds	Avg	TD
Wilder	407	1544	3.8	13
DeBerg	28	59	2.1	2
Carver	11	44	4.0	0
J. Thompson	5	35	7.0	0
Armstrong	10	34	3.4	2
Morton	16	27	1.7	0
Carter	1	16	16.0	0
Dierking	3	14	4.7	0
Peoples	1	2	2.0	0
Owens	1	1	1.0	0

RECEIVING

Last Name	No.	Yds	Avg	TD
Wilder	85	685	8.1	0
House	76	1005	13.2	5
Carter	60	816	13.6	5
J. Bell	29	397	13.7	4
Giles	24	310	12.9	2
T. Bell	22	350	15.9	0
Armstrong	22	180	8.2	3
Dixon	5	69	13.8	0
Carroll	5	50	10.0	1
Carver	3	27	9.0	0
Owens	2	13	6.5	1
Dierking	1	5	5.0	0

PUNT RETURNS

Last Name	No.	Yds	Avg	TD
Bright	23	173	7.5	0
Holt	7	19	2.7	0
T. Bell	3	8	2.7	0

KICKOFF RETURNS

Last Name	No.	Yds	Avg	TD
Morton	38	835	22.0	0
Owens	8	168	21.0	0
Bright	16	300	18.8	0
Wood	5	43	8.6	0
Spradlin	1	5	5.0	0

PASSING — PUNTING — KICKING

PASSING	Att	Cmp	%	Yds	Yd/Att	TD	Int-	%	RK
DeBerg	509	308	61	3554	7.0	19	18-	4	8
Thompson	52	25	48	337	6.5	2	5-	10	
Wilder	1	1	100	16	16.0	1	0-	0	
Garcia	1	0	0	0	0.0	0	0-	0	

PUNTING	No	Avg
Garcia	68	41.9

KICKING	XP	Att	%	FG	Att	%
Ariri	38	40	95	19	26	73

DETROIT LIONS

RUSHING

Last Name	No.	Yds	Avg	TD
Sims	130	687	5.3	5
J. Jones	137	532	3.9	3
Jenkins	78	358	4.6	1
Danielson	41	218	5.3	3
Bussey	32	91	2.8	0
D'Addio	7	46	6.6	0
Witkowski	7	33	4.7	0
Nichols	3	27	9.0	0
Martin	1	14	14.0	0
Chadwick	1	12	12.0	1
Machurek	1	9	9.0	0
Hipple	2	3	1.5	0
Black	3	-6	-2.0	0
Thompson	3	-7	-2.3	0

RECEIVING

Last Name	No.	Yds	Avg	TD
J. Jones	77	662	8.6	5
L. Thompson	50	773	15.5	6
Chadwick	37	540	14.6	2
Nichols	34	744	21.9	1
Sims	31	239	7.7	0
Jenkins	21	246	11.7	0
Lewis	16	236	14.8	3
Rubick	14	188	13.4	1
Bussey	9	63	7.0	0
Mandley	3	38	12.7	0
McCall	3	15	5.0	0
Danielson	1	22	22.0	1
D'Addio	1	12	12.0	0
Martin	1	9	9.0	0

PUNT RETURNS

Last Name	No.	Yds	Avg	TD
Martin	25	210	8.4	0
Hall	7	30	4.3	0
Jenkins	1	1	1.0	0
Mandley	2	0	0.0	0
Johnson	1	0	0.0	0

KICKOFF RETURNS

Last Name	No.	Yds	Avg	TD
Jenkins	18	396	22.0	0
Hall	19	385	20.3	0
Mandley	22	390	17.7	0
Martin	10	144	14.4	0
Meade	4	32	8.0	0
D'Addio	1	0	0.0	0

PASSING — PUNTING — KICKING

PASSING	Att	Cmp	%	Yds	Yd/Att	TD	Int-	%	RK
Danielson	410	252	62	3076	7.5	17	15-	4	7
Hipple	38	16	42	246	6.5	1	1-	3	
Witkowski	34	13	38	210	6.2	0	0-	0	
Machurek	43	14	33	193	4.5	0	0-	0	

PUNTING	No	Avg
Black	76	41.6

KICKING	XP	Att	%	FG	Att	%
Murray	31	31	100	20	27	74

MINNESOTA VIKINGS

RUSHING

Last Name	No.	Yds	Avg	TD
Anderson	201	773	3.8	2
Brown	98	442	4.5	3
Dar. Nelson	80	406	5.1	3
Rice	14	58	4.1	1
Jones	4	45	11.3	0
Manning	11	42	3.8	0
Wilson	9	30	3.3	0
Waddy	3	24	8.0	0
Coleman	2	11	5.5	0
Lewis	2	11	5.5	0
Kramer	15	9	0.6	0
Jordan	1	4	4.0	1
Dav. Nelson	1	3	3.0	0
Collins	3	-14	-4.7	0

RECEIVING

Last Name	No.	Yds	Avg	TD
Lewis	47	830	17.7	4
Brown	46	349	7.6	3
Jones	38	591	15.6	1
Jordan	38	414	10.9	2
Dar. Nelson	27	162	6.0	1
White	21	399	19.0	1
Anderson	17	102	6.0	1
Senser	15	110	7.3	0
Mularkey	14	134	9.6	2
Collins	11	143	13.0	1
Rice	4	59	14.8	1
Kramer	1	20	20.0	1
Hasselbeck	1	10	10.0	0
LeCount	1	14	14.0	0

PUNT RETURNS

Last Name	No.	Yds	Avg	TD
Dar. Nelson	23	180	7.8	0
Lewis	4	31	7.8	0
Bess	2	9	4.5	0
Teal	1	0	0.0	0
Waddy	1	-3	-3.0	0

KICKOFF RETURNS

Last Name	No.	Yds	Avg	TD
Dar. Nelson	39	891	22.8	0
Anderson	30	639	21.3	0
Waddy	3	64	21.3	0
Lewis	1	31	31.0	0
Bess	3	47	15.7	0
Smith	2	26	13.0	0
Rice	3	34	11.3	0
Rouse	2	22	11.0	0
Turner	2	21	10.5	0
Dav. Nelson	1	0	0.0	0

PASSING — PUNTING — KICKING

PASSING	Att	Cmp	%	Yds	Yd/Att	TD	Int-	%	RK
Kramer	236	124	53	1678	7.1	9	10-	4	13
Wilson	195	102	52	1019	5.2	5	11-	6	17
Manning	94	52	55	545	5.8	2	3-	3	
Anderson	7	3	43	95	13.6	2	1-	14	
Coleman	1	0	0	0	0.0	0	0-	0	

PUNTING	No	Avg
Coleman	82	42.4

KICKING	XP	Att	%	FG	Att	%
Stenerud	30	31	97	20	23	87

SAN FRANCISCO 49ERS 15-1-0 Bill Walsh

Scores of Each Game		
30	Detroit	27
37	WASHINGTON	31
30	NEW ORLEANS	20
21	Phiadelphia	9
14	ATLANTA	5
31	N.Y.Giants	10
17	PITTSBURGH	20
34	Houston	21
33	L.A.Rams	0
23	CINCINNATI	17
41	Cleveland	7
24	TAMPA BAY	17
35	New Orleans	3
35	Atlanta	17
51	MINNESOTA	7
19	L.A.RAMS	16

Use Name	Pos.	Hgt	Wgt	Age	Int	Pts
Keith Fahnhorst	OT	6'6"	273	32		
Allan Kennedy	OT	6'7"	275	26		
Bubba Paris	OT	6'6"	295	23		
Billy Shields	OT	6'7"	279	31		
John Ayers	OG	6'5"	265	31		
Randy Cross	OG	6'3"	265	30		
Guy McIntyre	OG	6'3"	271	23		
Jesse Sapolu	OG	6'4"	260	23		
John Macauley	C	6'3"	254	25		
Fred Quillan	C	6'5"	266	28		
Dwaine Board	DE	6'5"	250	27		
Fred Dean	DE	6'3"	232	32		
Jeff Stover	DE	6'5"	275	26		
Jim Stuckey	DE	6'4"	251	26		
Michael Carter	NT	6'2"	281	23		
Gary Johnson (from SD)	NT	6'2"	261	32		8
Louis Kelcher	NT	6'5"	310	31		
Lawrence Pillers	NT-DE	6'3"	250	31		
Manu Tuiasosopo	NT	6'3"	252	27		
Dan Bunz	LB	6'4"	225	28	1	
Riki Ellison	LB	6'2"	220	24		
Jim Fahnhorst	LB	6'4"	230	25	2	
Ron Ferrari	LB	6'	212	25		
Milt McColl	LB	6'6"	230	25		
Blanchard Montgomery	LB	6'2"	236	23		
Jack Reynolds	LB	6'1"	232	36		
Todd Shell	LB	6'4"	225	22	3	6
Keena Turner	LB	6'2"	219	25	4	
Michael Walter	LB	6'3"	238	23		
Mario Clark	DB	6'2"	195	30	1	
Jeff Fuller	DB	6'2"	216	22	1	
Dwight Hicks	DB	6'1"	189	28	3	
Tom Holmoe	DB	6'2"	180	24		
Ronnie Lott	DB	6'	199	25	4	
Dana McLemore	DB	5'10"	183	24	2	12
Carlton Williamson	DB	6'	204	26	2	
Eric Wright	DB	6'1"	180	25	2	
Matt Cavanaugh	QB	6'2"	212	27		
Joe Montana	QB	6'2"	195	28		12
Derrick Harmon	HB	5'10"	202	21		6
Carl Monroe	HB	5'8"	166	24		6
Wendell Tyler	HB	5'10"	200	29		54
Roger Craig	FB	6'	222	24		60
Bill Ring	FB	5'10"	205	27		18
Dwight Clark	WR	6'4"	215	27		36
Renaldo Nehemiah	WR	6'1"	183	25		12
Freddie Solomon	WR	5'11"	185	31		66
Mike Wilson	WR	6'3"	210	25		6
Earl Cooper	TE	6'2"	227	25		24
Al Dixon	TE	6'5"	235	30		
Russ Francis	TE	6'6"	242	31		12
John Frank	TE	6'3"	225	22		6
Tom Orosz	K	6'1"	204	24		
Max Runager	K	6'1"	189	28		
Ray Wersching	K	5'11"	210	34		131

Allen Fleming - Knee Injury
John Harty - Foot Injury

Tim Collier - Achilles Tendon Injury
Mark Bonner - Neck Injury
Danny Fulton - Shoulder Injury
Don Dow - Neck Injury

LOS ANGELES RAMS 10-6-0 John Robinson

Scores of Each Game		
13	DALLAS	20
20	CLEVELAND	17
14	Pittsburgh	24
24	Cincinnati	14
33	N.Y.GIANTS	12
28	ATLANTA	30
28	New Orleans	10
24	Atlanta	10
0	SAN FRANCISCO	33
16	St.Louis	13
29	CHICAGO	13
6	Green Bay	31
34	Tampa Bay	33
34	NEW ORLEANS	21
27	HOUSTON	16
16	San Francisco	19

Use Name	Pos.	Hgt	Wgt	Age	Int	Pts
Bill Bain	OT	6'4"	290	32		
Irv Pankey	OT	6'4"	267	25		
Jackie Slater	OT	6'4"	271	30		
Russ Bolinger	OG	6'5"	255	29		
Dennis Harrah	OG	6'5"	265	31		
Kent Hill	OG	6'5"	260	27		
Joe Shearin	OG	6'4"	250	24		
Doug Smith	C	6'3"	253	27		
Reggie Doss	DE	6'4"	263	27		
Gary Jeter	DE	6'4"	260	29		
Doug Reed	DE	6'3"	250	24		
Booker Reese (from TB)	DE	6'6"	260	24		
Jack Youngblood	DE	6'4"	242	34		
Charles DeJurnett	NT	6'4"	260	32		
Greg Meisner	NT	6'3"	253	25		
Shawn Miller	NT	6'4"	255	23		
George Andrews	LB	6'3"	225	28		
Ed Brady	LB	6'2"	228	24		
Jim Collins	LB	6'2"	230	26	2	
Carl Ekern	LB	6'3"	222	30		
Mark Jerue	LB	6'3"	229	24		
John Kamana	LB	6'	215	22		
Jim Laughlin	LB	6'	222	26		
Mike McDonald	LB	6'1"	235	26		
Mel Owens	LB	6'2"	224	25	1	
Norwood Vann	LB	6'1"	225	22		2
Mike Wilcher	LB	6'3"	235	24		
Jim Youngblood	LB	6'3"	231	34		
Nolan Cromwell	DB	6'1"	200	29	3	6
David Croudip	DB	5'8"	183	25		
Gary Green	DB	5'11"	191	28	3	
Eric Harris	DB	6'3"	202	29		
LeRoy Irvin	DB	5'11"	184	26	5	12
Johnnie Johnson	DB	6'1"	183	27	2	
Vince Newsome	DB	6'1"	179	23	1	
Ivory Sully	DB	6'	201	27		2
Steve Dils (from MIN)	QB	6'1"	191	28		
Vince Ferragamo	QB	6'3"	212	30		
Jeff Kemp	QB	6'	201	25		6
Eric Dickerson	HB	6'3"	220	23		84
A.J.Jones	HB	6'1"	202	25		
Mike Pleasant	HB	6'1"	195	26		
Barry Redden	HB-FB	5'10"	205	24		
Dwayne Crutchfield	FB	6'	235	24		12
Mike Guman	FB	6'2"	218	26		6
Ron Brown	WR	5'11"	181	23		24
Drew Hill	WR	5'9"	170	27		24
Henry Ellard	WR	5'11"	170	23		48
George Farmer	WR	5'10"	175	25		
Otis Grant	WR	6'3"	197	23		
Mike Barber	TE	6'3"	237	31		
Chris Faulkner	TE	6'4"	257	24		
David Hill	TE	6'2"	228	30		6
James McDonald	TE	6'5"	230	23		
Mike Lansford	K	6'	183	26		112
John Misko	K	6'5"	207	29		

Kirk Collins - Died of cancer
Doug Barnett - Knee Injury
Gary Kowalski - Knee Injury

NEW ORLEANS SAINTS 7-9-0 Bum Phillips

Scores of Each Game		
28	ATLANTA	36
17	TAMPA BAY	13
20	San Francisco	30
34	ST.LOUIS	24
27	Houston	10
7	Chicago	20
10	L.A.RAMS	28
27	Dallas	*30
16	Cleveland	14
13	GREEN BAY	23
17	Atlanta	13
27	PITTSBURGH	24
3	SAN FRANCISCO	35
21	L.A.Rams	34
21	CINCINNATI	24
10	N.Y.Giants	3

Use Name	Pos.	Hgt	Wgt	Age	Int	Pts
Stan Brock	OT	6'6"	285	26		
Angelo Fields	OT	6'6"	314	26		
Dave Lafary	OT	6'7"	285	29		
Chris Ward	OT	6'3"	267	28		
Kelvin Clark	OG	6'3"	273	28		
Brad Edelman	OG	6'6"	262	23		
Steve Korte	OG	6'2"	270	24		
Louis Oubre	OG	6'4"	272	26		
David Carter (from HOU)	OG-C	6'2"	275	30		
Joel Hilgenberg	C	6'3"	250	22		
John Hill	C	6'2"	260	34		
Jim Pietrzak	C	6'5"	260	31		
Bruce Clark	DE	6'3"	281	26	1	
Reggie Lewis	DE	6'2"	248	30		
Frank Warren	DE	6'4"	275	24		
Jim Wilks	DE	6'5"	265	26		
Tony Elliott	NT	6'2"	280	25		
James Geathers	NT	6'7"	267	24		
Derland Moore	NT	6'4"	273	32		
Don Thorpe	NT	6'4"	260	22		
James Haynes	LB	6'2"	230	24		
Rickey Jackson	LB	6'2"	239	26	1	
Jim Kovach	LB	6'2"	239	28	1	
Whitney Paul	LB	6'3"	220	28		
Scott Pelluer	LB	6'2"	227	25		
Glen Redd	LB	6'1"	231	26		
Dennis Winston	LB	6'1"	244	28	2	12
Jitter Fields	DB	5'8"	188	22		
Russell Gary	DB	5'11"	195	25		
Greg Harding	DB	6'2"	197	24		
Terry Hoage	DB	6'3"	197	22		
Bobby Johnson	DB	6'	187	24	1	
Rodney Lewis	DB	5'11"	186	25		
Johnnie Poe	DB	6'1"	194	25	1	
Frank Wattelet	DB	6'	185	25	2	12
Dave Waymer	DB	6'1"	188	26	4	
Ken Stabler	QB	6'3"	210	38		
Richard Todd	QB	6'2"	212	30		
Dave Wilson	QB	6'3"	210	25		
Tyrone Anthony	HB	5'11"	212	22		6
George Rogers	HB	6'2"	229	25		12
Jimmy Rogers	HB	5'10"	195	29		
Earl Campbell (from HOU)	FB	5'11"	233	29		6
Hokie Gajan	FB	5'11"	226	24		42
Tim Wilson	FB	6'3"	235	30		
Wayne Wilson	FB	6'3"	220	26		24
Kenny Duckett	WR	6'	179	24		
Eugene Goodlow	WR	6'2"	181	25		18
Jeff Groth	WR	5'10"	181	27		
Guido Merkens	WR-QB	6'1"	197	29		
Lindsay Scott	WR	6'1"	200	23		6
Tyrone Young	WR	6'6"	190	24		18
Hoby Brenner	TE	6'4"	245	25		36
Larry Hardy	TE	6'3"	245	28		6
Junior Miller	TE	6'4"	244	26		6
John Tice	TE	6'5"	242	24		6
Morten Andersen	K	6'2"	205	24		94
Brian Hansen	K	6'3"	218	23		

Michael Dellocono - Back Injury
Gary Lewis - Non-Football Illness

ATLANTA FALCONS 4-12-0 Dan Henning

Scores of Each Game		
36	New Orleans	28
24	DETROIT	*27
20	Minnesota	27
42	HOUSTON	10
5	San Francisco	14
30	L.A.Rams	28
7	N.Y.GIANTS	19
10	L.A.RAMS	24
10	Pittsburgh	35
14	Washington	27
13	NEW ORLEANS	17
7	CLEVELAND	23
14	Cincinnati	35
17	SAN FRANCISCO	35
6	Tampa Bay	23
26	PHILADELPHIA	10

Use Name	Pos.	Hgt	Wgt	Age	Int	Pts
Mike Kenn	OT	6'7"	266	28		
Brett Miller	OT	6'7"	285	25		
Eric Sanders	OT	6'7"	280	25		
Dan Dufour	OG	6'5"	280	23		
Joe Pellegrini	OG-C	6'4"	258	27		
R.C.Thielemann	OG	6'4"	262	29		
Mike Chapman	C-OG	6'4"	250	23		
John Scully	C	6'6"	255	26		
Jeff Van Note	C	6'2"	250	38		
Gary Burley	DE	6'3"	290	31		
Roy Harris	DE	6'2"	266	23		
Mike Pitts	DE	6'5"	268	23		
Jeff Yeates	DE	6'3"	257	33		
Dan Benish	DT	6'5"	265	22		
Rick Bryan	DT	6'4"	260	22		2
Andrew Provence	DT	6'3"	260	23		
Don Smith	DT	6'5"	270	27		
Thomas Benson	LB	6'2"	235	22		
Buddy Curry	LB	6'4"	228	26		
David Frye	LB	6'2"	213	23		
Jeff Jackson	LB	6'1"	228	22	1	6
Fulton Kuykendall	LB	6'5"	225	31		
Dave Levenick	LB	6'3"	220	25		
Rydell Malancon	LB	6'2"	219	22		
John Rade	LB	6'1"	225	24		
Al Richardson	LB	6'2"	222	26		
Johnny Taylor	LB	6'4"	239	24		
James Britt	DB	6'	185	23	1	
Bobby Butler	DB	5'11"	175	25	2	
Scott Case	DB	6'	178	22		2
Blane Gaison	DB	6'	185	26		
Steve Haworth	DB	5'11"	190	22		
Kenny Johnson	DB	5'10"	172	26	5	
Tom Pridemore	DB	5'10"	186	28	2	
Gerald Small	DB	5'11"	192	28	1	
David Archer	QB	6'2"	206	22		
Steve Bartkowski	QB	6'4"	218	31		
Mike Moroski	QB	6'4"	200	26		
Cliff Austin	HB	6'	190	24		
Lynn Cain	HB	6'1"	205	28		18
Sylvester Stamps	HB	5'7"	166	23		
Rodney Tate	HB	5'11"	190	25		
Tim Tyrrell	HB-FB	6'1"	201	23		
Allama Matthews	FB	6'2"	230	23		
Gerald Riggs	FB	6'1"	230	23		78
Stacey Bailey	WR	6'	157	24		36
Willie Curran	WR	5'10"	175	24		
Floyd Hodge	WR	6'	195	25		
Alfred Jackson	WR	5'11"	190	29		12
Billy Johnson	WR	5'9"	177	32		18
Perry Tuttle (from TB)	WR	6'	178	25		
Cliff Benson	TE	6'4"	234	23		
Arthur Cox	TE	6'2"	255	23		18
Mike Landrum	TE	6'2"	231	22		
Ralph Giacomarro	K	6'1"	192	23		
Mick Luckhurst	K	6'	183	26		91

William Andrews - Knee Injury
Stan Gay - Knee Injury

* Overtime

SAN FRANCISCO 49ERS

RUSHING

Last Name	No.	Yds	Avg	TD
Tyler	246	1262	5.1	7
Craig	155	649	4.2	7
D. Harmon	39	192	4.9	1
Ring	38	162	4.3	3
Montana	39	118	3.0	2
Solomon	6	72	12.0	1
Monroe	3	13	4.3	0
Cooper	3	13	4.3	0
Runager	1	-5	-5.0	0
Cavanaugh	4	-11	-2.8	0

RECEIVING

Last Name	No.	Yds	Avg	TD
Craig	71	675	9.5	3
D. Clark	52	880	16.9	6
Cooper	41	459	11.2	4
Solomon	40	737	18.4	10
Tyler	28	230	8.2	2
Francis	23	285	12.4	2
Nehemiah	18	357	19.8	2
Wilson	17	245	14.4	1
Monroe	11	139	12.6	1
Frank	7	60	8.6	1
Ring	3	10	3.3	0
Harmon	1	2	2.0	0

PUNT RETURNS

Last Name	No.	Yds	Avg	TD
McLemore	45	521	11.6	1

KICKOFF RETURNS

Last Name	No.	Yds	Avg	TD
Monroe	27	561	20.8	0
Harmon	13	357	27.5	0
McLemore	3	80	26.7	0
Ring	1	27	27.0	0
Wilson	1	14	14.0	0
Cooper	1	0	0.0	0
McIntyre	1	0	0.0	0

PASSING — PUNTING — KICKING

PASSING	Att	Cmp	%	Yds	Yd/Att	TD	Int-	%	RK
Montana	432	279	65	3630	8.4	28	10-	2	1
Cavanaugh	61	33	54	449	7.4	4	0-	0	
Harmon	2	0	0	0	0.0	0	0-	0	
D. Clark	1	0	0	0	0.0	0	0-	0	

PUNTING	No	Avg
Runager	56	41.8
Orosz	5	39.0

KICKING	XP	Att	%	FG	Att	%
Wersching	56	56	100	25	35	71

LOS ANGELES RAMS

RUSHING

Last Name	No.	Yds	Avg	TD
Dickerson	379	2105	5.6	14
Crutchfield	73	337	4.6	1
Redden	45	247	5.5	0
Kemp	34	153	4.5	1
Brown	2	25	12.5	0
Guman	1	2	2.0	0
Ferragamo	4	0	0.0	0
Ellard	3	-5	-1.7	0

RECEIVING

Last Name	No.	Yds	Avg	TD
Ellard	34	622	18.3	6
Da. Hill	31	300	9.7	1
Brown	23	478	20.8	4
Dickerson	21	139	6.6	0
Guman	19	161	8.5	0
Dr. Hill	14	390	27.9	4
Grant	9	64	7.1	0
Farmer	7	75	10.7	0
Barber	7	42	6.0	0
McDonald	4	55	13.8	0
Redden	4	39	9.8	0
Crutchfield	2	11	5.5	1
Faulkner	1	6	6.0	0

PUNT RETURNS

Last Name	No.	Yds	Avg	TD
Ellard	30	403	13.4	2
Irvin	9	83	9.2	0
Johnson	1	3	3.0	0

KICKOFF RETURNS

Last Name	No.	Yds	Avg	TD
Redden	23	530	23.0	0
Dr. Hill	26	543	20.9	0
Pleasant	2	48	24.0	0
Irvin	2	33	16.5	0
Ellard	2	24	12.0	0
Guman	1	43	43.0	1
Crutchfield	1	20	20.0	0
Sully	1	3	3.0	0

PASSING — PUNTING — KICKING

PASSING	Att	Cmp	%	Yds	Yd/Att	TD	Int-	%	RK
Kemp	284	143	50	2021	7.1	13	7-	3	9
Ferragamo	66	29	44	317	4.8	2	8-	12	
Dils	7	4	57	44	6.3	1	1-	14	
Dickerson	1	0	0	0	0.0	0	1-	100	

PUNTING	No	Avg
Misko	74	38.7

KICKING	XP	Att	%	FG	Att	%
Lansford	37	38	97	25	33	76

NEW ORLEANS SAINTS

RUSHING

Last Name	No.	Yds	Avg	TD
G. Rogers	239	914	3.8	2
Gajan	102	615	6.0	5
Campbell	146	468	3.2	4
W. Wilson	74	261	3.5	1
Todd	28	111	4.0	0
Anthony	20	105	5.3	1
T. Wilson	2	8	4.0	0
Goodlow	1	5	5.0	0
Stabler	1	-1	-1.0	0
Duckett	1	-3	-3.0	0
D. Wilson	3	-7	-2.3	0
Hansen	2	-27	-13.5	0

RECEIVING

Last Name	No.	Yds	Avg	TD
Gajan	35	288	8.2	2
Groth	33	487	14.8	0
W. Wilson	33	314	9.5	3
Young	29	597	20.6	3
Brenner	28	554	19.8	6
Goodlow	22	281	12.8	3
Scott	21	278	13.2	1
Anthony	12	113	9.4	0
G. Rogers	12	76	6.3	0
Miller	8	81	10.1	1
Tice	6	55	9.2	1
Hardy	4	50	12.5	1
Duckett	3	24	8.0	0
Campbell	3	27	9.0	0

PUNT RETURNS

Last Name	No.	Yds	Avg	TD
Fields	27	236	8.7	0
Groth	6	32	5.3	0

KICKOFF RETURNS

Last Name	No.	Yds	Avg	TD
Anthony	22	490	22.3	0
Duckett	29	580	20.0	0
Fields	19	356	18.7	0
W. Wilson	1	23	23.0	0
T. Wilson	1	16	16.0	0

PASSING — PUNTING — KICKING

PASSING	Att	Cmp	%	Yds	Yd/Att	TD	Int-	%	RK
Todd	312	161	52	2178	7.0	1	19-	6	15
D. Wilson	93	51	55	647	7.0	7	4-	4	
Stabler	70	33	47	339	4.8	2	5-	7	
Gajan	1	1	100	34	34.0	1	0-	0	

PUNTING	No	Avg
Hansen	69	43.8

KICKING	XP	Att	%	FG	Att	%
Andersen	34	34	100	20	27	74

ATLANTA FALCONS

RUSHING

Last Name	No.	Yds	Avg	TD
Riggs	353	1486	4.2	13
Cain	77	276	3.6	3
Moroski	21	98	4.7	0
Archer	6	38	6.3	0
Bartkowski	15	34	2.3	0
Hodge	2	17	8.5	0
Stamps	3	15	5.0	0
C. Benson	3	8	2.7	0
B. Johnson	3	8	2.7	0
Austin	4	7	1.8	0
Pridemore	1	7	7.0	0
Giacomarro	1	0	0.0	0

RECEIVING

Last Name	No.	Yds	Avg	TD
Bailey	67	1138	17.0	6
A. Jackson	52	731	14.1	2
Riggs	42	277	6.6	0
Cox	34	329	9.7	3
C. Benson	26	244	9.4	0
B. Johnson	24	371	15.5	3
Hodge	24	234	9.8	0
Cain	12	87	7.3	0
Landrum	6	66	11.0	0
Stamps	4	48	12.0	0
Curran	1	7	7.0	0
Matthews	1	7	7.0	0
Tuttle	1	7	7.0	0

PUNT RETURNS

Last Name	No.	Yds	Avg	TD
B. Johnson	15	152	10.1	0
K. Johnson	10	79	7.9	0
Curran	9	21	2.3	0

KICKOFF RETURNS

Last Name	No.	Yds	Avg	TD
Stamps	19	452	23.8	0
K. Johnson	19	359	18.9	0
Curran	11	219	19.9	0
Austin	4	77	19.3	0
B. Johnson	2	39	19.5	0
Tate	9	148	16.4	0
Gaison	1	15	15.0	0
Matthews	1	3	3.0	0
Malancon	1	0	0.0	0
Tyrrell	1	0	0.0	0

PASSING — PUNTING — KICKING

PASSING	Att	Cmp	%	Yds	Yd/Att	TD	Int-	%	RK
Bartkowski	269	181	67	2158	8.0	1	10-	4	4
Moroski	191	102	53	1207	6.3	2	9-	5	16
Archer	18	1	61	181	10.1	1	1-	6	

PUNTING	No	Avg
Giacomarro	68	42.0

KICKING	XP	Att	%	FG	Att	%
Luckhurst	31	31	100	20	27	74

1984 A.F.C. Moving with the Cover of Darkness

Al Davis' courtroom success stripped the N.F.L. of its ability to govern franchise shifts. The fallout was quick in coming. Bob Irsay was wooed by Indianapolis and Phoenix and decided to move his Colts to Indiana. The move was publicly announced only after the Colts had packed their goods and driven away in the middle of a spring night in Baltimore. While Indianapolis merited an N.F.L. team, Baltimore suffered the loss of a cultural pillar, a team which traditionally had been one of the league's strongest. As the 1984 season wore down, Phoenix almost lured the Philadelphia Eagles to Arizona. Only direct intervention by government officials kept the Eagles where they had played for more than 50 years.

EASTERN DIVISION

Miami Dolphins — An opening-day triumph over Washington launched the Dolphins on a season of white-hot excellence. The spotlight hugged the spectacular Miami passing game. In his second pro season, Dan Marino threw for touchdowns at a record clip. His quick delivery was matched by the quick feet of the Marks Brothers — Duper and Clayton, a brace of long-distance receivers. The offense scintillated despite David Overstreet's death in a car accident, Bob Kuechenberg's eye injury, and knee injuries to Andra Franklin and Eric Laakso. With the Killer Bee defense doing its share, the Dolphins blew away their first 11 foes before losing in overtime at San Diego. By then, Miami's fourth straight playoff trip was assured.

New England Patriots — Despite a 5-2 start, all was not well with the Paticts. Head coach Ron Meyer had angered his players with public criticism. The dissension came to a boil when Meyer fired defensive coordinator Rod Rust after a 44-22 loss to Miami. In the wake of the uproar, Meyer was fired and replaced by Raymond Berry. The new coach's first move was rehiring Rust. The Patriots won three of their first four games under Berry, but then dropped three straight to sabotage their playoff drive. Out of the disappointing season, the Patriots came up with a new starting quarterback in Tony Eason, an effective new runner in U.S.F.L. refugee Craig James, and a newly blossomed defensive star in Andre Tippett.

New York Jets — After last year's flop, the Jets unloaded players in wholesale fashion. The playoffs seemed far off in training camp with new men in key spots. The Jets shot out to a surprising 6-2 start, with veterans Freeman McNeil and Mark Gastineau leading their new mates. Pat Ryan settled comfortably into the quarterback job in the early drive. In mid-season, however, he suffered two concussions and lost his job to Ken O'Brien. At the same time, injuries decimated the secondary to a paper-thin state. The playoff hopes died in a six-game losing streak, which killed the optimism of October. A 41-21 loss at Tampa Bay ended the season on a sour note.

Indianapolis Colts — The Colts opened a new chapter by moving into the Hoosier Dome. Once they started playing, they looked exactly like the Baltimore Colts of recent years. The offense scored 10 points or less in half the games, with Frank Kush shuffling his quarterbacks like cards. Kush moved his best offensive lineman, Chris Hinton, from guard to tackle, then lost him to a broken leg in October. The hometown fans got a sobering view of their new team in a 50-17 defeat to the Patriots. When three straight losses followed, Kush resigned to take the coaching job of the U.S.F.L. Arizona team. Without Kush, the Colts kept their stride by losing at New England 16-10.

Buffalo Bills — The Bills lost games nonstop until mid-November. Sporting an 0-11 record, they welcomed the Dallas Cowboys to Rich Stadium. On the first play from scrimmage, rookie Greg Bell dashed 85 yards for a touchdown. With a quick lead in hand, the Buffalo defense stifled the Dallas offense and engineered a 14-3 upset. That victory was the high point of a brutally bad season. The offense suffered as Joe Cribbs jumped to the U.S.F.L., Frank Lewis retired, Jerry Butler injured a knee, and Joe Ferguson lost his effectiveness to ankle and arm woes. The offensive line and defensive secondary especially plagued coach Kay Stephenson.

CENTRAL DIVISION

Pittsburgh Steelers — Even as the old guard departed, Chuck Noll kept the Steelers atop the Central Division. Mel Blount retired, joined by Terry Bradshaw and his dead passing arm. Franco Harris was shockingly cut in the middle of a training-camp holdout for a better contract. On opening day, Jack Lambert severely injured a toe and missed most of the season. The Steelers absorbed the changes in stride in the A.F.C.'s weakest division. Although only 6-6 in mid-November, they still held a two-game lead over Cincinnati. By winning three of their remaining four games, the Steelers earned their third straight playoff ticket. With Lambert hurt, linebackers Robin Cole and Mike Merriweather emerged as leaders on defense. Veterans John Stallworth and Mike Webster starred on offense, joined by brilliant rookie receiver Louis Lipps. David Woodley began the year at quarterback, but when he suffered two concussions and a leg injury, Mark Malone stepped in and played well.

Cincinnati Bengals — The Bengals took awhile getting used to new coach Sam Wyche. Before he settled into his seat, the team had lost four of its first five games. Mid-season brought relief in games against Houston and Cleveland. A 22-20 victory over the Steelers on November 11 brought the Bengals within two games of the top, but even a strong finish would not gain the playoffs. Wyche kept his offense moving despite Dan Ross' departure to the U.S.F.L. and Pete Johnson's trade to San Diego. Ken Anderson suffered back and shoulder ills, giving Turk Schonert and rookie Boomer Esiason a chance to run the attack. A 52-21 victory over Buffalo in the finale fueled hope for the future.

Cleveland Browns — An opening-day debacle at Seattle made Brian Sipe's absence seem fatal. As the losses piled up, rumors flew as to coach Sam Rutigliano's job security. An October 7 game against New England brought brickbats crashing into the coach. Trailing 17-16, the Browns drove deep into Patriot territory. With 23 seconds left on the clock, Rutigliano eschewed a field goal to call a pass play. The Patriots promptly intercepted Paul McDonald's pass to end the game. After two more losses, Rutigliano was fired and replaced by assistant Marty Schottenheimer. With his defense holding firm, Schottenheimer coaxed four victories out of his men in the remaining eight games.

Houston Oilers — The Oilers added one Campbell and subtracted another. Hugh Campbell became head coach after a long career in Canada and one season in the U.S.F.L. In October, he sent Earl Campbell to New Orleans for a first-round draft pick, parting with the team's offensive workhorse since 1978. The new offensive hub was Warren Moon, a C.F.L. quarterback lured to Texas with a rich contract. The team's new look didn't prevent 10 losses in the first 10 games, with offense and defense sharing the blame. The offense did not run well, and the defense failed to rush enemy passers. The Oilers improved and won half of their final six games. Starring on offense were guard Mike Munchak and receiver Tim Smith.

WESTERN DIVISION

Denver Broncos — A 27-0 embarrassment at Chicago on September 9 was the only game the Broncos didn't win of their first dozen. The unexpected rise to the top came on the strong back of the defense. Even with Randy Gradishar retired and Bob Swenson injured, the defense created turnovers and evoked memories of the old Orange Crush defense. Veteran linebacker Tom

FINAL TEAM STATISTICS

OFFENSE

	BUFF.	CIN.	CLEV.	DEN.	HOU.	IND.	K.C.	L.A.	MIA.	N.E.	NY J	PIT.	S.D.	SEA.
FIRST DOWNS:														
Total	263	339	295	299	284	254	295	301	387	315	310	302	374	287
by Rushing	98	135	89	121	95	114	88	114	115	104	118	117	106	94
by Passing	149	179	180	152	164	117	178	162	243	186	176	167	240	171
by Penalty	16	25	26	26	25	23	29	25	29	25	16	18	28	22
RUSHING:														
Number	398	540	489	508	433	510	408	516	484	482	504	574	456	495
Yards	1643	2179	1696	2076	1656	2025	1527	1886	1918	2032	2189	2179	1654	1645
Average Yards	4.1	4.0	3.5	4.1	3.8	4.0	3.7	3.7	4.0	4.2	4.3	3.8	3.6	3.3
Touchdowns	9	18	10	12	13	13	12	19	18	15	17	13	18	10
PASSING:														
Attempts	588	496	495	475	487	411	593	491	572	500	488	443	662	497
Completions	298	306	273	263	282	206	305	266	367	292	272	240	401	283
Completion Pct.	50.7	61.7	55.2	55.4	57.9	50.1	51.4	54.2	64.2	58.4	55.7	54.2	60.6	56.9
Passing Yards	3252	3659	3490	3116	3610	2543	3869	3718	5146	3685	3341	3519	4928	3751
Avg. Yds per Att.	5.5	7.4	7.1	6.6	7.4	6.2	6.5	7.6	9.0	7.4	6.9	7.9	7.4	7.6
Avg. Yds per Comp.	10.9	12.0	12.8	11.9	12.8	12.3	12.7	14.0	14.0	12.6	12.3	14.7	12.3	13.3
Times Tackled	60	45	55	35	49	58	33	54	14	66	52	35	36	42
Yds Lost Tackled	554	358	358	257	382	436	301	360	128	454	382	278	285	328
Net Yards	2698	3301	3132	2859	3228	2107	3568	3358	5018	3231	2959	3241	4643	3423
Touchdowns	18	17	14	22	14	13	21	21	49	26	20	25	25	32
Interceptions	30	22	23	17	15	22	22	28	18	14	21	25	21	26
Pct. Intercepted	5.1	4.4	4.6	3.6	3.1	5.4	3.7	5.7	3.1	2.8	4.3	5.6	3.2	5.2
PUNTS:														
Number	90	67	76	96	88	98	98	91	51	92	75	70	66	95
Average	41.1	42.3	42.3	40.1	39.6	44.7	44.9	41.9	44.7	42.4	39.1	41.2	42.0	37.5
PUNT RETURNS														
Number	33	38	40	41	26	38	42	67	39	48	35	61	33	44
Yards	297	473	322	318	152	278	346	667	365	430	324	696	212	484
Average Yards	9.0	12.4	8.1	7.8	5.8	7.3	8.2	10.0	9.4	9.0	9.3	11.4	6.4	11.0
Touchdowns	1	0	0	0	0	0	0	1	0	0	0	1	1	1
KICKOFF RET.:														
Number	76	61	61	45	69	69	56	56	44	63	65	54	63	54
Yards	1422	1155	1157	897	1352	1331	1061	1216	799	1246	1498	1026	1319	1007
Average Yards	18.7	18.9	19.0	19.9	19.6	19.3	18.9	21.7	18.2	19.8	23.0	19.0	20.9	18.6
Touchdowns	0	0	0	0	0	1	0	0	0	0	1	0	0	0
INTERCEPT RET.:														
Number	16	25	20	31	13	18	30	20	24	17	15	31	19	38
Yards	233	368	236	510	139	190	465	339	478	210	152	433	499	697
Average Yards	14.6	14.7	11.8	16.5	10.7	10.6	15.5	17.0	19.9	12.4	10.1	14.0	26.3	18.3
Touchdowns	0	4	0	4	0	1	2	2	2	0	0	4	4	7
PENALTIES:														
Number	121	85	111	78	99	95	98	143	67	86	96	112	112	128
Yards	997	693	928	636	813	798	801	1209	527	674	779	948	1023	1179
FUMBLES:														
Number	31	32	31	36	36	35	34	42	26	29	26	40	35	24
Number Lost	14	17	16	17	16	16	15	20	10	15	13	15	17	13
POINTS:														
Total	250	339	250	353	240	239	314	368	513	362	332	387	394	418
PAT Attempts	31	37	25	42	28	28	35	44	70	42	40	45	47	51
PAT Made	31	37	25	38	27	27	35	40	66	42	39	45	46	50
FG Attempts	21	31	35	28	19	23	33	27	19	28	24	32	29	24
FG Made	11	22	25	21	15	14	23	20	9	22	17	24	20	20
Percent FG Made	52.4	71.0	71.4	75.0	78.9	60.9	69.7	74.1	47.4	78.6	70.8	75.0	69.0	83.3
Safeties	0	1	0	0	0	1	0	2	0	1	1	0	0	1

DEFENSE

	BUFF.	CIN.	CLEV.	DEN.	HOU.	IND.	K.C.	L.A.	MIA.	N.E.	NY J	PIT.	S.D.	SEA.
FIRST DOWNS:														
Total	345	322	270	311	345	343	335	297	314	311	341	282	322	288
by Rushing	134	115	103	90	158	124	121	107	130	109	117	87	109	99
by Passing	186	191	145	206	168	194	192	147	172	182	198	167	189	160
by Penalty	25	16	22	15	19	25	22	43	12	20	26	28	24	29
RUSHING:														
Number	531	477	494	435	596	559	523	517	458	498	497	454	457	475
Yards	2106	1868	1945	1664	2789	2007	1980	1892	2155	1886	2064	1617	1851	1789
Average Yards	4.0	3.9	3.9	3.8	4.7	3.6	3.8	3.7	4.7	3.8	4.2	3.6	4.1	3.8
Touchdowns	19	21	10	10	27	16	10	12	16	11	16	12	23	11
PASSING:														
Attempts	495	517	458	631	447	515	586	508	551	513	511	515	531	521
Completions	300	302	261	346	271	298	332	254	310	283	312	299	323	265
Completion Pct.	60.6	58.4	57.0	54.8	60.6	57.9	56.7	50.0	56.3	55.2	61.1	58.1	60.8	50.9
Passing Yards	3667	3689	3049	4453	3446	3890	4009	3268	3604	3666	3862	3689	4303	3572
Avg. Yds per Att.	7.4	7.1	6.7	7.1	7.7	7.6	6.8	6.4	6.5	7.1	7.6	7.2	8.1	6.9
Avg. Yds per Comp.	12.2	12.2	11.7	12.9	12.7	13.1	12.1	12.9	11.6	13.0	12.4	12.3	13.3	13.5
Times Tackled	26	40	43	57	32	42	50	64	42	55	44	47	33	55
Yds Lost Tackled	191	298	353	430	267	320	364	516	339	452	360	390	218	398
Net Yards	3476	3391	2696	4023	3179	3570	3645	2752	3265	3214	3502	3299	4085	3174
Touchdowns	32	15	15	16	23	31	19	19	22	25	24	19	27	18
Interceptions	16	25	20	31	13	18	30	20	24	17	15	31	19	38
Pct. Intercepted	3.2	4.8	4.4	4.9	2.9	3.5	5.1	3.9	4.4	3.3	2.9	6.0	3.6	7.3
PUNTS:														
Number	72	67	77	81	64	80	91	117	83	83	67	90	73	83
Average	39.1	41.4	40.6	41.5	42.2	42.0	40.0	43.3	41.9	40.3	42.6	42.4	39.6	40.3
PUNT RETURNS														
Number	52	38	43	44	60	62	60	34	17	45	37	37	43	32
Yards	597	310	489	335	618	600	461	345	138	442	242	351	399	205
Average Yards	11.5	8.2	11.4	7.6	10.3	9.7	7.7	10.1	8.1	9.8	6.5	9.5	9.3	6.4
Touchdowns	0	0	0	0	0	0	0	0	0	1	0	1	0	1
KICKOFF RET.:														
Number	44	69	52	55	51	42	64	61	66	73	48	61	72	67
Yards	958	1446	1159	1181	986	849	1354	1063	1368	1373	1030	1338	1437	1116
Average Yards	21.8	21.0	22.3	21.5	19.3	20.2	21.2	17.4	20.7	18.8	21.5	21.9	20.0	16.7
Touchdowns	0	1	0	0	0	0	0	0	0	0	0	1	0	0
INTERCEPT RET.:														
Number	30	22	23	17	15	22	22	28	18	14	21	25	21	26
Yards	416	364	518	189	214	423	683	300	377	237	207	371	180	333
Average Yards	13.9	16.5	22.5	11.1	14.3	19.2	31.1	10.7	20.9	16.9	9.9	14.8	8.6	12.8
Touchdowns	4	2	3	0	2	2	7	2	1	3	0	1	0	3
PENALTIES:														
Number	87	90	108	104	105	98	108	121	93	87	87	107	108	114
Yards	734	743	765	891	876	813	951	1061	772	773	723	945	905	883
FUMBLES:														
Number	36	27	34	44	24	29	18	28	23	33	34	30	34	47
Number Lost	21	15	15	24	11	13	11	14	12	8	18	11	17	25
POINTS:														
Total	454	339	297	241	437	414	324	278	298	352	364	310	413	282
PAT Attempts	56	39	30	26	53	50	38	33	38	42	41	35	51	34
PAT Made	56	37	30	26	51	47	37	29	37	37	40	34	50	34
FG Attempts	28	27	33	33	30	23	27	21	17	31	37	28	25	22
FG Made	20	22	29	19	22	21	19	17	9	21	26	22	19	14
Percent FG Made	71.4	81.5	87.9	57.6	73.3	91.3	70.4	81.0	52.9	67.7	70.3	78.6	76.0	63.6
Safeties	1	1	0	1	1	2	1	0	0	0	0	0	0	1

Jackson led by example while Dennis Smith achieved stardom in the secondary. The less brilliant offense showcased runner Sammy Winder and receiver Steve Watson. With Steve DeBerg gone in a trade, John Elway was secure in the quarterback job and played well. Three victories over the Raiders and Seahawks displayed a new strength of the Broncos.

Seattle Seahawks — A severe knee injury to Curt Warner marred a 33-0 whitewash of Cleveland on opening day. With their ace runner gone for the season, the Seattle offense appeared to be in trouble. Chuck Knox allowed no relapse and drove the Seahawks into the playoffs with a passing attack and marvelous defense. Dave Krieg threw frequently and successfully to slick Steve Largent and rookie Daryl Turner, a speedburner who perfectly complemented Largent. The defense posted three shutouts. Linemen Jacob Green, Joe Nash and Jeff Bryant starred in the 3-4 defense, as did Dave Brown and Kenny Easley in the secondary. Brown returned two interceptions for touchdowns in a 45-0 trouncing of Kansas City. Losses to the Chiefs and Broncos in December cost the Seahawks a divisional title and forced them into a wild-card berth.

Los Angeles Raiders — Even with Ted Hendricks retired, the Raider defense mauled enemy offenses. Howie Long and Lyle Alzado starred in the line, backed wonderfully by Rod Martin and Matt Millen. Lester Hayes, Mike Haynes and Vann McElroy earned honors in the secondary. The offense had to adjust to a new quarterback, as Jim Plunkett pulled a stomach muscle on October 7 and sat out most of the season. Marc Wilson kept Marcus Allen and Todd Christensen busy, protected by Henry lawrence and the rest of the strong blockers. After a 7-1 start, the Raiders ran into a three-game losing streak in mid-season. A late resurgence included a 45-34 victory over Miami.

Kansas City Chiefs — The Chiefs won their first two games and last three games and struggled in between. The glaring flaw on offense was a weak running game in which rookie Herman Heard got the most work. Coming off his best season, quarterback Bill Kenney broke his thumb in the pre-season and missed the early games. Todd Blackledge ran the offense until Kenney returned in relief in a 31-13 victory over San Diego on October 14. The defense lost Gary Green in a trade with the Rams but still had veteran stars in Art Still and Deron Cherry. Bill Maas and Kevin Ross made strong contributions as rookies. The start of November brought back-to-back humiliations, a 45-0 loss to Seattle and a 17-16 defeat to winless Houston.

San Diego Chargers — The Chargers beat Minnesota 42-13 on opening day, won four of their first six games, and beat the undefeated Dolphins 34-28 on November 18. Despite the high moments, the Chargers suffered through a disappointing campaign in which Chuck Muncie and Kellen Winslow contributed little. Don Coryell found Muncie's attitude objectionable and traded him to the Dolphins in September; Muncie failed a drug test in Miami, was returned to San Diego and spent the year on suspension. Winslow left the team after the opening game to force renegotiation of his contract. He returned after missing only one game, only to suffer a season-ending knee injury on October 21. The inexperienced defense was not up to carrying the wounded offense. Discovered in the offensive flux was Earnest Jackson, who stepped into Muncie's shoes and ran for more than 1,100 yards.

MIAMI DOLPHINS 14-2-0 Don Shula

Scores of Each Game		
35	Washington	17
28	NEW ENGLAND	7
21	Buffalo	17
44	INDIANAPOLIS	7
36	St.Louis	28
31	Pittsburgh	7
28	HOUSTON	10
44	New England	24
38	BUFFALO	7
31	N.Y.Jets	17
24	PHILADELPHIA	23
28	San Diego	*34
28	N.Y.JETS	17
34	L.A.RAIDERS	45
35	Indianapolis	17
28	DALLAS	21

Use Name	Pos.	Hgt	Wgt	Age	Int	Pts
Jon Giesler	OT	6'5"	260	27		
Cleveland Green	OT	6'3"	262	26		
Eric Laakso	OT	6'4"	265	27		
Roy Foster	OG-OT	6'4"	275	24		
Ronnie Lee	OG-OT	6'4"	265	27		
Ed Newman	OG	6'2"	255	33		
Jeff Toews	C-OG	6'3"	255	26		
Dwight Stephenson	C	6'2"	255	26		
Bill Barnett	DE	6'4"	260	28		
Charles Benson	DE	6'3"	267	23		
Doug Betters	DE	6'7"	265	28		
Kim Bokamper	DE	6'6"	255	29		
Bob Baumhower	NT	6'5"	265	29		6
Mike Charles	NT	6'4"	283	21		
Steve Clark	NT	6'4"	255	24		
Charles Bowser	LB	6'3"	235	24		
Jay Brophy	LB	6'3"	233	24		
Mark Brown	LB	6'2"	225	23		
Bob Brudzinski	LB	6'4"	230	29	1	
A.J.Duhe	LB	6'4"	235	28	1	
Ed Judie	LB	6'2"	230	25		
Earnest Rhone	LB	6'2"	224	31		
Jackie Shipp	LB	6'2"	236	22		
Sanders Shiver	LB	6'2"	235	29		
Rodell Thomas	LB	6'2"	225	26		
Glenn Blackwood	DB	6'	190	27	6	
Lyle Blackwood	DB	6'	190	33	3	
Bud Brown	DB	6'	194	23	1	
William Judson	DB	6'1"	190	25	4	6
Mike Kozlowski	DB	6'	198	28	1	
Paul Lankford	DB	6'1"	184	25	3	
Don McNeal	DB	5'11"	192	26	3	6
Robert Sowell	DB	5'11"	175	23	1	
Fulton Walker	DB	5'10"	193	26		
Dan Marino	QB	6'4"	214	22		
Don Strock	QB	6'5"	220	33		
Joe Carter	HB	5'11"	196	22		6
Eddie Hill	HB	6'2"	210	27		
Tony Nathan	HB	6'	206	27		18
Woody Bennett	FB	6'2"	222	29		48
Andra Franklin	FB	5'10"	225	25		
Pete Johnson (from SD)	FB	6'	255	30		72
Jimmy Cefalo	WR	5'11"	188	27		12
Mark Clayton	WR	5'9"	172	23		108
Mark Duper	WR	5'9"	187	25		48
Vince Heflin	WR	6'	185	25		
Jim Jensen	WR	6'4"	212	25		12
Nat Moore	WR	5'9"	188	32		36
John Chesley	TE	6'5"	225	22		
Bruce Hardy	TE	6'5"	230	28		30
Dan Johnson	TE	6'3"	240	24		18
Joe Rose	TE	6'3"	230	27		12
Reggie Roby	K	6'2"	243	23		12
Uwe von Schamann	K	6'	188	28		93

David Overstreet - Died in auto accident, June 24
Ron Hester - Knee Injury
Tommy Vigorito - Knee Injury
Bob Kuechenberg - Injury

NEW ENGLAND PATRIOTS 9-7-0 Ron Meyer, Raymond Berry

Scores of Each Game		
21	Buffalo	17
7	Miami	28
38	SEATTLE	23
10	WASHINGTON	26
28	N.Y.Jets	21
17	Cleveland	16
20	CINCINNATI	14
24	MIAMI	44
30	N.Y.JETS	21
19	Denver	26
38	BUFFALO	10
50	Indianapolis	17
17	Dallas	20
10	ST.LOUIS	33
17	Philadelphia	27
16	INDIANAPOLIS	10

Use Name	Pos.	Hgt	Wgt	Age	Int	Pts
Darryl Haley	OT	6'4"	275	23		
Brian Holloway	OT	6'7"	288	25		
Steve Moore	OT	6'4"	285	23		
Paul Fairchild	OG	6'4"	270	23		
John Hannah	OG	6'2"	265	33		
Ron Wooten	OG	6'4"	273	25		
Pete Brock	C	6'5"	275	30		
Guy Morriss	C	6'4"	255	33		
Julius Adams	DE	6'3"	270	36		
Doug Rogers	DE	6'5"	270	24		
Kenneth Sims	DE	6'5"	271	24		
Scott Virkus(from BUF,to IND)	DE	6'5"	248	24		
Toby Williams	DE	6'3"	260	24		
Luther Henson	NT	6'	275	25		
Dennis Owens	NT	6'1"	258	24		
Lester Williams	NT	6'3"	272	25		
Don Blackmon	LB	6'3"	235	26	1	
Tim Golden	LB	6'1"	220	24		
Brian Ingram	LB	6'4"	235	24		
Larry McGrew	LB	6'5"	233	27		
Steve Nelson	LB	6'2"	230	33	1	
Johnny Rembert	LB	6'3"	234	23		
Ed Reynolds	LB	6'5"	230	22		
Andre Tippett	LB	6'3"	241	24		
Clayton Weishuhn	LB	6'2"	220	24		
Ed Williams	LB	6'4"	244	23		
Raymond Clayborn	DB	6'1"	186	29	3	
Paul Dombroski	DB	6'	185	28	1	
Ernest Gibson	DB	5'10"	185	22	2	
Roland James	DB	6'2"	191	26	2	2
Keith Lee	DB	5'11"	193	26		
Ronnie Lippett	DB	5'11"	180	23	3	
Fred Marion	DB	6'2"	191	25	2	
Rod McSwain	DB	6'1"	198	22		
Rick Sanford	DB	6'1"	192	27	2	
Tony Eason	QB	6'4"	212	24		30
Steve Grogan	QB	6'4"	210	31		
Mike Kerrigan	QB	6'3"	205	24		
Tony Collins	HB	5'11"	212	25		30
Jonathan Williams	HB	5'9"	205	23		
Greg Hawthorne	FB	6'2"	225	27		
Craig James	FB	6'	215	23		6
Bo Robinson	FB	6'2"	235	28		6
Mosi Tatupu	FB	6'	227	29		24
Robert Weathers	FB	6'2"	222	23		
Irving Fryar	WR	6'	200	21		6
Cedric Jones	WR	6'	184	24		18
Stanley Morgan	WR	5'11"	181	29		30
Stephen Starring	WR	5'10"	172	23		24
Clarence Weathers	WR	5'9"	170	22		12
Lin Dawson	TE	6'3"	240	25		24
Derrick Ramsey	TE	6'5"	235	27		42
Rich Camarillo	K	5'11"	191	24		
Tony Franklin	K	5'8"	182	27		108
Luke Prestridge	K	6'4"	235	27		

George Crump - Knee Injury
Darryal Wilson - Knee Injury

NEW YORK JETS 7-9-0 Joe Walton

Scores of Each Game		
23	Indianapolis	14
17	PITTSBURGH	23
43	CINCINNATI	23
28	Buffalo	26
21	NEW ENGLAND	28
17	Kansas City	16
24	Cleveland	20
28	KANSAS CITY	7
20	New England	30
17	MIAMI	31
5	INDIANAPOLIS	9
20	Houston	31
17	Miami	28
10	N.Y.GIANTS	20
21	BUFFALO	17
21	Tampa Bay	41

Use Name	Pos.	Hgt	Wgt	Age	Int	Pts
Reggie McElroy	OT	6'6"	270	24		
Marvin Powell	OT	6'5"	271	29		
Guy Bingham	C-OG-OT	6'3"	255	26		
Stan Waldemore	OG-OT	6'4"	269	29		
Dan Alexander	OG	6'4"	260	29		
Jim Sweeney	OG-C	6'4"	260	22		
Ted Banker	OG-C	6'2"	255	23		
Joe Fields	C	6'2"	253	30		
George Lilja (to CLE)	OT-C	6'4"	262	26		
Mark Gastineau	DE	6'5"	265	27		6
Marty Lyons	DE-DT	6'5"	269	27		
Tom Baldwin	DT	6'4"	270	23		
Barry Bennett	DT-DE	6'4"	260	28		
Ron Faurot	DT-DE	6'7"	262	22		
Joe Klecko	DT-DE	6'3"	263	30		
Ben Rudolph	DT-DE	6'5"	270	27		
Bobby Bell	LB	6'3"	217	22		
Greg Buttle	LB	6'3"	232	30	2	6
Kyle Clifton	LB	6'4"	233	22	1	
Bob Crable	LB	6'3"	234	24		
Jim Eliopulos	LB	6'2"	229	25		
Rusty Guilbeau	LB	6'4"	237	25		
Lance Mehl	LB	6'3"	235	26		
John Woodring	LB	6'2"	232	25		
Russell Carter	DB	6'2"	195	22	4	
Mike Dennis (from SD)	DB	5'10"	195	26		
George Floyd	DB	5'11"	190	23		
Harry Hamilton	DB	6'	193	21		
Bobby Jackson	DB	5'9"	180	27		
Skip Lane (to KC)	DB	6'1"	208	24		
Johnny Lynn	DB	6'	198	27	2	
Davlin Mullen	DB	6'1"	177	24	1	
Darrol Ray	DB	6'1"	198	26	2	
Ken Schroy	DB	6'2"	198	31	2	
Kirk Springs	DB	6'	192	26	1	
Bob Avellini (from CHI)	QB	6'2"	210	31		
Glenn Inverso	QB	6'1"	199	26		
Ken O'Brien	QB	6'4"	210	23		
Mark Reed	QB	6'3"	204	25		
Pat Ryan	QB	6'3"	210	28		1
Dennis Bligen	HB	5'11"	215	22		
Bruce Harper	HB	5'8"	177	29		6
Johnny Hector	HB	5'11"	197	23		6
Freeman McNeil	HB	5'11"	212	25		36
Cedric Minter	HB	5'10"	200	25		12
Marion Barber	FB	6'3"	224	24		12
Tony Paige	FB	5'10"	230	21		48
Nick Bruckner	WR	5'11"	185	23		
Frenanza Burgess (to MIA)	WR	6'1"	210	24		
Chy Davidson	WR	5'11"	175	25		
Derrick Gaffney	WR	6'1"	182	29		
Bobby Humphrey	WR	5'10"	170	23		12
Johnny "Lam" Jones	WR	5'11"	180	26		6
Kurt Sohn	WR	5'11"	180	27		
Wesley Walker	WR	6'	182	29		42
Glenn Dennison	TE	6'3"	225	22		6
Rocky Klever	TE	6'3"	225	25		6
Mickey Shuler	TE	6'3"	231	28		36
Pat Leahy	K	6'	193	33		89
Chuck Ramsey	K	6'2"	194	32		

Mike Augustyniak - Knee Injury

INIANAPOLIS COLTS 4-12-0 Frank Kush, Hal Hunter

Scores of Each Game		
14	N.Y.JETS	23
35	Houston	21
33	ST.LOUIS	34
7	Miami	44
31	BUFFALO	17
7	WASHINGTON	35
7	Philadelphia	16
17	PITTSBURGH	16
3	Dallas	22
10	SAN DIEGO	38
9	N.Y.Jets	5
17	NEW ENGLAND	50
7	L.A.Raiders	21
15	Buffalo	21
17	MIAMI	35
10	New England	16

Use Name	Pos.	Hgt	Wgt	Age	Int	Pts
Kevin Call	OT	6'7"	289	22		
Andy Ekern	OT	6'6"	265	23		
Jim Mills	OT	6'9"	281	22		
Ted Petersen (from CLE)	OT	6'5"	253	29		
Steve Wright	OT	6'6"	250	25		
Ellis Gardner	OT-OG	6'5"	250	22		
Mark Kirchner	OT-OG	6'3"	261	24		
Chris Hinton	OG	6'4"	283	23		
Ron Solt	OG	6'3"	275	22		
Ben Utt	OG	6'5"	280	25		
Don Bailey	C	6'4"	257	23		
Ray Donaldson	C	6'3"	273	26		
Steve Parker	DE	6'4"	262	24		
Chris Scott	DE	6'5"	253	22		
Byron Smith	DE	6'5"	264	21		
Donnell Thompson	DE	6'4"	263	25		
Henry Waechter (to CHI)	DE	6'5"	260	25		
Blaise Winter	DE	6'3"	262	22		
Brad White	NT	6'2"	260	26		
Leo Wisniewski	NT	6'1"	259	24		
Greg Bracelin	LB	6'1"	216	27		
Johnie Cooks	LB	6'4"	243	25		
Steve Hathaway	LB	6'4"	238	22		
Mike Humiston	LB	6'3"	238	25		2
Barry Krauss	LB	6'3"	249	27	3	
Vernon Maxwell	LB	6'2"	238	23		
Cliff Odom	LB	6'2"	235	25		
Gary Padjen	LB	6'2"	241	26		
Kim Anderson	DB	5'11"	182	27		
Larry Anderson	DB	5'11"	194	27		
James Burroughs	DB	6'1"	187	26	3	
Eugene Daniel	DB	5'11"	179	23	6	
Preston Davis	DB	5'11"	180	22	1	
Nesby Glasgow	DB	5'10"	180	27	1	
Mark Kafentzis	DB	5'10"	200	26	1	6
Bo Metcalf	DB	6'2"	193	23		
George Radachowsky	DB	5'11"	178	21		
Tate Randle	DB	6'	196	25	3	
Vaughan Williams	DB	6'2"	193	22		
Mark Herrmann	QB	6'4"	190	25		
Mike Pagel	QB	6'2"	205	23		6
Art Schlichter	QB	6'3"	210	24		6
Curtis Dickey	HB	6'1"	222	27		18
Frank Middleton	HB	5'11"	201	23		12
Alvin Moore	HB	6'	198	25		12
George Wonsley	HB	5'10"	212	23		
Randy McMillan	FB	6'	212	25		30
Matt Bouza	WR	6'3"	211	25		
Ray Butler	WR	6'3"	195	28		36
Bernard Henry	WR	6'1"	179	24		12
Tracy Porter	WR	6'1"	202	25		12
Phil Smith	WR	6'3"	188	23		6
Mark Bell	TE-DE	6'4"	246	27		
Tim Sherwin	TE	6'6"	245	26		
Dave Young	TE	6'5"	243	25		12
Raul Allegre	K	5'10"	165	25		47
Dean Biasucci	K	6'	188	22		22
Rohn Stark	K	6'3"	203	25		

Ricky Jones - Injury
Victor Oatis - Thigh Injury
Karl Baldischwiler - Neck Injury
Pat Beach - Ankle Injury
Newton Williams - Ankle Injury

BUFFALO BILLS 2-14-0 Kay Stephenson

Scores of Each Game		
17	NEW ENGLAND	21
7	St.Louis	37
17	MIAMI	21
26	N.Y.JETS	28
17	Indianapolis	31
17	PHILADELPHIA	27
28	Seattle	31
7	DENVER	37
7	Miami	38
10	CLEVELAND	13
10	New England	38
14	DALLAS	3
14	Washington	41
21	INDIANAPOLIS	15
17	N.Y.Jets	21
21	Cincinnati	52

Use Name	Pos.	Hgt	Wgt	Age	Int	Pts
Justin Cross	OT	6'6"	265	25		
Joe Devlin	OT	6'5"	250	30		
Ken Jones	OT	6'5"	260	31		
Jon Borchardt	OG	6'5"	255	27		
Tom Lynch	OG	6'5"	250	29		
Jim Ritcher	OG-C	6'3"	251	26		
Will Grant	C	6'3"	255	30		
Tim Vogler	C	6'3"	245	27		
Ken Johnson	DE	6'5"	253	29		
Sean McNanie	DE	6'5"	252	22		
Dean Prater	DE	6'4"	245	25		
Ben Williams	DE	6'3"	260	30		
Bill Acker	NT	6'3"	255	27		
Fred Smerlas	NT	6'3"	270	27	1	
Joe Azelby	LB	6'1"	225	22		
Stan David	LB	6'3"	210	22		6
Jim Haslett	LB	6'3"	232	27		
Chris Keating	LB	6'2"	233	26		6
Eugeen Marve	LB	6'2"	230	24		
Steve Potter	LB	6'3"	235	26		
Lucius Sanford	LB	6'2"	216	28		6
Darryl Talley	LB	6'4"	235	24	1	
Al Wenglikowski	LB	6'1"	220	24		
Martin Bayless (from STL)	DB	6'2"	195	21		
Rodney Bellinger	DB	5'8"	181	22	1	
Brian Carpenter (from WAS)	DB	5'10"	170	23	3	
Steve Freeman	DB	5'11"	185	31	3	
Rod Hill	DB	6'	188	25		
Lawrence Johnson(from CLE)	DB	5'11"	204	26		
Rod Kush	DB	6'	188	27	1	
Charles Romes	DB	6'1"	190	29	5	
Garry Thompson	DB	6'	180	25		
Marco Tongue	DB	5'9"	180	24		
Len Walterscheid	DB	5'11"	190	29		
Don Wilson	DB	6'2"	190	23		6
Joe Dufek	QB	6'4"	215	23		6
Joe Ferguson	QB	6'1"	195	34		
Matt Kofler	QB	6'3"	192	25		
Robb Riddick	HB	6'	195	27		
Van Williams	HB	6'	208	25		6
Greg Bell	FB	5'10"	210	22		48
Booker Moore	FB	5'11"	224	25		
Speedy Neal	FB	6'2"	254	22		6
Mitchell Brookins	WR	5'11"	196	23		6
Julius Dawkins	WR	6'1"	196	23		12
Preston Dennard	WR	6'1"	183	28		42
Byron Franklin	WR	6'1"	181	25		24
Mike Mosley	WR	6'2"	188	26		
Craig White	WR	6'1"	194	22		
Buster Barnett	TE	6'5"	235	25		
Mark Brammer	TE	6'3"	235	26		
Tony Hunter	TE	6'4"	237	24		12
Ulysses Norris	TE	6'4"	232	27		
Joe Danelo	K	5'9"	166	30		41
John Kidd	K	6'3"	201	23		
Chuck Nelson	K	6'	175	24		23

Jerry Butler - Knee Injury
Jeff Nixon - Knee Injury

* Overtime

MIAMI DOLPHINS

RUSHING

Last Name	No.	Yds	Avg	TD
Bennett	114	606	4.2	7
Nathan	118	558	4.7	1
Carter	100	495	5.0	1
P. Johnson	87	205	2.4	12
Franklin	20	74	3.7	0
Clayton	3	35	11.7	0
Moore	1	3	3.0	0
Strock	2	-5	-2.5	0
Marino	28	-7	-0.3	0

RECEIVING

Last Name	No.	Yds	Avg	TD
Clayton	73	1389	19.0	18
Duper	71	1306	18.4	8
Nathan	61	579	9.5	2
Moore	43	573	13.3	6
D. Johnson	34	426	12.5	3
Hardy	28	257	9.2	5
Cefalo	18	185	10.3	2
Jensen	13	139	10.7	2
Rose	12	195	16.3	2
Carter	8	53	6.6	0
Bennett	6	44	7.3	1
P. Johnson	2	7	3.5	0

PUNT RETURNS

Last Name	No.	Yds	Avg	TD
Walker	21	169	8.0	0
Clayton	8	79	9.9	0
Heflin	6	76	12.7	0
Kozlowski	4	41	10.3	0

KICKOFF RETURNS

Last Name	No.	Yds	Avg	TD
Walker	29	617	21.3	0
Heflin	9	130	14.4	0
Clayton	2	15	7.5	0
Kozlowski	2	23	11.5	0
Duhe	1	0	0.0	0
Hill	1	14	14.0	0

PASSING — PUNTING — KICKING

PASSING	Att	Cmp	%	Yds	Yd/Att	TD	Int-	%	RK
Marino	564	362	64	5084	9.01	48	17-	3	1
Strock	6	4	67	27	4.50	0	0-	0	
Clayton	1	0	0	0	0.0	0	1-	100	
Jensen	1	1	100	35	35.0	1	0-	0	

PUNTING	No.	Avg
Roby	51	44.7

KICKING	XP	Att	%	FG	Att	%
von Schamann	66	70	94	9	19	47

NEW ENGLAND PATRIOTS

RUSHING

Last Name	No.	Yds	Avg	TD
C. James	160	790	4.9	1
Tatupu	133	553	4.2	4
Collins	138	550	4.0	5
Eason	40	154	3.9	5
Grogan	7	12	1.7	0
Fryar	2	-11	-5.5	0
Starring	2	-16	-8.0	0

RECEIVING

Last Name	No.	Yds	Avg	TD
D. Ramsey	66	792	12.0	7
Starring	46	657	14.3	4
Dawson	39	427	10.9	4
Morgan	38	709	18.7	5
C. James	22	159	7.2	0
Jones	19	244	12.8	2
Tatupu	16	159	9.9	0
Collins	16	100	6.3	0
Fryar	11	164	14.9	1
C. Weathers	8	115	14.4	2
Hawthorne	7	127	18.1	0
Robinson	4	32	8.0	1

PUNT RETURNS

Last Name	No.	Yds	Avg	TD
Fryar	36	347	9.6	0
Starring	10	73	7.3	0
C. Weathers	1	7	7.0	0
Gibson	1	3	3.0	0

KICKOFF RETURNS

Last Name	No.	Yds	Avg	TD
Collins	25	544	21.8	0
J. Williams	23	461	20.0	0
Fryar	5	95	19.0	0
Lee	3	43	14.3	0
Robinson	3	38	12.7	0
Jones	1	20	20.0	0
Hawthorne	1	14	14.0	0
Tatupu	1	9	9.0	0

PASSING — PUNTING — KICKING

PASSING	Att	Cmp	%	Yds	Yd/Att	TD	Int-	%	RK
Eason	431	259	60	3228	7.5	23	8-	2	2
Grogan	68	32	47	444	6.53	3	6-	9	
Kerrigan	1	1	100	13	13.0	0	0-	0	

PUNTING	No	Avg
Prestridge	44	42.8

KICKING	XP	Att	%	FG	Att	%
Franklin	42	42	100	22	28	79

NEW YORK JETS

RUSHING

Last Name	No.	Yds	Avg	TD
McNeil	229	1070	4.7	5
Hector	124	531	4.3	1
Barber	31	148	4.8	2
Minter	34	136	4.0	1
Paige	35	130	3.7	7
Ryan	23	92	4.0	0
Harper	10	48	4.8	1
O'Brien	16	29	1.8	0
Dennison	1	4	4.0	0
Walker	1	1	1.0	0
Avellini	3	-5	-1.7	0

RECEIVING

Last Name	No.	Yds	Avg	TD
Shuler	68	782	11.5	6
Walker	41	623	15.2	7
Jones	32	470	14.7	1
McNeil	25	294	11.8	1
Hector	20	182	9.1	0
Gaffney	19	285	15.0	0
Dennison	16	141	8.8	1
Humphrey	14	206	14.7	1
Minter	10	109	10.9	1
Barber	10	79	7.9	0
Paige	6	31	5.2	1
Harper	5	71	14.2	0
Klever	3	29	9.7	1
Sohn	2	28	14.0	0
Bruckner	1	11	11.0	0

PUNT RETURNS

Last Name	No.	Yds	Avg	TD
Springs	28	247	8.8	0
Minter	4	44	11.0	0
Bruckner	2	25	12.5	0
Mullen	1	8	8.0	0

KICKOFF RETURNS

Last Name	No.	Yds	Avg	TD
Humphery	22	675	30.7	1
Springs	23	521	22.7	0
Minter	10	224	22.4	0
Mullen	2	34	17.0	0
Paige	3	7	2.3	0
Bruckner	1	17	17.0	0
Davidson	1	9	9.0	0
Gaffney	1	6	6.0	0
Banker	1	5	5.0	0
Shuler	1	0	0.0	0

PASSING — PUNTING — KICKING

PASSING	Att	Cmp	%	Yds	Yd/Att	TD	Int-	%	RK
O'Brien	203	116	57	1402	6.91	6	7-	3	11
Ryan	285	156	55	1939	6.80	14	14-	5	13
Avellini	53	30	57	288	5.43	0	3-	6	

PUNTING	No	Avg
Ramsey	74	39.7

KICKING	XP	Att	%	FG	Att	%
Leahy	38	39	97	17	24	71

INDIANAPOLIS COLTS

RUSHING

Last Name	No.	Yds	Avg	TD
McMillan	163	705	4.3	5
Dickey	131	523	4.0	3
Middleton	92	275	3.0	1
Moore	38	127	3.3	2
Wonsley	37	111	3.0	0
Pagel	26	149	5.7	1
Schlichter	19	145	7.6	1
P.Smith	2	-10	-5.0	0
Stark	2	0	0.0	0

RECEIVING

Last Name	No.	Yds	Avg	TD
Butler	43	664	15.4	6
Porter	39	590	15.1	2
Bouza	22	270	12.3	0
McMillan	19	201	10.6	0
Middleton	15	112	7.5	1
Young	14	164	11.7	2
Dickey	14	135	9.6	0
Henry	11	139	12.6	2
Sherwin	11	169	15.4	0
Moore	9	52	5.8	0
Wonsley	9	47	5.2	0

PUNT RETURNS

Last Name	No.	Yds	Avg	TD
L. Anderson	27	182	6.7	0
Glasgow	7	79	11.3	0
Bouza	3	17	5.7	0
Padjen	1	0	0.0	0

KICKOFF RETURNS

Last Name	No.	Yds	Avg	TD
L. Anderson	22	525	23.9	0
P. Smith	32	651	20.3	1
Kafentzis	5	69	13.8	0
Wonsley	4	52	13.0	0
Moore	2	19	9.5	0
Hathaway	1	2	2.0	0
Radachowsky	1	0	0.0	0
Middleton	1	11	11.0	0
Sherwin	1	2	2.0	0

PASSING — PUNTING — KICKING

PASSING	Att	Cmp	%	Yds	Yd/Att	TD	Int-	%	RK
Pagel	212	114	54	1426	6.73	8	8-	4	14
Schlichter	140	62	44	702	5.01	3	7-	5	
Herrman	56	29	52	352	6.30	1	6-	11	
Dickey	1	1	100	63	63.0	1	0-	0	

PUNTING	No	Avg
Stark	98	44.7

KICKING	XP	Att	%	FG	Att	%
Allegre	14	14	100	11	18	61
Biasucci	13	14	93	3	5	60

BUFFALO BILLS

RUSHING

Last Name	No.	Yds	Avg	TD
Bell	262	1100	4.2	7
Neal	49	175	3.6	1
Ferguson	19	102	5.4	0
Moore	24	84	3.5	0
Kofler	10	80	8.0	0
V. Williams	18	51	2.8	0
Brookins	2	27	13.5	0
Dufek	9	22	2.4	1
Hunter	1	6	6.0	0
Riddick	3	3	1.0	0
Franklin	1	-7	-7.0	0

RECEIVING

Last Name	No.	Yds	Avg	TD
Franklin	69	862	12.5	4
Bell	34	277	8.1	1
Hunter	33	331	10.0	2
Moore	33	172	5.2	0
Dennard	30	417	13.9	7
Riddick	23	276	12.0	0
Dawkins	21	295	14.1	2
Brookins	18	318	17.7	1
Neal	9	76	8.4	0
Barnett	8	67	8.4	0
Bramer	7	49	7.0	0
V. Williams	5	46	9.2	1
White	4	28	7.0	0
Mosley	4	38	9.5	0

PUNT RETURNS

Last Name	No.	Yds	Avg	TD
Wilson	33	297	9.0	1

KICKOFF RETURNS

Last Name	No.	Yds	Avg	TD
V. Williams	39	820	21.0	0
Wilson	34	576	16.9	0
Bell	1	15	15.0	0
David	1	6	6.0	0
White	1	5	5.0	0

PASSING — PUNTING — KICKING

PASSING	Att	Cmp	%	Yds	Yd/Att	TD	Int-	%	RK
Ferguson	344	191	56	1991	5.79	12	17-	5	18
Dufek	150	74	49	829	5.53	4	8-	5	
Kofler	93	33	36	432	4.65	2	5-	5	
Mosley	1	0	0	0	0.0	0	0-	0	

PUNTING	No	Avg
Kidd	88	42.0

KICKING	XP	Att	%	FG	Att	%
Danelo	17	17	100	8	16	50
Nelson	14	14	100	3	5	60

PITTSBURGH STEELERS 9-7-0 Chuck Noll

Scores of Each Game		
27	KANSAS CITY	37
23	N.Y.Jets	17
24	L.A.RAMS	14
10	Cleveland	20
38	CINCINNATI	17
7	MIAMI	31
20	San Francisco	17
16	Indianapolis	17
35	ATLANTA	10
35	HOUSTON	7
20	Cincinnati	22
24	New Orleans	27
52	SAN DIEGO	24
20	Houston	*23
23	CLEVELAND	20
13	L.A.Raiders	7

Use Name	Pos.	Hgt	Wgt	Age	Int	Pts
Steve August (from SEA)	OT	6'5"	258	29		
Larry Brown	OT	6'4"	270	35		
Mark Catano	OT	6'3"	265	22		
Tunch Ilkin	OT	6'3"	253	26		
Pete Rostosky	OT	6'4"	255	23		
Terry Long	OG	5'11"	272	25		
Ray Snell	OG	6'4"	265	26		
Blake Wingle	OG	6'2"	267	24		
Craig Wolfley	OG	6'1"	255	26		
Emil Boures	C-OG	6'1"	261	24		
Randy Rasmussen	C-OG	6'2"	253	23		
Mike Webster	C	6'1"	250	32		
Keith Gary	DE	6'3"	260	24		
John Goodman	DE	6'6"	255	25		
Keith Willis	DE	6'1"	260	25		
Gary Dunn	NT	6'3"	265	31		
Edmund Nelson	NT-DE	6'3"	270	24		
Craig Bingham	LB	6'2"	220	24		
Robin Cole	LB	6'2"	225	28	1	
Terry Echols	LB	6'	220	22		
Bryan Hinkle	LB	6'2"	220	25	3	6
Bob Kohrs	LB	6'3"	235	25		
Jack Lambert	LB	6'4"	220	32		
David Little	LB	6'1"	230	25		
Mike Merriweather	LB	6'2"	215	23	2	
Todd Seabaugh	LB	6'4"	225	23		
Chris Brown	DB	6'	195	22	1	
Harvey Clayton	DB	5'9"	180	23	1	
Ron Johnson	DB	5'10"	200	28		
Donnie Shell	DB	5'11"	190	32	7	6
Sam Washington	DB	5'8"	180	24	6	12
Eric Williams	DB	6'1"	183	24	3	
Robert Williams	DB	5'11"	202	21		
Dwayne Woodruff	DB	6'	198	27	5	12
Rick Woods	DB	6'	191	24	2	
Scott Campbell	QB	6'	201	22		
Mark Malone	QB	6'4"	218	25		18
David Woodley	QB	6'2"	204	25		
Walter Abercrombie	HB	6'	210	24		6
Rich Erenberg	HB	5'10"	200	22		18
Fernandars Gillespie	HB	5'10"	185	22		
Todd Spenser	HB	6'	200	22		
Anthony Corley	FB	6'	210	24		
Frank Pollard	FB	5'10"	218	27		36
Elton Veals	FB	5'11"	230	23		
Wayne Capers	WR	6'2"	193	23		
Gregg Garrity (to PHI)	WR	5'10"	171	23		
Louis Lipps	WR	5'10"	190	22		66
John Stallworth	WR	6'2"	191	32		66
Calvin Sweeney	WR	6'2"	190	29		
Weegie Thompson	WR	6'6"	210	23		18
Bennie Cunningham	TE	6'4"	255	29		6
Chris Kolodziejski	TE	6'3"	231	23		
Darrell Nelson	TE	6'2"	235	22		
John Rodgers	TE	6'2"	238	24		
Gary Anderson	K	5'11"	170	25		117
Craig Colquitt	K	6'2"	182	30		

CINCINNATI BENGALS 8-8-0 Sam Wyche

Scores of Each Game		
17	Denver	20
22	KANSAS CITY	27
23	N.Y.Jets	43
14	L.A.RAMS	24
17	Pittsburgh	38
13	HOUSTON	3
14	New England	20
12	CLEVELAND	9
31	Houston	13
17	San Francisco	23
22	PITTSBURGH	20
6	SEATTLE	26
35	ATLANTA	14
20	Cleveland	*17
24	New Orleans	21
52	BUFFALO	21

Use Name	Pos.	Hgt	Wgt	Age	Int	Pts
Brain Blados	OT	6'4"	295	22		
Anthony Munoz	OT	6'6"	278	26		6
Bruce Reimers	OT	6'7"	280	23		
Mike Wilson	OT	6'5"	271	29		
Max Montoya	OG	6'5"	275	28		
Gary Smith	OG	6'2"	265	24		
Bruce Kozerski	C	6'4"	275	22		
Dave Rimington	C	6'3"	288	22		
Ross Browner	DE	6'3"	261	30		
Glen Collins	DE	6'6"	265	25		
Eddie Edwards	DE	6'5"	256	30		
Jerry Boyarsky	NT	6'3"	290	25		
Pete Koch	NT	6'6"	265	22		
Tim Krumrie	NT	6'2"	262	24		
Leo Barker	LB	6'1"	221	24		
Glenn Cameron	LB	6'2"	228	31	1	
Guy Frazier	LB	6'2"	221	25		
Steve Maidlow	LB	6'2"	234	24		
Brian Pillman	LB	5'10"	228	22		
Rick Razzano	LB	5'11"	227	28		
Jeff Schuh	LB	6'2"	228	26	1	
Ron Simpkins	LB	6'1"	235	26		
Reggie Williams	LB	6'1"	228	29	2	
Ralph Battle	DB	6'2"	205	23		
Louis Breeden	DB	5'11"	185	30	4	
James Griffin	DB	6'2"	197	22	1	6
Ray Griffin	DB	5'10"	186	28	2	
Ray Horton	DB	5'11"	190	24	3	6
Robert Jackson	DB	5'10"	184	25	4	6
Bobby Kemp	DB	6'	191	25	4	
John Simmons	DB	5'11"	192	25	2	6
Jimmy Turner	DB	6'	187	25	1	
Ken Anderson	QB	6'1"	212	35		
Bryan Clark	QB	6'2"	196	24		
Boomer Esiason	QB	6'4"	220	23		12
Turk Schonert	QB	6'1"	190	27		6
James Brooks	HB	5'10"	182	25		24
John Farley	HB	5'10"	202	23		
Stanford Jennings	HB	6'1"	205	22		30
Stanley Wilson	HB-FB	5'10"	210	23		
Charles Alexander	FB	6'1"	226	27		12
Larry Kinnebrew	FB	6'1"	252	25		60
Cris Collinsworth	WR	6'5"	192	25		36
Isaac Curtis	WR	6'	192	33		
Steve Kreider	WR	6'3"	192	26		6
Mike Martin	WR	5'10"	186	23		
Clay Pickering	WR	6'5"	215	23		
David Verser	WR	6'1"	200	26		
Gary Williams	WR	6'2"	215	24		
M.L.Harris	TE	6'5"	238	30		12
Rodney Holman	TE	6'3"	230	24		6
Don Kern	TE	6'4"	225	22		
Jim Breech	K	5'6"	161	28		103
Pat McInally	K	6'6"	212	31		

Mike Obrovac - Knee Injury

CLEVELAND BROWNS 5-11-0 Sam Rutigliano, Marty Schottenheimer

Scores of Each Game		
0	Seattle	33
17	L.A.RAMS	20
14	Denver	24
20	PITTSBURGH	10
6	Kansas City	10
16	NEW ENGLAND	17
20	N.Y.JETS	24
9	Cincinnati	12
14	NEW ORLEANS	16
13	Buffalo	10
7	SAN FRANCISCO	41
23	Atlanta	7
27	HOUSTON	10
17	CINCINNATI	20
20	Pittsburgh	*23
27	Houston	20

Use Name	Pos.	Hgt	Wgt	Age	Int	Pts
Bill Contz	OT	6'5"	260	23		
Doug Dieken	OT	6'5"	252	35		
Paul Farren	OT	6'5"	260	23		
Robert Sikora	OT	6'8"	285	22		
Joe DeLamielleure	OG	6'3"	260	33		
Robert Jackson	OG	6'5"	260	31		
Mike Baab	C	6'4"	270	24		
Tom DeLeone	C	6'2"	254	34		
Keith Baldwin	DE	6'4"	270	23		
Reggie Camp	DE	6'4"	270	23		
Elvis Franks	DE	6'4"	265	27		
Carl Hairston	DE	6'3"	260	31		
Bob Golic	NT	6'2"	260	26		
Dave Puzzuoli	NT	6'3"	260	23		
Stuart Anderson (from WAS)	LB	6'1"	224	24		
Chip Banks	LB	6'4"	233	24	1	
Tom Cousineau	LB	6'3"	225	27	2	
Jim Dumont	LB	6'1"	224	23		
Eddie Johnson	LB	6'1"	215	25	2	
David Marshall	LB	6'3"	220	23		
Clay Matthews	LB	6'2"	235	28		
Scott Nicolas	LB	6'3"	226	24		
Curtis Weathers	LB	6'5"	230	27		
Greg Best	DB	5'10"	185	24		
Larry Braziel	DB	6'	184	29		
Clinton Burrell	DB	6'2"	192	27		
Hanford Dixon	DB	5'11"	182	25	5	
Al Gross	DB	6'3"	186	23	5	
Frank Minnifield	DB	5'9"	180	24	1	
Chris Rockins	DB	6'	195	22	1	
Don Rogers	DB	6'1"	206	21	1	
Tom Flick	QB	6'3"	190	26		
Paul McDonald	QB	6'2"	185	26		6
Terry Nugent	QB	6'4"	218	22		
James Black	HB	5'11"	198	22		
Dwight Walker	HB	5'10"	185	25		
Charles White	HB	5'10"	190	26		
Earnest Byner	FB	5'10"	215	21		18
Johnny Davis	FB	6'1"	235	28		6
Boyce Green	FB	5'11"	215	24		6
Mike Pruitt	FB	6'	225	30		36
Willis Adams	WR	6'2"	200	28		
Brian Brennan	WR	5'9"	178	22		18
Preston Brown	WR	5'11"	187	26		
Bruce Davis	WR	5'8"	160	21		125
Ricky Feacher	WR	5'10"	180	30		6
Duriel Harris (to DAL)	WR	5'11"	184	29		12
Glen Young	WR	6'2"	205	23		
Ricky Bolden	TE	6'6"	250	22		
Harry Holt	TE	6'4"	230	26		
Darryl Lewis	TE	6'6"	232	23		
Ozzie Newsome	TE	6'2"	232	28		30
Tim Stracka	TE	6'3"	225	24		
Matt Bahr	K	5'10"	175	28		97
Steve Cox	K	6'4"	195	26		3

Cody Risien - Knee Injury
Mike Whitwell - Knee Injury
Dick Ambrose - Ankle Injury

HOUSTON OILERS 3-13-0 Hugh Campbell

Scores of Each Game		
14	L.A.RAIDERS	24
21	INDIANAPOLIS	35
14	San Diego	31
10	Atlanta	42
10	NEW ORLEANS	27
3	Cincinnati	13
10	Miami	28
21	SAN FRANCISCO	34
13	CINCINNATI	31
7	Pittsburgh	35
17	Kansas City	16
31	N.Y.JETS	20
10	Cleveland	27
23	PITTSBURGH	*20
16	L.A.Rams	27
20	CLEVELAND	27

Use Name	Pos.	Hgt	Wgt	Age	Int	Pts
Eric Moran	OT	6'5"	280	24		
Harvey Salem	OT	6'6"	285	23		
Dean Steinkuhler	OT	6'3"	273	23		
Pat Howell	OG	6'5"	265	27		
Mike Munchak	OG	6'3"	286	24		
John Schuhmacher	OG	6'3"	277	28		
Bruce Matthews	C	6'4"	280	23		
Jim Romano (from RAID)	C	6'3"	255	24		
Jesse Baker	DE	6'5"	272	27		
Bryan Caldwell	DE	6'4"	248	24		
Jerome Foster	DE	6'2"	263	24		
Bob Hamm	DE	6'4"	263	25		
Mike Johnson	DE	6'5"	253	22		
Mark Studaway	DE	6'3"	269	23		
Brian Sochia	NT	6'3"	254	23		
Mike Stensrud	NT	6'5"	280	28		
Robert Abraham	LB	6'1"	230	24	1	
Gregg Bingham	LB	6'1"	232	33		
Robert Brazile	LB	6'4"	253	31	1	
John Grimsley	LB	6'2"	232	22		
Daryl Hunt	LB	6'3"	239	27		
Tim Joiner	LB	6'4"	248	23		
Robert Lyles	LB	6'1"	223	23		
Johnny Meads	LB	6'2"	225	23		
Avon Riley	LB	6'3"	236	25		
Ted Thompson	LB	6'1"	218	31		
Patrick Allen	DB	5'10"	173	23	1	
Keith Bostic	DB	6'1"	212	23		6
Steve Brown	DB	5'11"	188	24	1	
Jeff Donaldson	DB	6'	193	22		
Bo Eason	DB	6'2"	200	23	1	
Carter Hartwig	DB	6'	210	28	3	
Mike Kennedy	DB	6'	195	25		
Allen Lyday	DB	5'10"	186	23	1	
Darryl Meadows	DB	6'1"	199	23		
Willie Tullis	DB	6'	195	26	4	
Oliver Luck	QB	6'2"	198	24		6
Warren Moon	QB	6'3"	208	27		6
Brian Ransom	QB	6'3"	202	24		
Willie Joyner	HB	5'10"	200	22		
Richard Williams (from ATL)	HB	6'	205	24		
Donnie Craft	FB	6'	205	24		
Stan Edwards	FB	6'	210	24		6
Larry Moriarty	FB	6'1"	240	26		42
Steve Bryant	WR	6'2"	197	24		
Mike Holston	WR	6'3"	192	26		6
Eric Mullins	WR	5'11"	181	22		6
Carl Roaches	WR	5'8"	170	30		
Tim Smith	WR	6'2"	206	27		24
Herkie Walls	WR	5'8"	160	23		6
Chris Dressel	TE	6'4"	238	23		12
Mike McCloskey	TE	6'5"	246	23		6
Jamie Williams	TE	6'4"	232	24		18
Joe Cooper	K	5'10"	175	24		46
John James	K	6'3"	196	35		
Florian Kempf	K	5'9"	170	28		26

Doug France - Shoulder Injury

* Overtime

PITTSBURGH STEELERS

RUSHING

Last Name	No.	Yds	Avg	TD
Pollard	213	851	4.0	6
Abercrombie	145	610	4.2	1
Erenberg	115	405	3.5	2
Corley	18	89	4.9	0
Veals	31	87	2.8	0
Lipps	3	71	23.7	1
Malone	25	42	1.7	3
Gillespie	7	18	2.6	0
Woodley	11	14	1.3	0
Colquitt	1	0	0.0	0
Spencer	1	0	0.0	0
Capers	1	-3	-3.0	0
Campbell	3	-5	-1.7	0

RECEIVING

Last Name	No.	Yds	Avg	TD
Stallworth	80	1395	17.4	11
Lipps	45	860	19.1	9
Erenberg	38	358	9.4	1
Pollard	21	186	8.9	0
Thompson	17	291	17.1	3
Abercrombie	16	135	8.4	0
Capers	7	81	11.6	0
Kolodziejski	5	59	11.8	0
Cunningham	4	64	16.0	1
D. Nelson	2	31	15.5	0
Sweeney	2	25	12.5	0
Garrity	2	22	11.0	0
Gillespie	1	12	12.0	0

PUNT RETURNS

Last Name	No.	Yds	Avg	TD
Lipps	53	656	12.4	1
Woods	6	40	6.7	0
Clayton	1	0	0.0	0
Long	1	0	0.0	0

KICKOFF RETURNS

Last Name	No.	Yds	Avg	TD
Spencer	18	373	20.7	0
Erenberg	28	575	20.5	0
Veals	4	40	10.0	0
C. Brown	1	11	11.0	0
Catano	1	0	0.0	0
Corley	1	15	15.0	0
Gillespie	1	12	12.0	0

PASSING — PUNTING — KICKING

PASSING	Att	Cmp	%	Yds	Yd/Att	TD	Int-	%	RK
Malone	272	147	54	2137	7.86	16	17-	6	9
Woodley	156	85	55	1273	8.16	8	7-	5	12
Campbell	15	8	53	109	7.27	1	1-	7	

PUNTING	No	Avg
Colquitt	70	41.2

KICKING	XP	Att	%	FG	Att	%
Anderson	45	45	100	24	32	75

CINCINNATI BENGALS

RUSHING

Last Name	No.	Yds	Avg	TD
Kinnebrew	154	623	4.0	9
Alexander	132	479	3.6	2
Brooks	103	396	3.8	2
Jennings	79	379	4.8	2
Schonert	13	77	5.9	1
S. Wilson	17	74	4.4	0
Esiason	19	63	3.3	2
Anderson	11	64	5.8	0
Farley	7	11	1.6	0
Collinsworth	1	7	7.0	0
Martin	1	3	3.0	0
Verser	2	5	2.5	2
Harris	1	-2	-2.0	0

RECEIVING

Last Name	No.	Yds	Avg	TD
Collinsworth	64	989	15.5	6
Harris	48	759	15.8	2
Jennings	35	346	9.9	3
Brooks	34	268	7.9	2
Alexander	29	203	7.0	0
Holman	21	239	11.4	1
Kreider	20	243	12.2	1
Kinnebrew	19	159	8.4	1
Curtis	12	135	11.3	0
Martin	11	164	14.9	0
Kern	2	14	7.0	0
Verser	6	113	18.8	0
Farley	2	11	5.5	0
Wilson	2	15	7.5	0
Munoz	1	1	1.0	1

PUNT RETURNS

Last Name	No.	Yds	Avg	TD
Martin	24	376	15.7	0
Simmons	12	98	8.2	0
Horton	2	-1	-0.5	0

KICKOFF RETURNS

Last Name	No.	Yds	Avg	TD
Jennings	22	452	20.5	0
Martin	19	386	20.3	0
Brooks	7	144	20.6	0
Farley	6	93	15.5	0
Verser	3	46	15.3	0
Simmons	1	15	15.0	0
Kinnebrew	1	7	7.0	0
Harris	1	12	12.0	0
Williams	1	0	0.0	0

PASSING — PUNTING — KICKING

PASSING	Att	Cmp	%	Yds	Yd/Att	TD	Int-	%	RK
Anderson	275	175	64	2107	7.66	10	12-	4	7
Schonert	117	78	67	945	8.08	4	7-	6	
Esiason	102	51	50	530	5.20	3	3-	3	
McInally	2	2	100	77	38.50	0	0-	0	

PUNTING	No	Avg
McInally	67	42.3

KICKING	XP	Att	%	FG	Att	%
Breech	37	37	100	22	31	71

CLEVELAND BROWNS

RUSHING

Last Name	No.	Yds	Avg	TD
Green	202	673	3.3	0
Pruitt	163	506	3.1	6
Byner	72	426	5.9	2
White	24	62	2.6	0
J. Davis	3	15	5.0	1
Holt	1	12	12.0	0
B. Davis	1	6	6.0	0
McDonald	22	4	0.2	1
Walker	1	-8	-8.0	0

RECEIVING

Last Name	No.	Yds	Avg	TD
Newsome	89	1001	11.2	5
Brennan	35	455	13.0	3
Harris	32	512	16.0	2
Feacher	22	382	17.4	1
Adams	21	261	12.4	0
Holt	20	261	13.1	0
Green	12	124	10.3	1
Byner	11	118	10.7	0
Walker	10	122	12.2	0
B. Davis	7	119	17.0	2
White	5	29	5.8	0
Pruitt	5	29	5.8	0
Young	1	47	47.0	0
Bolden	1	19	19.0	0
Stracka	1	15	15.0	0
McDonald	1	4	4.0	0

PUNT RETURNS

Last Name	No.	Yds	Avg	TD
Brennan	29	199	8.0	0
Harris	9	73	8.1	0
Walker	6	50	8.3	0

KICKOFF RETURNS

Last Name	No.	Yds	Avg	TD
B. Davis	18	369	20.5	0
Byner	22	415	18.9	0
P. Brown	8	136	17.0	0
Young	5	134	26.8	0
White	5	80	16.0	0
Nicolas	1	12	12.0	0
Contz	1	10	10.0	0
Holt	1	1	1.0	0

PASSING — PUNTING — KICKING

PASSING	Att	Cmp	%	Yds	Yd/Att	TD	Int-	%	RK
McDonald	493	271	55	3472	7.0	14	23-	5	17
Flick	1	1	100	2	2.0	0	0-	0	
Cox	1	1	100	16	16.0	0	0-	0	

PUNTING	No	Avg
Cox	74	43.4

KICKING	XP	Att	%	FG	Att	%
Bahr	25	25	100	24	32	75
Cox	0	0	0.0	1	3	33

HOUSTON OILERS

RUSHING

Last Name	No.	Yds	Avg	TD
Moriarty	189	785	4.2	6
Edwards	60	267	4.5	1
Moon	58	211	3.6	1
Luck	10	75	7.5	1
Walls	4	20	5.0	0
Joyner	14	22	1.6	0
Mullins	1	0	0.0	0
Cooper	1	-2	-2.0	0

RECEIVING

Last Name	No.	Yds	Avg	TD
Smith	69	1141	16.5	4
J. Williams	41	545	13.3	3
Dressel	40	378	9.5	2
Moriarty	31	206	6.6	1
Holston	22	287	13.0	1
Edwards	20	151	7.6	0
Bryant	19	278	14.6	0
Walls	18	291	16.2	1
McCloskey	9	152	16.9	1
Mullins	6	85	14.2	1
Roaches	4	69	17.3	0

PUNT RETURNS

Last Name	No.	Yds	Avg	TD
Roaches	26	152	5.8	0

KICKOFF RETURNS

Last Name	No.	Yds	Avg	TD
Roaches	30	679	22.6	0
Walls	15	289	19.3	0
Allen	11	210	19.1	0
R. Williams	5	84	16.8	0
Joyner	3	57	19.0	0
Brown	3	17	5.7	0
Thompson	1	16	16.0	0
J. Williams	1	0	0.0	0

PASSING — PUNTING — KICKING

PASSING	Att	Cmp	%	Yds	Yd/Att	TD	Int-	%	RK
Moon	450	259	58	3338	7.42	12	14-	3	8
Luck	36	22	61	256	7.11	2	1-	3	
Moriarty	1	1	100	16	16.0	0	0-	0	

PUNTING	No	Avg
James	88	39.6

KICKING	XP	Att	%	FG	Att	%
Cooper	13	13	100	11	13	85
Kempf	14	14	100	4	6	67

DENVER BRONCOS 13-3-0 Dan Reeves

Scores of Each Game		
20	CINCINNATI	17
0	Chicago	27
24	Cleveland	14
21	KANSAS CITY	0
16	L.A.RAIDERS	13
28	Detroit	7
17	GREEN BAY	14
37	Buffalo	7
22	L.A.Raiders	*19
26	NEW ENGLAND	19
16	San Diego	13
42	MINNESOTA	21
24	SEATTLE	27
13	Kansas City	16
16	SAN DIEGO	13
31	Seattle	14

Use Name	Pos.	Hgt	Wgt	Age	Int	Pts
Mark Cooper	OT	6'5"	267	24		
Marsharne Graves	OT	6'4"	272	22		
Ken Lanier	OT	6'3"	269	25		
Dave Studdard	OT	6'4"	260	28		
Mike Freeman	OG	6'3"	256	22		
Winford Hood	OG	6'3"	262	22		
Paul Howard	OG	6'3"	260	33		
Keith Bishop	C-OG	6'3"	265	27		
Bill Bryan	C	6'2"	255	28		
Walt Bowyer	DE	6'4"	252	23		
Barney Chavous	DE	6'3"	258	33		
Rulon Jones	DE	6'6"	260	26		
Andre Townsend	DE-NT	6'3"	265	21		
Rubin Carter	NT	6'	256	31		
Scott Garnett	NT	6'2"	271	21		
Steve Busick	LB	6'4"	227	25	2	
Darren Comeaux	LB	6'1"	227	24	1	
Rick Dennison	LB	6'3"	220	26		
Ricky Hunley	LB	6'2"	238	22		
Tom Jackson	LB	5'11"	220	33		
Karl Mecklenburg	LB	6'3"	250	24	2	
Jim Ryan	LB	6'1"	215	27	1	
Aaron Smith	LB	6'2"	223	22		
Ken Woodard	LB	6'1"	218	24	1	6
Steve Foley	DB	6'2"	190	30	6	12
Mike Harden	DB	6'1"	192	26	6	6
Roger Jackson	DB	6'	186	25	1	
Tony Lilly	DB	6'	199	22	1	
Randy Robbins	DB	6'2"	189	21	2	6
Dennis Smith	DB	6'3"	200	25	3	6
Steve Wilson	DB	5'10"	195	27	4	
Louis Wright	DB	6'2"	200	31	1	6
John Elway	QB	6'3"	202	24		6
Gary Kubiak	QB	6'	192	23		6
Scott Stankavage	QB	6'1"	192	22		
Chris Brewer	HB	6'1"	193	22		
Gene Lang	HB	5'10"	196	22		18
Sammy Winder	HB	5'11"	203	25		36
Jesse Myles	FB-HB	5'10"	210	23		
Rick Parros	FB	5'11"	200	26		12
Gerald Willhite	FB	5'10"	200	25		12
Ray Alexander	WR	6'4"	195	22		6
Butch Johnson	WR	6'1"	187	30		36
Dave Logan	WR	6'4"	216	30		
Clint Sampson	WR	5'11"	183	23		6
Zach Thomas (to TB)	WR	6'	182	23		
Steve Watson	WR	6'4"	195	27		42
Clarence Kay	TE	6'2"	237	23		18
John Sawyer	TE	6'2"	230	31		
Don Summers	TE	6'4"	226	23		
James Wright	TE	6'3"	240	28		6
Rich Karlis	K	6'	180	25		101
Chris Norman	K	6'2"	198	22		

Bob Swenson - Knee Injury
Wilbur Myers - Knee Injury

SEATTLE SEAHAWKS 12-4-0 Chuck Knox

Scores of Each Game		
33	CLEVELAND	0
31	SAN DIEGO	17
23	New England	38
38	CHICAGO	9
20	Minnesota	12
14	L.A.Raiders	28
31	BUFFALO	28
30	Green Bay	24
24	San Diego	0
45	KANSAS CITY	0
17	L.A.RAIDERS	14
26	Cincinnati	6
27	Denver	24
38	DETROIT	17
7	Kansas City	34
14	DENVER	31

Use Name	Pos.	Hgt	Wgt	Age	Int	Pts
Sid Abramowitz	OT-OG	6'6"	279	24		
Ron Essink	OT	6'6"	275	26		
Brian Millard	OT	6'5"	284	24		
Edwin Bailey	OG	6'4"	265	25		
Bob Cryder	OG	6'4"	282	27		
Reggie McKenzie	OG	6'4"	255	34		
Robert Pratt	OG	6'4"	250	33		
Adam Schreiber	OG	6'4"	280	22		
Blair Bush	C	6'3"	252	27		
Kani Kauahi	C	6'2"	260	24		
Jeff Bryant	DE	6'5"	270	24	1	2
Jacob Green	DE	6'3"	255	27		
Randy Edwards	NT	6'4"	255	23		
Mike Fanning	NT	6'6"	255	31		
Dino Mangiero	NT	6'2"	270	25		
Joe Nash	NT	6'2"	250	23		6
Chuck Butler	LB	6'	220	22		
Keith Butler	LB	6'4"	238	28		
Greg Gaines	LB	6'3"	220	25	1	
Michael Jackson	LB	6'1"	220	27		
John Kaiser	LB	6'3"	221	22		
Sam Merriman	LB	6'3"	225	23		
Shelton Robinson	LB	6'2"	233	23		
Bruce Scholtz	LB	6'6"	240	25	1	
Fredd Young	LB	6'1"	225	22		
Dave Brown	DB	6'1"	190	31	8	12
Don Dufek	DB	6'	195	30		
Kenny Easley	DB	6'3"	206	25	10	12
John Harris	DB	6'2"	200	28	6	
Terry Jackson	DB	5'10"	197	28	4	6
Paul Moyer	DB	6'1"	201	23		
Keith Simpson	DB	6'1"	195	28	4	12
Terry Taylor	DB	5'10"	175	23	3	
Ray Wilmer	DB	6'2"	190	22		
Dave Kreig	QB	6'1"	185	25		18
Jim Zorn	QB	6'2"	200	31		
Zachary Dixon	HB	6'1"	204	27		12
Eric Lane	HB	6'	195	25		30
Randall Morris	HB	6'	190	23		
Curt Warner	HB	5'11"	205	23		
Cullen Bryant	FB	6'1"	236	33		
Dan Doornink	FB	6'3"	210	28		12
Franco Harris	FB	6'2"	225	34		
David Hughes	FB	6'	220	25		12
Chris Castor	WR	6'	170	24		
Paul Johns	WR	5'11"	180	25		12
Steve Largent	WR	5'11"	184	29		72
Dwight Scales	WR	6'2"	182	31		
Paul Skansi	WR	5'11"	190	23		
Daryl Turner	WR	6'3"	198	22		60
Bryon Walker	WR	6'4"	190	24		6
Pete Metzelaars	TE	6'7"	240	24		
Mike Tice	TE	6'7"	250	25		18
Charle Young	TE	6'4"	234	33		6
Norm Johnson	K	6'2"	193	24		110
Jeff West	K	6'3"	205	31		

Mark Hicks - Knee Injury
Eugene Williams - Stress Fracture of Leg
Joe Norman - Knee Injury

LOS ANGELES RAIDERS 11-5-0 Tom Flores

Scores of Each Game		
24	Houston	14
28	GREEN BAY	7
22	Kansas City	20
33	SAN DIEGO	30
13	Denver	16
28	SEATTLE	14
23	MINNESOTA	20
44	San Diego	37
19	DENVER	*22
6	Chicago	17
14	Seattle	17
17	KANSAS CITY	7
21	INDIANAPOLIS	7
42	Miami	34
24	Detroit	3
7	PITTSBURGH	13

Use Name	Pos.	Hgt	Wgt	Age	Int	Pts
Warren Bryant (from ATL)	OT	6'7"	285	28		
Bruce Davis	OT	6'6"	280	28		
Shelby Jordan	OT	6'7"	280	32		
Henry Lawrence	OT	6'4"	270	32		
Ed Muransky	OT	6'7"	275	24		
Charley Hannah	OG	6'5"	260	29		
Curt Marsh	OG	6'5"	270	25		
Mickey Marvin	OG	6'4"	265	28		
Dave Dalby	C	6'2"	255	34		
Don Mosebar	C-OG	6'6"	260	22		
Dwight Wheeler	C	6'3"	274	29		
Lyle Alzado	DE	6'3"	260	35		
Greg Boyd (from SF)	DE	6'6"	280	31		
Sean Jones	DE	6'7"	265	21		
Howie Long	DE	6'5"	270	24		
Bill Pickel	DE-NT	6'5"	260	24		
Greg Townsend	DE-NT	6'3"	240	22		
Reggie Kinlaw	NT	6'2"	245	27		
Stanley Adams	LB	6'2"	215	24		
Jeff Barnes	LB	6'2"	230	29	1	
Darryl Byrd	LB	6'1"	220	23		
Tony Caldwell	LB	6'1"	225	23		
Rod Martin	LB	6'2"	225	30	2	14
Larry McCoy	LB	6'2"	240	23		
Mark Merrill (from BUF)	LB	6'4"	234	29		
Matt Millen	LB	6'2"	250	26		
Bob Nelson	LB	6'4"	235	31		
Jack Squirek	LB	6'4"	230	25		
Brad Van Pelt	LB	6'5"	235	33	1	
James Davis	DB	6'	190	27	1	
Mike Davis	DB	6'3"	205	28	2	
Lester Hayes	DB	6'	200	29	1	
Mike Haynes	DB	6'2"	190	31	6	6
Vann McElroy	DB	6'2"	190	24	4	
Odis McKinney	DB	6'2"	190	27	1	
Stacey Toran	DB	6'2"	200	22		
Ted Watts	DB	6'	190	26	1	
Jerry Goldsteyn	QB	6'4"	210	30		
David Humm	QB	6'2"	190	32		
Jim Plunkett	QB	6'3"	220	36		6
Marc Wilson	QB	6'6"	205	27		6
Marcus Allen	HB	6'2"	205	24		108
Joe McCall	HB-FB	6'	200	22		
Greg Pruitt	HB	5'10"	190	33		
Jimmy Smith(from WAS)	HB	6'	205	23		
Chester Willis	HB	5'11"	200	26		
Frank Hawkins	FB	5'9"	210	25		18
Kenny King	FB	5'11"	205	27		
Malcolm Barnwell	WR	5'11"	185	26		12
Cliff Branch	WR	5'11"	170	36		
Cle Montgomery	WR	5'8"	180	26		6
Sam Seale	WR-DB	5'9"	175	21		
Dokie Williams	WR	5'11"	180	24		24
Dave Casper	TE	6'4"	240	32		12
Todd Christensen	TE	6'3"	230	28		42
Derrick Jensen	TE-FB	6'1"	215	28		12
Andy Parker	TE	6'5"	240	22		
Chris Bahr	K	5'10"	170	31		100
Ray Guy	K	6'3"	195	34		

KANSAS CITY CHIEFS 8-8-0 John Mackovic

Scores of Each Game		
37	Pittsburgh	27
27	Cincinnati	22
0	L.A.RAIDERS	22
0	Denver	21
10	CLEVELAND	6
16	N.Y.JETS	17
31	SAN DIEGO	13
7	N.Y.Jets	28
24	TAMPA BAY	20
0	Seattle	45
16	HOUSTON	17
7	L.A.Raiders	17
27	N.Y.Giants	28
16	DENVER	13
34	SEATTLE	7
45	San Diego	21

Use Name	Pos.	Hgt	Wgt	Age	Int	Pts
John Alt	OT	6'7"	278	22		
Scott Auer	OT-OG	6'5"	255	22		
Rich Baldinger	OT-OG	6'4"	285	24		
Matt Herkenhoff	OT	6'4"	275	33		
David Lutz	OT	6'6"	285	24		
Jim Rourke	OT-OG	6'5"	263	27		
Brad Budde	OG	6'4"	260	26		
Tom Condon	OG	6'3"	275	31		
Adam Lingner	C-OG	6'4"	250	23		
Bob Rush	C	6'5"	264	29		
Mike Bell	DE	6'4"	250	27		
Eric Holle	DE	6'5"	250	23		
Dave Lindstrom	DE	6'6"	255	29		
Art Still	DE	6'7"	257	28		
Mike Dawson	NT	6'4"	254	30		
Ken Kremer	NT	6'4"	260	27	1	
Bill Maas	NT	6'5"	265	22		
Jerry Blanton	LB	6'1"	236	27	1	
Calvin Daniels	LB	6'3"	236	25	2	
Charles Jackson	LB	6'2"	222	29	1	
Ken Jolly	LB	6'2"	220	22		
Ken McAlister	LB	6'5"	230	24	2	
Jeff Paine	LB	6'2"	224	23		
Scott Radecic	LB	6'3"	240	22	2	6
Gary Spani	LB	6'2"	228	28		
John Zamberlin	LB	6'2"	226	28		
Lloyd Burruss	DB	6'	202	26	2	
Deron Cherry	DB	5'11"	190	24	7	
Greg Hill	DB	6'1"	189	23	2	
Van Jakes	DB	6'	185	23		
Albert Lewis	DB	6'2"	190	23	4	
Kerry Parker	DB	6'1"	195	28		
Mark Robinson	DB	5'11"	206	21		
Kevin Ross	DB	5'9"	180	22	6	6
Todd Blackledge	QB	6'3"	225	23		6
Bill Kenney	QB	6'4"	211	29		
Sandy Osiecki	QB	6'5"	202	24		
David Whitehurst	QB	6'2"	204	29		
Herman Heard	HB	5'10"	184	22		24
Billy Jackson	HB	5'10"	215	24		12
Lawrence Ricks	HB	5'9"	194	23		
Theotis Brown	FB	6'2"	225	27		24
Mike Gunter	FB	5'11"	206	23		
Ken Lacy	FB	6'	222	23		
Carlos Carson	WR	5'11"	180	25		24
Anthony Hancock	WR	6'	200	24		6
Henry Marshall	WR	6'2"	220	30		24
Stephone Paige	WR	6'2"	180	22		24
J.T.Smith	WR	6'2"	185	28		
Walt Arnold (from WAS)	TE	6'3"	234	26		6
Ed Beckman	TE	6'4"	227	29		6
Dave Little	TE	6'2"	239	23		
Willie Scott	TE	6'4"	245	25		18
Jim Arnold	K	6'2"	212	23		
Nick Lowery	K	6'4"	189	28		104

Ken Thomas - Knee Injury

SAN DIEGO CHARGERS 7-9-0 Don Coryell

Scores of Each Game		
42	Minnesota	13
17	Seattle	31
31	HOUSTON	14
30	L.A.Raiders	33
27	DETROIT	24
34	Green Bay	28
13	Kansas City	31
37	L.A.RAIDERS	44
0	SEATTLE	24
38	Indianapolis	10
13	DENVER	16
34	MIAMI	*28
24	Pittsburgh	52
20	CHICAGO	7
13	Denver	16
21	KANSAS CITY	42

Use Name	Pos.	Hgt	Wgt	Age	Int	Pts
Sam Claphan	OT	6'6"	282	27		
Andrew Gissinger	OT	6'5"	279	25		
Chuck Loewen	OT-OG	6'3"	268	27		
Bill Elko	OG	6'5"	280	24		
Ed White	OG	6'2"	284	37		
Doug Wilkerson	OG	6'2"	253	37		
Derrel Gofourth	OG-C	6'3"	250	29		
Don Macek	C-OG	6'3"	260	30		
Dennis McKnight	C-OG	6'3"	272	24		
Chuck Ehin	DE	6'4"	260	23		
Keith Ferguson	DE	6'5"	255	25		
Fred Robinson	DE	6'4"	240	22		
Lee Williams	DE	6'6"	270	21	1	
Richard Ackerman (to RAID)	NT	6'4"	262	25		
Tony Chickillo	NT	6'3"	257	24		
Keith Guthrie	NT	6'3"	267	22		
Rickey Hogood	NT	6'2"	286	23		
Carlos Bradley	LB	6'	226	24		
Mike Green	LB	6'	239	23		
Linden King	LB	6'4"	250	29	2	
Woodrow Lowe	LB	6'	219	30	3	
Derrie Nelson	LB	6'2"	238	26		
Vince Osby	LB	5'11"	220	23		
Ray Preston	LB	6'	220	30		
Billy Ray Smith	LB	6'3"	231	23	3	
Cliff Thrift	LB	6'2"	237	28		
Eric Williams	LB	6'2"	235	29		
Gill Byrd	DB	5'11"	191	23	4	12
Scott Byers	DB	5'11"	170	23		
Tim Fox	DB	5'11"	186	30		
Ken Greene	DB	6'3"	196	28		
Bob Gregor	DB	6'2"	190	27		
Reuben Henderson	DB	6'1"	196	25		
Miles McPherson	DB	5'11"	191	24		
Lucious Smith (from BUF)	DB	5'10"	190	27		
Johnny Ray Smith	DB	5'9"	185	26		
John Turner	DB	6'	193	28	2	
Danny Walters	DB	6'1"	180	23		
Andre Young	DB	6'	190	23	2	
Dan Fouts	QB	6'3"	205	33		
Ed Luther	QB	6'3"	210	27		
Bruce Mathison	QB	6'3"	203	25		
Earnest Jackson	HB	5'9"	208	24		54
Lionel James	HB	5'7"	171	22		
Buford McGee	HB	6'	206	24		36
Wayne Morris	FB	6'	210	30		
Chuck Muncie	FB	6'3"	228	31		
Jewerl Thomas	FB	5'10"	230	26		12
Jesse Bendross	WR	6'	197	23		
Wes Chandler	WR	6'	183	28		36
Bobby Duckworth	WR	6'3"	197	25		24
Charlie Joiner	WR	5'11"	180	36		36
Ron Egloff	TE	6'5"	227	28		
Pete Holohan	TE	6'4"	249	25		
Bobby Micho	TE	6'3"	227	22		
Eric Sievers	TE	6'4"	236	25		18
Kellen Winslow	TE	6'5"	242	26		12
Rolf Benirschke	K	6'1"	184	29		92
Maury Buford	K	6'1"	191	24		
Benny Ricardo	K	5'10"	170	30		14

* Overtime

DENVER BRONCOS

RUSHING

Last Name	No.	Yds	Avg	TD
Winder	296	1153	3.9	4
Willhite	77	371	4.8	2
Elway	56	237	4.2	1
Parros	46	208	4.5	2
Lang	8	42	5.3	2
Brewer	10	28	2.8	0
Kubiak	9	27	3.0	1
Myles	5	7	1.4	0
Johnson	1	3	3.0	0

RECEIVING

Last Name	No.	Yds	Avg	TD
Watson	69	1170	17.0	7
Winder	44	288	6.5	2
Johnson	42	587	14.0	6
Willhite	27	298	11.0	0
Sawyer	17	122	7.2	0
Kay	16	136	8.5	3
J. Wright	11	118	10.7	1
Sampson	9	123	13.7	1
Alexander	8	132	16.5	1
Parros	6	25	4.2	0
Lang	4	24	6.0	1
Summers	3	32	10.7	0
Myles	2	22	11.0	0
Brewer	2	20	10.0	0
Kubiak	1	20	20.0	0
Logan	1	3	3.0	0
Studdard	1	-4	-4.0	0

PUNT RETURNS

Last Name	No.	Yds	Avg	TD
Thomas	21	125	6.0	0
Wilhite	20	200	10.0	0
Wilson	1	0	0.0	0

KICKOFF RETURNS

Last Name	No.	Yds	Avg	TD
Lang	19	404	21.3	0
Thomas	18	351	19.5	0
Willhite	4	109	27.3	0
Dennison	2	27	13.5	0
Harden	1	4	4.0	0
A. Smith	1	2	2.0	0

PASSING — PUNTING — KICKING

PASSING	Att	Cmp	%	Yds	Yd/Att	TD	Int-	% RK
Elway	380	214	56	2598	6.84	18	15-	4
Kubiak	75	44	59	440	5.87	4	1-	1
Stankavage	18	4	22	58	3.22	0	1-	6
Willhite	2	1	50	20	10.0	0	0-	0

PUNTING	No	Avg
Norman	96	40.1

KICKING	XP	Att	%	FG	Att	%
Karlis	38	41	93	21	28	75

SEATTLE SEAHAWKS

RUSHING

Last Name	No.	Yds	Avg	TD
Hughes	94	327	3.5	1
Lane	80	299	3.7	4
Doornink	57	215	3.8	0
Morris	58	189	3.3	0
Krieg	46	186	4.0	3
F. Harris	68	170	2.5	0
Dixon	52	149	2.9	2
C. Bryant	20	58	2.9	0
Warner	10	40	4.0	0
Largent	2	10	5.0	0
C. Young	1	5	5.0	0
Zorn	7	-3	-0.4	0

RECEIVING

Last Name	No.	Yds	Avg	TD
Largent	74	1164	15.7	12
Turner	35	715	20.4	10
C. Young	33	337	10.2	1
Doornink	31	365	11.8	2
Hughes	22	121	5.5	1
Johns	17	207	12.2	1
Walker	13	236	18.2	1
Lane	11	101	9.2	1
Morris	9	61	6.8	0
Tice	8	90	11.1	0
Castor	8	89	11.1	0
Skansi	7	85	12.1	0
Metzelaars	5	80	16.0	0
C. Bryant	3	20	6.7	0
Scales	2	22	11.0	0
Dixon	2	6	3.0	0
Pratt	1	30	30.0	0
Warner	1	19	19.0	0
F. Harris	1	3	3.0	0

PUNT RETURNS

Last Name	No.	Yds	Avg	TD
Easley	16	194	12.1	0
Skansi	16	145	9.1	0
Johns	11	140	12.7	1
Dixon	1	5	5.0	0

KICKOFF RETURNS

Last Name	No.	Yds	Avg	TD
Hughes	17	348	20.5	0
Dixon	25	446	17.8	0
Morris	8	153	19.1	0
C. Bryant	3	53	17.7	0
J. Harris	1	7	7.0	0

PASSING — PUNTING — KICKING

PASSING	Att	Cmp	%	Yds	Yd/Att	TD	Int-	% RK
Krieg	480	276	58	3671	7.7	32	24-	5
Zorn	17	7	41	80	4.7	0	2-	12

PUNTING	No	Avg
West	95	37.5

KICKING	XP	Att	%	FG	Att	%
N. Johnson	50	51	98	20	24	83

LOS ANGELES RAIDERS

RUSHING

Last Name	No.	Yds	Avg	TD
Allen	275	1168	4.2	15
Hawkins	108	376	3.5	3
King	67	254	3.8	0
Wilson	30	56	1.9	1
Plunkett	16	14	0.9	1
Humm	2	7	3.5	0
Willis	5	4	0.8	0
McCall	1	3	3.0	0
Jensen	3	3	1.0	1
Pruitt	8	0	0.0	0
Montgomery	1	1	1.0	0

RECEIVING

Last Name	No.	Yds	Avg	TD
Christensen	80	1007	12.6	7
Allen	64	758	11.8	5
Barnwell	45	851	18.9	2
Branch	27	401	14.9	0
Williams	22	509	23.1	4
King	14	99	7.1	0
Hawkins	7	51	7.3	0
Casper	4	29	7.3	2
Pruitt	2	12	6.0	0
Jensen	1	1	1.0	1

PUNT RETURNS

Last Name	No.	Yds	Avg	TD
Pruitt	53	473	8.9	0
Montgomery	14	194	13.9	1

KICKOFF RETURNS

Last Name	No.	Yds	Avg	TD
Williams	24	621	25.9	0
Montgomery	26	555	21.3	0
Pruitt	3	16	5.3	0
Willis	1	13	13.0	0
Jensen	1	11	11.0	0
McKinney	1	0	0.0	0

PASSING — PUNTING — KICKING

PASSING	Att	Cmp	%	Yds	Yd/Att	TD	Int-	% RK
Plunkett	198	108	55	1473	7.4	6	10-	5
Wilson	282	153	54	2151	7.6	15	17-	6
Humm	7	4	57	56	8.0	0	1-	14
Allen	4	1	25	38	9.5	0	0-	0

PUNTING	No	Avg
Guy	91	41.9

KICKING	XP	Att	%	FG	Att	%
Bahr	40	42	95	20	27	74

KANSAS CITY CHIEFS

RUSHING

Last Name	No.	Yds	Avg	TD
Heard	165	684	4.1	4
Brown	97	337	3.5	4
B. Jackson	50	225	4.5	1
Lacy	46	165	3.6	2
Blackledge	18	102	5.7	1
Paige	3	19	6.3	0
Gunter	15	12	0.8	0
Ricks	2	1	0.5	0
J. Arnold	1	0	0.0	0
Osiecki	1	-2	-2.0	0
Kenney	9	-8	-0.9	0
Carson	1	-8	-8.0	0

RECEIVING

Last Name	No.	Yds	Avg	TD
Marshall	62	912	14.7	4
Carson	57	1078	18.9	4
Brown	38	236	6.2	0
Paige	30	541	18.0	4
Scott	28	253	9.0	3
Heard	25	223	8.9	0
B. Jackson	15	101	6.7	1
Lacy	13	87	6.7	2
W. Arnold	11	95	8.6	1
Hancock	10	217	21.7	1
J.T. Smith	8	69	8.6	0
Beckman	7	44	6.3	1
Little	1	13	13.0	0

PUNT RETURNS

Last Name	No.	Yds	Avg	TD
J.T. Smith	39	332	8.5	0
Hancock	3	14	4.7	0

KICKOFF RETURNS

Last Name	No.	Yds	Avg	TD
J.T. Smith	19	391	20.6	0
Paige	27	544	20.1	0
Ricks	5	83	16.6	0
Hancock	2	32	16.0	0
Scott	1	9	9.0	0
Carson	1	2	2.0	0
Cherry	1	0	0.0	0

PASSING — PUNTING — KICKING

PASSING	Att	Cmp	%	Yds	Yd/Att	TD	Int-	% RK
Kenney	282	151	54	2098	7.4	15	10-	4
Blackledge	294	147	50	1707	5.8	6	11-	4
Osiecki	17	7	41	64	3.8	0	1-	6

PUNTING	No	Avg
J. Arnold	98	44.9

KICKING	XP	Att	%	FG	Att	%
Lowery	35	35	100	23	33	70

SAN DIEGO CHARGERS

RUSHING

Last Name	No.	Yds	Avg	TD
Jackson	296	1179	4.0	8
McGee	67	226	3.4	4
James	25	115	4.6	0
Muncie	14	51	3.6	0
Thomas	14	43	3.1	2
Morris	5	12	2.4	1
Luther	4	11	2.8	0
Fouts	12	--29	-2.4	0

RECEIVING

Last Name	No.	Yds	Avg	TD
Joiner	61	793	13.0	6
Holohan	56	734	13.1	1
Winslow	55	663	12.1	2
Chandler	52	708	13.6	6
Sievers	41	438	10.7	3
Jackson	39	222	5.7	1
Duckworth	25	715	28.6	4
James	23	206	9.0	0
Bendross	16	213	13.3	0
Egloff	11	92	8.4	0
McGee	9	76	8.4	2
Muncie	4	38	9.5	0
Gissinger	1	3	3.0	0
Fouts	1	0	0.0	0

PUNT RETURNS

Last Name	No.	Yds	Avg	TD
James	30	208	6.9	1
Henderson	1	0	0.0	0
L. Smith	1	0	0.0	0

KICKOFF RETURNS

Last Name	No.	Yds	Avg	TD
James	43	959	22.3	0
McGee	14	315	22.5	0
Egloff	2	20	10.0	0
Jackson	1	10	10.0	0

PASSING — PUNTING — KICKING

PASSING	Att	Cmp	%	Yds	Yd/Att	TD	Int-	% RK
Fouts	507	317	63	3740	7.4	19	17-	3
Luther	151	83	55	1163	7.7	5	3-	2
Holohan	2	1	50	25	12.5	1	0-	0
James	2	0	0	0	0.0	0	1-	50

PUNTING	No	Avg
Buford	66	42.0

KICKING	XP	Att	%	FG	Att	%
Benirschke	41	41	100	17	26	65
Ricardo	5	6	83	3	3	100

1984 A.F.C. PLAYOFFS — FIRST ROUND

1984 N.F.C.—PLAYOFFS

December 23, at Anaheim, Calif. (Attendance 67,037)

SCORING

N.Y. GIANTS	10	0	6	0	16
L.A. RAMS	0	3	7	3	13

First Quarter
- N.Y.G. — Haji-Sheikh, 37 yard field goal
- N.Y.G. — Carpenter, 1 yard rush; PAT—Haji-Sheikh (kick)

Second Quarter
- L.A. Rams — Lansford, 38 yard field goal

Third Quarter
- N.Y.G. — Haji-Sheikh, 39 yard field goal
- L.A. Rams — Dickerson, 14 yard rush; PAT—Lansford (kick)
- N.Y.G. — Haji-Sheikh, 36 yard field goal

Fourth Quarter
- L.A. Rams — Lansford, 22 yard field goal

TEAM STATISTICS

N.Y.G.		L.A.
16	First Downs-Total	12
5	First Downs-Rushing	5
8	First Downs-Passing	5
3	First Downs-Penalty	2
3	Fumbles-Number	2
0	Fumbles-Lost Ball	2
5	Penalty-Number	10
81	Yards Penalized	75
0	Missed Field Goals	0
62	Offensive Plays	43
192	Net Yards	214
3.1	Average Gain	5.0
0	Giveaways	2
2	Takeaways	0
+2	Difference	-2

INDIVIDUAL STATISTICS

N.Y. GIANTS	No.	Yds.	Avg.	L.A. RAMS	No.	Yds.	Avg.
RUSHING							
Morris	10	21	2.1	Dickerson	23	107	4.7
Carpenter	13	20	1.5	Kemp	1	2	2.0
Simms	4	-1	-0.3	Crutchfield	2	-2	-1.0
	27	20	1.5		26	107	4.1
RECEIVING							
Carpenter	7	23	3.3	Brown	3	32	10.7
Mowatt	7	73	10.4	Barber	3	31	10.3
Manuel	3	52	17.3	Ellard	2	22	11.0
Gray	2	20	10.0	McDonald	2	18	9.0
Johnson	1	6	6.0	Da. Hill	1	6	6.0
Galbreath	1	3	3.0		11	109	9.9
Morris	1	2	2.0				
	22	179	8.1				
PUNTING							
Jennings	4		38.8	Misko	4		37.8
PUNT RETURNS							
Manuel	3	25	8.3	Ellard	2	17	8.5
KICKOFF RETURNS							
Hill	3	49	16.3	Redden	5	92	18.4
Cephous	1	20	20.0				
	4	69	17.3				
INTERCEPTION RETURNS							
none				none			

PASSING

	Att.	Cmp	Cmp Pct	Yds	Int	Yds./Att	Yds./Cmp
N.Y. GIANTS							
Simms	31	22	71	179	0	5.8	8.1
L.A. RAMS							
Kemp	15	11	73	109	0	7.3	9.9

December 29 at San Francisco, Calif. (Attendance 60,303)

SCORING

N.Y. GIANTS	0	10	0	0	10
SAN FRANCISCO	14	7	0	0	21

First Quarter
- S.F. — Clark, 21 yard pass from Montana; PAT—Wersching (kick)
- S.F. — Francis, 9 yard pass from Montana; PAT—Wersching (kick)

Second Quarter
- N.Y.G. — Haji-Sheikh, 46 yard field goal
- N.Y.G. — Carson, 14 yard interception return
- S.F. — Solomon, 29 yard pass from Montana; PAT—Wersching (kick)

TEAM STATISTICS

N.Y.G.		S.F.
18	First Downs-Total	22
7	First Downs-Rushing	5
10	First Downs-Passing	16
1	First Downs-Penalty	1
2	Fumbles-Number	0
1	Fumble-Lost Ball	0
2	Penalties-Number	5
25	Yards Penalized	29
1	Missed Field Goals	2
75	Offensive Plays	71
260	Net Yards	412
3.5	Average Gain	5.8
3	Giveaways	3
3	Takeaways	3
0	Difference	0

INDIVIDUAL STATISTICS

N.Y. GIANTS	No.	Yds.	Avg.	SAN FRANCISCO	No.	Yds.	Avg.
RUSHING							
Morris	17	46	2.7	Montana	3	63	21.0
Galbreath	4	34	8.5	Tyler	14	35	2.5
Carpenter	3	4	1.3	Craig	10	34	3.4
Simms	1	3	3.0	Harmon	1	-1	-1.0
	25	87	3.5		28	131	4.7
RECEIVING							
Mowatt	5	49	9.8	D. Clark	9	112	12.4
Morris	4	45	11.3	Solomon	4	94	23.5
Manuel	2	32	16.0	Wilson	3	37	12.3
Galbreath	4	25	6.3	Craig	4	31	7.8
Johnson	3	23	7.7	Tyler	2	26	13.0
Carpenter	5	22	4.4	Francis	1	9	9.0
Mullady	2	22	11.0	Cooper	2	0	0.0
	25	218	8.7		25	309	12.4
PUNTING							
Jennings	6		37.7	Runager	5		42.0
PUNT RETURNS							
Manuel	3	22	7.3	McLemore	2	7	3.5
KICKOFF RETURNS							
Hill	4	109	27.3	Monroe	2	26	13.0
				Harmon	1	14	14.0
					3	40	13.3
INTERCEPTION RETURNS							
Reasons	2	33	16.5	Lott	1	38	38.0
Carson	1	14	14.0	Ellison	1	12	12.0
	3	47	15.7		2	50	25.0

PASSING

	Att.	Comp.	Cmp. Pct	Yds	Int	Yds/. Att.	Yds/ Comp
N.Y. GIANTS							
Simms	44	25	57	218	2	5.0	8.7
SAN FRANCISCO							
Montana	39	25	64	309	3	7.9	12.4

December 30, at Washington, D.C. (Attendance 55,431)

SCORING

CHICAGO	0	10	13	0	23
WASHINGTON	3	0	14	2	19

First Quarter
- Wash. — Moseley, 25 yard field goal

Second Quarter
- Chicago — B. Thomas, 34 yard field goal
- Chicago — Dunsmore, 19 yard pass from Payton; PAT—B. Thomas (kick)

Third Quarter
- Chicago — Gault, 75 yard pass from Fuller; PAT—kick failed
- Wash. — Riggins, 1 yard rush; PAT—Moseley (kick)
- Chicago — McKinnon, 16 yard pass from Fuller; PAT—B. Thomas (kick)
- Wash. — Riggins, 1 yard rush; PAT—Moseley (kick)

Fourth Quarter
- Wash. — Safety, Finzer stepped out of endzone

TEAM STATISTICS

CHI.		WASH.
13	First Downs-Total	22
5	First Downs-Rushing	6
7	First Downs-Passing	14
1	First Downs-Penalty	2
2	Fumbles-Number	3
1	Fumbles-Lost Ball	2
6	Penalties-Number	7
34	Yards Penalized	55
0	Missed Field Goals	1
57	Offensive Plays	76
310	Net Yards	336
5.4	Average Gain	4.4
1	Giveaways	3
3	Takeaways	1
+2	Difference	-2

INDIVIDUAL STATISTICS

CHICAGO	No.	Yds.	Avg.	WASHINGTON	No.	Yds.	Avg.
RUSHING							
Payton	24	104	4.3	Riggins	21	50	2.4
Suhey	7	7	1.0	Theismann	5	38	7.6
C. Thomas	1	5	5.0	J. Washington	1	5	5.0
Fuller	2	5	2.5		27	93	3.4
Finzer	1	-7	-7.0				
	35	114	3.3				
RECEIVING							
McKinnon	4	72	18.0	Monk	10	122	12.2
Gault	1	75	75.0	Muhammad	5	62	12.4
Suhey	1	33	33.0	Didier	4	85	21.2
Dunsmore	1	19	19.0	Washington	2	12	6.0
C. Thomas	1	13	13.0	Warren	1	11	11.0
Payton	1	12	12.0		22	292	13.3
Moorehead	1	6	6.0				
	10	230	23.0				
PUNTING							
Finzer	5		39.4	Hayes	5		36.8
PUNT RETURNS							
Fisher	2	17	8.5	Nelms	3	29	9.7
KICKOFF RETURNS							
Gault	3	74	24.7	Nelms	4	77	19.3
				Kane	1	10	10.0
				Griffin	1	0	0.0
				Coleman	0	25	—
					6	112	18.7
INTERCEPTION RETURNS							
Richardson	1	0	0.0	none			

PASSING

	Att.	Comp.	Comp. Pct.	Yds.	Int.	Yds./ Att.	Yds./ Comp.
CHICAGO							
Fuller	15	9	60	211	0	14.1	23.4
Payton	2	1	50	19	0	9.5	19.0
	17	10	59	230	0	13.5	23.0
WASHINGTON							
Theismann	42	22	52	292	1	7.0	13.3

1984 A.F.C.—PLAYOFFS

December 22, at Seattle, Wa. (Attendance 62,049)

SCORING

L.A. RAIDERS	0	0	0	7-	7
SEATTLE	0	7	3	3-	13

Second Quarter		
	Seattle	Turner, 26 yard pass from Krieg PAT—N. Johnson (kick)
Third Quarter		
	Seattle	N. Johnson, 35 yard field goal
Fourth Quarter		
	Seattle	N. Johnson, 44 yard field goal
	L.A. Raiders	Allen, 46 yard pass from Plunkett PAT—Bahr (kick)

TEAM STATISTICS

RAID.		SEA.
14	First Downs-Total	17
5	First Downs-Rushing	12
8	First Downs-Passing	4
1	First Downs-Penalty	1
2	Fumbles-Number	0
1	Fumbles-Lost Ball	0
8	Penalty-Number	7
68	Yards Penalized	55
0	Missed Field Goals	0
58	Offensive Plays	63
240	Net Yards	248
4.1	Average Gain	3.9
3	Giveaways	0
0	Takeaways	3
-3	Difference	+3

INDIVIDUAL STATISTICS

RAIDERS	No.	Yds.	Avg.	SEATTLE	No.	Yds.	Avg.
RUSHING							
Allen	17	61	3.6	Doornink	27	123	4.6
Hawkins	6	34	5.7	Hughes	14	54	3.9
Pruitt	1	6	6.0	Lane	4	17	4.3
King	1	4	4.0	Krieg	3	10	3.3
	25	105	4.2	Largent	1	-2	-2.0
					49	202	4.1
RECEIVING							
Allen	5	90	18.0	Turner	1	26	26.0
Hawkins	4	27	6.8	Tice	1	20	20.0
Barnwell	3	34	11.3	Doornink	1	14	14.0
Christensen	1	21	21.0	Hughes	1	10	10.0
King	1	12	12.0		4	70	17.5
	14	184	13.1				
PUNTING							
Guy	8		41.9	West	8		37.8
PUNT RETURNS							
Montgomery	3	5	1.7	Easley	5	52	10.4
KICKOFF RETURNS							
Pruitt	2	28	14.0	Hughes	2	38	19.0
INTERCEPTION RETURNS							
none				Haris	1	0	0.0
				Easley	1	21	21.0
					2	21	10.5

PASSING

L.A. RAIDERS	Att.	Comp.	Comp. Pct.	Yds.	Int.	Yds./ Att.	Yds./ Comp.
Plunkett	27	14	52	184	2	6.8	13.1
SEATTLE							
Krieg	10	4	40	70	0	7.0	17.5

December 29, at Miami, Fl. (Attendance 73,469)

SCORING

SEATTLE	0	10	0	0-	10
MIAMI	7	7	14	3-	31

First Quarter		
	Miami	Nathan, 14 yard rush PAT—von Schamann (kick)
Second Quarter		
	Seattle	N. Johnson, 27 yard field goal
	Miami	Cefalo, 34 yard pass from Marino PAT—von Schamann (kick)
	Seattle	Largent, 56 yard pass from Krieg PAT—N. Johnson (kick)
Third Quarter		
	Miami	Hardy, 3 yard pass from Marino PAT—von Schamann (kick)
	Miami	Clayton, 33 yard pass from Marino PAT—von Schamann (kick)
Fourth Quarter		
	Miami	von Schamann, 37 yard field goal

TEAM STATISTICS

SEA.		MIA.
8	First Downs-Total	22
2	First Downs-Rushing	8
6	First Downs-Passing	12
0	First Downs-Penalty	2
1	Fumbles-Number	0
1	Fumbles-Lost Ball	0
4	Penalties-Number	1
20	Yards Penalized	5
1	Missed Field Goals	2
55	Offensive Plays	70
267	Net Yards	405
4.9	Average Gain	5.8
1	Giveaways	2
2	Takeaways	1
+1	Difference	-1

INDIVIDUAL STATISTICS

SEATTLE	No.	Yds.	Avg.	MIAMI	No.	Yds.	Avg.
RUSHING							
Doornink	10	35	3.5	Nathan	18	76	4.2
Hughes	7	14	2.0	Bennett	11	41	3.7
Krieg	1	2	2.0	P. Johnson	6	22	3.7
	18	51	2.8	Carter	1	4	4.0
					36	143	4.0
RECEIVING							
Largent	6	128	21.3	Clayton	5	75	15.0
Doornink	6	23	3.8	Nathan	4	20	5.0
Turner	3	38	12.7	Hardy	3	48	16.0
Skansi	2	31	15.5	Duper	3	32	10.7
Hughes	1	8	8.0	Cefalo	2	43	21.5
C. Young	1	5	5.0	Moore	2	11	5.5
Krieg	1	1	1.0	Bennett	1	20	20.0
	20	234	11.7	Rose	1	13	13.0
					21	262	12.5
PUNTING							
West	7		37.0	Roby	3		37.0
PUNT RETURNS							
Easley	1	5	5.0	Walker	3	30	10.0
KICKOFF RETURNS							
Bryant	2	43	21.5	Walker	2	30	15.0
Hughes	1	21	21.0	Hardy	1	21	21.0
Tice	1	13	13.0		3	51	17.0
	4	77	19.3				
INTERCEPTIONS RETURNS							
J. Harris	2	45	22.5				

PASSING

SEATTLE	Att.	Comp.	Comp. Pct.	Yds.	Int.	Yds./ Att.	Yds./ Comp.
Krieg	35	20	57	234	0	6.7	11.7
MIAMI							
Marino	34	21	62	262	2	7.7	12.5

December 30, at Denver, Co. (Attendance 74,981)

SCORING

PITTSBURGH	0	10	7	7-	24
DENVER	7	0	10	0-	17

First Quarter		
	Denver	Wright, 9 yard pass from Elway PAT—Karlis (kick)
Second Quarter		
	Pitt.	Anderson, 28 yard field goal
	Pitt.	Pollard, 1 yard rush PAT—Anderson (kick)
Third Quarter		
	Denver	Karlis, 21 yard field goal
	Denver	Watson, 20 yard pass from Elway PAT—Karlis (kick)
	Pitt.	Lipps, 10 yard pass from Malone PAT—Anderson (kick)
Fourth Quarter		
	Pitt.	Pollard, 2 yard rush PAT—Anderson (kick)

TEAM STATISTICS

PITT.		DEN.
25	First Downs-Total	15
12	First Downs-Rushing	4
13	First Downs-Passing	11
0	First Downs-Penalty	0
3	Fumbles Number	2
2	Fumbles-Lost Ball	0
4	Peanlties-Number	1
30	Yards Penalized	5
3	Missed Field Goals	2
70	Offensive Plays	64
381	Net Yards	250
5.4	Average Gain	3.9
2	Giveaways	2
2	Takeaways	2
0	Difference	0

INDIVIDUAL STATISTICS

PITTSBURGH	No.	Yds.	Avg.	DENVER	No.	Yds.	Avg.
RUSHING							
Pollard	16	99	6.2	Winder	15	37	2.5
Abercrombie	17	75	4.4	Elway	4	16	4.0
Veals	1	1	1.0	Willhite	1	1	1.0
Lipps	1	0	0.0	Parros	1	0	0.0
Malone	5	-6	-1.2	Watson	1	-3	-3.0
	40	169	4.2		22	51	2.3
RECEIVING							
Lipps	5	86	17.2	Watson	11	177	16.1
Pollard	4	48	12.0	Winder	4	22	5.5
Stallworth	3	38	12.7	Wright	2	16	8.0
Abercrombie	3	18	6.0	Willhite	2	12	6.0
Cunningham	1	19	19.0	Alexander	1	9	9.0
Thompson	1	15	15.0		20	236	11.8
	17	224	13.2				
PUNTING							
Colquitt	3		28.3	Norman	4		42.3
PUNT RETURNS							
Lipps	3	9	3.0	Willhite	2	17	8.5
KICKOFF RETURNS							
Erenberg	1	29	29.0	Willhite	2	56	28.0
Lipps	3	73	24.3				
	4	102	25.5				
INTERCEPTIONS RETURNS							
E. Williams	1	28	28.0	none			
Dunn	1	6	6.0				
	2	34	17.0				

PASSING

PITTSBURGH	Att.	Comp.	Comp. Pct.	Yds.	Int.	Yds./ Att.	Yds./ Comp.
Malone	28	17	61	224	0	8.0	13.2
DENVER							
Elway	37	19	51	184	2	5.0	9.7
Willhite	1	1	100	52	0	52.0	52.0
	38	20	53	236	2	6.2	11.8

1984 Championship Games

NFC CHAMPIONSHIP GAME

January 6, 1985 at San Francisco

(Attendance 61,040)

SCORING

CHICAGO	0	0	0	0-	0
SAN FRANCISCO	3	3	7	10-	23

First Quarter	
S.F.	Wersching, 22 yard field goal
Second Quarter	
S.F.	Wersching, 22 yard field goal
Third Quarter	
S.F.	Tyler, 9 yard rush PAT—Wersching (kick)
Fourth Quarter	
S.F.	Solomon, 10 yard pass from Montana PAT—Wersching (kick)
S.F.	Wersching, 34 yard field goal

TEAM STATISTICS

CHI.		S.F.
13	First Downs-Total	25
9	First Downs-Rushing	9
3	First Downs-Passing	14
1	First Downs-Penalty	2
1	Fumbles-Number	1
0	Fumbles-Lost Ball	0
7	Penalties-Number	3
50	Yards Penalized	20
1	Missed Field Goals	0
63	Offensive Plays	67
186	Net Yards	387
3.0	Average Gain	5.8
1	Giveaways	2
2	Takeaways	1
+1	Difference	-1

The 49ers brimmed with confidence as they faced the Bears before a raucous San Francisco crowd. While the 49ers had talent in all sectors, the Bears got this far on the strength of their spirited defense, which overwhelmed foes with novel deployments.

Steve Fuller had returned from an injury to quarterback Chicago to an upset victory over the Redskins en route to San Francisco.

The Chicago defense played well in the first half despite three 49er penetrations into their territory. Twice they held the Niners to field goals, and once they covered a Joe Montana fumble on the two-yard line. While the Chicago defense held the 49ers to six first-half points, the San Francisco defense blanked the Bear offense.

In the second half, the Niners continued their incessant pressure on Fuller. On offense, they rigged up new blocking assignments, which gave Montana room to move. They drove to two touchdowns and a field goal for a 23-0 victory and a trip to the Super Bowl.

Although the Chicago defense had the bigger reputation, the San Francisco defense left the field with nine sacks and a shutout.

INDIVIDUAL STATISTICS

CHICAGO	No.	Yds.	Avg.	SAN FRANCISCO	No.	Yds.	Avg.
RUSHING							
Payton	22	92	4.2	Tyler	10	68	6.8
Fuller	6	39	6.5	Craig	8	44	5.5
Suhey	3	16	5.3	Montana	5	22	4.4
C. Thomas	1	2	2.0	Harmon	3	18	6.0
	32	149	4.7	Ring	2	5	2.5
				Cavanaugh	1	2	2.0
					29	159	5.5
RECEIVING							
McKinnon	3	48	16.0	D. Clark	4	83	20.8
Moorehead	2	14	7.0	Solomon	7	73	10.4
Suhey	4	11	2.8	Wilson	2	25	12.5
Payton	3	11	3.7	Tyler	2	22	11.0
Dunsmore	1	3	3.0	Francis	2	20	10.0
	13	87	6.7	Nehemiah	1	10	10.0
				Harmon	1	3	3.0
					19	236	12.4
PUNTING							
Finzer	7		43.1	Runager	3		39.0
PUNT RETURNS							
Fisher	2	12	6.0	McLemore	4	69	17.3
KICKOFF RETURNS							
Gentry	3	49	16.3	Harmon	1	15	15.0
Gault	1	18	18.0				
	4	67	16.8				
INTERCEPTIONS RETURNS							
Fencik	2	5	2.5	Hicks	1	0	0.0

PASSING

	Att.	Comp.	Comp. Pct.	Yds.	Int.	Yds./ Att.	Yds./ Comp.
CHICAGO							
Fuller	22	13	59	87	1	4.0	6.7
SAN FRANCISCO							
Montana	34	18	53	233	2	6.9	12.9
Cavanaugh	1	1	100	3	0	3.0	3.0
	35	19	54	236	2	6.7	12.4

AFC CHAMPIONSHIP GAME

January 6, 1985 at Miami

(Attendance 76,029)

SCORING

PITTSBURGH	7	7	7	7-	28
MIAMI	7	17	14	7-	45

First Quarter	
Miami	Clayton, 40 yard pass from Marino PAT—von Schamann (kick)
Pitt.	Erenberg, 7 yard run PAT—Anderson (kick)
Second Quarter	
Miami	von Schamann, 26 yard field goal
Pitt.	Stallworth, 65 yard pass from Malone PAT—Anderson (kick)
Miami	Duper, 41 yard pass from Marino PAT—von Schamann (kick)
Miami	Nathan, 2 yard rush PAT—von Schamann (kick)
Third Quarter	
Miami	Duper, 36 yard pass from Marino PAT—von Schamann (kick)
Pitt.	Stallworth, 19 yard pass from Malone PAT—Anderson (kick)
Miami	Bennett, 1 yard rush PAT—von Schamann (kick)
Fourth Quarter	
Miami	Moore, 6 yard pass from Marino PAT—von Schamann (kick)
Pitt.	Capers, 29 yard pass from Malone PAT—Anderson (kick)

TEAM STATISTICS

PITT.		MIA.
22	First Downs-Total	28
8	First Downs-Rushing	10
14	First Downs-Passing	18
2	Fumbles-Number	1
1	Fumbles-Lost Ball	1
3	Penalties-Number	3
30	Yards Penalized	25
1	Missed Field Goals	1
68	Offensive Plays	71
455	Net Yards	569
6.7	Average Gain	8.0
4	Giveaways	2
2	Takeaways	4
-2	Difference	+2

The Miami passing attack had blown all opponents away, but Pittsburgh coach Chuck Noll had a game plan to defuse it. The Steelers would rely on a grinding ground game to minimize Dan Marino's time on the field. When the Dolphins did have the ball, Pittsburgh would torment them with blitzes.

It was a good plan with limited success. The Steelers did drive downfield early in the game, only to lose the ball on a goalline interception by William Judson. Four plays later, Marino hit Mark Clayton for a 40-yard touchdown. The Steelers drove back on the ground to tie the game at the end of the second quarter, and Pittsburgh took the lead on a Mark Malone pass to John Stallworth.

Eighty-two seconds later, Mark Duper carried a Marino pass into the endzone. A Lyle Blackwood interception set up another Miami touchdown late in the first half for a 24-14 lead.

Forced to play catch-up ball in the second half, the Steelers had less success on the ground and were unable to ignite their passing game. Although the Steelers did score two second-half touchdowns, the Dolphins scored three.

The 45-28 Miami victory featured Marino's four touchdown passes, which negated Noll's best-laid plans.

INDIVIDUAL STATISTICS

PITTSBURGH	No.	Yds.	Avg.	MIAMI	No.	Yds.	Avg.
RUSHING							
Abercrombie	15	68	4.5	Nathan	19	64	3.4
Pollard	11	48	4.4	Johnson	10	39	3.9
Erenberg	6	27	4.5	Bennett	8	33	4.1
	32	143	4.5	Strock	1	-2	-2.0
					38	134	3.5
RECEIVING							
Stallworth	4	111	27.8	Nathan	8	114	14.3
Lipps	3	45	15.0	Duper	5	148	29.6
Sweeney	3	42	14.0	Clayton	4	95	23.8
Pollard	3	13	4.3	Moore	2	34	17.0
Erenberg	5	59	11.8	Hardy	2	16	8.0
Capers	1	29	29.0	Rose	1	28	28.0
Abercrombie	1	13	13.0		22	435	19.8
	20	312	15.6				
PUNTING							
Colquitt	3		43.7	Roby	2		42.5
PUNT RETURNS							
Lipps	1	7	7.0	Walker	2	10	5.0
				Kozlowski	1	2	2.0
					3	12	4.0
KICKOFF RETURNS							
Erenberg	5	106	21.2	Walker	3	62	20.7
INTERCEPTIONS RETURNS							
Shell	1	18	18.0	L. Blackwood	1	4	4.0
				Judson	1	34	34.0
				G. Blackwood	1	4	4.0
					3	42	14.0

PASSING

	Att.	Comp.	Comp. Pct.	Yds.	Int.	Yds./ Att.	Yds./ Comp.
PITTSBURGH							
Malone	36	20	56	312	3	8.7	15.6
MIAMI							
Marino	32	21	66	421	1	13.2	20.0
Nathan	1	1	100	14	0	14.0	14.0
	33	22	67	435	1	13.2	19.8

January 21, 1985 at Stanford, Calif.

(Attendance 84,059)

Montana & Co. Beat the Killer Bees and Marino

The league's best two teams squared off for the championship. The Dolphins had the Killer Bee defense and a killer passing attack featuring Dan Marino and the Marks Brothers. The 49ers had a versatile offense and a mobile defense, both devised by strategic master Bill Walsh. On the same day that Ronald Reagan took his second presidential oath, Stanford Stadium rocked with the cheers of 84,059 fans.

Marino lived up to his advance notices in the first quarter. He completed 9-of-10 passes for 103 yards and a touchdown. Miami twice launched sustained drives and had a 10-7 lead after 15 minutes. The second quarter brought a shift in momentum. The 49ers adjusted their defense by using five defensive backs and playing Fred Dean in a four-man line. The new alignment blanketed Mark Duper and Mark Clayton and kept a steady pressure on Marino. With their offense stalled, the Dolphins had the misfortune of several bad punts by Reggie Roby. After a 37-yard punt, the Niners took four plays to reach the endzone. On the next Miami drive, Roby kicked a 40-yard line drive that Dana McLemore returned 28 yards to the San Francisco 45-yard line. Six plays later, Joe Montana dashed six yards for another touchdown. Another weak Roby punt set up a nine-play San Francisco drive, giving the 49ers a 28-10 lead. The Dolphins did respond with a field goal 22 seconds before halftime. On the perfunctory kickoff, San Francisco guard Guy McIntyre picked up the squib kick and promptly fumbled it away. The Dolphins rushed their field-goal team onto the field and closed the gap to 28-16 at the half.

In need of a big second half, the Dolphins couldn't keep the momentum generated by McIntyre's blunder. The 49ers gave Marino little time to throw and sacked him three times early in the third quarter. The San Francisco offense, meanwhile, continued its steady advance against the Killer Bee defense. It added a field goal and a touchdown to run the score to 38-16 by the end of the period. Neither team scored in the fourth quarter.

Kudos were due for many of the 49ers. The San Francisco defense held Miami to 25 rushing yards and sacked Marino four times. Fullback Roger Craig set a Super Bowl record by scoring three touchdowns, less with heroics than by fitting perfectly into the balanced offense. Leading that offense was Montana, the MVP of the game. He passed for a record 331 yards, threw three touchdowns and ran for 59 yards, more than double the Miami team total.

LINEUPS

MIAMI		S.F
	OFFENSE	
Duper	WR	Clark
Giesler	LT	Paris
Foster	LG	Ayers
Stephenson	C	Quillan
Newman	RG	Cross
Green	RT	Fahnhorst
Hardy	TE	Francis
Clayton	WR	Solomon
Marino	QB	Montana
Nathan	RB	Tyler
Bonnott	FB	Craig
	DEFENSE	
Betters	LE	Pillers
Baumhower	NT	Tuiasosopo
Bokamper	RE	Board
Brudzinski	LOLB	Bunz
Brophy	LILB	Ellison
Brown	RILB	Reynolds
Bowser	ROLB	Turner
McNeal	LCB	Lott
Judson	RCB	Wright
G. Blackwood	SS	Williamson
L. Blackwood	FS	Hicks

SUBSTITUTES

MIAMI		
	OFFENSE	
Carter	Jensen	Rose
Cefalo	D. Johnson	Strock
Heflin	Moore	
	DEFENSE	
Barnett	Hill	Shipp
Benson	Kozlowski	Shiver
B. Brown	Lankford	Sowell
Charles	Lee	Toews
Clark	Rhone	Walker
Duhe		
	KICKERS	
Roby	von Schamann	
SAN FRANCISCO		
	OFFENSE	
Cooper	Monroe	Ring
Harmon	Nehemiah	Wilson
	DEFENSE	
Carter	Kennedy	Shell
Dean	McColl	Shields
Fuller	McIntyre	Stover
Holmoe	McLemore	Stuckey
Johnson	Montgomery	Walter
Kelcher		
	KICKERS	
Runager	Wersching	

SCORING

MIAMI	10	6	0	0- 16
SAN FRAN.	7	21	10	0- 38

First Quarter
- Miami — von Schamann, 37 yard field goal
- S.F. — Monroe, 33 yard pass from Montana; PAT—Wersching (kick)
- Miami — D. Johnson, 2 yard pass from Marino; PAT—von Schamann (kick)

Second Quarter
- S.F. — Craig, 8 yard pass from Montana; PAT—Wersching (kick)
- S.F. — Montana, 6 yard run; PAT—Wersching (kick)
- S.F. — Craig, 2 yard run; PAT—Wersching (kick)
- Miami — von Schamann, 31 yard field goal
- Miami — von Schamann, 30 yard field goal

Third Quarter
- S.F. — Wersching, 27 yard field goal
- S.F. — Craig, 16 yard pass from Montana; PAT—Wersching (kick)

TEAM STATISTICS

MIA.		S.F.
19	First Downs-Total	31
2	First Downs-Rushing	16
17	First Downs-Pasiing	15
0	First Downs-Penalty	0
1	Fumbles-Number	2
0	Fumbles-Lost Ball	2
1	Penaties-Number	2
10	Yards Penalized	10
0	Missed Field Goals	0
63	Offensive Plays	76
314	Net Yards	537
5.0	Average Gain	7.1
2	Giveaways	2
2	Takeaways	2
0	Difference	0

INDIVIDUAL STATISTICS

MIAMI	No.	Yds.	Avg.	SAN FRANCISCO	No.	Yds.	Avg.
RUSHING							
Nathan	5	18	3.6	Tyler	13	65	5.0
Bennett	3	7	2.3	Montana	5	59	11.8
Marino	1	0	0.0	Craig	15	58	3.9
	9	25	2.8	Harmon	5	20	4.0
				Solomon	1	5	5.0
				Cooper	1	4	4.0
					40	211	5.3
RECEIVING							
Nathan	10	83	8.3	Craig	7	77	11.0
Clayton	6	92	15.3	D. Clark	6	77	12.8
Rose	6	73	12.2	Francis	5	60	12.0
D. Johnson	3	28	9.3	Tyler	4	70	17.5
Moore	2	17	8.5	Monroe	1	33	33.0
Cefalo	1	14	14.0	Solomon	1	14	14.0
Duper	1	11	11.0		24	331	13.8
	29	318	11.0				
PUNTING							
Roby	6		39.3	Runager	3		32.7
PUNT RETURNS							
Walker	2	15	7.5	McLemore	5	51	10.2
KICKOFF RETURNS							
Walker	4	93	23.3	Harmon	2	24	12.0
Hardy	2	31	15.5	Monroe	1	16	16.0
Hill	1	16	16.0	McIntyre	1	0	0.0
	7	140	20.0		4	40	10.0
INTERCEPTIONS RETURNS							
none				Wright	1	0	0.0
				Williamson	1	0	0.0
					2	0	0.0

PASSING

	Att.	Comp.	Comp. Pct.	Yds.	Int.	Yds./ Att.	Yds./ Comp.	Yards Lost Tackled
MIAMI								
Marino	50	29	58	318	2	6.4	11.0	4-29
SAN FRANCISCO								
Montana	35	24	69	331	0	9.5	13.8	1-5

1985 N.F.C. The Midway's New Monsters

Coach Mike Ditka's Bears were *the* pro football story of 1985 and deserved to be. They had all the elements. For those who like intrigue, there were constant rumors of friction between Ditka and defensive coordinator Buddy Ryan, architect of the Bears' much-publicized "46" defense, the league's best. For nostalgia, Walter Payton padded his all-time record rushing total with 1,551 yards and looked toward his first Super Bowl. Flaky Jim McMahon was the N.F.L.'s most inspirational leader, the N.F.C.'s second-best passer and football's most unpredictable character. For comic relief, 308-pound defensive tackle William "The Refrigerator" Perry became a national hero by moving into the backfield as a blocker on short-yardage plays and then scoring three touchdowns, one on a pass reception. Suspense was added when the Bears won their first 12 games, raising the question — answered by Miami in week 13 — of whether they could go all the way undefeated.

EASTERN DIVISION

Dallas Cowboys — Although the Cowboys returned to the playoffs as N.F.C. East champs, success was catching up to them. All those years of drafting near the end of the pack had produced few stars to replace the aging nucleus of the team. Of the first draft choices from the previous eight years, only defensive end Jim Jeffcoat was a starter. Coach Tom Landry got the team away and winging with a big 44-14 win over the arch-rival Redskins in the Monday night opener, and the Cowboys stood 7-3 after 10 weeks. Then, on November 17, the Bears came to Dallas and crushed them 44-0, ending the N.F.L.'s second-longest non-shutout skein at 218 games, and showing the Cowboys had slipped badly. A later 50-24 thrashing by Cincinnati confirmed the diagnosis. Tony Dorsett, Danny White, Randy White, Too Tall Jones and several others were past 30. Of the younger players, only Jeffcoat, middle linebacker Eugene Lockhart and cornerback Everson Walls had established themselves. Walls became the N.F.L.'s first three-time interception leader with nine steals.

New York Giants — Clearly, the Giants were a team on the rise. For the second straight year, New York made the playoffs as a wild-card team, and only a pair of frustrating defeats by the Cowboys kept them from the N.F.C. East title. Of the team's six losses, only one was by as many as seven points. The defense, led by all-world linebacker Lawrence Taylor, had been getting raves for years. In 1985, coach Bill Parcells found an offense. Stubby running back Joe Morris emerged as one of the N.F.L.'s top threats with 1,336 yards and 21 touchdowns. Trouble loomed when tight end Zeke Mowatt went out with a knee injury, but Mark Bavaro proved a more-than-adequate replacement. Phil Simms showed continued improvement at quarterback, and — equally important — good health. His 3,829 passing yards put him into the Pro Bowl where he was MVP.

Washington Redskins — On Monday night, November 18, America watched the end of Joe Theismann's career, when a Lawrence Taylor sack snapped his right leg. After Theismann was carried off, a new star appeared for the Skins, who were only 5-5 going into the game. Young Jay Schroeder rallied the team to a 23-21 win over the Giants and four more victories in the last five games. In the only loss, he passed for 348 yards against San Francisco. Although Washington could not overcome its stumbling start — it lost three of its first four games — the final 10-6 record was the same as the Cowboys and Giants posted. Only a tiebreaker kept them out of the playoffs. In another changing of the guard, George Rogers replaced sore-backed John Riggins as the No. 1 runner. Some things stayed the same. Receiver Art Monk caught 91 passes, and the celebrated Hogs' offensive line continued to block no matter who was in the backfield.

Philadelphia Eagles — For the third straight year, the Eagles' record improved, but the progress wasn't fast enough for new owners Norman Braman and Ed Leibowitz. Coach Marion Campbell was fired with a game left on the schedule. A streak of five wins in six games at mid-season raised too many hopes for Campbell to survive the inevitable collapse. The Eagles' defense, led by Pro Bowl safety Wes Hopkins, was respectable, but the offense creaked, despite the presence of well-named wide receiver Mike Quick. A 99-yard Ron Jaworski-to-Quick pass in overtime against Atlanta produced one of Philadelphia's wins. The main culprit was the offensive line, which was offensive only to lovers of good blocking. Somehow, new running back Earnest Jackson gained 1,028 yards and Jaworski survived.

St. Louis Cardinals — Big things were expected of the Big Red after a 9-7 year in '84, and three victories in the first four games did nothing to diminish confidence. Then, injuries to receiver Roy Green and back Ottis Anderson put the team into a tailspin — losing 10 of the remaining 12 games and costing Jim Hanifan, the coach since 1980, his job. Stump Mitchell did a good job as Anderson's replacement, but, without Green or Anderson in his arsenal, quarterback Neil Lomax regressed to just another thrower. In a fashion note, the team played its December 8 game with New Orleans in knee-length maroon socks. Possibly from embarrassment, but more likely because of Mitchell's 158 rushing yards, the Cardinals won their only game in the final seven weeks. The league office quickly ruled the socks out of bounds, and the much-relieved Cards went back to losing in traditional garb.

CENTRAL DIVISION

Chicago Bears — The Bears reached near-perfection in mid-November as they annihilated Detroit, Dallas and Atlanta by an aggregate 104-3. When Miami finally stopped them 38-24 on a Monday night at the Orange Bowl, Chicago was already focusing on the playoffs. William Perry, Walter Payton and Jim McMahon were the media darlings, but the heart of the team was its defense. Linebackers Mike Singletary and Otis Wilson, linemen Richard Dent and Dan Hampton, and safety Dave Duerson were Pro Bowlers, but several other Bear defenders could have been equally honored. They led the league in fewest points allowed, rushing defense, overall defense, interceptions, fewest points allowed, and takeaway-giveaway ratio. Dent led the N.F.C. in sacks for the second consecutive year with 17. Although safety Gary Fencik's 118 tackles topped the team, the leader of the impregnable defense was Singletary, voted United Press International's defensive player of the year. About the only thing they couldn't defend against was media backlash. When a Bears' rock-video hit the charts, some fans were ready to cry, "Enough!"

Green Bay Packers — The Packers' .500 finish was their second under Forrest Gregg, third in a row and fourth in five years. The only time they missed 8-8 during that stretch was the strike-shortened '82 season. The roster, with the exception of receiver James Lofton, was mostly middling in quality. Lofton caught 69 passes for 1,153 yards, even though he was double- and triple-covered. The offensive line was less than average. QB Lynn Dickey finally tired of being sacked and asked to be benched for the fourth game. After that, Randy Wright, Jim Zorn and Dickey took turns at signal-calling. Regardless, the Packers' offense consisted of short passes to tight end Paul Coffman and bombs to Lofton.

Minnesota Vikings — Easygoing Bud Grant's return as coach lasted only one season, but it was enough to get the Vikings back to respectability. The encouraging 7-9 season was accomplished with much the same crew that floundered to 3-13 in '84. QB Tommy Kramer, still the model of inconsistency, threw for a bundle of yards one week and a bunch of interceptions the next. One of his best nights came in a losing effort when he zinged the Bears' all-everything defense for 436 yards and three touchdowns. Little Darrin Nelson was a versatile runner-receiver, and U.S.F.L. refugee Anthony Carter gave Kramer a consistent deep threat, but the team's bread-and-butter pass catcher was tight end Steve Jordan. With the Vikings on the right track again, Grant turned the reins over to long-time assistant Jerry Burns and retired again.

Detroit Lions — Had the Lions been able to play all their games at the Pontiac Silverdome, they might have challenged the Bears. Under new coach Darryl Rogers, they won their first six home games before a pair of losses dropped them to 6-2. Among the victims were Dallas, San Francisco and Miami. On the road, the Lions were a dreadful 1-7, losing to Tampa Bay and Indianapolis, among others. Eric Hipple was at quarterback most of the time, but he was adequate, at best. Billy Sims, nursing his injured knee, didn't play all year, putting the pressure on James Jones, who gained a respectable 886 yards.

FINAL TEAM STATISTICS

OFFENSE

	ATL.	CHI.	DALL.	DET.	G.B.	L.A.	MINN.	N.O.	NY G	PHIL.	STL.	S.F.	T.B.	WASH.
FIRST DOWNS:														
Total	296	343	336	259	318	258	317	250	356	292	301	340	291	319
by Rushing	149	176	95	89	114	115	95	83	138	82	108	137	95	147
by Passing	132	145	208	150	172	131	189	148	192	188	171	179	162	157
by Penalty	15	22	33	20	32	12	33	19	26	22	22	24	34	15
RUSHING:														
Number	560	610	462	452	470	503	406	431	581	428	417	477	434	571
Yards	2466	2761	1741	1538	2208	2057	1516	1683	2451	1630	1974	2232	1644	2523
Average Yards	4.4	4.5	3.8	3.4	4.7	4.1	3.7	3.9	4.2	3.8	4.7	4.7	3.8	4.4
Touchdowns	14	27	11	13	16	15	19	4	24	8	14	20	11	20
PASSING:														
Attempts	462	432	587	462	513	403	576	508	497	567	534	550	508	512
Completions	254	237	344	254	267	234	311	260	275	290	296	331	269	280
Completion Pct.	55.0	54.9	58.6	55.0	52.0	58.1	54.0	51.2	55.3	51.1	55.4	60.2	53.0	54.7
Passing Yards	3025	3303	4236	3316	3552	2872	3931	3257	3829	4036	3581	3987	3423	3243
Avg. Yds per Att.	4.7	6.5	6.1	5.7	5.6	5.4	5.9	4.9	6.3	5.8	5.2	6.2	5.7	5.0
Avg. Yds per Comp.	11.9	13.9	12.3	13.1	13.3	12.3	12.6	12.5	13.9	13.9	12.1	12.1	12.7	11.6
Times Tackled	69	43	44	53	50	57	45	58	52	55	65	42	40	52
Yds Lost Tackled	531	227	375	378	389	409	296	461	396	450	469	299	301	428
Net Yards	2494	3076	3861	2938	3163	2463	3635	2796	3433	3586	3112	3688	3122	2815
Touchdowns	13	17	27	19	21	16	22	20	22	19	19	28	22	13
Interceptions	20	16	25	21	27	14	29	23	20	28	18	14	26	21
Pct. Intercepted	4.3	3.7	4.3	4.5	5.3	3.5	5.0	4.5	4.0	4.9	3.4	2.5	5.1	4.1
PUNTS:														
Number	89	69	83	73	82	88	67	89	81	91	87	87	79	73
Average	42.2	41.6	41.4	41.8	39.8	42.7	42.8	42.3	42.9	41.5	40.7	39.3	40.9	40.7
PUNT RETURNS														
Number	31	54	40	38	38	38	25	30	53	45	40	38	25	47
Yards	223	503	237	403	370	501	250	215	442	393	393	258	229	508
Average Yards	7.2	9.3	5.9	10.6	9.7	13.2	10.0	7.2	8.3	8.7	9.8	6.8	9.2	10.8
Touchdowns	0	0	0	1	0	1	0	0	0	0	0	0	0	0
KICKOFF RET.:														
Number	72	43	62	68	67	56	68	71	50	56	78	58	80	60
Yards	1406	1089	1210	1494	1318	1394	1576	1547	866	1160	1421	1269	1622	1349
Average Yards	19.5	25.3	19.5	22.0	19.7	24.9	23.2	21.8	17.3	20.7	18.2	21.9	20.3	22.5
Touchdowns	1	2	0	0	0	3	0	0	0	0	0	1	0	0
INTERCEPT RET.:														
Number	22	34	33	18	15	29	22	21	24	18	13	18	18	23
Yards	247	512	263	136	262	359	283	312	339	125	240	310	146	220
Average Yards	11.2	15.1	8.0	7.6	17.5	12.4	12.9	14.9	14.1	6.9	18.5	17.2	8.1	9.6
Touchdowns	1	4	4	0	2	4	1	2	2	2	1	1	0	0
PENALTIES:														
Number	126	104	100	104	101	97	88	98	80	98	101	105	103	74
Yards	1149	912	759	741	798	730	690	805	781	736	816	868	751	596
FUMBLES:														
Number	23	24	29	36	39	35	27	23	36	25	38	29	37	27
Number Lost	10	15	16	20	18	21	18	13	18	12	16	20	22	19
POINTS:														
Total	282	456	357	307	337	340	346	294	399	286	278	411	294	297
PAT Attempts	30	51	43	33	40	39	43	29	48	30	34	53	33	33
PAT Made	30	51	42	31	38	38	41	27	45	29	33	52	30	31
FG Attempts	31	37	28	31	26	29	26	35	33	30	28	21	32	35
FG Made	24	31	19	26	19	22	15	31	22	25	13	13	22	22
Percent FG Made	77.4	83.8	67.9	83.9	73.1	75.9	57.7	88.6	66.7	83.3	46.4	61.9	68.8	62.9
Safeties	0	3	0	0	1	1	1	0	0	1	1	1	0	1

DEFENSE

	ATL.	CHI.	DALL.	DET.	G.B.	L.A.	MINN.	N.O.	NY G	PHIL.	STL.	S.F.	T.B.	WASH.
FIRST DOWNS:														
Total	329	236	312	359	310	281	324	335	258	307	314	293	351	244
by Rushing	112	74	98	179	111	104	139	125	77	122	115	89	146	94
by Passing	181	141	193	156	178	155	163	188	163	160	169	183	185	134
by Penalty	36	21	21	24	21	22	22	22	18	25	30	21	20	16
RUSHING:														
Number	437	359	465	560	494	444	542	508	419	526	552	435	547	424
Yards	2052	1319	1853	2685	2047	1586	2223	2162	1482	2205	2378	1683	2430	1734
Average Yards	4.7	3.7	4.0	4.8	4.1	3.6	4.1	4.3	3.5	4.2	4.3	3.9	4.4	4.1
Touchdowns	24	6	18	19	17	9	16	19	9	17	11	10	28	11
PASSING:														
Attempts	535	522	549	478	509	548	490	529	· 535	478	461	621	505	465
Completions	289	249	279	283	295	296	280	306	278	251	253	346	318	239
Completion Pct.	54.0	47.7	50.8	59.2	58.0	54.0	57.1	57.8	52.0	52.5	54.9	55.7	63.0	51.4
Passing Yards	4129	3299	4214	3242	3509	3483	3464	3975	3377	3289	3257	3965	3955	3124
Avg. Yds per Att.	6.6	4.8	6.2	5.6	5.6	5.1	6.2	6.4	4.7	5.5	6.1	5.2	6.8	5.3
Avg. Yds per Comp.	14.3	13.3	15.1	11.5	11.9	11.8	12.4	13.0	12.2	13.1	12.9	11.5	12.4	13.1
Times Tackled	42	64	62	45	48	56	33	46	68	53	32	60	35	52
Yds Lost Tackled	331	483	459	336	383	421	223	322	539	359	254	457	277	378
Net Yards	3798	2816	3755	2906	3126	3062	3241	3653	2838	2930	3003	3508	3678	2746
Touchdowns	32	16	20	16	22	19	20	26	20	18	34	11	18	19
Interceptions	22	34	33	18	15	29	22	21	24	18	13	18	18	23
Pct. Intercepted	4.1	6.5	6.0	3.8	2.9	5.3	4.5	4.0	4.5	3.8	2.8	2.9	3.6	4.9
PUNTS:														
Number	69	90	78	64	77	89	65	81	107	92	75	92	59	85
Average	42.0	40.4	41.3	40.2	42.7	42.0	41.4	42.2	40.8	42.6	40.9	39.6	44.4	43.8
PUNT RETURNS														
Number	52	23	44	44	46	43	36	45	29	41	51	33	47	32
Yards	417	203	286	420	411	297	328	397	247	462	456	294	519	205
Average Yards	8.0	8.8	6.5	9.5	8.9	6.9	9.1	8.8	8.5	11.3	8.9	8.9	11.0	8.9
Touchdowns	0	0	0	0	0	0	0	0	0	1	0	1	0	0
KICKOFF RET.:														
Number	62	78	68	60	71	66	68	43	79	65	56	72	51	53
Yards	1135	1827	1310	1313	1570	1253	1491	968	1697	1293	1150	1485	1187	1186
Average Yards	18.3	23.4	19.3	21.9	22.1	19.0	21.9	22.5	21.5	19.9	20.5	20.6	23.3	22.4
Touchdowns	0	0	0	1	2	0	0	1	0	0	0	1	0	2
INTERCEPT RET.:														
Number	20	16	25	21	27	14	29	23	20	28	18	14	26	21
Yards	172	99	319	247	326	138	311	251	285	474	245	80	368	215
Average Yards	8.6	6.2	12.8	11.8	12.1	9.9	10.7	10.9	14.3	16.9	13.6	5.7	14.2	10.2
Touchdowns	0	1	2	1	1	1	2	1	4	2	1	1	4	2
PENALTIES:														
Number	97	118	108	105	102	72	123	108	106	99	88	106	114	89
Yards	738	944	990	729	797	529	1000	837	821	834	742	778	945	699
FUMBLES:														
Number	18	30	24	35	44	30	37	24	36	27	28	31	37	28
Number Lost	12	20	15	18	25	17	22	16	13	14	14	17	22	11
POINTS:														
Total	452	198	333	366	355	277	359	401	283	310	414	263	448	312
PAT Attempts	57	23	40	40	43	30	39	48	33	39	47	26	50	35
PAT Made	55	22	37	40	41	28	38	48	31	37	46	24	50	34
FG Attempts	23	19	27	36	31	29	37	28	21	29	38	35	43	28
FG Made	17	12	18	28	16	23	29	21	18	13	28	27	32	22
Percent FG Made	73.9	63.2	66.7	77.8	51.6	79.3	78.4	75.0	85.7	44.8	73.7	77.1	74.4	78.6
Safeties	2	1	1	1	4	0	0	1	0	0	1	1	1	1

Some improvement in the offensive line and on the defense gave hope for the future.

Tampa Bay Buccaneers — The Bucs were the Central Division omega to the Bears' alpha. By mid-season, Chicago looked like it would never lose, and Tampa Bay looked like it would never win. After new coach Leeman Bennett's team topped St. Louis in the 10th week and then was stomped 62-28 the next week by the Jets, he switched from Steve DeBerg to ex-U.S.F.L. QB Steve Young. The result was an 19-16 overtime win over Detroit. Four more losses resulted in a 2-14 finish. Tight end Jimmie Giles and running back James Wilder played tough all year, and Young gave promise for the future, but the general talent level indicated several coming years of early draft positions.

WESTERN DIVISION

Los Angeles Rams — The Rams signed Dieter Brock out of the Canadian Football League where he was twice MVP, hoping the 34-year-old "rookie" could finally give them some passing punch. In camp, Brock won the starting job from Jeff Kemp, but, after that, his short passes satisfied virtually no one. Eric Dickerson, the Rams' most important weapon, held out until the third game while free agent Charles White filled in admirably. Once signed, Dickerson, though inconsistent, rushed for 1,234 yards and 12 scores, a good season for anyone else. The team won its first seven games, then lost four of its next six. The lead over San Francisco was down to a game, but, on December 9, Ron Brown's TD kickoff return and Gary Green's interception runback for another score sparked a 27-20 victory over the 49ers to lock up the West title.

San Francisco 49ers — The defense slumped badly and quarterback Joe Montana got off to a slow start. The '84 Super Bowl champs slipped below .500 after seven games. Five victories in the next half-dozen games got them back into the race and eventually to a wild-card berth. The defense was unreliable to the end, but Montana came back to lead the N.F.C. in passing. Reliable Dwight Clark and tight end Russ Francis were steady receivers, and rookie Jerry Rice gave Montana an exciting long-ball threat. Running back Roger Craig had a gangbuster year, rushing for 1,050 yards and catching a league-leading 92 passes for another 1,106, to become the first player ever to gain a thousand yards both ways.

New Orleans Saints — For the 19th consecutive year, the Saints failed to finish above .500. Kicker Morten Andersen provided most of the offense with 31 field goals out of 35 attempts. In the spring, the Saints handed Earl Campbell the running back job by trading George Rogers to Washington, but Campbell showed he was past his prime. The quarterback situation was never completely settled, although ex-U.S.F.L.er Bobby Hebert showed promise. The defense had been the best thing coach Bum Phillips had going for him, but it fell apart. After the Saints upset Minnesota on November 24, Phillips resigned. His son Wade, the team's defensive coordinator, replaced him on an interim basis. The team responded with a second upset, over the Rams, and then dropped its last three games to finish 5-11.

Atlanta Falcons — The Falcons signed first-round draft choice Bill Fralic, a guaranteed future all-pro. Once the season opened, they dropped like a rock to the bottom of the division by losing their first six games. Quarterback David Archer replaced an injured Steve Bartkowski after five weeks, but Atlanta had little luck passing the ball. Billy "White Shoes" Johnson, at 34 years old, was the only receiver with more than 30 catches. The one-dimensional offense was almost all Gerald Riggs. He was excellent, leading the N.F.C. in rushing with 1,719 yards, but the so-so defense couldn't make up for the lack of a passing attack.

DALLAS COWBOYS 10-6 Tom Landry

Scores of Each Game		
44	WASHINGTON	14
21	Detroit	26
20	CLEVELAND	7
17	Houston	10
30	N.Y.Giants	29
27	PITTSBURGH	13
14	Philadelphia	16
24	ATLANTA	10
10	St.Louis	21
13	Washington	7
0	CHICAGO	44
34	PHILADELPHIA	17
35	ST.LOUIS	17
24	Cincinnati	50
28	N.Y.GIANTS	21
16	San Francisco	31

Use Name	Pos.	Hgt	Wgt	Age	Int	Pts
Jim Cooper	OT	6'5"	274	29		
Phil Pozderac	OT	6'9"	282	25		
Chris Schultz	OT	6'8"	288	25		
Crawford Ker	OG	6'3"	293	23		
Kurt Petersen	OG	6'4"	278	28		
Howard Richards	OG-OT	6'6"	262	26		
Broderick Thompson	OG	6'5"	280	25		
Glen Titensor	OG	6'4"	261	27		
Tom Rafferty	C	6'3"	264	31		
Mark Tuinel	C	6'5"	270	25		
Kevin Brooks	DE	6'6"	270	22		
Jim Jeffcoat	DE	6'5"	263	24	1	6
Too Tall Jones	DE	6'9"	287	34		
John Dutton	DT	6'7"	268	34		
David Ponder	DT	6'3"	250	23		
Don Smerek	DT	6'7"	265	27		
Randy White	DT	6'4"	272	32		

Dowe Aughtman - Shoulder Injury
Brian Baldinger - Knee Injury

Use Name	Pos.	Hgt	Wgt	Age	Int	Pts
Vince Albritton	LB	6'2"	213	23		
Steve DeOssie	LB	6'2"	245	22		
Mike Hegman	LB	6'1"	228	32	1	
Eugene Lockhart	LB	6'2"	234	24	1	6
Jesse Penn	LB	6'3"	217	22		6
Jeff Rohrer	LB	6'3"	230	26		
Brian Salonen	LB	6'3"	226	24		
Bill Bates	DB	6'1"	199	24	4	
Dextor Clinkscale	DB	5'11"	195	27	3	
Michael Downs	DB	6'3"	204	26	3	
Ricky Easmon (to TB)	DB	5'10"	160	22		
Ron Fellows	DB	6'	180	26	4	
Victor Scott	DB	6'	196	23	2	6
Dennis Thurmna	DB	5'11"	179	29	5	6
Everson Walls	DB	6'1"	194	25	9	

Use Name	Pos.	Hgt	Wgt	Age	Int	Pts
Steve Pelluer	QB	6'4"	208	23		
Danny White	QB	6'2"	196	33		12
Gary Hogeboom	QB	6'4"	207	27		6
Tony Dorsett	HB	5'11"	185	31		60
James Jones	HB	5'10"	203	26		
Robert Lavette	HB	5'11"	199	21		
John Williams (to SEA)	HB	5'11"	219	24		
Todd Fowler	FB	6'3"	218	23		
Timmy Newsome	FB	6'1"	237	27		18
Gordon Banks	WR	5'10"	173	27		
Kenny Duckett (from NO)	WR	6'	183	25		
Leon Gonzales	WR	5'10"	162	21		
Tony Hill	WR	6'2"	202	29		42
Karl Powe	WR	6'2"	175	23		
Mike Renfro	WR	6'	189	30		48
Fred Cornwell	TE	6'6"	233	24		6
Doug Cosbie	TE	6'6"	245	29		36
Mike Saxon	K	6'3"	187	23		
Rafael Septien	K	5'10"	179	31		99

NEW YORK GIANTS 10-6 Bill Parcells

Scores of Each Game		
21	PHILADELPHIA	0
20	Green Bay	23
27	ST.LOUIS	17
16	Philadelphia	*10
29	DALLAS	30
30	Cincinnati	35
17	WASHINGTON	3
21	New Orleans	13
22	TAMPA BAY	20
24	L.A.RAMS	19
21	Washington	23
34	St.Louis	3
33	CLEVELAND	35
35	Houston	14
21	Dallas	28
28	PITTSBURGH	10

Use Name	Pos.	Hgt	Wgt	Age	Int	Pts
Brad Benson	OT	6'3"	270	29		
Conrad Goode	OT-C	6'6"	285	23		
Gordon King	OT	6'6"	275	29		
Karl Nelson	OT	6'6"	285	25		
Billy Ard	OG	6'3"	270	26		
Chris Godfrey	OG	6'3"	265	27		
David Jordan	OG	6'6"	276	23		
Bart Oates	C	6'3"	265	26		
Dee Hardison	DE	6'4"	274	29		
Leonard Marshall	DE	6'3"	285	23	1	
George Martin	DE	6'4"	255	32	1	6
Curtis McGriff	DE	6'5"	276	27		
Casey Merrill	DE	6'4"	260	28		
Jim Burt	NT	6'1"	260	26		
Jerome Sally	NT	6'3"	270	26		

Use Name	Pos.	Hgt	Wgt	Age	Int	Pts
Carl Banks	LB	6'4"	235	23		
Harry Carson	LB	6'2"	240	31		
Andy Headen	LB	6'5"	242	25	2	
Byron Hunt	LB	6'5"	242	26		
Robbie Jones	LB	6'2"	230	25		
Gary Reasons	LB	6'4"	234	23	1	
Lawrence Taylor	LB	6'3"	243	26		
Tyrone Davis	DB	6'1"	190	23		
Bill Currier	DB	6'	196	30	1	
Larry Flowers (to NYJ)	DB	6'1"	195	27		
Mark Haynes	DB	5'11"	195	26		
Kenny Hill	DB	6'	195	27	2	
Terry Kinard	DB	6'1"	200	25	5	
Elvis Patterson	DB	5'11"	188	24	6	6
Ted Watts	DB	6'	190	27	1	
Herb Welch	DB	5'11"	180	24	2	
Perry Williams	DB	6'2"	203	24	2	

Kenny Daniel - Broken Hand
Zeke Mowatt - Knee Injury

Use Name	Pos.	Hgt	Wgt	Age	Int	Pts
Jeff Hostetler	QB	6'3"	212	24		
Jeff Rutledge	QB	6'1"	195	28		
Phil Simms	QB	6'3"	214	28		
Joe Morris	HB	5'7"	195	24		126
Lee Rouson	HB	6'1"	210	22		
George Adams	FB	6'1"	225	22		24
Rob Carpenter	FB	6'1"	226	30		
Maurice Carthon	FB	6'1"	225	24		
Tony Galbreath	FB	6'	228	31		6
Bobby Johnson	WR	5'11"	171	23		48
Lionel Manuel	WR	5'11"	175	23		30
Phil McConkey	WR	5'10"	170	28		6
Stacy Robinson	WR	5'11"	186	23		
Byron Williams	WR	6'2"	183	24		
Mark Bavaro	TE	6'4"	245	22		24
Don Jasselbeck	TE	6'7"	245	30		6
Vyto Kab (from PHI)	TE	6'5"	240	25		
Jess Atkinson (to STL)	K	5'9"	165	23		53
Ali Haji-Sheikh	K	6'	170	24		11
Sean Landetta	K	6'	200	23		
Eric Schubert	K	5'8"	193	23		53

WASHINGTON REDSKINS 10-6 Joe Gibbs

Scores of Each Game		
14	Dallas	44
16	HOUSTON	13
6	PHILADELPHIA	19
10	Chicago	45
27	ST.LOUIS	10
24	DETROIT	3
3	N.Y.Giants	17
14	Cleveland	7
44	Atlanta	10
7	DALLAS	13
23	N.Y.GIANTS	21
30	Pittsburgh	23
8	SAN FRANCISCO	35
17	Philadelphia	12
27	CINCINNATI	24
27	St.Louis	16

Use Name	Pos.	Hgt	Wgt	Age	Int	Pts
Joe Jacoby	OT	6'7"	305	26		
Mark May	OT	6'6"	295	25		
Dan McQuaid	OT	6'7"	278	24		
Russ Grimm	OG	6'3"	275	26		
Ken Huff	OG	6'4"	265	32		
Raleigh McKenzie	OG	6'2"	262	22		
R.C. Thielemann	OG	6'4"	262	30		
Jeff Bostic	C-OG	6'2"	260	26		
Rick Donnalley	C	6'2"	257	26		
Doug Barnett	DE	6'3"	250	25		
Steve Hamilton	DE	6'4"	255	23		
Todd Liebenstein	DE	6'6"	255	25		
Dexter Manley	DE	6'3"	250	26		
Charles Mann	DE	6'6"	260	24		
Tom Beasley	DT-DE	6'5"	248	31		
Dave Butz	DT	6'7"	295	35		
Darryl Grant	DT	6'1"	275	25		
Dean Hamel	DT	6'3"	275	24		

Use Name	Pos.	Hgt	Wgt	Age	Int	Pts
Stuart Anderson	LB	6'1"	255	25		
Monte Coleman	LB	6'2"	230	27		
Pete Cronan	LB	6'2"	238	30		
Mel Kaufman	LB	6'2"	218	27	3	
Chris Keating	LB	6'2"	233	27		
Rich Milot	LB	6'4"	237	28	2	
Neal Olkewicz	LB	6'	233	28	1	
Raphel Cherry	DB	6'	194	23	2	
Vernon Dean	DB	5'11"	178	26	5	
Darrel Green	DB	5'8"	170	25	2	
Curtis Jordan	DB	6'2"	205	31	5	
Tony Peters	DB	6'1"	190	32	2	
Barry Willburn	DB	6'3"	186	21	1	
Greg Williams	DB	5'11"	185	26		
Kevin Williams	DB	5'9"	169	23		

Ken Coffey - Knee Injury

Use Name	Pos.	Hgt	Wgt	Age	Int	Pts
Babe Laufenberg (from SD)	QB	6'2"	195	25		
Jay Schroeder	QB	6'4"	215	24		
Joe Theismann	QB	6'	198	35		12
Keith Griffin	HB	5'8"	185	23		18
Ken Jenkins	HB	5'8"	185	26		
Michael Morton	HB	5'8"	180	25		
Otis Wonsley	HB-FB	5'10"	214	28		
Reggie Branch	FB	5'11"	227	22		
John Riggins	FB	6'2"	240	36		48
George Rogers	FB	6'2"	229	26		42
Malcolm Barnwell (to NO)	WR	5'11"	185	27		
Gary Clark	WR	5'9"	173	23		30
Mark McGrath	WR	5'11"	175	27		
Art Monk	WR	6'3"	209	27		12
Calvin Muhammad	WR	6'	190	26		6
Joe Phillips	WR	5'9"	188	22		
Clint Didier	TE	6'5"	240	26		24
Anthony Jones	TE	6'3"	248	25		
Rick Walker	TE	6'3"	245	30		
Don Warren	TE	6'4"	242	29		6
Steve Cox	K	6'4"	195	27		
Jeff Hayes	K	5'11"	175	26		
Mark Moseley	K	5'11"	204	37		97

PHILADELPHIA EAGLES 7-9 Marion Campbell (6-9), Fred Bruney (1-0)

Scores of Each Game		
0	N.Y.Giants	21
6	L.A.RAMS	17
19	Washington	6
10	N.Y.GIANTS	*16
21	New Orleans	23
30	ST.LOUIS	7
16	DALLAS	14
21	BUFFALO	17
13	San Francisco	24
23	ATLANTA	*17
24	St.Louis	14
17	Dallas	34
23	MINNESOTA	28
12	WASHINGTON	17
14	San Diego	20
37	Minnesota	35

Use Name	Pos.	Hgt	Wgt	Age	Int	Pts
Kevin Allen	OT	6'5"	284	22		
Tom Jelesky	OT	6'6"	275	24		
Leonard Mitchell	OT	6'7"	295	26		
Ken Reeves	OT-OG	6'5"	268	23		
Ron Baker	OG	6'4"	274	30		
Steve Kenney	OG	6'4"	274	29		
Mark Dennard	C	6'1"	262	29		
Gerry Feehery	C	6'2"	270	25		
Greg Brown	DE	6'5"	265	28		
Smiley Creswell	DE	6'4"	251	25		
Byron Darby	DE	6'4"	262	25		
Thomas Strauthers	DE	6'4"	264	24		
Ken Clarke	DT	6'2"	272	29		
Joe Drake	DT	6'2"	290	22		
Dwaine Morris	DT	6'2"	255	22		
Reggie White	DT	6'5"	285	23		

Use Name	Pos.	Hgt	Wgt	Age	Int	Pts
Aaron Brown	LB	6'2"	235	29		
Garry Cobb	LB	6'2"	228	28		
Tim Golden	LB	6'1"	220	25		
Anthony Griggs	LB	6'3"	230	25		
Dwayne Jiles	LB	6'4"	242	21		
Jon Kimmel	LB	6'4"	240	25		
Rich Kraynak	LB	6'1"	230	24	1	
Tom Polley	LB	6'3"	242	23		
Mike Reichenbach	LB	6'2"	238	23	1	
Reggie Wilkes	LB	6'4"	242	29		
Joel Williams	LB	6'1"	227	28		
Evan Cooper	DB	5'11"	184	23	2	
Herman Edwards	DB	6'	194	31	3	6
Ray Ellis	DB	6'1"	196	26	4	
Elbert Foules	DB	5'11"	185	24		
Wes Hopkins	DB	6'1"	212	23	6	6
Andre Waters	DB	5'11"	185	23		
Brenard Wilson	DB	6'	185	30		
Roynell Young	DB	6'1"	185	27	1	

Jody Schulz - Knee Injury

Use Name	Pos.	Hgt	Wgt	Age	Int	Pts
Jeff Christensen	QB	6'3"	202	25		
Randall Cunningham	QB	6'4"	192	22		
Ron Jaworski	QB	6'2"	199	34		12
Herman Hunter	HB	6'1"	193	24		12
Earnest Jackson	HB	5'9"	208	25		36
Major Everett	FB	5'10"	218	25		
Michael Haddix	FB	6'2"	227	23		
Hubie Oliver	FB	5'10"	212	27		
Jairo Penaranda	FB	5'11"	218	27		
Keith Baker	WR	5'10"	185	28		
Gregg Garrity	WR	5'10"	169	24		
Kenny Jackson	WR	6'	177	23		6
Ron Johnson	WR	6'3"	186	26		
Mike Quick	WR	6'2"	190	26		66
John Goode	TE	6'2"	243	22		
Dave Little	TE	6'2"	232	24		6
John Spagnola	TE	6'4"	238	28		30
Mike Horan	K	5'11"	190	26		
Paul McFadden	K	5'11"	163	23		104

ST. LOUIS CARDINALS 5-11 Jim Hanifan

Scores of Each Game		
27	Cleveland	*24
41	CINCINNATI	27
17	N.Y.Giants	27
43	GREEN BAY	28
10	Washington	27
7	Philadelphia	30
10	Pittsburgh	23
10	HOUSTON	20
21	DALLAS	10
0	Tampa Bay	16
14	PHILADELPHIA	24
3	N.Y.GIANTS	34
17	Dallas	35
28	NEW ORLEANS	16
14	L.A.Rams	46
16	WASHINGTON	27

Use Name	Pos.	Hgt	Wgt	Age	Int	Pts
Scott Bergold	OT	6'7"	263	23		
Tootie Robbins	OT	6'5"	302	27		
Carlos Scott	OT-C	6'4"	285	25		
Luis Sharpe	OT	6'4"	260	25		
Joe Bostic	OG	6'3"	268	28		
Doug Dawson	OG	6'3"	267	23		
Lance Smith	OG	6'2"	262	22		
Randy Clark	C	6'3"	270	28		
Rob Monaco	C	6'3"	283	23		
Al Baker	DE	6'6"	270	28		
Curtis Greer	DE	6'4"	258	27		
Stafford Mays	DE	6'2"	255	27		
Mark Duda	DT	6'3"	279	24		
David Galloway	DT	6'3"	279	26		
Elois Grooms	DT	6'4"	250	32		

Dan Ralph - Back Injury

Use Name	Pos.	Hgt	Wgt	Age	Int	Pts
Charlie Baker	LB	6'2"	234	27		
Bob Harris	LB	6'2"	223	24		
Tom Howard	LB	6'2"	220	31		
E.J.Junior	LB	6'3"	235	25	5	
Niko Noga	LB	6'1"	235	23		
Freddie Joe Nunn	LB	6'4"	228	23		
Danny Spradlin	LB	6'1"	235	26		
Jeff Griffin	DB	6'	185	27		
Liffort Hobley	DB	6'	207	22		
Bobby Johnson	DB	6'	187	25		
Cedric Mack	DB	6'	194	24	2	
Lee Nelson	DB	5'10"	185	31		
Benny Perrin	DB	6'2"	175	25		
Leonard Smith	DB	5'11"	202	24	2	
Wayne Smith	DB	6'	170	28		
Lionel Washington	DB	6'	188	24	1	6
Lonnie Young	DB	6'1"	182	22	3	

Use Name	Pos.	Hgt	Wgt	Age	Int	Pts
Scott Brunner	QB	6'5"	215	28		
Neil Lomax	QB	6'3"	215	26		
Rick McIvor	QB	6'4"	210	24		
Perry Harrington	HB	5'11"	216	27		6
Randy Love	HB	6'1"	224	28		
Stump Mitchell	HB	5'9"	188	26		60
Tony Mumford	HB	6'	215	22		
Ottis Anderson	FB	6'2"	225	28		24
Earl Ferrell	FB	6'	224	27		24
Ron Wolfley	FB	6'	222	22		
Clyde Duncan	WR	6'2"	211	24		6
Earnest Gray	WR	6'3"	195	28		
Roy Green	WR	6'	195	28		30
Jay Novacek	WR	6'4"	217	22		
J.T.Smith	WR	6'2"	185	29		6
Pat Tilley	WR	5'10"	178	32		36
Greg LaFleur	TE	6'4"	236	26		
Doug Marsh	TE	6'3"	238	27		6
Carl Birdsong	K	6'	192	26		
Novo Bojovic	K	5'10"	172	25		20
Neil O'Donoghue	K	6'6"	210	32		49

Quentin Walker - Wrist Injury

* Overtime

DALLAS COWBOYS

RUSHING

Last Name	No.	Yds	Avg	TD
Dorsett	305	1307	4.3	7
Newsome	88	252	2.9	2
Hogeboom	8	48	6.0	1
D. White	22	44	2.0	1
Williams	14	42	3.0	0
Lavette	13	34	2.6	0
Fowler	7	25	3.6	0
J. Jones	1	0	0.0	0
Banks	1	-1	-1.0	0
Pelluer	3	-2	-0.7	0
Hill	1	-6	-6.0	0

RECEIVING

Last Name	No.	Yds	Avg	TD
Hill	74	1113	15.0	7
Cosbie	64	793	12.4	6
Renfro	60	955	15.9	8
Dorsett	46	449	9.8	3
Newsome	46	361	7.8	1
J. Jones	24	179	7.5	0
Powe	14	237	16.9	0
Cornwell	6	77	12.8	1
Fowler	5	24	4.8	0
Gonzales	3	28	9.3	0
D. White	1	12	12.0	1
Lavette	1	8	8.0	0

PUNT RETURNS

Last Name	No.	Yds	Avg	TD
Bates	22	152	6.9	0
Gonzales	15	58	3.9	0
Banks	3	27	9.0	0

KICKOFF RETURNS

Last Name	No.	Yds	Avg	TD
Lavette	34	682	20.1	0
Duckett	9	173	19.2	0
J. Jones	9	161	17.9	0
Williams	6	129	21.5	0
Fowler	3	48	16.0	0
Powe	1	17	17.0	0

PASSING — PUNTING — KICKING

PASSING	Att	Cmp	%	Yds	Yd/Att	TD	Int—	%	RK
D. White	450	267	59	3157	7.0	21	17—	4	
Hogeboom	126	70	56	978	7.8	5	7—	6	
Pelluer	8	5	63	47	5.9	0	0—	0	
J. Jones	2	1	50	12	6.0	1	1—	50	
Hill	1	1	100	42	42.0	0	0—	0	

PUNTING	No	Avg
Saxon	81	41.9
D. White	1	43.0

KICKING	XP	Att	%	FG	Att	%
Septien	42	43	98	19	28	68

NEW YORK GIANTS

RUSHING

Last Name	No.	Yds	Avg	TD
Morris	294	1336	4.5	21
Adams	128	498	3.9	2
Carpenter	60	201	3.4	0
Galbreath	29	187	6.4	0
Sims	37	132	3.6	0
Carthon	27	70	2.6	0
B. Williams	2	18	9.0	0
Atkinson	1	14	14.0	1
Rouson	1	1	1.0	0
Rutledge	2	-6	-3.0	0

RECEIVING

Last Name	No.	Yds	Avg	TD
Manuel	49	859	17.5	5
Bavaro	37	511	13.8	4
Johnson	33	533	16.2	8
Adams	31	389	12.5	2
Galbreath	30	327	10.9	1
McConkey	25	404	16.2	1
Morris	22	212	9.6	0
Carpenter	20	162	8.1	0
B. Williams	15	280	18.7	0
Carthon	8	81	10.1	0
Hasselbeck	5	71	14.2	1

PUNT RETURNS

Last Name	No.	Yds	Avg	TD
McConkey	53	442	8.3	0

KICKOFF RETURNS

Last Name	No.	Yds	Avg	TD
Adams	14	241	17.2	0
McConkey	12	234	19.5	0
Hill	11	186	16.9	0
Galbreath	7	120	17.1	0
Rouson	2	35	17.5	0
Morris	2	25	12.5	0
Hasselbeck	1	21	21.0	0
Sally	1	4	4.0	0

PASSING — PUNTING — KICKING

PASSING	Att	Cmp	%	Yds	Yd/Att	TD	Int—	%	RK
Simms	495	275	56	3829	7.7	22	20—	4	
Adams	1	0	0	0	0.0	0	0—	0	
Landeta	1	0	0	0	0.0	0	0—	0	

PUNTING	No	Avg
Landeta	81	42.9

KICKING	XP	Att	%	FG	Att	%
Atkinson	14	15	93	10	15	67
Schubert	26	27	96	10	13	77
Haji-Sheikh	5	5	100	2	5	40

WASHINGTON REDSKINS

RUSHING

Last Name	No.	Yds	Avg	TD
Rogers	231	1093	4.7	7
Riggins	176	677	3.8	8
Griffin	102	473	4.6	3
Theismann	25	115	4.6	2
Monk	7	51	7.3	0
Jenkins	2	39	19.5	0
Schroeder	17	30	1.8	0
Walker	3	16	5.3	0
Clark	2	10	5.0	0
Wonsley	4	8	2.0	0
Green	1	6	6.0	0
Warren	1	5	5.0	0

RECEIVING

Last Name	No.	Yds	Avg	TD
Monk	91	1226	13.5	2
Clark	72	926	12.9	5
Didier	41	433	10.6	4
Griffin	37	285	7.7	0
Warren	15	163	10.9	1
Muhammad	9	116	12.9	1
Riggins	6	18	3.0	0
Rogers	4	29	7.3	0
Barnwell	3	28	9.3	0
Cherry	1	11	11.0	0
Walker	1	8	8.0	0

PUNT RETURNS

Last Name	No.	Yds	Avg	TD
Jenkins	26	272	10.5	0
Green	16	214	13.4	0
Cherry	4	22	5.5	0
Dean	1	0	0.0	0

KICKOFF RETURNS

Last Name	No.	Yds	Avg	TD
Jenkins	41	1018	24.8	0
Griffin	7	142	20.3	0
Morton	6	131	21.8	0
Wonsley	2	26	13.0	0
Hamel	1	14	14.0	0
Cherry	1	9	9.0	0
Keating	1	9	9.0	0
Jones	1	0	0.0	0

PASSING — PUNTING — KICKING

PASSING	Att	Cmp	%	Yds	Yd/Att	TD	Int—	%	RK
Theismann	301	167	56	1774	5.9	8	16—	5	
Schroeder	209	112	54	1458	6.9	5	5—	2	
Cox	1	1	100	11	11.0	0	0—	0	
Riggins	1	0	0	0	0.0	0	0—	0	

PUNTING	No	Avg
Cox	52	41.8
Hayes	16	41.6
Schroeder	4	33.0
Theismann	1	1.0

KICKING	XP	Att.	%	FG	Att	%
Moseley	31	33	94	22	34	65
Cox				0	1	0

PHILADELPHIA EAGLES

RUSHING

Last Name	No.	Yds	Avg	TD
E. Jackson	282	1028	3.6	5
Haddix	67	213	3.2	0
Cunningham	29	205	7.1	0
Hunter	27	121	4.5	1
Jaworski	17	35	2.1	2
Everett	4	13	3.3	0
Horan	1	12	12.0	0
Oliver	1	3	3.0	0

RECEIVING

Last Name	No.	Yds	Avg	TD
Quick	73	1247	17.1	11
Spagnola	64	772	12.1	5
Haddix	43	330	7.7	0
K. Jackson	40	692	17.3	1
Hunter	28	405	14.5	1
Johnson	11	186	16.9	0
E. Jackson	10	126	12.6	1
Garrity	7	142	20.3	0
Little	7	82	11.7	0
Everett	4	25	6.3	0
K. Baker	2	25	12.5	0
Oliver	1	4	4.0	0

PUNT RETURNS

Last Name	No.	Yds	Avg	TD
Cooper	43	364	8.5	0
Waters	1	23	23.0	0
Hunter	1	6	6.0	0

KICKOFF RETURNS

Last Name	No.	Yds	Avg	TD
Hunter	48	1047	21.8	0
Waters	4	74	18.5	0
Cooper	3	32	10.7	0
Foules	1	7	7.0	0

PASSING — PUNTING — KICKING

PASSING	Att	Cmp	%	Yds	Yd/Att	TD	Int—	%	RK
Jaworski	484	255	53	3450	7.1	17	20—	4	
Cunningham	81	34	42	584	6.8	1	8—	10	
Hunter	2	1	50	38	19	1	0—	0	

PUNTING	No	Avg
Horan	91	41.5

KICKING	XP	Att	%	FG	Att	%
McFadden	29	29	100	25	30	83

ST. LOUIS CARDINALS

RUSHING

Last Name	No.	Yds	Avg	TD
Mitchell	183	1006	5.5	7
Anderson	117	479	4.1	4
Ferrell	46	208	4.5	2
Lomax	32	125	3.9	0
Wolfley	24	64	2.7	0
Harrington	7	42	6.0	1
J.T. Smith	3	36	12.0	0
Brunner	3	8	2.7	0
Love	1	4	4.0	0
Green	1	2	2.0	0

RECEIVING

Last Name	No.	Yds	Avg	TD
Green	50	693	13.9	5
Tilley	49	726	14.8	6
Mitchell	47	502	10.7	3
J.T. Smith	43	581	13.5	1
Marsh	37	355	9.6	1
Ferrell	25	277	11.1	2
Anderson	23	225	9.8	0
LaFleur	9	119	13.2	0
Duncan	4	39	9.8	1
Gray	3	22	7.3	0
Wolfley	2	18	9.0	0
Love	2	4	2.0	0
Mack	1	16	16.0	0
Novacek	1	4	4.0	0

PUNT RETURNS

Last Name	No.	Yds	Avg	TD
J.T. Smith	26	283	10.9	0
Mitchell	11	97	8.8	0
Nelson	2	14	7.0	0
Tilley	1	-1	-1.0	0

KICKOFF RETURNS

Last Name	No.	Yds	Avg	TD
Duncan	28	550	19.6	0
Mitchell	19	345	18.2	0
Wolfley	13	234	18.0	0
Le. Smith	5	68	13.6	0
Harrington	4	77	19.3	0
J.T. Smith	4	59	14.8	0
Nelson	3	49	16.3	0
Novacek	1	20	20.0	0
Mumford	1	19	19.0	0

PASSING — PUNTING — KICKING

PASSING	Att	Cmp	%	Yds	Yd/Att	TD	Int—	%	RK
Lomax	471	265	56	3214	6.8	18	12—	3	
Brunner	60	30	50	336	5.6	1	6—	10	
Mitchell	2	1	50	31	15.5	0	0—	0	
Birdsong	1	0	0	0	0.0	0	0—	0	

PUNTING	No	Avg
Birdsong	85	41.7

KICKING	XP	Att	%	FG	Att	%
O'Donoghue	19	19	100	10	18	56
Bojovic	11	12	92	3	7	43

CHICAGO BEARS 15-1 Mike Ditka

Scores of Each Game		
38	TAMPA BAY	28
20	NEW ENGLAND	7
33	Minnesota	24
45	WASHINGTON	10
27	Tampa Bay	19
26	San Francisco	10
23	GREEN BAY	7
27	MINNESOTA	9
16	Green Bay	10
24	DETROIT	3
44	Dallas	0
36	ATLANTA	0
24	Miami	38
17	INDIANAPOLIS	10
19	N.Y.Jets	6
37	Detroit	17

Use Name	Pos.	Hgt	Wgt	Age	Int	Pts
Jim Covert	OT	6'4"	271	25		
Andy Frederick	OT	6'6"	265	31		
Keith Van Horne	OT	6'6"	280	27		
Kurt Becker	OG	6'5"	270	26		
Mark Bortz	OG	6'6"	269	24		
Stefan Humphries	OG	6'3"	263	23		
Tom Thayer	OG-C	6'4"	261	24		
Tom Andrews	C	6'4"	267	23		
Jay Hilgenberg	C	6'3"	258	26		
Richard Dent	DE	6'5"	263	24	2	6
Mike Hartenstine	DE	6'3"	254	32		
Tyrone Keys	DE	6'7"	267	25		
Dan Hampton	DT	6'5"	267	27		
Steve McMichael	DT	6'2"	260	27		2
Wiliam Perry	DT-FB	6'2"	308	22		18
Henry Waechter	DT	6'5"	275	26		2
Brian Cabral	LB	6'	227	29		
Wilber Marshall	LB	6'1"	225	23	4	
Jim Morrissey	LB	6'3"	215	22		
Ron Rivera	LB	6'3"	239	23	1	6
Mike Singletary	LB	6'	228	26	1	
Cliff Thrift	LB	6'2"	230	29		
Otis Wilson	LB	6'2"	232	27	3	8
Dave Duerson	DB	6'1"	203	24	5	
Gary Fencik	DB	6'1"	196	31	5	
Leslie Frazier	DB	6'	187	26	6	6
Shaun Gayle	DB	5'11"	193	23		
Reggie Phillips	DB	5'10"	170	24		
Mike Richardson	DB	6'	188	24	4	6
Ken Taylor	DB	6'1"	185	21	3	
Steve Fuller	QB	6'4"	195	28		30
Jim McMahon	QB	6'1"	190	26		24
Mike Tomczak	QB	6'1"	195	22		
Dennis Gentry	HB	5'8"	181	26		18
Walter Payton	HB	5'11"	202	31		66
Thomas Sanders	FB	5'11"	203	23		6
Matt Suhey	FB	5'11"	216	27		12
Calvin Thomas	FB	5'11"	245	25		24
Brad Anderson	WR	6'2"	198	24		
Willie Gault	WR	6'	183	25		12
James Maness	WR	6'1"	174	22		
Ken Margerum	WR	6'	180	26		12
Dennis McKinnon	WR	6'1"	185	24		42
Keith Ortego	WR	6'	180	22		
Emery Moorehead	TE	6'2"	220	31		6
Tim Wrightman	TE	6'3"	237	25		6
Maury Buford	K	6'1"	190	25		
Kevin Butler	K	6'1"	204	23		144

Brian Baschnagel - Knee Injury
Pat Dunsmore - Thigh Injury
Mitch Krenk - Back Injury

Todd Bell - Holdout
Al Harris - Holdout
Dan Rains - Knee Injury

GREEN BAY PACKERS 8-8 Forrest Gregg

Scores of Each Game		
20	New England	26
23	N.Y. GIANTS	20
3	N.Y.JETS	24
28	St.Louis	43
43	DETROIT	10
20	MINNESOTA	17
7	Chicago	23
10	Indianapolis	37
10	CHICAGO	16
27	Minnesota	17
38	NEW ORLEANS	14
17	L.A.Rams	34
21	TAMPA BAY	0
24	MIAMI	34
26	Detroit	23
20	Tampa Bay	17

Use Name	Pos.	Hgt	Wgt	Age	Int	Pts
Tim Huffman	OT	6'5"	282	26		
Greg Koch	OT	6'4"	276	30		
Ken Ruettgers	OT	6'5"	267	23		
Karl Swanke	OT-C	6'6"	262	27		
Ron Hallstrom	OG	6'6"	283	26		
Keith Uecker	OG-OT	6'5"	270	25		
Mark Cannon	C	6'3"	258	23		
Blake Moore	C-OG	6'5"	272	27		6
Rich Moran	C-OG	6'3"	272	23		
Robert Brown	DE	6'2"	250	25		2
Mike Butler	DE	6'5"	269	31		
Alphonso Carreker	DE	6'6"	260	23		
Tony Degrate	DE	6'3"	280	23		
Donnie Humphrey	DE	6'3"	275	24		
Ezra Johnson	DE	6'4"	259	29		
Charles Martin	NT-DE	6'4"	270	26		
Mark Shumate (from NYJ)	NT	6'5"	265	25		
John Anderson	LB	6'3"	229	29	2	
George Cumby	LB	6'	224	29		
John Dorsey	LB	6'3"	235	25		
Mike Douglass	LB	6'	214	30	2	6
Brian Noble	LB	6'3"	237	23		
Guy Prather	LB	6'2"	229	27		
Randy Scott	LB	6'1"	222	26	2	
Ronnie Burgess	DB	5'11"	175	22		
Mossy Cade	DB	6'1"	195	23	1	
Chuck Clanton	DB	5'11"	192	23		
Tom Flynn	DB	6'	195	23	1	
Gary Hayes	DB	5'10"	180	28		
Daryll Jones	DB	6'	190	23		
Mark Lee	DB	5'11"	188	27	1	
Tim Lewis	DB	5'11"	191	23	4	6
Mike McLeod	DB	6'	180	27		
Mark Murphy	DB	6'2"	201	27	2	6
Ken Stills	DB	5'10"	185	21		
Lynn Dickey	QB	6'4"	203	35		6
Joe Shield	QB	6'1"	185	23		
Randy Wright	QB	6'2"	194	24		
Jim Zorn	QB	6'2"	200	32		
Harlan Huckleby	HB	6'1"	201	27		
Eddie Lee Ivery	HB	6'1"	214	28		24
Jessie Clark	FB	6'	233	25		42
Gary Ellerson	FB	5'11"	220	22		12
Gerry Ellis	FB	5'11"	225	27		30
Preston Dennard	WR	6'1"	183	29		12
Phillip Epps	WR	5'10"	165	25		24
James Lofton	WR	6'3"	197	29		24
Walter Stanley	WR	5'9"	180	22		
Paul Coffman	TE	6'3"	225	29		36
Mark Lewis	TE	6'2"	218	24		
Ed West	TE	6'1"	242	24		6
Don Bracken	K	6'	205	23		
Al Del Greco	K	5'10"	195	23		95
Joe Prokop	K	6'3"	225	25		

MINNESOTA VIKINGS 7-9 Bud Grant

Scores of Each Game		
28	SAN FRANCISCO	21
31	Tampa Bay	16
24	CHICAGO	33
27	Buffalo	20
10	L.A.Rams	13
17	Green Bay	20
21	SAN DIEGO	17
9	Chicago	27
16	DETROIT	13
17	GREEN BAY	27
21	Detroit	41
23	NEW ORLEANS	30
28	Philadelphia	23
26	TAMPA BAY	7
13	Atlanta	14
35	PHILADELPHIA	37

Use Name	Pos.	Hgt	Wgt	Age	Int	Pts
Tim Irwin	OT	6'6"	289	26		
Tery Tausch	OT	6'5"	275	26		
Brent Boyd	OG	6'3"	276	28		
Jim Hough	OG	6'2"	276	29		
Dave Huffman	OG	6'6"	283	28		
Mark MacDonald	OG	6'4"	267	24		
Curtis Rouse	OG	6'3"	322	25		
Kirk Lowdermilk	C	6'3"	263	22		
Dennis Swilley	C	6'3"	257	30		
Neil Elshire	DE	6'6"	270	27		2
Doug Martin	DE	6'3"	270	28		
Keith Millard	DE	6'5"	260	23		
Mark Mullaney	DE	6'6"	246	32	1	
Robert Smith	DE	6'5"	255	22		
Tim Newton	NT	6'	283	22	2	
Matt Blair	LB	6'5"	242	34		
Chris Doleman	LB	6'5"	250	23	1	
Dennis Fowlkes	LB	6'2"	234	24		
David Howard	LB	6'2"	228	23		
Chris Martin	LB	6'2"	233	24		
Fred McNeill	LB	6'2"	230	33		
Tim Meamber	LB	6'3"	231	22		
Scott Studwell	LB	6'2"	228	31	2	
Rufus Bess	DB	5'9"	187	29	2	
Joey Browner	DB	6'2"	212	25	2	6
Issiac Holt	DB	6'1"	197	22	1	
Carl Lee	DB	6'	184	24	3	
Keith Nord	DB	6'	192	28		
Ted Rosnagle	DB	6'3"	207	23		
Willie Teal	DB	5'10"	190	27	3	6
John Turner	DB	6'	196	29	5	
Steve Bono	QB	6'4"	216	23		
Tommy Kramer	QB	6'2"	207	30		
Wade Wilson	QB	6'3"	208	26		
Darrin Nelson	HB	5'9"	183	26		36
Allen Rice	HB	5'10"	203	23		24
Maurice Turner (to GB)	HB	5'11"	199	24		
Alfred Anderson	FB	6'1"	219	24		30
Ted Brown	FB	5'10"	212	28		60
Anthony Carter	WR	5'11"	166	24		48
Mike Jones	WR	5'11"	183	25		24
Leo Lewis	WR	5'8"	171	28		18
Buster Rhymes	WR	6'2"	216	23		
Sammy White	WR	5'11"	210	31		
Jay Carroll	TE	6'4"	232	23		
Steve Jordan	TE	6'4"	236	24		
Mike Mularkey	TE	6'4"	238	23		6
Greg Coleman	K	6'	181	30		
Jan Stenerud	K	6'2"	190	42		86

Wes Hamilton - Back Injury

Walker Lee Ashley - Achilles Tendon

DETROIT LIONS 7-9 Darryl Rogers

Scores of Each Game		
28	Atlanta	27
26	DALLAS	21
6	Indianapolis	14
30	TAMPA BAY	9
10	Green Bay	43
3	Washington	24
23	SAN FRANCISCO	21
31	MIAMI	21
13	Minnesota	16
3	Chicago	24
41	MINNESOTA	21
16	Tampa Bay	*19
31	N.Y.JETS	20
6	New England	23
23	GREEN BAY	26
17	CHICAGO	37

Use Name	Pos.	Hgt	Wgt	Age	Int	Pts
Lomas Brown	OT	6'4"	282	22		
Rich Stenger	OT	6'7"	276	25		
Chris Dieterich	OG-OT	6'3"	260	27		
Keith Dorney	OG-OT	6'5"	270	27		
Don Greco	OG	6'3"	265	26		
Larry Lee (to MIA)	OG-C	6'2"	263	25		
Mark Stevenson	OG-C	6'3"	285	27		
Kevin Glover	C-OG	6'2"	267	22		
David Jones	C-OG	6'3"	260	23		
Steve Mott	C	6'3"	265	24		
Tom Turnure	C-OG	6'4"	253	28		
Leon Evans	DE	6'5"	282	23		
William Gay	DE	6'5"	260	30	1	
Martin Moss	DE	6'4"	255	26		
Steve Baack	NT-DE	6'4"	265	24		
Doug English	NT	6'5"	258	32		
Curtis Green	NT-DE	6'3"	258	28		
Eric Williams	NT	6'4"	280	23		
Kurt Allerman	LB	6'3"	231	30		
Roosevelt Barnes	LB	6'2"	228	27	1	
Dan Bunz	LB	6'4"	225	29	1	
Mike Cofer	LB	6'5"	245	25		
August Curley	LB	6'3"	226	25		
Ken Fantetti	LB	6'2"	232	28		
James Harrell	LB	6'1"	230	28	1	
June James	LB	6'1"	218	22		
Angelo King	LB	6'1"	222	27		
Vernon Maxwell	LB	6'2"	235	23		
Jimmy Williams	LB	6'3"	230	24		
John Bostic	DB	5'10"	178	22		
Arnold Brown	DB	5'10"	185	23		
Clarence Chapman	DB	5'10"	195	31		
William Frizzell	DB	6'3"	198	22	1	
Duane Galloway	DB	5'8"	181	23		
William Graham	DB	5'11"	191	25	3	
Alvin Hall	DB	5'10"	184	27		
Demetrious Johnson	DB	5'11"	190	24	3	
Bruce McNorton	DB	5'11"	175	26	2	
Bobby Watkins	DB	5'10"	184	25	5	
Joe Ferguson	QB	6'1"	195	35		6
Eric Hipple	QB	6'2"	198	27		12
A.J. Jones (from LA)	HB	6'1"	202	26		
Rick Kane	HB	5'11"	200	30		
Wilbert Montgomery	HB	5'10"	194	30		
Alvin Moore	HB	6'	194	26		30
James Jones	FB	6'2"	229	24		54
Mike Meade	FB	5'11"	227	25		
Carl Bland	WR	5'11"	182	24		
Jeff Chadwick	WR	6'3"	190	24		18
Pet Mandley	WR	5'10"	191	24		6
Mark Nichols	WR	6'2"	208	25		24
Leonard Thompson	WR	5'11"	192	33		30
David Lewis	TE	6'3"	235	24		18
Reese McCall	TE	6'7"	245	29		
Rob Rubick	TE	6'3"	234	24		
Mike Black	K	6'2"	197	24		
Eddie Murray	K	5'10"	175	29		109

Kirk Dodge - Shoulder Injury

Dave D'Addio - Ankle Injury

TAMPA BAY BUCCANEERS 2-14 Leeman Bennett

Scores of Each Game		
28	Chicago	38
16	MINNESOTA	31
13	New Orleans	20
9	Detroit	30
19	CHICAGO	27
27	L.A.RAMS	31
38	Miami	41
14	NEW ENGLAND	32
20	N.Y.Giants	22
16	ST.LOUIS	0
28	N.Y.Jets	62
19	DETROIT	*16
0	Green Bay	21
7	Minnesota	26
23	INDIANAPOLIS	31
17	GREEN BAY	20

Use Name	Pos.	Hgt	Wgt	Age	Int	Pts
Ron Heller	OT	6'6"	280	23		
Ken Kaplan	OT	6'4"	275	25		
Gene Sanders	OT	6'3"	285	28		
Steve Courson	OG	6'1"	275	29		
Sean Farrell	OG	6'3"	260	25		
Rick Mallory	OG	6'2"	260	24		
Joe Shearin	OG	6'4"	250	25		
George Yarno	OG-OT	6'2"	265	28		
Steve Wilson	C	6'3"	270	31		
Randy Grimes	C	6'4"	270	25		
John Cannon	DE	6'5"	260	25		
Don Fielder	DE	6'3"	260	26		
Ron Holmes	DE	6'4"	255	22		
Chris Lindstrom	DE	6'7"	260	25		
Mark Studaway	DE	6'4"	275	24		
David Logan	NT	6'2"	250	22		
Karl Morgan	NT	6'1"	255	24		
Scot Brantley	LB	6'1"	230	27		
Keith Browner	LB	6'5"	240	23	1	
Jeff Davis	LB	6'	230	25	1	
Cecil Johnson	LB	6'2"	235	30	1	
Dennis Johnson (from MIN)	LB	6'3"	235	27		
Larry Kubin (from BUF)	LB	6'2"	238	26		
Ervin Randle	LB	6'1"	250	22	1	
Chris Washington	LB	6'4"	230	23		
Paul Dombroski	DB	6'	185	29		
Carl Howard (to NYJ)	DB	6'2"	190	23		
Bret Clark	DB	6'2"	200	24		
Jeremiah Castille	DB	5'10"	175	24	7	
Craig Curry	DB	6'	190	24		
David Greenwood	DB	6'3"	210	25	5	
John Holt	DB	5'11"	180	26	1	
Mike Prior	DB	6'	200	21		
Ivory Sully	DB	6'	200	28	1	
Steve DeBerg	QB	6'2"	210	31		
Alan Risher	QB	6'2"	190	24		
Steve Young	QB	6'2"	200	23		6
Leon Bright	HB	5'9"	190	30		
Melvin Carver	HB	5'11"	225	26		
George Peoples	HB	6'	215	25		
Adger Armstrong	FB	6'	230	28		6
Ron Springs	FB	6'2"	225	28		
James Wilder	FB	6'3"	225	27		60
Theo Bell	WR	6'	195	31		
Gerald Carter	WR	6'1"	190	28		18
Phil Freeman	WR	5'11"	185	22		
Kevin House	WR	6'1"	185	27		30
David Verser	WR	6'1"	200	27		
Gene Branton	TE	6'4"	235	24		
Jerry Bell	TE	6'5"	230	26		12
K.D.Dunn	TE	6'3"	235	22		
Jimmie Giles	TE	6'3"	240	30		48
Calvin Magee	TE	6'3"	240	22		18
Mark Witte	TE	6'3"	235	25		
Frank Garcia	K	6'	210	28		
Donald Igwebuike	K	5'9"	185	24		96

John Janata - Elbow and wrist injuries

* Overtime

CHICAGO BEARS

RUSHING

Last Name	No.	Yds	Avg	TD
Payton	324	1551	4.8	9
Suhey	115	471	4.1	1
McMahon	47	252	5.4	3
Gentry	30	160	5.3	2
Thomas	31	125	4.0	4
Sanders	25	104	4.2	1
Fuller	24	77	3.2	5
Gault	5	18	3.6	0
Perry	5	7	1.4	2
Tomczak	2	3	1.5	0
McKinnon	1	0	0.0	0
Margerum	1	-7	-7.0	0

RECEIVING

Last Name	No.	Yds	Avg	TD
Payton	49	483	9.9	2
Moorehead	35	481	13.7	1
Gault	33	704	21.3	1
Suhey	33	295	8.9	1
McKinnon	31	555	17.9	7
Wrightman	24	407	17.0	1
Margerum	17	190	11.2	2
Gentry	5	77	15.4	0
Thomas	5	45	9.0	0
Maness	1	34	34.0	0
McMahon	1	13	13.0	1
Sanders	1	9	9.0	0
Anderson	1	6	6.0	0
Perry	1	4	4.0	1

PUNT RETURNS

Last Name	No.	Yds	Avg	TD
Taylor	25	198	7.9	0
Ortego	17	158	9.3	0
Duerson	6	47	7.8	0
McKinnon	4	44	11.0	0
Maness	2	9	4.5	0
Gentry	0	47	—	0

KICKOFF RETURNS

Last Name	No.	Yds	Avg	TD
Gault	22	577	26.2	1
Gentry	18	466	25.9	1
Taylor	1	18	18.0	0
McKinnon	1	16	16.0	0
Sanders	1	10	10.0	0
Marshall	0	2	—	0

PASSING — PUNTING — KICKING

PASSING	Att	Cmp	%	Yds	Yd/Att	TD	Int—	%	RK
McMahon	313	178	57	2392	7.6	15	11—	4	
Fuller	107	53	50	777	7.3	1	5—	5	
Tomczak	6	2	33	33	5.5	0	0—	0	
Payton	5	3	60	96	19.2	1	0—	0	
Buford	1	1	100	5	5.0	0	0—	0	

PUNTING	No	Avg
Buford	68	42.2

KICKING	XP	Att	%	FG	Att	%
Butler	51	51	100	31	37	84

GREEN BAY PACKERS

RUSHING

Last Name	No.	Yds	Avg	TD
Ivery	132	636	4.8	2
Clark	147	633	4.3	5
Ellis	104	571	5.5	5
Ellerson	32	205	6.4	2
Epps	5	103	20.6	1
Huckleby	8	41	5.1	0
Lofton	4	14	3.5	0
Zorn	10	9	0.9	0
Wright	8	8	1.0	0
Prather	1	0	0.0	0
West	1	0	0.0	0
Dickey	18	-12	-0.7	1

RECEIVING

Last Name	No.	Yds	Avg	TD
Lofton	69	1153	16.7	4
Coffman	49	666	13.6	6
Epps	44	683	15.5	3
Ivery	28	270	9.6	2
Clark	24	252	10.5	2
Ellis	24	206	8.6	0
Dennard	13	182	14.0	2
West	8	95	11.9	1
Huckleby	5	27	5.4	0
Ellerson	2	15	7.5	0
Moore	1	3	3.0	1

PUNT RETURNS

Last Name	No.	Yds	Avg	TD
Epps	15	146	9.7	0
Stanley	14	179	12.8	0
Flynn	7	41	5.9	0
Murphy	1	4	4.0	0
Hayes	1	0	0.0	0

KICKOFF RETURNS

Last Name	No.	Yds	Avg	TD
Ellerson	29	521	18.0	0
Ellis	13	247	19.0	0
Epps	12	279	23.3	0
Stanley	9	212	23.6	0
Flynn	1	20	20.0	0
Anderson	1	14	14.0	0
Stills	1	14	14.0	0
Jones	1	11	11.0	0

PASSING — PUNTING — KICKING

PASSING	Att	Cmp	%	Yds	Yd/Att	TD	Int—	%	RK
Dickey	314	172	55	2206	7.0	15	17—	5	
Zorn	123	56	46	794	6.5	4	6—	5	
Wright	74	39	53	552	7.5	2	4—	5	
Ellis	1	0	0	0	0.0	0	0—	0	
Ivery	1	0	0	0	0.0	0	0—	0	

PUNTING	No	Avg
Prokop	56	39.5
Bracken	26	40.5

KICKING	XP	Att	%	FG	Att	%
Del Greco	38	40	95	19	26	73

MINNESOTA VIKINGS

RUSHING

Last Name	No.	Yds	Avg	TD
Nelson	200	893	4.5	5
Brown	93	336	3.6	7
Anderson	50	121	2.4	4
Rice	31	104	3.4	3
Kramer	27	54	2.0	0
Jones	2	6	3.0	0
Lewis	1	2	2.0	0
Coleman	2	0	0.0	0

RECEIVING

Last Name	No.	Yds	Avg	TD
Jordan	68	795	11.7	0
Jones	46	641	13.9	4
Carter	43	821	19.1	8
Nelson	43	301	7.0	1
Brown	30	291	9.7	3
Lewis	29	442	15.2	3
Anderson	16	175	10.9	1
Mularkey	13	196	15.1	1
Rice	9	61	6.8	1
White	8	76	9.5	0
Rhymes	5	124	24.8	0
Carroll	1	8	8.0	0

PUNT RETURNS

Last Name	No.	Yds	Avg	TD
Nelson	16	133	8.3	0
Carter	9	117	13.0	0

KICKOFF RETURNS

Last Name	No.	Yds	Avg	TD
Rhymes	53	1345	25.4	0
Rice	4	70	17.5	0
M. Turner	4	61	15.3	0
Nelson	3	51	17.0	0
Bess	2	33	16.5	0
Brown	1	7	7.0	0
Browner	1	0	0.0	0
Mularkey	0	9	—	0

PASSING — PUNTING — KICKING

PASSING	Att	Cmp	%	Yds	Yd/Att	TD	Int—	%	RK
Kramer	506	277	55	3522	7.0	19	26—	5	
Wilson	60	33	55	404	6.7	3	3—	5	
Bono	10	1	10	5	0.5	0	0—	0	

PUNTING	No	Avg
Coleman	67	42.8

KICKING	XP	Att	%	FG	Att	%
Stenerud	41	43	95	15	26	58

DETROIT LIONS

RUSHING

Last Name	No.	Yds	Avg	TD
J. Jones	244	886	3.6	6
Montgomery	75	251	3.3	0
Moore	80	221	2.8	4
Hipple	32	89	2.8	2
Kane	11	44	4.0	0
Meade	3	18	6.0	0
Nichols	1	15	15.0	0
Ferguson	4	12	3.0	1
A.J. Jones	1	2	2.0	0
Black	1	0	0.0	0

RECEIVING

Last Name	No.	Yds	Avg	TD
Thompson	51	736	14.4	5
J. Jones	45	334	7.4	3
Nichols	36	592	16.4	4
Lewis	28	354	12.6	3
Chadwick	25	478	19.1	3
Moore	19	154	8.1	1
Mandley	18	316	17.6	0
Bland	12	157	13.1	0
Montgomery	7	55	7.9	0
Kane	5	56	11.2	0
Rubick	2	33	16.5	0
Meade	2	21	10.5	0
McCall	1	7	7.0	0

PUNT RETURNS

Last Name	No.	Yds	Avg	TD
Mandley	38	403	10.6	1

KICKOFF RETURNS

Last Name	No.	Yds	Avg	TD
Hall	39	886	22.7	0
Moore	13	230	17.7	0
A.J. Jones	10	226	22.6	0
Mandley	6	152	25.3	0

PASSING — PUNTING — KICKING

PASSING	Att	Cmp	%	Yds	Yd/Att	TD	Int—	%	RK
Hipple	406	223	55	2952	7.3	17	18—	4	
J. Ferguson	54	31	57	364	6.7	2	3—	6	
J. Jones	1	0	0	0	0.0	0	0—	0	
Moore	1	0	0	0	0.0	0	0—	0	

PUNTING	No	Avg
Black	73	41.8

KICKING	XP	Att	%	FG	Att	%
Murray	31	33	94	26	31	84

TAMPA BAY BUCCANEERS

RUSHING

Last Name	No.	Yds	Avg	TD
Wilder	365	1300	3.6	10
Young	40	233	5.8	1
Springs	16	54	3.4	0
DeBerg	9	28	3.1	0
Carter	1	13	13.0	0
Fisher	1	10	10.0	0
Armstrong	2	6	3.0	0

RECEIVING

Last Name	No.	Yds	Avg	TD
Wilder	53	341	6.4	0
House	44	803	18.3	5
Giles	43	673	15.7	8
J. Bell	43	496	11.5	2
Carter	40	557	13.9	3
Magee	26	288	11.1	3
T. Bell	12	184	15.8	0
Springs	3	44	14.7	0
Witte	3	28	9.3	0
Armstrong	2	4	2.0	1

PUNT RETURNS

Last Name	No.	Yds	Avg	TD
Prior	13	105	8.1	0
Bright	12	124	10.3	0

KICKOFF RETURNS

Last Name	No.	Yds	Avg	TD
Freeman	48	1085	22.6	0
Bright	11	213	19.4	0
Prior	10	131	13.1	0
Springs	5	112	22.4	0
Verser	4	61	15.3	0
Magee	2	20	10.0	0

PASSING — PUNTING — KICKING

PASSING	Att	Cmp	%	Yds	Yd/Att	TD	Int—	%	RK
DeBerg	370	197	53	2488	6.7	19	18—	5	
Young	138	72	52	935	6.8	3	8—	6	

PUNTING	No	Avg
Garcia	77	42.0

KICKING	XP	Att	%	FG	Att	%
Igwebuike	30	32	91	22	32	69

LOS ANGELES RAMS 11-5 John Robinson

Scores of Each Game		
20	DENVER	16
17	Philadelphia	6
35	Seattle	24
17	ATLANTA	6
13	MINNESOTA	10
31	Tampa Bay	27
16	Kansas City	0
14	SAN FRANCISCO	28
28	NEW ORLEANS	10
19	N.Y.Giants	24
14	Atlanta	30
34	GREEN BAY	17
3	New Orleans	29
27	San Francisco	20
46	ST.LOUIS	14
6	L.A.RAIDERS	16

Use Name	Pos.	Hgt	Wgt	Age	Int	Pts
Bill Bain	OT	6'4"	290	33		
Irv Pankey	OT	6'4"	267	26		
Jackie Slater	OT	6'4"	271	31		
Russ Bolinger	OG	6'5"	255	30		
Dennis Harrah	OG	6'5"	265	32		
Kent Hill	OG	6'5"	260	28		
Duval Love	OG	6'3"	263	22		
Tony Slaton	C	6'3"	265	24		
Doug Smith	C	6'3"	260	28		
Reggie Doss	DE	6'4"	263	28		2
Dennis Harrison	DE	6'8"	280	29		
Gary Jester	DE	6'4"	260	30		
Doug Reed	DE	6'3"	262	25		
Booker Reese	DE	6'6"	260	25		
Charles DeJurnett	NT	6'4"	260	33		
Greg Meisner	NT	6'3"	253	26		
Shawn Miller	NT	6'4"	255	24		

Use Name	Pos.	Hgt	Wgt	Age	Int	Pts
Ed Brady	LB	6'2"	235	25		
Jim Collins	LB	6'2"	230	27	2	
Carl Ekern	LB	6'3"	230	31	2	6
Kevin Greene	LB	6'3"	238	23		
Mark Jerue	LB	6'3"	232	25		
Jim Laughlin	LB	6'	222	27		
Mel Owens	LB	6'2"	224	26		
Norwood Vann	LB	6'1"	225	23		
Mike Wilcher	LB	6'3"	240	25	1	
Nolan Cromwell	DB	6'1"	200	30	2	
Tim Fox	DB	5'11"	186	31	2	
Jerry Gray	DB	6'	185	22		
Gary Green	DB	5'11"	191	29	6	6
Eric Harris	DB	6'3"	202	30		
LeRoy Irvin	DB	5'11"	184	27	6	6
Johnnie Johnson	DB	6'1"	183	28	5	6
Vince Newsome	DB	6'1"	179	24	3	

George Andrews - Knee Injury
Mike Pleasant - Leg Injury

Use Name	Pos.	Hgt	Wgt	Age	Int	Pts
Dieter Brock	QB	6'1"	195	34		
Steve Dils	QB	6'1"	191	29		
Jeff Kemp	QB	6'	201	26		
Lynn Cain	HB	6'1"	205	29		
Barry Redden	HB	5'10"	205	25		
Charles White	HB	5'10"	190	27		18
Eric Dickerson	FB	6'3"	220	24		72
Mike Guman	FB	6'2"	218	27		
Ron Brown	WR	5'11"	181	24		36
Bobby Duckworth	WR	6'3"	196	26		18
Henry Ellard	WR	5'11"	175	24		36
Michael Young	WR	6'1"	185	23		
David Hill	TE	6'2"	240	31		6
Tony Hunter	TE	6'4"	237	25		24
James McDonald (from DET)	TE	6'5"	230	24		
Dale Hatcher	K	6'2"	200	22		
Mike Lansford	K	6'	183	27		104

SAN FRANCISCO FORTY NINERS 10-6 Bill Walsh

Scores of Each Game		
21	Minnesota	28
35	ATLANTA	16
34	L.A.Raiders	10
17	NEW ORLEANS	20
38	Atlanta	17
10	CHICAGO	26
21	Detroit	23
28	L.A.Rams	14
24	PHILADELPHIA	13
16	Denver	17
31	KANSAS CITY	3
19	SEATTLE	6
35	Washington	8
20	L.A.RAMS	27
31	New Orleans	19
31	DALLAS	16

Use Name	Pos.	Hgt	Wgt	Age	Int	Pts
Bruce Collie	OT	6'6"	275	23		
Keith Fahnhorst	OT	6'6"	273	33		
Bubba Parris	OT	6'6"	299	24		
Vince Stroth	OT	6'4"	256	24		
John Ayers	OG	6'5"	265	32		
Randy Cross	OG	6'3"	265	31		
Guy McIntyre	OG	6'3"	264	24		6
John Hill	C	6'2"	260	34		
Jim Leonard (to SD)	C	6'3"	260	27		
Fred Quillan	C	6'5"	266	29		
Dwaine Board	DE	6'5"	248	28		
Fred Dean	DE	6'3"	232	33		
John Harty	DE	6'4"	260	26		2
Jeff Stover	DE	6'5"	275	27		
Jim Stuckey	DE	6'4"	253	27		
Michael Carter	NT	6'2"	285	25		
Gary Johnson	NT	6'2"	261	33		
Manu Tuiasosopo	NT	6'3"	262	28		

Allan Kennedy - Knee Injury
Jesse Sapolu - Broken foot

Use Name	Pos.	Hgt	Wgt	Age	Int	Pts
Riki Ellison	LB	6'2"	225	25		
Jim Fahnhorst	LB	6'4"	230	26		
Ron Ferrari	LB	6'	215	26		
Jim Kovach (from NO)	LB	6'2"	239	29	1	
Fulton Kuykendall	LB	6'5"	228	32		
Milt McColl	LB	6'6"	230	26		6
Todd Shell	LB	6'4"	225	23	1	
Keena Turner	LB	6'2"	222	26		6
Michael Walter	LB	6'3"	238	24	1	
Dwight Hicks	DB	6'1"	192	29	4	
Jeff Fuller	DB	6'2"	216	23	1	
Ronnie Lott	DB	6'	200	26	6	
Dana McLemore	DB	5'10"	183	25	1	
Tory Nixon	DB	5'11"	186	23		
Carlton Williamson	DB	6'	204	27	3	6
Eric Wright	DB	6'1"	185	26	1	

Tom Holmoe - Shoulder Injury

Use Name	Pos.	Hgt	Wgt	Age	Int	Pts
Matt Cavanaugh	QB	6'2"	212	28		
Joe Montana	QB	6'2"	195	29		18
Derrick Harmon	HB	5'10"	202	22		
Carl Monroe	HB	5'8"	180	25		6
Bill Ring	HB	5'10"	205	28		6
Wendell Tyler	HB	5'10"	207	30		48
Roger Craig	FB	6'	224	25		90
Freddie Solomon	WR	5'11"	188	32		6
Dwight Clark	WR	6'4"	215	28		60
Jerry Rice	WR	6'2"	200	22		24
Mike Wilson	WR	6'3"	215	26		12
Earl Cooper	TE	6'2"	232	27		
Russ Francis	TE	6'6"	242	32		18
John Frank	TE	6'3"	225	23		6
Max Runager	K	6'1"	189	29		
Ray Wersching	K	5'11"	215	35		91

NEW ORLEANS SAINTS 5-11 Bum Phillips (4-8) Wade Phillips (1-3)

Scores of Each Game		
27	KANSAS CITY	47
23	Denver	34
20	TAMPA BAY	13
20	San Francisco	17
23	PHILADELPHIA	21
13	L.A.Raiders	23
24	Atlanta	31
13	N.Y.GIANTS	21
10	L.A.Rams	28
3	SEATTLE	27
14	Green Bay	38
30	Minnesota	23
29	L.A.RAMS	3
16	St.Louis	28
19	SAN FRANCISCO	31
10	ATLANTA	16

Use Name	Pos.	Hgt	Wgt	Age	Int	Pts
Stan Brock	OT	6'6"	288	27		
Daren Gilbert	OT	6'6"	285	21		
Dave Lafary	OT	6'7"	285	30		
Jim Rourke	OT	6'5"	263	28		
Ralph Williams	OT	6'3"	270	27		
Kelvin Clark	OG	6'3"	273	29		
Brad Edelman	OG	6'6"	262	24		
Petey Perot	OG	6'2"	271	28		
Adam Schreiber	OG	6'4"	270	23		
David Carter	C-OG	6'2"	275	31		
Joel Hilgenberg	C-OG	6'3"	253	23		
Steve Korte	C	6'2"	271	25		
Bruce Clark	DE	6'3"	281	27		
James Geathers	DE	6'7"	267	25		
Frank Warren	DE	6'4"	278	25		12
Jim Wilks	DE	6'5"	265	27		
Tony Elliott	NT	6'2"	300	26		
Derland Moore	NT	6'4"	273	33		

Use Name	Pos.	Hgt	Wgt	Age	Int	Pts
Jack Del Rio	LB	6'4"	235	22	2	6
James Haynes	LB	6'2"	227	25		
Rickey Jackson	LB	6'2"	239	27		
Joe Kohlbrand	LB	6'4"	242	22		
Whitney Paul	LB	6'3"	218	29		
Scott Pelluer	LB	6'2"	227	26		
Glen Redd	LB	6'1"	231	27	1	
Alvin Toles	LB	6'1"	211	22		
Russell Gary	DB	5'11"	196	26		
Terry Hoage	DB	6'3"	199	23	4	6
Earl Johnson	DB	6'	190	21		
Brett Maxie	DB	6'2"	190	23		
Johnnie Poe	DB	6'1"	194	26	3	6
David Rackley	DB	5'9"	172	24		
Willie Tullis	DB	6'	190	27	2	
Frank Wattelet	DB	6'	185	26	2	
Dave Waymer	DB	6'1"	188	27	6	

Use Name	Pos.	Hgt	Wgt	Age	Int	Pts
Bobby Hebert	QB	6'4"	215	25		6
Guido Merkens	QB	6'1"	197	30		6
Richard Todd	QB	6'2"	212	31		
Dave Wilson	QB	6'3"	211	26		
Earl Campbell	HB	5'11"	233	30		6
Tyrone Anthony	FB	5'11"	212	23		
Bobby Fowler	FB	6'2"	230	24		
Hokie Gajan	FB	5'11"	226	25		12
Wayne Wilson	FB	6'3"	220	27		18
Eugene Goodlow	WR	6'2"	181	26		18
Jeff Groth	WR	5'10"	181	28		12
Eric Martin	WR	6'1"	195	23		24
Mike Miller	WR	6'	183	25		
Carl Roaches	WR	5'8"	165	31		
Lindsay Scott	WR	6'1"	200	24		
Hoby Brenner	TE	6'4"	245	26		18
Larry Hardy	TE	6'3"	246	29		12
John Tice	TE	6'5"	243	25		12
Morten Andersen	K	6'2"	205	25		120
Brian Hansen	K	6'3"	218	24		

Tyrone Young - Knee Injury

ATLANTA FALCONS 4-12 Dan Henning

Scores of Each Game		
27	DETROIT	28
16	San Francisco	35
28	DENVER	44
6	L.A.Rams	17
17	SAN FRANCISCO	38
26	Seattle	30
31	NEW ORLEANS	24
10	Dallas	24
10	WASHINGTON	44
17	Philadelphia	*23
30	L.A.RAMS	14
0	Chicago	36
24	L.A.RAIDERS	34
10	Kansas City	38
14	MINNESOTA	13
16	New Orleans	10

Use Name	Pos.	Hgt	Wgt	Age	Int	Pts
Glen Howe (from PIT)	OT	6'6"	292	23		
Mike Kenn	OT	6'7"	277	29		
Brett Miller	OT	6'7"	290	26		
Eric Sanders	OT	6'7"	280	26		
Bill Fralic	OG-OT	6'5"	280	22		
Jeff Kiewel	OG	6'4"	265	24		
Joe Pellegrini	OG-C	6'4"	264	28		
John Scully	OG	6'6"	265	27		
Jeff Van Note	C	6'2"	264	39		
Wayne Tadloff	C-OG	6'5"	263	24		
Chuck Thomas	C-OG	6'3"	277	24		
Rick Bryan	DE	6'4"	270	23		6
Mike Gann	DE	6'5"	265	21		6
Andrew Provence	DE	6'3"	267	24		
Lawrence Pillers	DE	6'3"	257	32		
Dan Benish	DT	6'5"	280	23		
Willard Goff	DT	6'3"	265	23		
Mike Pitts	DT	6'5"	277	24	1	
Roy Harris	DT	6'2"	266	24		

Use Name	Pos.	Hgt	Wgt	Age	Int	Pts
Thomas Benson	LB	6'2"	235	23		
Buddy Curry	LB	6'4"	222	27	1	
David Frye	LB	6'2"	218	24	1	
Jeff Jackson	LB	6'1"	228	23		
John Rade	LB	6'1"	220	25	2	6
Al Richardson	LB	6'2"	222	27		
Johnny Taylor	LB	6'4"	235	25		
Ronnie Washington	LB	6'1"	236	22		
James Britt	DB	6'	185	24	1	
Bobby Butler	DB	5'11"	170	26	5	
Scott Case	DB	6'	178	23	4	
Wendell Cason	DB	5'11"	183	22	3	
David Croudip (from SD)	DB	5'8"	180	26		
Tiger Greene	DB	6'	184	23	2	
Kenny Johnson	DB	5'10"	167	27		
Reggie Pleasant	DB	5'9"	175	23		
Tom Pridemore	DB	5'10"	186	29	2	
Sean Thomas (from CIN)	DB	5'11"	190	23		
Dan Wagoner	DB	5'10"	180	25		

Rydell Malancon - Knee Injury

Use Name	Pos.	Hgt	Wgt	Age	Int	Pts
Dave Archer	QB	6'2"	203	23		12
Bob Holly	QB	6'2"	205	25		6
Steve Bartkowski (to WAS)	QB	6'4"	218	32		
Cliff Austin	HB	6'	207	25		6
Sylvester Stamps	HB	5'7"	166	24		
Tim Tyrrell	HB	6'1"	201	24		
Joe Washington	HB	5'10"	179	31		12
Gerald Riggs	FB	6'1"	232	24		60
Anthony Allen	WR	5'11"	182	26		12
Stacey Bailey	WR	6'	157	25		
Charlie Brown	WR	5'10"	184	26		12
Billy Johnson	WR	5'9"	170	33		30
Cliff Benson	TE	6'4"	238	24		
Arthur Cox	TE	6'2"	255	24		12
Allama Matthews	TE	6'2"	230	24		6
Ken Whisenhunt	TE	6'2"	233	23		
Rick Donnelly	K	6'	184	23		
Ralph Giacomarro	K	6'1"	194	24		
Mick Luckhurst	K	6'	183	27		101

William Andrews - Knee Injury
Mike Landrum - Knee Injury

* Overtime

LOS ANGELES RAMS

RUSHING

Last Name	No.	Yds	Avg	TD
Dickerson	292	1234	4.2	12
Redden	87	380	4.4	0
White	70	310	4.4	3
Cain	11	46	4.2	0
Brock	20	38	1.9	0
Guman	11	32	2.9	0
Brown	2	13	6.5	0
Ellard	3	8	2.7	0
Kemp	5	0	0.0	0
Dils	2	-4	-2.0	0

RECEIVING

Last Name	No.	Yds	Avg	TD
Ellard	54	811	15.0	5
Hunter	50	562	11.2	4
D. Hill	29	271	9.3	1
Duckworth	25	422	16.9	3
Dickerson	20	126	6.3	0
Redden	16	162	10.1	0
Brown	14	215	15.4	3
Young	14	157	11.2	0
McDonald	5	81	16.2	0
Cain	5	24	4.8	0
Guman	3	23	7.7	0
White	1	12	12.0	0

PUNT RETURNS

Last Name	No.	Yds	Avg	TD
Ellard	37	501	13.5	1
White	1	0	0.0	0

KICKOFF RETURNS

Last Name	No.	Yds	Avg	TD
Brown	28	918	32.8	3
White	17	300	17.6	0
Cain	6	115	19.2	0
Guman	2	30	15.0	0
Slaton	1	18	18.0	0
Miller	1	10	10.0	0
Cromwell	1	3	3.0	0

PASSING — PUNTING — KICKING

PASSING	Att	Cmp	%	Yds	Yd/Att	TD	Int—	%	RK
Brock	365	218	60	2658	7.28	16	13—	4	
Kemp	38	16	42	214	5.63	0	1—	3	

PUNTING	No	Avg
Hatcher	87	43.2

KICKING	XP	Att	%	FG	Att	%
Lansford	38	39	97	22	29	80

SAN FRANCISCO FORTY NINERS

RUSHING

Last Name	No.	Yds	Avg	TD
Craig	214	1050	4.9	9
Tyler	171	867	5.1	6
Montana	42	153	3.6	3
Harmon	28	92	3.3	0
Rice	6	26	4.3	1
Ring	8	23	2.9	1
Cooper	2	12	6.0	0
Cavanaugh	4	5	1.3	0
Soloman	2	4	2.0	0

RECEIVING

Last Name	No.	Yds	Avg	TD
Craig	92	1016	11.0	6
Clark	54	705	13.1	10
Rice	49	927	18.9	3
Francis	44	478	10.9	3
Solomon	25	259	10.4	1
Tyler	20	154	7.7	2
Harmon	14	123	8.8	0
Wilson	10	165	16.5	2
Monroe	10	51	5.1	0
Frank	7	50	7.1	1
Cooper	4	45	11.3	0
Ring	2	14	7.0	0

PUNT RETURNS

Last Name	No.	Yds	Avg	TD
McLemore	38	258	6.8	0

KICKOFF RETURNS

Last Name	No.	Yds	Avg	TD
Monroe	28	717	25.6	1
Harmon	23	467	20.3	0
McLemore	4	76	19.0	0
Rice	1	6	6.0	0
Lott	1	2	2.0	0
Frank	1	1	1.0	0

PASSING — PUNTING — KICKING

PASSING	Att	Cmp	%	Yds	Yd/Att	TD	Int—	%	RK
Montana	494	303	61	3653	7.4	27	13—	3	
Cavanaugh	54	28	52	334	6.2	1	1—	2	
Harmon	1	0	0	0	0.0	0	0—	0	
Solomon	1	0	0	0	0.0	0	0—	0	

PUNTING	No	Avg
Runager	86	39.8

KICKING	XP	Att	%	FG	Att	%
Wersching	52	53	98	13	21	62

NEW ORLEANS SAINTS

RUSHING

Last Name	No.	Yds	Avg	TD
W. Wilson	168	645	3.8	1
Campbell	158	643	4.1	1
Gajan	50	251	5.0	2
Anthony	17	65	3.8	0
Wattelet	2	42	21.0	0
Hebert	12	26	2.2	0
D. Wilson	18	7	0.4	0
Fowler	2	4	2.0	0
Goodlow	1	3	3.0	0
Martin	2	-1	-0.5	0
Merkens	1	-2	-2.0	0

RECEIVING

Last Name	No.	Yds	Avg	TD
Brenner	42	652	15.5	3
W.Wilson	38	228	6.0	2
Martin	35	522	14.9	4
Goodlow	32	603	18.8	3
Anthony	28	185	6.6	0
Tice	24	266	11.1	2
Groth	15	238	15.9	2
Hardy	15	208	13.9	2
Gajan	8	87	10.9	0
Scott	7	61	8.7	0
Campbell	6	88	14.7	0
Fowler	5	43	8.6	0
Merkens	3	61	20.3	1
Haynes	1	8	8.0	0
Hebert	1	7	7.0	1

PUNT RETURNS

Last Name	No.	Yds	Avg	TD
Tullis	17	141	8.3	0
Martin	8	53	6.6	0
Roaches	4	21	5.3	0
Groth	1	0	0.0	0

KICKOFF RETURNS

Last Name	No.	Yds	Avg	TD
Anthony	23	476	20.7	0
Tullis	23	470	20.4	0
Martin	15	384	25.6	0
Fowler	4	78	19.5	0
Roaches	4	76	19.0	0
Rackley	1	63	63.0	0
Merkens	1	0	0.0	0

PASSING — PUNTING — KICKING

PASSING	Att	Cmp	%	Yds	Yd/Att	TD	Int—	%	RK
D. Wilson	293	145	50	1843	6.3	11	15—	5	
Hebert	181	97	54	1208	6.7	5	4—	2	
Todd	32	16	50	191	6.0	3	4—	13	
Hansen	1	1	100	8	8.0	0	0—	0	
Merkens	1	1	100	7	7.0	1	0—	0	

PUNTING	No	Avg
Hansen	89	42.3

KICKING	XP	Att	%	FG	Att	%
Anderson	27	29	93	31	35	89

ATLANTA FALCONS

RUSHING

Last Name	No.	Yds	Avg	TD
Riggs	397	1719	4.3	10
Archer	70	347	5.0	2
J. Washington	52	210	4.0	1
Austin	20	110	5.5	0
Pridemore	1	48	48.0	0
Holly	3	36	12.0	1
Bartkowski	5	9	1.8	0
Whisenhunt	1	3	3.0	0
Bailey	1	-3	-3.0	0
Donnelly	2	-5	-2.5	0
B. Johnson	8	-8	-1.0	0

RECEIVING

Last Name	No.	Yds	Avg	TD
B. Johnson	62	830	13.4	5
J. Washington	37	328	8.9	1
Cox	33	454	13.8	2
Riggs	33	267	8.1	0
Bailey	30	364	12.1	0
Brown	24	412	17.2	2
Allen	14	207	14.8	2
Benson	10	37	3.7	0
Matthews	7	57	8.1	1
Whisenhunt	3	48	16.0	0
Austin	1	21	21.0	0

PUNT RETURNS

Last Name	No.	Yds	Avg	TD
Allen	21	141	6.7	0
B. Johnson	10	82	8.2	0

KICKOFF RETURNS

Last Name	No.	Yds	Avg	TD
Austin	39	838	21.5	1
Wagoner	13	262	20.2	0
Allen	8	140	17.5	0
Stamps	4	89	22.3	0
Whisenhunt	4	33	8.3	0
K. Johnson	1	20	20.0	0
Tyrrell	1	13	13.0	0
Matthews	1	11	11.0	0
R. Washington	1	0	0.0	0

PASSING — PUNTING — KICKING

PASSING	Att	Cmp	%	Yds	Yd/Att	TD	Int—	%	RK
Archer	312	161	52	1992	6.4	7	17—	5	
Bartkowski	111	69	62	738	6.3	5	1—	1	
Holly	39	24	62	295	7.6	1	2—	5	

PUNTING	NO	Avg
Donnelly	59	43.6
Giacomarro	29	39.9
Luckhurst	1	26.0

KICKING	XP	Att	%	FG	Att	%
Luckhurst	29	29	100	24	31	77

1985 A.F.C. The Arms of Youth

The American Football Conference standings looked like a bowl in 1985, and not the Super variety. The Eastern Division had three strong teams in the Dolphins, Jets and Patriots. Out west, the other high points were called Raiders and Broncos. In the middle, at the bottom of the bowl, was the Central Division, once the pride of the conference. Because the Central champ automatically went to the playoffs, Denver at 11-5 stayed home to watch Cleveland at 8-8.

There was a general feeling that the A.F.C. had slipped behind the N.F.C. in quality. As evidence, only the Raiders had been able to win the Super Bowl in the '80s. Some suggested the A.F.C. teams had spent their time nurturing spectacular young quarterbacks to the detriment of the rest of their programs. That was opinion; fact was that the A.F.C. did have a multitude of spectacular young quarterbacks. Heading the list was record-breaking Dan Marino, but close on his heels were Ken O'Brien, John Elway, Boomer Esiason, Bernie Kosar and Tony Eason. Another fact: most of the really awful defenses in pro football were in the A.F.C.

EASTERN DIVISION

Miami Dolphins — The Dolphins struggled early, in part due to Dan Marino's holdout through training camp and an injury that limited key wide receiver Mark "Super" Duper. With half of the Mark II receivers laid up, defenders concentrated on Mark Clayton, reducing his effectiveness. After nine games, Miami stood at only 5-4. The Killer Bee defense hadn't shown much sting and, as usual, the Miami running game was so-so, despite the estimable blocking of all-world center Dwight Stephenson. Then, while no one was looking, Shula got the act together and the Dolphins won the last seven regular-season games — including the only victory over the Bears all season — to take their third straight Eastern Division crown. Marino finished with 4,137 passing yards and 31 TD tosses — both N.F.L. highs — and it was considered an off year.

New York Jets — In the year Joe Namath was elected to the Pro Football Hall of Fame, the Jets finally appeared to have found his successor. Ken O'Brien, in his third season, emerged as the top quarterback while helping turn the Jets from losers to an 11-5 wild-card team. O'Brien was still criticized for holding the ball too long, contributing to a record 62 sacks, but his effective passing put him on top of the N.F.L.'s pass-rating system. Wide receivers Wesley Walker and spectacular rookie Al Toon helped a lot, as did tight end Mickey Shuler. Running back Freeman McNeil stayed healthy most of the time and rushed for 1,331 yards, but only three touchdowns. An improved defense that cut opponents' points by 100 from 1984 was as important as O'Brien and McNeil in the Jets' resurgence. Nose tackle Joe Klecko was the leader, with able assistance from end Mark Gastineau and outside linebacker Lance Mehl.

New England Patriots — After years of being tagged talented underachievers, the Patriots began to live up to their ability. Tony Eason began the season at quarterback and, when he went down injured, Steve Grogan stepped in to do a, bang-up job. Both had the benefit of a line boasting all-pro Brian Holloway and all-universe John Hannah, excellent receivers in revitalized Stanley Morgan and meteoric Irving Fryar, and a strong running attack led by Craig James and Tony Collins. Andre Tippett keyed a tough linebacking crew, and cornerback Raymond Clayborn and free safety Fred Marion were among the A.F.C.'s better defenders. In the next-to-last game, New England had a shot at the division crown but lost to Miami for the 18th consecutive time in the Orange Bowl. A win over Cincinnati in the last game gave the Pats a wild-card berth.

Indianapolis Colts — When the punter is the only player on the roster selected to the Pro Bowl, your team is in trouble. The Colts actually ran the ball well for new coach Rod Dowhower, finishing first in the A.F.C. through the efforts of running back Randy McMillan and a young offensive line. The passing attack was awful. Art Schlichter opened the season at quarterback and he was cut after four games. Mike Pagel got the job by default, but did nothing to excite the fans. The defense improved slightly, but not nearly enough. Ah, but Rohn Stark's punts were fine!

Buffalo Bills — A team that scores fewer than 10 points in seven of its games has offensive problems. A team that gives up 49 points to the Colts has defensive troubles. A team that did both of these in '85 was Buffalo. After opening with four straight losses, coach Kay Stephenson was replaced by Hank Bullough, known for his malaprops and his defensive expertise. The Bills responded to him by handing the Colts those 49 points. The only position where help wasn't needed was running back, where young Greg Bell rushed for 883 yards. So, who came back from the U.S.F.L.? Joe Cribbs.

CENTRAL DIVISION

Cleveland Browns — When the Browns won the division crown with a modest 8-8 record, critics said it showed how weak the Central had become. In Cleveland, they took it as a preview of coming attractions. Coach Marty Schottenheimer had a tough defense led by Chip Banks, one of the few linebackers mentionable in the same breath as Lawrence Taylor, and an undersized nose tackle in Bob Golic. He also had a talented but raw rookie quarterback in Bernie Kosar. Predictably, Schottenheimer chose to keep the ball on the ground all season while Kosar learned the ropes. Running backs Kevin Mack and Earnest Byner became the third tandem to each rush for more than 1,000 yards in a season. Despite the paucity of passes, Ozzie Newsome caught 62 and became the all-time top receiver among tight ends.

Cincinnati Bengals — The party line in Cincinnati was that another slow start under coach Sam Wyche — three straight losses — cost them the division title. But the Bengals also dropped their last two when the crown was within their grasp. A hulking offensive line, led by all-pro tackle Anthony Munoz, made it easier for lefty Boomer Esiason to blossom as a premier quarterback. Rookie receiver Eddie Brown and vet Cris Collinsworth gave him two ace targets for his passes, and the Bengals put a team-record 441 points on the scoreboard. No matter, possibly the least effective defensive unit since the Polish cavalry used horses against the Panzurs also set a team record, giving up 437 points.

Pittsburgh Steelers — The Steelers started off with a 45-3 win over the Colts as quarterback Mark Malone threw five touchdown passes. Then Malone got hurt, backup David Woodley showed why Miami had let him go, and third-string Scott Campbell proved he deserved to be only third-string. Receiver John Stallworth made a remarkable comeback to catch 75 passes, and Louis Lipps was a Pro Bowler at the other wideout position. Frank Pollard and Walter Abercrombie formed a strong, if unspectacular, rushing duo. Mike Merriweather was a standout at linebacker. But the team fell under .500 for the first time since 1971 and was obviously just going through the motions by the end.

Houston Oilers — The reason for the Oilers' inability to win was a multiple-choice quiz. The answer was: (a) coach Hugh Campbell's offense lacked inventiveness; (b) quarterback Warren Moon could not read defenses; (c) running back Mike Rozier had left his running ability in Nebraska with his Heisman Trophy; (d) all those high draft choices on the offensive line had been overrated; (e) the defense was lousy no matter what the offense did; or (f) all of the above. General manager Ladd Herzeg chose (a) and fired Campbell with two games left, replacing him with defensive coordinator Jerry Glanville.

WESTERN DIVISION

Los Angeles Raiders — The Raiders take pride in doing things differently, but they were not pleased to be the only strong A.F.C. team without an impressive young quarterback. After six seasons, they'd just about given up on Marc Wilson. Ancient Jim Plunkett was reduced by age and injuries to part-

FINAL TEAM STATISTICS

OFFENSE

	BUFF.	CIN.	CLEV.	DEN.	HOU.	IND.	K.C.	L.A.	MIA.	N.E.	NY J	PIT.	S.D.	SEA.
FIRST DOWNS:														
Total	256	344	271	339	270	282	258	304	361	294	344	315	380	299
by Rushing	86	125	119	113	96	131	79	111	116	126	121	125	92	96
by Passing	151	191	128	192	149	130	158	167	218	153	201	165	259	179
by Penalty	19	28	24	34	25	21	21	26	27	15	22	25	29	24
RUSHING:														
Number	412	503	533	497	428	485	428	532	444	565	564	541	440	462
Yards	1611	2183	2285	1851	1570	2439	1486	2262	1729	2331	2312	2177	1665	1644
Average Yards	3.9	4.3	4.3	3.7	3.7	5.0	3.5	4.3	3.9	4.1	4.1	4.0	3.8	3.6
Touchdowns	13	20	16	20	13	22	10	18	19	15	18	14	20	9
PASSING:														
Attempts	517	518	414	617	512	468	511	506	576	457	497	512	632	575
Completions	263	302	222	329	277	235	267	269	343	255	303	254	386	304
Completion Pct.	50.9	58.3	53.6	53.3	54.1	50.2	52.3	53.2	59.5	55.8	61.0	49.6	61.1	52.9
Passing Yards	3331	4082	2885	3952	3523	2811	3726	3481	4278	3483	3983	3397	5175	3820
Avg. Yds per Att.	5.3	6.7	5.9	5.6	5.4	5.1	6.1	5.7	6.9	6.4	6.4	5.8	7.3	5.4
Avg. Yds per Comp.	12.7	13.5	13.0	12.0	12.8	12.0	14.0	12.9	12.5	13.7	13.2	13.4	13.4	12.6
Times Tackled	42	41	36	38	58	35	43	43	19	39	62	33	39	53
Yds Lost Tackled	347	365	249	307	441	244	335	335	164	315	399	224	305	457
Net Yards	2984	3717	2636	3645	3082	2567	3391	3146	4114	3168	3584	3173	4870	3363
Touchdowns	9	31	17	23	18	15	23	20	31	20	25	23	37	28
Interceptions	31	13	13	23	22	20	23	24	21	22	8	27	30	23
Pct. Intercepted	6.0	2.5	3.1	3.7	4.3	4.3	4.5	4.7	3.6	4.8	1.6	5.3	4.7	4.0
PUNTS:														
Number	92	63	81	94	84	80	95	89	59	92	74	79	68	91
Average	41.5	40.7	40.3	40.0	41.5	44.8	40.3	40.8	43.7	43.0	40.2	39.1	42.4	40.3
PUNT RETURNS														
Number	38	32	47	46	30	42	43	71	39	42	39	49	25	53
Yards	293	268	371	429	250	449	381	785	319	530	386	483	213	483
Average Yards	7.7	8.4	7.9	9.3	8.3	10.7	8.9	11.1	8.2	12.6	9.9	9.9	8.5	9.1
Touchdowns	0	0	1	0	0	1	0	0	0	2	0	2	0	0
KICKOFF RET.:														
Number	68	67	53	52	67	67	59	54	52	57	53	65	71	58
Yards	1334	1385	1217	1203	1515	1403	1117	1132	1177	1119	1043	1337	1494	1166
Average Yards	19.6	20.7	23.0	23.1	22.6	20.9	18.9	21.0	22.6	19.6	19.7	20.6	21.0	20.1
Touchdowns	0	0	0	0	0	0	0	0	0	0	0	0	1	0
INTERCEPT RET.:														
Number	20	19	18	24	15	16	27	17	23	23	22	20	26	24
Yards	225	283	254	290	144	75	298	235	265	427	127	211	461	272
Average Yards	11.3	14.9	14.1	12.1	9.6	4.7	11.0	13.8	11.5	18.6	5.8	10.6	17.7	11.3
Touchdowns	0	2	1	1	0	0	1	3	1	1	1	1	2	3
PENALTIES:														
Number	132	110	99	85	127	87	87	116	77	114	119	85	100	102
Yards	965	795	753	677	1150	678	666	962	637	842	907	665	937	827
FUMBLES:														
Number	36	35	40	24	41	27	22	27	31	37	35	31	44	34
Number Lost	21	16	23	8	15	14	11	14	20	20	21	9	19	18
POINTS:														
Total	200	441	287	380	284	320	317	354	428	362	393	379	467	349
PAT Attempts	23	53	35	45	32	39	35	42	52	41	45	40	60	44
PAT Made	23	49	35	41	29	36	35	40	50	40	43	40	53	41
FG Attempts	17	33	18	38	27	26	27	32	27	30	34	42	28	25
FG Made	13	24	14	23	21	16	24	20	22	24	26	33	18	14
Percent FG Made	76.5	72.7	77.8	60.5	77.8	61.5	88.9	62.5	81.5	80.0	76.5	78.6	64.3	56.0
Safeties	0	1	0	0	0	1	0	1	0	2	1	0	0	1

DEFENSE

	BUFF.	CIN.	CLEV.	DEN.	HOU.	IND.	K.C.	L.A.	MIA.	N.E.	NY J	PIT.	S.D.	SEA.
FIRST DOWNS:														
Total	320	337	297	290	356	330	336	273	314	284	276	273	364	290
by Rushing	142	118	106	103	150	124	129	73	135	92	85	105	122	90
by Passing	159	194	172	168	158	192	184	166	160	168	154	144	218	179
by Penalty	19	25	19	19	48	14	23	34	19	24	37	24	24	21
RUSHING:														
Number	569	461	497	475	588	539	513	461	509	466	433	470	470	473
Yards	2462	1999	1851	1973	2814	2145	2169	1605	2256	1655	1516	1876	1972	1837
Average Yards	4.3	4.3	3.7	4.2	4.8	4.0	4.2	3.5	4.4	3.6	3.5	4.0	4.2	3.9
Touchdowns	20	23	14	10	21	20	18	7	15	15	10	19	25	12
PASSING:														
Attempts	477	518	509	547	462	504	576	511	487	525	507	484	595	496
Completions	265	297	289	277	260	275	332	251	257	262	267	287	357	273
Completion Pct.	55.6	57.3	56.8	50.6	56.3	54.6	57.6	49.1	52.8	49.9	52.7	59.3	60.0	55.0
Passing Yards	3301	3998	3460	3584	3654	3721	3752	3486	3789	3393	3626	3088	4597	3787
Avg. Yds per Att.	6.1	6.6	5.6	5.4	6.6	6.4	5.7	5.2	6.7	5.3	5.9	5.6	6.8	6.0
Avg. Yds per Comp.	12.5	13.5	12.0	12.9	14.1	13.5	11.3	13.9	14.7	13.0	13.6	10.8	12.9	13.9
Times Tackled	25	40	44	47	41	36	37	65	38	51	40	36	40	61
Yds Lost Tackled	223	334	353	378	313	267	263	488	278	334	370	305	304	464
Net Yards	3078	3664	3107	3206	3341	3454	3489	2998	3511	3059	3256	2783	4293	3323
Touchdowns	24	26	18	22	29	24	22	22	21	14	17	18	28	22
Interceptions	20	19	18	24	15	16	27	17	23	23	22	20	26	24
Pct. Intercepted	4.2	3.7	3.5	4.4	3.2	3.2	4.7	3.3	4.7	4.4	4.3	4.1	4.4	4.8
PUNTS:														
Number	81	60	91	94	68	72	75	104	73	97	88	86	70	97
Average	40.5	41.3	42.2	41.1	39.4	41.4	41.2	41.9	40.7	40.5	41.8	40.9	38.8	42.1
PUNT RETURNS														
Number	49	42	36	38	45	43	48	26	27	56	36	43	36	47
Yards	438	554	304	325	345	572	530	159	371	598	319	380	274	374
Average Yards	8.9	13.2	8.4	8.6	7.7	13.3	11.0	6.1	13.7	10.7	8.9	8.8	7.6	8.0
Touchdowns	1	1	0	0	0	1	1	0	1	0	1	0	0	0
KICKOFF RET.:														
Number	41	81	51	64	39	59	69	59	63	76	58	65	68	47
Yards	798	1734	884	1346	970	1189	1626	1165	1370	1434	1135	1566	1363	918
Average Yards	19.5	21.4	17.3	21.0	24.9	20.2	23.6	19.7	21.7	18.9	19.6	24.1	20.0	19.5
Touchdowns	0	0	0	1	0	0	0	0	0	0	0	0	0	0
INTERCEPT RET.:														
Number	31	13	13	23	22	20	23	24	21	22	8	27	30	23
Yards	418	199	217	332	267	232	251	365	100	243	101	409	268	389
Average Yards	13.5	15.3	16.7	14.4	12.1	11.6	10.9	15.2	4.7	11.0	12.6	15.1	8.9	16.9
Touchdowns	4	0	1	2	1	0	0	1	0	2	1	5	0	1
PENALTIES:														
Number	107	84	102	91	121	90	89	109	112	83	113	89	86	106
Yards	870	731	773	953	908	699	77	856	854	699	868	679	703	840
FUMBLES:														
Number	36	34	28	22	35	32	25	27	36	36	42	34	37	39
Number Lost	15	19	9	12	20	17	14	13	18	24	20	14	16	20
POINTS:														
Total	381	437	294	329	412	386	360	308	320	290	264	355	435	303
PAT Attempts	50	51	34	36	51	45	41	34	38	32	30	43	55	35
PAT Made	45	51	33	35	49	41	39	32	35	30	30	40	51	31
FG Attempts	15	34	29	33	34	31	30	35	28	25	25	25	30	28
FG Made	12	26	19	26	19	25	25	24	19	22	18	19	18	20
Percent FG Made	80.0	76.5	65.5	78.8	55.9	80.6	83.3	68.6	67.9	88.0	72.0	76.0	60.0	71.4
Safeties	0	1	0	0	0	0	0	0	0	1	0	0	0	1

time status or less. Nevertheless, they won the Western Division title with a six-game winning streak at season's end, riding a sensational year by Marcus Allen and an intimidating defense. Allen led the N.F.L. with 1,759 rushing yards, caught 67 passes and scored 14 touchdowns. Tight end Todd Christensen took some of the pressure off Allen with 82 ball-control catches. The defense kept the pressure on with linemen Howie Long and Bill Pickel. Cornerback Mike Haynes regained his reputation as one of the best in football. The conference-leading 65 sacks was matched by a less-than-50 percent pass-completion mark for opponents.

Denver Broncos — Two overtime three-point losses to the Raiders within a three-week span late in the season cost the Broncos the division title and, on tie-breakers, a trip to the playoffs. Their 11-5 record was the best ever for an excluded team. John Elway took several strides toward becoming the superstar Denver bet he would. Sammy Winder was a useful all-around running back, but, with no dominant runner, the offense relied mainly on Elway throwing to Steve Watson and others. Karl Mecklenburg emerged as a defensive star without a position as he shifted among various line and linebacking spots. End Rulon Jones and cornerback Louis Wright also helped make the essentially no-name defense highly effective.

Seattle Seahawks — Curt Warner was back, perhaps a half step slower from knee surgery, but still good for 1,094 yards. Receiver Steve Largent caught 79 passes for a league-leading 1,287 yards, while extending his consecutive-game receiving mark to 123. The defense, boasting linemen Jacob Green, Jeff Bryant and Joe Nash, and safety Kenny Easley, was one of the best. Yet, the Seahawks slipped to .500, alternating every two wins with two losses. Most of the blame was heaped on the erratic play of quarterback Dave Krieg. His 20 interceptions helped reduce the turnover ratio from plus-24 in 1984 to plus-3 in '85. At times, he just couldn't move the team, causing a loss of confidence in him by the coaches and by himself.

San Diego Chargers — Nothing new this year. Once again, quarterback Dan Fouts threw a ton of passes; receivers Wes Chandler and Charlie Joiner, running back Lionel James, and others caught a high percentage of them for many yards. James caught the most of anyone in the A.F.C. with 86. Runner Earnest Jackson was traded away, so the Chargers only ran the ball when the moon was in the right phase. The offense scored lots of points. Then they turned the ball over to the other team and let them score lots of points. Another season of Air Coryell and the Little Defense That Couldn't.

Kansas City Chiefs — Take a seven-game losing streak out of the heart of the season, and the Chiefs had a good year. Let quarterback Bill Kenney play an entire season without injuries, and he's one of the best. Ditto for defensive end Art Still. Give this team something remotely resembling a running attack and ... get the picture? The Chiefs end almost every season with "might-have-beens." In the real world of the Chiefs, free safety Deron Cherry was all-pro and intercepted four passes in one game against Seattle. Receiver Stephone Paige broke an N.F.L. record with 309 yards on eight receptions in the season finale. And Kansas City missed post-season play for the 14th consecutive year.

MIAMI DOLPHINS 12-4 Don Shula

Scores of Each Game		
23	Houston	26
30	INDIANAPOLIS	13
31	KANSAS CITY	0
30	Denver	26
30	PITTSBURGH	20
7	N.Y.Jets	23
41	TAMPA BAY	38
21	Detroit	31
13	New England	17
21	N.Y.JETS	17
34	Indianapolis	20
23	Buffalo	14
38	CHICAGO	24
34	Green Bay	24
30	NEW ENGLAND	27
28	BUFFALO	0

Use Name	Pos.	Hgt	Wgt	Age	Int	Pts
Jeff Dellenbach	OT	6'6"	280	22		
Jon Giesler	OT	6'5"	260	28		
Cleveland Green	OT	6'3"	262	27		
Steve Clark	OG	6'4"	255	25		
Roy Foster	OG	6'4"	275	25		
Ronnie Lee	OG	6'3"	265	28		
Dwight Stephenson	C	6'2"	255	27		
Jeff Toews	C-OG	6'3"	255	27		
Bill Barnett	DE-NT	6'4"	260	29		
Doug Betters	DE	6'7"	265	29		
Kim Bokamper	DE	6'6"	255	30		
Mack Moore	DE	6'4"	258	26		
Mike Charles	NT	6'4"	285	22		
George Little	NT	6'4"	278	22		
Charles Bowser	LB	6'3"	235	25		
Jay Brophy	LB	6'3"	233	25	1	
Mark Brown	LB	6'2"	225	24	1	
Bob Brudzinski	LB	6'4"	223	30	1	6
Hugh Green (from TB)	LB	6'2"	225	26	1	
Alex Moyer	LB	6'1"	221	21	1	
Robin Sendlein	LB	6'3"	225	26		
Jackie Shipp	LB	6'2"	236	23	1	
Sanders Shiver	LB	6'2"	230	30		
Glenn Blackwood	DB	6'	190	28	6	
Lyle Blackwood	DB	6'	190	34	1	
Bud Brown	DB	6'	194	24	2	
William Judson	DB	6'1"	190	26	4	6
Mike Kozlowski	DB	6'	198	29		
Paul Lankford	DB	6'1"	184	27	4	
Don McNeal	DB	5'11"	192	27		
Mike Smith	DB	6'	171	22		
Robert Sowell	DB	5'11"	175	24		
Dan Marino	QB	6'4"	214	23		
Don Strock	QB	6'5"	220	34		
Joe Carter	HB	5'11"	196	23		
Lorenzo Hampton	HB	6'	212	23		18
Tony Nathan	HB	6'	206	28		36
Woody Bennett	FB	6'2"	225	30		6
Ron Davenport	FB	6'2"	230	22		78
Mark Clayton	WR	5'9"	175	24		24
Mark Duper	WR	5'9"	187	26		18
Duriel Harris	WR	5'11"	176	30		
Vince Heflin	WR	6'	185	26		6
Jim Jensen	WR	6'4"	215	26		6
Frank Lockett	WR	6'	200	28		
Nat Moore	WR	5'9"	188	33		42
Tommy Vigorito	WR	5'10"	190	25		
Bruce Hardy	TE	6'5"	232	29		24
Dan Johnson	TE	6'3"	240	25		18
Joe Rose	TE	6'3"	230	28		24
Fuad Reveiz	K	5'11"	222	22		116
Reggie Roby	K	6'2"	243	24		

Bob Baumhower - Knee Injury
Ed Newman - Knee Injury
Joe Pisarcik - Injury

NEW YORK JETS 11-5 Joe Walton

Scores of Each Game		
0	L.A.Raiders	31
42	BUFFALO	3
24	Green Bay	3
25	INDIANAPOLIS	20
29	Cincinnati	20
23	MIAMI	7
13	New England	20
17	SEATTLE	14
35	Indianapolis	17
17	Miami	21
62	TAMPA BAY	28
16	NEW ENGLAND	*13
20	Detroit	31
27	Buffalo	7
6	CHICAGO	19
37	CLEVELAND	10

Use Name	Pos.	Hgt	Wgt	Age	Int	Pts
Ted Banker	OT-OG	6'2"	255	24		
Reggie McElroy	OT	6'6"	270	25		
Marvin Powell	OT	6'5"	270	30		
Billy Shields	OT	6'8"	284	32		
Sid Abramowitz	OG	6'6"	280	25		
Dan Alexander	OG	6'4"	260	30		
Guy Bingham	OG-OT	6'3"	255	27		
Jim Sweeney	OG-OT	6'4"	266	23		
Joe Fields	C	6'2"	253	31		
Barry Bennett	DE-DT	6'4"	260	29		
Mark Gastineau	DE	6'5"	265	28		
Ron Faurot	DE	6'7"	262	23		
Marty Lyons	DE-DT	6'5"	269	28		
Ben Rudolph	DE	6'5"	271	28		
Tom Baldwin	DT	6'4"	275	24		6
Joe Klecko	DT-DE	6'3"	263	31		
Kyle Clifton	LB	6'4"	233	23	3	
Bob Crable	LB	6'3"	228	25		
Jim Eliopulos	LB	6'2"	229	26		
Rusty Guilbeau	LB	6'4"	237	26		
Charles Jackson	LB	6'2"	224	30		
Lance Mehl	LB	6'3"	233	27	3	
Matt Monger	LB	6'1"	235	23		
John Woodring	LB	6'2"	232	26		
Russell Carter	DB	6'2"	195	23		
Donnie Elder	DB	5'9"	175	22		
Kerry Glenn	DB	5'9"	175	23	4	6
Harry Hamilton	DB	6'	193	22	2	
Bobby Jackson	DB	5'9"	180	28	4	
Lester Lyles	DB	6'3"	209	22		
Johnny Lynn	DB	6'	198	28	1	
Rich Miano	DB	6'	200	22	2	
Davlin Mullen	DB	6'1"	177	25	3	
Kirk Springs	DB	6'	197	27		
Ken O'Brien	QB	6'4"	208	24		
Pat Ryan	QB	6'3"	210	29		
Dennis Bligen	HB	5'11"	209	23		6
Johnny Hector	HB	5'11"	197	24		36
Freeman McNeil	HB	5'11"	212	26		30
Cedric Minter	HB	5'10"	200	26		
Marion Barber	FB	6'3"	224	25		
Tony Paige	FB	5'10"	220	22		60
Nick Bruckner	WR	5'11"	185	24		
Chy Davidson	WR	5'11"	175	26		
Bobby Humphrey	WR	5'10"	180	24		
Kurt Sohn	WR	5'11"	180	28		24
Al Toon	WR	6'4"	200	22		18
JoJo Townsell	WR	5'9"	180	24		
Wesley Walker	WR	6'	182	30		32
Billy Griggs	TE	6'3"	230	23		
Rocky Klever	TE	6'3"	225	26		12
Mickey Shuler	TE	6'3"	231	29		42
Dave Jennings	K	6'4"	200	33		
Pat Leahy	K	6'	193	34		121

Stan Waldemore - Knee Injury
Glenn Dennison - Back Injury
Johnny "Lam" Jones - Finger Injury

NEW ENGLAND PATRIOTS 11-5 Raymond Berry

Scores of Each Game		
26	GREEN BAY	20
7	Chicago	20
17	Buffalo	14
20	L.A.RAIDERS	35
20	Cleveland	24
14	BUFFALO	3
20	N.Y.JETS	13
32	Tampa Bay	14
17	MIAMI	13
34	INDIANAPOLIS	15
20	Seattle	13
13	N.Y.Jets	*16
32	Indianapolis	31
23	DETROIT	6
27	Miami	30
34	CINCINNATI	23

Use Name	Pos.	Hgt	Wgt	Age	Int	Pts
Brian Holloway	OT	6'7"	288	26		
Art Plunkett	OT	6'7"	260	26		
Tom Condon	OG	6'1"	275	32		
Paul Fairchild	OG	6'4"	270	23		
John Hannah	OG	6'2"	265	34		
Steve Moore	OG-OT	6'4"	285	24		
Ron Wooten	OG	6'4"	273	26		
Pete Brock	C	6'5"	275	31		
Trevor Matich	C	6'4"	270	23		
Guy Morriss	C-OG	6'4"	255	34		
Julius Adams	DE	6'3"	265	37		
Kenneth Sims	DE	6'5"	271	25		
Ben Thomas	DE	6'4"	280	24		
Garin Veris	DE	6'4"	255	22		
Toby Williams	DE	6'3"	254	25		
Dennis Owens	NT	6'1"	258	25		
Lester Williams	NT	6'3"	272	26		
Don Blackmon	LB	6'3"	235	27	1	4
Brian Ingram	LB	6'4"	235	25		
Larry McGrew	LB	6'5"	233	28	1	
Steve Nelson	LB	6'2"	230	34		
Johnny Rembert	LB	6'3"	234	24		6
Ed Reynolds	LB	6'5"	230	23		
Andre Tippett	LB	6'3"	241	25		6
Ed Williams	LB	6'4"	244	24		
Jim Bowman	DB	6'2"	210	21		
Raymond Clayborn	DB	6'1"	186	30	6	6
Ernest Gibson	DB	5'10"	185	23		
Roland James	DB	6'2"	191	27	4	
Ronnie Lippett	DB	5'11"	180	24	3	
Fred Marion	DB	6'2"	191	26	7	
Rod McSwain	DB	6'1"	198	23	1	
Tony Eason	QB	6'4"	212	25		6
Steve Grogan	QB	6'4"	210	32		12
Tom Ramsey	QB	6'1"	189	24		
Craig James	HB	6'	215	24		42
Tony Collins	HB	5'11"	212	26		30
Mosi Tatupu	FB	6'	227	30		12
Robert Weathers	FB	6'2"	222	24		6
Irving Fryar	WR	6'	220	22		60
Greg Hawthorne	WR-HB	6'2"	225	28		6
Cedric Jones	WR	6'1"	184	25		18
Stanley Morgan	WR	5'11"	181	30		30
Stephen Starring	WR	5'10"	172	24		
Derwin Williams	WR	6'1"	170	24		
Lin Dawson	TE	6'3"	240	26		
Derrick Ramsey	TE	6'5"	235	28		6
Rich Camarillo	K	5'11"	185	25		
Tony Franklin	K	5'8"	182	28		112

Darryl Haley - Colitus
Clayton Weishuhn - Knee Injury
Eric Jordan - Jaw Injury
Bo Robinson - Groin Injury
Jon Williams - Knee Injury

INDIANAPOLIS COLTS 5-11 Rod Dowhower

Scores of Each Game		
3	Pittsburgh	45
13	Miami	30
14	DETROIT	6
20	N.Y.Jets	25
49	BUFFALO	17
10	DENVER	15
9	Buffalo	21
37	GREEN BAY	10
17	N.Y.JETS	35
15	New England	34
20	MIAMI	34
7	Kansas City	20
31	NEW ENGLAND	38
10	Chicago	17
31	Tampa Bay	23
34	HOUSTON	16

Use Name	Pos.	Hgt	Wgt	Age	Int	Pts
Karl Baldischwiler	OT	6'5"	276	29		
Kevin Call	OT	6'7"	288	23		
Roger Caron	OT	6'5"	292	23		
Chris Hinton	OG	6'4"	285	24		
Ron Solt	OG	6'3"	283	23		
Ben Utt	OG	6'5"	281	26		
Don Bailey	C	6'4"	268	24		
Ray Donaldson	C	6'3"	281	27		
Charles Benson	DE	6'3"	267	24		
Willie Broughton	DE	6'5"	282	20		
Chris Scott	DE	6'5"	271	23		
Byron Smith	DE	6'5"	271	22		
Donnell Thompson	DE	6'4"	269	26		
Scott Virkus	DE	6'5"	283	25		
George Achica	NT	6'4"	275	24		
Brad White	NT	6'2"	261	27		
Dave Ahrens	LB	6'3"	245	26		
Duane Bickett	LB	6'5"	244	22	1	
Johnie Cooks	LB	6'4"	243	26	1	
Lamonte Hunley	LB	6'2"	238	22		
Barry Krauss	LB	6'3"	253	28	1	
Orlando Lowry	LB	6'4"	238	24		
Cliff Odom	LB	6'2"	241	26		
Don Anderson	DB	5'10"	197	22	1	
Leonard Coleman	DB	6'2"	211	23		
Eugene Daniel	DB	5'11"	184	24	8	
Preston Davis	DB	5'11"	180	23	2	
Nesby Glasgow	DB	5'10"	191	28		
Keith Lee	DB	5'11"	200	27		
George Radachowsky	DB	5'11"	178	22		
Tate Randle	DB	6'	204	26	1	2
Anthony Young	DB	5'11"	196	21	1	6
Matt Kofler	QB	6'3"	203	26		6
Mike Pagel	QB	6'2"	211	24		12
Art Schlichter	QB	6'3"	210	25		
Albert Bentley	HB	5'11"	215	25		12
Frank Middleton	HB	5'11"	201	24		6
George Wonsley	HB	5'10"	221	24		36
Curtis Dickey (to CLE)	FB	6'1"	220	28		
Owen Gill	FB	6'1"	230	23		12
Randy McMillan	FB	6'	220	26		42
Matt Bouza	WR	6'3"	215	26		12
Ray Butler (to SEA)	WR	6'3"	203	28		12
Wayne Capers	WR	6'2"	203	24		30
Bernard Henry	WR	6'1"	180	25		
Robbie Martin	WR	5'8"	187	26		6
Ricky Nichols	WR	5'10"	176	23		
Oliver Williams	WR	6'3"	192	24		6
Pat Beach	TE	6'4"	244	25		36
Mark Boyer	TE	6'4"	232	22		
Keli McGregor (from DEN)	TE	6'6"	253	22		
Tim Sherwin	TE	6'6"	246	27		
Raul Allegre	K	5'10"	167	26		84
Rohn Stark	K	6'3"	212	26		

Mark Kirchner - Injury
Jim Mills - Shoulder Injury
Blaise Winter - Shoulder Injury
Leo Wisniewski - Knee Injury

BUFFALO BILLS 2-14 Kay Stephenson (0-4), Hank Bullough (2-10)

Scores of Each Game		
9	SAN DIEGO	14
3	N.Y.Jets	42
14	NEW ENGLAND	17
20	MINNESOTA	27
17	Indianapolis	49
3	New England	14
21	INDIANAPOLIS	9
17	Philadelphia	21
17	CINCINNATI	23
20	HOUSTON	0
7	Cleveland	17
14	MIAMI	23
7	San Diego	40
7	N.Y.JETS	27
24	Pittsburgh	30
0	Miami	28

Use Name	Pos.	Hgt	Wgt	Age	Int	Pts
Justin Cross	OT	6'6"	265	26		
Joe Devlin	OT	6'5"	267	31		
Dale Hellestrae	OT	6'5"	261	23		
Ken Jones	OT	6'5"	279	32		
Greg Christy	OG	6'4"	279	23		
Joe DeLamielleure	OG	6'3"	260	34		
Jim Richer	OG	6'3"	258	27		
Mark Traynowicz	OG	6'5"	272	22		
Tim Vogler	OG	6'3"	267	28		
Will Grant	C	6'3"	264	31		
Sean McNanie	DE	6'5"	265	23		
Dean Prater	DE	6'4"	256	26		
Bruce Smith	DE	6'4"	279	22		
Ben Williams	DE	6'3"	266	31		
Fred Smerlas	NT	6'3"	268	28		
Don Smith	NT	6'5"	262	28		
Anthony Dickerson	LB	6'2"	222	28		
Guy Frazier	LB	6'2"	217	26	1	
Hal Garner	LB	6'4"	220	23		
Jim Haslett	LB	6'3"	228	27	1	
Steve Maidlow	LB	6'2"	238	25		
Eugene Marve	LB	6'2"	240	29		
Lucius Sanford	LB	6'2"	220	29		
Darryl Talley	LB	6'4"	227	25		
Larry Kubin	LB	6'2"	238	26		
Eric Wilson	LB	6'1"	247	23		
Martin Bayless	DB	6'2"	195	22	2	
Rodney Bellinger	DB	5'8"	189	23	2	
Derrick Burroughs	DB	6'1"	180	23	2	
Steve Freeman	DB	5'11"	185	32		
Rod Hill	DB	6'	188	26	2	
Lawrence Johnson	DB	5'11"	202	27	1	
Jim Perryman	DB	6'	175	24		
Charles Romes	DB	6'1"	188	30	7	
Don Wilson	DB	6'2"	190	24	2	6
Bruce Mathison	QB	6'3"	205	26		6
Frank Reich	QB	6'3"	208	23		
Vince Ferragamo (to GB)	QB	6'3"	217	31		6
Joe Cribbs	HB	5'11"	193	27		6
Anthony Hutchison	HB	5'10"	186	24		
Van Williams	HB	6'	208	26		
Greg Bell	FB	5'10"	210	23		54
Booker Moore	FB	5'11"	222	26		6
Anthony Steels (from SD)	FB	5'9"	200	26		
Mitchell Brookins	WR	5'11"	196	24		
Chris Burkett	WR	6'4"	198	23		
Jerry Butler	WR	6'	178	27		12
Andre Reed	WR	6'	186	20		30
Eric Richardson	WR	6'1"	185	23		
Jimmy Teal	WR	5'10"	170	23		
Pete Metzelaars	TE	6'7"	243	25		6
Eason Ramson	TE	6'2"	234	29		6
Ulysses Norris	TE	6'4"	232	28		
John Kidd	K	6'3"	208	24		
Scott Norwood	K	6'	205	25		62

Stan David - Torn back muscle
Robb Riddick - Knee Injury

* Overtime

MIAMI DOLPHINS

RUSHING

Last Name	No.	Yds	Avg	TD
Nathan	143	667	4.7	5
Davenport	98	370	3.8	11
Hampton	105	369	3.5	3
Bennett	54	256	4.7	0
Carter	14	76	5.4	0
N. Moore	1	11	11.0	0
Clayton	1	10	10.0	0
Strock	2	-6	-3.0	0
Marino	26	-24	-0.9	0

RECEIVING

Last Name	No.	Yds	Avg	TD
Nathan	72	651	9.0	1
Clayton	70	996	14.2	4
N. Moore	51	701	13.7	7
Hardy	39	409	10.5	4
Duper	35	650	18.6	3
Rose	19	306	16.1	4
Johnson	13	192	14.8	3
Davenport	13	74	5.7	2
Bennett	10	101	10.1	1
Hampton	8	56	7.0	0
Heflin	6	98	16.3	1
Harris	3	24	8.0	0
Carter	2	7	3.5	0
Vigorito	1	9	9.0	0
Jensen	1	4	4.0	1

PUNT RETURNS

Last Name	No.	Yds	Avg	TD
Vigorito	22	197	9.0	0
Kozlowski	7	65	9.3	0
Lockett	5	23	4.6	0
G. Blackwood	3	20	6.7	0
Clayton	2	14	7.0	0

KICKOFF RETURNS

Last Name	No.	Yds	Avg	TD
Hampton	45	1020	22.7	0
Carter	4	82	20.5	0
L. Blackwood	2	32	16.0	0
Hardy	1	11	11.0	0
Kozlowski	0	32	—	0

PASSING — PUNTING — KICKING

PASSING	Att	Cmp	%	Yds	Yd/Att	TD	Int—	%	RK
Marino	567	336	59	4137	7.3	30	21—	4	
Strock	9	7	78	141	15.7	1	0—	0	

PUNTING	No	Avg
Roby	59	43.7

KICKING	XP	Att	%	FG	Att	%
Reveiz	50	52	96	22	27	81

NEW YORK JETS

RUSHING

Last Name	No.	Yds	Avg	TD
McNeil	294	1331	4.5	3
Hector	145	572	3.9	6
Paige	55	158	2.9	8
Bligen	22	107	4.9	1
O'Brien	25	58	2.3	0
Barber	9	41	4.6	0
Minter	8	23	2.9	0
Sohn	1	12	12.0	0
Humphery	1	10	10.0	0
Toon	1	5	5.0	0
Ryan	3	-5	-1.7	0

RECEIVING

Last Name	No.	Yds	Avg	TD
Shuler	76	879	11.6	7
Toon	46	662	14.4	3
Sohn	39	534	13.7	4
McNeil	38	427	11.2	2
Walker	34	725	21.3	5
Paige	18	120	6.7	2
Hector	17	164	9.6	0
Klever	14	183	13.1	2
Townsell	12	187	15.6	0
Bligen	5	43	8.6	0
Barber	3	46	15.3	0
Minter	1	13	13.0	0

PUNT RETURNS

Last Name	No.	Yds	Avg	TD
Sohn	16	149	9.3	0
Springs	14	147	10.5	0
Townsell	6	65	10.8	0
Minter	2	25	12.5	0
Humphery	1	0	0.0	0

KICKOFF RETURNS

Last Name	No.	Yds	Avg	TD
Humphery	17	363	21.4	0
Hector	11	274	24.9	0
Springs	10	227	22.7	0
Glenn	5	71	14.2	0
Elder	3	42	14.0	0
Sohn	3	7	2.3	0
Townsell	2	42	21.0	0
Minter	1	14	14.0	0
Klever	1	3	3.0	0

PASSING — PUNTING — KICKING

PASSING	Att	Cmp	%	Yds	Yd/Att	TD	Int—	%	RK
O'Brien	488	297	61	3888	8.0	25	8—	2	
Ryan	9	6	67	95	10.6	0	0—	0	

PUNTING	No	Avg
Jennings	74	40.2

KICKING	XP	Att	%	FG	Att	%
Leahy	43	45	96	26	34	77

NEW ENGLAND PATRIOTS

RUSHING

Last Name	No.	Yds	Avg	TD
C. James	263	1227	4.7	5
Collins	163	657	4.0	3
Weathers	41	174	4.2	1
Tatupu	47	152	3.2	2
Eason	22	70	3.2	1
Grogan	20	29	1.5	2
Fryar	7	27	3.9	1
Morgan	1	0	0.0	0
Franklin	1	-5	-5.0	0

RECEIVING

Last Name	No.	Yds	Avg	TD
Collins	52	549	10.6	2
Morgan	39	760	19.5	5
Fryar	39	670	17.2	7
D. Ramsey	28	285	10.2	1
C.James	27	360	13.3	2
Jones	21	237	11.3	2
Dawson	17	148	8.7	0
Starring	16	235	14.7	0
D. Williams	9	163	18.1	0
Hawthorne	3	42	14.0	1
Weathers	2	18	9.0	0
Tatupu	2	16	8.0	0

PUNT RETURNS

Last Name	No.	Yds	Avg	TD
Fryar	37	520	14.1	2
R. James	2	13	6.5	0
Starring	2	0	0.0	0
Bowman	1	-3	-3.0	0

KICKOFF RETURNS

Last Name	No.	Yds	Avg	TD
Starring	48	1012	21.1	0
Fryar	3	-39	-13.0	0
Jones	3	37	12.3	0
Weathers	1	18	18.0	0
Hawthorne	1	13	13.0	0
C. James	1	0	0.0	0

PASSING — PUNTING — KICKING

PASSING	Att	Cmp	%	Yds	Yd/Att	TD	Int—	%	RK
Eason	299	168	56	2156	7.2	11	17—	6	
Grogan	156	85	55	1311	8.4	7	5—	3	
C. James	2	2	100	16	8.0	2	0—	0	

PUNTING	No	Avg
Camarillo	92	43.0

KICKING	XP	Att	%	FG	Att	%
Franklin	40	41	98	24	30	80

INDIANAPOLIS COLTS

RUSHING

Last Name	No.	Yds	Avg	TD
McMillan	190	858	4.5	7
Wonsley	138	716	5.2	6
Bentley	54	288	5.3	2
Gill	45	262	5.8	2
Pagel	25	160	6.4	2
Dickey	11	40	3.6	0
Middleton	13	35	2.7	1
Kofler	4	33	8.3	1
Martin	1	23	23.0	0
Capers	3	18	6.0	1
Schlichter	2	13	6.5	0
Butler	1	-1	-1.0	0

RECEIVING

Last Name	No.	Yds	Avg	TD
Beach	36	376	10.4	6
Wonsley	30	257	8.6	0
Bouza	27	381	14.1	2
Capers	25	438	17.5	4
Boyer	25	274	11.0	0
McMillan	22	115	5.2	0
Butler	19	345	18.2	2
Bentley	11	85	7.7	0
Martin	10	128	12.8	0
Williams	9	175	19.4	1
Sherwin	5	64	12.8	0
Middleton	5	54	10.8	0
Gill	5	52	10.4	0
Dickey	3	30	10.0	0
Henry	2	31	15.5	0
Pagel	1	6	6.0	0

PUNT RETURNS

Last Name	No.	Yds	Avg	TD
Martin	40	443	11.1	1
Daniel	1	6	6.0	0
Lowrey	1	0	0.0	0

KICKOFF RETURNS

Last Name	No.	Yds	Avg	TD
Bentley	27	674	25.0	0
Martin	32	638	19.9	0
Williams	3	44	14.7	0
Young	2	15	7.5	0
Middleton	1	20	20.0	0
Gill	1	6	6.0	0
Lee	1	6	6.0	0

PASSING — PUNTING — KICKING

PASSING	Att	Cmp	%	Yds	Yd/Att	TD	Int—	%	RK
Pagel	393	199	51	2414	6.1	14	15—	4	
Kofler	48	23	48	284	5.9	1	3—	6	
Schlichter	25	12	48	107	4.3	0	2—	8	
Bentley	1	1	100	6	6.0	0	0—	0	
Stark	1	0	0	0	0.0	0	0—	0	

PUNTING	No	Avg
Stark	78	45.9

KICKING	XP	Att	%	FG	Att	%
Allegre	36	39	92	16	26	62

BUFFALO BILLS

RUSHING

Last Name	No.	Yds	Avg	TD
Bell	223	883	4.0	8
Cribbs	122	399	3.3	1
Mathison	27	231	8.6	1
Steels	10	38	3.8	0
Moore	15	23	1.5	1
Ferragamo	8	15	1.9	1
Hutchison	2	11	5.5	0
B. Smith	1	0	0.0	0
Reed	3	-1	-0.3	1

RECEIVING

Last Name	No.	Yds	Avg	TD
Bell	58	576	9.9	1
Reed	48	637	13.3	4
Butler	41	770	18.8	2
Ramson	37	369	10.0	1
Burkett	21	371	17.7	0
Cribbs	18	142	7.9	0
Richardson	12	201	16.8	0
Metzelaars	12	80	6.7	1
Moore	7	44	6.3	0
Brookins	3	71	23.7	0
Norris	2	30	15.0	0
Steels	2	9	4.5	0
Teal	1	24	24.0	0
V. Williams	1	7	7.0	0

PUNT RETURNS

Last Name	No.	Yds	Avg	TD
D. Wilson	16	161	10.1	0
Hill	16	120	7.5	0
Reed	5	12	2.4	0
E. Wilson	1	0	0.0	0

KICKOFF RETURNS

Last Name	No.	Yds	Avg	TD
D. Wilson	22	465	21.1	0
Steels	30	561	18.7	0
Hutchison	12	239	19.9	0
Brookins	6	152	25.3	0
Richardson	3	69	23.0	0
Moore	3	31	10.3	0
Teal	1	20	20.0	0
V. Williams	1	20	20.0	0

PASSING — PUNTING — KICKING

PASSING	Att	Cmp	%	Yds	Yd/Att	TD	Int—	%	RK
Ferragamo	287	149	52	1677	5.8	5	17—	6	
Mathison	228	113	50	1635	7.2	4	14—	6	
Reich	1	1	100	19	19.0	0	0—	0	
Bell	1	0	0	0	0.0	0	0—	0	
Kidd	0	0	0	-9	-9.0	0	0—	0	

PUNTING	No	Avg
Kidd	92	41.5

KICKING	XP	Att	%	FG	Att	%
Norwood	23	23	100	13	17	77

CLEVELAND BROWNS 8-8 Marty Schottenheimer

Scores of Each Game		
24	ST.LOUIS	*27
17	PITTSBURGH	7
7	Dallas	20
21	San Diego	7
24	NEW ENGLAND	20
21	Houston	6
20	L.A.RAIDERS	21
7	WASHINGTON	14
9	Pittsburgh	10
10	Cincinnati	27
17	BUFFALO	7
24	CINCINNATI	6
35	N.Y.Giants	33
13	Seattle	31
28	HOUSTON	21
10	N.Y.Jets	37

Use Name	Pos.	Hgt	Wgt	Age	Int	Pts
Scott Bolzan	OT	6'3"	270	23		
Bill Contz	OT	6'5"	270	24		
Paul Farren	OT	6'5"	270	24		
Cody Risien	OT	6'7"	280	28		
Dan Fike	OG-OT	6'7"	280	24		
George Lilja	OG-C	6'4"	270	27		
Robert Jackson	OG	6'5"	260	32		
Mike Baab	C	6'4"	270	25		
Keith Baldwin	DE	6'4"	270	24		
Reggie Camp	DE	6'4"	270	24		
Sam Clancy	DE	6'7"	260	27		
Carl Hairston	DE	6'3"	260	32		
Bob Golic	NT	6'2"	260	27		
Dave Puzzuoli	NT	6'3"	260	24		
Chip Banks	LB	6'4"	233	25		
Tom Cousineau	LB	6'3"	225	28	1	
Eddie Johnson	LB	6'1"	225	26	1	
Clay Matthews	LB	6'2"	235	29		
Scott Nicolas	LB	6'3"	226	25		
Curtis Weathers	LB	6'5"	230	28	1	
Larry Braziel	DB	6'	184	30	2	
Hanford Dixon	DB	5'11"	186	26	3	
Al Gross	DB	6'3"	195	24	5	6
D.D.Hoggard	DB	6'	188	24		
Frank Minnifield	DB	5'9"	180	25	1	
Chris Rockins	DB	6'	195	23	1	
Don Rogers	DB	6'1"	206	22	1	
Harry Skipper	DB	5'11"	175	25		
Felix Wright	DB	6'2"	190	26	2	
Gary Danielson	QB	6'2"	196	33		
Bernie Kosar	QB	6'5"	210	21		
Paul McDonald	QB	6'2"	185	27		
Greg Allen	HB	5'11"	200	22		
Herman Fontenot	HB	6'	206	21		
Boyce Green	HB	5'11"	215	25		
Kevin Mack	HB	6'	212	23		60
Earnest Byner	FB	5'10"	215	22		60
Johnny Davis	FB	6'1"	235	29		
Willie Adams	WR	6'2"	200	29		
Fred Banks	WR	5'10"	177	23		12
Brian Brennan	WR	5'9"	178	23		6
John Jefferson	WR	6'1"	204	29		
Reggie Langhorne	WR	6'2"	195	22		
Clarence Weathers	WR	5'9"	170	23		18
Glen Young	WR	6'2"	205	24		6
Harry Holt	TE	6'4"	230	27		6
Ozzie Newsome	TE	6'2"	232	29		30
Travis Tucker	TE	6'3"	227	21		
Matt Bahr	K	5'10"	175	29		77
Jeff Gossett	K	6'2"	200	28		

CINCINNATI BENGALS 7-9 Sam Wyche

Scores of Each Game		
24	SEATTLE	28
27	St.Louis	41
41	SAN DIEGO	44
37	Pittsburgh	24
20	N.Y.JETS	29
35	N.Y.GIANTS	30
27	Houston	44
26	PITTSBURGH	21
23	Buffalo	17
27	CLEVELAND	10
6	L.A.Raiders	13
6	Cleveland	24
45	HOUSTON	27
50	DALLAS	24
24	Washington	27
23	New England	34

Use Name	Pos.	Hgt	Wgt	Age	Int	Pts
Anthony Munoz	OT	6'6"	278	27		
Bruce Riemers	OT	6'7"	280	24		
Joe Walter	OT	6'6"	290	22		
Mike Wilson	OT	6'5"	271	30		
Brian Blados	OG	6'4"	295	23		
Max Montoya	OG	6'5"	275	29		
Bruce Kozerski	C	6'4"	275	23		
Dave Rimington	C	6'3"	288	23		
Ross Browner	DE	6'3"	265	31		2
Glen Collins	DE	6'6"	265	26		
Eddie Edwards	DE	6'5"	256	31		
Jerry Boyarsky	NT	6'3"	290	26		
Tim Krumrie	NT	6'2"	262	25		
Leo Barker	LB	6'1"	221	25		
Glenn Cameron	LB	6'2"	228	32		
Tom Dinkel	LB	6'3"	240	29		
Emanuel King	LB	6'4"	245	22		
Jeff Schuh	LB	6'2"	234	27		
Ron Simpkins	LB	6'1"	235	27		
Reggie Williams	LB	6'1"	228	30		
Carl Zander	LB	6'2"	235	22		
Louis Breeden	DB	5'11"	185	31	2	
Lee Davis	DB	5'11"	198	22		
James Griffin	DB	6'2"	197	23	7	6
Ray Horton	DB	5'11"	190	25	2	
Robert Jackson	DB	5'10"	186	26	6	6
Bobby Kemp	DB	6'	192	26	1	
John Simmons	DB	5'11"	192	26		
Sean Thomas	DB	6'	190	23		
Jimmy Turner	DB	6'	187	26		1
Sam Washington (from PIT)	DB	5'8"	180	25		
Ken Anderson	QB	6'3"	212	36		
Boomer Esiason	QB	6'4"	220	24		6
Turk Schonert	QB	6'1"	190	28		
James Brooks	HB	5'10"	182	26		72
Stanford Jennings	HB	6'1"	205	23		24
Charles Alexander	FB	6'1"	226	28		12
Bill Johnson	FB	6'2"	230	24		
Larry Kinnebrew	FB	6'1"	255	26		60
Eddie Brown	WR	6'	185	22		48
Cris Collinsworth	WR	6'5"	192	26		30
Steve Kreider	WR	6'3"	192	27		7
Mike Martin	WR	5'10"	186	24		
Clay Pickering	WR	6'5"	215	24		
M.L.Harris	TE	6'5"	238	31		6
Rodney Holman	TE	6'3"	232	25		42
Don Kern	TE	6'4"	225	23		
Jim Breech	K	5'6"	161	29		120
Pat McInally	K	6'6"	212	32		

Stanley Wilson - Suspended by N.F.L.

PITTSBURGH STEELERS 7-9 Chuck Noll

Scores of Each Game		
45	INDIANAPOLIS	3
7	Cleveland	17
20	HOUSTON	0
24	CINCINNATI	37
20	Miami	24
13	Dallas	27
23	ST.LOUIS	10
21	Cincinnati	26
10	CLEVELAND	9
36	Kansas City	28
30	Houston	7
23	WASHINGTON	30
23	DENVER	31
44	San Diego	54
30	BUFFALO	24
10	N.Y.Giants	28

Use Name	Pos.	Hgt	Wgt	Age	Int	Pts
Tunch Ilkin	OT	6'3"	262	27		
Ray Pinney	OT-C	6'4"	262	31		
Pete Rostosky	OT	6'4"	252	24		
Ray Snell (to DET)	OT-OG	6'4"	265	27		
Emil Boures	OG-C	6'1"	260	25		
Terry Long	OG	5'11"	265	26		
Randy Rasmussen	OG-C	6'2"	254	24		
Blake Wingle (to GB)	OG	6'2"	267	25		
Craig Wolfley	OG	6'1"	265	27		
Dan Turk	C	6'4"	270	23		
Mike Webster	C	6'1"	260	33		
Keith Gary	DE	6'3"	265	25		
John Goodman	DE-NT	6'6"	258	26		
Edmund Nelson	DE-NT	6'3"	277	25		
Darryl Sims	DE	6'3"	265	24		
Keith Willis	DE	6'1"	258	26		
Mark Catano	DT-NT	6'3"	267	23		
Gary Dunn	NT	6'3"	275	32		
Gregg Carr	LB	6'1"	216	23		
Robin Cole	LB	6'2"	225	29	1	
Bryan Hinkle	LB	6'2"	218	26		
Bob Kohrs	LB	6'3"	235	26		
David Little	LB	6'1"	238	26	2	
Mike Merriweather	LB	6'2"	216	24	2	6
Fred Small	LB	5'11"	230	22		
Dennis Winston (from NO)	LB	6'	238	29		
Chris Brown	DB	6'	205	23		
Harvey Clayton	DB	5'9"	179	24		
Dave Edwards	DB	6'	192	23		
Donnie Shell	DB	5'11"	198	33	4	
John Swain (from MIA)	DB	6'1"	192	25	2	
Anthony Tuggle	DV	6'1"	210	21		
Eric Williams	DB	6'1"	190	25	4	
Dwayne Woodruff	DB	6'	198	28	5	
Rick Woods	DB	6'	195	25		
Scott Campbell	QB	6'	194	23		
Mark Malone	QB	6'4"	220	26		6
David Woodley	QB	6'2"	211	26		12
Walter Abercrombie	HB	6'	208	25		54
Rich Erenberg	HB	5'10"	195	23		18
Tod Spencer	HB	6'	200	23		
Steve Morse	FB	5'11"	211	22		
Frank Pollard	FB	5'10"	223	28		18
Louis Lipps	WR	5'10"	185	23		90
Frank Pokorny	WR	6'	205	22		
John Stallworth	WR	6'2"	202	33		30
Calvin Sweeney	WR	6'2"	202	30		
Weegie Thompson	WR	6'6"	209	24		6
Bennie Cunningham	TE	6'4"	260	30		
Preston Gothard	TE	6'4"	237	23		
Darrell Nelson	TE	6'2"	235	23		
Gary Anderson	K	5'11"	174	26		139
Harry Newsome	K	6'	185	22		

HOUSTON OILERS 5-11 Hugh Campbell

Scores of Each Game		
26	MIAMI	23
13	Washington	16
0	Pittsburgh	20
10	DALLAS	17
20	Denver	31
6	CLEVELAND	21
44	CINCINNATI	27
20	St.Louis	10
23	KANSAS CITY	20
0	Buffalo	20
7	PITTSBURGH	30
37	SAN DIEGO	35
27	Cincinnati	45
14	N.Y.GIANTS	35
21	Cleveland	28
16	Indianapolis	34

Use Name	Pos.	Hgt	Wgt	Age	Int	Pts
Bruce Matthews	OT	6'4"	280	24		
Eric Moran	OT	6'5"	282	25		
Harvey Salem	OT	6'6"	285	24		
Pat Howell	OG	6'5"	265	28		
Mike Munchak	OG	6'3"	286	25		
John Schuhmacher	OG	6'3"	277	29		
Mike Kelley	C-OG	6'5"	266	23		
Jim Romano	C	6'3"	255	25		
Jesse Baker (from DAL)	DE	6'5"	271	28		
Ray Childress	DE	6'6"	267	22		
Bob Hamm	DE	6'4"	263	26		
Richard Byrd	NT	6'3"	255	23		
Doug Smith	NT	6'5"	285	26		
Brian Sochia	NT	6'3"	254	24		
Mike Stensrud	NT	6'5"	280	29	1	
Robert Abraham	LB	6'1"	230	25		
Tom Briehl	LB	6'3"	247	22		
Frank Bush	LB	6'1"	218	22		
John Grimsley	LB	6'2"	232	23		
Robert Lyles	LB	6'1"	223	24		
Johnny Meads	LB	6'2"	225	24		
Avon Riley	LB	6'3"	236	27	1	
Patrick Allen	DB	5'10	185	24		
Keith Bostic	DB	6'1"	210	24	3	
Steve Brown	DB	5'11"	189	25	5	
Jeff Donaldson	DB	6'	193	23		
Bo Eason	DB	6'2"	200	24	3	
Richard Johnson	DB	6'1"	195	21		
Rod Kush	DB	6'	195	28	2	
Allen Lyday	DB	5'10"	186	24		
Audrey McMillian	DB	6'	190	23		
Oliver Luck	QB	6'2"	196	25		
Warren Moon	QB	6'3"	208	28		
Mike Moroski	QB	6'4"	200	27		
Brian Ransom	QB	6'3"	202	25		
Stan Edwards	HB	6'	210	25		6
Mike Rozier	HB	5'10"	198	24		48
Steve Tasker	HB	5'9"	185	23		
Larry Moriarty	FB	6'1"	240	27		18
Butch Woolfolk	FB	6'1"	212	25		30
Mike Akiu	WR	5'9"	185	23		6
Steve Bryant	WR	6'2"	197	25		
Willie Drewrey	WR	5'7"	158	22		
Drew Hill	WR	5'9"	170	28		54
Tim Smith	WR	6'2"	206	28		12
Herkie Walls	WR	5'8"	160	24		
Chris Dressel	TE	6'4"	238	24		6
Mike McCloskey	TE	6'5"	246	24		6
Jamie Williams	TE	6'4"	232	25		6
Lee Johnson	K	6'2"	204	23		
Tony Zendejas	K	5'8"	160	25		92

Mike Johnson - Knee Injury

Dean Steinkuhler - Knee Injury

Dwayne Crutchfield - Knee Injury

* Overtime

CLEVELAND BROWNS

RUSHING

Last Name	No.	Yds	Avg	TD
Mack	222	1104	5.0	7
Byner	244	1002	4.1	8
Danielson	25	126	5.0	0
Allen	8	32	4.0	0
Cl. Weathers	1	18	18.0	0
Davis	4	9	2.3	0
Baab	1	0	0.0	0
Kosar	26	-12	-0.5	1

RECEIVING

Last Name	No.	Yds	Avg	TD
Newsome	62	711	11.5	5
Byner	45	460	10.2	2
Brennan	32	487	15.2	0
Mack	29	297	10.2	3
Cl. Weathers	16	449	28.1	3
Adams	10	132	13.2	0
Holt	10	95	9.5	1
Young	5	111	22.2	1
F. Banks	5	62	12.4	2
Jefferson	3	30	10.0	0
Tucker	2	20	10.0	0
Fontenot	2	19	9.5	0
Langhorne	1	12	12.0	0

PUNT RETURNS

Last Name	No.	Yds	Avg	TD
Cl. Weathers	28	218	7.8	0
Brennan	19	153	8.1	1

KICKOFF RETURNS

Last Name	No.	Yds	Avg	TD
Young	35	898	25.7	0
Fontenot	8	215	26.9	0
Langhorne	3	46	15.3	0
Green	2	20	10.0	0
Puzzuoli	2	8	4.0	0
Cl. Weathers	1	17	17.0	0
Nicolas	1	9	9.0	0
Allen	1	4	4.0	0

PASSING — PUNTING — KICKING

PASSING	Att	Cmp	%	Yds	Yd/Att	TD	Int—	%	RK
Kosar	248	124	50	1578	6.4	8	7—	3	
Danielson	163	97	60	1274	7.8	8	6—	4	
Brennan	1	1	100	33	33.0	1	0—	0	
Fontenot	1	0	0	0	0.0	0	0—	0	
Gossett	1	0	0	0	0.0	0	0—	0	

PUNTING	No	Avg
Gossett	81	40.3

KICKING	XP	Att	%	FG	Att	%
Bahr	35	35	100	14	18	77

CINCINNATI BENGALS

RUSHING

Last Name	No.	Yds	Avg	TD
Brooks	192	929	4.8	7
Kinnebrew	170	714	4.2	9
Alexander	44	156	3.5	2
Brown	14	129	9.2	0
Jennings	31	92	3.0	1
Esiason	33	79	2.4	1
Johnson	8	44	5.5	0
Schonert	8	39	4.9	0
Collinsworth	1	3	3.0	0
Anderson	1	0	0.0	0
McInally	1	-2	-2.0	0

RECEIVING

Last Name	No.	Yds	Avg	TD
Collinsworth	65	1125	17.3	5
Brooks	55	576	10.5	5
Brown	53	942	17.8	8
Holman	38	479	12.6	7
Kinnebrew	22	187	8.5	1
Alexander	15	110	7.3	0
Martin	14	187	13.4	0
Jennings	12	101	8.4	3
Kreider	10	184	18.4	1
Harris	10	123	12.3	1
Blados	1	4	4.0	0
Munoz	1	1	1.0	0

PUNT RETURNS

Last Name	No.	Yds	Avg	TD
Martin	32	268	8.4	0

KICKOFF RETURNS

Last Name	No.	Yds	Avg	TD
Martin	48	1104	23.0	0
Jennings	13	218	16.8	0
Brooks	3	38	12.7	0
Zander	1	19	19.0	0
Brown	1	6	6.0	0
Griffin	1	0	0.0	0

PASSING — PUNTING — KICKING

PASSING	Att	Cmp	%	Yds	Yd/Att	TD	Int—	%	RK
Esiason	431	251	58	3443	8.0	27	12—	3	
Schonert	51	33	65	460	9.0	1	0—	0	
Anderson	32	16	50	170	5.3	2	0—	0	
Brooks	1	1	100	8	8.0	1	0—	0	
Kreider	1	1	100	1	1.0	0	0—	0	
Collinsworth	1	0	0	0	0.0	0	1—	100	
McInally	1	0	0	0	0.0	0	0—	0	

PUNTING	No	Avg
McInally	57	42.3
Breech	5	30.6

KICKING	XP	Att	%	FG	Att	%
Breech	48	50	96	24	33	73

PITTSBURGH STEELERS

RUSHING

Last Name	No.	Yds	Avg	TD
Pollard	233	991	4.3	3
Abercrombie	227	851	3.7	7
Malone	15	80	5.3	1
Woodley	17	71	4.2	2
Erenberg	17	67	3.9	0
Spencer	13	56	4.3	0
Campbell	9	28	3.1	0
Morse	8	17	2.1	0
Lipps	2	16	8.0	1

RECEIVING

Last Name	No.	Yds	Avg	TD
Stallworth	75	937	12.5	5
Lipps	59	1134	19.2	12
Erenberg	33	326	9.9	3
Pollard	24	250	10.4	0
Abercrombie	24	209	8.7	2
Sweeney	16	234	14.6	0
Thompson	8	138	17.3	1
Gothard	6	83	13.8	0
Cunningham	6	61	10.2	0
Spencer	3	25	8.3	0

PUNT RETURNS

Last Name	No.	Yds	Avg	TD
Lipps	36	437	12.1	2
Woods	13	46	3.5	0

KICKOFF RETURNS

Last Name	No.	Yds	Avg	TD
Spencer	27	617	22.9	0
Erenberg	21	441	21.0	0
Lipps	13	237	18.2	0
Washington	3	34	11.3	0
Tuggle	1	8	8.0	0

PASSING — PUNTING — KICKING

PASSING	Att	Cmp	%	Yds	Yd/Att	TD	Int—	%	RK
Malone	233	117	50	1428	6.1	13	7—	3	
Woodley	183	94	51	1357	7.4	6	14—	8	
Campbell	96	43	45	612	6.4	4	6—	6	

PUNTING	No	Avg
Newsome	78	39.6

KICKING	XP	Att	%	FG	Att	%
Anderson	40	40	100	33	42	79

HOUSTON OILERS

RUSHING

Last Name	No.	Yds	Avg	TD
Rozier	133	462	3.5	8
Woolfolk	103	392	3.8	1
Moriarty	106	381	3.6	3
Moon	39	130	3.3	0
Edwards	25	96	3.8	1
Luck	15	95	6.3	0
Tasker	2	16	8.0	0
Moroski	2	2	1.0	0
L. Johnson	1	0	0.0	0
Drewrey	2	-4	-2.0	0

RECEIVING

Last Name	No.	Yds	Avg	TD
Woolfolk	80	814	10.2	4
Hill	64	1169	18.3	9
T. Smith	46	660	14.3	2
Williams	39	444	11.4	1
Moriarty	17	112	6.6	0
Rozier	9	96	10.7	0
Edwards	7	71	10.1	0
McCloskey	4	29	7.3	1
Dressel	3	17	5.7	1
Akiu	2	32	16.0	0
Drewrey	2	28	14.0	0
Tasker	2	19	9.5	0
Walls	1	7	7.0	0

PUNT RETURNS

Last Name	No.	Yds	Avg	TD
Drewrey	24	215	9.0	0
Donaldson	6	35	5.8	0

KICKOFF RETURNS

Last Name	No.	Yds	Avg	TD
Drewrey	26	642	24.7	0
Tasker	17	447	26.3	0
Walls	12	234	19.5	0
Donaldson	5	93	18.6	0
Brown	2	45	22.5	0
Williams	2	21	10.5	0
Hill	1	22	22.0	0
Lyday	1	6	6.0	0
Briehl	1	5	5.0	0

PASSING — PUNTING — KICKING

PASSING	Att	Cmp	%	Yds	Yd/Att	TD	Int—	%	RK
Moon	377	200	53	2709	7.2	15	19—	5	
Luck	100	56	56	572	5.7	2	2—	2	
Moroski	34	20	59	249	7.3	1	1—	3	
Zendejas	1	1	100	-7	-7.0	0	0—	0	

PUNTING	No	Avg
L. Johnson	83	41.7
T. Smith	1	26.0

KICKING	XP	Att	%	FG	Att	%
Zendejas	29	31	94	21	27	78

LOS ANGELES RAIDERS 12-4 Tom Flores

Scores of Each Game		
31	N.Y.JETS	0
20	Kansas City	36
10	SAN FRANCISCO	34
35	New England	20
19	KANSAS CITY	10
23	NEW ORLEANS	13
21	Cleveland	20
34	SAN DIEGO	21
3	Seattle	33
34	San Diego	*40
13	CINCINNATI	6
31	DENVER	*28
34	Atlanta	24
17	Denver	*14
13	SEATTLE	3
16	L.A.Rams	6

Use Name	Pos.	Hgt	Wgt	Age	Int	Pts
Bruce Davis	OT	6'6"	280	29		
Shelby Jordan	OT	6'7"	280	33		
Henry Lawrence	OT	6'4"	275	33		
Kevin Belcher	OG	6'5"	285	23		
Charley Hannah	OG	6'5"	260	30		
Curt Marsh	OG	6'5"	275	26		
Mickey Marvin	OG	6'4"	265	29		
Dave Dalby	C	6'2"	250	34		
Don Mosebar	C	6'6"	270	23		
Lyle Alzado	DE	6'3"	260	36		8
Elvis Franks	DE	6'4"	270	28		
Sean Jones	DE	6'7"	275	22		
Howie Long	DE	6'5"	270	25		
Greg Townsend	DE	6'3"	250	23		
Bill Pickel	NT	6'5"	260	25		
Mitch Willis	NT	6'7"	275	23		
Dave Stalls	NT	6'4"	250	29		
Randy Van Divier - Injury						
Jeff Barnes	LB	6'2"	230	30	1	
Tony Caldwell	LB	6'1"	220	24		
Rod Martin	LB	6'2"	225	31	1	
Reggie McKenzie	LB	6'1"	240	22		
Matt Millen	LB	6'2"	245	27		
Jerry Robinson	LB	6'2"	225	28		
Jack Squirek	LB	6'4"	235	26	1	
Brad Van Pelt	LB	6'5"	235	34	1	
Don Bessillieu	DB	6'1"	190	29		
James Davis	DB	6'	200	28		
Mike Davis	DB	6'3"	205	29		
Lester Hayes	DB	6'	200	30	4	6
Mike Haynes	DB	6'2"	190	32	4	
Vann McElroy	DB	6'2"	195	25	2	
Odis McKinney (from KC)	DB	6'2"	190	28	1	
Sam Seale	DB	5'9"	175	22	1	6
Stacey Toran	DB	6'2"	200	23	1	6
Fulton Walker (from MIA)	DB	5'10"	200	27		
Ricky Williams	DB	6'1"	195	25		
Bob Nelson - Knee Injury						
Rusty Hilger	QB	6'4"	200	23		
Russ Jensen	QB	6'2"	215	24		
Jim Plunkett	QB	6'3"	225	37		
Marc Wilson	QB	6'6"	205	28		12
Marcus Allen	HB	6'2"	205	25		84
Frank Hawkins	HB	5'9"	210	26		24
Derrick Jensen	FB	6'1"	220	29		
Kenny King	FB	5'11"	205	28		
Steve Strachan	FB	6'1"	215	22		
Cliff Branch	WR	5'11"	170	37		
Jessie Hester	WR	5'11"	170	22		30
Tim Moffett	WR	6'2"	180	23		
Cle Montgomery	WR	5'8"	180	29		
Jim Smith	WR	6'2"	205	30		6
Dokie Williams	WR	5'11"	180	25		30
Todd Christensen	TE	6'3"	230	29		36
Trey Junkin	TE	6'2"	225	24		6
Andy Parker	TE	6'5"	240	23		
Chris Bahr	K	5'10"	170	32		100
Ray Guy	K	6'3"	200	35		

DENVER BRONCOS 11-5 Dan Reeves

Scores of Each Game		
16	L.A.Rams	20
34	NEW ORLEANS	23
44	Atlanta	28
26	MIAMI	30
31	HOUSTON	20
15	Indianapolis	10
13	SEATTLE	*10
30	Kansas City	10
10	San Diego	30
17	SAN FRANCISCO	16
30	SAN DIEGO	*24
28	L.A.Raiders	*31
31	Pittsburgh	23
14	L.A.RAIDERS	*17
14	KANSAS CITY	13
27	Seattle	24

Use Name	Pos.	Hgt	Wgt	Age	Int	Pts
Winford Hood	OT	6'3"	262	23		
Ken Lanier	OT	6'3"	269	26		
Dean Miraldi	OT	6'5"	285	27		
Dave Studdard	OT	6'4"	260	29		
Mark Cooper	OG-OT	6'5"	267	25		
Paul Howard	OG	6'3"	260	34		
Glenn Hyde	OG-C	6'3"	255	34		
Keith Bishop	C-OG	6'3"	265	28		
Billy Bryan	C	6'2"	255	29		
Barney Chavous	DE	6'3"	258	34		
Simon Fletcher	DE	6'5"	240	23		
Rulon Jones	DE	6'6"	260	27		
Andre Townsend	DE-NT	6'3"	265	22		
Rubin Carter	NT	6'	256	32		
Greg Kragen	NT	6'3"	245	23		
Mike Freeman - Knee Injury						
Marsharne Graves - Knee Injury						
Steve Busick	LB	6'4"	227	26		
Darren Comeaux	LB	6'1	227	25		
Rick Dennison	LB	6'3"	220	27		
Ricky Hunley	LB	6'2"	238	23		
Tom Jackson	LB	5'11"	220	34		
Karl Mecklenburg	LB	6'3"	230	25		
Jim Ryan	LB	6'1"	218	28		
Ken Woodard	LB	6'1"	218	25	1	
Steve Foley	DB	6'2"	190	31	3	
Mike Harden	DB	6'1"	192	27	5	6
Daniel Hunter	DB	5'11"	175	23	1	
Roger Jackson	DB	6'	186	26		
Tony Lilly	DB	6'	199	23	2	
Randy Robbins	DB	6'2"	189	22	1	
Dennis Smith	DB	6'3"	200	26	3	
Steve Wilson	DB	5'10"	195	28	3	
Louis Wright	DB	6'2"	200	32	5	6
Aaron Smith - Knee Injury						
John Elway	QB	6'3"	210	25		
Gary Kublak	QB	6'	192	24		
Scott Stankavage	QB	6'1"	194	23		
Gene Lang	HB	5'10"	196	23		42
Gerald Willhite	HB	5'10"	200	26		24
Sammy Winder	HB	5'11"	203	26		48
Nathan Poole	FB	5'9"	212	28		
Steve Sewell	FB	6'3"	210	22		30
Butch Johnson	WR	6'1"	187	31		18
Vance Johnson	WR	5'11"	185	22		18
Clint Sampson	WR	5'11"	183	24		24
Steve Watson	WR	6'4"	195	28		30
Mike Barber (from LA)	TE	6'3"	237	32		
Clarence Kay	TE	6'2"	237	24		18
Keli McGregor	TE	6'7"	252	22		
Don Summers	TE	6'4"	226	24		
James Wright	TE	6'3"	240	29		6
Rich Karlis	K	6'	180	26		110
Chris Norman	K	6'2"	198	23		
Al Hill - Shoulder Injury						
John Sawyer - Broken hand						

SEATTLE SEAHAWKS 8-8 Chuck Knox

Scores of Each Game		
28	Cincinnati	24
49	San Diego	35
24	L.A.RAMS	35
7	Kansas City	28
26	SAN DIEGO	21
30	ATLANTA	26
10	Denver	*13
14	N.Y.Jets	17
33	L.A.RAIDERS	3
27	New Orleans	3
13	NEW ENGLAND	20
6	San Francisco	19
24	KANSAS CITY	6
31	CLEVELAND	13
3	L.A.Raiders	13
24	DENVER	27

Use Name	Pos.	Hgt	Wgt	Age	Int	Pts
Bob Cryder	OT	6'4"	286	28		
Ron Essink	OT	6'6"	279	27		
Edwin Bailey	OG	6'4"	265	26		
Jon Borchardt	OG	6'5"	270	28		
Bryan Millard	OG	6'5"	284	25		
Robert Pratt	OG	6'4"	250	34		
Blair Bush	C	6'3"	257	28		
Kani Kauahi	C	6'2"	254	25		
Jeff Bryant	DE	6'5"	270	25		
Randy Edwards	DE	6'4"	266	24		
Jacob Green	DE	6'3"	257	28	1	12
Reggie Kinlaw	NT	6'2"	249	28		
Joe Nash	NT	6'2"	257	24		
Keith Butler	LB	6'4"	238	29	2	
Greg Gaines	LB	6'3"	222	26		
Michael Jackson	LB	6'1"	228	28		
John Kaiser	LB	6'3"	227	23		
Sam Merriman	LB	6'3"	229	24		6
Shelton Robinson	LB	6'2"	236	24		
Bruce Scholtz	LB	6'6"	240	26		
Fredd Young	LB	6'1"	233	23		
Dave Brown	DB	6'1"	197	32	6	6
Kenny Easley	DB	6'3"	206	26	2	
John Harris	DB	6'2"	204	29	7	
Terry Jackson	DB	5'10"	197	28		
Paul Moyer	DB	6'1"	201	24		
Eugene Robinson	DB	6'	186	22	2	
Rick Sanford	DB	6'1"	192	28		
Keith Simpson	DB	6'1"	195	29		
Terry Taylor	DB	5'10"	188	24	4	12
Gale Gilbert	QB	6'3"	206	23		
Dave Krieg	QB	6'1"	196	26		6
Eric Lane	HB	6'	197	26		
Randall Morris	HB	6'	199	24		
Rick Parros	HB	5'11"	202	27		
Curt Warner	HB	5'11"	205	24		54
Dan Doornink	FB	6'3"	210	29		
Andre Hardy	FB	6'1"	233	23		
David Hughes	FB	6'	220	26		
Byron Franklin	WR	6'1"	181	26		
Danny Greene	WR	5'11"	190	23		6
Steve Largent	WR	5'11"	191	30		37
Paul Skansi	WR	5'11"	183	24		6
Daryl Turner	WR	6'3"	191	23		78
Byron Walker	WR	6'4"	188	25		18
Dan Ross (from CIN)	TE	6'4"	234	28		12
Mike Tice	TE	6'7"	247	26		
Charle Young	TE	6'4"	234	34		12
Jimmy Colquitt	K	6'4"	208	22		
Dave Finzer	K	6'1"	196	26		
Norm Johnson	K	6'2"	194	25		82
Jeff West	K	6'3"	205	32		

SAN DIEGO CHARGERS 8-8 Don Coryell

Scores of Each Game		
14	Buffalo	9
35	SEATTLE	49
44	Cincinnati	41
7	CLEVELAND	21
21	Seattle	26
31	KANSAS CITY	20
17	Minnesota	21
21	L.A.Raiders	34
30	DENVER	10
40	L.A.RAIDERS	*34
24	Denver	*30
35	Houston	37
40	BUFFALO	7
54	PITTSBURGH	44
20	PHILADELPHIA	14
34	Kansas City	38

Use Name	Pos.	Hgt	Wgt	Age	Int	Pts
Sam Claphan	OT	6'6"	282	28		
Gary Kowalski	OT	6'6"	290	25		
Jim Lachey	OT	6'6"	288	22		
Rich Umphrey	OG-C	6'3"	270	26		
Ken Dallafior	OG	6'4"	262	26		
Bill Searcey	OG	6'1"	281	26		
Ed White	OG	6'2"	284	38		
Jerry Doerger	C-OT	6'5"	270	25		
Don Macek	C	6'3"	260	31		
Dennis McKnight	C-OG	6'3"	273	25		
Keith Ferguson (to DET)	DE	6'5"	255	26		
Fred Robinson	DE	6'4"	242	23		
Tony Simmons	DE	6'5"	270	22		
Lee Williams	DE	6'6"	273	22	1	
Earl Wilson	DE	6'4"	267	26		
Tony Chickillo	NT-OG	6'3"	259	25		
Chuck Ehin	NT	6'4"	265	24		
Scott Garnett (from SF)	NT	6'2"	271	22		
James Lockette - Knee Injury						
Craig Bingham	LB	6'2"	220	25		
Carlos Bradley	LB	6'	222	25	2	
Mike Douglass	LB	6'	214	31		
Mark Fellows	LB	6'1"	222	22		
Mike Guendling	LB	6'3"	238	23		
Mike Green	LB	6'	239	24	2	
Linden King	LB	6'4"	247	30	2	
Woodrow Lowe	LB	6'	229	31	3	
Derrie Nelson	LB	6'2"	234	27		
Vince Osby	LB	5'11"	221	24		
Billy Ray Smith	LB	6'3"	231	24	1	
Gill Byrd	DB	5'11"	201	24	1	
Jeffrey Dale	DB	6'3"	214	22	2	6
Wayne Davis	DB	5'11"	175	22	2	
John Hendy	DD	5'10"	196	22	4	6
Terry Lewis	DB	5'11"	193	23		
Miles McPherson	DB	5'11"	186	25	1	
Ronnie O'Bard	DB	5'9"	190	27		
Jim Rockford	DB	5'10"	180	23		
Lucious Smith	DB	5'10"	190	28		
Danny Walters	DB	6'1"	180	24	5	
Shane Nelson - Achillies tendon injury						
Joe Dufek (from BUF)	QB	6'4"	215	24		
Dan Fouts	QB	6'3"	205	34		
Mark Herrmann	QB	6'4"	209	26		
Curtis Adams	HB	6'	198	23		6
Gary Anderson	HB	6'1"	190	24		42
Anthony Corley	HB	6'	210	25		
Lionel James	HB	5'7"	170	23		48
Buford McGee	FB	6'	203	25		18
Tim Spencer	FB	6'1"	220	24		60
Jesse Bendross	WR	6'	197	24		12
Wes Chandler	WR	6'	182	29		60
Trumaine Johnson	WR	6'1"	196	25		6
Charlie Joiner	WR	5'11"	177	37		42
Chris Faulkner	TE	6'4"	250	25		
Pete Holohan	TE	6'4"	244	26		18
Eric Sievers	TE	6'4"	236	26		36
Kellen Winslow	TE	6'5"	242	27		
Rolf Benirschke	K	6'1"	183	30		2
Ralf Mojsiejenko	K	6'3"	198	22		
Bob Thomas	K	5'10"	177	33		105
Bob Micho - Foot Injury						

KANSAS CITY CHIEFS 6-10 John Mackovic

Scores of Each Game		
47	New Orleans	27
36	L.A.RAIDERS	20
0	Miami	31
28	SEATTLE	7
10	L.A.Raiders	19
20	San Diego	31
0	L.A.RAMS	16
10	DENVER	30
20	Houston	23
28	PITTSBURGH	36
3	San Francisco	31
20	INDIANAPOLIS	7
6	Seattle	24
38	ATLANTA	10
13	Denver	14
38	SAN DIEGO	34

Use Name	Pos.	Hgt	Wgt	Age	Int	Pts
John Alt	OT	6'7"	282	23		
Matt Herkenhoff	OT	6'4"	286	34		
David Lutz	OT	6'6"	287	25		
Billy Shields	OT	6'7"	280	32		
Scott Auer	OG-OT	6'5"	255	23		
Rich Baldinger	OG-OT	6'4"	281	25		
Brad Budde	OG	6'4"	271	27		
Rob Fada	OG	6'2"	259	24		
Bob Olderman	OG	6'5"	262	23		
Adam Lingner	C-OG	6'4"	260	24		
Bob Rush	C	6'5"	270	30		
Mike Bell	DE	6'4"	259	28		
Bob Hamm	DE	6'4"	257	26		
Eric Holle	DE-NT	6'5"	258	24		
Pete Koch	DE	6'6"	265	23		
Dave Lindstrom	DE	6'6"	258	30		
Hal Stephens (from DET)	DE-NT	6'4"	252	24		
Art Still	DE	6'7"	254	29		
Bill Maas	NT-DE	6'5"	259	23		
Jerry Blanton	LB	6'1"	229	28		
Louis Cooper	LB	6'2"	235	22		
Calvin Daniels	LB	6'3"	241	26		
Ken Jolly	LB	6'2"	220	23		
Jeff Paine	LB	6'2"	224	24		
Scott Radecic	LB	6'3"	246	23	1	
Gary Spani	LB	6'2"	229	29		
Lloyd Burruss	DB	6'	209	27	1	
Deron Cherry	DB	5'11"	196	25	7	6
Sherman Cocroft	DB	6'1"	188	24	3	
Greg Hill	DB	6'1"	199	24	3	
Garcia Lane	DB	5'9"	180	23		
Albert Lewis	DB	6'2"	192	24	8	6
Mark Robinson	DB	5'11"	206	22	1	
Kevin Ross	DB	5'9"	182	23	3	
Kevin McAlister - Knee Injury						
Todd Blackledge	QB	6'3"	225	24		
Bill Kenney	QB	6'4"	211	30		6
Herman Heard	HB	5'10"	182	23		36
E.J.Jones	HB	5'11"	219	23		
Jeff Smith	HB	5'9"	201	23		12
Ethan Horton	FB	6'3"	228	22		24
Bruce King	FB	6'1"	219	22		
Ken Lacy	FB	6'	222	24		
Mike Pruitt (from BUF)	FB	6'	225	31		12
Carlos Carson	WR	5'11"	182	26		24
Anthony Hancock	WR	6'	204	25		12
Mike Holston (from HOU)	WR	6'3"	188	27		
Henry Marshall	WR	6'2"	213	31		
Stephone Paige	WR	6'2"	191	23		60
George Shorthose	WR	6'	198	23		
Walt Arnold	TE	6'3"	225	27		6
Jonathan Hayes	TE	6'5"	234	23		6
Willie Scott	TE	6'4"	245	26		
Jim Arnold	K	6'2"	220	24		
Nick Lowery	K	6'4"	189	29		107

* Overtime

LOS ANGELES RAIDERS

Rushing

Last Name	No.	Yds	Avg	TD
Allen	380	1759	4.6	11
Hawkins	84	269	3.2	4
Wilson	24	98	4.1	2
King	16	67	4.2	0
D. Jensen	16	35	2.2	0
Hester	1	13	13.0	1
Plunkett	5	12	2.4	0
Hilger	3	8	2.7	0
Strachan	2	1	0.5	0
Guy	1	0	0.0	0

Receiving

Last Name	No.	Yds	Avg	TD
Christensen	82	987	12.0	6
Allen	67	555	8.3	3
D. Williams	48	925	19.3	5
Hester	32	665	20.8	4
Hawkins	27	174	6.4	0
Moffett	5	90	18.0	0
King	3	49	16.3	0
Smith	3	28	9.3	1
Junkin	2	8	4.0	1

Punt Returns

Last Name	No.	Yds	Avg	TD
Walker	62	692	11.2	0
Montgomery	8	84	10.5	0
Haynes	1	9	9.0	0

Kickoff Returns

Last Name	No.	Yds	Avg	TD
Walker	21	467	22.2	0
Seale	23	482	21.0	0
Montgomery	7	150	21.4	0
D. Williams	1	19	19.0	0
Hawkins	1	14	14.0	0
Hayes	1	0	0.0	0

Passing — Punting — Kicking

PASSING	Att	Cmp	%	Yds	Yd/Att	TD	Int—	%	RK
Wilson	388	193	50	2608	6.7	16	21—	5	
Plunkett	103	71	69	803	7.8	3	3—	3	
Hilger	13	4	31	54	4.2	1	0—	0	
Allen	2	1	50	16	8.0	0	0—	0	

PUNTING	No	Avg
Guy	89	40.8

KICKING	XP	Att	%	FG	Att	%
Bahr	40	42	95	20	32	63

DENVER BRONCOS

Rushing

Last Name	No.	Yds	Avg	TD
Winder	199	714	3.6	8
Lang	84	318	3.8	5
Sewell	81	275	3.4	4
Elway	51	253	5.0	0
Willhite	66	237	3.6	3
V. Johnson	10	36	3.6	0
Poole	4	12	3.0	0
Kubiak	1	6	6.0	0
Norman	1	0	0.0	0

Receiving

Last Name	No.	Yds	Avg	TD
Watson	61	915	15.0	5
V. Johnson	51	721	14.1	3
Willhite	35	297	8.5	1
Winder	31	197	6.4	0
Kay	29	339	11.7	3
J. Wright	28	246	8.8	1
Sampson	26	432	16.6	4
Sewell	24	224	9.3	1
Lang	23	180	7.8	2
B. Johnson	19	380	20.0	3
Barber	2	37	18.5	0
Cooper	1	13	13.0	0

Punt Returns

Last Name	No.	Yds	Avg	TD
V. Johnson	30	260	8.7	0
Willhite	16	169	10.6	0

Kickoff Returns

Last Name	No.	Yds	Avg	TD
V. Johnson	30	740	24.7	0
Lang	17	361	21.2	0
Willhite	2	40	20.0	0
Hunter	2	33	16.5	0
Sewell	1	29	29.0	0

Passing — Punting — Kicking

PASSING	Att	Cmp	%	Yds	Yd/Att	TD	Int—	%	RK
Elway	605	327	54	3891	6.4	22	23—	4	
Kubiak	5	2	40	61	12.2	1	0—	0	
Willhite	3	0	0	0	0.0	0	0—	0	
V. Johnson	1	0	0	0	0.0	0	0—	0	
Norman	1	0	0	0	0.0	0	0—	0	
Winder	1	0	0	0	0.0	0	0—	0	
Sewell 1	0	0	0	0	0.0	0	0—	0	

PUNTING	No	Avg
Norman	92	40.9

KICKING	XP	Att	%	FG	Att	%
Karlis	41	44	93	23	38	61

SEATTLE SEAHAWKS

Rushing

Last Name	No.	Yds	Avg	TD
Warner	291	1094	3.8	8
Morris	55	236	4.3	0
Hughes	40	128	3.2	0
Krieg	35	121	3.5	1
Lane	14	32	2.3	0
Parros	8	19	2.4	0
Franklin	1	5	5.0	0
Hardy	5	5	1.0	0
Gilbert	7	4	0.6	0
Doornink	4	0	0.0	0
Finzer	1	-2	-2.0	0

Receiving

Last Name	No.	Yds	Avg	TD
Largent	79	1287	16.3	6
Warner	47	307	6.5	1
Turner	34	670	19.7	13
C. Young	28	351	12.5	2
Skansi	21	269	12.8	1
Walker	19	285	15.0	2
Hughes	19	184	9.7	0
Ross	16	135	8.4	2
Lane	15	153	10.2	0
Franklin	10	119	11.9	0
Doornink	8	52	6.5	0
Morris	6	14	2.3	0
Hardy	3	7	2.3	0
Tice	2	13	6.5	0
Greene	2	10	5.0	1
Parros	1	27	27.0	0

Punt Returns

Last Name	No.	Yds	Avg	TD
Skansi	31	312	10.1	0
Greene	11	60	5.5	0
Easley	8	87	10.9	0
Harris	3	24	8.0	0

Kickoff Returns

Last Name	No.	Yds	Avg	TD
Morris	31	636	20.5	0
Skansi	19	358	18.8	0
Greene	5	144	28.8	0
Tice	1	17	17.0	0
E. Robinson	1	10	10.0	0
Lane	1	1	1.0	0

Passing — Punting — Kicking

PASSING	Att	Cmp	%	Yds	Yd/Att	TD	Int—	%	RK
Krieg	532	285	54	3602	6.8	27	20—	4	
Gilbert	40	19	48	218	5.5	1	2—	5	
Finzer	1	0	0	0	0.0	0	1—	100	
Largent	1	0	0	0	0.0	0	0—	0	
Morris	1	0	0	0	0.0	0	0—	0	

PUNTING	No	Avg
Finzer	68	40.7
Colquitt	12	40.1
West	11	38.2

KICKING	XP	Att	%	FG	Att	%
Johnson	40	41	93	14	25	56

SAN DIEGO CHARGERS

Rushing

Last Name	No.	Yds	Avg	TD
James	105	516	4.9	2
Spencer	124	478	3.9	10
Anderson	116	429	3.7	4
McGee	42	181	4.3	3
Adams	16	49	3.1	1
Chandler	1	9	9.0	0
Mojsiejenko	1	0	0.0	0
Fouts	11	-1	-0.1	0
Hermann	18	-8	-0.4	0

Receiving

Last Name	No.	Yds	Avg	TD
James	86	1027	11.9	6
Chandler	67	1199	17.9	10
Joiner	59	932	15.8	7
Holohan	42	458	10.9	3
Sievers	41	438	10.7	6
Anderson	35	422	12.1	2
Winslow	25	318	12.7	0
Bendross	11	156	14.2	2
Spencer	11	135	12.3	0
Johnson	4	51	12.8	1
McGee	3	15	5.0	0
Adams	1	12	12.0	0
Faulkner	1	12	12.0	0

Punt Returns

Last Name	No.	Yds	Avg	TD
James	25	213	8.5	0

Kickoff Returns

Last Name	No.	Yds	Avg	TD
James	36	779	21.6	0
Anderson	13	302	23.2	1
McGee	7	135	19.3	0
Adams	2	50	25.0	0
Sievers	1	3	3.0	0
Bendross	1	2	2.0	0
Holohan	1	0	0.0	0

Passing — Punting — Kicking

PASSING	Att	Cmp	%	Yds	Yd/Att	TD	Int—	%	RK
Fouts	430	254	59	3638	8.5	27	20—	5	
Herrmann	201	132	66	1537	7.7	10	10—	5	
Holohan	1	0	0	0	0.0	0	0—	0	

PUNTING	No	Avg
Mojsiejenko	68	42.4

KICKING	XP	Att	%	FG	Att	%
Thomas	51	55	93	18	28	64
Benirschke	2	2	100	0	0	0

KANSAS CITY CHIEFS

Rushing

Last Name	No.	Yds	Avg	TD
Heard	164	595	3.6	4
Pruitt	112	390	3.5	2
Horton	48	146	3.0	3
Smith	30	118	3.9	0
Blackledge	17	97	5.7	0
King	28	83	3.0	0
Carson	3	25	8.3	0
Lacy	6	21	3.5	0
Jones	12	19	1.6	0
Paige	1	15	15.0	0
Kenney	14	1	0.1	1

Receiving

Last Name	No.	Yds	Avg	TD
Carson	47	843	17.9	4
Paige	43	943	21.9	10
Heard	31	257	8.3	2
W. Arnold	28	339	12.1	1
Horton	28	185	6.6	1
Marshall	25	446	17.8	0
Smith	18	157	8.7	2
Hancock	15	286	19.1	2
King	7	45	6.4	0
Pruitt	7	43	6.1	0
Holston	6	76	12.7	0
Scott	5	61	12.2	0
Hayes	5	39	7.8	1
Jones	3	31	10.3	0

Punt Returns

Last Name	No.	Yds	Avg	TD
Lane	43	381	8.9	0

Kickoff Returns

Last Name	No.	Yds	Avg	TD
Smith	33	654	19.8	0
Lane	13	269	20.7	0
Hancock	6	125	20.8	0
Paige	2	36	18.0	0
W. Arnold	2	9	4.5	0
King	1	13	13.0	0
Shorthose	1	11	11.0	0
Hayes	1	0	0.0	0

Passing — Punting — Kicking

PASSING	Att	Cmp	%	Yds	Yd/Att	TD	Int—	%	RK
Kenney	338	181	54	2536	7.5	17	9—	3	
Blackledge	172	86	50	1190	6.9	6	14—	8	
Horton	1	0	0	0	0.0	0	0—	0	

PUNTING	No	Avg
J. Arnold	93	41.2

KICKING	XP	Att	%	FG	Att	%
Lowery	35	35	100	24	27	88

1985 N.F.C.—PLAYOFFS

December 29, 1985 at East Rutherford (Attendance 75,131)

SCORING

SAN FRANCISCO	0	3	0	0- 3
N.Y. GIANTS	3	7	7	0- 17

First Quarter
N.Y.G. — Schubert, 47 yard field goal

Second Quarter
N.Y.G. — Bavaro, 18 yard pass from Simms
PAT—Schubert (kick)
S.F. — Wersching, 21 yard field goal

Third Quarter
N.Y.G. — Hasselbeck, 3 yard pass from Simms
PAT—Schubert (kick)

TEAM STATISTICS

S.F.		N.Y.G.
19	First Downs- Total	21
6	First Downs- Rushing	9
10	First Downs- Passing	11
3	First Downs- Penalty	1
2	Fumbles- Number	0
1	Fumbles- Lost Ball	0
6	Penalties- Number	5
41	Yards Penalized	45
0	Missed Field Goals	3
74	Offensive Plays	72
362	Net Yards	355
4.9	Average Gain	4.9
2	Giveaways	1
1	Takeaways	2
-1	Difference	+1

INDIVIDUAL STATISTICS

SAN FRANCISCO — NEW YORK

RUSHING

SAN FRANCISCO	No.	Yds.	Avg.	NEW YORK	No.	Yds.	Avg.
Tyler	10	61	6.1	Morris	28	141	5.0
Craig	9	23	2.6	Carpenter	4	25	6.3
Monroe	1	10	10.0	Adams	4	13	3.3
Harmon	1	0	0.0	Simms	5	-5	-1.0
Montana	1	0	0.0		41	174	4.2
	22	94	4.3				

RECEIVING

SAN FRANCISCO	No.	Yds.	Avg.	NEW YORK	No.	Yds.	Avg.
Clark	8	120	15.0	Bavaro	5	67	13.4
Rice	4	45	11.3	Manuel	3	56	18.7
Francis	4	39	9.8	Carpenter	3	36	12.0
Frank	3	25	8.3	Galbreath	1	9	9.0
Craig	2	18	9.0	Adams	1	5	5.0
Ring	3	19	6.3	Morris	1	5	5.0
Harmon	1	16	16.0	Hasselbeck	1	3	3.0
Wilson	1	14	14.0		15	181	12.1
	26	296	11.4				

PUNTING

Runager	6		38.0	Landeta	5		36.5

PUNT RETURNS

McLemore	1	5	5.0	McConkey	4	29	7.3

KICKOFF RETURNS

Monroe	3	42	14.0	Galbreath	1	17	17.0
				Rouson	1	18	18.0
					2	35	17.5

INTERCEPTION RETURNS

Williamson	1	2	2.0	Kinard	1	15	15.0

PASSING

SAN FRANCISCO

	Att.	Comp.	Comp. Pct.	Yds.	Int.	Yds./ Att.	Yds./ Comp.
Montana	47	26	55.3	296	1	6.3	11.4
Rice	1	0	0.0	0	0	0.0	0.0
	48	26	54.2	296	1	6.2	11.4

NEW YORK

	Att.	Comp.	Comp. Pct.	Yds.	Int.	Yds./ Att.	Yds./ Comp.
Simms	31	15	48.4	181	1	5.8	12.1

January 4, 1986 at Anaheim (Attendance 66,581)

SCORING

DALLAS	0	0	0	0- 0
L.A. RAMS	3	0	10	7- 20

First Quarter
L.A. — Lansford, 33 yard field goal

Third Quarter
L.A. — Dickerson, 55 yard rush
PAT—Lansford (kick)
L.A. — Lansford, 34 yard field goal

Fourth Quarter
L.A. — Dickerson, 40 yard rush
PAT—Lansford (kick)

TEAM STATISTICS

DAL.		L.A.
15	First Downs- Total	15
3	First Downs- Rushing	11
12	First Downs- Passing	3
0	First Downs- Penalty	1
3	Fumbles- Number	3
3	Fumbles- Lost Ball	1
5	Penalties- Number	4
30	Yards Penalized	29
0	Missed Field Goals	0
66	Offensive Plays	64
243	Net Yards	316
3.7	Average Gain	4.9
6	Giveaways	2
2	Takeaways	6
-4	Difference	+4

INDIVIDUAL STATISTICS

DALLAS — LOS ANGELES

RUSHING

DALLAS	No.	Yds.	Avg.	LOS ANGELES	No.	Yds.	Avg.
Dorsett	17	58	3.4	Dickerson	34	248	7.3
Newsome	1	3	3.0	Redden	6	21	3.5
	18	61	3.4	Brock	1	0	0.0
					41	269	6.6

RECEIVING

DALLAS	No.	Yds.	Avg.	LOS ANGELES	No.	Yds.	Avg.
Dorsett	8	80	10.0	Ellard	2	33	16.5
Cosbie	6	61	10.2	Redden	1	15	15.0
T. Hill	5	41	8.2	D. Hill	1	3	3.0
Newsome	3	10	3.4	Hunter	1	3	3.0
Powe	1	19	19.0	Dickerson	1	-4	-4.0
J. Jones	1	6	6.0		6	50	8.3
	24	217	9.0				

PUNTING

Saxon	7		46.9	Hatcher	7		40.7

PUNT RETURNS

Banks	4	30	7.5	Ellard	4	37	9.3

KICKOFF RETURNS

Duckett	4	99	24.8	White	1	14	14.0
J. Jones	1	11	11.0				
	5	110	22.0				

INTERCEPTION RETURNS

Walls	1	20	20.0	Irvin	1	55	55.0
				Gray	1	10	10.0
				Green	1	1	1.0
					3	66	22.0

PASSING

DALLAS

	Att.	Comp.	Comp. Pct.	Yds.	Int.	Yds./ Att.	Yds./ Comp.
D. White	43	24	55.8	217	3	5.0	9.0

LOS ANGELES

	Att.	Comp.	Comp. Pct.	Yds.	Int.	Yds./ Att.	Yds./ Comp.
Brock	22	6	27.3	50	1	2.3	8.3

January 5, 1986 at Chicago (Attendance 65,670)

SCORING

N.Y. GIANTS	0	0	0	0- 0
CHICAGO	7	0	14	0- 21

First Quarter
Chi. — Gayle, 5 yard punt return
PAT—Butler (kick)

Third Quarter
Chi. — McKinnon, 23 yard pass from McMahon
PAT—Butler (kick)
Chi. — McKinnon, 20 yard pass from McMahon
PAT—Butler (kick)

TEAM STATISTICS

N.Y.G.		CHI.
10	First Downs- Total	17
1	First Downs- Rushing	9
8	First Downs- Passing	8
1	First Downs- Penalty	0
3	Fumbles- Number	0
1	Fumbles- Lost Ball	0
4	Penalties- Number	2
25	Yards Penalized	20
1	Missed Field Goals	3
55	Offensive Plays	65
181	Net Yards	363
3.3	Average Gain	5.6
1	Giveaways	0
0	Takeaways	1
-1	Difference	+1

INDIVIDUAL STATISTICS

NEW YORK — CHICAGO

RUSHING

NEW YORK	No.	Yds.	Avg.	CHICAGO	No.	Yds.	Avg.
Morris	12	32	2.7	Payton	27	93	3.4
Galbreath	1	9	9.0	Suhey	6	33	5.5
B. Williams	1	-9	-9.0	McMahon	5	18	3.6
	14	32	2.3	Thomas	4	11	2.8
				Gentry	1	-1	-1.0
				McKinnon	1	-7	-7.0
					44	147	3.3

RECEIVING

NEW YORK	No.	Yds.	Avg.	CHICAGO	No.	Yds.	Avg.
Bavaro	4	36	9.0	Gault	3	68	22.7
Adams	3	65	21.7	McKinnon	3	52	17.3
Carpenter	3	24	8.0	Suhey	2	5	2.5
B. Williams	1	33	33.0	Wrightman	1	46	46.0
McConkey	1	23	23.0	Gentry	1	41	41.0
Johnson	1	17	17.0	Payton	1	4	4.0
Galbreath	1	11	11.0		11	216	19.6
	14	209	14.9				

PUNTING

Landeta	9		38.1	Buford	6		37.3

PUNT RETURNS

McConkey	2	9	4.5	Ortego	5	22	4.4
				Gayle	1	5	5.0
					6	27	4.5

KICKOFF RETURNS

Rouson	2	58	29.0	Gault	1	21	21.0
Hasselbeck	1	20	20.0				
Galbreath	1	17	17.0				
	4	95	23.8				

INTERCEPTION RETURNS

none — none

PASSING

NEW YORK

	Att.	Comp.	Comp. Pct.	Yds.	Int.	Yds./ Att.	Yds./ Comp.
Simms	35	14	40.0	209	0	6.0	14.9

CHICAGO

	Att.	Comp.	Comp. Pct.	Yds.	Int.	Yds./ Att.	Yds./ Comp.
McMahon	21	11	52.4	216	0	10.3	19.6

December 28, 1985 at East Rutherford (Attendance 75,945)

SCORING

NEW ENGLAND	3	10	10	3- 26
N.Y. JETS	0	7	7	0- 14

First Quarter
- N.E. — Franklin, 33 yard field goal

Second Quarter
- N.Y.J. — Hector, 11 yard pass from O'Brien
  PAT—Leahy (kick)
- N.E. — Franklin, 41 yard field goal
- N.E. — Morgan, 36 yard pass from Eason
  PAT—Franklin (kick)

Third Quarter
- N.E. — Franklin, 20 yard field goal
- N.E. — Rembert, 15 yard fumble return
  PAT—Franklin (kick)
- N.Y.J. — Shuler, 12 yard pass from Ryan
  PAT—Leahy (kick)

Fourth Quarter
- N.E. — Franklin, 26 yard field goal

TEAM STATISTICS

N.E.		N.Y.J.
12	First Downs- Total	15
5	First Downs- Rushing	3
6	First Downs- Passing	12
1	First Downs- Penalty	0
2	Fumbles- Number	3
0	Fumbles- Lost Ball	2
1	Penalties- Number	6
10	Yards Penalized	48
1	Missed Field Goals	0
58	Offensive Plays	60
258	Net Yards	250
4.4	Average Gain	4.2
0	Giveaways	4
4	Takeaways	0
+4	Difference	-4

INDIVIDUAL STATISTICS

NEW ENGLAND	No.	Yds.	Avg.	N.Y. Jets	No.	Yds.	Avg.
RUSHING							
James	22	49	2.2	McNeil	16	41	2.6
Collins	11	36	3.3	Hector	4	13	3.3
Eason	6	14	2.3	O'Brien	1	4	4.0
	39	99	2.5		21	58	2.8
RECEIVING							
Morgan	4	62	15.5	Toon	9	93	10.3
Fryar	2	47	23.5	Shuler	5	53	10.6
James	2	36	18.0	Walker	4	54	13.5
Dawson	2	20	10.0	McNeil	3	13	4.3
Collins	2	14	7.0	Hector	1	11	11.0
	12	179	14.9	Klever	1	9	9.0
					23	233	10.1
PUNTING							
Camarillo	5		40.0	Jennings	5		38.4
PUNT RETURNS							
Fryar	4	12	3.0	Sohn	1	3	3.0
KICKOFF RETURNS							
Starring	1	19	19.0	Hector	6	115	19.2
C. Jones	1	11	11.0	Humphrey	1	50	50.0
	2	30	15.0		7	165	23.6
INTERCEPTION RETURNS							
Marion	1	28	28.0	none			
Veris	1	18	18.0				
	2	46	23.0				

PASSING

NEW ENGLAND

	Att.	Comp.	Comp. Pct.	Yds.	Int.	Yds./ Att.	Yds./ Comp.
Eas	16	12	75	179	0	11.2	14.9

NE / YORK

	Att.	Comp.	Comp. Pct.	Yds.	Int.	Yds./ Att.	Yds./ Comp.
C' ien	17	13	76	149	1	8.8	11.5
R n	17	10	59	84	1	4.9	8.4
	34	23	68	233	2	6.9	10.1

January 4, 1986 at Miami (Attendance 74,667)

SCORING

CLEVELAND	7	7	7	0- 21
MIAMI	3	0	14	7- 24

First Quarter
- MIA. — Reveiz, 51 yard field goal
- CLE. — Newsome, 16 yard pass from Kosar
  PAT—Bahr (kick)

Second Quarter
- CLE. — Byner, 21 yard rush
  PAT—Bahr (kick)

Third Quarter
- CLE. — Byner 66 yard rush
  PAT—Bahr (kick)]
- MIA. — N. Moore, 6 yard pass from Marino
  PAT—Reveiz (kick)
- MIA. — Davenport, 31 yard rush
  PAT—Reveiz (kick)

Fourth Quarter
- MIA. — Davenport, 1 yard rush
  PAT—Reveiz (kick)

TEAM STATISTICS

CLE.		MIA.
17	First Downs- Total	20
11	First Downs- Rushing	6
5	First Downs- Passing	13
1	First Downs- Penalty	1
1	Fumbles- Number	1
0	Fumbles- Lost Ball	0
6	Penalties- Number	2
49	Yards Penalized	20
0	Missed Field Goals	1
57	Offensive Plays	64
313	Net Yards	330
5.5	Average Gain	5.2
1	Giveaways	1
1	Takeaways	1
0	Difference	0

INDIVIDUAL STATISTICS

CLEVELAND	No.	Yds.	Avg.	MIAMI	No.	Yds.	Avg.
RUSHING							
Byner	16	161	10.1	Davenport	6	48	8.0
Mack	13	56	4.3	Nathan	7	21	3.0
Dickey	6	28	4.7	Bennett	4	17	4.3
Kosar	2	6	3.0	Carter	2	6	3.0
	37	251	6.8		19	92	4.8
RECEIVING							
Byner	4	25	6.3	Nathan	10	101	10.1
Newsome	2	22	11.0	Hardy	5	51	10.2
Holt	2	2	1.0	N. Moore	4	29	7.3
Cl. Weathers	1	12	12.0	Johnson	2	17	8.5
Fontenot	1	5	5.0	Rose	1	17	17.0
	10	66	6.6	Clayton	1	15	15.0
				Bennett	1	6	6.0
				Carter	1	2	2.0
					25	238	9.5
PUNTING							
Gossett	6		37.2	Roby	5		41.6
PUNT RETURNS							
Brennan	1	1	1.0	Vigorito	3	23	7.7
				Kozlowski	1	0	0.0
					4	23	5.8
KICKOFF RETURNS							
Young	3	75	25.0	Vigorito	1	19	19.0
				Hampton	3	70	23.3
					4	89	22.3
INTERCEPTION RETURNS							
Rogers	1	45	45.0	Lankford	1	2	2.0

PASSING

CLEVELAND

	Att.	Comp.	Comp. Pct.	Yds.	Int.	Yds./ Att.	Yds./ Comp.
Kosar	19	10	53	66	1	3.5	6.6

MIAMI

	Att.	Comp.	Comp. Pct.	Yds.	Int.	Yds./ Att.	Yds./ Comp.
Marino	45	25	56	238	1	5.3	9.5

January 5, 1986 at Los Angeles (Attendance 87,163)

SCORING

NEW ENGLAND	7 10	10	0-	27
L.A. RAIDERS	3 17	0	0-	20

First Quarter
- N.E. — Dawson, 13 yard pass from Eason
  PAT—Franklin (kick)
- L.A. — Bahr, 29 yard field goal

Second Quarter
- L.A. — Hester, 16 yard pass from Wilson
  PAT—Bahr (kick)
- L.A. — Allen, 11 yard rush
  PAT—Bahr (kick)
- N.E. — C. James, 2 yard rush
  PAT—Franklin (kick)
- N.E. — Franklin, 45 yard field goal
- L.A. — Bahr, 32 yard field goal

Third Quarter
- N.E. — Franklin, 32 yard field goal
- N.E. — Bowman, fumble recovery in end zone
  PAT—Franklin (kick)

TEAM STATISTICS

N.E.		RAID.
15	First Downs- Total	17
9	First Downs- Rushing	11
5	First Downs- Passing	6
1	First Downs- Penalty	0
3	Fumbles- Number	5
2	Fumbles- Lost Ball	3
6	Penalties- Number	6
45	Yards Penalized	53
0	Missed Field Goals	1
67	Offensive Plays	56
254	Net Yards	287
3.8	Average Gain	5.1
2	Giveaways	6
6	Takeaways	2
+4	Difference	-4

INDIVIDUAL STATISTICS

NEW ENGLAND	No.	Yds.	Avg.	L.A. RAIDERS	No.	Yds.	Avg.
RUSHING							
C. James	23	104	4.5	Allen	22	121	5.5
Collins	9	18	2.0	Hawkins	4	33	8.3
Weathers	9	18	2.0	Wilson	1	9	9.0
Tatupu	4	17	4.3		27	163	6.0
Fryar	1	3	3.0				
Eason	3	-4	-1.3				
	49	156	3.2				
RECEIVING							
C. James	3	48	16.0	Christensen	4	78	19.5
D. Ramsey	2	34	17.0	Williams	3	33	11.0
Morgan	1	22	22.0	Allen	3	8	2.7
Dawson	1	13	13.0	Hester	1	16	16.0
Collins	1	8	8.0		11	135	12.3
	8	125	15.6				
PUNTING							
Camarillo	5		45.0	Guy	2		34.0
PUNT RETURNS							
none				Walker	4	36	9.0
KICKOFF RETURNS							
Starring	2	45	22.5	Walker	3	59	19.7
Jones	2	9	4.5	Seale	2	7	3.5
	4	54	13.5		5	66	13.2
INTERCEPTION RETURNS							
Marion	1	22	22.0	none			
Lippett	2	1	0.5				
	3	23	7.7				

PASSING

NEW ENGLAND

	Att.	Comp.	Comp. Pct.	Yds.	Int.	Yds./ Att.	Yds./ Comp.
Eason	14	7	50	117	0	8.4	16.7
C. James	1	1	100	8	0	8.0	8.0
	15	8	53	125	0	8.3	15.6

LOS ANGELES

	Att.	Comp.	Comp. Pct.	Yds.	Int.	Yds./ Att.	Yds./ Comp.
Wilson	27	11	41	135	3	5.0	12.3

1985 Championship Games

NFC CHAMPIONSHIP GAME

January 12, 1986 at Chicago

(Attendance 63,522)

SCORING

L.A. RAMS	0	0	0	0-	0
CHICAGO	10	0	7	7-	24

First Quarter

Chi. McMahon, 16 yard rush
PAT—Butler (kick)

Chi Butler, 34 yard field goal

Third Quarter

Chi. Gault, 22 yard pass from McMahon
PAT—Butler (kick)

Fourth Quarter

Chi. Marshall, 52 yard fumble recovery return
PAT—Butler (kick)

TEAM STATISTICS

LA		CHI
9	First Downs-Total	13
5	First Downs-Rushing	5
3	First Downs-Passing	8
1	First Downs-Penalty	0
4	Fumbles-Number	3
2	Fumbles-Lost Ball	1
4	Penalties-Number	6
25	Yards Penalized	48
0	Missed Field Goals	0
60	Offensive Plays	61
130	Net Yards	232
2.2	Average Gain	3.8
3	Giveaways	1
1	Takeaways	3
-2	Difference	+2

A week after shutting out the New York Giants 21-0 in a near-perfect defensive performance, the Chicago Bears hosted the Los Angeles Rams for the NFC title in cool, gusty Soldier Field.

Excellent defenders themselves, the Rams had also posted a shutout the previous week, 20-0 over the Cowboys. But the Bears waded through Los Angeles on their first possession to score the only points they needed for victory. Bear QB Jim McMahon capped a five-play, 66-yard drive with a 16-yard scramble to make it 7-0. When the Rams couldn't move, Chicago got the ball back, and Kevin Butler kicked a 34-yard field goal, making it 10-0.

Chicago shut down Ram workhorse Eric Dickerson and harried QB Dieter Brock with a devastating pass rush led by DE Richard Dent. Late in the first half, the Rams recovered a fumble at the Bear 21 but failed to score before time ran out.

Having lost their chance to change the momentum, the Rams were flattened in the second half. Chicago built its lead to 17-0 in the third quarter on a McMahon-to-Willie Gault, 22-yard scoring pass. Then, as snow began to fall in the fourth quarter, Chicago's defense appropriately added the final points. Dent forced Brock to fumble, and LB Wilber Marshall grabbed the ball and raced 52 yards for a touchdown.

The awesome Bear defense held Dickerson to 46 yards and pressured Brock to a net gain of only 44 yards passing. Not since the Eagles in the NFL championship games of 1948 and 1949 had a team posted two consecutive shutouts in postseason play.

INDIVIDUAL STATISTICS

L.A. RAMS	No.	Yds.	Avg.	CHICAGO	No.	Yds.	Avg.
RUSHING							
Dickerson	17	46	2.7	Payton	18	32	1.8
Redden	9	40	4.4	McMahon	4	28	7.0
	26	86	3.3	Suhey	6	23	3.8
				Gentry	2	9	4.5
				Thomas	3	-1	-0.3
					33	91	2.8
RECEIVING							
Hunter	3	29	9.7	Payton	7	48	6.9
Dickerson	3	10	3.3	Gault	4	56	14.0
Brown	2	14	7.0	Moorehead	2	28	14.0
Duckworth	1	8	8.0	McKinnon	1	17	17.0
Ellard	1	5	5.0	Wrightman	1	8	8.0
	10	66	6.6	Suhey	1	7	7.0
					16	164	10.3
PUNTING							
Hatcher	11		39.2	Buford	10		36.3
PUNT RETURNS							
Johnson	2	6	3.0	Ortego	4	21	5.3
Ellard	1	6	6.0	Phillips	1	0	0.0
Irvin	1	4	4.0	Duerson	0	0	0.0
	4	16	4.0		5	21	4.2
KICKOFF RETURNS							
Brown	3	63	21.0	Gentry	1	22	22.0
Redden	1	13	13.0				
	4	76	19.0				
INTERCEPTION RETURNS							
none				Frazier	1	-3	-3.0

PASSING

L.A. RAMS	Att.	Comp.	Comp Pct.	Yds.	Int.	Yds./ Att.	Yds./ Comp.
Brock	31	10	32.2	66	1	2.1	6.6
CHICAGO							
McMahon	25	16	64.0	164	0	6.6	10.3

AFC CHAMPIONSHIP GAME

January 12, 1986 at Miami

(Attendance 74,978)

SCORING

NEW ENGLAND	3	14	7	7-	31
MIAMI	0	7	0	7-	14

First Quarter

N.E. Franklin, 23 yard field goal

Second Quarter

Mia. Johnson, 10 yard pass from Marino
PAT—Reveiz (kick)

N.E. Collins, 4 yard pass from Eason
PAT—Franklin (kick)

N.E. D. Ramsey, 1 yard pass from Eason
PAT—Franklin (kick)

Third Quarter

N.E. Weathers, 2 yard pass from Eason
PAT—Franklin (kick)

Fourth Quarter

Mia. Nathan, 10 yard pass from Marino
PAT—Reveiz (kick)

N.E. Tatupu, 1 yard rush
PAT—Franklin (kick)

TEAM STATISTICS

NE		MIA
21	First Downs- Total	18
15	First Downs- Rushing	3
6	First Downs- Passing	15
0	First Downs- Penalty	0
2	Fumbles- Number	5
2	Fumbles- Lost Ball	4
2	Penalties- Number	4
15	Yards Penalized	35
1	Missed Field Goals	1
71	Offensive Plays	62
326	Net Yards	302
4.6	Average Gain	4.9
2	Giveaways	6
6	Takeaways	2
+4	Difference	-4

The Miami Dolphins were Eastern Division champions, whereas the New England Patriots were only wild-card qualifiers playing their third straight game on the road. Moreover, the Dolphins had never lost an AFC title game and had beaten the Patriots 18 consecutive times in the Orange Bowl.

But, on the first play from scrimmage, New England DE Garin Veris recovered Dolphin Tony Nathan's fumble to set the tone of the game. Six plays later, Tony Franklin delivered a 23-yard field goal to put the Patriots in front 3-0.

Miami took the lead on a 10-yard pass from Dan Marino to Dan Johnson, but the Patriots bounced right back with a 66-yard drive to regain the lead on a four-yard, Tony Eason-to-Tony Collins pass. Two plays after the ensuing kickoff, Marino fumbled and the Patriots recovered again. A few moments later, Eason hit Derrick Ramsey with a one-yard TD to give New England a 17-7 halftime lead.

Miami's giveaway problems continued as Lorenzo Hampton fumbled the second-half kickoff and, shortly afterward, Eason threw to Weathers for a touchdown.

Behind 24-7, Marino began throwing on every down, but the best he could do was a single 10-yard TD toss to Nathan. New England matched that with Mosi Tatupu's one-yard plunge.

INDIVIDUAL STATISTICS

NEW ENGLAND	No.	Yds.	Avg.	MIAMI	No.	Yds.	Avg.
RUSHING							
C. James	22	105	4.8	Carter	6	56	9.3
Weathers	16	87	5.4	Davenport	3	6	2.0
Collins	12	61	5.1	Nathan	2	4	2.0
Tatupu	6	9	1.5	Bennett	1	2	2.0
Eason	3	-7	-2.3	Marino	1	0	0.0
	59	255	4.3		13	68	5.2
RECEIVING							
D. Ramsey	3	18	6.0	Nathan	5	57	11.4
Collins	3	15	5.0	Hardy	3	52	17.3
Morgan	2	30	15.0	Duper	3	45	15.0
Tatupu	1	6	6.0	Clayton	3	41	13.7
Weathers	1	2	2.0	Davenport	3	23	7.7
	10	71	7.1	Johnson	1	10	10.0
				Moore	1	10	10.0
				Rose	1	10	10.0
					20	248	12.4
PUNTING							
Camarillo	5		40.2	Roby	4		41.3
PUNT RETURNS							
R. James	2	2	1.0	Vigorito	1	8	8.0
KICKOFF RETURNS							
Starring	3	67	22.3	Hampton	6	91	15.2
INTERCEPTION RETURNS							
Marion	1	21	21.0	none			
Clayborn	1	0	0.0				
	2	21	10.5				

PASSING

NEW ENGLAND	Att.	Comp.	Comp. Pct.	Yds.	Int.	Yds./ Att.	Yds./ Comp.
Eason	12	10	83.3	71	0	5.9	7.1
MIAMI							
Marino	48	20	41.7	248	2	5.2	12.4

SUPER BOWL XX

January 26, 1986 at New Orleans

(Attendance 73,818)

Cinderella and the 45 Bears

The 20th Super Bowl had the makings of one of the all-time David-and-Goliath stories. On one side were the Chicago Bears with a 15-1 regular-season record and fresh off two post-season shutouts to win the N.F.C. crown hands down, as just about everyone expected they would. The Bears, with their bone-crushing defense, unpredictable quarterback and ground-eating running game, were cast inevitably as Goliath. As David: the New England Patriots, a respectable 11-5 on the season but barely in the playoffs as the second wild-card team. After winning three road games against supposedly stronger opponents, the Patriots needed only a victory over the ferocious Bears to become the ultimate Cinderella team. But midnight struck early in the Louisiana Superdome. Goliath took away David's rocks and buried him in the most one-sided Super Bowl ever.

On the second play of the game, Chicago's Walter Payton fumbled, and the Patriots' Don Blackmon recovered on the Chicago 19. The Patriots had gotten to the Super Bowl by taking advantage of opponents' miscues. Three incomplete passes later, it was fourth-and-10. Tony Franklin, New England's barefoot kicker, booted a 36-yard field goal to give the Patriots a 3-0 lead, the high point of their day.

As though shocked to have someone finally score against them, the Bears roared back. Jim McMahon's 43-yard pass to Willie Gault put them in New England territory, and Matt Suhey picked up another first down on two carries. When the Patriots stiffened, Kevin Butler tied the score at 3-3 with a 28-yard field goal.

New England suddenly developed fumble-itis. Super Bowl MVP Richard Dent sacked Tony Eason, who fumbled at the 13. Butler put the Bears in front with a successful 24-yard boot. As soon as the Patriots got the ball back, Craig James fumbled and Mike Singletary recovered, again at the 13. Two plays later, when Suhey burst 11 yards for a touchdown, the game was as good as over.

The Bears tacked on 10 more points in the second quarter. McMahon's two-yard run capped a 59-yard scoring drive to make it 20-3. Eason was 0-for-6 with his passes, and coach Raymond Berry sent in veteran Steve Grogan at quarterback. It didn't help. Chicago held the ball for 11 plays on a 72-yard drive before Butler kicked his third field goal, this one from 24 yards.

In piling up a 23-3 lead, the Bears had gained 236 total yards to the Patriots' minus-14!

The second half was only slightly better statistically for the Patriots, who saw the score go to 44-3 before they finally crossed the Bear goalline. After a short drive at the opening of the third quarter, New England punted to the Bear four. On first down, McMahon trashed the Pats with a 60-yard bomb to Gault. From there, the Bears drove in, with McMahon sneaking over from the one. Three plays later, Chicago reserve cornerback Reggie Phillips stepped in front of a Grogan pass and ran it back 28 yards for another touchdown. Still another New England fumble gave the Bears the ball again. Chicago drove 30 yards to the Patriot one. William "The Refrigerator" Perry had gained national notoriety by occasionally masquerading as a roly-poly fullback, and the Bears now satisfied his fans as he took the ball into the endzone on a one-yard smash.

In the final quarter, with the game more than lost, the Patriots put on their only sustained drive of the day against the Bears' second-stringers: 76 yards to an eight-yard Grogan-to-Irving Fryar scoring pass. But the Bears had the last word. With four minutes left, Henry Waechter tackled Grogan behind the goalline for a safety.

LINEUPS

CHICAGO		NEW ENGLAND
	OFFENSE	
Gault	WR	Morgan
Covert	LT	Holloway
Bortz	LG	Hannah
Hilgenberg	C	Brock
Thayer	RG	Wooten
Van Horne	RT	Moore
Moorehoad	TE	Dawson
McKinnon	WR	Starring
McMahon	QB	Eason
Payton	RB	Collins
Suhey	RB	James
	DEFENSE	
Hampton	LE	Veris
McMichael	LT/NT	Williams
Perry	RT/RE	Adams
Dent	RE/LOLB	Tippett
Wilson	LLB/LILB	Nelson
Singletary	MLB/RILB	McGrew
Marshall	RLB/ROLB	Blackmon
Richardson	LCB	Lippett
Frazier	RCB	Clayborn
Duerson	SS	James
Fencik	FS	Marion

SUBSTITUTES

CHICAGO

	OFFENSE	
Andrews	Humphries	Thomas
Frederick	Margerum	Tomczak
Fuller	Ortego	Wrightman
Gentry	Sanders	
	DEFENSE	
Cabral	Keys	Rivera
Gayle	Morrissey	Taylor
Hartenstine	Phillips	Thrift
	KICKERS	
Buford	Butler	

NEW ENGLAND

	OFFENSE	
Fairchild	Jones	Ramsey
Fryar	Morriss	Tatupu
Grogan	Plunkett	Weathers
Hawthorne		
	DEFENSE	
Bowman	McSwain	Reynolds
Creswell	Owens	Thomas
Gibson	Ramsey	Williams
Ingram	Rembert	
	KICKERS	
Camarillo	Franklin	

SCORING

CHICAGO	13	10	21	2-	46
NEW ENGLAND	3	0	0	7-	10

First Quarter
- N.E. Franklin, 36 yard field goal
- Chi. Butler, 28 yard field goal
- Chi. Butler, 24 yard field goal
- Chi. Suhey, 11 yard rush
  PAT—Butler (kick)

Second Quarter
- Chi. McMahon, 2 yard rush
  PAT—Butler (kick)
- Chi. Butler, 24 yard field goal

Third Quarter
- Chi. McMahon, 1 yard rush
  PAT—Butler (kick)
- Chi. Phillips, 28 yard interception return
  PAT—Butler (kick)
- Chi. Perry, 1 yard rush
  PAT—Butler (kick)

Fourth Quarter
- N.E. Fryar, 8 yard pass from Grogan
  PAT—Franklin (kick)
- Chi. Safety, Waechter tackled Grogan in end zone

TEAM STATISTICS

CHI		NE
23	First Downs- Total	12
13	First Downs- Rushing	1
9	First Downs- Passing	10
1	First Downs- Penalty	1
3	Fumbles- Number	4
2	Fumbles- Lost Ball	4
7	Penalties- Number	5
40	Yards Penalized	35
0	Missed Field Goals	0
76	Offensive Plays	54
408	Net Yards	123
5.4	Average Gain	2.3
2	Giveaways	6
6	Takeaways	2
+4	Difference	-4

INDIVIDUAL STATISTICS

CHICAGO	No.	Yds.	Avg.	NEW ENGLAND	No.	Yds.	Avg
RUSHING							
Payton	22	61	2.8	C. James	5	1	0.2
Suhey	11	52	4.7	Collins	3	4	0.8
McMahon	5	14	2.8	Grogan	1	3	3.0
Sanders	4	15	3.8	Weathers	1	3	3.0
Gentry	3	15	5.0	Hawthorne	1	-4	-4.0
Thomas	2	8	4.0		11	7	0.6
Fuller	1	1	1.0				
Perry	1	1	1.0				
	49	167	3.4				
RECEIVING							
Gault	4	129	32.3	Morgan	7	70	10.0
Gentry	2	41	20.5	Starring	2	39	19.5
Margerum	2	36	18.0	Fryar	2	24	12.0
Moorehead	2	22	11.0	Collins	2	19	9.5
Suhey	1	24	24.0	Ramsey	2	16	8.0
Thomas	1	4	4.0	C. James	1	6	6.0
	12	256	21.3	Weathers	1	3	3.0
					17	177	10.4
PUNTING							
Buford	4		43.3	Camarillo	6		43.8
PUNT RETURNS							
Ortego	2	20	10.0	Fryar	2	22	11.0
KICKOFF RETURNS							
Gault	4	49	12.3	Starring	7	153	21.9
INTERCEPTION RETURNS							
Morrissey	1	47	47.0	none			
Phillips	1	28	28.0				
	2	75	37.5				

PASSING

	Att.	Comp.	Comp. Pct.	Yds.	Int.	Yds./ Att.	Yds./ Comp.	Yards Lost Tackled
CHICAGO								
McMahon	20	12	60.0	256	0	12.8	21.3	3-15
Fuller	4	0	0.0	0	0	0.0	0.0	0-0
	24	12	50.0	256	0	10.7	21.3	3-15
NEW ENGLAND								
Grogan	30	17	56.7	177	2	5.9	10.4	4-33
Eason	6	0	0.0	0	0	0.0	0.0	3-28
	36	17	47.2	177	2	4.9	10.4	7-61

1986 N.F.C. In a Gatorade Shower

It didn't start as New York's year. Running back Joe Morris held out for contract renegotiation until four hours before the first game, and then the Giants dropped the opener to arch-rival Dallas 31-28. Top wide receiver Lionel Manuel was injured most of the time. Still, coach Bill Parcells' men won their next five before losing at Seattle. After that, they just kept on winning, rolling to the Eastern Division championship. In addition to N.F.L. foes, they had to face constant comparison with outstanding Giants' teams of the 1950s and early '60s that had not won the Big One. Much of that stopped after a December 1 meeting at San Francisco when the Giants trailed 17-0 at the half and came back to win 21-17. Quarterback Phil Simms wasn't selected to the Pro Bowl, but eight other Giants were. By season's end, one of TV's most familiar scenes was Harry Carson's ceremonial dumping of a tub full of Gatorade on Parcells after every New York victory.

EASTERN DIVISION

New York Giants — Morris rushed for 1,516 yards and scored 14 touchdowns. Simms picked up 3,487 yards passing and proved he was a team leader. The offensive line was young and cohesive, and tight end Mark Bavaro blocked brilliantly and caught 66 passes for 1,001 yards. The Giants had a more-than-adequate offense. But the defense was still the key to success. Lawrence Taylor led the N.F.L. in sacks with 20 1/2 from his linebacker position and was named league MVP. Carl Banks, on the other side, was almost his equal, and Carson held his own, too. The front three also came in for recognition: end George Martin was steady and his counterpart, Leonard Marshall, had a Pro Bowl year, as did classic overachiever Jim Burt, the nose tackle.

Washington Redskins — Quarterback Jay Schroeder proved the promise he showed in the final five games of '85 was no fluke, throwing for a club-record 4,109 yards and pulling out six victories after his team trailed going into the fourth quarter. George Rogers rumbled for 1,203 yards and 18 touchdowns, and U.S.F.L. refugee Kelvin Bryant was an excellent all-purpose back after recovering from an early-season injury. Receivers Art Monk and Gary Clark provided a potent one-two punch with more than 70 catches and 1,000 yards apiece. Free-spirit defensive end Dexter Manley led an aggressive defense with 18 1/2 sacks, another club record. Even though nearly a third of the roster was new, the Skins would have won the division if they'd been able to beat the Giants. Two losses to New York left them second, but with a wild-card berth.

Dallas Cowboys — The Cowboys never recovered from a mid-season 17-14 loss to the Giants in which quarterback Danny White suffered a broken wrist. Defensive tackle Randy White and running back Tony Dorsett were also slowed by injuries, others began to show their age, and the team dropped seven of its last eight games to finish below .500 for the first time since 1965. The tailspin spoiled an impressive N.F.L. debut for Herschel Walker, about the only bright spot on coach Tom Landry's roster. Lining up at several positions, Walker topped the team in receiving, finished a close second to Dorsett in rushing, and scored 14 touchdowns.

Philadelphia Eagles — New coach Buddy Ryan began the season predicting a playoff berth, but the Eagles retreated from also-rans to also-staggereds. Ryan tore the '85 roster apart, cutting 20 players, including nine starters. The result was disaster. The offensive line gave up an incredible 104 sacks, shattering the league record of 70. Veteran QB Ron Jaworski was buffeted regularly and finally put out permanently in game 10. His replacement, Randall Cunningham, survived only because he was a faster runner. Wide receiver Mike Quick managed 60 catches, and defensive end Reggie White went to the Pro Bowl. Ryan went back to the drawing board.

St. Louis Cardinals — Injured, undermanned and inexperienced, the Cardinals were never in the race and seldom interesting, as witness their league-low attendance. The team MVP was 31-year-old journeyman receiver J.T. Smith, whose 80 catches were a pleasant surprise. Vai Sikahema had plenty of opportunity to return kicks and took two punts back for touchdowns in the final game to provide one of the team's four wins. All-time leading rusher Ottis Anderson was traded to the Giants. Quarterback Neil Lomax continued to slump and was replaced at mid-season by Cliff Stoudt for a while. Nothing helped.

CENTRAL DIVISION

Chicago Bears — Quarterback Jim McMahon injured his shoulder in the opening game, was in and out of the lineup, and went out for good in week 12 after a controversial late hit. Even though coach Mike Ditka's men lost only twice, fans blamed McMahon's injury for the team's failure to blow out opponents. The Bears tried Mike Tomczak and Steve Fuller at quarterback, and ended with mid-season acquisition Doug Flutie, but none could provide McMahon's magic. The shaky quarterback situation offset a typical Walter Payton year (1,333 yards) and a record-setting performance by the defense. Mike Singletary, Wilber Marshall, Steve McMichael, et al., held opponents to just 187 points, the lowest ever for a 16-game season.

Minnesota Vikings — The Vikings continued to improve in '86, reaching the status of playoff contender. They would have made it to participant had they not blown fourth-quarter leads to Cleveland, the Giants and Washington. Quarterback Tommy Kramer enjoyed the best season of his 10-year career, leading the N.F.C. in passing. He credited his improved throwing to eating oysters the night before games, but most observers felt the nucleus of young talent the Vikings had stockpiled to surround him had more to do with it. Running back Darrin Nelson and receivers Anthony Carter and Steve Jordan continued to gain respect. Former U.S.F.L. offensive tackle Gary Zimmerman helped solidify the offensive line, and Keith Millard was marked a coming star at defensive tackle.

Detroit Lions — The Lions, who were 6-2 at home in '85, collapsed to 1-7 and were booed viciously. In a chicken-or-egg controversy, the Lions blamed the fans' booing for their poor play. The defense had an embarrassing habit of giving up big plays, especially late in the game, as happened when it blew 10- and 14-point leads in the final quarter to lose 44-40 in the nationally televised Thanksgiving Day game with Green Bay. Among the few highlights: a young and talented offensive line led by Lomas Brown, a pair of tough running backs in James Jones and Garry James, and some hope for the future in rookie quarterback Chuck Long's limited end-of-season play. The former Iowa All-American tossed a 34-yard touchdown on his first N.F.L. pass.

Green Bay Packers — After the Pack had finished at .500 in four of the past five years, coach Forrest Gregg decided the only way to move up was to tear the team apart and start over. He cut veterans Lynn Dickey, Paul Coffman and other regulars, and installed youngsters. Not surprisingly, the Packers were winless after six weeks. However, Gregg's drastic prescription began to look better as the season wore on. Three of the team's four victories came in the last six games. Quarterback Randy Wright, cornerback Mark Lee, kick returner Walter Stanley and a few others gave evidence that they just might make it in the N.F.L.

Tampa Bay Buccaneers — The Bucs spent their No. 1 pick in the '86 draft on Heisman Trophy winner Bo Jackson, but he opted to play baseball instead. The defense lost both ends to

FINAL TEAM STATISTICS

	OFFENSE													
	ATL.	CHI.	DAL.	DET.	G.B.	L.A.	MINN.	N.O.	NY G	PHIL.	STL.	S.F.	T.B.	WASH.
FIRST DOWNS:														
Total	305	305	325	287	286	269	321	275	324	287	273	**346**	273	312
by Rushing	149	**166**	98	100	96	139	114	109	127	113	102	114	100	112
by Passing	137	118	199	156	172	105	186	137	171	150	149	**213**	142	177
by Penalty	19	21	28	**31**	18	25	21	29	26	24	22	19	**31**	23
RUSHING:														
Number	578	**606**	447	470	424	578	461	505	558	499	419	510	455	474
Yards	2524	**2700**	1969	1771	1614	2457	1738	2074	2245	2002	1787	1986	1863	1732
Average Yards	4.4	**4.5**	4.4	3.8	3.8	4.3	3.8	4.1	4.0	4.0	4.3	3.9	4.1	3.7
Touchdowns	12	21	21	13	8	16	14	15	18	8	8	16	12	**23**
PASSING:														
Attempts	452	415	547	500	565	403	519	425	472	514	516	**582**	459	542
Completions	246	208	319	286	305	194	290	232	260	268	293	**353**	245	276
Completion Pct.	54.4	50.1	58.3	57.2	54.0	48.1	55.9	54.6	55.1	52.1	56.8	**60.7**	53.4	50.9
Passing Yards	3046	2912	4003	3107	3708	2380	4185	2893	3500	3248	3140	**4299**	2892	4109
Avg. Yds per Att.	5.1	6.3	5.8	5.2	5.7	5.9	**7.0**	5.9	6.1	4.1	4.7	6.7	4.9	6.8
Avg. Yds per Comp.	12.4	14.0	12.6	10.9	12.2	12.3	14.4	12.5	13.5	12.1	10.7	12.2	11.8	**14.9**
Times Tackled	56	**24**	60	39	37	27	44	27	46	104	59	26	56	28
Yds Lost Tackled	464	**153**	498	323	261	184	272	225	367	708	424	203	394	240
Net Yards	2582	2759	3505	2784	3447	2196	3913	2668	3133	2540	2716	**4096**	2498	3869
Touchdowns	14	12	21	18	18	15	**31**	13	22	19	17	21	13	22
Interceptions	17	25	24	20	27	**15**	**15**	25	22	17	19	20	25	22
Pct. Intercepted	3.8	6.0	4.4	4.0	4.8	3.7	**2.9**	5.9	4.7	3.3	3.7	3.4	5.4	4.1
PUNTS:														
Number	79	70	87	85	75	98	73	82	79	**111**	92	85	78	75
Average	43.3	40.7	40.2	39.9	37.7	38.2	40.0	42.1	**44.8**	41.0	37.1	40.6	40.2	43.6
PUNT RETURNS														
Number	44	**57**	46	43	33	42	31	47	41	44	45	43	26	51
Yards	292	482	252	420	316	361	215	377	287	374	528	397	110	**550**
Average Yards	6.6	8.5	5.5	9.8	9.6	8.6	6.9	8.0	7.0	8.5	**11.7**	9.2	4.2	10.8
Touchdowns	0	0	0	1	1	0	0	0	0	1	**2**	1	0	0
KICKOFF RET.:														
Number	54	50	59	67	**76**	59	56	55	50	53	70	42	**75**	60
Yards	1035	1115	1208	1321	1470	1160	1200	1332	**868**	945	**1548**	757	1302	1175
Average Yards	19.2	22.3	20.5	19.7	19.3	19.7	21.4	**24.2**	17.4	17.8	22.1	18.0	17.4	19.6
Touchdowns	0	**2**	0	0	0	0	0	1	0	0	0	0	0	0
INTERCEPT RET.:														
Number	22	31	17	22	20	28	24	26	24	23	10	**39**	13	19
Yards	294	370	183	190	147	458	319	235	296	124	121	**578**	128	126
Average Yards	13.4	11.9	10.8	8.6	7.4	**16.4**	13.3	9.0	12.3	5.4	12.1	14.8	9.8	6.6
Touchdowns	2	1	1	0	1	3	2	1	1	0	0	**5**	0	0
PENALTIES:														
Number	99	98	112	84	128	84	96	109	96	102	116	95	**83**	94
Yards	763	765	936	658	949	**603**	890	855	738	901	932	691	661	860
FUMBLES:														
Number	31	36	44	30	35	39	31	33	31	34	**25**	32	36	29
Number Lost	16	22	17	17	18	22	14	18	10	10	10	**9**	17	10
POINTS:														
Total	280	352	346	277	254	309	**398**	288	371	256	218	374	239	368
PAT Attempts	30	38	43	32	29	36	**48**	30	42	27	27	43	27	45
PAT Made	29	36	43	31	29	34	**44**	30	41	26	23	41	26	38
FG Attempts	36	**41**	21	25	27	24	28	30	37	31	24	35	24	32
FG Made	23	**28**	15	18	17	17	22	26	26	20	11	25	17	18
Percent FG Made	63.9	68.3	71.4	72.0	63.0	70.8	78.6	**86.7**	70.3	64.5	45.8	71.4	70.8	56.3
Safeties	1	**2**	0	0	0	1	0	0	0	1	0	0	0	0

	DEFENSE													
	ATL.	CHI.	DAL.	DET.	G.B.	L.A.	MINN.	N.O.	NY G	PHIL.	STL.	S.F.	T.B.	WASH.
FIRST DOWNS:														
Total	268	**241**	286	298	313	272	286	331	284	278	304	285	362	316
by Rushing	111	**67**	118	134	135	93	106	104	78	97	125	97	162	103
by Passing	**139**	151	148	148	151	169	155	197	177	156	149	169	177	181
by Penalty	18	23	20	16	27	**10**	25	30	29	25	30	19	23	32
RUSHING:														
Number	485	427	500	519	565	460	481	486	**350**	458	560	406	558	459
Yards	1916	1463	2200	2349	2095	1681	1796	1559	**1284**	1989	2227	1555	2648	1805
Average Yards	4.0	3.4	4.4	4.5	3.7	3.7	3.7	**3.2**	3.7	4.3	4.0	3.8	4.7	3.9
Touchdowns	10	**4**	17	15	16	9	10	11	10	14	17	8	31	14
PASSING:														
Attempts	453	513	464	468	448	539	494	576	587	532	**436**	604	484	532
Completions	241	243	226	279	267	313	276	331	334	260	**215**	324	289	302
Completion Pct.	53.2	**47.4**	48.7	59.6	59.6	58.1	55.9	57.5	56.9	48.3	49.3	53.6	59.7	56.8
Passing Yards	3169	3170	3149	3090	3142	3482	3475	3886	3887	3641	**2992**	3773	3838	3916
Avg. Yds per Att.	6.3	**4.6**	5.4	5.5	6.1	5.5	6.1	5.7	5.4	5.5	5.5	5.1	7.3	6.0
Avg. Yds per Comp.	13.2	13.1	14.0	**11.1**	11.8	**11.1**	12.6	11.7	11.6	14.0	13.9	11.7	13.3	13.0
Times Tackled	26	**62**	53	41	28	39	38	47	59	53	41	51	19	55
Yds Lost Tackled	177	**503**	364	290	222	292	259	343	414	406	355	448	153	424
Net Yards	2992	2667	2785	2800	2920	3190	3216	3543	3473	3235	**2637**	3325	3685	3492
Touchdowns	19	**12**	21	14	31	17	16	21	15	21	21	18	23	21
Interceptions	22	31	17	22	20	28	24	26	24	23	10	**39**	13	19
Pct. Intercepted	4.9	6.0	3.7	4.7	4.5	5.2	4.9	4.5	4.1	4.3	2.3	**6.5**	2.7	3.6
PUNTS:														
Number	83	100	87	68	70	96	75	78	89	97	83	91	**59**	95
Average	41.4	40.9	41.6	41.7	39.6	41.4	40.3	42.5	39.3	**38.7**	42.3	41.4	41.3	41.3
PUNT RETURNS														
Number	47	**23**	41	39	44	47	40	37	41	63	44	49	39	36
Yards	477	**110**	301	517	287	416	356	234	386	634	296	373	414	220
Average Yards	10.1	**4.8**	7.3	13.3	6.5	8.9	8.9	6.3	9.4	10.1	6.7	7.6	10.6	6.1
Touchdowns	3	0	0	2	0	0	0	0	0	2	0	0	3	0
KICKOFF RET.:														
Number	59	64	60	56	62	64	79	**35**	70	62	50	71	46	50
Yards	1190	1376	1358	1096	1181	1282	1532	**662**	1362	1261	886	1598	1009	1005
Average Yards	20.2	21.5	20.6	19.6	19.0	20.0	19.4	18.9	19.5	20.3	**17.7**	22.5	21.9	20.1
Touchdowns	0	0	0	0	0	0	0	0	0	0	0	1	1	0
INTERCEPT RET.:														
Number	17	25	24	20	27	**15**	**15**	25	22	17	19	20	25	22
Yards	198	115	331	311	357	128	**88**	362	218	192	271	205	236	186
Average Yards	11.6	**4.6**	13.8	15.6	13.2	8.5	5.9	14.5	9.9	11.3	14.3	10.3	9.4	8.5
Touchdowns	1	1	2	2	**3**	0	0	0	1	1	2	0	1	0
PENALTIES:														
Number	106	111	91	99	**79**	92	99	104	119	115	86	89	116	115
Yards	834	866	822	781	657	804	806	791	988	884	682	**653**	941	1026
FUMBLES:														
Number	30	27	29	36	32	25	32	37	36	30	**40**	31	39	21
Number Lost	14	16	18	**19**	12	15	18	17	**19**	13	12	10	**19**	9
POINTS:														
Total	280	**187**	337	326	418	267	273	287	236	312	351	247	473	296
PAT Attempts	34	**20**	41	36	52	27	27	34	26	39	40	29	58	35
PAT Made	31	**19**	39	36	48	27	24	32	26	37	37	28	56	35
FG Attempts	26	**22**	30	35	25	31	33	27	25	26	32	25	30	24
FG Made	15	16	16	24	18	24	27	17	18	**13**	24	15	21	17
Percent FG Made	57.7	72.7	53.3	68.6	72.0	77.4	81.8	63.0	72.0	**50.0**	75.0	60.0	70.0	70.8
Safeties	0	0	2	1	2	0	0	0	0	1	1	0	0	0

injury. At mid-season, coach Leeman Bennett cut Pro Bowl tight end Jimmie Giles and wide receiver Kevin House, his best long-distance receiver. The defense gave up 473 points and held opponents to no fewer than 20. Although quarterback Steve Young showed progress, the offense didn't and generally got worse as the season wound down. On merit, Tampa Bay won the right to pick first again in the '87 draft. This time, however, new coach Ray Perkins would make the pick, following the firing of Bennett.

WESTERN DIVISION

San Francisco 49ers — Quarterback Joe Montana aggravated a chronic back injury in the opener and underwent surgery amid predictions that his season and possibly his career had ended. Although Jeff Kemp filled in well and wide receiver Jerry Rice emerged as the league's most dangerous breakaway threat, the 49ers struggled. They were only 5-3-1 when Montana, against his doctor's advice, returned to the lineup. It was a miraculous comeback. He sparked the 49ers to the top of the division in a drive that included wins over three playoff teams in the final three weeks. With all of Montana's heroics, the team lived by its defense, where free safety Ronnie Lott was an inspirational leader, topping the N.F.L. with 10 interceptions, including one he returned for a touchdown against Green Bay after he'd suffered a hairline fracture of his leg.

Los Angeles Rams —Last year's quarterback, Dieter Brock, was out for the year with injuries. Oft-injured Steve Bartkowski tried to get through one more season and lasted less than half. Steve Dils showed he wasn't the answer, though he did beat the Bears in November. When the Rams traded all-pro guard Kent Hill and three draft choices to Houston for the rights to highly touted Jim Everett, they hoped to have their quarterback of the future, then had to rush him into action in week 11. Everett did well behind one of football's best offensive lines. He also had a strong defense to give him the ball and Eric Dickerson to run with it. Dickerson gained more than 1,800 yards for the third time in four years. Still, the Rams dropped their last two games to let themselves be nosed out of the division crown.

Atlanta Falcons — After six weeks, the Falcons were 5-1 and being hailed as a playoff contender. Then the roof fell in. They went 2-7-1 the rest of the way, out of the money, including an embarrassing loss on a blocked punt in week 14 that gave the Colts their first victory. The defense, led by cornerback Scott Case and first-round nose tackle Tony Casillas, played well all season, and guard Bill Fralic was all-pro on offense. But running back Gerald Riggs was less effective than the year before, and quarterback David Archer was erratic and ultimately was injured. After the first three games, the offense averaged less than two touchdowns per game. When the season ended, coach Dan Henning was fired and replaced by his defensive coordinator, Marion Campbell, a former Falcon head man.

New Orleans Saints — Jim Finks, who'd built winners in Minnesota and Chicago, had become New Orleans general manager. Jim Mora, the U.S.F.L.'s most successful coach, took over on the sideline. And the Saints limped out of the starting gate at 1-4. Mora handed out fines, benched and cut starters and, in general, proved to his minions that he was in charge. Under his harsh hand, the Saints became a respectable 6-5 the rest of the way. Running back Rueben Mayes, a third-round draft choice, was the N.F.C.'s top rookie, and linebacker Rickey Jackson played back to his Pro Bowl standard. The team still had never had a winning season, but there was hope.

NEW YORK GIANTS 14-2 Bill Parcells

Scores of Each Game		
28	Dallas	31
20	SAN DIEGO	7
14	L.A.Raiders	9
20	NEW ORLEANS	17
13	St.Louis	6
35	PHILADELPHIA	3
12	Seattle	17
27	WASHINGTON	20
17	DALLAS	14
17	Philadelphia	14
22	Minnesota	20
19	DENVER	16
21	San Francisco	17
24	Washington	14
27	ST.LOUIS	7
55	GREEN BAY	24

Use Name	Pos.	Hgt	Wgt	Age	Int	Pts
Brad Benson	OT	6'3"	270	30		
Damian Johnson	OT-OG	6'5"	290	23		
Karl Nelson	OT	6'6"	285	26		
William Roberts	OT	6'5"	280	24		
Billy Ard	OG	6'3"	270	27		
Chris Godfrey	OG	6'3"	265	28		
Brian Johnston	C	6'3"	275	23		
Bart Oates	C	6'3"	265	27		
Eric Dorsey	DE	6'5"	280	22		
Leonard Marshall	DE	6'3"	285	24		
George Martin	DE	6'4"	255	33	1	6
John Washington	DE	6'4"	275	23		
Jim Burt	NT	6'1"	260	27		
Erik Howard	NT	6'4"	268	21		
Jerome Sally	NT	6'3"	270	27		

Use Name	Pos.	Hgt	Wgt	Age	Int	Pts
Carl Banks	LB	6'4"	235	24		
Harry Carson	LB	6'2"	240	32	1	
Andy Headen	LB	6'5"	242	26	1	
Byron Hunt	LB	6'5"	242	27		
Pepper Johnson	LB	6'3"	248	22	1	
Robbie Jones	LB	6'2"	230	26		
Gary Reasons	LB	6'4"	234	24	2	
Lawrence Taylor	LB	6'3"	243	27		
Mark Collins	DB	5'10"	190	22	1	
Kenny Hill	DB	6'	195	28	3	
Terry Kinard	DB	6'1"	200	26	4	
Greg Lasker	DB	6'	200	21	1	
Elvis Patterson	DB	5'11"	188	25	2	
Herb Welch	DB	5'11"	180	25	2	
Perry Wiliams	DB	6'2"	203	25	4	

George Adams - Knee Injury
Tyrone Davis - Back Injury
David Jordan - Broken Ankle
Curtis McGriff - Leg Injury

Use Name	Pos.	Hgt	Wgt	Age	Int	Pts
Jeff Hostetler	QB	6'3"	212	25		
Jeff Rutledge	QB	6'1"	195	29		
Phil Simms	QB	6'3"	214	29		6
Joe Morris	HB	5'7"	195	25		90
Lee Rouson	HB	6'1"	222	23		18
Maurice Carthon	FB	6'1"	225	25		
Tony Galbreath	FB	6'	228	32		
Bobby Johnson	WR	5'11"	171	24		30
Lionel Manuel	WR	5'11"	180	24		18
Phil McConkey (from GB)	WR	5'10"	170	29		6
Solomon Miller	WR	6'1"	185	21		12
Stacy Robinson	WR	5'11"	186	24		12
Vince Warren	WR	6'	180	23		
Mark Bavaro	TE	6'4"	245	23		24
Zeke Mowatt	TE	6'3"	240	25		12
Raul Allegre	K	5'10"	167	27		105
Joe Cooper	K	5'10"	175	25		
Sean Landeta	K	6'	200	24		
Bob Thomas	K	5'10"	175	34		4

WASHINGTON REDSKINS 12-4 Joe Gibbs

Scores of Each Game		
41	PHILADELPHIA	14
10	L.A.RAIDERS	6
30	San Diego	14
19	SEATTLE	14
14	New Orleans	6
6	Dallas	30
28	ST.LOUIS	21
20	N.Y.Giants	27
44	MINNESOTA	*38
16	Green Bay	7
14	SAN FRANCISCO	6
41	DALLAS	14
20	St.Louis	17
14	N.Y.GIANTS	24
30	Denver	31
21	Philadelphia	14

Use Name	Pos.	Hgt	Wgt	Age	Int	Pts
Joe Jacoby	OT	6'7"	305	27		
Mark May	OT	6'6"	295	26		
Dan McQuaid	OT	6'7"	278	25		
Russ Grimm	OG	6'3"	275	27		
Raleigh McKenzie	OG	6'2"	262	23		
R.C.Thielemann	OG	6'4"	262	31		
Ron Tilton	OG	6'4"	250	23		
Jeff Bostic	C	6'2"	260	27		
Tom Beasley	DE	6'5"	248	32		
Steve Hamilton	DE-DT	6'4"	255	24		
Markus Koch	DE	6'5"	275	23		
Dexter Manley	DE	6'3"	257	27		6
Charles Mann	DE	6'6"	270	25		
Dave Butz	DT	6'7"	295	36		
Darryl Grant	DT	6'1"	275	26		
Dean Hamel	DT	6'3"	275	25		

Use Name	Pos.	Hgt	Wgt	Age	Int	Pts
Shawn Burks	LB	6'1"	230	23		
Monte Coleman	LB	6'2"	230	28		
Calvin Daniels	LB	6'3"	241	27	1	
Mel Kaufman	LB	6'2"	218	28		
Joe Krakowski	LB	6'1"	224	23		
Rich Milot	LB	6'4"	237	29	2	
Neal Olkewicz	LB	6'	233	29	1	
Jeff Paine	LB	6'2"	224	25		
Angelo Snipes (to SD)	LB	6'	215	23		
Todd Bowles	DB	6'2"	203	22	2	
Ken Coffey	DB	6'	198	25	2	
Vernon Dean	DB	5'11"	178	27	1	
Darrell Green	DB	5'8"	170	26	5	
Curtis Jordan	DB	6'2"	205	32	3	
Tim Morrison	DB	6'1"	195	23		
Alvin Walton	DB	6'	180	22		
Barry Wilburn	DB	6'3"	186	22	2	

Use Name	Pos.	Hgt	Wgt	Age	Int	Pts
Jay Schroeder	QB	6'4"	215	25		6
Doug Williams	QB	6'4"	220	31		
Kelvin Bryant	HB	6'2"	195	25		42
Dwight Garner	HB	5'8"	183	21		
Keith Griffin	HB	5'8"	185	24		
Ken Jenkins	HB	5'8"	185	27		
George Rogers	HB	6'2"	229	27		108
Ricky Sanders	HB	5'11"	180	24		12
Rick Badanjek	FB	5'8"	217	24		
Reggie Branch	FB	5'11"	227	23		
Gary Clark	WR	5'9"	173	24		42
Derek Holloway	WR	5'7"	166	25		
Art Monk	WR	6'3"	209	28		24
James Noble	WR	6'	193	23		
Clarence Verdin	WR	5'8"	160	23		
Eric Yarber	WR	5'8"	156	22		
Clint Didier	TE	6'5"	240	27		24
Todd Frain	TE	6'2"	235	24		
Anthony Jones	TE	6'3"	248	26		
Terry Orr	TE	6'3"	227	24		6
Don Warren	TE	6'4"	242	30		6
Jess Atkinson	K	5'9"	168	24		3
Steve Cox	K	6'4"	195	28		9
Mark Moseley (to CLE)	K	5'11"	204	38		91
Max Zendejas	K	5'11"	184	22		50

DALLAS COWBOYS 7-9 Tom Landry

Scores of Each Game		
31	N.Y.GIANTS	28
31	Detroit	7
35	ATLANTA	37
31	St.Louis	7
14	Denver	29
30	WASHINGTON	6
17	Philadelphia	14
37	ST.LOUIS	6
11	N.Y.Giants	17
13	L.A.RAIDERS	17
24	San Diego	21
14	Washington	41
14	SEATTLE	31
10	L.A.Rams	29
21	PHILADELPHIA	23
10	CHICAGO	24

Use Name	Pos.	Hgt	Wgt	Age	Int	Pts
Jim Cooper	OT	6'5"	268	30		
Phil Pozderac	OT	6'9"	283	26		
Howard Richards	OT	6'6"	269	27		
Brian Baldinger	OG	6'4"	262	27		
Crawford Ker	OG	6'3"	285	24		
Nate Nelson	OG	6'3"	317	24		
Glen Titensor	OG	6'4"	270	28		
Tom Rafferty	C	6'3"	262	32		
Mark Tuinei	C	6'5"	283	26		
Jesse Baker	DE	6'5"	271	29		
Kevin Brooks	DE	6'6"	273	23		
Jim Jeffcoat	DE	6'5"	260	25		
Too Tall Jones	DE	6'9"	273	25		
Bob Otto	DE	6'6"	251	23		
Kurt Ploeger (to BUF)	DE	6'5"	259	23		
John Dutton	DT	6'7"	261	35		
Don Smerek	DT	6'7"	262	28		
Randy White	DT	6'4"	265	33		

Use Name	Pos.	Hgt	Wgt	Age	Int	Pts
Steve DeOssie	LB	6'2"	245	23		
Mike Hegman	LB	6'1"	227	33		
Garth Jax	LB	6'2"	225	22		
Eugene Lockhart	LB	6'2"	235	25	1	
Jesse Penn	LB	6'3"	218	23		
Jeff Rohrer	LB	6'3"	227	27		
Vince Albritton	DB	6'2"	210	24		
Bill Bates	DB	6'1"	204	25		
Michael Downs	DB	6'3"	204	27	6	
Ron Fellows	DB	6'	173	27	5	6
Cornell Gowdy	DB	6'	192	22		
Manny Hendrix	DB	5'10"	178	21		
Johnny Holloway	DB	5'11"	182	22	1	
Victor Scott	DB	6'	203	24	1	
Everson Walls	DB	6'1"	193	26	3	

Norm Granger - Hamstring Injury
Brian Salonen - Groin Injury
Kurt Petersen - Knee Injury

Use Name	Pos.	Hgt	Wgt	Age	Int	Pts
Regie Collier	QB	6'3"	207	25		
Paul McDonald	QB	6'2"	185	28		
Steve Pelluer	QB	6'4"	208	24		6
Danny White	QB	6'2"	197	34		6
Darryl Clack	HB	5'10"	218	22		
Tony Dorsett	HB	5'11"	189	32		36
Robert Lavette	HB	5'11"	190	22		6
Herschel Walker	HB	6'1"	223	24		84
Todd Fowler	FB	6'3"	221	24		
Timmy Newsome	FB	6'1"	237	28		30
Gordon Banks	WR	5'10"	173	28		
Tony Hill	WR	6'2"	205	30		18
Karl Powe	WR	6'2"	178	24		
Mike Renfro	WR	6'	187	31		18
Mike Sherrard	WR	6'2"	187	23		30
Thornton Chandler	TE	6'5"	245	22		12
Doug Cosbie	TE	6'6"	238	30		6
Mike Saxon	K	6'3"	188	24		
Rafael Septien	K	5'10"	176	32		88

PHILADELPHIA EAGLES 5-10-1 Buddy Ryan

Scores of Each Game		
14	Washington	41
10	Chicago	13
7	DENVER	33
34	L.A.RAMS	20
16	Atlanta	0
3	N.Y.Giants	35
14	DALLAS	17
23	SAN DIEGO	7
10	St.Louis	13
14	N.Y.GIANTS	17
11	DETROIT	13
20	Seattle	24
33	L.A.Raiders	*27
10	ST.LOUIS	*10
23	Dallas	21
14	WASHINGTON	21

Use Name	Pos.	Hgt	Wgt	Age	Int	Pts
Mike Black	OT-OG	6'4"	290	22		
Joe Conwell	OT	6'5"	275	25		
Jim Gilmore	OT	6'5"	262	23		
Tom Jelesky	OT	6'6"	275	25		
Leonard Mitchell	OT	6'7"	295	27		
Ron Baker	OG	6'4"	274	31		
Nick Haden	OG-C	6'2"	270	23		
Bob Landsee	OG-OT	6'4"	273	22		
Ken Reeves	OG-OT	6'5"	275	24		
Adam Schreiber	OG-C	6'4"	270	24		
Matt Darwin	C	6'4"	260	23		
Gerry Feehery	C	6'2"	270	26		
Greg Brown	DE	6'5"	265	29		2
Clyde Simmons	DE	6'6"	258	22		
Thomas Strauthers	DE	6'4"	264	25		
Jeff Tupper	DE	6'5"	269	23		
Reggie White	DE-DT	6'5"	285	24		
Ken Clarke	DT	6'2"	275	30		
Reggie Singletary	DT	6'3"	272	22		

Use Name	Pos.	Hgt	Wgt	Age	Int	Pts
Garry Cobb	LB	6'2"	230	29	1	
Dwayne Jiles	LB	6'4"	242	24		
Alonzo Johnson	LB	6'3"	222	23	3	
Seth Joyner	LB	6'2"	241	21	1	
Rich Kraynak	LB	6'1"	230	25		
Byron Lee	LB	6'2"	230	21		
Mike Reichenbach	LB	6'2"	238	24		
Jody Schulz	LB	6'3"	235	26	1	
Evan Cooper	DB	5'11"	184	24	3	
Elbert Foules	DB	5'11"	185	25	1	
William Frizzell	DB	6'3"	198	23		
Terry Hoage	DB	6'3"	198	24	1	
Wes Hopkins	DB	6'1"	212	24		
Andre Waters	DB	5'11"	185	24	6	
Brenard Wilson	DB	6'	185	31		
Roynell Young	DB	6'1"	185	28	6	

Use Name	Pos.	Hgt	Wgt	Age	Int	Pts
Matt Cavanaugh	QB	6'2"	212	29		
Randall Cunningham	QB	6'4"	192	23		30
Ron Jaworski	QB	6'2"	199	35		
Kyle Mackey	QB	6'3"	219	24		
Keith Byars	HB	6'1"	230	22		6
Charles Crawford	HB	6'2"	235	22		6
Junior Tautalatasi	HB	5'10"	205	24		12
Michael Haddix	FB	6'2"	227	24		
Anthony Toney	FB	6'	227	23		6
Mike Waters	FB	6'2"	225	24		
Gregg Garrity	WR	5'10"	169	24		6
Kenny Jackson	WR	6'	180	24		36
Ron Johnson	WR	6'3"	186	27		6
Phil Smith	WR	6'3"	186	25		
Mike Quick	WR	6'2"	190	27		54
Byron Darby	TE	6'4"	262	26		
Dave Little	TE	6'2"	236	25		
John Spagnola	TE	6'4"	242	29		6
Paul McFadden	K	5'11"	163	24		86
John Teltschik	K	6'2"	215	22		

ST. LOUIS CARDINALS 4-11-1 Gene Stallings

Scores of Each Game		
10	L.A.RAMS	16
13	Atlanta	33
10	Buffalo	17
7	DALLAS	31
6	N.Y.GIANTS	13
30	Tampa Bay	19
21	Washington	28
6	Dallas	37
13	PHILADELPHIA	10
17	San Francisco	43
7	NEW ORLEANS	16
23	KANSAS CITY	14
17	WASHINGTON	20
10	Philadelphia	*10
7	N.Y.Giants	27
21	TAMPA BAY	17

Use Name	Pos.	Hgt	Wgt	Age	Int	Pts
Ray Brown	OT-OG	6'5"	257	23		
Tootie Robbins	OT	6'5"	302	28		
Luis Sharpe	OT	6'4"	260	26		
Lance Smith	OT	6'2"	262	22		
Joe Bostic	OG	6'3"	268	29		
Doug Dawson	OG	6'3"	267	24		
Derek Kennard	OG	6'3"	285	23		
Gene Chilton	C	6'3"	271	22		
Randy Clark	C	6'3"	270	29		
Rob Monaco	C	6'3"	283	24		
Mike Ruether	C	6'4"	275	23		
Al Baker	DE	6'6"	270	29		
Bob Clasby	DE	6'5"	260	25		
Gary Dulin	DE	6'4"	275	29		
Van Hughes	DE	6'3"	280	25		
Stafford Mays	DE	6'2"	255	28		
Mark Duda	NT	6'3"	279	25		
David Galloway	NT	6'3"	279	27		

Use Name	Pos.	Hgt	Wgt	Age	Int	Pts
Charlie Baker	LB	6'2"	234	28		
Anthony Bell	LB	6'3"	231	22		
Rick DiBernardo	LB	6'3"	225	22		
E.J.Junior	LB	6'3"	235	26		
Ron Monaco	LB	6'1"	225	23		
Niko Noga	LB	6'1"	235	24		
Freddie Joe Nunn	LB	6'4"	228	24		
Carl Carter	DB	5'11"	180	22	2	
Cedric Mack	DB	6'	194	25	4	
Leonard Smith	DB	5'11"	202	25	1	
Wayne Smith	DB	6'	170	29	1	
Dennis Thurman	DB	5'11"	179	30		
Lionel Washington	DB	6'	188	25	2	
Lonnie Young	DB	6'1"	182	23		

Bob Harris - Ankle Injury
Scott Bergold - Back Injury
Curtis Greer - Knee Injury
Randy Love - Back Injury
Lee Nelson - Back Injury

Use Name	Pos.	Hgt	Wgt	Age	Int	Pts
Kent Austin	QB	6'1"	195	23		
Neil Lomax	QB	6'3"	215	27		6
Cliff Stoudt	QB	6'4"	215	31		
Ottis Anderson (to NYG)	HB	6'2"	225	29		2
Stump Mitchell	HB	5'9"	188	27		30
Vai Sikahema	HB	5'9	191	24		18
Earl Ferrell	FB	6'	224	28		18
Broderick Sargent	FB	5'10"	215	23		
Ron Wolfley	FB	6'	222	23		
Chas Fox	WR	5'11"	180	22		6
Roy Green	WR	6'	195	29		36
Scott Holman	WR	6'2"	195	23		
Ron Holmes	WR	5'10"	180	25		
Troy Johnson	R	6'1"	175	23		
J.T.Smith	WR	6'2"	185	30		36
Eric Swanson	WR	5'11"	186	23		
Pat Tilley	WR	5'10"	178	33		
Cap Boso	TE	6'3"	224	23		
Doug Marsh	TE	6'3"	238	28		
Jay Novacek	TE	6'4"	217	23		
Robert Stallings	TE	6'6"	250	22		
Evan Arapostathis	K	5'9"	160	22		
Greg Cater	K	6'	191	29		
John Lee	K	5'11"	182	22		38
Eric Schubert	K	5'8"	193	24		18

* Overtime

NEW YORK GIANTS

RUSHING

Last Name	No.	Yds	Avg	TD
Morris	341	1516	4.4	14
Carthon	72	260	3.6	0
Rouson	54	179	3.3	2
Simms	43	72	1.7	1
Galbreath	16	61	3.8	0
B. Johnson	2	28	14.0	0
Manuel	1	25	25.0	0
Rutledge	3	19	6.3	0
Miller	1	3	3.0	0
Hostetler	1	1	1.0	0

RECEIVING

Last Name	No.	Yds	Avg	TD
Bavaro	66	1001	15.2	4
Galbreath	33	268	8.1	0
B. Johnson	31	534	17.2	5
Robinson	29	494	17.0	2
Morris	21	233	11.1	1
McConkey	16	279	17.4	1
Carthon	16	67	4.2	0
Manuel	11	181	16.5	3
Mowatt	10	119	11.9	2
Miller	9	144	16.0	2
Rouson	8	121	15.1	1
Carson	1	13	13.0	1

PUNT RETURNS

Last Name	No.	Yds	Avg	TD
McConkey	32	253	7.9	0
Manuel	3	22	7.3	0
Collins	3	11	3.7	0
Galbreath	3	1	0.3	0

KICKOFF RETURNS

Last Name	No.	Yds	Avg	TD
McConkey	24	471	19.6	0
Collins	11	204	18.5	0
Miller	7	111	15.9	0
Hill	5	61	12.2	0
Rouson	2	21	10.5	0
Lasker	1	0	0.0	0

PASSING — PUNTING — KICKING

PASSING	Cmp	Att	%	Yds	Yd/Att	TD	Int—	%	Rk
Simms	468	259	55	3487	7.45	21	22—	5	3
Rutledge	3	1	33	13	4.33	1	0—	0	
Galbreath	1	0	0	0	0.00	0	0—	0	

PUNTING	No	Avg
Landeta	79	44.8

KICKING	XP	Att	%	FG	Att	%
Allegre	33	33	100	24	32	67
Thomas	4	4	100	0	1	0
Cooper	4	4	100	2	4	50

WASHINGTON REDSKINS

RUSHING

Last Name	No.	Yds	Avg	TD
Rogers	303	1203	4.0	18
Bryant	69	258	3.7	4
Griffin	62	197	3.2	0
Schroeder	36	47	1.3	1
Monk	4	27	6.8	0

RECEIVING

Last Name	No.	Yds	Avg	TD
Clark	74	1265	17.1	7
Monk	73	1068	14.6	4
Bryant	43	449	10.4	3
Didier	34	691	20.3	4
Warren	20	164	8.2	1
Sanders	14	286	20.4	2
Griffin	11	110	10.0	0
Orr	3	45	15.0	1
Rogers	3	24	8.0	0
Holloway	1	7	7.0	0

PUNT RETURNS

Last Name	No.	Yds	Avg	TD
Jenkins	28	270	9.6	0
Green	12	120	10.0	0
Yarber	9	143	15.9	0
Clark	1	14	14.0	0
Milot	1	3	3.0	0

KICKOFF RETURNS

Last Name	No.	Yds	Avg	TD
Jenkins	27	554	20.5	0
Verdin	12	240	20.0	0
Griffin	8	156	19.5	0
Garner	7	142	20.3	0
Holloway	3	44	14.7	0
Orr	2	31	15.5	0
Krakowski	1	8	8.0	0

PASSING — PUNTING — KICKING

PASSING	Att	Cmp	%	Yds	Yd/Att	TD	Int—	%	Rk
Schroeder	541	276	51	4109	7.60	22	22—	4	4
Williams	1	0	0	0	0.0	0	0—	0	

PUNTING	No	Avg
Cox	75	43.6

KICKING	XP	ATT	%	FG	ATT	%
Zendejas	23	28	82	9	14	64
Cox	0	0	0	3	6	50

DALLAS COWBOYS

RUSHING

Last Name	No.	Yds	Avg	TD
Dorsett	184	748	4.1	5
Walker	151	737	4.9	12
Pelluer	41	255	6.2	1
Newsome	34	110	3.2	2
Collier	6	53	8.8	0
Clack	4	19	4.8	0
D. White	8	16	2.0	1
Sherrard	2	11	5.5	0
Cosbie	1	9	9.0	0
Lavette	10	6	0.6	0
Fowler	6	5	0.8	0

RECEIVING

Last Name	No.	Yds	Avg	TD
Walker	76	837	11.0	2
Hill	49	770	15.7	3
Newsome	48	421	8.8	3
Sherrard	41	744	18.1	5
Cosbie	28	312	11.1	1
Dorsett	25	267	10.7	1
Renfro	22	325	14.8	3
Banks	17	202	11.9	0
Chandler	6	57	9.5	2
Lavette	5	31	6.2	1
Fowler	1	19	19.0	0
Clack	1	18	18.0	0

PUNT RETURNS

Last Name	No.	Yds	Avg	TD
Banks	27	160	5.9	0
Lavette	18	92	5.1	0
Holloway	1	0	0.0	0

KICKOFF RETURNS

Last Name	No.	Yds	Avg	TD
Lavette	36	699	19.4	0
Clack	19	421	22.2	0
Banks	1	56	56.0	0
Newsome	2	32	16.0	0
Tuinei	1	0	0.0	0

PASSING — PUNTING — KICKING

PASSING	Att	Cmp	%	Yds	Yd/Att	TD	Int—	%	Rk
Pelluer	378	215	57	2727	7.21	8	17—	5	9
D. White	153	95	62	1157	7.56	12	5—	3	
Collier	15	8	53	96	6.40	1	2—	13	
Renfro	1	1	100	23	23.00	0	0—	0	

PUNTING	No	Avg
Saxon	87	40.2

KICKING	XP	Att	%	FG	Att	%
Septien	43	43	100	15	21	71

PHILADELPHIA EAGLES

RUSHING

Last Name	No.	Yds	Avg	TD
Byars	177	577	3.3	1
Cunningham	66	540	8.2	5
Toney	69	285	4.1	1
Haddix	79	276	3.5	0
Tautalatasi	51	163	3.2	0
Crawford	28	88	3.1	1
Jaworski	13	33	2.5	0
Cavanaugh	9	26	2.9	0
M. Waters	5	8	1.6	0
K. Jackson	1	6	6.0	0
Teltschik	1	0	0.0	0

RECEIVING

Last Name	No.	Yds	Avg	TD
Quick	60	939	15.7	9
Tautalatasi	41	325	7.9	2
Spagnola	39	397	10.2	1
K. Jackson	30	506	16.9	6
Haddix	26	150	5.8	0
Little	14	132	9.4	0
Toney	13	177	13.6	0
Garrity	12	227	18.9	0
R. Johnson	11	207	18.8	1
Byars	11	44	4.0	0
Smith	6	94	15.7	0
M. Waters	2	27	13.5	0
Darby	2	16	8.0	0

PUNT RETURNS

Last Name	No.	Yds	Avg	TD
Garrity	17	187	11.0	1
Cooper	16	139	8.7	0
M. Waters	7	30	4.3	0
Smith	4	18	4.5	0

KICKOFF RETURNS

Last Name	No.	Yds	Avg	TD
Crawford	27	497	18.4	0
Tautalatasi	18	344	19.1	0
Byars	2	47	23.5	0
Cooper	2	42	21.0	0
Quick	2	6	3.0	0
Schulz	1	9	9.0	0
Simmons	1	0	0.0	0

PASSING — PUNTING — KICKING

PASSING	Att	Cmp	%	Yds	Yd/Att	TD	Int—	%	Rk
Jaworski	245	128	52	1405	5.73	8	6—	2	8
Cunningham	209	111	53	1391	6.66	8	7—	3	
Cavanaugh	58	28	48	397	6.84	2	4—	7	
Byars	2	1	50	55	27.50	1	0—	0	

PUNTING	No	Avg
Teltschik	109	41.2
Cunningham	2	27.0

KICKING	XP	Att	%	FG	Att	%
McFadden	26	27	96	20	31	65

ST. LOUIS CARDINALS

RUSHING

Last Name	No.	Yds	Avg	TD
Mitchell	174	800	4.6	5
Ferrell	124	548	4.4	0
Anderson	75	237	3.2	3
Lomax	35	148	4.2	1
Sikahema	16	62	3.9	0
Stoudt	7	53	7.6	0
Wolfley	8	19	2.4	0
Marsh	1	5	5.0	0
Green	2	-4	-2.0	0
Austin	1	0	0.0	0

RECEIVING

Last Name	No.	Yds	Avg	TD
J. Smith	80	1014	12.7	6
Ferrell	56	434	7.8	3
Green	42	517	12.3	6
Mitchell	41	276	6.7	0
Marsh	25	313	12.5	0
T. Johnson	14	203	14.5	0
Anderson	19	137	7.2	0
Fox	5	59	11.8	1
Sikahema	10	99	9.9	1
Tilley	3	51	17.0	0
Holman	3	41	13.7	0
Wolfley	2	32	16.0	0
Sargent	1	8	8.0	0
Novacek	1	2	2.0	0

PUNT RETURNS

Last Name	No.	Yds	Avg	TD
Sikahema	43	522	12.1	2
J. Smith	1	6	6.0	0
Carter	1	0	0.0	0

KICKOFF RETURNS

Last Name	No.	Yds	Avg	TD
Sikahema	37	847	22.9	0
Swanson	10	206	20.6	0
Mitchell	6	203	33.8	0
Fox	6	161	26.8	0
Johnson	3	46	15.3	0
Ferrell	3	41	13.7	0
Sargent	2	27	13.5	0
Carter	2	21	10.5	0
Holmes	1	2	2.0	0
Wolfley	0	-6	-6.0	0

PASSING — PUNTING — KICKING

PASSING	Att	Cmp	%	Yds	Yd/Att	TD	Int—	%	Rk
Lomax	421	240	57	2583	6.14	13	12—	3	4
Stoudt	91	52	57	542	5.96	3	7—	8	
Mitchell	3	1	33	15	5.00	1	0—	0	
Arapostathis	1	0	0	0	0.0	0	0—	0	

PUNTING	No	Avg
Cater	62	36.6
Arapostathis	30	38.0

KICKING	XP	Att	%	FG	Att	%
Lee	14	17	82	8	13	62
Schubert	9	10	90	3	11	27

CHICAGO BEARS 14-2 Mike Ditka

Scores of Each Game		
41	CLEVELAND	31
13	PHILADELPHIA	*10
25	Green Bay	12
44	Cincinnati	7
23	MINNESOTA	0
20	Houston	7
7	Minnesota	23
13	DETROIT	7
17	L.A.RAMS	20
23	Tampa Bay	3
13	Atlanta	10
12	GREEN BAY	10
13	PITTSBURGH	*10
48	TAMPA BAY	14
16	Detroit	13
24	Dallas	10

Use Name	Pos.	Hgt	Wgt	Age	Int	Pts
Paul Blair	OT	6'4"	295	23		
Jim Covert	OT	6'4"	271	26		
Keith Van Horne	OT	6'6"	280	28		
Kurt Becker	OG	6'5"	267	27		
Mark Bortz	OG	6'6"	269	25		
Stefan Humphries	OG	6'3"	268	24		
Tom Thayer	OG-C	6'4"	261	25		
Jay Hilgenberg	C	6'3"	258	27		
Larry Rubens	C	6'1"	262	27		
Richard Dent	DE	6'5"	263	25		
Dan Hampton	DE	6'5"	267	28		2
Mike Hartenstine	DE	6'3"	254	33		
Steve McMichael	DT	6'2"	260	28	1	2
William Perry	DT	6'2"	325	23		
Henry Waechter	DT	6'5"	275	27		
Brian Cabral	LB	6'1"	232	30		
Al Harris	LB	6'5"	253	29		
Wilber Marshall	LB	6'1"	225	24	5	12
Jim Morrissey	LB	6'3"	215	23		
Dan Rains	LB	6'1"	232	30		
Ron Rivera	LB	6'3"	239	24		
Mike Singletary	LB	6'	228	27	1	
Otis Wilson	LB	6'2"	232	28	2	
Todd Bell	DB	6'1"	205	27	1	
Maurice Douglass	DB	5'11"	200	22		
Dave Duerson	DB	6'1"	203	25	6	
Gary Fencik	DB	6'1"	196	32	3	
Shaun Gayle	DB	5'11"	193	24	1	
Vestee Jackson	DB	6'	196	23	3	
Reggie Phillips	DB	5'10"	170	25	1	
Mike Richardson	DB	6'	188	25	7	
Doug Flutie	QB	5'9"	176	24		6
Steve Fuller	QB	6'4"	195	29		
Jim McMahon	QB	6'1"	190	27		6
Mike Tomczak	QB	6'1"	195	23		18
Neal Anderson	HB	5'11"	210	22		6
Dennis Gentry	HB-WR	5'8"	181	27		18
Walter Payton	HB	5'11"	202	32		66
Thomas Sanders	HB	5'11"	203	24		30
Matt Suhey	FB	5'11"	216	28		12
Calvin Thomas	FB	5'11"	245	26		
Lew Barnes	WR	5'8"	163	23		6
Willie Gault	WR	6'	183	25		30
Keith Ortego	WR	6'	180	23		12
Clay Pickering	WR	6'5"	215	25		
Emery Moorehead	TE	6'2"	220	32		6
Tim Wrightman	TE	6'3"	237	26		
Maury Buford	K	6'1"	196	26		
Kevin Butler	K	6'1"	195	24		120

Doug Donley - Wrist Injury
Leslie Frazier - Knee Injury
Andy Frederick - Foot Injury
Dennis McKinnon - Knee Injury

MINNESOTA VIKINGS 9-7 Jerry Burns

Scores of Each Game		
10	DETROIT	13
23	Tampa Bay	10
31	PITTSBURGH	7
42	GREEN BAY	7
0	Chicago	23
27	San Francisco	*24
23	CHICAGO	7
20	CLEVELAND	23
38	Washington	*44
24	Detroit	10
20	N.Y.GIANTS	22
20	Cincinnati	24
45	TAMPA BAY	13
32	Green Bay	6
10	Houston	23
33	NEW ORLEANS	17

Use Name	Pos.	Hgt	Wgt	Age	Int	Pts
Dave Huffman	OT	6'6"	284	29		
Tim Irwin	OT	6'6"	288	27		
Gary Zimmerman	OT	6'6"	277	24		
Brent Boyd	OG	6'3"	280	29		
Mark MacDonald	OG	6'4"	267	25		
Curtis Rouse	OG	6'3"	335	26		
Terry Tausch	OG	6'5"	276	27		
Jim Hough	C-OG	6'2"	269	30		
Kirk Lowdermilk	C	6'3"	269	23		
Dennis Swilley	C	6'3"	266	31		
Doug Martin	DE	6'3"	264	29		
Mark Mullaney	DE	6'6"	248	33		
Gerald Robinson	DE	6'3"	256	23		
Neil Elshire	DT	6'6"	262	28		
Keith Millard	DT	6'5"	262	24	1	
Tim Newton	DT	6'	287	23		
Joe Phillips	DT	6'5"	278	23		
Mike Stensrud	DT	6'5"	280	30		
Walker Lee Ashley	LB	6'	237	26		
Chris Doleman	LB	6'5"	250	24	1	6
David Howard	LB	6'2"	232	24		
Chris Martin	LB	6'2"	239	25		
Jesse Solomon	LB	6'	235	22	2	
Scott Studwell	LB	6'2"	230	32	1	
Rufus Bess	DB	5'9"	189	30	1	
Joey Browner	DB	6'2"	212	26	4	6
David Evans	DB	6'	178	27		
Neal Guggemos	DB	6'1"	187	22		
John Harris	DB	6'2"	198	30	3	
Issiac Holt	DB	6'1"	200	23	8	
Carl Lee	DB	6'	187	25	3	
Mike Lush (from IND)	DB	6'1"	195	28		
Kyle Morrell	DB	6'2"	189	22		
Willie Teal	DB	5'10"	192	28		
Steve Bono	QB	6'4"	211	24		
Tommy Kramer	QB	6'2"	205	31		6
Wade Wilson	QB	6'3"	213	27		6
Darrin Nelson	HB	5'9"	189	27		42
Allen Rice	HB	5'10"	204	24		30
Alfred Anderson	FB	6'1"	220	25		24
Ted Brown	FB-HB	5'10"	212	29		24
Wayne Wilson (to NO)	FB	6'3"	220	28		
Anthony Carter	WR	5'11"	175	25		42
Jim Gustafson	WR	6'1"	181	25		12
Hassan Jones	WR	6'	195	22		24
Leo Lewis	WR	5'8"	170	29		12
Buster Rhymes	WR	6'2"	218	24		
Carl Hilton	TE	6'3"	232	22		
Steve Jordan	TE	6'4"	239	25		36
Mike Mularkey	TE	6'4"	234	24		12
Greg Coleman	K	6'	184	31		
Chuck Nelson	K	6'	172	26		110

DETROIT LIONS 5-11 Darryl Rogers

Scores of Each Game		
13	Minnesota	10
7	DALLAS	31
20	TAMPA BAY	24
21	Cleveland	24
24	HOUSTON	13
21	Green Bay	14
10	L.A.Rams	14
7	Chicago	13
17	CINCINNATI	24
10	MINNESOTA	24
13	Philadelphia	11
38	Tampa Bay	17
40	GREEN BAY	44
17	Pittsburgh	27
13	CHICAGO	16
6	ATLANTA	20

Use Name	Pos.	Hgt	Wgt	Age	Int	Pts
Lomas Brown	OT	6'4"	282	23		
Harvey Salem (from HOU)	OT-OG	6'6"	285	25		
Rich Strenger	OT	6'7"	285	26		
Scott Barrows	OG-C	6'2"	278	23		
Chris Dieterich	OG-OT	6'3"	275	28		
Keith Dorney	OG-OT	6'5"	285	28		
Steve Kenney	OG	6'4"	262	30		
Kevin Glover	C-OG	6'2"	267	23		
Steve Mott	C	6'3"	270	25		
Tom Turnure	C	6'4"	253	29		
Leon Evans	DE	6'5"	282	24		
Keith Ferguson	DE	6'5"	260	27	1	
William Gay	DE	6'5"	260	31		
Curtis Green	DE-DT	6'3"	265	29		
Steve Baack	NT-OG	6'4"	265	25		
Eric Williams	NT	6'4"	280	24	1	
Paul Butcher	LB	6'	219	22		
Mike Cofer	LB	6'5"	245	26		
August Curley	LB	6'3"	226	26		
James Harrell	LB	6'1"	230	29		
James Johnson	LB	6'2"	236	24		
Angelo King	LB	6'1"	222	28		
Vernon Maxwell	LB	6'2"	235	24		
Shelton Robinson	LB	6'2"	236	25		
Jimmy Williams	LB	6'3"	230	25	2	
John Bostic	DB	5'10"	178	23	1	
Duane Galloway	DB	5'8"	181	24	4	
William Graham	DB	5'11"	191	26		
James Griffin	DB	6'2"	197	24	2	
Demetrious Johnson	DB	5'11"	190	25	2	
Bruce McNorton	DB	5'11"	175	27	4	
Devon Mitchell	DB	6'1"	194	23	5	
Bobby Watkins	DB	5'10"	184	26		
Joe Ferguson	QB	6'1"	195	36		
Eric Hipple	QB	6'2"	196	28		
Chuck Long	QB	6'4"	211	23		
Herman Hunter	HB	6'1"	193	25		6
Gary James	HB	5'10"	214	22		18
Alvin Moore	HB	6'	194	27		
Oscar Smith	HB	5'9"	203	23		
James Jones	FB	6'2"	229	25		54
Scott Williams	FB	6'2"	234	24		12
Carl Bland	WR	5'11"	182	25		12
Jeff Chadwik	WR	6'3"	190	25		30
Pete Mandley	WR	5'10"	191	25		6
Leonard Thompson	WR	5'11"	192	34		30
Jimmie Giles (from TB)	TE	6'3"	240	31		18
David Lewis	TE	6'3"	235	25		6
Rob Rubick	TE	6'3"	234	25		
Jim Arnold	K	6'3"	211	25		
Mike Black	K	6'2"	197	25		
Eddie Murray	K	5'10"	175	30		85

Arnold Brown - Broken Arm
Mark Nichols - Knee Injury

GREEN BAY PACKERS 4-12 Forrest Gregg

Scores of Each Game		
3	HOUSTON	31
10	New Orleans	24
12	CHICAGO	25
7	Minnesota	42
28	CINCINNATI	34
14	DETROIT	21
17	Cleveland	14
17	SAN FRANCISCO	31
3	Pittsburgh	27
7	WASHINGTON	16
31	TAMPA BAY	7
10	Chicago	12
44	Detroit	40
6	MINNESOTA	32
21	Tampa Bay	7
24	N.Y.Giants	55

Use Name	Pos.	Hgt	Wgt	Age	Int	Pts
Greg Feasel	OT	6'7"	301	27		
Ruben Mendoza	OT	6'4"	290	23		
Tom Neville	OT-OG	6'5"	306	24		
Ken Ruettgers	OT	6'5"	280	24		
Karl Swanke	OT-C	6'6"	262	28		
Alan Veingrad	OT-OG	6'5"	277	23		
Ron Hallstrom	OG	6'6"	290	27		
Bill Cherry	C-OG	6'4"	277	25		
Rich Moran	C-OG	6'3"	275	24		
Mark Cannon	C	6'3"	258	24		
Robert Brown	DE	6'2"	267	26		
Alphonso Carreker	DE	6'6"	271	24		
Donnie Humphrey	DE	6'3"	296	25		
Ezra Johnson	DE	6'4"	265	30		
Matt Koart	DE	6'5"	258	22		
Ben Thomas (from NE)	DE-NT	6'4"	275	25		
Charles Martin	NT	6'4"	280	27		
John Anderson	LB	6'3"	229	30	1	
Burnell Dent	LB	6'1"	236	23		
John Dorsey	LB	6'3"	243	26		
Tim Harris	LB	6'5"	236	21		
Bobby Leopold	LB	6'1"	224	28	1	
Brian Noble	LB	6'3"	253	23		
Jeff Schuh (to MIN)	LB	6'2"	234	28		
Randy Scott	LB	6'1"	228	27		
Miles Turpin	LB	6'4"	232	22		
Mike Weddington	LB	6'4"	245	25		
Ed Berry	DB	5'10"	183	22		
Mossy Cade	DB	6'1"	198	24	4	
Tom Flynn (to NYG)	DB	6'	194	24	2	
Tiger Greene	DB	6'	194	24	2	
David Greenwood	DB	6'3"	210	26		
Gary Hayes	DB	5'10"	180	29		
Mark Lee	DB	5'11"	189	28	9	
Tim Lewis	DB	5'11"	195	24		
Ken Stills	DB	5'10"	187	22	1	6
Elbert Watts	DB	6'2"	205	23	1	
Vince Ferragamo	QB	6'3"	217	32		
Chuck Fusina	QB	6'1"	195	29		
Joe Shield	QB	6'1"	185	24		
Randy Wright	QB	6'2"	203	25		6
Paul Ott Carruth	HB	6'1"	220	25		24
Kenneth Davis	HB	5'10"	209	24		6
Gary Ellerson	HB	5'11"	219	23		18
Eddie Lee Ivery	HB	6'1"	206	29		6
Jessie Clark	FB	6'	228	26		
Gerry Ellis	FB	5'11"	235	28		12
Phillip Epps	WR	5'10"	165	26		24
Nolan Franz	WR	6'2"	183	26		
James Lofton	WR	6'3"	197	30		24
Walter Stanley	WR	5'9"	179	23		18
Mark Lewis	TE	6'2"	237	25		12
Mike Moffitt	TE	6'4"	211	23		
Dan Ross	TE	6'4"	240	29		
Ed West	TE	6'1"	243	25		6
Al Del Greco	K	5'10"	191	24		80
Bill Renner	K	6'	198	27		
Don Braken	K	6'	211	24		

Daryll Jones - Injury
Mark Murphy - Foot Injury
Keith Uecker - Knee Injury

TAMPA BAY BUCCANEERS 2-14 Leeman Bennett

Scores of Each Game		
7	SAN FRANCISCO	31
10	MINNESOTA	23
24	Detroit	20
20	ATLANTA	*23
20	L.A.Rams	*26
19	ST.LOUIS	30
7	New Orleans	38
20	Kansas City	27
34	BUFFALO	28
3	CHICAGO	23
7	Green Bay	31
17	DETROIT	38
13	Minnesota	45
14	Chicago	48
7	GREEN BAY	21
17	St. Louis	21

Use Name	Pos.	Hgt	Wgt	Age	Int	Pts
Ron Heller	OT	6'6"	280	24		6
J.D.Maarleveld	OT	6'6"	300	24		
Marvin Powell	OT	6'5"	270	31		
Greg Robinson	OT	6'5"	285	23		
Rob Taylor	OT	6'6"	290	25		
Sean Farrell	OG	6'3"	260	26		
Rick Mallory	OG	6'2"	265	25		
George Yarno	OG	6'2"	265	29		
Randy Grimes	C	6'4"	270	26		
John Cannon	DE	6'5"	260	26		
Ron Holmes	DE	6'4"	265	23		
Kevin Kellin	DE	6'6"	265	26		
Tyrone Keys	DE	6'7"	270	26		
David Logan	NT	6'2"	250	29		
Karl Morgan	NT	6'1"	255	25		
Bob Nelson	NT	6'4"	265	27		
Scot Brantley	LB	6'1"	230	28	2	
Keith Browner	LB	6'6"	245	24	1	
Jeff Davis	LB	6'	230	26	1	
Kevin Murphy	LB	6'2"	230	22		
Ervin Randle	LB	6'1"	250	23		
Jackie Walker	LB	6'5"	245	23		
Chris Washington	LB	6'4"	230	24	1	
Jeremiah Castille	DB	5'10"	175	25		
Craig Curry	DB	6'	190	25	2	
Ricky Easmon	DB	5'10"	160	23		
Bobby Futrell	DB	5'11"	190	24		
Rod Jones	DB	6'	175	22	1	
Vito McKeever	DB	6'	180	24	3	
Ivory Sully	DB	6'	200	29		
Craig Swoope	DB	6'1"	200	22	1	
Kevin Walker	DB	5'11"	180	22		
Steve DeBerg	QB	6'2"	210	32		
Steve Young	QB	6'2"	200	24		30
Greg Allen	HB	5'11"	200	23		
Bobby Howard	HB	6'	210	22		6
James Wilder	HB	6'3"	225	28		18
Nathan Wonsley	HB	5'10"	190	22		18
Mack Boatner	FB	6'	220	27		
Pat Franklin	FB	6'1"	230	23		12
Ron Springs	FB	6'2"	225	29		
Gerald Carter	WR	6'1"	190	29		12
Phil Freeman	WR	5'11"	185	23		12
Willie Gillespie	WR	5'9"	170	24		
Leonard Harris	WR	5'8"	155	25		
Vince Heflin	WR	6'	185	27		6
Kevin House (to LA)	WR	6'1"	185	28		12
David Williams	WR	6'3"	190	23		
Jerry Bell	TE	6'5"	230	27		
K.D. Dunn	TE	6'3"	235	23		
Calvin Magee	TE	6'3"	240	23		30
Jeff Spek	TE	6'3"	240	25		
Frank Garcia	K	6'	210	29		
Donald Igwebuike	K	5'9"	185	25		77

Joe McCall - Knee Injury
Mike Prior - Wrist Injury
Don Fiedler - Knee Injury
Nat Hudson - Knee Injury
Ken Kaplan - Elbow Injury

* Overtime

CHICAGO BEARS

RUSHING

Last Name	No.	Yds	Avg	TD
Payton	321	1333	4.2	8
Suhey	84	270	3.2	2
Sanders	27	224	8.3	5
Thomas	56	224	4.0	0
McMahon	22	152	6.9	1
Anderson	35	146	4.2	0
Tomczak	23	117	5.1	3
Gentry	11	103	9.4	1
Gault	8	79	9.9	0
Flutie	9	36	4.0	1
Fuller	8	30	3.8	0
Perry	1	-1	-1.0	0
Buford	1	-13	-13.0	0

RECEIVING

Last Name	No.	Yds	Avg	TD
Gault	42	818	19.5	5
Payton	37	382	10.3	3
Moorehead	26	390	15.0	1
Suhey	24	235	9.8	0
Ortego	23	430	18.7	2
Wrightman	22	241	11.0	0
Gentry	19	238	12.5	0
Anderson	4	80	20.0	1
Barnes	4	54	13.5	0
Thomas	4	18	4.5	0
Sanders	2	18	9.0	0
Bortz	1	8	8.0	0

PUNT RETURNS

Last Name	No.	Yds	Avg	TD
Barnes	57	482	8.5	0

KICKOFF RETURNS

Last Name	No.	Yds	Avg	TD
Gentry	20	576	28.8	1
Sanders	22	399	18.1	0
Anderson	4	26	6.5	0
Barnes	3	94	31.3	1
G ault	1	20	20.0	0

PASSING — PUNTING — KICKING

PASSING	Att	Cmp	%	Yds	Yd/Att	TD	Int-	%	RK
Tomczak	151	74	49	1105	7.32	2	10—	7	
McMahon	150	77	51	995	6.63	5	8—	5	
Fuller	64	34	53	451	7.05	2	4—	6	
Flutie	46	23	50	361	7.85	3	2—	4	
Payton	4	0	0	0	0.00	0	1—	25	

PUNTING	No	Avg
Buford	70	40.7

KICKING	XP	Att	%	FG	Att	%
Butler	37	37	97	28	41	68

MINNESOTA VIKINGS

RUSHING

Last Name	No.	Yds	Avg	TD
D. Nelson	191	793	4.2	4
Anderson	83	347	4.2	2
Brown	63	251	4.0	4
Rice	73	220	3.0	2
Kramer	23	48	2.1	1
Coleman	2	46	23.0	0
W. Wilson	10	19	1.9	0
Jones	1	14	14.0	0
Carter	1	12	12.0	0
Wilson	13	9	0.7	1
Lewis	3	-16	-5.3	0

RECEIVING

Last Name	No.	Yds	Avg	TD
Jordan	58	859	14.8	6
D. Nelson	53	593	11.2	3
Carter	38	686	18.1	7
Lewis	32	600	18.8	2
Rice	30	391	13.0	3
Jones	28	570	20.4	4
Anderson	17	179	10.5	2
Brown	15	132	8.8	0
Mularkey	11	89	8.1	2
Gustafson	5	61	12.2	2
Rhymes	3	25	8.3	0
W. Wilson	1	-3	-3.0	0

PUNT RETURNS

Last Name	No.	Yds	Avg	TD
Bess	23	162	7.0	0
Lewis	7	53	7.6	0
Rice	1	0	0.0	0

KICKOFF RETURNS

Last Name	No.	Yds	Avg	TD
Bess	31	705	22.7	0
Rhymes	9	213	23.7	0
Rice	5	88	17.6	0
D. Nelson	3	105	35.0	0
Anderson	3	38	12.7	0
W. Wilson	2	33	16.5	0
Brown	2	18	9.0	0
Irwin	1	0	0.0	0

PASSING — PUNTING — KICKING

PASSING	Att	Cmp	%	Yds	Yd/Att	TD	Int-	%	RK
Kramer	372	208	56	3000	8.06	24	10—	3	1
Wilson	143	80	56	1165	8.15	7	5—	4	
Anderson	2	1	50	17	8.50	0	0—	0	
Bono	1	1	100	3	3.00	0	0—	0	
Rice	1	0	0	0	0.00	0	0—	0	

PUNTING	No	Avg
Coleman	67	41.4
Wilson	3	25.3
C. Nelson	3	24.0

KICKING	XP	Att	%	FG	Att	%
C. Nelson	44	47	94	22	28	79

DETROIT LIONS

RUSHING

Last Name	No.	Yds	Avg	TD
Jones	252	903	3.6	8
James	159	688	4.3	3
Moore	19	73	3.8	0
Hipple	16	46	2.9	0
J. Ferguson	5	25	5.0	0
S. Williams	13	22	1.7	2
Hunter	3	22	7.3	0
Long	2	0	0.0	0
Black	1	-8	-8.0	0

RECEIVING

Last Name	No.	Yds	Avg	TD
Jones	54	334	6.2	1
Chadwick	53	995	18.8	5
Bland	44	511	11.6	2
Giles	35	376	10.7	4
James	34	219	6.4	0
Thompson	25	320	12.8	5
Hunter	25	218	8.7	1
Lewis	10	88	8.8	1
Moore	8	47	5.9	0
Mandley	7	106	15.1	0
Rubick	5	62	12.4	0
S. Williams	2	9	4.5	0

PUNT RETURNS

Last Name	No.	Yds	Avg	TD
Mandley	43	420	9.8	1

KICKOFF RETURNS

Last Name	No.	Yds	Avg	TD
Hunter	48	1007	20.6	0
Bland	6	114	19.0	0
Smith	5	81	16.2	0
Graham	3	72	24.0	0
Mandley	2	37	18.5	0
Evans	1	0	0.0	0

PASSING — PUNTING — KICKING

PASSING	Att	Cmp	%	Yds	Yd/Att	TD	Int—	%	Rk
Hipple	305	192	63	1919	6.29	9	11—	4	4
J. Ferguson	155	73	47	941	6.07	7	7—	5	
Long	40	21	53	247	6.18	2	2—	5	

PUNTING	No	Avg
Black	47	38.7
Arnold	37	41.4
Murray	1	37.0

KICKING	XP	Att	%	FG	Att	%
Murray	31	32	97	18	25	72

GREEN BAY PACKERS

RUSHING

Last Name	No.	Yds	Avg	TD
Davis	114	519	4.6	0
Ellis	84	345	4.1	2
Carruth	81	308	3.8	2
Ellerson	90	287	3.2	3
Wright	18	41	2.3	1
Clark	18	41	2.3	0
Ivery	4	25	6.3	0
Stanley	1	19	19.0	0
Epps	4	18	4.5	0
Fusina	7	11	1.6	0
Renner	1	0	0.0	0
Swanke	1	0	0.0	0
Ferragamo	1	0	0.0	0

RECEIVING

Last Name	No.	Yds	Avg	TD
Lofton	64	840	13.1	4
Epps	49	612	12.5	4
Stanley	35	723	20.7	2
Ivery	31	385	12.4	1
Ellis	24	258	10.8	0
Carruth	24	134	5.6	2
Davis	21	142	6.8	1
Ross	17	143	8.4	1
West	15	199	13.3	1
Ellerson	12	130	10.8	0
Clark	6	41	6.8	0
Moffitt	4	87	21.8	0
M. Lewis	2	7	3.5	2
Franz	1	7	7.0	0

PUNT RETURNS

Last Name	No.	Yds	Avg	TD
Stanley	33	316	9.6	1

KICKOFF RETURNS

Last Name	No.	Yds	Avg	TD
Stanley	28	559	20.0	0
Watts	12	239	19.9	0
Davis	12	231	19.3	0
Stills	10	209	20.9	0
Ellerson	7	154	22.0	0
Carruth	4	40	10.0	0
Epps	1	21	21.0	0
Berry	1	16	16.0	0
Noble	1	1	1.0	0

PASSING — PUNTING — KICKING

PASSING	Att	Cmp	%	Yds	Yd/Att	TD	Int—	%	Rk
Wright	492	263	54	3247	6.60	17	23—	5	10
Ferragamo	40	23	58	283	7.08	1	3—	8	
Fusina	32	19	59	178	5.56	0	1—	3	
Lofton	1	0	0	0	0.0	0	0—	0	

PUNTING	No	Avg
Bracken	57	38.6
Renner	18	34.6

KICKING	XP	Att	%	FG	Att	%
Del Greco	29	29	100	17	27	63

TAMPA BAY BUCCANEERS

RUSHING

Last Name	No.	Yds	Avg	TD
Wilder	190	704	3.7	2
Young	74	425	5.7	5
Wonsley	73	339	4.6	3
Springs	74	285	3.9	0
Howard	30	110	3.7	1
Franklin	7	7	1.0	0
House	2	5	2.5	0
DeBerg	2	1	0.5	0
Allen	1	3	3.0	0
Carter	1	-5	-5.0	0
Garcia	1	-11	-11.0	0

RECEIVING

Last Name	No.	Yds	Avg	TD
Magee	45	564	12.5	5
Wilder	43	326	7.6	1
Carter	42	640	15.2	2
Springs	24	187	7.8	0
House	18	384	21.3	2
Giles	18	178	9.9	1
Freeman	14	229	16.4	2
Bell	10	120	12.0	0
Wonsley	8	57	7.1	0
Franklin	7	29	4.1	1
Williams	6	91	15.2	0
Howard	5	60	12.0	0
Dunn	3	83	27.7	0
Harris	3	52	17.3	0
Heflin	3	42	14.0	0
Gillespie	1	18	18.0	0
Mallory	1	9	9.0	0
Heller	1	1	1.0	1

PUNT RETURNS

Last Name	No.	Yds	Avg	TD
Futrell	14	67	4.8	0
Walker	9	27	3.0	0
Harris	3	16	5.3	0

KICKOFF RETURNS

Last Name	No.	Yds	Avg	TD
Freeman	31	582	18.8	0
Wonsley	10	208	20.8	0
K. Walker	8	146	18.3	0
Futrell	5	115	23.0	0
Howard	4	71	17.8	0
Harris	4	63	15.8	0
Williams	2	29	14.5	0
Franklin	3	23	7.7	0
Magee	2	21	10.5	0
Allen	1	21	21.0	0
Heflin	1	15	15.0	0
Curry	1	6	6.0	0
Boatner	1	2	2.0	0
Randle	1	0	0.0	0
Dunn	1	0	0.0	0

PASSING — PUNTING — KICKING

PASSING	Att	Cmp	%	Yds	Yd/Att	TD	Int—	%	Rk
Young	363	195	54	2382	6.29	8	13—	4	12
DeBerg	96	50	52	610	6.35	5	12—	13	

PUNTING	No	Avg
Garcia	77	40.1
Springs	1	43.0

KICKING	XP	Att	%	FG	Att	%
Igwebuike	26	27	96	17	24	71

SAN FRANCISCO FORTY-NINERS 10-5-1 Bill Walsh

Scores of Each Game		
31	Tampa Bay	7
13	L.A. Rams	16
26	NEW ORLEANS	17
31	Miami	16
35	INDIANAPOLIS	14
24	MINNESOTA	*27
10	Atlanta	*10
31	Green Bay	17
10	New Orleans	23
43	ST.LOUIS	17
6	Washington	14
20	ATLANTA	0
17	GIANTS	21
24	N.Y.JETS	10
29	New England	24
24	L.A.RAMS	14

Use Name	Pos.	Hgt	Wgt	Age	Int	Pts
Bruce Collie	OT-OG	6'6"	275	24		
Keith Fahnhorst	OT	6'6"	273	34		
Bubba Paris	OT	6'6	299	25		
Steve Wallace	OT	6'5"	276	21		
John Ayers	OG	6'5"	265	33		
Randy Cross	OG	6'3"	265	32		
Michael Durrette	OG	6'4"	280	29		
Guy McIntyre	OG	6'3"	264	25		
Fred Quillan	C	6'5"	266	30		
Dwaine Board	DE	6'5"	248	29		
Charls Haley	DE	6'5"	230	22		
John Harty	DE	6'4"	260	27		
Larry Roberts	DE	6'3"	264	23		
Doug Rogers	DE	6'5"	280	26		
Jeff Stover	DE	6'5"	275	28		
Jim Stuckey	DE	6'4"	253	28		
Michael Carter	NT	6'2"	285	25		
Manu Tulasosopo	NT	6'3"	262	29		
Pete Kugler	NT-DE	6'4"	255	27		
Tom Cousineau	LB	6'3"	225	29	1	
Riki Ellison	LB	6'2"	225	26		
Jim Fahnhorst	LB	6'4"	230	27	4	
Ron Ferrari	LB	6'	215	27		
Milt McColl	LB	6'6"	230	27		
Todd Shell	LB	6'4"	225	24		
Keena Turner	LB	6'2"	222	27	1	
Michael Walter	LB	6'3"	238	25		
Jeff Fuller	DB-LB	6'2"	216	24	4	
Don Griffin	DB	6'	176	22	3	
Tom Holmoe	DB	6'2"	195	26	3	12
Ronnie Lott	DB	6'	200	27	10	6
Tim McKyer	DB	6'	174	22	6	6
Tory Nixon	DB	5'11"	186	24	2	6
Carlton Williamson	DB	6'	204	28	3	
Eric Wright	DB	6'1"	185	27		
Bob Gagliano	QB	6'3"	195	27		
Jeff Kemp	QB	6'	201	27		
Joe Montana	QB	6'2"	195	30		
Mike Moroski	QB	6'4"	200	28		6
Tony Cherry	HB	5'7"	187	23		
Joe Cribbs	HB	5'11"	193	28		30
Derrick Harmon	HB	5'10"	202	23		6
Carl Monroe	HB-WR	5'8"	180	26		
Wendell Tyler	HB	5'10"	207	31		
Roger Craig	FB	6'	224	26		42
Tom Rathman	FB	6'1"	232	23		6
Bill Ring	FB	5'10	205	29		
Dwight Clark	WR	6'4"	215	29		12
Derrick Crawford	WR	5'10"	185	25		
Ken Margerum	WR	6'	180	27		
Jerry Rice	WR	6'2"	200	23		96
Mike Wilson	WR	6'3"	215	27		6
Russ Francis	TE	6'6"	242	33		6
John Frank	TE	6'3"	225	24		12
Max Runager	K	6'1"	189	30		
Ray Wersching	K	5'11"	215	36		116

Wymon Henderson - Foot Injury
Jesse Sapolu - Leg Injury
Jimmy Rogers - Knee Injury

LOS ANGELES RAMS 10-6 John Robinson

Scores of Each Game		
16	St.Louis	10
16	SAN FRANCISCO	13
24	Indianapolis	7
20	Philadelphia	34
26	TAMPA BAY	*20
14	Atlanta	26
14	DETROIT	10
14	ATLANTA	7
20	Chicago	17
0	New Orleans	6
28	NEW ENGLAND	30
26	NEW ORLEANS	13
17	N.Y.Jets	3
29	DALLAS	10
31	MIAMI	*37
14	San Francisco	24

Use Name	Pos.	Hgt	Wgt	Age	Int	Pts
Irv Pankey	OT	6'4"	267	28		
Jackie Slater	OT	6'4"	271	32		
Dennis Harrah	OG	6'5"	265	33		
Kent Hill	OG	6'5"	260	29		
Duval Love	OG	6'3"	263	23		
Tom Newberry	OG	6'2"	279	23		6
Tony Slaton	C	6'3"	265	25		
Doug Smith	C	6'3"	253	29		
Reggie Doss	DE	6'4"	263	29		
Gary Jeter	DE	6'4"	260	31		2
Doug Reed	DE	6'3"	262	26		
Charles DeJurnett	NT	6'4"	260	34		
Greg Meisner	NT	6'3"	253	27		
Shawn Miller	NT	6'4"	255	25		
Alvin Wright	NT	6'2"	285	25		
Steve Busick	LB	6'4"	227	27		
Carl Ekern	LB	6'3"	230	32		
Kevin Greene	LB	6'3"	238	24		
Mark Jerue	LB	6'3"	232	26	2	6
Jim Laughlin	LB	6'	222	28		
Mike McDonald	LB	6'1"	230	28		
Mel Owens	LB	6'2"	224	27		
Cliff Thrift	LB	6'2"	235	30		
Norwood Vann	LB	6'1"	225	24		
Mike Wilcher	LB	6'3"	240	26	1	
Nolan Cromwell	DB	6'1"	200	31	5	6
Herman Edwards	DB	5'10"	190	32		
Tim Fox	DB	5'11"	186	32		
Jerry Gray	DB	6'	185	23	8	
LeRoy Irvin	DB	5'11"	184	28	6	6
Johnnie Johnson	DB	6'1"	183	29	1	
Vince Newsome	DB	6'1"	179	25	3	
Mickey Sutton	DB	5'8"	165	26		
Steve Bartkowski	QB	6'4"	218	33		
Steve Dils	QB	6'1"	191	30		
Jim Everett	QB	6'5"	212	23		6
Eric Dickerson	HB	6'3"	218	25		66
Charles White	HB	5'10"	190	28		
Rob Carpenter	FB	6'1"	230	31		
Mike Guman	FB	6'2"	218	28		
Barry Redden	FB	5'10"	205	26		30
Tim Tyrrell (from ATL - HB)	FB	6'1"	201	25		
Ron Brown	WR	5'11"	181	25		18
Bobby Dickworth (to PHI)	WR	6'3"	196	27		
Henry Ellard	WR	5'11"	175	25		24
Chuck Scott	WR	6'2"	202	23		
Michael Young	WR	6'1"	185	24		
David Hill	TE	6'2"	240	32		6
Tony Hunter	TE	6'4"	237	26		
Damone Johnson	TE	6'4"	230	24		
Darren Long	TE	6'3	240	27		
Dale Hatcher	K	6'2"	200	23		
Mike Lansford	K	6'	183	28		85

Jim Collins - Shoulder Injury
Dieter Brock - Back Injury

ATLANTA FALCONS 7-8-1 Dan Henning

Scores of Each Game		
31	New Orleans	10
33	ST.LOUIS	13
37	Dallas	35
23	Tampa Bay	*20
0	PHILADELPHIA	16
26	L.A.RAMS	14
10	SAN FRANCISCO	*10
7	L.A.Rams	14
17	New England	25
14	N.Y.JETS	28
10	CHICAGO	13
0	San Francisco	20
20	Miami	14
23	INDIANAPOLIS	28
9	NEW ORLEANS	14
20	Detroit	6

Use Name	Pos.	Hgt	Wgt	Age	Int	Pts
Bill Fralic	OT-OG	6'5"	280	23		
Glen Howe	OT	6'7"	298	24		
Mike Kenn	OT	6'7"	277	30		
Brett Miller	OT	6'7"	300	27		
Eric Sanders (to DET)	OT-OG	6'7"	288	27		
Jamie Dukes	OG	6'1"	270	22		
Joe Pellegrini	OG-C	6'4"	265	29		
John Scully	OG	6'6"	270	28		
Wayne Radloff	C-OG	6'5"	277	25		
Jeff Van Note	C	6'2"	268	40		
Rick Bryan	DE	6'4"	265	24		
Mike Gann	DE	6'5"	265	22		2
Dennis Harrison (from SF)	DE	6'8"	280	30		
Mike Pitts	DE	6'5"	277	25		6
Andrew Provence	DE	6'3"	267	25		
Dan Benish	NT	6'5"	280	24		
Tony Casillas	NT	6'3"	280	22		
Aaron Brown	LB	6'2"	238	30		
Joe Costello	LB	6'3"	250	26		
Buddy Curry	LB	6'4"	222	28	1	
Tim Green	LB	6'2"	249	22		
Ray Phillips	LB	6'3"	245	22		
John Rade	LB	6'1"	240	26	1	
Johnny Taylor (to MIA)	LB	6'4"	235	26		
Reggie Wilkes	LB	6'4"	242	30	2	
Joel Williams	LB	6'1"	227	29	2	6
James Britt	DB	6'	185	25		6
Bobby Butler	DB	5'11"	182	27	1	1
Scott Case	DB	6'	178	24	4	
Wendell Cason	DB	5'11"	197	23	1	
Bret Clark	DB	6'3"	198	25	5	
David Croudip	DB	5'8"	185	27	2	
Herman Edwards	DB	6'	194	32		
Kenny Johnson (to HOU)	DB	5'10"	175	28		
Robert Moore	DB	5'11"	190	22	1	
Dennis Woodberry	DB	5'10"	183	25	2	
David Archer	QB	6'2"	208	24		
Turk Schonert	QB	6'1"	196	29		6
Tony Baker (to CLE)	HB	5'10"	175	21		
Sylvester Stamps	HB	5'7"	175	25		6
William Andrews	FB	6'	220	30		6
Cliff Austin	FB	6'	213	26		6
Gerald Riggs	FB	6'1"	232	25		54
Anthony Allen	WR	5'11"	182	27		12
Stacey Bailey	WR	6'	157	26		
Charlie Brown	WR	5'10"	184	27		24
Floyd Dixon	WR	5'9"	170	22		12
Billy Johnson	WR	5'9"	170	34		
Joey Jones	WR	5'8"	165	23		
Aubrey Matthews	WR	5'7"	165	23		
Keith Williams	WR-RB	5'10"	173	21		6
Arthur Cox	TE	6'2"	262	25		6
Ron Middleton	TE	6'2"	252	21		
Ken Whisenhunt	TE	6'2"	233	24		18
Rick Donnelly	K	6'	190	24		1
Ali Haji-Sheikh	K	6'	172	25		34
Mick Luckhurst	K	6'	178	28		63

Jeff Kiewel - Knee Injury
Dan Wagoner - Knee Injury

Mike Landrum - Knee Injury
Dan Sharp - Shoulder Injury
Bobby Jackson - Hamstring Injury

NEW ORLEANS SAINTS 7-9 Jim Mora

Scores of Each Game		
10	ATLANTA	31
24	GREEN BAY	10
17	San Francisco	26
17	N.Y.Giants	20
6	WASHINGTON	14
17	Indianapolis	14
38	TAMPA BAY	7
23	N.Y.Jets	28
23	SAN FRANCISCO	10
6	L.A.RAMS	0
16	St.Louis	7
13	L.A.Rams	26
20	NEW ENGLAND	21
27	MIAMI	31
14	Atlanta	9
17	Minnesota	33

Use Name	Pos.	Hgt	Wgt	Age	Int	Pts
Stan Brock	OT	6'6"	292	28		
Bill Contz (from CLE)	OT	6'5"	270	25		
Jim Dombrowski	OT	6'5"	298	22		
Daren Gilbert	OT	6'6"	295	22		
Chuck Commiskey	OG	6'4"	290	28		
Brad Edelman	OG	6'6"	270	25		
Pat Saindon	OG	6'3"	273	25		
Ralph Williams	OG	6'3"	298	28		
Joel Hilgenberg	C-OG	6'3"	252	24		
Steve Korte	C	6'2"	269	26		
Bruce Clark	DE	6'3"	274	28		
Jonathan Dumbauld	DE	6'4"	259	23		
James Geathers	DE	6'7"	290	26		
Casey Merrill	DE	6'4"	250	29		
Frank Warren	DE	6'4"	290	26		
Jim Wilks	DE	6'5"	266	28		
Sheldon Andrus	NT	6'1"	271	23		
Tony Elliott	NT	6'2"	285	27		
Jack Del Rio	LB	6'4"	238	23		
James Haynes	LB	6'2"	233	26	1	6
Rickey Jackson	LB	6'2"	243	28	1	
Vaughn Johnson	LB	6'3"	235	24		
Joe Kohlbrand	LB	6'4"	242	23		
Sam Mills	LB	5'9"	225	27		
Pat Swilling	LB	6'3"	242	21		
Alvin Toles	LB	6'1"	227	23		
Russell Gary (to PHI)	DB	5'11"	195	27	1	
Antonio Gibson	DB	6'3"	204	24	2	
Van Jakes	DB	6'	190	25		
Bobby Johnson (from STL)	DB	6'	187	26		
Brett Maxie	DB	6'2"	194	24	2	
Dana McLemore (from SF)	DB	5'10"	183	26		
Johnnie Poe	DB	6'1"	194	27	4	
Willie Tullis	DB	6'	194	28		
Frank Wattelet	DB	6'	186	27	3	
Dave Waymer	DB	6'1"	188	28	9	
Bobby Hebert	QB	6'4"	215	26		
Babe Laufenberg	QB	6'2"	196	26		
Dave Wilson	QB	6'3"	206	27		6
Mel Gray	HB	5'9"	166	25		6
Dalton Hilliard	HB	5'8"	204	22		30
Rueben Mayes	HB	5'11"	200	23		48
Buford Jordan	FB	6'	223	24		6
Wayne Wilson	FB	6'3"	220	28		
John Williams	FB	5'11"	213	25		
Kelvin Edwards	WR	6'2"	197	22		
Eugene Goodlow	WR	6'2"	186	27		12
Herbert Harris	WR	6'1"	206	25		
Mike Jones	WR	5'11"	183	26		18
Eric Martin	WR	6'1"	207	24		30
Hoby Brenner	TE	6'4"	245	27		
John Tice	TE	6'5"	249	26		18
Morten Andersen	K	6'2"	221	26		108
Brian Hansen	K	6'3"	209	25		

Dave Lafary - Toe Injury

Earl Johnson - Shoulder Injury
Tim Joiner - Shoulder Injury
Guido Merkens - Knee Injury

Bobby Fowler - Knee Injury
Hokie Gajan - Knee Injury
Mike Miller - Achilles Tendon Injury

* Overtime

SAN FRANCISCO FORTY-NINERS

RUSHING

Last Name	No.	Yds	Avg	TD
Craig	204	830	4.1	7
Cribbs	152	590	3.9	5
Rathman	33	138	4.2	1
Tyler	31	127	4.1	0
Harmon	27	77	2.9	1
Rice	10	72	7.2	1
Kemp	15	49	3.3	0
Cherry	11	42	3.8	0
Montana	17	38	2.2	0
Moroski	6	22	3.7	1
Ring	3	4	1.3	0
Frank	1	-3	-3.0	0

RECEIVING

Last Name	No.	Yds	Avg	TD
Rice	86	1570	18.3	15
Craig	81	624	7.7	0
Clark	61	794	13.0	2
Francis	41	505	12.3	1
Cribbs	35	346	9.9	0
Rathman	13	121	9.3	0
Wilson	9	104	11.6	1
Frank	9	61	6.8	2
Harmon	8	78	9.8	0
Crawford	5	70	14.0	0
Margerum	2	12	6.0	0
Monroe	2	6	3.0	0
Ring	1	8	8.0	0

PUNT RETURNS

Last Name	No.	Yds	Avg	TD
Griffin	38	377	9.9	1
Crawford	4	15	3.8	0
McKyer	1	5	5.0	0

KICKOFF RETURNS

Last Name	No.	Yds	Avg	TD
Crawford	15	280	18.7	0
Monroe	8	139	17.4	0
Griffin	5	97	19.4	0
Harmon	4	82	20.5	0
Rathman	3	66	22.0	0
Cherry	2	29	14.5	0
Frank	2	24	12.0	0
McKyer	1	15	15.0	0
Ring	1	15	15.0	0
Wilson	1	10	10.0	0

PASSING — PUNTING — KICKING

PASSING	Att	Cmp	%	Yds	Yd/Att	TD	Int—	%	RK
Montana	307	191	62	2236	7.28	8	9—	3	2
Kemp	200	119	60	1554	7.77	11	8—	4	
Moroski	73	42	58	493	6.75	2	3—	4	
Rice	2	1	50	16	8.00	0	0—	0	

PUNTING	No	Avg
Runager	83	41.6

KICKING	XP	Att	%	FG	Att	%
Wersching	41	42	98	25	35	72

LOS ANGELES RAMS

RUSHING

Last Name	No.	Yds	Avg	TD
Dickerson	404	1821	4.5	11
Redden	110	467	4.2	4
White	22	126	5.7	0
Everett	16	46	2.9	1
Brown	4	5	1.3	0
Dils	10	5	0.5	0
Carpenter	2	3	1.5	0
Bartkowski	6	3	0.5	0
Guman	2	2	1.0	0
Hunter	1	-6	-6.0	0
Ellard	1	-15	-15.0	0

RECEIVING

Last Name	No.	Yds	Avg	TD
Ellard	34	447	13.1	4
Redden	28	217	7.8	1
Dickerson	26	205	7.9	0
Brown	25	396	15.8	3
Hunter	15	206	13.7	0
Young	15	181	12.1	3
Hill	14	202	14.4	1
Duckworth	10	148	14.8	1
Guman	9	68	7.6	0
Scott	5	76	15.2	0
Long	5	47	9.4	0
Tyrrell	1	9	9.0	0
White	1	7	7.0	0

PUNT RETURNS

Last Name	No.	Yds	Avg	TD
Ellard	14	127	9.1	0
Sutton	28	234	8.4	0

KICKOFF RETURNS

Last Name	No.	Yds	Avg	TD
Brown	36	794	22.1	0
White	12	216	18.0	0
Sutton	5	91	18.2	0
Guman	2	28	14.0	0
Carpenter	2	19	9.5	0
Ellard	1	18	18.0	0
Love	1	-6	-6.0	0

PASSING — PUNTING — KICKING

PASSING	Att	Cmp	%	Yds	Yd/Att	TD	Int—	%	RK
Everett	147	73	50	1018	6.93	8	8—	5	
Dils	129	59	46	693	5.37	4	4—	3	
Bartkowski	126	61	48	654	5.19	2	3—	2	
Dickerson	1	1	100	15	15.0	1	0—	0	

PUNTING	No	Avg
Hatcher	98	38.2

KICKING	XP	Att	%	FG	Att	%
Landsford	34	35	97	17	24	71

ATLANTA FALCONS

RUSHING

Last Name	No.	Yds	Avg	TD
Riggs	343	1327	3.9	9
Archer	52	398	5.7	0
Austin	62	280	4.5	1
Stamps	30	220	7.3	0
Andrews	52	214	4.1	1
Dixon	11	67	6.1	0
B. Johnson	6	25	4.2	0
Whisenhunt	1	20	20.0	0
K. Williams	3	18	6.0	0
Matthews	1	12	12.0	0
Schonert	11	12	1.1	1
Clark	2	8	4.0	0
Jones	1	7	7.0	0
Bailey	1	6	6.0	0
Baker	1	3	3.0	0

RECEIVING

Last Name	No.	Yds	Avg	TD
C. Brown	63	918	14.6	4
Dixon	42	617	14.7	2
Cox	24	301	12.5	1
Riggs	24	136	5.7	0
Stamps	20	221	11.1	1
Whisenhunt	20	184	9.2	3
K. Williams	12	164	13.7	1
Allen	10	156	15.6	2
Jones	7	141	20.1	0
B. Johnson	6	57	9.5	0
Middleton	6	31	5.2	0
Andrews	5	35	7.0	0
Bailey	3	39	13.0	0
Austin	3	21	7.0	0
Matthews	1	25	25.0	0

PUNT RETURNS

Last Name	No.	Yds	Avg	TD
Dixon	26	151	5.8	0
B. Johnson	8	87	10.9	0
Jones	7	36	5.1	0
Allen	2	10	5.0	0
Stamps	1	8	8.0	0

KICKOFF RETURNS

Last Name	No.	Yds	Avg	TD
Stamps	24	514	21.4	0
K. Williams	14	255	18.2	0
Austin	7	120	17.1	0
Andrews	4	71	17.8	0
Matthews	3	42	14.0	0
Croudip	1	20	20.0	0
Dixon	1	13	13.0	0

PASSING — PUNTING — KICKING

PASSING	Att	Cmp	%	Yds	Yd/Att	TD	Int—	%	RK
Archer	294	150	51	2007	6.83	10	9—	3	7
Schonert	154	95	62	1032	6.70	4	8—	5	
Riggs	1	0	0	0	0.00	0	0—	0	

PUNTING	No	Avg
Donnelly	79	43.3

KICKING	XP	Att	%	FG	Att	%
Luckhurst	21	21	100	14	24	58
Donnelly	1	1	100	0	0	0
Haji-Sheikh	7	8	88	9	12	75

NEW ORLEANS SAINTS

RUSHING

Last Name	No.	Yds	Avg	TD
Mayes	286	1353	4.7	8
Hilliard	121	425	3.5	5
Jordan	68	207	3.0	1
Gray	6	29	4.8	0
D. Wilson	14	19	1.4	1
Del Rio	1	16	16.0	0
Hebert	5	14	2.8	0
Edwards	1	6	6.0	0
Hansen	1	0	0.0	0

RECEIVING

Last Name	No.	Yds	Avg	TD
Jones	48	625	13.0	3
Martin	37	675	18.2	5
Tice	37	330	8.9	3
Goodlow	20	306	15.3	2
Brenner	18	286	15.9	0
Hilliard	17	107	6.3	0
Mayes	17	96	5.6	0
Harris	11	148	13.5	0
Jordan	11	127	11.5	0
Edwards	10	132	13.2	0
Gray	2	45	22.5	0
Waymer	1	13	13.0	0
J. Williams	1	5	5.0	0
Hebert	1	1	1.0	0

PUNT RETURNS

Last Name	No.	Yds	Avg	TD
Martin	24	227	9.5	0
McLemore	10	67	6.7	0
Poe	8	71	8.9	0
Edwards	3	2	0.7	0
Tullis	2	10	5.0	0

KICKOFF RETURNS

Last Name	No.	Yds	Avg	TD
Gray	31	866	27.9	1
Mayes	10	213	21.3	0
Harris	7	122	17.4	0
Martin	3	64	21.3	0
McLemore	2	39	19.5	0
Tullis	2	28	14.0	0

PASSING — PUNTING — KICKING

PASSING	Att	Cmp	%	Yds	Yd/Att	TD	Int-	%	RK
D. Wilson	342	189	55	2353	6.88	10	17—	5	11
Hebert	79	41	52	498	6.30	2	8—	10	
Hilliard	3	1	33	29	29.00	1	0—	0	
Wattelet	1	1	100	13	13.00	0	0—	0	

PUNTING	No	Avg
Hansen	82	42.1

KICKING	XP	Att	%	FG	Att	%
Andersen	30	30	100	26	30	87

1986 A.F.C. Caught in the Draft

The N.F.L. draft is slow but inexorable. Nothing in the league is surer than that a team drafting near the end, year after year, will eventually stock its roster with a number of athletes of lesser quality than those on teams that consistently draft near the top. It's not so certain that all teams with high draft choices every year will eventually come up winners. A team may make poor choices, key players can be injured, or luck can take a hand. But, on the other end of the scale, any team that must yearly choose its players after 20 or so others have had their picks is going to finally suffer for it. Some teams stave off the inevitable for a while with shrewd choices, clever trading or good luck, but, sooner or later, every dynasty must be rebuilt.

Several of the strongest teams of the 1970s found themselves struggling in 1986, primarily because their low draft positions had not allowed them to replace aging stars with newcomers of equal talent. The Steelers and Chargers had been crumbling for several seasons and may have hit bottom. The Dolphins and Raiders slipped to .500 ballclubs in '86, each with nearly a whole platoon in need of replacement. In the N.F.C., the Cowboys suffered their first losing season since 1965.

EASTERN DIVISION

New England Patriots — The Patriots were 3-3 when they went on a seven-game winning streak to move past the Jets into first place in the East. Then, two late-season losses brought their chances down to a final game at the Orange Bowl where they'd finally broken an 18-year jinx in the 1985 A.F.C. championship game. To the surprise of any who'd questioned the Patriots' chips-down courage, the Steve Grogan-to-Stanley Morgan pass combo led them to a 34-27 win over the Dolphins. Morgan had the best season of his 10-year career, but the running game evaporated with the retirement of all-world guard John Hannah. As a team, the Patriots averaged only 2.9 yards per carry, and none of the regular runners could top that figure. Linebackers Don Blackmon and Andre Tippett and cornerbacks Ronnie Lippett and Raymond Clayborn led a generally satisfactory defense.

New York Jets — For the first 11 weeks, the Jets were the best team in the A.F.C. At 10-1, Ken O'Brien looked like the next great quarterback, wide receiver Al Toon was an unstoppable weapon, and the defense, led by nose tackle Joe Klecko, was strong. Then, injuries to Klecko, linebacker Lance Mehl, running back Freeman McNeil, center Joe Fields and others caught up to coach Joe Walton's club. The offense all but disappeared — O'Brien was finally replaced by Pat Ryan — and, by the end of the season, the defense had also collapsed, giving up 97 points in the last two games. But, despite closing with a five-game losing streak, the Jets still had enough wins in the till to qualify as a wild-card team.

Miami Dolphins — The Dolphins had half of a great team — the offense. Appropriately, they halved their schedule, going 8-8. The offense, despite a sporadic running game, was awesome as Dan Marino set N.F.L. records for pass attempts (623) and completions (392), while posting marks in yardage (4,746) and touchdowns (44) that had been exceeded only by Marino himself in 1984. His prime receivers, the Marks Brothers — Duper and Clayton — accounted for 127 catches, 2,463 yards and 21 scores between them. But, when they turned the ball over to their opponents, the Dolphins were terrible, particularly in the beginning of the season when they gave up 176 points during a 1-4 start.

Buffalo Bills — The much-heralded arrival of quarterback Jim Kelly from the U.S.F.L. increased home attendance by about 30,000 per game and turned the Bills into respectable losers. Besides drawing fans back to the park, Kelly gave the team two things: strong passing and on-field leadership. Despite Kelly's considerable efforts, his supporting cast doomed the Bills to another losing season. They did, however, win two more games than in 1985 and stayed close in most of the losses. Not close enough to save coach Hank Bullough's job, however; he was replaced after nine games by Marv Levy.

Indianapolis Colts — The Colts were sailing along at 0-13, nearly certain of earning the first draft pick in 1987 and with an excellent chance of becoming the first team to lose 16 games in a season. Then, Ron Meyer replaced Rod Dowhower as head coach, he reinstalled Gary Hogeboom (injured in week two) at quarterback and, with the help of a last-second blocked punt, won a game. Even more surprising, the Colts won two more, losing their top draft spot but raising hopes of their fans. Until then, the play of rookie wide receiver Bill Brooks, the solid running of Randy McMillan, Rohn Stark's punting, and strong blocking from Chris Hinton and Ray Donaldson were the few bright spots.

CENTRAL DIVISION

Cleveland Browns — The Browns won the Central Division title for the second straight year, but the '86 team was very different from the '85 club that sneaked in at 8-8. In 1985, Cleveland used a strong running attack and tough defense to grind out wins. The defense was back in '86, but struggled early because of the death of safety Don Rogers and the pre-season holdout of linebacker Chip Banks. Cornerback Hanford Dixon emerged as an outstanding defender. The offense changed completely under the tutelage of new coordinator Lindy Infante. Both Earnest Byner and Kevin Mack, the 1,000-yard rushers of '85, were injured at various times and played together for only eight quarters. But young Bernie Kosar became one of the A.F.C.'s most effective passers, gaining 3,854 yards through the air.

Cincinnati Bengals — The Bengals were consistently inconsistent, scoring a ton of points one week and yet being unable to score 10 points three times. The high-tech passing game boasted Boomer Esiason as one of football's top bombers and Cris Collinsworth and Eddie Brown as speedy targets. Back James Brooks rushed for 1,087 yards and caught 54 passes. The mountainous offensive line out-muscled everybody. Even the defense improved to nearly adequate. In week 15, the Bengals needed only a victory over the Browns to win the division, but Kosar completed a 66-yard pass on the first play of the game and Cincinnati never recovered, dropping two straight.

Pittsburgh Steelers — Chuck Noll's Steelers came out of the gate belly-up and were 1-6 after New England gave them a 34-0 humiliation, their worst-ever loss at Three Rivers Stadium. But waiver pick Earnest Jackson gave them a strong running attack, receivers Louis Lipps and John Stallworth and center Mike Webster got healthy, and much-maligned quarterback Mark Malone went to an effective short passing game. Pittsburgh was 5-4 down the stretch, with two of the losses in overtime to playoff teams.

Houston Oilers — Coach Jerry Glanville let the Oilers stumble to 1-8 before he admitted his conservative offense was not working. The team's strength was its pair of burner receivers, rookie Ernest Givins and veteran Drew Hill. Disappointing quarterback Warren Moon opened up for the remainder of the schedule and the Oilers went 4-3. The end-of-the-season spurt helped improve upon the offensive and defensive stats from 1985, but turnovers and penalties hurt them all year.

WESTERN DIVISION

Denver Broncos — The Broncos' offense was almost all John Elway. The "franchise" quarterback passed for 3,485 yards and was also his team's most dangerous runner. With an under-

FINAL TEAM STATISTICS

OFFENSE

	BUFF.	CIN.	CLEV.	DENV.	HOU.	IND.	K.C.	L.A.	MIA.	N.E.	NY J	PIT.	S.D.	SEA.
FIRST DOWNS:														
Total	291	348	302	319	299	278	264	302	351	314	319	292	334	291
by Rushing	101	134	102	94	101	77	83	97	84	77	104	125	98	123
by Passing	152	183	175	184	179	173	152	186	250	202	191	140	212	158
by Penalty	38	31	25	41	19	28	29	19	17	35	24	27	24	10
RUSHING:														
Number	419	521	470	455	490	407	432	475	349	469	490	584	471	513
Yards	1654	2533	1650	1678	1700	1491	1468	1790	1545	1373	1729	2223	1576	2300
Average Yards	3.9	4.9	3.5	3.7	3.5	3.7	3.4	3.8	4.4	2.9	3.5	3.9	3.3	4.5
Touchdowns	9	24	20	17	13	10	10	6	9	10	16	18	19	15
PASSING:														
Attempts	499	497	538	549	551	586	521	530	645	557	537	491	604	453
Completions	294	287	315	306	288	300	257	281	392	340	334	238	339	268
Completion Pct.	58.9	57.7	58.6	55.7	52.3	51.2	49.3	53.0	60.8	61.0	62.2	48.5	56.1	59.2
Passing Yards	3697	4160	4018	3811	3843	3615	3122	3973	4898	4321	4032	2747	4045	3424
Avg. Yds per Att.	6.2	7.5	6.5	6.0	5.8	5.0	4.8	5.9	7.2	6.6	6.3	5.1	5.9	6.3
Avg. Yds per Comp.	12.6	14.5	12.8	12.5	13.3	12.1	12.2	14.1	12.5	12.7	122.1	11.5	11.9	12.8
Times Tackled	45	28	39	38	48	53	50	64	17	47	45	20	32	39
Yds Lost Tackled	334	203	274	273	394	406	372	464	119	367	386	159	265	315
Net Yards	3363	3957	3744	3538	3449	3209	2750	3509	4779	3954	3646	2588	3780	3109
Touchdowns	22	25	18	22	14	16	23	27	46	29	27	16	21	24
Interceptions	19	20	11	16	31	24	18	25	23	13	21	20	33	14
Pct. Intercepted	3.8	4.0	2.0	2.9	5.6	4.1	3.5	4.7	3.6	2.3	3.9	4.1	5.5	3.1
PUNTS:														
Number	75	59	83	86	89	81	99	90	56	92	85	89	79	79
Average	40.4	33.8	41.2	39.3	41.1	44.7	40.7	40.2	44.2	40.7	39.4	38.7	40.4	38.6
PUNT RETURNS														
Number	32	29	41	48	43	35	35	56	40	42	39	36	37	39
Yards	247	235	350	552	341	250	265	484	297	396	341	310	334	457
Average Yards	7.7	8.1	8.5	11.5	7.9	7.1	7.6	8.6	7.4	9.4	8.7	8.6	9.0	11.7
Touchdowns	1	0	1	2	0	0	0	1	1	1	0	0	0	1
KICKOFF RET.:														
Number	55	63	62	53	59	74	56	64	65	58	63	66	65	64
Yards	1074	1389	1213	1094	1139	1443	1117	1252	1185	1147	1189	1304	1137	1322
Average Yards	19.5	22.0	19.6	20.6	19.3	19.5	19.9	19.6	18.2	19.8	18.9	19.8	17.5	20.7
Touchdowns	0	0	1	0	0	0	1	0	0	0	2	0	0	0
INTERCEPT RET.:														
Number	10	17	18	18	16	16	31	26	13	21	20	20	15	22
Yards	89	146	184	318	100	166	567	275	152	312	164	218	274	216
Average Yards	8.9	8.6	10.2	17.7	16.7	10.4	18.3	10.6	11.7	14.9	8.2	10.9	18.3	10.8
Touchdowns	0	1	0	2	0	0	4	1	0	1	0	1	1	1
PENALTIES:														
Number	121	111	101	104	121	99	97	114	72	87	131	104	119	98
Yards	878	847	807	910	1018	880	829	951	609	672	981	853	977	813
FUMBLES:														
Number	40	31	31	24	28	41	27	36	37	27	37	27	29	29
Number Lost	20	16	13	13	12	20	17	24	14	11	16	16	16	13
POINTS:														
Total	287	409	391	378	274	229	358	323	430	412	364	307	335	366
PAT Attempts	34	51	45	45	30	27	43	37	56	45	45	35	41	43
PAT Made	32	50	43	44	28	26	43	36	52	44	44	32	39	42
FG Attempts	27	32	33	28	27	25	26	28	22	41	19	32	25	35
FG Made	17	17	26	20	22	13	19	21	14	32	16	21	16	22
Percent FG Made	63.0	53.1	78.8	71.4	81.5	52.0	73.1	75.0	63.6	78.0	84.2	65.6	64.0	62.9
Safeties	0	1	0	2	0	1	0	1	0	1	1	1	1	0

DEFENSE

	BUFF.	CIN.	CLEV.	DENV.	HOU.	IND.	K.C.	L.A.	MIA.	N.E.	NY J	PIT.	S.D.	SEA.
FIRST DOWNS:														
Total	334	336	302	291	285	334	310	283	337	286	349	303	308	310
by Rushing	100	134	113	93	102	123	111	85	144	118	92	97	104	93
by Passing	204	171	171	177	137	185	173	168	177	153	216	176	182	192
by Penalty	30	31	18	21	46	26	26	30	16	15	41	30	22	25
RUSHING:														
Number	465	514	494	432	532	517	485	439	540	510	450	471	475	471
Yards	1721	2122	1981	1681	2035	1962	1739	1728	2493	2203	1661	1872	1678	1759
Average Yards	3.7	4.1	4.0	3.8	3.8	3.8	3.6	3.9	4.6	4.3	3.7	4.0	3.5	3.7
Touchdowns	18	23	12	13	13	14	13	19	23	19	12	10	14	12
PASSING:														
Attempts	570	495	518	545	490	510	569	501	485	473	603	536	509	535
Completions	343	278	291	301	228	306	303	271	290	255	348	311	288	301
Completion Pct.	60.2	56.2	56.2	55.2	46.5	60.0	53.3	54.1	59.8	53.9	57.7	578.0	56.6	56.3
Passing Yards	4069	3520	3546	3755	3200	3933	3555	3539	3825	3324	4567	3669	4128	3888
Avg. Yds per Att.	6.3	5.9	6.0	5.6	5.8	7.0	5.2	5.5	6.9	5.7	7.0	5.8	6.5	6.2
Avg. Yds per Comp.	11.9	12.7	12.2	12.5	14.0	12.9	11.7	13.1	13.2	13.0	13.1	11.8	14.3	12.9
Times Tackled	36	42	35	49	32	24	44	63	33	48	28	43	62	47
Yds Lost Tackled	267	368	258	459	201	194	360	463	268	346	178	289	440	306
Net Yards	3802	3152	3288	3296	2999	3739	3195	3076	3557	2978	4389	3380	3688	3582
Touchdowns	21	17	21	21	25	28	21	21	22	15	35	22	27	20
Interceptions	10	17	18	18	16	16	31	26	13	21	20	20	15	22
Pct. Intercepted	1.8	3.4	3.5	3.3	3.3	3.1	5.4	5.2	2.7	4.4	3.3	3.7	2.9	4.1
PUNTS:														
Number	83	77	80	86	94	67	83	97	64	90	75	82	81	81
Average	38.1	39.8	37.9	42.9	39.5	40.7	37.0	42.1	41.4	39.8	39.7	39.0	40.8	40.4
PUNT RETURNS														
Number	32	19	44	40	40	52	52	42	23	60	36	34	43	38
Yards	260	182	268	362	303	533	572	357	200	565	165	364	370	298
Average Yards	8.1	9.6	6.1	9.1	7.6	10.3	11.0	8.5	8.7	9.4	4.6	10.7	8.6	7.8
Touchdowns	0	0	0	0	0	1	1	1	0	0	0	0	1	0
KICKOFF RET.:														
Number	56	80	78	65	32	43	71	63	53	81	62	56	60	59
Yards	1157	1611	1476	1299	695	827	1278	1064	997	1480	1307	1362	1088	1002
Average Yards	20.7	20.1	18.9	20.0	21.7	19.2	18.0	16.9	18.8	18.3	21.1	24.3	18.1	17.0
Touchdowns	0	1	1	0	0	0	0	0	0	0	0	3	0	0
INTERCEPT RET.:														
Number	19	20	11	16	31	24	18	25	23	13	21	20	33	14
Yards	284	189	136	363	325	310	181	282	221	151	230	244	421	216
Average Yards	15.0	9.5	12.3	22.7	10.5	12.9	10.0	11.3	9.6	11.6	11.0	12.2	12.8	15.4
Touchdowns	0	0	1	2	1	2	1	1	1	0	1	2	2	1
PENALTIES:														
Number	128	93	101	127	85	100	114	118	82	106	102	109	108	81
Yards	1098	840	754	1034	674	728	965	868	596	866	795	904	918	652
FUMBLES:														
Number	19	30	36	32	31	41	26	33	32	38	48	31	42	26
Number Lost	8	11	19	17	16	19	18	12	14	19	18	13	22	14
POINTS:														
Total	348	394	310	327	329	400	326	346	405	307	386	336	396	293
PAT Attempts	40	47	36	36	38	47	39	43	47	35	48	39	47	34
PAT Made	38	44	34	35	38	46	36	40	45	34	48	36	45	32
FG Attempts	33	30	29	32	29	35	31	21	31	28	27	39	31	28
FG Made	22	22	20	24	19	24	20	16	26	21	16	22	23	19
Percent FG Made	66.7	73.3	69.0	75.0	65.5	68.6	64.5	76.2	83.9	75.0	59.3	56.4	74.2	67.9
Safeties	2	1	0	2	0	0	1	0	0	0	1	0	0	0

sized offensive line that could block better for passing than running and a group of backs that was ordinary at best, Elway took over the attack with his arm and feet and led Denver to the Western Division title. They got out in front with a 6-0 start and then alternated wins and losses to hold on. The defense, bulwarked by linebackers Karl Mecklenburg and Ricky Hunley, end Rulon Jones and cornerback Louis Wright, was strong early but slumped badly at season's end.

Kansas City Chiefs — The Chiefs had their first winning season since 1981 and earned a playoff berth for the first time since 1971, so, naturally, they fired the coach at the end of the season. John Mackovic was blamed for the team's poor offense and general disharmony. His successor, special-teams coach Frank Gansz, had produced a unit that blocked 11 kicks (four by Albert Lewis) and had six touchdown returns. In the final game against Pittsburgh, needing a win to make the playoffs, the special teams accounted for all three touchdowns in a 24-19 win.

Seattle Seahawks — The Seahawks stood 5-3 after losing at Denver on October 26, but they'd been inconsistent. Coach Chuck Knox benched quarterback Dave Krieg, replacing him with Gale Gilbert, and the team became *very* inconsistent. They lost three straight with only a single touchdown in each outing. When Krieg was restored as the starter, Seattle won its final five and just missed the playoffs. During the final month, Krieg's pass rating was a sensational 138.2. Running back Curt Warner proved he was fully recovered from knee surgery by leading the A.F.C. in rushing with 1,481 yards and 13 scores. Receiver Steve Largent set an N.F.L. record after catching passes in 139 consecutive games. Defensive end Jacob Green had an outstanding year with 12 sacks, but the defense was hurt when safety Kenny Easley went out with injuries.

Los Angeles Raiders — The Raiders began to show their age in '86. The offensive line was blitzed for 64 sacks, which didn't help a shaky quarterback situation. By mid-season, coach Tom Flores benched Marc Wilson in favor of ancient Jim Plunkett, who played well until he was injured. Running back Marcus Allen had a terrible year, gaining only 759 yards — exactly 1,000 fewer than he gained in '85 — and fumbling at inopportune times. Even the defense, long a source of pride, showed some slippage, although cornerback Mike Haynes and nose tackle Bill Pickel were outstanding. Todd Christensen's 92 pass receptions broke his own record for tight ends.

San Diego Chargers — The resignation of coach Don Coryell with the team at 1-7 did not mark a great turnaround in the Chargers' fortunes, but new coach Al Saunders promised a change from the team's point-a-minute defenses of the past. Indeed, in the three games won under Saunders, the Chargers held their opponents without a touchdown. Linebacker Billy Ray Smith, with 11 sacks and 110 tackles, was the leading light in the defensive improvement. Quarterback Dan Fouts showed he could play Saunder's ball-control, short passing game but suffered a couple of concussions along the way. Running back Gary Anderson led the team in both rushing and receiving.

NEW ENGLAND PATRIOTS 11-5 Raymond Berry

Scores of Each Game		
33	INDIANAPOLIS	3
20	N.Y.Jets	6
31	SEATTLE	38
20	Denver	27
34	MIAMI	7
24	N.Y.JETS	31
34	Pittsburgh	0
23	Buffalo	3
25	ATLANTA	17
30	Indianapolis	21
30	L.A.Rams	28
22	BUFFALO	19
21	New Orleans	20
7	CINCINNATI	31
24	SAN FRANCISCO	29
34	Miami	27

Use Name	Pos.	Hgt	Wgt	Age	Int	Pts
Bill Bain (from NYJ)	OT	6'4"	290	34		
Brian Holloway	OT	6'7"	288	27		
Darryl Haley	OT-OG	6'4"	265	25		
Steve Moore	OT	6'4"	305	25		
Paul Fairchild	OG	6'4"	270	24		
Ron Wooten	OG	6'4"	273	27		
Guy Morriss	OG-C	6'4"	275	35		
Pete Brock	C	6'5"	275	32		
Trevor Matich	C	6'4"	270	24		
Milford Hodge (from NO)	DE-NT	6'3"	278	25		
Kenneth Sims	DE	6'5"	271	26		
Garin Veris	DE	6'4"	255	23		
Toby Williams	DE-NT	6'3"	270	26		
Brent Williams	DE-NT	6'3"	278	21		6
Dennis Owens	NT	6'1"	258	26		
Mike Ruth	NT	6'1"	266	22		
Mel Black	LB	6'2"	228	24		
Don Blackman	LB	6'3"	235	28		
Steve Doig	LB	6'2"	240	26		
Larry McGrew	LB	6'5"	233	29	2	
Steve Nelson	LB	6'2"	230	25	2	
Johnny Rembert	LB	6'3"	234	25	1	6
Ed Reynolds	LB	6'5"	242	24		
Andre Tippett	LB	6'3"	241	26		
Clayton Weishuhn	LB	6'2"	220	25		
Ed Williams	LB	6'4"	245	25		
Jim Bowman	DB	6'2"	210	22		
Raymond Clayborn	DB	6'1"	186	31	3	
Ernest Gibson	DB	5'10"	185	24		
Roland James	DB	6'2"	191	28	2	
Ronnie Lippett	DB	5'11"	180	25	8	
Fred Marion	DB	6'2"	191	27	2	6
Rod McSwain	DB	6'1"	198	24	1	6
Eugene Profit	DB	5'10"	165	21		
Tony Eason	QB	6'4"	212	26		
Steve Grogan	QB	6'4"	210	33		6
Tom Ramsey	QB	6'1"	189	25		
Tony Collins	HB	5'11"	212	27		48
Reggie Dupard	HB	5'11"	205	22		
Craig James	HB	6'	215	25		24
Mosi Tatupu	FB	6'	227	31		12
Robert Weathers	FB	6'2"	222	25		6
Irving Fryar	WR	6'	200	23		42
Cedric Jones	WR	6'1"	184	26		6
Stanley Morgan	WR	5'11"	181	31		60
Stephen Starring	WR	5'10"	172	25		12
Derwin Williams	WR	6'1"	185	25		
Greg Baty	TE	6'5"	241	22		12
Greg Hawthorne	TE	6'2"	235	29		
Willie Scott	TE	6'4"	245	27		18
Rich Camarillo	K	5'11"	185	26		
Tony Franklin	K	5'8"	182	29		140

Lin Dawson - Knee Injury
Art Plunkett - Knee Injury

NEW YORK JETS 10-6 Joe Walton

Scores of Each Game		
28	Buffalo	24
6	NEW ENGLAND	20
51	MIAMI	*45
26	Indianapolis	7
14	BUFFALO	13
31	New England	24
22	DENVER	10
28	NEW ORLEANS	23
38	Seattle	7
28	Atlanta	14
31	INDIANAPOLIS	16
3	Miami	45
3	L.A.RAMS	17
10	San Francisco	24
24	PITTSBURGH	45
21	Cincinnati	52

Use Name	Pos.	Hgt	Wgt	Age	Int	Pts
Gordon King	OT-OG	6'6"	270	30		
Reggie McElroy	OT	6'6"	275	26		
Jim Sweeney	OT-OG	6'4"	260	24		
Dan Alexander	OG	6'4"	270	31		
Ted Banker	OG-OT-C	6'2"	265	25		
Mike Haight	OG-OT	6'4"	270	23		
Guy Bingham	C-OT-OG	6'3"	260	28		
Joe Fields	C	6'2"	253	32		
Barry Bennett	DE-DT	6'4"	260	30		
Mark Gastineau	DE	6'5"	270	29		
Marty Lyons	DE-DT	6'5"	269	29		
Ben Rudolph	DE	6'5"	271	29		
Tom Baldwin	DT	6'4"	275	25		
Joe Klecko	NT-DT-DE	6'3"	265	32		
Derland Moore (from NO)	NT	6'4"	273	34		
Rogers Alexander	LB	6'3"	220	22		
Troy Benson	LB	6'2"	235	23		
Kyle Clifton	LB	6'4"	230	24	2	
Bob Crable	LB	6'3"	230	26	1	
Rusty Guilbeau	LB	6'4"	235	27		
Charles Jackson	LB	6'2"	225	31		
Kevin McArthur	LB	6'2"	230	23		
Lance Mehl	LB	6'3"	233	28		
Matt Monger	LB	6'1"	238	24		
Russell Carter	DB	6'2"	195	24		
Robert Ducksworth	DB	5'11"	200	23		
Harry Hamilton	DB	6'	195	23	1	
Jerry Holmes	DB	6'2"	175	28	6	
Carl Howard	DB	6'2"	190	24		
Bobby Humphery	DB	5'10"	180	25		8
Kerry Glenn	DB	5'9"	175	24		
Lester Lyles	DB-LB	6'3"	218	23	5	
Johnny Lynn	DB	6'	198	29	5	
Rich Milano	DB	6'	200	23		
Devlin Mullen	DB	6'1"	177	26		
Ken O'Brien	QB	6'4"	208	25		
Pat Ryan	QB	6'3"	210	30		
Richard Todd	QB	6'2"	212	32		
Dennis Bilgen (to TB)	HB	5'11"	215	24		6
Johnny Hector	HB	5'11"	200	25		48
Freeman McNeil	HB	5'11"	214	27		36
Marion Barber	FB	6'3"	228	26		
Nuu Faaola	FB	5'11"	215	22		
Tony Paige	FB	5'10"	225	23		12
Michael Harper	WR	5'10"	180	25		
Kurt Sohn	WR	5'11"	180	29		12
Al Toon	WR	6'4"	205	23		48
JoJo Townsell	WR	5'9"	180	25		6
Wesley Walker	WR	6'	182	31		72
Billy Griggs	TE	6'3"	230	24		
Rocky Klever	TE	6'3"	228	27		
Mickey Shuler	TE	6'3"	231	30		24
Pat Leahy	K	6'	200	35		92
Dave Jennings	K	6'4"	200	34		

Johnny "Lam" Jones - Finger Injury
Kirk Springs - Back Injury
Stan Waldemore - Knee Injury
Nick Bruckner - Shoulder Injury

MIAMI DOLPHINS 8-8 Don Shula

Scores of Each Game		
28	San Diego	50
30	INDIANAPOLIS	10
45	N.Y.Jets	*51
16	SAN FRANCISCO	31
7	New England	34
27	BUFFALO	14
28	L.A.RAIDERS	30
17	Indianapolis	13
28	HOUSTON	7
16	Cleveland	26
34	Buffalo	24
45	N.Y.JETS	3
14	ATLANTA	20
31	New Orleans	27
37	L.A.Rams	31
27	NEW ENGLAND	34

Use Name	Pos.	Hgt	Wgt	Age	Int	Pts
Jeff Dellenbach	OT	6'6"	280	23		
Jon Giesler	OT	6'5"	265	29		
Cleveland Green	OT	6'3"	263	28		
Greg Koch	OT	6'4"	276	31		
Tom Toth	OT	6'5"	275	24		
Roy Foster	OG	6'4"	275	26		
Ronnie Lee	OG	6'3"	265	29		
Larry Lee	C	6'2"	263	26		
Dwight Stephenson	C	6'2"	255	28		
Doug Betters	DE	6'7"	265	30		
Jerome Foster (to NYJ)	DE	6'2"	275	26		
George Little	DE	6'4"	278	23		
Mack Moore (to SD)	DE	6'4"	258	27		
T.J.Turner	DE	6'4"	265	23		
Bob Baumhower	NT	6'5"	265	31		
Mike Charles	NT	6'4"	287	23	1	
Brian Sochia	NT	6'3"	274	25		
Jay Brophy	LB	6'3"	233	26		
Mark Brown	LB	6'2"	230	25		
Bob Brudzinski	LB	6'4"	223	31		
David Frye	LB	6'2"	227	25		
Hugh Green	LB	6'2"	225	27		
Andy Hendel	LB	6'1"	230	25		
Larry Kolic	LB	6'1"	242	23		
Alex Moyer	LB	6'1"	221	22		
John Offerdahl	LB	6'3"	232	22	1	
Jackie Shipp	LB	6'2"	236	24		
Jack Squirek	LB	6'4"	235	27		
Glenn Blackwood	DB	6'	190	29	2	
Lyle Blackwood	DB	6'	190	35	1	
Bud Brown	DB	6'	194	25	1	
William Judson	DB	6'1"	190	27	2	
Mike Kozlowski	DB	6'	198	30	1	
Paul Lankford	DB	6'1"	184	28		
Don McNeal	DB	5'11"	192	28	2	
Donovan Rose	DB	6'1"	190	29	2	
Mike Smith	DB	6'	171	23		
Reyna Thompson	DB	5'11"	194	23		
Dan Marino	QB	6'4"	214	24		
Don Strock	QB	6'5"	225	35		
Joe Carter	HB	5'11"	198	24		
Craig Ellis	HB	5'11"	180	25		
Lorenzo Hampton	HB	6'	212	24		72
Tony Nathan	HB	6'	206	29		12
Woody Bennett	FB	6'2"	225	30		
Ron Davenport	FB	6'2"	230	23		6
Mark Clayton	WR	5'9"	175	25		60
Mark Duper	WR	5'9"	187	27		66
Jim Jensen	WR	6'4"	215	27		6
Nat Moore	WR	5'9"	188	34		42
James Pruitt	WR	6'3"	199	22		18
Bruce Hardy	TE	6'5"	232	30		30
Dan Johnson	TE	6'3"	240	26		24
Fuad Reveiz	K	5'11"	222	23		94
Reggie Roby	K	6'2"	243	25		

Joe Rose - Leg Injury
Robin Sendlein - Knee Injury
Steve Clark - Injury
Charles Bowser - Ankle Injury

BUFFALO BILLS 4-12 Hank Bullough (2-7) Marv Levy (2-5)

Scores of Each Game		
24	N.Y.JETS	28
33	Cincinnati	*36
17	ST.LOUIS	10
17	KANSAS CITY	20
13	N.Y.Jets	14
14	Miami	27
24	INDIANAPOLIS	13
3	NEW ENGLAND	23
28	Tampa Bay	34
16	PITTSBURGH	12
24	MIAMI	34
19	New England	22
17	Kansas City	14
17	CLEVELAND	21
14	Indianapolis	24
7	Houston	16

Use Name	Pos.	Hgt	Wgt	Age	Int	Pts
Justin Cross	OT	6'6"	265	27		
Joe Devlin	OT	6'5"	280	32		
Dale Hellestrae	OT	6'5"	275	24		
Ken Jones	OT	6'5"	285	34		
Will Wolford	OT	6'5"	276	22		
Jim Ritcher	OG	6'3"	265	28		
Mark Traynowicz	OG	6'5"	275	23		
Tim Vogler	OG	6'3"	285	29		
Leonard Burton	C	6'3"	252	22		
Kent Hull	C	6'4"	262	25		
Mike Hamby	DE	6'4"	270	23		
Sean McNanie	DE	6'5"	270	24		
Dean Prater	DE	6'4"	280	23		
Bruce Smith	DE	6'4"	280	23		
Jerry Boyarsky (to GB)	NT	6'3"	290	27		
Mark Catano	NT	6'3"	267	24		
Fred Smerlas	NT	6'3"	280	29	1	
Don Smith	NT	6'5"	262	29		
Ray Bentley	LB	6'2"	250	25		
George Cumby	LB	6'	224	30		
Guy Frazier	LB	6'2"	217	27		
Tony Furjanic	LB	6'1"	228	22		
Hal Garner	LB	6'4"	225	24		
Eugene Marve	LB	6'2"	240	26		
Lucius Sanford	LB	6'2"	220	30		
Darryl Talley	LB	6'4"	227	26		
Martin Bayless	DB	6'2"	195	23	1	
Rodney Bellinger	DB	5'8"	189	24	1	6
Derrick Burroughs	DB	6'1"	180	24	2	
Dwight Drane	DB	6'1"	200	24		
Steve Freeman	DB	5'11"	185	33	1	
Rod Hill (to DET)	DB	6'	188	27		
Mark Kelso	DB	5'11"	177	23		
Ron Pitts	DB	5'10"	175	23		6
Charles Romes	DB	6'1"	190	32	4	
Kevin Williams	DB	5'9"	170	24		
Stan Gelbaugh	QB	6'3"	207	23		
Jim Kelly	QB	6'3"	215	26		
Frank Reich	QB	6'3"	208	24		
Greg Bell	HB	5'10"	210	24		36
Ronnie Harmon	HB	5'11"	192	22		6
Robb Riddick	HB	6'	195	29		30
Carl Byrum	FB	6'	232	23		
Bruce King (from KC)	FB	6'1"	219	23		
Ricky Moore	FB	5'11"	230	23		6
Gary Wilkins	FB	6'1"	235	22		
Walter Broughton	WR	5'10"	180	23		
Chris Burkett	WR	6'4"	198	24		24
Jerry Butler	WR	6'	178	28		12
Andre Reed	WR	6'	186	23		42
Eric Richardson	WR	6'1"	185	24		
Steve Tasker (from HOU)	WR	5'9"	185	24		
Jimmy Teal	WR	5'10"	170	24		6
Don Kern	TE	6'4"	235	24		
Pete Metzelaars	TE	6'7"	243	26		24
Butch Rolle	TE	6'3"	242	22		
John Kidd	K	6'3"	208	25		
Scott Norwood	K	6'	207	26		83

Greg Christy - Neck Injury
Jim Haslett - Knee Injury
Lawrence Johnson - Leg Injury
Mitchell Brookins - Knee Injury

INDIANAPOLIS COLTS 3-13 Rod Dowhower (0-13) Ron Meyer (3-0)

Scores of Each Game		
3	New England	33
10	Miami	30
7	L.A.RAMS	24
7	N.Y.JETS	26
14	San Francisco	35
14	NEW ORLEANS	17
13	Buffalo	24
13	MIAMI	17
9	CLEVELAND	24
21	NEW ENGLAND	30
16	N.Y.Jets	31
16	Houston	31
3	SAN DIEGO	17
28	Atlanta	23
24	BUFFALO	14
30	L.A.Raiders	24

Use Name	Pos.	Hgt	Wgt	Age	Int	Pts
Karl Baldischwiler	OT	6'5"	276	30		
Bob Brotzki	OT	6'5"	269	23		
Kevin Call	OT	6'7"	293	24		
Roger Caron	OT	6'5"	272	24		
Chris Hinton	OT	6'4"	288	25		
Mark Kirchner	OG	6'3"	265	26		
Ron Solt	OG	6'3"	279	24		
Ben Utt	OG	6'5"	281	27		
Ray Donaldson	C	6'3"	282	28		
Willie Broughton	DE	6'5"	277	21		
Jon Hand	DE	6'7"	280	22	1	
Donnell Thompson	DE	6'4"	272	27		
John Haines	DE-DT-NT	6'6"	266	24		
Scott Kellar	DT	6'3"	278	22		
Harvey Armstrong	NT	6'3"	261	26	1	
Dave Ahrens	LB	6'3"	245	27		
Duane Bickett	LB	6'5"	241	23	2	
Johnie Cooks	LB	6'4"	251	27	1	
Lamonte Hunley	LB	6'2"	241	23		
Barry Krauss	LB	6'3"	253	29		
Jeff Leiding	LB	6'3"	232	24		2
Orlando Lowry	LB	6'4"	237	25		
Cliff Odom	LB	6'2"	241	28		
Glenn Redd (from NO)	LB	6'1"	232	28		
Pat Ballage	DB	6'1"	200	22		
Dextor Clinkscale	DB	5'11"	195	28		
Leonard Coleman	DB	6'2"	197	24	4	
Eugene Daniel	DB	5'11"	178	25	3	6
Kenny Daniel	DB	5'10"	180	26	1	
Preston Davis	DB	5'11"	180	24		
Nesby Glasgow	DB	5'10"	186	29		
Dwight Hicks	DB	6'1"	192	30	2	
John Holt	DB	5'11"	180	27	1	
Victor Jackson	DB	6'	205	26		
Tate Randle	DB	6'	204	27		
Tommy Sims	DB	6'	190	21		
Gary Hogeboom	QB	6'4"	207	28		6
Blair Kiel	QB	6'	200	24		
Ed Luther	QB	6'3"	210	29		
Jack Trudeau	QB	6'3"	211	23		6
Albert Bentley	HB	5'11"	210	26		18
George Wonsley	HB	5'10"	220	25		6
Owen Gill	FB	6'1"	230	24		6
Randy McMillan	FB	6'	216	27		18
Hubie Oliver (to HOU)	FB	5'10"	230	28		
Matt Bouza	WR	6'3"	208	28		30
Bill Brooks	WR	5'11"	190	22		48
Wayne Capers	WR	6'2"	203	25		
James Harbour	WR	6'1"	192	23		
Robbie Martin	WR	5'8"	187	27		
Walter Murray	WR	6'4"	200	23		
Pat Beach	TE	6'4"	244	26		6
Mark Boyer	TE	6'4"	239	23		6
Greg LaFleur (from STL)	TE	6'4"	236	27		
Tim Sherwin	TE	6'6"	246	28		6
Dean Biasucci	K	6'	198	24		65
Rohn Stark	K	6'3"	202	27		

* Overtime

NEW ENGLAND PATRIOTS

RUSHING

Last Name	No.	Yds	Avg	TD
C. James	154	427	2.8	4
Collins	156	412	2.6	3
Tatupu	71	172	2.4	1
Eason	35	170	4.9	0
Fryar	4	80	20.0	0
Weathers	21	58	2.8	1
Dupard	15	39	2.6	0
Grogan	9	23	2.6	1
Hawthorne	1	5	5.0	0
Starring	1	0	0.0	0
Ramsey	1	-6	-6.0	0
Jones	1	-7	-7.0	0

RECEIVING

Last Name	No.	Yds	Avg	TD
Morgan	84	1491	17.8	10
Collins	77	684	8.9	5
Fryar	43	737	17.1	6
Baty	37	331	8.9	2
Hawthorne	24	192	8.0	0
C. James	18	129	7.2	0
Starring	16	295	18.4	2
Tatupu	15	145	9.7	0
Jones	14	222	15.9	1
Scott	8	41	5.1	3
D. Williams	2	35	17.5	0
Weathers	1	14	14.0	0
Holloway	1	5	5.0	0

PUNT RETURNS

Last Name	No.	Yds	Avg	TD
Fryar	35	366	10.5	1
Starring	6	18	3.0	0
Marion	1	12	12.0	0

KICKOFF RETURNS

Last Name	No.	Yds	Avg	TD
Starring	36	802	22.3	0
Fryar	10	192	19.2	0
Jones	4	63	15.8	0
Dupard	3	50	16.7	0
Rembert	3	27	9.0	0
Hawthorne	2	13	6.5	0

PASSING — PUNTING — KICKING

PASSING	Att	Cmp	%	Yds	Yd/Att	TD	Int-	%	RK
Eason	448	276	62	3328	7.4	19	10-	2	3
Grogan	102	62	61	976	9.6	9	2-	2	
C. James	4	1	25	10	2.5	1	1-	25	
Ramsey	3	1	33	7	2.3	0	0-	0	

PUNTING	No	Avg
Camarillo	89	42.1

KICKING	XP	Att	%	FG	Att	%
Franklin	44	45	98	32	41	78

NEW YORK JETS

RUSHING

Last Name	No.	Yds	Avg	TD
McNeil	214	856	4.0	5
Hector	164	605	3.7	8
Paige	47	109	2.3	2
Bligen	20	65	3.3	1
O'Brien	17	46	2.7	0
Ryan	8	28	3.5	0
Barber	11	27	2.5	0
Faaola	3	5	1.7	0
Townsell	1	2	2.0	0
Jennings	1	0	0.0	0
Toon	2	-3	-1.5	0
Sohn	2	-11	-5.5	0

RECEIVING

Last Name	No.	Yds	Avg	TD
Toon	85	1176	13.8	8
Shuler	69	675	9.8	4
Walker	49	1016	20.7	12
McNeil	49	410	8.4	1
Hector	33	302	9.2	0
Paige	18	121	6.7	0
Klever	15	150	10.0	0
Sohn	8	129	16.1	2
Barber	5	36	7.2	0
Bligen	2	6	3.0	0
Townsell	1	11	11.0	0

PUNT RETURNS

Last Name	No.	Yds	Avg	TD
Sohn	35	289	8.3	0
Townsell	4	52	13.0	0

KICKOFF RETURNS

Last Name	No.	Yds	Avg	TD
Humphery	28	655	23.4	1
Townsell	13	322	24.8	1
Sohn	7	124	17.7	0
Harper	7	71	10.1	0
Rudolph	3	17	5.7	0
Baldwin	2	3	1.5	0
Shuler	2	-3	-1.5	0
Lynn	1	0	0.0	0

PASSING — PUNTING — KICKING

PASSING	Att	Cmp	%	Yds	Yd/Att	TD	Int-	%	RK
O'Brien	482	300	62	3690	7.7	25	20-	4	5
Ryan	55	34	62	342	6.2	2	1-	2	

PUNTING	No	Avg
Jennings	85	39.4

KICKING	XP	Att	%	FG	Att	%
Leahy	44	44	100	16	19	84

MIAMI DOLPHINS

RUSHING

Last Name	No.	Yds	Avg	TD
Hampton	186	830	4.5	9
Davenport	75	314	4.2	0
Nathan	27	203	7.5	0
Bennett	36	162	4.5	0
Clayton	2	33	16.5	0
Carter	4	18	4.5	0
Ellis	3	6	2.0	0
Strock	1	0	0.0	0
Marino	12	-3	-0.3	0
Roby	2	-8	-4.0	0
Duper	1	-10	-10.0	0

RECEIVING

Last Name	No.	Yds	Avg	TD
Duper	67	1313	19.6	11
Hampton	61	446	7.3	3
Clayton	60	1150	19.2	10
Hardy	54	430	8.0	5
Nathan	48	457	9.5	2
N. Moore	38	431	11.3	7
Davenport	20	177	8.9	1
Johnson	19	170	8.9	4
Pruitt	15	235	15.7	2
Jensen	5	50	10.0	1
Bennett	4	33	8.3	0
Carter	1	6	6.0	0

PUNT RETURNS

Last Name	No.	Yds	Avg	TD
Ellis	24	149	6.2	0
Pruitt	11	150	13.6	1
G. Blackwood	1	0	0.0	0
L. Blackwood	1	0	0	0
Clayton	1	0	0.0	0
Thompson	1	0	0.0	0
N. Moore	1	-2	-2.0	0

KICKOFF RETURNS

Last Name	No.	Yds	Avg	TD
Ellis	25	541	21.6	0
Davenport	16	285	17.8	0
Hampton	9	182	20.2	0
Carter	9	133	14.8	0
Hardy	3	39	13.0	0
L. Lee	1	5	5.0	0
Johnson	1	0	0.0	0
Toth	1	0	0.0	0

PASSING — PUNTING — KICKING

PASSING	Att	Cmp	%	Yds	Yd/Att	TD	Int-	%	RK
Marino	623	378	61	4746	7.6	44	23-	4	1
Strock	20	14	70	152	7.6	2	0-	0	
Jensen	2	0	0	0	0.0	0	0-	0	

PUNTING	No	Avg
Roby	56	44.2

KICKING	XP	Att	%	FG	Att	%
Reveiz	52	55	95	14	22	64

BUFFALO BILLS

RUSHING

Last Name	No.	Yds	Avg	TD
Riddick	150	632	4.2	4
Bell	90	377	4.2	4
Kelly	41	199	4.9	0
Harmon	54	172	3.2	0
Byrum	38	156	4.1	0
Moore	33	104	3.2	1
Wilkins	3	18	6.0	0
King	4	10	2.5	0
Kidd	1	0	0.0	0
Reich	1	0	0.0	0
Broughton	1	-6	-6.0	0
Reed	3	-8	-2.7	0

RECEIVING

Last Name	No.	Yds	Avg	TD
Reed	53	739	13.9	7
Metzelaars	49	485	9.9	3
Riddick	49	468	9.6	1
Burkett	34	778	22.9	4
Moore	23	184	8.0	0
Harmon	22	185	8.4	1
Butler	15	302	20.1	2
Byrum	13	104	8.0	1
Bell	12	142	11.8	2
Wilkins	8	74	9.3	0
Teal	6	60	10.0	1
Rolle	4	56	14.0	0
Broughton	3	71	23.7	0
Richardson	3	49	16.3	0

PUNT RETURNS

Last Name	No.	Yds	Avg	TD
Pitts	18	194	10.8	1
Broughton	12	53	4.4	0
Hill	1	0	0.0	0
Richardson	1	0	0.0	0

KICKOFF RETURNS

Last Name	No.	Yds	Avg	TD
Harmon	18	321	17.8	0
Tasker	12	213	17.8	0
Broughton	11	243	22.1	0
Riddick	8	200	25.0	0
Richardson	6	123	20.5	0
Bellinger	2	32	16.0	0
Pitts	1	7	7.0	0

PASSING — PUNTING — KICKING

PASSING	Att	Cmp	%	Yds	Yd/Att	TD	Int-	%	RK
Kelly	480	285	59	3593	7.5	22	17-	4	7
Reich	19	9	47	104	5.5	0	2-	11	

PUNTING	No	Avg
Kidd	75	40.4

KICKING	XP	Att	%	FG	Att	%
Norwood	32	34	94	17	27	63

INDIANAPOLIS COLTS

RUSHING

Last Name	No.	Yds	Avg	TD
McMillan	189	609	3.2	3
Bentley	73	351	4.8	3
Gill	53	228	4.3	1
Wonsley	60	214	3.6	1
Trudeau	13	21	1.6	1
Kiel	3	20	6.7	0
Hogeboom	10	20	2.0	1
Bouza	1	12	12.0	0
Capers	1	11	11.0	0
Brooks	4	5	1.3	0

RECEIVING

Last Name	No.	Yds	Avg	TD
Bouza	71	830	11.7	5
Brooks	65	1131	17.4	8
McMillan	34	289	8.5	0
Beach	25	265	10.6	1
Bentley	25	230	9.2	0
Boyer	22	237	10.8	1
Wonsley	16	175	10.9	0
Gill	16	137	8.6	0
Capers	9	118	13.1	0
LaFleur	7	56	8.0	0
Harbour	4	46	11.5	0
Sherwin	3	26	8.7	1
Murray	2	34	17.0	0
Martin	1	41	41.0	0

PUNT RETURNS

Last Name	No.	Yds	Avg	TD
Brooks	18	141	7.8	0
Martin	17	105	6.4	0

KICKOFF RETURNS

Last Name	No.	Yds	Avg	TD
Bentley	32	687	21.5	0
Martin	21	385	18.3	0
Brooks	8	143	17.9	0
K. Daniel	5	109	21.8	0
Gill	5	73	14.6	0
Wonsley	2	31	15.5	0
Williams	1	15	15.0	0

PASSING — PUNTING — KICKING

PASSING	Att	Cmp	%	Yds	Yd/Att	TD	Int-	%	RK
Trudeau	417	204	49	2225	5.3	8	18-	4	15
Hogeboom	144	85	59	1154	8.0	6	6-	4	
Kiel	25	11	44	236	9.4	2	0-	0	

PUNTING	No	Avg
Stark	76	45.2
Kiel	5	38.0

KICKING	XP	Att	%	FG	Att	%
Biasucci	26	27	96	13	25	52

CLEVELAND BROWNS 12-4 Marty Schottenheimer

Scores of Each Game		
31	Chicago	41
23	Houston	20
13	CINCINNATI	30
24	DETROIT	21
27	Pittsburgh	24
20	KANSAS CITY	7
14	GREEN BAY	17
23	Minnesota	20
24	Indianapolis	9
26	MIAMI	16
14	L.A.Raiders	27
37	PITTSBURGH	*31
13	HOUSTON	*10
21	Buffalo	17
34	Cincinnati	3
47	SAN DIEGO	17

Use Name	Pos.	Hgt	Wgt	Age	Int	Pts
Rickey Bolden	OT-OG	6'6"	280	24		
Bob Gruber	OT	6'5"	270	28		
Cody Risien	OT	6'7"	280	29		
Paul Farren	OG-OT	6'5"	280	25		
Dan Fike	OG-OT	6'7"	280	25		
Larry Williams	OG	6'5"	290	23		
George Lilja	OG-C	6'4"	270	28		
Jeff Wiska	OG	6'3"	260	26		
Mike Baab	C	6'4"	270	26		
Keith Baldwin	DE	6'4"	270	25		
Reggie Camp	DE	6'4"	280	25		
Sam Clancy	DE	6'7"	260	28		
Carl Hairston	DE	6'3"	260	33		
Ralph Malone	DE	6'5"	225	22		
Bob Golic	NT	6'2"	270	28		
Dave Puzzuoli	NT	6'3"	260	25		

Use Name	Pos.	Hgt	Wgt	Age	Int	Pts
Chip Banks	LB	6'4"	233	26		
Anthony Griggs	LB	6'3"	230	26		
Eddie Johnson	LB	6'1"	225	27		
Mike Johnson	LB	6'1"	228	23		
Clay Matthews	LB	6'2"	235	30	2	
Scott Nicolas	LB	6'3"	226	26		
Brad Van Pelt	LB	6'5"	235	35		
Hanford Dixon	DB	5'11"	186	27	5	
Ray Ellis	DB	6'1"	196	27	2	
Al Gross	DB	6'3"	195	25		6
Mark Harper	DB	5'9"	174	24	1	
D.D.Hoggard	DB	6'	188	25		
Frank Minnifield	DB	5'9"	180	26	3	6
Chris Rockins	DB	6'	195	24	2	
Felix Wright	DB	6'2"	190	27	3	6

Keith Baldwin - Knee Injury
Gary Danielson - Ankle Injury
Curtis Weathers - Knee Injury

Use Name	Pos.	Hgt	Wgt	Age	Int	Pts
Gary Danielson	QB	6'2"	196	34		
Bernie Kosar	QB	6'5"	210	22		
Mike Pagel	QB	6'2"	200	25		
Earnest Byner	HB	5'10"	215	23		24
Curtis Dickey	HB	6'1"	220	29		36
Herman Fontenot	HB	6'	206	22		12
Johnny Davis	FB	6'1"	235	30		
Major Everett	FB	5'10"	218	26		
Kevin Mack	FB	6'	212	24		60
Brian Brennan	WR	5'9"	178	24		42
Terry Greer	WR	6'1"	192	28		
Reggie Langhorne	WR	6'2"	195	23		6
Gerald McNeil	WR	5'7"	140	24		12
Webster Slaughter	WR	6'	170	21		30
Clarence Weathers	WR	5'9"	170	24		
Harry Holt	TE	6'4"	240	28		12
Ozzie Newsome	TE	6'2"	232	30		18
Travis Tucker	TE	6'3"	240	22		
Matt Bahr	K	5'10"	175	30		90
Jeff Gossett	K	6'2"	200	29		

CINCINNATI BENGALS 10-6 Sam Wyche

Scores of Each Game		
14	Kansas City	24
36	BUFFALO	*33
30	Cleveland	13
7	CHICAGO	44
34	Green Bay	28
24	PITTSBURGH	22
31	HOUSTON	28
9	Pittsburgh	30
24	Detroit	17
28	Houston	32
34	SEATTLE	7
24	MINNESOTA	20
28	Denver	34
31	New England	7
3	CLEVELAND	34
52	N.Y.JETS	21

Use Name	Pos.	Hgt	Wgt	Age	Int	Pts
David Douglas	OT	6'4"	280	23		
Anthony Munoz	OT	6'6"	278	28		12
Bruce Riemers	OT	6'7"	280	25		
Joe Walter	OT	6'6"	290	23		
Brian Blados	CG	6'5"	295	24		
Max Montoya	OG	6'5"	275	30		
Bruce Kozerski	C	6'4"	275	24		
Dave Rimington	C	6'3"	288	24		
Ross Browner	DE	6'3"	265	32		
Eddie Edwards	DE	6'5"	256	32		6
Mike Hammerstein	DE	6'4"	270	23		
Jim Show	DE	6'3"	250	23		
Tim Krumrie	NT	6'2"	262	26		

Use Name	Pos.	Hgt	Wgt	Age	Int	Pts
Leo Barker	LB	6'2"	227	26	2	
Ed Brady	LB	6'2"	235	26		
Kiki DeAyala	LB	6'1"	225	24		
Joe Kelly	LB	6'2"	227	21	1	
Emanuel King	LB	6'4"	251	23		
Ron Simpkins	LB	6'1"	235	28		
Leon White	LB	6'2"	236	22		2
Reggie Williams	LB	6'1"	228	31		
Carl Zander	LB	6'2"	235	21		
Lewis Billups	DB	5'1"	190	22		
Louis Breeden	DB	5'11"	185	32	7	6
Barney Bussey	DB	6'	195	24	1	
David Fulcher	DB	6'3"	228	21	4	
Ray Horton	DB	5'11"	190	26	1	
Robert Jackson	DB	5'10"	186	27		
Bobby Kemp	DB	6'	191	27	1	
John Simmons (to GB)	DB	5'11"	192	27	6	
Jimmy Turner (to ATL)	DB	6'	187	27		

Use Name	Pos.	Hgt	Wgt	Age	Int	Pts
Ken Anderson	QB	6'3"	212	37		
Boomer Esiason	QB	6'4"	220	25		6
Doug Gaynor	QB	6'2"	205	23		
James Brooks	HB	5'10"	182	27		54
Stanford Jennings	HB	6'1"	205	24		6
Bill Johnson	FB	6'2"	230	25		
Larry Kinnebrew	FB	6'1"	255	27		54
Stanley Wilson	FB	5'10"	210	25		48
Eddie Brown	WR	6'	185	23		24
Cris Collinsworth	WR	6'5"	192	27		60
Steve Kreider	WR	6'3"	192	28		
Mike Martin	WR	5'10"	186	25		
Tim McGee	WR	5'10"	175	22		6
Rodney Holman	TE	6'3"	238	26		12
Eric Kattus	TE	6'5"	235	23		6
Jim Breech	K	5'6"	161	30		101
Jeff Hayes	K	5'11"	175	27		6

PITTSBURGH STEELERS 6-10 Chuck Noll

Scores of Each Game		
0	Seattle	30
10	DENVER	21
7	Minnesota	31
22	Houston	*16
24	CLEVELAND	27
22	Cincinnati	24
0	NEW ENGLAND	34
30	CINCINNATI	9
27	GREEN BAY	3
12	Buffalo	16
21	HOUSTON	10
31	Cleveland	*37
10	Chicago	*31
27	DETROIT	17
45	N.Y.Jets	24
19	KANSAS CITY	24

Use Name	Pos.	Hgt	Wgt	Age	Int	Pts
Mark Behning	OT	6'6"	290	24		
Tunch Ilkin	OT	6'3"	265	28		
Ray Pinney	OT	6'4"	265	32		
Pete Rostosky	OT	6'4"	270	25		
Terry Long	OG	5'11"	265	27		
John Rienstra	OG	6'5"	273	23		
Craig Wolfley	OG	6'1"	260	28		
Dan Turk	C	6'4"	265	24		
Mike Webster	C	6'1"	260	34		
Randy Rasmussen	C-OG	6'2"	254	26		
Keith Gary	DE	6'3"	265	26		
Edmund Nelson	DE-NT	6'3"	277	26		
Darryl Sims	DE-NT	6'3"	275	25		
Keith Willis	DE	6'1"	255	27		
Gary Dunn	NT	6'3"	275	33		
Gerald Williams	NT	6'3"	270	22		

Use Name	Pos.	Hgt	Wgt	Age	Int	Pts
Gregg Carr	LB	6'2"	220	24		
Robin Cole	LB	6'2"	225	30		
Anthony Henton	LB	6'1"	218	23		
Bryan Hinkle	LB	6'2"	220	27	3	
David Little	LB	6'1"	240	27		
Mike Merriweather	LB	6'2"	215	26	2	
Larry Station	LB	5'11"	227	22		
Dennis Winston	LB	6'	224	30		
Harvey Clayton	DB	5'9"	180	25	3	
Dave Edwards	DB	6'	195	24		2
Donnie Elder (to DET)	DB	5'9"	175	23		
Lupe Sanchez	DB	5'10"	192	24	3	6
Chris Sheffield	DB	6'1"	185	23		
Donnie Shell	DB	5'11"	198	34	3	
John Swain	DB	6'1"	192	26		
Eric Williams	DB	6'1"	190	26	3	
Rick Woods	DB	6'	195	26	3	

Dwayne Woodruff - Knee Injury

Use Name	Pos.	Hgt	Wgt	Age	Int	Pts
Bubby Brister	QB	6'3"	184	24		6
Scott Campbell (to ATL)	QB	6'	195	24		
Mark Malone	QB	6'4"	220	27		30
Walter Abercrombie	HB	6'	210	26		48
Rich Erenberg	HB	5'10"	205	24		24
Earnest Jackson	HB	5'9"	208	26		30
David Hughes	FB	6'	220	27		
Frank Pollard	FB	5'10"	223	29		
Dan Reeder	FB	5'11"	235	25		
Chuck Sanders	FB	6'1"	233	22		
Jessie Britt	WR	6'4"	198	23		
Louis Lipps	WR	5'10"	185	24		18
John Stallworth	WR	6'2"	202	34		6
Calvin Sweeney	WR	6'2"	192	31		6
Weegie Thompson	WR	6'6"	210	25		30
Preston Gothard	TE	6'4"	240	24		6
Warren Seitz	TE	6'4"	223	23		
Gary Anderson	K	5'11"	170	27		95
Harry Newsome	K	6'	186	23		

HOUSTON OILERS 5-11 Jerry Glanville

Scores of Each Game		
31	Green Bay	3
20	CLEVELAND	23
13	Kansas City	27
16	PITTSBURGH	*22
13	Detroit	24
7	CHICAGO	20
28	Cincinnati	31
17	L.A.RAIDERS	28
7	Miami	28
32	CINCINNATI	28
10	Pittsburgh	21
31	INDIANAPOLIS	17
10	Cleveland	*13
0	San Diego	27
23	MINNESOTA	10
16	BUFFALO	7

Use Name	Pos.	Hgt	Wgt	Age	Int	Pts
Bruce Matthews	OT	6'4"	283	25		
Don Maggs	OT-OG	6'5"	279	24		
Eric Moran	OT-OG	6'5"	294	26		
Dean Steinkuhler	OT-OG	6'3"	275	25		
Doug Williams	OT-OG	6'5"	285	23		
Kent Hill	OG	6'5"	260	29		
Mike Munchak	OG	6'3"	286	26		6
Jay Pennison	C	6'1"	265	24		
Jim Romano	C	6'3"	264	26		
Jesse Baker	DE	6'5"	271	29		
Ray Childress	DE	6'6"	276	23		
William Fuller	DE	6'3"	255	24		
Lynn Madsen	DE	6'4"	260	26		
Malcolm Taylor	DE	6'6"	280	26		
Richard Byrd	DT	6'3"	264	24		
Mike Golic	DT	6'5"	272	23		
Karl Morgan	DT	6'1"	255	25		
Doug Smith	NT	6'5"	285	27		

Use Name	Pos.	Hgt	Wgt	Age	Int	Pts
Robert Abraham	LB	6'1"	236	26		
Frank Bush	LB	6'1"	218	23		
Kirk Dodge	LB	6'1"	232	24		
Eric Fairs	LB	6'3"	235	22		
John Grimsley	LB	6'2"	235	24		
Robert Lyles	LB	6'1"	225	25	2	6
Johnny Meads	LB	6'2"	235	25		
Avon Riley	LB	6'3"	240	28		
Patrick Allen	DB	5'10	179	25	3	
Keith Bostic	DB	6'1"	223	25		
Steve Brown	DB	5'11"	187	26	2	
Jeff Donaldson	DB	6'	194	24	1	6
Bo Eason	DB	6'2"	200	25	2	
Larry Griffin	DB	6'	190	23		
Richard Johnson	DB	6'1"	190	22	2	
Allen Lyday	DB	5'10"	197	25	3	
Audrey McMillian	DB	6'	190	24		

Tom Briehl - Ankle Injury
Mike Kelley - Neck Injury
Rod Kush - Knee Injury

Use Name	Pos.	Hgt	Wgt	Age	Int	Pts
Oliver Luck	QB	6'2"	196	26		
Warren Moon	QB	6'3"	210	29		12
John Witkowski	QB	6'1"	205	24		
Stan Edwards	HB	6'	210	26		
Allen Pinkett	HB	5'9"	185	22		18
Mike Rozier	HB	5'10"	211	25		24
Butch Woolfolk	HB	6'1"	207	26		12
Chuck Banks	FB	6'2"	225	22		
Ray Wallace	FB	6'	221	22		30
Mike Akiu	WR	5'9"	182	24		
Willie Drewrey	WR	5'7"	164	23		
Ernest Givins	WR	5'9"	174	21		24
Drew Hill	WR	5'9"	168	30		30
Tim Smith	WR	6'2"	206	29		
Chris Dressel	TE	6'4"	239	25		
Jeff Parks	TE	6'4"	236	21		
Jamie Williams	TE	6'4"	245	26		6
Lee Johnson	K	6'2"	199	24		
Tony Zendejas	K	5'8"	165	26		94

* Overtime

CLEVELAND BROWNS

RUSHING

Last Name	No.	Yds	Avg	TD
Mack	174	665	3.8	10
Dickey	135	523	3.9	6
Byner	94	277	2.9	2
Fontenot	25	105	4.2	1
Everett	12	43	3.6	0
Kosar	24	19	0.8	0
Holt	1	16	16.0	1
McNeil	1	12	12.0	0
Slaughter	1	1	1.0	0
Pagel	2	0	0.0	0
Langhorne	1	-11	-11.0	0

RECEIVING

Last Name	No.	Yds	Avg	TD
Brennan	55	838	15.2	6
Fontenot	47	559	11.9	1
Slaughter	40	577	14.4	4
Langhorne	39	678	17.4	1
Newsome	39	417	10.7	3
Byner	37	328	8.9	2
Mack	28	292	10.4	0
Dickey	10	78	7.8	0
Weathers	9	100	11.1	0
Holt	4	61	15.3	1
Greer	3	51	17.0	0
Tucker	2	29	14.5	0
McNeil	1	9	9.0	0
Kosar	1	1	1.0	0

PUNT RETURNS

Last Name	No.	Yds	Avg	TD
McNeil	40	348	8.7	1
Slaughter	1	2	2.0	0

KICKOFF RETURNS

Last Name	No.	Yds	Avg	TD
McNeil	47	997	21.2	1
Fontenot	7	99	14.1	0
Langhorne	4	57	14.3	0
Nicolas	3	28	9.3	0
Puzzuoli	1	32	32.0	0

PASSING — PUNTING — KICKING

PASSING	Att	Cmp	%	Yds	Yd/Att	TD	Int—	%	Rk
Kosar	531	310	58	3854	7.3	17	10—	2	6
Pagel	3	2	67	53	17.7	0	0—	0	
Gossett	2	1	50	30	15.0	0	1—	50	
Fontenot	1	1	100	46	46.0	1	0—	0	
Brennan	1	1	100	35	35.0	0	0—	0	

PUNTING	Att	Avg
Gossett	83	41.2

KICKING	XP	Att.	%	FG	Att	%
Bahr	30	30	100	20	26	77
Moseley	25	28	89	12	19	63

CINCINNATI BENGALS

RUSHING

Last Name	No.	Yds	Avg	TD
Brooks	205	1087	5.3	5
Kinnebrew	131	519	4.0	3
Wilson	68	379	5.6	8
Johnson	39	226	5.8	0
Esiason	44	146	3.3	1
Hayes	3	92	30.7	1
Jennings	16	54	3.4	1
Brown	8	32	4.0	0
McGee	4	10	2.5	0
Gaynor	1	4	4.0	0
Collinsworth	2	-16	-8.0	0

RECEIVING

Last Name	No.	Yds	Avg	TD
Collinsworth	62	1024	16.5	10
Brown	58	964	16.6	4
Brooks	54	686	12.7	4
Holman	40	570	14.3	2
McGee	16	276	17.3	1
Johnson	13	103	7.9	1
Kinnebrew	13	136	10.5	0
Kattus	11	99	9.0	1
Jennings	6	86	14.3	0
Kreider	5	96	19.2	0
Wilson	4	45	11.3	0
Martin	3	68	22.7	0
Munoz	2	7	3.5	2

PUNT RETURNS

Last Name	No.	Yds	Avg	TD
Horton	11	111	10.1	0
Martin	13	96	7.4	0
McGee	3	21	7.0	0
Simmons	2	7	3.5	0

KICKOFF RETURNS

Last Name	No.	Yds	Avg	TD
McGee	43	1007	23.4	0
Jennings	12	257	21.4	0
Martin	4	83	20.8	0
Simpkins	2	24	12.0	0
Holman	1	18	18.0	0
Simmons	1	0	0.0	0

PASSING — PUNTING — KICKING

PASSING	Att	Cmp	%	Yds	Yd/Att	TD	Int—	%	Rk
Esiason	469	273	58	3959	8.4	24	17—	4	4
Anderson	23	11	48	171	7.4	1	2—	9	
Gaynor	3	3	100	30	10.0	0	0—	0	
Brooks	1	0	0	0	0.0	0	0—	0	
Kreider	1	0	0	0	0.0	0	1—	100	

PUNTING	Att	Avg
Hayes	56	35.1
Esiason	1	31.0

KICKING	XP	Att	%	FG	Att	%
Breech	50	51	98	17	32	53

PITTSBURGH STEELERS

RUSHING

Last Name	No.	Yds	Avg	TD
Jackson	216	910	4.2	5
Abercrombie	214	877	4.1	6
Erenberg	42	170	4.0	1
Malone	31	107	3.5	5
Pollard	24	86	3.6	0
Hughes	14	32	2.3	0
Reeder	6	20	3.3	0
Sanders	4	12	3.0	0
Brister	6	10	1.7	1
Campbell	1	7	7.0	0
Seitz	3	2	0.7	0
Lipps	4	-3	-0.8	0

RECEIVING

Last Name	No.	Yds	Avg	TD
Abercrombie	47	395	8.4	2
Lipps	38	590	15.5	3
Stallworth	34	466	13.7	1
Erenberg	27	217	8.0	3
Sweeney	21	337	16.0	1
Gothard	21	246	11.7	1
Thompson	17	191	11.2	5
Jackson	17	169	9.9	0
Hughes	10	98	9.8	0
Sanders	2	19	9.5	0
Pollard	2	15	7.5	0
Reeder	2	4	2.0	0

PUNT RETURNS

Last Name	No.	Yds	Avg	TD
Woods	33	294	8.9	0
Lipps	3	16	5.3	0

KICKOFF RETURNS

Last Name	No.	Yds	Avg	TD
Sanchez	25	591	23.6	0
Elder	22	435	19.8	0
Sanders	8	148	18.5	0
Reeder	4	52	13.0	0
Hughes	2	16	8.0	0
Seitz	2	25	12.5	0
Merriweather	1	27	27.0	0
Rostosky	1	3	3.0	0
Sweeney	1	0	0.0	0
Woods	1	17	17.0	0

PASSING — PUNTING — KICKING

PASSING	Att	Cmp	%	Yds	Yd/Att	TD	Int—	%	Rk
Malone	425	216	51	2444	5.8	15	18—	4	13
Brister	60	21	35	291	4.9	0	2—	3	
Campbell	7	1	14	7	1.0	0	0—	0	
Newsome	2	1	50	12	6.0	1	0—	0	

PUNTING	Att	Avg
Newsome	86	40.1

KICKING	XP	Att	%	FG	Att	%
Anderson	32	32	100	21	32	66

HOUSTON OILERS

RUSHING

Last Name	No.	Yds	Avg	TD
Rozier	199	662	3.3	4
Moriarty	90	252	2.8	1
Pinkett	77	225	2.9	2
Wallace	52	218	4.2	3
Moon	42	157	3.7	2
Givins	9	148	16.4	1
Banks	29	80	2.8	0
Woolfolk	23	57	2.5	0
Luck	2	12	6.0	0
Edwards	1	3	3.0	0
Oliver	1	1	1.0	0

RECEIVING

Last Name	No.	Yds	Avg	TD
D. Hill	65	1112	17.1	5
Givins	61	1062	17.4	3
Pinkett	35	248	7.1	1
Woolfolk	28	314	11.2	2
Rozier	24	180	7.5	0
J. Williams	22	227	10.3	1
Drewery	18	299	16.6	0
Wallace	17	177	10.4	2
Banks	7	71	10.1	0
T. Smith	4	72	18.0	0
Akiu	4	67	16.8	0
Oliver	1	-2	-2.0	0

PUNT RETURNS

Last Name	No.	Yds	Avg	TD
Drewery	34	262	7.7	0
Givins	8	80	10.0	0
Pinkett	1	-1	-1.0	0

KICKOFF RETURNS

Last Name	No.	Yds	Avg	TD
Drewrey	25	500	20.0	0
Pinkett	26	519	20.0	0
Riley	2	17	8.5	0
Woolfolk	2	38	19.0	0
Madsen	1	0	0.0	0

PASSING — PUNTING — KICKING

PASSING	Att	Cmp	%	Yds	Yd/Att	TD	Int—	%	Rk
Moon	488	256	53	3489	7.2	13	26—	5	14
Luck	60	31	52	341	5.7	1	5—	8	
Givins	2	0	0	0	0.0	0	0—	0	
Rozier	1	1	100	13	13.0	0	0—	0	

PUNTING	Att	Avg
L. Johnson	88	41.2
Zendejas	1	36.0

KICKING	XP	Att	%	FG	Att	%
Zendejas	28	29	97	22	27	82

DENVER BRONCOS 11-5 Dan Reeves

Scores of Each Game		
38	L.A.RAIDERS	36
21	Pittsburgh	10
33	Philadelphia	7
27	NEW ENGLAND	20
29	DALLAS	14
31	San Diego	14
10	N.Y.Jets	22
20	SEATTLE	13
21	L.A.Raiders	10
3	SAN DIEGO	9
38	KANSAS CITY	17
16	N.Y.Giants	19
34	CINCINNATI	28
10	Kansas City	37
31	WASHINGTON	30
16	Seattle	41

Use Name	Pos.	Hgt	Wgt	Age	Int	Pts
Winford Hood	OT	6'3"	262	24		
Ken Lanier	OT	6'3"	269	27		
Dan Remsberg	OT	6'6"	275	24		
Dave Studdard	OT	6'4"	260	30		
Mark Cooper	OG	6'5"	267	26		
Mike Freeman	OG	6'3"	256	24		
Paul Howard	OG	6'3"	260	35		
Keith Bishop	C-OG	6'3"	265	29		
Billy Bryan	C	6'2"	255	30		
Simon Fletcher	DE	6'5"	240	24		
Freddie Gilbert	DE	6'4"	275	24		
Rulon Jones	DE	6'6"	260	28		2
Karl Macklenburg	DE-LB	6'3"	230	26		
Andre Townsend	DE-NT	6'3"	265	23		6
Rubin Carter	NT	6'	256	33		
Tony Colorito	NT	6'5"	260	21		
Greg Kragen	NT	6'3"	245	24		
Darren Comeaux	LB	6'1	227	26		
Rick Dennison	LB	6'3"	220	28	1	
Ricky Hunley	LB	6'2"	238	24	1	
Tom Jackson	LB	5'11"	220	35		
Jim Ryan	LB	6'1"	218	29		
Ken Woodard	LB	6'1"	218	26		6
Steve Foley	DB	6'2"	190	32	2	
Mike Harden	DB	6'1"	192	28	6	18
Mark Haynes	DB	5'11"	195	27		
Daniel Hunter (to SD)	DB	5'11"	180	23		
Tony Lilly	DB	6'	199	24	3	
Randy Robbins	DB	6'2"	189	23		
Dennis Smith	DB	6'3"	200	27	1	
Steve Wilson	DB	5'10"	195	29	1	6
Louis Wright	DB	6'2"	200	33	3	
John Elway	QB	6'3"	210	26		12
Gary Kublak	QB	6'	192	25		
Ken Bell	HB	5'10"	190	21		
Tony Boddie	HB	5'11"	198	25		
Gene Lang	HB	5'10"	196	24		18
Gerald Willhite	HB	5'10"	200	27		54
Sammy Winder	HB	5'11"	203	27		84
Steve Sewell	FB-WR	6'3"	210	23		12
Mark Jackson	WR	5'9"	174	23		6
Vance Johnson	WR	5'11"	185	22		12
Clint Sampson	WR	5'11"	183	25		
Steve Watson	WR	6'4"	195	29		18
Joey Hackett	TE	6'5"	267	28		
Clarence Kay	TE	6'2"	237	25		6
Bobby Micho	TE	6'3"	240	24		
Orson Mobley	TE	6'5"	256	23		6
Rich Karlis	K	6'	180	27		104
Mike Horan	K	5'11	190	27		
Chris Norman	K	6'2"	198	24		
Jack Weil	K	5'11"	175	24		

KANSAS CITY CHIEFS 10-6 John Mackovic

Scores of Each Game		
24	CINCINNATI	14
17	Seattle	23
27	HOUSTON	13
20	Buffalo	17
17	L.A.RAIDERS	24
7	Cleveland	20
42	SAN DIEGO	41
27	TAMPA BAY	20
24	San Diego	23
27	SEATTLE	7
17	Denver	38
14	St.Louis	23
14	BUFFALO	17
37	DENVER	10
20	L.A.Raiders	17
24	Pittsburgh	19

Use Name	Pos.	Hgt	Wgt	Age	Int	Pts
John Alt	OT	6'7"	282	24		
Irv Eastman	OT	6'7"	293	25		
Brian Jozwiak	OT	6'5"	308	23		
David Lutz	OT	6'6"	295	26		
Jim Rourke	OT	6'5"	263	29		
Rich Baldinger	OG-OT	6'4"	285	26		
Mark Adickes	OG	6'4"	274	25		
Brad Budde	OG	6'4"	271	28		
Adam Lingner	OG-C	6'4"	260	25		
Tom Baugh	C	6'3"	274	22		
Rick Donnalley	C	6'2"	270	27		
Gary Baldinger	DE-NT	6'3"	260	22		
Leonard Griffin	DE	6'4"	252	26		
Eric Holle	DE-NT	6'5"	265	25		
Pete Koch	DE	6'6"	275	24		
Kit Lathrop	DE	6'5"	261	30		
Art Still	DE	6'7"	255	30		
Bill Maas	NT	6'5"	268	24		
Tim Cofield	LB	6'2"	245	23		
Louis Cooper	LB	6'2"	235	23		
Dino Hackett	LB	6'3"	225	22	1	
Ken McAlister	LB	6'5"	220	26		
Whitney Paul	LB	6'3"	219	32		
Aaron Pearson	LB	6'	183	23		
Scott Radecic	LB	6'3"	242	24	1	
Gary Spani	LB	6'2"	229	30	1	
Lloyd Burruss	DB	6'	209	28	5	24
Deron Cherry	DB	5'11"	196	26	9	12
Sherman Cocroft	DB	6'1"	195	25	3	
Greg Hill	DB	6'1"	199	25	3	6
Albert Lewis	DB	6'2"	192	25	4	
J.C.Pearson	DB	5'11"	183	23		
Mark Robinson	DB	5'11"	206	23		
Kevin Ross	DB	5'9"	182	24	4	6
Todd Blackledge	QB	6'3"	223	25		
Bill Kenney	QB	6'4"	211	31		
Frank Seurer	QB	6'1"	195	24		
Herman Heard	HB	5'10"	190	24		12
Jeff Smith	HB	5'9"	201	24		36
Boyce Green	FB	5'11"	215	26		24
Larry Moriarty (from Hou)	FB	6'1"	237	28		6
Mike Pruitt	FB	6'	225	32		12
Chris Smith	FB	6'	222	23		
Carlos Carson	WR	5'11"	184	27		24
Anthony Hancock	WR	6'	224	26		
Emile Harry	WR	5'11"	175	23		6
Henry Marshall	WR	6'2"	216	32		6
Stephone Paige	WR	6'2"	183	24		66
Walt Arnold	TE	6'3"	224	28		12
Paul Coffman	TE	6'3"	225	30		12
Jonathan Hayes	TE	6'5"	236	24		
Lewis Colbert	K	5'11"	180	23		
Nick Lowery	K	6'4"	189	30		100

Mike Bell - Suspended by N.F.L.

SEATTLE SEAHAWKS 10-6 Chuck Knox

Scores of Each Game		
30	PITTSBURGH	0
23	KANSAS CITY	17
38	New England	31
14	Washington	19
33	SAN DIEGO	7
10	L.A.Raiders	14
17	N.Y.GIANTS	12
13	Denver	20
7	N.Y.JETS	38
7	Kansas City	27
7	Cincinnati	34
24	PHILADELPHIA	20
31	Dallas	14
37	L.A.RAIDERS	0
34	San Diego	24
41	DENVER	16

Use Name	Pos.	Hgt	Wgt	Age	Int	Pts
Bob Cryder	OT	6'4"	236	29		
Ron Mattes	OT	6'6"	306	23		
Curt Singer	OT	6'5"	275	24		
Mike Wilson	OT	6'5"	280	31		
Edwin Bailey	OG	6'4"	276	27		
Jon Borchardt	OG	6'5"	272	29		
Bryan Millard	OG	6'5"	284	25		
Blair Bush	C	6'3"	272	29		
Will Grant	C	6'3"	268	32		
Glenn Hyde	C	6'3"	255	35		
Kani Kauahi	C	6'2"	261	26		
Jeff Bryant	DE	6'5"	272	26		
Randy Edwards	DE	6'4"	267	25		
Jacob Green	DE	6'3"	252	29		
Alonzo Mitz	DE	6'3"	275	23		
Reggie Kinlaw	NT	6'2"	249	29		
Joe Nash	NT	6'2"	257	25		
Keith Butler	LB	6'4"	239	30		
Greg Gaines	LB	6'3"	222	27	1	
Michael Jackson	LB	6'1"	228	29		
John Kaiser	LB	6'3"	233	24		
Sam Merriman	LB	6'3"	232	25		
Bruce Scholtz	LB	6'6"	244	27	2	
Fredd Young	LB	6'1"	233	24		
Eddie Anderson	DB	6'1"	199	23		
Dave Brown	DB	6'1"	197	33	5	6
Kenny Easley	DB	6'3"	206	27	2	
Patrick Hunter	DB	5'11"	185	21		
Greggory Johnson	DB	6'1"	195	27		
Kerry Justin	DB	5'11"	175	31	4	
Paul Moyer	DB	6'1"	203	25	3	6
Eugene Robinson	DB	6'	186	23	3	
Terry Taylor	DB	5'10"	191	25	2	
Gale Gilbert	QB	6'3"	206	24		
Dave Krieg	QB	6'1"	196	27		6
Sean Salisbury	QB	6'5"	215	23		
Bobby Joe Edmonds	HB	5'11"	186	21		6
Randall Morris	HB	6'	200	24		6
Curt Warner	HB	5'11"	204	25		78
Eric Lane	FB	6'	201	27		2
John L. Williams	FB	5'11"	226	21		
Ray Butler	WR	6'3"	206	29		24
Byron Franklin	WR	6'1"	183	28		12
Steve Largent	WR	5'11"	191	31		54
Paul Skansi	WR	5'11"	183	25		
Daryl Turner	WR	6'3"	194	24		42
Byron Walker	WR	6'4"	188	26		
Gordon Hudson	TE	6'4"	241	24		6
Jim Laughton	TE	6'5"	225	26		
Mike Tice	TE	6'7"	247	27		
Vince Gamache	K	5'11"	170	24		
Norm Johnson	K	6'2"	194	26		108

Ron Essink - Broken Arm
Danny Greene - Broken Finger

LOS ANGELES RAIDERS 8-8 Tom Flores

Scores of Each Game		
36	Denver	38
6	Washington	10
9	N.Y.GIANTS	14
17	SAN DIEGO	13
24	Kansas City	17
14	SEATTLE	10
30	Miami	28
28	Houston	17
10	DENVER	21
17	Dallas	13
27	CLEVELAND	14
37	San Diego	*31
27	PHILADELPHIA	*33
0	Seattle	37
17	KANSAS CITY	20
24	INDIANAPOLIS	30

Use Name	Pos.	Hgt	Wgt	Age	Int	Pts
Bruce Davis	OT	6'6"	285	30		
Shelby Jordan	OT	6'7"	285	34		
Henry Lawrence	OT	6'4"	275	34		
Chris Riehm	OT	6'6"	275	25		
Charley Hannah	OG	6'5"	265	31		
Curt Marsh	OG	6'5"	275	27		
Mickey Marvin	OG	6'4"	265	30		
Bill Lewis	C	6'7"	270	23		
Don Mosebar	C	6'6"	275	25		
Elvis Franks (to NYJ)	DE	6'4"	265	29		
Sean Jones	DE	6'7"	265	23		
Howie Long	DE	6'5"	270	26		
Greg Townsend	DE	6'3"	250	24		6
Mike Wise	DE	6'7"	260	22		
Bill Pickel	NT	6'5"	260	26		
Mitch Willis	NT	6'8"	275	24		
Jeff Barnes	LB	6'2"	230	31	2	
Jamie Kimmel	LB	6'3"	235	24		
Linden King	LB	6'4"	250	31		
Rod Martin	LB	6'2"	225	32	1	
Reggie McKenzie	LB	6'1"	240	23	1	
Matt Millen	LB	6'2"	245	28		
Jerry Robinson	LB	6'2"	225	29	4	12
Stefon Adams	DB	5'10"	185	23	1	
James Davis	DB	6'	195	29		
Lester Hayes	DB	6'	200	31	2	6
Mike Haynes	DB	6'2"	190	33	2	
Vann McElroy	DB	6'2"	195	26	7	
Odis McKinney	DB	6'2"	190	29		
Sam Seale	DB	5'9"	180	23	4	
Stacey Toran	DB	6'2"	200	24	2	
Fulton Walker	DB	5'10"	195	28		6
Rusty Hilger	QB	6'4"	205	24		
Jim Plunkett	QB	6'3"	220	38		
Marc Wilson	QB	6'6"	205	29		
Marcus Allen	HB	6'2"	205	26		42
Napoleon McCallum	HB	6'2"	215	22		6
Vance Mueller	HB	6'	205	22		
Steve Strachan	HB - FB	6'1"	220	23		
Frank Hawkins	FB	5'9"	215	27		
Rod Barksdale	WR	6'	185	23		12
Jessie Hester	WR	5'11"	170	23		36
Tim Moffett	WR	6'2"	180	24		
Mark Pattison (from LA)	WR	6'2"	190	24		
Dokie Williams	WR	5'11"	180	26		48
Todd Christensen	TE	6'3"	230	30		48
Earl Cooper	TE	6'2"	232	28		
Derrick Jensen	TE	6'1"	220	30		
Trey Junkin	TE	6'2"	225	25		
Andy Parker	TE	6'5"	240	24		6
Chris Bahr	K	5'10"	175	33		99
Ray Guy	K	6'3"	205	36		

Gene Branton - Injury
Mike Davis - Injury

SAN DIEGO CHARGERS 4-12 Don Coryell (1-7) Al Saunders (3-5)

Scores of Each Game		
50	MIAMI	28
7	N.Y.Giants	20
27	WASHINGTON	30
13	L.A.Raiders	17
7	Seattle	33
14	DENVER	31
41	Kansas City	42
7	Philadelphia	23
23	KANSAS CITY	24
9	Denver	3
21	DALLAS	24
31	L.A.RAIDERS	*37
17	Indianapolis	3
27	HOUSTON	0
24	SEATTLE	34
17	Cleveland	47

Use Name	Pos.	Hgt	Wgt	Age	Int	Pts
Sam Claphan	OT	6'6"	288	30		
James FitzPatrick	OT	6'8"	302	22		
Jim Lachey	OT	6'6"	284	23		
Ken Dallafior	OG	6'4"	277	27		
Curt DiGiacomo	OG	6'4"	275	22		
Gary Kowalski	OG-OT	6'6"	280	26		
Dennis McKnight	OG-C	6'3"	270	26		
Jeff Walker	OG	6'4"	295	23		
Jim Leonard	C-OG	6'3"	270	28		
Don Macek	C	6'3"	270	32		
Dee Hardison	DE	6'4"	274	30		
Leslie O'Neal	DE	6'4"	255	22	2	6
Lee Williams	DE	6'6"	263	23		
Lester Williams	DE	6'3"	272	27		
Earl Wilson	DE	6'4"	280	27		
Blaise Winter	DE	6'3"	274	24		
Chuck Ehin	NT	6'4"	257	25		
Terry Unrein	NT	6'5"	283	23		
Ty Allert	LB	6'2"	233	23		
Thomas Benson	LB	6'2"	235	24		
Mike Douglass	LB	6'	214	31		
Mark Fellows	LB	6'2"	233	23		
Andy Hawkins	LB	6'2"	230	28		
Woodrow Lowe	LB	6'1"	229	32		
Derrie Nelson	LB	6'2"	239	28		
Gary Plummer	LB	6'2"	230	26		
Fred Robinson (to MIA)	LB	6'4"	238	24		
Billy Ray Smith	LB	6'3"	236	25		
Donald Brown (to MIA)	DB	5'11"	189	22	1	
Gill Byrd	DB	5'11"	194	25	5	
Jeffrey Dale	DB	6'3"	213	23	4	
Wayne Davis	DB	5'11"	175	23		
Vencie Green (from NE)	DB	6'	183	21	2	
David Martin	DB	5'9"	187	27		
John Sullivan (from GB)	DB	6'1"	190	24		
Ken Taylor	DB	6'1"	186	22	1	
Danny Walters	DB	6'1"	200	25		
Kevin Wyatt	DB	5'10"	190	22		
Tom Flick	QB	6'3"	191	28		6
Dan Fouts	QB	6'3"	204	35		
Mark Herrmann	QB	6'4"	199	27		
Bruce Mathison	QB	6'3"	205	27		
Curtis Adams	HB	6'	194	24		24
Gary Anderson	HB-WR	6'1"	180	25		54
Lionel James	HB-WR	5'7"	170	24		
Buford McGee	HB	6'	206	26		42
Tim Spencer	FB	6'2"	227	25		36
Wes Chandler	WR	6'	188	30		24
Trumaine Johnson	WR	6'1"	191	26		6
Charlie Joiner	WR	5'11"	183	38		12
Timmie Ware	WR	5'10"	171	23		
Pete Holohan	TE	6'4"	232	27		6
Eric Sievers	TE	6'4"	235	27		
Kellen Winslow	TE	6'5"	250	28		30
Rolf Benirschke	K	6'2"	180	31		87
Ralf Mosjsiejenko	K	6'3"	210	23		

Tony Simmons - Knee Injury

John Hendy - Knee Injury

* Overtime

DENVER BRONCOS

RUSHING

Last Name	No.	Yds	Avg	TD
Winder	240	789	3.3	9
Willhite	85	365	4.3	5
Elway	52	257	4.9	1
Sewell	23	123	5.3	1
Lang	29	94	3.2	1
Kubiak	6	22	3.7	0
Bell	9	17	1.9	0
Johnson	5	15	3.0	0
M. Jackson	2	6	3.0	0
Boddie	1	2	2.0	0
Horan	1	0	0.0	0
Mobley	1	-1	-1.0	0
Norman	1	-11	-11.0	0

RECEIVING

Last Name	No.	Yds	Avg	TD
Willhite	64	529	8.3	3
Watson	45	699	15.5	3
M. Jackson	38	738	19.4	1
Johnson	31	363	11.7	2
Winder	26	171	6.6	5
Sewell	23	294	12.8	1
Mobley	22	332	15.1	1
Sampson	21	259	12.3	0
Kay	15	195	13.0	1
Lang	13	105	8.1	2
Hackett	3	48	16.0	0
Bell	2	10	5.0	0
Wilson	1	43	43.0	1
Elway	1	23	23.0	1
Studdard	1	2	2.0	1

PUNT RETURNS

Last Name	No.	Yds	Avg	TD
Willhite	42	468	11.1	1
Johnson	3	36	12.0	0
M. Jackson	2	7	3.5	0
Harden	1	41	41.0	1

KICKOFF RETURNS

Last Name	No.	Yds	Avg	TD
Bell	23	531	23.1	0
Lang	21	480	22.9	0
Willhite	3	35	11.7	0
Johnson	2	21	10.5	0
Hunley	2	11	5.5	0
M. Jackson	1	16	16.0	0
Ryan	1	0	0.0	0

PASSING — PUNTING — KICKING

PASSING	Att	Cmp	%	Yds	Yd/Att	TD	Int-	%	RK
Norman	1	1	100	43	43.0	1	0-	0	
Sewell	1	1	100	23	23.0	1	0-	0	
Elway	504	280	56	3485	6.9	19	13-	3	9
Kubiak	38	23	61	249	6.6	1	3-	8	
Willhite	4	1	25	11	2.8	0	0-	0	
Johnson	1	0	0	0	0.0	0	0-	0	

PUNTING	No	Avg
Weil	34	39.5
Norman	30	38.9
Horan	21	41.1

KICKING	XP	Att	%	FG	Att	%
Karlis	44	45	98	20	28	71

KANSAS CITY CHIEFS

RUSHING

Last Name	No.	Yds	Avg	TD
Pruitt	139	448	3.2	2
Green	90	314	3.5	3
Heard	71	295	4.2	2
Smith	54	238	4.4	3
Blackledge	23	60	2.6	0
Kenney	18	0	0.0	0
Paige	2	-2	-1.0	0

RECEIVING

Last Name	No.	Yds	Avg	TD
Paige	52	829	15.9	11
Marshall	46	652	14.2	1
Smith	33	230	7.0	3
Carson	21	497	23.7	4
Arnold	20	169	8.5	1
Green	19	137	7.2	0
Heard	17	83	4.9	0
Coffman	12	75	6.3	2
Harry	9	211	23.4	1
Moriarty	9	67	7.4	0
Hayes	8	69	8.6	0
Pruitt	8	56	7.0	0
Hancock	4	63	15.8	0
Kenney	1	0	0.0	0

PUNT RETURNS

Last Name	No.	Yds	Avg	TD
Smith	29	245	8.4	0
Harry	6	20	3.3	0

KICKOFF RETURNS

Last Name	No.	Yds	Avg	TD
Smith	29	557	19.2	0
Green	10	254	25.4	1
Harry	6	115	19.2	0
Carson	5	88	17.6	0
Moriarty	4	80	20.0	0
Cocroft	1	23	23.0	0
Pearson	1	0	0.0	0

PASSING — PUNTING — KICKING

PASSING	Att	Cmp	%	Yds	Yd/Att	TD	Int-	%	RK
Kenney	308	161	52	1922	6.2	13	11—	4	11
Blackledge	211	96	46	1200	5.7	10	6—	3	
Green	1	0	0	0	0.0	0	1—	100	
Marshall	1	0	0	0	0.0	0	0—	0	

PUNTING	No	Avg
Colbert	99	40.7

KICKING	XP	Att	%	FG	Att	%
Lowery	43	43	100	19	26	73

SEATTLE SEAHAWKS

RUSHING

Last Name	No.	Yds	Avg	TD
Warner	319	1481	4.6	13
Williams	129	538	4.2	0
Morris	19	149	7.8	1
Krieg	35	122	3.5	1
Lane	6	11	1.8	0
Gilbert	3	8	2.7	0
Franklin	1	2	2.0	0
Edmonds	1	-11	-11.0	0

RECEIVING

Last Name	No.	Yds	Avg	TD
Largent	70	1070	15.3	9
Warner	41	342	8.3	0
Franklin	33	547	16.6	2
Williams	33	219	6.6	0
Skansi	22	271	12.3	0
R. Butler	19	351	18.5	4
Turner	18	334	18.6	7
Tice	15	150	10.0	0
Hudson	13	131	10.1	1
Lane	3	6	2.0	1
Bailey	1	3	3.0	0

PUNT RETURNS

Last Name	No.	Yds	Avg	TD
Edmonds	34	419	12.3	1
Skansi	5	38	7.6	0

KICKOFF RETURNS

Last Name	No.	Yds	Avg	TD
Edmonds	34	764	22.5	0
Morris	23	465	20.2	0
Scholtz	3	39	13.0	0
Skansi	1	21	21.0	0
Tice	1	17	17.0	0
Edwards	1	13	13.0	0
Lane	1	3	3.0	0

PASSING — PUNTING — KICKING

PASSING	Att	Cmp	%	Yds	Yd/Att	TD	Int-	%	RK
Krieg	375	225	60	2921	7.8	21	11-	3	2
Gilbert	76	42	55	485	6.4	3	3-	4	
Largent	1	1	100	18	18.0	0	0-	0	
Morris	1	0	0	0	0.0	0	0-	0	

PUNTING	No	Avg
Gamache	79	38.6

KICKING	XP	Att	%	FG	Att	%
N. Johnson	42	42	100	22	35	63

LOS ANGELES RAIDERS

RUSHING

Last Name	No.	Yds	Avg	TD
Allen	208	759	3.6	5
McCallum	142	536	3.8	1
Hawkins	58	245	4.2	0
Strachan	18	53	2.9	0
Hilger	6	48	8.0	0
Plunkett	12	47	3.9	0
Wilson	14	45	3.2	0
Mueller	13	30	2.3	0
Williams	3	27	9.0	0
Guy	1	0	0.0	0

RECEIVING

Last Name	No.	Yds	Avg	TD
Christensen	95	1153	12.1	8
Allen	46	453	9.8	2
Williams	43	843	19.6	8
Hawkins	25	166	6.6	0
Hester	23	632	27.5	6
Barksdale	18	434	24.1	2
McCallum	13	103	7.9	0
Moffett	6	77	12.8	0
Mueller	6	54	9.0	0
Junkin	2	38	19.0	0
Pattison	2	12	6.0	0
Parker	2	8	4.0	1

PUNT RETURNS

Last Name	No.	Yds	Avg	TD
Walker	49	440	9.0	1
McCallum	7	44	6.3	0

KICKOFF RETURNS

Last Name	No.	Yds	Avg	TD
Adams	27	573	21.2	0
Walker	23	368	16.0	0
McCallum	8	183	22.9	0
Millen	3	40	13.3	0
Mueller	2	73	36.5	0
Hawkins	1	15	15.0	0

PASSING — PUNTING — KICKING

PASSING	Att	Cmp	%	Yds	Yd/Att	TD	Int-	%	RK
Plunkett	252	133	53	1986	7.9	14	9-	4	8
Wilson	240	129	54	1721	7.2	12	15-	6	11
Hilger	38	19	50	266	7.0	1	1-	3	

PUNTING	No.	Avg.
Guy	90	3620

KICKING	XP	Att	%	FG	Att	%
Bahr	36	36	100	21	28	75

SAN DIEGO CHARGERS

RUSHING

Last Name	No.	Yds	Avg	TD
Anderson	127	442	3.5	1
Adams	118	366	3.1	4
Spencer	99	350	3.5	6
James	51	224	4.4	0
McGee	63	187	3.0	7
Herrmann	2	6	3.0	0
Flick	6	5	.8	1
Mathison	1	-1	-1.0	0
Fouts	4	-3	-.8	0

RECEIVING

Last Name	No.	Yds	Avg	TD
Anderson	80	871	10.9	8
Winslow	64	728	11.4	5
Chandler	56	874	15.6	4
Joiner	34	440	12.9	2
Johnson	30	399	13.3	1
Holohan	29	356	12.3	1
James	23	173	7.5	0
McGee	10	105	10.5	0
Spencer	6	48	8.0	0
Adams	4	26	6.5	0
Sievers	2	14	7.0	0
Ware	1	11	11.0	0

PUNT RETURNS

Last Name	No.	Yds	Avg	TD
Anderson	25	227	9.1	0
James	9	94	10.4	0
Chandler	3	13	4.3	0

KICKOFF RETURNS

Last Name	No.	Yds	Avg	TD
Anderson	24	482	20.1	0
James	18	315	17.5	0
Adams	5	100	20.0	0
Spencer	5	81	16.2	0
Wyatt	5	74	14.8	0
Johnson	3	48	16.0	0
Winslow	2	11	5.5	0
McGee	1	15	15.0	0
Chandler	1	11	11.0	0
Plummer	1	0	0.0	0

PASSING — PUNTING — KICKING

PASSING	Att	Cmp	%	Yds	Yd/Att	TD	Int-	%	RK
Fouts	430	252	59	3031	7.1	16	22-	5	10
Herrmann	97	51	53	627	6.5	2	3-	3	
Flick	73	33	45	361	5.0	2	8-	0	
Anderson	1	1	100	4	4.0	1	0-	0	
Holohan	2	1	50	21	10.5	0	0-	0	
McGee	1	1	100	1	1.0	0	0-	0	

PUNTING	No	Avg
Mojsiejenko	72	42.0
Chandler	5	33.4

KICKING	XP	Att	%	FG	Att	%
Benirschke	39	41	95	16	25	64

1986 N.F.C.—PLAYOFFS

December 28, 1986 at RFK Stadium (Attendance 54,180)

SCORING

L.A. RAMS	0	0	0	7-	7
WASHINGTON	10	3	3	3-	19

First Quarter
- Wash. — Atkinson, 25 yard field goal
- Wash. — Bryant, 14 yard pass from Schroeder
  PAT—Atkinson (kick)

Second Quarter
- Wash. — Atkinson, 20 yard field goal

Third Quarter
- Wash. — Atkinson, 38 yard field goal

Fourth quarter
- L.A. — House, 12 yard pass from Everett
  PAT— Lansford (kick)
- Wash. — Atkinson, 19 yard field goal

TEAM STATISTICS

L.A.		WASH.
16	First Downs	15
9	First Downs-Rushing	9
6	First Downs-Passing	5
1	First Downs-Penalty	1
4	Fumbles	1
1	Fumbles-Lost Ball	0
8	Penalties-Number	6
78	Yards Penalized	45
1	Missed Field Goals	0
53	Offensive Plays	64
324	Net Yards	228
6.1	Average Gain	3.6
3	Giveaways	0
0	Takeaways	3
-3	Difference	+3

INDIVIDUAL STATISTICS

L.A. RAMS	No.	Yds.	Avg.	WASHINGTON	No.	Yds.	Avg.
RUSHING							
Dickerson	26	158	6.1	Rogers	29	115	4.0
Redden	7	28	4.0	Bryant	4	17	4.3
Everett	1	12	12.0	Griffin	5	8	1.6
	34	198	5.8	Schroeder	3	-2	-0.7
					41	138	3.4
RECEIVING							
Ellard	1	14	14.0	Monk	5	34	6.8
Redden	1	20	20.0	Bryant	2	18	9.0
Hill	3	27	9.0	Didier	1	4	4.0
Long	1	5	5.0	Clark	1	8	8.0
House	3	70	23.3	Sanders	2	15	7.5
	9	136	15.1	Warren	1	7	7.0
				Rogers	1	4	4.0
					13	90	6.9
PUNTING							
Hatcher	3		38.3	Cox	5		42.2
PUNT RETURNS							
Ellard	2	23	11.5	Yarber	2	8	4.0
KICKOFF RETURNS							
White	3	42	14	Garner	2	27	13.5
Sutton	2	37	18.5				
McDonald	1	7	7.0				
	6	86	14.3				
INTERCEPTION RETURNS							
none				Walton	1	16	16.0
				Wilburn	1	2	2.0
					2	18	9.0

PASSING

L.A. RAMS	Att.	Comp.	Comp. Pct.	Yds.	Int.	Yds./Att.	Yds./Comp.
Everett	18	9	50	136	2	7.6	15.1
WASHINGTON							
Schroeder	23	13	57	90	0	3.9	6.9

January 3, 1987 at Chicago (Attendance 65,141)

SCORING

WASHINGTON	7	0	7	13-	27
CHICAGO	0	13	0	0-	13

First Quarter
- Wash. — Monk, 28 yard pass from Schroeder
  PAT—Atkinson (kick)

Second Quarter
- Chicago — Gault, 50 yard pass from Flutie
- Chicago — Butler, 23 yard field goal
- Chicago — Butler, 41 yard field goal

Third Quarter
- Wash. — Monk, 23 yard pass from Schroeder
  PAT—Atkinson (kick)

Fourth Quarter
- Wash. — Rogers, 1 yard run
  PAT—Atkinson (kick)
- Wash. — Atkinson, 35 yard field goal
- Wash. — Atkinson, 25 yard field goal

TEAM STATISTICS

WASH.		CHI.
19	First Downs	14
8	First Downs-Rushing	8
8	First Downs-Passing	5
3	First Downs-Penalty	1
2	Fumbles_Number	3
0	Fumbles-Lost	2
8	Penalties-Number	4
65	Yards Penalized	42
1	Missed Field Goals	1
73	Offensive Plays	56
302	Net Yards	220
4.1	Average Gain	3.9
1	Giveaways	4
4	Takeaways	1
+3	Difference	-3

INDIVIDUAL STATISTICS

WASHINGTON	No.	Yds.	Avg.	CHICAGO	No.	Yds.	Avg.
RUSHING							
Rogers	28	72	2.6	Payton	14	38	2.7
Bryant	8	16	2.0	Suhey	4	14	3.5
Schroeder	3	16	5.3	Thomas	3	18	6.0
	39	104	2.7	Anderson	1	11	11.0
				Flutie	2	12	6.0
					24	93	3.9
RECEIVING							
Monk	5	81	16.2	Gault	5	82	16.4
Clark	5	37	7.4	Ortego	2	36	18.0
Bryant	4	61	15.3	Wrightman	2	16	8.0
Warren	1	5	5.0	Suhey	1	2	2.0
	15	184	12.3	Payton	1	-2	-2.0
					11	134	12.2
PUNTING							
Cox	7		39.3	Buford	5		40.6
PUNT RETURNS							
Yarber	3	22	7.3	Barnes	5	27	5.4
KICKOFF RETURNS							
Garner	3	71	23.7	Gentry	3	127	42.3
				Thomas	2	15	7.5
				Anderson	1	17	17.0
					6	159	26.5
INTERCEPTION RETURNS							
Dean	1	16	16.0	Richardson	1	43	43.0
Green	1	17	17.0				
	2	33	16.5				

PASSING

WASHINGTON	Att.	Comp.	Comp. Pct.	Yds.	Int.	Yds./Att.	Yds./Comp.
Schroeder	32	15	47	184	1	5.8	12.3
CHICAGO							
Flutie	31	11	35	134	2	4.3	12.2

January 4, 1987 at East Rutherford, N.J. (Attend. 76,034)

SCORING

SAN FRANCISCO	3	0	0	0-	3
N.Y. GIANTS	7	21	21	0-	49

First Quarter
- N.Y.G. — Bavaro, 24 yard pass from Simms
  PAT—Allegre (kick)
- S.F. — Wersching, 26 yard field

Second Quarter
- N.Y.G. — Morris, 45 yard run
  PAT—Allegre (kick)
- N.Y.G. — B. Johnson, 15 yard pass from Simms
  PAT—Allegre (kick)
- N.Y.G. — Taylor, 34 yard interception return
  PAT—Allegre (kick)

Third Quarter
- N.Y.G. — McConkey, 28 yard pass from Simms
  PAT—Allegre (kick)
- N.Y.G. — Mowatt, 29 yard pass from Simms
  PAT—Allegre (kick)
- N.Y.G. — Morris, 2 yard run
  PAT—Allegre (kick)

TEAM STATISTICS

S.F.		N.Y.G.
9	First Downs-Total	21
2	First Downs-Rushing	12
6	First Downs-Passing	6
1	First Downs-Penalty	3
2	Fumbles-Number	0
1	Fumbles-Lost Ball	0
11	Penalties-Number	3
62	Yards Penalized	23
0	Missed Field Goals	0
58	Offensive Plays	65
184	Net Yards	366
3.2	Average Gain	5.6
4	Giveaways	0
0	Takeaways	4
-4	Difference	+4

INDIVIDUAL STATISTICS

SAN FRANCISCO	No.	Yds.	Avg.	N.Y. GIANTS	No.	Yds.	Avg.
RUSHING							
Craig	5	17	3.4	Morris	24	159	6.6
Cribbs	12	4	0.3	Carthon	6	17	2.8
Rathman	3	8	2.7	Simms	1	15	15.0
	20	29	1.5	Rouson	8	28	3.5
				Anderson	4	2	0.5
				Manuel	1	-5	-5.0
					44	216	4.9
RECEIVING							
Rice	3	48	16.0	Bavaro	2	47	23.5
Clark	3	52	17.3	B. Johnson	1	15	15.0
Margerum	1	12	12.0	Galbreath	1	9	9.0
Francis	3	26	8.7	Mowatt	1	29	29.0
Craig	4	22	5.5	Carthon	1	7	7.0
Cribbs	1	2	2.0	Morris	1	2	2.0
	15	162	10.8	Rouson	2	22	11.0
				McConkey	1	28	28.0
					10	159	15.9
PUNTING							
Runager	10		40.0	Landeta	7		43.9
PUNT RETURNS							
Griffin	2	11	5.5	McConkey	7	57	8.1
KICKOFF RETURNS							
Cribbs	3	71	22.7	Rouson	1	17	17.0
Craig	4	48	12.0	Hill	1	15	15.0
	7	119	17.0		2	32	16.0
INTERCEPTION RETURNS							
none				Taylor	1	34	34.0
				P. Johnson	1	27	27.0
				Welch	1	0	0.0
					3	61	20.3

PASSING

SAN FRANCISCO	Att.	Comp.	Comp. Pct.	Yds.	Int.	Yds./Att.	Yds./Comp.
Montana	15	8	53	98	2	6.5	12.3
Kemp	22	7	32	64	1	2.9	9.1
	37	15	41	162	3	4.4	10.8
N.Y. GIANTS							
Simms	19	9	47	136	0	7.2	15.1
Rutledge	1	1	100	23	0	23.0	23.0
	20	10	50	159	0	7.95	15.9

1986 A.F.C.— PLAYOFFS

December 28, 1986 at East Rutherford (Attendance 69,307)

SCORING

KANSAS CITY	6	0	0	9- 15
N.Y. JETS	7	14	7	7- 35

First Quarter
- K.C. — J. Smith, 1 yard run; PAT—kick failed
- N.Y.J. — McNeil, 4 yard run; PAT—Leahy (kick)

Second Quarter
- N.Y.J. — McNeil, 1 yard pass from Ryan; PAT—Leahy (kick)
- N.Y.J. — Toon, 11 yard pass from Ryan; PAT—Leahy (kick)

Third Quarter
- N.Y.J. — McArthur, 21 yard interception return; PAT—Leahy (kick)

Fourth Quarter
- K.C. — Lewis, recovered blocked punt in endzone; PAT—Lowery (kick)
- N.Y.J. — Griggs, 6 yard pass from Ryan; PAT—Leahy (kick)
- K.C. — Safety, Jennings ran out of endzone

TEAM STATISTICS

K.C.		N.Y.J.
15	First Downs- Total	19
4	First Downs- Rushing	9
8	First Downs-Passing	10
3	First Downs-Penalty	0
2	Fumbles- Number	0
1	Fumbles- Lost Ball	0
1	Penalties- Number	8
5	Yards Penalized	54
0	Missed Field Goals	0
59	Offensive Plays	61
241	Net Yards	306
4.1	Average Gain	5.0
3	Giveaways	0
0	Takeaways	3
- 3	Difference	+ 3

INDIVIDUAL STATISTICS

KANSAS CITY	No.	Yds.	Avg.	N.Y. JETS	No.	Yds.	Avg.
RUSHING							
Moriarty	2	7	3.5	McNeil	31	135	4.4
Green	8	15	1.9	Paige	2	3	1.5
Heard	1	1	1.0	Ryan	2	30	15.0
Smith	4	12	3.0	Jennings	1	-3	-31.0
Blackledge	4	33	8.2		36	165	4.6
Paige	1	-2	-2.0				
	20	67	3.4				
RECEIVING							
Marshall	6	72	12.0	Toon	4	48	12.0
Green	5	7	1.2	Shuler	4	28	7.0
Coffman	3	12	4.0	McNeil	3	16	5.2
Carson	2	43	21.5	Walker	2	45	22.5
J. Smith	2	12	6.0	Sohn	1	11	11.0
Moriarty	1	16	16.0	Griggs	1	7	7.0
Heard	1	15	15.0	Alexander	1	1	-1.0
	20	174	8.7		16	141	8.8
PUNTING							
Colbert	3		41.3	Jennings	4		29.0
PUNT RETURNS							
J. Smith	3	5	1.6	Sohn	1	4	4.0
KICKOFF RETURNS							
J. Smith	3	50	16.7	Paige	1	7	7.0
Moriarty	2	35	17.5	Townsell	1	13	13.0
	5	85	17.0		2	20	10.0
INTERCEPTION RETURNS							
none				McArthur	1	21	21.0
				Carter	1	12	12.0
					2	23	11.5

PASSING

	Att.	Comp.	Comp. Pct.	Yds.	Int.	Yds./Att.	Yds./Comp.
KANSAS CITY							
Kenney	16	8	50.0	97	0	6.1	12.2
Blackledge	21	12	57.1	80	2	3.9	6.7
	37	20	54.2	177	2	4.8	8.9
N.Y. JETS							
Ryan	23	16	69.5	153	0	6.7	9.6

January 4, 1987 at Cleveland (Attendance 78,106)

SCORING

N.Y. JETS	7	3	3	7	0	0- 17
CLEVELAND	7	3	0	10	0	3- 20

First Quarter
- N.Y.J. — Walker, 42 yard pass from Ryan; PAT—Leahy (kick)
- Cle. — Fontenot, 37 yard pass from Kosar; PAT-Moseley (kick)

Second Quarter
- Cle. — Moseley, 38 yard field goal
- N.Y.J. — Leahy, 46 yard field goal

Third Quarter
- N.Y.J — Leahy, 37 yard field goal

Fourth Quarter
- N.Y.J. — McNeil, 25 yard run; PAT—Leahy (kick)
- Cle. — Mack, 1 yard run; PAT—Moseley (kick)
- Cle. — Moseley, 22 yard field goal

Second Overtime
- Cle. — Moseley, 27 yard field goal

TEAM STATISTICS

N.Y.J.		CLE.
14	First Downs- Total	33
6	First Downs-Rushing	6
8	First Downs-Passing	21
0	First Downs-Penalty	6
0	Fumbles- Number	2
0	Fumbles-Lost Ball	0
10	Penalties- Number	4
94	Yards Penalized	40
0	Missed Field Goals	3
71	Offensive Plays	96
287	Net Yards	558
4.0	Average Gain	5.8
0	Giveaways	2
2	Takeaways	0
+2	Difference	- 2

INDIVIDUAL STATISTICS

N.Y. JETS	No.	Yds.	Avg.	CLEVELAND	No.	Yds.	Avg.
RUSHING							
McNeil	25	71	2.9	Mack	20	63	3.1
O'Brien	3	22	7.1	Fontenot	3	8	2.6
Paige	3	11	3.8	Dickey	3	4	1.3
	31	104	3.4	Kosar	1	0	0.0
					27	75	2.8
RECEIVING							
Toon	5	93	18.6	Newsome	6	114	19.0
Shuler	4	43	10.8	Slaughter	6	86	14.3
McNeil	4	35	8.8	Fontenot	5	62	12.1
Walker	2	49	24.5	Mack	5	51	10.0
Paige	1	10	10.0	Brennan	4	69	17.3
Sohn	1	7	7.0	Langhorne	4	65	16.3
	17	237	13.9	Holt	2	42	21.0
				Weathers	1	3	3.0
				Dickey	1	2	2.0
					34	483	15.6
PUNTING							
Jennings	14		37.9	Gossett	8		38.8
PUNT RETURNS							
Sohn	1	9	9.0	McNeil	7	65	9.3
McNeil	2	14	7.0				
	3	23	7.7				
KICKOFF RETURNS							
Townsell	4	83	20.8	McNeil	3	37	12.3
Bingham	1	8	8.0	Puzzuoli	1	6	6.0
	5	91	18.2	Nicolas	1	3	3.0
					5	46	9.2
INTERCEPTION RETURNS							
Carter	1	0	0.0	none			
Holmes	1	0	0.0				
	2	0	0.0				

PASSING

	Att.	Comp.	Comp. Pct.	Yds.	Int.	Yds./Att.	Yds./Comp.
N.Y. JETS							
O'Brien	19	11	57.8	134	0	7.1	12.2
Ryan	11	6	54.5	103	0	9.4	17.2
	30	17	56.7	237	0	7.9	13.9
CLEVELAND							
Kosar	64	33	51.5	483	2	7.5	14.6

January 4, 1987 at Denver (Attendance 76,105)

SCORING

NEW ENGLAND	0	10	7	0- 17
DENVER	3	7	10	2- 22

First Quarter
- Den. — Karlis, 27 yard field goal

Second Quarter
- Den. — Elway, 22 yard run; PAT—Karlis (kick)
- N.E. — Franklin, 38 yard field goal
- N.E. — Morgan, 19 pass from Eason; PAT—Franklin (kick)

Third Quarter
- Den. — Karlis, 22 yard field goal
- N.E. — Morgan, 45 yard pass from Eason; PAT—Franklin (kick)
- Den. — Johnson, 48 yard pass from Elway; PAT—Franklin (kick)

Fourth Quarter
- Den. — Safety, Eason tackled in endzone by Jones

TEAM STATISTICS

N.E.		DEN.
12	First Downs- Total	21
6	First Downs-Rushing	12
6	First Downs-Passing	9
0	First Down-Penalty	0
1	Fumbles- Number	0
0	Fumbles- Lost Ball	0
5	Penalties- Number	3
45	Yards Penalized	20
0	Missed Field Goals	0
54	Offensive Plays	75
271	Net Yards	441
5.0	Average Gain	5.9
0	Giveaways	2
2	Takeaways	0
+2	Difference	-2

INDIVIDUAL STATISTICS

NEW ENGLAND	No.	Yds.	Avg.	DENVER	No.	Yds.	Avg.
RUSHING							
C. James	10	31	3.1	Winder	19	102	5.4
Collins	5	46	9.1	Lang	11	44	4.0
Dupard	5	18	3.6	Elway	5	18	3.6
Eason	2	23	11.5	Willhite	3	4	1.3
Fryar	1	-2	-2.0	Bell	2	12	6.0
Hawthorne	1	5	5.0	Sewell	2	8	4.0
	24	121	5.0		42	188	4.5
RECEIVING							
Morgan	3	100	3.3	Johnson	4	89	22.3
Collins	4	46	11.5	Sewell	3	41	13.7
Baty	3	31	8.0	Mobley	2	69	34.5
Hawthorne	1	6	6.0	Watson	1	21	21.0
Fryar	2	11	5.5	Winder	1	16	16.0
	13	150	11.5	Micho	1	20	20.0
				Lang	1	1	1.0
					13	253	19.5
PUNTING							
Camarillo	9		50.2	Horan	5		49.0
				Elway	1		31.0
					6		46.0
PUNT RETURNS							
Fryar	2	13	6.5	Johnson	3	26	8.7
				Willhite	1	9	9.0
					4	35	8.8
KICKOFF RETURNS							
Starring	2	13	6.5	Lang	1	21	21.0
				Bell	3	63	21.0
					4	84	21.0
INTERCEPTION RETURNS							
McSwain	1	2	2.0	none			
Rembert	1	0	0.0				
	2	2	1.0				

PASSING

	Att.	Comp.	Comp. Pct.	Yds.	Int.	Yds./Att.	Yds./Comp.
NEW ENGLAND							
Eason	24	13	54.2	194	0	8.1	14.9
DENVER							
Elway	32	13	40.6	257	2	8.0	19.8

1986 Championship Games

NFC CHAMPIONSHIP GAME

January 11, 1987 at East Rutherford, N.J.
(Attendance 76,633)

SCORING

WASHINGTON	0	0	0	0-	0
N.Y. GIANTS	10	7	0	0-	17

First Quarter
- N.Y. G. — Allegre, 47 yard field goal
- N.Y. G. — Manuel, 11 yard pass from Simms
  PAT—Allegre (kick)

Second Quarter
- N.Y. G. — Morris, 1 yard run
  PAT—Allegre (kick)

TEAM STATISTICS

WAS.		N.Y.G.
12	First Downs-Total	12
2	First Downs-Rushing	8
7	First Downs-Passing	3
3	First Downs-Penalty	1
3	Fumbles-Number	4
1	Fumbles-Ball Lost	3
3	Penalties-Number	6
15	Yards Penalized	48
0	Missed Field Goals	0
70	Offensive Plays	61
190	Net Yards	199
2.7	Average Gain	3.3
2	Giveaways	3
3	Takeaways	2
+1	Difference	-1

With the wind gusting to 33 miles per hour, New York coach Bill Parcells took the wind when his team won the coin toss. It was a sound decision; the Redskins' passing game was stymied during the first period by a rugged combination of New Jersey breeze and Giant blue. Redskin QB Jay Schroeder could get only two first downs while the Giants put 10 points on the scoreboard: Raul Allegre's 47-yard field goal, to open the scoring, and a' Phil Simms-to-Lionel Manuel TD pass.

Trailing 10-0 early in the second quarter, but with the wind now at their backs, the Redskins had a chance to get back into the game. Schroeder completed a 48-yard pass to Art Monk to take his team out of a deep hole. A few moments later, the Redskins lined up for a 51-yard field-goal try by Jess Atkinson, but the snap was bad and the scoring opportunity over. Then, the Giants crushed the Skins by marching to a touchdown against the wind.

There was no scoring in the second half, as the "Big Blue Wrecking Crew" Giant defense continued to dominate and the offense ate up the clock with a conservative running game. Schroeder completed only 20-of-50 passes for an average gain of a mere 3.8 per attempt. LB Carl Banks took over as the defense's big-play man when Lawrence Taylor was forced out of action with an injury.

INDIVIDUAL STATISTICS

RUSHING

WASHINGTON	No.	Yds.	Avg.	N.Y. GIANTS	No.	Yds.	Avg.
Rogers	9	15	1.7	Morris	29	87	3.0
Bryant	6	25	4.2	Carthon	7	28	4.0
Schroeder	1	0	0.0	Rouson	1	2	2.0
	16	40	2.5	Anderson	1	3	3.0
				Simms	7	-2	-0.3
				Galbreath	1	-1	-1.0
					46	117	2.5

RECEIVING

WASHINGTON	No.	Yds.	Avg.	N.Y. GIANTS	No.	Yds.	Avg.
Monk	8	126	15.8	Bavaro	2	36	18.0
Didier	1	7	7.0	Manuel	2	36	18.0
Warren	3	9	3.0	Carthon	3	18	6.0
Bryant	7	45	6.4		7	72	10.3
Griffin	1	8	8.0				
	20	195	9.8				

PUNTING

WASHINGTON	No.	Yds.	Avg.	N.Y. GIANTS	No.	Yds.	Avg.
Cox	9		35.6	Landeta	6		42.3

PUNT RETURNS

WASHINGTON	No.	Yds.	Avg.	N.Y. GIANTS	No.	Yds.	Avg.
Yarber	3	19	6.3	McConkey	5	27	5.4

KICKOFF RETURNS

WASHINGTON	No.	Yds.	Avg.	N.Y. GIANTS	No.	Yds.	Avg.
Orr	1	10	10.0	none			
Branch	1	5	5.0				
	2	15	7.5				

INTERCEPTION RETURNS

WASHINGTON	No.	Yds.	Avg.	N.Y. GIANTS	No.	Yds.	Avg.
none				Reasons	1	15	15.0

PASSING

	Att.	Comp.	Comp. Pct.	Yds.	Int.	Yds./Att.	Yds./Comp.
WASHINGTON							
Schroeder	50	20	40.0	195	1	3.9	9.8
N.Y. GIANTS							
Simms	14	7	50.0	90	0	6.4	12.8

AFC CHAMPIONSHIP GAME

January 11, 1987 at Cleveland
(Attendance 79,915)

SCORING

DENVER	0	10	3	7	3-	23
CLEVELAND	7	3	0	10	0-	20

First Quarter
- Cle. — Fontenot, 3 yard pass from Kosar
  PAT—Moseley (kick)

Second Quarter
- Den. — Karlis, 19 yard field goal
- Den. — Willhite, 1 yard run
  PAT—Moseley (kick)
- Cle. — Moseley, 29 yard field goal

Third Quarter
- Den. — Karlis, 26 yard field goal

Fourth Quarter
- Cle. — Moseley, 24 yard field goal
- Cle. — Brennan, 48 yard pass from Kosar
  PAT — Moselet (kick)
- Den. — M. Jackson, 5 yard pass from Elway
  PAT — Karlis (kick)

Overtime
- Den. — Karlis, 33 yard field goal

TEAM STATISTICS

DEN.		CLE.
22	First Downs- Total	17
6	First Downs- Rushing	4
13	First Downs- Passing	12
3	First Downs- Penalty	1
2	Fumbles- Number	3
0	Fumbles- Lost Ball	1
6	Penalties- Number	9
39	Yards Penalized	76
0	Missed Field Goals	0
77	Offensive Plays	66
374	Net Yards	356
4.9	Average Gain	5.4
1	Giveaways	3
3	Takeaways	1
+2	Difference	-2

Before nearly 80,000 partisan Clevelanders, the Broncos made a remarkable comeback to win the AFC title in a seesaw overtime battle. Cleveland got off to a 7-0 lead in the first quarter with an 86-yard drive that culminated in Bernie Kosar's three-yard TD pass to Herman Fontenot. Then, turnovers stopped Cleveland through most of the remainder of the half. The Broncos were able to capitalize for a 19-yard field goal by barefoot Rich Karlis and a one-yard scoring smash by Gerald Willhite. Cleveland's Mark Moseley tied the score at 10-10 just before halftime.

Karlis' 26-yard field goal was the only score of the third quarter. Early in the fourth quarter, Moseley tied it again. With less than six minutes left, Kosar hit Brian Brennan on a 48-yard TD pass to give Cleveland a 20-13 lead. When Denver's Gene Lang mishandled the ensuing kickoff before recovering at the Denver two, the Broncos were 98 yards from a tie. Denver had been unable to sustain a long drive during the half, but John Elway patiently began moving the Broncos downfield. With 1:47 remaining, he faced a 3rd-and-18 situation at the Cleveland 48. A 20-yard toss to Mark Jackson gave the Broncos new life and, five plays later, a five-yard flip to Jackson brought the touchdown.

Cleveland received the overtime kickoff but couldn't move. Then Elway and the Broncos roared downfield. With 5:48 gone, Karlis lined up for a field goal at the Browns' 23-yard line. His kick curved dangerously toward the left upright but was good, making Denver the AFC champions.

INDIVIDUAL STATISTICS

RUSHING

DENVER	No.	Yds.	Avg.	CLEVELAND	No.	Yds.	Avg.
Winder	26	83	3.2	Mack	26	94	3.6
Elway	4	56	14.0	Kosar	4	3	3.0
Lang	3	9	3.0	Fontenot	3	3	1.0
Willhite	3	0	0.0		33	100	3.3
Sewell	1	1	1				
	37	149	4.9				

RECEIVING

DENVER	No.	Yds.	Avg.	CLEVELAND	No.	Yds.	Avg.
Johnson	3	25	6.3	Fontenot	7	66	9.5
Watson	3	55	18.3	Brennan	4	72	18.0
Sewell	3	47	15.6	Langhorne	2	35	17.5
Mobley	3	36	12.0	Mack	2	20	10.0
Kay	2	23	11.5	Weathers	1	42	42.0
Willhite	2	20	10.0	Slaughter	1	20	20.0
Winder	2	2	1.0	Byner	1	4	4.0
Jackson	2	25	12.5		18	256	14.2
Sampson	1	10	10.0				
Lang	1	1	1.0				
	22	225	10.2				

PUNTING

DENVER	No.	Yds.	Avg.	CLEVELAND	No.	Yds.	Avg.
Horan	6		40.7	Gossett	6		43.2
Elway	1		19.0				
	7		37.6				

PUNT RETURNS

DENVER	No.	Yds.	Avg.	CLEVELAND	No.	Yds.	Avg.
Willhite	3	10	3.3	McNeil	3	37	12.3

KICKOFF RETURNS

DENVER	No.	Yds.	Avg.	CLEVELAND	No.	Yds.	Avg.
Lang	2	14	7.0	McNeil	4	80	20.0
Bell	2	10	5.0	Fontenot	2	25	12.5
Freeman	1	9	9.0				
	5	33	6.6				

INTERCEPTION RETURNS

DENVER	No.	Yds.	Avg.	CLEVELAND	No.	Yds.	Avg.
Hunley	1	14	14.0.0	Harper	1	0	0.0
Ryan	1	26	26.0				
	2	40	20.0				

PASSING

	Att.	Comp.	Comp. Pct.	Yds.	Int.	Yds./Att.	Yds./Comp.
DENVER							
Elway	38	22	57.8	244	1	6.4	11.1
CLEVELAND							
Kosar	32	18	56.2	259	2	8.1	14.4

SUPER BOWL XXI

January 25, 1987 at Pasadena, Calif.

(Attendance 101,643)

Two for the Price of One

Under sunny skies and with a 76-degree temperature, the Denver Broncos and New York Giants played two different Super Bowls. One game, encompassing the first half, was probably the most evenly played matchup of the 21 played. The second game, the second half, was in the tradition of the one-sided blowouts that Super Bowls too often exhibit. Indeed, it may have been the most one-sided yet, other than the Bears' win a year before. Had both teams, and all of the 101,643 in attendance at the Rose Bowl, gone home at intermission, the game would have gone down as the best. Instead, the Giants' complete dominance of the second half left only the impression of a terrible mismatch.

On the game's opening drive, Denver went 45 yards in eight plays to set up a Rich Karlis field goal, the key being a 24-yard John Elway-to-Mark Jackson pass. Karlis' barefoot boot from 48 yards matched the longest in Super Bowl history. The Giants came right back to take the lead on a 78-yard drive. Phil Simms, who was 6-for-6 on the drive, hit three crucial passes to account for most of the yardage, and his short toss to Mark Bavaro brought the score to 7-3. Back came Denver. Ken Bell returned the kickoff 28 yards to the Bronco 42. Elway passed to Orson Mobley and Sammy Winder for a total of 25 yards. Then, on a nine-yard screen pass to Winder, Giant linebacker Harry Carson was called for a late hit and, when teammate Lawrence Taylor complained too vociferously, a second penalty was tacked on to put the ball at the six. Three plays later, Elway ran up the middle on a quarterback draw to score.

The Broncos launched another drive as soon as they got the ball back. Elway's 54-yard strike to Vance Johnson was the big play as they stormed to a first-and-goal at the one. At last, the vaunted New York defense awoke. On first down, Elway was caught for a two-yard loss on a rollout. Then, Gerald Willhite gained nothing up the middle. On third down, Winder lost three around left end. On the 23-yard field-goal try, Karlis set a Super Bowl record — for the shortest miss. Most observers tagged the four-play goalline stand as the game's turning point. After a couple of first downs by the Giants, Sean Landeta punted to the Denver 15. On third-and-12, Giant defensive end Leonard Marshall sacked Elway for a safety. There was no more scoring in the first half, although Karlis missed again on a 34-yard attempt with 18 seconds left.

The Giants took the second-half kickoff and drove to their own 47 where they faced a fourth-and-1. Instead of punting, New York coach Bill Parcells sent in backup quarterback Jeff Rutledge, who ran a sneak for two yards and the first down. New York completed the 63-yard drive with a 13-yard touchdown pass from Simms to Bavaro. Before the quarter ended, the Giants had built their lead to 26-10 on a 21-yard field goal by Raul Allegre and a one-yard touchdown plunge by Joe Morris. A feature of the TD drive was a 44-yard Simms pass to Phil McConkey off a flea-flicker.

The fourth quarter saw two more New York touchdowns, the first for six yards on McConkey's catch of a deflected pass, and the other on a two-yard run by Ottis Anderson. Denver, fighting to the end, saw Karlis connect on a 28-yard field goal, and, with just over two minutes remaining, Elway hit Vance Johnson for a 47-yard TD.

Although Elway passed for 304 yards, the Broncos' running game was shut down, with Elway also the leading rusher with 27 yards. Simms was the MVP, completing 22-of-25 passes for a record 88 percent. Also standing out among the many Giant luminaries was linebacker Carl Banks, who had 10 solo tackles.

LINEUPS

DENVER		N.Y. GIANTS
	OFFENSE	
Johnson	WR	Johnson
Studdard	LT	Benson
Bishop	LG	Ard
Bryan	C	Oates
Howard	RG	Godfrey
Lanier	RT	Nelson
Mobley	TE	Bavaro
Watson	WR	Robinson
Elway	QB	Simms
Winder	RB	Morris
Willhite	RB	Carthon
	DEFENSE	
Jones	LE	Martin
Kragen	NT	Howard
Townsend	RE	Marshall
Ryan	LOLB	Banks
Mecklenburg	LILB	Reasons
Hunley	RILB	Carson
Jackson	ROLB	Taylor
Wright	LCB	Collins
Harden	RCB	Williams
Foley	FS	Welch
Smith	SS	Hill

SUBSTITUTES

DENVER		
	OFFENSE	
Bell	Hackett	Micho
Bishop	Jackson	Remsberg
Cooper	Kubiak	Sampson
Freeman	Lang	Sewell
	DEFENSE	
Colorito	Gilbert	Robinson
Comeaux	Haynes	Wilson
Dennison	Lilly	Woodard
Fletcher		
	KICKERS	
Horan	Karlis	
NEW ENGLAND		
	OFFENSE	
Anderson	Manuel	Roberts
Galbreath	McConkey	Rouson
Johnson	Miller	Rutledge
Johnston	Mowatt	
	DEFENSE	
Burt	Headen	Lasker
Collins	Hunt	Patterson
Dorsey	Johnson	Sally
Flynn	Jones	
	KICKERS	
Allegre	Landeta	

SCORING

DENVER	10	0	0	10-	20
N.Y. GIANTS	7	2	17	13-	39

First Quarter
- Denver — Karlis, 48-yard field goal
- N.Y.G. — Mowatt, 6 yard pass from Simms. PAT—Allegre (kick)
- Denver — Elway, 4 yard run. PAT—Karlis (kick)

Second Quarter
- N.Y.G. — Safety, Martin tackled Elway in endzone

Third Quarter
- N.Y.G. — Bavaro, 13 yard pass from Simms. PAT—Allegre (kick)
- N.Y.G. — Allegre, 21 yard field goal
- N.Y.G. — Morris, 1 yard run. PAT—Allegre (kick)

Fourth Quarter
- N.Y.G. — McConkey, 6 yard pass from Simms. PAT—Allegre (kick)
- Denver — Karlis, 28 yard field goal
- N.Y.G. — Anderson, 2 yard run. PAT—kick failed
- Denver — V. Johnson, 47 yard pass from Elway. PAT—Karlis (kick)

TEAM STATISTICS

DEN		NYG
23	First Downs-Total	24
5	First Downs-Rushing	10
16	First Downs-Passing	13
2	First Downs-Penalty	1
2	Fumbles-Number	0
0	Fumbles-Lost Ball	0
4	Penalties Number	6
28	Yards Penalized	48
2	Missed Field Goals	0
64	Offensive Plays	64
372	Net Yards	399
5.8	Average Gain	6.2
1	Giveaways	0
0	Takeaways	1
-1	Difference	+1

INDIVIDUAL STATISTICS

DENVER	No.	Yds.	Avg.	N.Y. GIANTS	No.	Yds.	Avg.
RUSHING							
Elway	6	27	4.5	Morris	20	67	3.3
Willhite	4	19	4.8	Simms	3	25	8.3
Sewell	3	4	1.3	Rouson	3	22	7.3
Lang	2	2	1.0	Galbreath	4	17	4.3
Winder	4	0	0.0	Carthon	3	4	1.3
	19	52	2.7	Anderson	2	1	0.5
				Rutledge	3	0	0.0
					38	136	3.6
RECEIVING							
V. Johnson	5	121	24.2	Bavaro	4	51	12.8
Willhite	5	39	7.8	Morris	4	20	5.0
Winder	4	34	8.5	Carthon	4	13	3.3
M. Jackson	3	51	17.0	Robinson	3	62	20.7
Watson	2	54	27.0	Manuel	3	43	14.3
Sampson	2	20	10.0	McConkey	2	50	25.0
Mobley	2	17	8.5	Rouson	1	23	23.0
Sewell	2	12	6.0	Mowatt	1	6	6.0
Lang	1	4	4.0		22	268	12.2
	26	252	9.7				
PUNTING							
Horan	2		41.0	Landeta	3		46.0
PUNT RETURNS							
Willhite	1	9	9.0	McConkey	1	25	25.0
KICKOFF RETURNS							
Bell	3	48	16.0	Rouson	3	56	18.7
Lang	2	36	18.0	Flynn	1	-3	-3.0
	5	84	16.8		4	53	13.3
INTERCEPTION RETURNS							
none				Patterson	1	-7	-7.0

PASSING

DENVER	Att.	Comp.	Comp. Pct.	Yds.	Int.	Yds./ Att.	Yds./ Comp.	Yards Lost Tackled
Elway	37	22	59.5	304	1	8.2	13.8	4-26
Kubiak	4	4	100.0	48	0	12.0	12.0	0-0
	41	26	63.4	352	1	8.6	13.5	4-26
N.Y. GIANTS								
Simms	25	22	88	268	0	10.7	12.2	1-5

1987 N.F.C. The Second Page

All 1987 pro football stories finished far behind the strike as news, but the N.F.C. had its share of second-page features.

On the upbeat side was the Joe Montana-to-Jerry Rice touchdown connection that kept San Francisco aglow — and winning — all season. Then there was the story in New Orleans that it was actually possible for the Saints to win more games than they lost, a revelation that took two decades to arrive.

There was Walter Payton's final season — on the whole, a graceful exit. And there was the slow and often painful progress toward stardom made by several young quarterbacks, including Tampa Bay's Vinny Testaverde, the 1986 Heisman Trophy winner and No. 1 choice in the draft.

On the downside was the utter collapse of the New York Giants, the continuing erosion of the Dallas Cowboys, strained relations among the Chicago Bears and the total ineptness of the Atlanta Falcons.

EASTERN DIVISION

Washington Redskins — The Skins went through most of the season a la Rodney Dangerfield, getting little respect. They won, but seldom convincingly. Quarterback Jay Schroeder, the prodigy of '85, was erratic and twice was replaced by Doug Williams, who won in relief. Running back George Rogers nursed a toe injury in training camp and, in the regular season, ran as if he feared for the other nine toes. Age was creeping into both lines, but the Hogs were still fearsome blockers. Defensive end Charles Mann emerged as a star, and defensive end Dexter Manley, though inconsistent, was devastating much of the time. Barry Wilburn was a pleasant surprise at cornerback, but the secondary gave up more air yards than the offense gained. Fortunately, the issue was never in doubt in a division that held the Redskins and four losing teams. When the Redskins beat the Giants in Game 11, after trailing at the half, it was all over in the NFC East.

Dallas Cowboys — Herschel Walker was terrific, leading the league with 1,606 combined yards (891 rushing, 715 receiving) and making Tony Dorsett an unhappy benchwarmer. But he couldn't do it alone, and the Cowboys finished with another losing record. Quarterback Danny White still hadn't recovered from his '86 broken wrist, but substitute Steve Pelluer seldom looked capable of taking over. After an embarrassing 21-10 loss to Atlanta in Week 12, owner Bum Bright — in a "what have you done for me lately" move — blasted head coach Tom Landry, saying he was "horrified" at Landry's play-calling.

St. Louis Cardinals — Owner Bill Bidwill spent much of the season shopping for a new city for his Cardinals while a lot of St. Louis fans stayed home and voted nolo contendre. Nevertheless, the Cardinals showed signs of life on the field, as quarterback Neil Lomax made an excellent comeback that landed him in the Pro Bowl. Top receiver J.T. Smith was unaccountably absent from the Pro Bowl despite leading the league in catches (91) and accounting for 1,117 yards. Only defensive end Freddie Joe Nunn, with nine sacks, did much on defense. In March of '88, Bidwill received the NFL's permission to move the team to Phoenix after 28 years in St. Louis without a championship.

Philadelphia Eagles — Head coach Buddy Ryan was openly disdainful of the replacement players who lost three straight games, but his attitude may have helped build team unity among the regulars. The Eagles won three straight after the strike and were 7-5 in union games. Perhaps more important than Ryan's attitude was quarterback Randall Cunningham's improvement from a shaky question mark to a plus, passing for 2,786 yards and 23 TDs. He was less skittish in the pocket but still became the first quarterback to lead his team in rushing since Bobby Douglass in 1972. Defensive end Reggie White had 21 sacks but, overall, the defense was subpar — surprising in view of Ryan's reputation as a defensive genius.

New York Giants — The Giants' collapse wasn't likely to sell many of the books that so many of them authored after their '86 Super Bowl season. When offensive tackle Karl Nelson went out for the season with Hodgkin's disease in August and offensive guard Chris Godfrey was sidelined with a sprained knee the next month, the Giants lost their running game. An 0-3 replacement team and some in-house backbiting didn't help either. Without a line in front of him, Joe Morris looked like just another undersized runner. Through a long season, tight end Mark Bavaro, linebacker Carl Banks, cornerback Mark Collins and quarterback Phil Simms continued to perform as all-stars.

CENTRAL DIVISION

Chicago Bears — Walter Payton's final season might have been one of appropriate sweetness, and Payton himself finished up as a gentleman. But other Bears scarred the year with bitter controversy. Head coach Mike Ditka called his striking regulars "prima donnas" and "egomaniacs." The players responded with criticism of the coach. Cracks in the once-great defense were blamed on a lack of intensity, even by some Bears themselves. But, when Ditka benched regulars Todd Bell and William Perry (who had ballooned up to 362 pounds) before the playoffs, there were more flare-ups. For once, the big Bear news wasn't quarterback Jim McMahon or his injuries.

Minnesota Vikings — Although quarterback Tommy Kramer didn't play a full game all season because of a recurring pinched nerve in his shoulder, Wade Wilson did a good job as a backup, and wide receiver Anthony Carter emerged as one of the top threats in the league with a 24.3-yard average per catch. Chris Doleman, a bust at linebacker, became a Pro Bowler at defensive end. Together with defensive tackle Keith Millard, he helped revive memories of the Purple People Eaters. The Vikings stumbled into the playoffs despite losing all three replacement games and three of their last four regular-season contests.

Green Bay Packers — No. 1 draft pick Brent Fullwood was a disappointment. When he wasn't in the training room, he was forgetting plays, missing blocks, dropping passes or making gaffes like asking Forrest Gregg, "Coach, did you ever play in this league?" On the other hand, quarterback Don Majkowski, the 255th player taken in the '87 draft, started five games and gave evidence that he could develop. Veteran cornerback Dave Brown, obtained from Seattle for next-to-nothing, made a fine comeback to anchor a surprisingly strong defense.

Tampa Bay Buccaneers — The Bucs started November talking playoffs with a 4-3 record. On November 8, they led the Cardinals 28-3 in the fourth quarter, yet lost 31-28, as the Cards made the biggest final-quarter comeback in NFL history. Shocked, the Bucs lost their last seven games. "If I believed in a turning point," new coach Ray Perkins admitted, "I'd say that was probably it." Still, Perkins' troops showed improvement over the abject ineptitude of '86 that had earned them the first choice in the '87 draft. All-world, $8.2 million draft choice Vinny Testaverde started at quarterback in the last four games after veteran Steve DeBerg had done an excellent job paving the way.

Detroit Lions — It was another long season for Detroit, which has won only one division title (1983) in the past 30 years. Quarterback Chuck Long began to develop into the player

FINAL TEAM STATISTICS

OFFENSE

	ATL.	CHI.	DALL.	DET.	G.B.	L.A.	MINN.	N.O.	NY G	PHIL.	STL.	S.F.	T.B.	WASH.
FIRST DOWNS:														
Total	230	319	293	270	248	276	293	304	266	289	325	357	263	301
by Rushing	73	121	93	81	97	118	129	128	80	112	115	134	62	119
by Passing	139	156	176	156	133	136	136	151	168	154	189	202	168	153
by Penalty	18	42	24	33	18	22	28	25	18	23	21	21	33	29
RUSHING:														
Number	333	485	465	398	464	512	482	569	440	509	462	524	394	500
Yards	1298	1954	1865	1435	1801	2097	1983	2190	1457	2027	1873	2237	1365	2102
Average Yards	3.9	4.0	4.0	3.6	3.9	4.1	4.1	3.8	3.3	4.0	4.1	4.3	3.5	4.2
Touchdowns	5	13	17	9	13	15	20	20	4	12	15	11	7	18
PASSING:														
Attempts	501	493	500	509	455	420	446	411	499	520	529	501	517	478
Completions	247	272	288	275	234	220	232	227	265	283	305	322	264	247
Completion Pct.	49.3	55.2	57.6	54.0	51.4	52.4	52.0	55.2	53.1	54.4	57.7	64.3	51.1	51.7
Passing Yards	3108	3420	3594	3150	2977	2750	3185	2987	3645	3561	3650	3955	3377	3718
Avg. Yds per Att.	6.2	6.9	7.2	6.2	6.5	6.5	7.1	7.3	7.3	6.8	7.3	7.9	6.5	7.8
Avg. Yds per Comp.	12.6	12.6	12.5	11.5	12.7	12.5	13.7	13.2	13.8	12.6	12.6	12.3	12.8	15.1
Times Tackled	46	48	52	26	45	25	52	29	61	72	54	29	43	27
Yds Lost Tackled	340	330	403	194	296	196	359	213	443	511	397	205	361	223
Net Yards	2768	3090	3191	2956	2681	2554	2826	2774	3202	3050	3453	3750	3016	3495
Touchdowns	17	23	19	16	15	16	21	23	26	26	25	44	22	27
Interceptions	32	24	20	26	17	18	23	12	22	16	15	14	17	18
Pct. Intercepted	6.4	4.9	4.0	5.1	3.7	4.3	5.2	2.9	4.4	3.1	2.8	2.8	3.3	3.8
PUNTS:														
Number	83	62	84	70	93	77	79	63	91	102	70	68	88	78
Average	40.7	39.3	39.6	41.8	39.3	40.8	38.9	41.1	39.6	37.0	38.0	37.4	39.3	39.1
PUNT RETURNS														
Number	31	50	41	35	35	40	36	41	55	34	44	34	31	56
Yards	221	484	353	303	245	245	420	468	448	202	550	365	257	615
Average Yards	7.1	9.7	8.6	8.7	7.0	6.1	11.7	11.4	8.1	5.9	12.5	10.7	8.3	11.0
Touchdowns	0	2	0	0	0	0	1	0	0	0	1	1	0	0
KICKOFF RET.:														
Number	79	57	64	71	59	63	71	55	56	66	63	55	56	59
Yards	1700	1193	1295	1428	1032	1282	1421	1149	1128	1112	1317	1144	1037	1139
Average Yards	21.5	20.9	20.2	20.1	17.5	20.3	20.0	20.9	20.1	16.8	20.9	20.8	18.5	19.3
Touchdowns	1	1	0	0	0	1	0	0	0	0	0	1	0	0
INTERCEPT RET.:														
Number	15	13	23	19	18	16	26	30	20	21	14	25	16	23
Yards	182	69	208	290	220	305	303	280	263	197	167	205	248	329
Average Yards	12.1	5.3	9.0	15.3	12.2	19.1	11.7	9.3	13.2	9.4	11.9	8.2	15.5	14.3
Touchdowns	0	2	2	1	0	2	0	0	1	0	1	0	2	1
PENALTIES:														
Number	98	103	131	86	135	91	96	107	100	116	101	88	115	82
Yards	807	821	1091	737	1103	677	814	994	835	919	797	792	894	691
FUMBLES:														
Number	27	33	30	29	35	26	28	33	38	44	23	25	35	26
Number Lost	17	20	20	11	18	15	10	16	20	19	12	12	14	19
POINTS:														
Total	205	356	340	269	255	317	336	422	280	337	362	459	286	379
PAT Attempts	24	42	37	27	27	38	41	46	32	40	46	59	33	47
PAT Made	23	38	37	27	24	36	40	43	28	38	44	55	31	43
FG Attempts	17	32	29	39	29	21	29	42	32	31	27	23	24	29
FG Made	12	22	25	26	21	17	14	33	20	19	14	16	19	18
Percent FG Made	70.6	68.8	86.2	66.7	72.4	81.0	48.3	78.6	62.5	61.3	51.9	69.6	79.2	62.1
Safeties	1	0	0	1	0	1	1	2	0	1	0	1	0	0

DEFENSE

	ATL.	CHI.	DALL.	DET.	G.B.	L.A.	MINN.	N.O.	NY G	PHIL.	STL.	S.F.	T.B.	WASH.
FIRST DOWNS:														
Total	354	261	294	314	296	279	281	270	275	301	306	250	314	296
by Rushing	162	77	85	122	118	95	95	81	97	85	116	95	124	104
by Passing	164	158	175	162	152	162	159	155	148	186	168	132	163	177
by Penalty	28	26	34	30	26	22	27	34	30	30	22	23	27	15
RUSHING:														
Number	600	412	459	504	521	419	440	388	493	428	492	429	500	441
Yards	2734	1413	1617	2070	1920	1732	1724	1550	1768	1643	2001	1611	2038	1679
Average Yards	4.6	3.4	3.5	4.1	3.7	4.1	3.9	4.0	3.6	3.8	4.1	3.8	4.1	3.8
Touchdowns	24	5	19	18	15	8	9	6	14	16	16	8	18	10
PASSING:														
Attempts	453	507	502	459	469	504	498	489	508	561	490	467	457	527
Completions	243	255	269	259	279	281	278	246	292	305	276	224	271	276
Completion Pct.	53.6	50.3	53.6	56.4	59.5	55.8	55.8	50.3	57.5	54.4	56.3	48.0	59.3	52.4
Passing Yards	3291	3286	3781	3558	3200	3693	3407	3155	3272	4058	3668	2771	3255	3767
Avg. Yds per Att.	7.3	6.5	7.5	7.8	6.8	7.3	6.8	6.5	6.4	7.2	7.5	5.9	7.1	7.1
Avg. Yds per Comp.	13.5	12.9	14.1	13.7	11.5	13.1	12.3	12.8	11.2	13.3	13.3	12.4	12.0	13.7
Times Tackled	17	70	51	42	34	38	41	47	55	57	41	37	39	53
Yds Lost Tackled	118	484	337	355	197	304	307	355	382	452	285	287	306	424
Net Yards	3173	2802	3444	3203	3003	3389	3100	2800	2890	3606	3383	2484	2949	3343
Touchdowns	26	24	21	23	14	31	24	25	17	29	30	13	23	19
Interceptions	15	13	23	19	18	16	26	30	20	21	14	25	16	23
Pct. Intercepted	3.3	2.6	4.6	4.1	3.8	3.2	5.2	6.1	3.9	3.7	2.9	5.4	3.5	4.4
PUNTS:														
Number	60	86	75	65	77	83	74	73	96	88	74	72	64	91
Average	39.7	39.6	40.6	37.9	40.1	37.3	39.9	37.5	38.1	37.1	41.2	39.6	41.2	39.2
PUNT RETURNS														
Number	48	26	45	34	54	43	44	29	51	54	36	29	50	37
Yards	541	339	376	177	422	317	424	199	811	469	489	195	621	231
Average Yards	11.3	13.0	8.4	5.2	7.8	7.4	9.6	6.9	15.9	8.7	13.6	6.7	12.4	6.2
Touchdowns	1	1	1	0	0	0	0	0	2	0	1	0	1	0
KICKOFF RET.:														
Number	44	58	65	56	61	57	64	55	68	59	59	76	61	63
Yards	915	1054	1281	1089	1140	1112	1173	1115	1463	1276	1063	1598	1242	1352
Average Yards	20.8	18.2	19.7	19.4	18.7	19.5	18.3	20.3	21.5	21.6	18.0	21.0	20.4	21.5
Touchdowns	1	0	0	0	0	0	0	0	0	0	0	1	0	1
INTERCEPT RET.:														
Number	32	24	20	26	17	18	23	12	22	16	15	14	17	18
Yards	342	334	279	335	115	226	399	173	164	68	227	258	227	193
Average Yards	10.7	13.9	14.0	12.9	6.8	12.6	17.3	14.4	7.5	4.3	15.1	18.4	13.4	10.7
Touchdowns	2	1	0	2	1	1	3	1	1	0	0	0	0	1
PENALTIES:														
Number	92	120	100	115	104	100	107	84	97	105	88	80	125	97
Yards	729	1108	851	907	852	888	964	685	802	830	718	660	926	801
FUMBLES:														
Number	18	37	29	36	42	28	30	31	31	41	34	30	42	22
Number Lost	12	11	20	13	24	11	11	18	14	27	19	13	20	11
POINTS:														
Total	436	282	348	384	300	361	335	283	312	380	368	253	360	285
PAT Attempts	54	33	41	43	31	43	38	35	35	46	48	26	44	33
PAT Made	51	30	39	42	29	40	35	35	33	44	45	25	42	30
FG Attempts	30	31	29	34	36	24	31	18	34	29	18	35	30	28
FG Made	19	18	19	28	27	21	24	12	23	18	11	24	18	19
Percent FG Made	63.3	58.1	65.5	82.4	75.0	87.5	77.4	66.7	67.6	62.1	61.1	68.6	60.0	67.9
Safeties	2	0	0	0	2	0	0	1	0	0	1	0	0	0

the Lions expected, but first-round pick, defensive end Reggie Rogers was out for 30 days in midseason for emotional counseling, and his future was in doubt. Several key players were out for various amounts of time with more visible injuries. Punter Jim Arnold was chosen for the Pro Bowl after getting plenty of opportunities to practice his specialty. Still, with a roster of young talent, the Lions considered their future to be bright.

WESTERN DIVISION

San Francisco 49ers — The 49ers had the best regular-season record in the league, thanks in no small part to wide receiver Jerry Rice, who set an NFL record with 22 TD catches and was voted Player of the Year. Quarterback Joe Montana, who won the league passing title, had one of his best seasons. He seemed fully recovered from his back injury of '86, but the team had a quarterback controversy gestating, as backup Steve Young was terrific in his few opportunities. Montana, Rice, Young, running back Roger Craig and the rest helped San Francisco lead the league in total offense, despite a wave of injuries that caused wholesale shuffling of the offensive line. Nose tackle Michael Carter was a standout and free safety Ronnie Lott called signals for the NFL's top-rated defense. The only apparent weakness was age in a few key spots.

New Orleans Saints — Owner Tom Benson cracked, "When you're 21, you become a man!" In the 21st year of their existence, the Saints had both their first winning record and their first playoff berth. Fans went Saint-happy and Benson danced on the sideline after each victory. They were all in ecstasy during a nine-game win streak that ended the regular season. Coach of the Year Jim Mora went with underrated quarterback Bobby Hebert, who finished with the best QB rating in Saints history. Running back Rueben Mayes slumped from his rookie highs, but Dalton Hilliard picked up the slack, and Morten Andersen (121 points) remained the NFL's best kicker. Despite some soft spots in the secondary, the team's strength was its defense. Linebackers Vaughan Johnson, Rickey Jackson, Sam Mills and Pat Swilling formed one of the NFL's best units.

Los Angeles Rams — Running back Charles White had a magnificent season, gaining 1,324 yards rushing — only four fewer than the total for his previous six years. He got his chance after the blockbuster trade which sent contract-unhappy Eric Dickerson to Indianapolis for a trunk full of draft choices. Quarterback Jim Everett made only marginal progress toward being the passer the Rams expected, and the team really never came together after a 1-7 start. Winning five in a row put them temporarily in the playoff picture, but they lost their last two, including a 48-0 crushing by the 49ers that ended the season on a downer. For head coach John Robinson, the team's 6-9 mark was his first losing season, either college or pro. All-Pro offensive guard Dennis Harrah learned he'd been named to the Pro Bowl for the sixth time on the same day he announced his retirement.

Atlanta Falcons — Marion Campbell made his reputation as a defensive coach, but his Falcons gave up an NFL-high 436 points. That was compounded by the fact that they scored the fewest points (205). And, for a clean sweep of the booby prizes, they had the league's lowest attendance, in part because they played all three strike games at home. Quarterback Scott Campbell showed why he'd been unable to win a starting job in Pittsburgh. Top draft pick Chris Miller, the heir apparent at quarterback, wasn't signed until October 30 and had some rough moments once he started to play, but at least he gave some hope for the future.

WASHINGTON REDSKINS 11-4 Joe Gibbs

Scores of Each Game		
34	PHILADELPHIA	24
20	Atlanta	21
28	ST.LOUIS	21
38	N.Y.Giants	12
13	Dallas	7
17	N.Y.JETS	16
27	Buffalo	7
27	Philadelphia	31
20	DETROIT	13
26	L.A.RAMS	30
23	N.Y.GIANTS	19
34	St.Louis	17
24	DALLAS	20
21	Miami	23
27	Minnesota	*24

Use Name	Pos.	Hgt	Wgt	Age	Int	Pts
#Mark Carlson	OT	6'6"	284	24		
Joe Jacoby	OT	6'7"	305	28		
Mark May	OT	6'6"	295	27		
Dan McQuaid	OT	6'7"	278	26		
#Willard Scissum	OT-OG	6'3"	275	24		
Ed Simmons	OT-OG	6'5"	275	23		
Darrick Britz	OG	6'3"	264	23		
#Frank Frazier	OG	6'5"	290	27		
Rick Kehr	OG	6'3"	285	28		
Raleigh McKenzie	OG-C	6'2"	270	24		
#Phil Pettey	OG	6'4"	274	25		
R.C. Thielemann	OG	6'4"	262	32		
Jeff Bostic	C	6'2"	260	28		
#John Cowne	C	6'2"	245	25		
#Eric Coyle	C	6'3"	260	23		
Russ Grimm	C-OG	6'3"	275	28		
Ray Hitchcock	C	6'2"	289	22		
#Mike Wooten	C	6'3"	260	24		
#Alec Gibson	DE	6'4"	270	23		
Steve Hamilton	DE-DT	6'4"	270	25		
Markus Koch	DE	6'5"	275	24		
#Kit Lathrop	DE	6'5"	261	31		
Dexter Manley	DE	6'3"	257	28		
Charles Mann	DE	6'6"	270	26		
#Steve Martin	DE	6'3"	260	22		
#Curtis McGriff	DE	6'5"	275	29		
#Dan Benish	DT	6'5"	275	26		
Dave Butz	DT	6'7"	295	37		
Darryl Grant	DT	6'1"	275	27		
Dean Hamel	DT	6'3"	290	26		
#Ted Karras	DT	6'2"	265	22		
#Anthony Sagnella	DT	6'5"	260	23		
#Steve Thompson	DT	6'2"	275	22		
#Henry Waechter	DT	6'5"	275	28		

Use Name	Pos.	Hgt	Wgt	Age	Int	Pts
#Derek Bunch	LB	6'3"	215	25		
Ravin Caldwell	LB	6'3"	229	24		
Monte Coleman	LB	6'2"	230	29	2	
Anthony Copeland	LB	6'2"	250	24		
#Bobby Curtis	LB	6'3"	235	22		
Kurt Gouveia	LB	6'1"	227	22		
Mel Kaufman	LB	6'2"	218	29		
#Jon Kimmel	LB	6'4"	240	27		
Rich Milot	LB	6'4"	237	30		
Neal Olkewicz	LB	6'	233	30		
#Carlton Rose	LB	6'2"	220	25		
#Tony Settles	LB	6'3"	210	23		
#Eric Wilson	LB	6'1"	245	25		
#David Windham	LB	6'2"	240	26		
Todd Bowles	DB	6'2"	203	23	4	
#Danny Burmeister	DB	6'2"	201	23		
#Joe Cofer	DB	6'	200	24		
Brian Davis	DB	6'2"	190	24		
Vernon Dean	DB	5'11"	178	28		
#David Etherly	DB	6'1"	190	24		
Steve Gage	DB	6'3"	210	23	1	
Darrell Green	DB	5'8"	185	27	3	6
#Charles Jackson	DB	6'4"	210	24		
#Garry Kimble	DB	5'11"	184	24		
#Skip Lane	DB	6'1"	210	27		
#Michael Mitchell	DB	5'10"	180	25	1	
Tim Morrison	DB	6'1"	195	24		
Gary Thompson	DB	6'	180	28		
Clarence Vaughn	DB	6'	202	23		
Alvin Walton	DB	6'	180	23	3	
Barry Wilburn	DB	6'3"	186	23	9	6
Dennis Woodberry	DB	5'10"	183	26		

Use Name	Pos.	Hgt	Wgt	Age	Int	Pts
Babe Laufenberg	QB	6'2'	195	27		
#Tony Robinson	QB	6'3"	200	23		
#Ed Rubbert	QB	6'5"	225	22		
Mark Rypien	QB	6'4"	234	24		
Jay Schroeder	QB	6'4"	214	26		18
#Jack Stanley	QB	6'3"	207	23		
Doug Williams	QB	6'4"	220	32		6
Kelvin Bryant	HB	6'2"	195	26		36
Keith Griffin	HB	5'8"	185	25		6
Tim Jessie	HB	5'11"	190	24		6
Timmy Smith	HB	5'11"	216	23		
#Lionel Vital	HB	5'9"	195	24		12
Reggie Branch	FB	5'11"	235	24		6
#Allen Harvin	FB	5'9"	200	28		
#Walter Holman	FB	5'10"	208	27		
George Rogers	FB	6'2"	229	28		36
#Wayne Wilson	FB	6'3"	220	29		12
Anthony Allen	WR	5'11"	182	27		18
#Keiron Bigby	WR	5'10"	177	21		
Gary Clark	WR	5'9"	173	25		42
#Richard Johnson	WR	5'7"	178	25		
Art Monk	WR	6'3"	209	29		36
#Joe Phillips	WR	5'9"	188	24		
Ricky Sanders	WR	5'11"	180	25		18
#Derrick Shepard	WR	5'10"	183	23		
Clarence Verdin	WR	5'8"	160	24		
#Ted Wilson	WR	5'9	170	23		12
Eric Yarber	WR	5'8"	156	23		
Joe Caravello	TE	6'3"	270	24		
Glenn Dennison	TE	6'3"	225	25		
Clint Didier	TE	6'5"	240	28		6
#K.D.Dunn	TE	6'3"	235	24		
Anthony Jones	TE	6'3"	248	27		
Craig McEwen	TE	6'1"	220	21		
Terry Orr	TE	6'3"	227	25		
#Dave Truitt	TE	6'4"	232	23		
Don Warren	TE	6'4"	242	31		
#Marvin Williams	TE	6'3"	235	23		
#Obed Ariri	K	5'8"	165	31		15
Jess Atkinson	K	5'9"	168	25		4
Steve Cox	K	6'4"	195	29		6
Ali Haji-Sheikh	K	6'	172	26		68
#Brendan Tolbin	K	6'	205	23		4
#Jack Weil	K	5'11"	175	25		

ST. LOUIS CARDINALS 7-8 Gene Stallings

Scores of Each Game		
24	DALLAS	13
24	San Diego	28
21	Washington	28
24	NEW ORLEANS	19
28	San Francisco	34
7	N.Y.Giants	30
23	PHILADELPHIA	28
31	TAMPA BAY	28
24	L.A.RAMS	27
31	Philadelphia	19
34	Atlanta	21
17	WASHINGTON	34
27	N.Y.GIANTS	24
31	Tampa Bay	14
16	Dallas	21

Use Name	Pos.	Hgt	Wgt	Age	Int	Pts
Ray Brown	OT-OG	6'5"	280	24		
Gene Chilton	OT	6'3"	271	23		
#Victor Perry	OT	6'5"	278	23		
Tootie Robbins	OT	6'5"	302	29		
Luis Sharpe	OT	6'4"	260	27		
#Tom Welter	OT-OG	6'5"	280	23		
#Joe Bock	OG	6'4"	254	28		
Joe Bostic	OG	6'3"	268	30		
Michael Morris	OG	6'5"	275	26		
#Ron Pasquale	OG	6'2"	266	23		
Todd Peat	OG	6'2"	294	23		
Mike Ruether	OG-C	6'4"	275	24		
Lance Smith	OG-OT	6'2"	262	23		
#Charles Vatterott	OG-OT	6'4"	263	23		
Derek Kennard	C-OG	6'3"	285	24		
#Keith Radecic	C	6'1"	260	23		
#Ron Bohm	DE-DT	6'3"	250	22		
#Victor Burnett	DE	6'5"	250	24		
David Galloway	DE	6'3"	279	28		
Curtis Greer	DE	6'4"	258	29		
Freddie Joe Nunn	DE	6'4"	255	25		
Rod Saddler	DE	6'5"	276	21	1	
Steve Alvord	DT	6'4"	272	22		
#Anthony Burke	DT	6'3"	262	22		
Bob Clasby	DT	6'5"	260	26		
Mark Duda	DT	6'3"	279	26		
#Gary Dulin	DT-DE	6'4"	275	30		
Mark Garalczyk	DT	6'5"	272	22		
Collin Scotts	DT	6'5"	263	24		

Use Name	Pos.	Hgt	Wgt	Age	Int	Pts
Charlie Baker	LB	6'2"	234	29		
Anthony Bell	LB	6'3"	231	23	1	
#Tony Buford	LB	6'2"	222	23		
#Jimmie Carter	LB	6'1"	220	26	1	
Wayne Davis	LB	6'1"	213	23		
#Phil Forney	LB	6'2"	230	23		
Ilia Jarostchuk	LB	6'3"	231	23		
E.J. Junior	LB	6'3"	235	27	1	
Terence Mack	LB	6'3"	240	23		
Niko Noga	LB	6'1"	235	25		6
#Peter Noga	LB	6'	212	23	1	6
#Jeff Paine	LB	6'2"	224	26		
#Dwayne Anderson	DB	6'	205	25		
#Terrence Anthony	DB	5'10"	183	22		
Carl Carter	DB	5'11"	180	23		
Travis Curtis	DB	5'10"	180	21	5	
Johnny Holloway	DB	5'11"	182	23		
Mark Jackson	DB	5'9"	180	25		6
Greggory Johnson	DB	6'1"	195	28		
Cedric Mack	DB	6'	194	26	2	
#Mark Mathis	DB	5'9"	178	22	1	
#Tony Mayes	DB	6'	200	23		
Tim McDonald	DB	6'2"	207	22		
John Preston	DB	6'	207	25		
#Ed Scott	DB	5'10"	182	26		
#Ken Sims	DB	5'9"	177	23		
Leonard Smith	DB	5'11"	202	26		6
Charles Wright	DB	5'9"	178	23		
Lonnie Young	DB	6'1"	182	24	1	

Use Name	Pos.	Hgt	Wgt	Age	Int	Pts
#Sammy Garza	QB	6'1"	184	21		6
#Shawn Halloran	QB	6'4"	217	23		
Neil Lomax	QB	6'3"	215	28		
Cliff Stoudt	QB	6'4"	215	32		
#Gregg Tipton	QB	6'3"	191	23		
Derrick McAdoo	HB	5'10"	198	22		24
Stump Mitchell	HB	5'9"	188	28		30
Val Sikahema	HB	5'9"	191	25		6
Earl Ferrell	FB	6'	224	29		42
#Don Goodman	FB	5'11"	214	28		
Broderick Sargent	FB	5'10"	215	24		
Ron Wolfley	FB	6'	222	24		6
Ron Brown	WR	5'10"	186	24		
#Clarence Collins	WR	6'1"	180	25		
Roy Green	WR	6'	190	30		24
Don Holmes	WR	5'10"	180	26		
Troy Johnson	WR	6'1"	175	24		12
#Adrian McBride	WR	6'	195	24		
J.T.Smith	WR	6'2"	185	31		48
Rob Awalt	TE	6'5"	248	23		36
William Harris	TE	6'4"	243	22		
#Bob Keseday	TE	6'4"	225	25		
Jay Novacek	TE	6'4"	235	24		18
Greg Cater	K	6'	205	30		
Jim Gallery	K	6'1"	190	25		57
Greg Horne (from CIN)	K	6'	188	22		
#Mark Royals (to PHI)	K	6'5"	216	24		
#Jason Staurovsky	K	5'9"	167	24		9

PHILADELPHIA EAGLES 7-8 Buddy Ryan

Scores of Each Game		
24	Washington	34
27	NEW ORLEANS	17
3	CHICAGO	35
22	Dallas	41
10	Green Bay	*16
37	DALLAS	20
28	St. Louis	23
31	WASHINGTON	27
17	N.Y.GIANTS	20
19	ST.LOUIS	31
34	New England	*31
20	N.Y.Giants	*23
10	MIAMI	28
38	N.Y.Jets	27
17	BUFFALO	7

* Overtime

Use Name	Pos.	Hgt	Wgt	Age	Int	Pts
David Alexander	OT-OG	6'3"	279	23		
Joe Conwell	OT	6'5"	275	26		
Matt Darwin	OT	6'4"	260	24		
#Mike Perrino	OT	6'5"	285	23		
Ken Reeves	OT-OG	6'5"	275	25		
#Jeff Wenzel	OT	6'7"	270	23		
#Jim Angelo	OG	6'3"	275	24		
Ron Baker	OG	6'4"	274	32		
Bob Landsee	OG	6'4"	273	23		
#Scott Leggett	OG-OT	6'3"	285	24		
#Mike Nease	OG	6'3"	272	25		
Adam Schreiber	OG	6'4"	270	25		
Reggie Singletary	OG	6'3"	272	23		
#Pete Walters	OG	6'2"	265	28		
Gerry Feehery	C	6'2"	270	27		
#Matt Long	C	6'3"	270	26		
#Paul Ryczek	C	6'3"	235	25		
Ben Tamburello	C-OG	6'3"	278	22		
#Jim Auer	DE	6'7"	275	25		
#Marvin Ayres	DE	6'5"	265	23		
Jonathan Dumbauld	DE	6'4"	259	24		
#Elois Grooms	DE-DT	6'4"	250	34		
John Klingel	DE	6'3"	260	23		
#Greg Liter	DE	6'6"	275	23		
#Tim Mooney	DE	6'2"	265	25		
#Ray Phillips	DE-LB	6'3"	240	23		
Clyde Simmons	DE-DT	6'6"	258	23		
Reggie White	DE	6'5"	285	25		6
#Gary Bolden	DT	6'1"	275	25		
Jerome Brown	DT	6'2"	292	22	2	
Ken Clarke	DT	6'2"	275	31		
#Ray Conlin	DT	6'2"	258	25		
Mike Golic (from HOU)	DT-DE	6'5"	275	24		
#Skip Hamilton	DT	6'2"	265	28		
#Randall Mitchell	DT	6'1"	275	23		
Mike Pitts	DT-DE	6'5"	277	26		

Use Name	Pos.	Hgt	Wgt	Age	Int	Pts
Ty Allert (from SD)	LB	6'2"	233	24		
#Matt Battaglia	LB	6'2"	225	21		
#Carlos Bradley	LB	6'	222	27		
#Dave Brown	LB	6'2"	215	23		
Garry Cobb	LB	6'2"	230	30		
#George Cumby	LB	6'	224	31		
Byron Evans	LB	6'2"	225	23	1	
#Chuck Gorecki	LB	6'4"	237	23		
Dwayne Jiles	LB	6'4"	242	25		
Alonzo Johnson	LB	6'3"	222	24		
Seth Joyner	LB	6'2"	241	22	2	6
#Kelly Kirchbaum	LB	6'2"	240	30		
#Byron Lee	LB	6'2"	230	22		
Mike Reichenbach	LB	6'2"	238	25		
Jody Schulz	LB	6'3"	235	27		
#Fred Smalls	LB	6'3"	225	24		
#Victor Bellamy	DB	6'1"	195	24		
Cedrick Brown	DB	5'10"	178	22	1	
#Thomas Caterbone	DB	5'8"	175	23		
Evan Cooper	DB	5'11"	184	25	2	
Elbert Foules	DB	5'11"	185	26	4	
William Frizzell	DB	6'3"	198	24		
Russell Gary	DB	5'11"	200	28		
#Chris Gerhard	DB	5'10"	185	23		
#Jeff Griffin	DB	6'	185	29		
#Greg Harding	DB	6'2"	197	27		
Terry Hoage	DB	6'3"	199	25	2	
#Angelo James	DB	6'	180	25		
#Christopher Johnson	DB	6'4"	225	26		
#Michael Kullman	DB	6'1"	185	25	2	
#Mike Ulmer	DB	6'	201	32		
Andre Waters	DB	5'11"	185	25	3	
#Troy West	DB	6'1"	205	26	1	
Roynell Young	DB	6'1"	185	29	1	

Wes Hopkins - Knee Injury
Nick Haden - Ankle Injury

Use Name	Pos.	Hgt	Wgt	Age	Int	Pts
Matt Cavanaugh	QB	6'2"	212	30		
Randall Cunningham	QB	6'4"	192	24		18
#Marty Horn	QB	6'2"	206	24		
#Guido Merkens	QB	6'1"	195	32		
#Scott Tinsley	QB	6'2"	195	27		
#Topper Clemons	HB	5'11"	205	23		6
Bobby Morse	HB	5'10"	201	21		
Alan Reid	HB	5'8"	190	26		
Junior Tautalatasi	HB	5'10"	205	25		
#Willie Turrall	HB	5'10"	190	23		
#Reggie Brown	FB	5'11"	211	27		
Keith Byars	FB	6'1"	230	23		24
Charles Crawford	FB	6'2"	235	23		
Michael Haddix	FB	6'2"	227	25		
#Jacque Robinson	FB	5'11"	215	25		
#Alvin Ross	FB	5'11"	235	24		6
Anthony Toney	FB	6'	227	24		36
#Jesse Bendross	WR	6'	196	25		
#Kevin Bowman	WR	6'3"	205	25		6
Cris Carter	WR	6'3"	194	21		12
Gregg Garrity	WR	5'10"	169	25		12
#Otis Grant	WR	6'3"	197	26		
Kenny Jackson	WR	6'	180	25		18
Ron Johnson	WR	6'3"	186	28		
Mike Quick	WR	6'2"	190	27		66
#Mike Siano	WR	6'4"	215	23		6
#Eric Bailey	TE	6'5"	240	25		
#Ron Fazio	TE	6'4"	242	25		
Jimmie Giles (from DET)	TE	6'3"	240	32		6
Dave Little	TE	6'2"	236	26		
Mike McCloskey	TE	6'5"	246	26		
#Jay Repko	TE	6'3"	240	28		
John Spagnola	TE	6'4"	242	30		12
#Dave Jacobs	K	5'7"	151	30		11
Paul McFadden	K	5'11"	163	25		64
John Teltschik	K	6'2"	215	23		

- on the active roster for strike replacement games only

WASHINGTON REDSKINS

RUSHING

Last Name	No.	Yds	Avg	TD
Rogers	163	613	3.8	6
Bryant	77	406	5.3	1
Vital	80	346	4.3	2
Griffin	62	242	3.9	0
Smith	29	126	4.3	0
Schroeder	26	120	4.6	3
Monk	6	63	10.5	0
W. Wilson	18	55	3.1	2
Jessie	10	37	3.7	1
Rubbert	9	31	3.4	0
T. Wilson	2	28	14.0	1
Verdin	1	14	14.0	0
Branch	4	9	2.3	0
D. Williams	7	9	1.3	1
Holman	2	7	3.5	0
Clark	1	0	0.0	0
Robinson	2	0	0.0	0
Sanders	1	-4	-4.0	0

RECEIVING

Last Name	No.	Yds	Avg	TD
Clark	56	1066	19.0	7
Bryant	43	490	11.4	5
Monk	38	483	12.7	6
Sanders	37	630	17.0	3
Allen	13	337	25.9	3
Didier	13	178	13.7	1
McEwen	12	164	13.7	0
Warren	7	43	6.1	0
T. Wilson	5	112	22.4	1
Rogers	4	23	5.8	0
Orr	3	35	11.7	0
Griffin	3	13	4.3	1
Verdin	2	62	31.0	0
Caravello	2	29	14.5	0
W. Wilson	2	16	8.0	0
Dennison	2	8	4.0	0
Vital	1	13	13.0	0
Jessie	1	8	8.0	0
Johnson	1	5	5.0	0
Yarber	1	5	5.0	0
Smith	1	-2	-2.0	0

PUNT RETURNS

Last Name	No.	Yds	Avg	TD
Yarber	37	273	7.4	0
T. Wilson	8	143	17.9	0
Shepard	6	146	24.3	0
Green	5	53	10.6	0

KICKOFF RETURNS

Last Name	No.	Yds	Avg	TD
Griffin	25	478	19.1	0
Verdin	12	244	20.3	0
Branch	4	61	15.3	0
Jessie	4	73	18.3	0
Orr	4	62	15.5	0
Sanders	4	118	29.5	0
Vital	2	31	15.5	0
W. Wilson	2	32	16.0	0
Shepard	1	20	20.0	0
T. Wilson	1	20	20.0	0

PASSING — PUNTING — KICKING

PASSING	Att	Cmp	%	Yds	Yd/Att	TD	Int—	%	RK
Schroeder	267	129	48.3	1878	7.0	12	10—	3.7	21
D. Williams	143	81	56.6	1156	8.1	11	5—	3.5	
Rubbert	49	26	53.1	532	10.9	4	1—	2.0	
Robinson	18	11	61.1	152	8.4	0	2—	11.1	
Bryant	1	0	0.0	0	0.0	0	0—	0.0	

PUNTING	No	Avg
Cox	64	40.2
Weil	14	34.4

KICKING	XP	Att	%	FG	Att	%
Haji-Sheikh	29	32	94	13	19	68
Ariri	6	6	100	3	5	60
Cox	3	3	100	1	1	100
Atkinson	1	1	100	1	1	100
Toibin	4	4	100	0	2	0

ST. LOUIS CARDINALS

RUSHING

Last Name	No.	Yds	Avg	TD
Mitchell	203	781	3.8	3
Ferrell	113	512	4.5	7
McAdoo	53	230	4.3	3
Lomax	29	107	3.7	0
Sargent	18	90	5.0	0
Wolfley	26	87	3.3	1
Green	2	34	17.0	0
Garza	8	31	3.9	1
Ro. Brown	1	9	9.0	0
T. Johnson	1	9	9.0	0
Cater	2	3	1.5	0
Stoudt	1	-2	-2.0	0
Awalt	2	-9	-4.5	0
Halloran	3	-9	-3.0	0

RECEIVING

Last Name	No.	Yds	Avg	TD
J. Smith	91	1117	12.3	8
Mitchell	45	397	8.8	2
Green	43	731	17.0	4
Awalt	42	526	12.5	6
Ferrell	23	262	11.4	0
Novacek	20	254	12.7	3
T. Johnson	15	308	20.5	2
Holmes	11	132	12.0	0
Wolfley	8	68	8.5	0
Sargent	2	19	9.5	0
Ro. Brown	2	16	8.0	0
McAdoo	2	12	6.0	0
Harris	1	8	8.0	0

PUNT RETURNS

Last Name	No.	Yds	Avg	TD
Sikahema	44	550	12.5	1

KICKOFF RETURNS

Last Name	No.	Yds	Avg	TD
Sikahema	34	761	22.4	0
McAdoo	23	444	19.3	0
Sargent	3	37	12.3	0
Ro. Brown	1	40	40.0	0
Ferrell	1	10	10.0	0
Holmes	1	25	25.0	0

PASSING — PUNTING — KICKING

PASSING	Att	Cmp	%	Yds	Yd/Att	TD	Int—	%	Rk
Lomax	463	275	59.4	3387	7.3	24	12—	2.6	5
Halloran	42	18	42.9	263	6.3	0	1—	2.4	
Garza	20	11	55.0	183	9.2	1	2—	10.0	
Mitchell	3	1	33.3	17	5.7	0	0—	0.0	
Stoudt	1	0	0.0	0	0.0	0	0—	0.0	

PUNTING	No	Avg
Horne	43	40.2
Cater	40	36.8
Royals	11	39.2

KICKING	XP	Att	%	FG	Att	%
Gallery	30	31	97	9	19	47
Staurovsky	6	6	100	1	3	33

PHILADELPHIA EAGLES

RUSHING

Last Name	No.	Yds	Avg	TD
Cunningham	76	505	6.6	3
Toney	127	473	3.7	5
Byars	116	426	3.7	3
Haddix	59	165	2.8	0
R. Brown	39	136	3.5	0
Robinson	24	114	4.8	0
Tautalatasi	26	69	2.7	0
Ross	14	54	3.9	1
Teltschik	3	32	10.7	0
Jackson	6	27	4.5	0
Grant	1	20	20.0	0
Morse	6	14	2.3	0
Tinsley	4	2	0.5	0
Clemons	3	0	0.0	0
Horn	1	0	0.0	0
Cavanaugh	1	-2	-2.0	0
Merkens	3	-8	-2.7	0

RECEIVING

Last Name	No.	Yds	Avg	TD
Quick	46	790	17.2	11
Toney	39	341	8.7	1
Spagnola	36	350	9.7	2
Tautalatasi	25	176	7.0	0
Jackson	21	471	22.4	3
Byars	21	177	8.4	1
Grant	16	280	17.5	0
Giles	13	157	12.1	1
Garrity	12	242	20.2	2
Siano	9	137	15.2	1
Bailey	8	69	8.6	0
R. Brown	8	53	6.6	0
Haddix	7	58	8.3	0
Bowman	6	127	21.2	1
Carter	5	84	16.8	2
Repko	5	46	9.2	0
Ross	5	41	8.2	0
Robinson	2	9	4.5	0
Clemons	1	13	13.0	1
Little	1	8	8.0	0
Morse	1	8	8.0	0
Cunningham	1	-3	-3.0	0
Singletary	1	-11	-11.0	0

PUNT RETURNS

Last Name	No.	Yds	Avg	TD
Morse	20	121	6.1	0
Bowman	4	43	10.8	0
Garrity	4	16	4.0	0
Caterbone	2	13	6.5	0
Ulmer	2	10	5.0	0
C. Brown	1	-1	-1.0	0
A. Johnson	1	0	0.0	0

KICKOFF RETURNS

Last Name	No.	Yds	Avg	TD
Morse	24	386	16.1	0
Carter	12	241	20.1	0
Bowman	7	153	21.9	0
Cooper	5	86	17.2	0
Reid	4	58	14.5	0
Tautalatasi	3	53	17.7	0
Haddix	2	16	8.0	0
Turrall	1	21	21.0	0
R. Brown	1	20	20.0	0
C. Brown	1	13	13.0	0
Siano	1	13	13.0	0
Ulmer	1	8	8.0	0
Alexander	1	6	6.0	0
Clemons	1	0	0.0	0
Reeves	0	1	—	0

PASSING — PUNTING — KICKING

PASSING	Att	Cmp	%	Yds	Yd/Att	TD	Int—	%	Rk
Cunningham	406	223	54.9	2786	6.9	23	12—	3.0	13
Tinsley	86	48	55.8	637	7.4	3	4—	4.7	
Merkens	14	7	50.0	70	5.0	0	0—	0.0	
Horn	11	5	45.5	68	6.2	0	0—	0.0	
Carter	1	0	0.0	0	0.0	0	0—	0.0	
Grant	1	0	0.0	0	0.0	0	0—	0.0	
Toney	1	0	0.0	0	0.0	0	0—	0.0	

PUNTING	No	Avg
Teltschik	83	37.7
Jacobs	11	33.5
Merkens	3	20.3

KICKING	XP	Att	%	FG	Att	%
McFadden	36	36	100	16	26	62
Jacobs	2	4	50	3	5	60

DALLAS COWBOYS 7-8 Tom Landry

Scores of Each Game		
13	St. Louis	24
16	N.Y.Giants	14
38	N.Y.Jets	24
41	PHILADELPHIA	22
7	WASHINGTON	13
20	Philadelphia	37
33	N.Y.GIANTS	24
17	Detroit	27
23	New England	*17
14	MIAMI	20
38	MINNESOTA	*44
10	ATLANTA	21
20	Washington	24
29	L.A.Rams	21
21	ST.LOUIS	16

Use Name	Pos.	Hgt	Wgt	Age	Int	Pts
Brian Baldinger	OT-OG	6'4"	266	28		
#Dave Burnette	OT	6'6"	278	26		
#Steve Cisowaki	OT	6'5"	275	24		
Kevin Gogan	OT	6'7"	310	22		
Phil Pozderac	OT	6'9"	283	27		
#Jon Shields	OT	6'5"	293	23		
Daryle Smith	OT	6'5"	278	23		
Mark Tuinei	OT	6'5"	282	27		
#Sal Cesario	OG	6'4"	255	24		
Crawford Ker	OG	6'3"	283	25		
Nate Newton	OG	6'3"	315	25		
#Gary Walker	OG	6'3"	283	23		
Bob White	OG	6'5"	270	24		
Jeff Zimmerman	OG	6'3"	310	22		
George Lilja	C	6'4"	282	29		
Tom Rafferty	C	6'3"	262	33		
Joe Shearin	C	6'4"	265	27		
#Mike Zentic	C	6'3"	255	23		
Jim Jeffcoat	DE	6'5"	263	26	1	6
Too Tall Jones	DE	6'9"	275	36		
#Ray Perkins	DE	6'5"	242	21		
Don Smerek	DE-DT	6'7"	262	29		
Randy Watts	DE-DT	6'6"	275	24		
Kevin Brooks	DT	6'6"	278	24		
John Dutton	DT	6'7"	261	36		
#Mike Dwyer	DT	6'3"	280	24		
#Walter Johnson	DT	6'1"	250	21		
Danny Noonan	DT	6'4"	270	22		
Mark Walen	DT-DE	6'5"	265	24		
Randy White	DT	6'4"	263	34	1	

Use Name	Pos.	Hgt	Wgt	Age	Int	Pts
Ron Burton	LB	6'1"	250	23		
Steve DeOssie	LB	6'2"	249	24		
#Chris Duliban	LB	6'2"	216	24		
#Harry Flaherty	LB	6'1"	232	25		
Mike Hegman	LB	6'1"	236	34		
Jeff Hurd	LB	6'2"	245	23		
Garth Jax	LB	6'2"	225	23		
#Dale Jones	LB	6'1"	234	24		
Eugene Lockhart	LB	6'2"	235	26	1	
Jesse Penn	LB	6'3"	224	24	1	
Jeff Rohrer	LB	6'3"	222	28		
#Victor Simmons	LB	6'2"	230	23		
#Russ Swan	LB	6'4"	225	24		
#Kirk Timmer	LB	6'3"	242	23		
#Vince Albritton	DB	6'2"	217	25		
#Jimmy Armstrong	DB	5'8"	165	25		
Bill Bates	DB	6'1"	204	26	3	
#Anthony Coleman	DB	6'	185	23		
Michael Downs	DB	6'3"	212	28	4	
Ron Francis	DB	5'9"	199	23	2	6
#Alex Green	DB	6'1"	194	21	1	
#Tommy Haynes	DB	6'	190	24	3	
Manny Hendrix	DB	5'10"	181	22		
#Bill Hill	DB	5'9"	172	26		
#Bruce Livingston	DB	5'10"	169	24		
Victor Scott	DB	6'	203	25	1	
Everson Walls	DB	6'1"	192	27	5	
Robert Williams	DB	5'10"	195	24		

Kurt Petersen - Knee Injury
Robert Smith - Arm Injury
Glen Titensor - Knee Injury
Brian Salonen - Groin Injury
Ray Alexander - Wrist Injury
Mike Sherrard - Broken Leg

Use Name	Pos.	Hgt	Wgt	Age	Int	Pts
Paul McDonald	QB	6'2"	182	29		
Steve Pelluer	QB	6'4"	208	25		6
#Loran Snyder	QB	6'4"	207	23		
#Kevin Sweeney	QB	6'	191	23		
Danny White	QB	6'2"	198	35		6
#David Adams	HB	5'6"	170	23		6
#Alvin Blount	HB	5'9"	197	22		18
Tony Dorsett	HB	5'11"	188	33		12
Robert Lavette (to PHI)	HB	5'11"	190	23		
Herschel Walker	HB	6'1"	223	25		48
Darryl Clack	FB	5'10"	218	23		
Todd Fowler	FB	6'3"	222	25		
#E.J.Jones	FB	5'11"	212	25		
Timmy Newsome	FB	6'1"	235	29		24
#Gerald White	FB	5'11"	223	22		
Gordon Banke	WR	5'10"	170	29		6
Ron Barksdale	WR	6'	193	24		6
#Cornell Burbage	WR	5'10"	181	22		12
#Vince Courville	WR	5'9"	170	27		
Kelvin Edwards	WR	6'2"	205	23		24
Kelvin Martin	WR	5'9"	163	22		
Mike Renfro	WR	6'	184	32		24
#Chuck Scott	WR	6'2"	195	24		
#Sebron Spivey	WR	5'11"	180	23		
#Rich Borreson	TE	6'5"	252	23		
Thornton Chandler	TE	6'5"	245	23		6
Doug Cosbie	TE	6'6"	241	31		18
Steve Folsom	TE	6'5"	236	29		
#Tim Hendrix	TE	6'5"	241	21		
#Kerry Brady	K	6'1'	205	24		
Roger Ruzek	K	6'1"	190	26		92
#Buzz Sawyer	K	6'1"	201	24		
Mike Saxon	K	6'3"	193	25		
#Luis Zendejas	K	5'9"	160	25		19

NEW YORK GIANTS 6-9 Bill Parcells

Scores of Each Game		
19	Chicago	34
14	DALLAS	16
21	SAN FRANCISCO	41
12	WASHINGTON	38
3	Buffalo	*6
30	ST.LOUIS	7
24	Dallas	33
17	NEW ENGLAND	10
20	Philadelphia	17
14	New Orleans	23
19	Washington	23
23	PHILADELPHIA	*20
24	St.Louis	27
20	GREEN BAY	10
20	N.Y.JETS	7

Use Name	Pos.	Hgt	Wgt	Age	Int	Pts
Brad Benson	OT	6'3"	270	31		
#Mike Black	OT	6'4"	280	23		
#Kevin Meuth	OT	6'5"	270	23		
Doug Riesenberg	OT	6'5"	275	22		
William Roberts	OT	6'5"	280	25		
#Frank Sutton	OT	6'3"	280	23		
#Gregg Swartwoudt	OT	6'3"	275	23		
Billy Ard	OG	6'3"	270	28		
#Kelvin Davis	OG	6'2"	260	24		
#Bill Dugan	OG-OT	6'4"	290	28		
Chris Godfrey	OG	6'3"	265	29		
Damian Johnson	OG	6'5"	290	24		
#Dan Morgan	OG	6'6"	285	23		
#Scott Urch	OG	6'2"	270	22		
Brian Johnston	C	6'3"	275	24		
#Chris Jones	C	6'3"	263	23		
#Russell Mitchell	C	6'5"	288	26		
Bart Oates	C	6'3"	265	28		
#Reggie Carr	DE	6'3"	300	24		
Eric Dorsey	DE	6'5"	280	23		
#Curtis Garrett	DE	6'5"	302	25		
Leonard Marshall	DE	6'3"	285	25		
George Martin	DE	6'4"	255	34		
#Brian Sisley	DE	6'4"	235	23		
#Torin Smith	DE	6'4"	320	25		
#Joe Taibi	DE	6'5"	265	24		
John Washington	DE	6'4"	275	24		
#Dennis Borcky	NT	6'4"	284	22		
Jim Burt	NT	6'1"	260	28		
#Anthony Howard	NT	6'3"	267	27		
Erik Howard	NT	6'4"	268	22		

Use Name	Pos.	Hgt	Wgt	Age	Int	Pts
Carl Banks	LB	6'4"	235	25	1	
#Charlie Burgess	LB	6'	230	24		
Harry Carson	LB	6'2"	240	33		
#Chris Davis	LB	6'1"	225	24		
#Dan DeRose	LB	6'	230	25	1	
Andy Headen	LB	6'5"	242	27	2	
Byron Hunt	LB	6'5"	242	28		
Pepper Johnson	LB	6'3"	248	23		
Robbie Jones	LB	6'2"	230	27		
#Jerry Kimmel	LB	6'2"	240	24		
#Frank Nicholson	LB	6'2"	205	26		
Gary Reasons	LB	6'4"	234	25		
Lawrence Taylor	LB	6'3"	243	28	3	
#Warren Thompson	LB	6'3"	241	23		
#Jeff Tootie	LB	6'2"	240	25		
#Don Brown	DB	5'11"	189	23	1	
#Boris Byrd	DB	6'	210	25		
Harvey Clayton	DB	5'9"	186	26		
Mark Collins	DB	5'10"	190	23	2	
Tom Flynn	DB	6'	195	25		6
Wayne Haddix	DB	6'1"	203	22		
Kenny Hill	DB	6'	195	29	1	
Terry Kinard	DB	6'1"	200	27	5	6
Greg Lasker	DB	6'	200	22		
#Pat Morrison	DB	6'2"	194	22		
#Jimmy Norris	DB	5'11"	188	22		
#Robert Porter	DB	6'2"	210	25		
#Steve Rehage	DB	6'1"	190	23	1	
#Doug Smith	DB	6'	192	24		
Herb Welch	DB	5'11"	180	26	2	
Adrian White	DB	6'	200	23		
Perry Williams	DB	6'2"	203	26	1	
#Jim Yarbrough	DB	6'	195	23		

Karl Nelson - Hodgkin's disease

Use Name	Pos.	Hgt	Wgt	Age	Int	Pts
#Mike Busch	QB	6'4"	214	24		
#Jim Crocicchia	QB	6'2"	209	23		
Jeff Hostetler	QB	6'3"	212	26		
#Paul Kelly	QB	6'1"	205	23		
Jeff Rutledge	QB	6'1"	195	30		
Phil Simms	QB	6'3"	214	30		
Ottis Anderson	HB	6'2"	225	30		
#Earl Beecham	HB	5'6"	180	21		
#Robert DiRico	HB	5'10"	202	23		
Joe Morris	HB	5'7"	195	26		18
#Van Williams	HB	6'1"	215	28		
George Adams	FB	6'1"	225	24		12
Maurice Carthon	FB	6'1"	225	26		
#Jamie Covington	FB	6'1"	234	24		
#Fred DiRenzo	FB	5'11"	234	26		
Tony Galbreath	FB	6'	228	33		
#Kaulana Park	FB	6'2"	230	25		
Lee Rouson	FB	6'1"	222	24		6
#Beau Almodobar	WR	5'9"	180	24		
Stephen Baker	WR	5'8"	160	23		12
#Lewis Bennett	WR	5'11"	175	24		6
#Mack Cummings	WR	6'	195	27		
Mark Ingram	WR	5'10"	188	22		
#Edwin Lovelady	WR	5'9"	180	24		12
Lionel Manuel	WR	5'11"	180	25		36
Phil McConkey	WR	5'10"	170	30		
#Reggie McGowan	WR	5'8"	165	22		6
Stacy Robinson	WR	5'11"	186	25		12
#Warren Seitz	WR	6'4"	210	24		
Odessa Turner	WR	6'3"	205	22		6
Mark Bavaro	TE	6'4"	245	25		48
#Charles Coleman	TE	6'4"	222	23		
Zeke Mowatt	TE	6'3"	240	26		6
#Jeff Smith	TE	6'4"	230	24		
Raul Allegre	K	5'10"	167	28		76
#George Benyola	K	5'10"	195	22		12
Sean Landeta	K	6'	200	25		
#Jim Miller	K	5'11"	183	30		
#Dana Moore	K	5'10"	180	25		

Central Division

CHICAGO BEARS 11-4 Mike Ditka

Scores of Each Game		
34	N.Y.GIANTS	19
20	TAMPA BAY	3
35	Philadelphia	3
27	MINNESOTA	7
17	NEW ORLEANS	19
27	Tampa Bay	26
31	KANSAS CITY	28
26	Green Bay	24
29	Denver	31
30	DETROIT	10
23	GREEN BAY	10
30	Minnesota	24
0	San Francisco	41
21	SEATTLE	34
6	L.A.Raiders	3

* Overtime

\# - on the active roster for replacement games only

Use Name	Pos.	Hgt	Wgt	Age	Int	Pts
#John Arp	OT	6'5"	275	22		
Paul Blair	OT	6'4"	295	24		
Jim Covert	OT	6'4"	275	27		
#Jack Oliver	OT	6'3"	281	25		
#Stuart Rindy	OT-OG	6'5"	266	23		
Keith Van Horne	OT	6'6"	285	29		
Kurt Becker	OG	6'5"	280	28		
Mark Bortz	OG	6'6"	275	26		
#Jon Roehik	OG	6'2"	257	26		
Tom Thayer	OG	6'4"	280	26		
John Wojciechowski	OG-OT	6'4"	262	24		
John Adickes	C	6'3"	264	23		
Jay Hilgenberg	C	6'3"	260	27		
#Brent Johnson	C	6'2"	255	24		
Mark Rodenhauser	C	6'5"	260	26		
Richard Dent	DE	6'5"	263	26		
Dan Hampton	DE-DT	6'5"	267	29		
Al Harris	DE	6'5"	270	30		
#Sean McInerney	DE	6'3"	255	26		
Jon Norris	DE-DT	6'3"	260	24	1	
Sean Smith	DE	6'4"	275	22		
Jim Althoff	DT	6'3"	278	25		
Dick Chapura	DT	6'3"	280	23		
#Greg Fitzgerald	DT	6'4"	265	24		
Steve McMichael	DT	6'2"	265	29		
William Perry	DT	6'2"	315	24		
#Eugene Rowell	DT	6'3"	265	29		
#Guy Teafatiller	DT	6'2"	260	23		

Use Name	Pos.	Hgt	Wgt	Age	Int	Pts
#Bobby Bell	LB	6'3"	217	25		
#Mike January	LB	6'1"	234	23		
Will Johnson	LB	6'4"	242	23		
Wilber Marshall	LB	6'1"	230	25		
Paul Migliazzo	LB	6'1"	228	23		
#Eldridge Milton	LB	6'1"	235	25		
#Raymond Morris	LB	5'10"	222	26		
Jim Morrissey	LB	6'3"	222	24		
Jay Norvell	LB	6'2"	232	24		
Ron Rivers	LB	6'3"	235	25	2	
#Doug Rothschild	LB	6'2"	231	22		
Mike Singletary	LB	6'	235	28		
Otis Wilson	LB	6'2"	227	29		
Egypt Allen	DB	6'	203	23		
Todd Bell	DB	6'1"	212	28		
Maurice Douglass	DB	5'11"	200	23	2	
#George Duarte	DB	5'9"	172	23		
Dave Duerson	DB	6'1"	210	26	3	
Gary Fencik	DB	6'1"	193	33		
Shaun Gayle	DB	5'11"	193	25	1	6
#Mike Hintz	DB	6'1"	190	22		
Vestee Jackson	DB	6'	186	24		
#Eric Jeffries	DB	5'10"	161	23	1	
#Lorenzo Lynch	DB	5'9"	197	23		
#Bruce McCray	DB	5'9"	181	24	1	6
Reggie Phillips	DB	5'10"	170	26	2	
Mike Richardson	DB	6'	188	26		
Garland Rivers	DB	6'1"	181	22		
#Mike Stoops	DB	6'1"	185	22		
#Steve Trimble	DB	5'10"	190	29		

Larry Rubens - Knee Injury
Lew Barnes - Leg Injury
Steve Fuller - Shoulder Injury
Tim Wrightman - Knee Injury

Use Name	Pos.	Hgt	Wgt	Age	Int	Pts
#Steve Bradley	QB	6'2"	216	24		
Jim Harbaugh	QB	6'3"	202	23		
#Mike Hohensee	QB	6'	205	26		
Jim McMahon	QB	6'1"	190	28		12
#Sean Payton	QB	5'11"	200	23		
Mike Tomczak	QB	6'1"	195	24		6
#Darryl Clark	HB	5'11"	204	26		
#Frank Harris	HB	6'1"	196	23		
#Anthony Mosley	HB	5'9"	204	22		6
Walter Payton	HB	5'11"	205	33		30
Thomas Sanders	HB	5'11"	203	25		6
Neal Anderson	FB-HB	5'11"	210	23		36
#Chris Brewer	FB	6'1"	203	25		18
#Lakei Heimuli	FB	5'11"	219	22		6
Matt Suhey	FB	5'11"	216	29		
Calvin Thomas	FB	5'11"	245	27		
#Al Wolden	FB	6'3"	232	22		
#Todd Black	WR	5'11"	174	23		
Willie Gault	WR	6'	183	26		42
Dennis Gentry	WR	5'8"	180	28		12
#Herbert Johnson	WR	5'11"	182	23		
#Ken Knapczyk	WR	5'11"	190	24		
#Glen Kozlowski	WR	6'1"	190	24		18
Dennis McKinnon	WR	6'1"	185	26		18
Ron Morris	WR	6'1"	187	22		6
#Gary Mullen	WR	5'11"	174	24		
Keith Ortego	WR	6'	180	24		
#Lawrence White	WR	6'2"	187	24		
Cap Boso	TE	6'3"	224	24		12
#Sam Bowers	TE	6'4"	250	29		
#Brian Glasgow	TE	6'2"	230	26		
#Don Kindt	TE	6'6"	242	26		6
Emery Moorehead	TE	6'2"	225	33		6
#Kevin Brown	K	6'2"	178	24		
Kevin Butler	K	6'1"	204	25		85
#Tim Leshar	K	5'9"	160	22		19
Bryan Wagner	K	6'2"	195	25		

DALLAS COWBOYS

RUSHING

Last Name	No.	Yds	Avg	TD
Walker	209	891	4.3	7
Dorsett	130	456	3.5	1
Pelluer	25	142	5.7	1
Blount	46	125	2.7	3
Newsome	25	121	4.8	2
Edwards	2	61	30.5	1
Adams	7	49	7.0	1
D. White	10	14	1.4	1
Sweeney	5	8	1.6	0
E.J. Jones	2	7	3.5	0
Snyder	2	0	0.0	0
G. White	1	-4	-4.0	0
Cosbie	1	-5	-5.0	0

RECEIVING

Last Name	No.	Yds	Avg	TD
Walker	60	715	11.9	1
Renfro	46	662	14.4	4
Cosbie	36	421	11.7	3
Edwards	34	521	15.3	3
Newsome	34	274	8.1	2
Dorsett	19	177	9.3	1
Banks	15	231	15.4	1
Barksdale	12	165	13.8	1
Burbage	7	168	24.0	2
Martin	5	103	20.6	0
G. White	5	46	9.2	0
Chandler	5	25	5.0	1
E.J. Jones	3	16	5.3	0
Spivey	2	34	17.0	0
C. Scott	1	11	11.0	0
Adams	1	8	8.0	0
Fowler	1	6	6.0	0
Lavette	1	6	6.0	0
Blount	1	5	5.0	0

PUNT RETURNS

Last Name	No.	Yds	Avg	TD
Martin	22	216	9.8	0
Edwards	8	75	9.4	0
Banks	5	33	6.6	0
Burbage	5	29	5.8	0
Livingston	1	0	0.0	0

KICKOFF RETURNS

Last Name	No.	Yds	Avg	TD
Clack	29	635	21.9	0
Martin	12	237	19.8	0
Edwards	7	155	22.1	0
Adams	6	113	18.8	0
Lavette	6	109	18.2	0
Spivey	2	49	24.5	0
Newsome	2	22	1.0	0
Chandler	1	7	7.0	0
Borresen	1	5	5.0	0

PASSING — PUNTING — KICKING

PASSING	Att	Cmp	%	Yds	Yd/Att	TD	Int—	%	Rk
D. White	362	215	59.4	2617	7.2	12	17—	4.7	19
Pelluer	101	55	54.5	642	6.4	3	2—	2.0	
Sweeney	28	14	50.0	291	10.4	4	1—	3.6	
Snyder	9	4	44.4	44	4.9	0	0—	0.0	

PUNTING	No	Avg
Saxon	68	39.5
Sawyer	16	39.9

KICKING	XP	Att	%	FG	Att	%
Ruzek	26	26	100	22	25	88
Zendejas	10	10	100	3	4	75

NEW YORK GIANTS

RUSHING

Last Name	No.	Yds	Avg	TD
Morris	193	658	3.4	3
Adams	61	169	2.8	1
Rouson	41	155	3.8	0
V. Williams	29	108	3.7	0
DiRico	25	90	3.6	0
Galbreath	10	74	7.4	0
Carthon	26	60	2.3	0
Simms	14	44	3.1	0
Rutledge	15	31	2.1	0
Beecham	5	22	4.4	0
Baker	1	18	18.0	0
Lovelady	2	11	5.5	0
Park	6	11	1.8	0
Anderson	2	6	3.0	0
Crocicchia	4	5	1.3	0
DiRenzo	1	5	5.0	0
Covington	4	0	0.0	0
Manuel	1	-10	-10.0	0

RECEIVING

Last Name	No.	Yds	Avg	TD
Bavaro	55	867	15.8	8
Adams	35	298	8.5	1
Manuel	30	545	18.2	6
Galbreath	26	248	9.5	0
Baker	15	277	18.5	2
McConkey	11	186	16.9	0
Rouson	11	129	11.7	1
Morris	11	114	10.4	0
Turner	10	195	19.5	1
Bennett	10	184	18.4	1
Lovelady	10	125	12.5	2
Carthon	8	71	8.9	0
J. Smith	6	72	12.0	0
Robinson	6	58	9.7	2
V. Williams	5	36	7.2	0
McGowan	4	111	27.8	1
Mowatt	3	39	13.0	1
Ingram	2	32	16.0	0
DiRico	2	22	11.0	0
Anderson	2	16	8.0	0
Covington	1	9	9.0	0
Park	1	6	6.0	0
Coleman	1	5	5.0	0

PUNT RETURNS

Last Name	No.	Yds	Avg	TD
McConkey	42	394	9.4	0
Lovelady	10	38	3.8	0
Baker	3	16	5.3	0

KICKOFF RETURNS

Last Name	No.	Yds	Avg	TD
Rouson	22	497	22.6	0
Adams	9	166	18.4	0
Ingram	6	114	19.0	0
Byrd	4	99	24.8	0
Norris	4	70	17.5	0
Beecham	3	70	23.3	0
DiRico	2	31	15.5	0
Coleman	1	20	20.0	0
Bavaro	1	16	16.0	0
Dorsey	1	13	13.0	0
Urch	1	13	13.0	0
Cummings	1	11	11.0	0
McConkey	1	8	8.0	0

PASSING — PUNTING — KICKING

PASSING	Att	Cmp	%	Yds	Yd/Att	TD	Int—	%	Rk
Simms	282	163	57.8	2230	7.9	17	9—	3.2	3
Rutledge	155	79	51.0	1048	6.8	5	11—	7.1	
Busch	47	17	36.2	278	5.9	3	2—	4.3	
Crocicchia	15	6	40.0	89	5.9	1	0—	0.0	

PUNTING	No	Avg
Landeta	66	42.0
Moore	15	32.4
Miller	10	34.5

KICKING	XP	Att	%	FG	Att	%
Allegre	25	26	96	17	27	63
Benyola	3	3	100	3	5	60

CHICAGO BEARS

RUSHING

Last Name	No.	Yds	Avg	TD
Anderson	129	586	4.5	3
W. Payton	146	533	3.7	4
Heimuli	34	128	3.8	0
Sanders	23	122	5.3	1
McMahon	22	88	4.0	2
Thomas	25	88	3.5	0
Mosley	18	80	4.4	0
Hohensee	9	56	6.2	0
Brewer	24	55	2.3	2
Tomczak	18	54	3.0	1
Gentry	6	41	6.8	0
S. Payton	1	28	28.0	0
Suhey	7	24	3.4	0
F. Harris	6	23	3.8	0
Gault	2	16	8.0	0
Harbaugh	4	15	3.8	0
Clark	5	11	2.2	0
Wolden	2	8	4.0	0
Marshall	1	1	1.0	0
Brown	1	0	0.0	0
Perry	1	0	0.0	0
Bradley	1	-3	-3.0	0

RECEIVING

Last Name	No.	Yds	Avg	TD
Anderson	47	467	9.9	3
Gault	35	705	20.1	7
W. Payton	33	217	6.6	1
McKinnon	27	406	15.0	1
Moorehead	24	269	11.2	1
Ro. Morris	20	379	19.0	1
Boso	17	188	11.1	2
Gentry	17	183	10.8	1
Kozlowski	15	199	13.3	3
Suhey	7	54	7.7	0
Brewer	5	56	11.2	1
Heimuli	5	51	10.2	1
Kindt	5	34	6.8	1
Knapczyk	4	62	15.5	0
Sanders	3	53	17.7	0
Mullen	2	33	16.5	0
Glasgow	2	16	8.0	0
Mosley	2	16	8.0	0
Wolden	1	26	26.0	0
Bowers	1	6	6.0	0

PUNT RETURNS

Last Name	No.	Yds	Avg	TD
McKinnon	40	405	10.1	2
Duarte	8	64	8.0	0
Duerson	1	10	10.0	0
Jeffries	1	5	5.0	0

KICKOFF RETURNS

Last Name	No.	Yds	Avg	TD
Gentry	25	621	24.8	1
Sanders	20	349	17.5	0
Kozlowski	3	72	24.0	0
Lynch	3	66	22.0	0
T. Bell	1	18	18.0	0
Mosley	1	17	17.0	0
White	1	17	17.0	0
Knapczyk	1	14	14.0	0
Milton	1	10	10.0	0
Suhey	1	9	9.0	0

PASSING — PUNTING — KICKING

PASSING	Att	Cmp	%	Yds	Yd/Att	TD	Int—	%	Rk
McMahon	210	125	59.5	1639	7.8	12	8—	3.8	7
Tomczak	178	97	54.5	1220	6.9	5	10—	5.6	
Hohensee	52	28	53.8	343	6.6	4	1—	1.9	
S. Payton	23	8	34.8	79	3.4	0	1—	4.3	
Bradley	18	6	33.3	77	4.3	2	3—	16.7	
Harbaugh	11	8	72.7	62	5.6	0	0—	0.0	
W. Payton	1	0	0.0	0	0.0	0	1—	100	

PUNTING	No	Avg
Wagner	37	39.5
Brown	19	39.1

KICKING	XP	Att	%	FG	Att	%
Butler	28	30	93	19	28	68
Lasher	10	10	100	3	4	75

MINNESOTA VIKINGS 8-7 Jerry Burns

Scores of Each Game		
34	DETROIT	19
21	L.A.Rams	16
16	GREEN BAY	23
7	Chicago	27
10	Tampa Bay	20
34	DENVER	27
17	Seattle	28
31	L.A.RAIDERS	20
23	TAMPA BAY	17
24	ATLANTA	13
44	Dallas	*38
24	CHICAGO	30
10	Green Bay	16
17	Detroit	14
24	WASHINGTON	*27

Use Name	Pos.	Hgt	Wgt	Age	Int	Pts
#Derek Burton	OT	6'2"	270	24		
Tim Irwin	OT	6'6"	290	28		
#John Scardina	OT	6'4"	265	29		
Gary Zimmerman	OT	6'6"	284	25		
#Mark Hanson	OG	6'2"	260	22		
Dave Huffman	OG	6'6"	285	30		
Wayne Jones	OG	6'4"	270	27		
Greg Koch (from MIA)	OG	6'4"	276	32		
Mark MacDonald	OG	6'4"	265	26		
#Mike McCurry	OG	6'3"	258	24		
#Ted Million	OG	6'4"	260	24		
#Frank Ori	OG	6'2"	255	23		
Terry Tausch	OG	6'5"	276	28		
#Mike Turner	OG	6'3"	255	27		
Chris Foote	C	6'3"	265	30		
Kirk Lowdermilk	C	6'3"	264	24		
Randy Rasmussen	C-OG	6'2"	254	26		
#Ron Selesky	C	6'1"	266	21		
Dennis Swilley	C	6'3"	266	32		
#Kevin Webster	C	6'2"	260	25		
#Daniel Coleman	DE	6'4"	249	25		
Chris Doleman	DE	6'5"	262	25		
Mike Hartenstine	DE	6'3"	254	34		
Doug Martin	DE	6'3"	258	30		
#Phil Micech	DE	6'5"	265	26		
#Tony Norman	DE	6'5"	270	32		
Gerald Robinson	DE	6'3"	261	24		
#Don Bramlett	DT	6'2"	270	24		
Stafford Mays	DT-DE	6'2"	264	29		
Keith Millard	DT	6'5"	264	25		
#Fred Molden	DT	6'2"	272	24		
Tim Newton	DT	6'	297	24		
#Kurt Ploeger	DT	6'5"	260	24		
#Joe Stepanek	DT	6'5"	268	23		2
Henry Thomas	DT	6'2"	268	22	1	
#Jimmy Walker	DT	6'2"	265	30		
#Brad White	DT	6'2"	261	29		

Use Name	Pos.	Hgt	Wgt	Age	Int	Pts
#Steve Ache	LB	6'3"	229	25		
Sam Anno (from LA)	LB	6'2"	230	22		
Walker Lee Ashley	LB	6'	232	27		
Ray Berry	LB	6'2"	230	23		
#Tim Bryant	LB	6'1"	217	25		
#Fabray Collins	LB	6'2"	215	25		
#Jim Dick	LB	6'1"	230	23		
David Howard	LB	6'2"	234	25	1	
Chris Martin	LB	6'2"	231	26		
Peter Najarian	LB	6'2"	233	23		
#Kelly Quinn	LB	6'1"	220	24		
#Randy Scott	LB	6'1"	228	28		
Jesse Solomon	LB	6'	236	23	1	
Scott Studwell	LB	6'2"	230	33	2	
#Rufus Bess	DB	5'9"	189	31		
Joey Browner	DB	6'2"	210	27	6	
#David Evans	DB	6'	178	28		
#Jamie Fitzgerald	DB	6'	180	22		
Steve Freeman	DB	5'11"	185	34		
Neal Guggemos	DB	6'1"	190	23	1	
John Harris	DB	6'2"	197	31	3	
Wymon Henderson	DB	5'10"	186	25	4	
Issiac Holt	DB	6'2"	199	24	2	
Carl Lee	DB	6'	188	26	3	
#Fletcher Louallen	DB	6'	195	24	1	
#Terry Love	DB	6'2"	205	29		
#Ted Rosnagle	DB	6'3"	202	25		
Reggie Rutland	DB	6'1"	195	23		
#Mike Slaton	DB	6'2"	194	22		
Wayne Smith	DB	6'	170	30	1	
#Timothy Starks	DB	5'9"	175	23		
#John Turner	DB	6'	193	31		

Mark Mullaney - Neck Injury
Buster Rhymes - Ankle Injury

Use Name	Pos.	Hgt	Wgt	Age	Int	Pts
#Tony Adams	QB	6'	195	37		
#Keith Bishop	QB	6'4"	190	24		
Rich Gannon	QB	6'3"	197	21		
Tommy Kramer	QB	6'2"	202	32		12
#Todd Krueger	QB	6'4"	210	30		
#Larry Miller	QB	6'4"	220	25		
Wade Wilson	QB	6'3"	206	28		30
D.J.Dozier	HB	6'	198	21		42
#Phil Frye	HB	5'11"	180	26		
#Steve Harris	HB	5'11"	194	24		
Darrin Nelson	HB	5'9"	185	28		12
#Jimmy Smith	HB	5'11"	190	26		
#Andre Thomas	HB	6'	205	26		
#Jeff Womack	HB	5'9"	188	24		6
Alfred Anderson	FB	6'1"	217	26		12
Rick Fenney	FB	6'1"	240	22		12
#Sam Harrell	FB	6'2"	213	29		
#Leonard Moore	FB	6'	222	24		
Allen Rice	FB	5'10"	206	25		12
#Adam Walker	FB	5'11"	220	24		
#Brett Wilson	FB	6'	220	26		
#James Brim	WR	6'3"	187	24		18
#Larry Brown	WR	5'11"	180	23		
Anthony Carter	WR	5'11"	174	26		42
#Ron Daugherty	WR	6'3"	185	29		
#Steve Finch	WR	6'	200	26		
#Willie Gillespie	WR	5'9"	170	25		
Jim Gustafson	WR	6'1"	178	26		
Hassan Jones	WR	6'	198	23		12
#Keith Kidd	WR	6'1"	195	24		
#Terry LeCount	WR	5'10"	176	31		
Leo Lewis	WR	5'8"	167	30		18
#Rickey Parks	WR	6'1"	179	23		
Greg Richardson	WR	5'7"	172	22		
#Clifton Eley	TE	6'5"	230	26		
Carl Hilton	TE	6'3"	236	23		12
Steve Jordan	TE	6'4"	235	26		12
#Marc May	TE	6'4"	230	29		
Mike Mularkey	TE	6'4"	236	25		
#Ed Schenk	TE	6'4"	230	26		
#Dave Bruno	K	6'1"	235	24		
Greg Coleman	K	6'	185	32		
#Dale Dawson	K	6'	213	22		7
Chuck Nelson	K	6'	175	27		75
Bucky Scribner	K	6'	205	27		

GREEN BAY PACKERS 5-9-1 Forrest Gregg

Scores of Each Game		
0	L.A.RAIDERS	20
17	DENVER	*17
23	Minnesota	16
16	DETROIT	19
16	PHILADELPHIA	10
34	Detroit	33
17	TAMPA BAY	23
24	CHICAGO	26
13	Seattle	24
23	Kansas City	3
10	Chicago	23
12	SAN FRANCISCO	23
16	MINNESOTA	10
10	N.Y.Giants	20
24	New Orleans	33

* Overtime

Use Name	Pos.	Hgt	Wgt	Age	Int	Pts
Steve Collier	OT	6'7"	342	27		
#Bob Gruber	OT	6'5"	280	29		
#Greg Jensen	OT	6'3"	266	25		
#Ed Konopasek	OT	6'6"	289	23		
#Jim Meyer	OT	6'5"	290	24		
Tom Neville	OT-OG	6'5"	306	25		
Tommy Robison	OT	6'4"	290	25		
Ken Ruettgers	OT	6'5"	280	25		
Keith Uecker	OT-OG	6'5"	284	27		
Alan Veingrad	OT-OG	6'5"	277	24		
#Mike Estep	OG	6'4"	265	23		
Ron Hallstrom	OG	6'6"	290	28		
#Perry Hartnett	OG	6'5"	285	27		
#Jim Hobbins	OG	6'6"	275	23		
#John McGarry	OG	6'5"	288	23		
Rich Moran	OG	6'3"	275	25		
#Travis Simpson	OG	6'3"	272	23		
Mark Cannon	C	6'3"	258	25		
Bill Cherry	C-OG	6'4"	277	26		
#Vince Rafferty	C-OG	6'4"	285	26		
#Warren Bone	DE	6'4"	260	22		
Robert Brown	DE	6'2"	267	27		
Alphonso Carreker	DE	6'6"	271	25	1	
Ezra Johnson	DE	6'4"	265	31		
#Tony Leiker	DE	6'5"	250	22		
#Sylvester McGrew	DE	6'4"	257	27		
#Carl Sullivan	DE	6'4"	248	25		
#Calvin Wallace	DE	6'3"	230	22		
Jerry Boyarsky	NT	6'3"	290	28		
Ross Browner	NT-DE	6'3"	265	33		
#David Caldwell	NT	6'1"	261	22		
#Jeff Drost	NT	6'5"	286	23		
David Logan	NT	6'2"	250	30		
#Stan Mataele	NT	6'2"	278	24		
#Vince Villanucci	NT	6'2"	265	23		

Use Name	Pos.	Hgt	Wgt	Age	Int	Pts
#Aric Anderson	LB	6'2"	220	22		
John Anderson	LB	6'3"	229	31	2	
#Todd Auer	LB	6'1"	230	22		
#Putt Choate	LB	6'	225	30		
Burnell Dent	LB	6'1"	236	24		
John Dorsey	LB	6'3"	243	27		
Tim Harris	LB	6'5"	236	22		
Johnny Holland	LB	6'2"	221	22	2	
#Kenneth Jordan	LB	6'2"	235	23		
#Rydell Malancon	LB	6'2"	230	25		
#James Melka	LB	6'1"	235	25	1	
#John Miller	LB	6'2"	218	26		
#Ron Monaco	LB	6'2"	240	24		
Brent Moore	LB	6'5"	242	24		
Brian Noble	LB	6'3"	252	24	1	
#John Pointer	LB	6'2"	225	29		
Scott Stephen	LB	6'2"	232	23		
Mike Weddington	LB	6'4"	245	26		
Clayton Weishuhn	LB	6'2"	218	27		
Dave Brown	DB	6'1"	197	34	3	
#Chuck Compton	DB	5'10"	190	22		
#Tony Elliott	DB	5'10"	195	23		
Tiger Greene	DB	6'	194	25	1	
#Anthony Harrison	DB	6'1"	195	21	1	
Norman Johnson	DB	5'10"	183	23		
Kenneth Johnson	DB	6'	185	23	1	
#David King	DB	5'9"	175	24		
#Don King	DB	6'	200	23		
Mark Lee	DB	5'11"	189	29	1	
Chris Mandeville	DB	6'1"	213	22		
#Von Mansfield	DB	5'11"	183	27	1	
Jim Bob Morris	DB	6'3"	211	26	3	
Mark Murphy	DB	6'2"	201	29		
#Lou Rash	DB	5'9"	190	27		
Ken Stills	DB	5'10"	187	23		
#Chuck Washington	DB	5'11"	186	23		

Mossy Cade - Prison
David Greenwood - Groin Injury
Bobby Leopold - Back Injury
Elbert Watts - Knee Injury
Ben Thomas - Knee Injury
Eddie Lee Ivery - Back Injury

Use Name	Pos.	Hgt	Wgt	Age	Int	Pts
#Willie Gillus	QB	6'4"	215	24		
Don Majkowski	QB	6'2"	197	23		
#John McCarthy	QB	6'4"	212	26		
Alan Risher	QB	6'2"	190	26		6
Randy Wright	QB	6'2"	203	26		
Kenneth Davis	HB	5'10"	209	25		18
Brent Fullwood	HB	5'11"	209	23		30
#Larry Morris	HB	5'7"	207	25		
#John Sterling	HB	6'2"	203	22		
#Lavale Thomas	HB	6'	205	23		6
#Kevin Willhite	HB	5'11"	206	24		
Paul Ott Carruth	FB	6'1"	220	26		24
Jessie Clark	FB	6'	228	27		6
Kelly Cook	FB	5'11"	225	25		
#Jim Hargrove	FB	6'2"	232	28		6
#Tony Hunter	FB	5'9"	215	24		
#Freddie Parker	FB	5'10"	215	25		
#Lee Weigel	FB	5'11"	220	23		
Phillip Epps	WR	5'10"	165	27		12
#Derrick Harden	WR	6'1"	175	23		
Lee Morris	WR	5'11"	180	23		6
Frankie Neal	WR	6'1"	202	21		18
Keith Paskett	WR	5'11"	180	22		6
#Cornelius Redick	WR	6'	185	23		
Patrick Scott	WR	5'10"	170	22		
#Wes Smith	WR	6'	190	24		
Walter Stanley	WR	5'9"	179	24		18
#Kevin Fitzgerald	TE	6'3"	235	23		
Joey Hackett	TE	6'5"	267	28		
#Craig Jay	TE	6'4"	257	24		
#Don Summers	TE	6'4"	235	26		6
Ed West	TE	6'1"	243	26		6
Don Bracken	K	6'	211	25		
Al Del Greco (to STL)	K	5'10"	191	25		46
#Bill Renner	K	6'	198	28		
Max Zendejas	K	5'11"	184	23		61

- on the active roster for strike replacement games only

MINNESOTA VIKINGS

RUSHING

Last Name	No.	Yds	Avg	TD
D. Nelson	131	642	4.9	2
Anderson	68	319	4.7	2
W. Wilson	41	263	6.4	5
Dozier	69	257	3.7	5
Fenney	42	174	4.1	2
Rice	51	131	2.6	1
Kramer	10	44	4.4	2
Brim	2	36	18.0	1
Adams	11	31	2.8	0
A. Walker	5	24	4.8	0
Womack	9	20	2.2	0
B. Wilson	5	16	3.3	0
J. Smith	7	13	1.9	0
Moore	4	11	2.8	0
Harrell	5	8	1.6	0
Frye	4	4	1.0	0
A. Thomas	6	4	0.7	0
S. Harris	4	3	0.8	0
Miller	1	-1	-1.0	0
Gustafson	1	-2	-2.0	0
Lewis	5	-7	-1.4	0
Scribner	1	-7	-7.0	0

RECEIVING

Last Name	No.	Yds	Avg	TD
Carter	38	922	24.3	7
Jordan	35	490	14.0	2
D. Nelson	26	129	5.0	0
Lewis	24	383	16.0	2
Rice	19	201	10.6	1
Brim	18	282	15.7	2
Dozier	12	89	7.4	2
H. Jones	7	189	27.0	2
Anderson	7	69	9.9	0
Fenney	7	27	3.9	0
Womack	5	46	9.2	1
Gustafson	4	55	13.8	0
Finch	3	54	18.0	0
Parks	3	46	15.3	0
Frye	3	25	8.3	0
Harrell	3	20	6.7	0
Gillespie	2	28	14.0	0
Daugherty	2	21	10.5	0
S. Harris	2	17	8.5	0
Hilton	2	16	8.0	0
B. Wilson	2	14	7.0	0
A. Thomas	2	13	6.5	0
A. Walker	2	3	1.5	0
May	1	22	22.0	0
Schenk	1	10	10.0	0
Moore	1	8	8.0	0
Mularkey	1	6	6.0	0

PUNT RETURNS

Last Name	No.	Yds	Avg	TD
Lewis	22	275	12.5	1
Bess	7	86	12.3	0
Richardson	4	19	4.8	0
Carter	3	40	13.3	0

KICKOFF RETURNS

Last Name	No.	Yds	Avg	TD
Guggemos	36	808	22.4	0
Bess	10	169	16.9	0
D. Nelson	7	164	23.4	0
Womack	5	77	15.4	0
Richardson	4	76	19.0	0
Smith	2	42	21.0	0
Rice	2	29	14.5	0
Dozier	2	23	11.5	0
Mularkey	1	16	16.0	0
Hilton	1	13	13.0	0
Harrell	1	4	4.0	0

PASSING — PUNTING — KICKING

PASSING	Att	Cmp	%	Yds	Yd/Att	TD	Int—	%	Rk
Wade Wilson	264	140	53.0	2106	8.0	14	13—	4.9	16
Adams	89	49	55.1	607	6.8	3	5—	5.6	
Kramer	81	40	49.4	452	5.6	4	3—	3.7	
Gannon	6	2	33.3	18	3.0	0	1—	16.7	
Miller	6	1	16.7	2	0.3	0	1—	16.7	

PUNTING	No	Avg
Coleman	46	38.8
Scribner	20	41.3
Bruno	13	35.7

KICKING	XP	Att	%	FG	Att	%
C. Nelson	36	37	97	13	24	54
Dawson	4	4	100	1	5	20

GREEN BAY PACKERS

RUSHING

Last Name	No.	Yds	Avg	TD
Davis	109	413	3.8	3
Fullwood	84	274	3.3	5
Willhite	53	251	4.7	0
Clark	56	211	3.8	0
Carruth	64	192	3.0	3
Majkowski	15	127	8.5	0
Wright	13	70	5.4	0
Risher	11	64	5.8	1
Stanley	4	38	9.5	0
Hargrove	11	38	3.5	1
Parker	8	33	4.1	0
Weigel	10	26	2.6	0
Sterling	5	20	4.0	0
Larry Morris	10	20	2.0	0
Thomas	5	19	3.8	0
Cook	2	3	1.5	0
Lee Morris	2	2	1.0	0
Scott	1	2	2.0	0
Epps	1	0	0.0	0
Hunter	1	0	0.0	0
Neal	1	0	0.0	0

RECEIVING

Last Name	No.	Yds	Avg	TD
Stanley	38	672	17.7	3
Neal	36	420	11.7	3
Epps	34	516	15.2	2
Clark	22	119	5.4	1
West	19	261	13.7	1
Lee Morris	16	259	16.2	1
Davis	14	110	7.9	0
Paskett	12	188	15.7	1
Carruth	10	78	7.8	1
Scott	8	79	9.9	0
Summers	7	83	11.9	1
Willhite	6	37	6.2	0
Parker	3	22	7.3	0
Thomas	2	52	26.0	1
Harden	2	29	14.5	0
Fullwood	2	11	5.5	0
Redick	1	18	18.0	0
Weigel	1	17	17.0	0
Hargrove	1	6	6.0	0

PUNT RETURNS

Last Name	No.	Yds	Avg	TD
Stanley	28	173	6.2	0
Scott	6	71	11.8	0
Lee Morris	1	1	1.0	0

KICKOFF RETURNS

Last Name	No.	Yds	Avg	TD
Fullwood	24	510	21.3	0
Cook	10	147	14.7	0
Lee Morris	6	104	17.3	0
Harden	4	72	18.0	0
Neal	4	44	11.0	0
Scott	2	32	16.0	0
Jefferson	2	30	15.0	0
Carruth	1	8	8.0	0
Weishuhn	1	1	1.0	0
Sterling	1	0	0.0	0
Willhite	0	37	0	0

PASSING — PUNTING — KICKING

PASSING	Att	Cmp	%	Yds	Yd/Att	TD	Int—	%	Rk
Wright	247	132	53.4	1507	6.1	6	11—	4.5	26
Majkowski	127	55	43.3	875	6.9	5	3—	2.4	
Risher	74	44	59.5	564	7.6	3	3—	4.1	
Gillus	5	2	40.0	28	5.6	0	0—	0.0	
Carruth	1	1	100	3	3.0	1	0—	0.0	
Neal	1	0	0.0	0	0.0	0	0—	0.0	

PUNTING	No	Avg
Bracken	73	40.4
Renner	20	35.6

KICKING	XP	Att.	%	FG	Att	%
Zendejas	13	15	87	16	19	84
Del Greco	19	20	95	9	15	60

TAMPA BAY BUCCANEERS 4-11 Ray Perkins

Scores of Each Game		
48	ATLANTA	10
3	Chicago	20
31	Detroit	27
13	SAN DIEGO	17
20	MINNESOTA	10
26	CHICAGO	27
23	Green Bay	17
28	St.Louis	31
17	Minnesota	23
10	SAN FRANCISCO	24
3	L.A.Rams	35
34	New Orleans	44
10	DETROIT	20
14	ST.LOUIS	31
6	Indianapolis	24

Use Name	Pos.	Hgt	Wgt	Age	Int	Pts
Mark Cooper (from DEN)	OT-OG	6'5"	270	27		
#Dave Heffernan	OT	6'4"	255	24		
Ron Heller	OT	6'6"	280	25		
#Hoss Johnson	OT	6'4"	295	24		
J.D. Maarleveld	OT	6'6"	300	25		
Marvin Powell	OT	6'5"	270	32		
#Donald Pumphrey	OT	6'4"	275	23		
#Reggie Smith	OT	6'5"	295	25		
Rob Taylor	OT	6'6"	290	26		
Rufus Brown	OG	6'2"	295	25		
Conrad Goode	OG-OT	6'6"	285	25		
#Jim Huddleston	OG-OT	6'4"	280	24		
#John Hunt	OG	6'5"	245	24		
David Jordan	OG	6'6"	270	25		
Rick Mallory	OG	6'2"	265	26		
#Paul O'Connor	OG	6'3"	270	24		
George Yarno	OG	6'2"	265	30		
Randy Grimes	C	6'4"	270	27		
#Charles Pitcock	C	6'4"	272	29		
Dan Turk	C-OG	6'4"	260	25		
John Cannon	DE	6'5"	260	27		
#Walter Carter	DE	6'4"	276	29		
#Mike Clark	DE	6'4"	268	28		
#Roy Harris	DE	6'2"	260	26		
Ron Holmes	DE	6'4"	255	24		
Curt Jarvis	DE-DT	6'2"	266	22		
Kevin Kellin	DE	6'6"	265	27		
Tyrone Keys	DE	6'7"	270	27		
Tom McHale	DE	6'4"	275	24		
#Jim Ramey	DE	6'4"	275	30		
#Charles Riggins	DE	6'5"	295	25		
Harry Swayne	DE	6'5"	268	22		
#Calvin Turner	DE	6'4"	270	27		
#Fred Nordgren	NT	6'	240	27		
Dan Sileo	NT	6'2"	282	23		
Mike Stensrud	NT	6'5"	280	31		
Scot Brantley	LB	6'1"	230	29		
Jeff Davis	LB	6'	230	27		
Brian Gant	LB	6'	235	21	1	
Don Graham	LB	6'2"	244	23		
#Cam Jacobs	LB	6'2"	230	25		
#Fred McCallister	LB	6'1'	250	25		
#Sankar Montoute	LB	6'3"	230	26	1	
Winston Moss	LB	6'3"	235	21		6
Kevin Murphy	LB	6'2"	230	22		
#Leon Pennington	LB	6'1"	225	23		
Ervin Randle	LB	6'1"	250	24		
#Pat Teague	LB	6'1"	228	23		
#Miles Turpin	LB	6'4"	232	23		
Jackie Walker	LB	6'5"	245	24		
Chris Washington	LB	6'4"	230	25		
Don Anderson	DB	5'10"	195	24		
#Torin Clark	DB	6'1"	175	23		
#Ivory Curry	DB	5'11"	185	26		
Bobby Futrell	DB	5'11"	190	25	2	
#Jeff George	DB	6'1"	185	28		
Sonny Gordon	DB	5'11"	192	22		
Ray Isom	DB	5'9"	190	21	2	
Rod Jones	DB	6'	175	23	2	
Bobby Kemp	DB	6'	190	28	1	
#Tim King	DB	6'2"	190	27		
Vito McKeever	DB	6'	180	25		
#Lee Paige	DB	6'	197	26		
Ricky Reynolds	DB	5'11"	182	22		
Paul Tripoli	DB	6'	197	25	3	6
#Kevin Walker	DB	5'11"	180	23	2	6
Rick Woods	DB	6'	195	27	2	
Steve DeBerg	QB	6'2"	210	33		
#Mike Hold	QB	6'	190	24		
#John Reaves	QB	6'3"	210	37		
Vinny Testaverde	QB	6'5"	220	23		6
#Jim Zorn	QB	6'2"	200	34		
Steve Bartalo	HB	5'9"	200	23		6
#Greg Boone	HB	5'9"	196	25		
#Charles Gladman	HB	5'11"	205	21		
Bobby Howard	HB	6'	210	23		6
#Dan Land	HB	6'	190	22		
#Harold Ricks	HB	5'10"	200	24		6
Cliff Austin	FB	6'	213	27		6
Jeff Smith	FB	5'9"	204	25		24
#Derrick Thomas	FB	6'	232	22		
James Wilder	FB	6'3"	225	29		6
#Adrian Wright	FB	6'1"	230	25		6
Mark Carrier	WR	6'	182	21		18
Gerald Carter	WR	6'1"	190	30		30
#Steve Carter	WR	5'10"	170	24		
#Dwayne Dixon	WR	6'1"	203	25		
Phil Freeman	WR	5'11"	185	24		12
Bruce Hill	WR	6'	175	23		12
Derek Holloway	WR	5'7"	188	26		
#David Jackson	WR	5'8"	175	22		
Solomon Miller	WR	6'1"	185	22		
#Stanley Shakespeare	WR	5'11"	190	25		
#Eric Streater	WR	5'11"	165	23		12
Gene Taylor	WR	6'2"	189	24		
Herkie Walls	WR	5'8"	160	26		
Ron Hall	TE	6'4"	238	23		6
Steve Holloway	TE	6'3"	235	23		
Calvin Magee	TE	6'3"	240	24		18
#Jeff Modesitt	TE	6'5"	245	23		
#Arthur Wells	TE	6'4"	235	24		6
#Ray Criswell	K	6'	189	24		
Frank Garcia	K	6'	210	30		
Donald Igwebuike	K	5'9"	185	26		66
#Van Tiffin (to MIA)	K	5'9"	155	21		22

Ricky Easmon - Knee Injury
Quentin Walker - Achilles Tendon Injury
Nathan Wonsley - Neck Injury

DETROIT LIONS 4-11 Darryl Rogers

Scores of Each Game		
19	Minnesota	34
7	L.A.Raiders	27
27	TAMPA BAY	31
19	Green Bay	*16
14	SEATTLE	37
33	GREEN BAY	34
0	Denver	34
27	DALLAS	17
13	Washington	20
10	Chicago	30
20	KANSAS CITY	27
16	L.A.RAMS	37
20	Tampa Bay	10
14	MINNESOTA	17
30	Atlanta	13

Use Name	Pos.	Hgt	Wgt	Age	Int	Pts
Lomas Brown	OT	6'4"	282	24		
#Rick Johnson	OT	6'6"	255	23		
#Jerry Quaerna	OT	6'6"	275	23		
Harvey Salem	OT-OG	6'6"	285	26		
Eric Sanders	OT-OG	6'7"	280	28		
Rich Strenger	OT	6'7"	285	27		
#Jim Warne	OT	6'7"	315	22		
Steve Baack	OG	6'4"	265	26		
Scott Barrows	OG-C	6'2"	278	24		
Keith Dorney	OG	6'5"	285	29		
#Joe Felton	OG	6'2"	266	22		
#Chris Geile	OG	6'4"	305	23		
Kevin Glover	OG-C	6'2"	267	24		
#Paul Kiser	OG	6'4"	270	23		
Joe Milinichik	OG-OT	6'5"	275	24		
#Greg Orton	OG	6'1"	265	25		
#Patrick Cain	C-OG	6'2"	260	24		
Steve Mott	C	6'3"	270	26		
#Chuck Steele	C	6'1"	255	23		
#Bob Beemer	DE	6'5"	231	24		
#Charles Benson	DE	6'3"	267	26	1	
Keith Ferguson	DE	6'5"	260	28		
William Gay	DE	6'5"	260	32		
Curtis Green	DE-NT	6'3"	265	30		
#George McDuffie	DE	6'6"	270	24		
Reggie Rogers	DE	6'6"	272	23		
Eric M.Williams	DE-NT	6'4"	280	25		
Jerry Ball	NT	6'1"	283	22		
#Jerome Davis	NT	6'1"	260	25		
#Jeff Kacmarek	NT	6'2"	240	24		
Dan Saleaumua	NT	6'	285	21		
#Stuart Tolle	NT	6'3"	245	25		
#Ernie Adams	LB	6'2"	226	28		
#Steve Boadway	LB	6'4"	240	24		
#Thomas Boyd	LB	6'3"	210	27		
Paul Butcher	LB	6'	219	23		
#Carl Carr	LB	6'3"	230	23		
Mike Cofer	LB	6'5"	245	27		
Dennis Gibson	LB	6'2"	240	23	1	
#Mark Hicks	LB	6'2"	245	26		
George Jamison	LB	6'1"	226	24		2
#Angelo King	LB	6'1"	222	29		6
Danny Lockett	LB	6'2"	228	23		
Vernon Maxwell	LB	6'2"	235	25		
#Anthony Office	LB	6'2"	250	27		
Shelton Robinson	LB	6'2"	236	26		
#Tom Ross	LB	6'5"	225	28		
#Robert Thompson	LB	6'3"	225	27		
Jimmy Williams	LB	6'3"	230	26	2	
John Bostic	DB	5'10"	178	24		
Raphel Cherry	DB	6'	194	25	1	
#Dexter Clark	DB	6'	190	23		
#Creig Federico	DB	6'2"	205	24		
#Anthony Fields	DB	6'1"	192	23		
Duane Galloway	DB	5'8"	181	25	3	
William Graham	DB	5'11"	191	27		
James Griffin	DB	6'2"	197	25	6	
#Alvin Hall	DB	5'10"	184	29	1	
#Maurice Harvey	DB	5'10"	190	31		
#Ivan Hicks	DB	6'2"	185	24		
#Steve Hirsch	DB	6'	195	25		
#Bob McDonough	DB	6'1"	170	24		
Bruce McNorton	DB	5'11"	175	28	3	
Chris Sheffield (from PIT)	DB	6'1"	200	24	1	
Ivory Sully	DB	6'	201	30		
Bobby Watkins	DB	5'10"	184	27		
Eric T. Williams	DB	6'1'	190	27		
Joe Ferguson	QB	6'1"	195	37		
#Brendon Folmer	QB	6'1"	200	23		
#Todd Hons	QB	6'1"	195	25		
Chuck Long	QB	6'4"	211	24		
Karl Bernard	HB	5'11"	205	22		12
Garry James	HB	5'10"	214	23		24
#Cleve Wester	HB	5'8"	188	23		
Butch Woolfolk	HB	6'1"	212	27		
#Tony Dollinger	FB	5'11"	205	24		
#Stan Edwards	FB	6'	214	28		
Gary Ellerson	FB	5'11"	220	24		24
James Jones	FB	6'2"	229	26		
#Nick Kowgios	FB	6'	216	24		
Tony Paige	FB	5'10"	230	24		
Scott Williams	FB	6'2"	234	25		6
Carl Bland	WR	5'11"	182	26		6
#Danny Bradley	WR	5'9"	175	24		12
Jeff Chadwick	WR	6'3"	190	26		
#Darrell Grymes	WR	6'2"	182	24		12
#Melvin Hoover	WR	6'	185	27		
#Gilvanni Johnson	WR	6'1"	195	23		
Gary Lee	WR	6'1"	202	22		
Pete Mandley	WR	5'10"	191	26		42
Mark Nichols	WR	6'2"	208	27		
Ricky Smith	WR-DB	6'	188	27	1	6
#Eric Truvillion	WR	6'4"	205	28		6
#Jerry Diorio	TE	6'3"	245	25		
Vyto Kab	TE	6'5"	240	27		
Mark Lewis (from GB)	TE	6'2"	250	26		
Derrick Ramsey	TE	6'5"	235	30		
Rob Rubick	TE	6'3"	234	26		6
#Mark Wheeler	TE	6'2"	232	23		
#Mark Witte	TE	6'3"	240	27		
Jim Arnold	K	6'3"	211	26		
#Mike Black	K	6'2"	197	26		
Russell Erxleben	K	6'4"	238	30		
#Matt Kinzer	K	6'3"	225	24		
#John Misko	K	6'5"	207	32		
Eddie Murray	K	5'10"	175	31		81
#Mike Prindle	K	5'9"	160	23		24

Donnie Elder - Hamstring Injury
Devon Mitchell - Knee Injury
Bob Cryder - Knee Injury
Leon Evans - Knee Injury
Dave D'Addio - Knee Injury
Eric Hipple - Thumb Injury

Western Division

SAN FRANCISCO 49ERS 13-2 Bill Walsh

Scores of Each Game		
17	Pittsburgh	30
27	Cincinnati	26
41	N.Y.Giants	21
25	Atlanta	17
34	ST.LOUIS	28
24	New Orleans	22
31	L.A.Rams	10
27	HOUSTON	20
24	NEW ORLEANS	26
24	Tampa Bay	10
38	CLEVELAND	24
23	Green Bay	12
41	CHICAGO	0
35	ATLANTA	7
48	L.A.RAMS	0

Use Name	Pos.	Hgt	Wgt	Age	Int	Pts
Harris Barton	OT	6'3"	280	23		
#Mark Cochran	OT	6'5"	284	24		
Bruce Collie	OT-OG	6'6"	275	25		
Keith Fahnhorst	OT	6'6"	273	35		
#Gary Hoffman	OT	6'7"	285	25		
Bubba Paris	OT	6'6"	299	26		
Steve Wallace	OT	6'5"	276	22		
Jeff Bregel	OG	6'4"	280	23		
#Michael Durrette	OG	6'4"	280	30		
#Tracy Franz	OG	6'5"	270	27		
Guy McIntyre	OG	6'3"	264	26		
#Limbo Parks	OG	6'3"	265	22		
#Kevin Reach	OG-C	6'3"	270	23		
Jesse Sapolu	OG-C	6'4"	260	26		
Randy Cross	C-OG	6'3"	265	33		
#Tim Long	C	6'6"	295	24		
Fred Quillan	C	6'5"	266	31		
Chuck Thomas	C-OG	6'3"	280	26		
Dwaine Board	DE	6'5"	248	30		
#Glen Collins	DE	6'6"	270	28		
Kevin Fagan	DE	6'4"	260	24		
Clyde Glover	DE	6'6"	280	27		
Pete Kugler	DE-NT	6'4"	255	28		
#Greg Liter	DE	6'6"	275	23		
#Elston Ridgle	DE	6'6"	260	24		
Larry Roberts	DE	6'3"	264	24		
Jeff Stover	DE	6'5"	275	29		
Michael Carter	NT	6'2"	285	26		
#Joe Drake	NT	6'2"	290	24		
Doug Mikolas	NT	6'1"	270	25		
#Reno Patterson	NT	6'3"	275	26		
Darren Comeaux	LB	6'1"	227	27		
George Cooper	LB	6'2"	225	28		
Tom Cousineau	LB	6'3"	225	30	1	
Kevin Dean	LB	6'1"	235	22		
Riki Ellison	LB	6'2"	225	27		
Jim Fahnhorst	LB	6'4"	230	28	1	
#Ron Hadley	LB	6'2"	240	23		
Charles Haley	LB-DE	6'5"	230	23		
#James Johnson (to SD)	LB	6'2"	235	25		
#Jerry Keebie	LB	6'3"	230	24		
#Carl Keever	LB	6'2"	236	26		
#Mark Korff	LB	6'1"	230	24		
Milt McColl	LB	6'6"	230	28	1	
Todd Shell	LB	6'4"	225	25	1	
Keena Turner	LB	6'2"	222	28	1	
Michael Walter	LB	6'3"	238	26	1	
#John Butler	DB	6'1"	200	22		
#Matt Courtney	DB	5'11"	194	25	1	
#John Faylor	DB	6'1"	197	24		
Jeff Fuller	DB-LB	6'2"	216	25		8
Don Griffin	DB	6'	176	23	5	
Tom Holmoe	DB	6'2"	195	27	1	
Ronnie Lott	DB	6'	200	28	5	
#Derrick Martin	DB	6'	185	30	1	
Tim McKyer	DB	6'	174	23	2	
Dana McLemore	DB	5'10"	183	27	2	1
Tory Nixon	DB	5'11"	186	25	1	
#Darryl Pollard	DB	5'11"	187	23		
#Jonathan Shelley	DB	6'	176	23		
#John Sullivan	DB	6'1"	190	25		
Carlton Williamson	DB	6'	204	29	1	
Eric Wright	DB	6'1"	185	28		
#Ed Blount	QB	6'	195	23		
Bob Gagliano	QB	6'3"	195	28		
Joe Montana	QB	6'2"	195	31		6
#Mark Stevens	QB	6'1"	190	25		6
Steve Young	QB	6'2"	200	25		6
#Ray Brown	HB	5'9"	185	22		
#Tony Cherry	HB	5'7"	187	24		6
Joe Cribbs	HB	5'11"	193	29		12
Doug DuBose	HB	5'11"	190	23		
Terrence Flagler	HB	6'	200	22		
Del Rodgers	HB	5'10"	203	27		6
Roger Craig	FB-HB	6'	224	27		24
#Andre Hardy	FB	6'1"	230	25		
Tom Rathman	FB	6'1"	232	24		24
Harry Sydney	FB	6'	217	28		
#Mike Varajon	FB	6'1"	232	23		
Dwight Clark	WR	6'4"	215	30		30
#Tony Gladney	WR	6'3"	200	23		
#Terry Greer	WR	6'1"	192	29		6
#Thomas Henley	WR	5'11"	185	22		
Ken Margerum	WR	6'	180	28		
#Carl Monroe	WR	5'8"	180	27		6
Jerry Rice	WR	6'2"	200	24		138
John Taylor	WR	6'1"	185	25		6
Mike Wilson	WR	6'3"	215	28		30
#Chris Dressel	TE	6'4"	240	26		
Russ Francis (to NE)	TE	6'6"	242	34		
John Frank	TE	6'3"	225	25		18
Ron Heller	TE	6'3"	235	23		18
Brent Jones	TE	6'4"	230	24		
#Mike Wells	TE	6'3"	233	25		6
#Jim Asmus	K	6'2"	195	24		
#Jeff Brockhaus	K	6'2"	212	28		20
Max Runager	K	6'1"	189	31		
Ray Wersching	K	5'11"	215	37		83

Sean Thomas - Ankle Injury
Derrick Crawford - Foot Injury

* Overtime

- on the active roster for strike replacement games only

TAMPA BAY BUCCANEERS

RUSHING

Last Name	No.	Yds	Avg	TD
Wilder	106	488	4.6	0
Smith	100	309	3.1	2
Wright	37	112	3.0	0
Howard	30	100	3.3	1
Ricks	24	76	3.2	1
Hold	7	69	9.9	0
Testaverde	13	50	3.8	1
Austin	19	32	1.7	1
Bartalo	9	30	3.3	1
Gladman	12	29	2.4	0
Land	9	20	2.2	0
Streater	1	5	5.0	0
Zord	4	4	1.0	0
Hill	3	3	3.0	0
Boone	1	2	2.0	0
Thomas	1	2	2.0	0
Freeman	1	1	1.0	0
Criswell	1	0	0.0	0
DeBerg	8	-8	-1.0	0

RECEIVING

Last Name	No.	Yds	Avg	TD
Carter	38	586	15.4	5
Magee	34	424	12.5	3
Carrier	26	423	16.3	3
Hill	23	403	17.5	2
Wilder	40	328	8.2	1
Smith	20	197	9.9	2
Hall	16	169	10.6	1
Freeman	8	141	17.6	2
Holloway	10	127	12.7	0
Howard	10	123	12.3	0
Wright	13	98	7.5	1
Streater	5	117	23.4	2
Miller	5	97	19.4	0
Austin	5	51	10.2	0
Taylor	2	21	10.5	0
Gladman	2	8	4.0	0
Dixon	1	18	18.0	0
Walls	1	13	13.0	0
Carter	1	12	12.0	0
Ricks	1	12	12.0	0
Bartalo	1	5	5.0	0

PUNT RETURNS

Last Name	No.	Yds	Avg	TD
Futrell	24	213	8.9	0
Walls	4	12	3.0	0
Curry	3	32	10.7	0

KICKOFF RETURNS

Last Name	No.	Yds	Avg	TD
Futrell	31	609	19.6	0
Walls	6	136	22.7	0
Smith	5	84	16.8	0
Miller	3	68	22.7	0
Curry	3	53	17.7	0
Ricks	1	26	26.0	0
Wright	1	17	17.0	0
Gladman	1	16	16.0	0
Bartalo	1	15	15.0	0
Hill	1	8	8.0	0
Howard	1	5	5.0	0
Carrier	1	0	0.0	0
Walker	1	0	0.0	0

PASSING — PUNTING — KICKING

PASSING	Att	Cmp	%	Yds	Yd/Att	TD	Int—	%	Rk
DeBerg	275	159	57.8	1891	6.9	14	7—	2.5	9
Testaverde	165	71	43.0	1081	6.6	5	6—	3.6	
Zorn	36	20	55.6	199	5.5	0	2—	4.3	
Hold	24	8	33.3	123	5.1	2	1—	4.2	
Reaves	16	6	37.5	83	5.2	1	0—	0.0	
Bartalo	1	0	0.0	0	0.0	0	1—	100	

PUNTING	No	Avg
Garcia	62	38.9
Criswell	26	40.2

KICKING	XP	Att	%	FG	Att	%
Igwebuike	24	26	92	14	18	78
Tiffin	11	11	100	5	7	71

DETROIT LIONS

RUSHING

Last Name	No.	Yds	Avg	TD
Jones	96	342	3.6	0
James	82	270	3.3	4
Ellerson	47	196	4.2	3
Bernard	45	187	4.2	2
Wester	33	113	3.4	0
Woolfolk	12	82	6.8	0
Edwards	32	69	2.2	0
Long	22	64	2.9	0
Hons	5	49	9.8	0
Williams	8	29	3.6	0
Dollinger	8	22	2.8	0
Paige	4	13	3.3	0
Mandley	1	3	3.0	0
Kowgios	1	2	2.0	0
Black	1	0	0.0	0
Chadwick	1	-6	-6.0	0

RECEIVING

Last Name	No.	Yds	Avg	TD
Mandley	58	720	12.4	7
Jones	34	262	7.7	0
Chadwick	30	416	13.9	0
Lee	19	308	16.2	0
Woolfolk	19	166	8.7	0
James	16	215	13.4	0
Rubick	13	147	11.3	1
Bernard	13	91	7.0	0
Truvillion	10	184	18.4	1
Grymes	9	140	15.6	2
Nichols	7	87	12.4	0
Edwards	7	82	11.7	0
Ellerson	7	71	10.1	1
Bradley	7	50	7.1	2
Kab	5	54	10.8	0
Dollinger	3	25	8.3	0
Witte	1	19	19.0	0
Wheeler	2	17	8.5	0
Williams	4	16	4.0	1
Bland	2	14	7.0	1
Paige	2	1	0.5	0
Kowgios	1	3	3.0	0

PUNT RETURNS

Last Name	No.	Yds	Avg	TD
Mandley	23	250	10.9	0
Bradley	12	53	4.4	0

KICKOFF RETURNS

Last Name	No.	Yds	Avg	TD
Lee	32	719	22.5	0
Woolfolk	11	219	19.9	0
Bradley	9	188	20.9	0
Hall	6	105	17.5	0
Bernard	4	54	13.5	0
Saleaumua	3	57	19.0	0
Bland	2	44	22.0	0
Ball	2	23	11.5	0
Glover	1	19	19.0	0

PASSING — PUNTING — KICKING

PASSING	Att	Cmp	%	Yds	Yd/Att	TD	Int—	%	Rk
Long	416	232	55.8	2598	6.3	11	20—	4.8	25
Hons	92	43	46.7	552	6.0	5	5—	5.4	
Jones	1	0	0.0	0	0.0	0	1—	100	

PUNTING	No	Avg
Arnold	46	43.6
Kinzer	7	34.0
Black	6	38.8
Misko	6	40.3
Murray	4	38.8
Erxleben	1	52.0

KICKING	XP	Att	%	FG	Att	%
Murray	21	21	100	20	32	63
Prindle	6	6	100	6	7	86

SAN FRANCISCO 49ers

RUSHING

Last Name	No.	Yds	Avg	TD
Craig	215	815	3.8	3
Cribbs	70	300	4.3	1
Rathman	62	257	4.1	1
Young	26	190	7.3	1
Montana	35	141	4.0	1
Sydney	29	125	4.3	0
Varajon	18	82	4.6	0
Cherry	13	65	5.0	1
Rice	8	51	6.4	1
Hardy	7	48	6.9	0
Rodgers	11	46	4.2	1
Stevens	10	45	4.5	1
DuBose	10	33	3.3	0
Monroe	2	26	13.0	0
Flagler	6	11	1.8	0
Frank	1	2	2.0	0
Blount	1	0	0.0	0

RECEIVING

Last Name	No.	Yds	Avg	TD
Craig	66	492	7.5	1
Rice	65	1078	16.6	22
Rathman	30	329	11.0	3
Wilson	29	450	15.5	5
Frank	26	296	11.4	3
Clark	24	290	12.1	5
Francis	22	202	9.2	0
Heller	12	165	13.8	3
Taylor	9	151	16.8	0
Cribbs	9	70	7.8	0
Greer	6	111	18.5	1
Gladney	4	60	15.0	0
DuBose	4	37	9.3	0
Monroe	3	66	22.0	1
Varajon	3	25	8.3	0
Rodgers	2	45	22.5	0
Jones	2	35	17.5	0
Flagler	2	28	14.0	0
Dressel	1	8	8.0	0
Hardy	1	7	7.0	0
Margerum	1	7	7.0	0
Sydney	1	3	3.0	0

PUNT RETURNS

Last Name	No.	Yds	Avg	TD
McLemore	21	265	12.6	1
Griffin	9	79	8.8	0
Martin	2	12	6.0	0
Taylor	1	9	9.0	0
Pollard	1	0	0.0	0

KICKOFF RETURNS

Last Name	No.	Yds	Avg	TD
Rodgers	17	358	21.1	0
Cribbs	13	327	25.2	1
Sydney	12	243	20.3	0
Monroe	5	91	18.2	0
Flagler	3	31	10.3	0
Rathman	2	37	18.5	0
McLemore	1	23	23.0	0
Henley	1	21	21.0	0
Varajon	1	13	13.0	0

PASSING — PUNTING — KICKING

PASSING	Att	Cmp	%	Yds	Yd/Att	TD	Int—	%	RK
Montana	398	266	66.8	3054	7.7	31	13—	3.3	1
Young	69	37	53.6	570	8.3	10	0—	0.0	
Gagliano	29	16	55.2	229	7.9	1	1—	3.4	
Stevens	4	2	50.0	52	13.0	1	0—	0.0	
Sydney	1	1	100.0	50	50.0	1	0—	0.0	

PUNTING	No	Avg
Runager	56	38.5
Asmus	12	32.0

KICKING	XP	Att	%	FG	Att	%
Wersching	44	46	96	13	17	76
Brockhaus	11	13	85	3	6	50

NEW ORLEANS SAINTS 12-3 Jim Mora

Scores of Each Game			
28	CLEVELAND	21	
17	Philadelphia	27	
37	L.A.RAMS	10	
19	St.Louis	24	
19	Chicago	17	
22	SAN FRANCISCO	24	
38	Atlanta	0	
31	L.A.Rams	14	
26	San Francisco	24	
23	N.Y.GIANTS	14	
20	Pittsburgh	16	
44	TAMPA BAY	34	
24	HOUSTON	10	
41	Cincinnati	24	
33	GREEN BAY	24	

Use Name	Pos.	Hgt	Wgt	Age	Int	Pts
Stan Brock	OT	6'6"	292	29		
Bill Contz	OT	6'5"	270	26		
Jim Dombrowski	OT	6'5"	298	23		
Daren Gilbert	OT	6'6"	295	23		
#Walter Housman	OT-OG	6'5"	285	24		
Ken Kaplan	OT	6'4"	270	27		
James Campen	OG-C	6'3"	260	23		
Chuck Commiskey	OG	6'4"	290	29		
Brad Edelman	OG	6'6"	270	26		
#Bill Leach	OG-OT	6'5"	280	23		
#Greg Loberg	OG-OT	6'4"	264	25		
#Henry Thomas	OG	6'2"	275	23		
Steve Trapilo	OG	6'5"	281	22		
Joel Hilgenberg	C	6'3"	252	25		
#Phillip James	C-OG	6'2"	265	22		
Steve Korte	C	6'2"	260	27		
#Robert Brannon (from CLE)	DE	6'7"	245	26		
Bruce Clark	DE	6'3"	275	29		2
James Geathers	DE	6'7"	290	27		
Shawn Knight	DE	6'6"	288	23		
Patrick Swoopes	DE-NT	6'4"	280	23		
Frank Warren	DE	6'4"	290	27		
Jim Wilks	DE	6'5"	266	29		
#Kevin Young	DE	6'5"	265	22		
#Sheldon Andrus	NT	6'1"	270	24		
#Ted Elliott	NT	6'6"	275	22		
Tony Elliott	NT	6'2"	295	28		

Use Name	Pos.	Hgt	Wgt	Age	Int	Pts
#Joe DeForest	LB	6'1"	240	22		
#Keith Fourcade	LB	5'11"	225	25		
James Haynes	LB	6'2"	233	27		
Rickey Jackson	LB	6'2"	243	29	2	
Vaughan Johnson	LB	6'3"	235	25	1	
Joe Kohlbrand	LB	6'4"	242	24		
#Scott Leach	LB	6'2"	221	23	1	
#Ken Marchiol	LB	6'2"	248	22		
#Larry McCoy	LB	6'2"	240	26		
Sam Mills	LB	5'9"	225	28		
#Bill Roe	LB	6'3"	235	29		
Pat Swilling	LB	6'3"	242	22	1	
Alvin Toles	LB	6'1"	227	24		6
#Ron Weissenofer	LB	6'3"	235	23		
Michael Adams	DB	5'10"	195	23		
Gene Atkins	DB	6'1"	200	23	3	
Toi Cook	DB	5'11"	188	22		
Antonio Gibson	DB	6'3"	204	25	1	
Van Jakes	DB	6'	190	26	3	
Milton Mack	DB	5'11"	182	23	4	
Brett Maxie	DB	6'2"	194	25	3	2
Johnnie Poe	DB	6'1"	194	28	1	6
#John Sutton	DB	6'1"	195	30		
Reggie Sutton	DB	5'10"	180	22	5	6
#Derrick Taylor	DB	5'11"	186	23		
#Junior Thurman	DB	6'	180	22		
#Darrel Toussaint	DB	6'	175	28		
Dave Waymer	DB	6'1"	188	29	5	
#Scott Woerner	DB	6'	185	28		

Hokie Gajan - Knee Injury

Use Name	Pos.	Hgt	Wgt	Age	Int	Pts
John Fourcade	QB	6'1"	208	26		
Bobby Hebert	QB	6'4"	215	27		
#Kevin Ingram	QB	6'	178	25		
#Tim Riordan	QB	6'1"	185	27		
Dave Wilson	QB	6'3"	206	28		
#Dwight Beverly	HB	5'11"	205	25		12
Mel Gray	HB	5'9"	166	26		6
#Nate Johnson	HB	6'2"	224	23		
Rueben Mayes	HB	5'11"	200	24		30
#Vincent Alexander	FB	5'10"	205	23		6
Dalton Hilliard	FB	5'8"	204	23		48
#Garland Jean-Batiste	FB	6'	208	22		
Buford Jordan	FB	6'	223	25		12
#Jeff Rodenberger	FB	6'3"	235	27		
Barry Word	FB	6'2"	220	23		12
Robert Clark	WR	5'11"	175	22		
#Stacey Dawsey	WR	5'9"	154	21		
Herbert Harris	WR	6'1"	206	26		
#Vic Harrison	WR	5'9"	184	26		
Lonzell Hill	WR	6'	189	21		12
Mike Jones	WR	5'11"	183	27		18
Eric Martin	WR	6'1"	207	25		42
Mark Pattison	WR	6'2"	190	25		
#Curtland Thomas	WR	6'	183	25		
#Joe Thomas	WR	5'11"	175	25		
#Dwight Walker	WR	5'10"	190	28		
Cliff Benson (from WAS)	TE	6'4"	240	26		
Hoby Brenner	TE	6'4"	240	28		12
#Darren Gottschalk	TE	6'4"	225	22		
#Ken O'Neal	TE	6'3"	240	25		6
#Malcolm Scott	TE	6'5"	245	26		
John Tice	TE	6'5"	249	27		36
Mike Waters	TE	6'2"	230	25		6
Morten Andersen	K	6'2"	221	27		121
Tommy Barnhardt (to CHI)	K	6'3"	205	24		
#Mike Cofer	K	6'1"	197	27		8
Brian Hansen	K	6'3"	209	26		
#Florian Kempf	K	5'9"	170	31		13

LOS ANGELES RAMS 6-9 John Robinson

Scores of Each Game			
16	Houston	20	
16	MINNESOTA	21	
10	New Orleans	37	
31	PITTSBURGH	21	
20	Atlanta	24	
17	Cleveland	30	
10	SAN FRANCISCO	31	
14	NEW ORLEANS	31	
27	St.Louis	24	
30	Washington	26	
35	TAMPA BAY	3	
37	Detroit	16	
33	ATLANTA	0	
21	DALLAS	29	
0	San Francisco	48	

Use Name	Pos.	Hgt	Wgt	Age	Int	Pts
Robert Cox	OT	6'5"	258	23		
#Hank Goebel	OT	6'7"	270	22		
Irv Pankey	OT	6'4"	280	29		
#Greg Sinnott	OT	6'7"	280	23		
Jackie Slater	OT	6'4"	275	23		
#Kelly Thomas	OT	6'6"	265	26		
Dennis Harah	OG	6'5"	265	35		
Duval Love	OG-OT	6'3"	280	24		
#Christopher Matau	OG	6'3"	310	23		
#Joe Murray	OG	6'4"	265	26		
Tom Newberry	OG	6'2"	279	24		
#Tom Taylor	OG	6'3"	265	24		
#Tom Cox	C	6'5"	260	24		
Tony Slaton	C	6'3"	265	26		
Doug Smith	C	6'3"	260	30		
#Navy Tuiasosopo	C	6'2"	285	22		
Reggie Doss	DE	6'4"	263	30		
#Dennis Edwards	DE	6'4"	253	27		
Donald Evans	DE	6'2"	262	23		
Gary Jeter	DE	6'4"	260	32		
Shawn Miller	DE	6'4"	255	26		
#Dave Purling	DE	6'5"	240	25		
Doug Reed	DE	6'3"	250	27		
Fred Stokes	DE	6'3"	253	23		
#Marion Knight	NT	6'2"	265	23		
Greg Meisner	NT	6'3"	265	28		
#Chris Pacheco	NT	6'	250	23		
Alvin Wright	NT-DE	6'2"	265	26		

Use Name	Pos.	Hgt	Wgt	Age	Int	Pts
#David Aupiu	LB	6'2"	235	26		
#Kyle Borland	LB	6'3"	232	26		
Richard Brown	LB	6'3"	240	21		
#Dan Clark	LB	6'2"	233	24		
Jim Collins	LB	6'2"	230	29		
#Rick DiBernardo	LB	6'3"	234	23		
Carl Ekern	LB	6'3"	222	33	1	
Kevin Greene	LB	6'3"	238	25	1	6
#Neil Hope	LB	6'2"	235	24		
Mark Jerue	LB	6'3"	229	27		
#Jim Kalafat	LB	6'	235	22		
Larry Kelm	LB	6'4"	226	22		
Mike McDonald	LB	6'1"	235	29		
Mel Owens	LB	6'2"	224	28	1	
Norwood Vann	LB	6'1"	237	25		
#Cary Whittingham	LB	6'2"	230	23		
#Kyle Whittingham	LB	6'	232	27		
Mike Wilcher	LB	6'3"	235	27	1	6
Nolan Cromwell	DB	6'1"	200	32	2	
Jerry Gray	DB	6'	185	24	2	6
#Darryl Hall	DB	5'11"	185	27		
Clifford Hicks	DB	5'10"	188	23	1	
LeRoy Irvin	DB	5'11"	184	29	2	6
Kirby Jackson	DB	5'9"	177	22	1	6
#Holbert Johnson	DB	5'9"	180	27	1	
Johnnie Johnson	DB	6'1"	183	30	1	6
Vince Newsome	DB	6'1"	179	26		
#Reggie Richardson	DB	6'	180	24		
#Craig Rutledge	DB	6'	190	23		
Michael Stewart	DB	5'11"	195	22		2
Mickey Sutton	DB	5'8"	165	27	1	
Frank Wattelet (from N.O.)	DB	6'	190	28		
#Greg Williamson	DB	5'11"	185	23	1	
#Ed Zeman	DB	6'1"	195	23		

Jeff Walker - Knee Injury

Use Name	Pos.	Hgt	Wgt	Age	Int	Pts
Steve Dils	QB	6'1"	191	31		
Jim Everett	QB	6'5"	212	24		6
Hugh Millen	QB	6'5"	216	23		
#Bernard Quarles	QB	6'2"	215	27		
Greg Bell (from BUF)	HB	5'10"	210	25		6
Jon Francis	HB	5'11"	207	23		12
Buford McGee	HB	6'	206	27		6
Tim Tyrrell	HB	6'1"	201	26		
Charles White	HB	5'10"	190	29		66
#Alonzo Williams	HB	5'9"	190	24		
#Cullen Bryant	FB	6'1"	244	36		
Owen Gill	FB	6'1"	236	25		
Mike Guman	FB	6'2"	218	29		6
#Casey Tiumalu	FB	5'8"	206	26		
Ron Brown	WR	5'11"	181	26		18
Henry Ellard	WR	5'11"	175	26		18
#Bernard Henry	WR	6'	187	27		
Kevin House	WR	6'1"	185	29		6
#Samuel Johnson	WR	5'11"	180	22		
#Stacey Mobley	WR	5'8"	170	21		6
Michael Young	WR	6'1"	185	25		6
Jon Embree	TE	6'2"	230	21		
David Hill	TE	6'2"	235	33		
Damone Johnson	TE	6'4"	230	25		12
James McDonald	TE	6'5"	245	26		12
#Malcolm Moore	TE	6'3"	240	26		6
#Don Noble	TE	6'2"	253	21		
#Joe Rose	TE	6'3"	230	30		
Dale Hatcher	K	6'2"	200	24		
Mike Lansford	K	6'	190	29		87

ATLANTA FALCONS 3-12 Marion Campbell

Scores of Each Game			
10	Tampa Bay	48	
21	WASHINGTON	20	
12	PITTSBURGH	28	
17	SAN FRANCISCO	25	
24	L.A.RAMS	20	
33	Houston	37	
0	NEW ORLEANS	38	
3	Cleveland	38	
10	CINCINNATI	16	
13	Minnesota	24	
21	ST.LOUIS	34	
21	Dallas	10	
0	L.A.Rams	33	
7	San Francisco	35	
13	DETROIT	30	

* Overtime

Use Name	Pos.	Hgt	Wgt	Age	Int	Pts
#Randy Clark	OT	6'3"	270	30		
Mike Kenn	OT	6'7"	277	31		
#Doug Mackie	OT	6'4"	280	29		
Brett Miller	OT	6'7"	300	28		
Leonard Mitchell	OT	6'7"	295	28		
#Greg Quick	OT	6'4"	280	23		
#Don Robinson	OT	6'5"	280	21		
Jamie Dukes	OG	6'1"	278	23		
Bill Fralic	OG	6'5"	280	24		
#Lawrence Jackson	OG	6'1"	275	23		
Jeff Kiewel	OG	6'4"	277	26		
#Pat Saindon	OG	6'3"	273	26		
John Scully	OG	6'6"	270	29		
Doug Barnett	C	6'3"	260	27		
#James Hendley	C	6'3"	257	22		
Wayne Radloff	C-OG	6'5"	277	26		
#Eric Wiegand	C	6'2"	260	23		
#Dwight Bingham	DE	6'6"	265	26		
Greg Brown	DE-DT	6'5"	265	30		
Rick Bryan	DE-DT	6'4"	265	25		
Mike Gann	DE	6'5"	275	23		
Dennis Harrison	DE	6'8"	280	31		
#Buddy Moor	DE	6'5"	250	28		2
Mark Mraz	DE	6'4"	255	22		
Andrew Provence	DE-DT	6'3"	267	26		
#Mark Studaway	DE	6'3"	275	26		
#Leonard Wingate	DE	6'3"	265	25		
#Mitchell Young	DE	6'4"	260	26		
Tony Casillas	NT-DT	6'3"	280	23		
#Dwaine Morris	NT-DE	6'2"	260	24		
#Emanuel Weaver	NT	6'4"	263	27		

Use Name	Pos.	Hgt	Wgt	Age	Int	Pts
#Ken Bowen	LB	6'1"	220	24		
Aaron Brown	LB	6'2"	238	31		
Joe Costello	LB	6'3"	244	27		
Buddy Curry	LB	6'4"	228	29		
#Paul Gray	LB	6'2"	231	25		
Tim Green	LB	6'2"	245	23		
#James Hall	LB	6'1"	252	24		
Rich Kraynak	LB	6'1"	230	26		
Jim Laughlin	LB	6'	222	29		
#Art Price	LB	6'3"	227	25		
John Rade	LB	6'1"	240	27		
Michael Reid	LB	6'2"	226	23		
#Herb Spencer	LB	6'3"	230	27		
Jessie Tuggle	LB	5'11"	225	22		
Reggie Wilkes	LB	6'4"	242	31		
Joel Williams	LB	6'1"	227	30		
James Britt	DB	6'	185	26	1	
Bobby Butler	DB	5'11"	175	28	4	
Scott Case	DB	6'	178	25	1	
Wendell Cason	DB	5'11"	192	24		
Bret Clark	DB	6'3"	198	26		
David Croudip	DB	5'8"	183	28	2	
Tim Gordon	DB	6'	188	22	2	
#Charles Huff	DB	5'11"	195	24	2	
#Lydell Jones	DB	5'9"	175	25		
#Leander Knight	DB	6'1"	193	24		
#Mike Lush	DB	6'1"	195	29		
Robert Moore	DB	5'11"	190	23	2	6
#Gary Moss	DB	5'10"	192	23	1	
#Jerome Norris	DB	6'	187	23		
Elbert Shelley	DB	5'11"	180	22		
#Struggy Smith	DB	6'2"	190	23		
#Leon Thomasson	DB	5'11"	190	24		
Jimmy Turner	DB	5'11"	187	28		
Brenard Wilson (from PHI)	DB	6'	185	32		

Joey Jones - Knee Injury

Use Name	Pos.	Hgt	Wgt	Age	Int	Pts
David Archer	QB	6'2"	208	25		
Scott Campbell	QB	6'	195	25		12
#Erik Kramer	QB	6'	192	22		
Chris Miller	QB	6'2"	195	22		
#Jeff Van Raaphorst	QB	6'1"	210	23		
#Jerry Butler	HB	5'11"	193	24		
Larry Emery	HB	5'9"	195	23		
Kenny Flowers	HB	6'	210	23		
Steve L. Griffin	HB	5'10"	185	22		
#Joe McIntosh	HB	5'10"	192	24		6
#Darryl Oliver	HB	5'10"	194	23		
Sylvester Stamps	HB	5'7"	171	26		6
#Rick Badanjek	FB	5'8"	217	25		6
#Norm Granger	FB	5'9"	222	25		
#Shelley Poole	FB	5'7"	219	22		
Gerald Riggs	FB	6'1"	232	26		12
John Settle	FB	5'9"	207	22		
#Michael Williams	FB	6'2"	218	26		
Stacey Bailey	WR	6'	157	27		18
#Milton Barney	WR	5'9"	156	23		12
Charlie Brown	WR	5'10"	184	28		
Floyd Dixon	WR	5'9"	170	23		30
#Leon Gonzalez	WR	5'10"	160	23		
#Steve B. Griffin	WR	5'11"	198	23		
#Kwante Hampton	WR	6'1"	182	23		
Billy Johnson	WR	5'9"	172	35		
Aubrey Matthews	WR	5'7"	165	24		18
#James Shibest	WR	5'10"	187	22		
#Lenny Taylor	WR	5'10"	183	26		6
#Sylvester Byrd	TE	6'2"	225	24		
Arthur Cox	TE	6'2"	262	26		
#John Evans	TE	6'2"	243	23		
#John Kamana	TE	6'	230	26		6
Ron Middleton	TE	6'2"	252	22		
Dan Sharp	TE	6'2"	235	25		
Ken Whisenhunt	TE	6'3"	240	25		6
#Geno Zimmerlink	TE	6'3"	222	24		
#Louis Berry	K	6'	193	22		
#Greg Davis	K	5'11"	197	21		15
Rick Donnelly	K	6'	190	25		
Mick Luckhurst	K	6'	183	29		44
#John Starnes	K	6'3"	185	24		

- on the active roster for strike replacement games only

NEW ORLEANS SAINTS

RUSHING

Last Name	No.	Yds	Avg	TD
Mayes	243	917	3.8	5
Hilliard	123	508	4.1	7
Beverly	62	217	3.5	2
J. Fourcade	19	134	7.1	0
Word	36	133	3.7	2
Hebert	13	95	7.3	0
Alexander	21	71	3.4	1
Gray	8	37	4.6	1
Jordan	12	36	3.0	2
Rodenberger	17	35	2.1	0
Jean-Batiste	8	18	2.3	0
Ingram	2	14	7.0	0
Riordan	1	3	3.0	0
Hansen	2	-6	-3.0	0
Hill	1	-9	-9.0	0
Barnhardt	1	-13	-13.0	0

RECEIVING

Last Name	No.	Yds	Avg	TD
Martin	44	778	17.7	7
M. Jones	27	420	15.6	3
Hilliard	23	264	11.5	1
Brenner	20	280	14.0	2
Hill	19	322	16.9	2
Tice	16	181	11.3	6
Mayes	15	68	4.5	0
Dawsey	13	142	10.9	0
Pattison	9	132	14.7	0
Word	6	54	9.0	0
Scott	6	35	5.8	0
Gray	6	30	5.0	0
Waters	5	140	28	1
Clark	3	38	12.7	0
O'Neal	3	10	3.3	1
Rodenberger	2	17	8.5	0
Alexander	2	15	7.5	0
Walker	2	15	7.5	0
Jordan	2	13	6.5	0
Benson	2	11	5.5	0
C. Thomas	1	14	14.0	0
Beverly	1	8	8.0	0

PUNT RETURNS

Last Name	No.	Yds	Avg	TD
Gray	24	352	14.7	0
Martin	14	88	6.3	0
Jordan	1	13	13.0	0
Maxie	1	12	12.0	0
Cook	1	3	3.0	0

KICKOFF RETURNS

Last Name	No.	Yds	Avg	TD
Gray	30	636	21.2	0
Hilliard	10	248	24.8	0
Adams	4	52	13.0	0
Word	3	100	33.3	0
Beverly	3	46	15.3	0
Jordan	2	28	14.0	0
Martin	1	15	15.0	0
Brock	1	11	11.0	0
Thomas	1	11	11.0	0

PASSING — PUNTING — KICKING

PASSING	Att	Cmp	%	Yds	Yd/Att	TD	Int—	%	RK
Hebert	294	164	55.8	2119	7.2	15	9—	3.1	14
J. Fourcade	89	48	53.9	597	6.7	4	3—	3.4	
Wilson	24	13	54.2	243	10.1	2	0—	0.0	
Ingram	2	1	50.0	5	2.5	1	0—	0.0	
Hilliard	1	1	100.0	23	23.0	1	0—	0.0	
Riordan	1	0	0.0	0	0.0	0	0—	0.0	

PUNTING	No	Avg
Hansen	52	40.5
Barnhardt	17	42.3

KICKING	XP	Att	%	FG	Att	%
Andersen	37	37	100	28	36	78
Cofer	5	7	71	1	1	100
Kempf	1	1	100	4	5	80

LOS ANGELES RAMS

RUSHING

Last Name	No.	Yds	Avg	TD
White	324	1374	4.2	11
Francis	35	138	3.9	0
Guman	36	98	2.7	1
Bell	22	86	3.9	0
Everett	18	83	4.6	1
Tyrrell	11	44	4.0	0
Ro. Brown	2	22	11.0	0
Evans	3	10	3.3	0
Williams	2	9	4.5	0
Quarles	1	8	8.0	0
McGee	3	6	2.0	1
Ellard	1	4	4.0	0
Bryant	1	2	2.0	0
Dils	7	-4	-0.6	0

RECEIVING

Last Name	No.	Yds	Avg	TD
Ellard	51	799	15.7	3
Ro. Brown	26	521	20.0	2
White	23	121	5.3	0
Guman	22	263	12.0	0
D. Johnson	21	198	9.4	2
Hill	11	105	9.5	0
Bell	9	96	10.7	1
Mobley	8	107	13.4	1
Francis	8	38	4.8	2
McGee	7	40	5.7	0
Moore	6	107	17.8	1
House	6	63	10.5	1
Tyrrell	6	59	9.8	0
Young	4	56	14.0	1
McDonald	4	31	7.8	2
Smith	3	95	31.7	0
Henry	1	13	13.0	0

PUNT RETURNS

Last Name	No.	Yds	Avg	TD
Ellard	15	107	7.1	0
Hicks	13	110	8.5	0
S. Johnson	4	-4	-1.0	0
Rutledge	3	10	3.3	0
Smith	2	5	2.5	0
Mobley	1	12	12.0	0
J. Johnson	1	5	5.0	0
Irvin	1	0	0.0	0

KICKOFF RETURNS

Last Name	No.	Yds	Avg	TD
Ro. Brown	27	581	21.5	1
Tiumalu	8	158	19.8	0
Tyrrell	6	116	19.3	0
Williams	5	114	22.8	0
Hicks	4	119	29.8	0
White	3	73	24.3	0
McDonald	3	31	10.3	0
Sutton	2	37	18.5	0
Guman	2	18	9.0	0
Ri. Brown	1	15	15.0	0
Cox	1	12	12.0	0
Ellard	1	8	8.0	0

PASSING — PUNTING — KICKING

PASSING	Att	Cmp	%	Yds	Yd/Att	TD	Int—	%	RK
Everett	302	162	53.6	2064	6.8	10	13—	4.3	23
Dils	114	56	49.1	646	5.7	5	4—	3.5	
Quarles	3	1	33.3	40	13.3	1	1—	33.3	
Millen	1	1	100.0	0	0.0	0	0—	0.0	

PUNTING	No	Avg
Hatcher	77	40.8

KICKING	XP	Att	%	FG	Att	%
Lansford	36	38	95	17	21	81

ATLANTA FALCONS

RUSHING

Last Name	No.	Yds	Avg	TD
Riggs	203	875	4.3	2
Campbell	21	102	4.9	2
Badanjek	29	87	3.0	1
Settle	19	72	3.8	0
Flowers	14	61	4.4	0
M. Williams	14	49	3.5	0
C. Miller	4	21	5.3	0
Granger	6	12	2.0	0
McIntosh	5	11	2.2	0
Kramer	2	10	5.0	0
Archer	2	8	4.0	0
Stamps	1	6	6.0	0
Van Raaphorst	1	6	6.0	0
Emery	1	5	5.0	0
J. Butler	1	1	1.0	0
Oilver	1	0	0.0	0
Griffin	1	-2	-2.0	0
Dixon	3	-3	-1.0	0
Matthews	1	-4	-4.0	0
Donnelley	3	-6	-2.0	0
Taylor	1	-13	-13.0	0

RECEIVING

Last Name	No.	Yds	Avg	TD
Dixon	36	600	16.7	5
Matthews	32	537	16.8	3
Riggs	25	199	8.0	0
Bailey	20	325	16.3	3
Whisenhunt	17	145	8.5	1
Taylor	12	171	14.3	1
Settle	11	153	13.9	0
Cox	11	101	9.2	0
Barney	10	175	17.5	2
M. Williams	9	70	7.8	0
Johnson	8	84	10.5	0
Byrd	7	125	17.9	0
Kamana	7	51	7.3	1
Flowers	7	50	7.1	0
Badanjek	6	35	5.8	0
C. Brown	5	103	20.6	0
Emery	5	31	6.2	0
Stamps	4	40	10.0	0
Gonzalez	3	40	13.3	0
McIntosh	3	15	5.0	1
Granger	2	34	17.0	0
J. Butler	2	7	3.5	0
Sharp	2	6	3.0	0
Evans	1	8	8.0	0
Oliver	1	2	2.0	0
Middleton	1	1	1.0	0

PUNT RETURNS

Last Name	No.	Yds	Avg	TD
Johnson	21	168	8.0	0
Barney	5	28	5.6	0
Moss	3	15	5.0	0
J. Butler	2	10	5.0	0

KICKOFF RETURNS

Last Name	No.	Yds	Avg	TD
Stamps	24	660	27.5	1
Emery	21	440	21.0	0
Settle	10	158	15.8	0
Oliver	5	90	18.0	0
Flowers	4	72	18.0	0
McIntosh	3	108	36.0	0
Babanjek	2	27	13.5	0
M. Williams	2	15	7.5	0
Moss	1	23	23.0	0
Griffin	1	21	21.0	0
Croudip	1	18	18.0	0
J. Butler	1	13	13.0	0
Cox	1	11	11.0	0
Sharp	1	11	11.0	0

PASSING — PUNTING — KICKING

PASSING	Att	Cmp	%	Yds	Yd/Att	TD	Int—	%	RK
Campbell	260	136	52.3	1728	6.7	11	14—	5.4	24
Kramer	92	45	48.9	559	6.1	4	5—	5.4	
C. Miller	92	39	42.4	552	6.0	1	9—	9.8	
Van Raaphorst	34	18	52.9	174	5.1	1	2—	5.9	
Archer	23	9	39.1	95	4.1	0	2—	8.7	

PUNTING	No	Avg
Donnelly	63	42.7
Berry	7	36.9
Starnes	6	33.8
Davis	6	31.8
Luckhurst	1	37.0

KICKING	XP	Att	%	FG	Att	%
Luckhurst	17	17	100	9	13	69

1987 A.F.C. The Best Defense

The A.F.C. provided the best possible defense against fan backlash after the strike by putting on tight races in all three divisions. In the East, four of the five teams had a chance for at least a wild-card playoff berth until the last two weeks of the season. Cleveland was clearly the class of the Central Division, but Houston stayed in the race, and even Pittsburgh could have made the playoffs had they beaten the Browns in the season's final game. The West saw San Diego race to the front, only to be overtaken by Denver and Seattle. After being accused of falling behind the N.F.C. in quality for several years — underscored by one-sided Super Bowl losses — the A.F.C. improved its image by nearly splitting interconference play with 22 wins, 23 losses and one tie.

EASTERN DIVISION

Indianapolis Colts —The Colt defense improved by seven points a game, largely through the efforts of linebackers Duane Bickett and Johnie Cooks and some exotic sets by defensive coordinator George Hill. Suddenly finding themselves with a chance for the playoffs, the Colts made the "deal of the century," sending unsigned No. 1 draft choice Cornelius Bennett to Buffalo and a gaggle of high draft choices to the Rams to get the unhappy running machine, Eric Dickerson. After being cheered up by a new contract, Dickerson joined the club on Halloween and did what was expected — ran for an AFC-leading 1,011 yards behind a powerful offensive line led by center Ray Donaldson. Perhaps equally important, the trade proved to the other Colt players that the front office sincerely wanted a winner. Despite another injury-plagued season for quarterback Gary Hogeboom, the Colts, who had seemed hopeless until the last three games in '86, barged into the '87 playoffs.

Miami Dolphins —The Dolphins had a new home, Joe Robbie Stadium, and an old problem, no defense. They finished 26th overall in that department, wasting another typical year by quarterback Dan Marino (3,245 yards and 26 touchdowns). Although wide receivers Mark Duper and Mark Clayton slumped by nearly 50 receptions from the previous year, rookie running back Troy Stradford turned out to be an excellent receiver. Stradford also put some punch in the Miami rushing attack (619 yards), but it still ranked only 23rd. Nevertheless, Marino kept the team in the playoff picture right up to the end.

New England Patriots — The Pats were inconsistent most of the season and missed the playoffs for the first time in head coach Raymond Berry's three-year regime. A continuing question of whether the Sullivan family would — or could — sell the team didn't help matters. None of the blame was placed on quarterback Steve Grogan, who finally received some credit for the leadership and clutch play he'd shown for years. The insertion of four rookies into the starting offense for the final three games brought some improvement to what had been a nearly invisible running attack, and the Pats finished on a high note with three straight wins.

Buffalo Bills —Once linebacker Cornelius Bennett was acquired from the Colts, the Bills became a surprisingly good defensive team. Defensive and Bruce Smith, with 12 sacks, was a Pro Bowler. Linebacker Shane Conlan was picked by several selectors as the top rookie defender, and Bennett, in only eight games, was being compared to the best in football. Just when it looked like Buffalo might finish with a winning record, quarterback Jim Kelly went into an unaccountable slump. The offense produced only one touchdown in the final two games — both losses.

New York Jets — The Jets continued the slide which they started in '86. They were suddenly old. Nose tackle Joe Klecko played back to some of his pre-injury form but was "asked" to retire by the Jets at season's end. Jet fans asked the same of embattled coach Joe Walton all year. Walton also riled some of his players by damning them one day and praising them the next. Defensive end Mark Gastineau alienated teammates by crossing the picket line, for which he was pelted with eggs. The onetime king of sacks struggled to only 4 1/2. All told, the team managed only 29 sacks while giving up 66, the worst differential in the league.

CENTRAL DIVISION

Cleveland Browns — The Browns won their third consecutive Central Division crown in Bernie Kosar's third season as quarterback. It was more than mere coincidence. Few quarterbacks look as awkward running an offense as Kosar, but even fewer could run one as well. In addition to throwing for 3,033 yards and 22 TDs while leading the A.F.C. in passing, Kosar was a master at using his running backs, Kevin Mack and Earnest Byner, to maximum effect. The Cleveland defense improved its ranking, despite trading away star linebacker Chip Banks. Most of the credit went to linebacker Clay Matthews and cornerbacks Frank Minnifield and Hanford Dixon.

Houston Oilers —After six years of high draft choices, the Oilers finally came through with a winning season and their first playoff berth since 1980. Key players were quarterback Warren Moon (2,806 yards and 21 TDs), running back Mike Rozier (957 rushing yards) and wide receivers Drew Hill and Ernest Givins, who combined for 102 catches, 1,922 yards and 12 TDs. The Oilers got a break when the replacement players defeated Cleveland and Denver. Despite the new-found success, attendance in the Astrodome dipped, owner Bud Adams flirted with moving the team to Jacksonville, Fla., and head coach Jerry Glanville was criticized by the local press for errors and by Steeler head coach Chuck Noll for allegedly teaching dirty play.

Pittsburgh Steelers —The Steelers were in the playoff picture until the final game of the season, thanks to an opportunistic defense that scored or set up 143 of the team's 285 points. Rookie defensive backs Delton Hall, Thomas Everett and Rod Woodson turned a weak secondary into a strong point, and linebacker Mike Merriweather played back to his '85 form. The offense was often dreadful. Quarterback Mark Malone, the league's lowest-rated passer, threw for only one TD and 11 interceptions in the last seven games. He got no encouragement from the fans. Malone couldn't have been more thoroughly booed at Three Rivers Stadium had he profaned motherhood and apple pie. Wide receiver Louis Lipps and running back Walter Abercrombie also disappointed, and running back Earnest Jackson was injured much of the time.

Cincinnati Bengals — The Bengals expected to challenge for a playoff berth but, instead, they invented new ways to lose. The worst loss came against San Francisco when the Bengals led 26-20 with six seconds to go. They chose not to punt, failed to run out the clock on a fourth-down sweep at their 30 and then allowed the 49ers to pass for the winning TD. Almost as bad, the Bengals, locked in a 20-20 tie with the Jets, attemped a late field goal which missed. But kicker Jim Breech got a second try because the whistle had blown for the two-minute warning. This time, his kick was blocked and returned for a Jet touchdown. Some improvement by the defense was more than offset by an offense that floundered, with running back James Brooks and wide receiver Cris Collinsworth injured and quarterback Boomer Esiason slumping.

WESTERN DIVISION

Denver Broncos — Quarterback John Elway was the league's

FINAL TEAM STATISTICS

OFFENSE

	BUFF.	CIN.	CLEV.	DENV.	HOU.	IND.	K.C.	L.A.	MIA.	N.E.	NYJ	PIT.	S.D.	SEA.
FIRST DOWNS:														
Total	294	319	310	331	294	285	265	300	331	266	292	263	264	301
by Rushing	111	130	110	132	118	122	97	107	109	84	97	114	68	120
by Passing	151	159	171	173	150	138	141	158	197	158	169	126	175	154
by Penalty	32	30	29	26	26	25	27	35	25	24	26	23	21	27
RUSHING:														
Number	465	538	474	510	486	497	419	475	408	513	458	517	396	496
Yards	1840	2164	1745	1970	1923	2143	1799	2197	1662	1771	1671	2144	1308	2023
Average Yards	4.0	4.0	3.7	3.9	4.0	4.3	4.3	4.6	4.1	3.5	3.6	4.1	3.3	4.1
Touchdowns	9	13	16	18	12	14	7	13	16	12	17	11	11	13
PASSING:														
Attempts	516	475	482	530	482	447	432	457	584	440	517	429	516	405
Completions	292	255	291	285	240	255	236	247	338	236	302	198	303	237
Completion Pct.	56.6	53.7	60.4	53.8	49.8	57.0	54.6	54.0	57.9	53.6	58.4	46.2	58.7	58.5
Passing Yards	3246	3468	3625	3874	3534	3042	2985	3429	3977	2929	3402	2464	3602	3028
Avg. Yds per Att.	6.3	7.3	7.5	7.3	7.3	6.8	6.9	7.5	6.8	6.7	6.6	5.7	7.0	7.5
Avg. Yds per Comp.	11.1	13.6	12.5	13.6	14.7	11.9	12.6	13.9	11.8	12.4	11.3	12.4	11.9	12.8
Times Tackled	37	32	29	30	30	24	48	53	13	33	66	27	39	36
Yds Lost Tackled	345	255	170	220	234	190	366	359	101	246	443	198	322	316
Net Yards	2901	3213	3455	3654	3300	2852	2619	3070	3876	2683	2959	2266	3280	2712
Touchdowns	21	17	27	24	24	16	17	19	29	22	18	13	13	31
Interceptions	19	20	12	19	23	16	17	18	20	18	15	25	23	21
Pct. Intercepted	3.7	4.2	2.5	3.6	4.8	3.6	3.9	3.9	3.4	4.1	2.9	5.8	4.5	5.2
PUNTS:														
Number	83	73	57	65	75	78	69	71	63	89	82	82	84	61
Average	38.2	41.0	36.9	39.9	39.1	37.7	40.4	39.4	38.5	37.6	37.1	40.2	42.0	38.9
PUNT RETURNS														
Number	31	34	44	48	37	38	32	44	37	25	42	36	45	32
Yards	232	293	487	486	249	210	346	356	290	213	497	244	508	322
Average Yards	7.5	8.6	11.1	10.1	6.7	5.5	10.8	8.1	7.8	8.5	11.8	6.8	11.3	10.1
Touchdowns	0	0	0	1	0	0	1	1	0	0	2	0	1	0
KICKOFF RET.:														
Number	45	67	48	46	67	55	70	60	54	48	65	56	62	64
Yards	872	1161	846	952	1225	1115	1437	1174	952	901	1221	1060	1137	1236
Average Yards	19.4	17.3	17.6	20.7	18.3	20.3	20.5	19.6	17.6	18.8	18.8	18.9	18.3	19.3
Touchdowns	0	0	0	0	0	0	2	0	0	0	0	0	0	0
INTERCEPT RET.:														
Number	17	14	23	28	23	20	11	13	16	21	18	27	13	17
Yards	93	187	366	403	274	212	140	178	135	307	239	336	291	289
Average Yards	5.5	13.4	15.9	14.4	11.9	10.6	12.7	13.7	8.4	14.6	13.3	12.4	22.4	17.0
Touchdowns	0	0	2	2	1	0	0	2	0	2	0	5	2	1
PENALTIES:														
Number	94	99	100	95	114	90	108	114	76	64	135	105	98	79
Yards	762	791	857	812	1029	742	861	1048	634	506	1055	801	743	668
FUMBLES:														
Number	41	29	33	29	32	36	41	24	37	36	33	37	38	31
Number Lost	24	12	17	17	14	18	24	13	17	13	19	8	20	15
POINTS:														
Total	270	285	390	379	345	300	273	301	362	320	334	285	253	371
PAT Attempts	33	30	47	45	38	31	30	35	47	39	38	31	29	46
PAT Made	32	28	45	44	37	31	30	34	44	38	38	31	27	44
FG Attempts	20	32	31	29	32	32	25	30	16	28	26	29	28	22
FG Made	12	25	21	21	26	27	21	19	12	16	20	22	16	17
Percent FG Made	60.0	78.1	67.7	72.4	81.3	84.4	84.0	63.3	75.0	57.1	76.9	75.9	57.1	77.3
Safeties	2	1	0	1	1	1	0	0	0	0	1	1	2	0

DEFENSE

	BUFF.	CIN.	CLEV.	DENV.	HOU.	IND.	K.C.	L.A.	MIA.	N.E.	NYJ	PIT.	S.D.	SEA.
FIRST DOWNS:														
Total	297	286	251	277	287	276	344	267	314	293	300	289	280	297
by Rushing	114	99	86	103	98	97	139	98	115	112	117	94	120	133
by Passing	162	169	134	148	153	161	172	135	176	159	153	170	136	148
by Penalty	21	18	31	26	36	18	33	34	23	22	30	25	24	16
RUSHING:														
Number	541	441	401	454	446	463	535	469	498	490	476	455	522	472
Yards	2052	1641	1433	2017	1848	1790	2333	1637	2198	1778	1835	1610	2171	2201
Average Yards	3.8	3.7	3.6	4.4	4.1	3.9	4.4	3.5	4.4	3.6	3.9	3.5	4.2	4.7
Touchdowns	11	15	7	16	10	6	16	12	18	13	15	8	14	14
PASSING:														
Attempts	447	456	467	456	495	501	484	425	494	520	488	481	441	445
Completions	249	267	246	261	266	250	279	224	295	273	260	290	227	255
Completion Pct.	55.7	58.6	52.7	57.2	53.7	49.9	57.6	52.7	59.7	52.5	53.3	60.3	51.5	57.3
Passing Yards	3121	3359	3088	3040	3416	3073	3473	3088	3430	3438	3412	3506	3080	3196
Avg. Yds per Att.	7.0	7.4	6.6	6.7	6.9	6.1	7.2	7.3	6.9	6.6	7.0	7.3	7.0	7.2
Avg. Yds per Comp.	12.5	12.6	12.6	11.7	12.8	12.3	12.5	13.8	11.6	12.6	13.1	12.1	13.6	12.5
Times Tackled	34	40	34	31	35	39	26	44	21	43	29	26	45	37
Yds Lost Tackled	267	303	257	244	271	313	167	361	183	339	206	196	298	238
Net Yards	2854	3056	2831	2796	3145	2760	3306	2727	3247	3099	3206	3310	2782	2958
Touchdowns	25	24	15	15	25	19	25	18	21	17	27	22	19	20
Interceptions	17	14	23	28	23	20	11	13	16	21	18	27	13	17
Pct. Intercepted	3.8	3.1	4.9	6.1	4.6	4.0	2.3	3.1	3.2	4.0	3.7	5.6	2.9	3.8
PUNTS:														
Number	88	75	81	75	77	82	56	78	71	77	80	70	89	63
Average	36.7	40.2	37.5	42.1	39.4	37.2	40.4	42.6	38.8	38.1	38.4	39.2	41.5	39.1
PUNT RETURNS														
Number	35	42	17	34	43	39	43	34	26	41	33	46	43	32
Yards	179	299	93	424	454	376	442	256	141	397	162	395	429	251
Average Yards	5.1	7.1	5.5	12.5	10.6	9.6	10.3	7.5	5.4	9.7	4.9	8.6	10.0	7.8
Touchdowns	0	0	0	2	0	0	0	0	0	0	0	0	1	1
KICKOFF RET.:														
Number	43	62	72	61	57	60	55	59	67	63	54	65	50	67
Yards	679	1145	1343	1168	1177	1068	1263	1136	1222	1130	1013	1083	985	1379
Average Yards	15.8	18.5	18.7	19.1	20.6	17.8	23.0	19.3	18.2	17.9	18.8	16.7	19.7	20.6
Touchdowns	0	0	0	0	0	0	1	0	0	0	0	0	1	1
INTERCEPT RET.:														
Number	19	20	12	19	23	16	17	18	20	18	15	25	23	21
Yards	177	336	173	362	225	181	141	371	298	160	210	330	266	146
Average Yards	9.3	16.8	14.4	19.1	9.8	11.3	8.3	20.6	14.9	8.9	14.0	13.2	11.6	7.0
Touchdowns	0	2	2	2	1	1	0	2	2	2	0	1	1	0
PENALTIES:														
Number	103	79	120	96	101	85	112	95	103	110	96	95	107	104
Yards	840	669	1008	785	874	689	936	652	850	846	881	771	869	890
FUMBLES:														
Number	37	26	26	35	37	43	24	28	32	42	23	41	26	38
Number Lost	14	12	13	19	14	25	17	15	16	21	11	17	15	21
POINTS:														
Total	305	370	239	288	349	238	368	289	335	293	360	299	317	314
PAT Attempts	37	43	26	35	37	28	45	33	41	33	43	34	37	36
PAT Made	36	43	26	32	35	25	44	31	41	33	42	31	36	35
FG Attempts	20	26	25	21	36	26	35	29	22	27	29	26	29	26
FG Made	15	23	17	14	30	15	24	20	14	18	20	20	19	21
Percent FG Made	75.0	88.5	68.0	66.7	83.3	57.7	68.6	69.0	63.6	66.7	69.0	76.9	65.5	80.8
Safeties	1	0	3	2	1	0	1	0	0	1	0	2	1	0

most potent weapon, and he became more dangerous when the Broncos went to the shotgun in their ninth game. It opened his view of the field and gave him greater opportunity for scrambling. Surprisingly, the running game improved out of what was considered a passing formation. Elway was aided by the "Three Amigos" — big-play wide receivers Vance Johnson, Mark Jackson and Ricky Nattiel. A spate of injuries and retirements caused a major overhaul on the defense, but linebacker Karl Mecklenburg and defensive end Rulon Jones continued their stellar play and, for the second straight year, the Broncos made it to the Super Bowl.

Seattle Seahawks — Although the media flocked to the "Boz" — colorful rookie linebacker Brian Bosworth — the Seahawk defense was disappointing, with only linebacker Fredd Young having a strong year. In an up-and-down season, the team won with running backs Curt Warner (985 yards) and John L. Williams (500 yards) running behind an outstanding offensive line. Quarterback Dave Krieg had nine games in which he passed for less than 200 yards, in part because of head coach Chuck Knox's decision to go with a ball-control attack. That didn't stop wide receiver Steve Largent from becoming the all-time leader in receptions with 752.

San Diego Chargers —With their replacement players winning three straight, the Chargers took eight of their first nine games. The defense, so often the team's Achilles' heel, was mainly patchwork, culled from other teams but generally effective. Linebacker Chip Banks helped, and linebacker Billy Ray Smith was outstanding. The team needed only two wins in its last six starts to cinch a playoff spot. Then, in a dive worthy of Greg Louganis, San Diego lost its last six to finish out of the playoffs. Longtime quarterback Dan Fouts, looking his age, could get the offense only seven touchdowns in the final eight games.

Los Angeles Raiders —Despite a midseason offensive transfusion from running back Bo Jackson, the Raiders were doomed by a seven-game losing streak — the team's longest since 1962. Rusty Hilger got the job at quarterback but didn't get the job done. Marc Wilson relieved him in all but two of his starts and took over permanently in November. Although Wilson had his best season for the Raiders, he was still considered a lame duck. But, when Jackson arrived after the baseball season to join Marcus Allen in the backfield, the running attack moved up to No. 1 in the league. A sprained ankle put Jackson out of the last three games, and the Raider rushing average dropped to 86.6 yards per game.

Kansas City Chiefs — Under new head coach Frank Gansz, the architect of the great Chief special teams of '86, Kansas City won its opening game and then plunged into a franchise-record nine-game losing streak. The defense, with the exception of nose tackle Bill Maas, was no great shakes, plummeting to 27th in the league. The offense showed some spark with running back Christian Okoye leading all rookie runners with 660 yards. Wide receiver Carlos Carson was terrific, gaining 1,044 yards on 55 catches. Quarterback Bill Kenney had an OK season after regaining his starting job.

Eastern Division

INDIANAPOLIS COLTS 9-6 Ron Meyer

Scores of Each Game		
21	CINCINNATI	23
10	MIAMI	23
47	Buffalo	6
6	N.Y.JETS	0
7	Pittsburgh	21
30	NEW ENGLAND	16
19	N.Y.Jets	14
13	SAN DIEGO	16
40	Miami	21
0	New England	24
51	HOUSTON	27
9	Cleveland	7
3	BUFFALO	27
20	San Diego	7
24	TAMPA BAY	6

Use Name	Pos.	Hgt	Wgt	Age	Int	Pts
#Sid Abramowitz	OT	6'5"	285	27		
Mark Boggs	OT	6'5"	301	23		
Bob Brotzki	OT	6'5"	293	24		
Kevin Call	OT	6'7"	302	25		
#Milt Carthens	OT	6'4"	305	26		
Randy Dixon	OT	6'3"	293	22		
#Marsharne Graves	OT	6'4"	265	25		
Chris Hinton	OT	6'4"	295	26		
Joel Patten	OT	6'7"	307	29		
Steve Knight	OG	6'4"	298	25		
#Jeff Criswell	OG	6'7"	265	24		
Ron Solt	OG	6'3"	285	25		
Ben Utt	OG	6'5"	286	28		
Ray Donaldson	C	6'3"	288	28		
Ron Plantz	C	6'4"	272	23		
Bob Hamm	DE	6'4"	265	28		
Jon Hand	DE	6'7"	280	28		
#Marcus Jackson	DE-NT	6'5"	260	30		
#Frank Mattlace	DE-NT	6'1"	264	26		
#Jim Merritts	DE-NT	6'3"	255	26		
Chris Scott	DE	6'5"	256	25		
Donnell Thompson	DE	6'4"	275	28		6
Don Thorpe	DE-NT	6'4"	260	25		
Harvey Armstrong	NT	6'3"	268	27		
Byron Darby	NT-DE	6'4"	260	27		
#Bill Elko	NT	6'5"	280	27		
Scott Kellar	NT	6'3"	285	23		
Jerome Sally	NT	6'3"	270	28		
Dave Ahrens	LB	6'3"	249	28		
Duane Bickett	LB	6'5"	243	25		
#Brian Bulluck	LB	6'3"	236	22		
#Ricky Chatman	LB	6'2"	230	25		
Johnie Cooks	LB	6'4"	252	22	1	
Kevin Hancock	LB	6'2"	225	25		
June James	LB	6'1"	236	24		
Barry Krauss	LB	6'3"	255	30		
Orlando Lowry	LB	6'4"	236	26		
Cliff Odom	LB	6'2"	245	28		
#Bob Ontko	LB	6'3"	237	23		
#Gary Padjen	LB	6'2"	237	28		
#Roger Remo	LB	6'3"	237	23		
#Brad Saar	LB	6'1"	220	24		
#Pat Ballage	DB	6'1"	208	23		
Leonard Coleman	DB	6'2"	202	25		
#Craig Curry	DB	6'	187	26	1	
Eugene Daniel	DB	5'11"	178	26	2	
#Kenny Daniel	DB	5'10"	180	27		
#Lee Davis	DB	5'11"	201	24	1	
Nesby Glasgow	DB	5'10"	187	30	1	
Chris Goode	DB	6'	193	23		
John Holt	DB	5'11"	179	28		
#Bryant Jones	DB	5'11'	186	23	2	6
Jim Perryman	DB	6'	187	26	1	
Mike Prior	DB	6'	200	23	6	
Freddie Robinson	DB	6'1"	191	23	2	
#John Simmons	DB	5'11"	192	28		
Craig Swoope (from TB)	DB	6'1"	200	23		
Willie Tullis	DB	6'	195	29	3	
Terry Wright	DB	6'	195	22		
Gary Hogeboom	QB	6'4"	206	29		
Blair Kiel	QB	6'	216	25		
Terry Nugent	QB	6'4"	214	25		
Sean Salisbury	QB	6'5"	215	24		
Jack Trudeau	QB	6'3"	213	24		
Albert Bentley	HB	5'11"	214	27		54
#Gordon Brown	HB	5'11"	220	24		6
Eric Dickerson (from LA)	HB	6'3"	217	26		30
George Wonsley	HB	5'10"	219	26		6
#Chuck Banks	FB	6'2"	227	23		
Melvin Carver	FB	5'11"	225	28		
Chris McLemore (to RAID)	FB	6'1"	235	23		
John Williams	FB	5'11"	205	26		
Roy Banks	WR	5'10"	190	23		
Mark Bellini	WR	5'11"	185	23		
Matt Bouza	WR	6'3"	212	29		24
Bill Brooks	WR	6'	197	23		18
#Steve Bryant	WR	6'2"	195	27		
#Kelley Johnson	WR	5'8"	168	25		
#Tim Kearse	WR	5'11"	186	27		
Walter Murray	WR	6'4"	200	24		18
#James Noble	WR	6'	196	24		12
Pat Beach	TE	6'4"	252	27		
Mark Boyer	TE	6'4"	242	24		
John Brandes	TE	6'2"	237	23		
#Greg Hawthorne	TE	6'2"	238	30		
Joe Jones	TE	6'5"	255	25		6
Keith Lester	TE	6'5"	235	25		
Tim Sherwin	TE	6'5"	252	29		6
Mark Walczak (from BUF)	TE	6'6"	246	25		
Dean Biasucci	K	6'	191	25		96
#Steve Jordan	K	5'10"	205	24		16
Rohn Stark	K	6'3"	204	28		

Willie Broughton - Knee Injury
Randy McMillan - Knee Injury

NEW ENGLAND PATRIOTS 8-7 Raymond Berry

Scores of Each Game		
28	MIAMI	21
24	N.Y.Jets	43
10	CLEVELAND	20
14	BUFFALO	7
21	Houston	7
16	Indianapolis	30
26	L.A.RAIDERS	23
10	N.Y.Giants	17
17	DALLAS	*23
24	INDIANAPOLIS	0
31	PHILADELPHIA	*34
20	Denver	31
42	N.Y.JETS	20
13	Buffalo	7
24	Miami	10

Use Name	Pos.	Hgt	Wgt	Age	Int	Pts
Bruce Armstrong	OT	6'4"	284	21		
George Colton	OT	6'4"	279	24		
Steve Moore	OT	6'4"	305	26		
Art Plunkett	OT	6'7"	282	27		
#Greg Robinson	OT	6'5"	275	24		
Danny Villa	OT	6'5"	305	22		
Sean Farrell	OG	6'3"	260	27		
#Todd Sandham	OG	6'3"	255	23		
Ron Wooten	OG	6'4"	273	28		
Pete Brock	C	6'5"	275	32		
Paul Fairchild	C-OG	6'4"	270	25		
Trevor Matich	C	6'4"	270	25		
Guy Morriss	C-OG	6'4"	275	36		
#Eric Stokes	C-OG	6'4"	255	25		
Darren Twombly	C	6'4"	270	22		
Julius Adams	DE	6'3"	265	38		
Milford Hodge	DE	6'3"	278	26		
#Ben Reed	DE	6'5"	265	24		
Kenneth Sims	DE	6'5"	271	27		
#Bill Turner	DE	6'4"	245	27		
Garin Veris	DE	6'4"	255	24		
#Steve Wilburn	DE	6'4"	266	26		
Brent Williams	DE	6'3"	278	22		
#John Guzik	NT-DE	6'4"	270	24		
#Dino Mangiero	NT	6'2"	270	28		
#Tom Porrell	NT	6'3"	275	22		
Mike Ruth	NT	6'1"	266	23		
#Murray Wichard	NT-DE	6'2"	260	23		
Toby Williams	NT	6'3"	270	27		
#Rogers Alexander	LB	6'3"	225	23		
#Mel Black	LB	6'2"	228	25		
Don Blackmon	LB	6'3"	235	29		
#Rico Corsetti	LB	6'1"	225	24		
Steve Doig	LB	6'2"	242	27		
Tim Jordan	LB	6'3"	226	23		
#Jerry McCabe	LB	6'1"	225	22		
#Joe McHale	LB	6'2"	227	23		
Larry McGrew	LB	6'5"	233	30		
#Greg Moore	LB	6'1"	240	22		
Steve Nelson	LB	6'2"	230	36		
Johnny Rembert	LB	6'3"	234	26	1	
Ed Reynolds	LB	6'5"	242	25		
#Frank Sacco	LB	6'4"	240	23		
#Randy Sealby	LB	6'2"	230	27		
Andre Tippett	LB	6'3"	241	27		6
Ed Williams	LB	6'4"	244	25	1	
#Ricky Atkinson	DB	6'	175	22		
Jim Bowman	DB	6'2"	210	23	2	
Raymond Clayborn	DB	6'1"	186	32	2	6
#Duffy Cobbs	DB	5'11"	178	23		
Ernest Gibson	DB	5'10"	185	25	2	
#David Hendley	DB	6'	188	23		
Darryl Holmes	DB	6'2"	190	22	1	
Roland James	DB	6'2"	191	29	1	
Ronnie Lippett	DB	5'11"	180	26	3	12
Fred Marion	DB	6'2"	191	28	4	
Rod McSwain	DB	6'1"	196	25	1	
#Joe Peterson	DB	5'10"	185	23	1	
Eugene Profit	DB	5'10"	175	22		
#Jon Sawyer	DB	5'9"	175	23		
#Ron Shegog	DB	5'11"	190	24	1	
#Perry Williams	DB	6'1"	200	23	1	
#Bob Bleier	QB	6'3"	210	23		6
Tony Eason	QB	6'4"	212	27		
Doug Flutie (from CHI)	QB	5'9"	176	24		
Steve Grogan	QB	6'4"	210	34		12
Tom Ramsey	QB	6'1"	189	26		6
#Todd Whitten	QB	6'	185	22		
#Frank Bianchini	HB	5'8"	190	26		
Tony Collins	HB	5'11"	212	28		36
Elgin Davis	HB	5'10"	192	21		
Reggie Dupard	HB	5'11"	205	23		18
Michael LeBlanc	HB	5'11"	199	25		6
#Chuck McSwain	HB	6'	198	26		
#Carl Woods	HB	5'11"	200	22		6
Bruce Hansen	FB	6'1"	225	26		
Craig James	FB	6'	215	26		
Bob Perryman	FB	6'1"	233	23		
Mosi Tatupu	FB	6'	227	32		
#Brian Carey	WR	6'	200	23		
#Wayne Coffey	WR	5'7"	158	23		
Irving Fryar	WR	6'	200	24		30
#Dennis Gadbois	WR	6'1"	183	23		
Cedric Jones	WR	6'1"	184	27		18
#Larry Linne	WR	6'1"	185	25		12
Stanley Morgan	WR	5'11"	181	32		18
Stephen Starring	WR	5'10"	172	26		18
Darwin Williams	WR	6'1"	185	26		
Greg Baty (from LA)	TE	6'5"	240	23		12
Lin Dawson	TE	6'3"	240	28		
#Todd Frain	TE	6'3"	240	25		
#Arnold Franklin	TE	6'3"	246	23		
Willie Scott	TE	6'4"	245	28		12
Rich Camarillo	K	5'11"	185	27		
Tony Franklin	K	5'8"	182	29		82
#Alan Herline	K	6'	168	22		
#Eric Schubert	K	5'8"	193	25		4

Robert Weathers - Ankle Injury

MIAMI DOLPHINS 8-7 Don Shula

Scores of Each Game		
21	New England	28
23	Indianapolis	10
20	Seattle	24
42	KANSAS CITY	0
31	N.Y.Jets	*37
31	BUFFALO	*34
35	PITTSBURGH	24
20	Cincinnati	14
21	INDIANAPOLIS	40
20	Dallas	14
0	Buffalo	27
37	N.Y.JETS	28
28	Philadelphia	10
23	WASHINGTON	21
10	NEW ENGLAND	24

Use Name	Pos.	Hgt	Wgt	Age	Int	Pts
#Bill Bealles	OT	6'7"	290	24		
#Greg Cleveland	OT	6'5"	295	23		
Jeff Dellenbach	OT-C	6'6"	280	24		
Mark Dennis	OT	6'6"	291	22		
Jon Giesler	OT	6'5"	265	30		
#Scott Kehoe	OT	6'4"	282	22		
Ronnie Lee	OT	6'3"	265	30		
Chris Conlin	OG	6'4"	290	22		
Roy Foster	OG	6'4"	275	27		
#Jim Gilmore	OG	6'5"	275	24		
#Steve Jacobson	OG	6'3"	255	24		
Doug Marrone	OG	6'5"	269	23		
#Louis Oubre	OG	6'4"	274	29		
Tom Toth	OG	6'5"	275	25		
Jeff Wiska	OG	6'3"	265	27		
#Greg Ours	C	6'5"	279	23		
Dwight Stephenson	C	6'2"	258	29		
#Charles Bennett	DE	6'5"	257	24		
Doug Betters	DE	6'7"	265	31		
John Bosa	DE	6'4"	263	23		
George Little	DE	6'4"	270	24		
#Stanley Scott	DE	6'3"	255	23		
T.J.Turner	DE	6'4"	275	24		
#Derek Wimberly	DE	6'4"	270	23		
Jackie Cline (from PIT)	NT-DE	6'5"	276	27		
Mike Lambrecht	NT	6'1"	271	24		
#Ike Readon	NT	6'	273	24		
Brian Sochia	NT	6'3"	274	26		
Mark Brown	LB	6'2"	235	26		
Bob Brudzinski	LB	6'4"	223	32		
#Laz Chavez	LB	6'	220	23		
#Dennis Fowlkes	LB	6'2"	245	26		
David Frye	LB	6'2"	227	26		
Rick Graf	LB	6'5"	239	24		
Hugh Green	LB	6'2"	225	28		
Larry Kolic	LB	6'1"	238	24		
#Steve Lubischer	LB	6'3"	240	25		
#David Marshall	LB	6'3"	220	26		
#Victor Morris	LB	6'1"	243	23		
Scott Nicolas	LB	6'3"	226	27		
John Offerdahl	LB	6'3"	232	23		
#Tim Pidgeon	LB	6'	233	21		
#Duke Schamel	LB	6'3"	235	24		
Jackie Shipp	LB	6'2"	236	25		
#Greg Storr	LB	6'2"	225	26		
Glenn Blackwood	DB	6'	190	30	3	
Bud Brown	DB	6'	194	26	1	
#Marvell Burgess	DB	6'3"	195	21		
Liffort Hobley	DB	6'	199	25		
#Trell Hooper	DB	5'11"	182	25	2	6
#Mark Irvin	DB	5'10"	190	22		
Demetrious Johnson	DB	5'11"	190	26		
William Judson	DB	6'1"	190	27	2	
Paul Lankford	DB	6'1"	184	29	3	
Don McNeal	DB	5'11"	192	29		
#Floyd Raglin	DB	5'9"	180	26		
#Tate Randle	DB	6'	202	28	2	
Donovan Rose	DB	6'1"	190	30		
Mike Smith	DB	6'	175	24		
#Robert Sowell	DB	5'11"	180	26	1	
#John Swain	DB	6'2"	200	27		
Reyna Thompson	DB	5'11"	194	24		
Ron Jaworski	QB	6'2"	195	36		
#Kyle Mackey	QB	6'3"	215	25		12
Dan Marino	QB	6'4"	214	26		6
#Scott Stankavage	QB	6'1"	192	25		
Don Strock	QB	6'5"	225	36		
Lorenzo Hampton	HB	6'	203	25		
#Mark Konecny	HB	5'11"	197	24		
Tony Nathan	HB	6'	210	30		
#Ronald Scott	HB	5'11"	200	21		18
Troy Stradford	HB	5'9"	191	22		42
#John Tagliaferri	HB	5'11"	195	23		6
#Clarence Bailey	FB	5'11"	220	24		
Woody Bennett	FB	6'2"	244	31		
Tom Brown	FB	6'1"	218	22		
Ron Davenport	FB	6'2"	230	24		12
#Rickey Isom	FB	6'	224	23		6
#Pete Roth	FB	5'11"	210	23		
Fred Banks	WR	5'10"	180	25		6
#Mark Caterbone	WR	5'11"	175	25		
#Eddie Chavis	WR	6"	182	24		
Mark Clayton	WR	5'9"	175	26		42
#Leland Douglas	WR	6'	179	23		6
Mark Duper	WR	5'9"	187	28		48
George Farmer	WR	5'10"	175	28		
#Todd Feldman	WR	5'10"	184	25		
Jim Jensen	WR	6'4"	215	28		6
James Pruitt	WR	6'3"	199	23		18
#Dameon Reilly	WR	5'11"	180	24		
Scott Schwedes	WR	6'	181	22		
Bruce Hardy	TE	6'5"	234	31		12
Dan Johnson	TE	6'3"	245	27		12
David Lewis	TE	6'3"	235	26		6
#Lawrence Sampleton	TE	6'5"	235	25		6
#Rich Siler	TE	6'4"	240	23		
#Willie Smith	TE	6'2"	235	23		6
#Joel Williams	TE	6'3"	242	22		
#Willie Beecher	K	5'10"	170	24		21
#Stacy Gore	K	6'	200	25		
#Jeff Hayes	K	5'11"	175	28		
Fuad Reveiz	K	5'11"	217	24		55
Reggie Roby	K	6'2"	242	26		

Andy Hendel - Leg Injury
Robin Sendlein - Eye Injury

* Overtime

- on the active roster for strike replacement games only

INDIANAPOLIS COLTS

RUSHING

Last Name	No.	Yds	Avg	TD
Dickerson	283	1288	4.6	6
Bentley	142	631	4.4	7
Banks	50	245	4.9	0
Brown	19	85	4.5	1
Wonsley	18	71	3.9	1
McLemore	17	58	3.4	0
Kiel	4	30	7.5	0
Trudeau	15	7	.5	0
Carver	2	3	1.5	0
Hogeboom	3	3	1.0	0
Nugent	2	1	.5	0
Brooks	2	-2	-1.0	0

RECEIVING

Last Name	No.	Yds	Avg	TD
Brooks	51	722	14.2	3
Bouza	42	569	13.5	4
Bentley	34	447	13.1	2
Beach	28	239	8.5	0
Murray	20	339	17.0	3
Dickerson	18	171	9.5	0
Noble	10	78	7.8	2
Boyer	10	73	7.3	0
Sherwin	9	92	10.2	1
Banks	9	50	5.6	0
Bellini	5	69	13.8	0
Wonsley	5	48	9.6	0
Brandes	5	35	7.0	0
Kearse	3	51	17.0	0
Hawthorne	3	41	17.0	0
Jones	3	25	8.3	0
McLemore	2	9	4.5	0
Johnson	1	15	15.0	0
Bryant	1	12	12.0	0
Utt	1	-4	-4.0	0

PUNT RETURNS

Last Name	No.	Yds	Avg	TD
Brooks	22	136	6.2	0
Johnson	9	42	4.7	0
Tullis	4	27	6.8	0
Simmons	2	5	2.5	0
Ahrens	1	0	0.0	0

KICKOFF RETURNS

Last Name	No.	Yds	Avg	TD
Bentley	22	500	22.7	0
Daniel	10	225	22.5	0
Johnson	6	98	16.3	0
Prior	3	47	15.7	0
Noble	2	35	17.5	0
Wonsley	1	19	19.0	0
Perryman	1	4	4.0	0

PASSING — PUNTING — KICKING

PASSING	Att	Cmp	%	Yds	Yd/Att	TD	Int—	%	RK
Trudeau	229	128	56	1587	6.9	6	6—	3	
Hogeboom	168	99	59	1145	6.8	9	5—	3	
Kiel	33	17	52	195	5.9	1	3—	9	
Salisbury	12	8	67	68	5.7	0	2—	17	
Nugent	5	3	60	47	9.4	0	0—	0	

PUNTING	No	Avg
Stark	63	38.7
Kiel	12	36.7
Colquitt	3	20.3

KICKING	XP	Att	%	FG	Att	%
Biasucci	24	24	100	24	27	89
Jordan	7	7	100	3	5	60

NEW ENGLAND PATRIOTS

RUSHING

Last Name	No.	Yds	Avg	TD
Collins	147	474	3.2	3
Dupard	94	318	3.4	3
Tatupu	79	248	3.1	0
Perryman	41	187	4.6	0
LeBlanc	49	170	3.5	1
Ramsey	13	75	5.8	1
Fryar	9	52	5.8	0
Hansen	16	44	2.8	0
Davis	9	43	4.8	0
Flutie	6	43	7.2	0
Grogan	20	37	1.9	2
Eason	3	25	8.3	0
C. McSwain	9	23	2.6	0
Woods	4	20	5.0	0
Starring	2	13	6.5	0
James	4	10	2.5	0
Camarillo	1	0	0.0	0
Bleier	5	-5	-1.0	1
Whitten	2	-6	-3.0	0

RECEIVING

Last Name	No.	Yds	Avg	TD
Collins	44	347	7.9	3
Morgan	40	672	16.8	3
Fryar	31	467	15.1	5
Jones	25	388	15.5	3
Baty	18	175	9.7	2
Starring	17	289	17.0	3
Tatupu	15	136	9.1	0
Dawson	12	81	6.8	0
Linne	11	158	14.4	2
Scott	5	35	7.0	1
Coffey	3	66	22.0	0
Gadbois	3	51	17.0	0
D. Williams	3	30	10.0	0
Perryman	3	13	4.3	0
Dupard	3	1	0.3	0
Frain	2	22	11.0	0
LeBlanc	2	3	1.5	0
Hansen	1	22	22.0	0
Pickering	1	10	10.0	0

PUNT RETURNS

Last Name	No.	Yds	Avg	TD
Fryar	18	174	9.7	0
Linne	5	22	4.4	0
Starring	1	17	17.0	0
Marion	1	0	0.0	0

KICKOFF RETURNS

Last Name	No.	Yds	Avg	TD
Starring	23	445	19.3	0
Fryar	6	119	19.8	0
Davis	5	134	26.8	0
Dupard	4	61	15.3	0
Perryman	3	43	14.3	0
C. McSwain	2	32	16.0	0
LeBlanc	2	31	15.0	0
Collins	1	18	18.0	0
Hansen	1	14	14.0	0
Alexander	1	4	4.0	0

PASSING — PUNTING — KICKING

PASSING	Att	Cmp	%	Yds	Yd/Att	TD	Int-	%	RK
Grogan	161	93	57.8	1183	7.4	10	9—	6	
Ramsey	134	71	53.0	898	6.7	6	6—	5	
Eason	79	42	53.2	453	5.7	3	2—	3	
Bleier	39	14	35.9	181	4.6	1	1—	3	
Flutie	25	15	60.0	199	8.0	1	0—	0	
Jones	1	0	0.0	0	0.0	0	0—	0	
Tatupu	1	1	100.0	15	15.0	1	0—	0	

PUNTING	No	Avg
Camarillo	63	39.5
Herline	26	33.1

KICKING	XP	Att	%	FG	Att	%
Franklin	37	38	97	15	26	58
Schubert	1	1	100	1	2	50

MIAMI DOLPHINS

RUSHING

Last Name	No.	Yds	Avg	TD
Stradford	145	619	4.3	6
Hampton	75	289	3.9	1
Scott	47	199	4.2	3
Davenport	32	114	3.6	1
Bennett	25	102	4.1	0
Mackey	17	98	5.8	2
Bailey	10	55	5.5	0
Konecny	6	46	7.7	0
Tagliaferri	13	45	3.5	1
Isom	9	41	4.6	1
Nathan	4	20	5.0	0
Jensen	4	18	4.5	0
Roth	3	10	3.3	0
Clayton	2	8	4.0	0
Brown	3	3	1.0	0
Roby	1	0	0.0	0

RECEIVING

Last Name	No.	Yds	Avg	TD
Stradford	48	457	9.5	1
Clayton	46	776	16.9	7
Duper	33	597	18.1	8
Davenport	27	249	9.2	1
Pruitt	26	404	15.5	3
Jensen	26	221	8.5	1
Hampton	23	223	9.7	0
Tagliaferri	12	117	9.8	0
Nathan	10	77	7.7	0
Douglas	9	92	10.2	1
Sampleton	8	64	8.0	0
Chavis	7	108	15.4	0
Lewis	6	53	14.5	1
Konecny	6	26	4.3	0
Reilly	5	70	14.0	0
Bennett	4	18	4.5	0
Caterbone	2	46	23.0	0
Smith	2	13	6.5	1
Scott	2	7	3.5	0
Isom	1	11	11.0	0
Banks	1	10	10.0	1
Brown	1	6	6.0	0

PUNT RETURNS

Last Name	No.	Yds	Avg	TD
Schwedes	24	203	8.5	0
Caterbone	9	78	8.7	0
Brown	2	8	4.0	0
Blackwood	1	1	1.0	0
Hooper	1	0	0.0	0

KICKOFF RETURNS

Last Name	No.	Yds	Avg	TD
Hampton	16	304	19.0	0
Stradford	14	258	18.4	0
Schwedes	9	177	19.7	0
Hardy	5	62	12.4	0
Farmer	3	56	18.7	0
Roth	2	49	24.5	0
Johnson	2	13	6.5	0
Scott	1	22	22.0	0
Isom	1	11	11.0	0
Lewis	1	0	0.0	0

PASSING — PUNTING — KICKING

PASSING	Att	Cmp	%	Yds	Yd/Att	TD	Int-	%	RK
Marino	444	263	59	3245	7.3	26	13—	3	4
Mackey	109	57	52	604	5.5	3	5—	5	
Strock	23	13	57	114	5.0	0	1—	4	
Stankavage	7	4	57	8	1.1	0	1—	14	
Stradford	1	1	100	6	6.0	0	0—	0	

PUNTING	No	Avg
Roby	32	42.8
Hayes	8	34.3
Gore	14	35.9
Strock	9	30.8

KICKING	XP	Att	%	FG	Att	%
Reveiz	28	30	93	9	11	82
Beecher	12	12	100	3	4	75

BUFFALO BILLS 7-8 Marv Levy

Scores of Each Game			
28	N.Y.JETS	31	
34	HOUSTON	30	
6	INDIANAPOLIS	47	
7	New England	14	
6	N.Y.GIANTS	*3	
34	Miami	*31	
7	WASHINGTON	27	
21	DENVER	14	
21	Cleveland	27	
17	N.Y.Jets	14	
27	MIAMI	0	
21	L.A.Raiders	34	
27	Indianapolis	3	
7	NEW ENGLAND	13	
7	Philadelphia	17	

Use Name	Pos.	Hgt	Wgt	Age	Int	Pts
#Tony Brown	OT	6'5"	285	23		
Leonard Burton	OT-C	6'3"	275	23		
#Glen Campbell	OT	6'4"	280	26		
Joe Devlin	OT	6'5"	280	34		
#Don Sommer	OT	6'4"	290	23		
Will Wolford	OT	6'5"	276	23		
#Sean Dowling	OG-OT	6'4"	280	24		
#Mike Estep	OG-OT	6'4"	270	23		
Mitch Frerotte	OG	6'3"	280	22		
#Kevin Lamar	OG	6'4"	260	25		
#Rick Schulte	OG-OT	6'2"	270	24		
Jim Ritcher	OG	6'3"	265	29		
Mark Traynowicz	OG-C	6'5"	280	24		
Tim Vogler	OG	6'3"	280	30		
#Joe Bock	C	6'4"	254	28		
#Will Grant	C	6'3"	264	33		
Kent Hull	C	6'4"	275	26		
Adam Lingner	C	6'4"	260	26		
#Erik Rosenmeier	C	6'4"	240	22		
#Mark Shupe	C	6'5"	285	25		
#Joe Silipo	C	6'3"	295	28		
#Jack Bravyak	DE	6'3"	255	27		
#Arnold Campbell	DE	6'3"	260	24		
#Scott Garnett	DE-NT	6'2"	265	24		
Sean McNanie	DE	6'5"	270	25		6
Dean Prater	DE	6'4"	260	28		
Leon Seals	DE	6'4"	265	23		
Bruce Smith	DE	6'4"	285	24		
#Richard Tharpe	DE-NT	6'3"	255	26		
#Billy Wilt	DE	6'5"	265	23		
#Ira Albright	NT-FB	6'	285	28		
#Scott Hernandez	NT	6'	250	27		
#Joe McGrail	NT	6'3"	280	23		
Bruce Mesner	NT	6'5"	280	23		
Fred Smerlas	NT	6'3"	280	30		
Cornelius Bennett	LB	6'2"	235	21		
Ray Bentley	LB	6'2"	245	26		
#Will Cokeley	LB	6'2"	220	26	1	
Shane Conlan	LB	6'3"	230	23		
Tony Furjanic	LB	6'1"	228	23		
John Kaiser	LB	6'3"	227	25		
#Mike Jones	LB	6'4"	224	23		
#Bob LeBlanc	LB	6'2"	243	24		
#Steve Maidlow	LB	6'2"	240	27		
Eugene Marve	LB	6'2"	240	27		
Mark Pike	LB	6'4"	257	23		
Scott Radecic	LB	6'3"	242	25	2	
#Scott Schankweiler	LB	6'	225	23	1	
Darryl Talley	LB	6'4"	227	27		
#Craig Walls	LB	6'1"	215	29		
#Scott Waters	LB	6'2"	230	22		
#Al Wenglikowski	LB	6'1"	210	27		
#John Armstrong	DB	5'9"	190	24		
#Gerald Bess	DB	6'	188	29		
Derrick Burroughs	DB	6'1"	180	25	2	
#Bill Callahan	DB	6'	200	23		
#Steve Clark	DB	6'2"	190	25	1	
Wayne Davis	DB	5'11"	175	24		
Dwight Drane	DB	6'2"	205	25		
#Larry Friday	DB	6'4"	215	28		
Lawence Johnson	DB	5'11"	202	29		
Mark Kelso	DB	5'11"	177	24	6	6
#John Lewis	DB	5'10"	175	25		
#David Martin	DB	5'9"	195	28		
Roland Mitchell	DB	5'11"	180	23		
#Chip Nuzzo	DB	5'11'	190	22		
Nate Odomes	DB	5'10"	188	22		
#Kerry Parker	DB	6'1"	188	31		
Ron Pitts	DB	5'10"	175	24	3	
Durwood Roquemore	DB	6'1"	190	26		
Jim Kelly	QB	6'3"	218	27		
#Dan Manucci	QB	6'2"	199	29		
#Bran McClure	QB	6'6"	222	23		
#Mark Miller	QB	6'2"	210	24		
Frank Reich	QB	6'3"	208	25		
#Willie Totten	QB	6'2"	195	25		
#Joe Chetti	HB	5'9"	205	23		
Ronnie Harmon	HB	5'11"	192	23		24
#Mike Panepinto	HB	5'11"	202	21		
Kerry Porter	HB	6'1"	210	22		
Ricky Porter	HB	5'11"	205	27		
Robb Riddick	HB	6'	195	30		50
#Johnny Shepherd	HB	5'10"	185	30		
#Leonard Williams	HB	6'	205	23		
Carl Byrum	FB	6'	235	24		
#Bruce King	FB	6'1"	225	24		
#Warren Loving	FB	6'1"	230	25		
Jamie Mueller	FB	6'1"	225	22		12
#Gary Wilkins	FB	6'1"	235	23		
Walter Broughton	WR	5'10"	180	24		
#Marc Brown	WR	6'2"	195	26		6
Chris Burkett	WR	6'4"	210	25		24
#Reggie Bynum	WR	6'1"	185	23		
#Sheldon Gaines	WR	5'9"	155	23		
#Kris Haines	WR	5'11"	180	30		
Trumaine Johnson	WR	6'1"	196	27		
#Thad McFadden	WR	6'2"	200	25		6
Andre Reed	WR	6'	190	23		30
Steve Tasker	WR	5'9"	185	25		2
#Veno Belk	TE	6'3"	233	24		
#Keith McKeller	TE	6'6"	230	23		
Pete Metzelaars	TE	6'7"	243	27		
Butch Rolle	TE	6'3"	242	23		12
John Kidd	K	6'3"	208	24		
Scott Norwood	K	6'	207	27		61
#Rick Partridge	K	6'1"	175	30		
#Todd Schlopy	K	5'10"	165	26		7

Mike Hamby - Hip Injury
Dale Hellestrae - Hip Injury
Clint Sampson - Knee Injury

Jerry Butler - Knee Injury
Greg Christy - Neck Injury
Chas Fox - Injury
Hal Garner - Knee Injury
Stam Gelbaugh - Elbow Injury

NEW YORK JETS 6-9 Joe Walton

Scores of Each Game			
31	Buffalo	28	
43	NEW ENGLAND	24	
24	DALLAS	38	
0	Indianapolis	6	
37	MIAMI	*31	
16	Washington	17	
14	INDIANAPOLIS	19	
30	SEATTLE	14	
16	Kansas City	9	
14	BUFFALO	17	
27	CINCINNATI	20	
28	Miami	37	
20	New England	42	
27	PHILADELPHIA	38	
7	N.Y.Giants	20	

Use Name	Pos.	Hgt	Wgt	Age	Int	Pts
#Chris Brown	OT	6'1"	295	24		
Ken Jones	OT	6'5"	285	34		
Gordon King	OT-OG	6'6"	270	31		
Reggie McElroy	OT	6'6"	275	27		
Jim Sweeney	OT	6'4"	275	25		
#John Thomas	OT	6'4"	280	23		
Dan Alexander	OG-OT	6'4"	274	32		
Ted Banker	OG-C	6'2"	275	25		
#Anthony Corvino	OG-OT	6'1"	262	21		
Joe Fields	OG-C	6'2"	253	33		
Mike Haight	OG-OT	6'4"	270	24		
#Tom Humphrey	OG-OT	6'3"	280	24		
#Vince Jasper	OG	6'4"	270	22		
#Pete McCartney	OG	6'6"	260	25		
Guy Bingham	C-OG	6'3"	260	29		
#Martin Cornelson	C	6'1"	230	26		
#Eric Coss	C	6'3"	270	24		
Don Baldwin	DE	6'3"	263	23		
Barry Bennett	DE-DT	6'4"	260	31		
Jerome Foster	DE-DT	6'2"	275	27		
#Tony Garbarczyk	DE	6'4"	275	23		
Mark Gastineau	DE	6'5"	255	30		
Marty Lyons	DE-DT	6'5"	269	30		2
Scott Mersereau	DE-NT	6'3"	278	22		
Don Smith	DE	6'5"	262	30		
#Tony Chickillo	NT-DE	6'4"	270	27		
Joe Klecko	NT	6'3"	263	34		
Gerald Nichols	NT	6'2"	261	23		
#Lynwood Alford	LB	6'3"	220	24		
Troy Benson	LB	6'2"	235	24		
#Jay Brophy	LB	6'3"	233	27		
Kyle Clifton	LB	6'4"	236	25		
Bob Crable	LB	6'3"	230	27	1	
Onzy Elam	LB	6'2"	225	23		
Alex Gordon	LB	6'5"	246	22		
#Jim Haslett	LB	6'3"	236	30	1	
Kevin McArthur	LB	6'2"	245	24		
Lance Mehl	LB	6'3"	233	29		
Matt Monger	LB	6'1"	238	25		
Ken Rose	LB	6'1"	215	26	1	
#Henry Walls	LB	6'2"	220	23		
#Ladell Wills	LB	6'3"	240	25		
#Mike Witteck	LB	6'2"	225	23		
Russell Carter	DB	6'2"	195	25		
#Trent Collins	DB	6'1"	187	26		
Sean Dykes	DB	5'10"	170	23		
Kerry Glenn	DB	5'9"	175	25		
Harry Hamilton	DB	6'	195	24	3	
#Jo Jo Heath	DB	5'10"	178	30	1	
#Marc Hogan	DB	6'	180	25	1	
Jerry Holmes	DB	6'2"	175	29	1	
Carl Howard	DB	6'2"	190	25	3	
Bobby Humphrey	DB	5'10"	180	26		6
Sid Lewis	DB	5'11"	180	23		
Lester Lyles	DB	6'3"	218	24		
Rich Miano	DB	6'	200	24	3	6
George Radachowsky	DB	5'11"	192	24	2	
#Larry Robinson	DB	5'9"	194	25	1	
#Treg Songy	DB	6'2"	200	25		
Mike Zordich	DB	5'11"	207	23		
#Walter Briggs	QB	6'1"	205	22		
#Tom Flick	QB	6'3"	190	28		
#David Norris	QB	6'4"	220	23		
Ken O'Brien	QB	6'4"	208	26		
Pat Ryan	QB	6'3"	210	31		6
Dennis Bligen	HB	5'11"	215	25		6
#Joe Burke	HB	6'	200	26		
Nuu Faaola	HB	5'11"	210	23		12
#Derrick Foster	HB	5'11"	205	23		
Johnny Hector	HB-FB	5'11"	200	26		66
#Eddie Hunter (to TB)	HB	5'10"	205	22		12
Freeman McNeil	HB	5'11"	214	28		6
#Maurice Turner	HB	5'11"	207	26		
Marion Barber	FB	6'3"	228	27		
#John Chirico	FB	6'	220	22		
#Tim Newman	FB	6'	220	23		
Roger Vick	FB	6'3"	232	23		6
#Derrick Gaffney	WR	6'1"	182	32		
#Michael Harper	WR	5'10"	180	26		12
#Scott Holman	WR	6'2"	193	24		
#Stan Hunter	WR	6'2"	184	23		6
#Tracy Martin	WR	6'3"	205	22		
Reggie Smith	WR	5'4"	168	31		
Kurt Sohn	WR	5'11"	180	30		12
Al Toon	WR	6'4"	205	24		30
JoJo Townsell	WR	5'9"	180	26		6
Wesley Walker	WR	6'	182	32		6
Billy Griggs	TE	6'3"	230	27		
Rocky Klever	TE	6'3"	230	28		
#Jamie Kurisko	TE	6'4"	236	23		6
#Eric Riley	TE	6'3"	230	22		
Mickey Shuler	TE	6'3"	231	31		18
#Tony Sweet	TE	6'4"	230	23		
Dave Jennings	K	6'4"	200	35		
Pat Leahy	K	6'	193	36		85
#Tom O'Connor	K	6'1"	190	24		
#Pat Ragusa	K	5'8"	180	24		13

Tom Baldwin - Knee Injury

Central Division

CLEVELAND BROWNS 10-5 Marty Schottenheimer

Scores of Each Game			
21	New Orleans	28	
34	PITTSBURGH	10	
20	New England	10	
10	HOUSTON	15	
34	Cincinnati	0	
30	L.A.RAMS	17	
24	San Diego	*27	
38	ATLANTA	3	
27	BUFFALO	21	
40	Houston	7	
24	San Francisco	38	
7	INDIANAPOLIS	9	
38	CINCINNATI	24	
24	L.A.Raiders	17	
19	Pittsburgh	13	

* Overtime

Use Name	Pos.	Hgt	Wgt	Age	Int	Pts
Rickey Bolden	OT	6'6"	280	25		
#Keith Bosley	OT	6'5"	320	24		
Paul Farren	OT-OG	6'5"	280	26		
Darryl Haley	OT-OG	6'4"	265	26		
Gregg Rakoczy	OT	6'6"	290	22		
Cody Risien	OT	6'7"	280	30		
#Ralph Van Dyke	OT	6'6"	273	23		
Dan Fike	OG	6'7"	280	26		
#Mark Krerowicz	OG	6'3"	285	24		
#Dave Sparenberg	OG	6'3"	267	28		
Larry Williams	OG	6'5"	290	24		
#Blake Wingle	OG	6'2"	260	27		
Mike Baab	C	6'4"	270	27		
#Mike Katolin	C	6'3"	255	29		
#Mike Teifke	C	6'4"	255	23		
Frank Winters	C	6'3"	290	23		
Al Baker	DE	6'6"	270	30		
Reggie Camp	DE	6'4"	280	25		
#Alex Carter	DE	6'3"	255	24		
Sam Clancy	DE	6'7"	260	29		
#Scott Cooper	DE	6'5"	285	23		
Carl Hairston	DE	6'3"	260	34		
Marlon Jones	DE	6'4"	260	23		
#Aaron Moog	DE	6'4"	260	25		
Darryl Sims	DE	6'3"	282	26		
Bob Golic	NT	6'2"	270	29		
Dave Puzzuoli	NT	6'3"	260	26		
#Mike Rusinek	NT	6'3"	250	24		
#Dave Butler	LB	6'4"	225	22		
#James Capers	LB	6'4"	232	28		
#Tim Crawford	LB	6'4"	245	25		
David Grayson	LB	6'2"	229	23		6
Anthony Griggs	LB	6'3"	230	27		
Rusty Guilbeau	LB	6'4"	235	28		
#Cliff Hanneman	LB	6'2"	235	23		
Eddie Johnson	LB	6'1"	225	28	1	
Mike Johnson	LB	6'1"	228	24	1	
Mike Junkin	LB	6'3"	247	22		
#Mike Kovaleski	LB	6'2"	225	22		
Clay Matthews	LB	6'2"	235	30	4	6
Nick Miller	LB	6'2"	238	23		
#Stevan Nave	LB	6'2"	250	24		
#Jerry Parker	LB	6'	227	22		
#Tom Polley	LB	6'3"	250	25		
Lucius Sanford	LB	6'2"	216	31		
#Vincent Barnett	DB	6'1"	200	22		
Stephen Braggs	DB	5'9"	173	22		
#Vince Carreker	DB	6'	183	24		
Hanford Dixon	DB	5'11"	186	28	3	
#Brian Dudley	DB	6'1"	180	27		
Ray Ellis	DB	6'1"	196	28		6
Al Gross	DB	6'3"	195	26		
Mark Harper	DB	5'9"	174	25	2	
D.D. Hoggard	DB	6'	188	22		
#Alvin Horn	DB	5'11"	185	26	1	
#Enis Jackson	DB	5'9"	180	24		
Frank Minnifield	DB	5'9"	180	27	4	
#Billy Robinson	DB	6'1"	200	24		
#DeJuan Robinson	DB	5'10"	185	22	1	
Chris Rockins	DB	6'	195	25	2	
Troy Wilson	DB	5'10"	170	21	1	
#Felix Wright	DB	6'2"	190	28	4	6
#Jeff Christensen	QB	6'3"	202	27		
Gary Danielson	QB	6'2"	196	35		
#Homer Jordan	QB	6'	183	27		
Bernie Kosar	QB	6'5"	210	23		6
Mike Pagel	QB	6'2"	206	27		
#Mike Crawford	HB	5'10"	215	23		
#Stacey Driver	HB	5'7"	190	23		
Major Everett (to ATL)	HB	5'10"	218	27		
#Kirk Jones	HB	5'10"	210	22		
#Larry Mason	HB	5'11"	205	26		
Earnest Byner	FB	5'10"	215	24		60
#Johnny Davis	FB	6'1"	235	31		
Herman Fontenot	FB	6'	206	23		
Kevin Mack	FB	6'	225	25		36
Tim Manoa	FB	6'1"	227	22		
George Swarn	FB	5'10"	205	23		
#Clayton Beauford	WR	5'11"	190	24		
Brian Brennan	WR	5'9"	178	25		36
#Perry Kemp	WR	5'11"	170	25		
Reggie Langhorne	WR	6'2"	195	24		6
Gerald McNeil	WR	5'7"	147	25		12
#Steve Pierce	WR	5'10"	190	23		
Webster Slaughter	WR	6'	170	22		42
#Keith Tinsley	WR	5'9"	184	22		
#David Verser	WR	6'1"	202	29		
#Louis Watson	WR	5'11'	175	24		
Remi Watson	WR	6'	174	22		
Clarence Weathers	WR	5'9"	170	25		12
Glen Young	WR	6'2"	205	26		
#Donnie Echols	TE	6'3"	240	29		
#Chris Kelley	TE	6'4"	239	22		
Ozzie Newsome	TE	6'2"	232	31		
Derek Tennell	TE	6'5"	245	23		18
Travis Tucker	TE	6'3"	240	23		
Matt Bahr	K	5'10"	175	31		21
#Brian Franco	K	5'8"	165	27		
Jeff Jaeger	K	5'11"	189	22		75
#Goran Lingmerth	K	5'8"	160	22		
Jeff Gossett (to HOU)	K	6'2"	200	30		
#Dale Walters	K	6'	200	26		
George Winslow	K	6'4"	205	24		

Tony Baker - Wrist Injury
Robert Stallings - Ankle Injury

\# - on the active roster for strike replacement games only

BUFFALO BILLS

RUSHING

Last Name	No.	Yds	Avg	TD
Harmon	116	485	4.2	3
Mueller	82	354	3.8	1
Byrum	66	280	4.2	0
Riddick	59	221	3.7	5
R. Porter	47	177	3.8	0
Kelly	29	133	4.6	0
Shepherd	12	42	3.5	0
King	9	28	3.1	0
L. Williams	9	25	2.8	0
Partridge	1	13	13.0	0
Totten	12	11	0.9	0
Manucci	4	6	1.5	0
McClure	2	4	2.0	0
Reed	1	1	1.0	0
K. Porter	2	0	0.0	0

RECEIVING

Last Name	No.	Yds	Avg	TD
Reed	57	752	13.2	5
Burkett	56	765	13.7	4
Harmon	56	477	8.5	2
Metzelaars	28	290	10.4	0
T. Johnson	15	186	12.4	2
Riddick	15	96	6.4	3
M.Brown	9	120	13.3	1
Gaines	9	115	12.8	0
McKeller	9	80	8.9	0
R. Porter	9	70	7.8	0
Broughton	5	90	18.0	1
McFadden	4	41	10.3	1
Byrum	3	23	7.7	0
Mueller	3	13	4.3	0
Bynum	2	24	12.0	0
Rolle	2	6	3.0	2
Kelly	1	35	35.0	0
Chetti	1	9	9.0	0
Belk	1	7	7.0	0
Williams	1	5	5.0	0
King	1	3	3.0	0
Shepherd	1	2	2.0	0

PUNT RETURNS

Last Name	No.	Yds	Avg	TD
Pitts	23	149	6.5	0
McFadden	8	83	10.4	0

KICKOFF RETURNS

Last Name	No.	Yds	Avg	TD
Tasker	11	197	17.9	0
R. Porter	8	219	27.4	0
Riddick	7	151	21.6	0
McFadden	7	121	17.3	0
Mueller	5	74	14.8	0
Brown	2	35	17.5	0
Armstrong	2	25	12.5	0
Harmon	1	30	30.0	0
Radecic	1	14	14.0	0
Rolle	1	6	6.0	0

PASSING — PUNTING — KICKING

PASSING	Att	Cmp	%	Yds	Yd/Att	TD	Int—	%	RK
Kelly	419	250	60	2798	6.7	19	11—	3	11
McClure	38	20	53	181	4.8	0	3—	8	
Totten	33	13	39	155	4.7	2	2—	6	
Manucci	21	7	33	68	3.2	0	2—	10	
Miller	3	1	33	9	3.0	0	1—	33	
Kidd	1	0	0	0	0.0	0	0—	0	
Riddick	1	1	100	35	35.0	0	0—	0	

PUNTING	No	Avg
Kidd	64	39.0
Partridge	19	35.7

KICKING	XP	Att	%	FG	Att	%
Norwood	31	31	100	10	15	67
Schlopy	1	2	50	2	5	40

NEW YORK JETS

RUSHING

Last Name	No.	Yds	Avg	TD
McNeil	121	530	4.4	0
Hector	111	435	3.9	11
Vick	77	257	3.3	1
E. Hunter	56	210	3.8	0
Bligen	31	128	4.1	1
O'Brien	30	61	2.0	0
Faaola	14	43	3.1	2
Chirico	12	22	1.8	1
D. Foster	1	9	9.0	0
Jennings	2	5	2.5	0
Norrie	5	5	1.0	0
Ryan	4	5	1.3	1
Briggs	1	4	4.0	0
Townsell	1	-2	-2.0	0

RECEIVING

Last Name	No.	Yds	Avg	TD
Toon	68	976	14.4	5
Shuler	43	434	10.1	3
Hector	32	249	7.8	0
McNeil	24	262	10.9	1
Sohn	23	261	11.3	2
Harper	18	225	12.5	1
Holman	15	155	10.3	0
Klever	14	152	10.9	0
Vick	13	108	8.3	0
Bligen	11	81	7.4	0
Walker	9	190	21.1	1
E. Hunter	7	28	4.0	2
S. Hunter	6	50	8.3	1
E. Riley	4	42	10.5	0
Townsell	4	37	9.3	0
Chirico	4	18	4.5	0
Sweet	3	45	15.0	0
Griggs	2	17	8.5	1
Dennison	2	8	4.0	0
Kunsko	1	41	41.0	1
Faaola	1	16	16.0	0
Gaffney	1	10	10.0	0
D. Foster	1	9	9.0	0

PUNT RETURNS

Last Name	No.	Yds	Avg	TD
Townsell	32	381	11.9	1
Harper	4	93	23.3	1
D. Foster	2	8	4.0	0
R. Smith	2	9	4.5	0
Collins	1	0	0.0	0
Sohn	1	6	6.0	0

KICKOFF RETURNS

Last Name	No.	Yds	Avg	TD
Humphery	18	357	19.8	0
Townsell	11	272	24.7	0
E. Hunter	8	123	15.4	0
Martin	8	180	22.5	0
Klever	5	85	17.0	0
Harper	4	75	18.8	0
R. Smith	4	60	15.0	0
Sohn	3	47	15.7	0
Barber	2	5	2.5	0
Faaola	1	4	4.0	0
Griggs	1	13	13.0	0

PASSING — PUNTING — KICKING

PASSING	Att	Cmp	%	Yds	Yd/Att	TD	Int—	%	RK
O'Brien	393	234	60	2696	6.86	13	8—	2	14
Norrie	68	35	52	376	5.5	1	4—	6	
Ryan	53	32	60	314	5.9	4	2—	4	
Briggs	2	0	0	0	0.0	0	1—	50	
Jennings	1	1	100	16	16.0	0	0—	0	

PUNTING	No	Avg
Jennings	64	38.2
O'Connor	18	33.4

KICKING	XP	Att	%	FG	Att	%
Leahy	31	31	100	18	22	82
Ragusa	7	7	100	2	4	50

CLEVELAND BROWNS

RUSHING

Last Name	No.	Yds	Avg	TD
Mack	201	735	3.7	5
Byner	105	432	4.1	8
Mason	56	207	3.7	2
Manoa	23	116	5.0	0
Everett	34	95	2.8	0
Christensen	11	41	3.7	0
Fontenot	15	33	2.2	1
Driver	9	31	3.4	0
Kosar	15	22	1.5	1
McNeil	1	17	17.0	0
Verser	1	9	9.0	0
Davis	1	7	7.0	0
Danielson	1	0	0.0	0
Katolin	1	0	0.0	0

RECEIVING

Last Name	No.	Yds	Avg	TD
Byner	52	552	10.6	2
Slaughter	47	806	17.1	7
Brennan	43	607	14.1	6
Newsome	34	375	11.0	0
Mack	32	223	7.0	1
Langhorne	20	288	14.4	1
Kemp	12	224	18.7	2
Weathers	11	153	13.9	2
Tennell	9	102	11.3	3
McNeil	8	120	15.0	2
Everett	8	41	5.1	0
Mason	5	26	5.2	1
Fontenot	4	40	10.0	0
Pierce	2	21	10.5	0
Tinsley	1	17	17.0	0
R. Watson	1	13	13.0	0
L. Watson	1	9	9.0	0
Manoa	1	8	8.0	0

PUNT RETURNS

Last Name	No.	Yds	Avg	TD
McNeil	34	386	11.4	0
Wilson	10	101	10.1	0

KICKOFF RETURNS

Last Name	No.	Yds	Avg	TD
Young	18	412	22.9	0
McNeil	11	205	18.6	0
Fontenot	9	130	14.4	0
Everett	2	33	16.5	0
Tinsley	2	31	15.5	0
Manoa	2	14	7.0	0
Beauford	1	22	22.0	0
Driver	1	16	16.0	0
Langhorne	1	8	8.0	0
Grayson	1	6	6.0	0
Byner	1	2	2.0	0
Mason	1	0	0.0	0

PASSING — PUNTING — KICKING

PASSING	Att	Cmp	%	Yds	Yd/Att	TD	Int—	%	RK
Kosar	389	241	62.0	3033	7.80	22	9—	2	2
Danielson	33	25	75.8	281	8.52	4	0—	0	
Christensen	58	24	41.4	297	5.12	1	3—	5	
Fontenot	1	1	100	14	14.00	0	0—	0	
Jaeger	1	0	0.0	0	0.00	0	0—	0	

PUNTING	No	Avg
Gossett	45	39.5
Winslow	18	34.2
Walters	11	36.4

KICKING	XP	Att	%	FG	Att	%
Jaeger	33	33	100	14	22	64
Bahr	9	10	90	4	5	80
Franco	2	2	100	3	4	75
Kelley	1	1	100	0	0	0

HOUSTON OILERS 9-6 Jerry Glanville

Scores of Each Game		
20	L.A.RAMS	16
30	Buffalo	34
40	Denver	10
15	Cleveland	10
7	NEW ENGLAND	21
37	ATLANTA	33
31	Cincinnati	29
20	San Francisco	27
23	Pittsburgh	3
7	CLEVELAND	40
27	Indianapolis	51
33	SAN DIEGO	18
10	New Orleans	24
24	PITTSBURGH	16
21	CINCINNATI	17

Use Name	Pos.	Hgt	Wgt	Age	Int	Pts
Bruce Davis (from RAID)	OT	6'6"	280	31		
John Davis	OT-OG	6'4"	304	22		
#Jerrell Franklin	OT	6'3"	287	28		
Mike Kelley	OT-OG	6'5"	280	25		
Bruce Matthews	OT-OG	6'4"	280	26		
#Clay Miller	OT-OG	6'4"	273	24		
Barry Pettyjohn	OT-C	6'5	285	23		
Dean Steinkuhler	OT	6'3"	278	26		
Doug Williams	OT-OG	6'5"	288	24		
#Scott Boucher	OG	6'3"	260	29		
Kent Hill	OG	6'5"	265	30		
#Doug Kellermeyer	OG-OT	6'3"	275	26		
Mike Munchak	OG	6'3"	280	27		
Vince Stroth	OG	6'4"	270	26		
#Almon Young	OG	6'3"	290	25		
Billy Kidd	C	6'4"	270	26		
Jay Pennison	C	6'1"	275	25		
#Brett Petersmark	C	6'3"	280	24		
Jesse Baker	DE	6'5"	260	30		2
Richard Byrd	DE	6'4"	265	25		
Ray Childress	DE	6'6"	276	24		
Rayford Cooks	DE	6'3"	245	25		
William Fuller	DE	6'3"	260	25		
#Eric Larkin	DE	6'4"	265	23		
Kenny Neil	DE	6'4"	249	28		
#Bob Otto	DE	6'6"	255	24		
Joe Dixon	NT	6'3"	275	23		
Charles Martin (from GB)	NT	6'4"	280	28		
Doug Smith	NT	6'5"	282	28		
#Dwaine Turner	NT	6'	290	23		
Robert Abraham	LB	6'1"	236	27		
#Tom Briehl	LB	6'3"	248	24		
Toby Caston	LB	6'1"	235	22		
Eric Fairs	LB	6'3"	240	23		
#Scott Fox	LB	6'2"	222	23		
John Grimsley	LB	6'2"	236	25		
#Thad Jefferson	LB	5'11"	225	23		
#Byron Johnson	LB	6'1"	220	25		
Walter Johnson	LB	6'	241	23		
Robert Lyles	LB	6'1"	223	26	2	6
Johnny Meads	LB	6'2"	230	26		
Eugene Seale	LB	5'10"	250	23	1	6
Al Smith	LB	6'1"	230	22		
#Larry Smith	LB	6'1"	210	22		
#Paul Vogel	LB	6'1"	220	23		
#Earl Allen	DB	5'11"	193	21		
Patrick Allen	DB	5'10"	180	26	1	
#Craig Birdsong	DB	6'2"	217	23		
Keith Bostic	DB	6'1"	223	26	6	
Sonny Brown	DB	6'2"	200	23		
Steve Brown	DB	5'11'	187	27	2	
Domingo Bryant	DB	6'4"	175	23	4	
#Charles Clinton	DB	5'8"	170	25		
Jeff Donaldson	DB	6'	194	25	4	
Bo Eason	DB	6'2"	205	26		
Kenny Johnson	DB	5'10"	175	29		
Richard Johnson	DB	6'1"	190	23	1	
#Larry Joyner	DB	6'	207	23		
Kurt Kafentzis	DB	6'2"	190	24		
Allen Lyday	DB	5'10"	192	26		
Audrey McMillian	DB	6'	190	23	1	
Tony Newsom	DB	5'8"	175	22	1	
#Donovan Small	DB	5'11"	190	23	1	
#Emmuel Thompson	DB	5'11'	180	27		
#Robert White	DB	6'2"	180	24		
Cody Carlson	QB	6'3"	203	24		
Warren Moon	QB	6'3"	210	31		
Brent Pease	QB	6'2"	200	22		6
#John Witkowski	QB	6'1"	195	25		
#Eric Cobble	HB	5'10"	205	23		
#Herman Hunter	HB	6'1"	205	26		
Andrew Jackson	HB	5'10"	190	23		6
Allen Pinkett	HB	5'9"	185	23		
Mike Rozier	HB	5'10"	211	26		
Spencer Tillman	HB	5'11"	206	23		6
Ira Valentine	HB	6'	212	24		
Alonzo Highsmith	FB	6'1"	235	22		18
#Ricky Moore	FB	5'11"	230	24		
Ray Wallace	FB	6'	220	23		
#Chris Darrington	WR	5'10"	180	23		
Willie Drewrey	WR	5'7"	164	24		
Curtis Duncan	WR	5'11"	184	22		30
Ernest Givins	WR	5'9"	170	31		36
#Leonard Harris	WR	5'8"	165	26		
Drew Hill	WR	5'9"	170	31		36
Haywood Jeffires	WR	6'2"	198	22		
#Keith McDonald	WR	5'9"	170	23		6
Joey Walters	WR	5'11"	175	29		
#Oliver Williams	WR	6'3"	195	26		6
Mitch Daum	TE	6'5"	250	23		
#Scott Eccles	TE	6'5"	245	24		
Mark Gehring	TE	6'4"	235	23		6
#Arrike James	TE	6'4"	238	23		
Jeff Parks	TE	6'4"	240	23		
Jamie Williams	TE	6'4"	245	27		18
#John Diettrich	K	6'2"	190	24		23
Lee Johnson (to CLE)	K	6'2"	198	25		
Steve Superick	K	5'11"	204	23		
Tony Zendejas	K	5'8"	165	27		92

PITTSBURGH STEELERS 8-7 Chuck Noll

Scores of Each Game		
30	SAN FRANCISCO	17
10	Cleveland	34
28	Atlanta	12
21	L.A.Rams	31
21	INDIANAPOLIS	7
23	CINCINNATI	20
24	Miami	35
17	Kansas City	16
3	HOUSTON	23
30	Cincinnati	16
16	NEW ORLEANS	20
13	SEATTLE	9
20	San Diego	16
16	Houston	24
13	CLEVELAND	19

Use Name	Pos.	Hgt	Wgt	Age	Int	Pts
Buddy Aydelette	OT-C	6'4"	262	31		
#Jim Boyle	OT	6'5"	270	25		
Tunch Ilkin	OT	6'3"	265	29		
#Jeff Lucas	OT	6'7"	288	23		
Ray Pinney	OT	6'4"	270	33		
Jerry Quick	OT	6'5"	279	23		
#Robert Washington	OT	6'4"	251	24		
Brian Blankenship	OG	6'1"	281	24		
#Charlie Dickey	OG	6'3"	270	24		
#Ben Lawrence	OG	6'1"	325	23		
Terry Long	OG	5'11"265		28		
#Ted Petersen	OG-OT	6'5"	235	32		
John Rienstra	OG	6'5"	275	23		
Craig Wolfley	OG-OT	6'1"	268	29		
#John Lott	C-OG	6'2"	260	23		
Paul Oswald	C	6'3"	273	23		
Mike Webster	C	6'1"	260	35		
#Tommy Dawkins	DE	6'3"	260	22		
Keith Gary	DE	6'3"	265	27		
Tim Johnson	DE	6'3"	260	22		
Edmund Nelson	DE-DT	6'3"	275	27		
#Brett Shugarts	DE	6'2"	250	27		
#Xavier Warren	DE	6'1"	250	23		
Gerald Williams	DE-DT	6'3"	270	23		
Keith Willis	DE	6'1"	263	28		
Gary Dunn	NT	6'3"	275	31		
Lorenzo Freeman	NT-DT	6'5"	270	23		
#Alan Huff	NT	6'4"	265	23		
#Michael Minter	NT	6'3"	275	22		
#David Opfar	NT	6'4"	270	27		
#Steve Apke	LB	6'1"	222	22		
#Craig Bingham	LB	6'2"	227	27		
Gregg Carr	LB	6'2"	220	25		2
Robin Cole	LB	6'2"	225	31	1	
Bryan Hinkle	LB	6'2"	220	28	3	
Darryl Knox	LB	6'3"	220	24		
#David Little	LB	6'1"	240	28		
Mike Merriweather	LB	6'2"	219	26	2	
Hardy Nickerson	LB	6'2"	219	22		
#Avon Riley	LB	6'3"	242	29	1	
Tyronne Stowe	LB	6'1"	235	22		
#Albert Williams	LB	6'3"	229	27		
#Joe Williams	LB	6'4"	237	22		
Ken Woodard	LB	6'1"	218	27		
#Dave Edwards	DB	6'	202	25	1	
Thomas Everett	DB	5'9"	179	23	3	
Cornell Gowdy	DB	6'1"	195	23	2	6
Larry Griffin	DB	6'	190	24	2	
Delton Hall	DB	6'1"	195	22	3	12
Bruce Jones	DB	6'1"	197	22		
Kelvin Middleton	DB	6'	186	25		
#Rock Richmond	DB	5'10"	180	23		
#Cameron Riley	DB	6'1"	195	23		
Lupe Sanchez	DB	5'10"	192	25		
Donnie Shell	DB	5'11"	198	35	1	12
#Anthony Tuggle	DB	6'1"	211	23		
#Ray Williams	DB	5'11"	198	21	1	
Dwayne Woodruff	DB	6'	198	30	5	6
Rod Woodson	DB	6'	195	22	1	6
Steve Bono	QB	6'4"	216	25		6
Bubby Brister	QB	6'3"	200	25		
#Reggie Collier	QB	6'3"	207	26		
Mark Malone	QB	6'4"	216	28		18
Walter Abercrombie	HB	6'	210	27		12
Rodney Carter	HB	6'	222	22		18
#Spark Clark	HB	5'7"	182	22		
Earnest Jackson	HB	5'9"	225	27		6
Dwight Stone	HB	6'	188	23		
Frank Pollard	FB	5'10"	230	30		18
Merril Hoge	FB	6'2"	212	22		6
#Dan Reeder	FB	5'11"	235	26		
Chuck Sanders	FB	6'1"	233	23		6
#Lyneal Alston	WR	6'1"	205	23		12
Melvin Anderson	WR	5'11"	175	22		
Joey Clinkscales	WR	6'	199	23		6
#Moses Ford	WR	6'2"	220	23		
#Russell Hairston	WR	6'3"	206	24		6
Louis Lipps	WR	5'10"	187	25		
Charles Lockett	WR	6'	175	21		6
John Stallworth	WR	6'2"	206	35		12
Calvin Sweeney	WR	6'2"	192	32		
Weegie Thompson	WR	6'6"	210	26		6
#Ralph Britt	TE	6'3"	240	22		
Preston Gothard	TE	6'4"	242	25		6
Danzell Lee	TE	6'2"	232	24		
Theo Young	TE	6'2"	237	22		
Gary Anderson	K	5'11"	179	28		87
#John Bruno	K	6'2"	190	22		
Harry Newsome	K	6'	189	24		
#David Trout	K	5'6"	169	29		10

Mark Behning - Achilles Tendon Injury
Rich Erenberg - Knee Injury
Anthony Henton - Knee Injury

CINCINNATI BENGALS 4-11 Sam Wyche

Scores of Each Game		
23	Indianapolis	21
26	SAN FRANCISCO	27
9	SAN DIEGO	10
17	Seattle	10
0	CLEVELAND	34
20	Pittsburgh	23
29	HOUSTON	31
14	MIAMI	20
16	Atlanta	10
16	PITTSBURGH	30
20	N.Y.Jets	27
30	KANSAS CITY	*27
24	Cleveland	38
24	NEW ORLEANS	41
17	Houston	21

Use Name	Pos.	Hgt	Wgt	Age	Int	Pts
#Keith Cupp	OT	6'6"	301	23		
Anthony Munoz	OT	6'6"	278	29		6
#Bob Riley	OT	6'5"	276	23		
#Tom Richey	OT	6'4"	274	26		
#Mark Tigges	OT	6'3"	290	23		
Joe Walter	OT	6'6"	290	24		
Doug Aronson	OG	6'3"	293	22		
Brian Blados	OG	6'5"	295	25		
#John Fletcher	OG	6'3"	293	22		
Bruce Kozerski	OG	6'4"	275	25		
Max Montoya	OG	6'5"	275	31		
#Bill Poe	OG	6'3"	280	23		
Bruce Reimers	OG-OT	6'7"	280	26		
#Ken Smith	OG	6'1"	285	26		
David Douglas	C-OG	6'4"	280	24		
#Sam Manos	C	6'3"	265	25		
Dave Rimington	C	6'3"	288	25		
Jason Buck	DE	6'5"	264	24		
Eddie Edwards	DE	6'5"	256	33		
#Willie Fears	DE	6'3"	278	23		
Mike Hammerstein	DE	6'4"	270	24		
Skip McClendon	DE	6'7"	270	23		
#Jeff Reinke	DE	6'4"	262	24		
Jim Skow	DE	6'3"	250	24		
#Jeff Smith	DE	6'4"	248	25		
#Bill Berthusen (to NYG)	NT	6'5"	290	23		
#James Eaddy	NT	6'2"	280	24		
Tim Krumrie	NT	6'2"	262	27		
Leo Barker	LB	6'2"	227	27		
Ed Brady	LB	6'2"	235	27		
#Toney Catchings	LB	6'3"	236	22		
Kiki DeAyala	LB	6'1"	225	25		
#Tom Flaherty	LB	6'3"	223	22		
Tim Inglis	LB	6'3"	232	23		
Joe Kelly	LB	6'2"	227	22		
Emanuel King	LB	6'4"	251	24		
#Scott Schutt	LB	6'4"	218	24		2
#Lance Sellers	LB	6'1"	230	24		
#David Ward	LB	6'2"	230	23		
Leon White	LB	6'2"	236	23		
Reggie Williams	LB	6'1"	228	32		
Carl Zander	LB	6'2"	235	24		
#Chris Barber	DB	6'	187	23		
Lewis Billups	DB	5'11"	190	23		
#Nate Borders	DB	5'10"	190	24		
Louis Breeden	DB	5'11"	185	34	2	
Barney Bussey	DB	6'	195	25	1	
David Fulcher	DB	6'3"	228	23	3	
Ray Horton	DB	5'11"	190	27		
Gary Hunt	DB	5'11"	175	23		
Robert Jackson	DB	5'10"	186	28	3	
#Mark Johnson	DB	6'1"	194	23		
#Aaron Manning	DB	5'10"	178	26		
#Rob Niehoff	DB	6'2"	205	23	1	
#Daryl Smith	DB	5'9"	185	24	2	
Eric Thomas	DB	5'11"	175	22	1	
Solomon Wilcots	DB	5'11"	180	22	1	
#Ben Bennett	QB	6'1"	200	25		
#Adrian Breen	QB	6'4"	183	22		
Boomer Esiason	QB	6'4"	220	26		
Mike Norseth	QB	6'2"	200	23		
Turk Schonert	QB	6'1"	196	30		
#Dave Walter	QB	6'3"	230	23		
James Brooks	HB	5'10"	182	27		18
Stanford Jennings	HB	6'1"	205	25		18
#Marc Logan	HB	5'11"	204	22		6
#Pat Franklin	FB	6'1"	230	24		
Bill Johnson	FB	6'2"	230	26		6
Larry Kinnebrew	FB	6'1"	258	28		48
#David McCluskey	FB	6'1"	227	23		6
#Dan Rice	FB	6'1"	241	23		
Dana Wright	FB	6'1"	219	24		
Eddie Brown	WR	6'	185	24		18
#Ken Brown	WR	5'8"	175	22		
#Tom Brown	WR	6'4"	190	23		
Cris Collinsworth	WR	6'5"	192	28		
Ira Hillary	WR	5'11"	190	24		
Mike Martin	WR	5'10"	186	26		18
Tim McGee	WR	5'10"	175	23		6
#Greg Meehan	WR	6'	191	24		
#Marquis Pleasant	WR	6'2"	172	22		
#Rodney Tweet	WR	6'1"	195	23		
Rodney Holman	TE	6'3"	238	27		12
#Curtis Jeffries	TE	6'4"	236	22		
Eric Kattus	TE	6'5"	235	24		
Jim Riggs	TE	6'5"	245	23		
#Dave Romasko	TE	6'3"	241	23		
#Wade Russell	TE	6'4"	250	24		6
#Reggie Sims	TE	6'4"	253	23		
Jim Breech	K	5'6"	161	31		97
Scott Fulhage	K	5'11"	191	25		
#Massimo Manca	K	5'10"	211	23		

Stanley Wilson - Suspended by N.F.L.

* Overtime

- on the active roster for strike replacement games only

HOUSTON OILERS

RUSHING

Last Name	No.	Yds	Avg	TD
Rozier	229	957	4.2	3
Jackson	60	232	3.9	1
Pinkett	31	149	4.8	2
Hunter	34	144	4.2	0
Moon	34	112	3.3	3
Highsmith	29	106	3.7	1
Wallace	19	102	5.4	0
Pease	15	33	2.2	1
Tillman	12	29	2.4	1
Cobble	9	23	2.6	0
Moore	7	22	3.1	0
Valentine	5	10	2.0	0
Harris	1	17	17.0	0
Givins	1	-13	-13.0	0

RECEIVING

Last Name	No.	Yds	Avg	TD
Givins	53	933	17.6	6
D. Hill	49	989	20.2	6
Rozier	27	192	7.1	0
Duncan	13	237	18.2	5
J. Williams	13	158	12.2	3
O. Williams	11	165	15.0	1
Drewrey	11	148	13.5	0
Harris	10	164	16.4	0
Jackson	10	44	4.4	0
Jeffires	7	89	12.7	0
Wallace	7	34	4.9	0
Walters	5	99	19.8	0
Gehring	5	64	12.8	1
McDonald	4	56	14.0	1
Highsmith	4	55	13.8	1
Moore	3	21	7.0	0
Hunter	3	17	5.7	0
Valentine	2	10	5.0	0
Darrington	1	38	38.0	0
James	1	14	14.0	0
Pinkett	1	7	7.0	0

PUNT RETURNS

Last Name	No.	Yds	Avg	TD
K. Johnson	24	196	8.2	0
Duncan	8	23	2.9	0
Drewrey	3	11	3.7	0
Walters	2	19	9.5	0

KICKOFF RETURNS

Last Name	No.	Yds	Avg	TD
Duncan	28	546	19.5	0
Pinkett	17	322	18.9	0
Drewrey	8	136	17.0	0
Hunter	4	79	19.8	0
Harris	3	87	29.0	0
K. Johnson	2	24	12.0	0
Walters	1	18	18.0	0
Valentine	1	13	13.0	0
J. Davis	1	0	0.0	0
Fuller	1	0	0.0	0
Tillman	1	0	0.0	0

PASSING — PUNTING — KICKING

PASSING	Att	Cmp	%	Yds	Yd/Att	TD	Int—	%	RK
Moon	368	184	50	2806	7.6	21	18—	5	18
Pease	113	56	50	728	6.4	3	5—	4	
D. Hill	1	0	0	0	0.0	0	0—	0	

PUNTING	No	Avg
Johnson	41	40.3
Superick	8	33.6

KICKING	XP	Att	%	FG	Att	%
Zendejas	32	33	97	20	26	77
Dietrich	5	5	100	6	6	100

PITTSBURGH STEELERS

RUSHING

Last Name	No.	Yds	Avg	TD
Jackson	180	696	3.9	1
Pollard	128	536	4.2	3
Abercrombie	123	459	3.7	2
Malone	34	162	4.8	3
Stone	17	135	7.9	0
Sanders	11	65	5.9	1
Bono	8	27	3.4	1
Collier	4	20	5.0	0
Newsome	2	16	8.0	0
Carter	5	12	2.4	0
Hoge	3	8	2.7	0
Reeder	2	8	4.0	0

RECEIVING

Last Name	No.	Yds	Avg	TD
Stallworth	41	521	12.7	2
Abercrombie	24	209	8.7	0
Thompson	17	313	18.4	1
Sweeney	16	217	13.6	0
Carter	16	180	11.3	3
Pollard	14	77	5.5	0
Clinkscales	13	240	18.5	1
Lee	12	124	10.3	0
Lipps	11	164	14.9	0
Lockett	7	116	16.6	1
Hoge	7	97	13.9	1
Jackson	7	52	7.4	0
Alston	3	84	28.0	2
Hairston	2	16	8.0	1
Young	2	10	5.0	0
Gothard	2	9	4.5	1
Stone	1	22	22.0	0
Sanders	1	11	11.0	0
Bono	1	2	2.0	0
Boyle	1	0	0.0	0

PUNT RETURNS

Last Name	No.	Yds	Avg	TD
Woodson	16	135	8.4	0
Lipps	7	46	6.6	0
Anderson	7	38	5.4	0
Everett	4	22	5.5	0
Lockett	2	3	1.5	0

KICKOFF RETURNS

Last Name	No.	Yds	Avg	TD
Stone	28	568	20.3	0
Woodson	13	290	22.3	0
Sanchez	6	116	19.3	0
Jones	2	38	19.0	0
Britt	2	9	4.5	0
Clark	1	18	18.0	0
Hoge	1	13	13.0	0
Gowdy	1	0	0.0	0
Riley	1	0	0.0	0

PASSING — PUNTING — KICKING

PASSING	Att	Cmp	%	Yds	Yd/Att	TD	Int—	%	RK
Malone	336	156	46	1896	5.6	6	19—	6	27
Bono	74	34	46	438	5.9	5	2—	3	
Brister	12	4	33	20	1.7	0	3—	25	
Collier	7	4	57	110	15.7	2	1—	14	

PUNTING	No	Avg
Newsome	65	41.2
Bruno	17	36.4

KICKING	XP	Att	%	FG	Att	%
Anderson	21	21	100	22	27	82
Trout	10	10	100	0	2	0

CINCINNATI BENGALS

RUSHING

Last Name	No.	Yds	Avg	TD
Kinnebrew	145	570	3.9	8
Jennings	70	314	4.5	1
Brooks	94	290	3.1	1
Esiason	52	241	4.6	0
B. Johnson	39	205	5.3	1
Logan	37	203	5.5	1
McCluskey	29	94	3.2	1
Wright	24	74	3.1	0
Rice	18	59	3.3	0
D. Walter	16	70	4.4	0
Meehan	4	19	4.8	0
Breen	6	18	3.0	0
Bennett	2	17	8.5	0
Brown	1	0	0.0	0
McGee	1	-10	-10.0	0

RECEIVING

Last Name	No.	Yds	Avg	TD
E. Brown	44	608	13.8	3
Jennings	35	277	7.9	2
Collinsworth	31	494	15.9	0
Holman	28	438	15.6	2
McGee	23	408	17.7	1
Brooks	22	272	12.4	2
Martin	20	394	19.7	3
Kattus	18	217	12.1	2
Kinnebrew	9	114	12.7	0
Hillary	5	65	13.0	0
Wright	4	28	7.0	0
Meehan	3	25	8.3	0
B. Johnson	3	19	6.3	0
Logan	3	14	4.7	0
Pleasant	2	45	22.5	0
Russell	2	27	13.5	1
Munoz	2	15	7.5	1
McCluskey	1	8	8.0	0

PUNT RETURNS

Last Name	No.	Yds	Avg	TD
Martin	28	277	9.9	0
K. Brown	5	16	3.2	0
Horton	1	0	0.0	0

KICKOFF RETURNS

Last Name	No.	Yds	Avg	TD
Bussey	21	406	19.3	0
McGee	15	242	16.1	0
Wright	13	266	20.5	0
K. Brown	3	45	15.0	0
Logan	3	31	10.3	0
Martin	3	51	17.0	0
Brooks	2	42	21.0	0
Jennings	2	32	16.0	0
Kattus	2	22	11.0	0
Hillary	1	15	15.0	0
Meehan	1	9	9.0	0
Fulcher	1	0	0.0	0

PASSING — PUNTING — KICKING

PASSING	Att	Cmp	%	Yds	Yd/Att	TD	Int—	%	RK
Esiason	440	240	55	3321	7.6	16	19—	4	20
D. Walter	21	10	48	113	5.4	0	0—	0	
Breen	8	3	38	9	1.1	1	0—	0	
Bennett	6	2	33	25	4.2	0	1—	17	

PUNTING	No.	Avg.
Fulhage	52	41.7
Esiason	2	34.0

KICKING	XP	Att	%	FG	Att	%
Breech	25	27	93	24	30	80
Manca	3	3	100	1	2	50

Western Division

DENVER BRONCOS 10-4-1 Dan Reeves

Scores of Each Game		
40	SEATTLE	17
17	Green Bay	*17
10	HOUSTON	40
30	L.A.RAIDERS	14
26	Kansas City	17
27	Minnesota	34
34	DETROIT	0
14	Buffalo	21
31	CHICAGO	29
23	L.A.Raiders	17
31	San Diego	17
31	NEW ENGLAND	20
21	Seattle	28
20	KANSAS CITY	17
24	SAN DIEGO	0

Use Name	Pos.	Hgt	Wgt	Age	Int	Pts
Kevin Belcher	OT	6'5"	310	25		
Archie Harris	OT	6'6"	270	22		
Keith Kartz	OT	6'4"	270	24		
Ken Lanier	OT	6'3"	269	28		
Dan Remsberg	OT	6'6"	275	25		
Dave Studdard	OT	6'4"	260	31		
John Ayers	OG	6'5"	265	34		
Keith Bishop	OG-C	6'3"	265	30		
#Winford Hood	OG	6'3"	265	25		
Stefan Humphries	OG	6'3"	268	25		
Billy Bryan	C	6'2"	255	31		
Mike Freeman	C-OG	6'3"	256	25		
David Jones	C	6'3"	266	25		
Larry Lee	C-OG	6'2"	263	27		
#Jack Peavey	C	6'2"	260	24		
Walt Bowyer	DE	6'4"	260	26		
Steve Bryan	DE-NT	6'2"	256	23		
Freddie Gilbert	DE	6'4"	275	25		
Rulon Jones	DE	6'6"	260	29		
#Bill Lobenstein	DE-NT	6'3"	261	26		
#Ron McLean	DE-NT	6'3"	267	24		
Greg Kragen	NT	6'3"	245	25		
Karl Mecklenburg	DE-LB	6'3"	230	27	3	
Andre Townsend	DE-NT	6'3"	265	24		
Jeff Tupper	NT	6'5"	269	24		
Michael Brooks	LB	6'1"	235	22		
Rick Dennison	LB	6'3"	220	29	1	
#Kirk Dodge	LB	6'1"	233	25	2	6
Simon Fletcher	LB	6'5"	240	25		
Ricky Hunley	LB	6'2"	238	25	2	6
#Tim Joiner	LB	6'4"	235	25		
Bruce Klostermann	LB	6'4"	225	24		
#Mike Knox	LB	6'2"	240	24		
Tim Lucas	LB	6'3"	230	26	1	
#Dan MacDonald	LB	6'2"	230	23		
Marc Munford	LB	6'2"	231	22		
Jim Ryan	LB	6'1"	225	30	3	
#Matt Smith	LB	6'2"	234	22		
#Bryant Winn	LB	6'4"	231	26		
Tyrone Braxton	DB	5'11"	174	22		
Jeremiah Castille	DB	5'10"	175	26		
Kevin Clark	DB	5'10"	185	23	3	6
#Steve Fitzhugh	DB	5'11"	188	24		
Mike Harden	DB	6'1"	192	28	4	
Mark Haynes	DB	5'11"	195	28	3	6
#Roger Jackson	DB	6'	185	28		
#Earl Johnson	DB	6'	200	23		
#Darryl Jones	DB	6'	193	25		
Tony Lilly	DB	6'	199	25	3	
#Lyle Pickens	DB	5'10"	175	22		
Bruce Plummer	DB	6'1"	197	23		
Randy Robbins	DB	6'2"	189	24	3	
#Martin Rudolph	DB	5'10"	183	22		
#Darryl Russell	DB	6'	190	22		
Dennis Smith	DB	6'3"	200	28	2	
Steve Wilson	DB	5'10"	195	30		
John Elway	QB	6'3"	210	26		24
#Ken Karcher	QB	6'3"	205	24		
Gary Kubiak	QB	6'	192	25		
#Dean May	QB	6'5"	220	25		
#Monte McGuire	QB	6'4"	202	23		
Ken Bell	HB	5'10"	190	22		
Tony Boddie	HB	5'11"	198	26		6
#Scott Caldwell	HB	5'10"	196	25		
#Joe Dudek	HB	6'	181	23		12
Gene Lang	HB	5'10"	196	25		24
#Nathan Poole	HB	5'9"	212	30		6
Gerald Willhite	HB	5'10"	200	28		
Samy Winder	HB	5'11"	203	28		42
Warren Marshall	FB	6'	216	23		
Bobby Micho	FB	6'3"	240	25		12
Steve Sewell	FB	6'3"	210	24		18
#Laron Brown	WR	5'9"	172	23		
Sam Graddy	WR	5'10"	165	23		
Mark Jackson	WR	5'9"	174	24		12
Vance Johnson	WR	5'11"	185	24		42
Rick Massie	WR	6'1"	190	27		24
Ricky Nattiel	WR	5'9"	180	21		12
#Shane Swanson	WR	5'9"	200	24		6
#Robert Thompson	WR	5'9"	168	23		
Steve Watson	WR	6'4"	195	30		6
Mitch Andrews	TE	6'2"	239	23		
Clarence Kay	TE	6'2"	237	26		
#Kerry Locklin	TE	6'3"	242	27		
Orson Mobley	TE	6'5"	256	24		6
#Russell Payne	TE	6'1"	240	22		
#Mike Clendenen	K	5'11"	190	24		16
#Ralph Giacomarro	K	6'1"	196	26		
Mike Horan	K	5'11"	180	27		
Rich Karlis	K	6'	180	27		91

Tony Colorito - Knee Injury

SEATTLE SEAHAWKS 9-6 Chuck Knox

Scores of Each Game		
17	Denver	40
43	KANSAS CITY	14
24	MIAMI	20
10	CINCINNATI	17
37	Detroit	14
35	L.A.Raiders	13
28	MINNESOTA	17
14	N.Y.Jets	30
24	GREEN BAY	13
34	SAN DIEGO	3
14	L.A.RAIDERS	37
9	Pittsburgh	13
28	DENVER	21
34	Chicago	21
20	Kansas City	41

Use Name	Pos.	Hgt	Wgt	Age	Int	Pts
John Borchardt	OT	6'5"	272	30		
#Tim Burnham	OT	6'5"	280	24		
Ron Mattes	OT	6'6"	306	24		
#Howard Richards	OT	6'6"	272	28		
#Ron Scoggins	OT	6'6"	305	27		
Mike Wilson	OT	6'5"	280	32		
Edwin Bailey	OG	6'4"	276	28		
#Matt Hanousek	OG-OT	6'4"	265	24		
Bryan Millard	OG	6'5"	284	26		
Alvin Powell	OG	6'5"	291	27		
#Jack Sims	OG	6'3"	260	25		
#Garth Thomas	OG	6'3"	260	23		
#Tom Andrews	C-OG	6'4"	267	25		
Blair Bush	C	6'3"	272	30		
Stan Eisenhooth	C	6'5"	300	24		
Grant Feasel	C	6'7"	280	27		
Doug Hire	C	6'2"	245	22		
#Dean Perryman	C	6'3"	260	23		
Jeff Bryant	DE	6'5"	272	30		
#Dale Dorning	DE	6'5"	260	25		
Wes Dove	DE	6'7"	270	23		
Randy Edwards	DE	6'4"	267	26		
#Don Fairbanks	DE	6'3"	253	23		
Jacob Green	DE	6'3"	252	30		
#Doug Hollie	DE	6'4"	265	26		
#Van Hughes	DE	6'3"	280	26		
Alonzo Mitz	DE	6'3"	273	24		
#Greg Ramsey	DE	6'3"	244	23		
Roland Barbay	NT	6'4"	260	22		
#John Eisenhooth	NT	6'2"	265	25		
#David Graham	NT	6'6"	250	28		
Joe Nash	NT	6'2"	257	26		
#Charles Wiley	NT	6'2"	268	22		
#Lester Williams	NT	6'3"	290	28		
Brian Bosworth	LB	6'2"	248	22		
Keith Butler	LB	6'4"	239	31		
#Tony Caldwell	LB	6'1"	220	26	1	
#Julio Cortes	LB	6'	226	26		
#Rob DeVita	LB	6'2"	222	28		
Greg Gaines	LB	6'3"	222	28		
#Joe Jackson	LB	6'1"	225	24		
M.L.Johnson	LB	6'3"	225	24		
Paul Lavine	LB	6'2"	207	25		
#John McVeigh	LB	6'1"	226	24		
Sam Merriman	LB	6'3"	232	26		
#Fred Orns	LB	6'2"	230	25		
Bruce Scholtz	LB	6'6"	241	28		
#Joe Terry	LB	6'2"	222	25		
#Rico Tipton	LB	6'2"	240	26		
Tony Woods	LB	6'4"	244	21		
David Wyman	LB	6'2"	231	23		
Fredd Young	LB	6'1"	233	25	1	6
#Harvey Allen	DB	6'3"	215	22		
#Curtis Baham	DB	5'11"	180	24		
#Anthony Blue	DB	5'9"	185	22		
#Arnold Brown	DB	5'10"	185	25		
#Fred Davis	DB	5'10"	182	23		
Kenny Easley	DB	6'3"	198	28	4	
#Charles Glaze	DB	5'11"	200	21	2	
David Hollis	DB	5'11"	175	22		
Patrick Hunter	DB	5'11"	185	22	1	
Melvin Jenkins	DB	5'10"	170	25	3	
Kerry Justin	DB	5'11"	185	32		
#Kim Mack	DB	6'	190	25		
Mark Moore	DB	6'	194	22		
Paul Moyer	DB	6'1"	201	25	1	
Eugene Robinson	DB	6'	186	24	3	
#Dallis Smith	DB	5'11"	170	22		
Terry Taylor	DB	5'10"	191	26	1	
#Ricky Thomas	DB	6'	185	22		
#Chris White	DB	6'3"	200	25		
#Renard Young	DB	5'10"	184	26		
Jeff Kemp	QB	6'	201	27		
Dave Krieg	QB	6'1"	196	28		12
#David Lindley	QB	6'	190	22		
#Bruce Mathison	QB	6'3"	205	28		
Bobby Joe Edmonds	HB	5'11"	186	22		
#Boyce Green	HB	5'11"	215	27		
#Alvin Moore	HB	6'	190	28		
Randall Morris	HB	6'	200	25		
#Michael Morton	HB	5'8"	175	27		
#Rick Parros	HB	5'11"	202	29		6
Curt Warner	HB	5'11"	205	26		60
Tony Burse	FB	6'	220	22		
#Mike Hagen	FB	6'	240	28		
Eric Lane	FB	6'	201	28		
#Chad Stark	FB	6'1"	220	22		
#James Williams	FB	5'10"	210	23		
John L.Williams	FB	5'11"	226	22		24
#Brent Bengen	WR	5'8"	172	23		
Ray Butler	WR	6'3"	206	23		
Louis Clark	WR	6'1"	193	23		
#Russell Evans	WR	5'8"	165	22		
Byron Franklin	WR	6'1"	183	28		
#Kevin Juma	WR	6'2"	195	25		
Steve Largent	WR	5'11"	191	32		48
#Curt Pardridge	WR	5'10"	175	23		
Paul Skansi	WR	5'11"	190	26		
#Donald Snell	WR	6'2"	177	22		
Jimmy Teal	WR	5'10"	175	25		12
Daryl Turner	WR	6'3"	194	25		36
#Chris Corley	TE	6'4"	285	23		
#John O'Callaghan	TE	6'4"	245	23		
#Ken Sager	TE	6'4"	228	23		
Wilbur Strozier	TE	6'4"	255	22		
Mike Tice	TE	6'7"	247	28		12
#Barry Bowman	K	5'11"	180	22		
#Russell Griffith	K	5'11"	175	22		
#Scott Hagler	K	5'8"	160	23		
Norm Johnson	K	6'2"	200	22		85
Ruben Rodriguez	K	6'2"	198	26		

Gale Gilbert - Knee Injury
Curt Singer - Ankle Injury

SAN DIEGO CHARGERS 8-7 Al Saunders

Scores of Each Game		
13	Kansas City	20
28	ST.LOUIS	24
10	Cincinnati	9
17	Tampa Bay	13
23	L.A.Raiders	17
42	KANSAS CITY	21
27	CLEVELAND	*24
16	Indianapolis	13
16	L.A.RAIDERS	14
3	Seattle	34
17	DENVER	31
18	Houston	33
16	PITTSBURGH	20
7	INDIANAPOLIS	20
0	Denver	24

Use Name	Pos.	Hgt	Wgt	Age	Int	Pts
#Greg Feasel	OT	6'7"	301	29		
Gary Kowalski	OT-OG	6'6"	280	27		
Jim Lachey	OT	6'6"	289	24		
#Emil Slovacek	OT	6'3"	300	24		
Curtis Rouse	OT-OG	6'3"	340	27		
Sam Claphan	OG-OT	6'6"	288	30		
Ken Dallafior	OG	6'4"	278	28		
James FitzPatrick	OG-OT	6'8"	286	23		
Dennis McKnight	OG-C	6'3"	270	33		
Dan Rosado	OG	6'3"	280	28		
Broderick Thompson	OG-OT	6'5"	290	27		
#David Diaz-Infante	C-OG	6'2"	272	23		
Don Macek	C	6'3"	270	33		
#John Stadnik	C	6'4"	275	27		
Keith Baldwin	DE	6'4"	270	26		
#Monte Bennett	DE	6'3"	270	28		
#Willard Goff	DE	6'4"	265	25		
Dee Hardison	DE	6'4"	291	31		
Les Miller	DE	6'7"	285	22		6
#Duane Pettitt	DE	6'4"	265	22		
Joe Phillips	DE	6'5"	275	24		
Tony Simmons	DE	6'5"	268	24		
Terry Unrein	DE-NT	6'5"	280	24		
Lee Williams	DE	6'6"	263	24		2
Earl Wilson	DE	6'4"	280	28		
Karl Wilson	DE	6'4"	268	22		
Mike Charles	NT	6'4"	287	24		
Chuck Ehin	NT-LB	6'4"	266	25		2
#Blaisie Winter	NT	6'3"	274	25		
Chip Banks	LB	6'4"	236	27	1	
Thomas Benson	LB	6'2"	235	25		
David Brandon	LB	6'4"	225	24		6
Steve Busick	LB	6'4"	227	27		
Andy Hawkins	LB	6'2"	230	29		
Mike Humiston	LB	6'3"	245	28		
#Brian Ingram	LB	6'4"	245	27		
Jeff Jackson	LB	6'1"	230	25		
Randy Kirk	LB	6'2"	235	22		
Gary Plummer	LB	6'2"	240	27	1	
Billy Ray Smith	LB	6'3"	236	26	5	
Johnny Taylor	LB	6'4"	237	27		
Anthony Anderson	DB	6'2"	205	22		
Martin Bayless	DB	6'2"	200	24		
#Ed Berry	DB	5'10"	183	24		
#Carl Brazley	DB	6'	180	30	1	
Gill Byrd	DB	5'11"	195	26		
Vencie Glenn	DB	6'	187	22	4	6
#Walter Harris	DB	6'1"	195	23		
Darrell Hopper	DB	6'1"	196	23		
Mike Hudson	DB	6'	202	23		
Daniel Hunter	DB	5'11"	178	25		
Elvis Patterson (from NYG)	DB	5'11"	198	26	1	6
#Stacey Price	DB	6'2"	194	25		
Charles Romes	DB	6'1"	190	32		
#King Simmons	DB	6'2"	199	24		
Danny Walters	DB	6'1"	200	26		
Ted Watts	DB	6'	205	29		
Dan Fouts	QB	6'3"	210	35		12
Mark Herrmann	QB	6'4"	207	28		
#Mike Kelley	QB	6'3"	195	27		
#Rick Neuheisel	QB	6'1"	190	26		7
Mark Vlasic	QB	6'3"	206	23		
Curtis Adams	HB	6'	194	25		6
Gary Anderson	HB	6'1"	188	26		30
#Keyvan Jenkins	HB	5'10"	190	26		
#Frank Middleton	HB	5'11"	210	26		6
#Jeff Powell	HB	5'10"	185	24		
#Martin Sartin	HB	5'10"	202	24		6
#Todd Spencer	HB	6'	209	25		
#Anthony Steels	HB	5'9"	200	28		
Barry Redden	FB	5'10"	219	27		
Tim Spencer	FB	6'2"	227	26		
#Ken Zachary	FB	6'	222	23		
Wes Chandler	WR	6'	188	31		
Jamie Holland	WR	6'2"	186	23		
Lionel James	WR	5'7"	170	25		36
#Tim Moffett	WR	6'2"	180	25		6
#Calvin Muhammad	WR	6'	195	28		
#Tag Rome	WR	5'9"	175	25		
Timmie Ware	WR	5'10"	170	24		
#Al Williams	WR	5'10"	180	25		6
Rod Bernstine	TE	6'3"	235	22		6
#Kevin Ferguson	TE	6'2"	223	22		
Pete Holohan	TE	6'4"	235	28		
#Harry Holt	TE	6'4"	250	30		
Eric Sievers	TE	6'4"	230	28		
Kellen Winslow	TE	6'5"	251	29		18
Vince Abbott	K	6'	206	29		
#Jeff Gaffney	K	6'2"	195	22		13
Ralf Mojsiejenko	K	6'3"	212	24		
#Joe Prokop	K	6'3"	235	27		

Jeffrey Dale - Back Injury
Woodrow Lowe - Knee Injury
Leslie O'Neal - Knee Injury

* Overtime

- on the active roster for strike replacement only

DENVER BRONCOS

RUSHING

Last Name	No.	Yds	Avg	TD
Winder	196	741	3.8	6
Elway	66	304	4.6	4
Lang	89	303	3.4	2
Dudek	35	154	4.4	2
Willhite	26	141	5.4	0
Poole	28	126	4.5	1
Sewell	19	83	4.4	2
Caldwell	16	53	3.3	0
Bell	13	43	3.3	0
Nattiel	2	13	6.5	0
Micho	4	8	2.0	0
Boddie	3	7	2.3	1
Karcher	9	3	0.3	0
Kubiak	1	3	3.0	0
May	2	-4	-2.0	0
V. Johnson	1	-8	-8.0	0

RECEIVING

Last Name	No.	Yds	Avg	TD
V. Johnson	42	684	16.3	7
Nattiel	31	630	20.3	2
Kay	31	440	14.2	0
Jackson	26	436	16.8	2
Micho	25	242	9.7	2
Lang	17	130	7.6	2
Mobley	16	228	14.3	1
Winder	14	74	5.3	1
Massie	13	244	18.8	4
Sewell	13	209	16.1	1
Watson	11	167	15.2	1
Boddie	9	85	9.4	0
Willhite	9	25	2.8	0
Dudek	7	41	5.9	0
Swanson	6	87	14.5	1
Andrews	4	53	13.3	0
Brown	4	40	10.0	0
Caldwell	4	34	8.5	0
Poole	1	9	9.0	0
Payne	1	8	8.0	0
Bell	1	8	8.0	

PUNT RETURNS

Last Name	No.	Yds	Avg	TD
Clark	18	233	12.9	1
Nattiel	12	73	6.1	0
Swanson	9	132	14.7	0
Willhite	4	22	5.5	0
Harden	2	11	5.5	0
Lilly	2	6	3.0	0
V. Johnson	1	9	9.0	0

KICKOFF RETURNS

Last Name	No.	Yds	Avg	TD
Bell	15	323	21.5	0
Swanson	9	234	26.0	0
Johnson	7	140	20.0	0
Lang	4	78	19.5	0
Nattiel	4	78	19.5	0
Brown	3	57	19.0	0
Clark	2	33	16.5	0
Ryan	2	9	4.5	0

PASSING — PUNTING — KICKING

PASSING	Att	Cmp	%	Yds	Yd/Att	TD	Int—	%	RK
Elway	410	224	55	3198	7.8	19	12—	3	12
Karcher	102	56	55	628	6.2	5	4—	3	
McGuire	3	2	67	23	7.7	0	0—	0	
Lang	1	0	0	0	0.0	0	0—	0	
Willhite	1	0	0	0	0.0	0	0—	0	
V. Johnson	1	0	0	0	0.0	0	0—	0	
Kubiak	7	3	43	25	3.6	0	2—	29	
May	5	0	0	0	0.0	0	1—	20	

PUNTING	No	Avg
Horan	46	39.3
Giacomarro	18	42.1
Elway	1	31.0

KICKING	XP	Att	%	FG	Att	%
Karlis	37	37	100	18	25	72
Clendenen	7	7	100	3	4	75

SEATTLE SEAHAWKS

RUSHING

Last Name	No.	Yds	Avg	TD
Warner	234	985	4.2	8
Williams	113	500	4.4	1
Krieg	36	155	4.3	2
B. Green	21	77	3.7	0
Morris	21	71	3.4	0
Morton	19	52	2.7	1
Lane	13	40	3.1	0
Burse	7	36	5.1	0
Largent	2	33	16.5	0
Parros	13	32	2.5	1
A. Moore	3	15	5.0	0
Mathison	5	15	3.0	0
Kemp	5	9	1.8	0
Hagen	2	3	1.5	0
Griffith	1	0	0.0	0
Rodriguez	1	0	0.0	0

RECEIVING

Last Name	No.	Yds	Avg	TD
Largent	58	912	15.7	8
Jo. Williams	38	420	11.1	3
R. Butler	33	465	14.1	5
Skansi	19	207	10.9	1
Warner	17	167	9.8	2
Teal	14	198	14.1	2
Turner	14	153	10.9	6
Tice	14	106	7.6	2
Pardridge	8	145	18.1	1
Juma	7	95	13.6	0
Lane	4	30	7.5	0
Bengen	2	33	16/5	0
Franklin	1	7	7.0	0
Parros	1	7	7.0	0
Millard	1	-5	-5.0	0

PUNT RETURNS

Last Name	No.	Yds	Avg	TD
Edmonds	20	251	12.6	0
Hollis	6	33	5.5	0
Teal	6	38	6.3	0

KICKOFF RETURNS

Last Name	No.	Yds	Avg	TD
Edmonds	27	564	20.9	0
Hollis	10	263	26.3	0
Morris	9	149	16.6	0
Teal	6	95	15.8	0
Bengen	2	47	23.5	0
Lane	2	34	17.0	0
Pardridge	2	29	14.5	0
Powell	2	23	11.5	0
B. Green	1	20	20.0	0
Scholtz	1	11	11.0	0
Burse	1	1	1.0	0
Hunter	1	0	0.0	0

PASSING — PUNTING — KICKING

PASSING	Att	Cmp	%	Yds	Yd/Att	TD	Int—	%	RK
Krieg	294	178	61	2131	7.3	23	15—	5	6
Mathison	76	36	47	501	6.6	3	5—	7	
Kemp	33	23	70	396	12.0	5	1—	3	
Largent	2	0	0	0	0.0	0	0—	0	

PUNTING	No	Avg
Rodriguez	47	40.0
Griffith	11	35.1
Bowman	3	34.7

KICKING	XP	Att	%	FG	Att	%
Johnson	40	40	100	15	20	75
Hagler	4	4	100	2	2	100

SAN DIEGO CHARGERS

RUSHING

Last Name	No.	Yds	Avg	TD
Adams	90	343	3.8	1
Anderson	80	260	3.3	3
Tim Spencer	73	228	3.1	0
James	27	102	3.8	2
Jenkins	22	88	4.0	0
Middleton	28	74	2.6	1
Sartin	19	52	2.7	1
Neuheisel	6	41	6.8	1
Redden	11	36	3.3	0
Todd Spencer	14	24	1.7	0
Kelley	4	17	4.3	0
Holland	1	17	17.0	0
Bernstine	1	9	9.0	0
Steels	1	3	3.0	0
Zachary	1	3	3.0	0
Moffett	1	1	1.0	0
Fouts	12	0	0.0	2
Herrmann	4	-1	-0.2	0

RECEIVING

Last Name	No.	Yds	Avg	TD
Winslow	53	519	9.8	3
Anderson	47	503	10.7	3
James	41	593	14.5	3
Chandler	39	617	15.8	2
Holohan	20	239	12.0	0
Tim Spencer	17	123	7.2	0
Williams	12	247	20.6	1
Bernstine	10	76	7.6	1
Middleton	8	43	5.4	0
Jenkins	8	40	5.0	0
Holt	7	56	8.0	0
Redden	7	46	6.6	0
Holland	6	138	23.0	0
Rome	6	49	8.2	0
Sartin	6	19	3.2	0
Moffett	5	80	16.0	1
Adams	4	38	9.5	0
Mohammad	2	87	43.5	0
Tom Spencer	2	47	23.5	0
Ware	2	38	19.0	0
Steels	1	4	4.0	0

PUNT RETURNS

Last Name	No.	Yds	Avg	TD
James	32	400	12.5	1
Williams	10	96	9.6	0
Rome	3	12	4.0	0

KICKOFF RETURNS

Last Name	No.	Yds	Avg	TD
Anderson	22	433	19.7	0
Holland	19	410	21.6	0
Sartin	5	117	23.4	0
Adams	4	32	8.0	0
Kirk	3	15	5.0	0
Jenkins	2	46	23.0	0
James	2	41	20.5	0
Rome	2	28	14.0	0
Bernstine	1	13	13.0	0
Zachary	1	2	2.0	0
Hunter	1	0	0.0	0

PASSING — PUNTING — KICKING

PASSING	Att	Cmp	%	Yds	Yd/Att	TD	Int-	%	RK
Fouts	364	206	57	2517	6.9	10	15—	4	22
Neuheisel	59	40	68	367	6.2	1	1—	2	
Herrmann	57	37	65	405	7.1	1	5—	9	
Kelley	29	17	59	305	10.5	1	0—	0	
Vlasic	6	3	50	8	1.3	0	1—	17	
Smith	1	0	0	0	0.0	0	1—	100	

PUNTING	No	Avg
Mojsiejenko	67	42.9
Prokop	17	38.5

KICKING	XP	Att	%	FG	Att	%
Abbott	22	23	96	13	22	59
Gaffney	4	5	80	3	6	50

LOS ANGELES RAIDERS 5-10 Tom Flores

Scores of Each Game		
20	Green Bay	0
27	DETROIT	7
35	KANSAS CITY	17
14	Denver	30
17	SAN DIEGO	23
13	SEATTLE	35
23	New England	26
20	Minnesota	31
14	San Diego	16
17	DENVER	23
37	Seattle	14
34	BUFFALO	21
10	Kansas City	16
17	CLEVELAND	24
3	CHICAGO	6

Use Name	Pos.	Hgt	Wgt	Age	Int	Pts
John Clay	OT	6'5"	295	23		
Brian Holloway	OT	6'7"	275	28		
#David Pyles	OT	6'5"	275	26		
#John Tautolo	OT	6'4"	280	28		
Steve Wright	OT-OG	6'6"	280	28		
#Andy Dickerson	OG	6'5"	260	24		
John Gesek	OG	6'5"	275	24		
Charley Hannah	OG	6'5"	270	32		
Bill Lewis	OG	6'7"	275	24		
Mickey Marvin	OG	6'4"	265	31		
Dean Miraldi	OG	6'5"	280	28		
Chris Riehm	OG	6'6"	275	26		
Bruce Wilkerson	OG-OT	6'5"	280	23		
#Jon Zogg	OG	6'4"	290	26		
#Paul Dufault	C	6'4"	255	23		
Don Mosebar	C	6'6"	275	25		
#Shawn Regent	C	6'5"	280	24		
Dwight Wheeler (to SD)	C-OG	6'3"	285	32		
#Brian Belway	DE	6'6"	265	23		
Bob Buczkowski	DE	6'5"	260	23		
#Ted Chapman	DE	6'3"	260	23		
#Rick Goltz	DE	6'4"	255	32		
Sean Jones	DE	6'7"	265	24		
Howie Long	DE	6'5"	265	27		
Greg Townsend	DE	6'3"	250	25		
Mike Wise	DE	6'7"	265	23		
Richard Ackerman	NT-DE	6'4"	260	28		
Bill Pickel	NT	6'5"	260	28		
Mike Rodriguez	NT	6'1"	275	26		
Malcolm Taylor	NT	6'6"	280	27		
Mitch Willis	NT	6'8"	280	25		

Use Name	Pos.	Hgt	Wgt	Age	Int	Pts
Jeff Barnes	LB	6'2"	230	32		
#Keith Browner (from SF)	LB	6'6"	245	25		
#Darryl Byrd	LB	6'1"	225	26		
#Joe Cormier	LB	6'6"	230	24		
#Jim Ellis	LB	6'3"	240	23		
#Darryl Goodlow	LB	6'2	235	26		
#Leonard Jackson (from CHI)	LB	6'	240	22		
Jamie Kimmel	LB	6'3"	235	25		
Linden King	LB	6'4"	250	32	1	
Rod Martin	LB	6'2"	225	33		
Reggie McKenzie	LB	6'1"	235	23		
#Dan McMillen (from PHI-DE)	LB	6'4"	240	23		
Matt Millen	LB	6'2"	245	29	1	
#Mike Noble	LB	6'4"	220	23		
Jerry Robinson	LB	6'2"	225	30		
#Ronnie Washington	LB	6'1"	245	24		
Stefon Adams	DB	5'10"	190	24	1	
Eddie Anderson	DB	6'1"	200	24	1	
#Chetti Carr	DB	5'9"	185	24		
James Davis	DB	6'	200	30		
Ron Fellows	DB	6'	175	28		
#Ron Foster	DB	6'	200	23		
#Lance Harkey	DB	5'10"	180	22		
Mike Haynes	DB	6'2"	190	34	2	
Rod Hill	DB	6'	185	28		
#Victor Jackson	DB	6'	205	27		
Vann McElroy	DB	6'2"	195	27	4	6
Sam Seale	DB	5'9"	185	24		
#Willie Teal	DB	5'10"	180	29		
Stacey Toran	DB	6'2"	200	25	3	6
#Tony Tillmon	DB	5'10"	170	23		
Lionel Washington	DB	6'	185	26		
Demise Williams	DB	6'1"	225	23		
#Ricky Williams	DB	6'1"	200	27		

Lester Hayes - foot injury
Shelby Jordan - triceps injury
Curt Marsh - ankle injury
Jim Plunkett - shoulder injury

Use Name	Pos.	Hgt	Wgt	Age	Int	Pts
Vince Evans	QB	6'2"	210	32		6
Rusty Hilger	QB	6'4"	205	25		
Marc Wilson	QB	6'6"	205	30		
#Scott Woolf	QB	6'1"	190	25		
Marcus Allen	HB	6'2"	205	27		30
#Rick Calhoun	HB	5'7"	190	24		6
#Craig Ellis	HB	5'11"	190	26		12
Frank Hawkins	HB	5'9"	210	28		
Bo Jackson	HB	6'1"	230	24		36
Vance Mueller	HB	6'	210	23		6
Steve Strachan	HB	6'1"	220	24		
#Jim Browne	FB	6'1"	215	25		
#Rob Harrison	FB	6'2"	220	24		6
Ethan Horton	FB	6'4"	220	24		6
Zeph Lee (from DEN)	FB	6'3"	215	24		
Steve Smith	FB	6'1"	235	23		
#Carl Aikens	WR	6'1"	185	25		18
Mervyn Fernandez	WR	6'3"	200	27		
Jessie Hester	WR	5'11"	170	24		
#Greg Lathan	WR	6'1"	195	22		
#Wade Lockett	WR	6'1"	190	23		
James Lofton	WR	6'3"	196	31		30
#David Williams	WR	6'3"	190	24		
Dokie Williams	WR	5'11"	180	27		30
Chris Woods	WR	5'11"	190	25		
Todd Christensen	TE	6'3"	230	31		12
Trey Junkin	TE	6'2"	230	26		
Andy Parker	TE	6'5"	250	25		
#Mario Perry	TE	6'6"	240	23		6
#Ron Wheeler	TE	6'5"	235	27		
Chris Bahr	K	5'10"	170	34		84
#Vince Gamache	K	5'11"	170	25		
#David Hardy	K	5'7"	180	28		
Stan Talley	K	6'5"	220	28		

KANSAS CITY CHIEFS 4-11 Frank Gansz

Scores of Each Game		
20	SAN DIEGO	13
14	Seattle	43
17	L.A. Raiders	35
0	Miami	42
17	DENVER	26
21	San Diego	42
28	Chicago	31
16	PITTSBURGH	17
9	N.Y. JETS	16
3	GREEN BAY	23
27	Detroit	20
27	Cincinnati	30
16	L.A. RAIDERS	10
17	Denver	20
41	SEATTLE	20

* Overtime

Use Name	Pos.	Hgt	Wgt	Age	Int	Pts
John Alt	OT	6'7"	290	25		
#Dan Doubiago	OT	6'5"	283	26		
Irv Eatman	OT	6'7"	293	26		
#Doug Hoppock	OT-OG	6'4"	280	27		
David Lutz	OT	6'6	290	27		
#Mark Nelson	OT	6'4"	270	23		
#Steve Rogers	OT	6'5"	260	28		
Mark Adickes	OG	6'4"	270	26		6
Rich Baldinger	OG-OT	6'4"	285	27		
#Lee Getz	OG	6'3"	250	23		
#James Harvey	OG-OT	6'3"	265	21		
Byron Ingram	OG	6'2"	295	22		
Brian Jozwiak	OG	6'5"	310	24		
Arland Thompson	OG	6'3"	265	29		
#Kevin Adkins	C	6'1"	250	23		
Tom Baugh	C	6'3"	274	23		
Rick Donnalley	C	6'2"	260	28		
Glenn Hyde	C	6'3"	252	36		
#Jim Pietrzak	C	6'5"	263	34		
Gary Baldinger	DE	6'3"	260	23		
Mike Bell	DE	6'4"	260	30		
James Black	DE	6'4"	280	28		
#Tony Holloway	DE-LB	6'2"	222	23		
#Ken Johnson	DE	6'5"	260	32		
#Chris Lindstrom	DE	6'7"	261	27		
#Lloyd Mumphrey	DE	6'3"	260	26		
Art Still	DE	6'7"	255	31		
Ray Woodard (from DEN)	DE	6'6"	290	26		
#John Walker	NT-DT	6'6"	270	26		
#Bill Acker	DT	6'3"	255	31		
#Jeff Faulkner	NT-DE	6'3"	270	23		
Leonard Griffin	NT-DE	6'4"	258	24		
Eric Holle	NT	6'5"	265	26		
Pete Koch	NT	6'6"	265	26		
Bill Maas	NT	6'5"	268	28		6

Use Name	Pos.	Hgt	Wgt	Age	Int	Pts
Tim Cofield	LB	6'2"	245	24		
Louis Cooper	LB	6'2"	240	24	1	
Jack Del Rio	LB	6'4"	238	24		
#Randy Frazier	LB	6'3"	235	23		
Dino Hackett	LB	6'3"	228	23		
James Harrell	LB	6'1"	240	30		
#Bob Harris	LB	6'2"	223	27		6
#Bruce Holmes	LB	6'2"	235	22		
Todd Howard	LB	6'2"	235	22		
#Fred Jones	LB	6'3"	240	22		
Ken McAlister	LB	6'5"	220	27		
#Gary Moten	LB	6'1"	210	26		
Aaron Pearson	LB	6'	240	23		
Angelo Snipes (from SD)	LB	6'	220	24		
#Gary Spann	LB	6'1"	218	24		
#Trent Bryant	DB	5'10"	180	28	1	
Lloyd Burruss	DB	6'	209	30		
Deron Cherry	DB	5'11"	193	27	3	
Sherman Cocroft	DB	6'1"	192	26		
#Jeff Colter	DB	5'10"	171	26		
#Cornelius Dozier	DB	6'2"	190	23		
#Jack Epps	DB	6'	197	24		
Jitter Fields (from IND)	DB	5'8"	180	25		6
Greg Hill (from RAID)	DB	6'1"	197	26		
#Garcia Lane	DB	5'9"	180	25		
Albert Lewis	DB	6'2"	192	26	1	
#Ted Nelson	DB	5'10"	203	22		
J.C. Pearson	DB	5'11"	183	24		
Mark Robinson	DB	5'11"	206	24	2	
Kevin Ross	DB	5'9"	182	25	3	6
#Blane Smith	DB	5'10"	190	27		
Carlton Thomas	DB	6'	200	23		
#Kevin Wyatt	DB	5'10"	208	23		

Brad Budde - Stomach Injury
Emile Harry - Shoulder Separation
Gary Spani - Knee Injury

Use Name	Pos.	Hgt	Wgt	Age	Int	Pts
Todd Blackledge	QB	6'3"	219	26		
#Alex Espinoza	QB	6'1"	193	23		
Doug Hudson	QB	6'2"	201	22		
Bill Kenney	QB	6'4"	207	32		
Frank Seurer	QB	6'1"	195	25		
#Matt Stevens	QB	6'	190	23		
Michael Clemens	HB	5'5"	166	22		
#Steve Griffin	HB	5'10"	205	23		
Herman Heard	HB	5'10"	182	25		18
Paul Palmer	HB	5'9"	184	22		12
Robert Parker	HB	6'1"	201	24		
James Evans	FB	6'	220	24		
#Ken Lacey	FB	6'	220	26		
Larry Moriarty	FB	6'1"	237	29		6
Christian Okoye	FB	6'1"	253	26		18
#Woodie Pippens	FB	5'11"	225	24		
#Chris Smith	FB	6'	242	24		
#Ralph Stockemer	FB	6'1"	212	24		
Eric Brown	WR	6'2"	180	23		
Carlos Carson	WR	5'11"	185	29		42
Darre;; Colbert	WR	5'10"	174	22		
#Richard Estell	WR	6'2"	210	25		
#Eric Hodges	WR	6'1"	189	23		
Henry Marshall	WR	6'2"	216	33		
David Montagne	WR	6'2"	184	23		
Kenny Nash	WR	6'2"	195	25		
#Stephone Paige	WR	6'2"	185	25		24
#John Trahan	WR	5'9"	160	26		
Wait Arnold	TE	6'3"	225	29		
Paul Coffman	TE	6'3"	225	31		6
Jonathan Hayes	TE	6'5"	240	25		12
#Rod Jones	TE	6'4"	242	23		6
Mark Keel (from SEA)	TE	6'4"	228	25		6
#Stein Koss	TE	6'2"	225	24		
#Riley Walton	TE	6'4"	245	24		
Lewis Colbert	K	5'11"	180	24		
Kelly Goodburn	K	6'2"	195	25		
#James Hamrick	K	5'11"	177	24		10
Nick Lowery	K	6'4"	189	31		83

- on the active roster for strike replacement games only

L.A. RAIDERS

RUSHING

Last Name	No.	Yds	Avg	TD
Allen	200	754	3.8	5
Jackson	81	554	6.8	4
Mueller	37	175	4.7	1
Evans	11	144	13.1	1
Strachan	28	108	3.9	0
Horton	31	95	3.1	0
Wilson	17	91	5.4	0
Harrison	9	49	5.4	0
Calhoun	7	36	5.1	0
Hawkins	4	24	6.0	0
Smith	5	18	3.6	0
Hilger	8	8	1.0	0
Aikens	1	1	1.0	0
Browne	2	1	0.5	0
Lofton	1	1	1.0	0

RECEIVING

Last Name	No.	Yds	Avg	TD
Allen	51	410	8.0	0
Christensen	47	663	14.1	2
Lofton	41	880	21.5	5
Williams	21	330	15.7	5
Jackson	16	136	8.5	2
Fernandez	14	236	16.9	0
Mueller	11	95	8.6	0
Aikens	8	134	16.8	3
Lathan	5	98	19.6	0
Ellis	5	39	7.8	0
Williams	4	106	26.0	0
Strachan	4	42	10.5	0
Wheeler	3	61	20.3	0
Smith	3	46	15.3	0
Horton	3	44	14.7	1
Harrison	2	18	9.0	0
Junkin	2	15	7.5	0
Hester	1	30	30.0	0
Calhoun	1	17	17.0	0
Woods	1	14	14.0	0
Hawkins	1	6	6.0	0
Perry	1	3	3.0	0

PUNT RETURNS

Last Name	No.	Yds	Avg	TD
Woods	26	189	7.3	0
Calhoun	8	92	11.5	1
Adams	5	39	7.8	0
Fellows	2	19	9.5	0
Harkey	2	17	8.5	0
Davis	1	0	0.0	0

KICKOFF RETURNS

Last Name	No.	Yds	Avg	TD
Mueller	27	588	21.8	0
Williams	14	221	15.8	0
Calhoun	9	217	24.1	0
Adams	3	61	20.3	0
Woods	3	55	18.3	0
Harkey	1	20	20.0	0
Foster	1	12	12.0	0
Millen	1	0	0.0	0
R. Washington	1	0	0.0	0

PASSING — PUNTING — KICKING

PASSING	Att	Cmp	%	Yds	Yd/Att	TD	Int—	%	RK
Wilson	266	152	57	2070	7.8	12	8—	3	10
Hilger	106	55	52	706	6.7	2	6—	6	
Evans	83	39	47	630	7.6	5	5—	0	
Allen	2	1	50	23	11.5	0	0—	0	

PUNTING	No	Avg
Talley	57	39.9
Gamache	14	37.1

KICKING	XP	Att	%	FG	Att	%
C. Bahr	27	28	96	19	29	66
Hardy	7	7	100	0	1	0

KANSAS CITY CHIEFS

RUSHING

Last Name	No.	Yds	Avg	TD
Okoye	157	660	4.2	3
Heard	82	466	5.7	3
Palmer	24	155	6.5	0
Parker	47	150	3.2	1
C. Smith	26	114	4.4	0
Moriarty	30	107	3.6	0
Lacy	14	49	3.7	0
Seurer	9	33	3.7	0
Blackledge	5	21	4.2	0
Goodburn	1	16	16.0	0
Pippens	3	16	5.3	0
Clemons	2	7	3.5	0
Stevens	3	7	2.3	0
Espinoza	1	5	5.0	0
Stockemer	1	2	2.0	0
Hudson	1	0	0.0	0
Kenney	12	-2	-0.2	0
Carson	1	-7	-7.0	0

RECEIVING

Last Name	No.	Yds	Avg	TD
Carson	55	1044	19.0	7
Paige	43	707	16.4	4
Okoye	24	169	7.0	0
Hayes	21	272	13.3	2
Heard	14	118	8.4	0
Marshall	10	126	12.6	0
Moriarty	10	37	3.7	1
Keel	8	97	12.1	1
R. Jones	8	76	9.5	1
Parker	7	44	6.3	0
Brown	5	69	13.8	0
Montagne	5	47	9.4	0
Coffman	5	42	8.4	1
Trahan	4	40	10.0	0
Palmer	4	27	6.8	0
Arnold	3	26	8.7	0
Estell	3	24	8.0	1
D. Colbert	3	21	7.0	0
Koss	2	25	12.5	0
Nash	2	22	11.0	0
C. Smith	2	21	10.5	0
Pippens	2	12	6.0	0
Stockemer	1	4	4.0	0
Adickes	1	3	3.0	1

PUNT RETURNS

Last Name	No.	Yds	Avg	TD
Clemons	19	162	8.5	0
Fields	8	161	20.1	1
Wyatt	2	4	2.0	0
Cocroft	1	0	0.0	0
D. Colbert	1	11	11.0	0
Montagne	1	8	8.0	0

KICKOFF RETURNS

Last Name	No.	Yds	Avg	TD
Palmer	38	923	24.3	2
Moriarty	6	102	17.0	0
Robinson	5	97	19.4	0
Wyatt	5	121	24.2	0
Lacy	4	44	11.0	0
Parker	3	49	16.3	0
Lane	2	37	18.5	0
A. Pearson	2	4	2.0	0
Clemons	1	3	3.0	0
D. Colbert	1	18	18.0	0
Fields	1	13	13.0	0
S. Griffin	1	16	16.0	0
B. Smith	1	10	10.0	0

PASSING — PUNTING — KICKING

PASSING	Att	Cmp	%	Yds	Yd/Att	TD	Int—	%	RK
Kenney	273	154	56	2107	7.7	15	9—	3	8
Stevens	57	32	56	315	5.5	1	1—	2	
Seurer	55	26	47	340	6.2	0	4—	7	
Blackledge	31	15	48	154	5.0	1	1—	3	
Espinoza	14	9	64	69	4.9	0	2—	14	
Hudson	1	0	0	0	0.0	0	0—	0	
Palmer	1	0	0	0	0.0	0	0—	0	

PUNTING	No	Avg
Goodburn	59	40.9
L. Colbert	10	37.7

KICKING	XP	Att	%	FG	Att	%
Lowery	26	26	100	19	23	83
Hamrick	4	4	100	2	2	100

1987 N.F.C.—PLAYOFFS

Jan. 3, 1988 at New Orleans (Attendance 68,127)

SCORING

MINNESOTA	10	21	3	10	-44
NEW ORLEANS	7	3	0	0	-10

First quarter

N.O.	Martin, 10 yard pass from Hebert PAT — Andersen (kick)
Minn.	C. Nelson, 42 yard field goal
Minn.	Carter, 84 yard punt return PAT — C. Nelson (kick)

Second quarter

Minn.	Jordan, 5 yard pass from Wilson PAT — C. Nelson (kick)
Minn.	Carter, 10 yard pass from Rice PAT — C. Nelson (kick)
N.O.	Andersen, 40 yard field goal
Minn.	Jones, 44 yard pass from Wilson PAT — C. Nelson (kick)

Third quarter

Minn.	C. Nelson, 42 yard field goal

Fourth quarter

Minn.	C. Nelson, 19 yard field goal
Minn.	Dozier, 18 yard run PAT — C. Nelson (kick)

TEAM STATISTICS

MINN.		N.O.
28	First Downs	9
14	First Downs-Rushing	0
14	First Downs-Passing	7
0	First Downs-Penalty	2
4	Fumbles	3
2	Fumbles-Lost Ball	2
5	Penalties-Number	4
42	Yards Penalized	26
0	Missed Field Goals	0
86	Offensive Plays	47
417	Net Yards	149
4.8	Average Gain	3.2
2	Giveaways	6
6	Takeaways	2
+4	Difference	-4

INDIVIDUAL STATISTICS

MINNESOTA	No.	Yds.	Avg.	NEW ORLEANS	No.	Yds.	Avg.
RUSHING							
D. Nelson	17	73	4.3	Hilliard	8	39	4.9
Anderson	7	49	7.0	Mayes	3	11	3.7
Dozier	8	45	5.6	Hebert	2	2	1.0
Fenney	7	20	2.9	Jordan	1	1	1.0
Rice	4	10	2.5		14	53	3.8
Kramer	2	5	2.5				
Wilson	2	5	2.5				
Gannon	3	3	1.0				
	50	210	4.2				
RECEIVING							
Carter	6	79	13.2	Brenner	2	33	16.5
Nelson	2	50	25.0	Pattison	2	18	9.0
Lewis	2	27	13.5	Hill	2	15	7.5
Rice	2	17	8.5	Hilliard	2	15	7.5
Jordan	2	17	8.5	Tice	2	13	6.5
H. Jones	1	44	44.0	Martin	1	10	10.0
Gustafson	1	12	12.0		11	96	8.7
Anderson	1	-3	-3.0				
	17	207	12.2				
PUNTING							
Scribner	3		32.0	Hansen	6		44.2
PUNT RETURNS							
Carter	6	143	23.8	Gray	1	0	0.0
KICKOFF RETURNS							
none				Word	4	53	19.2
				Adams	1	19	19.0
				Gray	1	16	16.0
				Brock	1	13	13.0
					7	101	14.4
INTERCEPTION RETURNS							
Holt	1	0	0.0				
Harris	1	15	15.0				
Rutland	1	0	0.0				
Freeman	1	30	30.0				
	4	45	11.3				

PASSING

MINNESOTA	Att.	Comp.	Comp Pct.	Yds.	Int.	Yds./Att.	Yds./Comp.
Kramer	9	5	56	50	0	5.6	10.0
Wilson	20	11	55	189	0	14.5	18.5
Rice	1	1	100	10	0	10.0	10.0
	30	17	57	249	0	8.3	14.6
NEW ORLEANS							
Hebert	19	9	47	84	2	4.4	9.3
Wilson	12	2	17	20	2	1.7	10.0
	31	11	35	104	4	3.4	9.5

Jan. 9, 1988, at San Francisco (Attendance 62, 457)

SCORING

MINNESOTA	3	17	10	6	-36
SAN FRANCISCO	3	0	14	7	-24

First Quarter

Minn.	C. Nelson, 21 yard field goal
S.F.	Wersching, 43 yard field goal

Second Quarter

Minn.	Hilton, 7 yard pass from Wilson PAT — C. Nelson (kick)
Minn.	C. Nelson, 23 yard field goal
Minn.	Rutland, 45 yard interception return PAT — C. Nelson (kick)

Third Quarter

S.F.	Fuller, 48 yard interception return PAT—Wersching (kick)
Minn.	H. Jones, 5 yard pass from Wilson PAT — C. Nelson (kick)
S.F.	Young, 5 yard run PAT — Wersching (kick)
Minn.	C. Nelson, 40 yard field goal

Fourth Quarter

Minn.	C. Nelson, 40 yard field goal
S.F.	Frank, 16 yard pass from Young PAT — Wersching (kick)
Minn.	C. Nelson, 23 yard field goal

TEAM STATISTICS

MINN.		S.F.
22	First Downs	17
5	First Downs-Rushing	6
15	First Down-Passing	10
2	First Downs-Penalty	1
0	Fumbes- Number	1
0	Fumbles-Lost	0
2	Penalties-Number	8
20	Yards Penalized	75
0	Missed Field Goals	2
70	Offensive Plays	66
397	Net Yards	358
5.7	Average Gain	5.4
1	Giveaways	2
2	Takeaways	1
+1	Difference	-1

INDIVIDUAL STATISTICS

MINNESOTA	No.	Yds.	Avg.	SAN FRANCISCO	No.	Yds.	Avg.
RUSHING							
D. Nelson	11	42	3.8	Young	6	72	12.0
W. Wilson	6	30	5.0	Montana	3	20	6.7
Carter	1	30	30.0	Craig	7	17	2.4
Anderson	7	9	1.3	Rathman	1	12	12.0
Rice	6	8	1.3	Cribbs	1	-6	-6.0
Dozier	3	-2	-0.7		18	115	6.4
	34	117	3.4				
RECEIVING							
Carter	10	227	22.7	Craig	9	78	8.7
Rice	4	39	9.8	Wilson	5	50	10.0
D. Nelson	2	17	8.5	Rice	3	28	9.3
Hilton	1	7	7.0	Taylor	2	28	14.0
H. Jones	1	5	5.0	Rathman	2	18	9.0
Lewis	1	5	5.0	Frank	1	16	16.0
Anderson	1	-2	-2.0	Clark	1	13	13.0
	20	280	14.0	Cribbs	1	7	7.0
				Jones	1	7	7.0
				Young	0	2	—
					24	257	10.7
PUNTING							
Scribner	5		36.4	Runager	6		40.8
PUNT RETURNS							
Carter	2	21	10.5	McLemore	3	17	5.7
Lewis	1	8	8.0				
	3	29	9.7				
KICKOFF RETURNS							
D. Nelson	2	56	28.0	Rathman	3	45	15.0
Rice	1	20	20.0	Cribbs	3	28	9.3
	3	76	25.3	Sydney	2	28	14.0
				Taylor	0	29	—
					8	130	16.3
INTERCEPTION RETURNS							
Rutland	1	45	45.0	Fuller	1	48	48.0
Lee	1	-5	-5.0				
	2	40	20.0				

PASSING

MINNESOTA	Att.	Comp.	Comp. Pct.	Yds.	Int.	Yds./Att.	Yds./Comp.
W. Wilson	34	20	59	298	1	8.8	14.9
SAN FRANCISCO							
Montana	26	12	46	109	1	4.2	9.1
Young	17	12	71	158	1	9.3	13.2
	43	24	56	267	2	6.2	11.1

Jan. 10, 1988 at Chicago (Att. 58,153)

SCORING

WASHINGTON	0	14	7	0	-21
CHICAGO	7	7	3	0	-17

First Quarter

Chicago	Thomas, 2 yard run PAT — Butler (kick)

Second Quarter

Chicago	Morris, 14 yard pass from McMahon PAT — Butler (kick)
Wash.	Rogers, 3 yard run PAT — Haji-Sheikh (kick)
Wash.	Didier, 18 yard pass from Williams PAT — Haji-Sheikh (kick)

Third Quarter

Wash.	Green, 52 yard punt return PAT—Haji-Sheikh (kick)
Chicago	Butler, 25 yard field goal

TEAM STATISTICS

WASH.		CHI.
17	First Downs-Total	15
4	First Downs-Rushing	8
11	First Downs-Passing	7
2	First Downs-Penalty	0
1	Fumbles-Number	1
1	Fumbles-Lost Ball	0
3	Penalties-Number	5
20	Yards Penalized	50
0	Missed Field Goals	1
59	Offensive Plays	64
272	Net Yards	280
4.6	Average Gain	4.4
2	Giveaways	3
3	Takeaways	2
+1	Difference	-1

INDIVIDUAL STATISTICS

WASHINGTON	No.	Yds.	Avg.	CHICAGO	No.	Yds.	Avg.
RUSHING							
Rogers	6	13	2.2	Payton	18	85	4.7
Bryant	3	8	2.7	Suhey	4	8	2.0
Clark	1	-6	-6.0	Thomas	2	3	1.5
Smith	16	66	4.1	Gentry	2	5	2.5
Schroeder	1	-8	-8.0	McMahon	2	5	2.5
Williams	2	-1	-0.5	Sanders	2	4	2.0
	29	72	2.5		30	110	3.7
RECEIVING							
Sanders	6	92	15.3	Gentry	3	43	14.3
Rogers	1	11	11.0	Boso	3	19	6.3
Clark	4	56	14.0	Morris	2	47	23.5
Didier	2	32	16.0	Suhey	1	6	6.0
Warren	1	16	16.0	Payton	3	20	6.7
	14	207	14.8	Gault	1	44	44.0
				Sanders	1	2	2.0
				McKinnon	1	16	16.0
					15	297	19.8
PUNTING							
Cox	4		42.3	Barnhardt	4		36.3
PUNT RETURNS							
Yarber	2	13	6.5	McKinnon	2	12	6.0
Green	1	52	52.0				
	3	65	21.7				
KICKOFF RETURNS							
Sanders	2	25	12.5	Gentry	2	74	37.0
Smith	1	19	19.0	Gault	1	29	29.0
Branch	1	12	12.0		3	103	34.3
	4	56	14.0				
INTERCEPTION RETURNS							
Davis	1	23	23.0	Richardson	1	0	0.0
Wilburn	1	0	0.0				
Woodbury	1	0	0.0				
	3	23	7.7				

PASSING

WASHINGTON	Att.	Comp.	Comp. Pct.	Yds.	Int.	Yds./Att.	Yds./Comp.
Williams	29	14	48	207	1	7.1	14.8
CHICAGO							
McMahon	29	15	52	197	3	6.8	13.1

1987 A.F.C.—PLAYOFFS

January 3, 1988 at Houston (Attendance 49,622)

SCORING

SEATTLE	7	3	3	7	0-	20
HOUSTON	3	10	7	0	3-	23

First Quarter
Sea. Largent, 20 yard pass from Krieg
PAT-N. Johnson (kick)
Hou. Zendejas, 47 yard field goal

Second Quarter
Hou. Rozier, 1 yard rush
PAT—Zendejas (kick)
Hou. Zendejas, 49 yard field goal
Sea. Johnson, 33 yard field goal

Third Quarter
Sea. Johnson, 41 yard field goal
Hou. Drewrey, 29 pass from Moon
PAT—Zendejas (kick)

Fourth Quarter
Sea. Largent, 12 yard pass from Krieg
PAT—N. Johnson (kick)

Overtime
Hou. Zendejas, 42 yard field goal

TEAM STATISTICS

SEA.		HOU.
11	First Downs-Total	27
1	First Downs-Rushing	9
10	First Downs-Passing	12
0	First Downs-Penalty	0
1	Fumbles-Number	2
1	Fumbles-Lost Ball	1
3	Penalties-Number	4
20	Yards Penalized	25
0	Missed Field Goals	2
52	Offensive Plays	84
250	Net Yards	437
4.8	Average Gain	5.2
1	Giveaways	2
2	Takeaways	1
+1	Difference	-1

INDIVIDUAL STATISTICS

SEATTLE	No.	Yds.	Avg.	HOUSTON	No.	Yds.	Avg.
RUSHING							
J. Williams	7	27	3.9	Rozier	21	66	3.1
Morris	4	2	0.5	Highsmith	12	74	6.2
	11	29	2.6	Wallace	2	11	5.5
				Moon	4	-2	-.5
				Pinkett	11	29	2.6
					50	178	3.6
RECEIVING							
Largent	7	132	18.9	Givins	7	89	12.7
R. Butler	3	73	24.3	Drewrey	3	62	20.7
Tice	1	8	8.0	D. Hill	6	84	14.0
Skansi	2	13	6.5	McNeil	3	13	4.3
Williams	2	5	2.5	Highsmith	2	17	8.5
Morris	1	6	6.0	Wallace	1	11	11.0
	16	221	13.8	Rozier	1	7	7.0
				Pinkett	1	3	3.0
					21	259	12.3
PUNTING							
Rodriguez		7	44.3	Jennings		3	35.0
PUNT RETURNS							
Edmonds	2	66	33.0	K. Johnson	4	27	6.8
KICKOFF RETURNS							
Edmonds	2	66	33.0	Pinkett	4	65	16.8
Hollis	1	23	23.0				
	3	89	26.3				
INTERCEPTION RETURNS							
Jenkins	1	28	28.0	none			

PASSING

SEATTLE	Att.	Comp.	Comp. Pct.	Yds.	Int.	Yds./Att.	Yds./Comp.
Krieg	38	16	42	237	1	6.2	14.8
J. Williams	1	0	0	0	0	0.0	0.0
	39	16	41	237	1	6.1	14.8
HOUSTON							
Moon	32	21	66	237	1	8.5	13.0

January 9, 1988 at Cleveland (Attendance 78,586)

SCORING

INDIANAPOLIS	7	7	0	7-	21
CLEVELAND	7	7	7	17-	38

First Quarter
Cle. Byner, 10 yard pass from Kosar
PAT—Bahr (kick)
Ind. Beach, 2 yard pass form Trudeau
PAT—Biasucci (kick)

Second Quarter
Cle. Langhorne, 39 yard pass from Kosar
PAT—Bahr (kick)
Ind. Dickerson, 19 yard pass from Trudeau
PAT—Biasucci (kick)

Third Quarter
Cle. Byner 2 yard rush
PAT—Bahr (kick)]

Fourth Quarter
Cle. Bahr, 22 field goal
Cle. Brennan, 2 yard pass from Kosar
PAT—Bahr (kick)
Ind. Bentley, 1 yard rush
PAT—Biasucci (kick)
Cle. Minnifield, 48 interception return
PAT—Bahr (kick)

TEAM STATISTICS

IND.		CLE.
23	First Downs-Total	25
4	First Downs-Rushing	10
16	First Downs-Passing	13
3	First Downs-Penalty	2
1	Fumbles-Number	2
0	Fumbles-Lost Ball	0
7	Penalties-Number	4
75	Yards Penalized	20
0	Missed Field Goals	0
62	Offensive Plays	65
301	Net Yards	404
5.1	Average Gain	6.2
2	Giveaways	1
1	Takeaways	2
-1	Difference	+1

INDIVIDUAL STATISTICS

INDIANAPOLIS	No.	Yds.	Avg.	CLEVELAND	No.	Yds.	Avg.
RUSHING							
Dickerson	15	50	3.3	Byner	23	122	5.3
Bentley	4	6	1.5	Mack	6	38	6.3
Trudeau	2	4	2.0	Manoa	4	10	2.5
	21	60	2.9		33	170	5.2
RECEIVING							
Dickerson	7	65	9.3	Newsome	4	65	16.3
Brooks	5	78	15.6	Byner	4	36	9.0
Bentley	4	47	11.8	Brennan	3	25	8.3
Bouza	2	24	12.0	Mack	3	17	5.7
Beach	2	6	3.0	Fontenot	2	20	10.0
Murray	1	25	25.0	Langhorne	1	39	39.0
Bellini	1	21	21.0	Slaughter	1	14	14.0
	22	266	12.1	McNeil	1	8	8.0
				Weathers	1	5	5.0
					20	229	11.5
PUNTING							
Stark	4		43.8	L. Johnson	1	37	37.0
PUNT RETURNS							
none				McNeil	3	32	10.0
KICKOFF RETURNS							
Bentley	6	114	19.0	Fontentot	1	3	3.0
Ahrens	1	10	10.0	McNeil	1	18	18.0
					2	21	11.5
INTERCEPTION RETURNS							
Robinson	1	0	0.0	Minnifield	1	48	48.0

PASSING

INDIANAPOLIS	Att.	Comp.	Comp. Pct.	Yds.	Int.	Yds./Att.	Yds./Comp.
Trudeau	33	21	64	251	1	7.6	12.0
Salisbury	6	1	17	15	1	2.5	15.0
	39	22	56	266	2	6.8	12.1
CLEVELAND							
Kosar	31	20	65	229	1	7.4	11.5

January 10, 1988 at Denver (Attendance 75,968)

SCORING

HOUSTON	0	3	0	7-	10
DENVER	14	10	3	7-	34

First Quarter
Den. Lang, 1 yard rush
PAT—Karlis (kick)
Den. Kay, 27 yard pass from Elway
PAT—Karlis (kick)

Second Quarter
Den. Karlis, 43 yard field goal
Hou. Zendejas, 46 yard field goal
Den. Kay, 1 yard pass from Elway
PAT—Karlis (kick)

Third Quarter
Den. Karlis, 23 yard field goal

Fourth Quarter
Hou. Givins, 19 yard pass from Moon
PAT—Zendejas (kick)
Den. Elway, 3 yard rush
PAT—Karlis (kick)

TEAM STATISTICS

HOU.		DEN.
20	First Downs-Total	19
5	First Downs-Rushing	9
14	First Downs-Passing	9
1	First Downs-Penalty	1
2	Fumbles-Number	0
1	Fumbles-Lost Ball	0
10	Penalties-Number	4
73	Yards Penalized	35
0	Missed Field Goals	0
69	Offensive Plays	55
337	Net Yards	312
4.9	Average Gain	5.7
3	Giveaways	1
1	Takeaways	3
-2	Difference	+2

INDIVIDUAL STATISTICS

HOUSTON	No.	Yds.	Avg.	DENVER	No.	Yds.	Avg.
RUSHING							
Rozier	9	25	2.8	Winder	13	46	3.5
Pinkett	6	20	3.3	Sewell	5	9	1.8
Moon	5	15	3.0	Elway	4	8	2.0
Highsmith	5	13	2.6	Bell	2	7	3.5
Givins	1	0	0.0	Kubiak	2	-3	-1.5
	26	73	2.8	Lang	3	-6	-2.0
					29	61	2.1
RECEIVING							
Givins	6	84	17.0	Johnson	4	105	26.3
D. Hill	5	93	18.6	Kay	3	57	19.0
Duncan	4	32	8.0	Sewell	3	41	13.7
Highsmith	4	20	5.0	Lang	1	25	25.0
Drewrey	2	17	8.5	Boddie	1	15	15.0
Williams	1	7	7	Mobley	1	9	9.0
Rozier	1	6	6	Nattiel	1	7	7.0
Pinkett	1	5	5		14	255	18.2
	24	264	12				
PUNTING							
Gossett	3		44.7	Horan	2		46.0
PUNT RETURNS							
none				Clark	2	15	7.5
KICKOFF RETURNS							
Pinkett	3	62	20.7	Bell	1	28	28.0
				Clark	1	0	0.0
					2	28	14.0
INTERCEPTION RETURNS							
Allen	1	2	2.0	Mecklenburg	1	18	18.0
				Haynes	1	57	57.0
					2	75	37.5

PASSING

HOUSTON	Att.	Comp.	Comp. Pct.	Yds.	Int.	Yds./Att.	Yds./Comp.
Moon	43	24	56	264	2	6.1	11.0
DENVER							
Elway	25	14	56	259	1	10.4	18.5

1987 Championship Games

NFC CHAMPIONSHIP GAME

January 17, 1988 at Washington, D.C.
(Attendance 55,212)

SCORING

MINNESOTA	0	7	0	3-	10
WASHINGTON	7	0	3	7-	17

First Quarter	Wash.	Bryant, 42 yard pass from Williams PAT — Haji-Sheikh (kick)
Second Quarter	Minn.	Lewis, 23 yard pass from Wilson PAT—C. Nelson (kick)
Third quarter	Wash.	Haji-Sheikh, 28 yard field goal
Fourth quarter	Minn.	C. Nelson, 18 yard field goal
	Wash.	Clark, 7 yard pass from Williams PAT — Haji-Sheikh (kick)

TEAM STATISTICS

Minn.		Wash.
16	First Downs-Total	11
5	First Downs-Rushing	7
10	First Downs-Passing	4
1	First Downs-Penalty	0
0	Fumbles-Number	0
0	Fumbles-Ball Lost	0
2	Penalties-Number	3
10	Yards Penalized	18
0	Missed Field Goals	0
68	Offensive Plays	60
259	Net Yards	280
3.8	Average Gain	4.7
1	Giveaways	0
0	Takeaways	1
-1	Difference	+1

The Washington Redskins used a clutch defense to ruin the Minnesota Vikings' Cinderella story 17-10. The Vikes got to the title game by upsetting both New Orleans and San Francisco, the NFC teams with the best regular-season records. A Viking victory would have made them only the third wild-card team in history to reach the Super Bowl.

The Redskins drove 98 yards for a touchdown, the score coming on Doug Williams' 42-yard pass to Kelvin Bryant on a 3rd-and-10 play. The Vikings were held in check through most of the first half but drove 71 yards to score with two minutes left. Wade Wilson passed 23 yards to wide receiver Leo Lewis for the TD.

Wilson was sacked eight times on the day, one short of the title game record. But, in the fourth quarter, he led the Vikes down to the goalline. The Redskin defense stopped Minnesota on two straight shots from the one and forced the Vikings to settle for a tie score on Chuck Nelson's 18-yard field goal with 10:06 to play.

Williams completed only 9-of-26 passes for 119 yards on the day, but, following the kickoff, he took his team 70 yards for the go-ahead touchdown. His seven-yard toss to Gary Clark on an improvised play culminated the drive. Again, Minnesota drove down the field, reaching the Redskin six-yard line. And, again, Washington stopped the Vikes short of a touchdown. On fourth down, Darrin Nelson dropped Wilson's pass at the goalline.

INDIVIDUAL STATISTICS

MINNESOTA	No.	Yds.	Avg.	WASHINGTON	No.	Yds.	Avg.
RUSHING							
Wilson	4	28	7.0	Smith	13	72	5.5
Anderson	4	25	6.3	Rogers	12	49	4.1
D. Nelson	8	15	1.9	Sanders	1	28	28.0
Rice	1	8	8.0	Williams	4	7	1.8
Fenney	2	2	1.0	Clark	1	5	5.0
Dozier	2	-2	-1.0	Bryant	3	3	1.0
	21	76	3.6		34	161	4.7
RECEIVING							
Carter	7	85	12.1	Bryant	4	47	11.8
Lewis	4	54	13.5	Clark	3	57	19.0
Jordan	3	56	18.7	Allen	1	9	9.0
D. Nelson	3	25	8.3	Warren	1	6	6.0
Rice	1	15	15.0		9	119	13.2
Anderson	1	8	8.0				
	19	243	12.8				
PUNTING							
Scribner	10		33.2	Cox	8		39.1
PUNT RETURNS							
Carter	4	57	14.3	Dean	1	0	0.0
				Green	1	1	1.0
				Yarber	1	9	9.0
				Davis	1	0	0.0
					4	10	2.5
KICKOFF RETURNS							
D. Nelson	2	43	21.5	Sanders	2	30	15.0
Rice	1	15	15.0	Smith	1	24	24.0
	3	58	19.3		3	54	18.0
INTERCEPTION RETURNS							
none				Kaufman	1	10	10.0

PASSING

MINNESOTA	Att.	Comp.	Comp. Pct.	Yds.	Int.	Yds./ Att.	Yds./ Comp.
W. Wilson	39	19	49	243	1	6.2	12.8
WASHINGTON							
Williams	26	9	35	119	0	4.6	13.2

AFC CHAMPIONSHIP GAME

January 17, 1988 at Denver
(Attendance 75,993)

SCORING

CLEVELAND	0	3	21	9-	33
DENVER	14	7	10	7-	38

First Quarter	DEN.	Nattiel, 8 yard pass from Elway PAT—Karlis (kick)
	DEN.	Sewell, 1 yard rush PAT—Karlis (kick)
Second Quarter	CLE.	Bahr, 24 yard field goal
	DEN.	Lang, 1 yard rush PAT—Karlis (kick)
Third Quarter	CLE.	Langhorne, 18 yard pass from Kosar PAT—Bahr (kick)
	DEN.	Jackson, 80 yard pass from Elway PAT—Karlis (kick)
	CLE.	Byner, 32 yard pass from Kosar PAT—Bahr(kick)
	CLE.	Byner, 4 yard rush PAT—Bahr (kick)
Fourth Quarter	CLE.	Slaughter, 4 pass from Kosar PAT— Bahr (kick)
	DEN.	Winder, 20 yard pass from Elway PAT—Karlis (kick)
	CLE.	Safety, Horan ran out of endzone

TEAM STATISTICS

CLE.		DEN.
25	First Downs-Total	24
8	First Downs-Rushing	10
15	First Downs-Passing	11
2	First Downs-Penalty	3
3	Fumbles-Number	2
3	Fumbles-Lost Ball	0
7	Penalties-Number	7
59	Yards Penalized	44
1	Missed Field Goals	1
70	Offensive Plays	61
444	Net Yards	232
6.6	Average Gain	3.8
4	Giveaways	1
1	Takeaways	4
+3	Difference	-3

In what may have been the most exciting game played in the NFL all season, the Denver Broncos edged the Cleveland Browns 38-33 to go to the Super Bowl for the second straight year. The same two teams had waged a classic battle in the 1986 title game, but this one was even more dramatic.

The first half was Denver's. After a diving interception by DE Freddie Gilbert, Bronco QB John Elway hit WR Ricky Nattiel with an eight-yard TD pass. Cleveland CB Frank Minnifield was caught holding in the endzone on a third-down incompletion, and RB Steve Sewell went over from the one on a reverse, giving the Broncos the impetus for a 21-3 lead at the half.

Bernie Kosar brought the Browns back with ample help from RB Earnest Byner. Kosar's TD passes to Reggie Langhorne and Byner, plus Byner's TD run, cut the gap to 31-24 entering the final period.

Kosar connected with Byner on a 53-yard pass to spark an 86-yard drive. Webster Slaughter's four-yard TD catch tied the score. But Elway's 20-yard pass to Sammy Winder put Denver ahead again. Back came Cleveland on a length-of-the-field drive. But, on second down at the Denver eight, Byner burst off tackle. At the two he was stripped of the ball by Denver's Jeremiah Castille, and the Broncos recovered. As time ran out, Denver elected to take a safety rather than punt out of its own endzone, making the final score 38-33.

INDIVIDUAL STATISTICS

CLEVELAND	No.	Yds.	Avg.	DENVER	No.	Yds.	Avg.
RUSHING							
Byner	15	67	4.5	Winder	20	72	3.6
Mack	12	61	5.1	Elway	11	36	3.3
	27	128	4.7	Lang	5	51	5.2
				Sewell	1	1	1.0
				Boddie	1	8	8.0
				Horan	1	-12	-12.0
					39	156	4.0
RECEIVING							
Byner	7	120	17.7	Nattiel	5	95	19.0
Slaughter	4	53	13.3	Jackson	4	134	33.5
Brennan	4	48	12.0	Winder	3	34	11.3
Mack	4	28	7.0	Sewell	1	10	10.0
Newsome	3	35	11.6	Mobley	1	8	8.0
Langhorne	2	48	24.0		14	256	18.3
Tennell	1	5	5.0				
Weathers	1	19	19.0				
	26	336	12.9				
PUNTING							
L. Johnson	2		48.0	Horan	2		41.5
				Elway	1		18.0
					3		33.7
PUNT RETURNS							
McNeil	2	24	12.0	Clark	2	13	6.5
KICKOFF RETURNS							
McNeil	5	94	18.8	Bell	3	43	14.3
INTERCEPTION RETURNS							
Wright	1	13	13.0	Gilbert	1	0	0.0

PASSING

CLEVELAND	Att	Comp	Comp Pct	Yds	Int	Yds./ Att	Yds./ Comp
Kosar	41	26	63.4	336	1	8.2	12.9
DENVER							
Elway	26	14	53.8	281	1	10.8	20.1

SUPER BOWL XXII

January 31, 1988 at San Diego, Calif.
(Attendance 73,302)

Size Disadvantage Stymies Broncos Again

For the fourth consecutive year, the Super Bowl resulted in a rout of the AFC by the NFC. For the second year in a row, the victim was Denver. The consensus opinion was that Washington, a good big team, had proven superior to a fair small team with one great player — Denver's John Elway.

In spite of the 42-10 score, Super Bowl XXII had its share of drama, including the biggest single-quarter offensive explosion in Super Bowl history. The most publicized element in the two weeks prior to the game was that of Washington's Doug Williams being the first black to start a Super Bowl and inevitable comparisons of his abilities and those of Elway.

Largely because of the perceived advantage the Broncos had with Elway, Denver entered the game as a 3 1/2-point favorite. Williams, who gained the Redskins' starting job only at the end of the regular season, handled the pregame media blitz with grace, even when fielding such inane questions as, "How long have you been a black quarterback?"

The Broncos broke on top when Elway hit wide receiver Ricky Nattiel with a 56-yard touchdown bomb after only 1:57 of the first quarter. Elway looked off Redskin cornerback Barry Wilburn until the last second before turning to Nattiel. On Denver's next possession, a trick pass — Steve Sewell to Elway — helped the Broncos drive close to the Washington goalline before settling for Rich Karlis' 24-yard field goal.

Meanwhile, Washington seemed unable to muster a consistent offense. Near the end of the quarter, Williams slipped on the turf and twisted his knee, forcing him to leave the field for a play.

The Redskins entered the second quarter trailing 10-0 and with a limping quarterback. They proceeded to put together the most remarkable 15 minutes in Super Bowl history. First, Williams hit Ricky Sanders for an 80-yard TD, tying the S.B. record for the longest reception. The play, which many regarded as the turning point, was designed to go short, but, when Sanders was bumped at the line of scrimmage, he adjusted by going long. Next, Williams threw to Gary Clark for 27 yards to put the Skins in front 14-10. Moments later, rookie running back Timmy Smith broke away for 58 yards on a counter play to widen the lead. The next possession saw the Williams-to-Sanders combination click for a 50-yard TD. Tight end Clint Didier scored the Redskins' fifth touchdown with 1:04 left in the period on an eight-yard toss from Williams.

The Redskins' 35 points in one quarter was a record for a postseason game. They totaled 356 yards on only 18 plays. Individual marks for the quarter included Smith's 122 rushing yards (on five carries), Sanders' 168 receiving yards (on five catches) and Williams' 228 passing yards (on 9-of-11 completions). His four TD passes set a record for one quarter and tied the S.B. record for a game.

The second half was anticlimactic. The Redskins kept mainly to the ground. Smith, who was not told he would start until shortly before game time, scored the only touchdown of the second half on a four-yard run at 1:51 of the fourth quarter. For the game, Smith broke Marcus Allen's S.B. record with 204 yards on 22 carries. Other S.B. records were broken by Williams (340 passing yards), Sanders (193 receiving yards) and kicker Ali Haji-Sheikh (six extra points). The Redskins' 602 net yards was also a S.B. record.

Meanwhile, Denver was held completely in check. With Elway forced to pass on most plays in a futile attempt to catch up, the Redskins sacked him five times. He completed only 14-of-38 attempts for 257 yards and had three intercepted — two by Wilburn. Williams, who completed 18-of-29, was chosen the game's Most Valuable Player, certainly the most effective answer to those who questioned the ability of a black quarterback to win a Super Bowl.

LINEUPS

DENVER		WASHINGTON
	OFFENSE	
Jackson	WR	Clark
Studdard	LT	Jacoby
Bishop	LG	McKenzie
Freeman	C	Bostic
Humphries	RG	Thielemann
Lanier	RT	May
Kay	TE	Warren
Nattiel	WR	Sanders
Elway	QB	Williams
Winder	RB-TE	Didier
Lang	RB	Smith
	DEFENSE	
Townsend	LE	Mann
Kragen	NT-DLT	Butz
	DRT	Grant
Jones	DRE	Manley
Fletcher	LOLB	Kaufman
Mecklenburg	LILB	
	MLB	Olkewicz
Hunley	RILB	
Ryan	ROLB	Coleman
Haynes	LCB	Green
Wilson	RCB	Wilburn
Lilly	FS	Bowles
Smith	SS	Walton

SUBSTITUTES

DENVER

	OFFENSE	
Bell	Johnson	Mobley
Boddie	Kartz	Sewell
Bowyer	Kubiak	Watson
Braxton	Micho	
	DEFENSE	
Brooks	Fletcher	Plummer
Castille	Gilbert	Robbins
Clark	Klosterman	Woodard
Dennison	Lucas	
	KICKERS	
Horan	Karlis	

WASHINGTON

	OFFENSE	
Branch	Jones	Rogers
Bryant	Kehr	Schroeder
Griffin	Monk	Vaughn
Grimm	Orr	Yarber
	DEFENSE	
Caldwell	Gouveia	Koch
Davis	Hamel	Milot
Dean	Hamilton	Woodberry
	KICKERS	
Cox	Haji-Sheikh	

SCORING

WASHINGTON	0	35	0	7-	42
DENVER	10	0	0	0-	10

First Quarter
Denver — Nattiel, 56 yard pass from Elway
PAT — Karlis (kick)
Denver — Karlis, 24 yard field goal

Second Quarter
Wash. — Sanders, 80 yard pass from Williams
PAT — Haji-Sheikh (kick)
Wash. — Clark, 27 yard pass from Williams
PAT — Haji-Sheikh (kick)
Wash. — Smith, 58 yard run
PAT — Haji-Sheikh (kick)
Wash. — Sanders, 50 yard pass from Williams
PAT — Haji-Sheikh (kick)
Wash. — Didier, 8 yard pass from Williams
PAT — Haji-Sheikh (kick)

Fourth Quarter
Wash. — Smith, 4 yard run
PAT — Haji-Sheikh (kick)

TEAM STATISTICS

WASH.		DEN
25	First Downs-Total	18
13	First Downs-Rushing	6
11	First Downs-Passing	10
1	First Downs-Penalty	2
1	Fumbles-Number	0
0	Fumbles-Lost Ball	0
6	Penalties Number	5
65	Yards Penalized	26
0	Missed Field Goals	0
72	Offensive Plays	61
602	Net Yards	327
8.4	Average Gain	5.4
1	Giveaways	3
3	Takeaways	1
+2	Difference	-2

INDIVIDUAL STATISTICS

WASHINGTON	No.	Yds.	Avg.	DENVER	No.	Yds.	Avg
RUSHING							
Smith	22	204	9.3	Lang	5	38	7.6
Bryant	8	38	4.8	Elway	3	32	10.7
Clark	1	25	25.0	Winder	8	30	3.8
Rogers	5	17	3.4	Sewell	1	-3	-3.0
Griffin	1	2	2.0		17	97	5.7
Sanders	1	-4	-4.0				
Williams	2	-2	-2.0				
	40	280	7.0				
RECEIVING							
Sanders	9	193	21.4	Jackson	4	76	19.0
Clark	3	55	18.3	Sewell	4	41	10.3
Warren	2	15	7.5	Nattiel	2	69	24.5
Monk	1	40	40.0	Kay	2	38	19.0
Bryant	1	20	20.0	Winder	1	26	26.0
Smith	1	9	9.0	Elway	1	23	23.0
Didier	1	8	8.0	Lang	1	7	7.0
	18	340	18.9		15	280	18.7
PUNTING							
Cox	4		37.5	Horan	7		36.1
PUNT RETURNS							
Green	1	0	0.0	Clark	2	18	9.0
KICKOFF RETURNS							
Sanders	3	46	15.3	Bell	5	88	17.6
INTERCEPTION RETURNS							
Wilburn	2	11	5.5	Castille	1	0	0.0
Davis	1	0	0.0				
	3	33	3.7				

PASSING

	Att.	Comp.	Comp. Pct.	Yds.	Int.	Yds./Att.	Yds./Comp.	Yards Lost Tackled
WASHINGTON								
Williams	29	18	62	340	1	11.7	18.9	1-10
Schroeder	1	0	0	0	0	0	0	1-8
	30	18	60	340	1	11.3	18.9	2-18
DENVER								
Elway	38	14	37	257	3	6.8	18.4	5-50
Sewell	1	1	100	23	0	23.0	23.0	0-0
	39	15	38	280	3	7.2	18.7	5-50

N.F.C. 1988 Ready for Prime Time

Charisma — that indefiniable quality that separates the stars from the merely starring — was attributed to the N.F.C. over the A.F.C. in 1988, both in a widely-quoted poll of "experts" conducted by a Houston newspaper and on television by ESPN. The Houston respondents named the Bears the most charismatic team, with the Redskins, 49ers and Cowboys also ranked high. Cumulatively, the N.F.C. teams came in ahead of the A.F.C 's, although Atlanta finished dead last. ESPN agreed in general that the N.F.C. had the better of it in "star quality," citing the conference's recent Super Bowl successes and pointing out that the most consistently successful teams of the 1980s were in the N.F.C. Another factor, however, was that the N.F.C. had a larger share of the major television markets.

Charsima or not, the A.F.C. finished on top in interconference games for the second straight year, 30-22. In fact, the charismatic N.F.C. had come out in victories against the mundane A.F.C. only once since 1971.

EASTERN DIVISION

Philadelphia Eagles — Word before the season was that coach Buddy Ryan had to get the Eagles into the playoffs — or else. He had one big weapon. QB Randall Cunningham was a unique force, leading the team in rushing for the second straight year and passing for 3,808 yards. He was the key to an offense that usually had just enough to win. The running backs were not much of a factors except as receivers, and WR Mike Quick missed half of the season with a broken ankle. Rookie TE Keith Jackson came straight from a ground-bound attack at Oklahoma to catch 81 passes for Philadelphia. Except for DE Reggie White, the Eagles' defense was ordinary only on paper, but it played tough all season. The Eagles knocked off the Giants twice — the second time on a touchdown scored after New York had blocked an overtime field-goal try. When the Giants dropped their final game to the Jets, the Eagles had the division title, and Ryan was in the playoffs.

New York Giants — The Giants had a soft schedule and were primed for a playoff berth. Phil Simms had another strong year, aided by healthy WR Lionel Manuel. However, TE Mark Bavaro was only so-so. RB Joe Morris gained over 1,000 yards rushing again, but most of them came in the last four games, when the offensive line finally gelled, with the play of rookies OG Eric Moore and OT John Elliott. The defense was okay, but never as dominant as it had been in the last few seasons. OLB Lawrence Taylor missed the first four games with a drug suspension, ILB Harry Carson missed the last four with an injury, and OLB Carl Banks never for rolling after holding out at the beginning of the season.

Washington Redskins — One quarterback controversey was defused when Jay Schroeder was traded to the Raiders after the first game, but another debate soon arose. QB Doug Williams underwent an emergency appendectomy, and unheralded Mark Rypien played so well in his stead that whichever played from then on, he was the "wrong quarterback" for most Redskins fans. The Redskins stayed close enough through two-thirds of the season, then faded. The quarterbacks both played well, but the offensive line was hurt by constant shuffling in an attempt to find a healthy, effective combination. RB Timmy Smith, the Super Bowl hero, flopped as an overweight regular, and Kelvin Bryant, who replaced Smith as the one-back, went out with a knee injury in Game 10. The secondary was also hit with injuries and the linebackers and rush line by age.

Phoenix Cardinals — Owner Bill Bidwell had a bonanza at Sun Devil Stadium, with team-record attendances and league-record ticket prices. The team looked like a winner, too, with a 7-4 record through Week 12. QB Neil Lomax continued the fine comeback he'd begun in 1987, RB's Earl Ferrell and Stump Mitchell provided a steady running attack, and J.T. Smith and Roy Green were among the top receivers. The defense was adequate. The the plug was pulled, and Phoenix collapsed like a — well — house of Cards, losing their last five games. Part of the problem was a flare-up of Lomax's arthritic hip that sidelined him for a couple of games, part of it was injuries and mistakes, but most of the nose dive was simply that the other teams had more talent.

Dallas Cowboys — Dallas fans with long memories insisted the season was worse than 1960, when the Cowboys went through their first NFL season winless. Fans with short memories blasted coach Tom Landry, and one newsman even accused him of senility in print. More rational fans recognized an offensive line torn up by injuries, a defense longer on youth than talent, and a quarterback, in Steve Pelluer, who had fair statistics but a penchant for making the big mistake. Through the debacle that included a 10-game losing streak, Herschel Walker was terrific. He led the NFC with 1,514 rushing yards (and had 505 more on 53 pass receptions. The team was up for sale, but no one was racing to pick up the $150 milliion asked.

CENTRAL DIVISION

Chicago Bears — The Bears rode their great defense to a fifth straight NFC Central championship, despite losing OLB's Wilbur Marshall to Washington through free agency and Otis Wilson to a season-ending knee injury in preseason. DE Richard Dent was having one of his best seasons (10.5 sacks) until he, too, went out with a broken ankle. Still, Mike Singletary, Dave Duerson, Steve McMichael, Dan Hampton and a host of rookies stuffed opponents for a league-low 215 points. QB Jim McMahon had his annual injury at midseason, but Mike Tomczak played well in relief. RB Neal Anderson emerged as a star in his third season. The biggest Bears' story was coach Mike Ditka's midseason heart attack. He returned to the sideline after missing only one game, promising a calmer, more patient demeanor.

Minnesota Vikings — The Vikings were clearly the coming power of the NFC Central. Their defense, led by DT Keith Millard, DE Chris Doleman, LB Scott Studwell, CB Carl Lee and SS Joey Browner was being compared to the Bears' — and some said it was better. QB Wade Wilson led the NFC in passing, although veteran Tommy Kramer won a couple of early-season games. Wilson caused some ripples when he complained about being benched in the second half of the final-game win over Chicago. Both quarterbacks were aided immeasurably by WR's Anthony Carter (1,225 yards) and Hassan Jones and TE Steve Jodan. The passing game had to carry the attack because none of the runners were able to gain consistently.

Tampa Bay Buccaneers — Vinny Testaverde was handed the quarterback job in his second season. He threw far too many interceptions (35) and his pass rating was a horrible 48.8. Nevertheless, he showed some progress, along with the other eight first- or second-year players starting on offense. Particularlty impressive were WR Bruce Hill and rookie OT Paul Gruber. When the improving defense held the last three opponents to a total of 25 points, the Bucs were able to win twice.

Green Bay Packers — When Forrest Gregg resigned to return to his alma mater, Southern Methodist, Lindy Infante was brought in as coach. Infante has earned an enviable reputation as an offensive coordinator, most recently with Cleveland. The young Pack had problems with the new system, and the offense lagged all season, wasting several strong efforts by a good defense. LB Tim Haris was exceptional. He, the other linebackers and a slow but cagey secondary, made up for a lack of a pass rush up front. But, with a flat offense, the Packers were set for the No. 1 draft choice in 1989 until they blew it with a victory over Phoenix in the final game.

Detroit Lions — The Lions were bad, slow and dull. QB Chuck Long seemed to regress and they was kayoed in the sixth game. With Eric

FINAL TEAM STATISTICS

OFFENSE

	ATL	CHI	DAL	DET	G.B.	L.A.	MINN	N.O.	NYG	PHIL	PHX	S.F.	T.B.	WASH
FIRST DOWNS:														
Total	257	303	311	226	280	333	318	306	317	318	336	326	295	307
by Rushing	106	137	112	63	78	114	112	108	123	105	122	141	91	88
by Passing	136	134	175	141	175	203	187	179	168	179	195	167	173	202
by Penalty	15	32	24	22	27	16	19	19	26	34	19	18	31	17
RUSHING:														
Number	478	555	469	391	385	507	501	512	493	464	480	527	452	437
Yards	2016	2319	1995	1243	1379	2003	1806	2046	1689	1945	2027	2523	1753	1543
Average Yards	4.2	4.2	4.3	3.2	3.6	4.0	3.6	4.0	3.4	4.2	4.2	4.8	3.9	3.5
Touchdowns	11	25	10	7	14	16	22	9	15	17	15	18	11	8
PASSING:														
Attempts	481	461	555	477	582	522	520	498	525	581	562	502	512	592
Completions	250	248	307	213	319	312	294	286	290	309	322	293	253	327
Completion Pct.	52.0	53.8	55.3	44.7	54.8	59.8	56.5	57.4	55.2	53.2	57.3	58.4	49.4	55.2
Passing Yards	2914	3173	3727	2572	3609	4002	4100	3256	3716	3927	4191	3675	3608	4339
Avg. Yds per Att.	4.9	6.2	5.9	4.1	5.2	6.9	6.7	5.9	5.6	5.5	6.1	6.2	6.1	6.7
Avg. Yds per Comp.	11.7	12.8	12.1	12.1	11.3	12.8	14.0	11.4	12.8	12.7	13.0	12.5	14.3	13.3
Times Tackled	43	24	35	52	51	28	47	24	60	57	60	47	34	24
Yds Lost Tackled	348	175	239	410	324	197	311	171	450	442	411	298	300	203
Net Yards	2566	2998	3488	2162	3285	3805	3789	3085	3266	3485	3780	3377	3308	4136
Touchdowns	13	13	21	13	13	31	20	21	22	25	26	21	16	33
Interceptions	19	15	27	18	24	18	18	16	14	17	19	14	36	25
Pct. Intercepted	4.0	3.3	4.9	3.8	4.1	3.4	3.5	3.2	2.7	2.9	3.4	2.8	7.0	4.2
PUNTS:														
Number	98	79	80	97	86	76	86	73	81	104	80	80	68	67
Average	40.0	41.5	40.9	42.4	38.2	39.5	39.4	39.9	39.9	39.7	40.3	38.7	36.4	38.2
PUNT RETURNS														
Number	42	38	45	42	35	49	59	35	47	33	52	54	36	52
Yards	343	294	360	346	208	322	553	413	359	233	463	612	328	377
Average Yards	8.2	7.7	8.0	8.2	5.9	6.6	9.4	11.8	7.6	7.1	8.9	11.3	9.1	7.3
Touchdowns	0	0	0	0	1	0	0	1	0	0	0	2	0	0
KICKOFF RET.:														
Number	59	45	69	59	64	59	56	70	62	59	60	55	64	74
Yards	1057	896	1410	1154	1181	1191	1160	1408	1154	1028	1106	978	1345	1355
Average Yards	17.9	19.9	20.4	19.6	18.5	20.2	20.7	20.1	18.6	17.4	18.4	17.8	21.0	18.3
Touchdowns	0	0	0	0	0	0	0	0	0	0	0	0	0	0
INTERCEPT RET.:														
Number	24	26	10	15	20	22	36	17	15	32	16	22	21	14
Yards	185	237	67	247	224	281	589	295	292	371	88	88	283	193
Average Yards	7.7	9.1	6.7	16.5		11.2	16.4	17.4	19.5	11.6	5.5	4.0	13.5	13.8
Touchdowns	1	0	1	2	0	1	5	0	2	0	0	0	1	0
PENALTIES:														
Number	67	88	141	94	94	78	118	101	88	115	99	115	102	96
Yards	542	644	1148	804	785	587	998	821	660	907	790	986	816	817
FUMBLES:														
Number	29	37	22	31	44	28	22	29	32	29	34	27	27	34
Number Lost	18	19	13	15	26	16	12	16	13	9	16	12	16	21
POINTS:														
Total	244	312	265	220	240	407	406	312	359	379	344	369	261	345
PAT Attempts	27	38	32	23	29	48	49	33	41	43	44	41	28	41
PAT Made	25	37	32	22	23	45	48	32	39	42	42	40	28	40
FG Attempts	30	19	25	21	25	32	25	36	30	32	21	38	30	26
FG Made	19	15	13	20	13	24	20	26	24	23	12	27	21	19
Percent FG Made	63.3	78.9	52.0	95.2	52.0	75.0	80.0	72.2	80.0	71.9	57.1	71.1	70.0	73.1
Safeties	0	1	1	0	2	1	2	2	1	2	1	1	1	1

DEFENSE

	ATL	CHI	DAL	DET	G.B.	L.A.	MINN	N.O.	NYG	PHIL	PHX	S.F.	T.B.	WASH
FIRST DOWNS:														
Total	312	264	297	334	281	289	243	286	291	311	301	277	293	294
by Rushing	124	76	93	128	130	100	85	97	95	85	111	90	104	113
by Passing	168	158	180	179	136	166	132	167	177	199	170	160	169	153
by Penalty	20	30	24	27	15	23	26	22	19	27	20	27	20	28
RUSHING:														
Number	518	389	454	511	514	414	435	442	454	466	467	441	478	442
Yards	2319	1326	1858	2037	2110	1686	1602	1779	1759	1652	1925	1588	1551	1745
Average Yards	4.5	3.4	4.1	4.0	4.1	4.1	3.7	4.0	3.9	3.5	4.1	3.6	3.2	3.9
Touchdowns	14	5	13	16	17	12	10	7	8	11	19	8	21	17
PASSING:														
Attempts	504	545	523	513	474	571	480	505	566	578	508	530	527	497
Completions	281	245	264	337	256	307	219	277	294	309	264	292	304	261
Completion Pct.	55.8	45.0	50.5	65.7	54.0	53.8	45.6	54.9	51.9	53.5	52.0	55.1	57.7	52.5
Passing Yards	3584	3399	3883	3672	2949	3694	2763	3579	3755	4443	3539	3284	3744	3744
Avg. Yds per Att.	6.3	5.2	6.3	5.9	5.4	5.3	4.8	6.2	5.4	6.7	5.9	5.2	6.6	6.4
Avg. Yds per Comp.	12.8	13.9	14.7	10.9	11.5	12.0	12.0	12.9	12.8	14.4	13.4	11.3	12.3	14.3
Times Tackled	30	43	46	47	30	56	37	31	52	42	39	42	20	43
Yds Lost Tackled	211	365	327	393	216	394	274	252	428	296	295	297	140	305
Net Yards	3373	3034	3556	3279	2733	3300	2489	3327	3327	4147	3244	2987	3604	3439
Touchdowns	17	18	30	17	12	17	12	19	23	23	30	25	19	24
Interceptions	24	26	10	15	20	22	36	17	15	32	16	22	21	14
Pct. Intercepted	4.8	4.8	1.9	2.9	4.2	3.9	7.5	3.4	2.7	5.5	3.1	4.2	4.0	2.8
PUNTS:														
Number	73	90	86	74	76	93	96	70	93	85	83	86	77	79
Average	39.6	40.2	41.6	39.4	37.6	39.9	42.3	40.2	39.8	37.8	41.1	41.0	39.0	39.4
PUNT RETURNS														
Number	51	40	37	57	39	43	39	39	38	47	41	47	38	39
Yards	297	447	239	483	314	347	405	248	303	393	416	426	273	448
Average Yards	5.8	11.2	6.5	8.5	8.1	8.1	10.4	6.4	8.0	8.4	10.1	9.1	7.2	11.5
Touchdowns	0	0	0	1	0	0	0	0	0	0	1	0	0	1
KICKOFF RET.:														
Number	48	56	56	56	49	81	81	43	73	63	65	73	52	61
Yards	982	1130	1060	1076	966	1563	1622	823	1269	1266	1379	1362	1129	1111
Average Yards	20.5	20.2	18.9	19.2	19.7	19.3	20.0	19.1	17.4	20.1	21.2	18.7	21.7	18.2
Touchdowns	0	0	0	0	0	1	0	0	0	0	1	0	0	0
INTERCEPT RET.:														
Number	19	15	27	18	24	18	18	16	14	17	19	14	36	25
Yards	214	175	314	159	386	138	212	226	116	98	264	185	486	271
Average Yards	11.3	11.7	11.6	8.8	16.1	7.7	11.8	14.1	8.3	5.8	13.9	13.2	13.5	10.8
Touchdowns	2	1	0	0	4	1	1	2	0	0	0	1	2	0
PENALTIES:														
Number	92	102	92	106	112	111	91	77	116	115	103	76	105	91
Yards	761	804	772	869	903	937	753	628	902	897	770	603	872	711
FUMBLES:														
Number	29	17	24	35	33	36	36	27	36	28	27	30	29	23
Number Lost	14	9	9	21	21	15	17	15	18	12	13	16	12	8
POINTS:														
Total	315	215	381	313	315	293	233	283	304	319	398	294	350	387
PAT Attempts	34	25	44	34	34	35	24	29	32	37	51	34	42	46
PAT Made	31	22	41	32	34	35	22	28	31	35	47	34	42	43
FG Attempts	36	22	29	29	35	23	25	34	33	29	22	24	30	36
FG Made	26	13	24	25	25	16	21	27	25	20	13	18	18	22
Percent FG Made	72.2	59.1	82.8	86.2	71.4	69.6	84.0	79.4	75.8	69.0	59.1	75.0	60.0	61.1
Safeties	1	2	2	1	1	0	2	0	0	1	3	1	1	1

Hipple also out injured, Raiders' reject Rusty Hilger became the starter in his first week with the team. While the offense evaporated, the defense had some bright spots in rookies LB Chris Spielman and SS Bennie Blades and veteran LB Mike Cofer. That wasn't nearly enough to save Darryl Rogers' job. He was replaced by defensive coordinator Wayne Fontes with five games to go. The Lions won two of the remaining games.

WESTERN DIVISION

San Francisco 49ers — Coach Bill Walsh lit a quarterback controversey by declaring the competition open for the No. 1 spot before training camp. Then, after Joe Montana had apparently won his job, he was kept on the bench longer than he or other observers deemed necessary when he was injured. Roger Craig had his greatest season, but Jerry Rice nursed a bad ankle through most of the schedule and the offensive line also struggled early. The 'Niners were 6-5 with five games to go. Then everything came together. San Francisco reeled off four straight victories to clinch the division title and make what might have been a showdown with the Rams academic. Down the stretch, Montana was strong, Craig kept going and the line became cohesive. The defense, led by Ronnie Lott, Michael Carter and Charles Haley, was tough all the way.

Los Angeles Rams — The Rams roared to a 7-2 record after nine games. The defense was on a record sack pace. Jim Everett had an All-Pro first half-season, as did Greg Bell, the runner picked up from Buffalo as part of 1987's Eric Dickerson trade. WR Henry Ellard was also enjoying his best season. Then the wheels came off the defense and Los Angeles dropped four straight to slip to third place. When the defense magically returned in Week 14, coach John Robinson's team rallied for three straight wins, including victories over the Bears and 49ers, to gain a playoff berth for the fifth time in six years.

New Orleans Saints — The Saints had their second consecutive winning season and only the second in their history — but 1988 was nevertheless disappointing. Saints fans were primed for a division title and a second trip to the playoffs. Instead, the Saints tripped coming down the stretch, losing three straight before winning the finale over Atlanta by a single point. Injuries cut into a squad that wasn't very deep, and one game was lost to the Giants when Morten Andersen, the nonpareil, missed a 29-yard field goal. The defense depended on the outstanding linebackers both to stop the run and rush the passer, and when opponents could neutralize Rickey Jackson, Vaughan Johnson, Sam Mills and Pat Swilling, the Saints are in trouble.

Atlanta Falcons — The Falcons went through another losing season in 1988, but finished up more hopeful than in recent season's past. The offense gave signs of respectability. Young quarterback Chris Miller made definite progress both in passing and leadership. When Gerald Riggs was forced out with an injury, second-year free-agent John Settle settled in for a 1,000-yard seaosn. OG Bill Fralic and OT Mike Kenn had banner seasons. The defense cut over 100 points from its largess, as Scott Case led the league in interceptions and rookie LB Aundray Bruce played like a star in the making on occasions. The Falcons also had the league's most tragic event — DB David Croudip died October 10 of an apparent drug overdose.

PHILADELPHIA EAGLES 10-6 Buddy Ryan

Score of Each Game		
41	Tampa Bay	14
24	CINCINNATI	28
10	Washington	17
21	Minnesota	23
32	HOUSTON	23
24	N.Y. GIANTS	13
3	Cleveland	19
24	DALLAS	23
24	ATLANTA	27
30	L.A. RAMS **	24
27	Pittsburgh	26
23	N.Y. Giants	*17
31	PHOENIX	21
19	WASHINGTON	20
23	Phoenix	17
23	Dallas	7

Use Name	Pos.	Hgt	Wgt	Age	Int	Pts
Matt Darwin	OT	6'4"	275	25		
Ron Heller	OT	6'3"	280	26		
Ken Reeves	OT-OG	6'5"	270	27		
David Alexander	OG-C	6'3"	275	23		
Ron Baker	OG	6'4"	274	34		
Reggie Singletary	OG-OT	6'3"	280	24		
Ron Solt (from IND)	OG	6'3"	285	26		
Ben Tamburello	OG-C	6'3"	278	23		
Dave Rimington	C	6'3"	288	28		
Doug Bartlett	DE-DT	6'2"	255	25		
Jonathan Dumbauld (to NO)	DE	6'4"	259	25		
Donald Evans	DE	6'2"	241	24		
John Klingel	DE	6'3"	267	24		
Clyde Simmons	DE	6'6"	276	24		8
Reggie White	DE-DT	6'5"	285	26		
Jerome Brown	DT	6'2"	288	23	1	
Mike Golic	DT	6'5"	275	26		
Mike Pitts	DT	6'5"	277	28		
Ty Allert	LB	6'2"	233	25		
Todd Bell	LB	6'1"	212	30		
Scott Curtis	LB	6'1"	230	24		
Byron Evans	LB	6'2"	225	24		
Dwayne Jiles	LB	6'4"	250	27		
Seth Joyner	LB	6'2"	248	24	4	
Mike Reichenbach	LB	6'2"	230	27		
Eric Allen	DB	5'10"	183	21	5	
Eric Everett	DB	5'10"	161	22	1	
William Frizzell	DB	6'3"	205	26	3	
Terry Hoage	DB	6'3"	201	26	8	6
Wes Hopkins	DB	6'1"	212	27	5	
Izel Jenkins	DB	5'10"	191	23	2	
Andre Waters	DB	5'11"	195	26	3	
Roynell Young	DB	6'1"	185	30	2	
Matt Cavanaugh	QB	6'2"	210	32		
Randall Cunningham	QB	6'4"	203	25		36
Don McPherson	QB	6'1"	183	23		
Walter Abercrombie	HB	6'	210	29		
Keith Byars	HB	6'1"	238	25		60
Mark Konecny	HB	5'11"	200	25		
Junior Tautalatasi	HB-FB	5'10"	210	26		
Michael Haddix	FB	6'2"	227	27		
Anthony Toney	FB	6'	227	25		30
Shawn Beals	WR	5'10"	178	22		
Cris Carter	WR	6'3"	194	23		42
Gregg Garrity	WR	5'10"	169	26		6
Kenny Jackson	WR	6'	180	26		
Ron Johnson	WR	6'3"	186	30		12
Mike Quick	WR	6'2"	190	27		24
Jimmie Giles	TE	6'3"	240	34		6
Keith Jackson	TE	6'2"	250	23		36
Dave Little	TE	6'2"	226	27		
Dean Dorsey (to GB)	K	5'11"	195	31		27
John Teltschik	K	6'2"	209	24		
Luis Zendejas (from DAL)	K	5'9"	160	26		95

Bob Landsee — Knee Injury
Eric Bailey — Back Injury

NEW YORK GIANTS 10-6 Bill Parcells

Score of Each Game		
27	WASHINGTON	20
17	SAN FRANCISCO	20
12	Dallas	10
31	L.A. RAMS	45
24	Washington	23
13	Philadelphia	24
30	DETROIT	10
23	Atlanta	16
13	Detroit	*10
29	DALLAS	21
17	Phoenix	24
17	PHILADELPHIA	*23
13	New Orleans	12
44	PHOENIX	7
28	KANSAS CITY	12
21	N.Y. Jets	27

Use Name	Pos.	Hgt	Wgt	Age	Int	Pts
John Elliott	OT	6'7"	305	23		
Eric Moore	OT	6'5"	290	23		
Karl Nelson	OT	6'6"	285	28		
Doug Riesenberg	OT	6'5"	275	23		
William Roberts	OT	6'5"	280	26		
Billy Ard	OG	6'3"	270	29		
Damian Johnson	OG-OT	6'5"	290	25		
Joe Fields	C	6'2"	253	34		
Bart Oates	C	6'3"	265	29		
Eric Dorsey	DE	6'5"	280	24		
Leonard Marshall	DE	6'3"	285	26		
George Martin	DE	6'4"	255	35		
John Washington	DE	6'4"	275	25		
Robb White	DE	6'4"	270	23		
Jim Burt	NT	6'1"	260	29		6
Erik Howard	NT	6'4"	268	23		
Carl Banks	LB	6'4"	235	26	1	6
Harry Carson	LB	6'2"	240	34	2	
Johnie Cooks (from IND)	LB	6'4"	251	29		
Andy Headen	LB	6'5"	242	28		
Byron Hunt	LB	6'5"	242	29		
Pepper Johnson	LB	6'3"	248	24	1	6
Gary Reasons	LB	6'4"	234	26	1	
Ricky Shaw	LB	6'4"	240	23		
Lawrence Taylor	LB	6'3"	243	29		
Mark Collins	DB	5'10"	190	24	1	2
Tom Flynn	DB	6'	195	26		6
Neal Guggemos	DB	6'1"	190	24		
Wayne Haddix	DB	6'1"	203	23		
Kenny Hill	DB	6'	195	30		
Terry Kinard	DB	6'1"	200	28	3	
Greg Lasker (to CHI and PHX)	DB	6'	200	23		
Adrian White	DB	6'	200	24	1	
Sheldon White	DB	5'11"	188	23	4	
Perry Williams	DB	6'2"	203	27	1	
Jeff Hostetler	QB	6'3"	212	27		
Jeff Rutledge	QB	6'1"	195	31		
Phil Simms	QB	6'3"	214	31		
Ottis Anderson	HB	6'2"	225	31		48
Joe Morris	HB	5'7"	195	27		30
George Adams	FB	6'1"	225	25		
Maurice Carthon	FB	6'1"	225	27		18
Lee Rouson	FB	6'1"	222	25		
Stephen Baker	WR	5'8"	160	24		42
Mark Ingram	WR	5'10"	188	23		6
Lionel Manuel	WR	5'11"	180	26		24
Phil McConkey	WR	5'10"	170	31		
Stacy Robinson	WR	5'11"	186	26		18
Odessa Turner	WR	6'3"	205	23		6
Mark Bavaro	TE	6'4"	245	25		24
Brad Beckman	TE	6'2"	236	23		
Zeke Mowatt	TE	6'3"	240	27		6
Tim Sherwin	TE	6'5"	252	30		
Raul Allegre	K	5'10"	167	29		44
Maury Buford	K	6'1"	195	28		
Sean Landeta	K	6'	200	26		
Paul McFadden	K	5'11"	166	26		67

Herb Welch — Leg Injury

WASHINGTON REDSKINS 7-9 Joe Gibbs

Score of Each Game		
20	N.Y. Giants	27
30	PITTSBURGH	29
17	PHILADELPHIA	10
21	Phoenix	30
23	N.Y. GIANTS	24
35	Dallas	17
33	PHOENIX	17
20	Green Bay Mil.)	17
17	Houston	41
27	NEW ORLEANS	24
14	CHICAGO	34
21	San Francisco	37
13	CLEVELAND	17
20	Philadelphia	19
17	DALLAS	24
17	Cincinnati	*20

Use Name	Pos.	Hgt	Wgt	Age	Int	Pts
Joe Jacoby	OT	6'7"	305	29		
Jim Lachey (from RAID)	OT	6'6"	290	25		
Mark May	OT-OG	6'6"	295	28		
Ed Simmons	OT	6'5"	280	24		
Russ Grimm	OG	6'3"	275	29		
Raleigh McKenzie	OG-C	6'2"	270	25		
R.C. Thielemann	OG	6'4"	272	33		
Jeff Bostic	C	6'2"	260	29		
Dave Harbour	C	6'4"	265	22		
Mike Scully	C	6'5"	280	22		
Steve Hamilton	DE-DT	6'4"	270	26		
Markus Koch	DE	6'5"	275	25		
Dexter Manley	DE	6'3"	257	29		
Charles Mann	DE	6'6"	270	27		
Dave Butz	DT	6'7"	295	39		
Darryl Grant	DT	6'1"	275	28		
Dean Hamel	DT	6'3"	280	27		
Ravin Caldwell	LB	6'3"	229	25		2
Monte Coleman	LB	6'2"	230	30	1	
Kurt Gouveia	LB	6'1"	227	23		
Mel Kaufman	LB	6'2"	230	30		
Greg Manusky	LB	6'1"	242	22		
Wilber Marshall	LB	6'1"	230	26	3	
Neal Olkewicz	LB	6'	230	31		
Todd Bowles	DB	6'2"	203	24	1	
Brian Davis	DB	6'2"	190	25	1	
Steve Gage	DB	6'3"	210	24		
Darrell Green	DB	5'8"	170	28	1	
Johnny Thomas	DB	5'9"	190	24		
Clarence Vaughn	DB	6'	202	24		
Alvin Walton	DB	6'	180	24	3	
Barry Wilburn	DB	6'3"	186	24	4	
Kevin Williams	DB	5'9"	169	26		
Dennis Woodberry	DB	5'10"	183	27		
David Archer	QB	6'2"	208	26		
Mark Rypien	QB	6'4"	234	25		6
Doug Williams	QB	6'4"	220	33		6
Kelvin Bryant	HB	6'2"	195	27		36
Keith Griffin	HB	5'8"	185	26		6
Jamie Morris	HB	5'7"	188	23		12
Mike Oliphant	HB	5'10"	183	25		
Timmy Smith	HB-FB	5'11"	216	24		18
Anthony Allen	WR	5'11"	182	29		6
Gary Clark	WR	5'9"	173	25		42
Billy Johnson	WR	5'9"	170	36		
Art Monk	WR	6'3"	209	30		30
Ricky Sanders	WR	5'11"	180	26		72
Derrick Shepard	WR	5'10"	187	24		
Joe Caravello	TE	6'3"	270	25		
Anrthony Jones (to SD)	TE	6'3"	248	28		
Craig McEwen	TE	6'1"	220	22		
Ron Middleton	TE	6'2"	252	23		
Terry Orr	TE	6'3"	227	26		12
Don Warren	TE	6'4"	242	32		
Tommy Barnhardt	K	6'3"	205	25		
Greg Coleman	K	6'	184	33		
Steve Cox	K	6'4"	195	30		
Chip Lohmiller	K	6'3"	213	22		97

Dan Benish — Knee Injury
Blake Hitchcock — Knee Injury
Rick Kehr — Knee Injury
Eric Yarber — Knee Injury

PHOENIX CARDINALS 7-9 Gene Stallings

Score of Each Game		
14	Cincinnati	21
14	DALLAS	17
30	Tampa Bay	24
30	WASHINGTON	21
41	L.A. Rams	27
31	PITTSBURGH	14
17	Washington	33
21	CLEVELAND	29
16	Dallas	10
24	SAN FRANCISCO	23
24	N.Y. GIANTS	17
20	Houston	38
21	Philadelphia	31
7	N.Y. Giants	44
17	PHILADELPHIA	23
17	GREEN BAY	26

Use Name	Pos.	Hgt	Wgt	Age	Int	Pts
Ray Brown	OT-OG	6'5"	280	25		
Tootie Robbins	OT	6'5"	302	30		
Luis Sharpe	OT	6'4"	260	28		
Joe Bostic	OG	6'3"	268	31		
Scott Dill	OG	6'5"	272	22		
Todd Peat	OG	6'2"	294	24		
Lance Smith	OG-OT	6'2"	262	24		
Mark Traynowicz (from BUF)	OG	6'5"	280	26		
Derek Kennard	C-OG	6'3"	285	25		
David Galloway	DE	6'3"	279	29		
Sean McNanie	DE	6'5"	270	26		
Freddie Joe Nunn	DE	6'4"	255	26		
Rod Saddler	DE	6'5"	276	22		6
Steve Alvord	DT	6'4"	272	23		
Bob Clasby	DT	6'5"	280	27	1	
Anthony Bell	LB	6'3"	231	24		
Wayne Davis	LB	6'1"	213	24		
Ken Harvey	LB	6'2"	225	23		2
Ricky Hunley	LB	6'2"	250	26		
Tyrone Jones	LB	6'	220	25		
E.J. Junior	LB	6'3"	235	28	1	6
Niko Noga	LB	6'1"	235	26		
Michael Brim	DB	6'	186	22		
Carl Carter	DB	5'11"	180	24	3	
Travis Curtis	DB	5'10"	180	22	1	
Lester Lyles	DB	6'3"	205	25	2	
Cedric Mack	DB	6'	194	27	3	6
Tim McDonald	DB	6'2"	207	23	2	
Roland Mitchell	DB	5'11"	180	24	1	
Reggie Phillips	DB	5'10"	175	27		
Lonnie Young	DB	6'1"	182	25	1	
Neil Lomax	QB	6'3"	215	29		6
Cliff Stoudt	QB	6'4"	215	33		
Tom Tupa	QB	6'4"	220	21		
Tony Jeffery	HB	5'11"	208	24		
Tony Jordan	HB	6'2"	220	23		18
Derrick McAdoo (from TB)	HB	5'10"	195	23		
Stump Mitchell	HB	5'9"	188	29		30
Vai Sikahema	HB	5'9"	191	26		
Jessie Clark (from DET)	FB	6'	228	28		
Earl Ferrell	FB	6'	240	30		54
Ricky Moore	FB	5'11"	253	25		
Ron Wolfley	FB	6'	222	25		
Roy Green	WR	6'	195	31		42
Don Holmes	WR	5'10"	180	27		
Ernie Jones	WR	5'11"	186	23		18
Andy Schillinger	WR	5'11"	179	23		
J.T. Smith	WR	6'2"	185	32		30
Rob Awalt	TE	6'5"	248	24		
Greg Baty	TE	6'5"	242	24		
Jay Novacek	TE	6'4"	235	25		24
Mark Walczak	TE	6'6"	246	26		
Al Del Greco	K	5'10"	191	26		78
Greg Horne	K	6'	188	23		

Curtis Greer — Back Injury
Michael Morris — Knee Injury
Colin Scotts — Shoulder Injury

DALLAS COWBOYS 3-13 Tom Landry

Score of Each Game		
21	Pittsburgh	24
17	Phoenix	14
10	N.Y. GIANTS	12
26	ATLANTA	20
17	New Orleans	20
17	WASHINGTON	35
7	Chicago	17
23	Philadelphia	24
10	PHOENIX	16
21	N.Y. Giants	29
3	MINNESOTA	43
24	CINCINNATI	38
17	HOUSTON	25
21	Cleveland	24
24	Washington	17
7	PHILADELPHIA	23

Use Name	Pos.	Hgt	Wgt	Age	Int	Pts
Bob Brotzki (from IND)	OT	6'5"	280	25		
Kevin Gogan	OT	6'7"	306	23		
Daryle Smith	OT	6'5"	276	24		
Mark Tuinei	OT	6'5"	282	28		
Dave Widell	OT	6'6"	300	23		
Crawford Ker	OG	6'3"	290	26		
Nate Newton	OG	6'3"	314	26		
Glen Titensor	OG	6'4"	270	30		
Jeff Zimmerman	OG	6'6"	313	23		
Tom Rafferty	C	6'3"	264	34		
Bob White	C	6'5"	273	25		
Jim Jeffcoat	DE	6'5"	262	27		
Too Tall Jones	DE	6'9"	278	37		
Kevin Brooks	DT	6'6"	284	25		
Danny Noonan	DT	6'4"	266	23	1	8
Mark Walen	DT-DE	6'5"	267	25		
Randy White	DT	6'4"	272	35		
Ron Burton	LB	6'1"	245	24		
Garry Cobb	LB	6'2"	233	31		
Steve DeOssie	LB	6'2"	246	25		
Garth Jax	LB	6'2"	230	24		
Eugene Lockhart	LB	6'2"	235	27		
Ken Norton	LB	6'2"	236	21		
Sean Scott	LB	6'1"	226	22		
Vince Albritton	DB	6'2"	220	26		
Bill Bates	DB	6'1"	200	27	1	
Michael Downs	DB	6'3"	215	29	2	
Ron Francis	DB	5'9"	201	24	1	
Manny Hendrix	DB	5'10"	181	23	1	
Billy Owens	DB	6'1"	207	22		
Victor Scott	DB	6'	203	26		
Everson Walls	DB	6'1"	193	28	2	
Robert Williams	DB	5'10"	186	25	2	
Charles Wright (from TB)	DB	5'9"	178	24		
Steve Pelluer	QB	6'4"	212	26		12
Scott Secules	QB	6'3"	219	23		
Kevin Sweeney	QB	6'	193	24		
Danny White	QB	6'2"	200	36		
Mark Higgs	HB	5'7"	196	22		
Herschel Walker	HB-FB	6'1"	226	26		42
Darryl Clack	FB	5'10"	220	24		6
Todd Fowler	FB	6'3"	226	26		
Timmy Newsome	FB	6'1"	236	30		18
Ray Alexander	WR	6'4"	193	26		36
Cornell Burbage	WR	5'10"	189	23		
Kelvin Edwards	WR	6'2"	204	24		
Everett Gay	WR	6'2"	209	23		6
Michael Irvin	WR	6'2"	202	22		30
Kelvin Martin	WR	5'9"	163	23		18
Thornton Chandler	TE	6'5"	240	24		6
Doug Cosbie	TE	6'6"	244	32		
Steve Folsom	TE	6'5"	240	30		12
Roger Ruzek	K	6'1"	195	27		63
Mike Saxon	K	6'3"	198	26		

Jeff Hurd — Knee Injury
Jeff Rohrer — Back Injury
Rod Barksdale — Knee Injury
Mike Sherrard — Leg Injury

PHILADELPHIA EAGLES

RUSHING

Last Name	No.	Yds	Avg	TD
Cunningham	93	624	6.7	6
Byars	152	517	3.4	6
Toney	139	502	3.6	4
Haddix	57	185	3.2	0
Hoage	1	38	38.0	1
Teltschik	2	36	18.0	0
Tautalatasi	14	28	2.0	0
Abercrombie	5	14	2.8	0
Carter	1	1	1.0	0

RECEIVING

Last Name	No.	Yds	Avg	TD
Kei. Jackson	81	869	10.7	6
Byars	72	705	9.8	4
Carter	39	761	19.5	6
Toney	34	256	7.5	1
Quick	22	508	23.1	4
Johnson	19	417	21.9	2
Garrity	17	208	12.2	1
Haddix	12	82	6.8	0
Giles	6	57	9.5	1
Tautalatasi	5	48	9.6	0
Konecny	1	18	18.0	0
Abercrombie	1	-2	-2.0	0

PUNT RETURNS

Last Name	No.	Yds	Avg	TD
Konecny	33	233	7.1	0

KICKOFF RETURNS

Last Name	No.	Yds	Avg	TD
Beals	34	625	18.4	0
Konecny	17	276	16.2	0
Abercrombie	5	87	17.4	0
Byars	2	20	10.0	0
Jenkins	1	20	20.0	0

PASSING — PUNTING — KICKING

PASSING	Att	Cmp	%	Yds	Yd/Att	TD	Int—%	RK
Cunningham	560	301	53.8	3808	6.80	24	16—2.9	7
Cavanaugh	16	7	43.8	101	6.31	1	1—6.3	
Teltschik	3	1	33.3	18	6.00	0	0—0.0	
Byars	2	0	0.0	0	0.00	0	0—0.0	

PUNTING	No.	Avg.
Teltschik	101	39.2
Cunningham	3	55.7

KICKING	XP	ATT	%	FG	ATT	%
Zendejas	35	36	97	20	27	74
Dorsey	12	13	92	5	10	50

NEW YORK GIANTS

RUSHING

Last Name	No.	Yds	Avg	TD
Morris	307	1083	3.5	5
Anderson	65	208	3.2	8
Simms	33	152	4.6	0
Carthon	46	146	3.2	2
Adams	29	76	2.6	0
Manuel	4	27	6.8	0
Rouson	1	1	1.0	0
Rutledge	3	-1	-0.3	0
Hostetler	5	-3	-0.6	0

RECEIVING

Last Name	No.	Yds	Avg	TD
Manuel	65	1029	15.8	4
Bavaro	53	672	12.7	4
Baker	40	656	16.4	7
Adams	27	174	6.4	0
Morris	22	166	7.5	0
Carthon	19	194	10.2	1
Mowatt	15	196	13.1	1
Ingram	13	158	12.2	1
Turner	10	128	12.8	1
Anderson	9	57	6.3	0
Robinson	7	143	20.4	3
McConkey	5	72	14.4	0
Rouson	4	61	15.3	0
Hostetler	1	10	10.0	0

PUNT RETURNS

Last Name	No.	Yds	Avg	TD
McConkey	40	313	7.8	0
Baker	5	34	6.8	0
Kinard	1	8	8.0	0
Flynn	1	4	4.0	0

KICKOFF RETURNS

Last Name	No.	Yds	Avg	TD
Guggemos	17	344	20.2	0
Hill	13	262	20.2	0
Ingram	8	129	16.1	0
Rouson	8	130	16.3	0
Haddix	6	123	20.5	0
Collins	4	67	16.8	0
S. White	3	62	20.7	0
McConkey	2	30	15.0	0
Beckman	1	7	7.0	0

PASSING — PUNTING — KICKING

PASSING	Att	Cmp	%	Yds	Yd/Att	TD	Int—%	RK
Simms	479	263	54.9	3359	7.01	21	11—2.3	5
Hostetler	29	16	55.2	244	8.41	1	2—3.4	
Rutledge	17	11	64.7	113		0	1— 5.9	

PUNTING	No.	Avg.
Buford	75	40.2
Landeta	6	37.0

KICKING	XP	ATT	%	FG	ATT	%
McFadden	25	27	93	14	19	74
Allegre	14	14	100	10	11	91

WASHINGTON REDSKINS

RUSHING

Last Name	No.	Yds	Avg	TD
Bryant	108	498	4.6	1
Smith	155	470	3.0	3
Morris	126	437	3.5	2
Monk	7	46	6.6	0
Rypien	9	31	3.4	1
Oliphant	8	30	3.8	0
Griffin	6	23	3.8	0
Sanders	2	14	7.0	0
Clark	2	6	3.0	0
Archer	3	1	0.3	0
D. Williams	9	0	0.0	0
G. Coleman	2	-13	-6.5	0

RECEIVING

Last Name	No.	Yds	Avg	TD
Sanders	73	1148	15.7	12
Monk	72	946	13.1	5
Clark	59	892	15.1	7
Bryant	42	447	10.6	5
McEwen	23	323	14.0	0
Oliphant	15	111	7.4	0
Warren	12	112	9.3	0
Orr	11	222	20.2	2
Smith	8	53	6.6	0
Allen	5	48	9.6	1
Jones	3	21	7.0	0
Caravello	2	15	7.5	0
Griffin	2	9	4.5	1
Morris	1	3	3.0	0

PUNT RETURNS

Last Name	No.	Yds	Avg	TD
Shepard	12	104	8.7	0
Allen	10	62	6.2	0
Green	9	103	11.4	0
Clark	8	48	6.0	0
Oliphant	7	24	3.4	0
Johnson	3	26	8.7	0
Orr	2	10	5.0	0
Caldwell	1	0	0.0	0
Gage	0	0	0.0	0

KICKOFF RETURNS

Last Name	No.	Yds	Avg	TD
Morris	21	413	19.7	0
Sanders	19	362	19.1	0
Shepard	16	329	20.6	0
Oliphant	7	127	18.1	0
Gage	5	60	12.0	0
Griffin	3	45	15.0	0
Jones	1	13	13.0	0
Hamilton	1	7	7.0	0
Harbour	1	6	6.0	0
Orr	1	6	6.0	0

PASSING — PUNTING — KICKING

PASSING	Att	Cmp	%	Yds	Yd/Att	TD	Int—%	RK
D. Williams	380	213	56.1	2609	6.87	15	12—3.2	8
Rypien	208	114	54.8	1730	8.32	18	13—6.3	
Archer	2	0	0.0	0	0.00	0	0—0.0	
G. Coleman	1	0	0.0	0	0.00	0	0—0.0	
Monk	1	0	0.0	0	0.00	0	0—0.0	

PUNTING	No.	Avg.
Coleman	39	38.6
Barnhardt	15	41.9
Cox	7	31.6
Lohmiller	6	34.7

KICKING	XP	ATT	%	FG	ATT	%
Lohmiller	40	41	98	19	26	73

PHOENIX CARDINALS

RUSHING

Last Name	No.	Yds	Avg	TD
Ferrell	202	924	4.6	7
S. Mitchell	164	726	4.4	4
Jordan	61	160	2.6	3
Stoudt	14	57	4.1	0
Lomax	17	55	3.2	1
Wolfley	9	43	4.8	0
Horne	3	20	6.7	0
J. Smith	1	15	15.0	0
Novacek	1	10	10.0	0
Del Greco	1	8	8.0	0
Jeffery	3	8	2.7	0
Green	4	1	0.3	0

RECEIVING

Last Name	No.	Yds	Avg	TD
J. Smith	83	986	11.9	5
Green	68	1097	16.1	7
Awalt	39	454	11.6	4
Novacek	38	569	15.0	4
Ferrell	38	315	8.3	2
S. Mitchell	25	214	8.6	1
Jones	23	496	21.6	3
Jordan	4	24	6.0	0
Wolfley	2	11	5.5	0
Moore	1	15	15.0	0
Holmes	1	10	10.0	0

PUNT RETURNS

Last Name	No.	Yds	Avg	TD
Sikahema	33	341	10.3	0
J. Smith	17	119	7.0	0
Hunley	1	3	3.0	0
McAdoo	1	0	0.0	0
McDonald	0	0	0.0	0

KICKOFF RETURNS

Last Name	No.	Yds	Avg	TD
Sikahema	23	475	20.7	0
McAdoo	13	311	23.9	0
Jones	11	147	13.4	0
S. Mitchell	10	221	22.1	0
Ferrell	2	25	12.5	0
Jeffery	1	11	11.0	0
Clark	2	10	5.0	0
Schillinger	1	10	10.0	0
Phillips	1	4	4.0	0

PASSING — PUNTING — KICKING

PASSING	Att	Cmp	%	Yds	Yd/Att	TD	Int—%	RK
Lomax	443	255	57.6	3395	7.66	20	11—2.5	4
Stoudt	113	63	55.8	747	6.61	6	8—7.1	
Tupa	6	4	66.7	49	8.17	0	0—0.0	

PUNTING	No.	Avg.
Horne	80	40.4

KICKING	XP	Att	%	FG	Att	%
Del Greco	42	44	95	12	21	57

DALLAS COWBOYS

RUSHING

Last Name	No.	Yds	Avg	TD
Walker	361	1514	4.2	5
Pelluer	51	314	6.2	2
Newsome	32	75	2.3	3
Clack	11	54	4.9	0
Sweeney	6	34	5.7	0
Fowler	3	6	2.0	0
Irvin	1	2	2.0	0
Martin	4	-4	-1.0	0

RECEIVING

Last Name	No.	Yds	Avg	TD
Alexander	54	788	14.6	6
Walker	53	505	9.5	2
Martin	49	622	12.7	3
Irvin	32	654	20.4	5
Newsome	30	236	7.9	0
Chandler	18	186	10.3	1
Clack	17	126	7.4	1
Gay	15	205	13.7	1
Cosbie	12	112	9.3	0
Fowler	10	64	6.4	0
Folsom	9	84	9.3	2
Edwards	5	93	18.6	0
Burbage	2	50	25.0	0
Newton	1	2	2.0	0

PUNT RETURNS

Last Name	No.	Yds	Avg	TD
Martin	44	360	8.2	0
Walls	1	0	0.0	0

KICKOFF RETURNS

Last Name	No.	Yds	Avg	TD
Burbage	20	448	22.4	0
Clack	32	690	21.6	0
Martin	12	210	17.5	0
Higgs	2	31	15.5	0
Smith	2	24	12.0	0
B. White	1	7	7.0	0

PASSING — PUNTING — KICKING

PASSING	Att	Cmp	%	Yds	Yd/Att	TD	Int—%	RK
Pelluer	435	245	56.3	3139	7.22	17	19—4.4	9
Sweeney	78	33	42.3	314	4.03	3	5—6.4	
D. White	42	29	69.1	274	6.52	1	3—7.1	

PUNTING	No.	Avg.
Saxon	80	40.9

KICKING	XP	Att.	%	FG	Att	%
Ruzek	27	27	100	12	22	55

CHICAGO BEARS 12-4 Mike Ditka

Scores of Each Game		
34	MIAMI	7
17	Indianapolis	13
7	MINNESOTA	31
24	Green Bay	6
24	BUFFALO	3
24	Detroit	7
17	DALLAS	7
10	SAN FRANCISCO	9
7	New England	30
28	TAMPA BAY	10
34	Washington	14
27	Tampa Bay	15
16	GREEN BAY	0
3	L.A. Rams	23
13	DETROIT	12
27	Minnesota	28

Use Name	Pos.	Hgt	Wgt	Age	Int	Pts
Jim Covert	OT	6'4"	278	28		
Caesar Rentie	OT	6'3"	291	23		
Keith Van Horne	OT	6'6"	283	30		
John Wojciechowski	OT	6'4"	270	25		
Kurt Becker	OG	6'5"	280	29		
Mart Bortz	OG	6'6"	272	27		
Tom Thayer	OG	6'4"	270	27		
John Adickes	C	6'3"	264	24		
Jay Hilgenberg	C	6'3"	260	28		
Richard Dent	DE	6'5"	268	27		
Al Harris	DE	6'5"	270	31		
William Perry	DE	6'2"	320	25		
Sean Smith	DE-DT	6'4"	290	23		
Dick Chapura	DT	6'3"	275	24		
Dan Hampton	DT	6'5"	274	30		
Steve McMichael	DT	6'2"	268	30		6
John Shannon	DT	6'3"	269	23		
Greg Clark	LB	6'	221	23		
Troy Johnson	LB	6'	236	23		
Dante Jones	LB	6'1"	236	23		
Jim Morrissey	LB	6'3"	227	25	3	
Mickey Pruitt	LB	6'1"	206	23		
Ron Rivera	LB	6'3"	240	26	2	
Mike Singletary	LB	6'	230	29	1	
Maurice Douglass	DB	5'11"	200	24	1	
Dave Duerson	DB	6'1"	212	27	2	
Shaun Gayle	DB	5'11"	194	26	1	
Vestee Jackson	DB	6'	186	25	8	
Todd Krumm	DB	6'	189	22	2	
Lorenzo Lynch	DB	5'9"	199	25		
Mike Richardson	DB	6'	181	27	2	
Lemuel Stinson	DB	5'9"	159	22		
David Tate	DB	6'	177	23	4	
Ben Bennett	QB	6'1"	200	26		
Jim Harbaugh	QB	6'3"	204	24		6
Jim McMahon	QB	6'1"	198	29		24
Mike Tomczak	QB	6'1"	198	25		6
Neal Anderson	HB	5'11"	210	24		72
Thomas Sanders	HB	5'11"	203	26		18
Brad Muster	FB	6'3"	231	23		6
Matt Suhey	FB	5'11"	213	30		12
Wendell Davis	WR	5'11"	188	22		
Dennis Gentry	WR-HB	5'8"	180	29		24
Glen Kozlowski	WR	6'1"	205	25		
Dennis McKinnon	WR	6'1"	177	27		24
Ron Morris	WR	6'1'	195	23		24
Cap Boso	TE	6'3"	240	24		
Emery Moorehead	TE	6'2"	230	34		12
Brent Novoselsky	TE	6'3"	232	22		
Jim Thornton	TE	6'2"	242	23		
Kevin Butler	K	6'1"	204	26		82
Bryan Wagner	K	6'2"	200	26		

Paul Blair — Knee Injury

Otis Wilson — Knee Injury

MINNESOTA VIKINGS 11-5 Jerry Burns

Scores of Each Game		
10	Buffalo	13
36	NEW ENGLAND	6
31	Chicago	7
23	PHILADELPHIA	21
7	Miami	24
14	TAMPA BAY	13
14	GREEN BAY	34
49	Tampa Bay	20
21	San Francisco	24
44	DETROIT	17
43	Dallas	3
12	INDIANAPOLIS	3
23	Detroit	0
45	NEW ORLEANS	3
6	Green Bay	18
28	CHICAGO	27

Use Name	Pos.	Hgt	Wgt	Age	Int	Pts
Tim Irwin	OT	6'6"	285	29		
Gary Zimmerman	OT	6'6"	286	26		
Dave Huffman	OG-OT	6'6"	284	32		
Todd Kalis	OG	6'5"	284	23		
Mark MacDonald (to PHX)	OG	6'4"	265	27		
Randall McDaniel	OG	6'3"	271	23		
Terry Tausch	OG	6'5"	273	29		
Chris Foote	C	6'3"	255	31		
Kirk Lowdermilk	C	6'3"	267	25		
Randy Rasmussen	C-OG	6'2"	254	28		
Al Baker	DE	6'6"	280	31		2
Barry Bennett (from NYJ)	DE	6'4"	257	32		
Chris Doleman	DE	6'5"	262	26		2
William Gay	DE	6'5"	260	33		
Doug Martin	DE	6'3"	258	31		
Stafford Mays	DE	6'2"	264	30		
Keith Millard	DT	6'5"	262	26		
Tim Newton	DT	6'	277	25		
Al Noga	DT-DE	6'1"	261	22		
Henry Thomas	DT	6'2"	267	23	1	6
Sam Anno	LB	6'2"	230	23		
Walker Lee Ashley	LB	6'	230	28	1	6
Ray Berry	LB	6'2"	225	24		
David Howard	LB	6'2"	232	26	3	
Chris Martin (to KC)	LB	6'2"	231	27		6
Jesse Solomon	LB	6'	232	24	4	6
Scott Studwell	LB	6'2"	228	34		
Joey Browner	DB	6'2"	210	28	5	
Brad Edwards	DB	6'1"	200	22	2	6
Darrell Fullington	DB	6'1"	197	24	3	
John Harris	DB	6'2"	199	32	3	
Wymon Henderson	DB	5'10"	185	26	1	
Issiac Holt	DB	6'2"	202	25	2	2
Carl Lee	DB	6'	183	27	8	12
Reggie Rutland	DB	6'1"	194	24	3	
Rich Gannon	QB	6'3"	199	22		
Tommy Kramer	QB	6'2"	202	33		12
Wade Wilson	QB	6'3"	208	29		
D.J. Dozier	HB	6'	198	22		12
Darryl Harris	HB	5'10"	178	22		6
Darrin Nelson	HB	5'9"	184	28		6
Allen Rice	HB	5'10"	204	26		36
Alfred Anderson	FB	6'1"	223	26		48
Rick Fenney	FB	6'1"	232	28		18
Anthony Carter	WR	5'11"	177	27		36
Jim Gustafson	WR	6'1"	174	27		6
Hassan Jones	WR	6'	192	24		30
Leo Lewis	WR	5'8"	172	31		6
Paul Coffman	TE	6'3"	225	32		
Carl Hilton	TE	6'3"	230	24		6
Steve Jordan	TE	6'4"	239	27		30
Mike Mularkey	TE	6'4"	240	26		
Chuck Nelson	K	6'	172	28		108
Bucky Scribner	K	6'	213	28		

TAMPA BAY BUCCANEERS 5-11 Ray Perkins

Scores of Each Game		
14	PHILADELPHIA	41
13	Green Bay	10
24	PHOENIX	30
9	New Orleans	13
27	GREEN BAY	24
13	Minnesota	14
31	Indianapolis	35
20	MINNESOTA	49
14	MIAMI	17
10	Chicago	28
23	Detroit	20
15	CHICAGO	27
10	Atlanta	17
10	BUFFALO	5
7	New England	10
21	DETROIT	10

Use Name	Pos.	Hgt	Wgt	Age	Int	Pts
Mark Cooper	OT	6'5"	280	28		
Paul Gruber	OT	6'5"	290	23		
Rob Taylor	OT	6'6"	295	27		
John Bruhin	OG	6'3"	280	23		
Rick Mallory	OG	6'2"	265	27		
Tom McHale	OG	6'4"	275	25		
Dan Turk	OG	6'4"	260	26		
Randy Grimes	C	6'4"	275	28		
Kevin Thomas	C	6'2"	265	24		
John Cannon	DE-NT	6'5"	260	28		
Reuben Davis	DE	6'4"	290	23		
Robert Goff	DE	6'3"	270	22		
Ron Holmes	DE	6'4"	265	25		
Kevin Kellin	DE	6'6"	270	28		
Harry Swayne	DE	6'5"	270	23		
Curt Jarvis	NT	6'2"	265	23		
Shawn Lee	NT	6'2"	290	21		
Sidney Coleman	LB	6'2"	250	24		
Victor Jones	LB	6'2"	250	21		
Eugene Marve	LB	6'2"	240	28	1	
Winston Moss	LB	6'3"	235	22		
Kevin Murphy	LB	6'2"	235	24	1	6
Peter Najarian	LB	6'2"	230	24		
Ervin Randle	LB	6'1"	250	25		
Henry Rolling	LB	6'2"	225	22		
Jackie Walker	LB	6'5"	255	25		
Chris Washington	LB	6'4"	240	26		
Selwyn Brown	DB	5'11"	205	22		
Donnie Elder	DB	5'9"	175	24	3	
Bobby Futrell	DB	5'11"	190	26	1	
Harry Hamilton	DB	6'	195	25	6	
Odie Harris	DB	6'	190	22	2	
Ray Isom	DB	5'9"	190	22		
Rod Jones	DB	6'	185	24	1	
Ricky Reynolds	DB	5'11"	190	23	4	
Mark Robinson	DB	5'11"	200	25	2	
Joe Ferguson	QB	6'1"	190	38		
Vinny Testaverde	QB	6'5"	215	24		6
Kerry Goode	HB	5'11"	200	22		6
Don Smith	HB-WR	5'11"	195	24		6
Jeff Smith	HB	5'9"	205	26		
Lars Tate	HB	6'2"	215	22		48
Bobby Howard	FB	6'	220	24		
William Howard	FB-HB	6'	240	24		6
James Wilder	FB-HB	6'3"	225	30		6
Mark Carrier	WR	6'	185	22		30
Bruce Hill	WR	6'	180	24		54
Frank Pillow	WR	5'10"	170	23		6
Greg Richardson	WR	5'7"	170	23		
Stephen Starring (to DET)	WR	5'10"	172	27		
Gene Taylor	WR	6'2"	190	25		
Ron Hall	TE	6'4"	245	24		
Calvin Magee	TE	6'3"	245	25		
Jeff Parks	TE	6'4"	240	23		
John Carney	K	5'11"	160	24		12
Ray Criswell	K	6'	195	25		1
Donald Igwebuike	K	5'9"	175	27		78

DETROIT LIONS 4-12 Darryl Rogers (2-9), Wayne Fontes (2-3)

Scores of Each Game		
31	ATLANTA	17
10	L.A. Rams	17
14	NEW ORLEANS	22
10	N.Y. JETS	17
13	San Francisco	20
7	CHICAGO	24
10	N.Y. Giants	30
7	Kansas City	6
10	N.Y. GIANTS	13
17	Minnesota	44
20	TAMPA BAY	23
19	Green Bay (Mil.)	9
0	MINNESOTA	23
30	GREEN BAY	14
12	Chicago	13
10	Tampa Bay	21

Use Name	Pos.	Hgt	Wgt	Age	Int	Pts
Lomas Brown	OT	6'4"	275	25		
Harvey Salem	OT	6'6"	285	27		
Eric Sanders	OT-OG	6'7"	280	29		
Curt Singer	OT	6'5"	279	26		
Eric Andolsek	OG	6'2"	277	22		
Scott Barrows	OG-C	6'2"	280	25		
Kevin Glover	OG-C	6'2"	275	25		
Joe Milinichik	OG-OT	6'5"	275	25		
Steve Mott	C	6'3"	265	27		
Keith Ferguson	DE	6'5"	260	29		
Curtis Green	DE-NT	6'3"	265	31		
Reggie Rogers	DE	6'6"	285	24		
Thomas Strauthers	DE	6'4"	264	27		
Eric Williams	DE	6'4"	286	26		
Gary Hadd	DT-NT	6'4"	270	22		
Jerry Ball	NT	6'1"	292	23		
Dan Saleaumua	NT	6'	285	22		
Dave Ahrens	LB	6'3"	245	29		
Paul Butcher	LB	6'	219	24		
Mike Cofer	LB	6'5"	245	28		
Dennis Gibson	LB	6'2"	240	24		
George Jamison	LB	6'1"	226	25	3	12
Danny Lockett	LB	6'2"	250	24		
Shelton Robinson	LB	6'2"	236	27		
Chris Spielman	LB	6'	247	27		
Jimmy Williams	LB	6'3"	230	27	1	
Bennie Blades	DB	6'1"	221	21	2	
Lou Brock (from SEA)	DB	5'10"	175	24		
Raphel Cherry	DB	6'	190	26	2	
James Griffin	DB	6'2"	203	26	2	
Jerry Holmes	DB	6'2"	175	30	1	
Bruce McNorton	DB	5'11"	175	29	1	
Devon Mitchell	DB	6'1"	194	25	3	6
Bobby Watkins	DB	5'10"	180	28		
William White	DB	5'10"	191	22		
Rusty Hilger	QB	6'4"	205	26		
Eric Hipple	QB	6'2"	198	30		
Chuck Long	QB	6'4"	221	25		
John Witkowski	QB	6'1"	205	26		
Garry James	HB	5'10"	214	24		42
Carl Painter	HB	5'9"	185	24		
Butch Woolfolk	HB	6'1"	212	28		
James Jones	FB	6'2"	230	27		
Tony Paige	FB	5'10"	235	25		
Scott Williams	FB	6'2"	234	26		6
Carl Bland	WR	5'11"	180	27		12
Jeff Chadwick	WR	6'3"	190	27		18
Paco Craig	WR	5'10"	170	23		
Gary Lee	WR	6'1"	201	23		6
Pete Mandley	WR	5'10"	195	27		30
Ray Roundtree	WR	6'	180	22		
Pat Carter	TE	6'4"	250	22		
Mark Lewis	TE	6'2"	250	27		6
Rob Rubick	TE	6'3"	234	27		
Jim Arnold	K	6'3"	211	27		
Eddie Murray	K	5'10"	180	32		82

Steve Baack — Hip Injury

Karl Bernard — Knee Injury
Vyto Kab — Knee Injury

GREEN BAY PACKERS 4-12 Lindy Infante

Scores of Each Game		
7	L.A. RAMS	34
10	TAMPA BAY	13
17	Miami	24
6	CHICAGO	24
24	Tampa Bay	27
45	NEW ENGLAND (Mil.)	3
34	Minnesota	14
17	WASHINGTON (Mil.)	20
0	Buffalo	28
0	Atlanta	20
13	INDIANAPOLIS	20
9	DETROIT (Mil.)	19
0	Chicago	16
14	Detroit	30
18	MINNESOTA	6
26	Phoenix	17

Use Name	Pos.	Hgt	Wgt	Age	Int	Pts
Dave Croston	OT	6'5"	280	24		
Darryl Haley	OT	6'5"	265	27		
Tom Neville	OT-OG	6'5"	306	26		
Ken Ruettgers	OT	6'5"	280	26		
Keith Uecker	OT	6'5"	284	28		
Ron Hallstrom	OG	6'6"	290	29		
Rich Moran	OG	6'3"	275	26		
Mark Cannon	C	6'3"	258	26		
Kani Kauahi	C	6'2"	271	28		
Robert Brown	DE	6'2"	267	28		
Alphonso Carreker	DE	6'6"	271	26		
Nate Hill (to MIA)	DE	6'4"	273	22		
Shawn Patterson	DE-NT	6'5"	261	23		
Blaise Winter	DE-NT	6'3"	275	26		
Jerry Boyarsky	NT	6'3"	290	29		
Bob Nelson	NT	6'4"	275	29		
John Anderson	LB	6'3"	228	32		
John Corker	LB	6'5"	240	29		
Burnell Dent	LB	6'1"	236	25		
John Dorsey	LB	6'3"	243	28		
Tim Harris	LB	6'5"	235	23		10
Johnny Holland	LB	6'2"	221	23		
Brian Noble	LB	6'3"	252	25		
Ron Simpkins	LB	6'1"	234	30		
Scott Stephen	LB	6'2"	232	24		
Mike Weddington	LB	6'4"	245	27		
Dave Brown	DB	6'1"	187	35	3	
Chuck Cecil	DB	6'	184	23	4	
Tiger Greene	DB	6'	194	26		
Norman Jefferson	DB	5'10"	183	24		
Mark Lee	DB	5'11"	189	30	3	
Mark Murphy	DB	6'2"	201	30	5	
Ron Pitts	DB	5'10"	175	25	2	6
Gary Richard	DB	5'9"	171	22		
Ken Stills	DB	5'10"	186	24	3	
Blair Kiel	QB	6'	214	26		
Randy Wright	QB	6'2"	203	27		12
Don Majkowski	QB	6'2"	197	24		6
Patrick Collins	HB	5'9"	177	22		
Kenneth Davis	HB	5'10"	209	26		6
Lavale Thomas	HB	6'	205	24		
Keith Woodside	HB	5'11"	203	24		30
Paul Ott Carruth	FB	6'1"	220	27		
Brent Fullwood	FB-HB	5'11"	209	24		48
Larry Mason	FB	5'11"	205	27		6
Albert Bell	WR	6'	170	24		
Scott Bolton	WR	6'	188	23		
Phillip Epps	WR	5'10"	165	28		
Perry Kemp	WR	5'11"	170	26		
Aubrey Matthews (from ATL)	WR	5'7"	165	25		12
Patrick Scott	WR	5'10"	170	23		6
Sterling Sharpe	WR	5'11"	202	23		6
Walter Stanley	WR	5'9"	179	25		
Clint Didier	TE	6'5"	240	29		6
Joey Hackett	TE	6'5"	267	29		6
Ed West	TE	6'1"	243	27		18
Don Bracken	K	6'1"	211	26		
Curtis Burrow	K	5'11"	185	25		2
Dale Dawson (from PHI)	K	6'	213	23		13
Max Zendejas	K	5'11"	184	24		44

Tommy Robison — Groin Injury
Alan Veingrad — Hip Injury

Kenneth Johnson — Back Injury
Brent Moore — Knee Injury

CHICAGO BEARS

RUSHING

Last Name	No.	Yds	Avg	TD
Anderson	249	1106	4.4	12
Sanders	95	332	3.5	3
Suhey	87	253	2.9	2
Muster	44	197	4.5	0
Harbaugh	19	110	5.8	1
McMahon	26	104	4.0	4
Gentry	7	86	12.3	1
Morris	3	40	13.3	0
Tomczak	13	40	3.1	1
McKinnon	3	25	8.3	1
Davis	1	3	3.0	0
Kozlowski	1	3	3.0	0
Wagner	2	0	0.0	0

RECEIVING

Last Name	No.	Yds	Avg	TD
McKinnon	45	704	15.6	3
Anderson	39	371	9.5	0
Gentry	33	486	14.7	3
Morris	28	498	17.8	4
Muster	21	236	11.2	1
Suhey	20	154	7.7	0
Davis	15	220	14.7	0
Thornton	15	135	9.0	0
Moorehead	14	133	9.5	2
Sanders	9	94	10.4	0
Boso	6	50	8.3	0
Kozlowski	3	92	30.7	0

PUNT RETURNS

Last Name	No.	Yds	Avg	TD
McKinnon	34	277	8.1	0
Davis	3	17	5.7	0
Kozlowski	1	0	0.0	0

KICKOFF RETURNS

Last Name	No.	Yds	Avg	TD
Gentry	27	578	21.4	0
Sanders	13	248	19.1	0
Muster	3	33	11.0	0
Kozlowski	2	37	18.5	0

PASSING — PUNTING — KICKING

PASSING	Att	Cmp	%	Yds	Yd/Att	TD	Int— %	RK
McMahon	192	114	59.4	1346	7.01	6	7—3.6	
Tomczak	170	86	50.6	1310	7.71	7	6—3.5	
Harbaugh	97	47	48.5	514	5.30	0	2—2.1	
Wagner	1	1	100.0	3	3.00	0	0—0.0	
Anderson	1	0	0.0	0	0.00	0	0—0.0	

PUNTING	No.	Avg.
Wagner	79	41.5

KICKING	XP	ATT	%	FG	ATT	%
Butler	37	38	97	15	19	79

MINNESOTA VIKINGS

RUSHING

Last Name	No.	Yds	Avg	TD
D. Nelson	112	380	3.4	1
Rice	110	322	2.9	6
Anderson	87	300	3.4	7
Fenney	55	271	4.9	3
Dozier	42	167	4.0	2
D. Harris	34	151	4.4	1
Wilson	36	136	3.8	2
Carter	4	41	10.3	0
Gannon	4	29	7.3	0
Kramer	14	8	0.6	0
Jones	1	7	7.0	0
Scribner	1	0	0.0	0
Mularkey	1	-6	-6.0	0

RECEIVING

Last Name	No.	Yds	Avg	TD
Carter	72	1225	17.0	6
Jordan	57	756	13.3	5
Jones	40	778	19.5	5
Rice	30	279	9.3	0
Anderson	23	242	10.5	1
D. Nelson	16	105	6.6	0
Gustafson	15	231	15.4	1
Fenney	15	224	14.9	0
Lewis	11	141	12.8	1
D. Harris	6	30	5.0	0
Dozier	5	49	9.8	0
Mularkey	3	39	13.0	0
Hilton	1	1	1.0	1

PUNT RETURNS

Last Name	No.	Yds	Avg	TD
Lewis	58	550	9.5	0
Carter	1	3	3.0	0

KICKOFF RETURNS

Last Name	No.	Yds	Avg	TD
D. Harris	39	833	21.4	0
D. Nelson	9	210	23.3	0
Dozier	5	105	21.0	0
Lewis	1	12	12.0	0
Rice	1	0	0.0	0
Carter	1	0	0.0	0

PASSING — PUNTING — KICKING

PASSING	Att	Cmp	%	Yds	Yd/Att	TD	Int— %	RK
Wilson	332	204	61.4	2746	8.27	15	9—2.7	1
Kramer	173	83	48.0	1264	7.31	5	9—5.2	
Gannon	15	7	46.7	90	6.00	0	0—0.0	

PUNTING	No.	Avg.
Scribner	86	39.4

KICKING	XP	ATT	%	FG	ATT	%
Nelson	48	49	98	20	25	80

TAMPA BAY BUCCANEERS

RUSHING

Last Name	No.	Yds	Avg	TD
Tate	122	467	3.8	7
W. Howard	115	452	3.9	1
Wilder	86	343	4.0	1
Goode	62	231	3.7	0
Testaverde	28	138	4.9	1
J. Smith	20	87	4.4	0
D. Smith	13	46	3.5	1
Criswell	2	0	0.0	0
Ferguson	1	0	0.0	0
Hill	2	-11	-5.5	0

RECEIVING

Last Name	No.	Yds	Avg	TD
Hill	58	1040	17.9	9
Carrier	57	970	17.0	5
Hall	39	555	14.2	0
J. Smith	16	134	8.4	0
Pillow	15	206	13.7	1
Wilder	15	124	8.3	0
D. Smith	12	138	11.5	0
W. Howard	11	97	8.8	0
Magee	9	103	11.4	0
Starring	8	164	20.5	0
Goode	7	68	9.7	0
G. Taylor	5	53	10.6	0
Tate	5	23	4.6	1
Parks	1	22	22.0	0

PUNT RETURNS

Last Name	No.	Yds	Avg	TD
Futrell	27	283	10.5	0
J. Smith	8	45	5.6	0
Elder	1	0	0.0	0

KICKOFF RETURNS

Last Name	No.	Yds	Avg	TD
Elder	34	772	22.7	0
J. Smith	10	180	18.0	0
D. Smith	9	188	20.9	0
Starring	8	130	16.3	0
Pillow	3	38	12.7	0
Futrell	2	38	19.0	0
Howard	2	21	10.5	0

PASSING — PUNTING — KICKING

PASSING	Att	Cmp	%	Yds	Yd/Att	TD	Int— %	RK
Testaverde	466	222	47.6	3240	6.95	13	35—7.5	14
Ferguson	46	31	67.4	368	8.00	3	1—2.2	

PUNTING	No.	Avg.
Criswell	68	36.4

KICKING	XP	ATT	%	FG	ATT	%
Igwebuike	21	21	100	19	25	76
Carney	6	6	100	2	5	40
Criswell	1	1	100	0	0	0

DETROIT LIONS

RUSHING

Last Name	No.	Yds	Avg	TD
James	182	552	3.0	5
Jones	96	314	3.3	0
Paige	52	207	4.0	0
Mandley	6	44	7.3	1
Painter	17	42	2.5	0
Hilger	18	27	1.5	0
Long	7	22	3.1	0
S. Williams	9	22	2.4	1
Hipple	1	5	5.0	0
Woolfolk	1	4	4.0	0
Bland	1	4	4.0	0
Witkowski	1	0	0.0	0

RECEIVING

Last Name	No.	Yds	Avg	TD
Mandley	44	617	14.0	4
James	39	382	9.8	2
Jones	29	259	8.9	0
Lee	22	261	11.9	1
Bland	21	307	14.6	2
Chadwick	20	304	15.2	3
Carter	13	145	11.2	0
Paige	11	100	9.1	0
S. Williams	3	46	15.3	0
Lewis	3	32	10.7	1
Craig	2	29	14.5	0
Painter	1	1	1.0	0

PUNT RETURNS

Last Name	No.	Yds	Avg	TD
Mandley	37	287	7.8	0
Bland	5	59	11.8	0

KICKOFF RETURNS

Last Name	No.	Yds	Avg	TD
Lee	18	355	19.7	0
Painter	17	347	20.4	0
Bland	8	179	22.4	0
Woolfolk	4	99	24.8	0
Andolsek	1	3	3.0	0
Saleaumua	1	0	0.0	0

PASSING — PUNTING — KICKING

PASSING	Att	Cmp	%	Yds	Yd/Att	TD	Int— %	RK
Hilger	306	126	41.2	1558	5.09	7	12—3.9	13
Long	141	75	53.2	856	6.07	6	6—4.3	
Hipple	27	12	44.4	158	5.85	0	0—0.0	
Arnold	1	0	0.0	0	0.00	0	0—0.0	
Witkowski	1	0	0.0	0	0.00	0	0—0.0	
Jones	1	0	0.0	0	0.00	0	0—0.0	

PUNTING	No.	Avg.
Arnold	97	42.4

KICKING	XP	Att	%	FG	Att	%
Murray	22	23	96	20	21	95

GREEN BAY PACKERS

RUSHING

Last Name	No.	Yds	Avg	TD
Fullwood	101	483	4.8	7
Majkowski	47	225	4.8	1
Woodside	83	195	2.3	3
Mason	48	194	4.0	0
Davis	39	121	3.1	1
Carruth	49	114	2.3	0
Wright	8	43	5.4	2
Matthews	3	3	1.0	0
Collins	2	2	1.0	0
Stanley	1	1	1.0	0
Sharpe	4	-2	-0.5	0

RECEIVING

Last Name	No.	Yds	Avg	TD
Sharpe	55	791	14.4	1
Kemp	48	620	12.9	0
Woodside	39	352	9.0	2
West	30	276	9.2	3
Stanley	28	436	15.6	0
Carruth	24	211	8.8	0
Scott	20	275	13.8	1
Fullwood	20	128	6.4	1
matthews	15	167	11.1	2
Epps	11	99	9.0	0
Davis	11	81	7.4	0
Mason	8	84	10.5	1
Didier	5	37	7.4	1
Bolton	2	33	16.5	0
Collins	2	17	8.5	0
Hackett	1	2	2.0	1

PUNT RETURNS

Last Name	No.	Yds	Avg	TD
Pitts	9	93	10.3	1
Sharpe	9	48	5.3	0
Stanley	12	52	4.3	0
Jefferson	5	15	3.0	0

KICKOFF RETURNS

Last Name	No.	Yds	Avg	TD
Fullwood	21	421	20.0	0
Woodside	19	343	18.1	0
Scott	12	207	17.3	0
Jefferson	4	116	29.0	0
Stanley	2	39	19.5	0
Pitts	1	17	17.0	0
Sharpe	1	17	17.0	0
Hackett	1	9	9.0	0
Winter	1	7	7.0	0
Stills	1	4	4.0	0
Hill	1	1	1.0	0

PASSING — PUNTING — KICKING

PASSING	Att	Cmp	%	Yds	Yd/Att	TD	Int— %	RK
Majkowski	336	178	53.0	2119	6.31	9	11—3.3	10
Wright	244	141	57.8	1490	6.11	4	13—5.3	12
Carruth	2	0	0.0	0	0.00	0	0— 0	

PUNTING	No.	Avg.
Bracken	86	38.2

KICKING	XP	Att.	%	FG	Att	%
Zendejas	17	19	89	9	16	56
Dawson	4	5	80	3	6	50
Burrow	2	4	50	0	1	0

SAN FRANCISCO 49ERS 10-6 Bill Walsh

Scores of Each Game		
34	New Orleans	33
20	N.Y. Giants	17
17	ATLANTA	34
38	Seattle	7
20	DETROIT	13
13	DENVER	16
24	L.A. Rams	21
9	Chicago	10
24	MINNESOTA	21
23	Phoenix	24
3	L.A. RAIDERS	9
37	WASHINGTON	21
48	San Diego	10
13	Atlanta	3
30	NEW ORLEANS	17
16	L.A. RAMS	38

Use Name	Pos.	Hgt	Wgt	Age	Int	Pts
Harris Barton	OT	6'4"	280	24		
Bubba Paris	OT	6'6"	306	27		
Steve Wallace	OT	6'5"	276	23		
Jeff Bregel	OG	6'4"	280	24		
Bruce Collie	OG-OT	6'6"	275	26		
Guy McIntyre	OG	6'3"	265	27		6
Jesse Sapolu	OG-C	6'4"	260	27		
Randy Cross	C	6'3"	265	34		
Chuck Thomas	C	6'3"	280	27		
Kevin Fagan	DE	6'4"	265	25		
Pierce Holt	DE	6'4"	280	26		
Pete Kugler	DE	6'4"	255	29		
Larry Roberts	DE	6'3"	275	25		
Jeff Stover	DE	6'5"	275	30		
Danny Stubbs	DE	6'4"	260	23		
Kevin Lilly	NT-DE	6'4"	265	25		
Michael Carter	NT-DT	6'2"	285	27	1	

Mark Cochran — Knee Injury

Use Name	Pos.	Hgt	Wgt	Age	Int	Pts
Riki Ellison	LB	6'2"	225	28		
Jim Fahnhorst	LB	6'4"	230	29		
Ron Hadley	LB	6'2"	240	24		
Charles Haley	LB-DE	6'5"	230	24		2
Sam Kennedy	LB	6'3"	235	24		
Bill Romanowski	LB	6'4"	231	22		
Keena Turner	LB	6'2"	222	29	1	
Michael Walter	LB	6'3"	238	27		
Chet Brooks	DB	5'11"	191	22		
Greg Cox	DB	6'	223	23		
Jeff Fuller	DB	6'2"	216	26	4	
Don Griffin	DB	6'	176	24		
Tom Holmoe	DB	6'2"	195	28	2	
Ronnie Lott	DB	6'	200	29	5	
Tim McKyer	DB	6'	174	24	7	
Tory Nixon	DB	5'11"	186	26		
Darryl Pollard	DB	5'11"	187	23		
Eric Wright	DB	6'1"	185	29	2	

Todd Shell — Neck Injury
Carlton Williamson — Knee Injury

Use Name	Pos.	Hgt	Wgt	Age	Int	Pts
Joe Montana	QB	6'2"	195	32		18
John Paye	QB	6'3"	205	23		
Todd Santos	QB	6'2"	207	24		
Steve Young	QB	6'2"	200	26		6
Roger Craig	HB	6'	224	28		60
Doug DuBose	HB	5'11"	190	24		12
Terrence Flagler	HB	6'	200	23		
Del Rodgers	HB	5'10"	203	28		
Steve Bartalo	FB	5'9"	200	24		
Tom Rathman	FB	6'1"	232	25		12
Harry Sydney	FB	6'	217	29		
Wes Chandler	WR	6'	188	32		
Terry Greer	WR	6'1"	192	30		
Calvin Nicholas	WR	6'4"	208	24		
Jerry Rice	WR	6'2"	200	25		60
John Taylor	WR	6'1"	185	26		24
Mike Wilson	WR-HB	6'3"	215	28		18
John Frank	TE	6'3"	225	26		18
Ron Heller	TE	6'3"	235	24		
Brent Jones	TE	6'4"	230	25		12
Mike Cofer	K	6'1"	190	24		121
Barry Helton	K	6'3"	205	23		

Mike Sherrard — Broken Leg

LOS ANGELES RAMS 10-6 John Robinson

Scores of Each Game		
34	Green Bay	7
17	DETROIT	10
22	L.A. Raiders	17
45	N.Y. Giants	31
27	PHOENIX	41
33	Atlanta	0
21	SAN FRANCISCO	24
31	SEATTLE	10
12	New Orleans	10
24	Philadelphia	30
10	NEW ORLEANS	14
24	SAN DIEGO	38
24	Denver	35
23	CHICAGO	3
22	ATLANTA	7
38	San Francisco	16

Use Name	Pos.	Hgt	Wgt	Age	Int	Pts
Robert Cox	OT	6'5"	270	24		
Irv Pankey	OT	6'4"	267	30		
Jackie Slater	OT	6'4"	275	34		
Duval Love	OG	6'3"	280	25		
Tom Newberry	OG	6'2"	279	25		
Mike Schad	OG	6'5"	290	24		
Tony Slaton	OG-C	6'3"	265	27		
Doug Smith	C	6'3"	260	31		
Gary Jeter	DE	6'4"	260	33		
Shawn Miller	DE-NT	6'4"	255	27		
Doug Reed	DE	6'3"	250	28		
Fred Stokes	DE	6'3"	265	24		
Greg Meisner	NT	6'3"	265	29	1	
Alvin Wright	NT	6'2"	256	27		

Use Name	Pos.	Hgt	Wgt	Age	Int	Pts
Jim Collins	LB	6'2"	233	30		
Carl Ekern	LB	6'3"	222	34		
Brett Faryniarz	LB	6'3"	225	23		
Kevin Greene	LB	6'3"	238	26	1	2
Mark Jerue	LB	6'3"	234	28	1	
Larry Kelm	LB	6'4"	226	23	2	
Mike McDonald	LB	6'1"	235	30		
Mel Owens	LB	6'2"	224	29	1	
Fred Strickland	LB	6'2"	224	22		
Mike Wilcher	LB	6'3"	240	28		
Jerry Gray	DB	6'	185	25	3	6
Clifford Hicks	DB	5'10"	188	24		
LeRoy Irvin	DB	5'11"	184	30	3	
Johnnie Johnson	DB	6'1"	183	31	4	
Anthony Newman	DB	6'	199	22	2	
Vince Newsome	DB	6'1"	183	27		
Michael Stewart	DB	5'11"	195	23	2	
Mickey Sutton	DB	5'8"	165	28	1	
James Washington	DB	6'1"	191	23	1	
Frank Wattelet	DB	6'	190	29		

Use Name	Pos.	Hgt	Wgt	Age	Int	Pts
Jim Everett	QB	6'5"	212	25		
Mark Herrmann	QB	6'4"	186	29		
Greg Bell	HB	5'10"	210	26		108
Gaston Green	HB	5'10"	189	22		
Charles White	HB	5'10"	193	30		
Robert Delpino	FB	6'	205	22		12
Mike Guman	FB	6'2"	216	30		
Buford McGee	FB	6'	206	28		18
Tim Tyrrell	FB	6'1"	206	27		
Willie Anderson	WR	6'	169	23		
Ron Brown	WR	5'11"	181	27		
Aaron Cox	WR	5'9"	174	23		30
Henry Ellard	WR	5'11"	175	27		60
Michael Young	WR	6'1"	183	26		
Jon Embree	TE	6'2"	237	23		
Pete Holohan	TE	6'4"	232	29		18
Damone Johnson	TE	6'4"	230	26		36
Rich Camarillo	K	5'11"	185	28		
Dale Hatcher	K	6'2"	211	25		
Mike Lansford	K	6'	183	30		117

NEW ORLEANS SAINTS 10-6 Jim Mora

Scores of Each Game		
33	SAN FRANCISCO	34
29	Atlanta	21
22	Detroit	14
13	TAMPA BAY	9
20	DALLAS	17
23	San Diego	17
20	Seattle	19
20	L.A. RAIDERS	6
10	L.A. RAMS	12
24	Washington	27
14	L.A. Rams	10
42	DENVER	0
12	N.Y. GIANTS	13
3	Minnesota	45
17	San Francisco	30
10	ATLANTA	9

Use Name	Pos.	Hgt	Wgt	Age	Int	Pts
Stan Brock	OT	6'6"	290	30		
Bill Contz	OT	6'5"	280	27		
Jim Dombrowski	OT	6'5"	298	25		
Daren Gilbert	OT	6'6"	280	24		
Jeff Walker	OT	6'4"	295	25		
Chuck Commiskey	OG	6'4"	290	30		
Brad Edelman	OG	6'6"	270	27		
Joel Hilgenberg	OG-C	6'3"	252	26		
Steve Trapilo	OG	6'5"	295	23		
James Campen	C-OG	6'3"	260	24		
Steve Korte	C	6'2"	260	28		
Dwaine Board (from SF)	DE	6'5"	248	31		
Bruce Clark	DE	6'3"	275	30		
James Geathers	DE	6'7"	290	28		
Frank Warren	DE	6'4"	290	28		
Jim Wilks	DE	6'5"	266	30		
Tony Elliott	NT	6'2"	295	29		
Ted Gregory	NT	6'1"	260	23		

Use Name	Pos.	Hgt	Wgt	Age	Int	Pts
Brian Forde	LB	6'2"	225	24		
James Haynes	LB	6'2"	233	28		
Rickey Jackson	LB	6'2"	243	30	1	2
Vaughan Johnson	LB	6'3"	235	26	1	
Joe Kohlbrand	LB	6'4"	242	25		
Sam Mills	LB	5'9"	225	29		
Pat Swilling	LB	6'3"	242	23		
Alvin Toles	LB	6'1"	227	25		
Michael Adams	DB	5'10"	195	24		
Gene Atkins	DB	6'1"	200	24	4	
Toi Cook	DB	5'11"	188	23	1	
Antonio Gibson	DB	6'3"	204	26		
Van Jakes	DB	6'	190	27	3	
Milton Mack	DB	5'11"	182	24	1	
Brett Maxie	DB	6'2"	194	26		
Reggie Sutton	DB	5'10"	180	23	3	
Dave Waymer	DB	6'1"	188	30	3	6

Use Name	Pos.	Hgt	Wgt	Age	Int	Pts
John Fourcade	QB	6'1"	208	27		
Bobby Hebert	QB	6'4"	215	28		
Dave Wilson	QB	6'3"	206	29		
Mel Gray	HB	5'9"	166	27		6
Dalton Hilliard	HB	5'8"	204	24		36
Rueben Mayes	HB	5'11"	200	25		18
Craig Heyward	FB	5'11"	251	21		6
Buford Jordan	FB	6'	223	26		6
Barry Word	FB	6'2"	220	24		
Robert Clark	WR	5'11"	175	23		12
Lonzell Hill	WR	6'	189	22		42
Eric Martin	WR	6'1"	207	26		42
Mark Pattison	WR	6'2"	198	26		
Brett Perriman	WR	5'9"	175	22		12
Cliff Benson	TE	6'4"	240	27		
Hoby Brenner	TE	6'4"	240	29		
Greg Scales	TE	6'4"	253	22		6
John Tice	TE	6'5"	249	28		6
Morten Andersen	K	6'2"	221	28		110
Brian Hansen	K	6'3"	209	27		

Mike Waters — Back Injury

ATLANTA FALCONS 5-11 Marion Campbell

Scores of Each Game		
17	Detroit	31
21	NEW ORLEANS	29
34	San Francisco	17
20	Dallas	26
20	SEATTLE	31
0	L.A. RAMS	33
14	Denver	30
16	N.Y. GIANTS	23
27	Philadelphia	24
20	GREEN BAY	0
7	SAN DIEGO	10
12	L.A. Raiders	6
17	TAMPA BAY	10
3	SAN FRANCISCO	13
7	L.A. Rams	22
9	New Orleans	10

Use Name	Pos.	Hgt	Wgt	Age	Int	Pts
Stan Clayton	OT-OG	6'3"	265	23		
Houston Hoover	OT	6'2"	285	23		
Mike Kenn	OT	6'7"	277	32		
Brett Miller	OT	6'7"	300	29		
Jamie Dukes	OG	6'1"	278	24		
Bill Fralic	OG	6'5"	280	25		
Paul Oswald (from DAL)	OG	6'3"	275	24		
John Scully	OG	6'6"	270	30		
Wayne Radloff	C	6'5"	277	27		
George Yarno	C-OG	6'2"	265	31		
Greg Brown	DE	6'5"	265	31		
Rick Bryan	DE	6'4"	265	26		
Reggie Camp	DE	6'4"	280	27		
Mike Gann	DE	6'5"	275	24		6
Mitch Willis (from RAID)	NT	6'8"	280	26		
Tony Casillas	NT	6'3"	280	24		
Charles Martin	NT	6'4"	280	29		

Use Name	Pos.	Hgt	Wgt	Age	Int	Pts
Aundray Bruce	LB	6'5"	245	22	2	
Joe Costello	LB	6'3"	244	28		
Marcus Cotton	LB	6'3"	225	22		
Tim Green	LB	6'2"	245	24		
John Rade	LB	6'1"	240	28		
Michael Reid	LB	6'2"	226	24		
Jessie Tuggle	LB	5'11"	225	23		6
Joel Williams	LB	6'1"	227	31		
Vinson Smith	DB	6'	219	23		
Bobby Butler	DB	5'11"	175	29	1	
Scott Case	DB	6'	178	26	10	
Bret Clark	DB	6'3"	198	27	4	
Evan Cooper	DB	5'11"	194	26		
David Croudip	DB	5'8"	183	29		
Charles Dimry	DB	6'	175	22		
Tim Gordon	DB	6'	188	23	2	
Leander Knight	DB	6'1"	193	25		
Robert Moore	DB	5'11"	190	24	5	6
Elbert Shelley	DB	5'11"	180	23		

Use Name	Pos.	Hgt	Wgt	Age	Int	Pts
Kerwin Bell	QB	6'2"	205	23		
Steve Dils	QB	6'1"	191	32		6
Hugh Millen	QB	6'5"	216	24		
Chris Miller	QB	6'2"	195	23		6
Gene Lang	HB	5'10"	206	26		6
James Primus	HB	5'11"	196	24		6
John Settle	HB-FB	5'9"	207	23		48
Sylvester Stamps	HB-WR	5'7"	171	27		
Rick Badanjek	FB-HB	5'8"	217	26		
Gerald Riggs	FB-HB	6'1"	232	27		6
Stacey Bailey	WR	6'	157	28		12
Lew Barnes	WR	5'8"	163	25		
Floyd Dixon	WR	5'9"	170	24		12
Michael Haynes	WR	6'	180	22		24
Jessie Hester	WR	5'11"	170	25		
James Milling	WR	5'9"	156	23		
Alex Higdon	TE	6'5"	247	21		12
Danzell Lee	TE	6'2"	237	25		
Ken Whisenhunt	TE	6'3"	240	26		6
Gary Wilkins	TE	6'	235	24		
Greg Davis	K	5'11"	197	22		82
Rick Donnelly	K	6'	190	26		

Scott Campbell — Knee Injury
Kenny Flowers — Knee Injury

SAN FRANCISCO 49ERS

RUSHING

Last Name	No.	Yds	Avg	TD
Craig	310	1502	4.8	9
Rathman	102	427	4.2	2
Young	27	184	6.8	1
Montana	38	132	3.5	3
DuBose	24	116	4.8	2
Rice	13	107	8.2	1
Sydney	9	50	5.6	0
Flagler	3	5	1.7	0
Helton	1	0	0.0	0

RECEIVING

Last Name	No.	Yds	Avg	TD
Craig	76	534	7.0	1
Rice	64	1306	20.4	9
Rathman	42	382	9.1	0
Wilson	33	405	12.3	3
Frank	16	195	12.2	3
Taylor	14	325	23.2	2
Heller	14	140	10.0	0
Greer	8	120	15.0	0
Jones	8	57	7.1	2
DuBose	6	57	9.5	0
Flagler	4	72	18.0	0
Chandler	4	33	8.3	0
Sydney	2	18	9.0	0
McIntyre	1	17	17.0	1
Nicholas	1	14	14.0	0

PUNT RETURNS

Last Name	No.	Yds	Avg	TD
Taylor	44	556	12.6	2
Chandler	6	28	4.7	0
Griffin	4	28	7.0	0

KICKOFF RETURNS

Last Name	No.	Yds	Avg	TD
DuBose	32	608	19.0	0
Taylor	12	225	18.8	0
Rodgers	6	98	16.3	0
Craig	2	32	16.0	0
Sydney	1	8	8.0	0
Thomas	1	5	5.0	0
Wilson	1	2	2.0	0

PASSING — PUNTING — KICKING

PASSING	Att	Cmp	%	Yds	Yd/Att	TD	Int— %	RK
Montana	397	238	59.9	2981	7.51	18	10— 2.5	3
Young	101	54	53.5	680	6.73	3	3— 3.0	
Rice	3	1	33.3	14	4.67	0	1—33.3	
Sydney	1	0	0.0	0	0.00	0	0— 0.0	

PUNTING	No.	Avg.
Helton	79	38.8

KICKING	XP	ATT	%	FG	ATT	%
Cofer	40	41	98	27	38	71

LOS ANGELES RAMS

RUSHING

Last Name	No.	Yds	Avg	TD
Bell	288	1212	4.2	16
White	88	323	3.7	0
Delpino	34	147	4.3	0
Green	35	117	3.3	0
Everett	34	105	3.1	0
McGee	22	69	3.1	0
Brown	3	24	8.0	0
Ellard	1	7	7.0	0
Guman	1	1	1.0	0
Herrmann	1	-1	-1.0	0

RECEIVING

Last Name	No.	Yds	Avg	TD
Ellard	86	1414	16.4	10
Holohan	59	640	11.1	3
D. Johnson	42	350	8.3	6
Delpino	30	312	10.4	2
Cox	28	590	21.1	5
Bell	24	124	5.2	2
McGee	16	117	7.3	3
Anderson	11	319	29.0	0
Green	6	57	9.5	0
White	6	36	6.0	0
Young	2	27	13.5	0
Brown	2	16	8.0	0

PUNT RETURNS

Last Name	No.	Yds	Avg	TD
Hicks	25	144	5.8	0
Ellard	17	119	7.0	0
Sutton	3	52	17.3	0
J. Johnson	2	4	2.0	0
Irvin	1	2	2.0	0
Gray	1	1	1.0	0

KICKOFF RETURNS

Last Name	No.	Yds	Avg	TD
Brown	19	401	21.1	0
Delpino	14	333	23.8	0
Green	17	345	20.3	0
Sutton	2	41	20.5	0
White	2	38	18.5	0
McDonald	3	34	11.3	0
McGee	1	0	0.0	0
Stewart	1	0	0.0	0

PASSING — PUNTING — KICKING

PASSING	Att	Cmp	%	Yds	Yd/Att	TD	Int— %	RK
Everett	517	308	59.6	3964	7.66	31	18— 3.5	2
Herrmann	5	4	80.0	38	7.60	0	0— 0.0	

PUNTING	No.	Avg.
Hatcher	36	39.6
Camarillo	40	39.5

KICKING	XP	ATT	%	FG	ATT	%
Lansford	45	48	94	24	32	75

NEW ORLEANS SAINTS

RUSHING

Last Name	No.	Yds	Avg	TD
Hilliard	204	823	4.0	5
Mayes	170	628	3.7	3
Heyward	74	355	4.8	1
Jordan	19	115	6.1	0
Hebert	37	79	2.1	0
Perriman	3	17	5.7	0
Martin	2	12	6.0	0
Hansen	1	10	10.0	0
Hill	2	7	3.5	0

RECEIVING

Last Name	No.	Yds	Avg	TD
Martin	85	1083	12.7	7
Hill	66	703	10.7	7
Hilliard	34	335	9.9	1
Tice	26	297	11.4	1
Clark	19	245	12.9	2
Perriman	16	215	13.4	2
Heyward	13	105	8.1	0
Mayes	11	103	9.4	0
Jordan	5	70	14.0	0
Brenner	5	67	13.4	0
Scales	2	20	10.0	1
Hebert	2	0	0.0	0
Pattison	1	8	8.0	0
Benson	1	5	5.0	0

PUNT RETURNS

Last Name	No.	Yds	Avg	TD
Gray	25	305	12.2	1
Hill	10	108	10.8	0

KICKOFF RETURNS

Last Name	No.	Yds	Avg	TD
Atkins	20	424	21.2	0
Gray	32	670	20.9	0
Mayes	7	132	18.9	0
Hilliard	6	111	18.5	0
Martin	3	32	10.7	0
Waymer	2	39	19.5	0

PASSING — PUNTING — KICKING

PASSING	Att	Cmp	%	Yds	Yd/Att	TD	Int— %	RK
Hebert	478	280	58.6	3156	6.60	20	15— 3.1	6
Wilson	16	5	31.3	73	4.56	0	1— 6.3	
Hilliard	2	1	50.0	27	13.50	1	0— 0.0	
Fourcade	1	0	0.0	0	0.00	0	0— 0.0	
Hill	1	0	0.0	0	0.00	0	0— 0.0	

PUNTING	No.	Avg.
Hansen	73	39.9

KICKING	XP	ATT	%	FG	ATT	%
Andersen	32	33	97	26	36	72

ATLANTA FALCONS

RUSHING

Last Name	No.	Yds	Avg	TD
Settle	232	1024	4.4	7
Riggs	113	488	4.3	1
Lang	53	191	3.6	0
Miller	31	138	4.5	1
Primus	35	95	2.7	1
Dixon	7	69	9.9	0
Millen	1	7	7.0	0
Hester	1	3	3.0	0
Dils	2	1	0.5	1
Stamps	3	0	0.0	0

RECEIVING

Last Name	No.	Yds	Avg	TD
Settle	68	570	8.4	1
Lang	38	398	10.8	1
Dixon	28	368	13.1	2
Riggs	22	171	7.8	0
Bailey	17	437	25.7	2
Whisenhunt	16	174	10.9	1
Haynes	13	232	17.8	4
Hester	12	176	14.7	0
Wilkins	11	134	12.2	0
Primus	8	42	5.3	0
Milling	5	66	13.2	0
Stamps	5	22	4.4	0
Higdon	3	60	20.0	2

PUNT RETURNS

Last Name	No.	Yds	Avg	TD
Barnes	34	307	9.0	0
Matthews	6	26	4.3	0
Cooper	2	10	5.0	0

KICKOFF RETURNS

Last Name	No.	Yds	Avg	TD
Cooper	16	331	20.7	0
Gordon	14	209	14.9	0
Stamps	12	219	18.3	0
Barnes	6	142	23.7	0
Haynes	6	113	18.8	0
Dukes	1	13	13.0	0
Primus	1	13	13.0	0
Lang	1	12	12.0	0
Shelley	2	5	2.5	0

PASSING — PUNTING — KICKING

PASSING	Att	Cmp	%	Yds	Yd/Att	TD	Int— %	RK
Miller	351	184	52.4	2133	52.4	11	12— 3.4	11
Dils	99	49	49.5	566	5.72	2	5— 5.1	
Millen	31	17	54.8	215	6.94	0	2— 6.5	

PUNTING	No.	Avg.
Donnelly	98	40.0

KICKING	XP	Att	%	FG	Att	%
Davis	25	27	93	19	30	63

A.F.C. No. 1 In The Recovery Ward

The major NFL story through the first half of the season was the rash of quarterback injuries. Nearly every week a quarterback or two or three went on the injury list, and commentators seriously discussed what new rules might be necessary to protect what was becoming an endangered species.

The N.F.C. lost Joe Montana for a few games, Chuck Long for the last 10 weeks and, as usual, Jim McMahon for half a season. Doug Williams was temporarily kayoed by an appendectomy and Neil Lomax by an arthritic hip. The A.F.C. was hit even harder. The most extreme example was in Cleveland, where no less than four signalcallers were sidelined at one time or another. Three quarterbacks suffered serious injuries in Indianapolis. Denver lost superstar John Elway for one game with arm and ankle hurts, and he never was at the top of his game. New England had to completely retool its offense when Steve Grogan was stopped by a neck injury. Seattle's Dave Krieg missed half of the season. San Diego installed a new quarterback in Mark Vlasic in Week 10, only to lose him in Week 13. Houston's Warren Moon was knocked out for four games with a shoulder injury. Pittsburgh's Bubby Brister missed games with a broken hand.

Not surprisingly, the two A.F.C. teams with the best records — Cincinnati and Buffalo — kept their quarterbacks in good health all season.

EASTERN DIVISION

Buffalo Bills — The Bills' defense was the class of the AFC. Cornelius Bennett and Shane Conlan were landslide Pro Bowlers. NT Fred Smerlas had one of his best seasons. DE Bruce Smith missed the first four games on drug suspension, but still managed 11 sacks. Veteran Art Still, picked up for a song from the Chiefs, filled in admirably in Smith's absence and played close to his old form the rest of the way. S Mark Kelso was a good ballhawk. The offense got just enough points to win most of the time. Jim Kelly was solid at quarterback. Rookie Thurman Thomas was the best of an ordinary group of runners, but the running attack by committee did the job most days. An injury to Shane Conlan precipitated a late slump, but, by then, the Bills had the division race wrapped up.

Indianapolis Colts — The Colts had a lot of unhappy players early in the season , and they played like it. Several linemen felt they deserved more pay to block for wealthy Eric Dickerson. When Indianapolis acquired high-priced LB Fredd Young, the other linebackers also felt underpaid. Gary Hogeboom felt under-played after being replaced at quarterback by Jack Trudeau and then rookie Chris Chandler. Coach Ron Meyer finally got everyone pulling in the same direction, and the Colts made a good, if unsuccessful, try for the playoffs in the second half of the season. One of the year's most interesting innovations was the occasional incorporation into the attack of a collegiate wishbone formation, with free-agent Ricky Turner at quarterback.

New England Patriots — The Patriots' ownership was settled during the season with the sale to Victor Kiam, the "I bought the company" head of Rimington. The team's on-field leadership was never finalized. Steve Grogan opened at quarterback with a wide-open attack, but after an opening win, New England lost three straight. Tom Ramsey was ineffective in Week Five against the Colts, and Doug Flutie won the starting slot with a fourth-quarter rally. The Patriots won six of eight with Flutie throwing rare rollout passes and most of the attack based on the running of super-rookie John Stephens. Then Tony Eason was given the starting job for the last two games in an effort to improve the passing attack. Instead, the New England offense hibernated, and any chance to make the playoffs was lost.

New York Jets — Joe Klecko was gone, but Mark Gastineau won his old defensive end spot back and by midseason led the conference in sacks. Then he suddenly retired to go to ailing girlfriend Brigitte Nielson. Gastineau's defection left the Jets without a pass rush and the largely rookie secondary was suddenly porous, although Erik McMillan still finished as Rookie of the Year. Al Toon and Mickey Shuler were great possession receivers, but the only deep threat was Wesley Walker, who seldom saw the ball. For the third year in a row, Pat Ryan replaced Ken O'Brien at quarterback late in the season. But O'Brien was back to engineer a comeback win over the Giants in the last game. Coach Joe Walton, rumored on his way out all season, was given a new three-year contract.

Miami Dolphins — What had been Dan Marino, the Marks Duper and Clayton, a subpar defense and a poor running game, became Marino and Clayton — period — in 1988. Duper was off his game for most of the season and was suspended for drugs near the end. The defense, particularly against opponents' runners, was pitiful. A Miami running game simply did not exist. Coach Don Shula opted to throw two passes for every run. His strategy was sometimes spectacular and kept the Dolphins dangerous, but it produced few victories. The team was generally considered the weakest he'd ever put on the field.

CENTRAL DIVISION

Cincinnati Bengals — The Bengals jumped from last to first in the division and put up one of the league's three 12-4 records. The offense deserved most of the credit. Boomer Esiason was the NFL MVP by passing judiciously but with great effectiveness to Eddie Brown, Rodney Holman and Tim McGee. James Brooks ran for 931 yards, but the new star was Ickey Woods, with 1,066 yards and 15 touchdowns. After each score, the rookie performed the "Ickey Shuffle," setting the art of the dance back to pre-minuet days. The burly offensive line, led by Anthony Munoz, Max Montoya and Joe Walter, made it all happen. The defense was less effective, although NT Tim Krumrie was exceptional and S David Fulcher was strong against the run. Coach Sam Wyche, nearly fired after the disaster of '87, was the toast of Cincinnati.

Cleveland Browns — The Browns went through quarterbacks like Kleenex. Bernie Kosar injured his arm in the opening quarter of the first game; backup Gary Danielson broke his leg the next week; and third-string Mike Pagel, lasted to Week Six. That left 38-year-old Don Strock, signed for emergencies, as the only healthy signallcaller when the Browns beat the Eagles in Week Seven. Kosar returned, but was knocked out again in the Week 15 loss to Miami. But Strock won the finale against Houston to put the Browns into the playoffs for the fourth straight season. CB Frank Minnifield was the defensive star, as Hanford Dixon had his own injury problems. Coach Marty Schottenheimer, whose play-calling was roundly criticized, resigned after the season rather than name a new offensive coordinator.

Houston Oilers — Coach Jerry Glanville brought smiles all season with his joke of leaving tickets at the gate for Elvis Presley and other deceased celebrities, but his roughhouse defense and special teams were unamusing to opponents. The Astrodome was nicknamed "The House of Pain" for the bruises dealt out there. With a strong offense led by QB Warren Moon, 1,000-yard runner Mike Rozier, and two of the best receivers in the league in Drew Hill and Ernest Givins, the Oilers were one of the AFC's best teams at home. However, their inability to win on the road kept them from mounting a serious challenge to Cincinnati.

Pittsburgh Steelers — Bubby Brister was installed at quarterback, and his passing and fiery leadership provided most of the rare good moments for the Steelers. LB Mike Merriweather held out the entire season, DE Keith Willis went out for the year after being injured during training camp, and No. 1 draft choice Aaron Jones bombed as a pass rusher. With the Steelers putting little pressure on rival quarterbacks, the young secondary became easy pickings. Coach Chuck Noll was berated by fans

FINAL TEAM STATISTICS

OFFENSE

	BUFF	CIN	CLEV	DEN	HOU	IND	K.C.	L.A.	MIA	N.E.	NYJ	PITT	S.D.	SEA
FIRST DOWNS:														
Total	313	351	294	338	308	311	289	283	321	264	331	292	255	291
by Rushing	137	159	93	106	141	153	104	116	77	126	118	120	115	125
by Passing	161	165	177	196	148	130	161	145	218	112	181	150	116	139
by Penalty	15	27	24	36	19	28	24	22	26	26	32	22	24	27
RUSHING:														
Number	528	563	440	464	558	545	448	493	335	588	514	499	438	517
Yards	2133	2710	1575	1815	2249	2249	1713	1852	1205	2120	2132	2228	2041	2086
Average Yards	4.0	4.8	3.6	3.9	4.0	4.1	3.8	3.8	3.6	3.6	4.1	4.5	4.7	4.0
Touchdowns	15	27	10	13	26	23	8	15	11	17	19	17	11	14
PASSING:														
Attempts	454	392	537	581	428	403	528	496	621	389	538	489	468	437
Completions	271	225	313	324	218	222	282	219	363	199	299	226	241	245
Completion Pct.	59.7	57.4	58.3	55.8	50.9	55.1	53.4	44.2	58.5	51.2	55.6	46.2	51.5	56.1
Passing Yards	3411	3592	3686	3941	3166	2865	3484	3503	4557	2333	3374	3307	2628	2979
Avg. Yds per Att.	6.6	8.0	6.0	6.0	6.5	6.0	5.5	5.7	7.2	5.3	5.3	5.6	4.8	5.9
Avg. Yds per Comp.	12.6	16.0	11.8	12.2	14.5	12.9	12.4	16.0	12.6	11.7	11.3	14.6	10.9	12.2
Times Tackled	30	30	36	32	24	34	43	46	7	23	42	42	31	29
Yds Lost Tackled	229	245	250	250	210	244	353	394	41	160	291	331	240	223
Net Yards	3182	3347	3436	3691	2956	2621	3131	3109	4516	2173	3083	2976	2388	2756
Touchdowns	15	28	19	24	21	15	16	21	29	12	20	15	11	22
Interceptions	17	14	17	22	18	22	21	20	23	28	11	20	20	20
Pct. Intercepted	3.7	3.6	3.2	4.7	3.2	5.5	4.0	4.0	3.7	4.8	2.1	4.1	4.6	4.6
PUNTS:														
Number	62	64	67	68	65	64	76	91	64	91	85	71	86	70
Average	39.5	36.7	38.5	43.8	38.8	43.5	40.3	41.8	43.0	38.3	38.9	41.5	43.5	40.8
PUNT RETURNS														
Number	26	32	40	53	36	26	32	55	27	38	38	39	35	37
Yards	152	244	325	451	225	254	215	480	260	308	418	322	314	340
Average Yards	5.8	76	8.1	8.5	6.3	9.8	6.7	8.9	9.6	10.5	11.0	8.3	9.0	9.2
Touchdowns	0	0	0	0	0	1	0	0	0	0	1	0	0	0
KICKOFF RET.:														
Number	50	57	55	58	60	52	56	62	65	57	72	74	60	62
Yards	935	1054	1159	1198	1232	1033	925	1407	1365	1248	1404	1575	1510	1352
Average Yards	18.7	18.5	21.1	20.7	20.5	19.9	16.5	22.7	21.0	21.9	19.5	21.3	25.2	21.8
Touchdowns	0	1	0	0	1	0	0	1	0	1	0	2	2	0
INTERCEPT RET.:														
Number	15	22	20	16	22	15	18	17	16	20	24	20	16	22
Yards	244	181	319	200	302	189	166	278	219	244	228	381	179	280
Average Yards	16.3	8.2	16.0	12.5	13.7	12.6	9.2	16.3	13.7	12.2	9.5	19.1	11.2	12.7
Touchdowns	1	1	1	0	2	1	0	1	0	0	3	2	1	1
PENALTIES:														
Number	109	82	110	85	125	89	85	102	99	87	115	99	118	89
Yards	824	647	875	717	1150	657	636	762	845	665	931	803	1039	790
FUMBLES:														
Number	26	28	32	34	33	20	21	33	26	19	32	40	26	29
Number Lost	16	13	16	12	17	8	12	13	12	10	16	19	12	14
POINTS:														
Total	329	448	304	327	424	354	254	325	319	250	372	336	231	339
PAT Attempts	33	59	33	37	51	40	24	39	41	31	43	36	27	39
PAT Made	33	56	32	36	48	39	23	37	37	25	43	34	27	39
FG Attempts	37	18	29	36	34	32	32	29	23	24	28	36	20	28
FG Made	32	12	24	23	22	25	27	18	12	13	23	28	14	22
Percent FG Made	86.5	66.7	82.8	63.9	64.7	78.1	84.4	62.1	52.2	54.2	82.1	77.7	70.0	78.6
Safeties	1	1	1	0	2	0	3	0	0	0	1	1	0	0

DEFENSE

	BUFF	CIN	CLEV	DEN	HOU	IND	K.C.	L.A.	MIA	N.E.	NYJ	PITT	S.D.	SEA
FIRST DOWNS:														
Total	299	322	301	316	304	315	318	310	359	272	310	319	335	321
by Rushing	114	126	114	140	94	109	162	124	155	119	123	110	135	134
by Passing	146	177	162	161	170	184	136	165	173	138	162	181	173	171
by Penalty	39	19	25	15	40	22	20	21	31	15	25	28	27	16
RUSHING:														
Number	477	493	498	552	431	447	609	533	557	496	517	516	521	509
Yards	1854	2048	1920	2538	1592	1694	2592	2208	2506	2099	2124	1864	2133	2286
Average Yards	3.9	4.2	3.9	4.6	3.7	3.8	4.3	4.1	4.5	4.2	4.1	3.6	4.1	4.5
Touchdowns	14	18	13	21	20	14	23	17	22	20	15	20	15	14
PASSING:														
Attempts	448	524	474	467	512	539	410	483	491	436	476	532	517	501
Completions	250	283	245	262	281	321	214	265	298	234	244	309	274	280
Completion Pct.	55.8	54.0	51.7	56.1	54.9	59.6	52.2	54.9	60.7	53.7	51.3	58.1	53.0	55.9
Passing Yards	3046	3508	3102	3168	3619	3803	2591	3471	3442	2801	3823	4086	3525	3618
Avg. Yds per Att.	5.5	5.5	5.6	5.8	5.9	6.3	5.6	6.1	6.4	5.6	6.7	7.2	6.0	6.3
Avg. Yds per Comp.	12.2	12.4	12.7	12.1	12.9	11.9	12.1	13.1	11.6	12.0	15.7	13.2	12.9	12.9
Times Tackled	46	42	37	36	42	30	23	40	24	29	45	19	34	30
Yds Lost Tackled	322	374	255	235	353	201	157	300	167	219	314	145	240	265
Net Yards	2724	3134	2847	2933	3266	3602	2434	3171	3275	2582	3509	3941	3285	3353
Touchdowns	14	19	13	18	22	21	12	23	19	13	28	25	22	21
Interceptions	15	22	20	16	22	15	18	17	16	20	24	20	16	22
Pct. Intercepted	3.3	4.2	4.2	3.4	4.3	2.8	4.4	3.5	3.3	4.6	5.0	3.8	3.1	4.4
PUNTS:														
Number	75	65	69	84	80	68	63	94	58	86	72	67	71	66
Average	39.7	39.9	39.4	43.4	37.2	39.4	40.2	41.4	41.8	42.2	38.1	40.7	39.3	42.1
PUNT RETURNS														
Number	36	32	32	33	35	37	48	47	35	37	34	40	56	36
Yards	222	280	304	364	206	418	473	397	318	217	201	418	558	202
Average Yards	6.2	8.8	9.5	11.0	5.9	11.3	9.9	8.4	9.1	5.9	5.9	10.5	10.0	5.6
Touchdowns	0	0	1	1	0	1	0	0	0	0	0	0	0	0
KICKOFF RET.:														
Number	69	61	58	52	69	67	57	61	53	45	70	63	47	66
Yards	1117	1335	973	1035	1362	1480	1380	1299	1109	888	1491	1351	1055	1207
Average Yards	16.2	21.9	16.8	19.9	19.7	22.1	24.2	21.3	20.9	19.7	21.3	21.4	22.4	18.3
Touchdowns	0	0	0	0	1	1	2	0	0	0	0	1	1	0
INTERCEPT RET.:														
Number	17	14	17	22	18	22	21	20	23	28	11	20	20	20
Yards	202	185	190	344	280	201	206	219	390	286	126	367	307	195
Average Yards	11.9	13.2	11.2	15.6	16.1	13.2	9.8	10.0	17.3	10.2	11.5	18.4	15.4	9.8
Touchdowns	1	0	2	1	1	1	1	0	4	0	0	1	0	1
PENALTIES:														
Number	90	95	100	116	118	118	106	94	103	108	89	79	74	111
Yards	713	873	789	966	947	965	854	823	734	858	757	705	619	861
FUMBLES:														
Number	28	28	23	23	33	32	30	31	31	29	35	35	25	31
Number Lost	17	14	11	13	20	20	13	17	15	15	16	13	10	18
POINTS:														
Total	237	329	288	352	365	315	320	369	380	284	354	421	332	329
PAT Attempts	29	39	30	41	46	38	39	41	45	33	43	49	38	38
PAT Made	27	38	30	41	43	36	38	40	44	33	36	47	36	38
FG Attempts	24	24	34	27	18	25	24	29	28	26	30	32	36	32
FG Made	12	17	26	21	14	17	16	27	22	17	20	26	22	21
Percent FG Made	50.0	70.8	76.5	77.7	77.7	68.0	66.7	93.1	78.6	65.4	66.7	81.3	61.1	65.6
Safeties	0	3	0	1	2	0	0	1	0	1	0	1	1	0

and press with short memories.

WESTERN DIVISION

Seattle Seahawks — When the Seahawks defeated the Raiders 43-37 in a see-saw finale to win their first AFC West title, coach Chuck Knox had completed a hat trick in winning division crowns for each NFL team he'd coached. FB John L. Williams became a full-fledged running and receiving star, and Curt Warner topped 1,000 yards in rushing again. The key man was QB Dave Krieg, who missed half of the season with an injury, but was sensational coming down the stretch, finishing with the AFC's second-best pass rating. The defense, led by Jacob Greene's nine sacks, was effective but small; it could be outmuscled by the league's bigger offensive lines.

Denver Broncos — John Elway's sore arm crippled the offense. New RB Tony Dorsett, who was past his prime, couldn't give the Broncos a viable running game to pick up the slack, and injuries among the receivers exacerbated the problems with the pass attack. But none of these hurt Denver as much as a defense that could no longer get by on quickness instead of heft. The team was especially vulnerable when star LB Karl Mecklenburg was out or playing at less than 100 percent because of a hand injury. After the season, coach Dan Reeves fired most of the defensive coaches, including coordinator Joe Collier, who'd been with the Broncos for 20 years.

Los Angeles Raiders — The Raiders had two new quarterbacks in rookie Steve Beuerlein and Redskins' emigree Jay Schroeder, four of the league's highest-priced receivers in Rookie of the Year Tim Brown, Canadian import Mervyn Fernandez, former Bear Willie Gault and ex-Packer James Lofton, and two Heisman Trophy runners in veteran Marcus Allen and, for half of the season, Bo Jackson. Yet, new coach Mike Shanahan's offense sputtered. The line was unsettled and the offense had too many new players in a new system and too many disappointing performances. The defense had injuries, most notably to DE Howie Long, but the major dilemma there was age.

San Diego Chargers — Gary Anderson rushed for 1,119 yards and a 5.0 average, but the Chargers went through three quarterbacks before settling on much-criticized Mark Malone by default. The wide receivers lacked experience, and the offensive line was made up of four free agents and a rookie. DE Lee Williams had 11 sacks, but the defense lost LB Billy Ray Smith for most of the season with injuries and LB Chip Banks for all of the season to a holdout. Still, coach Al Saunders' club won four of its last six games. It wasn' enough to save his job. He was fired the day ater the season ended.

Kansas City Chiefs — When Bill Kenney couldn't move the team, journeyman Steve DeBerg took over at quarterback. He passed for 2,935 yards, but had almost ne help from the runners, as Christian Okoye struggled with injuries. S Deron Cherry had an All-Pro year, but the other Pro Bowlers in the secondary, Lloyd Burrus and Albert Lewis, also had injury problems. DE Art Still was shuffled off to Buffalo at the beginning of the season, and when NT Bill Maas went out after eight games, the Chiefs lost any ability to stop opponent's runners.

BUFFALO BILLS 12-4 Marv Levy

Scores of Each Game		
13	MINNESOTA	10
9	MIAMI	6
16	New England	14
36	PITTSBURGH	28
3	Chicago	24
34	INDIANAPOLIS	23
37	N.Y. Jets	14
23	NEW ENGLAND	20
28	GREEN BAY	0
13	Seattle	3
31	Miami	6
9	N.Y. JETS	*6
21	Cincinnati	35
5	Tampa Bay	10
37	L.A. RAIDERS	21
14	Indianapolis	17

Use Name	Pos.	Hgt	Wgt	Age	Int	Pts
Howard Ballard	OT	6'6"	300	24		
Leonard Burton	OT	6'3"	275	24		
Joe Devlin	OT	6'5"	280	35		
Dale Hellestrae	OT	6'5"	280	26		
Will Wolford	OT-OG	6'5"	280	24		
Jim Ritcher	OG	6'3"	265	30		
Tim Vogler	OG	6'3"	285	31		
Kent Hull	C	6'4"	275	27		
Mark Pike	DE	6'4"	272	24		
Dean Prater	DE	6'4"	260	29		
Leon Seals	DE	6'4"	265	24		6
Bruce Smith	DE	6'4"	285	25		2
Art Still	DE	6'7"	255	32		
Fred Smerlas	NT	6'3"	280	31		
Jeff Wright	NT	6'2"	270	25		
Carlton Bailey	LB	6'2"	240	23		
Cornelius Bennett	LB	6'2"	235	22	2	
Ray Bentley	LB	6'2"	235	27	1	
Shane Conlan	LB	6'3"	235	24	1	
Tom Erlandson	LB	6'1"	220	22		
Hal Garner	LB	6'4"	235	26		
Don Graham	LB	6'2"	244	24		
Scott Radecic	LB	6'3"	242	26		
Darryl Talley	LB	6'4"	235	28		
Derrick Burroughs	DB	6'1"	180	26		
Sherman Cocroft	DB	6'1"	190	27	1	
Wayne Davis	DB	5'11"	180	25	1	
Dwight Drane	DB	6'2"	205	26		
John Hagy	DB	5'11"	190	22		
Kirby Jackson	DB	5'10"	180	23		
Mark Kelso	DB	5'11"	185	25	7	6
Nate Odomes	DB	5'10"	188	23	1	
Leonard Smith (from PHX)	DB	5'11"	202	27	2	
Erroll Tucker	DB	5'8"	170	24		
Stan Gelbaugh	QB	6'3"	207	25		
Jim Kelly	QB	6'3"	218	28		
Frank Reich	QB	6'4"	210	26		
Ronnie Harmon	HB	5'11"	200	24		24
Robb Riddick	HB	6'	195	31		84
Thurman Thomas	HB	5'10"	198	22		12
Carl Byrum	FB	6'	235	25		
Jamie Mueller	FB	6'1"	225	23		
Walter Broughton	WR	5'10"	180	25		
Chris Burkett	WR	6'4"	210	26	6	
Flip Johnson	WR	5'10"	185	25	6	
Trumaine Johnson	WR	6'1"	196	28		
Andre Reed	WR	6'	190	24		36
Steve Tasker	WR	5'9"	185	26		
Keith McKeller	TE	6'6"	245	24		
Pete Metzelaars	TE	6'7"	250	28	6	
Butch Rolle	TE	6'3"	242	24		12
John Kidd	K	6'3"	208	27		
Scott Norwood	K	6'	207	28		129

Rich Strenger — Knee Injury
Bruce Mesner — Knee Injury
Elston Ridgle — Ankle Injury
Tony Brown — Injury

INDIANAPOLIS COLTS 9-7 Ron Meyer

Scores of Each Game		
14	HOUSTON	*17
13	CHICAGO	17
17	Cleveland	23
15	MIAMI	13
17	New England	21
23	Buffalo	34
35	TAMPA BAY	31
16	San Diego	0
55	DENVER	23
38	N.Y. JETS	14
20	Green Bay	13
3	Minnesota	12
24	NEW ENGLAND	21
31	Miami	28
16	N.Y. Jets	34
17	BUFFALO	14

Use Name	Pos.	Hgt	Wgt	Age	Int	Pts
Brian Baldinger	OT	6'4"	268	29		
Kevin Call	OT	6'7"	302	26		
Chris Hinton	OT	6'4"	295	27		
Dan McQuaid (from MIN)	OT-OG	6'7"	278	27		
Joel Patten	OT	6'7"	301	30		
Randy Dixon	OG-OT	6'3"	290	23		
Ben Utt	OG	6'5"	286	29		
Ray Donaldson	C	6'3"	288	30		
Jon Hand	DE	6'7"	298	24		
Ezra Johnson	DE	6'4"	250	32		
Donnell Thompson	DE	6'4"	275	29		
Byron Darby	NT	6'4"	260	28		
Joe Klecko	NT	6'3"	265	34		
O'Brien Alston	LB	6'6"	246	22		
Harvey Armstrong	LB	6'3"	268	28		
Duane Bickett	LB	6'5"	243	25	3	
Jeff Herrod	LB	6'	243	22		
Barry Krauss	LB	6'3"	248	31	1	
Orlando Lowry	LB	6'4"	236	27		
Cliff Odom	LB	6'2"	245	30		
Fredd Young	LB	6'1"	233	26		
Michael Ball	DB	6'	216	24		
Eugene Daniel	DB	5'11"	178	27	2	6
Chris Goode	DB	6'	193	24	2	
John Holt	DB	5'11"	179	29		
Chuckie Miller	DB	5'10"	180	23		
Mike Prior	DB	6'	204	24	3	
Freddie Robinson	DB	6'1"	190	24		
Craig Swoope	DB	6'1"	214	24		
Keith Taylor	DB	5'11"	193	23		
Willie Tullis	DB	6'	195	30	4	
Terry Wright	DB	6'	195	23		
Chris Chandler	QB	6'4"	210	22		12
Bob Gagliano	QB	6'3"	195	29		
Gary Hogeboom	QB	6'4"	217	30		6
Bill Ransdell	QB	6'2"	212	25		
Jack Trudeau	QB	6'3"	214	25		
Ricky Turner	QB	6'	190	26		12
Albert Bentley	HB-FB	5'11"	214	28		18
Eric Dickerson	HB	6'3"	217	27		90
Mark Boyer	HB-TE	6'4"	242	25		18
George Wonsley	HB-FB	5'10"	219	27		6
Roy Banks	WR	5'10"	193	22		
Mark Bellini	WR	5'11"	182	24		
Matt Bouza	WR	6'3"	212	30		24
Bill Brooks	WR	6'	191	24		18
Clarence Verdin	WR	5'8"	163	25		30
Pat Beach	TE	6'4"	252	27		
John Brandes	TE	6'2"	255	24		
Donnie Dee	TE	6'4"	247	23		
Jess Atkinson	K	5'9"	168	26		
Dean Biasucci	K	6'	191	26		114
Kerry Brady	K	6'1"	205	25		
Rohn Stark	K	6'3"	204	29		

Steve Knight — Knee Injury

NEW ENGLAND PATRIOTS 9-7 Raymond Berry

Scores of Each Game		
28	N.Y. JETS	3
6	Minnesota	36
14	BUFFALO	16
6	Houston	31
21	INDIANAPOLIS	17
3	Green Bay (Mil.)	45
27	CINCINNATI	21
20	Buffalo	23
30	CHICAGO	7
21	MIAMI	10
14	N.Y. Jets	13
6	Miami	3
21	Indianapolis	14
13	SEATTLE	7
10	TAMPA BAY	*7
10	Denver	21

Use Name	Pos.	Hgt	Wgt	Age	Int	Pts
Bruce Armstrong	OT	6'4"	284	•22		
Tom Rehder	OT	6'7"	280	23		
Danny Villa	OT	6'5"	305	23		
Paul Fairchild	OG	6'4"	270	26		
Sean Farrell	OG	6'3"	260	28		
Ron Wooten	OG	6'4"	273	29		
Mike Baab	C	6'4"	270	28		
Trevor Matich	C	6'4"	270	26		
Milford Hodge	DE	6'3"	278	27		
Edmund Nelson	DE-DT	6'3"	275	28		
Kenneth Sims	DE	6'5"	271	28		
Verin Garis	DE	6'4"	255	25		
Tim Goad	NT	6'3"	280	22		
Brent Williams	NT-DE	6'3"	278	23		
Toby Williams	NT	6'3"	275	28		
Thomas Benson	LB	6'2"	245	26		
Vincent Brown	LB	6'2"	245	23		
Tim Jordan	LB	6'3"	226	24	1	
Larry McGrew	LB	6'5"	233	31	1	
Eric Naposki	LB	6'2"	230	21		
Johnny Rembert	LB	6'3"	234	27	2	
Ed Reynolds	LB	6'5"	242	26		
Andre Tippett	LB	6'3"	241	28		
Jim Bowman	DB	6'2"	210	24	1	
Raymond Clayborn	DB	6'1"	186	33	4	
Ernest Gibson	DB	5'10"	185	26		
Darryl Holmes	DB	6'2"	190	23		
Roland James	DB	6'2"	191	30	4	
Ronnie Lippett	DB	5'11"	180	27	1	
Fred Marion	DB	6'2"	191	29	4	
Rod McSwain	DB	6'1"	198	26	2	
Eugene Profit	DB	5'10"	165	23		
Tony Eason	QB	6'4"	212	28		
Doug Flutie	QB	5'9"	175	25		6
Steve Grogan	QB	6'4"	210	35		6
Tom Ramsey	QB	6'1"	188	27		
Marvin Allen	HB	5'10"	215	22		
Elgin Davis	HB	5'10"	192	22		
Reggie Dupard	HB	5'11"	205	24		12
John Stephens	HB	6'1"	220	22		30
Craig James	FB	6'	215	27		6
Bob Perryman	FB	6'1"	233	23		36
Mosi Tatupu	FB	6'	227	33		12
Irving Fryar	WR	6'	200	25		30
Dennis Gadbois	WR	6'1"	183	24		
Cedric Jones	WR	6'1"	184	28		6
Sammy Martin	WR	5'11"	175	23		6
Stanley Morgan	WR	5'11"	181	33		24
Lin Dawson	TE	6'3"	240	29		12
Russ Francis	TE	6'6"	242	35		
Steve Johnson	TE	6'6"	245	23		
Willie Scott	TE	6'4"	245	29		
Jeff Feagles	K	6'	198	22		
Teddy Garcia	K	5'10"	190	24		29
Jason Staurovsky	K	5'9"	170	25		35

David Ward — Shoulder Injury
Ed Williams — Knee Injury

Tony Collins — Suspended by N.F.L.

NEW YORK JETS 8-7-1 Joe Walton

Scores of Each Game		
3	New England	28
23	Cleveland	3
45	HOUSTON	3
17	Detroit	10
17	KANSAS CITY	*17
19	Cincinnati	36
14	BUFFALO	37
44	Miami	30
24	PITTSBURGH	20
14	Indianapolis	38
13	NEW ENGLAND	14
6	Buffalo	*9
38	MIAMI	34
34	Kansas City	38
34	INDIANAPOLIS	16
27	N.Y. GIANTS	21

Use Name	Pos.	Hgt	Wgt	Age	Int	Pts
Dave Cadigan	OT	6'4"	285	23		
Jeff Criswell	OT-OG	6'7"	284	24		
Reggie McElroy	OT	6'6"	276	28		
Dan Alexander	OG	6'4"	274	33		
Ted Banker	OG-C	6'2"	275	27		
Mike Haight	OG-OT	6'4"	281	25		
Adam Schreiber (from PHI)	OG	6'4"	277	26		
Ron Tilton	OG	6'4"	250	25		
Mike Withycombe	OG-OT	6'5"	295	23		
Guy Bingham	C-OG	6'3"	260	30		
Jim Sweeney	C-OT-OG	6'4"	270	26		
Paul Frase	DE-NT	6'5"	273	23		
Mark Gastineau	DE	6'5"	255	31		
Marty Lyons	DE-NT	6'5"	269	31		2
Tom Baldwin	NT-DE	6'4"	275	27		
Mark Garalczyk (from PHX)	DT-DE	6'5"	272	23		
Scott Mersereau	NT	6'3"	273	23		
Gerald Nichols	NT	6'2"	267	24		
Troy Benson	LB	6'2"	235	25	1	
Kyle Clifton	LB	6'4"	236	26		
Robin Cole	LB	6'2"	225	32		
Onzy Elam	LB	6'2"	225	23		
John Galvin	LB	6'3"	226	23		
Alex Gordon	LB	6'5"	246	23		
Steve Hammond	LB	6'4"	225	28		
Kevin McArthur	LB	6'2"	250	25	1	
Ken Rose	LB	6'1"	204	26		
John Booty	DB	6'	179	22	3	
James Hasty	DB	6'	200	23	5	
Carl Howard	DB	6'2"	190	26	2	
Bobby Humphery	DB	5'10"	180	27	1	
Erik McMillan	DB	6'2"	197	23	8	12
Rich Miano	DB	6'	200	25	2	
George Radachowsky	DB	5'11"	190	25		
Terry Williams	DB	5'11"	197	22		
Mike Zordich	DB	5'11"	199	24	1	6
Ken O'Brien	QB	6'4"	200	27		
Pat Ryan	QB	6'3"	210	32		
Johnny Hector	HB	5'11"	202	27		60
Freeman McNeil	HB	5'11"	209	29		42
Marion Barber	FB-TE	6'3"	228	28		
Nuu Faaola	FB	5'11"	220	24		
Roger Vick	FB	6'3"	228	24		18
Michael Harper	WR	5'10"	180	27		
Kurt Sohn	WR	5'11"	180	31		12
Al Toon	WR	6'4"	205	25		30
JoJo Townsell	WR	5'9"	180	27		6
Wesley Walker	WR	6'	182	33		42
K.D. Dunn	TE	6'3"	237	25		
Billy Griggs	TE	6'3"	234	26		
Keith Neubert	TE	6'5"	250	23		
Mickey Shuler	TE	6'3"	231	32		30
Pat Leahy	K	6'	196	37		112
Joe Prokop	K	6'2"	224	28		

Michael Mitchell — Hip Injury

Bob Crable — Knee Injury
Matt Monger — Forearm Injury
Kerry Glenn — Knee Injury
Bobby Curtis — Injury

Rocky Klever — Back Injury
Jamie Kurisko — Hamstring Injury
Kyle Mackey — Shoulder Injury
Tracy Martin — Quadriceps Injury

MIAMI DOLPHINS 6-10 Don Shula

Scores of Each Game		
7	Chicago	34
6	Buffalo	9
24	GREEN BAY	17
13	Indianapolis	15
24	MINNESOTA	7
24	L.A. Raiders	14
31	SAN DIEGO	28
30	N.Y. JETS	44
17	Tampa Bay	14
10	New England	21
6	BUFFALO	31
3	NEW ENGLAND	6
34	N.Y. Jets	38
28	INDIANAPOLIS	31
38	CLEVELAND	31
24	Pittsburgh	40

Use Name	Pos.	Hgt	Wgt	Age	Int	Pts
Louis Cheek	OT	6'6"	295	23		
Mark Dennis	OT	6'6"	290	23		
Jon Giesler	OT	6'5"	272	31		
Ronnie Lee	OT	6'3"	275	31		
Roy Foster	OG	6'4"	275	28		
Harry Galbreath	OG	6'1"	275	23		
Greg Johnson	OG	6'4"	295	23		
Tom Toth	OG	6'5"	282	26		
Jeff Dellenbach	C	6'6"	280	25		
John Bosa	DE	6'4"	273	24		
Jackie Cline	DE-NT	6'5"	280	28		
Jeff Cross	DE	6'4"	270	22		
T.J. Turner	DE	6'4"	280	25		
Eric Kumerow	DE-LB	6'7"	260	23		
Mike Lambrecht	NT	6'1"	274	25		
Brian Sochia	NT	6'3"	275	27		
Mark Brown	LB	6'2"	238	27	2	
Bob Brudzinski	LB	6'4"	235	33		
David Frye	LB	6'2"	227	27		
Tony Furjanic	LB	6'1"	228	24		
Chris Gaines	LB	6'	238	24		
Rick Graf	LB	6'5"	249	25	1	
Hugh Green	LB	6'2"	228	29		
Ilia Jarostchuk	LB	6'3"	231	24		
Larry Kolic	LB	6'1"	239	25		
John Offerdahl	LB	6'3"	237	24	2	
Jackie Shipp	LB	6'2"	238	26		
Bud Brown	DB	6'	193	27		
Liffort Hobley	DB	6'	202	26		6
William Judson	DB	6'1"	192	29	4	
Paul Lankford	DB	6'1"	190	30	1	
Don McNeal	DB	5'11"	193	30	1	
Rodney Thomas	DB	5'10"	190	22	1	
Reyna Thompson	DB	6'	193	25		
Jarvis Williams	DB	5'11"	196	23	4	
Ron Jaworski	QB	6'1"	205	37		
Dan Marino	QB	6'4"	222	26		
Joe Cribbs (from IND)	HB	5'11"	190	30		
Lorenzo Hampton	HB	6'	208	26		72
Troy Stradford	HB	5'9"	192	23		18
Woody Bennett	FB	6'2"	244	33		
Ron Davenport	FB	6'2"	232	25		
Fred Banks	WR	5'10"	180	26		12
Mark Clayton	WR	5'9"	184	27		84
Mark Duper	WR	5'9"	190	29		6
Jim Jensen	WR-FB	6'4"	220	29		30
James Pruitt (to IND)	WR	6'3"	198	24		
Scott Schwedes	WR	6'	182	23		
Ferrell Edmunds	TE	6'6"	248	23		18
Bruce Hardy	TE	6'5"	234	32		
Brian Kinchen	TE	6'2"	238	23		
Tony Franklin	K	5'8"	182	30		18
Fuad Reveiz	K	5'11"	220	25		55
Reggie Roby	K	6'2"	242	27		

Chris Scott — Knee Injury
Dwight Stephenson — Knee Injury
Chris Conlin — Knee Injury

Scott Nicholas — Knee Injury
Glenn Blackwood — Knee Injury

Dan Johnson — Back Injury

RUSHING

Last Name	No.	Yds	Avg	TD
BUFFALO BILLS				
Thomas	207	881	4.3	2
Riddick	111	438	3.9	12
Mueller	81	296	3.7	0
Harmon	57	212	3.7	1
Kelly	35	154	4.4	0
Byrum	28	91	3.3	0
Reed	6	64	10.7	0
Reich	3	-3	-1.0	0
INDIANAPOLIS COLTS				
Dickerson	388	1659	4.3	14
Bentley	45	230	5.1	2
Chandler	46	139	3.0	0
Verdin	8	77	9.6	0
Brooks	5	62	12.4	0
Wonsley	26	48	1.8	1
Turner	16	42	2.6	2
Hogeboom	11	-8	-0.7	1
NEW ENGLAND PATRIOTS				
Stephens	297	1168	3.9	4
Perryman	146	448	3.1	6
Flutie	38	179	4.7	1
Dupard	52	151	2.9	2
Tatupu	22	75	3.4	2
Allen	7	40	5.7	0
Eason	5	18	3.6	0
C. James	4	15	3.8	1
Fryar	6	12	2.0	0
Grogan	6	12	2.0	1
Ramsey	3	8	2.7	0
Feagles	1	0	0.0	0
Morgan	1	-6	-6.0	0
NEW YORK JETS				
McNeil	219	944	4.3	6
Hector	137	561	4.1	10
Vick	128	540	4.2	3
O'Brien	21	25	1.2	0
Ryan	5	22	4.4	0
Faaola	1	13	13.0	0
Walker	1	12	12.0	0
Leahy	1	10	10.0	0
Toon	1	5	5.0	0
MIAMI DOLPHINS				
Hampton	117	414	3.5	9
Stradford	95	335	3.5	2
Davenport	55	273	5.0	0
Bennett	31	115	3.7	0
Jensen	10	68	6.8	0
Cribbs	5	21	4.2	0
Clayton	1	4	4.0	0
Edmunds	1	-8	-8.0	0
Marino	20	-17	-0.9	0

RECEIVING

Last Name	No.	Yds	Avg	TD
BUFFALO BILLS				
Reed	71	968	13.6	6
T. Johnson	37	514	13.9	0
Harmon	37	427	11.5	3
Metzelaars	33	438	13.3	1
Burkett	23	354	15.4	1
Thomas	18	208	11.6	0
F. Johnson	9	170	18.9	1
Mueller	8	42	5.3	0
Rolle	2	3	1.5	2
Byrum	2	0	0.0	0
Kelly	1	5	5.0	0
INDIANAPOLIS COLTS				
Brooks	54	867	16.1	3
Dickerson	36	377	10.5	1
Boyer	27	256	9.5	2
Bentley	26	252	9.7	1
Beach	26	235	9.0	0
Bouza	25	342	13.7	4
Verdin	20	437	21.9	4
Bellini	5	64	12.8	0
Baldinger	1	37	37.0	0
Hinton	1	1	1.0	0
Donaldson	1	-3	-3.0	0
NEW ENGLAND PATRIOTS				
Dupard	34	232	6.8	0
Fryar	33	490	14.8	5
Morgan	31	502	16.2	4
Jones	22	313	14.2	1
Perryman	17	134	7.9	0
C. James	14	171	12.2	0
Stephens	14	98	7.0	0
Francis	11	161	14.6	0
Dawson	8	106	13.3	2
Tatupu	8	58	7.3	0
Martin	4	51	12.8	0
Scott	1	8	8.0	0
Johnson	1	5	5.0	0
Farrell	1	4	4.0	0
NEW YORK JETS				
Toon	93	1067	11.5	5
Shuler	70	805	11.5	5
McNeil	34	288	8.5	1
Walker	26	551	21.2	7
Hector	26	237	9.1	0
Vick	19	120	6.3	0
Griggs	14	133	9.5	0
Sohn	7	66	9.4	2
Dunn	6	67	11.2	0
Townsell	4	40	10.0	0
MIAMI DOLPHINS				
Clayton	86	1129	13.1	14
Jensen	58	652	11.2	5
Stradford	56	426	7.6	1
Duper	39	626	16.1	1
Edmunds	33	575	17.4	3
Devenport	30	282	9.4	0
Banks	23	430	18.7	2
Hampton	23	204	8.9	3
Schwedes	6	130	21.7	0
Hardy	4	46	11.5	0
Pruitt	2	38	19.0	0
Bennett	2	16	8.0	0
Kinchen	1	3	3.0	0

PUNT RETURNS

Last Name	No.	Yds	Avg	TD
BUFFALO BILLS				
F. Johnson	16	72	4.5	0
Tucker	10	80	8.0	0
INDIANAPOLIS COLTS				
Verdin	22	239	10.9	1
Brooks	3	15	5.0	0
Prior	1	0	0.0	0
NEW ENGLAND PATRIOTS				
Fryar	38	398	10.5	0
Bowman	0	0	0.0	0
NEW YORK JETS				
Townsell	35	409	11.7	1
Sohn	3	9	3.0	0
MIAMI DOLPHINS				
Schwedes	24	230	9.6	0
Williams	3	29	9.7	0

KICKOFF RETURNS

Last Name	No.	Yds	Avg	TD
BUFFALO BILLS				
Tucker	15	310	20.7	0
F. Johnson	14	250	17.9	0
Harmon	11	249	22.6	0
Riddick	6	100	16.7	0
Rolle	1	12	12.0	0
Byrum	2	9	4.5	0
Pike	1	5	5.0	0
INDIANAPOLIS COLTS				
Bentley	39	775	19.9	0
Verdin	7	145	20.7	0
Banks	4	56	14.0	0
Beach	1	35	35.0	0
Wright	1	22	22.0	0
NEW ENGLAND PATRIOTS				
Martin	31	735	23.7	1
Allen	18	391	21.7	0
Davis	6	106	17.7	0
Tatupu	1	13	13.0	0
Fryar	1	3	3.0	0
NEW YORK JETS				
Humphery	21	510	24.3	0
Townsell	31	601	19.4	0
Sohn	9	159	17.7	0
Harper	7	114	16.3	0
Faaola	2	9	4.5	0
Barber	1	11	11.0	0
Rose	1	0	0.0	0
MIAMI DOLPHINS				
Cribbs	41	863	21.0	0
Hampton	9	216	24.0	0
Williams	8	159	19.9	0
Schwedes	3	49	16.3	0
Davenport	2	41	20.5	0
Edmunds	1	20	20.0	0
Hardy	1	17	17.0	0
Hill	1	1	1.0	0

PASSING — PUNTING — KICKING

BUFFALO BILLS

PASSING	Att	Cmp	%	Yds	Yd/Att	TD	Int-	%	RK
Kelly	452	269	59.5	3380	7.48	15	17—	3.8	7
Riddick	2	2	100.0	31	15.50	0	0—	0.0	

PUNTING	No.	Avg.
Kidd	62	39.5

KICKING	XP	ATT	%	FG	ATT	%
Norwood	33	33	100	32	37	86

INDIANAPOLIS COLTS

PASSING	Att	Cmp	%	Yds	Yd/Att	TD	Int-	%	RK
Chandler	233	129	55.4	1619	6.95	8	12—	5.2	10
Hogeboom	131	76	58.0	996	7.60	7	7—	5.3	
Trudeau	34	14	41.2	158	4.65	0	3—	8.8	
Turner	4	3	75.0	92	23.00	0	0—	0.0	
Bentley	1	0	0.0	0	0.00	0	0—	0.0	

PUNTING	No.	Avg.
Stark	64	43.5

KICKING	XP	ATT	%	FG	ATT	%
Biasucci	39	40	98	25	32	78

NEW ENGLAND PATRIOTS

PASSING	Att	Cmp	%	Yds	Yd/Att	TD	Int—	%	RK
Flutie	179	92	51.4	1150	6.42	8	10—	5.6	
Grogan	140	67	47.9	834	5.96	4	13—	9.3	
Eason	43	28	65.1	249	5.79	0	2—	4.7	
Ramsey	27	12	44.4	100	3.70	0	3—	11.1	

PUNTING	No.	Avg.
Feagles	91	38.3

KICKING	XP	ATT	%	FG	ATT	%
Staurovsky	14	15	93	7	11	63
Garcia	11	16	69	6	13	46

NEW YORK JETS

PASSING	Att	Cmp	%	Yds	Yd/Att	TD	Int—	%	RK
O'Brien	424	236	55.7	2567	6.05	15	7—	1.7	6
Ryan	113	63	55.8	807	7.14	5	4—	3.5	
Hector	1	0	0.0	0	0.0	0	0—	0.0	

PUNTING	No.	Avg.
Prokop	85	38.9

KICKING	XP	Att	%	FG	Att	%
Leahy	43	43	100	23	28	82

MIAMI DOLPHINS

PASSING	Att	Cmp	%	Yds	Yd/Att	TD	Int—	%	RK
Marino	606	354	58.4	4434	7.32	28	23—	3.8	5
Jaworski	14	9	64.3	123	8.79	1	0—	0.0	
Stradford	1	0	0.0	0	0.0	0	0—	0.0	

PUNTING	No.	Avg.
Roby	64	43.0

KICKING	XP	Att.	%	FG	Att	%
Reveiz	21	32	97	8	12	67
Franklin	6	7	86	4	11	36

CINCINNATI BENGALS 12-4 Sam Wyche

Scores of Each Game		
21	PHOENIX	14
28	Philadelphia	24
17	Pittsburgh	12
24	CLEVELAND	17
45	L.A. Raiders	21
36	N.Y. JETS	19
21	New England	27
44	HOUSTON	21
16	Cleveland	23
42	PITTSBURGH	7
28	Kansas City	31
38	Dallas	24
35	BUFFALO	21
27	SAN DIEGO	10
6	Houston	41
20	WASHINGTON	*17

Use Name	Pos.	Hgt	Wgt	Age	Int	Pts
David Douglas	OT	6'4"	280	25		
Anthony Munoz	OT	6'6"	278	30		
Dave Smith	OT	6'7"	290	23		
Joe Walter	OT	6'6"	290	25		
Brian Blados	OG	6'5"	295	26		
Max Montoya	OG	6'5"	275	32		
Bruce Reimers	OG	6'7"	280	27		
Bruce Kozerski	C-OG	6'4"	275	26		
Jason Buck	DE	6'5"	264	25		
Eddie Edwards	DE	6'5"	256	34		
Curtis Maxey	DE	6'3"	298	23		
Skip McClendon	DE	6'7"	275	24		
Jim Skow	DE	6'3"	255	25		
David Grant	NT	6'4"	277	22		
Tim Krumrie	NT	6'2"	268	28		

Mike Hammerstein — Knee Injury

Use Name	Pos.	Hgt	Wgt	Age	Int	Pts
Leo Barker	LB	6'2"	227	28		6
Ed Brady	LB	6'2"	235	28		
Tim Inglis	LB	6'3"	232	24		
Joe Kelly	LB	6'2"	231	23		
Emanuel King	LB	6'4"	251	25		
Rich Romer	LB	6'3"	222	22		
Kevin Walker	LB	6'2"	238	22		
Leon White	LB	6'3"	245	24		
Reggie Williams	LB	6'1"	232	33		
Carl Zander	LB	6'2"	235	25	1	
Lewis Billups	DB	5'11"	190	24	4	6
Barney Bussey	DB	6'	195	26		
Ellis Dillahunt	DB	5'11"	200	23		
Rickey Dixon	DB	5'11"	181	21	1	
David Fulcher	DB	6'3"	228	26	5	6
Ray Horton	DB	5'11"	190	28	3	
Daryl Smith	DB	5'9"	188	25		
Eric Thomas	DB	5'11"	181	23	7	
Solomon Wilcots	DB	5'11"	185	23	1	

Chris Barber — Arm Injury

Use Name	Pos.	Hgt	Wgt	Age	Int	Pts
Boomer Esiason	QB	6'4"	225	27		6
Mike Norseth	QB	6'2"	200	24		
Turk Schonert	QB	6'1"	196	31		
James Brooks	HB	5'10"	182	29		84
Stanford Jennings	HB	6'1"	205	26		12
Marc Logan	HB	5'11"	207	23		
Stanley Wilson	FB	5'10"	212	27		18
Ickey Woods	FB	6'2"	232	22		90
Eddie Brown	WR	6'	185	25		54
Cris Collinsworth	WR	6'5"	192	29		6
Ira Hillary	WR	5'11"	190	25		6
Mike Martin	WR	5'10"	186	27		6
Tim McGee	WR	5'10"	175	24		36
Carl Parker	WR	6'2"	201	23		
Rodney Holman	TE	6'3"	238	28		18
Eric Kattus	TE	6'5"	235	25		
Jim Riggs	TE	6'5"	245	24		
Jim Breech	K	5'6"	161	32		89
Scott Fulhage	K	5'11"	191	23		
Lee Johnson (from CLE)	K	6'2"	198	26		3

CLEVELAND BROWNS 10-6 Marty Schottenheimer

Scores of Each Game		
6	Kansas City	3
3	N.Y. JETS	23
23	INDIANAPOLIS	17
17	Cincinnati	24
23	Pittsburgh	9
10	SEATTLE	16
19	PHILADELPHIA	3
29	Phoenix	21
23	CINCINNATI	21
17	Houston	24
7	Denver	30
27	PITTSBURGH	7
17	Washington	13
24	DALLAS	21
31	Miami	38
28	HOUSTON	23

Use Name	Pos.	Hgt	Wgt	Age	Int	Pts
Rickey Bolden	OT	6'6"	280	26		6
Paul Farren	OT	6'5"	280	27		
Cody Risien	OT	6'7"	280	31		
Dan Fike	OG	6'7"	280	27		
Tony Jones	OG	6'5"	280	22		
Larry Williams	OG	6'5"	290	25		
Gregg Rakoczy	C	6'6"	290	23		
Frank Winters	C	6'3"	280	24		
Charles Buchanan	DE	6'3"	245	23		2
Sam Clancy	DE	6'7"	275	30		
Carl Hairston	DE-LB	6'3"	280	35		
Michael Dean Perry	DE-DT	6'1"	285	23		
Darryl Sims	DE-NT	6'3"	290	27		
Marlon Jones	DT-DE	6'4"	260	24		
Bob Golic	NT-DE	6'2"	265	30		

Use Name	Pos.	Hgt	Wgt	Age	Int	Pts
Clifford Charlton	LB	6'3"	240	23		
Dave Grayson	LB	6'2"	230	24		
Anthony Griggs	LB	6'3"	230	28		
Eddie Johnson	LB	6'1"	225	28	2	
Mike Johnson	LB	6'1"	225	25	2	
Mike Junkin	LB	6'3"	238	23		
Clay Matthews	LB	6'2"	245	32		
Van Waiters	LB	6'4"	240	23		
Anthony Blaylock	DB	5'11"	190	23		
Stephen Braggs	DB	5'10"	180	23		
Hanford Dixon	DB	5'11"	195	29	2	
Thane Gash	DB	6'	200	23		
Mark Harper	DB	5'9"	185	26	2	
Will Hill	DB	6'	200	25		
Frank Minnifield	DB	5'9"	185	28	4	6
Brian Washington	DB	6'	210	22	3	6
Felix Wright	DB	6'2"	190	29	5	

Use Name	Pos.	Hgt	Wgt	Age	Int	Pts
Gary Danielson	QB	6'2"	196	36		
Bernie Kosar	QB	6'5"	210	24		6
Mike Pagel	QB	6'2"	211	27		
Steve Slayden	QB	6'1"	185	22		
Don Strock	QB	6'5"	225	37		
Tony Baker	HB	5'10"	180	24		
Earnest Byner	HB	5'10"	215	25		18
Herman Fontenot	HB	6'	206	24		12
Kevin Mack	FB	6'	235	26		18
Tim Manoa	FB	6'1"	227	23		12
Brian Brennan	WR	5'9"	178	26		6
Reggie Langhorne	WR	6'2"	200	25		48
Gerald McNeil	WR	5'7"	147	26		
Webster Slaughter	WR	6'	170	23		12
Clarence Weathers	WR	5'9"	170	26		6
Glen Young	WR	6'2"	205	27		
Ozzie Newsome	TE	6'2"	232	32		12
Derek Tennell	TE	6'5"	245	24		6
Matt Bahr	K	5'10"	175	32		100
Max Runager (from SF)	K	6'1"	189	32		

Jeff Jaeger — Foot Injury
Jeff Modesitt — Shoulder Injury
George Swarn — Ankle Injury

HOUSTON OILERS 10-6 Jerry Glanville

Scores of Each Game		
17	Indianapolis	*14
38	L.A. RAIDERS	35
3	N.Y. Jets	45
31	NEW ENGLAND	6
23	Philadelphia	32
7	KANSAS CITY	6
34	Pittsburgh	14
21	Cincinnati	44
41	WASHINGTON	17
24	CLEVELAND	17
24	Seattle	27
38	PHOENIX	20
25	Dallas	17
34	PITTSBURGH	37
41	CINCINNATI	6
23	Cleveland	28

Use Name	Pos.	Hgt	Wgt	Age	Int	Pts
Bruce Davis	OT	6'6"	315	32		
Don Maggs	OT-OG	6'5"	285	26		
Dean Steinkuhler	OT	6'3"	291	27		
Vince Stroth	OT-TE	6'4"	275	27		
Bruce Matthews	OG	6'4"	293	27		
Mike Munchak	OG	6'3"	284	28		
John Davis	C-OT	6'4"	293	23		
Jay Pennison	C	6'1"	282	26		
Robert Banks	DE	6'5"	263	24		
Richard Byrd	DE-NT	6'4"	267	26	1	
Ray Childress	DE	6'6"	270	25		
William Fuller	DE	6'3"	269	26	1	
Sean Jones	DE	6'7"	273	25		
Doug Mikolas (from SF)	NT	6'1"	270	26		
Doug Smith	NT	6'5"	282	29	1	

Doug Williams — Leg Injury
Almon Young — Hand Injury

Use Name	Pos.	Hgt	Wgt	Age	Int	Pts
Toby Caston	LB	6'1"	240	23		
Eric Fairs	LB	6'3"	240	24		2
John Grimsley	LB	6'2"	238	26	1	
Walter Johnson	LB	6'	240	24		
Robert Lyles	LB	6'1"	230	27	2	
Johnny Meads	LB	6'2"	235	27		
Eugene Seale	LB	5'10"	240	24	1	2
Al Smith	LB	6'1"	236	23		
Patrick Allen	DB	5'10"	182	27	1	
Keith Bostic	DB	6'1"	215	27	1	
Steve Brown	DB	5'11"	192	28	2	6
Domingo Bryant	DB	6'4"	178	24	3	6
Cris Dishman	DB	6'	180	23		6
Jeff Donaldson	DB	6'	190	26	4	
Kenny Johnson	DB	5'10"	172	30	1	
Richard Johnson	DB	6'1"	190	24	3	
Quintin Jones	DB	5'11'	193	22		
Calvin Loveall (to KC and ATL)	DB	5'9"	180	26		

Audrey McMillian — Knee Injury

Use Name	Pos.	Hgt	Wgt	Age	Int	Pts
Cody Carlson	QB	6'3"	199	24		6
Warren Moon	QB	6'3"	210	31		30
Brent Pease	QB	6'2"	204	23		6
Allen Pinkett	HB	5'9"	192	24		54
Mike Rozier	HB	5'10"	213	27		66
Lorenzo White	HB	5'11"	209	22		6
Alonzo Highsmith	FB	6'1"	234	23		12
Spencer Tillman	FB	5'11"	208	24		
Willie Drewrey	WR	5'7"	164	25		6
Curtis Duncan	WR	5'11"	185	23		6
Ernest Givins	WR	5'9"	172	23		30
Leonard Harris	WR	5'8"	162	27		
Drew Hill	WR	5'9"	175	31		60
Haywood Jeffires	WR	6'2"	198	23		6
Chris Verhulst	TE	6'2"	249	22		
Jamie Williams	TE	6'4"	255	28		
Greg Montgomery	K	6'3"	213	23		
Tony Zendejas	K	5'8"	165	28		114

Ray Wallace — Ankle Injury

PITTSBURGH STEELERS 5-11 Chuck Noll

Scores of Each Game		
24	DALLAS	21
29	Washington	30
12	CINCINNATI	17
28	Buffalo	36
9	CLEVELAND	23
14	Phoenix	31
14	HOUSTON	34
39	DENVER	21
20	N.Y. Jets	24
7	Cincinnati	42
26	PHILADELPHIA	27
7	Cleveland	27
16	KANSAS CITY	10
37	Houston	34
14	San Diego	20
40	MIAMI	24

Use Name	Pos.	Hgt	Wgt	Age	Int	Pts
Jim Boyle	OT	6'5"	275	26		
Tunch Ilkin	OT	6'3"	266	30		
John Jackson	OT	6'6"	282	23		
Craig Wolfley	OT-OG	6'1"	269	30		
Brian Blankenship	OG-C	6'1"	275	25		
Dermontti Dawson	OG	6'2"	271	23		
Terry Long	OG	5'11"	275	29		
John Rienstra	OG	6'5"	268	25		
Chuck Lanza	C	6'2"	263	23		
Mike Webster	C	6'1"	254	36		
Keith Gary	DE	6'3"	268	28		
Tim Johnson	DE-DT	6'3"	261	23		
Aaron Jones	DE-LB	6'5"	257	21		
Jerry Reese	DE	6'2"	267	24		
Ben Thomas	DE	6'4"	275	27		
Rollin Putzier	DT	6'4"	281	22		
Lorenzo Freeman	NT-DT	6'5"	298	24		
Gerald Williams	NT-DT	6'3"	262	24		

Buddy Aydelette — Knee Injury
Keith Willis — Neck Injury

Use Name	Pos.	Hgt	Wgt	Age	Int	Pts
Gregg Carr	LB	6'2"	222	26	1	
Anthony Henton	LB	6'1"	230	25		
Bryan Hinkle	LB	6'2"	222	29	1	
Darin Jordan	LB-DE	6'1"	235	23	1	6
David Little	LB	6'1"	230	29	1	
Greg Lloyd	LB	6'2"	224	23		
Hardy Nickerson	LB	6'2"	229	23	1	
Tyronne Stowe	LB	6'1"	236	23		
Thomas Everett	DB	5'9"	179	23	3	
Cornell Gowdy	DB	6'1"	202	24	1	
Larry Griffin	DB	6'	200	25	2	
Delton Hall	DB	6'1"	205	23		
Greg Lee	DB	6'1"	207	23		
Lupe Sanchez	DB	5'10"	195	26	1	
Dwayne Woodruff	DB	6'	198	31	4	6
Rod Woodson	DB	6'	199	23	4	6

Mike Merriweather — Holdout

Use Name	Pos.	Hgt	Wgt	Age	Int	Pts
Todd Blackledge	QB	6'3"	227	27		6
Steve Bono	QB	6'4"	215	26		
Bubby Brister	QB	6'3"	205	26		36
Rodney Carter	HB	6'	216	23		30
Dwight Stone	HB	6'	188	24		12
Warren Williams	HB	6'	202	23		6
Merril Hoge	FB	6'2"	226	23		36
Earnest Jackson	FB-HB	5'9"	222	28		18
Frank Pollard	FB	5'10"	229	31		
Joey Clinkscales (to TB)	WR	6'	203	24		
Troy Johnson	WR	6'1"	185	25		
Louis Lipps	WR	5'10"	190	26		36
Charles Lockett	WR	6'	181	22		6
Weegie Thompson	WR	6'6"	216	27		6
Preston Gothard	TE	6'4"	235	26		6
Mike Hinnant	TE	6'3"	258	21		
Jeff Markland	TE	6'3"	245	22		
Gary Anderson	K	5'11"	175	29		118
Harry Newsome	K	6'	188	25		

CINCINNATI BENGALS

RUSHING

Last Name	No.	Yds	Avg	TD
Woods	203	1066	5.3	15
Brooks	182	931	5.1	8
Wilson	112	398	3.6	2
Esiason	43	248	5.8	1
Jennings	17	47	2.8	1
Logan	2	10	5.0	0
Schonert	2	10	5.0	0
Norseth	1	5	5.0	0
Brown	1	-5	-5.0	0

RECEIVING

Last Name	No.	Yds	Avg	TD
Brown	53	1273	24.0	9
Holman	39	527	13.5	3
McGee	36	686	19.1	6
Brooks	29	287	9.9	6
Woods	21	199	9.5	0
Collinsworth	13	227	17.5	1
Wilson	9	110	12.2	1
Riggs	9	82	9.1	0
Hillary	5	76	15.2	1
Jennings	5	75	15.0	0
Martin	2	22	11.0	1
Logan	2	20	10.0	0
Kattus	2	8	4.0	0

PUNT RETURNS

Last Name	No.	Yds	Avg	TD
Hillary	17	166	9.8	0
Brown	10	48	4.8	0
Martin	5	30	6.0	0

KICKOFF RETURNS

Last Name	No.	Yds	Avg	TD
Jennings	32	684	21.4	1
Hillary	12	195	16.3	0
Bussey	7	83	11.9	0
Logan	4	80	20.0	0
Dixon	1	18	18.0	0
Brooks	1	-6	-6.0	0
Riggs	0	0	—	0

PASSING — PUNTING — KICKING

PASSING	Att	Cmp	%	Yds	Yd/Att	TD	Int— %	RK
Esiason	388	223	57.5	3572	9.21	28	14—3.6	1
Schonert	4	2	50.0	20	5.00	0	0—0.0	

PUNTING	No.	Avg.
Johnson	31	39.9

KICKING	XP	Att.	%	FG	Att	%
Breech	56	59	95	11	16	69
Johnson				1	2	50

CLEVELAND BROWNS

RUSHING

Last Name	No.	Yds	Avg	TD
Byner	157	576	3.7	3
Mack	123	485	3.9	3
Manoa	99	389	3.9	2
Fontenot	28	87	3.1	0
Langhorne	2	26	13.0	1
Baker	3	19	6.3	0
Danielson	4	3	0.8	0
Pagel	4	1	.03	0
Runager	1	0	0.0	0
Kosar	12	-1	-0.1	1
Strock	6	-2	-0.3	0
Bahr	1	-8	-8.0	0

RECEIVING

Last Name	No.	Yds	Avg	TD
Byner	59	576	9.8	2
Langhorne	57	780	13.7	7
Brennan	46	579	12.6	1
Newsome	35	343	9.8	2
Slaughter	30	462	15.4	3
Weathers	29	436	15.0	1
Fontenot	19	170	8.9	1
Mack	11	87	7.9	0
Manoa	10	54	5.4	0
Tennell	9	88	9.8	1
McNeil	5	74	14.8	0
Young	2	34	17.0	0
Bolden	1	3	3.0	1

PUNT RETURNS

Last Name	No.	Yds	Avg	TD
McNeil	38	315	8.3	0
Weathers	2	10	5.0	0

KICKOFF RETURNS

Last Name	No.	Yds	Avg	TD
Young	29	635	21.9	0
Fontenot	45	879	19.5	0
McNeil	2	38	19.5	0
Braggs	1	27	27.0	0
Perry	1	13	13.0	0
Tennell	1	11	11.0	0

PASSING — PUNTING — KICKING

PASSING	Att	Cmp	%	Yds	Yd/Att	TD	Int— %	RK
Kosar	259	156	60.2	1890	7.30	10	7—2.7	4
Pagel	134	71	53.0	736	5.49	3	4—3.0	
Strock	91	55	60.4	736	8.09	6	5—5.5	
Danielson	52	31	59.6	324	6.23	0	1—1.9	
Fontenot	1	0	0.0	0	0.00	0	0—0.0	

PUNTING	No.	Avg.
Runager	47	40.1

KICKING	XP	Att.	%	FG	Att	%
Bahr	32	33	97	24	29	83

HOUSTON OILERS

RUSHING

Last Name	No.	Yds	Avg	TD
Rozier	251	1002	4.0	10
Pinkett	122	513	4.2	7
Highsmith	94	466	5.0	2
White	31	115	3.7	0
Moon	33	88	2.7	5
Carlson	12	36	3.0	1
Givins	4	26	6.5	0
Tillman	3	5	1.7	0
Pease	8	-2	-0.3	1

RECEIVING

Last Name	No.	Yds	Avg	TD
Hill	72	1141	15.8	10
Givins	60	976	16.3	5
Duncan	22	302	13.7	1
Highsmith	12	131	10.9	0
Pinkett	12	114	9.5	2
Drewrey	11	172	15.6	1
Rozier	11	99	9.0	1
Harris	10	136	13.6	0
Williams	6	46	7.7	0
Jeffires	2	49	24.5	0

PUNT RETURNS

Last Name	No.	Yds	Avg	TD
K. Johnson	30	170	5.7	0
Duncan	4	47	11.8	0
Drewrey	2	8	4.0	0

KICKOFF RETURNS

Last Name	No.	Yds	Avg	TD
Harris	34	678	19.9	0
White	8	196	24.5	1
Pinkett	7	137	19.6	0
K. Johnson	6	157	26.2	0
Duncan	1	34	34.0	0
Tillman	1	13	13.0	0
Drewrey	1	10	10.0	0
Donaldson	1	5	5.0	0
R. Johnson	1	2	2.0	0

PASSING — PUNTING — KICKING

PASSING	Att	Cmp	%	Yds	Yd/Att	TD	Int— %	RK
Moon	294	160	54.4	2327	7.91	17	8—2.7	3
Carlson	112	52	46.4	775	6.92	4	6—5.4	
Pease	22	6	27.3	64	2.91	0	4—18.2	

PUNTING	No.	Avg.
Montgomery	65	38.8

KICKING	XP	ATT	%	FG	ATT	%
Zendejas	48	50	96	22	34	65

PITTSBURGH STEELERS

RUSHING

Last Name	No.	Yds	Avg	TD
Hoge	170	705	4.1	3
W. Williams	87	409	4.7	0
E. Jackson	74	315	4.3	3
Carter	36	216	6.0	3
Brister	45	209	4.6	6
Lipps	6	129	21.5	1
Stone	40	127	3.2	0
Pollard	31	93	3.0	0
Blackledge	8	25	3.1	1
Newsome	2	0	0.0	0

RECEIVING

Last Name	No.	Yds	Avg	TD
Lipps	50	973	19.5	5
Hoge	50	487	9.7	3
Carter	32	363	11.3	2
Lockett	22	365	16.6	1
Thompson	16	370	23.1	1
Gothard	12	121	10.1	1
Stone	11	196	17.8	1
W. Williams	11	66	6.0	1
Tr. Johnson	10	237	23.7	0
E. Jackson	9	84	9.3	0
Pollard	2	22	11.0	0
Hinnant	1	23	23.0	0

PUNT RETURNS

Last Name	No.	Yds	Avg	TD
Woodson	33	281	8.5	0
Lipps	4	30	7.5	0
Sanchez	2	11	5.5	0

KICKOFF RETURNS

Last Name	No.	Yds	Avg	TD
Woodson	37	850	23.0	1
Stone	29	610	21.0	1
Sanchez	4	71	21.0	0
Boyle	1	19	19.0	0
J. Jackson	1	10	10.0	0
W. Williams	1	10	10.0	0
Blankenship	1	5	5.0	0

PASSING — PUNTING — KICKING

PASSING	Att	Cmp	%	Yds	Yd/Att	TD	Int— %	RK
Brister	370	175	47.3	2634	7.12	11	14—3.8	13
Blackledge	79	38	48.1	494	6.25	2	3—3.8	
Bono	35	10	28.6	110	3.14	1	2—5.7	
Carter	3	2	66.7	56	18.67	0	0—0.0	
Lipps	2	1	50.0	13	6.50	1	1—50.0	

PUNTING	No.	Avg.
Newsome	71	41.5

KICKING	XP	Att	%	FG	Att	%
Anderson	34	35	97	28	36	78

SEATTLE SEAHAWKS 9-7 Chuck Knox

Scores of Each Game		
21	Denver	14
31	KANSAS CITY	10
6	San Diego	17
7	SAN FRANCISCO	38
31	Atlanta	20
16	Cleveland	10
19	NEW ORLEANS	20
10	L.A. Rams	31
17	SAN DIEGO	14
3	BUFFALO	13
27	HOUSTON	24
24	Kansas City	27
35	L.A. RAIDERS	27
7	New England	13
42	DENVER	14
43	L.A. Raiders	37

Use Name	Pos.	Hgt	Wgt	Age	Int	Pts
Ron Mattes	OT	6'6"	302	25		
Mike Wilson	OT	6'5"	274	33		
Edwin Bailey	OG	6'4"	270	29		
Tim Burnham	OG	6'5"	280	25		
Chris Godfrey	OG	6'3"	265	30		
Bryan Millard	OG-OT	6'5"	281	27		
Alvin Powell	OG	6'5"	296	28		
Blair Bush	C	6'3"	272	31		
Stan Eisenhooth	C-OT	6'5"	274	25		
Grant Feasel	C	6'7"	277	28		
Jeff Bryant	DE	6'5"	268	28		
Jacob Green	DE	6'3"	254	31		6
Doug Hollie	DE	6'4"	265	27		
Alonzo Mitz	DE	6'3"	271	25		
Ken Clarke	NT	6'2"	271	32		
Joe Nash	NT	6'2"	269	27		

Roland Barbay — Knee Injury

Use Name	Pos.	Hgt	Wgt	Age	Int	Pts
Brian Bosworth	LB	6'2"	248	23		
Darren Comeaux	LB	6'1"	227	28	1	
Greg Gaines	LB	6'3"	229	29		
M.L. Johnson	LB	6'3"	229	24		
Darrin Miller	LB	6'1"	227	23	1	
Bruce Scholtz	LB	6'6"	241	29		
Tony Woods	LB	6'4"	244	22		
David Wyman	LB	6'2"	234	24		
Rufus Porter	LB	6'1"	207	23		
Vernon Dean	DB	5'11'	180	29	1	6
Nesby Glasgow	DB	5'10"	187	31	2	
Dwayne Harper	DB	5'11"	165	22		
David Hollis (to and from KC)	DB	5'11"	180	23	2	
Patrick Hunter	DB	5'11"	185	23		
Melvin Jenkins	DB	5'10"	173	26	3	
Paul Moyer	DB	6'1"	196	27	6	
Eugene Robinson	DB	6'	183	25	1	
Terry Taylor	DB	5'10"	191	27	5	6

Sam Merriman — Knee Injury

Use Name	Pos.	Hgt	Wgt	Age	Int	Pts
Jeff Kemp	QB	6'	198	29		
Dave Krieg	QB	6'1"	192	29		
Bruce Mathison	QB	6'3"	205	29		
Kelly Stouffer	QB	6'3"	210	24		
Bobby Joe Edmonds	HB	5'11"	184	23		
Kevin Harmon	HB	6'	190	22		
Randall Morris (to DET)	HB	6'	200	26		
Curt Warner	HB	5'11"	205	27		72
Tommie Agee	FB	6'	218	24		
John L. Williams	FB	5'11"	226	23		42
Brian Blades	WR	5'11"	182	23		48
Ray Butler	WR	6'3"	204	32		24
Louis Clark	WR	6'1"	193	24		6
Tommy Kane	WR	5'11"	180	24		
Steve Largent	WR	5'11"	191	33		12
Paul Skansi	WR	5'11"	184	27		6
Jimmy Teal	WR	5'11"	175	26		
John Spagnola	TE	6'4"	242	31		6
Mike Tice	TE	6'7"	244	29		
Norm Johnson	K	6'2"	197	28		105
Ruben Rodriguez	K	6'2"	214	23		

DENVER BRONCOS 8-8 Dan Reeves

Scores of Each Game		
14	SEATTLE	21
34	SAN DIEGO	3
13	Kansas City	20
27	L.A. RAIDERS	*30
12	San Diego	0
16	San Francisco	*13
30	ATLANTA	14
21	Pittsburgh	39
23	Indianapolis	55
17	KANSAS CITY	11
30	CLEVELAND	7
0	New Orleans	42
35	L.A. RAMS	24
20	L.A. Raiders	21
14	Seattle	42
21	NEW ENGLAND	10

Use Name	Pos.	Hgt	Wgt	Age	Int	Pts
Jim Juriga	OT-OG	6'6"	269	23		
Ken Lanier	OT	6'3"	269	29		
Gerald Perry	OT	6'6"	305	23		
Dave Studdard	OT	6'4"	260	32		
Keith Bishop	OG-C	6'3"	265	31		
Winford Hood	OG	6'3"	262	26		
Stefan Humphries	OG	6'3"	268	26		
Keith Kartz	OG-OT	6'4"	270	25		
Larry Lee	OG-C	6'2"	263	28		
Billy Bryan	C	6'2"	255	32		
Mike Ruether	C	6'4"	275	25		
Walt Bowyer	DE	6'4"	260	27	1	
Freddie Gilbert	DE	6'4"	275	26		
Rulon Jones	DE	6'6"	260	30		
Shawn Knight	DE	6'6"	288	24		
Andre Townsend	DE-NT	6'3"	265	25		
Greg Kragen	NT	6'3"	260	26		

Andrew Provence — Foot Injury

Use Name	Pos.	Hgt	Wgt	Age	Int	Pts
Michael Brooks	LB	6'1"	235	23		
Steve Bryan	LB-DE	6'2"	256	24		
Rick Dennison	LB	6'3"	220	30	1	
Simon Fletcher	LB-DE	6'5"	240	26	1	
Bruce Klostermann	LB	6'4"	232	25		
Tim Lucas	LB	6'3"	230	27		
Karl Mecklenburg	LB-DE	6'3"	230	28		
Marc Munford	LB	6'2"	231	23		
Jim Ryan	LB	6'1"	225	31		
Tyrone Braxton	DB	5'11"	174	23	2	
Jeremiah Castille	DB	5'10"	175	27	3	
Kevin Clark	DB	5'10"	185	24		
Kevin Guidry	DB	6'	176	24		
Mike Harden	DB	6'1"	192	29	4	
Mark Haynes	DB	5'11"	195	29	1	
Bruce Plummer (to MIA)	DB	6'1"	197	24		
Randy Robbins	DB	6'2"	189	24	2	
Dennis Smith	DB	6'3"	200	29		
Steve Wilson	DB	5'10"	195	31	1	

Use Name	Pos.	Hgt	Wgt	Age	Int	Pts
John Elway	QB	6'3"	210	28		6
Ken Karcher	QB	6'3"	205	25		
Gary Kubiak	QB	6'	192	27		
Ken Bell	HB	5'10"	190	23		
Tony Dorsett	HB	5'11"	189	34		30
Sammy Winder	HB	5'11"	203	29		30
Steve Sewell	FB-WR	6'3"	210	25		36
Calvin Thomas (from CHI)	FB	5'11"	245	28		
Gerald Willhite	FB	5'10"	200	29		12
Sam Graddy	WR	5'10"	165	24		
Mark Jackson	WR	5'9"	180	25		36
Jason Johnson	WR	5'10"	178	22		
Vance Johnson	WR	5'11"	185	25		30
Rick Massie	WR	6'1"	190	28		
Ricky Nattiel	WR	5'9"	180	22		6
Clarence Kay	TE	6'2"	237	27		24
Pat Kelly	TE	6'6"	252	22		
Orson Mobley	TE	6'5"	256	25		12
Mike Horan	K	5'11"	190	29		
Rich Karlis	K	6'	180	29		105

Steve Watson — Neck Injury

LOS ANGELES RAIDERS 7-9 Mike Shanahan

Scores of Each Game		
24	SAN DIEGO	13
35	Houston	38
17	L.A. RAMS	22
30	Denver	*27
21	CINCINNATI	45
14	MIAMI	24
27	Kansas City	17
6	New Orleans	20
17	KANSAS CITY	10
13	San Diego	3
9	San Francisco	3
6	ATLANTA	12
27	Seattle	35
21	DENVER	20
21	Buffalo	37
37	SEATTLE	43

Use Name	Pos.	Hgt	Wgt	Age	Int	Pts
Rory Graves	OT	6'6"	285	25		
Brian Holloway	OT-OG	6'7"	285	29		
Don Mosebar	OT	6'6"	280	26		
Steve Wright	OT	6'6"	280	29		
Charley Hannah	OG	6'5"	270	33		
Chris Riehm	OG	6'6"	280	27		
Dwight Wheeler	OG	6'3"	280	33		
Bruce Wilkerson	OG	6'5"	285	24		
Mike Freeman	C-OG	6'3"	265	26		
John Gesek	C-OG	6'5"	275	25		
Bill Lewis	C	6'7"	275	25		
Ron Brown	DE	6'4"	225	24		
Scott Davis	DE-LB	6'7"	270	23		
Howie Long	DE	6'5"	265	28	1	
Greg Townsend	DE-NT	6'3"	250	26	1	12
Mike Wise	DE	6'7"	280	24		
Malcolm Taylor	NT-DE	6'6"	280	28		
Bill Pickel	NT-DT	6'5"	265	28		

Use Name	Pos.	Hgt	Wgt	Age	Int	Pts
Linden King	LB	6'4"	245	33		
Rod Martin	LB	6'2"	225	34		
Milt McColl	LB	6'6"	230	29		
Reggie McKenzie	LB	6'1"	240	25	1	
Matt Millen	LB	6'2"	250	30		
Jerry Robinson	LB	6'2"	230	31		
Norwood Vann	LB	6'1"	227	26		
Stefon Adams	DB	5'10"	190	25		
Eddie Anderson	DB	6'1"	195	25	2	
Russell Carter	DB	6'2"	200	26		
Ron Fellows	DB	6'	175	29	2	
David Greenwood	DB	6'3"	210	28		
Mike Haynes	DB	6'2"	190	35	3	
Zeph Lee	DB	6'3"	205	25	1	
Terry McDaniel	DB	5'10"	175	23		
Vann McElroy	DB	6'2"	195	28	3	
Dennis Price	DB	6'1"	175	23	2	
Stacey Toran	DB	6'2"	200	26		
Lionel Washington	DB	6'	185	27	1	

Jamie Kimmel — Knee Injury

Use Name	Pos.	Hgt	Wgt	Age	Int	Pts
Steve Beuerlein	QB	6'2"	205	23		
Vince Evans	QB	6'2"	205	33		
Jay Schroeder	QB	6'4"	215	27		6
Marcus Allen	HB	6'2"	205	28		48
Bo Jackson	HB	6'1"	225	25		18
Chris McLemore	FB	6'1"	230	24		
Vance Mueller	FB	6'	215	24		
Steve Smith	FB	6'1"	230	24		54
Steve Strachan	FB	6'1"	225	25		6
Tim Brown	WR	6'	195	22		42
Mervyn Fernandez	WR	6'3"	200	28		24
Willie Gault	WR	6'	180	27		12
James Lofton	WR	6'3"	190	32		
Chris Woods	WR	5'11"	190	26		
Todd Christensen	TE	6'3"	230	32		
Trey Junkin	TE	6'2"	230	27		12
Andy Parker	TE	6'5"	250	26		
Chris Bahr	K	5'10"	170	35		91
Jeff Gossett	K	6'2"	195	31		

SAN DIEGO CHARGERS 6-10 Al Saunders

Scores of Each Game		
13	L.A. Raiders	24
3	Denver	34
17	SEATTLE	6
24	Kansas City	23
0	DENVER	12
17	NEW ORLEANS	23
28	Miami	31
0	INDIANAPOLIS	16
14	Seattle	17
3	L.A. RAIDERS	13
10	Atlanta	7
38	L.A. Rams	24
10	SAN FRANCISCO	48
10	Cincinnati	27
20	PITTSBURGH	14
24	KANSAS CITY	13

Use Name	Pos.	Hgt	Wgt	Age	Int	Pts
John Clay	OT	6'5"	305	24		
Ken Dallafior	OT-OG	6'4"	275	29		
Chris Gambol (from IND)	OT	6'6"	303	23		
Gary Kowalski	OT-OG	6'6"	288	28		
David Richards	OT	6'5"	310	22		
Darrick Brilz	OG-OT	6'3"	270	24		
James FitzPatrick	OG-OT	6'8"	310	24		
Dennis McKnight	OG-C	6'3"	280	28		
Broderick Thompson	OG-OT	6'5"	295	28		
Don Macek	C	6'3"	278	34		
Dan Rosado	C-OG	6'3"	280	29		
Keith Baldwin	DE	6'4"	270	27		
George Hinkle	DE	6'5"	267	23		
Tyrone Keys	DE	6'7"	291	27		
Les Miller	DE	6'7"	293	23		
Leslie O'Neal	DE	6'4"	259	24		
Lee Williams	DE	6'6"	271	25		
Karl Wilson	DE-LB	6'4"	275	23		
Joe Phillips	NT-DE	6'5"	275	25		
Mike Charles	NT	6'4"	296	25		

Use Name	Pos.	Hgt	Wgt	Age	Int	Pts
David Brandon	LB	6'4"	230	23		
Keith Browner	LB	6'6"	266	26	2	6
Joe Campbell	LB	6'4"	245	21		
Chuck Faucette	LB	6'3"	242	24	1	
Cedric Figaro	LB	6'2"	255	22		
Jeff Jackson	LB	6'1"	242	26		
Randy Kirk	LB	6'2"	227	23		
Gary Plummer	LB	6'2"	240	28		
Billy Ray Smith	LB	6'3"	236	27	1	
Ken Woodard	LB	6'1"	220	28		
Martin Bayless	DB	6'2"	212	25		
Roy Bennett	DB	6'2"	195	27	1	6
Gill Byrd	DB	5'11"	198	27	7	
Leonard Coleman	DB	6'2"	202	26	2	
Jeffery Dale	DB	6'3"	207	25		
Vencie Glenn	DB	6'	192	23	1	
Pat Miller	DB	6'1"	206	24		
Elvis Patterson	DB	5'11"	198	27	1	
Sam Seale	DB	5'9"	185	25		6

Demetrious Johnson — Achilles' Tendon Injury

Use Name	Pos.	Hgt	Wgt	Age	Int	Pts
Steve Fuller	QB	6'4"	196	31		
Babe Laufenberg	QB	6'3"	205	28		
Mark Malone	QB	6'4"	222	29		24
Mark Vlasic	QB	6'3"	203	24		
Curtis Adams	HB	6'	207	26		6
Gary Anderson	HB-WR	6'1"	184	27		18
Lionel James	HB	5'7"	170	26		6
Kevin Scott	HB	5'9"	180	24		
Barry Redden	FB	5'10"	220	28		18
Tim Spencer	FB	6'2"	223	27		
Quinn Early	WR	6'	188	23		24
Darren Flutie	WR	5'10"	184	21		12
Jamie Holland	WR-HB	6'2"	195	24		12
Anthony Miller	WR	5'11"	185	23		24
Rod Bernstine	TE-FB	6'3"	238	23		
Arthur Cox	TE	6'2"	277	27		
Eric Sievers (to LA)	TE	6'4"	238	29		
Wilbur Strozier	TE	6'4"	255	23		
Vince Abbott	K	6'	208	29		39
Steve DeLine	K	5'11"	185	27		30
Ralf Mojsiejenko	K	6'3"	213	25		

KANSAS CITY CHIEFS 4-11-1 Frank Gansz

Scores of Each Game		
3	CLEVELAND	6
10	Seattle	31
20	DENVER	13
23	SAN DIEGO	24
17	N.Y. Jets	*17
6	Houston	7
17	L.A. RAIDERS	27
6	DETROIT	7
10	L.A. Raiders	17
11	Denver	17
31	CINCINNATI	28
27	SEATTLE	24
10	Pittsburgh	16
38	N.Y. JETS	34
12	N.Y. Giants	28
13	San Diego	24

Use Name	Pos.	Hgt	Wgt	Age	Int	Pts
John Alt	OT	6'7"	290	26		
Irv Eatman	OT	6'7"	294	27		
David Lutz	OT-OG	6'6"	290	28		
Mark Adickes	OG	6'4"	273	27		
Rich Baldinger	OG-OT	6'4"	285	28		
Curt DiGiacomo	OG-C	6'4"	265	23		
James Harvey	OG	6'3"	265	22		
Byron Ingram	OG	6'2"	295	23		
Brian Jozwiak	OG	6'5"	293	25		
Tom Baugh	C	6'3"	290	24		
Gerry Feehery	C	6'2"	270	28		
Adam Lingner	C	6'4"	265	27		
Gary Baldinger	DE-NT	6'3"	265	24		
Mike Bell	DE	6'4"	260	30		
Leonard Griffin	DE	6'4"	270	25		
Neil Smith	DE	6'4"	270	22		
Dee Hardison	NT	6'4"	291	32		
Bill Maas	NT	6'5"	268	26		2
Ron McLean	NT	6'3"	274	25		
Jerome Sally	NT	6'3"	270	29		
Mike Stensrud	DE-NT	6'5"	280	32	1	
Don Thorp (from IND)	DE-NT	6'4"	260	26		

Pete Koch — Broken Wrist

Use Name	Pos.	Hgt	Wgt	Age	Int	Pts
Tim Cofield	LB	6'2"	242	25	1	
Louis Cooper	LB	6'2"	245	24		
Jack Del Rio	LB	6'4"	238	25	1	
Dino Hackett	LB	6'3"	228	24		2
Andy Hawkins	LB	6'2"	244	30		
Todd Howard	LB	6'2"	244	23		
Jerry McCabe	LB	6'1"	225	23		
Aaron Pearson	LB	6'	240	23		
Angelo Snipes	LB	6'	227	25		
Troy Stedman	LB	6'3"	243	23		
Lloyd Burruss	DB	6'	205	30	2	
Deron Cherry	DB	5'11"	203	28	7	
Greg Hill	DB	6'1"	202	27	1	
Sidney Johnson	DB	5'9"	175	23		
Albert Lewis	DB	6'2"	198	27	1	2
J.C. Pearson	DB	5'11"	190	24	2	
Kevin Porter	DB	5'10"	215	22		
Kevin Ross	DB	5'9"	182	26	1	

Use Name	Pos.	Hgt	Wgt	Age	Int	Pts
Steve DeBerg	QB	6'2"	210	34		6
Bill Kenney	QB	6'4"	217	33		
Danny McManus	QB	6'	200	23		
Kenny Gamble	HB-DB	5'10"	197	23	1	
Herman Heard	HB	5'10"	190	26		
Keyvan Jenkins	HB	5'10"	192	27		
Paul Palmer	HB	5'9"	181	23		36
Larry Moriarty	FB	6'1"	237	30		
Christian Okoye	FB	6'1"	253	27		18
James Saxon	FB	5'11"	215	22		12
Carlos Carson	WR	5'11"	190	29		18
Darrell Colbert	WR	5'10"	174	23		
Emile Harry	WR	5'11"	176	25		6
Mike Jones	WR	5'11"	183	28		
Stephone Paige	WR	6'2"	185	26		42
Kitrick Taylor	WR	5'10"	197	24		
Jonathan Hayes	TE	6'5"	239	25		6
Rod Jones	TE	6'4"	241	24		
Alfredo Roberts	TE	6'3"	250	23		
Kelly Goodburn	K	6'2"	198	26		
Nick Lowery	K	6'4"	189	32		104

SEATTLE SEAHAWKS

RUSHING

Last Name	No.	Yds	Avg	TD
Warner	266	1025	3.9	10
Williams	189	877	4.6	4
Krieg	24	64	2.7	0
Kemp	6	51	8.5	0
Stouffer	19	27	1.4	0
Blades	5	24	4.8	0
Harmon	2	13	6.5	0
Morris	3	6	2.0	0
Agee	1	2	2.0	0
Rodriguez	1	0	0.0	0
Largent	1	-3	-3.0	0

RECEIVING

Last Name	No.	Yds	Avg	TD
Williams	58	651	11.2	3
Blades	40	682	17.1	8
Largent	39	645	16.5	2
Tice	29	244	8.4	0
Skansi	24	238	9.9	1
Warner	22	154	7.0	2
Butler	18	242	13.4	4
Kane	6	32	5.3	0
Spagnola	5	40	8.0	1
Agee	3	31	10.3	0
Clark	1	20	20.0	1

PUNT RETURNS

Last Name	No.	Yds	Avg	TD
Edmunds	35	340	9.7	0
Glasgow	1	0	0.0	0
Hunter	1	0	0.0	0

KICKOFF RETURNS

Last Name	No.	Yds	Avg	TD
Edmonds	40	900	22.5	0
Hollis	13	261	20.1	0
Morris	13	259	19.9	0
Harmon	3	62	20.7	0
Tice	1	17	17.0	0

PASSING - PUNTING - KICKING

PASSING	Att	Cmp	%	Yds	Yd/Att	TD	Int—	%	RK
Krieg	228	134	58.8	1741	7.64	18	8—	3.5	2
Stouffer	173	98	56.6	1106	6.39	4	6—	3.5	
Kemp	35	13	37.1	132	3.77	0	5—	14.3	
Agee	1	0	0.0	0	0.00	0	1—	100	

PUNTING	No.	Avg.
Rodriguez	70	40.8

KICKING	XP	ATT	%	FG	ATT	%
N. Johnson	39	39	100	22	28	79

DENVER BRONCOS

RUSHING

Last Name	No.	Yds	Avg	TD
Dorsett	181	703	3.9	5
Winder	149	543	3.6	4
Elway	54	234	4.3	1
Sewell	32	135	4.2	1
Kubiak	17	65	3.8	0
Nattiel	5	51	10.2	0
Willhite	13	39	3.0	2
Bell	9	36	4.0	0
Thomas	6	20	3.3	0
Jackson	1	5	5.0	0
J. Johnson	1	3	3.0	0
V. Johnson	1	1	1.0	0

RECEIVING

Last Name	No.	Yds	Avg	TD
V. Johnson	68	896	13.2	5
Jackson	46	852	18.5	6
Nattiel	46	574	12.5	1
Sewell	38	507	13.3	5
Kay	34	352	10.4	4
Willhite	32	238	7.4	0
Mobley	21	218	10.4	2
Winder	17	103	6.1	1
Dorsett	16	122	7.6	0
Massey	3	39	13.0	0
Graddy	1	30	30.0	0
Johnson	1	6	6.0	0
Kelly	1	4	4.0	0

PUNT RETURNS

Last Name	No.	Yds	Avg	TD
Nattiel	22	218	9.9	0
Clark	13	115	8.8	0
Willhite	13	90	6.9	0
Harden	2	14	7.0	0
Massey	1	5	5.0	0
Johnson	1	5	5.0	0
Bell	1	4	4.0	0
Johnson	0	0	0.0	0

KICKOFF RETURNS

Last Name	No.	Yds	Avg	TD
Bell	36	762	21.2	0
Johnson	14	285	20.4	0
Nattiel	6	124	20.7	0
Winder	1	11	11.0	0
Harden	1	9	9.0	0

PASSING - PUNTING - KICKING

PASSING	Att	Cmp	%	Yds	Yd/Att	TD	Int—	%	RK
Elway	496	274	55.2	3309	6.67	17	19—	3.8	9
Kubiak	69	43	62.3	497	7.20	5	3—	4.3	
Karcher	12	6	50.0	128	10.67	1	0—	0.0	
Dorsett	2	1	50.0	7	3.50	1	0—	0.0	
Sewell	1	0	0.0	0	0.00	0	0—	0.0	
Nattiel	1	0	0.0	0	0.00	0	0—	0.0	

PUNTING	No.	Avg.
Horan	65	44.0
Elway	3	39.0

KICKING	XP	ATT	%	FG	ATT	%
Karlis	36	37	97	23	36	64

LOS ANGELES RAIDERS

RUSHING

Last Name	No.	Yds	Avg	TD
Allen	223	831	3.7	7
Jackson	136	580	4.3	3
Smith	38	162	4.3	3
Schroeder	29	109	3.8	1
Mueller	17	60	3.5	0
T. Brown	14	50	3.6	1
Beuerlein	30	35	1.2	0
Strachan	4	12	3.0	0
Fernandez	1	9	9.0	0
Gault	1	4	4.0	0

RECEIVING

Last Name	No.	Yds	Avg	TD
T. Brown	43	725	16.9	5
Allen	34	303	8.9	1
Fernandez	31	805	26.0	4
Lofton	28	549	19.6	0
Smith	26	299	11.5	6
Gault	16	392	24.5	2
Christensen	15	190	12.7	0
Jackson	9	79	8.8	0
Mueller	5	63	12.6	0
Parker	4	33	8.3	0
Junkin	4	25	6.3	2
Strachan	3	19	6.3	1
Beuerlein	1	21	21.0	0

PUNT RETURNS

Last Name	No.	Yds	Avg	TD
T. Brown	49	444	9.1	0
Adams	6	45	7.5	0

KICKOFF RETURNS

Last Name	No.	Yds	Avg	TD
T. Brown	41	1098	26.8	1
Adams	8	132	16.5	0
Mueller	5	97	19.4	0
Smith	3	46	15.3	0
Toran	2	0	0.0	0
Woods	1	20	20.0	0
Carter	1	14	14.0	0
Lee	1	0	0.0	0

PASSING - PUNTING - KICKING

PASSING	Att	Cmp	%	Yds	Yd/Att	TD	Int—	%	RK
Schroeder	256	113	44.1	1839	7.18	13	13—	5.1	12
Beuerlein	238	105	44.1	1643	6.90	8	7—	2.9	11
Allen	2	1	50.0	21	10.50	0	0—	0.0	

PUNTING	No.	Avg.
Gossett	91	41.8

KICKING	XP	ATT	%	FG	ATT	%
Bahr	37	39	95	18	29	62

SAN DIEGO CHARGERS

RUSHING

Last Name	No.	Yds	Avg	TD
Anderson	225	1119	5.0	3
Spencer	44	215	4.9	0
Malone	37	169	4.6	4
Adams	38	149	3.9	1
Laufenberg	31	120	3.9	0
James	23	105	4.6	0
Early	7	63	9.0	0
A, Miller	7	45	6.4	0
Redden	19	30	1.6	3
Holland	3	19	6.3	0
Bernstine	2	7	3.5	0
Vlasic	2	0	0.0	0

RECEIVING

Last Name	No.	Yds	Avg	TD
Holland	39	536	13.7	1
A. Miller	36	526	14.6	3
James	36	279	7.8	1
Anderson	32	182	5.7	0
Early	29	375	12.9	4
Bernstine	29	340	11.7	0
Flutie	18	208	11.6	2
Cox	18	144	8.0	0
Spencer	1	14	14.0	0
Redden	1	11	11.0	0
Sievers	1	2	2.0	0

PUNT RETURNS

Last Name	No.	Yds	Avg	TD
James	28	278	9.9	0
Flutie	7	36	5.1	0

KICKOFF RETURNS

Last Name	No.	Yds	Avg	TD
Holland	31	810	26.1	1
A. Miller	25	648	25.9	1
Spencer	1	16	16.0	0
Adams	1	13	13.0	0
Flutie	1	10	10.0	0

PASSING - PUNTING - KICKING

PASSING	Att	Cmp	%	Yds	Yd/Att	TD	Int—	%	RK
Malone	272	147	54.0	1580	5.81	6	13—	4.8	14
Laufenberg	144	69	47.9	778	5.40	4	5—	3.5	
Vlasic	52	25	48.1	270	5.19	1	2—	3.8	

PUNTING	No.	Avg.
Mojsiejenko	86	43.5

KICKING	XP	Att	%	FG	Att	%
Abbott	15	15	100	8	12	67
DeLine	12	12	100	6	8	75

KANSAS CITY CHIEFS

RUSHING

Last Name	No.	Yds	Avg	TD
Okoye	105	473	4.5	3
Palmer	134	452	3.4	2
Heard	106	438	4.1	0
Saxon	60	236	3.9	2
Moriarty	20	62	3.1	0
DeBerg	18	30	1.7	1
Goodburn	1	15	15.0	0
Kenney	2	4	2.0	0
Taylor	1	2	2.0	0
Carson	1	1	1.0	0

RECEIVING

Last Name	No.	Yds	Avg	TD
Paige	61	902	14.8	7
Palmer	53	611	11.5	4
Carson	46	711	15.5	3
Harry	25	362	13.9	1
Hayes	22	233	10.6	1
Heard	20	198	9.9	0
Saxon	19	177	9.3	0
Roberts	10	104	10.4	0
Taylor	9	105	11.7	0
Okoye	8	51	6.4	0
Moriarty	6	40	6.7	0
Colbert	1	-3	-3.0	0
Gamble	1	-7	-7.0	0

PUNT RETURNS

Last Name	No.	Yds	Avg	TD
Taylor	29	187	6.4	0
Hollis	3	28	9.3	0

KICKOFF RETURNS

Last Name	No.	Yds	Avg	TD
Palmer	23	364	15.8	0
Gamble	15	291	19.4	0
Taylor	5	80	16.0	0
Saxon	2	40	20.0	0
Ingram	2	16	8.0	0
Jenkins	2	12	6.0	0
Porter	1	16	16.0	0

PASSING - PUNTING - KICKING

PASSING	Att	Cmp	%	Yds	Yd/Att	TD	Int—	%	RK
DeBerg	414	224	54.1	2935	7.09	16	16—	3.9	8
Kenney	114	58	50.9	549	4.82	0	5—	4.4	

PUNTING	No.	Avg.
Goodburn	76	40.3

KICKING	XP	Att.	%	FG	Att	%
Lowery	23	23		27	32	84

1988 N.F.C.—PLAYOFFS

December 26, 1988 at Minneapolis (Attendance 57,666)

SCORING

L.A. RAMS	0	7	3	7	- 17
MINNESOTA	14	0	7	7	- 28

First Quarter
- Minn. — Anderson, 7 yard run; PAT—C. Nelson (kick)
- Minn. — Rice, 17 yard run; PAT—C. Nelson (kick)

Second Quarter
- L.A. Rams — D. Johnson, 3 yard pass from Everett; PAT—Lansford (kick)

Third Quarter
- Minn. — Anderson, 1 yard run; PAT—C. Nelson (kick)
- L.A. Rams — Lansford, 33 yard field goal

Fourth Quarter
- Minn. — Hilton, 5 yard pass from Wilson; PAT—C. Nelson (kick)
- L.A. Rams — Holohan, 11 yard pass from Everett; PAT—Lansford (kick)

TEAM STATISTICS

L.A. RAMS		MINN.
19	First Downs- Total	20
4	First Downs- Rushing	7
15	First Downs- Passing	11
0	First Downs- Penalty	2
0	Fumbles- Number	1
0	Fumbles- Lost Ball	1
10	Penalties- Number	6
54	Yards Penalized	40
1	Missed Field Goals	1
70	Offensive Plays	66
342	Net Yards	310
4.9	Average Gain	3.7
3	Giveaways	0
0	Takeaways	3
- 3	Difference	+ 3

INDIVIDUAL STATISTICS

RUSHING

L.A. RAMS	No.	Yds.	Avg.	MINNESOTA	No.	Yds.	Avg.
Bell	17	91	5.4	Rice	17	79	4.6
Delpino	3	4	1.3	Anderson	6	9	1.5
Everett	2	4	2.0	Nelson	3	9	3.0
White	1	2	2.0	Fenney	2	5	2.5
Ellard	1	2	2.0	Wilson	5	1	0.2
	24	107	4.5		33	103	3.1

RECEIVING

L.A. RAMS	No.	Yds.	Avg.	MINNESOTA	No.	Yds.	Avg.
Ellard	4	54	13.5	Carter	4	102	25.5
Holohan	3	44	14.6	Fenney	3	19	6.3
D. Johnson	3	27	9.0	Gustafson	2	52	26.0
Delpino	2	33	16.5	Jones	2	28	14.0
W. Anderson	2	29	14.5	Anderson	2	10	5.0
Brown	1	26	26.0	Jordan	1	19	19.0
	19	247	13.0	Rice	1	12	12.0
				Nelson	1	6	6.0
				Hilton	1	5	5.0
					17	253	14.9

PUNTING

L.A. RAMS	No.	Yds.	Avg.	MINNESOTA	No.	Yds.	Avg.
Hatcher	5		48.2	Scribner	7		41.6

PUNT RETURNS

L.A. RAMS	No.	Yds.	Avg.	MINNESOTA	No.	Yds.	Avg.
Hicks	4	46	11.5	Carter	1	1	1.0
Sutton	1	14	14.0	Lewis	1	14	14.0
	5	60	12.0		2	15	7.5

KICKOFF RETURNS

L.A. RAMS	No.	Yds.	Avg.	MINNESOTA	No.	Yds.	Avg.
Brown	4	71	17.8	Harris	3	58	19.3
Delpino	1	35	35.0				
	5	106	21.2				

INTERCEPTION RETURNS

L.A. RAMS	No.	Yds.	Avg.
Browner	2	40	20.0
Studwell	1	0	0.0
	3	40	13.3

PASSING

	Att.	Comp.	Comp. Pct.	Yds.	Int.	Yds./Att.	Yds./Comp.
L.A. RAMS							
Everett	45	19	42.2	247	3	5.5	13.0
MINNESOTA							
Wilson	28	17	60.7	253	0	9.0	14.9

December 31, 1988 at Chicago (Attendance 65,534)

SCORING

PHILADELPHIA	3	6	3	0	- 12
CHICAGO	7	10	0	3	- 20

First Quarter
- Chi. — McKinnon, 64 yard pass from Tomczak; PAT—Butler (kick)
- Phil. — Zendejas, 42 yard field goal

Second Quarter
- Phil. — Zendejas, 29 yard field goal
- Chi. — Anderson, 4 yard run; PAT—Butler (kick)
- Chi. — Butler, 46 yard field goal
- Phil. — Zendejas, 30 yard field goal

Third Quarter
- Phil. — Zendejas, 35 yard field goal

Fourth Quarter
- Chi. — Butler, 27 yard field goal

TEAM STATISTICS

PHIL.		CHI
22	First Downs- Total	14
1	First Downs- Rushing	8
21	First Downs- Passing	6
0	First Downs- Penalty	0
0	Fumbles- Number	1
0	Fumbles- Lost Ball	1
7	Penalties- Number	1
60	Yards Penalized	5
1	Missed Field Goals	2
75	Offensive Plays	57
430	Net Yards	341
5.7	Average Gain	6.0
3	Giveaways	4
4	Takeaways	3
+ 1	Difference	- 1

INDIVIDUAL STATISTICS

RUSHING

PHILADELPHIA	No.	Yds.	Avg.	CHICAGO	No.	Yds.	Avg.
Byars	7	34	4.9	Sanders	8	94	11.8
Toney	5	3	0.6	Anderson	14	54	3.9
Cunningham	3	12	4.0	Muster	6	12	2.0
Haddix	1	3	3.0	Gentry	1	6	6.0
	16	52	3.3	Suhey	1	0	0.0
				McMahon	2	-2	-1.0
					33	164	5.0

RECEIVING

PHILADELPHIA	No.	Yds.	Avg.	CHICAGO	No.	Yds.	Avg.
Byars	9	103	11.4	McKinnon	4	108	27.0
Jackson	7	142	20.2	Boso	2	9	4.5
Quick	5	82	16.4	Gentry	2	9	4.5
Haddix	2	23	11.5	Moris	1	27	27.0
Toney	2	9	4.5	Davis	1	11	11.0
R. Johnson	1	31	31.0	Sanders	1	8	8.0
Carter	1	7	7.0	Anderson	1	6	6.0
	27	407	15.1		12	185	15.4

PUNTING

PHILADELPHIA	No.	Yds.	Avg.	CHICAGO	No.	Yds.	Avg.
Teltschik	4		32.5	Wagner	2		43.0

PUNT RETURNS

PHILADELPHIA	No.	Yds.	Avg.	CHICAGO	No.	Yds.	Avg.
Garrity	1	1	1.0	McKinnon	1	0	0.0

KICKOFF RETURNS

PHILADELPHIA	No.	Yds.	Avg.	CHICAGO	No.	Yds.	Avg.
Jenkins	5	101	20.2	Gentry	4	63	15.8
				Kozlowski	1	23	23.0
					5	86	17.2

INTERCEPTION RETURNS

PHILADELPHIA	No.	Yds.	Avg.	CHICAGO	No.	Yds.	Avg.
Hoage	1	12	12.0	Jackson	1	51	51.0
Joyner	1	8	8.0	Douglass	1	47	47.0
	2	20	10.0	Pruitt	1	0	0.0
					3	98	32.7

PASSING

	Att.	Comp.	Comp. Pct.	Yds.	Int.	Yds./Att.	Yds./Comp.
PHILADELPHIA							
Cunningham	54	27	50.0	407	3	7.5	15.1
Carter	1	0	0.0	0	0	0.0	0.0
CHICAGO							
Tomczak	20	10	50.0	172	3	8.6	17.2
McMahon	3	2	66.7	13	0	4.3	6.5

January 1, 1989 at San Francisco (Attendance 61,848)

SCORING

MINNESOTA	3	0	6	0	- 9
SAN FRANCISCO	7	14	0	13	- 34

First Quarter
- Minn. — Nelson, 47 yard field goal
- S.F. — Rice, 2 yard pass from Montana; PAT—Cofer (kick)

Second Quarter
- S.F. — Rice, 4 yard pass from Montana; PAT—Cofer (kick)

Third Quarter
- Minn. — H. Jones, 5 yard pass from Wilson; PAT—kick failed

Fourth Quarter
- S.F. — Craig, 4 yard run; PAT—Cofer (kick)
- S.F. — Craig, 80 yard run; PAT—kick failed

TEAM STATISTICS

MINN.		S.F.
20	First Downs- Total	20
4	First Downs- Rushing	7
14	First Downs- Passing	11
2	First Downs- Penalty	2
1	Fumbles- Number	2
1	Fumbles- Lost Ball	1
9	Penalties- Number	6
90	Yards Penalized	60
0	Missed Field Goals	1
66	Offensive Plays	62
262	Net Yards	372
4.0	Average Gain	6.0
3	Giveaways	1
1	Takeaways	3
- 2	Difference	+ 2

INDIVIDUAL STATISTICS

RUSHING

MINNESOTA	No.	Yds.	Avg.	SAN FRANCISCO	No.	Yds.	Avg.
Rice	5	20	4.0	Craig	21	135	6.4
Fenney	6	20	6.3	Rathman	3	29	9.7
Anderson	3	9	3.0	Rice	1	21	21.0
Nelson	2	3	1.5	Montana	3	18	6.0
Wilson	3	2	0.7	Sydney	1	1	1.0
	19	54	2.8	Young	3	1	0.3
				Flagler	2	-4	-2.0
					34	201	5.9

RECEIVING

MINNESOTA	No.	Yds.	Avg.	SAN FRANCISCO	No.	Yds.	Avg.
Jones	7	71	10.1	Rice	5	61	12.2
Rice	4	26	6.5	Taylor	3	42	14.0
Carter	3	45	15.0	Craig	3	26	8.7
Jordan	3	44	14.6	Rathman	2	20	10.0
Anderson	3	36	12.0	B. Jones	2	17	8.5
Lewis	1	19	19.0	Wilson	1	12	12.0
Gustafson	1	18	18.0	Sydney	1	-12	-12.0
Fenney	1	4	4.0		17	177	10.4
	23	255	11.1				

PUNTING

MINNESOTA	No.	Yds.	Avg.	SAN FRANCISCO	No.	Yds.	Avg.
Scribner	7		39.3	Helton	5		36.2

PUNT RETURNS

MINNESOTA	No.	Yds.	Avg.	SAN FRANCISCO	No.	Yds.	Avg.
Carter	2	15	7.5	Taylor	2	27	13.5
Lewis	1	12	12.0				
	3	27	9.0				

KICKOFF RETURNS

MINNESOTA	No.	Yds.	Avg.	SAN FRANCISCO	No.	Yds.	Avg.
Harris	3	55	18.3	Rodgers	3	39	13.0
Nelson	2	37	18.5				
Jordan	1	4	4.0				
	6	96	16.0				

INTERCEPTION RETURNS

MINNESOTA	No.	Yds.	Avg.	SAN FRANCISCO	No.	Yds.	Avg.
Browner	1	0	0.0	Lott	2	10	5.0

PASSING

	Att.	Comp.	Comp. Pct.	Yds.	Int.	Yds./Att.	Yds./Comp.
MINNESOTA							
Wilson	47	23	48.9	255	2	5.4	11.1
SAN FRANCISCO							
Montana	27	16	59.3	178	1	6.6	11.1
Young	1	1	100.0	-1	0	-1.0	-1.0

1988 A.F.C.—PLAYOFFS

December 24, 1988 at Cleveland (Attendance 74,977)

SCORING

HOUSTON	0	14	0	10	- 24
CLEVELAND	3	6	7	7	- 23

First Quarter
- Clev. — Bahr, 33 yard field goal

Second Quarter
- Hous. — Pinkett, 14 yard pas from Moon; PAT—Zebdejas (kick)
- Clev. — Bahr, 26 yard field goal
- Clev. — Bahr, 28 yard field goal

Third Quarter
- Clev. — Slaughter, 14 yard pass from Pagel; PAT—Bahr (kick)

Fourth Quarter
- Hous. — White, 1 yard run; PAT—Zendejas (kick)
- Hous. — Zendejas, 49 yard field goal
- Clev. — Slaughter, 2 yard pass from Pagel; PAT—Bahr (kick)

TEAM STATISTICS

HOUS.		CLEV
19	First Downs- Total	19
7	First Downs- Rushing	4
12	First Downs- Passing	11
0	First Downs- Penalty	4
2	Fumbles- Number	1
0	Fumbles- Lost Ball	1
13	Penalties- Number	9
118	Yards Penalized	75
0	Missed Field Goals	0
62	Offensive Plays	54
334	Net Yards	260
3.8	Average Gain	4.5
3	Giveaways	2
2	Takeaways	3
- 1	Difference	+ 1

INDIVIDUAL STATISTICS

RUSHING

HOUSTON	No.	Yds.	Avg.	CLEVELAND	No.	Yds.	Avg.
Pinkett	14	82	5.9	Byner	9	57	6.3
White	12	30	2.5	Mack	12	14	1.2
Moon	6	16	2.7	Strock	1	0	0.0
Highsmith	2	3	1.5	Pagel	1	-1	-1.0
Givins	1	-2	-2.0	Fontenot	3	-2	-0.7
	35	129	3.7		26	68	2.6

RECEIVING

HOUSTON	No.	Yds.	Avg.	CLEVELAND	No.	Yds.	Avg.
Hill	5	73	14.6	Langhorne	6	57	9.5
Jeffires	3	52	17.3	Slaughter	5	58	1.6
Duncan	2	33	16.5	Byner	3	40	13.3
Pinkett	2	24	12.0	Brennan	2	34	17.0
Williams	1	14	14.0	Weathers	2	27	13.5
Givins	1	8	8.0	Mack	1	6	6.0
Highsmith	1	8	8.0		19	192	10.1
White	1	1	1.0				
	16	213	13.3				

PUNTING

Montgomery	3		37.6	Runager	3		35.3

PUNT RETURNS

Duncan	0	0	0.0	McNeil	3	27	9.0

KICKOFF RETURNS

White	4	72	18.0	Young	2	58	29.0
Pinkett	1	0	0.0	McNeil	1	17	17.0
	5	72	14.4		3	75	25.0

INTERCEPTION RETURNS

R. Johnson	1	0	0.0	Wright	2	32	16.0
				Harper	1	17	17.0
					3	49	16.3

PASSING

	Att.	Comp.	Comp. Pct.	Yds.	Int.	Yds./ Att.	Yds./ Comp.
HOUSTON							
Moon	26	16	61.5	213	3	8.2	13.3
CLEVELAND							
Pagel	25	17	68.0	179	1	7.2	10.5
Strock	3	2	67.0	13	0	4.3	6.5

December 31, 1988 at Cincinnati (Attendance 58,560)

SCORING

SEATTLE	0	0	0	13	- 13
CINCINNATI	7	14	0	0	- 21

First Quarter
- Cin. — Wilson, 3 yard run; PAT—Breech (kick)

Second Quarter
- Cin. — Wilson, 3 yard run; PAT—Breech (kick)
- Woods. — Woods, 1 yard run; PAT—Breech (kick)

Fourth Quarter
- Sea. — Williams, 7 yard pass from Krieg; PAT—N. Johnson (kick)
- Sea. — Krieg, 1 yard run; PAT—kick failed

TEAM STATISTICS

SEA.		CIN.
19	First Downs- Total	22
1	First Downs- Rushing	17
16	First Downs- Passing	5
2	First Downs- Penalty	0
1	Fumbles- Number	3
1	Fumbles- Lost Ball	2
5	Penalties- Number	2
45	Yards Penalized	29
0	Missed Field Goals	0
69	Offensive Plays	68
294	Net Yards	345
4.3	Average Gain	5.1
3	Giveaways	2
2	Takeaways	3
- 1	Difference	+ 1

INDIVIDUAL STATISTICS

RUSHING

SEATTLE	No.	Yds.	Avg.	CINCINNATI	No.	Yds.	Avg.
Warner	8	11	1.4	Woods	23	126	5.5
Williams	8	6	0.8	Brooks	13	72	5.5
Krieg	1	1	1.0	Wilson	7	45	6.4
	17	18	1.0	Esiason	4	11	2.8
					47	254	5.4

RECEIVING

SEATTLE	No.	Yds.	Avg.	CINCINNATI	No.	Yds.	Avg.
Williams	11	137	12.5	Holman	3	44	14.7
Blades	5	78	15.6	Collinsworth	1	30	30.0
Butler	2	40	20.0	Brown	1	23	23.0
Largent	2	17	8.5	Brooks	1	9	9.0
Skansi	1	11	11.0	Riggs	1	2	2.0
L. Clark	1	8	8.0		7	108	15.4
Spagnola	1	7	7.0				
Warner	1	-1	-1.0				
	24	297	12.4				

PUNTING

Rodriguez	6		44.2	L. Johnson	6		46.0

PUNT RETURNS

Edmonds	5	30	6.0	Hillary	3	19	6.3

KICKOFF RETURNS

Edmonds	2	40	20.0	Brooks	1	23	23.0
Harmon	1	26	26.0	Jennings	1	18	18.0
	3	66	22.0	Hillary	1	13	13.0
					3	54	18.0

INTERCEPTION RETURNS

				Thomas	1	0	0.0
				Wilcots	1	0	0.0
					2	0	0.0

PASSING

	Att.	Comp.	Comp. Pct.	Yds.	Int.	Yds./ Att.	Yds./ Comp.
SEATTLE							
Krieg	50	24	48.0	297	2	5.9	12.4
CINCINNATI							
Esiason	7	7	100.0	108	0	15.4	15.4

January 1, 1989 at Orchard Park, N.Y. (Attendance 79,532)

SCORING

HOUSTON	0	3	0	7	- 10
BUFFALO	0	7	7	3	- 17

Second Quarter
- Buff. — Riddick, 1 yard run; PAT—Norwood (kick)
- Hous. — Zendejas, 35 yard field goal

Third Quarter
- Buff. — Thomas, 11 yard run; PAT—Norwood (kick)

Fourth Quarter
- Buff. — Norwood, 27 yard field goal
- Hous. — Rozier, 1 yard run; PAT—Zendejas (kick)

TEAM STATISTICS

HOUS.		BUFF.
20	First Downs- Total	18
6	First Downs- Rushing	6
12	First Downs- Passing	9
2	First Downs- Penalty	3
5	Fumbles- Number	1
2	Fumbles- Lost Ball	0
8	Penalties- Number	8
60	Yards Penalized	57
2	Missed Field Goals	2
61	Offensive Plays	63
351	Net Yards	372
5.7	Average Gain	5.9
4	Giveaways	1
1	Takeaways	4
- 3	Difference	+ 3

INDIVIDUAL STATISTICS

RUSHING

HOUSTON	No.	Yds.	Avg.	BUFFALO	No.	Yds.	Avg.
Highsmith	5	57	11.4	Thomas	7	75	10.7
Rozier	13	44	3.4	Mueller	7	24	3.4
Pinkett	3	13	4.3	Kelly	3	18	6.0
Moon	5	11	2.2	Riddick	9	12	1.3
	26	125	4.9	Harmon	1	7	7.0
				Byrum	1	0	0.0
				Reed	1	-1	-1.0
					29	135	4.7

RECEIVING

HOUSTON	No.	Yds.	Avg.	BUFFALO	No.	Yds.	Avg.
Jeffires	5	78	15.6	Reed	6	91	15.2
Hill	4	64	16.0	Harmon	5	58	11.6
Pinkett	2	21	10.5	Burkett	3	55	18.3
Harris	2	44	22.0	Johnson	3	31	10.3
Highsmith	2	3	1.5	Metzelaars	1	7	7.0
Givins	1	23	23.0	Mueller	1	2	2.0
Duncan	1	9	9.0		19	244	12.8
	17	242	14.2				

PUNTING

Montgomery	6		37.2	Kidd	4		39.2

PUNT RETURNS

Duncan	1	6	6.0	Tucker	4	56	14.0

KICKOFF RETURNS

Tillman	2	31	15.5				
White	2	27	13.5				
	4	58	14.5				

INTERCEPTION RETURNS

Eaton	1	0	0.0	Kelso	1	28	28.0

PASSING

	Att.	Comp.	Comp. Pct.	Yds.	Int.	Yds./ Att.	Yds./ Comp.
HOUSTON							
Moon	33	17	51.5	240	1	7.3	14.1
BUFFALO							
Kelly	33	19	57.6	244	1	7.4	12.8

1988 Championship Games

AFC CHAMPIONSHIP GAME

January 8, 1989 at Cincinnati, Oh.

(Attendance59,747)

The Cincinnati defense that received little respect all season stole the thunder from the heralded offense, as the Central Division champs humbled Buffalo at Riverfront Stadium. The Bills were held to a mere 181 total yards and were unable to convert any third-down situations. On its first three possessions in the first half and first four in the second half, Buffalo was unable to gain a first down. The defense that held Seattle to only 18 rushing yards a week before stuffed Buffalo for only 45 yards.

The Bengals stuck to a bread-and-butter diet of crunching rushes by FB Ickey Woods, who gained 102 yards on 29 carries. He scored Cincinnati's first touchdown on a one-yard plunge in the opening quarter. Buffalo came back to tie the game early in the second period on a short pass from Jim Kelly to Andre Reed. Then, after Cincinnati regained the lead on one of Boomer Esiason's infrequent passes, a 10-yarder to James Brooks, the Bills closed the gap to 14-10 on Scott Norwood's 39-yard field goal.

Despite their dominance, the Bengals were unable to put the game away until Buffalo helped them twice on a long drive midway through the second half. Facing a fourth-and-four at the Buffalo 33, Cincinnati fooled the Bills on a fake punt for the first down. Moments later, the drive seemed to stall, but Buffalo CB Derrick Burroughs was called for slugging Tim McGee in the endzone, and Cincinnati was given a first down at the Buffalo four-yard line. Two plays later, Woods crashed over for his second touchdown.

SCORING

BUFFALO	0	10	0	0	- 10
CINCINNATI	7	7	0	7	- 21

First Quarter
- Cin. — Woods, 1 yard run; PAT—Breech (kick)

Second Quarter
- Buff. — Reed, 9 yard pas from Kelly; PAT—Norwood (kick)
- Cin. — Brooks, 10 yard pass from Esiason; PAT—Breech (kick)
- Buff. — Norwood, 39 yard field goal

Fourth Quarter
- Cin. — Woods, 1 yard run; PAT—Breech (kick)

TEAM STATISTICS

BUFF.		CIN.
10	First Downs- Total	23
2	First Downs- Rushing	15
8	First Downs- Passing	5
0	First Downs- Penalty	3
0	Fumbles- Number	2
0	Fumbles- Lost Ball	0
5	Penalties- Number	4
50	Yards Penalized	45
1	Missed Field Goals	0
50	Offensive Plays	73
181	Net Yards	249
3.6	Average Gain	3.4
3	Giveaways	2
2	Takeaways	3
- 1	Difference	+ 1

INDIVIDUAL STATISTICS

BUFFALO	No.	Yds.	Avg.	CINCINNATI	No.	Yds.	Avg.
RUSHING							
Mueller	8	21	2.6	Woods	29	102	3.5
Kelly	2	10	5.0	Wilson	5	29	5.8
Thomas	4	6	1.5	Esiason	7	26	3.7
Riddick	1	4	4.0	Jennings	2	12	6.0
Byrum	1	3	3.0	Brooks	7	6	0.9
Harmon	1	1	1.0		50	175	3.5
	17	45	2.6				
RECEIVING							
Reed	5	55	11.0	Holman	4	38	9.5
Harmon	3	18	6.0	Riggs	2	16	8.0
Riddick	3	28	9.3	Brooks	2	21	10.5
T. Johnson	2	48	24.0	McGee	2	14	7.0
Metzelaars	1	14	14.0	Collinsworth	1	5	5.0
	14	163	11.6		11	94	8.5
PUNTING							
Kidd	6		45.1	Johnson	6		36.8
PUNT RETURNS							
Tucker	1	2	2.0	Hillary	2	24	12.0
				Dixon	1	0	0.0
					3	24	8.0
KICKOFF RETURNS							
Harmon	2	45	22.5	Jennings .	1	19	19.0
Tucker	1	12	12.0	Hillary	2	11	5.5
	3	57	19.0		3	30	10.0
INTERCEPTION RETURNS							
Kelso	1	25	25.0	Thomas	1	26	26.0
Bentley	1	0	0.0	Fulcher	1	0	0.0
	2	25	12.5	Billups	1	-3	-3.0
					3	23	7.7

PASSING

	Att.	Comp.	Comp. Pct.	Yds.	Int.	Yds./ Att.	Yds./ Comp.
BUFFALO							
Kelly	30	14	46.7	163	3	5.4	11.6
CINCINNATI							
Esiason	20	11	55.0	94	2	4.7	8.5

1988 Championship Games

NFC CHAMPIONSHIP GAME

January 8, 1989 at Chicago, Ill.

(Attendance 64,830)

The Bears' defense that was the best in the NFL proved easy pickings for Joe Montana and Jerry Rice at Soldier Field, as the 49ers moved to within a step of their third league championship in the 1980s. The temperature hovered around 17 degrees, but the Montana-to-Rice combination was red-hot. San Francisco coach Bill Walsh said of Montana, who completed 17 of 27 passes, "It may have been his greatest game under the conditions." Rice scored two TD's and had a third called back on a penalty.

With abouth three-and-a-half minutes left in the first quarter, Montana caught the Bears in single coverage on Rice and fired a short pass to him near the sideline. Rice leaped and took the ball away from Bears CB Mike Richardson, then out-raced Richardson and Vestee Jackson into the endzone. In the second quarter, Montana-to-Rice connected again. This time, Rice took a pass off his shoetops to victimize Jackson. The Bears got their only score near the end of the first half on a 25-yard field goal by Kevin Butler to make it 14-3.

San Francisco took the second-half kickoff and marched 78 yards in 13 plays to widen the lead to 21-3. Montana passed five yards to TE John Frank for the score.

Although the 49ers' defense registered no sacks, Chicago's Jim McMahon, making his first start since mid-October, was pressured all day and was unable to complete anything but short passes. He was 14 of 29, but gained only 121 yards and was replaced by Mike Tomczak. The 49ers defense held the Bears to 267 total yards on the day, and only 97 yards rushing.

In the final period, the 49ers ended the *coup de grace* on Tom Rathman's four-yard smash.

SCORING

SAN FRANCISCO	7	7	7	7	- 28
CHICAGO	0	3	0	0	- 3

First Quarter
- S.F. — Rice, 61 yard pass from Montana; PAT—Cofer (kick)

Second Quarter
- S.F. — Rice, 27 yard pas from Montana; PAT—Cofer (kick)
- Chi. — Butler, 25 yard field goal

Third Quarter
- S.F. — Frank, 5 yard pass from Montana; PAT—Cofer (kick)

Fourth Quarter
- S.F. — Rathman, 4 yard run; PAT—Cofer (kick)

TEAM STATISTICS

S.F.		CHI.
21	First Downs- Total	15
9	First Downs- Rushing	8
12	First Downs- Passing	7
0	First Downs- Penalty	0
1	Fumbles- Number	2
1	Fumbles- Lost Ball	1
0	Penalties- Number	3
0	Yards Penalized	35
0	Missed Field Goals	0
66	Offensive Plays	66
406	Net Yards	267
6.2	Average Gain	4.0
1	Giveaways	2
2	Takeaways	1
+1	Difference	- 1

INDIVIDUAL STATISTICS

SAN FRANCISCO	No.	Yds.	Avg.	CHICAGO	No.	Yds.	Avg.
RUSHING							
Craig	18	68	3.8	Anderson	14	59	4.2
Rathman	10	36	3.6	Sanders	7	22	3.1
Montana	3	12	4.0	McMahon	1	9	9.0
Sydney	2	12	6.0	Suhey	1	3	3.0
Flagler	3	7	2.3	Muster	1	2	2.0
Rice	1	3	3.0	McKinnon	1	-4	-4.0
	37	138	3.7		25	91	3.6
RECEIVING							
Rice	5	133	26.6	Anderson	5	31	6.2
Rathman	5	51	10.2	Thornton	4	52	13.5
Taylor	3	51	17.0	McKinnon	4	32	8.0
Craig	2	33	16.5	Morris	2	25	12.5
Frank	2	20	10.0	Suhey	2	8	4.0
	17	288	16.9	Sanders	1	12	12.0
				Muster	1	9	9.0
				Gentry	1	7	7.0
					20	176	8.8
PUNTING							
Helton	6		34.5	Wagner	7		31.4
PUNT RETURNS							
Taylor	4	24	6.0	McKinnon	1	1	1.0
KICKOFF RETURNS							
Sydney	1	14	14.0	Sanders	2	31	15.5
Taylor	1	22	22.0	Muster	1	21	21.0
	2	36	18.0	Gentry	1	19	19.0
				Stinson	1	18	18.0
					5	89	17.8
INTERCEPTION RETURNS							
Fuller	1	0	0.0				

PASSING

	Att.	Comp.	Comp. Pct.	Yds.	Int.	Yds./ Att.	Yds./ Comp.
SAN FRANCISCO							
Montana	27	17	63.0	288	0	10.7	16.9
CHICAGO							
McMahon	29	14	48.3	121	1	4.2	8.6
Tomczak	12	6	50.0	55	0	4.2	9.2

SUPER BOWL XXIII

January 22, 1989 at Miami, Fla.

(Attendance 75,179)

One Worth Watching

After several Super Bowls that were mostly hype followed by few thrills, No. 23 turned out to be better than its advance billing. During the preceding week, the traditional media overkill was somewhat upstaged by a real killing, as Miami was the scene of bloody riots precipitated by a police shooting. The tragic events put the importance of a football game — even the Super Bowl — into perspective.

Nevertheless, more than 75,000 paid $8.1 million for tickets to Joe Robbie Stadium to watch the Bengals and 49ers, and advertisers shelled out $675,000 for each 30-second chance to reach more than 100 million television fans. For once, the money may have been well spent.

The first half was a defensive struggle, punctuated by two key injuries. On the first series after the kickoff, San Francisco OT Steve Wallace was sidelined with a broken ankle, depriving the 49ers of one of their best blockers. After an exchange of punts, Cincinnati's All-Pro NT Tim Krumrie was injured on a freak play when he planted his foot and his left leg snapped in two places. The injury came on the first play of a 73-yard, 13-play San Francisco drive that culminated in Mike Cofer's 41-yard field goal. At the end of the first quarter, the 49ers started another drive from their 30 that finished at the Cincinnati two. But Cofer's attempt at a second field goal was foiled by a bad snap.

The Bengals tied the score late in the second quarter on Jim Breech's 34-yard field goal after a short drive from midfield.

The defensive battle continued into the third period. The Bengals took the kickoff and drove 61 yards, despite three penalties. Two passes from Boomer Esiason to Cris Collinsworth paced the drive. When Cincinnati stalled at the 49er 25, Breech kicked his second field goal to make the score 6-3.

San Francisco came back to tie the game late in the third quarter. Rookie LB Bill Romanowski intercepted Esiason at the 23 with 2:22 remaining. Four plays later, Cofer kicked a 32-yard field goal to knot the score again. The tie lastes until the kickoff. The Bengals' Stanford Jennings took the ball at his seven and burst 93 yards to a touchdown to put Cincinnati back in front 13-6.

Joe Montana led his team downfield in four plays from his own 15, completing a 31-yard pass to Jerry Rice and a 40-yarder to Roger Craig. From the Cincinnati 14, Montana threw into the endzone and into the hands of Bengals CB Lewis Billups, but he dropped the ball. On the next play, Montana threw left to Rice for a touchdown to tie the score again at 13-13.

Cincinnati was unable to gain and punted to San Francisco at the 49ers 18. On the first play, Montana hit Rice for 44 yards. When two running plays and a pass failed to pick up the first down, Cofer tried for a field goal from the Cincinnati 49, but his attempt was wide right. The Bengals drove to the San Francisco 22, with the key play being a 3rd-and-12 pass from Esiason to Ira Hillary. Breech kicked his third field goal, a 40-yarder, to give the Bengals a 16-13 lead with 3:20 remaining.

It was time for the drive of the game. Montana started from his own eight with short passes to John Frank and Rice. At the 35, he connected with Rice for 17 yards to move the ball into Cincinnati territory. A 13-yarder to Craig put the ball at the 35, but a penalty sent the 49ers back to the 45. With 1:15 on the clock and a 2nd-and-20 situation, Montana threw over the middle to Rice, who was finally hauled down at the Bengals' 18. A quick pass over the middle to Craig gained eight. Then Montana hit John Taylor in the endzone for the winning touchdown, completing an 11-play, 92-yard drive. Cincinnati was unable to do anything in the 34 seconds they had left, and San Francisco had its third Super Bowl victory of the 1980s.

LINEUPS

CIN.		S.F
	OFFENSE	
McGee	WR	Taylor
Munoz	LT	Wallace
Reimers	LG	Sapolu
Kozerski	C	Cross
Montoya	RG	McIntyre
Blados	RT	Barton
Holman	TE	Frank
Brown	WR	Rice
Esiason	QB	Montana
Brooks	RB	Craig
Woods	FB	Rathman
	DEFENSE	
Skow	LE	Roberts
Krumrie	NT	Carter
Buck	RE	Fagan
White	LOLB	Haley
Zander	LILB	Fahnhorst
Kelly	RILB	Walter
Williams	ROLB	Turner
Billups	LCB	McKyer
Thomas	RCB	Griffin
Fulcher	SS	Fuller
Wilcots	FS	Lott

SUBSTITUTES

CINCINNATI		
	OFFENSE	
Norseth	Schonert	Logan
Jennings	D. Smith	Douglas
Rourke	Collinsworth	Parker
Riggs	Hillary	
	DEFENSE	
Horton	Smith	Bussey
Dixon	Barker	Brady
McClendon	Eddwards	King
Grant		
	KICKERS	
Breech	L. Johnson	
SAN FRANCISCO		
	OFFENSE	
Young	Sydney	Pollard
Flagler	Thomas	Collie
Paris	Greer	B. Jones
Wilson	Heller	
	DEFENSE	
Wright	Cox	Holmoe
Ellison	Kennedy	Romanowski
Kugler	Stover	Holt
Stubbs		
	KICKERS	
Cofer	Helton	

SCORING

CINCINNATI	0	3	10	3	- 16
SAN FRANCISCO	3	0	3	14	- 20

First Quarter
S.F. Cofer, 41 yard field goal

Second Quarter
Cin. Breech, 34 yard field goal

Third Quarter
Cin. Breech, 43 yard field goal
S.F. Cofer, 32 yard field goal
Cin. Jennings, 93 yard kickoff return
PAT—Breech (kick)

Fourth Quarter
S.F. Rice, 14 yard pass from Montana
PAT—Cofer (kick)
Cin. Breech, 40 yard field goal
S.F. Taylor, 10 yard pass from Montana
PAT—Cofer (kick)

TEAM STATISTICS

CIN.		S.F.
13	First Downs-Total	23
7	First Downs-Rushing	6
6	First Downs-Pasiing	16
0	First Downs-Penalty	1
1	Fumbles-Number	4
0	Fumbles-Lost Ball	1
7	Penaties-Number	4
65	Yards Penalized	32
0	Missed Field Goals	2
64	Offensive Plays	67
229	Net Yards	454
3.6	Average Gain	6.8
1	Giveaways	1
1	Takeaways	1
0	Difference	0

INDIVIDUAL STATISTICS

CINCINNATI	No.	Yds.	Avg.	SAN FRANCISCO	No.	Yds.	Avg.
RUSHING							
Woods	20	79	3.9	Craig	17	74	4.4
Brooks	6	24	4.0	Rathman	5	23	4.6
Jennings	1	3	3.0	Montana	5	9	1.8
Esiason	1	0	0.0	Rice	1	5	5.0
	28	106	3.8		28	111	4.0
RECEIVING							
Brown	4	44	11.0	Rice	11	215	19.5
Collinsworth	3	40	13.3	Craig	8	101	12.6
McGee	2	23	11.5	Frank	2	15	7.5
Brooks	1	20	20.0	Rathman	1	16	16.0
Hillary	1	17	17.0	Taylor	1	10	10.0
	11	144	13.1		23	357	15.5
PUNTING							
L. Johnson	5		44.6	Helton	4		37.0
PUNT RETURNS							
Horton	1	5	5.0	Taylor	3	56	18.7
Hillary	1	0	0.0				
	2	5	2.5				
KICKOFF RETURNS							
Jennings	2	117	58.5	Rodgers	3	53	17.7
Brooks	1	15	15.0	Taylor	1	13	13.0
	3	132	44.0	Sydney	1	11	11.0
					5	77	15.4
INTERCEPTIONS RETURNS							
none				Romanowski	1	0	0.0

PASSING

	Att.	Comp.	Comp. Pct.	Yds.	Int.	Yds./ Att.	Yds./ Comp.	Yards Lost Tackled
CINCINNATI								
Esiason	25	11	44.0	144	1	5.8	13.9	5-21
SAN FRANCISCO								
Montana	36	23	63.9	357	0	9.9	15.5	3-14

1989 N.F.C. Who Was That Hitman?

In a year that saw the Bears' defense collapse, the Packers mount a stirring playoff drive, the Lions improve, the Saints slip, Herschel Walker traded and Joe Montana canonized, the Talk of the NFC — at least for a couple of weeks — was "bounty hunting." After Dallas lost to Philadelphia on Thanksgiving, Cowboys' coach Jimmy Johnson accused the Eagles of putting a price on the head of Luis Zendejas, the Dallas placekicker. Zendejas, an ex-Eagle kayoed by a former teammate in a kickoff collission, insisted he had proof in the form of a taped telephone conversation with a Philadelphia assistant coach. Amid charge and counter-charge, Eagle coach Buddy Ryan wondered rhetorically why anyone would want to knock a placekicker who'd been in a six-week slump out of a game.

EASTERN DIVISION

New York Giants— The Giants put together their second-best won-lost record in 26 years, yet were a mere 1-4 against playoff teams, including a pair of losses to the second-place Eagles. The surprise of the season was veteran running back Ottis Anderson, who stepped in for the injured Joe Morris and produced the sixth 1,000-yard rushing season of his career (but first since 1984). Considered at the end of his days before the season, Anderson combined with a hefty young line to produce a strong power running game. Rookie Dave Meggett was another pleasant surprise, making the Pro Bowl with his jitterbug kick returning and occasional long-distance pass catching. Phil Simms was steady throughout, except for a horrible two-game stretch against the 49ers and Eagles when he committed a mind-boggling seven turnovers, six of which produced points for the opposition. Linebackers Lawrence Taylor, with 15 sacks, and Carl Banks, making a comeback after a so-so season, led an adequate defense. Banks was named the team's MVP by the players.

Philadelphia Eagles — Randall Cunningham led the team in rushing for the third straight year, something no quarterback has done since the T-formation became the basic pro offense in the 1940s. However, it was a subpar season for the fifth-year pro who signed an $18 million, five-year contract extension in October. After a holdout, defensive end Reggie White wasn't up to his usual standard, either, although he still made most All-Pro teams. Star receiver Mike Quick was lost in October to double-knee surgery. Nevertheless, Buddy Ryan's Eagles still won 11 games to qualify for a wild-card spot. The slack was taken up by an improved running game and the blossoming of defensive linemen Clyde Simmons and Jerome Brown, who combined for 26 sacks. Cornerback Eric Allen led the NFC with eight interceptions.

Washington Redskins — Coach Joe Gibbs' Redskins missed the playoffs in consecutive years for the first time in his nine years as boss. Washington hit its first season low by being the only team to lose to Dallas and its second when veteran defensive end Dexter Manley was permanently banned for drug use. Heralded trade acquisition Gerald Riggs missed most of six games with injuries. Mark Rypien, who started most of the time at quarterback, was erratic and showed an alarming tendency to fumble when he was sacked. Another rash of injuries to the offensive line didn't help either. Yet, through it all, the Redskins were improved over 1989, largely because of the stellar play of the wide receivers. Art Monk, Gary Clark and Ricky Sanders each gained more than 1,000 yards on pass receptions.

Phoenix Cardinals— The season began with the bad news that veteran quarterback Neil Lomax's arthritic hip would keep him from playing. He retired after the season, but by then the Cardinals had suffered through many more disasters. Injuries caused starters to miss a combined total of 77 games. Substance-abuse suspensions took care of a few others. Coach Gene Stallings somehow got the club to 5-6 with bailing wire and spit, but when he announced he would not seek a contract extension, he was fired. Under interim coach Hank Kuhlmann, Phoenix lost its last five games with seldom a whimper. Meanwhile, empty seats became the norm at Sun Devil Stadium; the club suffered an astounding 26.9 percent drop in attendance.

Dallas Cowboys — New owner Jerry Jones and new coach Jimmy Johnson decided on the new-book approach and swept out or aside most of the Cowboys of yore in favor of youth, even trading super-running back Herschel Walker to Minnesota for a posse of draft choices and several players. Youth must be served, but the Dallas youth was mostly served on a plate. No. 1 draft choice Troy Aikman showed promise as a quarterback and leader, but he had few tools to work with — especially after wide receiver Michael Irvin went out with a knee injury. With Aikman as the future, it was hard to figure the Dallas decision to grab quarterback Steve Walsh in the supplemental draft. It cost Dallas the first pick in the 1990 draft when the team flopped to a 1-15 record. Through the debacle, middle linebacker Eugene Lockhart performed heroically and closed 1989 with more than 200 tackles.

CENTRAL DIVISION

Minnesota Vikings— Despite winning their division, the Vikings were generally disappointing, losing six of eight games away from the friendly Metrodome. The big trade that brought Herschel Walker from the Cowboys after Week Five looked like a steal wehn Walker opened his Viking career by rushing for 148 yards in his first game, but after that he performed at only an ordinary pace. The offense was also dragged down by quarterback Wade Wilson's inconsistency and nagging injuries to wide receiver Athony Carter. It was the league-leading defense that kept Minnesota afloat. Defensive end Chris Doleman topped the NFL with 21 sacks and defensive tackl· Keith Millard was close behind with 18. The team sack total of 71 was only one behind the record set by the '84 Bears. An ugly early-season incident that saw some team members involved in contract disputes — one accused GM Mike Lynn of racism — didn't do anything for team morale.

Green Bay Packers — The Pack was back — almost. Their 10-6 mark tied Minnesota in percentage but not in the NFL's tie-breaking system. Under the expanded playoff system of 1990, Green Bay would have made postseason play. Nevertheless, it was a fine year for coach Lindy Infante, who received most of the Coach of the Year laurels. Much of the Packers' improvement was credited to the development of quarterback Don Majkowski, who went from erratic to the "Magic Man" and led several remarkable comeback victories and helped Green Bay win six games by a total of 11 points. Wide receiver Sterling Sharpe was another sensation, leading the league in receiving; he also had 12 TD's. The defense ranked in the lower echelon, but linebacker Tim Harris was an All-Pro, registering 19.5 sacks. Cornerback Dave Brown, at 36 years old, led the team with six interceptions.

Detroit Lions — Heisman Trophy winner Barry Sanders, coming out of college as a junior, led the NFC in rushing, but through a 1-8 start, it all seemed for naught. Then coach Wayne Fontes' troops roared down the stretch to finish a respectable 7-9. Free-agent quarterback Bob Gagliano's improvement was the big factor in the turnaround. Ironically, the Lions' new run-and-shoot offense, dubbed the "Silver Stretch," was geared to a passing attack, yet Sanders made the attack go on the ground and quarterbacks Gagliano and Rodney Peete accounted for almost as many touchdowns with their running as with their passing, nine to 11. Veteran placekicker Eddie Murray made the Pro Bowl after duplicating his '88 success on 20-of-21 field-goal attempts.

Chicago Bears — Jim McMahon was traded to San Diego before the season began, but the Bears still couldn't settle on a quarterback as both Mike Tomczak and Jim Harbaugh started games. Neither received much help from a crew of receivers that was, at best, ordinary. Meanwhile, Neal Anderson became a star of the first order with 1,275 rushing yards. Anderson led the team in rushing, receiving and scoring. Although the offense was undependable, it was the once-invincible Bear defense that really let them down, finishing 25th in the league and three times blowing leads in the final two minutes. Chicago started the season with four victories, but then defensive tackle Dan Hampton was lost for the year with surgery on both knees. In the absence of Hampton, opponents concentrated on stopping Richard Dent's pass rush and isolating middle linebacker Mike Singletary. Then, without a pass rush, the defensive backs became easy pickings. The Bears lost 10 of their last 12 games, including the final six.

FINAL TEAM STATISTICS

OFFENSE

	ATL	CHI	DAL	DET	G.B.	L.A.	MINN	N.O.	NYG	PHIL	PHX	S.F.	T.B.	WASH
FIRST DOWNS:														
Total	261	302	246	274	342	321	326	304	298	321	262	350	288	338
by Rushing	75	136	78	117	114	107	126	108	118	120	83	124	84	101
by Passing	173	147	145	139	207	197	172	167	157	171	157	209	174	217
by Penalty	13	19	23	18	21	17	28	29	23	30	22	17	30	20
RUSHING:														
Number	318	516	355	421	397	472	514	502	556	540	407	493	412	514
Yards	1155	2287	1409	2053	1732	1909	2066	1948	1889	2208	1361	1966	1507	1904
Average Yards	3.6	4.4	4.0	4.9	4.4	4.0	4.0	3.9	3.4	4.1	3.3	4.0	3.7	3.7
Touchdowns	11	22	7	23	13	19	12	19	17	14	10	14	10	14
PASSING:														
Attempts	578	484	513	450	600	523	499	461	444	538	523	483	570	581
Completions	312	267	266	229	354	308	272	284	248	294	279	339	302	337
Completion Pct.	54.0	55.2	51.9	50.9	59.0	58.9	54.5	61.6	55.9	54.6	53.3	70.2	53.0	58.0
Passing Yards	3903	3262	3124	3282	4325	4369	3468	3651	3355	3455	3659	4584	3666	4476
Avg. Yds per Att.	6.0	6.0	5.3	5.8	6.3	7.5	5.9	6.8	6.3	5.3	5.7	8.2	5.4	7.2
Avg. Yds per Comp.	12.5	12.2	11.7	14.3	12.2	14.2	12.8	12.9	13.5	11.8	13.1	13.5	12.1	13.3
Times Tackled	51	28	30	57	48	32	40	36	46	45	56	45	43	21
Yds Lost Tackled	389	174	239	343	277	236	279	271	281	343	379	282	331	127
Net Yards	3514	3088	2885	2939	4048	4133	3189	3380	3074	3112	3280	4302	3335	4349
Touchdowns	17	21	14	11	27	29	17	23	17	23	17	35	23	24
Interceptions	12	25	27	24	20	18	19	19	16	16	30	11	28	17
Pct. Intercepted	2.1	5.2	5.3	5.3	3.3	3.4	3.8	4.1	3.6	3.0	5.7	2.3	4.9	2.9
PUNTS:														
Number	85	72	82	83	66	74	72	71	70	87	82	56	86	63
Average	40.8	39.5	39.8	42.6	40.6	38.3	39.8	39.1	43.1	39.0	43.6	39.8	38.5	42.3
PUNT RETURNS														
Number	32	32	31	47	35	35	45	53	46	37	40	39	32	26
Yards	341	220	197	572	289	332	448	428	582	331	469	429	296	226
Average Yards	10.7	6.9	6.4	12.2	8.3	9.5	10.0	8.1	12.7	8.9	11.7	11.0	9.3	8.7
Touchdowns	1	0	0	0	0	0	0	1	1	0	0	0	0	0
KICKOFF RET.:														
Number	80	73	77	61	69	67	51	63	51	49	83	51	62	58
Yards	1509	1539	1709	1272	1239	1328	1122	1284	926	828	1650	954	1055	1176
Average Yards	18.9	21.1	22.2	20.9	18.0	19.8	22.0	20.4	18.2	16.9	19.9	18.7	17.0	20.3
Touchdowns	0	1	1	0	0	0	1	1	0	0	0	0	0	1
INTERCEPT RET.:														
Number	20	26	7	16	25	21	18	21	22	30	16	21	21	27
Yards	285	268	37	107	232	372	264	226	330	375	275	262	234	284
Average Yards	14.3	10.3	5.3	6.7	9.3	17.7	14.7	10.8	15.0	12.5	17.2	12.5	11.1	10.5
Touchdowns	0	1	0	1	0	3	2	2	2	2	2	0	2	3
PENALTIES:														
Number	82	95	100	121	81	102	119	90	83	114	113	109	104	105
Yards	671	846	771	977	666	823	974	676	675	938	856	922	881	881
FUMBLES:														
Number	26	23	29	37	35	26	28	28	30	43	24	32	21	32
Number Lost	11	17	15	24	13	11	14	12	14	16	14	14	9	20
POINTS:														
Total	279	358	204	312	362	426	351	386	348	342	258	442	320	386
PAT Attempts	30	45	25	36	42	51	36	46	37	40	29	51	36	42
PAT Made	30	43	24	36	42	51	35	44	35	40	28	49	34	41
FG Attempts	32	19	20	21	28	30	44	29	38	33	26	36	28	40
FG Made	23	15	10	20	22	23	32	20	29	20	18	29	22	29
Percent FG Made	71.9	78.9	50.0	95.2	78.6	76.7	72.7	69.0	76.3	60.6	69.2	80.6	78.6	72.5
Safeties	0	0	0	0	1	0	2	3	2	1	1	0	2	3

DEFENSE

	ATL	CHI	DAL	DET	G.B.	L.A.	MINN	N.O.	NYG	PHIL	PHX	S.F.	T.B.	WASH
FIRST DOWNS:														
Total	336	332	321	314	307	306	266	293	266	281	329	283	317	274
by Rushing	156	118	116	98	116	101	100	79	90	81	113	76	115	72
by Passing	163	191	183	189	179	181	140	198	159	171	185	178	170	177
by Penalty	17	23	22	27	12	24	26	16	17	29	31	29	32	25
RUSHING:														
Number	572	446	543	454	460	404	462	373	421	426	539	372	479	384
Yards	2471	1897	1991	1621	2008	1543	1683	1326	1539	1605	2302	1383	2023	1344
Average Yards	4.3	4.3	3.7	3.6	4.4	3.8	3.6	3.6	3.7	3.8	4.3	3.7	4.2	3.5
Touchdowns	26	21	17	18	15	13	14	10	10	6	12	9	18	9
PASSING:														
Attempts	437	554	488	570	476	577	488	577	486	529	531	564	515	530
Completions	259	307	301	370	302	345	252	320	273	258	286	316	301	277
Completion Pct.	59.3	55.4	61.7	64.9	63.4	59.8	51.6	55.5	56.2	48.8	53.9	56.0	58.4	52.3
Passing Yards	3737	4079	3748	4193	3553	4302	3003	4222	3427	3713	3794	3568	3659	3875
Avg. Yds per Att.	7.6	6.5	6.9	6.4	6.6	6.5	4.5	6.2	6.0	5.6	6.4	5.3	6.3	6.3
Avg. Yds per Comp.	14.4	13.3	12.5	11.3	11.8	12.5	12.0	13.2	12.6	14.4	13.3	11.3	12.2	14.0
Times Tackled	31	39	29	40	34	42	71	47	39	62	30	43	33	40
Yds Lost Tackled	183	247	183	277	214	278	502	362	302	424	219	333	222	304
Net Yards	3554	3832	3565	3916	3339	4024	2501	3860	3125	3289	3575	3235	3437	3571
Touchdowns	19	21	21	19	22	24	18	23	16	26	24	15	29	25
Interceptions	20	26	7	16	25	21	18	21	22	30	16	21	21	27
Pct. Intercepted	4.6	4.7	1.4	2.8	5.3	4.4	3.7	3.6	4.5	5.7	3.0	3.7	4.1	5.1
PUNTS:														
Number	56	67	73	80	65	81	95	75	74	85	76	74	69	76
Average	41.8	39.6	39.9	41.2	40.7	41.5	40.6	39.4	40.1	42.0	41.5	38.9	40.3	40.1
PUNT RETURNS														
Number	43	30	38	46	30	34	32	35	29	37	46	35	54	34
Yards	460	262	334	373	416	315	300	244	236	215	371	361	492	383
Average Yards	10.7	8.7	8.8	8.1	13.9	9.3	9.4	7.0	8.1	5.8	8.1	10.3	9.1	11.3
Touchdowns	0	0	1	0	0	1	0	0	0	0	0	0	0	0
KICKOFF RET.:														
Number	60	68	46	65	63	84	68	55	73	60	57	76	55	74
Yards	1188	1375	853	1037	1389	1633	1287	983	1306	1307	1193	1435	1143	1532
Average Yards	19.8	20.2	18.5	16.0	22.0	19.4	18.9	17.9	17.9	21.8	20.9	18.9	20.8	20.7
Touchdowns	0	0	0	1	0	0	0	0	0	1	0	0	0	1
INTERCEPT RET.:														
Number	12	25	27	24	20	18	19	19	16	16	30	11	28	17
Yards	85	182	396	447	321	207	138	265	240	147	327	140	240	229
Average Yards	7.1	7.3	14.7	18.6	16.1	11.5	7.3	13.9	15.0	9.2	10.9	12.7	8.6	13.5
Touchdowns	0	1	3	3	2	0	2	1	2	0	3	0	2	1
PENALTIES:														
Number	79	94	102	107	105	93	116	105	109	118	106	75	109	98
Yards	682	802	723	993	851	798	903	850	800	956	916	581	869	796
FUMBLES:														
Number	26	24	22	28	28	38	29	35	38	44	18	34	30	24
Number Lost	12	12	10	16	15	15	18	18	15	26	11	16	18	15
POINTS:														
Total	437	377	393	364	356	344	275	301	252	274	377	253	419	308
PAT Attempts	49	43	44	42	41	38	33	35	30	33	41	26	51	38
PAT Made	48	41	43	41	39	36	32	34	30	30	40	26	51	38
FG Attempts	36	36	35	33	30	29	21	24	21	26	40	31	24	23
FG Made	31	26	28	23	23	26	13	19	14	14	29	23	20	14
Percent FG Made	86.1	72.2	80.0	69.7	76.7	89.7	61.9	79.2	66.7	53.8	72.5	74.2	83.3	60.9
Safeties	1	0	1	1	1	1	0	0	0	2	2	1	1	0

Tampa Bay Buccaneers — The Buccaneers stood 3-2 and were talking of a winning season again when apparent-patsy Detroit came to town — and left with a 17-16 victory. Tampa Bay then went into a dive, augmented by injuries, and crawled to another 5-11 season. Wide receiver Mark Carrier became one of the NFL's best, catching 86 passes for 1,422 yards and nine touchdowns. But fans were at a loss to explain why he wasn't selected to the Pro Bowl (although he made it as a replacement). Quarterback Vinny Testaverde still lacked the consistency needed to rank amont the league's elite, but he cut his interceptions to 22 and upped his touchdowns to 20. Coach Ray Perkins' Bucs had a subpar running game and a defense dinged for 419 points.

WESTERN DIVISION

San Francisco 49ers — Coach Bill Walsh moved into the broadcasting booth, but the 49ers kept right on rolling under former defensive coordinator George Seifert, even improving on their 1988 record, to become everybody's choice as the "Team of the '80s." Quarterback Joe Montana had his best season ever statistically, as he set a new mark with a 112.4 pass rating. Premier receiver Jerry Rice broke the team record for TD catches in only his fifth season, and John Taylor emerged as a dangerous running mate. The offensive line survived a rash of injuries, as Roger Craig again rushed for over 1,000 yards. The defense, led by strong safety Ronnie Lott, performed admirably despite a career-ending injury to free safety Jeff Fuller.

Los Angeles Rams — The Rams' aerial attack brought back memories of the Van Brocklin-Waterfield days of the early 1950s, as quarterback Jim Everett passed for over 4,000 yards and a league-high 29 touchdowns. His chief targets were veteran Henry Ellard and second-year star Willie "Flipper" Anderson. Both gained over 1,000 yards, and Anderson set a single-game NFL record with 336 yards (on 15 receptions). Greg Bell topped 1,000 yards rushing with the help of of a 221-yard game against Green Bay in Week Three and a 21-yard outing in the season finale against New England. Linebacker Kevin Greene had 16.5 sacks, but the defense faltered when several other linebackers were injured. That led to a four-game losing streak after the Rams opened the season with five straight wins.

New Orleans Saints — Coach Jim Mora's team won one less game than in 1988 and finished out of the playoffs again, but the 9-7 mark was still a winning season, something the Saints struggled 20 years to accomplsih. Rickey Jackson's injury in an auto accident and Pat Swilling's holdout cost New Orleans its two most dominant defenders at the start of the season, and by the time the two star linebackers rounded into shape, the Saints were 1-4. Running back Dalton Hilliard was brilliant all along, rushing for 1,262 yards and scoring 18 touchdowns. But the key to the three victories in the final three games was former Arena Football League quarterback John Fourcade, who stepped in for slipping Bobby Hebert to throw seven touchdowns, run for one and ignite a dormant attack.

Atlanta Falcons — The Falcons hoped for improvement in the standings on the strength of the strong, end-of-the-season defense in '88. Instead, Atlanta finished dead last in the NFL in total defense. With the team at 3-8, coach Marion Campbell resigned. Interim coach Jim Hanifan couldn't pull the Falcons out of the dive, and they lost the last five games. Leading to the defensive shortcomings was a foot injury that kept cornerback Scott Case sidelined for more than half of the season and the disappointing play of young (and expensive) linebackers Aundray Bruce and Marcus Cotton. Running back John Settle also slipped form his 1988 level. But most tragic for this seemingly jinxed team was the in-season deaths of rookie offensive tackle Ralph Norwood and reserve tight end Brad Beckman in auto accidents within a month of each other. New 1990 coach Jerry Glanville took over a team with a losing heritage and a defensive back in Deion Sanders who is even better at grabbing media attention than Glanville himself.

NEW YORK GIANTS 12-4 Bill Parcells

Scores of Each Game		
27	Washington	24
24	DETROIT	14
35	PHOENIX	7
30	Dallas	13
19	Philadelphia	21
20	WASHINGTON	17
20	San Diego	13
24	MINNESOTA	14
20	Phoenix	13
10	L.A. Rams	31
15	SEATTLE	3
24	San Francisco	34
17	PHILADELPHIA	24
14	Denver	7
15	DALLAS	0
34	L.A. RAIDERS	17

Use Name	Pos.	Hgt	Wgt	Age	Int	Pts
John Elliott	OT	6'7"	305	24		
Eric Moore	OT	6'5"	290	24		
Doug Riesenberg	OT	6'5"	275	24		
Bob Kratch	OG	6'3"	288	23		
Damian Johnson	OG	6'5"	290	26		
William Roberts	OG	6'5"	280	27		
Brian Williams	OG-C	6'5"	300	23		
Bart Oates	C	6'3"	265	30		
Frank Winters	C	6'3"	280	25		
Eric Dorsey	DE	6'5"	280	25		
Mark Duckens	DE	6'4"	270	24		
Leonard Marshall	DE	6'3"	285	27		2
John Washington	DE	6'4"	275	26		
Robb White	DE	6'4"	270	24		
Erik Howard	NT	6'4"	268	24		
Carl Banks	LB	6'4"	235	27	1	6
Johnie Cooks	LB	6'4"	251	30		
Steve DeOssie	LB	6'2"	248	26		
Dwayne Jiles (from PHI)	LB	6'4"	245	27		
Pepper Johnson	LB	6'3"	248	25	3	6
Gary Reasons	LB	6'4"	234	27	1	2
Lawrence Taylor	LB	6'3"	243	30		
Mark Collins	DB	5'10"	190	25	2	
Greg Cox	DB	6'	223	24		
Myron Guyton	DB	6'1"	205	22	2	
Greg Jackson	DB	6'1"	200	23		
Terry Kinard	DB	6'1"	200	29	5	6
Reyna Thompson	DB	6'	193	26		
Adrian White	DB	6'	200	25	2	
Sheldon White	DB	5'11"	188	24	2	
Perry Williams	DB	6'2"	203	28	3	
Jeff Hostetler	QB	6'3"	212	28		
Jeff Rutledge	QB	6'1"	195	32		
Phil Simms	QB	6'3"	214	32		6
Ottis Anderson	HB	6'2"	225	32		84
Dave Meggett	HB	5'7"	180	23		30
Lewis Tillman	HB	6'	195	23		
George Adams	FB	6'1"	225	26		
Maurice Carthon	FB	6'1"	225	28		
Lee Rouson	FB	6'1"	222	26		
Stephen Baker	WR	5'8"	160	25		12
Mark Ingram	WR	5'10"	188	24		6
Lionel Manuel	WR	5'11"	180	27		
Stacy Robinson	WR	5'11"	186	27		
Odessa Turner	WR	6'3"	205	24		24
Mark Bavaro	TE	6'4"	245	26		18
Howard Cross	TE	6'5"	245	22		6
Zeke Mowatt	TE	6'3"	240	28		
Raul Allegre	K	5'10"	167	30		83
Sean Landeta	K	6'	200	27		
Bjorn Nittmo	K	5'11"	185	23		39

Joe Morris — Foot Injury

PHILADELPHIA EAGLES 11-5 Buddy Ryan

Scores of Each Game		
31	SEATTLE	7
42	Washington	37
28	SAN FRANCISCO	38
13	Chicago	27
21	N.Y. GIANTS	19
17	Phoenix	5
10	L.A. RAIDERS	7
28	Denver	24
17	San Diego	20
3	WASHINGTON	10
10	MINNESOTA	9
27	Dallas	0
24	N.Y. Giants	17
20	DALLAS	10
20	New Orleans	30
31	PHOENIX	14

Use Name	Pos.	Hgt	Wgt	Age	Int	Pts
Matt Darwin	OT	6'4"	275	26		
Ron Heller	OT	6'6"	280	27		
Ken Reeves	OT-OG	6'5"	270	28		
Mike Schad	OG	6'5"	290	25		
Reggie Singletary	OG-OT	6'3"	280	25		
Ron Solt	OG	6'3"	285	27		
Ben Tamburello	OG-C	6'3"	278	24		
David Alexander	C-OT	6'3"	275	24		
Dave Rimington	C	6'3"	288	29		
Steve Kaufusi	DE-DT	6'4"	274	25		
Clyde Simmons	DE	6'6"	276	25	1	6
Reggie White	DE-DT	6'5"	285	27		
Jerome Brown	DT	6'2"	288	24		
Mike Golic	DT	6'5"	275	27	1	
Mike Pitts	DT	6'5"	277	29		
Ty Allert	LB	6'2"	233	26		
Todd Bell	LB	6'1"	212	31	1	
Byron Evans	LB	6'2"	225	25	3	
Britt Hager	LB	6'1"	222	23		
Al Harris	LB	6'5"	265	32	2	2
Seth Joyner	LB	6'2"	248	24	4	
Mike Reichenbach	LB	6'2"	230	28		
Ricky Shaw (from NYG)	LB	6'4"	240	24		
Jessie Small	LB	6'3"	239	22		
Eric Allen	DB	5'10"	183	22	8	
Alan Dial	DB	6'1"	188	24		
Eric Everett	DB	5'10"	161	23	4	6
William Frizzell	DB	6'3"	205	27	4	
Terry Hoage	DB	6'3"	201	27		
Wes Hopkins	DB	6'1"	212	28		
Izel Jenkins	DB	5'10"	191	24	4	
Tyrone Jones	DB	6'4"	223	22		
Sammy Lilly	DB	5'9"	178	24		
Andre Waters	DB	5'11"	195	27	1	6
Matt Cavanaugh	QB	6'2"	210	33		
Randall Cunningham	QB	6'4"	203	26		24
Don McPherson	QB	6'1"	183	24		
Keith Byars	HB	6'1"	238	26		30
Robert Drummond	HB	6'1"	205	22		6
Mark Higgs	FB	5'7"	200	23		
Heath Sherman	FB-HB	6'	190	22		12
Anthony Toney	FB	6'	227	26		18
Cris Carter	WR	6'3"	194	24		66
Anthony Edwards	WR	5'11"	195	23		
Gregg Garrity	WR	5'10"	169	27		12
Ron Johnson	WR	6'3"	186	31		6
Mike Quick	WR	6'2"	190	30		12
Henry Williams	WR	5'6"	185	27		
Jimmie Giles	TE	6'3"	240	35		12
Keith Jackson	TE	6'2"	250	24		18
Dave Little	TE	6'2"	226	28		6
Steve DeLine	K	5'11"	185	28		12
Max Runager	K	6'1"	189	33		
John Teltschik	K	6'2"	209	25		
Rick Tuten	K	6'2"	220	24		
Luis Zendejas (to DAL)	K	5'9"	160	27		75

WASHINGTON REDSKINS 10-6 Joe Gibbs

Scores of Each Game		
24	N.Y. GIANTS	27
37	PHILADELPHIA	42
30	Dallas	7
16	New Orleans	14
30	PHOENIX	28
17	N.Y. Giants	20
32	TAMPA BAY	28
24	L.A. Raiders	37
3	DALLAS	13
10	Philadelphia	3
10	DENVER	14
38	CHICAGO	14
29	Phoenix	10
26	SAN DIEGO	21
31	Atlanta	30
29	Seattle	0

Use Name	Pos.	Hgt	Wgt	Age	Int	Pts
Ray Brown	OT	6'5"	280	26		
Joe Jacoby	OT	6'7"	305	30		
Jim Lachey	OT	6'6"	290	26		
Mark May	OT-OG	6'6"	295	29		
Ed Simmons	OT	6'5"	280	25		
Russ Grimm	OG	6'3"	275	30		
Raleigh McKenzie	OG-C	6'2"	270	26		
Jeff Bostic	C	6'2"	260	30		
Dave Harbour	C	6'4"	265	23		
Mark Schlereth	C	6'3"	285	23		
Markus Koch	DE	6'5"	275	26		
Dexter Manley	DE	6'3"	257	30		2
Charles Mann	DE	6'6"	270	28		
Lybrant Robinson	DE	6'4"	250	25		
Fred Stokes	DE	6'3"	262	25		2
Darryl Grant	DT	6'1"	275	29	2	
Tracy Rocker	DT	6'3"	288	23		
Mike Stensrud	DT	6'5"	280	33		
Brian Bonner	LB	6'2"	225	23		
Ravin Caldwell	LB	6'3"	229	26		
Monte Coleman	LB	6'2"	230	31	2	6
Kurt Gouveia	LB	6'1"	227	24	1	
Don Graham	LB	6'2"	245	25		
Greg Manusky	LB	6'1"	242	23		
Wilber Marshall	LB	6'1"	230	27	1	
Neal Olkewicz	LB	6'	230	32		
Todd Bowles	DB	6'2"	203	25	3	
Brian Davis	DB	6'2"	190	26	4	
Wayne Davis (from BUF)	DB	5'11"	180	26	1	
Darrell Green	DB	5'8"	170	29	2	
A.J. Johnson	DB	5'8"	176	22	4	6
Chris Mandeville	DB	6'1"	213	24		
Martin Mayhew	DB	5'8"	172	23		
Clarence Vaughn	DB	6'	202	25		
Alvin Walton	DB	6'	180	25	4	6
Herb Welch	DB	5'11"	180	28		
Barry Wilburn	DB	6'3"	186	25	3	
Stan Humphries	QB	6'2"	223	24		
Mark Rypien	QB	6'4"	234	26		6
Doug Williams	QB	6'4"	220	34		
Reggie Branch	HB-FB	5'11"	235	26		
Jamie Morris	HB-FB	5'7"	188	24		12
Gerald Riggs	HB-FB	6'1"	232	28		24
Earnest Byner	FB-HB	5'10"	215	26		54
Joe Mickles	FB	5'10"	221	23		
Gary Clark	WR	5'9"	173	26		54
Carl Harry	WR	5'9"	168	23		
Joe Howard	WR	5'8"	170	26		6
Art Monk	WR	6'3"	209	31		48
Ricky Sanders	WR	5'11"	180	27		24
Jimmie Johnson	TE	6'2"	246	21		
Terry Orr	TE	6'3"	227	27		
Mike Tice	TE	6'7"	247	30		
Don Warren	TE	6'4"	242	33		6
Chip Lohmiller	K	6'3"	213	23		128
Ralf Mojsiejenko	K	6'2"	212	26		

Eugene Profit — Leg Injury

Kelvin Bryant — Knee Injury

Ken Whisenhunt — Leg Injury

PHOENIX CARDINALS 5-11 Gene Stallings (5-6), Hank Kuhlmann (0-5)

Scores of Each Game		
16	Detroit	13
34	Seattle	24
7	N.Y. Giants	35
13	SAN DIEGO	24
28	Washington	30
5	PHILADELPHIA	17
34	ATLANTA	20
19	Dallas	10
13	N.Y. GIANTS	20
24	DALLAS	20
14	L.A. Rams	37
13	TAMPA BAY	14
10	WASHINGTON	29
14	L.A. Raiders	16
0	DENVER	37
14	Philadelphia	31

Use Name	Pos.	Hgt	Wgt	Age	Int	Pts
Tootie Robbins	OT	6'5"	302	31		
Luis Sharpe	OT	6'4"	260	29		
Scott Dill	OG	6'5"	272	23		
Todd Peat	OG	6'2"	294	25		
Lance Smith	OG	6'2"	262	25		
Mark Traynowicz	OG	6'5"	280	27		
Joe Wolf	OG-OT	6'5"	279	22		
Mike Zandofsky	OG	6'2"	285	23		
Kani Kauahi	C	6'2"	270	29		
Derek Kennard	C	6'3"	285	26		
Bob Buczkowski	DE	6'5"	260	25		
David Galloway	DE	6'3"	279	30		
Freddie Gilbert	DE	6'4"	275	27		
Shawn Knight	DE	6'6"	290	25		
Freddie Joe Nunn	DE	6'4"	255	27		
Rod Saddler	DE	6'5"	276	23		
Karl Wilson	DE	6'4"	275	24		2
Bob Clasby	DT	6'5"	260	28		
Gary Hadd	DT	6'4"	278	24		
Jim Wahler	DT	6'4"	268	23	1	
Anthony Bell	LB	6'3"	231	25		
Ron Burton (from DAL)	LB	6'1"	245	25	1	
Ken Harvey	LB	6'2"	225	24		
Eric Hill	LB	6'1"	248	22		
Ilia Jarostchuk	LB	6'3"	231	25		
Garth Jax	LB	6'2"	229	25		
Randy Kirk	LB	6'2"	231	24		
Michael Adams	DB	5'10"	195	25		
Michael Downs	DB	6'3"	212	30	1	
Carl Carter	DB	5'11"	180	25	1	
Kevin Guidry	DB	6'	176	25		
Cedric Mack	DB	6'	194	28	4	
Tim McDonald	DB	6'2"	207	24	7	6
Roland Mitchell	DB	5'11"	180	25		
Jay Taylor	DB	5'9"	170	21		
Marcus Turner	DB	6'	190	23		
Lonnie Young	DB	6'1"	182	26	1	
Mike Zordich	DB	5'11"	197	25	1	6
Gary Hogeboom	QB	6'4"	207	31		6
Timm Rosenbach	QB	6'2"	210	22		
Tom Tupa	QB-K	6'4"	220	22		
Tony Baker	HB	5'10"	190	25		
Tony Jordan	HB	6'2"	220	24		12
Stump Mitchell	HB	5'9"	188	30		
Vai Sikahema	HB	5'9"	191	27		
Lydell Carr	FB	6'1"	228	24		
Jessie Clark (to MIN)	FB	6'	233	29		
Earl Ferrell	FB	6'	240	31		36
Ron Wolfley	FB	6'	222	26		6
Roy Green	WR	6'	195	32		42
Don Holmes	WR	5'10"	180	28		6
Ernie Jones	WR	5'11"	186	24		18
Phil McConkey (to SD)	WR	5'10"	170	32		
J.T. Smith	WR	6'2"	185	33		30
Darryl Usher (from SD)	WR	5'8"	170	24		
Rob Awalt	TE	6'5"	248	25		
Jay Novacek	TE	6'4"	235	26		6
Walter Reeves	TE	6'4"	249	23		
Rich Camarillo	K	5'11"	193	28		
Al Del Greco	K	5'10"	191	27		82

Joe Bostic — Knee Injury

Reggie McKenzie — Knee Injury

Neil Lomax — Hip Injury

Andy Schillinger — Knee Injury

DALLAS COWBOYS 1-15 Jimmy Johnson

Scores of Each Game		
0	New Orleans	28
21	Atlanta	27
7	WASHINGTON	30
13	N.Y. GIANTS	30
13	Green Bay	31
14	SAN FRANCISCO	31
28	Kansas City	36
10	PHOENIX	19
13	Washington	3
20	Phoenix	24
14	MIAMI	17
0	PHILADELPHIA	27
31	L.A. RAMS	35
10	Philadelphia	20
0	N.Y. Giants	15
10	GREEN BAY	20

Use Name	Pos.	Hgt	Wgt	Age	Int	Pts
Kevin Gogan	OT	6'7"	309	24		
Mark Tuinei	OT	6'5"	282	29		
Dave Widell	OT	6'6"	300	24		
Crawford Ker	OG	6'3"	290	27		
Nate Newton	OG	6'3"	314	27		
Mark Stepnoski	OG-C	6'2"	269	22		
Jeff Zimmerman	OG	6'3"	313	24		
Tom Rafferty	C	6'3"	264	35		
Bob White	C	6'5"	273	26		
Willie Broughton	DE	6'5"	275	25		
Jim Jeffcoat	DE	6'5"	262	28		6
Too Tall Jones	DE	6'9"	278	38		
Tony Tolbert	DE	6'6"	241	21		
Jon Carter	DT	6'4"	273	24		
Dean Hamel	DT	6'3"	276	28		
Danny Noonan	DT	6'4"	266	24		
Garry Cobb	LB	6'2"	233	32		
Jack Del Rio	LB	6'4"	236	26		6
Onzy Elam	LB	6'2"	225	24		
David Howard (from MIN)	LB	6'2"	230	27		
Eugene Lockhart	LB	6'2"	235	28	2	6
Ken Norton	LB	6'2"	236	22		
Randy Shannon	LB	6'1"	221	23		
Jesse Solomon (from MIN)	LB	6'	235	25		
Ken Tippins	LB	6'1"	226	23		
Vince Albritton	DB	6'2"	220	27	1	
Scott Ankrom	DB	6'1"	194	23		
Bill Bates	DB	6'1"	200	28	1	
Eric Brown	DB	5'11"	177	22		
Ron Francis	DB	5'9"	201	25	1	
Manny Hendrix	DB	5'10"	181	24		
Issiac Holt (from MIN)	DB	6'2"	200	26	1	6
Ray Horton	DB	5'11"	187	29	1	
Tim Jackson	DB	5'11"	192	23		
Tony Lilly	DB	6'	199	27		
Everson Walls	DB	6'1"	193	29		
Robert Williams	DB	5'10"	186	26		
Troy Aikman	QB	6'4"	216	22		
Babe Laufenberg	QB	6'3"	205	29		
Steve Walsh	QB	6'2"	200	22		
Paul Palmer (from DET)	HB	5'9"	181	24		12
Kevin Scott	HB	5'9"	177	25		
Curtis Stewart	HB	5'11"	208	26		
Darryl Clack	FB	5'10"	220	25		12
Daryl Johnston	FB	6'2"	234	23		18
Broderick Sargent	FB	5'10"	220	26		6
Curtis Stewart	FB	5'11"	208	23		
Junior Tautalatasi	FB-HB	5'11"	208	27		
Ray Alexander	WR	6'4"	193	27		
Cornell Burbage	WR	5'10"	189	24		
James Dixon	WR	5'10"	181	22		18
Bernard Ford	WR	5'9"	168	23		6
Michael Irvin	WR	6'2"	202	22		30
Kelvin Martin	WR	5'9"	163	25		12
Derrick Shepard (from NO)	WR	5'10"	187	25		6
Thornton Chandler	TE	6'5"	240	25		
Steve Folsom	TE	6'5"	240	31		12
Keith Jennings	TE	6'4"	251	23		
Mike Saxon	K	6'3"	198	27		
Roger Ruzek (to PHI)	K	6'1"	195	28		67

Jeff Hurd — Knee Injury

Mark Walen — Knee Injury

NEW YORK GIANTS

RUSHING

Last Name	No.	Yds	Avg	TD
Anderson	325	1023	3.1	14
Tillman	79	290	3.7	0
Carthon	57	153	2.7	0
Simms	32	141	4.4	1
Meggett	28	117	4.2	0
Hostetler	11	71	6.5	2
Rouson	11	51	4.6	0
Adams	9	29	3.2	0
Turner	2	11	5.5	0
Reasons	1	2	2.0	0
Ingram	1	1	1.0	0

RECEIVING

Last Name	No.	Yds	Avg	TD
Turner	38	467	12.3	4
Meggett	34	531	15.6	4
Manuel	33	539	16.3	1
Anderson	28	268	9.6	0
Mowatt	27	288	10.7	0
Bavaro	22	278	12.6	3
Ingram	17	290	17.1	1
Carthon	15	132	8.8	0
Baker	13	255	19.6	2
Rouson	7	121	17.3	0
Cross	6	107	17.8	1
Robinson	4	41	10.3	0
Adams	2	7	3.5	0
Banks	1	22	22.0	1
Tillman	1	9	9.0	0

PUNT RETURNS

Last Name	No.	Yds	Avg	TD
Megett	46	582	12.7	1

KICKOFF RETURNS

Last Name	No.	Yds	Avg	TD
Meggett	27	577	21.4	0
Ingram	22	332	15.1	0
Rouson	1	17	17.0	0
Collins	1	0	0.0	0

PASSING—PUNTING—KICKING

PASSING	Att	Cmp	%	Yds	Yd/Att	TD	Int—	%	RK
Simms	405	228	56.3	3061	7.56	14	14—	3.5	6
Hostetler	39	20	51.3	294	7.54	3	2—	5.1	

PUNTING	No.	Avg.
Landeta	70	43.1

KICKING	XP	ATT	%	FG	ATT	%
Allegre	23	24	96	20	26	77
Nittmo	12	13	92	9	12	75

PHILADELPHIA EAGLES

RUSHING

Last Name	No.	Yds	Avg	TD
Cunningham	104	621	6.0	4
Toney	172	582	3.4	3
Byars	133	452	3.4	5
Higgs	49	184	3.8	0
Sherman	40	177	4.4	2
Drummond	32	127	4.0	0
Reichenbach	1	30	30.0	0
Teltschik	1	23	23.0	0
Carter	2	16	8.0	0
Runager	2	5	2.5	0
Johnson	1	3	3.0	0
Cavanaugh	2	-3	-1.5	0

RECEIVING

Last Name	No.	Yds	Avg	TD
Byars	68	721	10.6	0
Jackson	63	648	10.3	3
Carter	45	605	13.4	11
Johnson	20	295	14.8	1
Toney	19	124	6.5	0
Drummond	17	180	10.6	1
Giles	16	225	14.1	2
Quick	13	228	17.5	2
Garrity	13	209	16.1	2
Sherman	8	85	10.6	0
Williams	4	32	8.0	0
Higgs	3	9	3.0	0
Edwards	2	75	37.0	0
Little	2	8	4.0	1

PUNT RETURNS

Last Name	No.	Yds	Avg	TD
Williams	30	267	8.9	0
Edwards	7	64	9.1	0

KICKOFF RETURNS

Last Name	No.	Yds	Avg	TD
Higgs	16	293	18.3	0
Williams	14	249	17.8	0
Sherman	13	222	17.1	0
Edwards	3	23	7.7	0
Little	2	14	7.0	0
Byars	1	27	27.0	0

PASSING—PUNTING—KICKING

PASSING	Att	Cmp	%	Yds	Yd/Att	TD	Int—	%	RK
Cunningham	532	290	54.5	3400	6.39	21	15—	2.8	8
Cavanaugh	5	3	60.0	33	6.60	1	1—	20.0	
Ruzek	1	1	100.0	22	22.00	1	0—	0.0	

PUNTING	No.	Avg.
Teltschik	57	39.4
Cunningham	6	53.2
Tuten	7	36.6
Runager	17	33.4

KICKING	XP	ATT	%	FG	ATT	%
Zendejas	33	33	100	14	24	58
DeLine	3	3	100	3	7	43

WASHINGTON REDSKINS

RUSHING

Last Name	No.	Yds	Avg	TD
Riggs	201	834	4.1	4
Byner	134	580	4.3	7
Morris	124	336	2.7	2
Rypien	26	56	2.2	1
Clark	2	19	9.5	0
Sanders	4	19	4.8	0
Humphries	5	10	2.0	0
Monk	3	8	2.7	0
Coleman	1	-1	-1.0	0
Williams	1	-4	-4.0	0

RECEIVING

Last Name	No.	Yds	Avg	TD
Monk	86	1186	13.8	8
Sanders	80	1138	14.2	4
Clark	79	1229	15.6	9
Byner	54	458	8.5	2
Warren	15	167	11.1	1
Morris	8	65	8.1	0
Riggs	7	67	9.6	0
J. Johnson	4	84	21.0	0
Orr	3	80	26.7	0
Tice	1	2	2.0	0

PUNT RETURNS

Last Name	No.	Yds	Avg	TD
Howard	21	200	9.5	0
Sanders	2	12	6.0	0
Green	1	11	11.0	0
B. Davis	1	3	3.0	0
Mayhew	1	0	0.0	0

KICKOFF RETURNS

Last Name	No.	Yds	Avg	TD
Howard	21	522	24.9	1
A. Johnson	24	504	21.0	0
Sanders	9	134	14.9	0
Mandeville	1	10	10.0	0
Branch	1	6	6.0	0
Gouveia	1	0	0.0	0
Orr	1	0	0.0	0

PASSING—PUNTING—KICKING

PASSING	Att	Cmp	%	Yds	Yd/Att	TD	Int—	%	RK
Rypien	476	280	58.8	3768	7.92	22	13—	2.7	3
Williams	93	51	54.8	585	6.29	1	3—	3.2	
Humphries	10	5	50.0	91	9.10	1	1—	10.0	
Sanders	1	1	100.0	32	32.00	0	0—	0.0	
Byner	1	0	0.0	0	0.00	0	0—	0.0	

PUNTING	No.	Avg.
Mojsiejenko	63	42.3

KICKING	XP	ATT	%	FG	ATT	%
Lohmiller	41	41	100	29	40	73

PHOENIX CARDINALS

RUSHING

Last Name	No.	Yds	Avg	TD
Ferrell	149	502	3.4	6
Jordan	83	211	2.5	2
S. Mitchell	43	165	3.8	0
Sikahema	38	145	3.8	0
Clark	20	99	5.0	0
Hogeboom	27	89	3.3	1
Tupa	15	75	5.0	0
Wolfley	13	36	2.8	1
Baker	20	31	1.6	0
Rosenbach	6	26	4.3	0
J.T. Smith	2	21	10.5	0
Jones	1	18	18.0	0

RECEIVING

Last Name	No.	Yds	Avg	TD
J. Smith	62	778	12.5	5
Jones	45	838	18.6	3
Green	44	703	16.0	7
Awalt	33	360	10.9	0
Sikahema	23	245	10.7	0
Novacek	23	225	9.8	1
Ferrell	18	122	6.8	0
Holmes	13	271	20.8	1
Jordan	6	20	3.3	0
Wolfley	5	38	7.6	0
Baker	2	18	9.0	0
McConkey	2	18	9.0	0
S. Mitchell	1	10	10.0	0
Usher	1	8	8.0	0
Reeves	1	5	5.0	0

PUNT RETURNS

Last Name	No.	Yds	Avg	TD
Sikahema	37	433	11.7	0
McConkey	15	124	8.3	0
Usher	4	25	6.3	0
Jones	1	13	13.0	0

KICKOFF RETURNS

Last Name	No.	Yds	Avg	TD
Sikahema	43	874	20.3	0
Usher	27	506	18.7	0
Baker	11	245	22.3	0
Jones	7	124	17.7	0
McConkey	2	40	20.0	0
Carr	1	15	15.0	0
Reeves	1	5	5.0	0
Clark	2	6	3.0	0

PASSING—PUNTING—KICKING

PASSING	Att	Cmp	%	Yds	Yd/Att	TD	Int—	%	RK
Hogeboom	364	204	56.0	2591	7.12	14	19—	5.2	10
Tupa	134	65	48.5	973	7.26	3	9—	6.7	
Rosenbach	22	9	40.9	95	4.32	0	1—	4.5	
Camarillo	1	1	100.0	0	0.00	0	0—	0.0	
Sikahema	1	0	0.0	0	0.00	0	0—	0.0	
Awalt	1	0	0.0	0	0.00	0	1—	100.0	

PUNTING	No.	Avg.
Camarillo	76	43.4
Tupa	6	46.7

KICKING	XP	Att	%	FG	Att	%
Del Greco	28	29	97	18	26	69

DALLAS COWBOYS

RUSHING

Last Name	No.	Yds	Avg	TD
Palmer	112	446	4.0	2
Aikman	38	302	7.9	0
Johnston	67	212	3.2	0
Sargent	20	87	4.4	1
Clack	14	40	2.9	2
Dixon	3	30	10.0	0
Walsh	6	16	2.7	0
Tautalatasi	6	15	2.5	0
Shepard	3,	12	4.0	0
Irvin	1	6	6.0	0
Saxon	1	1	1.0	0
Bates	1	0	0.0	0
Scott	2	-4	-2.0	0

RECEIVING

Last Name	No.	Yds	Avg	TD
Martin	46	644	14.0	2
Folsom	28	265	9.5	2
Irvin	26	378	14.5	2
Dixon	24	477	19.9	2
Shepard	20	304	15.2	1
Tautalatasi	17	157	9.2	0
Burbage	17	134	7.9	0
Palmer	17	93	5.5	0
Johnston	16	133	8.3	3
Scott	9	63	7.0	0
Ford	7	78	11.1	1
Sargent	6	50	8.3	0
Jennings	6	47	7.8	0
Clack	4	69	17.3	0
Alexander	1	16	16.0	0
Ruzek	1	4	4.0	0
Aikman	1	-13	-13.0	0

PUNT RETURNS

Last Name	No.	Yds	Avg	TD
Shepard	31	251	8.1	1
Martin	4	32	8.0	0
Burbage	3	5	1.7	0

KICKOFF RETURNS

Last Name	No.	Yds	Avg	TD
Dixon	47	1181	25.1	1
Shepard	27	529	19.6	0
Clack	3	56	18.7	0
Burbage	3	55	18.3	0
Ankrom	2	6	3.0	0
Tautalatasi	1	9	9.0	0
Chandler	1	8	8.0	0
Sargent	1	0	0.0	0

PASSING—PUNTING—KICKING

PASSING	Att	Cmp	%	Yds	Yd/Att	TD	Int—	%	RK
Aikman	293	155	52.9	1749	5.97	9	18—	6.1	14
Walsh	219	110	50.2	1371	6.26	5	9—	4.1	
Saxon	1	1	100.0	4	4.00	0	0—	0.0	

PUNTING	No.	Avg.
Saxon	81	39.9
Ruzek	1	28.0

KICKING	XP	Att.	%	FG	Att	%
Ruzek	28	29	97	13	22	59

MINNESOTA VIKINGS 10-6 Jerry Burns

Scores of Each Game		
38	HOUSTON	7
7	Chicago	38
14	Pittsburgh	27
17	TAMPA BAY	3
24	DETROIT	17
26	GREEN BAY	14
20	Detroit	7
14	N.Y. Giants	24
23	L.A. RAMS	* 21
24	Tampa Bay	10
9	Philadelphia	10
19	Green Bay (Mil.)	20
27	CHICAGO	16
43	ATLANTA	17
17	Cleveland	* 23
29	CINCINNATI	21

Use Name	Pos.	Hgt	Wgt	Age	Int	Pts
Brian Habib	OT	6'7"	282	24		
Tim Irwin	OT	6'6"	285	30		
Gary Zimmerman	OT	6'6"	286	27		
Dave Huffman	OG	6'6"	284	33		
Todd Kalis	OG	6'5"	284	24		
Randall McDaniel	OG	6'3"	271	24		
John Adickes	C	6'3"	264	25		
Chris Foote	C	6'3"	255	32		
Kirk Lowdermilk	C	6'3"	267	26		
Mark Rodenhauser	C	6'5"	262	28		
Chris Doleman	DE	6'5"	262	27		
Doug Martin	DE	6'3"	258	32		
Al Noga	DE	6'1"	248	22		
Thomas Strauthers	DE	6'4"	262	28		
Ken Clarke	DT	6'2"	281	33		
Keith Millard	DT	6'5"	262	27	1	6
Tim Newton	DT	6'	277	26		6
Henry Thomas	DT	6'2"	267	24		6

Randy Rasmussen — Back Injury

Use Name	Pos.	Hgt	Wgt	Age	Int	Pts
Ray Berry	LB	6'2"	225	25		2
David Braxton	LB	6'1"	232	24		
Mark Dusbabek	LB	6'3"	230	25	1	
John Galvin	LB	6'3"	226	24		
Mike Merriweather	LB	6'2"	222	28	3	8
Scott Studwell	LB	6'2"	228	35	1	
Michael Brim (from DET)	DB	6'	186	23		
Joey Browner	DB	6'2"	210	29	5	
Travis Curtis	DB	5'10"	183	23		
Brad Edwards	DB	6'1"	200	23	1	
Darrell Fullington	DB	6'1"	197	25	1	
Ken Johnson	DB	6'2"	197	22		
Carl Lee	DB	6'	183	28	2	
Audrey McMillian	DB	6'	189	27		
Reggie Rutland	DB	6'1"	194	25	2	6
Daryl Smith	DB	5'9"	185	26		

Use Name	Pos.	Hgt	Wgt	Age	Int	Pts
Rich Gannon	QB	6'3"	199	23		
Tommy Kramer	QB	6'2"	202	34		
Wade Wilson	QB	6'3"	208	30		6
D.J. Dozier	HB	6'	198	23		
Allen Rice	HB	5'10"	204	26		36
Herschel Walker (from DAL)	HB-FB	6'1"	226	27		60
Alfred Anderson	FB-HB	6'1"	223	27		12
Rick Bayless	FB	6'	202	24		
Rick Fenney	FB	6'1"	232	24		36
Anthony Carter	WR	5'11"	177	28		24
Jim Gustafson	WR	6'1"	174	28		12
Hassan Jones	WR	6'	192	25		6
Leo Lewis	WR	5'8"	172	32		6
Carl Hilton	TE	6'3"	230	25		
Darryl Ingram	TE	6'2"	230	23		6
Steve Jordan	TE	6'4"	239	28		18
Brent Novoselsky	TE	6'3"	232	23		12
Teddy Garcia	K	5'10"	190	25		11
Rich Karlis	K	6'	180	30		120
Bucky Scribner	K	6'	213	29		

GREEN BAY PACKERS 10-6 Lindy Infante

Scores of Each Game		
21	TAMPA BAY	23
35	NEW ORLEANS	34
38	L.A. Rams	41
23	ATLANTA (Mil.)	21
31	DALLAS	13
14	Minnesota	26
20	Miami	23
23	DETROIT (Mil.)	* 20
14	CHICAGO	13
22	Detroit	31
21	San Francisco	17
20	MINNESOTA (Mil.)	19
17	Tampa Bay	16
3	KANSAS CITY	21
40	Chicago	28
20	Dallas	10

Use Name	Pos.	Hgt	Wgt	Age	Int	Pts
Mike Ariey	OT	6'5"	285	25		
Tony Mandarich	OT	6'5"	300	22		
Ken Ruettgers	OT	6'5"	280	27		
Alan Veingrad	OT	6'5"	277	26		
Billy Ard	OG	6'3"	270	30		
Ron Hallstrom	OG	6'6"	290	30		
Rich Moran	OG	6'3"	275	27		
Blair Bush	C	6'3"	272	32		
James Campen	C-OG	6'3"	270	25		
Matt Brock	DE	6'5"	267	23		
Robert Brown	DE	6'2"	267	29		
Mark Hall	DE	6'4"	285	23		
Shawn Patterson	DE	6'5"	261	24		
Blaise Winter	DE-NT	6'3"	275	27		
Jerry Boyarsky	NT	6'3"	290	30		
Bob Nelson	NT	6'4"	275	30		

Dave Croston — Shoulder Injury
Keith Uecker — Knee Injury

Use Name	Pos.	Hgt	Wgt	Age	Int	Pts
John Anderson	LB	6'3"	228	33	1	
Burnell Dent	LB	6'1"	236	26	1	
Tim Harris	LB	6'5"	235	24		
Johnny Holland	LB	6'2"	221	24	1	
Brian Noble	LB	6'3"	252	26		
Scott Stephen	LB	6'2"	232	25	2	
Mike Weddington	LB	6'4"	245	28		
Dave Brown	DB	6'1"	187	36	6	
Chuck Cecil	DB	6'	184	24	1	
Tiger Greene	DB	6'	194	27	1	
Van Jakes	DB	6'	190	28	1	
Mark Lee	DB	5'11"	189	31	2	
Michael McGruder	DB	5'11"	180	27		
Mark Murphy	DB	6'2"	201	31	3	
Ron Pitts	DB	5'10"	175	26	1	
Ken Stills	DB	5'10"	186	25	3	

John Dorsey — Knee Injury

Use Name	Pos.	Hgt	Wgt	Age	Int	Pts
Anthony Dilweg	QB	6'3"	215	24		
Blair Kiel	QB	6'	214	27		
Don Majkowski	QB	6'2"	197	25		30
Herman Fontenot	HB	6'	206	25		24
Keith Woodside	HB	5'11"	203	25		6
Vince Workman	HB	5'10	193	21		6
Michael Haddix	FB	6'2"	227	27		6
Brent Fullwood	FB-HB	5'11"	209	25		30
Carl Bland	WR	5'11"	182	27		12
Perry Kemp	WR	5'11"	170	27		12
Aubrey Matthews	WR	5'7"	165	26		
Jeff Query	WR	6'	165	22		12
Sterling Sharpe	WR	5'11"	202	24		78
Clint Didier	TE	6'5"	240	30		6
John Spagnola	TE	6'4"	242	32		
Ed West	TE	6'1"	243	28		30
Don Bracken	K	6'1"	211	27		
Chris Jacke	K	6'	197	23		108

DETROIT LIONS 7-9 Wayne Fontes

Scores of Each Game		
13	PHOENIX	16
14	N.Y. Giants	24
27	CHICAGO	47
3	PITTSBURGH	23
17	Minnesota	24
17	Tampa Bay	16
7	MINNESOTA	20
20	Green Bay (Mil.)	* 23
31	Houston	35
31	GREEN BAY	22
7	Cincinnati	42
13	CLEVELAND	10
21	NEW ORLEANS	14
27	Chicago	17
33	TAMPA BAY	7
31	Atlanta	24

Use Name	Pos.	Hgt	Wgt	Age	Int	Pts
Lomas Brown	OT	6'4"	275	26		
Chris Gambol	OT	6'6"	303	24		
Harvey Salem	OT	6'6"	285	28		
Eric Sanders	OT-OG	6'7"	280	30		
Eric Andolsek	OG	6'2"	277	23		
Ken Dallafior	OG-C	6'4"	279	30		
Kevin Glover	OG-C	6'2"	275	26		
Joe Milinichik	OG-OT	6'5"	275	26		
Mike Utley	OG-OT	6'6"	288	23		
Trevor Matich	C	6'4"	270	27		
Keith Ferguson	DE	6'5"	260	30		
Curtis Green	DE-NT	6'3"	265	32		
James Cribbs	DE	6'3"	269	23		
Byron Darby	DE	6'4"	260	29		
Eric Williams	DE	6'4"	286	27		
Kevin Brooks	DT-DE	6'6"	278	26		
Jerry Ball	NT	6'1"	298	24		
Lawrence Pete	NT	6'	282	23		

Steve Mott — Neck Injury

Use Name	Pos.	Hgt	Wgt	Age	Int	Pts
Mark Brown	LB	6'2"	240	27		
Toby Caston	LB	6'1"	243	24		
Mike Cofer	LB	6'5"	245	29		
Dennis Gibson	LB	6'2"	240	25	1	
George Jamison	LB	6'1"	226	26		
Victor Jones	LB	6'2"	240	22		
Keith Karpinski	LB	6'3"	225	22		
Niko Noga	LB	6'1"	235	27	1	
Chris Spielman	LB	6'	247	28		
Jimmy Williams	LB	6'3"	230	28	5	
Bruce Alexander	DB	5'9"	169	23		
Bennie Blades	DB	6'1"	221	22		
Ray Crockett	DB	5'9"	181	22	1	
James Griffin	DB	6'2"	203	27		
Jerry Holmes	DB	6'2"	175	31	6	6
Bruce McNorton	DB	5'11"	175	30		
John Miller	DB	6'1"	195	23		
Terry Taylor	DB	5'10"	191	28	1	
William White	DB	5'10"	191	23	1	6
Jerry Woods	DB	5'10"	187	23		

Use Name	Pos.	Hgt	Wgt	Age	Int	Pts
Bob Gagliano	QB	6'3"	196	30		24
Eric Hipple	QB	6'2"	198	31		6
Chuck Long	QB	6'4"	221	26		
Rodney Peete	QB	6'	193	23		24
Carl Painter	HB	5'9"	185	25		
Barry Sanders	HB-FB	5'8"	203	21		84
Tony Paige	FB	5'10"	235	26		
Robert Clark	WR	5'11"	173	24		12
John Ford	WR	6'2"	204	23		
Mel Gray	WR	5'9"	162	28		
Richard Johnson	WR	5'7"	185	27		48
Troy Johnson	WR	6'1"	185	26		
Keith McDonald	WR	5'9"	159	25		
Stacey Mobley	WR	5'8"	165	23		
Jason Phillips	WR	5'7"	168	22		6
Walter Stanley	WR	5'9"	180	26		
Mike Williams	WR	5'10"	177	22		
Jim Arnold	K	6'3"	211	28		
Eddie Murray	K	5'10"	180	33		96

CHICAGO BEARS 6-10 Mike Ditka

Scores of Each Game		
17	CINCINNATI	14
38	MINNESOTA	7
47	Detroit	27
27	PHILADELPHIA	13
35	Tampa Bay	42
28	HOUSTON	33
7	Cleveland	27
20	L.A. RAMS	10
13	Green Bay	14
20	Pittsburgh	0
31	TAMPA BAY	32
14	Washington	38
16	Minnesota	27
17	DETROIT	27
28	GREEN BAY	40
0	San Francisco	26

Use Name	Pos.	Hgt	Wgt	Age	Int	Pts
Jim Covert	OT	6'4"	278	29		
Chris Dyko	OT	6'6"	295	23		
Keith Van Horne	OT	6'6"	283	31		
John Wojciechowski	OT	6'4"	270	26		
Dave Zawatson	OT	6'4"	274	23		
Mark Bortz	OG	6'6"	272	28		
Jerry Fontenot	OG	6'3"	272	22		
Tom Thayer	OG	6'4"	270	28		
Jay Hilgenberg	C	6'3"	260	29		
Trace Armstrong	DE	6'4"	259	23		
Richard Dent	DE	6'5"	268	28	1	
Tony Woods	DE-DT	6'4"	274	23		
William Perry	DT	6'2"	320	26		
Dick Chapura	DT	6'3"	275	25		
Dan Hampton	DT	6'5"	274	31		
Steve McMichael	DT	6'2"	268	31		
John Shannon	DT-DE	6'3"	269	24		

Use Name	Pos.	Hgt	Wgt	Age	Int	Pts
LaSalle Harper (from NYG)	LB	6'	226	22		
Steve Hyche	LB	6'3"	236	26		
Troy Johnson	LB	6'	236	24		
Dante Jones	LB	6'1"	236	24		
Jim Morrissey	LB	6'3"	227	26	2	
Mickey Pruitt	LB	6'1"	206	24		
Ron Rivera	LB	6'3"	240	27	2	
John Roper	LB	6'1"	228	23	2	
Mike Singletary	LB	6'	230	30		
Maurice Douglass	DB	5'11"	200	25	1	
Dave Duerson	DB	6'1"	212	28	1	
Shaun Gayle	DB	5'11"	194	27	3	
Vestee Jackson	DB	6'	186	26	2	
Lorenzo Lynch	DB	5'9"	199	26	3	
Markus Paul	DB	6'2"	199	23	1	
Lemuel Stinson	DB	5'9"	159	23	4	6
George Streeter	DB	6'2"	212	22		
David Tate	DB	6'	177	24	1	
Donnell Woolford	DB	5'9"	187	23	3	

Use Name	Pos.	Hgt	Wgt	Age	Int	Pts
Jim Harbaugh	QB	6'3"	204	25		18
Mike Tomczak	QB	6'1"	198	26		6
Neal Anderson	HB	5'11"	210	25		90
Mark Green	HB	5'11"	184	22		6
Thomas Sanders	HB	5'11"	203	27		12
Brian Taylor	HB	5'10"	175	22		
Brad Muster	FB	6'3"	231	24		48
Matt Suhey	FB	5'11"	213	31		12
Wendell Davis	WR	5'11"	188	23		18
Dennis Gentry	WR-HB	5'8"	180	30		6
Glen Kozlowski	WR	6'1"	205	26		
Dennis McKinnon	WR	6'1"	177	28		18
Ron Morris	WR	6'1"	195	24		6
Tom Waddle	WR	6'	181	22		
Cap Boso	TE	6'3"	240	25		6
Jim Thornton	TE	6'2"	242	24		18
Maury Buford	K	6'1"	198	29		
Kevin Butler	K	6'1"	204	27		88

TAMPA BAY BUCCANEERS 5-11 Ray Perkins

Scores of Each Game		
23	Green Bay	21
16	SAN FRANCISCO	20
20	NEW ORLEANS	10
3	Minnesota	17
42	CHICAGO	35
16	DETROIT	17
28	Washington	32
23	Cincinnati	56
31	CLEVELAND	42
10	MINNESOTA	24
32	Chicago	31
14	Phoenix	13
16	GREEN BAY	17
17	Houston	20
7	Detroit	33
22	PITTSBURGH	31

Use Name	Pos.	Hgt	Wgt	Age	Int	Pts
Paul Gruber	OT	6'5"	290	24		
Rob Taylor	OT	6'6"	295	28		
Harry Swayne	OT	6'5"	270	24		
Carl Bax	OG-OT	6'4"	290	23		
John Bruhin	OG	6'3"	280	24		
Sam Anno	C	62"	235	24		
Mark Cooper	OG-OT	6'5"	280	29		
Byron Ingram	OG	6'2"	295	24		
Tom McHale	OG	6'4"	275	26		
Mike Simmonds	OG	6'4"	285	25		
Dan Graham	C	6'2"	270	24		
Randy Grimes	C	6'4"	275	29		
John Cannon	DE	6'5"	260	29		
Reuben Davis	DE	6'4"	290	24	1	6
Robert Goff	DE	6'3"	270	23		
Rhondy Weston	DE	6'5"	275	23		
Curt Jarvis	NT	6'2"	265	24		
Shawn Lee	NT	6'2"	290	22		
Ray Seals	NT	6'3"	270	24		

Use Name	Pos.	Hgt	Wgt	Age	Int	Pts
Sam Anno	LB	6'2"	235	24		
Sidney Coleman	LB	6'2"	250	25		
Eugene Marve	LB	6'2"	240	29		
Winston Moss	LB	6'3"	235	23		
Kevin Murphy	LB	6'2"	235	25		
Peter Najarian	LB	6'2"	230	25		
Ervin Randle	LB	6'1"	250	26		
Henry Rolling	LB	6'2"	225	23		
Broderick Thomas	LB-DE	6'4"	245	22		
Sherman Cocroft	DB	6'1"	205	28		2
Donnie Elder	DB	5'9"	175	25	1	
Bobby Futrell	DB	5'11"	190	27	1	
Harry Hamilton	DB	6'	195	26	6	
Odie Harris	DB	6'	190	23	1	
Rod Jones	DB	6'	185	25		
Ricky Reynolds	DB	5'11"	190	24	5	12
Mark Robinson	DB	5'11"	200	26	6	

Use Name	Pos.	Hgt	Wgt	Age	Int	Pts
Kerwin Bell	QB	6'3"	205	24		
Joe Ferguson	QB	6'1"	190	39		
Vinny Testaverde	QB	6'5"	215	25		
Don Smith	HB-WR	5'11"	195	25		
Sylvester Stamps	HB	5'7"	180	28		6
Lars Tate	HB	6'2"	215	23		54
Jamie Lawson	FB	5'10"	240	23		
Alvin Mitchell	FB	6'	235	25		
William Howard	FB-HB	6'	240	25		12
James Wilder	FB-HB	6'3"	225	31		18
Mark Carrier	WR	6'	185	23		54
Willie Drewrey	WR	5'7"	170	26		6
Everett Gay	WR	6'2"	209	24		
Bruce Hill	WR	6'	180	25		30
Danny Peebles	WR	5'11"	180	23		
Frank Pillow	WR	5'10"	170	24		
Ron Hall	TE	6'4"	245	25		12
William Harris	TE	6'4"	235	24		6
Jackie Walker	TE	6'5"	255	26		
John Carney	K	5'11"	160	25		
Donald Igwebuike	K	5'9"	175	28		99
Chris Mohr	K	6'4"	220	23		1

MINNESOTA VIKINGS

RUSHING

Last Name	No.	Yds	Avg	TD
Walker	250	915	3.7	7
Fenney	151	588	3.9	4
Dozier	46	207	4.5	0
Anderson	52	189	3.6	2
Wilson	32	132	4.1	1
Jones	1	37	37.0	0
Rice	6	25	4.3	0
Carter	3	18	6.0	0
Lewis	1	11	11.0	0
Kramer	12	9	0.8	0

RECEIVING

Last Name	No.	Yds	Avg	TD
Carter	65	1066	16.4	4
Jones	42	694	16.5	1
Walker	40	423	10.6	2
Jordan	35	506	14.5	3
Fenney	30	254	8.5	2
Anderson	20	193	9.7	0
Dozier	14	148	10.6	0
Gustafson	14	144	10.3	2
Lewis	12	148	12.3	1

PUNT RETURNS

Last Name	No.	Yds	Avg	TD
Lewis	44	446	10.1	0
Carter	1	2	2.0	0

KICKOFF RETURNS

Last Name	No.	Yds	Avg	TD
Walker	13	374	28.8	1
Dozier	12	258	21.5	0
Anderson	5	75	15.0	0
Lewis	2	30	15.0	0
Carter	1	19	19.0	0
Curtis	1	18	18.0	0
Rice	1	13	13.0	0
Fenney	1	12	12.0	0

PASSING — PUNTING — KICKING

PASSING	Att	Cmp	%	Yds	Yd/Att	TD	Int— %	RK
Wilson	362	194	53.6	2543	7.02	9	12—3.3	9
Kramer	136	77	56.6	906	6.66	7	7—5.1	
Dozier	1	1	100.0	19	19.00	1	0—0.0	

PUNTING	No.	Avg.
Scribner	72	39.8

KICKING	XP	ATT	%	FG	ATT	%
Garcia	8	8	100	1	5	20
Karlis	27	28	96	31	39	79

GREEN BAY PACKERS

RUSHING

Last Name	No.	Yds	Avg	TD
Fullwood	204	821	4.0	5
Majkowski	75	358	4.8	5
Woodside	46	273	5.9	1
Haddix	44	135	3.1	0
Fontenot	17	69	4.1	1
Kemp	5	43	8.6	0
Sharpe	2	25	12.5	0
Workman	4	8	2.0	1

RECEIVING

Last Name	No.	Yds	Avg	TD
Sharpe	90	1423	15.8	12
Woodside	59	527	8.9	0
Kemp	48	611	12.7	2
Fontenot	40	372	9.3	3
Query	23	350	15.2	2
West	22	269	12.2	5
Fullwood	19	214	11.3	0
Matthews	18	200	11.1	0
Haddix	15	111	7.4	1
Bland	11	164	14.9	1
Didier	7	71	10.1	1
Spagnola	2	13	6.5	0

PUNT RETURNS

Last Name	No.	Yds	Avg	TD
Query	30	247	8.2	0

KICKOFF RETURNS

Last Name	No.	Yds	Avg	TD
Workman	33	547	16.6	0
Bland	13	256	19.7	0
Fullwood	11	243	22.1	0
Query	6	125	20.8	0
Woodside	2	38	19.0	0
Fontenot	2	30	15.0	0
Didier	1	0	0.0	0
Mandarich	1	0	0.0	0

PASSING — PUNTING — KICKING

PASSING	Att	Cmp	%	Yds	Yd/Att	TD	Int— %	RK
Majkowski	599	353	58.9	4318	7.21	27	20—3.3	5
Dilweg	1	1	100.0	7	7.00	0	0—0.0	

PUNTING	No.	Avg.
Bracken	66	40.6

KICKING	XP	Att.	%	FG	Att	%
Jacke	42	42	100	22	28	79

DETROIT LIONS

RUSHING

Last Name	No.	Yds	Avg	TD
B. Sanders	280	1470	5.3	14
Gagliano	41	192	4.7	4
Peete	33	148	4.5	4
Paige	3-	105	3.5	0
Painter	15	64	4.3	0
R. Johnson	12	38	3.2	0
Gray	3	22	7.3	0
Hipple	2	11	5.5	1
L. Brown	1	3	3.0	0
Long	3	2	0.7	0
McDonald	1	-2	-2.0	0

RECEIVING

Last Name	No.	Yds	Avg	TD
R. Johnson	70	1091	15.6	8
Clark	41	748	18.2	2
Phillips	30	352	11.7	1
Stanley	24	304	12.7	0
B. Sanders	24	282	11.8	0
Mobley	13	158	12.2	0
McDonald	12	138	11.5	0
Ford	5	56	11.2	0
Painter	3	41	13.7	0
Gray	2	47	23.5	0
T. Johnson	2	29	13.5	0
Paige	2	27	13.5	0

PUNT RETURNS

Last Name	No.	Yds	Avg	TD
Stanley	36	496	13.8	0
Gray	11	76	6.9	0
Woods	0	0	0.0	0
Miller	0	0	0.0	0

KICKOFF RETURNS

Last Name	No.	Yds	Avg	TD
Gray	24	640	26.7	0
Palmer	11	255	23.2	0
Stanley	9	95	10.6	0
B. Sanders	5	118	23.6	0
Alexander	5	100	20.0	0
Woods	2	28	14.0	0
Dallafior	2	13	6.5	0
Painter	1	14	14.0	0
Crockett	1	8	8.0	0

PASSING — PUNTING — KICKING

PASSING	Att	Cmp	%	Yds	Yd/Att	TD	Int— %	RK
Gagliano	232	117	50.4	1671	7.20	6	12—5.2	13
Peete	195	103	52.8	1479	7.58	5	9—4.6	
Hipple	18	7	38.9	90	5.00	0	0—16.7	
Long	5	2	40.0	42	8.40	0	0—0.0	

PUNTING	No.	Avg.
Arnold	83	42.6

KICKING	XP	Att	%	FG	Att	%
Murray	36	36	100	20	21	95

CHICAGO BEARS

RUSHING

Last Name	No.	Yds	Avg	TD
Anderson	274	1275	4.7	11
Muster	82	327	4.0	5
Harbaugh	45	276	6.1	3
Sanders	41	127	3.1	0
Gentry	17	106	6.2	0
Tomczak	24	71	3.0	1
Suhey	20	51	2.6	1
Green	5	46	9.2	1
Taylor	2	7	3.5	0
Buford	1	6	6.0	0
McKinnon	3	5	1.7	0
Thornton	1	4	4.0	0
Morris	1	-14	-14.0	0

RECEIVING

Last Name	No.	Yds	Avg	TD
Anderson	50	434	8.7	4
Gentry	39	463	11.9	1
Muster	32	259	8.1	3
Morris	30	486	16.2	1
McKinnon	28	418	14.9	3
Davis	26	397	15.3	3
Thornton	24	392	16.3	3
Boso	17	182	10.7	1
Suhey	9	73	8.1	1
Green	5	48	9.6	0
Kozlowski	3	74	24.7	0
Sanders	3	28	9.3	1
Waddle	1	8	8.0	

PUNT RETURNS

Last Name	No.	Yds	Avg	TD
Green	16	141	8.8	0
McKinnon	10	67	6.7	0
Kozlowski	4	-2	-0.5	0
Woolford	1	12	12.0	0
Waddle	1	2	2.0	0

KICKOFF RETURNS

Last Name	No.	Yds	Avg	TD
Gentry	28	667	23.8	0
Sanders	23	491	21.3	1
Green	11	239	21.7	0
Suhey	6	93	15.5	0
Pruitt	2	17	8.5	0
Kozlowski	1	12	12.0	0
Tate	1	12	12.0	0
Chapura	1	8	8.0	0

PASSING — PUNTING — KICKING

PASSING	Att	Cmp	%	Yds	Yd/Att	TD	Int— %	RK
Tomczak	306	156	51.0	2058	6.73	16	16—5.2	12
Harbaugh	178	111	62.4	1204	6.76	5	9—5.1	

PUNTING	No.	Avg.
Buford	72	39.5

KICKING	XP	ATT	%	FG	ATT	%
Butler	43	45	96	15	19	79

TAMPA BAY BUCCANEERS

RUSHING

Last Name	No.	Yds	Avg	TD
Tate	167	589	3.5	8
Howard	108	357	3.3	1
Wilder	70	244	3.5	0
Stamps	29	141	4.9	1
Testaverde	25	139	5.6	0
D. Smith	7	37	5.3	0
Ferguson	4	6	1.5	0
Peebles	2	-6	-3.0	0

RECEIVING

Last Name	No.	Yds	Avg	TD
Carrier	86	1422	16.5	9
Hill	50	673	13.5	5
Wilder	36	335	9.3	3
Hall	30	331	11.0	2
Howard	30	188	6.3	1
Stamps	15	82	5.5	0
Drewrey	14	157	11.2	1
Peebles	11	180	16.4	0
W. Harris	11	102	9.3	1
Tate	11	75	6.8	1
D. Smith	7	110	15.7	0
Mitchell	1	11	11.0	0

PUNT RETURNS

Last Name	No.	Yds	Avg	TD
Drewrey	20	220	11.0	0
Futrell	12	76	6.3	0

KICKOFF RETURNS

Last Name	No.	Yds	Avg	TD
Elder	40	685	17.1	0
Stamps	9	145	16.1	0
Howard	5	82	16.4	0
Futrell	4	58	14.5	0
Wilder	2	42	21.0	0
Drewrey	1	26	26.0	0
Pillow	1	17	17.0	0

PASSING — PUNTING — KICKING

PASSING	Att	Cmp	%	Yds	Yd/Att	TD	Int— %	RK
Testaverde	480	258	53.8	3133	6.53	20	22—4.6	11
Ferguson	90	44	48.9	533	5.92	3	6—6.7	

PUNTING	No.	Avg.
Mohr	86	38.5

KICKING	XP	ATT	%	FG	ATT	%
Igwebuike	33	35	94	22	28	79
Mohr	1	1	100	0	0	0

SAN FRANCISCO 49ERS 14-2 George Seifert

Scores of Each Game		
30	Indianapolis	24
20	Tampa Bay	16
38	Philadelphia	28
12	L.A. RAMS	13
24	New Orleans	20
31	Dallas	14
37	NEW ENGLAND	20
23	N.Y. Jets	10
31	NEW ORLEANS	13
45	ATLANTA	3
17	GREEN BAY	21
34	N.Y. GIANTS	24
23	Atlanta	10
30	L.A. Rams	27
21	BUFFALO	10
26	CHICAGO	0

Use Name	Pos.	Hgt	Wgt	Age	Int	Pts
Harris Barton	OT-OG	6'4"	280	25		
Dave Cullity	OT	6'7"	275	25		
Bubba Paris	OT	6'6"	306	28		
Steve Wallace	OT	6'5"	276	24		
Jeff Bregel	OG	6'4"	280	25		
Bruce Collie	OG	6'6"	275	27		
Guy McIntyre	OG	6'3"	265	28		
Terry Tausch	OG	6'5"	276	30		
Jesse Sapolu	C	6'4"	260	28		
Chuck Thomas	C-OG	6'3"	280	28		
Kevin Fagan	DE	6'4"	265	26		
Pierce Holt	DE	6'4"	280	27		
Pete Kugler	DE	6'4"	255	30		
Larry Roberts	DE	6'3"	275	26		
Danny Stubbs	DE	6'4"	260	24		
Kevin Lilly (from DAL)	DT-DE	6'4"	265	26		
Jim Burt	NT	6'1"	260	30		
Michael Carter	NT-DT	6'2"	285	28		
Rollin Putzier	NT	6'4"	279	23		

Use Name	Pos.	Hgt	Wgt	Age	Int	Pts
Keith DeLong	LB	6'2"	235	22	1	
Jim Fahnhorst	LB	6'4"	230	30		
Antonio Goss	LB	6'4"	228	23		
Charles Haley	LB-DE	6'5"	230	25		6
Steve Hendrickson (to DAL)	LB	6'	245	23		
Matt Millen	LB	6'2"	245	31	1	
Bill Romanowski	LB	6'4"	231	23	1	
Keena Turner	LB	6'2"	222	30	1	
Michael Walter	LB	6'3"	238	28		
Chet Brooks	DB	5'11"	191	23	3	
Jeff Fuller	DB	6'2"	216	27		
Don Griffin	DB	6'	176	25	2	
Tom Holmoe	DB	6'2"	195	29	1	
Johnny Jackson	DB	6'1"	204	22	2	6
Ronnie Lott	DB	6'	200	30	5	
Tim McKyer	DB	6'	174	25	1	
Darryl Pollard	DB	5'11"	187	24	1	
Mike Richardson	DB	6'	188	28		
Eric Wright	DB	6'1"	185	30	2	

Riki Ellison — Knee Injury
Chris Washington — Broken Leg

Use Name	Pos.	Hgt	Wgt	Age	Int	Pts
Steve Bono	QB	6'4"	215	27		
Joe Montana	QB	6'2"	195	33		18
Steve Young	QB	6'2"	200	27		12
Roger Craig	HB-FB	6'	224	29		42
Terrence Flagler	HB	6'	200	24		6
Spencer Tillman	HB	5'11"	206	25		
Keith Henderson	FB	6'1"	220	23		6
Tom Rathman	FB	6'1"	232	26		12
Harry Sydney	FB	6'	217	30		
Mike Barber	WR	5'10"	172	22		
Terry Greer	WR	6'1"	192	31		
Jerry Rice	WR	6'2"	200	26		102
John Taylor	WR	6'1"	185	27		60
Mike Wilson	WR	6'3"	215	30		6
Brent Jones	TE	6'4"	230	26		24
Wesley Walls	TE	6'5"	246	23		6
Jamie Williams	TE	6'4"	245	29		
Mike Cofer	K	6'1"	190	25		136
Barry Helton	K	6'3"	205	24		

Mike Sherrard — Leg Injury (played in playoffs)

LOS ANGELES RAMS 11-5 John Robinson

Scores of Each Game		
31	Atlanta	21
31	INDIANAPOLIS	17
41	GREEN BAY	38
13	San Francisco	12
26	ATLANTA	14
20	Buffalo	23
21	NEW ORLEANS	40
10	Chicago	20
21	Minnesota	* 23
31	N.Y. GIANTS	10
37	PHOENIX	14
20	New Orleans	* 17
35	Dallas	31
27	SAN FRANCISCO	30
38	N.Y. JETS	14
24	New England	20

Use Name	Pos.	Hgt	Wgt	Age	Int	Pts
Robert Cox	OT	6'5"	270	25		
Irv Pankey	OT	6'4"	267	31		
Jackie Slater	OT	6'4"	275	35		
Kurt Becker	OG	6'5"	280	29		
Duval Love	OG	6'3"	280	26		
Tom Newberry	OG	6'2"	279	26		
Tony Slaton	C	6'3"	265	28		
Doug Smith	C	6'3"	260	32		
Shawn Miller	DT-NT-DE	6'4"	255	28	1	
Doug Reed	DE-DT	6'3"	250	29		
Bill Hawkins	DT	6'6"	268	23		
Mark Piel	DT	6'4"	263	23		
Sean Smith (from DAL, TB)	DT-DE	6'4"	275	24		2
Alvin Wright	NT-DE-DT	6'2"	256	28		

Use Name	Pos.	Hgt	Wgt	Age	Int	Pts
George Bethune	LB	6'4"	240	22		
Richard Brown	LB	6'3"	240	23		
Brett Faryniarz	LB	6'3"	225	24		
Kevin Greene	LB-DE	6'3"	238	27		
Mark Jerue	LB	6'3"	234	29		
Larry Kelm	LB	6'4"	226	24		
Mike McDonald	LB	6'1"	235	31		
Mark Messner	LB	6'2"	256	23		
Mel Owens	LB	6'2"	224	30	1	
Brian Smith	LB	6'6"	242	23		
Frank Stams	LB	6'2"	240	24	1	
Fred Strickland	LB	6'2"	224	23	2	
Mike Wilcher	LB	6'3"	240	29	1	
Jerry Gray	DB	6'	185	26	6	6
Darryl Henley	DB	5'9"	170	22	1	
Clifford Hicks	DB	5'10"	188	25	2	
LeRoy Irvin	DB	5'11"	184	31	3	
Alfred Jackson	DB	6'	177	22		
Anthony Newman	DB	6'	199	23		
Vince Newsome	DB	6'1"	183	28	1	6
Michael Stewart	DB	5'11"	195	24	2	6
James Washington	DB	6'1"	191	24		

Use Name	Pos.	Hgt	Wgt	Age	Int	Pts
Steve Dils	QB	6'1"	191	33		
Jim Everett	QB	6'5"	212	26		6
Mark Herrmann	QB	6'4"	186	30		
Greg Bell	HB	5'10"	210	27		90
Cleveland Gary	HB	6'	226	23		6
Gaston Green	HB	5'10"	189	23		
Robert Delpino	FB	6'	205	23		12
Mel Farr Jr.	FB	6'	223	23		
Buford McGee	FB	6'	206	29		30
Willie Anderson	WR	6'	169	24		30
Ron Brown	WR	5'11"	181	28		6
Aaron Cox	WR	5'9"	174	24		18
Henry Ellard	WR	5'11"	175	28		48
Pat Carter	TE	6'4"	250	23		
Pete Holohan	TE	6'4"	232	30		12
Damone Johnson	TE	6'4"	230	27		30
Dale Hatcher	K	6'2"	211	26		
Mike Lansford	K	6'	183	31		120

NEW ORLEANS SAINTS 9-7 Jim Mora

Scores of Each Game		
28	DALLAS	0
34	Green Bay	35
10	Tampa Bay	20
14	WASHINGTON	16
20	SAN FRANCISCO	24
29	N.Y. JETS	14
40	L.A. Rams	21
20	ATLANTA	13
13	San Francisco	31
28	New England	24
26	Atlanta	17
17	L.A. RAMS	* 20
14	Detroit	21
22	Buffalo	19
30	PHILADELPHIA	20
41	INDIANAPOLIS	6

Use Name	Pos.	Hgt	Wgt	Age	Int	Pts
Stan Brock	OT	6'6"	290	31		
Glenn Derby	OT	6'6"	290	25		
Jim Dombrowski	OT-OG	6'5"	298	26		
Kevin Haverdink	OT	6'5"	285	23		
Jeff Walker	OT	6'4"	295	26		
Brad Edelman	OG	6'6"	270	28		
Steve Trapilo	OG	6'5"	295	24		
Joel Hilgenberg	C-OG	6'3"	252	26		
Steve Korte	C	6'2"	260	29		
Doug Marrone	C-OT	6'5"	269	25		
James Geathers	DE	6'7"	290	29		
Wayne Martin	DE	6'5"	275	23		
Michael Simmons	DE	6'4"	269	23		
Frank Warren	DE	6'4"	290	29		2
Patrick Swoopes	NT	6'4"	280	25		
Jim Wilks	NT-DE	6'5"	266	31		

Use Name	Pos.	Hgt	Wgt	Age	Int	Pts
Brian Forde	LB	6'2"	225	25		2
James Haynes	LB	6'2"	233	29		
Rickey Jackson	LB	6'2"	243	31		
Vaughan Johnson	LB	6'3"	235	27		
Walter Johnson	LB	6'	240	25		
Joe Kohlbrand	LB	6'4"	242	26		
Sam Mills	LB	5'9"	225	30		
Pat Swilling	LB	6'3"	242	24	1	
Gene Atkins	DB	6'1"	200	25	1	
Toi Cook	DB	5'11"	188	24	3	6
Antonio Gibson	DB	6'3"	204	27		
Milton Mack	DB	5'11"	182	25	2	
Robert Massey	DB	5'10"	182	22	5	
Brett Maxie	DB	6'2"	194	27	3	6
Michael Mayes	DB	5'10"	182	23		
Calvin Nicholson	DB	5'9"	183	22		
Kim Phillips	DB	5'9"	188	21		
Bennie Thompson	DB	6'	200	26		
Dave Waymer	DB	6'1"	188	31	6	

Alvin Toles — Knee Injury

Use Name	Pos.	Hgt	Wgt	Age	Int	Pts
John Fourcade	QB	6'1"	208	28		6
Bobby Hebert	QB	6'4"	215	29		
Dave Wilson	QB	6'3"	206	30		
Paul Frazier	HB	5'8"	188	21		6
Dalton Hilliard	HB	5'8"	204	25		108
Craig Heyward	FB	5'11"	260	22		6
Buford Jordan	FB	6'	223	27		18
Bobby Morse	FB	5'10"	213	22		6
Rod Harris	WR	5'10"	183	22		
Lonzell Hill	WR	6'	189	23		24
Undra Johnson (to ATL)	WR	5'9"	199	23		
Mike Jones	WR	5'11"	180	29		
Eric Martin	WR	6'1"	207	27		48
Brett Perriman	WR	5'9"	175	23		
Floyd Turner	WR	5'11"	188	23		6
Hoby Brenner	TE	6'4"	240	30		24
Greg Scales	TE	6'4"	253	23		6
John Tice	TE	6'5"	249	29		6
Morten Andersen	K	6'2"	221	29		104
Tommy Barnhardt	K	6'3"	205	26		
George Winslow	K	6'4"	201	26		

Rueben Mayes — Achilles' Tendon Injury

ATLANTA FALCONS 3-13 Marion Campbell (3-9), Jim Hanifan (0-4)

Scores of Each Game		
21	L.A. RAMS	31
27	DALLAS	21
9	Indianapolis	13
21	Green Bay (Mil.)	23
14	L.A. Rams	26
16	NEW ENGLAND	15
20	Phoenix	34
13	New Orleans	20
30	BUFFALO	28
3	San Francisco	45
17	NEW ORLEANS	26
7	N.Y. Jets	27
10	SAN FRANCISCO	23
17	Minnesota	43
30	WASHINGTON	31
24	DETROIT	31

Use Name	Pos.	Hgt	Wgt	Age	Int	Pts
Houston Hoover	OT	6'2"	285	24		
John Hunter	OT	6'8"	296	24		
Mike Kenn	OT	6'7"	277	33		
* Ralph Norwood	OT	6'7"	285	23		
Stan Clayton	OG-OT	6'3"	265	24		
Bill Fralic	OG	6'5"	280	26		
Wayne Radloff	OG	6'5"	277	28		
Tommy Robison	OG	6'4"	290	27		
Guy Bingham	C-OG	6'3"	260	31		
Jamie Dukes	C	6'1"	278	25		
Rick Bryan	DE	6'4"	265	27		
Mike Gann	DE	6'5"	275	25		
Curtis Maxey	DE-DT	6'3"	298	24		
Malcolm Taylor	DE	6'6"	280	29		
Ben Thomas	DE	6'4"	275	28		
Tony Bowick	NT	6'2"	265	22		
Tony Casillas	NT	6'3"	280	25		

* died Nov. 24, 1989 in automobile accident

John Scully — Holdout

Use Name	Pos.	Hgt	Wgt	Age	Int	Pts
Aundray Bruce	LB	6'5"	245	23	1	
Marcus Cotton	LB	6'3"	225	23		
Tim Green	LB	6'2"	245	25		
John Rade	LB	6'1"	240	29		
Michael Reid	LB	6'2"	226	25		
Galand Thaxton	LB	6'1"	242	24		
Jessie Tuggle	LB	5'11"	225	24		
Joel Williams	LB	6'1"	227	32		
Bobby Butler	DB	5'11"	175	30		6
Scott Case	DB	6'	178	27	2	
Evan Cooper	DB	5'11"	194	27	4	
Charles Dimry	DB	6'	175	23	2	
Tim Gordon	DB	6'	188	24	4	
Brian Jordan	DB	5'11"	202	22		
Robert Moore	DB	5'11"	190	25		
Deion Sanders	DB	6'	187	22	5	6
Elbert Shelley	DB	5'11"	180	24	1	
Tony Zackery	DB	6'2"	195	22	1	

Use Name	Pos.	Hgt	Wgt	Age	Int	Pts
Scott Campbell	QB	6'	195	27		
Hugh Millen	QB	6'5"	216	25		
Chris Miller	QB	6'2"	195	23		3
Kenny Flowers	HB	6'	210	25		6
Keith Jones	HB-FB	6'1"	210	23		36
Gene Lang	HB	5'10"	206	27		12
James Primus	HB	5'11"	196	25		
John Settle	HB-FB	5'9"	207	24		30
Greg Paterra	FB	5'11"	211	22		
Stacey Bailey	WR	6'	157	29		
Shawn Collins	WR	6'2"	207	22		18
Floyd Dixon	WR	5'9"	170	25		12
Michael Haynes	WR	6'	180	23		24
George Thomas	WR	5'9"	169	25		
* Brad Beckman	TE	6'3"	240	24		6
Ron Heller	TE	6'3"	238	25		6
Gary Wilkins	TE	6'1"	235	25		18
Scott Fulhage	K	5'11"	193	27		
Paul McFadden	K	5'11"	166	27		63

Rick Donnelly — Back Injury
Alex Higdon — Knee Injury

* died Dec. 18, 1989 in autmobile accident

SAN FRANCISCO 49ERS

RUSHING

LastName	No.	Yds	Avg	TD
Craig	271	1054	3.9	6
Rathman	79	305	3.9	1
Montana	49	227	4.6	3
Flagler	33	129	3.9	1
Young	38	126	3.3	2
Sydney	9	56	6.2	0
Rice	5	33	6.6	0
Henderson	7	30	4.3	1
Taylor	1	6	6.0	0
Helton	1	0	0.0	0

RECEIVING

LastName	No.	Yds	Avg	TD
Rice	82	1483	18.1	17
Rathman	73	616	8.4	1
Taylor	60	1077	18.0	10
Craig	49	473	9.7	1
Jones	40	500	12.5	4
Wilson	9	103	11.4	1
Sydney	9	71	7.9	0
Flagler	6	51	8.5	0
Walls	4	16	4.0	1
Henderson	3	130	43.3	0
Williams	3	38	12.7	0
Greer	1	26	26.0	0

PUNT RETURNS

LastName	No.	Yds	Avg	TD
Taylor	36	417	11.6	0
Griffin	1	9	9.0	0
Greer	1	3	3.0	0
Romanowski	1	0	0.0	0

KICKOFF RETURNS

LastName	No.	Yds	Avg	TD
Flagler	32	643	20.1	0
Tillman	10	206	20.6	0
Sydney	3	16	5.3	0
Taylor	2	51	25.5	0
Henderson	2	21	10.5	0
Greer	1	17	17.0	0
Jackson	1	0	0.0	0

PASSING—PUNTING—KICKING

PASSING	Att	Cmp	%	Yds	Yd/Att	TD	Int—	%	RK
Montana	386	271	70.2	3521	9.12	28	8—	2.1	1
Young	92	64	69.6	1001	10.88	8	3—	3.3	
Bono	5	4	80.0	62	12.40	1	0—	0.0	

PUNTING	No.	Avg.
Helton	56	39.8

KICKING	XP	ATT	%	FG	ATT	%
Cofer	49	51	96	29	36	81

LOS ANGELES RAMS

RUSHING

LastName	No.	Yds	Avg	TD
Bell	272	1137	4.2	15
Delpino	78	368	4.7	1
Gary	37	163	4.4	1
McGee	21	99	4.7	1
Green	26	73	2.8	0
Everett	25	31	1.2	1
Ro. Brown	6	27	4.5	0
Ellard	2	10	5.0	0
Holohan	1	3	3.0	0
Hatcher	1	0	0.0	0
Anderson	1	-1	-1.0	0
Herrmann	2	-1	-0.5	0

RECEIVING

LastName	No.	Yds	Avg	TD
Ellard	70	1382	19.7	8
Holohan	51	510	10.0	2
Anderson	44	1146	26.0	5
McGee	37	303	8.2	4
Delpino	34	334	9.8	1
Johnson	25	148	5.9	5
A. Cox	20	340	17.0	3
Bell	19	85	4.5	0
Ro. Brown	5	113	22.6	1
Gary	2	13	6.5	0
Green	1	-5	-5.0	0

PUNT RETURNS

LastName	No.	Yds	Avg	TD
Henley	29	273	9.4	0
Hicks	24	39	9.8	0
Ellard	2	20	10.0	0
Irvin	0	0	0.0	0

KICKOFF RETURNS

LastName	No.	Yds	Avg	TD
Ro. Brown	47	968	20.6	0
Delpino	17	334	19.6	0
McDonald	2	22	11.0	0
Gary	1	4	4.0	0

PASSING—PUNTING—KICKING

PASSING	Att	Cmp	%	Yds	Yd/Att	TD	Int—	%	RK
Everett	518	304	58.7	4310	8.32	29	17—	3.3	2
Herrmann	5	4	80.0	59	11.80	0	1—	20.0	

PUNTING	No.	Avg.
Hatcher	74	38.3

KICKING	XP	ATT	%	FG	ATT	%
Lansford	51	51	100	23	30	77

NEW ORLEANS SAINTS

RUSHING

LastName	No.	Yds	Avg	TD
Hilliard	344	1262	3.7	13
Heyward	49	183	3.7	1
Jordan	38	179	4.7	3
Frazier	25	112	4.5	1
Fourcade	14	91	6.5	1
Hebert	25	87	3.5	0
Morse	2	43	21.5	0
Turner	2	8	4.0	0
Winslow	1	0	0.0	0
Hill	1	-7	-7.0	0
Perriman	1	-10	-10.0	0

RECEIVING

LastName	No.	Yds	Avg	TD
Martin	68	1090	16.0	8
Hilliard	52	514	9.9	5
Hill	48	636	13.3	4
Brenner	34	398	11.7	4
Turner	22	279	12.7	1
Perriman	20	356	17.8	0
Heyward	13	69	5.3	0
Tice	9	98	10.9	1
Scales	8	89	11.1	0
Jordan	4	53	13.3	0
Shepard	2	36	18.0	0
Cook	1	8	8.0	0

PUNT RETURNS

LastName	No.	Yds	Avg	TD
Harris	27	196	7.3	0
Morse	10	29	2.9	0
Hill	7	41	5.9	0
Perriman	1	10	10.0	0
Turner	1	7	7.0	0
Massey	0	54	—	0

KICKOFF RETURNS

LastName	No.	Yds	Avg	TD
Harris	19	378	19.9	0
Atkins	12	245	20.4	0
Morse	10	278	27.8	1
Frazier	8	157	19.6	0
U. Johnson	2	34	17.0	0
Phillips	1	24	24.0	0
Hilliard	1	20	20.0	0
Hill	1	13	13.0	0
Scales	1	0	0.0	0

PASSING—PUNTING—KICKING

PASSING	Att	Cmp	%	Yds	Yd/Att	TD	Int—	%	RK
Hebert	353	222	62.9	2686	7.61	15	15—	4.2	4
Fourcade	107	61	57.0	930	8.69	7	4—	3.7	
Hilliard	1	1	100.0	35	35.00	1	0—	0.0	

PUNTING	No.	Avg.
Barnhardt	55	39.6
Winslow	16	37.2

KICKING	XP	ATT	%	FG	ATT	%
Andersen	44	45	98	20	29	69

ATLANTA FALCONS

RUSHING

LastName	No.	Yds	Avg	TD
Settle	179	689	3.8	3
Jones	52	202	3.9	6
Lang	47	176	3.7	1
Haynes	4	35	8.8	0
Paterra	9	32	3.6	0
Flowers	13	24	1.8	1
Miller	10	20	2.0	0
Fulhage	1	0	0.0	0
Millen	1	0	0.0	0
Dixon	2	-23	-11.5	0

RECEIVING

LastName	No.	Yds	Avg	TD
Collins	58	862	14.9	3
Jones	41	396	9.7	0
Haynes	40	681	17.0	4
Lang	39	436	11.2	1
Settle	39	316	8.1	2
Heller	33	324	9.8	1
Dixon	25	357	14.3	2
Beckman	11	102	9.3	1
Wilkins	8	179	22.4	3
Bailey	8	170	21.3	0
Paterra	5	42	8.4	0
G. Thomas	4	46	11.5	0
Sanders	1	-8	-8.0	0

PUNT RETURNS

LastName	No.	Yds	Avg	TD
Sanders	28	307	11.0	1
Jordan	4	34	8.5	0

KICKOFF RETURNS

LastName	No.	Yds	Avg	TD
Sanders	35	725	20.7	0
Jones	23	440	19.1	0
Paterra	8	129	16.1	0
G. Thomas	7	142	20.3	0
Jordan	3	27	9.0	0
Beckman	2	15	7.5	0
Primus	1	16	16.0	0
Bruce	1	15	15.0	0

PASSING—PUNTING—KICKING

PASSING	Att	Cmp	%	Yds	Yd/Att	TD	Int—	%	RK
Miller	526	280	53.2	3459	6.58	16	10—	1.9	7
Millen	50	31	62.0	432	8.64	1	2—	4.0	
Fulhage	1	1	100.0	12	12.00	0	0—	0.0	
Jones	1	0	0.0	0	0.00	0	0—	0.0	

PUNTING	No.	Avg.
Fulhage	85	40.8

KICKING	XP	Att	%	FG	Att	%
McFadden	18	18	100	15	20	75
Miller	0	0	0	1	1	100

1989 A.F.C. A Question of Strength or Weakness

Although it took until the final week of the regular season for the N.F.C. to finally forge ahead of the A.F.C. in victories in games between the two conferences (for only the second time since 1970), the A.F.C. was general perceived as the weaker group of teams. Some commentators even went as far as to urge a new playoff format leading to the Super Bowl, arguing that at least five N.F.C. teams were stronger than the best A.F.C. club.

Serious analysts argued with some cause that the N.F.C. had stronger defenses, at least with its better teams. This, they said, gave the top National Conference teams a distinct advantage in "chips-down" games. Recent Super Bowls were cited as proof.

A.F.C. fans could admit their conference had not 49ers but that it didn"t have the Cowboys and Falcons, either. Eleven of the 14 A.F.C. teams were in the playoff hunt up to the final week. If there were no super teams, there was a balance of power that was the very soul of parity. None of the American Conference division winners had records equal to their counterparts in the N.F.C.. But, whether this denoted strength or weakness was a matter of opinion.

EASTERN DIVISION

Buffalo Bills — It was a rough season in Buffalo. All-Pro linebackers Shane Conlan and Cornelius Bennett missed time with injuries, cornerback Derrick Burroughs was diagnosed to have a career-ending spinal condition in September, and quarterback Jim Kelly was knocked out for three games. Frank Reich, a virtually unknown backup, rode to Kelly's rescue, leading the Bills to three victories, and it wasn't long before Buffalo fans were calling for him, not Kelly. But the defense wasn't up to its 1988 level. Distractions included Kelly's criticism of his teammates, the teammates criticism of Kelly, fan criticism of some of the players' attitudes, and even a fight between two assistant coaches. Almost lost in the mess were outstanding seasons by running back Thurman Thomas and wide receiver Andre Reed, and that the Bills repeated as division champs for the first time since the 1960s.

Indianapolis Colts — Like a bad rerun, the Colts lost their starting quarterback early in the season for the fourth straight year when Chris Chandler tore up his knee in Game Three. Jack Trudeau was OK as the replacement, but he played hurt, and having Eric Dickerson slowed all season with a hamstring injury didn't help, either. Despite his nagging injury, Dickerson became the first player to top 1,000 yards rushing in seven consecutive seasons, finishing with 1,311 yards. Bill Brooks and Andre Rison gave Trudeau a pair of dangerous receivers, but the much-balleyhooed offensive line didn't live up to expectations. DE Jon Hand, with 10 sacks, and linebackers Duane Bickett and Jeff Herrod were the strengths of an up-and-down defense.

Miami Dolphins — An inept running game and mediocre defense kept the Dolphins out of the playoffs for the fourth straight year, their longest dry spell since Don Shula took over as coach in 1970. No. 1 draft pick Sammie Smith showed promise as a runner but was obviously hurt by his training camp holdout and a so-so offensive line. The Dolphins finished 27th in rushing and 24th in defense to waste the usual aerial fireworks by Dan Marino. Plagued by an assortment of injuries all season, Marino still came within three yards of throwing for 4,000. Miami seemed headed for the playoffs with a 7-4 mark after 11 games, but they blew a 14-0 lead to the Steelers at home and went on to lose four of their last five games. Owner Joe Robbie died Jan. 7.

New England Patriots — The Patriots lost three defensive starters for the year in the final preseason game — linebacker Andre Tippett, defensive end Garin Veris and cornerback Ronnie Lippett. That crippled the defense. Wide receiver Stanely Morgan missed six games with a broken leg and Irving Fryar was out five with assorted injuries, but the offense never really jelled, as coach Raymond Berry started four different quarterbacks, with castoff Marc Wilson the apparent final choice by default. Second-year running back John Stephens didn't play up to his rookie standard, but the ineptitude of the passing game allowed opponents to concentrate on stopping his runs. Management fired Berry in February when he balked at hiring offensive and defensive coordinators. New coach Rod Rust inherited a mending squad, but one that still lacked a proven quarterback.

New York Jets — The Jets fell apart in 1989; only the inept Cowboys presented a weaker aggregation to suffering fans. No single area could be blamed for the Jets' disaster because there was enough culpability for all. However, a string of holdouts, spawned by management's hardball position, got the team off and limping on the wrong foot. The young secondary was again victimized by a poor pass rush. Star wide receiver Al Toon played only six full games. And coach Joe Walton played his annual game of musical chairs at quarterback, even starting rookie Kyle Mackey at one point. Mostly, though, the Jets didn't have the horses. At the end of the season, the front office underwent a long-needed house cleaning, with Dick Steinberg being brought in from New England as GM. His first move was to fire Walton.

CENTRAL DIVISION

Cleveland Browns — New coach Bud Carson brought the Browns their fifth division championship of the decade, but it took close wins over Minnesota and Houston in the final two games to do the trick. The offense never hit on all cylinders all season. Quarterback Bernie Kosar's arm wasn't sound after an early-season injury, causing much speculation as to how permanent was the condition. Fullback Kevin Mack missed the first 12 games after a drug arrest led to a suspension and prison sentence. The offensive line seldom played top quality. Rookie running back Eric Metcalf was an early sensation with his tricky, twisting runs, but even he tailed off late. A couple of new stars emerged on the defense in defensive tackle Michael Dean Perry and free safety Thane Gash. Added to linebackers Clay Matthews and Mike Johnson, cornerback Frank Minnifield and strong safety Felix Wright, they made a strong unit.

Houston Oilers — The Oilers were favored to win the division title going in and needed only a victory in either of their last two games to earn their first undisputed Central crown. Instead, the suffered the worst defeat in their history to Cincinnati 61-7, and then booted the finale to Cleveland with 39 seconds left. Then they were knocked out of the playoffs in overtime by the Steelers. The losses cost coach Jerry Glanville his job (although officially he resigned). Glanville was faulted for failure to settle on Alonzo Highsmith, Mike Rozier, Allen Pinkett or Lorenzo White as the main running threat, and for the team's often mindless penalties — a team record 148. But Glanville couldn't personally rush opposing passers, something his team lacked. Nor could he cover in the secondary, where the Oilers were beaten all season despite high marks for rookie Bubba McDowell. Jack Pardee left the University of Houston to replace Glanville.

Pittsburgh Steelers — After the Steelers lost their first two games by a combined score of 92-10, they were the league's laughing stock. Coach Chuck Noll held together a roster that was one-fourth rookies, and Pittsburgh roared down the stretch to win five of their last six games and make the playoffs. Heralded rookie Tim Worley was a long holdout and untracked slowly, but he rushed for 417 yards in the last five games. Fullback Merril Hoge was steady once he recovered from an early rib injury and the offensive line regained its health. Quarterback Bubby Brister was unspectacular in passing statistics but a major plus in leadership, and wide receiver Louis Lipps had another fine year. The strength of the team was a gritty defense that came back from the early blowouts to hang tough when it had to.

Cincinnati Bengals — After coming within 34 seconds of a Super Bowl victory, the Bengals had high hopes for 1989 — until fullback Ickey Woods' season ended with a knee injury in Game Two. Cincinnati got to 4-1, then blew early leads to lose two straight. They staggered home as a model of inconsistency. Veteran breakaway runner James Brooks was a sensation, posting a league-high 5.6-yard rushing average, but without Woods, the Bengals couldn't run between the tackles. Wide receiver Tim McGee joined Eddie Brown as a solid deep threat for Boomer Esiason's passes, but the team that scored 61 points against Houston was held five times under 15. Although oversized strong safety

FINAL TEAM STATISTICS

OFFENSE

	BUFF	CIN	CLEV	DEN	HOU	IND	K.C.	L.A.	MIA	N.E.	NYJ	PITT	S.D.	SEA
FIRST DOWNS:														
Total	334	348	285	308	327	273	304	259	310	335	292	244	267	290
by Rushing	136	136	101	125	112	118	120	93	88	114	91	106	95	86
by Passing	177	183	161	163	185	140	165	143	201	187	189	117	149	180
by Penalty	21	29	23	20	30	15	19	23	21	34	12	21	23	24
RUSHING:														
Number	532	529	448	554	495	458	559	454	400	485	400	500	432	405
Yards	2264	2483	1609	2092	1928	1853	2227	2038	1330	1749	1596	1818	1873	1392
Average Yards	4.3	4.7	3.6	3.8	3.9	4.0	4.0	4.5	3.3	3.6	4.0	3.6	4.3	3.4
Touchdowns	15	17	14	15	16	11	18	9	10	12	11	17	13	5
PASSING:														
Attempts	478	513	529	474	496	493	435	414	601	610	570	404	515	559
Completions	281	288	309	256	295	253	259	201	331	302	338	210	270	316
Completion Pct.	58.8	56.1	58.4	54.0	59.5	51.3	59.5	48.6	55.1	49.5	59.3	52.0	52.4	56.5
Passing Yards	3831	3950	3625	3352	3786	3134	3220	3277	4302	3972	3892	2662	3291	3583
Avg. Yds per Att.	7.0	6.5	6.1	5.8	6.6	5.7	6.6	6.4	6.9	7.8	5.4	4.8	5.5	5.3
Avg. Yds per Comp.	13.6	13.7	11.7	13.1	12.8	12.4	12.4	16.3	13.0	13.2	11.5	12.7	12.2	11.3
Times Tackled	35	41	34	43	37	28	23	44	10	34	62	51	39	46
Yds Lost Tackled	242	332	192	351	287	174	182	326	86	265	477	484	254	379
Net Yards	3586	3618	3433	3001	3499	2960	3038	2951	4216	3707	3415	2178	3037	3204
Touchdowns	32	32	20	21	23	18	14	21	26	17	14	10	15	21
Interceptions	20	13	15	20	16	17	23	22	25	27	24	13	19	23
Pct. Intercepted	4.2	2.5	2.8	4.2	3.2	3.4	5.3	5.3	4.2	4.4	4.2	3.2	3.7	4.1
PUNTS:														
Number	67	65	97	80	58	80	67	67	59	64	87	83	84	76
Average	38.3	38.5	39.4	39.8	41.8	42.4	40.1	40.5	41.7	37.4	39.4	40.6	39.5	39.4
PUNT RETURNS														
Number	33	36	49	45	19	26	44	40	33	45	33	40	38	30
Yards	301	209	496	344	122	322	331	378	338	379	299	278	272	251
Average Yards	9.1	5.8	10.1	7.6	6.4	12.4	7.5	9.5	10.2	8.4	9.1	7.0	7.2	8.4
Touchdowns	0	0	0	0	0	1	0	0	1	0	0	0	0	0
KICKOFF RET.:														
Number	53	54	50	43	74	60	52	54	61	69	75	56	64	65
Yards	1058	941	932	876	1285	1164	915	1002	1153	1462	1309	1304	1235	1246
Average Yards	20.0	17.4	18.6	20.4	17.4	19.4	17.6	18.6	18.9	21.2	17.5	23.3	19.3	19.2
Touchdowns	0	0	0	0	0	0	0	0	1	0	0	1	1	1
INTERCEPT RET.:														
Number	23	21	27	21	21	21	15	18	15	16	15	21	25	9
Yards	269	204	300	318	263	391	133	362	126	118	261	261	224	57
Average Yards	11.7	9.7	11.1	15.1	12.5	18.6	8.9	20.1	8.4	7.4	17.4	12.4	9.0	6.3
Touchdowns	1	1	4	2	0	2	0	3	0	1	2	0	0	0
PENALTIES:														
Number	103	85	128	83	149	89	116	132	83	63	116	116	122	79
Yards	831	637	973	594	1153	704	878	1105	614	509	953	986	906	738
FUMBLES:														
Number	30	29	23	26	39	33	32	28	30	26	32	32	24	43
Number Lost	21	19	15	12	17	10	18	12	16	12	17	18	17	14
POINTS:														
Total	409	404	334	362	365	298	318	315	331	297	253	265	266	241
PAT Attempts	48	52	40	40	41	33	35	35	39	30	30	29	31	28
PAT Made	46	50	40	39	40	31	34	34	38	27	29	28	29	28
FG Attempts	30	20	24	33	37	27	33	34	26	40	21	30	25	25
FG Made	23	14	16	27	25	21	24	23	19	30	14	21	17	15
Percent FG Made	76.7	70.0	66.7	81.8	67.6	77.8	72.7	67.6	73.1	75.0	66.7	70.0	68.0	60.0
Safeties	0	0	0	1	2	0	1	1	1	0	1	0	0	0

DEFENSE

	BUFF	CIN	CLEV	DEN	HOU	IND	K.C.	L.A.	MIA	N.E.	NYJ	PITT	S.D.	SEA
FIRST DOWNS:														
Total	299	280	276	246	314	336	252	308	337	297	328	323	295	293
by Rushing	117	114	93	90	119	126	92	121	139	110	127	112	102	119
by Passing	156	151	161	142	165	192	140	160	180	176	178	177	172	158
by Penalty	26	15	22	14	30	18	20	27	18	11	23	34	21	16
RUSHING:														
Number	484	482	446	426	437	507	445	504	493	495	517	498	479	520
Yards	1840	2162	1670	1580	1669	2077	1766	1940	2153	1978	2136	2008	1813	2118
Average Yards	3.8	4.5	3.7	3.7	3.8	4.1	4.0	3.8	4.4	4.0	4.1	4.0	3.8	4.1
Touchdowns	15	9	8	10	20	10	9	15	19	19	16	16	13	11
PASSING:														
Attempts	508	482	540	504	467	556	471	506	513	449	514	548	513	445
Completions	255	256	269	268	269	322	236	277	315	259	282	290	283	252
Completion Pct.	50.2	53.1	49.8	53.2	57.6	57.9	50.1	54.7	61.4	57.7	54.9	52.9	55.2	56.6
Passing Yards	3495	3383	3520	3201	3819	3918	2821	3311	3811	3905	4035	3721	3311	3332
Avg. Yds per Att.	5.9	6.1	5.4	5.1	7.0	5.9	5.0	5.7	6.4	7.6	7.1	6.1	5.2	6.5
Avg. Yds per Comp.	13.7	13.2	13.1	11.9	14.2	12.2	12.0	12.0	12.1	15.1	14.3	12.8	11.7	13.2
Times Tackled	38	33	45	47	36	46	36	35	39	31	28	31	48	32
Yds Lost Tackled	289	248	359	374	277	384	294	248	208	239	177	180	360	235
Net Yards	3206	3135	3161	2827	3542	3534	2527	3063	3543	3666	3858	3541	2951	3097
Touchdowns	14	22	20	13	28	15	16	18	21	27	31	17	15	23
Interceptions	23	21	27	21	21	21	15	18	15	16	15	21	25	9
Pct. Intercepted	4.5	4.4	5.0	4.2	4.5	3.8	3.2	3.6	2.9	3.6	2.9	3.8	4.9	2.0
PUNTS:														
Number	75	75	94	84	56	65	82	72	62	81	69	69	79	74
Average	38.3	39.1	40.4	41.0	37.6	41.6	39.1	40.3	39.0	42.1	39.8	40.5	38.6	39.2
PUNT RETURNS														
Number	25	33	49	28	24	51	40	41	26	38	34	45	43	41
Yards	227	323	418	370	191	558	325	301	256	346	257	361	451	334
Average Yards	9.1	9.8	8.5	13.2	8.0	10.9	8.1	7.3	9.8	9.1	7.6	8.0	10.5	8.1
Touchdowns	0	0	0	0	0	1	0	1	0	0	1	0	0	0
KICKOFF RET.:														
Number	75	55	58	72	59	63	55	59	63	61	47	53	57	44
Yards	1187	1203	1175	1256	1024	1208	1156	1001	1215	1199	1029	1096	1249	814
Average Yards	15.8	21.9	20.3	17.4	17.4	19.2	21.0	17.0	19.3	19.7	21.9	20.7	21.9	18.5
Touchdowns	0	0	0	0	1	0	2	2	0	0	0	0	1	0
INTERCEPT RET.:														
Number	20	13	15	20	16	17	23	22	25	27	24	13	19	23
Yards	364	42	306	194	171	345	269	298	335	338	282	103	179	248
Average Yards	18.2	3.2	20.4	9.7	10.7	20.3	11.7	13.5	13.4	12.5	11.8	7.9	9.4	10.8
Touchdowns	2	0	1	1	0	2	2	0	1	2	2	1	0	2
PENALTIES:														
Number	87	122	122	102	109	103	102	105	106	111	90	96	93	118
Yards	616	1060	985	823	903	772	797	867	831	954	675	785	741	809
FUMBLES:														
Number	31	26	32	43	25	34	32	40	19	22	32	40	21	26
Number Lost	13	16	11	22	16	15	18	18	8	12	9	21	13	13
POINTS:														
Total	317	285	254	226	412	301	286	297	379	391	411	326	290	327
PAT Attempts	34	32	29	25	51	29	32	36	43	48	50	38	29	37
PAT Made	33	31	29	25	49	29	31	36	42	46	46	37	27	35
FG Attempts	37	27	28	27	21	43	26	21	33	26	31	27	41	32
FG Made	26	20	15	17	17	32	21	15	25	19	21	19	29	22
Percent FG Made	70.3	74.1	53.6	63.0	81.0	74.4	80.8	71.4	75.8	73.1	67.7	70.4	70.7	68.8
Safeties	1	1	0	0	0	1	0	0	2	0	1	2	1	2

David Fulcher was a terror, the otherwise undersized defense couldn't stop the run nor put up much of a pass rush.

WESTERN DIVISION

Denver Broncos — After barely hitting .500 in 1988, the Broncos compiled the best record in the A.F.C. in 1989 and wrapped up the home-field playoff advantage early. The major improvement came in the revamping of the defense by coach Dan Reeves and new defensive coordinator Wade Phillips. To stalwarts such as linebackers Karl Mecklenburg and Simon Fletcher, Denver added Plan B free-agents cornerback Wymon Henderson and defensive end Alphonso Carreker and top draft pick Steve Atwater. Just as important, the Broncos installed a simpler, more aggressive scheme that allowed 126 fewer points than in '88. Quarterback John Elway had only a mediocre season, but the offense benefitted from a 1,000-yard seaosn by rookie running back Bobby Humphrey.

Kansas City Chiefs — The Chiefs, after making wholesale roster changes under new coach Marty Schottenheimer, staggered out of the starting gate. In the first six games, they lost eight fumbles and their quarterbacks threw 13 interceptions. Not surprisingly, they were 2-4 and far behind Denver. Once Kansas City settled down, however, they turned into one of the A.F.C.'s better teams. Fullback Christian Okoye, a 260-pound native Nigerian, led the NFL in rushing with 1,480 yards and 12 touchdowns. Veteran quarterback Steve DeBerg was twice benched early in the season but finished up strong. Rookie linebacker Derrick Thomas, with 10 sacks, keyed a defense that ranked first in the conference. Four victories in the last five games gave Kansas City only its third winning season in the last 16 years.

Los Angeles Raiders — When the Raiders limped off to a 1-3 start, coach Mike Shanahan was replaced by Art Shell, the Hall of Fame offensive tackle. Shell thus became the NFL's first black head coach in the modern era. The move was a popular one with the team which played better football the rest of the season. Bo Jackson took over at running back after his baseball season ended, and Steve Beuerlein won the quarterback job from costly acquisition Jay Schroeder. But the Raiders still were lacking an offense with receiver-returner Tim Brown sidelined all season and Willie Gault used mostly as a decoy. Only once in the final seven games did the Raiders score as many as three touchdowns.

Seattle Seahawks —The key to the Seahawks' disappointing season was a club-record 43 fumbles while intercepting a mere nine opponents' passes. The minus-15 turnover ratio was too much for Seattle's undersized defense and slumping running game to overcome — even in the AFc's weak West Division. Quarterback Dave Krieg was benched in midseason, and — as usual — he came back strong down the stretch in leading the team to three victories in its last four games. Brian Blades became the premier receiver in Steve Largent's final season. Largent retired with his consecutive-game streat intact at 177 games and the all-time records for total receptions, yardage and touchdowns.

San Diego Chargers — The Chargers' defense gave them hope for the future, holding all but one opponent to 20-or-less points over the last 14 games. Outstanding were pass-ruser Lee Williams, rookie Burt Grossman, linebackers Leslie O'Neal, Billy Ray Smith and Gary Plummer and cornerback Gill Bryd. Unfortunately, good efforts by the defense were more often than not offset by woeful special-teams play and a creaky offense. Breakaway star Gary Anderson was a season-long holdout, crippling the running game. Former Bears quarterback Jim McMahon was disappointing and eventually benched, and got more attention for his sometimes boorish off-the-field behavior than anything he did on the field. Wide receiver Anthony Miller emerged as the team's most potent threat. After the season, owner Alex Spanos hired former Redskins' GM Bobby Beathard to lead the Chargers back to the playoffs.

BUFFALO BILLS 9-7 Marv Levy

Scores of Each Game		
27	Miami	24
14	DENVER	28
47	Houston	* 41
31	NEW ENGLAND	10
14	Indianapolis	37
23	L.A. RAMS	20
34	N.Y. JETS	3
31	MIAMI	17
28	Atlanta	30
30	INDIANAPOLIS	7
24	New England	33
24	CINCINNATI	7
16	Seattle	17
19	NEW ORLEANS	22
10	San Francisco	21
37	N.Y. Jets	0

Use Name	Pos.	Hgt	Wgt	Age	Int	Pts
Howard Ballard	OT	6'6"	300	25		
Leonard Burton	OT	6'3"	275	25		
John Davis	OT	6'4"	310	24		
Will Wolford	OT	6'5"	280	25		
Joe Devlin	OG	6'5"	280	36		
Jim Ritcher	OG	6'3"	265	31		
Kent Hull	C	6'4"	275	28		
Adam Lingner	C	6'4"	268	27		
Mark Pike	DE	6'4"	272	25		
Leon Seals	DE	6'4"	265	25		
Bruce Smith	DE	6'4"	285	26		
Art Still	DE	6'7"	255	33	1	
Fred Smerlas	NT	6'3"	280	32		
Jeff Wright	NT	6'2"	270	26		

Mitch Frerotte — Back Injury
Bruce Mesner — Knee Injury
Tim Vogler — Knee Injury

Use Name	Pos.	Hgt	Wgt	Age	Int	Pts
Carlton Bailey	LB	6'2"	240	24	1	
Cornelius Bennett	LB	6'2"	235	23	2	
Ray Bentley	LB	6'2"	235	27		
Tim Cofield (from NYJ)	LB	6'2"	242	26		
Shane Conlan	LB	6'3"	235	24	1	
Matt Monger	LB	6'1"	240	27		
Scott Radecic	LB	6'3"	242	27		
Darryl Talley	LB	6'4"	235	29		
Derrick Burroughs	DB	6'1"	180	27		
Dwight Drane	DB	6'2"	205	27	1	
John Hagy	DB	5'11"	190	23		
Chris Hale	DB	5'7"	161	23		
Kirby Jackson	DB	5'10"	180	23	2	6
Mark Kelso	DB	5'11"	185	26	6	6
Nate Odomes	DB	5'10"	188	23	5	
Leonard Smith	DB	5'11"	202	28	2	
Mickey Sutton (from GB)	DB	5'9"	172	29	1	

Hal Garner — Suspended by N.F.L.

Use Name	Pos.	Hgt	Wgt	Age	Int	Pts
Stan Gelbaugh	QB	6'3"	207	26		
Jim Kelly	QB	6'3"	218	29		12
Frank Reich	QB	6'4"	210	27		
Kenneth Davis	HB	5'10"	209	27		18
Ronnie Harmon	HB	5'11"	200	25		24
Thurman Thomas	HB	5'10"	198	23		72
Larry Kinnebrew	FB	6'1"	256	29		36
Jamie Mueller	FB	6'1"	225	24		
Don Beebe	WR	5'11"	177	24		12
Flip Johnson	WR	5'10"	185	26		6
James Lofton	WR	6'3"	190	33		18
Andre Reed	WR	6'	190	24		54
Steve Tasker	WR	5'9"	185	27		
Keith McKeller	TE	6'6"	245	25		12
Pete Metzelaars	TE	6'7"	250	29		12
Butch Rolle	TE	6'3"	242	24		6
Kerry Brady	K	6'1"	215	26		
John Kidd	K	6'3"	208	28		
Scott Norwood	K	6'	207	29		115

Robb Riddick — Knee Injury

MIAMI DOLPHINS 8-8 Don Shula

Scores of Each Game		
24	BUFFALO	27
24	New England	10
33	N.Y. JETS	40
7	Houston	39
13	CLEVELAND	* 10
20	Cincinnati	13
23	GREEN BAY	20
17	Buffalo	31
19	INDIANAPOLIS	13
31	N.Y. Jets	23
17	Dallas	14
14	PITTSBURGH	34
21	Kansas City	26
31	NEW ENGLAND	10
13	Indianapolis	42
24	KANSAS CITY	27

Use Name	Pos.	Hgt	Wgt	Age	Int	Pts
Louis Cheek	OT	6'6"	295	24		
Jeff Dellenbach	OT-C	6'6"	280	26		
Mark Dennis	OT	6'6"	290	24		
Ronnie Lee	OT	6'3"	275	32		
Roy Foster	OG	6'4"	275	29		
Harry Galbreath	OG	6'1"	275	24		
Alvin Powell	OG	6'5"	296	29		
Tom Toth	OG	6'5"	282	27		
Jeff Uhlenhake	C	6'3"	282	23		
John Bosa	DE	6'4"	273	25		
Jackie Cline	DE-NT	6'5"	280	29		
Jeff Cross	DE	6'4"	270	23		
T.J. Turner	DE	6'4"	280	26		
Mike Lambrecht	NT	6'1"	274	26		
Brian Sochia	NT	6'3"	275	28		

Jon Giesler — Knee Injury
Greg Johnson — Knee Injury

Use Name	Pos.	Hgt	Wgt	Age	Int	Pts
Dave Ahrens	LB	6'4"	247	31		
Bob Brudzinski	LB	6'4"	235	34		
Greg Clark	LB	6'1"	234	24		
David Frye	LB	6'2"	227	28		
Rick Graf	LB	6'5"	249	26		
Hugh Green	LB	6'2"	228	30		
David Griggs	LB-TE	6'3"	239	22		
E.J. Junior	LB	6'3"	242	29		
Barry Krauss	LB	6'3"	248	32		
Eric Kumerow	LB-DE	6'7"	268	24		
John Offerdahl	LB	6'3"	237	25		
J.B. Brown	DB	6'	192	23		
Ernest Gibson	DB	5'10"	185	27		
Liffort Hobley	DB	6'	202	27	1	
William Judson	DB	6'1"	192	29	2	
Paul Lankford	DB	6'1"	190	31	1	
Don McNeal	DB	5'11"	193	31	3	
Louis Oliver	DB	6'2"	226	23	4	
Rodney Thomas	DB	5'10"	190	23	2	
Jarvis Williams	DB	5'11"	196	24	2	

Use Name	Pos.	Hgt	Wgt	Age	Int	Pts
Dan Marino	QB	6'4"	222	27		12
Scott Secules	QB	6'3"	219	24		
Cliff Stoudt	QB	6'4"	218	34		
Kerry Goode	HB	5'11'	200	24		
Sammie Smith	HB	6'2"	226	22		36
Lorenzo Hampton	HB	6'	208	27		72
Willard Reaves (from WAS)	HB	5'11"	200	30		
Troy Stradford	HB	5'9"	192	24		6
Tom Brown	FB	6'1"	228	25		
Nuu Faaola (from NYJ)	FB	5'11"	220	24		
Ron Davenport	FB	6'2"	232	26		6
Marc Logan	FB	5'11"	220	24		12
Fred Banks	WR	5'10"	180	27		6
Andre Brown	WR	6'3"	210	23		30
Mark Clayton	WR	5'9"	184	28		54
Mark Duper	WR	5'9"	190	30		6
Jim Jensen	WR-FB	6'4"	220	30		36
Scott Schwedes	WR	6'	182	24		12
Ferrell Edmunds	TE	6'6"	248	24		18
Bruce Hardy	TE	6'5"	234	33		
Brian Kinchen	TE	6'2"	238	24		
Pete Stoyonovich	K	5'10"	180	22		95
Reggie Roby	K	6'2"	242	28		

INDIANAPOLIS COLTS 8-8 Ron Meyer

Scores of Each Game		
24	SAN FRANCISCO	30
17	L.A. Rams	31
13	ATLANTA	9
17	N.Y. Jets	10
37	BUFFALO	14
3	Denver	14
23	Cincinnati	12
20	NEW ENGLAND	* 23
13	Miami	19
7	Buffalo	30
27	N.Y. JETS	10
10	SAN DIEGO	6
16	New England	22
23	CLEVELAND	* 17
42	MIAMI	13
6	New Orleans	41

Use Name	Pos.	Hgt	Wgt	Age	Int	Pts
Kevin Call	OT	6'7"	302	27		
Chris Hinton	OT	6'4"	295	28		
Zefross Moss	OT	6'6"	315	23		
Brian Baldinger	OG	6'4"	272	30		
Randy Dixon	OG	6'3"	290	24		6
Ben Utt	OG	6'6"	286	30		
Ray Donaldson	C	6'3"	288	31		
Stan Eisenhooth	C	6'5"	290	26		
Sam Clancy	DE	6'7"	284	31		
Jon Hand	DE	6'7"	298	25		
Ezra Johnson	DE	6'4"	250	33		
Donnell Thompson	DE	6'4"	275	30		
Mitchell Benson	NT	6'3"	302	22		
Harvey Armstrong	NT	6'3"	282	29		

Steve Knight — Knee Injury

Use Name	Pos.	Hgt	Wgt	Age	Int	Pts
O'Brien Alston	LB	6'6"	246	23		
Chip Banks	LB	6'4"	245	29	2	
Duane Bickett	LB	6'5"	243	26	1	
Jeff Herrod	LB	6'	243	23		
Kurt Larson	LB	6'4"	236	23		
Orlando Lowry (to NE)	LB	6'4"	236	28		
Quintus McDonald	LB	6'3	240	22		
Dan Murray	LB	6'1"	240	22		
Eric Naposki (from NE)	LB	6'2"	230	22		
Cliff Odom	LB	6'2"	245	31		
Ronnie Washington	LB	6'1"	250	26		
Fredd Young	LB	6'1"	233	27	2	
Michael Ball	DB	6'	216	25	1	
John Baylor	DB	6'	203	24		
Eugene Daniel	DB	5'11"	178	28	1	
Chris Goode	DB	6'	193	25		
Anthony Parker	DB	5'10"	181	23		
Bruce Plummer	DB	6'1"	203	25	1	
Mike Prior	DB	6'	204	25	6	6
Keith Taylor	DB	5'11'	193	24	7	6
Charles Washington	DB	6'1"	208	22		

Use Name	Pos.	Hgt	Wgt	Age	Int	Pts
Chris Chandler	QB	6'4"	210	23		6
Wayne Johnson	QB	6'4"	221	23		
Tom Ramsey	QB	6'1"	188	28		
Don Strock	QB	6'5"	225	38		
Jack Trudeau	QB	6'3"	214	26		12
Albert Bentley	HB-FB	5'11"	214	29		30
Eric Dickerson	HB	6'3"	224	28		48
Ivy Joe Hunter	FB-HB	6'	237	22		
Matt Bouza	WR	6'3"	212	31		
Bill Brooks	WR	6'	191	25		24
James Pruitt	WR	6'3"	201	25		6
Andre Rison	WR	5'10"	185	22		24
Clarence Verdin	WR	5'8"	163	26		12
Pat Beach	TE	6'4"	252	28		12
Mark Boyer	TE	6'4"	242	26		12
John Brandes	TE	6'2"	255	25		
Dean Biasucci	K	6'	191	26		94
Rohn Stark	K	6'3"	204	30		

NEW ENGLAND PATRIOTS 5-11 Raymond Berry

Scores of Each Game		
27	N.Y. Jets	24
10	MIAMI	24
3	SEATTLE	24
10	Buffalo	31
23	HOUSTON	13
15	Atlanta	16
20	San Francisco	37
23	Indianapolis	* 20
26	N.Y. JETS	27
24	NEW ORLEANS	28
33	BUFFALO	24
21	L.A. Raiders	24
22	INDIANAPOLIS	16
10	Miami	31
10	Pittsburgh	28
20	L.A. RAMS	24

Use Name	Pos.	Hgt	Wgt	Age	Int	Pts
Bruce Armstrong	OT	6'4"	284	23		
Tom Rehder	OT-OG	6'7"	280	24		
David Viaene	OT	6'5"	300	24		
Danny Villa	OT	6'5"	305	24		
David Douglas	OG-OT	6'4"	280	26		
Paul Fairchild	OG	6'4"	270	27		
Sean Farrell	OG	6'3"	260	29		
Mike Baab	C	6'4"	270	29		
Mike Morris (from KC)	C-OG	6'5"	275	28		
Milford Hodge	DE	6'3"	278	28		
Gary Jeter	DE	6'4"	260	34		
Peter Shorts	DE	6'8"	278	23		
Kenneth Sims	DE	6'5"	271	29		
Tim Goad	NT	6'3"	280	23		
Emanuel McNeil	NT	6'3"	285	22		
Brent Williams	NT-DE	6'3"	278	24		

Garin Veris — Knee Injury

Use Name	Pos.	Hgt	Wgt	Age	Int	Pts
Vincent Brown	LB	6'2"	245	24	1	
Terrence Cooks	LB	6'	230	22		
Tim Jordan	LB	6'3"	226	25		
Larry McGrew	LB	6'5"	233	32	1	
Johnny Rembert	LB	6'3"	234	28	1	
Ed Reynolds	LB	6'5"	242	27		
Bruce Scholtz	LB	6'6"	244	30		
David Ward	LB	6'2"	232	25		
Jim Bowman	DB	6'2"	210	25		
Raymond Clayborn	DB	6'1"	186	34	1	
Eric Coleman	DB	6'	190	22	1	
Howard Feggins	DB	5'10"	190	24	1	
Darryl Holmes	DB	6'2"	190	24		
Maurice Hurst	DB	5'10"	185	21	5	6
Roland James	DB	6'2"	191	31	2	
Fred Marion	DB	6'2"	191	30	2	
Rod McSwain	DB	6'1"	198	27	1	
Rodney Rice	DB	5'8"	180	23		
Erroll Tucker (from BUF)	DB	5'8"	170	25		

Andre Tippett — Shoulder Injury
Ronnie Lippett — Foot Injury
Ed Williams — Knee Injury

Use Name	Pos.	Hgt	Wgt	Age	Int	Pts
Tony Eason (to NYJ)	QB	6'4"	212	28		
Doug Flutie	QB	5'9"	175	26		
Steve Grogan	QB	6'4"	210	36		
Marc Wilson	QB	6'6"	205	32		
Marvin Allen	HB	5'10"	215	23		6
Patrick Egu	HB	5'11"	205	22		6
Reggie Dupard (to WAS)	HB-TE	5'11"	205	25	6	
John Stephens	HB	6'1"	220	23		42
Bob Perryman	FB	6'1"	233	24		12
Mosi Tatupu	FB	6'	227	34		
George Wonsley	FB	5'10"	219	28		
Glenn Antrum	WR	5'11"	175	23		
Hart Lee Dykes	WR	6'4"	218	22		30
Irving Fryar	WR	6'	200	26		18
Cedric Jones	WR	6'1"	184	29		36
Sammy Martin	WR	5'11"	175	24		
Stanley Morgan	WR	5'11"	181	34		18
Kitrick Taylor	WR	5'11"	190	25		
Michael Timpson	WR	5'10"	175	22		
Marv Cook	TE	6'4"	234	23		
Lin Dawson	TE	6'3"	240	30		
Eric Sievers	TE	6'4"	238	31		
Greg Davis (to ATL)	K	5'11"	197	23		61
Jeff Feagles	K	6'	198	23		
Jason Staurovsky	K	5'9"	170	26		56

Russ Francis — Knee Injury
Tony Collins — Suspended by N.F.L.

NEW YORK JETS 4-12 Joe Walton

Scores of Each Game		
24	NEW ENGLAND	27
24	Cleveland	38
40	Miami	33
10	INDIANAPOLIS	17
7	L.A. RAIDERS	14
14	New Orleans	29
3	Buffalo	34
10	SAN FRANCISCO	23
27	NEW ENGLAND	26
23	MIAMI	31
10	INDIANAPOLIS	27
27	ATLANTA	7
20	San Diego	17
0	PITTSBURGH	13
14	L.A. RAMS	38
0	BUFFALO	37

Use Name	Pos.	Hgt	Wgt	Age	Int	Pts
Dave Cadigan	OT	6'4"	285	24		
Jeff Criswell	OT-OG	6'7"	284	25		
Reggie McElroy	OT	6'6"	276	29		
Jeff Oliver	OT-OG	6'4"	292	24		
Curt Singer	OT	6'5"	279	27		
Dan Alexander	OG	6'4"	274	34		
Mike Haight	OG	6'4"	281	26		
Adam Schreiber	OG-C	6'4"	277	27		
Mike Withycombe	OG-OT	6'5"	295	24		
Jim Sweeney	C	6'4"	270	27		
Dennis Byrd	DE	6'5"	270	22		
Ron Stallworth	DE	6'5"	262	23		
Marvin Washington	DE-DT	6'6"	260	23		
Paul Frase	NT-DE	6'5"	273	24		
Marty Lyons	DE-NT	6'5"	269	32		
Gerald Nichols	DT-DE	6'2"	267	25		
Scott Mersereau	NT	6'3"	273	24	1	

Use Name	Pos.	Hgt	Wgt	Age	Int	Pts
Troy Benson	LB	6'2"	235	26		
Adam Bob	LB	6'2"	240	21		
Kyle Clifton	LB	6'4"	236	27		
Alex Gordon	LB	6'5"	246	24	1	
Jeff Lageman	LB-DE	6'5"	250	22		
Kevin McArthur	LB	6'2"	250	26		
Joe Mott	LB	6'4"	253	23		
Ken Rose	LB	6'1"	204	27		
John Booty	DB	6'	179	23	1	
Kerry Glenn	DB	5'9"	175	27	1	
James Hasty	DB	6'	200	24	5	6
Carl Howard	DB	6'2"	190	27		
Bobby Humphery	DB	5'10"	180	28		
Leander Knight	DB	6'1"	196	26		
Erik McMillan	DB	6'2"	197	24	6	18
Rich Miano	DB	6'	200	26		
Michael Mitchell	DB	5'9"	192	27		
George Radachowsky	DB	5'11"	190	26		6
Terry Williams	DB	5'11"	197	23		

Use Name	Pos.	Hgt	Wgt	Age	Int	Pts
Kyle Mackey	QB	6'3"	216	26		
Mark Malone	QB	6'4"	222	30		
Ken O'Brien	QB	6'4"	200	28		
Pat Ryan	QB	6'3"	210	33		
A.B. Brown	HB	5'9"	212	23		
Johnny Hector	HB	5'11"	202	28		30
Freeman McNeil	HB	5'11"	209	30		18
Brad Baxter	FB	6'1"	231	22		
Roger Vick	FB	6'3"	228	25		42
Sanjay Beach	WR	6'	189	23		
Chris Burkett (from BUF)	WR	6'4"	210	27		6
Titus Dixon (to IND)	WR	5'6"	152	23		
Phillip Epps	WR	5'10"	165	29		
Michael Harper	WR	5'10"	180	28		
Al Toon	WR	6'4"	205	26		12
JoJo Townsell	WR	5'9"	180	28		30
Wesley Walker	WR	6'	182	34		
K.D. Dunn	TE	6'2"	237	26		
Billy Griggs	TE	6'3"	234	27		
Keith Neubert	TE	6'5"	250	24		6
Mickey Shuler	TE	6'3"	231	33		
Greg Werner	TE	6'4"	236	22		
Pat Leahy	K	6'	196	38		71
Joe Prokop	K	6'3"	224	29		6

Mark Konecny — Knee Injury

BUFFALO BILLS

RUSHING

Last Name	No.	Yds	Avg	TD
Thomas	298	1244	4.2	6
Kinnebrew	131	533	4.1	6
K. Davis	29	149	5.1	1
Kelly	29	137	4.7	2
Harmon	17	99	5.8	0
Mueller	16	44	2.8	0
Reed	2	31	15.5	0
Reich	9	30	3.3	0
Gelbaugh	1	-3	-3.0	0

RECEIVING

Last Name	No.	Yds	Avg	TD
Reed	88	1312	14.9	9
Thomas	60	669	11.2	6
Harmon	29	363	12.5	4
Johnson	25	303	12.1	1
McKeller	20	341	17.1	2
Metzelaars	18	179	9.9	2
Beebe	17	317	18.6	2
Lofton	8	166	20.8	3
K. Davis	6	92	15.3	2
Kinnebrew	5	60	12.0	0
Mueller	1	8	8.0	0
Rolle	1	1	1.0	1

PUNT RETURNS

Last Name	No.	Yds	Avg	TD
Sutton	31	273	8.8	0
Johnson	1	7	7.0	0

KICKOFF RETURNS

Last Name	No.	Yds	Avg	TD
Harmon	18	409	22.7	0
Beebe	16	353	22.1	0
K. Davis	3	52	17.3	0
Rolle	2	20	10.0	0
Tasker	2	39	19.5	0
Mueller	1	19	19.0	0
Jackson	1	0	0.0	0

PASSING—PUNTING—KICKING

PASSING	Att	Cmp	%	Yds	Yd/Att	TD	Int—	%	RK
Kelly	301	228	58.3	3130	8.01	25	18—	4.6	3
Reich	87	53	60.9	701	8.06	7	2—	2.3	

PUNTING	No.	Avg.
Kidd	67	38.3

KICKING	XP	ATT	%	FG	ATT	%
Norwood	46	47	98	23	30	77

MIAMI DOLPHINS

RUSHING

Last Name	No.	Yds	Avg	TD
Smith	200	659	3.3	6
Stradford	66	240	3.6	1
Logan	57	201	3.5	0
Davenport	14	56	4.0	1
Jensen	8	50	6.3	0
Hampton	17	47	2.8	0
Secules	4	39	9.8	0
T. Brown	13	26	2.0	0
Faaola	2	10	5.0	0
Clayton	3	9	3.0	0
Roby	2	0	0.0	0
Reaves	1	-1	-1.0	0
Marino	14	-7	-0.5	2

RECEIVING

Last Name	No.	Yds	Avg	TD
Clayton	64	1011	15.8	9
Jensen	61	557	9.1	6
Duper	49	717	14.6	1
Edmunds	32	382	11.9	3
Banks	30	520	17.3	1
Stradford	25	233	9.3	0
A. Brown	24	410	17.1	5
T. Brown	13	117	9.0	0
Hampton	8	25	3.1	0
Schwedes	7	174	24.9	1
Smith	7	81	11.6	0
Logan	5	34	6.8	0
Davenport	3	19	6.3	0
Kinchen	1	12	12.0	0
Faaola	1	8	8.0	0
Hardy	1	2	2.0	0

PUNT RETURNS

Last Name	No.	Yds	Avg	TD
Schwedes	18	210	11.7	1
Stradford	14	129	9.2	0
Gibson	1	-1	-1.0	0
Williams	0	0	0.0	0

KICKOFF RETURNS

Last Name	No.	Yds	Avg	TD
Logan	24	613	25.5	1
Hampton	17	303	17.8	0
Reaves	6	84	14.0	0
Schwedes	3	24	8.0	0
Faaola	2	30	15.0	0
Kinchen	2	26	13.0	0
A. Brown	2	9	4.5	0
Williams	1	21	21.0	0
Davenport	1	19	19.0	0
Ahrens	1	10	10.0	0
Goode	1	8	8.0	0
Brudzinski	1	6	6.0	0

PASSING—PUNTING—KICKING

PASSING	Att	Cmp	%	Yds	Yd/Att	TD	Int—	%	RK
Marino	550	308	56.0	3997	7.27	24	22—	4.0	5
Secules	50	22	44.0	286	5.72	1	3—	6.0	
Jensen	1	1	100.0	19	19.00	0	0—	0.0	

PUNTING	No.	Avg.
Roby	59	41.7

KICKING	XP	Att.	%	FG	Att	%
Stoyonovich	38	39	97	19	26	73

INDIANAPOLIS COLTS

RUSHING

Last Name	No.	Yds	Avg	TD
Dickerson	314	1311	4.2	7
Bentley	75	299	4.0	1
Trudeau	35	91	2.6	2
Chandler	7	57	8.1	1
Hunter	13	47	3.6	0
Verdin	4	39	9.8	0
Rison	3	18	6.0	0
Ramsey	4	5	1.3	0
Brooks	2	-3	-1.5	0
Stark	1	-11	-11.0	0

RECEIVING

Last Name	No.	Yds	Avg	TD
Brooks	63	919	14.6	4
Rison	52	820	15.8	4
Bentley	52	525	10.1	3
Dickerson	30	211	7.0	1
Verdin	20	381	19.1	1
Beach	14	87	6.2	2
Boyer	11	58	5.3	2
Pruitt	5	71	14.2	1

PUNT RETURNS

Last Name	No.	Yds	Avg	TD
Verdin	23	296	12.9	1
Rison	2	20	10.0	0
C. Washington	1	6	6.0	0
Prior	0	0	0.0	0

KICKOFF RETURNS

Last Name	No.	Yds	Avg	TD
Verdin	19	371	19.5	0
Bentley	17	328	19.3	0
Pruitt	12	257	21.4	0
Rison	8	150	18.8	0
Hunter	4	58	14.5	0

PASSING—PUNTING—KICKING

PASSING	Att	Cmp	%	Yds	Yd/Att	TD	Int—	%	RK
Trudeau	362	190	52.5	2317	6.40	15	13—	3.6	12
Chandler	80	39	48.8	537	6.71	2	3—	3.8	
Ramsey	50	24	48.0	280	5.60	1	1—	2.0	
Bentley	1	0	0.0	0	0.00	0	0—	0.0	

PUNTING	No.	Avg.
Stark	80	42.4

KICKING	XP	ATT	%	FG	ATT	%
Biasucci	31	32	97	21	27	78

NEW ENGLAND PATRIOTS

RUSHING

Last Name	No.	Yds	Avg	TD
Stephens	244	833	3.4	7
Perryman	150	562	3.7	2
Dupard	37	111	3.0	1
Flutie	16	87	5.4	0
Allen	11	51	4.6	1
Wilson	7	42	6.0	0
Tatupu	11	38	3.5	0
Egu	3	20	6.7	1
Martin	2	20	10.0	0
Grogan	9	19	2.1	0
Fryar	2	15	7.5	0
C. Jones	1	3	3.0	0
Eason	3	-2	-0.7	0
Wonsley	2	-2	-1.0	0

RECEIVING

Last Name	No.	Yds	Avg	TD
Sievers	54	615	11.4	0
Dykes	49	795	16.2	5
C. Jones	48	670	14.0	6
Fryar	29	537	18.5	3
Perryman	29	195	6.7	0
Morgan	28	486	17.4	3
Stephens	21	207	9.9	0
Martin	13	229	17.6	0
Dawson	12	101	8.4	0
Tatupu	10	54	5.4	0
Dupard	6	70	11.7	0
Cook	3	13	4.3	0

PUNT RETURNS

Last Name	No.	Yds	Avg	TD
Martin	19	164	8.6	0
Tucker	19	165	8.7	0
Fryar	12	107	8.9	0
Hurst	1	6	6.0	0
Taylor	0	0	0.0	0

KICKOFF RETURNS

Last Name	No.	Yds	Avg	TD
Martin	24	584	24.3	0
Tucker	23	436	19.0	0
Rice	11	242	22.0	0
Allen	6	124	20.7	0
Taylor	3	52	17.3	0
Wonsley	3	69	23.0	0
Egu	2	26	13.0	0
Hodge	2	19	9.5	0
Timpson	2	13	6.5	0
Fryar	1	47	47.0	0
Rehder	1	14	14.0	0
Tatupu	1	2	2.0	0

PASSING—PUNTING—KICKING

PASSING	Att	Cmp	%	Yds	Yd/Att	TD	Int—	%	RK
Grogan	261	133	51.0	1697	6.50	9	14—	5.4	13
Wilson	150	75	50.0	1006	6.71	3	5—	3.3	
Eason	141	79	56.0	1016	7.21	4	6—	4.3	
Flutie	91	36	39.6	493	5.42	2	4—	4.4	
Feagles	2	0	0.0	0	0.00	0	0—	0.0	
Tatupu	1	1	100.0	15	15.00	0	0—	0.0	

PUNTING	No.	Avg.
Feagles	64	37.4

KICKING	XP	ATT	%	FG	ATT	%
Davis	25	28	89	23	34	68
Staurovsky	14	14	100	14	17	82

NEW YORK JETS

RUSHING

Last Name	No.	Yds	Avg	TD
Hector	177	702	4.0	3
Vick	112	434	3.9	5
McNeil	80	352	4.4	2
Brown	12	63	5.3	0
O'Brien	9	18	2.0	0
Prokop	1	17	17.0	1
Epps	1	14	14.0	0
Harper	1	3	3.0	0
Mackey	2	3	1.5	0
Malone	1	0	0.0	0
Ryan	1	-1	-1.0	0
Burkett	1	-4	-4.0	0
Lageman	1	-5	-5.0	0

RECEIVING

Last Name	No.	Yds	Avg	TD
Toon	63	693	11.0	2
Townsell	45	787	17.5	5
Hector	38	330	8.7	2
Vick	34	241	7.1	2
McNeil	31	310	10.0	1
Shuler	29	322	11.1	0
Neubert	28	302	10.8	1
Burkett	24	298	12.4	1
Griggs	9	112	12.4	0
Werner	8	115	14.4	0
Epps	8	108	13.5	0
Walker	8	89	11.1	0
Harper	7	127	18.1	0
Brown	4	10	2.5	0
Dunn	2	13	6.5	0

PUNT RETURNS

Last Name	No.	Yds	Avg	TD
Townsell	33	299	9.1	0

KICKOFF RETURNS

Last Name	No.	Yds	Avg	TD
Townsell	34	653	19.2	0
Humphery	24	414	17.3	0
Epps	9	154	17.1	0
Dixon	4	67	16.8	0
Nichols	2	9	4.5	0
Washington	1	11	11.0	0
Byrd	1	1	1.0	0

PASSING—PUNTING—KICKING

PASSING	Att	Cmp	%	Yds	Yd/Att	TD	Int—	%	RK
O'Brien	477	288	60.4	3346	7.01	12	18—	3.8	8
Ryan	30	15	50.0	153	5.10	1	3—	10.0	
Mackey	25	11	44.0	125	5.00	0	1—	4.0	
Malone	2	2	100.0	13	6.50	0	0—	0.0	

PUNTING	No.	Avg.
Prokop	87	39.4

KICKING	XP	Att	%	FG	Att	%
Leahy	29	30	97	14	21	67

CLEVELAND BROWNS 9-6-1 Bud Carson

Scores of Each Game		
51	Pittsburgh	0
38	N.Y. JETS	24
14	Cincinnati	21
16	DENVER	13
10	Miami	*13
7	PITTSBURGH	17
27	CHICAGO	7
28	HOUSTON	17
42	Tampa Bay	31
17	Seattle	7
10	KANSAS CITY	*10
10	Detroit	13
0	CINCINNATI	21
17	Indianapolis	*23
23	MINNESOTA	*17
24	Houston	20

Use Name	Pos.	Hgt	Wgt	Age	Int	Pts
Rickey Bolden	OT	6'6"	280	27		
Paul Farren	OT	6'5"	280	28		
Mike Graybill	OT	6'7"	275	22		
Cody Risien	OT	6'7"	280	32		
Kevin Robbins	OT	6'6"	286	22		
Kevin Simons	OT	6'3"	315	22		
Daryle Smith	OT	6'5"	278	25		
Ted Banker	OG	6'2"	290	28		
Dan Fike	OG	6'7"	280	28		
Tony Jones	OG-OT	6'5"	280	23		
Tom Baugh	C	6'4"	290	25		
Gregg Rakoczy	C	6'3"	290	24		
Al Baker	DE	6'6"	280	32		
Robert Banks	DE	6'5"	255	25		
Tom Gibson	DE	6'7"	250	25		
Marlon Jones	DE	6'4"	270	25		
Andrew Stewart	DE	6'5"	265	23		
Carl Hairston	DT	6'3"	280	36		
Michael Dean Perry	DT	6'1"	285	24		
Chris Pike	DT	6'8"	290	25		

Darryl Sims — Knee Injury

Use Name	Pos.	Hgt	Wgt	Age	Int	Pts
Clifford Charlton	LB	6'3"	240	24		
David Grayson	LB	6'2"	230	25	2	12
Eddie Johnson	LB	6'1"	225	29		
Mike Johnson	LB	6'1"	225	26	3	
Clay Matthews	LB	6'2"	245	33	1	6
Van Waiters	LB	6'4"	240	24		6
TonyBlaylock	DB	5'11"	190	24		
Stephen Braggs	DB	5'10"	180	24		
Hanford Dixon	DB	5'11"	195	30	1	
Thane Gash	DB	6'	200	24	3	12
Mark Harper	DB	5'9"	185	27	3	
Kyle Kramer	DB	6'3"	190	22	1	
Robert Lyons	DB	6'1"	195	23	1	
Frank Minnifield	DB	5'9"	185	29	3	
Felix Wright	DB	6'2"	190	30	9	6

Use Name	Pos.	Hgt	Wgt	Age	Int	Pts
Bernie Kosar	QB	6'5"	210	25		6
Mike Pagel	QB	6'2"	211	28		
Keith Jones	HB	5'10"	190	23		6
Eric Metcalf	HB-WR	5'10"	185	21		60
Mike Oliphant	HB	5'10"	183	26		6
Kevin Mack	FB	6'	235	27		6
Tim Manoa	FB	6'1"	227	24		30
Barry Redden	FB-HB	5'10"	219	29		6
Brian Brennan	WR	5'9"	178	27		
Vernon Joines	WR	6'2"	200	23		
Reggie Langhorne	WR	6'2"	200	26		12
Gerald McNeil	WR	5'7"	147	27		
Webster Slaughter	WR	6'	170	24		36
Lawyer Tillman	WR	6'5"	230	23		18
Ron Middleton	TE	6'2"	252	24		6
Ozzie Newsome	TE	6'2"	232	33		6
Derek Tennell	TE	6'5"	245	25		6
Matt Bahr	K	5'10"	175	33		99
Bryan Wagner	K	6'2"	200	27		

HOUSTON OILERS 9-7 Jerry Glanville

Scores of Each Game		
7	Minnesota	38
34	San Diego	27
41	BUFFALO	*47
39	MIAMI	7
13	New England	23
33	Chicago	28
27	PITTSBURGH	0
17	Cleveland	28
35	DETROIT	31
26	CINCINNATI	24
23	L.A. RAIDERS	7
0	Kansas City	34
23	Pittsburgh	16
20	TAMPA BAY	17
7	Cincinnati	61
20	CLEVELAND	24

Use Name	Pos.	Hgt	Wgt	Age	Int	Pts
Bruce Davis	OT	6'6"	315	33		
Don Maggs	OG-OT	6'5"	285	27		
Dean Steinkuhler	OT	6'3"	291	28		
David Williams	OT	6'5"	292	23		
Bruce Matthews	OG-C	6'4"	293	28		
Mike Munchak	OG	6'3"	284	29		
Jay Pennison	C	6'1"	282	27		
George Yarno	C-OG	6'2"	270	32		
Richard Byrd	DE-NT	6'4"	267	27		
Ray Childress	DE-NT	6'6"	274	26		
William Fuller	DE	6'3"	269	27		
Sean Jones	DE	6'7"	273	26		
* Anthony Spears	DE	6'5"	260	23		
Glenn Montgomery	NT	6'	274	22		
Doug Smith	NT	6'5"	282	30		

Mark Garalczyk — Ankle Injury

* played only in playoff game

Use Name	Pos.	Hgt	Wgt	Age	Int	Pts
John Brantley	LB	6'2"	245	22		
Eric Fairs	LB	6'3"	240	25		
John Grimsley	LB	6'2"	238	27		
Scott Kozak	LB	6'3"	226	23		
Robert Lyles	LB	6'1"	230	28	4	
Johnny Meads	LB	6'2"	235	28		
Eugene Seale	LB	5'10"	240	25		6
Al Smith	LB	6'1"	236	24		
Billy Bell	DB	5'10"	170	28		
Patrick Allen	DB	5'10"	182	28		
Steve Brown	DB	5'11"	192	29	5	
Cris Dishman	DB	6'	180	24	4	6
Jeff Donaldson	DB	6'	190	27		
Tracey Eaton	DB	6'1"	195	24	3	
Kenny Johnson	DB	5'10"	172	31		
Richard Johnson	DB	6'1"	190	25	1	
Bubba McDowell	DB	6'1"	195	22	4	2

Use Name	Pos.	Hgt	Wgt	Age	Int	Pts
Cody Carlson	QB	6'3"	199	25		
Warren Moon	QB	6'3"	210	32		24
Allen Pinkett	HB	5'9"	192	25		12
Mike Rozier	HB	5'10"	213	28		12
Lorenzo White	HB	5'11"	209	23		30
Steve Avery	FB	6'1"	216	23		
Alonzo Highsmith	FB	6'1"	234	24		36
Tracy Johnson	FB	6'	232	22		
Curtis Duncan	WR	5'11"	185	24		30
Ernest Givins	WR	5'9"	172	24		18
Leonard Harris	WR	5'8"	162	28		12
Drew Hill	WR	5'9"	175	32		48
Kenny Jackson	WR	6'	183	27		
Haywood Jeffires	WR	6'2"	198	24		12
Bob Mrosko	TE	6'6"	265	23		
Chris Verhulst	TE	6'2"	249	23		
Greg Montgomery	K	6'3"	213	24		
Tony Zendejas	K	5'8"	165	29		115

PITTSBURGH STEELERS 9-7 Chuck Noll

Scores of Each Game		
0	CLEVELAND	51
10	Cincinnati	41
27	MINNESOTA	14
23	Detroit	3
16	CINCINNATI	26
17	Cleveland	7
0	Houston	27
23	KANSAS CITY	17
7	Denver	34
0	CHICAGO	20
20	SAN DIEGO	17
34	Miami	14
16	HOUSTON	23
13	N.Y. Jets	0
28	NEW ENGLAND	10
31	Tampa Bay	22

Use Name	Pos.	Hgt	Wgt	Age	Int	Pts
Tunch Ilkin	OT	6'3"	266	31		
John Jackson	OT	6'6"	282	24		
Craig Wolfley	OT-OG	6'1"	269	31		
Brian Blankenship	OG	6'1"	275	26		
Terry Long	OG	5'11"	275	30		
Tom Ricketts	OG	6'5"	298	23		
John Rienstra	OG	6'5"	268	26		
Dermontti Dawson	C	6'2"	271	24		
Chuck Lanza	C	6'2"	263	24		
Tim Johnson	DE	6'3"	261	24		
Aaron Jones	DE-LB	6'5"	257	22		
Keith Willis	DE	6'1"	263	30		
Lorenzo Freeman	NT	6'5"	298	25		
Gerald Williams	NT	6'3"	262	25		

Use Name	Pos.	Hgt	Wgt	Age	Int	Pts
Bryan Hinkle	LB	6'2"	222	30	1	
A.J. Jenkins	LB-DE	6'2"	237	23		
David Little	LB	6'1"	230	30	3	
Greg Lloyd	LB	6'2"	224	24	3	
Hardy Nickerson	LB	6'2"	229	24		
Jerry Olsavsky	LB	6'1"	222	22		
* Tracy Simien	LB	6'1"	245	22		
Tyronne Stowe	LB	6'1"	236	24		
Jerrol Williams	LB	6'5"	242	22		
David Arnold	DB	6'3"	208	22		
Thomas Everett	DB	5'9"	179	24	3	
Larry Griffin	DB	6'	200	26	1	
Delton Hall	DB	6'1"	205	24	1	
David Johnson	DB	6'	185	23	1	
Carnell Lake	DB	6'1"	205	22	1	
Dwayne Woodruff	DB	6'	198	32	4	6
Rod Woodson	DB	6'	199	24	3	6

Vinson Smith — Foot Injury

* played only in playoff game

Use Name	Pos.	Hgt	Wgt	Age	Int	Pts
Todd Blackledge	QB	6'3"	227	28		
Bubby Brister	QB	6'3"	205	27		
Rick Strom	QB	6'2"	210	24		
Rodney Carter	HB	6'	216	24		24
Dwight Stone	HB-WR	6'	188	25		
Eric Wilkerson	HB-WR	5'9"	185	22		
Warren Williams	HB	6'	202	24		6
Tim Worley	HB	6'2"	228	22		30
Merril Hoge	FB	6'2"	226	24		48
Tim Tyrrell	FB	6'1"	215	28		
Ray Wallace	FB	6'	230	26		6
Derek Hill	WR	6'1"	193	21		6
Jason Johnson	WR	5'11"	180	23		
Louis Lipps	WR	5'10"	190	27		36
Mark Stock	WR	5'11"	177	23		
Weegie Thompson	WR	6'6"	216	28		
Mike Hinnant	TE	6'3"	258	22		
Mike Mularkey	TE	6'4"	237	27		6
Terry O'Shea	TE	6'4"	236	22		
Gary Anderson	K	5'11"	175	30		91
Harry Newsome	K	6'	188	26		

CINCINNATI BENGALS 8-8 Sam Wyche

Scores of Each Game		
14	Chicago	17
41	PITTSBURGH	10
21	CLEVELAND	14
21	Kansas City	17
26	Pittsburgh	16
13	MIAMI	20
12	INDIANAPOLIS	23
56	TAMPA BAY	23
7	L.A. Raiders	28
24	Houston	26
42	DETROIT	7
7	Buffalo	24
21	Cleveland	0
17	SEATTLE	24
61	HOUSTON	7
21	Minnesota	29

Use Name	Pos.	Hgt	Wgt	Age	Int	Pts
Scott Jones	OT	6'5"	278	23		
Ken Moyer	OT	6'6"	292	22		
Anthony Munoz	OT	6'6"	278	31		
Joe Walter	OT	6'6"	290	26		
Paul Jetton	OG	6'4"	295	24		
Brian Blados	OG-C	6'5"	295	27		
Max Montoya	OG	6'5"	275	33		
Bruce Reimers	OG	6'7"	280	28		
Bruce Kozerski	C-OG	6'4"	275	27		
Jason Buck	DE	6'5"	264	26		
Mike Hammerstein	DE	6'4"	272	26		
Skip McClendon	DE	6'7"	275	25		
Jim Skow	DE	6'3"	255	26		
Natu Tuatagaloa	DE	6'4"	265	23		
David Grant	NT	6'4"	277	23		
Tim Krumrie	NT	6'2"	268	29		
Dana Wells	NT	6'	270	23		

Use Name	Pos.	Hgt	Wgt	Age	Int	Pts
Leo Barker	LB	6'2"	227	29		
Ed Brady	LB	6'2"	235	29		
Joe Kelly	LB	6'2"	231	24	1	
Rich Romer	LB	6'3"	222	23		
Kevin Walker	LB	6'2"	238	23		
Leon White	LB	6'3"	245	25	1	6
Reggie Williams	LB	6'1"	232	34		
Carl Zander	LB	6'2"	235	26		
Chris Barber	DB	6'	187	25		
Lewis Billups	DB	5'11"	190	25	2	
Barney Bussey	DB	6'	195	27	1	6
Richard Carey	DB	5'9"	185	21	1	
Rickey Dixon	DB	5'11"	181	22	3	
David Fulcher	DB	6'3"	228	27	8	
Robert Jackson	DB	5'10"	186	30		
Eric Thomas	DB	5'11"	181	24	4	6
Solomon Wilcots	DB	5'11"	185	24		

Use Name	Pos.	Hgt	Wgt	Age	Int	Pts
Boomer Esiason	QB	6'4"	225	28		
Turk Schonert	QB	6'1"	196	32		
Erik Wilhelm	QB	6'3"	210	23		
Eric Ball	HB-FB	6'2"	211	23		18
James Brooks	HB	5'10"	182	30		54
John Holifield	HB	6'	202	25		
Stanford Jennings	HB-FB	6'1"	205	27		18
Craig Taylor	FB	5'11"	224	23		30
Ickey Woods	FB	6'2"	232	23		12
Eddie Brown	WR	6'	185	26		36
John Garrett	WR	5'11"	180	24		
Kendal Smith	WR	5'9"	189	23		6
Ira Hillary	WR	5'11"	190	26		6
Mike Martin	WR	5'10"	186	28		12
Tim McGee	WR	5'10"	175	25		48
Carl Parker	WR	6'2"	201	24		
Rodney Holman	TE	6'3"	238	29		54
Eric Kattus	TE	6'5"	235	26		
Jim Riggs	TE	6'5"	245	25		
Jim Breech	K	5'6"	161	33		73
Jim Gallery	K	6'1"	190	28		19
Lee Johnson	K	6'2"	198	27		

Stanley Wilson — Suspended by N.F.L.

CLEVELAND BROWNS

RUSHING

Last Name	No.	Yds	Avg	TD
Metcalf	187	633	3.4	6
Manoa	87	289	3.3	3
Redden	40	180	4.5	1
K. Jones	43	160	3.7	1
Mack	37	130	3.5	1
Oliphant	15	97	6.5	1
Kosar	30	70	2.3	1
McNeil	2	32	16.0	0
Langhorne	5	19	3.8	0
Pagel	2	-1	-0.5	0

RECEIVING

Last Name	No.	Yds	Avg	TD
Slaughter	65	1236	19.0	6
Langhorne	60	749	12.5	2
Metcalf	54	397	7.4	4
Newsome	29	324	11.2	1
Brennan	28	289	10.3	0
Manoa	27	241	8.9	2
K. Jones	15	126	8.4	0
McNeil	10	114	11.4	0
Tillman	6	70	11.7	2
Redden	6	34	5.7	0
Oliphant	3	22	7.3	0
Mack	2	7	3.5	0
Waiters	1	14	14.0	1
Middleton	1	5	5.0	1
Tennell	1	4	4.0	1
Kosar	1	-7	-7.0	0

PUNT RETURNS

Last Name	No.	Yds	Avg	TD
McNeil	49	496	10.1	0

KICKOFF RETURNS

Last Name	No.	Yds	Avg	TD
Metcalf	31	718	23.2	0
Oliphant	5	69	13.8	0
McNeil	4	61	15.3	0
K. Jones	4	42	10.5	0
Braggs	2	20	10.0	0
Redden	2	2	1.0	0
Joines	1	12	12.0	0
E. Johnson	1	8	8.0	0

PASSING — PUNTING — KICKING

PASSING	Att	Cmp	%	Yds	Yd/Att	TD	Int— %	RK
Kosar	513	303	59.1	3533	6.89	18	14— 2.7	4
Pagel	14	5	35.7	60	4.29	1	1— 7.1	
Metcalf	2	1	50.0	32	16.00	1	0— 0.0	

PUNTING	No.	Avg.
Wagner	97	39.4

KICKING	XP	ATT	%	FG	ATT	%
M. Bahr	40	40	100	16	24	67

HOUSTON OILERS

RUSHING

Last Name	No.	Yds	Avg	TD
Highsmith	128	531	4.1	4
Pinkett	94	449	4.8	1
White	104	349	3.4	5
Rozier	88	301	3.4	2
Moon	70	268	3.8	4
Gr. Montgomery	3	17	5.7	0
T. Johnson	4	16	4.0	0
Duncan	1	0	0.0	0
Carlson	3	-3	-1.0	0

RECEIVING

Last Name	No.	Yds	Avg	TD
Hill	66	938	14.2	8
Givins	55	794	14.4	3
Jeffires	47	619	13.2	2
Duncan	43	613	14.3	5
Pinkett	31	239	7.7	1
Highsmith	18	201	11.2	2
Harris	13	202	15.5	2
White	6	37	6.2	0
Verhulst	4	48	12.0	0
Jackson	4	31	7.8	0
Rozier	4	28	7.0	0
Mrosko	3	28	9.3	0
T. Johnson	1	8	8.0	0

PUNT RETURNS

Last Name	No.	Yds	Avg	TD
K. Johnson	19	122	6.4	0

KICKOFF RETURNS

Last Name	No.	Yds	Avg	TD
K. Johnson	21	372	17.7	0
White	17	303	17.8	0
Harris	14	331	23.6	0
T. Johnson	13	224	17.2	0
Mrosko	3	46	15.3	0
Williams	2	8	4.0	0
Fairs	1	1	1.0	0
Lyles	1	0	0.0	0
Gl. Montgomery	1	0	0.0	0
Verhulst	1	0	0.0	0

PASSING — PUNTING — KICKING

PASSING	Att	Cmp	%	Yds	Yd/Att	TD	Int— %	RK
Moon	464	280	60.3	3631	7.83	23	14— 3.0	2
Carlson	31	15	48.4	155	5.00	0	1— 3.2	
Zendejas	1	0	0.0	0	0.00	0	1—100.0	

PUNTING	No.	Avg.
Montgomery	58	41.8

KICKING	XP	ATT	%	FG	ATT	%
Zendejas	40	40	100	25	37	68

PITTSBURGH STEELERS

RUSHING

Last Name	No.	Yds	Avg	TD
Worley	195	770	3.9	5
Hoge	186	621	3.3	8
Lipps	13	180	13.8	1
W. Williams	37	131	3.5	1
Stone	10	53	5.3	0
Brister	27	25	0.9	0
Blackledge	9	20	2.2	0
Carter	11	16	1.5	1
Wallace	5	10	2.0	1
Tyrrell	1	3	3.0	0
Strom	4	-3	-0.8	0
Newsome	2	-8	-4.0	0

RECEIVING

Last Name	No.	Yds	Avg	TD
Lipps	50	944	18.9	5
Carter	38	267	7.0	3
Hoge	34	271	8.0	0
Hill	28	455	16.3	1
Mularkey	22	326	14.8	1
Worley	15	113	7.5	0
Stone	7	92	13.1	0
W. Williams	6	48	8.0	0
Stock	4	74	18.5	0
Thompson	4	74	18.5	0
O'Shea	1	8	8.0	0
Brister	1	-10	10.0	0

PUNT RETURNS

Last Name	No.	Yds	Avg	TD
Woodson	29	207	7.1	0
Hill	5	22	4.4	0
Lipps	4	27	6.8	0
J. Johnson	2	22	11.0	0

KICKOFF RETURNS

Last Name	No.	Yds	Avg	TD
Woodson	36	982	27.3	1
Stone	7	173	24.7	0
Thompson	4	41	10.3	0
J. Williams	4	31	7.8	0
J. Johnson	3	43	14.3	0
Griffin	1	21	21.0	0
Hinnant	1	13	13.0	0

PASSING — PUNTING — KICKING

PASSING	Att	Cmp	%	Yds	Yd/Att	TD	Int— %	RK
Brister	342	187	54.7	2365	6.92	9	10— 2.9	11
Blackledge	60	22	36.7	282	4.70	1	3— 5.0	
Carter	1	1	100.0	15	15.00	0	0— 0.0	
Strom	1	0	0.0	0	0.00	0	0— 0.0	

PUNTING	No.	Avg.
Newsome	83	40.6

KICKING	XP	Att	%	FG	Att	%
Anderson	28	28	100	21	30	70

CINCINNATI BENGALS

RUSHING

Last Name	No.	Yds	Avg	TD
Brooks	221	1239	5.6	7
Ball	98	391	4.0	3
Jennings	83	293	3.5	2
Esiason	47	278	5.9	0
Taylor	30	111	3.7	3
Woods	29	94	3.2	2
McGee	2	36	18.0	0
Wilhelm	6	30	5.0	0
Holifield	11	20	1.8	0
Hillary	1	-2	-2.0	0
Johnson	1	-7	-7.0	0

RECEIVING

Last Name	No.	Yds	Avg	TD
McGee	65	1211	18.6	8
Brown	52	814	15.7	6
Holman	50	736	14.7	9
Brooks	37	306	8.3	2
Hillary	17	162	9.5	1
Martin	15	160	10.7	2
Kattus	12	93	7.8	0
Smith	10	140	14.0	1
Jennings	10	119	11.9	1
Ball	6	44	7.3	0
Riggs	5	29	5.8	0
Taylor	4	44	11.0	2
Garrett	2	29	14.5	0
Holifield	2	18	9.0	0
Parker	1	45	45.0	0

PUNT RETURNS

Last Name	No.	Yds	Avg	TD
Martin	15	107	7.1	0
Smith	12	54	4.5	0
Hillary	6	19	3.2	0
Carey	3	29	9.7	0

KICKOFF RETURNS

Last Name	No.	Yds	Avg	TD
Jennings	26	525	20.2	0
Hillary	14	223	15.9	0
Carey	6	104	17.3	0
Smith	5	65	13.0	0
Ball	1	19	19.0	0
Taylor	1	5	5.0	0
Holifield	1	0	0.0	0

PASSING — PUNTING — KICKING

PASSING	Att	Cmp	%	Yds	Yd/Att	TD	Int— %	RK
Esiason	455	258	56.7	3525	7.75	28	11— 2.4	1
Wilhelm	56	30	53.6	425	7.59	4	2— 3.6	
Schonert	2	0	0.0	0	0.00	0	0— 0.0	

PUNTING	No.	Avg.
Johnson	63	38.8
Breech	2	29.0

KICKING	XP	ATT	%	FG	ATT	%
Breech	37	38	97	12	14	81
Jim Gallery	13	13	100	2	6	33
Johnson	0	1	0	0	0	—

DENVER BRONCOS 11-5 Dan Reeves

Scores of Each Game		
34	KANSAS CITY	20
28	Buffalo	14
31	L.A. RAIDERS	21
13	Cleveland	16
16	SAN DIEGO	10
14	INDIANAPOLIS	3
24	Seattle	* 21
24	PHILADELPHIA	28
34	PITTSBURGH	7
16	Kansas City	13
14	Washington	10
41	SEATTLE	14
13	L.A. Raiders	* 16
7	N.Y. GIANTS	14
37	Phoenix	0
16	San Diego	19

Use Name	Pos.	Hgt	Wgt	Age	Int	Pts
Jim Juriga	OT-OG	6'6"	269	24		
Ken Lanier	OT	6'3"	269	30		
Gerald Perry	OT	6'6"	305	23		
Keith Bishop	OG-C	6'3"	265	32		
Monte Smith	OG	6'5"	270	22		
Doug Widell	OG	6'4"	287	22		
Keith Kartz	C	6'4"	270	26		
Mike Ruether	C	6'4"	275	26		
Alphonso Carreker	DE	6'6"	272	27		
Brad Henke	DE-NT	6'3"	275	23		
Ron Holmes	DE	6'4"	265	26		
Jake McCullough	DE	6'5"	270	24		
Warren Powers	DE	6'6"	287	24		
Andre Townsend	DE-NT	6'3"	265	26		
Greg Kragen	NT	6'3"	260	27		6

Billy Bryan — Knee Injury
Andrew Provence — Hip Injury

Use Name	Pos.	Hgt	Wgt	Age	Int	Pts
Michael Brooks	LB	6'1"	235	24		2
Scott Curtis	LB	6'1"	230	24		
Rick Dennison	LB	6'3"	220	31	1	
Simon Fletcher	LB-DE	6'5"	240	27		
Bruce Klostermann	LB	6'4"	232	26		
Tim Lucas	LB	6'3"	230	28		
Karl Mecklenburg	LB	6'3"	230	29		6
Marc Munford	LB	6'2"	231	24	2	
Steve Atwater	DB	6'3"	217	22	3	
Tyrone Braxton	DB	5'11"	174	24	6	6
Darren Carrington	DB	6'1"	189	22	1	
Kip Corrington	DB	6'	175	24	1	
Mark Haynes	DB	5'11"	195	30		
Wymon Henderson	DB	5'10"	186	27	3	
Randy Robbins	DB	6'2"	189	25	2	6
Richard Shelton	DB	5'10"	180	23		
Dennis Smith	DB	6'3"	200	30	2	

Use Name	Pos.	Hgt	Wgt	Age	Int	Pts
John Elway	QB	6'3"	210	29		18
Gary Kubiak	QB	6'	192	28		
Bobby Humphrey	HB	6'1"	201	22		48
Jeff Alexander	FB	6'	232	24		12
Melvin Bratton	FB	6'1"	225	24		24
Sammy Winder	FB	5'11"	203	30		12
Steve Sewell	FB-WR	6'3"	210	26		18
Ken Bell	WR	5'10"	190	24		
Mark Jackson	WR	5'9"	180	26		12
Vance Johnson	WR	5'11"	185	26		42
Ricky Nattiel	WR	5'9"	180	23		6
Chris Woods	WR	5'11"	190	27		
Michael Young	WR	6'1"	183	27		12
Clarence Kay	TE	6'2"	237	28		12
Pat Kelly	TE	6'6"	252	23		
Orson Mobley	TE	6'5"	256	26		
Mike Horan	K	5'11"	190	30		
David Treadwell	K	6'1"	175	22		120

Tony Dorsett — Knee Injury

KANSAS CITY CHIEFS 8-7-1 Marty Schottenheimer

Scores of Each Game		
20	Denver	34
24	L.A. RAIDERS	19
6	San Diego	21
17	CINCINNATI	21
20	Seattle	16
14	L.A. Raiders	20
36	DALLAS	28
17	Pittsburgh	23
20	SEATTLE	10
13	DENVER	16
10	Cleveland	* 10
34	HOUSTON	0
26	MIAMI	21
21	Green Bay	3
13	SAN DIEGO	20
27	Miami	24

Use Name	Pos.	Hgt	Wgt	Age	Int	Pts
John Alt	OT	6'7"	290	27		
Irv Eatman	OT	6'7"	294	28		
David Lutz	OT-OG	6'6"	290	29		
Mark Adickes	OG	6'4"	273	28		
Rich Baldinger	OG-OT	6'4"	285	29		
Mark Cannon (from GB)	C	6'3"	258	27		
Gene Chilton	C-OG	6'3"	286	25		
Michael Harris	C-OG	6'4"	306	23		
Mike Webster	C	6'1"	260	37		
Bruce Clark	DE	6'3"	275	31		
Mike Bell	DE	6'4"	260	31		
Leonard Griffin	DE	6'4"	270	26		
Neil Smith	DE	6'4"	270	23		6
Greg Meisner	DE-NT	6'3"	271	30		
Bill Maas	NT	6'5"	268	27		6
Dan Saleaumua	NT	6'	289	23	1	

Use Name	Pos.	Hgt	Wgt	Age	Int	Pts
Walker Lee Ashley	LB	6'	230	29	1	
Louis Cooper	LB	6'2"	245	25		
Dino Hackett	LB	6'3"	228	25		
Stacy Harvey	LB	6'4"	245	24		
Mike Junkin	LB	6'3"	238	24		
Chris Martin	LB	6'2"	231	28		
Rob McGovern	LB	6'2"	223	23		2
Angelo Snipes	LB	6'	227	26	1	
Derrick Thomas	LB	6'3"	234	22		
Lloyd Burruss	DB	6'	205	31	1	
Deron Cherry	DB	5'11"	203	29	2	
Danny Copeland	DB	6'2"	210	23		
Kenny Hill	DB	6'	195	31	1	
Albert Lewis	DB	6'2"	198	28	4	
J.C. Pearson	DB	5'11"	190	25		
Stan Petry	DB	5'11"	175	23		
Kevin Porter	DB	5'10"	215	23		
Kevin Ross	DB	5'9"	182	27		

Jerry McCabe — Broken Arm

Use Name	Pos.	Hgt	Wgt	Age	Int	Pts
Steve DeBerg	QB	6'2"	210	35		
Mike Elkins	QB	6'3"	225	23		
Ron Jaworski	QB	6'2"	205	38		
Steve Pelluer	QB	6'4"	212	27		12
Paul Ott Carruth	HB	6'1"	220	28		
Kenny Gamble	HB	5'10"	197	24		6
Herman Heard	HB	5'10"	190	27		6
Todd McNair	HB	6'1"	185	24		6
Tommie Agee	FB	6'	218	25		
Christian Okoye	FB	6'1"	253	28		72
James Saxon	FB-HB	5'11"	215	23		18
Lew Barnes	WR	5'8"	163	26		
Carlos Carson (to PHI)	WR	5'11"	190	30		6
Emile Harry	WR	5'11"	176	26		12
Pete Mandley	WR	5'10"	195	28		6
Stephone Paige	WR	6'2"	185	27		12
Robb Thomas	WR	5'11"	171	23		12
Clarence Weathers (from IND)	WR	5'9"	172	27		
Naz Worthen	WR	5'8"	177	23		
Chris Dressel (to NYJ)	TE	6'4"	245	27		6
Jonathan Hayes	TE	6'5"	239	26		12
Alfredo Roberts	TE	6'3"	250	24		6
Kelly Goodburn	K	6'2"	198	27		
Nick Lowery	K	6'4"	189	33		106

LOS ANGELES RAIDERS 8-8 Mike Shanahan (1-3), Art Shell (7-5)

Scores of Each Game		
40	SAN DIEGO	14
19	Kansas City	24
21	Denver	31
20	SEATTLE	24
14	N.Y. Jets	7
20	KANSAS CITY	14
7	Philadelphia	10
37	WASHINGTON	24
28	CINCINNATI	7
12	San Diego	14
7	Houston	23
24	NEW ENGLAND	21
16	DENVER	* 13
16	PHOENIX	14
17	Seattle	23
17	New York Giants	34

Use Name	Pos.	Hgt	Wgt	Age	Int	Pts
Rory Graves	OT	6'6"	285	26		
Tim Rother	OT	6'7"	285	23		
Bruce Wilkerson	OT	6'5"	285	25		
Steve Wright	OT-OG-TE	6'6"	280	30		
John Gesek	OG	6'5"	275	26		
Steve Wisniewski	OG	6'4"	280	25		
Don Mosebar	C	6'6"	280	27		
Dan Turk	C	6'4"	270	27		
Scott Davis	DE	6'7"	270	24		
Pete Koch	DE	6'6"	275	27		
Howie Long	DE	6'5"	265	29		
Mark Mraz	DE	6'4"	260	24		
Greg Townsend	DE-LB	6'3"	250	27		
Mike Wise	DE	6'7"	280	25		
Bob Golic	NT	6'2"	280	31		
Bill Pickel	DE-NT	6'5"	265	29		

Dale Hellestrae — Broken Leg
Sam Graddy — Knee Injury

Use Name	Pos.	Hgt	Wgt	Age	Int	Pts
Thomas Benson	LB	6'2"	240	27	2	
Joe Costello	LB	6'3"	244	29		
Ricky Hunley	LB	6'2"	250	28		
Emanuel King	LB	6'4"	251	26		
Linden King	LB	6'4"	245	34		6
Jerry Robinson	LB	6'2"	230	32		
Jackie Shipp	LB	6'2"	236	27		
Otis Wilson	LB	6'2"	227	31		
Stefon Adams	DB	5'10"	190	26		2
Eddie Anderson	DB	6'1"	195	26	5	12
Russell Carter	DB	6'2"	200	27		
Mike Harden	DB	6'1"	195	30	2	
Mike Haynes	DB	6'2"	190	36		
Dan Land	DB	6'	190	24		
Zeph Lee	DB	6'3"	205	26		
Terry McDaniel	DB	5'10"	175	24	3	
Vann McElroy	DB	6'2"	195	29	2	
Dennis Price	DB	6'1"	175	24		
Lionel Washington	DB	6'	185	28	3	12

Stacey Toran — Died in Offseason Automobile Accident

Use Name	Pos.	Hgt	Wgt	Age	Int	Pts
Steve Beuerlein	QB	6'2"	205	24		
Vince Evans	QB	6'2"	205	34		
Jay Schroeder	QB	6'4"	215	28		
Marcus Allen	HB	6'2"	205	29		12
Bobby Joe Edmonds	HB	5'11"	186	24		
Bo Jackson	HB	6'1"	225	26		24
Kerry Porter	HB	6'1"	220	24		
Derrick Crudup	FB	6'2"	225	24		
Vance Mueller	FB	6'	215	25		24
Steve Smith	FB	6'1"	230	25		6
Steve Strachan	FB	6'1"	225	26		
Mike Alexander	WR	6'3"	195	24		
Tim Brown	WR	6'	195	23		
Mervyn Fernandez	WR	6'3"	200	29		54
Willie Gault	WR	6'	180	28		24
Timmie Ware	WR	5'10"	171	26		
Mike Dyal	TE	6'2"	240	26		12
Ethan Horton	TE	6'4"	240	26		6
Trey Junkin	TE	6'2"	230	28		12
Jeff Gossett	K	6'2"	195	32		
Jeff Jaeger	K	5'11"	195	24		103

SEATTLE SEAHAWKS 7-9 Chuck Knox

Scores of Each Game		
7	Philadelphia	31
24	PHOENIX	34
24	New England	3
24	L.A. Raiders	20
16	KANSAS CITY	20
17	San Diego	16
21	DENVER	* 24
10	SAN DIEGO	7
10	Kansas City	20
7	CLEVELAND	17
3	N.Y. Giants	15
14	Denver	41
17	BUFFALO	16
24	Cincinnati	17
23	L.A. RAIDERS	17
0	WASHINGTON	29

Use Name	Pos.	Hgt	Wgt	Age	Int	Pts
Andy Heck	OT	6'6"	291	22		
Ron Mattes	OT	6'6"	302	26		
Mike Wilson	OT	6'5"	274	34		
Edwin Bailey	OG	6'4"	270	30		
Darrick Brilz	OG	6'3"	270	25		
Bryan Millard	OG	6'5"	281	28		
Warren Wheat	OG	6'6"	274	22		
Joe Tofflemire	C	6'2"	274	24		
Grant Feasel	C	6'7"	277	29		
Jeff Bryant	DE	6'5"	268	29		
Jethro Franklin	DE	6'1"	258	23		
Jacob Green	DE	6'3"	254	32		
Elston Ridgle (from BUF)	DE	6'6"	270	26		
Alonzo Mitz	DE-LB	6'3"	271	25		
Roy Hart	NT	6'1"	280	24		
Joe Nash	NT	6'2"	269	28		

Use Name	Pos.	Hgt	Wgt	Age	Int	Pts
Brian Bosworth	LB	6'2"	248	24		
Joe Cain	LB	6'1"	228	24		
Darren Comeaux	LB	6'1"	227	29	1	
M.L. Johnson	LB	6'3"	229	25		
Vernon Maxwell	LB	6'2"	235	27		
Darrin Miller	LB	6'1"	227	24		
Rufus Porter	LB-DE	6'1"	207	24		
Rod Stephens	LB	6'1"	237	23		
Tony Woods	LB	6'4"	244	23		
David Wyman	LB	6'2"	234	25		
Nesby Glasgow	DB	5'10"	187	32		6
Dwayne Harper	DB	5'11"	165	23	2	
David Hollis	DB	5'11"	180	24		
Patrick Hunter	DB	5'11"	185	24		
James Jefferson	DB	6'1"	199	25		6
Melvin Jenkins	DB	5'10"	173	27		
Johnnie Johnson	DB	6'1"	183	32	1	
Thom Kaumeyer	DB	5'11"	187	22		
Paul Moyer	DB	6'1"	196	28		
Eugene Robinson	DB	6'	183	26	5	

Use Name	Pos.	Hgt	Wgt	Age	Int	Pts
Jeff Kemp	QB	6'	198	30		
Dave Krieg	QB	6'1"	192	30		
Kelly Stouffer	QB	6'3"	210	25		
Derrick Fenner	HB	6'3"	229	22		6
Kevin Harmon	HB	6'	190	22		
Curt Warner	HB	5'11"	205	28		24
Elroy Harris	FB	5'9"	218	23		
James Jones	FB	6'2"	230	28		
John L. Williams	FB	5'11"	226	24		42
Brian Blades	WR	5'11	182	24		30
Willie Bouyer	WR	6'3"	200	22		
Jeff Chadwick (from DET)	WR	6'3"	190	29		
Louis Clark	WR	6'1"	193	25		6
Tommy Kane	WR	5'11"	180	25		
Steve Largent	WR	5'11"	191	34		19
Paul Skansi	WR	5'11"	184	28		30
Donnie Dee (from IND)	TE	6'4"	247	24		
Rod Jones	TE	6'5"	245	25		
Harper LeBel	TE	6'4"	251	26		
Travis McNeal	TE	6'3"	248	22		
Robert Tyler	TE	6'5"	257	23		
Norm Johnson	K	6'2"	197	29		72
Ruben Rodriguez	K	6'2"	214	24		

SAN DIEGO CHARGERS 6-10 Dan Henning

Scores of Each Game		
14	L.A. Raiders	40
27	HOUSTON	34
21	KANSAS CITY	6
24	Phoenix	13
10	Denver	16
16	SEATTLE	17
13	N.Y. GIANTS	20
7	Seattle	10
20	PHILADELPHIA	17
14	L.A. RAIDERS	12
17	Pittsburgh	20
6	Indianapolis	10
17	N.Y. JETS	20
21	Washington	26
20	Kansas City	13
19	DENVER	16

Use Name	Pos.	Hgt	Wgt	Age	Int	Pts
James FitzPatrick	OT	6'8"	310	25		
Joey Howard	OT	6'6"	305	23		
Brett Miller	OT	6'7"	300	30		
Joel Patten	OT	6'7"	307	31		
David Richards	OG	6'5"	310	23		
Broderick Thompson	OG	6'5"	295	29		
Courtney Hall	C	6'2"	269	21		
Don Macek	C	6'3"	278	35		
Burt Grossman	DE	6'6"	270	22		
George Hinkle	DE	6'5"	267	24		
Les Miller	DE	6'7"	293	24		
Gerald Robinson	DE	6'3"	262	26		
Lee Williams	DE	6'6"	271	26		
Joe Phillips	NT	6'5"	275	26		
Mike Charles	NT	6'4"	296	26		

Dennis McKnight — Knee Injury
Larry Williams — Shoulder Injury

Use Name	Pos.	Hgt	Wgt	Age	Int	Pts
David Brandon	LB	6'4"	230	24		
Joe Campbell	LB	6'4"	245	22		
Jim Collins	LB	6'2"	233	31		
Cedric Figaro	LB	6'2"	255	23	1	
Leslie O'Neal	LB-DE	6'4"	259	25		
Gary Plummer	LB	6'2"	240	29		
Billy Ray Smith	LB	6'3"	236	28	1	6
Ken Woodard	LB	6'1"	220	29		
Martin Bayless	DB	6'2"	212	26	1	
Roy Bennett	DB	6'2"	195	28	3	
Michael Brooks	DB	6'	195	22		
Gill Byrd	DB	5'11"	198	28	7	
Leonard Coleman	DB	6'2"	202	27		
Vencie Glenn	DB	6'	192	24	4	6
Lester Lyles	DB	6'3"	200	26	2	
Elvis Patterson	DB	5'11"	198	28	2	
Sam Seale	DB	5'9"	185	25	4	
Elliot Smith	DB	6'2"	192	22		
Johnny Thomas	DB	5'9"	185	25		

Use Name	Pos.	Hgt	Wgt	Age	Int	Pts
David Archer	QB	6'2"	208	27		
Jim McMahon	QB	6'1"	198	30		
Billy Joe Tolliver	QB	6'1"	218	24		
Victor Floyd	HB	6'1"	201	23		
Darrin Nelson (from MIN)	HB	5'9"	184	29		
Marion Butts	FB	6'1"	248	23		54
Tim Spencer	FB	6'2"	223	28		18
Anthony Allen	WR	5'11"	182	30		
Dana Brinson	WR	5'9"	167	24		
Quinn Early	WR	6'	188	24		
Jamie Holland	WR-HB	6'2"	195	25		
Anthony Miller	WR	5'11"	185	24		66
Wayne Walker	WR	5'8"	162	22		6
Rod Bernstine	TE-FB	6'3"	238	24		12
Joe Caravello	TE	6'3"	270	26		
Arthur Cox	TE	6'2"	277	28		12
Chris Gannon	TE	6'6"	265	23		
Craig McEwen	TE	6'1"	220	23		
Andy Parker	TE	6'5"	245	27		6
Mark Walczak	TE	6'6"	246	27		
Chris Bahr	K	5'10"	170	36		80
Lewis Colbert	K	5'11"	185	26		
Hank Ilesic	K	6'1"	210	29		

Gary Anderson — Holdout
Mark Vlasic — Knee Injury

DENVER BRONCOS

RUSHING

Last Name	No.	Yds	Avg	TD
Humphrey	294	1151	3.9	7
Winder	110	351	3.2	2
Elway	48	244	5.1	3
Alexander	45	146	3.2	2
Bratton	30	108	3.6	1
Sewell	7	44	6.3	0
Kubiak	15	35	2.3	0
Jackson	5	13	2.6	0

RECEIVING

Last Name	No.	Yds	Avg	TD
V. Johnson	76	1095	14.4	7
Jackson	28	446	15.9	2
Sewell	25	416	16.6	3
Young	22	402	18.3	2
Humphrey	22	156	7.1	1
Kay	21	197	9.4	2
Mobley	17	200	11.8	0
Winder	14	91	6.5	0
Nattiel	10	183	18.3	1
Bratton	10	69	6.9	3
Alexander	8	84	10.5	0
Kelly	3	13	4.3	0

PUNT RETURNS

Last Name	No.	Yds	Avg	TD
Bell	21	143	6.8	0
Johnson	12	118	9.8	0
Nattiel	9	77	8.6	0
Woods	2	6	3.0	0
Carrington	1	0	0.0	0

KICKOFF RETURNS

Last Name	No.	Yds	Avg	TD
Bell	30	602	20.1	0
Carrington	6	152	25.3	0
Humphrey	4	86	21.5	0
Bratton	2	19	9.5	0
Woods	1	17	17.0	0

PASSING—PUNTING—KICKING

PASSING	Att	Cmp	%	Yds	Yd/Att	TD	Int— %	RK
Elway	416	223	53.6	3051	7.33	18	18—4.3	9
Kubiak	55	32	58.2	284	5.16	2	2—3.6	
Humphrey	2	1	66.7	17	8.50	1	0—0.0	
Johnson	1	0	0.0	0	0.00	0	0—0.0	

PUNTING	No.	Avg.
Horan	77	40.4
Elway	1	34.0
Kubiak	2	21.5

KICKING	XP	ATT	%	FG	ATT	%
Treadwell	39	40	98	27	33	82

KANSAS CITY CHIEFS

RUSHING

Last Name	No.	Yds	Avg	TD
Okoye	**370**	**1480**	4.0	**12**
Saxon	58	233	4.0	3
Heard	63	216	3.4	0
Pelluer	17	143	8.4	2
McNair	23	121	5.3	0
Gamble	6	24	4.0	1
Harry	1	9	9.0	0
Jaworski	4	5	1.3	0
Agee	1	3	3.0	0
Mandley	2	1	0.5	0
DeBerg	14	-8	-0.6	0
Carson	1	-9	-9.0	0

RECEIVING

Last Name	No.	Yds	Avg	TD
Paige	44	759	17.3	2
Mandley	35	476	13.6	1
McNair	34	372	10.9	1
Harry	33	430	13.0	2
Heard	25	246	9.8	1
Weathers	23	254	11.0	0
Hayes	18	229	12.7	2
Saxon	11	86	7.8	0
Dressel	12	191	15.9	1
R. Thomas	8	58	7.3	2
Roberts	8	55	6.9	1
Carson	8	107	13.4	1
Worthen	5	69	13.8	0
Okoye	2	12	6.0	0
Carruth	1	3	3.0	0
Gamble	2	2	1.0	0

PUNT RETURNS

Last Name	No.	Yds	Avg	TD
Mandley	19	151	7.9	0
Worthen	19	133	7.0	0
Barnes	2	41	20.5	0
Harry	2	6	3.0	0
Ross	2	0	0.0	0

KICKOFF RETURNS

Last Name	No.	Yds	Avg	TD
Copeland	26	466	17.9	0
McNair	13	257	19.8	0
Worthen	5	113	22.6	0
Gamble	3	55	18.3	0
Saxon	3	16	5.3	0
Saleaumua	1	8	8.0	0
Mandley	1	0	0.0	0

PASSING—PUNTING—KICKING

PASSING	Att	Cmp	%	Yds	Yd/Att	TD	Int— %	RK
DeBerg	324	196	2529	60.5	7.81	11	16—4.9	6
Jaworski	61	36	59.0	385	6.31	2	5—8.2	
Pelluer	47	26	55.3	301	6.40	1	0—0.0	
Elkins	2	1	50.0	5	2.50	0	1—50.0	
Saxon	1	0	0.0	0	0.00	0	1—100.0	

PUNTING	No.	Avg.
Goodburn	67	40.1

KICKING	XP	Att.	%	FG	Att	%
Lowery	34	35	97	24	33	73

LOS ANGELES RAIDERS

RUSHING

Last Name	No.	Yds	Avg	TD
Jackson	173	950	5.5	4
Smith	117	471	4.0	1
Allen	69	293	4.2	2
Mueller	48	161	3.4	2
Porter	13	54	4.2	0
Beuerlein	16	39	2.4	0
Schroeder	15	38	2.5	0
Evans	1	16	16.0	0
Fernandez	2	16	8.0	0

RECEIVING

Last Name	No.	Yds	Avg	TD
Fernandez	57	1069	18.8	9
Gault	28	690	24.6	4
Dyal	27	499	18.5	2
Allen	20	191	9.6	0
Smith	19	140	7.4	0
Mueller	18	240	7.4	0
Alexander	15	295	19.7	1
Jackson	9	69	7.7	0
Horton	4	44	11.0	1
Junkin	3	32	10.7	2
Brown	1	8	8.0	0

PUNT RETURNS

Last Name	No.	Yds	Avg	TD
Adams	19	156	8.2	0
Edmonds	16	168	10.5	0
Brown	4	43	10.8	0
Harden	1	11	11.0	0

KICKOFF RETURNS

Last Name	No.	Yds	Avg	TD
Adams	22	425	19.3	0
Edmonds	14	271	19.4	0
Mueller	5	120	24.0	0
Ware	4	86	21.5	0
Brown	3	63	21.0	0
Smith	2	19	9.5	0
Gault	1	16	16.0	0
Turk	1	2	2.0	0
Junkin	1	0	0.0	0
Lee	1	0	0.0	0

PASSING—PUNTING—KICKING

PASSING	Att	Cmp	%	Yds	Yd/Att	TD	Int— %	RK
Beuerlein	217	108	49.8	1677	7.73	13	9—4.1	
Schroeder	194	91	46.9	1550	7.99	8	13—6.7	
Evans	2	2	100.0	50	25.00	0	0—0.0	
Gossett	1	0	0.0	0	0.00	0	0—0.0	

PUNTING	No.	Avg.
Gossett	67	40.5

KICKING	XP	ATT	%	FG	ATT	%
Jaeger	34	34	100	23	34	68

SEATTLE SEAHAWKS

RUSHING

Last Name	No.	Yds	Avg	TD
Warner	194	631	3.3	3
Williams	146	499	3.4	1
Krieg	40	160	4.0	0
Fenner	11	41	3.7	1
Harmon	1	24	24.0	0
Harris	8	23	2.9	0
Stouffer	2	11	5.5	0
Blades	1	3	3.0	0
Kemp	1	0	0.0	0
Rodriguez	1	0	0.0	0

RECEIVING

Last Name	No.	Yds	Avg	TD
Blades	77	1063	13.8	5
Williams	76	657	8.6	6
Skansi	39	488	12.5	5
Largent	28	403	14.4	3
Clark	25	260	10.4	1
Warner	23	153	6.7	1
Tyler	14	148	10.6	0
Chadwick	9	104	11.6	0
Kane	7	94	13.4	0
Harris	3	26	8.7	0
Fenner	3	23	7.7	0
Buoyer	1	9	9.0	0
J. Jones	1	8	8.0	0
Feasel	1	5	5.0	0
Glasgow	1	4	4.0	0

PUNT RETURNS

Last Name	No.	Yds	Avg	TD
Hollis	18	164	9.1	0
Jefferson	12	87	7.3	0

KICKOFF RETURNS

Last Name	No.	Yds	Avg	TD
Jefferson	22	511	23.2	1
Harris	18	334	18.6	0
Hollis	15	247	16.5	0
Harmon	6	84	14.0	0
Clark	1	31	31.0	0
McNeal	1	17	17.0	0
Woods	1	13	13.0	0
Comeaux	1	9	9.0	0

PASSING—PUNTING—KICKING

PASSING	Att	Cmp	%	Yds	Yd/Att	TD	Int— %	RK
Krieg	499	286	57.3	3309	6.63	21	20—4.0	7
Stouffer	59	29	49.2	270	4.58	0	3—5.1	
Rodriguez	1	1	100.0	4	4.00	0	0—0.0	

PUNTING	No.	Avg.
Rodriguez	76	39.4

KICKING	XP	ATT	%	FG	ATT	%
N. Johnson	27	27	100	15	25	60
Largent	1	1	100	0	0	0

SAN DIEGO CHARGERS

RUSHING

Last Name	No.	Yds	Avg	TD
Butts	170	683	4.0	9
Spencer	134	521	3.9	3
Nelson	67	321	4.8	0
McMahon	29	141	4.9	0
Bernstine	15	137	9.1	1
Brinson	17	64	3.8	0
Holland	6	46	7.7	0
A. Miller	4	21	5.3	0
Early	1	19	19.0	0
Floyd	8	15	1.9	0
Archer	2	14	7.0	0
Walker	1	9	9.0	0
Plummer	1	6	6.0	0
Caravello	1	0	0.0	0
Tolliver	7	0	0.0	0

RECEIVING

Last Name	No.	Yds	Avg	TD
A. Miller	75	1252	16.7	**10**
Nelson	38	380	10.0	0
Holland	26	336	12.9	0
Walker	24	395	16.5	1
Cox	22	200	9.1	2
Bernstine	21	222	10.6	1
Spencer	18	112	6.2	0
Brinson	12	71	5.9	0
Early	11	126	11.5	0
Caravello	10	95	9.5	0
McEwen	7	99	14.1	0
Butts	7	21	3.0	0
Allen	2	19	9.5	0
Parker	2	5	2.5	0
Floyd	1	6	6.0	0
McMahon	1	4	4.0	0

PUNT RETURNS

Last Name	No.	Yds	Avg	TD
Brinson	11	112	10.2	0
Walker	6	31	5.2	0
Allen	2	3	1.5	0
Figaro	1	0	0.0	0
Lyles	1	0	0.0	0
Byrd	0	0	0.0	0

KICKOFF RETURNS

Last Name	No.	Yds	Avg	TD
A. Miller	21	533	25.4	1
Holland	29	510	17.6	0
Nelson	14	317	22.6	0
Floyd	3	12	4.0	0
Figaro	1	21	21.0	0

PASSING—PUNTING—KICKING

PASSING	Att	Cmp	%	Yds	Yd/Att	TD	Int— %	RK
McMahon	318	176	55.3	2132	6.70	10	10—3.1	10
Tolliver	185	89	48.1	1097	5.93	5	8—4.3	
Archer	12	5	41.7	62	5.17	0	1—8.3	

PUNTING	No.	Avg.
Ilesic	76	40.1
Colbert	8	33.3

KICKING	XP	Att	%	FG	Att	%
C. Bahr	29	30	97	17	25	68

December 31, 1989 at Houston (Attendance 58,306)

SCORING

PITTSBURGH	7	3	3	10	3	- 26
HOUSTON	0	6	3	14	0	- 23

First Quarter
- Clev. — Worley, 9 yard run; PAT — Anderson (kick)

Second Quarter
- Hous. — Zendejas, 26 yard field goal
- Hous. — Zendejas, 35 yard field goal
- Pitt. — Anderson, 25 yard field goal

Third Quarter
- Hous. — Zendejas, 26 yard field goal
- Pitt. — Anderson, 30 yard field goal

Fourth Quarter
- Pitt. — Anderson, 40 yard field goal
- Hous. — Givins, 18 yard pass from Moon; PAT — Zendejas (kick)
- Hous. — Givins, 9 yard pass from Moon; PAT — Zendejas (kick)
- Pitt. — Hoge, 2 yard run; PAT — Anderson (kick)

Overtime
- Pitt. — Anderson, 50 yard field goal

TEAMSTATISTICS

PITT.		HOUS.
17	First Downs- Total	22
8	First Downs- Rushing	2
9	First Downs- Passing	18
0	First Downs- Penalty	2
1	Fumbles- Number	3
1	Fumbles- Lost Ball	2
5	Penalties- Number	8
40	Yards Penalized	45
0	Missed Field Goals	1
64	Offensive Plays	73
289	Net Yards	380
4.5	Average Gain	5.2
1	Giveaways	2
2	Takeaways	1
+1	Difference	-1

INDIVIDUALSTATISTICS

RUSHING

PITTSBURGH	No.	Yds.	Avg.	HOUSTON	No.	Yds.	Avg.
Hoge	17	100	5.9	Pinkett	8	26	3.3
Worley	11	54	4.9	White	7	13	1.9
Stone	1	22	22.0	Moon	3	12	4.0
Brister	1	1	1.0	Rozier	5	12	2.4
				Highsmith	2	2	1.0
	30	177	5.9		25	65	2.6

RECEIVING

PITTSBURGH	No.	Yds.	Avg.	HOUSTON	No.	Yds.	Avg.
Worley	4	23	5.8	Givins	11	136	12.4
Mularkey	3	40	13.3	Hill	6	98	16.3
Hoge	3	26	8.7	Pinkett	3	24	8.0
Lipps	3	24	8.0	Highsmith	3	21	7.0
Stock	1	7	7.0	Jeffires	3	16	5.3
Hill	1	7	7.0	Duncan	2	15	7.5
				Rozier	1	5	5.0
	16	213	13.3		19	192	10.1

PUNTING

PITTSBURGH	No.	Avg.	HOUSTON	No.	Avg.
Newsome	6	25.0	Montgomery	4	33.0

PUNT RETURNS

PITTSBURGH	No.	Yds.	Avg.	HOUSTON	No.	Yds.	Avg.
Woodson	2	20	10.0	K. Johnson	1	0	0.0

KICKOFF RETURNS

PITTSBURGH	No.	Yds.	Avg.	HOUSTON	No.	Yds.	Avg.
Woodson	4	74	18.5	K. Johnson	1	18	18.0
Thompson	1	11	11.0	L. White	1	9	9.0
Stone	1	14	14.0		2	27	13.5
	6	99	15.0				

INTERCEPTION RETURNS

None — None

PASSING

	Att.	Comp.	Comp. Pct.	Yds.	Int.	Yds./Att.	Yds./Comp.
PITTSBURGH							
Brister	33	15	45.5	127	0	3.8	8.5
HOUSTON							
Moon	48	29	60.4	315	0	6.6	10.9

January 6, 1990 at Cleveland (Attendance 77,706)

SCORING

BUFFALO	7	7	7	9	- 30
CLEVELAND	3	14	14	3	- 34

First Quarter
- Buff. — Reed, 72 yard pass from Kelly; PAT — Norwood (kick)
- Clev. — Bahr, 45 yard field goal

Second Quarter
- Clev. — Slaughter, 52 yard pass from Kosar; PAT — Bahr (kick)
- Buff. — Lofton, 33 yard pass from Kelly; PAT — Norwood (kick)
- Clev. — Middleton, 3 yard pass from Kosar; PAT — Bahr (kick)

Third Quarter
- Clev. — Slaughter 44 yard pass from Kosar; PAT — Bahr (kick)
- Buff. — Thomas, 6 yard pass from Kelly; PAT — Norwood (kick)
- Clev. — Metcalf, 90 yard kickoff return; PAT — Bahr (kick)

Fourth Quarter
- Buff. — Norwood, 30 yard field goal
- Clev. — Bahr, 47 yard field goal
- Buff. — Thomas, 3 yard pass from Kelly; PAT — Norwood (kick)

TEAMSTATISTICS

BUFF.		CLEV.
24	First Downs- Total	18
2	First Downs- Rushing	10
20	First Downs- Passing	8
2	First Downs- Penalty	0
2	Fumbles- Number	1
1	Fumbles- Lost Ball	1
6	Penalties- Number	5
35	Yards Penalized	30
0	Missed Field Goals	1
73	Offensive Plays	61
453	Net Yards	325
6.2	Average Gain	5.3
3	Giveaways	1
1	Takeaways	3
-2	Difference	+2

INDIVIDUALSTATISTICS

RUSHING

BUFFALO	No.	Yds.	Avg.	CLEVELAND	No.	Yds.	Avg.
Thomas	10	27	2.7	Mack	12	62	5.2
Kinnebrew	7	17	2.4	Redden	6	13	2.2
Kelly	1	5	5.0	Tillman	1	8	8.0
	18	49	2.7	Manoa	3	6	2.0
				Metcalf	4	2	0.5
				Langhorne	1	0	0.0
				Kosar	3	-1	-0.3
					30	90	3.0

RECEIVING

BUFFALO	No.	Yds.	Avg.	CLEVELAND	No.	Yds.	Avg.
Thomas	13	150	11.5	Langhorne	6	48	8.0
Reed	6	115	19.2	Newsome	4	35	8.8
Harmon	4	50	12.5	Slaughter	3	114	38.0
Lofton	3	56	18.7	Middleton	3	12	4.0
Beebe	1	17	17.0	Mack	2	19	9.5
Kinnebrew	1	7	7.0	Brennan	1	15	15.0
	28	405	14.5	Metcalf	1	8	8.0
					20	251	12.6

PUNTING

BUFFALO	No.	Avg.	CLEVELAND	No.	Avg.
Kidd	3	41.3	Wagner	3	37.7

PUNT RETURNS

BUFFALO	No.	Yds.	Avg.	CLEVELAND	No.	Yds.	Avg.
Sutton	1	4	4.0	McNeil	1	0	0.0

KICKOFF RETURNS

BUFFALO	No.	Yds.	Avg.	CLEVELAND	No.	Yds.	Avg.
Harmon	3	52	17.3	Metcalf	4	159	39.8
Beebe	2	53	26.5	Oliphant	2	21	10.5
	5	105	21.0		6	180	30.0

INTERCEPTION RETURNS

CLEVELAND	No.	Yds.	Avg.
Harper	1	0	0.0
Matthews	1	0	0.0
	2	0	0.0

PASSING

	Att.	Comp.	Comp. Pct.	Yds.	Int.	Yds./Att.	Yds./Comp.
BUFFALO							
Kelly	54	28	51.9	405	2	7.5	14.5
CLEVELAND							
Kosar	20	20	69.0	251	0	8.7	12.6

January 7, 1990 at Denver, Colo. (Attendance 75,868)

SCORING

PITTSBURGH	3	14	3	3	- 23
DENVER	0	10	7	7	- 24

First Quarter
- Pitt. — Anderson, 32 yard field goal

Second Quarter
- Pitt. — Worley, 7 yard run; PAT — Anderson (kick)
- Den. — Bratton, 1 yard run; PAT — Treadwell (kick)
- Pitt. — Lipps, 9 yard pass from Brister; PAT — Anderson (kick)
- Den. — Treadwell, 43 yard field goal

Third Quarter
- Den. — V. Johnson, 37 yard pass from Elway; PAT — Treadwell (kick)
- Pitt. — Anderson, 35 yard field goal

Fourth Quarter
- Pitt. — Anderson, 32 yard field goal
- Den. — Bratton, 1 yard run; PAT — Treadwell (kick)

TEAMSTATISTICS

PITT.		DEN.
19	First Downs- Total	19
7	First Downs- Rushing	8
12	First Downs- Passing	9
0	First Downs- Penalty	2
2	Fumbles- Number	1
2	Fumbles- Lost Ball	0
8	Penalties- Number	2
50	Yards Penalized	19
0	Missed Field Goals	0
61	Offensive Plays	52
404	Net Yards	364
6.6	Average Gain	7.0
2	Giveaways	1
1	Takeaways	2
-1	Difference	+1

INDIVIDUALSTATISTICS

RUSHING

PITTSBURGH	No.	Yds.	Avg.	DENVER	No.	Yds.	Avg.
Hoge	16	120	7.5	Humphrey	18	85	4.7
Worley	13	50	3.8	Elway	7	44	6.3
Brister	2	4	2.0	Bratton	4	3	0.8
Lipps	1	1	1.0	Sewell	1	6	6.0
	32	175	5.5	Winder	1	0	0.0
					31	138	4.5

RECEIVING

PITTSBURGH	No.	Yds.	Avg.	DENVER	No.	Yds.	Avg.
Hoge	8	60	7.5	Jackson	5	111	22.2
Lipps	3	29	9.7	Johnson	3	85	28.3
Stone	3	18	6.0	Young	2	22	11.0
Mularkey	2	36	18.0	Nattiel	1	15	15.0
Worley	1	33	33.0	Humphrey	1	6	6.0
Stock	1	30	30.0		12	239	19.9
Thompson	1	23	23.0				
	19	229	12.1				

PUNTING

PITTSBURGH	No.	Avg.	DENVER	No.	Avg.
Newsome	2	43.0	Horan	3	44.3
			Elway	1	17.0
				4	37.5

PUNT RETURNS

PITTSBURGH	No.	Yds.	Avg.	DENVER	No.	Yds.	Avg.
Woodson	1 FC			Johnson	1	6	6.0

KICKOFF RETURNS

PITTSBURGH	No.	Yds.	Avg.	DENVER	No.	Yds.	Avg.
Woodson	2	33	16.5	Bell	2	62	31.0
				Carrington	2	51	25.5
				Bratton	1	6	6.0
					5	119	23.8

INTERCEPTION RETURNS

PITTSBURGH	No.	Yds.	Avg.
Everett	1	26	26.0

PASSING

	Att.	Comp.	Comp. Pct.	Yds.	Int.	Yds./Att.	Yds./Comp.
PITTSBURGH							
Brister	29	19	65.5	229	0	7.9	12.1
DENVER							
Elway	20	12	60.0	239	1	12.0	19.9

1989 N.F.C. — PLAYOFFS

December 31, 1989 at Philadelphia (Attendance 57,869)

SCORING

L.A. RAMS	14	0	0	7	- 21
PHILADELPHIA	0	0	0	7	- 7

First Quarter
- L.A. Rams — Ellard, 39 yard pass from Everett; PAT — Lansford (kick)
- L.A. Rams — Johnson, 4 yard pass from Everett; PAT — Lansford (kick)

Fourth Quarter
- Phil. — Toney, 1 yard run; PAT — Ruzek (kick)
- L.A. Rams — Bell, 7 yard run; PAT — Lansford (kick)

TEAMSTATISTICS

L.A. RAMS		PHIL.
19	First Downs- Total	14
6	First Downs- Rushing	6
12	First Downs- Passing	8
1	First Downs- Penalty	0
1	Fumbles- Number	6
1	Fumbles- Lost Ball	2
1	Penalties- Number	4
5	Yards Penalized	35
1	Missed Field Goals	1
71	Offensive Plays	62
409	Net Yards	306
5.5	Average Gain	4.5
3	Giveaways	3
3	Takeaways	3
0	Difference	0

INDIVIDUALSTATISTICS

L.A. RAMS	No.	Yds.	Avg.	PHILADELPHIA	No.	Yds.	Avg.
RUSHING							
Bell	27	124	4.6	Toney	5	12	2.4
Everett	7	2	0.3	Cunningham	6	39	6.5
McGee	2	18	9.0	Sherman	9	44	4.9
	36	144	4.0		20	95	4.8
RECEIVING							
Delpino	3	31	10.3	Byars	9	68	7.6
Ellard	4	87	21.8	Toney	4	35	8.8
Holohan	4	37	9.3	Jackson	3	47	15.7
McGee	3	33	11.0	R. Johnson	2	38	19.0
Anderson	2	77	38.5	Sherman	2	18	9.0
Bell	1	23	23.0	Carter	2	16	8.0
D. Johnson	1	4	4.0	Garrity	2	16	8.0
	18	281	15.6		24	238	9.9
PUNTING							
Hatcher	7	37.0		Tuten	9		36.3
				Cunningham	1		20.0
					10		34.7
PUNT RETURNS							
Henley	3	15	5.0	Edwards	2	5	2.5
KICKOFF RETURNS							
Delpino	1	0	0.0	Edwards	3	37	12.3
Brown	1	14	14.0	Higgs	1	15	15.0
	2	14	7.0		4	52	13.5
INTERCEPTION RETURNS							
Irvin	1	0	0.0	Jenkins	1	33	33.0
				Joyner	1	1	1.0
					2	34	17.0

PASSING

	Att.	Comp.	Comp. Pct.	Yds.	Int.	Yds./ Att.	Yds./ Comp.
L.A. RAMS							
Everett	33	18	54.5	281	2	8.5	15.6
PHILADELPHIA							
Cunningham	40	24	60.0	238	1	6.0	9.9

Januaru 6, 1990 at San Francisco (Attendance 64,585)

SCORING

MINNESOTA	3	0	3	7	- 13
SAN FRANCISCO	7	20	0	14	- 41

First Quarter
- Minn. — Karlis, 38 yard field goal
- S.F. — Rice, 72 yard pass from Montana; PAT — Cofer (kick)

Second Quarter
- S.F. — Jones, 8 yard pass from Montana; PAT — Cofer (kick)
- S.F. — Taylor, 8 yard pass from Montana; PAT — Cofer (kick)
- S.F. — Rice, 13 yard pass from Montana; PAT — kick failed

Third Quarter
- Minn. — Karlis, 44 yard field goal

Fourth Quarter
- S.F. — Lott, 58 yard interception return; PAT — Cofer (kick)
- S.F. — Craig, 4 yard run; PAT — Cofer (kick)
- Minn. — Fenney, 3 yard run; PAT — Karlis (kick)

TEAMSTATISTICS

MINN.		S.F.
25	First Downs- Total	22
7	First Downs- Rushing	10
17	First Downs- Passing	11
1	First Downs- Penalty	1
1	Fumbles- Number	1
1	Fumbles- Lost Ball	1
4	Penalties- Number	9
31	Yards Penalized	65
0	Missed Field Goals	2
79	Offensive Plays	57
385	Net Yards	403
4.9	Average Gain	7.1
5	Giveaways	1
1	Takeaways	5
- 4	Difference	+ 4

INDIVIDUALSTATISTICS

MINNESOTA	No.	Yds.	Avg.	SAN FRANCISCO	No.	Yds.	Avg.
RUSHING							
Wilson	3	39	13.0	Craig	18	125	6.9
Walker	9	29	3.2	Rathman	7	24	3.4
Fenney	4	8	2.0	Flagler	5	13	2.6
Gannon	2	7	3.5	Montana	2	0	0.0
Dozier	3	13	4.3		32	162	5.1
	21	86	4.1				
RECEIVING							
Jordan	9	149	16.6	Rice	6	114	19.0
Carter	4	44	11.0	Taylor	3	50	16.7
Fenney	4	15	3.8	Rathman	3	29	9.7
Anderson	3	18	6.0	Jones	3	24	8.0
Dozier	3	15	5.0	Henderson	2	24	12.0
Gustafson	2	46	23.0		17	241	14.2
Lewis	2	19	9.5				
Jones	2	18	9.0				
Walker	2	14	7.0				
	31	338	10.9				
PUNTING							
Scribner	4		32.0	Helton	4	30.8	
PUNT RETURNS							
Lewis	2	18	9.0	Taylor	2	6	3.0
KICKOFF RETURNS							
Walker	5	97	19.4	Tillman	2	26	13.0
Dozier	1	19	19.0	Flagler	1	58	58.0
Lewis	1	14	14.0	Rathman	1	0	0.0
	7	130	18.6		4	84	21.0
INTERCEPTION RETURNS							
				Lott	1	58	58.0
				Brooks	1	28	28.0
				MyKyer	1	41	41.0
				Griffin	1	0	0.0
					4	127	31.8

PASSING

	Att.	Comp.	Comp. Pct.	Yds.	Int.	Yds./ Att.	Yds./ Comp.
MINNESOTA							
Wilson	17	9	52.9	84	2	4.9	9.3
Kramer	19	9	47.4	110	1	5.8	12.2
Gannon	18	13	72.2	144	1	8.0	11.1
	54	31	57.4	338	4	6.3	10.9
SAN FRANCISCO							
Montana	24	17	70.8	241	0	10.0	14.2
Young	1	0	0.0	0	0	0.0	0.0
	25	17	68.0	241	0	9.6	14.2

January 7, 1990 at East Rutherford, N.J. (Attendance 76,325)

SCORING

L.A. RAMS	0	7	0	6	6	- 19
N.Y. GIANTS	6	0	7	0	0	- 13

First Quarter
- N.Y.G. — Allegre, 35 yard field goal
- N.Y.G. — Allegre, 41 yard field goal

Second Quarter
- L.A. Rams — Anderson, 20 yard pass from Everett; PAT — Lansford (kick)

Third Quarter
- N.Y.G. — Anderson, 2 yard run; PAT — Allegre (kick)

Fourth Quarter
- L.A. Rams — Lansford, 31 yard field goal
- L.A. Rams — Lansford, 22 yard field goal

Overtime
- L.A. Rams — Anderson, 30 yard pass from Everett

TEAMSTATISTICS

L.A.RAMS		N.Y.G.
26	First Downs- Total	20
6	First Downs- Rushing	11
18	First Downs- Passing	8
2	First Downs- Penalty	1
1	Fumbles- Number	3
1	Fumbles- Lost Ball	0
5	Penalties- Number	4
35	Yards Penalized	59
0	Missed Field Goals	0
70	Offensive Plays	67
448	Net Yards	344
5.0	Average Gain	5.1
2	Giveaways	1
1	Takeaways	2
- 1	Difference	+ 1

INDIVIDUALSTATISTICS

L.A. RAMS	No.	Yds.	Avg.	N.Y. GIANTS	No.	Yds.	Avg.
RUSHING							
Bell	19	87	4.6	O. Anderson	24	120	5.0
McGee	3	34	11.3	Tillman	7	25	3.6
Everett	2	25	12.5	Simms	3	16	5.3
	24	146	6.1	Meggett	1	7	7.0
				Carthon	1	3	3.0
					36	171	4.8
RECEIVING							
Ellard	8	125	15.6	Meggett	4	52	13.0
Holohan	5	48	9.6	Mowatt	3	52	17.3
Brown	3	35	11.7	Anderson	3	-2	-0.7
Johnson	3	15	5.0	Baker	2	46	23.0
Anderson	2	50	25.0	Manuel	1	24	24.0
McGee	2	31	15.5	Carthon	1	8	8.0
Bell	2	11	5.5		14	180	12.9
	25	315	12.6				
PUNTING							
Hatcher	4		30.3	Landeta	5		37.2
PUNT RETURNS							
Irvin	1	3	3.0	Meggett	1	0	0.0
Henley	2	-4	-2.0				
	3	-1	-0.3				
KICKOFF RETURNS							
Delpino	4	60	15.0	Ingram	2	41	20.5
Brown	1	38	38.0	Meggett	1	25	25.0
	5	98	19.6	Cross	1	9	9.0
					4	75	18.8
INTERCEPTION RETURNS							
Stewart	1	19	19.0	Collins	1	0	0.0

PASSING

	Att.	Comp.	Comp. Pct.	Yds.	Int.	Yds./ Att.	Yds./ Comp.
L.A. RAMS							
Everett	44	25	56.8	315	1	7.2	12.6
N.Y. GIANTS							
Simms	29	14	48.3	180	1	6.2	12.9
Meggett	1	0	0.0	0	0	0.0	0.0
	30	14	46.7	180	1	6.0	12.9

1989 Championship Games

A.F.C. CHAMPIONSHIP GAME

January 14, 1990 at Denver, Colo.
(Attendance 76,005)

The Broncos and Browns met for the A.F.C. championship for the third time in four years, but this game was not to be decided on last-minute heroics like the previous two. Denver's John Elway had, by his own admission, the game of his life. He completed 20-of-36 passes for 385 yards and three touchdowns and even led his team in rushing. Cleveland's Bernie Kosar, playing with arm miseries, was ineffective in the first half, hitting on only 7-of-23.

Denver started slowly with a 29-yard field goal by David Treadwell after safety Dennis Smith intercepted an errant Kosar pass. Early in the second quarter, Denver's arsenal was reduced when star runner Bobby Humphrey was knocked out with broken ribs, courtesy of a hit by Cleveland cornerback Frank Minnifield. But a few minutes later, Minnifield was the goat as he was burned by Michael Young for a 70-yard touchdown pass and a 10-0 Denver lead.

A little over three minutes into the third quarter, Kosar hit Brian Brennan for a 27-yard TD, but Elway answered by with an 80-yard drive capped by a five-yard scoring pass to Orson Mobley. A 60-yard drive followed, ending in Sammy Winder's seven-yard scoring scamper.

Kosar closed the gap with another touchdown pass to Brennan. Then Browns safety Felix Wright grabbed Melvin Bratton's fumble at the 26 and ran it to the one. Tim Manoa plunged over to cut the lead to 24-21. But Elway was brilliant in directing another 80-yard drive with a 39-yard pass to Sammy Winder shortly into the fourth quarter to give Denver 31-21 breathing room. Treadwell sealed the game with two field goals after interceptions of desperate Kosar passes.

SCORING

CLEVELAND	0	0	21	0	- 21
DENVER	3	7	14	13	- 37

First Quarter
Den. Treadwell, 29 yard field goal

Second Quarter
Den. Young, 70 yard pass from Elway
PAT — Treadwell (kick)

Third Quarter
Clev. Brennan, 27 yard pass from Kosar
PAT — Bahr (kick)
Den. Mobley, 5 yard pass from Elway
PAT — Treadwell (kick)
Den. Winder, 7 yard run
PAT — Treadwell (kick)
Clev. Brennan, 10 yard pass from Kosar
PAT — Bahr (kick)
Clev. Manoa, 2 yard run
PAT — Bahr (kick)

Fourth Quarter
Den. Winder, 39 yard pass from Elway
PAT — Treadwell (kick)
Den. Treadwell, 34 yard field goal
Den. Treadwell, 31 yard field goal

TEAM STATISTICS

CLEV.		DEN.
14	First Downs- Total	22
3	First Downs- Rushing	6
11	First Downs- Passing	14
0	First Downs- Penalty	2
3	Fumbles- Number	2
0	Fumbles- Lost Ball	2
8	Penalties- Number	1
55	Yards Penalized	5
0	Missed Field Goals	0
62	Offensive Plays	76
256	Net Yards	497
4.1	Average Gain	6.5
3	Giveaways	2
2	Takeaways	3
- 1	Difference	+ 1

INDIVIDUAL STATISTICS

CLEVELAND	No.	Yds.	Avg.	DENVER	No.	Yds.	Avg.
RUSHING							
Mack	6	36	6.0	Elway	5	39	7.8
Kosar	2	22	11.0	Winder	21	37	1.8
Manoa	2	5	2.5	Humphrey	8	23	2.9
Metcalf	3	4	1.3	Sewell	4	17	4.3
Langhorne	1	-1	-1.0	Bratton	1	4	4.0
	14	66	4.7		39	120	3.1
RECEIVING							
Langhorne	5	48	9.6	V. Johnson	7	91	13.0
Brennan	5	58	11.6	Sewell	3	55	18.3
Slaughter	3	36	12.0	Young	2	123	61.5
Mack	2	8	4.0	Winder	2	39	19.5
Metcalf	2	7	3.5	M. Jackson	2	25	12.5
Tillman	1	15	15.0	Mobley	2	22	11.0
Manoa	1	8	8.0	Humphrey	1	23	23.0
	19	210	11.1	Bratton	1	7	7.0
					20	385	19.3
PUNTING							
Wagner	8		42.3	Horan	5		46.4
PUNT RETURNS							
McNeil	1	7	7.0	V. Johnson	4	36	9.0
KICKOFF RETURNS							
Metcalf	6	119	19.8				
K. Jones	1	12	12.0				
	7	130	18.6				
INTERCEPTION RETURNS							
				D. Smith	2	13	6.5
				Corrington	1	1	1.0
					5	14	2.8

PASSING

	Att.	Comp.	Comp. Pct.	Yds.	Int.	Yds./ Att.	Yds./ Comp.
CLEVELAND							
Kosar	44	19	43.2	210	3	47.7	11.1
DENVER							
Elway	35	20	57.1	385	0	11.0	19.3

N.F.C. CHAMPIONSHIP GAME

January 14, 1990 at San Francisco, Calif.
(Attendance 64,769)

The Rams beat the 49ers in October and came close in December, but it was no contest this time before a record crowd at Candlestick Park as San Francisco rolled over Los Angeles. The Rams offense, which had averaged 428 yards in two playoff victories, managed a paltry 156 against the 49ers. "Special Lark," a new defense installed by coach George Seifert to take away deep passes to Ram receivers Henry Ellard and Flipper Anderson, worked so well that Rams quarterback Jim Everett was completely befuddled. He completed only 16-of-36 passes, nine of them short tosses to his backs, for 141 yards and was intercepted three times.

Meanwhile, 49ers quarterback Joe Montana ripped through the Rams for 262 yards and two touchdowns, completing 26-of-30 passes.

The Rams had the better of the first quarter but couldn't take full advantage. After driving 44 yards on their first possession, they had to settle for Mike Lansford's 23-yard field goal. San Francisco fumbled and Everett had Anderson open for a possible touchdown, but 49ers safety Ronnie Lott batted the ball away at the last second. After that, it was all 49ers.

In the second quarter, Montana threw a 20-yard TD pass to Brent Jones, and Roger Craig plunged for another score. With 3:10 left in the first half, the 49ers took the ball at their own 13. They drove 87 yards, with the Montana-to-John Taylor scoring pass coming with only nine seconds left. In the second half, the 49ers widened their lead on three Mike Cofer field goals, and the Rams were held to a mere 33 yards.

SCORING

L.A. RAMS	3	0	0	0	- 3
SAN FRANCISCO	0	21	3	6	- 30

First Quarter
L.A. Rams Lansford, 23 yard field goal

Second Quarter
S.F. Jones, 20 yard pass from Montana
PAT — Cofer (kick)
S.F. Craig, 1 yard run
PAT — Cofer (kick)
S.F. Taylor, 18 yard pass from Montana
PAT — Cofer (kick)

Third Quarter
S.F. Cofer, 28 yard field goal

Fourth Quarter
S.F. Cofer, 36 yard field goal
S.F. Cofer, 25 yard field goal

TEAM STATISTICS

L.A. RAMS		S.F.
9	First Downs- Total	29
0	First Downs- Rushing	12
9	First Downs- Passing	16
0	First Downs- Penalty	1
1	Fumbles- Number	3
0	Fumbles- Lost Ball	2
1	Penalties- Number	4
10	Yards Penalized	40
0	Missed Field Goals	1
47	Offensive Plays	76
156	Net Yards	442
3.1	Average Gain	5.8
3	Giveaways	2
2	Takeaways	3
-1	Difference	+ 1

INDIVIDUAL STATISTICS

L.A. RAMS	No.	Yds.	Avg.	SAN FRANCISCO	No.	Yds.	Avg.
RUSHING							
Bell	8	20	2.5	Craig	23	93	4.0
Gary	1	3	3.0	Rathman	10	63	6.3
Delpino	1	3	3.0	Flagler	8	19	2.4
	10	26	2.6	Montana	1	4	4.0
				Henderson	1	1	1.0
				Young	1	-1	-1.0
					44	179	4.1
RECEIVING							
McGee	7	53	7.6	Rice	6	55	9.2
Holohan	3	26	8.7	Rathman	6	48	8.0
Bell	3	23	7.7	Jones	4	46	11.5
Ellard	2	18	9.0	Taylor	4	45	11.3
Anderson	1	14	14.0	Craig	3	40	13.3
Johnson	1	7	7.0	Sherrard	2	21	10.5
	16	141	8.8	Wilson	1	7	7.0
				Williams	1	6	6.0
					27	268	9.9
PUNTING							
Hatcher	7		31.4	Helton	2		31.0
PUNT RETURNS							
Irvin	1	10	10.0	Taylor	1	4	4.0
KICKOFF RETURNS							
Delpino	4	95	23.8	Flagler	1	19	19.0
Brown	2	51	25.5	Tillman	1	16	16.0
	6	146	24.3		2	35	17.5
INTERCEPTION RETURNS							
				McKyer	1	27	27.0
				Turner	1	15	15.0
				Lott	1	14	14.0
					3	56	18.7

PASSING

	Att.	Comp.	Comp. Pct.	Yds.	Int.	Yds./ Att.	Yds./ Comp.
L.A. RAMS							
Everett	36	16	44.4	141	3	3.9	10.1
SAN FRANCISCO							
Montana	30	26	86.7	262	0	8.7	10.1
Young	1	1	100.0	6	0	6.0	6.0

January 28, 1990 at New Orleans, La.

(Attendance 72,919)

Super: Dome, Joe and the 49ers

It was possibly the best Super Bowl ever — for one team. Joe Montana and the San Francisco 49ers carved a niche in football history at the Louisiana Superdome by winning their fourth championship of the decade. Moreover, Super Bowl XXIV made them the first back-to-back winners since the Steelers of the '70s. To say they did it convincingly is the greatest understatement since Noah's weatherman predicted "possible showers." This time it was the Broncos who were deluged. San Francisco's 55-10 victory represented both the biggest margin in Super Bowl history and the most points scored by a Super Bowl team.

Meanwhile, Denver suffered its fourth loss in as many Super Bowl appearances. Ironically, a few weeks before the game, 54 percent of Denver fans responding to a survey hoped their team would *not* go to the Super Bowl and thus avoid another embarrassing defeat. The Broncos didn't listen, and apparently 100 percent of the 49ers hoped they would show up.

The Broncos, 12-point underdogs, were expected to run the ball to try to keep Montana & Co. off the field. Instead, John Elway came out throwing and the combination of the 49er pass rush and coverage, some misdirected passes and drops by receivers put Denver into a quick hole. Less than five minutes into the contest, Montana hit Jerry Rice for a 20-yard touchdown that put San Francisco ahead to stay. Denver came back to score on a 43-yard David Treadwell field goal, but the dam was about to burst. Montana's seven-yard toss to Brent Jones widened the lead with three seconds left in the first quarter.

When Tom Rathman cracked over from thc one midway through the second quarter, the game was over for all purposes except counting up the score. Montana connected with Rice again for a 38-yard TD with less than a minute left in the first half to make the score 27-3, and much of America's TV fans decided it was time to check out other channels.

If they neglected to return for the second half, they missed Rice scoring on a 28-yarder from Montana and John Taylor taking a 35-yarder for another score. The 49ers stayed on the ground in the fourth period, as Rathman and Roger Craig scored the last touchdowns. In between 49er scores, Elway directed a Bronco offense that was mostly "three downs and out," although he did run three yards for a third-quarter score that made the score "only" 41-10 at the time.

In a 55-10 game, it's difficult to find one play that makes a significant difference, however the Broncos were making a run at the 49ers midway through the first quarter when they had a first down at their own 49-yard line and trailing only 7-3. Bobby Humphrey took a handoff from Elway and attempted to run behind left tackle Gerald Perry. But 49ers defensive end Kevin Fagan wrapped up Humphrey and stripped the ball away from him. Chet Brooks recovered for San Francisco and the game was effectively over.

"The most we gave up all year was 28 points," said Denver defensive coordinator Wade Phillips, who received considerable praise for upgrading the defense (before the game). "Today they got 27 in the first half only because they missed a point (on a missed conversion), and 28 more in the second half. They have a great killer instinct. You make a mistake and they go for the big play."

Rice caught seven passes for 148 yards and three TD's, all better marks than he registered in earning MVP honors a year earlier. But the day belonged to Montana, whose 22-of-29 passing, 13 consecutive completions at one point, 297 yards and five touchdowns earned him his third Super Bowl MVP award. Amazingly, in 122 Super Bowl passes, hc'd completed 68 percent and never thrown an interception.

LINEUPS

S.F.		DEN.
	OFFENSE	
Taylor	WR	V. Johnson
Paris	LT	Perry
McIntyre	LG	Juriga
Sapolu	C	Kartz
Collie	RG	Widell
Barton	RT	Lanier
Jones	TE	Mobley
Rice	WR	M. Jackson
Montana	QB	Elway
Craig	RB	Humphrey
Rathman	FB	Sewell
	DEFENSE	
Holt	LE	Carreker
Carter	NT	Kragen
Fagan	RE	Holmes
Haley	LOLB	Brooks
Millen	LILB	Dennison
Walter	RILB	Mecklenburg
Turner	ROLB	Fletcher
Pollard	LCB	Braxton
Griffin	RCB	Henderson
Brooks	SS	Smith
Lott	FS	Atwater

SUBSTITUTES

SAN FRANCISCO		
	OFFENSE	
Young	Tillman	Sydney
Flagler	C. Thomas	Tausch
Wallace	J. Williams	Wilson
Sherrard	Walls	
	DEFENSE	
Wright	McKyer	J. Jackson
Romanowski	Hendrickson	DeLong
Burt	Kugler	Roberts
Stubbs		
	KICKERS	
Cofer	Helton	

DENVER		
	OFFENSE	
Kubiak	Winder	Bratton
Bell	Bishop	M. Smith
Young	Nattiel	Green
Kay		
	DEFENSE	
Corrington	Carrington	Haynes
Robbins	Munford	Curtis
Lucas	Townsend	Henke
Powers	Klostermann	
	KICKERS	
Horan	Treadwell	

SCORING

SAN FRANCISCO	13	14	14	14	-	55
DENVER	3	0	7	0	-	10

First Quarter
- S.F. Rice, 20 yard pass from Montana
  PAT — Cofer (kick)
- Den. Treadwell, 42 yard field goal
- S.F. Jones, 7 yard pass from Montana
  PAT — kick failed

Second Quarter
- S.F. Rathman, 1 yard run
  PAT — Cofer (kick)
- S.F. Rice, 38 yard pass from Montana
  PAT — Cofer (kick)

Third Quarter
- S.F. Rice, 28 yard pas from Montana
  PAT — Cofer (kick)
- S.F. Taylor, 35 yard pass from Montana
  PAT — Cofer (kick)
- Den. Elway, 3 yard run
  PAT — Treadwell (kick)

Fourth Quarter
- S.F. Rathman, 4 yard run
  PAT — Cofer (kick)
- S.F. Craig, 1 yard run
  PAT — Cofer (kick)

TEAM STATISTICS

S.F.		DEN.
28	First Downs-Total	12
14	First Downs-Rushing	5
14	First Downs-Pasiing	6
0	First Downs-Penalty	1
0	Fumbles-Number	3
0	Fumbles-Lost Ball	2
4	Penaties-Number	0
38	Yards Penalized	0
0	Missed Field Goals	0
77	Offensive Plays	52
461	Net Yards	167
6.0	Average Gain	3.2
0	Giveaways	4
4	Takeaways	0
+4	Difference	-4

INDIVIDUAL STATISTICS

SAN FRANCISCO	No.	Yds.	Avg.	DENVER	No.	Yds.	Avg.
RUSHING							
Craig	20	69	3.5	Humphrey	12	61	5.1
Montana	2	15	7.5	Elway	4	8	2.0
Rathman	11	38	3.5	Winder	1	-5	-5.0
Flagler	6	14	2.3		17	64	3.8
Sydney	1	2	2.0				
Young	4	6	1.5				
	44	144	3.3				
RECEIVING							
Rice	7	148	21.1	Humphrey	3	38	12.7
Craig	5	34	6.8	Sewell	2	22	11.0
Rathman	4	43	10.8	Johnson	2	21	10.5
Taylor	3	49	16.3	Nattiel	1	28	28.0
Sherrard	1	13	13.0	Bratton	1	14	14.0
Walls	1	9	9.0	Winder	1	7	7.0
Jones	1	7	7.0	Kay	1	6	6.0
Williams	1	7	7.0		11	136	12.4
Sydney	1	7	7.0				
	24	317	13.2				
PUNTING							
Helton	4		39.5	Horan	6		38.5
PUNT RETURNS							
Taylor	3	38	12.7	Johnson	2	11	5.5
KICKOFF RETURNS							
Flagler	3	49	16.3	Carrington	6	146	24.3
				Bell	2	41	20.5
				Bratton	1	9	9.0
					9	196	21.7
INTERCEPTIONS RETURNS							
Walter	1	4	4.0	None			
Brooks	1	38	38.0				
	2	42	20.5				

PASSING

SAN FRANCISCO	Att.	Comp.	Comp. Pct.	Yds.	Int.	Yds./ Att.	Yds./ Comp.	Yards Lost Tackled
Montana	29	22	75.9	297	0	10.2	13.5	0-0
Young	3	2	66.7	20	0	6.7	10.0	1-0
	32	24	75.0	317	0	9.9	13.2	1-0
DENVER								
Elway	26	10	38.5	108	2	4.1	10.8	6-33
Kubiak	3	1	33.3	28	0	9.3	28.0	0-0
	29	11	37.9	136	2	4.7	12.4	6-33

1990 N.F.C. Being Best Can Be Boring

While most critics insisted the NFC had moved ahead of the AFC in football prowess, citing the superior defense played in the former, the sad truth was that the NFC had little to offer fans in title races during the 1990 season. In the East, the Giants forged to the front early and were never in real danger of losing their lead to either Philadelphia or Washington, the only NFC teams to post winning records without wining a division title. The Central Division was a cakewalk by the Bears combined with the collapse of the Vikings and Packers. And in the West, San Francisco needed barely to work up a sweat as the Rams submerged and the Saints struggled all season to get to .500.

With the division races all but settled by midseason, interests focused on the playoffs and the 49ers' chances for a third consecutive Super Bowl championship. The game of the season was a December 3 meeting at San Francisco between the Giants and 49ers. It was widely viewed as a preview of the NFC championship game, and, indeed, it turned out to be just that. San Francisco scored the only touchdown in what NFC fans called "a great defensive battle" and AFC fans called dull. The Niners won 7-3.

EASTERN DIVISION

New York Giants — Under Bill Parcells, the Giants had earned a reputation for a conservative offense over the past few years. After a few adjustments in 1990, they set an NFL record for fewest turnovers with a measly 14 — less than one per game. A 10-game winning streak from the opening of the season locked up the division title quickly. The huge offensive line, bulwarked by tackle Jumbo Elliott, opened holes for ageless Ottis Anderson, Dave Meggett and rookie Rodney Hampton all season, and the Lawrence Taylor-led defense finished first overall in the NFC. Even three defeats in the last four games and the loss of starting quarterback Phil Simms to a sprained foot and Hampton to a leg injury couldn't knock the Giants off track. Anderson continued to grind out yards, and Jeff Hostetler proved to be a capable backup for Simms.

Philadelphia Eagles — The Eagles bounced back from a 1-3 start to make the playoffs for the third straight year. They were criticized around the league for taunting, cheap shots, and dirty play, but coach Buddy Ryan defended his troops as merely aggressive. Whatever, it worked. The defense was spotty against the pass and the special teams weren't up to their previous efforts, but Randall Cunningham remained the league's top offensive threat. He just missed becoming the first quarterback to both run and pass for over 1,000 yards each. Although he led the Eagles in rushing for the fourth straight season, he got help from his running backs for a change, particularly Heath Sherman. Ryan was fired after the season for the team's failure to win a playoff game and for inspiring his team's ruffian reputation.

Washington Redskins — Coach Joe Gibbs' club never was able to put together a victory streak so they were never candidates for more than a wild-card berth in the playoffs. Gibbs complained he never knew who would show up for a game: "Elmer and the boys or a pretty good football team," he said. The most inconsistent position on the Redskins was quarterback, where Mark Rypien, Stan Humphries, and Jeff Rutledge all had excellent moments mixed with disasters and injuries. The supporting cast was strong. Wide receivers Art Monk, Gary Clark and Ricky Sanders combined for 199 receptions. Running back Gerald Riggs was hobbled with an arch injury, but Earnest Byner turned in a terrific season, rushing for 1,219 yards.

Dallas Cowboys — The Cowboys' season gave Jimmy Johnson NFC Coach of the Year honors. From 1-15 in '89, Dallas improved to a point where they had a shot at a .500 season and the playoffs until the last week of the season. The key to the improvement was a no-name defense that finished first in the NFC in pass defense and fourth overall. Emmitt Smith gave Dallas a running threat with a near-1,000-yard season, and Troy Aikman continued to make progress towards becoming a top pro quarterback. Aikman won seven starts before he separated his shoulder against Philadelphia in Week 15. Unfortunately for the Cowboys' playoff aspirations, the efforts of his replacement, Babe Laufenberg, were, well, lauf-able.

Phoenix Cardinals — Although the Cardinals fell into last place with the same 5-11 mark they'd had in 1989, the outlook was hopeful. Under new coach Joe Bugel, the Cards made progress on offense. Second-year quarterback Timm Rosenbach improved as the season went on, finishing with over 3,000 yards passing. In the final two games, he threw for 682 yards and six touchdowns. Wide receiver Ricky Proehl caught more passes than any rookie in the league, blending nicely with veterans Roy Green and Ernie Jones. Rookie running back Johnny Johnson was a revelation. And, when he was injured, second-round draft choice Anthony Thompson came on strong. Luis Sharpe and the rest of the veteran offensive line played well. But, for all the optimism generated by the offense, the defense — which gave up 50 touchdowns — still was in need of a transfusion.

CENTRAL DIVISION

Chicago Bears — The famed Bears defense was back. Defensive tackle Dan Hampton returned for his 12th and final season to anchor the line with inspirational play. Richard Dent, Steve McMichael, and Mike Singletary were other strengths, and rookie free safety Mark Carrier made the Pro Bowl. His 10 interceptions broke a club record. The Bears lacked a premier wide receiver, but Jim Harbaugh took over as quarterback and played reasonably well until sidelined by a shoulder separation in the 14th game. Neal Anderson also had injury problems but still managed another 1,000-yard season. Tragedy struck when rookie defensive lineman Fred Washington was killed in an auto accident in December.

Detroit Lions — A leaky defense kept the Lions from taking advantage of their increasingly potent offense. Linebackers Mike Cofer and Chris Spielman and cornerback Ray Crockett were defenders of promise, but Detroit ended dead last in the NFC in defense. The line desperately needed a pass rusher. Cofer blitzed often enough to lead the team in sacks with 10. One knock on the "Silver Stretch" offense, Detroit's name for the run-and-shoot, was that it couldn't protect a lead. This was never more evident than in the November 4 game against the Redskins when the Lions piled up 38 points only to see Washington come back to tie and then win in overtime. Barry Sanders remained the NFC's top runner and Rodney Peete showed improvement at quarterback.

Tampa Bay Buccaneers — A 3-1 start fueled hopes for the Bucs' first winning season since 1982, but a six-game losing streak brought those dreams crashing down and cost coach Ray Perkins his job. Ironically, Perkins' ouster came after the team finally broke the loss streak. Vinny Testaverde was still inconsistent amid more and more whispers that he'd never be the franchise quarterback Tampa Bay expected when they drafted him No. 1 in 1987. Much was expected from running backs Gary Anderson and Reggie Cobb, but the ground game still sputtered. A bright spot was the play of free-agent cornerback Wayne Haddix, who ended in the Pro Bowl. Overall, the Bucs were next-to-last in offense, next-to-last in defense and dead last in disappointment.

Green Bay Packers — Instead of building on their 10-6 record of 1989, the Packers spun back toward the bottom of the division in 1990. The primary bugaboos were training-camp holdouts, injuries, and the complete lack of a running game. Sixteen veterans, including 13 starters, sat out a total of 302 days in various contract disputes. Quartback Don Majkowski the "Magic Man" of 1989, missed 45 days as a holdout and then, after eight starts, was knocked out for the season with a career-threatening rotator cuff tear. Backup Anthony Dilwig played well at times, badly at others, and was eventually sidelined, too. Receiver Sterling Sharpe caught 23 fewer passes than in '89 due to cracked ribs and the revolving quarterback situation. Michael Haddix, the leading Packer rusher, ranked 58th in the NFL.

Minnesota Vikings — The Vikings went from the penthouse to the outhouse in one season, struggling to the fourth-worst record in their history. Major factors in the plunge were injuries to quarterback Wade

OFFENSE

	ATL	CHI	DAL	DET	G.B.	L.A.	MINN	N.O.	NYG	PHIL	PHX	S.F.	T.B.	WASH
FIRST DOWNS:														
Total	273	295	250	278	276	311	288	253	273	325	270	324	238	327
by Rushing	84	142	88	112	72	89	106	107	120	132	115	107	83	117
by Passing	168	134	135	152	183	191	164	133	135	170	135	201	142	193
by Penalty	21	19	27	14	21	31	18	13	18	23	20	16	13	17
RUSHING:														
Number	420	551	393	366	350	422	455	464	541	540	452	454	410	515
Yards	1594	2436	1500	1927	1369	1612	1867	1850	2049	2556	1912	1718	1626	2083
Average Yards	3.8	4.4	3.8	5.3	3.9	3.8	4.1	4.0	3.8	4.7	4.2	3.8	4.0	4.0
Touchdowns	11	22	13	19	5	17	10	14	17	10	13	12	7	16
PASSING:														
Attempts	528	430	475	460	541	561	497	447	398	479	439	583	448	536
Completions	293	229	254	242	302	310	265	226	231	281	238	360	245	301
Completion Pct.	55.5	53.3	53.5	52.6	55.8	55.3	53.3	50.6	58.0	58.7	54.2	61.7	54.7	56.2
Passing Yards	3726	2827	2898	3328	3696	4016	3445	2757	2898	3582	3118	4371	3282	3611
Avg. Yds per Att.	6.0	5.4	5.0	6.1	5.5	6.5	5.8	6.2	6.5	5.9	5.9	6.7	5.7	6.2
Avg. Yds per Comp.	12.7	12.3	11.4	13.8	12.2	13.0	13.0	12.2	12.6	12.8	13.1	12.1	13.4	12.0
Times Tackled	46	43	43	44	62	30	40	20	29	50	43	37	53	22
Yds Lost Tackled	265	283	317	278	390	198	278	131	142	438	285	194	433	132
Net Yards	3461	2544	2581	3050	3306	3818	3167	2626	2756	3144	2833	4177	2849	3479
Touchdowns	21	14	12	24	20	24	25	15	18	34	16	28	18	22
Interceptions	18	12	24	20	21	17	24	23	5	13	18	16	24	22
Pct. Intercepted	3.4	2.8	5.1	4.3	3.9	3.0	4.8	5.1	1.3	2.7	4.1	2.7	5.4	4.1
PUNTS:														
Number	70	78	79	63	65	69	79	71	75	74	67	70	72	55
Average	41.6	39.4	43.2	40.6	37.4	38.6	41.8	42.1	44.1	40.9	42.8	36.2	40.3	37.5
PUNT RETURNS														
Number	35	36	39	35	32	35	33	45	43	40	40	48	23	48
Yards	279	399	250	361	308	346	225	400	467	315	342	356	184	388
Average Yards	8.0	11.1	6.4	10.3	9.6	9.9	6.8	8.9	10.9	7.9	8.6	7.4	8.0	8.1
Touchdowns	1	1	0	0	0	0	0	0	1	0	0	0	0	0
KICKOFF RET.:														
Number	58	54	54	70	63	63	66	58	46	54	60	53	63	62
Yards	1229	879	1102	1466	1303	1279	1249	1205	884	965	1068	965	1175	1113
Average Yards	21.2	16.3	20.4	20.9	20.7	20.3	18.9	20.8	19.2	17.9	17.8	18.2	18.7	18.0
Touchdowns	1	0	1	0	1	1	0	0	0	0	0	0	0	0
INTERCEPT RET.:														
Number	17	31	11	17	16	12	22	8	23	19	16	17	25	21
Yards	237	268	126	273	154	105	358	158	116	271	274	171	487	271
Average Yards	13.9	8.6	11.5	16.1	9.6	8.8	16.3	19.8	5.0	14.3	17.1	10.0	19.5	12.9
Touchdowns	3	1	1	1	1	1	2	1	2	3	2	0	3	2
PENALTIES:														
Number	125	75	98	88	84	87	83	108	83	120	96	104	77	102
Yards	1004	615	729	711	669	632	565	829	655	981	883	828	651	824
FUMBLES:														
Number	40	29	27	29	37	25	30	29	21	32	25	24	38	14
Number Lost	21	14	9	16	22	14	13	16	9	15	14	14	19	6
POINTS:														
Total	348	348	244	373	271	345	351	274	335	396	268	353	264	381
PAT Attempts	40	38	27	46	29	43	39	30	39	48	31	40	28	41
PAT Made	40	36	26	46	28	42	38	29	38	45	31	39	27	41
FG Attempts	33	37	25	26	30	24	28	27	28	29	27	36	27	40
FG Made	22	26	18	17	23	15	25	21	21	21	17	24	23	30
Percent FG Made	66.7	70.3	72.0	65.4	76.7	62.5	89.3	77.8	75.0	72.4	63.0	66.7	85.2	75.0
Safeties	1	0	1	0	0	0	2	1	0	0	0	1	0	2

DEFENSE

	ATL	CHI	DAL	DET	G.B.	L.A.	MINN	N.O.	NYG	PHIL	PHX	S.F.	T.B.	WASH
FIRST DOWNS:														
Total	300	256	280	334	286	286	257	279	245	251	306	250	313	267
by Rushing	79	91	109	142	113	93	107	91	90	59	140	77	129	77
by Passing	179	147	153	173	160	175	136	167	139	169	146	157	168	166
by Penalty	42	18	18	19	13	18	14	21	16	23	20	16	16	24
RUSHING:														
Number	413	391	482	532	475	418	503	410	388	337	521	353	496	382
Yards	1357	1572	1976	2388	2059	1649	2074	1559	1459	1169	2318	1258	2223	1587
Average Yards	3.3	4.0	4.1	4.5	4.3	3.9	4.1	3.8	3.8	3.5	4.4	3.6	4.5	4.2
Touchdowns	11	10	18	22	16	17	12	8	9	9	20	7	20	8
PASSING:														
Attempts	537	495	470	507	479	501	422	534	496	566	402	522	471	514
Completions	297	258	271	319	256	296	218	316	278	273	233	265	263	281
Completion Pct.	55.3	52.1	57.7	62.9	53.4	59.1	51.7	59.2	56.0	48.2	58.0	50.8	55.8	54.7
Passing Yards	4127	3220	2931	3625	3555	3942	2920	3584	2933	3771	3130	3278	3460	3483
Avg. Yds per Att.	6.9	5.5	5.2	6.1	6.7	7.1	5.6	5.8	5.2	5.7	6.6	5.3	6.5	5.6
Avg. Yds per Comp.	13.9	12.5	10.8	11.4	13.9	13.3	13.4	11.3	10.6	13.8	13.4	12.4	13.2	12.4
Times Tackled	33	41	36	41	27	30	47	42	30	45	36	44	34	45
Yds Lost Tackled	214	300	292	279	172	180	277	265	186	280	232	263	204	340
Net Yards	3913	2920	2639	3346	3383	3762	2643	3319	2747	3491	2898	3015	3256	3143
Touchdowns	31	19	12	21	20	30	20	21	12	23	29	17	22	21
Interceptions	17	31	11	17	16	12	22	8	23	19	16	17	25	21
Pct. Intercepted	3.2	6.3	2.3	3.4	3.3	2.4	5.2	1.5	4.6	3.4	4.0	3.3	5.3	4.1
PUNTS:														
Number	74	74	70	62	69	66	77	74	76	86	63	82	55	76
Average	40.2	37.9	40.9	40.8	39.1	41.4	39.4	40.9	41.3	40.3	43.6	40.0	40.5	43.3
PUNT RETURNS														
Number	39	39	43	29	34	46	44	43	41	37	41	30	39	30
Yards	314	322	438	233	266	420	513	302	291	338	258	215	352	205
Average Yards	8.1	8.3	10.2	8.0	7.8	9.1	11.7	7.0	7.1	9.1	6.3	7.2	9.0	6.8
Touchdowns	0	0	1	0	0	0	0	0	0	1	0	0	0	0
KICKOFF RET.:														
Number	49	73	55	70	56	68	62	36	65	74	56	66	43	58
Yards	814	1494	1136	1229	1125	1406	1350	583	1245	1408	1060	1284	1036	1008
Average Yards	16.6	20.5	20.7	17.6	20.1	20.7	21.8	16.2	19.2	19.0	18.9	19.5	24.1	17.4
Touchdowns	0	0	1	1	0	0	0	0	1	0	0	0	0	0
INTERCEPT RET.:														
Number	18	12	24	20	21	17	24	23	5	13	18	16	24	22
Yards	368	164	353	346	293	204	260	283	54	88	201	176	346	271
Average Yards	7.1	7.3	14.7	18.6	16.1	11.5	7.3	13.9	15.0	9.2	10.9	12.7	8.6	13.5
Touchdowns	2	0	4	3	2	2	1	0	1	0	1	1	2	5
PENALTIES:														
Number	95	84	104	97	109	109	100	87	83	94	96	85	78	90
Yards	811	676	911	788	854	968	787	655	569	706	834	641	617	712
FUMBLES:														
Number	26	38	32	31	26	32	25	35	28	32	28	21	33	24
Number Lost	18	14	19	18	14	19	11	19	11	11	11	14	17	12
POINTS:														
Total	365	280	308	413	347	412	326	275	211	299	396	239	367	301
PAT Attempts	44	31	36	48	40	49	34	30	23	33	50	26	45	35
PAT Made	42	28	36	48	39	46	32	30	23	32	48	26	43	35
FG Attempts	28	28	26	30	34	31	36	35	22	32	20	23	27	23
FG Made	19	22	18	23	22	24	30	21	16	23	16	19	18	18
Percent FG Made	67.9	78.6	69.2	76.7	64.7	77.4	83.3	60.0	72.7	71.9	80.0	82.6	66.7	78.3
Safeties	1	0	1	1	1	0	0	1	1	0	0	0	0	1

Wilson and defensive tackle Keith Millard that crippled both the offense and defense. The continued disappointing play of running back Herschel Walker was another element. After a 1-6 start, Minnesota won five in a row before collapsing down the stretch. Although safety Joey Browner, receiver Anthony Carter, guard Randall McDaniel and a few others continued to play well through what Wilson called "a season for hell," the general diagnosis of the flop was that the team wasn't nearly as talented as it had been given credit with being. Offensive coordinator Bob Schnelker and defensive coordinator Floyd Peters were fired after the season, but an injection of new players was called for by disappointed fans.

WESTERN DIVISION

San Francisco 49ers — The 1988 and '89 champs went for a "three-peat" in '90, an their 14-2 regular-season record — the best in the NFL — indicated they were right in line. But the record was deceiving as holes began to show. Mostly it was age finally catching up with some fine players, particularly in the secondary. Safety Ronnie Lott missed five games for the second year in a row. The running attack completely disappeared as age and injuries ruined Roger Craig's season. Rookie Dexter Carter was a helpful replacement but he proved to be too small for continuous pounding. But the passing game carried all, or nearly all, through the year to give the 49ers home-field advantage for the playoffs. The Joe Montana-to-Jerry Rice connection cemented their eventual enshrinements in the Hall of Fame.

New Orleans Saints — The Saints spent the season trying to get to .500, a mark they finally achieved with two straight wins at the end. Quarterback Bobby Hebert spent the season holding out. New Orleans opened with John Fourcade at quarterback, but the surprise of '89 was a flop in '90. After three games, general manager Jim Finks mortgaged the future by sending three high draft picks to Dallas for Steve Walsh. Although the team had a winning record after Walsh's acquisition, his play was inconsistent. His critics derided his arm strength, while his defenders argued he needed time to learn a new offense. The strength of the team remained its defense, particularity the linebackers.

Los Angeles Rams — After reaching the playoffs in six of the previous seven seasons, the Rams' 1990 nosedive came as a shock. A rash of preseason injuries and holdouts got them off to a bad start. Several of the 16 second- and third-year players didn't play up to expectations. Quarterback Jim Everett threw for nearly 4,000 yards, but he was not as sharp as in previous seasons. The running game didn't help much. Cleveland Gary had fumble problems, Curt Warner was washed up, and Marcus Dupree, attempting a comeback after five years away from football, wasn't ready. The worst problem was the undersized, underachieving defense. Cornerback Jerry Gray was injured most of the year, and the defensive line was embarrassing porous. Only linebacker Kevin Greene, with 13 sacks, was a bright spot.

Atlanta Falcons — Under new coach Jerry Glanville the Falcons improved their record by two wins, but that was scant consolation to fans who'd hoped for a .500 season. A seven-game losing streak that began with the first game in November ruined any chance of breaking even. Chris Miller, the "franchise quarterback" prospect, never quite lived up to that billing and then was lost in the 12th game with a broken collarbone. The best that could be said was that Atlanta kept most games close and the players' morale was higher than in '89. Bright spots on an improved defense were the play of end Mike Gann and cornerback Deion Sanders. The Falcons' MVP was receiver Andre Rison, who set team records with 82 catches, 1,208 yards, and 10 touchdowns. Mike Rozier, acquired early in the season for Houston, ran for over 100 yards in each of the last two games.

NEW YORK GIANTS 13-3 Bill Parcells

Scores of Each Game		
27	PHILADELPHIA	20
28	Dallas	7
20	MIAMI	3
31	DALLAS	17
24	Washington	20
20	PHOENIX	19
21	WASHINGTON	10
24	Indianapolis	7
31	L.A. Rams	7
20	DETROIT	0
13	Philadelphia	31
3	San Francisco	7
23	MINNESOTA	15
13	BUFFALO	17
24	Phoenix	21
13	New England	10

Use Name	Pos.	Hgt	Wgt	Age	Int	Pts
John Elliott	OT	6'7"	305	25		
Eric Moore	OT-OG	6'5"	290	25		
Doug Riesenberg	OT	6'5"	275	25		
Bob Kratch	OG	6'3"	288	24		
Tom Rehder	OG-OT	6'7"	290	25		
William Roberts	OG	6'5"	280	28		
Brian Williams	OG-C	6'5"	300	24		
Bart Oates	C	6'3"	265	31		
Eric Dorsey	DE	6'5"	280	26		
Mike Fox	DE	6'6"	275	23		
Leonard Marshall	DE	6'3"	285	28		
John Washington	DE	6'4"	275	27		
Erik Howard	NT	6'4"	268	25		
Kent Wells	NT	6'4"	295	25		

Use Name	Pos.	Hgt	Wgt	Age	Int	Pts
Bobby Abrams	LB	6'3"	230	23		
Carl Banks	LB	6'4"	235	28		
Johnie Cooks	LB	6'4"	251	31		
Steve DeOssie	LB	6'2"	248	27		
Pepper Johnson	LB	6'3"	248	26	1	
Larry McGrew	LB	6'5"	250	33		
Gary Reasons	LB	6'4"	234	28	3	
Lawrence Taylor	LB	6'3"	243	31	1	6
Roger Brown	DB	6'	196	23		
Mark Collins	DB	5'10"	190	26	2	
Dave Duerson	DB	6'1"	208	29	1	6
Myron Guyton	DB	6'1"	205	23	1	
Greg Jackson	DB	6'1"	200	24	5	
Reyna Thompson	DB	6'	193	27		
Everson Walls	DB	6'1"	194	30	6	6
David Whitmore	DB	6'	235	23		
Perry Williams	DB	6'2"	203	29	3	

Adrain White — Knee Injury

Use Name	Pos.	Hgt	Wgt	Age	Int	Pts
Matt Cavanaugh	QB	6'2"	210	33		
Jeff Hostetler	QB	6'3"	212	29		12
Phil Simms	QB	6'3"	214	33		6
Ottis Anderson	HB	6'2"	225	33		66
Rodney Hampton	HB	5'11"	215	21		24
Dave Meggett	HB	5'7"	180	24		12
Lewis Tillman	HB	6'	195	24		6
Maurice Carthon	FB	6'1"	225	29		
Lee Rouson	FB	6'1"	222	27		
Stephen Baker	WR	5'8"	160	26		24
Mark Ingram	WR	5'10"	188	25		30
Troy Kyles	WR	6'	180	22		
Lionel Manuel	WR	5'11"	180	28		
Stacy Robinson	WR	5'11"	186	28		
Odessa Turner	WR	6'3"	205	25		
Mark Bavaro	TE	6'4"	245	27		
Howard Cross	TE	6'5"	245	23		
Bob Mrosko	TE	6'6"	270	24		6
Raul Allegre	K	5'10"	167	31		21
Matt Bahr	K	5'10"	175	34		80
Sean Landeta	K	6'	200	28		

PHILADELPHIA EAGLES 10-6 Buddy Ryan

Scores of Each Game		
20	N.Y. Giants	27
21	PHOENIX	23
27	L.A. Rams	21
23	INDIANAPOLIS	24
32	MINNESOTA	24
7	Washington	13
21	Dallas	20
48	NEW ENGLAND	20
28	WASHINGTON	14
24	Atlanta	23
31	N.Y. GIANTS	13
23	Buffalo	30
20	Miami	* 23
31	GREEN BAY	0
17	DALLAS	3
23	Phoenix	21

Use Name	Pos.	Hgt	Wgt	Age	Int	Pts
Matt Darwin	OT	6'4"	275	27		
Ron Heller	OT	6'6"	280	28		
Daryle Smith	OT	6'5"	278	26		
Bruce Collie	OG	6'6"	275	28		
Cecil Gray	OG-DT	6'4"	274	22		
Mike Schad	OG	6'5"	290	26		
Ron Solt	OG	6'3"	285	28		
Ben Tamburello	OG-C	6'3"	278	25		
David Alexander	C	6'3"	282	25		
David Bailey	DE	6'4"	240	24		
Steve Kaufusi	DE	6'4"	274	26		
Clyde Simmons	DE	6'6"	276	26		6
Reggie White	DE-DT	6'5"	285	28		
Jerome Brown	DT	6'2"	295	25		
Dick Chapura (from PHX)	DT	6'3"	280	26		
Mike Golic	DT	6'5"	275	28	1	
Mike Pitts	DT	6'5"	277	30		

Use Name	Pos.	Hgt	Wgt	Age	Int	Pts
Byron Evans	LB	6'2"	225	26	1	6
Britt Hager	LB	6'1"	222	24		
Al Harris	LB	6'5"	265	33		
Maurice Henry	LB	5'11"	220	23		
Seth Joyner	LB	6'2"	248	25		
Ken Rose (from CLE)	LB	6'1"	216	28		
Ricky Shaw	LB	6'4"	240	25		
Jessie Small	LB	6'3"	239	23		
Eric Allen	DB	5'10"	183	23	3	6
William Frizzell	DB	6'3"	205	28	3	6
Terry Hoage	DB	6'3"	201	28	1	
Wes Hopkins	DB	6'1"	212	29	5	
Izel Jenkins	DB	5'10"	191	25		
Sammy Lilly (to SD)	DB	5'9"	178	25		
Ben Smith	DB	5'11"	183	23	3	
Andre Waters	DB	5'11"	195	28		

Use Name	Pos.	Hgt	Wgt	Age	Int	Pts
Randall Cunningham	QB	6'4"	203	27		30
Jim McMahon	QB	6'1"	190	31		
Keith Byars	HB	6'1"	238	27		18
Robert Drummond	HB	6'1"	205	23		6
Thomas Sanders	HB	5'11"	203	28		6
Heath Sherman	FB-HB	6'	190	23		24
Anthony Toney	FB	6'	227	27		24
Roger Vick	FB	6'3"	235	26		6
Fred Barnett	WR	6'	203	24		48
Mike Bellamy	WR	6'	195	24		
Anthony Edwards	WR	5'11"	195	24		
Marvin Hargrove	WR	5'10"	178	22		6
Kenny Jackson	WR	6'	180	28		
Mike Quick	WR	6'2"	190	31		6
Calvin Williams	WR	5'11"	181	23		54
Keith Jackson	TE	6'2"	250	25		36
Harper LeBel	TE	6'4"	251	27		
Mickey Shuler	TE	6'3"	231	34		
Jeff Feagles	K	6'	198	24		
Roger Ruzek	K	6'1"	195	29		108

John Teltschik — Leg Injury
Ron Johnson — Did Not Report

WASHINGTON REDSKINS 10-6 Joe Gibbs

Scores of Each Game		
31	PHOENIX	0
13	San Francisco	26
19	DALLAS	15
38	Phoenix	10
20	N.Y. GIANTS	24
13	PHILADELPHIA	7
10	N.Y. Giants	21
41	Detroit	* 38
14	Philadelphia	28
31	NEW ORLEANS	17
17	Dallas	27
42	MIAMI	20
10	CHICAGO	9
25	New England	10
28	Indianapolis	35
29	BUFFALO	14

Use Name	Pos.	Hgt	Wgt	Age	Int	Pts
Joe Jacoby	OT	6'7"	305	31		
Jim Lachey	OT	6'6"	290	27		
Ed Simmons	OT	6'5"	280	26		
Mark Adickes	OG	6'4"	275	29		
Russ Grimm	OG	6'3"	275	31		
Raleigh McKenzie	OG-C	6'2"	270	27		
Mark Schlereth	OG	6'3"	285	24		
Jeff Bostic	C	6'2"	260	31		
James Geathers	DT	6'7"	290	30		
Markus Koch	DE	6'5"	275	27		
Charles Mann	DE	6'6"	270	29		
Fred Stokes	DE	6'3"	262	26		
Darryl Grant	DT	6'1"	275	30		
Tim Johnson	DT	6'3"	261	25		
Tracy Rocker	DT	6'3"	288	24		
Eric Williams	DT	6'4"	286	28		

Mark May — Knee Injury

Use Name	Pos.	Hgt	Wgt	Age	Int	Pts
Ravin Caldwell	LB	6'3"	229	27		
Monte Coleman	LB	6'2"	230	32	1	
Andre Collins	LB	6'1"	230	22		
Kurt Gouveia	LB	6'1"	227	25		6
Randy Kirk	LB	6'2"	235	24		
Greg Manusky	LB	6'1"	242	24		
Wilber Marshall	LB	6'1"	230	28	1	
Todd Bowles	DB	6'2"	203	26	3	
Brian Davis	DB	6'2"	190	27		
Wayne Davis	DB	5'11"	180	27		
Brad Edwards	DB	6'1"	196	24	2	
Darrell Green	DB	5'8"	170	30	4	6
A.J. Johnson	DB	5'8"	176	23	1	
Sidney Johnson	DB	5'9"	175	25		
Martin Mayhew	DB	5'8"	172	24	7	
Alvoid Mays	DB	5'9"	180	24		
Johnny Thomas	DB	5'9"	185	26		
Clarence Vaughn	DB	6'	202	26		
Alvin Walton	DB	6'	180	26	2	6

Use Name	Pos.	Hgt	Wgt	Age	Int	Pts
Gary Hogeboom	QB	6'4"	207	32		
Stan Humphries	QB	6'2"	223	25		12
Jeff Rutledge	QB	6'1"	195	33		6
Mark Rypien	QB	6'4"	234	27		
Kelvin Bryant	HB	6'2"	195	30		6
Reggie Dupard	HB	5'11"	205	26		
Brian Mitchell	HB	5'10"	195	22		6
Gerald Riggs	HB-FB	6'1"	232	29		36
Earnest Byner	FB-HB	5'10"	215	27		42
Gary Clark	WR	5'9"	173	27		48
Stephen Hobbs	WR	5'11"	195	24		6
Joe Howard	WR	5'8"	170	27		
Art Monk	WR	6'3"	209	32		30
Ricky Sanders	WR	5'11"	180	28		18
Walter Stanley	WR	5'9"	180	27		
John Brandes	TE	6'2"	250	26		
Jimmie Johnson	TE	6'2"	246	22		12
Ron Middleton	TE	6'2"	255	25		
Don Warren	TE	6'4"	242	34		6
Kelvin Whisenhuint	TE	6'3"	240	28		
Kelly Goodburn (from KC)	K	6'2"	202	28		
Chip Lohmiller	K	6'3"	213	24		131
Ralf Mojsiejenko	K	6'3"	212	27		

Reggie Branch — Ankle Injury
Tom Brown — Knee Injury
Charles Lockett — Quadriceps Injury

DALLAS COWBOYS 7-9 Jimmy Johnson

Scores of Each Game		
17	SAN DIEGO	14
7	N.Y. GIANTS	28
15	Washington	19
17	N.Y. Giants	31
14	TAMPA BAY	10
3	Phoenix	20
17	Tampa Bay	13
20	PHILADELPHIA	21
9	N.Y. Jets	24
6	SAN FRANCISCO	24
24	L.A. Rams	21
27	WASHINGTON	17
17	NEW ORLEANS	13
41	PHOENIX	10
3	Philadelphia	17
7	Atlanta	26

Use Name	Pos.	Hgt	Wgt	Age	Int	Pts
Louis Cheek (to PHI)	OT	6'6"	295	25		
Kevin Gogan	OT	6'7"	311	25		
Mark Tuinei	OT	6'5"	293	30		
John Gesek	OG	6'5"	283	27		
Dale Hellestrae	OG-C	6'5"	275	28		
Crawford Ker	OG	6'3"	283	28		
Nate Newton	OG	6'3"	322	28		
Tony Slaton	OG	6'3"	280	29		
Mark Stepnoski	OG	6'2"	266	23		
Jeff Zimmerman	OG	6'6"	332	25		
Lester Brinkley	DE	6'6"	270	25		
Jim Jeffcoat	DE	6'5"	264	29		
Danny Stubbs	DE	6'4"	264	25		
Tony Tolbert	DE	6'6"	254	22		
Willie Broughton	DT	6'5"	280	26		
Dean Hamel	DT	6'3"	271	29		
Jimmie Jones	DT	6'4"	272	24		
Danny Noonan	DT	6'4"	266	25		
Mitch Willis	DT	6'8"	285	28		

Use Name	Pos.	Hgt	Wgt	Age	Int	Pts
Willis Crockett	LB	6'3"	234	24		
Jack Del Rio	LB	6'4"	236	27		
Dave Harper	LB	6'1"	220	24		
David Howard	LB	6'2"	233	28		
Eugene Lockhart	LB	6'2"	235	29		
Ken Norton	LB	6'2"	236	23		
Randy Shannon	LB	6'1"	221	24		
Vinson Smith	LB	6'2"	225	25		
Jesse Solomon	LB	6'	235	26		
Vince Albritton	DB	6'2"	220	28		
Bill Bates	DB	6'1"	200	29	1	
Michael Brooks (from SD)	DB	6'	195	23		
Ron Francis	DB	5'9"	201	26		
Kenneth Gant	DB	5'11"	181	23	1	
Manny Hendrix	DB	5'10"	185	25	1	
Issiac Holt	DB	6'2"	202	27	3	6
Ray Horton	DB	5'11"	187	30	1	
Stan Smagala	DB	5'10"	184	22		
James Washington	DB	6'1"	195	25	3	
Robert Williams	DB	5'10"	186	27	1	

Scott Ankrum — Knee Injury

Use Name	Pos.	Hgt	Wgt	Age	Int	Pts
Troy Aikman	QB	6'4"	216	23		6
Babe Laufenberg	QB	6'3"	205	30		
Cliff Stoudt	QB	6'4"	218	35		
James Dixon	HB-WR	5'10"	184	23		
Emmitt Smith	HB	5'9"	203	21		66
Timmy Smith	HB	5'11"	216	26		
Tommie Agee	FB	6'	223	26		6
Alonzo Highsmith	FB	6'1"	237	25		
Daryl Johnston	FB	6'2"	234	24		12
Rod Harris (to PHI)	WR	5'10"	183	23		
Michael Irvin	WR	6'2"	202	23		30
Kelvin Martin	WR	5'9"	163	26		
Dennis McKinnon (to MIA)	WR	6'1"	177	29		6
Derrick Shepard	WR	5'10"	181	26		
Alexander Wright	WR	6'	189	23		6
Robert Awalt	TE	6'5"	238	26		
Steve Folsom	TE	6'5"	240	32		
Jay Novacek	TE	6'4"	230	27		24
Mike Saxon	K	6'3"	200	28		
Ken Willis	K	5'11"	189	23		80

Keith Jones — Knee Injury

PHOENIX CARDINALS 5-11 Joe Bugel

Scores of Each Game		
0	Washington	31
23	Philadelphia	21
7	New Orleans	28
10	WASHINGTON	38
20	DALLAS	3
19	N.Y. Giants	20
21	CHICAGO	31
3	Miami	23
14	Buffalo	45
21	GREEN BAY	24
34	NEW ENGLAND	14
20	INDIANAPOLIS	17
24	Atlanta	13
10	Dallas	41
21	N.Y. GIANTS	24
21	PHILADELPHIA	23

Use Name	Pos.	Hgt	Wgt	Age	Int	Pts
Tootie Robbins	OT	6'5"	302	32		
Luis Sharpe	OT	6'4"	290	30		6
Joe Wolf	OT	6'5"	283	23		
Derek Kennard	OG	6'3"	319	27		
Lance Smith	OG	6'2"	285	26		
Vernice Smith	OG-OT	6'2"	289	24		
Kani Kauahi	C	6'2"	274	30		
Bill Lewis	C	6'7"	278	27		
Dexter Manley	DE	6'3"	257	31		
Freddie Joe Nunn	DE	6'4"	250	28		
Elston Ridgle	DE	6'5"	270	27		
Rod Saddler	DE	6'5"	280	24		
Carl Hairston	DT	6'2"	280	37		
Bob Clasby	DT	6'5"	276	29		
Craig Patterson	NT	6'5"	310	26		
Jim Wahler	NT-DT	6'4"	276	24		

Jeff Walker — Knee Injury

Use Name	Pos.	Hgt	Wgt	Age	Int	Pts
David Bavaro	LB	6'	236	23		
Anthony Bell	LB	6'3"	231	26	1	
David Braxton (from MIN)	LB	6'1"	232	25		
Ken Harvey	LB	6'2"	228	25		
Eric Hill	LB	6'1"	248	25		
Garth Jax	LB	6'2"	229	26	2	
Eldonta Osbourne	LB	6'	226	23		
Jeroy Robinson (from DEN)	LB	6'1"	241	22		
Chris Washington	LB	6'4"	240	28		
Stanley Blair	DB	6'	192	26		
Tracy Eaton	DB	6'1"	191	25		
Lorenzo Lynch	DB	5'9"	200	27		
Cedric Mack	DB	6'	194	29	2	
Tim McDonald	DB	6'2"	207	25	4	
Jay Taylor	DB	5'9"	170	22	4	
Marcus Turner	DB	6'	191	23	1	12
Lonnie Young	DB	6'1"	182	27	2	
Mike Zordich	DB	5'11"	197	26	1	

Use Name	Pos.	Hgt	Wgt	Age	Int	Pts
Timm Rosenbach	QB	6'2"	215	23		18
Tom Tupa	QB	6'4"	220	23		
Larry Centers	HB	5'11"	203	22		
Terrence Flagler	HB	6'	200	25		12
Johnny Johnson	HB	6'2"	216	22		30
Vai Sikahema	HB	5'9"	184	28		
Dennis Smith	HB	6'	230	23		
Anthony Thompson	HB	5'11"	207	23		24
Ron Wolfley	FB	6'	222	27		
Roy Green	WR	6'	195	33		24
Don Holmes	WR	5'10"	182	29		
John Jackson	WR	5'10"	175	23		
Ernie Jones	WR	5'11"	186	25		24
Ricky Proehl	WR	5'10"	185	22		24
J.T. Smith	WR	6'2"	185	34		12
Tim Jordan	TE	6'2"	220	23		
Dave Little	TE	6'2"	230	29		
Walter Reeves	TE	6'4"	262	24		
Rich Camarillo	K	5'11"	193	29		
Al Del Greco	K	5'10"	191	28		82

Darren Flutie — Foot Injury

NEW YORK GIANTS

RUSHING

Last Name	No.	Yds	Avg	TD
Anderson	225	784	3.5	11
Hampton	109	455	4.2	2
Tillman	84	231	2.8	1
Hostetler	39	190	4.9	2
Meggett	22	164	7.5	0
Carthon	36	143	4.0	0
Simms	21	61	2.9	1
Rouson	3	14	4.7	0
Ingram	1	4	4.0	0
Baker	1	3	3.0	0

RECEIVING

Last Name	No.	Yds	Avg	TD
Meggett	39	140	10.5	1
Bavaro	33	393	11.9	5
Hampton	32	274	8.6	2
Baker	26	541	20.8	4
Ingram	26	499	19.2	5
Anderson	18	139	7.7	0
Carthon	14	151	10.8	0
Manuel	11	169	15.4	0
Cross	8	106	13.3	0
Tillman	8	18	2.3	0
Turner	6	69	11.5	0
Kyles	4	77	19.3	0
Mrosko	3	27	9.0	1
Robinson	2	13	6.5	0
Rouson	1	12	12.0	0

PUNT RETURNS

Last Name	No.	Yds	Avg	TD
Megett	43	467	10.9	1

KICKOFF RETURNS

Last Name	No.	Yds	Avg	TD
Meggett	21	492	23.4	0
Hampton	20	340	17.0	0
Ingram	3	42	14.0	0
Cross	1	10	10.0	0
Whitmore	1	0	0.0	0

PASSING—PUNTING—KICKING

PASSING	Att	Cmp	%	Yds	Yd/Att	TD	Int— %	RK
Simms	311	184	59.2	2284	7.34	15	4—1.3	1
Hostetler	87	47	54.0	614	7.06	3	1—1.1	

PUNTING	No.	Avg.
Landeta	75	44.1

KICKING	XP	ATT	%	FG	ATT	%
Allegre	9	9	100	4	5	80
M. Bahr	29	30	97	17	23	74

PHILADELPHIA EAGLES

RUSHING

Last Name	No.	Yds	Avg	TD
Cunningham	118	942	8.0	5
Sherman	164	685	4.2	1
Toney	132	452	3.4	1
Sanders	56	208	3.7	1
Byars	37	141	3.8	0
Vick	16	58	3.6	1
Drummond	8	33	4.1	1
Williams	2	20	10.0	0
Barnett	2	13	6.5	0
Feagles	2	3	1.5	0
McMahon	3	1	0.3	0

RECEIVING

Last Name	No.	Yds	Avg	TD
Byars	81	819	10.1	3
Kei. Jackson	50	670	13.4	6
Williams	37	602	16.3	9
Barnett	36	721	20.0	8
Sherman	23	167	7.3	3
Shuler	18	190	10.6	0
Toney	17	133	7.8	3
Quick	9	135	15.0	1
Drummond	5	39	7.8	0
Sanders	2	20	10.0	0
Ken. Jackson	1	43	43.0	0
Hargrove	1	34	34.0	0
LeBel	1	9	9.0	0

PUNT RETURNS

Last Name	No.	Yds	Avg	TD
Hargrove	12	83	6.9	0
Edwards	8	60	7.5	0
Bellamy	2	22	11.0	0
Williams	2	-1	-0.5	0

KICKOFF RETURNS

Last Name	No.	Yds	Avg	TD
Hargrove	19	341	17.9	0
Sanders	15	299	19.9	0
Ken. Jackson	6	125	20.8	0
Barnett	4	65	16.3	0
Edwards	3	36	12.0	0
Vick	2	22	11.0	0
Bellamy	1	17	17.0	0
Jenkins	1	14	14.0	0
Allen	1	2	2.0	0
Hager	1	0	0.0	0

PASSING—PUNTING—KICKING

PASSING	Att	Cmp	%	Yds	Yd/Att	TD	Int— %	RK
Cunningham	465	271	58.3	3466	7.45	30	13—2.8	2
McMahon	9	6	66.7	63	7.00	0	0—0.0	
Byars	4	4	100.0	53	13.25	4	0—0.0	
Feagles	1	0	0.0	0	0.00	0	0—0.0	

PUNTING	No.	Avg.
Feagles	74	40.9

KICKING	XP	ATT	%	FG	ATT	%
Ruzek	45	48	94	21	29	72

WASHINGTON REDSKINS

RUSHING

Last Name	No.	Yds	Avg	TD
Byner	297	1219	4.1	6
Riggs	123	475	3.9	6
Humphries	23	106	4.6	2
Dupard	19	85	4.5	0
Mitchell	15	81	5.4	1
Monk	7	59	8.4	0
Bryant	6	24	4.0	0
Sanders	4	17	4.3	0
Rutledge	4	12	3.0	1
Goodburn	1	5	5.0	0
Rypien	15	4	0.3	0
Clark	1	1	1.0	0
Mojsiejenko	1	0	0.0	0

RECEIVING

Last Name	No.	Yds	Avg	TD
Clark	75	1112	14.8	8
Monk	68	770	11.3	5
Sanders	56	727	13.0	3
Byner	31	279	9.0	1
Bryant	26	248	9.5	1
J. Johnson	15	218	14.5	2
Warren	15	123	8.2	1
Riggs	7	60	8.6	0
Howard	3	36	12.0	0
Stanley	2	15	7.5	0
Mitchell	2	5	2.5	0
Hobbs	1	18	18.0	1

PUNT RETURNS

Last Name	No.	Yds	Avg	TD
Stanley	24	176	7.3	0
Mitchell	12	107	8.9	0
Howard	10	99	9.9	0
Green	1	6	6.0	0
Thomas	1	0	0.0	0

KICKOFF RETURNS

Last Name	No.	Yds	Avg	TD
Howard	22	427	19.4	0
Mitchell	18	365	20.3	0
Stanley	9	177	19.7	0
Hobbs	6	92	15.3	0
Gouveia	2	23	11.5	0
Sanders	1	22	22.0	0
Middleton	1	7	7.0	0
Dupard	2	0	0.0	0
Bowles	1	0	0.0	0

PASSING—PUNTING—KICKING

PASSING	Att	Cmp	%	Yds	Yd/Att	TD	Int— %	RK
Rypien	304	166	54.6	2070	6.81	16	11—3.6	8
Humphries	156	91	58.3	1015	6.51	3	10—6.4	
Rutledge	68	40	58.8	455	6.69	2	1—1.5	
Mitchell	6	3	50.0	40	6.67	0	0—0.0	
Byner	2	1	50.0	31	15.50	1	0—0.0	

PUNTING	No.	Avg.
Mojsiejenko	44	38.3
Goodburn	11	36.8

KICKING	XP	ATT	%	FG	ATT	%
Lohmiller	41	41	100	30	40	75

DALLAS COWBOYS

RUSHING

Last Name	No.	Yds	Avg	TD
E. Smith	241	937	3.9	11
Agee	53	213	4.0	0
Aikman	40	172	4.3	1
Highsmith	19	48	2.5	0
Dixon	11	43	3.9	0
Johnston	10	35	3.5	1
Wright	3	26	8.7	0
Saxon	1	20	20.0	0
Laufenberg	2	6	3.0	0
T. Smith	6	6	1.0	0
Bates	1	4	4.0	0
Martin	4	-2	-0.5	0
McKinnon	1	-8	-8.0	0

RECEIVING

Last Name	No.	Yds	Avg	TD
Martin	64	732	11.4	0
Novacek	59	657	11.1	4
Agee	30	272	9.1	1
E. Smith	24	228	9.5	0
Irvin	20	413	20.7	5
McKinnon	14	172	12.3	1
Johnston	14	148	10.6	1
Awalt	13	133	10.2	0
Wright	11	104	9.5	0
Highsmith	3	13	4.3	0
Dixon	2	26	13.0	0

PUNT RETURNS

Last Name	No.	Yds	Avg	TD
Harris	28	214	7.6	0
Shepard	20	121	6.1	0
Martin	5	46	9.2	0
McKinnon	2	20	10.0	0

KICKOFF RETURNS

Last Name	No.	Yds	Avg	TD
Dixon	36	736	20.4	0
Wright	12	276	23.0	1
Shepard	4	75	18.8	0
Harris	2	44	22.0	0
Stepnoski	1	15	15.0	0

PASSING—PUNTING—KICKING

PASSING	Att	Cmp	%	Yds	Yd/Att	TD	Int— %	RK
Aikman	399	226	56.6	2579	6.46	11	18—4.5	14
Laufenberg	67	24	35.8	279	4.16	1	6—9.0	

PUNTING	No.	Avg.
Saxon	79	43.2

KICKING	XP	Att.	%	FG	Att	%
Willis	26	26	100	18	25	72

PHOENIX CARDINALS

RUSHING

Last Name	No.	Yds	Avg	TD
Johnson	234	926	4.0	5
Rosenbach	86	470	5.5	3
Thompson	106	390	3.7	4
Flagler	13	85	6.5	1
Jones	4	33	8.3	0
Sikahema	3	8	2.7	0
Proehl	1	4	4.0	0
J. Smith	1	4	4.0	0
Wolfley	2	3	1.5	0
Tupa	1	0	0.0	0
Camarillo	1	-11	-11.0	0

RECEIVING

Last Name	No.	Yds	Avg	TD
Proehl	56	802	14.3	4
Green	53	797	15.0	4
Jones	43	724	16.8	4
Johnson	25	241	9.6	0
J. Smith	18	225	12.5	2
Reeves	18	126	7.0	0
Flagler	13	130	10.0	1
Sikahema	7	51	7.3	0
Thompson	2	11	5.5	0
Jorden	2	10	5.0	0
Sharpe	1	1	1.0	1

PUNT RETURNS

Last Name	No.	Yds	Avg	TD
Sikahema	36	306	8.5	0
J. Smith	3	34	11.3	0
Proehl	1	2	2.0	0

KICKOFF RETURNS

Last Name	No.	Yds	Avg	TD
Sikahema	27	544	20.1	0
Centers	16	272	17.0	0
Flagler	10	167	16.7	0
Proehl	4	53	13.3	0
Jax	2	17	8.5	0
Green	1	15	15.0	0

PASSING—PUNTING—KICKING

PASSING	Att	Cmp	%	Yds	Yd/Att	TD	Int— %	RK
Rosenbach	437	237	54.2	3098	7.09	16	17—3.9	11
Green	1	1	100.0	20	20.00	0	0—0.0	
Johnson	1	0	0.0	0	0.00	0	1—100.0	

PUNTING	No.	Avg.
Camarillo	67	42.8

KICKING	XP	Att	%	FG	Att	%
Del Greco	31	31	100	17	27	63

CHICAGO BEARS 11-5 Mike Ditka

Scores of Each Game		
17	SEATTLE	0
31	Green Bay	13
19	MINNESOTA	16
10	L.A. Raiders	24
27	GREEN BAY	13
38	L.A. RAMS	9
31	Phoenix	21
26	Tampa Bay	6
30	ATLANTA	24
16	Denver	* 13
13	Minnesota	41
23	DETROIT	* 17
9	Washington	10
21	Detroit	38
27	TAMPA BAY	14
10	KANSAS CITY	21

Use Name	Pos.	Hgt	Wgt	Age	Int	Pts
Jim Covert	OT	6'4"	278	30		
Keith Van Horne	OT	6'6"	283	32		
John Wojciechowski	OT	6'4"	270	27		
Kurt Becker	OG	6'5"	269	31		
Mark Bortz	OG	6'6"	272	28		
Jerry Fontenot	OG	6'3"	272	23		
Tom Thayer	OG	6'4"	270	29		
Jay Hilgenberg	C	6'3"	260	30		
Trace Armstrong	DE	6'4"	259	24		
Richard Dent	DE	6'5"	268	29	3	6
Terry Price	DE	6'4"	272	22		
Tim Ryan	DE	6'4"	268	22		
Dan Hampton	DT	6'5"	274	32		
Steve McMichael	DT	6'2"	268	32		
William Perry	DT	6'2"	315	27		
* Fred Washington	DT	6'2"	277	23		
Ron Cox	LB	6'2"	242	22		
Dante Jones	LB	6'1"	236	25		
Jim Morrissey	LB	6'3"	227	27	2	
Mickey Pruitt	LB	6'1"	206	25		
Ron Rivera	LB	6'3"	240	28	2	
John Roper	LB	6'1"	228	24		
Glenell Sanders	LB	6'	224	23		
Mike Singletary	LB	6'	230	31		
Mark Carrier	DB	6'1"	180	22	10	
Maurice Douglass	DB	5'11"	200	26		
Shaun Gayle	DB	5'11"	194	28	2	
Vestee Jackson	DB	6'	186	27	1	6
John Mangum	DB	5'10"	173	23		
Markus Paul	DB	6'2"	199	24	2	
Lemuel Stinson	DB	5'9"	159	24	6	
David Tate	DB	6'	177	25		
Donnell Woolford	DB	5'9"	187	24	3	
Jim Harbaugh	QB	6'3"	220	25		24
Mike Tomczak	QB	6'1"	198	27		12
Peter Tom Willis	QB	6'2"	188	23		
Neal Anderson	HB	5'11"	210	26		78
Johnny Bailey	HB	5'8"	180	23		6
Mark Green	HB	5'11"	184	23		6
Lars Tate	HB	6'2"	215	24		
Brad Muster	FB	6'3"	231	25		36
James Rouse	FB	6'	220	23		
Wendell Davis	WR	5'11"	188	24		18
Dennis Gentry	WR-HB	5'8"	180	31		12
Glen Kozlowski	WR	6'1"	205	27		
Ron Morris	WR	6'1'	195	25		18
Quintin Smith	WR	5'10"	172	22		
Tom Waddle	WR	6'	181	23		
Cap Boso	TE	6'3"	240	26		6
James Coley	TE	6'3"	270	23		
Jim Thornton	TE	6'2"	242	25		6
Maury Buford	K	6'1"	198	30		
Kevin Butler	K	6'1"	190	28		114

* died Dec. 21 in automobile accident

TAMPA BAY BUCCANEERS 6-10 Ray Perkins (5-8), Richard Williamson (1-2)

Scores of Each Game		
38	Detroit	21
14	L.A. RAMS	35
23	DETROIT	20
23	Minnesota	* 20
10	Dallas	14
26	GREEN BAY	14
13	DALLAS	17
10	San Diego	41
6	CHICAGO	26
7	New Orleans	35
7	San Francisco	31
10	Green Bay	20
23	ATLANTA	17
26	MINNESOTA	13
14	Chicago	27
14	N.Y. JETS	16

Use Name	Pos.	Hgt	Wgt	Age	Int	Pts
Paul Gruber	OT	6'5"	290	25		
Harry Swayne	OT	6'5"	270	25		
Rob Taylor	OT	6'6"	290	29		
Carl Bax	OG	6'4"	290	24		
Ian Beckles	OG	6'1"	295	23		
John Bruhin	OG	6'3"	285	25		
Scott Dill	OG	6'5"	272	24		
Tom McHale	OG	6'4"	280	27		
Randy Grimes	C	6'4"	275	30		
Tony Mayberry	C	6'4"	285	22		
John Cannon	DE	6'5"	265	30		
Reuben Davis	DE	6'4"	285	25		
Benji Roland	DE	6'3"	260	23		
Jim Skow	DE	6'3"	250	27		
Robb White	DE	6'4"	280	25		
Curt Jarvis	NT	6'2"	265	25		
Tim Newton	NT	6'	277	27		
Ray Seals (to IND)	NT	6'3"	270	25		
Willie Wyatt	NT	5'11"	275	22		
Sam Anno	LB	6'2"	235	25		
Sidney Coleman	LB	6'2"	250	26		
Eugene Marve	LB	6'2"	240	30		
Keith McCants	LB	6'3"	255	21		
Winston Moss	LB	6'3"	235	24		
Kevin Murphy	LB	6'2"	235	26		
Ervin Randle	LB	6'1"	250	27		
Broderick Thomas	LB	6'4"	245	23		
Eric Everett	DB	5'10"	170	24	4	
Bobby Futrell	DB	5'11"	190	28		
Wayne Haddix	DB	6'1"	205	27	7	18
Harry Hamilton	DB	6'	195	27	5	
Odie Harris	DB	6'	190	24		
Ricky Reynolds	DB	5'11"	190	25	3	
Rodney Rice	DB	5'8"	180	24	2	
Mark Robinson	DB	5'11"	200	27	4	
Jeff Carlson	QB	6'3"	215	24		
Chris Chandler	QB	6'4"	220	24		6
Vinny Testaverde	QB	6'5"	215	26		6
Gary Anderson	HB	6'	190	29		30
Derrick Douglas	HB	5'10"	205	22		
John Harvey	HB	5'11"	185	23		6
Reggie Cobb	FB	6'	225	22		12
Jamie Lawson (to NE)	FB	5'10"	240	24		
Bruce Perkins	FB	6'2"	230	23		
Terry Anthony	WR	6'	200	22		
Mark Carrier	WR	6'	185	24		24
Willie Drewrey	WR	5'7"	170	27		6
Chris Ford	WR	6'1"	185	23		
Bruce Hill	WR	6'	180	26		30
Danny Peebles	WR	5'11"	180	25		6
Frank Pillow	WR	5'10"	170	25		
Jesse Anderson	TE	6'2"	245	24		
Ron Hall	TE	6'4"	245	26		12
Ed Thomas	TE	6'3"	235	24		
Steve Christie	K	6'	185	22		96
Mark Royals	K	6'5"	215	26		

DETROIT LIONS 6-10 Wayne Fontes

Scores of Each Game		
21	TAMPA BAY	38
21	ATLANTA	14
20	Tampa Bay	23
21	GREEN BAY	24
34	Minnesota	27
24	Kansas City	43
27	New Orleans	10
38	WASHINGTON	* 41
7	MINNESOTA	17
0	N.Y. Giants	20
40	DENVER	27
17	Chicago	* 23
31	L.A. RAIDERS	38
38	CHICAGO	21
24	Green Bay	17
10	Seattle	30

Use Name	Pos.	Hgt	Wgt	Age	Int	Pts
Lomas Brown	OT	6'4"	287	27		
Harvey Salem	OT	6'6"	285	29		
Eric Sanders	OT-OG	6'7"	286	31		
Eric Andolsek	OG	6'2"	286	24		
Ken Dallafior	OG	6'4"	279	31		
Mike Utley	OG-OT	6'6"	279	24		
Kevin Glover	C	6'2"	282	27		
Dennis McKnight	C-OG	6'3"	280	30		
Kevin Brooks	DE	6'6"	278	27		
Jackie Cline	DE	6'5"	280	30		
Mark Duckens	DE	6'4"	270	25		
Keith Ferguson	DE	6'5"	260	31		
Jeff Hunter	DE	6'5"	285	24		
Dan Owens	DE	6'3"	268	23		
Marc Spindler	DE	6'5"	277	20		
Jerry Ball	NT	6'1"	298	25		
Lawrence Pete	NT	6'	282	24		
Mark Brown	LB	6'2"	240	28		
Toby Caston	LB	6'1"	243	25		
Mike Cofer	LB	6'5"	245	30	1	
Dennis Gibson	LB	6'2"	240	26		
Tracy Hayworth	LB	6'3"	250	22		
George Jamison	LB	6'1"	226	27		
Victor Jones	LB	6'2"	240	23	1	
Niko Noga	LB	6'1"	235	28		
Chris Spielman	LB	6'	247	29	1	
Jimmy Williams (to MIN)	LB	6'3"	230	29		6
Bruce Alexander	DB	5'9"	169	24		
Bennie Blades	DB	6'1"	221	23	2	
Darren Carrington	DB	6'1"	189	23		
Ray Crockett	DB	5'9"	181	23	3	6
LeRoy Irvin	DB	5'11"	184	32	1	
Bruce McNorton	DB	5'11"	175	31	1	
John Miller	DB	6'1"	195	24		
Chris Oldham	DB	5'9"	183	21	1	
Terry Taylor	DB	5'10"	191	29		
Herb Welch	DB	5'11"	180	29	1	
Sheldon White	DB	5'11"	188	25		
William White	DB	5'10"	191	24	5	6
Bob Gagliano	QB	6'3"	196	31		
Rodney Peete	QB	6'	193	24		36
Barry Sanders	HB-FB	5'8"	203	22		96
James Wilder (from WAS)	HB-FB	6'2"	225	32		6
Jeff Campbell	WR	5'8"	167	22		12
Robert Clark	WR	5'11"	173	25		48
Mike Farr	WR	5'10"	192	23		
Mel Gray	WR	5'9"	162	29		
Terry Greer	WR	6'1"	192	32		18
Richard Johnson	WR	5'7"	185	28		36
Aubrey Matthews	WR	5'7"	165	27		6
Jason Phillips	WR	5'7"	168	23		
Jim Arnold	K	6'3"	211	29		
Rich Karlis	K	6'	180	31		24
Eddie Murray	K	5'10"	180	34		73

GREEN BAY PACKERS 6-10 Lindy Infante

Scores of Each Game		
36	L.A. RAMS	24
13	CHICAGO	31
3	KANSAS CITY	17
24	Detroit	21
13	Chicago	27
14	Tampa Bay	26
24	MINNESOTA	10
20	SAN FRANCISCO	24
29	L.A. Raiders	16
24	Phoenix	21
20	TAMPA BAY	10
7	Minnesota	23
14	SEATTLE	20
0	Philadelphia	31
17	DETROIT	24
13	Denver	22

Use Name	Pos.	Hgt	Wgt	Age	Int	Pts
Tony Mandarich	OT	6'5"	295	23		
Ken Ruettgers	OT	6'5"	288	28		
Alan Veingrad	OT	6'5"	281	27		
Billy Ard	OG	6'3"	273	31		
Ron Hallstrom	OG	6'6"	297	31		
Rich Moran	OG	6'3"	283	28		
Keith Uecker	OG	6'5"	295	39		
Blair Bush	C	6'3"	272	33		
Lester Archambeau	DE	6'4"	274	23		
James Campen	C	6'3"	270	26		
Matt Brock	DE	6'5"	285	24		
Robert Brown	DE	6'2"	270	30		
Mark Hall	DE	6'4"	280	24		
Shawn Patterson	DE	6'5"	270	25	1	6
Blaise Winter	DE	6'3"	282	28		
Bob Nelson	NT	6'4"	275	31		
Tony Bennett	LB	6'2"	233	23		
Burnell Dent	LB	6'1"	234	27		
Tim Harris	LB	6'5"	258	25		
Johnny Holland	LB	6'2"	221	25	1	
Bobby Houston	LB	6'2"	234	22		
Brian Noble	LB	6'3"	252	27		
Bryce Paup	LB	6'5"	245	22		
Scott Stephen	LB	6'2"	232	26	2	
Mike Weddington	LB	6'4"	245	29		
LeRoy Butler	DB	6'	192	22	3	
Chuck Cecil	DB	6'	184	25	1	
Tiger Greene	DB	6'	194	28		6
Jerry Holmes	DB	6'2"	176	32	3	
Mark Lee	DB	5'11"	189	32	1	
Mark Murphy	DB	6'2"	201	32	3	
Ron Pitts	DB	5'10"	175	27	1	
Jerry Woods	DB	5'8"	193	24		
Anthony Dilweg	QB	6'3"	215	25		
Blair Kiel	QB	6'	214	28		6
Don Majkowski	QB	6'2"	197	26		6
Mike Norseth	QB	6'2"	202	26		
Herman Fontenot	HB	6'	206	26		6
Keith Woodside	HB	5'11"	203	26		6
Vince Workman	HB	5'10	193	22		6
Michael Haddix	FB	6'2"	227	28		12
Brent Fullwood (to CLE)	FB-HB	5'11"	209	26		6
Darrell Thompson	FB	6'	215	22		12
Carl Bland	WR	5'11"	182	28		
Perry Kemp	WR	5'11"	170	28		12
Jeff Query	WR	6'	165	23		18
Sterling Sharpe	WR	5'11"	202	25		36
Clarence Weathers	WR	5'9"	182	28		6
Charles Wilson	WR	5'9"	174	22		
Jackie Harris	TE	6'3"	240	22		
William Harris	TE	6'4"	243	25		
Ed West	TE	6'1"	243	29		30
Don Bracken	K	6'1"	211	28		
Chris Jacke	K	6'	197	24		97

Dave Brown — Achilles' Injury

MINNESOTA VIKINGS 6-10 Jerry Burns

Scores of Each Game		
21	Kansas City	24
32	NEW ORLEANS	3
16	Chicago	19
20	TAMPA BAY	* 23
27	DETROIT	34
24	Philadelphia	32
10	Green Bay	24
27	DENVER	22
17	Detroit	7
24	Seattle	21
41	CHICAGO	13
23	GREEN BAY	7
15	N.Y. Giants	23
13	Tampa Bay	26
24	L.A. RAIDERS	28
17	SAN FRANCISCO	20

Use Name	Pos.	Hgt	Wgt	Age	Int	Pts
-Paul Blair	OT	6'4"	280	27		
-Brian Habib	OT	6'7"	288	25		
-Tim Irwin	OT	6'6"	295	31		
-Gary Zimmerman	OT	6'6"	286	28		
-Dave Huffman	OG	6'6"	284	34		
-Todd Kalis	OG	6'5"	286	25		
-Randall McDaniel	OG	6'3"	271	25		
-Craig Wolfley	OG	6'1"	277	32		
-Chris Foote	C	6'3"	266	33		
-Kirk Lowdermilk	C	6'3"	267	27		
-Adam Schrieber	C-OG	6'4"	288	28		
-Chris Doleman	DE	6'5"	262	28	1	2
-Willie Fears	DE	6'3"	278	26		
-Al Noga	DE	6'1"	248	23	1	12
-John Randle	DE	6'1"	248	22		
-Thomas Strauthers	DT-DE	6'4"	262	29		
-Ken Clarke	DT	6'2"	280	34		
-Keith Millard	DT	6'5"	262	28		
-Henry Thomas	DT	6'2"	267	25		
-Walker Lee Ashley	LB	6'	232	30		
-Ray Berry	LB	6'2"	226	26		
-David Braxton	LB	6'1"	230	25		2
-Mark Dusbabek	LB	6'3"	230	26		2
John Galvin	LB	6'3"	226	24		
-William Kirksey	LB	6'2"	221	24		
-Mike Merriweather	LB	6'2"	222	29	3	6
-Scott Studwell	LB	6'2"	228	36		
-Michael Brim	DB	6'	186	24	2	
-Joey Browner	DB	6'2"	210	30	7	6
-Pat Eilers	DB	5'11"	195	23		
-Darrell Fullington	DB	6'1"	197	26	1	
-Alonzo Hampton	DB	5'10"	191	23		
-Ken Johnson	DB	6'2"	197	23		
-Carl Lee	DB	6'	183	29	2	
-Audrey McMillian	DB	6'	189	28	3	
-Reggie Rutland	DB	6'1"	194	26	2	
-Ken Stills	DB	5'10"	186	26		
Rich Gannon	QB	6'3"	202	24		6
Sean Salisbury	QB	6'5"	208	27		
Wade Wilson	QB	6'3"	208	31		
D.J. Dozier	HB	6'	198	24		
Allen Rice	HB	5'10"	204	27		
Herschel Walker	HB-FB	6'1"	226	28		54
Alfred Anderson	FB	6'1"	223	28		12
Jessie Clark	FB	6'	233	30		
Rick Fenney	FB	6'1"	232	25		12
Cedric Smith	FB	5'10"	223	22		
Anthony Carter	WR	5'11"	177	29		48
Cris Carter	WR	6'3"	200	24		18
Ira Hillary	WR	5'11"	190	27		
Hassan Jones	WR	6'	192	26		42
Leo Lewis (from CLE)	WR	5'8"	172	33		
Pat Newman	WR	5'11"	189	21		
Mike Jones	TE	6'3"	255	23		
Steve Jordan	TE	6'4"	239	29		18
Brent Novoselsky	TE	6'3"	232	24		
Jim Gallery	K	6'1"	190	28		
Donald Igwebuike	K	5'9"	190	29		61
Harry Newsome	K	6'	188	27		
Fuad Reveiz (from SD)	K	5'11"	216	27		65

Jim Gustafson — Neck Injury

CHICAGO BEARS

RUSHING

Last Name	No.	Yds	Avg	TD
Anderson	260	1078	4.1	10
Muster	141	664	4.7	6
Harbaugh	51	321	6.3	4
Green	27	126	4.7	0
Bailey	26	86	3.3	0
Rouse	16	56	3.5	0
Gentry	11	43	3.9	0
Tomczak	12	41	3.4	2
Morris	2	26	13.0	0
L. Tate	3	5	1.7	0
Perry	1	-1	-1.0	-
Buford	1	-9	-9.0	0

RECEIVING

Last Name	No.	Yds	Avg	TD
Muster	47	452	9.6	0
Anderson	42	484	11.5	3
Davis	39	572	14.7	3
Morris	31	437	14.1	3
Gentry	23	320	13.9	2
Thornton	19	254	13.4	1
Boso	11	135	12.3	1
Kozlowski	7	83	11.9	0
Green	4	26	6.5	1
Waddle	2	32	16.0	0
Smith	2	20	10.0	0
Coley	1	7	7.0	0
Tomczak	1	5	5.0	0

PUNT RETURNS

Last Name	No.	Yds	Avg	TD
Bailey	36	399	11.1	1

KICKOFF RETURNS

Last Name	No.	Yds	Avg	TD
Bailey	23	363	15.8	0
Gentry	18	388	21.6	0
Green	7	112	16.0	0
Rouse	3	17	5.7	0
Roper	1	0	0.0	0
L. Tate	1	0	0.0	0
Ryan	1	-1	-1.0	0

PASSING — PUNTING — KICKING

PASSING	Att	Cmp	%	Yds	Yd/Att	TD	Int— %	RK
Harbaugh	312	180	57.7	2178	6.98	10	6—1.9	4
Tomczak	104	39	37.5	521	5.01	3	5—4.8	
Willis	13	9	69.2	106	8.15	1	1—7.7	
Bailey	1	1	100.0	22	22.00	0	0—0.0	

PUNTING	No.	Avg.
Buford	78	39.4

KICKING	XP	ATT	%	FG	ATT	%
Butler	36	37	97	26	37	70

TAMPA BAY BUCCANEERS

RUSHING

Last Name	No.	Yds	Avg	TD
G. Anderson	166	646	3.9	3
Cobb	151	480	3.2	2
Testaverde	38	280	7.4	1
Harvey	27	113	4.2	0
Chandler	13	71	5.5	1
Perkins	13	36	2.8	0
Carlson	1	0	0.0	0
Hill	1	0	0.0	0

RECEIVING

Last Name	No.	Yds	Avg	TD
Carrier	49	813	16.6	4
Hill	42	641	15.3	5
Cobb	39	299	7.7	0
G. Anderson	38	464	12.2	2
Hall	31	464	15.0	2
Harvey	11	86	7.8	1
Pillow	8	118	14.8	0
Perkins	8	85	10.6	2
Drewrey	7	182	26.0	1
Peebles	6	50	8.3	1
J. Anderson	5	77	15.4	0
Testaverde	1	3	3.0	0

PUNT RETURNS

Last Name	No.	Yds	Avg	TD
Drewrey	23	184	8.0	0

KICKOFF RETURNS

Last Name	No.	Yds	Avg	TD
Peebles	18	369	20.5	0
Drewrey	14	244	17.4	0
Harvey	12	207	17.3	0
Cobb	11	223	20.3	0
G. Anderson	6	123	20.5	0
Coleman	1	9	9.0	0
Hall	1	0	0.0	0

PASSING — PUNTING — KICKING

PASSING	Att	Cmp	%	Yds	Yd/Att	TD	Int— %	RK
Testaverde	365	2-3	55.6	2818	**7.72**	17	18—4.9	9
Chandler	83	42	50.6	464	5.59	1	6—7.2	

PUNTING	No.	Avg.
Royals	72	40.3

KICKING	XP	ATT	%	FG	ATT	%
Christie	27	27	100	23	27	85
Team	0	1	0	0	0	0

DETROIT LIONS

RUSHING

Last Name	No.	Yds	Avg	TD
B. Sanders	255	**1304**	5.1	13
Peete	48	365	7.6	6
Gagliano	46	145	3.2	0
Ware	7	64	9.1	0
Wilder	11	51	4.6	0

RECEIVING

Last Name	No.	Yds	Avg	TD
Johnson	64	727	11.4	6
Clark	53	932	17.6	8
B. Sanders	35	462	13.2	3
Matthews	30	349	11.6	1
Greer	20	332	16.6	3
Campbell	19	236	12.4	2
Farr	12	170	14.2	0
Phillips	8	112	14.0	0
Wilder	1	8	8.0	1

PUNT RETURNS

Last Name	No.	Yds	Avg	TD
Gray	34	362	10.6	0
Campbell	1	0	0.0	0

KICKOFF RETURNS

Last Name	No.	Yds	Avg	TD
Gray	41	939	22.9	0
Oldham	13	234	18.0	0
Campbell	12	238	19.8	0
Phillips	2	43	21.5	0
Andolsek	1	12	12.0	0
McKnight	1	0	0.0	0

PASSING — PUNTING — KICKING

PASSING	Att	Cmp	%	Yds	Yd/Att	TD	Int— %	RK
Peete	271	142	52.4	1974	7.28	13	8—3.0	5
Gagliano	159	87	54.7	1190	7.48	10	10—6.3	
Ware	30	13	43.3	164	5.47	1	2—6.7	

PUNTING	No.	Avg.
Arnold	63	40.6

KICKING	XP	Att	%	FG	Att	%
Murray	34	34	100	13	19	68
Karlis	12	12	100	4	7	57

GREEN BAY PACKERS

RUSHING

Last Name	No.	Yds	Avg	TD
Haddix	98	311	3.2	0
Thompson	76	264	3.5	1
Majkowski	29	186	6.4	1
Woodside	46	182	4.0	1
Fullwood	44	124	2.8	1
Dilweg	21	114	5.4	0
Fontenot	17	76	4.5	0
Workman	8	51	6.4	0
Query	3	39	13.0	0
Sharpe	2	14	7.0	0
Kiel	5	9	1.8	1
Kemp	1	-1	-1.0	0

RECEIVING

Last Name	No.	Yds	Avg	TD
Sharpe	67	1105	16.5	6
Kemp	44	527	12.0	2
Query	34	458	13.5	2
Weathers	33	390	11.8	1
Fontenot	31	293	9.55	1
West	27	356	13.2	5
Woodside	24	184	7.7	0
J. Harris	12	157	13.1	0
Wilson	7	84	12.0	0
Workman	4	30	7.5	1
Fullwood	3	17	5.7	0
Thompson	3	1	0.3	0

PUNT RETURNS

Last Name	No.	Yds	Avg	TD
Query	32	308	9.6	0
Pitts	0	0	0.0	0

KICKOFF RETURNS

Last Name	No.	Yds	Avg	TD
Wilson	35	798	22.8	0
Workman	14	210	15.0	0
Fullwood	6	119	19.8	0
Bland	7	104	14.9	0
Thompson	3	103	34.3	1
Fontenot	3	88	29.3	0
West	1	0	0.0	0

PASSING — PUNTING — KICKING

PASSING	Att	Cmp	%	Yds	Yd/Att	TD	Int— %	RK
Majkowski	264	150	56.8	1925	7.29	10	12—4.5	10
Dilweg	192	101	52.6	1267	6.60	8	7—3.6	
Kiel	85	51	60.0	504	5.93	2	2—2.4	

PUNTING	No.	Avg.
Bracken	65	37.4

KICKING	XP	Att.	%	FG	Att	%
Jacke	28	29	97	23	30	77

MINNESOTA VIKINGS

RUSHING

Last Name	No.	Yds	Avg	TD
Walker	184	770	4.2	5
Fenney	87	376	4.3	2
Gannon	52	268	5.2	1
Anderson	59	207	3.5	2
Wilson	12	79	6.6	0
Rice	22	74	3.4	0
Clark	16	49	3.1	0
Smith	9	19	2.1	0
A. Carter	3	16	5.3	0
Dozier	6	12	2.0	0
C. Carter	2	6	3.0	0
Newsome	2	-2	-1.0	0
H. Jones	1	-7	-7.0	0

RECEIVING

Last Name	No.	Yds	Avg	TD
Carter	70	1008	14.4	8
H. Jones	51	810	15.9	7
Jordan	45	636	14.1	3
Walker	35	315	9.0	4
C. Carter	27	413	15.3	3
Fenney	17	112	4.6	0
Anderson	13	80	6.2	0
Rice	4	46	11.5	0
Dozier	1	12	12.0	0
Lewis	1	9	9.0	0
Clark	1	4	4.0	0

PUNT RETURNS

Last Name	No.	Yds	Avg	TD
Lewis	33	236	7.2	0
Hillary	8	45	5.6	0
A. Carter	0	0	0.0	0

KICKOFF RETURNS

Last Name	No.	Yds	Avg	TD
Walker	**44**	**966**	22.0	0
Rice	12	176	14.7	0
Anderson	3	44	14.7	0
Lewis	3	39	13.0	0
Smith	1	16	16.0	0
Hillary	1	6	6.0	0
Schrieber	1	5	5.0	0
Jordan	1	-3	-3.0	0

PASSING — PUNTING — KICKING

PASSING	Att	Cmp	%	Yds	Yd/Att	TD	Int— %	RK
Gannon	349	182	52.1	2278	6.53	16	16—4.6	12
Wilson	146	82	56.2	1155	7.91	9	8—5.5	
Walker	2	1	50.0	12	6.00	0	0—0.0	

PUNTING	No.	Avg.
Newsome	79	41.8

KICKING	XP	ATT	%	FG	ATT	%
Reveiz	26	27	96	13	19	68
Igwebuike	19	19	**100**	14	16	**88**

SAN FRANCISCO 49ERS 14-2 George Seifert

Scores of Each Game		
13	New Orleans	12
26	WASHINGTON	13
19	ATLANTA	13
24	Houston	21
45	Atlanta	35
27	PITTSBURGH	7
20	CLEVELAND	17
24	Green Bay	20
24	Dallas	6
31	TAMPA BAY	7
17	L.A. RAMS	28
7	N.Y. GIANTS	3
20	Cincinnati	* 17
26	L.A. Rams	10
10	NEW ORLEANS	13
20	Minnesota	17

Use Name	Pos.	Hgt	Wgt	Age	Int	Pts
Harris Barton	OG-OT	6'4"	280	26		
Frank Pollack	OT	6'4"	277	22		
Bubba Paris	OT	6'6"	306	29		
Steve Wallace	OT-OG	6'5"	276	25		
Guy McIntyre	OG	6'3"	265	29		
Ricky Siglar	OG	6'7"	296	24		
Jesse Sapolu	C	6'4"	260	29		
Chuck Thomas	C	6'3"	280	29		
Dennis Brown	DE	6'4"	290	22		
Kevin Fagan	DE	6'4"	260	27		
Pierce Holt	DE	6'4"	280	28		
Larry Roberts	DE	6'3"	275	27		
Jim Burt	NT	6'1"	260	31		
Michael Carter	NT	6'2"	285	29		
Pete Kugler	NT-DE	6'4"	255	31		
Fred Smerlas	NT	6'3"	288	33		
Keith DeLong	LB	6'2"	235	23		
LeRoy Etienne	LB	6'2"	245	24		
Jim Fahnhorst	LB	6'4"	230	31		
Charles Haley	LB-DE	6'5"	230	26		
Martin Harrison	LB-DE	6'5"	240	22		
Matt Millen	LB	6'2"	245	32	1	
Bill Romanowski	LB	6'4"	231	24		
Keena Turner	LB	6'2"	222	31		2
Michael Walter	LB	6'3"	238	29		
Chet Brooks	DB	5'11"	191	24		
Greg Cox	DB	6'	223	25		
Eric Davis	DB	5'11"	178	22	1	
Don Griffin	DB	6'	176	26	3	
Johnny Jackson	DB	6'1"	204	23		
Kevin Lewis	DB	5'11"	173	23	1	
Ronnie Lott	DB	6'	200	31	3	
Darryl Pollard	DB	5'11"	187	25	1	
Dave Waymer	DB	6'1"	188	32	7	
Eric Wright	DB	6'1"	185	31		
Steve Bono	QB	6'4"	215	28		
Joe Montana	QB	6'2"	195	34		6
Steve Young	QB	6'2"	200	28		
Dexter Carter	HB	5'9"	170	22		6
Roger Craig	HB	6'	224	30		6
Spencer Tillman	HB	5'11"	206	26		
Keith Henderson	FB	6'1"	220	24		
Tom Rathman	FB	6'1"	232	27		42
Harry Sydney	FB	6'	217	31		18
Ronald Lewis	WR	5'11"	173	22		
Jerry Rice	WR	6'2"	200	27		78
Mike Sherrard	WR	6'2"	187	27		12
John Taylor	WR	6'1"	185	28		42
Mike Wilson	WR	6'3"	215	31		
Brent Jones	TE	6'4"	230	27		30
Wesley Walls	TE	6'5"	246	24		
Jamie Williams	TE	6'4"	245	30		
Mike Cofer	K	6'1"	190	26		111
Barry Helton	K	6'3"	205	25		

Dave Cullity — Shoulder Injury
Wayne Radloff — Knee Injury

NEW ORLEANS SAINTS 8-8 Jim Mora

Scores of Each Game		
12	SAN FRANCISCO	13
3	Minnesota	32
28	PHOENIX	7
27	Atlanta	28
25	CLEVELAND	20
10	Houston	23
10	DETROIT	27
21	Cincinnati	7
35	TAMPA BAY	7
17	Washington	31
10	ATLANTA	7
13	Dallas	17
24	L.A. Rams	20
6	PITTSBURGH	9
13	San Francisco	10
20	L.A. RAMS	17

Use Name	Pos.	Hgt	Wgt	Age	Int	Pts
Stan Brock	OT	6'6"	290	32		
Richard Cooper	OT	6'4"	285	25		
Glenn Derby	OT-OG	6'6"	290	26		
Kevin Haverdink	OT	6'5"	285	24		
Jim Dombrowski	OG	6'5"	298	27		
Steve Trapilo	OG	6'5"	281	25		
Joel Hilgenberg	C	6'3"	252	27		
Steve Korte	C	6'2"	260	30		
Brad Leggett	C	6'4"	270	24		
Wayne Martin	DE	6'5"	275	24		
Michael Simmons	DE	6'4"	269	24		
Joel Smeenge	DE	6'5"	250	22		
Renaldo Turnbull	DE	6'4"	248	24		
Jim Wilks	DE-NT	6'5"	275	32		
Travis Davis	NT	6'2"	274	24		
Robert Goff	NT	6'3"	270	24		
Brian Forde	LB	6'2"	225	26		
Rickey Jackson	LB	6'2"	243	32		
Vaughan Johnson	LB	6'3"	235	28		
Sam Mills	LB	5'9"	225	31		
Pat Swilling	LB	6'3"	242	25		
James Williams	LB	6'	230	21		
DeMond Winston	LB	6'2"	239	21		
Gene Atkins	DB	6'1"	200	26	2	
Vince Buck	DB	6'	198	22		
Toi Cook	DB	5'11"	188	25	2	
Milton Mack	DB	5'11"	182	26		
Robert Massey	DB	5'10"	182	23		
Brett Maxie	DB	6'2"	194	28	2	6
Ernest Spears	DB	5'11"	192	22		
Bennie Thompson	DB	6'	200	27	2	
Mike Buck	QB	6'3"	227	23		
John Fourcade	QB	6'1"	208	29		6
Tommy Kramer	QB	6'2"	202	35		
Steve Walsh	QB	6'2"	200	23		
Gill Fenerty	HB	6'	205	27		12
Dalton Hilliard	HB	5'8"	204	26		6
Rueben Mayes	HB	5'11"	200	27		42
Craig Heyward	FB	5'11"	270	23		24
Buford Jordan	FB	6'	223	28		
Bobby Morse	FB	5'10"	213	23		
Gerald Alphin	WR	6'3"	200	26		
Lonzell Hill	WR	6'	189	24		
Eric Martin	WR	6'1"	207	28		30
Brett Perriman	WR	5'9"	175	24		12
Floyd Turner	WR	5'11"	188	24		24
Hoby Brenner	TE	6'4"	240	31		12
Greg Scales	TE	6'4"	253	24		6
John Tice	TE	6'5"	249	30		
Morten Andersen	K	6'2"	221	30		92
Tommy Barnhardt	K	6'3"	205	27		

Bobby Hebert — Holdout

LOS ANGELES RAMS 5-11 John Robinson

Scores of Each Game		
24	Green Bay	36
35	Tampa Bay	14
21	PHILADELPHIA	27
31	CINCINNATI	* 34
9	Chicago	38
44	ATLANTA	24
10	Pittsburgh	41
17	HOUSTON	13
7	N.Y. GIANTS	31
21	DALLAS	24
28	San Francisco	17
38	Cleveland	23
20	NEW ORLEANS	24
10	SAN FRANCISCO	26
13	Atlanta	20
17	New Orleans	20

Use Name	Pos.	Hgt	Wgt	Age	Int	Pts
Robert Cox	OT	6'5"	285	26		
Jeff Mickel	OT	6'6"	300	24		
Irv Pankey	OT	6'4"	267	32		
Jackie Slater	OT	6'4"	275	36		
Duval Love	OG	6'3"	287	27		
Joe Milinichik	OG	6'5"	275	27		
Tom Newberry	OG	6'2"	279	27		
Bern Brostek	C-OG	6'3"	300	23		
Doug Smith	C	6'3"	260	33		
Doug Reed	DE-DT	6'3"	250	30		
Bill Hawkins	DT	6'6"	268	24		
Mark Piel	DT	6'4"	263	24		
Brian Smith	DT	6'6"	268	24		
Alvin Wright	NT-DE	6'2"	256	29		
George Bethune	LB	6'4"	240	23		
Paul Butcher	LB	6'	230	26		
Greg Clark	LB	6'1"	232	25		
Brett Faryniarz	LB	6'3"	232	25		
Kevin Greene	LB-DE	6'3"	238	28		
Larry Kelm	LB	6'4"	226	25		
Bruce Klostermann	LB	6'4"	236	27		
Mike McDonald	LB	6'1"	235	32		
Frank Stams	LB	6'2"	240	24		
Fred Strickland	LB	6'2"	224	25		
Mike Wilcher	LB	6'3"	240	30		
Latin Berry	DB	5'10"	196	23		
Jerry Gray	DB	6'	185	27		
Darryl Henley	DB	5'9"	170	23	1	
Bobby Humphery	DB	5'10"	180	29	4	6
Alfred Jackson	DB	6'	177	23		
Anthony Newman	DB	6'	199	24	2	
Vince Newsome	DB	6'1"	183	29	4	
Michael Stewart	DB	5'11"	195	25		
Mickey Sutton	DB	5'8"	172	30		
Pat Terrell	DB	6'	195	22	1	
Jim Everett	QB	6'5"	212	27		6
Chuck Long	QB	6'4"	221	27		
Marcus Dupree	HB	6'2"	225	26		
Cleveland Gary	HB	6'	226	24		90
Gaston Green	HB	5'10"	189	24		12
Curt Warner	HB	5'11"	205	29		6
Robert Delpino	FB	6'	205	24		24
Buford McGee	FB	6'	206	30		30
Willie Anderson	WR	6'	169	25		24
Aaron Cox	WR	5'9"	174	25		
Henry Ellard	WR	5'11"	175	29		24
Derrick Faison	WR	6'4"	200	23		6
Tony Lomack	WR	5'8"	180	22		
Richard Ashe	TE	6'4"	260	23		
Pat Carter	TE	6'4"	250	24		
Pete Holohan	TE	6'4"	232	31		12
Damone Johnson	TE	6'4"	230	28		18
Keith English	K	6'3"	220	24		
Mike Lansford	K	6'	183	32		87

Mel Owens — Back Injury

ATLANTA FALCONS 5-11 Jerry Glanville

Scores of Each Game		
47	HOUSTON	27
14	Detroit	21
13	San Francisco	19
28	NEW ORLEANS	27
35	SAN FRANCISCO	45
24	L.A. Rams	44
38	CINCINNATI	17
9	Pittsburgh	21
24	Chicago	30
23	PHILADELPHIA	24
7	New Orleans	10
17	Tampa Bay	23
13	PHOENIX	24
10	Cleveland	13
20	L.A. RAMS	13
26	DALLAS	7

Use Name	Pos.	Hgt	Wgt	Age	Int	Pts
Chris Hinton	OT	6'4"	300	29		
John Hunter	OT	6'8"	296	25		
Mike Kenn	OT	6'7"	277	34		
Bill Fralic	OG	6'5"	280	27		
Houston Hoover	OG-OT	6'2"	290	25		
John Scully	OG	6'6"	270	32		
Guy Bingham	C	6'3"	260	32		
Jamie Dukes	C	6'1"	285	26		
Mike Ruether	C	6'4"	275	27		
Rick Bryan	DE-NT-DT-LB	6'4"	265	28		
Mike Gann	DE	6'5"	270	26		
Oliver Barnett	DE	6'3"	288	24		
Tony Casillas	NT	6'3"	280	26		
Tory Epps	NT	6'	280	23		
Aundray Bruce	LB	6'5"	245	24		
Darion Conner	LB	6'2"	256	22		
Marcus Cotton (to CLE)	LB	6'3"	225	24		
Tim Green	LB	6'2"	245	26		2
Robert Lyles (from HOU)	LB	6'1"	230	29		
John Rade	LB	6'1"	240	30		
Michael Reid	LB	6'2"	226	26		
Kenny Tippins	LB	6'1"	230	24		
Jessie Tuggle	LB	5'11"	225	25		6
Eric Bergeson	DB	5'11"	192	24		
Bobby Butler	DB	5'11"	175	31	3	12
Scott Case	DB	6'	178	28	3	6
Charles Dimry	DB	6'	175	24	3	
William Evers	DB	5'10"	175	21		
Tim Gordon	DB	6'	188	25		
Brian Jordan	DB	5'11"	202	23	3	
Roland Mitchell	DB	5'11"	180	26	2	
Ricky Royal	DB	5'9"	187	24		
Deion Sanders	DB	6'	187	23	3	18
Elbert Shelley	DB	5'11"	180	25		
Scott Campbell	QB	6'	195	28		
Hugh Millen	QB	6'5"	216	26		
Chris Miller	QB	6'2"	195	24		6
Steve Broussard	HB	5'7"	201	23		24
Gene Lang	HB	5'10"	206	28		
Mike Pringle	HB	5'8"	186	22		
Mike Rozier (from HOU)	HB	5'10"	213	29		18
John Settle	FB	5'9"	207	25		
Tracy Johnson	FB	6'	230	24		24
Keith Jones	FB	6'1"	210	24		6
Stacey Bailey	WR	6'	157	30		
Shawn Collins	WR	6'2"	207	23		12
Floyd Dixon	WR	5'9"	170	26		24
Michael Haynes	WR	6'	180	24		
James Milling	WR	5'9"	156	25		6
Andre Rison	WR	6'	191	23		60
George Thomas	WR	5'9"	169	26		6
Troy Sadowski	TE	6'5"	265	24		
Gary Wilkins	TE	6'1"	235	26		12
Greg Davis	K	5'11"	197	24		106
Scott Fulhage	K	5'11"	193	28		

Galand Thaxton — Ankle Injury

SAN FRANCISCO 49ERS

RUSHING

Last Name	No.	Yds	Avg	TD
D. Carter	114	460	4.0	1
Craig	141	439	3.1	1
Rathman	101	318	3.1	7
Sydney	35	166	4.7	2
Montana	40	162	4.1	1
Young	15	159	10.6	0
Henderson	6	14	2.3	0
Rice	2	0	0.0	0

RECEIVING

Last Name	No.	Yds	Avg	TD
Rice	100	1502	15.0	13
Jones	56	747	13.3	5
Taylor	49	748	15.3	7
Rathman	48	327	6.8	0
D. Carter	25	217	8.7	0
Craig	25	201	8.0	0
Sherrard	17	264	15.5	2
Sydney	10	116	11.6	1
Williams	9	54	6.0	0
Wilson	7	89	12.7	0
R. Lewis	5	44	8.8	0
Walls	5	27	5.4	0
Henderson	4	35	8.8	0

PUNT RETURNS

Last Name	No.	Yds	Avg	TD
Taylor	26	212	8.2	0
Griffin	16	105	6.6	0
Davis	5	38	7.6	0
Wilson	1	1	1.0	0

KICKOFF RETURNS

Last Name	No.	Yds	Avg	TD
D. Carter	41	783	19.1	0
Tillman	6	111	18.5	0
Sydney	2	33	16.5	0
Walls	1	16	16.0	0
Griffin	1	15	15.0	
Williams	2	7	3.5	0

PASSING — PUNTING — KICKING

PASSING	Att	Cmp	%	Yds	Yd/Att	TD	Int— %	RK
Montana	520	321	61.7	3944	7.58	26	16— 3.1	3
Young	62	38	61.3	427	6.89	2	0— 0.0	
Helton	1	1	100.0	0	0.00	0	0— 0.0	

PUNTING	No.	Avg.
Helton	70	36.2

KICKING	XP	ATT	%	FG	ATT	%
Cofer	39	39	100	24	36	67

NEW ORLEANS SAINTS

RUSHING

Last Name	No.	Yds	Avg	TD
Heyward	129	599	4.6	4
Mayes	138	510	3.7	7
Fenerty	73	355	4.9	2
Hilliard	90	284	3.2	0
Fourcade	15	77	5.1	1
Walsh	20	25	1.3	0

RECEIVING

Last Name	No.	Yds	Avg	TD
E. Martin	63	912	14.5	5
Perriman	36	382	10.6	2
Turner	21	396	18.9	4
Fenerty	18	209	11.6	0
Heyward	18	121	6.7	0
Brenner	17	213	12.5	2
Hilliard	14	125	8.9	1
Mayes	12	121	10.1	0
Tice	11	113	10.3	0
Scales	8	64	8.0	1
Alphin	4	57	14.3	0
Hill	3	35	11.7	0
Hilgenberg	1	9	9.0	0

PUNT RETURNS

Last Name	No.	Yds	Avg	TD
V. Buck	28	572	20.4	0
Morse	8	95	11.9	0

KICKOFF RETURNS

Last Name	No.	Yds	Avg	TD
Fenerty	28	572	20.4	0
Atkins	19	471	24.8	0
Morse	4	56	14.0	0
V. Buck	3	38	12.7	0
Mayes	2	39	19.5	0
Mack	1	17	17.0	0
Heyward	1	12	12.0	0

PASSING — PUNTING — KICKING

PASSING	Att	Cmp	%	Yds	Yd/Att	TD	Int— %	RK
Walsh	336	179	53.3	2010	5.98	12	13— 3.9	13
Fourcade	116	50	43.1	785	6.77	3	8— 6.9	
Kramer	3	1	33.3	2	0.67	0	1—33.3	
Heyward	1	0	0.0	0	0.00	0	1—100.0	

PUNTING	No.	Avg.
Barnhardt	71	42.1

KICKING	XP	ATT	%	FG	ATT	%
Andersen	29	29	100	21	27	78

LOS ANGELES RAMS

RUSHING

Last Name	No.	Yds	Avg	TD
Gary	204	808	4.0	14
Green	68	261	3.8	0
McGee	44	234	5.3	1
Warner	49	139	2.8	1
Dupree	19	72	3.8	0
Delpino	13	52	4.0	0
Everett	20	31	1.6	1
Ellard	2	21	10.5	0
Anderson	1	13	13.0	0
English	2	-19	-9.5	0

RECEIVING

Last Name	No.	Yds	Avg	TD
Ellard	76	1294	17.0	4
Anderson	51	1097	21.5	4
Holohan	49	475	9.7	2
McGee	47	388	8.3	4
Gary	30	150	5.0	1
Cox	17	266	15.6	0
Delpino	15	172	11.5	4
Johnson	12	66	5.5	3
Carter	8	58	7.3	0
Faison	3	27	9.0	1
Green	2	23	11.5	1

PUNT RETURNS

Last Name	No.	Yds	Avg	TD
Henley	19	195	10.3	0
Sutton	14	136	9.7	0
Ellard	2	15	7.5	0

KICKOFF RETURNS

Last Name	No.	Yds	Avg	TD
Green	25	560	22.4	1
Delpino	20	389	19.5	0
Berry	17	315	18.5	0
McDonald	1	15	15.0	0

PASSING — PUNTING — KICKING

PASSING	Att	Cmp	%	Yds	Yd/Att	TD	Int— %	RK
Everett	554	307	55.4	3989	7.20	23	17— 3.1	6
Long	5	1	20.0	4	0.80	0	0— 0.0	
McGee	2	2	100.0	23	11.50	1	0— 0.0	

PUNTING	No	Avg.
English	68	39.2

KICKING	XP	ATT	%	FG	ATT	%
Lansford	42	43	98	15	24	63

ATLANTA FALCONS

RUSHING

Last Name	No.	Yds	Avg	TD
Rozier	163	717	4.4	3
Broussard	126	454	3.6	4
Jones	49	185	3.8	0
Johnson	30	106	3.5	3
Miller	26	99	3.8	1
Campbell	9	38	4.2	0
Lang	9	24	2.7	0
Settle	9	16	1.8	0
Pringle	2	9	4.5	0
Millen	7	-12	-1.7	0

RECEIVING

Last Name	No.	Yds	Avg	TD
Rison	82	1208	14.7	10
Dixon	38	399	10.5	4
Collins	34	503	14.8	2
Haynes	31	445	14.4	0
Broussard	24	160	6.7	0
Thomas	18	383	21.3	1
Milling	18	161	8.9	1
Rozier	13	105	8.1	0
Jones	13	103	7.9	0
Wilkins	12	175	14.6	2
Johnson	10	79	7.9	1
Bailey	4	44	11.0	0
Lang	1	7	7.0	0

PUNT RETURNS

Last Name	No.	Yds	Avg	TD
Sanders	29	250	8.6	1
Jordan	2	19	9.5	0
Rison	2	10	5.0	0
Mitchell	1	0	0.0	0
Reid	1	0	0.0	0

KICKOFF RETURNS

Last Name	No.	Yds	Avg	TD
Sanders	39	851	21.8	0
Jones	8	236	29.5	1
Broussard	3	45	15.0	0
Gordon	1	43	43.0	0
Lang	1	18	18.0	0
Pringle	1	14	14.0	0
Wilkins	1	7	7.0	0
Case	1	13	13.0	0
Johnson	2	2	1.0	0
Dixon	1	0	0.0	0
Haynes	1	0	0.0	0

PASSING — PUNTING — KICKING

PASSING	Att	Cmp	%	Yds	Yd/Att	TD	Int— %	RK
Miller	388	222	57.2	2735	7.05	17	14— 3.6	7
Campbell	76	36	47.4	527	6.93	3	4— 5.3	
Millen	63	34	54.0	427	6.78	1	0— 0.0	
Jones	1	1	100.0	37	37.00	0	0— 0.0	

PUNTING	No.	Avg.
Fulhage	70	41.6

KICKING	XP	Att	%	FG	Att	%
David	40	40	100	22	33	67

1990 A.F.C. A Public Black Eye

For much of the season, interest around the AFC centered on three good division races, the resurgence of the Raiders, and Buffalo's chances in the Super Bowl. But, for a couple of weeks in September, attention was focused on New England where a lockerroom incident produced one of the uglier stories of the year. According to news accounts and the NFL's subsequent investigation, *Boston Herald* reporter Lisa Olson was lewdly harassed by New England's Zeke Mowatt and several other Patriots players in the team lockerroom where she was pursuing an interview. Reportedly the players exposed themselves and made indecent remarks.

In the aftermath, team owner Victor Kiam worsened the NFL's image by suggesting that Olson had precipitated the situation. He later apologized, claiming he'd been given wrong information. Although a new debate was sparked over the rights of women reporters to have access to lockerrooms, few defended the Patriots' boorish behavior.

EASTERN DIVISION

Buffalo Bills — While winning the Eastern title for the third straight year, the Bills established themselves as the AFC's most complete team. Gone were the personal problems that often disrupted the squad in the past. The defense, with end Bruce Smith and linebackers Cornelius Bennett, Shane Colan, and Darryl Talley stifled the opposition. Coach Marv Levy was criticized as "too conservative," but Buffalo put together the most potent offense in the conference. Running back Thurman Thomas ran and caught passes brilliantly, and Andre Reed established himself as perhaps the AFC's best receiver. Many felt that quarterback Jim Kelly was the NFL's Player of the Year. And, when Kelly was out with a knee injury, Frank Reich filled in capably. The season's must-win game was against Miami two days before Christmas. With Kelly on the sideline, Reich completed 15 of 21 passes for 234 yards to insure victory.

Miami Dolphins — Don Shula got the Dolphins turned around and came within a late-season loss to the Bills of winning the division. Foremost in Miami's improvement were a new, tougher defense and a more balanced offense. Cornerback Tim McKyer keyed the defensive upswing, bringing attitude and competence to the secondary. Linebackers John Offerdahl and Hugh Green were also factors. Although it slipped toward the end, the defense carried the Dolphins through the early season. Rookie offensive tackle Richmond Webb gave the line a big, aggressive blocker, and running back Sammie Smith supplied a ground punch that had been missing for years. With the new firepower at his command, quarterback Don Marino reestablished himself as one of the best passers in NFL history.

Indianapolis Colts — Eric Dickerson held out for a contract renegotiation and then was suspended for the first five games for failure to report. Albert Bentley was a workman-like replacement, but he lacked Dickerson's ability to dominate a game. Even after his return, Dickerson showed only flashes of his old running powers. Meanwhile, the offense was entrusted to expensive rookie quarterback Jeff George, who struggled early. Jack Trudeau replaced him as the starter in the fourth game. The offense perked up slightly but, after four games, he went down with his usual season-ending injury. George improved steadily upon his return, leading the Colts to five wins in the last eight games. Clearly, Indianapolis was paying the price for trading away Andre Rison, Chris Hinton, and some draft choices, but the late rally was probably enough to save coach Ron Meyer's job.

New York Jets — Although it was hardly a banner year for the Jets, new coach Bruce Coslett made progress in both attitude and record. The team improved its win-loss record by two and was blown out in only three of its 10 losses. Inconsistency was the stumbling point. Quarterback Ken O'Brien started well and then tailed off. Running back Blair Thomas started slowly — partly because of a protracted holdout. Receiver Al Toon was bothered by injuries, and the defense was erratic. Defensive tackle Dennis Byrd showed signs of becoming a premier pass rusher. Runner Freeman McNeil had a strong comeback season, but the team voted as its MVP veteran placekicker Pat Leahy. In the season's 11th game, with an outside shot at the playoffs, the Jets led the Colts 14-3 when safety Erik McMillan picked off an Indianapolis pass but then lost the ball on an ill-conceived lateral. The Colts scored and went on to win.

New England Patriots — The pitiful Patriots suffered through one of the worst seasons ever experienced by a modern NFL team. Ironically, they began well under new coach Rod Rust, losing in the final minute to Miami and trouncing Indianapolis. Then everything collapsed. The team's public relations were destroyed when the Lisa Olson incident made ugly headlines all over the country. Owner Victor Kiam further aggravated the situation by at first criticizing Olson. A few days later, receiver Irving Fryer and Hart Lee Dykes were injured in a barroom brawl. Meanwhile, a serious neck injury took quarterback Steve Grogan out of play and sank the Patriots' offense. After veteran Marc Wilson was tried and found wanting, rookie Tommy Hodson showed promise but little polish. The 181 points registered by the offense were the fewest by any team since the league went to a 16-game schedule.

CENTRAL DIVISION

Cincinnati Bengals — Three straight wins got the Bengals off on the right foot, but they were 4-7 through the next 11 games before winning their final two. A porous defense and inconsistency of their own passing game were blamed for Cincinnati's lack of dominance, along with the off-field controversy coach Sam Wyche stirred up when he barred women reporters from his lockerroom in the wake of the Lisa Olson incident in New England. Quarterback Boomer Esiason threw 24 touchdown passes but also had 22 interceptions. Running back Ickey Woods came back from his 1989 injury pretty well, but James Brooks was a sensation with another 1,000-yard season. The offensive line was hurt early by the Plan B defection of guard Max Montoya and late injuries to tackle Anthony Munoz and guard Bruce Reimers.

Houston Oilers — Under new coach Jack Pardee, the Oilers staggered out of the starting gate with a pair of road losses. Once Houston's run-and-shoot offense began to roll, however, quarterback Warren Moon and receivers Drew Hill, Haywood Jeffires, Ernest Givins and Curtis Duncan terrorized the league. Yet, the team had an ugly habit of coming up empty against weak teams, losing to the Jets, Rams and Seahawks when the offense faltered. Moon was on a pace to set new league passing records when he dislocated his thumb in the 15th game, a blowout by the Bengals. Substitute Cody Carlson was brilliant in the season-ending, must-win victory over the Steelers that put Houston into the playoffs.

Pittsburgh Steelers — Joe Walton was hired as offensive coordinator to redesign the offense, but his system was so complex that the Steelers didn't scored an offensive touchdown until the fourth game. Once Walton's system was simplified, the team began to win. Quarterback Bubby Brister, although still erratic, had his best season, throwing 20 touchdowns passes. Fullback Merril Hoge was a steady running and receiving threat. Eric Green set a Steelers record for tight end with seven TD catches. Mostly the team depended on a defense that moved to the top of the league in fewest yards allowed. The secondary, led by cornerback Rod Woodson, was particularly effective. A victory in the final game would have given Pittsburgh the division title.

Cleveland Browns — The Browns suffered through the worst season in their history, setting team records for most losses and most points allowed. They were shut out three times. The offseason signing of 35-year-old Raymond Clayborn as a Plan B free agent caused training-camp holdouts by five starters. Frank Minnifield didn't appear until four games into the schedule. Tackle Cody Risen and guard Rickey Bolden were surprise retirements in training camp, crippling an already suspect offensive line. Quarterback Bernie Kosar was rushed and ineffective. With little offense and a fading defense, Coach John Carson lasted through nine games and seven losses. Interim coach Jim Shofner went 1-6 before escaping to the front office.

WESTERN DIVISION

OFFENSE

	BUFF	CIN	CLEV	DEN	HOU	IND	K.C.	L.A.	MIA	N.E.	NYJ	PITT	S.D.	SEA
FIRST DOWNS:														
Total	302	277	259	323	376	245	280	258	303	239	295	263	272	284
by Rushing	123	107	74	126	97	81	104	110	90	65	128	93	112	112
by Passing	161	151	167	170	251	142	153	133	190	156	143	150	142	154
by Penalty	18	19	18	27	28	22	23	15	23	18	24	20	18	18
RUSHING:														
Number	479	484	345	462	328	335	504	496	420	383	476	456	484	457
Yards	2080	2120	1220	1872	1417	1282	1948	2028	1535	1398	2127	1880	2257	1749
Average Yards	4.3	4.4	3.5	4.1	4.3	3.8	3.9	4.1	3.7.	3.7	4.5	4.1	4.7	3.8
Touchdowns	20	16	10	19	10	9	11	20	13	4	16	11	14	18
PASSING:														
Attempts	425	425	573	527	639	488	449	336	539	514	451	408	472	448
Completions	263	237	301	305	399	269	260	183	310	274	246	237	246	265
Completion Pct.	61.9	55.8	52.5	57.9	62.4	55.1	57.9	54.5	57.5	53.3	54.5	58.1	52.1	59.2
Passing Yards	3404	3152	3407	3671	5072	3297	3458	2885	3611	3208	3059	2887	2840	3194
Avg. Yds per Att.	7.1	6.4	5.1	5.8	7.1	5.3	6.9	7.4	6.3	4.8	5.6	6.0	5.5	5.8
Avg. Yds per Comp.	12.9	13.3	11.3	12.0	12.7	12.3	13.3	15.8	11.6	11.7	12.4	12.2	11.5	12.1
Times Tackled	27	34	42	46	39	51	22	29	16	58	40	33	20	40
Yds Lost Tackled	208	209	260	330	267	424	191	197	99	443	300	242	157	360
Net Yards	3196	2943	3147	3341	4805	2873	3267	2688	3512	2765	2759	2645	2683	2834
Touchdowns	28	25	13	15	37	22	23	19	21	14	14	20	18	15
Interceptions	11	23	23	18	15	21	5	10	12	20	11	15	19	20
Pct. Intercepted	2.6	5.4	4.0	3.4	2.3	4.3	1.1	3.0	2.2	3.9	2.4	3.7	4.0	4.5
PUNTS:														
Number	58	65	78	60	34	72	81	62	72	92	61	66	62	67
Average	39.3	42.1	36.9	43.5	45.0	42.8	38.7	37.3	42.0	40.8	39.3	37.2	39.4	40.6
PUNT RETURNS														
Number	25	30	31	33	30	36	37	34	39	29	30	39	35	36
Yards	177	255	209	256	172	402	254	295	233	134	319	398	336	337
Average Yards	7.1	8.5	6.7	7.8	5.7	11.2	6.9	8.7	6.0	4.6	10.6	10.2	9.6	9.4
Touchdowns	0	1	0	0	0	0	0	0	0	0	1	1	2	0
KICKOFF RET.:														
Number	51	62	71	66	47	65	46	64	43	77	61	50	55	50
Yards	1040	1266	1276	1260	861	1189	784	1237	780	1395	1129	956	1188	985
Average Yards	20.4	20.4	18.0	19.1	18.3	18.3	17.0	19.3	18.1	18.1	18.5	19.1	21.6	19.7
Touchdowns	0	0	2	0	0	0	0	0	0	0	0	0	0	0
INTERCEPT RET.:														
Number	18	15	13	10	21	9	20	13	19	14	18	24	19	12
Yards	151	146	212	190	295	173	250	102	288	194	205	385	188	182
Average Yards	8.4	9.7	16.3	19.0	14.0	19.2	12.5	7.8	15.2	13.9	11.4	16.0	9.9	15.2
Touchdowns	2	1	1	1	1	1	1	1	2	0	0	1	0	0
PENALTIES:														
Number	92	83	122	108	135	79	111	97	64	99	101	110	103	89
Yards	683	627	922	775	1009	590	886	682	486	744	848	928	886	746
FUMBLES:														
Number	17	25	37	30	34	23	30	24	33	33	28	40	24	32
Number Lost	10	12	23	14	21	10	14	14	15	16	13	17	13	16
POINTS:														
Total	428	360	228	331	405	281	369	337	336	181	295	292	315	306
PAT Attempts	53	44	27	36	49	33	38	42	39	19	32	33	36	34
PAT Made	50	41	24	34	46	32	37	40	37	19	32	32	34	33
FG Attempts	29	22	20	34	32	24	37	20	25	22	26	25	28	32
FG Made	20	17	14	25	21	17	34	15	21	16	23	20	21	23
Percent FG Made	69.0	77.3	70.0	73.5	65.6	70.8	91.9	75.0	84.0	72.7	88.5	80.0	75.0	71.9
Safeties	0	2	0	3	1	0	1	0	1	0	1	1	1	0

DEFENSE

	BUFF	CIN	CLEV	DEN	HOU	IND	K.C.	L.A.	MIA	N.E.	NYJ	PITT	S.D.	SEA
FIRST DOWNS:														
Total	288	308	314	306	279	320	268	266	268	307	318	257	268	280
by Rushing	105	116	117	110	88	130	85	95	110	151	112	102	92	86
by Passing	159	180	169	181	160	176	164	152	145	139	186	130	152	171
by Penalty	24	12	28	15	31	14	19	19	13	17	20	25	24	23
RUSHING:														
Number	483	442	511	456	392	513	373	439	461	565	423	446	424	413
Yards	1808	2085	2105	1963	1575	2212	1640	1716	1831	2676	2018	1615	1515	1605
Average Yards	3.7	4.7	4.1	4.3	4.0	4.3	4.4	3.9	4.0	4.7	4.8	3.6	3.6	3.9
Touchdowns	13	15	21	16	12	12	12	4	11	29	15	13	10	7
PASSING:														
Attempts	455	543	444	479	460	492	512	437	462	374	516	460	462	504
Completions	254	300	253	284	267	301	267	246	257	218	311	236	254	300
Completion Pct.	55.8	55.2	57.0	59.3	58.0	61.2	52.1	56.3	55.6	58.3	60.3	51.3	55.0	59.5
Passing Yards	3125	3725	3296	3671	3332	3605	3662	3032	3064	3245	3745	2728	3255	3256
Avg. Yds per Att.	5.6	6.2	6.5	6.6	6.1	6.5	5.7	5.6	5.4	7.4	6.2	5.1	5.7	5.6
Avg. Yds per Comp.	12.3	12.4	13.0	12.9	12.5	12.0	13.7	12.3	11.9	14.9	12.0	11.6	12.8	10.9
Times Tackled	43	25	32	34	38	29	60	48	45	33	38	34	45	33
Yds Lost Tackled	326	205	211	289	272	203	421	335	348	224	308	228	345	252
Net Yards	2799	3520	3085	3382	3060	3402	3241	2697	2716	3021	3437	2500	2910	3004
Touchdowns	17	24	32	22	18	20	16	20	14	21	23	9	22	19
Interceptions	18	15	13	10	21	9	20	13	19	14	18	24	19	12
Pct. Intercepted	4.0	2.8	2.9	2.1	4.6	1.8	3.9	3.0	4.1	3.7	3.5	5.2	4.1	2.4
PUNTS:														
Number	66	63	68	62	62	58	72	64	75	56	56	64	70	77
Average	38.2	41.8	38.1	41.4	38.7	42.0	37.0	38.2	40.0	40.8	41.4	40.9	41.2	41.9
PUNT RETURNS														
Number	31	36	41	22	23	42	44	24	40	50	35	16	28	29
Yards	227	323	418	370	191	558	325	301	256	346	257	361	451	334
Average Yards	8.1	9.8	10.4	7.2	8.1	8.0	9.3	6.4	9.9	10.1	7.7	6.6	4.7	8.8
Touchdowns	0	1	0	0	1	0	2	0	0	0	0	0	0	2
KICKOFF RET.:														
Number	73	43	45	69	71	49	81	49	53	38	61	56	62	51
Yards	1129	945	805	1319	1329	961	1391	1026	1092	665	1185	1245	1048	910
Average Yards	15.5	22.0	17.9	19.1	18.7	19.6	17.2	20.9	20.6	17.5	19.4	22.2	16.9	17.8
Touchdowns	0	0	0	0	1	0	0	0	0	0	1	1	0	0
INTERCEPT RET.:														
Number	11	23	23	18	15	21	5	10	12	20	11	15	19	20
Yards	156	233	422	169	237	221	86	100	184	143	186	124	310	252
Average Yards	14.2	10.1	18.3	9.4	15.8	10.5	17.2	10.0	15.3	7.2	16.9	8.3	16.3	12.6
Touchdowns	0	1	3	3	2	1	0	0	0	0	0	0	1	0
PENALTIES:														
Number	107	101	95	105	134	104	122	86	95	73	106	89	87	108
Yards	839	824	684	819	1015	781	859	710	759	488	876	719	720	766
FUMBLES:														
Number	31	26	32	43	25	34	32	40	19	22	32	40	21	26
Number Lost	13	16	11	22	16	15	18	18	8	12	9	21	13	13
POINTS:														
Total	263	352	462	374	307	353	257	268	242	446	345	240	281	286
PAT Attempts	30	41	59	43	37	36	30	26	26	52	39	26	33	32
PAT Made	29	40	56	38	34	35	29	25	26	51	35	26	33	32
FG Attempts	24	29	27	33	21	43	20	33	29	31	32	28	21	27
FG Made	18	22	16	26	17	32	16	29	20	27	24	18	16	20
Percent FG Made	75.0	75.9	59.3	78.8	81.0	74.4	80.0	87.9	69.0	87.1	75.0	64.3	76.2	74.1
Safeties	0	0	2	0	0	3	0	0	0	1	2	2	1	1

Los Angeles Raiders — Art Shell received several Coach of the Year honors for restoring the Raiders to a dominant position in the AFC West. His emphasis on traditional Raiders virtues — an aggressive, physical defense and long-range scoring on offense —pushed Los Angeles to the title. Quarterback Jay Schroeder showed signs of playing back to the level of his best days with the Redskins. After going 0-for-November in touchdown passes, he rallied to connect for 11 TDs down the stretch. Running back Marcus Allen put together a solid season, and, once the baseball season ended, Bo Jackson was in top form. His 88-yard run against the Bengals made everyone's highlight film.

Kansas City Chiefs — In his second year as coach, Marty Schottenheimer got the Chiefs to the playoffs for only the second time since 1971. Much of the success was due to an opportunistic defense that accounted for 60 sacks, six blocked punts, 25 fumble recoveries and 20 pass interceptions. Linebacker Derrick Thomas led with 20 sacks, and safety Deron Cherry made a strong comeback from injury. Quarterback Steve DeBerg had a fabulous year despite playing the last couple of games with a broken finger on his passing hand. He connected for 23 touchdowns and only four interceptions. Christian Okoye, the 1989 rushing leader, was bothered by injuries much of the season, but Barry Word came on strong to take up much of the slack.

Seattle Seahawks — The Seahawks started 0-3 but hung tough in enough close games to finish with a winning record and were in the playoffs until the final weekend. No fewer than six games were decided in the final play and the lead changed hands in the last three minutes of two other contests. Although it ranked as the team's strength, the defense had to survive eight serious injuries to linebackers (including the shoulder problem which caused Brian Bosworth to retire in the offseason). Fullback John L. Williams, who caught 73 passes, and halfback Derrick Fenner, who scored 14 touchdowns, formed a strong running tandem, but quarterback Dave Krieg did not have a vintage year. His 20 interceptions helped put the Seahawks at minus-6 in the giveaway column.

San Diego Chargers — The arrival of general manager Bobby Beathard and relatively easy schedule gave the Chargers hope for an improved record, but, when the smoke cleared, they were 6-10 once again. A solid secondary and strong pass rush from ends Lee Williams and Burt Grossman and linebacker Leslie O'Neal kept San Diego in most games, but the offense was inconsistent. Anthony Miller was the only receiving threat, and Billy Joe Tolliver never showed enough consistency to prove that he was the quarterback for the future. Twice during the season he was replaced as the starter. The season's most pleasant surprise was the blooming of fullback Marion Butts, who came from nowhere to become — until a late season injury put him on I.R. — the AFC's leading rusher.

Denver Broncos — After getting to the Super Bowl in three of the four previous seasons, the Broncos got busted in 1990. The season began on a worrisome note, with coach Dan Reeves undergoing surgery to clear blocked arteries. He soon returned to the sideline, but Denver's performance did little to elevate his health. The team stood 2-1 when it took a 21-9 lead into the fourth quarter at Buffalo. The Bills rallied to win by a point, and the next week Denver lost to Cleveland — again by a point. Seven of the Broncos' 11 losses were by a total of 23 points. Much of the blame fell on quarterback John Elway, who had a poor year, but the teams' problems stemmed from injuries, especially on defense . Running back Bobby Humphrey got off to a terrific start with four 100-yard games in the first five, but a sprained ankle reduced his effectiveness the rest of the way.

BUFFALO BILLS 13-3 Marv Levy

Scores of Each Game		
26	INDIANAPOLIS	10
7	Miami	30
30	N.Y. Jets	7
29	DENVER	28
38	L.A. RAIDERS	24
30	N.Y. JETS	27
27	New England	10
42	Cleveland	0
45	PHOENIX	14
14	NEW ENGLAND	0
24	Houston	27
30	PHILADELPHIA	23
31	Indianapolis	7
17	N.Y. Giants	13
24	MIAMI	14
14	Washington	29

Use Name	Pos.	Hgt	Wgt	Age	Int	Pts
Howard Ballard	OT	6'6"	325	26		
Will Wolford	OT	6'5"	295	26		
John Davis	OG-OT	6'4"	310	24		
Mitch Freotte	OG	6'3"	285	25		
Glenn Parker	OG-OT	6'5"	304	24		
Jim Ritcher	OG	6'3"	275	31		
Kent Hull	C	6'4"	275	29		
Adam Lingner	C	6'4"	263	28		
Jeff Hunter	DE	6'5"	285	24		
Mike Lodish	DE	6'3"	270	23		
Mark Pike	DE	6'4"	272	26		
Leon Seals	DE	6'4"	270	26	1	
Bruce Smith	DE	6'4"	275	27		
Gary Baldinger (from IND)	NT	6'3"	270	26		
Jeff Wright	NT	6'2"	270	26		

Leonard Burton — Knee Injury

Use Name	Pos.	Hgt	Wgt	Age	Int	Pts
Carlton Bailey	LB	6'2"	240	25		
Cornelius Bennett	LB	6'2"	235	24		6
Ray Bentley	LB	6'2"	235	28	1	
Shane Conlan	LB	6'3"	235	25		
Hal Garner	LB	6'4"	238	28		
Matt Monger	LB	6'1"	235	28		
Marvcus Patton	LB	6'2"	223	23		
Darryl Talley	LB	6'4"	235	30	2	6
Richard Carey	DB	5'9"	185	22		
Dwight Drane	DB	6'2"	205	28		
John Hagy	DB	5'11"	190	24	2	
Chris Hale	DB	5'7"	161	24		
Clifford Hicks (from LA)	DB	5'10"	188	26		
Kirby Jackson	DB	5'10"	180	24	3	
Mark Kelso	DB	5'11"	185	27	2	
Nate Odomes	DB	5'10"	188	24	1	6
Kim Phillips	DB	5'9"	188	22		
David Pool	DB	5'9"	188	23	1	
Leonard Smith	DB	5'11"	202	29	2	6
James Williams	DB	5'10"	175	23	2	6

Use Name	Pos.	Hgt	Wgt	Age	Int	Pts
Gale Gilbert	QB	6'3"	210	28		
Jim Kelly	QB	6'3"	218	30		
Frank Reich	QB	6'4"	210	28		
Kenneth Davis	HB	5'10"	209	28		30
Thurman Thomas	HB	5'10"	198	24		78
Carwell Gardner	FB	6'2"	235	23		
Larry Kinnebrew	FB	6'1"	256	30		6
Jamie Mueller	FB	6'1"	225	25		18
Don Smith	FB-HB	5'11"	200	26		12
Don Beebe	WR	5'11"	177	25		6
Al Edwards	WR	5'8"	168	23		
James Lofton	WR	6'3"	190	34		24
Andre Reed	WR	6'	190	25		48
Steve Tasker	WR	5'9"	185	28		12
Vernon Turner	WR	5'8"	185	23		
Keith McKeller	TE	6'6"	245	26		30
Pete Metzelaars	TE	6'7"	250	30		6
Butch Rolle	TE	6'3"	242	25		18
John Nies	K	6'2"	199	23		
Scott Norwood	K	6'	207	30		110
Rick Tuten	K	6'2"	218	25		

Robb Riddick — Knee Injury

MIAMI DOLPHINS 12-4 Don Shula

Scores of Each Game		
27	New England	24
30	BUFFALO	7
3	N.Y. Giants	20
28	Pittsburgh	6
20	N.Y. JETS	16
17	NEW ENGLAND	10
27	Indianapolis	7
23	PHOENIX	3
17	N.Y. Jets	3
10	L.A. RAIDERS	13
30	Cleveland	13
20	Washington	42
23	PHILADELPHIA	20
24	SEATTLE	17
14	Buffalo	24
23	INDIANAPOLIS	17

Use Name	Pos.	Hgt	Wgt	Age	Int	Pts
Jeff Dellenbach	OT-C	6'6"	280	27		
Mark Dennis	OT	6'6"	295	25		
Richmond Webb	OT	6'6"	298	23		
Roy Foster	OG	6'4"	284	30		
Harry Galbreath	OG	6'1"	275	25		
Keith Sims	OG	6'2"	305	23		
Jeff Uhlenhake	C	6'3"	282	24		
Bert Weidner	C	6'3"	284	23		
Jeff Cross	DE	6'4"	272	24		
Greg Mark (to PHI)	DE-LB	6'3"	252	23		
T.J. Turner	DE	6'4"	280	27		
Karl Wilson	DE	6'4"	275	26		
Shawn Lee	NT	6'2"	285	23		
Alfred Oglesby	NT	6'3"	278	23		
Brian Sochia	NT	6'3"	275	29		6

John Bosa — Knee Injury

Use Name	Pos.	Hgt	Wgt	Age	Int	Pts
Rick Graf	LB	6'5"	249	27		
Hugh Green	LB	6'2"	228	31		
David Griggs	LB-TE	6'3"	239	23		
E.J. Junior	LB	6'3"	242	30		
Eric Kumerow	LB-DE	6'7"	268	25	1	
Cliff Odom	LB	6'2"	243	32		6
John Offerdahl	LB	6'3"	237	26	1	
Mike Reichenbach	LB	6'2"	240	28		
J.B. Brown	DB	6'	192	24		
Kerry Glenn	DB	5'9"	178	28	2	6
African Grant	DB	6'	200	25		
Bobby Harden	DB	6'	192	23		
Liffort Hobley	DB	6'	202	28	1	
Paul Lankford	DB	6'1"	190	32		
Michael McGruder	DB	5'11"	180	28		
Tim McKyer	DB	6'	177	26	4	
Stevon Moore	DB	5'11"	204	23		
Louis Oliver	DB	6'2"	226	24	5	
Rodney Thomas	DB	5'10"	190	24		
Jarvis Williams	DB	5'11"	196	25	5	6

Barry Krauss — Knee Injury

Use Name	Pos.	Hgt	Wgt	Age	Int	Pts
Dan Marino	QB	6'4"	222	28		
Scott Secules	QB	6'3"	219	25		
Tony Collins	HB	5'11"	212	31		
Mark Higgs	HB	5'7"	196	24		6
Sammie Smith	HB	6'2"	226	23		54
Troy Stradford	HB	5'9"	192	25		6
Garrett Limbrick	FB	6'2"	240	24		
Marc Logan	FB	5'11"	220	25		12
Tony Paige	FB	5'10"	235	27		36
Fred Banks	WR	5'10"	180	28		
Andre Brown	WR	6'3"	210	24		
Mark Clayton	WR	5'9"	184	29		30
Mark Duper	WR	5'9"	190	31		30
Jim Jensen	WR-FB	6'4"	220	31		6
Tony Martin	WR	6'	180	24		12
James Pruitt	WR	6'2"	201	26		18
Scott Schwedes (to, from SD)	WR	6'	182	25		6
Greg Baty	TE	6'5"	240	26		
Ferrell Edmunds	TE	6'6"	248	25		6
Brian Kinchen	TE	6'2"	238	25		
Reggie Roby	K	6'2"	242	29		
Pete Stoyonovich	K	5'10"	180	23		100

INDIANAPOLIS COLTS 7-9 Ron Meyer

Scores of Each Game		
10	Buffalo	26
14	NEW ENGLAND	16
10	Houston	24
24	Philadelphia	23
23	KANSAS CITY	19
17	DENVER	27
7	MIAMI	27
7	N.Y. GIANTS	24
13	New England	10
17	N.Y. JETS	14
34	Cincinnati	20
17	Phoenix	20
7	BUFFALO	31
29	N.Y. Jets	21
35	WASHINGTON	28
17	Miami	23

Use Name	Pos.	Hgt	Wgt	Age	Int	Pts
Joey Banes	OT	6'7"	282	23		
Kevin Call	OT	6'7"	302	28		
Pat Cunningham	OT	6'6"	295	21		
Zefross Moss	OT	6'6"	338	23		
William Schultz	OT	6'5"	293	23		
Brian Baldinger	OG-OT	6'4"	278	31		
Chris Conlin	OG	6'4"	287	25		
Randy Dixon	OG	6'3"	302	25		
Pat Tomberlin	OG	6'2"	330	24		
Ray Donaldson	C	6'3"	300	32		
Sam Clancy	DE	6'7"	284	32		
Jeff Faulkner	DE	6'3"	280	26		
Jon Hand	DE	6'7"	301	26		
Ralph Jarvis	DE	6'4"	255	25		
Sean McNanie	DE	6'5"	270	28		
Donnell Thompson	DE	6'4"	280	31		
Harvey Armstrong	NT	6'3"	282	30		
Mitchell Benson	NT	6'3"	302	23		
Tony Siragusa	NT	6'3"	291	23		

Use Name	Pos.	Hgt	Wgt	Age	Int	Pts
Chip Banks	LB	6'4"	245	30		
Duane Bickett	LB	6'5"	243	27	1	
Jeff Herrod	LB	6'	243	24	1	
Kurt Larson	LB	6'4"	236	23		
Quintus McDonald	LB	6'3	263	23		
Scott Radecic	LB	6'3"	236	28		
Matt Vanderbeek	LB	6'3"	258	23		
Tony Walker	LB	6'3"	235	22		
Fredd Young	LB	6'1"	233	27		
Michael Ball	DB	6'	216	26		
John Baylor	DB	6'	203	25		
Eugene Daniel	DB	5'11"	178	29		
Chris Goode	DB	6'	193	26	1	6
Alan Grant	DB	5'10"	187	23	1	6
Cornell Holloway	DB	5'11"	182	24		
Mike Prior	DB	6'	204	26	3	
George Streeter	DB	6'2"	212	23		
Keith Taylor	DB	5'11'	193	25	2	

O'Brien Alston — Knee Injury

Use Name	Pos.	Hgt	Wgt	Age	Int	Pts
Joe Ferguson	QB	6'1"	190	40		
Jeff George	QB	6'4"	221	22		6
Mark Herrmann	QB	6'4"	186	31		
Rusty Hilger	QB	6'4"	205	28		
Jack Trudeau	QB	6'3"	214	27		
Albert Bentley	HB-FB	5'11"	214	30		36
Eric Dickerson	HB	6'3"	224	29		24
Ken Clark	FB	5'9"	201	24		
Ivy Joe Hunter	FB-HB	6'	237	23		
Anthony Johnson	FB	6'	222	22		12
Bill Brooks	WR	6'	191	26		30
Jessie Hester	WR	5'11"	172	27		36
Stanley Morgan	WR	5'11"	185	35		30
Stacey Simmons	WR	5'9"	183	22		
Clarence Verdin	WR	5'8"	163	27		6
Eugene Riley	TE	6'2"	236	23		
Pat Beach	TE	6'4"	252	29		6
Dean Biasucci	K	6'	191	27		83
Rohn Stark	K	6'3"	204	31		

NEW YORK JETS 6-10 Bruce Coslet

Scores of Each Game		
20	Cincinnati	25
24	CLEVELAND	21
7	BUFFALO	30
37	New England	13
16	Miami	20
3	SAN DIEGO	39
27	Buffalo	30
17	Houston	12
24	DALLAS	9
3	MIAMI	17
14	Indianapolis	17
7	PITTSBURGH	24
17	San Diego	38
21	INDIANAPOLIS	29
42	NEW ENGLAND	7
16	Tampa Bay	14

Use Name	Pos.	Hgt	Wgt	Age	Int	Pts
Jeff Criswell	OT	6'7"	291	25		
Scott Jones	OT	6'5"	282	24		
Brett Miller	OT	6'7"	293	31		
Dave Cadigan	OG	6'4"	285	25		
Mike Haight	OG	6'4"	279	27		
Trevor Matich	OG-C-OT	6'4"	282	28		
Dwayne White	OG	6'2"	312	23		
Dave Zawatson	OG-OT	6'4"	287	24		
Roger Duffy	C	6'3"	285	23		
Jim Sweeney	C-OG	6'4"	275	28		
Darrell Davis	DE	6'2"	258	24		6
Jeff Lageman	DE	6'5"	255	23		
Ron Stallworth	DE-DT	6'5"	260	24		
Marvin Washington	DE-DT	6'6"	276	24		
Dennis Byrd	DT	6'5"	270	23		2
Emanuel McNeil	DT	6'3"	277	23		
Scott Mersereau	DT	6'3"	273	25		
Gerald Nichols	DT-DE	6'2"	260	26		

Marty Lyons — Arm Injury
Paul Frase — Hyperthyroid Illness

Use Name	Pos.	Hgt	Wgt	Age	Int	Pts
Kyle Clifton	LB	6'4"	236	28	3	
John Galvin	LB	6'3"	230	25		
Troy Johnson	LB	6'2"	236	25		
Joe Kelly	LB	6'2"	235	25		
Joe Mott	LB	6'4"	253	24		
Dan Murray	LB	6'1"	240	23		
Mac Stephens	LB	6'3"	220	22		
John Booty	DB	6'	179	24		
Travis Curtis	DB	5'10"	180	24	2	
James Hasty	DB	6'	200	25	2	
Carl Howard	DB	6'2"	190	28		
Ken Johnson	DB	6'2"	208	23		
Michael Mayes	DB	5'10"	173	24	1	
Erik McMillan	DB	6'2"	197	25	5	
Don Odegard	DB	6'	180	23		
Tony Stargell	DB	5'11"	190	24	2	
Brian Washington	DB	6'1"	220	24	3	

Troy Benson — Neck Injury
Dennis Price — Shoulder Injury
Terry Williams — Knee Injury

Use Name	Pos.	Hgt	Wgt	Age	Int	Pts
Tony Eason	QB	6'4"	212	30		
Ken O'Brien	QB	6'4"	200	29		
Troy Taylor	QB	6'4"	200	22		6
A.B. Brown	HB	5'9"	212	24		
Johnny Hector	HB	5'11"	202	29		12
Freeman McNeil	HB	5'11"	209	31		36
Blair Thomas	HB	5'10"	195	22		12
Brad Baxter	FB	6'1"	231	23		
Chris Burkett	WR	6'4"	210	28		
Dale Dawkins	WR	6'1"	190	23		
Terance Mathis	WR	5'10"	170	23		6
Rob Moore	WR	6'3"	205	21		36
Al Toon	WR	6'4"	205	27		36
JoJo Townsell	WR	5'9"	180	29		6
Mark Boyer	TE	6'4"	242	27		6
Chris Dressel	TE	6'4"	239	29		
Pat Kelly	TE	6'6"	252	24		
Doug Wellsandt	TE	6'3"	248	23		
Pat Leahy	K	6'	196	39		101
Joe Prokop	K	6'3"	224	30		

Patrick Egu — Arm Injury

NEW ENGLAND PATRIOTS 1-15 Rod Rust

Scores of Each Game		
24	MIAMI	27
16	Indianapolis	14
7	Cincinnati	41
13	N.Y. JETS	37
20	SEATTLE	33
10	Miami	17
10	BUFFALO	27
20	Philadelphia	48
10	INDIANAPOLIS	13
0	Buffalo	14
14	Phoenix	34
7	KANSAS CITY	37
3	Pittsburgh	24
10	WASHINGTON	25
7	N.Y. Jets	42
10	N.Y. GIANTS	13

Use Name	Pos.	Hgt	Wgt	Age	Int	Pts
Bruce Armstrong	OT	6'4"	284	24		
Stan Clayton	OT-OG	6'3"	265	25		
David Viaene	OT	6'5"	300	25		
Danny Villa	OT-C	6'5"	305	25		
Paul Fairchild	OG-C	6'4"	270	28		
Chris Gambol	OG-OT	6'6"	303	25		
Damian Johnson	OG	6'5"	290	27		
Gene Chilton	C	6'3"	286	26		
Elbert Crawford	C-OG	6'3"	280	24		
David Douglas	C-OG	6'4"	280	27		
Ray Agnew	DE	6'3"	272	22		
Chris Gannon	DE	6'6"	260	24		
Marion Hobby	DE	6'4"	277	23		
Sean Smith	DE	6'4"	280	23		
Garin Veris	DE	6'4"	255	27		
Fred DeRiggi	NT	6'2"	268	23		
Tim Goad	NT	6'3"	280	24		
Brent Williams	DE	6'3"	278	25		6

Bob White — Knee Injury

Use Name	Pos.	Hgt	Wgt	Age	Int	Pts
Vincent Brown	LB	6'2"	245	25		
Richard Harvey	LB	6'1"	227	23		
Ilia Jarostchuk	LB	6'3"	245	26		
Johnny Rembert	LB	6'3"	234	29	2	
Ed Reynolds	LB	6'5"	242	28		
Chris Singleton	LB	6'2"	247	23		
Richard Tardits	LB	6'2"	218	25		
Andre Tippett	LB	6'3"	241	30		
Ed Williams	LB	6'4"	244	28		
Eric Coleman	DB	6'	190	23		
Tim Hauck	DB	5'11"	185	23		
Maurice Hurst	DB	5'10"	185	22	4	
Brian Hutson	DB	6'1"	198	25		
Roland James	DB	6'2"	191	32		
Ronnie Lippett	DB	5'11"	180	29	4	
Fred Marion	DB	6'2"	191	31	4	
Rod McSwain	DB	6'1"	198	28		
Junior Robinson	DB	5'9"	181	22		
Mickey Washington	DB	5'9"	187	22		
Tony Zackery	DB	6'2"	195	23		

Use Name	Pos.	Hgt	Wgt	Age	Int	Pts
Steve Grogan	QB	6'4"	210	37		
Tom Hodson	QB	6'3"	195	23		
Marc Wilson	QB	6'6"	205	33		
Marvin Allen	HB	5'10"	215	24		6
Jamie Morris	HB	5'7"	188	25		
Don Overton	HB	6'	221	22		
John Stephens	HB	6'1"	220	24		18
George Adams	FB	6'1"	225	27		6
Bob Perryman (to DAL)	FB	6'1"	233	25		6
Mosi Tatupu	FB	6'	227	35		
Pat Coleman	WR	5'7"	173	23		
Hart Lee Dykes	WR	6'4"	218	23		12
Irving Fryar	WR	6'	200	27		24
Cedric Jones	WR	6'1"	184	30		
Sammy Martin	WR	5'11"	175	25		6
Greg McMurtry	WR	6'2"	207	22		
Michael Timpson	WR	5'10"	175	23		
Marv Cook	TE	6'4"	234	24		30
Lin Dawson	TE	6'3"	240	31		
Zeke Mowatt	TE	6'3"	240	29		
Eric Sievers	TE	6'4"	238	32		
Brian Hansen	K	6'4"	220	29		
Jason Staurovsky	K	5'9"	170	27		67

1990 A.F.C. — Eastern Division

BUFFALO BILLS

RUSHING

Last Name	No.	Yds	Avg	TD
Thomas	271	1297	4.8	11
K. Davis	64	302	4.7	4
Mueller	59	207	3.5	2
D. Smith	20	82	4.1	2
Kelly	22	63	2.9	0
Gardner	15	41	2.7	0
Reich	15	24	1.6	0
Beebe	1	23	23.0	0
Reed	3	23	7.7	0
Kinnebrew	9	18	2.0	1

RECEIVING

Last Name	No.	Yds	Avg	TD
Reed	71	945	13.3	8
Thomas	49	532	10.9	2
Lofton	35	712	20.3	4
McKeller	34	464	13.6	5
D. Smith	21	225	10.7	0
Mueller	16	106	6.6	1
Beebe	11	221	20.1	1
Metzelaars	10	60	6.0	1
K. Davis	9	78	8.7	1
Rolle	3	6	2.0	3
Tasker	2	44	22.0	2
Edwards	2	11	5.5	0

PUNT RETURNS

Last Name	No.	Yds	Avg	TD
Edwards	14	92	6.6	0
Hale	10	76	7.6	0
Odomes	1	9	9.0	0

KICKOFF RETURNS

Last Name	No.	Yds	Avg	TD
D. Smith	32	643	20.1	0
Edwards	11	256	23.3	0
Beebe	6	119	19.8	0
Rolle	2	22	11.0	0

PASSING — PUNTING — KICKING

PASSING	Att	Cmp	%	Yds	Yd/Att	TD	Int— %	RK
Kelly	346	219	63.3	2829	8.18	24	9—2.6	1
Reich	63	36	57.1	469	7.44	2	0—0.0	
Gilbert	15	8	53.3	106	7.07	2	2—13.3	
D. Smith	1	0	0.0	0	0.00	0	0—0.0	

PUNTING	No.	Avg.
Tuten	53	39.8

KICKING	XP	ATT	%	FG	ATT	%
Norwood	50	52	96	20	29	69

MIAMI DOLPHINS

RUSHING

Last Name	No.	Yds	Avg	TD
Smith	226	831	3.7	8
Logan	79	317	4.0	2
Stradford	37	138	3.7	1
Paige	32	95	3.0	2
Higgs	10	67	6.7	0
Secules	8	34	4.3	0
Marino	16	29	1.8	0
Limbrick	5	14	2.8	0
Martin	1	8	8.0	0
Jensen	4	6	1.5	0
Banks	1	3	3.0	0
Edmunds	1	-7	-7.0	0

RECEIVING

Last Name	No.	Yds	Avg	TD
Duper	52	810	15.6	5
Jensen	44	365	8.3	1
Paige	35	247	7.1	4
Clayton	32	406	12.7	3
Edmunds	31	446	14.4	1
Stradford	30	257	8.6	0
Martin	29	388	13.4	2
Pruitt	13	235	18.1	3
Banks	13	131	10.1	0
Smith	11	134	12.2	1
Logan	7	54	7.7	0
Schwedes	6	66	11.0	1
Limbrick	4	23	5.8	0
A. Brown	3	49	16.3	0

PUNT RETURNS

Last Name	No.	Yds	Avg	TD
Martin	26	140	5.4	0
Schwedes	14	122	9.7	0
Stradford	3	4	1.3	0
Williams	1	5	5.0	0

KICKOFF RETURNS

Last Name	No.	Yds	Avg	TD
Logan	20	367	18.4	0
Higgs	10	210	21.0	0
Stradford	3	56	18.7	0
Collins	2	30	15.0	0
Schwedes	2	52	26.0	0
Paige	1	18	18.0	0
Kinchen	1	16	16.0	0
Sims	1	9	9.0	0
Graf	1	6	6.0	0

PASSING — PUNTING — KICKING

PASSING	Att	Cmp	%	Yds	Yd/Att	TD	Int— %	RK
Marino	531	306	57.6	3563	6.71	21	11—2.1	5
Secules	7	3	42.9	17	2.43	0	1—14.3	
Jensen	1	1	100.0	31	31.00	0	0—0.0	

PUNTING	No.	Avg.
Roby	72	42.0

KICKING	XP	Att.	%	FG	Att	%
Stoyonovich	37	37	100	21	25	84

INDIANAPOLIS COLTS

RUSHING

Last Name	No.	Yds	Avg	TD
Dickerson	166	677	4.1	4
Bentley	137	556	4.1	4
Trudeau	10	28	2.8	0
Clark	7	10	1.4	0
Hester	4	9	2.3	0
George	11	2	0.2	1

RECEIVING

Last Name	No.	Yds	Avg	TD
Bentley	71	664	9.4	2
Brooks	62	823	13.3	5
Hester	54	924	17.1	6
Morgan	23	364	15.8	5
Dickerson	18	92	5.1	0
Verdin	14	178	12.7	1
Beach	12	124	10.3	1
Johnson	5	32	6.4	2
Clark	5	23	4.6	0
Simmons	4	33	4.6	0
Prior	1	40	40.0	0

PUNT RETURNS

Last Name	No.	Yds	Avg	TD
Verdin	31	396	12.8	0
Grant	2	6	3.0	0
Prior	2	0	0.0	0
Daniel	1	0	0.0	0

KICKOFF RETURNS

Last Name	No.	Yds	Avg	TD
Simmons	19	348	18.3	0
Verdin	18	350	19.4	0
Grant	15	280	18.7	0
Bentley	11	211	19.2	0
Ball	1	0	0.0	0
Jarvis	1	0	0.0	0

PASSING — PUNTING — KICKING

PASSING	Att	Cmp	%	Yds	Yd/Att	TD	Int— %	RK
George	334	181	54.2	2152	6.44	16	13—3.9	10
Trudeau	144	84	58.3	1078	7.49	6	6—4.2	
Ferguson	8	2	25.0	21	2.63	0	2—25.0	
Herrmann	1	1	100.0	6	6.00	0	0—0.0	
Stark	1	1	100.0	40	40.00	0	0—0.0	

PUNTING	No.	Avg.
Stark	72	42.8

KICKING	XP	ATT	%	FG	ATT	%
Biasucci	32	33	97	17	24	71

NEW YORK JETS

RUSHING

Last Name	No.	Yds	Avg	TD
Thomas	123	620	5.0	1
Baxter	124	539	4.3	6
F. McNeil	99	458	4.6	6
Hector	91	377	4.1	2
O'Brien	21	72	3.4	0
Eason	7	29	4.1	0
Taylor	2	20	10.0	1
Mathis	2	9	4.5	0
Brown	1	8	8.0	0
Prokop	3	2	0.7	0
Wellsandt	1	-3	-3.0	0
Moore	2	-4	-2.0	0

RECEIVING

Last Name	No.	Yds	Avg	TD
Toon	57	757	13.3	6
Moore	44	692	15.7	6
Boyer	40	334	8.4	1
Thomas	20	204	10.2	1
Mathis	19	245	12.9	0
F. McNeil	16	230	14.4	0
Burkett	14	204	14.6	0
Baxter	8	73	9.1	0
Hector	8	72	9.0	0
Dressel	6	66	11.0	0
Dawkins	5	68	13.6	0
Wellsandt	5	57	11.4	0
Townsell	4	57	14.3	0

PUNT RETURNS

Last Name	No.	Yds	Avg	TD
Townsell	17	154	9.1	0
Mathis	11	165	15.0	1
Hasty	1	0	0.0	0
Odegard	1	0	0.0	0

KICKOFF RETURNS

Last Name	No.	Yds	Avg	TD
Mathis	43	787	18.3	0
Townsell	7	158	22.6	0
Odegard	5	89	17.8	0
Nichols	2	3	1.5	0
Brown	1	63	63.0	0
Boyer	1	14	14.0	0
Duffy	1	8	8.0	0
Dressel	1	7	7.0	0

PASSING — PUNTING — KICKING

PASSING	Att	Cmp	%	Yds	Yd/Att	TD	Int— %	RK
O'Brien	411	226	55.0	2855	6.95	13	10—2.4	8
Eason	28	13	46.4	155	5.54	0	1—3.6	
Taylor	10	7	70.0	49	4.90	1	0—0.0	
Toon	2	0	0.0	0	0.00	0	0—0.0	

PUNTING	No.	Avg.
Prokop	59	40.1

KICKING	XP	Att	%	FG	Att	%
Leahy	32	32	100	23	26	88

NEW ENGLAND PATRIOTS

RUSHING

Last Name	No.	Yds	Avg	TD
Stephens	212	808	3.8	2
Allen	63	237	3.8	1
Adams	28	111	4.0	0
Perryman	32	97	3.0	1
Hodson	12	79	6.6	0
Tatupu	16	56	3.5	0
Overton	5	8	1.6	0
Wilson	5	7	1.4	0
Morris	2	4	2.0	0
Gannon	1	0	0.0	0
Hansen	1	0	0.0	0
Fryar	2	-4	-2.0	0
Grogan	4	-5	-1.3	0

RECEIVING

Last Name	No.	Yds	Avg	TD
Fryar	54	856	15.9	4
Cook	51	455	8.9	5
Dykes	34	549	16.1	2
Stephens	28	196	7.0	1
McMurtry	22	240	10.9	0
Jones	21	301	14.3	0
Adams	16	146	9.1	1
Perryman	15	88	5.9	0
Sievers	8	77	9.6	0
Mowatt	6	67	11.2	0
Allen	6	48	8.0	0
Timpson	5	91	18.2	0
Martin	4	65	16.3	1
Overton	2	19	9.5	0
Tatupu	2	10	5.0	0

PUNT RETURNS

Last Name	No.	Yds	Avg	TD
Fryar	28	133	4.8	0
Martin	1	1	1.0	0

KICKOFF RETURNS

Last Name	No.	Yds	Avg	TD
Martin	25	515	20.6	0
Allen	11	168	15.3	0
Morris	11	202	18.4	0
Robinson	11	211	19.2	0
Overton	10	188	18.8	0
Timpson	3	62	20.7	0
Jones	2	24	12.0	0
P. Coleman	2	18	9.0	0
Adams	1	7	7.0	0
McSwain	1	0	0.0	0

PASSING — PUNTING — KICKING

PASSING	Att	Cmp	%	Yds	Yd/Att	TD	Int— %	RK
Wilson	265	139	52.5	1625	6.13	6	11—4.2	14
Hodson	156	85	54.5	968	6.21	4	5—3.2	
Grogan	92	50	54.3	615	6.68	4	3—3.3	
Stephens	1	0	0.0	0	0.00	0	1—100.0	

PUNTING	No.	Avg.
Hansen	92	40.8

KICKING	XP	ATT	%	FG	ATT	%
Staurovsky	19	19	100	16	22	73

1990 A.F.C. — Central Division

CINCINNATI BENGALS 9-7 Sam Wyche

Scores of Each Game		
25	N.Y. JETS	20
21	San Diego	16
41	NEW ENGLAND	7
16	Seattle	31
34	L.A. Rams	* 31
17	Houston	48
34	Cleveland	13
17	Atlanta	38
7	NEW ORLEANS	21
27	PITTSBURGH	3
20	INDIANAPOLIS	34
16	Pittsburgh	12
17	SAN FRANCISCO	* 20
7	L.A. Raiders	24
40	HOUSTON	20
21	CLEVELAND	14

Use Name	Pos.	Hgt	Wgt	Age	Int	Pts
Mike Brennan	OT	6'5"	274	23		
Anthony Munoz	OT	6'6"	284	32		
Kirk Scrafford	OT	6'6"	255	23		
Joe Walter	OT	6'6"	292	27		
Paul Jetton	OG	6'4"	288	25		
Brian Blados	OG	6'5"	295	28		
Ken Moyer	OG	6'6"	297	23		
Bruce Reimers	OG	6'7"	298	29		
Bruce Kozerski	C	6'4"	287	28		
Jason Buck	DE-DT	6'5"	264	27		
David Grant	DE-NT	6'4"	278	24		
Mike Hammerstein	DE-DT-NT	6'4"	272	27		
Skip McClendon	DE	6'7"	287	26		
Natu Tuatagaloa	DE	6'4"	274	24		
Tim Krumrie	NT-DT	6'2"	274	30		
Leo Barker	LB	6'2"	227	30		
Ed Brady	LB	6'2"	235	30		
Bernard Clark	LB	6'2"	248	23		
James Francis	LB	6'5"	252	22	1	8
Craig Ogletree	LB	6'2"	236	22		
Kevin Walker	LB	6'2"	238	24		
Leon White	LB	6'3"	245	26	1	
Carl Zander	LB	6'2"	235	27		
Lewis Billups	DB	5'11"	190	26	3	
Barney Bussey	DB	6'	195	28	4	6
Carl Carter	DB	5'11"	180	26		
Rickey Dixon	DB	5'11"	181	23		
David Fulcher	DB	6'3"	228	28	4	2
Rod Jones	DB	6'	185	26		
Mitchell Price	DB	5'9"	181	23	1	6
Eric Thomas	DB	5'11"	181	25		
Solomon Wilcots	DB	5'11"	195	25		
Boomer Esiason	QB	6'4"	225	29		
Todd Philcox	QB	6'4"	209	23		
Erik Wilhelm	QB	6'3"	210	24		
Eric Ball	HB-FB	6'2"	211	24		12
James Brooks	HB	5'10"	182	31		54
Harold Green	HB	6'2"	222	22		12
Stanford Jennings	HB-FB	6'1"	205	28		6
Craig Taylor	FB	5'11"	224	24		18
Ickey Woods	FB	6'2"	232	24		36
Mike Barber	WR	5'11"	172	23		6
Eddie Brown	WR	6'	185	27		54
Lynn James	WR	6'	191	23		
Kendal Smith	WR	5'9"	189	24		
Tim McGee	WR	5'10"	175	26		6
Rodney Holman	TE	6'3"	238	30		30
Eric Kattus	TE	6'5"	235	27		12
Jim Riggs	TE	6'5"	245	26		
Jim Breech	K	5'6"	161	34		92
Lee Johnson	K	6'2"	198	28		

HOUSTON OILERS 9-7 Jack Pardee

Scores of Each Game		
27	Atlanta	47
9	Pittsburgh	20
24	INDIANAPOLIS	10
17	San Diego	7
21	SAN FRANCISCO	24
48	CINCINNATI	17
23	NEW ORLEANS	10
12	N.Y. JETS	17
13	L.A. Rams	17
35	Cleveland	23
27	BUFFALO	24
10	Seattle	* 13
58	CLEVELAND	14
27	Kansas City	10
20	Cincinnati	40
34	PITTSBURGH	14

Use Name	Pos.	Hgt	Wgt	Age	Int	Pts
Don Maggs	OT-OG	6'5"	290	28		
Dean Steinkuhler	OT	6'3"	287	29		
David Williams	OT	6'5"	292	24		
Doug Dawson	OG-C	6'2"	288	28		
Bruce Matthews	OG-C	6'4"	291	29		
Mike Munchak	OG	6'3"	284	30		
Erik Norgard	C-OG	6'1"	278	24		
Jay Pennison	C	6'1"	274	28		
William Fuller	DE	6'3"	265	28		
Sean Jones	DE	6'7"	264	27		
Willis Peguese	DE	6'4"	267	23		
Jeff Alm	DT	6'6"	269	22		
Ray Childress	DT-DE	6'6"	272	27		2
Ezra Johnson	DT-DE	6'4"	257	34		
Glenn Montgomery	DT	6'	268	23		
Doug Smith	DT	6'5"	314	31		
Eric Fairs	LB	6'3"	244	26		
John Grimsley	LB	6'2"	238	28		
Scott Kozak	LB	6'3"	222	24		
Lamar Lathon	LB	6'3"	244	22		
Johnny Meads	LB	6'2"	226	29	1	
Eugene Seale	LB	5'10"	253	26		
Al Smith	LB	6'1"	244	25		
Patrick Allen	DB	5'10"	182	29	1	
Steve Brown	DB	5'11"	190	30		
Cris Dishman	DB	6'	180	25	4	
Richard Johnson	DB	6'1"	195	26	8	6
Quintin Jones	DB	5'11"	193	24		
Terry Kinard	DB	6'1"	198	30	4	
Leander Knight	DB	6'1"	192	27	1	
Bubba McDowell	DB	6'1"	195	23	2	
Bo Orlando	DB	5'10"	180	24		
Dee Thomas	DB	5'10"	176	22		
Cody Carlson	QB	6'3"	199	26		
Warren Moon	QB	6'3"	210	33		12
Reggie Slack	QB	6'1"	221	22		
Victor Jones	HB-FB	5'8"	212	22		
Allen Pinkett	HB	5'9"	192	26		
Lorenzo White	HB	5'11"	209	24		72
Curtis Duncan	WR	5'11"	184	25		6
Bernard Ford	WR	5'9"	171	24		6
Ernest Givins	WR	5'9"	172	25		54
Leonard Harris	WR	5'8"	162	29		18
Drew Hill	WR	5'9"	172	33		30
Haywood Jeffires	WR	6'2"	201	25		48
Tony Jones	WR	5'7"	139	24		36
Gerald McNeil	WR	5'7"	142	28		
Teddy Garcia	K	5'10"	172	26		68
Greg Montgomery	K	6'3"	213	25		
Tony Zendejas	K	5'8"	165	30		41

PITTSBURGH STEELERS 9-7 Chuck Noll

Scores of Each Game		
3	Cleveland	13
20	HOUSTON	9
3	L.A. Raiders	20
6	MIAMI	28
36	SAN DIEGO	14
34	Denver	17
7	San Francisco	27
41	L.A. RAMS	10
21	ATLANTA	9
3	Cincinnati	27
24	N.Y. Jets	7
12	CINCINNATI	16
24	NEW ENGLAND	3
9	New Orleans	6
35	CLEVELAND	0
14	Houston	34

Use Name	Pos.	Hgt	Wgt	Age	Int	Pts
Tunch Ilkin	OT	6'3"	274	32		
John Jackson	OT	6'6"	290	25		
Tom Ricketts	OT-OG	6'5"	293	24		
Justin Strzelczyk	OT	6'5"	291	22		
Brian Blankenship	OG-C	6'1"	280	27		
Calton Haselrig	OG	6'1"	291	24		
Terry Long	OG	5'11"	278	31		
John Rienstra	OG	6'5"	272	27		
Dermontti Dawson	C	6'2"	279	25		
Kenny Davidson	DE	6'5"	272	23		
Donald Evans	DE	6'2"	265	26		
Aaron Jones	DE	6'5"	269	24	1	
Keith Willis	DE	6'1"	263	31	1	
Lorenzo Freeman	NT	6'5"	319	26		
Craig Veasey	NT-DE	6'2"	280	23		
Gerald Williams	NT	6'3"	291	26		
Bryan Hinkle	LB	6'2"	222	31	1	
A.J. Jenkins	LB-DE	6'2"	237	24		
David Little	LB	6'1"	236	31	1	
Greg Lloyd	LB	6'2"	224	25	1	
Eddie Miles	B	6'1"	233	21		
Hardy Nickerson	LB	6'2"	229	25		
Jerry Olsavsky	LB	6'1"	222	23		
Tyronne Stowe	LB	6'1"	236	25		2
Jerrol Williams	LB	6'5"	242	22		
Thomas Everett	DB	5'9"	179	25	3	
Larry Griffin	DB	6'	200	27	4	
Delton Hall	DB	6'1"	205	25	1	
David Johnson	DB	6'	185	24	2	6
Gary Jones	DB	6'1"	203	22		
Carnell Lake	DB	6'1"	205	23	1	
Richard Shelton	DB	5'10"	180	24		
Dwayne Woodruff	DB	6'	198	33	3	
Rod Woodson	DB	6'	199	25	5	6
Bubby Brister	QB	6'3"	208	28		
Neil O'Donnell	QB	6'3"	221	24		
Rick Strom	QB	6'2"	210	25		
Richard Bell	HB	6'	200	23		6
Barry Foster	HB	5'10"	223	21		6
Warren Williams	HB	6'	202	25		24
Tim Worley	HB	6'2"	228	23		
Merril Hoge	FB	6'2"	226	25		60
Chris Calloway	WR	5'10"	185	22		6
Lorenzo Davis	WR	5'11"	185	22		
Derek Hill	WR	6'1"	193	22		
Louis Lipps	WR	5'10"	190	28		18
Dwight Stone	WR-HB	6'	188	26		6
Eric Green	TE	6'5"	274	23		42
Mike Mularkey	TE	6'4"	237	28		18
Terry O'Shea	TE	6'4"	236	23		
Gary Anderson	K	5'11"	184	31		92
Dan Stryzinski	K	6'1"	193	25		

Chuck Lanza — Triceps Injury

CLEVELAND BROWNS 3-13 Bud Carson (2-7), Jim Shofner (1-6)

Scores of Each Game		
13	PITTSBURGH	3
21	N.Y. Jets	24
14	SAN DIEGO	24
0	Kansas City	34
30	Denver	29
20	New Orleans	25
13	CINCINNATI	34
17	San Francisco	20
0	BUFFALO	42
23	HOUSTON	35
13	MIAMI	30
23	L.A. RAMS	38
14	Houston	58
13	ATLANTA	10
0	Pittsburgh	35
14	Cincinnati	21

Use Name	Pos.	Hgt	Wgt	Age	Int	Pts
Paul Farren	OT	6'5"	270	29		
Tony Jones	OT	6'5"	290	24		
Ken Reeves	OT	6'5"	277	28		
Dan Fike	OG	6'7"	285	29		
Ben Jefferson	OG	6'9"	330	24		
Gregg Rakoczy	OG	6'6"	295	25		
Kevin Robbins	OG	6'6"	295	23		
Ralph Tamm	OG	6'4"	280	24		
Mike Baab	C	6'4"	275	30		
Michael Morris (from SEA)	C	6'5"	285	29		
Al Baker	DE	6'6"	260	33		
Robert Banks	DE	6'5"	255	26		
Rob Burnett	DE	6'4"	270	23		
Bob Buczkowski	DT	6'5"	260	26		
Tom Gibson	DT-DE	6'7"	270	26		
Anthony Pleasant	DE	6'5"	258	23		
Michael Dean Perry	DT-DE	6'1"	285	24		
Chris Pike	DT	6'8"	300	26		
David Grayson	LB	6'2"	230	26	1	
Eddie Johnson	LB	6'1"	225	30		
Mike Johnson	LB	6'1"	225	27	1	6
Jock Jones	LB	6'2"	230	22		
Clay Matthews	LB	6'2"	245	34		
Van Waiters	LB	6'4"	240	25	1	
Stefon Adams (to MIA)	DB	5'10"	190	27		
Harlon Barnett	DB	5'11"	200	23		
Tony Blaylock	DB	5'11"	190	25	2	6
Keith Bostic	DB	6'1"	223	29		
Stephen Braggs	DB	5'10"	180	25	2	
Raymond Clayborn	DB	6'	190	35		
Thane Gash	DB	6'	200	25	1	
Mark Harper	DB	5'9"	185	28		
Randy Hilliard	DB	5'11"	160	23		
Frank Minnifield	DB	5'9"	185	30	2	
Felix Wright	DB	6'2"	190	31	3	
Jeff Francis	QB	6'4"	225	24		
Bernie Kosar	QB	6'5"	210	26		
Mike Pagel	QB	6'2"	211	29		
Eric Metcalf	HB-WR	5'10"	185	22		24
Derrick Gainer	FB	5'11"	235	24		6
Leroy Hoard	FB-HB	5'11"	230	22		18
Kevin Mack	FB	6'	235	28		42
Barry Redden	FB-HB	5'10"	219	30		
Brian Brennan	WR	5'9"	178	28		12
Vernon Joines	WR	6'2"	200	24		
Reggie Langhorne	WR	6'2"	200	27		12
Eugene Rowell	WR	6'1"	180	22		
Webster Slaughter	WR	6'	170	25		24
Scott Galbraith	TE	6'3"	260	23		
Ozzie Newsome	TE	6'2"	232	34		12
John Talley	TE	6'5"	245	25		
Jerry Kauric	K	6'	210	27		66
Bryan Wagner	K	6'2"	200	28		

Ted Banker — Knee Injury
Marlon Jones — Broken Foot
Rhony Weston — Knee Injury

Kyle Kramer — Shoulder Injury
Tom Manoa — Elbow Injury
Mike Oliphant — Hamstring Injury
Lawyer Tillman — Leg Injury

CINCINNATI BENGALS

RUSHING

Last Name	No.	Yds	Avg	TD
Brooks	195	1004	5.1	5
Green	83	353	4.3	1
Woods	64	268	4.2	6
Taylor	51	216	4.2	2
Esiason	50	157	3.1	0
Ball	22	72	3.3	1
Jennings	12	46	3.8	1
James	1	11	11.0	0
Wilhelm	6	6	1.0	0
Barber	1	-13	-13.0	0

RECEIVING

Last Name	No.	Yds	Avg	TD
Brown	44	706	16.0	9
McGee	43	737	17.1	1
Holman	40	596	14.9	5
Brooks	26	269	10.3	4
Woods	20	162	8.1	0
Barber	14	196	14.0	1
Green	12	90	7.5	1
Kattus	11	145	13.2	2
Riggs	8	79	9.9	0
Smith	7	45	6.4	0
Jennings	4	23	5.8	0
James	3	36	12.0	0
Taylor	3	22	7.3	1
Ball	2	46	23.0	1

PUNT RETURNS

Last Name	No.	Yds	Avg	TD
Price	29	251	8.7	1
Smith	1	4	4.0	0

KICKOFF RETURNS

Last Name	No.	Yds	Avg	TD
Jennings	29	584	20.1	0
Ball	16	366	22.9	0
Price	10	191	19.1	0
Smith	2	35	17.5	0
James	1	43	43.0	0
Taylor	1	16	16.0	0
Barber	1	14	14.0	0
Kattus	1	10	10.0	0
Riggs	1	7	7.0	0

PASSING — PUNTING — KICKING

PASSING	Att	Cmp	%	Yds	Yd/Att	TD	Int—	%	RK
Esiason	402	224	55.7	3031	7.54	24	22—	5.5	9
Wilhelm	19	12	63.2	117	6.16	0	0—	0.0	
Philcox	2	0	0.0	0	0.00	0	1—	50.0	
Johnson	1	1	100.0	4	4.00	1	0—	0.0	
James	1	0	0.0	0	0.00	0	0—	0.0	

PUNTING	No.	Avg.
Johnson	64	42.3
Breech	1	34.0

KICKING	XP	ATT	%	FG	ATT	%
Breech	41	44	93	17	21	81
Johnson	0	0	0	0	1	0

HOUSTON OILERS

RUSHING

Last Name	No.	Yds	Avg	TD
L. White	168	702	4.2	8
Pinkett	66	268	4.1	0
Moon	55	215	3.9	2
V. Jones	14	75	5.4	0
Givins	3	65	21.7	0
Carlson	11	52	4.7	0
T. Jones	1	-2	-2.0	0

RECEIVING

Last Name	No.	Yds	Avg	TD
Jeffires	74	1048	14.2	8
Hill	74	1019	13.8	5
Givins	72	979	13.6	9
Duncan	66	785	11.9	1
White	39	368	9.4	4
T. Jones	30	409	13.6	6
Harris	13	172	13.2	3
Pinkett	11	85	7.7	0
Ford	10	98	9.8	1
McNeil	5	63	12.6	0

PUNT RETURNS

Last Name	No.	Yds	Avg	TD
McNeil	30	172	5.7	0
Duncan	0	0	0.0	0

KICKOFF RETURNS

Last Name	No.	Yds	Avg	TD
McNeil	27	551	20.4	0
Ford	14	219	15.6	0
Pinkett	4	91	22.8	0
Norgard	2	0	0.0	0

PASSING — PUNTING — KICKING

PASSING	Att	Cmp	%	Yds	Yd/Att	TD	Int—	%	RK
Moon	584	362	62.0	4689	8.03	33	13—	2.2	2
Carlson	55	37	67.3	383	6.96	4	2—	3.6	

PUNTING	No.	Avg.
Montgomery	34	45.0

KICKING	XP	ATT	%	FG	ATT	%
Zendejas	20	21	95	7	12	58
Garcia	26	28	93	14	20	70

PITTSBURGH STEELERS

RUSHING

Last Name	No.	Yds	Avg	TD
Hoge	203	772	3.8	7
Worley	109	418	3.8	0
W. Williams	68	389	5.7	3
Foster	36	203	5.6	1
Brister	25	64	2.6	0
Bell	5	18	3.6	0
Stryzinski	3	17	5.7	0
Strom	4	10	2.5	0
Lipps	1	-5	-5.0	0
Stone	2	-6	-3.0	0

RECEIVING

Last Name	No.	Yds	Avg	TD
Lipps	50	682	13.6	3
Hoge	40	342	8.6	3
Green	34	387	11.4	7
Mularkey	32	365	11.4	3
Hill	25	391	15.6	0
Stone	19	332	17.5	1
Bell	12	137	11.4	1
Calloway	10	124	12.4	1
Worley	8	70	8.8	0
W. Williams	5	42	8.4	1
O'Shea	1	13	13.0	0
Foster	1	2	2.0	0

PUNT RETURNS

Last Name	No.	Yds	Avg	TD
Woodson	38	398	10.5	1
Hill	1	0	0.0	0

KICKOFF RETURNS

Last Name	No.	Yds	Avg	TD
Woodson	35	764	21.8	0
Stone	5	91	18.2	0
Foster	3	29	9.7	0
J. Williams	3	31	10.3	0
Griffin	2	16	8.0	0
Green	1	16	16.0	0
Lipps	1	9	9.0	0

PASSING — PUNTING — KICKING

PASSING	Att	Cmp	%	Yds	Yd/Att	TD	Int—	%	RK
Brister	387	223	57.6	2725	7.04	20	14—	3.6	6
Strom	21	14	66.7	162	7.71	0	1—	4.8	

PUNTING	No.	Avg.
Stryzinski	66	37.2

KICKING	XP	Att	%	FG	Att	%
Anderson	32	32	100	20	25	80

CLEVELAND BROWNS

RUSHING

Last Name	No.	Yds	Avg	TD
Mack	158	702	4.4	5
Metcalf	80	248	3.1	1
Hoard	58	149	2.6	3
Gainer	30	81	2.7	1
Slaughter	5	29	5.8	0
Kosar	10	13	1.3	0
Redden	1	-1	-1.0	0
Pagel	3	-1	-0.3	0

RECEIVING

Last Name	No.	Yds	Avg	TD
Slaughter	59	847	14.4	4
Metcalf	57	452	7.9	1
Langhorne	45	585	13.0	2
Brennan	45	568	12.6	2
Mack	42	360	8.6	2
Newsome	23	240	10.4	2
Hoard	10	73	7.3	0
Gainer	7	85	12.1	0
Joines	6	86	14.3	0
Galbraith	4	62	15.5	0
Talley	2	28	14.0	0
Kauric	1	21	21.0	0

PUNT RETURNS

Last Name	No.	Yds	Avg	TD
Adams	13	81	6.2	0
Brennan	9	72	8.0	0
Lewis	8	56	7.0	0
Waiters	1	0	0.0	0

KICKOFF RETURNS

Last Name	No.	Yds	Avg	TD
Metcalf	52	1052	20.2	2
Adams	3	33	11.0	0
Galbraith	3	16	5.3	0
Hoard	2	18	9.0	0
E. Johnson	2	17	8.5	0
Barnett	1	15	15.0	0
Talley	1	6	6.0	0
Gainer	1	0	0.0	0

PASSING — PUNTING — KICKING

PASSING	Att	Cmp	%	Yds	Yd/Att	TD	Int—	%	RK
Kosar	423	230	54.4	2562	6.06	10	15—	3.5	13
Pagel	148	69	46.6	819	5.53	3	8—	5.4	
Francis	2	2	100.0	26	13.00	0	0—	0.0	

PUNTING	No.	Avg.
Wagner	78	36.9

KICKING	XP	ATT	%	FG	ATT	%
Kauric	24	27	89	14	20	70

LOS ANGELES RAIDERS 12-4 Art Shell

Scores of Each Game		
14	DENVER	9
17	Seattle	13
20	PITTSBURGH	3
24	CHICAGO	10
24	Buffalo	38
24	SEATTLE	17
24	San Diego	9
7	Kansas City	9
16	GREEN BAY	29
13	Miami	10
24	KANSAS CITY	27
23	Denver	20
38	Detroit	31
24	CINCINNATI	7
28	Minnesota	24
17	SAN DIEGO	12

Use Name	Pos.	Hgt	Wgt	Age	Int	Pts
James FitzPatrick	OT	6'8"	310	26		
Rory Graves	OT	6'6"	295	27		
Tim Rother	OT	6'7"	285	24		
Bruce Wilkerson	OT	6'5"	295	26		
Steve Wright	OT-TE	6'6"	280	31		
Max Montoya	OG	6'5"	290	34		
Todd Peat	OG	6'2"	315	26		
Steve Wisniewski	OG	6'4"	280	26		
Don Mosebar	C	6'6"	280	28		
Dan Turk	C	6'4"	275	28		
Howie Long	DE-DT	6'5"	270	30		
Greg Townsend	DE	6'3"	250	28	1	6
Mike Wise	DE	6'7"	270	26		
Mike Charles	DT	6'4"	287	27		
Scott Davis	DT-DE	6'7"	270	25		
Bob Golic	DT	6'2"	275	32		
Bill Pickel	DT	6'5"	260	30		

Use Name	Pos.	Hgt	Wgt	Age	Int	Pts
Thomas Benson	LB	6'2"	240	28		
Ron Burton	LB	6'1"	245	26		
Riki Ellison	LB	6'2"	230	30	1	
Alex Gordon	LB	6'5"	245	25		
Ricky Hunley	LB	6'2"	250	29		
A.J. Jimerson	LB	6'2"	230	22		
Jerry Robinson	LB	6'2"	230	33	1	6
Aaron Wallace	LB	6'3"	230	23		
Eddie Anderson	DB	6'1"	205	27	3	
Ron Brown	DB	5'11"	190	29		
Torin Dorn	DB	6'	190	22		
Mike Harden	DB	6'1"	195	31	3	
Dan Land	DB	6'	190	25		
Garry Lewis	DB	5'11"	185	23		
Terry McDaniel	DB	5'10"	175	25	3	6
Elvis Patterson	DB	5'11"	195	29		
Lionel Washington	DB	6'	185	29	1	

Use Name	Pos.	Hgt	Wgt	Age	Int	Pts
Steve Beuerlein	QB	6'2"	205	25		
Vince Evans	QB	6'2"	205	35		
Jay Schroeder	QB	6'4"	215	29		
Marcus Allen	HB	6'2'	205	31		78
Greg Bell	HB	5'10"	210	28		6
Bo Jackson	HB	6'1"	225	27		30
Napoleon McCallum	HB	6'2"	220	26		
Vance Mueller	FB	6'	215	26		
Steve Smith	FB	6'1"	230	26		30
Tim Brown	WR	6'	195	24		18
Mervyn Fernandez	WR	6'3"	200	30		30
Willie Gault	WR	6'	180	29		18
Sam Graddy	WR	5'10"	175	26		6
Jamie Holland	WR	6'2"	195	26		
Rich Bartlewski	TE	6'5"	250	23		
Mike Dyal	TE	6'2"	240	24		
Ethan Horton	TE	6'4"	240	27		18
Andy Parker	TE	6'5"	245	28		
Jeff Gossett	K	6'2"	195	33		
Jeff Jaeger	K	5'11"	195	25		85

Mike Alexander — Knee Injury

KANSAS CITY CHIEFS 11-5 Marty Schottenheimer

Scores of Each Game		
24	MINNESOTA	21
23	Denver	24
17	Green Bay	3
34	CLEVELAND	0
19	Indianapolis	23
43	DETROIT	24
7	Seattle	19
9	L.A. RAIDERS	7
16	SEATTLE	17
27	SAN DIEGO	10
27	L.A. Raiders	24
37	New England	7
31	DENVER	20
10	HOUSTON	27
24	San Diego	21
21	Chicago	10

Use Name	Pos.	Hgt	Wgt	Age	Int	Pts
John Alt	OT	6'7"	296	28		
Rich Baldinger	OT	6'4"	291	30		
Irv Eatman	OT	6'7"	295	29		
Derrick Graham	OT	6'4"	306	23		
David Lutz	OG	6'6"	305	30		
David Szott	OG	6'4"	278	22		
Frank Winters	OG-C	6'3"	285	26		
Tim Grunhard	C	6'2"	302	22		
Mike Webster	C	6'1"	260	38		
Mike Bell	DE	6'4"	266	32		
Leonard Griffin	DE	6'4"	275	27		
Neil Smith	DE	6'4"	275	24		
Greg Meisner	DE-NT	6'3"	271	31		
Bill Maas	DE-NT	6'5"	270	28		2
Dan Saleaumua	NT	6'	285	24		6

Use Name	Pos.	Hgt	Wgt	Age	Int	Pts
Louis Cooper	LB	6'2"	245	26		
Dino Hackett	LB	6'3"	230	26		
Chris Martin	LB	6'2"	231	29		6
Rob McGovern	LB	6'2"	223	24		
Tracy Rogers	LB	6'2"	241	23		
Percy Snow	LB	6'2"	248	22	1	
Derrick Thomas	LB	6'3"	244	23		
Lloyd Burruss	DB	6'	205	32	1	
Deron Cherry	DB	5'11"	203	30	3	
Danny Copeland	DB	6'2"	210	24		
Jeff Donaldson	DB	6'	188	28	3	
Albert Lewis	DB	6'2"	198	29	2	
J.C. Pearson	DB	5'11"	190	27	1	
Stan Petry	DB	5'11"	175	24	3	6
Kevin Porter	DB	5'10"	215	24	1	
Kevin Ross	DB	5'9"	182	28	5	6
Charles Washington		6'1"	210	23		

Use Name	Pos.	Hgt	Wgt	Age	Int	Pts
Steve DeBerg	QB	6'2"	210	36		
Mike Elkins	QB	6'3"	225	24		
Steve Pelluer	QB	6'4"	212	28		
Kenny Gamble	HB	5'10"	197	25		
Bill Jones	HB	5'11"	228	23		30
Todd McNair	HB	6'1"	185	25		12
Barry Word	HB	6'2"	240	26		24
Christian Okoye	FB	6'1"	253	29		42
James Saxon	FB-HB	5'11"	215	24		
J.J. Birden	WR	5'9"	160	25		18
Emile Harry	WR	5'11"	188	27		12
Fred Jones	WR	5'9"	175	23		
Pete Mandley	WR	5'10"	195	29		
Stephone Paige	WR	6'2"	185	28		30
Robb Thomas	WR	5'11"	171	24		24
Naz Worthen	WR	5'8"	177	24		
Jonathan Hayes	TE	6'5"	239	27		6
Alfredo Roberts	TE	6'3"	250	25		
Danta Whitaker	TE	6'4"	248	26		6
Bryan Barker	K	6'1"	187	26		
Nick Lowery	K	6'4"	189	34		139

SEATTLE SEAHAWKS 9-7 Chuck Knox

Scores of Each Game		
0	Chicago	17
13	L.A. RAIDERS	17
31	Denver	* 34
31	CINCINNATI	16
33	New England	20
17	L.A. Raiders	24
19	KANSAS CITY	7
14	SAN DIEGO	31
17	Kansas City	16
21	MINNESOTA	24
13	San Diego	* 10
13	HOUSTON	* 10
20	Green Bay	14
17	Miami	24
17	DENVER	12
30	DETROIT	10

Use Name	Pos.	Hgt	Wgt	Age	Int	Pts
Andy Heck	OT	6'6"	286	23		
Ronnie Lee	OT	6'3"	295	33		
Ron Mattes	OT	6'6"	302	27		
Edwin Bailey	OG	6'4"	279	31		
Darrick Brilz	OG	6'3"	281	26		
Bryan Millard	OG	6'5"	277	29		
Joe Tofflemire	C	6'2"	273	25		
Grant Feasel	C	6'7"	279	30		
Jeff Bryant	DT-DE	6'5"	281	30		
Jacob Green	DE	6'3"	256	33		
Eric Hayes	DT	6'3"	297	22		
Cortez Kennedy	DT	6'3"	293	22		
Joe Nash	DT	6'2"	278	29		

Use Name	Pos.	Hgt	Wgt	Age	Int	Pts
Dave Ahrens	LB	6'4"	247	31		
Ricky Andrews	LB	6'2"	236	24		
Ned Bolcar	LB	6'1"	245	23	1	
Joe Cain	LB	6'1"	228	25		
Darren Comeaux	LB	6'1"	227	30		
Donald Miller	LB	6'2"	223	26		
Richard Newbill (from MIN)	LB	6'1"	240	22		
Rufus Porter	LB	6'1"	207	25		
Rod Stephens	LB	6'1"	237	24		
Terry Wooden	LB	6'3"	232	23		
Tony Woods	LB	6'4"	244	24		
David Wyman	LB	6'2"	234	26	1	
Robert Blackmon	DB	6'	198	23		
Nesby Glasgow	DB	5'10"	187	33		
Dwayne Harper	DB	5'11"	165	24	3	
Patrick Hunter	DB	5'11"	185	25	1	
James Jefferson	DB	6'1"	199	26	1	
Melvin Jenkins	DB	5'10"	173	28	1	
Thom Kaumeyer	DB	5'11"	187	23		
Vann McElroy (from RAID)	DB	6'2"	190	30		
Eugene Robinson	DB	6'	183	27	3	6

Use Name	Pos.	Hgt	Wgt	Age	Int	Pts
Jeff Kemp	QB	6'	198	31		
Dave Krieg	QB	6'1"	192	31		
Kelly Stouffer	QB	6'3"	210	26		
Derrick Fenner	HB	6'3"	228	23		90
Derek Loville	HB	5'9"	196	22		
Chris Warren	HB	6'2"	225	23		6
James Jones	FB	6'2"	230	29		
John L. Williams	FB	5'11"	226	25		18
Brian Blades	WR	5'11	182	25		18
Jeff Chadwick	WR	6'3"	190	30		24
Louis Clark	WR	6'1"	193	26		
Tommy Kane	WR	5'11"	180	26		24
Paul Skansi	WR	5'11"	184	29		12
Ron Heller	TE	6'3"	242	26		6
Trey Junkin	TE	6'2"	240	29		
Travis McNeal	TE	6'3"	248	23		
Mike Tice	TE	6'7"	247	31		
Rick Donnelly	K	6'	209	28		
Norm Johnson	K	6'2"	197	30		102

SAN DIEGO CHARGERS 6-10 Dan Hening

Scores of Each Game		
14	Dallas	17
16	CINCINNATI	21
24	Cleveland	14
7	HOUSTON	17
14	Pittsburgh	36
39	N.Y. Jets	3
9	L.A. RAIDERS	24
41	TAMPA BAY	10
31	Seattle	14
19	DENVER	7
10	Kansas City	27
10	SEATTLE	* 13
38	N.Y. JETS	17
10	Denver	20
21	KANSAS CITY	24
12	L.A. Raiders	17

Use Name	Pos.	Hgt	Wgt	Age	Int	Pts
Eric Floyd	OT	6'5"	300	24		
Leo Goeas	OT	6'4"	285	24		
Joel Patten	OT	6'7"	307	32		
Courtney Hall	OG-C	6'2"	269	22		
David Richards	OG	6'5"	310	24		
Broderick Thompson	OG	6'5"	295	30		
Tom Toth	OG	6'5"	282	28		
Mike Zandofsky	OG	6'2"	285	24		
Frank Cornish	C	6'4"	295	22		
Mark Rodenhauser	C	6'5"	263	29		
Burt Grossman	DE	6'6"	255	23		2
George Hinkle	DE-NT	6'5"	267	25		
Gerald Robinson	DE	6'3"	262	27		
Lee Williams	DE	6'6"	271	27		
Les Miller	NT	6'7"	300	25		12
Joe Phillips	NT	6'5"	300	27		
Tony Savage	NT	6'3"	300	23		

Mike Simmonds — Knee Injury

Use Name	Pos.	Hgt	Wgt	Age	Int	Pts
Richard Brown	LB	6'3"	240	24		
Steve Hendrickson	LB	6'	250	24		
Cedric Figaro	LB	6'2"	250	24		
Jeff Mills (to DEN)	LB	6'3"	241	21		
Leslie O'Neal	LB	6'4"	259	26		
Gary Plummer	LB	6'2"	240	30		12
Henry Rolling	LB	6'2"	225	24	1	
Junior Seau	LB	6'3"	250	21		
Billy Ray Smith	LB	6'3"	236	29		
Martin Bayless	DB	6'2"	212	27	1	
Gill Byrd	DB	5'11"	198	29	7	
Donnie Elder	DB	5'9"	178	26	1	
Donald Frank	DB	6'	200	24	2	
Joe Fuller	DB	5'11"	180	25	1	
Vencie Glenn	DB	6'	192	25	1	
Lester Lyles	DB	6'3"	200	27	1	
Sam Seale	DB	5'9"	185	27	2	
Anthony Shelton	DB	6'1"	195	22		

David Brandon — Knee Injury

Use Name	Pos.	Hgt	Wgt	Age	Int	Pts
John Friesz	QB	6'4"	209	23		
Billy Joe Tolliver	QB	6'1"	218	25		
Mark Vlasic	QB	6'3"	206	26		
Rod Bernstine	HB-FB	6'3"	238	25		24
Ronnie Harmon	HB	5'11"	200	26		12
Jerry Mays	HB	5'7"	176	22		
Darrin Nelson	HB	5'9"	184	30		
Marion Butts	FB	6'1"	248	24		48
Joe Mickles	FB	5'10"	221	24		
Tim Spencer	FB	6'2"	223	29		
Nate Lewis	WR	5'11"	189	23		18
Quinn Early	WR	6'	188	25		6
Anthony Miller	WR	5'11"	185	25		42
Kitrick Taylor	WR	5'10"	191	26		6
Walter Wilson	WR	5'10"	185	23		
Derrick Walker	TE	6'1"	244	23		6
Joe Caravello	TE	6'3"	270	27		6
Arthur Cox	TE	6'2"	277	29		6
Craig McEwen	TE	6'1"	220	24		18
Terry Orr (from WAS)	TE	6'2"	235	28		
John Carney (from LA)	K	5'11"	170	26		84
John Kidd	K	6'3"	208	29		

Wayne Walker — Knee Injury

DENVER BRONCOS 5-11 Dan Reeves

Scores of Each Game		
9	L.A. Raiders	14
24	KANSAS CITY	23
34	SEATTLE	* 31
28	Buffalo	29
29	CLEVELAND	30
17	PITTSBURGH	34
27	Indianapolis	17
22	Minnesota	27
7	San Diego	19
13	CHICAGO	* 16
27	Detroit	40
20	L.A. RAIDERS	23
20	Kansas City	31
20	SAN DIEGO	10
12	Seattle	17
22	GREEN BAY	13

Use Name	Pos.	Hgt	Wgt	Age	Int	Pts
Darrell Hamilton	OT	6'5"	298	25		
Ken Lanier	OT	6'3"	290	31		
Gerald Perry	OT	6'6"	305	24		
Dave Widell	OT	6'6"	292	25		
Scott Beavers	OG	6'4"	277	23		
Jeff Davidson	OG	6'5"	309	22		
Sean Farrell	OG	6'3"	260	30		
Jim Juriga	OG	6'6"	275	25		
Doug Widell	OG	6'4"	287	23		
Keith Kartz	C	6'4"	270	27		
David Galloway	DE	6'3"	265	31		
Ron Holmes	DE	6'4"	265	27		
Jake McCullough	DE	6'5"	270	25		
Warren Powers	DE	6'6"	287	25		
Jim Szymanski	DE	6'5"	268	23		
Andre Townsend	DE-NT	6'3"	265	27		
Greg Kragen	NT	6'3"	265	28		

Alphonso Carreker — Knee Injury
Monte Smith — Foot Injury

Use Name	Pos.	Hgt	Wgt	Age	Int	Pts
Ty Allert (to SEA)	LB	6'2"	238	27		
Michael Brooks	LB	6'1"	235	25		
Scott Curtis	LB	6'1"	230	25		
Rick Dennison	LB	6'3"	220	32		
Simon Fletcher	LB	6'5"	240	28		2
Ronnie Haliburton	LB	6'4"	230	22		
Tim Lucas	LB	6'3"	230	29		
Karl Mecklenburg	LB	6'3"	240	30		8
Marc Munford	LB	6'2"	231	25		
Anthony Thompson	LB	6'1"	227	23		
Steve Atwater	DB	6'3"	217	23	2	
Tyrone Braxton	DB	5'11"	174	25	1	
Kevin Clark	DB	5'10"	185	26		
Kip Corrington	DB	6'	175	25		
Wymon Henderson	DB	5'10"	186	28	2	6
Le-Lo Lang	DB	5'11"	185	23	1	
Alton Montgomery	DB	6'	195	22	2	
Bruce Plummer (to SF)	DB	6'1"	203	26	1	
Randy Robbins	DB	6'2"	189	26		
Dennis Smith	DB	6'3"	200	31	1	
Elliott Smith	DB	6'2"	192	22		

Use Name	Pos.	Hgt	Wgt	Age	Int	Pts
John Elway	QB	6'3"	210	30		18
Gary Kubiak	QB	6'	192	29		
Blake Ezor	HB	5'9"	183	22		
Bobby Humphrey	HB	6'1"	201	23		42
Melvin Bratton	FB	6'1"	225	25		24
Kerry Porter	FB	6'1"	220	25		
Sammy Winder	FB	5'11"	203	31		12
Steve Sewell	FB-WR	6'3"	210	27		18
Mark Jackson	WR	5'10"	180	27		30
Vance Johnson	WR	5'11"	185	27		18
Ricky Nattiel	WR	5'9"	180	24		12
Shannon Sharpe	WR-TE	6'2"	225	22		6
Tim Stallworth	WR	5'10"	185	24		
Michael Young	WR	6'1"	183	28		24
Clarence Kay	TE	6'2"	237	29		
Orson Mobley (to IND)	TE	6'5"	256	27		
Chris Verhulst	TE	6'2"	249	24		
Mike Horan	K	5'11"	190	31		
David Treadwell	K	6'1"	175	23		109

LOS ANGELES RAIDERS

RUSHING

Last Name	No.	Yds	Avg	TD
Jackson	125	698	5.6	5
Allen	179	682	3.8	12
Smith	81	327	4.0	2
Bell	47	164	3.5	1
Schroeder	37	81	2.2	0
Mueller	13	43	3.3	0
McCallum	10	25	2.5	0
Fernandez	3	10	3.3	0
Evans	1	-2	-2.0	0

RECEIVING

Last Name	No.	Yds	Avg	TD
Fernandez	52	839	16.1	5
Gault	50	985	19.7	3
Horton	33	404	12.2	3
T. Brown	18	265	14.7	3
Allen	15	189	12.6	1
Jackson	6	68	11.3	0
Smith	4	30	7.5	3
Dyal	3	51	17.0	0
Graddy	1	47	47.0	1
Bell	1	7	7.0	0

PUNT RETURNS

Last Name	No.	Yds	Avg	TD
T. Brown	34	295	8.7	0

KICKOFF RETURNS

Last Name	No.	Yds	Avg	TD
Holland	32	655	20.5	0
R. Brown	30	575	19.2	0
McCallum	1	7	7.0	0
Turk	1	0	0.0	0

PASSING — PUNTING — KICKING

PASSING	Att	Cmp	%	Yds	Yd/Att	TD	Int— %	RK
Schroeder	334	182	54.5	2849	8.53	19	9—2.7	4
Evans	1	1	100.0	36	36.00	0	0—0.0	
Allen	1	0	0.0	0	0.00	0	1—100.0	

PUNTING	No.	Avg.
Gossett	62	37.3

KICKING	XP	ATT	%	FG	ATT	%
Jaeger	40	42	95	15	20	75

KANSAS CITY CHIEFS

RUSHING

Last Name	No.	Yds	Avg	TD
Word	204	1015	5.0	4
Okoye	245	805	3.3	7
McNair	14	61	4.4	0
B. Jones	10	47	4.7	0
Saxon	3	15	5.0	0
Pelluer	5	6	1.2	0
F. Jones	1	-1	-1.0	0
DeBerg	21	-5	-0.2	0

RECEIVING

Last Name	No.	Yds	Avg	TD
Paige	65	1021	15.7	5
R. Thomas	41	545	13.3	4
Harry	41	519	12.7	2
McNair	40	507	12.7	2
B. Jones	19	137	7.2	5
Birden	15	352	23.5	3
Roberts	11	119	10.8	0
Hayes	9	83	9.2	1
Mandley	7	97	13.9	0
Word	4	28	7.0	0
Okoye	4	23	5.8	0
Whitaker	2	17	8.5	1
F. Jones	1	5	5.0	0
Saxon	1	5	5.0	0

PUNT RETURNS

Last Name	No.	Yds	Avg	TD
Worthen	25	180	7.2	0
Birden	10	72	7.2	0
Harry	1	2	2.0	0
Whitaker	1	0	0.0	0

KICKOFF RETURNS

Last Name	No.	Yds	Avg	TD
McNair	14	227	16.2	0
Worthen	11	226	20.5	0
F. Jones	9	175	19.4	0
Saxon	5	81	16.2	0
Mandley	4	51	12.8	0
Birden	1	14	14.0	0
Word	1	10	10.0	0
Roberts	1	0	0.0	0

PASSING — PUNTING — KICKING

PASSING	Att	Cmp	%	Yds	Yd/Att	TD	Int— %	RK
DeBerg	444	258	58.1	3444	7.76	23	4—0.9	3
Pelluer	5	2	40.0	14	2.80	0	1—20.0	

PUNTING	No.	Avg.
Barker	64	38.7

KICKING	XP	Att.	%	FG	Att	%
Lowery	37	38	97	34	37	92

SEATTLE SEAHAWKS

RUSHING

Last Name	No.	Yds	Avg	TD
Fenner	215	859	4.0	14
Williams	187	714	3.8	3
Krieg	32	115	3.6	0
Jones	5	20	4.0	0
Blades	3	19	6.3	0
Loville	7	12	1.7	0
Warren	6	11	1.8	1
McNeal	1	2	2.0	0
Chadwick	1	-3	-3.0	0

RECEIVING

Last Name	No.	Yds	Avg	TD
Williams	73	699	9.6	0
Kane	52	776	14.9	4
Blades	49	525	10.7	3
Chadwick	27	478	17.7	4
Skansi	22	257	11.7	2
Fenner	17	143	8.4	1
Heller	13	157	12.1	1
McNeal	10	143	14.3	0
Jones	1	22	22.0	0
Krieg	1	-6	-6.0	0

PUNT RETURNS

Last Name	No.	Yds	Avg	TD
Warren	28	269	9.6	0
Jefferson	8	68	8.5	0

KICKOFF RETURNS

Last Name	No.	Yds	Avg	TD
Warren	23	478	20.8	0
Loville	18	359	19.9	0
Jefferson	4	96	24.0	0
McNeal	2	29	14.5	0
Jones	2	21	10.5	0
Glasgow	1	2	2.0	0

PASSING — PUNTING — KICKING

PASSING	Att	Cmp	%	Yds	Yd/Att	TD	Int— %	RK
Krieg	448	265	59.2	3194	7.13	15	20—4.5	11

PUNTING	No.	Avg.
Donnelley	67	40.6

KICKING	XP	ATT	%	FG	ATT	%
N. Johnson	33	34	97	23	32	72

SAN DIEGO CHARGERS

RUSHING

Last Name	No.	Yds	Avg	TD
Butts	265	1225	4.6	8
Bernstine	124	589	4.8	4
Harmon	66	363	5.5	0
Lewis	4	25	6.3	1
Tolliver	14	22	1.6	0
Nelson	3	14	4.7	0
A. Miller	3	13	4.3	0
Friesz	1	3	3.0	0
Plummer	2	3	1.5	1
Vlasic	1	0	0.0	0
Wilson	1	0	0.0	0

RECEIVING

Last Name	No.	Yds	Avg	TD
A. Miller	63	933	14.8	7
Harmon	46	511	11.1	2
McEwen	29	325	11.2	3
Walker	23	240	10.4	1
Butts	16	117	7.3	0
Early	15	238	15.9	1
Lewis	14	192	13.7	1
Cox	14	93	6.6	1
Wilson	10	87	8.7	0
Bernstine	8	40	5.0	0
Nelson	4	29	7.3	0
Caravello	2	21	10.5	1
Hendrickson	1	12	12.0	0
Plummer	1	2	2.0	1

PUNT RETURNS

Last Name	No.	Yds	Avg	TD
Lewis	13	117	9.0	1
Mays	7	30	4.3	0
Taylor	6	112	18.7	1
Nelson	3	44	14.7	0
Lyles	1	0	0.0	0

KICKOFF RETURNS

Last Name	No.	Yds	Avg	TD
Elder	24	571	23.8	0
Lewis	17	383	22.5	0
Frank	8	172	21.5	0
Nelson	4	36	9.0	0
A. Miller	1	13	13.0	0
Orr	1	13	13.0	0

PASSING — PUNTING — KICKING

PASSING	Att	Cmp	%	Yds	Yd/Att	TD	Int— %	RK
Tolliver	410	216	52.7	2574	6.28	16	16—3.09	12
Vlasic	40	19	47.5	168	4.20	1	2—5.0	
Friesz	22	11	50.0	98	4.45	1	1—4.5	

PUNTING	No.	Avg.
Kidd	62	39.4

KICKING	XP	Att	%	FG	Att	%
Carney	27	28	96	19	21	90

DENVER BRONCOS

RUSHING

Last Name	No.	Yds	Avg	TD
Humphrey	288	1202	4.2	7
Elway	50	258	5.2	3
Winder	42	120	2.9	2
Bratton	27	82	3.0	3
Ezor	23	81	3.5	0
Kubiak	9	52	5.8	0
Sewell	17	46	2.7	3
Jackson	5	28	5.6	1
Porter	1	3	3.0	0

RECEIVING

Last Name	No.	Yds	Avg	TD
Jackson	57	926	16.2	4
Johnson	54	747	13.8	3
Kay	29	282	9.7	0
Bratton	29	276	9.5	1
Young	28	385	13.8	4
Sewell	26	268	10.3	0
Humphrey	24	152	6.3	0
Nattiel	18	297	16.5	2
Winder	17	145	8.5	0
Mobley	8	41	5.1	0
Sharpe	7	99	14.1	1
Porter	4	44	11.0	0
Verhulst	3	13	4.3	0
Lanier	1	-4	-4.0	0

PUNT RETURNS

Last Name	No.	Yds	Avg	TD
Clark	21	159	7.6	0
Johnson	11	92	8.4	0
Nattiel	1	5	5.0	0

KICKOFF RETURNS

Last Name	No.	Yds	Avg	TD
Clark	20	505	25.3	0
Montgomery	14	286	20.4	0
Ezor	13	214	16.5	0
Johnson	6	126	21.0	0
Winder	4	55	13.8	0
Bratton	3	37	12.3	0
Jackson	1	18	18.0	0
Kay	2	10	5.0	0
Mobley	1	9	9.0	0
Nattiel	1	0	0.0	0
Atwater	1	0	0.0	0

PASSING — PUNTING — KICKING

PASSING	Att	Cmp	%	Yds	Yd/Att	TD	Int— %	RK
Elway	502	294	58.6	3526	7.02	15	14—2.87	
Kubiak	22	11	50.0	145	6.59	0	4—18.2	
Humphrey	2	0	0.0	0	0.00	0	0—0.0	
Sewell	1	0	0.0	0	0.00	0	0—0.0	

PUNTING	No.	Avg.
Horan	59	43.6
Elway	1	37.0

KICKING	XP	ATT	%	FG	ATT	%
Treadwell	34	36	94	25	34	74

1990 A.F.C. PLAYOFFS — FIRST ROUND

January 5, 1991 at Miami (Attendance 67,276)

SCORING

KANSAS CITY	3	7	6	0	- 16
MIAMI	0	3	0	14	- 17

First Quarter
K.C. — Lowery, 27 yard field goal

Second Quarter
Mia. — Stoyanovich, 58 yard field goal
K.C. — Paige, 26 yard pass from DeBerg
PAT — Lowery (kick)

Third Quarter
K.C. — Lowery, 25 yard field goal
K.C. — Lowery, 38 yard field goal

Fourth Quarter
Mia. — Paige, 1 yard pass from Marino
PAT — Stoyanovich (kick)
Mia. — Clayton, 12 yard pass from Marino
PAT — Stoyanovich (kick)

TEAMSTATISTICS

K.C.		MIA.
15	First Downs- Total	23
4	First Downs- Rushing	7
11	First Downs- Passing	14
1	First Downs- Penalty	2
0	Fumbles- Number	2
0	Fumbles- Lost Ball	2
4	Penalties- Number	2
35	Yards Penalized	22
1	Missed Field Goals	1
55	Offensive Plays	64
367	Net Yards	311
6.7	Average Gain	4.8
1	Giveaways	2
2	Takeaways	1
+ 1	Difference	- 1

INDIVIDUALSTATISTICS

RUSHING

KANSAS CITY	No.	Yds.	Avg.	MIAMI	No.	Yds.	Avg.
Okoye	13	83	6.4	Smith	20	82	4.1
Word	9	13	1.4	Logan	7	17	2.4
McNair	2	7	3.5	Paige	1	2	2.0
	24	103	4.3	Marino	4	-3	-0.8
					32	98	3.1

RECEIVING

KANSAS CITY	No.	Yds.	Avg.	MIAMI	No.	Yds.	Avg.
Paige	8	142	17.8	Clayton	5	66	13.2
McNair	3	22	7.3	Paige	5	30	6.0
Harry	2	59	29.5	Duper	3	36	12.0
Roberts	2	26	13.0	Edmunds	2	49	24.5
R. Thomas	1	15	15.0	Smith	2	22	11.0
Hayes	1	5	5.0	Jensen	1	11	11.0
	17	269	15.8	Martin	1	7	7.0
					19	221	11.6

PUNTING

KANSAS CITY	No.	Yds.	Avg.	MIAMI	No.	Yds.	Avg.
Barker	4		35.0	Roby	2		59.5

PUNT RETURNS

KANSAS CITY	No.	Yds.	Avg.	MIAMI	No.	Yds.	Avg.
Harry	2	16	8.0				

KICKOFF RETURNS

KANSAS CITY	No.	Yds.	Avg.	MIAMI	No.	Yds.	Avg.
F. Jones	3	59	19.7	Pruitt	2	18	9.0
				Logan	1	24	24.0
					3	42	14.0

INTERCEPTION RETURNS

KANSAS CITY	No.	Yds.	Avg.	MIAMI	No.	Yds.	Avg.
None				Williams	1	0	0.0

PASSING

	Att.	Comp.	Comp. Pct.	Yds.	Int.	Yds./ Att.	Yds./ Comp.
KANSAS CITY							
DeBerg	30	17	56.7	269	1	9.0	15.8
MIAMI							
Marino	30	19	63.3	221	0	7.4	11.6

January 6, 1991 at Cincinnati (Attendance 60,012)

SCORING

HOUSTON	0	0	7	7	- 14
CINCINNATI	10	10	14	7	- 41

First Quarter
Cin. — Woods, 1 yard run
PAT — Breech (kick)
Cin. — Breech, 27 yard field goal

Second Quarter
Cin. — Green, 2 yard pass from Esiason
PAT — Breech (kick)
Cin. — Breech, 30 yard field goal

Third Quarter
Cin. — Ball, 3 yard run
PAT — Breech (kick)
Cin. — Esiason, 10 yard run
PAT — Breech (kick)
Hous. — Givins, 16 yard pass from Carlson
PAT — Garcia (kick)

Fourth Quarter
Cin. — Kattus, 9 yard pass from Esiason
PAT — Breech (kick)
Hous. — Givins, 5 yard pass from Carlson
PAT — Garcia (kick)

TEAMSTATISTICS

HOU.		CIN.
13	First Downs- Total	24
4	First Downs- Rushing	15
9	First Downs- Passing	7
0	First Downs- Penalty	2
2	Fumbles- Number	1
1	Fumbles- Lost Ball	0
5	Penalties- Number	4
33	Yards Penalized	40
0	Missed Field Goals	0
47	Offensive Plays	69
226	Net Yards	349
4.8	Average Gain	5.1
2	Giveaways	0
0	Takeaways	2
- 2	Difference	+ 2

INDIVIDUALSTATISTICS

RUSHING

HOUSTON	No.	Yds.	Avg.	CINCINNATI	No.	Yds.	Avg.
White	4	2	0.5	Woods	6	11	1.8
Carlson	4	22	5.5	Brooks	6	17	2.8
Pinkett	5	43	8.6	Esiason	5	57	11.4
	13	67	5.2	Ball	7	33	4.7
				Green	11	55	5.0
				Jennings	6	16	2.7
				Wilhelm	3	-2	-0.7
					44	187	4.3

RECEIVING

HOUSTON	No.	Yds.	Avg.	CINCINNATI	No.	Yds.	Avg.
Givins	6	60	10.0	Holman	2	51	25.5
Harris	4	37	9.3	McGee	2	23	11.5
Jeffires	2	33	16.5	Kattus	2	19	9.5
Duncan	1	15	15.0	Jennings	2	15	7.5
Pinkett	1	10	10.0	Green	2	15	7.5
White	1	5	5.0	Brown	2	14	7.0
Hill	1	5	5.0	Woods	2	13	6.5
	16	165	10.3	Barber	1	12	12.0
					15	162	10.8

PUNTING

HOUSTON	No.	Yds.	Avg.	CINCINNATI	No.	Yds.	Avg.
Montgomery	6		42.6	Johnson	3		45.0

PUNT RETURNS

HOUSTON	No.	Yds.	Avg.	CINCINNATI	No.	Yds.	Avg.
McNeil	1	19	19.0	Price	3	42	14.0

KICKOFF RETURNS

HOUSTON	No.	Yds.	Avg.	CINCINNATI	No.	Yds.	Avg.
Ford	3	57	19.0	Ball	1	28	28.0
Pinkett	2	48	24.0	Jennings	1	18	18.0
Norgard	1	9	9.0	Brown	1	12	12.0
	6	114	19.0		3	58	19.3

INTERCEPTION RETURNS

HOUSTON	No.	Yds.	Avg.	CINCINNATI	No.	Yds.	Avg.
None				Fulcher	1	43	43.0

PASSING

	Att.	Comp.	Comp. Pct.	Yds.	Int.	Yds./ Att.	Yds./ Comp.
HOUSTON							
Carlson	33	16	48.5	165	1	5.0	10.3
CINCINNATI							
Esiason	20	14	70.0	150	0	7.5	10.7
Wilhelm	5	1	20.0	12	0	2.4	12.0
	25	15	60.0	162	0	6.5	10.8

1990 N.F.C. PLAYOFFS — FIRST ROUND

January 5, 1991 at Philadelphia (Attendance 65,287)

SCORING

WASHINGTON	0	10	10	0	- 20
PHILADELPHIA	3	3	0	0	- 6

First Quarter
Phil. Ruzek, 37 yard field goal

Second Quarter
Phil. Ruzek, 28 yard field goal
Wash. Monk, 16 yard pass from Rypien
PAT — Lohmiller (kick)
Wash. Lohmiller, 20 yard field goal

Third Quarter
Wash. Lohmiller, 19 yard field goal
Wash. Clark, 3 yard pass from Rypien
PAT — Lohmiller (kick)

TEAMSTATISTICS

WASH.		PHIL.
15	First Downs- Total	16
3	First Downs- Rushing	6
12	First Downs- Passing	8
0	First Downs- Penalty	2
2	Fumbles- Number	2
1	Fumbles- Lost Ball	2
3	Penalties- Number	4
23	Yards Penalized	40
0	Missed Field Goals	0
66	Offensive Plays	65
299	Net Yards	318
4.5	Average Gain	4.9
2	Giveaways	3
3	Takeaways	2
+1	Difference	-1

INDIVIDUALSTATISTICS

RUSHING

WASHINGTON	No.	Yds.	Avg.	PHILADELPHIA	No.	Yds.	Avg.
Byner	18	49	2.7	Sherman	17	53	3.1
Riggs	14	45	3.2	Cunningham	7	80	11.4
Sanders	1	3	3.0	Toney	2	3	1.5
Rypien	2	-4	-2.0	Sanders	2	12	6.0
	35	93	2.7		28	148	5.3

RECEIVING

WASHINGTON	No.	Yds.	Avg.	PHILADELPHIA	No.	Yds.	Avg.
Sanders	2	22	11.0	Kei. Jackson	5	116	23.2
Clark	4	63	15.8	Sherman	2	15	7.5
Monk	2	44	22.0	Byars	2	18	9.0
Byner	7	77	11.0	Williams	1	9	9.0
	15	206	13.7	Sanders	5	47	9.4
					15	205	13.7

PUNTING

WASHINGTON	No.	Yds.	Avg.	PHILADELPHIA	No.	Yds.	Avg.
Goodburn	9		36.9	Feagles	7		39.1

PUNT RETURNS

WASHINGTON	No.	Yds.	Avg.	PHILADELPHIA	No.	Yds.	Avg.
Howard	0	0	0.0	Harris	4	33	8.3
Green	1	10	10.0				
Mitchell	4	31	7.8				
	5	41	8.2				

KICKOFF RETURNS

WASHINGTON	No.	Yds.	Avg.	PHILADELPHIA	No.	Yds.	Avg.
Mitchell	1	17	17.0	Sanders	4	52	13.0
Howard	2	21	10.5				
	3	38	12.7				

INTERCEPTION RETURNS

WASHINGTON	No.	Yds.	Avg.	PHILADELPHIA	No.	Yds.	Avg.
Green	1	0	0.0	Allen	1	3	3.0

PASSING

WASHINGTON

	Att.	Comp.	Comp. Pct.	Yds.	Int.	Yds./ Att.	Yds./ Comp.
Rypien	31	15	48.4	206	1	6.6	13.7

PHILADELPHIA

	Att.	Comp.	Comp. Pct.	Yds.	Int.	Yds./ Att.	Yds./ Comp.
Cunningham	29	15	51.7	205	1	7.1	13.7
McMahon	3	0	0.0	0	0	0.0	0.0
	32	15	46.9	205	1	6.4	13.7

January 6, 1991 at Chicago (Attendance 60,767)

SCORING

NEW ORLEANS	0	3	0	3	- 6
CHICAGO	3	7	3	3	- 16

First Quarter
Chi. Butler, 19 yard field goal

Second Quarter
Chi. Thornton, 18 yard pass from Tomczak
PAT — Butler (kick)
N.O. Andersen, 47 yard field goal

Third Quarter
Chi. Butler, 22 yard field goal

Fourth Quarter
N.O. Andersen, 38 yard field goal
Chi. Butler, 21 yard field goal

TEAMSTATISTICS

N.O.		CHI.
11	First Downs- Total	18
2	First Downs- Rushing	9
7	First Downs- Passing	8
2	First Downs- Penalty	1
1	Fumbles- Number	2
0	Fumbles- Lost Ball	1
2	Penalties- Number	7
10	Yards Penalized	57
1	Missed Field Goals	1
54	Offensive Plays	71
193	Net Yards	365
3.6	Average Gain	5.1
3	Giveaways	1
1	Takeaways	3
-2	Difference	+2

INDIVIDUALSTATISTICS

RUSHING

NEW ORLEANS	No.	Yds.	Avg.	CHICAGO	No.	Yds.	Avg.
Heyward	4	10	2.5	Anderson	27	102	3.8
Fenerty	8	29	3.6	Muster	12	71	5.9
Fourcade	2	13	6.5	Tomczak	2	8	4.0
Hilliard	4	13	3.3	Green	2	8	4.0
	18	65	3.6		43	189	4.4

RECEIVING

NEW ORLEANS	No.	Yds.	Avg.	CHICAGO	No.	Yds.	Avg.
Fenerty	4	22	5.5	Anderson	4	42	10.5
Martin	2	47	23.5	Thornton	2	43	21.5
Scales	1	31	31.0	Gentry	2	41	20.5
Tice	1	19	19.0	Morris	2	28	14.0
Brenner	1	17	17.0	Muster	2	21	10.5
Perriman	1	11	11.0	Davis	1	13	13.0
Turner	1	6	6.0		13	175	13.5
	11	153	13.9				

PUNTING

NEW ORLEANS	No.	Yds.	Avg.	CHICAGO	No.	Yds.	Avg.
Barnhardt	3		30.0	Buford	2		27.5

PUNT RETURNS

NEW ORLEANS	No.	Yds.	Avg.	CHICAGO	No.	Yds.	Avg.
Buck	1	2	2.0	Bailey	1	13	13.0
				Jackson	1	0	0.0
					2	13	6.5

KICKOFF RETURNS

NEW ORLEANS	No.	Yds.	Avg.	CHICAGO	No.	Yds.	Avg.
Fenerty	2	33	16.5	Gentry	1	39	39.0
Hilliard	1	21	21.0				
Jordan	1	17	17.0				
Heyward	1	14	14.0				
	5	85	17.0				

INTERCEPTION RETURNS

NEW ORLEANS	No.	Yds.	Avg.	CHICAGO	No.	Yds.	Avg.
None				Mangum	1	9	9.0
				Gayle	1	27	27.0
				Carrier	1	0	0.0
					3	36	12.0

PASSING

NEW ORLEANS

	Att.	Comp.	Comp. Pct.	Yds.	Int.	Yds./ Att.	Yds./ Comp.
Walsh	16	6	37.5	74	1	4.6	12.3
Fourcade	18	5	2.8	79	2	4.4	15.8
	34	11	32.4	153	3	4.5	13.9

CHICAGO

	Att.	Comp.	Comp. Pct.	Yds.	Int.	Yds./ Att.	Yds./ Comp.
Tomczak	25	12	48.0	166	0	6.4	13.8
Anderson	1	1	100.0	22	0	22.0	22.0
	26	13	50.0	188	0	7.2	13.8

1990 A.F.C. PLAYOFFS — SECOND ROUND

January 12, 1991 at Orchard Park, N.Y. (Attendance 77,087)

SCORING

MIAMI	3	14	3	14	- 34
BUFFALO	13	14	3	14	- 44

First Quarter

Buff.	Reed, 40 yard pass from Kelly PAT — Norwood (kick)
Mia.	Stoyanovich, 49 yard field goal
Buff.	Norwood, 40 yard field goal
Buff.	Norwood, 22 yard field goal

Second Quarter

Buff.	Thomas, 5 yard run PAT — Norwood (kick)
Mia.	Duper, 64 yard pass from Marino PAT — Stoyanovich (kick)
Buff.	Lofton, 13 yardd pass from Kelly PAT — Norwood (kick)
Mia.	Marino, 2 yard run PAT — Stoyanovich (kick)

Third Quarter

Mia.	Stoyanovich, 22 yard field goal
Buff.	Norwood, 28 yard field goal
Mia.	Foster, 2 yard pass from Marino PAT — Stoyanovich (kick)

Fourth Quarter

Buff.	Thomas, 5 yard run PAT — Norwood (kick)
Buff.	Reed , 26 yard pass from Kelly PAT — Norwood (kick)
Mia.	Martin, 8 yard pass from Marino PAT — Stoyanovich (kick)

TEAMSTATISTICS

MIA.		BUFF.
24	First Downs- Total	24
9	First Downs- Rushing	7
13	First Downs- Passing	16
2	First Downs- Penalty	1
1	Fumbles- Number	3
1	Fumbles- Lost Ball	1
4	Penalties- Number	4
32	Yards Penalized	30
0	Missed Field Goals	0
76	Offensive Plays	66
430	Net Yards	493
5.6	Average Gain	7.5
3	Giveaways	2
2	Takeaways	3
-1	Difference	+1

INDIVIDUALSTATISTICS

MIAMI	No.	Yds.	Avg.	BUFFALO	No.	Yds.	Avg.
RUSHING							
Smith	21	99	4.7	Thomas	32	117	3.7
Logan	5	6	1.2	Kelly	5	37	7.4
Marino	1	2	2.0		37	154	4.2
	27	107	3.9				
RECEIVING							
Clayton	4	82	20.5	Lofton	7	149	21.3
Martin	4	44	11.0	Reed	4	123	30.8
Jensen	4	38	9.5	Thomas	3	38	12.7
Duper	3	113	37.7	McKeller	3	15	5.0
Edmunds	3	21	7.0	Edwards	1	12	12.0
Logan	2	8	4.0	K. Davis	1	3	3.0
Smith	1	9	9.0		19	339	17.8
Paige	1	6	6.0				
Foster	1	2	2.0				
	23	323	14.0				
PUNTING							
Roby	2		40.0	Tuten	1		47.0
PUNT RETURNS							
Clayton	1	3	3.0	Edwards	2	17	8.5
KICKOFF RETURNS							
Logan	8	138	17.3	D. Smith	3	51	17.0
Adams	1	13	13.0	Edwards	2	51	25.5
	9	151	16.8	Rolle	1	14	14.0
					6	116	19.3
INTERCEPTION RETURNS							
Williams	1	0	0.0	Odomes	1	9	9.0
				Kelso	1	0	0.0
					2	9	4.5

PASSING

	Att.	Comp.	Comp. Pct.	Yds.	Int.	Yds./ Att.	Yds./ Comp.
MIAMI							
Marino	49	23	46.9	323	2	6.6	14.0
BUFFALO							
Kelly	29	19	65.5	339	1	11.7	17.8

January 13, 1991 at Los Angeles (Attendance 92,045)

SCORING

CINCINNATI	0	3	0	7	- 10
L.A. RAIDERS	0	7	3	10	- 20

Second Quarter

Cin.	Breech, 27 yard field goal
L.A.	Fernandez, 13 yard pass from Schroeder PAT — Jaeger (kick)

Third Quarter

L.A.	Jaeger, 49 yard field goal

Fourth Quarter

Cin.	Jennings, 8 yard pass from Esiason PAT — Breech (kick)
L.A.	Horton, 41 yard pass from Schroeder PAT — Jaeger (kick)
L.A.	Jaeger, 25 yard field goal

TEAMSTATISTICS

CIN.		L.A.
12	First Downs- Total	20
7	First Downs- Rushing	11
5	First Downs- Passing	9
0	First Downs- Penalty	0
1	Fumbles- Number	0
0	Fumbles- Lost Ball	0
1	Penalties- Number	0
5	Yards Penalized	0
0	Missed Field Goals	0
48	Offensive Plays	56
182	Net Yards	389
3.8	Average Gain	6.9
0	Giveaways	1
1	Takeaways	0
+1	Difference	-1

INDIVIDUALSTATISTICS

CINCINNATI	No.	Yds.	Avg.	L.A. RAIDERS	No.	Yds.	Avg.
RUSHING							
Woods	11	73	6.6	Allen	21	140	6.7
Brooks	11	26	2.4	Jackson	6	77	12.8
Ball	5	14	2.8	Smith	5	18	3.6
Esiason	2	11	5.5		32	235	7.3
	29	124	4.3				
RECEIVING							
Holman	2	51	25.5	Horton	4	77	19.3
Brown	2	18	9.0	T. Brown	3	42	14.0
Brooks	1	22	22.0	Fernandez	2	24	12.0
Jennings	1	8	8.0	Allen	1	24	24.0
Woods	1	5	5.0	Smith	1	5	5.0
McGee	1	0	0.0		11	172	15.6
	8	104	13.0				
PUNTING							
Johnson	5		51.6	Gossett	2		39.5
PUNT RETURNS							
None				T. Brown	3	40	13.3
KICKOFF RETURNS							
Jennings	3	68	22.7	R. Brown	1	18	18.0
Ball	1	14	14.0				
	4	82	20.5				
INTERCEPTION RETURNS							
Fulcher	1	11	11.0	None			

PASSING

	Att.	Comp.	Comp. Pct.	Yds.	Int.	Yds./ Att.	Yds./ Comp.
BUFFALO							
Esiason	15	8	5.3	104	0	6.9	13.0
CLEVELAND							
Schroeder	21	11	52.4	172	1	8.2	15.6

1990 N.F.C. PLAYOFFS — SECOND ROUND

January 12, 1991 at San Francisco (Attendance 65,292)

SCORING

	1	2	3	4	Total
WASHINGTON	10	0	0	0	10
SAN FRANCISCO	7	14	0	7	28

First Quarter
- Wash. — Monk, 31 yard pass from Rypien; PAT — Lohmiller (kick)
- S.F. — Rathman, 1 yard run; PAT — Cofer (kick)
- Wash. — Lohmiller, 44 yard field goal

Second Quarter
- S.F. — Rice, 10 yard pass from Montana; PAT — Cofer (kick)
- S.F. — Sherrard, 8 yard pass from Montana; PAT — Cofer (kick)

Fourth Quarter
- S.F. — M. Carter, 61 yard interception return; PAT — Cofer (kick)

TEAMSTATISTICS

WASH.		S.F.
25	First Downs- Total	20
6	First Downs- Rushing	3
18	First Downs- Passing	16
1	First Downs- Penalty	1
0	Fumbles- Number	0
0	Fumbles- Lost Ball	0
1	Penalties- Number	4
15	Yards Penalized	25
0	Missed Field Goals	0
72	Offensive Plays	58
441	Net Yards	338
6.1	Average Gain	5.8
3	Giveaways	1
1	Takeaways	3
- 2	Difference	+ 2

INDIVIDUALSTATISTICS

WASHINGTON	No.	Yds.	Avg.	SAN FRANCISCO	No.	Yds.	Avg.
RUSHING							
Byner	12	51	4.3	Craig	12	20	1.7
Riggs	10	18	1.8	Sydney	7	19	2.7
Monk	1	9	9.0	Rathman	4	6	1.5
Mitchell	1	2	2.0	Montana	1	1	1.0
	24	80	3.3		24	46	1.9
RECEIVING							
Monk	10	163	16.3	Rice	6	68	11.3
Clark	6	63	10.5	Jones	4	103	25.8
Sanders	4	78	19.5	Sydney	4	10	2.5
Mitchell	3	25	8.3	Craig	3	54	18.0
Hobbs	1	13	13.0	Sherrard	3	16	5.3
Warren	1	11	1..0	Taylor	2	38	19.0
Riggs	1	8	8.0	Williams	1	13	13.0
Byner	1	0	0.0		23	302	13.1
	27	361	13.4				
PUNTING							
Goodburn	4		33.0	Helton	5		41.8
PUNT RETURNS							
Howard	2	15	7.5	Taylor	1	-4	-4.0
Green	1	5	5.0				
	3	20	6.7				
KICKOFF RETURNS							
Howard	2	37	18.5	D. Carter	1	19	19.0
Mitchell	2	37	18.5				
	4	74	18.5				
INTERCEPTION RETURNS							
Coleman	1	15	15.0	M. Carter	1	61	61.0
				Jackson	1	0	0.0
				Pollard	1	0	0.0
					3	61	20.3

PASSING

WASHINGTON	Att.	Comp.	Comp. Pct.	Yds.	Int.	Yds./ Att.	Yds./ Comp.
Rypien	48	27	56.3	361	3	7.5	13.4
SAN FRANCISCO							
Montana	31	22	71.0	274	1	8.8	12.5
Sydney	1	1	100.0	28	0	28.0	28.0
	32	23	71.9	302	1	9.4	13.1

January 13, 1991 at East Rutherford, N.J. (Attendance 77,025)

SCORING

	1	2	3	4	Total
CHICAGO	0	3	0	0	3
N.Y. GIANTS	10	7	7	7	31

First Quarter
- NYG — Bahr, 46 yard field goal
- NYG — Baker, 21 yard pass from Hostetler; PAT — Bahr (kick)

Second Quarter
- Chi. — Butler, 33 yard field goal
- NYG. — Cross, 5 yard pass from Hostetler; PAT — Bahr (kick)

Third Quarter
- NYG — Hostetler, 3 yard run; PAT — Bahr (kick)

Fourth Quarter
- NYG — Carthon, 1 yard run; PAT — Bahr (kick)

TEAMSTATISTICS

CHI.		NYG
11	First Downs- Total	23
0	First Downs- Rushing	16
11	First Downs- Passing	7
0	First Downs- Penalty	0
0	Fumbles- Number	1
0	Fumbles- Lost Ball	1
4	Penalties- Number	2
30	Yards Penalized	15
0	Missed Field Goals	0
52	Offensive Plays	68
232	Net Yards	288
4.5	Average Gain	4.2
2	Giveaways	1
1	Takeaways	2
- 1	Difference	+ 1

INDIVIDUALSTATISTICS

CHICAGO	No.	Yds.	Avg.	N.Y. GIANTS	No.	Yds.	Avg.
RUSHING							
Anderson	12	19	1.6	O. Anderson	21	80	3.8
Muster	4	8	2.0	Hostetler	6	43	7.2
	16	27	1.7	Tillman	9	31	3.4
				Carthon	8	19	2.4
				Meggett	2	18	9.0
				Hampton	2	3	1.5
					48	194	4.0
RECEIVING							
Anderson	4	23	5.8	Baker	3	58	19.3
Davis	3	76	25.3	Bavaro	3	25	8.3
Thornton	3	28	9.3	Ingram	1	12	12.0
Muster	3	21	7.0	Mrosko	1	6	6.0
Gentry	2	23	11.5	O. Anderson	1	6	6.0
Kozlowski	1	10	10.0	Cross	1	5	5.0
Morris	1	24	24.0	Metcalf	1	8	8.0
	17	205	12.1		10	112	11.2
PUNTING							
Buford	2		42.0	Landeta	3		40.7
PUNT RETURNS							
Bailey	2	3	1.5	Meggett	1	13	13.0
KICKOFF RETURNS							
Bailey	2	61	30.5	Ingram	1	18	18.0
Gentry	2	42	21.0				
Rouse	1	9	9.0				
	5	112	22.4				
INTERCEPTION RETURNS							
				Walls	1	37	37.0
				Collins	1	11	11.0
					2	48	24.0

PASSING

CHICAGO	Att.	Comp.	Comp. Pct.	Yds.	Int.	Yds./ Att.	Yds./ Comp.
Tomczak	36	17	47.2	205	2	5.7	12.1
N.Y. GIANTS							
Hostetler	17	10	58.8	112	0	6.6	11.2

1990 Championship Games

A.F.C. CHAMPIONSHIP GAME

January 20, 1991 at BUFFALO, N.Y.
(Attendance 80,324)

SCORING

L.A. RAIDERS	3	0	0	0	- 3
BUFFALO	21	20	0	10	- 51

First Quarter

Buf.	Lofton, 13 yard pass from Kelly PAT — Norwood (kick)
L.A.Rd.	Jaeger, 41 yard field goal
Buf.	Thomas, 12 yard run PAT — Norwood (kick)
Buf.	Talley, 27 yard interception return PAT — Norwood (kick)

Second Quarter

Buf.	K. Davs, 1 yard run (kick blocked)
Buf.	K. Davis, 3 yard run PAT — Norwood (kick)
Buf.	Lofton, 8 yard pass from Kelly PAT — Norwood (kick)

Fourth Quarter

Buf.	K. Davis, 1 yard run PAT — Norwood (kick)
Buf.	Norwood, 39 yard field goal

The Buffalo Bills were nearly perfect in dismantling the Los Angeles Raiders for the A.F.C. title. The Bills' 41-points set a record for the biggest first-half splurge in championship game history. And, even though Buffalo concentrated on conservative, run-out-the-clock football in the second half, the 48-point margin was the second biggest ever — behind only the Bears' legendary 73-0 beating of the Redskins in 1940.

Buffalo jumped out to a 7-0 lead at 3:30 of the first quarter when Jim Kelly's 13-yard pass to Jim Lofton capped a 75-yard drive. The Raiders came right back with a 41-yard field goal by Jeff Jaeger'sl. But it took the Bills only a little over a minute to score a second TD on a 12-yard run by Thurman Thomas, with a 41-yard Kelly-to-Lofton pass the key play in the 66-yard drive.

Trailing 14-3, the Raiders self-destructed. Jay Schroeder's pass was intercepted at the 27 by Darryl Talley, who raced into the end zone with Buffalo's third score of the first quarter. Schroeder was intercepted four more times.

Buffalo scored three more TD's in the second quarter, all of them on drives of more than 50 yards. Backup Kenneth Davis scored two of his three touchdowns on short runs and Lofton took another Kelly pass for the final first-half score.

The Bills stayed mainly on the ground in the second half, but at the top of the fourth quarter Davis scored his third TD to finish off a 78-yard drive. Scott Norwood ended the scoring with a 39-yard field goal a few minutes later.

TEAM STATISTICS

L.A.Rd.		BUF.
21	First Downs- Total	30
12	First Downs- Rushing	14
8	First Downs- Passing	15
1	First Downs- Penalty	1
1	Fumbles- Number	3
1	Fumbles- Lost Ball	3
2	Penalties- Number	6
28	Yards Penalized	32
0	Missed Field Goals	1
68	Offensive Plays	69
320	Net Yards	502
4.7	Average Gain	7.3
7	Giveaways	1
1	Takeaways	7
- 6	Difference	+ 6

INDIVIDUAL STATISTICS

L.A. RAIDERS	No.	Yds.	Avg.	BUFFALO	No.	Yds.	Avg.
RUSHING							
Bell	5	36	7.2	Thomas	25	138	5.5
Evans	4	33	8.3	Gardner	1	23	23.0
Schroeder	4	33	8.3	K. Davis	10	21	2.1
Allen	10	26	2.6	Kelly	2	12	6.0
Smith	4	19	4.8	Mueller	3	6	2.0
McCallum	1	4	4.0	D. Smith	3	3	1.0
	28	151	5.4	Reich	2	-1	-1.0
					46	202	4.4
RECEIVING							
Fernandez	4	57	14.3	Lofton	5	113	22.6
Gault	2	32	16.0	Thomas	5	61	12.2
Horton	3	23	7.7	McKeller	3	44	13.3
Bell	2	26	13.0	Tasker	2	53	26.5
Allen	2	19	9.5	Reed	2	29	14.5
T. Brown	2	17	8.5		17	300	17.6
	15	174	11.7				
PUNTING							
Gossett	3		40.3	Tuten	2		37.5
PUNT RETURNS							
Patterson	1	17	17.0	Odomes	1	18	18.0
T. Brown	1	5	5.0	Edwards	1	12	12.0
	2	22	11.0		2	30	15.0
KICKOFF RETURNS							
Holland	6	60	10.0	D. Smith	1	19	19.0
R. Brown	3	59	19.7	Edwards	1	11	11.0
	9	119	13.2		2	30	15.0
INTERCEPTION RETURNS							
Lewis	1	0	0.0	Talley	2	48	24.0
				Bentley	1	32	32.0
				L. Smith	1	24	24.0
				Odomes	1	9	9.0
				Kelso	1	0	0.0
					6	113	18.8

PASSING

	Att.	Comp.	Comp. Pct.	Yds.	Int.	Yds./ Att.	Yds./ Comp.
L.A. RAIDERS							
Schroeder	31	13	41.9	150	5	4.8	11.5
Evans	8	2	25.0	26	1	3.3	13.0
BUFFALO							
Kelly	23	17	73.9	300	1	13.0	17.6

N.F.C. CHAMPIONSHIP GAME

January 20, 1991 at San Francisco, Calif.
(Attendance 65,750)

SCORING

N.Y. GIANTS	3	3	3	6	- 15
SAN FRANCISCO	3	3	7	0	- 13

First Quarter

S.F.	Cofer, 47 yard field goal
NYG	Bahr, 28 yard field goal

Second Quarter

NYG	Bahr, 42 yard field goal
S.F.	Cofer, 35 yard field goal

Third Quarter

S.F.	Taylor, 61 yard pass from Montana PAT — Cofer (kick)
NYG	Bahr, 46 yard field goal

Fourth Quarter

NYG	Bahr, 38 yard field goal
NYG	Bahr, 42 yard field goal

The New York Giants ended the San Francisco 49ers' dreams of a third-straight Super Bowl championship in a game that had seven field goals and only one touchdown. Five of the field goals were kicked by the Giants' Matt Bahr to offset the 49ers' touchdown and pair of goals. The same two teams met a month earlier on the same field, with San Francisco collecting the only touchdown in that game, too, but holding New York to only one field goal for a 7-3 win.

With regular quarterback Phil Simms injured, the Giants used a conservative ground attack to keep the pressure off reserve Jeff Hostetler, who nevertheless hit on several key passes to help set up field-goal attempts.

San Francisco jumped off to a 3-0 lead in the first quarter with a field goal of its own, 47 yards by Mike Cofer. Bahr tied the game before the end of the period with a 28-yarder. In the second quarter, the teams again exchanged field goals, Bahr from 42 yards and Cofer from 35.

Less than five minutes into the third quarter, a 61-yard pass from Joe Montana to John Taylor gave the 49ers a 13-6 lead. Giants cornerback Everson Walis gambled on an interception on the play and was burned. Bahr hit a 46-yard field goal to narrow the gap before the period ended.

Montana was sacked and knocked from the game with a broken finger with 9:42 remaining. Trailing 13-9, the Giants surprised the 49ers with a fake punt with Gary Reasons running 30 yards to set up a 38-yard Bahr field goal to bring New York to within a point of San Francisco.

Under substitute Steve Young, the 49ers tried to control the ball on the ground as time ran down, but Roger Craig fumbled and New York's Lawrence Taylor recovered with 2:36 left. The Giants drove to within a field-goal range on a pair of Hostetler passes. Then, as time ran out, Bahr hit field goal No. 5 for the winner.

TEAM STATISTICS

NYG		S.F.
20	First Downs- Total	13
8	First Downs- Rushing	1
8	First Downs- Passing	11
4	First Downs- Penalty	1
0	Fumbles- Number	3
0	Fumbles- Lost Ball	1
5	Penalties- Number	9
45	Yards Penalized	63
1	Missed Field Goals	0
68	Offensive Plays	41
311	Net Yards	240
4.6	Average Gain	5.9
0	Giveaways	1
1	Takeaways	0
+1	Difference	- 1

INDIVIDUAL STATISTICS

N.Y. GIANTS	No.	Yds.	Avg.	SAN FRANCISCO	No.	Yds.	Avg.
RUSHING							
Anderson	20	67	3.4	Craig	8	26	3.3
Meggett	10	36	3.6	Montana	2	9	4.5
Reasons	1	30	30.0	Rathman	1	4	4.0
Hostetler	3	11	3.7		11	39	3.5
Carthon	2	8	4.0				
	36	152	4.2				
RECEIVING							
Ingram	5	82	16.4	Taylor	2	75	37.5
Bavaro	5	54	10.8	Rice	5	54	10.8
Baker	2	22	11.0	Jones	3	46	15.3
Meggett	2	15	7.5	Craig	3	16	5.3
Anderson	1	3	3.0	Rathman	4	16	4.0
	15	176	9.8	Sherrard	2	8	4.0
					19	215	11.3
PUNTING							
Landeta	3		41.3	Helton	5		40.0
PUNT RETURNS							
Meggett	5	42	8.4	Taylor	2	40	20.0
KICKOFF RETURNS							
Meggett	2	36	18.0	Carter	3	74	24.7
Cross	1	3	3.0	Tillman	1	11	11.0
	3	39	13.0		4	85	21.3
INTERCEPTION RETURNS							
				None			
					3	56	18.7

PASSING

	Att.	Comp.	Comp. Pct.	Yds.	Int.	Yds./ Att.	Yds./ Comp.
N.Y. GIANTS							
Hostetler	27	15	55.5	176	0	6.5	11.7
Meggett	1	0	0.0	0	0	0.0	0.0
Cavanaugh	1	0	0.0	0	0	0.0	0.0
SAN FRANCISCO							
Montana	26	18	69.2	190	0	7.3	10.6
Young	1	1	100.0	25	0	25.0	

SUPER BOWL XXV

January 12, 1991 at Tampa, Fla.
(Attendance 73,813)

Worth Waiting For

The Silver Anniversary Super Bowl deserved no worse than a silver medal in the "best-ever" sweepstakes. Certainly it was the closest Super Bowl, with a one-point margin separating the winning New York Giants from the losing Buffalo Bills. It had the virtue of having the underdog triumph — the Bills were favored by about a touchdown, even though the AFC hadn't won a Super Bowl since XVIII. And, the decision came down to the last play of the game.

After Buffalo failed to move after the opening kickoff, New York took over on its own 31. The Giants drove to the Bills' 11 in 11 plays before settling for a 28-yard field goal by Matt Bahr. A Jeff Hostetler-to-Mark Ingram third-down pass for 16 yards was the key play of the drive.

When Buffalo got the ball back, Jim Kelly threw a 61-yard pass to James Lofton to move to the Giants' 8-yard-line, but the drive stalled. Scott Norwood tied the game with a 23-yard field goal.

Late in the first quarter, Buffalo began a drive at its own 20. In 12 plays, including passes by Kelly for 20 yards to Andre Reed and 16 yards to Thurman Thomas, the Bills drove for a touchdown. Don Smith scored on a one-yard slash.

After an exchange of punts, New York found itself in trouble when Dave Meggett elected to fair catch at the Giants' 7-yard-line. A few seconds later, Hostetler tripped over Ottis Anderson's foot while dropping back to pass and sprawled into the end zone. He scrambled to his feet but couldn't avoid Buffalo's Bruce Smith, who pulled him down for a safety. With New York kicking to them and leading 12-3, the Bills seemed about to take control, but three passes by Kelly fell incomplete. Neither team could put together a scoring drive until the Giants started from their 13 with 3:49 left in the second quarter. Hostetler mixed passes with the running of Anderson and Meggett to move the ball to the Buffalo 14, where a Hostetler-to-Stephen Baker scoring pass completed the 87-yard drive.

Trailing 12-10, the Giants began the second half with a long drive — a 75-yard, 14-play, grind-'em-out one that took 9:29 off the clock. Anderson's one-yard run put New York in front. Key plays were Hostetler's 11-yard pass to Meggett on a 3rd-and-8 and Anderson's 24-yard burst on a 3rd-and-1.

With the Giants' two long drives plus extended halftime, the Bills hadn't run anything more than a first-half-ending kneel-down in more than an hour, and it took them a while to get on-track. But, with 1:19 left in the third quarter, they started a drive from their 37 that ended in Thurman Thomas' 31-yard TD run on the first play of the fourth quarter.

Down 19-17, the Giants put together their third long, time-consuming drive of the game — 74 yards in 14 plays — with Bahr's 21-yard field goal giving New York back the lead, 20-19. Again, a clutch Hostetler pass, 16 yards to Mark Bavaro, salvaged a third-down situation.

But Buffalo wasn't finished. In the final two minutes, the Bills drove from their own 10 to the New York 29, but Norwood's attempt for a 47-yard, game-winning field goal sailed wide right.

LINEUPS

BUFF.		NYG
	OFFENSE	
Lofton	WR	Ingram
Wolford	LT	Elliott
Ritcher	LG	Roberts
Hull	C	Oates
Davis	RG	Moore
Ballard	RT	Riesenberg
McKeller	TE	Bavaro
Reed	WR	Baker
Kelly	QB	Hostetler
Thomas	RB	O. Anderson
Mueller	FB	Carthon
	DEFENSE	
Seals	LE	Dorsey
Wright	NT	Howard
B. Smith	RE	Marshall
Bennett	LOLB	Banks
Conlan	LILB	DeOssie
Bentley	RILB	Johnson
Talley	ROLB	Taylor
Jackson	LCB	Collins
Odomes	RCB	Walls
Smith	SS	Jackson
Kelso	FS	Guyton

SUBSTITUTES

BUFFALO		
	OFFENSE	
Reich	K. Davis	D. Smith
Gardner	Freotte	Lingner
G. Parker	Edwards	Rolle
Metzelaars	Tasker	G. Baldinger
Gilbert		
	DEFENSE	
Hagy	Hicks	J. Williams
Drane	Bailey	Lodish
Pike	Garner	
	KICKERS	
Norwood	Tuten	
N.Y. GIANTS		
	OFFENSE	
Rouson	Meggett	Tillman
B. Williams	Kratch	Mrosko
Robinson	Kyles	Cross
Cavanaugh		
	DEFENSE	
Thompson	P. Williams	Duerson
Whitmore	R. Brown	Abrams
Reasons	McGrew	Washington
Fox	Cooks	
	KICKERS	
Bahr	Landeta	

SCORING

BUFFALO	3	9	0	7	- 19
N.Y. GIANTS	3	7	7	3	- 20

First Quarter
- NYG — Bahr, 28 yard field goal
- Buff. — Norwood, 23 yard field goal

Second Quarter
- Buff. — D. Smith, 1 yard run; PAT — Norwood (kick)
- Buff. — Hostetler, sacked by B. Smith for a safety
- NYG — Baker, 14 yard pass from Hostetler; PAT — Bahr (kick)

Third Quarter
- NYG — Anderson, 1 yard run; PAT — Bahr (kick)

Fourth Quarter
- Buff. — Thomas, 31 yard run; PAT — Norwood (kick)
- NYG — Bahr, 21 yard field goal

TEAM STATISTICS

BUFF.		NYG
18	First Downs-Total	24
8	First Downs-Rushing	10
9	First Downs-Pasiing	13
1	First Downs-Penalty	1
1	Fumbles-Number	0
0	Fumbles-Lost Ball	0
6	Penaties-Number	5
35	Yards Penalized	31
1	Missed Field Goals	0
56	Offensive Plays	73
371	Net Yards	386
6.6	Average Gain	5.3
0	Giveaways	0
0	Takeaways	0
+ 0	Difference	+ 0

INDIVIDUAL STATISTICS

SBUFFALO	No.	Yds.	Avg.	N.Y. GIANTS	No.	Yds.	Avg.
				RUSHING			
Thomas	15	135	9.0	Anderson	21	102	4.9
Kelly	6	23	3.8	Meggett	9	48	5.3
Davis	2	4	2.0	Carthon	3	12	4.0
Mueller	1	3	3.0	Hostetler	6	10	1.7
	25	166	6.6		39	172	4.4
				RECEIVING			
Reed	8	62	7.8	Ingram	5	74	14.8
Thomas	5	55	11.0	Bavaro	5	50	10.0
Davis	2	23	11.5	Cross	4	39	9.8
McKeller	2	11	5.5	Baker	2	31	15.5
Lofton	1	61	61.0	Meggett	2	18	9.0
	18	212	11.8	Anderson	1	7	7.0
				Carthon	1	3	3.0
					20	222	11.1
				PUNTING			
Tuten	6		38.8	Landeta	4		43.8
				PUNT RETURNS			
Edwards	0	0	0.0	Meggett	3	37	18.5
				KICKOFF RETURNS			
D. Smith	4	66	16.5	Meggett	2	26	13.0
Edwards	2	48	24.0	Duerson	1	22	22.0
	6	114	19.0		3	48	16.0
				INTERCEPTIONS RETURNS			
None				None			

PASSING

	Att.	Comp.	Comp. Pct.	Yds.	Int.	Yds./ Att.	Yds./ Comp.	Yards Lost Tackled
BUFFALO								
Kelly	30	18	60.0	212	0	7.1	11.8	1-7
N.Y. GIANTS								
Hostetler	32	20	62.5	222	0	6.9	11.1	2-8

1991 N.F.C. Thumbs Up for Lions and Utley

The NFC won its eighth consecutive Super Bowl when the Redskins trounced the Bills in Super Bowl XXVI, which was played in Minneapolis, only the second in a northern city. But the big story of the 1991 season was the rejuvenation of the Lions coming on the heels of a tragic accident to one of their teammates. In Week 12, with Detroit's season on the line, guard Mike Utley fell forward while blocking and landed head-first on the Silverdome's artificial turf, tearing a ligament and bursting a spinal disk. Utley, 25, was paralyzed from the neck down. However, while being carried off the field on a stretcher, Utley gave his teammates the thumbs-up sign, galvanizing his teammates to five straight victories and the NFC Central Division championship.

The Lions made it all the way to the NFC championship game, where Washington knocked them back into reality. That was a lot farther than several perennial playoff teams got. The 49ers, playing without Joe Montana, missed the playoffs. So did the Eagles, who lost Randall Cunningham in the first game, and the Giants, who slumped to an 8-8 record on the heels of their Super Bowl XXV championship following a coaching change.

EASTERN DIVISION

Washington Redskins — The Redskins went into the season unsure if Mark Rypien was an NFL-caliber quarterback and came out of it knowing he was the best quarterback in the league. Feeding off the team's stellar running game and throwing behind one of the league's biggest offensive lines (he was sacked only seven times all season), Rypien was able to open it up and throw long to a corps of receivers that included future Hall of Famer Art Monk, Gary Clark and Ricky Sanders. The running attack was fueled by Earnest Byner (1,048 yards), rookie Ricky Ervins (680 yards) and Gerald Riggs (11 touchdowns, and six more in the playoffs). Four Plan B free agents started on the league's second-best defense that included All-Pro's Wilber Marshall and Darrell Green. Placekicker Chip Lohmiller led the NFL with 149 points.

Dallas Cowboys — Two years of wheeling and dealing by owner Jerry Jones and coach Jimmy Johnson paid big dividends in 1991 as the Cowboys made the playoffs for the first time since 1985 and advanced to the second round of the playoffs. An explosive offense was led by running back Emmitt Smith, who led the NFL in rushing yards and carries (365 for 1,563) and wide receiver Michael Irvin, who caught 93 passes for a league-high 1,523 yards in his first injury-free season in the pros. Troy Aikman was the NFL's hottest quarterback over the first half of the season, and, when he went down with a sprained knee in the 12th game, the team's hopes didn't go down the tubes like they did in '90 because backup Steve Beuerlein kept the team in the playoff hunt. Defensive tackle Russell Maryland, the No. 1 pick in the 1991 draft, led an improved defense.

Philadelphia Eagles — Coach Rich Kotite knew his team's chances to make the the playoffs were shattered when quarterback Randall Cunningham suffered a season-ending knee injury only 18 minutes into the first game. Backup Jim McMahon battled numerous injuries and rallied the Eagles back into playoff contention. But, when he wasn't in the lineup, the Eagles were forced to start reclaimed veteran Pat Ryan and rookie Brad Goebel through a four-game losing streak and then waiver pickup Jeff Kemp for the last two games. But the big story in Philadelphia was the defense. The Eagles defense led the league in fewest total yards, fewest rushing yards and fewest passing yards — only the fifth team ever to achieve that rare triple.

New York Giants — When Bill Parcells resigned as head coach in May, everyone knew changes were in store for the defending Super Bowl champions. But nobody thought a .500 record and "home for the holidays" would be some of the changes. New coach Ray Handley's first decision was to decide the starting quarterback, and he chose Jeff Hostetler, who led the Giants to their victory in Super Bowl XXV. However, Hostetler was ineffective and eventually suffered a back injury and was replaced by veteran Phil Simms. Ottis Anderson was finally sent to the bench, and a star was born in the name of Rodney Hampton, who gained 1,059 yards rushing. The Giants' defense was still tough, but age was starting to show in the play of Lawrence Taylor, Carl Banks and some other veterans.

Phoenix Cardinals — The Cardinals got off to a quick start with victories in their first two games, but then the bottom fell out as they won only two more games in the remaining 14 contests, and the team lost its most games in franchise history. Starter Timm Rosenbach suffered a season-ending knee injury in the final preseason game, so the quarterbacking was done by Tom Tupa, Stan Gelbaugh (the Most Valuable Player in the World League of American Football) and Chris Chandler (who was cut by Tampa Bay). But, while the Phoenix defense was improved, the Cards scored no touchdowns in five games and only one in seven others. Defensive end Eric Swann, the top draft pick who didn't play college football, wasn't much help, but cornerback Aeneas Williams, a third-rounder, was one of the league's best.

CENTRAL DIVISION

Detroit Lions — After years of struggling in mediocrity, the Lions broke free and did something special in 1991. They survived a 45-0 loss to Washington on Opening Day and the loss of five starters, and they rallied around a partially paralyzed teammate — guard Mike Utley — to record the best record in club history and the Central Division title. When Rodney Peete was injured in the eighth game, free-agent Erik Kramer took over and led the Lions to six straight victories to close out the season and then a thrashing of Dallas in the first round of the playoffs before the Redskins ended the season almost as it began. Detroit had gone 8-0 at home during the regular season. Barry Sanders rushed for 1,548 yards, second-most in the league, and the team's wide receivers — specifically Brett Perriman, Robert Clark and Mike Farr — blossomed.

Chicago Bears — Move over running game — the Bears turned into a passing team in 1991! However, Chicago lost its firm grip on the division crown by losing three of their final five games after winning five straight at midseason. Running backs Neal Anderson and Brad Muster were never 100 percent after suffering nagging injuries, and the Bears defense and special teams were inconsistent too many times. However, quarterback Jim Harbaugh did show that he could bring the team from behind, as he led them to last-minute victories over the Giants and Jets in Weeks Three and Four. Harbaugh, who set team records for passing attempts and completions, was the first Bears quarterback to start every game since 1981. And Wendell Davis had the most receptions and receiving yardage of any Bears receiver since 1970.

Minnesota Vikings — The Vikings had their second straight dismal season, finishing 8-8 and out of the playoffs. The quarterback situation was again the problem, as neither Wade Wilson nor Rich Gannon were effective. Running back Herschel Walker again seemed to be a disappointment, but he still rushed for 825 yards and scored 10 touchdowns. Cris Carter had the biggest year of the receivers, catching 72 passes for 962 yards and five scores. The defense, which fell apart in the second half of the season, was riddled by injuries on the line, few big plays from the linebackers and too many mistakes by the secondary men. As the season wound down, coach Jerry Burns announced his retirement.

Green Bay Packers — The Packers again refused to run the football, and, since neither Don Majkowski nor Mike Tomczak could spark anything at quarterback, Green Bay suffered through a 4-12 season, leading to the dismissal of head coach Lindy infante. Darrell Thompson showed some flashes at running back, but still gained only 471 yards while averaging 3.3 yards per carry. Backup Vince Workman scored 11 touchdowns but few people considered him as anything more than a role player. Run defense was the team's specialty. The Packers yielded only 96.6 yards per game, the lowest for a Green Bay team since 1940. Still, the Packers didn't have a Pro Bowl player on defense for the 13th time in 14 seasons. After the season, Ron Wolf was hired from the Jets to be Green Bay's new general manager, and Mike Holmgren came in from the 49ers as head coach.

OFFENSE

	ATL	CHI	DAL	DET	G.B.	L.A.	MINN	N.O.	NYG	PHIL	PHX	S.F.	T.B.	WASH
FIRST DOWNS:														
Total	258	317	304	280	259	270	300	267	280	249	237	336	249	302
by Rushing	82	120	89	116	88	75	125	93	120	86	73	112	79	107
by Passing	162	168	191	148	150	180	158	157	148	142	143	197	147	179
by Penalty	14	29	24	16	21	15	17	17	12	21	21	27	23	16
RUSHING:														
Number	410	502	433	454	381	388	464	483	487	446	391	440	371	540
Yards	1664	1949	1711	1930	1389	1285	2201	1709	2064	1396	1295	1861	1429	2049
Average Yards	4.1	3.9	4.0	4.3	3.6	3.3	4.7	3.5	4.2	3.1	3.3	4.2	3.9	3.8
Touchdowns	6	18	15	19	12	11	18	15	16	8	6	19	9	21
PASSING:														
Attempts	500	497	500	459	514	518	477	506	428	513	492	522	495	447
Completions	260	286	305	252	272	289	284	292	261	285	254	325	250	261
Completion Pct.	52.0	57.5	61.0	54.9	52.9	55.8	59.5	57.7	61.0	55.6	51.6	62.3	50.5	58.4
Passing Yards	3524	3292	3663	2974	3213	3610	3016	3419	3025	3169	3039	4167	2955	3771
Avg. Yds per Att.	6.5	6.0	6.3	5.9	5.3	6.2	5.7	6.2	6.1	5.2	5.0	7.3	4.7	8.1
Avg. Yds per Comp.	14.0	11.5	12.0	11.8	11.8	12.5	10.6	11.7	11.6	11.1	12.0	12.8	11.8	14.5
Times Tackled	31	26	38	25	45	30	28	19	36	45	43	24	56	9
Yds Lost Tackled	185	172	273	116	270	200	133	160	181	263	372	170	383	79
Net Yards	3449	3120	3390	2858	2943	3410	2883	3259	2844	2906	2667	3997	2572	3692
Touchdowns	30	16	16	16	17	13	16	20	13	17	10	29	13	30
Interceptions	22	17	12	17	19	20	16	15	8	27	25	12	29	11
Pct. Intercepted	4.4	3.4	2.4	3.7	3.7	3.9	3.4	3.0	1.9	5.3	5.1	2.3	5.9	2.5
PUNTS:														
Number	82	70	57	75	86	75	68	87	64	88	77	56	84	55
Average	42.6	40.2	42.6	41.2	40.4	38.1	45.5	43.0	43.3	41.4	44.7	39.2	40.3	37.6
PUNT RETURNS														
Number	35	47	29	26	41	37	30	44	36	53	41	42	39	46
Yards	286	340	309	385	396	320	225	317	336	416	307	320	361	610
Average Yards	8.2	7.2	10.7	14.8	9.7	8.6	7.5	7.2	9.3	7.8	7.5	7.6	9.3	13.3
Touchdowns	0	0	1	1	0	0	0	0	1	0	0	0	0	2
KICKOFF RET.:														
Number	52	45	52	57	60	59	44	50	50	47	52	50	60	49
Yards	997	763	1127	1170	1197	1070	899	879	917	764	972	1028	1047	926
Average Yards	19.2	17.0		20.5	20.0	18.1	20.4	17.6	18.3	16.3	18.7	20.6	17.5	18.9
Touchdowns	1	0	1	0	1	0	0	0	0	0	0	1	0	0
INTERCEPT RET.:														
Number	19	17	12	19	15	11	17	29	12	26	17	12	11	27
Yards	225	225	167	286	234	175	242	482	122	280	187	125	63	279
Average Yards	13.9	8.6	11.5	16.1	9.6	8.8	16.3	19.8	5.0	14.3	17.1	10.0	19.5	12.9
Touchdowns	1	1	2	2	0	1	2	2	0	1	1	0	0	3
PENALTIES:														
Number	113	80	74	93	98	108	88	101	92	111	78	114	88	90
Yards	929	662	610	799	834	774	675	801	719	839	661	902	780	798
FUMBLES:														
Number	19	25	23	25	41	32	21	24	33	34	31	33	30	26
Number Lost	14	16	12	13	17	20	10	15	15	16	14	19	18	12
POINTS:														
Total	361	299	342	339	273	234	301	341	281	285	196	393	199	485
PAT Attempts	42	34	37	40	31	26	36	38	30	29	19	50	22	56
PAT Made	40	32	37	40	31	25	34	38	29	27	19	49	22	56
FG Attempts	26	29	39	28	24	17	24	32	31	33	30	28	20	43
FG Made	21	19	27	19	18	17	17	25	24	28	21	14	15	31
Percent FG Made	80.8	65.5	69.2	67.9	75.0	100.0	70.8	78.1	77.4	84.8	70.0	50.0	75.0	72.1
Safeties	3	0	1	1	1	1	0	0	0	0	0	1	0	0

DEFENSE

	ATL	CHI	DAL	DET	G.B.	L.A.	MINN	N.O.	NYG	PHIL	PHX	S.F.	T.B.	WASH
FIRST DOWNS:														
Total	278	254	299	305	298	286	301	214	257	206	301	260	295	242
by Rushing	94	77	103	93	99	105	106	63	103	53	132	86	120	72
by Passing	157	164	180	189	177	162	172	139	138	133	156	155	147	151
by Penalty	27	13	16	23	22	19	23	12	16	20	13	19	28	19
RUSHING:														
Number	466	389	400	444	457	469	456	334	414	383	493	399	512	348
Yards	1953	1580	1571	1760	1546	1659	1837	1213	1726	1136	2136	1512	2107	1346
Average Yards	4.2	4.1	3.9	4.0	3.4	3.5	4.0	3.6	4.2	3.0	4.3	3.8	4.1	3.9
Touchdowns	13	9	11	16	10	19	17	6	11	4	27	8	21	11
PASSING:														
Attempts	481	513	540	534	531	434	499	491	440	467	447	499	438	549
Completions	252	286	320	315	305	259	286	259	251	206	268	267	257	292
Completion Pct.	52.4	55.8	59.3	59.0	57.4	59.7	57.3	52.7	57.0	44.1	60.0	53.5	58.7	53.2
Passing Yards	3532	3184	3646	3523	3573	3657	3396	3057	3128	2807	3069	3254	3130	3292
Avg. Yds per Att.	6.5	5.3	6.2	5.8	5.7	7.9	6.0	5.0	6.1	4.6	6.2	5.7	6.0	4.9
Avg. Yds per Comp.	14.0	11.1	11.4	11.2	11.7	14.1	11.9	11.8	12.5	13.6	11.5	12.2	12.2	11.3
Times Tackled	29	40	23	30	45	17	33	50	34	55	25	31	39	50
Yds Lost Tackled	237	257	151	237	307	112	217	337	254	394	153	212	258	345
Net Yards	3295	2927	3495	3286	3266	3545	3179	2720	2874	2413	2916	3042	2872	2947
Touchdowns	28	19	17	16	20	25	16	12	17	16	12	16	15	13
Interceptions	19	17	12	19	15	11	17	29	12	26	17	12	11	27
Pct. Intercepted	4.0	3.3	2.2	3.6	2.8	2.5	3.4	5.9	2.7	5.6	3.8	2.4	2.5	4.9
PUNTS:														
Number	79	81	61	67	76	68	67	88	74	86	71	82	71	85
Average	40.3	41.3	38.8	39.2	42.1	41.6	42.7	42.3	40.5	42.7	45.2	41.0	42.9	41.7
PUNT RETURNS														
Number	45	28	28	35	35	33	42	50	35	42	48	30	49	31
Yards	387	205	231	340	375	292	426	470	350	431	313	239	559	190
Average Yards	8.6	7.3	8.3	9.7	10.7	8.8	10.1	9.4	10.0	10.3	6.5	8.0	11.4	6.1
Touchdowns	0	0	0	1	1	0	0	0	1	1	0	0	1	0
KICKOFF RET.:														
Number	67	58	69	63	47	39	43	35	55	60	42	66	32	66
Yards	1419	1134	1169	1095	942	671	851	851	940	1146	958	1288	720	1153
Average Yards	21.2	19.6	16.9	17.4	20.5	17.2	19.8	24.3	17.1	19.1	22.8	19.5	22.5	17.5
Touchdowns	1	0	1	0	0	0	0	2	0	0	1	1	0	0
INTERCEPT RET.:														
Number	22	17	12	17	19	20	16	15	8	27	25	12	29	11
Yards	279	145	244	229	185	297	203	257	36	432	399	82	349	109
Average Yards	12.7	8.5	20.3	13.5	9.7	14.9	12.7	17.1	4.5	16.0	16.0	6.8	12.0	9.9
Touchdowns	1	0	2	1	1	1	1	2	0	2	1	0	1	1
PENALTIES:														
Number	100	94	97	94	106	83	92	95	80	105	94	84	110	94
Yards	802	891	801	704	777	743	709	711	622	881	734	782	925	767
FUMBLES:														
Number	27	25	23	32	31	17	24	34	27	43	37	32	27	22
Number Lost	16	13	11	17	14	8	11	19	9	22	21	16	16	14
POINTS:														
Total	338	269	310	295	313	390	306	211	297	244	344	239	365	224
PAT Attempts	43	29	32	34	35	47	35	23	30	24	43	25	41	26
PAT Made	41	29	31	34	34	46	34	22	30	23	41	23	40	26
FG Attempts	26	30	39	28	31	28	29	21	30	33	23	25	35	18
FG Made	13	22	29	19	23	20	20	17	29	25	15	22	25	14
Percent FG Made	50.0	73.3	74.4	67.9	74.2	71.4	69.0	81.0	96.7	75.8	65.2	88.0	71.4	77.8
Safeties	0	0	0	0	0	1	1	0	0	1	0	0	2	0

Tampa Bay Buccaneers — The Buccaneers were just plain lousy from start to finish in 1991. The offense scored only 199 points, as quarterback Vinny Testaverde again did little to show why he was the first pick in the 1987 NFL draft. Testaverde was benched twice, but both times regained his starting job. Reggie Cobb came on in the second half of the season at running back, and rookie wide receiver Lawrence Dawsey led the Bucs in receiving. Even though the defense outperformed the offense, it had a big weakness in its inability to create turnovers and make big plays. Still, Tampa Bay is a team with talent at the skill positions and on defense, where linebacker Broderick Thomas began to shine. That's good news for new head coach Sam Wyche, who came over from Cincinnati at the end of the season to replace Richard Williamson.

WESTERN DIVISION

New Orleans Saints — For the first time in their 15-year history, the Saints won a division championship with an 11-5 record. However, after that brief highlight, the team lost its third playoff game in three tries. Bobby Hebert returned from a one-year holdout and led New Orleans to a 9-2 record. However, the Saints were only 2-3 when he was injured and Steve Walsh was in the lineup. Floyd Turner blossomed into a fine wide receiver, scoring eight touchdowns. But the running attack was lethergic, with nobody gaining even 500 yards. The strength of the team was the defense, which led the NFL in fewest points allowed. Linebacker Pat Swilling led the NFL in sacks and was voted the league's Defensive Player of the Year.

Atlanta Falcons — For a change, the Falcons backed up their boasts in 1991, finishing 10-6 and ahead of the 49ers in the NFC West. Atlanta ranked fifth in the NFL in points scored, thanks to a potent run-and-shoot offense led by quarterback Chris Miller, who threw 26 touchdown passes. Wide receiver Michael Haynes caught only 50 passes but averaged a league-high 22.4 yards per reception and scored 12 times. Andre Rison chipped in with 11 TD's. They were the NFL's most explosive receiving duo. But, again, it was a matter of the offense outscoring the opponents, because the Atlanta defense showed some holes. Cornerbacks Deion Sanders and Tim McKyer might have been the NFL's best pair, but the Falcons couldn't stop the run.

San Francisco 49ers — The headlines read no Montana and no playoffs for the 49ers in 1991. For the first time in more than a decade, Joe Montana wasn't around to take the 49ers under his wing, as he missed the season after elbow surgery. Steve Young won the NFL passing title and rushed for 415 yards, but was only 5-5 as a starter and eventually was knocked out of the lineup with a sprained knee. That put journeyman Steve Bono into the lineup, and he responded with his finest showing ever and a 5-1 record. The running game again had nobody to depend on, but wide receivers Jerry Rice and John Taylor came through in typical fashion and 23 touchdowns between them. But, in the end, San Francisco missed departed veterans Ronnie Lott and Roger Craig, and it received terrible plackicking from Mike Cofer.

Los Angeles Rams — The Rams started off the '91 season 3-3 before losing their final nine games for a 3-13 record (and 8-24 over two seasons). Quarterback Jim Everett plummeted to mediocrity, finishing as the league's 14th-ranked passer and throwing a career-high 20 interceptions. Robert Delpino looked good at running back early in the season, but down the stretch nobody could hold down the job, and the Rams finished 27th in the NFL in rushing. And the defense didn't have enough talent to fit into coordinator Jeff Fisher's attacking schemes. Los Angeles allowed an NFC-high 390 points and finished last in the NFL with 17 sacks and 19 takeaways. When the season was over, the John Robinson era ended, giving way to the Chuck Knox era, Part Two.

WASHINGTON REDSKINS 14-2 Joe Gibbs

Scores of Each Game		
45	DETROIT	0
33	Dallas	31
34	PHOENIX	0
34	Cincinnati	27
23	PHILADELPHIA	0
20	Chicago	7
42	CLEVELAND	17
17	N.Y. Giants	13
16	HOUSTON	* 13
56	ATLANTA	17
41	Pittsburgh	14
21	DALLAS	24
27	L.A. Rams	6
20	Phoenix	14
34	N.Y. GIANTS	17
22	Philadelphia	24

Use Name	Pos.	Hgt.	Wgt.	Age	Int	Pts
Joe Jacoby	OT-OG	6'7"	314	31		
Jim Lachey	OT	6'6"	294	28		
Ed Simmons	OT	6'5"	300	27		
Mark Adickes	OG	6'4"	285	30		
Russ Grimm	OG	6'3"	284	32		
Raleigh McKenzie	OG-C	6'2"	279	28		
Mark Schlereth	OG	6'3"	283	25		
Ralph Tamm (from CLE, to CIN)	OG	6'4"	280	25		
Jeff Bostic	C	6'2"	278	32		
Jason Buck	DE	6'4"	265	28		
Markus Koch	DE	6'5"	275	28		
Charles Mann	DE	6'6"	272	30		
Fred Stokes	DE	6'3"	274	27	1	
James Geathers	DE	6'7"	289	31		
Tim Johnson	DT	6'3"	283	26	1	
Eric Williams	DT	6'4"	290	29		
Bobby Wilson	DT	6'2"	283	23		

Ray Brown — Elbow Injury

Use Name	Pos.	Hgt.	Wgt.	Age	Int	Pts
Ravin Caldwell	LB	6'3"	240	28		
Monte Coleman	LB	6'2"	245	33	1	
Andre Collins	LB	6'1"	233	23	2	6
Kurt Gouveia	LB	6'1"	228	26	1	
Wilber Marshall	LB	6'1"	231	29	5	6
Matt Millen	LB	6'2"	245	33		
Danny Copeland	DB	6'2"	213	25	1	
Travis Curtis	DB	5'10"	180	25		
Brad Edwards	DB	6'1"	207	25	4	
Darrell Green	DB	5'8"	170	31	5	
Terry Hoage	DB	6'2"	201	29		
A.J. Johnson	DB	5'8"	170	24		
Sidney Johnson	DB	5'9"	175	26	2	
Martin Mayhew	DB	5'8"	172	25	3	6
Alvoid Mays	DB	5'9"	180	25	1	
Clarence Vaughn	DB	6'	202	27		
Alvin Walton	DB	6'	180	27		

Use Name	Pos.	Hgt.	Wgt.	Age	Int	Pts
Stan Humphries	QB	6'2"	223	26		
Jeff Rutledge	QB	6'1"	193	34		
Mark Rypien	QB	6'4"	234	28		6
Earnest Byner	HB-FB	5'10"	218	28		30
Ricky Ervins	HB	5'7"	200	22		24
Brian Mitchell	HB	5'10"	209	23		12
Gerald Riggs	HB-FB	6'1"	240	30		66
Gary Clark	WR	5'9"	173	29		60
Stephen Hobbs	WR	5'11"	200	25		
Joe Johnson	WR	5'8"	170	28		
Art Monk	WR	6'3"	210	33		48
Ricky Sanders	WR	5'11"	180	29		36
John Brandes	TE	6'2"	249	27		
James Jenkins	TE	6'2"	234	24		
Jimmie Johnson	TE	6'2"	246	24		12
Ron Middleton	TE	6'2"	270	26		
Terry Orr	TE	6'2"	235	29		24
Don Warren	TE	6'4"	242	35		
Kelly Goodburn	K	6'2"	199	29		
Chip Lohmiller	K	6'3"	210	25		149

John Settle — Rib Injury

DALLAS COWBOYS 11-5 Jimmy Johnson

Scores of Each Game		
26	Cleveland	14
31	WASHINGTON	33
9	PHILADELPHIA	24
17	Phoenix	9
21	N.Y. GIANTS	16
20	Green Bay	17
35	CINCINNATI	23
10	Detroit	34
27	PHOENIX	7
23	Houston	* 26
9	N.Y. Giants	22
24	Washington	21
20	PITTSBURGH	10
23	NEW ORLEANS	14
25	Philadelphia	13
31	ATLANTA	27

Use Name	Pos.	Hgt.	Wgt.	Age	Int	Pts
Nate Newton	OT	6'3"	332	29		
Mark Tuinei	OT	6'5"	299	31		
Erik Williams	OT	6'6"	319	22		
John Gesek	OG	6'5"	279	28		
Kevin Gogan	OG	6'7"	317	26		
Dale Hellestrae	OG-C	6'5"	285	29		
Alan Veingrad	OG-OT	6'5"	280	28		
Mark Stepnoski	C	6'2"	269	24		
Tony Hill	DE	6'6"	242	22		
Jim Jeffcoat	DE	6'5"	274	30		
Danny Stubbs (to CIN)	DE	6'4"	264	26		
Tony Tolbert	DE	6'6"	265	23		
Tony Cassillas	DT	6'3"	277	27		
Jimmie Jones	DT	6'4"	276	25		
Leon Lett	DT	6'6"	287	22		
Russell Maryland	DT-DE	6'1"	277	21		
Danny Noonan	DT	6'4"	275	26		

Use Name	Pos.	Hgt.	Wgt.	Age	Int	Pts
Darrick Brownlow	LB	5'10"	237	22		
Reggie Cooper	LB	6'2"	215	23		
Jack Del Rio	LB	6'4"	240	28		
Dixon Edwards	LB	6'1"	224	23	1	6
Godfrey Myles	LB	6'1"	241	22		
Ken Norton	LB	6'2"	238	24		
Mickey Pruitt	LB	6'1"	218	26		
Vinson Smith	LB	6'2"	231	26		
Vince Albritton	DB	6'2"	216	29		
Bill Bates	DB	6'1"	205	30		
Larry Brown	DB	5'11"	182	21	2	
Kenneth Gant	DB	5'11"	188	24	1	
Manny Hendrix	DB	5'10"	187	26		2
Issiac Holt	DB	6'2"	201	28	4	
Ray Horton	DB	5'11"	190	31	1	12
Stan Smagala	DB	5'10"	184	23		
Donald Smith	DB	5'11"	189	23		
James Washington	DB	6'1"	197	26	2	
Robert Williams	DB	5'10"	190	28	1	6

Michael Brooks — Knee Injury

Use Name	Pos.	Hgt.	Wgt.	Age	Int	Pts
Troy Aikman	QB	6'4"	222	24		6
Steve Beuerlein	QB	6'2"	209	26		
James Dixon	HB-WR	5'10"	184	24		
Curvin Richards	HB	5'9"	195	22		
Emmitt Smith	HB	5'9"	203	22		78
Tommie Agee	FB	6'	225	27		6
Ricky Blake	FB	6'2"	244	24		6
Daryl Johnston	FB	6'2"	236	25		6
Alvin Harper	WR	6'3"	203	24		6
Michael Irvin	WR	6'2"	199	25		48
Kelvin Martin	WR	5'9"	162	26		6
Derrick Shepard	WR	5'10"	183	27		
Alexander Wright	WR	6'	190	24		6
Robert Awalt	TE	6'5"	245	27		
Jay Novacek	TE	6'4"	231	28		24
Alfredo Roberts	TE	6'3"	252	26		6
Mike Saxon	K	6'3"	202	29		
Ken Willis	K	5'11"	185	24		18

PHILADELPHIA EAGLES 10-6 Rich Kotite

Scores of Each Game		
20	Green Bay	3
10	PHOENIX	26
24	Dallas	0
23	PITTSBURGH	14
0	Washington	23
13	Tampa Bay	14
6	NEW ORLEANS	13
7	SAN FRANCISCO	23
30	N.Y. GIANTS	7
32	Cleveland	30
17	CINCINNATI	10
34	Phoenix	14
13	Houston	6
19	N.Y. Giants	14
13	DALLAS	25
24	WASHINGTON	22

Use Name	Pos.	Hgt.	Wgt.	Age	Int	Pts
Antone Davis	OT	6'4"	325	24		
Cecil Gray	OT-OG	6'4"	275	23		
Ron Heller	OT	6'6"	280	29		
Daryle Smith	OT	6'5"	276	27		
Bruce Collie	OG	6'6"	275	29		
John Hudson	OG-C	6'2"	275	23		
Dennis McKnight	OG-C	6'3"	280	31		
Rob Selby	OG-OT	6'3"	286	23		
Ron Solt	OG	6'3"	275	29		
David Alexander	C	6'3"	275	27		
Mike Flores	DE	6'3"	256	24		
Andy Harmon	DE	6'4"	265	22		
Clyde Simmons	DE	6'6"	280	27		6
Reggie White	DE-DT	6'5"	285	29	1	
Jerome Brown	DT	6'2"	295	26		
Mike Golic	DT	6'5"	275	28	1	
Mike Pitts	DT	6'5"	280	30		

Mike Schad — Back Injury
Ben Tamburello — Knee Injury

Use Name	Pos.	Hgt.	Wgt.	Age	Int	Pts
Byron Evans	LB	6'2"	235	27	2	
Britt Hager	LB	6'1"	225	25		
Seth Joyner	LB	6'2"	235	26	3	6
Scott Kowalkowski	LB	6'2"	228	23		
Ken Rose	LB	6'1"	215	29		
Jessie Small	LB	6'3"	240	24		
William Thomas	LB	6'2"	218	23		
Eric Allen	DB	5'10"	180	25	5	
John Booty	DB	6'	180	25		
Wes Hopkins	DB	6'1"	215	29	5	
Izel Jenkins	DB	5'10"	190	27		
Rich Miano	DB	6'1"	200	28	3	
Bruce Plummer	DB	6'	198	27		
Ben Smith	DB	5'11"	183	24	2	
Otis Smith	DB	5'11"	184	25	2	6
Andre Waters	DB	5'11"	200	29	1	

Use Name	Pos.	Hgt.	Wgt.	Age	Int	Pts
Randall Cunningham	QB	6'4"	203	28		
Brad Goebel	QB	6'3"	198	23		
Jim McMahon	QB	6'1"	195	32		6
Pat Ryan	QB	6'3"	210	35		
Keith Byars	HB	6'1"	238	27		24
Robert Drummond	HB	6'1"	205	24		12
James Joseph	HB-FB	6'	222	23		18
Thomas Sanders	HB	5'11"	203	29		6
Heath Sherman	FB-HB	6'	205	24		
Fred Barnett	WR	6'	199	25		24
Roy Green	WR	6'1"	195	34		
Rod Harris	WR	5'10"	185	24		
Kenny Jackson	WR	6'	180	29		
Calvin Williams	WR	5'11"	190	24		18
Keith Jackson	TE	6'2"	250	26		30
Maurice Johnson	TE	6'2"	243	24		6
Mickey Shuler	TE	6'3"	231	35		
Jeff Feagles	K	6'	205	25		
Roger Ruzek	K	6'1"	200	30		111

NEW YORK GIANTS 8-8 Ray Handley

Scores of Each Game		
16	SAN FRANCISCO	14
13	L.A. RAMS	19
17	Chicago	20
13	CLEVELAND	10
16	Dallas	21
20	PHOENIX	9
23	Pittsburgh	20
13	WASHINGTON	17
7	Philadelphia	30
21	Phoenix	14
22	DALLAS	9
21	Tampa Bay	14
24	Cincinnati	27
14	PHILADELPHIA	19
17	Washington	34
24	HOUSTON	20

Use Name	Pos.	Hgt.	Wgt.	Age	Int	Pts
John Elliott	OT	6'7"	305	26		
Clarence Jones	OT	6'6"	280	23		
Doug Riesenberg	OT	6'5"	275	26		
Bob Kratch	OG	6'3"	288	25		
Eric Moore	OG-OT	6'5"	290	26		
William Roberts	OG	6'5"	280	29		
Brian Williams	OG-C	6'5"	300	25		
Bart Oates	C	6'3"	265	32		
Eric Dorsey	DE	6'5"	280	27		
Mike Fox	DE	6'6"	275	24		
Leonard Marshall	DE	6'3"	285	29		
Greg Meisner	DE-NT	6'3"	271	32		
Lorenzo Freeman	NT	6'5"	319	27		
Erik Howard	NT	6'4"	268	26		
John Washington	NT	6'4"	275	28		

Use Name	Pos.	Hgt.	Wgt.	Age	Int	Pts
Bobby Abrams	LB	6'3"	230	24		
Carl Banks	LB	6'4"	235	29		
Steve DeOssie	LB	6'2"	248	28		
Pepper Johnson	LB	6'3"	248	27	2	
Kanavis McGhee	LB	6'4"	257	22		
Corey Miller	LB	6'2"	225	22		
Gary Reasons	LB	6'4"	234	29		
Lawrence Taylor	LB	6'3"	243	32		
Roger Brown	DB	6'	196	24		
Mark Collins	DB	5'10"	190	27	4	
A.J. Greene	DB	5'8"	167	25		
Myron Guyton	DB	6'1"	205	24		
Greg Jackson	DB	6'1"	200	25	1	
Lamar McGriggs	DB	6'3"	210	23		
Reyna Thompson	DB	6'	193	28		
Everson Walls	DB	6'1"	194	31	4	
Adrian White	DB	6'	200	27	1	
Perry Williams	DB	6'2"	203	30		

Thom Kaumeyer — Knee Injury

Use Name	Pos.	Hgt.	Wgt.	Age	Int	Pts
Matt Cavanaugh	QB	6'2"	210	34		
Jeff Hostetler	QB	6'3"	212	30		12
Phil Simms	QB	6'3"	214	35		6
Ottis Anderson	HB	6'2"	225	34		6
Rodney Hampton	HB	5'11"	215	22		60
Dave Meggett	HB	5'7"	180	25		30
Lewis Tillman	HB	6'	195	25		6
Jarrod Bunch	FB	6'2"	248	23		
Maurice Carthon	FB	6'1"	225	30		
Stephen Baker	WR	5'8"	160	27		24
Mark Ingram	WR	5'10"	188	26		18
Ed McCaffrey	WR	6'5"	215	23		
Joey Smith	WR	5'10"	177	22		
Odessa Turner	WR	6'3"	205	26		
Howard Cross	TE	6'5"	245	24		12
Zeke Mowatt	TE	6'3"	240	30		6
Raul Allegre (to NYJ)	K	5'10"	167	32		22
Matt Bahr	K	5'10"	175	35		90
Sean Landeta	K	6'	210	29		

PHOENIX CARDINALS 4-12 Joe Bugel

Scores of Each Game		
24	L.A. Rams	14
26	Philadelphia	10
0	Washington	34
9	DALLAS	17
24	NEW ENGLAND	10
9	N.Y. Giants	20
7	Minnesota	34
16	ATLANTA	10
0	MINNESOTA	28
7	Dallas	27
14	N.Y. GIANTS	21
10	San Francisco	14
14	PHILADELPHIA	34
14	WASHINGTON	20
19	Denver	24
3	NEW ORLEANS	27

Use Name	Pos.	Hgt.	Wgt.	Age	Int	Pts
Tootie Robbins	OT	6'5"	310	33		
Luis Sharpe	OT	6'4"	295	31		
Willie Williams	OT	6'6"	300	24		6
Mike Brennan (from CIN, to BUF)	OG	6'5"	274	24		
Lance Smith	OG	6'2"	290	28		
Vernice Smith	OG-OT	6'2"	298	25		
Joe Wolf	OG	6'5"	296	24		
Kani Kauahi	C	6'2"	275	31		
Bill Lewis	C	6'7"	290	28		
Scott Evans	DE	6'3"	261	23		
Jeff Faulkner	DE	6'4"	305	27		
Mike Jones	DE	6'4"	285	22		
Craig Patterson	DE	6'5"	317	27	1	
Eric Swann	DE	6'4"	310	21		
Rod Saddler (to CIN)	DE	6'5"	280	25		6
Jim Wahler	NT-DT	6'4"	275	25		
Chris Williams	NT	6'3"	304	22		

Use Name	Pos.	Hgt.	Wgt.	Age	Int	Pts
David Braxton	LB	6'1"	230	26		
Sidney Coleman	LB	6'2"	250	27		
Ken Harvey	LB	6'2"	230	26		
Eric Hill	LB	6'1"	250	24		6
Steve Hyche	LB	6'2"	226	28		
Garth Jax	LB	6'2"	240	27		
Freddie Joe Nunn	LB-DE	6'4"	250	29		
Tyronne Stowe	LB	6'1"	249	26		
Dave Duerson	DB	6'1"	208	30	1	
Dexter Davis	DB	5'10"	190	21		
Steve Lofton	DB	5'9"	180	22		
Lorenzo Lynch	DB	5'9"	200	28	3	6
Robert Massey	DB	5'10"	185	24		
Tim McDonald	DB	6'2"	215	26	5	
Chris Oldham	DB	5'9"	183	22		
Jay Taylor	DB	5'9"	175	23		
Marcus Turner	DB	6'	190	25		
Aeneas Williams	DB	5'10"	187	22	6	
Mike Zordich	DB	5'11"	200	27	1	

Use Name	Pos.	Hgt.	Wgt.	Age	Int	Pts
Stan Gelbaugh	QB	6'3"	207	28		
Craig Kupp (to DAL)	QB	6'4"	215	24		
Tom Tupa	QB	6'4"	215	25		6
Larry Centers	HB	5'11"	200	23		
Terrence Flagler	HB	6'	200	26		
Johnny Johnson	HB	6'2"	220	23		36
Anthony Thompson	HB	5'11"	210	24		6
Ron Wolfley	FB	6'	230	28		
Anthony Edwards	WR	5'9"	190	25		
Arnod Field	WR	5'11"	181	23		
Randal Hill	WR	5'10"	177	21		6
John Jackson	WR	5'10"	183	24		
Ernie Jones	WR	5'11"	200	26		24
Tony Lomack	WR	5'8"	180	23		
Ricky Proehl	WR	5'10"	190	23		12
Tim Jorden	TE	6'2"	235	24		
Walter Reeves	TE	6'4"	266	25		
Rich Camarillo	K	5'11"	195	31		
Greg Davis	K	6'	200	25		82

Timm Rosenbach — Knee Injury

WASHINGTON REDSKINS

RUSHING Last Name	No.	Yds	Avg	TD
Byner	274	1048	3.8	5
Ervins	145	680	4.7	3
Riggs	78	248	3.2	11
Sanders	7	47	6.7	1
Monk	9	19	2.1	0
Mitchell	3	14	4.7	0
Rypien	15	6	0.4	1
Clark	1	0	0.0	0
Rutledge	8	-13	-1.6	0

RECEIVING Last Name	No.	Yds	Avg	TD
Monk	71	1049	14.8	8
Clark	70	1340	19.1	10
Sanders	45	580	12.9	5
Byner	34	308	9.1	0
Ervins	16	181	11.3	1
Orr	10	201	20.1	4
Warren	5	51	10.2	0
Middleton	3	25	8.3	0
Hobbs	3	24	8.0	0
Ji. Johnson	3	7	2.3	2
Riggs	1	5	5.0	0

PUNT RETURNS Last Name	No.	Yds	Avg	TD
Mitchell	45	600	13.3	2
Hobbs	1	10	10.0	0

KICKOFF RETURNS Last Name	No.	Yds	Avg	TD
Mitchell	29	583	20.1	0
Ervins	11	232	21.1	0
Jo. Johnson	5	83	16.6	0
Gouveia	3	12	4.0	0
Hobbs	1	16	16.0	0

PASSING	Att	Cmp	%	Yds	Yd/Att	TD	Int—%	RK
Rypien	421	249	59.1	3564	8.47	28	11—2.6	2
Rutledge	22	11	50.0	109	8.50	1	0—0.0	
Byner	4	1	25.0	18	4.50	1	0—0.0	

PUNTING	No.	Avg.
Goodburn	55	37.6

KICKING	XP	ATT	%	FG	ATT	%
Lohmiller	56	56	100	31	43	73

DALLAS COWBOYS

RUSHING Last Name	No.	Yds	Avg	TD
E. Smith	365	1563	4.3	12
Blake	15	80	5.3	1
Johnston	17	54	3.2	0
Agee	9	20	2.2	1
Aikman	16	5	0.3	1
Richards	2	4	2.0	0
Wright	2	-1	-0.5	0
Beuerlein	7	-14	-2.0	0

RECEIVING Last Name	No.	Yds	Avg	TD
Irvin	93	1523	16.4	8
Novacek	59	664	11.3	4
E. Smith	49	258	5.3	1
Johnston	28	244	8.7	1
Harper	20	326	16.3	1
Martin	16	243	15.2	0
Roberts	16	136	8.5	1
Wright	10	170	17.0	0
Agee	7	43	6.1	0
Awalt	5	57	11.4	0
Blake	1	5	5.0	0
Aikman	1	-6	-6.0	0

PUNT RETURNS Last Name	No.	Yds	Avg	TD
Martin	21	244	11.6	1
Shepard	6	57	9.5	0
Horton	1	8	8.0	0
Brownlow	1	0	0.0	0

KICKOFF RETURNS Last Name	No.	Yds	Avg	TD
Wright	21	514	24.5	1
Dixon	18	398	22.1	0
Gant	6	114	19.0	0
Shepard	3	54	18.0	0
Martin	3	47	15.7	0
Horton	1	0	0.0	0

PASSING	Att	Cmp	%	Yds	Yd/Att	TD	Int—%	RK
Aikman	363	237	65.3	2754	7.59	11	10—2.8	4
Beuerlein	137	68	49.6	909	6.64	5	2—1.5	

PUNTING	No.	Avg.
Saxon57	42.6	

KICKING	XP	Att.	%	FG	Att	%
Willis	37	37	100	27	39	69

PHILADELPHIA EAGLES

RUSHING Last Name	No.	Yds	Avg	TD
Joseph	135	440	3.3	3
Byars	94	383	4.1	1
Sherman	106	279	2.6	0
Sanders	54	122	2.3	1
McMahon	22	55	2.5	1
Drummond	12	27	2.3	2
Ken. Jackson	1	18	18.0	0
Goebel	1	2	2.0	0
Barnett	1	0	0.0	0
Feagles	3	-1	-0.3	0
Ryan	1	-2	-2.0	0

RECEIVING Last Name	No.	Yds	Avg	TD
Barnett	62	948	15.3	4
Byars	62	564	9.1	3
Kei. Jackson	48	569	11.9	5
Williams	33	326	9.9	3
Green	29	364	12.6	0
Sherman	14	59	4.2	0
Joseph	10	64	6.4	0
Sanders	8	62	7.8	0
Shuler	6	91	15.2	0
M. Johnson	6	70	11.7	2
Ken. Jackson	4	29	7.3	0
Harris	2	28	14.0	0
McMahon	1	-5	-5.0	0

PUNT RETURNS Last Name	No.	Yds	Avg	TD
Harris	53	416	7.8	0

KICKOFF RETURNS Last Name	No.	Yds	Avg	TD
Harris	28	473	16.9	0
Sanders	10	160	16.0	0
Green	5	70	14.0	0
Sherman	4	61	15.3	0

PASSING	Att	Cmp	%	Yds	Yd/Att	TD	Int—%	RK
McMahon	311	187	60.1	2239	7.20	12	11—3.5	8
Goebel	56	30	53.6	267	4.77	0	6—10.7	
Ryan	26	10	38.5	98	3.77	0	4—15.4	
Cunningham	4	1	25.0	19	4.75	0	0—0.0	
Byars	2	0	0.0	0	0.00	0	1—50.0	

PUNTING	No.	Avg.
Feagles	88	41.4

KICKING	XP	ATT	%	FG	ATT	%
Ruzek	27	29	93	28	33	85

NEW YORK GIANTS

RUSHING Last Name	No.	Yds	Avg	TD
Hampton	256	1059	4.1	10
Tillman	65	287	4.4	1
Hostetler	42	273	6.5	2
Meggett	29	153	5.3	1
Anderson	53	141	2.7	1
Carthon	32	109	3.4	0
Simms	9	42	4.7	1
Bunch	1	0	0.0	0

RECEIVING Last Name	No.	Yds	Avg	TD
Ingram	51	824	16.2	3
Meggett	50	412	8.2	3
Hampton	43	283	6.6	0
Baker	30	525	17.5	4
Turner	21	356	17.0	0
Cross	20	283	14.2	2
McCaffrey	16	146	9.1	0
Anderson	11	41	3.7	0
Carthon	7	39	5.6	0
Mowatt	5	78	15.6	1
Tillman	5	30	6.0	0
Bunch	2	8	4.0	0

PUNT RETURNS Last Name	No.	Yds	Avg	TD
Meggett	28	287	10.3	1
Ingram	8	49	6.1	0

KICKOFF RETURNS Last Name	No.	Yds	Avg	TD
Meggett	25	514	20.6	0
Hampton	10	204	20.4	0
Ingram	8	125	15.6	0
Smith	3	34	11.3	0
Tillman	2	29	14.5	0
Cross	1	11	11.0	0
Freeman	1	0	0.0	0

PASSING	Att	Cmp	%	Yds	Yd/Att	TD	Int—%	RK
Hostetler	285	179	62.8	2032	7.13	5	4—1.4	5
Simms	141	82	58.2	993	7.04	8	4—2.8	
Ingram	1	0	0.0	0	0.00	0	0—0.0	
Meggett	1	0	0.0	0	0.00	0	0—0.0	

PUNTING	No.	Avg.
Landeta	64	43.3

KICKING	XP	ATT	%	FG	ATT	%
Bahr	24	25	96	22	29	76
Allegre	7	7	100	5	6	83

PHOENIX CARDINALS

RUSHING Last Name	No.	Yds	Avg	TD
Johnson	196	666	3.4	4
Thompson	126	376	3.0	1
Tupa	28	97	3.5	1
Centers	14	44	3.1	0
E. Jones	5	24	4.8	0
Gelbaugh	9	23	2.6	0
Proehl	3	21	7.0	0
Flagler	1	7	7.0	0
Kupp	1	5	5.0	0

RECEIVING Last Name	No.	Yds	Avg	TD
E. Jones	61	957	15.7	4
Proehl	55	766	13.9	2
R. Hill	43	495	11.5	1
Johnson	29	225	7.8	2
Centers	19	176	9.3	0
Jorden	15	127	8.5	0
Jackson	8	108	13.5	0
Flagler	8	85	10.6	0
Reeves	8	45	5.6	0
Thompson	7	52	7.4	0
W. Williams	1	3	3.0	1

PUNT RETURNS Last Name	No.	Yds	Avg	TD
Jackson	31	244	7.9	0
Centers	5	30	6.0	0
Proehl	4	26	6.5	0
Edwards	1	7	7.0	0

KICKOFF RETURNS Last Name	No.	Yds	Avg	TD
Centers	16	330	20.6	0
Edwards	13	261	20.1	0
Flagler	12	208	17.3	0
R. Hill	9	146	16.2	0
Jackson	2	41	20.5	0
Lomack	1	19	19.0	0

PASSING	Att	Cmp	%	Yds	Yd/Att	TD	Int—%	RK
Tupa	315	165	52.4	2053	6.52	6	13—4.1	15
Gelbaugh	118	61	51.7	674	5.71	3	10—8.5	
Kupp	7	3	42.9	23	3.29	0	0—0.0	
Camarillo	1	0	0.0	0	0.00	0	0—0.0	
Thompson	1	0	0.0	0	0.00	0	0—0.0	

PUNTING	No.	Avg.
Camarillo	77	44.7

KICKING	XP	Att	%	FG	Att	%
Davis	19	19	100	21	30	70

DETROIT LIONS 12-4 Wayne Fontes

Scores of Each Game		
0	Washington	45
23	GREEN BAY	14
17	MIAMI	13
33	Indianapolis	24
31	TAMPA BAY	3
24	MINNESOTA	20
3	San Francisco	35
34	DALLAS	10
10	Chicago	20
21	Tampa Bay	30
21	L.A. RAMS	10
34	Minnesota	14
16	CHICAGO	6
34	N.Y. JETS	20
21	Green Bay	17
17	Buffalo	*14

UseName	Pos.	Hgt.	Wgt.	Age	Int	Pts
Lomas Brown	OT	6'4"	287	28		
Roman Fortin	OT	6'5"	290	24		
Eric Sanders	OT-OG	6'7"	286	32		
Eric Andolsek	OG	6'2"	291	25		
Shawn Bouwens	OG	6'4"	290	23		
Scott Conover	OG	6'4"	285	22		
Ken Dallafior	OG-C	6'4"	285	32		
Mike Utley	OG-OT	6'6"	290	25		
Kevin Glover	C	6'2"	282	28		
Darryl Milburn	DE	6'3"	260	22		
Dan Owens	DE	6'3"	280	24		
Kelvin Pritchett	DE	6'2"	281	21		
Marc Spindler	DE	6'5"	290	21		
Jerry Ball	NT	6'1"	298	26		2
Lawrence Pete	NT	6'	295	25		

UseName	Pos.	Hgt.	Wgt.	Age	Int	Pts
Anthony Bell	LB	6'3"	235	27		
Mark Brown	LB	6'2"	240	28		
Toby Caston	LB	6'1"	243	26		
Mike Cofer	LB	6'5"	244	31		
Dennis Gibson	LB	6'2"	243	27		
Tracy Hayworth	LB	6'3"	260	23	1	6
George Jamison	LB	6'1"	228	28	3	
Victor Jones	LB	6'2"	250	24		
Niko Noga	LB	6'1"	235	29		
Chris Spielman	LB	6'	247	25		
Bruce Alexander	DB	5'9"	169	25	1	
Bennie Blades	DB	6'1"	221	24	1	
Ray Crockett	DB	5'9"	181	24	6	6
Melvin Jenkins	DB	5'10"	173	29		
Kevin Scott	DB	5'9"	175	22		
Terry Taylor	DB	5'10"	191	30	4	
Herb Welch	DB	5'11"	180	30		
Sheldon White	DB	5'11"	188	26	2	6
William White	DB	5'10"	191	25	1	

UseName	Pos.	Hgt.	Wgt.	Age	Int	Pts
Erik Kramer	QB	6'1"	195	26		6
Chuck Long	QB	6'4"	217	28		
Andre Ware	QB	6'2"	205	23		
Rodney Peete	QB	6'	193	25		12
D.J. Dozier	HB	6'	205	25		
Barry Sanders	HB-FB	5'8"	203	23		102
Cedric Jackson	FB-HB	5'11"	229	23		
Don Overton	FB-HN	6'	221	23		
Reggie Barrett	WR	6'3"	215	22		
Jeff Campbell	WR	5'8"	167	23		
Robert Clark	WR	5'11"	173	26		36
Mike Farr	WR	5'10"	192	24		6
Mel Gray	WR	5'9"	162	30		6
Willie Green	WR	6'2"	179	25		42
Aubrey Matthews	WR	5'7"	165	28		
Herman Moore	WR	6'3"	205	21		
Brett Perriman	WR	5'9"	180	25		6
David Little	TE	6'2"	226	30		
Eugene Riley	TE	6'3"	238	24		
Derek Tennell	TE	6'5"	270	27		
Jim Arnold	K	6'3"	211	30		
Eddie Murray	K	5'10"	180	35		97

CHICAGO BEARS 11-5 Mike Ditka

Scores of Each Game		
10	MINNESOTA	6
21	Tampa Bay	20
20	N.Y. GIANTS	17
19	N.Y. JETS	*13
20	Buffalo	35
7	WASHINGTON	20
10	Green Bay	0
20	New Orleans	17
20	DETROIT	10
34	Minnesota	17
31	Indianapolis	17
13	MIAMI	*16
6	Detroit	16
27	GREEN BAY	13
27	TAMPA BAY	0
14	San Francisco	52

UseName	Pos.	Hgt.	Wgt.	Age	Int	Pts
Ron Mattes	OT	6'6"	300	28		
Stan Thomas	OT	6'5"	302	22		
Keith Van Horne	OT	6'6"	283	33		
John Wojciechowski	OT	6'4"	270	28		
Mark Bortz	OG	6'6"	272	30		
Jerry Fontenot	OG	6'3"	272	24		
Tom Thayer	OG	6'4"	270	30		
Jay Hilgenberg	C	6'3"	260	31		
Trace Armstrong	DE	6'4"	259	25		
Richard Dent	DE	6'5"	268	30	1	
Tim Ryan	DE-DT	6'4"	268	23		
James Williams	DE	6'7"	305	23		
Steve McMichael	DT	6'2"	268	33		
William Perry	DT	6'2"	350	28		
Chris Zorich	DT	6'1"	267	22		

Jim Covert — Back Injury
Eric Kumerow — Broken Ankle

UseName	Pos.	Hgt.	Wgt.	Age	Int	Pts
Ron Cox	LB	6'2"	242	23		
Dante Jones	LB	6'1"	236	26		
Jim Morrissey	LB	6'3"	227	28	1	
Ron Rivera	LB	6'3"	240	29		
John Roper	LB	6'1"	228	25		
Mike Singletary	LB	6'	230	32		
Mike Stonebreaker	LB	6'	226	24		
Mark Carrier	DB	6'1"	180	23	2	
Maurice Douglass	DB	5'11"	200	27		
Shaun Gayle	DB	5'11"	194	29	1	
John Hardy	DB	5'10"	166	23		
John Mangum	DB	5'10"	173	24	1	
Markus Paul	DB	6'2"	199	25	3	
Lemuel Stinson	DB	5'9"	159	25	4	6
David Tate	DB	6'	177	26	2	
Donnell Woolford	DB	5'9"	187	25	2	

UseName	Pos.	Hgt.	Wgt.	Age	Int	Pts
Jim Harbaugh	QB	6'3"	220	26		12
Peter Tom Willis	QB	6'2"	200	24		
Neal Anderson	HB	5'11"	210	27		54
Johnny Bailey	HB	5'8"	180	24		6
Mark Green	HB	5'11"	184	24		18
Darren Lewis	HB-FB	5'10"	219	22		6
Brad Muster	FB	6'3"	231	26		42
James Rouse	FB	6'	220	24		
Wendell Davis	WR	5'11"	188	25		36
Dennis Gentry	WR-HB	5'8"	180	32		
Glen Kozlowski	WR	6'1"	190	28		
Anthony Morgan	WR	6'1"	195	23		12
Ron Morris	WR	6'1'	195	26		
Tom Waddle	WR	6'	181	24		18
Cap Boso	TE	6'3"	240	27		
Keith Jennings	TE	6'4"	251	25		
Jim Thornton	TE	6'2"	242	26		6
Maury Buford	K	6'1"	198	31		
Kevin Butler	K	6'1"	190	29		89
Chris Gardocki	K	6'1"	194	21		

Quintin Smith — Leg Injury

MINNESOTA VIKINGS 8-8 Jerry Burns

Scores of Each Game		
6	Chicago	10
20	Atlanta	19
17	SAN FRANCISCO	14
0	New Orleans	26
6	DENVER	13
20	Detroit	24
34	PHOENIX	7
23	New England	*26
28	Phoenix	0
28	TAMPA BAY	13
17	CHICAGO	34
35	Green Bay	21
14	DETROIT	34
26	Tampa Bay	24
20	L.A. RAMS	14
7	GREEN BAY	27

UseName	Pos.	Hgt.	Wgt.	Age	Int	Pts
Brian Habib	OT	6'7"	292	26		
Tim Irwin	OT	6'6"	301	32		
Gary Zimmerman	OT	6'6"	286	29		
Todd Kalis	OG	6'5"	285	26		
Randall McDaniel	OG	6'3"	271	26		
Craig Wolfley	OG	6'1"	265	33		
Chris Foote	C	6'3"	266	34		
Kirk Lowdermilk	C	6'3"	270	28		
Mike Morris	C	6'5"	268	30		
Adam Schrieber	C-OG	6'4"	280	29		
Chris Doleman	DE	6'5"	266	29		
Al Noga	DE	6'1"	264	25		
John Randle	DE	6'1"	264	23		
Thomas Strauthers	DE	6'4"	263	30		
Ken Clarke	DT	6'2"	279	35		
Mike Teeter	DT	6'2"	269	24		
Henry Thomas	DT	6'2"	269	26		

Keith Millard — Knee Injury

UseName	Pos.	Hgt.	Wgt.	Age	Int	Pts
Ray Berry	LB	6'2"	227	27	1	
Ivan Caesar	LB	6'1"	241	24		
Mark Dusbabek	LB	6'3"	230	27		
Carlos Jenkins	LB	6'3"	222	23		
Greg Manusky	LB	6'1"	236	25		
Mike Merriweather	LB	6'2"	226	30	1	6
Mac Stephens	LB	6'3"	220	23		
Jimmy Williams	LB	6'3"	221	30		
Joey Browner	DB	6'2"	231	31	5	
Pat Eilers	DB	5'11"	192	24		
Carl Lee	DB	6'	183	30	1	
Mike Myes	DB	5'10"	179	25		
Audrey McMillian	DB	6'	190	29	4	
Reggie Rutland	DB	6'1"	191	27	3	6
Todd Scott	DB	5'10"	190	23		
Solomon Wilcots	DB	5'11"	200	26		
Felix Wright	DB	6'2"	197	32	2	

UseName	Pos.	Hgt.	Wgt.	Age	Int	Pts
Rich Gannon	QB	6'3"	203	25		12
Sean Salisbury	QB	6'5"	213	28		
Wade Wilson	QB	6'3"	205	32		
Terry Allen	HB	5'10"	189	23		18
Darrin Nelson	HB	5'9"	180	32		12
Herschel Walker	HB-FB	6'1"	220	29		60
Alfred Anderson	FB	6'1"	219	30		6
Randy Baldwin	FB	5'10"	210	24		
Rick Fenney	FB	6'1"	233	26		
Anthony Carter	WR	5'11"	176	30		36
Cris Carter	WR	6'3"	198	25		30
Hassan Jones	WR	6'	196	27		6
Leo Lewis	WR	5'8"	163	34		
Terry Obee	WR	5'10"	190	23		
Jake Reed	WR	6'3"	216	23		
Mike Jones	TE	6'3"	256	24		12
Steve Jordan	TE	6'4"	238	30		12
Brent Novoselsky	TE	6'3"	236	25		
Harry Newsome	K	6'	189	28		
Fuad Reveiz	K	5'11"	225	28		85

GREEN BAY PACKERS 4-12 Lindy Infante

Scores of Each Game		
3	PHILADELPHIA	20
14	Detroit	23
15	TAMPA BAY	13
13	Miami	16
21	L.A. Rams	23
17	DALLAS	20
0	CHICAGO	10
27	Tampa Bay	0
16	N.Y. Jets	*19
24	BUFFALO	34
21	MINNESOTA	35
14	INDIANAPOLIS	10
31	Atlanta	35
13	Chicago	27
17	DETROIT	21
27	Minnesota	7

UseName	Pos.	Hgt.	Wgt.	Age	Int	Pts
Louis Cheek	OT-OG	6'7"	286	26		
Steve Gabbard	OT	6'4"	297	25		
Scott Jones	OT	6'5"	282	25		
Tony Mandarich	OT	6'5"	310	24		
Ken Ruettgers	OT	6'5"	286	29		
Billy Ard	OG	6'3"	273	32		
Ron Hallstrom	OG	6'6"	305	32		
Rich Moran	OG	6'3"	280	29		
Keith Uecker	OG	6'5"	299	31		
Blair Bush	C	6'3"	275	34		
James Campen	C	6'3"	277	27		
Lester Archambeau	DE	6'4"	271	24		
Matt Brock	DE	6'5"	290	25		
Robert Brown	DE	6'2"	278	31	1	
Don Davey	DE	6'4"	273	23		
Shawn Patterson	DE	6'5"	273	27		
John Jurkovic	NT	6'2"	297	24		
Esera Tuaolo	NT	6'2"	284	23	1	

UseName	Pos.	Hgt.	Wgt.	Age	Int	Pts
Tony Bennett	LB	6'2"	242	24		
Reggie Burnette	LB	6'2"	240	23		
Burnell Dent	LB	6'1"	233	28		
Johnny Holland	LB	6'2"	232	26		
Kurt Larson	LB	6'4"	241	25		
Brian Noble	LB	6'3"	250	28		6
Bryce Paup	LB	6'5"	247	23		2
Scott Stephen	LB	6'2"	243	27	1	
LeRoy Butler	DB	6'	195	23	3	
Chuck Cecil	DB	6'	190	26	3	
Vinnie Clark	DB	6'	194	22	2	
Joe Fuller	DB	5'11"	186	26		
Tim Hauck	DB	5'11"	181	24		
Jerry Holmes	DB	6'2"	178	33	1	
Roland Mitchell	DB	5'11"	198	27		
Mark Murphy	DB	6'2"	209	33	3	

UseName	Pos.	Hgt.	Wgt.	Age	Int	Pts
Blair Kiel	QB	6'	209	29		
Don Majkowski	QB	6'2"	206	27		12
Mike Tomczak	QB	6'1"	204	28		6
Vai Sikahema	HB	5'9"	196	29		
Keith Woodside	HB	5'11"	217	27		6
Vince Workman	HB	5'10	201	23		66
Steve Avery	FB	6'1"	225	25		
Walter Dean	FB	5'10"	216	23		
Allen Rice	FB	5'11"	206	29		
Darrell Thompson	FB	6'	227	23		6
Chuck Webb	FB	5'9"	201	22		
Erik Affholter	WR	6'	187	25		
Perry Kemp	WR	5'11"	163	29		12
Jeff Query	WR	6'	165	24		
Sterling Sharpe	WR	5'11"	205	26		24
Clarence Weathers	WR	5'9"	169	29		
Charles Wilson	WR	5'9"	178	23		12
Jackie Harris	TE	6'3"	243	23		18
Ed West	TE	6'1"	244	30		18
Chris Jacke	K	6'	197	25		85
Paul McJulien	K	5'10"	190	26		

TAMPA BAY BUCCANEERS 3-13 Richard Williamson

Scores of Each Game		
13	N.Y. Jets	16
20	CHICAGO	21
13	Green Bay	15
10	BUFFALO	17
3	Detroit	31
14	PHILADELPHIA	13
7	New Orleans	23
0	GREEN BAY	27
13	Minnesota	28
30	DETROIT	21
7	Atlanta	43
14	N.Y. GIANTS	21
14	Miami	33
24	MINNESOTA	26
0	Chicago	27
17	INDIANAPOLIS	3

UseName	Pos.	Hgt.	Wgt.	Age	Int	Pts
Scott Dill	OT	6'5"	285	25		
Paul Gruber	OT	6'5"	290	26		
Charles McRae	OT	6'7"	290	22		
Rob Taylor	OT	6'6"	290	30		
Ian Beckles	OG	6'1"	295	24		
John Bruhin	OG	6'3"	285	26		
Tom McHale	OG	6'4"	280	28		
Tim Ryan	OG	6'2"	280	22		
Tony Mayberry	C	6'4"	285	23		
Al Chamblee	DE	6'1"	240	22		
Dexter Manley	DE	6'4"	270	32		
Keith McCants	DE	6'3"	265	23		
Ray Seals	DE	6'3"	270	26		
Reuben Davis	DT-DE	6'4"	285	26		
Darryl Grant	DT	6'1"	275	31		
Rhett Hall	DT	6'2"	260	22		
Tim Newton	DT	6'	275	28		
Gerald Nichols	DT	6'2"	260	27		

Randy Grimes — Elbow Injury

UseName	Pos.	Hgt.	Wgt.	Age	Int	Pts
Sam Anno	LB	6'2"	235	26		
Eugene Marve	LB	6'2"	240	31	1	
Kevin Murphy	LB	6'2"	235	27		
Maurice Oliver	LB	6'3"	235	24		
Jesse Solomon	LB	6'	235	27		
Broderick Thomas	LB	6'4"	245	24		
Calvin Tiggle	LB	6'1"	235	22		
Carl Carter	DB	5'11"	180	27	1	
Marty Carter	DB	6'1"	200	21	1	
Tony Covington	DB	5'11"	190	23	3	
William Frizzell	DB	6'3"	205	28		
Darrell Fullington (from NE)	DB	6'1"	195	27	2	
Harry Hamilton	DB	6'	195	28		
Alonzo Hampton	DB	5'10"	195	24	1	
Roger Jones	DB	5'9"	175	22		
Ricky Reynolds	DB	5'11"	190	26	2	
Glenn Rogers	DB	6'	185	22		

Mark Robinson — Shoulder Injury

UseName	Pos.	Hgt.	Wgt.	Age	Int	Pts
Jeff Carlson	QB	6'3"	215	25		
Chris Chandler (to PHX)	QB	6'4"	220	25		
Vinny Testaverde	QB	6'5"	215	27		
Gary Anderson	HB	6'	190	30		6
Reggie Cobb	HB-FB	6'	215	23		42
Robert Hardy	HB	5'10"	210	24		
Alonzo Highsmith (from DAL)	FB	6'1"	235	26		
Chuck Weatherspoon	FB	5'7"	230	23		
Robert Wilson	FB	6'	240	22		12
Terry Anthony	WR	6'	200	23		
Mark Carrier	WR	6'	185	25		12
Lawrence Dawsey	WR	6'	195	23		18
Willie Drewrey	WR	5'7"	170	28		12
Bruce Hill	WR	6'	180	27		12
Jesse Anderson	TE	6'2"	245	25		12
Ron Hall	TE	6'4"	245	27		
Ed Thomas	TE	6'3"	245	25		
Steve Christie	K	6'	185	23		67
Mark Royals	K	6'5"	215	27		

DETROIT LIONS

RUSHING

Last Name	No.	Yds	Avg	TD
B. Sanders	342	1548	4.5	16
Peete	25	125	5.0	2
Overton	14	59	4.2	0
Jackson	17	53	3.1	0
Dozier	9	48	5.3	0
Arnold	2	42	21.0	0
Kramer	34	21	0.6	1
Gray	2	11	5.5	0
Perriman	4	10	2.5	0
Ware	4	6	1.5	0

RECEIVING

Last Name	No.	Yds	Avg	TD
Perriman	52	668	12.8	1
Clark	47	640	13.6	6
Farr	42	431	10.3	1
Sanders	41	307	7.5	1
Green	39	592	15.2	7
Moore	11	135	12.3	0
Tennell	4	43	10.8	0
Overton	4	38	9.4	0
Gray	3	42	14.0	0
Matthews	3	21	7.0	0
Campbell	2	49	24.5	0
Fortin	1	4	4.0	0
Riley	1	3	3.0	0
Dozier	1	3	3.0	0
Jackson	1	-2	-2.0	0

PUNT RETURNS

Last Name	No.	Yds	Avg	TD
Gray	25	385	15.4	1
Jenkins	1	0	0.0	0

KICKOFF RETURNS

Last Name	No.	Yds	Avg	TD
Gray	36	929	25.8	0
Campbell	9	85	9.4	0
Overton	4	71	17.8	0
Dozier	4	60	15.0	0
Scott	1	16	16.0	0
Jackson	1	9	9.0	0
Clark	1	0	0.0	0
Bell	1	0	0.0	0

PASSING — PUNTING — KICKING

PASSING	Att	Cmp	%	Yds	Yd/Att	TD	Int— %	RK
Kramer	265	136	51.3	1635	6.17	11	8—3.0	13
Peete	194	116	59.8	1339	6.90	5	9—4.6	

PUNTING	No.	Avg.
Arnold	75	41.2

KICKING	XP	Att	%	FG	Att	%
Murray	40	40	100	19	28	68

CHICAGO BEARS

RUSHING

Last Name	No.	Yds	Avg	TD
Anderson	210	747	3.6	6
Muster	90	412	4.6	6
Harbaugh	70	338	4.8	2
Green	61	217	3.6	3
Rouse	24	74	2.7	0
Gentry	9	58	6.4	0
Bailey	15	43	2.9	1
Lewis	15	36	2.4	0
Morgan	3	18	6.0	0
Willis	2	6	3.0	0

RECEIVING

Last Name	No.	Yds	Avg	TD
Davis	61	945	15.5	6
Waddle	55	599	10.9	3
Anderson	47	368	7.8	3
Muster	35	287	8.2	1
Thornton	17	278	16.4	1
Gentry	16	149	9.3	0
Rouse	15	93	6.2	0
Morgan	13	211	16.2	2
Morris	8	147	18.4	0
Jennings	8	109	13.6	0
Green	6	54	9.0	0
Boso	3	36	12.0	0
Kozlowski	2	16	8.0	0

PUNT RETURNS

Last Name	No.	Yds	Avg	TD
Bailey	36	281	7.8	0
Waddle	5	31	6.2	0
Morgan	3	19	6.3	0
Green	3	9	3.0	0

KICKOFF RETURNS

Last Name	No.	Yds	Avg	TD
Bailey	16	311	19.4	0
Gentry	13	227	17.5	0
Morgan	8	133	16.6	0
Green	4	69	17.3	0
Lewis	2	13	6.5	0
Rouse	2	10	5.0	0

PASSING — PUNTING — KICKING

PASSING	Att	Cmp	%	Yds	Yd/Att	TD	Int— %	RK
Harbaugh	478	275	57.5	3121	6.53	15	16—3.3	11
Willis	18	11	61.1	171	9.50	1	1—5.6	
Anderson	1	0	0.0	0	0.00	0	0—0.0	

PUNTING	No.	Avg.
Buford	70	40.2

KICKING	XP	ATT	%	FG	ATT	%
Butler	32	34	94	19	29	66

MINNESOTA VIKINGS

RUSHING

Last Name	No.	Yds	Avg	TD
Walker	198	825	4.2	10
Allen	120	563	4.7	2
Gannon	43	236	5.5	2
Nelson	28	210	7.5	2
Anderson	26	118	4.5	1
A. Carter	13	117	9.0	1
Fenney	23	99	4.3	0
Wilson	13	33	2.5	0

RECEIVING

Last Name	No.	Yds	Avg	TD
C. Carter	72	962	13.4	5
Jordan	57	638	11.2	2
A. Carter	51	553	10.8	5
Walker	33	204	6.2	0
H. Jones	32	384	12.0	1
Nelson	19	142	7.5	0
Allen	6	49	8.2	1
Lewis	4	36	9.0	0
Novoselsky	4	27	6.8	0
Fenney	2	11	5.5	0
M. Jones	2	8	4.0	2
Anderson	1	2	2.0	0
Gannon	1	0	0.0	0

PUNT RETURNS

Last Name	No.	Yds	Avg	TD
Lewis	30	225	7.5	0

KICKOFF RETURNS

Last Name	No.	Yds	Avg	TD
Nelson	31	682	22.0	0
Eilers	5	99	19.8	0
Walker	5	83	16.6	0
Allen	1	14	14.0	0
Baldwin	1	14	14.0	0
Anderson	1	7	7.0	0

PASSING — PUNTING — KICKING

PASSING	Att	Cmp	%	Yds	Yd/Att	TD	Int— %	RK
Gannon	354	211	59.6	2166	6.12	12	6—1.7	6
Wilson	122	72	59.0	825	6.76	3	10—8.2	
Nelson	1	1	100.0	25	25.00	1	0—0.0	

PUNTING	No.	Avg.
Newsome	68	45.5

KICKING	XP	ATT	%	FG	ATT	%
Reveiz	34	35	97	17	24	71

GREEN BAY PACKERS

RUSHING

Last Name	No.	Yds	Avg	TD
Thompson	141	471	3.3	1
Woodside	84	326	3.9	1
Workman	71	237	3.3	7
Majkowski	25	108	4.3	2
Rice	30	100	3.3	0
Tomczak	17	93	5.5	1
Kiel	4	46	11.5	0
Sharpe	4	4	1.0	0
Wilson	3	3	1.0	0
Harris	1	1	1.0	0
McJulien	1	0	0.0	0

RECEIVING

Last Name	No.	Yds	Avg	TD
Sharpe	69	961	13.9	4
Workman	46	371	8.1	4
Kemp	42	583	13.9	2
Harris	24	264	11.0	3
Woodside	22	185	8.4	0
Wilson	19	305	16.1	1
West	15	151	10.1	3
Weathers	12	150	12.5	0
Query	7	94	13.4	0
Thompson	7	71	10.1	0
Affholter	7	68	9.7	0
Rice	2	10	5.0	0

PUNT RETURNS

Last Name	No.	Yds	Avg	TD
Sikahema	26	239	9.2	0
Query	14	157	11.2	0

KICKOFF RETURNS

Last Name	No.	Yds	Avg	TD
Wilson	23	522	22.7	1
Sikahema	15	325	21.7	0
Workman	8	139	17.4	0
Thompson	7	127	18.1	0
Rice	3	36	12.0	0
Webb	2	40	20.0	0
Davey	1	8	8.0	0
Dean	1	0	0.0	0

PASSING — PUNTING — KICKING

PASSING	Att	Cmp	%	Yds	Yd/Att	TD	Int— %	RK
Tomczak	238	128	53.8	1490	6.26	11	9—3.8	12
Majkowski	226	115	50.9	1362	6.03	3	8—3.5	16
Kiel	50	29	58.0	361	7.22	3	2—4.0	

PUNTING	No.	Avg.
McJulien	86	40.4

KICKING	XP	Att.	%	FG	Att	%
Jacke	31	31	100	18	24	75

TAMPA BAY BUCCANEERS

RUSHING

Last Name	No.	Yds	Avg	TD
Cobb	196	752	3.8	7
G. Anderson	72	263	3.7	1
Wilson	42	179	4.3	0
Chandler	26	111	4.3	0
Testaverde	32	101	3.2	0
Carlson	5	25	5.0	0
Highsmith	5	21	4.2	0

RECEIVING

Last Name	No.	Yds	Avg	TD
Dawsey	55	818	14.9	3
Carrier	47	698	14.9	2
Ro. Hall	31	284	9.2	0
Drewrey	26	375	14.4	2
G. Anderson	25	184	7.4	0
Wilson	20	121	6.1	2
Hill	17	185	10.9	2
Cobb	15	111	7.4	0
J. Anderson	6	73	12.2	2
E. Thomas	4	55	13.8	0
Anthony	4	51	12.8	0

PUNT RETURNS

Last Name	No.	Yds	Avg	TD
Drewrey	38	360	9.5	0
Carter	1	1	1.0	0

KICKOFF RETURNS

Last Name	No.	Yds	Avg	TD
G. Anderson	34	643	18.9	0
Drewrey	12	246	20.5	0
Hardy	8	119	14.9	0
Wilson	2	19	9.5	0
Cobb	2	15	7.5	0
Ryan	1	4	4.0	0
Ro. Hall	1	1	1.0	0

PASSING — PUNTING — KICKING

PASSING	Att	Cmp	%	Yds	Yd/Att	TD	Int— %	RK
Testaverde	326	166	50.9	1994	6.12	8	15—4.6	17
Chandler	154	78	50.6	846	5.49	5	10—4.0	

PUNTING	No.	Avg.
Royals	84	40.3

KICKING	XP	ATT	%	FG	ATT	%
Christie	22	22	100	15	20	75

NEW ORLEANS SAINTS 11-5 Jim Mora

Scores of Each Game		
27	SEATTLE	24
17	Kansas City	10
24	L.A. RAMS	7
26	MINNESOTA	0
27	Atlanta	6
13	Philadelphia	6
23	TAMPA BAY	7
17	CHICAGO	20
24	L.A. Rams	17
10	SAN FRANCISCO	3
21	San Diego	24
20	ATLANTA	*23
24	San Francisco	38
14	Dallas	23
27	L.A. RAIDERS	0
27	Phoenix	3

UseName	Pos.	Hgt.	Wgt.	Age	Int	Pts
Stan Brock	OT	6'6"	278	33		
Richard Cooper	OT	6'4"	290	26		
Kevin Haverdink	OT	6'5"	285	25		
Mike Keim	OT	6'7"	285	25		
Jim Dombrowski	OG	6'5"	298	27		
Derek Kennard	OG	6'3"	300	28		
Chris Port	OG	6'5"	290	23		
Larry Williams	OG-C	6'5"	294	28		
Joel Hilgenberg	C	6'3"	252	29		
Brad Leggett	C	6'4"	270	25		
Wayne Martin	DE	6'5"	275	25		
Les Miller	DE	6'7"	285	26		
Renaldo Turnbull	DE	6'4"	255	25		
Jim Wilks	NT	6'5"	275	33		
Robert Goff	NT	6'3"	270	25		
Frank Warren	DE	6'4"	290	31		

Steve Trapilo — Knee Injury

UseName	Pos.	Hgt.	Wgt.	Age	Int	Pts
Brian Forde	LB	6'2"	235	27		
Rickey Jackson	LB	6'2"	243	33		
Vaughan Johnson	LB	6'3"	235	29	1	
Sam Mills	LB	5'9"	225	32	2	
Scott Ross	LB	6'1"	235	22		
Joel Smeenge	DE	6'5"	255	23		
Pat Swilling	LB	6'3"	242	26	1	6
James Williams	LB	6'	230	22		
Gene Atkins	DB	6'1"	200	26	5	
Vince Buck	DB	6'	198	23	5	
Toi Cook	DB	5'11"	188	26	3	
Vencie Glenn	DB	6'	192	26	4	
Reggie Jones	DB	6'1"	202	22	3	
Milton Mack	DB	5'11"	182	27		
Brett Maxie	DB	6'2"	194	29	3	6
Calvin Nicholson	DB	5'9"	183	34		
Stan Petry (from KC)	DB	5'11"	180	25	1	
Bennie Thompson	DB	6'	200	28	1	

DeMond Winston — Knee Injury

UseName	Pos.	Hgt.	Wgt.	Age	Int	Pts
Mike Buck	QB	6'3"	227	24		
Bobby Hebert	QB	6'4"	215	31		
Steve Walsh	QB	6'2"	204	24		
Gill Fenerty	HB	6'	205	28		30
Dalton Hilliard	HB	5'8"	204	27		30
Stanford Jennings	HB	6'1"	212	29		
Fred McAfee	HB	5'10"	193	23		12
Craig Heyward	FB	5'11"	260	24		30
Buford Jordan	FB	6'	223	29		18
Bobby Morse	FB	5'10"	213	24		
Cedric Smith	FB	5'10"	223	23		
Gerald Alphin	WR	6'3"	200	27		
Wesley Carroll	WR	6'	183	23		6
Quinn Early	WR	6'	190	26		12
Eric Martin	WR	6'1"	207	29		24
Pat Newman	WR	5'11"	189	22		
Floyd Turner	WR	5'11"	188	25		48
Hoby Brenner	TE	6'4"	245	32		
Greg Scales	TE	6'4"	253	25		
John Tice	TE	6'5"	249	31		
Frank Wainright	TE	6'3"	236	23		
Morten Andersen	K	6'2"	221	31		113
Tommy Barnhardt	K	6'3"	207	28		

ATLANTA FALCONS 10-6 Jerry Glanville

Scores of Each Game		
3	Kansas City	14
19	MINNESOTA	20
13	San Diego	10
21	L.A. RAIDERS	17
6	NEW ORLEANS	27
39	San Francisco	34
10	Phoenix	16
31	L.A. RAMS	14
17	SAN FRANCISCO	14
17	Washington	56
43	TAMPA BAY	7
23	New Orleans	*20
35	GREEN BAY	31
31	L.A. Rams	14
26	SEATTLE	13
27	Dallas	31

UseName	Pos.	Hgt.	Wgt.	Age	Int	Pts
Chris Hinton	OT	6'4"	300	30		
John Hunter	OT	6'8"	300	26		
Mike Kenn	OT	6'7"	280	35		
Reggie Redding	OT	6'3"	290	22		
Joe Sims	OT	6'3"	294	22		
Bill Fralic	OG	6'5"	280	28		
Houston Hoover	OG	6'2"	295	26		
Mike Ruether	OG-C	6'4"	286	28		
Guy Bingham	C	6'3"	260	33		
Jamie Dukes	C	6'1"	285	27		
Rick Bryan	DE	6'4"	265	29		
Mike Gann	DE	6'5"	270	27	1	
Oliver Barnett	DE	6'3"	285	25		6
Tim Green	DE	6'2"	245	27		
Tory Epps	NT	6'	270	24		
Moe Gardner	NT	6'2"	258	23		

UseName	Pos.	Hgt.	Wgt.	Age	Int	Pts
Aundray Bruce	LB-TE	6'5"	250	25		
Darion Conner	LB	6'2"	250	23		
Robert Lyles	LB	6'1"	230	30		
Wes Pritchett	LB	6'4"	234	24		
John Rade	LB	6'1"	240	31		
Michael Reid	LB	6'2"	235	27		
Kenny Tippins	LB	6'1"	230	25	1	6
Jessie Tuggle	LB	5'11"	230	26	1	6
Bobby Butler	DB	5'11"	175	32		
Scott Case	DB	6'	188	29	2	
Jeff Donaldson	DB	6'	190	29		
Tracey Eaton	DB	6'1"	195	26		
William Evers	DB	5'10"	175	22		
Joe Fishback	DB	5'11"	198	23		6
Brian Jordan	DB	5'11"	205	24	2	4
Tim McKyer	DB	6'	174	27	6	
Brian Mitchell	DB	5'9"	164	22		
Bruce Pickens	DB	5'11"	190	23		
Deion Sanders	DB	6'	185	24	6	12
Elbert Shelley	DB	5'11"	185	26		

UseName	Pos.	Hgt.	Wgt.	Age	Int	Pts
Brett Favre	QB	6'2"	220	21		
Chris Miller	QB	6'2"	205	26		
Billy Joe Tolliver	QB	6'1"	218	25		
Steve Broussard	HB	5'7"	201	24		30
Erric Pegram	HB	5'9"	188	22		6
Mike Rozier	HB	5'10"	213	30		
Pat Chaffey	FB	6'1"	218	24		6
Tracy Johnson	FB	6'	230	25		
Keith Jones	FB	6'1"	210	25		
Shawn Collins	WR	6'2"	204	24		
Floyd Dixon	WR	5'9"	170	27		6
Michael Haynes	WR	6'	180	25		66
Jason Phillips	WR	5'7"	168	22		
Mike Pritchard	WR	5'11"	180	21		12
Andre Rison	WR	6'	188	24		72
George Thomas	WR	5'9"	169	27		12
Rich Bartlewski	TE	6'5"	255	24		
Harper LeBel	TE	6'4"	245	28		
Gary Wilkins	TE	6'1"	248	27		6
Scott Fulhage	K	5'11"	193	29		
Norm Johnson	K	6'2"	203	31		95

SAN FRANCISCO 49ERS 10-6 George Seifert

Scores of Each Game		
14	N.Y. Giants	16
34	SAN DIEGO	14
14	Minnesota	17
27	L.A. RAMS	10
6	L.A. Raiders	12
34	ATLANTA	39
35	DETROIT	3
23	Philadelphia	7
14	Atlanta	17
3	New Orleans	10
14	PHOENIX	10
33	L.A. Rams	10
38	NEW ORLEANS	24
24	Seattle	22
28	KANSAS CITY	14
52	CHICAGO	14

UseName	Pos.	Hgt.	Wgt.	Age	Int	Pts
Harris Barton	OG-OT	6'4"	280	27		
Frank Pollack	OT-OG	6'4"	285	23		
Steve Wallace	OT	6'5"	276	26		
Roy Foster	OG	6'4"	290	31		
Guy McIntyre	OG	6'3"	265	30		
Tom Neville	OG	6'5"	298	29		
Jesse Sapolu	C	6'4"	260	30		
Chuck Thomas	C	6'3"	280	30		
Dennis Brown	DE	6'4"	290	23		
Kevin Fagan	DE	6'4"	260	28		
Pierce Holt	DE	6'4"	280	29		
Greg Joelson	DE	6'3"	270	25		
Larry Roberts	DE	6'3"	275	28		
Jim Burt	NT	6'1"	270	32		
Michael Carter	NT	6'2"	285	30		
Ted Washington	NT-DE	6'4"	299	23		

UseName	Pos.	Hgt.	Wgt.	Age	Int	Pts
Keith DeLong	LB	6'2"	235	24		
Mitch Donahue	LB	6'2"	254	23		
Antonio Goss	LB	6'4"	228	25		
Charles Haley	LB-DE	6'5"	230	27		
Tim Harris	LB-DE	6'6"	258	26		
John Johnson	LB	6'3"	230	23		
Darin Jordan	LB	6'2"	245	26		2
Bill Romanowski	LB	6'4"	231	25	1	
Michael Walter	LB	6'3"	238	30		
Todd Bowles	DB	6'2"	205	27	1	
Greg Cox	DB	6'	223	25		
Eric Davis	DB	5'11"	178	23		
Don Griffin	DB	6'	176	27	1	6
Merton Hanks	DB	6'2"	185	23		
Johnny Jackson	DB	6'1"	204	24	1	
Mark Lee (to NO)	DB	6'	197	33	1	
Kevin Lewis	DB	5'11"	173	24	2	
Dave Waymer	DB	6'1"	188	33	4	
David Whitmore	DB	6'	235	24		

UseName	Pos.	Hgt.	Wgt.	Age	Int	Pts
Steve Bono	QB	6'4"	215	29		
Bill Musgrave	QB	6'2"	196	23		
Steve Young	QB	6'2"	200	29		24
Dexter Carter	HB	5'9"	170	23		24
Spencer Tillman	HB	5'11"	206	27		
Keith Henderson	FB	6'1"	220	25		12
Tom Rathman	FB	6'1"	232	28		36
Harry Sydney	FB	6'	217	32		42
Sanjay Beach	WR	6'1"	190	25		
Jerry Rice	WR	6'2"	200	28		84
Mike Sherrard	WR	6'2"	187	28		12
John Taylor	WR	6'1"	185	29		54
Brent Jones	TE	6'4"	230	28		
Wesley Walls	TE	6'5"	246	25		
Jamie Williams	TE	6'4"	245	31		6
Mike Cofer	K	6'1"	160	27		91
Ralf Mojsiejenko	K	6'3"	212	28		
Joe Prokop	K	6'2"	225	31		

Joe Montana — Elbow Injury
Darryl Pollard — Ankle Injury
Ronald Lewis — Back Injury

LOS ANGELES RAMS 3-13 John Robinson

Scores of Each Game		
14	PHOENIX	24
19	N.Y. Giants	13
7	New Orleans	24
10	San Francisco	27
23	GREEN BAY	21
30	SAN DIEGO	24
17	L.A. Raiders	20
14	Atlanta	31
17	NEW ORLEANS	24
20	KANSAS CITY	27
10	Detroit	21
10	SAN FRANCISCO	33
6	WASHINGTON	27
14	ATLANTA	31
14	Minnesota	20
9	Seattle	23

UseName	Pos.	Hgt.	Wgt.	Age	Int	Pts
Robert Jenkins	OT	6'5"	285	27		
Gerald Perry	OT	6'6"	305	26		
Jackie Slater	OT	6'4"	287	37		
Bern Brostek	OG-C	6'3"	300	24		
Duval Love	OG-OT	6'3"	287	28		
Joe Milinichik	OG	6'5"	290	28		
Jeff Pahukoa	OG-OT	6'2"	298	22		
Tom Newberry	C-OG	6'2"	285	28		
Doug Smith	C	6'3"	272	34		
Tom Gibson	DE	6'8"	275	27		
Kevin Greene	DE-LB	6'3"	247	29		2
Gerald Robinson	DE-DT	6'3"	262	28		
Ben Thomas	DE	6'3"	275	30		
Karl Wilson	DE	6'4"	275	27		
Mike Charles	DT	6'4"	305	28		
Bill Hawkins	DT	6'6"	269	25		
Mark Piel	DT	6'4"	270	25		
Chris Pike	DT	6'8"	300	27		
David Rocker	DT	6'4"	267	22		
Alvin Wright	DT	6'2"	285	30		
Robert Young	DT	6'6"	273	22		

UseName	Pos.	Hgt.	Wgt.	Age	Int	Pts
Paul Butcher	LB	6'	230	27		
Terry Crews	LB	6'2"	244	23		
Brett Faryniarz	LB	6'3"	232	26		
Larry Kelm	LB	6'4"	240	26		
Mike McDonald	LB	6'1"	240	33		
Roman Phifer	LB	6'6"	305	23		
Glenell Sanders	LB	6'	224	24		
Frank Stams	LB	6'2"	237	26		
Fred Strickland	LB	6'2"	250	25		
Robert Bailey	DB	5'9"	176	22		
Jerry Gray	DB	6'	185	28	3	6
Darryl Henley	DB	5'9"	172	24	3	
Sammy Lilly	DB	5'9"	178	26		
Todd Lyght	DB	6'	186	22	1	
Anthony Newman	DB	6'	199	25	1	6
Michael Stewart	DB	5'11"	199	26	2	
Pat Terrell	DB	6'	195	23	1	
Rodney Thomas	DB	5'10"	190	25		

UseName	Pos.	Hgt.	Wgt.	Age	Int	Pts
Jim Everett	QB	6'5"	212	28		
Mike Pagel	QB	6'2"	220	30		
Marcus Dupree	HB	6'2"	225	27		6
Cleveland Gary	HB	6'	226	25		6
David Lang	HB	5'11"	201	24		
Robert Delpino	FB	6'	205	25		60
Buford McGee	FB	6'	210	31		
Mosi Tatupu	FB	6'	227	36		
Ernie Thompson	FB	5'11"	230	21		6
Willie Anderson	WR	6'	175	26		6
Ron Brown	WR	5'11"	185	30		
Aaron Cox	WR	5'9"	178	26		
Henry Ellard	WR	5'11"	182	30		18
Jimmy Raye	WR	5'9"	165	22		
Vernon Turner	WR	5'8"	185	24		6
Pat Carter	TE	6'4"	255	25		12
Damone Johnson	TE	6'4"	250	29		12
Jim Price	TE	6'4"	247	28		12
Dale Hatcher	K	6'2"	220	28		
Barry Helton	K	6'3"	205	26		
Tony Zendejas	K	5'8"	165	31		76

RUSHING

Last Name	No.	Yds	Avg	TD
NEW ORLEANS SAINTS				
McAfee	109	494	4.5	2
Fenerty	139	477	3.4	3
Heyward	76	260	3.4	4
Hilliard	79	252	3.2	4
Jordan	47	150	3.2	2
Hebert	18	56	3.1	0
Early	3	13	4.3	0
Morse	3	7	2.3	0
Barnhardt	1	0	0.0	0
Walsh	8	0	0.0	0
ATLANTA FALCONS				
Broussard	99	449	4.5	4
Rozier	96	361	3.8	0
Pegram	101	349	3.5	1
Miller	32	229	7.2	0
Chaffey	29	127	4.4	1
Jones	35	126	3.6	0
T. Johnson	8	26	3.3	0
Tolliver	9	6	0.7	0
Rison	1	-9	-9.0	0
SAN FRANCISCO 49ERS				
Henderson	137	561	4.1	2
Young	66	415	6.3	4
D. Carter	85	379	4.5	2
Sydney	57	245	4.3	5
Rathman	63	183	2.9	6
Bono	17	46	2.7	0
Tillman	13	40	3.1	0
Rice	1	2	2.0	0
Prokop	1	-10	-10.0	0
LOS ANGELES RAMS				
Delpino	214	688	3.2	9
Gary	68	245	3.6	1
Dupree	49	179	3.7	1
McGee	19	65	3.4	0
Everett	27	44	1.6	0
Turner	7	44	6.3	0
Brown	2	11	5.5	0
Thompson	2	9	4.5	0

RECEIVING

Last Name	No.	Yds	Avg	TD
NEW ORLEANS SAINTS				
E. Martin	66	803	12.2	4
Turner	64	927	14.5	8
Early	32	541	16.9	2
Fenerty	26	235	9.0	2
Tice	22	230	10.5	0
Hilliard	21	127	6.0	1
Carroll	18	184	10.2	1
Brenner	16	179	11.2	0
Jordan	15	92	6.1	1
Heyward	4	34	8.5	1
Newman	3	33	11.0	0
Scales	3	23	7.7	0
McAfee	1	8	8.0	0
Wainright	1	3	3.0	0
ATLANTA FALCONS				
Rison	81	976	12.0	12
Haynes	50	1122	22.4	11
Pritchard	50	624	12.5	2
Thomas	28	365	13.0	2
Dixon	12	146	12.2	1
Broussard	12	120	10.0	1
Phillips	6	73	12.2	0
Jones	6	58	9.7	0
Collins	3	37	12.3	0
T. Johnson	3	27	9.0	0
Wilkins	3	22	7.3	1
Rozier	2	15	7.5	0
Ruether	1	22	22.0	0
Sanders	1	17	17.0	0
Bruce	1	11	11.0	0
Pegram	1	-1	-1.0	0
SAN FRANCISCO 49ERS				
Rice	80	1206	15.1	14
Taylor	64	1011	15.8	9
Rathman	34	286	8.4	0
Henderson	30	303	10.1	0
Jones	27	417	15.4	0
Sherrard	24	296	12.3	2
D. Carter	23	253	11.0	1
Williams	22	235	10.7	1
Sydney	13	90	6.9	2
Beach	4	43	10.8	0
Walls	2	24	12.0	0
Tillman	2	3	1.5	0
LOS ANGELES RAMS				
Ellard	64	1052	16.4	3
Delpino	55	617	11.2	1
Price	35	410	11.7	2
Anderson	32	530	16.6	1
Johnson	32	253	7.9	2
McGee	20	160	8.0	0
Cox	15	216	14.4	0
Gary	13	110	8.5	0
Carter	8	69	8.6	2
Dupree	6	46	7.7	0
Brown	3	52	17.3	0
Turner	3	41	13.7	1
Thompson	2	35	17.5	1
Raye	1	19	19.0	0

PUNT RETURNS

Last Name	No.	Yds	Avg	TD
NEW ORLEANS SAINTS				
V. Buck	31	260	8.4	0
Fenerty	12	55	4.6	0
Morse	1	2	2.0	0
ATLANTA FALCONS				
Sanders	21	170	8.1	0
Jordan	14	116	8.3	0
SAN FRANCISCO 49ERS				
Taylor	31	267	8.6	0
Beach	10	53	5.3	0
K. Lewis	1	0	0.0	0
LOS ANGELES RAMS				
Turner	23	201	8.7	0
Henley	13	110	8.5	0
Gray	1	9	9.0	0

KICKOFF RETURNS

Last Name	No.	Yds	Avg	TD
NEW ORLEANS SAINTS				
Atkins	20	368	18.4	0
Jennings	12	213	17.8	0
Early	9	168	18.7	0
Morse	3	60	20.0	0
Fenerty	2	28	14.0	0
Jordan	2	18	9.0	0
McAfee	1	14	14.0	0
Glenn	1	10	10.0	0
ATLANTA FALCONS				
Sanders	26	576	22.2	1
Pegram	16	260	16.3	0
Jordan	5	100	20.0	0
Fishback	3	29	9.7	0
Pritchard	1	18	18.0	0
Chaffey	1	14	14.0	0
SAN FRANCISCO 49ERS				
D. Carter	37	839	22.7	1
Tillman	9	132	14.7	0
Beach	2	37	18.5	0
Sydney	1	13	13.0	0
Whitmore	1	7	7.0	0
LOS ANGELES RAMS				
Turner	24	457	19.0	0
Brown	12	256	21.3	0
Lang	12	194	16.2	0
Delpino	4	54	13.5	0
McDonald	3	32	10.7	0
Raye	2	57	28.5	0
Carter	1	18	18.0	0
Sanders	1	2	2.0	0

PASSING—PUNTING—KICKING

NEW ORLEANS SAINTS

PASSING	Att	Cmp	%	Yds	Yd/Att	TD	Int—	%	RK
Walsh	255	141	55.3	1638	6.42	11	6—	2.4	9
Hebert	248	149	60.1	1676	6.76	9	8—	3.2	10
M. Buck	2	1	50.0	61	30.50	0	1—	50.0	
Heyward	1	1	100.0	44	44.00	0	0—	0.0	

PUNTING	No.	Avg.
Barnhardt	87	43.0

KICKING	XP	ATT	%	FG	ATT	%
Andersen	38	38	100	25	32	78

ATLANTA FALCONS

PASSING	Att	Cmp	%	Yds	Yd/Att	TD	Int—	%	RK
Miller	413	220	53.3	3103	7.51	26	18—	4.4	7
Tolliver	82	40	48.8	531	6.48	4	2—	2.4	
Favre	5	0	0.0	0	0.00	0	2—	40.0	

PUNTING	No.	Avg.
Fulhage	81	42.8

KICKING	XP	Att	%	FG	Att	%
N. Johnson	38	39	97	19	23	83

SAN FRANCISCO 49ERS

PASSING	Att	Cmp	%	Yds	Yd/Att	TD	Int—	%	RK
Young	279	180	64.5	2517	9.02	17	8—	2.9	1
Bono	237	141	59.5	1617	6.82	11	4—	1.7	3
Musgrave	5	4	80.0	141	6.60	1	0—	0.0	
Sydney	1	0	0.0	0	0.00	0	0—	0.0	

PUNTING	No.	Avg.
Mojsiejenko	16	41.0
Prokop	40	38.5

KICKING	XP	ATT	%	FG	ATT	%
Cofer	49	50	98	14	28	50

LOS ANGELES RAMS

PASSING	Att	Cmp	%	Yds	Yd/Att	TD	Int—	%	RK
Everett	490	277	56.5	3438	7.02	11	20—	4.1	14
Pagel	27	11	40.7	150	5.56	2	0—	0.0	
Helton	1	1	100.0	22	22.00	0	0—	0.0	

PUNTING	No.	Avg.
Hatcher	63	38.1
Helton	12	37.8

KICKING	XP	ATT	%	FG	ATT	%
Zendejas	25	26	96	17	17	100

1991 A.F.C. Coaching Carousel Continues All Season

The 1991 NFL season began in a strange way in April when Raghib "Rocket" Ismail, the Heisman Trophy winner, decided to play football in Canada. That was just a preview of things to come, as the entire rookie class produced not one impact player among the several hundred who made NFL rosters. The Rookies of the Year were New England running back Leonard Russell, who gained 959 yards but averaged only 3.6 yards per carry and scored just four touchdowns, and Denver linebacker Mike Croel, who had 10 sacks but played mostly in pass-rushing situations. Several AFC clubs started on the comeback trail, most notably New England under Dick MacPherson, the Jets with Bruce Coslet and Cleveland under Bill Belichick.

And the season ended with the league's biggest turnover among head coaches in 13 years. Nine teams changed head coaches. Indianapolis fired both Ron Meyer and interim coach Rick Venturi. Also let go were Dan Henning (San Diego), Lindy Infante (Green Bay), Richard Williamson (Tampa Bay) and Sam Wyche (Cincinnati). Resigning were Jerry Burns (Minnesota), John Robinson (Rams) and Chuck Knox (Seattle). And Pittsburgh's Chuck Noll decided he had had enough, too.

EASTERN DIVISION

Buffalo Bills — The Bills went to their second straight Super Bowl before falling soundly to the Redskins 37-24 and becoming the third team to lose consecutive Super Bowls. Buffalo won 10 of its first 11 games behind a no-huddle offense that dominated the NFL. Quarterback Jim Kelly led the league with 33 touchdown passes, and running back Thurman Thomas was named the league's Most Valuable Player. He rushed for 1,407 yards, caught 61 passes for 631 yards and scored 12 touchdowns. Andre Reed led the receivers again with 81 catches and 10 TD's, and 36-year-old James Lofton chipped in with 57 receptions for 1,072 yards and eight scores. But the Bills had problems on defense. End Bruce Smith missed most of the season with a knee injury, and the team finished 27th in the NFL in yards allowed. It showed in the Super Bowl.

New York Jets — The Jets came a long way 1991, finishing with an 8-8 record and making the wild-card round of the playoffs. But they seemed to come up just a bit short all season, blowing at least three games they should've won(including one that was the Colts' only victory all season). Ken O'Brien had too many costly interceptions inside the opponents' 20-yard line, and running back Blair Thomas slumped in his second season, running tentatively after a costly fumble lost the Chicago game. Wide receiver Al Toon had 74 receptions but no touchdowns, and Rob Moore caught 70 passes. A bright light was fullback Brad Baxter, who scored 11 times in goal line situations.

Miami Dolphins — Twenty years ago, the Dolphins were famed for their "No-Name" defense. In 1991, the Dolphins had no defense. Miami ranked 25th overall and 27th against the run, allowing 21.8 points per game. Even though they salvaged an 8-8 record, they finished out of the playoffs for the fifth time in six seasons after losing their final two games (a victory in either of which would have clinched the playoffs). Quarterback Dan Marino starred again with 25 touchdown passes and 3,970 yards passing. And the Marks Brothers — Duper and Clayton — each caught 70 passes for over 1,000 yards and 17 touchdowns combined. Running back Sammie Smith was benched after fumbling twice on the goal line, and the Miami running game would have been sunk if Mark Higgs hadn't come out of nowhere to gain 905 yards rushing.

New England Patriots — Coach Dick MacPherson came over from Syracuse University and infused lots of spirit and motivation into a team that badly needed it. In turn, the Patriots gave MacPherson — and the NFL — a few surprises, finishing with a 6-10 record on the heels of a 1-15 season in 1990. Hugh Millen took over at quarterback after three games (all losses) and passed for 3,073 yards while leading the Patriots to a series of frantic finishes near midseason. Wide receiver Irving Fryar had his best season as a pro with 1,014 yards receiving, and tight end Marv Cook was the NFL's best with 82 receptions. Running back Leonard Russell was the NFL Offensive Rookie of the Year, as he rushed for 959 yards.

Indianapolis Colts — The Colts were the most inept team in the NFL in 1991. The offense scored only 143 points — the fewest ever for an NFL team in a 16-game season. A tidal wave of injuries sank the Colts from the start. The offensive line leaked like a sieve, leaving quarterback Jeff George running for his life. Running back Eric Dickerson continued to cause problems, until he was finally suspended for five games for "insubordination." On defense, Indianapolis finished last in three categories and in the bottom five in eight others. Coach Ron Meyer was fired after five games — all losses — but interim coach Rick Venturi didn't do much better, guiding the Colts to a 1-10 record. After the season, Venturi was replaced by Ted Marchibroda, who came back for his second tour of duty with the Colts.

CENTRAL DIVISION

Houston Oilers — The Oilers won the Central Division title outright for the first time ever and became the only team to make the playoffs every year from 1987-91. But, for the fifth straight time they failed to get past the second round. The defense made great strides, allowing the second-fewest points in the conference, and the team put a league-high eight players in the Pro Bowl. Quarterback Warren Moon was the NFL's most prolific passer, setting league records for attempts (655) and completions (404) — but he matched a career-worst with 21 interceptions. Wide receiver Haywood Jeffires became only the fifth player in NFL history to reach 100 receptions in a season. But a 4-4 record the second half of the season and a 1-1 mark in the playoffs left fans wondering if the Oilers wouild ever get to the Super Bowl.

Pitt burgh Steelers — An era ended when Chuck Noll announced his retirement following the 1991 season. The only coach to win four Super Bowls called the '91 season the most disappointing of his career. The Steelers expected to make the playoffs but were out of contention by midseason, as they failed to beat winning teams for the third straight season. The biggest shock of 1991 was the fall of the defense, which was first in the league in '90. Offensively, the Steelers again failed to adapt to coordinator Joe Walton's complicated offense, and a quarterback duo began with Bubby Brister and Neil O'Donnell sharing the duties. Once again, tight end Eric Green was the team's best offensive weapon, until he was injured in Game Nine. Noll was replaced by Kansas City defensive coordinator Bill Cowher.

Cleveland Browns — The Browns showed signs of life under new coach Bill Belichick. They won four of their first eight games and started priming for a playoff run until injuries and a thin bench caused a 2-6 record after midseason. Quarterback Bernie Kosar had a fine comeback season, keeping the Browns in games with his gutsy performances behind a revamped offensive line that did little to help. Running back Leroy Hoard was the Browns' surprise player of the year by scoring 11 touchdowns, nine of them on receptions. He was joined in the backfield by Kevin Mack, who chipped in 10 scores and 726 yards rushing despite being hampered by injuries all season. The defense sliced its points allowed per game from 28.8 points in '90 to 18.6 in '91.

Cincinnati Bengals — Cincinnati lost its first eight games of the season as head coach Sam Wyche was losing his composure on the sideline. At the end of the season, Wyche lost his job and was replaced by 32-year-old Dave Shula, Don's son who became the youngest head coach in modern NFL history. Most of the Bengals had disappointing seasons, including quarterback Boomer Esiason, running backs James Brooks and Ickey Woods and wide receivers Eddie Brown and Tim McGee. The offense failed to score a touchdown in two games and scored only one in six others. And the defense finished last in total defense, pass defense and scoring defense. Second-year running back Harold Green had a promising season with 731 yards rushing.

WESTERN DIVISION

Denver Broncos — After going 5-11 in 1990, the Broncos made the

OFFENSE

	BUFF	CIN	CLEV	DEN	HOU	IND	K.C.	L.A.	MIA	N.E.	NYJ	PITT	S.D.	SEA
FIRST DOWNS:														
Total	359	286	265	284	353	236	322	248	312	259	331	254	285	253
by Rushing	128	96	82	117	99	55	127	97	91	93	133	82	114	80
by Passing	208	162	163	150	236	163	172	132	205	155	169	158	155	159
by Penalty	23	28	20	17	18	18	23	19	16	11	29	14	16	14
RUSHING:														
Number	505	449	389	507	331	354	521	446	379	433	523	394	464	394
Yards	2381	1811	1360	2015	1366	1169	2217	1706	1352	1467	2160	1627	2248	1426
Average Yards	4.7	4.0	3.5	4.0	4.1	3.3	4.3	3.8	3.6	3.4	4.1	4.1	4.8	3.6
Touchdowns	16	11	12	16	16	3	14	8	8	9	17	8	16	11
PASSING:														
Attempts	516	511	503	459	667	512	479	414	563	481	5023	476	511	488
Completions	332	290	312	246	411	305	284	220	327	284	295	259	272	290
Completion Pct.	64.3	56.8	62.0	53.6	61.6	59.6	59.3	53.1	58.1	59.0	58.6	54.4	53.2	59.4
Passing Yards	4140	3413	3547	3310	4804	3066	3281	2977	4077	3442	3429	3313	2983	3371
Avg. Yds per Att.	7.0	5.8	6.1	5.9	6.7	4.5	6.2	6.1	6.6	5.5	5.9	5.7	5.0	5.9
Avg. Yds per Comp.	12.5	11.8	11.4	13.5	11.7	10.1	11.6	13.5	12.5	12.1	11.6	12.8	11.0	11.6
Times Tackled	35	33	42	46	24	57	21	33	28	63	33	45	35	42
Yds Lost Tackled	269	255	243	313	183	487	177	258	188	436	273	359	236	263
Net Yards	3871	3158	3304	2997	4621	2579	3104	2719	3889	3006	3156	2954	2747	3108
Touchdowns	39	14	19	13	24	10	19	20	26	11	12	20	13	15
Interceptions	19	22	10	12	21	16	14	18	14	22	12	16	16	26
Pct. Intercepted	3.7	4.3	2.0	2.6	3.1	3.1	2.9	4.4	2.5	4.6	2.4	3.4	3.1	5.3
PUNTS:														
Number	54	65	80	74	53	82	57	67	57	82	64	75	77	76
Average	38.6	43.5	42.5	41.2	41.7	42.6	40.4	44.2	44.8	39.0	39.4	39.9	39.8	40.6
PUNT RETURNS														
Number	26	29	31	41	36	27	34	29	30	31	23	39	33	38
Yards	281	280	251	284	244	171	258	330	258	211	157	373	328	325
Average Yards	10.8	9.7	8.1	6.9	6.8	6.3	7.6	11.4	8.6	6.8	6.8	9.6	9.9	8.6
Touchdowns	0	1	0	0	0	0	0	1	0	0	0	1	0	1
KICKOFF RET.:														
Number	52	69	55	37	46	55	48	52	50	56	58	67	55	60
Yards	970	1225	888	687	835	1061	978	928	890	1108	1003	1314	1171	1280
Average Yards	18.7	17.8	16.1	18.6	18.2	19.3	20.4	17.8	17.8	19.8	17.3	19.6	21.3	21.3
Touchdowns	1	0	0	0	0	1	0	0	0	1	0	0	1	0
INTERCEPT RET.:														
Number	23	17	15	23	20	15	15	18	12	12	18	19	19	18
Yards	276	169	260	379	255	202	216	155	135	93	283	329	227	302
Average Yards	12.0	9.9	17.3	16.5	12.8	10.1	14.4	8.6	11.3	7.8	15.7	17.3	11.9	16.8
Touchdowns	1	1	3	2	2	0	0	0	0	0	2	2	1	2
PENALTIES:														
Number	113	107	108	94	99	85	94	117	62	97	103	116	96	85
Yards	865	845	872	715	784	689	724	1013	516	667	814	933	799	682
FUMBLES:														
Number	25	31	18	31	33	31	22	20	23	34	28	37	24	26
Number Lost	16	20	8	13	19	15	8	13	14	20	13	14	12	17
POINTS:														
Total	458	263	293	304	386	143	322	298	343	211	314	292	274	276
PAT Attempts	58	27	34	32	46	14	35	30	35	21	32	31	31	29
PAT Made	56	27	33	31	41	14	35	29	34	19	32	31	31	27
FG Attempts	29	32	22	36	31	26	30	34	39	29	43	33	29	31
FG Made	18	24	16	27	23	15	25	29	33	20	30	23	19	25
Percent FG Made	62.1	75.0	72.7	75.0	74.2	57.7	83.3	85.3	84.6	69.0	69.8	69.7	65.6	80.6
Safeties	0	1	1	0	0	0	1	1	0	0	0	0	0	0

DEFENSE

	BUFF	CIN	CLEV	DEN	HOU	IND	K.C.	L.A.	MIA	N.E.	NYJ	PITT	S.D.	SEA
FIRST DOWNS:														
Total	335	308	298	242	280	305	275	305	327	312	208	320	292	262
by Rushing	138	100	100	81	94	140	88	108	133	94	94	98	94	91
by Passing	166	191	179	147	163	152	168	176	177	199	185	194	181	159
by Penalty	31	17	19	14	23	13	19	21	17	19	19	28	17	12
RUSHING:														
Number	519	454	447	411	407	544	417	447	499	460	379	466	430	435
Yards	2044	1662	1875	1794	1540	2327	1770	1889	2301	1579	1442	1582	1666	1684
Average Yards	3.9	3.7	4.2	4.4	3.8	4.3	4.2	4.2	4.6	3.4	3.8	3.4	3.9	3.9
Touchdowns	20	20	12	8	8	23	8	13	17	5	8	14	15	4
PASSING:														
Attempts	536	505	522	476	532	388	471	513	485	565	540	535	503	517
Completions	299	303	312	246	310	240	279	295	300	335	331	334	300	296
Completion Pct.	55.8	60.0	59.8	51.7	58.3	61.9	59.2	57.5	61.9	59.3	61.3	62.4	59.6	57.3
Passing Yards	3660	4119	3445	3101	3522	3002	3532	3559	3353	4035	3765	3843	3628	3288
Avg. Yds per Att.	6.0	7.6	5.8	5.2	5.6	6.7	6.3	5.9	6.0	6.5	6.2	6.3	6.5	5.5
Avg. Yds per Comp.	12.2	13.6	11.0	12.6	11.4	12.5	12.7	12.1	11.2	12.0	11.4	11.5	12.1	11.1
Times Tackled	31	21	35	52	45	29	39	42	35	25	35	38	28	36
Yds Lost Tackled	246	129	236	346	314	202	304	283	248	183	226	257	183	269
Net Yards	3414	3990	3209	2755	3208	2800	3228	3276	3105	3852	3539	3586	3445	3019
Touchdowns	12	26	20	12	17	22	17	18	18	25	21	21	22	18
Interceptions	23	17	15	23	20	15	15	18	12	12	18	19	19	18
Pct. Intercepted	4.3	3.4	2.9	4.8	3.8	3.9	3.2	3.5	2.5	2.1	3.3	3.6	3.8	3.5
PUNTS:														
Number	70	57	61	79	74	59	60	61	65	69	56	65	76	79
Average	39.1	42.0	41.3	44.5	42.1	41.4	42.5	38.7	39.8	42.2	40.6	41.6	40.3	39.1
PUNT RETURNS														
Number	15	38	40	28	29	47	27	41	30	37	29	29	32	40
Yards	53	456	3988	170	192	516	190	341	332	303	164	210	267	289
Average Yards	3.5	12.0	9.7	6.1	6.6	11.0	7.0	8.3	11.1	8.2	5.7	7.2	8.3	7.2
Touchdowns	0	2	0	0	0	1	0	0	0	1	0	0	0	0
KICKOFF RET.:														
Number	62	38	50	62	63	33	57	58	66	51	60	43	52	51
Yards	1266	741	1022	1096	1071	573	1171	1059	1270	850	921	825	1034	858
Average Yards	20.4	19.5	20.4	17.7	17.0	17.4	20.5	18.3	19.2	16.7	15.4	19.2	19.9	16.8
Touchdowns	0	0	0	0	0	0	0	1	0	0	1	0	0	0
INTERCEPT RET.:														
Number	19	22	10	12	21	16	14	18	14	22	12	16	16	26
Yards	320	331	95	101	296	184	251	374	217	154	105	182	183	334
Average Yards	16.8	15.0	9.5	8.4	14.1	11.5	17.9	20.8	15.5	7.0	8.8	11.4	11.4	12.8
Touchdowns	2	3	1	0	0	1	2	2	2	0	0	2	1	2
PENALTIES:														
Number	110	94	103	105	109	88	110	111	91	83	93	84	87	108
Yards	938	808	770	848	797	645	827	905	684	608	774	685	718	845
FUMBLES:														
Number	26	23	33	26	27	21	27	24	19	32	38	27	22	34
Number Lost	14	14	18	10	18	13	18	13	9	19	19	11	9	21
POINTS:														
Total	318	435	298	235	251	381	252	297	349	305	293	344	342	261
PAT Attempts	34	52	33	22	26	46	27	36	40	31	30	38	38	25
PAT Made	33	49	32	22	26	46	25	33	40	30	29	38	37	25
FG Attempts	35	31	30	33	29	23	28	28	33	42	38	41	29	32
FG Made	27	22	22	27	23	17	21	16	23	29	26	26	23	28
Percent FG Made	77.1	71.0	73.3	81.8	79.3	73.9	75.0	57.1	69.7	69.0	68.4	63.4	79.3	87.5
Safeties	0	1	1	0	0	1	1	0	0	1	0	0	1	1

most dramatic improvement in team history, finishing 12-4 and winning the AFC West title. The difference was a 9-3 record in games decided by a touchdown or less in 1991 as compared to a 2-7 mark the year before. The Denver defense led the AFC in virtually every category, including touchdowns allowed, points allowed, sacks, third-down conversions and passing yards allowed. With Bobby Humphrey holding out and being banished to the bench upon his return, Gaston Green went from being a bust with the Rams to a 1,000-yard rusher with the Broncos. But the team's leader once again was quarterback John Elway. Despite mediocre statistics of 13 touchdowns and 12 interceptions, he had his best season since 1987, capped off by "The Drive II" in the playoffs.

Kansas City Chiefs — In an up-and-down season, the Chiefs could go only as far as quarterback Steve DeBerg could take them, which was a lot farther than they thought when he was benched in Game 15. However, replacement quarterback Mark Vlasic injured himself within two quarters and DeBerg came back on to rally the Chiefs to the second round of the playoffs. The offense showed an inability to make big plays, so the Chiefs relied on their ground game. The combination of running backs Christian Okoye and Barry Word had 1,715 yards rushing and 13 touchdowns, but it was rookie Harvey Williams who drew the praise in limited playing time. The defense was strong overall, with end Neil Smith and linebacker Derrick Thomas starring in front of a secondary that hid its age well.

Los Angeles Raiders — Teams only one game away from the playoffs don't usually switch from a veteran quarterback to an untested rookie, but that's what the Raiders did in 1991, benching Jay Schroeder in favor of Todd Marinovich for Game 16 and the wild-card playoff. Although Marinovich won his first game and lost the playoff, he proved to be the team's future. Injuries hampered the running backs who rushed for 107 yards a game without a dominant performer. Eight players were chosen for the Pro Bowl, including Plan B pickup Ronnie Lott, who solidified the defense and led the NFL with eight interceptions. But the team was sparked by its kickers — Jeff Gossett led the NFL in punting, and Jeff Jaeger won two games with kicks and set a team record by hitting 29 of 34 field goals, usually when the offense failed near the end zone.

Seattle Seahawks — Seattle suffered a season of hard knocks, and then coach Chuck Knox bolted for the Rams when it ended. He was replaced by Tom Flores. In stumbling to a 7-9 record, the Seahawks saw three quarterbacks start games — none of them effectively — and four different halfbacks who could combine for only 2.9 yards per carry and 31.4 yards per game. Fullback John L. Williams led the offense with 1,240 yards rushing and receiving, and Brian Blades led the receivers with 70 catches for 1,003 yards but only two scores. But the offense averaged only 17.3 points and scored more than 24 points just twice, and an AFC-high 43 turnovers was impossible to overcome. The defense set team records for fewest points allowed (261) and was the only one in the AFC not to allow a 100-yard rusher or a 300-yard passer.

San Diego Chargers — The Chargers suffered through their eighth non-winning season in nine years and ninth straight out of the playoffs — the longest drought in the AFC. Coach Dan Henning was fired when it was over and replaced by Bobby Ross. The offense packed a powerful one-two punch from running backs Marion Butts (834 yards and six touchdowns) and Rod Bernstine (766 yards and eight TD's). Another back, Ronnie Harmon, led the team with 59 receptions. But quarterback John Friesz, who had one start before the '91 season, was the lowest-rated passer in the conference. His lack of experience showed in close games, and San Diego had a 2-8 record in games decided by a touchdown or less.

BUFFALO BILLS 13-3 Marv Levy

Scores of Each Game		
35	MIAMI	31
52	PITTSBURGH	34
23	N.Y. Jets	20
17	at Tampa Bay	10
35	CHICAGO	20
6	Kansas City	33
42	INDIANAPOLIS	6
35	CINCINNATI	16
22	NEW ENGLAND	17
34	Green Bay	24
41	Miami	27
13	New England	16
24	N.Y. JETS	13
30	L.A. Raiders	* 27
35	Indianapolis	7
14	DETROIT	* 17

Use Name	Pos.	Hgt.	Wgt.	Age	Int	Pts
Howard Ballard	OT	6'6"	325	27		
Joe Staysniak	OT	6'5"	296	24		
Will Wolford	OT	6'5"	295	27		
John Davis	OG	6'4"	310	26		
Mitch Frerotte	OG	6'3"	285	26		
Glenn Parker	OG-OT	6'5"	301	25		
Jim Ritcher	OG	6'3"	273	33		
Kent Hull	C	6'4"	275	30		
Adam Lingner	C	6'4"	263	30		
Phil Hansen	DE	6'5"	258	23		
Mark Pike	DE	6'4"	272	27		
Reggie Rogers	DE	6'6"	280	27		
Leon Seals	DE	6'4"	270	27		
Bruce Smith	DE	6'4"	275	28		
Gary Baldinger	NT	6'3"	270	27		
Odell Haggins	NT	6'2"	278	24		
Mike Lodish	NT-DE	6'3"	265	24		
Jeff Wright	NT	6'2"	270	28		
Carlton Bailey	LB	6'2"	240	26		
David Bavaro	LB	6'	235	24		
Cornelius Bennett	LB	6'2"	236	26		6
Ray Bentley	LB	6'2"	235	30	1	
Shane Conlan	LB	6'3"	235	27		
Hal Garner	LB	6'4"	235	29		
Marvcus Patton	LB	6'2"	226	24		
Darryl Talley	LB	6'4"	235	31	5	
Dwight Drane	DB	6'2"	205	29		
Chris Hale	DB	5'7"	165	25	1	
Clifford Hicks	DB	5'10"	188	27	1	
Kirby Jackson	DB	5'10"	180	26	4	
Henry Jones	DB	5'11"	197	23		
Mark Kelso	DB	5'11"	185	28	2	
Nate Odomes	DB	5'10"	188	26	5	6
Leonard Smith	DB	5'11"	202	30	3	
Brian Taylor	DB	5'10"	195	24		
James Williams	DB	5'10"	172	24	1	
Gale Gilbert	QB	6'3"	210	29		
Jim Kelly	QB	6'3"	218	31		6
Frank Reich	QB	6'4"	210	29		
Kenneth Davis	HB	5'10"	209	29		30
Eddie Fuller	HB	5'9"	201	23		
Thurman Thomas	HB	5'10"	198	25		72
Carwell Gardner	FB	6'2"	232	24		24
Mike Alexander	WR	6'3"	185	26		
Don Beebe	WR	5'11"	183	26		36
Al Edwards	WR	5'8"	171	24		12
James Lofton	WR	6'3"	190	35		48
Andre Reed	WR	6'	190	27		60
Steve Tasker	WR	5'9"	183	29		6
Keith McKeller	TE	6'6"	245	27		18
Pete Metzelaars	TE	6'7"	250	31		12
Butch Rolle	TE	6'3"	245	27		12
Brad Daluiso	K	6'2"	208	23		8
Chris Mohr	K	6'5"	215	25		
Scott Norwood	K	6'	207	31		110

Jamie Mueller— Nerve Injury

NEW YORK JETS 8-8 Bruce Coslet

Scores of Each Game		
16	TAMPA BAY	13
13	Seattle	20
20	BUFFALO	23
13	Chicago	* 19
41	MIAMI	23
17	Cleveland	14
20	HOUSTON	23
17	Indianapolis	6
19	GREEN BAY	* 16
27	INDIANAPOLIS	28
28	New England	21
24	SAN DIEGO	3
13	Buffalo	24
20	Detroit	34
3	NEW ENGLAND	6
23	Miami	* 20

Use Name	Pos.	Hgt.	Wgt.	Age	Int	Pts
Jeff Criswell	OT	6'7"	291	27		
Irv Eatman	OT	6'7"	298	30		
Brett Miller	OT	6'7"	286	32		
Dave Cadigan	OG	6'4"	285	26		
Mike Haight	OG-OT	6'4"	291	28		
Trevor Matich	OG-C-OT	6'4"	297	29		6
Dwayne White	OG	6'2"	305	24		
Roger Duffy	C	6'3"	285	24		
Jim Sweeney	C-OG	6'4"	286	29		
Darrell Davis	DE	6'2"	258	25		
Mark Gunn	DE	6'5"	292	23		
Jeff Lageman	DE	6'5"	266	24		
Marvin Washington	DE	6'6"	272	25		
Dennis Byrd	DT	6'5"	266	24		
Paul Frase	DT-DE	6'5"	270	26		
Scott Mersereau	DT	6'3"	275	26	2	
Bill Pickel	DT	6'5"	265	31		
Kyle Clifton	LB	6'4"	236	29	1	
John Galvin	LB	6'3"	230	26		
Bobby Houston	LB	6'2"	235	23		
Troy Johnson	LB	6'2"	236	26		
Joe Kelly	LB	6'2"	235	26	2	
Mo Lewis	LB	6'3"	240	21		
Michael Brim	DB	6'	192	25	4	
James Hasty	DB	6'	201	26	3	
R.J. Kors	DB	6'	195	25	1	
Erik McMillan	DB	6'2"	200	26	3	12
Don Odegard	DB	6'	180	24		
Tony Stargell	DB	5'11"	180	25		
Brian Washington	DB	6'1"	212	25	1	
Lonnie Young	DB	6'1"	192	28	1	
Browning Nagle	QB	6'3"	225	23		
Ken O'Brien	QB	6'4"	212	30		
Troy Taylor	QB	6'4"	200	23		
A.B. Brown	HB	5'9"	215	25		6
Johnny Hector	HB	5'11"	214	30		
Freeman McNeil	HB	5'11"	208	32		12
Blair Thomas	HB	5'10"	195	23		24
Brad Baxter	FB	6'1"	235	24		66
Chris Burkett	WR	6'4"	200	29		30
Dale Dawkins	WR	6'1"	190	24		
Terance Mathis	WR	5'10"	170	24		6
Rob Moore	WR	6'3"	205	22		30
Al Toon	WR	6'4"	205	28		
Mark Boyer	TE	6'4"	242	28		
Chris Dressel	TE	6'4"	239	30		
Pat Kelly	TE	6'6"	252	25		
Ken Whisenhunt	TE	6'3"	240	29		
Louis Aguiar	K	6'2"	200	25		
Pat Leahy	K	6'	200	40		108

Joe Mott — Knee Injury
Dennis Price — Knee Injury
Patrick Egu — Knee Injury

MIAMI DOLPHINS 8-8 Don Shula

Scores of Each Game		
31	Buffalo	35
17	INDIANAPOLIS	6
13	Detroit	17
16	GREEN BAY	13
23	N.Y. Jets	41
20	New England	10
7	Kansas City	42
13	HOUSTON	17
10	Indianapolis	6
30	NEW ENGLAND	20
27	BUFFALO	41
16	Chicago	* 13
33	TAMPA BAY	14
37	CINCINNATI	13
30	San Diego	38
20	N.Y. JETS	* 23

Use Name	Pos.	Hgt.	Wgt.	Age	Int	Pts
Jeff Dellenbach	OT-C	6'6"	285	28		
Mark Dennis	OT	6'6"	295	26		
Richmond Webb	OT	6'6"	298	24		
Harry Galbreath	OG	6'1"	275	26		
Keith Sims	OG	6'2"	305	24		
Gene Williams	OG	6'2"	308	22		
Dave Zawatson	OG-OT	6'5"	287	25		
Jeff Uhlenhake	C	6'3"	284	25		
Bert Weidner	C	6'3"	284	24		
Jeff Cross	DE	6'4"	272	25		
Donnie Gardner	DE	6'3"	260	23		
Alfred Oglesby	DE-NT	6'3"	278	24		
T.J. Turner	DE-NT	6'4"	280	28		
Chuck Klingbeil	NT	6'1"	260	25		6
Shawn Lee	NT	6'2"	285	24	1	
Ned Bolcar	LB	6'1"	235	24		
Louis Cooper	LB	6'2"	238	28		
Bryan Cox	LB	6'3"	235	23		
Hugh Green	LB	6'2"	230	32		
David Griggs	LB-TE	6'3"	248	24		
E.J. Junior	LB	6'3"	242	31		
Cliff Odom	LB	6'2"	243	33	1	
John Offerdahl	LB	6'3"	237	27		
Mike Reichenbach	LB	6'2"	240	29	1	
J.B. Brown	DB	6'	192	25	1	
Kerry Glenn	DB	5'9"	178	29		
Chris Green	DB	5'11"	188	23		
Bobby Harden	DB	6'	192	24	2	
Mike Iaquaniello	DB	6'3"	208	23		
Vestee Jackson	DB	6'	186	28		
Paul Lankford	DB	6'1"	191	33		
Michael McGruder	DB	5'11"	190	27		
Louis Oliver	DB	6'2"	226	25	5	
Jarvis Williams	DB	5'11"	196	26	1	
Dan Marino	QB	6'4"	224	29		6
Scott Mitchell	QB	6'6"	236	23		
Scott Secules	QB	6'3"	219	26		6
Aaron Craver	HB	5'11"	215	21		6
Mark Higgs	HB	5'7"	195	25		24
Sammie Smith	HB	6'2"	226	24		6
Marc Logan	FB	5'11"	222	26		
Tony Paige	FB	5'10"	235	28		6
Fred Banks	WR	5'10"	180	29		6
Mark Clayton	WR	5'9"	185	30		72
Mark Duper	WR	5'9"	192	32		30
Jim Jensen	WR-FB	6'4"	224	32		12
Tony Martin	WR	6'	180	25		12
Scott Miller	WR	5'10"	179	22		
James Pruitt	WR	6'2"	201	27		
Mike Williams	WR	5'10"	177	24		
Greg Baty	TE	6'5"	240	27		6
Ferrell Edmunds	TE	6'6"	254	26		12
Charles Henry	TE	6'4"	230	27		
Reggie Roby	K	6'2"	246	30		
Pete Stoyonovich	K	5'10"	185	24		**121**

Terry Price — Elbow Injury
John Grimsley — Knee Injury
Bruce McNorton — Wrist Injury
Stevon Moore — Knee Injury
Garrett Limbrick — Shoulder Injury

NEW ENGLAND PATRIOTS 6-10 Dick MacPherson

Scores of Each Game		
16	Indianapolis	7
0	CLEVELAND	20
6	Pittsburgh	20
24	HOUSTON	20
10	Phoenix	24
10	MIAMI	20
26	MINNESOTA	* 23
6	DENVER	9
17	Buffalo	22
20	Miami	30
21	N.Y. JETS	28
16	BUFFALO	13
3	Denver	20
23	INDIANAPOLIS	* 17
6	N.Y. Jets	3
7	Cincinnati	29

Use Name	Pos.	Hgt.	Wgt.	Age	Int	Pts
Bruce Armstrong	OT	6'4"	284	25		
Fred Childress	OT	6'4"	333	23		6
Pat Harlow	OT	6'6"	290	22		
Jon Melander	OT	6'7"	280	24		
Danny Villa	OG-C	6'5"	305	26		
Stan Clayton	OG	6'3"	265	26		
Gene Chilton	C	6'3"	286	27		
Elbert Crawford	C-OG	6'3"	280	25		
Gregg Rakoczy	C-OG	6'5"	280	26		
Ray Agnew	DE	6'3"	272	23		
Chris Gannon	DE	6'6"	260	25		
Marion Hobby	DE	6'4"	277	24		
Sean Smith	DE	6'4"	280	24		
Garin Veris	DE	6'4"	255	28		
Brent Williams	DE	6'3"	275	26		
Tim Goad	NT	6'3"	280	25		
Fred Smerlas	NT	6'4"	291	34		
Vincent Brown	LB	6'2"	245	26		
Richard Harvey	LB	6'1"	227	24		
David Howard	LB	6'1"	230	29		
Eugene Lockhart	LB	6'2"	233	30		
Johnny Rembert	LB	6'3"	234	30		
Ed Reynolds	LB	6'5"	242	29		
Chris Singleton	LB	6'2"	247	24		
Richard Tardits	LB	6'2"	235	25		
Andre Tippett	LB	6'3"	241	31	1	
Harry Colon	DB	5'11"	203	22		
Tim Gordon	DB	6'	188	26		
Jerome Henderson	DB	5'10"	189	22	2	
Maurice Hurst	DB	5'10"	185	23	3	
David Key	DB	5'10"	198	23		
Ronnie Lippett	DB	5'11"	180	30	2	
Fred Marion	DB	6'2"	191	32	2	
David Pool	DB	5'9"	182	24		
Mickey Washington	DB	5'9"	187	23	2	
Tony Zackery	DB	6'2"	195	24		
Tom Hodson	QB	6'3"	195	24		
Hugh Millen	QB	6'5"	216	27		6
Marvin Allen	HB	5'10"	208	25		
Leonard Russell	HB	6'2"	235	21		24
John Stephens	HB-FB	6'1"	215	25		12
Jon Vaughn	HB	5'9"	203	21		18
George Adams	FB	6'1"	225	28		
Ivy Joe Hunter	FB-HB	6'1"	248	24		
Rob Carpenter	WR	6'2"	215	23		
Irving Fryar	WR	6'	200	28		18
Greg McMurtry	WR	6'2"	207	23		12
Gene Taylor	WR	6'2"	289	28		
Michael Timpson	WR	5'10"	175	24		12
Ben Coates	TE	6'4"	245	22		6
Marv Cook	TE	6'4"	234	25		18
Charlie Baumann	K	6'1"	203	24		42
Shawn McCarthy	K	6'6"	227	23		
Jason Staurovsky	K	5'9"	170	28		49
Bryan Wagner	K	6'2"	200	29		

David Viaene — Knee Injury
Ilia Jarostchuk — Bicep Injury
Hart Lee Dykes — Knee Injury

INDIANAPOLIS COLTS 1-15 Ron Meyer (0-5), Rick Venturi (1-10)

Scores of Each Game		
7	NEW ENGLAND	16
6	Miami	17
0	L.A. Raiders	16
24	DETROIT	33
3	Seattle	31
3	PITTSBURGH	21
6	Buffalo	42
6	N.Y. JETS	17
6	MIAMI	10
28	N.Y. Jets	27
17	CHICAGO	31
10	Green Bay	14
0	CLEVELAND	31
17	New England	* 23
7	BUFFALO	35
3	Tampa Bay	17

Use Name	Pos.	Hgt.	Wgt.	Age	Int	Pts
Kevin Call	OT	6'7"	308	29		
Jack Linn	OT	6'5"	295	24		
Zefross Moss	OT	6'6"	338	25		
Irv Pankey	OT-OG	6'5"	295	33		
Darin Shoulders	OT	6'3"	288	23		
Mark Vander Poel	OT	6'7"	303	23		
Brian Baldinger	OG-C	6'4"	278	32		
Brian Blados (from CIN)	OG	6'3"	296	29		
Chris Conlin	OG	6'4"	290	26		
Randy Dixon	OG	6'3"	302	27		
Bubba Paris (to DET)	OG-OT	6'6"	299	30		
William Schultz	OG-OT	6'5"	305	24		
Mark Cannon	C	6'3"	258	29		
Ray Donaldson	C	6'3"	300	33		
Mel Agee	DE	6'5"	290	22		
Sam Clancy	DE	6'7"	300	33		
Shane Curry	DE	6'5"	270	23		
Jon Hand	DE	6'7"	301	27		
Donnell Thompson	DE	6'4"	280	32		
Travis Davis	NT	6'2"	283	25		
Frank Giannetti	NT	6'2"	267	24		
Tony Siragusa	NT-LB	6'3"	303	24		
Chip Banks	LB	6'4"	254	31		
Duane Bickett	LB	6'5"	251	28		
Jeff Herrod	LB	6'	246	25	1	
Matt Jaworski	LB	6'1"	226	23		
Brian Jones	LB	6'1"	240	23		
Quintus McDonald	LB	6'3	263	24		
Scott Radecic	LB	6'3"	236	29	1	
Pat Snyder	LB	6'1"	225	28		
Matt Vanderbeek	LB	6'3"	258	24		
Tony Walker	LB	6'3"	235	23		
Michael Ball	DB	6'	220	27		
John Baylor	DB	6'	203	26	4	
Eugene Daniel	DB	5'11"	188	30	3	
Chris Goode	DB	6'	196	27	2	
Alan Grant	DB	5'10"	187	24		
Cornell Holloway	DB	5'11"	182	25	1	
Dave McCloughan	DB	6'1"	180	24		
Mike Prior	DB	6'	210	27	3	
Keith Taylor	DB	5'11'	206	26		
Jeff George	QB	6'4"	221	23		
Mark Herrmann	QB	6'4"	220	32		
Rusty Hilger	QB	6'4"	209	29		
Jack Trudeau	QB	6'3"	219	28		
Albert Bentley	HB-FB	5'11"	217	31		
Ken Clark	HB-FB	5'9"	204	25		
Eric Dickerson	HB	6'3"	224	30		18
Brian Lattimore	HB	6'1"	202	28		
Bruce Perkins	HB-FB	6'2"	230	24		
Anthony Johnson	FB	6'	222	23		
Tim Manoa	FB	6'1"	245	26		6
Bill Brooks	WR	6'	189	27		24
Jessie Hester	WR	5'11"	172	28		30
Darvell Huffman	WR	5'8"	158	24		
Sammy Martin (from NE)	WR	5'11"	175	26		
Reggie Thornton	WR	5'10"	170	23		
Clarence Verdin	WR	5'8"	162	28		6
Pat Beach	TE	6'4"	249	30		
Kerry Cash	TE	6'4"	247	22		
James Coley	TE	6'3"	270	24		
Bob Mrosko	TE	6'5"	260	25		
Dean Biasucci	K	6'	190	29		59
Rohn Stark	K	6'3"	203	32		

Mark Garalczyk — Neck Injury
Pat Tomberlin — Leg Injury

RUSHING — RECEIVING — PUNT RETURNS — KICKOFF RETURNS — PASSING — PUNTING — KICKING Statistics

BUFFALO BILLS

RUSHING

Last Name	No.	Yds	Avg	TD
Thomas	288	1407	4.9	7
K. Davis	129	624	4.8	4
Gardner	42	146	3.5	4
Reed	12	136	11.3	0
Kelly	20	45	2.3	1
Edwards	1	17	17.0	0
Reich	13	6	0.5	0

RECEIVING

Last Name	No.	Yds	Avg	TD
Reed	81	1113	13.7	10
Thomas	62	631	10.2	5
Lofton	57	1072	18.8	8
McKeller	44	434	9.9	3
Beebe	32	414	12.9	6
Edwards	22	228	10.4	1
K. Davis	20	118	5.9	1
Metzelaars	5	54	10.8	2
Gardner	3	20	6.7	0
Rolle	3	10	3.3	2
Tasker	2	39	19.5	1
Alexander	1	7	7.0	0

PUNT RETURNS

Last Name	No.	Yds	Avg	TD
Hicks	12	203	16.9	0
Edwards	13	69	5.3	0
Odomes	1	9	9.0	0

KICKOFF RETURNS

Last Name	No.	Yds	Avg	TD
Edwards	31	623	20.1	1
Fuller	8	125	15.6	0
Beebe	7	121	17.3	0
K. Davis	4	73	18.3	0
Taylor	1	18	18.0	0
Gardner	1	10	10.0	0

PASSING	Att	Cmp	%	Yds	Yd/Att	TD	Int— %	RK
Kelly	474	304	64.1	3844	8.11	33	17—3.6	1
Reich	41	27	65.9	305	7.44	6	2—4.9	
Mohr	1	1	100.0	9	9.00	0	0—0.0	

PUNTING	No.	Avg.
Mohr	54	38.6

KICKING	XP	ATT	%	FG	ATT	%
Norwood	56	58	97	18	29	62

NEW YORK JETS

RUSHING

Last Name	No.	Yds	Avg	TD
Thomas	189	728	3.9	3
Baxter	184	666	3.6	11
Hector	62	345	5.6	0
McNeil	51	300	5.9	2
O'Brien	23	60	2.6	0
Taylor	7	23	3.3	0
Mathis	1	19	19.0	0
Aguiar	1	18	18.0	0
Brown	3	4	1.3	1
Nagle	1	-1	-1.0	0
Burkett	1	-2	-2.0	0

RECEIVING

Last Name	No.	Yds	Avg	TD
Toon	74	963	13.0	0
Moore	70	987	14.1	5
Thomas	30	195	6.5	1
Mathis	28	329	11.8	1
Burkett	23	327	14.2	4
Dressel	17	122	7.2	0
Boyer	16	153	9.6	0
Baxter	12	124	10.3	0
McNeil	7	56	8.0	0
Hector	7	51	7.3	0
Whisenhunt	4	34	8.5	0
Dawkins	3	38	12.7	0
Matich	3	23	7.7	1
O'Brien	1	27	27.0	0

PUNT RETURNS

Last Name	No.	Yds	Avg	TD
Mathis	23	157	6.8	0

KICKOFF RETURNS

Last Name	No.	Yds	Avg	TD
Mathis	29	599	20.7	0
Brown	10	100	10.0	0
Hector	8	172	21.5	0
Odegard	6	106	17.7	0
Dawkins	2	22	11.0	0
P. Kelly	1	4	4.0	0
Boyer	1	0	0.0	0
Dressel	1	0	0.0	0

PASSING	Att	Cmp	%	Yds	Yd/Att	TD	Int— %	RK
O'Brien	489	287	58.7	3300	6.75	10	11—2.2	8
Eason	28	13	46.4	155	5.54	0	1—3.6	
Taylor	10	7	70.0	49	4.90	1	0—0.0	
Toon	2	0	0.0	0	0.00	0	0—0.0	

PUNTING	No.	Avg.
Prokop	59	40.1

KICKING	XP	Att	%	FG	Att	%
Leahy	30	30	100	26	37	70

MIAMI DOLPHINS

RUSHING

Last Name	No.	Yds	Avg	TD
Higgs	231	905	3.9	4
S. Smith	83	297	3.6	1
Craver	20	58	2.9	1
Marino	27	32	1.2	1
Secules	4	30	7.5	1
Paige	10	25	2.5	0
Logan	4	5	1.3	0

RECEIVING

Last Name	No.	Yds	Avg	TD
Duper	70	1085	15.5	5
Clayton	70	1053	15.0	12
Paige	57	469	8.2	1
Martin	27	434	16.1	2
Jensen	21	183	8.7	2
Baty	20	269	13.5	1
S. Smith	14	95	6.8	0
Edmunds	11	118	10.7	2
Higgs	11	80	7.3	0
Banks	9	119	13.2	1
Craver	8	67	8.4	0
Miller	4	49	12.3	0
Pruitt	2	30	15.0	0
Henry	2	17	8.5	0
Sims	1	9	9.0	0

PUNT RETURNS

Last Name	No.	Yds	Avg	TD
Miller	28	248	8.9	0
Junior	1	0	0.0	0
Martin	1	0	0.0	0

KICKOFF RETURNS

Last Name	No.	Yds	Avg	TD
Craver	32	615	19.2	0
Logan	12	191	15.9	0
Paige	2	31	15.5	0
Henry	1	13	13.0	0
J. Williams	1	7	7.0	0
Dellenbach	1	0	0.0	0

PASSING	Att	Cmp	%	Yds	Yd/Att	TD	Int— %	RK
Marino	549	318	57.9	3970	7.23	25	13—2.4	3
Secules	13	8	61.5	90	6.92	1	1—7.7	
Jensen	1	1	100.0	17	17.00	0	0—0.0	

PUNTING	No.	Avg.
Roby	55	44.8

KICKING	XP	Att.	%	FG	Att	%
Stoyonovich	28	29	97	31	37	84

NEW ENGLAND PATRIOTS

RUSHING

Last Name	No.	Yds	Avg	TD
Russell	266	959	3.6	4
Stephens	63	163	2.6	2
Vaughn	31	146	4.7	2
Millen	31	92	3.0	1
Hunter	18	53	2.9	0
Allen	13	50	3.8	0
Fryar	2	11	5.5	0
Adams	2	3	1.5	0
Chilton	1	0	0.0	0
Hodson	4	0	0.0	0
Timpson	1	-4	-4.0	0
Coates	1	-6	-6.0	0

RECEIVING

Last Name	No.	Yds	Avg	TD
Cook	82	808	9.9	3
Fryar	68	1014	14.9	3
McMurtry	41	614	15.0	2
Timpson	25	471	18.8	2
Russell	18	81	4.5	0
Stephens	16	119	7.4	0
Hunter	11	97	8.8	0
Coates	10	95	9.5	1
Vaughn	9	89	9.9	0
Carpenter	3	45	15.0	0
Allen	1	9	9.0	0

PUNT RETURNS

Last Name	No.	Yds	Avg	TD
Henderson	27	201	7.4	0
Fryar	2	10	5.0	0
Pool	1	0	0.0	0
Zackery	1	0	0.0	0

KICKOFF RETURNS

Last Name	No.	Yds	Avg	TD
Vaughn	34	717	21.1	1
Allen	8	161	20.1	0
Timpson	2	37	18.5	0
Hobby	2	0	0.0	0
Rakoczy	1	9	9.0	0
Coates	1	6	6.0	0

PASSING	Att	Cmp	%	Yds	Yd/Att	TD	Int— %	RK
Millen	409	246	60.1	3073	7.51	9	18—4.4	12
Hodson	68	36	52.9	345	5.07	1	4—5.9	
Vaughn	2	1	50.0	13	6.50	1	0—0.0	
McCarthy	1	1	100.0	11	11.00	0	0—0.0	
Fryar	1	0	0.0	0	0.00	0	0—0.0	

PUNTING	No.	Avg.
McCarthy	66	39.0

KICKING	XP	ATT	%	FG	ATT	%
Staurovsky	10	11	91	13	19	68
Baumann	15	16	94	9	12	75

INDIANAPOLIS COLTS

RUSHING

Last Name	No.	Yds	Avg	TD
Dickerson	167	536	3.2	2
Clark	114	366	3.2	0
Manoa	27	144	5.3	1
Johnson	22	94	4.3	0
George	16	36	2.3	0
Perkins	4	11	2.8	0
Verdin	1	4	4.0	0
Herrmann	1	-1	-1.0	0
Huffman	1	-8	-8.0	0
Stark	1	-13	-13.0	0

RECEIVING

Last Name	No.	Yds	Avg	TD
Brooks	72	888	12.3	4
Hester	60	753	12.6	5
Johnson	42	344	8.2	0
Dickerson	41	269	6.6	1
Clark	33	245	7.4	0
Verdin	21	214	10.2	0
Mrosko	8	90	11.3	0
Bentley	7	42	6.0	0
Martin	5	79	15.8	0
Beach	5	56	11.2	0
Huffman	3	14	4.7	0
Perkins	3	-2	-0.7	0
Manoa	2	5	2.5	0
Thornton	1	38	38.0	0
Cash	1	18	18.0	0
Coley	1	13	13.0	0

PUNT RETURNS

Last Name	No.	Yds	Avg	TD
Verdin	25	163	6.5	0
Clark	1	6	6.0	0
Grant	1	2	2.0	0

KICKOFF RETURNS

Last Name	No.	Yds	Avg	TD
Martin	20	483	24.2	0
Verdin	36	689	19.1	1
Grant	3	20	6.7	0
McCloughan	2	35	17.5	0
Mrosko	1	9	9.0	0
McDonald	1	3	3.0	0

PASSING	Att	Cmp	%	Yds	Yd/Att	TD	Int— %	RK
George	485	292	60.2	2910	6.00	10	12—2.5	10
Herrmann	19	11	57.9	137	7.21	0	3—15.8	
Trudeau	7	2	28.6	19	2.71	0	1—14.3	
Hilger	1	0	0.0	0	0.00	0	0—0.0	

PUNTING	No.	Avg.
Stark	82	42.6

KICKING	XP	ATT	%	FG	ATT	%
Biasucci	14	14	100	15	26	58

1991 A.F.C. — Central Division

HOUSTON OILERS 11-5 Jack Pardee

Scores of Each Game		
47	L.A. RAIDERS	17
30	Cincinnati	7
17	KANSAS CITY	7
20	New England	24
42	DENVER	14
23	N.Y. Jets	20
17	Miami	13
35	CINCINNATI	3
13	Washington	* 16
26	DALLAS	* 23
28	CLEVELAND	24
14	Pittsburgh	26
6	PHILADELPHIA	13
31	PITTSBURGH	6
17	Cleveland	14
20	N.Y. Giants	24

UseName	Pos.	Hgt.	Wgt.	Age	Int	Pts
Kevin Donnalley	OT	6'5"	290	23		
Don Maggs	OT-OG	6'5"	290	29		
Dean Steinkuhler	OT	6'3"	287	30		
David Williams	OT	6'5"	292	25		
Doug Dawson	OG-C	6'2"	288	29		
John Flannery	OG-C	6'3"	304	22		
Mike Munchak	OG	6'3"	284	31		
Bruce Matthews	C-OG	6'4"	291	30		
William Fuller	DE	6'3"	274	29		
Sean Jones	DE	6'7"	264	28		
Willis Peguese	DE	6'4"	267	24		
Jeff Alm	DT	6'6"	289	23		
Ray Childress	DT-DE	6'6"	272	28		
Ezra Johnson	DT-DE	6'4"	257	35		
Lee Williams	DE-DT	6'6"	271	28		
Glenn Montgomery	DT	6'	272	24		
Doug Smith	DT	6'5"	309	32		

Erik Norgard — Shoulder Injury

UseName	Pos.	Hgt.	Wgt.	Age	Int	Pts
Eric Fairs	LB	6'3"	244	27		
Rick Graf	LB	6'5"	244	27		
Scott Kozak	LB	6'3"	222	25		
Lamar Lathon	LB	6'3"	250	23	1	6
Johnny Meads	LB	6'2"	226	30		
Eugene Seale	LB	5'10"	253	27		
Al Smith	LB	6'1"	251	26	1	6
Herbie Anderson	DB	5'9"	183	22		
Cris Dishman	DB	6'	178	26	6	6
Mike Dumas	DB	5'11"	178	22	1	6
Steve Jackson	DB	5'8"	182	22		
Richard Johnson	DB	6'1"	195	27		
Darryll Lewis	DB	5'9"	188	22	1	6
Bubba McDowell	DB	6'1"	198	24	4	6
Bo Orlando	DB	5'10"	180	25	4	
Marcus Robertson	DB	5'11"	197	21		

UseName	Pos.	Hgt.	Wgt.	Age	Int	Pts
Cody Carlson	QB	6'3"	202	27		
Warren Moon	QB	6'3"	212	34		12
Gary Brown	HB-FB	5'11"	224	22		6
Victor Jones	HB-FB	5'8"	212	23		
Allen Pinkett	HB	5'9"	196	27		60
Lorenzo White	HB	5'11"	222	25		24
Pat Coleman	WR	5'7"	173	24		6
Curtis Duncan	WR	5'11"	184	26		24
Ernest Givins	WR	5'9"	172	26		30
Leonard Harris	WR	5'8"	162	30		
Drew Hill	WR	5'9"	172	34		24
Haywood Jeffires	WR	6'2"	201	26		42
Alex Johnson	WR	5'9"	167	23		
Tony Jones	WR	5'7"	139	25		12
Frank Miotke	WR	6'	175	25		
Al Del Greco	K	5'10"	200	29		46
Ian Howfield	K	6'2"	196	25		64
Greg Montgomery	K	6'3"	215	26		
Kent Sullivan	K	5'10"	197	27		

PITTSBURGH STEELERS 7-9 Chuck Noll

Scores of Each Game		
26	SAN DIEGO	20
34	Buffalo	52
20	NEW ENGLAND	6
14	Philadelphia	23
21	Indianapolis	3
20	N.Y. GIANTS	23
7	SEATTLE	27
14	Cleveland	17
13	Denver	20
33	Cincinnati	* 27
14	WASHINGTON	41
26	HOUSTON	14
10	Dallas	20
6	Houston	31
17	CINCINNATI	10
17	CLEVELAND	10

UseName	Pos.	Hgt.	Wgt.	Age	Int	Pts
Tunch Ilkin	OT	6'3"	273	33		
John Jackson	OT	6'6"	289	26		
Tom Ricketts	OT-OG	6'5"	288	25		
Ariel Solomon	OT-OG	6'5"	271	23		
Justin Strzelczyk	OT	6'5"	297	23		
Brian Blankenship	OG-C	6'1"	280	28		
Dean Caliguire (from SF)	OG-C	6'2"	280	24		
Calton Haselrig	OG	6'1"	295	25		
Terry Long	OG	5'11"	284	32		
Dermontti Dawson	C	6'2"	275	26		
Kenny Davidson	DE	6'5"	264	24		
Donald Evans	DE	6'2"	258	27		
Aaron Jones	DE	6'5"	257	24		
Keith Willis	DE	6'1"	260	32		
Craig Veasey	NT-DT-DE	6'2"	285	24		
Gerald Williams	NT	6'3"	282	27		

UseName	Pos.	Hgt.	Wgt.	Age	Int	Pts
Jeff Brady	LB	6'1"	224	22		
Bryan Hinkle	LB	6'2"	224	32	2	6
David Little	LB	6'1"	236	32	1	
Greg Lloyd	LB	6'2"	223	26	1	
Rob McGovern	LB	6'2"	223	24		
Hardy Nickerson	LB	6'2"	227	26		
Jerry Olsavsky	LB	6'1"	219	24		
Huey Richardson	LB-DE	6'5"	233	23		
Jerrol Williams	LB	6'5"	237	24		6
Thomas Everett	DB	5'9"	183	26	4	
Larry Griffin	DB	6'	200	28	1	
Delton Hall	DB	6'1"	204	26		
David Johnson	DB	6'	181	25	1	
Gary Jones	DB	6'1"	208	23	1	
Carnell Lake	DB	6'1"	207	24		
Richard Shelton	DB	5'10"	196	25	3	6
Kevin Smith	DB	5'11"	204	24		
Shawn Vincent	DB	5'10"	180	23	2	
Sammy Walker	DB	5'11"	197	22		
Rod Woodson	DB	6'	197	26	3	

UseName	Pos.	Hgt.	Wgt.	Age	Int	Pts
Bubby Brister	QB	6'3"	217	29		
Neil O'Donnell	QB	6'3"	223	25		6
Barry Foster	HB	5'10"	218	22		12
Warren Williams	HB	6'	213	26		24
Tim Worley	HB	6'2"	216	24		
Merril Hoge	FB	6'2"	222	26		18
Leroy Thompson	FB	5'10"	215	22		
Chris Calloway	WR	5'10"	190	23		6
Jeff Graham	WR	6'1"	195	22		
Louis Lipps	WR	5'10"	185	29		12
Ernie Mills	WR	5'11"	178	22		12
Dwight Stone	WR-HB	6'	190	27		30
Keith Cash	TE	6'4"	235	22		6
Adrian Cooper	TE	6'5"	259	23		12
Eric Green	TE	6'5"	280	24		36
Mike Mularkey	TE	6'4"	240	29		
Gary Anderson	K	5'11"	179	32		100
Dan Stryzinski	K	6'1"	189	26		

CLEVELAND BROWNS 6-10 Bill Belichick

Scores of Each Game		
14	DALLAS	26
20	New England	0
14	CINCINNATI	13
10	N.Y. Giants	13
14	N.Y. JETS	17
17	Washington	42
30	San Diego	* 24
17	PITTSBURGH	14
21	Cincinnati	23
30	PHILADELPHIA	32
24	Houston	28
20	KANSAS CITY	15
31	Indianapolis	0
7	DENVER	17
14	HOUSTON	17
10	Pittsburgh	17

UseName	Pos.	Hgt.	Wgt.	Age	Int	Pts
Leonard Burton	OT	6'3"	277	27		
Paul Farren	OT-OG	6'5"	270	30		
Dan Fike	OT-OG	6'7"	285	30		
Tony Jones	OT	6'5"	290	25		
Rob Woods	OT	6'5"	295	25		
Ed King	OG	6'4"	303	21		
John Rienstra	OG	6'5"	275	28		
Mike Baab	C	6'4"	275	31		
Chris Thome	C	6'4"	280	22		
Rob Burnett	DE	6'4"	270	24		
Ernie Logan	DE	6'3"	271	23		
Pio Sagapolutele	DE	6'6"	297	21		
Anthony Pleasant	DE	6'5"	258	23		
Mike Wise	DE	6'7"	270	27		
Frank Conover	DT	6'5"	317	23		
James Jones	DT-NT	6'2"	294	22		8
Michael Dean Perry	DT	6'1"	285	26		
John Thornton	DT	6'3"	303	22		

UseName	Pos.	Hgt.	Wgt.	Age	Int	Pts
David Brandon	LB	6'4"	230	26	2	6
Richard Brown	LB	6'3"	240	25	1	
Johnie Cooks	LB	6'4"	251	32		
Cedric Figaro	LB	6'3"	255	24	1	
Mike Johnson	LB	6'1"	230	28	1	
Jock Jones (to PHX)	LB	6'2"	230	23		
Clay Matthews	LB	6'2"	245	35	1	
Van Waiters	LB	6'4"	250	26		
Harlon Barnett	DB	5'11"	200	24		
Latin Berry	DB	5'10"	196	24		
Anthony Blaylock (to SD)	DB	5'11"	190	26		
Stephen Braggs	DB	5'10"	180	26	3	
Raymond Clayborn	DB	6'	190	36		
Anthony Florence	DB	6'	185	25		
Odie Harris	DB	6'	190	25		
Alfred Jackson	DB	6'	180	24	1	
Joe King (from CIN)	DB	6'2"	202	23		
Frank Minnifield	DB	5'9"	180	31		
Vince Newsome	DB	6'1"	185	30	1	6
Eric Turner	DB	6'1"	207	22	2	6

Thane Gash — Neck Injury
Mark Harper — Heel Injury

UseName	Pos.	Hgt.	Wgt.	Age	Int	Pts
Bernie Kosar	QB	6'5"	215	27		
Todd Philcox	QB	6'4"	225	24		
Eric Metcalf	HB-WR	5'10"	190	23		
Joe Morris	HB	5'9"	195	30		12
Derrick Douglas	FB	5'10"	222	23		
Leroy Hoard	FB-HB	5'11"	230	23		66
Kevin Mack	FB	6'	230	29		60
Lee Rouson	FB	6'1"	222	28		
Brian Brennan	WR	5'9"	185	29		6
Darryl Ingram	WR	6'3"	240	25		
Michael Jackson	WR	6'4"	195	24		12
Lynn James	WR	6'	190	26		
Reggie Langhorne	WR	6'2"	205	28		12
Mike Oliphant	WR-HB	5'9"	171	28		
Danny Peebles	WR	5'11"	180	25		
Tyrone Shavers	WR	6'3"	210	23		
Webster Slaughter	WR	6'	170	26		18
Scott Galbraith	TE	6'3"	260	24		
Brian Kinchen	TE	6'2"	232	26		
Bruce McGonnigal	TE	6'4"	230	23		
John Talley	TE	6'5"	245	26		
Brian Hansen	K	6'4"	220	30		
Matt Stover	K	5'11"	178	23		81

Lawyer Tillman — Ankle Injury

CINCINNATI BENGALS 3-13 Sam Wyche

Scores of Each Game		
14	Denver	45
7	HOUSTON	30
13	Cleveland	14
27	WASHINGTON	34
7	SEATTLE	13
23	Dallas	35
16	Buffalo	35
3	Houston	35
23	CLEVELAND	21
27	PITTSBURGH	* 33
10	Philadelphia	17
14	L.A. RAIDERS	38
27	N.Y. GIANTS	24
13	Miami	37
10	Pittsburgh	17
29	NEW ENGLAND	7

UseName	Pos.	Hgt.	Wgt.	Age	Int	Pts
Scott Jones	OT	6'6"	280	25		
Anthony Munoz	OT	6'6"	284	33		
Kirk Scrafford	OT	6'6"	255	24		
Joe Walter	OT-OG	6'6"	292	28		
Mike Withycombe	OT	6'5"	310	26		
Paul Jetton	OG	6'4"	288	26		
Ken Moyer	OG	6'6"	297	24		
Bruce Reimers	OG	6'7"	298	30		
Mike Arthur	C	6'3"	271	23		
Bruce Kozerski	C-OG	6'4"	287	29		
Jason Buck	DE-DT	6'5"	264	27		
David Grant	DE	6'4"	278	25	1	
Alonzo Mitz	DE	6'4"	278	28	1	
Skip McClendon (to SD)	DE	6'7"	287	27		
Lamar Rogers	DE	6'4"	292	23		
Natu Tuatagaloa	DE	6'4"	274	25		
Tim Krumrie	NT-DT	6'2"	274	31		

Andrew Stewart — Knee Injury

UseName	Pos.	Hgt.	Wgt.	Age	Int	Pts
Leo Barker	LB	6'2"	230	31	1	
Ed Brady	LB	6'2"	236	31		
Bernard Clark (to, from SEA)	LB	6'2"	248	24		
James Francis	LB	6'5"	252	23	1	
Alex Gordon	LB	6'5"	245	26		2
Kevin Walker	LB	6'2"	238	25		
Leon White	LB	6'3"	242	27		
Alfred Williams	LB	6'6"	240	22		
Carl Zander	LB	6'2"	235	28		
Antoine Bennett	DB	5'11"	185	23		
Lewis Billups	DB	5'11"	190	27		
Barney Bussey	DB	6'	210	29	2	
Rickey Dixon	DB	5'11"	191	24	2	
Richard Fain (to PHX)	DB	5'10"	183	23	1	
David Fulcher	DB	6'3"	238	26	4	6
Wayne Haddix (from TB)	DB	6'1"	205	28		
Rod Jones	DB	6'	185	27		
Mitchell Price	DB	5'9"	181	24	1	6
Eric Thomas	DB	5'11"	181	26	3	
Fernandus Vinson	DB	5'10"	197	22		

UseName	Pos.	Hgt.	Wgt.	Age	Int	Pts
Boomer Esiason	QB	6'4"	220	30		
Donald Hollas	QB	6'3"	215	23		
Erik Wilhelm	QB	6'3"	210	25		
Eric Ball	HB-FB	6'2"	211	25		6
James Brooks	HB	5'10"	182	32		24
Harold Green	HB	6'2"	222	23		12
Mike Dingle	FB	6'2"	240	22		6
Craig Taylor	FB	5'11"	228	25		12
Ickey Woods	FB	6'2"	232	25		24
Mike Barber	WR	5'11"	172	24		6
Eddie Brown	WR	6'	185	28		12
Shane Garrett	WR	5'11"	185	23		
Lynn James	WR	6'	191	24		6
Tim McGee	WR	5'10"	183	27		24
Reggie Rembert	WR	6'5"	200	24		6
Rodney Holman	TE	6'3"	238	31		12
Eric Kattus	TE	6'5"	251	28		
Jim Riggs	TE	6'5"	245	27		
Jim Breech	K	5'6"	161	35		96
Lee Johnson	K	6'2"	200	29		3

HOUSTON OILERS

RUSHING

Last Name	No.	Yds	Avg	TD
Pinkett	171	720	4.2	9
White	110	465	4.2	4
Brown	8	85	10.6	1
Moon	33	68	2.1	2
Givins	4	30	7.5	0
Hill	1	1	1.0	0
Carlson	4	-3	-0.8	0

RECEIVING

Last Name	No.	Yds	Avg	TD
Jeffires	100	1181	11.8	7
Hill	90	1109	12.3	4
Givins	70	996	14.2	5
Duncan	55	588	10.7	4
Pinkett	29	228	7.9	1
White	27	211	7.8	0
T. Jones	19	251	13.2	2
Coleman	11	138	12.5	1
Harris	8	101	12.6	0
Brown	2	1	0.5	0

PUNT RETURNS

Last Name	No.	Yds	Avg	TD
Coleman	22	138	6.3	0
Givins	11	107	9.7	0
Duncan	1	-1	-1.0	0
Jackson	1	0	0.0	0
Robertson	1	0	0.0	0

KICKOFF RETURNS

Last Name	No.	Yds	Avg	TD
Pinkett	26	508	19.5	0
Coleman	13	256	19.7	0
Brown	3	30	10.0	0
Harris	2	34	17.0	
Flannery	1	0	0.0	0
V. Jones	1	7	7.0	0

PASSING — PUNTING — KICKING

PASSING	Att	Cmp	%	Yds	Yd/Att	TD	Int—	%	RK
Moon	655	404	61.7	4690	7.16	23	21—	3.2	5
Carlson	12	7	58.3	114	9.50	1	0—	0.0	

PUNTING	No.	Avg.
Montgomery	50	42.1
Sullivan	3	32.3

KICKING	XP	ATT	%	FG	ATT	%
Howfield	25	29	86	13	18	72
Del Greco	16	16	100	10	13	77

PITTSBURGH STEELERS

RUSHING

Last Name	No.	Yds	Avg	TD
Hoge	165	610	3.7	2
Foster	96	488	5.1	1
W. Williams	57	262	4.6	4
Worley	22	117	5.3	0
O'Donnell	18	82	4.6	1
Thompson	20	60	3.0	0
Brister	11	17	1.5	0
Stone	1	2	2.0	0
Stryzinski	4	-11	-2.8	0

RECEIVING

Last Name	No.	Yds	Avg	TD
Lipps	55	671	12.2	2
Hoge	49	379	7.7	1
Green	41	582	14.2	6
Stone	32	649	20.3	5
Calloway	15	254	10.9	1
W. Williams	15	139	9.3	0
Thompson	14	118	8.4	0
Cooper	11	147	13.4	2
Foster	9	117	13.0	1
Cash	7	90	12.9	1
Mularkey	6	67	11.2	0
Mills	3	79	26.3	1
Graham	2	21	10.5	0

PUNT RETURNS

Last Name	No.	Yds	Avg	TD
Woodson	28	320	11.4	0
Graham	8	46	5.8	0
Cash	1	6	6.0	0
Mills	1	0	0.0	0
Vincent	1	0	0.0	0

KICKOFF RETURNS

Last Name	No.	Yds	Avg	TD
Woodson	44	880	20.0	0
Mills	11	284	25.8	0
Stone	6	75	12.5	0
Graham	3	48	16.0	0
J. Williams	1	19	19.0	0
Thompson	1	8	8.0	0
McGovern	1	0	0.0	0

PASSING — PUNTING — KICKING

PASSING	Att	Cmp	%	Yds	Yd/Att	TD	Int—	%	RK
O'Donnell	286	156	54.5	1963	6.86	11	7—	2.4	7
Brister	190	103	54.2	1350	7.11	9	9—	4.7	

PUNTING	No.	Avg.
Stryzinski	75	39.9

KICKING	XP	Att	%	FG	Att	%
Anderson	31	31	100	23	33	70

CLEVELAND BROWNS

RUSHING

Last Name	No.	Yds	Avg	TD
Mack	197	726	3.7	8
Morris	93	289	3.1	2
Hoard	37	154	4.2	2
Metcalf	30	107	3.6	0
Kosar	26	74	2.8	0
Rouson	3	14	4.7	0
Philcox	1	-1	-1.0	0
Hansen	2	-3	-1.5	0

RECEIVING

Last Name	No.	Yds	Avg	TD
Slaughter	64	906	14.2	3
Hoard	48	567	11.8	9
Mack	40	255	6.4	2
Langhorne	39	505	12.9	2
Brennan	31	325	10.5	1
Metcalf	29	294	10.1	0
Galbraith	27	328	12.1	0
Jackson	17	268	15.8	2
Morris	13	76	5.8	0
James	7	103	14.7	1
Rouson	2	9	4.5	0
Talley	1	13	13.0	0
Kosar	1	1	1.0	0

PUNT RETURNS

Last Name	No.	Yds	Avg	TD
Slaughter	17	112	6.6	0
Metcalf	12	100	8.3	0
Brennan	2	11	5.5	0
James	1	0	0.0	0

KICKOFF RETURNS

Last Name	No.	Yds	Avg	TD
Metcalf	23	351	15.3	0
Morris	18	310	17.2	0
Peebles	8	149	18.6	0
James	8	143	17.9	0
Galbraith	2	13	6.5	0
Rouson	1	16	16.0	0

PASSING — PUNTING — KICKING

PASSING	Att	Cmp	%	Yds	Yd/Att	TD	Int—	%	RK
Kosar	494	307	62.1	3487	7.06	18	9—	1.8	2
Philcox	8	4	50.0	49	6.13	0	1—	12.5	
Hansen	1	1	100.0	11	11.00	1	0—	0.0	

PUNTING	No.	Avg.
Hansen	80	42.5

KICKING	XP	ATT	%	FG	ATT	%
Stover	33	34	97	16	22	73

CINCINNATI BENGALS

RUSHING

Last Name	No.	Yds	Avg	TD
Green	158	731	4.6	2
Brooks	152	571	3.8	2
Taylor	33	153	4.6	2
Woods	36	97	2.7	4
Dingle	21	91	4.3	0
Esiason	24	66	2.8	0
Hollas	12	66	5.5	0
Ball	10	21	2.1	1
Wilhelm	1	9	9.0	0
Brown	1	8	8.0	0
Johnson	1	-2	-2.0	0

RECEIVING

Last Name	No.	Yds	Avg	TD
Brown	59	827	14.0	2
McGee	51	802	15.7	4
Brooks	40	348	8.7	2
Holman	31	445	14.4	2
Barber	23	255	11.1	1
Taylor	21	122	5.8	0
Green	16	136	8.5	0
Kattus	12	136	11.3	0
Rembert	9	117	13.0	1
James	7	103	14.7	1
Woods	6	36	6.0	0
Dingle	5	23	4.6	1
Riggs	4	14	3.5	0
Garrett	3	32	10.7	0
Ball	3	17	5.7	0

PUNT RETURNS

Last Name	No.	Yds	Avg	TD
Price	14	203	14.5	1
Barber	13	70	5.4	0
Garrett	1	7	7.0	0
James	1	0	0.0	0

KICKOFF RETURNS

Last Name	No.	Yds	Avg	TD
Ball	13	262	20.2	0
Garrett	13	214	16.5	0
Brooks	11	190	17.3	0
James	8	143	17.9	0
Dingle	7	176	25.1	0
Price	5	91	18.2	0
Green	4	66	16.5	0
King	3	34	11.3	0
Riggs	2	28	14.0	0
Holman	1	15	15.0	0
Barber	1	7	7.0	0
Thomas	1	-1	-1.0	0

PASSING — PUNTING — KICKING

PASSING	Att	Cmp	%	Yds	Yd/Att	TD	Int—	%	RK
Esiason	413	233	56.4	2883	6.98	13	16—	3.9	11
Hollas	55	32	58.2	310	5.64	1	4—	7.3	
Wilhelm	42	24	57.1	217	5.17	0	2—	4.8	
Johnson	1	1	100.0	3	3.00	0	0—	0.0	

PUNTING	No.	Avg.
Johnson	64	43.7
Breech	1	33.0

KICKING	XP	ATT	%	FG	ATT	%
Breech	27	27	100	23	29	79
Johnson	0	0	0	1	3	33

DENVER BRONCOS 12-4 Dan Reeves

Scores of Each Game		
45	CINCINNATI	14
13	L.A. Raiders	16
16	SEATTLE	10
27	SAN DIEGO	19
13	Minnesota	6
14	Houston	42
19	KANSAS CITY	16
9	New England	6
20	PITTSBURGH	13
16	L.A. RAIDERS	17
24	Kansas City	20
10	Seattle	13
20	NEW ENGLAND	3
17	Cleveland	7
24	PHOENIX	19
17	San Diego	14

UseName	Pos.	Hgt.	Wgt.	Age	Int	Pts
Jeff Davidson	OT	6'5"	309	23		
Darrell Hamilton	OT	6'5"	298	26		
Ken Lanier	OT	6'3"	290	32		
Harvey Salem	OT	6'6"	289	30		
Nick Subis	OT-C	6'4"	278	23		
Sean Farrell	OG	6'3"	260	31		
Crawford Ker	OG	6'3"	285	29		
Dave Widell	OG	6'6"	292	26		
Doug Widell	OG	6'4"	287	24		
Keith Kartz	C	6'4"	270	28		
Alphonso Carreker	DE	6'6"	272	31		
Ron Holmes	DE	6'4"	265	28		
Warren Powers	DE	6'6"	287	26		6
Jim Szymanski	DE	6'5"	268	24		
Kenny Walker	DE	6'3"	260	24		
Greg Kragen	NT	6'3"	265	29		
Brian Sochia (from MIA)	NT-DE	6'3"	278	30		
Michael Brooks	LB	6'1"	235	26	2	
Mike Croel	LB	6'3"	231	22		
Simon Fletcher	LB	6'5"	240	29		
Ronnie Haliburton	LB	6'4"	230	23		
Tim Lucas	LB	6'3"	230	30		
Karl Mecklenburg	LB	6'3"	235	31		
Jeff Mills	LB	6'3"	238	22		
Mark Murray	LB	6'2"	240	23		
Keith Traylor	LB	6'2"	260	21		
Steve Atwater	DB	6'3"	217	24	5	
Tyrone Braxton	DB	5'11"	185	26	4	6
Kevin Clark	DB	5'10"	185	27		
Charles Dimry	DB	6'	175	25	3	6
Wymon Henderson	DB	5'10"	186	29	2	
Le-Lo Lang	DB	5'11"	185	24	1	
Alton Montgomery	DB	6'	195	23		
Randy Robbins	DB	6'2"	189	28	1	
Dennis Smith	DB	6'3"	200	32	5	
John Elway	QB	6'3"	215	31		36
Gary Kubiak	QB	6'	192	30		
Gaston Green	HB	5'11"	192	25		24
Bobby Humphrey	HB	6'1"	201	24		
Greg Lewis	HB-FB	5'10"	214	22		24
Bob Perryman	FB	6'1"	233	27		
Reggie Rivers	FB	6'1"	215	23		
Steve Sewell	FB-WR	6'3"	210	28		24
Mark Jackson	WR	5'10"	174	28		6
Barry Johnson	WR	6'2"	197	24		
Vance Johnson	WR	5'11"	185	28		18
Ricky Nattiel	WR	5'9"	180	25		12
Derek Russell	WR	6'	179	22		6
Michael Young	WR	6'1"	183	29		6
Reggie Johnson	TE	6'2"	256	23		6
Clarence Kay	TE	6'2"	237	30		
Shannon Sharpe	TE-WR	6'2"	230	23		6
Mike Horan	K	5'11"	190	32		
David Treadwell	K	6'1"	180	24		112

Jim Juriga — Back Injury

KANSAS CITY CHIEFS 10-6 Marty Schottenheimer

Scores of Each Game		
14	ATLANTA	3
10	NEW ORLEANS	17
7	Houston	17
20	SEATTLE	13
14	San Diego	13
33	BUFFALO	6
42	MIAMI	7
16	Denver	19
24	L.A. RAIDERS	21
27	L.A. Rams	20
20	DENVER	24
15	Cleveland	20
19	Seattle	6
20	SAN DIEGO	* 17
14	San Francisco	28
27	L.A. Raiders	21

UseName	Pos.	Hgt.	Wgt.	Age	Int	Pts
John Alt	OT	6'7"	296	29		
Rich Baldinger	OT	6'4"	293	31		
Derrick Graham	OT	6'4"	306	24		
David Lutz	OG	6'6"	305	31		
David Szott	OG	6'4"	275	23		
Frank Winters	OG-C	6'3"	285	27		
Tim Grunhard	C	6'2"	299	23		
Mike Bell	DE	6'4"	266	33		
Leonard Griffin	DE	6'4"	278	28		
Neil Smith	DE	6'4"	275	25		
Bill Maas	DE-NT	6'5"	275	28		
Dan Saleaumua	NT	6'	295	26		2
Tom Sims	NT	6'2"	285	24		
Pat Swoopes (to MIA)	NT	6'3"	277	27		
Dino Hackett	LB	6'3"	230	27		
Chris Martin	LB	6'2"	241	30	1	6
Lonnie Marts	LB	6'1"	243	22		
Ervin Randle	LB	6'1"	250	28		
Tracy Rogers	LB	6'2"	241	24		
Tracy Simien	LB	6'1"	245	24		
Derrick Thomas	LB	6'3"	236	24		6
Billy Bell	DB	5'10"	161	30	1	
Lloyd Burruss	DB	6'	214	33	1	
Deron Cherry	DB	5'11"	203	31	4	
Eric Everett	DB	5'10"	170	25		
Albert Lewis	DB	6'2"	195	30	3	
Anthony Parker	DB	5'9"	175	25		
J.C. Pearson	DB	5'11"	186	28	3	
Kevin Porter	DB	5'10"	214	25		
Kevin Ross	DB	5'9"	182	29	1	
Charles Washington	DB	6'1"	210	23	1	
Steve DeBerg	QB	6'2"	217	37		
Mark Vlasic	QB	6'3"	205	27		
Kimble Anders	HB	5'11"	219	24		
Bill Jones	HB	5'11"	227	24		6
Todd McNair	HB	6'1"	190	26		6
Troy Stradford	HB-WR	5'9"	194	26		
Harvey Williams	HB	6'2"	222	24		18
Barry Word	HB	6'2"	242	27		24
Christian Okoye	FB	6'1"	260	30		54
James Saxon	FB-HB	5'11"	234	25		
Tim Barnett	WR	6'1"	209	23		30
J.J. Birden	WR	5'9"	170	26		12
Willie Davis	WR	6'	170	23		
Emile Harry	WR	5'11"	186	28		18
Fred Jones	WR	5'9"	182	24		
Stephone Paige	WR	6'2"	188	29		
Robb Thomas	WR	5'11"	175	25		6
Jonathan Hayes	TE	6'5"	248	29		12
Pete Holohan	TE	6'4"	247	32		12
Troy Sadowski	TE	6'5"	258	25		
Bryan Barker	K	6'1"	187	27		
Nick Lowery	K	6'4"	205	35		10

Percy Snow — Ankle Injury

Stump Mitchell — Knee Injury

LOS ANGELES RAIDERS 9-7 Art Shell

Scores of Each Game		
17	Houston	47
16	DENVER	13
16	INDIANAPOLIS	0
17	Atlanta	21
12	SAN FRANCISCO	6
13	SAN DIEGO	21
23	Seattle	* 20
20	L.A. RAMS	17
21	Kansas City	24
17	Denver	16
31	SEATTLE	7
38	Cincinnati	14
9	San Diego	7
27	BUFFALO	* 30
0	New Orleans	27
21	KANSAS CITY	27

UseName	Pos.	Hgt.	Wgt.	Age	Int	Pts
James FitzPatrick	OT-OG	6'8"	320	27		
Rory Graves	OT	6'6"	295	28		
Joel Patten	OT	6'7"	290	33		
Bruce Wilkerson	OT	6'5"	295	27		
Steve Wright	OT-TE	6'6"	280	32		
Reggie McElroy	OG-OT	6'6"	295	31		
Max Montoya	OG	6'5"	295	35		
Steve Wisniewski	OG	6'4"	285	24		
Don Mosebar	C	6'6"	285	29		
Dan Turk	C	6'4"	270	29		
Nolan Harrison	DE-DT	6'5"	290	22		
A.J. Jimerson	DE-LB	6'3"	235	23		
Howie Long	DE	6'5"	270	31		
Anthony Smith	DE	6'3"	265	24		
Greg Townsend	DE	6'3"	265	29	1	
Scott Davis	DT-DE	6'7"	275	26		
Bob Golic	DT	6'2"	275	33		
Roy Hart	DT	6'	285	26		
Thomas Benson	LB	6'2"	240	29	1	
Riki Ellison	LB	6'2"	225	31		
Mike Jones	LB	6'1"	225	22		
Winston Moss	LB	6'3"	240	25		
Jerry Robinson	LB	6'2"	230	34		
Aaron Wallace	LB	6'3"	235	24		
Eddie Anderson	DB	6'1"	210	28	2	
Derrick Crudup	DB	6'2"	220	26		
Torin Dorn	DB	6'	190	23		2
Dan Land	DB	6'	196	26	1	
Garry Lewis	DB	5'11"	180	24		
Ronnie Lott	DB	6'	205	32	8	
Terry McDaniel	DB	5'10"	180	26		
Elvis Patterson	DB	5'11"	195	30		6
Lionel Washington	DB	6'	185	30	5	
Vince Evans	QB	6'2"	210	36		
Todd Marinovich	QB	6'4"	215	22		
Jay Schroeder	QB	6'4"	210	30		
Marcus Allen	HB	6'2'	210	31		12
Nick Bell	HB	6'2"	255	23		18
Roger Craig	HB	6'	215	31		6
Napoleon McCallum	HB	6'2"	225	27		6
Marcus Wilson	HB	6'1"	200	23		
Doug Lloyd	FB	6'1"	220	26		
Steve Smith	FB	6'1"	240	27		12
Tim Brown	WR	6'	190	25		36
Mervyn Fernandez	WR	6'3"	200	31		6
Willie Gault	WR	6'	175	30		24
Sam Graddy	WR	5'10"	180	27		6
Jamie Holland	WR	6'2"	195	27		
Andrew Glover	TE	6'6"	245	24		18
Ethan Horton	TE	6'4"	240	28		30
Jeff Gossett	K	6'2"	195	34		
Jeff Jaeger	K	5'11"	195	26		116

Vance Mueller — Knee Injury
Mike Dyal — Hamstring Injury

SEATTLE SEAHAWKS 7-9 Chuck Knox

Scores of Each Game		
24	New Orleans	27
20	N.Y. JETS	13
10	Denver	16
13	Kansas City	20
31	INDIANAPOLIS	3
13	Cincinnati	7
20	L.A. RAIDERS	* 23
27	Pittsburgh	7
20	SAN DIEGO	9
14	San Diego	17
7	L.A. Raiders	31
13	DENVER	10
6	KANSAS CITY	19
22	SAN FRANCISCO	24
13	Atlanta	26
23	L.A. RAMS	9

UseName	Pos.	Hgt.	Wgt.	Age	Int	Pts
Andy Heck	OT	6'6"	289	24		
Bill Hitchcock	OT	6'6"	291	24		
Ronnie Lee	OT	6'3"	296	34		
Edwin Bailey	OG	6'4"	284	32		
Darrick Brilz	OG	6'3"	287	27		
Bryan Millard	OG	6'5"	277	30		
Curt Singer	OG	6'5"	281	29		
Warren Wheat	OG	6'6"	286	24		
Grant Feasel	C	6'7"	283	31		
Jeff Bryant	DT-DE	6'5"	281	31		
Jacob Green	DE	6'3"	263	34	1	
Jim Skow	DE	6'3"	250	28		
Tony Woods	DE	6'4"	269	25		
Eric Hayes	DT	6'3"	288	23		
Cortez Kennedy	DT	6'3"	293	23		
Joe Nash	DT	6'2"	278	30		
Joe Cain	LB	6'1"	233	26	1	
Darren Comeaux	LB	6'1"	239	31		
Marcus Cotton	LB	6'3"	233	25		
Richard Newbill	LB	6'1"	240	23		
Rufus Porter	LB	6'1"	227	26	1	
Rod Stephens	LB	6'1"	237	25		
Terry Wooden	LB	6'3"	236	24		
David Wyman	LB	6'2"	248	27		
Robert Blackmon	DB	6'	197	24	3	
Brian Davis	DB	6'2"	187	28	1	6
Dedrick Dodge	DB	6'2"	184	24		
Nesby Glasgow	DB	5'10"	187	34	1	
Dwayne Harper	DB	5'11"	174	25	4	
Patrick Hunter	DB	5'11"	186	26	1	6
James Jefferson	DB	6'1"	199	27		
Eugene Robinson	DB	6'	191	28	5	
Jeff Kemp (to PHIL)	QB	6'	198	32		
Dave Krieg	QB	6'1"	192	32		
Dan McGwire	QB	6'8"	243	23		
Kelly Stouffer	QB	6'3"	214	27		
Derrick Fenner	HB	6'3"	228	24		24
Derek Loville	HB	5'9"	198	23		
Chris Warren	HB	6'2"	225	24		6
James Jones	FB	6'2"	232	30		18
John L. Williams	FB	5'11"	231	26		30
Brian Blades	WR	5'11	189	26		12
Jeff Chadwick	WR	6'3"	189	30		18
Louis Clark	WR	6'1"	198	27		12
David Daniels	WR	6'1"	190	21		
Tommy Kane	WR	5'11"	181	27		12
Paul Skansi	WR	5'11"	184	30		
Doug Thomas	WR	5'10"	178	21		
Trey Junkin	TE	6'2"	237	30		
Travis McNeal	TE	6'3"	244	24		6
Mike Tice	TE	6'7"	249	32		24
Rick Donnelly	K	6'	209	29		
John Kasay	K	5'10"	189	21		102
Rick Tuten	K	6'2"	218	26		
Alex Waits	K	6'2"	208	23		

Joe Tofflemire — Back Injury

Vann McElroy — Ankle Injury

SAN DIEGO CHARGERS 4-12 Dan Henning

Scores of Each Game		
20	Pittsburgh	26
14	San Francisco	34
10	ATLANTA	13
19	Denver	27
13	KANSAS CITY	14
21	L.A. Raiders	13
24	L.A. Rams	30
24	CLEVELAND	* 30
9	Seattle	20
17	SEATTLE	14
24	NEW ORLEANS	21
3	N.Y. Jets	24
7	L.A. RAIDERS	9
17	Kansas City	* 20
38	MIAMI	30
14	DENVER	17

UseName	Pos.	Hgt.	Wgt.	Age	Int	Pts
Leo Goeas	OT-OG	6'4"	292	25		
Harry Swayne	OT	6'5"	290	26		
Broderick Thompson	OT	6'5"	295	31		
Eric Floyd	OG-OT	6'5"	310	25		
Mark May	OG-OT	6'6"	296	31		
Eric Moten	OG	6'2"	306	23		
David Richards	OG	6'5"	310	25		
Mike Zandofsky	OG	6'2"	305	25		
Frank Cornish	C-OG	6'4"	289	23		
Courtney Hall	C	6'2"	281	23		
Mark Rodenhauser	C	6'5"	283	30		
Burt Grossman	DE	6'6"	255	24		
George Hinkle	DE	6'5"	269	26		
Mitchell Benson	NT-DT	6'4"	300	24		
Joe Phillips	NT	6'5"	315	28		
George Thornton	NT-DT	6'3"	300	23		
Greg Clark (from GB)	LB	6'	226	26		
David Grayson	LB	6'3"	233	27		
Randy Kirk	LB	6'2"	230	26		
Leslie O'Neal	LB	6'4"	259	27		
Gary Plummer	LB	6'2"	244	31		
Henry Rolling	LB	6'2"	225	25	2	
Junior Seau	LB	6'3"	250	22		
Billy Ray Smith	LB	6'3"	236	30	2	
Galand Thaxton	LB	6'1"	240	26		
Mike Wilcher	LB	6'3"	245	31		
Martin Bayless	DB	6'2"	212	28	1	
Gill Byrd	DB	5'11"	198	30	6	
Darren Carrington	DB	6'2"	200	24	3	
Donnie Elder	DB	5'9"	178	27	1	
Floyd Fields	DB	6'	208	22		
Donald Frank	DB	6'	192	25	1	6
Cedric Mack	DB	5'11"	190	30		
Stanley Richard	DB	6'2"	197	23	2	
Sam Seale	DB	5'9"	185	28		
Anthony Shelton	DB	6'1"	195	23	1	
John Friesz	QB	6'4"	218	24		
Bob Gagliano	QB	6'3"	205	32		
Rod Bernstine	HB-FB	6'3"	238	26		48
Eric Bieniemy	HB	5'7"	210	22		
Ronnie Harmon	HB	5'11"	207	27		12
Chris Samuels	HB-FB	5'10"	202	22		
Marion Butts	FB-HB	6'1"	248	25		42
Shawn Jefferson	WR	5'11"	172	22		6
Nate Lewis	WR	5'11"	198	24		24
Anthony Miller	WR	5'11"	189	26		18
Kitrick Taylor	WR	5'10"	191	27		
Yancey Thigpen	WR	6'1"	208	22		
Steve Hendrickson	TE-FB	6'	258	25		12
Derrick Walker	TE	6'1"	250	24		
Arthur Cox (to MIA, CLE)	TE	6'2"	277	30		
Craig McEwen	TE	6'1"	226	25		18
Mark Walczak	TE	6'6"	246	29		
Duane Young	TE	6'1"	276	23		
John Carney	K	5'11"	170	27		88
John Kidd	K	6'3"	208	30		

DENVER BRONCOS

RUSHING

Last Name	No.	Yds	Avg	TD
Green	261	1037	4.0	4
Lewis	99	376	3.8	4
Elway	54	258	4.8	6
Sewell	50	211	4.2	2
Perryman	21	45	2.1	0
Humphrey	11	33	3.0	0
Jackson	2	18	9.0	0
Sharpe	1	15	15.0	0
Kubiak	3	11	3.7	0
Horan	2	9	4.5	0
Rivers	2	5	2.5	0

RECEIVING

Last Name	No.	Yds	Avg	TD
Young	44	629	14.3	2
Sewell	38	436	11.5	2
Jackson	33	603	18.3	1
Sharpe	22	322	14.6	1
Russell	21	317	15.1	1
V. Johnson	21	208	9.9	3
Perryman	17	171	10.1	0
Nattiel	16	288	18.0	2
Green	13	78	6.0	0
Kay	11	139	12.6	0
R. Johnson	6	73	12.2	1
Lewis	2	9	4.5	0
Elway	1	24	24.0	0
B. Johnson	1	13	13.0	0

PUNT RETURNS

Last Name	No.	Yds	Avg	TD
V. Johnson	24	174	7.3	0
Nattiel	10	43	4.3	0
Clark	7	67	9.6	0

KICKOFF RETURNS

Last Name	No.	Yds	Avg	TD
Montgomery	26	488	18.8	0
Russell	7	120	17.1	0
Clark	2	45	22.5	0
Lewis	1	20	20.0	0
Sewell	1	14	14.0	0

PASSING — PUNTING — KICKING

PASSING	Att	Cmp	%	Yds	Yd/Att	TD	Int— %	RK
Elway	451	242	53.7	3253	7.21	13	12—2.7	9
Kubiak	5	3	60.0	33	6.60	0	0—0.0	
Sewell	3	1	33.0	24	8.00	0	0—0.0	

PUNTING	No.	Avg.
Horan	72	41.3
Elway	1	34.0

KICKING	XP	ATT	%	FG	ATT	%
Treadwell	31	32	97	27	36	75

KANSAS CITY CHIEFS

RUSHING

Last Name	No.	Yds	Avg	TD
Okoye	225	1031	4.6	9
Word	160	684	4.3	4
Williams	97	447	4.6	1
McNair	10	51	5.1	0
Saxon	6	13	2.2	0
Stradford	1	7	7.0	0
Vlasic	1	-1	-1.0	0
DeBerg	21	-15	-0.7	0

RECEIVING

Last Name	No.	Yds	Avg	TD
R. Thomas	43	495	11.5	1
Barnett	41	564	13.8	5
McNair	37	342	36	1
Harry	35	431	12.3	3
Birden	27	465	17.2	2
Hayes	19	208	10.9	2
Williams	16	147	9.2	2
B. Jones	14	97	6.9	1
Holohan	13	113	8.7	2
Saxon	6	55	9.2	0
Paige	9	111	12.3	0
Okoye	3	34	11.3	0
Stradford	9	91	10.1	0
Anders	2	30	15.0	0
F. Jones	8	85	10.6	0
Word	2	13	6.5	0

PUNT RETURNS

Last Name	No.	Yds	Avg	TD
Stradford	22	150	6.8	0
F. Jones	12	108	9.0	0

KICKOFF RETURNS

Last Name	No.	Yds	Avg	TD
Williams	24	524	21.8	0
Stradford	14	292	20.9	0
McNair	4	66	16.5	0
Saxon	4	56	14.0	0
F. Jones	2	40	20.0	0

PASSING — PUNTING — KICKING

PASSING	Att	Cmp	%	Yds	Yd/Att	TD	Int— %	RK
DeBerg	434	256	59.0	2965	6.83	17	14—3.2	6
Vlasic	44	28	63.6	316	7.18	2	0—0.0	
Williams	1	0	0.0	0	0.00	0	0—0.0	

PUNTING	No.	Avg.
Barker	57	40.4

KICKING	XP	Att.	%	FG	Att	%
Lowery	35	35	100	25	30	83

LOS ANGELES RAIDERS

RUSHING

Last Name	No.	Yds	Avg	TD
Craig	162	590	3.5	1
Bell	78	307	3.9	3
Allen	63	287	4.6	2
S. Smith	62	265	4.3	1
McCallum	31	110	3.5	1
Schroeder	28	76	2.7	0
Wilson	6	21	3.5	0
Evans	8	20	2.5	0
Brown	5	16	3.2	0
Marinovich	3	14	4.7	0

RECEIVING

Last Name	No.	Yds	Avg	TD
Horton	53	650	12.3	5
Fernandez	46	694	15.1	1
Brown	36	554	15.4	5
Gault	20	346	17.3	4
Craig	17	136	8.0	0
Allen	15	131	8.7	0
S. Smith	15	130	8.7	1
Graddy	6	195	32.5	1
Bell	6	62	10.3	0
Glover	5	45	9.0	5
Patterson	1	34	34.0	0

PUNT RETURNS

Last Name	No.	Yds	Avg	TD
T. Brown	29	330	11.4	1

KICKOFF RETURNS

Last Name	No.	Yds	Avg	TD
Holland	22	421	19.1	0
Graddy	22	373	17.0	0
McCallum	5	105	21.0	0
Brown	1	29	29.0	0
S. Smith	1	0	0.0	0
Turk	1	0	0.0	0

PASSING — PUNTING — KICKING

PASSING	Att	Cmp	%	Yds	Yd/Att	TD	Int— %	RK
Schroeder	356	189	53.1	2562	7.20	15	16—4.2	13
Marinovich	40	23	57.5	243	6.08	3	0—0.0	
Evans	14	6	42.9	127	7.07	1	2—14.3	
Allen	2	1	50.0	11	5.50	1	0—0.0	
Gossett	1	1	100.0	34	34.00	0	0—0.0	

PUNTING	No.	Avg.
Gossett	67	44.2

KICKING	XP	ATT	%	FG	ATT	%
Jaeger	29	30	97	29	34	85

SEATTLE SEAHAWKS

RUSHING

Last Name	No.	Yds	Avg	TD
Williams	188	741	3.9	4
Fenner	91	267	2.9	4
Jones	45	154	3.4	3
Kemp	38	179	4.7	0
Loville	22	69	3.1	0
Krieg	13	59	4.5	0
Blades	2	17	8.5	0
Warren	11	13	1.2	0

RECEIVING

Last Name	No.	Yds	Avg	TD
Blades	70	1003	14.3	2
Williams	61	499	8.2	1
Kane	50	763	15.3	2
Chadwick	22	255	11.6	3
L. Clark	21	228	10.9	2
McNeal	17	208	12.2	1
Fenner	11	72	6.5	0
Jones	10	103	10.3	0
Tice	10	70	7.0	4
Skansi	9	96	10.7	0
Daniels	4	38	9.5	0
Thomas	3	27	9.0	0
Warren	2	9	4.5	0

PUNT RETURNS

Last Name	No.	Yds	Avg	TD
Warren	32	298	9.3	1
Loville	3	16	5.3	0
Harper	1	5	5.0	0
Skansi	1	5	5.0	0
B. Davis	1	1	1.0	0

KICKOFF RETURNS

Last Name	No.	Yds	Avg	TD
Warren	35	792	22.6	0
Loville	18	412	22.9	0
McNeal	4	30	7.5	0
Tice	3	46	15.3	0

PASSING — PUNTING — KICKING

PASSING	Att	Cmp	%	Yds	Yd/Att	TD	Int— %	RK
Krieg	285	187	65.6	2080	7.30	11	12—4.2	4
Kemp	295	151	51.2	1753	5.94	9	17—5.8	18
Stouffer	15	6	40.0	57	3.80	0	1—6.7	
McGwire	7	3	42.9	27	3.86	0	1—14.3	

PUNTING	No.	Avg.
Donnelley	13	38.8
Tuten	49	43.0
Waits	14	33.9

KICKING	XP	ATT	%	FG	ATT	%
Kasay	27	28	96	25	31	81

SAN DIEGO CHARGERS

RUSHING

Last Name	No.	Yds	Avg	TD
Butts	193	834	4.3	6
Bernstine	159	766	4.8	8
Harmon	89	544	6.1	1
Jefferson	1	27	27.0	0
Gagliano	3	19	6.3	0
Friesz	10	18	1.8	0
Bieniemy	3	17	5.7	0
Lewis	3	10	3.3	0
Samuels	2	10	5.0	0
Hendrickson	1	3	3.0	0

RECEIVING

Last Name	No.	Yds	Avg	TD
Harmon	59	555	9.4	1
Miller	44	649	14.8	3
Lewis	42	554	13.2	3
McEwen	37	399	10.8	3
Taylor	24	218	9.1	0
Walker	20	134	6.7	0
Jefferson	12	125	10.4	1
Bernstine	11	124	11.3	0
Butts	10	91	9.1	1
Cox	5	53	10.6	0
Hendrickson	4	36	9.0	1
Samuels	2	33	16.5	0
Young	2	12	6.0	0

PUNT RETURNS

Last Name	No.	Yds	Avg	TD
Taylor	28	269	9.6	0
Lewis	5	59	11.8	0

KICKOFF RETURNS

Last Name	No.	Yds	Avg	TD
Lewis	23	578	25.1	1
Elder	27	535	19.8	0
Harmon	2	25	12.5	0
Bernstine	1	7	7.0	0
Benson	1	2	2.0	0
Butts	1	0	0.0	0
Carrington	0	24	—	0

PASSING — PUNTING — KICKING

PASSING	Att	Cmp	%	Yds	Yd/Att	TD	Int— %	RK
Friesz	487	262	53.8	2896	5.95	12	15—3.1	14
Gagliano	23	9	39.1	76	3.30	0	1—4.3	
Bernstine	1	1	100.0	11	11.00	1	0—0.0	

PUNTING	No.	Avg.
Kidd	77	39.8

KICKING	XP	Att	%	FG	Att	%
Carney	31	31	100	19	29	66

1991 A.F.C. PLAYOFFS — FIRST ROUND

December 28, 1991 at Kansas City (Attendance 75,827)

SCORING

L.A. RAIDERS	0	3	3	0	- 6
KANSAS CITY	0	7	0	3	- 10

Second Quarter
K.C. — Jones, 11 yard pass from DeBerg
PAT — Lowery (kick)
L.A.Rd. — Jaeger, 32 yard field goal

Third Quarter
L.A.Rd. — Jaeger, 26 yard field goal

Fourth Quarter
K.C. — Lowery, 18 yard field goal

TEAM STATISTICS

L.A.Rd.		K.C.
16	First Downs- Total	16
7	First Downs- Rushing	10
7	First Downs- Passing	5
2	First Downs- Penalty	1
2	Fumbles- Number	2
2	Fumbles- Lost Ball	1
9	Penalties- Number	3
75	Yards Penalized	20
0	Missed Field Goals	2
55	Offensive Plays	55
276	Net Yards	204
5.0	Average Gain	3.7
6	Giveaways	2
2	Takeaways	6
- 4	Difference	+ 4

INDIVIDUAL STATISTICS

L.A. RAIDERS / **KANSAS CITY**

RUSHING

L.A. RAIDERS	No.	Yds.	Avg.	KANSAS CITY	No.	Yds.	Avg.
Bell	20	107	5.4	Word	33	130	3.9
Allen	7	39	5.6	H. Williams	2	4	2.0
S. Smith	3	6	2.0	Okoye	1	2	2.0
	30	152	5.1	DeBerg	3	-5	-1.7
					39	131	3.4

RECEIVING

L.A. RAIDERS	No.	Yds.	Avg.	KANSAS CITY	No.	Yds.	Avg.
T. Brown	4	45	11.3	R. Thomas	3	18	6.0
Horton	3	59	19.7	B. Jones	2	25	12.5
Fernandez	2	12	6.0	F. Jones	2	20	10.0
Gault	1	11	11.0	Birden	1	18	18.0
S. Smith	1	9	9.0	Word	1	8	8.0
Allen	1	4	4.0		9	89	9.9
	12	140	11.7				

PUNTING

BGossett	1		20.0	Barker	2		46.0

PUNT RETURNS

T. Brown	2	23	11.5	

KICKOFF RETURNS

Holland	3	46	15.3	Stradford	2	33	16.5

INTERCEPTION RETURNS

Lott	1	35	35.0	Cherry	2	46	23.0
				Everett	1	23	23.0
				Marts	1	7	7.0
					4	76	19.0

PASSING

	Att.	Comp.	Comp. Pct.	Yds.	Int.	Yds./ Att.	Yds./ Comp.
L.A. RAIDERS							
Marinovich	23	12	52.2	140	4	6.1	11.7
KANSAS CITY							
DeBerg	14	9	64.3	89	1	6.4	9.9

December 29, 1991 at Houston (Attendance 61,485)

SCORING

N.Y. JETS	0	10	0	0	- 10
HOUSTON	7	7	0	3	- 17

First Quarter
Hou. — Givins, 5 yard pass from Moon
PAT — Del Greco (kick)

Second Quarter
NYJ — Toon, 10 yard pass from O'Brien
PAT — Allegre (kick)
Hou. — Givins, 20 yard pass from Moon
PAT — Del Greco (kick)
NYJ — Allegre, 33 yard field goal

Fourth Quarter
Hou. — Del Greco, 53 yard field goal

TEAM STATISTICS

NYJ		HOU.
18	First Downs- Total	21
1	First Downs- Rushing	5
4	First Downs- Passing	15
3	First Downs- Penalty	1
0	Fumbles- Number	3
0	Fumbles- Lost Ball	1
5	Penalties- Number	8
45	Yards Penalized	55
0	Missed Field Goals	1
55	Offensive Plays	64
285	Net Yards	303
5.2	Average Gain	4.7
3	Giveaways	2
2	Takeaways	3
- 1	Difference	+ 1

INDIVIDUAL STATISTICS

N.Y. JETS / **HOUSTON**

RUSHING

N.Y. JETS	No.	Yds.	Avg.	HOUSTON	No.	Yds.	Avg.
Hector	12	46	3.8	White	17	65	3.8
Baxter	5	14	2.8	Moon	3	6	2.0
O'Brien	2	10	5.0		20	71	3.6
McNeil	4	1	0.3				
	23	71	3.1				

RECEIVING

N.Y. JETS	No.	Yds.	Avg.	HOUSTON	No.	Yds.	Avg.
Toon	8	96	12.0	Hill	9	77	8.6
R. Moore	4	70	17.5	Givins	6	83	13.8
McNeil	4	23	5.8	Jeffires	4	49	12.8
Boyer	3	20	6.7	White	4	31	7.8
Mathis	2	12	6.0	Duncan	4	24	6.0
	21	221	10.5	Harris	1	7	7.0
					28	271	9.7

PUNTING

Aguiar	2		36.0	Montgomery	2	4	4.5

PUNT RETURNS

Coleman 2FC

KICKOFF RETURNS

Brown	2	44	22.0	Montgomery	1	0	0.0
Mathis	1	10	10.0				
	3	54	18.0				

INTERCEPTION RETURNS

McMillan	1	0	0.0	McDowell	2	32	16.0
				Orlando	1	0	1.0
					3	32	10.7

PASSING

	Att.	Comp.	Comp. Pct.	Yds.	Int.	Yds./ Att.	Yds./ Comp.
N.Y. JETS							
O'Brien	31	21	67.7	221	3	7.1	10.5
HOUSTON							
Moon	40	28	70.0	271	1	6.8	9.7

December 28, 1991 at New Orleans (Attendance 68,794)

SCORING

ATLANTA	0	10	7	10	- 27
NEW ORLEANS	7	6	0	7	- 20

First Quarter
- N.O. — Turner, 26 yard pass from Hebert; PAT — Andersen (kick)

Second Quarter
- N.O. — Andersen, 45 yard field goal
- Atl. — Rison, 24 yard pass from Miller; PAT — Johnson (kick)
- Atl. — Johnson, 44 yard field goal
- N.O. — Andersen, 35 yard field goal

Third Quarter
- Atl. — Haynes, 20 yard pass from Miller; PAT — Johnson (kick)

Fourth Quarter
- N.O. — Hilliard, 1 yard run; PAT — Andersen (kick)
- Atl. — Johnson, 36 yard field goal
- Atl. — Haynes, 61 yard pass from Miller; PAT — Johnson (kick)

TEAM STATISTICS

ATL.		N.O.
20	First Downs- Total	23
6	First Downs- Rushing	3
13	First Downs- Passing	16
1	First Downs- Penalty	4
3	Fumbles- Number	2
1	Fumbles- Lost Ball	1
6	Penalties- Number	5
48	Yards Penalized	49
1	Missed Field Goals	0
57	Offensive Plays	67
334	Net Yards	330
5.9	Average Gain	4.9
2	Giveaways	3
3	Takeaways	2
+ 1	Difference	- 1

INDIVIDUAL STATISTICS

RUSHING

ATLANTA	No.	Yds.	Avg.	NEW ORLEANS	No.	Yds.	Avg.
Rozier	7	35	5.0	McAfee	14	49	3.5
Pegram	11	26	2.4	Hebert	1	9	9.0
Miller	4	18	4.5	Hilliard	4	5	1.3
	22	79	3.6	Jordan	3	2	0.7
					22	65	3.0

RECEIVING

ATLANTA	No.	Yds.	Avg.	NEW ORLEANS	No.	Yds.	Avg.
Haynes	6	144	24.0	Martin	7	83	11.9
Pritchard	5	63	12.6	Turner	5	75	15.0
Rison	4	56	14.0	Early	5	41	8.2
Thomas	1	19	19.0	Hilliard	5	33	6.7
Pegram	1	5	5.0	Carroll	2	23	11.5
Dixon	1	4	4.0	Tice	1	13	13.0
	18	291	16.2	Jordan	1	5	5.0
					26	273	10.5

PUNTING

ATLANTA	No.	Yds.	Avg.	NEW ORLEANS	No.	Yds.	Avg.
Fulhage	1		42.0	Barnhardt	3		54.0

PUNT RETURNS

ATLANTA	No.	Yds.	Avg.	NEW ORLEANS	No.	Yds.	Avg.
Sanders	1	22	22.0	Fenerty	1FC		

KICKOFF RETURNS

ATLANTA	No.	Yds.	Avg.	NEW ORLEANS	No.	Yds.	Avg.
Sanders	2	32	16.0	McAfee	4	98	24.5
Fishback	1	0	0.0				
	3	32	10.7				

INTERCEPTION RETURNS

ATLANTA	No.	Yds.	Avg.	NEW ORLEANS	No.	Yds.	Avg.
Sanders	1	31	31.0	Glenn	1	0	0.0
McKyer	1	0	0.0				
	2	31	15.5				

PASSING

	Att.	Comp.	Comp. Pct.	Yds.	Int.	Yds./ Att.	Yds./ Comp.
ATLANTA							
Miller	30	18	60.0	291	1	9.7	16.2
NEW ORLEANS							
Hebert	44	26	59.1	273	2	6.2	10.5

December 29, 1991 at Chicago (Attendance 62,594)

SCORING

DALLAS	10	0	7	0	- 17
CHICAGO	0	3	3	7	- 13

First Quarter
- Dal. — Willis, 27 yard field goal
- Dall. — E. Smith, 1 yard run; PAT — Willis (kick)

Second Quarter
- Chi. — Butler, 19 yard field goal

Third Quarter
- Chi. — Butler, 43 yard field goal
- Dal. — Novacek, 3 yard pass from Beuerlein; PAT — Willis (kick)

Fourth Quarter
- Chi. — Waddle, 6 yard pass from Harbaugh; PAT — Butler (kick)

TEAM STATISTICS

DAL.		CHI.
15	First Downs- Total	26
6	First Downs- Rushing	12
7	First Downs- Passing	14
2	First Downs- Penalty	0
2	Fumbles- Number	1
0	Fumbles- Lost Ball	1
2	Penalties- Number	4
16	Yards Penalized	16
2	Missed Field Goals	0
48	Offensive Plays	82
288	Net Yards	372
6.0	Average Gain	4.5
0	Giveaways	3
3	Takeaways	0
+ 3	Difference	- 3

INDIVIDUAL STATISTICS

RUSHING

DALLAS	No.	Yds.	Avg.	CHICAGO	No.	Yds.	Avg.
Smith	26	105	4.0	Lewis	9	65	7.2
Beuerlein	4	3	0.8	Anderson	13	34	2.6
	30	108	3.6	Harbaugh	7	26	3.7
				Muster	5	25	5.0
					34	150	4.4

RECEIVING

DALLAS	No.	Yds.	Avg.	CHICAGO	No.	Yds.	Avg.
Irvin	4	83	20.8	Waddle	9	104	11.6
Harper	3	88	29.3	Davis	7	79	11.3
Johnston	1	6	6.0	Anderson	3	5	1.7
Novacek	1	3	3.0	Lewis	2	18	9.0
	9	180	20.0	Rivera	1	15	15.0
				Thornton	1	12	12.0
					23	233	10.1

PUNTING

DALLAS	No.	Yds.	Avg.	CHICAGO	No.	Yds.	Avg.
Saxon	3		44.7	Buford	1		0.0

PUNT RETURNS

DALLAS	No.	Yds.	Avg.	CHICAGO	No.	Yds.	Avg.
				Woolford	2	5	2.5

KICKOFF RETURNS

DALLAS	No.	Yds.	Avg.	CHICAGO	No.	Yds.	Avg.
Wright	1	18	18.0	Lewis	3	44	13.3
Gant	1	16	16.0	Green	1	15	15.0
	2	34	12.0		4	59	14.8

INTERCEPTIONS

DALLAS	No.	Yds.	Avg.
Bates	1	7	7.0
Brown	1	0	0.0
	2	7	3.5

PASSING

	Att.	Comp.	Comp. Pct.	Yds.	Int.	Yds./ Att.	Yds./ Comp.
DALLAS							
Beuerlein	18	9	50.0	180	0	10.0	20.0
CHICAGO							
Harbaugh	44	22	50.0	218	2	4.9	9.9
Buford	1	1	100.0	15	0	15.0	15.0
	45	23	51.1	233	2	5.2	10.1

1991 A.F.C. PLAYOFFS — SECOND ROUND

January 4, 1992 at Denver (Attendance 75,301)

SCORING

HOUSTON	14	7	0	3	- 24
DENVER	6	7	3	10	- 26

First Quarter
- Hou. Jeffires, 15 yard pass from Moon
  PAT — Del Greco (kick)
- Hou. Hill, 9 yard pass from Moon
  PAT — Del Greco (kick)
- Den. V. Johnson, 10 yard pass from Elway
  PAT — Treadwell kick failed

Second Quarter
- Hou. Duncan, 6 yard pass from Moon
  PAT — Del Greco (kick)
- Den. Lewis, 1 yard run
  PAT — Treadwell (kick)

Third Quarter
- Den. Treadwell, 49 yard field goal

Fourth Quarter
- Hou. Del Greco, 25 yard field goal
- Den. Lewis, 1 yard run
  PAT — Treadwell (kick)
- Den. Treadwell, 28 yard field goal

TEAMSTATISTICS

HOU.		DEN.
23	First Downs- Total	26
7	First Downs- Rushing	13
14	First Downs- Passing	12
2	First Downs- Penalty	1
0	Fumbles- Number	3
0	Fumbles- Lost Ball	0
13	Penalties- Number	6
85	Yards Penalized	70
1	Missed Field Goals	0
55	Offensive Plays	65
422	Net Yards	418
7.7	Average Gain	6.4
1	Giveaways	1
1	Takeaways	1
0	Difference	0

INDIVIDUALSTATISTICS

HOUSTON	No.	Yds.	Avg.	DENVER	No.	Yds.	Avg.
RUSHING							
L. White	17	79	4.6	Green	17	59	3.5
Moon	2	18	9.0	Sewell	4	48	12.0
	19	97	5.1	Elway	6	39	6.5
				Rivers	1	3	3.0
				Lewis	3	2	0.7
					31	151	4.9
RECEIVING							
Jeffires	7	99	14.1	V. Johnson	5	78	15.6
Givins	6	111	18.5	Young	4	85	21.3
Duncan	6	40	6.7	Sewell	3	28	9.3
L. White	5	35	7.0	Sharpe	3	20	6.7
Hill	2	21	10.5	Nattiel	2	27	13.5
T. Jones	1	19	19.0	Russell	1	20	20.0
	27	325	12.0	Kay	1	8	8.0
				Green	1	1	1.0
					20	267	13.4
PUNTING							
Montgomery	1		44.0	Horan	2		40.5
PUNT RETURNS							
Coleman	1FC						
KICKOFF RETURNS							
Pinkett	3	46	15.3	Montgomery	4	88	22.0
Coleman	3	36	12.0				
	6	82	13.7				
INTERCEPTION RETURNS							
R. Johnson	1	25	25.0	Atwater	1	0	0.0

PASSING

HOUSTON	Att.	Comp.	Comp. Pct.	Yds.	Int.	Yds./ Att.	Yds./ Comp.
Moon	36	27	75.0	325	1	9.0	12.0
DENVER							
Elway	33	19	57.6	257	1	77.9	13.5
Sewell	1	1	100.0	10	0	10.0	10.0
	34	20	58.8	267	1	7.8	13.4

January 6, 1992 at Buffalo (Attendance 80,182)

SCORING

KANSAS CITY	0	0	7	7	- 14
BUFFALO	7	10	7	13	- 37

First Quarter
- Buff. Reed, 25 yard pass from Kelly
  PAT — Norwood (kick)

Second Quarter
- Buff. Reed, 53 yard pass from Kelly
  PAT — Norwood (kick)
- Buff. Norwood, 33 yard field goal

Third Quarter
- Buff. Lofton, 10 yard pass from Kelly
  PAT — Norwood (kick)
- K.C. Word, 3 yard run
  PAT — Lowery (kick)

Fourth Quarter
- Buff Norwood, 20 yard field goal
- Buff. Norwood, 47 yard field goal
- Buff. Davis, 5 yard run
  PAT — Norwood (kick)
- K.C. F. Jones, 20 yard pass from Vlasic
  PAT — Lowery (kick)

TEAMSTATISTICS

K.C.		BUFF.
14	First Downs- Total	29
4	First Downs- Rushing	13
9	First Downs- Passing	12
1	First Downs- Penalty	4
3	Fumbles- Number	0
0	Fumbles- Lost Ball	0
10	Penalties- Number	6
59	Yards Penalized	40
0	Missed Field Goals	0
54	Offensive Plays	82
213	Net Yards	448
3.9	Average Gain	5.5
4	Giveaways	3
3	Takeaways	4
- 1	Difference	+ 1

INDIVIDUALSTATISTICS

KANSAS CITY	No.	Yds.	Avg.	BUFFALO	No.	Yds.	Avg.
RUSHING							
Word	15	50	3.3	Thomas	22	100	4.5
Williams	8	24	3.0	K. Davis	19	75	3.9
McNair	1	3	3.0	Reed	1	6	6.0
	24	77	3.2	Kelly	1	2	2.0
				Reich	3	-3	-1.0
					46	180	3.9
RECEIVING							
McNair	5	52	10.4	Beebe	6	77	12.8
F. Jones	3	31	10.3	McKeller	5	34	6.8
Birden	2	19	9.5	Reed	4	100	25.0
Hayes	1	21	21.0	Thomas	4	21	5.3
Barnett	1	20	20.0	Lofton	3	34	11.3
B. Jones	1	2	2.0	Edwards	1	7	7.0
Thomas	1	1	1.0		23	273	11.9
	14	146	10.4				
PUNTING							
Barker	7		40.3	Mohr	3		33.3
PUNT RETURNS							
Stradford	1	11	11.0	Hicks	4	43	8.0
KICKOFF RETURNS							
Williams	3	48	16.0	Edwards	1	24	24.0
Birden	1	0	0.0	Beebe	1	0	0.0
	4	48	12.0		2	24	12.0
INTERCEPTION RETURNS							
Everett	1	15	15.0	K. Jackson	2	6	3.0
Marts	1	12	12.0	L. Smith	1	0	0.0
Cherry	1	1	1.0	Hicks	1	0	0.0
	3	28	9.3		4	6	1.5

PASSING

KANSAS CITY	Att.	Comp.	Comp. Pct.	Yds.	Int.	Yds./ Att.	Yds./ Comp.
DeBerg	9	5	55.6	22	0	2.4	4.4
Vlasic	20	9	45.0	124	4	6.2	13.8
	29	14	48.3	146	4	5.0	10.4
BUFFALO							
Kelly	35	23	65.7	273	3	7.8	11.9

1991 N.F.C. PLAYOFFS — SECOND ROUND

January 4, 1992 at Washington (Attendance 55,181)

SCORING

ATLANTA	0	7	0	0	- 7
WASHINGTON	0	14	3	7	- 24

Second Quarter
- Wash. — Ervins, 17 yard run; PAT — Lohmiller (kick)
- Wash. — Riggs, 2 yard run; PAT — Lohmiller (kick)
- Atl. — T. Johnson, 1 yard run; PAT — Johnson (kick)

Third Quarter
- Wash. — Lohmiller, 24 yard field goal

Fourth Quarter
- Wash — Riggs, 1 yard run; PAT — Lohmiller (kick)

TEAMSTATISTICS

ATL.		WASH.
12	First Downs- Total	22
2	First Downs- Rushing	10
9	First Downs- Passing	11
1	First Downs- Penalty	1
3	Fumbles- Number	0
2	Fumbles- Lost Ball	0
3	Penalties- Number	4
19	Yards Penalized	23
1	Missed Field Goals	3
50	Offensive Plays	74
193	Net Yards	332
3.9	Average Gain	4.5
6	Giveaways	1
1	Takeaways	6
- 5	Difference	+ 5

INDIVIDUALSTATISTICS

ATLANTA	No.	Yds.	Avg.	WASHINGTON	No.	Yds.	Avg.
RUSHING							
T. Johnson	8	33	4.1	Ervins	23	104	4.5
Chaffey	3	8	2.7	Byner	14	57	4.1
Pegram	3	2	0.7	Riggs	4	7	1.8
	14	43	3.1	Monk	1	-2	-2.0
				Rypien	3	-4	-0.8
					45	162	3.6
RECEIVING							
Rison	7	62	8.9	Clark	6	64	10.7
Pritchard	5	56	11.2	Monk	3	45	15.0
Dixon	2	19	9.5	Ervins	3	24	8.0
Haynes	1	15	15.0	Sanders	1	26	26.0
Thomas	1	15	15.0	Byner	1	11	11.0
Phillips	1	11	11.0		14	170	12.1
	17	178	10.5				
PUNTING							
Fulhage	4		42.3	Goodburn	4		38.8
PUNT RETURNS							
Sanders	2	11	5.5	Mitchell	3	28	9.3
				Green	1FC		
KICKOFF RETURNS							
Sanders	4	92	23.0	Mitchell	2	51	25.5
INTERCEPTION RETURNS							
Jordan	1	4	4.0	Copeland	1	19	19.0
				Gouveia	1	6	6.0
				Mayhew	1	2	2.0
				Coleman	1	0	0.0
					4	27	6.8

PASSING

	Att.	Comp.	Comp. Pct.	Yds.	Int.	Yds./ Att.	Yds./ Comp.
ATLANTA							
Miller	32	17	53.1	178	4	5.6	10.5
WASHINGTON							
Rypien	29	14	48.3	170	1	5.8	12.1

January 5, 1992 at Detroit (Attendance 78,290)

SCORING

DALLAS	3	3	0	0	- 6
DETROIT	7	10	14	7	- 38

First Quarter
- Det. — Green, 31 yard pass from Kramer; PAT — Murray (kick)
- Dall. — Willis, 28 yard field goal

Second Quarter
- Det. — Jenkins, 41 yard interception return; PAT — Murray (kick)
- Dall. — Willis, 28 yard field goal
- Det. — Murray, 36 yard field goal

Third Quarter
- Det. — Green, 9 yard pass from Kramer; PAT — Murray (kick)
- Det. — Moore, 7 yard pass from Kramer; PAT — Murray (kick)

Fourth Quarter
- Det. — Sanders, 47 yard run; PAT — Murray (kick)

TEAMSTATISTICS

DAL.		DET.
16	First Downs- Total	23
4	First Downs- Rushing	3
11	First Downs- Passing	19
1	First Downs- Penalty	1
3	Fumbles- Number	0
2	Fumbles- Lost Ball	0
3	Penalties- Number	4
19	Yards Penalized	39
0	Missed Field Goals	0
54	Offensive Plays	55
276	Net Yards	421
5.1	Average Gain	7.7
3	Giveaways	0
0	Takeaways	3
- 3	Difference	+ 3

INDIVIDUALSTATISTICS

DALLAS	No.	Yds.	Avg.	DETROIT	No.	Yds.	Avg.
RUSHING							
E. Smith	15	80	5.3	Sanders	12	69	5.8
Agee	3	12	4.0	Overton	3	17	5.7
Johnston	1	3	3.0	Ware	1	-2	-2.0
Beuerlein	1	2	2.0		16	84	5.3
Aikman	2	0	0.0				
	22	97	4.4				
RECEIVING							
Irvin	5	84	16.8	Green	8	115	14.4
Harper	4	56	14.0	Moore	6	87	14.5
Novacek	4	55	13.8	Farr	5	62	12.4
Wright	1	7	7.0	Sanders	5	30	6.0
Johnston	1	3	3.0	Perriman	3	18	6.0
Awalt	1	2	2.0	Clark	2	29	14.5
E. Smith	1	2	2.0		29	341	11.8
Agee	1	-4	-4.0				
	18	205	11.4				
PUNTING							
Saxon	5		44.8	Arnold	5		46.2
PUNT RETURNS							
Martin	1	18	18.0	Gray	2	26	13.0
KICKOFF RETURNS							
Gant	2	54	27.0	Gray	2	35	17.0
Martin	2	36	18.0	Dozier	1	14	14.0
Wright	1	12	12.0		3	49	16.3
Pruitt	1	6	6.0				
	6	108	18.0				
INTERCEPTION RETURNS							
None				Jenkins	1	41	41.0
				Spielman	1	0	0.0
					2	41	20.5

PASSING

	Att.	Comp.	Comp. Pct.	Yds.	Int.	Yds./ Att.	Yds./ Comp.
DALLAS							
Beuerlein	13	7	53.8	91	1	7.0	13.0
Aikman	16	11	68.8	114	1	7.1	10.4
DETROIT							
Kramer	38	29	76.3	341	0	9.0	11.8

1991 Championship Games

A.F.C. CHAMPIONSHIP GAME

January 12, 1992 at Buffalo, N.Y.
(Attendance 80,272)

SCORING

DENVER	0	0	0	7	- 7
BUFFALO	0	0	7	3	- 10

Third Quarter
Buff. — Bailey, 11 yard interception return
PAT — Norwood (kick)

Fourth Quarter
Buff. — Norwood, 44 yard field goal
Den. — Kubiak, 3 yard run
PAT — Treadwell (kick)

TEAM STATISTICS

DEN.		BUFF.
20	First Downs- Total	12
6	First Downs- Rushing	5
13	First Downs- Passing	5
1	First Downs- Penalty	2
4	Fumbles- Number	0
1	Fumbles- Lost Ball	0
4	Penalties- Number	6
20	Yards Penalized	35
3	Missed Field Goals	0
69	Offensive Plays	61
304	Net Yards	213
4.4	Average Gain	3.5
2	Giveaways	2
2	Takeaways	2
--	Difference	--

Unheralded linebacker Carlton Bailey emerged as the hero of a defensive drama in the AFC championship game with an 11-yard interception return for a touchdown that sent the Buffalo Bills to their second straight Super Bowl with a 10-7 triumph over the Denver Broncos.

Denver held the high-powered Bills without an offensive touchdown, but the Broncos' offense was shackled by the 27th-ranked defense.

Denver's hopes began to fade when quarterback John Elway suffered a bruised right thigh and limped out of the game 2:20 into the fourth quarter with his team trailing 7-0.

Gary Kubiak, who a week earlier had announced he would retire at the end of the season, replaced Elway and was able to draw the Broncos within three points with 1:28 to play.

The Broncos then recovered an onside kick and had a chance to pull out an improbable victory, but after Kubiak hit Steve Sewell inside Buffalo territory, Sewell fumbled the ball and Buffalo's Kirby Jackson recovered to clinch the victory with 1:28 to play.

After a surprising first half in which the Broncos wasted one scoring chance after another, the game seemed likely to turn on a defensive play. And it did. With the game still scoreless in the third quarter, Elway tried to throw a screen pass down the middle of the field to Sewell. But Jeff Wright tipped the ball and it went right to Bailey, who broke an attemped tackle by Elway and ran 11 yards for the breakthrough score with 9:32 to play in the period.

The Bills went up 10-0 at 4:18 of the fourth quarter on Scott Norwood's 44-yard field goal.

Kubiak scrambled three yards for Denver's only score after driving the Broncos 85 yards.

INDIVIDUAL STATISTICS

RUSHING

DENVER	No.	Yds.	Avg.	BUFFALO	No.	Yds.	Avg.
Green	19	53	2.8	Thomas	26	72	2.8
Kubiak	3	22	7.3	Reed	1	16	16.0
Elway	4	10	2.5	Kelly	2	9	4.5
Sewell	4	3	0.8	K. Davis	6	7	1.2
SV. Johnson	2	-7	-3.5		35	104	3.0
	32	81	2.5				

RECEIVING

DENVER	No.	Yds.	Avg.	BUFFALO	No.	Yds.	Avg.
V. Johnson	8	104	13.0	McKeller	3	39	13.0
Sewell	7	78	11.1	T. Thomas	3	15	5.0
Sharpe	3	40	13.3	Reed	2	19	9.5
Young	3	25	8.3	K. Davis	2	13	6.5
Nattiel	1	10	10.0	Metzelaars	1	14	14.0
	22	257	11.7	Lofton	1	11	1..0
				Beebe	1	6	6.0
					13	117	9.0

PUNTING

DENVER	No.	Yds.	Avg.	BUFFALO	No.	Yds.	Avg.
Horan	6		43.7	Mohr		8	38.0

PUNT RETURNS

DENVER	No.	Yds.	Avg.	BUFFALO	No.	Yds.	Avg.
V. Johnson	3	36	12.0	Hicks	1FC		

KICKOFF RETURNS

DENVER	No.	Yds.	Avg.	BUFFALO	No.	Yds.	Avg.
Montgomery	2	34	17.0	Edwards	1	24	24.0
Russell	1	15	15.0				
	3	49	16.3				

INTERCEPTION RETURNS

DENVER	No.	Yds.	Avg.	BUFFALO	No.	Yds.	Avg.
Braxton	1	5	5.0	Bailey	1	11	11.0
Kragen	1	0	0.0				
	2	5	2.5				

PASSING

	Att.	Comp.	Comp. Pct.	Yds.	Int.	Yds./ Att.	Yds./ Comp.
DENVER							
Elway	21	11	52.4	121	1	5.8	11.0
Kubiak	12	11	91.7	136	0	11.3	12.4
	33	22	66.7	257	1	7.8	11.7
BUFFALO							
Kelly	25	13	52.0	117	2	4.7	9.0

N.F.C. CHAMPIONSHIP GAME

January 12, 1992 at Washington D.C.
(Attendance 55,585)

SCORING

DETROIT	0	10	0	0	- 10
WASHINGTON	10	7	10	14	- 41

First Quarter
Wash. — Riggs, 2 yard run
PAT — Lohmiller (kick)
Wash. — Lohmiller, 20 yard field goal

Second Quarter
Det. — Green, 18 yard pass from Kramer
PAT — Murray (kick)
Wash. — Riggs, 3 yard run
PAT — Lohmiller (kick)
Det. — Murray, 30 yard field goal

Third Quarter
Wash. — Lohmiller, 28 yard field goal
Wash. — Clark, 45 yard pass from Rypien
PAT — Lohmiller (kick)

Fourth Quarter
Wash. — Monk, 21 yard pass from Rypien
PAT — Lohmiller (kick)
Wash. — Green, 32 yard interception return
PAT — Lohmiller (kick)

TEAM STATISTICS

DET.		WASH.
20	First Downs- Total	17
6	First Downs- Rushing	6
12	First Downs- Passing	10
2	First Downs- Penalty	1
3	Fumbles- Number	0
1	Fumbles- Lost Ball	0
7	Penalties- Number	4
46	Yards Penalized	46
1	Missed Field Goals	1
65	Offensive Plays	52
304	Net Yards	345
4.7	Average Gain	6.6
3	Giveaways	0
0	Takeaways	3
- 2	Difference	+ 2

The Redskins turned two early turnovers into 10 points and Mark Rypien threw two long second-half touchdown passes, lifting Washington to a 41-10 rout of the Detroit Lions and into the Super Bowl for the fourth time in 10 years.

Washington jumped on two turnovers by Detroit quarterback Erik Kramer in the opening minutes as the Redskins built a seven-point halftime lead. Then Rypien threw touchdown passes of 45 yards to Gary Clark and 21 yards to Ark Monk.

The Redskins' four Super Bowl trips in the last decade have all come under the guidance of coach Joe Gibbs.

The Lions, 13-5, suffered a devastating ending to what had been a surprisingly successful season. Detroit won its last six regular-season games to capture the NFC Central title, then defeated Dallas in its first playoff game. The Lions' surge was inspired by a paralyzing injury to guard Mike Utley in a Nov. 17 game against the Los Angeles Rams.

The Redskins extended their winning streak over Detroit to 15 games and ran their record against the Lions to a perfect 16-0 in Washington. The Redskins are 11-1 in playoff games at home.

Detroit remains one of nine NFL teams never to have played in the Super Bowl.

Rypien completed 12 of 17 passes for 228 yards, completing four straight during one span in the second half for 110 yards and two touchdowns.

INDIVIDUAL STATISTICS

RUSHING

DETROIT	No.	Yds.	Avg.	WASHINGTON	No.	Yds.	Avg.
Sanders	11	44	4.0	Byner	17	62	3.6
Ware	2	25	12.5	Ervins	13	53	4.1
Kramer	4	4	1.0	Riggs	2	5	2.5
Long	1	-1	-1.0	Rypien	3	-3	-1.0
	18	72	4.0		35	117	3.3

RECEIVING

DETROIT	No.	Yds.	Avg.	WASHINGTON	No.	Yds.	Avg.
Farr	6	73	12.2	Monk	5	94	18.8
Perriman	5	43	8.6	Clark	4	77	19.3
Moore	4	69	17.3	Sanders	2	12	6.0
Green	4	54	13.5	Orr	1	45	45.0
Sanders	4	15	3.8		12	228	19.0
Overton	2	10	5.0				
	25	264	10.6				

PUNTING

DETROIT	No.	Yds.	Avg.	WASHINGTON	No.	Yds.	Avg.
Arnold	3		47.0	Goodburn	3		35.7

PUNT RETURNS

DETROIT	No.	Yds.	Avg.	WASHINGTON	No.	Yds.	Avg.
Gray	3	13	4.3	Mitchell	1	13	13.0

KICKOFF RETURNS

DETROIT	No.	Yds.	Avg.	WASHINGTON	No.	Yds.	Avg.
Gray	5	134	26.8	Ervins	3	59	19.7
Dozier	1	21	21.0				
Alexander	1	15	15.0				
	7	170	24.3				

INTERCEPTION RETURNS

DETROIT	No.	Yds.	Avg.	WASHINGTON	No.	Yds.	Avg.
None				Gouveia	1	38	38.0
				Green	1	32	32.0
					2	70	35.0

PASSING

	Att.	Comp.	Comp. Pct.	Yds.	Int.	Yds./ Att.	Yds./ Comp.
DETROIT							
Kramer	33	21	63.6	249	1	7.5	11.9
Ware	9	4	44.4	15	1	1.7	3.8
	42	25	59.5	264	2	6.3	10.6
WASHINGTON							
Rypien	17	12	70.6	228	0	13.4	19.0

SUPER BOWL XXVI

January 26, 1992 at Minneapolis, Minn.

(Attendance 63,130)

Redskins Let 'Er Rip

Super Bowl XXVI was played like most of the last 10 or so — with the NFC champions soundly thrashing the best from the AFC. The only thing different about Washington's 37-24 victory over Buffalo was the script.

In the end, the Redskins defeated the Bills with what the losers do best — a no-huddle offense. The Redskins also stole another page from the Bills' playbook, perfecting the multiple-wide receiver offense while shutting down that of Buffalo. A little-known running back from Washington outrushed the NFL's Offensive Player of the Year from Buffalo. And a sixth-round draft pick outperformed the league's top quarterback and, in turn, was named the game's Most Valuable Player.

Still, Super Bowl XXVI was just like most of its predecessors — a super blowout that was pretty much decided by halftime. It was an embarassment for the losers that left many of the 63,000 fans in attendance and another 120 million or so watching scross the country wondering why the Super Bowl is usually a super bore.

Redskins head coach Joe Gibbs, who became the third NFL coach to win three Super Bowls, didn't think so. "It was kind of a dream game for us," he said.

It was just the opposite for the Bills, who became the third team to lose consecutive Super Bowls. "I said before the game we need to go out and make history," said Buffalo defensive end Bruce Smith. "We did it the wrong damn way."

In the beginning of the game, it was Washington doing things the wrong way. Three times the Redskins had easy scoring chances and three times put no points on the scoreboard. And, while the Bills weren't in the game after halftime, there were four times that, if things had gone the other way, might have changed the outcome. The first turning point followed the first scoreless first quarter in 15 Super Bowls. Redskins quarterback, the game's Most Valuable Player, connected with Ricky Sanders on a 41-yard pass on the second play of the second period. Four plays later, Chip Lohmiller kicked the first of his three field goals, and Washington had the lead for good. Washington then scored on Earnest Byner's 10-yard reception and Gerald Riggs' one yard run — 17 points in a period of 5:45. Rypien completed 18 of 33 passes for 292 yards.

The Redskins intercepted Buffalo quarterback Jim Kelly four times and forced him to fumble once. Kelly's four interceptions tied the Super Bowl record, and his 58 pass attempts set a record. And Bills running back Thurman Thomas managed only 13 yards on 10 carries.

On the first play of the second half, Kelly was intercepted, and, on the next play, Riggs scored his second touchdown of the game. Buffalo then scored 10 points on its next two possessions on a one-yard run by Thomas and a field goal by Scott Norwood. But Washington responded with an 11-play, 79-yard drive that iced the game when Gary Clark caught a 30-yard touchdown pass from Rypien. Lohmiller kicked two more field goals for the Redskins. Finally, the Bills, down 37-10, scored two touchdowns in a stretch of 2:04 late in the fourth quarter, helped by the recovery of an onside kick.

LINEUPS

WASH.		BUFF.
	OFFENSE	
Clark	WR	Lofton
Middleton	TE	Metzelaars
Lachey	LT	Wolford
McKenzie	LG	Ritcher
Bostic	C	Hull
Schlereth	RG	Parker
Jacoby	RT	Ballard
Warren	TE	McKeller
Monk	WR	Reed
Rypien	QB	Kelly
Byner	RB	K. Davis
	DEFENSE	
Mann	LE	Seals
E. Williams	LT/NT	Wright
T. Johnson	RT/RE	B. Smith
Stokes	RE/LOLB	Bennett
Marshall	LLB/LILB	Conlan
Gouveia	MLB/RILB	Bailey
Collins	RLB/ROLB	Talley
Mayhew	LCB	K. Jackson
Green	RCB	Odomes
Copeland	SS	Drane
Edwards	FS	Kelso

SUBSTITUTES

WASHINGTON		
	OFFENSE	
Rutledge	B. Mitchell	Ervins
Riggs	Adickes	Grimm
Simmons	Brandes	Sanders
Hobbs	Jenkins	Orr
	DEFENSE	
Mays	Hoage	S. Johnson
A. Johnson	Caldwell	Coleman
B. Wilson	Geathers	Buck
	KICKERS	
Goodburn	Lohmiller	

BUFFALO		
	OFFENSE	
Reich	T. Thomas	Gardner
Frerotte	Lingner	Staysniak
Beebe	Edwards	Rolle
Tasker		
	DEFENSE	
H. Jones	Hale	Hicks
J. Williams	Bentley	Patton
Lodish	Hansen	Pike
Garner		
	KICKERS	
Daluiso	Mohr	Norwood

SCORING

WASHINGTON	0	17	14	6	- 37
BUFFALO	0	0	10	14	- 24

Second Quarter
- Wash. Lohmiller, 34 yard field goal
- Wash. Byner, 10 yard pass from Rypien
  PAT — Lohmiller (kick)
- Wash. Riggs, 1 yard run
  PAT — Lohmiller (kick)

Third Quarter
- Wash. Riggs, 2 yard run
  PAT — Lohmiller (kick)
- Buff. Norwood, 21 yard field goal
- Buff. Thomas, 1 yard run
  PAT — Norwood (kick)
- Wash. Clark, 30 yard pass from Rypien
  PAT — Lohmiller (kick)

Fourth Quarter
- Wash. Lohmiller, 25 yard field goal
- Wash. Lohmiller, 39 yard field goal
- Buff. Metzelaars, 2 yard pass from Kelly
  PAT — Norwood (kick)
- Buff. Beebe, 4 yard pass from Kelly
  PAT — Norwood (kick)

TEAM STATISTICS

WASH.		BUFF.
24	First Downs-Total	25
10	First Downs-Rushing	4
12	First Downs-Pasiing	18
2	First Downs-Penalty	3
1	Fumbles-Number	6
0	Fumbles-Lost Ball	1
5	Penaties-Number	6
82	Yards Penalized	50
0	Missed Field Goals	0
73	Offensive Plays	82
417	Net Yards	283
5.7	Average Gain	3.5
1	Giveaways	5
5	Takeaways	1
+ 4	Difference	- 4

INDIVIDUAL STATISTICS

WASHINGTON	No.	Yds.	Avg.	BUFFALO	No.	Yds.	Avg.
				RUSHING			
Ervins	13	72	5.5	K. Davis	4	17	4.3
Byner	14	49	3.5	Kelly	3	16	5.3
Riggs	5	7	1.4	Thomas	10	13	1.3
Sanders	1	1	1.0	Lofton	1	-3	-3.0
Rutledge	1	0	0.0		18	43	2.4
Rypien	6	-4	-0.7				
	40	125	3.1				
				RECEIVING			
Clark	7	114	16.3	Lofton	7	92	13.1
Monk	7	113	16.1	Reed	5	34	6.8
Byner	3	24	8.0	Beebe	4	61	15.3
Sanders	1	41	41.0	Davis	4	38	9.5
	18	292	16.2	Thomas	4	27	6.8
				McKeller	2	29	14.5
				Edwards	1	11	11.0
				Metzelaars	1	2	2.0
				Kelly	1	-8	-8.0
					29	286	9.9
				PUNTING			
Goodburn	4		37.5	Mohr	6		35.0
				PUNT RETURNS			
Mitchell	2FC			Hicks	3	9	3.0
				KICKOFF RETURNS			
Mitchell	1	16	16.0	Edwards	4	77	19.3
				INTERCEPTIONS RETURNS			
Edwards	2	56	28.0	Jackson	1	4	4.0
Gouveia	1	23	23.0				
Green	1	0	0.0				
	4	79	19.8				

PASSING

	Att.	Comp.	Comp. Pct.	Yds.	Int.	Yds./ Att.	Yds./ Comp.	Yards Lost Tackled
WASHINGTON								
Rypien	33	18	54.5	292	1	8.8	16.2	0-0
BUFFALO								
Kelly	58	28	48.3	275	4	47.4	9.8	5-46
Reich	1	1	100.0	11	0	11.0	11.0	0-0

1992 N.F.C. A New Era Comes to Pro Football

A new era came to the National Football League in 1992 as the owners and players were forced into settling their six-year-long dispute. The owners lost the first round in September, when Federal District Judge David Doty declared four players immediate free agents.

Then, as the regular season ended in December, because of a 24-hour imposed time limit on negotiations, the two sides finally came to a settlement of all the litigation on the more than 20 suits that had been filed since the last collective bargaining agreement had expired in 1987. The players won their long sought-after free agency, and all players with five years or more in the league were given the freedom to change teams when their contracts expired. But the owners also received what they had wanted, a salary cap tied to percentage of gross revenues that guaranteed them financial stability. The draft was also shortened to eight rounds.

In the NFC, the Dallas Cowboys, the youngest team in the NFL, showed that they might have the makings of a dynasty after winning Super Bowl XXVII in a rout of the Buffalo Bills.

EASTERN DIVISION

Dallas Cowboys — The Cowboys culminated one of the most remarkable comebacks in NFL history, going from 1-15 in 1989 to 13-3 and the Super Bowl championship in 1992. Dallas had several of the biggest impact players in the NFL. Troy Aikman passed for 23 TD's and was the Super Bowl MVP, Emmitt Smith led the NFL in rushing with 1,713 yards and touchdowns with 19, Michael Irvin caught 78 passes for 1,396 yards and seven scores and Jay Novacek led the league's tight ends with 68 catches. Nearly 20 players were rotated in and out of the lineup on one of the league's best defenses, although none of them made the Pro Bowl. Charles Haley and Thomas Everett, who were obtained in preseason trades, were the impact players on defense. In the end, coach Jimmy Johnson was getting doused with ice water and Jerry Jones was enjoying every second as owner of the finest team in the land.

Philadelphia Eagles — Keith Jackson held out and was awarded free agency, eventually signing with Miami, and by the end of the year, Reggie White, Seth Joyner and Clyde Simmons had already been declared free agents. Quarterback Randall Cunningham experienced a splendid comeback from the knee injury that caused him to miss the 1991 season, throwing 19 TD passes. Philadelphia obtained Herschel Walker in a June trade, and he responded with over 1,000 yards rushing and 10 touchdowns. The defense was again one of the league's best, but it missed tackle Jerome Brown, who was killed in a car accident before training camp began. So a season that began so promising with the Super Bowl as the goal ended with free agency destined to destroy continuity.

Washington Redskins — The Redskins followed up their Super Bowl season in 1991 by slipping into the playoffs, but the talk in the nation's capital was about what happened to Mark Rypien. After a long training camp holdout, the quarterback finished as the lowest-rated passer in the NFC. Art Monk became pro football's all-time leading receiver, but he had a mediocre season. Gary Clark led the team in receptions but also dropped more balls than an amateur juggler. Want more? Earnest Byner gained 1,000 yards rushing, then lost a few yards and was injured, ending with 998. The offense scored 185 fewer points than in '91, but positions on both sides of the ball were riddled with injuries. Two months after the season ended, coach Joe Gibbs surprised everyone with his retirement, leaving defensive coordinator Richie Petitbon in charge.

New York Giants — Maybe the highlight of the Ray Handley era was that he wasn't the first coach fired after the season. The shortest reign of any coach in New York history — 19 months — spelled the end of Handley, and some time later Dan Reeves moved east from Denver to take over. Future Hall of Famer Lawrence Taylor was planning to retire, but then he suffered a season-ending injury which caused him to re-think his plans. There was a merry-go-round at quarterback with three different starters because of injuries and a defense that aged quickly. Halfback Rodney Hampton proved to be one of the league's top runners with 1,141 yards and 14 touchdowns. Six losses in the final seven games and a season full of turmoil meant changes in New York as 1993 approached.

Phoenix Cardinals — The Cardinals were probably the best once-gain last-place team in the NFL. Playing hard, stopping enemy running games and strong special-teams play were components of every Cardinals game. Phoenix defeated playoff teams Washington and San Francisco for two of its four wins. Quarterback Timm Rosenbach was injured again, and Chris Chandler took over and showed that he deserved the starting job. The defense had a couple of stars in Tim McDonald (who led the team in tackles for the fourth time in five years), Eric Swann and Freddie Joe Nunn. But with six losses in the last seven games, when the season ended coach Joe Bugel and general manager Larry Wilson were given one more year to turn things around.

CENTRAL DIVISION

Minnesota Vikings — New head coach Dennis Green turned whiners into winners and captured the division title by providing tough, prove-it-or-lose-it leadership that was desperately needed. He shipped out Herschel Walker, Joey Browner, Keith Millard and Wade Wilson, But Green couldn't decide on a quarterback, flip-flopping back and forth between Rich Gannon and journeyman Sean Salisbury late in the season when the playoffs were on the line. The Vikings defense was a force all year, and it provided the team with a couple of victories with some of the eight turnovers that were returned for touchdowns. Defensive end Chris Doleman had a resurgence, and Audray McMillian and Todd Scott provided fireworks from the secondary. Terry Allen rushed for a club-record 1,102 yards and scored 15 touchdowns.

Green Bay Packers — Brett Favre and Sterling Sharpe were the big stories in Green Bay, as the Packers contended for a playoff spot until the final weekend of the season. In his second season after being obtained in an offseason trade with Atlanta, Favre mastered the ball-control passing game of new coach Mike Holmgren and threw for 3,227 yards and 18 touchdowns after replacing Don Majkowski. Sharpe was on the receiving end of many of Favre's passes, as he set an NFL single-season record with 108 receptions. He also led the league with 1,461 receiving yards and 13 touchdowns. Other than tight end Jackie Harris (55 catches), the Packers were devoid of stars. The Green Bay defense wasn't dominant but certainly respectable, led by safety Chuck Cecil and linebacker Tony Bennett, who had 12.5 sacks.

Tampa Bay Buccaneers — New head coach Sam Wyche had high hopes after the Buccaneers started out 3-1. But then they were subjected to a slow death, as they lost 10 of their last 12 games. Following a strong start, Vinny Testaverde's interception problems returned, and he did little to convince Wyche that he should be brought back for another season. Offensive bright spots were running back Reggie Cobb (1,058 yards rushing and nine touchdowns) and receiver Lawrence Dawsey (58 catches). Defensively, the Bucs had their usual problems. They finished 21st in team defense and were especially vulnerable against the pass, although cornerback Ricky Reynolds was one of the league's best. Two top rookies were linemen Santana Dotson and Mark Wheeler, while veterans Broderick Thomas and Keith McCants were disappointments.

Chicago Bears — Da Bears hit Da Skids with one of the biggest collapses in the team's 73-year history, losing seven of their last eight games. Coach Mike Ditka provided a steady supply of controversy all season and was fired after it ended. The biggest problems were an aging defense and an offense that had trouble generating points. Paramount to all the Bears' troubles was the lack of players on either side of the ball who could make things happen. Jim Harbaugh entered the season as the division's best quarterback, but he slumped to a point where backups Peter Tom Willis and Will Furrer got opportunities to show what they could do (and it wasn't much). Neal Anderson had another subpar year at halfback, even losing his starting job for a time to Darren Lewis.

Detroit Lions — The Lions slumped from division champs to the

FINAL TEAM STATISTICS

OFFENSE

	ATL	CHI	DAL	DET	G.B.	L.A.	MINN	N.O.	NYG	PHIL	PHX	S.F.	T.B.	WASH
FIRST DOWNS:														
Total	273	282	324	241	291	278	288	267	271	292	277	**344**	281	276
by Rushing	67	101	119	83	101	83	115	92	120	**138**	88	135	100	104
by Passing	**194**	157	183	133	171	174	157	155	119	138	161	192	165	160
by Penalty	12	24	22	25	19	21	16	20	**32**	16	28	17	16	12
RUSHING:														
Number	322	427	500	378	420	393	497	454	458	**516**	395	482	438	483
Yards	1270	1871	2121	1644	1555	1659	2030	1628	2077	**2388**	1491	2315	1706	1727
Average Yards	3.9	4.4	4.2	4.3	3.7	4.2	4.1	3.6	4.5	4.6	3.8	**4.8**	3.9	3.6
Touchdowns	3	15	20	9	7	12	19	10	20	19	11	**22**	12	10
PASSING:														
Attempts	**548**	479	491	406	527	495	458	426	433	429	517	480	511	485
Completions	336	266	314	231	**340**	289	258	251	232	255	298	319	299	272
Completion Pct.	61.3	55.5	64.0	56.9	64.5	58.4	56.3	58.9	53.6	59.4	57.6	**66.6**	58.5	56.1
Passing Yards	3892	3334	3597	3150	3498	3422	3162	3297	2628	3054	3344	**4054**	3399	3339
Avg. Yds per Att.	6.2	5.9	6.8	6.0	5.7	6.2	5.8	7.2	4.9	5.3	5.6	**7.6**	5.5	6.2
Avg. Yds per Comp.	11.6	12.5	11.5	**13.6**	10.3	11.8	12.3	13.1	11.3	12.0	11.2	12.7	11.4	12.3
Times Tackled	40	45	23	59	43	26	40	**15**	45	64	36	32	45	23
Yds Lost Tackled	259	284	**112**	354	208	204	293	119	283	462	258	174	334	176
Net Yards	3633	3070	3485	2796	3230	3218	2869	3178	2345	2592	3086	**3880**	3065	3163
Touchdowns	**33**	17	23	16	20	23	18	19	14	20	15	29	17	15
Interceptions	15	24	15	21	15	20	15	16	10	13	24	**9**	20	17
Pct. Intercepted	2.7	5.0	3.1	5.2	2.8	4.0	3.3	3.8	2.3	3.0	4.6	**1.9**	3.9	3.5
PUNTS:														
Number	70	79	61	66	68	76	73	67	85	82	58	**49**	74	65
Average	40.8	42.9	43.0	43.1	38.4	41.1	**44.4**	44.0	40.6	42.2	42.8	39.1	40.7	39.3
PUNT RETURNS														
Number	29	23	44	21	35	39	33	45	27	**47**	33	40	26	37
Yards	196	176	550	190	315	345	336	231	240	**555**	364	389	160	355
Average Yards	6.8	7.7	**12.5**	9.0	9.0	8.8	10.2	5.1	8.9	11.8	11.0	9.7	6.2	9.6
Touchdowns	0	0	**2**	1	1	**2**	0	0	0	1	0	1	0	**2**
KICKOFF RET.:														
Number	**64**	56	37	59	54	63	45	42	56	48	51	42	50	48
Yards	**1532**	1143	699	1193	1017	1054	874	815	1098	987	1127	879	881	973
Average Yards	**23.9**	20.4	18.9	20.2	18.8	16.7	19.4	19.4	19.6	20.6	22.1	20.9	17.6	20.3
Touchdowns	**2**	1	0	1	0	0	0	0	1	0	0	0	0	0
INTERCEPT RET.:														
Number	11	14	17	21	15	18	**28**	18	14	24	16	17	20	23
Yards	135	188	158	255	222	283	**502**	254	192	307	298	172	234	485
Average Yards	12.3	13.4	9.3	12.1	14.8	15.7	17.9	14.1	13.7	12.8	18.6	10.1	11.7	**21.1**
Touchdowns	0	0	1	0	1	1	**6**	3	1	2	3	1	1	2
PENALTIES:														
Number	78	93	91	122	88	79	99	**60**	87	101	85	80	91	84
Yards	656	776	650	903	749	592	809	**567**	647	807	722	636	754	741
FUMBLES:														
Number	30	23	**16**	26	41	30	29	27	25	25	26	29	19	18
Number Lost	14	10	9	15	21	17	17	13	13	15	18	13	9	**7**
POINTS:														
Total	327	295	409	273	276	313	374	330	306	354	243	**431**	267	300
PAT Attempts	39	34	48	30	30	38	45	35	36	44	29	**54**	33	30
PAT Made	39	34	47	30	30	38	45	33	36	40	28	**53**	33	30
FG Attempts	22	26	35	26	29	20	25	34	23	25	26	27	22	**40**
FG Made	18	19	24	21	22	15	19	29	18	16	13	18	12	**30**
Percent FG Made	81.8	73.1	68.6	80.8	75.9	75.0	76.0	**85.3**	78.3	64.0	50.0	66.7	54.5	75.0
Safeties	0	0	1	0	0	1	1	0	0	1	1	0	0	0

DEFENSE

	ATL	CHI	DAL	DET	G.B.	L.A.	MINN	N.O.	NYG	PHIL	PHX	S.F.	T.B.	WASH
FIRST DOWNS:														
Total	304	274	241	308	277	319	293	246	287	**242**	281	277	296	249
by Rushing	109	109	**68**	119	89	130	113	86	115	73	101	90	100	89
by Passing	172	144	147	168	170	175	154	146	155	146	163	174	175	**138**
by Penalty	23	21	26	21	18	14	26	14	17	23	17	**13**	21	22
RUSHING:														
Number	464	468	**345**	460	406	467	438	381	458	387	436	351	441	406
Yards	2294	1948	**1244**	1841	1821	2230	1733	1605	2012	1481	1635	1418	1675	1696
Average Yards	4.9	4.2	**3.6**	4.0	4.5	4.8	4.0	4.2	4.4	3.8	3.8	4.0	3.8	4.2
Touchdowns	20	14	11	14	12	22	11	8	17	**4**	13	5	15	11
PASSING:														
Attempts	**439**	442	484	487	483	507	508	511	440	517	452	551	508	466
Completions	277	261	263	296	277	305	320	287	270	263	276	320	293	**258**
Completion Pct.	63.1	59.0	54.3	60.8	57.3	60.2	63.0	56.2	61.4	**50.9**	61.1	58.1	57.7	55.4
Passing Yards	3496	3290	3034	3402	3496	3481	3124	**2846**	3228	3316	3687	3642	3740	3021
Avg. Yds per Att.	6.9	6.2	5.1	6.2	6.3	6.1	5.0	**4.4**	6.5	5.1	7.3	5.7	6.5	5.4
Avg. Yds per Comp.	12.6	12.6	11.5	11.5	12.6	11.4	**9.8**	9.9	12.0	12.6	13.4	11.4	12.8	11.7
Times Tackled	31	43	44	29	34	31	51	**57**	25	55	27	41	36	39
Yds Lost Tackled	241	286	347	185	219	188	342	376	197	**385**	196	273	230	279
Net Yards	3255	3004	2687	3217	3277	3293	2702	**2470**	3031	2931	3491	3369	3510	2742
Touchdowns	24	20	16	20	16	18	**12**	13	22	20	24	20	25	15
Interceptions	11	14	17	21	15	18	28	18	14	**24**	16	17	20	23
Pct. Intercepted	2.5	3.2	3.3	4.3	3.1	3.6	**5.5**	3.5	3.2	4.6	3.5	3.1	3.9	4.9
PUNTS:														
Number	61	70	87	**55**	68	66	76	89	64	85	62	76	64	73
Average	41.5	40.6	42.1	41.1	43.3	42.1	41.9	41.2	38.7	41.5	42.8	41.2	41.3	42.8
PUNT RETURNS														
Number	44	38	34	30	26	48	34	31	46	36	**22**	23	**22**	27
Yards	482	351	397	356	230	522	339	218	548	295	141	177	**117**	332
Average Yards	11.0	9.2	11.7	11.9	8.8	10.9	10.0	7.0	11.9	8.2	6.4	7.7	**5.3**	12.3
Touchdowns	4	1	**0**	**0**	1	1	1	**0**	2	**0**	**0**	**0**	**0**	1
KICKOFF RET.:														
Number	55	50	60	45	57	55	50	**40**	64	53	42	66	49	54
Yards	1059	1027	1217	948	901	1128	925	923	1207	1027	**767**	1273	1236	1074
Average Yards	19.3	20.5	20.3	21.1	**15.8**	20.5	18.5	23.1	18.9	19.4	18.3	19.3	25.2	19.9
Touchdowns	**0**	**0**	**0**	**0**	**0**	**0**	**0**	**0**	**0**	1	**0**	**0**	1	1
INTERCEPT RET.:														
Number	15	24	15	21	15	20	15	16	10	13	24	**9**	20	17
Yards	246	612	300	294	198	305	164	280	190	**77**	279	126	211	318
Average Yards	16.4	25.5	20.0	14.0	13.2	15.3	10.9	17.5	19.0	**5.9**	11.6	14.0	10.6	18.7
Touchdowns	3	6	**0**	1	1	1	1	2	2	**0**	1	2	1	2
PENALTIES:														
Number	92	90	94	**111**	98	102	98	77	93	86	100	79	74	85
Yards	761	780	727	**871**	830	778	768	729	744	683	826	651	563	709
FUMBLES:														
Number	24	34	25	25	32	26	23	**37**	27	27	25	23	19	23
Number Lost	16	13	11	17	14	8	11	19	**9**	**22**	21	16	16	14
POINTS:														
Total	414	361	243	332	296	383	249	202	367	245	332	236	365	255
PAT Attempts	51	43	29	38	32	43	27	**24**	46	26	40	27	43	30
PAT Made	51	43	27	38	32	41	27	**22**	44	26	38	26	43	29
FG Attempts	31	25	**17**	35	27	34	25	**17**	21	32	28	20	30	21
FG Made	19	20	14	22	24	28	20	**12**	15	21	18	16	20	14
Percent FG Made	**61.3**	80.0	82.4	62.9	88.9	82.4	80.0	70.6	71.4	65.6	64.3	80.0	66.7	66.7
Safeties	**0**	**0**	**0**	**0**	**0**	**0**	**0**	**0**	1	**0**	**0**	**0**	2	2

cellar with tragedies, injuries and quarterback controversies all year long. The offensive line was the No. 1 headache, especially for the quarterbacks who were batted around like a beach ball. On top of Mike Utley's injury that left him paralyzed in 1991, guard Eric Andolsek was killed before the '92 season began, and two other starters were lost by midseason. Thus, running back Barry Sanders was a marked man all season, although he did overcome a slow start to become only the third player to rush for 1,000 yards in each of his first four seasons. Receivers Herman Moore and Brett Perriman and kicker Jason Hanson were solid performers, but quarterbacks Rodney Peete, Erik Kramer and Andre Ware were mostly ineffective.

WESTERN DIVISION

San Francisco 49ers — Joe Montana played only 30 minutes of the season and it was a much-celebrated event in the season finale. But Steve Young is the quarterback of the present in San Francisco, and all he did was lead the NFL in passing with 25 touchdowns and only seven interceptions as well as running for 537 yards and four scores. Jerry Rice was his usual fantastic self (84 catches, 11 TD's), and the 49ers found a new star at running back in Ricky Watters, who rushed for 1,013 yards. The defense, particularly a young secondary, was ravaged in a 34-31 loss to Buffalo in Week Two, but it improved as the season progressed. In the end, Young failed to win the Super Bowl, which left many 49ers fans wondering what Montana might have done.

New Orleans Saints — The Saints would have won the division title, but they couldn't defeat the 49ers, dropping both games, as well as contests with the Eagles and Bills, by a total of 13 points. New Orleans sent an unprecedented four linebackers to the Pro Bowl — Rickey Jackson, Vaughan Johnson, Sam Mills and Pat Swilling — and end Wayne Martin emerged as a pass-rushing force. But the offense remained average at best. When hot, quarterback Bobby Hebert formed a dangerous combination with Eric Martin (68 catches, five touchdowns). But for the most part, coach Jim Mora's troops relied on a ground game that was anything but spectacular. Rookie Vaughn Dunbar led the team with 565 yards rushing, but he lost his starting job by midseason. Morten Andersen tied for the NFC lead with 120 points.

Atlanta Falcons — The team that believed it was too legit looked as if it wanted to quit by the end of a season that became what fans had learned to expect from a Jerry Glanville-coached team: respectable but hardly a Super Bowl contender. Deion Sanders played both baseball and football in the fall, sometimes both on the same day, but the Atlanta defense struggled and ranked last in the conference. The gambling style too often resulted in big scores for the opponents. Quarterback Chris Miller was second in the NFC in passing when he was injured in Week Eight and knocked out for the rest of the year. Ex-Viking Wade Wilson looked fantastic in the final three games. The Falcons didn't have a running game to speak of, but receivers Andre Rison (93 catches, 11 TD's) and Michael Haynes 48 and 10) kept the pressure on opponents.

Los Angeles Rams — Jim Everett began to break out of his two-year doldrums, throwing for 3,323 yards and 22 touchdowns. As expected, Chuck Knox bolstered what had been an anemic running game. Cleveland Gary returned to form, and rushed for 1,125 yards and topped the team with 52 receptions. Flipper Anderson scored seven touchdowns, and Henry Ellard caught 47 passes to lead the wideouts. Another Ram who rebounded in 1992 was Kevin Greene, who led the team in tackles and sacks after switching back to linebacker. For the most part, the Rams' defensive woes, which saw them rank next to last in the NFC, were a product of their inexperience. Two rookies, Sean Gilbert and Marc Boutte, started up front. The last game saw running back David Lang score three TD's and Todd Kinchen return two punts for scores.

DALLAS COWBOYS 13-3 Jimmy Johnson

Scores of Each Game		
23	WASHINGTON	10
34	N.Y. Giants	28
31	PHOENIX	20
7	Philadelphia	31
27	SEATTLE	0
17	KANSAS CITY	10
28	L.A. Raiders	13
20	PHILADELPHIA	10
37	Detroit	3
23	L.A. RAMS	27
16	Phoenix	10
30	N.Y. GIANTS	3
31	Denver	27
17	Washington	20
41	Atlanta	17
27	CHICAGO	14

Use Name	Pos.	Hgt.	Wgt.	Age	Int	Pts
Mark Tuinei	OT	6'5"	298	32		
Erik Williams	OT	6'6"	321	23		
John Gesek	OG	6'5"	282	29		
Kevin Gogan	OG-OT	6'7"	319	27		
Dale Hellestrae	OG-C	6'5"	283	30		
Nate Newton	OG	6'3"	303	30		
Alan Veingrad	OG-OT	6'5"	280	29		
Frank Cornish	C-OG	6'4"	285	24		
Mark Stepnoski	C	6'2"	269	25		
Charles Haley	DE	6'5"	245	28		
Tony Hill	DE	6'6"	242	23		
Jim Jeffcoat	DE	6'5"	276	31		
Tony Tolbert	DE	6'6"	265	24		
Tony Casillas	DT	6'3"	273	28		
Chad Hennings	DT	6'6"	267	26		
Jimmie Jones	DT	6'4"	276	26		
Leon Lett	DT	6'6"	292	23		
Russell Maryland	DT-DE	6'1"	275	22		6
Bobby Abrams (to CLE, NYG)	LB	6'3"	230	25		
Dixon Edwards	LB	6'1"	224	24		
Robert Jones	LB	6'2"	238	22		
Godfrey Myles	LB	6'1"	242	23	1	
Ken Norton	LB	6'2"	241	25		
Mickey Pruitt	LB	6'1"	218	27		
Vinson Smith	LB	6'2"	237	27		
Bill Bates	DB	6'1"	205	31		
Larry Brown	DB	5'11"	185	22	1	
Thomas Everett	DB	5'9"	183	27	2	
Kenneth Gant	DB	5'11"	191	25	3	
Clayton Holmes	DB	5'10"	181	23		
Issiac Holt	DB	6'2"	198	29	2	2
Ray Horton	DB	5'11"	188	32	2	6
Kevin Smith	DB	5'11"	177	22	2	
James Washington	DB	6'1"	203	27	3	
Robert Williams	DB	5'10"	186	29		6
Darren Woodson	DB	6'1"	215	23		
Troy Aikman	QB	6'4"	222	25		6
Steve Beuerlein	QB	6'2"	213	27		
Derrick Gainer (from RAID)	HB	5'11"	240	26		
Curvin Richards	HB	5'9"	195	23		6
Emmitt Smith	HB	5'9"	209	23		114
Tommie Agee	FB	6'	227	28		
Daryl Johnston	FB	6'2"	238	26		12
Alvin Harper	WR	6'3"	207	25	1	24
Michael Irvin	WR	6'2"	199	26		42
Kelvin Martin	WR	5'9"	165	27		30
Jimmy Smith	WR	6'1"	205	23		
Jay Novacek	TE	6'4"	231	29		36
Alfredo Roberts	TE	6'3"	252	27		
Lin Elliott	K	6'	182	23		119
Mike Saxon	K	6'3"	200	30		

PHILADELPHIA EAGLES 11-5 Rich Kotite

Scores of Each Game		
15	NEW ORLEANS	13
31	Phoenix	14
30	DENVER	0
31	DALLAS	7
17	Kansas City	24
12	Washington	16
7	PHOENIX	3
10	Dallas	20
31	L.A. RAIDERS	10
24	Green Bay	27
47	N.Y. Giants	34
14	San Francisco	20
28	MINNESOTA	17
20	Seattle	* 17
17	WASHINGTON	13
20	N.Y. GIANTS	10

Use Name	Pos.	Hgt.	Wgt.	Age	Int	Pts
Brian Baldinger	OT-C	6'4"	278	32		
Antone Davis	OT	6'4"	325	25		
Ron Heller	OT	6'6"	280	30		
Daryle Smith	OT	6'5"	276	28		
Eric Floyd	OG-OT	6'5"	310	26		
John Hudson	OG-C	6'2"	275	24		
Mike Schad	OG	6'5"	290	28		
Rob Selby	OG-OT	6'3"	286	24		
David Alexander	C	6'3"	275	28		
Mike Flores	DE	6'3"	256	25		
Clyde Simmons	DE	6'6"	280	28		
Reggie White	DE	6'5"	305	30		
Mike Golic	DT	6'5"	275	29		
Andy Harmon	DT	6'4"	265	23		
Tommy Jeter	DT	6'5"	282	22		
Mike Pitts	DT	6'5"	280	31		
Leon Seals	DT	6'5"	270	28		
Ephesians Bartley	LB	6'2"	213	23		
Byron Evans	LB	6'2"	235	28	4	
Britt Hager	LB	6'1"	225	26		
Seth Joyner	LB	6'2"	235	27	4	12
Scott Kowalkowski	LB	6'2"	228	24		
Ken Rose	LB	6'1"	215	30		6
William Thomas	LB	6'2"	218	24		
Eric Allen	DB	5'10"	180	26	4	
John Booty	DB	6'	180	26	3	
William Frizzell	DB	6'3"	206	29		
Tom Gerhart	DB	6'1"	195	27		
Wes Hopkins	DB	6'1"	215	30	3	
Izel Jenkins	DB	5'10"	190	28		
Mark McMillian	DB	5'7"	162	22	1	
Rich Miano	DB	6'1"	200	29	1	
Otis Smith	DB	5'11"	184	26	1	
Andre Waters	DB	5'11"	200	30		
David Archer	QB	6'2"	208	30		
Randall Cunningham	QB	6'4"	205	29		30
Jim McMahon	QB	6'1"	195	33		
Tony Brooks	HB	6'	230	23		
James Joseph	HB-FB	6'	222	24		
Heath Sherman	HB-FB	6'	205	25		36
Siran Stacy	HB	5'11"	203	24		
Herschel Walker	HB	6'1"	225	30		60
Fred Barnett	WR	6'	199	26		36
Floyd Dixon	WR	5'9"	170	28		
Roy Green	WR	6'1"	195	35		
Vai Sikahema	WR	5'9"	196	30		6
Jeff Sydner	WR	5'6"	170	22		
Calvin Williams	WR	5'11"	190	25		42
Pat Beach	TE	6'4"	250	32		12
Keith Byars	TE-HB	6'1"	238	28		18
Maurice Johnson	TE	6'2"	243	25		
Jeff Feagles	K	6'	205	26		
Roger Ruzek	K	6'1"	200	31		88

Jerome Brown — Died in Offseason Automobile Accident

Ben Smith — Knee Injury

WASHINGTON REDSKINS 9-7 Joe Gibbs

Scores of Each Game		
10	Dallas	23
24	ATLANTA	17
13	DETROIT	10
24	Phoenix	27
34	DENVER	3
16	PHILADELPHIA	12
15	Minnesota	13
7	N.Y. GIANTS	24
16	Seattle	3
16	Kansas City	35
3	New Orleans	20
41	PHOENIX	3
28	N.Y. Giants	10
20	DALLAS	17
13	Philadelphia	17
20	L.A. RAIDERS	21

Use Name	Pos.	Hgt.	Wgt.	Age	Int	Pts
Ray Brown	OT	6'5"	280	29		
Mo Elewonibi	OT	6'4"	310	27		
Mike Haight	OT	6'4"	291	29		
Joe Jacoby	OT-OG	6'7"	314	32		
Jim Lachey	OT	6'6"	294	29		
Ed Simmons	OT	6'5"	300	28		
Raleigh McKenzie	OG-C-OT	6'2"	279	29		
Tom Myslinski	OG	6'2"	291	24		
Mark Schlereth	OG	6'3"	283	26		
Guy Bingham	C	6'3"	260	34		
Jeff Bostic	C	6'2"	278	33		
Matt Elliott	C	6'1"	265	23		
Jason Buck	DE	6'4"	265	29		
Shane Collins	DE	6'3"	267	23		
Charles Mann	DE	6'6"	272	31		
Fred Stokes	DE	6'3"	274	28		
James Geathers	DT	6'7"	289	32		
Tim Johnson	DT	6'3"	283	26		
Jim Wahler (from PHX)	DT-NT	6'4"	275	26		
Eric Williams	DT	6'4"	290	30		
Bobby Wilson	DT	6'2"	283	24		
Tony Barker	LB	6'2"	230	23		
John Brantley	LB	6'3"	240	26		
Ravin Caldwell	LB	6'3"	240	29		
Monte Coleman	LB	6'2"	245	34		
Andre Collins	LB	6'1"	233	24	1	
Kurt Gouveia	LB	6'1"	228	27	3	
Wilber Marshall	LB	6'1"	231	30	2	6
Todd Bowles	DB	6'2"	205	28	1	
Danny Copeland	DB	6'2"	213	26		6
Brad Edwards	DB	6'2"	207	26	6	6
Pat Eilers	DB	5'11"	195	25		
Darrell Green	DB	5'8"	170	32	1	
David Gulledge	DB	6'1"	203	25		
A.J. Johnson	DB	5'8"	170	25	3	
Sidney Johnson	DB	5'9"	175	27	1	
Martin Mayhew	DB	5'8"	172	26	3	
Alvoid Mays	DB	5'9"	180	26	2	
Johnny Thomas	DB	5'9"	191	28		
Mickey Washington	DB	5'9"	187	24		
Cary Conklin	QB	6'4"	215	24		
Jeff Rutledge	QB	6'1"	193	35		
Mark Rypien	QB	6'4"	234	29		12
Earnest Byner	HB-FB	5'10"	218	29		42
Ricky Ervins	HB	5'7"	200	23		12
Robert Green	HB	5'8"	207	21		
Brian Mitchell	HB	5'10"	209	24		6
Gary Clark	WR	5'9"	173	30		30
Carl Harry	WR	5'9"	170	24		
Stephen Hobbs	WR	5'11"	200	26		
Desmond Howard	WR	5'9"	183	22		6
Art Monk	WR	6'3"	210	34		18
Ricky Sanders	WR	5'11"	180	30		18
James Jenkins	TE	6'2"	234	25		
Ron Middleton	TE	6'2"	270	27		
Terry Orr	TE	6'2"	235	30		18
Ray Rowe	TE	6'2"	256	23		
Don Warren	TE	6'4"	242	36		
Kelly Goodburn	K	6'2"	199	30		
Chip Lohmiller	K	6'3"	210	26		**120**

Mark Adickes — Back Injury

Terry Hoage — Arm Injury
Clarence Vaughn — Knee Injury

John Settle — Knee Injury

NEW YORK GIANTS 6-10 Ray Handley

Scores of Each Game		
14	SAN FRANCISCO	31
28	DALLAS	34
27	Chicago	14
10	L.A. Raiders	13
31	PHOENIX	21
17	L.A. Rams	38
23	SEATTLE	10
24	Washington	7
27	GREEN BAY	7
13	Denver	27
34	PHILADELPHIA	47
3	Dallas	30
10	WASHINGTON	28
0	Phoenix	19
35	KANSAS CITY	21
10	Philadelphia	20

Use Name	Pos.	Hgt.	Wgt.	Age	Int	Pts
John Elliott	OT	6'7"	305	27		
Clarence Jones	OT	6'6"	280	24		
Doug Riesenberg	OT	6'5"	275	27		
Bob Kratch	OG	6'3"	288	26		
Eric Moore	OG-OT	6'5"	290	27		
William Roberts	OG	6'5"	280	30		
Bart Oates	C	6'3"	265	33		
Brian Williams	C-OG	6'5"	300	26		
Stacey Dillard	DE	6'5"	288	23		
Eric Dorsey	DE	6'5"	280	28		
Mike Fox	DE	6'6"	275	25		
Keith Hamilton	DE	6'6"	280	21		
Leonard Marshall	DE	6'3"	285	30		
Corey Widmer	DT	6'3"	276	23		
Erik Howard	NT	6'4"	268	27		
John Washington (to ATL)	NT	6'4"	275	29		
Carl Banks	LB	6'4"	235	30		
Steve DeOssie	LB	6'2"	248	29		
Pepper Johnson	LB	6'3"	248	28	2	
Kanavis McGhee	LB	6'4"	257	23		
Corey Miller	LB	6'2"	225	23		
Ed Reynolds	LB	6'5"	242	30		
Lawrence Taylor	LB	6'3"	243	33		
Jesse Campbell	DB	6'1"	215	23		
Mark Collins	DB	5'10"	190	28	1	
Myron Guyton	DB	6'1"	205	25		
Greg Jackson	DB	6'1"	200	26	4	
Lamar McGriggs	DB	6'3"	210	24		
Corey Raymond	DB	5'11"	180	23		
Phillippi Sparks	DB	5'11"	186	23	1	
Reyna Thompson	DB	6'	193	29	2	6
Perry Williams	DB	6'2"	203	31	1	
Dave Brown	QB	6'5"	215	22		
Kent Graham	QB	6'5"	220	23		
Jeff Hostetler	QB	6'3"	212	31		18
Phil Simms	QB	6'3"	214	36		
Ottis Anderson	HB	6'2"	225	35		
Rodney Hampton	HB	5'11"	215	23		84
Dave Meggett	HB	5'7"	180	26		18
Lewis Tillman	HB	6'	195	26		
Jarrod Bunch	FB	6'2"	248	24		24
Stephen Baker	WR	5'8"	160	28		12
Chris Calloway	WR	5'10"	185	24		6
Mark Ingram	WR	5'10"	188	27		6
Ed McCaffrey	WR	6'5"	215	24		30
Joey Smith	WR	5'10"	177	23		
John Brandes (from WAS)	TE	6'2"	249	28		
Derek Brown	TE	6'6"	252	22		
Howard Cross	TE	6'5"	245	25		12
Aaron Pierce	TE	6'5"	246	22		
Matt Bahr	K	5'10"	175	36		77
Sean Landeta	K	6'	210	30		

Thom Kaumeyer — Knee Injury

PHOENIX CARDINALS 4-12 Joe Bugel

Scores of Each Game		
7	Tampa Bay	23
14	PHILADELPHIA	31
20	Dallas	31
27	WASHINGTON	24
21	N.Y. Giants	31
21	NEW ORLEANS	30
3	Philadelphia	7
24	SAN FRANCISCO	14
20	L.A. Rams	14
17	Atlanta	20
10	DALLAS	16
3	Washington	41
21	SAN DIEGO	27
19	N.Y. GIANTS	0
13	Indianapolis	16
3	TAMPA BAY	7

Use Name	Pos.	Hgt.	Wgt.	Age	Int	Pts
Rob Baxley	OT	6'5"	287	23		
Rick Cunningham	OT	6'6"	307	25		
Luis Sharpe	OT	6'4"	280	32		
Danny Villa	OT-C	6'5"	300	27		
Joe Wolf	OT	6'5"	296	25		
Mark May	OG-OT	6'6"	300	32		
Lance Smith	OG	6'2"	286	29		
Vernice Smith	OG	6'2"	290	22		
Ed Cunningham	C	6'3"	290	23		
Bill Lewis	C	6'7"	290	29		
Reuben Davis (from TB)	DE	6'4"	292	27		
Jeff Faulkner	DE	6'4"	290	28		
Mike Jones	DE	6'4"	287	23		
Eric Swann	DE	6'4"	299	22		2
Michael Bankston	NT	6'2"	290	22		
Keith Rucker	NT	6'3"	325	23		
David Braxton	LB	6'1"	240	27		
Ken Harvey	LB	6'2"	230	27		
Eric Hill	LB	6'1"	260	25		
Steve Hyche	LB	6'2"	245	29		
Garth Jax	LB	6'2"	250	28		
Jock Jones	LB	6'2"	245	24	1	
Freddie Joe Nunn	LB	6'4"	250	30		
Jessie Small	LB	6'3"	240	25		
Tyronne Stowe	LB	6'1"	247	27		
Dexter Davis	DB	5'10"	190	22	2	
Dave Duerson	DB	6'1"	208	31		
Odie Harris (from CLE)	DB	6'	190	26		
Steve Lofton	DB	5'9"	180	23		
Lorenzo Lynch	DB	5'9"	200	29		
Robert Massey	DB	5'10"	188	25	5	18
Tim McDonald	DB	6'2"	222	27	2	
Chris Oldham	DB	5'9"	183	23		
Aeneas Williams	DB	5'10"	192	23	3	
Mike Zordich	DB	5'11"	200	28	3	
Chris Chandler	QB	6'4"	220	26		6
Timm Rosenbach	QB	6'1"	215	25		
Tony Sacca	QB	6'5"	230	22		
Johnny Bailey	HB	5'8"	187	25		18
Eric Blount	HB	5'9"	190	21		
Ivory Lee Brown	HB-FB	6'2"	245	23		12
Larry Centers	HB	5'11"	212	24		12
Johnny Johnson	HB	6'2"	215	24		36
Anthony Edwards	WR	5'9"	188	26		6
Randal Hill	WR	5'10"	180	22		18
John Jackson	WR	5'10"	183	25		6
Ernie Jones	WR	5'11"	200	27		24
Ricky Proehl	WR	5'10"	190	24		18
Walter Reeves	TE	6'4"	265	26		
Butch Rolle	TE	6'4"	250	28		
Derek Ware	TE	6'2"	255	24		
Willie Wright	TE	6'6"	295	25		
Rich Camarillo	K	5'11"	195	32		
Greg Davis	K	6'	195	26		67

Willie Williams — Knee Injury

Jay Taylor — Bicep Injury

DALLAS COWBOYS

RUSHING

Last Name	No.	Yds	Avg	TD
E. Smith	**373**	**1713**	4.6	18
Richards	49	176	3.6	1
Aikman	37	105	2.8	1
Johnston	17	61	3.6	0
Agee	16	54	3.4	0
Harper	1	15	15.0	0
Martin	2	13	6.5	0
Beuerlein	4	-7	-1.8	0
Irvin	1	-9	-9.0	0

RECEIVING

Last Name	No.	Yds	Avg	TD
Irvin	78	1396	17.9	7
Novacek	68	630	9.3	6
E. Smith	59	335	5.7	1
Harper	35	562	16.1	4
Martin	32	359	11.2	3
Johnston	32	249	7.8	2
Roberts	3	36	12.0	0
Agee	3	18	6.0	0
Richards	3	8	2.7	0
Gesek	1	4	4.0	0

PUNT RETURNS

Last Name	No.	Yds	Avg	TD
Martin	**42**	**532**	12.7	**2**
K. Smith	1	17	17.0	0
Horton	1	1	1.0	0

KICKOFF RETURNS

Last Name	No.	Yds	Avg	TD
Martin	24	503	21.0	0
Holmes	3	70	23.3	0
K. Smith	1	9	9.0	0
Edwards	1	0	0.0	0

PASSING — PUNTING — KICKING

PASSING	Att	Cmp	%	Yds	Yd/Att	TD	Int—	%	RK
Aikman	473	**302**	63.8	3445	7.28	23	14—	3.0	0
Beuerlein	18	12	66.7	152	8.44	0	1—	5.6	

PUNTING	No.	Avg.
Saxon	61	43.0

KICKING	XP	Att.	%	FG	Att	%
Elliott	47	48	98	24	35	69

PHILADELPHIA EAGLES

RUSHING

Last Name	No.	Yds	Avg	TD
Walker	267	1070	4.0	8
Sherman	112	583	5.2	5
Cunningham	87	549	6.3	5
Byars	41	176	4.3	1
McMahon	6	23	3.8	0
Sikahema	2	2	1.0	0
Barnett	1	-15	-15.0	0

RECEIVING

Last Name	No.	Yds	Avg	TD
Barnett	67	1083	16.2	6
Byars	56	502	9.0	2
Williams	42	14.2	7	
Walker	38	278	7.3	2
Sherman	18	219	12.2	1
Sikahema	13	142	10.9	0
Green	8	105	13.1	0
Beach	8	75	9.4	2
F. Dixon	3	36	12.0	0
Johnson	2	16	8.0	0

PUNT RETURNS

Last Name	No.	Yds	Avg	TD
Sikahema	40	503	12.6	1
Sydner	7	52	7.4	0

KICKOFF RETURNS

Last Name	No.	Yds	Avg	TD
Sikahema	26	528	20.3	0
Sydner	17	368	21.6	0
Walker	3	69	23.0	0
Booty	1	11	11.0	0
Brooks	1	11	11.0	0

PASSING — PUNTING — KICKING

PASSING	Att	Cmp	%	Yds	Yd/Att	TD	Int—	%	RK
Cunningham	384	233	60.7	2775	7.23	19	11—	2.9	4
McMahon	43	22	51.2	279	6.49	1	2—	4.7	
Byars	1	0	0.0	0	0.00	0	0—	0.0	
Walker	1	0	0.0	0	0.00	0	0—	0.0	

PUNTING	No.	Avg.
Feagles	**82**	42.2

KICKING	XP	ATT	%	FG	ATT	%
Ruzek	40	44	91	16	25	64

WASHINGTON REDSKINS

RUSHING

Last Name	No.	Yds	Avg	TD
Byner	262	998	3.8	6
Ervins	151	495	3.3	2
Mitchell	6	70	11.7	0
Rypien	36	50	1.4	2
R. Green	8	46	5.8	0
Monk	6	45	7.5	0
Clark	2	18	9.0	0
Howard	3	14	4.7	0
Goodburn	2	1	0.5	0
Conklin	3	-4	-1.3	0
Sanders	4	-6	-1.5	0

RECEIVING

Last Name	No.	Yds	Avg	TD
Clark	64	912	14.3	5
Sanders	51	707	13.9	3
Monk	46	644	14.0	3
Byner	39	338	8.7	1
Ervins	32	252	7.9	0
Orr	22	356	16.2	3
Middleton	7	50	7.1	0
Warren	4	25	6.3	0
Mitchell	3	30	10.0	0
Howard	3	20	6.7	0
R. Green	1	5	5.0	0

PUNT RETURNS

Last Name	No.	Yds	Avg	TD
Mitchell	29	271	9.3	1
Howard	6	84	14.0	1
S. Johnson	1	0	0.0	0
Thomas	1	0	0.0	0

KICKOFF RETURNS

Last Name	No.	Yds	Avg	TD
Mitchell	23	492	21.4	0
Howard	22	462	21.0	0
R. Green	1	9	9.0	0
Gouveia	1	7	7.0	0
Orr	1	3	3.0	0

PASSING — PUNTING — KICKING

PASSING	Att	Cmp	%	Yds	Yd/Att	TD	Int—	%	RK
Rypien	**479**	269	56.2	3282	6.85	13	17—	3.5	12
Byner	3	1	33.3	41	13.67	1	0—	0.0	
Conklin	2	2	100.0	16	8.00	1	0—	0.0	
Mitchell	1	0	0.0	0	0.00	0	0—	0.0	

PUNTING	No.	Avg.
Goodburn	65	39.3

KICKING	XP	ATT	%	FG	ATT	%
Lohmiller	30	30	**100**	**30**	**40**	75

NEW YORK GIANTS

RUSHING

Last Name	No.	Yds	Avg	TD
Hampton	257	1141	4.4	14
Bunch	104	501	4.8	3
Hostetler	34	172	5.1	3
Meggett	32	167	5.2	0
Graham	6	36	6.0	0
Anderson	10	31	3.1	0
Simms	6	17	2.8	0
Tillman	6	13	2.2	0
Da. Brown	2	-1	-0.5	0

RECEIVING

Last Name	No.	Yds	Avg	TD
McCaffrey	49	610	12.4	5
Meggett	38	229	6.0	2
Hampton	28	215	7.7	0
Ingram	27	408	15.1	1
Cross	27	357	13.2	2
Calloway	27	335	12.4	1
Baker	17	333	19.6	2
Bunch	11	50	4.5	1
De. Brown	4	31	7.8	0
Smith	3	45	15.0	0
Tillman	1	15	15.0	0

PUNT RETURNS

Last Name	No.	Yds	Avg	TD
Meggett	27	240	8.9	0

KICKOFF RETURNS

Last Name	No.	Yds	Avg	TD
Meggett	20	455	22.8	1
Smith	30	564	18.8	0
Calloway	2	29	14.5	0
Bunch	2	27	13.5	0
Sparks	2	23	11.5	0

PASSING — PUNTING — KICKING

PASSING	Att	Cmp	%	Yds	Yd/Att	TD	Int—	%	RK
Hostetler	192	103	53.6	1225	6.38	8	3—	1.6	
Simms	137	83	60.6	912	6.66	5	3—	2.2	
Graham	97	42	43.3	470	4.85	1	4—	4.1	
Da. Brown	7	4	57.1	21	3.00	0	0—	0.0	

PUNTING	No.	Avg.
Landeta	55	42.1

KICKING	XP	ATT	%	FG	ATT	%
Bahr	29	29	**100**	16	21	76

PHOENIX CARDINALS

RUSHING

Last Name	No.	Yds	Avg	TD
Johnson	178	734	4.1	6
Bailey	52	233	4.5	1
Brown	68	194	2.9	2
Chandler	36	149	4.1	1
Centers	37	139	3.8	0
Proehl	3	23	7.7	0
Rosenbach	9	11	1.2	0
R. Hill	1	4	4.0	0
Blount	1	-1	-1.0	0
E. Jones	2	-3	-1.5	0

RECEIVING

Last Name	No.	Yds	Avg	TD
Proehl	60	744	12.4	3
R. Hill	58	861	14.8	3
Centers	50	417	8.3	2
E. Jones	38	559	14.7	4
Bailey	33	331	10.0	1
Edwards	14	147	10.5	1
Johnson	14	103	7.4	0
Rolle	13	64	4.9	0
Brown	7	54	7.7	0
Reeves	6	28	4.7	0
Blount	3	18	6.0	0
Ware	1	13	13.0	0
Jackson	1	5	5.0	0

PUNT RETURNS

Last Name	No.	Yds	Avg	TD
Bailey	20	263	**13.2**	0
Blount	13	101	7.8	0

KICKOFF RETURNS

Last Name	No.	Yds	Avg	TD
Bailey	28	690	24.6	0
Blount	11	251	22.8	0
Edwards	8	143	17.9	0
L. Smith	2	16	8.0	0
Jackson	1	17	17.0	0
Rolle	1	10	10.0	0

PASSING — PUNTING — KICKING

PASSING	Att	Cmp	%	Yds	Yd/Att	TD	Int—	%	RK
Chandler	413	245	59.3	2832	6.86	15	15—	3.6	8
Rosenbach	92	49	53.3	483	5.25	0	6—	6.5	
Sacca	11	4	36.4	29	2.64	0	2—	18.2	
Proehl	1	0	0.0	0	0.00	0	1—	100.0	

PUNTING	No.	Avg.
Camarillo	54	42.9
G. Davis	4	36.8

KICKING	XP	Att	%	FG	Att	%
Davis	28	28	**100**	13	26	50z

MINNESOTA VIKINGS 11-5 Dennis Green

Scores of Each Game		
23	Green Bay	*20
17	Detroit	31
26	TAMPA BAY	20
42	Cincinnati	7
21	CHICAGO	20
31	DETROIT	14
13	WASHINGTON	15
38	Chicago	10
35	Tampa Bay	7
13	HOUSTON	17
17	CLEVELAND	13
31	L.A. Rams	17
17	Philadelphia	28
17	SAN FRANCISCO	20
6	Pittsburgh	3
27	GREEN BAY	7

UseName	Pos.	Hgt.	Wgt.	Age	Int	Pts
Scott Adams	OT	6'5"	281	25		
Tim Irwin	OT	6'6"	297	33		
Gary Zimmerman	OT	6'6"	294	30		
Bernard Dafney	OG	6'5"	317	22		
Brian Habib	OG	6'7"	299	27		
Randall McDaniel	OG	6'3"	280	27		
Adam Schreiber	OG-C	6'4"	290	30		
Kirk Lowdermilk	C	6'3"	280	29		
Mike Morris	C	6'5"	273	31		
Chris Doleman	DE	6'5"	275	30	1	8
Robert Harris	DE	6'4"	285	23		
Al Noga	DE	6'1"	269	26		
Roy Barker	DT	6'4"	292	23		
Brad Culpepper	DT	6'1"	267	24		
George Hinkle	DT	6'5"	269	27		
John Randle	DT	6'1"	270	24		
Henry Thomas	DT	6'2"	285	27		
Esera Tuaolo (from GB)	DT	6'2"	275	24		

Lorenzo Freeman — Knee Injury
Todd Kalis — Knee Injury

UseName	Pos.	Hgt.	Wgt.	Age	Int	Pts
David Bavaro	LB	6'	228	25		
Ray Berry	LB	6'2"	227	28		
Jack Del Rio	LB	6'4"	250	29	2	6
Carlos Jenkins	LB	6'3"	222	24	1	12
Greg Manusky	LB	6'1"	237	26		
Ed McDaniel	LB	5'11"	232	23		
Mike Merriweather	LB	6'2"	226	31		
Van Waiters	LB	6'4"	250	27		
Eric Everett	DB	5'11"	170	25		
Vencie Glenn	DB	6'	189	27	5	
Carl Lee	DB	6'	182	31	2	
Audrey McMillian	DB	6'	190	30	8	12
Anthony Parker	DB	5'10"	179	26	3	6
Todd Scott	DB	5'10"	191	24	5	6
Tripp Welbourne	DB	6'	205	23		
David Wilson (from NE)	DB	5'10"	192	22		
Felix Wright	DB	6'2"	197	33	1	

Najee Mustafaa — Back Injury

UseName	Pos.	Hgt.	Wgt.	Age	Int	Pts
Rich Gannon	QB	6'3"	208	26		
Sean Salisbury	QB	6'5"	217	29		
Terry Allen	HB	5'10"	197	24		90
Roger Craig	HB	5'11"	181	31		24
Keith Henderson (from SF)	HB	6'1"	220	26		6
Darrin Nelson	HB	5'9"	180	33		
Anthony Carter	WR	5'11"	181	31		18
Cris Carter	WR	6'3"	198	26		36
Joe Johnson	WR	5'8"	170	29		6
Hassan Jones	WR	6'	202	28		24
Jake Reed	WR	6'3"	216	24		
Ronnie West	WR	6'1"	215	24		
Steve Jordan	TE	6'4"	240	31		12
Brent Novoselsky	TE	6'3"	237	26		
Derek Tennell (to DAL)	TE	6'5"	270	28		
Mike Tice	TE	6'7"	253	33		6
Danta Whitaker	TE	6'4"	254	28		
Harry Newsome	K	6'	185	29		
Fuad Reveiz	K	5'11"	226	29		102

GREEN BAY PACKERS 9-7 Mike Holmgren

Scores of Each Game		
20	MINNESOTA	*23
3	Tampa Bay	31
24	CINCINNATI	23
17	PITTSBURGH	3
10	Atlanta	24
6	Cleveland	17
10	CHICAGO	30
27	Detroit	13
7	N.Y. Giants	27
27	PHILADELPHIA	24
17	Chicago	3
19	TAMPA BAY	14
38	DETROIT	10
16	Houston	14
28	L.A. RAMS	13
7	Minnesota	27

UseName	Pos.	Hgt.	Wgt.	Age	Int	Pts
Cecil Gray	OT	6'4"	292	24		
Tootie Robbins	OT	6'5"	315	34		
Ken Ruettgers	OT	6'5"	286	30		
Harvey Salem	OT	6'6"	289	31		
Joe Sims	OT-OG	6'3"	294	23		
Ron Hallstrom	OG	6'6"	310	33		
Rich Moran	OG	6'3"	280	30		
Tom Neville	OG	6'5"	288	30		
Frank Winters	OG-C	6'3"	290	28		
David Viaene	OG-OT	6'5"	300	27		
James Campen	C	6'3"	280	28		
Lester Archambeau	DE	6'4"	275	25		
Sebastian Barrie	DE	6'3"	270	22		
Matt Brock	DE	6'5"	290	26		
Robert Brown	DE	6'2"	280	32		
Don Davey	DE	6'4"	280	24		
Keith Millard (from SEA)	DT	6'5"	263	30		
Danny Noonan (from DAL)	DT	6'4"	275	27		
John Jurkovic	NT	6'2"	300	25		
Alfred Oglesby	NT	6'3"	285	25		

Tony Mandarich — Thyroid Illness
Shawn Patterson — Knee INjury

UseName	Pos.	Hgt.	Wgt.	Age	Int	Pts
Tony Bennett	LB	6'2"	243	25		6
Jeff Brady	LB	6'1"	235	23		
Brett Collins	LB	6'1"	226	23		
Burnell Dent	LB	6'1"	238	29		
Mark D"Onofrio	LB	6'2"	235	23		
Johnny Holland	LB	6'2"	235	27	3	
George Koonce	LB	6'1"	238	23		
Brian Noble	LB	6'3"	250	29		
Bryce Paup	LB	6'5"	247	24		
Lewis Billups	DB	5'11"	182	28		
Terrell Buckley	DB	5'9"	174	21	3	12
LeRoy Butler	DB	6'	200	24	1	
Carl Carter	DB	5'11"	190	28		
Chuck Cecil	DB	6'	190	27	4	
Vinnie Clark	DB	6'	194	23	2	
Tim Hauck	DB	5'11"	181	25		
Dave McCloughan	DB	6'1"	185	25		
Buford McGee	FB					
Roland Mitchell	DB	5'11"	195	28	2	
Adrian White	DB	6'	205	28		

UseName	Pos.	Hgt.	Wgt.	Age	Int	Pts
Ty Detmer	QB	6'	183	24		
Brett Favre	QB	6'2"	220	22		6
Don Majkowski	QB	6'2"	203	28		
Darrell Thompson	HB	6'	222	24		18
Marcus Wilson	HB	6'1"	210	24		
Vince Workman	HB	5'10	205	24		12
Edgar Bennett	FB	6'	223	23		
Buford McGee	FB	6'	210	32		
Dexter McNabb	FB	6'2"	245	23		
Harry Sydney	FB	6'	217	33		18
Sanjay Beach	WR	6'1"	194	26		6
Robert Brooks	WR	6'	171	22		6
Corey Harris (from HOU)	WR	5'11"	195	22		
Ron Lewis (from SF)	WR	5'11"	180	24		
Sterling Sharpe	WR	5'11"	205	27		78
Kitrick Taylor	WR	5'11"	189	28		6
Jackie Harris	TE	6'3"	243	24		12
Darryl Ingram	TE	6'3"	250	26		
Ed West	TE	6'1"	244	31		
Chris Jacke	K	6'	197	26		96
Paul McJulien	K	5'10"	190	27		
Bryan Wagner	K	6'2"	200	30		

TAMPA BAY BUCCANEERS 5-11 Sam Wyche

Scores of Each Game		
23	PHOENIX	7
31	GREEN BAY	3
20	Minnesota	26
27	Detroit	23
14	INDIANAPOLIS	24
14	Chicago	31
7	DETROIT	38
21	New Orleans	23
7	MINNESOTA	35
20	CHICAGO	17
14	San Diego	29
14	Green Bay	19
27	L.A. RAMS	31
7	ATLANTA	35
14	San Francisco	21
7	Phoenix	3

UseName	Pos.	Hgt.	Wgt.	Age	Int	Pts
Scott Dill	OT	6'5"	285	26		
Paul Gruber	OT	6'5"	290	27		
Charles McRae	OT-OG	6'7"	300	23		
Rob Taylor	OT	6'6"	290	31		
Ian Beckles	OG	6'1"	295	25		
Brian Blados	OG	6'5"	296	30		
Tom McHale	OG	6'4"	290	29		
Bruce Reimers	OG	6'7"	300	31		
Tim Ryan	OG	6'2"	280	23		
Mike Sullivan	OG	6'3"	290	24		
Randy Grimes	C	6'4"	275	32		
Tony Mayberry	C	6'4"	290	24		
Al Chamblee	DE	6'1"	240	23		
Santana Dotson	DE	6'5"	270	22		6
Mark Duckens	DE-DT	6'4"	270	27		
Keith McCants	DE	6'3"	265	24		
Reggie Rogers	DE	6'6"	280	28		
Ray Seals	DE	6'3"	270	27		
David Grant	DT	6'5"	278	26		
Rhett Hall	DT	6'2"	260	23		
Mark Wheeler	NT-DT	6'2"	280	22		
Corey Mayfield	NT-DT	6'3"	280	22		

UseName	Pos.	Hgt.	Wgt.	Age	Int	Pts
Elijah Alexander	LB	6'2"	230	22		
Ed Brady	LB	6'2"	235	30		
Darrick Brownlow	LB	6'	235	23		
Reggie Burnette	LB	6'2"	240	23		
Sidney Coleman	LB	6'2"	250	28		
Broderick Thomas	LB	6'4"	250	25	2	6
Calvin Tiggle	LB	6'1"	235	23		
Jimmy Williams	LB	6'3"	230	31	2	
Darren Anderson (from NE)	DB	5'10"	180	23		
Chris Barber	DB	6'	187	28		
Joey Browner	DB	6'2"	231	32		
Marty Carter	DB	6'1"	200	22	3	
Tony Covington	DB	5'11"	190	24		
Darrell Fullington	DB	6'1"	200	28	3	
Rogerick Green	DB	5'10"	180	22		
Roger Jones	DB	5'9"	175	23		6
Joe King	DB	6'2"	200	24	2	
Garry Lewis	DB	5'11"	185	25	1	
Milton Mack	DB	5'11"	185	28	3	
Darryl Pollard	DB	5'11"	185	28	2	
Ricky Reynolds	DB	5'11"	190	27	2	6

UseName	Pos.	Hgt.	Wgt.	Age	Int	Pts
Steve DeBerg	QB	6'3"	215	38		
Craig Erickson	QB	6'2"	200	23		
Mike Pawlawski	QB	6'1"	205	23		
Vinny Testaverde	QB	6'5"	220	28		12
Gary Anderson	HB	6'	190	31		6
Reggie Cobb	HB-FB	6'	215	24		54
Stanford Jennings	HB	6'1"	210	30		6
Alonzo Highsmith	FB	6'1"	235	27		
Anthony McDowell	FB	5'11"	230	23		12
Mazio Royster	FB	6'1"	205	22		
Mike Barber	WR	5'11"	172	25		
Mark Carrier	WR	6'	185	26		24
Willie Culpepper	WR	5'11"	155	25		
Lawrence Dawsey	WR	6'	195	24		6
Willie Drewrey	WR	5'7"	170	29		12
Courtney Hawkins	WR	5'9"	180	22		12
Jeff Parker	WR	5'10"	185	23		
Charles Wilson	WR	5'10"	180	24		
Tyji Armstrong	TE	6'4"	255	21		6
Ron Hall	TE	6'4"	245	28		24
Todd Harrison	TE	6'4"	260	23		
Dave Moore (from MIA)	TE	6'2"	245	22		
Eddie Murray (from KC)	K	5'11"	185	36		28
Dan Stryzinski	K	6'1"	195	27		
Ken Willis (to NYG)	K	5'11"	190	25		57

CHICAGO BEARS 5-11 Mike Ditka

Scores of Each Game		
27	DETROIT	24
6	New Orleans	28
14	N.Y. GIANTS	27
41	ATLANTA	31
20	Minnesota	21
31	TAMPA BAY	14
30	Green Bay	10
10	MINNESOTA	38
28	CINCINNATI	*31
17	Tampa Bay	20
3	GREEN BAY	17
14	Cleveland	27
7	Houston	24
30	PITTSBURGH	6
3	Detroit	16
14	Dallas	27

UseName	Pos.	Hgt.	Wgt.	Age	Int	Pts
Louis Age	OT	6'7"	350	22		
Troy Auzenne	OT	6'7"	282	23		
Stan Thomas	OT	6'5"	290	23		
Keith Van Horne	OT	6'6"	290	34		
Mark Bortz	OG	6'6"	280	31		
Tom Thayer	OG	6'4"	280	31		
John Wojciechowski	OG-OT	6'4"	280	29		
Jerry Fontenot	C	6'3"	280	25		
Jay Leeuwenburg	C	6'2"	290	23		
Mark Rodenhauser	C	6'5"	265	31		
Trace Armstrong	DE	6'4"	275	26		
Richard Dent	DE	6'5"	265	31		
Alonzo Spellman	DE-DT	6'4"	280	20		
Steve McMichael	DT	6'2"	270	34		
William Perry	DT	6'2"	320	29		
Tim Ryan	DT-DE	6'4"	270	24		
James Williams	DT	6'7"	305	24		
Chris Zorich	DT	6'1"	267	23		6

UseName	Pos.	Hgt.	Wgt.	Age	Int	Pts
Ron Cox	LB	6'2"	242	24		
Dante Jones	LB	6'1"	240	27		
Jim Morrissey	LB	6'3"	227	29	1	
Ron Rivera	LB	6'3"	230	30		
John Roper	LB	6'1"	240	26		
Jim Schwantz	LB	6'2"	231	22		
Mike Singletary	LB	6'	240	33	1	
Mark Carrier	DB	6'1"	192	24		
Maurice Douglass	DB	5'11"	200	28		
Richard Fain	DB	5'10"	180	24		
Shaun Gayle	DB	5'11"	202	30	2	
John Mangum	DB	5'10"	178	25		
Markus Paul	DB	6'2"	205	26	1	
Lemuel Stinson	DB	5'9"	170	26	2	
David Tate	DB	6'	200	27		
Donnell Woolford	DB	5'9"	194	26	7	

UseName	Pos.	Hgt.	Wgt.	Age	Int	Pts
Will Furrer	QB	6'3"	208	24		
Jim Harbaugh	QB	6'3"	215	27		6
Peter Tom Willis	QB	6'2"	200	25		
Neal Anderson	HB	5'11"	218	28		66
Mark Green	HB	5'11"	195	25		12
Darren Lewis	HB-FB	5'10"	225	23		30
Bob Christian	FB	5'10"	215	23		
Brad Muster	FB	6'3"	235	27		30
Wendell Davis	WR	5'11"	194	26		12
Dennis Gentry	WR-HB	5'8"	180	33		
Glen Kozlowski	WR	6'1"	205	29		
Anthony Morgan	WR	6'1"	195	24		12
Ron Morris	WR	6'1'	200	27		
Tom Waddle	WR	6'	185	25		24
Barry Wagner	WR	6'3"	213	24		
Eric Wright	WR	6'	196	23		
Kelly Blackwell	TE	6'1"	255	23		
Keith Jennings	TE	6'4"	265	26		6
Kevin Butler	K	6'1"	190	30		91
Chris Gardocki	K	6'1"	196	22		

Jim Thornton — Arch Injury

DETROIT LIONS 5-11 Wayne Fontes

Scores of Each Game		
24	Chicago	27
31	MINNESOTA	17
10	Washington	13
23	TAMPA BAY	27
7	NEW ORLEANS	13
14	Minnesota	31
38	Tampa Bay	7
13	GREEN BAY	27
3	DALLAS	37
14	Pittsburgh	17
19	Cincinnati	13
21	HOUSTON	24
10	Green Bay	38
24	CLEVELAND	14
16	CHICAGO	3
6	San Francisco	24

UseName	Pos.	Hgt.	Wgt.	Age	Int	Pts
Lomas Brown	OT	6'4"	287	29		
Scott Conover	OT	6'4"	285	23		
Eric Sanders	OT-OG	6'7"	286	33		
Larry Tharpe	OT	6'4"	299	21		
Shawn Bouwens	OG	6'4"	290	24		
Ken Dallafior	OG	6'4"	283	33		
Jack Linn	OG-OT	6'5"	285	25		
Dennis McKnight	OG	6'3"	280	32		
Leonard Burton	C	6'3"	275	28		
Kevin Glover	C	6'2"	282	29		
Brad Leggett	C	6'4"	270	26		
Blake Miller	C	6'1"	282	24		
Dan Owens	DE	6'3"	280	25		
Robert Porcher	DE	6'3"	283	23		
Kelvin Pritchett	DE	6'2"	281	22		
Marc Spindler	DE	6'5"	290	21		
Jerry Ball	NT	6'1"	298	27		6
Lawrence Pete	NT	6'	290	26		

Eric Andolsek — Died in Offseason Accident

UseName	Pos.	Hgt.	Wgt.	Age	Int	Pts
Toby Caston	LB	6'1"	243	27		
Mike Cofer	LB	6'5"	244	32		
John Derby	LB	6"	232	24		
Dennis Gibson	LB	6'2"	243	28		
Tracy Hayworth	LB	6'3"	260	24		
George Jamison	LB	6'1"	235	29		
Troy Johnson	LB	6'2"	230	27		
Andre Jones	LB	6'2"	245	23		
Victor Jones	LB	6'2"	250	25		
Mike McDonald	LB	6'1"	240	34		
Tracy Scroggins	DB	6'2"	255	22		
Chris Spielman	LB	6'	247	26		
Bennie Blades	DB	6'1"	221	25	3	6
Willie Clay	DB	5'9"	184	21		
Harry Colon	DB	6'	203	23		
Ray Crockett	DB	5'9"	181	25	4	
Melvin Jenkins	DB	5'10"	173	30	4	6
Junior Robinson	DB	5'9"	181	24		
Kevin Scott	DB	5'9"	175	23	4	
Sheldon White	DB	5'11"	188	27	2	
William White	DB	5'10"	191	26	4	

UseName	Pos.	Hgt.	Wgt.	Age	Int	Pts
Erik Kramer	QB	6'1"	199	27		
Rodney Peete	QB	6'	193	26		
Andre Ware	QB	6'2"	205	24		
Eric Lynch	HB	5'10"	224	22		
Barry Sanders	HB-FB	5'8"	203	24		60
Troy Stradford (from LA)	HB	5'9"	194	27		
Don Overton	FB-HB	6'	221	24		
Ed Tillison	FB-HB	6'	225	23		
Reggie Barrett	WR	6'3"	215	23		6
Jeff Campbell	WR	5'8"	173	24		6
Mike Farr	WR	5'10"	181	25		
Mel Gray	WR	5'9"	162	31		12
Willie Green	WR	6'2"	181	26		30
Aubrey Matthews	WR	5'7"	165	29		
Herman Moore	WR	6'3"	210	22		24
Brett Perriman	WR	5'9"	180	26		24
Mike Hinnant	TE	6'3"	280	25		
Jimmie Johnson	TE	6'2"	255	25		
Thomas McLemore	TE	6'5"	245	22		
Jim Arnold	K	6'3"	211	31		
Jason Hanson	K	5'11"	183	22		93

Chuck Long — Shoulder Injury

MINNESOTA VIKINGS

RUSHING

Last Name	No.	Yds	Avg	TD
Allen	266	1201	4.5	13
Craig	105	416	4.0	4
Gannon	45	187	4.2	0
Henderson	44	150	3.4	1
A. Carter	16	66	4.1	1
J. Johnson	4	26	6.5	0
C. Carter	5	15	3.0	0
Nelson	10	5	0.5	0
Jones	1	1	1.0	0
Salisbury	11	0	0.0	0

RECEIVING

Last Name	No.	Yds	Avg	TD
C. Carter	53	681	12.8	6
Allen	49	478	9.8	2
A. Carter	41	580	14.1	2
Jordan	28	394	14.1	2
Jones	22	308	14.0	4
Craig	22	164	7.5	0
J. Johnson	21	211	10.0	1
Reed	6	142	23.7	0
Tice	5	65	13.0	1
Henderson	5	64	12.8	0
Novoselsky	4	63	15.8	0
Tennell	2	12	6.0	0
Whitaker	1	4	4.0	0

PUNT RETURNS

Last Name	No.	Yds	Avg	TD
Parker	33	336	10.2	0

KICKOFF RETURNS

Last Name	No.	Yds	Avg	TD
Nelson	29	626	21.6	0
Henderson	5	111	22.2	0
J. Johnson	5	79	15.8	0
Parker	2	30	15.0	0
West	2	27	13.5	0
Reed	1	1	1.0	0
Adams	1	0	0.0	0

PASSING — PUNTING — KICKING

PASSING	Att	Cmp	%	Yds	Yd/Att	TD	Int— %	RK
Gannon	279	159	57.0	1905	6.83	12	13—4.7	11
Salisbury	175	97	55.4	1203	6.87	5	2—1.1	
Henderson	1	1	100.0	36	36.00	1	0—0.0	
Jones	1	1	100.0	18	18.0	0	0—0.0	
A. Carter	1	0	0.0	0	0.00	0	0—0.0	
Newsome	1	0	0.0	0	0.00	0	0—0.0	

PUNTING	No.	Avg.
Newsome	73	44.4

KICKING	XP	ATT	%	FG	ATT	%
Reveiz	45	45	100	19	25	76

GREEN BAY PACKERS

RUSHING

Last Name	No.	Yds	Avg	TD
Workman	159	631	4.0	2
Thompson	76	255	3.4	2
E. Bennett	61	214	3.5	0
Favre	47	198	4.2	1
Sydney	51	163	3.2	2
Majkowski	8	33	4.1	0
McGee	8	19	2.4	0
Brooks	2	14	7.0	0
McNabb	2	11	5.5	0
C. Harris	2	10	5.0	0
Sharpe	4	8	2.0	0

RECEIVING

Last Name	No.	Yds	Avg	TD
Sharpe	108	1461	13.5	13
J. Harris	55	595	10.8	2
Sydney	49	384	7.8	1
Workman	47	290	6.2	0
Beach	17	122	7.2	1
Lewis	13	152	11.7	0
Thompson	13	129	9.9	1
E. Bennett	13	93	7.2	0
Brooks	12	126	10.5	1
McGee	6	60	10.0	0
West	4	30	7.5	0
Taylor	2	63	31.5	1
Favre	1	-7	-7.0	0

PUNT RETURNS

Last Name	No.	Yds	Avg	TD
Buckley	21	211	10.0	1
Brooks	11	102	9.3	0
C. Harris	6	17	2.8	0
Lewis	4	23	5.8	0
Hauck	1	2	2.0	0
Cecil	1	0	0.0	0
Clark	1	0	0.0	0

KICKOFF RETURNS

Last Name	No.	Yds	Avg	TD
C. Harris	33	691	20.9	0
Brooks	18	338	18.8	0
E. Bennett	5	104	20.8	0
Jurkovic	3	39	13.0	0
Workman	1	17	17.0	0
McNabb	1	15	15.0	0
Sims	1	11	11.0	0
Davey	1	8	8.0	0
West	1	0	0.0	0

PASSING — PUNTING — KICKING

PASSING	Att	Cmp	%	Yds	Yd/Att	TD	Int— %	RK
Favre	471	302	64.1	3227	6.85	18	13—2.8	5
Majkowski	55	38	69.1	271	4.93	2	2—3.6	
McJulian	1	0	0.0	0	0.00	0	0—0.0	

PUNTING	No.	Avg.
McJulien	38	36.5
Wagner	30	40.7

KICKING	XP	Att.	%	FG	Att	%
Jacke	30	30	100	22	20	76

TAMPA BAY BUCCANEERS

RUSHING

Last Name	No.	Yds	Avg	TD
Cobb	310	1171	3.8	9
Testaverde	36	197	5.5	2
G. Anderson	55	194	3.5	1
McDowell	14	81	5.8	0
Jennings	5	25	5.0	0
Highsmith	8	23	2.9	0
Stryzinski	1	7	7.0	0
DeBerg	3	3	1.0	0
Erickson	1	-1	-1.-	0

RECEIVING

Last Name	No.	Yds	Avg	TD
Dawsey	60	776	12.9	1
Carrier	56	692	12.4	4
Hall	39	351	9.0	4
G. Anderson	34	284	8.4	0
McDowell	27	258	9.6	2
Cobb	21	156	7.4	0
Hawkins	20	336	16.8	2
Drewrey	16	237	14.8	2
Jennings	9	69	7.7	1
Armstrong	7	138	19.7	1
Highsmith	5	28	5.6	0
Barber	1	32	32.0	0
Parker	1	12	12.0	0
Fullington	1	12	12.0	0
Moore	1	10	10.0	0
Royster	1	8	8.0	0

PUNT RETURNS

Last Name	No.	Yds	Avg	TD
Hawkins	13	53	4.1	0
Drewrey	7	62	8.9	0
Anderson	6	45	7.5	0

KICKOFF RETURNS

Last Name	No.	Yds	Avg	TD
G. Anderson	29	564	19.4	0
Hawkins	9	118	13.1	0
Ryan	2	24	12.0	0
Mayfield	2	22	11.0	0
Wilson	1	23	23.0	0
Chamblee	1	9	9.0	0

PASSING — PUNTING — KICKING

PASSING	Att	Cmp	%	Yds	Yd/Att	TD	Int— %	RK
Testaverde	358	206	57.5	2554	7.13	14	16—4.5	10
DeBerg	125	76	60.8	710	5.68	3	4—3.2	
Erickson	26	15	57.7	121	4.65	0	0—0.0	
Stryzinski	2	2	100.0	14	7.00	0	0—0.0	

PUNTING	No.	Avg.
Stryzinski	74	40.7

KICKING	XP	ATT	%	FG	ATT	%
Murray	13	13	100	4	8	50

CHICAGO BEARS

RUSHING

Last Name	No.	Yds	Avg	TD
Anderson	156	582	3.7	5
Muster	98	414	4.2	3
Lewis	90	382	4.2	4
Harbaugh	47	272	5.8	1
Green	23	107	4.7	2
Morgan	3	68	22.7	0
Davis	4	42	10.5	0
Gentry	5	2	0.4	0
Willis	1	2	2.0	0

RECEIVING

Last Name	No.	Yds	Avg	TD
Davis	54	734	13.6	2
Waddle	46	674	14.7	4
Anderson	42	399	9.5	6
Muster	34	389	11.4	2
Jennings	23	264	11.5	1
Lewis	18	175	9.7	0
Morgan	14	323	23.1	2
Gentry	12	114	9.5	0
Green	7	85	12.1	0
Wright	5	56	11.2	0
Blackwell	5	54	10.8	0
Morris	4	44	11.0	0
Wagner	1	16	16.0	0
Kozlowski	1	7	7.0	0

PUNT RETURNS

Last Name	No.	Yds	Avg	TD
Woolford	12	127	10.6	0
Waddle	8	28	3.5	0
Morgan	3	21	7.0	0

KICKOFF RETURNS

Last Name	No.	Yds	Avg	TD
Lewis	23	511	22.2	1
Gentry	16	330	20.6	0
Green	11	224	20.4	0
Morgan	4	71	17.8	0
Leeuwenburg	1	7	7.0	0
Rivera	1	0	0.0	0

PASSING — PUNTING — KICKING

PASSING	Att	Cmp	%	Yds	Yd/Att	TD	Int— %	RK
Harbaugh	358	202	56.4	2486	6.94	13	12—3.4	9
Willis	92	54	58.7	716	7.78	4	8—8.7	
Furrer	25	9	36.0	89	3.56	0	3—12.0	
Gardocki	3	1	33.3	43	14.33	0	0—0.0	
Muster	1	0	0.0	0	0.00	0	0—100.0	

PUNTING	No.	Avg.
Gardocki	79	42.9

KICKING	XP	ATT	%	FG	ATT	%
Butler	34	34	100	19	26	73

DETROIT LIONS

RUSHING

Last Name	No.	Yds	Avg	TD
B. Sanders	312	1352	4.3	9
Ware	20	124	6.2	0
Peete	21	83	4.0	0
Stradford	12	41	3.4	0
Kramer	12	34	2.8	0
Tillison	4	22	5.5	0

RECEIVING

Last Name	No.	Yds	Avg	TD
Perriman	69	810	11.7	4
Moore	51	966	18.9	4
Green	33	586	17.8	5
Sanders	29	225	7.8	1
Farr	15	115	7.7	0
Matthews	9	137	15.2	0
Campbell	8	155	19.4	1
J. Johnson	6	34	5.7	0
Barrett	4	67	16.8	1
Hinnant	3	28	9.3	0
Stradford	2	15	7.5	0
McLemore	2	12	6.0	0

PUNT RETURNS

Last Name	No.	Yds	Avg	TD
Gray	18	175	9.7	1
Campbell	3	15	5.0	0
Stradford	1	1	1.0	0

KICKOFF RETURNS

Last Name	No.	Yds	Avg	TD
Gray	42	1006	24.0	1
Stradford	7	94	13.4	0
Campbell	4	61	15.3	0
Perriman	4	59	14.8	0
Scott	3	5	1.7	0
Tillison	1	27	27.0	0
J. Johnson	1	0	0.0	0

PASSING — PUNTING — KICKING

PASSING	Att	Cmp	%	Yds	Yd/Att	TD	Int— %	RK
Peete	213	123	57.7	1702	7.99	9	9—4.2	
Kramer	106	58	54.7	771	7.27	4	8—7.5	
Ware	86	50	58.1	677	7.87	3	4—4.7	
Sanders	1	0	0.0	0	0.00	0	0—0.0	

PUNTING	No.	Avg.
Arnold	66	43.1

KICKING	XP	Att	%	FG	Att	%
Hanson	30	30	100	21	26	81

SAN FRANCISCO 49ERS 14-2 George Seifert

Scores of Each Game		
31	N.Y. Giants	14
31	BUFFALO	34
31	N.Y. Jets	14
16	New Orleans	10
27	L.A. RAMS	24
24	New England	12
56	ATLANTA	17
14	Phoenix	24
41	Atlanta	3
21	NEW ORLEANS	20
27	L.A. Rams	10
20	PHILADELPHIA	14
27	MIAMI	3
20	Minnesota	17
21	TAMPA BAY	14
24	DETROIT	6

UseName	Pos.	Hgt.	Wgt.	Age	Int	Pts
Harris Barton	OT	6'4"	286	28		
Harry Boatswain	OT	6'4"	295	23		
Steve Wallace	OT	6'5"	280	27		
Brian Bollinger	OG	6'5"	285	23		
Roy Foster	OG	6'4"	290	32		
Guy McIntyre	OG	6'3"	276	31		
Ralph Tamm	OG-C	6'4"	280	26		
Jesse Sapolu	C	6'4"	278	31		
Chuck Thomas	C	6'3"	280	31		
Dennis Brown	DE	6'4"	290	24	1	
Kevin Fagan	DE	6'4"	265	29		
Jacob Green	DE	6'3"	263	35		
Pierce Holt	DE	6'4"	280	30		
Larry Roberts	DE	6'3"	275	29	1	
Garin Veris	DE	6'4"	255	29		
Michael Carter	NT-DT	6'2"	285	31		
Ted Washington	NT-DE	6'4"	295	24		

UseName	Pos.	Hgt.	Wgt.	Age	Int	Pts
Keith DeLong	LB	6'2"	250	25	1	
Mitch Donahue	LB	6'2"	254	24		
Antonio Goss	LB	6'4"	228	26		
Tim Harris	LB-DE	6'6"	258	27		
Martin Harrison	LB	6'5"	240	24		
John Johnson	LB	6'3"	230	24	1	6
Darin Jordan	LB	6'2"	245	27		
Reggie McKenzie	LB	6'1"	239	29		
Bill Romanowski	LB	6'4"	240	26		
Michael Walter	LB	6'3"	246	31		
David Wilkins	LB	6'4"	240	23		
Eric Davis	DB	5'11"	178	24	3	
Thane Gash	DB	5'11"	198	26		
Alan Grant	DB	5'10"	187	25		
Don Griffin	DB	6'	180	28	5	
Dana Hall	DB	6'2"	206	23	2	
Merton Hanks	DB	6'2"	185	24	2	6
Johnny Jackson (to GB)	DB	6'1"	204	25		
Michael McGruder	DB	5'10"	190	28		
David Whitmore	DB	6'	217	25	1	

Kevin Lewis — Neck Injury
Rodney Thomas — Knee Injury

UseName	Pos.	Hgt.	Wgt.	Age	Int	Pts
Steve Bono	QB	6'4"	211	30		
Joe Montana	QB	6'2"	195	36		
Bill Musgrave	QB	6'2"	196	24		
Steve Young	QB	6'2"	205	30		24
Dexter Carter	HB	5'9"	170	24		6
Amp Lee	HB	5'11"	200	20		24
Marc Logan	HB	6'	212	27		6
Adam Walker	HB	6'1"	210	24		
Ricky Watters	HB	6'1"	212	23		66
Tom Rathman	FB	6'1"	232	29		54
Jerry Rice	WR	6'2"	200	29		66
Mike Sherrard	WR	6'2"	187	29		6
John Taylor	WR	6'1"	185	30		18
Odessa Turner	WR	6'3"	215	27		12
Chris Dressel	TE	6'4"	239	31		
Brent Jones	TE	6'4"	230	29		24
Jamie Williams	TE	6'4"	245	32		6
Mike Cofer	K	6'1"	190	28		107
Klaus Wilmsmeyer	K	6'1"	210	24		

Wesley Walls — Shoulder Injury

NEW ORLEANS SAINTS 12-4 Jim Mora

Scores of Each Game		
13	Philadelphia	15
28	CHICAGO	6
10	Atlanta	7
10	SAN FRANCISCO	16
13	Detroit	7
13	L.A. RAMS	10
30	Phoenix	21
23	TAMPA BAY	21
31	New England	14
20	San Francisco	21
20	WASHINGTON	3
24	MIAMI	13
22	ATLANTA	14
37	L.A. Rams	14
16	BUFFALO	20
20	N.Y. Jets	0

UseName	Pos.	Hgt.	Wgt.	Age	Int	Pts
Stan Brock	OT	6'6"	285	34		
Richard Cooper	OT	6'4"	290	27		
Jim Dombrowski	OG	6'5"	298	28		
Derek Kennard	OG	6'3"	300	29		
Chris Port	OG-OT	6'5"	290	24		
Steve Trapilo	OG	6'5"	289	27		
Joel Hilgenberg	C	6'3"	252	30		
Paul Jetton	C-OG	6'4"	288	27		
Gene McGuire	C	6'2"	284	22		
Wayne Martin	DE	6'5"	275	26		
Frank Warren	DE	6'4"	290	32		
Les Miller	NT-DE	6'7"	285	27		
Jim Wilks	NT	6'5"	275	33		
Robert Goff	NT-DE	6'3"	270	26		12

Kevin Haverdink — Back Injury

UseName	Pos.	Hgt.	Wgt.	Age	Int	Pts
Rickey Jackson	LB	6'2"	243	34		
Vaughan Johnson	LB	6'3"	235	30		
Sam Mills	LB	5'9"	225	33	1	6
Joel Smeenge	LB	6'5"	255	24		
Pat Swilling	LB	6'3"	242	27		
Renaldo Turnbull	DE	6'4"	255	26		
James Williams	LB	6'	230	23		
DeMond Winston	LB	6'2"	239	23		
Gene Atkins	DB	6'1"	200	27	3	
Vince Buck	DB	6'	198	24	2	6
Toi Cook	DB	5'11"	188	27	6	6
Antonio Gibson	DB	6'2"	210	30		
Reggie Jones	DB	6'1"	202	23	2	6
Tyrone Legette	DB	5'9"	177	22		
Sean Lumpkin	DB	6'	206	22		
Cedric Mack (from KC)	DB	5'11"	190	31		
Brett Maxie	DB	6'2"	194	30	2	
Jimmy Spencer	DB	5'9"	180	23		
Keith Taylor	DB	5'11"	206	27	2	

UseName	Pos.	Hgt.	Wgt.	Age	Int	Pts
Mike Buck	QB	6'3"	227	25		
Bobby Hebert	QB	6'4"	215	32		
Steve Walsh	QB	6'2"	210	25		
Vaughn Dunbar	HB	5'10"	204	23		18
Dalton Hilliard	HB	5'8"	204	28		42
Fred McAfee	HB	5'10"	193	24		6
Craig Heyward	FB	5'11"	260	25		18
Buford Jordan	FB	6'	223	30		
Wesley Carroll	WR	6'	183	24		12
Marcus Dowdell	WR	5'10"	179	22		
Quinn Early	WR	6'	190	27		30
Louis Lipps	WR	5'10"	193	30		
Eric Martin	WR	6'1"	207	30		30
Pat Newman	WR	5'11"	189	23		
Torrance Small	WR	6'3"	201	21		18
Floyd Turner	WR	5'11"	188	26		
Hoby Brenner	TE	6'4"	245	33		
Tommie Stowers	TE	6'3"	240	25		
John Tice	TE	6'5"	249	32		
Frank Wainright	TE	6'3"	236	24		
Morten Andersen	K	6'2"	221	32		**120**
Tommy Barnhardt	K	6'3"	207	29		

Allen Pinkett — Knee Injury

ATLANTA FALCONS 6-10 Jerry Glanville

Scores of Each Game		
20	N.Y. JETS	17
17	Washington	24
7	NEW ORLEANS	10
31	Chicago	41
24	GREEN BAY	10
17	Miami	21
17	San Francisco	56
30	L.A. RAMS	28
3	SAN FRANCISCO	41
20	PHOENIX	17
14	Buffalo	41
34	NEW ENGLAND	0
14	New Orleans	22
35	Tampa Bay	7
17	DALLAS	41
27	L.A. Rams	38

UseName	Pos.	Hgt.	Wgt.	Age	Int	Pts
Chris Hinton	OT	6'4"	300	31		
Mike Kenn	OT	6'7"	280	36		
Bob Whitfield	OT	6'5"	291	20		
John Buddenberg	OG	6'6"	270	23		
Roman Fortin	OG	6'5"	285	25		
Bill Fralic	OG	6'5"	280	29		
Houston Hoover	OG	6'2"	295	27		
Jamie Dukes	C	6'1"	285	28		
Mike Ruether	C	6'4"	286	29		
Mike Gann	DE	6'5"	270	28		
Oliver Barnett	DE-DT	6'3"	288	26		
Tim Green	DE	6'2"	245	28		
Chuck Smith	DE	6'2"	242	22		
Tory Epps	NT	6'	280	25		
Moe Gardner	NT	6'2"	258	24		
Bill Goldberg	NT	6'2"	266	22		

Rick Bryan — Neck Injury
Dave Zawatson — Elbow Injury

UseName	Pos.	Hgt.	Wgt.	Age	Int	Pts
Darion Conner	LB	6'2"	245	24		
Eric Fairs	LB	6'3"	244	28		
Michael Reid	LB	6'2"	235	28		
Jesse Solomon	LB	6'	235	28	1	
Kenny Tippins	LB	6'1"	230	26		
Jessie Tuggle	LB	5'11"	230	27	1	6
Bobby Butler	DB	5'11"	175	33		
Scott Case	DB	6'	188	30	2	
Jeff Donaldson	DB	6'	190	30		
Joe Fishback (from NYJ)	DB	6'	212	24		
Tim McKyer	DB	6'	174	28	1	
Brian Mitchell	DB	5'9"	164	23	1	
Bruce Pickens	DB	5'11"	190	24	2	
Terry Ray	DB	6'1"	187	22		
Louis Riddick	DB	6'2"	216	23		
Deion Sanders	DB	6'	185	25	3	18
Elbert Shelley	DB	5'11"	185	27		
Charles Washington	DB	6'1"	217	25		

Brian Forde — Knee Injury
John Rade — Knee Injury
Tracey Eaton — Knee Injury

UseName	Pos.	Hgt.	Wgt.	Age	Int	Pts
Chris Miller	QB	6'2"	205	27		
Billy Joe Tolliver	QB	6'1"	218	26		
Wade Wilson	QB	6'3"	210	33		
Steve Broussard	HB	5'7"	201	25		12
Erric Pegram	HB	5'9"	188	23		
Tony Smith	HB	6'1"	214	22		12
Keith Jones	FB	6'1"	210	26		
Michael Haynes	WR	6'	180	26		60
Drew Hill	WR	5'9"	172	35		18
Tony Jones	WR	5'7"	145	26		6
James Milling	WR	5'9"	160	27		
Jason Phillips	WR	5'7"	166	25		6
Mike Pritchard	WR	5'11"	180	22		30
Andre Rison	WR	6'	188	25		66
George Thomas (to TB)	WR	5'9"	169	28		
Harper LeBel	TE	6'4"	245	29		
Scott Fulhage	K	5'11"	193	30		
Norm Johnson	K	6'2"	203	32		93

LOS ANGELES RAMS 6-10 Chuck Knox

Scores of Each Game		
7	Buffalo	40
14	NEW ENGLAND	0
10	Miami	26
18	N.Y. JETS	10
24	San Francisco	27
10	New Orleans	13
38	N.Y. GIANTS	17
28	Atlanta	30
14	PHOENIX	20
27	Dallas	23
10	SAN FRANCISCO	27
17	MINNESOTA	31
31	Tampa Bay	27
14	NEW ORLEANS	37
13	Green Bay	28
38	ATLANTA	27

UseName	Pos.	Hgt.	Wgt.	Age	Int	Pts
Robert Jenkins	OT	6'5"	285	28		
Gerald Perry	OT	6'6"	305	27		
Jackie Slater	OT	6'4"	287	38		
Joe Milinichik	OG	6'5"	290	29		
Tom Newberry	OG	6'2"	285	29		
Jeff Pahukoa	OG-OT	6'2"	298	23		
Bern Brostek	C	6'3"	300	25		
Blair Bush	C	6'3"	275	35		
Bill Hawkins	DE	6'6"	269	26		
Warren Powers	DE	6'6"	287	27		
Gerald Robinson	DE	6'3"	262	29		
Jim Skow (from SD)	DE	6'3"	250	29		
Robert Young	DE	6'6"	277	23		
Marc Boutte	DT	6'4"	298	23		
Sean Gilbert	DT	6'4"	315	22		
Eric Hayes	DT	6'3"	288	24		
Mark Piel	DT	6'4"	270	26		
David Rocker	DT	6'4"	267	23		

UseName	Pos.	Hgt.	Wgt.	Age	Int	Pts
Paul Butcher	LB	6'	230	28		
Kevin Greene	LB	6'3"	247	30		2
Larry Kelm	LB	6'4"	240	27	1	
Roman Phifer	LB	6'2"	230	24	1	
Scott Stephen	LB	6'3"	243	28		
Fred Strickland	LB	6'2"	250	26		
Leon White	LB	6'3"	242	28	2	
Robert Bailey	DB	5'9"	176	23	3	6
Chris Crooms	DB	6'2"	211	23		
Darryl Henley	DB	5'9"	172	25	4	
Steve Israel	DB	5'10"	186	23		
Sammy Lilly	DB	5'9"	178	27		
Todd Lyght	DB	6'	185	23	3	
Anthony Newman	DB	6'	199	26	4	
Michael Stewart	DB	5'11"	195	27		
Pat Terrell	DB	6'	195	24		

UseName	Pos.	Hgt.	Wgt.	Age	Int	Pts
Jim Everett	QB	6'5"	212	29		
Mike Pagel	QB	6'2"	220	31		
Cleveland Gary	HB	6'	226	26		60
David Lang	HB-FB	5'11"	201	25		36
Anthony Thompson (from PHX)	HB	6'	210	25		6
Robert Delpino	FB	6'	205	26		6
Tim Lester	FB	5'9"	215	24		
Willie Anderson	WR	6'	175	27		42
Jeff Chadwick	WR	6'3"	185	31		18
Aaron Cox	WR	5'9"	178	27		
Henry Ellard	WR	5'11"	182	31		18
Todd Kinchen	WR	6'	187	23		12
Vernon Turner	WR	5'8"	185	25		
Pat Carter	TE	6'4"	255	26		18
Damone Johnson	TE	6'4"	250	30		
Travis McNeal	TE	6'3"	244	25		
Jim Price	TE	6'4"	247	29		12
Don Bracken	K	6'1"	211	30		
Tony Zendejas	K	5'8"	165	32		83

SAN FRANCISCO 49ERS

RUSHING

Last Name	No.	Yds	Avg	TD
Watters	206	1013	4.9	9
Young	76	537	7.1	4
Lee	91	362	4.0	2
Rathman	57	194	3.4	5
Rice	9	58	6.4	1
Logan	8	44	5.5	1
Montana	3	28	9.3	0
Bono	15	23	1.5	0
Taylor	1	10	10.0	0
D. Carter	4	9	2.3	0
Wilmsmeyer	2	0	0.0	0

RECEIVING

Last Name	No.	Yds	Avg	TD
Rice	84	1201	14.3	10
Jones	45	628	14.0	4
Rathman	44	343	7.8	4
Watters	43	405	9.4	2
Sherrard	38	607	16.0	0
Taylor	25	428	17.1	3
Lee	20	102	5.1	2
Turner	9	200	22.2	2
Williams	7	76	10.9	1
Logan	2	17	8.5	0
D. Carter	1	43	43.0	1

PUNT RETURNS

Last Name	No.	Yds	Avg	TD
Grant	29	249	8.6	0
Griffin	6	69	11.5	0
Hanks	1	48	48.0	1

KICKOFF RETURNS

Last Name	No.	Yds	Avg	TD
Logan	22	478	21.7	0
Lee	14	276	19.7	0
Grant	3	70	23.3	0
D. Carter	2	55	27.5	0
Turner	1	0	0.0	0

PASSING — PUNTING — KICKING

PASSING	Att	Cmp	%	Yds	Yd/Att	TD	Int—	%	RK
Young	402	268	66.7	3465	8.62	25	7—	1.7	1
Bono	56	36	64.3	463	8.27	2	2—	3.6	
Montana	21	15	71.4	126	6.00	2	0—	0.0	
Watters	1	0	0.0	0	0.00	0	0—	0.0	

PUNTING	No.	Avg.
Wilmsmeyer	49	39.1

KICKING	XP	ATT	%	FG	ATT	%
Cofer	53	54	98	18	27	67

NEW ORLEANS SAINTS

RUSHING

Last Name	No.	Yds	Avg	TD
Dunbar	154	565	3.7	3
Hilliard	115	445	3.9	3
Heyward	104	416	4.0	3
McAfee	39	114	2.9	1
Hebert	32	95	3.0	0
Early	3	-1	-0.3	0
Barnhardt	4	-2	-0.5	0
M. Buck	3	-4	-1.3	0

RECEIVING

Last Name	No.	Yds	Avg	TD
E. Martin	68	1041	15.3	5
Hilliard	48	465	9.7	4
Early	30	566	18.9	5
Small	23	278	12.1	3
Heyward	19	159	8.4	0
Carroll	18	292	16.2	2
Brenner	12	161	13.4	0
Wainright	9	143	15.9	0
Dunbar	9	62	6.9	0
Turner	5	43	8.6	0
Stowers	4	23	5.8	0
Newman	3	21	7.0	0
McAfee	1	16	16.0	0
Dowdell	1	6	6.0	0
Lipps	1	1	1.0	0
Cooper	0	20	—	0

PUNT RETURNS

Last Name	No.	Yds	Avg	TD
Newman	23	158	6.9	0
Dowdell	12	37	3.1	0
Lipps	5	22	4.4	0
Turner	3	10	3.3	0
V. Buck	2	4	2.0	0

KICKOFF RETURNS

Last Name	No.	Yds	Avg	TD
McAfee	19	393	20.7	0
Dunbar	10	187	18.7	0
Hilliard	7	130	18.6	0
Newman	3	62	20.7	0
Jordan	1	18	18.0	0
Heyward	1	14	14.0	0
Kennard	1	11	11.0	0

PASSING — PUNTING — KICKING

PASSING	Att	Cmp	%	Yds	Yd/Att	TD	Int—	%	RK
Hebert	422	249	59.0	3287	7.79	19	16—	3.8	6
M. Buck	4	2	50.0	10	2.50	0	0—	0.0	

PUNTING	No.	Avg.
Barnhardt	67	44.0

KICKING	XP	ATT	%	FG	ATT	%
Andersen	33	34	97	29	34	85

ATLANTA FALCONS

RUSHING

Last Name	No.	Yds	Avg	TD
Broussard	84	363	4.3	1
T. Smith	87	329	3.8	2
K. Jones	79	278	3.5	0
Miller	23	89	3.9	0
Pegram	21	89	4.2	0
Wilson	15	62	4.1	0
Pritchard	5	37	7.4	0
Tolliver	4	15	3.8	0
Solomon	2	12	6.0	0
Fulhage	1	0	0.0	0
Sanders	1	-4	-4.0	0

RECEIVING

Last Name	No.	Yds	Avg	TD
Rison	93	1121	12.1	11
Pritchard	77	827	10.7	5
Hill	60	623	10.4	3
Haynes	48	808	16.8	10
T. Jones	14	138	9.9	1
K. Jones	12	94	7.8	0
Broussard	11	96	8.7	1
Thomas	6	54	9.0	0
Phillips	4	26	6.5	1
Sanders	3	45	15.0	1
Milling	3	25	8.3	0
Pegram	2	25	12.5	0
T. Smith	2	14	7.0	0
Hinton	1	-2	-2.0	0

PUNT RETURNS

Last Name	No.	Yds	Avg	TD
T. Smith	16	155	9.7	0
Sanders	13	41	3.2	0

KICKOFF RETURNS

Last Name	No.	Yds	Avg	TD
Sanders	40	1067	26.7	2
Pegram	9	161	17.9	0
T. Smith	7	172	24.6	0
K. Jones	6	114	19.0	0
Barnett	1	13	13.0	0
Fortin	1	5	5.0	0

PASSING — PUNTING — KICKING

PASSING	Att	Cmp	%	Yds	Yd/Att	TD	Int—	%	RK
Miller	253	152	60.1	1739	6.87	15	6—	2.4	2
Wilson	163	111	68.1	1368	8.39	13	4—	2.5	
Tolliver	131	73	55.7	787	6.01	5	5—	3.8	
K. Jones	1	0	0.0	0	0.00	0	0—	0.0	

PUNTING	No.	Avg.
Fulhage	69	40.8
Johnson	1	37.0

KICKING	XP	Att	%	FG	Att	%
N. Johnson	39	39	100	18	22	82

LOS ANGELES RAMS

RUSHING

Last Name	No.	Yds	Avg	TD
Gary	279	1125	4.0	7
Lang	33	203	6.2	5
Everett	32	133	4.2	0
Delpino	32	115	3.6	0
Thompson	19	65	3.4	1
Turner	2	14	7.0	0
Pagel	1	0	0.0	0

RECEIVING

Last Name	No.	Yds	Avg	TD
Gary	52	293	5.6	3
Ellard	47	727	15.5	3
Anderson	38	657	17.3	7
Price	34	324	9.5	2
Chadwick	29	362	12.5	3
Carter	20	232	11.6	3
Lang	18	283	15.7	1
Cox	18	261	14.5	0
Delpino	18	139	7.7	1
Turner	5	42	8.4	0
Thompson	5	11	2.2	0
McNeal	4	79	19.8	0

PUNT RETURNS

Last Name	No.	Yds	Avg	TD
Turner	28	207	7.4	0
Kinchen	4	103	25.8	2

KICKOFF RETURNS

Last Name	No.	Yds	Avg	TD
Turner	29	569	19.6	0
Lang	13	228	17.5	0
Delpino	6	83	13.8	0
Thompson	4	34	8.5	0
Kinchen	4	63	15.8	0
Stephen	2	12	6.0	0
Anderson	1	9	9.0	0
Israel	1	-3	-3.0	0

PASSING — PUNTING — KICKING

PASSING	Att	Cmp	%	Yds	Yd/Att	TD	Int—	%	RK
Everett	475	281	59.2	3323	7.00	22	18—	3.8	7
Pagel	20	8	40.0	99	4.95	1	2—	10.0	

PUNTING	No.	Avg.
Bracken	76	41.1

KICKING	XP	ATT	%	FG	ATT	%
Zendejas	38	38	100	15	20	75

1992 A.F.C. New Coaches Are A Big Success

Beginner's luck became a part of pro football in 1992, with most of the nine new head coaches having very successful debuts. Three of them led their teams to division titles — San Diego's Bobby Ross, Pittsburgh's Bill Cowher and Minnesota's Dennis Green. Two other coaches — the Colts' Ted Marchibroda and the Packers' Mike Holmgren — had their teams in the playoff race until late in the season. Other new coaches were Cincinnati's Dave Shula, Seattle's Tom Flores, Tampa Bay's Sam Wyche and the Rams' Chuck Knox.

When the season ended, all nine of them still had their jobs, but four others had been fired — Chicago's Mike Ditka, New England's Dick MacPherson, the Giants' Ray Handley and Denver's Dan Reeves. Washington's Joe Gibbs retired after three Super Bowls.

Tragedy continued to impose upon the NFL. In the offseason, Philadelphia's Jerome Brown and Detroit's Eric Andolsek were killed in traffic accidents, and Indianapolis' Shane Curry was shot and killed by a teenager in a parking lot. During the season, the Jets' Dennis Byrd was paralyzed during a game. It was the second straight season a player has had his life changed because of a football injury.

EASTERN DIVISION

Miami Dolphins — The Dolphins won their first division title since 1985. With a 6-0 start, they brought back memories of the 1972 unbeaten team. Then reality struck, as they lost five of seven games before ending with three consecutive victories. The October acquisition of free-agent Keith Jackson was a big lift for the team and gave quarterback Dan Marino another weapon in his arsenal. However, the Dolphins offense struggled late in the season, scoring only six touchdowns in the last five and a half games. The Dolphins found a defense in 1992, with new stars such as Troy Vincent, Marco Coleman and Bryan Cox. They won their first playoff game in seven years, shutting out San Diego, before falling to the eventual AFC champion Bills. Head coach Don Shula got his 300th NFL victory in Week 16, and was less than a full season away from catching George Halas on the career victories list.

Buffalo Bills — Three years, three Super Bowls and three super losses. The Bills joined the Broncos and Vikings as kings of the Super Bowl losers, after being demolished by Dallas in Pasadena 52-17. They even failed to win the AFC East crown in 1992, losing out to Miami to a tiebreaker. But it was still a very successful season in Buffalo. The defense, led by league interception leader Henry Jones, improved, and Thurman Thomas led the league in total yards for the fourth straight year, breaking Jim Brown's record. Quarterback Jim Kelly was red-hot for half a season, but he threw a league-high 19 interceptions before getting injured. Backup quarterback Frank Reich will always be remembered for leading the Bills to a victory over Houston in the playoffs after trailing by 32 points in the third quarter.

Indianapolis Colts — The Colts completed one of the best turnarounds in NFL history, going from 1-15 to 9-7 under new head coach Ted Marchibroda. They won their last five games by a total of only 20 points. It was a remarkable comeback, considering quarterback Jeff George struggled and the running game was weak. Even Steve Emtman and Quentin Coryatt, who the Colts drafted with the first two overall picks in the draft, were injured and missed the last two months of the season. Both of them, however, proved to be impact players, as did rookie halfback Rodney Culver, who scored nine touchdowns. Backup quarterback Jack Trudeau was calm in the storm when George was injured for six games.

New York Jets — The Jets' rebuilding took a step backward in 1992. Overconfidence after a 5-0 preseason played a major role, and they lacked an impact player on either side of the ball. But other factors were out of their control. Wide receiver Al Toon retired after suffering too many concussions, and defensive end Dennis Byrd was paralyzed in a November game after colliding with teammate Scott Mersereau. Quarterback Browning Nagle was given the starting job in training camp but failed to excite. He passed for 366 yards in the season opener, then struggled mightily the rest of the year. Defensive end Jeff Lageman was lost in Week Two with a knee injury, and running back Blair Thomas was again disappointing, even before missing half of the year.

New England Patriots — The Patriots were 1992's version of Team Turmoil. Too much was expected of them from the start, and they didn't have the talent to match their 6-10 mark in 1991. Coach Dick MacPherson was hospitalized with diverticulitis and missed the next seven games. The team was shut out three games and was forced to start four quarterbacks (Hugh Millen, Tommy Hodson, Scott Zolak and Jeff Carlson). The running game — especially second-year back Leonard Russell — was abysmal, with only 1,550 yards and six TD's. Receivers Irving Fryar and Marv Cook were consistent. Chief executive officer Sam Jankovich fired MacPherson after the season ended, then quit himself a day later. Bill Parcells, who led the Giants to two Super Bowl titles, was hired as the next coach, and hopes were raised immediately.

CENTRAL DIVISION

Pittsburgh Steelers — New head coach Bill Cowher, only 35 years old, infused the team with new enthusiasm, and the Steelers won their first division title since 1984. It was also the Steelers' first 11-win season since 1979, when they last won a Super Bowl. But Barry Foster was the story of the year. He led the conference in rushing with 1,690 yards and 11 touchdowns. Besides breaking many of Franco Harris' team records, he tied Eric Dickerson's league record with 12 100-yard games in a season. Quarterback Neil O'Donnell was 9-3 as the starter before going out with a broken leg. Cornerback Rod Woodson was his usual All-Pro self, and solid showings were turned in by wide receiver Jeff Graham and rookie safety Darren Perry. Tight end Eric Green had his troubles and was suspended by the league for substance abuse.

Houston Oilers — Houston earned its NFL-best sixth straight postseason appearance during an up-and-down season. Like the Steelers, the Oilers operated down the stretch without their starting quarterback, with Cody Carlson taking over for the injured Warren Moon until the playoffs. Lorenzo White, who rushed for 1,226 yards, emerged as a star in a backfield that was far less crowded than in past years. With 90 catches, Haywood Jeffires led the AFC in receptions for the third straight year, and Ernest Givins led the AFC with 10 TD receptions. The Houston defense was again strong, ranking No. 1 in the AFC and No. 3 in the NFL. With an offense that finished second in the AFC, no other conference team could claim that kind of balance. But the season ended after Houston blew a 32-point lead against Buffalo in the playoffs.

Cleveland Browns — With a playoff berth at stake entering Week 15, the Browns promptly lost three straight games for their third consecutive losing season. They lacked any real explosiveness on offense, especially after quarterback Bernie Kosar went down with a broken ankle in the second game (and then again in the season finale). Todd Philcox was injured next, and then Mike Tomczak was signed for most of the rest of the season. No Cleveland players finished among the conference leaders in any major offensive category, especially the running backs who rotated all year long. Wide receiver Michael Jackson did catch seven touchdown passes. Linebacker Clay Matthews, the NFL's oldest defensive player, continued to set team marks for longevity and career sacks.

Cincinnati Bengals — Dave Shula took over as the youngest head coach in the league, and, even though a 2-0 start had everybody thinking he was as good as his father Don, the team finished with back-to-back 10-loss seasons for the first time in over a decade. Two five-game losing streaks were the main culprit. Boomer Esiason finished the season as the backup to rookie David Klingler, who became the team's quarterback of the present when he was surprisingly drafted early in the first round during the offseason. Another era ended when tackle Anthony Munoz announced his retirement following 13 seasons of dominating line play (though he was injured much of the season). Among the positives were running back Harold Green (who had 1,170 yards) and nose tackle Tim Krumrie, who led the defense with 97 tackles. Rookies Carl Pickens, Darryl Williams and Ricardo McDonald were impressive.

FINAL TEAM STATISTICS

OFFENSE

	BUFF	CIN	CLEV	DEN	HOU	IND	K.C.	L.A.	MIA	N.E.	NYJ	PITT	S.D.	SEA
FIRST DOWNS:														
Total	350	248	242	234	339	267	246	259	316	215	252	284	302	208
by Rushing	133	112	85	84	101	70	87	99	101	71	94	119	118	77
by Passing	192	114	141	135	217	174	134	139	194	130	137	143	161	114
by Penalty	25	22	16	15	21	23	25	21	21	14	21	22	23	17
RUSHING:														
Number	549	454	451	403	353	379	446	434	407	419	424	518	489	402
Yards	2436	1976	1607	1500	1626	1102	1532	1794	1525	1550	1752	2156	1875	1596
Average Yards	4.4	4.4	3.6	3.7	4.6	2.9	3.4	4.1	3.7	3.7	4.1	4.2	3.8	4.0
Touchdowns	18	11	7	11	10	8	14	7	9	6	8	13	18	4
PASSING:														
Attempts	509	435	398	473	573	546	413	471	563	444	495	431	496	476
Completions	293	227	238	258	373	305	230	233	332	244	251	249	282	230
Completion Pct.	57.6	52.2	59.8	54.5	65.1	55.9	55.7	49.5	59.0	55.0	50.7	57.8	56.9	48.3
Passing Yards	3678	2284	3102	3312	4231	3584	3115	2950	4148	2492	2962	3046	3614	2323
Avg. Yds per Att.	6.4	4.1	6.7	5.6	6.7	5.5	6.1	5.0	6.7	4.0	5.0	5.8	6.3	3.3
Avg. Yds per Comp.	12.6	10.1	13.0	12.8	11.3	11.8	13.5	12.7	12.5	10.2	11.8	12.2	12.8	10.1
Times Tackled	29	45	34	52	32	44	48	48	28	65	39	40	33	67
Yds Lost Tackled	221	341	217	382	202	318	323	360	173	458	283	290	268	545
Net Yards	3457	1943	2885	2930	4029	3266	2792	2590	3975	2034	2679	2750	3346	1778
Touchdowns	23	16	18	16	27	13	15	20	24	13	12	15	16	9
Interceptions	21	17	16	29	23	26	12	23	17	19	24	14	21	23
Pct. Intercepted	4.1	3.9	4.0	6.1	4.0	4.8	2.9	4.9	3.0	4.3	4.8	3.2	4.2	4.8
PUNTS:														
Number	60	76	75	85	55	83	86	77	61	103	73	74	68	108
Average	42.2	42.1	41.1	43.6	45.2	44.8	42.2	42.3	39.7	41.0	41.0	42.1	42.6	44.1
PUNT RETURNS														
Number	43	24	44	34	33	25	39	41	31	37	30	32	44	38
Yards	464	285	429	353	194	275	402	402	191	274	232	364	359	283
Average Yards	10.8	11.9	9.8	10.4	5.9	11.0	10.3	9.8	6.2	7.4	7.7	11.4	8.2	7.4
Touchdowns	0	1	1	0	0	2	2	0	0	0	0	1	0	0
KICKOFF RET.:														
Number	41	59	43	51	46	51	39	43	44	64	54	48	45	50
Yards	761	1058	880	1028	885	1001	722	744	838	1376	950	847	812	885
Average Yards	18.6	17.9	20.5	20.2	19.2	19.6	18.5	17.3	19.0	21.5	17.6	17.6	18.0	17.7
Touchdowns	0	0	0	0	0	0	0	0	0	1	0	0	0	0
INTERCEPT RET.:														
Number	23	16	13	15	20	20	24	12	18	14	21	22	25	20
Yards	325	205	222	210	181	302	403	339	458	285	269	384	405	324
Average Yards	14.1	12.8	17.1	14.0	9.1	15.1	16.8	28.3	25.4	20.4	12.8	17.5	16.2	16.2
Touchdowns	2	1	1	1	1	1	6	1	3	3	3	1	1	0
PENALTIES:														
Number	103	98	104	98	111	122	82	113	86	111	107	106	91	111
Yards	775	755	765	768	824	958	675	832	656	1051	873	941	813	918
FUMBLES:														
Number	31	32	19	29	28	24	28	25	31	43	28	28	26	37
Number Lost	17	10	12	14	12	11	9	15	17	26	15	18	12	18
POINTS:														
Total	381	274	272	262	352	216	348	249	340	205	220	299	335	140
PAT Attempts	44	31	30	29	41	24	40	29	36	25	23	31	36	14
PAT Made	43	31	29	28	41	24	39	28	34	22	23	29	35	14
FG Attempts	30	28	29	25	27	29	25	26	37	17	30	36	32	22
FG Made	24	19	21	20	21	16	23	15	30	11	19	28	26	14
Percent FG Made	80.0	67.9	72.4	80.0	77.8	55.2	92.0	57.7	81.1	64.7	63.3	77.8	81.3	63.6
Safeties	1	0	0	0	1	0	0	1	0	0	1	0	3	0

DEFENSE

	BUFF	CIN	CLEV	DEN	HOU	IND	K.C.	L.A.	MIA	N.E.	NYJ	PITT	S.D.	SEA
FIRST DOWNS:														
Total	278	319	281	283	254	314	256	264	273	292	276	266	250	247
by Rushing	77	126	86	105	93	129	97	104	92	112	110	99	80	96
by Passing	185	168	170	156	139	164	145	135	168	149	146	146	157	129
by Penalty	16	25	25	22	22	21	14	25	13	31	20	21	13	22
RUSHING:														
Number	427	490	429	489	412	495	441	478	428	521	460	435	365	513
Yards	1395	2007	1605	1963	1634	2174	1787	1683	1600	1951	1919	1841	1395	1922
Average Yards	3.3	4.1	3.7	4.0	4.0	4.4	4.1	3.5	3.7	3.7	4.2	4.2	3.8	3.7
Touchdowns	8	15	5	10	6	16	12	17	9	15	13	6	10	14
PASSING:														
Attempts	520	489	486	462	445	470	458	450	512	459	465	478	491	428
Completions	305	288	291	268	248	260	253	243	294	258	257	252	271	251
Completion Pct.	58.7	58.9	59.9	58.0	55.7	55.3	55.2	54.0	57.4	56.2	55.3	52.7	55.2	58.6
Passing Yards	3560	3620	3467	3437	2898	3236	2928	3153	3266	3211	3201	3065	3188	2978
Avg. Yds per Att.	5.7	6.2	5.9	6.1	5.2	5.7	5.0	5.7	5.4	6.5	5.9	5.5	5.2	5.6
Avg. Yds per Comp.	11.7	12.6	11.9	12.8	11.7	12.5	11.6	13.0	11.1	12.5	12.5	12.2	11.8	11.9
Times Tackled	44	45	48	50	50	39	50	46	36	20	36	36	51	46
Yds Lost Tackled	351	294	315	317	321	336	391	320	283	114	240	248	356	317
Net Yards	3209	3326	3152	3120	2577	2900	2537	2833	2983	3097	2961	2817	2832	2661
Touchdowns	19	24	23	21	20	14	19	11	16	22	19	15	17	11
Interceptions	23	16	13	15	20	20	24	12	18	14	21	22	25	20
Pct. Intercepted	4.4	3.3	2.7	3.2	4.5	4.3	5.2	2.7	3.5	3.1	4.5	4.6	5.1	4.7
PUNTS:														
Number	79	57	74	78	68	71	80	85	74	75	70	74	80	96
Average	43.9	41.8	44.5	43.3	43.2	42.5	43.1	42.5	40.1	40.6	40.9	42.0	44.6	41.8
PUNT RETURNS														
Number	22	32	27	39	31	45	40	40	33	59	26	39	24	56
Yards	185	284	234	382	255	313	320	385	382	499	189	308	244	416
Average Yards	8.4	8.9	8.7	9.8	8.2	7.0	8.2	9.6	11.6	8.5	7.3	7.9	10.2	7.4
Touchdowns	0	1	0	0	0	0	1	0	1	1	0	0	1	1
KICKOFF RET.:														
Number	60	46	51	13	63	36	64	35	65	45	33	52	54	36
Yards	1215	1079	907	254	989	630	1203	690	1380	749	552	1052	962	685
Average Yards	20.3	23.5	17.8	19.5	15.7	17.5	18.8	19.7	21.2	16.6	16.7	20.2	17.8	19.0
Touchdowns	1	2	0	0	0	0	0	0	0	0	0	0	0	0
INTERCEPT RET.:														
Number	21	17	16	29	23	26	12	23	17	19	24	14	21	23
Yards	423	127	213	567	367	461	162	345	446	232	347	235	241	231
Average Yards	20.1	7.5	13.3	19.6	16.0	17.7	13.5	15.0	26.2	12.2	14.5	16.8	11.5	10.0
Touchdowns	2	0	1	3	0	4	0	2	4	0	2	1	1	4
PENALTIES:														
Number	118	95	93	96	114	101	124	98	89	90	82	104	98	100
Yards	933	797	764	715	886	836	959	755	679	673	808	814	798	776
FUMBLES:														
Number	29	36	33	33	24	28	34	21	25	30	33	34	18	25
Number Lost	12	17	20	16	11	15	15	7	14	15	18	21	11	11
POINTS:														
Total	283	364	275	329	258	302	282	281	281	363	315	225	241	312
PAT Attempts	31	44	29	35	28	34	34	32	32	40	35	24	29	32
PAT Made	31	44	29	35	27	33	33	32	30	40	34	24	28	29
FG Attempts	30	30	29	38	26	28	21	30	26	41	31	28	16	36
FG Made	22	18	24	28	21	21	15	19	19	27	23	19	13	29
Percent FG Made	73.3	60.0	82.8	73.7	80.8	75.0	71.4	63.3	73.1	65.9	74.2	67.9	81.3	80.6
Safeties	0	1	0	0	0	1	0	0	1	1	1	0	0	2

WESTERN DIVISION

San Diego Chargers — The Chargers became the first team ever to go from 0-4 to the playoffs, and they won their first division title since 1981. After losing quarterback John Friesz in the preseason, San Diego acquired Stan Humphries in a trade with Washington. He took over as the starter in two games, and although the offense scored just 29 points in the first four games, the turnaround and eventual 11-1 finish under new head coach Bobby Ross was remarkable. Linebacker Junior Seau started to be recognized as one of the best defensive players in the game, but Leslie O'Neal, Chris Mims, Stanley Richard and others also spurred the comeback. Ronnie Harmon led NFL backs with 79 receptions, and Anthony Miller caught 72 passes for 1,060 yards and seven touchdowns.

Kansas City Chiefs — Quarterback Dave Krieg was supposed to be the missing piece to a Super Bowl puzzle. Instead, the Chiefs needed three defensive touchdowns in their last game to even make the playoffs. An 8-4 start evaporated into a struggle for the playoffs, and, even though they qualified for postseason play for the third straight year, the season was a disappointment. The offense was inconsistent at best, even with three solid runners in Barry Word, Christian Okoye and Harvey Williams. Each was capable of 1,000 yards, but they totaled only 1,317 yards between them. Neil Smith and Derrick Thomas, each of whom had 14.5 sacks, continued to be the center of attention on defense.

Denver Broncos — Dan Reeves was fired following an 8-8 season in which quarterback John Elway was injured and replaced by rotating quarterbacks in rookie Tommy Maddox and Shawn Moore. After a 7-3 start, Elway missed four starts, all losses, which killed any chances Denver had of making the playoffs. Without Elway, the offense fell apart, and the Broncos were outscored by 67 points in the 16 games. The running game, led by Gaston Green, failed to take some pressure off the passers, who were under siege when they dropped back, being sacked 52 times. Wideout Mark Jackson scored a team-high eight touchdowns, and linebacker Simon Fletcher had a team-record 16 sacks, making it 10 or more for him in four consecutive seasons. After the season, defensive coordinator Wade Phillips was promoted to head coach.

Los Angeles Raiders — The Raiders finished 7-9 while juggling three quarterbacks and three halfbacks, and their minus-19 turnover ratio was the worst in the league. Jay Schroeder and Todd Marinovich played most of the season, then long-time veteran Vince Evans took over in the last game. Eric Dickerson was acquired in a Draft Day trade, but he played like his best days were behind him, rushing for only 729 yards. And Marcus Allen, the wily veteran, was in Al Davis' doghouse and asked to be traded at the end of the year. The best player on offense was wide receiver Tim Brown, who led the team with 49 receptions and seven touchdowns. Veteran defensive lineman Howie Long continued to amaze, as he turned in another solid performance.

Seattle Seahawks — The Seahawks were clearly the worst team in the league with a horrible offense but a very good defense. The defensive players didn't mutiny against an offense that left them on the field too long, didn't take advantage of turnovers they created and yielded almost as many touchdowns (seven, plus two safeties) as it scored (13). Seattle scored only 140 points, the fewest by any team since the NFL went to a 16-game schedule in 1978. The Seahawks lost their top quarterbacks, Kelly Stouffer and Dan McGwire, to season-ending injuries. Stan Gelbaugh finished the year. A nice surprise on offense was halfback Chris Warren, who rushed for 1,017 yards. On defense, tackle Cortez Kennedy had 14 sacks and was named the league's Defensive Player of the Year.

MIAMI DOLPHINS 11-5 Don Shula

Scores of Each Game		
27	Cleveland	23
26	L.A. RAMS	10
19	Seattle	17
37	Buffalo	10
21	ATLANTA	17
38	NEW ENGLAND	17
20	INDIANAPOLIS	31
14	at N.Y. Jets	26
28	Indianapolis	0
20	BUFFALO	26
19	HOUSTON	16
13	New Orleans	24
3	San Francisco	27
20	L.A. RAIDERS	7
19	N.Y. JETS	17
16	New England	* 13

UseName	Pos.	Hgt.	Wgt.	Age	Int	Pts
Jeff Dellenbach	OT-C	6'6"	283	29		
Mark Dennis	OT	6'6"	292	27		
Richmond Webb	OT	6'6"	298	25		
Harry Galbreath	OG	6'1"	271	27		
Keith Sims	OG	6'2"	310	25		
Bert Weidner	OG-C	6'3"	284	26		
Gene Williams	OG	6'2"	308	23		
Jeff Uhlenhake	C	6'3"	284	26		
Marco Coleman	DE-LB	6'3"	259	22		
Jeff Cross	DE	6'4"	272	26		
Jeff Hunter (from DET)	DE	6'5"	293	26		
T.J. Turner	DE-NT	6'4"	280	29		
Larry Webster	DE	6'5"	285	23		
Chuck Klingbeil	NT	6'1"	265	26		
Roosevelt Collins	LB	6'4"	235	24		
Bryan Cox	LB	6'3"	235	24	1	
David Griggs	LB	6'3"	248	25		
John Grimsley	LB	6'2"	236	30		
Dwight Hollier	LB	6'2"	242	23		
Cliff Odom	LB	6'2"	241	34		
John Offerdahl	LB	6'3"	237	28		
Mark Sander	LB	6'2"	232	24		
Bruce Alexander	DB	5'8"	178	26	1	
Stephen Braggs	DB	5'9"	180	27		
J.B. Brown	DB	6'	189	26	4	6
Kerry Glenn	DB	5'9"	175	30		
Chris Green	DB	5'11"	188	24		
Bobby Harden	DB	6'	192	25		
Liffort Hobley	DB	6'	207	30		
Vestee Jackson	DB	6'	186	29	3	6
Darrell Malone (from KC)	DB	5'10"	177	24		
Louis Oliver	DB	6'2"	226	26	5	6
Troy Vincent	DB	6'	191	32	2	
Jarvis Williams	DB	5'11"	200	27	2	
Dan Marino	QB	6'4"	224	30		
Scott Mitchell	QB	6'6"	236	24		
Aaron Craver	HB	5'11"	215	22		
Mark Higgs	HB	5'7"	195	26		42
Bobby Humphrey	HB	6'1"	201	25		12
Bernie Parmalee	HB	5'11"	190	24		
Tony Paige	FB	5'10"	235	29		12
James Saxon	FB	5'11'	237	26		
Fred Banks	WR	5'10"	185	30		18
Robert Clark	WR	5'11"	175	27		
Mark Clayton	WR	5'9"	185	31		18
Mark Duper	WR	5'9"	192	33		42
Jim Jensen	WR-FB	6'4"	224	33		
Tony Martin	WR	6'	180	26		12
Scott Miller	WR	5'10"	179	23		
Mike Williams	WR	5'10"	178	25		
Greg Baty	TE	6'5"	240	28		6
Ferrell Edmunds	TE	6'6"	254	27		6
Keith Jackson	TE	6'2"	250	27		30
Joe Prokop (to NYG)	K	6'2"	225	32		
Reggie Roby	K	6'2"	243	31		
Pete Stoyonovich	K	5'10"	181	25		124

Ned Bolcar — Knee Injury

Scott Secules — Shoulder Injury

BUFFALO BILLS 11-5 Marv Levy

Scores of Each Game		
40	L.A. RAMS	7
34	San Francisco	31
38	INDIANAPOLIS	0
41	New England	7
10	MIAMI	37
3	L.A. Raiders	20
24	N.Y. Jets	20
16	NEW ENGLAND	7
28	PITTSBURGH	20
26	Miami	20
41	ATLANTA	14
13	Indianapolis	* 16
17	N.Y. JETS	24
27	DENVER	17
20	New Orleans	16
3	Houston	27

UseName	Pos.	Hgt.	Wgt.	Age	Int	Pts
Howard Ballard	OT	6'6"	325	28		
Jerry Crafts	OT	6'6"	333	24		
Will Wolford	OT	6'5"	297	28		
John Davis	OG	6'4"	311	27		
John Fina	OG-OT	6'4"	282	23		6
Mitch Frerotte	OG	6'3"	285	27		12
Glenn Parker	OG-OT	6'5"	305	26		
Jim Ritcher	OG	6'3"	273	34		
Kent Hull	C	6'4"	278	31		
Adam Lingner	C	6'4"	268	31		
Phil Hansen	DE	6'5"	275	24		
Mark Pike	DE	6'4"	272	28		
Bruce Smith	DE	6'4"	275	29		
Keith Willis	DE	6'1"	263	33		
Gary Baldinger	NT	6'3"	270	28		
Mike Lodish	NT	6'3"	272	25		6
Jeff Wright	NT	6'2"	270	29		
Carlton Bailey	LB	6'2"	235	27		
Cornelius Bennett	LB	6'2"	238	27		
Shane Conlan	LB	6'3"	230	28	1	
Keith Goganious	LB	6'2"	237	23		
Richard Harvey	LB	6'1"	235	25		
Mark Maddox	LB	6'1"	233	24		
Marvcus Patton	LB	6'2"	225	25		
Darryl Talley	LB	6'4"	235	32		
Matt Darby	DB	6'1"	200	23		
Chris Hale	DB	5'7"	165	26		2
Cliff Hicks	DB	5'10"	188	28		
Kirby Jackson	DB	5'10"	180	27		
Henry Jones	DB	5'11"	197	24	8	12
Mark Kelso	DB	5'11"	185	29	7	
Nate Odomes	DB	5'10"	188	27	5	
Kurt Schulz	DB	6'1"	206	23		
James Williams	DB	5'10"	172	25	2	
Gale Gilbert	QB	6'3"	210	29		
Jim Kelly	QB	6'3"	218	32		6
Frank Reich	QB	6'4"	210	30		
Kenneth Davis	HB	5'10"	208	30		36
Eddie Fuller	HB	5'9"	201	24		
Thurman Thomas	HB	5'10"	198	26		72
Carwell Gardner	FB	6'2"	232	25		12
Don Beebe	WR	5'11"	184	27		12
Al Edwards	WR	5'8"	173	25		
Brad Lamb	WR	5'10"	171	24		
James Lofton	WR	6'3"	190	36		36
Andre Reed	WR	6'	190	28		18
Steve Tasker	WR	5'9"	183	30		
Chris Walsh	WR	6'1"	185	23		
Rob Awalt	TE	6'5"	238	32		
Keith McKeller	TE	6'6"	245	28		
Pete Metzelaars	TE	6'7"	250	32		36
Chris Mohr	K	6'5"	215	26		
Steve Christie	K	6'	185	24		115

Ed Thomas — Knee Injury

INDIANAPOLIS COLTS 9-7 Ted Marchibroda

Scores of Each Game		
14	CLEVELAND	3
10	HOUSTON	20
0	Buffalo	38
24	Tampa Bay	14
6	N.Y. JETS	* 3
14	SAN DIEGO	34
31	Miami	20
0	San Diego	26
0	MIAMI	28
34	NEW ENGLAND	* 37
14	Pittsburgh	30
16	BUFFALO	* 13
6	New England	0
10	N.Y. Jets	6
16	PHOENIX	13
21	Cincinnati	17

UseName	Pos.	Hgt.	Wgt.	Age	Int	Pts
Kevin Call	OT	6'7"	308	30		
Ron Mattes	OT	6'6"	298	29		
Zefross Moss	OT	6'6"	338	26		
Irv Pankey	OT-OG	6'5"	295	34		
William Schultz	OT	6'5"	305	25		6
Mark Vander Poel	OT	6'7"	303	24		
Randy Dixon	OG	6'3"	305	28		
Trevor Matich	OG-C	6'4"	297	30		
Tom Ricketts	OG	6'5"	295	26		
Ron Solt	OG	6'3"	280	30		
Ray Donaldson	C	6'3"	300	34		
Mel Agee (to ATL)	DE	6'5"	290	22		
Sam Clancy	DE	6'7"	300	34		
Steve Emtman	DE	6'4"	290	22	1	6
Jon Hand	DE	6'7"	301	28		
Skip McClendon (from MIN)	DE	6'7"	302	28		
Willis Peguese (from HOU)	DE	6'4"	273	25		
Tony McCoy	NT	6'	279	23		
Tony Siragusa	NT	6'3"	303	25		
Chip Banks	LB	6'4"	254	32	1	
Duane Bickett	LB	6'5"	251	29	1	
Quentin Coryatt	LB	6'3"	250	22		
Steve Grant	LB	6'	231	22		
Jeff Herrod	LB	6'	249	26	1	
Scott Radecic	LB	6'3"	236	30	1	
Matt Vanderbeek	LB	6'3"	258	25		
Tony Walker	LB	6'3"	246	24		
Ashley Ambrose	DB	5'10"	177	21		
Michael Ball	DB	6'	220	28		
John Baylor	DB	6'	203	27	1	
Jason Belser	DB	5'9"	187	22	3	
Eugene Daniel	DB	5'11"	188	31	1	
Chris Goode	DB	6'	199	28	2	
Cornell Holloway	DB	5'11"	182	26		
Mike Prior	DB	6'	210	28	6	
Tony Stargell	DB	5'11"	189	26	2	
Jeff George	QB	6'4"	227	24		6
Mark Herrmann	QB	6'4"	220	33		
Jack Trudeau	QB	6'3"	227	29		
Tom Tupa	QB	6'4"	230	26		
Ken Clark	HB-FB	5'9"	204	26		
Rodney Culver	HB	5'9"	224	22		54
Anthony Johnson	HB-FB	6'	222	24		18
Ed Toner	HB	6'	240	24		
Maurice Carthon	FB	6'1"	240	31		
Bill Brooks	WR	6'	189	28		6
Jessie Hester	WR	5'11"	175	29		6
Reggie Langhorne	WR	6'2"	207	29		6
Eddie Miller	WR	6'	185	23		
Clarence Verdin	WR	5'8"	162	29		12
Charles Arbuckle	TE	6'3"	248	23		6
Kerry Cash	TE	6'4"	247	23		18
Dean Biasucci	K	6'	190	30		72
Rohn Stark	K	6'3"	203	33		

Shane Curry — Shot and Killed During Offseason

NEW YORK JETS 4-12 Bruce Coslet

Scores of Each Game		
17	Atlanta	20
10	Pittsburgh	27
14	SAN FRANCISCO	31
10	L.A. Rams	18
30	NEW ENGLAND	21
3	Indianapolis	* 6
20	BUFFALO	24
26	MIAMI	14
16	Denver	27
17	CINCINNATI	14
3	New England	24
7	KANSAS CITY	23
24	Buffalo	17
6	INDIANAPOLIS	10
17	Miami	19
0	NEW ORLEANS	20

UseName	Pos.	Hgt.	Wgt.	Age	Int	Pts
Jeff Criswell	OT	6'7"	291	28		
Irv Eatman	OT	6'7"	298	31		
Siupeli Malamala	OT	6'5"	313	23		
Brett Miller	OT	6'7"	286	33		
Dave Cadigan	OG	6'4"	285	27		
Dwayne White	OG	6'2"	305	25		
Cal Dixon	C	6'4"	284	22		
Roger Duffy	C	6'3"	285	25		
Jim Sweeney	C-OG	6'4"	286	30		
Dennis Byrd	DE	6'5"	266	25		
Jeff Lageman	DE	6'5"	266	25		
Marvin Washington	DE	6'6"	272	26		2
Karl Wilson	DE	6'4"	275	28		
Paul Frase	DT-DE	6'5"	270	27		
Mark Gunn	DT-DE	6'5"	285	24		
Mario Johnson	DT	6'3"	292	22		
Scott Mersereau	DT	6'3"	275	27		
Bill Pickel	DT	6'5"	265	32		
Kurt Barber	LB-DE	6'4"	241	23		
Glenn Cadrez	LB	6'3"	235	22		
Kyle Clifton	LB	6'4"	236	30	1	
Keo Coleman	LB	6'1"	255	22		
Bobby Houston	LB	6'2"	235	24	1	6
Don Jones	LB	6'	231	23		
Joe Kelly	LB	6'2"	235	27		
Mo Lewis	LB	6'3"	250	22	1	
Huey Richardson (from WAS)	LB	6'5"	245	24		
Michael Brim	DB	6'	198	26	6	6
James Hasty	DB	6'	201	27	2	
R.J. Kors	DB	6'	195	26		
Erik McMillan	DB	6'2"	200	27		
Dennis Price	DB	6'1"	182	27	1	
Marcus Turner	DB	6'	185	26		
Brian Washington	DB	6'1"	212	26	6	6
Lonnie Young	DB	6'1"	196	29		
Jeff Blake	QB	6'	202	21		
Browning Nagle	QB	6'3"	225	24		
Ken O'Brien	QB	6'4"	212	31		
A.B. Brown	HB	5'9"	215	26		
Sheldon Canley	HB	5'9"	195	24		
Scottie Graham	HB	5'9"	220	23		
Johnny Hector	HB	5'11"	214	31		
Freeman McNeil	HB	5'11"	208	33		
Blair Thomas	HB	5'10"	202	24		
Brad Baxter	FB	6'1"	235	25		36
Pat Chaffey	FB	6'1"	220	25		6
Chris Burkett	WR	6'4"	200	30		6
Rob Carpenter	WR	6'2"	190	24		6
Dale Dawkins	WR	6'1"	190	25		
Terance Mathis	WR	5'10"	170	25		24
Rob Moore	WR	6'3"	205	23		24
Al Toon	WR	6'4"	205	29		12
Mark Boyer	TE	6'4"	242	29		
Eric Kattus	TE	6'5"	251	29		
Johnny Mitchell	TE	6'3"	263	21		6
Troy Sadowski	TE	6'5"	250	26		
Ken Whisenhunt	TE	6'3"	240	30		
Louis Aguiar	K	6'2"	215	26		
Cary Blanchard	K	6'1"	225	23		65
Jason Staurovsky	K	5'9"	170	29		15

NEW ENGLAND PATRIOTS 2-14 Dick MacPherson

Scores of Each Game		
0	L.A. Rams	14
6	SEATTLE	10
7	BUFFALO	41
21	N.Y. Jets	30
12	SAN FRANCISCO	24
17	Miami	38
17	CLEVELAND	19
7	Buffalo	16
14	NEW ORLEANS	31
37	Indianapolis	* 34
24	N.Y. JETS	3
0	Atlanta	34
0	INDIANAPOLIS	6
20	Kansas City	27
10	Cincinnati	20
13	MIAMI	* 16

UseName	Pos.	Hgt.	Wgt.	Age	Int	Pts
Bruce Armstrong	OT	6'4"	284	26		
Pat Harlow	OT	6'6"	290	23		
Eugene Chung	OG-OT	6'5"	295	23		
Gregg Rakoczy	OG-C	6'5"	280	27		
Reggie Redding	OG-OT	6'4"	305	23		
Calvin Stephens	OG	6'2"	285	24		
Larry Williams	OG	6'5"	294	29		
Gene Chilton	C	6'3"	286	28		
Ray Agnew	DE	6'3"	272	24		
Tim Edwards	DE	6'1"	270	24		
Chris Gannon	DE	6'6"	260	26		
Marion Hobby	DE	6'4"	277	25		
Brent Williams	DE	6'3"	275	27		
Tim Goad	NT	6'3"	280	26		6
Fred Smerlas	NT	6'4"	291	35		
Vincent Brown	LB	6'2"	245	27	1	12
Todd Collins	LB	6'2"	242	22		
David Howard	LB	6'1"	230	30	1	
Eugene Lockhart	LB	6'2"	233	31		
Rob McGovern	LB	6'2"	234	25		
Johnny Rembert	LB	6'3"	234	30		
Dwayne Sabb	LB	6'4"	248	22		
Chris Singleton	LB	6'2"	247	25	1	6
Richard Tardits	LB	6'2"	235	26		
Andre Tippett	LB	6'3"	241	32		
Roger Brown	DB	6'	196	25		
Tim Gordon	DB	6'	188	27		
Jerome Henderson	DB	5'10"	189	23	3	
Maurice Hurst	DB	5'10"	185	24	3	
Dion Lambert	DB	6'	185	23		
David Pool	DB	5'9"	182	25	2	6
Randy Robbins	DB	6'2"	189	29	2	
Rod Smith	DB	5'11"	187	22	1	
Jeff Carlson	QB	6'3"	215	26		
Tom Hodson	QB	6'3"	195	25		
Hugh Millen	QB	6'5"	216	28		
Scott Zolak	QB	6'5"	222	24		
Scott Lockwood	HB	5'10"	196	24		
Leonard Russell	HB	6'2"	235	22		12
John Stephens	HB	6'1"	215	26		12
Jon Vaughn	HB	5'9"	203	22		12
Sam Gash	FB	5'11"	224	23		6
Kevin Turner	FB	6'	224	23		12
Irving Fryar	WR	6'	200	29		24
Greg McMurtry	WR	6'2"	207	24		6
Walter Stanley (from SD)	WR	5'10"	180	27		
Michael Timpson	WR	5'10"	175	25		6
Ben Coates	TE	6'4"	245	23		18
Marv Cook	TE	6'4"	234	26		12
Charlie Baumann	K	6'1"	203	25		55
Shawn McCarthy	K	6'6"	227	24		

Ivy Joe Hunter — Knee Injury

Hart Lee Dykes — Knee Injury

MIAMI DOLPHINS

RUSHING

Last Name	No.	Yds	Avg	TD
Higgs	256	915	3.6	7
Humphrey	102	471	4.6	1
Marino	20	66	3.3	0
Parmalee	6	38	6.3	0
Paige	7	11	1.6	1
Mitchell	8	10	1.3	0
Craver	3	9	3.0	0
Saxon	4	7	1.8	0
Martin	1	-2	-2.0	0

RECEIVING

Last Name	No.	Yds	Avg	TD
Humphrey	54	507	9.4	1
K. Jackson	48	594	12.4	5
Paige	48	399	8.3	1
Duper	44	762	17.3	7
Clayton	43	619	14.4	3
Martin	33	553	16.8	2
Banks	22	319	14.5	3
Higgs	16	142	8.9	0
Edmunds	10	91	9.1	1
Saxon	5	41	8.2	0
Clark	3	59	19.7	0
M. Williams	3	43	14.3	0
Baty	3	19	6.3	1

PUNT RETURNS

Last Name	No.	Yds	Avg	TD
Miller	24	175	7.3	0
Vincent	5	16	3.2	0
Martin	1	0	0.0	0
J. Williams	1	0	0.0	0

KICKOFF RETURNS

Last Name	No.	Yds	Avg	TD
M. Williams	19	328	17.3	0
Parmalee	14	289	20.6	0
Craver	8	174	21.8	0
Paige	2	29	14.5	0
Humphrey	1	18	18.0	0

PASSING — PUNTING — KICKING

PASSING	Att	Cmp	%	Yds	Yd/Att	TD	Int— %	RK
Marino	**554**	330	59.6	**4116**	7.43	**24**	16–2.9	2
Mitchell	8	2	25.0	32	4.00	0	1—12.5	
Martin	1	0	0.0	0	0.00	0	0—0.0	

PUNTING	No.	Avg.
Roby	35	41.2
Prokop	32	37.0
Stoyanovich	2	45.0

KICKING	XP	Att.	%	FG	Att	%
Stoyonovich	34	36	94	**30**	**37**	81

BUFFALO BILLS

RUSHING

Last Name	No.	Yds	Avg	TD
Thomas	312	1487	4.8	9
K. Davis	139	613	4.4	6
Gardner	40	166	4.2	2
Reed	8	65	8.1	0
Kelly	31	53	1.7	1
Fuller	6	39	6.5	0
Mohr	1	11	11.0	0
Tasker	1	9	9.0	0
Edwards	1	8	8.0	0
Beebe	1	-6	-6.0	0
Reich	9	-9	-1.0	0

RECEIVING

Last Name	No.	Yds	Avg	TD
Reed	65	913	14.0	3
Thomas	58	626	10.8	3
Lofton	51	786	15.4	6
Beebe	33	554	16.8	2
Metzelaars	30	298	9.9	6
K. Davis	15	80	5.3	0
McKeller	14	110	7.9	0
Lamb	7	139	19.9	0
Gardner	7	67	9.6	0
Awalt	4	34	8.5	0
Edwards	2	25	12.5	0
Tasker	2	24	12.0	0
Fuller	2	17	8.5	0
Frerotte	2	4	2.0	2
Fina	1	1	1.0	1

PUNT RETURNS

Last Name	No.	Yds	Avg	TD
Hicks	129	289	10.0	0
Hale	14	175	12.5	0

KICKOFF RETURNS

Last Name	No.	Yds	Avg	TD
K. Davis	14	251	17.9	0
Edwards	12	274	22.8	0
Fuller	8	134	16.8	0
Lamb	5	97	19.4	0
Hicks	1	5	5.0	0
Frerotte	1	0	0.0	0

PASSING — PUNTING — KICKING

PASSING	Att	Cmp	%	Yds	Yd/Att	TD	Int— %	RK
Kelly	462	269	58.2	3457	7.48	23	19—4.1	4
Reich	47	24	51.1	221	4.70	0	2—4.3	

PUNTING	No.	Avg.
Mohr	60	42.2

KICKING	XP	ATT	%	FG	ATT	%
Christie	**43**	**44**	98	24	30	80

INDIANAPOLIS COLTS

RUSHING

Last Name	No.	Yds	Avg	TD
Johnson	178	592	3.3	0
Culver	121	321	2.7	7
Clark	40	134	3.4	0
George	14	26	1.9	1
Brooks	2	14	7.0	0
Carthon	4	9	2.3	0
Trudeau	13	6	0.5	0
Tupa	3	9	3.0	0
Herrmann	3	-2	-0.7	0
Langhorne	1	-7	-7.0	0

RECEIVING

Last Name	No.	Yds	Avg	TD
Langhorne	65	811	12.5	1
Hester	52	792	15.2	1
Johnson	49	517	10.6	3
Brooks	44	468	10.6	1
Cash	43	521	12.1	3
Culver	26	210	8.1	2
Arbuckle	13	152	11.7	1
Clark	5	46	9.2	0
Verdin	3	37	12.3	0
Carthon	3	10	3.3	0
Prior	1	17	17.0	0
Schultz	1	3	3.0	1

PUNT RETURNS

Last Name	No.	Yds	Avg	TD
Verdin	24	268	11.2	**2**
Prior	1	12	12.0	0

KICKOFF RETURNS

Last Name	No.	Yds	Avg	TD
Verdin	**39**	**815**	20.9	0
Ambrose	8	126	15.8	0
Clark	3	54	18.0	0
Vanderbeek	1	6	6.0	0

PASSING — PUNTING — KICKING

PASSING	Att	Cmp	%	Yds	Yd/Att	TD	Int— %	RK
George	306	167	54.6	1963	6.42	7	15—4.9	10
Trudeau	181	105	58.0	1271	7.02	4	8—4.4	
Tupa	33	17	51.5	156	4.73	1	2—6.1	
Herrmann	24	15	62.5	177	7.38	1	1—4.2	
Stark	1	1	100.0	17	17.00	0	0—0.0	
Johnson	1	0	0.0	0	0.00	0	0—0.0	

PUNTING	No.	Avg.
Stark	83	44.8

KICKING	XP	ATT	%	FG	ATT	%
Biasucci	24	24	**100**	16	29	55

NEW YORK JETS

RUSHING

Last Name	No.	Yds	Avg	TD
Baxter	152	698	4.6	6
Thomas	97	440	4.5	0
Chaffey	27	186	6.9	1
McNeil	43	170	4.0	0
Hector	24	67	2.8	0
Nagle	24	57	2.4	0
Brown	24	42	1.8	0
Graham	14	29	2.1	0
Mathis	3	25	8.3	1
Moore	1	21	21.0	0
Canley	4	9	2.3	0
O'Brien	8	8	1.0	0
Carpenter	1	2	2.0	0
Blake	2	-2	-2.0	0

RECEIVING

Last Name	No.	Yds	Avg	TD
Burkett	57	724	12.7	1
Moore	50	726	14.5	4
Toon	31	311	10.0	2
Mathis	22	316	14.4	3
Boyer	19	149	7.8	0
Mitchell	16	210	13.1	1
McNeil	16	154	9.6	0
Carpenter	13	161	12.4	1
Chaffey	7	56	8.0	0
Thomas	7	49	7.0	0
Baxter	4	32	8.0	0
Brown	4	30	7.5	0
Hector	2	13	6.5	0
Whisenhunt	2	11	5.5	0
Sadowski	1	20	20.0	0

PUNT RETURNS

Last Name	No.	Yds	Avg	TD
Carpenter	28	208	7.4	0
Mathis	2	24	12.0	0

KICKOFF RETURNS

Last Name	No.	Yds	Avg	TD
Mathis	28	492	17.6	0
McMillan	22	420	19.1	0
Hector	1	15	15.0	0
Dawkins	1	10	10.0	0
Duffy	1	7	7.0	0
Dixon	1	6	6.0	0

PASSING — PUNTING — KICKING

PASSING	Att	Cmp	%	Yds	Yd/Att	TD	Int— %	RK
Nagle	387	192	49.6	2280	5.89	7	17—4.4	12
O'Brien	98	55	56.1	642	6.55	5	6—6.1	
Blake	9	4	44.4	40	4.44	0	1—11.1	
Carpenter	1	0	0.0	0	0.00	0	0—0.0	

PUNTING	No.	Avg.
Aguiar	73	41.0

KICKING	XP	Att	%	FG	Att	%
Blanchard	17	17	**100**	16	22	73
Staurovsky	6	6	100	3	8	38

NEW ENGLAND PATRIOTS

RUSHING

Last Name	No.	Yds	Avg	TD
Vaughn	113	451	4.0	1
Russell	123	390	3.2	2
J. Stephens	75	277	3.7	2
Lockwood	35	162	4.6	0
Millen	17	108	6.4	0
Zolak	18	71	3.9	0
Turner	10	40	4.0	0
Carlson	11	32	2.9	0
Hodson	5	11	2.2	0
Gash	5	7	1.4	1
Fryar	1	6	6.0	0
McMurtry	2	3	1.5	0
Coates	1	2	2.0	0
McCarthy	3	-10	-3.3	0

RECEIVING

Last Name	No.	Yds	Avg	TD
Fryar	55	791	14.4	4
Cook	52	413	7.9	2
McMurtry	35	424	12.1	1
Timpson	26	315	12.1	1
J. Stephens	21	161	7.7	0
Coates	20	171	8.6	3
Vaughn	13	84	6.5	0
Russell	11	24	2.2	0
Turner	7	52	7.4	2
Stanley	3	63	21.0	0
Hodson	1	-6	-6.0	0

PUNT RETURNS

Last Name	No.	Yds	Avg	TD
Stanley	28	227	8.1	0
Timpson	8	47	5.9	0
Lambert	1	0	0.0	0

KICKOFF RETURNS

Last Name	No.	Yds	Avg	TD
Vaughn	20	564	28.2	1
Stanley	29	529	18.2	0
Lockwood	11	233	21.2	0
Timpson	2	28	14.0	0
Turner	1	11	11.0	0
Hobby	1	11	11.0	0

PASSING — PUNTING — KICKING

PASSING	Att	Cmp	%	Yds	Yd/Att	TD	Int— %	RK
Millen	203	124	61.1	1203	5.93	8	10—4.9	
Zolak	100	52	52.0	561	5.61	2	4—4.0	
Hodson	91	50	54.9	496	5.45	2	2—2.2	
Carlson	49	18	36.7	232	4.73	1	3—6.1	
McMurtry	1	0	0.0	0	0.00	0	0—0.0	

PUNTING	No.	Avg.
McCarthy	103	40.9

KICKING	XP	ATT	%	FG	ATT	%
Baumann	22	24	92	11	17	65

PITTSBURGH STEELERS 11-5 Bill Cowher

Scores of Each Game		
29	Houston	24
27	N.Y. JETS	10
23	San Diego	6
3	Green Bay	17
9	Cleveland	17
20	CINCINNATI	0
27	Kansas City	3
21	HOUSTON	20
20	Buffalo	28
17	DETROIT	14
30	INDIANAPOLIS	14
21	Cincinnati	9
20	SEATTLE	14
6	Chicago	30
3	MINNESOTA	6
23	CLEVELAND	13

Use Name	Pos.	Hgt.	Wgt.	Age	Int	Pts
Tunch Ilkin	OT	6'3"	276	34		
John Jackson	OT	6'6"	290	27		
Leon Searcy	OT	6'3"	305	22		
Justin Strzelczyk	OT	6'5"	305	24		
Calton Haselrig	OG	6'1"	290	26		
Duval Love	OG	6'3"	291	29		
Dermontti Dawson	C	6'2"	288	27		
Kendall Gammon	C	6'4"	273	23		
Ariel Solomon	C-OT	6'5"	286	24		
Kenny Davidson	DE	6'5"	277	25		
Donald Evans	DE	6'2"	275	28		
Aaron Jones	DE	6'5"	257	25		
Garry Howe	NT	6'1"	298	24		
Joel Steed	NT	6'2"	290	23		
Gerald Williams	NT	6'3"	289	28		

Use Name	Pos.	Hgt.	Wgt.	Age	Int	Pts
Darryl Ford	LB	6'1"	225	26		
Bryan Hinkle	LB	6'2"	229	33		
Levon Kirkland	LB	6'	247	23		
David Little	LB	6'1"	239	33	2	
Greg Lloyd	LB	6'2"	223	27	1	
Hardy Nickerson	LB	6'2"	233	27		
Jerry Olsavsky	LB	6'1"	222	25		
Elnardo Webster	LB	6'2"	243	22		
Jerrol Williams	LB	6'5"	237	25	1	
Larry Griffin	DB	6'	200	29	3	6
David Johnson	DB	6'	181	26	5	
Carnell Lake	DB	6'1"	207	25		
Darren Perry	DB	5'10"	194	23	6	
Richard Shelton	DB	5'10"	196	25		
Sammy Walker	DB	5'11"	197	23		
Solomon Wilcots	DB	5'11"	202	27		
Rod Woodson	DB	6'	197	27	4	6

Gary Jones — Knee Injury

Use Name	Pos.	Hgt.	Wgt.	Age	Int	Pts
Bubby Brister	QB	6'3"	217	30		
Neil O'Donnell	QB	6'3"	223	26		6
Rick Strom	QB	6'2"	205	27		
Albert Bentley	HB	5'11"	217	32		
Barry Foster	HB	5'10"	217	23		66
Warren Williams	HB	6'	213	27		
Merril Hoge	FB	6'2"	222	27		6
Leroy Thompson	FB	5'10"	215	23		6
Charles Davenport	WR	6'3"	210	23		6
Mark Didio	WR	5'11"	181	23		
Jeff Graham	WR	6'1"	195	23		6
Ernie Mills	WR	5'11"	186	23		18
Darrick Owens	WR	6'2"	195	21		
Dwight Stone	WR-HB	6'	190	28		18
Yancey Thigpen	WR	6'1"	203	23		
Jesse Anderson (from TB)	TE	6'2"	245	26		
Russ Campbell	TE	6'5"	259	23		
Adrian Cooper	TE	6'5"	268	24		18
Eric Green	TE	6'5"	284	25		12
Tim Jorden	TE	6'3"	239	25		12
Gary Anderson	K	5'11"	179	33		113
Mark Royals	K	6'5"	212	28		

Tim Worley — Suspended by NFL

HOUSTON OILERS 10-6 Jack Pardee

Scores of Each Game		
24	PITTSBURGH	29
20	Indianapolis	10
23	KANSAS CITY	* 20
27	SAN DIEGO	0
38	Cincinnati	24
21	Denver	27
26	CINCINNATI	10
20	Pittsburgh	21
14	CLEVELAND	24
17	Minnesota	13
16	Miami	19
24	Detroit	21
24	CHICAGO	7
14	GREEN BAY	16
17	Cleveland	14
27	BUFFALO	3

Use Name	Pos.	Hgt.	Wgt.	Age	Int	Pts
Kevin Donnalley	OT	6'5"	305	24		
Don Maggs	OT	6'5"	296	30		
David Williams	OT	6'5"	292	26		
Doug Dawson	OG	6'2"	288	30		
John Flannery	OG-C	6'3"	304	23		
Mike Munchak	OG	6'3"	284	32		
Bruce Matthews	C	6'4"	291	31		
Erik Norgard	C-OG	6'1"	282	26		
William Fuller	DE	6'3"	274	30		6
Sean Jones	DE	6'7"	264	29	1	
Lee Williams	DE-DT	6'6"	271	29		
Jeff Alm	DT	6'6"	278	24		
Ray Childress	DT-DE	6'6"	272	29		6
Glenn Montgomery	DT	6'	272	25		
Tim Roberts	DT	6'6"	309	23		
Doug Smith	DT	6'5"	309	33		
Craig Veasey	DT	6'2"	286	26		

Use Name	Pos.	Hgt.	Wgt.	Age	Int	Pts
Joe Bowden	LB	5'11"	227	22		
Rick Graf	LB	6'5"	244	28	1	
Scott Kozak	LB	6'3"	222	26		
Lamar Lathon	LB	6'3"	250	24		
Johnny Meads (to WAS)	LB	6'2"	226	31		6
Eddie Robinson	LB	6'1"	242	22		
Eugene Seale	LB	5'10"	253	28		
Al Smith	LB	6'1"	251	27	1	
Tony Brown	DB	5'9"	183	22		
Cris Dishman	DB	6'	178	27	3	
Mike Dumas	DB	5'11"	178	23	1	
Jerry Gray	DB	6'	185	29	6	
Steve Jackson	DB	5'8"	182	23	3	
Richard Johnson	DB	6'1"	195	28		
Darryll Lewis	DB	5'9"	188	23		
Bubba McDowell	DB	6'1"	198	25	3	6
Bo Orlando	DB	5'10"	180	26		
Marcus Robertson	DB	5'11"	197	22	1	

Use Name	Pos.	Hgt.	Wgt.	Age	Int	Pts
Cody Carlson	QB	6'3"	202	28		6
Mike Elkins	QB	6'3"	225	26		
Warren Moon	QB	6'3"	212	35		6
Bucky Richardson	QB	6'1"	221	23		
Gary Brown	HB-FB	5'11"	229	23		6
Spencer Tillman	HB	5'11"	206	28		
Lorenzo White	HB	5'11"	222	26		48
Pat Coleman	WR	5'7"	173	25		
Curtis Duncan	WR	5'11"	184	27		6
Ernest Givins	WR	5'9"	172	27		60
Leonard Harris	WR	5'8"	162	31		12
Haywood Jeffires	WR	6'2"	201	27		54
Damon Mays	WR	5'9"	170	24		
Webster Slaughter	WR	6'1"	170	27		24
Gary Wellman	WR	5'9"	168	25		
Al Del Greco	K	5'10"	200	30		104
Greg Montgomery	K	6'3"	215	27		

CLEVELAND BROWNS 7-9 Bill Belichick

Scores of Each Game		
3	Indianapolis	14
23	MIAMI	27
28	L.A. Raiders	16
0	DENVER	12
17	PITTSBURGH	9
17	GREEN BAY	6
19	New England	17
10	Cincinnati	30
24	Houston	14
13	SAN DIEGO	14
13	Minnesota	17
27	CHICAGO	14
37	CINCINNATI	21
14	Detroit	24
14	HOUSTON	17
13	Pittsburgh	23

Use Name	Pos.	Hgt.	Wgt.	Age	Int	Pts
Freddie Childress	OT	6'4"	330	25		
Bob Dahl	OT	6'5"	285	23		
Dan Fike	OT-OG	6'7"	285	31		
Tony Jones	OT	6'5"	290	26		
Ed King	OG	6'4"	303	22		
John Rienstra	OG	6'5"	275	29		
Jay Hilgenberg	C	6'3"	260	33		
Chris Thome (to NYG)	C	6'4"	280	23		
Lance Zeno	C	6'4"	279	25		
Rob Burnett	DE	6'4"	270	25		
Ernie Logan	DE	6'3"	271	24		
Pio Sagapolutele	DE	6'6"	297	22		
Anthony Pleasant	DE	6'5"	258	24		
Bill Johnson	DT	6'4"	305	23		
James Jones	DT	6'2"	294	23		6
Michael Dean Perry	DT	6'1"	285	27		
Alvin Wright (from LA)	DT	6'2"	285	31		

Paul Farren — Back Injury
John Thornton — Leg Injury

Use Name	Pos.	Hgt.	Wgt.	Age	Int	Pts
David Brandon	LB	6'4"	230	27	2	12
Richard Brown	LB	6'3"	240	26		
Cedric Figaro	LB	6'3"	255	25		
Mike Johnson	LB	6'1"	230	29	1	6
Clay Matthews	LB	6'2"	245	36	1	
Frank Stams	LB	6'2"	240	26		
Harlon Barnett	DB	5'11"	200	25		
Latin Berry	DB	5'10'	196	25		
Fred Foggie	DB	6'	188	23		
Alan Haller (from PIT)	DB	5'11"	185	22		
Randy Hilliard	DB	5'11"	160	25		
Alfred Jackson	DB	6'	180	25		
Frank Minnifield	DB	5'9"	180	32	2	
Stevon Moore	DB	5'11"	205	25		6
Vince Newsome	DB	6'1"	185	31	3	
Terry Taylor	DB	5'10"	190	31	1	
Eric Turner	DB	6'1"	207	23	1	
Everson Walls (from NYG)	DB	6'1"	195	32	2	
Barry Wilburn	DB	6'3"	186	28		

Use Name	Pos.	Hgt.	Wgt.	Age	Int	Pts
Jeff Francis	QB	6'4"	225	26		
Brad Goebel	QB	6'3"	198	24		
Bernie Kosar	QB	6'5"	215	28		
Todd Philcox	QB	6'4"	225	25		
Mike Tomczak	QB	6'1"	204	29		
James Brooks (to TB)	HB	5'10"	180	33		
Eric Metcalf	HB	5'10"	190	24		42
Ron Wolfley	HB	6'	230	29		6
Randy Baldwin	FB	5'10"	216	25		
Leroy Hoard	FB-HB	5'11"	230	24		6
Kevin Mack	FB	6'	225	30		36
Tommy Vardell	FB	6'2"	238	23		
Shawn Collins (from ATL)	WR	6'2"	204	25		
Jamie Holland	WR	6'1"	195	28		
Michael Jackson	WR	6'4"	195	25		42
Keenan McCardell	WR	6'1"	185	22		
Rico Smith	WR	6'	185	23		
Lawyer Tillman	WR	6'5"	230	26		
Mark Bavaro	TE	6'4"	245	29		12
Scott Galbraith	TE	6'3"	260	25		6
Pete Holohan	TE	6'4"	247	33		
Brian Kinchen	TE	6'2"	232	27		
Brian Hansen	K	6'4"	220	31		
Matt Stover	K	5'11"	178	24		92

Derrick Douglas — Knee Injury

CINCINNATI BENGALS 5-11 Dave Shula

Scores of Each Game		
21	Seattle	3
24	L.A. RAIDERS	* 21
23	Green Bay	24
7	MINNESOTA	42
24	HOUSTON	38
0	Pittsburgh	20
10	Houston	26
30	CLEVELAND	10
31	Chicago	* 28
14	N.Y. Jets	17
13	DETROIT	19
9	PITTSBURGH	21
21	Cleveland	37
10	San Diego	27
20	NEW ENGLAND	10
17	INDIANAPOLIS	21

Use Name	Pos.	Hgt.	Wgt.	Age	Int	Pts
Anthony Munoz	OT	6'6"	284	34		
Tom Rayam	OT	6'6"	297	24		
Kevin Sargent	OT	6'6"	284	23		
Joe Walter	OT	6'6"	292	29		
Bruce Kozerski	OG	6'4"	287	30		
Jon Melander	OG	6'7"	280	25		
Kirk Scrafford	OG-OT	6'6"	255	25		
Mike Withycombe	OG-C	6'5"	297	27		
Mike Arthur	C	6'3"	280	24		
Mike Frier	DE	6'5"	299	23		
Alonzo Mitz	DE	6'4"	278	29	1	
Roosevelt Nix	DE	6'6"	315	25		
Elston Ridgle	DE	6'5"	277	29		
Lamar Rogers	DE	6'4"	292	24		
Danny Stubbs	DE-LB	6'4"	264	27		
Tim Krumrie	NT	6'2"	274	32		

Ken Moyer — Foot Injury

Use Name	Pos.	Hgt.	Wgt.	Age	Int	Pts
Ray Bentley	LB	6'2"	235	31		6
James Francis	LB	6'5"	252	24	3	6
Alex Gordon	LB	6'5"	245	27		
Randy Kirk	LB	6'2"	231	27		
Ricardo McDonald	LB	6'2"	235	22	1	
Gary Reasons	LB	6'4"	234	30		
Eric Shaw	LB	6'3"	248	20		
Brian Townsend	LB	6'3"	242	23		
Kevin Walker	LB	6'2"	238	26		
Alfred Williams	LB	6'6"	240	23		
Antoine Bennett	DB	5'11"	185	24		
Barney Bussey	DB	6'	210	30	1	
Rickey Dixon	DB	5'11"	191	25		
David Fulcher	DB	6'3"	238	27	3	
Rod Jones	DB	6'	185	28	2	
Mitchell Price	DB	5'9"	181	25		
Eric Thomas	DB	5'11"	181	27		
Fernandus Vinson	DB	5'10"	197	23		6
Leonard Wheeler	DB	5'11"	189	23	1	
Darryl Williams	DB	6'	191	22	4	

Use Name	Pos.	Hgt.	Wgt.	Age	Int	Pts
Boomer Esiason	QB	6'4"	220	31		
Donald Hollas	QB	6'3"	215	24		
David Klingler	QB	6'2"	205	23		
Eric Ball	HB-FB	6'2"	220	26		24
Harold Green	HB	6'2"	222	24		12
Derrick Fenner	FB-HB	6'3"	228	25		48
Ostell Miles	FB	6'	236	21		
Brian Brennan (to SD)	WR	5'10"	185	30		6
Tim McGee	WR	5'10"	183	28		18
Carl Pickens	WR	6'2"	206	22		12
Jeff Query	WR	6'	165	25		18
Reggie Rembert	WR	6'5"	200	25		
Milt Stegall	WR	6'	184	22		6
Rodney Holman	TE	6'3"	238	32		12
Jim Riggs	TE	6'5"	245	28		
Jeff Thomason	TE	6'4"	233	22		
Craig Thompson	TE	6'2"	244	23		12
Jim Breech	K	5'6"	161	36		88
Lee Johnson	K	6'2"	200	30		

Shane Garrett — Arm Injury
Eddie Brown — Neck Injury

PITTSBURGH STEELERS

RUSHING

Last Name	No.	Yds	Avg	TD
Foster	**390**	**1690**	4.3	**11**
Thompson	35	157	4.5	1
Hoge	41	150	3.7	0
Stone	12	118	9.8	0
Mills	1	20	20.0	0
Brister	10	16	1.6	0
O'Donnell	27	5	0.2	1
W. Williams	2	0	0.0	0

RECEIVING

Last Name	No.	Yds	Avg	TD
Graham	49	711	14.5	1
Foster	36	344	9.6	0
Stone	34	501	14.7	3
Mills	30	383	12.8	3
Hoge	28	231	8.3	1
Thompson	22	278	12.6	0
Cooper	16	197	12.3	3
Green	14	152	10.9	2
Davenport	9	136	15.1	0
Jorden	6	28	4.7	2
Didio	3	39	13.0	0
W. Williams	1	44	44.0	0
Thigpen	1	2	2.0	0

PUNT RETURNS

Last Name	No.	Yds	Avg	TD
Woodson	32	364	**11.4**	1

KICKOFF RETURNS

Last Name	No.	Yds	Avg	TD
Woodson	25	469	18.8	0
Stone	12	219	18.3	0
Thompson	2	51	25.5	0
Thigpen	2	44	22.0	0
Hoge	2	28	14.0	0
Bentley	1	17	17.0	0
Mills	1	11	11.0	0
Cooper	1	8	8.0	0
Campbell	1	0	0.0	0
W. Williams	1	0	0.0	0

PASSING — PUNTING — KICKING

PASSING	Att	Cmp	%	Yds	Yd/Att	TD	Int—	%	RK
O'Donnell	313	185	59.1	2283	7.29	13	9—	**2.9**	3
Brister	116	63	54.3	719	6.20	2	5—	4.3	
Royals	1	1	100.0	44	44.00	0	0—	0.0	
Foster	1	0	0.0	0	0.00	0	0—	0.0	

PUNTING	No.	Avg.
Royals	74	42.1

KICKING	XP	Att	%	FG	Att	%
Anderson	29	31	94	28	36	78

HOUSTON OILERS

RUSHING

Last Name	No.	Yds	Avg	TD
White	265	1226	4.6	7
Moon	27	147	5.4	1
G. Brown	19	87	4.6	1
Carlson	27	77	2.9	1
Givins	7	75	10.7	0
Slaughter	3	20	6.7	0
L. Harris	1	8	8.0	0
Tillman	1	1	1.0	0
Richardson	1	-1	-1.0	0
Gr. Montgomery	2	-14	-7.0	0

RECEIVING

Last Name	No.	Yds	Avg	TD
Jeffires	**90**	913	10.1	9
Duncan	82	954	11.6	1
Givins	67	787	11.7	**10**
White	57	641	11.2	1
Slaughter	39	486	12.5	4
L. Harris	35	435	12.4	2
Coleman	2	10	5.0	0
G. Brown	1	5	5.0	0

PUNT RETURNS

Last Name	No.	Yds	Avg	TD
Slaughter	20	142	7.1	0
Coleman	7	35	5.0	0

KICKOFF RETURNS

Last Name	No.	Yds	Avg	TD
Coleman	14	290	20.7	0
Tillman	10	157	15.7	0
Lewis	8	171	21.4	0
Slaughter	1	21	21.0	0
G. Brown	1	15	15.0	0
Gl. Montgomery	1	13	13.0	0
Flannery	1	12	12.0	0

PASSING — PUNTING — KICKING

PASSING	Att	Cmp	%	Yds	Yd/Att	TD	Int—	%	RK
Moon	346	224	64.7	2521	7.29	18	12—	3.5	**1**
Carlson	227	149	**65.6**	1710	7.53	9	11—	4.8	5

PUNTING	No.	Avg.
Montgomery	55	**45.2**

KICKING	XP	ATT	%	FG	ATT	%
Del Greco	41	41	**100**	21	27	78

CLEVELAND BROWNS

RUSHING

Last Name	No.	Yds	Avg	TD
Mack	169	543	3.2	6
Vardell	99	369	3.7	0
Metcalf	73	301	4.1	1
Hoard	54	236	4.4	0
Tomczak	24	39	1.6	0
Brooks	18	44	2.4	0
Baldwin	10	31	3.1	0
M. Jackson	1	21	21.0	0
Tillman	2	15	7.5	0
Kosar	5	12	2.4	0
Wolfley	1	2	2.0	0

RECEIVING

Last Name	No.	Yds	Avg	TD
M. Jackson	47	755	16.1	7
Metcalf	47	614	13.1	5
Hoard	26	310	11.9	1
Tillman	25	498	19.9	0
Bavaro	25	315	12.6	2
Holohan	20	170	8.5	0
Vardell	13	128	9.8	0
Mack	13	81	6.2	0
R. Smith	5	64	12.8	0
Galbraith	4	63	15.8	1
Collins	3	31	10.3	0
Baldwin	2	30	15.0	0
Holland	2	27	13.5	0
Wolfley	2	8	4.0	0
Brooks	2	-1	-0.5	0
McCardell	1	8	8.0	0
J. Jones	1	1	1.0	0

PUNT RETURNS

Last Name	No.	Yds	Avg	TD
Metcalf	**44**	**429**	9.8	1
Brooks	3	49	16.3	0

KICKOFF RETURNS

Last Name	No.	Yds	Avg	TD
Baldwin	30	675	22.5	0
Metcalf	9	157	17.4	0
Hoard	2	34	17.0	0
Vardell	2	14	7.0	0

PASSING — PUNTING — KICKING

PASSING	Att	Cmp	%	Yds	Yd/Att	TD	Int—	%	RK
Tomczak	211	120	56.9	1693	8.02	7	7—	3.3	
Kosar	155	103	66.5	1160	7.48	8	7—	4.5	
Philcox	27	13	48.1	217	8.04	3	1—	3.7	
Goebel	3	2	66.7	32	10.67	0	0—	0.0	
Metcalf	1	0	0.0	0	0.00	0	0—	0.0	
Stover	1	0	0.0	0	0.00	0	1—	100.0	

PUNTING	No.	Avg.
Hansen	75	41.1

KICKING	XP	ATT	%	FG	ATT	%
Stover	29	30	97	21	29	72

CINCINNATI BENGALS

RUSHING

Last Name	No.	Yds	Avg	TD
Green	265	1170	4.4	2
Fenner	112	500	4.5	7
Hollas	20	109	5.5	0
Esiason	21	66	3.1	0
Ball	16	55	3.4	2
Klingler	11	53	4.8	0
Miles	8	22	2.8	0
Query	1	1	1.0	0

RECEIVING

Last Name	No.	Yds	Avg	TD
Green	41	214	5.2	0
McGee	35	408	11.7	3
Pickens	26	326	12.5	1
Holman	26	266	10.2	2
Rembert	19	219	11.5	0
Thompson	19	194	10.2	2
Query	16	265	16.6	3
Brennan	19	188	9.9	1
Riggs	11	70	6.4	0
Fenner	7	41	5.9	1
Ball	6	66	11.0	2
Stegall	3	35	11.7	1
Thomason	2	14	7.0	0

PUNT RETURNS

Last Name	No.	Yds	Avg	TD
Pickens	18	229	12.7	1
Price	6	41	6.8	0

KICKOFF RETURNS

Last Name	No.	Yds	Avg	TD
Ball	20	411	20.6	0
Stegall	25	430	17.2	0
Miles	8	128	16.0	0
Fenner	2	38	19.0	0
Price	2	20	10.0	0
Bussey	1	18	18.0	0
Query	1	13	13.0	0

PASSING — PUNTING — KICKING

PASSING	Att	Cmp	%	Yds	Yd/Att	TD	Int—	%	RK
Esiason	278	144	51.8	1407	5.06	11	15—	5.4	11
Klingler	98	47	48.0	530	5.41	3	2—	2.0	
Hollas	58	35	60.3	335	5.78	2	0—	0.0	
Breech	1	1	100.0	12	12.00	0	0—	0.0	

PUNTING	Avg.	
Johnson	76	42.1

KICKING	XP	ATT	%	FG	ATT	%
Breech	31	31	**100**	19	27	70
Johnson	0	0	0	0	1	0

SAN DIEGO CHARGERS 11-5 Bobby Ross

Scores of Each Game		
10	KANSAS CITY	24
13	Denver	21
6	PITTSBURGH	23
0	Houston	27
17	SEATTLE	6
34	Indianapolis	14
24	DENVER	21
26	INDIANAPOLIS	0
14	Kansas City	16
14	Cleveland	13
29	TAMPA BAY	14
27	L.A. RAIDERS	3
27	Phoenix	21
27	CINCINNATI	10
36	L.A. Raiders	14
31	Seattle	14

UseName	Pos.	Hgt.	Wgt.	Age	Int	Pts
Leo Goeas	OT-OG	6'4"	292	26		
Harry Swayne	OT	6'5"	290	27		
Broderick Thompson	OT	6'5"	295	32		
Eric Moten	OG	6'2"	306	24		
David Richards	OG	6'5"	310	26		
Courtney Hall	C	6'2"	281	24		
Curtis Whitley	C	6'1"	288	23		
Mike Zandofsky	C-OG	6'2"	305	26		
Burt Grossman	DE	6'6"	270	25		4
Shawn Lee	DE	6'2"	280	25		
Chris Mims	DE	6'5"	270	21		2
Leslie O'Neal	DE	6'4"	259	28		
George Thornton	DT	6'3"	300	24		
Reggie White	DT	6'4"	291	22		
Blaise Winter	DT-NT	6'4"	278	30		
Tony Savage (to CIN)	NT	6'3"	300	25		

UseName	Pos.	Hgt.	Wgt.	Age	Int	Pts
Sam Anno	LB	6'3"	240	27		
Eugene Marve	LB	6'2"	240	32		
Kevin Murphy	LB	6'2"	235	28		
Gary Plummer	LB	6'2"	244	32	2	
Henry Rolling	LB	6'2"	247	26		
Junior Seau	LB	6'3"	250	23	2	
Billy Ray Smith	LB	6'3"	236	31		
Anthony Blaylock	DB	5'10"	185	27	2	
Gill Byrd	DB	5'11"	198	31	4	
Darren Carrington	DB	6'2"	200	25	6	6
Floyd Fields	DB	6'	208	23	1	
Donald Frank	DB	6'	192	26	4	
Delton Hall	DB	6'1"	211	27		
Marquez Pope	DB	5'10"	188	21		
Stanley Richard	DB	6'2"	197	24	3	
Sean Vanhorse	DB	5'10"	180	24		

David Grayson — Leg Injury

UseName	Pos.	Hgt.	Wgt.	Age	Int	Pts
Bob Gagliano	QB	6'3"	205	33		
Stan Humphries	QB	6'2"	223	27		24
Rod Bernstine	HB-FB-TE	6'3"	238	27		24
Eric Bieniemy	HB	5'7"	198	23		18
Ronnie Harmon	HB	5'11"	207	28		24
Peter Tuipulotu	HB-FB	5'11"	210	23		
Marion Butts	FB-HB	6'1"	248	26		24
Johnnie Barnes	WR	6'1"	180	24		
Robert Claiborne	WR	5'10"	175	25		
Shawn Jefferson	WR	5'11"	172	23		12
Nate Lewis	WR	5'11"	198	25		24
Anthony Miller	WR	5'11"	189	27		48
Steve Hendrickson	FB-LB	6'	250	26		
Deems May	TE	6'4"	250	23		
Alfred Pupunu	TE	6'2"	252	22		
Derrick Walker	TE	6'1"	244	25		12
Duane Young	TE	6'1"	260	24		
John Carney	K	5'11"	170	28		113
John Kidd	K	6'3"	208	31		

John Friesz — Knee Injury

KANSAS CITY CHIEFS 10-6 Marty Schottenheimer

Scores of Each Game		
24	San Diego	10
26	SEATTLE	7
20	Houston	* 23
27	L.A. RAIDERS	7
19	Denver	20
24	PHILADELPHIA	17
10	Dallas	17
3	PITTSBURGH	27
16	SAN DIEGO	14
35	WASHINGTON	16
24	Seattle	14
23	N.Y. Jets	7
7	L.A. Raiders	28
27	NEW ENGLAND	20
21	N.Y. Giants	35
42	DENVER	20

UseName	Pos.	Hgt.	Wgt.	Age	Int	Pts
John Alt	OT	6'7"	303	30		
Rich Baldinger	OT	6'4"	293	32		
Tom Dohring	OT	6'6"	290	24		
Derrick Graham	OT	6'4"	306	25		
Joe Staysniak	OT	6'5"	295	25		
Joe Valerio	OT-C	6'5"	293	23		
David Lutz	OG	6'6"	305	32		
Dave Szott	OG	6'4"	290	24		
Mike Baab	C	6'4"	278	32		
Tim Grunhard	C	6'2"	299	24		
Kani Kauahi	C	6'3"	275	32		
Leonard Griffin	DE	6'4"	278	29		
Neil Smith	DE	6'4"	275	26	1	6
Bill Maas	DE	6'5"	275	29		
Darren Mickel	DE	6'4"	268	22		
Mike Evans	DT-DE	6'3"	269	25		
Joe Phillips	DT	6'5"	300	29		
Dan Saleaumua	DT-NT	6'	295	27		
Tom Sims	DT	6'2"	291	25		

UseName	Pos.	Hgt.	Wgt.	Age	Int	Pts
Chris Martin	LB	6'2"	246	31		
Lonnie Marts	LB	6'1"	243	23	1	6
Ervin Randle	LB	6'1"	250	29		
Tracy Rogers	LB	6'2"	241	25		6
Tracy Simien	LB	6'1"	245	25	3	
Percy Snow	LB	6'2"	250	24		
Derrick Thomas	LB	6'3"	242	25		6
Martin Bayless	DB	6'2"	213	29	1	
Dale Carter	DB	6'1"	188	22	7	18
Albert Lewis	DB	6'2"	195	31	1	
Tahaun Lewis	DB	5'10"	175	23		
Charles Mincy	DB	5'11"	197	22	4	18
J.C. Pearson	DB	5'11"	186	29		
Kevin Porter (to NYJ)	DB	5'10"	214	26		
Kevin Ross	DB	5'9"	185	30	1	6
Doug Terry	DB	5'11"	192	22	1	
Bennie Thompson	DB	6'	214	29		

William Kirksey — Foot Injury
Dino Hackett — Ear Injury

UseName	Pos.	Hgt.	Wgt.	Age	Int	Pts
Matt Blundin	QB	6'6"	230	23		
Dave Krieg	QB	6'1"	202	33		12
Mark Vlasic	QB	6'3"	205	28		
Kimble Anders	HB	5'11"	221	25		
Bill Jones	HB	5'11"	227	25		
Todd McNair	HB	6'1"	202	27		12
Harvey Williams	HB	6'2"	229	25		6
Barry Word	HB	6'2"	245	28		24
Christian Okoye	FB	6'1"	260	31		36
Tim Barnett	WR	6'1"	201	24		24
J.J. Birden	WR	5'9"	170	27		18
Willie Davis	WR	6'	170	24		18
Tony Hargain	WR	6'	194	24		
Emile Harry (to LA)	WR	5'11"	186	29		
Fred Jones	WR	5'9"	182	25		
Michael Smith	WR	5'8"	160	21		
Keith Cash	TE	6'4"	245	23		12
Mike Dyal	TE	6'2"	240	26		
Jonathan Hayes	TE	6'5"	248	30		12
Bryan Barker	K	6'1"	187	28		
Nick Lowery	K	6'4"	205	36		105
Kent Sullivan	K	5'10"	197	28		

DENVER BRONCOS 8-8 Dan Reeves

Scores of Each Game		
17	L.A. RAIDERS	13
21	SAN DIEGO	13
0	Philadelphia	30
12	Cleveland	0
20	KANSAS CITY	19
3	Washington	34
27	HOUSTON	21
21	San Diego	24
27	N.Y. JETS	16
27	N.Y. GIANTS	13
0	L.A. Raiders	24
13	Seattle	* 16
27	DALLAS	31
17	Buffalo	27
10	SEATTLE	6
20	Kansas City	42

UseName	Pos.	Hgt.	Wgt.	Age	Int	Pts
Russell Freeman	OT	6'7"	290	22		
Chuck Johnson	OT	6'5"	275	23		
Ken Lanier	OT	6'3"	290	33		
Jeff Davidson	OG	6'5"	309	24		
Dave Widell	OT-C	6'6"	292	27		
Doug Widell	OG	6'4"	287	25		
Keith Kartz	C	6'4"	270	29		
Shane Dronett	DE	6'6"	275	21		
Ron Holmes	DE	6'4"	265	29		
Brian Sochia	DE	6'3"	278	31		
Kenny Walker	DE	6'3"	260	25		
Ron Geater	NT	6'6"	270	23		
Greg Kragen	NT	6'3"	265	30		

Frank Pollack — Back Injury

UseName	Pos.	Hgt.	Wgt.	Age	Int	Pts
Michael Brooks	LB	6'1"	235	27	1	6
Mike Croel	LB	6'3"	231	23		
Simon Fletcher	LB	6'5"	240	30		
John Kacherski	LB	6'3"	240	25		
Tim Lucas	LB	6'3"	230	31		
Karl Mecklenburg	LB	6'3"	235	32		
Jeff Mills	LB	6'3"	238	23		
John Sullins	LB	6'1"	225	22		
Keith Traylor	LB	6'2"	260	22		
Steve Atwater	DB	6'3"	217	25	2	
Tyrone Braxton	DB	5'11"	185	27	2	
Charles Dimry	DB	6'	175	26	1	
John Granby	DB	6'1"	198	23		
Wymon Henderson	DB	5'10"	186	30	4	6
Le-Lo Lang	DB	5'11"	185	25	1	
Alton Montgomery	DB	6'	195	24		
Muhammad Oliver	DB	5'11"	170	23		
Frank Robinson (from CIN)	DB	5'11"	174	23		
Dennis Smith	DB	6'3"	200	33	4	

Ronnie Haliburton — Neck Injury

UseName	Pos.	Hgt.	Wgt.	Age	Int	Pts
John Elway	QB	6'3"	215	32		12
Tommy Maddox	QB	6'4"	195	21		
Shawn Moore	QB	6'2"	214	24		
Gaston Green	HB	5'11"	192	26		12
Victor Jones	HB	5'8"	220	24		
Greg Lewis	HB-FB	5'10"	214	23		24
Sammie Smith	DB	6'2"	228	25		
Jeff Alexander	FB	6'	232	27		
Bob Perryman	FB	6'2"	233	28		
Reggie Rivers	FB	6'1"	215	24		24
Mark Jackson	WR	5'10"	180	29		48
Vance Johnson	WR	5'11"	185	29		12
Arthur Marshall	WR	5'11"	174	23		6
Ricky Nattiel	WR	5'9"	180	26		
Derek Russell	WR	6'	179	23		
Cedric Tillman	WR	6'2"	204	22		6
Michael Young	WR	6'1"	183	30		
Reggie Johnson	TE	6'2"	256	24		6
Clarence Kay	TE	6'2"	237	31		
Shannon Sharpe	TE	6'2"	230	24		12
Brad Daluiso	K	6'2"	207	24		
Mike Horan	K	5'11"	190	33		
Daren Parker	K	6'	185	23		
Ruben Rodriguez	K	6'2"	209	27		
David Treadwell	K	6'1"	180	25		88

Steve Sewell — Ankle Injury

LOS ANGELES RAIDERS 7-9 Art Shell

Scores of Each Game		
13	Denver	17
21	Cincinnati	* 24
16	CLEVELAND	28
7	Kansas City	27
13	N.Y. GIANTS	10
20	BUFFALO	3
19	Seattle	0
13	DALLAS	28
10	Philadelphia	31
20	SEATTLE	3
24	DENVER	0
3	San Diego	27
28	KANSAS CITY	7
7	Miami	20
14	SAN DIEGO	36
21	Washington	20

UseName	Pos.	Hgt.	Wgt.	Age	Int	Pts
Greg Skrepenak	OG	6'6"	315	22		
Bruce Wilkerson	OT	6'5"	295	28		
Steve Wright	OT	6'6"	285	33		
Reggie McElroy	OT	6'6"	290	32		
Max Montoya	OG	6'5"	295	36		
Todd Peat	OG	6'2"	305	28		
Steve Wisniewski	OG	6'4"	290	25		
Don Mosebar	C	6'6"	305	30		
Dan Turk	C	6'4"	305	30		
Aundray Bruce	DE	6'5'	260	26		
Howie Long	DE	6'5"	275	32		
Anthony Smith	DE	6'3"	265	25		
Greg Townsend	DE	6'3"	270	30		
Willie Broughton	DT	6'5"	280	27		
Bob Golic	DT	6'2"	280	34		
Nolan Harrison	DT	6'5"	280	23		2
Chester McGlockton	DT	6'4"	320	22		

James FitzPatrick — Knee Injury

UseName	Pos.	Hgt.	Wgt.	Age	Int	Pts
Anthony Bell	LB	6'3"	245	28		
Thomas Benson	LB	6'2"	240	30		
Riki Ellison	LB	6'2"	225	32		
Mike Jones	LB	6'1"	230	23		
Winston Moss	LB	6'3"	240	26		
Aaron Wallace	LB	6'3"	235	25		
Eddie Anderson	DB	6'1"	210	29	3	6
Torin Dorn	DB	6'	190	24	1	
Derrick Hoskins	DB	6'2"	200	21		
Dan Land	DB	6'	195	27	1	
Ronnie Lott	DB	6'	205	33	1	
Terry McDaniel	DB	5'10"	180	27	4	
Elvis Patterson	DB	5'11"	195	31		6
Sam Seale	DB	5'9"	185	29		
Lionel Washington	DB	6'	190	31	2	
Dave Waymer	DB	6'1"	205	34		

UseName	Pos.	Hgt.	Wgt.	Age	Int	Pts
Vince Evans	QB	6'2"	210	37		
Todd Marinovich	QB	6'4"	220	23		
Jay Schroeder	QB	6'4"	210	31		
Marcus Allen	HB	6'2'	210	32		18
Nick Bell	HB	6'2"	255	24		18
Eric Dickerson	HB	6'3"	220	31		18
Napoleon McCallum	HB	6'2"	230	28		
Steve Smith	FB	6'1"	240	28		6
Tim Brown	WR	6'	195	26		42
Mervyn Fernandez	WR	6'3"	205	32		
Willie Gault	WR	6'	175	31		24
Sam Graddy	WR	5'10"	180	28		6
Alexander Wright (from DAL)	WRT	6'	195	25		12
Andrew Glover	TE	6'6"	245	25		6
Ethan Horton	TE	6'4"	240	29		12
David Jones	TE	6'2"	220	23		
Kevin Smith	TE	6'4"	255	23		
Jeff Gossett	K	6'2"	195	35		
Jeff Jaeger	K	5'11"	195	27		73

SEATTLE SEAHAWKS 2-14 Tom Flores

Scores of Each Game		
3	CINCINNATI	21
7	Kansas City	26
10	New England	6
17	MIAMI	19
6	San Diego	17
0	Dallas	27
0	L.A. RAIDERS	19
10	N.Y. Giants	23
3	WASHINGTON	16
3	L.A. Raiders	20
14	KANSAS CITY	24
16	DENVER	* 13
14	Pittsburgh	20
17	PHILADELPHIA	* 20
6	Denver	10
14	SAN DIEGO	31

UseName	Pos.	Hgt.	Wgt.	Age	Int	Pts
Theo Adams	OT	6'4"	298	26		
Bill Hitchcock	OT	6'6"	291	25		
Mike Keim	OT	6'7"	285	26		
Ronnie Lee	OT	6'3"	296	35		
Ray Roberts	OT	6'6"	304	23		
Darrick Brilz	OG	6'3"	287	28		
Sean Farrell	OG	6'3"	260	32		
Andy Heck	OT	6'6"	298	25		
John Hunter	OG	6'8"	300	27		
Grant Feasel	C	6'7"	283	32		
Joe Tofflemire	C	6'3"	273	27		
Jeff Bryant	DE	6'5"	281	32		
Mike Sinclair	DE	6'4"	255	24		
Natu Tuatagaloa	DE	6'4"	274	26	1	
Tony Woods	DE	6'4"	269	26		
Cortez Kennedy	DT	6'3"	293	24		
Joe Nash	DT	6'2"	278	31		
Tyrone Rodgers	DT	6'3"	266	23		

Bryan Millard — Back Injury

UseName	Pos.	Hgt.	Wgt.	Age	Int	Pts
Joe Cain	LB	6'1"	233	27	2	
Greg Clark	LB	6'	226	27		
E.J. Junior (from TB)	LB	6'3"	242	32		
Richard Newbill	LB	6'1"	240	24		
Rufus Porter	LB	6'1"	227	27		
Bob Spitulski	LB	6'3"	235	22		
Rod Stephens	LB	6'1"	237	26		
Terry Wooden	LB	6'3"	236	25	1	
David Wyman	LB	6'2"	248	28		
Robert Blackmon	DB	6'	197	25	1	
Brian Davis	DB	6'2"	187	29	2	
Dedrick Dodge	DB	6'2"	184	25	1	
Malcolm Frank	DB	5'8"	182	23		
Nesby Glasgow	DB	5'10"	187	35		
Dwayne Harper	DB	5'11"	174	26	3	6
Patrick Hunter	DB	5'11"	186	27	2	
James Jefferson	DB	6'1"	199	28		
Eugene Robinson	DB	6'	191	29	7	
Rafael Robinson	DB	5'11"	200	23		

Marcus Cotton — Knee Injury
Vann McElroy — Ankle Injury

UseName	Pos.	Hgt.	Wgt.	Age	Int	Pts
Stan Gelbaugh	QB	6'3"	207	29		
Rusty Hilger	QB	6'4"	209	30		
Dan McGwire	QB	6'8"	243	24		
Kelly Stouffer	QB	6'3"	214	28		
Rueben Mayes	HB	5'11"	201	29		
Chris Warren	HB	6'2"	225	25		18
Tracy Johnson	FB	6'	230	25		
James Jones	FB-TE	6'2"	232	31		
John L. Williams	FB	5'11"	231	27		18
Brian Blades	WR	5'11	189	27		6
Louis Clark	WR	6'1"	198	28		6
David Daniels	WR	6'1"	190	22		
Tommy Kane	WR	5'11"	181	28		18
Doug Thomas	WR	5'10"	178	22		
Robb Thomas	WR	5'11"	175	26		
Brian Treggs	WR	5'9"	161	22		
Paul Green	TE	6'3"	230	25		6
Ron Heller	TE	6'3"	242	28		
Mike Jones	TE	6'3"	255	25		
Trey Junkin	TE	6'2"	237	31		6
John Kasay	K	5'10"	189	22		56
Rick Tuten	K	6'2"	218	27		

SAN DIEGO CHARGERS

RUSHING

Last Name	No.	Yds	Avg	TD
Butts	218	809	3.7	4
Bernstine	106	499	4.7	4
Bieniemy	74	264	3.6	3
Harmon	55	235	4.3	3
Humphries	28	79	2.8	4
Lewis	2	7	3.5	0
Miller	1	-1	-1.0	0
Gagliano	3	-4	-1.3	0
Kidd	2	-13	-6.5	0

RECEIVING

Last Name	No.	Yds	Avg	TD
Harmon	79	914	11.6	1
Miller	72	1060	14.7	7
Lewis	34	580	17.1	4
Walker	34	393	11.6	2
Jefferson	29	377	13.0	2
Bernstine	12	86	7.2	0
Butts	9	73	8.1	0
Bieniemy	5	49	9.8	0
Young	4	45	11.3	0
Claiborne	1	15	15.0	0

PUNT RETURNS

Last Name	No.	Yds	Avg	TD
Bieniemy	30	229	7.6	0
Lewis	13	127	9.8	0

KICKOFF RETURNS

Last Name	No.	Yds	Avg	TD
Lewis	10	402	21.2	0
Bieniemy	15	257	17.1	0
Harmon	7	96	13.7	0
Hendrickson	2	14	7.0	0
Miller	1	33	33.0	0

PASSING — PUNTING — KICKING

PASSING	Att	Cmp	%	Yds	Yd/Att	TD	Int—	%	RK
Humphries	454	263	57.9	3356	7.39	16	18	4.0	7
Gagliano	42	19	45.2	258	6.14	0	3	7.1	

PUNTING	No.	Avg.
Kidd	68	42.6

KICKING	XP	Att	%	FG	Att	%
Carney	35	35	100	26	32	81

KANSAS CITY CHIEFS

RUSHING

Last Name	No.	Yds	Avg	TD
Word	163	607	3.7	4
Okoye	144	448	3.1	6
Williams	78	262	3.4	1
McNair	21	124	5.9	1
Krieg	37	74	2.0	2
Harry	1	27	27.0	0
Anders	1	1	1.0	0
Davis	1	-11	-11.0	0

RECEIVING

Last Name	No.	Yds	Avg	TD
McNair	44	380	8.6	1
Birden	42	644	15.3	3
Davis	36	756	21.0	3
Barnett	24	442	18.4	4
F. Jones	18	265	14.7	0
Hargain	17	205	12.1	0
Cash	12	113	9.4	2
Word	9	80	8.9	0
Hayes	9	77	8.6	2
Anders	5	65	13.0	0
Harry	6	58	9.7	0
Williams	5	24	4.8	0
B. Jones	2	6	3.0	0
Dyal	1	7	7.0	0
Okoye	1	5	5.0	0

PUNT RETURNS

Last Name	No.	Yds	Avg	TD
Carter	38	398	10.5	2
Harry	6	34	5.7	0
Mincy	1	1	1.0	0

KICKOFF RETURNS

Last Name	No.	Yds	Avg	TD
Williams	21	405	19.3	0
Carter	11	190	17.3	0
F. Jones	3	51	17.0	0
McNair	2	20	10.0	0
Cash	1	36	36.0	0
Anders	1	20	20.0	0

PASSING — PUNTING — KICKING

PASSING	Att	Cmp	%	Yds	Yd/Att	TD	Int—	%	RK
Krieg	413	230	55.7	3115	7.54	15	12	2.9	6

PUNTING	No.	Avg.
Barker	76	42.7
Sullivan	6	41.2
Lowery	4	35.3

KICKING	XP	Att.	%	FG	Att	%
Lowery	39	39	100	22	24	92

DENVER BRONCOS

RUSHING

Last Name	No.	Yds	Avg	TD
Green	161	648	4.0	2
Rivers	74	282	3.8	3
Lewis	73	268	3.7	4
Elway	34	94	2.8	2
S. Smith	23	94	4.1	0
Marshall	11	56	5.1	0
Moore	8	39	4.9	0
Maddox	9	20	2.2	0
R. Johnson	2	7	3.5	0
M. Jackson	3	-1	-0.3	0
Perryman	3	-1	-0.3	0
Sharpe	2	-6	-3.0	0

RECEIVING

Last Name	No.	Yds	Avg	TD
Sharpe	53	640	12.1	2
M. Jackson	48	745	15.5	8
Rivers	45	449	10.0	1
Marshall	26	493	19.0	1
V. Johnson	24	294	12.3	2
Tillman	12	211	17.6	1
Russell	12	140	11.7	0
R. Johnson	10	139	13.9	1
Green	10	79	7.9	0
Kay	7	56	8.0	0
Lewis	4	30	7.5	0
Jones	3	17	5.7	0
Perryman	2	15	7.5	0
Young	1	11	11.0	0
Do. Widell	1	-7	-7.0	0

PUNT RETURNS

Last Name	No.	Yds	Avg	TD
Marshall	33	349	10.6	0
Dimry	1	4	4.0	0

KICKOFF RETURNS

Last Name	No.	Yds	Avg	TD
Montgomery	21	466	22.2	0
Marshall	8	132	16.5	0
Russell	7	154	22.0	0
Green	5	76	15.2	0
Robinson	4	89	22.3	0
R. Johnson	2	47	23.5	0
S. Smith	2	31	15.5	0
Oliver	1	20	20.0	0
Traylor	1	13	13.0	0

PASSING — PUNTING — KICKING

PASSING	Att	Cmp	%	Yds	Yd/Att	TD	Int—	%	RK
Elway	316	174	55.1	2242	7.09	10	17	5.4	8
Maddox	121	66	54.5	757	6.26	5	9	7.4	
Moore	34	17	50.0	232	6.82	0	3	8.8	
Marshall	1	1	100.0	81	81.00	1	0	0.0	
Lewis	1	0	0.0	0	0.00	0	0	0.0	

PUNTING	No.	Avg.
Horan	38	44.2
Rodriguez	47	40.6
Parker	12	40.9
Daluiso	10	40.7

KICKING	XP	ATT	%	FG	ATT	%
Treadwell	28	28	100	20	24	83

LOS ANGELES RAIDERS

RUSHING

Last Name	No.	Yds	Avg	TD
Dickerson	187	729	3.9	2
N. Bell	81	366	4.5	3
Allen	67	301	4.5	2
Schroeder	28	160	5.7	0
S. Smith	44	129	2.9	0
Evans	11	79	7.2	0
Marinovich	9	30	3.3	0
Gault	1	6	6.0	0
Brown	3	-4	-1.3	0
Gossett	1	-12	-12.0	0

RECEIVING

Last Name	No.	Yds	Avg	TD
Brown	49	693	14.1	7
Horton	33	409	12.4	2
Allen	28	277	9.9	1
S. Smith	28	217	7.8	1
Gault	27	508	18.8	4
Glover	15	178	11.9	1
Dickerson	14	85	6.1	1
A. Wright	12	175	14.6	2
Graddy	10	205	20.5	1
Fernandez	9	121	13.4	0
N. Bell	4	40	10.0	0
D. Jones	2	29	14.5	0
McCallum	1	13	13.0	0

PUNT RETURNS

Last Name	No.	Yds	Avg	TD
T. Brown	37	383	10.4	0
McCallum	4	19	4.8	0

KICKOFF RETURNS

Last Name	No.	Yds	Avg	TD
A. Wright	26	442	17.0	0
McCallum	14	274	19.6	0
Graddy	5	85	17.0	0
Land	2	27	13.5	0
Brown	2	14	7.0	0
N. Bell	1	16	16.0	0
Turk	1	3	3.0	0

PASSING — PUNTING — KICKING

PASSING	Att	Cmp	%	Yds	Yd/Att	TD	Int—	%	RK
Schroeder	253	123	48.6	1476	5.83	11	11	4.3	9
Marinovich	165	81	49.1	1102	6.68	5	9	5.3	
Evans	53	29	54.7	372	7.02	4	3	5.7	

PUNTING	No.	Avg.
Gossett	77	42.3

KICKING	XP	ATT	%	FG	ATT	%
Jaeger	28	29	97	15	26	58

SEATTLE SEAHAWKS

RUSHING

Last Name	No.	Yds	Avg	TD
Warren	223	1017	4.6	3
Williams	114	339	3.0	1
Gelbaugh	16	79	4.9	0
Mayes	28	74	2.6	0
Stouffer	9	37	4.1	0
Johnson	3	26	8.7	0
McGwire	3	13	4.3	0
D. Thomas	3	7	2.3	0
Blades	1	5	5.0	0
Tuten	1	0	0.0	0
R. Thomas	1	-1	-1.0	0

RECEIVING

Last Name	No.	Yds	Avg	TD
Williams	74	556	7.5	2
Kane	27	369	13.7	3
J. Jones	21	190	9.0	0
L. Clark	20	290	14.5	1
Blades	19	256	13.5	1
Warren	16	134	8.4	0
Heller	12	85	7.1	0
R. Thomas	11	136	12.4	0
P. Green	9	67	7.4	1
D. Thomas	8	85	10.6	0
Daniels	5	99	19.8	0
Junkin	3	25	8.3	1
M. Jones	3	18	6.0	0
Mayes	2	13	6.5	0

PUNT RETURNS

Last Name	No.	Yds	Avg	TD
Warren	34	252	7.4	0
Treggs	4	31	7.8	0

KICKOFF RETURNS

Last Name	No.	Yds	Avg	TD
Warren	28	524	18.7	0
Mayes	19	311	16.4	0
D. Thomas	1	19	19.0	0
J. Jones	1	16	16.0	0
Johnson	1	15	15.0	0

PASSING — PUNTING — KICKING

PASSING	Att	Cmp	%	Yds	Yd/Att	TD	Int—	%	RK
Gelbaugh	255	121	47.5	1307	5.13	6	11	4.3	13
Stouffer	190	92	48.4	900	4.74	3	9	4.7	
McGwire	30	17	56.7	116	3.87	0	3	10.0	
Tuten	1	0	0.0	0	0.00	0	0	0.0	

PUNTING	No.	Avg.
Tuten	108	44.1

KICKING	XP	ATT	%	FG	ATT	%
Kasay	14	14	100	14	22	64

1992 A.F.C. PLAYOFFS — FIRST ROUND

January 2, 1993 at San Diego (Attendance 58,278)

SCORING

KANSAS CITY	0	0	0	0	- 0
SAN DIEGO	0	0	10	7	- 17

Third Quarter
- S.D. — Butts, 54 yard run; PAT — Carney (kick)
- S.D. — Carney, 34 yard field goal

Fourth Quarter
- S.D. — Hendrickson, 5 yard run

TEAMSTATISTICS

K.C.		S.D.
17	First Downs- Total	18
5	First Downs- Rushing	8
10	First Downs- Passing	7
2	First Downs- Penalty	3
2	Fumbles- Number	2
1	Fumbles- Lost Ball	1
7	Penalties- Number	5
62	Yards Penalized	44
0	Missed Field Goals	1
60	Offensive Plays	63
251	Net Yards	342
4.2	Average Gain	5.4
3	Giveaways	1
1	Takeaways	3
- 2	Difference	+ 2

INDIVIDUALSTATISTICS

KANSAS CITY	No.	Yds.	Avg.	SAN DIEGO	No.	Yds.	Avg.
RUSHING							
Williams	12	35	2.9	Butts	15	119	7.9
McNair	3	18	6.0	Bieniemy	13	38	2.9
Krieg	2	4	2.0	Harmon	4	27	6.8
Word	2	4	2.0	Hendrickson	1	5	5.0
	19	61	3.2	Bernstine	1	3	3.0
				Humphries	1	0	0.0
					35	192	5.5
RECEIVING							
Birden	4	78	19.5	Harmon	4	21	5.3
McNair	4	35	8.8	Walker	3	60	20.0
Davis	3	30	10.0	Miller	2	58	29.0
Hargain	2	46	23.0	Butts	2	17	8.5
M. Smith	1	28	28.0	Lewis	1	39	39.0
Williams	1	11	11.0	Brennan	1	8	8.0
Cash	1	5	5.0	Bieniemy	1	-4	-4.0
	16	233	14.6		14	199	14.2
PUNTING							
Barker	8		45.0	Kidd	6		44.2
PUNT RETURNS							
Mincy	1	4	4.0	Lewis	4	35	8.8
Carter	1	1	1.0	Byrd	3FC		
	2	5	2.5				
KICKOFF RETURNS							
Carter	1	5	5.0	None			
INTERCEPTION RETURNS							
None				Carrington	1	40	40.0
				O'Neal	1	3	3.0
					2	43	21.5

PASSING

	Att.	Comp.	Comp. Pct.	Yds.	Int.	Yds./ Att.	Yds./ Comp.
KANSAS CITY							
Krieg	34	16	47.1	233	2	6.8	14.6
SAN DIEGO							
Humphries	23	14	60.9	199	0	8.7	14.2

January 3, 1993 at Orchard Park, N.Y. (Attendance 75,141)

SCORING

HOUSTON	7	21	7	3	0	- 38
BUFFALO	3	0	28	7	3	- 41

First Quarter
- Hou. — Jeffires, 3 yard pass from Moon; PAT — Del Greco (kick)
- Buff. — Christie, 36 yard field goal

Second Quarter
- Hou. — Slaughter, 7 yard pass from Moon; PAT — Del Greco (kick)
- Hou. — Duncan, 26 yard pass from Moon; PAT — Del Greco (kick)
- Hou. — Jeffires, 27 yard pass from Moon; PAT — Del Greco (kick)

Third Quarter
- Hou. — McDowell, 58 yard interception return; PAT — Del Greco (kick)
- Buff. — K. Davis, 1 yard run; PAT — Christie (kick)
- Buff. — Beebe, 38 yard pass from Reich; PAT — Christie (kick)
- Buff. — Reed, 26 yard pass from Reich; PAT — Christie (kick)
- Buff. — Reed, 18 yard pass from Reich; PAT — Christie (kick)

Fourth Quarter
- Buff. — Reed, 17 yard pass from Reich; PAT — Christie (kick)
- Hou. — Del Greco, 26 yard field goal

Overtime
- Buff — Christie, 32 yard field goal

TEAMSTATISTICS

HOU.		BUFF.
27	First Downs- Total	19
6	First Downs- Rushing	5
18	First Downs- Passing	13
3	First Downs- Penalty	1
2	Fumbles- Number	0
0	Fumbles- Lost Ball	0
4	Penalties- Number	4
30	Yards Penalized	30
0	Missed Field Goals	0
76	Offensive Plays	63
429	Net Yards	366
5.6	Average Gain	5.8
2	Giveaways	1
1	Takeaways	2
- 1	Difference	+ 1

INDIVIDUALSTATISTICS

HOUSTON	No.	Yds.	Avg.	BUFFALO	No.	Yds.	Avg.
RUSHING							
White	19	75	3.9	K. Davis	13	68	5.2
Moon	2	7	3.5	Thomas	11	26	2.4
Montgomery	1	0	0.0	Gardner	1	5	5.0
	22	82	3.7	Reich	1	-1	-1.0
					26	98	3.8
RECEIVING							
Givins	9	117	13.0	Reed	8	136	17.0
Jeffires	8	98	12.3	Beebe	4	64	16.0
Slaughter	8	73	9.1	Metzelaars	3	43	14.3
Duncan	8	57	7.1	K. Davis	2	25	12.5
Harris	2	15	7.5	Lofton	2	24	12.0
White	1	11	11.0	Thomas	2	-3	-1.5
	36	371	10.3		21	289	13.8
PUNTING							
Montgomery	2		24.5	Mohr	2		35.0
PUNT RETURNS							
Slaughter	1	7	7.0	None			
Slaughter	1FC						
KICKOFF RETURNS							
Tillman	1	15	15.0	K. Davis	2	33	16.5
D. Lewis	1	7	7.0	Lamb	1	22	22.0
Flannery	1	5	5.0	Schulz	1	0	0.0
T. Brown	1	0	0.0	Maddox	1	0	0.0
	4	27	6.8		5	55	11.0
INTERCEPTION RETURNS							
McDowell	1	58	58.0	Jones	1	15	15.0
				Odomes	1	2	2.0
					2	17	8.5

PASSING

	Att.	Comp.	Comp. Pct.	Yds.	Int.	Yds./ Att.	Yds./ Comp.
HOUSTON							
Moon	50	36	72.0	371	2	7.4	10.3
BUFFALO							
Reich	34	21	61.8	289	1	8.5	13.8

1992 N.F.C. PLAYOFFS — FIRST ROUND

January 2, 1993 at Minneapolis (Attendance 57,353)

SCORING

WASHINGTON	3	14	7	0	- 24
MINNESOTA	7	0	0	0	- 7

First Quarter

Minn.	Allen, 1 yard run PAT — Reveiz (kick)
Wash.	Lohmiller, 44 yard field goal

Second Quarter

Wash.	Byner, 3 yard run PAT — Lohmiller (kick)
Wash.	Mitchell, 8 yardrun PAT — Lohmiller (kick)

Third Quarter

Wash.	Clark, 24 yard pass from Rypien PAT — Lohmiller (kick)

TEAMSTATISTICS

WASH.		MINN.
24	First Downs- Total	9
12	First Downs- Rushing	9
9	First Downs- Passing	5
3	First Downs- Penalty	0
0	Fumbles- Number	1
0	Fumbles- Lost Ball	0
2	Penalties- Number	7
15	Yards Penalized	53
2	Missed Field Goals	0
73	Offensive Plays	41
358	Net Yards	148
4.9	Average Gain	3.6
1	Giveaways	2
2	Takeaways	1
+ 1	Difference	- 1

INDIVIDUALSTATISTICS

WASHINGTON	No.	Yds.	Avg.	MINNESOTA	No.	Yds.	Avg.
RUSHING							
Mitchell	16	109	6.8	Allen	10	48	4.8
Byner	20	62	3.1	Craig	5	23	4.6
Green	5	17	3.4	J. Johnson	1	2	2.0
Monk	3	7	2.3	Salisbury	1	0	0.0
Rypien	3	1	0.3		17	73	4.3
	47	196	4.2				
RECEIVING							
Clark	6	91	15.2	Carter	3	77	25.7
Monk	3	35	11.7	Allen	2	11	5.5
Mitchell	3	16	5.3	A. Carter	1	25	25.0
Byner	2	6	3.0		6	113	18.8
Middleton	1	19	19.0				
Sanders	1	5	5.0				
	16	172	10.8				
PUNTING							
Goodburn	3		37.0	Newsome	7		43.1
PUNT RETURNS							
Mitchell	3	70	23.3	Parker	1	13	13.0
Mitchell	3FC			Parker	1FC		
KICKOFF RETURNS							
Mitchell	1	14	14.0	Nelson	3	55	18.3
Copeland	1	6	6.0	J. Johnson	2	49	24.5
	2	20	10.0		5	104	20.8
INTERCEPTION RETURNS							
Mayhew	1	44	44.0	Scott	1	21	21.0
Edwards	1	6	6.0				
	2	50	25.0				

PASSING

WASHINGTON	Att.	Comp.	Comp. Pct.	Yds.	Int.	Yds./ Att.	Yds./ Comp.
Rypien	24	16	66.7	172	1	7.2	10.8
Byner	1	0	0.0	0	0	0.0	0.0
	25	16	64.0	172	1	6.9	10.8
MINNESOTA							
Salisbury	20	6	30.0	113	2	5.7	18.8

January 3, 1993 at New Orleans (Attendance 68,893)

SCORING

PHILADELPHIA	7	0	3	26	- 36
NEW ORLEANS	7	10	3	0	- 20

First Quarter

N.O.	Heyward, 1 yard run PAT — Andersen (kick)
Phil.	Barnett, 57 yard pass from Cunningham PAT — Ruzek (kick)

Second Quarter

N.O.	Andersen, 35 yard field goal
N.O.	Early, 7 yard pass from Hebert PAT — Andersen (kick)

Third Quarter

N.O.	Andersen, 42 yard field goal
Phil.	Ruzek, 40 yard field goal

Fourth Quarter

Phil.	Barnett, 35 yard pass from Cunningham PAT — Ruzek (kick)
Phil.	Sherman, 6 yard run PAT — Ruzek (kick)
Phil.	Safety, Hebert sacked by White in end zone
Phil.	Ruzek, 39 yard field goal
Phil	Allen, 18 yard interception return PAT — Ruzek (kick)

TEAMSTATISTICS

PHIL.		N.O.
19	First Downs- Total	20
10	First Downs- Rushing	3
8	First Downs- Passing	16
1	First Downs- Penalty	1
1	Fumbles- Number	1
1	Fumbles- Lost Ball	1
4	Penalties- Number	4
37	Yards Penalized	35
0	Missed Field Goals	0
64	Offensive Plays	60
349	Net Yards	360
5.5	Average Gain	6.0
1	Giveaways	4
4	Takeaways	1
+ 3	Difference	- 3

INDIVIDUALSTATISTICS

PHILADELPHIA	No.	Yds.	Avg.	NEW ORLEANS	No.	Yds.	Avg.
RUSHING							
Sherman	21	105	5.0	Dunbar	4	28	7.0
Cunningham	2	19	9.5	Heyward	10	23	2.3
Walker	5	12	2.4	Hebert	3	18	6.0
	28	136	4.9	Hilliard	3	7	2.3
					34	150	4.4
RECEIVING							
Byars	6	37	6.2	Early	7	93	13.3
Barnett	4	102	25.5	Martin	5	64	12.8
Williams	4	36	9.0	Dunbar	4	49	12.3
Sherman	3	29	9.7	Heyward	3	45	15.0
Green	1	14	14.0	Brenner	2	24	12.0
Walker	1	1	1.0	Hilliard	1	10	10.0
	19	219	11.5	Small	1	6	6.0
					23	291	12.7
PUNTING							
Feagles	5		51.2	Barnhardt	3		45.3
PUNT RETURNS							
Sikahema	2	8	4.0	Newman	3	31	10.3
				Newman	1FC		
KICKOFF RETURNS							
Sikahema	3	56	18.7	Dunbar	2	48	24.0
				Newman	1	16	16.0
					3	64	21.3
INTERCEPTIONS							
Allen	2	22	11.0	None			
Joyner	1	14	14.0				
	3	36	12.0				

PASSING

PHILADELPHIA	Att.	Comp.	Comp. Pct.	Yds.	Int.	Yds./ Att.	Yds./ Comp.
Cunningham	35	19	54.3	219	0	6.3	11.5
NEW ORLEANS							
Hebert	39	23	59.0	291	3	7.5	12.7

1992 A.F.C. PLAYOFFS — SECOND ROUND

January 9, 1993 at Pittsburgh (Attendance 60,407)

SCORING

BUFFALO	0	7	7	10	- 24
PITTSBURGH	3	0	0	0	- 3

First Quarter
Pit. — Anderson, 38 yard field goal

Second Quarter
Buff. — Frerotte, 1 yard pass from Reich
PAT — Christie (kick)

Third Quarter
Buff. — Lofton, 17 yard pass from Reich
PAT — Christie (kick)

Fourth Quarter
Buff. — Christie, 43 yard field goal
Buff. — Gardner, 1 yard run
PAT — Christie (kick)

TEAMSTATISTICS

BUFF.		PITT.
19	First Downs- Total	18
7	First Downs- Rushing	7
11	First Downs- Passing	10
1	First Downs- Penalty	1
0	Fumbles- Number	4
0	Fumbles- Lost Ball	1
4	Penalties- Number	2
33	Yards Penalized	23
0	Missed Field Goals	0
63	Offensive Plays	63
325	Net Yards	240
5.2	Average Gain	3.8
0	Giveaways	3
3	Takeaways	0
+3	Difference	-3

INDIVIDUALSTATISTICS

RUSHING

BUFFALO	No.	Yds.	Avg.	PITTSBURGH	No.	Yds.	Avg.
K. Davis	10	104	10.4	Foster	20	104	5.2
Thomas	19	54	2.8	O'Donnell	4	26	6.5
Gardner	7	22	3.1	Thompson	1	3	3.0
Reich	2	-3	-1.5	Royals	1	0	0.0
Reed	1	-8	-8.0	Stone	1	-4	-4.0
	39	169	4.3		27	129	4.8

RECEIVING

BUFFALO	No.	Yds.	Avg.	PITTSBURGH	No.	Yds.	Avg.
Beebe	6	72	12.0	Mills	8	93	11.6
Thomas	3	25	8.3	Davenport	3	54	18.0
Lofton	2	29	14.5	Foster	3	7	2.3
McKeller	2	22	11.0	Stone	1	9	9.0
Metzelaars	2	11	5.5		15	163	10.9
Frerotte	1	1	1.0				
	16	160	10.0				

PUNTING

BUFFALO	No.	Yds.	Avg.	PITTSBURGH	No.	Yds.	Avg.
Mohr	4		42.3	Royals	3		37.3

PUNT RETURNS

BUFFALO	No.	Yds.	Avg.	PITTSBURGH	No.	Yds.	Avg.
Hicks	1FC			Woodson	2	14	7.0
				Thigpen	1FC		

KICKOFF RETURNS

BUFFALO	No.	Yds.	Avg.	PITTSBURGH	No.	Yds.	Avg.
Lamb	1	24	24.0	Stone	3	65	21.7
Davis	1	18	18.0	Thompson	1	20	20.0
	2	42	21.0	Thigpen	1	14	14.0
					5	99	19.8

INTERCEPTION RETURNS

BUFFALO	No.	Yds.	Avg.
Odomes	1	1	1.0
Williams	1	0	0.0
	2	1	0.5

PASSING

BUFFALO	Att.	Comp.	Comp. Pct.	Yds.	Int.	Yds./ Att.	Yds./ Comp.
Reich	23	16	69.6	160	0	7.0	10.0
PITTSBURGH							
O'Donnell	29	15	51.7	163	2	5.6	10.9

January 10, 1993 at Miami (Attendance 71,224)

SCORING

SAN DIEGO	0	0	0	0	- 0
MIAMI	0	21	0	10	- 31

Second Quarter
Mia. — Paige, 1 yard pass from Marino
PAT — Stoyanovich (kick)
Mia. — Jackson, 9 yard pass from Marino
PAT — Stoyanovich (kick)
Mia. — Jackson, 30 yard pass from Marino
PAT — Stoyanovich (kick)

Fourth Quarter
Mia. — Stoyanovich, 22 yard field goal
Mia. — Craver, 25 yard run
PAT — Stoyanovich (kick)

TEAMSTATISTICS

S.D.		MIA.
10	First Downs- Total	18
3	First Downs- Rushing	9
7	First Downs- Passing	9
0	First Downs- Penalty	0
3	Fumbles- Number	3
1	Fumbles- Lost Ball	1
4	Penalties- Number	0
39	Yards Penalized	0
0	Missed Field Goals	0
62	Offensive Plays	69
202	Net Yards	324
3.3	Average Gain	4.7
5	Giveaways	1
1	Takeaways	5
- 4	Difference	+4

INDIVIDUALSTATISTICS

RUSHING

SAN DIEGO	No.	Yds.	Avg.	MIAMI	No.	Yds.	Avg.
Bieniemy	4	26	6.5	Craver	8	72	9.0
Butts	7	25	3.6	Humphrey	23	71	3.1
Humphries	1	10	10.0	Parmalee	5	18	3.6
Harmon	4	9	2.3	Clayton	1	0	0.0
	16	70	4.4	Mitchell	1	-1	-1.0
				Saxon	2	-3	-1.5
					40	157	3.9

RECEIVING

SAN DIEGO	No.	Yds.	Avg.	MIAMI	No.	Yds.	Avg.
Harmon	9	73	8.1	Paige	5	14	2.8
Walker	3	33	11.0	Jackson	4	53	13.3
Lewis	2	12	6.0	Humphrey	4	30	7.5
Miller	2	12	6.0	Duper	3	57	19.0
Jefferson	1	10	10.0	Craver	1	13	13.0
Butts	1	0	0.0		17	167	9.8
	18	140	7.8				

PUNTING

SAN DIEGO	No.	Yds.	Avg.	MIAMI	No.	Yds.	Avg.
Kidd	7		46.3	Roby	8		41.0

PUNT RETURNS

SAN DIEGO	No.	Yds.	Avg.	MIAMI	No.	Yds.	Avg.
Lewis	1	7	7.0	Miller	5	45	9.0
Lewis	2FC						

KICKOFF RETURNS

SAN DIEGO	No.	Yds.	Avg.	MIAMI	No.	Yds.	Avg.
Lewis	4	111	27.8	Craver	1	18	18.0
Bieniemy	1	14	14.0				
Pupunu	1	11	11.0				
	6	136	22.7				

INTERCEPTION RETURNS

SAN DIEGO	No.	Yds.	Avg.	MIAMI	No.	Yds.	Avg.
None				Vincent	2	2	1.0
				Oliver	1	21	21.0
				Cox	1	7	7.0
					4	30	7.5

PASSING

SAN DIEGO	Att.	Comp.	Comp. Pct.	Yds.	Int.	Yds./ Att.	Yds./ Comp.
Humphries	44	18	40.9	140	4	3.2	7.8
Kidd	1	0	0.0	0	0	0.0	0.0
	29	14	48.3	146	4	5.0	10.4
MIAMI							
Marino	29	17	58.6	167	0	5.8	9.8

1992 N.F.C. PLAYOFFS — SECOND ROUND

January 9, 1993 at San Francisco (Attendance 64,991)

SCORING

	1	2	3	4	Total
WASHINGTON	3	0	3	7	- 13
SAN FRANCISCO	7	10	0	3	- 20

First Quarter
- S.F. — Taylor, 5 yard pass from Young; PAT — Cofer (kick)
- Wash. — Lohmiller, 19 yard field goal

Second Quarter
- S.F. — Cofer, 23 yard field goal
- S.F. — Jones, 16 yard pass from Young; PAT — Cofer (kick)

Third Quarter
- Wash. — Lohmiller, 32 yard field goal

Fourth Quarter
- Wash. — Rypien , 1 yard run; PAT — Lohmiller (kick)
- S.F — Cofer, 33 yard field goal

TEAMSTATISTICS

WASH.		S.F.
20	First Downs- Total	22
4	First Downs- Rushing	10
15	First Downs- Passing	12
1	First Downs- Penalty	0
3	Fumbles- Number	4
2	Fumbles- Lost Ball	3
4	Penalties- Number	4
23	Yards Penalized	35
0	Missed Field Goals	0
67	Offensive Plays	63
323	Net Yards	401
4.8	Average Gain	6.4
4	Giveaways	4
4	Takeaways	4
0	Difference	0

INDIVIDUALSTATISTICS

WASHINGTON	No.	Yds.	Avg.	SAN FRANCISCO	No.	Yds.	Avg.
RUSHING							
Mitchell	8	38	4.8	Watters	18	83	4.6
Byner	9	29	3.2	Young	8	73	9.1
Rypien	3	3	1.0	Rathman	4	22	5.5
Monk	1	3	3.0	Rice	1	9	9.0
	21	73	3.5		31	107	6.0
RECEIVING							
Clark	7	100	14.3	Rice	6	88	14.7
Byner	3	45	15.0	Jones	4	64	16.0
Mitchell	3	39	13.0	Rathman	4	30	7.5
Sanders	3	33	11.0	Taylor	4	26	6.5
Monk	2	44	22.0	Watters	2	19	9.5
Thomas	1	10	10.0		20	227	11.4
Middleton	1	9	9.0				
	20	280	14.0				
PUNTING							
Goodburn	2		36.0	Wilmsmeyer	2		40.0
PUNT RETURNS							
None				None			
KICKOFF RETURNS							
Mitchell	4	75	18.8	Logan	2	27	13.5
Copeland	1	9	9.0				
	5	84	16.8				
INTERCEPTION RETURNS							
Johnson	1	0	0.0	Davis	1	2	2.0
				Whitmore	1	2	2.0
					2	4	2.0

PASSING

WASHINGTON	Att.	Comp.	Comp Pct.	Yds.	Int.	Yds./Att.	Yds./Comp.
Rypien	40	19	47.5	270	2	6.8	14.2
Goodburn	1	1	100.0	10	0	10.0	10.0
	41	20	48.8	280	2	6.8	14.0
SAN FRANCISCO							
Young	30	20	66.7	227	1	7.6	11.4

January 10, 1993 at Dallas (Attendance 63,721)

SCORING

	1	2	3	4	Total
PHILADELPHIA	3	0	0	7	- 10
DALLAS	7	10	10	7	- 34

First Quarter
- Phil. — Ruzek, 32 yard field goal
- Dall. — Tennell, 1 yard pass from Aikman; PAT — Elliott (kick)

Second Quarter
- Dall. — Novacek, 6 yard pass from Aikman; PAT — Elliott (kick)
- Dall. — Elliott, 20 yard field goal

Third Quarter
- Dall. — Smith, 23 yard run; PAT — Elliott (kick)
- Dall. — Elliott, 43 yard field goal

Fourth Quarter
- Dall. — Gainer, 1 yard run; PAT — Elliott (kick)
- Phil. — Williams, 18 yard pass from Cunningham; PAT — Ruzek (kick)

TEAMSTATISTICS

PHIL.		DAL.
12	First Downs- Total	22
5	First Downs- Rushing	10
6	First Downs- Passing	11
1	First Downs- Penalty	1
4	Fumbles- Number	2
2	Fumbles- Lost Ball	1
6	Penalties- Number	5
76	Yards Penalized	30
0	Missed Field Goals	0
52	Offensive Plays	65
178	Net Yards	346
3.4	Average Gain	5.3
2	Giveaways	1
1	Takeaways	2
-1	Difference	+1

INDIVIDUALSTATISTICS

PHILADELPHIA	No.	Yds.	Avg.	DALLAS	No.	Yds.	Avg.
RUSHING							
Walker	6	29	4.8	E. Smith	25	114	4.6
Cunningham	5	22	4.4	Gainer	9	29	3.2
Sherman	6	12	2.0	Aikman	3	13	4.3
	17	63	3.7	Johnston	1	4	4.0
					38	160	4.2
RECEIVING							
Walker	6	37	6.2	irvin	6	88	14.7
Williams	4	48	12.0	Novacek	3	36	12.0
Barnett	4	44	11.0	Martin	3	27	9.0
Byars	3	31	10.3	Harper	1	41	41.0
	17	160	9.4	Johnston	1	7	7.0
				Tennell	1	1	1.0
					15	200	13.3
PUNTING							
Feagles	7		40.9	Saxon	4		42.8
PUNT RETURNS							
Sikahema	4	24	6.0	Martin	1	5	5.0
				Washington1FC			
KICKOFF RETURNS							
Sikahema	5	81	16.2	Martin	2	60	30.0
Sydner	1	29	29.0	K. Smith	1	0	0.0
	6	110	18.3		3	60	20.0
INTERCEPTION RETURNS							
None				None			

PASSING

PHILADELPHIA	Att.	Comp.	Comp. Pct.	Yds.	Int.	Yds./Att	Yds./Comp.
Cunningham	30	17	56.7	160	0	5.3	9.4
DALLAS							
Aikman	25	15	60.0	200	0	8.0	13.3

1992 Championship Games

A.F.C. CHAMPIONSHIP GAME

January 17, 1993 at Miami, Fla.
(Attendance 72,703)

The Buffalo Bills qualified for a record-tying third straight Super Bowl with a convincing 29-10 victory over the Miami Dolphins.

The Bills became the fourth wild-card team to make it to the Super Bowl.

On defense, Buffalo end Bruce Smith played like Superman, with seven tackles, one and a half sacks, a forced fumble and a blocked pass.

On offense, Thurman Thomas, the NFL's total offense leader the last four seasons, showed why with 96 yards rushing and 70 more on five pass receptions.

And back on offense was quarterback Jim Kelly, after missing two and a half games with a knee injury. His 17-for-24 performance for 177 yards blunted any criticism of coach Marv Levy for starting him over Frank Reich, who had led the Bills to their first two playoff victories. Kelly threw a 17-yard TD pass to Thomas.

Kenneth Davis had a two-yard touchdown run and Steve Christie tied a playoff record with five field goals, from distances of 21, 33, 21, 31 and 38 yards.

The Buffalo defense was virtually inpenetrable, flustering Miami quarterback Dan Marino all game and sacking him four times.

The Dolphins, champions of the AFC East and seeking their first AFC title since 1984, hurt themselves with five turnovers. Marino was only 22 of 45 for 268 yards. He threw a 15-yard TD pass to Mark Duper.

"I think this team has really matured a lot and is ready to go out and win a Super Bowl," said Kelly.

SCORING

BUFFALO	3	10	10	6	- 29
MIAMI	3	0	0	7	- 10

First Quarter
- Buff. Christie, 21 yard field goal
- Mia. Stoyanovich, 51 yard field goal

Second Quarter
- Buff. Thomas, 17 yard pass from Kelly; PAT — Christie (kick)
- Buff. Christie, 33 yard field goal

Third Quarter
- Buff. Davis, 2 yard run; PAT — Christie (kick)
- Buff. Christie, 21 yard field goal

Fourth Quarter
- Buff. Christie, 31 yard field goal
- Mia. Duper, 15 yard pass from Marino; PAT — Stoyanovich (kick)
- Buff. Christie, 38 yard field goal

TEAMSTATISTICS

BUFF.		MIA.
20	First Downs- Total	15
10	First Downs- Rushing	1
8	First Downs- Passing	14
2	First Downs- Penalty	0
1	Fumbles- Number	4
0	Fumbles- Lost Ball	3
3	Penalties- Number	5
20	Yards Penalized	40
1	Missed Field Goals	0
73	Offensive Plays	60
358	Net Yards	276
4.9	Average Gain	4.6
2	Giveaways	5
5	Takeaways	2
+3	Difference	-3

INDIVIDUALSTATISTICS

BUFFALO	No.	Yds.	Avg.	MIAMI	No.	Yds.	Avg.
RUSHING							
Thomas	20	96	4.8	Humphrey	8	22	2.8
K. Davis	19	61	3.2	Craver	2	13	6.5
Lamb	1	16	16.0	Marino	1	-2	-2.0
Reed	2	6	3.0		11	33	3.0
Kelly	3	4	1.3				
Gardner	3	-1	-0.3				
	48	182	3.8				
RECEIVING							
Thomas	5	70	14.0	Jackson	5	71	14.2
K. Davis	4	52	13.0	Humphrey	5	41	8.2
Reed	3	25	8.3	Martin	3	55	18.3
Lofton	2	19	9.5	Clayton	3	32	10.7
McKeller	1	11	11.0	Duper	2	36	18.0
Metzelaars	1	6	6.0	Banks	2	18	9.0
Gardner	1	-6	-6.0	Craver	2	15	7.5
	17	177	10.4		22	268	12.2
PUNTING							
Mohr	2		34.5	Roby	4		37.0
PUNT RETURNS							
Hicks	1	16	16.0	Miller	1	14	14.0
Hale	1FC			Miller	1FC		
KICKOFF RETURNS							
Lamb	1	36	36.0	Craver	4	48	12.0
Davis	1	23	23.0	M. Williams	3	64	21.3
	2	59	29.5		7	112	16.0
INTERCEPTION RETURNS							
Hicks	1	31	31.0	Brown	1	32	32.0
Hansen	1	0	0.0	Oliver	1	0	0.0
	2	31	15.5		2	32	16.0

PASSING

	Att.	Comp.	Comp. Pct.	Yds.	Int.	Yds./ Att.	Yds./ Comp.
BUFFALO							
Kelly	24	17	70.8	177	2	7.4	10.4
MIAMI							
Marino	45	22	48.9	268	2	6.0	12.2

N.F.C. CHAMPIONSHIP GAME

January 17, 1993 at San Francisco, Calif.
(Attendance 64,920)

The Dallas Cowboys capped their rise from the NFL's depths at the same spot their downfall began. The Cowboys, the NFL's youngest team, qualified for their first Super Bowl in 14 years with a 30-20 victory over the San Francisco 49ers, the team that dominated the 1980s. Dallas was just 1-15 just three years ago.

Dallas' slide from the top to bottom began 11 years earlier in San Francisco when Dwight Clark made "The Catch" that put the 49ers in the first of the four Super Bowls they won.

Dallas got to its record sixth Super Bowl thanks in large part to Troy Aikman, Emmitt Smith and two perfect second-half touchdown drives with a San Francisco field goal sandwiched in between.

Those long drives broke open a game that was tied 10-10 at halftime. Aikman was 24 of 34 for 322 yards and two touchdowns.

For the 49ers, whose 14-2 regular-season record was the league's best, it was simply a case of not being able to stop the Dallas offense and not converting their own third downs. San Francisco also lost the ball four times on two interceptions and two fumbles.

The Cowboys' two drives in the second half were 78 yards in eight plays, capped by a three-yard TD run by Daryl Johnston, and then a nine-minute march that ended in a 16-yard TD pass from Aikman to Smith.

San Francisco had several early chances to break the game open but failed, including a touchdown that was called back on its first drive.

Steve Young, who completed 25 of 35 passes for 313 yards, ran for a touchdown and threw one to Jerry Rice.

For the first time since the first Super Bowl, the visiting teams won both conference title games.

SCORING

DALLAS	3	7	7	13	- 30
SAN FRANCISCO	7	3	3	7	- 20

First Quarter
- Dall. Elliott, 20 yard field goal
- S.F. Young, 1 yard run; PAT — Cofer (kick)

Second Quarter
- Dall. E. Smith, 4 yard run; PAT — Elliott (kick)
- S.F. Cofer, 28 yard field goal

Third Quarter
- Dall. Johnston, 3 yard run; PAT — Elliott (kick)
- S.F. Cofer, 42 yard field goal

Fourth Quarter
- Dall. E. Smith, 16 yard pass from Aikman; PAT — Elliott (kick)
- S.F. Rice, 5 yard pass from Young; PAT — Cofer (kick)
- Dall. Martin, 6 yard pass from Aikman; PAT — kick blocked

TEAMSTATISTICS

DALL.		S.F.
24	First Downs- Total	24
7	First Downs- Rushing	8
16	First Downs- Passing	16
1	First Downs- Penalty	0
1	Fumbles- Number	2
0	Fumbles- Lost Ball	2
4	Penalties- Number	4
25	Yards Penalized	38
1	Missed Field Goals	0
68	Offensive Plays	59
416	Net Yards	415
6.1	Average Gain	7.0
0	Giveaways	4
4	Takeaways	0
+ 4	Difference	- 4

INDIVIDUALSTATISTICS

DALLAS	No.	Yds.	Avg.	SAN FRANCISCO	No.	Yds.	Avg.
RUSHING							
E. Smith	24	114	4.8	Watters	11	69	6.3
Johnston	2	7	3.5	Young	8	33	4.1
Harper	1	3	3.0	Rathman	1	6	6.0
Aikman	3	-3	-3.0	Lee	1	6	6.0
	30	121	4.0		21	114	5.4
RECEIVING							
E. Smith	7	59	8.4	Rice	8	123	15.4
Irvin	6	86	14.3	Watters	6	69	11.5
Johnston	4	26	6.5	Rathman	4	33	8.3
Harper	3	117	39.0	Jones	3	40	13.3
Novacek	3	28	9.3	Taylor	3	33	11.0
K. Martin	1	6	6.0	Sherrard	1	15	15.0
	24	322	13.4		25	313	12.5
PUNTING							
Saxon	4		35.8	Wilmsmeyer	1		57.0
PUNT RETURNS							
K. Martin	1	8	8.0	Grant	3	30	10.0
				Grant	1FC		
KICKOFF RETURNS							
K. Martin	3	62	20.7	Logan	3	79	26.3
K. Smith	1	11	11.0	Grant	2	35	17.5
	4	73	18.3		5	114	22.8
INTERCEPTION RETURNS							
Washington	1	21	21.0	None			
Norton	1	14	14.0				
	2	35	17.5				

PASSING

	Att.	Comp.	Comp. Pct.	Yds.	Int.	Yds./ Att.	Yds./ Comp.
DALLAS							
Aikman	34	24	70.6	322	0	9.5	13.4
SAN FRANCISCO							
Young	35	25	71.4	313	2	8.9	12.5

SUPER BOWL XXVII

January 31, 1993 at Pasadena, Calif.

(Attendance 98,374)

Another Super Blowout

If the NFC team won …

If it was a blowout that was decided by halftime …

If the quarterback was the Most Valuable Player …

Then it had to be the Super Bowl.

Which means it wasn't all that super.

The Dallas Cowboys' 52-17 win over the Buffalo Bills in Super Bowl XXVII was another in a long list of NFC victories over the AFC — nine consecutive victories dating back to Super Bowl XVIII. It might also mark the start of a dynasty for Dallas.

For the Bills, it was another tragic loss in the nation's premier sports spectacle. They lost their quarterback and lost their spirit. And they lost in a Super Bowl for the third time in a row, the first team with that ignominious record.

Super Bowl XXVII had the makings of a truly great game until just before halftime. That's when Buffalo became unglued and Dallas turned an uneasy 14-10 lead into a 28-10 rout that continued throughout the second half.

Buffalo lost the ball nine times — five fumbles and four interceptions — and they led directly to five Dallas touchdowns. The most costly turnover was a Jim Kelly interception on a fourth-down play at the Dallas one-yard line early in the second quarter.

"You turn the ball over the way we did, there's no way you're going to win the game," said Kelly, who was injured in the second quarter and sat out the rest of the game. "It's a loss. It doesn't matter if you lose by three points or 30 or 20. Nobody likes to lose."

It was another story for the Cowboys, who returned to the Super Bowl after a 13-year absence and only three seasons removed from a 1-15 record.

Troy Aikman threw four touchdown passes on 22 of 30 passing for 273 yards and no interceptions and was voted the game's MVP. He threw TD passes of 18 and 19 yards to Michael Irvin, 23 yards to Jay Novacek and 45 yards to Alvin Harper.

"Troy was definitely in a zone," said Dallas running back Emmitt Smith, who rushed for 108 yards on 22 carries and scored on a 10-yard run.

But the Dallas defense was the story of the day. Defensive end Jimmie Jones scored on a two-yard return of a Kelly fumble, and linebacker Ken Norton ended the scoring on a nine-yard return of a Frank Reich fumble. Dallas' Leon Lett almost scored on a 65-yard fumble return, but he had the ball stripped from him just before he reached the goal line.

"Any time you have nine turnovers, you don't have a chance in the world, even if you have every great player in the league on your team," said Buffalo linebacker Cornelius Bennett.

Buffalo opened the scoring on a two-yard run by Thurman Thomas, who gained only 19 yards on 11 carries. Don Beebe scored Buffalo's other touchdown on a 40-yard pass from Reich, and Steve Christie added a 21-yard field goal.

Dallas' margin of victory was the third-largest in a Super Bowl.

LINEUPS

BUFF.		DALL.
	OFFENSE	
Lofton	WR	Harper
Wolford	LT	Tuinei
Ritcher	LG	Newton
Hull	C	Stepnoski
Parker	RG	Gesek
Ballard	RT	Williams
Metzelaars	TE	Novacek
Reed	WR	Irvin
Kelly	QB	Aikman
Thomas	RB	E. Smith
Beebe	WR/RB	Johnston
	DEFENSE	
Hansen	LE	Tolbert
Wright	NT/LT	Casillas
B. Smith	RE/RT	Maryland
Patton	LOLB/RE	Haley
Conlan	LILB/LLB	V. Smith
Bennett	RILB/MLB	R. Jones
Talley	ROLB/RLB	Norton
J. Williams	LCB	K. Smith
Odomes	RCB	L. Brown
Jones	SS	Washington
Kelso	FS	Everett

SUBSTITUTES

BUFFALO		
	OFFENSE	
Reich	K. Davis	Gardner
Frerotte	Lingner	J. Davis
Fina	Lamb	McKeller
Awalt	Tasker	
	DEFENSE	
Hale	Hicks	Darby
K. Jackson	Bailey	Maddox
Lodish	Pike	Goganious
	KICKERS	
Christie	Mohr	

DALLAS		
	OFFENSE	
Beuerlein	Agee	Gainer
Gogan	Cornish	Hellestrae
J. Smith	K. Martin	Tennell
	DEFENSE	
Horton	Woodson	Gant
Holt	Holmes	Pruitt
Edwards	Jeffcoat	Lett
Hennings	J. Jones	Myles
	KICKERS	
Elliott	Saxon	

SCORING

BUFFALO	7	3	7	0	- 17
DALLAS	14	14	3	21	- 52

First Quarter

Buff.	Thomas, 2 yard run PAT — Christie (kick)
Dall.	Novacek, 23 yard pass from Aikman PAT — Elliott (kick)
Dall.	J. Jones, 2 yard fumble return PAT — Elliott (kick)

Second Quarter

Buff.	Christie, 21 yard field goal
Dall.	Irvin, 19 yard pass from Aikman PAT — Elliott (kick)
Dall.	Irvin, 18 yard pass from Aikman PAT — Elliott (kick)

Third Quarter

Dall.	Elliott, 20 yard field goal
Buff.	Beebe, 40 yard pass from Reich PAT — Christie (kick)

Fourth Quarter

Dall.	Harper, 45 yard pass from Aikman PAT — Elliott (kick)
Dall.	E. Smith, 10 yard run PAT — Elliott (kick)
Dall.	Norton, 9 yard fumble return PAT — Elliott (kick)

TEAM STATISTICS

BUFF.		DALL.
22	First Downs-Total	20
7	First Downs-Rushing	9
11	First Downs-Pasiing	11
4	First Downs-Penalty	0
8	Fumbles-Number	4
5	Fumbles-Lost Ball	2
4	Penaties-Number	8
30	Yards Penalized	53
0	Missed Field Goals	0
71	Offensive Plays	60
362	Net Yards	408
5.1	Average Gain	6.8
9	Giveaways	2
2	Takeaways	9
- 7	Difference	+ 7

INDIVIDUAL STATISTICS

BUFFALO	No.	Yds.	Avg.	DALLAS	No.	Yds.	Avg.
RUSHING							
K. Davis	15	86	5.7	E. Smith	22	108	4.9
Thomas	11	19	1.7	Aikman	3	28	9.3
Gardner	1	3	3.0	Gainer	2	1	0.5
Reich	1	0	0.0	Johnston	1	0	0.0
	29	108	3.7	Beuerlein	1	0	0.0
					29	137	4.7
RECEIVING							
Reed	8	152	19.0	Novacek	7	72	10.3
Thomas	4	10	2.5	Irvin	6	114	19.0
K. Davis	3	16	5.3	E. Smith	6	27	4.5
Beebe	2	50	25.0	Johnston	2	15	7.5
Tasker	2	30	15.0	Harper	1	45	45.0
Metzelaars	2	12	6.0		22	273	12.4
McKeller	1	6	6.0				
	22	276	12.5				
PUNTING							
Mohr	3		45.3	Saxon	3		43.7
PUNT RETURNS							
Hicks	1	0	0.0	Martin	3	35	11.7
Hicks	1FC						
KICKOFF RETURNS							
Lamb	2	49	24.5	K. Martin	4	79	19.8
K. Davis	1	21	21.0				
Hicks	1	20	20.0				
	4	90	22.5				
INTERCEPTIONS RETURNS							
None				Everett	2	22	11.0
				Washington	1	13	13.0
				Brown	1	0	0.0
					4	35	8.8

PASSING

	Att.	Comp.	Comp. Pct.	Yds.	Int.	Yds./ Att.	Yds./ Comp.	Yards Lost Tackled
BUFFALO								
Kelly	7	4	57.1	82	2	11.7	20.5	2-10
Reich	31	18	58.1	194	2	6.3	10.8	2-12
DALLAS								
Aikman	30	22	73.3	273	0	9.1	12.4	1-2

1993 N.F.C. Free Agency Jolts NFL, But Cowboys Repeat

In five years of the Jerry Jones and Jimmy Johnson regime, the Cowboys have turned into the elite of the NFL, winning the last two Super Bowls and unquestionably being called the best team in the league. The Cowboys had not only the best lineup in the league, but one that was young and in little danger of reaching the salary cap that was placed on the 28 teams as the 1993 season came to an end. Jones even got Emmitt Smith to sign a new contract after the star running back missed the first two games of the season due to a holdout.

Dallas also entered the 1993 season virtually unhurt in free agency, which is why its nucleus and Smith, Troy Aikman, Michael Irvin and others were big favorites to win the Super Bowl.

Free agency was the story of 1993, as 120 players changed teams. Players with five or more years in the NFL were free to change teams when their contracts expired, and players with three or four years in the NFL could sign offer sheets that their present team had the option to match. The big names were defensive end Reggie White to Green Bay, safety Tim McDonald to San Francisco, running back Marcus Allen to Kansas City, wide receivers Mark Jackson and Mike Sherrard to the Giants and defensive tackle Pierce Holt to Atlanta. Several star players also changed teams through trades, the biggest being Eric Dickerson, who became a Falcon, and Joe Montana, who turned into a Chief.

EASTERN DIVISION

Dallas Cowboys — The Cowboys became the fifth team to win back-to-back Super Bowls, mainly behind the running of Emmitt Smith, who was named the NFL's Most Valuable Player and the Super Bowl MVP. Smith, who missed the first two games of the season — both Cowboy losses — rushed for 1,486 yards to lead the NFL for the third straight year. Quarterback Troy Aikman (only six interceptions) and wide receiver Michael Irvin (88 receptions, seven touchdowns) were equally masterful, but it still wasn't an easy season for the Cowboys. Smith's holdout and injuries to Aikman, Smith, defensive end Charles Haley and linebacker Ken Norton slowed them down. But, even with Smith ailing in the playoffs, Dallas rolled over the Packers and 49ers before facing the Bills again in the Super Bowl, a 30-13 victory. The Cowboys' fifth Super Bowl victory and seventh appearance overall were both records.

New York Giants — The Giants were one of the surprise teams of the NFL in 1993, going 11-5 and making the playoffs under new head coach Dan Reeves, who had come over from Denver. Quarterback Phil Simms also had a fine comeback, as he completed 61.8 percent of his passes for 3,038 yards and started every game for the first time in seven years. Reeves stuck to a combination of a strong running game and a powerful defense. Rodney Hampton rushed for 1,077 yards, while two free-agent newcomers, linebackers Carlton Bailey and Michael Brooks, were the defensive mainstays. Following six straight victories, New York was tied atop the division with Dallas at 11-4 going into the final game and looking for a first-round bye in the playoffs. But the Cowboys prevailed 16-13. After the season, Lawrence Taylor announced his retirement.

Philadelphia Eagles — Despite numerous free-agent losses, the Eagles surprised everybody when they won their first four games of the season and took a lead in the NFC East. Then disaster hit, as quarterback Randall Cunningham suffered a broken leg. Philadelphia then lost six straight games with Ken O'Brien and Bubby Brister at quarterback. Injuries also felled wide receiver Fred Barnett, linebacker Tim Harris and several other veterans. Brister finally hit his stride late in the season. He set a team record for fewest interceptions in a season and ranked fourth in the conference in passing. The Eagles won their final three games to finish with an 8-8 record. Eric Allen tied an NFL record when he returned four of his six interceptions for touchdowns.

Phoenix Cardinals — Before the season, owner Bill Bidwill issued an ultimatum to head coach Joe Bugel that the team had better win nine games or else he would be fired. Phoenix started the season 2-6 amid a plethora of injuries, and Bugel seemed as good as gone. Then the Cardinals went 5-3 over the second half to finish 7-9 and possibly save Bugel's job. Bidwill waited four weeks after the season ended before he finally pulled the trigger, canning Bugel and hiring Buddy Ryan. The Cardinals were better than they had been in any of their five seasons in Phoenix. Only the 49ers and Cowboys ranked ahead of them in yards and scoring, and the defense ranked fourth in points allowed. Quarterback Steve Beuerlein, a free-agent acquisition, passed for 3,164 yards and 18 touchdowns, and rookie Ron Moore rushed for 1,018 yards after he took over for injured first-round draft choice Garrison Hearst.

Washington Redskins — After Joe Gibbs surprised everybody with his retirement midway through the offseason, Richie Petitbon was elevated to head coach. Washington started the season with a convincing 35-16 victory over the Cowboys, but then the bottom fell out, as the Redskins suffered through their worst season in three decades. Washington lost six straight games at one point, had their most lopsided home loss since 1940 (41-7 to the Giants) and even lost one game 3-0. There were injuries to both lines and pitiful play from quarterback Mark Rypien, who threw only four TD passes. A bright spot was registered by rookie back Reggie Brooks, who rushed for 1,063 yards and had the two longest TD runs in the league. Petitbon was fired after the season and replaced by Dallas assistant Norv Turner.

CENTRAL DIVISION

Detroit Lions — Erik Kramer did it again. Two years after leading the Lions to the NFC Central Division championship and the conference title game, Kramer finally took over in December for quarterbacks Rodney Peete and Andre Ware and led Detroit to three victories in the final four games. And he did it without star running back Barry Sanders, who missed the final four games with a sprained knee. Sanders was the team MVP, as he rushed for over 1,000 yards for the fifth straight season, only the third player in NFL history to do so. Coach Wayne Fontes was under fire most of the season for his quarterback merry-go-round, until he righted the ship. The season ended quickly in the playoffs, with a loss to the Packers one week after beating them for the division title.

Minnesota Vikings — The Vikings were resilient in 1993, overcoming numerous injuries and free-agent losses to go 9-7 and make the playoffs. Quarterback Jim McMahon was in and out of the lineup on a frequent basis, though he was back starting by the playoffs (a 17-10 loss to the Giants). Minnesota see-sawed throughout the season with inconsistency, then, with McMahon back, won four of five games in December to squeeze into the playoffs. After top running back Terry Allen was lost for the season before it even began, Minnesota had trouble all year with its running game. Wide receiver Cris Carter was the offensive star, as he caught 86 passes for 1,071 yards and nine touchdowns. Defensively, the Vikings ranked first in the league. Defensive tackles Henry Thomas and John Randle combined for 21 sacks.

Green Bay Packers — The Packers had another 9-7 season, going to the playoffs for the first time since 1982 and having back-to-back winning seasons for the first time since 1966 and '67. Still, Green Bay was never a big threat in the division because it lost three of the first four games. Wide receiver Sterling Sharpe broke his own NFL record by catching 112 passes for 1,274 yards and 11 touchdowns. He had game-winning catches in three games. Defensive end Reggie White signed with Green Bay, the biggest free-agent signing in the league. White tied for the NFC lead with 13 sacks. The Green Bay defense was a pleasant surprise, as it ranked second in the NFL. Quarterback Brett Favre was the main man, however, as he threw for 19 touchdowns and 24 interceptions.

Chicago Bears — Unlike the top three teams in the division, who made the playoffs with late-season surges, the Bears fell apart when December rolled around. Winners of four straight games, three of them on the road, Chicago then lost its last four games to finish 7-9 and out of the playoffs for the second straight year. The Bears were improved in 1993, however, though nearly all of it was on defense. Defensive end Richard Dent, middle linebacker Dante Jones and cornerback Donnell Woolford were the defensive stars. New head coach Dave Wannstedt couldn't get much out out of an offense that ranked last in passing and

FINAL TEAM STATISTICS

OFFENSE

	ATL	CHI	DAL	DET	G.B.	L.A.	MINN	N.O.	NYG	PHIL	PHX	S.F.	T.B.	WASH
FIRST DOWNS:														
Total	292	226	322	248	282	279	283	264	300	302	295	372	241	255
by Rushing	91	98	120	101	98	117	85	94	127	103	107	104	80	92
by Passing	185	113	172	139	100	147	182	158	153	184	173	212	141	143
by Penalty	16	15	30	8	18	15	16	12	20	15	15	26	20	20
RUSHING:														
Number	395	477	490	456	448	449	447	414	560	456	452	463	402	396
Yards	1590	1677	2161	1944	1619	2014	1623	1766	2210	1761	1809	2133	1290	1726
Average Yards	4.0	3.5	4.4	4.3	3.6	4.5	3.6	4.3	3.9	3.9	4.0	4.6	3.2	4.4
Touchdowns	4	10	20	9	14	8	8	10	11	8	12	27	6	11
PASSING:														
Attempts	573	388	475	435	528	473	526	481	424	556	522	524	508	533
Completions	334	230	317	264	322	247	315	274	257	328	310	354	262	287
Completion Pct.	58.3	59.3	66.7	60.7	61.0	52.2	59.9	57.0	60.6	59.0	59.4	67.6	51.6	53.8
Passing Yards	3787	2270	3617	2943	3330	3021	3380	3183	3180	3463	3635	4480	3295	2764
Avg. Yds per Att.	6.6	5.9	7.6	6.8	6.3	6.4	6.4	6.6	7.5	6.2	7.0	8.6	6.5	5.2
Avg. Yds per Comp.	11.3	9.9	11.4	11.1	10.3	12.2	10.7	11.6	12.4	10.6	11.7	12.7	12.6	9.6
Times Tackled	40	48	29	46	30	31	35	40	40	42	33	35	39	40
Yds Lost Tackled	267	230	163	229	199	231	181	242	245	302	231	178	274	219
Net Yards	3520	2040	3454	2714	3131	2790	3199	2941	2935	3161	3404	4302	3021	2545
Touchdowns	28	7	18	15	19	16	18	18	17	22	21	29	19	11
Interceptions	25	16	6	19	24	19	14	21	9	13	20	17	25	21
Pct. Intercepted	4.4	4.1	1.3	4.4	4.5	4.0	2.7	4.4	2.1	2.3	3.8	3.2	4.9	3.9
PUNTS:														
Number	72	80	56	72	74	80	90	77	78	83	73	42	94	83
Average	43.3	38.5	41.8	44.5	42.9	40.9	42.8	43.6	41.9	40.0	43.7	40.9	40.1	43.9
PUNT RETURNS														
Number	35	35	37	40	45	19	39	38	32	33	47	35	38	35
Yards	276	289	381	349	404	102	280	517	331	284	384	411	311	245
Average Yards	7.9	8.3	10.3	8.4	9.0	5.4	7.2	13.6	10.3	8.6	8.3	11.7	8.2	7.0
Touchdowns	0	0	2	0	0	0	0	2	1	0	1	1	0	0
KICKOFF RET.:														
Number	55	45	36	52	60	49	55	62	32	53	45	41	58	59
Yards	1300	811	758	1204	1483	824	1086	1460	507	987	951	715	922	1166
Average Yards	23.6	18.0	21.0	23.2	24.7	16.8	19.7	23.5	15.8	18.6	21.1	17.4	15.9	19.8
Touchdowns	1	0	0	1	1	0	0	1	0	0	0	0	0	0
INTERCEPT RET.:														
Number	13	18	14	19	18	11	24	10	18	20	9	19	9	17
Yards	160	300	171	156	255	127	211	133	184	323	124	267	79	241
Average Yards	12.3	16.7	12.2	8.2	14.2	11.5	8.8	13.3	10.2	16.2	13.8	14.1	7.9	14.2
Touchdowns	0	2	1	1	0	0	2	0	1	4	1	3	2	2
PENALTIES:														
Number	111	68	94	93	85	71	109	81	90	101	77	95	89	90
Yards	838	587	744	665	734	526	806	663	586	758	644	800	765	596
FUMBLES:														
Number	31	29	33	29	26	20	15	24	19	32	23	31	28	24
Number Lost	17	14	16	13	10	11	10	13	8	21	11	13	11	10
POINTS:														
Total	316	234	376	298	340	221	277	317	288	293	326	473	237	230
PAT Attempts	34	22	41	28	36	25	28	33	30	33	37	61	27	26
PAT Made	34	21	40	28	35	23	27	33	28	30	37	59	27	24
FG Attempts	27	36	37	43	37	23	35	35	34	23	28	26	22	28
FG Made	26	27	30	34	31	16	26	28	26	16	21	16	16	16
Percent FG Made	96.2	75.0	81.1	79.1	83.8	69.6	74.3	80.0	76.5	69.6	75.0	61.5	72.7	57.1
Safeties	0	0	0	0	1	0	2	1	1	2	2	0	0	1

DEFENSE

	ATL	CHI	DAL	DET	G.B.	L.A.	MINN	N.O.	NYG	PHIL	PHX	S.F.	T.B.	WASH
FIRST DOWNS:														
Total	278	290	297	279	261	304	259	273	268	271	278	297	280	304
by Rushing	79	112	94	108	88	117	98	116	89	91	106	109	109	127
by Passing	180	163	176	154	157	179	139	145	161	155	158	171	152	157
by Penalty	19	15	27	17	16	8	22	12	18	25	14	17	19	20
RUSHING:														
Number	419	476	423	433	424	480	415	513	395	467	433	404	479	513
Yards	1784	1835	1651	1649	1582	1851	1534	2090	1547	2080	1861	1800	1994	2111
Average Yards	4.3	3.9	3.9	3.8	3.7	3.9	3.7	4.1	3.9	4.5	4.3	4.5	4.2	4.1
Touchdowns	14	9	7	12	6	18	14	7	7	11	13	6	15	14
PASSING:														
Attempts	505	504	555	514	529	488	478	444	514	463	495	564	503	483
Completions	308	306	334	309	290	299	310	259	298	251	281	314	300	291
Completion Pct.	61.0	60.7	60.2	60.1	54.8	61.3	64.9	58.3	58.0	54.2	56.8	55.7	59.6	60.2
Passing Yards	3786	3105	3347	3273	3201	3763	3146	2924	3354	3153	3511	3513	3384	3583
Avg. Yds per Att.	7.5	6.2	6.0	6.4	6.1	7.7	6.6	6.6	6.5	6.8	7.1	6.2	6.7	7.4
Avg. Yds per Comp.	12.3	10.1	10.0	10.6	11.0	12.6	10.1	11.3	11.3	12.6	12.5	11.2	11.3	12.3
Times Tackled	27	46	34	43	46	35	45	51	41	36	34	44	29	31
Yds Lost Tackled	149	287	231	253	301	203	276	318	238	214	205	316	132	197
Net Yards	3637	2818	3116	3020	2900	3560	2870	2606	3116	2939	3306	3197	3252	3386
Touchdowns	27	12	14	19	16	17	11	22	13	22	14	23	22	24
Interceptions	13	18	14	19	18	11	24	10	18	20	9	19	9	17
Pct. Intercepted	2.6	3.6	2.5	3.7	3.4	2.3	5.0	2.3	3.5	4.3	1.8	3.4	1.8	3.5
PUNTS:														
Number	74	78	78	81	79	58	78	80	80	75	78	68	76	73
Average	40.9	41.4	41.3	43.1	40.2	42.3	42.4	42.3	40.3	41.8	42.7	43.8	43.3	41.1
PUNT RETURNS														
Number	41	22	32	45	38	43	46	36	44	35	30	16	53	34
Yards	350	115	169	377	350	533	560	348	247	311	267	171	394	343
Average Yards	8.5	5.2	5.3	8.4	9.1	12.4	12.2	9.3	5.6	8.9	8.9	10.7	7.4	10.1
Touchdowns	0	0	0	0	0	2	1	1	0	1	0	0	0	2
KICKOFF RET.:														
Number	55	53	66	30	70	47	58	40	29	53	51	62	28	36
Yards	1064	918	1225	609	1407	984	1420	788	646	1133	994	1196	499	722
Average Yards	19.3	17.3	18.6	20.3	20.2	20.9	24.5	19.7	22.3	21.4	19.5	19.3	17.8	20.0
Touchdowns	0	0	1	0	0	0	1	0	0	0	0	0	0	0
INTERCEPT RET.:														
Number	25	16	6	19	24	19	14	21	9	13	20	17	25	21
Yards	345	105	47	177	437	347	166	444	175	107	143	157	280	209
Average Yards	13.8	6.6	7.8	9.3	18.2	18.3	11.9	21.1	19.4	8.2	7.2	9.2	11.2	10.0
Touchdowns	2	1	0	1	3	2	3	6	1	0	0	0	1	2
PENALTIES:														
Number	100	91	88	75	86	80	97	87	98	86	95	99	126	100
Yards	878	783	653	500	712	532	767	590	820	615	730	743	913	783
FUMBLES:														
Number	25	24	22	34	33	26	24	30	27	33	27	20	27	25
Number Lost	11	12	14	16	15	9	10	20	10	15	17	11	13	14
POINTS:														
Total	385	230	229	292	282	367	290	343	205	315	269	295	376	345
PAT Attempts	46	21	23	32	27	40	32	39	22	34	27	29	40	42
PAT Made	45	20	23	31	27	38	30	35	22	34	27	29	38	40
FG Attempts	31	34	27	30	40	37	33	30	23	34	35	30	35	22
FG Made	20	26	22	23	31	29	25	24	17	23	26	27	32	17
Percent FG Made	64.5	76.5	81.5	76.7	77.5	78.4	75.8	80.0	73.9	67.6	74.3	90.0	91.4	77.3
Safeties	2	0	1	0	0	1	0	1	0	1	1	2	1	1

scoring with only 14.6 points per game. Quarterback Jim Harbaugh and running backs Neal Anderson and Craig Heyward weren't much, and the receiving corps was either injured, inexperienced or ineffective.

Tampa Bay Buccaneers—Owning the NFL's worst record over the past 11 years, the Buccaneers had their 11th consecutive season with double-digit losses. The Bucs started the season losing seven of their first nine games by 15 or more points. Then, in the last seven outings, the Bucs won three times. There were some reasons for optimism, particularly the development of quarterback Craig Erickson and wide receiver Courtney Hawkins. And the defense, which had allowed an average of 362 yards in the first nine games, tightened to only 283 yards the final seven weeks. Erickson threw 21 interceptions but became the team's first 3,000-yard passer since 1989 and matured down the stretch. Middle linebacker Hardy Nickerson, a free-agent signee, led the Bucs with a team-record 214 tackles.

WESTERN DIVISION

San Francisco 49ers — Offense was again the story of the 49ers. Quarterback Steve Young became the first player in NFL history to lead the league in passing three straight years. Running back Ricky Watters rushed for 950 yards and scored 11 touchdowns. And Jerry Rice was his usual phenomenal self, catching 98 passes for 1,503 yards and 15 TD's. The team set a club record with 6,435 yards on offense and scored 473 points (29.6 per game), just two points shy of the team record. San Francisco shook off a 3-3 start to win its 10th division title in 13 years and extended a league record of 11 seasons with 10 or more victories. Still, the 49ers lost in the NFC title game for the third time in four years.

New Orleans Saints—The Saints seem to have fallen into a routine of starting off quickly before slipping and seemingly falling out of the playoff race. In 1993, New Orleans won its first five games, then hit the skids with losses in six of the next eight games before a season-ending victory. That left the team with an 8-8 mark and out of the playoffs. Quarterback Wade Wilson lived up to his reputation as a streaky passer. He threw only one interception in the first five games, then 14 in the next 11. After Vaughn Dunbar was injured in preseason, a new star developed in running back Derek Brown (705 yards). But the defense started to decline because of age and injuries, finishing 22nd in points allowed. Linebacker Renaldo Turnbull tied for the NFC lead with 13 sacks.

Atlanta Falcons — With Deion Sanders missing, the Falcons lost their first five games. Then, with Sanders playing both offense and defense, Atlanta won six of its next eight games. Finally, with the playoffs on the line, the Falcons lost their last three games. Sanders led the NFC with seven interceptions, but the defense allowed a league-worst 385 points. Quarterback Bobby Hebert passed for 2,978 yards and 24 touchdowns, and three receivers had 70 or more receptions — Andre Rison (86 catches and 15 touchdowns), Mike Pritchard (74 catches) and Michael Haynes (72). Erric Pegram replaced Eric Dickerson and rushed for 1,185 yards. Placekicker Norm Johnson set an NFL record with 26 field goals in 27 attempts. Coach Jerry Glanville was fired after the season and replaced by offensive coordinator June Jones.

Los Angeles Rams — Ground Chuck returned in the name of Jerome Bettis, the NFL's Offensive Rookie of the Year, who rushed for 1,429 yards, second in the league. It was the seventh-highest total ever for an NFL rookie. Bettis was almost the entire offense, as coach Chuck Knox went back and forth at quarterback between an ineffective Jim Everett and the inexperienced T.J. Rubley. Everett finished with a career-low 49.3 completion percentage and only eight touchdowns vs. 12 interceptions. But Rubley, a second-year player, wasn't much better. On defense, tackle Sean Gilbert registered 10.5 sacks.

DALLAS COWBOYS 12-4 Jimmy Johnson

Scores of Each Game		
16	Washington	35
10	BUFFALO	13
17	Phoenix	10
36	GREEN BAY	14
27	Indianapolis	3
26	SAN FRANCISCO	17
23	Philadelphia	10
31	N.Y. GIANTS	9
20	PHOENIX	15
14	Atlanta	27
14	MIAMI	16
23	PHILADELPHIA	17
37	Minnesota	20
28	N.Y. Jets	7
38	WASHINGTON	3
16	N.Y. Giants	*13

UseName	Pos.	Hgt	Wgt	Age	Int	Pts
Ron Stone	OT	6'5"	309	22		
Mark Tuinei	OT	6'5"	305	23		
Erik Williams	OT	6'6"	324	24		
John Gesek	OG	6'5"	285	30		
Kevin Gogan	OG-OT	6'7"	328	28		
Dale Hellestrae	OG-C	6'5"	275	31		
Nate Newton	OG	6'3"	325	31		
Frank Cornish	C-OG	6'4"	287	25		
Mark Stepnoski	C	6'2"	264	26		
Charles Haley	DE	6'5"	250	29		
Jim Jeffcoat	DE	6'5"	280	32		
Tony Tolbert	DE	6'6"	263	25		
Tony Casillas	DT	6'3"	279	29		
Chad Hennings	DT	6'6"	286	27		
Jimmie Jones	DT	6'4"	284	27		
Leon Lett	DT-DE	6'6"	285	24		
Russell Maryland	DT	6'1"	279	24		

UseName	Pos.	Hgt	Wgt	Age	Int	Pts
Bobby Abrams (to MIN)	LB	6'3"	230	26		
Dixon Edwards	LB	6'1"	222	25		
Robert Jones	LB	6'2"	237	23		
Godfrey Myles	LB	6'1"	242	24		
Ken Norton	LB	6'2"	240	26	1	
Darrin Smith	LB	6'1"	227	23		
Matt Vanderbeek	LB-DE	6'3"	243	26		
Bill Bates	DB	6'1"	205	32	2	
Larry Brown	DB	5'11"	182	23		
Thomas Everett	DB	5'9"	184	28	2	
Joe Fishback	DB	6'	212	25		
Kenneth Gant	DB	5'11"	189	26	1	
Chris Hall	DB	6'2"	184	23		
Brock Marion	DB	5'11"	189	23	1	
Elvis Patterson (from RAID)	DB	5'11"	195	32		
Kevin Smith	DB	5'11"	180	23	6	6
Dave Thomas	DB	6'2"	208	25		
James Washington	DB	6'1"	209	28	1	
Robert Williams	DB	5'10"	186	30		
Darren Woodson	DB	6'1"	215	24		

Clayton Holmes — Knee Injury

UseName	Pos.	Hgt	Wgt	Age	Int	Pts
Troy Aikman	QB	6'4"	228	26		
Jason Garrett	QB	6'2"	195	27		
Derrick Gainer	HB	5'11"	228	27		
Derrick Lassic	HB	5'10"	188	23		18
Emmitt Smith	HB	5'9"	209	24		60
Tommie Agee	FB	6'	235	29		
Lincoln Coleman	FB-HB	6'1"	249	24		12
Daryl Johnston	FB	6'2"	238	27		24
Alvin Harper	WR	6'3"	208	26		30
Michael Irvin	WR	6'2"	205	27		42
Kevin Williams	WR	5'9"	192	22		36
Tyrone Williams	WR	6'5"	220	23		
Kelly Blackwell	TE	6'1"	255	24		
Scott Galbraith	TE	6'2"	255	26		6
Joey Mickey	TE	6'5"	274	22		
Jay Novacek	TE	6'4"	232	30		12
Jim Price (from LA)	TE	6'4"	247	26		
Lin Elliott	K	6'	182	24		8
John Jett	K	6'	184	24		
Eddie Murray	K	5'11"	195	37		122

Jimmy Smith — Appendix
Alfredo Roberts — Foot Injury

NEW YORK GIANTS 11-5 Dan Reeves

Scores of Each Game		
26	Chicago	20
23	TAMPA BAY	7
20	L.A. RAMS	10
14	Buffalo	17
41	Washington	7
21	PHILADELPHIA	10
6	N.Y. JETS	10
9	Dallas	31
20	WASHINGTON	6
7	Philadelphia	3
19	PHOENIX	17
19	Miami	14
20	INDIANAPOLIS	6
24	New Orleans	14
6	Phoenix	17
13	DALLAS	*16

UseName	Pos.	Hgt	Wgt	Age	Int	Pts
Greg Bishop	OT	6'5"	298	22		
John Elliott	OT	6'7"	305	28		
Clarence Jones	OT	6'6"	280	25		
Eric Moore	OT-OG	6'5"	290	28		
Doug Riesenberg	OT	6'5"	275	28		
Scott Davis	OG	6'3"	289	23		
Bob Kratch	OG	6'3"	288	27		
William Roberts	OG	6'5"	280	31		
Bart Oates	C	6'3"	265	34		
Brian Williams	C	6'5"	300	27		
Mark Flythe	DE	6'7"	290	24		
Mike Fox	DE	6'6"	275	26		
Keith Hamilton	DE	6'6"	280	22		2
Mike Strahan	DE	6'4"	275	21		
George Thornton	DE	6'3"	300	25		
Stacey Dillard	NT	6'5"	288	24		
Erik Howard	NT	6'4"	268	28		

UseName	Pos.	Hgt	Wgt	Age	Int	Pts
Jessie Armstead	LB	6'1"	238	22	1	
Carlton Bailey	LB	6'3"	235	28		
Michael Brooks	LB	6'1"	235	29		
Marcus Buckley	LB	6'3"	235	22		
Steve DeOssie (to NYJ)	LB	6'2"	248	30		
Kanavis McGhee	LB	6'4"	257	24		
Corey Miller	LB	6'2"	255	24	2	
Andre Powell	LB	6'1"	226	24		
Lawrence Taylor	LB	6'3"	243	34		
Corey Widmer	DT	6'3"	276	24		
Willie Beamon	DB	5'11"	170	23	1	
Jesse Campbell	DB	6'1"	215	24	1	
Mark Collins	DB	5'10"	190	29	4	6
Myron Guyton	DB	6'1"	205	26	2	
Greg Jackson	DB	6'1"	200	27	4	
Izel Jenkins (from MIN)	DB	5'10"	190	29		
Corey Raymond	DB	5'11"	180	24	2	
Phillippi Sparks	DB	5'11"	186	24		
David Tate	DB	6'1"	200	28	1	
Perry Williams	DB	6'2"	203	32		

UseName	Pos.	Hgt	Wgt	Age	Int	Pts
Dave Brown	QB	6'5"	215	23		
Kent Graham	QB	6'5"	220	24		
Phil Simms	QB	6'3"	214	37		
Rodney Hampton	HB	5'11"	215	24		30
Dave Meggett	HB	5'7"	180	27		6
Lewis Tillman	HB	6'	195	27		18
Jarrod Bunch	FB	6'2"	248	25		18
Kenyon Rasheed	FB	5'10"	245	23		6
Chris Calloway	WR	5'10"	185	25		18
Keith Crawford	WR	6'2"	180	22		
Mark Jackson	WR	5'9"	180	30		24
Ed McCaffrey	WR	6'5"	215	25		12
Mike Sherrard	WR	6'2"	187	30		12
Derek Brown	TE	6'6"	252	23		
Howard Cross	TE	6'5"	245	26		30
Aaron Pierce	TE	6'5"	246	23		
Brad Daluiso	K	6'2"	207	25		3
Mike Horan	K	5'11"	190	34		
David Treadwell	K	6'1"	180	28		103

PHILADELPHIA EAGLES 8-8 Rich Kotite

Scores of Each Game		
23	PHOENIX	17
20	Green Bay	17
34	WASHINGTON	31
35	N.Y. Jets	30
6	Chicago	17
10	N.Y. Giants	21
10	DALLAS	23
3	Phoenix	16
14	MIAMI	19
3	N.Y. GIANTS	7
17	Washington	14
17	Dallas	23
7	BUFFALO	10
20	Indianapolis	10
37	NEW ORLEANS	26
37	San Francisco	*34

UseName	Pos.	Hgt	Wgt	Age	Int	Pts
Brian Baldinger	OT-OG	6'4"	278	33		
Antone Davis	OT	6'4"	325	26		
Ron Heller	OT	6'6"	280	31		
Broderick Thompson	OT	6'5"	295	33		
Eric Floyd	OG	6'5"	310	27		
Lester Holmes	OG	6'3"	301	23		
John Hudson	OG-C	6'2"	275	25		
Tom McHale	OG	6'4"	290	30		
Mike Schad	OG	6'5"	290	29		
Rob Selby	OG	6'3"	286	25		
David Alexander	C	6'3"	275	29		
Mike Chalenski	DE	6'4"	260	23		
Mike Flores	DE	6'3"	256	26		2
Tim Harris	DE	6'6"	258	28		
Clyde Simmons	DE	6'6"	280	29	1	
Andy Harmon	DT	6'4"	265	24		
Tommy Jeter	DT	6'5"	282	23		
Keith Millard	DT	6'5"	263	31		
Gerald Nichols (to WAS)	DT	6'2"	262	29		
William Perry (from CHI)	DT	6'2"	335	30		
Leonard Renfro	DT	6'2"	291	23		

UseName	Pos.	Hgt	Wgt	Age	Int	Pts
Louis Cooper	LB	6'1"	243	30		
Byron Evans	LB	6'2"	235	29	1	6
Britt Hager	LB	6'1"	225	27	1	
Seth Joyner	LB	6'2"	235	28	1	
Derrick Oden	LB	5'11"	230	22		
John Roper (from DAL)	LB	6'1"	235	27		
Ken Rose	LB	6'1"	215	31		
William Thomas	LB	6'2"	218	25	2	
Eric Allen	DB	5'10"	180	27	6	24
Corey Barlow	DB	5'9"	182	22		
William Frizzell	DB	6'3"	206	30		
Wes Hopkins	DB	6'1"	215	31	1	
Erik McMillan (to CLE, KC)	DB	6'2"	200	28		
Mark McMillian	DB	5'7"	162	23	2	
Rich Miano	DB	6'1"	200	30	4	
Mike Reid	DB	6'1"	218	22		
Ben Smith	DB	5'11"	185	26		
Otis Smith	DB	5'11"	184	27	1	
Andre Waters	DB	5'11"	200	31		

UseName	Pos.	Hgt	Wgt	Age	Int	Pts
Bubby Brister	QB	6'3"	207	31		
Randall Cunningham	QB	6'4"	205	30		6
Preston Jones	QB	6'3"	223	23		
Ken O'Brien	QB	6'4"	212	32		
Vaughn Hebron	HB	5'8"	196	22		18
James Joseph	HB-FB	6'	222	25		6
Heath Sherman	HB-FB	6'	205	26		12
Herschel Walker	HB	6'1"	225	31		24
Victor Bailey	WR	6'2"	196	23		6
Fred Barnett	WR	6'	199	27		
Reggie Lawrence	WR	6'	178	23		
James Lofton (from LA)	WR	6'3"	190	37		
Paul Richardson	WR	6'3"	204	24		
Vai Sikaherma	WR	5'9"	196	31		
Jeff Sydner	WR	5'6"	170	23		
Calvin Williams	WR	5'11"	190	26		60
Michael Young	WR	6'1"	183	31		12
Mark Bavaro	TE	6'4"	245	30		36
Maurice Johnson	TE	6'2"	243	26		
Matt Bahr	K	5'10"	175	37		67
Jeff Feagles	K	6'	205	27		
Roger Ruzek	K	6'1"	200	32		37

Tony Brooks — Back Injury

PHOENIX CARDINALS 7-9 Joe Bugel

Scores of Each Game		
17	Philadelphia	23
17	Washington	10
10	DALLAS	17
20	Detroit	26
21	NEW ENGLAND	23
36	WASHINGTON	6
14	San Francisco	28
17	NEW ORLEANS	20
16	PHILADELPHIA	3
15	Dallas	20
17	N.Y. Giants	19
38	L.A. RAMS	10
14	DETROIT	21
30	Seattle	*27
17	N.Y. GIANTS	6
27	Atlanta	10

UseName	Pos.	Hgt	Wgt	Age	Int	Pts
Ben Coleman	OT	6'6"	335	22		
Rick Cunningham	OT-OG	6'6"	320	26		
Ernest Dye	OT	6'6"	325	22		
Luis Sharpe	OT	6'4"	280	33		
Mark May	OG-C	6'6"	305	33		
Lance Smith	OG	6'2"	285	30		
Joe Wolf	OG-OT	6'6"	296	26		
Ed Cunningham	C	6'3"	285	24		
Kani Kauahi	C	6'3"	275	34		
Michael Bankston	DE	6'2"	280	23		
Chad Brown	DE	6'7"	265	22		
Reuben Davis	DE-DT	6'4"	320	28		
Mike Jones	DE	6'4"	295	24		
Freddie Joe Nunn	DE-LB	6'4"	255	31		
Eric Swann	DT-DE	6'4"	295	23		2
Chuckie Johnson	DT	6'4"	310	24		
Keith Rucker	DT	6'3"	360	24		

Rob Baxley — Knee Injury

UseName	Pos.	Hgt	Wgt	Age	Int	Pts
David Braxton	LB	6'1"	240	28		
Ken Harvey	LB	6'2"	245	28		
Eric Hill	LB	6'1"	255	26		
Steve Hyche	LB	6'2"	250	30		
Garth Jax	LB	6'2"	250	29		
Jock Jones	LB	6'2"	240	25		
Tyronne Stowe	LB	6'1"	250	28		
Brett Wallerstedt	LB	6'1"	240	22		
John Booty	DB	6'	180	27	2	
Chuck Cecil	DB	6'	185	28		
Dave Duerson	DB	6'1"	220	32		
Odie Harris	DB	6'	190	27		
Steve Lofton	DB	5'9"	185	24		
Lorenzo Lynch	DB	5'9"	200	30	3	6
Robert Massey	DB	5'10"	195	26		
Chris Oldham	DB	5'9"	195	24	1	
Aeneas Williams	DB	5'10"	190	25	2	12
Mike Zordich	DB	5'11"	201	29	1	

UseName	Pos.	Hgt	Wgt	Age	Int	Pts
Steve Beuerlein	QB	6'3"	210	28		
Chris Chandler	QB	6'4"	225	27		
Will Furrer	QB	6'3"	210	25		
Tony Sacca	QB	6'5"	235	23		
Johnny Bailey	HB	5'8"	190	26		12
Eric Blount	HB	5'9"	200	22		6
Larry Centers	HB	5'11"	215	25		18
Garrison Hearst	HB	5'11"	215	22		6
Ron Moore	HB-FB	5'10"	220	23		54
Gary Clark	WR	5'9"	175	31		24
Anthony Edwards	WR	5'9"	190	27		6
Randal Hill	WR	5'10"	180	23		24
Ricky Proehl	WR	5'10"	190	25		42
Pat Beach	TE	6'4"	250	33		
Chad Fann	TE	6'3"	250	23		
Walter Reeves	TE	6'4"	270	27		6
Butch Rolle	TE	6'4"	245	29		6
Derek Ware	TE	6'2"	250	25		
Rich Camarillo	K	5'11"	200	33		
Greg Davis	K	6'	205	27		100

WASHINGTON REDSKINS 4-12 Richie Petitbon

Scores of Each Game		
35	DALLAS	16
10	PHOENIX	17
31	Philadelphia	34
10	Miami	17
7	N.Y. GIANTS	41
6	Phoenix	36
10	Buffalo	24
30	INDIANAPOLIS	24
6	N.Y. Giants	20
6	L.A. Rams	10
14	PHILADELPHIA	17
23	Tampa Bay	17
0	N.Y. JETS	3
30	ATLANTA	17
3	Dallas	38
9	MINNESOTA	14

UseName	Pos.	Hgt	Wgt	Age	Int	Pts
Ray Brown	OT	6'5"	312	30		
Mo Elewonibi	OT	6'4"	286	27		
Joe Jacoby	OT	6'7"	314	33		
Ed Simmons	OT	6'5"	300	29		
Darryl Moore	OG	6'2"	292	24		
Mark Schlereth	OG	6'3"	278	27		
Guy Bingham	C	6'3"	260	35		
Jeff Bostic	C	6'2"	269	34		
Greg Huntington	C	6'3"	287	22		
Raleigh McKenzie	C-OG	6'2"	277	30		
Marc Raab	C	6'3"	265	24		
Jason Buck	DE	6'4"	274	30		
Shane Collins	DE	6'3"	267	24		
Jeff Faulkner (from NO)	DE	6'4"	305	29		
Charles Mann	DE	6'6"	272	32		
Al Noga	DE	6'1"	269	27		
Sterling Palmer	DE	6'5"	256	22		
Tim Johnson	DT	6'3"	275	27		
Jim Wahler	DT	6'4"	275	27		
Eric Williams	DT	6'4"	286	31		
Bobby Wilson	DT	6'2"	297	25		

Jim Lachey — Knee Injury
Matt Elliott — Knee Injury

UseName	Pos.	Hgt	Wgt	Age	Int	Pts
Carl Banks	LB	6'4"	249	31		
Monte Coleman	LB	6'2"	242	35	2	6
Andre Collins	LB	6'1"	231	25	1	
Kurt Gouveia	LB	6'1"	233	28	1	6
Rick Graf	LB	6'5"	244	29		
Rick Hamilton	LB	6'2"	241	23		
Lamont Hollinquest	LB	6'3"	245	22		
Todd Bowles	DB	6'2"	205	29		
Tom Carter	DB	5'11"	181	20	6	
Danny Copeland	DB	6'2"	210	27	1	
Brad Edwards	DB	6'2"	207	27	1	
Pat Eilers	DB	5'11"	195	26		
Darrell Green	DB	5'8"	170	33	4	6
A.J. Johnson	DB	5'8"	175	26	1	6
Alvoid Mays	DB	5'9"	172	27		
Darryl Morrison	CB	5'11"	185	22		
Johnny Thomas	DB	5'9"	191	29		

UseName	Pos.	Hgt	Wgt	Age	Int	Pts
Cary Conklin	QB	6'4"	225	25		
Rich Gannon	QB	6'3"	208	27		6
Mark Rypien	QB	6'4"	230	30		18
Reggie Brooks	HB	5'8"	202	22		18
Earnest Byner	HB-FB	5'10"	218	30		6
Ricky Ervins	HB	5'7"	195	24		
Brian Mitchell	HB	5'10"	205	25		18
Gregory Clifton	WR	5'11"	175	25		
Desmond Howard	WR	5'9"	180	23		
Tim McGee	WR	5'10"	174	29		18
Art Monk	WR	6'3"	202	35		12
Ricky Sanders	WR	5'11"	178	31		24
Mark Stock	WR	6'	180	27		
James Jenkins	TE	6'2"	241	26		
Ron Middleton	TE	6'2"	262	28		12
Terry Orr	TE	6'2"	235	31		
Jim Riggs	TE	6'5"	245	29		
Ray Rowe	TE	6'2"	256	24		
Frank Wycheck	TE	6'3"	235	21		
Kelly Goodburn	K	6'2"	199	31		
Chip Lohmiller	K	6'3"	215	27		72
Reggie Roby	K	6'2"	258	32		

Stephen Hobbs — Abdomen Injury

DALLAS COWBOYS

RUSHING

LastName	No.	Yds	Avg	TD
E. Smith	283	1486	5.3	9
Lassic	75	269	3.6	3
Coleman	34	132	3.9	2
Aikman	32	125	3.9	0
Johnston	24	74	3.1	3
Gainer	9	29	3.2	0
K. Williams	7	26	3.7	2
Agee	6	13	2.2	0
Irvin	2	6	3.0	0
Novacek	1	2	2.0	1
J. Garrett	8	-8	-1.0	0

RECEIVING

LastName	No.	Yds	Avg	TD
Irvin	88	1330	15.1	7
E. Smith	57	414	7.3	1
Johnston	50	372	7.4	1
Novacek	44	445	10.1	1
Harper	36	777	21.6	5
K. Williams	20	151	7.6	2
Lassic	9	37	4.1	0
Gainer	6	37	6.3	0
Coleman	4	24	6.0	0
T. Williams	1	25	25.0	0
Price	1	4	4.0	0
Galbraith	1	1	1.0	1

PUNT RETURNS

LastName	No.	Yds	Avg	TD
K. Williams	36	381	10.5	2
Washington	1	0	0.0	0

KICKOFF RETURNS

LastName	No.	Yds	Avg	TD
K. Williams	31	689	22.2	0
K. Smith	1	33	33.0	0
Gant	1	18	18.0	0
R. Jones	1	12	12.0	0
Hennings	1	7	7.0	0
Novacek	1	-1	-1.0	0
Vanderbeek	0	0	—	0

PASSING — PUNTING — KICKING

PASSING	Att	Cmp	%	Yds	Yd/Att	TD	Int— %	RK
Aikman	392	271	69.1	3100	7.91	15	6—1.5	2
J. Garrett	19	9	47.4	61	3.21	0	0—0.0	
Harper	1	1	100.0	46	46.00	0	0—0.0	

PUNTING	No.	Avg.
Jett	56	41.8

KICKING	XP	Att.	%	FG	Att	%
Murray	38	38	100	28	33	85
Elliott	2	3	67	2	4	50

NEW YORK GIANTS

RUSHING

LastName	No.	Yds	Avg	TD
Hampton	292	1077	3.7	5
Tillman	121	585	4.8	3
Meggett	69	329	4.8	0
Bunch	33	128	3.9	2
Rasheed	9	42	4.7	1
Simms	28	31	1.1	0
M. Jackson	3	25	8.3	0
Graham	2	-3	-1.5	0
Da. Brown	3	-4	-1.3	0

RECEIVING

LastName	No.	Yds	Avg	TD
M. Jackson	58	708	12.2	4
Meggett	38	319	8.4	0
Calloway	35	513	14.7	3
McCaffrey	27	335	12.4	2
Sherrard	24	433	18.0	2
Cross	21	272	13.0	5
Hampton	18	210	11.7	0
Bunch	13	98	7.5	1
Pierce	12	212	17.7	0
De. Brown	7	56	8.0	0
Tillman	1	21	21.0	0
Crawford	1	6	6.0	0
Rasheed	1	3	3.0	0
Simms	1	-6	-6.0	0

PUNT RETURNS

LastName	No.	Yds	Avg	TD
Meggett	32	331	10.3	1

KICKOFF RETURNS

LastName	No.	Yds	Avg	TD
Meggett	24	403	16.8	0
Calloway	6	89	14.8	0
Cross	2	15	7.5	0

PASSING — PUNTING — KICKING

PASSING	Att	Cmp	%	Yds	Yd/Att	TD	Int— %	RK
Simms	400	247	61.8	3038	7.60	15	9—2.3	3
Graham	22	8	36.4	79	3.59	0	0—0.0	
Meggett	2	2	100.0	63	31.50	2	0—0.0	

PUNTING	No.	Avg.
Horan	44	42.8

KICKING	XP	ATT	%	FG	ATT	%
Treadwell	28	29	97	25	31	81
Daluiso	0	0	—	1	3	33

PHILADELPHIA EAGLES

RUSHING

LastName	No.	Yds	Avg	TD
Walker	174	746	4.3	1
Sherman	115	406	3.5	2
Hebron	84	297	3.5	3
Joseph	39	140	3.6	0
Cunningham	18	110	6.1	1
Brister	20	39	2.0	0
O'Brien	4	17	4.3	0
Feagles	2	6	3.0	0

RECEIVING

LastName	No.	Yds	Avg	TD
Walker	75	610	8.1	3
Williams	60	725	12.1	10
Bavaro	43	481	11.2	6
Bailey	41	545	13.3	1
Joseph	29	291	10.0	1
Barnett	17	170	10.0	0
Young	14	186	13.3	2
Lofton	14	183	13.1	0
Sherman	12	78	6.5	0
Hebron	11	82	7.5	0
Johnson	10	81	8.1	0
Sydner	2	42	21.0	0
Lawrence	1	5	5.0	0

PUNT RETURNS

LastName	No.	Yds	Avg	TD
Sikahema	33	275	8.3	0
O. Smith	0	9	—	0

KICKOFF RETURNS

LastName	No.	Yds	Avg	TD
Sikahema	30	579	19.3	0
Walker	11	184	16.7	0
Sydner	9	158	17.6	0
Hebron	3	35	11.7	0
Johnson	1	7	7.0	0
O. Smith	0	24	—	0

PASSING — PUNTING — KICKING

PASSING	Att	Cmp	%	Yds	Yd/Att	TD	Int— %	RK
Brister	309	181	58.6	1905	6.17	14	5—1.6	4
O'Brien	137	71	51.8	708	5.17	4	3—2.2	
Cunningham	110	76	69.1	850	7.73	5	5—4.5	

PUNTING	No.	Avg.
Feagles	83	40.0

KICKING	XP	ATT	%	FG	ATT	%
Bahr	28	29	97	13	18	72
Ruzek	13	16	81	8	10	80

PHOENIX CARDINALS

RUSHING

LastName	No.	Yds	Avg	TD
Moore	263	1018	3.9	9
Hearst	76	264	3.5	1
Bailey	49	253	5.2	1
Centers	25	152	6.1	0
Proehl	8	47	5.9	0
Beuerlein	22	45	2.0	0
Blount	5	28	5.6	1
Chandler	3	2	0.7	0
Camarillo	1	0	0.0	0

RECEIVING

LastName	No.	Yds	Avg	TD
Centers	66	603	9.1	3
Proehl	65	877	13.5	7
Clark	63	818	13.0	4
R. Hill	35	519	14.8	4
Bailey	32	243	7.6	0
Edwards	13	326	25.1	1
Rolle	10	67	6.7	1
Reeves	9	67	7.4	1
Hearst	6	18	3.0	0
Blount	5	36	7.2	0
Ware	3	45	15.0	0
Moore	3	16	5.3	0

PUNT RETURNS

LastName	No.	Yds	Avg	TD
Bailey	35	282	8.1	1
Blount	9	90	10.0	0
Edwards	3	12	4.0	0

KICKOFF RETURNS

LastName	No.	Yds	Avg	TD
Bailey	31	699	22.5	0
Blount	8	163	20.4	0
Edwards	3	51	17.0	0
Lofton	1	18	18.0	0
Smith	1	11	11.0	0
Moore	1	9	9.0	0

PASSING — PUNTING — KICKING

PASSING	Att	Cmp	%	Yds	Yd/Att	TD	Int— %	RK
Beuerlein	418	258	61.7	3164	7.57	18	17—4.1	6
Chandler	103	52	50.5	471	4.57	3	2—2.9	
Hearst	1	0	0.0	0	0.00	0	1—100.0	

PUNTING	No.	Avg.
Camarillo	73	43.7

KICKING	XP	Att	%	FG	Att	%
Davis	37	37	100	21	28	75

WASHINGTON REDSKINS

RUSHING

LastName	No.	Yds	Avg	TD
Brooks	223	1063	4.8	3
Mitchell	63	246	3.9	3
Ervins	50	201	4.0	0
Byner	23	105	4.6	1
Gannon	21	88	4.2	1
Howard	2	17	8.5	0
Sanders	1	7	7.0	0
Rypien	9	2	0.2	3
Roby	1	0	0.0	0
Monk	1	-1	-1.0	0
Conklin	2	-2	-1.0	0

RECEIVING

LastName	No.	Yds	Avg	TD
Sanders	58	638	11.0	4
Monk	41	398	9.7	2
McGee	39	500	12.8	3
Byner	27	194	7.2	0
Middleton	24	154	6.4	2
Howard	23	286	12.4	0
Brooks	21	186	8.9	0
Mitchell	20	157	7.9	0
Ervins	16	123	7.7	0
Wycheck	16	113	7.1	0
Clifton	2	15	7.5	0

PUNT RETURNS

LastName	No.	Yds	Avg	TD
Mitchell	29	193	6.7	0
Howard	4	25	6.3	0
Green	1	27	27.0	0
Mays	1	0	0.0	0

KICKOFF RETURNS

LastName	No.	Yds	Avg	TD
Mitchell	33	678	20.5	0
Howard	21	405	19.3	0
Ervins	2	29	14.5	0
Bowles	1	27	27.0	0
Buck	1	15	15.0	0
Brooks	1	12	12.0	0

PASSING — PUNTING — KICKING

PASSING	Att	Cmp	%	Yds	Yd/Att	TD	Int— %	RK
Rypien	319	166	52.0	1514	4.75	4	10—3.1	14
Gannon	125	74	59.2	704	5.63	3	7—2.4	
Conklin	87	46	52.9	496	5.70	4	3—3.4	
Mitchell	2	1	50.0	50	25.00	0	1—50.0	

PUNTING	No.	Avg.
Roby	78	44.2
Goodburn	5	39.4

KICKING	XP	ATT	%	FG	ATT	%
Lohmiller	24	26	92	16	28	57

DETROIT LIONS 10-6 Wayne Fontes

Scores of Each Game		
30	ATLANTA	13
19	New England	*16
3	New Orleans	14
26	PHOENIX	20
10	Tampa Bay	27
30	SEATTLE	10
16	L.A. Rams	13
30	Minnesota	27
23	TAMPA BAY	0
17	Green Bay	26
6	CHICAGO	10
0	MINNESOTA	13
21	Phoenix	14
17	SAN FRANCISCO	55
20	Chicago	14
30	GREEN BAY	20

UseName	Pos.	Hgt	Wgt	Age	Int	Pts
Lomas Brown	OT	6'4"	287	30		
Scott Conover	OT	6'4"	285	24		
Jack Linn (to CIN)	OT	6'5"	285	26		
David Lutz	OT	6'6"	305	33		
Larry Tharpe	OT	6'4"	299	22		
Shawn Bouwens	OG	6'4"	290	25		
Bill Fralic	OG	6'5"	280	30		
David Richards	OG	6'5"	310	27		
Mike Compton	C-OG	6'6"	297	22		
Kevin Glover	C	6'2"	282	30		
Mark Rodenhauser	C	6'5"	280	32		
Dan Owens	DE	6'3"	280	26	1	
Robert Porcher	DE	6'3"	283	24		
Kelvin Pritchett	DE	6'2"	281	23		
Marc Spindler	DE-NT	6'5"	290	23		
Lawrence Pete	NT	6'	275	27		
Mack Travis	NT	6'1"	280	23		

UseName	Pos.	Hgt	Wgt	Age	Int	Pts
Toby Caston	LB	6'1"	243	28		
Darryl Ford	LB	6'1"	225	27		
Dennis Gibson	LB	6'2"	243	29	1	
Tracy Hayworth	LB	6'3"	260	25		
George Jamison	LB	6'1"	235	30	2	6
Victor Jones	LB	6'2"	250	26		
Antonio London	LB	6'2"	234	22		
Tracy Scroggins	LB	6'2"	255	23	1	
Chris Spielman	LB	6'	247	27	2	
Pat Swilling	LB	6'3"	242	28	3	
Bennie Blades	DB	6'1"	221	26		
Willie Clay	DB	5'9"	184	22		12
Harry Colon	DB	6'	203	24	2	
Ray Crockett	DB	5'9"	181	26	2	
Greg Jeffries	DB	5'9"	184	21		
Tim McKyer	DB	6'	174	29	2	
Ryan McNeil	DB	6'	175	22	2	
Kevin Scott	DB	5'9"	175	24		
William White	DB	5'10"	191	27	1	

Mike Cofer — Knee Injury

UseName	Pos.	Hgt	Wgt	Age	Int	Pts
Erik Kramer	QB	6'1"	199	28		
Rodney Peete	QB	6'	207	27		6
Andre Ware	QB	6'2"	205	25		
Eric Lynch	HB	5'10"	224	23		12
Derrick Moore	HB-FB	6'1"	227	25		24
Curvin Richards	HB	5'9"	195	24		
Barry Sanders	HB-FB	5'8"	203	25		18
Reggie Barrett	WR	6'3"	215	24		
Jeff Campbell	WR	5'8"	173	25		
Mel Gray	WR	5'9"	172	32		6
Willie Green	WR	6'2"	181	27		12
Aubrey Matthews	WR	5'7"	165	30		
Herman Moore	WR	6'3"	210	23		36
Brett Perriman	WR	5'9"	180	27		12
Vernon Turner (to TB)	WR	5'8"	185	26		
Ty Hallock	TE	6'3"	249	22		12
Rodney Holman	TE	6'3"	238	23		12
Jimmie Johnson	TE	6'2"	255	26		
Marty Thompson	TE	6'3"	243	23		
Jim Arnold	K	6'3"	211	32		
Jason Hanson	K	5'11"	183	23		130

Ed Tillison — Knee Injury

MINNESOTA VIKINGS 9-7 Dennis Green

Scores of Each Game		
7	L.A. Raiders	24
10	CHICAGO	7
15	GREEN BAY	13
19	San Francisco	38
15	TAMPA BAY	0
19	Chicago	12
27	DETROIT	30
17	SAN DIEGO	30
26	Denver	23
10	Tampa Bay	23
14	NEW ORLEANS	17
13	Detroit	0
20	DALLAS	37
21	Green Bay	17
30	KANSAS CITY	10
14	Washington	9

UseName	Pos.	Hgt	Wgt	Age	Int	Pts
Scott Adams	OT	6'5"	293	26		
Bernard Dafney	OT	6'5"	331	23		
Tim Irwin	OT	6'6"	297	34		
Everett Lindsay	OT	6'4"	290	22		
John Gerak	OG	6'3"	285	23		
Todd Kalis	OG	6'5"	289	28		
Randall McDaniel	OG	6'3"	275	28		
Jeff Christy	C	6'3"	277	24		
Mike Morris	C	6'5"	284	32		
Adam Schreiber	C	6'4"	288	31		
Chris Doleman	DE	6'5"	274	31	1	
James Harris	DE	6'4"	270	25		
Robert Harris	DE	6'4"	290	24		
Roy Barker	DT	6'4"	280	24		
Brad Culpepper	DT	6'1"	260	25		
John Randle	DT	6'1"	275	25		
Henry Thomas	DT	6'2"	277	28		2
Esera Tuaolo	DT	6'2"	275	25		

UseName	Pos.	Hgt	Wgt	Age	Int	Pts
Jack Del Rio	LB	6'4"	243	30	4	
Dave Garnett	LB	6'2"	219	22		
Bruce Holmes	LB	6'2"	237	27		
Carlos Jenkins	LB	6'3"	217	25	2	
Greg Manusky	LB	6'1"	233	27		
Ed McDaniel	LB	5'11"	230	24		
Ashley Sheppard	LB	6'3"	243	24		
Fred Strickland	LB	6'2"	245	27		
Ron Carpenter (to CIN)	DB	6'1"	188	23		
Vencie Glenn	DB	6'	201	28	5	
Shawn Jones	DB	6'1"	200	23		
Carl Lee	DB	6'	186	32	3	
Lamar McGriggs	DB	6'3"	210	25	1	6
Audrey McMillian	DB	6'	189	31	4	6
Anthony Parker	DB	5'10"	181	27	1	
Jayice Pearson	DB	5'11"	184	30	1	
Todd Scott	DB	5'10"	207	25	2	

UseName	Pos.	Hgt	Wgt	Age	Int	Pts
Jim McMahon	QB	6'1"	196	34		
Sean Salisbury	QB	6'5"	218	30		
Gino Torretta	QB	6'2"	215	23		
Roger Craig	HB	5'11"	211	33		12
Chuck Evans	HB	6'1"	226	26		
Scottie Graham	HB	5'9"	215	24		18
Robert Smith	HB	6'	195	21		12
Barry Word	HB	6'2"	242	30		12
Anthony Carter	WR	5'11"	168	32		30
Cris Carter	WR	6'3"	198	27		54
Eric Guliford	WR	5'8"	165	23		
Qadry Ismail	WR	6'	192	22		6
Jake Reed	WR	6'3"	212	25		
Olanda Truitt	WR	6'	186	22		
Steve Jordan	TE	6'4"	242	32		6
Brent Novoselsky	TE	6'3"	237	27		
Derek Tennell	TE	6'5"	251	29		
Mike Tice	TE	6'7"	264	34		6
Harry Newsome	K	6'	193	30		
Fuad Reveiz	K	5'11"	223	30		105

Terry Allen — Knee Injury
Ronnie West — Leg Injury

GREEN BAY PACKERS 9-7 Mike Holmgren

Scores of Each Game		
36	L.A. RAMS	6
17	PHILADELPHIA	20
13	Minnesota	15
14	Dallas	36
30	DENVER	27
37	Tampa Bay	14
17	CHICAGO	3
16	Kansas City	23
19	New Orleans	17
26	DETROIT	17
13	TAMPA BAY	10
17	Chicago	30
20	San Diego	13
17	MINNESOTA	21
28	L.A. RAIDERS	0
20	Detroit	30

UseName	Pos.	Hgt	Wgt	Age	Int	Pts
Earl Dotson	OT	6'4"	315	22		
Paul Hutchins	OT	6'5"	335	23		
Tunch Ilkin	OT	6'3"	272	35		
Tootie Robbins	OT	6'5"	315	35		
Ken Ruettgers	OT	6'5"	290	31		
Joe Sims	OT	6'3"	310	24		
Harry Galbreath	OG	6'1"	275	28		
Rich Moran	OG	6'3"	280	31		
Doug Widell	OG	6'4"	280	26		
James Campen	C	6'3"	280	29		
Frank Winters	C-OG	6'3"	285	29		
Lance Zeno (from CLE)	C	6'4"	279	26		
Matt Brock	DE	6'5"	280	27	1	
Don Davey	DE	6'4"	270	25		
David Grant	DE	6'4"	275	27		
Shawn Patterson	DE	6'5"	270	29		
Reggie White	DE	6'5"	290	31		
Gilbert Brown	NT	6'2"	330	22		
John Jurkovic	NT	6'2"	285	26		
Bill Maas	NT	6'5"	295	31		

Tom Neville — Achilles Injury

UseName	Pos.	Hgt	Wgt	Age	Int	Pts
Tony Bennett	LB	6'2"	243	26		
Keo Coleman	LB	6'1"	255	23		
Johnny Holland	LB	6'2"	235	28	2	
George Koonce	LB	6'1"	238	24		
Jim Morrissey (from CHI)	LB	6'3"	225	30		
Joe Mott	LB	6'4"	238	27		
Brian Noble	LB	6'3"	245	30		
Bryce Paup	LB	6'5"	247	25	1	
Wayne Simmons	LB	6'3"	240	23	2	
Keith Traylor	LB	6'2"	260	23		
James Willis	LB	6'2"	235	20		
Terrell Buckley	DB	5'9"	174	22	2	
LeRoy Butler	DB	6'	193	25	6	6
Doug Evans	DB	6'1"	188	23	1	
Corey Harris	DB-WR	5'11"	195	23		
Tim Hauck	DB	5'11"	185	26		
Roland Mitchell	DB	5'11"	195	29	1	
Muhammad Oliver (from KC)	DB	5'11"	170	24		
Mike Prior	DB	6'	215	29	1	
George Teague	DB	6'1"	187	22	1	
Sammy Walker	DB	5'1"	203	24		

Mark D'Onofrio — Hamstring Injury

UseName	Pos.	Hgt	Wgt	Age	Int	Pts
Mark Brunell	QB	6'1"	208	22		
Ty Detmer	QB	6'	190	25		
Brett Favre	QB	6'2"	218	23		6
Darrell Thompson	HB	6'	217	25		18
Kevin Williams	HB	6'	208	23		
Marcus Wilson	HB	6'1"	210	25		
Edgar Bennett	FB	6'	216	24		60
Dexter McNabb	FB	6'2"	245	24		
Robert Brooks	WR	6'	174	23		6
Mark Clayton	WR	5'9"	185	32		18
Shawn Collins	WR	6'2"	204	26		
Ron Lewis	WR	5'11"	189	25		
Anthony Morgan (from CHI)	WR	6'1"	195	25		
Sterling Sharpe	WR	5'11"	210	28		66
Mark Chmura	TE	6'5"	242	24		
Jackie Harris	TE	6'3"	243	25		24
Darryl Ingram	TE	6'3"	245	27		
Ed West	TE	6'1"	245	32		
Chris Jacke	K	6'	200	27		128
Bryan Wagner	K	6'2"	200	31		

James Milling — Concussion

CHICAGO BEARS 7-9 Dave Wannstedt

Scores of Each Game		
20	N.Y. GIANTS	26
7	Minnesota	10
47	TAMPA BAY	17
6	ATLANTA	0
17	Philadelphia	6
12	MINNESOTA	19
3	Green Bay	17
14	L.A. RAIDERS	16
16	San Diego	13
19	Kansas City	17
10	Detroit	6
30	GREEN BAY	17
10	Tampa Bay	13
3	DENVER	13
14	DETROIT	20
6	L.A. Rams	20

UseName	Pos.	Hgt	Wgt	Age	Int	Pts
Troy Auzenne	OT	6'7"	290	24		
Jay Leeuwenburg	OT	6'2"	288	24		
Keith Van Horne	OT	6'6"	290	35		
James Williams	OT	6'7"	330	25		
Mark Bortz	OG	6'6"	282	32		
Todd Perry	OG	6'5"	298	22		
Vernice Smith (to WAS)	OG	6'3"	298	27		
John Wojciechowski	OG-OT	6'4"	280	30		
Jerry Fontenot	C	6'3"	287	26		
Mark McGuire	C	6'2"	286	23		
Trace Armstrong	DE	6'4"	265	27		
Richard Dent	DE	6'5"	265	32	1	
Albert Fontenot	DE	6'4"	265	22		
Alonzo Spellman	DE	6'4"	282	21		
Tory Epps (from ATL)	DT	6'1"	280	26		
Steve McMichael	DT	6'2"	268	35	1	
Tim Ryan	DT-DE	6'4"	265	25		
Carl Simpson	DT	6'2"	282	23		
Chris Zorich	DT	6'1"	275	24		

UseName	Pos.	Hgt	Wgt	Age	Int	Pts
Myron Baker	LB	6'1"	228	22		12
Joe Cain	LB	6'1"	233	28		
Ron Cox	LB	6'2"	235	25		
Dante Jones	LB	6'1"	230	28	4	6
Barry Minter	LB	6'2"	242	23		
Vinson Smith	LB	6'2"	236	28		
Percy Snow	LB	6'2"	245	25		
Anthony Blaylock	DB	5'10"	185	28	2	
Mark Carrier	DB	6'1"	192	25	4	6
Maurice Douglass	DB	5'11"	202	29		
Shaun Gayle	DB	5'11"	202	31		
Keshon Johnson	DB	5'10"	179	23		
Jeremy Lincoln	DB	5'10"	180	24	3	6
John Mangum	DB	5'10"	182	26	1	
Kevin Miniefield	DB	5'9"	178	23		
Markus Paul (to TB)	DB	6'2"	205	27		
Donnell Woolford	DB	5'9"	188	27	2	

UseName	Pos.	Hgt	Wgt	Age	Int	Pts
Jim Harbaugh	QB	6'3"	215	29		24
Peter Tom Willis	QB	6'2"	204	26		
Neal Anderson	HB	5'11"	215	29		24
Robert Green	HB	5'8"	209	22		
Darren Lewis	HB	5'10"	225	24		
Tim Worley (from PIT)	HB	6'2"	226	26		12
Bob Christian	FB	5'10"	225	24		
Craig Heyward	FB	5'1"	290	26		
John Ivlow	FB	5'11"	226	23		
Fred Banks (from MIA)	WR	5'10"	185	31		
Curtis Conway	WR	6'	185	22		12
Wendell Davis	WR	5'11"	194	27		
Terry Obee	WR	5'10"	180	25		18
Tom Waddle	WR	6'	185	26		6
Chris Gedney	TE	6'5"	262	23		
Keith Jennings	TE	6'4"	265	27		
Ryan Wetnight	TE	6'2"	238	22		6
Danta Whitaker	TE	6'4"	254	29		
Kevin Butler	K	6'1"	204	31		102
Chris Gardocki	K	6'1"	188	23		

Glen Kozlowski — Knee Injury

TAMPA BAY BUCCANEERS 5-11 Sam Wyche

Scores of Each Game		
3	KANSAS CITY	27
7	N.Y. Giants	23
17	Chicago	47
27	DETROIT	10
0	Minnesota	15
14	GREEN BAY	37
31	Atlanta	24
0	Detroit	23
21	SAN FRANCISCO	45
23	MINNESOTA	10
10	Green Bay	13
17	WASHINGTON	23
13	CHICAGO	10
20	L.A. Raiders	27
17	Denver	10
17	SAN DIEGO	32

UseName	Pos.	Hgt	Wgt	Age	Int	Pts
Theo Adams	OT	6'4"	300	27		
Scott Dill	OT	6'5"	290	27		
Paul Gruber	OT	6'5"	290	28		
Charles McRae	OT-OG	6'7"	300	24		
Rob Taylor	OT	6'6"	290	32		
Ian Beckles	OG	6'1"	295	26		
Sean Love	OG	6'3"	295	25		
Bruce Reimers	OG	6'7"	300	32		
Tim Ryan	OG	6'2"	280	24		
Mike Sullivan	OG	6'3"	290	25		
Pat Tomberlin	OG-OT	6'2"	300	27		
Tony Mayberry	C	6'4"	290	25		
Chidi Ahanotu	DE	6'2"	280	22		
Eric Curry	DE	6'5"	270	23		
Santana Dotson	DE	6'5"	270	23		
Eric Hayes	DE-NT	6'3"	290	25		
Shawn Price	DE	6'5"	260	23		
Ray Seals	DE	6'3"	280	28	1	6
Rhett Hall	DT	6'2"	270	24		
Mark Wheeler	DT-NT	6'2"	280	23		
Bernard Wilson	NT-DT	6'2"	295	23		

Anthony Munoz — Shoulder Injury

UseName	Pos.	Hgt	Wgt	Age	Int	Pts
Ed Brady	LB	6'2"	235	31		
Darrick Brownlow	LB	6'	240	24		
Reggie Burnette	LB	6'2"	245	24		
Demetrious DuBose	LB	6'1"	240	22		
Hardy Nickerson	LB	6'2"	230	28	1	
Broderick Thomas	LB	6'4"	250	26		
Jimmy Williams	LB	6'3"	220	32		
Darren Anderson	DB	5'10"	180	24	1	
Curtis Buckley	DB-WR	6'	185	23		
Barney Bussey	DB	6'	210	31		
Marty Carter	DB	6'1"	200	23	1	
Jerry Gray	DB	6'	185	30		
Roger Jones	DB	5'9"	175	24		
Joe King	DB	6'2"	195	25	3	
John Lynch	DB	6'2"	220	21		
Milton Mack	DB	5'11"	195	29	1	6
Martin Mayhew	DB	5'8"	175	27		
Ricky Reynolds	DB	5'11"	190	28	1	

Tony Covington — Back Injury
Rogerick Green — Knee Injury
Darryl Pollard — Neck Injury

UseName	Pos.	Hgt	Wgt	Age	Int	Pts
Craig Erickson	QB	6'2"	205	24		
Mark Vlasic	QB	6'3"	205	29		
Casey Weldon	QB	6'1"	200	24		
Gary Anderson (to DET)	HB	6'	190	32		6
Reggie Cobb	HB	6'	215	25		24
Vince Workman	HB	5'10"	205	25		24
Rudy Harris	FB	6'1"	255	21		
Anthony McDowell	FB	5'11"	235	24		6
Mazio Royster	FB	6'1"	200	23		6
Robert Claiborne	WR	5'10"	175	26		
Horace Copeland	WR	6'2"	195	22		24
Lawrence Dawsey	WR	6'	195	25		
Courtney Hawkins	WR	5'9"	180	23		30
Lamar Thomas	WR	6'1"	170	23		12
Charles Wilson	WR	5'10"	185	25		
Tyji Armstrong	TE	6'4"	250	22		6
Ron Hall	TE	6'4"	245	29		6
Dave Moore	TE	6'2"	245	23		6
Michael Husted	K	6'	190	23		75
Dan Stryzinski	K	6'1"	195	28		

DETROIT LIONS

RUSHING

Last Name	No.	Yds	Avg	TD
Sanders	243	1115	4.6	3
D. Moore	88	405	4.6	3
Lynch	53	207	3.9	2
Peete	45	165	3.7	1
Ware	7	23	3.3	0
Perriman	4	16	4.0	0
Matthews	2	7	3.5	0
Kramer	10	5	0.5	0
Richards	4	1	0.3	0

RECEIVING

Last Name	No.	Yds	Avg	TD
H. Moore	61	935	15.3	6
Perriman	49	496	10.1	2
Sanders	36	205	5.7	0
Green	28	462	16.5	2
Holman	25	244	9.8	2
D. Moore	21	169	8.0	1
Lynch	13	82	6.3	0
Matthews	11	171	15.5	0
Hallock	8	88	11.0	2
Campbell	7	55	7.9	0
Johnson	2	18	9.0	0
Thompson	1	15	15.0	0
Turner	1	7	7.0	0
Fralic	1	-4	-4.0	0

PUNT RETURNS

Last Name	No.	Yds	Avg	TD
Gray	23	197	8.6	0
Turner	17	152	8.9	0

KICKOFF RETURNS

Last Name	No.	Yds	Avg	TD
Gray	28	688	24.6	1
Turner	15	330	22.0	0
Clay	2	34	17.0	0
D. Moore	1	68	68.0	0
Lynch	1	22	22.0	0
Hallock	1	11	11.0	0
Jamison	1	0	0.0	0

PASSING — PUNTING — KICKING Statistics

PASSING	Att	Cmp	%	Yds	Yd/Att	TD	Int—	%	RK
Peete	252	157	62.3	1670	6.63	6	14—	5.6	11
Kramer	138	87	63.0	1002	7.26	8	3—	2.2	
Ware	45	20	44.4	271	6.02	1	2—	4.4	

PUNTING	No.	Avg.
Arnold	72	44.8

KICKING	XP	Att	%	FG	Att	%
Hanson	28	28	100	34	43	79

MINNESOTA VIKINGS

RUSHING

Last Name	No.	Yds	Avg	TD
Graham	118	487	4.1	3
Word	142	458	3.2	2
Smith	82	399	4.9	2
Craig	38	119	3.1	1
McMahon	33	96	2.9	0
Evans	14	32	2.3	0
A. Carter	7	19	2.7	0
Ismail	3	14	4.7	0
Salisbury	10	-1	-0.1	0

RECEIVING

Last Name	No.	Yds	Avg	TD
C. Carter	86	1071	12.5	9
A. Carter	60	774	12.9	5
Jordan	56	542	9.7	1
Smith	24	111	4.6	0
Ismail	19	212	11.2	1
Craig	19	169	8.9	1
Tennell	15	122	8.1	0
Word	9	105	11.7	0
Graham	7	46	6.6	0
Tice	6	39	6.5	1
Reed	5	65	13.0	0
Evans	4	39	9.8	0
Truitt	4	40	10.0	0
Guliford	1	45	45.0	0

PUNT RETURNS

Last Name	No.	Yds	Avg	TD
Guliford	29	212	7.3	0
Parker	9	64	7.1	0
Smith	1	4	4.0	0

KICKOFF RETURNS

Last Name	No.	Yds	Avg	TD
Ismail	42	902	21.5	0
Guliford	5	101	20.2	0
Smith	3	41	13.6	0
Graham	1	16	16.0	0
Evans	1	11	11.0	0
Craig	1	11	11.0	0
Del Rio	1	4	4.0	0
McMillian	1	0	0.0	0

PASSING	Att	Cmp	%	Yds	Yd/Att	TD	Int—	%	RK
McMahon	331	200	60.4	1967	5.94	9	8—	2.4	7
Salisbury	195	115	59.0	1413	7.25	9	6—	3.1	

PUNTING	No.	Avg.
Newsome	90	42.9

KICKING	XP	ATT	%	FG	ATT	%
Reveiz	27	28	96	26	35	74

GREEN BAY PACKERS

RUSHING

Last Name	No.	Yds	Avg	TD
Thompson	169	654	3.9	2
E. Bennett	159	550	3.5	9
Favre	58	216	3.7	1
Brooks	3	17	5.7	0
Sharpe	4	8	2.0	0
Wilson	6	3	0.5	0
Detmer	1	-2	-2.0	0

RECEIVING

Last Name	No.	Yds	Avg	TD
Sharpe	**112**	1274	11.4	11
E. Bennett	59	457	7.7	1
J. Harris	42	604	14.4	4
Clayton	32	331	10.3	3
West	25	253	10.1	0
Brooks	20	180	9.0	0
Thompson	18	129	7.2	0
Lewis	2	21	10.5	0
Wilson	2	18	9.0	0
Chmura	2	13	6.5	0
C. Harris	2	11	5.5	0
Morgan	1	8	8.0	0

PUNT RETURNS

Last Name	No.	Yds	Avg	TD
Prior	17	194	11.4	0
Brooks	16	135	8.4	0
Buckley	11	76	6.9	0
Teague	1	-1	-1.0	0

KICKOFF RETURNS

Last Name	No.	Yds	Avg	TD
Brooks	23	611	**26.6**	1
C. Harris	16	482	30.1	0
Thompson	9	171	19.0	0
Wilson	9	197	21.9	0
Jurkovic	2	22	11.0	0
Chmura	1	0	0.0	0

PASSING	Att	Cmp	%	Yds	Yd/Att	TD	Int—	%	RK
Favre	**522**	**318**	60.9	3303	6.33	19	24—	4.6	8
Detmer	5	3	60.0	26	5.20	0	0—	0.0	
Sharpe	1	1	100.0	1	1.00	0	0—	0.0	

PUNTING	No.	Avg.
Wagner	74	42.9

KICKING	XP	Att.	%	FG	Att	%
Jacke	35	35	**100**	31	37	84

CHICAGO BEARS

RUSHING

Last Name	No.	Yds	Avg	TD
Anderson	202	646	3.2	4
Worley	120	470	3.9	2
Harbaugh	60	277	4.6	4
Heyward	68	206	3.0	0
Conway	5	44	8.8	0
Green	15	29	1.9	0
Christian	8	19	2.4	0
Lewis	7	13	1.9	0
Willis	2	6	3.0	0

RECEIVING

Last Name	No.	Yds	Avg	TD
Waddle	44	552	12.5	1
Anderson	31	160	5.2	0
Obee	26	351	13.5	3
Conway	19	231	12.2	2
Christian	16	160	10.0	0
Heyward	16	132	8.3	0
Jennings	14	150	10.7	0
Green	13	63	4.8	0
Davis	12	132	11.0	0
Worley	11	62	5.6	0
Gedney	10	98	9.8	0
Wetnight	9	93	10.3	1
Whitaker	6	53	8.8	0
Lewis	4	26	6.5	0
Banks	2	45	22.5	0
Harbaugh	1	1	1.0	0

PUNT RETURNS

Last Name	No.	Yds	Avg	TD
Obee	35	289	8.3	0

KICKOFF RETURNS

Last Name	No.	Yds	Avg	TD
Conway	21	450	21.4	0
Green	9	141	15.7	0
Obee	9	159	17.7	0
Worley	6	121	20.2	0
Heyward	1	12	12.0	0
A. Fontenot	1	8	8.0	0
Ryan	1	5	5.0	0
Mangum	1	0	0.0	0

PASSING	Att	Cmp	%	Yds	Yd/Att	TD	Int—	%	RK
Harbaugh	325	200	61.5	2002	6.16	7	11—	3.4	9
Willis	60	30	50.0	268	4.47	0	5—	8.3	
Gardocki	2	0	0.0	0	0.00	0	0—	0.0	
Anderson	1	0	0.0	0	0.00	0	0—	0.0	

PUNTING	No.	Avg.
Gardocki	80	38.5

KICKING	XP	ATT	%	FG	ATT	%
Butler	21	22	95	27	36	75

TAMPA BAY BUCCANEERS

RUSHING

Last Name	No.	Yds	Avg	TD
Cobb	221	658	3.0	3
Workman	78	284	3.6	2
Royster	33	115	3.5	1
Erickson	26	96	3.7	0
G. Anderson	28	56	2.0	0
Copeland	3	34	11.3	0
Harris	7	29	4.1	0
C. Wilson	2	7	3.5	0
McDowell	2	6	3.0	0
Armstrong	2	5	2.5	0

RECEIVING

Last Name	No.	Yds	Avg	TD
Hawkins	62	933	15.0	5
Workman	54	411	7.6	2
Copeland	30	633	21.1	4
Hall	23	268	11.7	1
C. Wilson	15	225	15.0	0
Dawsey	15	203	13.5	0
G. Anderson	11	89	8.1	1
Armstrong	9	86	9.6	1
Cobb	9	61	6.8	1
L. Thomas	8	186	23.3	2
McDowell	8	26	3.3	1
Claiborne	5	61	12.2	0
Royster	5	18	3.6	0
Harris	4	48	12.0	0
Moore	4	47	11.8	1

PUNT RETURNS

Last Name	No.	Yds	Avg	TD
G. Anderson	17	113	6.6	0
Hawkins	15	166	11.1	0
Claiborne	6	32	5.3	0

KICKOFF RETURNS

Last Name	No.	Yds	Avg	TD
C. Wilson	23	454	19.7	0
G. Anderson	12	181	15.1	0
Royster	8	102	12.8	0
Turner	6	61	10.2	0
Workman	5	67	13.4	0
Claiborne	4	57	14.3	0

PASSING	Att	Cmp	%	Yds	Yd/Att	TD	Int—	%	RK
Erickson	457	233	51.0	3054	6.68	18	21—	4.6	12
Weldon	11	6	54.5	55	5.00	0	1—	9.1	
Moore	1	0	0.0	0	0.00	0	0—	0.0	

PUNTING	No.	Avg.
Stryzinski	**94**	40.1

KICKING	XP	ATT	%	FG	ATT	%
Husted	27	27	**100**	16	22	73

SAN FRANCISCO 49ERS 10-6 George Seifert

	Scores of Each Game	
24	Pittsburgh	13
13	Cleveland	23
37	ATLANTA	30
13	New Orleans	16
38	MINNESOTA	19
17	Dallas	26
28	PHOENIX	14
40	L.A. RAMS	17
45	Tampa Bay	21
42	NEW ORLEANS	7
35	L.A. Rams	10
21	CINCINNATI	8
24	Atlanta	27
55	Detroit	17
7	HOUSTON	10
34	PHILADELPHIA	*37

Use Name	Pos.	Hgt	Wgt	Age	Int	Pts
Harris Barton	OT	6'4"	286	29		
Harry Boatswain	OT	6'4"	295	24		
James Parrish	OT	6'6"	315	25		
Steve Wallace	OT	6'5"	280	28		
Brian Bollinger	OG	6'5"	285	24		
Mike Dalman	OG-C	6'3"	285	23		
Roy Foster	OG	6'4"	290	33		
Guy McIntyre	OG	6'3"	276	32		
Ralph Tamm	OG	6'4"	280	27		6
Jesse Sapolu	C	6'4"	278	32		
Dennis Brown	DE	6'4"	290	25		
Kevin Fagan	DE	6'4"	265	30		
Martin Harrison	DE	6'5"	256	25		
Todd Kelly	DE	6'2"	259	22		
Matt LaBounty	DE	6'4"	254	24		
Larry Roberts	DE	6'3"	275	30		
Artie Smith	DE	6'4"	303	23		
Mark Thomas	DE	6'5"	273	24		
Troy Wilson	DE	6'4"	235	22		
Karl Wilson (from MIA)	DE	6'5"	277	28		
Dana Stubblefield	DT-NT	6'2"	302	22		
Ted Washington	DT-NT-DE	6'4"	295	25		
Keith DeLong	LB	6'2"	250	26		
Brett Faryniarz	LB	6'3"	230	28		
Antonio Goss	LB	6'4"	228	27		
John Johnson	LB	6'3"	230	25	1	
Darin Jordan	LB	6'2"	245	28		
Larry Kelm	LB	6'4"	240	28		
Bill Romanowski	LB	6'4"	240	27		
Michael Walter	LB	6'3"	246	32		
Eric Davis	DB	5'11"	178	25	4	12
Don Griffin	DB	6'	180	29	3	
Dana Hall	DB	6'2"	206	24		
Merton Hanks	DB	6'2"	185	25	3	6
Adrian Hardy	DB	5'11"	194	23		
Terry Hoage (to HOU)	DB	6'2"	201	31		
Tim McDonald	DB	6'2"	215	28	3	
Michael McGruder	DB	5'10"	190	29	5	6
Damien Russell	DB	6'1"	204	23		
Steve Bono	QB	6'4"	211	31		6
Bill Musgrave	QB	6'2"	205	25		
Steve Young	QB	6'2"	205	31		12
Dexter Carter	HB	5'9"	174	25		12
Amp Lee	HB	5'11"	200	21		18
Ricky Watters	HB	6'1"	212	24		66
Marc Logan	FB	6'	212	28		42
Tom Rathman	FB	6'1"	232	30		18
Adam Walker	FB	6'1"	210	25		
Sanjay Beach	WR	6'1"	194	27		6
Jerry Rice	WR	6'2"	200	30		96
Nate Singleton	WR	5'11"	190	25		6
John Taylor	WR	6'1"	185	31		30
Odessa Turner	WR	6'3"	215	28		
John Brandes	TE	6'2"	249	29		
Brent Jones	TE	6'4"	230	30		18
Wesley Walls	TE	6'5"	254	27		
Jamie Williams	TE	6'4"	245	33		6
Mike Cofer	K	6'1"	190	29		107
Klaus Wilmsmeyer	K	6'1"	210	25		

Thane Gash — Knee Injury
Brian Taylor — Knee Injury
Dave Waymer — Died in offseason

NEW ORLEANS SAINTS 8-8 Jim Mora

	Scores of Each Game	
33	HOUSTON	21
34	Atlanta	31
14	DETROIT	3
16	SAN FRANCISCO	13
37	L.A. Rams	6
14	Pittsburgh	37
15	ATLANTA	26
20	Phoenix	17
17	GREEN BAY	19
7	San Francisco	42
17	Minnesota	14
13	Cleveland	17
20	L.A. RAMS	23
14	N.Y. GIANTS	24
26	Philadelphia	37
20	CINCINNATI	13

Use Name	Pos.	Hgt	Wgt	Age	Int	Pts
Richard Cooper	OT	6'4"	290	28		
Willie Roaf	OT	6'4"	299	23		
Jim Dombrowski	OG-OT	6'5"	298	29		
Derek Kennard	OG-C	6'3"	300	30		
Chris Port	OG	6'5"	290	25		
Jay Hilgenberg	C	6'3"	270	34		
Joel Hilgenberg	C	6'3"	252	31		
Karl Dunbar	DE	6'4"	275	26		
Robert Goff	DE-NT	6'3"	270	27		
Wayne Martin	DE	6'5"	275	27		
Frank Warren	DE	6'4"	290	33		6
Ronnie Dixon	NT	6'2"	292	22		
Les Miller	NT-DE	6'7"	285	28		
Jim Wilks	NT-DE	6'5"	275	35		
Reggie Freeman	LB	6'1"	233	23		
Rickey Jackson	LB	6'2"	243	35		
Vaughan Johnson	LB	6'3"	240	31		
Sam Mills	LB	5'9"	225	34		6
Joel Smeenge	LB	6'5"	250	25		
Renaldo Turnbull	DE	6'4"	250	27	1	
James Williams	LB	6'	230	24		
DeMond Winston	LB	6'2"	239	24		
Gene Atkins	DB	6'1"	200	28	3	
Vince Buck	DB	6'	198	25	2	
Toi Cook	DB	5'11"	188	28	1	
Othello Henderson	DB	6'	192	31		
Tyrone Hughes	DB	5'9"	175	23		18
Reggie Jones	DB	6'1"	202	24	1	
Tyrone Legette	DB	5'9"	177	23		
Sean Lumpkin	DB	6'	206	23		
Cedric Mack	DB	5'11"	190	32		
Brett Maxie	DB	6'2"	194	31		
Jimmy Spencer	DB	5'9"	180	24		
Keith Taylor	DB	5'11"	206	28	2	
Mike Buck	QB	6'3"	227	26		
Steve Walsh	QB	6'2"	204	26		
Wade Wilson	QB	6'3"	206	34		
Derek Brown	HB	5'9"	186	22		18
Dalton Hilliard	HB	5'8"	204	29		18
Fred McAfee	HB	5'10"	195	25		6
Brad Muster	FB	6'4"	235	28		18
Lorenzo Neal	FB	5'10"	228	22		6
Derrick Ned	FB	6'1"	210	24		6
Marcus Dowdell	WR	5'10"	179	23		6
Quinn Early	WR	6'	190	28		36
Eric Martin	WR	6'1"	207	31		18
Pat Newman	WR	5'11"	189	24		6
Torrance Small	WR	6'3"	201	22		6
Floyd Turner	WR	5'11"	188	27		6
Jesse Anderson	TE	6'2"	245	27		
Hoby Brenner	TE	6'4"	245	34		6
Irv Smith	TE	6'3"	246	21		12
Tommie Stowers	TE	6'3"	240	26		2
Frank Wainright	TE	6'3"	245	25		
Morten Andersen	K	6'2"	221	33		117
Tommy Barnhardt	K	6'3"	207	30		

Vaughn Dunbar — Knee Injury

ATLANTA FALCONS 6-10 Jerry Glanville

	Scores of Each Game	
13	Detroit	30
31	NEW ORLEANS	34
30	San Francisco	37
17	PITTSBURGH	45
0	Chicago	6
30	L.A. RAMS	24
26	New Orleans	15
24	TAMPA BAY	31
13	L.A. Rams	0
27	DALLAS	14
17	CLEVELAND	14
17	Houston	33
27	SAN FRANCISCO	24
17	Washington	30
17	Cincinnati	21
10	PHOENIX	27

Use Name	Pos.	Hgt	Wgt	Age	Int	Pts
Mike Kenn	OT	6'7"	286	37		
Bob Whitfield	OT	6'5"	308	21		
Keith Alex	OG	6'4"	307	24		
Roman Fortin	OG-C	6'5"	295	26		
Chris Hinton	OG	6'4"	305	32		
Lincoln Kennedy	OG	6'6"	335	22		
Jamie Dukes	C	6'1"	292	29		
Mike Ruether	C-OG	6'4"	286	30		
Mel Agee	DE	6'5"	298	24		
Lester Archambeau	DE	6'5"	275	26		
Rick Bryan	DE	6'4"	270	31		
Mike Gann	DE	6'5"	270	29		
Tim Green	DE	6'2"	249	29		
Ernie Logan	DE	6'3"	285	25		
Chuck Smith	DE-LB	6'2"	254	23		
Moe Gardner	DT	6'2"	258	24		
James Geathers	DT	6'7"	290	33		
Bill Goldberg	DT-DE	6'2"	266	23		
Pierce Holt	DT	6'4"	275	31		
Darion Conner	LB	6'2"	245	25		
Howard Dinkins	LB	6'1"	230	24		
Ron George	LB	6'2"	225	23		
Dwayne Gordon	LB	6'1"	231	23		
Jesse Solomon	LB	6'	240	29		
Kenny Tippins	LB	6'1"	235	27		
Jessie Tuggle	LB	5'11"	230	28		
Scott Case	DB	6'	188	31		
Vinnie Clark	DB	6'	194	24	2	6
Jeff Donaldson	DB	6'	190	31		
Tracey Eaton	DB	6'1"	195	28	1	
Roger Harper	DB	6'2"	223	22		
Melvin Jenkins (to DET)	DB	5'10"	173	31		
Brian Mitchell	DB	5'9"	175	24		
Alton Montgomery	DB	6'	202	25		
Deion Sanders	DB	6'	185	26	7	6
Elbert Shelley	DB	5'11"	185	28		
Darnell Walker	DB	5'8"	164	23		
Charles Washington	DB	6'1"	217	26		
Bob Gagliano	QB	6'3"	205	34		
Bobby Hebert	QB	6'4"	215	33		
Chris Miller	QB	6'2"	212	28		
Billy Joe Tolliver	QB	6'1"	218	27		
Steve Broussard	HB-WR	5'7"	201	26		6
Eric Dickerson	HB	6'3"	220	32		
Erric Pegram	HB	5'9"	188	24		18
Tony Smith	HB	6'1"	224	23		6
Michael Haynes	WR	6'	184	27		24
Drew Hill	WR	5'9"	172	36		
David Mims	WR	5'8"	191	23		6
Jason Phillips	WR	5'7"	166	26		
Mike Pritchard	WR	5'11"	186	23		42
Andre Rison	WR	6'	188	26		90
Harper LeBel	TE	6'4"	248	30		
Mitch Lyons	TE	6'4"	255	23		
Harold Alexander	K	6'2"	224	22		
Norm Johnson	K	6'2"	203	33		112

LOS ANGELES RAMS 5-11 Chuck Knox

	Scores of Each Game	
6	Green Bay	36
27	PITTSBURGH	0
10	N.Y. Giants	20
28	Houston	13
6	NEW ORLEANS	37
24	Atlanta	30
13	DETROIT	16
17	San Francisco	40
0	ATLANTA	13
10	WASHINGTON	6
10	SAN FRANCISCO	35
10	Phoenix	38
23	New Orleans	20
3	Cincinnati	15
14	CLEVELAND	42
20	CHICAGO	6

Use Name	Pos.	Hgt	Wgt	Age	Int	Pts
Darryl Ashmore	OT	6'7"	300	23		
Irv Eatman	OT	6'7"	300	32		
Robert Jenkins	OT	6'5"	285	29		
Kevin Robbins	OT	6'4"	286	25		
Jackie Slater	OT	6'4"	285	39		
Leo Goeas	OG	6'4"	292	27		
Keith Loneker	OG	6'3"	330	22		
Tom Newberry	OG	6'2"	285	30		
Jeff Pahukoa	OG-OT	6'2"	298	24		
Bern Brostek	C	6'3"	300	26		
Blair Bush	C	6'3"	275	36		
Gerald Robinson	DE	6'3"	262	30		
Fred Stokes	DE	6'3"	274	29		
Tony Woods	DE	6'4"	269	27		
Robert Young	DE	6'6"	273	24		
Marc Boutte	DT	6'4"	298	24		
Sean Gilbert	DT	6'4"	315	23		
David Rocker	DT	6'4"	267	24		
Jeff Brady (to SD)	LB	6'1"	235	24		
Brett Collins (from GB)	LB	6'1"	234	24		
Shane Conlan	LB	6'3"	235	29	1	
Thomas Homco	LB	6'	245	23	1	
Chris Martin	LB	6'2"	241	32		
Roman Phifer	LB	6'2"	230	25		
Henry Rolling	LB	6'2"	225	27	2	
Leon White	LB	6'3"	242	29		
Robert Bailey	DB	5'9"	176	24	2	
Deral Boykin	DB	5'11"	196	22		6
Dexter Davis (from PHX)	DB	5'10"	185	23		
Courtney Griffin	DB	5'10"	180	26		
Wymon Henderson	DB	5'10"	188	31		
Darryl Henley	DB	5'9"	172	26		
Steve Israel	DB	5'10"	186	24		
Todd Lyght	DB	6'	186	24	2	
Anthony Newman	DB	6'	199	27		
Mitchell Price (from CIN)	DB	5'9"	181	26		
Sam Seale	DB	5'9"	185	30		
Michael Stewart	DB	5'11"	195	28	1	
Pat Terrell	DB	6'	195	25	2	
Jim Everett	QB	6'5"	212	30		
Mike Pagel	QB	6'2"	220	32		
T.J. Rubley	QB	6'3"	205	24		
Jerome Bettis	HB-FB	5'11"	243	21		42
Cleveland Gary	HB	6'	226	27		12
Howard Griffith	HB	6'	226	25		
David Lang	HB-FB	5'11"	213	25		
Russell White	HB	5'11"	186	22		
Tim Lester	FB	5'9"	215	25		
Willie Anderson	WR	6'	172	28		24
Richard Buchanan	WR	5'10"	178	24		
Henry Ellard	WR	5'11"	182	32		12
Ernie Jones	WR	6'	200	28		12
Todd Kinchen	WR	6'	187	24		6
Sean LaChapelle	WR	6'3"	205	23		
Pat Carter	TE	6'4"	250	27		6
Troy Drayton	TE	6'3"	255	23		24
Travis McNeal	TE	6'3"	244	26		6
Don Bracken	K	6'1"	211	31		
Sean Landeta (from NYG)	K	6'	210	31		
Paul McJulien	K	5'10"	190	28		
Tony Zendejas	K	5'8"	165	33		71

SAN FRANCISCO 49ERS

RUSHING

Last Name	No.	Yds	Avg	TD
Watters	208	**950**	4.6	**10**
Young	69	407	**5.9**	2
Logan	58	280	4.8	7
Lee	72	230	3.2	1
Rathman	19	80	4.2	3
Carter	10	72	7.2	1
Rice	3	69	23.0	1
J. Taylor	2	17	8.5	0
Walker	5	17	3.4	0
Bono	12	14	1.2	1
Wilmsmeyer	2	0	0.0	0
Musgrave	3	-3	-1.0	0

RECEIVING

Last Name	No.	Yds	Avg	TD
Rice	98	**1503**	15.3	**15**
Jones	68	735	10.8	3
J. Taylor	56	940	16.8	5
Logan	37	348	9.4	0
Watters	31	326	10.5	1
Williams	16	132	8.3	1
Lee	16	115	7.2	2
Rathman	10	86	8.6	0
Singleton	8	126	15.8	1
Beach	5	59	11.8	1
Turner	3	64	21.3	0
Carter	3	40	13.3	0
Young	2	2	1.0	0
Walker	1	4	4.0	0

PUNT RETURNS

Last Name	No.	Yds	Avg	TD
Carter	34	411	12.1	1
Kelm	1	0	0.0	0

KICKOFF RETURNS

Last Name	No.	Yds	Avg	TD
Carter	25	494	19.8	0
Lee	10	160	16.0	0
Walker	3	51	17.0	0
Brandes	1	10	10.0	0
Kelm	1	0	0.0	0
Walls	0	0	—	0
Williams	0	0	—	0

PASSING — PUNTING — KICKING

PASSING	Att	Cmp	%	Yds	Yd/Att	TD	Int	%	RK
Young	462	314	**68.0**	**4023**	**8.71**	**29**	16	3.5	1
Bono	61	39	63.9	416	6.82	0	1	1.6	
J. Taylor	1	1	100.0	41	41.00	0	0	0.0	

PUNTING	No.	Avg.
Wilmsmeyer	42	40.9

KICKING	XP	ATT	%	FG	ATT	%
Cofer	**59**	**61**	97	16	26	62

NEW ORLEANS SAINTS

RUSHING

Last Name	No.	Yds	Avg	TD
Brown	180	705	3.9	2
Wilson	31	230	7.4	0
Muster	64	214	3.3	3
Neal	21	175	8.3	1
Hilliard	50	165	3.3	2
McAfee	51	160	3.1	1
Ned	9	71	7.9	1
Early	2	32	16.0	0
Barnhardt	1	18	18.0	0
M. Buck	1	0	0.0	0
Walsh	4	-4	-1.0	0

RECEIVING

Last Name	No.	Yds	Avg	TD
E. Martin	66	950	14.4	3
Early	45	670	14.9	6
Hilliard	40	296	7.4	1
Muster	23	195	8.5	0
Brown	21	170	8.1	1
Smith	16	180	11.3	2
Small	16	164	10.3	1
Turner	12	163	13.6	1
Brenner	11	171	15.5	1
Ned	9	54	6.0	0
Newman	8	121	15.1	1
Dowdell	6	46	7.7	1
McAfee	1	3	3.0	0

PUNT RETURNS

Last Name	No.	Yds	Avg	TD
Hughes	37	**503**	**13.6**	**2**
Newman	1	14	14.0	0

KICKOFF RETURNS

Last Name	No.	Yds	Avg	TD
Hughes	30	753	25.1	**1**
McAfee	28	580	20.7	0
Brown	3	58	19.3	0
Hilliard	1	17	17.0	0
Dowdell	0	52	—	0

PASSING — PUNTING — KICKING

PASSING	Att	Cmp	%	Yds	Yd/Att	TD	Int	%	RK
Wilson	388	221	57.0	2457	6.33	12	15	3.9	10
M. Buck	54	32	59.3	448	8.30	4	3	5.6	
Walsh	38	20	52.6	271	7.13	2	3	7.9	
Barnhardt	1	1	100.0	7	7.00	0	0	0.0	

PUNTING	No.	Avg.
Barnhardt	77	43.6

KICKING	XP	ATT	%	FG	ATT	%
Andersen	33	33	**100**	28	35	80

ATLANTA FALCONS

RUSHING

Last Name	No.	Yds	Avg	TD
Pegram	292	1185	4.1	3
Broussard	39	206	5.3	1
Dickerson	26	91	3.5	0
Hebert	24	49	2.0	0
Tolliver	7	48	6.9	0
Miller	2	11	5.5	0
Pritchard	2	4	2.0	0
Mims	1	3	3.0	0
Alexander	2	-7	-3.5	0

RECEIVING

Last Name	No.	Yds	Avg	TD
Rison	86	1242	14.4	**15**
Pritchard	74	736	9.9	7
Haynes	72	778	10.8	4
Hill	34	384	11.3	0
Pegram	33	302	9.2	0
Mims	12	107	8.9	1
Lyons	8	63	7.9	0
Sanders	6	106	17.7	1
Dickerson	6	58	9.7	0
Phillips	1	15	15.0	0
Broussard	1	4	4.0	0
Hinton	1	-8	-8.0	0

PUNT RETURNS

Last Name	No.	Yds	Avg	TD
T. Smith	32	255	8.0	0
Sanders	2	21	10.5	0
Clark	1	0	0.0	0

KICKOFF RETURNS

Last Name	No.	Yds	Avg	TD
T. Smith	38	**948**	24.9	**1**
Sanders	7	169	24.1	0
Pegram	4	63	15.8	0
Montgomery	2	53	26.5	0
Phillips	2	38	19.0	0
Mims	1	22	22.0	0
Ruether	1	7	7.0	0

PASSING — PUNTING — KICKING

PASSING	Att	Cmp	%	Yds	Yd/Att	TD	Int	%	RK
Hebert	430	263	61.2	2978	6.93	24	17	4.0	5
Tolliver	76	39	51.3	464	6.11	3	5	6.6	
Miller	66	32	48.5	345	5.23	1	3	4.5	
Sanders	1	0	0.0	0	0.00	0	0	0.0	

PUNTING	No.	Avg.
Alexander	72	43.3

KICKING	XP	Att	%	FG	Att	%
N. Johnson	34	34	**100**	26	27	**96**

LOS ANGELES RAMS

RUSHING

Last Name	No.	Yds	Avg	TD
Bettis	**294**	1429	4.9	7
Gary	79	293	3.7	1
Rubley	29	102	3.5	0
Lester	11	74	6.7	0
Everett	19	38	2.0	0
Lang	9	29	3.2	0
Ellard	2	18	9.0	0
R. White	2	10	5.0	0
Kinchen	2	10	5.0	0
Drayton	1	7	7.0	0
Jones	1	4	4.0	0

RECEIVING

Last Name	No.	Yds	Avg	TD
Ellard	61	945	15.5	2
Anderson	37	552	14.9	4
Gary	36	289	8.0	1
Drayton	27	319	11.8	4
Bettis	26	244	9.4	0
Lester	18	154	8.6	0
Carter	14	166	11.9	1
Kinchen	8	137	17.1	1
McNeal	8	75	9.4	1
Jones	5	56	11.2	2
Lang	4	45	11.3	0
LaChapelle	2	23	11.5	0

PUNT RETURNS

Last Name	No.	Yds	Avg	TD
Buchanan	8	41	5.1	0
Kinchen	7	32	4.6	0
Ellard	2	18	9.0	0
Henley	1	8	8.0	0
Price	1	3	3.0	0

KICKOFF RETURNS

Last Name	No.	Yds	Avg	TD
Boykin	13	216	16.6	0
Griffith	8	169	21.1	0
Price	8	144	16.0	0
R. White	8	122	15.3	0
Kinchen	6	96	16.0	0
Israel	5	92	18.4	0
Drayton	1	-15	-15.0	0

PASSING — PUNTING — KICKING

PASSING	Att	Cmp	%	Yds	Yd/Att	TD	Int	%	RK
Rubley	189	108	57.1	1338	7.08	8	6	3.2	
Everett	274	135	49.3	1652	6.03	8	12	4.4	13
Pagel	9	3	33.3	23	2.56	0	1	11.1	
Gary	1	1	100.0	8	8.00	0	0	0.0	

PUNTING	No.	Avg.
Landeta	76	42.3
McJulien	21	37.9
Bracken	17	38.3

KICKING	XP	ATT	%	FG	ATT	%
Zendejas	23	25	92	16	2370	

1993 A.F.C. Shula Passes Halas as All-Time Winningest Coach

When Don Shula coached his first game in 1963, John F. Kennedy was still the president, three NFL head coaches were still in grade school and gasoline cost about a quarter a gallon. Times have changed, but Shula hasn't — he's still a winner. Shula got his 325th victory on November 14 to break George Halas' once-seemingly unbreakable record of 324 wins. The record victory was over the Jets, with Doug Pederson at quarterback in place of Scott Mitchell who was in place of Dan Marino.

But after that memorable milestone, Shula's Dolphins won only two more games before losing their final five and failing to make the playoffs. In other words, a tremendous achievement for Shula came in a season of disappointment.

In the AFC, the Bills became the first team in professional sports history to get to the championship game for four consecutive years without winning at least once. In the AFC championship game, they faced the Chiefs, who were led by quarterback Joe Montana, who was trying to make it to his fifth Super Bowl. Montana and Marcus Allen, another Kansas City acquisition in the offseason, were two of the biggest surprises in the conference — old veterans who still had it.

EASTERN DIVISION

Buffalo Bills — The fourth time wasn't a charm for the Bills, who, despite playing in the AFC championship game for a record-fourth straight year, lost for their fourth straight Super Bowl. Still, it was a very good year for the Bills, who improved on defense. Defensive end Bruce Smith was the NFL's Defensive Player of the Year and tied for the league lead with 13.5 sacks. But, on offense, the once-powerful, no-huddle machine seemed to have its problems. The Bills struggled to put points on the board early in the season and only a four-game winning streak in the final month gave them the home-field advantage in the playoffs. Quarterback Jim Kelly passed for 3,382 yards and 18 TD's, and running back Thurman Thomas led the AFC with 1,315 yards rushing.

Miami Dolphins — Don Shula began the season saying he wanted the coaching record for most victories to come in a season in which the Dolphins achieved success. It didn't happen. With a 9-2 record on Thanksgiving Day, the Dolphins had the best record in the NFL. Then they lost their final five games of the season to miss the playoffs again. Quarterback Dan Marino, who hadn't missed a game in eight years, suffered a torn Achilles tendon in the fifth game and was gone. Unproven Scott Mitchell took over and was the NFL's Player of the Month of October. Then he, too, was injured, leaving first-year pro Doug Pederson and pickup Steve DeBerg in charge until Mitchell returned. Rookie running back Terry Kirby led the team with 75 receptions, and free-agent wide receiver Irving Fryar caught 64 passes for 1,010 yards.

New York Jets — Quarterback Boomer Esiason was traded to the Jets during the offseason, and he quickly proved that he had a lot left by leading the team to a 7-4 mark. Esiason passed for 3,421 yards and 16 TD's, but losses in the final three games left the Jets out of the playoffs. Safety Ronnie Lott and running back Johnny Johnson (821 yards rushing and 67 catches) were other new faces on the Jets, who made strides to rebuild the team. They were vastly improved from their 4-12 mark in 1992, but missed opportunities all year eventually cost head coach Bruce Coslet his job. He was fired a few days after the end of the season and replaced by defensive coordinator Pete Carroll. Carroll's defense had improved to eighth overall in the league and allowed just 247 points.

New England Patriots — Bill Parcells returned to coaching and righted the Patriots sinking ship before it moved out of town. New England owned the first pick in the 1993 draft and chose quarterback Drew Bledsoe, who was quickly named the starter. The Patriots lost their first four games, won one and then lost seven more, though many of them were close. Then Parcells, Bledsoe and the Patriots got things into gear, and New England closed out the season with four consecutive victories. Bledsoe passed for 2,494 yards and 15 touchdowns, and Leonard Russell turned into a Parcells-type of dominating runner by rushing for 1,088 yards and seven scores. After the season, the team was sold by James Busch Orthwein to Robert Kraft, the owner of Foxboro Stadium.

Indianapolis Colts — Big things were expected from the Colts in 1993, but the season didn't go according to plan. First, quarterback Jeff George held out and asked to be traded and then was booed lustfully when he made his first appearance in the third game of the season. Defensive lineman Steve Emtman suffered another serious knee injury in the sixth game and was lost for the season. All year long the offense was unproductive and the defense was unable to play well in clutch situations. The result was a last-place, 4-12 finish. George did pass for 2,526 yards but with only eight TD passes. Wide receiver Reggie Langhorne led the AFC in receptions with 85 for 1,038 yards and three scores. And placekicker Dean Biasucci was again at the top of his game, with 26 field goals in 31 attempts to give the Colts 93 of their 189 points.

CENTRAL DIVISION

Houston Oilers — The Oilers made the playoffs again in 1993, but it was a season in which all anyone will remember is the punch defensive coordinator Buddy Ryan threw at offensive coordinator Kevin Gilbride during a nationally televised Sunday night game against the Jets. Ryan and Gilbride had feuded all season, and head coach Jack Pardee was unable to stop it. "Team Turmoil" started out 1-4, and Pardee's job was on the line. Then the Oilers reeled off 11 straight victories to win the AFC Central. It was the longest winning streak in the NFL since 1972. Ryan's defense was the league's best against the run and second in takeaways. Running back Gary Brown, who replaced an injured Lorenzo White, rushed for 1,002 yards in the last eight games, and helped quarterback Warren Moon, who had an off-year with 24 interceptions. Jeff Alm, a defensive tackle, committed suicide on December 14.

Pittsburgh Steelers — In their second year under head coach Bill Cowher, the Steelers again made the playoffs. But numerous mistakes by the NFL's worst special teams cost the Steelers at least two victories, and the 9-8 record (including postseason) really wasn't much better than .500. Running back Barry Foster suffered a season-ending ankle injury in the ninth game after rushing for 711 yards and scoring eight touchdowns. With Foster's big-play ability out of the lineup, the Steelers scored only eight touchdowns in the final seven games. Tight end Eric Green caught 63 passes for 942 yards, but the wide receivers might have been the league's worst, dropping far too many balls. Quarterback Neil O'Donnell fought season-long tendinitis in his throwing elbow but still broke Terry Bradshaw's team record for attempts and completions.

Cleveland Browns — November 8, 1993 is a day that will live in infamy for fans of the Browns. That's the day coach Bill Belichick cut quarterback and home-town favorite Bernie Kosar. Cleveland won its first three games of 1993 and had a 5-3 record — and first place in the AFC Central — under Kosar. But that wasn't good enough for Belichick, who cut Kosar, citing "diminishing skills" as the motive for the change. Because Vinny Testaverde was out injured, the offense was turned over temporarily to third-stringer Todd Philcox. Cleveland lost three straight and six of the final eight to finish 7-9 and third in the division. When he returned, Testaverde did play better than he had in past years in Tampa Bay, throwing more touchdowns than interceptions for the first time in his career. Running back Eric Metcalf helped, with a league-high 1,923 all-purpose yards and two punt-return touchdowns. And Kosar? He ended up on the Super Bowl champion Cowboys.

Cincinnati Bengals — One thing is for sure: Dave Shula is no Don Shula. The second-year head coach of the Bengals saw his team lose its first 10 games of 1993, though the team did win three of the final six. Still, the Bengals tied a team mark for the worst record — 3-13. Cincinnati got rid of most of its high-priced veterans before the start of the season, which left it inexperienced and lacking talent. The Bengals were abysmal on offense, scoring only 14 touchdowns the entire season and none in six games. Their 16-game total of 187 points was a record-low for the franchise. The main problem was one of the league's worst offensive lines and a woefully weak running game. That all meant second-year quarterback David Klingler was in a hole from the start, though he showed improvement, too, in the final six games.

OFFENSE

	BUFF	CIN	CLEV	DEN	HOU	IND	K.C.	L.A.	MIA	N.E.	NYJ	PITT	S.D.	SEA
FIRST DOWNS:														
Total	316	230	204	327	330	269	300	292	309	315	304	307	313	279
by Rushing	117	89	91	105	101	71	94	95	85	116	106	116	120	114
by Passing	176	133	152	187	208	180	180	168	207	169	173	180	171	144
by Penalty	23	17	21	35	21	18	26	29	17	30	25	11	22	21
RUSHING:														
Number	551	423	425	486	409	365	445	433	419	502	521	491	455	473
Yards	1943	1511	1701	1693	1792	1288	1655	1425	1459	1780	1880	2003	1824	2015
Average Yards	3.5	3.6	4.0	3.6	4.4	3.5	3.7	3.3	3.5	3.5	3.6	4.1	4.0	4.3
Touchdowns	12	3	8	13	11	4	14	10	10	9	14	13	14	13
PASSING:														
Attempts	497	510	478	553	614	594	490	495	581	566	489	540	563	498
Completions	304	272	262	350	357	332	287	281	342	289	294	299	301	280
Completion Pct.	61.2	53.3	54.8	63.3	58.1	55.9	58.6	56.8	58.9	51.1	60.1	55.4	53.5	56.2
Passing Yards	3535	2830	3328	4061	4145	3623	3384	3882	4564	3412	3492	3606	3383	2896
Avg. Yds per Att.	7.1	5.6	7.0	7.3	6.8	6.1	6.9	7.8	7.9	6.0	7.1	6.7	6.0	5.8
Avg. Yds per Comp.	11.6	10.4	12.7	11.6	11.6	10.9	11.8	13.8	13.3	11.8	11.9	12.1	11.2	10.3
Times Tackled	31	53	45	39	43	29	35	50	30	23	21	48	32	48
Yds Lost Tackled	218	289	289	293	279	206	204	293	211	127	160	374	240	242
Net Yards	3317	2541	3039	3768	3866	3417	3180	3589	4353	3285	3332	3232	3143	2654
Touchdowns	20	11	23	27	23	10	20	17	27	17	16	16	18	13
Interceptions	18	11	19	10	25	15	10	14	18	24	12	12	14	18
Pct. Intercepted	3.6	2.2	4.0	1.8	4.1	2.5	2.0	2.8	3.1	4.2	2.5	2.2	2.5	3.6
PUNTS:														
Number	74	90	84	68	56	83	77	71	58	76	73	89	74	91
Average	40.4	43.4	43.2	44.4	45.4	43.3	42.1	41.8	39.7	40.7	38.4	42.5	42.3	44.0
PUNT RETURNS														
Number	33	48	42	41	41	30	37	40	28	51	31	46	34	33
Yards	277	321	563	425	275	173	348	465	326	462	256	353	412	280
Average Yards	8.4	6.7	13.4	10.4	6.7	5.8	9.4	11.6	11.6	9.2	8.3	7.7	12.1	8.5
Touchdowns	1	0	3	0	0	0	0	1	2	0	0	0	0	0
KICKOFF RET.:														
Number	45	61	58	38	31	57	45	52	49	47	46	52	47	50
Yards	746	1211	1119	717	589	1124	875	1061	1068	819	675	878	901	931
Average Yards	16.6	19.9	19.1	18.9	18.9	19.7	19.4	20.7	21.8	17.4	14.7	16.9	19.2	18.6
Touchdowns	0	0	0	0	0	0	0	0	0	0	0	0	0	0
INTERCEPT RET.:														
Number	23	12	13	18	26	10	21	14	13	13	19	24	22	22
Yards	306	272	208	236	412	116	225	199	175	122	233	386	319	196
Average Yards	13.3	22.7	16.0	13.1	15.8	11.6	10.7	14.2	13.5	9.4	12.3	16.1	14.5	8.9
Touchdowns	3	2	1	1	3	0	0	1	1	0	1	1	1	1
PENALTIES:														
Number	95	105	121	112	132	94	121	148	81	64	86	100	87	99
Yards	630	773	842	822	1005	685	969	1181	663	468	555	861	699	745
FUMBLES:														
Number	26	24	27	29	37	34	28	23	30	30	38	27	13	25
Number Lost	17	9	17	18	20	20	18	11	14	10	16	15	5	13
POINTS:														
Total	329	187	304	373	368	189	328	306	349	238	270	308	322	280
PAT Attempts	37	16	36	42	40	16	37	29	37	25	31	32	36	29
PAT Made	36	13	36	41	39	15	37	27	37	25	31	32	31	29
FG Attempts	32	31	22	35	34	31	29	44	32	31	26	30	40	28
FG Made	23	24	16	26	29	26	23	35	24	19	17	28	31	23
Percent FG Made	71.9	77.4	72.7	74.3	85.3	83.9	79.3	79.5	75.0	61.3	65.4	93.3	77.5	82.1
Safeties	1	3	2	1	1	0	0	0	0	0	1	0	0	4

DEFENSE

	BUFF	CIN	CLEV	DEN	HOU	IND	K.C.	L.A.	MIA	N.E.	NYJ	PITT	S.D.	SEA
FIRST DOWNS:														
Total	331	306	290	280	289	334	300	302	332	269	266	267	299	322
by Rushing	114	134	94	86	73	151	103	111	103	97	93	74	86	106
by Passing	199	159	170	181	184	166	161	154	205	161	161	163	192	193
by Penalty	18	13	26	13	32	17	36	37	24	11	12	30	21	23
RUSHING:														
Number	500	521	451	397	369	575	453	494	460	505	420	399	414	452
Yards	1921	2220	1654	1418	1273	2521	1620	1865	1665	1951	1473	1368	1314	1660
Average Yards	3.8	4.3	3.7	3.6	3.4	4.4	3.6	3.8	3.6	3.9	3.5	3.4	3.2	3.7
Touchdowns	7	15	9	6	9	20	11	17	12	9	8	6	10	12
PASSING:														
Attempts	582	457	541	562	582	454	525	457	572	474	497	521	556	595
Completions	323	251	306	314	302	270	312	258	350	280	296	277	329	333
Completion Pct.	55.5	54.9	56.6	55.9	51.9	59.5	59.4	56.5	61.2	59.1	59.6	53.2	59.2	56.0
Passing Yards	3889	2952	3466	3969	3914	3238	3379	3141	3682	3087	3434	3440	3958	3897
Avg. Yds per Att.	6.7	6.5	6.4	7.1	6.7	7.1	6.4	6.9	6.4	6.5	6.9	6.6	7.1	6.6
Avg. Yds per Comp.	12.0	11.8	11.3	12.6	12.5	12.0	10.8	12.2	10.5	11.0	11.6	12.4	12.0	11.7
Times Tackled	37	22	48	46	52	21	35	45	29	34	32	42	32	38
Yds Lost Tackled	256	154	342	238	313	121	228	283	197	242	195	277	206	244
Net Yards	3633	2798	3124	3731	3601	3117	3151	2858	3485	2845	3239	3163	3752	3653
Touchdowns	18	20	19	21	16	22	18	17	26	20	15	16	17	16
Interceptions	23	12	13	18	26	10	21	14	13	13	19	24	22	22
Pct. Intercepted	4.0	2.6	2.4	3.2	4.5	2.2	4.0	3.1	2.3	2.7	3.8	4.6	4.0	3.7
PUNTS:														
Number	65	74	85	81	78	71	68	80	76	90	66	82	72	73
Average	41.8	42.2	42.4	43.7	43.7	40.2	44.6	42.1	41.3	41.2	43.3	44.0	42.1	42.4
PUNT RETURNS														
Number	29	47	48	33	28	41	43	35	32	34	26	50	36	47
Yards	247	416	438	337	249	352	352	301	359	313	156	678	292	475
Average Yards	8.5	8.9	9.1	10.2	8.9	8.6	8.2	8.6	11.2	9.2	6.0	13.7	8.2	10.2
Touchdowns	0	0	0	0	0	1	0	0	1	1	0	3	0	1
KICKOFF RET.:														
Number	43	38	46	63	60	37	49	45	62	44	47	54	64	52
Yards	850	831	814	1119	1062	551	1007	783	1239	921	911	1165	1063	967
Average Yards	19.8	21.9	17.7	18.0	17.7	14.9	20.6	17.4	20.0	20.9	19.4	21.4	16.6	18.6
Touchdowns	0	0	0	0	0	0	0	0	0	0	0	1	0	1
INTERCEPT RET.:														
Number	18	11	19	10	25	15	10	14	18	24	12	12	14	18
Yards	174	49	246	79	309	247	111	289	329	201	310	216	271	159
Average Yards	9.7	4.5	12.9	7.9	12.4	16.5	8.2	20,.5	18.3	8.4	25.8	18.0	19.4	8.8
Touchdowns	0	0	0	0	0	1	0	2	2	1	3	2	2	0
PENALTIES:														
Number	102	74	106	128	104	91	129	104	93	112	88	76	95	110
Yards	681	560	831	1019	786	610	1008	803	650	808	654	647	724	818
FUMBLES:														
Number	35	22	28	27	31	25	30	23	31	20	30	37	19	23
Number Lost	24	14	9	13	17	11	17	9	14	9	18	14	12	15
POINTS:														
Total	242	319	307	284	238	378	291	326	351	286	247	281	290	314
PAT Attempts	24	37	30	29	26	45	29	37	42	32	26	30	30	30
PAT Made	23	37	30	27	25	43	27	37	40	32	26	29	30	29
FG Attempts	35	28	38	36	28	30	32	33	27	24	26	29	33	39
FG Made	23	20	31	31	19	21	28	21	17	20	21	24	26	29
Percent FG Made	65.7	71.4	81.6	86.1	67.9	70.0	87.5	63.6	63.0	83.3	80.8	82.8	78.8	74.3
Safeties	0	0	2	1	0	1	0	2	1	0	1	0	1	2

WESTERN DIVISION

Kansas City Chiefs — The Chiefs advanced to the AFC championship game in 1993, further than at any time since 1969, when they won their only Super Bowl. After finishing 25th on offense in 1992, the Chiefs made wholesale changes for '93, bringing in offensive coordinator Paul Hackett, quarterback Joe Montana and running back Marcus Allen. Because of injuries, Montana missed five games and played in only 38 of 64 quarters, but he was the AFC's second-ranked passer. Allen was the NFL's Comeback Player of the Year, as he rushed for 764 yards and tied for a league-high 15 touchdowns. On the other side of the ball, defensive end Neil Smith recorded an NFL-best 15 sacks and had two blocked field goals in a three-point win over San Diego.

Los Angeles Raiders — The Raiders aren't what they used to be, but getting to the AFC divisional-playoff round in 1993 at least gave them their second postseason victory since 1983. They turned the corner by rebuilding through the free-agent market and the draft. Quarterback Jeff Hostetler was the best of the newcomers, as he added much-needed leadership and stability. He passed for 3,242 yards and 14 touchdowns and ran for another five TD's himself. Back Greg Robinson, an eighth-round draft pick, ran for a team-high 591 yards, despite being injured in early December. And undrafted rookie James Jett added to the Raiders' corps of speed receivers. Tim Brown caught 80 passes for an AFC-high 1,180 yards and seven touchdowns. Placekicker Jeff Jaeger tied a league record with 35 field goals for the season.

Denver Broncos — John Elway proved in 1993 how good he could really be if his talents were unleashed. With Dan Reeves gone and Wade Phillips in charge, Elway passed for a career-high 4,030 yards and 25 touchdowns. But the Broncos finished with a 9-7 record and a first-round playoff loss. Denver was the highest-scoring team in the conference, but the defense too often failed to hold onto leads and allowed too many big plays. The secondary ranked 27th in passing yards allowed. Shannon Sharpe, the brother of Green Bay's Sterling, had a sensational season with 81 catches for 995 yards and an AFC-best nine receiving touchdowns. Linebacker Simon Fletcher led the Broncos in sacks for the sixth straight season.

San Diego Chargers — Injuries were the story of the season for the Chargers in 1992. Quarterback Stan Humphries suffered a shoulder injury during the preseason and was replaced by John Friesz, who led the team to a 2-4 mark that kept people from thinking about the playoffs. Pro Bowl cornerback Gill Byrd missed the entire year, and guard Eric Moten, tight end Derrick Walker, defensive end Burt Grossman and linebacker Jerrol Williams missed large portions of it. The Chargers climbed back to 4-4, then lost two home games and eventually had to be satisfied with an 8-8 mark. There were some highlights, however. Placekicker John Carney set an NFL record by kicking 29 consecutive field goals over two seasons and 31 in 1993, and wide receiver Anthony Miller caught 84 passes for 1,162 yards and seven TD's.

Seattle Seahawks — A 6-10 record and last-place finish in the AFC West may not sound like reason for celebration in Seattle. But for the Seahawks they were cause for optimism. Rookie quarterback Rick Mirer, the No. 2 pick in the 1993 draft, completed 274 of 486 passes for 2,833 yards — all record numbers for a rookie. After scoring only 140 points in 1992, the Seahawks upped that total to 280 in '93, with Mirer providing a bright glimpse into the future. Back Chris Warren had his second consecutive 1,000-yard season, and having wide receiver Brian Blades (80 receptions for 945 yards) for an entire season helped. But the defense plummeted from top 10 the previous three seasons to No. 23 in 1993.

BUFFALO BILLS 12-4 Marv Levy

Scores of Each Game		
38	NEW ENGLAND	14
13	Dallas	10
13	MIAMI	22
17	N.Y. GIANTS	14
35	HOUSTON	7
19	N.Y. Jets	10
24	WASHINGTON	10
13	New England	*10
0	Pittsburgh	23
23	INDIANAPOLIS	9
7	Kansas City	23
24	L.A. RAIDERS	25
10	Philadelphia	7
47	Miami	34
16	N.Y. JETS	14
30	Indianapolis	10

UseName	Pos.	Hgt	Wgt	Age	Int	Pts
Howard Ballard	OT	6'6"	330	29		
Jerry Crafts	OT	6'6"	351	25		
John Fina	OT	6'4"	285	24		
John Davis	OG-C	6'4"	310	28		
Tom Myslinski (to CHI)	OG	6'2"	293	24		
Glenn Parker	OG-OT	6'5"	305	27		
Jim Ritcher	OG	6'3"	273	35		
Mike Devlin	C	6'1"	293	23		
Kent Hull	C	6'4"	284	32		
Adam Lingner	C	6'4"	268	32		
Oliver Barnett	DE	6'3"	292	27		
Phil Hansen	DE	6'5"	278	25		
John Parrella	DE	6'3"	296	23		
Mark Pike	DE	6'4"	272	29		
Bruce Smith	DE	6'4"	273	30	1	
Mike Lodish	NT	6'3"	280	26		
James Patton	NT	6'3"	287	23		
Jeff Wright	NT	6'2"	274	30		
Cornelius Bennett	LB	6'2"	238	28	1	
Monty Brown	LB	6'	228	23		
Keith Goganious	LB	6'2"	239	24		
Richard Harvey	LB	6'1"	242	26		
Mark Maddox	LB	6'1"	233	25		
Marvcus Patton	LB	6'2"	243	26	2	
Darryl Talley	LB	6'4"	235	33	3	6
Matt Darby	DB	6'1"	200	24	2	
Jerome Henderson (from NE)	DB	5'10"	189	24		
Henry Jones	DB	5'11"	197	25	2	8
Mark Kelso	DB	5'11"	180	30		
Nate Odomes	DB	5'10"	188	28	9	6
David Pool	DB	5'9"	182	26		
Kurt Schulz	DB	6'1"	208	22		
Thomas Smith	DB	5'11"	188	22		
Mickey Washington	DB	5'9"	191	25	1	6
James Williams	DB	5'10"	186	26	2	
Gale Gilbert	QB	6'3"	210	31		
Jim Kelly	QB	6'3"	226	33		
Frank Reich	QB	6'4"	205	31		
Kenneth Davis	HB	5'10"	208	31		36
Eddie Fuller	HB	5'9"	198	25		
Thurman Thomas	HB	5'10"	198	27		36
Carwell Gardner	FB	6'2"	244	26		6
Nate Turner	FB	6'1"	255	24		
Don Beebe	WR	5'11"	184	28		18
Bill Brooks	WR	6'	189	29		30
Russell Copeland	WR	6'	200	22		6
Brad Lamb	WR	5'10"	177	25		
Andre Reed	WR	6'	190	29		36
Steve Tasker	WR	5'9"	181	31		
Chris Walsh	WR	6'1"	185	24		
Rob Awalt	TE	6'5"	242	29		
Keith McKeller	TE	6'6"	242	29		6
Pete Metzelaars	TE	6'7"	254	33		24
Chris Mohr	K	6'5"	215	27		
Steve Christie	K	6'	185	25		105

Kirby Jackson — Knee Injury

Al Edwards — Shoulder Injury

MIAMI DOLPHINS 9-7 Don Shula

Scores of Each Game		
24	Indianapolis	20
14	N.Y. JETS	24
22	Buffalo	13
17	WASHINGTON	10
24	Cleveland	14
41	INDIANAPOLIS	27
30	KANSAS CITY	10
10	N.Y. Jets	27
19	Philadelphia	14
17	NEW ENGLAND	13
16	Dallas	14
14	N.Y. GIANTS	19
20	PITTSBURGH	21
34	BUFFALO	47
20	San Diego	45
27	New England	*33

UseName	Pos.	Hgt	Wgt	Age	Int	Pts
Mark Dennis	OT	6'6"	298	28		
Chris Gray	OT	6'4"	286	23		
Ron Heller	OT	6'6"	293	31		
Richmond Webb	OT	6'6"	298	26		
Keith Sims	OG	6'2"	310	26		
Tom Thayer	OG	6'4"	284	32		
Bert Weidner	OG-C	6'3"	290	27		
Jeff Dellenbach	C-OG	6'6"	297	30		
Jeff Uhlenhake	C	6'3"	284	27		
Marco Coleman	DE	6'3"	263	23		
Jeff Cross	DE	6'4"	274	27		
Jeff Hunter	DE	6'5"	291	27		
Mike Golic	DT	6'5"	275	30		
Chuck Klingbeil	DT	6'1"	295	27		
Craig Veasey (from HOU)	DT	6'2"	300	26		
Larry Webster	DT	6'5"	293	24		
Chuck Bullough	LB	6'1"	238	24		
Bryan Cox	LB	6'3"	241	25	1	
David Griggs	LB	6'3"	250	26		
John Grimsley	LB	6'2"	236	31		
Dwight Hollier	LB	6'2"	245	24		
David Merritt (to PHX)	LB	6'1"	237	21		
Cliff Odom	LB	6'2"	236	35		
John Offerdahl	LB	6'3"	238	29		
Chris Singleton (from NE)	LB	6'2"	247	26		
Bruce Alexander	DB	5'8"	178	27		
Stephen Braggs	DB	5'9"	177	28		
J.B. Brown	DB	6'	192	26	5	
Chris Green	DB	5'11"	189	25	2	
Bobby Harden	DB	6'	205	26		
Liffort Hobley	DB	6'	207	31	1	
Vestee Jackson	DB	6'	186	30		
Darrell Malone	DB	5'10"	182	25		
Louis Oliver	DB	6'2"	224	27	2	6
Frankie Smith	DB	5'9"	186	24		
Troy Vincent	DB	6'	191	33	2	
Jarvis Williams	DB	5'11"	200	28		
Steve DeBerg (from TB)	QB	6'2"	220	39		
Dan Marino	QB	6'4"	224	31		6
Scott Mitchell	QB	6'6"	230	25		
Doug Pederson	QB	6'3"	209	25		
Mark Higgs	HB	5'7"	198	27		18
Terry Kirby	HB	6'1"	221	23		36
Bernie Parmalee	HB	5'11"	201	25		
Keith Byars	FB	6'1"	255	29		36
James Saxon	FB	5'11'	237	27		
Irving Fryar	WR	6'	200	30		30
Mark Ingram	WR	5'11"	188	28		36
Tony Martin	WR	6'	181	27		18
O.J. McDuffie	WR	5'10"	191	22		12
Scott Miller	WR	5'10"	179	24		
Mike Williams	WR	5'10"	178	26		
Greg Baty	TE	6'5"	240	29		6
Keith Jackson	TE	6'2"	249	28		36
Ronnie Williams	TE	6'3"	259	27		
Dale Hatcher	K	6'2"	223	30		
Pete Stoyonovich	K	5'10"	181	26		109

Aaron Craver — Knee Injury

NEW YORK JETS 8-8 Bruce Coslet

Scores of Each Game		
20	DENVER	26
24	Miami	14
45	NEW ENGLAND	7
30	PHILADELPHIA	35
20	L.A. Raiders	24
10	BUFFALO	19
10	N.Y. Giants	6
27	MIAMI	10
31	Indianapolis	17
17	Cincinnati	12
6	New England	0
6	INDIANAPOLIS	9
3	Washington	0
7	DALLAS	28
14	Buffalo	16
0	Houston	24

UseName	Pos.	Hgt	Wgt	Age	Int	Pts
James Brown	OT	6'6"	231	23		
Jeff Criswell	OT	6'7"	291	29		
Siupeli Malamala	OT	6'5"	308	24		
Matt Willig	OT	6'8"	305	24		
Dave Cadigan	OG	6'4"	285	28		
Dwayne White	OG	6'2"	315	26		
Cal Dixon	C	6'4"	284	23		
Roger Duffy	C-OG	6'3"	285	26		
Jim Sweeney	C-OG	6'4"	286	31		
Jeff Lageman	DE	6'5"	266	26	1	
Coleman Rudolph	DE-DT	6'4"	270	22		
Marvin Washington	DE	6'6"	272	27		
Keith Willis (from WAS)	DE	6'1"	263	34		
Paul Frase	DT-DE	6'5"	270	28		
Mark Gunn	DT-DE	6'5"	279	25		
Leonard Marshall	DT	6'4"	288	31		
Scott Mersereau	DT	6'3"	275	28		
Bill Pickel	DT	6'5"	265	33		
Karl Wilson (to MIA, SF)	DT-DE	6'5"	277	28		
Kurt Barber	LB	6'4"	241	24		
Glenn Cadrez	LB	6'3"	240	23		
Kyle Clifton	LB	6'4"	236	31	1	
Bobby Houston	LB	6'2"	239	25	1	
Don Jones	LB	6'	231	24		
Marvin Jones	LB	6'2"	240	21		
Mo Lewis	LB	6'3"	250	23	2	
Mike Merriweather	LB	6'2"	224	32		
Victor Green	DB	5'9"	195	22		
James Hasty	DB	6'	201	28	2	
Cliff Hicks	DB	5'10"	195	29		
Ronnie Lott	DB	6'1"	203	34	3	
Damon Pieri	DB	6'	186	22		
Anthony Prior	DB	5'11"	185	23		
Eric Thomas	DB	5'11"	184	28	2	
Marcus Turner	DB	6'	190	27		
Brian Washington	DB	6'1"	206	27	6	6
Lonnie Young	DB	6'1"	196	30	1	
Boomer Esiason	QB	6'5"	220	32		6
Browning Nagle	QB	6'3"	225	25		
Johnny Johnson	HB	6'3"	220	25		24
Adrian Murrell	HB	5'11"	205	22		6
Blair Thomas	HB	5'10"	202	25		6
Richie Anderson	FB-HB	6'2"	215	21		
Brad Baxter	FB	6'1"	235	26		42
Pat Chaffey	FB	6'1"	220	26		6
Chris Burkett	WR	6'4"	200	31		24
Rob Carpenter	WR	6'2"	190	25		
Dale Dawkins	WR	6'1"	190	26		
Terance Mathis	WR	5'10"	177	26		6
Rob Moore	WR	6'3"	205	24		6
Fred Baxter	TE	6'3"	250	22		6
Johnny Mitchell	TE	6'3"	237	22		36
Troy Sadowski	TE	6'5"	250	27		
James Thornton	TE	6'2"	242	28		12
Louis Aguiar	K	6'2"	215	27		
Cary Blanchard	K	6'1"	225	24		82

Kevin Porter — Knee Injury

NEW ENGLAND PATRIOTS 5-11 Bill Parcells

Scores of Each Game		
14	Buffalo	38
16	DETROIT	*19
14	SEATTLE	17
7	N.Y. Jets	45
23	Phoenix	21
14	HOUSTON	28
9	Seattle	10
6	Indianapolis	9
10	BUFFALO	*13
13	Miami	17
0	N.Y. JETS	6
14	Pittsburgh	17
7	CINCINNATI	2
20	Cleveland	17
38	INDIANAPOLIS	0
33	MIAMI	*27

UseName	Pos.	Hgt	Wgt	Age	Int	Pts
Bruce Armstrong	OT	6'4"	284	27		
Pat Harlow	OT	6'6"	290	24		
Todd Jones	OT	6'3"	295	23		
Brandon Moore	OT	6'6"	290	23		
Rich Baldinger	OG	6'4"	293	33		
Eugene Chung	OG	6'4"	295	24		
Mike Gisler	OG	6'4"	300	24		
Todd Rucci	OG	6'5"	291	23		
Mike Arthur	C	6'3"	280	25		
Bill Lewis	C	6'6"	290	30		
Ray Agnew	DE	6'3"	272	25		
Aaron Jones	DE	6'5"	267	26		
Chris Gannon	DE	6'6"	260	27		
-Mike Pitts	DE	6'5"	277	32		
ohn Washington	DE	6'4"	290	30		
Brent Williams	DE	6'3"	275	28		
Tim Goad	NT	6'3"	280	27		
Mario Johnson	NT	6'3"	288	23		
David Bavaro	LB	6'	228	26		
Vincent Brown	LB	6'2"	245	28	1	
Jason Carthen	LB	6'3"	255	23		
Todd Collins	LB	6'2"	242	23	1	
Dwayne Sabb	LB	6'4"	248	23		
Chris Slade	LB	6'4"	232	22		
Andre Tippett	LB	6'3"	241	33		
David White	LB	6'2"	235	23		
Harlon Barnett	DB	5'11"	200	26	1	
Corwin Brown	DB	6'	192	23		
Maurice Hurst	DB	5'10"	185	25	4	
Dion Lambert	DB	6'	185	24	1	
Vernon Lewis	DB	5'10"	192	22		
Terry Ray	DB	6'1"	205	23	1	
Rod Smith	DB	5'11"	187	23		
Reyna Thompson	DB	6'	193	30	1	
Adrian White	DB	6'	205	29		
Darryl Wren	DB	6'	188	26	3	
Drew Bledsoe	QB	6'5"	233	21		
Scott Secules	QB	6'3"	223	28		
Scott Zolak	QB	6'5"	222	25		
Corey Croom	HB	5'11"	212	22		
Scott Lockwood	HB	5'10"	196	25		
Leonard Russell	HB	6'2"	235	23		42
Sam Gash	FB	5'11"	224	24		6
Burnie Legette	FB	6'	243	22		
Kevin Turner	FB	6'	224	24		12
Vincent Brisby	WR	6'1"	186	22		12
Troy Brown	WR	5'9"	183	22		
Ray Crittenden	WR	6'	188	23		6
Ronnie Harris	WR	5'10"	170	23		
Greg McMurtry	WR	6'2"	207	25		6
Michael Timpson	WR	5'10"	175	26		12
Ben Coates	TE	6'4"	245	24		48
Marv Cook	TE	6'4"	234	27		
Richard Griffith	TE	6'5"	256	24		
Mike Saxon	K	6'3"	202	31		
Scott Sisson	K	6'	197	22		57

INDIANAPOLIS COLTS 4-12 Ted Marchibroda

Scores of Each Game		
20	MIAMI	24
9	Cincinnati	6
23	CLEVELAND	10
13	Denver	35
3	DALLAS	27
27	Miami	41
9	NEW ENGLAND	6
24	Washington	30
17	N.Y. JETS	31
9	Buffalo	23
0	SAN DIEGO	31
9	N.Y. Jets	6
6	N.Y. Giants	20
10	PHILADELPHIA	20
0	New England	38
10	BUFFALO	30

UseName	Pos.	Hgt	Wgt	Age	Int	Pts
Kevin Call	OT	6'7"	308	31		
Cecil Gray	OT	6'4"	292	25		
Trevor Matich	OT-C	6'4"	297	31		
Zefross Moss	OT	6'6"	338	27		
John Ray	OT	6'8"	350	24		
Will Wolford	OT	6'5"	300	29		
Randy Dixon	OG	6'3"	305	28		
William Schultz	OG	6'5"	305	26		
Joe Staysniak	OG-OT	6'4"	296	26		
Kirk Lowdermilk	C	6'4"	280	30		
Michael Brandon	DE	6'4"	290	25		
Jon Hand	DE	6'7"	301	29		
Skip McClendon	DE	6'7"	302	29		
Willis Peguese	DE-DT	6'4"	273	26		
Steve Emtman	DT	6'4"	300	23		
Tom Sims	DT	6'2"	291	26		
Tony McCoy	DT-NT	6'	279	24		
Tony Siragusa	DT-NT	6'3"	303	26		
Duane Bickett	LB	6'5"	251	30		
Paul Butcher	LB	6'	230	29		
Quentin Coryatt	LB	6'3"	250	23		
Steve Grant	LB	6'	231	23		
Jeff Herrod	LB	6'	249	27	1	6
Devon McDonald	LB	6'4"	240	23		
Scott Radecic	LB	6'3"	240	31		
Ashley Ambrose	DB	5'10"	177	22		
Michael Ball	DB	6'	220	29		
John Baylor	DB	6'	208	28	3	
Jason Belser	DB	5'9"	187	23	1	
Ray Buchanan	DB	5'9"	193	21	4	
Eugene Daniel	DB	5'11"	188	32	1	
Chris Goode	DB	6'	199	29		
Derwin Gray	DB	5'10"	190	22		
Tony Stargell	DB	5'11"	189	27		
Jeff George	QB	6'4"	218	25		
Don Majkowski	QB	6'3"	203	29		
Jack Trudeau	QB	6'3"	218	30		
Rodney Culver	HB	5'9"	224	23		30
Anthony Johnson	HB-FB	6'	222	25		6
Ed Toner	HB	6'	240	25		
Warren Williams	HB	6'	218	28		
Roosevelt Potts	FB-HB	6'	258	22		
Aaron Cox	WR	5'10"	178	28		
Sean Dawkins	WR	6'4"	213	22		6
Jessie Hester	WR	5'11"	175	30		6
Reggie Langhorne	WR	6'2"	209	30		18
Eddie Miller	WR	6'	185	24		
Clarence Verdin	WR	5'8"	162	30		6
Charles Arbuckle	TE	6'3"	248	24		
Kerry Cash	TE	6'4"	252	24		18
Dean Biasucci	K	6'	190	31		93
Rohn Stark	K	6'3"	203	34		

Chip Banks — Shoulder Injury

Mark Vander Poel — Pectoral Injury
Ron Solt — Shoulder

BUFFALO BILLS

RUSHING

LastName	No.	Yds	Avg	TD
Thomas	**355**	**1315**	3.7	6
K. Davis	109	391	3.6	6
Kelly	36	102	2.8	0
Gardner	20	56	2.8	0
Turner	11	36	3.3	0
Brooks	3	30	10.0	0
Reed	9	21	2.3	0
Fina	1	-2	-2.0	0
Reich	6	-6	-1.0	0

RECEIVING

LastName	No.	Yds	Avg	TD
Metzelaars	68	609	9.0	4
Brooks	60	714	11.9	5
Reed	52	854	16.4	6
Thomas	48	387	8.1	0
Beebe	31	504	16.3	3
K. Davis	21	95	4.5	0
Copeland	13	242	18.6	0
Gardner	4	50	12.5	1
McKeller	3	35	11.7	1
Tasker	2	26	13.0	0
Awalt	2	19	9.5	0

PUNT RETURNS

LastName	No.	Yds	Avg	TD
Copeland	31	274	8.8	1
Brooks	1	3	3.0	0
Tasker	1	0	0.0	0

KICKOFF RETURNS

LastName	No.	Yds	Avg	TD
Copeland	24	436	18.2	0
Beebe	10	160	16.0	0
K. Davis	8	100	12.5	0
Lamb	2	40	20.0	0
Turner	1	10	10.0	0

PASSING — PUNTING — KICKING

PASSING	Att	Cmp	%	Yds	Yd/Att	TD	Int— %	RK
Kelly	470	288	61.3	3382	7.20	18	18—3.8	7
Reich	26	16	61.5	153	5.88	2	0—0.0	
Thomas	1	0	0.0	0	0.00	0	0—0.0	

PUNTING	No.	Avg.
Mohr	74	40.4

KICKING	XP	ATT	%	FG	ATT	%
Christie	36	37	97	23	32	72

MIAMI DOLPHINS

RUSHING

LastName	No.	Yds	Avg	TD
Higgs	186	693	3.7	3
Kirby	119	390	3.3	3
Byars	64	269	4.2	3
Mitchell	21	89	4.2	0
Parmalee	4	16	4.0	0
Saxon	5	13	2.6	0
Martin	1	6	6.0	0
Pederson	2	-1	-0.5	0
DeBerg	4	-4	-1.0	0
Fryar	3	-4	-1.3	0
Marino	9	-4	-0.4	1
McDuffie	1	-4	-4.0	0

RECEIVING

LastName	No.	Yds	Avg	TD
Kirby	75	874	11.7	3
Fryar	64	1010	15.8	5
Byars	61	613	10.0	3
Ingram	44	707	16.1	6
K. Jackson	39	613	15.7	6
Martin	20	347	17.4	3
McDuffie	19	197	10.4	0
Higgs	10	72	7.2	0
Baty	5	78	15.6	1
Miller	2	15	7.5	0
M. Williams	1	11	11.0	0
Parmalee	1	1	1.0	0

PUNT RETURNS

LastName	No.	Yds	Avg	TD
McDuffie	28	317	11.3	**2**
Vincent	0	9	—	0

KICKOFF RETURNS

LastName	No.	Yds	Avg	TD
McDuffie	32	755	23.6	0
M. Williams	8	180	22.5	0
Kirby	4	85	21.3	0
Miller	2	22	11.0	0
Fryar	1	10	10.0	0
Baty	1	7	7.0	0
Saxon	1	7	7.0	0
Vincent	0	2	—	0

PASSING — PUNTING — KICKING

PASSING	Att	Cmp	%	Yds	Yd/Att	TD	Int— %	RK
Mitchell	233	133	57.1	1773	7.61	12	8—3.4	5
DeBerg	227	136	59.9	1707	7.52	7	10—4.4	10
Marino	150	91	60.7	1218	8.12	8	3—2.0	
Pederson	8	4	50.0	41	5.13	0	0—0.0	
Byars	2	1	50.0	11	5.50	1	0—0.0	

PUNTING	No.	Avg.
Hatcher	58	39.7

KICKING	XP	Att.	%	FG	Att	%
Stoyonovich	37	37	**100**	24	32	75

NEW YORK JETS

RUSHING

LastName	No.	Yds	Avg	TD
J. Johnson	198	821	4.1	3
B. Baxter	174	559	3.2	7
B. Thomas	59	221	3.7	1
Murrell	34	157	4.6	1
Esiason	45	118	2.6	1
Mathis	2	20	10.0	1
Chaffey	5	17	3.4	0
Moore	1	-6	-6.0	0
Aguiar	3	-27	-9.0	0

RECEIVING

LastName	No.	Yds	Avg	TD
J. Johnson	67	641	9.6	1
Moore	64	843	13.2	1
Burkett	40	531	13.3	4
Mitchell	39	630	16.2	6
Mathis	24	352	14.7	0
B. Baxter	20	158	7.9	0
Thornton	12	108	9.0	2
B. Thomas	7	25	3.6	0
Carpenter	6	83	13.8	0
Murrell	5	12	2.4	0
Chaffey	4	55	13.8	1
F. Baxter	3	48	16.0	1
Sadowski	2	14	7.0	0
Esiason	1	-8	-8.0	0

PUNT RETURNS

LastName	No.	Yds	Avg	TD
Hicks	17	157	9.2	0
Mathis	14	99	7.1	0

KICKOFF RETURNS

LastName	No.	Yds	Avg	TD
Murrell	23	342	14.9	0
Prior	9	126	14.0	0
Mathis	7	102	14.6	0
R. Anderson	4	66	16.5	0
B. Thomas	2	39	19.5	0
Sadowski	1	0	0.0	0

PASSING — PUNTING — KICKING

PASSING	Att	Cmp	%	Yds	Yd/Att	TD	Int— %	RK
Esiason	473	288	60.9	3421	7.23	16	11—2.3	4
Nagle	14	6	42.9	71	5.07	0	0—0.0	
Aguiar	2	0	0.0	0	0.00	0	1—50.0	

PUNTING	No.	Avg.
Aguiar	73	38.4

KICKING	XP	Att	%	FG	Att	%
Blanchard	31	31	**100**	17	26	65

NEW ENGLAND PATRIOTS

RUSHING

LastName	No.	Yds	Avg	TD
Russell	300	1088	3.6	7
Turner	50	231	4.6	0
Croom	60	198	3.3	1
Gash	48	149	3.1	1
Bledsoe	32	82	2.6	0
Secules	8	33	4.1	0
Saxon	2	2	1.0	0
Zolak	1	0	0.0	0
Crittenden	1	-3	-3.0	0

RECEIVING

LastName	No.	Yds	Avg	TD
Coates	53	659	12.4	8
Brisby	45	626	13.9	2
Timpson	42	654	15.6	2
Turner	39	333	8.5	2
Russell	26	245	9.4	0
McMurtry	22	241	11.0	1
Cook	22	154	7.0	1
Crittenden	16	293	18.3	1
Gash	14	93	6.6	0
Croom	8	92	11.5	0
T. Brown	2	22	11.0	0

PUNT RETURNS

LastName	No.	Yds	Avg	TD
T. Brown	25	224	9.0	0
Harris	23	201	8.7	0
Crittenden	2	37	18.5	0
Smith	1	0	0.0	0

KICKOFF RETURNS

LastName	No.	Yds	Avg	TD
Crittenden	23	478	20.8	0
T. Brown	15	243	16.2	0
Harris	6	90	15.0	0
Sabb	2	0	0.0	0
Cook	1	8	8.0	0
Coates	0	0	—	0

PASSING — PUNTING — KICKING

PASSING	Att	Cmp	%	Yds	Yd/Att	TD	Int— %	RK
Bledsoe	429	214	49.9	2494	5.81	15	15—3.5	16
Secules	134	75	56.0	918	6.85	2	9—6.7	
Zolak	2	0	0.0	0	0.00	0	0—0.0	
Turner	1	0	0.0	0	0.00	0	0—0.0	

PUNTING	No.	Avg.
Saxon	76	40.7

KICKING	XP	ATT	%	FG	ATT	%
Sisson	15	15	100	14	26	54

INDIANAPOLIS COLTS

RUSHING

LastName	No.	Yds	Avg	TD
Potts	179	711	4.0	0
Johnson	95	331	3.5	1
Culver	65	150	2.3	3
George	13	39	3.0	0
Verdin	3	33	11.0	0
Stark	1	11	11.0	0
Toner	2	6	3.0	0
Majkowski	2	4	2.0	0
Trudeau	2	4	2.0	0

RECEIVING

LastName	No.	Yds	Avg	TD
Langhorne	**85**	1038	12.2	3
Hester	64	835	13.0	1
Johnson	55	443	8.1	0
Cash	43	402	9.3	3
Dawkins	26	430	16.5	1
Potts	26	189	7.3	0
Arbuckle	15	90	6.0	0
Culver	11	112	10.2	1
Cox	4	59	14.8	0
Verdin	2	20	10.0	1
Toner	1	5	5.0	0

PUNT RETURNS

LastName	No.	Yds	Avg	TD
Verdin	30	173	5.8	0

KICKOFF RETURNS

LastName	No.	Yds	Avg	TD
Verdin	**50**	**1050**	21.0	0
Culver	3	51	17.0	0
Butcher	2	2	1.0	0
Cash	1	11	11.0	0
Radecic	1	10	10.0	0

PASSING — PUNTING — KICKING

PASSING	Att	Cmp	%	Yds	Yd/Att	TD	Int— %	RK
George	407	234	57.5	2526	6.21	8	6—1.5	9
Trudeau	162	85	52.5	992	5.12	2	7—4.3	
Majkowski	24	13	54.2	105	4.38	0	1—4.2	
Johnson	1	0	0.0	0	0.00	0	1—100.0	

PUNTING	No.	Avg.
Stark	83	43.3

KICKING	XP	ATT	%	FG	ATT	%
Biasucci	15	16	94	26	31	84

HOUSTON OILERS 12-4 Jack Pardee

Scores of Each Game		
21	New Orleans	33
30	KANSAS CITY	0
17	San Diego	18
13	L.A. RAMS	28
7	Buffalo	35
28	New England	14
28	CINCINNATI	12
24	SEATTLE	14
38	Cincinnati	3
27	Cleveland	20
23	PITTSBURGH	3
33	ATLANTA	17
19	CLEVELAND	17
26	Pittsburgh	17
10	San Francisco	7
24	N.Y. JETS	0

UseName	Pos.	Hgt.	Wgt.	Age	Int	Pts
Kevin Donnalley	OT	6'5"	305	25		
Brad Hopkins	OT	6'3"	306	22		
Stan Thomas	OT	6'5"	295	24		
David Williams	OT	6'5"	292	27		
Doug Dawson	OG	6'2"	288	31		
Mike Munchak	OG	6'3"	284	33		
Erik Norgard	OG-C	6'1"	282	27		
Bruce Matthews	C	6'4"	291	31		
William Fuller	DE	6'3"	274	31		
Sean Jones	DE	6'7"	268	30		
Mike Teeter	DE	6'2"	260	25		
Ray Childress	DT-DE	6'6"	272	30		6
Glenn Montgomery	DT	6'	282	26		
Tim Roberts	DT	6'6"	318	24		
Lee Williams	DT-DE	6'6"	275	30		

John Flannery — Knee Injury
Jeff Alm — Committed Suicide in November 1993

UseName	Pos.	Hgt.	Wgt.	Age	Int	Pts
Micheal Barrow	LB	6'1"	236	23		
Joe Bowden	LB	5'11"	230	23		
Scott Kozak	LB	6'3"	222	27		
Lamar Lathon	LB	6'3"	252	25		
Wilber Marshall	LB	6'1"	240	31		
Keith McCants	LB	6'3"	265	25		
Eddie Robinson	LB	6'1"	245	23		
Al Smith	LB	6'1"	244	28		
Melvin Aldridge	DB	6'2"	195	23		
Blaine Bishop	DB	5'8"	197	23	1	
Tony Brown	DB	5'9"	183	23		
Cris Dishman	DB	6'	188	28	6	6
Steve Jackson	DB	5'8"	182	24	5	6
Darryll Lewis	DB	5'9"	188	24	1	6
Emanuel Martin	DB	5'11"	184	24		
Bubba McDowell	DB	6'1"	198	26	3	
Bo Orlando	DB	5'10"	180	27	3	6
Marcus Robertson	DB	5'11"	197	23	7	6

Mike Dumas — Foot Injury

UseName	Pos.	Hgt.	Wgt.	Age	Int	Pts
Cody Carlson	QB	6'3"	202	29		12
Warren Moon	QB	6'3"	212	36		6
Bucky Richardson	QB	6'1"	228	24		
Gary Brown	HB	5'11"	233	24		48
Le'Shai Maston	HB	6'1"	215	22		
Spencer Tillman	HB	5'11"	206	29		6
Lorenzo White	HB	5'11"	222	27		12
Reggie Brown	WR	6'1"	195	23		
Pat Coleman	WR	5'7"	176	26		
Willie Drewrey	WR	5'7"	164	30		
Curtis Duncan	WR	5'11"	184	28		18
Ernest Givins	WR	5'9"	178	28		24
Travis Hannah	WR	5'7"	161	23		
Leonard Harris	WR	5'8"	162	32		6
Haywood Jeffires	WR	6'2"	201	28		36
Tony Jones	WR	5'7"	148	27		
Webster Slaughter	WR	6'1"	170	28		30
Gary Wellman	WR	5'9"	173	26		6
John Henry Mills	TE	6'	222	22		
Al Del Greco	K	5'10"	202	31		126
Greg Montgomery	K	6'3"	210	28		

PITTSBURGH STEELERS 9-7 Bill Cowher

Scores of Each Game		
13	SAN FRANCISCO	24
0	L.A. Rams	27
34	CINCINNATI	7
45	Atlanta	17
16	SAN DIEGO	3
37	NEW ORLEANS	14
23	Cleveland	28
24	Cincinnati	16
23	BUFFALO	0
13	Denver	37
3	Houston	23
17	NEW ENGLAND	14
21	Miami	20
17	HOUSTON	26
6	Seattle	16
16	CLEVELAND	9

UseName	Pos.	Hgt.	Wgt.	Age	Int	Pts
John Jackson	OT	6'6"	297	28		
Leon Searcy	OT	6'3"	304	23		
Dan Fike	OG-OT	6'7"	285	32		
Calton Haselrig	OG	6'1"	295	27		
Duval Love	OG	6'3"	288	30		
Lonnie Palelei	OG	6'3"	311	22		
Justin Strzelczyk	OG-OT	6'5"	295	25		
Dermontti Dawson	C	6'2"	286	28		
Kendall Gammon	C	6'4"	286	24		
Ariel Solomon	C-OT	6'5"	290	25		
Kenny Davidson	DE	6'5"	275	26	1	6
Donald Evans	DE-DT	6'2"	277	29		
Kevin Henry	DE	6'4"	275	24	1	
Ricky Sutton	DE	6'2"	281	22		
Jeff Zgonina	DT	6'1"	284	23		
Joel Steed	NT	6'2"	295	24		
Gerald Williams	NT	6'3"	288	29		

UseName	Pos.	Hgt.	Wgt.	Age	Int	Pts
Reggie Barnes	LB	6'1"	235	23		
Chad Brown	LB	6'2"	240	23		
Kevin Greene	LB	6'3"	247	31		
Bryan Hinkle	LB	6'2"	229	34		
Dave Hoffmann	LB	6'2"	233	23		
Levon Kirkland	LB	6'	252	24		6
Greg Lloyd	LB	6'2"	226	28		
Rico Mack	LB	6'4"	239	22		
Jerry Olsavsky	LB	6'1"	224	26		
Deon Figures	DB	6'	200	23	1	
Larry Griffin	DB	6'	202	30		
Alan Haller	DB	5'11"	185	23		
David Johnson	DB	6'	187	27	3	
Gary Jones	DB	6'2"	214	25	2	
Carnell Lake	DB	6'1"	210	26	4	
Darren Perry	DB	5'10"	196	24	4	
Richard Shelton	DB	5'10"	202	27		
Willie Williams	DB	5'9"	188	22		
Rod Woodson	DB	6'	200	28	8	6

UseName	Pos.	Hgt.	Wgt.	Age	Int	Pts
Neil O'Donnell	QB	6'3"	230	27		
Rick Strom	QB	6'2"	205	28		
Mike Tomczak	QB	6'1"	195	30		
Barry Foster	HB	5'10"	218	24		54
Randy Cuthbert	FB	6'2"	225	23		
Merril Hoge	FB	6'2"	230	28		30
Victor Jones	FB	5'8"	215	25		
Leroy Thompson	FB	5'10"	217	24		18
Charles Davenport	WR	6'3"	210	24		
Jeff Graham	WR	6'1"	196	24		
Andre Hastings	WR	6'	188	22		
Ernie Mills	WR	5'11"	192	24		6
Dwight Stone	WR-HB	6'	180	29		18
Yancey Thigpen	WR	6'1"	207	24		18
Adrian Cooper	TE	6'5"	270	25		
Eric Green	TE	6'5"	280	26		30
Tim Jorden	TE	6'3"	240	26		
Craig Keith	TE	6'3"	262	22		
Gary Anderson	K	5'11"	179	34		116
Mark Royals	K	6'5"	215	29		

CLEVELAND BROWNS 7-9 Bill Belichick

Scores of Each Game		
27	CINCINNATI	14
23	SAN FRANCISCO	13
19	L.A. Raiders	16
10	Indianapolis	23
14	MIAMI	24
28	Cincinnati	17
28	PITTSBURGH	23
14	DENVER	29
5	Seattle	22
20	HOUSTON	27
14	Atlanta	17
17	NEW ORLEANS	13
17	Houston	19
17	NEW ENGLAND	20
42	L.A. Rams	14
9	Pittsburgh	16

UseName	Pos.	Hgt.	Wgt.	Age	Int	Pts
Herman Arvie	OT	6'4"	320	22		
Tony Jones	OT	6'5"	295	27		
Gene Williams	OT	6'2"	305	24		
Bob Dahl	OG-OT	6'5"	300	24		
Houston Hoover	OG	6'2"	300	28		
Ed King	OG	6'4"	300	23		
Steve Everitt	C	6'5"	292	23		
Wally Williams	C	6'2"	300	22		
Rob Burnett	DE	6'4"	280	26		
Dan Footmann	DE	6'5"	285	24		
Pio Sagapolutele	DE	6'6"	297	23		
Anthony Pleasant	DE	6'5"	273	25		
Jerry Ball	DT	6'1"	315	28		
Bill Johnson	DT-DE	6'4"	305	24		
James Jones	DT	6'2"	290	24		
Michael Dean Perry	DT	6'1"	285	28		

UseName	Pos.	Hgt.	Wgt.	Age	Int	Pts
Mike Caldwell	LB	6'2"	222	22		
Gerald Dixon	LB	6'3"	252	24		
Mike Johnson	LB	6'1"	230	30		
Pepper Johnson	LB	6'3"	248	29		
Clay Matthews	LB	6'2"	245	37		
Frank Stams	LB	6'2"	240	27		
Eddie Sutter	LB	6'3"	240	23		
Stacey Hairston	DB	5'9"	180	26		
Randy Hilliard	DB	5'11"	160	26		
Tim Jacobs	DB	5'10"	185	23		
Selwyn Jones	DB	6'	185	23		
Stevon Moore	DB	5'11"	205	26		
Najee Mustafaa	DB	6'1"	190	29		
Louis Riddick	DB	6'2"	216	24		
Del Speer	DB	6'	196	23		
Terry Taylor	DB	5'10"	190	32		
Eric Turner	DB	6'1"	207	24		
Everson Walls	DB	6'1"	195	33		

Richard Brown — Knee Injury
Thane Gash — Knee Injury

UseName	Pos.	Hgt.	Wgt.	Age	Int	Pts
Brad Goebel	QB	6'3"	198	25		
Bernie Kosar (to DAL)	QB	6'5"	215	29		
Todd Philcox	QB	6'4"	225	26		
Vinny Testaverde	QB	6'5"	215	29		
Eric Metcalf	HB	5'10"	190	25		
Ron Wolfley	HB	6'	230	30		
Randy Baldwin	FB	5'10"	216	26		
Leroy Hoard	FB-HB	5'11"	230	26		
Kevin Mack	FB	6'	225	31		
Tommy Vardell	FB	6'2"	233	24		
Clarence Williams	FB-TE	6'2"	240	24		
Mark Carrier	WR	6'	185	27		
Michael Jackson	WR	6'4"	195	24		
Keenan McCardell	WR	6'1"	175	23		
Patrick Rowe	WR	6'1"	195	24		
Rico Smith	WR	6'	185	24		
Lawyer Tillman	WR	6'5"	230	27		
Brian Kinchen	TE	6'2"	232	28		
Thomas McLemore	TE	6'5"	230	23		
Brian Hansen	K	6'4"	215	32		
Matt Stover	K	5'11"	178	25		

CINCINNATI BENGALS 3-13 Dave Shula

Scores of Each Game		
14	Cleveland	27
6	INDIANAPOLIS	9
7	Pittsburgh	34
10	SEATTLE	19
15	Kansas City	17
17	CLEVELAND	28
12	Houston	28
16	PITTSBURGH	24
3	HOUSTON	38
12	N.Y. Jets	17
16	L.A. RAIDERS	10
8	San Francisco	21
2	New England	7
15	L.A. RAMS	3
21	ATLANTA	17
13	New Orleans	20

UseName	Pos.	Hgt.	Wgt.	Age	Int	Pts
Chuck Bradley	OT	6'5"	296	23		
Donnell Johnson	OT	6'7"	310	23		
Dan Jones	OT	6'7"	304	23		
Tom Rayam	OT	6'6"	297	25		
Kevin Sargent	OT	6'6"	284	24		
Tom Scott	OT-OG	6'6"	330	23		
Joe Walter	OT	6'6"	292	30		
Scott Brumfield	OG-OT	6'8"	320	23		
Ken Moyer	OG-OT	6'7"	297	26		
Bruce Kozerski	C	6'4"	287	31		
Mike Frier	DE	6'5"	299	24		
George Hinkle	DE	6'5"	288	28		
Roosevelt Nix	DE	6'6"	315	26		
Danny Stubbs	DE-LB	6'4"	264	8		
John Copeland	DT	6'3"	286	22		
Ty Parten	DT	6'4"	272	23		
Garry Howe	NT	6'1"	298	25		
Tim Krumrie	NT	6'2"	274	33		

UseName	Pos.	Hgt.	Wgt.	Age	Int	Pts
James Francis	LB	6'5"	252	25	2	
Alex Gordon	LB	6'5"	245	28		
Randy Kirk	LB	6'2"	231	28		
Ricardo McDonald	LB	6'2"	235	23		
Karmeeleyah McGill	LB	6'3"	224	22		
Eric Shaw	LB	6'3"	248	21		
Brad Smith	LB	6'2"	228	22		
Steve Tovar	LB	6'3"	244	23	1	
Alfred Williams	LB	6'6"	240	24		2
Michael Brim	DB	6'	192	27	3	6
Alan Grant (from SF)	DB	5'10"	187	26	1	
Lance Gunn	DB	6'3"	222	23		
Rod Jones	DB	6'	185	29	1	
R.J. Kors	DB	6'	200	27		
Marcello Simmons	DB	6'1"	180	22		
Fernandus Vinson	DB	5'10"	197	24		
Leonard Wheeler	DB	5'11"	189	24		
Sheldon White	DB	5'11"	188	28	2	
Darryl Williams	DB	6'	191	23	2	6

UseName	Pos.	Hgt.	Wgt.	Age	Int	Pts
David Klingler	QB	6'2"	205	24		
Jay Schroeder	QB	6'4"	215	32		
Erik Wilhelm	QB	6'3"	217	27		
Eric Ball	HB-FB	6'2"	220	27		6
Ryan Benjamin	HB	5'7"	183	23		
Harold Green	HB	6'2"	222	25		
Derrick Fenner	FB-HB	6'3"	228	26		6
Ostell Miles	FB	6'	236	22		6
Wesley Carroll	WR	6'	183	25		
Allen Degraffenreid	WR	6'3"	200	23		
Carl Pickens	WR	6'2"	206	23		36
Jeff Query	WR	6'	165	26		24
Reggie Rembert	WR	6'5"	200	26		
Patrick Robinson	WR	5'8"	176	23		
Milt Stegall	WR	6'	184	23		
Reggie Thornton	WR	5'11"	173	25		
David Frisch	TE	6'7"	260	23		
Tony McGee	TE	6'3"	246	22		
Jeff Thomason	TE	6'4"	233	23		
Craig Thompson	TE	6'2"	244	24		6
Lee Johnson	K	6'2"	200	31		
Doug Pelfrey	K	5'11"	185	22		85

HOUSTON OILERS

RUSHING

Last Name	No.	Yds	Avg	TD
G. Brown	195	1002	5.1	6
White	131	465	3.5	2
Moon	48	145	3.0	1
Tillman	9	94	10.4	0
Carlson	14	41	2.9	2
Givins	6	19	3.2	0
Maston	1	10	10.0	0
Richardson	2	9	4.5	0
Wellman	2	6	3.0	0
Coleman	1	1	1.0	0

RECEIVING

Last Name	No.	Yds	Avg	TD
Slaughter	77	904	11.7	5
Givins	68	887	13.0	4
Jeffires	66	753	11.4	6
Duncan	41	456	11.1	3
White	34	229	6.7	0
Wellman	31	430	13.9	1
G. Brown	21	240	11.4	2
Coleman	9	129	14.3	0
Harris	4	53	13.3	1
R. Brown	2	30	15.0	0
Maston	1	14	14.0	0
Norgard	1	13	13.0	0
Tillman	1	4	4.0	0
Drewrey	1	3	3.0	0

PUNT RETURNS

Last Name	No.	Yds	Avg	TD
Drewrey	41	275	6.7	

KICKOFF RETURNS

Last Name	No.	Yds	Avg	TD
Drewrey	15	293	19.5	0
Mills	11	230	20.9	0
Coleman	3	37	12.3	0
G. Brown	2	29	14.5	0

PASSING — PUNTING — KICKING

PASSING	Att	Cmp	%	Yds	Yd/Att	TD	Int—	%	RK
Moon	520	303	58.3	3485	6.70	21	21—	4.0	11
Carlson	90	51	56.7	605	6.72	2	4—	4.4	
Richardson	4	3	75.0	55	13.75	0	0—	0.0	

PUNTING	No.	Avg.
Montgomery	54	45.6

KICKING	XP	ATT	%	FG	ATT	%
Del Greco	39	40	98	29	34	85

PITTSBURGH STEELERS

RUSHING

Last Name	No.	Yds	Avg	TD
Thompson	205	763	3.7	3
Foster	177	711	4.0	8
Hoge	51	249	4.9	1
Stone	12	121	10.1	1
O'Donnell	26	111	4.3	0
Mills	3	12	4.0	0
Cuthbert	1	7	7.0	0
Woodson	1	0	0.0	0
Tomczak	5	-4	-0.8	0

RECEIVING

Last Name	No.	Yds	Avg	TD
Green	63	942	15.0	5
Stone	41	587	14.3	2
Graham	38	579	15.2	0
Thompson	38	259	6.8	0
Hoge	33	247	7.5	4
Mills	29	386	13.3	1
Foster	27	217	8.0	1
Thigpen	9	154	17.1	3
Cooper	9	112	12.4	0
Davenport	4	51	12.8	0
Hastings	3	44	14.7	0
Jorden	1	12	12.0	0
Cuthbert	1	3	3.0	0

PUNT RETURNS

Last Name	No.	Yds	Avg	TD
Woodson	41	338	8.2	0
Figures	5	15	3.0	0

KICKOFF RETURNS

Last Name	No.	Yds	Avg	TD
Woodson	15	294	19.6	0
Hastings	12	177	14.8	0
Stone	11	168	15.3	0
Thompson	4	77	19.3	0
Hoge	3	33	11.0	0
Thigpen	1	23	23.0	0
W. Williams	1	19	19.0	0
Cooper	1	2	2.0	0

PASSING — PUNTING — KICKING

PASSING	Att	Cmp	%	Yds	Yd/Att	TD	Int—	%	RK
O'Donnell	486	270	55.6	3208	6.60	14	7—	1.4	8
Tomozak	54	29	53.7	398	7.37	2	5—	9.3	

PUNTING	No.	Avg.
Royals	89	42.5

KICKING	XP	Att	%	FG	Att	%
Anderson	32	32	100	28	30	93

CLEVELAND BROWNS

RUSHING

Last Name	No.	Yds	Avg	TD
Vardell	171	644	3.8	3
Metcalf	129	611	4.7	1
Hoard	56	227	4.1	0
Testaverde	18	74	4.1	0
Baldwin	18	61	3.4	0
Mack	10	33	3.3	1
Carrier	4	26	6.5	1
Kosar	23	26	1.1	0
Philcox	2	3	1.5	1
J. Jones	2	2	1.0	1
Jackson	1	1	1.0	0

RECEIVING

Last Name	No.	Yds	Avg	TD
Metcalf	63	539	8.6	2
Carrier	43	746	17.3	3
Jackson	41	756	18.4	8
Hoard	35	351	10.0	0
Kinchen	29	347	12.0	2
Vardell	19	151	7.9	1
McCardell	13	234	18.0	4
Tillman	5	68	13.6	1
Wolfley	5	25	5.0	1
Smith	4	55	13.8	0
Rowe	3	37	12.3	0
C. Williams	1	14	14.0	0
Baldwin	1	5	5.0	1

PUNT RETURNS

Last Name	No.	Yds	Avg	TD
Metcalf	36	464	12.9	2
Carrier	6	92	15.3	1
Turner	0	7	—	0

KICKOFF RETURNS

Last Name	No.	Yds	Avg	TD
Baldwin	24	444	18.5	0
Metcalf	15	318	21.2	0
Hoard	13	286	22.0	0
Vardell	4	58	14.5	0
R. Smith	1	13	13.0	0
Kinchen	1	0	0.0	0

PASSING — PUNTING — KICKING

PASSING	Att	Cmp	%	Yds	Yd/Att	TD	Int—	%	RK
Testaverde	230	130	56.5	1797	7.81	14	9—	3.9	3
Kosar	201	115	57.2	1217	6.05	8	3—	1.5	
Philcox	108	52	48.1	699	6.47	4	7—	6.5	
Jackson	1	1	100.0	25	25.00	0	0—	0.0	
Hoard	1	0	0.0	0	0.00	0	0—	0.0	

PUNTING	No.	Avg.
Hansen	84	43.2
Team	2	0.0

KICKING	XP	ATT	%	FG	ATT	%
Stover	36	36	100	16	22	73

CINCINNATI BENGALS

RUSHING

Last Name	No.	Yds	Avg	TD
Green	215	589	2.7	0
Fenner	121	482	4.0	1
Klingler	41	282	6.9	0
Miles	22	56	2.5	1
Schroeder	10	41	4.1	0
Ball	8	37	4.6	1
Query	2	13	6.5	0
Robinson	1	6	6.0	0
Benjamin	3	5	1.7	0

RECEIVING

Last Name	No.	Yds	Avg	TD
Query	56	654	11.7	4
Fenner	48	427	8.9	0
McGee	44	525	11.9	0
Pickens	43	565	13.1	6
Green	22	115	5.2	0
Thompson	17	87	5.1	1
Rembert	8	101	12.6	0
Robinson	8	72	9.0	0
Miles	6	89	14.8	0
Carroll	6	81	13.5	0
Frisch	6	43	7.2	0
Ball	4	39	9.8	0
Thomason	2	8	4.0	0
Benjamin	1	16	16.0	0
Stegall	1	8	8.0	0

PUNT RETURNS

Last Name	No.	Yds	Avg	TD
Robinson	43	305	7.1	0
Pickens	4	16	4.0	0
Simmons	1	0	0.0	0

KICKOFF RETURNS

Last Name	No.	Yds	Avg	TD
Robinson	30	567	18.9	0
Ball	23	501	21.8	0
Benjamin	4	78	19.5	0
Miles	4	65	16.3	0
Shaw	0	0	—	0

PASSING — PUNTING — KICKING

PASSING	Att	Cmp	%	Yds	Yd/Att	TD	Int—	%	RK
Klingler	343	190	55.4	1935	5.64	6	9—	2.6	15
Schroeder	159	78	49.1	832	5.23	5	2—	1.3	
Wilhelm	6	4	66.7	63	10.50	0	0—	0.0	
L. Johnson	1	0	0.0	0	0.00	0	0—	0.0	
Pickens	1	0	0.0	0	0.00	0	0—	0.0	

PUNTING	No.	Avg.
Johnson	90	43.9

KICKING	XP	ATT	%	FG	ATT	%
Pelfrey	13	16	81	24	31	77

KANSAS CITY CHIEFS 11-5 Marty Schottenheimer

Scores of Each Game		
27	Tampa Bay	3
0	Houston	30
15	DENVER	7
24	L.A. RAIDERS	9
17	CINCINNATI	15
17	San Diego	14
10	Miami	30
23	GREENBAY	16
31	L.A. Raiders	20
17	CHICAGO	19
23	BUFFALO	7
31	Seattle	16
21	Denver	27
28	SAN DIEGO	24
10	Minnesota	30
34	SEATTLE	24

UseName	Pos.	Hgt	Wgt	Age	Int	Pts
John Alt	OT	6'7"	307	31		
Derrick Graham	OT	6'4"	306	26		
Reggie McElroy	OT-OG	6'6"	290	33		
Ricky Siglar	OT	6'7"	304	27		
Joe Valerio	OT-C	6'5"	295	24		6
Tom Ricketts	OG	6'5"	305	27		
Will Shields	OG	6'2"	296	21		
Dave Szott	OG	6'4"	290	25		
Danny Villa	OG	6'5"	300	28		
Tim Grunhard	C	6'2"	299	25		
Leonard Griffin	DE	6'4"	278	30		
Pellom McDaniels	DE	6'3"	278	25		
Neil Smith	DE	6'4"	273	27	1	
Darren Mickel	DT	6'4"	280	23		
Tim Newton	DT	6'	269	30		
Joe Phillips	DT-NT	6'5"	300	30		
Dan Saleaumua	DT-DE	6'	300	28	1	6
Erick Anderson	LB	6'1"	235	24		
Jaime Fields	LB	5'11"	230	23		
Lonnie Marts	LB	6'1"	230	24	1	
Tracy Rogers	LB	6'2"	241	26		
Tracy Simien	LB	6'1"	250	26		
Santo Stephens	LB	6'4"	232	24		
Derrick Thomas	LB-DE	6'3"	242	26		6
Martin Bayless	DB	6'2"	219	30	2	
Dale Carter	DB	6'1"	188	23	1	
Albert Lewis	DB	6'2"	195	32	6	6
Garry Lewis	DB	5'11"	185	26		
Charles Mincy	DB	5'11"	197	23	5	
Bruce Pickens (from ATL, GB)	DB	5'11"	190	25		
Kevin Ross	DB	5'9"	185	31	2	
Jay Taylor	DB	5'10"	170	25	1	
Doug Terry	DB	5'11"	192	23	1	
Bennie Thompson	DB	6'	216	30		
Tim Watson	DB	6'1"	213	23		
David Whitmore	DB	6'	217	26		
Matt Blundin	QB	6'6"	233	24		
Dave Krieg	QB	6'1"	202	34		
Joe Montana	QB	6'2"	205	37		
Marcus Allen	HB	6'2"	210	33		90
Ron Dickerson	HB-WR	6'	211	23		
Todd McNair	HB	6'1"	197	27		12
John Stephens (from GB)	HB	6'1"	215	27		6
Harvey Williams	HB	6'2"	215	26		
Kimble Anders	FB	5'11"	221	26		6
Ernie Thompson	FB	5'11"	257	23		
Tim Barnett	WR	6'1"	200	25		6
J.J. Birden	WR	5'9"	165	28		12
Willie Davis	WR	6'	172	25		42
Danan Hughes	WR	6'1"	201	22		
Fred Jones	WR	5'9"	180	26		
Hassan Jones	WR	6'	202	29		
Mike Bartrum	TE	6'4"	234	23		
Keith Cash	TE	6'4"	240	24		24
Mike Dyal (to SD)	TE	6'2"	240	27		
Jonathan Hayes	TE	6'5"	252	31		6
Bryan Barker	K	6'1"	187	29		
Nick Lowery	K	6'4"	207	37		106

LOS ANGELES RAIDERS 10-6 Art Shell

Scores of Each Game		
24	MINNESOTA	7
17	Seattle	13
16	CLEVELAND	19
9	Kansas City	24
24	N.Y. JETS	20
23	Denver	20
23	SAN DIEGO	30
16	Chicago	14
20	Kansas City	31
12	San Diego	7
10	Cincinnati	16
25	Buffalo	24
27	SEATTLE	23
27	TAMPA BAY	20
0	Green Bay	28
33	DENVER	*30

UseName	Pos.	Hgt	Wgt	Age	Int	Pts
Ken Lanier	OT	6'3"	290	34		
Gerald Perry	OT	6'6"	300	28		
Rich Stephens	OT-OG	6'7"	300	27		
Bruce Wilkerson	OT	6'5"	295	29		
Max Montoya	OG	6'5"	295	37		
Todd Peat	OG	6'2"	305	29		
Steve Wisniewski	OG	6'4"	285	26		
Don Mosebar	C	6'6"	300	31		
Dan Turk	C	6'4"	290	31		
Aundray Bruce	DE	6'5	260	27		
Howie Long	DE	6'5"	275	33		
Anthony Smith	DE	6'3"	260	26		
Greg Townsend	DE	6'3"	270	31		
Willie Broughton	DT	6'5"	285	28		
Nolan Harrison	DT	6'5"	285	24		
Chester McGlockton	DT	6'4"	315	23	1	
Greg Biekert	LB	6'2"	235	24		
Mike Jones	LB	6'1"	230	24		
Joe Kelly	LB	6'2"	230	28		
Winston Moss	LB	6'3"	240	27		
Aaron Wallace	LB	6'3"	240	26		
Eddie Anderson	DB	6'1"	210	30	2	
Patrick Bates	DB	6'3"	220	22	1	
Rickey Dixon	DB	5'11"	185	26		
Torin Dorn	DB	6'	190	25		
David Fulcher	DB	6'3"	245	28		
Derrick Hoskins	DB	6'2"	205	23	2	
Dan Land	DB	6'	195	28		
Terry McDaniel	DB	5'10"	180	28	5	6
James Trapp	DB	6'	180	23	1	
Lionel Washington	DB	6'	185	32	2	
Vince Evans	QB	6'2"	215	38		
Billy Joe Hobert	QB	6'3"	225	11		
Jeff Hostetler	QB	6'3"	220	32		30
Nick Bell	HB	6'2"	250	25		6
Randy Jordan	HB	5'10"	205	23		
Napoleon McCallum	HB	6'2"	225	29		18
Tyrone Montgomery	HB	6'	190	23		
Greg Robinson	HB	5'10"	200	24		6
Steve Smith	FB	6'1"	240	29		
Tim Brown	WR	6'	195	27		48
Willie Gault	WR	6'	175	32		
Daryl Hobbs	WR	6'2"	180	25		
Raghib Ismail	WR	5'10"	180	23		6
James Jett	WR	5'10"	165	22		18
Alexander Wright	WR	6'	190	26		24
John Duff	TE	6'7"	250	26		
Andrew Glover	TE	6'6"	245	26		6
Ethan Horton	TE	6'4"	240	30		6
Kevin Smith	TE	6'4"	255	24		
Jeff Gossett	K	6'2"	195	36		
Jeff Jaeger	K	5'11"	190	28		132

Greg Skrepenak — Ankle Injury
Steve Wright — Knee Injury

Dave Waymer — Died in Offseason

DENVER BRONCOS 9-7 Wade Phillips

Scores of Each Game		
26	N.Y. Jets	20
34	SAN DIEGO	17
7	Kansas City	15
35	INDIANAPOLIS	13
27	Green Bay	30
20	L.A. RAIDERS	23
28	SEATTLE	17
29	Cleveland	14
23	MINNESOTA	26
37	PITTSBURGH	13
17	Seattle	9
10	San Diego	13
27	KANSAS CITY	21
13	Chicago	3
10	TAMPA BAY	17
30	L.A. Raiders	*33

UseName	Pos.	Hgt	Wgt	Age	Int	Pts
Russell Freeman	OT	6'7"	290	23		
Don Maggs	OT	6'5"	290	31		
Kirk Scrafford	OT	6'6"	265	26		
Gary Zimmerman	OT	6'6"	294	31		
Brian Habib	OG	6'7"	299	28		
Jon Melander	OG-OT	6'7"	280	26		
Dave Widell	OG-C	6'6"	292	28		
Keith Kartz	C	6'4"	270	30		
Bob Meeks	C	6'2"	279	24		
Shane Dronett	DE	6'6"	275	22	2	
Willie Oshodin	DE	6'4"	265	23		
Jeff Robinson	DE	6'4"	265	23		
Dan Williams	DE	6'4"	290	23		
Alphonso Taylor	DT	6'3"	350	23		
Darren Drozdov	NT	6'3"	280	23		
Greg Kragen	NT	6'3"	265	31		
Elijah Alexander	LB	6'2"	230	23		
Mike Croel	LB	6'3"	231	24	1	6
Mitch Donahue	LB	6'2"	254	25		
Simon Fletcher	LB	6'5"	240	31		
Tim Lucas	LB	6'3"	230	32		
Karl Mecklenburg	LB	6'3"	235	33		
Jeff Mills	LB	6'3"	250	24		
Dave Wyman	LB	6'2"	248	29	1	6
Steve Atwater	DB	6'3"	217	26	2	
Ronnie Bradford	DB	5'10"	188	22	1	
Tyrone Braxton	DB	5'11"	185	28	3	
Charles Dimry	DB	6'	175	27	1	
Darryl Hall	DB	6'2"	210	27	1	
Rondell Jones	DB	6'2"	210	22		
Le-Lo Lang	DB	5'11"	185	26	2	
Frank Robinson	DB	5'11"	174	24	1	
Dennis Smith	DB	6'3"	200	34	3	
John Elway	QB	6'3"	215	33		
Tommy Maddox	QB	6'4"	205	21		
Shawn Moore	QB	6'2"	214	24		
Rod Bernstine	HB-FB	6'3"	238	28		24
Robert Delpino	HB	6'	205	27		48
Glyn Milburn	HB	5'8"	177	22		18
Anthony Lynn	FB	6'3"	230	24		
Reggie Rivers	FB	6'1"	215	25		14
Melvin Bonner	WR	6'3"	207	23		
Vance Johnson	WR	5'11"	185	30		30
Tony Kimbrough	WR	6'2"	192	22		
Arthur Marshall	WR	5'11"	174	24		12
Barry Rose	WR	6'	185	25		
Derek Russell	WR	6'	195	24		24
Kitrick Taylor	WR	5'11"	189	29		
Cedric Tillman	WR	6'2"	204	23		12
Jerry Evans	TE	6'4"	250	24		
Reggie Johnson	TE	6'2"	256	25		6
Shannon Sharpe	TE	6'2"	230	25		54
Jason Elam	K	5'11"	192	23		119
Tom Rouen	K	6'3"	215	25		

SAN DIEGO CHARGERS 8-8 Bobby Ross

Scores of Each Game		
18	SEATTLE	12
17	Denver	34
18	HOUSTON	17
14	Seattle	31
3	Pittsburgh	16
14	KANSAS CITY	17
30	L.A. Raiders	23
30	Minnesota	17
13	CHICAGO	16
7	L.A. RAIDERS	12
31	Indianapolis	0
13	DENVER	10
13	GREEN BAY	20
24	Kansas City	28
45	MIAMI	20
32	Tampa Bay	17

UseName	Pos.	Hgt	Wgt	Age	Int	Pts
Stan Brock	OT	6'6"	295	35		
Eric Jonassen	OT	6'5"	310	25		
Mike Mooney	OT	6'6"	320	24		
Harry Swayne	OT	6'5"	295	28		
Joe Cocozzo	OG	6'4"	300	23		
Joe Milinichik	OG	6'5"	300	30		
Eric Moten	OG	6'2"	306	25		
Raymond Smoot	OG-OT	6'4"	300	23		
Mike Zandofsky	OG	6'2"	305	27		
Courtney Hall	C	6'2"	281	25		
Curtis Whitley	C	6'1"	285	24		
Burt Grossman	DE	6'6"	270	26		
Raylee Johnson	DE	6'3"	245	23		
Chris Mims	DE-DT	6'5"	290	22		
Leslie O'Neal	DE	6'4"	265	29		
Shawn Lee	DT	6'2"	300	26		
Reggie White	DT	6'4"	300	23		
Blaise Winter	DT	6'4"	295	31		
Sam Anno	LB	6'3"	240	28		
Lewis Bush	LB	6'2"	245	23		
Terry Crews	LB	6'2"	245	25		
Doug Miller	LB	6'3"	232	23		
Gary Plummer	LB	6'2"	247	33	2	
Junior Seau	LB	6'3"	250	24	2	
Jerrol Williams	LB	6'4"	240	26		
Darren Carrington	DB	6'2"	200	26	7	
Eric Castle	DB	6'3"	212	23		
Brian Davis	DB	6'2"	190	30	1	
Floyd Fields	DB	6'	208	24		
Donald Frank	DB	6'	192	27	3	6
James Fuller	DB	6'	208	24		
Darrien Gordon	DB	5'11"	182	22	1	
Marquez Pope	DB	5'10"	193	22	2	
Stanley Richard	DB	6'2"	197	25	1	
Sean Vanhorse	DB	5'10"	180	25	2	
John Friesz	QB	6'4"	218	26		
Stan Humphries	QB	6'2"	223	28		
Eric Bieniemy	HB	5'7"	198	24		6
Ronnie Harmon	HB	5'11"	207	29		12
Marion Butts	FB-HB	6'1"	248	27		24
Natrone Means	FB-HB	5'10"	245	21		48
Johnnie Barnes	WR	6'1"	180	25		
Shawn Jefferson	WR	5'11"	172	24		12
Nate Lewis	WR	5'11"	198	26		24
Anthony Miller	WR	5'11"	189	28		42
Mark Seay	WR	6'	175	26		
Steve Hendrickson	FB-LB	6'	250	27	1	
Deems May	TE	6'4"	263	24		
Alfred Pupunu	TE	6'2"	255	23		
Derrick Walker	TE	6'1"	250	26		6
Duane Young	TE	6'1"	270	25		12
John Carney	K	5'11"	170	29		124
John Kidd	K	6'3"	208	32		6
Kent Sullivan (to HOU)	K	5'10"	197	29		

Gill Byrd — Knee Injury

SEATTLE SEAHAWKS 6-10 Tom Flores

Scores of Each Game		
12	San Diego	18
13	L.A. RAIDERS	17
17	New England	14
19	Cincinnati	10
31	SAN DIEGO	14
10	Detroit	30
10	NEW ENGLAND	9
17	Denver	28
14	Houston	24
22	CLEVELAND	5
9	DENVER	17
16	KANSAS CITY	31
23	L.A. Raiders	27
27	PHOENIX	*30
16	PITTSBURGH	6
24	Kansas City	34

UseName	Pos.	Hgt	Wgt	Age	Int	Pts
Jason Childs	OT	6'4"	285	24		
Andy Heck	OT	6'6"	298	26		
Mike Keim	OT	6'7"	301	27		
Ray Roberts	OT	6'6"	304	24		
Rickie Shaw	OT	6'4"	294	23		
Jeff Blackshear	OG	6'6"	325	24		
Darrick Brilz	OG	6'3"	287	29		
Bill Hitchcock	OT	6'6"	291	28		
Ray Donaldson	C	6'3"	300	35		
Joe Tofflemire	C	6'3"	273	28		
Jeff Bryant	DE	6'5"	281	33		
Antonio Edwards	DE	6'3"	270	23		2
Michael McCrary	DE	6'4"	250	23		
Mike Sinclair	DE	6'4"	271	25		
Natu Tuatagaloa	DE	6'4"	274	27		
Cortez Kennedy	DT	6'3"	293	25		
Joe Nash	DT	6'2"	278	32	1	6
Tyrone Rodgers	DT	6'3"	266	24		
Ray Berry	LB	6'2"	230	29		
David Brandon (from CLE)	LB	6'4"	230	28		
Anthony Davis	LB	6'	231	24		
Dino Hackett	LB	6'3"	230	29		
E.J. Junior	LB	6'3"	242	33		
Kevin Murphy	LB	6'2"	235	29		
Rufus Porter	LB	6'1"	227	28	1	
Bob Spitulski	LB	6'3"	235	23		
Rod Stephens	LB	6'1"	237	27		10
Dean Wells	LB	6'3"	238	23		
Terry Wooden	LB	6'3"	239	26		
Brian Allred	DB	5'10"	175	24		
Robert Blackmon	DB	6'	197	26	2	6
Carlton Gray	DB	6'	191	22	3	
Dwayne Harper	DB	5'11"	174	27	1	
Patrick Hunter	DB	5'11"	186	28	4	
James Jefferson	DB	6'1"	199	29	1	
Dave McCloughan	DB	6'1"	185	26		
Eugene Robinson	DB	6'	191	30	9	
Rafael Robinson	DB	5'11"	200	24		
Stan Gelbaugh	QB	6'3"	207	30		
Dan McGwire	QB	6'8"	239	25		
Rick Mirer	QB	6'2"	216	23		18
Rueben Mayes	HB	5'11"	201	30		
Jon Vaughn	HB	5'9"	203	23		
Chris Warren	HB	6'2"	225	26		42
Tracy Johnson	FB	6'	230	26		6
John L. Williams	FB	5'11"	231	28		24
Michael Bates	WR	5'10"	189	23		
Brian Blades	WR	5'11	189	27		18
Kelvin Martin	WR	5'9"	162	28		30
Doug Thomas	WR	5'10"	178	23		
Robb Thomas	WR	5'11"	175	27		
Terrence Warren	WR	6'1"	200	24		
Ferrell Edmunds	TE	6'6"	254	28		12
Paul Green	TE	6'3"	230	26		6
Trey Junkin	TE	6'2"	237	32		
John Kasay	K	5'10"	189	23		98
Rick Tuten	K	6'2"	218	28		

Mitch Frerotte — Neck Injury
Grant Feasel — Knee Injury

KANSAS CITY CHIEFS

RUSHING

Last Name	No.	Yds	Avg	TD
Allen	206	764	3.7	**12**
Anders	75	291	3.9	0
McNair	51	278	5.5	2
Stephens	54	191	3.5	1
H. Williams	42	149	3.5	0
Montana	25	64	2.6	0
F. Jones	5	34	6.8	0
E. Thompson	11	28	2.5	0
Krieg	21	24	1.1	0
Barnett	1	3	3.0	0
Carter	1	2	2.0	0
Cash	1	0	0.0	0

RECEIVING

Last Name	No.	Yds	Avg	TD
Davis	52	909	17.5	7
Birden	51	721	14.1	2
Anders	40	326	8.2	1
Hayes	24	331	13.8	1
Cash	24	242	10.1	4
Barnett	17	182	10.7	1
McNair	10	74	7.4	0
F. Jones	9	111	12.3	0
H. Jones	7	91	13.0	0
Dyal	7	83	11.9	0
H. Williams	7	42	6.0	0
Stephens	5	31	6.2	0
E. Thompson	4	33	8.3	0
Valerio	1	1	1.0	1

PUNT RETURNS

Last Name	No.	Yds	Avg	TD
Carter	27	247	9.1	0
Birden	5	43	8.6	0
Hughes	3	49	16.3	0
Mincy	2	9	4.5	0

KICKOFF RETURNS

Last Name	No.	Yds	Avg	TD
Hughes	14	266	19.0	0
Dickerson	11	237	21.5	0
F. Jones	9	156	17.3	0
Stephens	5	88	17.6	0
H. Williams	3	53	17.7	0
Anders	1	47	47.0	0
McNair	1	28	28.0	0
Marts	1	0	0.0	0
Birden	0	0	—	0

PASSING — PUNTING — KICKING

PASSING	Att	Cmp	%	Yds	Yd/Att	TD	Int— %	RK
Montana	298	181	60.7	2144	7.19	13	7—2.3	2
Krieg	189	105	55.6	1238	6.55	7	3—1.6	
Blundin	3	1	33.3	2	0.67	0	0—0.0	
Anders	0	0	0.0	0	0.00	0	0—0.0	

PUNTING	No.	Avg.
Barker	77	42.1

KICKING	XP	Att.	%	FG	Att	%
Lowery	37	37	**100**	23	29	79

LOS ANGELES RAIDERS

RUSHING

Last Name	No.	Yds	Avg	TD
Robinson	156	591	3.8	1
Hostetler	55	202	3.7	5
Bell	67	180	2.7	1
S. Smith	47	156	3.3	0
McCallum	37	114	3.1	3
Montgomery	37	106	2.9	0
Evans	15	51	3.6	0
Jordan	12	33	2.8	0
Brown	2	7	3.5	0
Jett	1	0	0.0	0
Ismail	4	-5	-1.3	0
Gossett	1	-10	-10.0	0

RECEIVING

Last Name	No.	Yds	Avg	TD
Brown	80	**1180**	14.8	7
Horton	43	467	10.9	1
Jett	33	771	**23.4**	3
Wright	27	462	17.1	4
Ismail	26	353	13.6	1
S. Smith	18	187	10.4	0
Robinson	15	142	9.5	0
Bell	11	111	10.1	0
Montgomery	10	43	4.3	0
Gault	8	64	8.0	0
Glover	4	55	13.8	1
Jordan	4	42	10.5	0
McCallum	2	5	2.5	0

PUNT RETURNS

Last Name	No.	Yds	Avg	TD
T. Brown	40	**465**	11.6	1

KICKOFF RETURNS

Last Name	No.	Yds	Avg	TD
Ismail	25	605	**24.2**	0
Wright	10	167	16.7	0
Gault	7	187	26.7	0
Robinson	4	57	14.3	0
Peat	2	18	9.0	0
K. Smith	2	15	7.5	0
McCallum	1	12	12.0	0
Turk	1	0	0.0	0

PASSING — PUNTING — KICKING

PASSING	Att	Cmp	%	Yds	Yd/Att	TD	Int— %	RK
Hostetler	419	236	56.2	3242	7.71	14	10—2.4	6
Evans	76	45	59.2	640	8.42	3	4—5.3	

PUNTING	No.	Avg.
Gossett	71	41.8

KICKING	XP	ATT	%	FG	ATT	%
Jaeger	27	29	93	**35**	**44**	80

DENVER BRONCOS

RUSHING

Last Name	No.	Yds	Avg	TD
Bernstine	223	816	3.7	4
Delpino	131	445	3.4	8
Milburn	52	231	4.4	0
Elway	44	153	3.5	0
Rivers	15	50	3.3	1
Rouen	1	0	0.0	0
Maddox	2	-2	-1.0	0

RECEIVING

Last Name	No.	Yds	Avg	TD
Sharpe	81	995	12.3	**9**
Russell	44	719	16.3	3
Bernstine	44	372	8.5	0
Milburn	38	300	7.9	3
V. Johnson	36	517	14.4	5
Marshall	28	360	12.9	2
Delpino	26	195	7.5	0
R. Johnson	20	243	12.2	1
Tillman	17	193	11.4	2
Kimbrough	8	79	9.9	0
Rivers	6	59	9.8	1
K. Taylor	1	28	28.0	0
Wyman	1	1	1.0	1

PUNT RETURNS

Last Name	No.	Yds	Avg	TD
Milburn	40	425	10.6	0
Bradford	1	0	0.0	0

KICKOFF RETURNS

Last Name	No.	Yds	Avg	TD
Russell	18	374	20.8	0
Milburn	12	188	15.7	0
Delpino	7	146	20.9	0
Meeks	1	9	9.0	0
Sharpe	1	0	0.0	0

PASSING — PUNTING — KICKING

PASSING	Att	Cmp	%	Yds	Yd/Att	TD	Int— %	RK
Elway	**551**	**348**	**63.2**	**4030**	7.31	**25**	10—1.8	**1**
Maddox	1	1	100.0	1	1.00	1	0—0.0	
Marshall	1	1	100.0	30	30.00	1	0—0.0	

PUNTING	No.	Avg.
Rouen	68	44.4

KICKING	XP	ATT	%	FG	ATT	%
Elam	**41**	**42**	98	26	35	74

SAN DIEGO CHARGERS

RUSHING

Last Name	No.	Yds	Avg	TD
Butts	185	746	4.0	4
Means	160	645	4.0	8
Harmon	46	216	4.7	0
Bieniemy	33	135	4.1	1
Jefferson	5	53	10.6	0
Humphries	8	37	4.6	0
Friesz	10	3	0.3	0
Lewis	3	2	0.7	0
Hendrickson	1	0	0.0	0
Miller	1	0	0.0	0
Kidd	3	-13	-4.3	1

RECEIVING

Last Name	No.	Yds	Avg	TD
A. Miller	84	1162	13.8	7
Harmon	73	671	9.2	2
Lewis	38	463	12.2	4
Jefferson	30	391	13.0	2
Walker	21	212	10.1	1
Butts	15	105	7.0	0
Pupunu	13	142	10.9	0
Barnes	10	137	13.7	0
Means	10	59	5.9	0
Young	6	41	6.8	2
Bieniemy	1	0	0.0	0

PUNT RETURNS

Last Name	No.	Yds	Avg	TD
Gordon	31	395	12.7	0
Lewis	3	17	5.7	0

KICKOFF RETURNS

Last Name	No.	Yds	Avg	TD
Lewis	33	684	20.7	0
Bieniemy	7	110	15.7	0
A. Miller	2	42	21.0	0
Hendrickson	2	25	12.5	0
Means	2	22	11.0	0
Harmon	1	18	18.0	0

PASSING — PUNTING — KICKING

PASSING	Att	Cmp	%	Yds	Yd/Att	TD	Int— %	RK
Humphries	324	173	53.4	1981	6.11	12	10—3.1	13
Friesz	238	128	53.8	1402	5.89	6	4—2.5	12
Means	1	0	0.0	0	0.00	0	0—0.0	

PUNTING	No.	Avg.
Kidd	57	42.6
Sullivan	15	40.9
Carney	4	38.8

KICKING	XP	Att	%	FG	Att	%
Carney	31	33	94	31	40	78

SEATTLE SEAHAWKS

RUSHING

Last Name	No.	Yds	Avg	TD
C. Warren	273	1072	3.9	7
Williams	82	371	4.5	3
Mirer	68	343	5.0	3
Vaughn	36	153	4.3	0
Blades	5	52	10.4	0
Bates	2	12	6.0	0
Johnson	2	8	4.0	0
D. Thomas	1	4	4.0	0
Mayes	1	2	2.0	0
Martin	1	0	0.0	0
Gelbaugh	1	-1	-1.0	0
McGwire	1	-1	-1.0	0

RECEIVING

Last Name	No.	Yds	Avg	TD
Blades	80	945	11.8	3
Williams	58	450	7.8	1
Martin	57	798	14.0	5
Edmunds	24	239	10.0	2
Green	23	178	7.7	1
C. Warren	15	99	6.6	0
D. Thomas	11	95	8.6	0
R. Thomas	7	67	9.6	0
Johnson	3	15	5.0	1
Bates	1	6	6.0	0
Roberts	1	4	4.0	0

PUNT RETURNS

Last Name	No.	Yds	Avg	TD
Martin	32	270	8.4	0
McCloughan	1	10	10.0	0

KICKOFF RETURNS

Last Name	No.	Yds	Avg	TD
Bates	30	603	20.1	0
Vaughn	16	280	17.5	0
Martin	3	38	12.7	0
Tuatagaloa	1	10	10.0	0

PASSING — PUNTING — KICKING

PASSING	Att	Cmp	%	Yds	Yd/Att	TD	Int— %	RK
Mirer	486	274	56.4	2833	5.83	12	17—3.5	14
McGwire	5	3	60.0	24	4.80	1	0—0.0	
Gelbaugh	5	3	60.0	39	7.80	0	1—20.0	
Tuten	1	0	0.0	0	0.00	0	0—0.0	
Williams	1	0	0.0	0	0.00	0	0—0.0	

PUNTING	No.	Avg.
Tuten	**91**	44.0

KICKING	XP	ATT	%	FG	ATT	%
Kasay	29	29	**100**	23	28	82

1993 A.F.C. — WILD-CARD PLAYOFFS

January 8, 1994 at Kansas City, Mo. (Attendance 74,515)

SCORING

PITTSBURGH	7	10	0	7	0	- 24
KANSAS CITY	7	0	3	14	3	- 27

First Quarter
- Pitt. — Cooper, 10 yard pass from O'Donnell
  PAT — Anderson (kick)
- K.C. — Birden, 23 yard pass from Krieg
  PAT — Lowery (kick)

Second Quarter
- Pitt. — Anderson, 30 yard field goal
- Pitt. — Mills, 26 yard pass from O'Donnell
  PAT — Anderson (kick)

Third Quarter
- K.C. — Lowery, 23 yard field goal

Fourth Quarter
- K.C. — Allen, 2 yard run
  PAT — Lowery (kick)
- Pitt. — Green, 22 yard pass from O'Donnell
  PAT — Anderson (kick)
- K.C. — Barnett, 7 yard pass from Montana
  PAT — Lowery (kick)

Overtime
- K.C. — Lowery, 32 yard field goal

TEAMSTATISTICS

PITT.		K.C.
21	First Downs- Total	28
5	First Downs- Rushing	7
15	First Downs- Passing	19
1	First Downs- Penalty	2
1	Fumbles- Number	0
0	Fumbles- Lost Ball	0
5	Penalties- Number	5
40	Yards Penalized	25
0	Missed Field Goals	0
80	Offensive Plays	81
369	Net Yards	401
4.6	Average Gain	5.0
0	Giveaways	0
0	Takeaways	0
0	Difference	0

INDIVIDUALSTATISTICS

PITTSBURGH	No.	Yds.	Avg.	KANSAS CITY	No.	Yds.	Avg.
RUSHING							
Thompson	25	60	2.4	Allen	21	67	3.2
Hoge	6	27	4.5	Anders	5	27	5.4
Stone	3	11	3.7	Montana	4	13	3.3
O'Donnell	1	-1	-1.0	McNair	2	9	4.5
	35	97	2.8	F. Jones	1	9	9.0
					33	125	3.8
RECEIVING							
Graham	7	96	13.7	Cash	7	56	8.0
Mills	4	60	15.0	Birden	6	72	12.0
Hoge	3	43	14.3	Allen	4	29	7.3
Stone	3	36	12.0	Anders	3	30	10.0
Thompson	3	4	1.3	Barnett	3	30	10.0
Green	2	37	18.5	W. Davis	2	47	23.5
Cooper	1	10	10.0	Hayes	2	11	5.5
	23	286	11.4	Hughes	1	15	15.0
				McNair	1	9	9.0
					29	299	10.3
PUNTING							
Royals	6		44.7	Barker	6		44.8
PUNT RETURNS							
Woodson	3	18	6.0	Hughes	3	31	10.3
				Birden	1	5	5.0
					4	36	9.0
KICKOFF RETURNS							
Woodson	3	66	22.0	Stephens	3	72	24.0
Stone	1	18	18.0	Hughes	2	42	21.0
Cuthbert	1	13	13.0	McNair	1	13	13.0
	5	97	19.4		6	127	21.2
INTERCEPTION RETURNS							
None				None			

PASSING

PITTSBURGH	Att.	Comp.	Comp. Pct.	Yds.	Int.	Yds./ Att.	Yds./ Comp.
O'Donnell	42	23	54.8	286	0	6.8	12.4
KANSAS CITY							
Montana	43	28	65.1	276	0	6.4	12.4
Krieg	1	1	100.0	23	0	23.0	23.0
	44	29	65.9	299	0	6.8	10.3

January 9, 1994 at Los Angeles (Attendance 65,314)

SCORING

DENVER	7	14	0	3	- 24
L.A. RAIDERS	14	7	14	7	- 42

First Quarter
- L.A.Rd. — Horton, 9 yard pass from Hostetler
  PAT — Jaeger (kick)
- Den. — Sharpe, 23 yard pass from Elway
  PAT — Elam (kick)
- L.A.Rd. — T. Brown, 65 yard pass from Hostetler
  PAT — Jaeger (kick)

Second Quarter
- Den. — R. Johnson, 16 yard pass from Elway
  PAT — Elam (kick)
- L.A.Rd. — Jett, 54 yard pass from Hostetler
  PAT — Jaeger (kick)
- Den. — Russell, 6 yard pass from Elway
  PAT — Elway (kick)

Third Quarter
- L.A.Rd. — McCallum, 26 yard run
  PAT — Jaeger (kick)
- L.A.Rd. — McCallum, 2 yard run
  PAT — Jaeger (kick)

Fourth Quarter
- Den. — Elam, 33 yard field goal
- L.A.Rd. — McCallum, 1 yard run
  PAT — Jaeger (kick)

TEAMSTATISTICS

DEN.		L.A.Rd.
26	First Downs- Total	19
4	First Downs- Rushing	6
18	First Downs- Passing	10
4	First Downs- Penalty	3
2	Fumbles- Number	0
0	Fumbles- Lost Ball	0
10	Penalties- Number	17
97	Yards Penalized	130
0	Missed Field Goals	0
73	Offensive Plays	53
387	Net Yards	427
5.3	Average Gain	8.1
1	Giveaways	0
0	Takeaways	1
- 1	Difference	+ 1

INDIVIDUALSTATISTICS

DENVER	No.	Yds.	Avg.	L.A. RAIDERS	No.	Yds.	Avg.
RUSHING							
Delpino	9	32	3.6	McCallum	13	81	6.2
Elway	5	23	4.6	Montgomery	15	50	3.3
Rivers	1	2	2.0	Hostetler	4	5	1.3
Maddox	1	1	1.0		32	136	4.3
Milburn	2	-2	-1.0				
	18	56	3.1				
RECEIVING							
Sharpe	13	156	12.0	Jett	3	111	37.0
Marshall	5	69	13.8	T. Brown	3	86	28.7
Milburn	5	8	1.6	Horton	3	45	15.0
Russell	2	31	15.5	Montgomery	3	29	9.7
Tillman	2	25	12.5	Wright	1	23	23.0
R. Johnson	2	19	9.5		13	294	22.6
Taylor	1	13	13.0				
Rivers	1	8	8.0				
Evans	1	7	7.0				
	32	336	10.5				
PUNTING							
Rouen	4		33.8	Gossett	4		42.5
PUNT RETURNS							
Milburn	3	38	12.7	None			
KICKOFF RETURNS							
Milburn	6	85	14.2	Gault	4	55	13.8
INTERCEPTION RETURNS							
None				Dorn	1	1	1.0

PASSING

DENVER	Att.	Comp.	Comp. Pct.	Yds.	Int.	Yds./ Att.	Yds./ Comp.
Elway	47	29	61.7	302	1	6.4	10.4
Maddox	7	3	42.9	34	0	4.9	11.3
L.A. RAIDERS							
Hostetler	19	13	68.4	294	0	15.5	22.6

1993 N.F.C. — WILD-CARD PLAYOFFS

January 8, 1994 at Pontiac, Mich. (Attendance 68,479)

SCORING

	1	2	3	4	Final
GREEN BAY	0	7	14	7	28
DETROIT	3	7	7	7	24

First Quarter
- Det. — Lohmiller, 47 yard field goal

Second Quarter
- G.B. — Sharpe, 12 yard pass from Favre; PAT — Jacke (kick)
- Det. — Perriman, 1 yard pass from Kramer; PAT — Hanson (kick)

Third Quarter
- Det. — Jenkins, 15 yard interception return; PAT — Hanson (kick)
- G.B. — Sharpe, 28 yard pass from Favre; PAT — Jacke (kick)
- G.B. — Teague, 101 yard interception return; PAT — Jacke (kick)

Fourth Quarter
- Det. — D. Moore, 5 yard run; PAT — Hanson (kick)
- G.B. — Sharpe, 40 yard pass from Favre; PAT — Jacke (kick)

TEAMSTATISTICS

G.B.		DET.
16	First Downs- Total	25
6	First Downs- Rushing	9
10	First Downs- Passing	14
0	First Downs- Penalty	2
2	Fumbles- Number	2
0	Fumbles- Lost Ball	0
6	Penalties- Number	5
49	Yards Penalized	35
0	Missed Field Goals	0
51	Offensive Plays	64
293	Net Yards	410
5.7	Average Gain	6.4
1	Giveaways	2
2	Takeaways	1
+ 1	Difference	- 1

INDIVIDUALSTATISTICS

GREEN BAY	No.	Yds.	Avg.	DETROIT	No.	Yds.	Avg.
RUSHING							
Thompson	12	41	3.4	Sanders	27	169	6.3
Bennett	9	30	3.3	D. Moore	1	5	5.0
Favre	4	18	4.5	E. Kramer	1	1	1.0
	25	89	3.6		29	175	6.0
RECEIVING							
Sharpe	5	101	20.2	Perriman	10	150	15.0
West	3	40	13.3	D. Moore	4	14	3.5
Thompson	3	32	10.7	Holman	3	31	10.3
Bennett	2	21	10.5	Green	2	33	16.5
Clayton	1	9	9.0	Sanders	2	0	0.0
Brooks	1	1	1.0	H. Moore	1	20	20.0
	15	204	13.6		22	248	11.3
PUNTING							
Wagner	4		40.3	Arnold	3		48.3
PUNT RETURNS							
Brooks	2	43	21.5	Gray	1	22	22.0
KICKOFF RETURNS							
C. Harris	3	89	29.7	Gray	4	44	11.0
				D. Moore	1	20	20.0
					5	64	12.8
INTERCEPTION RETURNS							
Teague	1	101	101.0	Jenkins	1	15	15.0
Buckley	1	0	0.0				
	2	101	50.5				

PASSING

	Att.	Comp.	Comp. Pct.	Yds.	Int.	Yds./Att.	Yds./Comp.
GREEN BAY							
Favre	26	15	57.7	204	1	7.8	7.8
DETROIT							
Kramer	31	22	71.0	248	2	8.0	11.3

January 0, 1094 at East Rutherford, N.J. (Attendance 77,328)

SCORING

	1	2	3	4	Final
MINNESOTA	0	10	0	0	10
N.Y. GIANTS	3	0	14	0	17

First Quarter
- N.Y.G. — Treadwell, 26 yard field goal

Second Quarter
- Minn. — C. Carter, 40 yard pass from McMahon; PAT — Reveiz (kick)
- Minn. — Reveiz, 52 yard field goal

Third Quarter
- N.Y.G. — Hampton, 51 yard run; PAT — Treadwell (kick)
- N.Y.G — Hampton, 2 yard run; PAT — Treadwell (kick)

TEAMSTATISTICS

MINN.		N.Y.G.
11	First Downs- Total	17
4	First Downs- Rushing	10
6	First Downs- Passing	6
1	First Downs- Penalty	1
2	Fumbles- Number	0
1	Fumbles- Lost Ball	0
6	Penalties- Number	2
28	Yards Penalized	20
0	Missed Field Goals	1
59	Offensive Plays	67
260	Net Yards	270
4.4	Average Gain	4.0
1	Giveaways	0
0	Takeaways	1
- 1	Difference	+ 1

INDIVIDUALSTATISTICS

MINNESOTA	No.	Yds.	Avg.	NEW YORK GIANTS	No.	Yds.	Avg.
RUSHING							
Graham	19	69	3.6	Hampton	33	161	4.9
McMahon	1	5	5.0	Simms	4	14	3.5
A. Carter	1	4	4.0	Bunch	1	1	1.0
Craig	1	1	1.0	M. Jackson	1	1	1.0
	22	79	3.6	Tillman	2	-1	-0.5
					41	176	4.3
RECEIVING							
C. Carter	4	83	20.8	Hampton	6	24	4.0
Jordan	4	31	7.8	Meggett	4	12	3.0
A. Carter	2	37	18.5	Calloway	2	30	15.0
Graham	2	19	9.5	Cross	2	11	5.5
Reed	2	16	8.0	M. Jackson	2	9	4.5
Ismail	1	6	6.0	Pierce	1	8	8.0
	15	192	12.1		17	94	5.5
PUNTING							
Newsome	8		37.8	Horan	7		32.0
PUNT RETURNS							
A. Carter	2	22	11.0	Meggett	2	5	2.5
A. Parker	2FC						
KICKOFF RETURNS							
Ismail	4	47	11.8	Calloway	1	12	12.0
				Meggett	1	0	0.0
					2	12	6.0
INTERCEPTIONS							
None				None			

PASSING

	Att.	Comp.	Comp. Pct.	Yds.	Int.	Yds./Att.	Yds./Comp.
MINNESOTA							
McMahon	25	12	48.0	145	0	5.8	12.1
Salisbury	9	3	33.3	47	0	5.2	15.7
	34	15	44.1	192	0	5.6	12.8
NEW YORK GIANTS							
Simms	26	17	65.4	94	0	3.6	5.5

1993 A.F.C. — DIVISIONAL PLAYOFFS

January 15, 1994 at Orchard Park, N.Y. (Attendance 61,923)

SCORING

L.A. RAIDERS	0	17	6	0	- 23
BUFFALO	0	13	9	7	- 29

Second Quarter

L.A.Rd.	Jaeger, 30 yard field goal
Buff.	Davis, 1 yard run PAT — Christie (kick)
L.A.Rd.	McCallum, 1 yard run PAT — Jaeger (kick)
L.A. Rd.	McCallum, 1 yard run PAT — Jaeger (kick)
Buff.	Thomas, 8 yard run PAT — Christie (kick)

Third Quarter

Buff.	Brooks, 25 yard pass from Kelly PAT — Christie kick blocked
Buff.	Christie, 29 yard field goal
L.A. Rd.	T. Brown, 86 yard pass from Hostetler PAT — Jaeger kick no good

Fourth Quarter

Buff.	Brooks, 22 yard pass from Kelly PAT — Christie (kick)

TEAMSTATISTICS

L.A.Rd.		BUFF.
15	First Downs- Total	25
9	First Downs- Rushing	7
6	First Downs- Passing	14
0	First Downs- Penalty	4
2	Fumbles- Number	3
1	Fumbles- Lost Ball	1
9	Penalties- Number	2
77	Yards Penalized	15
1	Missed Field Goals	1
57	Offensive Plays	70
325	Net Yards	355
5.7	Average Gain	5.1
1	Giveaways	1
1	Takeaways	1
0	Difference	0

INDIVIDUALSTATISTICS

L.A. RAIDERS	No.	Yds.	Avg.	BUFFALO	No.	Yds.	Avg.
RUSHING							
Montgomery	9	22	2.4	Thomas	14	44	3.1
Hostetler	5	29	5.8	K. Davis	11	36	3.3
McCallum	19	56	2.9	Kelly	5	-5	-1.0
Bell	2	3	1.5		30	75	2.5
	35	110	3.1				
RECEIVING							
T. Brown	5	127	25.4	Brooks	6	96	16.0
Montgomery	3	26	8.7	Thomas	6	48	8.0
Horton	2	42	21.0	Metzelaars	5	43	8.6
McCallum	1	15	15.0	Reed	4	53	13.3
Bell	1	12	12.0	McKeller	3	21	7.0
Duff	1	5	5.0	K. Davis	1	16	16.0
Jett	1	3	3.0	Beebe	1	9	9.0
	14	230	16.4	Gardner	1	1	1.0
					27	287	10.6
PUNTING							
Gossett	6		37.0	Mohr	3		36.3
PUNT RETURNS							
T. Brown	3	7	2.3	Copeland	3	7	2.3
KICKOFF RETURNS							
Ismail	3	51	17.0	Tasker	1	67	67.0
Gault	2	22	11.0	Copeland	2	35	17.5
Turk	1	10	10.0	Beebe	1	9	9.0
	6	83	13.8		4	111	27.8
INTERCEPTION RETURNS							
None				None			

PASSING

	Att.	Comp.	Comp. Pct.	Yds.	Int.	Yds./ Att.	Yds./ Comp.
L.A. RAIDERS							
Hostetler	20	14	70.0	230	0	5.6	10.9
BUFFALO							
Kelly	37	27	73.0	287	0	7.8	10.6

January 16, 1994 at Houston (Attendance 64,011)

SCORING

KANSAS CITY	0	0	7	21	- 28
HOUSTON	10	0	0	10	- 20

First Quarter

Hou.	Del Greco, 49 yard field goal
Hou.	G. Brown, 2 yard run PAT — Del Greco (kick)

Third Quarter

K.C.	K. Cash, 7 yard pass from Montana PAT — Lowery (kick)

Fourth Quarter

Hou.	Del Greco, 43 yard field goal
K.C.	Birden, 11 yard pass from Montana PAT — Lowery (kick)
K.C.	W. Davis, 18 yard pass from Montana PAT — Lowery (kick)
Hou.	Givins, 7 yard pass from Moon PAT — Del Greco (kick)
K.C.	Allen, 21 yard run PAT — Lowery (kick)

TEAMSTATISTICS

K.C.		HOU.
18	First Downs- Total	19
3	First Downs- Rushing	4
14	First Downs- Passing	14
1	First Downs- Penalty	1
0	Fumbles- Number	7
0	Fumbles- Lost Ball	2
7	Penalties- Number	3
51	Yards Penalized	63
0	Missed Field Goals	0
58	Offensive Plays	66
354	Net Yards	277
6.1	Average Gain	4.2
2	Giveaways	3
3	Takeaways	2
+ 1	Difference	- 1

INDIVIDUALSTATISTICS

KANSAS CITY	No.	Yds.	Avg.	HOUSTON	No.	Yds.	Avg.
RUSHING							
Allen	14	74	5.3	Moon	3	22	7.3
Anders	1	0	0.0	G. Brown	11	17	1.5
Montana	1	-1	-1.0		14	39	2.8
Krieg	2	-2	-1.0				
	18	71	3.9				
RECEIVING							
Birden	6	60	10.0	Jeffires	9	88	9.8
W. Davis	5	96	19.2	Givins	7	63	9.0
K. Cash	4	80	20.0	Wellman	6	80	13.3
Barnett	2	24	12.0	Duncan	6	49	8.2
McNair	2	9	4.5	G. Brown	4	26	6.5
Allen	1	12	12.0		32	306	9.6
Hayes	1	9	9.0				
F. Jones	1	9	9.0				
	22	299	13.6				
PUNTING							
Barker	5		45.0	Montgomery	5		48.6
PUNT RETURNS							
Hughes	3	42	14.0	Drewrey	1	12	12.0
Birden	1	2	2.0				
	4	44	11.0				
KICKOFF RETURNS							
Stephens	2	38	19.0	Drewrey	2	39	19.5
				Hannah	1	11	11.0
					3	50	16.7
INTERCEPTION RETURNS							
Mincy	1	12	12.0	S. Jackson	1	14	14.0
				Hoage	1	0	0.0
					2	14	7.0

PASSING

	Att.	Comp.	Comp. Pct.	Yds.	Int.	Yds./ Att.	Yds./ Comp.
KANSAS CITY							
Montana	38	22	57.9	299	2	7.9	13.6
HOUSTON							
Moon	43	32	74.4	306	1	7.1	9.6

1993 N.F.C. — DIVISIONAL PLAYOFFS

January 15, 1994 at San Francisco (Attendance 67,143)

SCORING

N.Y. GIANTS	0	3	0	0	- 3
SAN FRANCISCO	9	14	14	7	- 44

First Quarter
S.F. Watters, 1 yard run
PAT — Cofer kick failed
S.F. Cofer, 29 yard field goal

Second Quarter
S.F. Watters, 1 yard run
PAT — Cofer (kick)
S.F. Watters, 2 yard run
PAT — Cofer (kick)
N.Y.G. Treadwell, 25 yard field goal

Third Quarter
S.F Watters, 6 yard run
PAT — Cofer (kick)
S.F. Watters, 2 yard run
PAT — Cofer (kick)

Fourth Quarter
S.F. Logan, 2 yard run
PAT — Cofer (kick)

TEAMSTATISTICS

N.Y.G.		S.F.
12	First Downs- Total	25
3	First Downs- Rushing	13
6	First Downs- Passing	11
3	First Downs- Penalty	1
0	Fumbles- Number	2
0	Fumbles- Lost Ball	1
4	Penalties- Number	6
24	Yards Penalized	50
0	Missed Field Goals	0
58	Offensive Plays	65
194	Net Yards	413
3.4	Average Gain	6.4
3	Giveaways	1
1	Takeaways	3
-2	Difference	+2

INDIVIDUALSTATISTICS

RUSHING

N.Y. GIANTS	No.	Yds.	Avg.	SAN FRANCISCO	No.	Yds.	Avg.
Hampton	7	12	1.7	Watters	24	118	4.9
Brown	1	8	8.0	Logan	9	40	4.4
Tillman	4	8	2.0	Young	3	17	5.7
Bunch	2	5	2.5	Rathman	2	7	3.5
Meggett	2	5	2.5	Lee	1	5	5.0
Simms	2	3	1.5	Rice	1	-9	-9.0
Jackson	1	0	0.0		40	178	4.5
	19	41	2.2				

RECEIVING

N.Y. GIANTS	No.	Yds.	Avg.	SAN FRANCISCO	No.	Yds.	Avg.
McCaffrey	5	59	11.8	Watters	5	46	9.2
Meggett	3	17	5.7	Jones	4	39	9.8
Cross	2	32	16.0	Rice	3	43	14.3
Calloway	2	24	12.0	Taylor	2	74	37.0
Jackson	2	16	8.0	Rathman	2	16	8.0
Hampton	2	11	5.5	Lee	2	15	7.5
Tillman	1	14	14.0	Logan	1	8	8.0
Pierce	1	7	7.0		19	241	12.7
	18	180	10.0				

PUNTING

N.Y. GIANTS	No.		Avg.	SAN FRANCISCO	No.		Avg.
Horan	5		39.8	Wilmsmeyer	3		44.7

PUNT RETURNS

N.Y. GIANTS	No.	Yds.	Avg.	SAN FRANCISCO	No.	Yds.	Avg.
Meggett	1	3	3.0	Carter	2	39	19.5

KICKOFF RETURNS

N.Y. GIANTS	No.	Yds.	Avg.	SAN FRANCISCO	No.	Yds.	Avg.
Meggett	4	80	20.0	None			
Calloway	1	25	25.0				
	5	105	21.0				

INTERCEPTION RETURNS

N.Y. GIANTS	No.	Yds.	Avg.	SAN FRANCISCO	No.	Yds.	Avg.
None				Caldwell	1	13	13.0
				Davis	1	4	4.0
				McDonald	1	4	4.0
					3	21	7.0

PASSING

N.Y. GIANTS	Att.	Comp.	Comp. Pct.	Yds.	Int.	Yds./ Att.	Yds./ Comp.
Simms	25	12	48.0	124	2	5.0	10.3
Brown	10	6	60.0	56	1	5.6	9.2
	35	18	51.4	180	3	5.1	10.0
SAN FRANCISCO							
Young	22	17	77.3	226	0	10.3	13.3
Bono	2	2	100.0	15	0	7.5	7.5
	24	19	79.2	241	0	10.0	12.7

January 16, 1994 at Dallas (Attendance 64,790)

SCORING

GREEN BAY	3	0	7	7	- 17
DALLAS	0	17	7	3	- 27

First Quarter
G.B. Jacke, 30 yard field goal

Second Quarter
Dal. Harper, 25 yard pass from Aikman
PAT — Murray (kick)
Dal. Murray, 41 yard field goal
Dal. Novacek, 6 yard pass from Aikman
PAT — Murray (kick)

Third Quarter
Dal. Irvin, 19 yard pass from Aikman
PAT — Murray (kick)
G.B. Brooks, 13 yard pass from Favre
PAT — Jacke (kick)

Fourth Quarter
Dal. Murray, 38 yard field goal
G.B. Sharpe, 29 yard pass from Favre
PAT — Jacke (kick)

TEAMSTATISTICS

G.B.		DAL.
19	First Downs- Total	23
2	First Downs- Rushing	6
17	First Downs- Passing	16
0	First Downs- Penalty	1
3	Fumbles- Number	2
2	Fumbles- Lost Ball	1
4	Penalties- Number	5
30	Yards Penalized	39
1	Missed Field Goals	0
60	Offensive Plays	68
358	Net Yards	381
6.0	Average Gain	5.6
4	Giveaways	3
3	Takeaways	4
-1	Difference	+1

INDIVIDUALSTATISTICS

RUSHING

GREEN BAY	No.	Yds.	Avg.	DALLAS	No.	Yds.	Avg.
Thompson	7	28	4.0	E. Smith	13	60	4.6
Bennett	6	3	0.5	Coleman	5	19	3.8
	13	31	2.4	Johnston	3	12	4.0
				Lassic	2	6	3.0
				Aikman	3	0	0.0
				Bates	1	0	0.0
					27	97	3.6

RECEIVING

GREEN BAY	No.	Yds.	Avg.	DALLAS	No.	Yds.	Avg.
Bennett	9	53	5.9	Irvin	9	126	14.0
Sharpe	6	128	21.3	Novacek	6	59	9.8
West	4	41	10.3	Johnston	6	43	7.2
Thompson	3	54	18.0	Harper	2	33	16.5
Brooks	3	39	13.0	E. Smith	2	27	13.5
Ingram	2	9	4.5	Coleman	2	6	3.0
Lewis	1	7	7.0	Lassic	1	8	8.0
	28	331	11.8		28	302	10.8

PUNTING

GREEN BAY	No.		Avg.	DALLAS	No.		Avg.
Wagner	3		39.0	Jett	3		43.7

PUNT RETURNS

GREEN BAY	No.	Yds.	Avg.	DALLAS	No.	Yds.	Avg.
Brooks	2	59	29.5	K. Williams	2	14	7.0

KICKOFF RETURNS

GREEN BAY	No.	Yds.	Avg.	DALLAS	No.	Yds.	Avg.
Brooks	2	36	18.0	K. Williams	1	20	20.0
C. Harris	2	15	7.5	Marion	1	14	14.0
Wilson	1	17	17.0	Novacek	0	0	0.0
Jurkovic	1	2	2.0		2	34	17.0
	6	70	11.7				

INTERCEPTION RETURNS

GREEN BAY	No.	Yds.	Avg.	DALLAS	No.	Yds.	Avg.
Butler	1	14	14.0	Woodson	1	5	5.0
Buckley	1	0	0.0	Haley	1	0	0.0
	2	14	7.0		2	5	2.5

PASSING

GREEN BAY	Att.	Comp.	Comp. Pct.	Yds.	Int.	Yds./ Att.	Yds./ Comp.
Favre	45	28	62.2	331	2	7.4	11.8
DALLAS							
Aikman	37	28	75.7	302	2	8.2	10.8

1993 Championship Games

A.F.C. CHAMPIONSHIP GAME

January 23, 1994 at Orchard Park, N.Y.
(Attendance 76,642)

Thurman Thomas may not be much in the Super Bowl, but he does just about everything to see that the Bills get there every year.

With most of the nation rooting against Buffalo and for Joe Montana to lead the Chiefs to the Super Bowl, Thomas almost single-handedly led the Bills to a 30-10 victory over Kansas City. Thomas carried the ball 33 times for 186 yards and three touchdowns, as the Bills earned their fourth consecutive Super Bowl trip.

Over and over, Buffalo quarterback Jim Kelly kept sticking the ball in Thomas' stomach while shouting, "Go!"

"He must have said that 15-16 times today," Thomas said. He knows that on certain plays I'm going to get a lot of yardage."

A Kansas City defense that had held Thomas to 44 yards eight weeks earlier was at a loss to explain how he quadrupled his total when it counted most.

"From where I was watching the game, it looked like everything Thurman tried worked, and almost nothing we tried worked," said Chiefs defensive tackle Joe Phillips. "We didn't stop him, and the final score shows it."

Montana was unable to work his magic, as he completed only 9 of 23 passes for 125 yards. He was knocked out of the game in the third quarter with a concussion, and backup Dave Krieg, while passing for 198 yards, could manage only one touchdown for the Chiefs.

The Chiefs also gained only 52 yards on the ground, a big difference from what Thomas was doing to them.

SCORING

KANSAS CITY	6	0	7	0	- 13
BUFFALO	7	13	0	10	- 30

First Quarter
Buff. — Thomas, 12 yard run
PAT — Christie (kick)
K.C. — Lowery, 31 yard field goal
K.C. — Lowery, 31 yard field goal

Second Quarter
Buff. — Thomas, 3 yard run
PAT — Christie (kick)
Buff. — Christie, 23 yard field goal
Buff. — Christie, 25 yard field goal

Third Quarter
K.C. — Allen, 1 yard run
PAT — Lowery (kick)

Fourth Quarter
Buff. — Christie, 18 yard field goal
Buff. — Thomas, 3 yard run
PAT — Christie (kick)

TEAMSTATISTICS

K.C.		BUFF.
22	First Downs- Total	30
3	First Downs- Rushing	17
18	First Downs- Passing	9
1	First Downs- Penalty	4
1	Fumbles- Number	1
0	Fumbles- Lost Ball	1
6	Penalties- Number	2
29	Yards Penalized	10
0	Missed Field Goals	0
77	Offensive Plays	73
338	Net Yards	389
4.4	Average Gain	5.3
2	Giveaways	1
1	Takeaways	2
+1	Difference	-1

INDIVIDUALSTATISTICS

KANSAS CITY	No.	Yds.	Avg.	BUFFALO	No.	Yds.	Avg.
RUSHING							
Allen	18	50	2.8	Thomas	33	186	5.6
Anders	2	1	0.5	K. Davis	10	32	3.2
Montana	1	1	1.0	Kelly	2	3	1.5
	21	52	2.5	Reed	1	8	8.0
					46	229	5.0
RECEIVING							
K. Cash	6	87	14.5	Reed	4	49	12.3
Davis	5	57	11.4	Brooks	4	34	8.5
Birden	4	60	15.0	Metzelaars	4	29	7.3
Allen	2	36	18.0	Thomas	2	22	11.0
McNair	2	33	16.5	Beebe	2	19	9.5
Hayes	2	14	7.0	McKeller	1	7	7.0
Thompson	1	12	12.0		17	160	9.4
Hughes	1	11	11.0				
Anders	1	7	7.0				
Szott	1	6	6.0				
	25	323	12.9				
PUNTING							
Barker	6		40.8	Mohr	4		33.3
PUNT RETURNS							
Hughes	1	11	11.0	Copeland	5	70	14.0
Hughes	1FC						
KICKOFF RETURNS							
Stephens	5	89	17.8	Copeland	4	68	17.0
INTERCEPTION RETURNS							
				Jones	1	15	15.0
				Williams	1	0	0.0
					2	15	7.5

PASSING

KANSAS CITY	Att.	Comp.	Comp. Pct.	Yds.	Int.	Yds./ Att.	Yds./ Comp.
Montana	23	9	39.1	125	1	5.4	13.9
Krieg	29	16	55.2	198	1	6.8	12.4
	52	25	48.1	323	2	6.2	12.9
BUFFALO							
Kelly	27	17	63.0	160	0	5.9	9.4

N.F.C. CHAMPIONSHIP GAME

January 23, 1994 at Dallas, Texas
(Attendance 64,902)

Football coaches don't like it when one of their players guarantees victories before games. But, in this instance, it was Dallas coach Jimmy Johnson who guaranteed victory over San Francisco … and he was right.

The Cowboys decisively beat the 49ers 38-21, as Emmitt Smith, who was playing with a separated shoulder, gained 88 yards on the ground while catching seven passes for 85 more yards. He scored two touchdowns.

"I thought Jimmy Johnson's comment was insane," said 49ers wide receiver Jerry Rice. "But I guess it was accurate."

Dallas scored touchdowns on four of its first five possessions and jumped out to a 28-7 lead. The 49ers gained only 74 yards in the first half.

San Francisco managed a slight comeback in the second half after Dallas quarterback Troy Aikman was hospitalized with a concussion, narrowing the lead to 28-14. However, Cowboys backup quarterback Bernie Kosar then threw a 42-yard TD pass to Alvin Harper and the game was no longer in much doubt.

Quarterback Steve Young again failed to advance the 49ers to the Super Bowl, as they lost in the conference championship game for the third time in four years. Young was sacked four times. "I never believed we'd be beaten by this score," he said.

The closest San Francisco came was when it tied the game 7-7 in the second quarter. After that, Dallas scored three touchdowns before halftime.

"The defense played a great game," said Cowboys defensive coordinator Butch Davis, "but the key was Emmitt. He controlled the ball and kept us off the field. That's what you have to have if you have a great defense."

SCORING

SAN FRANCISCO	0	7	7	7	- 21
DALLAS	7	21	7	3	- 38

First Quarter
Dall. — Smith, 5 yard run
PAT — Murray (kick)

Second Quarter
S.F. — Rathman, 7 yard pass from Young
PAT — Cofer (kick)
Dall. — Johnston, 4 yard run
PAT — Murray (kick)
Dall. — Smith, 11 yard pass from Aikman
PAT — Murray (kick)
Dall. — Novacek, 19 yard pass from Aikman
PAT — Murray (kick)

Third Quarter
S.F. — Watters, 4 yard run
PAT — Cofer (kick)
Dall. — Harper, 42 yard pass from Aikman
PAT — Murray (kick)

Fourth Quarter
Dall. — Murray, 50 yard field goal
S.F. — Young, 1 yard run
PAT — Cofer (kick)

TEAMSTATISTICS

S.F.		DALL.
24	First Downs- Total	24
5	First Downs- Rushing	9
15	First Downs- Passing	15
4	First Downs- Penalty	0
2	Fumbles- Number	0
0	Fumbles- Lost Ball	0
6	Penalties- Number	4
46	Yards Penalized	29
0	Missed Field Goals	0
70	Offensive Plays	63
359	Net Yards	377
5.1	Average Gain	6.0
1	Giveaways	0
0	Takeaways	1
- 1	Difference	+ 1

INDIVIDUALSTATISTICS

SAN FRANCISCO	No.	Yds.	Avg.	DALLAS	No.	Yds.	Avg.
RUSHING							
Young	7	38	5.4	Smith	23	88	3.8
Watters	12	37	3.1	Aikman	3	25	8.3
Rathman	2	9	4.5	Johnston	4	13	3.3
	21	84	4.0	Lassic	1	1	1.0
				Kosar	2	-3	-1.5
					33	124	3.8
RECEIVING							
Watters	7	33	4.7	Smith	7	85	12.1
Rice	6	83	13.8	Harper	4	78	19.5
Taylor	3	61	20.3	Novacek	4	57	14.3
Williams	3	44	14.7	Irvin	2	23	11.5
Jones	3	26	8.7	Johnston	2	17	8.5
Logan	3	21	7.0		19	260	13.7
Turner	1	12	12.0				
Rathman	1	7	7.0				
	27	287	10.6				
PUNTING							
Wilmsmeyer	4		45.5	Jett	4		41.0
PUNT RETURNS							
Carter	1	9	9.0	K. Williams	1	6	6.0
Carter	1FC			K. Williams	2FC		
KICKOFF RETURNS							
Carter	4	66	16.5	Marion	1	15	15.0
Logan	2	20	10.0	K. Williams	1	14	14.0
	4	73	18.3	Novacek	0	0	0.0
					2	29	14.5
INTERCEPTION RETURNS							
				Everett	1	14	14.0

PASSING

SAN FRANCISCO	Att.	Comp.	Comp. Pct.	Yds.	Int.	Yds./ Att.	Yds./ Comp.
Young	45	27	60.0	287	1	6.4	10.6
DALLAS							
Aikman	18	14	77.8	177	0	9.8	12.6
Kosar	9	5	55.6	83	0	9.2	16.6
Harper	1	0	0.0	0	0	0.0	0.0
	28	19	67.9	260	0	9.3	13.7

January 30, 1994 at Atlanta, Ga.

(Attendance 72,817)

Cowboys and Bills Do It Again

Dallas repeated and Buffalo four-peated. And, for a change, the Super Bowl wasn't a blowout. At least this one was close as the third quarter began. That's when the Cowboys went ahead and pulled away for a 30-13 victory over the Bills in Super Bowl XXVIII.

Emmitt Smith was the Most Valuable Player. The Dallas star running back rushed for 132 yards on 30 carries and scored two touchdowns.

But Dallas had a star on defense, too. James Washington, a backup safety who started in a nickel defense because Buffalo started three wide receivers, was responsible for three turnovers and one touchdown.

The Bills led 13-6 after two quarters. "At halftime, guys were looking at each other, saying, 'Damn, these boys came to play,' " Dallas wide receiver Michael Irvin said of the Bills, who had already lost three straight Super Bowls. "If they had taken the second-half kickoff and gone down and scored (to make it 20-6), we would have said, 'Man, this one's slipping away.' "

That's when Washington made the play of the game. Dallas defensive tackle Leon Lett stripped the ball from Buffalo running back Thurman Thomas, and Washington scooped it up and ran 46 yards for the tying touchdown.

"I don't think I've ever seen a play in any football game that ignited an attitude among a team like that play," said Cowboys defensive coordinator Butch Davis. "It set the tempo for the second half."

Earlier, Washington had forced a fumble that set up the Cowboys' second field goal. And, in the fourth quarter with Buffalo threatening to tie the game, Washington intercepted a Jim Kelly pass.

Following Washington's touchdown, Smith took over when Dallas got the ball back. He carried the ball seven out of eight plays and scored on a 15-yard run. In the fourth quarter, Smith scored from one yard out. Eddie Murray kicked three field goals for the Cowboys.

The Dallas defense limited the Bills to 87 yards on the ground and 5-of-17 efficiency on third downs. Thomas had his third straight miserable Super Bowl performance. He gained only 37 yards on 16 carries and fumbled twice. Later he admitted that his second fumble lost the game for the Bills. Kelly put the ball into the air 50 times, completing 31 of them, but he was unable to lead Buffalo to a score in the second half.

The Bills did look good in the first half, when Thomas scored on a four-yard run and Steve Christie kicked two field goals.

Again, I am disappointed that we lost the ballgame," said Bills defensive end Bruce Smith. "As far as embarassing, I think at any point and time that you sustain a loss, you have to hold your head up, especially if you gave it all you could. I think that is what we did today."

Emmitt Smith played with a separated shoulder. "The offensive line did a great job," he said. "They opened up holes for me to run the football. They controlled the whole line of scrimmage in the second half."

The Dallas victory was its fourth in a Super Bowl, tying a record held by Pittsburgh and San Francisco. The Cowboys have also played in a record seven Super Bowls. For Buffalo, the Super Bowl records are all negative ones. But at least they keep getting there.

LINEUPS

DALL.		BUFF.
	OFFENSE	
Harper	WR	Beebe
Tuinei	LT	Fina
Newton	LG	Parker
Gesek	C	Hull
Gogan	RG	Davis
E. Williams	RT	Ballard
Novacek	TE	Metzelaars
Irvin	WR	Reed
Aikman	QB	Kelly
E. Smith	RB	Thomas
D. Johnston	RB-WR	Brooks
	DEFENSE	
Tolbert	LE	Hansen
Casillas	LT/NT	Wright
Lett	RT/RE	B. Smith
Haley	RE/LOLB	Patton
Norton	MLB/LILB	Bennett
D. Smith	RLB/RILB	Maddox
Woodson	DB/ROLB	Talley
K. Smith	LCB	M. Washington
Brown	RCB	Odomes
Everett	SS	Jones
J. Washington	FS	Kelso

SUBSTITUTES

DALLAS		
	OFFENSE	
Kosar	Gainer	Coleman
Cornish	Hellestrae	K. Williams
Galbraith		
	DEFENSE	
Gant	Bates	D. Thomas
Patterson	Fishback	R. Jones
Edwards	Maryland	Jeffcoat
Vanderbeek	Hennings	Jones
Myles		
	KICKERS	
Murray	Jett	
BUFFALO		
	OFFENSE	
Reich	Davis	Gardner
Ritcher	Devlin	Lingner
Crafts	McKeller	Copeland
Tasker		
	DEFENSE	
Schulz	T. Smith	Henderson
Darby	Goganious	Harvey
Lodish	Barnett	Pike
M. Brown		
	KICKERS	
Christie	Mohr	

SCORING

DALLAS	6	0	14	10	- 30
BUFFALO	3	10	0	0	- 13

First Quarter
- Dall. Murray, 41 yard field goal
- Buff. Christie, 54 yard field goal
- Dall. Murray, 24 yard field goal

Second Quarter
- Buff. Thomas, 4 yard run
  PAT — Christie (kick)
- Buff. Christie, 28 yard field goal

Third Quarter
- Dall. J. Washington, 46 yard fumble return
  PAT — Murray (kick)
- Dall. E. Smith, 15 yard run
  PAT — Murray (kick)

Fourth Quarter
- Dall. E. Smith, 1 yard run
  PAT — Murray (kick)
- Dall. Murray, 20 yard run

TEAM STATISTICS

DALL.		BUFF.
20	First Downs-Total	22
6	First Downs-Rushing	6
14	First Downs-Pasiing	15
0	First Downs-Penalty	1
0	Fumbles-Number	3
0	Fumbles-Lost Ball	2
6	Penaties-Number	1
50	Yards Penalized	10
0	Missed Field Goals	0
64	Offensive Plays	80
341	Net Yards	314
5.3	Average Gain	3.9
1	Giveaways	3
3	Takeaways	1
+ 2	Difference	- 2

INDIVIDUAL STATISTICS

DALLAS	No.	Yds.	Avg.	BUFFALO	No.	Yds.	Avg.
				RUSHING			
E. Smith	30	132	4.4	K. Davis	9	38	4.2
K. Williams	1	6	6.0	Thomas	16	37	2.3
Aikman	1	3	3.0	Kelly	2	12	0.0
Johnston	1	0	0.0		27	87	3.2
Kosar	1	-1	-1.0				
Coleman	1	-3	-3.0				
	35	137	3.9				
				RECEIVING			
Irvin	5	66	13.2	Brooks	7	63	9.0
Novacek	5	26	5.2	Thomas	7	52	7.4
E. Smith	4	26	6.5	Reed	6	75	12.5
Harper	3	75	25.0	Beebe	6	60	10.0
Johnston	2	14	7.0	K. Davis	3	-5	-1.7
	19	207	10.9	Metzelaars	1	8	8.0
				McKeller	1	7	7.0
					31	260	8.4
				PUNTING			
Jett	4		43.8	Mohr	5		37.6
				PUNT RETURNS			
K. Williams	1	5	5.0	Copeland	1	5	5.0
K. Williams	1FC			Copeland	1FC		
				KICKOFF RETURNS			
K. Williams	1	50	50.0	Copeland	4	82	20.5
Gant	1	22	22.0	Beebe	2	62	31.0
	2	72	36.0		6	144	24.0
				INTERCEPTION RETURNS			
J. Washington	1	12	12.0	Odomes	1	41	41.0

PASSING

	Att.	Comp.	Comp. Pct.	Yds.	Int.	Yds./ Att.	Yds./ Comp.	Yards Lost Tackled
DALLAS								
Aikman	27	19	70.4	207	1	7.7	10.9	3
BUFFALO								
Kelly	50	31	62.0	260	1	5.1	8.4	33

UseName(Nickname)-Positions	Team by Year	See Section	Hgt.	Wgt.	College	Int	Pts
Abbott, Vince K	87-88SD	5	6'	207	Washington, Fullerton State		100
Abercrombie, Walter HB	82-87Pit 88Phi	23	6'	207	Baylor		174
Abraham, Robert LB	82-86Hou		6'1"	226	N. Carolina State	2	
Abramowitz, Sid OT-OG	83Bal 84Sea 85NYJ 87Ind		6'6"	281	Air Force, Tulsa		
Abrams, Bobby LB	90-91NYG 92Dal 92Cle 92NYG 93Dal 93Mia		6'3"	230	Michigan		
Ache, Steve LB	87Min		6'3"	229	SW Missouri State		
Achica, George DT	83-85USFL 85Ind		6'5"	260	Southern Calif.		
Acker, Bill NT-DT	80-81StL 82KC 83-84Buf 87KC		6'3"	255	Texas		
Ackerman, Richard DT	82-84SD 84,87Raid		6'4"	258	Memphis State		
Acorn, Fred DB	84TB		5'10"	185	Texas	1	
Adams, Curtis HB	86-87SD	2	6'0"	194	Central Michigan		30
Adams, David HB	87Dal		5'6"	170	Arizona		6
Adams, Ernie LB	87Det		6'2"	226	Illinois		
Adams, George FB	85NYG 86KJ 87-89NYG 90-91NE	2	6'1"	225	Kentucky		42
Adams, Michael DB	87-88NO 89Phx		5'10"	195	Arkansas State		
Adams, Scott OT	92-93Min		6'5"	287	Georgia		
Adams, Stanley LB	84Raid		6'2"	215	Memphis State		
Adams, Stefon DB	86-90Raid 90Cle 90Mia	3	5'10"	189	East Carolina	2	2
Adams, Theo OT	92Sea 93TB		6'4"	298	Hawaii		
Adams, Willis WR	79-85Cle	2	6'2"	196	Houston		12
Adickes, John C	87-88Chi 89Min		6'3"	264	Baylor		
Adickes, Mark OG	84-85USFL 86-89KC 90-91Was 92XJ		6'4"	278	Baylor		6
Adkins, Kevin C	87KC		6'1"	250	Oklahoma		
Adkins, Sam QB	77-83Sea	1	6'2"	214	Wichita State		
Affholter, Erik WR	91GB		6'	183	Southern Calif.		
Age, Louis OT	92Chi		6'7"	350	Southwestern La.		
Agee, Mel DE	91Ind 92-93Atl		6'5"	294	Illinois		
Agee, Tommie FB	88Sea 89KC 90-93Dal	2	6'	218	Auburn		12
Agnew, Ray DE	90-93NE		6'3"	272	N. Carolina State		
Aguiar, Louis K	91-93NYJ	4	6'2"	200	Utah State		3
Ahanotu, Chidi DE-DT	93TB		6'2"	280	California		
Ahrens, Dave LB	81-84StL 85-87Ind 88Det 89Mia 90Sea		6'3"	238	Wisconsin	1	6
Aikens, Carl WR	87Raid		6'1"	185	Northern Illinois		18
Aikman, Troy QB	89-93Dal	12	6'4"	216	Oklahoma, U.C.L.A.		6
Akiu, Mike WR	85-86Hou		5'9"	182	Hawaii		6
Albright, Ira NT-FB	87Buf		6'	285	Northeastern Okla.		
Albritton, Vince DB	84-91Dal		6'2"	215	Washington	1	
Aldridge, Jerry FB	80SF		6'2"	220	Angelo State		
Aldridge, Melvin DB	93Hou		6'2"	195	Murray State		
Alex, Keith OG	93Atl		6'4"	307	Texas A&M		
Alexander, Bruce DB	89-91Det 92-93Mia		5'9"	171	Stephen F. Austin	2	
Alexander, Charles HB-FB	79-85Cin	2	6'1"	224	Louisiana State		90
Alexander, Dan OG-OT	77-89NYJ		6'4"	261	Louisiana State		
Alexander, David OT-OG-C	87-93Phi		6'3"	276	Tulsa		
Alexander, Elijah LB	92TB 93Den		6'2"	230	Kansas State		
Alexander, Harold K	93Atl	4	6'2"	224	Appalachian State		
Alexander, Jeff FB	89,92Den	2	6'	232	Southern U.		12
Alexander, Mike WR	89Raid 90KJ 91Buf	2	6'3"	195	Penn State		6
Alexander, Ray WR	84Den 85-86CFL 87HJ 88-89Dal		6'4"	195	Florida A&M		42
Alexander, Robert HB	82-83LA 85USFL		6'	185	West Virginia		
Alexander, Rogers LB	86NYJ 87NE		6'3"	222	Penn State		
Alexander, Vincent FB	87NO		5'10"	205	Southern Miss.		6
Alexis, Alton WR	80Cin		6'	184	Tulane		
Alford, Lynwood LB	87NO		6'3"	220	Syracuse		
Allegre, Raul K	83Bal 84-85Ind 86-91NYG 91NYJ	5	5'10"	167	Montana, Texas		594
Allen, Anthony WR	83-85USFL 85-86Atl 87-88Was 89SD	2	5'11"	182	Washington		48
Allen, Carl DB	77-82StL 83-85USFL		6'	186	Southern Miss.	16	6
Allen, Earl DB	87Hou		5'11"	193	Houston		
Allen, Egypt DB	87Chi		6'	203	Texas Christian		
Allen, Eric DB	88-93Phi		5'10"	183	Arizona State	31	30
Allen, Gary HB	82Hou 83-84Dal	23	5'10"	183	Hawaii		12
Allen, Greg HB	85Cle 86TB		5'11"	200	Florida State		
Allen, Harvey DB	87SD		6'3"	215	Nevada-Las Vegas		
Allen, Jeff DB	80Mia 82SD		5'11'	190	Cal.-Davis	1	
Allen, Kevin OT	85Phi		6'5"	284	Indiana		
Allen, Marcus HB	82-92Raid 93KC	2	6'2"	205	Southern Calif.		678
Allen, Marvin HB	88-91NE	23	5'10"	215	Tulane		12
Allen, Patrick DB	84-90Hou	3	5'10"	180	Utah State	7	
Allen, Terry HB	91-912in 93KJ	2	5'10"	189	Clemson		108
Allerman, Kurt LB	77-79StL 80-81GB 82-84StL 85Det		6'3"	222	Penn State		
Allert, Ty LB	86-87SD 87-89Phi 90Den 90Sea		6'2"	233	Texas		
Allred, Brian DB	93Sea		5'10"	175	Sacramento State		
Alm, Jeff DT	90-93Hou		6'6"	284	Notre Dame		
	November 1993 — Committed suicide						
Almodobar, Beau WR	87NYG		5'9"	180	Norwich		
Alphin, Gerald WR	90-91		6'3"	220	Kansas State		
Alston, Lyneal WR	87Pit		6'1"	205	Southern Miss.		12
Alston, O'Brien LB	88-89Ind 90KJ		6'6"	246	Maryland		
Alt, John OT	84-93KC		6'8"	296	Iowa		
Althoff, Jim DT	87Chi		6'3"	278	Winona State		
Alvarez, Wilson K	81Sea	5	6'	165	Southeastern La.		23
Alvers, Steve TE-C	81Buf 82NYJ		6'4"	240	Miami (Fla.)		
Alvord, Steve DT	87StL 88Phx		6'4"	272	Washington		
Ambrose, Ashley DB	92-93Ind		5'10"	177	Miss. Valley St.		6
Anders, Kimble HB	91-93KC	2	5'11"	219	Houston		
Andersen, Morten K	82-93NO	5	6'2"	210	Michigan State		1202
Anderson, Alfred FB	84-91Min	23	6'1"	219	Baylor		162
Anderson, Aric LB	87GB		6'2"	200	Millikin		
Anderson, Anthony HB	79Pit 80Atl 83,85USFL		6'	197	Temple		6
Anderson, Anthony DB	87SD		6'2"	205	Grambling		
Anderson, Brad WR	84-85Chi		6'2"	197	Arizona		6
Anderson, Curtis DE	79KC 83-85USFL		6'6"	250	Central St.-Ohio		
Anderson, Darren DB	92NE 92-93TB		5'10"	180	Toledo	1	
Anderson, Don DB	85Ind 87TB		5'10"	196	Purdue	1	
Anderson, Dwayne DB	87StL		6'	205	S.M.U.		
Anderson, Eddie DB	86Sea 88-93Raid		6'1"	196	Fort Valley State	18	18
Anderson, Erick LB	93KC		6'1"	235	Michigan		
Anderson, Fred DE-DT	78Pit 79BH 80-82Sea 84USFL		6'4"	238	Oregon State, Prairie View		
Anderson, Gary HB-WR	83-85USFL 85-88SD 89HO 90-93TB 93Det	23	6'1"	185	Arkansas		192
Anderson, Gary K	82-93Pit	5	5'11'	169	Syracuse		1239
Anderson, Herbie DB	91Hou		5'9"	183	Texas A&I		
Anderson, Jesse TE	90-92TB 92Pit 93NO		6'2"	245	Mississippi State		12
Anderson, John LB	78-89GB		6'3"	226	Michigan	23	10
Anderson, Kim DB	80-83Bal 84Ind 85USFL	3	5'11"	183	Arizona State	7	6
Anderson, Larry DB	78-81Pit 82-83Bal 84Ind	3	5'11"	183	Louisiana Tech	2	6

UseName(Nickname)-Positions	Team by Year	See Section	Hgt.	Wgt.	College	Int	Pts
Anderson, Marcus WR	81Chi 83-85USFL		6'	178	Tulane		12
Anderson, Melvin WR	87Pit		5'11"	175	Minnesota		
Anderson, Neal HB	86-93Chi	2	5'11"	210	Florida		426
Anderson Ottis (O.J.) HB-FB	79-86StL 86-92NYG	2	6'2"	220	Miami (Fla.)		518
Anderson, Richie FB-HB	93NYJ		6'2"	215	Penn State		
Anderson, Stuart LB	82-83Was 84Cle 85Was		6'1"	238	Virginia		
Anderson, Vickey Ray FB	80GB 83USFL		6'	205	Oklahoma		
Anderson, Willie (Flipper) WR	88-93LA	2	6'	169	U.C.L.A.		126
Andolsek, Eric OG	88-91Det		6'2"	284	Louisiana State		
	June 1992 — killed in accident						
Andrews, George LB	79-84LA		6'3"	224	Nebraska	2	
Andrews, Ricky LB	90Sea		6'2"	236	Washington		
Angelo, Jim OG	87Phi		6'3"	275	Indiana (Pa.)		
Andrews, Mitch TE	87Den		6'2"	239	Louisiana State		
Andrews, Tom OT-C-OG	84-85Chi 87Sea		6'4"	265	Louisville		
Andrews, William FB	79-83Atl 84-85KJ 86Atl	2	6'	206	Auburn		246
Andrus, Sheldon DT-NT	86-87NO		6'1"	271	Nicholls State		
Ankrom, Scott DB	89Dal 90KJ		6'1"	194	Texas Christian		
Anno, Sam LB	87LA 87-88Min 89-91TB 92-93SD		6'2"	236	Southern Calif.		
Anthony, Terrence DB	87StL		5'10"	183	Iowa State		
Anthony, Terry WR	90-91TB		6'	200	Florida State		
Anthony, Tyrone HB-FB	84-85NO	23	5'11"	212	North Carolina		6
Antrum, Glenn WR	89NE		5'1"	175	Connecticut		
Apke, Steve LB	87Pit		6'1'	222	Pittsburgh		
Apuna, Ben LB	80NYG 83-84USFL		6'1"	222	Arizona State		
Arapostathis, Evan K	86StL	4	5'9"	160	Eastern Illinois		
Arbubakrr, Hasson DE	83TB 84Min		6'4"	250	Texas Tech		
Arbuckle, Charles TE	92-93Ind	2	6'2"	248	U.C.L.A.		6
Archambeau, Lester DE	90-92GB 93Atl		6'4"	274	Stanford		
Archer, David QB	84-87Atl 88Was 89SD 92Phi	12	6'2"	207	Iowa State		12
Ard, Billy OG	81-88NYG 89-91GB		6'3"	265	Wake Forest		
Ariey, Mike OT	89GB		6'5"	285	San Diego State		
Ariri, Obed K	83USFL 84TB 87Was	5	5'8"	168	Clemson		110
Armstead, Jessie LB	93NYG		6'1"	238	Miami (Fla.)	1	
Armstrong, Adger FB	80-82Hou 83-85TB	2	6'	213	Texas A&I		54
Armstrong, Bruce OT-OG	87-93NE		6'4"	284	Louisville		
Armstrong, Harvey NT	82-84Phi 86-90Ind		6'3"	265	S.M.U.	1	
Armstrong, Jimmy DB	87Dal		5'8"	166	Appalachian State		
Armstrong, John DB	87Buf		5'9"	190	Richmond		
Armstrong, Trace DE	89-93Chi		6'4"	270	Arizona State, Florida		
Armstrong, Tyji TE	92-93TB	2	6'4"	255	Mississippi		12
Arnold, David DB	89Pit		6'3"	208	Michigan		
Arnold, Jim K	83-85KC 86-93Det	4	6'2"	215	Vanderbilt		
Arnold, John WR	79-80Det 84-85USFL		5'10"	175	Wyoming		
Arnold, Walt TE	80-81LA 82-83Hou 84Was 84-87KC	2	6'3"	228	New Mexico		48
Aronson, Doug OG	87Cin		6'3"	293	San Diego State		
Arp, John OT	87Chi		6'5"	275	Lincoln		
Arthur, Mike C	91-92Cin 93NE		6'3"	277	Texas A&M		
Arvie, Herman OT	93Cle		6'4"	320	Grambling		
Ashe, Richard DE	90LA		6'4"	260	Humboldt State		
Ashley, Walker Lee LB	83-84Min 85LJ 86-88Min 89KC		6'	236	Penn State	2	6
Ashmore, Darryl OT	93LA		6'7"	300	Northwestern		
Asmus, Jim K	87SF		6'2"	195	Hawaii		
Atkins, Gene DB	87-93NO	3	6'1"	200	Florida A&M	17	
Atkins, Kelvin LB	83Chi		6'3"	235	Illinois		
Atkins, Steve FB-HB	79-81GB 81Phi	2	6'	216	Maryland		18
Atkinson, Jess K	85NYG 85StL 86-87Was 88Ind	5	5'9"	167	Maryland		60
Atkinson, Ricky DB	87NE		6'	175	Southern Conn. St.		
Atwater, Steve DB	89-93Den		6'3"	217	Arkansas	14	
Audick, Dan OT-OG	77StL 78-80SD 81-82SF 83-84StL		6'3"	252	Hawaii		
Auer, Jim DE	87Phi		6'7"	275	Georgia		
Auer, Scott OT-OG	84-85KC		6'5"	255	Michigan State		
Auer, Todd LB	87GB		6'1"	230	Western Illinois		
Aughtman, Dowe DE	84Dal		6'3"	260	Auburn		
August, Steve OT	77-84Sea 84Pit		6'5"	265	Tulsa		
Augustyniak, Mike FB	81-83NYJ 84KJ	2	5'11"	225	Purdue		48
Aupiu, David LB	87LA		6'2"	235	Brigham Young		
Austin, Cliff HB	83NO 84-86Atl 87TB	23	6'	203	Clemson		12
Austin, Kent QB	86StL		6'1"	195	Mississippi		
Auzenne, Troy OT	92-93Chi		6'7"	286	California		
Avery, Steve FB	89Hou 91GB		6'1"	216	Northern Michigan		
Awalt, Rob TE	87StL 88-89Phx 90-91Dal 92-93Buf	2	6'5"	248	Nevada-Reno, San Diego State		60
Aydelette, Buddy OT	80GB 81KJ 83-85USFL 87Pit 88KJ		6'4"	256	Alabama		
Ayers, John OG-OT	77-86SF 87Den		6'5"	258	Texas. West Texas State		
Ayers, Marvin DE	87Phi		6'5"	265	Grambling		
Azelby, Joe LB	84Buf		6'1"	225	Harvard		
Baab, Mike C	82-87Cle 88-89NE 90-91Cle 92KC		6'4"	270	Texas		
Baack, Steve DE-DT-NT-OG	84-87Det 88PJ		6'4"	264	Oregon		
Badanjek, Rick FB	86Was 87-88Atl	2	5'8"	217	Maryland		6
Baham, Curtis DB	87Sea		5'11"	180	Tulane		
Bahr, Chris K	76-79Cin 80-81Oak 82-88Raid 89SD	5	5'10"	172	Penn State		1213
Bahr, Matt K	79-80Pit 81SF 81-89Cle 90-92NYG 93Phi 93NE	5	5'10"	173	Penn State		1209
Bailey, Carlton LB	88-92Buf 93NYG		6'2"	239	North Carolina	1	
Bailey, Clarence FB	87Mia		5'11"	220	Hampton Institute		
Bailey, David DE	90Phi		6'4"	240	Oklahoma State		
Bailey, Don C	84-85 Ind		6'3"	264	Miami (Fla.)		
Bailey, Edwin OG	81-91Sea		6'4"	271	S. Carolina State		
Bailey, Elmer WR	80-81Mia 82Bal 84USFL		6'	195	Lincoln (Mo.), Macalester, Minnesota		
Bailey, Eric TE	87Phi 88XJ		6'5"	240	Kansas State		
Bailey, Harold WR	81-82Hou 83KJ		6'2"	195	Oklahoma State		
Bailey, Johnny HB	90-91Chi 92-93Phx	23	5'8"	180	Texas A&I		36
Bailey, Robert DB	91-93LA		5'9"	176	Miami (Fla.)	5	6
Bailey, Stacey WR	82-90Atl	2	6'	158	San Jose State		78
Bailey, Tom HB-FB	71-74Phi 75KJ	2	6'2"	211	Florida State		12
Bailey, Victor WR	93Phi	2	6'2"	196	Missouri		6
Bain, Bill OG-OT	75GB 76Den 77KJ 78Den 78NYG 79-85LA 86NYJ 86NE		6'4"	279	Colorado, Southern Calif.		
Baker, Al (Bubba) DE	80-82Det 83-86StL 87Cle 88Min 89-90Cle		6'6"	265	Colorado State	4	
Baker, Charlie LB	80-87StL		6'2"	226	New Mexico		
Baker, Jerry DT	83Den		6'2"	297	Tulane		
Baker, Jesse DE	79-85Hou 86Dal 86-87Hou		6'5"	269	Jacksonville State		8
Baker, Keith WR	85Phi		5'10"	185	Texas A&M, Texas Southern		
Baker, Myron LB	93Chi		6'1"	228	Louisiana Tech		12
Baker, Ron OG	78-79Bal 80-88Phi		6'4"	260	Oklahoma State		

UseName(Nickname)-Positions	Team by Year	See Section	Hgt	Wgt	College	Int	Pts
Baker, Stan WR	87Det		5'10"	165	Olivet		
Baker, Stephen WR	87-92NYG	2	5'8"	160	Fresno State		126
Baker, Tony HB	86Atl 86Cle 87BW 88Cle 89Phx		5'10"	182	East Carolina		
Baldinger, Brian C-OG-OT	82-84Dal 85KJ 86-87Dal 88-91Ind 92-93Phi		6'4"	271	Duke		
Baldinger, Gary DE-NT	86-88KC 90-92Buf		6'2"	264	Wake Forest		
Baldinger, Rich OT-OG	82-83NYG 83-92KC 93NE		6'4"	288	Wake Forest		
Baldischwiler, Karl OT	78-82Det 83Bal 84ZJ 85-86Ind		6'5"	267	Oklahoma		
Baldwin, Keith DE	82-85Cle 86KJ 87-88SD		6'4"	263	Texas A&M		
Baldwin, Don DE	87NYJ		6'3"	263	Purdue		
Baldwin, Randy FB-HB	91Min 92-93Cle	23	5'10"	216	Mississippi		6
Baldwin, Tom DT-NT-DE	84-86NYJ 87FJ 88NYJ		6'4"	274	Wisonsin, Tulsa		
Ball, Eric HB-FB	89-93Cin	23	6'2"	215	U.C.L.A.		66
Ball, Jerry NT-DT	87-93Det		6'1"	298	S.M.U.		8
Ball, Michael DB	88-93Ind		6'	216	Southern U.	1	6
Ballage, Pat DB	86-87Ind		6'1"	204	Notre Dame		
Ballard, Howard (House) OT	88-93Buf		6'6"	325	Alabama A&M		
Ballard, Quinton DT	83Bal		6'3"	289	Elon		
Banes, Joey OT	90Ind		6'7"	282	Houston		
Banker, Ted OG-C-OT	84-88NYJ 89Cle 90KJ		6'2"	270	SE Missouri St.		
Banks, Carl LB	84-92NYG 93Was		6'4"	238	Michigan State	3	6
Banks, Chip LB	82-86 Cle 87SD 88HO 89-92Ind 93SJ		6'4"	243	Southern Calif.	9	14
Banks, Chuck FB	86Hou 87Ind	2	6'2"	226	West Virginia Tech		
Banks, Fred WR	85Cle 87-93Mia 93Chi	2	5'10"	179	Liberty Baptist		60
Banks, Gordon WR	80-81NO 83-85USFL 85-87Dal	23	5'10"	174	Stanford		6
Banks, Robert DE	88 Hou 89-90Cle		6'5"	259	Notre Dame		
Banks, Roy WR	87-88Ind		5'10"	192	Eastern Illinois		
Bankston, Michael NT	92-93Phx		6'2"	285	Sam Houston State		
Barbaro, Gary DB	76-83KC 84-85USFL		6'4"	203	Nicholls State	42	24
Barbay, Roland NT	87Sea 88KJ		260	260	Louisiana State		
Barber, Chris DB	87Cin 88AJ 89Cin 92TB		6'	187	North Carolina A&T		
Barber, Kurt LB-DE	92-93NYJ		6'4"	241	Southern Calif.		
Barber, Marion FB	82-88NYJ	2	6'3"	226	Minnesota		24
Barber, Mike TE-WR	76-81Hou 82-85LA 85Den	2	6'3"	236	Louisiana Tech		102
Barber, Mike WR	89SF 89Phx 89SF 90-91Cin 92TB	2	5'10"	172	Marshall		12
Barker, Bryan K	90-93KC	4	6'1"	187	Santa Clara		
Barker, Leo LB	84-91Cin		6'2"	226	New Mexico State	3	6
Barker, Roy DT	92-93Min		6'4"	286	North Carolina		
Barker, Tony LB	92Was		6'2"	230	Rice		
Barksdale, Rod WR	86Raid 87Dal 88KJ	2	6'	189	Arizona		18
Barlow, Corey DB	93Phi		5'9"	182	Auburn		
Barnes, Earnest DE	83Bal		6'4"	260	Mississippi State		
Barnes, Jeff LB	77-81Oak 82-87Raid		6'2"	223	California	5	
Barnes, Johnnie WR	92-93SD	2	6'1"	180	Hampton U.		
Barnes, Lew WR	86Chi 87BL 88Atl 89KC	3	5'8"	163	Oregon		6
Barnes, Reggie LB	93Pit		6'1"	235	Oklahoma		
Barnes, Roosevelt LB	82-85Det		6'2"	224	Purdue	3	
Barnett, Bill DE-NT	80-85Mia		6'4"	258	Nebraska		
Barnett, Buster TE	81-84Buf		6'5"	228	Jackson State		6
Barnett, Dean TE	83Den		6'2"	225	Nevada-Las Vegas		
Barnett, Doug DE-C	82-83LA 84KJ 85Was 87Atl		6'3"	253	Azusa Pacific		
Barnett, Fred WR	90-93Phi	2	6'	203	Arkansas State		108
Barnett, Harlon DB	90-92Cle 93NE		5'11"	200	Michigan State	1	
Barnett, Oliver DE-DT-NT	90-92Atl 93Buf		6'3"	288	Kentucky		6
Barnett, Tim WR	91-93KC	2	6'1"	209	Jackson State		60
Barnett, Vincent DB	87Cle		6'1"	200	Arkansas State		
Barney, Milton WR	87Atl	2	5'9"	156	Alcorn State		12
Barnhardt, Tommy K	87NO 87Chi 88Was 89-93NO		6'3"	205	East Carolina, North Carolina		
Barnwell, Malcolm WR	81Oak 82-84Raid 85Was 85NO	2	5'11"	184	Virginia Union		24
Barrett, Dave FB	82TB 83KJ		6'	230	Houston		
Barrett, Reggie WR	91-93Det		6'3"	215	Texas-El Paso		6
Barrie, Sebastian DE	92GB		6'3"	270	Liberty		
Barrow, Micheal LB	93Hou		6'1"	236	Miami (Fla.)		
Barrows, Scott OG-C	86-88Det		6'2"	278	West Virginia		
Bartalo, Steve HB	87TB 88SF		5'9"	200	Colorado State		6
Bartkowski, Steve QB	75-85Atl 85Was 86LA	12	6'4"	215	California		66
Bartlett, Doug DE-DT	88Phi		6'2"	255	Northern Illinois		
Bartlewski, Rich TE	90Raid 91Atl		6'5"	250	Fresno State		
Bartley, Ephesians LB	92Phi		6'2"	213	Florida		
Barton, Harris OT	87-93SF		6'4"	282	North Carolina		
Bartrum, Mike TE	93KC		6'4"	234	Marshall		
Baschnagel, Brian WR-DB	76-84Chi 85KJ	23	5'11"	187	Ohio State		60
Bass, Don WR-TE	78-81Cin 82NO	2	6'2"	219	Houston		84
Bates, Bill DB	83-93Dal		6'1"	200	Tennessee	14	
Bates, Michael WR	93Sea	3	5'10"	189	Arizona		
Bates, Patrick DB	93Raid		6'3"	220	Texas A&M	1	
Battaglia, Matt LB	87Phi		6'2"	225	Louisville		
Battle, Ralph DB	84Cin		6'2"	205	Jacksonville State		
Battle, Ron TE	81-82LA		6'3"	220	North Texas State		6
Batton, Bobby HB	80NYJ	1	5'11"	185	Nev.-Las Vegas		
Baty, Greg TE	86-87NE 87LA 88Phx 90-93Mia	2	6'5"	241	Stanford		42
Bauer, Hank HB-FB	77-83SD	2	5'10"	200	Cal. Lutheran		120
Baugh, Tom C	86-88KC 89Cle		6'3"	274	Southern Illinois		
Baumann, Charlie K	91Mia 91-92NE	5	6'1"	203	West Virginia		97
Baumhower, Bob NT	77-84Mia 85KJ 86Mia		6'5"	261	Alabama	1	12
Bavaro, David LB	90Phx 91Buf 92Min 93NE		6'	234	Syracuse		
Bavaro, Mark TE	85-90NYG 92Cle 93Phi	2	6'4"	245	Notre Dame		216
Bax, Carl OG-OT	89-90TB		6'4"	290	Missouri		
Baxley, Rob OT	92Phx 93KJ		6'5"	287	Iowa		
Baxter, Brad FB	89-93NYJ	2	6'1"	233	Alabama State		180
Baxter, Fred TE	93NYJ		6'3"	250	Auburn		6
Bayless, Martin DB	84StL 84-86Buf 87-91SD 92-93KC		6'2"	202	Bowling Green	9	
Bayless, Rick FB	89Min		6'	202	Iowa		
Baylor, John DB	89-93Ind		6'	203	Southern Miss.	8	
Beach, Pat TE	82-83Bal 84NJ 85-91Ind 92Phi 93Phx	2	6'4"	247	Washington State		84
Beach, Sanjay WR	89NYJ 91SF 92GB 93SF	2	6'	189	Colorado State		12
Beals, Shawn WR	88Phi	3	5'10"	178	Idahoa State		
Bealles, Bill OT	87Mia		6'7"	290	Northern Iowa		
Beamon, Willie DB	93NYG		5'11"	170	Northern Iowa	1	
Beasley, Tom DT-DE-NT	78-83Pit 84-86Was		6'5"	250	Virginia Tech		
Beauford, Clayton WR	87Cle		5'11"	190	Auburn		
Beavers, Scott OG	90Den		6'4"	277	Georgia Tech		
Becker, Dave DB	80Chi		6'2"	190	Iowa		
Becker, Kurt OG	82-88Chi 89LA 90Chi		6'5"	271	Michigan		
Beckles, Ian OG	90-93TB		6'1"	295	Indiana		

UseName(Nickname)-Positions	Team by Year	See Section	Hgt	Wgt	College	Int	Pts
Beckman, Brad TE	88NYG 89Atl Dec. 18, 1989 — Died in Automobile Accident	2	6'3"	238	Nebraska-Omaha		6
Beckman, Ed TE	77-84KC	2	6'4"	229	Florida State		8
Beebe, Don WR	89-93Buf	23	5'11"	177	Western Illinois, Aurora, Chadron St.		84
Beecham, Earl HB	87NYG		5'8"	180	Bucknell		
Beecher, Willie K	87Mia	5	5'10"	170	Utah State		21
Beekley, Bruce LB	80GB 83USFL		6'2"	225	Oregon		
Beemer, Bob DE	87Det		6'5"	231	Toledo		
Beeson, Terry LB	77-81Sea 82SF 84-85USFL		6'3"	239	Kansas	1	
Behning, Mark OT	86Pit 87FJ		6'6"	290	Nebraska		
Belcher, Kevin OG	83-84NYG		6'3"	266	Texas-El Paso		
Belcher, Kevin OT	85Raid 87Den		6'6"	310	Wisconsin		
Belichick, Bill	HC91-93Cle				Wesleyan		
Belk, Rocky WR	83Cle		6'	187	Miami (Fla.)		
Belk, Veno TE	87Buf		6'3"	233	Michigan State		
Bell, Albert WR	88GB		6'	170	Alabama		
Bell, Anthony LB	86-87StL 88-90Phx 91Det 92Raid		6'3"	235	Michigan State	2	
Bell, Billy DB	89Hou 91KC		5'10"	170	Lamar	1	
Bell, Bobby LB	84NYJ 87Chi		6'3"	217	Missouri		
Bell, Greg HB	84-87Buf 87-89LA 90Raid	2	5'10"	210	Notre Dame		348
Bell, Jerry TE	82-86TB	2	6'5"	230	Arizona State		42
Bell, Ken HB-WR	86-89Den	23	5'10"	190	Boston College		
Bell, Kerwin QB	88Atl 89TB		6'2"	205	Florida		
Bell, Mark DE	79-80Sea 81KJ 82Sea 83Bal 84Ind		6'5"	241	Colorado State		
Bell, Mark WR	80-81StL		5'9"	175	Colorado State		
Bell, Mike DE	79-85KC 86SL 87-91KC		6'4"	257	Colorado State		
Bell, Nick HB	91-93Raid	2	6'2"	255	Iowa		42
Bell, Richard HB	90Pit	2	6'	200	Nebraska		6
Bell, Rick HB	83Min		6'	205	St. John's		
Bell, Ricky FB-HB	77-81TB 82-83SD	2	6'2"	218	Southern Calif.		114
Bell, Theo WR	76Pit 77FJ 78-80Pit 81-85TB	23	6-0	185	Arizona		48
Bell, Todd DB	81-84Chi 85HO 86-87Chi 88-89Phi		6'1"	208	Ohio State	7	12
Bellamy, Mike WR	90Phi		6'	195	Illinois		
Bellamy, Victor DB	87Phi		6'1"	195	Syracuse		
Bellinger, Rodney DB	84-86Buf		5'8"	186	Miami (Fla.)	4	6
Bellini, Mark WR	87-88Ind		5'11"	184	Brigham Young		
Belser, Jason DB	92-93Ind		5'9"	187	Oklahoma	4	
Belway, Brian DE	87Raid		6'6"	265	Calgary		
Bendross, Jesse WR	84-85SD 87Phi	2	6'	196	Alabama		
Bengen, Brant WR	87Sea		5'8"	172	Idaho		
Benirschke, Rolf K	77-86SD	5	6'	171	Cal.-Davis		766
Benish, Dan DT	83-86Atl 87Was 88KJ		6'5"	273	Clemson		
Benjamin, Guy QB	78-79Mia 80NO 81-83SF	1	6'4"	210	Stanford		
Benjamin, Ryan HB	93Cin		5'7"	183	U. of Pacific		
Bennett, Barry DT-NT-DE	78-81NO 82-88NYJ 88Min		6'4"	258	Concordia (Minn.)		
Bennett, Ben QB	84USFL 87Cin 88Chi		6'1"	200	Duke		
Benjamin, Bill LB	87Ind		6'3"	226	San Jose State		
Bennett, Antoine DB	91-92Cin		5'11"	185	New Mexico State		
Bennett, Charles DE	87Mia		6'5"	257	Southwestern La.		
Bennett, Cornelius LB	87-93Buf		6'2"	235	Alabama	10	12
Bennett, Edgar FB	92-93GB	2	6'	223	Florida State		60
Bennett, Leeman	HC77-82Atl HC85-86TB				Kentucky		
Bennett, Lewis WR	87NO	2	5'11"	175	Florida A&M		6
Bennett, Monte NT-DE	81NO 83-85USFL 87SD		6'5"	265	Kansas State		
Bennett, Roy DB	88-89SD		6'2"	195	Jackson State	4	6
Bennett, Tony LB	90-93GB		6'2"	240	Mississippi		6
Bennett, Woody FB	79-80NYJ 80-88Mia	23	6'2"	227	Miami (Fla.)		78
Benson, Brad OT-OG-C	77-87NYG		6'3"	262	Penn State		
Benson, Charles DE	83-84Mia 85Ind 87Det		6'3"	267	Baylor	1	
Benson, Cliff TE	84-85Atl 87Was 87-88NO	2	6'4"	238	Purdue		
Benson, Mitchell NT-DT	89-90Ind 91SD		6'4"	302	Texas Christian		
Benson, Thomas LB	84-85Atl 86-87SD 88NE 89-92Raid		6'2"	238	Oklahoma	1	
Benson, Troy LB	86-89NYJ 90ZJ		6'2"	235	Pittsburgh	1	
Bentley, Albert HB	84-85USFL 85-91Ind 92Pit	23	5'11"	213	Miami (Fla.)		168
Bentley, Ray LB	86-92Buf 92Cin		6'2"	240	Central Michigan	3	6
Benyola, George K	87NYG		5'10"	195	Louisiana Tech		12
Bergeson, Eric DB	90LA		5'11"	192	Brigham Young		
Bergold, Scott OT	85StL 86XJ		6'7"	263	Wisconsin		
Bernard, Karl HB	87Det 88KJ	2	5'11"	205	Southwestern La.		12
Berns, Rick HB	79-80 TB 82-83Raid	2	6'2"	206	Nebraska		
Bernstine, Rod TE-FB-HB	87-92SD 93Den	2	6'3"	237	Texas A&M		138
Berry, Ed DB	86GB 87SD		5'10"	183	Utah State		
Berry, Latin DB	90LA 91-92Cle		5'10"	196	Oregon		
Berry, Louis K	87Atl		6'	193	Florida State		
Berry, Ray LB	87-92Min 93Sea		6'2"	227	Baylor	1	2
Berthusen, Bill DE	87Cin 87NYG		6'5"	290	Iowa State		
Bess, Gerald DB	87Min		6'	188	Tuskegee Inst.		
Bess, Rufus DB	79Oak 80-81Buf 82-87Min		5'9"	184	S. Carolina State	11	
Bessillieu, Don DB	79-81Mia 82StL 83Raid 84-85USFL	3	6'1"	200	Georgia Tech	5	6
Best, Greg DB	83Pit 84Cle		5'10"	185	Kansas State		6
Bethea, Larry DT-DE	78-83Dal 84-85USFL		6'5"	251	Michigan State		
Bethune, George LB	89-90LA		6'4"	240	Alabama		
Betters, Doug DE	78-87Mia		6'7"	262	Montana, Nevada-Reno		
Bettis, Jerome HB-FB	93LA	2	5'11"	243	Notre Dame		42
Beuerlein, Steve QB	88-90Raid 91-92Dal 93Phx	12	6'2"	205	Notre Dame		
Beverly, Dwight HB	87NO	2	5'11"	205	Illinois		12
Bianchini, Frank HB	87NE		5'8"	190	Hofstra		
Biasucci, Dean K	84,86-93Ind	5	6'	192	Stanford		698
Bickett, Duane LB	85-93Ind		6'5"	247	Southern Calif.	9	
Biekert, Greg LB	93Raid		6'2"	235	Colorado		
Bieniemy, Eric HB-FB	91-93SD	23	5'7"	210	Colorado		24
Bigby, Keiron WR	87Was		5'10"	177	Brown		
Biles, Ed	HC81-83Hou				Miami-Ohio		
Billups, Lewis DB	86-91Cin 92GB		5'11"	190	North Alabama	9	6
Bingham, Craig LB	82-84Pit 85SD 87Pit		6'2"	218	Syracuse		
Bingham, Dwight DE	87Atl		6'6"	265	Mississippi		
Bingham, Guy C-OG-OT	80-88NYJ 89-91Atl 92-93Was		6'3"	257	Montana		
Bird, Steve WR	83-84StL 84SD		5'11"	171	Eastern Kentucky		
Birden, J.J. WR	90-93KC	2	5'9"	160	Oregon		60
Birdsong, Carl K	81-85StL	4	6'	192	Southwestern Okla.		
Birdsong, Craig DB	87Hou		6'2"	217	North Texas State		
Bishop, Blaine DB	93Hou		5'8"	197	all State	1	
Bishop, Greg OT	93NYG		6'5"	298	U of Pacific		
Bishop, Keith C-OG	80Den 81FJ 82-89Den		6'3"	263	Nebraska, Baylor		
Black, Barry OG	87Raid		6'2"	280	Boise State		

UseName(Nickname)- Positions	Team by Year	See Section	Hgt.	Wgt.	College	Int	Pts
Black, James DC	87KC		6'4"	280	S. Carolina State		
Black, James HB	84Cle		5'11"	198	Akron		
Black, Mel LB	86-87NE		6'2"	228	Eastern Illinois		
Black, Mike K	83-87Det	4	6'1"	197	Arizona State		
Black, Mike OT-OG	86Phi 87NYG		6'4"	285	Sacramento State		
Black, Todd WR	87Chi		5'11"	174	Concordia		
Blackledge, Todd QB	83-87KC 88-89Pit	12	6'3"	224	Penn State		12
Blackmon, Don LB	81-87NE		6'3"	235	Tulsa	5	4
Blackmon, Robert DB	90-93Sea		6'	198	Baylor	6	6
Blackmore, Richard DB	79-82Phi 83SF		5'10"	174	Mississippi State	5	6
Blackshear, Jeff OG	93Sea		6'6"	325	Northeast La.		
Blackwell, Kelly TE	92Chi 93Dal		6'1"	255	Texas Christian		
Blackwood, Glenn DB	79-87Mia 88KJ		6'	187	Texas	29	6
Blackwood, Lyle DB	73-75Cin 76Sea 77-80Bal 82-86Mia	3	6'1"	190	Texas Christian	35	12
Blades, Bennie DB	88-93Det		6'1"	221	Miami (Fla.)	8	6
Blades, Brian WR	88-93Sea	2	5'11"	184	Miami (Fla.)		132
Blados, Brian OT	84-90Cin 91Ind 92TB		6'5"	300	North Carolina		
Blair, Paul OT	86-87Ch 88KJ 90Mini		6'4"	295	Oklahoma State		
Blair, Stanley DB	90Phx		6'	192	Oklahoma State, Southeastern Okla.		
Blakes, Jeff QB	92-93NYJ		6'	202	East Carolina		
Blake, Ricky FB	91Dal		6'2"	244	Alabama A&M		6
Blanchard, Cary K	92-93NYJ	5	6'1"	225	Oklahoma State		147
Bland, Carl WR	84-88Det 89-90GB	23	5'11"	182	Michigan		42
Blankenship, Brian OG	87-91Pit		6'1"	277	Nebraska-Omaha		
Blanton, Jerry LB	79-85KC		6'1"	231	Kentucky	1	
Blaylock, Anthony DB	88-91Cle 91-92SD 93Chi		5'11"	190	Winston-Salem St.	6	6
Bledsoe, Curtis HB-FB	81-82KC 83-85USFL		5'11"	215	San Diego State		
Bledsoe, Drew QB	93NE	12	6'5"	233	Washington State		
Bleier, Bob QB	87NE	1	6'3"	210	Richmond		6
Bligen, Dennis HB	84-86NYJ 86TB 87NYJ	2	5'11"	214	St. John's (N.Y.)		12
Blinka, Stan LB	79-83NYJ 85USFL		6'2"	230	Sam Houston St.	3	
Blount, Alvin HB	87Dal	2	5'9"	197	Maryland		18
Blount, Ed QB	87SF		6'	195	Washington State		
Blount, Eric HB	92-93Phx		5'9"	190	North Carolina		6
Blount, Tony DB	80NYG 83USFL		6'1"	195	Virginia		
Blue, Anthony DB	87Sea		5'9	185	Nevada-Las Vegas		
Blundin, Matt QB	92-93KC		6'6"	230	Virginia		
Boadway, Steve LB	87Det		6'4"	240	Arizona		
Board, Dwaine DE	79-88SF 88NO		6'5"	248	N. Carolina A&T		6
Boatner, Mack HB	83-85USFL 86TB		6'	220	Southeastern La.		
Boatswain, Harry OT	92-93SF		6'4"	295	New Haven		
Bob, Adam LB	89NYJ		6'2"	240	Texas A&M		
Bock, Joe C	87StL 87Buf		6'4"	254	Virginia		
Boddie, Tony HB	86-87Den		5'11"	198	Montana State		6
Boggs, Mark OT	87Ind		6'5"	301	Ball State		
Bohannon, Fred DB	82-83Pit 84USFL		6'	201	Miss. Valley St.		
Bohm, Ron DT	87StL		6'3"	250	Illinois		
Bojovic, Novo K	83-84USFL 85StL	5	5'10"	172	Central Michigan		20
Bokamper, Kim LB-DE	77-85Mia		6'6"	250	Concordia (Minn.), San Jose State	6	8
Bolcar, Ned LB	90Sea 91Mia 92KJ		6'1"	240	Notre Dame	1	
Bolden, Gary (The Mule) DT	87Phi		6'1"	275	Southwestern Okla.		
Bolden, Rickey OT-TE	84Cle 85USFL 86-89Cle		6'6"	274	S.M.U.		6
Bolinger, Russ OG-OT	76-77Det 78KJ 79-82Det 83-84LA 85USFL 85LA		6'5"	255	Cal.-Riverside, Long Beach State		
Bollinger, Brian OG	92-93SF		6'5"	285	North Carolina		
Bolton, Scott WR	88GB		6'	188	Auburn		
Bolzan, Scott OG	85USFL 85Cle		6'3"	280	Northern Illinois		
Bone, Warren DE	87GB		6'4"	260	Texas Southern		
Bonner, Brian LB	89Was		6'2"	225	Wisconsin, Minnesota		
Bonner, Melvin WR	93Den		6'3"	207	Baylor		
Bono, Steve QB	85-86Min 87-88Pit 89-93SF	12	6'4"	215	U.C.L.A.		12
Boone, Greg HB	87TB		5'9"	196	Duke		
Booty, John DB	88-90NYJ 91-92Phi 93Phx		6'	179	Texas Christian	10	
Borchardt, Jon OT-OG	79-84Buf 85-87Sea		6'5"	260	Montana State		
Borcky, Dennis DT	87NYG		6'4"	284	Memphis State		
Borders, Nate DB	87Cin		5'10"	190	Indiana		
Borland, Kyle LB	87LA		6'3"	232	Wisconsin		
Borresen, Rich TE	87Dal		6'5"	252	Northwestern		
Bortz, Mark OG	83-93Chi		6'6"	275	Iowa		
Bosa, John DE	87-90Mia 90KJ		6'4"	270	Boston College		
Bosley, Keith OT	87Cle		6'5"	320	Eastern Kentucky		
Boso, Cap TE	86StL 87-91Chi	2	6'3"	232	Illinois		24
Bostic, Jeff C	80-93Was		6'2"	268	Clemson		
Bostic, Joe OG-OT	79-87StL 88Phx 89KJ		6'3"	266	Clemson		
Bostic, John DB	85-87Det		5'10"	178	Bethune-Cookman	1	
Bostic, Keith DB	83-88Hou 90Cle		6'1"	216	Michigan	13	6
Bosworth, Brian LB	87-89Sea		6'2"	248	Oklahoma		
Boucher, Scott OG	84-85USFL 87Hou		6'3"	260	Northeastern Okla.		
Boures, Emil C-OG	82-86Pit		6'1"	258	Pittsburgh		
Bouette, Marc DT	92-93LA		6'4"	298	Louisiana State		
Bouwens, Shawn OG	91-93Det		6'4"	290	Nebraska Wesleyan		
Bouyer, Willie WR	89Sea		6'3"	200	Michigan State		
Bouza, Matt WR	81SF 82-83Bal 84-89Ind	2	6'2"	211	California		102
Bowden, Joe LB	92-93Hou		5'11"	229	Oklahoma		
Bowen, Ken LB	87Atl		6'1"	220	East Tennesee St.		
Bowers, Sam TE	87Chi		6'4"	250	Fordham		
Bowick, Tony NT	89Atl		6'2"	265	Tenn.-Chattanooga		
Bowles, Todd DB	86-90Was 91-92SF 93Was		6'2"	203	Temple	15	
Bowman, Barry P	87Sea		5'11"	180	Louisiana Tech		
Bowman, Jim DB	85-89NE		6'2"	210	Central Michigan	3	
Bowman, Kevin WR	87Phi		6'3"	205	San Jose State		6
Bowser, Charles LB	82-85Mia 86NJ		6'3"	231	Duke		
Bowyer, Walt DE	83-84,87-88Den		6'4"	254	Arizona State	1	
Boyarsky, Jerry NT	81NO 82-85Cin 86Buf 86-89GB		6'3"	290	Pittsburgh		
Boyd, Brent OG	80-83Min 84LJ 85-86Min		6'3"	268	U.C.L.A.		
Boyd, Dennis DE-DT-OT-C	77-79Sea 80BA 81-82Sea		6'6"	255	Oregon State		6
Boyd, Greg DE	77-78NE 80-82Den 83GB 84SF 84Raid		6'6"	274	San Diego State		4
Boyd, Jerome LB	83Sea		6'2"	225	Oregon State		
Boyd, Thomas LB	87Det		6'3"	210	Alabama		
Boyer, Mark TE-HB	85-89Ind 90-92NYJ	2	6'4"	239	Southern Calif.		36
Boykin, Deral DB	93LA		5'11"	196	Louisville		6
Boyle, Jim OT	87Pit		6'5"	270	Tulane		
Bracelin, Greg LB	80Den 81Oak 82Raid 83Bal 84Ind		6'1"	214	California	3	
Bracken, Don K	85-90GB 92KC 93LA	4	6'	210	Michigan		
Bradord, Ronnie DB	93Den		5'10"	188	Colorado	1	
Bradley, Carlos LB	81-85SD 87Phi		6'	224	Wake Forest	2	
Bradley, Chuck LB	93Cin		6'5"	296	Kentucky		
Bradley, Danny WR	87Det		5'9"	175	Oklahoma		12
Bradley, Henry NT-DT	79-83Cle		6'2"	261	Alcorn State		
Bradley, Luther DB	78-81Det 83-85USFL		6'2"	194	Notre Dame	9	
Bradley, Steve QB	87Chi		6'2"	216	Indiana		
Bradshaw, Craig QB	80Hou		6'5"	215	Utah State		
Brady, Ed LB	84-85LA 86-91Cin 92-93TB		6'2"	234	Illinois		
Brady, Jeff LB	91Pit 92GB 93LA 93SD		6'1"	224	Kentucky		
Brady, Kerry K	87Dal 88Ind 89Buf		6'1"	208	Hawaii		1
Braggs, Byron DE	81-83GB 84TB		6'4"	290	Alabama		
Braggs, Stephen DB	87-91Cle 92-93Mia		5'10"	178	Texas	5	
Brammer, Mark TE	80-84Buf	2	6'3"	236	Michigan State		60
Bramlett, Don NT	87Min		6'2"	270	Carson-Newman		
Branch, Reggie FB	85-89Was 90NJ		5'11"	232	West Virginia St., East Carolina		6
Brandes, John TE	87-89Ind 90-92Was 92NYG 93SF		6'2"	249	Cameron		
Brandon, David LB	87-89SD 90KJ 91-93Cle 93Sea		6'4"	228	Memphis State	4	24
Brandon, Michael DE	93Ind		6'4"	290	Florida		
Brannon, Robert DE	87Cle 87NO		6'7"	245	Arkansas		
Brantley, John LB	89Hou 92Was		6'2"	245	Georgia		
Branstetter, Kent OT	73GB		6'3"	260	Houston		
Brantley, Scot LB	80-87TB		6'1"	230	Florida	8	
Branton, Gene WR	83TB 84LJ 85TB 86KJ		6'4"	223	Texas Southern		
Bratton, Melvin FB	89-90Den	2	6'1"	225	Miami (Fla.)		48
Braxton, David LB	89-90Min 90-93Phx		6'1"	236	Wake Forest		
Braxton, Tyrone DB	87-93Den		5'11"	177	N. Dakota State	18	12
Bravyak, Jack DE	87Buf		6'3"	255	Temple		
Braziel, Larry DB	79-81Bal 82-85Cle		6'	187	Southern Calif.	11	12
Brazley, Carl DB	87SD		6'	180	Western Kentucky	1	
Breech, Jim K	78-79Oak 80-92Cin	5	5'6"	160	California		1246
Breeden, Louis DB	78-87Cin		5'11"	185	N. Car. Central	33	12
Breen, Adrian QB	87Cin		6'4"	183	Morehead State		
Brennan, Brian WR	84-91Cle 92Cin 92SD	23	5'9"	179	Boston College		132
Brennan, Mike OT	90-91Cin 91Phx 91Buf		6'5"	274	Notre Dame		
Brenner, Hoby TE	81-93NO	2	6'4"	242	Southern Calif.		126
Brewer, Chris HB-FB	84Den 87Chi	2	6'1"	203	Arizona		18
Briehl, Tom LB	85Hou 86NJ 87Hou		6'3"	247	Illinois		
Briggs, Walter QB	87NYJ		6'1"	205	Montclair State		
Bright, Greg DB	80-81Cin		6'	208	Morehead State	1	
Bright, Leon HB	81-83NYG 84-85TB	23	5'9"	192	Florida State		12
Brilz, Darrick OG	87Was 88SD 89-93Sea		6'3"	279	Oregon		
Brim, James WR	87Min	2	6'3"	187	Wake Forest		18
Brim, Michael DB	88Phx 89Det 89-90Min 91-92NYJ 93Cin		6'	188	Virginia Union	15	12
Brinkley, Lester DE	90Dal		6'6"	270	Mississippi		
Brinson, Dana WR	89SD	2	5'9"	167	Nebraska		
Brisby, Vincent WR	93NE	2	6'1"	186	Northeast La.		12
Brister, Bubby QB	86-92Pit 93Phi	1	6'2"	203	Tulane, Northeast La.		42
Britt, James DB	84Atl 85BL 86-87Atl		6'	185	Louisiana State	3	6
Britt, Jessie WR	86Pit		6'4"	198	N. Carolina A&T		
Britt, Ralph TE	87Pit		6'3"	240	N. Carolina State		
Brock, Lou DB	88Sea 88Det		5'10"	175	Southern Calif.		
Brock, Dieter QB	85LA 86XJ	1	6'	195	Auburn, Jacksonville St.		
Brock, Matt DE-DT	89-93GB		6'5"	284	Oregon	1	
Brock, Pete C-OT-OG-TE	76-87NE		6'5"	267	Colorado		6
Brock, Stan OT	80-92NO 93SD		6'6"	288	Colorado		
Brockhaus, Jeff K	87SF	5	6'2"	218	Missouri		20
Brookins, Mitchell WR	84-85Buf 86KJ	2	5'11"	196	Illinois		6
Brooks, Bill WR	86-92Ind 93Buf	23	6'	192	Boston U.		198
Brooks, Chet DB	88-90SF		5'11"	191	Texas A&M	3	
Brooks, James HB	81-83SD 84-91Cin 92Cle 92TB	23	5'10"	181	Auburn		474
Brooks, Jon LB	79Det 80StL 80Atl 83-84USFL		6'2"	215	Clemson		
Brooks, Kevin DT	85-88Dal 89-90Det		6'6"	277	Michigan		
Brooks, Michael LB	87-92Den 93NYG		6'1"	235	Louisiana State	3	8
Brooks, Michael DB	89-90SD 90Dal 91KJ		6'	195	N. Carolina State		
Brooks, Perry DT	78-84Was		6'3"	264	Southern U.		
Brooks, Reggie HB	93Was	2	5'8"	202	Notre Dame		18
Brooks, Robert WR	92-93GB	23	6'	171	South Carolina		12
Brooks, Tony HB	92Phi 93XJ		6'	230	Notre Dame		
Brophy, Jay LB	84-86Mia 87NYJ		6'3"	233	Miami (Fla.)	1	
Brostek, Bern C-OG	90-93LA		6'3"	300	Washington		
Brotzki, Bob OT	86-88Ind 88Dal		6'5"	281	Syracuse		
Broughton, Walter WR	84-85USFL 86-88Buf		5'10"	180	Jacksonville St.		6
Broughton, Willie DE-DT	85-86Ind 87KJ 89-90Dal 92-93Raid		6'5"	279	Miami (Fla.)		
Broussard, Steve HB-WR	90-93Atl	2	5'7"	201	Washington State		72
Brown, A.B. HB	89-92NYJ	2	5'9"	212	Pittsburgh	6	
Brown, Aaron LB	78-80TB 82-84CFL 85Phi 86-87Atl		6'2"	236	Ohio State	1	
Brown, Andre WR	89-90Mia	2	6'3"	210	Miami (Fla.)		30
Brown, Arnold DB	85Det 86BA 87Sea		5'11"	185	N. Car. Central		
Brown, Bud DB	84-88Mia		6'	194	Southern Miss.	5	
Brown, Cedric DB	77-84TB		6'1"	199	Kent State	29	18
Brown, Cedrick DB	87Phi		5'10"	178	Washington State	1	
Brown, Chad LB	93Pit		6'2"	240	Colorado		
Brown, Chad DE	93Phx		6'7"	265	Mississippi		
Brown, Charlie WR	82-84Was 85-87Atl	2	5'10"	182	South Carolina		150
Brown, Chris DB	84-85Pit		6'	200	Notre Dame	1	
Brown, Chris OT	87NYJ		6'1	295	Lamar		
Brown, Clay TE	82Atl 83Den 84USFL		6'3"	225	Brigham Young		
Brown, Corwin DB	93NE		6'	192	Michigan		
Brown, Curtis FB-HB	77-82Buf 83Hou	23	5'10"	203	Missouri		90
Brown, Dave DB	75Pit 76-86Sea 87-89GB 90LJ	3	6'1"	192	Michigan	62	32
Brown, Dave LB	87Phi		6'2"	215	Miami-Ohio		
Brown, Dave QB	92-93NYG		6'5"	215	Duke		
Brown, Dennis DE	90-93SF		6'4"	290	Washington	1	
Brown, Derek TE	92-93NYG	2	6'6"	252	Notre Dame		
Brown, Derek HB	93NO	2	5'9"	186	Nebraska		18
Brown, Don OT	83SD		6'6"	262	Santa Clara		
Brown, Don DB	87NYG		5'11"	189	Maryland	1	
Brown, Donald DB	86SD 86Mia		5'11"	189	Oklahoma, Maryland	1	
Brown, Eddie WR	85-91Cin 92ZJ	2	6'	185	Miami (Fla.)		246
Brown, Eric WR	87KC		6'2"	180	Tulsa		
Brown, Eric DB	89Dal		5'11"	177	Savannah State		
Brown, Gary HB-FB	91-93Hou	2	5'11"	227	Penn State		60
Brown, Gilbert NT	93GB		6'2"	330	Kansas		
Brown, Gordon HB	87Ind		5'11"	220	Tulsa		6
Brown, Greg DE-DT	81-86Phi 87-88Atl		6'5"	254	Kansas State, Eastern Illinois		14

UseName(Nickname)-Positions	Team by Year	See Section	Hgt.	Wgt.	College	Int	Pts
Brown, Guy LB	77-82Dal		6'4"	223	Houston	1	
Brown, Ivory Lee HB	92Phx	2	6'2"	245	Ark.-Pine Bluff		
Brown, J.B. DB	89-93Mia		6'	192	Maryland	10	6
Brown, James OT	93Cle		6'6"	321	Virginia State		
Brown, Jerome DT	87-91Phi		6'2"	291	Miami (Fla.)	1	2
June 1992 — Died in Automobile Accident							
Brown, Ken WR	87Cin		5'8"	175	Southern Arkansas		
Brown, Kevin K	87Chi		6'2"	178	West Texas State		
Brown, Laron WR	87Den		5'9"	172	Texas		
Brown, Larry WR	87Min		5'11"	180	Mankato State		
Brown, Larry DB	91-93Dal		5'11"	184	Texas Christian	3	
Brown, Lomas OT	85-93Det		6'4"	283	Florida		
Brown, Marc WR	87Buf		6'2"	195	Towson State		6
Brown, Mark LB	83-88Mia 89-91Det		6'2"	230	Purdue	4	
Brown, Monty LB	93Buf		6'	228	Ferris State		
Brown, Norris TE	83Min 84-85USFL		6'3"	220	Southern Calif.		
Brown, Preston WR	80NE 81XJ 82NE 83NYJ 84Cle	3	5'10"	186	Vanderbilt		6
Brown, Ray OT-OG	86-87StL 88Phx 89Was 90KJ 91EJ 92-93Was		6'5"	289	Memphis State, Arizona State, Arkansas State		
Brown, Ray HB	87SF		5'9"	185	South Carolina		
Brown, Reggie FB	82-83Atl 84-85USFL 87Phi	23	5'11"	211	Oregon		
Brown, Reggie WR	93Hou		6'1"	195	Alabama State		
Brown, Richard LB	87,89LA 90SD 91-92Cle 93KJ		6'3"	240	San Diego State	1	
Brown, Robert DE	82-92GB		6'2"	268	Virginia Tech	2	8
Brown, Roger DB	90-91NYG 92NE		6'	196	Virginia Tech		
Brown, Ron WR-DB	84-89LA 90Raid 91LA	23	5'11"	181	Arizona State		84
Brown, Ron DE	88Raid		6'4"	225	Southern Calif.		
Brown, Ron WR	87StL		5'10"	186	Colorado		
Brown, Rufus OG	87TB		6'2"	295	Florida A&M		
Brown, Rush DE-NT-DT	80-83StL 84-85USFL		6'2"	259	Ball State	1	
Brown, Selwyn DB	88TB		5'11"	205	Miami (Fla.)		
Brown, Sonny DB	87Hou		6'2"	200	Oklahoma		
Brown, Steve DB	83-87Hou	3	5'11"	189	Oregon	19	12
Brown, Ted FB-HB	79-86Min	2	5'10"	206	N. Carolina State		318
Brown, Theotis FB-HB	79-81StL 81-83Sea 83-84KC	2	6'3"	225	U.C.L.A.		198
Brown, Thomas DE-NT	80Phi 81,83Cle		6'4"	247	Baylor		
Brown, Tim WR	88-93Raid	23	6'	195	Notre Dame		186
Brown, Tom FB	87Mia 88KJ 89Mia 90KJ	2	6'1"	223	Pittsburgh		
Brown, Tom WR	87Cin		6'4"	190	Augustana (S.D.)		
Brown, Tony OT	87Buf 88JJ		6'5"	285	Pittsburgh		
Brown, Tony DB	92-93Hou		5'9"	183	Fresno State		
Brown, Troy WR	93NE	3	5'9"	183	Marshall		
Brown, Vincent LB	89-93NE		6'2"	245	Miss. Valley St.	3	12
Browne, Jim HB	87Raid		6'1"	215	Boston College		
Browner, Jim DB	79-80Cin		6'1"	208	Notre Dame	1	
Browner, Joey DB	83-91Min		6'2"	221	Southern Calif.	37	18
Browner, Keith LB	84-86TB 87SF 87Raid 88SD		6'6"	245	Southern Calif.	4	6
Browner, Ross DE	78-84Cin 85USFL 85-86Cin 87GB		6'3"	262	Notre Dame	1	3
Browning, Dave DE	78-81Oak 82Raid 83NE 84-85USFL		6'5"	245	Washington	1	
Brownlow, Darrick LB	91Dal 92-93TB		5'10"	237	Illinois		
Bruce, Aundray LB-TE-DE	88-91Atl 92-93Raid		6'5"	253	Auburn	3	
Bruckner, Nick WR	83-85NYJ 86SJ		5'11"	185	Syracuse		
Brudzinski, Bob LB	77-80LA 81-89Mia		6'4"	229	Ohio State	9	12
Bruer, Bob TE	76Chi 77-78CFL 79-80SF 80-83Min 84KJ	2	6'5"	235	Mankato State		60
Bruhin, John OG	88-91TB		6'3"	282	Tennessee		
Brumfield, Scott OT	93Cin		6'8"	320	Brigham Young		
Brune, Larry DB	80Min		6'2"	202	Rice	2	
Brunell, Mark QB	93GB		6'1"	208	Washington		
Brunner, Scott QB	80-83NYG 84KJ 85StL	1	6'5"	203	Delaware		6
Bruno, Dave K	87Min		6'1"	235	Moraine Valley		
Bruno, John K	87Pit		6'2"	190	Penn State		
Bryan, Billy C-OG	77-88Den 89KJ		6'2"	251	Duke		
Bryan, Rick DT-DE-NT-LB	84-91Atl 92ZJ 93Atl		6'4"	265	Oklahoma		3
Bryan, Steve DE-NT-LB	87-88Den		6'2"	256	Oklahoma		
Bryant, Cullen FB-HB	73-82LA 83-84Sea 87LA	23	6'1"	234	Colorado		156
Bryant, Domingo DB	87-88Hou		6'4"	176	Texas A&M	3	6
Bryant, Jeff DE	82-93Sea		6'5"	276	Clemson	1	2
Bryant, Kelvin HB	86-88Was 89KJ 90Was	2	6'2"	195	North Carolina		120
Bryant, Steve WR	82-85Hou 87Ind	2	6'2"	195	Purdue		
Bryant, Tim LB	87Min		6'1"	217	Southern Miss.		
Bryant, Trent DB	81Was 82-83KC 84-85USFL 87KC		5'10"	180	Arkansas	2	
Bryant, Warren OT	77-84Atl 84Raid		6'6"	273	Kentucky		
Buben, Mark DE-NT	79NE 80JJ 81NE 82Cle 83-85USFL		6'3"	260	Tufts	1	
Buchanan, Charles DE	88Cle		6'3"	245	Tennessee State		2
Buchanan, Ray DB	93Ind		5'9"	193	Louisville	4	
Buchanan, Richard WR	93LA		5'10"	178	Northwestern		
Buck, Jason DE	87-90Cin 91-93Was		6'5"	268	Brigham Young		
Buck, Mike QB	90-93NO	1	6'3"	227	Maine		
Buck, Vince DB	90-93NO	3	6'	198	Central St.-Ohio	9	6
Buckley, Curtis DB-WR	93TB		6'	185	East Texas State		
Buckley, Marcus LB	93NYG		6'3"	235	Texas A&M		
Buckley, Terrell DB	92-93GB	3	5'9"	174	Florida State	5	12
Budde, Brad OG	80-86KC 87TJ		6'4"	262	Southern Calif.		
Buddenberg, John OG	92Atl		6'6"	270	Akron		
Buczkowski, Bob DE	87Raid 89Phx 90Cle		6'5"	260	Pittsburgh		
Buford, Maury K	82-84SD 85-86Chi 88NYG 89-91Chi	4	6'1"	191	Texas Tech		
Buford, Tony LB	87StL		6'2"	222	Tulsa		
Bugel, Joe	HC90-93Phx				Western Kentucky		
Bujnoch, Glenn OG	76-82Cin 83-84TB		6'5"	259	Texas A&M		6
Bullard, Louis OT	78-80Sea 83-85USFL		6'6"	265	Jackson State		
Bullough, Chuck LB	93Mia		6'1"	238	Michigan State		
Bulluck, Brian LB	87Ind		6'3"	236	N. Carolina State		
Bunch, Derrick LB	87Was		6'3"	215	Michigan State		
Bunch, Jarrod FB	91-93NYG	2	6'2"	248	Michigan		42
Bungarda, Ken OT	80SF 81KJ		6'6"	270	Missouri		
Bunz, Dan LB	78-84SF 85Det		6'4"	226	Long Beach State	4	
Burbage, Cornell WR	87-89Dal	2	5'10"	186	Kentucky		12
Burgess, Charlie LB	87NYG		6'	230	Carson-Newman		
Burgess, Fernanza WR	84NYJ 84Mia		6'1"	210	Miami (Fla.)		
Burgess, Marvell DB	87Mia		6'3"	195	Henderson State		
Burgess, Ronnie DB	85GB		5'11'	175	Wake Forest		
Burke, Anthony DT	87StL		6'3"	262	Minnesota		
Burke, Joe HB	87NYJ		6'	200	Rutgers		
Burke, Randy WR	78-81Bal 84USFL	2	6'2"	190	Kentucky		18
Burkett, Chris WR	85-89Buf 89-93NYJ	2	6'4"	205	Jackson State		120
Burks, Shawn LB	86Was		6'1"	230	Louisiana State		

UseName(Nickname)-Positions	Team by Year	See Section	Hgt.	Wgt.	College	Int	Pts
Burley, Gary DE	76-83Cin 84Atl		6'3"	272	Pittsburgh		
Burmeister, Danny DB	87Was		6'2"	201	North Carolina		
Burnett, Rob DE	90-93Cle		6'4"	275	Syracuse		
Burnett, Victor DE	87StL		6'5"	250	Fresno State		
Burnette, Dave OT	87Dal		6'6"	278	Arkansas, Central Arkansas		
Burnette, Reggie LB	91GB 92-93TB		6'2"	240	Houston		
Burnham, Tim OT	87-88Sea		6'5"	280	Washington		
Burns, Jerry	HC86-91Min				Michigan		
Burrell, Clinton DB	79-84Cle 85JJ		6'2"	192	Louisiana State	8	6
Burroughs, Derrick DB	85-89Buf		6'1"	180	Memphis State	6	
Burroughs, James DB	82-83Bal 84Ind		6'1"	192	Michigan State	6	6
Burrow, Curtis K	88GB		5'11"	185	Central Arkansas		2
Burruss, Lloyd DB	81-91KC		6'	204	Maryland	22	30
Burse, Tony FB	87Sea		6'	220	Middle Tenn. St.		
Burt, Jim NT-DT	81-88NYG 88-91SF		6'1"	260	Miami (Fla.)		6
Burton, Derek OG	87Min		6'2"	270	Oklahoma State		
Burton, Leonard C	86-89Buf 90KJ 91Cle 92Det		6'3"	269	South Carolina		
Burton, Ron LB	87-89Dal 89Phx 90Raid		6'1"	247	North Carolina	1	
Busch, Mike QB	87NYG	1	6'4"	214	S. Dakota State		
Bush, Blair C	78-82Cin 83-88Sea 89-91GB 92-93LA		6'3"	267	Washington		
Bush, Frank LB	85-86Hou		6'1"	218	N. Carolina State		
Bush, Lewis LB	93SD		6'2"	245	Washington State		
Busick, Steve LB	81-85Den 86LA 87SD		6'4"	227	Southern Calif.	2	
Bussey, Barney DB	84-85USFL 86-92Cin 93TB	3	6'	195	S. Carolina State	10	12
Butcher, Paul LB	86-88Det 89GJ 90-92LA 93Ind		6'	224	Wayne State		
Butler, Bobby DB	81-92Atl		5'11"	174	Florida State	28	18
Butler, Chuck LB	84Sea		6'	220	Boise State		
Butler, Dave LB	87Cle		6'4"	225	Notre Dame		
Butler, Jerry WR	79-83Buf 84KJ 85-86Buf 87KJ	2	6'	178	Clemson		174
Butler, Jerry HB	87Atl		5'11"	193	East Tennessee St.		
Butler, John DB	87SF		6'1"	200	Principia (Ill.)		
Butler, Keith LB	78-87Sea		6'4"	230	Memphis State	8	
Butler, Kevin K	85-93Chi	5	6'1"	195	Georgia		915
Butler, LeRoy DB	90-93GB		6'	192	Florida State	13	6
Butler, Mike DE	77-82GB 84-85USFL 85GB		6'5"	265	Kansas		6
Butler, Ray WR	80-83Bal 84-85Ind 85-88Sea	2	6'3"	200	Southern Calif.		198
Buttle, Greg LB	76-84NYJ		6'3"	232	Penn State	15	20
Butts, Marion FB	89-93SD	2	6'1"	248	Florida State		192
Butz, Dave DT-DE	73-74StL 75-88Was		6'7"	291	Purdue	2	
Byars, Keith HB	86-92Phi 93Mia	2	6'1	234	Ohio State		216
Byers, Scott DB	84SD		5'11"	170	Long Beach State		
Byner Earnest FB	84-88Cle 89-93Was	2	5'10"	215	East Carolina		360
Bynum, Reggie WR	87Buf		6'1"	185	Oregon State		
Byrd, Boris DB	87NYG		6'	210	Austin Peay		
Byrd, Darryl LB	83-84,87Raid		6'1"	222	Illinois		
Byrd, Dennis DE-DT	89-92NYJ		6'5"	270	Tulsa		2
November 1992 — Paralyzed in Game							
Byrd, Gill DB	83-92SD 93KJ		5'11"	195	San Jose State	42	12
Byrd, Richard DE	85-89Hou		6'3"	264	Southern Miss.		
Byrd, Sylvester TE	87Atl		6'2"	225	Kansas		
Byrum, Carl FB	86-88Buf	2	6'	234	Miss. Valley State		6
Cabral, Brian LB	79Atl 80GB 81-85Chi		6'1"	223	Colorado		
Caesar, Ivan LB	91Min		6'1"	241	Boston College		
Cade, Mossy DB	83USFL 85-86GB 87StL		6'1"	197	Texas	5	
Cadigan, Dave OT-OG	88-93NYJ		6'4"	285	Southern Calif.		
Cadrez, Glenn LB	92-93NYJ		6'3"	240	Houston		
Cain, Joe LB	89-92Sea 93Chi		6'1"	231	Stanford, Oregon Tech	3	
Cain, Lynn HB	79-84Atl 85LA	2	6'1"	205	Southern Calif.		150
Cain, Patrick C-OG	87Det		6'2"	260	Wichita State		
Caldwell, Bryan DE	84Dal 84Hou		6'4"	248	Arizona State		
Caldwell, Darryl OT	83Buf		6'5"	245	Tennessee State		
Caldwell, David NT	87GB		6'1"	261	Texas Christian		
Caldwell, Mike LB	93Cle		6'2"	222	Middle Tenn. State		
Caldwell, Ravin LB	87-92Was		6'3"	233	Arkansas		2
Caldwell, Scott HB	87Den		5'10"	196	Texas-Arlington		
Caldwell, Tony LB	83-85Raid 87Sea		6'1"	223	Washington		
Calhoun, Mike DT-DE	80TB 80SF		6'4"	260	Notre Dame		
Calhoun, Rick HB	87Raid		5'7"	190	Fullerton State		6
Caliguire, Dean OG-C	91SF 91Pit		6'2"	280	Pittsburgh		
Call, Kevin OT	84-93Ind		6'7"	302	Colorado State		
Callahan, Bill DB	87Buf		6'	200	Pittsburgh		
Callicut, Ken HB	78-82Det	3	6'	191	Clemson		
Calloway, Chris WR	90-91Pit 92-93NYG	2	5'10"	185	Michigan		36
Camarillo, Rich K	81-87NE 88LA 89-93Phx	4	5'11"	188	Washington		
Cameron, Glenn LB	75-85Cin		6'2"	226	Florida	5	
Cameron, Jack DB	84Chi		6'	182	Winston-Salem		
Camp, Reggie DE	83-87Cle 88Atl		6'4"	274	California		
Campbell, Arnold DE	87Buf		6'3"	260	Akron State		
Campbell, Earl HB-FB	78-83Hou 84-85NO	2	5'11"	232	Texas		444
Campbell, Gary LB	77-83Chi		6'1"	220	Colorado	4	
Campbell, Glen OT	87Buf		6'4"	280	Wake Forest		
Campbell, Hugh	HC84-85Hou				Washington State		
Campbell, Jack OT	82-83Sea		6'5"	277	Southern Calif., Utah		
Campbell, Jeff WR	90-93Det	23	5'8"	169	Colorado		18
Campbell, Jesse DB	92-93NYG		6'1"	215	N. Carolina State	1	
Campbell, Joe LB	88-89SD		6'4"	245	New Mexico State		
Campbell, Rich QB	81-84GB	1	6'4"	224	California		
Campbell, Russ TE	92Pit		6'5"	259	Kansas State		
Campbell, Scott QB	84-86Pit 86-87Atl 88KJ 89-90Atl	12	6'	196	Purdue		12
Campen, James C	87-88NO 89-93GB		6'3"	269	Tulane		
Campfield, Billy HB-FB	78-82Phi 83NYG 84-85USFL	23	5'11"	200	Kansas		78
Cancik, Phil LB	80NYG 81Den 83USFL		6'1"	228	Northern Arizona		
Canley, Sheldon HB	92NYJ		5'9"	195	San Jose State		
Cannon, Billy LB	84Dal		6'4"	231	Texas A&M		
Cannon, John DE-NT	82-90TB		6'5"	260	William & Mary	1	
Cannon, Mark C	84-89GB 89KC 91Ind		6'3"	258	Texas-Arlington		
Capece, Bill K	81-83TB	5	5'7	170	Florida State		196
Capers, James LB	87Cle		6'4"	232	Central Michigan		
Capers, Wayne WR	83-84Pit 85-86Ind	2	6'2"	198	Kansas		30
Carano, Glenn QB	77-83Dal 84USFL	1	6'3"	201	Nevada-Las Vegas		
Caravello, Joe TE	87-88Was 89-90SD	2	6'3"	270	Tulane		6
Carey, Brian WR	87NE		6'	200	American Inter.		
Carey, Richard DB	89Cin 90Buf		5'9"	185	Idaho	1	
Carlson, Cody QB	87-93Hou	12	6'3"	200	Baylor		24
Carlson, Jeff QB	90-91TB 92NE	1	6'3"	215	Weber State		
Carlson, Mark OT	87Was		6'6"	284	Southern Conn. St.		
Carney, John K	88-89TB 90LA 91-93SD	5	5'11"	160	Notre Dame		421

UseName(Nickname)-Positions	Team by Year	See Section	Hgt	Wgt	College	Int	Pts
Caron, Roger OT	85-86Ind		6'5"	282	Harvard		
Carpenter, Brian DB	82NYG 83-84Was 84Buf		5'10"	167	Michigan	4	
Carpenter, Rob FB-HB	77-81Hou 81-85NYG 86LA	2	6'1"	224	Miami-Ohio		204
Carpenter, Rob WR	91NE 92-93NYJ	23	6'2"	215	Notre Dame, Syracuse		6
Carpenter, Ron DB	93Min 93Cin		6'1"	188	Miami (Ohio)		
Carpenter, Steve DB	80NYJ 81StL		6'2"	195	Western Illinois		
Carr, Carl LB	87Det		6'3"	230	North Carolina		
Carr, Chetti DB	87Raid		5'9"	185	Northwestern Okla.		
Carr, Gregg LB	85-88Pit		6'1"	220	Auburn	1	2
Carr, Lydell FB	89Phx		6'1"	228	Oklahoma		
Carr, Reggie DT	87NYG		6'3"	300	Jackson State		
Carreker, Alphonso DE	84-88GB 89Den 90KJ 91Den		6'6"	268	Florida State	1	
Carreker, Vince DB	87Cle		6'	183	Cincinnati		
Carrier, Mark WR	87-92TB 93Cle	2	6'	184	Nicholls State		192
Carrier, Mark DB	90-93Chi		6'1"	188	Southern Calif.	16	6
Carrington, Darren DB	89Den 90Det 91-93SD		6'1"	189	Pittsburgh, Northern Arizona	17	6
Carroll, Jay TE	84TB 85Min		6'4"	231	Minnesota		6
Carroll, Wesley WR	91-92NO 93Cin	2	6'	183	Miami (Fla.)		18
Carruth, Paul Ott FB	85USFL 86-88GB 89KC	2	6'1"	220	Alabama		48
Carson, Bud	HC89-90Cle				North Carolina		
Carson, Carlos WR	80-89KC 89Phi	23	5'11"	180	Louisiana State		198
Carson, Harry LB	76-88NYG		6'2"	237	S. Carolina State	11	12
Carson, Howard LB	81-83LA 84-85USFL		6'2"	231	Howard Payne		
Carson, Malcolm OG	84Min		6'2"	260	Tenn.-Chattanooga		
Carter, Alex DE	87Cle		6'3"	255	Tennessee State		
Carter, Anthony WR	83-85USFL 85-93Min	2	5'11"	174	Michigan		324
Carter, Carl DB	86-87StL 88-89Phx 90Cin 91TB 92GB		5'11"	180	Texas Tech	5	
Carter, Cris WR	87-89Phi 90-93Min	2	6'3"	196	Ohio State		258
Carter, Dale DB	92-93KC	3	6'1"	188	Tennessee	8	18
Carter, David C-OG	77-83Hou 84-85NO		6'2"	250	Western Kentucky		
Carter, Dexter HB	90-93SF	23	5'9"	170	Florida State		48
Carter, Gerald WR	80NYJ 80-86TB	2	6'1"	190	Texas A&M		102
Carter, Jimmie LB	87StL		6'1"	220	New Mexico		
Carter, Joe HB	84-86Mia	2	5'11"	198	Alabama		6
Carter, Jon DT	89Dal		6'4"	273	Pittsburgh		
Carter, Larry DB	80Buf		5'11"	185	Kentucky		
Carter, Marty DB	91-93TB		6'1"	200	Middle Tenn. St.	4	
Carter, Michael NT	84-92SF		6'2"	285	S.M.U.	1	
Carter, M.L. DB	79-81KC 82CFL 83USFL		5'9"	173	Fullerton State, San Jose State	3	
Carter, Pat TE	88Det 89-93LA	2	6'4"	250	Florida State		36
Carter, Rodney HB	87-89Pit	2	6'	218	Purdue		72
Carter, Rubin NT-DT	75-86Den		6'	255	Miami (Fla.)		6
Carter, Russell DB	84-87NYJ 88-89Raid		6'2"	197	S.M.U.	4	
Carter, Steve WR	87TB		5'10"	170	Albany State		
Carter, Tom DB	93Was		5'11"	181	Notre Dame	6	
Carter, Walter DE	87TB		6'4"	276	Florida State		
Carthen, Jason LB	93NE		6'3"	255	Ohio U.		
Carthens, Milt OT	87Ind		6'4"	305	Michigan		
Carthon, Maurice FB	83-85USFL 85-91NYG 92Ind	2	6'1"	225	Arkansas State		18
Carver, Dale LB	83Cle		6'2"	225	Georgia		
Carver, Melvin FB	82-85TB 87Ind	2	5'11"	221	Nevada-Las Vegas		18
Case, Frank DE	81KC 83-84USFL		6'4"	243	Penn State		
Case, Scott DB	84-93Atl		6'	178	Oklahoma	28	8
Cash, Keith TE	91Pit 93KC	2	6'4"	235	Texas		42
Cash, Kerry TE	91-93Ind	2	6'4"	247	Texas		36
Casillas, Tony NT-DT	86-90Atl 91-93Dal		6'3"	280	Oklahoma		
Cason, Wendell DB	85-87Atl		5'11"	191	Oregon	4	
Cassidy, Ron WR	79-81GB 82SJ 83-84GB	2	6'	184	Utah State		
Castille, Jeremiah DB	83-86TB 87-88Den		5'10"	175	Alabama	14	6
Castle, Eric DB	93SD		6'3"	212	Oregon		
Caston, Toby LB	87-88Hou 89-93Det		6'1"	240	Louisiana State		
Castor, Chris WR	83-84Sea	2	6'	170	Duke		
Catano, Mark OT	84-85Pit 86Buf		6'3"	266	Valdosta State		
Catchings, Toney LB	87Cin		6'3"	236	Cincinnati		
Cater, Greg K	80-83Buf 85USFL 86-87StL	4	6'	193	Tenn.-Chattanooga		
Caterbone, Mike WR	87Mia		5'11"	175	Franklin & Marshall		
Caterbone, Thomas DB	87Phi		5'8"	175	Franklin & Marshall		
Cavanaugh, Matt QB	78-82NE 83-85SF 86-89Phi 90-91NYG	12	6'2"	211	Pittsburgh		18
Caver, James DB	83Det 85USFL		5'9"	175	Missouri		
Cecil, Chuck DB	88-92GB 93Phx		6'	186	Arizona	13	
Cefalo, Jimmy WR	78-84Mia	23	5'11"	189	Penn State		78
Celotto, Mario LB	78Buf 80-81Oak 81Bal 81LA		6'3"	228	Southern Calif.		
Centers, Larry HB-FB	90-93Phx	23	5'11"	209	Stephen F. Austin		30
Cephous, Frank HB	84NYG		5'10"	205	U.C.L.A.		
Cesare, Billy DB	78-79TB 80Mia 81-82Det 83-84USFL		5'11"	191	Miami (Fla.)		
Cesario, Sal OG	87Dal		6'4"	255	Cal. Poly.-S.L.O.		
Chadwick, Jeff WR	83-89Det 89-91Sea 92LA	2	6'3"	189	Grand Valley St.		168
Chaffey, Pat FB	91Atl 92-93NYJ	2	6'1"	218	Oregon State		18
Chalenski, Mike DB	93Phi		6'4"	260	U.C.L.A.		
Chamblee, Al DE	91-92TB		6'1"	240	Virginia Tech		
Chandler, Chris QB	88-89Ind 90-91TB 91-93Phx	12	6'4"	210	Washington		36
Chandler, Thornton TE	86-89Dal	2	6'5"	243	Florida A&M, Alabama		24
Chandler, Wes WR	78-81NO 81-87SD 88SF	23	6'	184	Florida		336
Chapman, Mike C-OG	84Atl		6'4"	250	Texas		
Chapman, Ted DE	87Raid		6'3"	260	Maryland		
Chapura, Dick DT	87-89Chi 90Phi 90Phx		6'3"	277	Missouri		
Charles, Mike NT-DT	83-86Mia 87-89SD 90Raid 91LA		6'4"	292	Syracuse	1	2
Charlton, Clifford LB	88-89Cle		6'3"	240	Florida		
Chatman, Cliff FB	82NYG 84USFL	2	6'2"	225	Central St.-Okla.		12
Chatman, Ricky LB	87Ind		6'2"	230	Louisiana State		
Chavez, Laz LB	87Mia		6'	220	Iowa		
Chavis, Eddie WR	87Mia		6'	182	Montclair State		
Cheek, Louis OT-OG	88-89Mia 90Dal 90Phx 91GB		6'6"	295	Texas A&M		
Cherry, Bill C-OG	86-87GB		6'4"	277	Middle Tenn. St.		
Cherry, Deron DB	81-91KC		5'11"	197	Rutgers	50	18
Cherry, Raphel DB	85Was 88Det		6'	194	Hawaii	5	
Cherry, Tony HB	86-87SF		5'7"	187	Oregon		6
Chesley, Al LB	79-81Phi 82Chi		6'3"	240	Pittsburgh	4	
Chesley, John TE	84Mia		6'5"	225	Oklahoma State		
Chetti, Joseph HB	87Buf		5'9"	205	C.W. Post		
Chickillo, Tony NT-DE-OG	84-85SD 87NYJ		6'2"	262	Miami (Fla.)		
Childress, Freddie OG-OT	91NE 92Cle		6'4"	331	Arkansas		6
Childress, Ray DE-DT-NT	85-93Hou		6'6"	274	Texas A&M		14
Childs, Jason OT	93Sea		6'4"	285	North Dakota		

UseName(Nickname)-Positions	Team by Year	See Section	Hgt	Wgt	College	Int	Pts
Chilton, Gene C-OT	86-87StL 89KC 90-92NE		6'3"	281	Texas		
Chmura, Mark TE	93GB		6'5"	242	Boston College		
Chirico, John FB	87NYJ		6'	220	Columbia		6
Choate, Putt LB	87GB		6'	225	S.M.U.		
Choma, John OG-OT-C	79KC 81-83SF		6'5"	256	Virginia		
Christiansen, Jeff QB	83Cin 84-85Phi 87Cle	1	6'3"	202	Eastern Illinois		
Christensen, Todd FB-TE	79NYG 79-81Oak 82-88Raid	2	6'3"	230	Brigham Young		254
Christian, Bob FB	92-93Chi	2	5'10"	220	Northwestern		
Christie, Steve K	90-91TB 92-93Buf	5	6'	180	William & Mary		383
Christopher, Herb DB	79-82KC		5'10"	195	Morris Brown	4	
Christy, Greg OT	85Buf 86-87ZJ		6'4"	285	Pittsburgh		
Christy, Jeff C	93Min		6'3"	277	Pittsburgh		
Chung, Eugene OT-OG	92-93NE		6'4"	295	Virginia Tech		
Churchman, Ricky DB	80-81SF		6'1"	193	Texas	4	
Cisowski, Steve OT	87Dal		6'5"	275	Santa Clara		
Clack, Darryl FB	86-89Dal	23	5'10"	219	Arizona State		18
Claiborne, Robert WR	92SD 93TB		5'10"	175	San Diego State		
Claitt, Rickey HB-FB	80-81Was 82KJ 83-85USFL	2	5'10"	206	Bethune-Cookman		12
Clancy, Sam DE-DT	83Sea 84-85USFL 85-88Cle 89-93Ind		6'6"	288	Pittsburgh		
Clanton, Chuck DB	84-85USFL 85GB		6'6"	280	Oklahoma		
Claphan, Sam OT-OG	81-87SD		6'7"	285	Oklahoma		
Clark, Allan HB	79-80NE 81KJ 82GB 82Buf 84-85USFL	23	5'10"	186	Northern Arizona		24
Clark, Bernard LB	90-91Cin 91Sea 91Cin		6'2"	248	Miami (Fla.)		
Clark, Bret DB	85USFL 86-88Atl		6'3"	198	Nebraska	9	
Clark, Brian OT	82Den		6'6"	260	Clemson		
Clark, Brian K	82TB		6'2"	190	Florida		
Clark, Bruce DE	82-88NO 89KC		6'3"	273	Penn State	1	2
Clark, Bryan QB	82SF 83SJ 84Cin		6'2"	196	Michigan State		
Clark, Calvin DE	81Was 83-85USFL		6'4"	260	Purdue		
Clark, Dan LB	87LA		6'2"	233	San Jose State		
Clark, Darryl HB	87Chi		5'11"	204	Texas		
Clark, Dexter DB	87Det		6'	190	Toledo		
Clark, Dwight WR	79-87SF	2	6'4"	211	Clemson		288
Clark, Gary WR	84-85USFL 85-92Was 93Phx	2	5'9"	173	James Madison		372
Clark, Greg LB	88Chi 89Mia 90LA 91GB 91SD 92Sea		6'1"	228	Arizona State		
Clark, Jessie FB	83-87GB 88Det 88-89Phx 89-90Min	2	6'	231	Arkansas		90
Clark, Ken FB-HB	90-92Ind	2	5'9"	203	Nebraska		
Clark, Kevin (K.C.) DB	87-88,90-91Den		5'10"	185	San Jose State	3	6
Clark, Kelvin OT-OG	79-81Den 82-85NO		6'3"	260	Nebraska		6
Clark, Louis WR	87-92Sea	2	6'1"	193	Mississippi State		30
Clark, Mario DB	76-83Buf 84SF		6'2"	194	Oregon	26	
Clark, Mike DE	81Was 82SF 84-85USFL 87TB		6'4"	253	Florida		
Clark, Randy C-DT-OG	80-86StL 87Atl		6'3"	260	Northern Illinois		
Clark, Randy DB	84TB		6'	204	Florida		
Clark, Robert WR	88NO 89-91Det 92Mia	2	5'11"	175	N. Car. Central		108
Clark, Spark HB	87Pit		5'7"	182	Akron		
Clark, Steve OT	81NE 82NJ		6'5"	258	Kansas State		
Clark, Steve DT-OG	82-86Mia		6'4"	255	Utah		
Clark, Steve DB	87Buf		6'2"	190	Liberty	1	
Clark, Torin DB	87TB		6'1"	175	West Virginia St.		
Clark, Vinnie DB	91-92GB 93Atl		6'	194	Ohio State	6	6
Clarke, Ken NT-DT	78-87Phi 88Sea 89-91Min		6'2"	268	Syracuse		2
Clasby, Bob DE-DT	84-85USFL 86-87StL 88-90Phx		6'5"	260	Notre Dame	1	
Clay, John OT	87Raid 88SD		6'5"	300	Missouri		
Clay, Willie DB	92-93Det		5'9"	184	Georgia Tech		12
Clayborn, Raymond DB	77-89NE 90Cle 91LJ	3	6'	187	Texas	36	32
Clayton, Harvey DB	83-86Pit 87NYG		5'9"	179	Florida	6	6
Clayton, Mark WR	83-92Mia 93GB	23	5'9"	177	Louisville		510
Clayton, Ralph WR-FB	81StL		6'3"	222	Michigan		
Clayton, Stan OG-OT	88-89Atl 90-91NE		6'3"	265	Penn State		
Clements, Tom QB	80KC		6'	183	Notre Dame		
Clemons, Michael HB	87KC		5'5"	166	William & Mary		
Clemons, Topper HB	87Phi		5'11"	205	Wake Forest		6
Clendenen, Mike K	87Den		5'11"	191	Houston		16
Cleveland, Greg OT	87Mia		6'5"	295	Florida		
Clifton, Gregory WR	93Was		5'11"	175	Johnson C. Smith		
Clifton, Kyle LB	84-93NYJ		6'4"	234	Texas Christian	12	
Cline, Jackie DE-NT	87Pit 87-89Mia		6'5"	279	Alabama		
Clinkscale, Dexter DB	80Dal 81FJ 82-85Dal 86Ind		5'11"	192	S. Carolina State	9	6
Clinkscales, Joey WR	87-88Pit 88TB	2	6'	201	Tennessee		6
Coates, Ben TE	91-93NE	2	6'4"	245	Livingstone		72
Cobb, Bob DE	81LA 82TB 83-84USFL		6'4"	248	Arizona		
Cobb, Garry LB	79-84Det 85-87Phi 88-89Dal		6'2"	227	Southern Calif.	10	
Cobb, Reggie HB	90-93TB	2	6'	225	Tennessee		132
Cobb, Robert OT-OG	84Min		6'2"	260	Texas		
Cobble, Eric HB	87Hou		5'10"	205	SW Texas State		
Cobbs, Duffy DB	87NE		5'11"	178	Penn State		
Cochran, Mark OT	87SF 88KJ		6'5"	284	Baylor		
Cocozzo, Joe OG	93Sea		6'4"	300	Michigan		
Cocroft, Sherman DB	85-87KC 88Buf 89TB		6'1"	195	San Jose State	7	2
Cofer, Joe DB	87Was		6'	200	Tennessee		
Cofer, Mike LB-DE	83-92Det 93KJ		6'5"	245	Tennessee	1	
Cofer, Mike K	87NO 88-93SF	5	6'2"	192	N. Carolina State		690
Coffey, Ken DB	83-84Was 85KJ 86Was		6'	193	SW Texas State	7	
Coffey, Wayne WR	87NE		5'7"	158	SW Texas State		
Coffman, Paul TE	78-85GB 86-87KC 88Min	2	6'3"	222	Kansas State		252
Cofield, Tim LB	86-88KC 89NYJ 89Buf		6'2"	245	Elizabeth City St.		
Cokeley, Will LB	87Buf		6'2"	220	Kansas State	1	
Colbert, Darrell WR	87-88KC		5'10"	174	Texas Southern		
Colbert, Lewis K	86-87KC 89SD	4	5'11"	182	Auburn		
Cole, Robin LB-DE	77-87Pit 88NYJ		6'2"	222	New Mexico	5	
Coleman, Anthony DB	87Dal		6'	185	Baylor		
Coleman, Ben OT	93Phx		6'6"	335	Wake Forest		
Coleman, Charles TE	87NYG		6'4"	222	Alcorn State		
Coleman, Daniel DE	87Min		6'4"	249	Murray State		
Coleman, Eric DB	89-90NE		6'	190	Wyoming	1	
Coleman, Greg K	77Cle 78-87Min 88Was	4	6'	182	Florida A&M		
Coleman, Keo LB	92NYJ 93GB		6'1"	255	Mississippi State		
Coleman, Leonard DB	85USFL 85-87Ind 88-89SD		6'2"	203	Vanderbilt	6	
Coleman, Lincoln FB	93Dal	2	6'1"	249	Baylor		12
Coleman, Marco DE-LB	92-93Mia		6'3"	261	Georgia Tech		
Coleman, Monte LB	79-93Was		6'3"	237	Central Arkansas	17	24
Coleman, Pat WR	90NE 91-93Hou	23	5'7"	173	Mississippi		6
Coleman, Sidney LB	88-90TB 91Phx 92TB		6'2"	250	Southern Miss.		
Coley, James TE	90Chi 91Ind		6'3"	270	Clemson		

UseName(Nickname)-Positions	Team by Year	See Section	Hgt	Wgt	College	Int	Pts
Collie, Bruce OT-OG	85-89SF 90-91Phi		6'6"	275	Texas-Arlington		
Collier, Reggie QB	83-85USFL 86Dal 87Pit		6'3"	207	Southern Miss.		
Collier, Steve OT-NT	87GB		6'7"	342	Bethune-Cookman		
Collier, Tim DB	76-79KC 80-82StL 82-83SF 84LJ		6'	172	East Texas State	15	12
Collins, Andre LB	90-93Was		6'1"	232	Central Arkansas	4	6
Collins, Brett LB	92-93GB 93LA		6'1"	226	Washington		
Collins, Clarence WR	87StL		6'1"	180	Illinois		
Collins, Dwight WR	84Min	2	6'1"	215	Pittsburgh		6
Collins, Fabray LB	87Min		6'2"	215	Southern Illinois		
Collins, George OG-OT	78-82StL 84-85USFL		6'2"	257	Georgia		
Collins, Glen DE	82-85Cin 87SF		6'6"	265	Mississippi		
Collins, Jim LB	81-85LA 86SJ 87-88LA 89SD		6'2"	231	Syracuse		
Collins, Kirk DB	81-83LA		5'11"	182	Baylor	5	
	1984 — Died from cancer						
Collins, Mark DB	86-93NYG		5'10"	190	Fullerton State	17	8
Collins, Patrick HB	88GB		5'9"	177	Oklahoma		
Collins, Roosevelt LB	92Mia		6'4"	235	Texas Christian		
Collins, Shawn WR	89-91Atl 92Cle 93GB	2	6'2"	207	Northern Arizona		30
Collins, Shane DE	92-93Was		6'3"	267	Arizona State		
Collins, Todd LB	92-93NE		6'2"	242	Carson-Newman		
Collins, Tony HB	81-87NE 88-89DR 90Mia	23	5'11"	208	East Carolina		264
Collins, Trent DB	87NYJ		6'1"	187	San Diego State		
Collinsworth, Cris WR	81-88Cin	2	6'5"	192	Florida		216
Colon, Harry DB	91NE 92Dal 93Det		5'11"	203	Missouri	2	
Colorito, Tony NT	86Den 87KJ		6'5"	260	Southern Calif.		
Colquitt, Craig K	78-81Pit 82LJ 83-84Pit	4	6'2"	183	Tennessee		
Colquitt, Jimmy K	85Sea		6'4"	208	Tennessee		
Colter, Jeff DB	84Min 87KC		5'10"	171	Kansas		
Colton, George OT	87NE		6'4"	279	Maryland		
Combs, Chris TE-OT	80-81StL 83-84USFL		6'4"	238	New Mexico		6
Comeaux, Darren LB	82-86Den 87SF 88-91Sea		6'1"	229	Arizona State	3	
Commiskey, Chuck OG	83-84USFL 86-88NO		6'4"	290	Mississippi		
Compton, Chuck DB	87GB		5'10"	190	Boise State		
Compton, Mike C-OG	93Det		6'6"	297	West Virginia		
Conklin, Cary QB	92-93Was	1	6'4"	220	Washington		
Conlan, Shane LB	87-92Buf 93LA		6'3"	233	Penn State	4	
Conlin, Chris OG	87Mia 88KJ 90-91Ind		6'4"	290	Penn State		
Conlin, Ray DT	87Phi		6'2"	258	Ohio State		
Connell, Mike K	78SF 80-81Was	4	6'1'	200	Cincinnati		
Conner, Darion LB	90-93Atl		6'2"	250	Jackson State		
Conover, Frank DT	91Cle		6'5"	317	Syracuse		
Conover, Scott OG-OT	91-93Det		6'4"	285	Purdue		
Contz, Bill OT	83-86Cle 86-88NO		6'5"	268	Penn State		
Conway, Curtis WR	93Chi	23	6'	185	Southern Calif.		12
Conwell, Joe OT	84-85USFL 86-87Phi		6'5"	275	North Carolina		
Cook, Charles DT	83NYG 85USFL		6'3"	255	Miami (Fla.)		
Cook, Kelly FB	87GB		5'11"	225	Oklahoma State		
Cook, Marv TE	89-93NE	2	6'4"	234	Iowa		60
Cook, Toi DB	87-93NO		5'11"	188	Stanford	16	12
Cooks, Johnie LB	82-83Bal 84-88Ind 88-90NYG 91Cle		6'4"	247	Mississippi State	4	6
Cooks, Rayford DE	87Hou		6'3"	245	North Texas State		
Cooks, Terrence LB	89NE		6'	230	Nicholls State		
Coombs, Larry OG-C	80NO		6'4"	260	Idaho		
Coombs, Tom TE	82-83NYJ		6'3"	234	Idaho		
Cooper, Adrian TE	91-93Pit	2	6'5"	259	Oklahoma		30
Cooper, Earl FB-TE	80-85SF 86Raid	2	6'2"	228	Rice		108
Cooper, Evan DB	84-87Phi 88-89Atl	3	5'11"	185	Michigan	11	
Cooper, George LB	87SF		6'2"	225	Michigan State		
Cooper, Jim OT-C-OG	77-86Dal		6'5"	262	Temple		
Cooper, Joe K	84Hou 86NYG	5	5'10"	175	Tulsa		56
Cooper, Louis LB	85-90KC 91Mia 93Phi		6'2"	240	Western Carolina	1	
Cooper, Mark OT	83-87Den 87-89TB		6'5"	271	Miami (Fla.)		
Cooper, Reggie LB	91Dal		6'2"	215	Nebraska		
Cooper, Richard OT	90-93NO		6'4"	288	Tennessee		
Cooper, Scott DE	87Cle		6'5"	285	Kearney State		
Copeland, Anthony LB	87Was		6'2"	250	Wichita State, Louisville		
Copeland, Danny DB	89-90KC 91-93Was	3	6'2"	210	Eastern Kentucky	2	6
Copeland, Horace WR	93TB	2	6'2"	195	Miami (Fla.)		24
Copeland, John DT	93Cin		6'3"	286	Alabama		
Copeland, Russell WR	93Buf	23	6'	200	Memphis State		6
Corker, John LB	80-82Hou 83-85USFL 88GB		6'5"	240	Oklahoma State		6
Corley, Anthony FB	84Pit 85SD		6'	210	Nevada-Reno		
Corley, Chris TE	87Sea		6'4"	285	South Carolina		
Cormier, Joe LB	87Raid		6'6"	230	Southern Calif.		
Cornish, Frank C-OG	90-91SD 92-93Dal		6'4"	292	U.C.L.A.		
Cornelson, Martin C	87NYJ		6'1"	230	N. Carolina State		
Cornwell, Fred TE	84-85Dal		6'6"	236	Southern Calif.		6
Corral, Frank K	78-81LA 83-85USFL	45	6'2"	224	U.C.L.A.		379
Correal, Chuck C	79-80Atl 81Cle 84USFL		6'3"	247	Penn State		
Corrington, Kip DB	89-90Den		6'	175	Texas A&M	1	
Corsetti, Rico LB	87NE		6'1"	225	Bates		
Cortes, Julio LB	87Sea		6'	226	Miami (Fla.)		
Corvino, Anthony OG-OT	87NYJ		6'1"	262	Southern Conn. St.		
Coryatt, Quentin LB	92-93Ind		6'3"	250	Texas A&M		
Coryell, Don	HC73-77StL HC78-86SD				Washington		
Cosbie, Doug TE	79-88Dal	2	6'6"	235	Santa Clara		180
Coss, Eric C	87NYJ		6'3"	270	Temple		
Costello, Joe LB	84-85USFL 86-88Atl 89Raid		6'3"	245	Central Conn. St.		
Cotney, Mark DB	75Hou 76-80TB 81KJ 82-84TB		6'	204	N. Mex. Highlands, Cameron	17	
Cotton, Barney OG	79Cin 80-81StL 82KJ		6'5"	264	Nebraska		
Cotton, Marcus LB	88-90Atl 90Cle 91Sea 92KJ		6'3"	225	Southern Calif.		
Courson, Steve OG	78-83Pit 84-85TB		6'1"	274	South Carolina		
Courtney, Matt DB	87SF		5'11"	194	Idaho State	1	
Courville, Vince WR	84-85USFL 87Dal		5'9"	170	Texas Southern, Rice		
Cousineau, Tom LB	79-81CFL 82-85Cle 86-87SF		6'3"	225	Ohio State	10	
Covert, Jim OT	83-90Chi 91XJ		6'4"	277	Pittsburgh		
Covington, Jamie FB	87NYG		6'1"	234	Syracuse		
Covington, Tony DB	91-92TB 93XJ		5'11"	190	Virginia	3	
Cowan, Larry HB	82Mia 82NE		5'11"	194	Jackson State		
Cowher, Bill LB	80Cle 81KJ 82Cle 83-84Phi HC92-93Pit		6'3"	226	N. Carolina State		
Cowne, John C	87Was		6'2"	245	Virginia Tech		
Cox, Aaron WR	88-92LA 93Ind	2	5'9"	174	Arizona State		48
Cox, Arthur TE	83-87Atl 88-91SD 91Mia 91Cle	2	6'3"	262	Texas Southern		60
Cox, Bryan LB	91-93Mia		6'3"	239	Western Illinois	2	
Cox, Greg DB	88SF 89NYG 90-91SF		6'	223	San Jose State		
Cox, Ron LB	90-93Chi		6'2"	240	Fresno State		

UseName(Nickname)-Positions	Team by Year	See Section	Hgt	Wgt	College	Int	Pts
Cox, Steve K	81-84Cle 85-88Was	45	6'4"	195	Arkansas		21
Cox, Tom C	87LA		6'5"	260	Southern Calif.		
Crable, Bob LB	82-87NYJ 88KJ		6'3"	230	Notre Dame	3	
Craft, Donnie FB	82-84Hou	2	6'	206	Louisville		24
Crafts, Jerry OT	92-93Buf		6'6"	341	Louisville		
Craig, Paco WR	88Det		5'10"	173	U.C.L.A.		
Craig, Roger FB-HB	83-90SF 91Raid 92-93Min	2	6'	224	Nebraska		438
Craver, Aaron HB	91-92Mia 93KJ	23	5'11"	215	Fresno State		6
Crawford, Charles FB	86-87Phi	23	6'2"	235	Oklahoma State		6
Crawford, Derrick WR	86SF 87FJ		5'10"	185	Memphis State		
Crawford, Elbert OG-C	90-91NE		6'3"	280	Arkansas		
Crawford, Keith WR	93NYG		6'2"	180	Howard Payne		
Crawford, Mike HB	87Cle		5'10"	215	Arizona State		
Crawford, Tim LB	87Cle 87Ind		6'4"	245	Texas Tech		
Creswell, Smiley DE	85Phi		6'4"	251	Michigan State		
Crews, Ron NT-DE	80Cle		6'3"	256	Nevada-Las Vegas		
Crews, Terry LB	91LA 93SD		6'2"	244	Western Michigan		
Cribbs, James DE	89Det		6'3"	269	Memphis State		
Cribbs, Joe HB	80-83Buf 84-85USFL 85Buf 86-87SF 88Ind 88Mia	23	5'11"	191	Auburn		258
Crissy, Cris DB	81Was 82JJ		5'11"	195	Princeton		
Criswell, Jeff OG-OT	87Ind 88-93NYJ		6'7"	289	Graceland		
Criswell, Kirby DE-LB	80-81StL		6'5"	238	Kansas		
Criswell, Ray K	87-88TB	4	6'	192	Florida		1
Crittenden, Ray WR	93NE	2	6'	188	Virginia Tech		6
Crocicchia, Jim QB	87NYG		6'2"	209	Pennsylvania		
Crockett, Ray DB	89-93Det		5'9"	181	Baylor	16	12
Crockett, Willis LB	90Dal		6'3"	234	Georgia Tech		
Croel, Mike LB	91-93Den		6'3"	231	Nebraska	1	6
Cromwell, Nolan DB	77-87LA		6'1"	199	Kansas	37	49
Cronan, Pete LB	77-79Sea 80ZJ 81Sea 81-85Was		6'2"	238	Boston College	2	
Croom, Corey HB	93NE	2	5'11"	212	Ball State		
Crooms, Chris DB	92LA		6'2"	211	Texas A&M		
Crosby, Cleveland DE	80Cle 82Bal 84-85USFL		6'4"	251	Purdue, Arizona		
Crosby, Ron LB	78NO 79-83NYJ 84-85USFL		6'3"	224	Penn State	2	
Cross, Howard TE	89-93NYG	2	6'5"	245	Alabama		60
Cross, Jeff DE	88-93Mia		6'4"	270	Missouri		
Cross, Justin OT	82-86Buf		6'6"	263	Western St. (Colo.)		
Cross, Randy OG-C	76-88SF		6'3"	259	U.C.L.A.		
Croston, Dave OT	88GB 89SJ		6'5"	280	Iowa		
Crouch, Terry OG	82Bal 84USFL		6'2"	278	Oklahoma		
Croudip, David DB	83-84USFL 84LA 85SD 85-88Atl		5'8"	183	San Diego State	4	
	October 10, 1988 — Died of drug overdose						
Crouse, Ray FB	84GB	2	5'11"	214	Oregon State		6
Crudup, Derrick DB-FB	89,91Raid		6'2"	225	Florida, Oklahoma		
Crump, George DE	82-83NE 84KJ		6'4"	260	East Carolina		2
Crutchfield, Dwayne FB	82-83NYJ 83Hou 84LA	2	6'	235	Iowa State		36
Cryder, Bob OG-OT	78-83NE 84-86Sea 87KJ		6'4"	275	Alabama		
Cullity, Dave OT	89SF 90SJ		6'7"	275	Utah		
Culpepper, Brad DT	92-93Min		6'1"	264	Florida		
Culpepper, Willie WR	92TB		5'11"	155	Southwestern La.		
Culver, Rodney HB	92-93Ind	2	5'9"	224	Notre Dame		84
Cumby, George LB	80-85GB 86Buf 87Phi		6'	220	Oklahoma	5	
Cummings, Mack WR	87NYG		6'	195	East Tennessee St.		
Cunningham, Bennie TE	76-85Pit	2	6'4"	254	Clemson		120
Cunningham, Ed C	92-93Phx		6'3"	290	Washington		
Cunningham, Eric OG	79NYJ 80StL 80NYJ		6'3"	257	Penn State		
Cunningham, Pat OT	90Ind		6'6"	295	Texas A&M		
Cunningham, Randall QB	85-93Phi	12	6'4"	196	Nevada-Las Vegas		174
Cunningham, Rick OT	92-93Phx		6'6"	312	Texas A&M		
Cupp, Keith OT	87Cin		6'6"	301	Findlay		
Curcio, Mike LB	81Phi 82NYG 82Phi 83GB		6'1"	235	Temple		
Curley, August LB	83-86Det		6'3"	226	Southern Calif.		
Curran, Willie WR	82-84Atl		5'10"	175	California		
Currier, Bill DB	77-79Hou 80NE 81-85NYG		6'	196	South Carolina	11	6
Curry, Buddy LB	80-87Atl		6'4"	224	North Carolina	7	12
Curry, Craig DB	84-86TB 87Ind		6'	189	Texas	3	
Curry, Eric DE	93TB		6'5"	270	Alabama		
Curry, Ivory DB	87TB		5'11"	185	Florida		
Curry, Shane DE	91Ind		6'5'	270	Georgia Tech, Miami (Fla.)		
	1992 — Killed in shooting						
Curtis, Bobby LB	87Was 88JJ		6'3"	235	Savannah State		
Curtis, Scott LB	88Phi 89-90Den		6'1"	230	New Hampshire		
Curtis, Travis DB	87StL 88Phx 88Was 89Min 90NYJ 91Was		5'10"	181	West Virginia	6	
Cuthbert, Randy FB	93Pit		6'3"	225	Duke		
D'Addio, Dave FB	84Det 85NJ 87KJ		6'2"	235	Maryland		
Dafney, Bernard OG-OT	92-93Min		6'5"	324	Tennessee		
Dahl, Bob OG-OT	92-93Cle		6'5"	293	Notre Dame		
Daluiso, Brad K	91Atl 91Buf 92Den 93NYG		6'2"	208	San Diego St., UCLA		11
Dale, Jeff DB	85-86SD 87XJ 88SD		6'3"	211	Louisiana State	6	6
Dallafior, Ken OG-OT-C	84USFL 85-88SD 89-92Det		6'4"	276	Minnesota		
Dalman, Chris OG-C	93SF		6'3"	285	Stanford		
Daniel, Eugene DB	84-93Ind		5'11"	179	Louisiana State	27	12
Daniel, Kenny DB	83-84USFL 84NYG 85BH 86-87Ind		5'10"	180	San Jose State	2	
Daniels, Calvin LB	82-85KC 86Was		6'3"	238	North Carolina	3	
Daniels, David WR	91-92Sea		6'1"	190	Penn State		
Danielson, Gary QB	76-78Det 79KJ 80-84Det 85Cle 86NJ 87-88Cle	12	6'2"	195	Purdue		48
Danmeier, Rick K	78-82Min 83XJ	5	6'	194	Sioux Falls		364
Darby, Byron DE-NT-TE	83-86Phi 87-88Ind 89Det		6'4"	260	Southern Calif.		
Darby, Matt DB	92-93Buf		6'1"	200	U.C.L.A.	2	
Dardar, Ramsey OG-OT	84StL		6'2"	264	Louisiana State		
Darns, Phil DE	84TB		6'3"	245	Miss. Valley St.		
Darrington, Chris WR	87Hou		5'10"	180	Weber State		
Darwin, Matt OT-C	86-89Phi		6'4"	268	Texas A&M		
Daugherty, Ron WR	87Min		6'3"	185	Northeastern		
Daum, Mike OT	81Was 84USFL		6'6"	256	Cal. Poly.-S.L.O		
Daum, Mitch TE	87Hou		6'5"	250	Wyoming		
Davenport, Charles WR	92-93Pit	2	6'3"	210	N. Carolina State		6
Davenport, Ron FB	85-89Mia	2	6'2"	230	Louisville		102
Davey, Don DE	91-93GB		6'4"	276	Wisconsin		
David, Stan LB	84Buf 85XJ		6'3"	210	Texas Tech		6
Davidson, Chy WR	84-85NYJ		5'11"	175	Rhode Island		
Davidson, Greg C	80-82Hou 84USFL		6'2"	250	North Texas		
Davidson, Jeff OG-OT	90-92Den		6'5"	309	Ohio State		
Davidson, Kenny DE	90-93Pit		6'5"	272	Louisiana State	1	6
Davis, Anthony LB	93Sea		6'	231	Utah		
Davis, Antone OT	91-93Phi		6'4"	325	Tennessee		
Davis, Billy LB	84StL		6'4"	210	Clemson		

UseName(Nickname)-Positions	Team by Year	See Section	Hgt.	Wgt.	College	Int	Pts
Davis, Brian DB	87-90Was 91-92Sea 93SD		6'2"	190	Nebraska	9	6
Davis, Bruce OT-OG	79-81Oak 82-87Raid 87-89Hou		6'6"	287	U.C.L.A.		
Davis, Bruce WR	84Cle		5'8"	160	Baylor		12
Davis, Chris LB	87NYG		6'1"	225	San Diego State		
Davis, Darrell DE	90-91NYJ		6'2"	258	Texas Christian		6
Davis, Dexter DB	91-92Phx 93LA	3	5'10"	190	Clemson	2	
Davis, Eric DB	90-93SF		5'11"	178	Jacksonville State	8	12
Davis, Elgin HB	87-88NE		5'10"	192	Central Florida		
Davis, Fred DB	87Sea		5'10"	182	Western Carolina		
Davis, Greg K	87-88Atl 89NE 89-90Atl 91-93Phx	5	5'11"	197	The Citadel		547
Davis, James DB	82-87Raid		6'	193	Southern U.	4	6
Davis, Jeff LB	82-87TB		6'	230	Clemson	3	
Davis, Jerome NT	87Det		6'1"	260	Ball State		
Davis, John OT-OG-C	87-88Hou 89-93Buf		6'4"	306	Georgia Tech		
Davis, Johnny FB	78-80TB 81SF 82-87Cle	2	6'1"	235	Alabama		90
Davis, Kelvin OG	87NYG		6'2"	260	Johnson C. Smith		
Davis, Kenneth HB	86-88GB 89-93Buf	23	5'10"	209	Texas Christian		180
Davis, Lee DB	85Cin 87Ind		5'11"	200	Mississippi	1	
Davis, Lorenzo WR	90Pit		5'11"	185	Youngstown State		
Davis, Mike DB	78-81Oak 82-85Raid 86JJ		6'3"	203	Colorado	11	6
Davis, Oliver DB	77-80Cle 81-82Cin 83-85USFL		6'"	203	Tennessee State	11	6
Davis, Paul LB	81-82Atl 83NYG 83StL		6'2"	221	North Carolina	1	
Davis, Preston DB	84-86Ind		5'11"	180	Baylor	3	
Davis, Reuben DE-DT	88-92TB 92-93Phx		6'4"	290	North Carolina	1	6
Davis, Russell FB	80-83Pit	2	6'1"	227	Michigan		12
Davis, Scott DE-LB-DT	88-91Raid		6'7"	272	Illinois		
Davis, Scott OG	93NYG		6'3"	289	Iowa		
Davis, Travis NT	90NO 91Ind		6'2"	279	Michigan State		
Davis, Tyrone DB	85NYG 86XJ		6'1"	190	Clemson		
Davis, Wayne DB	85-86SD 87-89Buf 89-90Was		5'11"	177	Indiana State	3	
Davis, Wayne LB	87StL 88Phx		6'1"	213	Alabama		
Davis, Wendell WR	88-93Chi	2	5'11"	188	Louisiana State		84
Davis, Willie WR	91-93KC	2	6'	170	Central Arkansas		60
Dawkins, Dale WR	90-93NYJ		6'1"	190	Miami (Fla.)		
Dawkins, Julius WR	83-84Buf	2	6'1"	196	Pittsburgh		18
Dawkins, Sean WR	93Ind	2	6'4"	213	California		6
Dawkins, Tommy DE	87Pit		6'3"	260	Appalachian State		
Dawsey, Lawrence WR	91-93TB	2	6'	195	Florida State		30
Dawsey, Stacey WR	87NO	2	5'9"	154	Indiana		
Dawson, Dale K	87Min 88Phi 88GB		6'	213	Eastern Kentucky		20
Dawson, Dermontti C-OG	88-93Pit		6'2"	279	Kentucky		
Dawson, Doug OG	84-86StL 90-93Hou		6'3"	279	Texas		
Dawson, Lin TE	81-85NE 86KJ 87-90NE	2	6'3"	240	N. Carolina State		48
Dawson, Mike NT-DT-DE	76-82StL 83Det 84KC		6'4"	269	Arizona	1	
Dean, Fred DE	75-81SD 81-85SF		6'3"	230	Louisiana Tech	1	12
Dean, Kevin LB	87SF		6'1"	235	Texas Christian		
Dean, Vernon DB	82-87Was 88Sea		5'11"	178	U.S. International, San Diego State	22	24
Dean, Walter FB	91GB		5'10"	216	Grambling		
DeAyala, Kiki LB	84-85USFL 86-87Cin		6'1"	225	Texas		
DeForest, Joe LB	87NO		6'1"	240	Southwestern La.		
DeBerg, Steve QB	77-80SF 81-83Den 84-87TB 88-91KC 92-93TB 93Mia	12	6'2"	207	San Jose State		42
deBruijn, Case K	82KC 84-85USFL	4	6'1"	176	Idaho State		
Dee, Donnie TE	88-89Ind 89Sea		6'4"	247	Tulsa		
DeGraffenreid, Allen WR	93Cin		6'3"	200	Ohio State		
Degrate, Tony DE	85GB		6'4"	280	Texas		
DeJurnett, Charles DE-DT-NT	76-80SD 81FJ 82-86LA		6'4"	263	San Jose State		
Delaney, Jeff DB	80LA 81Det 81TB 82-83Bal 84-85USFL		6'	195	Pittsburgh	4	
Delaney, Joe HB	81-82KC 83 — died in swimming accident	2	5'10"	184	Northwestern La.		18
Del Greco, Al K	84-87GB 87StL 88-90Phx 91-93Hou	5	5'10"	191	Auburn		800
DeLine, Steve K	88SD 89Phi	5	5'11"	185	Colorado State		42
Dellenbach, Jeff OT-C	85-93Mia		6'6"	281	Wisconsin		
DeLoach, Ralph DE	81NYJ		6'5"	254	California		
DeLong, Keith LB	89-93SF		6'2"	245	Tennessee	2	
Delpino, Robert FB-HB	88-92LA 93Den	23	6'	205	Missouri		162
Del Rio, Jack LB	85-86NO 87-88KC 89-91Dal 92-93Min		6'4"	238	Southern Calif.	9	6
Dennard, Mark C	79-83Mia 84-85Phi 86Cle		6'1"	253	Texas A&M		
Dennard, Preston WR	78-83LA 84Buf 85GB	2	6'1"	184	New Mexico		180
Dennis, Mark OT	87-93Mia		6'6"	292	Illinois		
Dennis, Mike DB	80-83NYG 84SD 84NYJ		5'10"	190	Wyoming	6	6
Dennison, Glenn TE	84NYJ 85XJ 87Was	2	6'3"	225	Miami (Fla.)		6
Dennison, Rick LB	82-90Den		6'3"	219	Colorado State	4	
Dent, Burnell LB	86-92GB		6'1"	236	Tulane	1	
Dent, Richard DE	83-93Chi		6'5"	264	Tennessee State	8	12
DeOssie, Steve LB	84-88Dal 89-93NYG 93NYJ		6'2"	247	Boston College	1	
Derby, Glenn OT-OG	89-90NO		6'6"	290	Wisconsin		
Derby, John LB	92Det		6'	232	Iowa		
DeRiggi, Fred NT	90NE		6'2"	268	Syracuse		
DeRoo, Brian WR	79-81Bal		6'3"	193	Redlands		6
DeRose, Dan LB	87NYG		6'	230	Southern Colorado	1	
Detmer, Ty QB	92-93GB		6'	183	Brigham Young		
DeVaughn, Dennis DB	82-83Phi 85USFL		5'10"	175	Bishop		
Devlin, Joe OT-OG	76-82Buf 83BN 84-89Buf		6'5"	261	Iowa		
Devlin, Mike C	93Buf		6'1"	293	Iowa		
DeVita, Rob LB	87Sea		6'2"	222	Illinois, Benedictine		
Dial, Alan DB	89Phi		6'1"	188	U.C.L.A.		
Diana, Rich FB	82Mia		5'9"	220	Yale		
Diaz-Infante, David C-OG	87SD		6'2"	272	San Jose State		
DiBernardo, Rick LB	86StL 87LA		6'3"	230	Notre Dame		
Dick, Jim LB	87Min		6'1"	230	N. Dakota State		
Dickerson, Andy OG	87Raid		6'5"	260	Cal. Lutheran		
Dickerson, Anthony LB	80-84Dal 85Buf		6'2"	220	S.M.U.	5	2
Dickerson, Eric HB-FB	83-87LA 87-91Ind 92Raid 93Atl	2	6'3"	220	S.M.U.		576
Dckerson, Ron HB-WR	93KC		6'	211	Arkansas		
Dickey, Charlie OG	87Pit		6'3"	270	Arizona		
Dickey, Curtis HB-FB	80-83Bal 84-85Ind85-86Cle	2	6'1"	213	Texas A&M		240
Didier, Clint TE	82-87Was 88-89GB	2	6'5"	240	Portland State		132
Didio, Mark WR	92Pit		5'11"	181	Connecticut		
Dierking, Scott HB-FB	77-83NYJ 84TB	2	5'10"	218	Purdue		138
Dieterich, Chris OT-OG	80-86Det		6'3"	262	N. Carolina State		
Diettrich, John K	87Hou		6'2"	190	Ball State		23
DiGiacomo, Curt OG-C	86SD 88KC		6'4"	270	Arizona		
Dill, Scott OG	88-89Phx 90-93TB		6'5"	282	Memphis State		
Dillard, Stacey DE-NT	92-93NYG		6'5"	288	Oklahoma		
Dils, Steve QB	79-84Min 84-87LA 88Atl 89LA	12	6'1"	191	Stanford		
Dilweg, Anthony QB	89-90GB	12	6'3"	215	Duke		

UseName(Nickname)-Positions	Team by Year	See Section	Hgt.	Wgt.	College	Int	Pts
Dimler, Rich NT-DT	79Cle 80GB 83-84USFL		6'6"	260	Southern Calif.		
Dimry, Charles DB	88-90Atl 91-93Den		6'	175	Nevada-Las Vegas	10	6
Dingle, Mike FB	91Cin	2	6'2"	240	South Carolina		6
Dinkel, Tom LB	78-83Cin 84-85USFL 85Cin		6'3"	240	Kansas	1	
Dinkins, Howard LB	93Atl		6'1"	230	Florida State		
Dion, Terry DE	80Sea		6'6"	254	Oregon		
Diorio, Jerry TE	87Det		6'3"	245	Michigan		
DiRenzo, Fred FB	87NYG		5'11"	234	New Haven		
DiRico, Robert HB	87NYG	2	5'10"	202	Kutztown		
Dishman, Cris DB	88-93Hou		6'	180	Purdue	23	24
Dixon, Al TE	77-79NYG 79-82KC 83Phi 84SD 84SF	2	6'5"	230	Iowa State		48
Dixon, Cal C	92-93NYJ		6'4"	284	Florida		
Dixon, Dwayne WR	84,87TB		6'1"	204	Florida		
Dixon, Floyd WR	86-91Atl 92Phi	23	5'9"	170	S.F. Austin State		96
Dixon, Gerald LB	93Cle		6'3"	252	South Carolina		
Dixon, Hanford DB	81-89Cle		5'11"	186	Southern Miss.	26	
Dixon, James WR-HB	89-91Dal	23	5'10"	181	Houston		18
Dixon, Joe NT	87Hou		6'3"	275	Tulsa		
Dixon, Randy OT-OG	87-93Ind		6'3"	299	Pittsburgh		6
Dixon, Rich LB	83Atl 85USFL		6'2"	235	California		
Dixon, Rickey DB	88-92Cin 93Raid		5'11"	183	Oklahoma	3	
Dixon, Ronnie NT	93NO		6'2"	292	Cincinnati		
Dixon, Titus WR	89NYJ 89Ind		5'6"	152	Troy State		
Dixon, Zachary HB	79Den 79NYG 80Phi 80-83Bal 83-84Sea 85KJ	23	6'	203	Temple		30
Dodge, Dedrick DB	91-92Sea		6'2"	184	Florida State	1	
Dodge, Kirk LB	84Det 85SJ 86Hou 87Den		6'1"	232	Nevada-Las Vegas		
Doerger, Jerry OT-C	82Chi 84-85USFL 85SD		6'5"	270	Wisconsin		
Dohring, Tom OT	92KC		6'6"	290	Michigan		
Doig, Steve LB	82-84Det 86-87NE		6'2"	242	New Hampshire		
Doleman, Chris DE-LB	85-93Min		6'5"	266	Pittsburgh	8	16
Dollinger, Tony FB	87Det		5'11"	205	Evangel		
Dombroski, Paul DB	80KC 81-84NE 85TB		6'	185	Linfield	2	
Dombrowski, Jim OT-OG	86-93NO		6'5"	298	Virginia		
Donahue, Mitch LB	91-92SF 93Den		6'2"	254	Wyoming		
Donaldson, Jeff DB	84-89Hou 90KC 91-93Atl		6'	192	Colorado	12	6
Donaldson, Ray C-OG	80-83Bal 84-92Ind 93Sea		6'3"	289	Georgia		
Donley, Doug WR	81-84Dal	2	6'	175	Ohio State		24
Donnalley, Kevin OT	91-93Hou		6'5"	299	Davidson, North Carolina		
Donnalley, Rick C-OG	82-83Pit 84-85Was 86-87KC		6'2"	261	North Carolina		
Donnelly, Rick K	85-88Atl 89XJ 90-91Sea	4	6'	190	Wyoming		1
D'Onofrio, Mark LB	92GB 93LJ		6'2"	235	Penn State		
Donovan, Tom WR	80NO 83-85USFL		5'11"	179	Penn State		
Doornink, Dan FB-HB	78NYG 79-85Sea	2	6'3"	210	Washington State		156
Dorn, Torin DB	90-93Raid		6'	190	North Carolina	1	2
Dornbrook, Thom OG-C	79Pit 80Mia 83-85USFL		6'2"	240	Kentucky		
Dorney, Keith OT-OG	79-87Det		6'5"	268	Penn State		
Dorning, Dale DE	87Sea		6'5"	260	Oregon		
Dorsett, Tony HB	77-87Dal 88Den 89KJ	2	5'11"	190	Pittsburgh		552
Dorsey, Dean K	88Phi 88GB	5	5'11"	190	Toronto		27
Dorsey, Eric DE	86-92NYG		6'5"	280	Notre Dame		
Dorsey, John LB	84-88GB 89KJ		6'3"	240	Connecticut		
Doss, Reggie DE-DT	78-87LA		6'4"	265	Hampton U.		
Dotson, Earl OT	93GB		6'4"	315	Texas A&I		
Dotson, Santana DE	92TB		6'5"	270	Baylor		6
Doubiago, Dan OT	87KC		6'5"	283	Utah		
Douglas, David OT-OG-C	86-88Cin 89-90NE		6'4"	280	Tennessee		
Douglas, Derrick FB	91Cle 92KJ		5'10"	222	Louisiana Tech		
Douglas, Leland WR	87Mia		6'	179	Baylor		6
Douglass, Mike LB	78-85GB 86SD		6'	220	Arizona State,	10	18
Douglass, Maurice DB	86-93Chi		5'11"	200	Kentucky	4	
Dove, Wes DE	87Sea		6'7"	270	Syracuse		
Dowdell, Marcus WR	92-93NO		5'10"	179	Tennessee State		6
Dowhower, Rod	HC85-86Ind				San Diego State		
Dowling, Sean OG-OT	87Buf		6'4"	280	C.W. Post		
Downing, Walt OG-C	78-83SF 85USFL		6'3"	259	Michigan		
Downs, Michael DB	81-88Dal		6'3"	205	Rice	35	18
Dozier, Cornelius DB	87KC		6'2"	190	S.M.U.		
Dozier, D.J. HB-FB	87-90Min 91Det 92 played major league baseball	2	6'	198	Penn State		54
Drake, Joe NT	85Phi 87SF		6'2"	290	Arizona		
Drane, Dwight DB	84-85USFL 86-91Buf		6'2"	204	Oklahoma	1	
Drayton, Troy TE	93LA	2	6'3"	255	Penn State		24
Dreschler, Dave OG	83-84GB		6'3"	264	North Carolina		
Dressel, Chris TE	83-86Hou 87SF 89KC 89-91NYJ 92SF	2	6'4"	239	Stanford		42
Drewrey, Willie WR	85-88Hou 89-92TB 93Hou	23	5'7"	164	West Virginia		42
Driver, Stacey HB	87Cle		5'7"	190	Clemson		
Dronett, Shane DE	92-93Den		6'6"	275	Texas	2	
Drost, Jeff NT	87GB		6'5"	286	Iowa		
Drozdov, Darren NT-DT	93Den		6'3"	280	Maryland		
Drummond, Robert HB	89-91Phi	2	6'1"	205	Syracuse		24
Duarte, George DB	87Chi		5'9"	172	Northern Arizona		
Dubois, Phil TE	79-80Was 81LA 83USFL		6'2"	220	San Diego State		
DuBose, Demetrious LB	93TB		6'1"	240	Notre Dame		
DuBose, Doug HB	87-88SF	23	5'11"	190	Nebraska		12
Duckens, Mark DE	89NYG 90Det 92TB		6'4"	270	Wichita State, Arizona State		
Duckett, Kenny WR	82-85NO 85Dal	23	6'	184	Wake Forest		24
Duckworth, Bobby WR	82-84SD 85-86LA 86Phi	2	6'3"	197	Arkansas		78
Ducksworth, Robert DB	86NYJ		5'11"	200	Southern Miss.		
Duda, Mark DT	83-87StL		6'3"	273	Maryland		
Dudek, Joe HB	87Den		6'	181	Plymouth State		12
Dudley, Brian DB	87Cle		6'1"	180	Bethune-Cookman		
Duerson, Dave DB	83-89Chi 90NYG 91-93Phx		6'1"	207	Notre Dame	20	6
Dufault, Paul C	87Raid		6'4"	255	New Hampshire		
Dufek, Don DB	76-77Sea 78KJ 79-84Sea		6'	195	Michigan	3	
Dufek, Joe QB	83-85Buf 85SD		6'4"	215	Yale		6
Duff, John TE	93Raid		6'7"	250	New Mexico		
Duffy, Roger C-OG	90-93NYJ		6'3"	285	Penn State		
Dufour, Dan OG	83-84Atl		6'5"	280	U.C.L.A.		
Dugan, Bill OG-OT	81-83Sea 84Min 85USFL 87NYG		6'4"	275	Penn State		
Duhe, A.J. DE-LB	77-84Mia		6'4"	247	Louisiana State	3	2
Dukes, Jamie OG-C	86-93Atl		6'1"	283	Florida State		
Duliban, Chris LB	87Dal		6'2"	216	Texas		
Dulin, Gary DT-DE	86-87StL		6'4"	275	Ohio State		
Dumas, Mike DB	91-92Hou 93FJ		5'11"	178	Indiana	2	6
Dumbauld, Jonathan DE	86NO 87-88Phi 88NO		6'4"	259	Kentucky		
Dumont, Jim LB	84Cle 85USFL		6'1"	224	Rutgers		
Dunaway, Craig TE	83Pit		6'2"	233	Michigan		

UseName(Nickname)-Positions	Team by Year	See Section	Hgt	Wgt	College	Int	Pts
Dunbar, Karl DE	93NO		6'4"	275	Louisiana State		
Dunbar, Vaughn HB	92NO 93KJ	2	5'10"	204	Indiana		18
Duncan, Clyde WR	84-85StL		6'1"	202	Tennessee	6	
Duncan, Curtis WR	87-93Hou	23	5'11"	185	Northwestern		120
Duncan, Frank DB	79-81SD 83-85USFL		6'1"	188	San Fran. State	1	
Dunek, Ken TE	80Phi 83-85USFL		6'6"	235	Memphis State		
Dunn, Gary DT-NT-DE	76Pit 77KJ 78-87Pit		6'3"	258	Miami (Fla.)		
Dunn, K.D. TE	85-86TB 87Was 88NYJ	2	6'3"	235	Clemson		
Dunsmore, Pat TE	83-84Chi 85LJ	2	6'3"	237	Drake		6
Dupard, Reggie HB-TE	86-89NE 89-90Was	2	5'11"	205	S.M.U.		66
Duper, Mark WR	82-92Mia	2	5'9"	188	Northwestern La.		354
Dupree, Marcus HB	90-91LA	2	6'2"	225	Oklahoma, Southern Miss.		6
Dupree, Myron DB	83Den		5'11"	180	N. Car. Central		
Durham, Darius WR	83SF		6'2"	185	San Diego State		
Durham, Steve DE	82Bal		6'5"	256	Clemson		
Durrette, Michael OG	86-87SF		6'4"	280	West Virginia		
Dusbabek, Mark LB	89-91Min		6'3"	230	Minnesota	1	2
Dutton, John DE-DT	74-78Bal 79-87Dal		6'7"	266	Nebraska	1	10
Dwyer, Mike DT	87Dal		6'3"	280	Massachusetts		
Dyal, Mike TE	89-90Raid 91LJ 92-93KC 93SD	2	6'2"	240	Texas A&I		12
Dye, Ernest OT	93Phx		6'6"	325	South Carolina		
Dykes, Donald DB	79-81NYJ 82SD 84-85USFL		5'11"	183	Southeastern La.	5	
Dykes, Hart Lee WR	89-90NE 91-92KJ	2	6'4"	218	Oklahoma State		42
Dykes, Sean DB	87NYJ		5'10"	170	Bowling Green		
Eaddy, James NT	87Cin		6'2"	280	New York Tech		
Earl, Robin FB-TE	77-82Chi 84-85USFL	2	6'5"	242	Washington		30
Early, Quinn WR	88-90SD 91-93NO	2	6'	188	Iowa		108
Easley, Kenny DB	81-87Sea	3	6'3"	206	U.C.L.A.	32	18
Easley, Walt FB	81-82SF 83-84USFL	2	6'1"	226	West Virginia		6
Easmon, Ricky DB	85Dal 85-86TB 87KJ		5'10"	160	Florida	1	
Eason, Bo DB	84-87Hou		6'2"	200	Cal.-Davis	6	
Eason, Tony QB	83-89NE 89-90NYJ	12	6'4"	212	Illinois		36
Eatman, Irv OT	83-85USFL 86-90KC 91-92NYJ 93LA		6'7"	296	U.C.L.A.		
Eaton, Tracey DB	89Hou 90Phx 91Atl 92KJ 93Atl		6'1"	195	Portland State	4	
Eccles, Scott TE	87Hou		6'5"	245	Eastern New Mexico		
Echols, Donnie TE	87Cle		6'3"	240	Oklahoma State		
Echols, Terry LB	84Pit		6'	220	Marshall		
Eckwood, Jerry HB-FB	79-81TB	2	6'	198	Arkansas		42
Eddings, Floyd WR	82-83NYG	2	5'11"	177	California		
Edelman, Brad OG	82-89NO		6'6"	265	Missouri		
Edmonds, Bobby Joe HB	86-88Sea 89Raid	3	5'11"	186	Arkansas		6
Edmunds, Ferrell TE	88-92Mia 93Sea	2	6'6"	252	Maryland		72
Edwards, Al WR	90-92Buf 93SJ	23	5'8"	168	Northwestern La.		12
Edwards, Anthony WR	89-90Phi 91-93Phx	23	5'11"	195	N. Mex. Highlands		12
Edwards, Antonio DE	93Sea		6'3"	270	Valdosta State		2
Edwards, Brad DB	88-89Min 90-93Was		6'1"	205	South Carolina	16	12
Edwards, Dave DB	85-87Pit		6'	196	Illinois	1	2
Edwards, Dennis DE	87LA		6'4"	253	Southern Calif.		
Edwards, Dixon LB	91-93Dal		6'1"	224	Michigan State	1	6
Edwards, Eddie DT-DE	77-88Cin		6'5"	256	Miami (Fla.)	1	6
Edwards, Herman DB	77-85Phi 86Atl		6'	192	California, San Diego State	30	6
Edwards, Kelvin WR	86NO 87-88Dal	2	6'2"	202	Liberty		24
Edwards, Randy DE-NT	84-87Sea		6'4"	264	Alabama		
Edwards, Stan FB-HB	82-86Hou 87Det	2	6'	210	Michigan		18
Edwards, Tim DE	92NE		6'1"	270	Delta State		
Egloff, Ron TE	77-83Den 84SD	2	6'5"	230	Wisconsin		24
Egu, Patrick HB	89NE 90AJ 91KJ		5'11"	205	Nevada-Reno		6
Ehin, Chuck DE-NT-LB	83-87SD		6'4"	261	Brigham Young		
Eilers, Pat DB	90-91Min 92-93Was		5'11"	195	Notre Dame		
Eisenhooth, Stan C-OT	87-88Sea		6'5"	287	Towson State		
Ekern, Andy OT	84Ind		6'6"	265	Missouri		
Ekern, Carl LB	76-78LA 79KJ 80-88LA		6'3"	223	San Jose State	6	
Elam, Jason K	93Den	5	5'11"	192	Hawaii		119
Elam, Onzy LB	87-88NYJ 89Dal		6'2"	225	Tennessee State		
Elder, Donnie DB	85NYJ 86Pit 86Det 88-89TB 90-91SD	3	5'9"	175	Memphis State	6	
Elewonibi, Mohammed OT	92-93Was		6'4"	298	Brigham Young		
Eley, Clifton TE	87Min		6'5"	230	Mississippi State		
Elias, Homer OG-OT	78-84Det		6'3"	255	Tennessee State		
Eliopulos, Jim LB	83StL 83-85NYJ		6'2"	229	Westminster (Mo.), Wyoming		
Elkins, Mike QB	89-90KC 92Hou		6'3"	225	Wake Forest		
Elko, Bill OG-NT	83-84SD 87Ind		6'5"	279	Arizona State, Louisiana State		
Ellard, Henry WR	83-93LA	23	5'11"	174	Fresno State		312
Ellerson, Gary FB-HB	85-86GB 87Det	2	5'11"	219	Wisconsin		54
Elliott, John (Jumbo) OT	88-93NYG		6'7"	305	Michigan		
Elliott, Lin K	92-93Dal 93Atl	5	6'	182	Texas Tech		127
Elliott, Matt C	92Was 93KJ		6'1"	265	Michigan		
Elliott, Ted NT	87NO		6'6"	275	Mankato State		
Elliott, Tony DB	87GB		5'10"	195	Central Michigan		
Elliott, Tony NT	82-88NO		6'2"	282	Wisconsin, North Texas		
Ellis, Craig HB	86Mia 87Raid	23	5'11"	185	San Diego State		12
Ellis, Gerry FB	80-86GB	2	5'11"	221	Missouri		210
Ellis, Jim LB	87Raid		6'3"	240	Boise State		
Ellis, Ray DB	81-85Phi 86-87Cle		6'1"	194	Ohio State	14	6
Ellison, Riki LB	83-88SF 89KJ 90-92Raid		6'2"	225	Southern Calif.		
Elshire, Neil DE	81-86Min		6'6"	260	Oregon		2
Elway, John QB	83-93Den	12	6'3"	208	Stanford		138
Embree, Jon TE	87-88LA		6'2"	234	Colorado		
Emery, Larry HB	87Atl		5'9"	195	Wisconsin		
Emtman, Steve DE	92-93Ind		6'4"	290	Washington	1	6
English, Doug DT-NT	75-79Det 80VR 81-85Det		6'5"	255	Texas		8
English, Keith K	90LA		6'3"	220	Colorado		
Epps, Jack DB	87KC		6'	197	Kansas State		
Epps, Phillip WR	82-88GB 89NYJ	23	5'10"	165	Texas Christian		84
Epps, Tory NT-DT	90-93Atl 93Chi		6'	277	Memphis State		
Erenberg, Rich HB	84-86Pit 87KJ	23	5'10"	200	Colgate		60
Erhardt, Ron	HC78-81NE				Jamestown		
Erickson, Craig QB	92-93TB	12	6'2"	200	Miami (Fla.)		
Erlandson, Tom LB	88Buf		6'1"	220	Washington		
Ervins, Ricky HB	91-93Was	2	5'7"	200	Southern Calif.		36
Erxleben, Russell K	79-83NO 87Det	4	6'4"	223	Texas		19
Esiason, Boomer QB	84-92Cin 93NYJ	12	6'4"	222	Maryland		36
Espinoza, Alex QB	87KC		6'1"	193	Iowa State		
Essink, Ron OT-TE	80-85Sea 86BA		6'6"	260	Grand Valley St.		6

UseName(Nickname)-Positions	Team by Year	See Section	Hgt	Wgt	College	Int	Pts
Estell, Richard WR	87KC		6'2"	210	Kansas		
Estep, Mike OG-OT	87Buf 87GB		6'4"	270	Bowling Green		
Etienne, Larry LB	90SF		6'2"	245	Nebraska		
Etherly, David DB	87Was		6'1"	190	Portland State		
Evans, Byron LB	87-93Phi		6'2"	233	Arizona	12	12
Evans, Chuck LB	80-81NO		6'3"	235	Stanford		
Evans, Chuck HB	93Min		6'1"	226	Clark-Atlanta		
Evans, David DB	83-85USFL 86-87Min		6'	178	Central Arkansas		
Evans, Donald DE-FB	87LA 88Phi 90-93Pit		6'2"	267	Winston-Salem St.		
Evans, Doug DB	93GB		6'1"	188	Louisiana Tech		
Evans, James FB	87KC		6'	220	Southern U.		
Evans, Jerry TE	93Den		6'4"	250	Toledo		
Evans, John TE	87Atl		6'2"	243	S.F. Austin State		
Evans, Leon DE	85-86Phi 87KJ		6'5"	282	Miami (Fla.)		
Evans, Mike DT-DE	92KC		6'3"	269	Michigan		
Evans, Reggie HB	83Was 85USFL		5'11"	201	Richmond		24
Evans, Scott DE	91Phx		6'3"	261	Oklahoma		
Evans, Russell WR	87Sea		5'8"	165	NE Missouri State		
Evans, Vince QB	77-83Chi 84-85USFL 87-93Raid	12	6'2"	211	Southern Calif.		84
Everett, Eric DB	88-89Phi 90TB 91-92KC		5'10"	163	Texas Tech	8	6
Everett, Jim QB	86-93LA	12	6'5"	212	Purdue		24
Everett, Major FB-HB	83-85Phi 86-87Cle 87Atl	2	5'10"	215	Mississippi		
Everett, Thomas DB	87-91Pit 92-93Dal		5'9"	179	Baylor	20	
Everitt, Steve C-OG	93Cle		6'5"	292	Michigan		
Evers, William DB	90-91Atl		5'10"	175	Florida A&M		
Eyre, Nick OT	81Hou 83USFL		6'5"	274	Brigham Young		
Ezor, Blake HB	90Den		5'9"	183	Michigan State		
Faaola, Nuu HB-FB	86-89NYJ 89Mia		5'11"	216	Hawaii		12
Fada, Rob OG	83-84Chi 85KC		6'2"	265	Pittsburgh		
Fagan, Kevin DE	87-93SF		6'4"	260	Miami (Fla.)		
Fahnhorst, Jim LB	83-84USFL 84-90SF		6'4"	230	Minnesota	3	
Fahnhorst, Keith OT	74-87SF		6'6"	266	Minnesota		
Fain, Richard DB	91Cin 91Phx 92Chi		5'10"	183	Florida	1	
Fairbanks, Don DE	87Sea		6'3"	253	Colorado		
Fairchild, Paul OG-C	84-90NE		6'4"	270	Kansas		
Fairs, Eric LB	86-91Hou 92Atl		6'3"	240	Memphis State		2
Faison, Derrick WR	90LA		6'4"	200	Howard		6
Fann, Chad TE	93Phx		6'3"	250	Florida A&M		
Fantetti, Ken LB	79-85Det		6'2"	230	Wyoming	6	
Farley, John HB	84Cin		5'10"	202	Sacramento State		
Farmer, George WR	82-84LA 87Mia	2	5'10"	175	Southern U.		42
Farr, Mel Jr. FB	89LA		6'	223	U.C.L.A.		
Farr, Mike WR	90-92Det	2	5'10"	192	U.C.L.A.		6
Farrell, Sean OG	82-86TB 87-89NE 90-91Den 92Sea		6'3"	260	Penn State		
Farren, Paul OT-OG	83-91Cle 92KJ		6'5"	272	Boston U.		
Faryniarz, Brett LB	88-91LA 93SF		6'3"	225	San Diego State		
Faucette, Chuck LB	88SD		6'3"	242	Maryland	1	
Faulkner, Chris OG-TE	84LA 85SD		6'4"	255	Florida		
Faulkner, Jeff NT-DE	87KC 90Ind 91-92Phx 93NO 93Was		6'3"	295	Southern U.		
Faurot, Ron DT-DE	84-85NYJ		6'7"	262	Arkansas		
Favre, Brett QB	91Atl 92-93GB	12	6'2"	220	Southern Miss.		12
Favron, Calvin LB	79-82StL 83BL		6'1"	225	Southeastern La.	1	
Faylor, John DB	87SF		6'1"	197	Santa Clara		
Fazio, Ron TE	87Phi		6'4"	242	Maryland		
Feacher, Ricky WR	76NE 76-84Cle	23	5'10"	175	Miss. Valley St.		90
Feagles, Jeff K	88-89NE 90-93Phi	4	6'	198	Miami (Fla.)		
Fears, Willie DE	87Cin 88-89CFL 90Min		6'3"	270	Northeast La.		
Feasel, Grant C	83Bal 84Ind 84Min 85KJ 87-92Sea 93KJ		6'7"	278	Abilene Christian		
Feasel, Greg OT	83-85USFL 86GB 87SD		6'7"	301	Abilene Christian		
Federico, Craig DB	87Det		6'2"	205	Illinois State		
Feehery, Gerry C-OG	83-87Phi 88KC		6'2"	269	Syracuse		
Feggins, Howard DB	89NE		5'10"	190	North Carolina	1	
Feldman, Todd WR	87Mia		5'10"	184	Kent State		
Fellows, Mark LB	86SD		6'2"	233	Montana State		
Fellows, Ron DB	81-86Dal 87-88Raid	3	6'	175	Missouri	19	18
Felton, Joe OG	87Det		6'2"	266	Albion		
Fencik, Gary DB	76-87Chi		6'1"	194	Yale	38	6
Fenerty, Gill HB	90-91NO	23	6'	205	Holy Cross		42
Fenner, Derrick HB	89-91Sea 92-93Cin	2	6'3"	229	North Carolina		174
Fenney, Rick FB	87-91Min	2	6'1"	235	Washington		78
Ferguson, Joe QB	73-84Buf 85-87Det 88-89TB 90Ind	12	6'1"	192	Arkansas		66
Ferguson, Keith DE	81-85SD 85-90Det		6'5"	252	Ohio State	1	
Ferguson, Kevin TE	87SD		6'2"	223	Virginia		
Ferguson, Vagas HB-FB	80-82NE 83Cle 83Hou 84USFL	2	6'1"	204	Notre Dame		30
Fernandez, Mervyn WR	82-86CFL 87-92Raid	2	6'3"	200	San Jose State		114
Ferragamo, Vince QB	77-80LA 81CFL 82-84LA 85Buf 85-86GB	12	6'3"	212	California, Nebraska		12
Ferrari, Ron LB	82-86SF		6'	213	Lakeland, Illinois		
Ferrell, Earl FB	82-87StL 88-89Phx	2	6'	225	East Tennessee St.		156
Fiedler, Don DE	83-85USFL 85TB 86KJ		6'3"	240	Kentucky		
Field, Amod WR	91Phx		5'11"	181	Montclair State		
Field, Doak LB	81StL 83-85USFL		6'2"	228	Baylor		
Fields, Angelo OT	80-81Hou 82GB		6'6"	321	Michigan State		
Fields, Anthony DB	87Det		6'1"	192	Eastern Michigan		
Fields, Floyd DB	91-93SD		6'	208	Arizona State	1	
Fields, Greg DE	79-80Bal 83-85USFL		6'7"	259	Grambling		
Fields, Jaime LB	93KC		5'11"	230	Washington		
Fields, Jitter DB	84NO 87Ind 87KC		5'8"	184	Texas		6
Fields, Joe C-OG	75-87NYJ 88NYG		6'2"	250	Rutgers-Camden, Widener		
Figaro, Cedric LB	88-90SD 91Ind 91-92Cle		6'2"	255	Notre Dame	2	
Figures, Deon DB	93Pit		6'	200	Colorado	1	
Fike, Dan OG-OT	84-85USFL 85-92Cle 93Pit		6'7"	282	Florida		
Fina, John OG-OT	92-93Buf		6'4"	282	Arizona		6
Finch, Steve WR	87Min		6'	200	Elmhurst		
Finzer, Dave K	84Chi 85Sea	4	6'1"	195	Illinois, DePauw		
Fishback, Joe DB	91Atl 92NYJ 92Atl 93Dal		5'11"	198	Carson-Newman		6
Fisher, Bob TE	80-81Chi 84USFL	2	6'3"	240	S.M.U.		12
Fisher, Jeff DB	81-84Chi	3	5'11"	190	Southern Calif.	5	6
Fisher, Mike WR	81StL 83-84USFL		5'11"	172	Baylor		
Fitzgerald, Greg DT	87Chi		6'4"	265	Iowa		
Fitzgerald, Jamie DB	87Min		6'	180	Idaho State		
Fitzgerald, Kevin TE	87GB		6'3"	235	Wis.-Eau Claire		
Fitzgerald, Mickey FB	81Atl 81Phi 84USFL		6'2"	235	Virginia Tech		
Fitzhugh, Steve DB	87Den		5'11"	188	Miami-Ohio		
Fitzkee, Scott WR	79-80Phi 81-82SD 83-85USFL	2	6'	187	Penn State		24
FitzPatrick, James OT-OG	86-89SD 90-91Raid 92KJ		6'8"	305	Southern Calif.		

UseName(Nickname)-Positions	Team by Year	See Section	Hgt	Wgt	College	Int	Pts
Flagler, Terrence HB	87-89SF 90-91Phx	23	6'	200	Clemson		18
Flaherty, Harry LB	87Dal		6'1"	232	Holy Cross		
Flaherty, Tom LB	87Cin		6'3"	223	Northwestern		
Flannery, John OG-C	91-93Hou		6'3"	304	Syracuse		
Fletcher, John OG	87Cin		6'3"	293	Texas A&I		
Fletcher, Simon DE-LB	85-93Den		6'5"	240	Houston	1	2
Flick, Tom QB	81Was 82NE 84Cle 86SD 87NYJ	1	6'3"	190	Washington		6
Flint, Judson DB	80-82Cle 83Buf		6'	201	California (Pa.),	3	
Flones, Brian LB	81-82Sea 83KJ		6'1"	228	Washington State		
Florence, Anthony DB	91Cle		6'	185	Bethune-Cookman		
Flores, Mike DE	91-93Phi		6'3"	256	Louisville		2
Flowers, Kenny HB	87Atl 88KJ 89Atl	2	6'	210	Clemson		6
Flowers, Larry DB	81-85NYG 85NYJ		6'1"	192	Texas Tech	2	
Floyd, Eric OT-OG	90-91SD 92-93Phi		6'5"	305	Auburn		
Floyd, George DB	82NYJ 83KJ 84NYJ		5'11"	190	Eastern Kentucky		
Floyd, John WR	79-80SD 81StL	2	6'1"	195	Northeast La.		12
Floyd, Victor HB	89SD		6'1"	201	Florida State		
Flutie, Darren WR	88SD 90FJ	2	5'10"	184	Boston College		12
Flutie, Doug QB	85USFL 86-87Chi 87-89NE	12	5'9"	176	Boston College		12
Flynn, Tom DB	84-86GB 86-88NYG		6'	195	Pittsburgh	10	18
Flythce, Mark DE	93NYG		6'7"	290	Penn State		
Foggie, Fred DB	92Cle		6'	188	Minnesota		
Foley, Steve DB	76-86Den		6'2"	189	Tulane	44	12
Foley, Tim OT	81Bal 82LJ		6'6"	275	Notre Dame		
Folmar, Brendon QB	87Det		6'1"	200	California (Pa.)		
Folsom, Steve TE	81Phi 82NYG 83-85USFL 87-90Dal	2	6'5"	235	Long Beach State, Utah		24
Fontenot, Albert DE	93Chi		6'4"	265	Baylor		
Fontenot, Herman HB-FB	85-88Cle 89-90GB	23	6'	206	Louisiana State		54
Fontenot, Jerry C-OG	89-93Chi		6'3"	278	Texas A&M		
Foote, Chris C-OG	80-81Bal 82-83NYG 84-85USFL 87-91Min		6'3"	253	Southern Calif.		
Footman, Dan DE	93Cle		6'5"	285	Florida State		
Ford, Bernard WR	89Dal 90Hou	2	5'9"	168	Central Florida		12
Ford, Chris WR	90TB		6'1"	185	Lamar		
Ford, Darryl LB	92Pit 92-93Det		6'1"	225	New Mexico State		
Ford, John WR	89Det		6'2"	204	Virginia		
Ford, Mike QB	81TB 84USFL		6'3"	220	S.M.U.		
Ford, Moses WR	87Pit		6'2"	220	Fayetteville St.		
Forde, Brian LB	88-91NO		6'2"	230	Washington State		2
Forney, Phil LB	87StL		6'2"	230	East Tennessee St.		
Fortin, Roman OT	91Det 92-93Atl		6'5"	290	Oregon, San Diego State		
Fortune, Hosea WR	83SD		6'	176	Rice		
Foster, Barry HB	90-93Pit	2	5'10"	223	Arkansas		138
Foster, Derrick HB	87NYJ		5'11"	205	Will. Patterson		
Foster, Jerome DE-DT	83-84Hou 86Mia 86-87NYJ		6'2"	266	Ohio State		
Foster, Ron DB	87Raid		6'	200	Northridge State		
Foster, Roy OG-OT	82-90Mia 91-93SF		6'4"	282	Southern Calif.		
Foules, Elbert DB	83-87Phi		5'11"	185	Alcorn State	10	
Fourcade, John QB	87-90NO	12	6'1"	208	Mississippi		12
Fourcade, Keith LB	87NO		5'11"	225	Mississippi		
Fouts, Dan QB	73-87SD	12	6'3"	204	Oregon		78
Fowler, Amos C-OG	78-84Det		6'3"	251	Southern Miss.		
Fowler, Bobby FB	85NO 86KJ		6'2"	230	Texas-El Paso, Louisiana Tech		
Fowler, Todd FB	83-84USFL 85-88Dal	2	6'3"	222	S.F. Austin State		
Fowlkes, Dennis LB	84-85Min 87Mia		6'2"	238	West Virginia		
Fox, Chas WR	86StL 87JJ		5'11"	180	Furman		6
Fox, Mike DE	90-93NYG		6'6"	275	West Virginia		
Fox, Scott LB	87Hou		6'2"	222	Austin Peay		
Fox, Tim DB	76-81NE 82-84SD 85-86LA		5'11"	188	Ohio State	26	
Frain, Todd TE	87NE		6'3"	240	Nebraska		
Fralic, Bill OG-OT	85-92Atl 93Det		6'5"	280	Pittsburgh		
Francis, James LB	90-93Cin		6'5"	252	Baylor	7	14
Francis, Jeff QB	90Cle 91SJ 92Cle		6'4"	225	Tennessee		
Francis, Jon HB	87LA	2	5'11"	207	Colorado State, Boise State		12
Francis, Phil FB-HB	79-80SF 81KJ	2	6'1"	205	Stanford		6
Francis, Ron DB	87-90Dal		5'9"	200	Baylor	4	6
Francis, Russ TE	75-80NE 81VR 82-87SF 87-88NE 89KJ	2	6'6"	242	Oregon		240
Franco, Brian K	87Cle		5'8"	165	Penn State		11
Frank, Donald DB	90-93SD		6'	197	Winston-Salem St.	10	12
Frank, John TE	84-88SF	2	6'3"	225	Ohio State		60
Frank, Malcolm DB	92Sea		5'8"	182	Baylor		
Franklin, Andra FB	81-84Mia	2	5'10"	225	Nebraska		138
Franklin, Arnold TE	87NE		6'3"	246	North Carolina		
Franklin, Byron WR	81Buf 82XJ 83-84Buf 85-87Sea	2	6'1"	181	Auburn		60
Franklin, Jerrell OT	87Hou		6'3"	287	Southern U.		
Franklin, Jethro DE	89Sea		6'1"	258	Fresno State		
Franklin, Pat FB	86TB 87Cin		6'1"	230	Houston, SW Texas State		12
Franklin, Tony K	79-83Phi 84-87NE 88Mia	5	5'8"	182	Texas A&M		872
Franks, Elvis DE	80-84Cle 85-86Raid 86NYJ		6'4"	252	Morgan State		
Franz, Nolan WR	86GB		6'2"	183	Tulane		
Franz, Tracy OG	87SF		6'5"	270	San Jose State		
Frase, Paul DE-NT-DT	88-89NYJ 90IL 91-93NYJ		6'5"	272	Syracuse		
Frazier, Frank OG	87Was		6'5"	290	Miami (Fla.)		
Frazier, Guy LB	81-84Cin 85-86Buf		6'2"	217	Wyoming	1	
Frazier, Leslie DB	81-85Chi 86KJ		6'	189	Alcorn State	20	12
Frazier, Paul HB	89NO	2	5'8"	188	Southwestern La.		6
Frazier, Randy LB	87KC		6'3"	235	Morehead State		
Frederick, Andy OT	77-81Dal 82Cle 83-85Chi 86FJ		6'6"	257	New Mexico		
Freeman, Lorenzo NT-DT	87-90Pit 91NYG 92KJ		6'5"	298	Pittsburgh		
Freeman, Mike OG-C	84Den 85KJ 86-87Den 88Raid		6'3"	256	Arizona		
Freeman, Phil WR	85-87TB	23	5'11"	185	Arizona		24
Freeman, Reggie LB	93NO		6'1"	233	Florida State		
Freeman, Russell OT	92-93Den		6'7"	290	Georgia Tech		
Freeman, Steve DB	75-86Buf 87Min		5'11"	185	Mississippi State	23	18
French, Ernest DB	82Pit 83KJ		5'11"	195	Alabama A&M		
Frerotte, Mitch OG	87Buf 89XJ 90-92Buf 93KJ		6'3"	281	Penn State		12
Friday, Larry DB	87Buf		6'4"	215	Mississippi State		
Friede, Mike WR	80Det 80-81NYG 83USFL	2	6'3"	203	Indiana		6
Frier, Mike DE	92-93Cin		6'5"	299	Appalachian State		
Friesz, John QB	90-91SD 92KJ 93SD	1	6'4"	209	Idaho		
Frisch, David TE	93Cin		6'7"	260	Colorado State		
Fritzche, Jim OT-OG	83Phi		6'8"	265	Purdue		
Frizzell, William DB	84-85Det 86-93Phi		6'3"	203	N. Car. Central	11	6
Fryar, Irving WR	84-92NE 93Mia	23	6'	200	Nebraska		282
Frye, David LB	83-85Atl 86-89Mia		6'2"	223	Purdue	1	
Frye, Phil HB	87Min		5'11"	180	Cal. Lutheran		

UseName(Nickname)-Positions	Team by Year	See Section	Hgt	Wgt	College	Int	Pts
Fulcher, David DB	86-92Cin 93Raid		6'3"	236	Arizona State	31	14
Fulhage, Scott K	87-88Cin 89-92Atl	4	5'11"	191	Kansas State		
Fuller, Eddie FB	91-93Buf		5'9"	201	Louisiana Tech		
Fuller, James DB	93SD		6'	208	Portland State		
Fuller, Jeff DB-LB	84-89SF		6'2"	216	Texas A&M	10	2
Fuller, Joe DB	90SD 91GB		5'11"	180	Northern Iowa	1	
Fuller, Steve QB	79-82KC 83LA 84-86Chi 87SJ 88SD	12	6'4"	197	Clemson		66
Fuller, William DE	84-85USFL 86-93Hou		6'3"	267	North Carolina	1	6
Fullington, Darrell DB	88-90Min 91NE 91-92TB		6'1"	197	Miami (Fla.)	10	
Fullwood, Brent FB-HB	87-90GB 90Cle	23	5'11"	209	Auburn		114
Fulton, Dan WR	79Buf 81-82Cle 84USFL		6'2"	184	Nebraska, Nebraska-Omaha		
Furjanic, Tony LB	86-87Buf		6'1"	228	Notre Dame		
Furrer, Will QB	92Chi 93Phx	1	6'3"	208	Virginia Tech		
Fusina, Chuck QB	79-81TB 83-85USFL 86GB	1	6'1"	197	Penn State		
Futrell, Bobby DB	84-85USFL 86-90TB	3	5'11"	190	Elizabeth City St.	4	
Gabbard, Steve OT	91GB		6'4"	297	Florida State		
Gadbois, Dennis WR	87-88NE		6'1"	183	Boston U.		
Gaffney, Derrick WR	78-84,87NYJ	2	6'1"	181	Florida		42
Gaffney, Jeff K	87SD		6'2"	195	Virginia		13
Gage, Steve DB	87-88Was		6'3"	210	Tulsa	1	
Gagliano, Bob QB	82-83KC 84-85USFL 86-87SF 88Ind 89-90Det 91-92SD 93Atl	12	6'3"	195	U.S. International, Utah State		
Gainer, Derrick FB	90Cle 92Raid 92Det 93Dal	2	5'11"	235	Texas A&M		6
Gaines, Chris LB	88Mia		6'	238	Vanderbilt		
Gaines, Greg LB	81Sea 82KJ 83-88Sea		6'3"	220	Tennessee	2	
Gaines, Sheldon WR	87Buf		5'9"	155	Long Beach State		
Gaison, Blane DB	81-84Atl		6'	185	Hawaii	2	6
Gajan, Hokie FB	82-85NO 86-87KJ	2	5'11"	220	Louisiana State		78
Galbraith, Scott TE	90-92Cle 93Dal	2	6'3"	260	Southern Calif.		12
Galbreath, Harry OG	88-92Mia 93GB		6'1"	275	Tennessee		
Galbreath, Tony FB-HB	76-80NO 81-83Min 84-87NYG	23	6'	228	Missouri		265
Gallery, Jim K	87StL 89Cin 90Min	5	6'1"	190	Minnesota		76
Galloway, David DT-DE	82-87StL 88-89Phx 90Den		6'3"	279	Florida	1	2
Galloway, Duane DB	85-87Det		5'8"	181	Arizona State	7	
Galvin, John LB	88NYJ 89Min 90-91NYJ		6'3"	226	Boston College		
Gamache, Vince K	86Sea 87Raid	4	5'11"	170	Fullerton State		
Gamble, Kenny HB-DB	88-90KC		5'10"	197	Colgate	1	6
Gambol, Chris OT-OG	88Ind 88SD 89Det 90NE		6'6"	303	Iowa		
Gammon, Kendall C	92-93Pit		6'4"	279	Pittsburg State		
Gann, Mike DE	85-93Atl		6'5"	271	Notre Dame	1	14
Gannon, Chris DE-TE	89SD 90-93NE		6'6"	263	Southwestern La.		
Gannon, Rich QB	87-92Min 93Was	12	6'3"	198	Delaware		24
Gansz, Frank	HC87-88KC				Navy		
Gant, Brian LB	87TB		6'	235	Illinois State	1	
Gant, Earl HB	79-80KC 83-85USFL	2	6'	207	Missouri		6
Gant, Kenneth DB	90-93Dal		5'11"	187	Albany State	6	
Garalczyk, Mark DT-DE	87StL 88Phx 88NYJ 89NJ 91ZJ		6'5"	272	Western Michigan		
Garbarczyk, Tony DE	87NYJ		6'4"	275	Wake Forest		
Garcia, Bubba WR	80-81KC 83USFL		5'11"	185	Texas-El Paso		6
Garcia, Eddie K	83-84GB	5	5'8"	178	S.M.U.		23
Garcia, Frank K	81Sea 83USFL 83-87TB	4	6'	205	Arizona State. Arizona		
Garcia, Teddy K	88NE 89Min 90Hou	5	5'10"	190	Northeast La.		108
Gardner, Carwell FB	90-93Buf	2	6'2"	235	Kentucky, Louisville		42
Gardner, Donnie DE	91Mia		6'3"	260	Kentucky		
Gardner, Ellis OT-OG	83KC 84Ind		6'5"	257	Georgia Tech		
Gardner, Moe NT-DE	91-93Atl		6'2"	258	Illinois		
Gardocki, Chris K	91-93Chi	4	6'1"	194	Clemson		
Garner, Dwight HB	86Was		5'8"	183	California		
Garner, Hal LB	85-86Buf 87KJ 88Buf 89DR 90-91Buf		6'4"	228	Utah State		
Garnett, Dave LB	93Min		6'2"	219	Stanford		
Garnett, Scott NT-DE	84Den 85SF 85SD 87Buf		6'2"	269	Washington		
Garrett, Alvin HB-WR	80-81NYG 81-84Was	3	5'7"	179	Angelo State		12
Garrett, Curtis DE	87NYG		6'5"	302	Illinois State		
Garrett, Jason QB	93Dal		6'2"	195	Princeton		
Garrett, John WR	89Cin		5'11"	180	Columbia, Princeton		
Garrett, Mike K	81Bal	4	6'1"	184	Georgia		
Garrett, Shane WR	91Cin 92AJ		5'11"	185	Texas A&M		
Garrity, Gregg WR	83-84Pit 84-89Phi	23	5'10"	170	Penn State		42
Gary, Cleveland HB	89-93LA	2	6'	226	Georgia, Miami (Fla.)		174
Gary, Keith DE	83-88Pit		6'3"	263	Oklahoma		
Gary, Russell DB	81-86NO 86-87Phi		5'11"	196	Nebraska	7	
Garza, Sammy QB	87StL		6'1"	184	Texas-El Paso		6
Gash, Sam FB	92-93NE	2	5'11"	224	Penn State		12
Gash, Thane DB	88-90Cle 91ZJ 92SF 93KJ		6'	200	East Tennessee St.	4	12
Gastineau, Mark DE	79-88NYJ		6'5"	266	Arizona State, E.C. Oklahoma		12
Gault, Willie WR	83-87Chi 88-93Raid	23	6'1"	181	Tennessee		270
Gay, Everett WR	88Dal 89TB	2	6'2"	209	Texas		6
Gay, William DT-DE-TE	78-87Det 88Min		6'5"	250	Southern Calif.	2	6
Gayle, Shaun DB	84-93Chi		5'11"	196	Ohio State	12	6
Gaynor, Doug QB	86Cin		6'2"	205	Long Beach State		
Geater, Ron NT	92Den		6'6"	270	Iowa		
Geathers, James (Jumpy) DE-NT-DT	84-89NO 90-92Was 93Atl		6'7"	283	Wichita State		
Gedney, Chris TE	93Chi	2	6'5"	262	Syracuse		
Gehring, Mark TE	87Hou		6'4"	235	Eastern Washington		6
Geile, Chris OG	87Det		6'4"	305	Eastern Illinois		
Gelbaugh, Stan QB	86Buf 87EJ 88-89Buf 91Phx 92-93Sea	12	6'3"	207	Maryland		
Gentry, Dennis HB-WR	82-92Chi	23	5'8"	180	Baylor		96
George, Jeff DB	87TB		6'1"	185	Illinois State		
George, Jeff QB	90-93Ind	12	6'4"	221	Purdue, Illinois		12
George, Ron LB	93Atl		6"	225	Stanford		
Gerak, John OG	93Min		6'3"	285	Penn State		
Gerhard, Chris DB	87Phi		5'10"	185	East Stroudsburg		
Gerhart, Tom DB	92Phi		6'1"	195	Ohio U.		
Gervais, Rick DB	81-83SF		5'11"	190	Stanford		
Gesek, John OG-C	87-89Raid 90-93Dal		6'5"	279	Sacramento State		
Getz, Lee OG	87KC		6'3"	250	Rutgers		
Giacomarro, Ralph K	83-85Atl	4	6'1"	192	Penn State		
Giannetti, Frank NT	91Ind		6'2"	267	Penn State		
Giaquinto, Nick HB-FB	80-81Mia 81-83Was	23	5'11"	204	Bridgeport, Connecticut		30
Gibbs, Joe	HC81-92Was				San Diego State		
Gibler, Andy TE	83Cin		6'4"	234	Missouri		
Gibson, Alec DE	87Was		6'4"	270	Illinois		
Gibson, Antonio DB	83-85USFL 86-89,92NO		6'3"	204	Cincinnati	3	
Gibson, Dennis LB	87-93Det		6'2"	240	Iowa State	3	
Gibson, Ernest DB	84-88NE 89Mia		5'10"	185	Furman	4	
Gibson, Tom DE-DT	89-90Cle 91LA		6'7"	257	Northern Arizona		

UseName(Nickname)-Positions	Team by Year	See Section	Hgt	Wgt	College	Int	Pts
Giddens, Frank OT	81-82Phi 84USFL		6'7"	300	New Mexico		
Giesler, Jon OT	79-88Mia 89KJ		6'5"	262	Michigan		
Gilbert, Daren OT	85-88NO		6'6"	289	Fullerton State		
Gilbert, Freddie DE	84-85USFL 86-88Den 89Phx		6'4"	275	Georgia		
Gilbert, Gale QB	85-86Sea 87KJ 90-93Buf	1	6'3"	206	California		
Gilbert, Lewis TE	78-79Atl 80Phi 80SF 81LA 83-85USFL		6'4"	225	Florida		
Gilbert, Sean DT	92-93LA		6'4"	315	Pittsburgh		
Giles, Jimmie TE	77Hou 78-86TB 86-87Det 87-89Phi	2	6'3"	239	Alcorn State		246
Gill, Owen FB	85-86Ind 87LA	2	6'1"	232	Iowa		18
Gillen, John LB	81-82StL 83NE 84-85USFL		6'3"	227	Illinois		
Gillespie, Fernandars (Scoop) HB	84Pit		5'10"	185	William Jewell		
Gillespie, Willie WR	86TB 87Min		5'9"	170	Tenn.-Chattanooga		
Gilmore, Jim OT-OG	86Phi 87Mia		6'5"	269	Ohio State		
Gillus, Willie QB	87GB		6'4"	215	Norfolk State		
Ginn, Tomie OG-C	80-81Det 82KJ		6'3"	253	Arkansas		
Gisler, Mike OG	93NE		6'4"	300	Houston		
Gissinger, Andrew OT	82-84SD 85JJ		6'5"	279	Syracuse		
Givins, Ernest WR	86-93Hou	2	5'9"	172	Louisville		276
Gladman, Charles HB	87TB		5'11"	205	Pittsburgh		
Gladney, Tony WR	87SF		6'3"	200	Nevada-Las Vegas		
Glanville, Jerry	HC85-89Hou 90-93Atl				Montana State, Northern Michigan		
Glasgow, Brian TE	87Chi		6'2"	230	Northern Illinois		
Glasgow, Nesby DB	79-83Bal 84-87Ind 88-92Sea	3	5'10"	185	Washington	15	12
Glass, Bill OG	80Cin		6'4"	261	Baylor		
Glaze, Charles DB	87Sea		5'11"	205	S. Carolina State	2	
Glazebrook, Bob DB	78-83Atl		6'1"	200	Fresno State	8	6
Glenn, Kerry DB	85-87NYJ 88KJ 89NYJ 90-92Mia		5'9"	175	Minnesota	7	12
Glenn, Vencie DB	86SD 86NE 87-90SD 91NO 92-93Min		6'	189	Indiana State	26	12
Glover, Andrew TE	91-93Raid	2	6'6"	245	Grambling		30
Glover, Clyde DE	87SF		6'6"	280	Fresno State		
Glover, Kevin C-OG	85-93Det		6'2"	276	Maryland		
Goad, Tim NT	88-93NE		6'3"	280	North Carolina		6
Godfrey, Chris OG-OT-DE-DT	80NYJ 81KJ 83USFL 84-87NYG 88Sea		6'3"	263	Michigan		
Goeas, Leo OT-OG	90-92SD 93LA		6'4"	289	Hawaii		
Goebel, Brad QB	91Phi 92-93Cle	1	6'3"	198	Baylor		
Goebel, Hank OT	87LA		6'7"	270	Fullerton State		
Goff, Robert (Pig) DE-NT	88-89TB 90-93NO		6'3"	270	Auburn		12
Goff, Willard DT	85Atl		6'4"	265	Illinois, West Texas State		
Gogan, Kevin OT-OG	87-93Dal		6'7"	313	Washington		
Goganious, Keith LB	92-93Buf		6'2"	237	Penn State		
Goldberg, Bill NT-DT	92-93Atl		6'2"	266	Georgia		
Golden, Tim LB	82-84NE 85Phil		6'1"	220	Florida		
Golic, Bob NT-LB-DE	79-82NE 83-88Cle 89-92Raid		6'2"	264	Notre Dame	1	6
Golic, Mike DT-NT-DE	86-87Hou 87-92Phi 93Mia		6'5"	274	Notre Dame	3	
Golsteyn, Jerry QB	77-78NYG 79Det 79Bal 82-83TB 84Raid 85USFL	1	6'4"	207	Northern Illinois		
Goltz, Rick DE	87Raid		6'4"	255	Simon Fraser		
Gonzales, Leon WR	85Dal 87Atl		5'10"	161	Bethune-Cookman		
Goodburn, Kelly K	87-90KC 90-93Was	4	6'2"	197	Iowa State, Emporia State		
Goode, Conrad OT-OG-C	84-85NYG 87TB		6'6"	285	Missouri		
Goode, Chris DB	87-93Ind		6'	195	North Alabama,	7	6
Goode, John TE	84StL 85Phi		6'2"	233	Alabama, Youngstown State		
Goode, Kerry HB	88TB 89Mia	2	5'11"	200	Alabama		2
Goodlow, Darryl LB	87Raid		6'2"	235	Arizona		
Goodlow, Eugene WR	83-86NO	2	6'2"	185	Kansas State		60
Goodman, Don FB	87StL		5'11"	214	Cincinnati		
Goodman, John DE-DT-NT	81-85Pit		6'6"	253	Oklahoma		
Goodson, John K	82Pit	5	6'3"	204	Texas		52
Goodspeed, Mark OT	80StL 83USFL		6'5"	270	Nebraska		
Gordon, Alex LB	87-89NYJ 90Raid 91-93Cin		6'5"	246	Cincinnati	1	2
Gordon, Darrien DB	93SD	3	5'11"	182	Stanford	1	
Gordon, Dwayne LB	93Atl		6'1"	231	New Hampshire		
Gordon, Sonny DB	87TB		5'11"	192	Ohio State		
Gordon, Tim DB	88-90Atl 91-92NE		6'	188	Tulsa	8	
Gore, Stacy K	87Mia		6'	200	Arkansas State		
Gorecki, Chuck LB	87Phi		6'4"	237	Boston College		
Goss, Antonio LB	89,91-93SF		6'4"	228	North Carolina		
Gossett, Jeff K	81-82KC 83Cle 84-85USFL 85-87Cle 87Hou 88-93Raid	4	6'2"	197	Eastern Illinois		
Gothard, Preston TE	85-88Pit	2	6'4"	239	Alabama		18
Gottschalk, Darren TE	87NO		6'4"	225	Cal. Lutheran		
Gouveia, Kurt LB	87-93Was		6'1"	229	Brigham Young	6	12
Gowdy, Cornell DB	86Dal 87-88Pit		6'1"	196	Morgan State	3	6
Graddy, Sam WR	87-88Den 89BL 90-92Raid	23	5'10"	165	Tennessee		18
Graf, Rick LB	87-90Mia 91-92Hou 93Was		6'5"	246	Wisconsin	2	
Graham, Dan C	89TB		6'2"	270	Northern Illinois		
Graham, David DE-NT	82Sea 84-85USFL 87Sea		6'6"	250	Morehouse		
Graham, Derrick OT	90-93KC		6'4"	306	Appalachian State		
Graham, Don LB	87TB 88Buf 89Was		6'2"	244	Penn State		
Graham, Jeff WR	91-93Pit	2	6'1"	195	Ohio State		6
Graham, Kent QB	92-93NYG	1	6'5"	220	Ohio State		
Graham, Scottie HB	92NYJ 93Min	2	5'9"	220	Ohio State		18
Graham, William DB	82-87Det		5'11"	191	Texas	6	
Granby, John DB	92Den		6'1"	198	Virginia Tech		
Granger, Norm FB	84Dal 86KJ 87Atl		5'19'	225	Iowa		
Grant, African DB	90Mia		6'	200	Illinois		
Grant, Alan DB	90-91Ind 92-93SF 93Cin	3	5'10"	187	Stanford	2	6
Grant, Darryl DT-OG-C-OT	81-91Was		6'1"	269	Rice	2	6
Grant, David NT-DE-LB	88-91Cin 92TB 93GB		6'4"	277	West Virginia		
Grant, Otis WR	83-84LA 87Phi	2	6'3"	197	Michigan State		6
Grant, Steve LB	92-93Ind		6'	231	West Virginia		
Grant, Will C	78-85Buf 86Sea 87Buf		6'3"	254	Idaho State, Kentucky		
Graves, Marsharne OT	84Den 87Ind		6'4"	268	Arizona		
Graves, Rory OT	88-91Raid		6'6"	288	Ohio State		
Gray, Carlton DB	93Sea		6'	191	U.C.L.A.	3	
Gray, Cecil OG-DT-OT	90-91Phi 92GB 93Ind		6'4"	269	North Carolina		
Gray, Chris OT	93Mia		6'4"	286	Auburn		
Gray, Derwin DB	93Ind		'10"	190	Brigham Young		
Gray, Earnest WR	79-84NYG 85StL	2	6'3"	195	Memphis State		162
Gray, Hector DB	81-83Det		6'1"	192	Florida State	2	
Gray, Jerry DB	85-91LA 92Hou 93TB		6'	185	Texas	28	24
Gray, Kevin DB	82NO		5'11"	179	Eastern Illinois		
Gray, Mel HB-WR	84-85USFL 86-88NO 89-93Det	3	5'9"	166	Purdue		42
Gray, Paul LB	87Atl		6'2"	231	Western Kentucky		
Graybill, Mike OT	89Cle		6'7"	275	Boston U.		

UseName(Nickname)-Positions	Team by Year	See Section	Hgt	Wgt	College	Int	Pts
Grayson, David LB	87-90Cle 91SD 92LJ		6'2"	230	Cal. Poly.-Pomona, Fresno State	3	18
Grbac, Elvis QB	93SF		6'5"	232	Michigan		
Greco, Don OG	82-85Det		6'3"	260	Western Illinois		
Green, Alex DB	87Dal		6'1"	194	Indiana	1	
Green, Boyce FB-HB	83-85Cle 86KC 87Sea	2	5'11"	215	Carson-Newman		54
Green, Bubba DT	81Bal		6'4"	278	N. Carolina State	1	
Green, Chris DB	91-93Mia		5'11"	188	Illinois	2	
Green, Cleveland OT	79-86Mia		6'3"	263	Southern U.		
Green, Curtis DT-DE-NT	81-89Det		6'3"	260	Alabama State		
Green, Darrell DB	83-93Was	3	5'8"	172	Texas A&I	34	24
Green, David HB	82Cle		5'10"	200	Edinboro		
Green, Dennis	HC92-93Min				Iowa		
Green, Eric TE	90-93Pit	2	6'5"	274	Liberty		120
Green, Gary DB	77-83KC 84-85LA		5'11"	187	Baylor	33	12
Green, Gaston HB	88-90LA 92Den	23	5'10"	189	U.C.L.A.		48
Green, Harold HB	90-93Cin	2	6'2"	222	South Carolina		36
Green, Hugh LB	81-85TB 85-91Mia		6'2"	225	Pittsburgh	6	12
Green, Jacob DE	80-91Sea 92SF		6'3"	253	Texas A&M	3	24
Green, Mark HB	89-92Chi	23	5'11"	184	Notre Dame		42
Green, Mike LB	83-85SD		6'	235	Oklahoma State	3	
Green, Paul TE	92-93Sea	2	6'3"	230	Southern Calif.		12
Green, Robert HB	92Was 93Chi	2	5'8"	207	William & Mary		
Green, Rogerick DB	92TB 93KJ		5'10"	180	Kansas State		
Green, Roy WR-DB	79-87StL 88-90Phx 91-92Phi	23	6'	193	Henderson State	4	414
Green, Tim LB-DE-DT	86-93Atl		6'2"	246	Syracuse		2
Green, Trent QB	93SD		6'3"	211	Indiana		
Green, Victor DB	93NYJ		5'9"	195	Akron		
Green, Willie WR	91-93Det	2	6'2"	179	Mississippi		84
Greene, A.J. DB	91NYG		5'8"	167	Wake Forest		
Greene, Danny WR	85Sea 86BG		5'11"	190	Washington		
Greene, Doug DB	78StL 79-80Buf 83-84USFL		6'2"	205	Texas A&I	1	
Greene, George (Tiger) DB	85Atl 86-90GB		6'	194	Western Carolina	5	6
Greene, Ken DB	78-82StL 83-84SD		6'3"	203	Washington State	15	
Greene, Kevin LB-DE	85-92LA 93Pit		6'3"	242	Auburn	2	12
Greene, Marcellus DB	84Min		6'	185	Arizona		
Greenwood, David DB	83-85USFL 85TB 86GB 87GJ 88Raid		6'3"	210	Wisconsin	5	
Greer, Curtis DE	80-85StL 86XJ 87StL 88XJ		6'4"	255	Michigan		
Greer, Terry WR	86Cle 87-89SF 90Det	2	6'1"	192	Alabama State		24
Gregor, Bob DB	81-84SD		6'2"	192	Washington State	4	
Gregory, Ted NT	88NO		6'1"	260	Syracuse		
Griffin, Courtney DB	93LA		5'10"	180	Fresno State		
Griffin, Don DB	86-93SF	3	6'	176	Middle Tenn. St.	22	12
Griffin, James DB	83-85Cin 86-89Det		6'2"	197	Middle Tenn. St.	19	18
Griffin, Jeff DB	81-85StL 87Phi		6'	185	Utah	4	
Griffin, Keith HB	84-88Was 88Atl	23	5'8"	185	Miami (Fla.)		30
Griffin, Larry DB	86Hou 87-92Pit		6'	195	North Carolina	13	6
Griffin, Leonard DE-NT	86-93KC		6'4"	268	Grambling		
Griffin, Ray DB	78-84Cin	3	5'10"	186	Ohio State	11	18
Griffin, Steve HB	87Atl		5'10"	185	Clemson		
Griffin, Steve WR	87Atl		5'11"	198	Purdue		
Griffith, Howard HB	93LA		6'	226	Illinois		
Griffith, Richard TE	93NE		6'5"	256	Arizona		
Griffith, Russell K	87Sea		5'11"	175	Weber State		
Griggs, Anthony LB	82-85Phi 86-88Cle		6'3"	227	Villanova, Ohio State	3	
Griggs, Billy TE	85-89NYJ	2	6'3"	232	Virginia		6
Griggs, David LB DE	89-93Mia		6'3"	245	Virginia		
Grimes, Randy C-OG	83-90TB 91EJ 92TB		6'4"	270	Baylor		
Grimm, Russ OG-C	81-91Was		6'3"	275	Pittsburgh		
Grimsley, John LB	84-90Hou 91KJ 92-93Mia		6'2"	235	Kentucky	1	
Grogan, Steve QB	75-90NE	12	6'4"	207	Kansas State		210
Grooms, Elois DE-DT	75-81NO 82-85StL 87Phi		6'4"	249	Tennessee Tech	3	14
Gross, Al DB	83-87Cle		6'3"	191	Arizona	11	12
Grossart, Kyle QB	80Oak 81NYJ		6'4"	210	Oregon State		
Grossman, Burt DE	89-93SD		6'6"	267	Pittsburgh		6
Groth, Jeff WR	79Mia 79-80Hou 81-85NO	23	5'10"	176	Bowling Green		18
Gruber, Bob OT	84-85USFL 86Cle 87GB		6'5"	275	Pittsburgh		
Gruber, Paul OT	88-93TB		6'5"	290	Wisconsin		
Grunhard, Tim C	90-93KC		6'2"	301	Notre Dame		
Grupp, Bob K	79-81KC 83-85USFL	4	5'11"	193	Duke		
Grymes, Darrell WR	87Det		6'2"	182	Central St.-Ohio		12
Guendling, Mike LB	85SD		6'3"	238	Northwestern		
Guggemos, Neal DB	86-87Min 88NYG	3	6'1"	189	St. Thomas	1	
Guidry, Kevin DB	88Den 89Phx		6'	176	Louisiana State		
Guilbeau, Rusty LB-DE	82-86NYJ 87Cle		6'4"	242	McNeese State		
Guliford, Eric WR	93Min	3	5'8"	165	Arizona State		
Gulledge, David DB	92Was		6'1"	203	Jacksonville State		
Guman, Mike FB-HB	80-88LA	2	6'2"	216	Penn State		96
Gunn, Lance DB	93Cin		6'3"	222	Texas		
Gunn, Mark DE-DT	91-93NYJ		6'5"	288	Pittsburgh		
Gunter, Mike FB	84KC		5'11"	206	Tulsa		
Gustafson, Jim WR	86-89Min 90ZJ	2	6'1"	177	St. Thomas		30
Guthrie, Keith NT	84SD		6'4"	264	Texas A&M		
Guyton, Myron DB	89-93NYG		6'1"	205	Eastern Kentucky	5	
Guzik, John NT-DE	87NE		6'4"	270	Ohio U.		
Habib, Brian OT-OG	89,91-92Min 93Den		6'7"	293	Washington		
Hackett, Dino LB	86-91KC 92IL 93Sea		6'3"	228	Appalachian State	1	2
Hackett, Joey TE	83-85USFL 86Den 87-88GB		6'5"	267	Elon		6
Hadd, Gary DT-NT	88Det 89Phx		6'4"	274	Minnesota		
Haddix, Michael FB	83-87Phi 89-90GB	2	6'2"	226	Memphis State		30
Haddix, Wayne DB	87-88NYG 90-91TB 91Cin		6'1"	203	Liberty	7	18
Haden, Nick OG-C	86Phi 87NJ		6'2"	270	Penn State		
Hadley, Ron LB	87-88SF		6'2"	240	Washington		
Hadnot, Jim FB	80-83KC 85USFL	2	6'2"	244	Texas Tech		30
Hagen, Mike FB	87Sea		6'	240	Montana		
Hager, Britt LB	89-93Phi		6'1"	223	Texas	1	
Haggins, Odell NT	91Buf		6'2"	278	Florida State		
Hagler, Scott K	87Sea		5'8"	160	South Carolina		10
Hagood, Rickey NT	84SD		6'2"	286	South Carolina		
Hagy, John DB	88-90Buf		5'11"	190	Texas	2	
Haight, Mike OG-OT	86-91NYJ 92Was		6'4"	281	Iowa		
Haines, John NT-DE-DT	84Min 86Ind		6'6"	266	Texas		
Haines, Kris WR	79Was 79-81Chi 83-85USFL 87Buf		5'11"	181	Notre Dame		
Hairston, Carl DE-DT-LB	76-83Phi 84-89Cle 90Phx		6'3"	260	Md. Eastern Shore	1	
Hairston, Russell WR	87Pit		6'3"	208	Kentucky		6
Hairston, Stacey DB	93Cle		5'9"	180	Ohio Northern		

UseName(Nickname)-Positions	Team by Year	See Section	Hgt.	Wgt.	College	Int	Pts
Haji-Sheikh, Ali K	83-85NYG 86Atl 87Was	5	6'	172	Michigan		323
Hakel, Chris QB	93Atl		6'2"	230	William & Mary		
Hale, Chris DB	90-92Buf	3	5'7"	163	Nebraska, Southern Calif.	1	2
Haley, Charles DE-LB	86-91SF 92-93Dal		6'5"	237	James Madison	1	8
Haley, Darryl OT-OG	82-84NE 85IL 86NE 87Cle 88GB		6'4"	269	Utah		
Haliburton, Ronnie LB	90-91Den 92ZJ		6'4"	230	Louisiana State		
Hall, Alvin DB	81-85,87Det	3	5'10"	185	Miami-Ohio	7	12
Hall, Chris DB	93Dal		6'2"	184	East Carolina		
Hall, Courtney C-OG	89-93SD		6'2"	277	Rice		
Hall, Dana DB	92-93SF		6'2"	206	Washington	2	
Hall, Darryl DB	93Den		6'2"	210	Washington	1	
Hall, Delton DB	87-91Pit 92SD		6'1"	202	Clemson	5	12
Hall, Dino HB	79-83Cle 85USFL	23	5'7"	165	Rowan		12
Hall, James LB	87Atl		6'1"	252	Northwestern La.		
Hall, Mark DE	89-90GB		6'4"	285	Louisiana State, Southwestern La.		
Hall, Rhett DT	91-93TB		6'2"	264	California		
Hall, Ron TE	87-93TB	2	6'4"	243	Cal. Poly.-Pomona, Hawaii		60
Haller, Alan DB	92Pit 92Cle 93Pit		5'11"	185	Michigan State		
Hallock, Ty TE	93Det		6'3"	249	Michigan State		12
Halloran, Shawn QB	87StL	1	6'4"	217	Boston College		
Hallstrom, Ron OT-OG	82-92GB 93Phi		6'6"	299	Iowa		
Hamel, Dean DT	85-88Was 89-90Dal		6'3"	279	Tulsa		
Hamilton, Darrell OT	89-91Den		6'5"	298	North Carolina		
Hamilton, Harry DB	84-87NYJ 88-91TB		6'	194	Penn State	23	
Hamilton, Keith DE	92-93NYG		6'6"	280	Pittsburgh		2
Hamilton, Rick LB	93Was		6'2"	241	Central Florida		
Hamilton, Skip DT	87Phi		6'2"	265	Southern		
Hamilton, Wes OG	76-84Min 85XJ		6'3"	261	Tulsa		
Hamilton, Steve DE-DT	85-88Was		6'4"	263	East Carolina		
Hamm, Bob DE	83-85Hou 87Ind		6'4"	260	Nevada-Reno		
Hammerstein, Mike DE-NT	86-87Cin 88KJ 89-90Cin		6'4"	270	Michigan		
Hammond, Steve LB	88NYJ		6'4"	225	Wake Forest		
Hampton, Alonzo DB	90Min 91TB		5'10"	191	Pittsburgh	1	
Hampton, Dan DE-DT	79-90Chi		6'5"	264	Arkansas		2
Hampton, Kwante WR	87Atl		6'1"	182	Long Beach State		
Hampton, Lorenzo HB	85-89Mia	23	6'	209	Florida		168
Hampton, Rodney HB	90-93NYG	23	5'11"	215	Georgia		198
Hamrick, James K	87KC		5'11"	177	Rice		10
Hancock, Anthony WR	82-86KC	23	6'	200	Tennessee		30
Hancock, Kevin LB	87Ind		6'2"	225	Baylor		
Hand, Jon DE	86-93Ind		6'7"	295	Alabama	1	
Handley, Ray	HC91-92NYG				Stanford		
Hanifan, Jim	HC80-85StL HC89Atl				California		
Hanks, Merton DB	91-93SF		6'2"	185	Iowa	5	12
Hannah, Charley OG-OT-DE	77-82TB 83-88Raid		6'5"	260	Alabama		
Hannah, Travis WR	93Hou		5'7"	161	Southern Calif.		
Hanneman, Cliff LB	87Cle		6'2"	235	Fresno State		
Hannon, Tom DB	77-84Min		5'11"	192	Michigan	15	10
Hannula, Jim OT	83Cin		6'6"	264	Northern Illinois		
Hanousek, Matt OG-OT	87Sea		6'4"	265	Drake, Utah State		
Hansen, Brian K	84-88NO 90NE 91-93Cle	4	6'3"	213	Sioux Falls		
Hansen, Bruce FB	87NE 88AJ		6'1"	225	Brigham Young		
Hansen, Phil DE	91-93Buf		6'5"	272	N. Dakota State		
Hanson, Jason K	92-93Det	5	5'11"	183	Washington State		223
Hanson, Mark OG	87Min		6'2"	260	Mankato State		
Harbaugh, Jim QB	87-93Chi	12	6'3"	203	Michigan		90
Harbour, Dave C	88-89Was		6'4"	265	Illinois		
Harbour, James WR	86Ind		6'1"	192	Mississippi		
Harden, Bobby DB	90-93Mia		6'	192	Miami (Fla.)		2
Harden, Derrick WR	87GB		6'1"	175	Eastern New Mexico		
Harden, Mike DB	80-88Den 89-90Raid	3	6'1"	192	Michigan	39	30
Harding, Greg DB	84NO 87Phi		6'2"	197	Nicholls State		
Hardison, Dee DE-DT-OT-NT	78-80Buf 81-85NYG 86-87SD 88KC		6'4"	274	North Carolina		
Hardy, Adrian DB	93SF		5'11"	194	NW State-La.		
Hardy, Andre FB	84Phi 85Sea 87SF	2	6'1"	232	Weber State, St. Mary's		
Hardy, Bruce TE-QB	78-89Mia	2	6'5"	232	Arizona State		150
Hardy, David K	87Raid		5'7"	180	Texas A&M		7
Hardy, John DB	91Chi		5'10"	166	California		
Hardy, Larry TE	78-85NO	2	6'3"	234	Jackson State		42
Hardy, Robert DT	79-82Sea 83BL		6'2"	250	Jackson State		
Hardy, Robert HB	91TB		5'10"	210	Carson-Newman		
Hargain, Tony WR	92KC	2	6'	194	Oregon		
Hargrove, Jim FB	81Cin 83-84USFL 87GB		6'2"	230	Wake Forest		12
Hargrove, Marvin WR	90Phi		5'10"	178	Richmond		6
Harkey, Lance DB	87Raid		5'10"	180	Illinois		
Harlow, Pat OT	91-93NE		6'6"	290	Southern Calif.		
Harmon, Andy DE-DT	91-93Phi		6'4"	265	Kent State		
Harmon, Clarence HB-FB	77-82Was84-85USFL	2	5'11"	204	Mississippi State		96
Harmon, Derrick HB	84-86SF	23	5'10"	202	Cornell		12
Harmon, Kevin HB	88-89Sea		6'	190	Iowa		
Harmon, Mike WR	83NYJ		6'	185	Mississippi		
Harmon, Ronnie HB	86-89Buf 90-93SD	23	5'11"	196	Iowa		138
Harper, Alvin WR	91-93Dal	2	6'3"	203	Tennessee		60
Harper, Bruce HB-WR	77-84NYJ	23	5'8"	176	Kutztown		126
Harper, Dave LB	90Dal		6'1"	220	Humboldt State		
Harper, Dwayne DB	88-93Sea		5'11"	168	S. Carolina State	13	6
Harper, John LB	83Atl 85USFL		6'3"	230	Southern Illinois		
Harper, LaSalle LB	89NYG 89Chi		6'1"	235	Arkansas		
Harper, Mark DB	84-85USFL 86-90Cle 91FJ		5'9"	170	Alcorn State	8	
Harper, Michael WR	86-89NYJ	2	5'10"	180	Southern Calif.		12
Harper, Roger DB	93Atl		6'2"	223	Ohio State		
Harrah, Dennis OG-C	75-87LA		6'5"	260	Miami (Fla.)		
Harrell, James LB	79-83Det 84USFL 85-86Det 87KC		6'1"	224	Florida	1	
Harrell, Sam FB	81-82Min 84-85USFL 87Min		6'2"	217	East Carolina		
Harrington, LaRue FB	80SD 83-84USFL		6'	210	Norfolk State		
Harrington, Perry FB-HB	80-83Phi 84-85StL	2	5'11"	210	Jackson State		36
Harris, Al DE-LB	79-84Chi 85HO 86-88Chi 89-90Phi		6'5"	253	Arizona State	4	8
Harris, Archie OT-OG	87Den		6'6"	270	William & Mary		
Harris, Bob LB	83-85StL 86NJ 87KC		6'2"	219	Auburn	3	6
Harris, Corey WR-CB	92Hou 92-93GB	3	5'11"	195	Vanderbilt		
Harris, Darryl HB	88Min	23	5'10"	178	Arizona State		6
Harris, Duriel WR	76-83Mia 84Cle 84Dal	23	5'11"	179	New Mexico State		120
Harris, Elroy FB	89Sea		5'9"	218	Eastern Kentucky		
Harris, Eric DB	80-82KC 83-85LA		6'3"	198	Memphis State	21	6

UseName(Nickname)-Positions	Team by Year	See Section	Hgt.	Wgt.	College	Int	Pts
Harris, Frank HB	87Chi		6'1"	196	N. Carolina State		
Harris, Herbert WR	86-87NO	2	6'1"	206	Lamar		
Harris, Jackie TE	90-93GB	2	6'3"	240	Northeastern La.		54
Harris, James DE	93Min		6'4"	270	Temple		
Harris, John DB	78-85Sea 86-88Min		6'2"	200	Arizona State	47	12
Harris, Leonard WR	84-85USFL 86TB 87-93Hou	23	5'8"	161	Austin, Texas Tech		48
Harris, Leotis OG	78-83GB 84KJ		6'1"	267	Arkansas		
Harris, Marshall DE-NT	80-82Cle 83NE 84USFL		6'6"	261	Texas Christian		
Harris, Michael C-OG	89KC		6'4"	306	Grambling		
Harris, M.L. TE	80-85Cin	2	6'5"	238	Tampa, Kansas St.		60
Harris, Odie DB	88-90TB 91-92Cle 92-93Phx		6'	190	Sam Houston St.	3	
Harris, Robert DE	92-93Min		6'4"	287	Southern U.		
Harris, Ronnie WR	93NE		5'10"	170	Oregon		
Harris, Rod WR	89NO 90Dal 90-91Phi	3	5'10"	183	Texas A&M		
Harris, Roy DE-NT	84-85Atl 87TB		6'2"	264	Florida		
Harris, Rudy FB	93TB		6'1"	255	Clemson		
Harris, Steve HB	87Min		5'11"	194	Northern Iowa		
Harris, Tim HB	83Pit		5'9"	206	Washington State		
Harris, Tim LB-DE	86-90GB 91-92SF 93Phi		6'5"	251	Memphis State		10
Harris, Walter DB	87SD		6'1"	195	Stanford		
Harris, William TE	87StL 89TB 90GB		6'4"	239	Texas, Bishop		6
Harrison, Anthony DB	87GB		6'1"	195	Georgia Tech	1	
Harrison, Dennis DE	78-84Phi 85LA 86SF 86-87Atl		6'8"	277	Vanderbilt	1	
Harrison, Martin LB-DE	90,92-93SF		6'5"	240	Washington		
Harrison, Nolan NT-DT	91-93Raid		6'5"	285	Indiana		2
Harrison, Rob FB	87Raid		6'2"	220	Sacramento State	1	
Harrison, Todd TE	92TB		6'4"	260	N. Carolina State		
Harrison, Vic WR	87NO		5'9"	184	North Carolina		
Harry, Carl WR	89,92Was		5'9"	168	Utah		
Harry, Emile WR	86KC 87SJ 88-92KC 92LA	2	5'11"	175	Stanford		36
Hart, Roy NT-DT	89Sea 91Raid		6'1"	280	South Carolina		
Hartenstine, Mike DE	75-86Chi 87Min		6'3"	251	Penn State		14
Hartley, Ken K	81NE 84-85USFL		6'2"	200	Catawba		
Hartnett, Perry OG	82-83Chi 84USFL 87GB		6'5"	278	S.M.U.		
Hartwig, Carter DB	79-84Hou		6'	203	Southern Calif.	9	
Harty, John NT-DE	81-83SF 84FJ 85-86SF		6'4"	260	Iowa		2
Harvey, James OG-OT	87-88KC		6'3"	265	Jackson State		
Harvey, John HB	90TB	2	5'11"	185	Texas-El Paso		6
Harvey, Ken LB	88-93Phx		6'2"	227	California		
Harvey, Marvin TE-WR	81KC 84-85USFL		6'3"	220	Southern Miss.		
Harvey, Maurice DB	78 Den 79KJ 80Den 81-83GB 83Det 84TB		5'10"	190	Ball State	9	6
Harvey, Richard LB	90-91NE 92-93Buf		6'1"	227	Tulane		
Harvey, Stacy LB	89KC		6'4"	245	Arizona State		
Harvin, Allen FB	87Det 87Was		5'9"	200	Cincinnati		
Haselrig, Carlton OG	90-93Pit		6'1"	293	Pittburgh-Johnstown		
Hasselbeck, Don TE	77-83NE 83Raid 84Min 85NYG	2	6'7"	245	Colorado		108
Haslett, Jim LB	79-85Buf 86KJ 87NYG		6'3"	233	Indiana (Pa.)	6	
Hastings, Andre WR	93Pit		6'	188	Georgia		
Hasty, James DB	88-93NYJ		6'	200	Central Washington, Washington State	19	6
Hatcher, Dale K	85-89,91LA 93Mia	4	6'2"	204	Clemson		
Hatchett, Derrick DB	80-83Bal 83Hou		5'11"	183	Texas	7	
Hathaway, Steve LB	84Ind		6'4"	238	West Virginia		
Hauck, Tim DB	90NE 91-93GB		5'11"	183	Pacific (Ore.), Montana		
Haverdink, Kevin OT	89-91NO		6'5"	285	Western Michigan		
Hawkins, Andy LB	80-83TB 84-85USFL 86-87SD 88KC		6'2"	225	Texas A&I	1	
Hawkins, Courtney WR	92-93TB	23	5'9"	180	Michigan State		42
Hawkins, Bill DT-DE	89-92LA		6'6"	268	Miami (Fla.)		
Hawkins, Frank FB-HB	81Oak 82-87Raid	2	5'9"	210	Nevada-Reno		108
Hawkins, Mike LB	78-81NE 82Raid 84-85USFL		6'2"	235	Texas A&I	5	6
Haworth, Steve DB	84Atl		5'11"	190	Oklahoma		
Hawthorne, Greg HB-FB-TE-WR	79-83Pit 84-86NE 87Ind	2	6'2"	228	Baylor		66
Hayes, Gary DB	84-86GB		5'10"	180	Fresno State		
Hayes, Eric DT	90-91Sea 92LA 93TB		6'3"	292	Florida State		
Hayes, Jeff K	82-85Was 86Cin 87Mia	4	5'11"	175	North Carolina		6
Hayes, Joe HB-WR	84Phi		5'9"	185	Texas A&I, Central State-Okla.		
Hayes, Jonathan TE	85-93KC	2	6'5"	240	Iowa		72
Hayes, Lester DB	77-81Oak 82-86Raid 87FJ		6'	200	Texas A&M	39	30
Haynes, James LB	84-89NO		6'2"	232	Miss. Valley St.	1	6
Haynes, Louis LB	82-83KC		6'	227	Bishop, North Texas		
Haynes, Mark DB	80-85NYG 86-89Den		5'11"	194	Colorado	17	6
Haynes, Michael WR	88-93Atl	2	6'	180	Northern Arizona		174
Haynes, Mike DB	76-82NE 83-89Raid	3	6'2"	192	Arizona State	46	30
Haynes, Tommy DB	87Dal		6'	190	Southern Calif.	3	
Hayworth, Tracy LB	90-93Det		6'3"	257	Tennessee	1	6
Headen, Andy LB	83-88NYG		6'5"	240	Clemson	5	6
Heard, Herman HB	84-89KC	2	5'10"	186	Fort Lewis, Southern Colorado		96
Hearst, Garrison HB	93Phx	2	5'11"	215	Georgia		6
Heater, Larry HB	80NYG 81BG 82-83NYG	2	5'11"	205	Arizona		18
Heath, JoJo DB	80Cin 81Phi 83CFL 84USFL 87NYJ		5'10"	181	Pittsburgh	1	
Hebert, Bobby QB	83-85USFL 85-89NO 90HO 91-92NO 93Atl	12	6'4"	215	Northwestern La.		6
Hebert, Bud DB	80NYG		6'	190	Oklahoma	1	
Hebron, Vaughn HB	93Phi	2	5'8"	196	Virginia Tech		18
Heck, Andy OT-OG	89-93Sea		6'6"	296	Notre Dame		
Hector, Johnny HB-FB	83-92NYJ	23	5'11"	200	Texas A&M		264
Heffernan, Dave OT	87TB		6'4"	255	Miami (Fla.)		
Heflin, Victor DB	83-84StL		6'	184	Central St.-Ohio	1	
Heflin, Vince WR	82-85Mia 86TB		6'	185	Arizona State		6
Hegman, Mike LB	76-87Dal		6'1"	227	Alabama A&M, Tennessee State	7	12
Heimkreiter, Steve LB	80Bal		6'2"	226	Notre Dame		
Heimuli, Lakei FB	87Chi	2	5'11"	219	Brigham Young		6
Heller, Ron OT	84-87TB 88-92Phi 93Mia		6'6"	282	Penn State		6
Heller, Ron TE	87-88SF 89Atl 90,92Sea	2	6'3"	236	Oregon State		30
Hellestrae, Dale OT	85-86Buf 87PJ 88Buf 89BL 90-93Dal		6'5"	277	S.M.U.		
Helton, Barry K	88-90SF 91LA	4	6'3"	205	Colorado		
Hemphill, Darryl DB	82Bal 84-85USFL		6'	195	West Texas State		
Hendel, Andy LB	84USFL 86Mia 87LJ		6'1"	230	North Carolina State		
Henderson, Jerome DB	91-93NE 93Buf	3	5'10"	189	Clemson	5	
Henderson, Keith FB	89-92SF 92Min	2	6'1"	220	Georgia		24
Henderson, Othello DB	93NO		6'	192	U.C.L.A.		
Henderson, Rueben DB	81-82Chi 83-84SD		6'1"	196	Oklahoma State, San Diego State	4	
Henderson, Wyatt DB	81SD 83-84USFL		5'10"	180	Fresno State		
Henderson, Wymon DB	87-88Min 89-92Den 93LA		5'10"	186	Nevada-Las Vegas	16	12
Henderson, Zac DB	78-79CFL 80Phi 82-83CFL 84-85USFL		6'1"	190	Oklahoma		

UseName(Nickname)-Positions	Team by Year	See Section	Hgt	Wgt	College	Int	Pts
Hendley, David DB	87NE		6'	188	Southern Conn. St.		
Hendley, James C	87Atl		6'3"	257	Florida State		
Hendrickson, Steve LB-TE	89SF 89Dal 90-93SD		6'	251	California	1	12
Hendrix, Manny DB	86-91Dal		5'10"	180	Utah	2	2
Hendrix, Tim TE	87Dal		6'5"	241	Tennessee		
Hendy, John DB	85SD 86KJ		5'10"	196	Long Beach State	4	6
Henke, Brad DE-NT	89Den		6'3"	275	Iowa State, Arizona		
Henley, Darryl DB	89-93LA	3	5'9"	170	U.C.L.A.	9	
Henley, Thomas WR	87SF		5'11"	185	Stanford		
Henning, Dan	HC83-86Atl 89-91SD				William & Mary		
Hennings, Chad DT	92-93Dal		6'6"	277	Air Force		
Henry, Bernard WR	82-83Bal 84-85Ind 87LA	2	6'1"	182	Arizona State		36
Henry, Kevin DE	93Pit		6'4"	275	Mississippi State	1	
Henry, Maurice LB	90Phi		5'11"	220	Kansas State		
Henry, Charles TE	91Mia		6'4"	230	Miami (Fla.)		
Henry, Steve DB	79StL 80NYG 81Bal		6'2"	190	Emporia State	1	
Henry, Wally WR	77-82Phi 83USFL	23	5'8"	175	U.C.L.A.		18
Henson, Luther NT	82-84NE		6'	275	Ohio State		
Henton, Anthony LB	86Pit 87KJ 88Pit		6'1"	224	Troy State		
Herkenhoff, Matt OT	76-85KC		6'4"	267	Minnesota		
Herline, Alan K	87NE	4	6'	168	Vanderbilt		
Herman, Chuck OG	80Atl		6'3"	250	Arkansas		
Hernandez, Matt OT	83Sea 84Min		6'6"	260	Purdue		
Herrmann, Mark QB	81-82Den 83Bal 84Ind 85-87SD 89LA 90-92Ind	12	6'4"	199	Purdue		6
Hernandez, Scott NT	87Buf		6'	250	Kent State		
Herrod, Jeff LB	88-93Ind		6'	246	Mississippi	4	6
Herron, Bruce LB	78-82Chi		6'2"	220	New Mexico		
Hester, Jessie WR	85-87Raid 88Atl 90-93Ind	2	5'11"	170	Florida State		144
Hester, Ron LB	82Mia 83-84KJ		6'2"	222	Florida State		
Hewko, Bob QB	83TB		6'3"	195	Florida		
Heyward, Craig (Ironhead) FB	88-92NO 93Chi	2	5'11"	254	Pittsburgh		84
Hicks, Bryan DB	80-82Cin 83SJ		6'	192	McNeese State	1	
Hicks, Cliff DB	87-90LA 90-92Buf 93NYJ	3	5'10"	188	Oregon	5	
Hicks, Dwight DB	79-85SF 86Ind	3	6'1"	190	Michigan	32	24
Hicks, Ivan DB	87Det		6'2"	185	Michigan		
Hicks, Mark LB	83Sea 87Det		6'2"	235	Arizona State		
Hicks, Victor TE	80LA 81FJ 83-84USFL	2	6'3"	250	Oklahoma		18
Higdon, Alex TE	88Atl		6'5"	247	Ohio State		12
Higgs, Mark HB-FB	88Dal 89Phi 90-93Mia	23	5'7"	198	Kentucky		90
Highsmith, Alonzo FB	87-89Hou 90-91Dal 91-92TB	2	6'1"	235	Miami (Fla.)		60
Hilgenberg, Jay C-OG	81-91Chi 92Cle 93NO		6'3"	259	Iowa		
Hilgenberg, Joel C-OG	84-93NO		6'3"	251	Iowa		
Hilger, Rusty QB	85-87Raid 88Det 90-91Ind 92Sea	12	6'4"	205	Oklahoma State		
Hill, Bill DB	87Dal		5'9"	172	Rutgers		
Hill, Bruce WR	87-91TB	2	6'	178	Arizona State		138
Hill, David TE	76-82Det 83-87LA	2	6'2"	229	Texas A&I		168
Hill, Derek WR	89-90Pit	2	6'1"	193	Arizona		6
Hill, Drew WR	79-82LA 83XJ 84LA 85-91Hou 92-93Atl	23	5'9"	171	Georgia Tech		366
Hill, Eddie HB	79-80LA 81-84Mia	2	6'2"	205	Memphis State		24
Hill, Eric LB	89-93Phx		6'1"	253	Louisiana State		6
Hill, Greg DB	83Hou 84-86KC 87Raid 87-88KC		6'1"	196	Oklahoma State	9	6
Hill, Kenny DB	81Oak 82-83Raid 84-88NYG 89KC	3	6'	194	Yale	6	
Hill, Kent OG-OT	79-86LA 87Hou		6'5"	260	Georgia Tech		
Hill, Lonzell (Mo) WR	87-90NO	2	6'	189	Washington		78
Hill, Nate DE	88GB 88Mia		6'4"	273	Auburn		
Hill, Randal WR	91Mia 91-93Phx	2	5'10"	177	Miami (Fla.)		48
Hill, Rod DB	82-83Dal 84-86Buf 86Det 87Raid	3	6'	186	Kentucky State	4	
Hill, Tony WR	77-86Dal	23	6'2"	199	Stanford		306
Hill, Tony DE	91-92Dal		6'6"	248	Tenn.-Chattanooga		
Hill, Will DB	88Cle		6'	200	Bishop		
Hillary, Ira WR	87-89Cin 90Min	23	5'11"	190	South Carolina		12
Hilliard, Dalton HB-FB	86-93NO	2	5'8"	204	Louisiana State		318
Hilliard, Randy DB	90-93Cle		5'11"	160	Northwestern La.	2	
Hilton, Carl TE	86-89Min		6'3"	232	Houston		18
Hines, Andre TE	80Sea 83USFL		6'6"	275	Stanford		
Hinkle, Bryan LB	82-93Pit		6'1"	222	Oregon	15	18
Hinkle, George DE-NT-DT	88-91SD 92Min 93Cin		6'5"	273	Arizona		
Hinnant, Mike TE	88-89Pit 92Det		6'3"	268	Temple		
Hinton, Chris OG-OT	83Bal 84-89Ind 90-93Atl		6'4"	295	Northwestern		
Hintz, Mike DB	87Chi		6'1"	190	Wis.-Platteville		
Hipp, I.M. HB	80Oak		5'10"	200	Nebraska		
Hipple, Eric QB	80-86Det 87RJ 88-89Det	12	6'2"	197	Utah State		78
Hire, Doug C	87Sea		6'2"	245	Linfield		
Hirsch, Steve DB	87Det		6'	195	Northern Illinois		
Hitchcock, Bill OT-OG	91-93Sea		6'6"	291	Purdue		
Hitchcock, Ray C-OG	87Was 88KJ		6'2"	289	Minnesota		
Hoage, Terry DB	84-85NO 86-90Phi 91Was 92AJ 93SF 93Hou		6'3"	199	Georgia	16	12
Hoard, Leroy FB	90-93Cle	2	5'11"	230	Michigan		84
Hobbs, Daryl WR	93Raid		6'2"	180	U. of Pacific		
Hobbs, Stephen WR	90-92Was 93TJ		5'11"	195	North Alabama		6
Hobby, Marion DE	90-92NE		6'4"	277	Tennessee		
Hobbins, Jim OG	87GB		6'6"	275	Minnesota		
Hobert, Billy Joe QB	93Raid		6'3"	225	Washington		
Hobley, Liffort DB	85StL 88-93Mia		6'	204	Louisiana State	5	12
Hodge, Floyd WR	82-84Atl	2	6'	193	Utah		24
Hodge, Milford DE-NT	86NO 86-89NE		6'3"	275	Washington State		
Hodges, Eric WR	87KC		6'1"	189	Florida		
Hodson, Tom QB	90-92NE	1	6'3"	195	Louisiana State		
Hoffman, Dave LB	93Pit		6'2"	233	Washington		
Hoffman, Gary OT	84GB 87SF		6'7"	284	Santa Clara		
Hogan, Mark DB	87NYJ		6'	180	Baruch	1	
Hoge, Merril HB-FB	87-93Pit	2	6'2"	224	Idaho State		204
Hogeboom, Gary QB	80-85Dal 86-88Ind 89Phx 90Was	12	6'4"	204	Central Michigan		24
Hoggard, D.D. DB	84USFL 85-87Cle		6'	188	N. Carolina State		
Hohensee, Mike QB	87Chi	1	6'	205	Minnesota		
Hoke, Jonathan DB	80Chi		5'11"	175	Ball State		
Hold, Mike QB	87TB		6'	190	South Carolina		
Holifield, John HB	89Cin		6'	202	West Virginia		
Holland, Jamie WR-HB	87-89SD 90-91Raid 92Cle	23	6'2"	192	Ohio State		12
Holland, Johnny LB	87-93GB		6'2"	231	Texas A&M	7	
Hollas, Donald QB	91-92Cin 93IL	12	6'3"	215	Rice		
Holle, Eric DE-NT	84-87KC		6'5"	260	Texas		
Hollie, Doug DE	87-88Sea		6'4"	265	S.M.U.		
Hollier, Dwight LB	92-93Mia		6'2"	242	North Carolina		
Hollis, David DB	87-88Sea 88KC 88-89Sea	3	5'11"	178	Nevada-Las Vegas	2	

UseName(Nickname)-Positions	Team by Year	See Section	Hgt	Wgt	College	Int	Pts
Hollingsworth, Shawn OT	83Den		6'2"	260	New Mexico		
Hollinquest, Lamont LB	93Was		6'3"	245	Southern Calif.		
Holloway, Brian OT-OG	81-86NE 87-88Raid		6'7"	284	Stanford		
Holloway, Cornell DB	90-92Ind		5'11"	182	Pittsburgh	1	
Holloway, Derek WR	83-85USFL 86Was 87FB		5'7"	166	Arkansas		
Holloway, Johnny DB	86Dal 87StL		5'11"	182	Kansas	1	
Holloway, Randy DE	78-84Min 84StL 85USFL		6'5"	250	Pittsburgh	1	8
Holloway, Steve TE	87TB	2	6'3"	235	Tennessee State		
Holloway, Stan LB	80NO		6'2"	218	California		
Holloway, Tony DE-LB	87KC		6'2"	222	Nebraska		
Holly, Bob QB	82-83Was 84Phi 84-85Atl	1	6'2"	197	Princeton		6
Holman, Rodney TE	82-92Cin 93Det	2	6'3"	235	Tulane		216
Holman, Scott WR	86StL 87NYJ	2	6'2"	194	Oregon		
Holman, Walter FB	87Was		5'10"	208	West Virginia State		
Holmes, Bruce LB	87KC		6'2"	235	Minnesota		
Holmes, Bruce LB	93Min		6'2"	237	Minnesota		
Holmes, Clayton DB	92Dal 93KJ		5'10"	181	Carson-Newman		
Holmes, Darryl DB	87-89NE		6'2"	190	Ft. Valley State	1	
Holmes, Don WR	86-87StL 88-90Phx	2	5'10"	180	Colorado, Mesa		6
Holmes, Jack FB-HB	78-82NO 83USFL	2	5'11"	210	Texas Southern		30
Holmes, Jerry DB	80-83NYJ 84-85USFL 86-87NYJ 88-89Det 90-91GB		6'2"	175	West Virginia	25	18
Holmes, Lester OG	93Phi		6'3"	301	Jackson State		
Holmes, Ron DE	85-88TB 89-92Den		6'4"	261	Washington		
Holmgren, Mike	HC92-93GB				Southern Calif.		
Holmoe, Tom DB	83-84SF 85SJ 86-89SF		6'2"	190	Brigham Young	7	12
Holohan, Pete TE	81-87SD 88-90LA 91KC 92Cle	2	6'4"	237	Notre Dame		96
Holston, Mike WR	81-85Hou 85KC	2	6'3"	189	Morgan State		24
Holt, Harry TE	83-86Cle 87SD	2	6'4"	236	Arizona		36
Holt, Issiac DB	85-89Min 89-92Dal		6'2"	200	Alcorn State	23	22
Holt, John DB	81-85TB 86-88Ind	3	5'11"	179	West Texas State	7	
Holt, Pierce DE-DT	88-92SF 93Atl		6'4"	280	Angelo State		
Holt, Robert WR	82Buf 83KJ		6'1"	182	Baylor		
Homco, Thomas LB	93LA		6'	245	Northwestern	1	
Hons, Todd QB	87Det	1	6'1"	195	Arizona State		
Hood, Estus DB	78-84GB		5'11"	183	Illinois State	11	6
Hood, Winford OG-OT	84-88Den		6'3"	262	Georgia		
Hooks, Alvin HB	81Phi 83USFL		5'11"	170	Northridge State		
Hooper, Trell DB	87Mia		5'11"	182	Memphis State	2	6
Hoover, Houston OT-OG	88-92Atl 93Cle		6'2"	293	Jackson State		
Hoover, Melvin WR	82-84Phi 87Det	2	6'	185	Arizona State		12
Hope, Neil LB	87LA		6'2"	235	Southern Calif.		
Hopkins, Brad OT	93Hou		6'3"	306	Illinois		
Hopkins, Thomas OT	83Cle		6'6"	260	Alabama A&M		
Hopkins, Wes DB	83-86Phi 87KJ 88-93Phi		6'1"	213	S.M.U.	30	6
Hopper, Darrel DB	87SD		6'1"	196	Southern Calif.		
Hoppock, Doug OT-OG	87KC		6'4"	280	Kansas State		
Horan, Mike K	84-85Phi 86-92Den 93NYG	4	5'11"	188	Long Beach State		
Horn, Alvin DB	87Cle		5'11"	185	Nevada-Las Vegas	1	
Horn, Bob LB	76-81SD 82-83SF 84USFL		6'3"	233	Oregon State	7	
Horn, Marty QB	87Phi		6'2"	206	Lehigh		
Horn, Rod NT	80-81Cin		6'4"	268	Nebraska		
Horne, Greg K	87Cin 87StL 88Phx		6'	188	Arkansas		
Horton, Ethan FB-TE	85KC 87,89-93Raid	2	6'4"	231	North Carolina		102
Horton, Ray DB	83-88Cin 89-92Dal		5'11"	190	Washington	19	30
Hoskins, Derrick DB	92-93Raid		6'2"	200	Southern Miss.	2	
Hostetler, Jeff QB	84-92NYG 93Raid	12	6'3"	212	West Virginia		84
Hough, Jim OG-C	78-86Min		6'2"	268	Utah State		
House, Kevin WR	80-86TB 86-87LA	2	6'1"	181	Southern Illinois		204
Housman, Walter OT-OG	87NO		6'5"	285	Iowa, Upsala		
Houston, Bobby LB	90GB 92-93NYJ		6'2"	236	N. Carolina State	2	6
Howard, Anthony NT	87NYG		6'3"	267	Tennessee		
Howard, Bobby HB-FB	86-88TB	2	6'	213	Indiana		12
Howard, Bryan DB	82Min 84-85USFL		6'	200	Tennessee State		
Howard, Carl DB	84Dal 85TB 85-90NYJ		6'2"	190	Rutgers	5	
Howard, David LB	84-85USFL 85-89Min 89-90Dal 91-92NE		6'1"	231	Oregon State, Long Beach State	5	
Howard, Desmond WR	92-93Was	23	5'9"	182	Michigan		6
Howard, Erik NT	86-93NYG		6'4"	268	Washington State		
Howard, Joey OT	89SD		6'6"	305	Tennessee		
Howard, Paul OG	73-75Den 76JJ 77-86Den		6'3"	260	Brigham Young		
Howard, Todd LB	87-88KC		6'2"	235	Texas A&M		
Howard, Tom LB	77-83KC 84-85StL		6'2"	213	Texas Tech	7	18
Howard, William FB-HB	88-89TB	2	6'	240	Tennessee		18
Howe, Garry NT	92Pit 93Cin		6'1"	298	Colorado		
Howe, Glen OT	85Pit 85-86Atl		6'7"	295	Southern Miss.		
Howell, Pat OG	79-83Atl 83-85Hou		6'5"	257	Southern Calif.		
Howell, Steve FB-TE	79-81Mia 83USFL	2	6'2"	227	Baylor		6
Howfield, Ian K	91Hou	5	6'2"	196	Tennessee		64
Hubach, Mike K	80-81NE	4	5'10"	185	Kansas		
Huckleby, Harlan HB	80-85GB	23	6'1"	200	Michigan		84
Huddleston, Jim OG-OT	87TB 87Mia		6'4"	280	Virginia		
Hudson, Doug QB	87KC		6'2"	201	Nicholls State		
Hudson, Gordon TE	84-85USFL 86Sea	2	6'4"	241	Brigham Young		6
Hudson, John OG-C	91-93Phi		6'2"	275	Auburn		
Hudson, Mike DB	87SD		6'	202	Oklahoma State		
Hudson, Nat OG	81NO 82Bal 84-85USFL		6'3"	268	Georgia		
Huff, Alan NT	87Pit		6'4"	265	Marshall		
Huff, Charles DB	87Atl		5'11"	195	Presbyterian	2	
Huff, Ken OG	75-82Bal 83-85Was		6'4"	260	North Carolina		
Huffman, Darvell WR	91Ind		5'8"	158	Boston U.		
Huffman, Dave OG-C-OT	79-83Min 84-85USFL 85-90Min		6'6"	271	Notre Dame		
Huffman, Tim OT-OG	81-85GB		6'5"	279	Notre Dame		
Hugger, Keith WR	83NYG		5'11"	175	Connecticut		
Hughes, Danan WR	93KC		6'1"	201	Iowa		
Hughes, David FB	81-85Sea 86Pit	2	6'	220	Boise State		42
Hughes, Ernie OG-C	78SF 79KJ 80SF 81-83NYG		6'3"	259	Notre Dame		
Hughes, Tyrone DB	93NO	3	5'9"	175	Nebraska		18
Hughes, Van DE	84-85USFL 86StL 87Sea		6'3"	280	SW Texas State		
Hull, Kent C	83-85USFL 86-93Buf		6'4"	276	Mississippi State		
Humiston, Mike LB	81Buf 82Bal 83NJ 84Ind 87SD		6'3"	240	Weber State		2
Humphery, Bobby WR-DB	84-89NYJ 90LA	23	5'10"	178	New Mexico State	5	32
Humphrey, Bobby HB	89-91Den 92Mia 93KJ	2	6'1"	201	Alabama		102
Humphrey, Donnie DE	84-86GB		6'3"	282	Auburn		
Humphrey, Tom OG-OT	87NYJ		6'3"	280	Iowa		
Humphries, Stan QB	89-91Was 92-93SD	12	6'2"	223	Louisiana State, Northwestern La.		36
Humphries, Stefan OG	84-86Chi 87-88Den		6'3"	266	Michigan		

UseName(Nickname)-Positions	Team by Year	See Section	Hgt.	Wgt.	College	Int	Pts
Hunley, Lamonte LB	85-86Ind		6'2"	240	Arizona		
Hunley, Ricky LB	84-87Den 88Phx 89-90Raid		6'2"	242	Arizona	3	6
Hunt, Byron LB	81-88NYG		6'5"	238	S.M.U.	2	
Hunt, Daryl LB	79-84Hou		6'3"	229	Oklahoma		
Hunt, Gary DB	87Cin		5'11"	175	Memphis State		
Hunt, John OG	87TB		6'5"	245	Florida		
Hunt, John OT	84Dal		6'4"	254	Florida		
Hunter, Daniel DB	85-86Den 86-87SD		5'11"	178	Henderson State	1	
Hunter, Eddie HB	87NYJ 87TB	2	5'11"	205	Virginia Tech		12
Hunter, Hal	HC84Ind				Pittsburgh		
Hunter, Herman HB	85Phi 86Det 87Hou	23	6'1"	197	Tennessee State		18
Hunter, Ivy Joe FB-HB	89-91Ind 92KJ	2	6'	237	Kentucky		
Hunter, James NT-DE	82Bal		6'5"	251	Southern Calif.		
Hunter, Jeff DE	90Buf 90-92Det 92-93Mia		6'2"	285	Albany State		
Hunter, John OT	89-91Atl 92Sea		6'8"	296	Brigham Young		
Hunter, Monty DB	82Dal 83StL		6'	202	Salem		
Hunter, Patrick DB	86-93Sea		5'11"	185	Nevada-Reno	9	6
Hunter, Stan WR	87NYJ		6'2"	184	Bowling Green		6
Hunter, Tony TE	83-84Buf 85-86LA	2	6'4'	237	Notre Dame		54
Hunter, Tony FB	87GB		5'9"	215	Minnesota		
Huntington, Greg C	93Was		6'3"	287	Penn State		
Hurd, Jeff LB	87Dal 88-89KJ		6'2"	245	Kansas State		
Hurley, Bill DB	81-83NO 83Buf		5'11"	195	Syracuse	1	6
Hurst, Maurice DB	89-93NE		5'10"	185	Southern U.	19	6
Hurt, Eric DB	80Dal		5'11"	171	San Jose State		
Husted, Michael K	93TB	5	6'	190	Virginia		75
Hutchins, Paul OT	93GB		6'5"	335	Western Michigan		
Hutchinson, Anthony HB	83-84Chi		5'10"	186	Texas Tech		12
Hutchinson, Scott DE	78-80Buf 81TB 83Buf 85USFL		6'4"	246	Florida		
Huther, Bruce LB	77-80Dal 81Cle 82Chi 83Dal 84USFL		6'1"	221	New Hampshire		
Hutson, Brian DB	90NE		6'1"	198	Mississippi State		
Hyche, Steve LB	89Chi 91-93Phx		6'3"	241	Livingston		
Hyde, Glenn OT-OG-C	74-75WFL 76-81Den 82Bal		6'3"	253	Pittsburgh		
	83USFL 85Den 86Sea 87KC						
Iaquiniello, Mike DB	91Mia		6'3"	208	Michigan State		
Igwebuike, Donald K	85-89TB 90Min	5	5'9"	181	Clemson		477
Ilesic, Hank K	89SD	4	6'1"	210	none		
Ilkin, Tunch OT-OG-C	80-92Pit 93GB		6'3"	263	Indiana State		
Infante, Lindy	HC88-91GB				Florida		
Inglis, Tim LB	87-88Cin		6'3"	232	Toledo		
Ingram, Brian LB	82-85NE 86KJ 87SD		6'4"	236	Tennessee		
Ingram, Byron OG	87-88KC 89TB		6'2"	295	Eastern Kentucky		
Ingram, Darryl TE	89Min 91Cle 92-93GB		6'2"	240	California		6
Ingram, Kevin QB	87NO		6'	178	East Carolina		
Ingram, Mark WR	87-92NYG 93Mia	23	5'10"	188	Michigan State		102
Inverso, Glenn QB	84NYJ		6'1"	199	Liberty		
Irvin, Darrell DE	80-82Buf 83Sea		6'4"	259	Oklahoma		
Irvin, LeRoy DB	80-89LA 90Det	3	5'11"	183	Kansas	35	66
Irvin, Mark DB	87Mia		5'10"	190	Bethune-Cookman		
Irvin, Michael WR	88-93Dal	2	6'2"	202	Miami (Fla.)		204
Irwin, Tim OT	81-93Min		6'6"	292	Tennessee		
Ismail, Quadry WR	93Min	23	6'	192	Syracuse		6
Ismail, Raghib (Rocket) WR	93Raid	23	5'10"	180	Notre Dame		6
Isom, Ray DB	87-88TB		5'9"	190	Penn State	2	
Isom, Rickey FB	87Mia		6'	224	N. Carolina State		6
Israel, Steve DB	92-93LA		5'10"	186	Pittsburgh		
Ivery, Eddie Lee HB-FB	79-86GB 87XJ	2	6'1"	210	Georgia Tech		180
Ivlow, John FB	93Chi		5'11"	226	Colorado State		
Jacke, Chris K	89-93GB	5	6'	197	Texas-El Paso		514
Jackson, Alfred WR	78-84Atl	2	5'11"	176	Texas		132
Jackson, Alfred DB	89-90LA 91-92Cle		6'	179	San Diego State	1	
Jackson, Andrew HB	87Hou	2	5'10"	190	Iowa State		6
Jackson, Bill DB	82Cle		6'1"	202	North Carolina		
Jackson, Billy FB-HB	81-84KC	2	5'10"	217	Alabama		108
Jackson, Bo HB	87-90Raid	2	6'1"	227	Auburn		108
	86-90,93 played major league baseball						
Jackson, Bobby DB	78-85NYJ		5'9"	178	Florida State	21	18
Jackson, Charles LB	78-84KC 85-86NYJ		6'2"	225	Washington	1	6
Jackson, Charles DB	87Was		6'4"	210	Texas Tech		
Jackson, Cedric HB-FB	91Det		5'11"	229	Texas Christian		
Jackson, Cleveland TE	79NYG 84USFL		6'4"	230	Nevada-Las Vegas		
Jackson, David WR	87TB		5'8"	175	SE Missouri St.		
Jackson, Earnest HB-FB	83-84SD 85Phi 86-88Pit	2	5'9"	213	Texas A&M		144
Jackson, Enis DB	87Cle		5'9"	180	Memphis State		
Jackson, Greg DB	89-93NYG		6'1"	200	Louisiana State	14	
Jackson, Jeff LB	84-85Atl 87-88SD		6'1"	232	Auburn	1	6
Jackson, Joe LB	87Sea		6'1"	225	San Fran. State		
Jackson, John OT	88-93Pit		6'6"	289	Eastern Kentucky		
Jackson, John WR	90-92Phx	3	5'10"	175	Southern Calif.		6
Jackson, Johnny DB	89-92SF 92GB		6'1"	204	Houston	3	6
Jackson, Keith TE	88-91Phi 92-93Mia	2	6'2"	250	Oklahoma		186
Jackson, Kenny WR	84-88Phi 89Hou 90-91Phi	2	6'	180	Penn State		66
Jackson, Kirby DB	87LA 88-92Buf 93KJ		5'10"	179	Mississippi State	6	12
Jackson, Lawrence OG	87Atl		6'1"	275	Presbyterian		
Jackson, Leonard LB	87Chi 87Raid		6'	240	Oklahoma State		
Jackson, Louis HB	81NYG 83-85USFL	2	5'11"	195	Cal. Poly.-S.L.O.		6
Jackson, Marcus DE-NT	87Ind		6'5"	260	Purdue		
Jackson, Mark WR	86-92Den 93NYG	2	5'9"	177	Purdue		174
Jackson, Mark DB	87StL		5'9"	180	Abilene Christian		6
Jackson, Michael LB	79-86Sea		6'1"	222	Washington	6	
Jackson, Michael WR	91-93Cle	2	6'4"	195	Southern Miss.		102
Jackson, Rickey LB	81-93NO		6'2"	239	Pittsburgh	7	2
Jackson, Robert LB	78-81Cle 82Atl		6'1"	230	Texas A&M	2	
Jackson, Robert DB	82-87Cin 88HO 89Cin		5'10"	186	Central Michigan	15	12
Jackson, Robert OG-OT-C	75-85Cle		6'5"	255	Duke		
Jackson, Roger DB	82-85,87Den		6'	186	Bethune-Cookman	2	
Jackson, Steve DB	91-93Hou		5'8"	185	Purdue	8	6
Jackson, Terry DB	78-83NYG 84-85Sea		5'10"	197	San Diego State	28	30
Jackson, Tim DB	89Dal		5'11"	192	Kansas State,		
					Nebraska		
Jackson, Vestee DB	86-90Chi 91-93Mia		6'	189	Washington	18	12
Jackson, Victor DB	86Ind 87Raid		6'	205	Bowie State		
Jacobs, Cam LB	87TB		6'2"	230	Kentucky		
Jacobs, Dave K	79NYJ 81Cle 83USFL 87Phi	5	5'7"	152	Syracuse		57
Jacobs, Tim DB	93Cle		5'10"	185	Delaware		
Jacobson, Steve OG	87Mia		6'3"	255	Abilene Christian		
Jacoby, Joe OT-OG	81-93Was		6'7"	305	Louisville		6
Jaeger, Jeff K	87Cle 88FJ 89-93Raid	5	5'11"	192	Washington		584

UseName(Nickname)-Positions	Team by Year	See Section	Hgt.	Wgt.	College	Int	Pts
Jakes, Van DB	83-84KC 85USFL 86-88NO 89GB		6'	188	Kent State	8	
James, Angelo DB	87Phi		6'	180	Sacramento State		
James, Arrike TE	87Hou		6'4"	238	Delta State		
James, Craig FB-HB	83-84USFL 84-88NE	2	6'	215	S.M.U.		114
James, Garry HB	86-88Det	2	5'10"	214	Louisiana State		84
James, June LB	85Det 87Ind		6'1"	227	Texas		
James, Lionel WR-HB	84-88SD	23	5'7"	170	Auburn		96
James, Lynn WR	90-91Cin 91Cle	2	6'	191	S.M.U., Arizona St.		6
James, Phillip C-OG	87NO		6'2"	265	Southern U.		
James, Roland DB	80-90NE	3	6'2"	190	Tennessee	29	8
Jamison, George LB	87-93Det		6'1"	230	Cincinnati	8	20
Janata, John OT	83Chi		6'7"	274	Illinois		
January, Mike LB	87Chi		6'1"	234	Texas		
Jarostchuk, Ilia LB	87StL 88Mia 89Phx 90NE 91AJ		6'3"	231	New Hampshire		
Jarvis, Curt DE-NT	87-90TB		6'2"	265	Alabama		
Jarvis, Ralph DE	90Ind		6'4"	255	Temple		
Jasper, Vince OG	87NYJ		6'4"	270	Iowa State		
Jaworski, Matt LB	91Ind		6'1"	226	Colgate		
Jaworski, Ron QB	74-76LA 77-86Phi 87-88Mia 89KC	12	6'2"	195	Youngstown State		96
Jax, Garth LB	86-88Dal 89-93Phx		6'2"	238	Florida State	2	
Jay, Craig TE	87GB		6'4"	257	Mt. Senario		
Jean-Batiste, Garland FB	87NO		6'	208	Louisiana State		
Jeffcoat, Jim DE	83-93Dal		6'5"	269	Arizona State	2	18
Jefferson, Ben OG	90Cle		6'9"	330	Maryland		
Jefferson, James DB	89-93Sea	3	6'1"	199	Texas A&I	2	6
Jefferson, John (J.J.) WR	78-80SD 81-84GB 85Cle	2	6'1"	198	Arizona State		282
Jefferson, Norman DB	87-88GB		5'10"	183	Louisiana State		
Jefferson, Shawn WR	91-93SD	2	5'11"	172	Central Florida		30
Jefferson, Thad LB	87Hou		5'11"	225	Hawaii		
Jeffery, Tony HB	88Phx		5'11"	208	Texas Christian		
Jeffires, Haywood WR	87-93Hou	2	6'2"	199	N. Carolina State		198
Jeffries, Curtis TE	87Cin		6'4"	236	Louisville		
Jeffries, Eric DB	87Chi		5'10"	161	Texas		
Jeffries, Greg DB	93Det		5'9"	184	Virginia		
Jelesky, Tom OT	85-86Phi		6'6"	275	Purdue		
Jenkins, A.J. LB-DE	89-90Pit		6'2"	237	Fullerton State		
Jenkins, Carlos LB	91-93Min		6'3"	222	Michigan State	3	12
Jenkins, Fletcher DE-NT	82Bal 84-85USFL		6'2"	258	Washington		
Jenkins, Izel DB	88-92Phi 93Min 93NYG		5'10"	191	N. Carolina State	4	2
Jenkins, James TE	91-93Was		6'2"	238	Rutgers		
Jenkins, Ken HB	83-84Det 85-86Was	23	5'8"	184	Bucknell		6
Jenkins, Keyvan HB	87SD 88KC		5'10"	191	Nevada-Las Vegas		
Jenkins, Melvin DB	87-90Sea 91-92Det 93Atl 93Det		5'10"	172	Cincinnati	11	6
Jenkins, Robert OT	87-93LA		6'5"	278	U.C.L.A.		
	(changed name from Robert Cox in 1991)						
Jennings, Dave K	74-84NYG 85-87NYJ	4	6'4"	203	St. Lawrence		
Jennings, Keith TE	89Dal 91-93Chi	2	6'4"	251	Clemson		6
Jennings, Stanford HB-FB	84-90Cin 91NO 92TB	23	6'1"	205	Furman		120
Jensen, Derrick FB-TE-HB	79-81Oak 82-86Raid	2	6'1"	221	Texas-Arlington		54
Jensen, Jim WR-QB-FB-TE	81-92Mia	2	6'4"	215	Boston U.		114
Jensen, Russ QB	83-85USFL 85Raid		6'2"	215	San Fran. State,		
					Cal. Lutheran		
Jerue, Mark LB	83-89LA		6'3"	231	Washington	2	
Jessie, Tim HB	87Was		5'11"	190	Auburn		6
Jeter, Gary DE-DT	77-82NYG 83-88LA 89NE		6'4"	259	Southern Calif.	2	
Jeter, Tommy DT	92-93Phi		6'5"	282	Texas		
Jett, James WR	93Raid	2	5'10"	165	West Virginia		18
Jett, John K	93Dal	4	6'	184	East Carolina		
Jetton, Paul OG-C	89-91Cin 92-93NO		6'4"	292	Texas		
Jiles, Dwayne LB	85-89Phi 89NYG		6'4"	244	Texas Tech		
Jimerson, A.J. LB	90-91Raid		6'3"	233	Norfolk State		
Jodat, Jim FB-HB	77-79LA 80-81Sea 82-83SD	23	5'11"	211	Carthage		60
Joelson, Greg DE	91SF		6'3"	270	Willamette,		
					Arizona State		
Johns, Paul WR	81-84Sea	23	5'11"	173	Tulsa		56
Johnson, A.J. DB	89-93Was	3	5'8"	176	SW Texas State	9	12
Johnson, Alex WR	91Hou		5'9"	167	Miami (Fla.)		
Johnson, Alonzo LB	86-87Phi		6'3"	222	Florida	3	
Johnson, Anthony FB-HB	90-93Ind	2	6'	222	Notre Dame		36
Johnson, Barry WR	91Cle		6'2"	197	Maryland		
Johnson, Bill FB	84-85USFL 85-87Cin	2	6'2"	230	Arkansas State		6
Johnson, Bill DT	92-93Cle		6'4"	305	Michigan State		
Johnson, Billy (White Shoes) WR	74-80Hou 81CFL	23	5'9"	170	Widener		210
	82-87Atl 88Was						
Johnson, Bobby DB	83-84NO 85-86StL 86NO		6'	190	Texas	3	6
Johnson, Bobby WR	84-86NYG	2	5'11"	171	Kansas		120
Johnson, Brad QB	93Min		6'5"	221	Florida State		
Johnson, Brent C	87Chi		6'2"	255	Tenn.-Chattanooga		
Johnson, Butch WR	76-83Dal 84-85Den	23	6'1"	189	Cal.-Riverside		168
Johnson, Byron LB	87Hou		6'1"	220	Baylor		
Johnson, Cecil LB	77-85TB		6'2"	230	Pittsburgh	9	
Johnson, Charles NT	77-81Phi 82-84Min		6'3"	266	Colorado	5	12
Johnson, Charles DB	79-80SF 81StL		5'10"	180	Grambling	2	
Johnson, Charles DT-NT	79-80GB 82LJ 83GB		6'1"	263	Maryland	1	
Johnson, Christopher DB	87Phi		6'4"	225	Millersville		
Johnson, Chuck OT	92Den		6'5"	275	Texas		
Johnson, Chuckie DT	93Phx		6'4"	310	Auburn		
Johnson, Damian OT-OG	86-89NYG 90NE		6'5"	290	Kansas State		
Johnson, Damone TE	86-92LA	2	6'4"	230	Cal.Poly.-S.L.O.		108
Johnson, Dan TE	83-87Mia 88XJ	2	6'3"	239	Iowa State		96
Johnson, David (D.J.) DB	89-93Pit		6'	185	Kentucky	12	6
Johnson, Demetrious DB	83-86Det 87Mia 88LJ		5'11"	190	Missouri	5	
Johnson, Dennis LB	80-85Min 85TB		6'3"	233	Southern Calif.		
Johnson, Donnell OT	93Cin		6'7"	310	Johnson C. Smith		
Johnson, Earl DB	85NO 87Den		6'	195	South Carolina		
Johnson, Eddie LB	81-90Cle		6'1"	220	Louisville	6	
Johnson, Ezra DE	77-87GB 88-89Ind 90-91Hou		6'4"	250	Morris Brown		
Johnson, Flip WR	88-89Buf	2	5'10"	185	McNeese State		12
Johnson, Gary (Big Hands) DT-NT	75-84SD 84-85SF		6'2"	256	Grambling	2	22
Johnson, Gary Don DT	80Bal 84USFL		6'4"	263	Baylor		
Johnson, Gilvanni WR	87Det		6'1"	195	Michigan		
Johnson, Greg OG	88Mia 89KJ		6'4"	295	Oklahoma		
Johnson, Greggory DB	81-83Sea 84-85USFL 86Sea		6'1"	191	Oklahoma State		6
	87StL						
Johnson, Henry LB	80-83Min		6'1"	235	Georgia Tech		
Johnson, Herbert WR	87Chi		5'11"	182	Missouri		
Johnson, Holbert DB	87LA		5'9"	180	New Mexico State	1	
Johnson, Hoss OT	87TB		6'4"	295	Alabama		
Johnson, James LB	86Det 87SF 87SD		6'2"	236	San Diego State		
Johnson, Jason WR	88Den 89Pit		5'10"	179	Illinois State		

UseName(Nickname)-Positions	Team by Year	See Section	Hgt	Wgt	College	Int	Pts
Johnson, Jesse DB	80-83NYJ 84USFL		6'3"	185	Colorado		
Johnson, Jimmie TE	89-91Was 92-93Det	2	6'2"	246	Howard		24
Johnson, Jimmy	HC89-93Dal				Arkansas		
Johnson, Joe WR	89-91Was 92Min	23	5'8"	170	Notre Dame		6
	(changed name from Joe Howard in 1991)						
Johnson, John LB	91-93SF		6'3"	230	Clemson	2	6
Johnson, Johnnie DB	80-88LA 89Sea		6'1"	183	Texas	22	30
Johnson, Johnny HB	90-92Phx 93NYJ	2	6'2"	218	San Jose State		126
Johnson, Kelly WR	87Ind		5'8"	168	Colorado		
Johnson, Ken DE	79-84Buf 87KC		6'5"	254	Knoxville		2
Johnson, Ken DB	89-90Min		6'2"	197	Florida A&M		
Johnson, Ken DB	90NYJ		6'2"	208	Florida A&M		
Johnson, Kenneth DB	87GB 88XJ		6'	185	Mississippi State	1	
Johnson, Kenny DB	80-86Atl 86-89Hou	3	5'10"	174	Mississippi State	17	24
Johnson, Keshon DB	93Chi		5'10"	179	Arizona		
Johnson, Lawrence DB	79-84Cle 84-85Buf 86KJ 87Buf		5'11"	204	Wisconsin	9	
Johnson, Lee K	85-87Hou 87-88Cle 88-93Cin	4	6'2"	199	Brigham Young		6
Johnson, M.L. LB	87-89Sea		6'3"	228	Hawaii		
Johnson, Mario DT	92NYJ 93NE		6'3"	292	Missouri		
Johnson, Mark DB	87Cin		6'1"	194	Western Kentucky		
Johnson, Maurice TE	91-93Phi	2	6'2"	243	Temple		12
Johnson, Mike DE	84Hou		6'5"	253	Illinois		
Johnson, Mike LB	84-85USFL 86-93Cle		6'1"	227	Virginia Tech	7	12
Johnson, Nate WR	80NYG		5'11"	192	Hillsdale		
Johnson, Nate HB	87NO		6'2"	224	Texas Southern		
Johnson, Norm K	82-90Sea 91-93Atl	5	6'2"	195	California		1110
Johnson, Pepper LB	86-92NYG 93Cle		6'3"	248	Ohio State	10	12
Johnson, Pete FB	77-83Cin 84SD 84Mia	2	6'	252	Ohio State		492
Johnson, Raylee DE	93SD		6'3"	245	Arkansas		
Johnson, Reggie TE	91-93Den	2	6'2"	256	Florida State		18
Johnson, Richard DB	85-92Hou		6'1"	192	Wisconsin	15	6
Johnson, Richard WR	87Was 89-90Det	2	5'7"	182	Colorado		84
Johnson, Rick OT	87Det		6'6"	255	Grand Valley St.		
Johnson, Ron WR	82-84CFL 85USFL 86-89Phi 90VR	2	6'0"	186	Long Beach State		24
Johnson, Ron DB	78-84Pit		5'10"	200	Eastern Michigan	13	6
Johnson, Samuel WR	87LA		5'11"	180	Prairie View		
Johnson, Sidney DB	88KC 90-92Was		5'9"	175	California	3	
Johnson, Steve TE	88NE		6'6"	245	Virginia Tech		
Johnson, Tim DE-DT	87-89Pit 90-93Was		6'3"	274	Penn State	1	
Johnson, Tracy FB	89Hou 90-91Atl 92-93Sea	2	6'	232	Clemson		30
Johnson, Troy WR	85USFL 86-87StL 88Pit 89Det	2	6'1"	180	Southern U.		12
Johnson, Troy LB-DE	88-89Chi 90-91NYJ 92Det		6'	236	Oklahoma		
Johnson, Trumaine WR	83-84USFL 85-86SD 87-88Buf	2	6'1"	195	Grambling		24
Johnson, Undra HB	89NO 80Atl		5'9"	199	West Virginia		
Johnson, Vance WR	85-93Den	23	5'11"	185	Arizona		222
Johnson, Vaughan LB	84-85USFL 86-93NO		6'3"	237	N. Carolina State	4	
Johnson, Walter LB	87-88Hou 89NO		6'	240	Louisiana Tech		
Johnson, Walter DT	87Dal		6'1"	250	Pittsburgh		
Johnson, Wayne QB	89Ind		6'4"	221	Georgia		
Johnson, Will LB	87Chi		6'4"	242	Northeast La.		
Johnston, Brian C	86NYG		6'3"	275	North Carolina		
Johnston, Daryl FB	89-93Dal	2	6'2"	234	Syracuse		72
Joiner, Tim LB	83-84Hou 87Den		6'4"	235	Louisiana Tech		
Joines, Vernon WR	89-90Cle		6'2"	200	Maryland		
Jolly, Ken LB	84-85KC		6'2"	220	Mid-Amer. Nazarene		
Jolly, Mike DB	80GB 81KJ 82-83GB		6'3"	188	Michigan	3	
Jonassen, Eric OT	93SD		6'5"	310	Bloomsburg		
Jones, A.J. FB-HB	82-85LA 85Det		6'1"	202	Texas		
Jones, Aaron DE-LB	88-92Pit 93NE		6'5"	259	Eastern Kentucky	1	
Jones, Andre LB	92Det		6'2"	245	Notre Dame		
Jones, Anthony TE	84-87Was		6'3"	248	Md.-Eastern Shore, Wichita State		
Jones, Arrington HB	81SF		6'	225	Winston-Salem St.		
Jones, Bill HB	90-92KC	2	5'11"	228	S.M.U., SW Texas State		36
Jones, Bobby WR	78-82NYJ 83Cle	2	5'11"	182	none		42
Jones, Boyd OT	84GB		6'3"	265	Texas Southern		
Jones, Brent TE	87-93SF	2	6'4"	230	Santa Clara		108
Jones, Brian LB	91Ind		6'1"	240	U.C.L.A., Texas		
Jones, Bruce DB	87Pit		6'1"	197	North Alabama		
Jones, Bryant DB	87Ind		5'11"	186	Toledo	2	
Jones, Cedric WR	82-90NE	2	6'1"	184	Duke		108
Jones, Clarence OT	91-93NYG		6'6"	280	Maryland		
Jones, Chris C	87NYG		6'3"	263	Delaware State		
Jones, Dale LB	87Dal		6'1"	234	Tennessee		
Jones, Dan OT	93Cin		6'7"	294	Maine		
Jones, Dante LB	88-93Chi		6'1"	236	Oklahoma	4	6
Jones, David C-OG	84-85Det 87Den		6'3"	262	Texas		
Jones, David TE	92Raid		6'2"	220	Delaware State		
Jones, Darryll DB	84-85GB 86ZJ 87Den		6'1"	191	Georgia		
Jones, Don LB	92-93NYJ		6'	231	Washington		
Jones, Earl DB	80-83Atl		6'	178	Norfolk State	4	
Jones, E.J. HB-FB	85KC 87Dal		5'11"	216	Kansas		
Jones, Ernie WR	88-92Phx 93LA	2	5'11"	186	Indiana		120
Jones, Fred LB	87KC		6'3"	240	Florida State		
Jones, Fred WR	90-93KC	2	5'9"	175	Grambling		
Jones, Gary DB	90-91Pit 92KJ 93Pit		6'1"	203	Texas A&M	3	
Jones, Gordon WR	79-82TB 83LA	2	6'	190	Pittsburgh		48
Jones, Hassan WR	86-92Min 93KC	2	6'	194	Florida State		144
Jones, Henry DB	91-93Buf		5'11"	197	Illinois	10	20
Jones, James HB-FB	80-82Dal 83KJ 84-85Dal	23	5'10"	201	Mississippi State		12
Jones, James FB-TE	83-88Det 89-92Sea	2	6'2"	229	Florida		216
Jones, James DT-NT	91-93Cle		6'2"	292	Northern Iowa	1	20
Jones, Jimmie DT	90-93Dal		6'4"	278	Miami (Fla.)		
Jones, Jock LB	90-91Cle 91-93Phx		6'2"	235	Virginia Tech	1	
Jones, Joe TE	87Ind		6'5"	255	Virginia Tech		6
Jones, Joey WR	84-85USFL 86Atl 87KJ		5'8"	165	Alabama		
Jones, Johnny (Lam) WR	80-84NYJ 85RJ 86LJ	2	5'11"	180	Texas		78
Jones, Keith HB	89Cle 90KJ		5'10"	190	Nebracka		6
Jones, Keith HB-FB	89-92Atl	23	6'1"	210	Illinois		42
Jones, Ken OT-DE	76-86Buf 87NYJ		6'5"	260	Arkansas State		
Jones, Lyndell DB	87Atl		5'9"	175	Hawaii		
Jones, Marlon DE-DT	87-89Cle 90FJ		6'4"	263	Central State-Ohio		
Jones, Marvin LB	93NYJ		6'2"	240	Florida State		
Jones, Melvin OG	81Was		6'2"	260	Houston		
Jones, Mike WR	83-85Min 86-87,89NO	2	5'11"	181	Tennessee State		66
Jones, Mike LB	87Buf		6'4"	224	Brockport State		
Jones, Mike TE	90-91Min 92Sea		6'3"	255	Michigan, Texas A&M		12
Jones, Mike LB	91-93Raid		6'1"	228	Missouri		
Jones, Mike DE	91-93Phx		6'4"	288	N. Carolina State		
Jones, Preston QB	93Phi		6'3"	223	Georgia		
Jones, Quinn FB	80Atl		6'1"	215	Tulsa		
Jones, Quintin DB	88,90Hou		5'11"	193	Pittsburgh		
Jones, Reggie DB	91-93NO		6'1"	202	Memphis State	4	
Jones, Ricky DB-LB	77-79Cle 80-83Bal 84JJ		6'1"	211	Tuskegee		
Jones, Robbie LB	84-87NYG		6'2"	230	Alabama		
Jones, Robert LB	92-93Dal		6'2"	238	East Carolina		
Jones, Rod DB	86-90TB 91-93Cin		6'	180	S.M.U.	7	
Jones, Rod TE	87-88KC 89Sea		6'4"	242	Washington		6
Jones, Roger DB	91-93TB		5'9"	175	Tennessee State		6
Jones, Rondell DB	93Den		6'2"	210	North Carolina		
Jones, Rulon DE	80-88Den		6'6"	260	Utah State		10
Jones, Scott OT	89Cin 90NYJ 91GB 91Cin		6'5"	281	Washington		
Jones, Sean DE	84-87Raid 88-93Hou		6'7"	269	Northeastern	1	
Jones, Selwyn DB	93Cle		6'	185	Colorado State	3	
Jones, Shawn DB	93Min		6'1"	200	Georgia Tech		
Jones, Terry NT-DT	78-84GB		6'2"	257	Alabama		
Jones, Todd OT	93NE		6'3"	295	Henderson State		
Jones, Tony OT-OG	88-93Cle		6'5"	288	Western Carolina		
Jones, Tony WR	90-91Hou 92Atl 93Hou	2	5'7"	139	Texas		54
Jones, Too Tall DE	74-78Dal 79VR 80-89Dal		6'9"	271	Tennessee State	3	
Jones, Tyrone LB	88Phx		6'	220	Southern U.		
Jones, Tyrone DB	89Phi		6'4"	223	Arkansas State		
Jones, Victor LB	88TB 89-93Det		6'2"	243	Virginia Tech	1	
Jones, Victor HB-FB	90-91Hou 92Den 93Pit		5'8"	214	Louisiana State		
Jones, Wayne OG	87Min		6'4"	270	Utah		
Jones, Willie DE	79-81Oak 82KJ		6'4"	244	Florida State		12
Jordan, Brian DB	89-91Atl		5'11"	202	Richmond	5	4
Jordan, Buford FB	84-85USFL 86-92NO	2	6'	223	McNeese State		60
Jordan, Curtis DB	76-80TB 81-86Was		6'2"	200	Texas Tech	17	12
Jordan, Darin LB-DE	88Pit 91-93SF		6'1"	239	Northeastern	1	8
Jordan, David OG	84-85NYG 86BN 87TB		6'6"	274	Auburn		
Jordan, Donald FB	84Chi	2	6'	210	Houston		
Jordan, Homer QB	87Cle		6'	183	Clemson		
Jordan, Kenneth LB	87GB		6'2"	235	Tuskegee		
Jordan, Randy FB	93Raid		5'10"	205	North Carolina		
Jordan, Shelby OT	75, 77NE 83-86Raid 87AJ		6'7"	275	Washington-St.L.		
	1976 — Ineligible to play pro football						
Jordan, Steve TE	82-93Min	2	6'4"	236	Brown		174
Jordan, Steve K	87Ind		5'10"	205	Southern Calif.		16
Jordan, Tony HB	88-89Phx	2	6'2"	220	Kansas State		30
Jordan, Tim LB	87-89NE		6'3"	226	Wisconsin	1	
Jorden, Tim TE	90-91Phx 92-93Pit	2	6'2"	235	Indiana		12
Joseph, James HB-FB	91-93Phi	2	6'	222	Auburn		24
Joyner, Seth LB	86-93Phi		6'2"	240	Texas-El Paso	17	30
Joyner, Willie HB	84Hou		5'10"	200	Maryland		
Jozwiak, Brian OG-OT	86-88KC		6'5"	304	West Virginia		
Judie, Ed LB	82-83SF 83TB 84Mia		6'2"	232	Northern Arizona		
Judson, William DB	82-89Mia 90Det		6'1"	189	S. Carolina State	24	12
Juma, Kevin WR	87Sea		6'2"	195	Idaho		
Junior, E.J. LB	81-87StL 88Phx 89-91Mia 92TB 92-93Sea		6'3"	237	Alabama	12	6
Junkin, Mike LB	87-88Cle 89KC		6'3"	241	Duke		
Junkin, Trey LB-TE	83-84Buf 84Was 85-89Raid 90-93Sea	2	6'2"	226	Louisiana Tech		36
Juriga, Jim OT-OG	88-90Den 91XJ		6'6"	269	Illinois		
Jurkovic, John NT	91-93GB		6'2"	297	Eastern Illinois		
Justin, Kerry DB	78-83Sea 84-85USFL 86-87Sea		5'11"	176	Oregon State	7	
Justin, Sid DB	79LA 81JJ 82Bal		5'10"	170	California	1	6
Kab, Vyto TE	82-85Phi 85NYG 87Det 88KJ	2	6'5"	243	Penn State		30
Kackerski, John LB	92Den		6'3"	240	Ohio State		
Kacmarek, Jeff NT	87Det		6'2"	240	Western Michigan		
Kafentzis, Kurt DB	87Hou		6'2"	190	Hawaii		
Kafentzis, Mark DB	82Cle 83Bal 84Ind		5'10"	190	Hawaii	1	6
Kaiser, John LB	84-86Sea 87Buf		6'3"	227	Arizona		
Kalafat, Jim LB	87LA		6'	235	Montana State		
Kalis, Todd OG	88-91Min 92KJ 93Min		6'5"	284	Arizona State		
Kamana, John LB-TE	84LA 87Atl		6'	223	Southern Calif.		6
Kane, Rick HB-FB	77-83Det 84Was 85Det	23	5'11"	200	Oregon, San Jose State		84
Kane, Tommy WR	88-92Sea	2	5'11"	180	Dawson (Que.), Syracuse		54
Kaplan, Ken OT	84-85TB 87NO		6'4"	272	New Hampshire		
Karcher, Ken QB	87-88Den	1	6'3"	205	Notre Dame, Tulane		
Karlis, Rich K	82-88Den 89Min 90Det	5	6'	180	Cincinnati		799
Karpinski, Keith LB	89Det		6'3"	225	Penn State		
Kartz, Keith OT-OG-C	87-93Den		6'4"	270	California		
Kasay, John K	91-93Sea	5	5'10"	189	Georgia		256
Katolin, Mike C	84-85USFL 87Cle		6'3"	255	San Jose State		
Kattus, Eric TE	86-91Cin 92NYJ	2	6'5"	240	Michigan		30
Kauahi, Kani C	82-86Sea 88GB 89-91Phx 92KC 93Phx		6'2"	268	Arizona State. Hawaii		
Kaufman, Mel LB	81-88Was		6'2"	221	Cal. Poly.-S.L.O.	7	12
Kaufusi, Steve DE-DT	89-90Phi		6'4"	274	Brigham Young		
Kaumeyer, Thom DB	89-90Sea 91-92KJ		5'11"	187	Oregon		
Kauric, Jerry K	90Cle	5	6'	210	Kennedy (Ontario)		66
Kay, Bill DB	81-83Hou 84Stl 84SD		6'1"	190	Purdue	4	
Kay, Clarence TE	84-92Den	2	6'2"	237	Georgia		78
Kearse, Tim WR	87Ind		5'11"	186	San Jose State		
Keating, Chris LB	79-84Buf 85Was		6'2"	223	Maine	3	6
Keeble, Jerry LB	87SF		6'3"	230	Minnesota		
Keel, Mark TE	87Sea 87KC		6'4"	228	Arizona		
Keever, Carl LB	87SF		6'2"	236	Oregon State, Boise State		
Kehoe, Scott OT	87Mia		6'4"	282	Illinois		
Kehr, Rick OG	87Was 88KJ		6'3"	285	Carthage		
Keim, Mike DT-OT	91NO 92-93Sea		6'7"	293	Brigham Young		
Keith, Craig TE	93Pit		6'3"	262	Lenoir-Rhyne		
Kellar, Bill WR	78KC 79SJ		5'11"	187	Stanford		
Kellar, Scott NT	86-87Ind		6'3"	282	Northern Illinois		
Kellermeyer, Doug OG-OT	87Hou		6'3"	275	Brigham Young		
Kelley, Chris TE	87Cle		6'4"	239	Akron		1
Kelley, Mike C-OG-OT	85Hou 86ZJ 87Hou		6'5"	273	Notre Dame		
Kelley, Mike QB	87SD		6'3"	195	Georgia Tech		
Kellin, Kevin DE	86-88TB		6'6"	267	Minnesota		
Kelly, Jim QB	83-85USFL 86-93Buf	12	6'3"	217	Miami (Fla.)		24
Kelly, Joe LB	86-89Cin 90-92NYJ 93Raid		6'2"	231	Washington	4	
Kelly, Paul QB	87NYG		6'1"	205	New Haven		

UseName(Nickname)-Positions	Team by Year	See Section	Hgt.	Wgt.	College	Int	Pts
Kelly, Pat TE	88-89Den 90-91NYJ		6'6"	252	Syracuse		
Kelly, Todd DE	93SF		6'2"	259	Tennessee		
Kelm, Larry LB	87-92LA 93SF		6'4"	236	Texas A&M	3	
Kelso, Mark DB	86-93Buf		5'11"	181	William & Mary	30	18
Kemp, Bobby DB	81-86Cin 87TB		6'	189	Fullerton State	10	
Kemp, Jeff QB	81-85LA 86SF 87-91Sea 91Phi	12	6'	200	Dartmouth		6
Kemp, Perry WR	87Cle 88-91GB	2	5'11"	170	California (Pa.)		48
Kempf, Florian K	82-84Hou 87NO	5	5'9"	170	Pennsylvania		151
Kenn, Mike OT	78-93Atl		6'7"	273	Michigan		
Kennard, Derek OG-C	84-85USFL 86-87StL 88-90Phx 91-93NO		6'3"	289	Nevada-Reno		
Kennard, Ken NT-DE	77-83Hou		6'2"	248	Angelo State		2
Kennedy, Allan OT	81SF 82NJ 83-84SF 85KJ		6'7"	273	Washington State		
Kennedy, Cortez DT	90-93Sea		6'3"	293	Miami (Fla.)		
Kennedy, Lincoln OG-OT	93Atl		6'6"	335	Washington		
Kennedy, Mike DB	83Buf 84Hou		6'	195	Toledo	1	6
Kennedy, Sam LB	88SF		6'3"	235	San Jose State		
Kenney, Bill QB	79-88KC	12	6'4"	211	Arizona State, Northern Colorado		30
Ker, Crawford OG	85-90Dal 91Den		6'3"	288	Florida		
Kern, Don TE	84-85Cin 86Buf		6'4"	228	Arizona State		
Kerrigan, Mike QB	83-84NE		6'3"	205	Northwestern		
Kersten, Wally OT	82LA		6'5"	270	Minnesota		
Keseday, Bob TE	87StL		6'4"	225	Texas-El Paso		
Key, David DB	91NE		5'10"	190	Michigan		
Keys, Tyrone DE	83-85Chi 86-87TB 88SD		6'7"	272	Mississippi State		
Kidd, Billy C	87Hou		6'4"	270	Houston		
Kidd, John K	84-89Buf 90-93SD	4	6'3"	207	Northwestern		6
Kidd, Keith WR	87Min		6'1"	195	Arkansas		
Kiel, Blair QB	84TB 86-87Ind 88-91GB	1	6'	209	Notre Dame		6
Kiewel, Jeff OG	83-84USFL 85Atl 86KJ 87Atl		6'4"	271	Arizona		
Kilson, David DB	83Buf		6'1"	200	Nevada-Reno		6
Kimball, Bruce OG	82NYG 83-84Was		6'2"	260	Massachusetts		
Kimble, Garry DB	87Was		5'11"	184	Sam Houston St.		
Kimbrough, Tony WR	93Den		6'2"	192	Jackson State		
Kimmel, Jamie LB	86-87Raid 88KJ		6'3"	235	Syracuse		
Kimmel, Jerry LB	87NYG		6'2"	240	Syracuse		
Kimmel, Jon LB	85Phi 87Was		6'4"	240	Colgate		
Kinard, Terry DB	83-89NYG 90Hou		6'1"	199	Clemson	31	18
Kinchen, Brian TE	88-90Mia 91-93Cle	2	6'2"	235	Louisiana State		12
Kinchen, Todd WR	92-93LA		6'	187	Louisiana State		18
Kindt, Don TE	87Chi		6'6"	242	Wis.-LaCrosse		6
King, Angelo LB	81-83Dal 84-87Det		6'1"	224	S. Carolina State		6
King, Bruce FB	85-86KC 86-87Buf	2	6'1"	221	Purdue		
King, David DB	87GB		5'9"	175	Auburn		
King, Don DB	87GB		6'	200	S.M.U.		
King, Ed OG-OT	91-93Cle		6'4"	303	Auburn		
King, Emanuel LB	85-88Cin 89Raid		6'4"	250	Alabama		
King, Gordon OT-OG	78-83NYG 84BA 85NYG 86-87NYJ		6'6"	274	Stanford		
King, Jerome DB	79-80Atl 80NYG 83USFL		5'10"	173	Purdue		
King, Joe DB	91Cin 91Cle 92-93TB		6'2"	212	Oklahoma State	5	
King, Kenny HB-FB	79Hou 80-81Oak 82-85Raid	2	5'11"	205	Oklahoma		48
King, Linden LB	82-85SD 86-89Raid		6'4"	247	Colorado State	8	6
King, Tim DB	87TB		6'2"	190	Delaware State		
Kinlaw, Reggie NT	79-81Oak 82-84Raid 85-86Sea		6'2"	245	Oklahoma		
Kinnebrew, Larry FB	83-87Cin 89-90Buf	2	6'1"	255	Tennessee State		282
Kinney, Steve OT-OG	80-85Phi 86Det		6'4"	265	Clemson		
Kinzer, Matt K	87Det		6'3"	225	Purdue		
87,90 played major league baseball							
Kirby, Terry HB	93Mia	2	6'1"	221	Virginia		36
Kirchbaum, Kelly LB	80KC 83-85USFL 87Phi		6'2"	240	Kentucky		
Kirchner, Mark OT-OG	83Pit 83KC 84Ind 85FJ 86Ind		6'3"	262	Baylor		
Kirk, Randy LB	87-88SD 89-90Phx 91Cle 91SD 92-93Cin		6'2"	231	San Diego State		
Kirkland, Levon LB	92-93Pit		6'	247	Clemson		6
Kirksey, William LB	90Min 92FJ		6'2"	221	Southern Miss.		
Kirtman, Mike WR	80Buf		6'1"	180	San Jose State		
Kiser, Paul OG	87Det		6'4"	270	Wake Forest		
Kitson, Syd OG-OT	80-81GB 82SJ 83-84GB 84Dal		6'4"	258	Wake Forest		
Klecko, Joe DE-DT-NT	77-87NYJ 88Ind		6'3"	263	Temple		
Klever, Rocky TE-FB	83-87NYJ 88XJ		6'3"	227	Montana		18
Klingbeil, Chuck NT	91-93Mia		6'1"	263	Northern Michigan		6
Klingel, John DE	87-88Phi		6'4"	267	Kentucky		
Klingler, David QB	92-93Cin	12	6'2"	205	Houston		
Klostermann, Bruce LB	87-90Den		6'4"	230	Iowa, S. Dakota St.		
Klug, Dave LB	81-83KC		6'4"	230	Concordia (Minn.)		6
Knafelc, Greg QB	83NO		6'4"	220	Notre Dame		
Knapczyk, Ken WR	87Chi		5'11"	190	Northern Iowa		
Knapple, Jeff QB	80Den 81CFL 83-84USFL		6'2"	200	Northern Colorado		
Knight, Leander DB	87-88Atl 89NYJ 90Hou		6'1"	194	Ferrum, Montclair State	1	
Knight, Marion DE	87LA		6'2"	265	Nevada-Las Vegas		
Knight, Shawn DE	87NO 88Den 89Phx		6'6"	288	Brigham Young		
Knight, Steve OG	87Ind 88-89KJ		6'4"	298	Tennessee		
Knox, Chuck	HC73-77LA HC78-82Buf HC83-91Sea HC92-93LA				Juniata		
Knox, Darryl LB	87Pit		6'3"	220	Nevada-Las Vegas		
Knox, Mike LB	87Den		6'2"	240	Nebraska		
Koart, Matt DE	86GB		6'5"	258	Southern Calif		
Koch, Greg OT-OG	77-85GB 86-87Mia 87Min		6'4"	270	Arkansas		
Koch, Markus DE	86-91Was		6'5"	270	Boise State		
Koch, Pete NT-DT	84Cin 85-87KC 88BW 89Raid		6'6"	269	Maryland		
Kofler, Matt QB	82-84Buf 85Ind	12	6'3"	194	San Diego State		
Kohlbrand, Joe LB	85-89NO		6'4"	242	Miami (Fla.)		
Kohrs, Bob DE-LB	81-85Pit		6'3"	239	Arizona State		2
Kolic, Larry LB	86-88Mia		6'1"	240	Ohio State		
Kolodziejski, Chris TE	84Pit		6'3"	231	Wyoming		
Komlo, Jeff QB	79-81Det 82Atl 83TB 84BJ	12	6'2"	200	Delaware		12
Konecny, Mark HB	87Mia 88Phi 89KJ	2	5'11"	199	Alma		
Konopasek, Ed OT	87GB		6'6"	289	Ball State		
Koonce, George LB	92-93GB		6'1"	238	East Carolina		
Korff, Mark LB	87SF		6'1"	230	Florida		
Kors, R.J. DB	91-92NYJ 93Cin		6'	195	Southern Calif., Long Beach State	2	
Korte, Steve OG-C	83-90NO		6'2"	265	Arkansas		6
Kosar, Bernie QB	85-93Cle 93Dal	12	6'5"	210	Miami (Fla.)		24
Koss, Stein TE	87KC		6'2"	225	Arizona State		
Kotite, Rich	HC91-93Phi				Wagner		
Kovach, Jim LB	79-85NO 85SF		6'2"	229	Kentucky	4	
Kovaleski, Mike LB	87Cle		6'2"	225	Notre Dame		
Kowalkowski, Scott LB	91-92Phi		6'2"	228	Notre Dame		
Kowalski, Gary OT-OG	83LA 84KJ 85-88SD		6'6"	280	Boston College		
Kowgios, Nick FB	87Det		6'	216	Lafayette		
Kozak, Scott LB	89-93Hou		6'3"	225	Oregon		
Kozerski, Bruce C-OG	84-93Cin		6'4"	279	Holy Cross		
Kozlowski, Glen WR	87-92Chi 93KJ	2	6'1"	200	Brigham Young		18
Kozlowski, Mike DB	79Mia 80NJ 81-86Mia	3	6'	196	San Diego State, Brigham Young, Colorado	8	18
Kragen, Greg NT	85-93Den		6'3"	259	Utah State		6
Krakoski, Joe LB	86Was		6'1"	224	Washington		
Kramer, Erik QB	87Atl 91-93Det	12	6'	192	N. Carolina State		6
Kramer, Kyle DB	89Cle 90SJ		6'3"	190	Bowling Green	1	
Kramer, Tommy QB	77-89Min 90NO	12	6'2"	202	Rice		48
Kratch, Bob OG-OT	89-93NYG		6'3"	288	Iowa		
Krauss, Barry LB	79-83Bal 84-88Ind 89Mia 90KJ		6'3"	245	Alabama	6	6
Kraynak, Rich LB	83-86Phi 87Atl		6'1"	227	Pittsburgh	1	6
Kreider, Steve WR	79-86Cin	2	6'3"	192	Lehigh		56
Kremer, Ken NT-DE	79-84KC		6'4"	252	Ball State	1	
Krenk, Mitch TE	84Chi		6'2"	225	Nebraska		
Krerowicz, Mark OG	87Cle		6'3"	285	Ohio State		
Krieg, Dave QB	80-91Sea 92-93KC	12	6'1"	190	Milton		72
Krimm, John DB	82NO 83KJ		6'1"	190	Notre Dame		
Krueger, Todd QB	87Min		6'4"	200	Northern Michigan		
Krumm, Todd DB	88Chi		6'	189	Michigan State	2	
Krumrie, Tim NT-DT	83-93Cin		6'2"	267	Wisconsin		
Kubiak, Gary QB	83-91Den	12	6'	192	Texas A&M		12
Kubin, Larry LB	82-84Was 85Buf 85TB		6'2"	235	Penn State		
Kuehn, Art C	76-82Sea 83NE 84-85USFL		6'3"	257	U.C.L.A.		
Kugler, Pete NT-DE	81-83SF 84-85USFL 86-90SF		6'4"	255	Penn State		
Kuhlmann, Hank	HC89Phx				Missouri		
Kullman, Michael DB	87Phi		6'1"	185	Kutztown	2	
Kumerow, Eric DE-LB	88-90Mia 91BN		6'7"	264	Ohio State	1	
Kunz, Lee LB	79-81Chi		6'2"	224	Nebraska		
Kupp, Craig QB	91Phx 91Dal		6'4"	215	Montana Tech, Pacific Lutheran		
Kurisko, Jamie TE	87NYJ 88LJ		6'4"	236	Southern Conn. St.		6
Kush, Frank	HC82-83Bal HC84Ind				Michigan State		
Kush, Rod DB	80-84Buf 85Hou 86KJ		6'	189	Nebraska-Omaha	4	
Kuykendall, Fulton (Captain Crazy) LB	75-84Atl 85SF		6'5"	225	U.C.L.A.	3	6
Kyles, Troy WR	90NYG		6'	180	Howard		
Laakso, Eric OT-OG	78-84Mia		6'4"	265	Tulane		
LaBeaux, Sandy DB	83TB 85USFL		6'3"	210	Hayward State		
LaBounty, Matt DE	93SF		6'4"	254	Oregon		
LaChapelle, Sean WR	93LA		6'3"	205	U.C.L.A.		
Lachey, Jim OT	85-87SD 88Raid 88-92Was 93KJ		6'6"	289	Ohio State		
Lacy, Ken FB	83-84USFL 84-85,87KC	2	6'	222	Tulsa		24
Lafary, Dave OT-OG	77-85NO		6'7"	280	Purdue		
LaFleur, Greg TE	81-86StL 86Ind	2	6'4"	236	Louisiana State		18
Lageman, Jeff LB-DE	89-93NYJ		6'5"	264	Virginia	1	
Lake, Carnell DB	89-93Pit		6'1"	205	UCLA	6	
Lamar, Kevin OG	87Buf		6'4"	260	Stanford		
Lamb, Brad WR	92-93Buf		5'10"	171	Anderson		
Lambert, Dion DB	92-93NE		6'	185	U.C.L.A.	1	
Lambrecht, Mike NT	87-89Mia		6'1"	273	St. Cloud State		
Land, Dan DB-HB	87TB 89-93Raid		6'	190	Albany State (Ga.)	2	
Land, Mel DE-LB	79Mia 80SF 82CFL 83USFL		6'3"	243	Michigan State		
Landeta, Sean K	83-85USFL 85-93NYG 93LA	4	6'	200	Towson State		
Landrum, Mike TE	84Atl 85-86KJ		6'2"	231	Southern Miss.		
Landsee, Bob C-OG	86-87Phi 88KJ		6'4"	273	Wisconsin		
Lane, Eric HB-FB	81-87Sea	2	6'	197	Brigham Young		42
Lane, Garcia DB	84-85USFL 85,87KC	3	5'9"	180	Ohio State		
Lane, Skip DB	84NYJ 84KC 87Was		6'1"	209	Mississippi		
Lang, David HB	91-93LA	23	5'11"	201	Northern Arizona		36
Lang, Gene HB	84-87Den 88-90Atl	23	5'10"	196	Louisiana State		120
Lang, Le-Lo DB	90-93Den		5'11"	185	Washington	5	
Langhorne, Reggie WR	85-91Cle 92-93Ind	2	6'2"	200	Elizabeth City St.		114
Lanier, Ken OT	81-92Den 93Raid		6'3"	279	Florida State		
Lankford, Paul DB	82-91Mia		6'1"	185	Penn State	13	
Lansford, Mike K	82-90LA	5	6'	183	Washington		789
Lanza, Chuck C	88-89Pit 90LJ		6'2"	263	Notre Dame		
Lapka, Myron NT-DE-DT	80NYG 81KJ 82-83LA		6'4"	258	Southern Calif.		
LaPoint, Ron TE	80Bal		6'2"	235	Penn State		
Largent, Steve WR	76-89Sea	2	5'11"	187	Tulsa		608
Larkin, Eric DE	87Hou		6'4"	265	Miami (Fla.)		
Larson, Kurt LB	89-90Ind 91GB		6'4"	236	Michigan State		
Lasher, Tim K	87Chi	5	5'9"	160	Oklahoma		19
Lasker, Greg DB	86-88NYG 88Chi 88Phx		6'	200	Arkansas		
Lassic, Derrick HB	93Dal	2	5'10"	188	Alabama		18
Laster, Donald OT	82Was 83ZJ 84Det 85JJ		6'5"	285	Tennessee State		
Lathan, Greg WR	87Raid		6'1"	195	Cincinnati		
Lathon, Lamar LB	90-93Hou		6'3"	249	Houston	3	6
Lathrop, Kit DE-NT	79Den 79-80GB 83-84USFL 86KC 87Was		6'5"	257	Arizona State		
Latimer, Al DB	79Phi 80SF 82-84Det		5'11"	176	Clemson	1	
Lattimore, Brian HB-FB	91Ind		6'1"	202	SE Missouri St.		
Laufenberg, Babe QB	83Was 84SJ 85SD 85Was 86NO 87Was 88SD 89-90Dal	12	6'2"	198	Stanford, Missouri, Indiana		
Laughlin, Jim LB	80-82Atl 83GB 84-86LA 87Atl		6'1"	222	Ohio State	2	
Laughton, Jim TE	86Sea		6'5"	225	San Diego State		
Lavette, Robert HB	85-87Dal 87Phi	3	5'11"	190	Georgia Tech		6
Lavine, Paul LB	87Sea		6'2"	207	Utah State		
Lawrence, Amos (Famous Amos) HB	81-82SF 84USFL	3	5'11"	180	North Carolina		12
Lawrence, Ben OG	87Pit		6'1"	325	Indiana (Pa.)		
Lawrence, Henry OT-OG	74-81Oak 82-86Raid		6'4"	272	Florida A&M		
Lawson, Jamie FB	89-90TB 90NE		5'10"	240	Louisiana State, Nicholls State		
Lawrence, Reggie WR	93Phi		6'	178	Carolina State		
Leach, Scott LB	87NO		6'2"	221	Ohio State	1	
Leach, Bill OG-OT	87NO		6'5"	280	Kentucky, N. Carolina State		
Leahy, Pat K	74-91NYJ	5	6'	194	St. Louis		1470
LeBel, Harper TE	89Sea 90Phi 91-93Atl		6'4"	251	Colorado State		
LeBlanc, Bob LB	87Buf		6'2"	243	Elon		
LeBlanc, Michael HB	87NE	2	5'11"	199	S.F. Austin State		6
LeCount, Terry WR	78-79SF 79-84,87Min	2	5'10"	178	Florida		36
Lee, Amp HB	92-93SF	2	5'11"	200	Florida State		42
Lee, Byron LB	86-87Phi		6'2"	230	Ohio State		
Lee, Carl DB	83-93Min		6'	185	Marshall	29	12
Lee, Danzell TE	87Pit 88Atl	2	6'2"	235	Lamar		
Lee, Gary WR	87-88Det	23	6'1"	202	Georgia Tech		6

UseName(Nickname)-Positions	Team by Year	See Section	Hgt	Wgt	College	Int	Pts
Lee, Greg DB	88Pit		6'1"	207	Arkansas State		
Lee, Jeff WR	80StL		6'2"	195	Nebraska		
Lee, John K	86StL	5	5'11"	182	U.C.L.A.		38
Lee, Keith DB	81-84NE 85Ind		5'11"	194	Colorado State	1	
Lee, Larry OG-C	81-85Det 85-86Mia 87-88Den		6'2"	265	U.C.L.A.		
Lee, Mark DB	80-90GB 91SF 91NO	3	5'11"	188	Washington	32	6
Lee, Oudious NT	80StL 83-84USFL		6'1"	253	Nebraska		
Lee, Ronnie TE-OT-OG	79-82Mia 83Atl 84-89Mia 90-92Sea	2	6'3"	266	Baylor		18
Lee, Shawn NT	88-89TB 90-91Mia 92-93SD		6'2"	294	North Alabama	1	
Lee, Zeph DB-FB	87Den 87-89Raid		6'3"	208	Southern Calif.	1	
Leewenburg, Jay C-OT	92-92Chi		6'2"	290	Colorado		
Legette, Burnie FB	93NE		6'	243	Michigan		
Legette, Tyrone DB	92-93NO		5'9"	177	Nebraska		
Leggett, Brad C	91NO 92Det		6'4"	270	Southern Calif.		
Leggett, Scott OG-OT	87Phi		6'3"	285	Central State-Okla.		
Leiding, Jeff LB	86Ind		6'3"	232	Texas		4
Leiker, Tony DE	87GB		6'5"	250	Stanford		
Leonard, Jim C-OG	80-82TB 83-85USFL 85SF 85-86SD		6'3"	258	Santa Clara		
Leopold, Bobby LB	80-83SF 84-85USFL 86GB 87XJ		6'1"	217	Notre Dame	5	
Lester, Keith TE	87Ind		6'5"	235	Murray State		
Lester, Tim FB-HB	92-93LA	2	5'9"	215	Eastern Kentucky		
Lett, Leon DT	91-93Dal		6'6"	290	Emporia State		
Levenick, Dave LB	83-84Atl		6'3"	220	Wisconsin		
Levy, Marv	HC78-82KC HC86-93Buf				Coe		
Lewis, Albert DB	83-93KC		6'2"	193	Grambling	38	14
Lewis, Bill C-OG	86-88Raid 90-92Phx 93NE		6'7"	285	Nebraska		
Lewis, Cliff LB	81-84GB		6'1"	226	Southern Miss.		
Lewis, Darryl TE	84Cle		6'6"	232	Texas-Arlington		
Lewis, Darren HB-FB	91-93Chi	23	5'10"	230	Texas A&M		30
Lewis, Darryll DB	91-93Hou		5'9"	188	Arizona	2	12
Lewis, Dave LB	77-81TB 82SD 83LA		6'4"	240	Southern Calif.	10	6
Lewis, David TE	84-86Det 87Mia	2	6'3"	234	California		48
Lewis, Gary TE-WR	81-83GB 84USFL 84GB	2	6'5"	234	Texas-Arlington		12
Lewis, Gary NT	83NO 84IL		6'3"	260	Oklahoma State		
Lewis, Garry DB	90-91Raid 92TB 93KC		5'11"	185	Alcorn State	1	
Lewis, Greg HB-FB	91-92Den	2	5'10"	214	Washington		48
Lewis, John DB	87Buf		5'10"	175	Pittsburgh		
Lewis, Kenny HB-FB	80-81NYJ 82USFL 83NYJ		6'	192	Virginia Tech		
Lewis, Kevin DB	90-91SF 92ZJ		5'11"	173	Nortthwestern La.	1	
Lewis, Leo WR	81-89Min 90Cle 90-91Min	23	5'8"	170	Missouri		102
Lewis, Mark TE	85-87GB 87-88Det		6'2"	239	Texas A&M		18
Lewis, Mo LB	91-93NYJ		6'3"	248	Georgia	3	
Lewis, Nate WR	90-93SD	23	5'11"	189	Oregon Tech		90
Lewis, Marvin FB	82NO		6'3"	208	Tulane		
Lewis, Reggie DE-NT	70 80TB 83USFL		6'3"	258	North Texas	1	6
Lewis, Reggie DE	82-84NO		6'2"	252	Oregon, San Diego State		
Lewis, Rodney DB	82-84NO		5'11"	189	Nebraska	1	
Lewis, Ron WR	90SF 91XJ 92SF 92-93GB	2	5'11"	173	Florida State		
Lewis, Sid DB	87NYJ		5'11"	180	Penn State		
Lewis, Tahaun DB	92KC		5'10"	175	Nebraska		
Lewis, Terry DB	85SD		5'11"	193	Michigan State		
Lewis, Tim DB	83-86GB		5'11"	192	Pittsburgh	16	6
Lewis, Vernon DB	93NE		5'10"	192	Pittsburgh		
Lewis, Will DB	80-81Sea 81KC 83-85USFL	3	5'9"	185	Millersville	6	
Lick, Dennis OT	78-82Chi		6'3"	266	Wisconsin		
Liebenstein, Todd DE	82-85Was		6'6"	253	Nevada-Las Vegas		
Liles, Alva NT-DT	80Oak 80Det 83USFL		6'3"	255	Boise State		
Lilja, George C-OG-OT	82LA 83-84NYJ 84-86Cle 87Dal		6'4"	264	Michigan		
Lilly, Kevin DE-NT-DT	88SF 89Dal 89SF		6'4"	265	Tulsa		
Lilly, Sammy DB	89-90Phi 90SD 91-92LA		5'9"	178	Georgia Tech		
Lilly, Tony DB	84-87Den 89Dal		6'	199	Florida	9	
Limbrick, Garrett FB	90Mia 91SJ		6'2"	240	Oklahoma State		
Lincoln, Jeremy DB	93Chi		5'10"	180	Tennessee	3	6
Lindley, David QB	87Sea		6'	190	Linfield		
Lindsay, Everett OT	93Min		6'4"	290	Mississippi		
Lindstrom, Chris DE	83Cin 84USFL 85TB 87KC		6'7"	260	Boston U.		
Lindstrom, Dave DE	78-85KC		6'6"	255	Boston U.		
Lingmerth, Goran K	87Cle		5'8"	160	Northern Arizona		
Lingner, Adam C-OG	83-86KC 87Buf 88KC 89-93Buf		6'4"	261	Illinois		
Linn, Jack OT-OG	91Ind 92-93Det 93Cin		6'5"	290	West Virginia		
Linne, Larry WR	87NE	2	6'1"	185	Texas-El Paso		12
Linnin, Chris DE	80NYG 84USFL		6'4"	255	Washington		
Lippett, Ronnie DB	83-88NE 89LJ 90-91NE		5'11"	180	Miami (Fla.)	24	12
Lipps, Louis WR	84-91Pit 92NO	23	5'10"	188	Southern Miss.		276
Lisch, Rusty QB	80-83StL 84Chi	1	6'3"	214	Notre Dame		
Liter, Greg DE	87SF 87Phi		6'6"	275	Iowa State		
Little, Dave TE	84KC 85-89Phi 90Phx 91Det	2	6'2"	233	Middle Tenn. St.		12
Little, David LB	81-92Pit		6'1"	232	Florida	10	
Little, George DE-NT	85-87Mia		6'4"	275	Iowa		
Livingston, Bruce DB	87Dal		5'10"	169	Arkansas Tech		
Lloyd, Doug FB	91Raid		6'1"	220	N. Dakota State		
Lloyd, Greg LB	88-93Pit		6'2"	224	Ft. Valley State	6	
Lobenstein, Bill DE-NT	87Den		6'3"	261	Wis.-Whitewater		
Loberg, Greg OG-OT	87NO		6'4"	264	California		
Lockett, Charles WR	87-88Pit 90LJ	2	6'	178	Long Beach State		12
Lockett, Danny LB	87-88Det		6'2"	239	Arizona		
Lockett, Frank WR	83-85USFL 85Mia		6'	200	Nebraska		
Lockett, Wade WR	87Raid		6'1"	190	Fullerton State		
Lockhart, Eugene LB	84-90Dal 91-92NE		6'2"	234	Houston	6	6
Locklin, Kerry TE	82LA 84USFL 87Den		6'3"	230	New Mexico State		
Lockwood, Scott HB	92-93NE	2	5'10"	196	Southern Cal		
Lodish, Mike DE	90-93Buf		6'3"	269	U.C.L.A.		6
Loewen, Chuck OT-OG	80-82SD 83XJ 84SD		6'3"	263	S. Dakota State		
Lofton, Steve DB	91-93Phx		5'9"	180	Texas A&M		
Lofton, James WR-DB	78-86GB 87-88Raid 89-92Buf 93LA 93Phi	2	6'3"	192	Stanford		456
Logan, Dave WR-DB	76-83Cle 84Den	2	6'4"	219	Colorado	1	144
Logan, David NT-DE	79-86TB 87GB		6'2"	250	Pittsburgh	1	24
Logan, Ernie DE	91-92Cle 93Atl		6'3"	276	East Carolina		
Logan, Marc HB-FB	87-88Cin 89-91Mia 92-93SF	23	5'11"	210	Kentucky		72
Lohmiller, Chip K	88-93Was	5	6'3"	213	Minnesota		697
Lomack, Tony WR	90LA 91Phx		5'8"	180	Florida		
Lomax, Neil QB	81-87StL 88Phx 89PJ	12	6'3"	215	Portland State		60
London, Antonio LB	93Det		6'2"	34	Alabama		
Loneker, Keith OG	93LA		6'3"	330	Kansas		
Long, Chuck QB	86-89Det 90LA 91Det	12	6'4"	216	Iowa		
Long, Darren TE	86LA		6'3"	240	Long Beach State		
Long, Howie DE-NT	81Oak 82-93Raid		6'5"	268	Villanova	1	
Long, Matt C	87Phi		6'3"	270	San Diego State		
Long, Terry OG	84-91Pit		5'11"	273	East Carolina		
Long, Tim C	87SF		6'6"	295	Memphis State		
Looney, Jim LB	81SF 83-84USFL		6'	225	Purdue		
Lott, John C-OG	87Pit		6'2"	260	North Texas		
Lott, Ronnie DB	81-90SF 92Raid 93NYJ		6'	200	Southern Calif.	63	30
Louallen, Fletcher DB	87Min		6'	195	Livingston	1	
Love, Duval OG-OT	85-92LA 93Pit		6'3"	281	Southern Calif., U.C.L.A.		
Love, Randy HB-FB	79-85StL 86XJ	2	6'1"	208	Houston		30
Love, Sean OG	93TB		6'3"	290	Penn State		
Love, Terry DB	87Min		6'2"	205	Murray State		
Loveall, Calvin DB	88Hou 88KC 88Atl		5'9"	180	Idaho		
Lovelady, Edwin WR	87NYG	2	5'9"	180	Memphis State		12
Loville, Derek HB	90-91Sea	23	5'9"	196	Oregon		
Loving, Warren FB	87Buf		6'1"	230	William Penn		
Lowdermilk, Kirk C	85-92Min 93Ind		6'3"	271	Ohio State		
Lowe, Woodrow LB	76-86SD 87KJ		6'	227	Alabama	21	24
Lowery, Nick K	78NE 80-93KC	5	6'4"	189	Dartmouth		1473
Lowry, Orlando LB	85-89Ind 89NE		6'4"	237	Ohio State		
Lowry, Quentin LB	81-83Was 83TB		6'3"	232	Youngstown State		
Loyd, Mike QB	79-80StL 84USFL	1	6'2"	216	Missouri Southern		
Lubischer, Steve LB	87Mia		6'3"	240	Boston College		
Lucas, Jeff OT	87Pit		6'7"	288	West Virginia		
Lucas, Tim LB	87-93Den		6'3"	230	California	1	
Luck, Oliver QB	82-86Hou	12	6'2"	196	West Virginia		6
Luckhurst, Mick K	81-87Atl	5	6'	181	St. Cloud State, California		558
Lumpkin, Joey LB	82-83Buf		6'2"	230	Arizona State		
Lumpkin, Sean DB	92-93NO		6'	206	Minnesota		
Luscinski, Jim OT-OG	82NYJ 83XJ		6'5"	275	Norwich		
Lush, Mike DB	83-85USFL 86Min 87Atl		6'1"	195	East Stroudsburg		
Luther, Ed QB	80-84SD 85USFL 86Ind	12	6'3"	207	San Jose State		
Lutz, David OT-OG	83-92KC 93Det		6'6"	297	Georgia Tech		
Lyday, Allen DB	84-87Hou		5'10"	190	Texas Southern, Nebraska	4	
Lyght, Todd DB	91-93LA		6'	186	Notre Dame	6	
Lyles, Lester DB-LB	85-87NYJ 88Phx 89-90SD		6'3"	210	Virginia	10	
Lyles, Robert LB	84-90Hou 90-91Atl		6'1"	226	Texas Christian	10	12
Lynch, Eric FB-HB	92-93Det	2	5'10"	224	Grand Valley St.		12
Lynch, John DB	93TB		6'2"	220	Stanford		
Lynch, Lorenzo DB	87-89Chi 90-93Phx		5'9"	198	Sacramento State	9	12
Lynch, Tom OG	77-80Sea 81-84Buf		6'5"	256	Boston College		
Lynn, Anthony FB	93Den		6'3"	230	Texas Tech		
Lynn, Johnny DB	79NYJ 80KJ 81-86NYJ		6'	196	U.C.L.A.	17	12
Lyons, Marty DT-DE-NT	79-89NYJ 90AJ		6'5"	265	Alabama		4
Lyons, Mitch TE	93Atl		6'4"	255	Michigan State		
Lyons, Robert DB	89Cle		6'1"	195	Akron	1	
Lytle, Rob HB-FB	77-83Den	2	6'1"	196	Michigan		84
Maarleveld, J.D. OT	86-87TB		6'6"	300	Notre Dame, Maryland		
Maas, Bill NT-DE	84-92KC 93GB		6'5"	270	Pittsburgh		16
Macaulay, John C	84SF		6'3"	254	Stanford		
MacDonald, Dan LB	87Den		6'2"	230	Idaho State		
MacDonald, Mark OG	85-88Min 88Phx		6'4"	266	Boston College		
Macek, Don C-OG	76-89SD		6'3"	261	Boston College		
Machurek, Mike QB	82-84Det		6'1"	205	Idaho State		
Mack, Cedric DB-WR	83-87StL 88-90Phx 91SD 92KC 92-93NO		6'	193	Baylor	20	6
Mack, Kevin FB-HB	84USFL 85-93Cle	2	6'	224	Clemson		324
Mack, Kim DB	87Sea		6'	190	Florida State		
Mack, Milton DB	87-91NO 92-93TB		5'11"	187	Alcorn State	8	6
Mack, Rico LB	93Pit		6'4"	239	Appalachian State		
Mack, Terence LB	87StL		6'3"	240	Clemson		
Mackey, Kyle QB	84StL 86Phi 87Mia 88SJ 89NYJ	1	6'3"	217	East Texas State		12
Mackie, Doug OT	87Atl		6'4"	280	Ohio State		
Mackovic, John	HC83-86KC				Wake Forest		
MacPherson, Dick	HC91-92NE				Springfield		
Maddox, Mark LB	92-93Buf		6'1"	233	Northern Michigan		
Maddox, Tommy QB	92-93Den	1	6'4"	200	U.C.L.A.		
Madsen, Lynn DE	84-85USFL 86Hou		6'4"	260	Washington		
Magee, Calvin TE	85-88TB	2	6'3"	240	Southern U.		66
Maggs, Don OT-OG-TE	84-85USFL 86,88-92Hou 93Den		6'5"	287	Tulane		
Maidlow, Steve LB	83-84Cin 85,87Buf		6'2"	235	Michigan State		
Majkowski, Don QB	87-92GB 93Ind	12	6'2"	197	Virginia		54
Malamala, Siupeli OT	92-93NYJ		6'5"	310	Washington		
Malancon, Rydell LB	84Atl 85KJ 87GB		6'2"	227	Louisiana State		
Malone, Darrell DB	92KC 92-93Mia		5'10"	177	Jacksonville St.		
Malone, Ralph DE	86Cle		6'5"	225	Georgia Tech		
Mallory, Rick OG	85-88TB		6'2"	264	Washington		
Malone, Mark QB-WR	80-87Pit 89NYJ	12	6'4"	221	Arizona State		114
Manca, Massimo K	87Cin		5'10"	211	Penn State	6	
Mandarich, Tony OT	89-91GB 92IL		6'5"	304	Michigan State		
Mandeville, Chris DB	87GB 89Was		6'1"	213	Cal.-Davis		
Mandley, Pete WR	84-88Det 89-90KC	23	5'10"	192	Northern Arizona		84
Maness, James WR	85Chi		6'1"	174	Texas Christian		
Mangum, John DB	90-93Chi		5'10"	176	Alabama	2	
Mangiero, Dino NT-DE	80-83KC 84Sea 87NE		6'2"	266	Rutgers	1	
Manley, Dexter DE	81-89Was 90Phx 91TB		6'3"	252	Oklahoma State	2	8
Mann, Charles DE	83-93Was		6'6"	268	Nevada-Reno		2
Manning, Aaron DB	87Cin		5'10"	178	Iowa State		
Manning, Wade DB-WR	79-80Dal 81-82Den	3	5'11"	190	Ohio State		
Manoa, Tim FB	87-89Cle 90EJ 91Ind	2	6'1"	227	Penn State		48
Manor, Brison DE	77-84Den 84TB		6'4"	248	Arkansas	1	
Manos, Sam C	87Cin		6'3"	265	Marshall		
Mansfield, Von DB	82Phi 84-85USFL 87GB		5'11"	184	Wisconsin		
Manucci, Dan QB	79-80Buf 81CFL 83USFL 87Buf		6'2"	196	Kansas State		
Manuel, Lionel WR	84-90NYG	2	5'11"	178	Pacific		138
Manumaleuga, Frank LB	79-81KC 83-85USFL		6'2"	245	U.C.L.A., San Jose State	6	6
Manusky, Greg LB	88-90Was 91-93Min		6'1"	240	Colgate		
Marchiol, Ken LB	87NO		6'2"	248	Mesa		
Margerum, Ken WR	81-83Chi 84KJ 85Chi 86-87SF	2	6'	176	Stanford		48
Marino, Dan QB	83-93Mia	12	6'4"	216	Pittsburgh		42
Marinovich, Todd QB	91-92Raid	1	6'4"	215	Southern Calif.		
Marion, Brock DB	93Dal		'11"	189	Nevada-Reno	1	
Marion, Frank LB	77-83NYG		6'3"	227	Florida A&M	1	
Marion, Fred DB	82-91NE		6'2"	192	Miami (Fla.)	29	6

UseName(Nickname)-Positions	Team by Year	See Section	Hgt	Wgt	College	Int	Pts
Mark, Greg DE-LB	90Mia 90Phi		6'3"	252	Miami (Fla.)		
Markham, Dale OT-DE	80NYG 81StL 83-85USFL		6'8"	280	North Dakota		
Markland, Jeff TE	88Pit		6'3"	245	Illinois		
Marrone, Doug OG-C-OT	87Mia 89NO		6'5"	269	Syracuse		
Marsh, Curt OG	81Oak 82Raid 83XJ 84-86Raid 87NJ		6'5"	273	Washington		
Marsh, Doug TE	80-86StL	2	6'3"	238	Michigan		114
Marshall, Arthur WR	92-93Den	23	5'11"	174	Georgia		18
Marshall, David LB	84Cle 87Mia		6'3"	220	Eastern Michigan		
Marshall, Henry WR	76-87KC	2	6'2"	214	Missouri		210
Marshall, James DB	80NO		6'	187	Jackson State	2	
Marshall, Leonard DE	83-92NYG 93NYJ		6'3"	285	Louisiana State	2	4
Marshall, Warren FB	87Den		6'	216	James Madison		
Marshall, Wilber LB	84-87Chi 88-92Was 93Hou		6'1"	228	Florida	21	24
Martin, Charles NT-DE	83USFL 84-87GB 87Hou 88Atl		6'4"	276	Livingston		
Martin, Chris LB	83NO 84-88Min 88-92KC 93LA		6'2"	234	Auburn	1	24
Martin, David DB	83-85USFL 86SD 87Buf		5'9"	191	Villanova		
Martin, Derrick DB	87SF		6'	185	San Jose State	1	
Martin, Doug DE-NT	80-89Min		6'3"	260	Washington	1	
Martin, Emanuel DB	93Hou		5'11"	184	Alabama State		
Martin, Eric WR	85-93NO	23	6'1"	205	Louisiana State		288
Martin, George DE-TE	75-88NYG		6'4"	247	Oregon	3	36
Martin, Jamie QB	93LA		6'2"	215	Weber State		
Martin, Kelvin WR	87-92Dal 93Sea	23	5'9"	163	Boston College		96
Martin, Mike WR	83-89Cin	23	5'10"	186	Illinois		36
Martin, Robbie WR	81-84Det 85-86Ind	3	5'8"	181	Cal. Poly.-S.L.O.		18
Martin, Rod LB	77-81Oak 82-88Raid		6'2"	218	Southern Calif.	15	38
Martin, Saladin DB	80NYJ 81SF 83USFL		6'	180	San Diego State	1	
Martin, Sammy WR	88-91NE 91Ind	23	5'11"	175	Louisiana State		12
Martin, Steve DE	87Was		6'3"	260	Jackson State		
Martin, Tony WR	90-93Mia	23	6'	180	Bishop, Mesa		54
Martin , Tracy WR	87NYJ 88LJ		6'3"	205	North Dakota		
Martin, Wayne DE	89-93NO		6'5"	275	Arkansas		
Martini, Rich WR	79-80Oak 81NO	2	6'2"	185	Cal.-Davis		12
Marts, Lonnie LB	91-93KC		6'1"	239	Tulane	2	6
Marve, Eugene LB	82-87Buf 88-91TB 92SD		6'2"	237	Saginaw Valley St.	3	
Marvin, Mickey OG	77-81Oak 82-86Raid 87KJ		6'4"	269	Tennessee		
Maryland, Russell DT-DE	91-93Dal		6'1"	277	Miami (Fla.)		6
Mason, Larry HB-FB	87Cle 88GB	2	5'11"	205	Troy State		18
Mason, Lindsey OT	78Oak 79KJ 80-81Oak 82SF 83Bal 84-85USFL		6'5"	265	Kansas		
Massey, Robert DB	89-90NO 91-93Phx		5'10"	189	N. Car. Central	10	18
Massie, Rick WR	87-88Den		6'1"	190	Kentucky		24
Maston, Le'Shai HB	93Hou		6'1"	215	Baylor		
Mataele, Stan NT	87GB		6'2"	278	Arizona		
Matau, Christopher OG	87LA		6'3"	310	Brigham Young		
Mathis, Mark DB	87StL		5'9"	178	Liberty	1	
Mathis, Reggie LB	79-80NO 85USFL		6'2"	220	Oklahoma	1	
Mathis, Terance WR	90-93NYJ	23	5'10"	170	New Mexico		42
Mathison, Bruce QB	83-84SD 85Buf 86SD 87-88Sea	12	6'3"	205	Nebraska		6
Matich, Trevor C-OG-TE-OT	85-88NE 89Det 90-91NYJ 92-93Ind		6'4"	277	Brigham Young		6
Mattes, Ron OT	86-90Sea 91Chi 92Ind		6'6"	304	Virginia		
Matthews, Allama TE-FB	83-85Atl	2	6'3"	230	Vanderbilt		6
Matthews, Aubrey WR	86-88Atl 88-89GB 90-93Det	2	5'7"	165	Delta State		36
Matthews, Bill LB	79-81NE 82KJ 84USFL		6'2"	235	S. Dakota State	1	
Matthews, Bruce OG-OT-C	83-93Hou		6'4"	288	Southern Calif.		
Matthews, Clay LB	78-93Cle		6'2"	238	Southern Calif.	14	12
Matthews, Ira HB-WR	79-81Oak 83USFL	23	5'8"	175	Wisconsin		6
Matthews, Shane QB	93Chi		6'3"	197	Florida		
Mattiace, Frank DE-NT	87Ind		6'1"	264	Holy Cross		
Mauti, Rich WR	77-80NO 81AJ 82-83NO 84Was	23	6'	190	Penn State		12
Maxey, Curtis DE-NT	88Cin 89Atl		6'3"	298	Grambling		
Maxie, Brett DB	85-93NO		6'2"	193	Texas Southern	15	20
Maxwell, Vernon LB	83Bal 84Ind 85-87Det 89Sea		6'2"	233	Arizona State	1	
May, Dean QB	84Phi 87Den		6'5"	220	Louisville		
May, Deems TE	92-93SD		6'4"	250	North Carolina		
May, Marc TE	87Min		6'4"	230	Purdue		
May, Mark OT-OG	81-89Was 90KJ 91SD 92-93Phx		6'6"	295	Pittsburgh		
Mayberry, James FB-HB	79-81Atl 83-85USFL	2	5'11"	210	Colorado	1	12
Mayberry, Tony C	90-93TB		6'4"	287	Wake Forest		
Mayes, Michael DB	89NO 90NYJ 91Min		5'10"	182	Louisiana State	1	
Mayes, Rueben HB	86-88NO 89KJ 90NO 92-93Sea	23	5'11"	200	Washington State		138
Mayes, Tony DB	87StL		6'	200	Kentucky		
Mayfield, Corey NT	92TB		6'3"	280	Oklahoma		
Mayhew, Martin DB	89-92Was 93TB		5'8"	172	Florida State	13	6
Mayock, Mike DB	82-83NYG		6'2"	195	Boston College		
Mays, Alvoid DB	90-93Was		5'9"	180	West Virginia	3	
Mays, Damon WR	92Hou		5'9"	170	Missouri		
Mays, Jerry HB	90SD		5'7"	176	Georgia Tech		
Mays, Stafford DE-NT	80-86StL 87-88Min		6'2"	252	Washington		
McAdoo, Derrick HB	87StL 88TB 88Phx	2	5'10"	197	Baylor		24
McAfee, Fred HB	91-93NO	23	5'10"	193	Mississippi Coll.		24
McAlister, Ken LB-DB	82-83Sea 83SF 84KC 85KJ 86-87KC		6'5"	220	San Francisco	2	
McArthur, Kevin LB	86-89NYJ		6'2"	244	Lamar	1	
McBride, Adrian WR	87StL		6'	195	Missouri		
McCabe, Jerry LB	87NE 88KC 89GA		6'1"	225	Holy Cross		
McCaffrey, Ed WR	91-93NYG	2	6'5"	215	Stanford		42
McCall, Joe HB-FB	84Raid		6'	200	Pittsburgh		
McCall, Reese TE	78-82Bal 83-85Det	2	6'7"	239	Auburn		78
McCallister, Fred LB	87TB		6'1"	250	Florida		
McCallum, Napoleon HB	86Raid 87-89MS 90-93Raid	23	6'2"	215	Navy		30
McCants, Keith LB-DE	90-92TB 93Hou		6'3"	260	Alabama		
McCardell, Keenan WR	92-93Cle	2	6'1"	185	Nevada-Las Vegas		24
McCarthy, John QB	87GB		6'4"	212	Williams		
McCarthy, Shawn K	91-92NE	4	6'6"	227	Purdue		
McCartney, Pete OG	87NYJ		6'6"	260	Louisville		
McClendon, Skip DE	87-91Cin 91SD 92Min 92-93Ind		6'6"	282	Northwestern, Arizona State		
McClendon, Willie HB-FB	79-82Chi 84USFL	2	6'1"	205	Georgia		12
McCloskey, Mike TE	83-85Hou 87Phi	2	6'5"	245	Penn State		18
McCloughan, Dave DB	91Ind 92GB 93Sea		6'1"	180	Colorado		
McClure, Brian QB	87Buf	1	6'6"	222	Bowling Green		
McCluskey, David FB	87Cin	2	6'1"	227	Georgia		6
McColl, Milt LB	81-87SF 88Raid		6'6"	248	Stanford	2	6
McConkey, Phil WR	84-85NYG 86GB 86-88NYG 89Phx 89SD	23	5'10"	170	Navy		18
McCoy, Larry LB	83USFL 84Raid 85USFL 87NO		6'2"	240	Lamar		
McCoy, Mike (M.C.) DB	76-83GB 84LJ	3	5'11"	183	Colorado	9	
McCoy, Tony NT	92-93Ind		6'	279	Florida		

UseName(Nickname)-Positions	Team by Year	See Section	Hgt	Wgt	College	Int	Pts
McCrary, Michael DE	93Sea		6'4"	250	Wake Forest		
McCray, Bruce DB	87Chi		5'9"	181	Western Illinois	1	6
McCullough, Jake DE	89-90Den		6'5"	270	Clemson		
McCurry, Mike OG	87Min		6'3"	258	Indiana		
McDaniel, Ed LB	92-93Min		5'11"	232	Clemson		
McDaniel, LeCharls DB	81-82Was 83NYG		5'9"	183	Cal. Poly.-S.L.O.		1
McDaniel, Orlando WR	82Den		6'	180	Louisiana State		
McDaniel, Randall OG	88-93Min		6'3"	274	Arizona State		
McDaniel, Terry DB	88-93Raid		5'10"	177	Tennessee	15	12
McDaniels, Pellom DE	93KC		6'3"	278	Oregon State		
McDole, Mardye WR	81-83Min		5'11"	198	Mississippi State		
McDonald, Devon LB	93Ind		6'4"	240	Notre Dame		
McDonald, James TE	83-84LA 85Det 85,87LA	2	6'5"	234	Southern Calif.		18
McDonald, Keith WR	87Hou 89Det	2	5'9"	170	San Jose State		6
McDonald, Mike LB	84,86-91LA 92Det		6'1"	238	Southern Calif.		
McDonald, Paul QB	80-85Cle 86-87Dal	12	6'2"	185	Southern Calif.		6
McDonald, Quintus LB	89-91Ind		6'3"	259	Penn State		
McDonald, Ricardo LB	92Cin		6'2"	235	Pittsburgh	1	
McDonald, Tim DB	87StL 88-92Phx 93SF		6'2"	210	Southern Calif.	23	6
McDonough, Bob DB	87Det		6'1"	170	California (Pa.)		
McDowell, Anthony FB	92-93TB	2	5'11"	230	Texas Tech		18
McDowell, Bubba DB	89-93Hou		6'1"	196	Miami (Fla.)	16	14
McDuffie, George DE	87Det		6'6"	270	Findlay		
McDuffie, O.J. WR	93Mia	23	5'10"	191	Penn State		12
McDouguld, Doug DE	80NE		6'5"	271	Virginia Tech		
McElroy, Reggie OT-OG	83-89NYJ 91-92Raid 93KC		6'6"	281	West Texas State		
McElroy, Vann DB	82-90Raid 90Sea 91-92NJ		6'2"	193	Baylor	31	6
McEwen, Craig TE	87-88Was 89-91SD	2	6'1"	222	Utah		36
McFadden, Paul K	84-87Phi 88NYG 89Atl	5	5'11"	163	Youngstown State		520
McFadden, Thad WR	87Buf		6'2"	200	Wisconsin		6
McGarry, John OG	87GB		6'5"	288	St. Joseph's		
McGee, Buford HB-FB	84-86SD 87-91LA 92GB	2	6'	205	Mississippi		180
McGee, Carl LB	80SD 83USFL		6'3"	228	Duke		
McGee, Tim WR	86-92Cin 93Was	23	5'10"	176	Tennessee		162
McGee, Tony TE	93Cin	2	6'3"	246	Michigan		
McGhee, Kanavis LB	91-93NYG		6'4"	257	Colorado		
McGill, Eddie TE	82-83StL 84KJ		6'6"	225	Western Carolina		
McGill, Karmeeleyah LB	93Cin		6'3"	224	Notre Dame		
McGlasson, Ed C	79NYJ 80LA 81NYG		6'4"	248	Youngstown State		
McGlockton, Chester DT	92-93Raid		6'4"	320	Clemson	1	
McGonnigal, Bruce TE	91Cle		6'4"	230	Virginia		
McGovern, Rob LB	89-90KC 91Pit 92NE		6'2"	223	Holy Cross		2
McGowan, Reggie WR	87NYG		5'8"	165	Abilene Christian		6
McGrail, Joe NT	87Buf		6'3"	280	Delaware		
McGrath, Mark WR	81Sea 83-85Was	2	5'11"	175	Montana State		6
McGregor, Keli TE	85Den 85Ind		6'6"	250	Colorado State		
McGrew, Larry LB	80NE 81KJ 82-89NE 90NYG		6'5"	233	Southern Calif.	6	
McGrew, Sylvester DE	87GB		6'4"	257	Tulane		
McGriff, Curtis DE-NT	80-85NYG 86LJ 87Was		6'5"	271	Alabama		
McGriff, Tyrone OG	80-82Pit 83-85USFL		6'	269	Florida A&M		
McGriggs, Lamar DB	91-92NYG 93Min		6'3"	210	Oklahoma State, Western Illinois	1	6
McGruder, Michael DB	89GB 90-91Mia 92-93SF		5'11"	186	Kent State	5	6
McGuire, Gene C	92NO 93Chi		6'2"	285	Notre Dame		
McGuire, Monte QB	87Den		6'4"	202	Texas Tech		
McGwire, Dan QB	91-93Sea	1	6'8"	243	Iowa, San Diego St		
McHale, Joe LB	87NE		6'2"	227	Delaware		
McHale, Tom DE-OG	87-92TB 93Phi		6'4"	282	Cornell		
McInally, Pat WR-K	76-85Cin	2 4	6'6"	210	Harvard		30
McInerney, Sean DE	87Chi		6'3"	255	Frostburg State		
McIntosh, Joe HB	87Atl		5'10"	192	N. Carolina State		6
McIntyre, Guy OG	84-93SF		6'3"	268	Georgia		12
McIntyre, Jeff LB	79SF 80StL 83-84USFL		6'3"	232	Arizona State		
McIvor, Rick QB	84-85StL		6'4"	210	Texas		
McJulien, Paul K	91-92GB 93LA	4	5'10"	190	Jackson State		
McKeever, Vito DB	86-87TB		6'	180	Florida	3	
McKeller, Keith TE	87-93Buf	2	6'6"	240	Jacksonville St.		66
McKenzie, Raleigh OG-C	85-93Was		6'2"	273	Tennessee		
McKenzie, Reggie LB	85-88Raid 89KJ 92SF		6'1"	239	Tennessee	2	
McKibben, Mike LB	79-80NYJ 81KJ		6'3"	228	Kent State	1	
McKinney, Odis DB	78-79NYG 80-81Oak 82-84Raid 85KC 85-86Raid		6'2"	189	Colorado	11	
McKinney, Zion WR	80Was		6'	200	South Carolina		
McKinnon, Dennis WR	83-85Chi 86KJ 87-89Chi 90Dal 90Mia	23	6'1"	182	Florida State		156
McKnight, Dennis C-OG	82-88SD 90KJ 90Det 91Phi 92Det		6'3"	271	Drake		
McKyer, Tim DB	86-89SF 90Mia 91-92Atl 93Det		6'	174	Texas-Arlington	29	6
McLaughlin, Joe LB	79GB 80-84NYG		6'1"	235	Massachusetts		
McLean, Ron NT-DE	87Den 88KC		6'3"	267	Fullerton State		
McLean, Scott LB	83Dal		6'4"	233	Florida State		
McLemore, Chris FB	87Ind 87-88Raid		6'1"	232	Colorado, Arizona		
McLemore, Dana DB	82-86SF 86NO 87SF	3	5'10"	183	Hawaii	5	30
McLemore, Thomas TE	92Det 93Cle		6'5"	245	Southern U.		
McLeod, Mike DB	84-85GB		6'	180	Minnesota	1	
McMahon, Jim QB	82-88Chi 89SD 90-92Phi 93Min	12	6'1"	191	Brigham Young		108
McManus, Danny QB	88KC		6'	200	Florida State		
McMichael, Steve (Mongo) DT-NT	80NE 81-93Chi		6'2"	263	Texas	2	6
McMillan, Erik DB	88-92NYJ 93Cle 93KC		6'2"	197	Missouri	22	42
McMillan, Randy FB	81-83Bal 84-86Ind	2	6'	219	Pittsburgh		156
McMillian, Audray DB	85-87Hou 88KJ 89-93Min		6'	190	Houston	19	18
McMillian, Mark DB	92-93Phi		5'7"	162	Alabama	3	
McMillen, Dan LB	87Phi87Raid		6'5"	240	Colorado		
McMurtry, Greg WR	90-93NE	2	6'2"	207	Michigan		18
McNair, Todd HB	89-93KC	23	6'1"	185	Temple		48
McNabb, Dexter FB	92-93GB		6'2"	245	Florida		
McNanie, Sean DE	84-87Buf 88Phx 90Ind		6'5"	265	Arizona State, San Diego State		6
McNeal, Don DB	80-82Mia 83LJ 84-89Mia		5'11"	192	Alabama	18	12
McNeal, Travis TE	89-91Sea 91-93LA	2	6'3"	248	Tenn.-Chattanooga		12
McNeil, Emanuel NT	89NE 90NYJ		6'3"	285	Tennessee-Martin		
McNeil, Gerald (Ice Cube) WR	86-89Cle 90Hou	23	5'7"	145	Baylor		24
McNeil, Freeman HB	81-92NYJ	2	5'11"	214	U.C.L.A.		300
McNeil, Ryan DB	93Det		6'	175	Miami (Fla.)	2	
McNorton, Bruce DB	82-90Det 91BW		5'11"	175	Georgetown (Ky.)	16	
McPherson, Don QB	88-89Phi 90Hou		6'1"	183	Syracuse		
McPherson, Miles DB	82-85SD		5'11"	184	New Haven	2	
McQuaid, Dan OT-OG	85-87Was 88Min 88Ind		6'7"	278	Nevada-Las Vegas		
McRae, Charles OT-OG	91-93TB		6'7"	295	Tennessee		

UseName(Nickname)-Positions	Team by Year	See Section	Hgt.	Wgt.	College	Int	Pts
McSwain, Chuck HB	83-84Dal 87NE		6'	193	Clemson	2	
McSwain, Rod DB	84-90NE		6'1"	198	Clemson	4	6
McVeigh, John LB	87Sea		6'1"	226	Kentucky, Miami (Fla.)		
Meade, Mike FB	82-83GB 84-85Det	2	5'11"	226	Penn State		18
Meadows, Darryl DB	83-84Hou		6'1"	199	Toledo		
Meads, Johnny LB	84-92Hou 92Was		6'2"	231	Nicholls State	1	6
Meamber, Tim LB	85Min		6'3"	231	Washington		
Means, Natrone FB-HB	93SD	2	5'10"	245	North Carolina		48
Mecklenburg, Karl LB-DE	83-93Den		6'3"	236	Augustana (S.D.), Minnesota	5	14
Meehan, Greg WR	87Cin		6'	191	Bowling Green		
Meeks, Bob C	93Den		6'2"	279	Auburn		
Meggett, Dave HB	89-93NYG	23	5'7"	180	Morgan State, Towson State		96
Mehl, Lance LB	80-87NYJ		6'3"	233	Penn State	15	6
Meisner, Greg NT-DE	81-88LA 89-90KC 91NYG		6'3"	257	Pittsburgh	1	
Melander, Jon OT-OG	91NE 92Cin 93Den		6'7"	280	Minnesota		
Melka, James LB	87GB		6'1"	235	Wisconsin	1	
Melontree, Andre LB	80Cin 83-85USFL		6'4"	228	Baylor		
Mendenhall, Mat DE	81-82Was 83IL		6'6"	254	Brigham Young		
Mendoza, Ruben OT	86GB		6'4"	290	Wayne State-Neb.		
Merkens, Guido WR-DB-QB	78-80Hou 80-85NO 87Phi	12	6'1"	200	Sam Houston St.		18
Merrill, Casey DE-DT	79-83GB 83-85NYG 86NO		6'4"	255	Cal.-Davis		
Merrill, Mark LB	78-79NYJ 79Chi 81-82Den 82GB 83-84Buf 84Raid		6'4"	236	Minnesota		
Merriman, Sam LB	83-87Sea 88KJ		6'3"	229	Idaho		6
Merrits, Jim DE-NT	87Ind		6'3"	255	West Virginia		
Merritt, David LB	93Mia 93Phx		6'1"	237	N. Carolina State		
Merriweather, Mike LB	82-87Pit 88HO 89-92Min 93NYJ		6'2"	219	Pacific	18	32
Mersereau, Scott NT-DE-DT	87-93NYJ		6'3"	275	Southern Conn. St.	3	
Mesner, Bruce NT	87Buf 88-89KJ		6'5"	280	Maryland		
Mesner, Mark LB	89LA		6'2"	256	Michigan		
Metcalf, Bo DB	84Ind		6'2"	193	Baylor		
Metcalf, Eric HB-WR	89-93Cle	23	5'10"	187	Texas		156
Metzelaars, Pete TE	82-84Sea 85-89-93Buf	2	6'7"	245	Wabash		132
Meuth, Kevin OT	87NYG		6'5"	270	SW Texas State		
Meyer, Jim OT	87GB		6'5"	290	Illinois State		
Meyer, Ron	HC82-84NE HC86-91Ind				Purdue		
Miano, Rich DB	85-89NYJ 91-93Phi		6'	200	Hawaii	15	6
Micech, Phil DE	87Min		6'5"	265	Wis.-Platteville		
Micho, Bobby TE-FB	84SD 85FJ 86-87Den	2	6'3"	236	Texas		12
Mickel, Jeff OT	90LA		6'6"	300	Eastern Washington		
Mickell, Darren DE	92-93KC		6'4"	274	Florida		
Mickey, Joey TE	93Dal		6'5"	274	Oklahoma		
Mickles, Joe FB	89Was 90SD		5'10"	221	Mississippi		
Middleton, Frank HB	84-85Ind 87SD	2	5'11"	204	Florida A&M		18
Middleton, Kelvin DB	87Pit		6'	186	Wichita State		
Middleton, Ron TE	86-87Atl 88Was 89Cle 90-93Was	2	6'2"	262	Auburn		18
Middleton, Terdell HB	77-81GB 82-83TB 84USFL	2	6'	198	Memphis State		114
Migliazzo, Paul LB	87Chi		6'1"	228	Oklahoma		
Milburn, Darryl DE	91Det		6'3"	260	Grambling		
Mikeska, Russ TE	79-83Atl		6'3"	225	Texas A&M		
Mikolas, Doug NT	87-88SF 88Hou		6'1"	270	Portland State		
Milburn, Glyn HB	93Den	23	5'8"	177	Stanford		18
Miles, Eddie LB	90Pit		6'1"	233	Minnesota		
Miles, Ostell HB	92-93Cin	2	6'	236	Houston		6
Milinichik, Joe OG-OT	87-89Det 90-92LA 93SD		6'5"	284	N. Carolina State		
Millard, Bryan OG-OT	83-84USFL 84-91Sea 92XJ		6'5"	283	Texas		
Millard, Keith DT-DE	85USFL 85-90Min 91KJ 92Sea 92GB 93Phi		6'5"	262	Washington State	2	6
Millen, Hugh QB	87LA 88-90Atl 91-92NE 93Mia	12	6'5"	216	Washington		6
Millen, Matt LB	80-81Oak 82-88Raid 89-90SF 91Was		6'2"	250	Penn State	9	
Miller, Anthony WR	88-93SD	23	5'11"	185	San Diego State, Tennessee		240
Miller, Blake C	92Det		6'1"	282	Louisiana State		
Miller, Brett OT	83-88Atl 89SD 90-92NYJ		6'7"	293	Iowa		
Miller, Chris QB	87-93Atl	12	6'2"	200	Oregon		15
Miller, Chuckie DB	88Ind		5'10"	180	U.C.L.A.		
Miller, Clay OT-OG	87Hou		6'4"	273	Michigan		
Miller, Corey LB	91-93NYG		6'2"	255	South Carolina	4	
Miller, Danny K	82NE 82Bal 84-85USFL	5	5'10"	172	Miami (Fla.)		27
Miller, Darrin LB	88-89Sea		6'1"	227	Tennessee	1	
Miller, Donald LB	90Sea		6'2"	223	Idaho State		
Miller, Doug LB	93SD		6'3"	232	S. Dakota State		
Miller, Eddie WR	92-93Ind		6'	185	South Carolina		
Miller, Jim K	80-82SF 83-84Dal 87NYG	4	5'11"	183	Mississippi		
Miller, John LB	87GB		6'2"	218	Mississippi State		
Miller, John DB	89-90Det		6'1"	195	Michigan State		
Miller, Junior TE	80-83Atl 84NO	2	6'4"	239	Nebraska		84
Miller, Larry QB	87Min		6'4"	220	Northern Iowa		
Miller, Les DE-NT	87-90SD 91-93NO		6'7	290	Kansas State, Ft. Hays State		18
Miller, Mark QB	87Buf		6'2"	210	Mesa		
Miller, Matt OT-OG	79Cle 80KJ 81-82Cle 84-85USFL		6'6"	270	Colorado		
Miller, Mike WR	83NYG 85NO 86LJ		6'	182	Tennessee		
Miller, Nick LB	87Cle		6'2"	238	Arkansas		
Miller, Pat DB	88SD		6'1"	206	Florida		
Miller, Scott WR	91-93Mia	3	5'10"	179	U.C.L.A.		
Miller, Shawn NT-DE-DT	84-89LA		6'4"	255	Utah State	1	
Miller, Soloman WR	86NYG 87TB	2	6'1"	185	Utah State		12
Miller, Terry HB	78-80Buf 81Sea 83-84USFL	23	5'10"	196	Oklahoma State		48
Milling, James WR	88,90,92Atl 93CJ	2	5'9"	156	Maryland		6
Million, Ted OT	87Min		6'4"	260	Duke		
Mills, Ernie WR	91-93Pit	2	5'11"	178	Florida		36
Mills, Jeff LB	90SD 90-93Den		6'3"	244	Nebraska		
Mills, Jim OT	83Bal 84Ind		6'9"	276	Hawaii		
Mills, John Henry TE	93Hou		6'	222	Wake Forest		
Mills, Sam LB	83-85USFL 86-93NO		5'9"	225	Montclair State	3	12
Milot, Rich LB	79-87Was		6'4"	234	Penn State	12	
Milton, Eldridge LB	87Chi		6'1"	235	Clemson		
Mims, Chris DE-DT	92-93SD		6'5"	280	Tennessee		2
Mims, David WR	93Atl	2	5'8"	191	Baylor		6
Mincy, Charles DB	92-93KC		5'11"	197	Washington	9	18
Miniefield, Kevin DB	93Chi		5'9"	178	Arizona State		
Minnifield, Frank DB	83-84USFL 84-92Cle		5'9"	182	Louisville	20	12
Minor, Vic DB	80-81Sea 84-85USFL		6'	198	Northeast La.	1	
Minter, Barry LB	93Chi		6'2"	242	Tulsa		
Minter, Cedric HB	84-85NYJ	2	5'10"	200	Boise State		12
Miotke, Frank WR	91Hou		6'	175	Grand Valley State		

UseName(Nickname)-Positions	Team by Year	See Section	Hgt.	Wgt.	College	Int	Pts
Miraldi, Dean OG-OT	81-84Phi 85Den 87Raid		6'5"	266	Long Beach State, Utah		
Mirer, Rick QB	93Sea	12	6'2"	216	Notre Dame		18
Misko, John K	82-84LA 87Det	4	6'5"	207	Oregon State		
Mistler, John WR	81-83NYG 84Buf 84NYG 85USFL	2	6'2"	186	Arizona State		18
Mitchell, Aaron DB	79-80Dal 81TB 83-84USFL		6'1"	196	Morris Brown, Nevada-Las Vegas	4	
Mitchell, Alvin FB	89TB		6'	235	Auburn		
Mitchell, Brian HB-QB	90-93Was	23	5'10"	199	Southwestern La.		42
Mitchell, Brian DB	91-93Atl		5'9"	164	Brigham Young	1	
Mitchell, Devon DB	86Det 87KJ 88Det		6'1"	194	Iowa	8	6
Mitchell, Johnny TE	92-93NYJ	2	6'3"	249	Nebraska		42
Mitchell, Leonard DE	81-86Phi 87Atl		6'7"	290	Houston		
Mitchell, Michael DB	87Was 88PJ 89NJ		5'10"	180	Howard Payne	1	
Mitchell, Randall DT	87Phi		6'1"	275	Tenn.-Chattanooga		
Mitchell, Roland DB-LB	87-88Buf 88-89Phx 90Atl 91-93GB		5'11"	180	Texas Tech	6	
Mitchell, Russell C	87NYG		6'5"	288	Mississippi		
Mitchell, Scott QB	91-93Mia	12	6'6"	236	Utah		
Mitchell, Stump HB	81-87StL 88-89Phx 91KJ	23	5'9"	188	The Citadel		252
Mitz, Alonzo DE-LB	86-89Sea 91-92Cin		6'3"	274	Florida	2	
Mobley, Orson TE	86-90Den 90Ind	2	6'5"	256	Florida State, Salem		24
Mobley, Stacey WR	87LA 89Det	2	5'8"	168	Jackson State		6
Modesitt, Jeff TE	87TB 88SJ		6'5"	245	Delaware		
Moffett, Tim WR	85-86Raid 87SD	2	6'2"	180	Mississippi		6
Moffitt, Mike TE	86GB		6'4"	211	Fresno State		
Mohr, Chris K	89TB 91-93Buf	4	6'4"	220	Alabama		1
Mohring, John LB	80Det 80Cle		6'3"	240	C.W. Post		
Mojsiejenko, Ralf K	85-88SD 89-90Was 91SF	4	6'3"	209	Michigan State		
Molden, Fred DT	87Min		6'2"	272	Jackson State		
Monaco, Rob C	85StL 86IL		6'3"	283	Vanderbilt		
Monaco, Ron LB	86StL		6'1"	225	South Carolina		
Monger, Matt LB	85-87NYJ 88AJ 89-90Buf		6'1"	238	Oklahoma State		
Monk, Art WR	80-93Was	2	6'3"	210	Syracuse		390
Monroe, Carl HB-WR	83-87SF	23	5'8"	164	Utah		12
Montagne, David WR	87KC		6'2"	184	Oregon State		
Montana, Joe QB	79-90SF 91EJ 92SF 93KC	12	6'2"	197	Notre Dame		120
Montgomery, Alton DB	90-92Den 93Atl	3	6'	195	Houston	2	
Montgomery, Blanchard LB	83-84SF		6'2"	236	U.C.L.A.		
Montgomery, Cle WR	80Cin 81Cle 81Oak 82-85Raid	3	5'8"	183	Abilene Christian		6
Montgomery, Glenn NT-DT	89-93Hou		6'	276	Houston		
Montgomery, Greg K	88-93Hou	4	6'3"	213	Penn State, Michigan State		
Montgomery, Tyrone HB	93Raid	2	6'	190	Mississippi		
Montgomery, Wilbert HB	77-84Phi 85Det	23	5'10"	195	Jackson State, Abilene Christian		348
Montoute, Sankar LB	87TB		6'3"	230	St. Leo	1	
Montoya, Max OG-OT	79-89Cin 90-93Raid		6'5"	282	U.C.L.A.		
Moog, Aaron DE	87Cle		6'4"	260	Nevada-Las Vegas		
Moon, Warren QB	84-93Hou	12	6'3"	210	Washington		126
Mooney, Mike OT	93SD		6'6"	320	Georgia Tech		
Mooney, Tim DE	87Phi		6'2"	265	Western Kentucky		
Moor, Buddy DE	87Atl		6'5"	250	Eastern Kentucky		2
Moore, Alvin HB	83Bal 84Ind 85-86Det 87Sea	2	6'	194	Arizona State		48
Moore, Blake C-OT-OG	80-83Cin 84-85GB		6'5"	267	Wooster		6
Moore, Brent LB	87GB 88KJ		6'5"	242	Southern Calif.		
Moore, Booker FB	82-85Buf	2	5'11"	224	Pennsylvania		12
Moore, Brandon OT	93NE		6'6"	290	Duke		
Moore, Dana K	87NYG		5'10"	180	Mississippi State		
Moore, Darryl OG	93Was		6'2"	292	Texas-El Paso		
Moore, Dave TE	92Mia 92-93TB		6'2"	245	Pittsburgh		6
Moore, Derrick HB-FB	93Det	2	6'1"	227	Northeastern Okla.		24
Moore, Eric OT-OG	88-93NYG		6'5"	293	Indiana		
Moore, Greg LB	87NE		6'1"	240	Tenn.-Chattanooga		
Moore, Herman WR	91-93Det	2	6'3"	208	Virginia		60
Moore, Jeff HB	79-81Sea 82-83SF 84Was	23	6'	195	Jackson State		78
Moore, Jeff WR	80-81LA	2	6'1"	194	Tennessee		6
Moore, Jimmy OG	81Bal		6'5"	268	Ohio State		
Moore, Leonard FB	87Min		6'	222	Jackson State		
Moore, Mack DE	85-86Mia 86SD		6'4"	258	Texas A&M		
Moore, Malcolm TE	87LA		6'3"	240	Southern Calif.		6
Moore, Mark DB	87Sea		6'	194	Oklahoma State		
Moore, Nat WR-HB	74-86Mia	23	5'9"	184	Tennessee-Martin, Florida		450
Moore, Ricky FB	86Buf 87Hou 88Phx	2	5'11"	234	Alabama		6
Moore, Rob WR	90-93NYJ	2	6'3"	205	Syracuse		96
Moore, Robert DB	86-89Atl		5'11"	190	Northwestern La.	7	12
Moore, Rocca OG-OT	80Chi		6'5"	276	Western Michigan		
Moore, Ron HB	93Phx	2	5'10"	220	Pittsburg State		54
Moore, Shawn QB	92-93Den	1	6'2"	214	Virginia		
Moore, Steve (Big House) OT-OG	83-87NE 88KJ		6'4"	293	Tennessee State		
Moore, Stevon DB	90Mia 91KJ 92-93Cle		5'11"	204	Mississippi		12
Moorehead, Emery TE-WR-HB-FB	77-79NYG 80Den 81-88Chi	23	6'2"	218	Colorado		90
Mora, Jim	HC86-93NO				Occidental		
Moran, Eric OT-OG	83USFL 84-86Hou		6'5"	285	Washington		
Moran, Rich OG-C	85-93GB		6'3"	276	San Diego State		
Morgan, Anthony WR	91-93Chi 93GB	2	6'1"	195	Tennessee		24
Morgan, Dan OG	87NYG		6'6"	285	Penn State		
Morgan, Karl DE-DT	84-86TB		6'1"	255	U.C.L.A.		
Morgan, Stanley WR	77-89NE 90Ind	23	5'11"	180	Tennessee		438
Moriarty, Larry FB	83-86Hou 86-88KC	2	6'1"	240	Notre Dame		90
Moroski, Mike QB	79-84Atl 85Hou 86SF	12	6'4"	200	Cal.-Davis		12
Morrell, Kyle DB	86Min		6'1"	189	Brigham Young		
Morris, Dwaine NT-DT	85Phi 87Atl		6'2"	260	Southwestern La.		
Morris, Jamie HB	88-90Was	23	5'7"	188	Michigan		24
Morris, Jim Bob DB	87GB		6'3"	211	Kansas State	3	
Morris, Joe HB	82-88NYG 89FJ 91Cle	23	5'7"	195	Syracuse		312
Morris, Larry HB	87GB		5'7"	207	Syracuse		
Morris, Lee WR	87GB	2	5'11"	180	Oklahoma		6
Morris, Michael OG-C	87StL 88KJ 89KC 89NE 90Sea 90Cle 91-93Min		6'5"	278	NE Missouri St.		
Morris, Mitchell DE	87KC		6'4"	255	Wichita State		
Morris, Randall HB	84-88Sea 88Det	23	6'	195	Tennessee		6
Morris, Raymond LB	87Chi		5'10"	222	Texas-El Paso		
Morris, Ron WR	87-92Chi	2	6'1"	187	S.M.U.		54
Morris, Thomas DB	82-83TB		5'11"	175	Michigan State		
Morris, Victor LB	87Mia		6'1"	243	Miami-Ohio		
Morris, Wayne FB-HB	76-83StL 84SD	2	6'	207	S.M.U.		258
Morrison, Darryl DB	93Was		5'11"	185	Arizona		
Morrison, Pat DB	87NYG		6'2"	194	Southern Conn. St.		

UseName(Nickname)-Positions	Team by Year	See Section	Hgt.	Wgt.	College	Int	Pts
Morrison, Tim DB	86-87Was		6'1"	195	North Carolina		
Morriss, Guy C-OG	73-83Phi 84-87NE		6'4"	257	Texas Christian		
Morrissey, Jim LB	85-93Chi 93GB		6'3"	223	Michigan State	9	
Morse, Bobby HB	87Phi 89-91NO	3	5'10"	207	Michigan State		6
Morse, Steve FB	85Pit		5'11"	211	Virginia		
Morton, Michael HB	82-84TB 85Was 87Sea	2	5'8"	179	Nevada-Las Vegas		12
Mosebar, Don C-OT-OG	83-93Raid		6'6"	288	Southern Calif.		
Moser, Rick HB	78-79Pit 80Mia 81KC 81-82Pit 82TB	2	6'	210	Rhode Island		12
Mosley, Anthony HB	87Chi		5'9"	204	Fresno State		6
Mosley, Mike WR	82-84Buf	2	6'2"	192	Texas A&M		18
Moss, Gary DB	87Atl		5'10"	192	Georgia	1	
Moss, Martin DT	82-85Det		6'4"	252	U.C.L.A.		
Moss, Winston LB	87-90TB 91-93Raid		6'3"	236	Miami (Fla.)	1	6
Moss, Zefross, OT	89-93Ind		6'6"	333	Alabama State		
Moten, Eric OG	91-93SD		6'2"	306	Michigan State		
Moten, Gary LB	83SF 85USFL 87KC		6'1"	210	S.M.U.		
Mott, Joe LB	89-90NYJ 91KJ 93GB		6'4"	253	Iowa		
Mott, Steve C	83-88Det 89ZJ		6'3"	266	Alabama		
Mowatt, Zeke TE	83-84NYG 85KJ 86-89NYG 90NE 91NYG	2	6'3"	239	Florida State		72
Moyer, Alex LB	85-86Mia		6'1"	221	Northwestern	1	
Moyer, Ken OT-OG	89-91Cin 92FJ 93Cin		6'6"	294	Toledo		
Moyer, Paul DB	83-89Sea		6'1"	200	Fullerton State	11	12
Mraz, Mark DE	87Atl 89Raid		6'4"	258	Utah State		
Mrosko, Bob TE	89Hou 90NYG 91Ind	2	6'6"	265	Penn State		6
Mueller, Jamie FB	87-90Buf 91JJ	2	6'1"	225	Benedictine		30
Mueller, Vance FB-HB	86-90Raid 91KJ	23	6'	211	Occidental		30
Muhammad, Calvin WR	82-83Raid 84-85Was 87SD	2	6'	190	Texas Southern		48
Mularkey, Mike TE	83-88Min 89-91Pit	2	6'4"	240	Florida		54
Mullady, Tom TE	79-84NYG	2	6'3"	232	Rhodes		24
Mullaney, Mark DE	75-86Min 87ZJ		6'6"	243	Colorado State	1	2
Mullen, Davlin DB	83-86NYJ		6'1"	177	Western Kentucky	4	
Mullen, Gary WR	87Chi		5'11"	174	West Virginia		
Mullins, Eric WR	84Hou		5'11"	181	Stanford		6
Mumford, Tony HB	85StL		6'	215	Penn State		
Mumphrey, Lloyd DE	87KC		6'3"	260	Miss. Valley St.		
Munchak, Mike OG	82-93Hou		6'3"	281	Penn State		6
Muncie, Chuck FB-HB	76-80NO 80-84SD	2	6'3"	227	California		444
Munford, Marc LB	87-90Den		6'2"	231	Nebraska	2	
Munoz, Anthony OT	80-92Cin 93SJ		6'6"	278	Southern Calif.		24
Muransky, Ed OT	82-84Raid 85USFL		6'7"	277	Michigan		
Murphy, James WR	81Atl 81KC		5'10"	177	Utah State		
Murphy, Kevin LB	86-91TB 92SD 93Sea		6'2"	233	Oklahoma	1	6
Murphy, Mark DB	77-84Was		6'4"	210	Colgate		27
Murphy, Mark DB	80-85GB 86FJ 87-91GB		6'2"	200	W. Liberty State	18	
Murphy, Phil DT	80-81LA 83USFL		6'5"	290	S. Carolina State		
Murray, Calvin HB	81-82Phi 83-84USFL	3	5'11"	185	Ohio State		
Murray, Dan LB	89Ind 90NYJ		6'1"	240	East Stroudsburg		
Murray, Eddie K	80-91Det 92KC 92TB 93Dal	5	5'10"	173	Tulane		1264
Murray, Joe OG	87LA		6'4"	265	Southern Calif.		
Murray, Mark LB	90Den		6'2"	240	Florida		
Murray, Walter WR	86-87Ind	2	6'4"	200	Hawaii		18
Murrell, Adrian HB	93NYJ	2	5'11"	205	West Virginia		6
Murtha, Greg OT	82Bal 83-84USFL		6'6"	268	Minnesota		
Musgrave, Bill QB	91-93SF		6'2"	196	Oregon		
Musser, Neal LB	81-83Atl		6'2"	220	N. Carolina State	1	
Mustafaa, Najee DB	87-91Min 92XJ 93Cle		6'1"	194	Georgia Tech	11	18
(changed name from Reggie Rutland in 1992)							
Muster, Brad FB	88-92Chi 93NO	2	6'3"	231	Stanford		180
Myers, Wilbur DB	83Den		5'11"	195	Delta State		
Myles, Godfrey LB	91-93Dal		6'1"	241	Florida	1	
Myles, Jesse HB-FB	83-84Den	2	5'10"	210	Louisiana State		6
Myslinski, Tom OG	92Was 93Buf 93Chi		6'2"	291	Tennessee		
Nagle, Browning	91-93NYJ	12	6'3"	225	West Virginia, Louisville		
Najarian, Peter LB	87Min 88-89TB		6'2"	231	Minnesota		
Nairne, Rob LB	77-80Den 81-83NO		6'4"	223	Oregon State	3	6
Naposki, Eric LB	88-89NE 89Ind		6'2"	230	Connecticut		
Nash, Joe NT-DT	82-93Sea		6'2"	269	Boston College	1	12
Nash, Kenny WR	87KC		6'2"	195	San Jose State		
Nattiel, Ricky WR	87-92Den	23	5'9"	180	Florida		48
Nathan, Tony HB-FB	79-87Mia	23	6'	206	Alabama		198
Nave, Stevan LB	87Cle		6'2"	250	Kansas		
Neal, Frankie WR	87GB	2	6'1"	202	Ft. Hays State, Florida		18
Neal, Lorenzo HB-FB	93NO		5'10"	228	Fresno State		6
Neal, Speedy FB	84Buf	2	6'2"	254	Miami (Fla.)		6
Nease, Mike OG	87Phi		6'3"	272	Tenn.-Chattanooga		
Ned, Derrick FB	93NO		6'1"	210	Grambling		6
Nehemiah, Renaldo WR	82-84SF	2	6'1"	181	Maryland		24
Neil, Kenny DE-DT	81-83NYJ 85USFL 87Hou		6'4"	245	Iowa State		
Neill, Bill NT	81-83NYG 84GB		6'4"	258	Pittsburgh		
Nelms, Mike DB	80-84Was	3	6'1"	188	Sam Houston St., Baylor	1	12
Nelson, Bob LB	75-77Buf 78JJ 79SF 80Oak 81SJ 82-84Raid 85KJ		6'4"	233	Nebraska	1	
Nelson, Bob NT	83-85USFL 86TB 88-90GB		6'4"	272	Miami (Fla.)		
Nelson, Chuck K	83LA 84Buf 86-88Min	5	6'	174	Washington		364
Nelson, Darrell TE	84-85Pit		6'2"	235	Memphis State		
Nelson, Darrin HB	82-89Min 89-90SD 91-92Min	23	5'9"	184	Stanford		138
Nelson, David FB	84Min		6'2"	230	Heidelberg		
Nelson, Derrie LB	83-86SD		6'2"	236	Nebraska		6
Nelson, Edmund DE-NT-DT	82-87Pit 88NE		6'3"	272	Auburn		
Nelson, Karl OT	84-86NYG 87IL 88NYG		6'6"	285	Iowa State		
Nelson, Lee DB	76-85StL 86XJ		5'10"	185	Florida State	7	6
Nelson, Mark OT	87KC		6'4"	270	Bowling Green		
Nelson, Steve LB	74-87NE		6'2"	230	Augsburg, N. Dakota State	18	
Nelson, Ted DB	87KC		5'10"	203	Nevada-Las Vegas		
Neubert, Keith TE	88-89NYJ	2	6'5"	250	Nebraska		6
Neuheisel, Rick QB	87SD	1	6'1"	190	U.C.L.A.		7
Neville, Tom OT-OG	86-88GB 91SF 92GB 93LA		6'5"	306	Weber State, Fresno State		
Newberry, Tom OG-C	86-93LA		6'2"	282	Wis.-La Crosse		6
Newbill, Richard LB	90Min 90-92Sea		6'1"	240	Miami (Fla.)		
Newman, Anthony DB	88-93LA		6'	199	Oregon	9	6
Newman, Pat WR	90Min 91-93NO	23	5'11"	189	Utah State		6
Newman, Tim HB	87NYJ		6'	220	Johnson C. Smith		
Newsom, Tony DB	87Hou		5'8"	175	S.F. Austin State	1	
Newsome, Harry K	85-89Pit 90-93Min	4	6'	187	Wake Forest		
Newsome, Ozzie TE	78-90Cle	2	6'2"	232	Alabama		294
Newsome, Timmy FB	80-88Dal	23	6'1"	232	Winston-Salem St.		180

UseName(Nickname)-Positions	Team by Year	See Section	Hgt.	Wgt.	College	Int	Pts
Newsome, Vince DB	83-90LA 91-92Cle		6'1"	180	Washington	16	12
Newton, Nate OG-OT	84-85USFL 86-93Dal		6'3"	318	Florida A&M		
Newton, Tim DT-NT	85-89Min 90-91TB 93KC		6'	280	Florida		6
Newton, Tom FB	77-82NYJ 84-85USFL	2	6'	212	California		54
Nicholas, Calvin WR	88SF		6'4"	208	Grambling		
Nichols, Gerald NT-DT-DE	87-90NYJ 91TB 93Phi 93Was		6'2"	265	Florida State		
Nichols, Mark WR	81-85Det 86KJ 87Det	2	6'2"	210	San Jose State		54
Nichols, Ricky WR	85Ind		5'10"	176	East Carolina		
Nicholson, Calvin DB	89,91NO		5'9"	183	Oregon State		
Nicholson, Frank LB	87NYG		6'2"	205	Delaware State		
Nickerson, Hardy LB	87-92Pit 93TB		6'2"	228	California	2	
Niehoff, Rob DB	87Cin		6'2"	205	Cincinnati	1	
Nies, John K	90Buf		6'2"	199	Arizona		
Nicolas, Scott LB	82-86Cle 87Mia 88KJ		6'3"	226	Miami (Fla.)		
Nielsen, Gifford QB	78-83Hou	12	6'4"	207	Brigham Young		
Nielsen, Hans K	81Chi		5'11"	165	Michigan State		8
Nittmo, Bjorn K	89NYG		5'11"	185	Appalachian State		39
Nix, Roosevelt DE	92-93Cin		6'6"	292	Central St.-Ohio		
Nixon, Fred WR	80-81GB 82KJ	3	5'11"	191	Oklahoma		
Nixon, Jeff DB	79-82Buf 83KJ		6'3"	190	Richmond	11	6
Nixon, Tory DB	86-88SF		5'11"	186	Arizona, San Diego State	3	6
Niziolek, Bob TE	81Det 83-85USFL		6'4"	220	Colorado		
Noble, Brian LB	85-93GB		6'3"	250	Arizona State	3	6
Noble, Don TE	87LA		6'2"	253	California		
Noble, James WR	86Was 87Ind	2	6'	195	S.F. Austin State		12
Noble, Mike LB	87Raid		6'4"	220	Stanford		
Noga, Al DT-DE	88-92Min 93Was		6'1"	265	Hawaii	1	2
Noga, Niko LB	84-87StL 88Phx 89-91Det		6'1"	234	Hawaii	1	6
Noga, Peter LB	87StL		6'	212	Hawaii	1	6
Noonan, Danny DT	87-92Dal 92GB		6'4"	270	Nebraska	1	8
Nord, Keith DB	79-83Min 84LJ 85Min		6'	195	St. Cloud State	1	6
Nordgren, Fred NT	87TB		6'	240	Portland State		
Norgard, Erik C-OG	90Hou 91SJ 92-93Hou		6'1"	278	Colorado		
Norman, Ben HB	80Den		6'	212	Colorado State		
Norman, Chris K	84-86Den	4	6'2"	198	South Carolina		
Norman, Joe LB	79-81Sea 82KJ 83Sea 84KJ		6'1"	220	Indiana	1	
Norman, Tim OG	83Chi		6'6"	270	Illinois		
Norman, Tony DE	87Min		6'5"	270	Iowa State		
Norrie, David QB	87NYJ	1	6'4"	220	U.C.L.A.		
Norris, Jerome DB	87Atl		6'	187	Furman		
Norris, Jimmy DB	87NYG		5'11"	188	Upsala		
Norris, Jon DT	87Chi		6'3"	260	American Inter.	1	
Norseth, Mike QB	87-88Cin 90GB		6'2"	200	Kansas		
Norris, Ulysses TE	79-83Det 84-85Buf	2	6'4"	230	Georgia		48
Norton, Ken LB	88-93Dal		6'2"	238	UCLA	1	
Norwood, Ralph OT	89Atl		6'7"	285	Louisiana State		
Died Nov. 24, 1989 in automobile accident							
Norwood, Scott K	83-84USFL 85-91Buf	5	6'	207	James Madison		670
Norvell, Jay LB	87Chi		6'2"	232	Iowa		
Novacek, Jay TE-WR	85-87StL 88-89Phx 90-93Dal	2	6'4"	228	Wyoming		144
Novoselsky, Brent TE	88Chi 89-93Min		6'3"	232	Pennsylvania		12
Nugent, Terry QB	84Cle 87Ind		6'4"	216	Colorado State		
Nunn, Freddie Joe DE-LB	85-87StL 88-93Phx		6'4"	249	Mississippi	2	
Nuzzo, Chip DB	87Buf		5'11"	190	Princeton		
Oates, Bart C	83-85USFL 85-93NYG		6'3"	265	Brigham Young		
Oatis, Victor WR	83Bal		6'	177	Northwestern La.		
O'Bard, Ronnie DB	85SD		5'9"	190	Idaho, Brigham Young		
Obee, Terry WR	91Min 93Chi	23	5'10"	190	Oregon		18
O'Brien, Ken QB	83-92NYJ 93Phi	12	6'4"	206	Sacramento State, Cal.-Davis		
Obrovac, Mike OT-OG	81-83Cin		6'6"	275	Bowling Green		
O'Callaghan, John TE	87Sea		6'4"	245	San Diego State		
O'Connor, Paul OG	87TB		6'3"	270	Miami (Fla.)		
O'Connor, Tom K	87NYJ		6'1"	190	South Carolina		
Odegard, Don DB	90-91NYJ		6'	180	Oregon State, Nevada-Las Vegas		
Oden, Derrick LB	93Phi		5'11"	230	Alabama		
Oden, McDonald TE	80-82Cle 83-84USFL		6'4"	234	Tennessee State		
Odom, Cliff LB	80Cle 82-83Bal 84-89Ind 90-93Mia		6'2"	237	Texas-Arlington	1	6
Odom, Henry HB	83Pit 85USFL	3	5'10"	200	S. Carolina State		
Odomes, Nate DB	87-93Buf		5'10"	188	Wisconsin	26	18
O'Donnell, Neil QB	90-93Pit	12	6'3"	221	Maryland		12
O'Donoghue, Neil K	77Buf 78-79TB 80-85StL	5	6'6"	208	St. Bernard, Auburn		576
Offerdahl, John LB	86-93Mia		6'3"	235	Western Michigan	4	
Office, Anthony LB	87Det		6'2"	250	Illinois State		
Oglesby, Alfred NT	90-92Mia 92GB		6'3"	278	Houston		
Ogletree, Craig LB	90Cin		6'2"	236	Auburn		
Ogrin, Pat DE-DT	81-82Was 84-85USFL		6'5"	265	Wyoming		
Okoye, Christian FB	87-92KC	2	6'1"	255	Azusa Pacific		240
Olderman, Bob OG	85KC		6'5"	262	Virginia		
Oldham, Chris DB	90Det 91Buf 91-93Phx		5'9"	183	Oregon	2	
Olenchalk, John LB-C	81-82KC		6'	228	Stanford		
Oliphant, Mike HB	88Was 89Cle 90LJ 91Cle	2	5'10"	183	Puget Sound		6
Oliver, Darryl HB	87Atl		5'10"	194	Miami (Fla.)		
Oliver, Hubie FB	81-85Phi 86Ind 86Hou	2	5'10"	215	Arizona		24
Oliver, Jack OT	87Chi		6'3"	281	Texas-El Paso, Memphis State		
Oliver, Jeff OT-OG	89NYJ		6'4"	292	Boston College		
Oliver, Louis DB	89-93Mia		6'2"	226	Florida	21	12
Oliver, Maurice LB	91TB		6'3"	235	Southern Miss.		
Oliver, Muhammad DB	92Den 93KC 93GB		5'11"	170	Oregon		
Olkewicz, Neal LB	79-89Was		6'	230	Maryland	6	6
Olsavsky, Jerry LB	89-93Pit		6'1"	222	Pittsburgh		
O'Neal, Leslie DE-LB	86SD 87KJ 88-93SD		6'4"	258	Oklahoma State	1	6
O'Neal, Ken TE	87NO		6'3"	240	Idaho State		6
Ontko, Bob LB	87Ind		6'3"	237	Penn State		
Opfar, David NT	87Pit		6'4"	270	Penn State		
Ori, Frank OG	87Min		6'2"	255	Northern Iowa		
Orlando, Bo DB	90-93Hou		5'10"	180	West Virginia	7	6
Orns, Fred LB	87Sea		6'2"	230	Chapman		
Orosz, Tom K	82Mia 83-84SF	4	6'1"	204	Ohio State		
Orr, Terry TE	86-90Was 90SD 91-93Was	2	6'3"	229	Texas		60
Orton, Greg OG	87Det		6'1"	265	Nebraska		
Ortego, Keith WR	85-87Chi	2	6'	180	McNeese State		6
Osbourne, Eldonta LB	90Phx		6'	226	Louisiana Tech		
Osby, Vince LB	84-85SD		5'11"	220	Illinois		
O'Shea, Terry TE	89-90Pit		6'4"	236	California (Pa.)		
Oshodin, Willie DE	93Den		6'4"	265	Villanova		
Osiecki, Sandy QB	84KC		6'5"	202	Arizona State		

UseName(Nickname)-Positions	Team by Year	See Section	Hgt.	Wgt.	College	Int	Pts
O'Steen, Dwayne DB	78-79LA 80-81Oak 82Bal 82-83TB 83-84GB		6'1"	193	California, San Jose State	8	
Oswald, Paul C-OG	87Pit 88Dal 88Atl		6'3"	274	Kansas		
Otto, Bob DE	86Dal 87Hou		6'6"	253	Idaho State		
Oubre, Louis OG	82-84NO 87Mia		6'4"	268	Oklahoma		
Ours, Greg C	87Mia		6'5"	279	Muskingum		
Overstreet, David HB-FB	83Mia	2	5'11"	208	Oklahoma		18
June 1984 — Killed in automobile accident							
Overton, Don HB	90NE 91-92Det		6'	221	Fairmont State		
Owens, Billy DB	88Dal		6'1"	207	Pittsburgh		
Owens, Dan DE	90-93Det		6'3"	277	Southern Calif.	1	
Owens, Darrick WR	92Pit		6'2"	195	Mississippi		
Owens, Dennis NT	82-86NE		6'1"	257	N. Carolina State		
Owens, James WR-HB-DB	79-80SF 81-84TB	23	5'11"	192	U.C.L.A.		78
Owens, Mel LB	81-89LA 90XJ		6'2"	224	Michigan	4	
Pacella, Dave C-OG	83-84USFL 84Phi		6'3"	266	Maryland		
Pacheco, Chris NT	87LA		6'	250	Fresno State		
Padjen, Gary LB	82-83Bal 84,87Ind		6'2"	244	Arizona State		
Pagel, Mike QB	82-83Bal 84-85Ind 86-90Cle 91-93LA	12	6'2"	206	Arizona State		24
Pahukoa, Jeff OG-OT	91-93LA		6'2"	298	Washington		
Paige, Lee DB	87TB		6'	197	Florida State		
Paige, Stephone WR	83-91KC	23	6'2"	184	Fresno State		294
Paige, Tony FB	84-86NYJ 87-89Det 90-92Mia	2	5'10"	228	Virginia Tech		174
Paine, Jeff LB	84-85KC 86 Was 87StL		6'2"	224	Texas A&M		
Painter, Carl HB	88-89Det	3	5'9"	185	Hampton U.		
Palelei, Lonnie OG	93Pit		6'3"	311	Nevada-Las Vegas		
Palmer, Paul HB	87-88KC 89Det 89Dal	23	5'9"	182	Temple		60
Palmer, Sterling DE	93Was		6'5"	256	Florida State		
Panepinto, Mike HB	87Buf		5'7"	180	Canisius		
Pankey, Irv OT	80-82LA 83LJ 84-90LA 91-92Ind		6'4"	277	Penn State		
Parcells, Bill	HC83-90NYG HC93NE				Wichita State		
Pardridge, Curt WR	87Sea		5'10"	175	Northern Illinois		6
Paris, Bubba OT	83-90SF 91Ind 91Det		6'6"	300	Michigan		
Park, Kaulana FB	87NYG		6'2"	230	Stanford		
Parker, Andy TE	84-88Raid 89SD 90Raid		6'5"	244	Utah		12
Parker, Anthony DB	89Ind 91KC 92-93Min	3	5'10"	181	Arizona State	4	6
Parker, Carl WR	88-89Cin		6'2"	201	Vanderbilt		
Parker, Daren K	92Den		6'	185	South Carolina		
Parker, Ervin LB	80-83Buf		6'4"	236	S. Carolina State		
Parker, Freddie FB	87GB		5'10"	215	Miss. Valley St.		
Parker, Glenn OT-OG	90-93Buf		6'5"	303	Arizona		
Parker, Jerry LB	87Cle		6'	227	Central St.-Ohio		
Parker, Jeff WR	92TB		5'10"	185	Bethune-Cookman		
Parker, Kerry DB	84KC 87Buf		6'1"	192	Grambling		
Parker, Robert RB	87KC	2	6'1"	201	Brigham Young		6
Parker, Rodney WR	80-81Phi 83-84USFL		6'1"	190	Tennessee State		18
Parker, Steve DE	80NO		6'6"	265	Idaho		
Parker, Steve DE	83Bal 84Ind		6'4"	256	Tennessee State		
Parks, Jeff TE	86-87Hou 88TB		6'4"	239	Auburn		
Parks, Limbo OG	87SF		6'3"	265	Arkansas		
Parks, Rickey WR	87Min		6'1"	179	Ark.-Pine Bluff		
Parlavecchio, Chet DB	83GB 83StL		6'2"	225	Penn State		
Parmalee, Bernie HB	92-93Mia		5'11"	190	Ball State		
Parrella, John DE	93Buf		6'3"	296	Nebraska		
Parrish, James OT	93SF		6'6"	315	Temple		
Parrish, Don NT-DE	78-82KC		6'2"	257	Pittsburgh		
Parros, Rick FB-HB	81-84Den 87Sea	2	5'11"	200	Utah State		72
Parten, Ty DT	93Cin		6'4"	272	Arizona		
Partridge, Rick K	79NO 80SD 83-85USFL 87Buf	4	6'1"	175	Utah		
Paschal, Doug FB	80Min 81KJ		6'2"	219	North Carolina		6
Paskett, Keith WR	87GB	2	5'11"	180	Western Kentucky		6
Pasquale, Ron OG	87StL		6'2"	266	Akron		
Paterra, Greg FB	89Atl		5'11"	211	Slippery Rock		
Patten, Joel OT	80Cle 81KJ 83-85USFL 87-88Ind 89-90SD 91Raid		6'7"	289	Duke		
Patterson, Craig NT	90-91Phx		6'5"	314	Brigham Young	1	
Patterson, Elvis DB	84-87NYG 87-89SD 90-93Raid 93Dal		5'11"	193	Kansas	10	24
Patterson, Reno NT	87SF		6'3"	275	Bethune-Cookman		
Patterson, Shawn DE-NT	88-91GB 92KJ 93GB		6'5"	265	Arizona State	1	6
Pattillo, Darrell DB	83SD 84-85USFL		5'10"	194	Long Beach State		
Pattison, Mark WR	86LA86Raid 87-88NO	2	6'2"	190	Washington		
Patton, James NT	93Buf		6'3"	287	Texas		
Patton, Marvcus LB	90-93Buf		6'2"	224	U.C.L.A.	2	
Patton, Ricky HB	78-79Atl 79GB 80-82SF	2	5'11"	190	Jackson State		42
Paul, Markus DB	89-93Chi 93TB		6'2"	199	Syracuse	7	
Paul, Whitney LB-DE	76-81KC 82-85NO 86KC		6'3"	220	Colorado	11	12
Paup, Bryce LB	90-93GB		6'5"	245	Northern Iowa	1	2
Pawlawski, Mike QB	92TB		6'1"	205	California		
Paye, John QB	88SF		6'3"	205	Stanford		
Payne, Russell TE	87Den		6'1"	240	Appalachian State		
Payton, Eddie (Sweet P) HB	77Cle 77Det 78KC 80-82Min	3	5'8"	176	Jackson State		18
Payton, Sean QB	87Chi		5'11"	200	Eastern Illinois		
Payton, Walter (Sweetness) HB	75-87Chi	12	5'11"	203	Jackson State		750
Peacock, Elvis HB-FB	79-80LA 81Cin	2	6'1"	212	Oklahoma		54
Pearson, Aaron LB	86-88KC		6'0"	239	Mississippi State		
Pearson, J.C. (Jayice) DB	86-92KC 93Min		5'11"	187	Cal. Poly.-Pomona, Washington	4	6
Pease, Brent QB	87-88Hou	12	6'2"	200	Montana		12
Peat, Todd OG-TE	87StL 88-89Phx 90,92-93Raid		6'2"	300	Northern Illinois		
Peavey, Jack C	87Den		6'2"	260	Troy State		
Pederson, Doug QB	93Mia		6'3"	209	Northeast La.		
Peebles, Danny WR	89-90TB 91Cle	23	5'11"	180	N. Carolina State		6
Peete, Rodney QB	89-92Det	12	6'	193	Southern Calif.		72
Pegram, Erric HB	91-93Atl	23	5'9"	188	North Texas		24
Peguese, Willis DE	90-92Hou 92-93Ind		6'4"	269	Miami (Fla.)		
Pelfrey, Doug K	93Cin	5	5'11"	185	Kentucky		85
Pellegrini, Joe OG-C	82-83NYJ 84-86Atl		6'4"	258	Harvard		
Pelluer, Scott LB	81-85NO		6'2"	219	Washington State		
Pelluer, Steve QB	84-88Dal 89-90KC	12	6'4"	209	Washington		36
Penaranda, Jairo FB	81LA 83-84USFL 85Phi		5'11"	217	U.C.L.A.		
Penn, Jesse LB	85-87Dal		6'3"	220	Virginia Tech	1	6
Pennington, Leon LB	87TB		6'1"	225	Florida		
Pennison, Jay C	85USFL 86-90Hou		6'1"	276	Nicholls State		
Peoples, George FB-HB	82Dal 83NE 84-85TB		6'	214	Auburn		
Perkins, Bruce FB	90TB 91Ind	2	6'2"	230	Arizona State		12
Perkins, Johnny WR	77-83NYG	2	6'2"	205	Abilene Christian		108
Perkins, Ray DE	87Dal		6'5"	242	Virginia		
Perko, Mike NT	82-83Atl 84-85USFL		6'4"	235	Gonzaga, Utah St.		
Perot, Petey OG	79-82Phi 83SJ 84Phi 85NO		6'2"	261	Northwestern La.		
Perriman, Brett WR	88-90NO 91-93Det	2	5'9"	175	Miami (Fla.)		66
Perrin, Benny DB	82-85StL		6'2"	178	Alabama	9	6
Perrino, Mike OT	87Phi		6'5"	285	Notre Dame		
Perry, Darren DB	92-93Pit		5'10"	194	Penn State	10	
Perry, Gerald OT	88-90Den 91-92LA 93Raid		6'6"	305	Southern U.		
Perry, Leon FB	80NYG 84-85USFL	2	5'11"	225	Mississippi		18
Perry, Mario TE	87Raid		6'6"	240	Mississippi		6
Perry, Michael Dean DT-DE-NT	88-93Cle		6'1"	285	Clemson		
Perry, Todd OG	93Chi		6'5"	298	Kentucky		
Perry, Vernon DB	79-82Hou 83NO		6'2"	211	Jackson State	11	
Perry, Victor OT	87StL		6'5"	278	Georgia		
Perry, William (The Refrigerator) DT-DE-FB	85-93Chi 93Phi		6'2"	326	Clemson		18
Perryman, Bob FB	87-90NE 90Dal 91-92Den	2	6'1"	233	Michigan		54
Perryman, Dean C	87Sea		6'3"	260	Washington		
Perryman, Jim DB	84USFL 85Buf 87Ind		6'0"	181	Millikin	1	
Pete, Lawrence NT	89-93Det		6'	285	Nebraska		
Petersen, Kurt OG	80-85Dal 86-87KJ		6'4"	264	Missouri		
Petersen, Tod OT-C-OG	77-83Pit 84Cle 84Ind 87Pit		6'5"	245	Eastern Illinois		
Petersmark, Brett C	87Hou		6'3"	280	Eastern Michigan		
Peterson, Joe DB	87NE		5'10"	185	Nevada-Reno	1	
Petry, Stan DB	89-90KC 91NO		5'11"	175	Texas Christian	3	6
Pettey, Phil OG	87Was		6'4"	274	Missouri		
Pettitt, Duane DE	87SD		6'4"	265	San Diego State		
Pettyjohn, Barry OT-C	87Hou		6'5"	285	Pittsburgh		
Petway, David DB	81GB		6'1"	207	Northern Illinois		
Phifer, Roman LB	91-93LA		6'2"	230	U.C.L.A.	1	
Philcox, Todd QB	90Cin 91-93Cle	1	6'4"	217	Syracuse		6
Phillips, Bum	HC75-80Hou HC81-85NO				S.F. Austin State		
Phillips, Irvin DB	81SD 83Raid		6'1"	191	Arkansas Tech		
Phillips, Jason WR	89-90Det 91-93Atl	2	5'7"	168	Houston		12
Phillips, Joe DE-NT-DT	86Min 87-91SD 92-93KC		6'5"	285	Oregon St., S.M.U.		
Phillips, Joe WR	85,87Was		5'9"	188	Kentucky		
Phillips, Kim DB	89NO 90Buf		5'9"	188	North Texas		
Phillips, Kirk WR	84Dal		6'1"	202	Tulsa		
Phillips, Ray LB-DE	86Atl 87Phi		6'3"	243	N. Carolina State		
Phillips, Reggie DB	85-87Chi 88Phx		5'10"	171	S.M.U.	3	
Phillips, Wade	HC85NO HC93Den				Houston		
Pickel, Bill NT-DE	83-90Raid 91-93NYJ		6'5"	263	Rutgers		
Pickering, Clay WR	84-85Cin 86Chi		6'5"	215	Maine		
Pickens, Bruce DB	91-93Atl 93GB 93KC		5'11"	190	Nebraska	2	
Pickens, Carl WR	92-93Cin	2	6'2"	206	Tennessee		48
Pickens, Lyle DB	87Den		5'10"	175	Colorado		
Pidgeon, Tim LB	87Mia		6'	233	Syracuse		
Piel, Mike DT	89-92LA		6'4"	268	Illinois		
Pierce, Aaron TE	92-93NYG	2	6'5"	246	Washington		
Pierce, Steve WR	87Cle		5'10"	190	Illinois		
Pieri, Damon DB	93NYJ		6'	186	San Diego State		
Pike, Chris DT	89-90Cle 91LA		6'8"	290	North Carolina, Tulsa		
Pike, Mark DE-LB	87-93Buf		6'4"	268	Georgia Tech		
Pillers, Lawrence DE-DT-NT	76-80NYJ 80-84SF 85Atl		6'3"	255	Alcorn State	1	
Pillman, Brian LB	84Cin		5'10"	228	Miami-Ohio		
Pillow, Frank WR	88-90TB	2	5'10"	170	Tennessee State		6
Pinkett, Allen HB	86-91Hou 92KJ	23	5'9"	189	Notre Dame		156
Pinney, Ray OT-C-OG	76-78Pit 79IL 80-82Pit 83-85USFL 85-87Pit		6'4"	251	Washington		
Pippens, Woodie FB	87KC		5'11"	225	Thiel		
Pisarcik, Joe QB	77-79NYG 80-84Phi	12	6'4"	220	New Mexico State		30
Pitcock, Charles C	87TB		6'4"	272	Tulane		
Pittman, Danny WR	80-83NYG 83-84StL	23	6'2"	205	Wyoming		6
Pitts, Mike DE-DT	83-86Atl 87-92Phi 93NE		6'5"	276	Alabama	1	6
Pitts, Ron DB	86-87Buf 88 00GB	3	5'10"	175	U.C.L.A.	7	12
Plantz, Ron C	87Ind		6'4"	272	Notre Dame		
Pleasant, Anthony DE	90-93Cle		6'5"	265	Tennessee State		2
Pleasant, Marquis WR	87Cin		6'2"	172	S.M.U.		
Pleasant, Mike HB	84LA		6'1"	195	Oklahoma		
Pleasant, Reggie DB	85Atl		5'9"	175	Clemson		
Ploeger, Kurt DE-DT	86Dal 86GB 87Min		6'5"	259	Gustavus Adolphus		
Plummer, Bruce DB	87-88Den 88Mia 89Ind 90Den 90SF 91Phi		6'1"	199	Mississippi	2	
Plummer, Gary LB	83-85USFL 86-93SD		6'2"	241	California	5	12
Plunkett, Art OT	81-84StL 85NE 86KJ 87NE 88KJ		6'7"	269	Nevada-Las Vegas		
Poe, Bill OG	87Cin		6'3"	280	Morehead State		
Poe, Johnnie DB	81-87NO		6'1"	190	Missouri	17	18
Pointer, John LB	87GB		6'2"	225	Vanderbilt		
Pokorny, Frank WR	85Pit		6'	198	Youngstown State		
Pollack, Frank OT-OG	90-91SF 92XJ		6'4"	281	Northern Arizona		
Pollard, Darryl DB	87-90SF 91AJ 92TB 93ZJ		5'11"	187	Weber State	4	
Pollard, Frank HB-FB	80-88Pit	2	5'10"	218	Baylor		120
Polley, Tom LB	85Phi 87Cle		6'3"	246	Nevada-Las Vegas		
Ponder, David DT	85Dal		6'3"	250	Florida State		
Pool, David DB	90Buf 91-92NE 93Buf		5'9"	186	Tennessee, Carson-Newman	3	6
Poole, Ken DE	81Mia 82XJ		6'3"	251	Northeast La.		
Poole, Nathan FB-HB	79-80Cin 82-83,85,87Den	2	5'9"	210	Louisville		30
Poole, Shelley FB	87Atl		5'7"	219	Temple		
Pope, Marquez DB	92-93SD		5'10"	188	Fresno State	2	
Porcher, Robert DE	92-93Det		6'3"	283	S. Carolina State		
Porell, Tom NT	87NE		6'3"	275	Boston College		
Port, Chris OG-OT	91-93NO		6'5"	290	Duke		
Porter, Kevin DB	88-92KC 92NYJ 93KJ		5'10"	215	Auburn	1	
Porter, Kerry HB-FB	87Buf 89Raid 90Den		6'1"	215	Washington State		
Porter, Ricky HB	82Det 83Bal 85USFL 87Buf	23	5'10"	198	Slippery Rock		
Porter, Robert DB	87NYG		6'2"	210	Holy Cross		
Porter, Rufus LB-DE	88-93Sea		6'1"	217	Southern		
Porter, Tracy WR	81-82Det 83Bal 84Ind	2	6'2"	190	Louisiana State		18
Potter, Kevin DB	83-84Chi		5'10"	186	Missouri		
Potter, Steve LB	81-82Mia 83KC 84Buf		6'3"	235	Virginia	1	
Potts, Roosevelt FB-HB	93Ind	2	6'	258	Northeast La.		
Powe, Karl WR	85-86Dal		6'2"	177	Alabama State		
Powell, Alvin OG	87-88Sea 89Mia		6'5"	294	Winston-Salem St.		
Powell, Andre LB	93NYG		6'1"	226	Penn State		
Powell, Jeff HB	87SD		5'10"	185	Tennessee		
Powell, Marvin OT	77-85NYJ 86-87TB		6'5"	268	Southern Calif.		
Powers, Warren DE	89-91Den 91LA		6'6"	287	Maryland		6
Pozderac, Phil OT	82-87Dal		6'9"	277	Notre Dame		
Prater, Dean DE	83KC 84-88Buf		6'54'	255	Oklahoma State		
Prather, Guy LB	81-85GB		6'2"	230	Grambling		

UseName(Nickname)-Positions	Team by Year	See Section	Hgt.	Wgt.	College	Int	Pts
Preston, Dave HB	78-83Den 84USFL	23	5'10"	195	Bowling Green		78
Preston, John DB	87StL		6'	207	Central St.-Okla.		
Preston, Ray LB	76-84SD		6'	218	Syracuse	6	
Prestridge, Luke K	79-83Den 84NE	4	6'4"	235	Baylor		
Price, Art LB	87Atl		6'3"	227	Wisconsin		
Price, Dennis DB	88-89Raid 90SJ 91KJ 92NYJ		6'1"	175	U.C.L.A.	3	
Price, Jim TE-WR	91-93LA 93Dal	2	6'4"	247	Stanford		24
Price, Mitchell DB	90-92Cin 92Phx 92-93Cin 93LA	3	5'9"	181	S.M.U., Tulane	2	12
Price, Shawn DE	93TB		6'5"	260	U. of Pacific		
Price, Terry DE	90Chi 91EJ		6'4"	272	Texas A&M		
Pridemore, Tom DB	78-85Atl		5'10"	186	West Virginia	21	6
Primus, James HB	88-89Atl	2	5'11"	196	U.C.L.A.		6
Prindle, Mike K	87Det		5'9"	160	Western Michigan		24
Pringle, Mike HB	90Atl		5'8"	186	Washington State, Fullerton State		
Prior, Anthony DB	93NYJ		5'11"	185	Washington State		
Prior, Mike DB	85TB 87-92Ind 93GB		6'	202	Illinois State	28	6
Pritchard, Mike WR	91-93Atl	2	5'11"	180	Colorado		84
Pritchett, Kelvin DE	91-93Det		6'2"	281	Mississippi		
Pritchett, Wes LB	91Atl		6'2"	234	Notre Dame		
Proehl, Ricky WR	90-93Phx	2	5'10"	185	Wake Forest		96
Profit, Eugene DB	86-88NE 89LJ		5'10"	168	Yale		
Prokop, Joe K	85GB 87SD 88-90NYJ 91SF 92Mia 92NYG	4	6'3"	227	Cal. Poly.-Pomona		6
Provence, Andrew DT-DE	83-87Atl 88FJ 89PJ		6'3"	265	South Carolina		
Pruitt, James WR	86-88Mia 88-89Ind 90-91Mia	2	6'3"	199	Fullerton State		60
Pruitt, Mickey LB-DB	88-90Chi 91-92Dal		6'1"	206	Colorado		
Pruitt, Mike FB	76-84Cle 85Buf 85-86KC	2	6'	222	Purdue		336
Puki, Craig LB	80-81SF 82StL		6'1"	231	Tennessee	1	
Pumphrey, Donald OT	87TB		6'4"	275	Valdosta State		
Pupunu, Alfred TE	92-93SD	2	6'2"	252	Weber State		
Purling, Dave DE	87LA		6'5"	240	Southern Calif.		
Putzier, Rollin DT-NT	88Pit 89SF		6'4"	280	Oregon		
Puzzuoli, Dave NT	83-87Cle		6'3"	260	Pittsburgh		
Pyles, David OT	87Raid		6'5"	275	Miami-Ohio		
Quaerna, Jerry OT	87Det		6'6"	275	Michigan		
Quarles, Bernard QB	87LA		6'2"	215	Hawaii		
Query, Jeff WR	89-91GB 92-93Cin	23	6'	165	Millikin		72
Quick, Greg OT	87Atl		6'4"	280	Catawba		
Quick, Jerry OT	87Pit		6'5"	279	Wichita State		
Quick, Mike WR	82-90Phi	2	6'2"	190	N. Carolina State		366
Quillan, Fred C	78-87SF		6'5"	261	Oregon		
Quinn, Jeff QB	82Pit 82TB 84USFL		6'3"	205	Nebraska		
Quinn, Kelly DE	87Min		6'1"	220	Michigan		
Raab, Marc C	93Was		6'3"	265	Southern Calif.		
Rackley, David DB	85NO		5'9"	172	Texas Southern		
Radachowsky, George DB	84-85Ind 87-89NYJ		5'11"	186	Boston College	2	6
Rade, John LB	83-91Atl		6'1"	232	Boise State	3	12
Radecic, Keith C	87StL		6'1"	260	Penn State		
Radecic, Scott LB	84-86KC 87-89Buf 90-91-93Ind		6'3"	241	Penn State	8	6
Radford, Bruce NT-DE	79Den 80TB 81StL		6'5"	257	Grambling		
Radloff, Wayne C-OG	83-84USFL 85-89Atl 90KJ		6'5"	274	Georgia		
Rafferty, Tom OG-C	76-89Dal		6'3"	256	Penn State		
Rafferty, Vince C-OG	87GB		6'4"	285	Colorado		
Raglin, Floyd DB	87Mia		5'9"	180	Southern U.		
Ragusa, Pat K	87NYJ		5'8"	180	St. John's (N.Y.)		13
Rains, Dan LB	82-84Chi 85KJ 86Chi		6'1"	224	Cincinnati		
Rakoczy, Gregg C-OT-OG	87-90Cle 91-92NE		6'6"	286	Miami (Fla.)		
Ralph, Dan DT	84StL 85XJ		6'4"	260	Colorado, Oregon		
Ramey, Jim DE	79StL 80-81CFL83-85USFL 87TB		6'4"	261	Kentucky		
Ramsey, Chuck K	77-84NYJ	4	6'2"	191	Wake Forest		
Ramsey, Derrick TE	78-81Oak 82-83Raid 83-85NE 87Det	2	6'5"	230	Kentucky		126
Ramsey, Greg DE	87Sea		6'3"	244	Fresno State		
Ramsey, Tom QB	85-88NE 89Ind	1	6'1"	189	U.C.L.A.		6
Ramson, Eason TE	78StL 79-83SF 85Buf	2	6'2"	232	Washington State		30
Randle, John DE-DT	90-93Min		6'1"	266	Texas A&I		
Randle, Ervin LB	85-90TB 91-92KC		6'1"	250	Baylor	1	
Randle, Tate DB	82-83Hou 83Bal 84-86Ind 87Mia		6'	202	Texas Tech	7	2
Ransdell, Bill QB	88Ind		6'2"	212	Kentucky		
Ransom, Brian QB	83-85Hou		6'3"	203	Tennessee State		
Rash, Lou DB	84Phi 87GB		5'9"	180	Miss. Valley St.		
Rasheed, Kenyon FB	93NYG		5'10"	245	Oklahoma		6
Rasmussen, Randy C-OG	84-86Pit 87-88Min		6'2"	254	Minnesota		
Rathman, Tom FB	86-93SF	2	6'1"	232	Nebraska		204
Ray, Darrol DB	80-84NYJ		6'1"	200	Oklahoma	21	24
Ray, John OT	93Ind		6'8"	350	West Virginia		
Ray, Ricky DB	79-81NO 81Mia 82-83CFL 84USFL		5'11"	180	Norfolk State	1	
Ray, Terry DB	92Atl 93NE		6'1"	187	Oklahoma	1	
Rayam, Thomas OT	92-93Cin		6'6"	297	Alabama		
Raye, Jimmy WR	91LA		5'9"	165	San Diego State		
Raymond, Corey DB	92-93NYG		5'11"	180	Louisiana State	2	
Razzano, Rick LB	80-84Cin		5'11"	227	Virginia Tech	1	
Reach, Kevin OG-C	87SF		6'3"	270	Utah		
Readon, Ike NT	87Mia		6'	273	Hampton U.		
Reasons, Gary LB	84-91NYG 92Cin		6'4"	234	Northwestern La.	10	2
Reaves, Willard HB	89Mia 89Was		5'11"	200	Northern Arizona		
Redd, Glen LB	81NO 82KJ 83-86NO 86Ind		6'1"	228	Brigham Young	2	
Redden, Barry HB-FB	82-86LA 87-88SD 89-90Cle	23	5'10"	210	Richmond		66
Redding, Reggie OT-OG	91Atl 92NE		6'3"	298	Fullerton State		
Redick, Cornelius WR	87GB		6'	185	Fullerton State		
Redwine, Jarvis HB	81-83Min	23	5'10"	203	Oregon State, Nebraska		
Reece, Beasley DB	76Dal 77-83NYG 83-84TB	3	6'1"	193	North Texas	19	6
Reed, Andre WR	85-93Buf	2	6'	188	Kutztown		354
Reed, Ben DE	87NE		6'5"	265	Mississippi		
Reed, Doug DE-DT	84-90LA		6'3"	254	San Diego State		
Reed, Jake WR	91-93Min	2	6'3"	216	Grambling		
Reed, Mark QB	82NYG 83Bal 84NYJ		6'3"	201	Moorhead State		
Reeder, Dan FB	86-87Pit		5'11"	235	Delaware		
Reese, Archie DE-DT-NT	78-81SF 82-83Raid 84USFL		6'3"	267	Clemson		
Reese, Booker DE	82-84TB 84-85LA		6'6"	260	Bethune-Cookman	2	
Reese, Jerry DE	88Pit		6'2"	267	Kentucky		
Reese, Jerry DB	79-80KC 83USFL		6'3"	192	Oklahoma		
Reeves, Ken OG-OT	85-89Phi 90Cle		6'5"	272	Texas A&M		
Reeves, Walter TE	89-93Phx	2	6'4"	255	Auburn		6
Regent, Shawn C	87Raid		6'5"	280	Boston College		
Rehage, Steve DB	87NYG		6'1"	190	Louisiana State	1	

UseName(Nickname)-Positions	Team by Year	See Section	Hgt.	Wgt.	College	Int	Pts
Rehder, Tom OT-OG	88-89NE 90NYG		6'7"	282	Notre Dame		
Reich, Frank QB	85-93Buf	12	6'3"	209	Maryland		
Reichenbach, Mike LB	84-89Phi 90-91Mia		6'2"	236	East S troudsburg	2	
Reid, Alan HB	87Phi		5'8"	190	Minnesota		
Reid, Michael LB	87-92Atl		6'2"	228	Wisconsin		
Reid, Mike DB	93Phi		6'1"	218	Clemson		
Reilly, Dameon WR	87Mia		5'11"	180	Rhode Island		
Reilly, Mike LB	82LA 83SL		6'4"	219	Oklahoma		
Reimers, Bruce OT-OG	84-91Cin 92-93TB		6'7"	285	Iowa State		
Reinke, Jeff DE	87Cin		6'4"	262	Mankato State		
Rembert, Johnny LB	83-92NE		6'3"	234	Clemson	7	12
Rembert, Reggie WR	91-93Cin	2	6'5"	200	West Virginia		6
Remo, Roger LB	87Ind		6'3"	237	Syracuse		
Remsberg, Dan OT	86-87Den		6'6"	275	Abilene Christian		
Renfro, Mike WR	78-83Hou 84-87Dal	2	6'	185	Texas Christian		150
Renfo, William DT	93Phi		6'2"	291	Colorado		
Rennaker, Terry LB	80Sea		6'6"	225	Stanford		
Renner, Bill K	86-87GB		6'	198	Virginia Tech		
Rentie, Caesar OT	88Chi		6'3"	291	Oklahoma		
Repko, Jay TE	87Phi		6'3"	240	Ursinus		
Reveiz, Fuad K	85-88Mia 90SD 90-93Min	5	5'11"	220	Tennessee		667
Reynolds, Ed LB	83-91NE 92NYG		6'5"	238	Virginia		
Reynolds, Ricky DB	87-93TB		5'11"	187	Washington State	17	18
Rhymes, Buster WR	85-86Min	3	6'2"	217	Oklahoma		
Ricardo, Benny K	76Buf 76Det 77SJ 78-79Det 80-81NO 83Min 84SD	5	5'10"	172	San Diego State		447
Rice, Allen HB-FB	84-90Min 91GB	23	5'10"	203	Baylor		114
Rice, Dan FB	87Cin		6'1"	241	Michigan		
Rice, Jerry WR	85-93SF	2	6'2"	200	Miss. Valley St.		744
Rice, Rodney DB	89NE 90TB		5'8"	180	Brigham Young	2	
Richard, Gary DB	88GB		5'9"	171	Pittsburgh		
Richard, Stanley DB	91-93SD		6'2"	197	Texas	6	
Richards, Curvin HB	91-92Dal 93Det		5'9"	195	Pittsburgh		6
Richards, David OT-OG	88-92SD 93Det		6'5"	310	S.M.U., U.C.L.A.		
Richards, Howard OG-OT	81-86Dal 87Sea		6'6"	263	Missouri		
Richardson, Al LB	80-85Atl		6'2"	211	Georgia Tech	9	6
Richardson, Bucky QB	92-93Hou		6'1"	221	Texas A&M		
Richardson, Eric WR	85-86Buf	2	6'1"	185	San Jose State		
Richardson, Greg WR	87Min 88TB		5'7"	171	Alabama		
Richardson, Huey LB-DE	91Pit 92Was 92NYJ		6'5"	233	Pittsburgh		
Richardson, Mike DB	83-88Chi		6'	187	Arizona State	20	6
Richardson, Paul WR	93Phi		6'3"	204	U.C.L.A.		
Richardson, Reggie DB	87LA		6'	180	Utah		
Richey, Tom OT	87Cin		6'4"	274	Kentucky		
Richmond, Rock DB	87Pit		5'10"	180	Oregon		
Ricketts, Tom OG-OT	89-91Pit 92Ind 93KC		6'5"	294	Pittsburgh		
Ricks, Harold HB	87TB		5'10"	200	Tenn.-Chattanooga		6
Ricks, Lawrence HB	83-84KC		5'9"	194	Michigan		
Riddick, Louis DB	92Atl 93Cle		6'2"	216	Pittsburgh		2
Riddick, Robb HB	81Buf 82KJ 83-84Buf 85KJ 86-88Buf 89-90KJ	23	6'	195	Millersville		164
Ridgle, Elston DE	87SF 88NJ 89Buf 89Sea 90Phx 92Cin		6'6"	265	Northern Arizona, Nevada-Reno		
Riehm, Chris OT-OG	84-85USFL 86Raid 87KJ 88Raid		6'6"	278	Ohio State		
Rienstra, John OG	86-90Pit 91-92Cle		6'5"	271	Temple		
Riesenberg, Doug OT	87-93NYG		6'5"	275	California		
Riggins, Charles DE	87TB		6'5"	295	Bethune-Cookman		
Riggs, Gerald FB-HB	82-88Atl 89-91Was	2	6'1"	231	Arizona State		414
Riggs, Jim TE	87-92Cin 93Was	2	6'5"	245	Clemson		
Riley, Avon LB	81-86Hou 87Pit		6'3"	230	U.C.L.A.	3	
Riley, Bob OT	87Cin		6'5"	276	Indiana		
Riley, Cameron DB	87Pit		6'1"	195	Missouri		
Riley, Eric TE	87NYJ		6'3"	230	Eastern Washington		
Riley, Eugene TE	90Ind 91Det		6'2"	236	Ball State		
Rimington, Dave C	83-87Cin 88-89Phi		6'3"	288	Nebraska		
Rindy, Stuart OT-OG	87Chi		6'5"	266	Wis.-Whitewater		
Riordan, Tim QB	87NO		6'1"	185	Temple		
Ring, Bill HB-FB	81-86SF	2	5'10"	208	Brigham Young		48
Risher, Alan QB	83-85USFL 85TB 87GB	1	6'2"	190	Louisiana State		6
Risien, Cody OT-OG	79-83Cle 84KJ 85-89Cle		6'7"	269	Texas A&M		
Rison, Andre WR	89Ind 90-93Atl	2	5'10"	185	Michigan State		312
Ritcher, Jim OG-C	80-93Buf		6'3"	265	N. Carolina State		
Rivera, Gabe NT	83Pit		6'2"	293	Texas Tech		
	1984 — Injured in automobile accident						
Rivera, Ron LB	84-92Chi		6'3"	239	California	8	6
Rivers, Nate FB	80NYG		6'3"	215	S. Carolina State		
Rivers, Garland DB	87Chi		6'1"	181	Michigan		
Rivers, Reggie FB	91-93Den	2	6'1"	215	Southwest Texas		38
Roaches, Carl WR	80-84Hou	3	5'8"	168	Texas A&M		12
Roaf, Willie OT	93NO		6'4"	299	Louisiana Tech		
Robbins, Kevin OT-OG	89-90Cle 93LA		6'6"	287	Wichita State, Michigan State		
Robbins, Randy DB	84-91Den 92NE		6'2"	189	Arizona	13	12
Robbins, Tootie OT	82-87StL 88-91Phx 92-93GB		6'5"	303	East Carolina		
Roberts, Alfredo TE	88-90KC 91-92Dal 93FJ	2	6'3"	250	Miami (Fla.)		12
Roberts, Bill OT	84NYG		6'5"	280	Ohio State		
Roberts, George K	78-80Mia 81SD 82Atl	4	6'	181	Virginia Tech		
Roberts, Greg OG	79-82TB 84USFL		6'3"	260	Oklahoma		
Roberts, Larry DE	86-93SF		6'3"	270	Alabama	1	
Roberts, Ray OT	92-93Sea		6'6"	304	Virginia		
Roberts, Tim DT	92-93Hou		6'6"	309	Southern Miss.		
Roberts, Wes DE	80NYJ 83USFL		6'6"	253	Texas Christian		
Roberts, William OT-OG	86-93NYG		6'5"	280	Ohio State		
Robertson, Marcus DB	91-93Hou		5'11"	197	Iowa State	8	6
Robinson, Billy DB	87Cle		6'1"	200	Arizona State		
Robinson, Bo FB-TE	79-80Det 81-83Atl 84NE 85GJ	2	6'2"	228	West Texas State		30
Robinson, DeJuan DB	87Cle		5'10"	185	Northern Arizona	1	
Robinson, Don OT	87Atl		6'5"	280	Baylor		
Robinson, Eddie LB	92-93Hou		6'1"	242	Alabama State		
Robinson, Eugene DB	85-93Sea		6'	185	Colgate	38	12
Robinson, Frank DB	92Cin 92-93Den		5'11"	174	Boise State	1	
Robinson, Fred DE-LB	84-86SD 86Mia		6'4"	240	Miami (Fla.)		
Robinson, Freddie DB	87-88Ind		6'1"	191	Alabama	2	
Robinson, Gerald DE-DT	86-87Min 89-90SD 91-93LA		6'3"	260	Auburn		
Robinson, Greg OT	86TB 87NE		6'5"	280	Nevada-Reno, Sacramento State		
Robinson, Greg HB	93Raid	2	5'10"	200	Northeast La.		6
Robinson, Jacque FB	87Phi		5'11"	215	Washington		
Robinson, Jeff DE	93Den		6'4"	265	Idaho		
Robinson, Jeroy LB	90Den 90Phx		6'1"	241	Texas A&M		

UseName(Nickname)-Positions	Team by Year	See Section	Hgt.	Wgt.	College	Int	Pts
Robinson, Jerry LB	79-84Phi 85-91Raid		6'2"	223	U.C.L.A.	12	24
Robinson, John	HC83-91LA				Oregon		
Robinson, Johnny NT	81Oak 82-83Raid		6'2"	258	Louisiana Tech		2
Robinson, Junior DB	90NE 92Det		5'9"	181	East Carolina		
Robinson, Larry DB	87NYJ		5'9"	194	Northwestern La.	1	
Robinson, Lybrant DE	89Was		6'4"	250	Delaware State		
Robinson, Mark DB	84-87KC 88-90TB 91SJ		5'11"	204	Penn State	15	
Robinson, Matt QB	77-79NYJ 80Den 81-82Buf	12	6'2"	196	Georgia		24
	84-85USFL						
Robinson, Mike DE	81-82Cle 84-85USFL		6'5"	265	Oklahoma State,		
					Arizona		
Robinson, Patrick WR	93Cin	3	5'8"	176	Tennessee State		
Robinson, Rafael DB	92-93Sea		5'11"	200	Wisconsin		
Robinson, Rex K	82NE		5'11"	205	Georgia		8
Robinson, Shelton LB	82-85Sea 86-88Det		6'2"	235	North Carolina	1	12
Robinson, Stacy WR	85-90NYG	2	5'11"	186	Prairie View,		42
					N. Dakota State		
Robinson, Tony QB	87Was		6'3"	200	Tennessee		
Robison, Tommy OT-OG	87GB 88GJ 89Atl		6'4"	290	Texas A&M		
Roby, Reggie K	83-92Mia 93Was	4	6'2"	243	Iowa		
Rocker, David DT	91-93LA		6'4"	267	Auburn		
Rocker, Tracy DT	89-90Was		6'3"	288	Auburn		
Rockford, Jim DB	85SD		5'10"	180	Oklahoma		
Rockins, Chris DB	84-87Cle		6'	195	Oklahoma State	6	
Rodenhauser, Mark C	87Chi 89Min 90-91SD 92Chi 93Det		6'5"	267	Illinois State		
Rodenberger, Jeff FB	87NO		6'3"	235	Maryland		
Rodgers, Del HB	82GB 83NJ 84GB 87-88SF	23	5'10"	201	Utah		30
Rodgers, John TE	82-84Pit		6'2"	226	Louisiana Tech		
Rodgers, Tyrone DT	92-93Sea		6'3"	266	Washington		
Rodriguez, Mike NT	87Raid		6'1"	275	Alabama		
Rodriguez, Ruben K	87-89Sea 92Den 92NYG	4	6'2"	209	Arizona		
Roe, Bill LB	80Dal 81BA 83-85USFL 87NO		6'3"	233	Colorado		
Roehlk, Jon OG	87Chi		6'2"	257	Iowa		
Rogers, Darryl	HC85-88Det				Fresno State		
Rogers, Don DB	84-85Cle		6'1"	206	U.C.L.A.	2	
	1986 — Died of cocaine overdose						
Rogers, Doug DE	82-83Atl 83-84NE 85SJ 86SF		6'5"	266	Stanford		
Rogers, George HB-FB	81-84NO 85-87Was	2	6'2"	228	South Carolina		324
Rogers, Glenn DB	91TB		6'	185	Memphis State		
Rogers, Jimmy HB	80-84NO	2	5'10"	191	Oklahoma		30
Rogers, Lamar DE	91-92Cin		6'4"	292	Auburn		
Rogers, Reggie DE	87-88Det 91Buf 92TB		6'6"	278	Washington		
Rogers, Steve OT	87KC		6'5"	260	Oregon State,		
					Brigham Young		
Rogers, Tracy LB	90-93KC		6'2"	241	Fresno State		6
Rohrer, Jeff LB	82-87Dal 88XJ		6'3"	228	Yale		
Roland, Benji DE	90TB		6'3"	260	Auburn		
Rolle, Butch TE	86-91Buf 92-93Phx	2	6'3"	242	Michigan State		66
Rolling, Henry LB	88-89TB 90-92SD 93LA		6'2"	232	Nevada-Reno	5	
Romano, Jim C	82-84Raid 84-86Hou		6'3"	258	Penn State		
Romanowski, Bill LB	88-93SF		6'4"	235	Boston College	2	
Romasko, Dave TE	87Cin		6'3"	241	Carroll (Wis.)		
Rome, Stan WR	79-82KC 83USFL	2	6'5"	212	Clemson		6
Rome, Tag WR	87SD		5'9"	175	Northwestern La.		
Romer, Rich LB	88-89Cin		6'3"	222	Union (N.Y.)		
Romes, Charles DB	77-86Buf 87SD		6'1"	190	N. Carolina State	28	12
Roopenian, Mark NT	82-83Buf		6'5"	254	Boston College		
Roper, John LB	89-92Chi 93Dal 93Phi		6'1"	232	Texas A&M	2	
Roquemore, Durwood DB	82-83KC 85USFL 87Buf		6'1"	183	Texas A&I	5	6
Rosado, Dan OG-C	87-88SD		6'3"	280	Northern Illinois		
Rose, Barry WR	93Den		6'	185	Wis.-Stevens Point		
Rose, Carlton LB	87Was		6'2"	220	Michigan		
Rose, Donovan DB	80KC 81-85CFL 86-87Mia		6'1"	187	Hampton U.	2	
Rose, Ken LB	87-89NYJ 90Cle 90-93Phi		6'1"	211	Nevada-Las Vegas	1	6
Rose, Joe TE	80-85Mia 86LJ 87LA	2	6'3"	228	California		54
Rosenbach, Timm QB	89-90Phx 91KJ 92Phx	12	6'2"	210	Washington State		18
Rosenmeier, Eric C	87Buf		6'4"	240	Colgate		
Rosnagle, Ted DB	85,87Min		6'3"	205	Portland State		
Ross, Alvin FB	87Phi		5'11"	235	Central St.-Okla.		6
Ross, Bobby	HC92-93SD				V.M.I.		
Ross, Dan TE	79-83Cin 84USFL 85Cin 85Sea 86GB	2	6'4"	236	Northeastern		114
Ross, Kevin DB	84-93KC		5'9"	182	Temple	30	30
Ross, Scott LB	91NO		6'1"	235	Southern Calif.		
Ross, Tom LB	87Det		6'5"	225	Bowling Green		
Rostosky, Pete OT-OG-C	84-86Pit		6'4"	259	Connecticut		
Roth, Pete FB	87Mia		5'11"	210	Northern Illinois		
Rother, Tim OT	89-90Raid		6'7"	285	Nebraska		
Rothschild, Doug LB	87Chi		6'2"	231	Wheaton		
Rouen, Tom K	93Den	4	6'3"	215	Colorado		
Roundtree, Ray WR	88Det		6'	180	Penn State		
Rourke, Jim OG-OT-C	80-84KC 85NO 86KC		6'5"	265	Boston College		
Rouse, Curtis OG-OT	82-86Min 87SD		6'3"	316	Tenn.-Chattanooga		
Rouse, James FB-HB	90-91Chi	2	6'	220	Arkansas		
Rouson, Lee FB-HB	85-90NYG 91Cle	23	6'1"	220	Colorado		24
Roveto, John K	81-82Chi 83USFL	5	5'11"	178	Southwestern La.		71
Rowe, Patrick WR	93Cle		6'1"	195	San Diego State		
Rowe, Ray TE	92-93Was		6'2"	256	San Diego State		
Rowell, Eugene DT	87Chi		6'3"	265	Dubuque		
Rowell, Eugene WR	90Cle		6'1"	180	Southern Miss.		
Royal, Ricky DB	90Atl		5'9"	187	Sam Houston St.		
Royals, Mark K	87StL 87Phi 90-91TB 92-93Pit		6'5"	216	Appalachian State		
Royster, Mazio FB	92-93TB	2	6'1"	205	Southern Calif.		6
Rozier, Mike HB	84-85USFL 85-90Hou 90-91Atl	2	5'10"	209	Nebraska		186
Rubbert, Ed QB	87Was	1	6'5"	225	Louisville		
Rubens, Larry C	82-83GB 85USFL 86Chi 87KJ		6'1"	255	Montana State		
Rubick, Rob TE	82-88Det	2	6'3"	232	Grand Valley St.		24
Rubley, T.J. QB	93LA	12	6'3"	205	Tulsa		
Rucker, Keith NT	92-93Phx		6'3"	325	Ohio Wesleyan		
Rucci, Todd OG	93NE		6'5"	291	Penn State		
Rudolph, Ben DT-DE	81-84NYJ 85USFL 85-86NYJ		6'5"	270	Long Beach State		
Rudolph, Coleman DE-DT	93NYJ		6'4"	270	Georgia Tech		
Rudolph, Martin DB	87Den		5'10"	183	Arizona		
Ruether, Mike C-OG-TE	84-85USFL 86-87StL 88-89Den		6'4"	279	Texas		
	90-93Atl						
Ruettgers, Ken OT	85-93GB		6'5"	283	Southern Calif.		
Ruff, Guy LB	82Pit 84USFL		6'1"	215	Syracuse		
Runager, Max K	79-83Phi 84-88SF 88Cle 89Phi	4	6'1"	189	South Carolina		
Rush, Bob C-OT	77SD 78KJ 79-82SD 83-85KC		6'5"	265	Memphis State		
Rusinek, Mike NT	87Cle		6'3"	250	California		

UseName(Nickname)-Positions	Team by Year	See Section	Hgt.	Wgt.	College	Int	Pts
Russell, Booker FB	78-79Oak 80SD 81Phi 83-84USFL	2	6'2"	233	SW Texas State		48
Russell, Damien DB	93SF		6'1"	204	Virginia Tech		
Russell, Darryle DB	87Den		6'	190	Appalachian State		
Russell, Derek WR	91-93Den	23	6'	179	Arkansas		30
Russell, Leonard HB	91-93NE	2	6'2"	235	Arizona State		78
Russell, Rusty OT	84Phi		6'5"	295	South Carolina		
Russell, Wade TE	87Cin		6'4"	250	Taylor		6
Rust, Rod	HC90NE				Iowa State		
Ruth, Mike NT	86-87NE		6'1"	266	Boston College		
Rutigliano, Sam	HC78-84Cle				Tulsa		
Rutledge, Craig DB	87LA		6'	190	U.C.L.A.		
Rutledge, Jeff QB	79-81LA 82-89NYG 90-92Was	12	6'1"	196	Alabama		6
Ruzek, Roger K	87-89Dal 89-93Phi	5	6'1"	195	Weber State		566
Ryan, Buddy	HC86-90Phi				Olahoma State		
Ryan, Jim LB	79-88Den		6'1"	217	William & Mary	5	2
Ryan, Pat QB	78-89NYJ 91Phi	12	6'3"	208	Tennessee		8
Ryan, Tim DE-DT	90-93Chi		6'4"	268	Southern Calif.		
Ryan, Tim OG	91-93TB		6'2"	280	Notre Dame		
Rypien, Mark QB	87-93Was	12	6'4"	234	Washington State		48
Saalfield, Kelly C	80NYG		6'3"	246	Nebraska		
Saar, Brad LB	87Ind		6'1"	220	Ball State		
Sabb, Dwayne LB	92-93NE		6'4"	248	New Hampshire		
Sacca, Tony QB	92-93Phx		6'5"	230	Penn State		
Sacco, Frank LB	87NE		6'4"	240	Fordham		
Saddler, Rod DE	87StL 88-91Phx 91Cin		6'5"	276	Texas A&M	1	12
Sadowski, Troy TE	90Atl 91KC 92-93NYJ		6'5"	255	Georgia		
Sagapolutele, Pio DE	91-93Cle		6'6"	297	San Diego State		
Sager, Ken TE	87Sea		6'4"	228	Western Washington		
Sagnella, Anthony DT	87Was		6'5"	260	Rutgers		
Saindon, Pat OG	86NO 87Atl		6'3"	273	Vanderbilt		
Saldi, Jay TE-WR	76-82Dal 83-84Chi	2	6'3"	225	South Carolina		48
Saleaumua, Dan NT	87-88Det 89-93KC		6'	292	Arizona State	2	14
Salem, Harvey OT-OG	83-86Hou 86-90Det 91Den 92GB		6'6"	283	California		
Salisbury, Sean QB	86Sea 87Ind 88-89CFL 90-93Min	1	6'5"	215	Southern Calif.		
Sally, Jerome NT	82-86NYG 87Ind 88KC		6'3"	267	Missouri		
Salonen, Brian LB-TE	84-85Dal 86-87GJ		6'3"	227	Montana		
Sampleton, Lawrence TE	82-84Phi 87Mia		6'5"	233	Texas		
Sampson, Clint WR	83-86Den 87KJ	2	5'11"	183	San Diego State		48
Sams, Ron OG	83GB 84Min		6'3"	262	Pittsburgh		
Samuels, Chris HB-FB	91SD		5'10"	202	Texas		
Sanchez, Lupe DB	84-85USFL 86-88Pit	3	5'10"	193	U.C.L.A.	4	6
Sander, Mark LB	92Mia		6'2"	232	Louisville		
Sanders, Barry HB-FB	89-93Det	2	5'8"	203	Oklahoma State		360
Sanders, Chuck FB	86-87Pit		6'1"	233	Slippery Rock		6
Sanders, Deion (Neon Deion) DB	89-93Atl	23	6'	187	Florida State	24	60
	89-93 played major league baseball						
Sanders, Eric OT-OG-C	81-86Atl 86-92Det		6'7"	282	Nevada-Reno		
Sanders, Gene OT-OG-DE-NT	79-85TB		6'3"	273	Washington,		
					Texas A&M		
Sanders, Glenell LB	90Chi 91LA		6'	224	Louisiana Tech		
Sanders, Ricky WR-HB	86-93Was	23	5'11"	182	SW Texas State		222
Sanders, Thomas HB	85-89Chi 90-91Phi	23	5'11"	203	Texas A&M		84
Sanford, Lucius LB	78-86Buf 87Cle		6'2"	217	Georgia Tech	5	18
Sanford, Rick DB	79-84NE 85Sea		6'1"	192	South Carolina	16	18
Santos, Todd QB	88SF		6'2"	207	San Jose State		
Sandham, Todd OG	87NE		6'3"	255	Northeastern		
Sapolu, Jesse OG-C	83-84SF 85BN 86LJ 87-93SF		6'4"	264	Hawaii		
Sargent, Broderick FB	86-87StL 89Dal	2	5'10"	217	Baylor		6
Sargent, Kevin OT	92-93Cin		6'6"	284	Eastern Washington		
Sartin, Martin HB	87SD		5'10"	202	Long Beach State		6
Saunders, Al	HC86-88SD				San Jose State		
Savage, Tony NT	90SD 91KJ 92SD 92Cin		6'3"	300	Washington State		
Sawyer, Buzz K	87Dal		6'1"	201	Baylor		
Sawyer, John TE	75-76Hou 77-78Sea 79LJ 80-82Sea	2	6'2"	230	Southern Miss.		12
	83Was 83-84Den						
Sawyer, Jon DB	87NE		5'9"	175	Cincinnati		
Saxon, James HB-FB	88-91KC 92-93Mia	2	5'11"	215	San Jose State		30
Saxon, Mike K	85-92Dal 93NE	4	6'3"	193	San Diego State		
Scales, Dwight WR	76-78LA 79NYG 81-83SD 84Sea	2	6'2"	178	Grambling		30
Scales, Greg TE	88-91NO	2	6'4"	253	Wake Forest		12
Scanlon, Jerry OT-OG	80-81Was		6'5"	270	Hawaii		
Scardina, John OT	87Min		6'4"	265	Lincoln (Mo.)		
Schad, Mike OG	88LA 89-90Phi 91XJ 92-93Phi		6'5"	290	Queens (Ont.)		
Schamel, Duke LB	87Mia		6'3"	235	South Dakota		
Schankweiler, Scott LB	87Buf		6'	225	Maryland	1	
Schenk, Ed TE	87Min		6'4"	230	Central Florida		
Schippang, Gary OT	86Min		6'4"	279	West Chester		
Schlichter, Art QB	82Bal 83SL 84-85Ind		6'2"	210	Ohio State		6
Schillinger, Andy WR	88Phx 89KJ		5'1"	179	Miami-Ohio		
Schlereth, Mark C-OG	89-93Was		6'3"	280	Idaho		
Schlopy, Todd K	87Buf		5'10"	165	Michigan		7
Schmitt, George DB	83StL 84XJ		5'11"	193	Delaware		
Scholtz, Bruce LB	82-88Sea 89NE		6'6"	241	Texas	5	6
Schonert, Turk QB	80-85Cin 86Atl 87-89Cin	12	6'1"	191	Stanford		24
Schreiber, Adam OG-C	84Sea 85NO 86-88Phi 88-89NYJ		6'4"	281	Texas		
	90-93Min						
Schroeder, Jay QB	84-87Was 88-92Raid 93Cin	12	6'4"	215	U.C.L.A.		30
Schroy, Ken DB	77-84NYJ 85SJ		6'2"	196	Maryland	16	6
Schubert, Eric K	84USFL 85NYG 86StL 87NE	5	5'8"	193	Pittsburgh		94
Schuh, Jeff LB	81-85Cin 86GB 86Min		6'2"	230	Minnesota	1	
Schuhmacher, John OG-OT	78Hou 79-80XJ 81-85Hou		6'3"	272	Southern Calif.		
Schulte, Rick OG-OT	87Buf		6'2"	270	Illinois		
Schultz, Chris OT	83Dal 84KJ 85Dal		6'8"	277	Arizona		
Schulz, Jody LB	83-84Phi 85KJ 86-87Phi		6'3"	235	East Carolina	1	
Schultz, Kurt DB	92-93Buf		6'1"	206	Eastern Washington		
Schultz, William OT-OG	90-93Ind		6'5"	303	Southern Calif.		6
Schutt, Scott LB	87Cin		6'4"	218	N. Dakota State		2
Schwants, Jim LB	92Chi		6'2"	231	Purdue		
Schwartz, Don DB	78-80NO 81StL 83-84USFL		6'1"	191	Washington State	2	
Schwedes, Scott WR	87-90Mia 90SD 90Mia	23	6'	182	Syracuse		12
Sciarra, John DB-QB	78-83Phi	3	5'11"	185	U.C.L.A.	4	12
Scissum, Willard OT-OG	87Was		6'3"	275	Alabama		
Scoggins, Eric LB	82SF 83-84USFL		6'2"	235	Southern Calif.		
Scoggins, Ron OT	87Sea		6'6"	305	Nevada-Las Vegas		
Scott, Carlos C-OT	83-85StL		6'4"	295	Texas-El Paso		
Scott, Chris DE	84-85,87Ind 88KJ		6'5"	260	Purdue		
Scott, Chuck WR	86LA 87Dal		6'2"	198	Vanderbilt		
Scott, Ed DB	87StL		5'10"	182	Grambling		
Scott, Kevin HB	88SD 89Dal		5'9"	179	Stanford		

UseName(Nickname)-Positions	Team by Year	See Section	Hgt.	Wgt.	College	Int	Pts
Scott, Kevin DB	91-93Det		5'9"	175	Stanford	4	
Scott, Lindsay WR	82-85NO	2	6'1"	195	Georgia		6
Scott, Malcolm TE	83NYG 87NO	2	6'5"	243	Louisiana State		
Scott, Patrick WR	87-88GB	2	5'10"	170	Grambling		6
Scott, Randy LB	81-86GB 87Min		6'1"	223	Alabama	3	
Scott, Ronald HB	87Mia	2	5'11"	200	Southern U.		18
Scott, Sean LB	88Dal		6'1"	226	Maryland		
Scott, Stanley DE	87Mia		6'3"	255	Florida State		
Scott, Todd DB	91-93Min		5'10"	190	Southwestern La.	7	6
Scott, Tom OT	93Cin		6'6"	330	East Carolina		
Scott, Victor DB	84-88Dal		6'	200	Colorado	5	6
Scott, Willie TE	81-85KC 86-88NE	2	6'4"	245	South Carolina		96
Scotts, Colin DT	87StL 88SJ		6'5"	263	Hawaii		
Scrafford, Kirk OT-OG	90-92Cin 93Den		6'6"	260	Montana		
Scribner, Bucky K	83-84GB 87-89Min	4	6'	207	Kansas		
Scroggins, Tracy LB	92-93Det		6'2"	255	Tulsa	1	
Scully, John C-OG	81-88Atl 89HO 90Atl		6'6"	262	Notre Dame		
Scully, Mike C	88Was		6'5"	280	Illinois		
Seabaugh, Todd LB	84Pit		6'4"	225	San Diego State		
Seale, Eugene LB	87-92Hou		5'10"	247	Lamar	2	8
Seale, Sam DB-WR	84-87Raid 88-91SD 92Raid 93LA		5'9"	182	Western St. (Colo.)	11	12
Sealby, Randy LB	87NE		6'2"	230	Missouri		
Seals, Leon DE	87-91Buf 92Phi		6'4"	266	Jackson State	1	6
Seals, Ray NT-DE	89-90TB 90Ind 91-93TB		6'3"	273	none	1	6
Searcey, Bill OG-C	83-84USFL 85SD		6'1"	281	Alabama		
Searcy, Leon OT	92-93Pit		6'3"	305	Miami (Fla.)		
Seau, Junior LB	90-93SD		6'3"	250	Southern Calif.	3	
Seay, Mark WR	93SD		6'	175	Long Beach State		
Seay, Virgil WR	81-84Was 84Atl	2	5'8"	175	Troy State		30
Secules, Scott QB	88Dal 89-91Mia 92SJ 93NE	12	6'3"	219	Virginia		6
Seifert, George	HC89-93SF				Utah		
Seitz, Warren TE-WR	86Pit 87NYG		6'4"	217	Missouri		
Selby, Rob OG-OT	91-93Phi		6'3"	286	Auburn		
Selesky, Ron C	87Min		6'1"	266	North Central		
Sellers, Lance LB	87Cin		6'1"	230	Boise State		
Selmon, Lee Roy DE	76-84TB		6'3"	256	Oklahoma		6
Sendlein, Robin LB	81-84Min 85Mia 86KJ 87IJ		6'3"	225	Texas		
Sensor, Joe TE	80-82Min 83KJ 84Min		6'4"	237	West Chester		96
Septien, Rafael K	77LA 78-86Dal	5	5'10"	176	Southwestern La.		960
Settle, John FB-HB	87-90Atl 91TJ 92KJ	2	5'9"	209	Appalachian State		78
Settles, Tony LB	87Was		6'3"	210	Elon		
Seurer, Frank QB	84-85USFL 86-87KC	1	6'1"	195	Kansas		
Sewell, Steve FB-WR	86-91Den 92NJ	2	6'3"	210	Oklahoma		126
Shaffer, Craig LB	82-84StL		6'	230	Indiana State		
Shakespeare, Stanley WR	87TB		5'11"	190	Miami (Fla.)		
Shanahan, Mike	HC88-89Raid				Eastern Illinois		
Shannon, John DT-DE	88-89Chi		6'3"	269	Kentucky		
Shannon, Randy LB	89-90Dal		6'1"	221	Miami (Fla.)		
Sharp, Dan TE	87Atl		6'2"	235	Texas Christian		
Sharpe, Luis OT	82-84StL 85USFL 85-87StL 88-93Phx		6'4"	275	U.C.L.A.		6
Sharpe, Shannon TE-WR	90-93Den	2	6'2"	228	Savannah State		78
Sharpe, Sterling WR	88-93GB	2	5'11"	202	South Carolina		288
Shavers, Tyrone WR	91Cle		6'3"	210	Lamar		
Shaw, Eric LB	92-93Cin		6'3"	248	Louisiana Tech		
Shaw, Rickie OT	93Sea		6'4"	294	North Carolina		
Shaw, Pete DB	77-81SD 82-84NYG		5'10"	181	Northwestern	12	
Shaw, Ricky LB	88-89NYG 89-90Phi		6'4"	240	Oklahoma State		
Shaw, Robert C-OG	79-81Dal 82KJ		6'4"	245	Tennessee		
Shearer, Brad DT	78Chi 79KJ 80-81Chi		6'3"	249	Texas		
Shearin, Joe OG-C	83-84LA 85TB 87Dal		6'4"	254	Texas		
Sheffield, Chris DB	86-87Pit 87Det		6'1"	193	Albany State (Ga.)	1	
Shegog, Ron DB	87NE		5'11"	190	Austin Peay	1	
Shell, Donnie DB	74-87Pit		5'11"	192	S. Carolina State	55	18
Shell, Todd LB	84-87SF 88ZJ		6'4"	225	Brigham Young	5	6
Shelley, Elbert DB	87-93Atl		5'11"	180	Arkansas State	1	
Shelley, Jonathan DB	87SF		6'	176	Mississippi		
Shelton, Anthony DB	90-91SD		6'1"	195	Tennessee State	1	
Shelton, Richard DB	89Den 90-93Pit		5'10"	180	Liberty	3	6
Shepard, Derrick WR	87-88Was 89NO 89-91Dal	23	5'10"	186	Oklahoma		12
Sheppard, Ashley LB	93Min		6'3"	243	Clemson		
Sheppard, Johnny HB	87Buf		5'10"	185	Livingston		
Sherman, Heath FB-HB	89-93Phi	2	6'	195	Texas A&I		84
Sherrard, Mike WR	86Dal 87-89BL 90-92SF 93NYG	2	6'2"	187	U.C.L.A.		72
Sherwin, Tim TE	81-83Bal 84-87Ind	2	6'6"	243	Boston College		18
Shibest, James WR	87Atl		5'10"	187	Arkansas		
Shield, Joe QB	86GB		6'1"	185	Trinity (Texas)		
Shields, Billy OT	75-83SD 84SF 85KC		6'7"	272	Georgia Tech		
Shields, Jon OG	87Dal		6'5	293	Portland State		
Shields, Will OG	93KC		6'2"	296	Nebraska		
Shipp, Jackie LB	84-88Mia 89Raid		6'2"	236	Oklahoma	1	
Shiver, Sanders LB	76-83Bal 84Mia		6'2"	227	Carson-Newman	5	6
Short, Laval NT	80Den 81TB 83-84USFL		6'3"	250	Colorado		
Shorthose, George WR	85KC		6'	198	Missouri		
Shorts, Peter DE	89NE		6'8"	278	Illinois State		
Shoulders, Darin OT	91Ind		6'3"	288	Tulane		
Shugarts, Bret DE	87Pit		6'2"	250	Indiana (Pa.)		
Shula, David WR	81Bal HC92-93Cin		5'11"	182	Dartmouth		
Shuler, Mickey TE	78-89NYJ 90-91Phi	2	6'3"	232	Penn State		222
Shull, Steve LB	80-82Mia 83KJ		6'1"	219	William & Mary		
Shumann, Mike WR	78-79SF 80TB 81SF 82-83StL	2	6'	178	Florida State		30
Shumate, Mark DE	85NYJ 85GB		6'5"	265	Wisconsin		
Shupe, Mark C	87Buf		6'5"	285	Arizona State		
Siano, Mike WR	87Phi		6'4"	220	Syracuse		
Sievers, Eric TE	81-88SD 88LA 89-90NE	2	6'4"	235	Maryland		60
Sigler, Ricky OG-OT	90SF 93KC		6'7"	296	San Jose State		
Sikahema, Vai HB	86-87StL 88-90Phx 91GB 92-93Phi	23	5'9"	191	Brigham Young		30
Sikora, Robert OT	84Cle		6'8"	285	Indiana		
Siler, Rich TE	87Mia		6'4"	240	Texas A&M		
Sileo, Dan NT	87TB		6'2"	282	Miami (Fla.)		
Silipo, Joe C	87Buf		6'3"	295	Tulane		
Simien, Tracy LB	91-93KC		6'1"	248	Texas Christian	3	
Simmonds, Mike OG	89TB 90KJ		6'4"	285	Indiana State		
Simmons, Bob OG-OT	77-83KC 84USFL		6'4"	260	Texas		
Simmons, Cleo TE	83Dal		6'2"	225	Jackson State		
Simmons, Clyde DE-DT	86-93Phi		6'6"	275	Western Carolina	2	26
Simmons, Dave LB	79GB 80Det 82Bal 83Chi 84-85USFL		6'4"	221	North Carolina		
Simmons, Ed OT-OG	87-93Was		6'5"	292	Eastern Washington		
Simmons, Jeff WR	83LA		6'3"	195	Southern Calif.		
Simmons, John DB	81-86Cin 86GB 87Ind	3	5'11"	192	S.M.U.	2	12
Simmons, King DB	87SD		6'2"	199	Texas Tech		
Simmons, Marcello DB	93Cin		6'1"	180	S.M.U.		
Simmons, Michael DE	89-90NO		6'4"	269	Mississippi State		
Simmons, Roy OG	79-81NYG 82VR 83Was 85USFL		6'3"	264	Georgia Tech		
Simmons, Stacy WR	90Ind		5'9"	183	Florida		
Simmons, Tony DE	85SD 86KJ 87SD		6'5"	269	Tennessee		
Simmons, Victor LB	87Dal		6'2"	230	Central St.-Ohio		
Simmons, Wayne LB	93GB		6'3"	240	Clemson	2	
Simms, Phil QB	79-81NYG 82KJ 83-93NYG	12	6'3"	215	Morehead State		30
Simons, Kevin OT	89Cle		6'3"	315	Tennessee		
Simpkins, Ron LB	80Cin 81LJ 82-86Cin 88GB		6'1"	235	Michigan		
Simpson, Carl DT	93Chi		6'2"	282	Florida State		
Simpson, Keith DB	78-85Sea		6'1"	195	Memphis State	19	18
Simpson, Travis OG	87GB		6'3"	272	Oklahoma		
Sims, Billy HB	80-84Det 85KJ	2	6'	212	Oklahoma		282
Sims, Darryl DE-NT	85-86Pit 87-88Cle 89KJ		6'3"	278	Wisconsin		
Sims, Jack OG	87Sea		6'3"	260	Hawaii		
Sims, Joe OT-OG	91Atl 92-93GB		6'3"	299	Nebraska		
Sims, Keith OG	90-93Mia		6'2"	308	Iowa State		
Sims, Ken DB	87StL		5'9"	177	Iowa		
Sims, Kenneth DE	82-89NE		6'5"	272	Texas		
Sims, Marvin FB	80-81Bal	2	6'4"	236	Clemson		12
Sims, Reggie TE	87Cin		6'4"	253	Northern Illinois		
Sims, Tom NT-DT	91-92KC 93Ind		6'2"	288	Western Michigan, Pittsburgh		
Sims, Tommy DB	86Ind		6'	190	Tennessee		
Sinclair, Mike DE	92-93Sea		6'4"	264	Eastern New Mexico		
Singer, Curt OT	86Sea 87NJ 88Det 89NYJ 91Sea		6'5"	278	Tennessee		
Singletary, Mike LB	81-92Chi		6'	230	Baylor	7	
Singletary, Reggie OT-OG-DT	86-90Phi		6'3"	279	N. Carolina State		
Singleton, Chris LB	90-93NE 93Mia		6'2"	247	Arizona	1	6
Singleton, Nate WR	93SF		5'11"	190	Grambling		6
Sinnott, Greg OT	87LA		6'7"	280	Utah State		
Sinnott, John OG-OT	80NYG 82Bal 83XJ		6'4"	275	Brown		
Siragusa, Tony NT-LB	90-93Ind		6'3"	301	Pittsburgh		
Sisley, Brian DE	87NYG		6'4"	235	S. Dakota State		
Sisson, Scott K	93NE	5	6'	197	Georgia Tech		57
Skansi, Paul WR	83Pit 84-91Sea	23	5'11"	186	Washington		60
Skaugstad, Daryle NT	81-82Hou 83SF 83GB		6'5"	254	California		
Skibinski, John FB	78-81Chi 83USFL		6'	226	Purdue		
Skladany, Tom K	78-82Det 83Phi	4	6'	192	Ohio State		
Skow, Jim DE	86-89Cin 90TB 91Sea 92SD 92LA		6'3"	253	Nebraska		
Skrepenak, Greg OT-OG	92Raid 93NJ		6'6"	315	Michigan		
Slack, Reggie QB	90Hou		6'1"	221	Auburn		
Slade, Chris LB	93NE		6'4"	232	Virginia		
Slater, Jackie OT-OG	76-93LA		6'4"	278	Jackson State		
Slater, Mark C	78SD 79-83Phi		6'2"	256	Minnesota		
Slaton, Mike DB	87Min		6'2"	194	South Dakota		
Slaton, Tony C-OG	85-90LA		6'3"	265	Southern Calif.		
Slaughter, Chuck OT	82NO 84USFL		6'5"	260	South Carolina		
Slaughter, Webster WR	86-91Cle 92-93Hou	23	6'	170	San Diego State		222
Slayden, Steve QB	88Cle		6'1"	185	Duke		
Slovacek, Emil OT	87SD		6'3"	300	S.F. Austin State		
Smagala, Stan DB	90-91Dal		5'10"	184	Notre Dame		
Small, Donovan DB	87Hou		5'11"	190	Minnesota	1	
Small, Fred LB	85Pit		5'1"	230	Washington		
Small, George NT	80NYG		6'2"	260	N. Carolina A&T		
Small, Gerald DB	78-83Mia 84Atl		5'11"	190	San Jose State	24	6
Small, Jessie LB	89-91Phi 92Phx		6'3"	239	Eastern Kentucky		
Small, Torrance WR	92-93NO	2	6'3"	201	Alcorn State		24
Smalls, Fred LB	87Phi		6'3"	225	West Virginia		
Smeenge, Joel LB-DE	90-93NO		6'5"	253	Western Michigan		
Smerek, Don DT-DE	81-87Dal		6'7"	258	Nevada-Reno		
Smerlas, Fred NT-DT	79-89Buf 90SF 91-92NE		6'3"	277	Boston College	2	6
Smigelsky, Dave K	82-83Atl 84USFL	4	5'11"	180	Virginia Tech		
Smith, Aaron LB	84Den		6'2"	223	Utah State		
Smith, Al LB	87-93Hou		6'1"	214	Cal. Poly.-Pomona, Utah State	2	6
Smith, Anthony DE-DT	91-93Raid		6'3"	265	Alabama, Arizona		
Smith, Art LB	80Den		6'1"	222	Hawaii		
Smith, Artie DE-DT	93SF		6'4"	303	Louisiana Tech		
Smith, Ben DB	90-91Phi 92KJ 93Phi		5'11"	184	Georgia	5	
Smith, Billy Ray LB	83-92SD		6'3"	235	Arkansas	14	6
Smith, Blane DB	87KC		5'10"	190	S.M.U.		
Smith, Brad LB	93Cin		6'2"	228	Texas Christian		
Smith, Brian LB-DT-DE	89-90LA		6'6"	242	Auburn		
Smith, Bruce DE	85-93Buf		6'4"	283	Virginia Tech	1	8
Smith, Byron DE	84-85Ind		6'5"	278	California		
Smith, Cedric FB	90Min 91NO		5'10"	223	Florida		
Smith, Chris FB	86-87KC	2	6'	232	Notre Dame		
Smith, Chuck DE-LB	92-93Atl		6'2"	248	Tennessee		
Smith, Dallis DB	87Sea		5'11"	170	Valdosta State		
Smith, Darrin LB	93Dal		6'1"	227	Miami (Fla.)		
Smith, Daryl DB	87-88Cin 89Min		5'9"	186	North Alabama	2	
Smith, Daryle OT	87-88Dal 89Cle 90-92Phi		6'5"	277	Tennessee		
Smith, Dave OT	88Cin		6'7"	290	Southern Illinois		
Smith, Dennis DB	81-93Den		6'3"	200	Southern Calif.	30	6
Smith, Dennis HB	90Phx		6'	230	Utah		
Smith, Don NT-DE-DT	79-84Atl 85-86Buf 87NYJ		6'5"	256	Miami (Fla.)		
Smith, Don HB-WR-FB	87KJ 88-89TB 90Buf	2	5'11"	195	Mississippi State		18
Smith, Donald DB	91Dal		5'11"	189	Liberty		
Smith, Doug NT-DT	84USFL 85-92Hou		6'4"	294	Auburn	1	
Smith, Doug C-OG-OT	78-91LA		6'3"	259	Bowling Green		
Smith, Doug DB	87NYG		6'	192	Ohio State		
Smith, Ed LB	80-81Bal 83-85USFL		6'2"	217	Vanderbilt	2	
Smith, Elliot DB	89SD 90Den		6'2"	192	Alcorn State		
Smith, Emmitt HB	90-93Dal	2	5'9"	203	Florida		318
Smith, Frankie DB	93Mia		5'9"	186	Baylor		
Smith, Franky OT	80KC 81-83CFL 84-85USFL		6'6"	279	Alabama A&M		
Smith, Gary OG	84Cin		6'2"	265	Virginia Tech		
Smith, Gregory NT	84Min		6'3"	261	Kansas		
Smith, Holden WR	82Bal 84USFL		6'1"	191	California		
Smith, Irv TE	93NO	2	6'3"	246	Notre Dame		12

UseName(Nickname)-Positions	Team by Year	See Section	Hgt	Wgt	College	Int	Pts
Smith, Jeff HB	85-86KC 88TB	23	5'9"	202	Nebraska		72
Smith, Jeff DE	87Cin		6'4"	248	Earlham		
Smith, Jeff TE	87NYG		6'3"	240	Tennessee		
Smith, Jerry TE-WR	65-77Was	2	6'2"	209	Arizona State		360
Smith, Jim WR	77-82Pit 83-85USFL 85 Raid	23	6'2"	205	Michigan		150
Smith, Jimmy HB	84Was 84Raid		6'	205	Elon		
Smith, Jimmy HB	87Min		5'11"	190	Purdue		
Smith, Jimmy WR	92Dal 93IL		6'1"	205	Jackson State		
Smith, Joey WR	91-92NYG	3	5'10"	177	Louisville		
Smith, Johnny Ray DB	82-83TB 84SD		5'9"	183	Lamar		
Smith, J.T. WR	78Was 78-84KC 85-87StL 88-90Phx	23	6'2"	185	North Texas		234
Smith, Ken OG	87Cin		6'1"	285	Miami-Ohio		
Smith, Kendal WR	89-90Cin	2	5'9"	189	Utah State		6
Smith, Kevin DB	91Pit		5'11"	204	Rhode Island		
Smith, Kevin TE	92-93Raid		6'4"	255	U.C.L.A.		
Smith, Kevin DB	92-93Dal		5'11"	177	Texas A&M	8	6
Smith, Lance OG-OT	86-87StL 88-93Phx		6'2"	279	Louisiana State		
Smith, Larry LB	87Hou		6'1"	210	Kentucky		
Smith, Leonard DB	83-87StL 88Phx 88-91Buf		5'11"	200	McNeese State	15	18
Smith, Lucious DB	80-82LA 83KC 84Buf 84-85SD		5'10"	190	San Diego State, Fullerton State	4	6
Smith, Matt LB	87Den		6'2"	234	West Virginia		
Smith, Michael WR	92KC		5'8"	160	Kansas State		
Smith, Mike WR	80Atl 83USFL		5'10"	194	Grambling		
Smith, Mike DB	85-87Mia		6'	172	Texas-El Paso		
Smith, Monte OG	89Den 90FJ		6'5"	270	North Dakota		
Smith, Neil DE	88-93KC		6'4"	271	Nebraska	2	12
Smith, Otis DB	91-93Phi		5'11"	184	Missouri	4	6
Smith, Phil WR	83Bal 84Ind 86Phi	3	6'3"	188	San Diego State		6
Smith, Quintin WR	90Chi 91LJ		5'10"	172	Kansas		
Smith, Reggie WR	80-81Atl 83USFL 87NYJ	3	5'4"	168	N.Car. Central		
Smith, Reggie OT	87TB		6'5"	295	Kansas		
Smith, Ricky DB-WR	82-84NE 84Was 87Det	3	6'	182	Alabama State	2	12
Smith, Rico WR	92-93Cle		6'	185	Colorado		
Smith, Robert DE	84USFL 85Min 87AJ		6'5"	255	Grambling		
Smith, Robert HB	93Min	2	6'	195	Ohio State		12
Smith, Rod DB	92-93NE		5'11"	187	Notre Dame	1	
Smith, Ron WR	78-79LA 80-81SD 81-83Phi 84USFL	2	6'	185	San Diego State		24
Smith, Sammie HB	89-91Mia 92Den	2	6'2"	226	Florida State		96
Smith, Sean DE-DT	87-88Chi 89Dal 89TB 89LA 90-91NE		6'4"	280	Grambling		2
Smith, Struggy DB	87Atl		6'2"	190	Appalachian State		
Smith, Steve OT-DE-TE	66Pit 68-70Min 71-74Phi		6'5"	246	Michigan		6
Smith, Steve FB	87-93Raid	2	6'1"	232	Penn State		108
Smith, Thomas DB	93Buf		5'11"	188	North Carolina		
Smith, Tim WR	80-86Hou	2	6'2"	201	Nebraska		72
Smith, Timmy FB-HB	87-88Was 90Dal	2	5'11"	216	Texas Tech		18
Smith, Tony HB	92-93Atl	23	6'1"	214	Southern Miss.		18
Smith, Torin DE	87NYG		6'4"	320	Mesa J.C.		
Smith, Vernice OG-OT	90-92Phx 93Chi 93Was		6'2"	295	Florida A&M		
Smith, Vinson LB	88Atl 89FJ 90-92Dal 93Chi		6'2"	228	East Carolina		
Smith, Waddell WR	84Dal		6'2"	180	Kansas		
Smith, Wayne DB	80-83Det 83-86StL 87Min		6'	171	Wis.-LaCrosse, Purdue	9	
Smith, Wes WR	87GB		6'	190	East Texas State		
Smith, Willie TE	87Mia		6'2"	235	Miami (Fla.)		6
Smoot, Raymond OG-OT	93SD		6'4"	305	Louisiana State		
Snell, Donald WR	87Sea		6'2"	177	Virginia Tech		
Snell, Ray OG-OT	80-83TB 84-85Pit 85Det		6'4"	262	Wisconsin		
Snipes, Angelo LB	85USFL 86Was 86-87SD 87-89KC		6'	222	West Georgia	1	
Snow, Percy LB	90KC 91BN 92KC 93Chi		6'2"	248	Michigan State	1	
Snyder, Loren QB	87Dal		6'4"	207	Northern Colorado		
Snyder, Pat LB	91Ind		6'1"	225	Purdue		
Sochia, Brian NT-DE	83-85Hou 86-91Mia 91-92Den		6'3"	270	Northwestern Okla.		6
Sohn, Kurt WR	81-82NYJ 83KJ 84-88NYJ	23	5'11"	179	N. Carolina State, Fordham		60
Solomon, Ariel OG-OT-C	91-93Pit		6'5"	283	Colorado		
Solomon, Freddie WR-QB-HB	75-77Mia 78-85SF	23	5'11"	185	Tampa		342
Solomon, Roland DB	80Dal 80Buf 81Den		6'	193	Utah		
Solomon, Jesse LB	86-89Min 89-90Dal 91TB 92-93Atl		6'	235	Florida State	8	6
Solt, Ron OG	84-88Ind 88-91Phi 92Ind 93SJ		6'3"	279	Maryland		
Sommer, Don OT	87Buf		6'4"	290	Texas-El Paso		
Songy, Treg DB	87NYJ		6'2"	200	Tulane		
Sowell, Robert DB	83-85,87Mia	3	5'11"	176	Howard	2	
Spagnola, John TE	79-82Phi 83XJ 84-87Phi 88Sea 89GB	2	6'4"	241	Yale		120
Spani, Gary LB	78-86KC		6'2"	229	Kansas State	2	18
Spann, Gary LB	87KC		6'1"	218	Texas Christian		
Sparenberg, Dave OG	87Cle		6'3"	267	Western Ontario		
Sparks, Phillipi DB	92-93NYG		5'11"	186	Arizona State	1	
Spears, Anthony DE	89Hou		6'5"	260	Portland State		
Spears, Ernest DB	90NO		5'11"	192	Southern Calif.		
Spears, Ron DE	82-83NE 83GB		6'6"	255	San Diego State		
Speer, Del DB	93Cle		6'	196	Florida	1	
Spek, Jeff TE	86TB		6'3"	240	San Diego State		
Spellman, Alonzo DE-DT	92-93Chi		6'4"	280	Ohio State		
Spencer, Herb LB	87Atl		6'3"	230	Newberry		
Spencer, Jimmy DB	92-93NO		5'9"	180	Florida		
Spencer, Tim FB	83-85USFL 85-90SD	2	6'2"	224	Ohio State		114
Spencer, Todd HB	84-85Pit 87SD	23	6'	203	Southern Calif.		
Spielman, Chris LB	88-93Det		6'	247	Ohio State	3	
Spindler, Marc DT-DE	90-93Det		6'5"	286	Pittsburgh		
Spitulski, Bob LB	92-93Sea		6'3"	235	Central Florida		
Spivey, Mike DB	77-79Chi 80Oak 80-81NO 82Atl		6'	197	Colorado		6
Spivey, Sebron WR	87Dal		5'11"	180	Southern Illinois		
Spradlin, Danny LB	81-82Dal 83-84TB 85StL		6'1"	235	Tennessee		
Springs, Kirk DB	81-85NYJ 86XJ	23	6'	193	Miami-Ohio	4	6
Springs, Ron FB-HB	79-84Dal 85-86TB	23	6'1"	213	Ohio State		228
Squirek, Jack LB	82-85Raid 86Mia		6'4"	230	Illinois	1	
Stachowicz, Ray K	81-82GB 83Chi	4	5'11"	187	Michigan State		
Stachowski, Rich NT	83Den		6'4"	245	California		
Stacy, Siran HB	92Phi		5'11"	203	Alabama		
Stadnik, John C	87SD		6'4"	275	Western Illinois		
Stallings, Gene	HC 86-87StL HC88-89Phx				Texas A&M		
Stallings, Robert TE	86StL 87NJ		6'6"	250	Southern Miss.		
Stalls, David DE-DT-NT	77-79Dal 80-83TB 83Raid 84USFL 85Raid		6'4"	247	Northern Colorado		
Stallworth, John WR	74-87Pit	2	6'2"	190	Alabama A&M		384
Stallworth, Ron DE	89-90NYJ		6'5"	262	Auburn		
Stallworth, Tim WR	90Den		5'10"	185	Washington State		
Stamps, Sylvester HB-WR	84-88Atl 89TB	23	5'7"	172	Jackson State		42
Stams, Frank LB	89-91LA 92-93Cle		6'2"	240	Notre Dame	1	

UseName(Nickname)-Positions	Team by Year	See Section	Hgt	Wgt	College	Int	Pts
Stanback, Harry DE	82 Bal		6'5"	255	North Carolina		
Stankavage, Scott QB	84Den 87Mia	1	6'1"	192	Florida A&M		
Stanley, Jack QB	87Was		6'3"	207	Nevada-Reno		
Stanley, Walter WR	85-88GB 89Det 90Was 92SD 92NE	23	5'9"	179	Colorado, Mesa		36
Stargell, Tony DB	90-91NYJ 92-93Ind		5'11"	190	Tennessee State	4	
Stark, Chad FB	87Sea		6'1"	220	N. Dakota State		
Stark, Rohn K	82-83Bal 84-93Ind	4	6'3"	203	Florida		
Starks, Timothy DB	87Min		5'9"	175	Kent State		
Starnes, John K	87Atl		6'3"	185	North Texas		
Starring, Stephen WR	83-87NE 88TB 88Det	23	5'10"	172	McNeese State		66
Station, Larry LB	86Pit		5'11"	227	Iowa		
Staurovsky, Jason K	87StL 88-91NE 92NYJ	5	5'9"	169	Tulsa		223
Staubach, Scott HB	81NO		5'11"	204	U.C.L.A.		
Staysniak, Joe OT	91Buf 92KC 93Ind		6'5"	298	Ohio State		
Steckel, Les	HC84Min				Navy		
Stedman, Troy LB	88KC		6'3"	243	Washburn		
Steed, Joel NT	92-93Pit		6'2"	290	Colorado		
Steele, Chuck C	87Det		6'1"	255	California		
Steels, Anthony HB-FB	83-84USFL 85SD 85Buf 87SD	3	5'9"	200	Nebraska		
Stegall, Milt WR	92-93Cin	3	6'	184	Miami-Ohio		6
Steinfeld, Al C-OG-OT	82KC 83Hou 83NYG		6'5"	256	C.W. Post		
Steinkuhler, Dean OT	84Hou 85KJ 86-91Hou		6'3"	283	Nebraska		
Stensrud, Mike NT-DT-DE	79-85Hou 86Min 87TB 88KC 89Was		6'5"	280	Iowa State	2	
Stepanek, Joe DT	87Min		6'5"	268	Minnesota		2
Stephen, Scott LB	87-91GB 92LA		6'2"	237	Arizona State	5	
Stephens, Calvin OG	92NE		6'2"	285	South Carolina		
Stephens, Hal DE	85Det 85KC		6'4"	252	East Carolina		
Stephens, John HB-FB	88-92NE 93GB 93KC	2	6'1"	220	Northwestern La.		114
Stephens, Mac LB	90NYJ 91Min		6'3"	220	Minnesota		
Stephens, Rich OG-OT	93Raid		6'7"	300	Tulsa		
Stephens, Rod LB	89-93Sea		6'1"	237	Georgia Tech		10
Stephens, Santo LB	93KC		6'4"	232	Temple		
Stephens, Steve TE	81NYJ 83USFL		6'3"	227	Oklahoma State		
Stephenson, Dwight C-OT	80-87Mia 88KJ		6'2"	255	Alabama		
Stepnoski, Mark OG-C	89-93Dal		6'2"	269	Pittsburgh		
Sterling, John HB	87GB		6'2"	203	Central St.-Okla.		
Stevens, Mark QB	87SF		6'1"	190	Utah		6
Stevens, Matt QB	87KC	1	6'	190	U.C.L.A.		
Stevenson, Mark OG-C	83USFL 85Det		6'3"	285	Missouri, Western Illinois		
Stewart, Andrew DE	89Cle 91KJ		6'5"	265	Cincinnati		
Stewart, Curtis HB	89Dal		5'11"	208	Auburn		
Stewart, Mark LB	84Min		6'3"	232	Washington		
Stewart, Michael DB	87-93LA		5'11"	195	Fresno State	7	8
Stief, Dave WR-DB	78-82StL 83Was 84USFL	2	6'3"	195	Portland State		30
Stieve, Terry OG	76-77NO 78-79StL 80KJ 81-84StL		6'2"	256	Wisconsin		
Still, Art DE	78-87KC 88-89Buf		6'7"	253	Kentucky	1	
Stills, Ken DB	85-89GB 90Min		5'10"	186	Wisconsin	7	6
Stinson, Lemuel DB	88-92Chi		5'9"	159	Texas Tech	16	12
Stock, Mark WR	89Pit 92LJ 93Was		5'11"	177	V.M.I.		
Stockemer, Ralph FB	87KC		6'1"	212	Baylor		
Stokes, Eric C-OG	87NE		6'4"	255	Northeastern		
Stokes, Fred DE	87-88LA 89-92Was 93LA		6'3"	268	Georgia Southern		2
Stone, Dwight HB-WR	87-93Pit	23	6'	188	Middle Tenn. St.		84
Stone, Ron OT	93Dal		6'5"	309	Boston College		
Stonebreaker, Mike LB	91Chi		6'	226	Notre Dame		
Stoops, Mike DB	87Chi		6'1"	185	Iowa		
Storr, Greg LB	87Mia		6'2"	225	Boston College		
Stoudt, Cliff QB	77-83Pit 84-85USFL 86-87StL 88Phx 89Mia 90Dal	12	6'4"	215	Youngstown State		24
Stouffer, Kelly QB	88-92Sea	12	6'3"	210	Colorado State		
Stover, Jeff DE	82-88SF		6'5"	275	Oregon		
Stover, Matt K	91-93Cle	5	5'11"	178	Louisiana Tech		257
Stowe, Tyronne LB	87-90Pit 91-93Phx		6'1"	242	Rutgers		2
Stowers, Tommie TE	92-93NO		6'3"	240	Missouri		
Stoyanovich, Pete K	89-93Mia	5	5'10"	180	Indiana		540
Strachan, Steve HB-FB	85-89Raid	2	6'1"	221	Boston College		6
Stracka, Tim TE	83-84Cle		6'3"	225	Wisconsin		
Stradford, Troy HB-WR	87-90Mia 91-92KC 92Det	23	5'9"	192	Boston College		72
Strahan, Mike DE	93NYG		6'4"	275	Texas Southern		
Strauthers, Thomas DE-DT	83-86Phi 88Det 89-91Min		6'4"	262	Jackson State		
Streater, Eric WR	87TB		5'11"	165	North Carolina		12
Strenger, Rich OT	83-87Det 88KJ		6'7"	278	Michigan		
Streeter, George DB	89Chi 90Ind		6'2"	212	Notre Dame		
Strickland, Fred LB	88-92LA 93Min		6'2"	243	Purdue	2	
Strock, Don QB	74-87Mia 88Cle 89Ind	12	6'5"	220	Virginia Tech		12
Strom, Rick QB	89-93Pit		6'2"	210	Georgia Tech		
Strong, Ray HB	78-82Atl	23	5'9"	184	Nevada-Las Vegas		18
Stroth, Vince OT-OG-TE	83-85USFL 85SF 87-88Hou		6'4"	267	Brigham Young		
Strozier, Wilbur TE	87Sea 88SD		6'4"	255	Georgia		
Stryzinski, Dan K	90-91Pit 92TB	4	6'1"	193	Indiana		
Strzelczyk, Justin OT	90-93Pit		6'5"	298	Maine		
Subblefield, Dana DT	93SF		6'2"	302	Kansas		
Stubbs, Danny DE-LB	88-89SF 90-91Dal 91-93Cin		6'4"	260	Miami (Fla.)		
Stuckey, Jim DE	80-86SF		6'4"	252	Clemson		2
Studaway, Mark DE	84Hou 85TB 87Atl		6'3"	273	Tennessee		
Studdard, Dave OT-OG-TE	79-88Den		6'4"	258	Texas		12
Studdard, Les C	82KC 83Hou		6'4"	260	Texas		
Studley, Chuck	HC83Hou				Illinois		
Studwell, Scott LB	77-90Min		6'2"	228	Illinois	11	
Subis, Nick OT-C	91Den		6'4"	278	Northwestern Okla.		
Suhey, Matt FB	80-89Chi	23	5'11"	215	Penn State		150
Sullins, John LB	92Den		6'1"	225	Alabama		
Sullivan, Carl DE	87GB		6'4"	248	San Jose State		
Sullivan, John DB	86GB 86SD 87SF		6'1"	190	California		
Sullivan, Kent K	91Hou 92KC 93SD 93Hou		5'10"	197	Cal. Lutheran		
Sullivan, Mike OG-C	92-93TB		6'3"	290	Miami (Fla.)		
Sully, Ivory DB	79-84LA 85-86TB 87Det		6'	198	Delaware	1	2
Summers, Don TE	84-85Den 87GB		6'4"	230	Oregon Tech, Boise State		6
Sunter, Ian K	80Cin	5	6'1"	215	none		48
Superick, Steve K	87Hou		5'11"	204	West Virginia		
Sutter, Ed LB	93Cle		6'3"	240	Northwestern		
Sutton, Frank OT	87NYG		6'3"	280	Jackson State		
Sutton, John DB	87NO		6'1"	195	New Mexico		
Sutton, Mickey DB	83CFL 84-85USFL 86-88LA 89GB 89Buf 90LA	3	5'8"	167	Montana	5	
Sutton, Reggie DB	87-88NO		5'10"	180	Miami (Fla.)	8	6
Sutton, Ricky DE	93Pit		6'2"	281	Auburn		

UseName(Nickname)-Positions	Team by Year	See Section	Hgt.	Wgt.	College	Int	Pts
Sverchek, Paul NT	84Min		6'3"	252	Cal. Poly.-S.L.O.		
Swain, John DB	81-84Min 85Mia 85-86Pit 87Mia		6'1"	194	Miami (Fla.)	14	
Swanke, Karl OT-C-OG	80-86GB		6'6"	257	Boston College		6
Swann, Eric DE-NT	91-93Phx		6'4"	310	none		2
Swanson, Eric WR	86StL		5'11"	186	Tennessee		
Swanson, Shane WR	87Den		5'9"	200	Nebraska		6
Swarn, George HB	87Cle 88NJ 90AJ		5'10"	205	Miami-Ohio		
Swartwoudt, Gregg OT	87NYG		6'3"	275	North Dakota		
Swayne, Harry DE-OT	87-90TB 91-93SD		6'5"	286	Rutgers		
Sweeney, Calvin WR	80-87Pit	2	6'2"	190	Southern Calif.		42
Sweeney, Jim OT-OG-C	84-93NYJ		6'4"	277	Pittsburgh		
Sweeney, Kevin QB	87-88Dal	1	6'	192	Fresno State		
Sweet, Tony TE	87NYJ		6'4"	230	Montclair State		
Swider, Larry K	79Det 80StL 81-82TB 84-85USFL	4	6'2"	195	Pittsburgh		
Swilley, Dennis C-OG-OT	77-83Min 84VR 85-87Min		6'3"	248	Texas A&M, North Texas		
Swilling, Pat LB	86-92NO 93Det		6'3"	242	Georgia Tech	6	6
Swoope, Craig DB	86-87TB 87-88Ind		6'1"	205	Illinois	1	
Swoopes, Patrick NT	87NO 88CFL 89NO 91KC 91Mia		6'4"	280	Mississippi State		
Sydner, Jeff WR	92-93Phi	3	5'6"	170	Hawaii		
Sydney, Harry FB	87-91SF 92GB	2	6'	217	Kansas		78
Sydnor, Willie WR	82Pit		5'11"	170	Northwestern, Villanova, Syracuse		
Sytsma, Stan LB	80Atl		6'2"	200	Minnesota		
Szott, David OG	90-93KC		6'4"	285	Penn State		
Szymanski, Jim DE	90-91Den		6'5"	268	Michigan State		
Tabor, Paul C-OG	80Chi 81KJ		6'4"	241	Oklahoma		
Tabor, Phil DE-NT-DT	79-82NYG		6'4"	255	Oklahoma		
Tagliaferri, John HB	87Mia	2	5'11"	195	Cornell		6
Taibi, Joe DE	87NYG		6'5"	265	Idaho		
Talley, Darryl LB	83-93Buf		6'4"	231	West Virginia	11	12
Talley, John TE	90-91Cle		6'5"	245	West Virginia		
Talley, Stan K	87Raid	4	6'5"	220	Texas Christian		
Talton, Ken HB	80KC 83-84USFL		6'	205	Cornell		
Tamburello, Ben OG-C	87-90Phi 91KJ		6'3"	278	Auburn		
Tamm, Ralph OG-C	90-91Cle 91Was 91Cin 92-93SF		6'4"	280	West Chester		6
Tardits, Richard LB	90-92NE		6'2"	228	Georgia		
Tasker, Steve WR	85-86Hou 86-93Buf	3	5'9"	185	Northwestern		20
Tate, David DB	88-92Chi 93NYG		6'	177	Colorado	8	
Tate, Lars HB	88-89TB 90Chi	2	6'2"	215	Georgia		102
Tate, Rodney HB	82-83Cin 84Atl	23	5'11"	190	Texas		
Tatupu, Mosi FB	78-90NE 91LA	2	6'	227	Southern Calif.		120
Tausch, Terry OT-OG	82-88Min 89SF		6'5"	275	Texas		
Tautalatasi, Junior HB-FB	86-88Phi 89Dal	2	5'10"	207	Washington State		12
Tautolo, John OG-OT	82-83NYG 85USFL 87Raid		6'3"	267	U.C.L.A.		
Tautolo, Terry LB	76-79Phi 80-81SF 81-82Det 83Mia 84Det		6'2"	232	U.C.L.A.	1	
Taylor, Alphonso DT	93Den		6'3"	350	Temple		
Taylor, Billy HB-FB	78-81NYG 81NYJ 83-84USFL	2	6'	215	Texas Tech		102
Taylor, Brian DB-HB	89Chi 91Buf 93KJ		5'10"	185	Oregon State		
Taylor, Craig FB	89-91Cin	2	5'11"	224	West Virginia		60
Taylor, Derrick DB	87NO		5'11"	186	N. Carolina State		
Taylor, Gene WR	87-88TB 89CFL 91NE		6'2"	189	Fresno State		
Taylor, Greg HB	82NE		5'8"	175	Virginia		
Taylor, Hosea DE	81Bal 82JJ 83Bal 84-85USFL		6'5"	255	Houston		2
Taylor, Jay DB	89-91Phx 92LJ 93KC		5'9"	170	San Jose State	4	
Taylor, Jim Bob QB	83Bal		6'2"	197	S.M.U.		
Taylor, John WR	87-93SF	23	6'1"	185	Delaware State		234
Taylor, Johnny LB	84-86Atl 86Mia 87SD		6'4"	237	Hawaii		
Taylor, J.T. OT	78-81NO 84USFL		6'4"	265	Missouri		
Taylor, Keith DB	88-91Ind 92-93NO		5'11"	193	Illinois	13	6
Taylor, Ken DB	85Chi 86SD	3	6'1"	186	Oregon State	4	
Taylor, Kitrick WR	88KC 89NE 90-91SD 92GB 93Den	23	5'10"	194	Washington State		12
Taylor, Lawrence (L.T.) LB	81-93NYG		6'3"	241	North Carolina	9	12
Taylor, Lenny WR	84GB 87Atl		5'10"	181	Tennessee		6
Taylor, Malcolm DE-NT	82-83Hou 84-85USFL 86Hou 87-88Raid 89Atl		6'6"	281	Tennessee State		
Taylor, Rob OT	83-85USFL 86-93TB		6'6"	293	Northwestern		
Taylor, Roger OT	81KC		6'6"	271	Oklahoma State		
Taylor, Terry DB	84-88Sea 89-91Det 92-93Cle		5'10"	188	Southern Illinois	21	18
Taylor, Tom OG	87LA		6'3"	265	Georgia Tech		
Taylor, Troy QB	90-91NYJ		6'4"	200	California		6
Teafatiller, Guy DT	87Chi		6'2"	260	Illinois		
Teague, George DB	93GB		6'1"	187	Alabama	1	
Teague, Matthew DE	80-81Atl		6'5"	240	Prairie View		
Teague, Pat LB	87TB		6'1"	225	N. Carolina State		
Teal, Jimmy WR	85-86Buf 87-88Sea	2	5'10"	171	Texas A&M		18
Teal, Willie DB	80-86Min 87Raid		5'10"	193	Louisiana State	12	6
Teeter, Mike DT	91Min 92Hou		6'2"	269	Michigan		
Teifke, Mike C	87Cle		6'4"	255	Akron		
Teltschik, John K	86-89Phi 90LJ	4	6'2"	212	Texas		
Tennell, Derek TE	87-89Cle 91Det 92-93Min	2	6'5"	245	U.C.L.A.		30
Terrell, Pat DB	90-93LA		6'	195	Notre Dame	4	
Terry, Doug DB	92-93KC		5'11"	192	Kansas	2	
Terry, Joe LB	87Sea		6'2"	230	Hayward State		
Testaverde, Vinny QB	87-92TB 93Cle	12	6'5"	217	Miami (Fla.)		30
Tharpe, Larry OT	92-93Det		6'4"	299	Tennessee State		
Tharpe, Richard DE-NT	87Buf		6'3"	255	Louisville		
Thaxton, Galand LB	89Atl 90AJ 91SD		6'1"	242	Wyoming		
Thayer, Tom OG-C	83-85USFL 85-92Chi 93Mia		6'4"	271	Notre Dame		
Theismann, Joe QB	74-85Was	12	6'	192	Notre Dame		122
Thielemann, R.C. OG-C	77-84Atl 85-88Was		6'4"	255	Arkansas		
Thigpen, Yancey WR	91SD 92-93Pit	2	6'1"	208	Winston-Salem St.		18
Thomas, Andre HB	87Min		6'	205	Mississippi		
Thomas, Ben DE-NT	85-86NE 86GB 87KJ 88Pit 89Atl 91LA		6'4"	276	Auburn		
Thomas, Blair HB	90-93NYJ	2	5'10"	195	Penn State		42
Thomas, Bob K	75-81Chi 82Det 82-84Chi 85SD 86NYG	5	5'10"	175	Notre Dame		756
Thomas, Broderick LB-DE	89-93TB		6'4"	248	Nebraska	2	6
Thomas, Carlton DB	87KC		6'	200	Elizabeth City St.		
Thomas, Calvin FB	82-88Chi 88Den	2	5'11"	239	Illinois		30
Thomas, Chuck C-OG	85Atl 87-92SF		6'3"	277	Oklahoma		
Thomas, Curtland WR	87NO		6'	183	Missouri		
Thomas, Dave DB	93Dal		6'2"	208	Tennessee		
Thomas, Dee DB	90Hou		5'10"	176	Nicholls State		
Thomas, Derrick FB	87TB		6'	232	Arkansas		
Thomas, Derrick LB	89-93KC		6'3"	237	Alabama		18
Thomas, Doug WR	91-93Sea	2	5'10"	178	Clemson		
Thomas, Ed TE	90-91TB 92KJ		6'3"	240	Houston		
Thomas, Eric DB	87-92Cin 93NYJ		5'11"	181	Tulane	16	6

UseName(Nickname)-Positions	Team by Year	See Section	Hgt.	Wgt.	College	Int	Pts
Thomas, Garth OG	87Sea		6'3"	260	Washington		
Thomas, George WR-FB-TE	89-92Atl 92TB	2	5'9"	169	Nevada-Las Vegas		18
Thomas, Henry DT	87-93Min		6'2"	273	Louisiana State	1	14
Thomas, Henry OG	87NO		6'2"	275	SW Texas State		
Thomas, Jewerl FB-HB	80-82LA 83KC 84SD	2	5'10"	229	San Jose State		30
Thomas, Joe WR	87NO		5'11"	175	Miss. Valley St.		
Thomas, John OT	87NYJ		6'4"	280	Toledo		
Thomas, Johnny DB	88Was 89SD 90,92-93Was		5'9"	188	Baylor		
Thomas, Kelly OT	83-84TB 87LA		6'6"	268	Southern Calif.		
Thomas, Ken HB	83KC 84KJ	2	5'9"	211	San Jose State		
Thomas, Kevin C	88TB		6'2"	265	Arizona State		6
Thomas, Lamar WR	93TB		6'1"	170	Miami (Fla.)		12
Thomas, Lavale HB	87-88GB		6'	205	Fresno State		6
Thomas, Lynn DB	81-82SF 84-85USFL		5'11"	181	Pittsburgh		
Thomas, Mark DE-LB	93SF		6'5"	273	N. Carolina State		
Thomas, Norris DB	77-79Mia 80-84TB		5'11"	179	Southern Miss.	9	6
Thomas, Ricky DB	87Sea		6'	185	Alabama		
Thomas, Robb WR	89-91KC 92-93Sea	2	5'11"	174	Oregon State		42
Thomas, Rodell LB	81Mia 81-82Sea 83-84Mia		6'2"	225	Alabama State		6
Thomas, Rodney DB	88-90Mia 91LA 92KJ		5'10"	190	Brigham Young	3	
Thomas, Sean DB	85Cin 85Atl 87NJ		5'11"	190	Texas Christian		
Thomas, Stan OT	91-92Chi 93Hou		6'5"	296	Texas		
Thomas, Thurman HB	88-93Buf	2	5'10"	198	Oklahoma State		342
Thomas, Todd C	81KC 83-84USFL		6'5"	262	North Dakota		
Thomas, William LB	91-93Phi		6'2"	218	Texas A&M	4	
Thomas, Zach WR	83-84Den 84TB	23	6'	182	S. Carolina State		6
Thomaselli, Rich FB-HB	81-82Hou		6'1"	199	West Va. Weslyan		
Thomason, Jeff TE	92-93Cin		6'4"	233	Oregon		
Thomasson, Leon DB	87Atl		5'11"	190	Texas Southern		
Thome, Chris C	91-92Cle 92NYG		6'4"	280	Minnesota		
Thompson, Anthony HB	90-92Phx 92LA	2	5'11"	207	Indiana		36
Thompson, Anthony LB	90Den		6'1"	227	East Carolina		
Thompson, Arland OG	80Den 81GB 82Bal 83-85USFL 87KC		6'3"	265	Baylor		
Thompson, Aundra WR-HB	77-81GB 81SD 81-82NO	23	6'1"	186	East Texas State		54
Thompson, Bennie DB	89-91NO 92-93KC		6'	200	Grambling	4	
Thompson, Broderick OG-OT	85USFL 85Dal 87-92SD 93Phi		6'5"	291	Kansas		
Thompson, Craig TE	92-93Cin	2	6'2"	244	N. Carolina A&T		18
Thompson, Darrell FB-HB	90-93GB	2	6'	215	Minnesota		54
Thompson, Del HB	82KC 83JJ	2	6'	203	Texas-El Paso, Texas		
Thompson, Donnell DE	81-83Bal 84-91Ind		6'4"	270	North Carolina		8
Thompson, Emmuel DB	87Hou		5'11"	180	Texas A&I		
Thompson, Ernie FB	91LA 93KC		5'11"	230	Indiana		6
Thompson, Gary DB	83-84Buf 87Was		6'	180	San Jose State		
Thompson, Jack QB	79-82Cin 83-84TB	12	6'3"	218	Washington State		36
Thompson, John TE	79-82GB 84USFL		6'3"	228	Weber State, Utah State		12
Thompson, Ken WR	82-83StL		6'1"	178	West Texas State, Utah State		
Thompson, Leonard WR-HB	75-86Det	23	5'11"	190	Oklahoma State		228
Thompson, Leroy HB	91-93Pit	2	5'10"	215	Penn State		24
Thompson, Marty DE	93Det		6'3"	243	Fresno State		
Thompson, Reyna DB	86-88Mia 89-92NYG 93NE		6'	194	Baylor	3	6
Thompson, Robert LB	83-84TB 87Det		6'3"	227	Michigan		
Thompson, Robert WR	87Den		5'9"	168	Youngstown State		
Thompson, Steve DT	87Was		6'2"	275	Minnesota		
Thompson, Vince FB	81Det 82JJ 83Det	2	6'	228	Villanova		12
Thompson, Warren LB	87NYG		6'3"	241	Oklahoma State		
Thompson, Weegie WR	84-89Pit	2	6'6"	212	Florida State		66
Thornton, Bruce DE-DT	79-81Dal 82StL 84-85USFL		6'5"	265	Illinois	1	
Thornton, George DE-DT	91-92SD 93NYG		6'3"	300	Alabama		
Thornton, Jim (Robocop) TE	88-91Chi 92FJ 93NYJ	2	6'2"	242	Fullerton State		42
Thornton, John DE-DT	91Cle 92LJ		6'3"	303	Cincinnati		
Thornton, Reggie WR	91Ind 93Cin		5'10"	170	Bowling Green		
Thornton, Sidney HB-FB	77-82Pit 84USFL	2	5'11"	230	Northwestern La.		144
Thorp, Don NT-DE	84NO 87-88Ind 88KC		6'4"	260	Illinois		
Thrift, Cliff LB	79-84SD 85Chi 86LA		6'2"	232	E. C. Oklahoma	3	
Thurman, Dennis DB	78-85Dal 86StL		5'11"	176	Southern Calif.	36	30
Thurman, Junior DB	87NO		6'	180	Southern Calif.		
Tice, John TE	83-92NO	2	6'5"	246	Maryland		90
Tice, Mike TE	81-88Sea 89Was 90-91Sea 92-93Min	2	6'7"	246	Maryland		66
Tiffin, Van K	87TB 87Mia		5'9"	155	Alabama		26
Tigges, Mark OT	87Cin		6'3"	290	Western Illinois		
Tiggle, Calvin LB	91-92TB		6'1"	235	Georgia Tech		
Tilley, Emmett LB	83Mia		5'11"	240	Duke		
Tilley, Pat WR	76-86StL	23	5'10"	176	Louisiana Tech		222
Tillison, Ed FB	92Det 93KJ		6'	225	NW Missouri St.		
Tillman, Cedric WR	92-93Den	2	6'2"	204	Alcorn State		18
Tillman, Lawyer WR	89Cle 90LJ 91-93Cle	2	6'5"	230	Auburn		24
Tillman, Lewis HB	89-93NYG	2	6'	195	Jackson State		30
Tillman, Spencer HB	87-88Hou 89-91SF 92-93Hou	23	5'11"	206	Oklahoma		12
Tillmon, Tony DB	87Raid		5'10"	170	Texas		
Tilton, Ron OG	86Was 88NYJ		6'4"	250	Tulane		
Times, Ken NT-DT	80SF 81StL		6'2"	246	Southern U.		
Timmer, Kirk LB	87Dal		6'3"	242	Montana State		
Timpson, Michael WR	89-93NE	2	5'10"	175	Kent State		30
Tinsley, Keith WR	87Cle		5'9"	184	Pittsburgh		
Tinsley, Scott QB	87Phi	1	6'2"	195	Southern Calif.		
Tippett, Andre LB	82-88NE 89SJ 90-93NE		6'3"	240	Iowa	1	12
Tippins, Ken LB	89Dal 90-93Atl		6'1"	229	Middle Tenn. St.	1	6
Tipton, Gregg QB	87StL		6'3"	191	Hawaii		
Tipton, Rico LB	87Sea		6'2"	240	Washington State		
Titensor, Glen OG-C	81-86Dal 87KJ 88Dal		6'4"	263	U.C.L.A., Brigham Young		
Tiumalu, Casey FB	87LA		5'8"	206	Brigham Young		
Tobin, Steve C	80NYG 83USFL		6'4"	258	Minnesota		
Todd, Richard QB	76-83NYJ 84-85NO 86NYJ	12	6'2"	207	Alabama		84
Toews, Jeff OG-C	79-85Mia		6'3"	255	Washington		
Toews, Loren LB	78-83Pit		6'3"	221	California	4	4
Tofflemire, Joe C	89-90Sea 91XJ 92-93Sea		6'2"	274	Arizona		
Toibin, Brendan K	87Was		6'	205	Richmond		4
Tolbert, Tony DE	89-93Dal		6'6"	261	Texas-El Paso		
Toler, Ken WR	81-82NE 84-85USFL		6'2"	193	Mississippi		12
Toles, Alvin LB	85-88NO		6'1"	223	Tennessee		6
Tolle, Stuart NT	87Det		6'3"	245	Bowling Green		
Tolliver, Billy Joe QB	89-90SD 91-93Atl	12	6'1"	218	Texas Tech		
Tomberlin, Pat OT-OG	90Ind 91LJ 93TB		6'2"	312	Florida State		
Tomczak, Mike QB	85-90Chi 91GB 92Cle 93Pit	12	6'1"	196	Ohio State		42

UseName(Nickname)-Positions	Team by Year	See Section	Hgt	Wgt	College	Int	Pts
Toner, Ed FB	92-93Ind		6'	240	Boston College		
Toney, Anthony FB-HB	86-90Phi	2	6'	227	Texas A&M		114
Tongue, Marco DB	83Bal 84Buf		5'9"	177	Bowie State		
Toon, Al WR	85-92NYJ	2	6'4"	205	Wisconsin		186
Toran, Stacey DB	84-88Raid		6'2"	200	Notre Dame	6	12
	Died in automobile accident — 1989						
Torretta, Gino QB	93Min		6'2"	215	Miami (Fla.)		
Toth, Tom OG-OT	86-89Mia 90SD		6'5"	279	Western Michigan		
Totten, Willie QB	87Buf	1	6'2"	195	Miss. Valley St.		
Toussaint, Darrel DB	87NO		6'	175	Northwestern La.		
Tovar, Steve LB	93Cin		6'3"	244	Ohio State		
Towns, Morris OT-OG	77-83Hou 84Was		6'4"	270	Missouri		
Townsell, JoJo WR	83-85USFL 85-90NYJ	23	5'9"	180	U.C.L.A.		42
Townsend, Andre DE-NT	84-90Den		6'3"	265	Mississippi		6
Townsend, Brian LB	92Cin		6'3"	242	Michigan		
Townsend, Greg DE-NT-LB	83-93Raid		6'3"	262	Texas Christian	3	32
Trahan, John WR	87KC		5'9"	160	Southern Colorado		
Traylor, Keith LB	91-92Den 93GB		6'2"	260	Oklahoma,		
					Central St.-Okla.		
Trapilo, Steve OG	87-90NO 91KJ 92NO		6'5"	290	Boston College		
Trapp, James DB	93Raid		6'	180	Clemson	1	
Travis, Mack NT	93Det		6'1"	280	California		
Traynowicz, Mark OG-C	85-88Buf 88-89Phx		6'5"	277	Nebraska		
Treadwell, David K	89-92Den 93NYG	5	6'1"	175	Clemson		532
Treggs, Brian WR	92Sea		5'9"	161	California		
Trimble, Steve DB	81-83Den 84-85USFL 87Chi		5'10"	183	Maryland		
Tripoli, Paul DB	87TB		6'	197	Alabama	3	6
Trocano, Rick QB-DB	81-83Cle		6'	188	Pittsburgh		
Trout, David K	81Pit 83-85USFL 87Pit	5	5'6"	167	Pittsburgh		84
Trudeau, Jack QB	86-93Ind	12	6'3"	213	Illinois		18
Truitt, Dave TE	87Was		6'4"	232	North Carolina		
Truitt, Olanda WR	93Min		6'	186	Mississippi State		
Truvillion, Eric WR	83-85USFL 87Det	2	6'4"	205	Florida A&M		6
Tuaolo, Esera NT	91-92GB 92-93Min		6'2"	284	Oregon State	1	
Tuatagaloa, Natu NT-DE-LB	89-91Cin 92-93Sea		6'4"	274	California	1	
Tucker, Errol DB	88-89Buf 89NE	3	5'8"	170	Utah		
Tucker, Travis TE	85-86Cle		6'3"	234	Southern Conn. St		
Tuggle, Anthony DB	87Pit		6'1"	211	Southern U.,		
					Nicholls State		
Tuggle, Jessie LB	87-93Atl		5'11"	226	Valdosta State	2	24
Tuggle, John FB	83NYG 84KJ		6'1"	210	California		6
Tuiasosopo, Manu NT-DT-DE	79-83Sea 84-86SF		6'3"	255	U.C.L.A.	1	
Tuiasosopo, Navy C	87LA		6'2"	285	Utah State		
Tuinei, Mark OT-C-DT	83-93Dal		6'5"	291	U.C.L.A., Hawaii		
Tuinei, Tom DT	80Det		6'4"	250	Hawaii		
Tuipulotu, Peter HB-FB	92SD		5'11"	210	Brigham Young		
Tullis, Willie DB	81-84Hou 85-86NO 87-88Ind	3	6'	193	Southern Miss.,	18	6
					Troy State		
Tupa, Tom QB-K	88-91Phx 92Ind	12	6'4"	220	Ohio State		6
Tupper, Jeff DE	86Phi 87Den		6'5"	269	Oklahoma		
Turk, Dan C-OG	86Pit 87-88TB 89-93Raid		6'4"	286	Drake, Wisconsin		
Turnbull, Renaldo DE	90-93NO		6'4"	252	West Virginia	1	
Turner, Bill DE	87NE		6'4"	245	Boston College		
Turner, Daryl WR	84-87Sea	2	6'3"	194	Michigan State		216
Turner, Dwain NT	87Hou		6'	290	Rice		
Turner, Eric DB	91-93Cle		6'1"	207	U.C.L.A.	8	6
Turner, Floyd WR	89-93NO	2	5'11"	188	Northwestern La.		84
Turner, Jimmie LB	84Dal		6'2"	220	Presbyterian		
Turner, Jimmy DB	83-86Cin 86-87Atl		6'	187	U.C.L.A.	2	
Turner, John DB	78-83Min 84SD 85,87Min		6'	197	Miami (Fla.)	24	6
Turner, J.T. OG-DT	77-83NYG 84Was 85USFL		6'3"	253	Duke		
Turner, Keena LB	80-90SF		6'2"	221	Purdue	11	8
Turner, Kevin LB	80NYG 81Was 81Sea 82Cle 84-85USFL		6'2"	225	U. of Pacific		
Turner, Kevin FB	92-93NE	2	6'	224	Alabama		24
Turner, Maurice HB-FB	84-85Min 85GB 87NYJ		5'11"	202	Utah State		
Turner, Mike OG	87Min		6'3"	255	Louisiana State		
Turner, Marcus DB	89-91Phx 92-93NYJ		6'	190	U.C.L.A.	3	12
Turner, Nate FB	93Buf		6'1"	255	Nebraska		
Turner, Odessa WR	87-91NYG 92-93SF	2	6'3"	205	Northwestern La		48
Turner, Richard NT	81-83GB		6'2"	260	Oklahoma		
Turner, Ricky QB	88Ind		6'	190	Washington State		6
Turner, T.J. DE-NT	86-92Mia		6'4"	276	Houston		
Turner, Vernon WR	90Buf 91-92LA 93Det 93TB	3	5'8"	185	Carson-Newman		6
Turnure, Tom C-OG	80-83Det 84USFL 85-86Det		6'4"	250	Washington		
Turpin, Miles LB	86GB 87TB		6'4"	232	California		
Turrall, Willie HB	87Phi		5'10"	190	New Mexico		
Tuten, Rick K	89Phi 90Buf 91-93Sea	4	6'2"	220	Miami (Fla.),		
					Florida State		
Tutson, Tom DB	83Atl		6'1"	180	S. Carolina State		
Tuttle, Perry WR	82-83Buf 84TB 84Atl	2	6'	178	Clemson		18
Tweet, Rodney WR	87Cin		6'1"	195	South Dakota		
Twombly, Darren C	87NE		6'4"	270	Boston College		
Tyler, Andre WR	83TB		6'	180	Stanford		
Tyler, Robert TE	89Sea	2	6'5"	257	S. Carolina State		
Tyler, Toussaint FB	81-82NO 84USFL	2	6'2"	220	Washington		
Tyler, Wendell HB	77-82LA 83-86SF	23	5'10"	197	U.C.L.A.		396
Tyrrell, Tim HB-FB	84-86Atl 86-88LA 89Pit		6'1"	204	Northern Illinois		
Uecker, Keith OT-OG	82-83Den 84-85GB 86KJ 87-88GB		6'5"	276	Auburn		
	89KJ 90-91GB						
Uhlenhake, Jeff C	89-93Mia		6'3"	282	Ohio State		
Ulmer, Mike DB	80Chi 81CFL 84-85USFL 87Phi		6'	196	Doane		
Umphrey, Rich C-OG	82-84NYG 85SD		6'3"	263	Utah, Colorado		
Unrein, Terry NT-DE	86-87SD		6'5"	281	Colorado State		
Urch, Scott OG	87NYG		6'2"	270	Virginia		
Usher, Darryl WR	89SD 89Phx	3	5'8"	170	Illinois		
Utley, Mike OG-OT	89-91Det		6'6"	288	Washington State		
	November 1991 — Paralyzed in game						
Utt, Ben OG	82-83Bal 84-88Ind		6'5"	275	Georgia Tech		
Valentine, Ira HB	87Hou		6'	212	Marshall (Tex.)		
Valentine, Zack LB	79-81Pit 82Phi 83KJ		6'2"	222	East Carolina		
Valerio, Joe OT-OG	92-93KC		6'5"	293	Pennsylvania		6
Vanderbeek, Matt LB-DE	90-92Ind 93Dal		6'3"	254	Michigan State		
Vander Poel, Mark OT	91-92Ind 93TJ		6'7"	303	Colorado		
Van Divier, Randy OT-OG	81Bal 82Raid 84-85USFL		6'5"	274	Washington		
Van Dyke, Ralph OT	87Cle		6'6"	273	Southern Illinois		
Van Horne, Keith OT	81-93Chi		6'6"	281	Southern Calif.		
Van Horse, Sean DB	92-93SD		5'10"	180	Howard	3	
Van Raaphorst, Jeff QB	87Atl	1	6'1"	210	Arizona State		
Vann, Norwood LB	84-87LA 88Raid		6'1"	228	East Carolina		
Varajon, Mike FB	87SF		6'1"	232	Toledo		
Vardell, Tommy FB	92-93Cle	2	6'2"	238	Stanford		24

UseName(Nickname)-Positions	Team by Year	See Section	Hgt	Wgt	College	Int	Pts
Vatterott, Charles OG-OT	87StL		6'4"	263	SW Texas State		
Vaughn, Clarence DB	87-91Was 92KJ		6'	202	Northern Illinois		
Vaughn, Jon HB	91-92NE 93Sea	23	5'9"	203	Michigan		30
Vaughn, Ruben DT-NT-DE	79SF 82Raid 84Min 85USFL		6'2"	261	Colorado		
Veals, Elton FB	84Pit	2	5'11"	230	Tulane		
Veasey, Craig DE-NT	90-91Pit 92-93Hou 93Mia		6'2"	283	Houston		
Veingrad, Alan OT-OG	86-87GB 88PJ 89-90GB 91-92Dal		6'5"	277	East Texas State		
Venturi, Rick	HC91Ind				Northwestern		
Venuto, Jay QB	81Bal 83USFL		6'1"	195	Wake Forest		
Verdin, Clarence WR	86-87Was 88-93Ind	23	5'8"	162	Southwestern La.		72
Verhulst, Chris TE	88-89Hou 90Den		6'2"	249	Chico State		
Veris, Garin DE	85-88NE 89KJ 90-91NE 92SF		6'4"	255	Stanford		
Verser, David WR	81-84Cin 85TB 87Cle	23	6'1"	200	Kansas		18
Viaene, David OT	89-90NE 91KJ 92GB		6'5"	300	Wis.-Platteville,		
					Minnesota-Duluth		
Vick, Roger FB	87-89NYJ 90Phi	2	6'3"	239	Texas A&M		72
Vigorito, Tommy HB-WR	81-83Mia 84KJ 85Mia	23	5'10"	193	Virginia		36
Villa, Danny OT-C-OG	87-91NE 92Phx 93KC		6'5"	305	Arizona State		
Villanucci, Vince NT	87GB		6'2"	265	Bowling Green		
Vincent, Shawn DB	91Pit		5'10"	180	Akron	2	
Vincent, Troy DB	92-93Mia		6'	191	Wisconsin	4	
Vinson, Fernandus DB	91-93Cin		5'10"	197	N. Carolina State		6
Virkus, Scott DE	83-84Buf 84NE 84-85Ind		6'5"	260	Purdue		
Visger, George DT	80SF 81KJ		6'4"	250	Colorado		
Vital, Lionel HB	87Was	2	5'9"	195	Nicholls State		12
Vitiello, Sandro K	80Cin 83-84USFL		6'2"	197	Massachusetts		1
Vlasic, Mark QB	87-88SD 89KJ 90SD 91-92KC 93TB	1	6'3"	205	Iowa		
Vogel, Paul LB	87Hou		6'1"	220	South Carolina		
Vogler, Tim C-OG	79-88Buf 89KJ		6'3"	259	Ohio State		
von Schamann, Uwe K	79-84Mia	5	6'	190	Oklahoma		540
Waddle, Tom WR	89-93Chi	2	6'	181	Boston College		48
Waddy, Billy WR	77-82LA 84Min	23	5'11"	187	Colorado		60
Waddy, Ray DB	79-80Was 81LJ 84USFL		5'11"	175	Texas A&I	1	
Waechter, Henry DE-DT	82Chi 83Bal 84Ind 84-86Chi		6'5"	271	Nebraska		2
	87Was						
Wagner, Barry WR	92Chi		6'3"	213	Alabama A&M		
Wagner, Bryan K	87-88Chi 89-90Cle 91NE 92-93GB	4	6'2"	198	Cal. Lutheran,		
					Northridge State		
Wagner, Ray OT	82Cin 84-85USFL		6'3"	290	Kent State		
Wagoner, Dan DB	82-84Det 84Min 85Atl 86KJ		5'10"	180	Kansas		
Wahler, Jim DT-NT	89-91Phx 92-93Was		6'4"	272	U.C.L.A.	1	
Wainright, Frank TE	91-93NO	2	6'3"	236	Northern Colorado		
Waiters, Van LB	88-91Cle 92Min		6'4"	243	Indiana	1	6
Waits, Alex K	91Sea		6'2"	208	Texas		
Walczak, Mark TE	87Buf 87Ind 88Phx 89,91SD		6'6"	246	Arizona		
Waldemore, Stan OG-C-OT	78-84NYJ 85-86KJ		6'4"	263	Nebraska		
Walen, Mark DT-DE	87-88Dal 89KJ		6'5"	266	U.C.L.A.		
Walker, Adam FB	87Min		5'11"	220	Carthage		
Walker, Adam HB-FB	92-93SF		6'1"	210	Pittsburgh		
Walker, Byron WR	82-86Sea	2	6'4"	190	The Citadel		48
Walker, Darnell DB	93Atl		5'8"	164	Oklahoma		
Walker, Derrick TE-FB	90-93SD	2	6'1"	244	Michigan		12
Walker, Dwight HB-WR	82-84Cle 87NO	23	5'10"	186	Nicholls State		6
Walker, Fulton DB	81-85Mia 85-86Raid	3	5'10"	195	West Virginia	5	12
Walker, Gary OG	87Dal		6'3"	283	Boston U.		
Walker, Herschel HB-FB	83-85USFL 86-89Dal 89-91Min	23	6'1"	225	Georgia		432
	92-93Phi						
Walker, Jackie LB-TE	86-89TB		6'5"	250	Jackson State		
Walker, James LB	83KC		6'1"	250	Kansas State		
Walker, Jeff OT-OG	86SD 87KJ 88-89NO 90KJ		6'4"	295	Memphis State		
Walker, Jimmy DT	87Min		6'2"	265	Arkansas		
Walker, John DE-DT	87KC		6'6"	270	Nebraska-Omaha		
Walker, Kenny LB-DE	91-92Den		6'3"	260	Nebraska		
Walker, Kevin DB	86-87TB		5'11"	180	East Carolina		
Walker, Kevin LB	88-92Cin		6'2"	238	Maryland		
Walker, Quentin FB	84StL 87LJ		6'1"	205	Virginia		
Walker, Rick TE	77-79Cin 80-85Was	2	6'3"	236	U.C.L.A.		54
Walker, Sammy DB	91-92Pit 93GB		5'11"	197	Texas Tech		
Walker, Tim LB	80Sea		6'1"	230	Savannah State		
Walker, Tony LB	90-91Ind		6'3"	235	SE Missouri St.		
Walker, Wayne (Bug) WR	89SD 90KJ	2	5'8"	162	Texas Tech		6
Walker, Wesley WR	77-89NYJ	2	6'	178	California		428
Wallace, Aaron LB	90-93Raid		6'3"	236	Texas A&M		
Wallace, Calvin DE	87GB		6'3"	230	West Virginia Tech		
Wallace, Ray FB	86-87Hou 88NJ 89Pit	2	6'	224	Purdue		36
Wallace, Steve OT-OG	86-93SF		6'5"	276	Auburn		
Wallerstedt, Brett LB	93Phx		6'1"	240	Arizona State		
Walls, Craig LB	87Buf		6'1"	215	Indiana		
Walls, Everson DB	81-89Dal 90-92NYG 92-93Cle		6'1"	194	Grambling	57	6
Walls, Henry LB	87NYJ		6'2"	220	Clemson		
Walls, Herkie WR	83-85Hou 87TB	23	5'8"	159	Texas		12
Walls, Wesley TE	89-91SF 92SJ 93SF	2	6'5"	246	Mississippi		6
Walsh, Bill	HC79-88SF				San Jose State		
Walsh, Chris WR	92-93Buf		6'1"	185	Stanford		
Walsh, Jim FB	80Sea		5'11"	220	San Jose State		
Walsh, Steve QB	89-90Dal 90-93NO	12	6'2"	200	Miami (Fla.)		
Walter, Dave QB	87Cin		6'3"	230	Michigan Tech		
Walter, Joe OT-OG	85-93Cin		6'6"	290	Texas Tech		
Walter, Michael LB	83Dal 84-93SF		6'3"	240	Oregon	2	
Walters, Dale K	87Cle		6'	200	Rice		
Walters, Danny DB	83-87SD		6'1"	189	Arkansas	12	
Walters, Joey WR	87Hou		5'11"	175	Clemson		
Walters, Pete OG	87Phi		6'2"	265	Western Kentucky		
Walterscheid, Len DB	77-82Chi 83-84Buf	3	5'11"	189	Southern Utah	7	6
Walton, Alvin DB	86-91Was		6'	180	Kansas	12	12
Walton, Riley TE	87KC		6'4"	245	Tennessee State		
Walton, Whip LB	80NYG		6'2"	225	San Diego State		
Wannstedt, Dave	HC93Chi				Pittsburgh		
Ward, Chris OT	78-83NYJ 84NO		6'3"	269	Ohio State		
Ward, David LB	87Cin 88SJ 89NE		6'2"	231	Southern Arkansas		
Ware, Andre QB	90-93Det	12	6'2"	205	Houston		
Ware, Derek TE	92-93Phx		6'2"	255	Central St.-Iowa		
Ware, Timmie WR	86-87SD 89Raid		5'10"	171	Southern Calif.		
Warne, Jim OT	87Det		6'7"	315	Arizona State		
Warner, Curt HB	83-89Sea 90LA	2	5'11"	205	Penn State		378
Warnke, David K	83TB	5	5'11"	185	Augsburg		1
Warren, Chris HB	90-93Sea	23	6'2"	225	Virginia, Ferrum		72
Warren, Don TE	79-92Was	2	6'4"	240	San Diego State		42

UseName(Nickname)-Positions	Team by Year	See Section	Hgt	Wgt	College	Int	Pts
Warren, Frank DE	81-89NO 90SL 91-93NO		6'4"	285	Auburn	1	14
Warren, John K	83-84Dal	4	6'	207	Tennessee		
Warren, Terrence WR	93Sea		6'1"	200	Hampton U.		
Warren, Vince WR	86NYG		6'	180	San Diego State		
Warren, Xavier DE	87Pit		6'1"	250	Tulsa		
Watters, Scott LB	87Buf		6'2"	230	Wittenberg		
Washington, Al LB	81NYJ		6'3"	235	Ohio State		
Washington, Anthony DB	81-82Pit 83-84Was		6'1"	204	California, Fresno State	8	
Washington, Brian DB	88Cle 90VR 90-93NYJ		6'	210	Nebraska	19	18
Washington, Charles DB	89Ind 90-91KC 92-93Atl		6'1"	208	Texas, Cameron	1	
Washington, Chris LB	84-88TB 89BL 90Phx		6'4"	231	Iowa State	1	
Washington, Chuck DB	87GB		5'11"	186	Arkansas		
Washington, Fred DT	90Chi		6'2"	277	Texas Christian		
Dec. 21, 1990 — Died in automobile accident							
Washington, James DB	88-89LA 90-93Dal		6'1"	196	U.C.L.A.	10	
Washington, Joe HB	77SD 78-80Bal 81-84Was 85Atl	2	5'10"	180	Oklahoma		186
Washington, John DE-NT	86-92NYG 92Atl 93NE		6'4"	280	Oklahoma State		
Washington, Lionel DB	83-86StL 87-93Raid		6'	186	Tulane	30	18
Washington, Marvin DE-DT	90-93NYJ		6'6"	270	Texas-El Paso, Idaho		2
Washington, Mickey DB	90-91NE 92Was 93Buf		5'9"	187	Texas A&M	3	6
Washington, Mike DB	76-84TB		6'3"	197	Alabama	28	24
Washington, Robert OT	87Pit		6'4"	251	Alcorn State		
Washington, Ronnie LB	85Atl 87Raid 89Ind		6'1"	244	Northeast La.		
Washington, Sam DB	82-85Pit 85Cin		5'8"	180	Miss. Valley St.	7	12
Washington, Ted NT-DE-DT	91-93SF		6'4"	299	Louisville		
Washington, Tim DB	82SF		5'9"	184	California, Fresno State		
Waters, Andre DB	84-93Phi		5'11"	189	Cheyney State	15	12
Waters, Mike FB-TE	86Phi 87NO 88XJ		6'2"	228	San Diego State		6
Watkins, Bobby DB	82-88Det		5'10"	184	SW Texas State	20	
Watson, Louis WR	87Cle		5'11"	175	Miss. Valley St.		
Watson, Remi WR	87Cle		6'	174	Bethune-Cookman		
Watson, Steve WR	79-87Den 88ZJ	2	6'4"	195	Temple		216
Watson, Tim DB	93KC		6'1"	213	Howard		
Wattelet, Frank DB	81-87NO 87-88LA		6'	186	Kansas	12	12
Watters, Ricky HB	91FJ 92-93SF	2	6'1"	212	Notre Dame		132
Watts, Elbert DB	86GB 87KJ		6'1"	205	Oklahoma, Southern Calif.	1	
Watts, Randy DE-DT	87Dal		6'6"	275	East Carolina, Catawba		
Watts, Rickey WR	79-83Chi 84JJ	2	6'1"	205	Tulsa		54
Watts, Ted DB	81Oak 82-84Raid 85NYG 87SD	3	6'	193	Texas Tech	5	6
Waymer, Dave DB	80-89NO 90-91SF 92Raid		6'1"	191	Notre Dame	48	6
Weathers, Clarence WR	83-84NE 85-88Cle 89Ind 89KC 90-91GB	23	5'9"	170	Delaware State		102
Weathers, Curtis LB-TE	79-85Cle 86KJ		6'5"	224	Mississippi	1	
Weathers, Robert FB	82-84NE	2	6'2"	220	Arizona State		24
Weatherspoon, Chuck FB	91TB		5'7"	230	Houston		
Weaver, Emanuel DT	82Cin 83KJ 85USFL 87Atl		6'4"	262	South Carolina		
Webb, Chuck FB	91GB		5'9"	201	Tennessee		
Webb, Richmond OT	90-93Mia		6'6"	298	Texas A&M		
Webster, Elnardo LB	92Pit		6'2"	243	Rutgers		
Webster, Kevin C	87Min		6'2"	260	Northern Iowa		
Webster, Larry DE	92-93Mia		6'5"	289	Maryland		
Webster, Mike C-OG	74-88Pit 89-90KC		6'1"	252	Wisconsin		
Weddington, Mike LB	86-90GB		6'4"	245	Oklahoma		
Weigel, Lee FB	87GB		5'11"	220	Wis.-Eau Claire		
Weidner, Bert C-OG	90-93Mia		6'3"	284	Kent State		
Weil, Jack K	86Den 87Was		5'11"	175	Temple		
Weishuhn, Clayton LB	82-84NE 85KJ 86NE 87GB		6'2"	220	Angelo State		6
Weissenhofer, Ron LB	87NO		6'3"	235	Notre Dame		
Welbourme, Tripp DB	92Min		6'	205	Michigan		
Welch, Herb DB	85-87NYG 88LJ 89Was 90-91Det		5'11"	180	U.C.L.A.	7	
Weldon, Casey QB	92-93TB		6'1"	200	Florida State		
Wellman, Gary WR	92Hou		5'9"	168	Southern Calif.		
Wells, Arthur TE	87TB		6'4"	235	Grambling		6
Wells, Dana NT	89Cin		6'	270	Arizona		
Wells, Dean LB	93Sea		6'3"	238	Kentucky		
Wells, Kent DT	90NYG		6'4"	295	Nebraska		
Wells, Mike TE	87SF		6'3"	233	San Diego State		6
Wells, Norm OG	80Dal 81-82KJ		6'5"	261	Northwestern		
Wellsandt, Doug TE	90NYJ		6'3"	248	Washington State		
Welter, Tom OT-OG	87StL		6'5"	280	Nebraska		
Wenglikowski, Al LB	84,87Buf		6'1"	215	Pittsburgh		
Wenzel, Jeff OT	87Phi		6'7"	270	Tulane		
Werner, Greg TE	89NYJ		6'4"	236	DePauw		
Wersching, Ray K	73-76SD 77-87SF	5	5'11"	213	California		1122
West, Ed TE	84-93GB	2	6'1"	243	Auburn		138
West, Jeff TE-K	75StL 76-79SD 81-85Sea	4	6'3"	212	Cincinnati		
West, Ronnie WR	92Min 93LJ		6'1"	215	Pittsburgh		
West, Troy DB	87Phi		6'1"	205	Southern Calif.	1	
Wester, Cleve HB	87Det	2	5'8"	188	Concordia (Minn.)		
Weston, Jeff OT-DT	79-82NYG		6'5"	259	Notre Dame		
Weston, Rhondy DE	89TB 90KJ		6'5"	275	Florida		
Wetnight, Ryan TE	93Chi		6'2"	228	Stanford		6
Wetzel, Marty LB	81NYJ		6'3"	235	Tulane		
Wetzel, Ron TE	83KC 84-85USFL		6'5"	242	Arizona State		
Wheat, Warren OG	89,91Sea		6'6"	274	Brigham Young		
Wheeler, Dwight OT-C-OG	78-83NE 84,87Raid 87SD 88Raid		6'3"	266	Tennessee State		
Wheeler, Leonard DB	92-93Cin		5'11"	189	Troy State	1	
Wheeler, Mark TE	87Det		6'2"	232	Kentucky		
Wheeler, Mark DT-NT	92-93TB		6'2"	280	Texas A&M		
Wheeler, Ron TE	87Raid		6'5"	235	Washington		
Whisenhunt, Ken TE	85-88Atl 89LJ 90Was 91-92NYJ	2	6'3"	237	Georgia Tech		30
Whitaker, Bill DB	81-82GB 83-84StL		6'	182	Missouri		
Whitaker, Danta TE-WR	90KC 92Min 93Chi	2	6'4"	248	Miss. Valley St.		6
White, Adrian DB	87-89NYG 90KJ 91NYG 92GB 93NE		6'	200	Southern Illinois, Florida	3	
White, Bob C-OG	87-89Dal 90KJ		6'5"	272	Rhode Island		
White, Brad NT-DT	81-83TB 84-85Ind 87Min		6'2"	256	Tennessee		
White, Charles HB	80-82Cle 83BN 84Cle 85-88LA	23	5'10"	188	Southern Calif.		144
White, Chris DB	87Sea		6'3"	200	Tennessee		
White, Craig WR	84Buf		6'1"	194	Missouri		
White, Danny QB	76-88Dal	12 4	6'2"	194	Arizona State		60
White, David LB	93NE		6'2"	235	Nebraska		
White, Dwayne OG	90-93NYJ		6'2"	311	Alcorn State		
White, Gerald FB	87Dal		5'11"	223	Michigan		
White, Lawrence WR	87Chi		6'2"	187	Dana		
White, Leon LB	86-91Cin 91-93LA		6'3"	240	Brigham Young	4	8
White, Lorenzo HB	88-93Hou	2	5'11"	209	Michigan State		192

UseName(Nickname)-Positions	Team by Year	See Section	Hgt	Wgt	College	Int	Pts
White, Lyman LB	81-82Atl		6'	217	Louisiana State		
White, Mike DE-DT-NT	79-80Cin 81-82Sea		6'5"	266	Albany State (Ga.)		
White, Randy DT-LB-DE	75-88Dal		6'4"	257	Maryland	1	
White, Reggie DE-DT	84-85USFL 85-92Phi 93GB		6'5"	285	Tennessee	2	12
White, Reggie DT	92-93SD		6'4"	296	N. Carolina A&T		
White, Robb DE-NT	88-89NYG 90TB		6'4"	270	South Dakota		
White, Robert DB	87Hou		6'2"	180	Lamar		
White, Russell HB	93LA		5'11"	216	California		
White, Sammy WR	76-85Min	2	5'11"	192	Grambling		300
White, Sheldon DB	88-89NYG 90-92Det 93Cin		5'11"	188	Miami-Ohio	11	6
White, William DB	88-93Det		5'10"	191	Ohio State	13	18
Whited, Mike OT	80Det		6'4"	250	U. of Pacific		
Whitfield, Bob OT	92-93Atl		6'5"	298	Stanford		
Whitehurst, David QB	77-83GB 84KC	12	6'2"	204	Furman		42
Whitley, Curtis C	92-93SD		6'1"	288	Clemson		
Whitley, Wilson DT-NT	77-82Cin		6'3"	265	Houston	1	
Whitmore, David DB	90-91NYG 92SF 93KC		6'	235	S.F. Austin State	2	
Whitten, Bobby OG	81Cin		6'3"	265	Kansas		
Whitten, Todd QB	87NE		6'	185	S.F. Austin State		
Whittington, Art HB	78-81Oak 82Buf 83-84USFL	23	5'11"	182	S.M.U.		96
Whittingham, Cary LB	87LA		6'2"	230	Brigham Young		
Whittingham, Kyle LB	87LA		6'	232	Brigham Young		
Whittington, Mike LB	80-83NYG 84-85USFL		6'2"	220	Notre Dame		
Whitwell, Mike WR-DB	82-83Cle 84KJ		6'	175	Texas A&M	3	
Wichard, Murray NT-DE	87NE		6'2"	260	Frostburg State		
Widell, Dave OT-OG	88-89Dal 90-93Den		6'6"	296	Boston College		
Widell, Doug OG	89-92Den 93GB		6'4"	287	Boston College		
Widmer, Corey DT	92-93NYG		6'3"	276	Montana State		
Wiegand, Eric C	87Atl		6'2"	260	Missouri-Rolla		
Wilburn, Barry DB	86-89Was 92Cle		6'3"	186	Mississippi	18	6
Wilburn, Steve DE	87NE		6'4"	266	Illinois State		
Wilcher, Mike LB	83-90LA 91SD		6'3"	238	North Carolina	4	6
Wilcots, Solomon DB	87-90Cin 91Min 92Pit		5'11"	189	Colorado	2	
Wilder, James FB-HB	81-89TB 90Was 90Det	2	6'3"	224	Missouri		282
Wiley, Charles NT	87Sea		6'2"	268	Nevada-Las Vegas		
Wilhelm, Erik QB	89-91,93Cin	1	6'3"	213	Oregon State		
Wilkerson, Bruce OG-OT	87-93Raid		6'5"	289	Tennessee		
Wilkerson, Daryl DE	81Bal 83-85USFL		6'4"	255	Houston		
Wilkerson, Eric HB-WR	89Pit		5'9"	185	Kent State		
Wilkes, Reggie LB	78-85Phi 86-87Atl		6'4"	235	Georgia Tech	8	1
Wilkins, David LB	92SF		6'4"	240	Eastern Kentucky		
Wilkins, Gary FB-TE	86-87Buf 88-91Atl	2	6'1"	235	Georgia Tech		36
Wilkinson, Jerry DE	79LA 80Cle 80SF 83USFL		6'9"	248	Oregon State		
Wilks, Jim DE-NT	81-93NO		6'5"	269	California, San Diego State		
Willhite, Gerald FB-HB	82-88Den	23	5'10"	200	San Jose State		138
Willhite, Kevin HB	87GB	2	5'11"	208	Oregon		
Williams, Aeneas DB	91-93Phx		5'10"	187	Southern	11	12
Williams, Al WR	87SD	2	5'10"	180	Nevada-Reno		6
Williams, Albert LB	87Pit		6'3"	229	Texas-El Paso		
Williams, Alfred LB	91-93Cin		6'6"	240	Colorado		2
Williams, Alonzo HB	87LA		5'9"	190	Mesa		
Williams, Ben DE-NT	76-85Buf		6'3"	251	Mississippi	2	2
Williams, Brent DE-NT	86-93NE		6'3"	278	Toledo		12
Williams, Brian TE	82NE 84-85USFL		6'5"	240	Southern U.		
Williams, Brian OG-C	89-93NYG		6'5"	300	Minnesota		
Williams, Brooks TE	78-81NO 81-82Chi 83NE	2	6'4"	226	North Carolina		12
Williams, Byron WR	83-85NYG	2	6'2"	182	Texas-Arlington		72
Williams, Calvin WR	90-93Phi	2	5'11"	181	Purdue		174
Williams, Chris DB	82-83Buf		6'	197	Louisiana Tech	3	
Williams, Chris NT	91Phx		6'3"	304	American Inter.		
Williams, Clarence HB-FB	93Cle		6'2"	240	Washington State		
Williams, Dan DE	93Den		6'4"	290	Toledo		
Williams, Darryl DB	92-93Cin		6'	191	Miami (Fla.)	6	6
Williams, David WR	86TB 87Raid		6'3"	190	Illinois		
Williams, David OT	89-93Hou		6'5"	292	Florida		
Williams, Demise DB	87Raid		6'1"	225	Oklahoma		
Williams, Derwin WR	85-87NE	2	6'1"	180	New Mexico		
Williams, Dokie WR	83-87Raid	23	5'11"	180	U.C.L.A.		150
Williams, Doug QB	78-82TB 84-85USFL 86-89Was	12	6'4"	218	Grambling		90
Williams, Doug OT-OG	86-87Hou 88LJ		6'5"	286	Texas A&M		
Williams, Ed LB	84-87NE 88-89KJ 90NE		6'4"	244	Texas	1	
Williams, Eric LB	77-81StL 82-83LA 84SD 85USFL		6'2"	227	Southern Calif.	5	
Williams, Eric T. DB	83-86Pit 87Det		6'1"	188	N. Carolina State	10	
Williams, Eric DT-NT-DT	84-89Det 90-93Was		6'4"	282	Washington State		
Williams, Erik OT	91-93Dal		6'6"	321	Central St.-Ohio		
Williams, Eugene LB	82-83Sea		6'1"	220	Texas	1	
Williams, Gardner DB	84Det		6'2"	199	St. Mary's		
Williams, Gary WR	84Cin		6'2"	215	Ohio State		
Williams, Gene OG-OT	91-92Mia 93Cle		6'2"	308	Iowa State		
Williams, Gerald NT-DE-DT	86-93Pit		6'3"	281	Auburn		
Williams, Greg DB	82-85Was		5'11"	185	Mississippi State	2	
Williams, Harvey HB	91-93KC	23	6'2"	226	Louisiana State		24
Williams, Henry (Gizmo) WR	89Phi	3	5'6"	185	East Carolina		
Williams, Henry DB	79Oak 81CFL 83LA 83SD 85USFL		5'10"	180	San Diego State	3	
Williams, Herb DB	80SF 81-82StL 84USFL		6'	199	Southern U.		
Williams, James FB	87Sea		5'10"	210	Fresno State		
Williams, James LB	90-93NO		6'	230	Mississippi State		
Williams, James (J.D.) DB	90-93Buf		5'10"	174	Fresno State	7	6
Williams, James (Big Cat) DE-OT	91-93Chi		6'7"	315	Cheyney		
Williams, Jamie TE	83StL 84TB 84-88Hou 89-93SF	2	6'4"	241	Nebraska		66
Williams, Jarvis DB	88-93Mia		5'11"	196	Florida	14	6
Williams, Jerrol LB	89-92Pit 93SD		6'5"	240	Purdue	1	6
Williams, Jimmy LB	82-90Det 90-91Min 92-93TB		6'3"	228	Nebraska	11	6
Williams, Joe LB	87Pit		6'4"	237	Grambling		
Williams, Joel LB	79-82Atl 83-85Phi 86-89Atl		6'1"	222	Wis.-La Crosse	5	20
Williams, Joel TE	87Mia		6'3"	242	Notre Dame		
Williams, John FB	83-85USFL 85Dal 85Sea 86NO 87Ind		5'11"	213	Wisconsin		
Williams, John L. FB	86-93Sea	2	5'11"	228	Florida		198
Williams, Jonathan HB	84NE 85KJ		5'9"	205	Penn State		
Williams, Keith WR-HB	86Atl 87KJ		5'10"	173	SW Missouri St.		6
Williams, Kendall DB	83Bal		5'9"	189	Arizona State	1	
Williams, Kevin WR	81Bal 83-85USFL		5'8"	164	Southern Calif.		
Williams, Kevin DB	85Was 86Buf 88Was		5'9"	170	Iowa State		
Williams, Kevin WR	93Dal	23	5'9"	192	Miami (Fla.)		36
Williams, Larry OG-C	86-88Cle 89SJ 91NO 92NE		6'5"	290	Notre Dame		
Williams, Lee DE-DT	84USFL 84-90SD 91-93Hou		6'6"	269	Bethune-Cookman	1	2

UseName(Nickname)-Positions	Team by Year	See Section	Hgt	Wgt	College	Int	Pts
Williams, Leonard HB	87Buf		6'	205	Western Carolina		
Williams, Lester NT-DE	82-85NE 86SD 87Sea		6'3"	275	Miami (Fla.)		
Williams, Marvin TE	87Was		6'3"	235	Fullerton State		
Williams, Michael FB	83-84Phi 87Atl	2	6'2"	220	Mississippi Coll.		
Williams, Mike FB-TE	79-81KC	2	6'3"	222	New Mexico		24
Williams, Mike TE	82-84Was		6'4"	249	Alabama A&M		
Williams, Mike WR	89Det 91-93Mia	3	5'10"	177	Northeastern		
Williams, Newton HB-FB	82SF 83Bal		5'10"	204	Arizona State		
Williams, Oliver WR	83-85USFL 85Ind 87Hou	2	6'3"	194	Illinois		12
Williams, Perry DB	87NE		6'1"	200	Clemson	1	
Williams, Perry DB	84-93NYG		6'2"	203	N. Carolina State	18	
Williams, Ray WR	80Det 81KJ	23	5'9"	170	Washington State		18
Williams, Ray DB	87Pit		5'11"	180	Rhode Island	1	
Williams, Ralph OT-OG	82-83Hou 84-85USFL 85-86NO		6'3"	280	Southern U.		
Williams, Reggie LB	76-89Cin		6'1"	228	Dartmouth	16	24
Williams, Richard HB	84Atl		6'	205	Memphis State		
Williams, Ricky DB	85,87Raid		6'1"	195	Langston		
Williams, Robert DB	84Pit		5'11"	202	Eastern Illinois		
Williams, Robert DB	87-92Dal		5'10"	188	Baylor	4	12
Williams, Ronnie TE	91Mia		6'3"	259	Oklahoma State		
Williams, Scott FB	86-88Det	2	6'2"	234	Georgia		24
Williams, Terry DB	88-89NYJ 90KJ		5'11"	197	Bethune-Cookman		
Williams, Toby DE-NT	83-88NE		6'3"	264	Nebraska		
Williams, Tyrone WR	93Dal		6'5"	220	Western Ontario		
Williams, Van HB	83-85Buf 87NYG	23	6'	210	East Tennessee St., Carson-Newman		6
Williams, Vaughn DB	84Ind		6'2"	193	Stanford		
Williams, Vince FB	82-83SF 85USFL	2	6'	231	Oregon		
Williams, Wally C	93Cle		6'2"	300	Florida A&M		
Williams, Walt DB	77-80Det 81-82Min 82-83Chi		6'	185	Ashland, New Mexico State	4	2
Williams, Warren HB	88-92Pit 93Ind	2	6'	209	Miami (Fla.)		60
Williams, Willie OT	91Phx 92KJ		6'6"	300	Louisiana State		6
Williams, Willie DB	93Pit		5'9"	188	Western Carolina		
Williamson, Carlton DB	81-87SF 88KJ		6'	204	Pittsburgh	17	6
Williamson, Greg DB	87LA		5'11"	185	Fresno State	1	
Williamson, Richard	HC90-91TB				Alabama		
Willig, Matt OT	93NYJ		6'8"	305	Southern Calif.		
Willis, Chester HB	81Oak 82-84Raid	2	5'11"	196	Auburn		6
Willis, James LB	93GB		6'2"	235	Auburn		
Willis, Keith DE-NT-DT	82-87Pit 88ZJ 89-91Pit 92Buf 93Was 93NYJ		6'1"	260	Northwestern	1	
Willis, Ken K	90-91Dal 92TB 92NYG	5	5'11"	189	Kentucky		255
Willis, Mitch NT	85-88Raid 88Atl 90Dal		6'8"	278	S.M.U.		
Willis, Peter Tom QB	90-92Chi	1	6'2"	188	Florida State		
Wills, Ladell LB	87NYJ		6'3"	240	Jackson State		
Wilmer, Ray DB	84Sea		6'2"	190	Colorado		
Wilmsmeyer, Klaus K	92-93SF	4	6'1"	210	Louisville		
Wilson, Bobby DT	91-93Was		6'2"	289	Michigan State		
Wilson, Bernard DT	93TB		6'2"	295	Tennessee State		
Wilson, Brenard DB	79-87Phi 87Atl		6'	178	Vanderbilt	17	
Wilson, Brett FB	87Min		6'	220	Illinois		
Wilson, Charles WR	90-91GB 92-93TB	23	5'9"	174	Memphis State		12
Wilson, Darrell DB	81NE		5'11"	180	Connecticut		
Wilson, Darryal WR	83NE 84KJ		6'	182	Tennessee		
Wilson, Dave QB	81NO 82KJ 83-89NO	12	6'3"	206	Illinois		12
Wilson, David DB	92NE 92Min		5'10"	192	California		
Wilson, Don DB	84-85Buf	3	6'2"	190	N. Carolina State	2	6
Wilson, Earl DE	85-87SD		6'4"	276	Kentucky		
Wilson, Eric LB	85Buf 87Was		6'1"	246	Maryland		
Wilson, Frank TE-FB	82Pit		6'2"	233	Rice		
Wilson, J.C. DB	78-83Hou		6'	178	Tampa, Pittsburgh	11	6
Wilson, Karl DE-LB	87-88SD 89Phx 90Mia 91LA 92-93NYJ 93Mia 93SF		6'4"	273	Louisiana State		2
Wilson, Marc QB	80-81Oak 82-87Raid 89-90NE	12	6'6"	207	Brigham Young		30
Wilson, Marcus HB	91Raid 92-93GB		6'1"	200	Virginia		
Wilson, Mike OT	78-85Cin 86-89Sea		6'5"	275	Georgia		
Wilson, Mike WR-HB	81-90SF	2	6'3"	213	Washington State		90
Wilson, Otis LB	80-87Chi 88KJ 89Raid		6'2"	227	Syracuse, Louisville	10	14
Wilson, Robert FB	91TB	2	6'	240	Texas A&M		12
Wilson, Stanley FB-HB	83-84,86,88Cin 85,87,89SL	2	5'10"	210	Oklahoma		78
Wilson, Steve C-OG-OT	76-85TB		6'3"	267	Georgia		
Wilson, Steve DB-WR	79-81Dal 82-88Den	3	5'10"	194	Howard	22	6
Wilson, Ted WR	87Was		5'9"	170	Central Florida		12
Wilson, Tim FB	77-82Hou 83-84NO	2	6'3"	226	Maryland		54
Wilson, Troy DB	87Cle		5'10"	170	Notre Dame	1	
Wilson, Troy DE	93SF		6'4"	235	Pittsburg State		
Wilson, Wade QB	81-91Min 91-92Atl 93NO	12	6'3"	211	East Texas State		54
Wilson, Walter WR	90SD	2	5'10"	185	East Carolina		
Wilson, Wayne FB-HB	79-85NO 86Min 86NO 87Was	23	6'3"	215	Shepherd		192
Wimberly, Derek DE	87Mia		6'4"	270	Purdue		
Wimmer, Gary LB	83Sea		6'2"	225	Stanford		
Winder, Sammy HB-FB	82-90Den	2	5'11"	203	Southern Miss.		288
Windham, David LB	87Was		6'2"	240	Jackson State		
Wingate, Leonard DE	87Atl		6'3"	265	S. Carolina State		
Wingle, Blake OG	83-85Pit 85GB 87Cle		6'2"	265	Cal. Poly.-S.L.O., U.C.L.A.		
Wingo, Rich LB	79GB 80XJ 81-84GB		6'1"	230	Alabama	4	1
Winn, Bryant LB	87Den		6'4"	231	Houston		
Winslow, George K	87Cle 89NO	4	6'4"	203	Villanova		
Winslow, Kellen TE	79-87SD	2	6'5"	250	Missouri		270
Winston, DeMond LB	90NO 91KJ 92-93NO		6'2"	239	Vanderbilt		
Winston, Dennis (Dirt) LB	77-81Pit 82-85NO 85-86Pit		6'	230	Arkansas	13	24
Winter, Blaise DE-NT	84Ind 85SJ 86-87SD 88-90GB 92-93SD		6'3"	279	Syracuse		
Winters, Chet HB	83GB		5'11"	204	Oklahoma		
Winters, Frank C-OG	87-88Cle 89NYG 90-91KC 92-93GB		6'3"	285	Western Illinois		
Wise, Mike DE-DT	86-90Raid 91Cle		6'7"	271	Cal.-Davis		
Wiska, Jeff OG	84-85USFL 86Cle 87Mia		6'3"	263	Michigan State		
Wisniewski, Leo NT	82-83Bal 84Ind 85KJ		6'1"	262	Penn State		
Wisniewski, Steve OG	89-93Raid		6'4"	285	Penn State		
Withycombe, Mike OG-OT	88-89NYJ 91Pit 91-92Cin		6'5"	295	Fresno State		
Witkowski, John QB	84Det 86-87Hou 88Det	1	6'1	201	Columbia		
Witte, Mark TE	83-85TB 87Det		6'3"	236	North Texas		
Witteck, Mike LB	87NYJ		6'2"	225	Northwestern		
Woerner, Scott DB	81Atl 83-85USFL 87NO	3	6'	190	Georgia		
Wojciechowski, John OG-OT	87-93Chi		6'4"	271	Michigan State		
Wolden, Al FB	87Chi		6'3"	232	Bemidji State		
Wolf, Joe OG-OT	89-93Phx		6'5"	288	Boston College		
Wolfley, Craig OG-OT	80-89Pit 90-91Min		6'1"	269	Syracuse		
Wolfley, Ron FB	85-87StL 88-91Phx 92-93Cle	2	6'	224	West Virginia		24

UseName(Nickname)-Positions	Team by Year	See Section	Hgt	Wgt	College	Int	Pts
Wolford, Will OT-OG	86-92Buf 93Ind		6'5"	289	Vanderbilt		
Womack, Jeff HB	87Min		5'9"	188	Memphis State		6
Wonsley, George HB-FB	84-88Ind 89NE	2	5'10"	218	Mississippi State		54
Wonsley, Nathan HB	86TB 87ZJ	2	5'10"	190	Mississippi		18
Wonsley, Otis FB-HB	81-85Was	2	5'10"	212	Alcorn State		30
Wood, Mike K	78Min 78-79StL 79-80SD 81-82Bal 83JJ	45	5'11"	199	SE Missouri St.		156
Wood, Richard (Batman) LB	75NYJ 76-84TB 85USFL		6'2"	224	Southern Calif.	9	18
Woodard, Ken LB	82-86Den 87Pit 88-89SD		6'1"	218	Tuskegee	3	12
Woodard, Ray DE	87Den 87KC		6'6"	290	Texas		
Woodberry, Dennis DB	86Atl 87-88Was		5'10"	183	Southern Arkansas	2	
Wooden, Terry LB	90-93Sea		6'3"	236	Syracuse	1	
Woodley, David QB	80-83Mia 84-85Pit	12	6'2"	204	Louisiana State		72
Woodring, John LB	81-85NYJ		6'2"	232	Brown		
Woodruff, Dwayne DB	79-85Pit 86KJ 87-90Pit		5'11"	195	Louisville	37	30
Woodruff, Tony WR	82-84Phi	2	6'	178	Fresno State		30
Woods, Carl HB	87NE		5'11"	200	Vanderbilt		6
Woods, Chris WR	84-86CFL 87-88Raid 89Den	3	5'11"	190	Auburn		
Woods, Ickey FB-HB	88-91Cin	2	6'2"	232	Nevada-Las Vegas		162
Woods, Jerry DB	89Det 90GB		5'10"	187	Northern Michigan		
Woods, Pete QB	80Mia		6'3"	214	Missouri		
Woods, Rick DB	82-86Pit 87TB	3	6'	195	Boise State	13	6
Woods, Rob OT	91Cle		6'5"	295	Eastern Washington, Cal.-Santa Barbara, Arizona		
Woods, Tony LB-DE	87-92Sea 93LA		6'4"	259	Pittsburgh		
Woods, Tony DE-DT	89Chi		6'4"	274	Oklahoma		
Woodside, Keith HB	88-91GB	2	5'11"	203	Texas A&M		48
Woodson, Darren DB	92-93Dal		6'1"	215	Arizona State		
Woodson, Rod DB	87-93Pit	3	6'	198	Purdue	27	36
Woolf, Scott QB	87Raid		6'1"	190	Mt. Union		
Woolford, Donnell DB	89-93Chi		5'9"	187	Clemson	17	
Woolfolk, Butch FB-HB	82-84NYG 85-86Hou 87-88Det	23	6'1"	210	Michigan		96
Woolford, Gary DB	80NYG		6'	182	Florida State	2	
Wooten, Mike C	87Was		6'3"	260	V.M.I.		
Wooten, Ron OG	82-88NE		6'4"	274	North Carolina		
Word, Barry FB-HB	87-88NO 90-92KC 93Min	2	6'2"	240	Virginia		96
Workman, Vince HB	89-92GB 93TB	23	5'10"	193	Ohio State		114
Worley, Tim HB	89-91Pit 92SL 93Pit 93Chi	2	6'2"	228	Georgia		42
Worthen, Naz WR	89-90KC	3	5'8"	177	N. Carolina State		
Wren, Darryl DB	93NE		6'	188	Pittsburg State	3	
Wright, Adrian FB	87TB	2	6'1"	230	Virginia Union		6
Wright, Alexander WR	90-92Dal 92-93Raid	23	6'	189	Auburn		48
Wright, Alvin NT-DE-DT	86-92LA 92Cle		6'2"	270	Jacksonville St.		
Wright, Brad QB	82Dal		6'2"	209	New Mexico		
Wright, Charles DB	87StL 88TB 88Dal		5'9"	178	Tulsa		
Wright, Dana HB	87Cin		6'1"	219	Kent State, Findlay		
Wright, Eric DB	81-90SF		6'1"	183	Missouri	18	12
Wright, Eric WR	92Chi		6'	196	S.F. Austin State		
Wright, Felix DB	85-90Cle 91-92Min		6'2"	190	Drake	28	18
Wright, James TE	78Atl 79KJ 80-85Den	2	6'3"	240	Texas Christian		24
Wright, Jeff NT	88-93Buf		6'2"	270	Tulsa, Central Missouri St.	1	
Wright, Johnnie FB	82Bal 84USFL		6'2"	210	South Carolina		
Wright, Louis DB	75-86Den		6'2"	198	Arizona State, San Jose State	26	24
Wright, Randy QB	84-88GB	12	6'2"	200	Wisconsin		18
Wright, Steve OT-OG-TE	81-82Dal 83Bal 84Ind 85USFL 87-92Raid 93KJ		6'6"	269	Northern Iowa		
Wright, Terry DB	87-88Ind		6'	195	Temple		
Wright, Willie TE	92Phx		6'4"	240	Wyoming		
Wrightman, Tim TE	83-84USFL 85-86Chi 87KJ	2	6'3"	237	U.C.L.A.		6
Wyatt, Kervin LB	80NYJ 81JJ		6'2"	235	Maryland		
Wyatt, Kevin DB	86SD 87KC		5'10"	199	Arkansas		
Wyatt, Willie NT	90TB		5'1"	275	Alabama		
Wycheck, Frank TE	93Was	2	6'3"	235	Maryland		
Wyman, David LB-DE	87-92Sea 93Den		6'2"	245	Stanford	3	6
Yakavonis, Ray NT	81-82Min 83KC		6'4"	248	East Stroudsburg		
Yarber, Eric WR	86-87Was 88KJ		5'8"	156	Idaho	3	
Yarbrough, Jim DB	87NYG		6'	195	Murray State		
Yarno, George OG-C-OT	79-83TB 84-85USFL 85-87TB 88Atl 89Hou		6'2"	261	Washington State		1
Yano, John C	77-82Sea 84Den		6'5"	251	Idaho		
Young, Almon OG	87Hou 88HJ		6'3"	290	Bethune-Cookman		
Young, Andre DB	82-84SD		6'	199	Louisiana Tech	6	6
Young, Anthony DB	85Ind 86ZJ		5'11"	187	Temple	1	6
Young, Ben TE	83Atl		6'4"	225	Texas-Arlington		6
Young, Dave TE	81NYG 83Bal 84Ind	2	6'5"	242	Purdue		18
Young, Duane TE	91-93SD	2	6'1"	266	Michigan State		12
Young, Fredd LB	84-87Sea 88-90Ind		6'1"	233	New Mexico State	3	6
Young, Glen WR	83Phi 84-85,87-88Cle	3	6'2"	205	Mississippi State		12
Young, Kevin DE	87NO		6'5"	265	Utah State		
Young, Lonnie DB	85-87StL 88-90Phx 91-93NYJ		6'1"	186	Michigan State	10	
Young, Michael WR	85-88LA 89-92Den 93Phi	2	6'1"	184	U.C.L.A.		84
Young, Mitchell DE	87Atl		6'4"	260	Arkansas State		
Young, Renard DB	87Sea		5'10"	184	Nevada-Las Vegas, San Diego State		
Young, Robert DE-DT	91-93LA		6'6"	275	Mississippi State		
Young, Roynell DB	80-88Phi		6'1"	183	Alcorn State	23	
Young, Steve QB	84-85USFL 85-86TB 87-93SF	12	6'2"	200	Brigham Young		120
Young, Theo TE	87Pit		6'2"	237	Arkansas		
Young, Tyrone WR	83-84NO	2	6'6"	190	Florida		36
Zachary, Ken FB	87SD		6'	222	Oklahoma State		
Zackery, Tony DB	89Atl 90-91NE		6'2"	195	Washington	1	
Zamberlin, John LB	79-82NE 83-84KC		6'2"	228	Pacific Lutheran	1	
Zander, Carl LB	85-91Cin		6'2"	235	Tennessee State	3	
Zandofsky, Mike OG-C	89Phx 90-93SD		6'2"	298	Washington		
Zawatson, Dave OG-OT	89Chi 90NYJ 91Mia		6'4"	275	California		
Zele, Mike NT-DT	79-83Atl		6'3"	239	Kent State		
Zeman, Ed DB	87LA		6'1"	195	Fort Lewis		
Zendejas, Joaquin K	83NE	5	5'11"	176	La Verne		3
Zendejas, Luis K	87-88Dal 88-89Phi 89Dal	5	5'9"	160	Arizona State		189
Zendejas, Max K	86Was 87-88GB	5	5'11"	184	Arizona		155
Zendejas, Tony K	84-85USFL 85-90Hou 91-93LA	5	5'8"	164	Nevada-Reno		778
Zeno, Lance C	92-93Cle 93GB		6'4"	279	U.C.L.A.		
Zentic, Mike C	87Dal		6'3"	255	Oklahoma State		
Zgonina, Jeff DT	93Pit		6'1"	284	Purdue		
Zimmerlink, Geno TE	87Atl		6'3"	222	Virginia		
Zimmerman, Gary OT	84-85USFL 86-92Min 93Den		6'6"	289	Oregon		
Zimmerman, Jeff OG	87-90Dal		6'3"	320	Florida		
Zogg, Jon OG	87Raid		6'4"	290	Boise State		

UseName(Nickname)-Positions	Team by Year	See Section	Hgt.	Wgt.	College	Int	Pts
Zolak, Scott QB	92-93NE	1	6'5"	222	Maryland		
Zordich, Mike DB	87-88NYJ 89-93Phx		5'11"	201	Penn State	8	12
Zorich, Chris DT	91-93Chi		6'1"	273	Notre Dame		6
Zorn, Jim QB	76-84Sea 85GB 87TB	12	6'2"	200	Cal. Poly.-Pomona		102

Lifetime Statistics- 1980- 1993 Players Section 1 — **PASSING**
(All men with 25 or more passing attempts)

Name	Years	Att.	Comp.	Comp. Pct.	Yards	Yds./ Att.	TD	Int.	Pct. Int.
Sam Adkins	77-82	39	17	43.6	232	5.9	2	4	10.3
Troy Aikman	89-93	1920	1191	62.0	13627	7.1	69	69	3.6
David Archer	84-89	661	336	50.8	4337	6.6	18	30	4.5
Steve Bartkowski	75-86	3456	1932	55.9	24124	7.0	156	144	4.2
Guy Benjamin	78-83	68	39	57.4	439	6.5	3	3	4.4
Steve Beuerlein	88-93	1028	551	53.6	7545	7.3	44	36	3.5
Todd Blackledge	83-89	881	424	48.1	5286	6.0	29	38	4.3
Drew Bledsoe	93	429	214	49.9	2494	5.8	15	15	3.5
Bob Bleier	87	39	14	35.9	181	4.6	1	1	2.6
Steve Bono	85-93	479	266	55.5	3117	6.5	20	10	2.1
Bubby Brister	86-93	1786	957	53.6	12009	6.7	65	62	3.5
Dieter Brock	85	365	218	59.7	2658	7.3	16	13	3.6
Scott Brunner	80-85	1046	512	48.9	6457	6.2	29	54	5.2
Mike Buck	90-93	58	34	58.6	458	7.9	4	3	5.2
Mike Busch	87	47	17	36.2	378	5.9	3	2	4.3
Rich Campbell	81-84	68	31	45.6	386	5.7	3	9	13.2
Scott Campbell	84-87,89-90	454	224	49.3	2983	6.6	19	25	5.5
Glenn Carano	77-83	57	21	36.8	304	5.3	3	1	1.8
Cody Carlson	87-93	527	311	59.0	3742	7.1	20	24	4.6
Jeff Carlson	90-92	114	49	43.0	636	5.6	2	9	7.9
Matt Cavanaugh	78-90	580	305	52.6	4332	7.5	28	30	5.2
Chris Chandler	88-93	1066	585	54.9	6769	6.3	34	48	4.5
Jeff Christensen	83-85,87	58	24	41.4	297	5.1	1	3	5.2
Cary Conklin	92-93	89	48	53.9	512	5.8	5	3	3.4
Randall Cunningham	85-93	2751	1540	56.0	19040	6.9	131	87	3.2
Gary Danielson	76-78,80-85,87-88	1932	1105	57.2	13764	7.1	81	78	4.0
Steve DeBerg	77-93	4965	2844	57.3	33872	6.8	193	203	4.1
Steve Dils	79-88	972	504	51.9	5816	6.0	27	32	3.3
Anthony Dilweg	89-90	193	102	52.8	1274	6.6	8	7	3.6
Joe Dufek	83-85	150	74	49.3	829	5.5	4	8	5.3
Tony Eason	83-90	1564	911	58.2	11142	7.1	61	51	3.3
John Elway	83-93	4890	2723	55.7	34246	7.0	183	167	3.4
Craig Erickson	92-93	483	248	51.3	3175	6.6	18	21	4.3
Boomer Esiason	84-93	3851	2185	56.7	29092	7.6	190	140	3.6
Vince Evans	77-83,87-93	1182	585	49.5	8027	6.8	44	67	5.7
Jim Everett	86-93	3277	1847	56.4	23758	7.2	142	123	3.8
Brett Favre	91-93	998	620	62.1	6530	6.5	37	39	3.9
Joe Ferguson	73-90	4519	2369	52.4	29817	6.6	196	209	4.6
Vince Ferragamo	77-80,82-86	1615	902	55.9	11336	7.0	76	91	5.6
Tom Flick	81-82,84,86	106	47	44.3	506	4.8	2	10	9.4
Doug Flutie	86-89	341	166	46.9	2203	6.5	14	16	4.7
John Fourcade	87-90	313	159	50.8	2312	7.4	14	15	4.8
Dan Fouts	73-87	5604	3297	58.8	43040	7.7	254	242	4.3
John Friesz	90-91-93	747	401	53.7	4396	5.9	19	20	2.7
Steve Fuller	79-86,88	1066	605	56.8	7156	6.7	28	41	3.8
Will Furrer	92	25	9	36.0	89	5.6	0	3	12.0
Chuck Fusina	79-81,86	37	22	59.5	198	5.4	1	2	5.4
Rich Gannon	87-93	1133	635	56.0	7161	6.3	43	43	3.8
Bob Gagliano	82-83,86-93	486	249	51.2	3431	7.1	17	27	5.6
Stan Gelbaugh	86,88-89,92-93	378	185	48.9	2020	5.3	9	22	5.8
Jeff George	90-93	1532	874	57.0	9552	6.2	41	46	3.0
Gale Gilbert	85-86,90-93	131	69	52.7	809	6.2	6	7	5.3
Brad Goebel	91-93	59	32	54.2	299	5.1	0	6	10.2
Jerry Golsteyn	77-79,82-83	217	92	42.4	1077	5.0	2	13	6.0
Kent Graham	92-93	119	50	42.0	549	4.6	1	4	3.4
Steve Grogan	75-90	3593	1879	52.3	26886	7.5	182	208	5.8
Shawn Halloran	87	42	18	42.9	263	6.3	0	1	2.4
Jim Harbaugh	87-93	1759	1023	58.2	11567	6.6	50	56	3.2
Bobby Hebert	85-89,91-93	2485	1465	59.0	17608	7.1	109	92	3.7
Mark Herrmann	82-92	561	334	59.5	4015	7.2	16	36	6.4
Rusty Hilger	85-88,90-91	464	202	43.5	2584	5.6	11	19	4.1
Eric Hipple	80-86,88-89	1546	830	53.7	10711	6.9	55	70	4.5
Tom Hodson	90-92	315	171	54.3	1809	5.7	7	11	3.5
Gary Hogeboom	80-89	1325	743	56.1	9436	7.1	49	60	4.5
Mike Hohensee	87	52	28	53.8	343	6.6	4	1	1.9
Donald Hollas	91-92	113	67	59.3	645	5.7	3	4	3.5
Bob Holly	82-85	40	25	62.5	300	7.5	1	2	5.0
Todd Hons	87	92	43	46.7	552	6.0	5	5	5.4
Jeff Hostetler	84-93	1051	601	57.2	7651	7.3	34	22	2.1
Stan Humphries	89-93	944	532	56.4	6443	6.8	32	39	4.1
Ron Jaworski	74-89	4117	2187	53.1	28190	6.8	179	164	4.0
Ken Karcher	87-88	114	62	54.4	756	6.6	6	4	3.5
Jim Kelly	86-93	3494	2112	60.4	26413	7.6	179	126	3.6
Jeff Kemp	81-91	916	479	52.3	6230	6.8	39	40	4.4
Bill Kenney	79-88	2430	1330	54.7	17277	7.1	105	86	3.5
Mike Kerrigan	83	14	6	42.9	72	5.1	0	1	7.1
Blair Kiel	84,86-87,89-91	193	108	55.9	1296	6.7	8	7	3.6
David Klingler	92-93	441	237	53.7	2465	5.6	9	11	2.5
Matt Kofler	83-85	202	91	45.0	1156	5.7	7	11	5.4
Jeff Komlo	79-81,83	437	218	49.9	2603	6.0	12	28	6.4
Bernie Kosar	85-93	3213	1889	58.9	22314	6.9	120	81	2.5
Erik Kramer	87,91-93	601	326	54.2	3967	6.6	27	24	4.0
Tommy Kramer	77-90	3651	2012	55.1	24777	6.8	159	158	4.3
Dave Krieg	80-93	4178	2431	58.2	30485	7.3	217	163	3.9
Gary Kubiak	83-91	298	173	58.1	1928	6.4	14	16	5.4
Babe Laufenberg	83,85-88,90	211	93	44.1	1057	5.0	5	11	5.2
Rusty Lisch	80-84	115	55	47.8	547	4.8	1	11	9.6
Neil Lomax	81-88	3153	1817	57.6	22771	7.2	136	90	2.9
Chuck Long	86-90	607	331	54.5	3747	6.2	19	28	4.6
Oliver Luck	83-86	413	233	56.4	2544	6.2	13	21	5.1
Ed Luther	80-84,86	460	245	53.3	3187	6.9	12	23	5.0
Mike Machurek	84	43	14	32.6	193	4.5	0	0	0.0
Kyle Mackey	84,86-87,89	134	68	50.7	729	5.4	3	6	4.5
Tommy Maddox	92-93	122	67	54.9	758	6.2	6	9	7.4
Don Majkowski	87-93	1667	902	54.1	10975	6.6	56	57	3.4
Mark Malone	80-89	1648	839	50.9	10175	6.2	60	81	4.8
Dan Marino	83-93	5434	3219	59.2	40720	7.5	298	168	3.1
Todd Marinovich	91-92	205	104	50.7	1345	6.6	8	9	4.4
Bruce Mathison	83-87	309	152	49.2	2177	7.0	7	20	6.5
Brian McClure	87	38	20	52.6	181	4.8	0	3	7.9
Paul McDonald	80-87	767	411	53.6	5269	6.9	24	37	4.8
Dan McGwire	91-93	42	23	53.5	167	4.0	1	4	9.5
Jim McMahon	82-93	2525	1465	58.0	17883	7.1	99	87	3.4
Guido Merkens	78-85,87	66	27	41.0	283	4.3	2	2	3.0
Hugh Millen	87-93	757	453	59.8	5350	7.1	19	32	4.2
Chris Miller	87-93	2089	1129	54.0	14066	6.7	87	72	3.4
Rick Mirer	93	486	274	56.4	2833	5.8	12	17	3.5
Scott Mitchell	91-93	241	135	56.0	1805	7.5	12	9	3.7
Joe Montana	79-90,92-93	4898	3110	63.5	37268	7.6	257	130	2.7
Warren Moon	84-93	4546	2632	57.9	33685	7.4	196	166	3.7
Shawn Moore	92	34	17	50.0	232	6.8	0	3	8.8
Mike Moroski	79-86	425	241	56.7	2864	6.7	8	18	4.2
Browning Nagle	91-93	403	199	49.4	2361	5.9	7	17	4.2
Rick Neuheisel	87	59	40	67.8	367	6.2	1	1	1.7
Gifford Nielsen	78-83	498	273	54.8	3255	6.5	20	22	4.4
David Norrie	87	68	35	51.5	376	5.5	1	4	5.9
Ken O'Brien	83-93	3602	2110	58.6	25094	7.0	128	98	2.7
Neil O'Donnell	90-93	1085	611	56.3	7454	6.9	38	23	2.1
Mike Pagel	82-93	1509	756	50.0	9414	6.2	49	63	4.2
Walter Payton	75-87	34	11	32.3	331	9.7	8	4	11.8
Brent Pease	87-88	135	62	45.9	792	5.9	3	9	6.7
Rodney Peete	89-93	1125	641	57.0	8164	7.3	38	49	4.4
Steve Pelluer	84-90	974	548	56.3	6870	7.1	29	39	4.0
Todd Philcox	90-93	145	69	47.6	965	6.7	7	10	6.9
Joe Pisarcik	77-84	898	425	47.3	5552	6.2	24	48	5.3
Tom Ramsey	85-89	214	108	50.5	1275	6.0	7	10	4.7
Frank Reich	85-93	284	166	58.4	1972	6.9	17	8	2.8
Alan Risher	85,87	74	44	59.5	564	7.6	3	3	4.1
Matt Robinson	77-82	523	244	46.7	3347	6.4	18	38	7.3
Timm Rosenbach	89-90,92	551	295	53.5	3676	6.7	16	24	4.4
Ed Rubbert	87	49	26	53.1	532	10.9	4	1	2.0
T.J. Rubley	93	189	108	57.1	1338	7.1	8	6	3.2
Jeff Rutledge	79-81,83-92	526	274	52.1	3628	6.9	16	29	5.5
Pat Ryan	78-89,91	657	364	55.4	4320	6.6	31	35	5.3
Mark Rypien	87-93	2207	1244	56.4	15928	7.2	101	75	3.4
Sean Salisbury	86-87,90-93	382	220	57.6	2684	7.0	14	10	2.6
Art Schlichter	82,84	202	91	45.0	1006	5.0	3	11	5.4
Turk Schonert	81-89	504	311	61.7	3788	7.5	11	20	4.0
Jay Schroeder	84-93	2569	1293	50.3	18553	7.2	110	101	3.9
Scott Secules	88-91,93	204	108	52.9	1311	6.4	4	14	6.0
Frank Seurer	86-87	55	26	47.3	340	6.2	0	4	7.3
Phil Simms	79-81,83-93	4047	2576	55.4	33462	7.2	199	157	3.4
Scott Stankavage	84,86-87	25	8	32.0	66	2.6	0	2	8.0
Matt Stevens	87	57	32	56.1	315	5.5	1	1	1.8
Cliff Stoudt	77-83,86-90	684	359	52.5	4506	6.6	23	43	6.3
Kelly Stouffer	88-92	437	225	51.5	2333	5.3	7	19	4.3
Don Strock	74-89	779	443	56.9	5349	6.9	45	42	5.4
Kevin Sweeney	87-88	106	47	44.3	605	5.7	7	6	5.7
Vinny Testaverde	87-93	2390	1256	52.6	16617	7.0	91	121	5.1
Joe Theismann	74-85	3602	2044	56.7	25206	7.0	160	138	3.8
Jack Thompson	79-84	845	449	53.1	5315	6.3	33	45	5.3
Scott Tinsley	87	86	48	55.8	637	7.4	3	4	4.7
Richard Todd	76-86	2967	1610	54.3	20610	6.9	124	161	5.4
Billy Joe Tolliver	89-93	884	457	51.7	5453	6.2	33	36	4.1
Mike Tomczak	85-93	1418	731	51.6	9828	6.9	53	68	4.9
Willie Totten	87	33	13	39.4	155	4.7	2	2	6.1
Jack Trudeau	86-93	1536	812	52.9	9647	6.3	41	62	4.0
Tom Tupa	88-92	488	251	51.4	3231	6.6	10	24	4.9
Jeff Van Raaphorst	87	34	18	52.9	174	5.1	1	2	5.9
Mark Vlasic	87-88,90-93	142	75	52.8	762	5.4	4	5	3.5
Steve Walsh	89-93	848	450	53.1	5290	6.2	30	31	3.7
Andre Ware	90-93	161	83	51.6	1112	6.9	5	8	5.0
Danny White	76-88	2950	1761	59.7	21959	7.4	155	132	4.4
David Whitehurst	77-84	980	504	51.4	6205	6.3	28	51	5.2
Erik Wilhelm	89-91,93	123	70	56.9	822	6.7	4	4	3.2
Doug Williams	78-82,86-89	2507	1240	49.5	16998	6.8	100	93	3.7
Peter Tom Willis	90-93	183	104	56.8	1261	6.9	6	15	8.2
Dave Wilson	81,83-89	1039	551	53.1	6987	6.7	36	55	5.3
Marc Wilson	80-87,89-90	2081	1085	52.1	14391	6.9	86	102	4.9
Wade Wilson	81-93	2216	1261	56.9	15960	7.2	91	94	4.2
John Witkowski	84-86,88	35	13	37.1	210	6.0	0	0	0.0
David Woodley	80-85	1300	687	52.8	8558	6.6	48	63	4.8
Randy Wright	84-88	1119	602	53.8	7106	6.4	31	57	5.1
Steve Young	85-93	1968	1222	62.1	15900	8.1	105	58	2.9
Scott Zolak	92-93	102	52	51.0	561	5.5	2	4	3.9
Jim Zorn	76-85,87	3149	1669	53.0	21115	6.7	111	141	4.5

		RUSHING				RECEIVING			
Name	**Years**	**Att.**	**Yards**	**Avg.**	**TD**	**Rec.**	**Yards**	**Avg.**	**TD**
Walter Abercrombie	82-88	847	3357	4.0	22	139	1351	9.7	7
Curtis Adams	86-88	246	858	3.4	6	8	64	8.0	0
George Adams	85-91	257	886	3.4	3	111	1014	9.1	4
Willie Adams	79-85	5	13	2.6	0	61	962	15.8	2
Tommie Agee	88-93	86	315	3.7	1	43	364	8.5	1
Troy Aikman	89-93	163	709	4.3	3	2	-19	-9.5	0
Charles Alexander	79-85	748	2645	3.5	13	165	1130	6.8	2
Jeff Alexander	89	45	146	3.2	2	8	84	10.5	0
Mike Alexander	89,91					16	302	18.9	1
Ray Alexander	84,88-89					63	936	14.9	7
Anthony Allen	85-89					44	667	15.2	8
Marcus Allen	82-93	2296	9309	4.1	91	480	4496	9.4	21
Marvin Allen	88-91	94	378	4.0	2	7	57	8.1	0
Terry Allen	91-92	386	1764	4.6	15	55	527	9.6	3
Kimble Anders	91-93	76	292	3.8	0	47	421	9.0	1
Alfred Anderson	84-91	626	2374	3.8	22	114	1044	9.2	5
Gary Anderson	85-88,90-93	869	3409	3.9	16	302	2999	9.9	15
Jesse Anderson	90-91					11	150	13.6	2
Ottis Anderson	79-92	2562	10273	4.0	81	376	3062	8.1	5
Neal Anderson	86-93	1515	6166	4.1	51	302	2763	9.1	20
Willie Anderson	88-93	2	12	6.0	0	213	4301	20.2	21
William Andrews	79-86	1315	5986	4.6	30	277	2647	9.6	11
Tyrone Anthony	84-85	37	170	4.6	1	40	298	7.5	0
Charles Arbuckle	92-93					28	242	8.6	1
David Archer	84-89,92	135	706	5.2	2				
Adger Armstrong	80-85	58	231	4.0	2	80	710	9.0	7
Tyji Armstrong	92-93	2	5	2.5	0	16	224	14.0	2
Walt Arnold	80-87					99	1053	10.6	8
Steve Atkins	79-81	121	488	4.0	2	18	138	7.7	1
Mike Augustyniak	81-83	153	567	3.7	7	52	404	7.8	1
Cliff Austin	83-87	109	445	4.1	2	11	118	10.7	0
Rob Awalt	87-93	2	-9	-4.5	0	138	1583	11.5	10
Rick Badanjek	86-87	29	87	3.0	1	6	35	5.8	0
Harold Bailey	81-82	1	13	13.0	0	26	367	14.1	0
Johnny Bailey	90-93	142	615	4.3	3	65	574	8.8	1
Stacey Bailey	82-90	4	-2	-0.5	0	208	3422	16.5	18
Victor Bailey	93					41	545	13.3	1
Stephen Baker	87-92	2	21	10.5	0	141	2587	18.3	21
Tony Baker	68-75	536	2087	3.9	15	82	685	8.4	2
Randy Baldwin	91-93	28	92	3.3	0	3	35	11.7	1
Eric Ball	89-93	154	516	3.7	8	21	212	10.1	3
Chuck Banks	86-87	79	325	4.1	0	16	121	7.6	0
Fred Banks	85,87-93					105	1636	15.6	10
Gordon Banks	80-81,85-87					35	458	13.1	1
Marion Barber	82-88	74	317	4.3	3	25	209	8.4	1
Mike Barber	76-85	5	19	8.9	0	222	2788	12.6	17
Mike Barber	89-92	1	-13	-13.0	0	38	483	12.7	2
Rod Barksdale	86-87					30	599	20.0	3
Johnnie Barnes	92-93					10	137	13.7	0
Buster Barnett	81-84					26	236	9.1	1
Fred Barnett	90-93	4	-2	-0.5	0	182	2922	16.1	18
Tim Barnett	91-93	1	3	3.0	0	82	1188	14.5	10
Milton Barney	87					10	175	17.5	2
Malcolm Barnwell	81-85	3	30	10.0	0	115	1969	17.1	4
Steve Bartkowski	75-86	178	259	1.5	11				
Brian Baschnagel	76-84	8	0	0.0	0	134	2024	15.1	9
Don Bass	78-82	6	40	6.7	0	117	1580	13.5	13
Greg Baty	86-88,90-93					83	872	10.5	7
Hank Bauer	77-83	123	377	3.1	18	12	97	8.1	2
Mark Bavaro	85-90,92-93					334	4518	13.5	36
Brad Baxter	89-93	634	2462	3.9	30	44	387	8.8	0
Pat Beach	82-93					163	1558	9.6	14
Sanjay Beach	89,91-93					26	224	8.6	2
Ed Beckman	77-84					23	198	8.6	1
Brad Beckman	88-89					11	102	9.3	1
Don Beebe	89-93	2	17	8.5	0	124	2010	16.2	14
Greg Bell	84-90	1204	4959	4.1	51	157	1307	8.3	6
Jerry Bell	82-86					101	1218	12.1	7
Ken Bell	86-89	31	96	3.1	0	3	18	6.0	0
Nick Bell	91-93	226	853	3.8	7	21	213	10.1	0
Richard Bell	90	5	18	3.6	0	12	137	11.4	1
Ricky Bell	77-83	822	3063	3.7	16	97	842	8.7	3
Theo Bell	76-85	2	12	6.0	0	136	2375	17.5	8
Mark Bellini	86-88					10	133	13.3	0
Jesse Bendross	84-86					27	369	13.7	2
Edgar Bennett	92-93	220	764	3.5	9	72	550	7.6	1
Lewis Bennett	87					10	184	18.4	1
Woody Bennett	79-88	424	1761	4.2	10	41	304	7.4	3
Albert Bentley	85-92	526	2355	4.4	19	226	2245	9.9	8
Cliff Benson	84-85,87-88	3	8	2.7	0	39	298	7.6	0
Karl Bernard	87	45	187	4.2	2	13	91	7.0	0
Rick Berns	79-83	68	255	3.8	0	6	46	7.7	0
Rod Bernstine	87-93	630	2823	4.5	21	135	1260	9.3	2
Jrome Bettis	93	294	1429	4.9	7	26	244	9.4	0
Steve Beuerlein	88-93	79	98	1.2	0	1	21	21.0	0
Dwight Beverly	87	62	217	3.5	2	1	8	8.0	0
Eric Bieniemy	91-93	110	416	3.8	4	6	49	8.2	0
J.J. Birden	90-93					135	2182	16.2	10
Todd Blackledge	83-89	81	325	4.0	2				
Brian Blades	88-93	21	120	5.7	0	325	4474	13.8	22
Carl Bland	84-90					90	1153	12.8	4
Drew Bledsoe	93	32	82	2.8	0				
Dennis Bligen	84-87	73	300	4.1	2	18	130	7.2	0
Alvin Blount	87	46	125	2.7	3	1	5	5.0	0
Steve Bono	85-93	52	110	2.1	2				
Cap Boso	86-91					54	591	10.9	4
Matt Bouza	81-89	1	12	12.0	0	234	3064	13.1	17
Mark Boyer	85-92					170	1534	9.0	6
Mark Brammer	80-84	3	25	8.3	0	116	1137	9.8	10
Melvin Bratton	89-90	57	190	3.3	4	39	345	8.8	4
Brian Brennan	84-92					334	4336	13.0	20
Hoby Brenner	81-93					267	3849	14.4	21
Chris Brewer	84,87	34	83	2.4	2	7	76	10.9	1
Leon Bright	81-85	53	204	3.9	2	32	343	10.7	0
James Brim	87	2	36	180	1	18	282	15.7	2

		RUSHING				RECEIVING			
Name	**Years**	**Att.**	**Yards**	**Avg.**	**TD**	**Rec.**	**Yards**	**Avg.**	**TD**
Dana Brinson	89	17	64	3.8	0	12	71	5.9	0
Vincent Brisby	93					45	626	13.9	2
Bubby Brister	86-93	144	380	2.6	7	1	-10	-10.0	0
Mitch Brookins	84	2	27	13.5	0	18	318	17.7	1
Bill Brooks	86-93	18	106	5.9	0	471	6532	13.9	33
James Brooks	81-92	1685	7962	4.7	49	383	3621	9.5	30
Reggie Brooks	93	223	1063	4.8	3	21	186	8.9	0
Robert Brooks	92-93	5	31	6.2	0	32	306	9.6	1
Steve Broussard	90-93	348	1472	4.2	10	48	380	7.9	2
A.B. Brown	89-92	40	117	2.9	1	8	40	5.0	0
Andre Brown	89-90					27	459	17.0	5
Charlie Brown	82-87	4	53	13.3	0	220	3548	16.1	25
Curtis Brown	77-83	567	2171	3.8	9	102	772	7.6	5
Derek Brown	92-93					11	87	7.9	0
Derek Brown	93	180	705	3.9	2	21	170	8.1	1
Eddie Brown	85-91	25	164	6.6	0	363	6134	16.9	41
Gary Brown	91-93	222	1174	5.3	8	24	246	10.3	2
Ivory Lee Brown	92	68	194	2.9	2	7	54	7.7	0
Reggie Brown	82-83,87	39	136	3.5	0				
Ron Brown	84-91	21	127	6.0	0	98	1791	18.3	13
Ted Brown	79-86	1117	4546	4.1	40	339	2850	8.4	13
Theotis Brown	79-84	549	2046	3.7	30	172	1558	9.1	3
Tim Brown	88-93	24	69	2.9	1	227	3425	15.1	27
Tom Brown	87,89	13	26	2.0	0	13	117	9.0	0
Bob Bruer	76, 79-83	5	-4	-0.8	0	72	709	9.9	8
Scott Brunner	80-83	69	129	1.9	1				
Cullen Bryant	73-84,87	849	3264	3.8	20	148	1176	8.0	3
Kelvin Bryant	86-88,90	260	1186	4.6	6	154	1634	10.6	14
Stephen Bryant	82-85					35	489	14.0	0
Jarrod Bunch	91-93	138	629	4.6	5	26	156	6.0	2
Cornell Burbage	87-89					26	352	13.5	2
Randy Burke	78-81					30	489	16.3	3
Chris Burkett	85-93	2	-6	-3.0	0	292	4352	14.9	19
Jerry Butler	79-83	4	32	8.0	0	278	4301	15.5	29
Ray Butler	80-88	4	9	2.3	0	239	3948	16.6	37
Marion Butts	89-93	1031	4297	4.2	31	57	407	7.1	0
Keith Byars	86-93	814	2941	3.6	20	432	4145	9.6	15
Earnest Byner	84-93	1662	6663	4.0	48	389	3611	9.3	12
Carl Byrum	86-88	132	527	4.0	0	18	127	7.1	1
Lynn Cain	79-85	615	2309	3.8	19	127	1061	8.4	6
Chris Calloway	90-93					87	1226	14.1	6
Earl Campbell	79-85	2187	9407	4.3	74	121	806	6.7	0
Jeff Campbell	90-93					36	495	13.8	3
Scott Campbell	84-87,89-90	43	170	4.0	2				
Billy Campfield	78-82	167	649	3.9	5	107	958	9.0	6
Wayne Capers	83-86	5	26	5.2	1	51	822	164	5
Joe Caravello	87-90	1	0	0.0	0	16	160	10.0	1
Cody Carlson	87-93	71	200	2.8	4				
Rob Carpenter	77-86	1172	4363	3.7	29	215	1707	7.9	5
Rob Carpenter	91-93	1	2	2.0	0	22	289	13.1	1
Mark Carrier	87-93	4	26	6.5	1	364	5764	15.8	30
Wesley Carroll	91-93					42	519	12.4	3
Paul Ott Carruth	86-89	194	614	3.2	5	59	426	7.2	3
Carlos Carson	80-89	12	62	5.2	0	353	6372	18.1	33
Anthony Carter	85-93	47	289	6.1	2	478	7635	16.0	52
Cris Carter	87-93	10	38	3.8	0	327	4550	13.9	42
Dexter Carter	90-93	213	920	4.3	4	52	553	10.6	2
Gerald Carter	80-87	4	24	6.0	0	239	3443	14.4	17
Joe Carter	84-86	118	589	5.0	1	11	66	6.0	0
Pat Carter	88-93					63	670	10.6	6
Rodney Carter	87-89	52	244	4.6	4	86	810	9.4	8
Maurice Carthon	85-92	300	950	3.2	2	90	745	8.3	1
Melvin Carver	82-84,87	197	624	3.2	1	39	335	8.6	2
Keith Cash	91-93	1	0	0.0	0	43	445	10.3	7
Kerry Cash	91-93					87	941	10.8	6
Ron Cassidy	79-84					14	233	16.6	0
Matt Cavanaugh	78-89	60	213	3.6	3	1	9	9.0	0
Jimmy Cefalo	78-84					93	1739	18.7	13
Larry Centers	90-93	76	335	4.4	0	135	1196	8.9	5
Jeff Chadwick	83-92	3	3	1.0	1	292	4549	15.6	27
Pat Chaffey	91-93	61	330	5.4	2	11	111	10.1	1
Chris Chandler	88-93	131	529	4.0	6				
Thornton Chandler	86-89					29	268	9.2	4
Wes Chandler	78-88	16	84	5.3	0	559	8966	16.0	56
Todd Christensen	79-88	1	-6	-6.0	0	461	5872	12.7	41
Bob Christian	92-93	8	19	2.4	0	16	160	10.0	0
Darryl Clack	86-89	29	113	3.9	2	22	213	9.7	1
Rickey Claitt	80-81	60	234	3.9	1	3	34	11.3	1
Allan Clark	79-81	28	140	5.0	3	2	35	17.5	0
Dwight Clark	79-87	6	50	8.3	0	506	6750	13.3	48
Gary Clark	85-93	11	54	4.9	0	612	9560	15.6	62
Jessie Clark	83-90	415	1736	4.2	9	102	943	9.2	6
Ken Clark	90-92	161	510	3.2	0	43	314	7.3	0
Louis Clark	87-92					67	798	11.9	3
Robert Clark	88-92					163	2624	16.1	18
Mark Clayton	83-93	14	108	7.7	0	582	8974	15.4	84
Joey Clinkscales	87					13	240	18.5	1
Ben Coates	91-93	2	-4	-2.0	0	83	925	11.1	12
Reggie Cobb	90-93	878	3061	3.5	21	84	627	7.5	1
Paul Coffman	78-87	1	3	3.0	0	339	4340	12.8	42
Lincoln Coleman	93	34	132	3.9	2	4	24	6.0	0
Pat Coleman	90-93	1	1	1.0	0	22	277	12.6	1
Dwight Collins	84	3	-14	-4.7	0	11	143	13.0	1
Shawn Collins	89-93					98	1433	14.6	5
Tony Collins	81-87,90	1191	4647	3.9	32	261	2356	9.0	12
Cris Collinsworth	81-88	7	-15	-2.6	0	417	6698	16.1	36
Curtis Conway	93	5	44	8.8	0	19	231	12.2	2
Marv Cook	89-93					210	1843	8.8	10
Adrian Cooper	91-92					36	456	12.7	5
Earl Cooper	80-86	298	1152	3.9	6	213	1908	9.0	12
Horace Copeland	93	3	34	11.3	0	30	633	21.1	4
Russell Copeland	93					13	242	18.6	0
Doug Cosbie	79-88	7	35	5.0	0	300	3728	12.4	30
Aaron Cox	88-93					102	1732	17.0	8
Arthur Cox	83-91					170	1758	10.3	10

		RUSHING				RECEIVING			
Name	**Years**	**Att.**	**Yards**	**Avg.**	**TD**	**Rec.**	**Yards**	**Avg.**	**TD**
Donnie Craft	82-83	73	189	2.6	3	35	329	9.4	1
Roger Craig	83-93	1991	8189	4.1	56	566	4911	8.7	17
Aaron Craver	91-92	23	67	2.9	1	8	67	8.4	0
Charles Crawford	86	28	88	3.1	1				
Joe Cribbs	80-83, 85-88	1299	5356	4.1	27	224	2199	9.8	15
Ray Crittenden	93	1	-3	-3.0	0	16	293	18.3	1
Corey Croom	93	60	198	3.3	1	8	92	11.5	0
Howard Cross	89-93					82	1125	13.7	10
Ray Crouse	84	53	169	3.2	0	9	93	10.3	1
Dwayne Crutchfield	82-85	235	993	4.3	5	21	144	6.9	1
Rodney Culver	92-93	186	471	2.5	10	37	322	8.7	3
Bennie Cunningham	76-85					202	2879	14.3	20
Randall Cunningham	85-93	591	4096	6.9	29	1	-3	-3.0	0
Gary Danielson	76-78, 80-85,88	186	857	4.6	7	1	22	22.0	1
Charles Davenport	92-93					13	187	14.4	0
Ron Davenport	85-89	274	1127	4.1	13	93	801	8.6	4
Johnny Davis	78-87	314	1094	3.5	15	22	106	4.8	0
Kenneth Davis	86-93	729	3132	4.3	25	117	796	6.8	5
Russell Davis	80-83	104	474	4.6	2	5	45	9.0	0
Wendell Davis	88-93	5	45	9.0	0	207	3000	14.5	14
Willie Davis	91-93	1	-11	-11.0	0	88	1665	18.9	10
Julius Dawkins	83-84					32	418	13.1	3
Sean Dawkins	93					26	430	16.5	1
Lawrence Dawsey	91-93	1	9	9.0	0	130	1797	13.8	4
Stacey Dawsey	87					13	142	10.9	0
Lin Dawson	81-85,88-89					117	1233	10.5	8
Steve DeBerg	77-93	196	210	1.1	7				
Joe Delaney	81-82	329	1501	4.6	3	33	299	9.1	0
Robert Delpino	88-93	502	1815	3.6	18	178	1769	9.9	9
Preston Dennard	78-85	12	81	6.8	0	232	3665	15.8	30
Glenn Dennison	84,87	1	4	4.0	0	20	149	7.5	1
Eric Dickerson	83-93	2996	13259	4.4	90	281	2137	7.6	6
Curtis Dickey	80-86	937	4019	4.3	32	134	1577	11.8	8
Clint Didier	82-89					141	1923	13.6	21
Scott Dierking	77-84	734	2915	4.0	18	124	1028	8.3	5
Steve Dils	80-88	45	71	1.6	1				
Anthony Dilweg	89-90	21	114	5.4	0				
Mike Dingle	91	21	91	4.3	0	5	23	4.6	1
Robert DiRico	87	25	90	3.6	0	2	22	11.0	0
Al Dixon	77-84	1	-5	-5.0	0	80	1194	14.9	8
Floyd Dixon	86-92	23	110	11.8	0	184	2523	13.7	16
James Dixon	89-91	14	73	5.2	0	26	503	19.3	2
Zachary Dixon	79-84	197	732	3.7	3	41	367	9.0	1
Doug Donley	81-86	2	5	2.5	0	55	898	16.3	4
Dan Doornink	78-85	523	1836	3.5	15	209	2006	9.6	11
Tony Dorsett	77-88	2936	12739	4.3	77	398	3554	8.9	13
D.J. Dozier	87-91	172	691	4.0	7	33	301	9.1	2
Troy Drayton	93	1	7	7.0	0	27	319	11.8	4
Chris Dressel	83-91	1	3	3.0	0	111	1098	9.9	8
Willie Drewrey	85-93	2	-4	-2.0	0	106	1601	15.1	7
Robert Drummond	89-91	52	187	3.6	3	22	219	10.0	1
Doug DuBose	87-88	34	149	4.4	2	10	94	9.4	0
Kenny Duckett	82-85	3	-19	-6.3	0	34	503	14.8	4
Bobby Duckworth	82-86					82	1784	21.7	13
Joe Dudek	87	35	154	4.4	2	7	41	5.9	0
Vaughn Dunbar	92	154	565	3.7	3	9	62	6.9	0
Curtis Duncan	87-93					322	3935	12.2	20
K.D. Dunn	85-89					11	163	14.8	0
Pat Dunsmore	83-84					17	208	12.2	1
Reggie Dupard	86-90	217	704	3.2	6	43	303	7.0	0
Mark Duper	82-92	1	-10	-10.0	0	511	8869	17.3	59
Marcus Dupree	90-91	68	251	3.7	1	6	46	7.7	0
Hart Lee Dykes	89-90					83	1344	16.2	7
Mike Dyal	89-90,92-93					38	640	16.8	2
Robin Earl	77-82	94	382	4.1	1	47	486	10.3	4
Quinn Early	88-93	16	126	7.9	0	162	2516	15.5	18
Walt Easley	81-82	76	224	2.9	1	9	62	6.9	0
Tony Eason	83-90	134	503	3.8	6				
Jerry Eckwood	79-81	515	1845	3.6	6	93	956	10.3	1
Floyd Eddings	82-83	3	15	5.0	0	28	506	18.1	0
Ferrell Edmunds	88-93	1	-8	-8.0	0	141	1851	13.1	12
Al Edwards	90-92	2	25	12.5	0	26	264	10.2	2
Anthony Edwards	89-93					29	547	18.9	2
Kelvin Edwards	86-88	3	67	22.3	1	49	746	15.2	3
Stan Edwards	82-87	149	533	3.6	2	52	436	8.4	1
Ron Egloff	77-84					75	839	11.2	4
Donnie Elder	85-86					25	477	19.1	0
Henry Ellard	83-93	18	55	3.1	0	593	9761	16.5	48
Gary Ellerson	85-87	169	688	4.1	8	21	216	10.3	1
Craig Ellis	86-87	26	144	4.0	2	5	39	7.8	0
Gerry Ellis	80-86	836	3826	4.6	25	267	2514	9.4	10
John Elway	83-93	537	2438	4.5	23	2	47	23.5	1
Phillip Epps	82-89	11	135	12.3	1	200	2992	15.0	14
Rich Erenberg	84-86	174	642	3.7	3	98	901	9.2	7
Craig Erickson	92-93	27	95	3.5	0				
Ricky Ervins	91-93	346	1376	4.0	5	64	556	8.7	1
Boomer Esiason	84-93	378	1462	3.9	6	1	-8	-8.0	0
Vince Evans	77-83,87-93	192	1069	5.6	14				
Jim Everett	86-93	191	510	2.7	4				
Major Everett	83-87	55	158	2.9	0	14	84	6.0	0
George Farmer	82-84,87	1	-9	-9.0	0	65	980	15.1	7
Mike Farr	90-92					69	716	10.4	1
Brett Favre	91-93	105	414	3.9	2	1	-7	-7.0	0
Ricky Feacher	76-84	2	-2	-1.0	0	113	2084	18.4	15
Gill Fenerty	90-91	212	832	3.9	5	44	444	10.1	2
Derrick Fenner	89-93	550	2149	3.9	27	86	706	8.2	2
Rick Fenney	87-91	358	1508	4.2	11	71	628	8.8	2
Joe Ferguson	73-90	351	1210	3.4	11	2	-9	-4.5	0
Vagas Ferguson	80-83	290	1163	4.0	5	26	212	8.2	0
Mervyn Fernandez	87-92	6	35	5.8	0	209	3764	18.0	19
Vince Ferragamo	77-86	75	134	1.8	2				
Earl Ferrell	82-89	682	2937	4.3	24	186	1628	8.8	8
Robert Fisher	80-81					12	203	16.9	3
Scott Fitzkee	79-82	1	15	15.0	0	17	321	18.9	4
Terrence Flagler	87-91	56	237	4.2	2	33	366	11.1	1
Kenny Flowers	87,89	27	85	3.1	1	7	50	7.1	0
John Floyd	79-81					14	215	15.4	2
Darren Flutie	88					18	208	11.6	2
Doug Flutie	86-89	59	281	4.8	2				
Steve Folsom	81-82,87-89					37	349	9.4	2
Herman Fontenot	85-90	102	370	3.6	2	143	1453	10.2	6
Bernard Ford	89-90					17	176	10.4	2
Barry Foster	90-93	699	3092	4.4	21	73	680	9.3	2
John Fourcade	87-90	48	302	6.3	2				
Dan Fouts	73-87	224	476	2.1	13				
Todd Fowler	86-88	16	36	2.3	0	17	113	7.6	0
Jon Francis	87	35	138	3.9	0	8	38	4.8	2
Phil Francis	79-80	38	154	4.1	1	35	221	6.3	0
Russ Francis	75-80,82-88	2	12	6.0	0	393	5262	13.4	40
John Frank	84-88	2	-1	-0.5	0	65	662	10.2	10
Andra Franklin	81-84	622	2232	3.6	22	6	15	2.5	1
Byron Franklin	81,83-87	5	-8	-1.6	0	145	2016	13.9	10
Paul Frazier	89	25	112	4.5	1	3	25	8.3	0
Phil Freeman	85-87	1	1	1.0	0	22	370	16.8	4
Mike Friede	80-81					40	621	15.5	1
Irving Fryar	84-93	38	184	4.8	1	427	6736	15.8	43
Steve Fuller	79-86	186	908	4.8	11				
Brent Fullwood	87-90	433	1702	3.9	18	44	370	8.4	1
Bob Gagliano	82-83,86-93	93	352	3.8	4				
Derrick Gaffney	78-84,87	2	-2	-1.0	0	156	2613	16.8	7
Derrick Gainer	90,92-93	41	120	2.9	1	13	122	9.4	0
Hokie Gajan	82-85	252	1358	5.4	11	63	515	8.2	2
Scott Galbraith	90-93					36	454	12.6	2
Tony Galbreath	76-87	1031	4072	3.9	34	490	4066	8.3	9
Rich Gannon	87-93	165	808	4.9	4	1	0	0.0	0
Earl Gant	79-80	65	228	3.5	1	24	169	7.0	0
Carwell Gardner	91-93	117	409	3.5	6	14	137	9.8	1
Alvin Garrett	80-84	12	33	2.8	0	32	412	12.9	2
Gregg Garrity	83-89					82	1329	16.2	6
Cleveland Gary	89-93	677	2634	3.9	14	133	857	6.4	5
Sam Gash	92-93	53	156	2.9	2	14	93	6.6	0
Willie Gault	83-93	21	154	7.3	0	333	6635	19.9	44
Everett Gay	88-89					15	205	13.7	1
Chris Gedney	93					10	98	9.8	0
Stan Gelbaugh	86,88-89,91-93	27	98	3.6	0				
Dennis Gentry	82-92	137	764	5.6	5	171	2076	12.1	7
Jeff George	90-93	54	103	1.9	2				
Nick Giaquinto	80-83	40	178	4.5	1	65	722	11.1	3
Jimmie Giles	77-89	5	-3	-0.6	0	350	5084	14.5	41
Ernest Givins	86-93	34	350	10.3	1	506	7414	14.7	45
Andrew Glover	91-93					24	278	11.6	5
Kerry Goode	88-89	63	231	3.7	0	7	68	9.7	0
Eugene Goodlow	83-86	2	8	4.0	0	115	1677	14.6	10
Preston Gothard	85-88					41	459	11.2	3
Sam Graddy	87-88,90-92					18	477	26.5	3
Jeff Graham	91-93					89	1311	14.7	1
Scottie Graham	91-93	132	516	3.9	3	7	46	6.6	1
Otis Grant	83-84,87	3	10	3.3	0	37	565	15.3	1
Earnest Gray	79-85	2	2	1.0	0	246	3790	15.4	27
Boyce Green	83-87	417	1561	3.7	6	56	428	7.6	2
Eric Green	90-93					152	2063	13.6	20
Gaston Green	88-92	551	2136	3.9	6	32	232	7.3	1
Harold Green	90-93	721	2843	3.9	5	91	555	6.1	1
Mark Green	89-92	116	496	4.3	6	22	213	9.7	1
Paul Green	92-93					32	245	7.7	2
Robert Green	92-93	23	75	3.3	0	14	68	4.9	0
Roy Green	79-92	23	140	6.1	1	559	8965	16.0	66
Willie Green	91-93					100	1640	16.4	14
Terry Greer	86-90	3	51	17.0	0	38	640	16.8	4
Keith Griffin	84-88	329	1343	4.1	3	61	460	7.5	2
Billy Griggs	85-89					25	262	10.5	1
Steve Grogan	75-90	445	2176	4.9	35	3	19	6.3	0
Jeff Groth	79-85	4	43	10.8	0	152	2126	14.0	5
Mike Guman	80-88	333	1286	3.9	11	150	1433	9.6	4
Jim Gustafson	85-89	1	-2	-2.0	0	38	491	12.9	5
Michael Haddix	83-90	543	1635	3.0	3	172	1310	7.6	3
James Hadnot	80-83	266	1029	3.9	5	54	426	7.9	0
Dino Hall	79-83	27	194	7.2	1	11	125	11.4	1
Ron Hall	87-93					209	2422	11.6	10
Lorenzo Hampton	85-89	503	1949	3.9	22	123	954	7.8	6
Rodney Hampton	90-93	914	3732	4.1	31	121	982	8.1	2
Anthony Hancock	82-86					73	1266	17.3	5
Jim Harbaugh	87-93	296	1609	5.4	15				
Andre Hardy	84-85,87	26	94	3.6	0	6	36	6.0	0
Bruce Hardy	78-89	1	2	2.0	0	256	2455	9.6	25
Larry Hardy	78-85					71	960	13.5	7
Tony Hargain	92					17	205	12.1	0
Clarence Harmon	77-82	360	1374	3.8	5	133	1383	10.4	11
Derrick Harmon	84-86	94	361	3.8	2	23	203	8.8	0
Ronnie Harmon	86-93	500	2326	4.7	7	421	4103	9.7	16
Alvin Harper	91-93	1	15	15.0	0	91	1665	18.3	10
Bruce Harper	77-84	374	1829	4.9	8	220	2409	11.0	12
Michael Harper	86-89	1	3	3.0	0	25	352	14.1	1
Perry Harrington	80-85	155	683	4.4	6	26	144	5.5	0
Darryl Harris	88	34	151	4.4	1	6	30	5.0	0
Duriel Harris	76-85	3	33	11.0	0	302	5055	16.7	20
Herbert Harris	86					11	148	13.5	0
Jackie Harris	90-93	1	1	1.0	0	133	1620	12.2	9
Leonard Harris	86-93	2	25	12.5	0	96	1315	13.7	8
M.L. Harris	80-85	3	-5	-1.7	0	99	1369	13.8	10
William Harris	87,89					12	110	7.6	1
Emile Harry	86,88-92	2	36	18.0	0	150	2011	13.4	9
John Harvey	90	27	113	4.2	0	11	86	7.8	1
Don Hasselbeck	77-85					107	1542	14.4	18
Courtney Hawkins	92-93					82	1269	15.5	7
Frank Hawkins	81-86	427	1635	3.8	15	96	685	7.1	4
Greg Hawthorne	79-86	137	527	3.8	7	89	1071	12.0	4
Jonathan Hayes	85-93					135	1541	11.4	12
Michael Haynes	88-93	4	35	8.8	0	254	4066	16.0	33
Herman Heard	83-89	651	2694	4.1	13	132	1125	8.5	3

Name	Years	RUSHING Att.	Yards	Avg.	TD	RECEIVING Rec.	Yards	Avg.	TD
Garrison Hearst	93	76	264	3.5	1	6	18	3.0	0
Larry Heater	80,82-83	114	373	3.3	3	12	154	12.8	0
Bobby Hebert	85-89,91-93	166	501	3.0	0	4	8	2.0	1
Vaughn Hebron	93	84	297	3.5	3	11	82	7.5	0
Johnny Hector	83-92	1051	4280	4.1	41	188	1661	8.8	3
Lakei Heimuli	87	34	128	3.8	0	5	51	10.2	1
Ron Heller	87-90,92					84	871	10.4	5
Keith Henderson	89-92	194	755	3.9	4	42	532	12.7	0
Bernard Henry	82-85					50	695	13.9	6
Wally Henry	77-82	2	-4	-2.0	0	15	229	15.3	2
Mark Herrmann	81-92	35	-2	-0.1	1				
Jessie Hester	85-88,90-93	6	25	4.3	1	298	4807	16.1	23
Craig Heyward	88-93	500	2019	4.0	13	83	620	7.5	1
Victor Hicks	80	1	19	19.0	0	23	318	13.4	3
Mark Higgs	88-93	730	2764	3.8	14	40	303	7.6	0
Alonzo Highsmith	87-92	283	1195	4.2	6	42	428	10.2	3
Rusty Hilger	85-88,90-91	35	91	2.6	0				
Bruce Hill	87-91	6	-8	-1.3	0	190	2942	15.5	23
David Hill	76-87	8	37	4.6	0	358	4212	11.8	28
Derek Hill	89-90					53	846	16.0	1
Drew Hill	79-93	3	19	6.3	0	634	9831	15.5	60
Eddie Hill	79-84	120	443	3.7	2	26	171	6.6	2
Tony Hill	77-86	14	84	6.0	0	479	7988	16.7	51
Lonzell Hill	87-90	4	-9	-2.3	0	136	1696	12.5	13
Randall Hill	91-93	1	4	4.0	0	136	1875	13.8	8
Ira Hillary	87-90	1	-2	-2.0	0	27	303	11.2	2
Dalton Hilliard	86-93	1126	4164	3.7	39	249	2233	9.0	14
Eric Hipple	80-86,88-89	145	550	3.8	13				
Leroy Hoard	90-93	205	766	3.7	5	119	1301	10.9	10
Floyd Hodge	82-84	4	28	7.0	0	63	674	10.7	4
Merril Hoge	87-93	819	3115	3.8	21	241	2054	8.5	23
Gary Hogeboom	80-89	83	181	2.2	4				
Jamie Holland	87-92	9	65	7.2	0	73	1037	14.2	1
Donald Hollas	91-92	32	175	5.5	0				
Steve Holloway	87					10	127	12.7	0
Rodney Holman	82-93					343	4573	13.3	36
Scott Holman	86-87					18	196	10.9	0
Don Holmes	86-90					25	413	16.5	1
Jack Holmes	78-82	117	393	3.4	4	71	453	6.4	1
Pete Holohan	81-92	1	3	3.0	0	363	3981	11.0	16
Mike Holston	81-85					74	1111	15.0	4
Harry Holt	83-87	5	36	5.0	1	70	895	12.8	5
Melvin Hoover	82-84	1	5	5.0	0	16	364	22.8	2
Ethan Horton	85,87,89-93	79	241	3.1	3	197	2203	11.2	13
Jeff Hostetler	84-93	187	906	4.8	14				
Kevin House	80-87	7	41	5.9	0	299	5169	17.3	34
Bobby Howard	86-87	60	210	3.5	2	15	183	12.2	0
Desmond Howard	92-93	5	31	6.2	0	26	306	11.8	0
William Howard	88-89	223	809	3.6	2	41	285	7.0	1
Steve Howell	79-81	68	235	3.5	1	10	70	7.0	0
Harlan Huckleby	80-85	242	779	3.2	10	53	411	7.8	3
Gordon Hudson	86					13	131	10.1	1
David Hughes	81-86	308	1041	3.4	2	107	864	8.1	5
Bobby Humphery	84-90	1	10	10.0	0	14	206	14.7	1
Bobby Humphrey	89-92	695	2857	4.1	15	100	815	8.2	2
Stan Humphries	89-93	64	232	3.6	6				
Eddie Hunter	87	56	209	3.7	0	7	28	4.0	2
Herman Hunter	85-87	64	287	4.5	1	56	646	11.5	2
Tony Hunter	83-86	4	28	7.0	0	134	1501	11.2	9
Mark Ingram	87-93	2	5	2.5	0	180	2918	16.2	17
Raghib Ismail	93	4	-5	-1.3	0	26	353	13.6	1
Quadry Ismail	93	3	14	4.7	0	19	212	11.2	1
Michael Irvin	88-93	5	5	1.0	0	337	5694	16.9	34
Eddie Lee Ivery	79-86	667	2933	4.4	23	162	1612	9.9	7
Alfred Jackson	79-84	3	9	3.0	0	188	3010	16.0	21
Andrew Jackson	87	50	208	4.2	1	5	14	2.8	0
Billy Jackson	81-84	399	1365	3.4	16	58	416	7.2	2
Bo Jackson	87-90	515	2782	5.4	16	40	352	8.8	2
Earnest Jackson	83-88	1059	4167	3.9	22	87	695	8.0	2
Keith Jackson	88-93					329	3963	12.0	31
Kenny Jackson	84-91	8	51	6.4	0	126	2170	17.2	11
Louis Jackson	81	27	68	2.5	1	3	25	8.3	0
Mark Jackson	86-93	21	94	4.5	0	334	5454	16.3	28
Michael Jackson	91-93	2	22	11.0	0	105	1779	16.9	17
Craig James	84-88	589	2479	4.2	11	81	819	10.1	2
Garry James	86-88	422	1502	3.6	12	89	816	9.2	2
Lionel James	84-88	231	1062	4.6	4	209	2278	10.9	10
Lynn James	90-91	1	11	11.0	0	10	139	13.9	1
Ron Jaworski	74-89	257	859	3.3	16				
John Jefferson	78-85	6	61	10.2	0	351	5714	16.3	47
Shawn Jefferson	91-93	6	80	13.3	0	71	893	12.6	5
Haywood Jeffires	87-93					386	4652	12.1	33
Ken Jenkins	83-86	80	397	5.0	1	21	246	11.7	0
Keith Jennings	89,91-93					51	570	11.2	1
Stanford Jennings	84-92	313	1250	4.0	9	116	1096	9.4	10
Derrick Jensen	79-86	224	780	3.5	5	44	384	8.7	3
Jim Jensen	81-92	26	142	5.5	0	229	2171	9.5	19
James Jett	93	1	0	0.0	0	33	771	23.4	3
Jim Jodat	77-83	226	866	3.8	7	35	265	7.6	2
Paul Johns	81-84	3	11	3.7	0	74	1058	14.3	7
Anthony Johnson	90-93	305	1017	3.3	1	151	1336	8.8	0
Bill Johnson	85-87	86	475	5.5	1	16	122	7.6	0
Billy "White Shoes" Johnson	74-87	56	316	5.6	2	337	4211	12.5	25
Bobby Johnson	84-86	2	28	14.0	0	112	1862	13.2	15
Butch Johnson	76-85	5	22	4.4	0	193	3091	16.0	28
Damone Johnson	87-92					132	1015	7.7	18
Dan Johnson	83-87					94	1012	10.8	16
Flip Johnson	88-89					34	473	13.9	2
Jimmie Johnson	89-93					30	361	12.0	4
Joe Johnson	89-92	4	26	6.5	0	24	247	10.3	1
Johnny Johnson	90-93	806	3147	3.9	18	135	1210	9.0	3
Maurice Johnson	91-93					18	167	9.3	2
Pete Johnson	77-84	1489	5626	3.8	76	175	1334	7.6	6
Reggie Johnson	91-93	2	7	3.5	0	36	455	12.6	3
Richard Johnson	87,89-90	12	38	3.2	0	135	1823	13.5	14

Name	Years	RUSHING Att.	Yards	Avg.	TD	RECEIVING Rec.	Yards	Avg.	TD
Ron Johnson	86-89	1	3	3.0	0	61	1105	18.1	4
Tracy Johnson	89-93	47	182	3.9	3	17	129	7.6	2
Troy Johnson	86-89					41	777	19.0	2
Trumaine Johnson	85-88					86	1150	13.4	4
Vance Johnson	85-93	17	44	2.6	0	403	5525	13.7	37
Daryl Johnston	89-93	135	436	3.2	4	140	1154	8.2	8
Bill Jones	90-92	10	47	4.7	0	35	240	6.9	6
Bobby Jones	78-83	2	23	11.5	0	89	1368	15.4	6
Brent Jones	87-93					246	3119	12.7	18
Cedric Jones	82-90	2	10	5.0	0	191	2703	14.1	16
Ernie Jones	88-93	12	76	6.3	0	215	3630	16.9	20
Fred Jones	90-93	6	33	5.5	0	36	466	12.9	0
Gordon Jones	79-83	2	2	1.0	0	97	1402	14.5	8
Hassan Jones	86-93	5	52	10.4	0	229	3824	16.7	24
James Jones	80-82,84-85	84	331	3.9	1	42	312	7.4	1
James Jones	83-92	1010	3626	3.6	26	318	2641	8.3	10
Johnny Lam Jones	80-84	9	17	1.9	0	138	2322	16.8	13
Keith Jones	89-92	180	665	3.7	6	66	593	9.0	0
Keith Jones	89	43	160	3.7	1	15	126	8.4	0
Mike Jones	83-89	7	60	8.6	0	123	2372	19.3	11
Tony Jones	90-93					63	798	12.7	9
Buford Jordon	86-91	184	687	3.7	8	37	355	9.6	2
Steve Jordan	82-93	1	4	4.0	1	495	6284	12.7	28
Tony Jordan	88-89	144	371	2.6	5	10	44	4.4	0
Tim Jorden	90-92					23	165	7.2	2
James Joseph	91-93	174	580	3.3	3	39	355	9.1	1
Trey Junkin	83-93					16	143	8.9	6
Vyto Kab	82-85,87					36	386	10.7	5
Rick Kane	77-85	409	1486	3.6	12	77	767	10.0	2
Tommy Kane	88-92					142	2034	14.3	9
Eric Kattus	86-92					66	698	10.6	5
Clarence Kay	84-92					193	2136	11.1	3
Jim Kelly	86-93	243	886	3.6	4	2	40	20.0	0
Jeff Kemp	83-91	109	448	4.1	1				
Perry Kemp	87-91	7	41	5.9	0	194	2565	13.2	8
Bill Kenney	79-88	123	191	1.6	5	2	0	0.0	0
Brian Kinchen	88-93					31	362	11.7	2
Bruce King	85-87	41	121	3.0	0	8	48	6.0	0
Kenny King	79-85	579	2477	4.3	7	89	715	8.0	1
Larry Kinnebrew	83-87,89-90	779	3133	4.0	44	70	660	9.4	3
Terry Kirby	93	119	390	3.3	3	75	874	11.7	3
Rocky Klever	83-87					46	514	11.1	3
David Klingler	92-93	52	335	6.4	0				
Jeff Komlo	79-83	38	121	3.2	2				
Bernie Kosar	85-93	171	223	1.3	4	3	-5	-1.2	0
Glen Kozlowski	87-92	1	3	3.0	0	31	471	15.2	3
Erik Kramer	87,91-93	58	70	1.2	1				
Tommy Kramer	77-90	214	531	2.5	8	1	23	23.0	1
Steve Kreider	79-86	4	23	5.8	0	150	2119	14.1	9
Dave Krieg	80-93	352	1188	3.4	12	2	5	2.5	0
Gary Kubiak	83-91	65	238	3.7	2				
Ken Lacy	84-85,87	56	235	3.6	2	13	87	6.7	2
Greg LaFleur	81-86					64	729	11.4	3
Eric Lane	81-87	129	405	3.1	4	42	357	8.5	2
David Lang	91-93	42	232	5.5	5	22	328	14.9	1
Gene Lang	84-90	319	1148	3.6	11	134	1244	9.3	9
Reggie Langhorne	85-93	9	27	3.0	1	411	5446	13.2	19
Steve Largent	76-89	17	83	4.9	1	819	13089	16.0	100
Derrick Lassic	93	75	269	3.6	3	9	37	4.1	0
Babe Laufenberg	83,85-90	33	126	3.6	0				
Michael LeBlanc	87	49	170	3.5	1	2	3	1.5	0
Terry LeCount	78-84	6	90	15.0	0	89	1354	15.2	7
Amp Lee	92-93	163	592	3.6	3	36	217	6.0	4
Danzell Lee	87					12	124	10.3	0
Gary Lee	87-88	41	569	13.9	1				
Ronnie Lee	79-89					25	167	6.7	3
Tim Lester	92-93	11	74	6.7	0	18	154	8.6	0
Darren Lewis	91-93	112	431	3.8	4	22	201	9.1	0
David Lewis	84-87					60	731	12.2	8
Gary Lewis	81-84	4	16	4.0	1	21	285	13.6	1
Greg Lewis	91-92	172	644	3.7	8	6	39	6.5	0
Leo Lewis	81-91	16	19	0.8	0	182	2924	16.1	16
Nate Lewis	90-93	12	44	3.7	1	128	1789	14.0	12
Ron Lewis	90,92-93					20	217	10.9	0
Louis Lipps	84-92	29	388	13.4	4	359	6019	16.8	39
Dave Little	84-91					25	243	9.7	1
Larry Linne	87					11	158	14.4	2
Charles Lockett	87-88					29	481	16.6	2
Scott Lockwood	92	35	162	4.6	0				
James Lofton	78-93	32	246	7.7	1	764	14004	18.3	75
Dave Logan	76-84					263	4250	16.2	24
Marc Logan	87-93	245	1060	4.3	11	56	487	8.7	0
Neil Lomax	81-88	222	969	4.4	10	1	10	10.0	0
Chuck Long	86-90	34	88	2.6	0				
Randy Love	79-86	65	211	3.2	3	15	95	6.3	2
Edwin Lovelady	87	2	11	5.5	0	10	125	12.5	2
Derek Loville	90-91	29	81	2.8	0				
Oliver Luck	83-86	44	237	5.4	1				
Ed Luther	80-84	20	-19	-1.0	0				
Eric Lynch	92-93	53	207	3.9	2	13	82	6.3	0
Rob Lytle	77-83	376	1451	3.9	12	61	562	9.2	2
Kevin Mack	85-93	1291	5123	4.0	46	197	1602	8.1	8
Calvin Magee	85-88					114	1379	12.1	11
Don Majkowski	87-93	189	929	4.9	9				
Mark Malone	80-89	159	628	3.9	18	1	90	90.0	1
Pete Mandley	84-90	9	48	5.3	1	172	2370	13.8	12
Tim Manoa	87-89,91	236	938	4.0	6	40	308	7.7	2
Lionel Manuel	84-90	9	44	4.9	0	232	3941	17.0	23
Ken Margerum	81-87	2	18	9.0	0	94	1336	14.2	8
Dan Marino	83-93	212	103	0.5	7				
Doug Marsh	80-86	2	0	0.0	0	166	2129	12.8	19
Arthur Marshall	92-93	11	56	5.1	0	54	853	16.0	3
Henry Marshall	76-87	24	257	10.7	2	416	6545	15.7	33
Eric Martin	85-93	4	11	2.8	0	532	7854	14.8	48
Kelvin Martin	87-93	11	7	0.6	0	269	3501	13.0	13

Lifetime Statistics- 1980-1993 Players Section 2 - **RUSHING and RECEIVING**
(All men with 25 or more rushing attempts or 10 or more receptions)

Name	Years	RUSHING Att.	Yards	Avg.	TD	RECEIVING Rec.	Yards	Avg.	TD
Mike Martin	83-89	3	24	8.0	0	67	1017	15.2	8
Sammy Martin	88-91	2	20	10.0	0	27	424	15.7	1
Tony Martin	90-93	3	12	4.0	0	109	1722	15.8	9
Rich Martini	79-81					33	367	11.1	2
Larry Mason	87-88	104	401	3.9	2	13	110	8.5	1
Rick Massie	87					13	244	18.8	4
Terance Mathis	90-93	8	73	9.1	2	93	1242	13.4	4
Ira Matthews	79-81	7	14	2.0	0	18	125	6.9	0
Bruce Mathison	83-87	34	245	7.2	1				
Allama Matthews	83-85					11	101	9.2	1
Aubrey Matthews	86-93	6	6	1.0	0	124	1671	13.5	6
Rich Mauti	77-83	1	2	2.0	0	21	314	15.0	2
James Mayberry	79-81	81	347	4.3	1	13	53	4.1	0
Rueben Mayes	86-88,90,92-93	866	3484	4.0	23	57	401	7.0	0
Derrick McAdoo	87-88	53	230	4.3	3	2	12	6.0	0
Fred McAfee	91-93	199	768	3.9	3	3	27	9.0	0
Ed McCaffrey	91-93					92	1091	11.9	7
Reece McCall	78-85					94	1366	14.5	12
Napoleon McCallum	86,90-93	220	785	3.6	2	16	121	7.6	0
Keenan McCardell	92-93					14	242	17.3	4
Willie McClendon	79-82	94	369	3.9	2	9	38	4.2	0
Mike McCloskey	83-85					29	318	11.0	3
David McCluskey	87	29	94	3.2	1	1	8	8.0	0
Phil McConkey	84-89					67	1118	16.6	2
James McDonald	83-85,87					14	168	12.0	3
Keith McDonald	87,89	1	-2	-2.0	0	16	194	12.1	1
Paul McDonald	82-87	37	10	0.3	1	1	-4	-4.0	0
Anthony McDowell	92-93	16	87	5.4	0	35	284	8.1	3
O.J. McDuffie	93	1	-4	-4.0	0	19	197	10.4	0
Craig McEwen	87-91					108	1010	12.1	6
Buford McGee	84-92	289	1086	3.8	17	155	1264	8.2	13
Tim McGee	86-93	7	36	5.1	0	308	5028	16.3	27
Tony McGee	93					44	525	11.9	0
Mark McGrath	81-85					15	171	11.4	1
Keith McKeller	87-93					115	1384	12.0	11
Dennis McKinnon	83-85,87-90	10	34	3.4	1	196	2925	14.9	22
Jim McMahon	82-93	329	1600	4.9	16	5	72	14.4	2
Randy McMillan	81-86	990	3876	3.9	24	164	1356	8.3	2
Greg McMurtry	90-93	2	3	1.5	0	120	1519	12.7	4
Todd McNair	89-93	119	635	5.3	3	165	1675	10.1	5
Travis McNeal	89-93	1	2	2.0	0	48	652	13.6	2
Freeman McNeil	81-92	1798	8074	4.5	38	295	2961	10.0	12
Gerald McNeil	86-90	4	61	15.3	0	29	380	13.1	2
Mike Meade	82-85	72	261	3.6	1	21	126	6.0	2
Natrone Means	93	160	645	4.0	8	10	59	5.9	0
Dave Meggett	89-93	180	932	5.2	1	199	1901	9.6	10
Guido Merkens	78-85,87	15	37	2.5	0	36	559	15.8	3
Eric Metcalf	89-93	499	1900	3.8	9	250	2296	9.2	12
Pete Metzelaars	82-93					280	2797	10.0	21
Bobby Micho	84,86-87	4	8	2.0	0	25	242	9.7	2
Frank Middleton	84-85,87	133	384	2.9	3	28	209	7.5	1
Ron Middleton	86-93					42	266	6.3	2
Terdell Middleton	77-83	561	2048	3.7	15	78	659	8.4	3
Glyn Milburn	93	52	231	4.4	0	38	300	7.9	3
Ostell Miles	92-93	30	78	2.6	1	6	89	14.8	0
Hugh Millen	87-93	57	195	3.5	1				
Anthony Miller	88-93	16	78	4.9	0	374	5582	14.9	37
Chris Miller	87-93	100	493	4.9	1				
Junior Miller	80-84	3	0	0.0	0	122	1409	11.5	14
Solomon Miller	86-87	1	3	3.0	0	14	241	17.2	2
Terry Miller	78-81	391	1583	4.0	8	35	382	10.9	0
James Milling	88,90,92					26	252	9.7	0
Ernie Mills	91-93	4	32	8.0	0	62	848	13.7	5
David Mims	93	1	3	3.0	0	12	107	8.9	1
Cedric Minter	84-85	42	159	3.8	1	11	122	11.1	1
Rick Mirer	93	68	343	5.0	3				
John Mistler	81-84					72	737	10.2	3
Brian Mitchell	90-93	87	411	4.7	4	25	192	7.7	0
Johnny Mitchell	92-93					55	840	15.3	7
Scott Mitchell	91-93	29	99	3.4	0				
Stump Mitchell	81-89	986	4649	4.7	32	209	1955	9.4	9
Orson Mobley	86-90	1	-1	-1.0	0	84	1019	12.1	4
Stacey Mobley	87,89					21	265	12.6	1
Tim Moffett	85-87	1	1	1.0	0	16	247	15.4	1
Art Monk	80-93	63	332	5.3	0	888	12026	13.5	65
Carl Monroe	83-87	15	62	4.1	0	28	323	11.5	2
Joe Montana	79-90,92-93	440	1659	3.8	20				
Tyrone Montgomery	93	37	106	2.9	0	10	43	4.3	0
Wilbert Montgomery	77-85	1540	6789	4.4	45	273	2502	9.2	12
Warren Moon	84-93	439	1541	3.5	21				
Alvin Moore	83-86	194	626	3.2	7	42	291	6.9	1
Booker Moore	82-85	115	420	3.7	1	75	423	5.6	1
Derrick Moore	93	88	405	4.6	3	21	169	8.0	1
Herman Moore	91-93					123	2036	16.6	10
Jeff Moore	79-83	208	722	3.5	7	115	1103	9.6	6
Jeff Moore	80-81					17	273	16.1	1
Nat Moore	74-86	40	249	6.2	1	510	7546	14.8	74
Ricky Moore	86-88	40	126	3.2	1	26	220	8.5	0
Rob Moore	90-93	4	11	2.8	0	228	3248	14.2	16
Ron Moore	93	263	1018	3.9	9	3	16	5.3	0
Emery Moorehead	77-88	47	114	2.4	0	224	2980	13.3	15
Anthony Morgan	91-93	6	86	14.3	0	28	542	19.3	4
Stanley Morgan	77-90	21	127	6.1	0	557	10716	19.2	72
Larry Moriarty	83-88	500	1908	3.8	13	77	494	6.4	2
Mike Moroski	79-86	37	182	4.9	2				
Jamie Morris	88-90	252	777	3.1	4	9	68	7.6	0
Joe Morris	82-88,91	1411	5585	4.0	50	111	960	8.2	2
Lee Morris	87	2	2	1.0	0	16	259	16.2	1
Randall Morris	84-88	156	651	4.2	1	9	61	6.8	0
Ron Morris	87-92	6	52	8.7	0	121	1991	16.4	9
Wayne Morris	76-84	899	3387	3.8	38	157	1201	7.6	5
Michael Morton	82-85,87	50	110	2.2	2	2	14	7.0	0
Rick Moser	78-82	54	190	3.5	1	3	10	3.3	1
Mike Moseley	82-84					27	314	11.6	3
Zeke Mowatt	83-84,86-91					135	1765	13.1	12

Name	Years	RUSHING Att.	Yards	Avg.	TD	RECEIVING Rec.	Yards	Avg.	TD
Bob Mrosko	89-91					14	145	10.4	1
Calvin Muhammad	82-85,87					69	1276	18.5	8
Mike Mularkey	84-91	1	-6	-6.0	0	102	1222	12.0	9
Jamie Mueller	87-90	238	901	3.8	4	28	169	6.0	1
Vance Mueller	86-90	128	469	3.7	3	40	452	11.3	2
Tom Mullady	79-84					84	1033	12.3	4
Chuck Muncie	76-84	1561	6702	4.3	71	263	2323	8.8	3
Walter Murray	86-87					22	373	17.0	3
Adrian Murrell	93	34	157	4.6	1	5	12	2.4	0
Brad Muster	88-93	519	2228	4.3	23	192	1818	9.5	7
Browning Nagle	91-93	25	56	2.2	0				
Tony Nathan	79-87	732	3543	4.8	16	383	3592	9.4	16
Ricky Nattiel	87-91	7	64	9.1	0	121	1972	16.3	8
Frankie Neal	87	1	0	0.0	0	36	420	11.7	3
Speedy Neal	84	49	175	3.6	1	9	76	8.4	0
Renaldo Nehemiah	82-84	1	-1	-1.0	0	43	754	17.5	4
Darrin Nelson	82-92	1020	4442	4.4	18	286	2559	8.9	5
Keith Neubert	88-89	28	302	10.8	1				
Pat Newman	90-93					14	175	12.5	1
Ozzie Newsome	78-90	18	135	7.5	2	662	7980	12.1	47
Timmy Newsome	80-88	342	1226	3.6	19	212	1966	9.3	11
Tom Newton	77-82	188	722	4.1	9	52	369	7.1	0
Mark Nichols	81-87	4	108	12.0	0	124	2228	18.0	9
Gifford Nielsen	78-83	29	89	3.1	0				
James Noble	86-87					10	78	7.8	2
Ulysses Norris	79-85					43	547	12.7	8
Jay Novacek	85-93	2	12	6.0	1	313	3450	11.0	23
Brent Novoselsky	88-93					12	101	8.4	2
Terry Obee	01,03					26	351	13.5	3
Ken O'Brien	83-93	174	394	2.3	0	1	27	27.0	0
Neil O'Donnell	90-93	71	198	2.8	2				
Christian Okoye	87-92	1246	4897	3.9	40	42	294	7.0	0
Mike Oliphant	88-89,91	23	127	5.5	1	18	133	7.4	0
Hubert Oliver	81-86	270	1030	3.8	2	93	602	6.5	2
Terry Orr	86-93					52	939	18.1	10
Keith Ortego	85-87					23	430	18.7	1
David Overstreet	83	85	392	4.6	1	8	55	6.9	2
James Owens	79-84	271	944	3.5	8	56	535	9.6	3
Mike Pagel	82-93	136	831	6.1	4				
Stephone Paige	83-91	6	32	5.3	0	377	6341	16.8	49
Tony Paige	84-92	272	853	3.1	20	197	1515	7.7	9
Carl Painter	88-89	32	106	3.3	0	4	42	10.5	0
Paul Palmer	87-89	280	1053	3.7	4	74	731	9.9	4
Robert Parker	87	47	150	3.2	1	7	44	6.3	0
Rodney Parker	80-81					17	316	18.6	3
Rick Parros	81-85,87	350	1381	3.9	7	82	660	8.0	5
Keith Pasketti	87					12	188	15.7	1
Mark Pattison	86-88					12	152	12.7	0
Rickey Patton	78-81	261	885	3.4	5	43	326	7.6	2
Walter Payton	75-87	3838	16726	4.4	110	492	4538	9.2	15
Elvis Peacock	79-81	216	1001	4.6	7	46	473	10.3	2
Danny Peebles	89-91	2	-6	-3.0	0	17	230	13.5	1
Rodney Peete	89-93	172	886	5.2	13				
Erric Pegram	91-93	414	1623	3.9	4	36	326	9.1	0
Steve Pelluer	84-90	143	858	6.0	6				
Bruce Perkins	90-91	17	47	2.8	0	11	83	7.5	0
Johnny Perkins	77-82	3	2	0.7	0	163	2611	16.0	18
Brett Perriman	88-93	12	33	2.8	0	242	2927	12.1	11
Leon Perry	80-82	134	543	4.1	1	22	223	10.1	2
Bob Perryman	87-92	393	1338	3.4	9	83	616	7.4	0
Jason Phillips	89-93					49	578	11.8	2
Carl Pickens	92-93					69	891	12.9	7
Aaron Pierce	92-93					12	212	17.7	0
Frank Pillow	88-90					23	324	14.1	1
Allen Pinkett	86-91	561	2324	4.1	21	119	921	7.7	5
Joe Pisarcik	77-84	65	147	2.3	5				
Danny Pittman	80-84	1	-7	-7.0	0	46	657	14.3	1
Frank Pollard	80-88	953	3989	4.2	20	104	872	8.4	0
Nathan Poole	79-83,85,87	126	423	3.4	5	24	179	7.5	0
Ricky Porter	82-83,87	47	177	3.8	0	9	70	7.8	0
Tracy Porter	81-84					79	1161	14.7	3
Roosevelt Potts	93	179	711	4.0	0	26	189	7.3	0
Jim Price	91-93					70	738	10.5	4
Dave Preston	78-83	479	1793	3.7	10	161	1423	8.8	3
James Primus	88	35	95	2.7	1	8	42	5.3	0
Mike Pritchard	91-93	7	41	5.9	0	201	2187	10.9	14
Ricky Proehl	90-93	15	95	6.4	0	236	3189	13.5	16
James Pruitt	86-91					63	1013	16.1	10
Mike Pruitt	76-86	1846	7378	4.0	51	270	1860	6.9	5
Jeff Query	89-93	6	53	8.8	0	136	1821	13.4	11
Alfred Pupunu	92-93					13	142	10.9	0
Mike Quick	82-90	1	-5	-5.0	0	363	6464	17.8	61
Derrick Ramsey	78-85					188	2364	12.6	21
Eason Ramson	78-83,85	5	9	1.8	0	104	983	9.5	5
Tom Rathman	86-93	516	1902	3.7	26	294	2490	8.5	8
Barry Redden	82-90	396	1735	4.4	10	10	88	8.8	1
Jarvis Redwine	81-83	17	70	4.1	0	1	4	4.0	0
Andre Reed	85-93	47	342	7.3	1	586	8233	14.0	58
Jake Reed	91-93					11	207	18.8	0
Walter Reeves	89-93					42	271	6.4	1
Frank Reich	85-93	56	42	0.8	0				
Reggie Rembert	91-93					30	437	12.1	1
Mike Renfro	78-87	3	24	8.0	0	323	4708	14.6	28
Allen Rice	84-91	337	1034	3.1	13	100	1067	10.7	6
Jerry Rice	85-93	57	428	7.5	6	708	11776	16.6	118
Curvin Richards	91-92	51	180	3.5	1	3	8	2.7	0
Eric Richardson	85-86					15	250	16.7	0
Robb Riddick	81,83-84,86-88	330	1341	4.1	21	120	1165	9.7	5
Gerald Riggs	82-91	1989	8188	4.1	69	201	1516	7.5	0
Jim Riggs	87-93					37	274	7.4	0
Bill Ring	81-86	183	732	4.0	7	45	336	7.5	1
Andre Rison	89-93	4	9	2.3	0	394	5367	13.6	52
Reggie Rivers	91-93	91	337	3.7	4	51	508	10.0	2
Alfredo Roberts	88-92					48	450	9.4	2
Bo Robinson	79-85	121	445	3.7	2	37	305	8.2	3

		RUSHING				RECEIVING			
Name	Years	Att.	Yards	Avg.	TD	Rec.	Yards	Avg.	TD
Greg Robinson	93	156	591	3.8	1	15	142	9.5	0
Matt Robinson	77-82	58	117	2.0	4				
Stacy Robinson	85-90					48	649	13.5	7
Del Rodgers	82-84,87-88	82	315	3.8	2	10	124	12.4	0
George Rogers	81-87	1692	7176	4.2	54	55	368	6.7	0
Jimmy Rogers	80-83	175	661	3.8	3	33	296	9.0	2
Butch Rolle	86-93					38	213	5.6	11
Stan Rome	79-82	1	-5	-5.0	0	20	261	13.1	1
Joe Rose	80-85					112	1493	13.3	13
Timm Rosenbach	89-90,92	101	507	5.0	3				
Dan Ross	79-83,85-86					290	3419	11.8	19
James Rouse	90-91	43	130	3.0	0	15	93	6.2	0
Mazio Royster	92-93	33	115	3.5	1	6	26	4.3	0
Lee Rouson	85-91	114	415	3.6	2	33	453	13.7	2
Mike Rozier	85-91	1159	4462	3.8	30	90	715	8.1	1
Robb Rubick	82-88	1	1	1.0	1	44	511	11.6	3
T.J. Rubley	93	29	102	3.5	0				
Booker Russell	78-81	90	419	4.7	8	7	74	10.6	0
Derek Russell	91-93					77	1176	15.3	4
Leonard Russell	91-93	689	2437	3.5	13	55	350	6.4	0
Jeff Rutledge	79-92	52	93	1.8	1				
Pat Ryan	78-89,91	53	156	2.9	1				
Mark Rypien	87-93	110	149	1.4	5				
Jay Saldi	76-84	2	18	9.0	0	84	913	10.9	7
Lawrence Sampleton	82-84,87					11	116	10.5	0
Clint Sampson	83-86					66	1014	15.4	8
Barry Sanders	89-93	1432	6789	4.7	55	165	1481	9.0	2
Deion Sanders	89-93	1	-4	-4.0	0	11	160	14.5	2
Ricky Sanders	86-93	23	94	4.1	1	414	5854	14.1	36
Thomas Sanders	85-91	321	1237	3.8	12	28	284	10.1	1
Broderick Sargent	86-87,89	38	177	4.7	1	9	77	8.6	0
John Sawyer	75-84					129	1496	11.6	2
James Saxon	88-93	136	517	3.8	5	42	364	8.7	0
Dwight Scales	76-79,81-84					56	1120	20.0	4
Greg Scales	88-91					21	196	9.3	2
Art Schlichter	82,84-85	22	161	7.3	1				
Turk Schonert	81-88	73	288	3.9	4				
Jay Schroeder	84-93	226	702	3.1	5				
Scott Schwedes	87-90					19	370	19.5	2
Lindsay Scott	82-85	1	-4	-4.0	0	69	864	12.5	1
Malcolm Scott	83,87					23	241	10.5	0
Patrick Scott	87-88					28	354	12.6	1
Ronald Scott	87	47	199	4.2	3	2	7	3.5	0
Willie Scott	81-88	1	1	1.0	0	89	766	8.6	15
Virgil Seay	81-84					43	792	8.4	5
Scott Secules	88-91,93	24	136	5.7	1				
Joe Senser	80-84	2	1	0.5	0	165	1822	11.0	16
John Settle	87-90	439	1801	4.1	10	118	1039	8.8	3
Steve Sewell	86-91	148	642	4.3	9	163	2160	13.3	12
Shannon Sharpe	90-93	3	9	3.0	0	163	2056	12.6	13
Sterling Sharpe	88-93	20	57	2.9	0	501	7015	14.0	47
Derrick Shepard	87-90	3	12	4.0	0	20	304	15.2	1
Heath Sherman	89-93	537	2130	4.0	10	75	608	8.1	4
Mike Sherrard	86,90-93	2	11	5.5	0	144	2344	16.3	11
Tim Sherwin	81-87					76	1002	13.2	2
Mickey Shuler	78-91					462	5100	11.0	37
Mike Shumann	78-83	1	19	19.0	0	62	760	12.3	5
Eric Sievers	81-90	1	-7	-7.0	0	214	2485	11.6	16
Vai Sikahema	86-93	59	217	3.7	0	53	537	10.1	1
Phil Simms	79-81, 83-93	349	1252	3.6	6	2	7	3.5	0
Billy Sims	80-84	1131	5106	4.5	42	186	2072	11.1	5
Marvin Sims	80-81	54	186	3.4	2	9	64	7.1	0
Paul Skansi	83-91					166	1950	11.7	10
Webster Slaughter	86-93	9	50	5.5	0	421	6224	14.8	36
Torrance Small	92-93					39	442	11.3	4
Chris Smith	86-87	26	114	4.4	0	2	21	10.5	0
Don Smith	88-90	40	165	4.1	3	40	473	11.8	0
Emmitt Smith	90-93	1262	5699	4.5	50	189	1235	6.5	3
Irv Smith	93					16	180	11.3	2
Jeff Smith	85-88	204	752	3.7	5	87	718	8.3	7
Jim Smith	77-82,85	2	27	13.5	0	113	2103	18.6	25
J.T. Smith	78-90	7	76	10.9	0	544	6974	12.8	35
Kendal Smith	89-90					17	185	10.9	1
Robert Smith	93	82	399	4.9	2	24	111	4.6	0
Ron Smith	78-83	1	7	7.0	0	62	1006	16.2	4
Sammie Smith	89-92	532	1881	3.5	15	32	310	9.7	1
Steve Smith	87-93	394	1528	3.9	7	113	1049	9.3	11
Tim Smith	83-86	2	16	8.0	0	206	3107	15.1	12
Timmy Smith	87-88,90	190	602	3.2	3	9	51	5.7	0
Tony Smith	92-93	87	329	3.8	2	2	14	7.0	0
Kurt Sohn	81-82,84-88	3	1	0.3	0	79	1016	12.9	10
Freddie Solomon	75-85	61	519	8.5	4	371	5846	15.8	48
John Spagnola	79-89					263	2886	11.0	15
Tim Spencer	85-89	474	1792	3.8	19	53	432	8.2	0
Todd Spencer	84-85,87	28	80	2.9	0	5	72	14.4	0
Ron Springs	79-84	694	2519	3.6	28	249	2259	7.1	10
John Stallworth	74-87	9	64	7.1	0	537	8723	16.2	63
Sylvester Stamps	84-89	66	382	5.8	1	48	413	8.6	1
Walter Stanley	85-90,92	6	58	9.7	0	130	2213	17.0	5
Stephen Starring	83-88	5	-3	-0.6	0	120	2029	16.9	11
John Stephens	88-93	945	3438	3.6	18	105	812	7.7	1
Dave Stief	78-81	2	0	0.0	0	67	1043	15.6	5
Dwight Stone	87-93	94	550	5.9	1	145	2379	16.4	12
Cliff Stoudt	82-83,86,88	122	661	5.4	4				
Kelly Stouffer	88-92	30	75	2.5	0				
Mike Strachan	75-80	472	1902	4.0	14	57	392	6.9	0
Troy Stradford	87-92	356	1370	3.8	10	170	1479	8.7	2
Don Strock	74-88	57	18	0.3	2				
Ray Strong	78-82	45	163	3.6	3	9	71	7.9	0
Matt Suhey	80-89	828	2946	3.6	20	260	2113	8.1	5
Don Summers	84-85,87					10	115	11.5	1
Calvin Sweeney	80-87	1	-2	-2.0	0	113	1775	15.7	7
Harry Sydney	87-92	190	805	4.2	9	84	682	8.1	4
John Tagliaferri	87	13	45	3.5	1	12	117	9.8	0
Steve Tasker	85-93					10	152	15.2	3

		RUSHING				RECEIVING			
Name	Years	Att.	Yards	Avg.	TD	Rec.	Yards	Avg.	TD
Lars Tate	88-90	292	1061	3.6	15	16	98	6.2	1
Rodney Tate	82-84	27	79	2.9	0	18	142	7.9	0
Mosi Tatupu	78-90	612	2415	3.9	18	96	843	8.8	2
Junior Tautalatasi	86-89	97	275	2.8	0	88	706	8.0	2
Billy Taylor	78-81	456	1641	3.6	13	78	647	8.3	4
Craig Taylor	89-91	114	480	4.2	7	28	188	6.7	2
John Taylor	87-93	4	33	8.3	0	277	4680	16.9	36
Kitrick Taylor	88-93	1	2	2.0	0	36	414	11.5	1
Lenny Taylor	84,87	1	-13	-13.0	0	13	179	13.8	1
Jimmy Teal	85-87					21	282	13.4	3
Derek Tennell	87-89,91-93					40	371	9.3	5
Vinny Testaverde	87-93	190	979	5.1	5	1	3	3.0	0
Joe Theismann	74-85	355	1815	5.1	17				
Yancey Thigpen	91-93					10	156	15.6	3
Blair Thomas	90-93	468	2009	4.3	5	64	473	7.4	2
Calvin Thomas	82-88	171	672	3.9	5	20	115	5.8	0
Charley Thomas	82-84	53	215	4.1	1	11	52	4.7	0
Doug Thomas	91-93	4	11	2.8	0	22	207	9.4	0
George Thomas	89-92					56	848	15.1	3
Jewerl Thomas	80-84	173	783	4.5	4	28	167	6.0	0
Ken Thomas	83	15	55	3.7	0	28	236	8.4	1
Robb Thomas	89-93	1	-1	-1.0	0	110	1301	11.8	5
Thurman Thomas	88-93	1731	7631	4.4	41	295	3053	10.3	16
Zach Thomas	83-84					12	182	15.2	0
Anthony Thompson	90-92	251	831	3.3	6	14	74	5.3	0
Aundra Thompson	77-82	13	16	1.2	0	109	1792	16.4	8
Craig Thompson	92-93					36	281	7.8	3
Darrell Thompson	90-93	462	1644	3.6	7	41	330	8.0	1
Jack Thompson	79-84	70	262	3.7	6				
Leonard Thompson	75-86	64	327	5.1	3	277	4682	16.9	35
Leroy Thompson	91-93	260	980	3.8	3	74	655	8.9	0
Vince Thompson	81, 83	75	349	4.7	2	8	56	7.0	0
Weegie Thompson	84-89					79	1377	17.4	11
Jim Thornton	88-91,93	1	4	4.0	0	87	1167	13.4	7
Sidney Thornton	77-82	356	1512	4.2	18	46	515	11.2	6
John Tice	83-92					158	1603	10.1	15
Mike Tice	81-93					104	872	8.4	11
Pat Tilley	76-86	1	32	32.0	0	468	7005	15.0	37
Cedric Tillman	92-93					29	404	13.9	3
Lawyer Tillman	89,91-93	2	15	7.5	0	36	626	17.4	3
Lewis Tillman	89-93	355	1406	4.0	5	16	93	5.8	0
Spencer Tillman	87-93	38	169	4.4	1	3	7	2.3	0
Michael Timpson	89-93	1	-4	-4.0	0	98	1515	14.5	5
Richard Todd	76-86	259	932	3.6	14	1	1	1.0	0
Billy Joe Tolliver	89-93	41	91	2.2	0				
Mike Tomczak	85-93	138	454	3.3	7	1	5	5.0	0
Anthoney Toney	86-90	639	2294	3.6	14	122	1031	8.5	5
Al Toon	85-92	4	7	1.8	0	517	6605	12.8	31
JoJo Townsell	85-89	2	0	0.0	0	66	1012	15.3	5
Jack Trudeau	86-93	91	156	1.7	3				
Eric Truvillion	87					10	184	18.4	1
Tom Tupa	89-92	47	181	3.9	1				
Daryl Turner	84-87					101	1872	18.5	36
Floyd Turner	89-93	2	8	4.0	0	124	1808	14.6	14
Kevin Turner	92-93	60	271	4.5	0	46	385	8.4	4
Odessa Turner	87-93	2	11	5.5	0	97	1479	15.2	8
Perry Tuttle	82-84					25	375	15.0	3
Robert Tyler	89					14	148	10.6	0
Toussaint Tyler	81-82	46	204	4.4	0	27	166	6.2	0
Wendell Tyler	77-86	1344	6378	4.7	50	202	1816	9.0	16
Tommy Vardell	92-93	270	1013	3.8	3	32	279	8.7	1
Jon Vaughn	91-93	180	750	4.2	3	22	173	7.9	0
Elton Veals	84	31	87	2.8	0				
Clarence Verdin	86-93	17	167	9.8	0	82	1329	16.2	6
David Verser	81-85	7	48	6.9	2	23	454	19.7	3
Roger Vick	87-90	333	1289	3.9	10	66	469	7.1	2
Tommy Vigorito	81-83, 85	54	215	4.0	2	59	439	7.4	2
Lionel Vital	87	80	346	4.3	2				
Tom Waddle	89-93					148	1865	12.6	8
Billy Waddy	77-82,84	10	53	5.3	0	120	1963	16.4	10
Frank Wainright	91-92					10	146	14.6	0
Byron Walker	82-86					54	925	17.1	7
Derrick Walker	90-93					98	979	10.0	4
Dwight Walker	82-84,87	20	92	4.6	0	49	546	11.1	1
Herschel Walker	86-93	1794	7468	4.2	55	410	3887	9.5	16
Rick Walker	77-85	10	36	3.6	0	70	673	9.6	9
Wayne Walker	89	1	9	9.0	0	24	395	16.5	1
Wesley Walker	77-89	6	35	5.8	0	438	8306	19.0	71
Ray Wallace	86-87,89	76	330	4.3	4	24	211	8.8	2
Herkie Walls	83-85,87	9	64	7.1	0	32	587	18.3	2
Wesley Walls	89-91					11	67	6.1	1
Steve Walsh	89-93	38	37	1.0	0				
Andre Ware	90-93	38	217	5.7	0				
Curt Warner	83-90	1698	6844	4.0	56	193	1467	7.6	7
Chris Warren	90-93	513	2113	4.1	11	33	242	7.3	0
Don Warren	79-92	1	5	5.0	0	244	2536	10.4	7
Joe Washington	76-85	1195	4839	4.0	12	395	3413	8.6	18
Steve Watson	79-87	6	19	3.2	0	353	6112	17.3	36
Ricky Watters	92-93	414	1963	4.7	19	74	731	9.9	3
Ricky Watts	79-82	3	-23	-7.7	0	81	1547	19.1	8
Clarence Weathers	83-91	2	46	23.0	0	160	2426	15.2	17
Robert Weathers	82-86	159	733	4.6	4	29	268	9.2	0
Gary Wellman	92-93	2	6	3.0	0	31	430	13.9	1
Ed West	84-93	2	2	1.0	1	171	1944	11.4	23
Cleve Wester	87	33	113	3.4	0				
Danta Whitaker	90,92-93					9	74	8.2	1
Ken Whisenhunt	85-88,90-92	2	23	11.5	0	62	596	9.6	5
Charles White	80-88	780	3075	3.9	23	114	860	7.5	1
Danny White	76-88	159	482	3.0	8	3	18	6.0	2
Lorenzo White	88-93	809	3322	4.1	27	163	1486	9.1	5
Sammy White	76-85	18	97	5.4	0	393	6400	16.3	50
David Whitehurst	77-83	77	242	3.1	7				
Art Whittington	78-82	448	1592	3.6	13	84	764	9.1	2
James Wilder	81-90	1586	6008	3.8	37	431	3500	8.1	10
Gary Wilkins	86-91	3	18	6.0	0	42	584	13.9	6

(All men with 25 or more rushing attempts or 10 or more receptions)

		RUSHING				RECEIVING			
Name	**Years**	**Att.**	**Yards**	**Avg.**	**TD**	**Rec.**	**Yards**	**Avg.**	**TD**
Gerald Willhite	82-88	380	1688	4.4	17	207	1767	8.5	5
Kevin Willhite	87	53	251	4.7	0	6	37	6.2	0
Al Williams	87	1	11	11.0	0	12	247	20.6	1
Brooks Williams	78-83					37	455	12.3	2
Byron Williams	83-85					84	1693	18.6	3
Calvin Williams	90-93	2	20	10.0	0	172	2251	13.1	29
David Williams	86-87					10	195	19.5	0
Derwin Williams	85-86					11	198	18.0	0
Dokie Williams	83-87	3	27	9.0	0	148	2886	19.4	25
Doug Williams	78-82,86-89	220	884	4.0	15				
Harvey Williams	91-93	217	858	4.0	2	28	213	7.6	2
Jamie Williams	84-93					178	1955	10.9	11
John L. Williams	86-93	1148	4579	4.0	17	471	4151	8.8	16
Keith Williams	86	3	18	6.0	0	12	164	13.7	1
Kevin Williams	93	7	26	3.7	2	20	151	7.6	2
Mike Williams	83-84,87	150	517	3.4	0	33	259	7.8	0
Mike Williams	79-81	71	261	3.7	1	19	141	7.4	3
Newton Williams	83	28	77	2.8	0	4	46	11.5	0
Oliver Williams	87					20	340	17.0	2
Ray Williams	80	2	17	8.5	1	10	148	14.6	1
Scott Williams	86-88	30	73	2.4	3	9	71	7.9	1
Van Williams	83-85,87	50	170	3.4	0	10	82	8.2	0
Vince Williams	82-84	41	130	3.2	0	9	79	8.8	1
Warren Williams	88-93	258	1191	4.6	8	37	295	8.0	1
Chester Willis	81-83	32	73	2.3	1	1	24	24.0	0
Charles Wilson	90-93	5	10	2.0	0	41	614	15.0	1
Dave Wilson	81,83-89	45	23	0.5	2				
Marc Wilson	80-87,89-90	141	551	3.9	5				
Mike Wilson	81-90					158	2199	13.9	15
Robert Wilson	91	42	179	4.3	0	20	121	6.1	2
Stanley Wilson	83-85,86,88	253	1118	4.4	11	28	277	9.6	2
Tim Wilson	77-84	398	1414	3.6	6	99	609	6.2	3
Wade Wilson	81-93	205	971	4.7	8				
Walter Wilson	90	1	0	0.0	0	10	87	8.7	0
Wayne Wilson	79-87	684	2531	3.7	19	181	1533	8.5	14
Sammy Winder	82-90	1495	5427	3.6	39	197	1302	6.6	9
Kellen Winslow	79-87					541	6741	12.5	45
Ron Wolfley	85-93	83	254	3.1	2	26	200	7.7	1
George Wonsley	84-89	281	1158	4.1	9				
Nate Wonsley	86	73	339	4.6	3	8	57	7.1	0
Otis Wonsley	81-85	61	181	3.0	4	2	6	3.0	1
David Woodley	80-85	201	856	4.3	11	2	21	10.5	1
Tony Woodruff	82-84					36	554	15.4	5
Keith Woodside	88-91	259	976	3.8	6	144	1248	8.7	2
Ickey Woods	88-91	332	1525	4.8	27	47	397	8.4	0
Butch Woolfolk	82-88	537	1923	3.6	8	187	1939	10.4	8
Barry Word	87-88,90-93	705	2897	4.1	16	30	280	9.3	0
Vince Workman	89-93	320	1211	3.8	12	151	1102	7.3	6
Tim Worley	89-91,93	446	1775	4.0	7	34	245	7.2	0
Adrian Wright	87	37	112	3.0	0	13	98	7.5	0
Alexander Wright	90-93	5	25	5.0	0	60	911	15.2	6
James Wright	78-85	3	-4	-1.3	0	66	666	10.1	4
Randy Wright	84-88	55	173	3.5	3				
Tim Wrightman	85-86					46	648	14.0	1
Frank Wycheck	93					16	113	7.1	0
Dave Young	81-84					19	213	11.2	3
Duane Young	91-93					12	98	8.2	0
Michael Young	85-93					144	2034	14.1	14
Steve Young	85-93	431	2676	6.2	20	2	2	1.0	0
Tyrone Young	83-84					36	682	18.9	6
Jim Zorn	76-85,87	322	1504	4.7	17	1	27	27.0	0

		PUNT RETURNS				KICKOFF RETURNS			
Name	**Years**	**No.**	**Yards**	**Avg.**	**TD**	**No.**	**Yards**	**Avg.**	**TD**
Stefon Adams	86-90	43	321	7.5	0	65	1240	19.1	0
Anthony Allen	85-89	35	216	6.2	0	8	140	17.5	0
Gary Allen	82-84	63	599	9.5	1	56	1136	20.3	0
Marvin Allen	88-91					43	844	19.6	0
Alfred Anderson	84-91					42	803	19.1	0
Gary Anderson	85-88,90-93	48	385	8.0	0	143	2779	19.4	1
Kim Anderson	80-81	5	7	1.4	0	40	779	19.5	0
Larry Anderson	78-84	75	582	7.8	0	189	4217	22.3	1
Tyrone Anthony	84-85					45	966	21.5	0
Gene Atkins	87-92					71	1508	21.2	0
Cliff Austin	83-87					57	1047	18.4	1
Johnny Bailey	90-93	127	1225	9.6	2	98	2063	21.1	0
Randy Baldwin	91-93					55	1133	20.6	0
Eric Ball	89-93					73	1559	21.4	0
Gordon Banks	85-87	37	220	5.9	0	1	56	56.0	0
Lew Barnes	86,88-89	93	830	8.9	0	9	236	26.2	1
Brian Baschnagel	76-84	6	58	9.7	0	89	2102	23.6	1
Michael Bates	93					30	603	20.1	0
Shawn Beals	88					34	625	18.4	0
Don Beebe	89-93					39	753	19.3	0
Ken Bell	86-89	25	147	5.9	0	104	2218	21.3	0
Theo Bell	76-85	189	1511	8.0	0	3	50	16.7	0
Albert Bentley	85-92					149	3192	21.4	0
Rufus Bess	79-87	55	432	7.9	0	48	998	20.8	0
Don Bessillieu	79-83	2	12	6.0	0	47	1024	21.6	0
Eric Bieniemy	91-93	30	229	7.6	0	22	367	16.7	0
Lyle Blackwood	73-86	69	319	4.6	0	19	388	20.4	0
Carl Bland	84-90	5	59	11.8	0	36	697	19.4	0
Brian Brennan	84-92	56	438	7.8	1	1	10	10.0	0
Leon Bright	81-85	141	1149	8.1	0	77	1544	20.1	0
Bill Brooks	86-93	44	295	6.7	0	8	143	17.9	0
James Brooks	81-92	52	565	10.9	0	130	2762	21.2	0
Robert Erooks	92-93	27	237	8.8	0	41	949	23.1	0
Bobby Brown	68-70	69	404	5.9	0	22	437	19.9	0
Curtis Brown	77-83	1	0	0.0	0	41	874	21.3	1
Dave Brown	75-90	35	291	8.3	0	6	126	21.0	0
Preston Brown	80-84	10	42	4.2	0	46	937	20.4	0
Reggie Brown	82-83,87					25	486	19.4	0
Ron Brown	84-91					199	4493	22.6	4
Tim Brown	88-93	193	1960	10.2	2	47	1204	25.6	1
Troy Brown	93	25	224	9.0	0	15	243	16.2	0
Steve Brown	83-86					36	857	23.8	1
Vince Buck	90-92	70	569	8.1	0	3	38	12.7	0
Terrell Buckley	92	21	211	10.0	1				
Barney Bussey	86-92					29	507	17.5	0
Ken Callicutt	78-81	5	25	5.0	0	44	742	16.9	0
Jack Cameron	84					26	485	18.7	0
Jeff Campbell	90-93	4	15	3.8	0	25	384	15.4	0
Billy Campfield	78-83					74	1566	21.2	1
Rob Carpenter	91-93	28	208	7.4	0				
Carlos Carson	80-89					57	1241	21.9	0
Dale Carter	92-93	65	645	9.9	2	11	190	17.3	0
Dexter Carter	90-93	34	411	11.7	1	105	2171	20.7	1
Jimmy Cefalo	78-84	30	242	8.1	0	2	40	20.0	0
Larry Centers	90-93	5	30	6.0	0	32	602	18.8	0
Wes Chandler	78-88	67	428	6.4	0	47	1021	21.7	0
Darryl Clack	86-89					83	1802	21.7	0
Allan Clark	79-82					44	912	20.7	0
Kevin Clark	87-88,90-91	59	575	9.7	0	22	550	25.0	0
Charles Crawford	86					27	497	18.4	0
Raymond Clayborn	77-88					57	1538	27.0	3
Mark Clayton	83-93	52	485	9.3	1	3	40	13.3	0
Pat Coleman	90-93	29	173	6.0	0	32	601	18.8	0
Tony Collins	81-87,90	3	15	5.0	0	67	1365	20.4	0
Curtis Conway	93					21	450	21.4	0
Evan Cooper	84-88	101	763	7.6	0	43	790	18.4	0
Danny Copeland	89					26	466	17.9	0
Russell Copeland	93	31	274	8.8	1	24	436	18.2	0
Aaron Craver	91-92					40	789	19.7	0
Joe Cribbs	80-83,85-88	29	154	5.3	0	56	1229	21.9	1
Kenneth Davis	86-93					41	707	17.2	0
Robert Delpino	88-93					68	1339	19.7	0
Floyd Dixon	86-91	26	151	5.8	0	2	13	6.5	0
James Dixon	89-91					101	2315	22.9	1
Zachary Dixon	79-84	1	5	5.0	0	128	2634	20.6	1
Willie Drewrey	85-93	192	1597	8.3	0	102	2097	20.6	0
Doug DuBose	87-88					32	608	19.0	0
Kenny Duckett	82-85					73	1511	20.7	0
Curtis Duncan	87-93	13	67	5.1	0	29	580	20.0	0
Jim Duncan	69-71					42	1369	32.6	2
Kenny Easley	81-87	26	302	11.6	0				
Bobby Joe Edmonds	86-89	105	1178	11.2	1	115	2549	22.2	0
Al Edwards	90-91	27	161	6.0	0	42	879	20.9	1
Anthony Edwards	88-93	19	143	7.5	0	30	514	17.1	0
Donnie Elder	85-86,89-91	1	0	0.0	0	150	3040	20.3	0
Henry Ellard	83-93	135	1527	11.3	4	19	364	19.2	0
Craig Ellis	86	24	149	6.2	0	25	541	21.6	0
Phillip Epps	82-89	100	819	8.2	1	34	686	20.2	0
Rich Erenberg	84					28	575	20.5	0
Ricky Feacher	76-84	15	157	10.5	0	37	821	22.2	0
Ron Fellows	81-87	48	325	6.8	0	73	1478	20.2	0
Gill Fenerty	90-91	12	55	4.6	0	30	600	20.0	0
Jitter Fields	84	27	236	8.7	0	19	356	18.7	0
Jeff Fisher	81-84	120	1125	9.4	1	14	204	14.6	0
Terrence Flagler	87-91					57	1049	18.4	0
Herman Fontenot	85-90					50	997	19.9	0
Phil Freeman	85-87					79	1667	21.1	0
Irving Fryar	84-93	206	2055	10.0	3	27	505	18.7	0
Brent Fullwood	87-90					62	1293	20.9	0
Bobby Futrell	86-90	77	639	8.3	0	42	820	19.5	0
Tony Galbreath	76-87	5	9	1.8	0	27	501	18.6	0
Gregg Garrity	83-89	21	203	9.7	1				
Alvin Garrett	80-84	43	344	8.0	0	50	1013	20.3	0
Willie Gault	83-93					45	1088	24.2	1
Dennis Gentry	82-92	15	77	5.1	1	192	4353	22.7	3
Nesby Glasgow	79-90	80	651	8.1	1	85	1906	22.4	0
Darrien Gordon	93	31	395	12.7	0				
Sam Graddy	87-88,90-92					27	458	17.0	0
Alan Grant	90-92	33	261	7.9	0	21	370	17.6	0
Mel Gray	86-93	160	1851	11.6	3	264	6374	24.1	3
Boyce Green	83-87					30	644	21.5	1
Darrell Green	83-93	51	576	11.3	0				
Gaston Green	88-92					47	981	20.9	1
Mark Green	89-92	19	150	7.9	0	33	644	19.5	0
Roy Green	80-92	27	230	8.5	1	89	2002	22.5	1
Don Griffin	86-93	74	667	9.1	1	41	848	20.7	0
Keith Griffin	84-88					52	985	18.9	0
Jeff Groth	79-85	105	887	8.4	0	16	287	17.9	0
Neal Guggemos	86-88					53	1152	21.7	0
Eric Guliford	93	29	212	7.3	0	5	101	20.2	0
Chris Hale	90-92	24	251	10.4	0				
Alvin Hall	81-85,87	15	139	9.3	0	128	2819	22.0	1
Dino Hall	79-83	111	901	8.1	0	151	3185	21.1	0
Lorenzo Hampton	85-89					96	2025	21.1	0
Rodney Hampton	90-93					30	544	18.1	0
Anthony Hancock	82-86	29	198	6.8	0	64	1281	20.0	0
Mike Harden	80-89	6	102	14.6	1	28	425	15.2	0
Derrick Harmon	84-87					40	906	22.7	0
Ronnie Harmon	86-93					58	1148	19.8	0
Bruce Harper	77-84	183	1784	9.8	1	243	5407	22.3	0
Corey Harris	92-93	6	17	2.8	0	49	1173	23.9	0
Darryl Harris	88					39	833	21.4	0
Duriel Harris	76-85	18	152	8.4	0	56	1416	25.3	0
Leonard Harris	86-93					57	1193	20.9	0
Rod Harris	89-91	108	826	7.6	0	49	897	18.3	0
Courtney Hawkins	92-93	28	219	7.8	0	9	118	13.1	0
Mike Haynes	76-88	112	1168	10.4	2				
Johnny Hector	83-92					34	735	21.6	0
Jerome Henderson	91	27	201	7.4	0				
Darryl Henley	89-93	61	579	9.5	0				
Wally Henry	77-82	148	1231	8.3	1	87	1950	22.4	0
Cliff Hicks	87-93	100	942	9.4	0	5	124	24.8	0
Dwight Hicks	79-86	54	403	7.7	0	3	58	19.3	0
Mark Higgs	88-93					28	534	19.1	0
Drew Hill	79-93	3	22	7.3	0	172	3460	20.1	1
Kenny Hill	81-88					50	1220	24.4	1
Rod Hill	82-87	51	391	7.7	0	14	243	17.4	0
Tony Hill	77-86	27	268	9.9	0	4	96	24.0	0
Ira Hillary	87-90	31	230	7.4	0	28	439	15.7	0
Jamie Holland	87-92					133	2806	21.1	0
David Hollis	87-89	27	225	8.3	0	38	771	18.7	1
John Holt	81-87	36	241	6.7	0	11	274	24.9	0
Desmond Howard	92-93	10	109	10.9	1	43	867	20.2	0
Harlan Huckleby	80-85					70	1300	18.6	0
David Hughes	81-86					32	663	20.7	0
Tyrone Hughes	93	37	503	13.6	2	30	753	25.1	1
Bobby Humphery	84-90	1	0	0.0	0	130	2974	22.9	2
Herman Hunter	85-87	1	6	6.0	0	100	2133	21.3	0
Ivy Joe Hunter	89-91	31	100	3.2	0	11	97	8.8	0
Mark Ingram	87-93	8	49	6.1	0	47	742	15.8	0
LeRoy Irvin	80-89	146	1451	9.9	4	4	60	15.0	0
Quadry Ismail	93					42	902	21.5	0
Raghib Ismail	93					25	605	24.2	0
John Jackson	90-92	31	244	7.9	0	3	58	19.3	0
Lionel James	84-88	124	1193	9.6	2	99	2094	21.2	0
Roland James	80-89	42	400	9.5	1				
James Jefferson	89-90	20	155	7.8	0	26	607	23.3	1
Ken Jenkins	83-86	78	773	9.9	0	108	2427	22.5	0
Stanford Jennings	84-92					148	2965	20.0	1
Jim Jodat	77-83					35	685	19.6	0
Paul Johns	81-84	74	843	11.4	2	8	13[illegible]	[illegible]7.3	0
A.J. Johnson	89-90					24	504	21.0	0
Billy "White Shoes" Johnson	74-88	282	3317	11.8	6	123	2941	23.9	2
Butch Johnson	76-85	146	1313	9.0	1	79	1832	23.2	0
Joe Johnson	89-92	31	209	9.7	0	53	1111	21.0	1
Kenny Johnson	80-89	110	854	7.8	0	60	1156	19.3	0
Vance Johnson	85-93	81	689	8.5	0	59	1312	22.2	0
James Jones	80-82,84-85	87	736	8.5	0	70	1444	20.6	0
Rick Kane	77-85	1	13	13.0	0	64	1370	21.4	0
Keith Jones	89-92					37	790	21.3	1
Mark Konecny	87-89	33	233	7.1	0	17	276	16.2	0
Eric Lane	81-86					27	442	16.4	0
Garcia Lane	85	43	381	8.9	0	13	269	20.7	0
David Lang	91-93					25	422	16.9	0
Gene Lang	84-90					63	1353	21.5	0
Robert Lavette	85-87	18	92	5.1	0	76	1490	19.6	0
Amos Lawrence	81-82					26	627	24.1	1
Amp Lee	92-93					24	436	18.2	0
Gary Lee	87-88					50	1074	21.5	0
Mark Lee	80-89	26	220	8.5	1	45	859	19.1	0
Darren Lewis	91-92					25	524	21.0	1
Leo Lewis	81-91	202	1868	9.2	1	6	81	13.5	0
Nate Lewis	90-93	34	320	9.4	0	92	2047	22.3	1
Will Lewis	80-81	56	449	8.0	1	45	963	21.4	0
Louis Lipps	84-92	112	1234	11.0	3	14	246	17.6	0
Marc Logan	87-93					85	1760	20.7	1
Derek Loville	90-91	3	16	5.3	0	36	771	21.4	0
Vaughn Lusby	80-81	36	274	7.6	0	6	92	15.3	0
Pete Mandley	84-90	165	1514	9.2	1	35	630	18.0	0
Wade Manning	79-82	51	433	8.5	0	48	1005	20.9	0
Arthur Marshall	92-93	33	349	10.6	0	8	132	16.5	0
Eric Martin	85-92	46	368	8.0	0	22	495	22.5	0
Kelvin Martin	87-93	170	1700	10.0	3	54	1035	19.2	0
Mike Martin	83-89	140	1381	9.9	0	75	1563	20.8	0
Robbie Martin	81-86	175	1670	9.5	2	113	2084	18.4	0
Sammy Martin	88-91	20	165	8.3	0	100	2317	23.2	1
Tony Martin	90-93	28	150	5.3	0				
Terance Mathis	90-93	50	445	8.9	1	107	1980	18.5	0
Ira Matthews	79-81	80	586	7.3	0	71	1602	22.6	1
Rich Mauti	77-84	75	610	8.1	0	124	2836	22.9	0

		PUNT RETURNS				KICKOFF RETURNS			
Name	**Years**	**No.**	**Yards**	**Avg.**	**TD**	**No.**	**Yards**	**Avg.**	**TD**
Rueben Mayes	86-88,90,92-93					38	695	18.3	0
Derrick McAdoo	87-88	1	0	0.0	0	36	755	21.0	0
Fred McAfee	91-93					48	987	20.6	0
Napoleon McCallum	86,90-93	11	63	5.7	0	29	574	19.8	0
Phil McConkey	84-89	218	1832	8.4	0	69	1324	19.2	0
Mike McCoy	76-83					54	1187	22.0	0
O.J. McDuffie	93	28	317	11.3	2	32	755	23.6	0
Tim McGee	86-93					58	1249	21.5	0
Willie McGee	73-78	6	56	9.3	0	50	1115	22.3	0
Dennis McKinnon	83-85,87-90	129	1191	9.2	3	3	58	19.3	0
Dana McLemore	82-87	152	1598	10.5	4	56	1147	20.5	0
Todd McNair	89-93					34	598	17.6	0
Gerald McNeil	86-90	191	1717	9.0	1	91	1852	20.4	1
Dave Meggett	89-93	178	1907	10.7	4	117	2441	20.9	1
Eric Metcalf	89-93	92	993	10.8	2	130	2596	20.0	2
Glyn Milburn	93	40	425	10.6	0	12	188	15.7	0
Anthony Miller	88-93					50	1269	25.4	2
Scott Miller	91-93	52	423	8.1	0	2	22	11.0	0
Terry Miller	78-81					25	480	19.2	0
Brian Mitchell	90-93	115	1171	10.2	3	103	2116	20.5	0
Stump Mitchell	81-89	156	1377	8.8	1	177	4007	22.6	0
Carl Monroe	83-87					76	1660	21.8	1
Alton Montgomery	90-93					63	1293	20.5	0
Cle Montgomery	80-85	70	622	8.9	1	132	2706	20.5	0
Wilbert Montgomery	77-85					32	814	25.4	1
Jeff Moore	79-83	10	90	9.0	0	40	784	19.6	0
Nat Moore	74-86	27	297	11.0	0	33	858	26.0	0
Emory Moorehead	77-88					31	627	20.2	0
Stanley Morgan	77-90	92	960	10.4	1	2	29	14.5	0
Jamie Morris	88-90					32	615	19.2	0
Joe Morris	82-88,91					40	659	16.5	0
Randall Morris	84-88					84	1662	19.8	0
Bobby Morse	87,89-91	39	247	6.3	0	41	780	19.0	0
Michael Morton	82-85					89	1885	21.2	0
Mike Mosley	82-83	11	61	5.5	0	27	723	26.8	0
Vance Mueller	86-90					39	878	22.5	0
Tony Nathan	79-87	51	484	9.5	1	50	1118	22.4	0
Ricky Nattiel	87-91	54	416	7.7	0	11	202	18.4	0
Mike Nelms	80-84	212	1948	9.2	2	175	4128	23.6	0
Darrin Nelson	82-92	42	357	8.5	0	163	3659	22.4	0
Pat Newman	90-93	24	158	6.6	0	3	62	20.7	0
Timmy Newsome	80-88					33	677	20.5	0
Fred Nixon	80-81	26	203	7.8	0	18	382	21.2	0
Terry Obee	91,93	35	289	8.3	0	9	159	17.7	0
Henry Odom	83					39	756	19.4	0
James Owens	79-84					127	2801	22.1	2
Stephone Paige	84-91					29	580	20.0	0
Paul Palmer	87-89					72	1542	21.4	2
Anthony Parker	89,91-93	42	400	9.5	0	2	30	15.0	0
Eddie Payton	77-78,80-82	156	1387	8.9	1	156	2676	17.1	2
Danny Peebles	89-91					26	518	19.9	0
Erric Pegram	91-93					29	484	16.7	0
Allen Pinkett	86-91	1	-1	-1.0	0	54	1069	19.8	0
Danny Pittman	80-84	10	50	5.0	0	37	778	21.0	0
Ron Pitts	86-90	50	436	8.7	1	2	24	12.0	0
Ricky Porter	82-83,87	14	104	7.4	0	26	559	21.5	0
Dave Preston	78-81	18	155	8.6	0	26	597	23.0	0
Mitchell Price	90-93	50	498	10.0	2	25	446	17.8	0
Mike Prior	85,87-93	34	306	9.0	0	13	178	13.7	0
Jeff Query	89-93	76	712	9.4	0	7	138	19.7	0
Barry Redden	82-90					66	1392	21.1	0
Jarvis Redwine	81-83					50	1124	22.5	0
Beasley Reece	76-84	5	18	3.6	0	40	775	19.4	0
Buster Rhymes	85-86					62	1558	25.1	0
Allen Rice	84-91	1	0	0.0	0	31	417	13.5	0
Robb Riddick	81,83-84,86-88	46	289	6.3	0	63	1276	20.3	0
Carl Roaches	80-85	155	1116	7.2	0	154	3352	21.8	2
Patrick Robinson	93	43	305	7.1	0	30	567	18.9	0
Del Rodgers	82-84,87-88					68	1445	21.3	1
Jimmy Rogers	80-84					77	1678	21.8	0
Lee Rouson	85-91					36	686	19.1	0
Derek Russell	91-93					32	648	20.3	0
Lupe Sanchez	86-88	2	11	5.5	0	35	778	22.2	0
Deion Sanders	89-93	93	789	8.5	2	147	3390	23.1	3
Ricky Sanders	86-93	2	12	6.0	0	36	619	17.2	0
Thomas Sanders	85-91					103	1946	18.9	1
Scott Schwedes	87-90	80	765	9.6	1	17	302	17.8	0
John Sciarra	78-83	117	909	7.8	0				
Pete Shaw	77-83	41	322	7.9	0	1	0	0.0	0
Derrick Shepard	87-91	75	679	9.1	1	51	1007	19.7	0
Vai Sikahema	86-93	292	3169	10.9	4	235	4933	21.0	0
John Simmons	83-87	46	307	6.7	0	17	342	20.1	0
Paul Skansi	83-91	91	863	9.5	0	20	379	19.0	0
Webster Slaughter	86-93	38	256	6.7	0	1	21	21.0	0
Don Smith	88-90					41	831	20.3	0
Jeff Smith	85-88	37	290	7.8	0	77	1475	19.2	0
Jim Smith	77-82,85	98	737	7.5	0	17	397	23.4	0
Joey Smith	91-92					33	598	17.0	0
J.T. Smith	78-90	267	2764	10.4	4	25	473	18.9	0
Phil Smith	83-84,86-87	6	23	3.8	0	32	651	20.3	1
Reggie Smith	80-81	39	361	9.3	0	72	1655	23.0	0
Ricky Smith	82-84	54	537	9.9	0	67	1505	22.5	1
Tony Smith	92-93	48	410	8.5	0	45	1120	24.9	1
Kurt Sohn	81-88	68	519	7.6	0	63	1164	18.5	0
Freddie Solomon	75-85	177	1614	9.1	4	32	694	21.7	0
Todd Spencer	84-85,87					45	990	22.0	0
Kirk Springs	81-84	51	534	10.5	1	49	885	18.1	0
Ron Springs	79-86					44	905	20.6	0
Sylvester Stamps	84-89	1	8	8.0	0	92	2079	22.6	1
Walter Stanley	85-90,92	175	1619	9.3	1	89	1658	18.6	0
Stephen Starring	83-88	19	108	5.7	0	115	2389	20.8	0
Anthony Steels	85,87	8	45	5.6	0	30	561	18.7	0
Milt Stegall	92					25	430	17.2	0
Dwight Stone	87-93					86	1685	19.6	1
Troy Stradford	87-92	40	284	7.1	0	38	700	18.4	0
Ray Strong	78-81					28	561	20.0	0
Matt Suhey	80-89	1	4	4.0	0	26	508	19.5	0
Mickey Sutton	86-90	76	695	9.1	0	9	169	18.8	0
Jeff Sydner	92-93	7	52	7.4	0	26	526	20.2	0
Steve Tasker	85-93	1	0	0.0	0	42	896	21.3	0
Rodney Tate	82-84					36	680	18.9	0
John Taylor	87-93	138	1461	10.6	2	14	276	19.7	0
Ken Taylor	85-86	25	198	7.9	0	1	18	18.0	0
Kitrick Taylor	88-93	63	568	9.0	1	8	132	16.5	0
Zach Thomas	83-84	54	493	9.1	1	46	924	20.1	0
Aundra Thompson	77-83					52	1090	21.0	1
Leonard Thompson	75-86	12	136	11.3	0	36	799	22.2	0
Pat Tilley	76-86	31	264	8.5	0				
Spencer Tillman	87-93					37	619	16.7	0
JoJo Townsell	85-90	127	1360	10.7	1	98	2048	20.9	1
Erroll Tucker	88-89	29	245	8.4	0	38	746	19.6	0
Willie Tullis	81-88	6	56	9.3	0	32	779	24.3	1
Vernon Turner	90-93	68	560	8.2	0	74	1417	19.1	0
Andre Tyler	83	27	208	7.7	0				
Wendell Tyler	77-86					27	570	21.1	0
Darryl Usher	89	4	25	6.3	0	27	506	18.7	0
Jon Vaughn	91-93					70	1561	22.3	0
Clarence Verdin	86-93	155	1537	9.9	5	209	4226	20.2	1
David Verser	81-85					65	1371	21.1	0
Tommy Vigorito	81-83,85	79	830	10.5	2	4	84	21.0	0
Billy Waddy	77-82,84	43	274	6.4	0				
Dwight Walker	82-84,87	28	177	6.3	0	42	922	22.0	0
Fulton Walker	81-86	145	1439	9.9	1	167	3769	22.6	1
Herschel Walker	86-93					76	1676	22.1	1
Herkie Walls	83-85,87	4	12	3.0	0	42	769	18.3	0
Len Walterscheid	77-84	57	424	7.4	0	34	833	24.5	0
Chris Warren	90-93	94	819	8.7	0	86	1794	20.9	0
Rickey Watts	79-84					34	710	20.9	1
Ted Watts	81-85	35	284	8.1	1				
Clarence Weathers	83-91	63	454	7.2	0	4	75	18.8	0
Charles White	80-88	1	14	14.0	0	52	970	18.7	0
Lorenzo White	88-89					25	499	20.0	1
Art Whittington	78-82	2	4	2.0	0	76	1513	19.9	1
Gerald Willhite	82-88	101	1054	10.4	1	26	521	20.0	0
Dokie Williams	83-87					44	949	21.6	0
Harvey Williams	91-93					48	982	20.5	0
Henry Williams	89	30	267	8.9	0	14	249	17.8	0
Kevin Williams	93	36	381	10.5	2	31	689	22.2	0
Mike Williams	89,91-93					27	508	18.8	0
Ray Williams	80	27	259	9.6	0	9	228	25.3	1
Van Williams	83-85,87	1	0	0.0	0	62	1334	21.5	0
Charles Wilson	90-93					82	1797	21.9	1
Don Wilson	84-85	49	458	9.3	1	56	1041	18.6	0
Steve Wilson	79-86	36	236	6.6	0	58	1107	19.1	0
Wayne Wilson	79-87					72	1630	22.6	0
Scott Woerner	81	33	278	8.4	0	10	210	21.0	0
Chris Woods	87-89	28	125	7.0	0	5	92	18.4	0
Rick Woods	82-86	70	568	8.1	0	1	17	17.0	0
Rod Woodson	87-93	217	2043	9.4	2	205	4529	22.1	2
Butch Woolfolk	82-88					53	1029	19.4	0
Vince Workman	89-93	1	0	0.0	0	61	980	16.1	0
Naz Worthen	89-90	44	313	7.1	0	16	339	21.2	0
Alexander Wright	90-93					69	1399	20.3	2
Eric Yarber	86-87	46	416	9.0	0				
Glen Young	83-85,87-88	14	93	6.6	0	113	2626	23.2	0

Lifetime Statistics - 1980- 1993 Section 4 - **PUNTING**
(All men with 25 or more punts)

Name	Years	No.	Avg.
Louie Aguiar	91-93	210	39.7
Harold Alexander	93	72	43.3
Evan Arapostathis	86	30	38.0
Jim Arnold	83-93	825	42.2
Bryan Barker	90-93	274	41.1
Tommy Barnhardt	87-93	389	42.6
Carl Birdsong	81-85	369	41.1
Mike Black	83-87	274	40.9
Don Bracken	85-90,92-93	466	39.6
Maury Buford	82-86,88-91	586	40.7
Rich Camarillo	81-93	859	42.7
Greg Cater	80-83,86-87	379	38.5
Lewis Colbert	86-87,89	117	40.0
Greg Coleman	77-88	823	40.4
Craig Colquitt	78-84	429	41.2
Mike Connell	78,80-81	254	38.7
Frank Corral	78-81	165	40.8
Steve Cox	81-88	393	41.2
Ray Criswell	87-88	94	37.5
Rick Donnelly	85-88,91	377	42.0
Keith English	90	68	39.2
Russell Erxleben	79-83,87	280	40.6
Jeff Feagles	88-93	482	40.1
Dave Finzer	84-85	153	39.9
Scott Fulhage	87-92	401	41.1
Vince Gamache	86-87	93	38.4
Frank Garcia	81,83-87	384	40.8
Chris Gardocki	91-93	159	40.9
Ralph Giacomarro	83-85,87	188	40.4
Kelly Goodburn	87-93	355	39.5
John Goodson	82	49	40.4
Jeff Gossett	81-83,85-93	776	40.9
Bob Grupp	79-81	214	40.9
Brian Hansen	84-88,90-93	697	41.7
Dale Hatcher	85-89,91,93	494	39.7
Jeff Hayes	82-87	279	37.5
Barry Helton	88-91	217	38.2
Alan Herline	87	26	33.1
Mike Horan	84-93	606	42.1
Greg Horne	87-88	123	40.3
Mike Hubach	80-81	82	38.0
Hank Ilesic	89	76	40.1
Dave Jennings	74-87	1163	40.9
John Jett	93	56	41.8
Lee Johnson	85-93	609	41.6
John Kidd	84-93	714	40.5
Sean Landeta	85-93	572	43.1
Shawn McCarthy	91-92	171	40.1
Pat McInally	76-85	709	41.3
Paul McJulien	91-93	145	39.0
Jim Miller	80-82	214	40.6
John Misko	82-84,87	207	40.4
Chris Mohr	89,91-93	274	39.8
Ralf Mojsiejenko	85-91	418	42.0
Greg Montgomery	88-93	316	42.8
Harry Newsome	85-93	697	42.3
Chris Norman	84-86	220	39.9
Tom Orosz	81-84	188	39.9
Rick Partridge	79-80,87	136	39.4
Luke Prestridge	79-84	421	41.9
Joe Prokop	85,87-92	376	39.1
Chuck Ramsey	77-84	553	40.0
Bill Renner	86-87	38	35.1
George Roberts	78-82	306	41.0
Reggie Roby	83-93	636	43.2
Ruben Rodriguez	87-89,92	239	40.4
Tom Rouen	93	68	44.4
Mark Royals	87,90-93	330	41.3
Max Runager	79-89	668	39.8
Mike Saxon	85-93	671	41.2
Bucky Scribner	83-84,87-89	342	39.5
Tom Skladany	78-83	295	42.2
Dave Smigelsky	82	26	38.5
Ray Stachowicz	81-83	136	40.2
Rohn Stark	82-93	918	43.7
Dan Stryzinski	90-93	309	39.6
Larry Swider	79-82	284	41.3
Stan Talley	87	57	39.9
John Teltschik	86-89	350	39.5
Rick Tuten	89-93	308	43.0
Bryan Wagner	87-93	409	40.0
John Warren	83-84	50	39.5
Jack Weil	86	34	39.5
Jeff West	75-79, 81-85	625	37.9
Danny White	78-86	612	39.8
Ron Widby	68-73	368	42.0
Klaus Wilmsmeyer	92-93	91	39.9
George Winslow	87,89	34	35.6
Mike Wood	78-81	82	36.8

Lifetime Statistics - 1980-1993 Section 5 - **KICKING**
(All men with 10 or more PAT or field goal attempts)

Name	Years	PAT	PAT Att.	PAT Pct.	FG	FG Att.	FG Pct.
Vince Abbott	87-88	37	38	97	21	34	62
Raul Allegre	83-91	183	190	96	137	186	74
Wilson Alvarez	81	14	15	93	3	7	30
Morten Andersen	82-93	380	386	98	274	350	78
Gary Anderson	82-93	384	388	99	285	364	78
Obed Ariri	84,87	44	46	96	22	31	71
Jess Atkinson	85-87	21	22	95	11	19	58
Chris Bahr	76-89	490	519	94	241	381	63
Matt Bahr	79-93	459	471	97	250	348	72
Charlie Baumann	91-92	37	40	93	20	29	69
Willie Beecher	87-88	12	12	100	3	4	75
Rolf Benirschke	77-86	328	353	93	146	208	70
Dean Biasucci	84,86-93	218	224	97	160	226	71
Cary Blanchard	92-93	48	48	100	33	48	69
Novo Bojovic	85	11	12	92	3	7	43
Jim Breech	79-92	517	539	96	243	340	71
Jeff Brockhaus	87	11	13	85	3	6	50
Kevin Butler	85-93	318	328	97	199	273	73
Bill Capece	81-83	67	72	93	43	70	61
John Carney	88-93	130	133	98	97	127	76
Steve Christie	90-93	128	130	98	85	109	78
Mike Cofer	87-93	294	303	97	129	192	67
Joe Cooper	84,86	17	17	100	13	17	76
Frank Corral	78-81	154	160	96	75	124	61
Steve Cox	81-87	3	3	100	6	12	50
Steve DeLine	88-89	15	15	100	9	15	60
Rick Danmeier	78-82	154	165	93	70	106	66
Greg Davis	87-93	180	185	97	122	185	66
Al Del Greco	84-93	317	324	98	161	228	71
Dean Dorsey	88	12	13	92	5	10	50
Jason Elam	93	41	42	98	26	35	74
Lin Elliott	92-93	49	51	96	26	39	67
Tony Franklin	79-88	341	355	96	177	264	67
Jim Gallery	87,89-90	43	44	98	11	25	44
Edgar Garcia	84	14	15	93	3	9	33
Teddy Garcia	88-90	45	52	87	21	38	55
Ali Haji-Sheikh	83-87	95	103	92	76	111	68
Jason Hanson	92-93	58	58	100	55	69	80
Ian Howfield	91	25	29	86	13	18	72
Michael Husted	93	27	27	100	16	22	73
Donald Igwebuike	85-90	153	160	96	108	143	76
Chris Jacke	89-93	166	167	99	116	148	78
Dave Jacobs	79,81,87	21	25	84	12	26	46
Jeff Jaeger	87,89-93	191	197	97	131	180	73
Norm Johnson	82-93	444	450	99	222	300	74
Rich Karlis	82-90	283	294	96	172	239	72
John Kasay	91-93	70	71	99	62	81	77
Jerry Kauric	90	24	27	89	14	20	70
Florian Kempf	82-84,87	64	67	96	29	38	76
Mike Lansford	82-90	315	325	97	158	217	73
Tim Lashar	87	10	10	100	3	4	75
Pat Leahy	74-91	558	584	96	304	426	71
John Lee	86	14	17	82	8	13	62
Chip Lohmiller	88-93	232	235	99	155	217	71
Nick Lowery	78,80-93	486	490	99	329	411	80
Mick Luckhurst	81-87	213	216	99	115	164	70
Paul McFadden	84-89	160	164	98	120	163	74
Eddie Murray	80-93	432	437	99	277	367	75
Chuck Nelson	83-84,86-88	175	184	95	63	93	68
Bjorn Nittmo	89	12	13	92	9	12	75
Scott Norwood	85-91	271	278	97	133	184	72
Neil O'Donoghue	77-85	240	257	93	112	189	59
Doug Pelfrey	93	13	16	81	24	31	77
Fuad Reveiz	85-88,90-93	293	304	96	128	175	73
Benny Ricardo	76-84	171	180	95	92	142	65
John Roveto	81-82	29	30	97	14	31	45
Roger Ruzek	87-93	206	219	94	120	166	72
Eric Schubert	85-87	36	38	95	18	36	50
Rafael Septien	77-86	420	433	97	180	256	70
Scott Sisson	93	15	15	100	14	26	54
Jason Staurovsky	87-92	69	71	97	54	80	68
Matt Stover	91-93	98	100	98	53	73	73
Pete Stoyanovich	89-93	174	178	98	125	157	80
Ian Sunter	80	15	15	100	11	20	55
Bob Thomas	75-86	303	330	92	151	239	63
David Treadwell	89-93	160	165	97	124	158	78
David Trout	81,87	48	56	86	12	19	63
Uwe von Schamann	79-84	237	250	95	101	149	68
Ray Wersching	73-87	456	477	96	222	329	67
Ken Willis	90-92	90	90	100	55	80	69
Mike Wood	78-82	69	77	90	29	49	59
Luis Zendejas	87-89	78	79	99	37	55	67
Max Zendejas	86-88	53	62	85	34	49	69
Tony Zendejas	85-93	283	293	97	165	223	74

Leaders and Features

The mention of any sport bring certain images to mind. When it comes to pro football the pictures are vivid and swift. Mostly, though, it is an extreme of functions. For those in love with risk and the dramatics of suddenness, there is nothing more serene than the aerial ballet of a 50-yard pass play. And for those who like to chew their fantasy in small, but certain chunks of yardage, there is nothing more pleasurable than the fullback who eludes a mammoth of flesh in search of four yards of daylight. Yet these two simplified illustrations have not always held true for pro football. If nothing else, football is a game of constant change. Unlike any other major sport, there is no way to compare the football athletes of today's two-platoon game with those men who needed a double set of talents in which to sustain their playing careers. This point, for example, could not be any sharper than when one considers Joe Namath attempting to play in the 1940's. But fortunately for Namath, and perhaps even the fans of today who would have been denied the excitement of his precision arm, football is no longer a game of one man for sixty minutes.

It is for this reason that many of the records which appear on the following pages have no continuity with the players of yesteryear and those of the modern game. Field goals, for example, are a modern phenomenon with no pre-1960 player on the list of the top single-season leaders. On the other hand, in the category of punters, Yale Lary, with a 48.9 average, is the only post-1960 player among the top single-season leaders. Of course, the changing hash marks and goal post positions are greatly responsible for these records.

Yet, beyond the comparison of any era, more important are the achievements of the men who made up their time, and the fact that whatever the criteria, each contributed the fullest and the best of his talents. It is on this basis that each must be measured and appreciated in the light of pro football's changing game.

Section Explanations

The following is an explanation of certain statistical matter which may be unfamiliar:

Yards per Game— In the category of Yards per Game for individuals, "per game" refers to games played by the team, because there is no available statistical information of the games played by the individual.

Passing Ranks— These ranks are determined by the formula used by the National Football League for its official rankings from 1960 to 1971. Each passer who qualifies by having a minimum number of passing attempts is ranked in four categories: Percent Completed, Percent Intercepted, Average Yards per Attempt, and Touchdowns. The four ranks are then added for each passer, and the totals are then ranked. This ranking of the sum of the four ranks is the passer's rank.

YEARLY CHAMPIONSHIP GAMES

NATIONAL FOOTBALL LEAGUE (CONFERENCE)

Year	Winner	Loser	Score
1933	CHICAGO BEARS	New York Giants	23-21
1934	NEW YORK GIANTS	Chicago Bears	30-13
1935	DETROIT LIONS	New York Giants	26- 7
1936	Green Bay Packers (at New York)	Boston Redskins	21- 6
1937	Washington Redskins	CHICAGO BEARS	28-21
1938	NEW YORK GIANTS	Green Bay Packers	23-17
1939	GREEN BAY PACKERS (at Milwaukee)	New York Giants	27- 0
1940	Chicago Bears	WASHINGTON REDSKINS	73- 0
1941	CHICAGO BEARS	New York Giants	37- 9
1942	WASHINGTON REDSKINS	Chicago Bears	14- 6
1943	CHICAGO BEARS	Washington Redskins	41-21
1944	Green Bay Packers	NEW YORK GIANTS	14- 7
1945	CLEVELAND RAMS	Washington Redskins	15-14
1946	Chicago Bears	NEW YORK GIANTS	24-14
1947	CHICAGO CARDINALS	Philadelphia Eagles	28-21
1948	PHILADELPHIA EAGLES	Chicago Cardinals	7- 0
1949	Philadelphia Eagles	LOS ANGELES RAMS	14- 0
1950	CLEVELAND BROWNS	Los Angeles Rams	30-28
1951	LOS ANGELES RAMS	Cleveland Browns	24-17
1952	Detroit Lions	CLEVELAND BROWNS	17- 7
1953	DETROIT LIONS	Cleveland Browns	17-16
1954	CLEVELAND BROWNS	Detroit Lions	56-10
1955	Cleveland Browns	LOS ANGELES RAMS	38-14
1956	NEW YORK GIANTS	Chicago Bears	47- 7
1957	DETROIT LIONS	Cleveland Browns	59-14
1958	Baltimore Colts	NEW YORK GIANTS	23-17
1959	BALTIMORE COLTS	New York Giants	31-16
1960	PHILADELPHIA EAGLES	Green Bay Packers	17-13
1961	GREEN BAY PACKERS	New York Giants	37- 0
1962	Green Bay Packers	NEW YORK GIANTS	16- 7
1963	CHICAGO BEARS	New York Giants	14-10
1964	CLEVELAND BROWNS	Baltimore Colts	27- 0
1965	GREEN BAY PACKERS	Cleveland Browns	23-12
1966	Green Bay Packers	DALLAS COWBOYS	34-27
1967	GREEN BAY PACKERS	Dallas Cowboys	21-17
1968	Baltimore Colts	CLEVELAND BROWNS	34- 0
1969	MINNESOTA VIKINGS	Cleveland Browns	27- 7
1970	Dallas Cowboys	SAN FRANCISCO 49ERS	17-10
1971	DALLAS COWBOYS	San Francisco 49ers	14- 3
1972	WASHINGTON REDSKINS	Dallas Cowboys	26- 3
1973	Minnesota Vikings	DALLAS COWBOYS	27-10
1974	MINNESOTA VIKINGS	Los Angeles Rams	14-10
1975	Dallas Cowboys	LOS ANGELES RAMS	37- 7
1976	MINNESOTA VIKINGS	Los Angeles Rams	24-13
1977	DALLAS COWBOYS	Minnesota Vikings	23- 6
1978	Dallas Cowboys	LOS ANGELES RAMS	28- 0
1979	Los Angeles Rams	TAMPA BAY BUCCANEERS	9- 0
1980	PHILADELPHIA EAGLES	Dallas Cowboys	20- 7
1981	SAN FRANCISCO 49ERS	Dallas Cowboys	28-27
1982	WASHINGTON REDSKINS	Dallas Cowboys	31-17
1983	WASHINGTON REDSKINS	San Francisco 49ers	24-21
1984	SAN FRANCISCO 49ERS	Chicago Bears	23- 0
1985	CHICAGO BEARS	Los Angeles Rams	24- 0
1986	NEW YORK GIANTS	Washington Redskins	17- 0
1987	WASHINGTON REDSKINS	Minnesota Vikings	17-10
1988	San Francisco 49ers	CHICAGO BEARS	28- 3
1989	SAN FRANCISCO 49ERS	Los Angeles Rams	30- 3
1990	New York Giants	SAN FRANCISCO 49ERS	15-13
1991	WASHINGTON REDSKINS	Detroit Lions	41-10
1992	Dallas Cowboys	SAN FRANCISCO 49ERS	30-20
1993	DALLAS COWBOYS	San Francisco 49ers	38-21

Home Team in Upper Case
*—Sudden Death Game

ALL-AMERICAN FOOTBALL CONFERENCE

Year	Winner	Loser	Score
1946	CLEVELAND BROWNS	New York Yankees	14- 9
1947	Cleveland Browns	NEW YORK YANKEES	14- 3
1948	CLEVELAND BROWNS	Buffalo Bills	49- 7
1949	CLEVELAND BROWNS	San Francisco 49ers	21- 7

AMERICAN FOOTBALL LEAGUE (CONFERENCE)

Year	Winner	Loser	Score
1960	HOUSTON OILERS	Los Angeles Chargers	24-16
1961	Houston Oilers	SAN DIEGO CHARGERS	10- 3
1962	Dallas Chiefs	HOUSTON OILERS	20-17
1963	SAN DIEGO CHARGERS	Boston Patriots	51-10
1964	BUFFALO BILLS	San Diego Chargers	20- 7
1965	Buffalo Bills	SAN DIEGO CHARGERS	23- 0
1966	Kansas City Chiefs	BUFFALO BILLS	31- 7
1967	OAKLAND RAIDERS	Houston Oilers	40- 7
1968	NEW YORK JETS	Oakland Raiders	27-23
1969	Kansas City Chiefs	OAKLAND RAIDERS	17- 7
1970	BALTIMORE COLTS	Oakland Raiders	27-17
1971	MIAMI DOLPHINS	Baltimore Colts	21- 0
1972	Miami Dolphins	PITTSBURGH STEELERS	21-17
1973	MIAMI DOLPHINS	Oakland Raiders	27-10
1974	Pittsburgh Steelers	OAKLAND RAIDERS	24-13
1975	PITTSBURGH STEELERS	Oakland Raiders	16-10
1976	OAKLAND RAIDERS	Pittsburgh Steelers	24- 7
1977	DENVER BRONCOS	Oakland Raiders	20-17
1978	PITTSBURGH STEELERS	Houston Oilers	34- 5
1979	PITTSBURGH STEELERS	Houston Oilers	27-13
1980	Oakland Raiders	SAN DIEGO CHARGERS	34-27
1981	CINCINNATI BENGALS	San Diego Chargers	27- 7
1982	MIAMI DOLPHINS	New York Jets	14- 0
1983	LOS ANGELES RAIDERS	Seattle Seahawks	30-14
1984	MIAMI DOLPHINS	Pittsburgh Steelers	45-28
1985	New England Patriots	MIAMI DOLPHINS	31-14
1986	Denver Broncos	CLEVELAND BROWNS	23-20
1987	DENVER BRONCOS	Cleveland Browns	38-33
1988	CINCINNATI BENGALS	Buffalo Bills	21-10
1989	DENVER BRONCOS	Cleveland Browns	37-21
1990	BUFFALO BILLS	Los Angeles Raiders	51- 3
1991	BUFFALO BILLS	Denver Broncos	10- 7
1992	Buffalo Bills	MIAMI DOLPHINS	29-10
1993	BUFFALO BILLS	Kansas City Chiefs	30-13

COMPOSITE STANDINGS
(All Leagues) Championship Games Only

Team	Games	Wins	Losses	Pct.
Cincinnati Bengals	2	2	0	1.000
Green Bay Packers	10	8	2	.800
Denver Broncos	5	4	1	.800
Philadelphia Eagles	5	4	1	.800
Buffalo Bills	8	6	2	.750
Kansas City Chiefs	3	3	1	.750
Miami Dolphins	7	5	2	.714
Detroit Lions	6	4	2	.667
Minnesota Vikings	6	4	2	.667
Indianapolis Colts	6	4	2	.667
Washington Redskins	12	7	5	.583
Pittsburgh Steelers	7	4	3	.571
Chicago Bears	13	7	6	.538
Chicago Cardinals	2	1	1	.500
New York Jets	2	1	1	.500
New England Patriots	2	1	1	.500
Dallas Cowboys	14	7	7	.500
Cleveland Browns	18	8	10	.471
San Francisco 49ers	10	4	6	.400
Oakland/L.A. Raiders	12	4	8	.333
Houston Oilers	6	2	4	.333
New York Giants	16	5	11	.313
Los Angeles Rams	12	3	9	.250
San Diego Chargers	7	1	6	.143
New York Yankees (AAFC)	2	0	2	.000
Buffalo Bills (AAFC)	1	0	1	.000
Tampa Bay Buccaneers	1	0	1	.000
Seattle Seahawks	1	0	1	.000

YEARLY CHAMPIONSHIP GAMES

SUPER BOWL

I at Los Angeles	Green Bay	7	7	14	7	- 35
	Kansas City	0	10	0	0	- 10
II at Miami	Green Bay	3	13	10	7	- 33
	Oakland	0	7	0	7	- 14
III at Miami	N.Y. Jets	0	7	6	3	- 16
	Baltimore	0	0	0	7	- 7
V at New Orleans	Kansas City	3	13	7	0	- 23
	Minnesota	0	0	7	0	- 7
V at Miami	Baltimore	0	6	0	10	- 16
	Dallas	3	10	0	0	- 13
VI at New Orleans	Dallas	3	7	7	7	- 24
	Miami	0	3	0	0	- 3
VII at Los Angeles	Miami	7	7	0	0	- 14
	Washington	0	0	0	7	- 7
VIII at Houston	Miami	14	3	7	0	- 24
	Minnesota	0	0	0	7	- 7
IX at New Orleans	Pittsburgh	0	2	7	7	- 16
	Minnesota	0	0	0	6	- 6
X at Miami	Pittsburgh	7	0	0	14	- 21
	Dallas	7	3	0	7	- 17
XI at Pasadena	Oakland	0	16	3	13	- 32
	Minnesota	0	0	7	7	- 14
XII at New Orleans	Dallas	10	3	7	7	- 27
	Denver	0	0	10	0	- 10
XIII at Miami	Pittsburgh	7	14	0	14	- 35
	Dallas	7	7	3	14	- 31
XIV at Los Angeles	Pittsburgh	3	7	7	14	- 31
	Los Angeles	7	6	6	0	- 19
XV at New Orleans	Oakland	14	0	10	3	- 27
	Philadelphia	0	3	0	7	- 10
XVI at Detroit	San Francisco	7	13	0	6	- 26
	Cincinnati	0	0	7	14	- 21
XVII at Pasadena	Washington	0	10	3	14	- 27
	Miami	7	10	0	0	- 17
XVIII at Tampa	L.A. Raiders	7	14	14	3	- 38
	Washington	0	3	6	0	- 9
XIX at Stanford	San Francisco	7	21	10	0	- 38
	Miami	10	6	0	0	- 16
XX at New Orleans	Chicago	13	10	21	2	- 46
	New England	3	0	0	7	- 10
XXI at Pasadena	N.Y. Giants	7	2	17	13	- 39
	Denver	10	0	0	10	- 20
XXII at San Diego	Washington	0	35	0	7	- 42
	Denver	10	0	0	0	- 10
XXIII at Miami	Cincinnati	0	3	10	3	- 16
	San Francisco	3	0	3	14	- 20
XXIV at New Orleans	San Francisco	13	14	14	14	- 55
	Denver	3	0	7	0	- 10
XXV at Tampa	Buffalo	3	9	0	7	- 19
	New York Giants	3	7	7	3	- 20
XXVI at Minneapolis	Washington Redskins	0	17	14	6	- 37
	Buffalo Bills	0	0	10	14	- 24
XXVII at Pasadena	Buffalo Bills	7	3	7	0	- 17
	Dallas Cowboys	14	14	3	21	- 52
XXVIII at Atlanta	Dallas Cowboys	6	0	14	10	- 30
	Buffalo Bills	3	10	0	0	- 13

SUPER BOWL COMPOSITE STANDINGS

Team	Games	Wins	Losses	Pct.
San Francisco 49ers	4	4	0	1.000
Pittsburgh Steelers	4	4	0	1.000
Green Bay Packers	2	0	0	1.000
New York Giants	2	2	0	1.000
Chicago Bears	1	1	0	1.000
New York Jets	1	1	0	1.000
Oakland/L.A. Raiders	4	3	1	.750
Washington Redskins	5	3	2	.600
Dallas Cowboys	7	4	3	571
Kansas City Chiefs	2	1	1	..500
Baltimore Colts	2	1	1	.500
Miami Dolphins	5	2	3	.400
Los Angeles Rams	1	0	1	.000
Philadelphia Eagles	1	0	1	.000
New England Patriots	1	0	1	.000
Cincinnati Bengals	1	0	1	.000
Buffalo Bills	4	0	4	.000
Denver Broncos	4	0	4	.000
Minnesota Vikings	4	0	4	000

YEARLY TEAM LEADERS

OFFENSE

YEAR	LGUE	POINTS-PTS/G	FIRST DOWNS	RUSH YARDS YDS/GAME	RUSH AVERAGE	RUSH TD	PASS COMPLETION PERCENTAGE	PASS YARDS YDS/GAME	PASS YARDS/ ATTEMPT	PASS TD	FEWEST INT.	LEAST INT.%	PUNTING AVERAGE	PUNT RETURN AVERAGE	KICKOFF RETURN AVERAGE	YEAR	LGUE
1933	NFL	NY G 244 17.4					Bkn. 46.7									1933	NFL
1934	NFL	ChiB 286 22.0					NY G 40.9									1934	NFL
1935	NFL	ChiB 192 16.0	ChiB 140	ChiB 2096 175		Det 15	NY G 44.8	G.B. 1545 129	G.B. 6.72	ChiB 13						1935	NFL
1936	NFL	G.B 248 20.7	Det 170	Det 2883 240	Det 4.73	Det 22	G.B. 42.4	G.B. 1629 136	ChiB 6.46	ChiB 17						1936	NFL
										G.B. 17							
1937	NFL	G.B. 220 20.0	Was 149	Det 2074 189	Det 4.30	Det 12	Was 44.6	G.B. 1397 127	ChiB 6.97	ChiB 16	NY G 11	NY G 5.42				1937	NFL
										G.B 16							
1938	NFL	G.B. 223 20.7	Was. 147	Det 1893 172	Det 4.01	NY G 12	NY G 48.9	Was. 1536 140	G.B. 6.98	G.B. 20	Bkn. 8	Bkn. 4.73				1938	NFL
1939	NFL	ChiB 298 27.1	G.B. 149	ChiB 2043 186	ChiB 4.66	ChiB 21	Was. 58.2	ChiB 1965 179	Was. 8.93	Was. 18	NY G 11	NY G 6.21				1939	NFL
1940	NFL	Was. 245 22.2	G.B. 154	ChiB 1818 165	Bkn. 3.92	ChiB 16	Was. 59.0	Was. 1887 172	ChiB 8.19	G.B. 18	Bkn. 13	Phi. 5.52				1940	NFL
										Was. 18							
1941	NFL	ChiB 396 36.0	ChiB 181	ChiB 2290 208	ChiB 4.63	ChiB 30	G.B. 52.6	ChiB 2002 182	**ChiB 10.21**	ChiB 19	ChiB 11	G.B. 5.14	Was. 45.9	**ChiB 20.2**	Det 26.5	1941	NFL
1942	NFL	ChiB 376 34.2	G.B. 176	ChiB 1911 174	ChiB 4.07	ChiB 23	Was. 53.3	G.B. 2407 219	ChiB 10.18	G.B. 28	Pit. 11	G.B. 5.45	Was. 44.3	Pit. 15.4	Was. 27.8	1942	NFL
1943	NFL	ChiB 303 30.3	ChiB 161	P-P 1730 173	ChiB 3.89	P-P 18	Was. 54.7	ChiB 2310 231	ChiB 10.09	ChiB 28	NY G 9	NY G 6.04	Was. 43.1	Det 13.6	Det 24.9	1943	NFL
1944	NFL	Phi. 267 26.7	G.B. 147	Phi. 1661 166	Phi. 3.92	Phi. 23	Was. 56.9	Was. 2021 202	ChiB 7.45	ChiB 21	Phi. 12	Was. 5.69	Det 40.5	Det 14.2	NY G 27.4	1944	NFL
1945	NFL	Phi. 272 27.2	ChiB 164	Cle. 1714 171	Cle 4.61	Phi 26	Was. 64.0	ChiB 1857 186	Cle. 8.88	Cle. 16	Was. 11	Was. 4.82	Was. 43.3	Det 14.4	Phi. 24.5	1945	NFL
1946	NFL	ChiB 289 26.3	L.A. 214	G.B. 1765 160	L.A. 4.17	ChiB 19	Phi. 53.5	L.A. 2080 189	ChiB 7.71	L.A. 19	Pit. 13	L.A. 7.36	L.A. 44.4	Pit. 13.5	NY G 26.0	1946	NFL
1946	AAFC	Cle. 423 30.2	L.A. 183	S.F. 2175 155	Buf. 4.08	Cle. 27	L.A. 54.7	Cle. 2266 162	Cle 9.56	Cle. 22	Cle. 7	Cle. 2.95	Bkn. 46.5	N.Y. 15.3	Chi. 24.5	1946	AAFC
1947	NFL	ChiB 363 30.3	ChiB 263	L.A. 2171 181	L.A. 4.73	ChiB 21	Was. 55.5	Was. 3336 278	ChiB 8.18	ChiB 29	Was. 18	Was. 4.33	G.B. 43.6	Bos. 15.1	Was. 22.1	1947	NFL
						Phi. 21											
1947	AAFC	Cle 410 29.8	S.F 218	N.Y 2930 209	N.Y 5.49	N.Y. 27	Cle 58.8	Cle. 2990 214	Cle 10.10	Cle 26	Cle. 12	Cle. 4.05	L.A. 45.0	Bal. 16.5	Buf 25.6	1947	AAFC
1948	NFL	ChiC 395 32.9	ChiB 242	ChiC 2560 213	ChiC 4.82	ChiC 25	Was. 56.1	Was 2861 238	Was. 7.95	L.A. 28	ChiC 12	ChiC 4.21	Phi 45.9	ChiC 19.1	ChiB 25.9	1948	NFL
1948	AAFC	S.F. 495 35.4	Cle. 243	**S.F. 3663 262**	**S.F. 6.07**	S.F. 35	S.F 56.3	Bal. 2899 207	Bal. 8.53	S.F. 30	Bal 13	Bal 3.82	L.A 47.2	Buf. 16.9	S.F 24.4	1948	AAFC
1949	NFL	Phi. 364 30.3	ChiB 248	Phi. 2607 217	ChiC 4.56	Phi. 25	L.A. 52.5	ChiB 3055 255	ChiB 7.94	ChiB 24	Phi. 14	Phi 5.56	L.A. 44.4	ChiC 18.2	NY G 26.0	1949	NFL
1949	AAFC	S.F. 416 34.7	Buf 184	S.F. 2798 233	S.F. 5.53	S.F 26	Buf. 57.1	Cle 2929 244	Cle. 9.90	S.F 28	Cle. 12	Cle. 4.05	S.F 45.5	S.F. 15.5	L.A. 23.7	1949	AAFC
1950	NFL	**L.A.** 466 **38.8**	L.A. 278	NY G 2336 195	NY Y 4.56	L.A. 28	L.A. 55.8	L.A. 3709 309	L.A. 8.19	L.A. 31	NY G 10	NY G 5.35	Cle. 43.2	G.B. 16.6	Det 26.7	1950	NFL
1951	NFL	L.A. 392 32.7	L.A. 272	ChiB 2408 201	L.A. 5.19	ChiB 24	Cle 55.7	L.A. 3296 275	L.A. 8.84	Det 29	Cle 7	L.A. 5.90	Cle. 45.5	Det 15.1	NY G 25.9	1951	NFL
1952	NFL	L.A. 349 29.1	Cle. 228	S.F. 1905 159	Cle. 4.53	L.A. 17	S.F. 51.8	Cle. 2839 237	G.B 7.98	G.B. 26	Phi. 19	Phi 5.26	Cle. 45.7	Det 14.9	Pit. 28.9	1952	NFL
1953	NFL	S.F. 372 31.0	Phi. 256	S.F. 2230 186	L.A 5.04	S.F. 26	Cle. 63.0	Phi. 3357 280	Cle. 10.10	Phi. 25	Cle. 9	Cle. 2.97	Pit 46.9	G.B 8.9	NY G 26.3	1953	NFL
1954	NFL	Det 337 28.1	L.A. 255	S.F. 2498 208	S.F 5.65	S.F 28	Cle 59.0	ChiB 3299 275	L.A. 9.91	Phi. 33	S.F. 12	S.F. 3.53	Pit 43.2	G.B 9.9	Cle. 25.3	1954	NFL
1955	NFL	Cle. 349 29.1	ChiB 235	ChiB 2388 199	ChiB 4.90	Cle. 20	Cle. 55.6	Phi. 2696 225	Cle. 9.51	Cle 21	Cle. 11	Cle. 4.70	L.A. 44.6	ChiC 12.0	Pit. 26.3	1955	NFL
1956	NFL	ChiB 363 30.3	Det 247	ChiB 2468 206	L.A. 5.15	ChiB 22	Bal. 56.6	L.A. 2601 217	ChiB 8.77	G.B. 21	ChiC 14	NY G 5.09	L.A. 43.1	ChiC 9.5	Pit. 26.1	1956	NFL
1957	NFL	L.A. 307 25.6	L.A. 235	L.A. 2142 179	L.A 4.52	Cle. 19	S.F. 62.6	Bal 2608 217	Cle. 9.61	Bal. 25	NY G 12	NY G 4.46	S.F. 44.7	Was. 10.5	S.F. 26.1	1957	NFL
1958	NFL	Bal. 381 31.8	Bal. 253	Cle. 2526 211	Cle. 5.32	Bal. 24	S.F. 58.2	L.A 2909 242	Pit 8.62	Bal. 26	Bal. 11	Bal. 3.11	Was. 45.4	Cle. 8.2	ChiB 25.8	1958	NFL
						Cle. 24											
1959	NFL	Bal. 374 31.2	Bal. 267	Cle. 2149 179	L.A 4.79	Cle. 20	Cle. 57.6	Bal. 2938 245	NY G 8.72	Bal. 33	Cle. 9	Cle. 3.26	NY G 46.6	ChiC 9.8	L.A 24.5	1959	NFL
1960	NFL	Cle. 362 30.2	G.B. 237	St.L. 2356 196	Cle. 5.04	G.B. 29	Cle. 60.6	Bal. 3164 264	Phi. 8.93	Phi. 29	**Cle. 5**	Cle. 1.89	St.L. 44.9	Cle. 9.9	S.F. 27.1	1960	NFL
1960	AFL	N.Y. 382 27.3	N.Y. 286	Dal. 1814 130	Dal. 3.76	Dal. 24	L.A. 51.9	Hou. 3371 241	Hou. 7.39	NY T 32	Dal. 19	Dal. 4.37	L.A. 39.7	Dal. 15.0	Hou. 25.5	1960	AFL
1961	NFL	G.B. 391 27.9	NY G 275	G.B. 2350 168	G.B. 4.96	G.B. 27	G.B. 57.8	Phi. 3824 273	Phi. 8.91	Phi. 34	Cle. 13	Cle 4.06	**Det 47.6**	G.B. 17.8	S.F. 26.6	1961	NFL
						S.F. 27											
1961	AFL	Hou 513 36.6	Hou. 293	Dal 2183 156	Dal. 4.97	S.D 24	Hou. 51.0	**Hou.** 4568 **326**	Hou. 9.17	Hou 48	Bos. 21	Bos. 5.00	Buf. 44.5	N.Y. 17.8	Dal. 27.6	1961	AFL
1962	NFL	G.B. 415 29.6	G.B. 281	G.B. 2460 176	G.B. 4.75	**G.B. 36**	G.B. 60.1	Phi. 3632 259	hi 8.49	NY G 35	G.B 13	G.B 4.18	S.F 45.6	Det 12.9	Was 28.2	1962	NFL
1962	AFL	Dal 389 27.8	Den. 270	Buf 2480 177	Buf 4.95	Dal. 21	Dal. 60.6	Den 3739 267	Dal. 8.77	Hou 32	Bos. 13	Bos. 3.40	Den. 42.9	N.Y. 12.3	Hou 25.9	1962	AFL
1963	NFL	NY G 448 32.0	NY G 278	Cle. 2639 189	Cle. 5.74	G.B. 22	Bal. 57.3	Bal. 3605 258	NY G 8.35	NY G 39	Bal. 12	Bal. 2.77	Chi 46.5	Was. 13.0	Was 26.8	1963	NFL
1963	AFL	S.D. 399 28.5	N/A	S.D. 2201 157	S.D. 5.57	Buf. 21	S.D. 56.4	Hou. 3478 248	Oak. 7.69	Oak. 31	K.C. 22	K.C. 5.01	Den. 44.3	Den. 12.9	Hou. 26.4	1963	AFL
1964	NFL	Bal. 428 30.6	St.L. 275	G.B. 2276 163	Cle. 4.97	Bal. 29	G.B. 57.9	Was. 3071 219	Bal. 8.83	Cle. 28	G.B. 6	G.B. 1.87	Min. 46.4	Cle. 15.2	G.B. 25.8	1964	NFL
1964	AFL	Buf. 400 28.6	Hou. 284	Buf. 2040 146	Oak. 4.47	Buf. 25	K.C. 55.3	Oak. 3886 276	Buf 8.62	K.C. 32	K.C. 21	Hou. 4.90	Den. 43.4	Oak. 13.5	Oak. 25.0	1964	AFL
1965	NFL	S.F. 421 30.1	S.F. 292	Cle. 2331 167	Cle. 4.90	ChiB 27	S.F. 59.9	S.F. 3633 260	Chi. 8.37	S.F 35	Min. 12	Min 3.23	S.F. 45.8	Cle. 11.9	Det 27.2	1965	NFL
1965	AFL	S.D. 340 24.3	S.D. 268	S.D. 1998 143	K.C. 4.19	Buf. 16	S.D. 50.6	S.D. 3379 241	S.D 8.43	Hou 25	Oak. 17	Oak. 3.94	NY J 45.3	S.D. 13.4	Den. 23.4	1965	AFL
1966	NFL	Dal. 445 31.8	Dal. 287	Cle 2166 155	Cle. 5.22	Dal. 24	G.B. 60.7	Dal. 3331 238	G.B 8.90	Cle 33	**G.B. 5**	**G.B. 1.57**	Bal 45.6	Det 10.4	Chi 27.9	1966	NFL
1966	AFL	K.C. 448 32.0	K.C. 266	K.C. 2274 162	K.C 5.18	Buf 19	K.C. 52.8	NY J 3556 254	K.C. 8.28	K.C 31	K.C. 15	S.D. 3.46	Den. 45.2	S.D. 12.2	Den 26.9	1966	AFL
						K.C 19					S.D. 15						
1967	NFL	L.A. 398 28.4	Bal. 289	Cle. 2139 153	Cle. 4.82	Bal. 21	Bal. 58.0	Was 3887 278	G.B. 8.33	NY G 33	L.A. 16	Was. 3.23	Atl 43.7	Cle. 10.2	G.B 27.0	1967	NFL
1967	AFL	Oak. 468 33.4	NY J 282	Hou. 2122 152	Hou. 4.46	Oak 19	K.C. 55.8	NY J 4128 295	NY J 8.02	Oak. 33	Den. 18	Den 4.81	Den. 44.9	Den. 13.5	Den. 25.3	1967	AFL
1968	NFL	Dal 431 30.8	Dal 297	Chi. 2377 170	Chi. 4.75	Dal 22	G.B. 59.1	Dal 3295 235	Bal. 8.62	Bal. 28	Det 15	Det 3.98	Atl. 44.3	Dal. 13.5	Bal. 26.4	1968	NFL
											G.B. 15						
1968	AFL	Oak. 453 32.4	Oak. 287	K.C. 2227 159	Oak 4.64	NY J 22	K.C. 57.8	S.D 3813 272	K.C 9.23	Oak 31	Cin. 11	Cin. 3.51	K.C 45.3	K.C. 14.5	Hou. 23.3	1968	AFL
1969	NFL	Min. 379 27.1	N.O. 282	Dal. 2276 163	Atl. 4.52	Cle. 17	Was. 61.9	S.F. 3379 241	Dal 9.05	L.A 25	L.A. 7	L.A. 1.68	Bal. 45.3	Det 11.0	Bal. 25.3	1969	NFL
						Dal. 17											
						St.L. 17											
1969	AFL	Oak. 377 26.9	S.D. 275	K.C. 2220 159	S.D 4.36	K.C 19	K.C. 55.8	Oak. 3375 241	Cin. 8.83	Oak 36	Cin. 15	S.D 4.73	S.D. 44.6	Den. 12.2	K.C. 26.6	1969	AFL
1970	NFC	S.F 352 25.1	NY G 257	Dal. 2300 164	St.L. 4.66	St.L. 18	Was. 59.4	S.F 2990 214	Dal. 8.23	S.F 25	S.F. 10	S.F. 2.61	N.O. 42.5	S.F. 11.5	L.A. 26.3	1970	NFC
1970	AFC	Bal 321 22.9	Oak. 270	Mia. 2082 149	Cin. 4.46	Den. 17	K.C. 53.3	Bal. 3087 221	Mia. 7.64	Oak. 28	Cin 11	Cin. 3.24	Cin. 46.2	K.C. 12.0	Bal. 25.8	1970	AFC
1971	NFC	Dal. 406 29.0	Dal 288	Det 2376 170	L.A. 4.65	Dal. 25	Atl. 58.6	NY G 3062 219	Atl 8.75	Dal 22	L.A. 11	L.A. 2.97	Phi 41.9	Was. 9.5	Dal. 27.5	1971	NFC
1971	AFC	Oak. 344 24.6	S.D. 264	Mia. 2429 174	Mia. 5.00	Bal 23	Cin 58.6	S.D. 3305 236	K.C 7.99	S.D. 23	Mia. 10	Cin 3.01	K.C 44.8	Mia. 10.5	Mia. 25.2	1971	AFC
1972	NFC	S.F. 353 25.2	NY G 265	Chi. 2360 169	L.A. 4.68	Det 20	NY G 59.9	S.F. 2888 206	Was. 8.03	S.F 27	G.B. 9	Min. 3.37	L.A. 44.2	G.B. 14.6	**Chi. 29.4**	1972	NFC
1972	AFC	Mia. 385 27.5	Oak. 297	Mia. 2960 211	Pit. 5.07	Mia. 26	Cin 57.0	NY J 2930 209	Mia. 8.63	Oak. 23	Cin. 11	Cin. 2.86	K.C 44.8	Den 11.1	Bal. 28.1	1972	AFC
1973	NFC	L.A. 388 27.7	L.A. 294	L.A. 2925 209	Dal. 4.46	Atl 18	Min 60.1	Phi. 3236 231	Dal. 8.11	Dal 26	Min 9	Phi. 2.71	S.F 43.8	S.F 10.6	Was 26.0	1973	NFC
						L.A. 18											
1973	AFC	Den. 354 25.3	Oak 288	Buf 3088 221	Buf. 5.10	Buf 20	Oak 58.1	Den 2706 193	Oak 7.40	Den. 22	Cin. 12	Cin 3.61	K.C 45.6	S.D 12.4	N.E. 24.1	1973	AFC
											Mia. 12						
1974	NFC	Was 320 22.9	Dal 295	Dal 2454 175	Dal. 4.53	Dal. 22	Was 61.5	Was. 2978 213	Dal. 7.42	Min 22	St.L 8	St.L 2.05	N.O 41.8	Det 12.6	Was 25.9	1974	NFC
										Was. 22							
1974	AFC	Oak 355 25.4	Pit 284	Pit 2417 173	Cin. 4.44	Mia 25	Cin. 63.5	Cin. 2804 200	Mia. 8.17	Oak. 28	Cin 13	Cin. 3.68	Oak 42.2	N.E 13.3	Cle 22.9	1974	AFC
1975	NFC	Min 377 26.9	Min 314	Dal. 2432 174	St.L. 4.33	St.L. 19	Min. 63.0	Min 3121 223	Dal 7.54	Was 28	Det 12	Min. 3.14	S.F 41.9	St.L 10.3	St.L 24.3	1975	NFC
1975	AFC	Buf 420 30.0	Buf. 318	Buf 2974 212	Buf 5.06	Bal. 28	Mia 60.9	Cin 3497 250	Cin 8.08	Buf 28	Bal 8	Bal. 2.26	Oak 43.8	Hou. 14.4	Oak 26.0	1975	AFC
						Oak 28											

Bold-designatesall-timeleader

YEARLY TEAM LEADERS

OFFENSE

YEAR	LGUE	POINTS-PTS/G			FIRST DOWNS		RUSH YARDS YDS/GAME			RUSH AVERAGE		RUSH TD		PASS COMPLETION PERCENTAGE		PASS YARDS YDS/GAME			PASS YARDS/ATTEMPT		PASS TD		FEWEST INT.		LEAST INT.%		PUNTING AVERAGE		PUNT RETURN AVERAGE		KICKOFF RETURN AVERAGE		YEAR	LGUE
1976	NFC	L.A.	351	25.1	St.L.	307	L.A.	2523	180	Det.	4.29	L.A.	23	Min.	61.1	Min.	2855	204	L.A.	8.35	Det.	20	Min.	10	Min.	2.26	Atl.	42.1	Was.	13.2	Dal.	24.5	1976	NFC
																					Was.	20												
1976	AFC	Bal.	417	29.8	Oak.	302	Pit.	2971	212	N.E.	4.99	Pit.	33	Oak.	63.3	K.C.	2929	209	Bal.	8.92	Oak.	33	Bal.	10	Bal.	2.77	Buf.	42.2	N.E.	13.1	Mia.	24.5	1976	AFC
1977	NFC	Dal.	345	24.6	Dal.	272	Chi.	2811	201	Chi.	4.7	Dal.	21	Min.	58.8	Min.	2692	192	Dal.	7.23	Min.	19	Dal.	10	Dal.	2.69	Atl.	41.2	Phi.	10.4	L.A.	18.9	1977	NFC
1977	AFC	Oak.	351	25.1	Oak.	305	Oak.	2627	188	Mia.	4.6	Oak.	20	Mia.	58.5	Buf.	2803	200	Pit.	7.72	Sea.	23	Bal.	12	Bal.	3.01	Oak.	43.3	Hou.	15.0	N.E.	26.9	1977	AFC
												Pit.	20										Den.	12										
1978	NFC	Dal.	384	24.0	Dal.	342	Dal.	2783	174	Dal.	4.5	Dal.	22	N.O.	61.4	Min.	3528	221	Dal.	7.58	Dal.	25	N.O.	16	N.O.	3.34	NY G	42.1	L.A.	10.6	Was.	23.3	1978	NFC
																					Min.	25	Phi.	16										
1978	AFC	Mia.	372	23.3	Sea.	345	N.E.	3165	198	N.E.	4.7	N.E.	30	Mia.	59.6	S.D.	3566	223	Pit.	7.79	Pit.	28	K.C.	16	K.C.	4.32	Cin.	42.4	NY J	12.5	K.C.	23.9	1978	AFC
1979	NFC	Dal.	371	23.2	Dal.	339	St.L.	2582	161	St.L.	4.6	N.O.	28	N.O.	60.0	Dal.	3883	243	Dal.	7.72	Dal.	29	Dal.	13	Dal.	2.58	NY G	42.7	Phi.	9.5	St.L.	22.7	1979	NFC
														S.F.	60.0								Phi.	13										
1979	AFC	Pit.	416	26.0	Cle.	350	NY J	2646	165	Pit.	4.6	Pit.	25	S.D.	62.5	S.D.	4138	259	Pit.	7.88	Cle.	28	Buf.	15	Buf.	3.22	K.C.	43.1	K.C.	10.6	Oak.	22.7	1979	AFC
												S.D.	25										Cin.	15										
1980	NFC	Dal.	454	28.4	Dal.	337	L.A.	2799	175	L.A.	4.6	Dal.	26	S.F.	60.8	N.O.	4010	251	Phi.	7.91	Atl.	31	Det.	12	Atl.	2.51	NY G	44.8	Was.	10.1	N.O.	22.4	1980	NFC
																					L.A.	31	Phi.	12										
1980	AFC	N.E.	441	27.6	S.D.	372	Hou.	2635	165	Hou.	4.6	Bal.	20	Hou.	63.9	S.D.	4741	296	N.E.	8.22	Cle.	30	Cle.	14	Cle.	2.52	Den.	43.9	K.C.	14.5	N.E.	22.9	1980	AFC
																					S.D.	30	K.C.	14										
1981	NFC	Atl.	426	26.6	Min.	343	Det.	2795	175	Det.	4.7	Det.	26	S.F.	63.4	Min.	4567	285	Det.	7.97	Atl.	30	S.F.	13	S.F.	2.51	Det.	43.5	L.A.	13.8	Was.	25.0	1981	NFC
1981	AFC	S.D.	478	29.9	Cle.	364	K.C.	2633	165	K.C.	4.3	S.D.	26	Cin.	60.4	S.D.	4873	305	Den.	8.23	S.D.	34	Cin.	12	Cin.	2.18	Cin.	44.8	S.D.	12.2	Hou.	23.9	1981	AFC
1982	NFC	Dal.	226	25.1	Atl.	190	Dal.	1313	146	Dal.	4.4	L.A.	13	Atl.	64.0	S.F.	2502	278	Dal.	8.33	S.F.	17	St.L.	6	St.L.	2.50	St.L.	43.8	Atl.	11.4	N.O.	22.2	1982	NFC
		G.B.	226	25.1										Was.	64.0																			
1982	AFC	S.D.	288	25.3	S.D.	233	Buf.	1371	152	Buf.	4.3	Raid.	15	S.D.	61.5	S.D.	2927	325	S.D.	8.94	S.D.	19	K.C.	8	Cin.	2.90	Den.	45.0	Den.	14.5	N.E.	23.1	1982	AFC
										NY J	4.3	S.D.	15																					
1983	NFC	**Was.**	**541**	33.8	Was.	353	Chi.	2727	170	Chi.	4.7	Was.	30	**S.F.**	**64.2**	G.B.	4365	272	G.B.	8.91	G.B.	33	Atl.	10	Atl.	1.97	T.B.	41.8	Det.	11.3	Min.	21.6	1983	NFC
1983	AFC	Raid.	442	27.6	Raid.	356	Balt.	2695	168	N.E.	4.8	Cin.	24	Cin.	63.9	S.D.	4661	291	Raid.	7.76	Buf.	30	Mia.	11	Mia.	2.49	Bal.	45.3	Raid.	11.5	Mia.	23.1	1983	AFC
1984	NFC	S.F.	475	29.7	S.F.	356	Chi.	2974	186	L.A.	5.3	Chi.	22	S.F.	62.9	St.L.	4257	266	S.F.	8.22	S.F.	32	S.F.	10	S.F.	2.01	N.O.	43.1	L.A.	12.2	S.F.	22.1	1984	NFC
1984	AFC	Mia.	513	32.1	**Mia.**	**387**	NY J	2189	137	NY J	4.3	Raid.	19	**Mia.**	**64.2**	**Mia.**	**5018**	314	Mia.	9.00	**Mia.**	**49**	N.E.	14	N.E.	2.80	K.C.	44.9	Cin.	12.4	NY J	23.0	1984	AFC
1985	NFC	Chi.	456	28.5	NY G	356	Chi.	2761	173	G.B.	4.7	Chi.	27	S.F.	60.2	Dal.	3861	241	NY G	7.70	S.F.	28	L.A.	14	S.F.	2.54	NY G	42.9	L.A.	13.2	Chi.	25.3	1985	NFC
										St.L.	4.7												S.F.	14										
										S.F.	4.7																							
1985	AFC	S.D.	467	29.2	S.D.	380	N.E.	2331	146	Ind.	5.0	Ind.	22	S.D.	61.1	S.D.	4870	304	S.D.	8.19	S.D.	37	NY J	8	NY J	1.61	Ind.	44.8	Raid.	11.1	Den.	23.1	1985	AFC
1986	NFC	Min.	398	24.9	S.F.	346	Chi.	2700	169	Chi.	4.5	Was.	23	Dal.	58.3	S.F.	4096	256	Min.	8.06	Min.	31	L.A.	15	Min.	2.89	NY G	44.8	St.L.	11.7	N.O.	24.2	1986	NFC
																							Min.	15										
1986	AFC	Mia.	430	26.9	S.D.	380	Cin.	2533	158	Cin.	4.9	Cin.	24	NY J	62.2	Mia.	4779	299	Cin.	8.37	Mia.	46	Cle.	11	Cle.	2.04	Ind.	44.7	Sea.	11.7	Cin.	22.0	1986	AFC
1987	NFC	S.F.	459	30.6	S.F.	357	S.F.	2237	149	S.F.	4.3	Min.	20	S.F.	64.3	S.F.	3750	250	S.F.	7.89	S.F.	44	N.O.	12	S.F.	2.79	Det.	41.8	St.L.	12.5	Atl.	21.5	1987	NFC
												N.O.	20																					
1987	AFC	Cle.	390	26.0	Den.	331	Raid.	2197	146	Raid.	4.6	Den.	18	Cle.	60.4	Mia.	3876	258	Cle.	7.52	Sea.	31	Cle.	12	Cle.	2.49	S.D.	42.0	NY J	11.8	Den.	20.7	1987	AFC
					Mia.	331																												
1988	NFC	L.A.	407	25.4	Phx.	336	S.F.	2523	158	S.F.	4.8	Chi.	25	L.A.	59.8	Wash.	4136	259	L.A.	6.92	Wash.	33	NYG	14	S.F.	2.67	Det.	42.4	N.O.	11.8	T.B.	21.0	1988	NFC
																							S.F.	14										
1988	AFC	Cin.	448	28.0	Cin.	351	Cin.	2710	169	Cin.	4.8	Cin.	27	Buf.	59.7	Mia.	4516	282	Cin.	7.93	Mia.	29	NYJ	11	NYJ	1.85	Den.	43.8	NYJ	11.0	S.D.	25.2	1988	AFC
1989	NFC	S.F.	442	27.6	S.F.	350	Chi.	2287	143	Det.	4.9	Det.	23	S.F.	70.2	S.F.	4302	269	S.F.	8.15	S.F.	35	S.F.	11	Atl.	2.08	Phx.	43.6	NYG	12.7	Dall.	22.2	1989	NFC
1989	AFC	Buf.	409	25.6	Cin.	348	Cin.	2483	155	Cin.	4.7	K.C.	18	Hou.	59.5	Mia.	4216	264	Buf.	7.00	Buf.	32	Cin.	13	Cin.	2.53	Ind.	42.4	Ind.	12.4	Pitt.	23.3	1989	AFC
														K.C.	59.5						Cin.	32	Pit.	13										
1990	NFC	Phi.	396	24.8	Was.	327	Phi.	2556	160	Det.	5.3	Chi.	22	S.F.	61.7	S.F.	4177	261	S.F.	6.74	Phi.	34	NYG	5	NYG	1.3	NYG	44.1	Chi.	11.1	Atl.	21.2	1990	NFC
1990	AFC	Buf.	428	26.8	Hou.	376	S.D.	2257	141	S.D.	4.7	Buff.	20	Hou.	62.4	Hou.	4805	300	Raid.	7.36	Hou.	37	K.C.	5	K.C.	1.1	Hou.	45.0	Ind.	11.2	S.D.	21.6	1990	AFC
												Raid.	20																					
1991	NFC	Wash.	485	30.3	S.F.	336	Minn.	2201	138	Minn.	4.7	Wash.	21	S.F.	62.3	S.F.	3997	250	Wash.	8.02	Wash.	30	NYG	8	NYG	1.9	Minn.	45.5	Det.	14.8	Dall.	21.7	1991	NFC
																					Atl.	30												
1991	AFC	Buff.	458	28.6	Buff.	359	Buff.	2381	149	S.D.	4.8	NYJ	17	Buff.	64.3	Hou.	4621	289	Buff.	7.03	Buff.	39	Clev.	10	Clev.	2.0	Mia.	44.8	L.A.Rd.	11.4	S.D.	21.3	1991	AFC
																															Sea.	21.3		
1992	NFC	S.F.	431	26.9	S.F.	344	Phil.	2388	149	S.F.	4.8	S.F.	22	S.F.	66.5	S.F.	3880	243	S.F.	7.58	Atl.	33	S.F.	9	S.F.	1.9	Minn.	44.4	Dall.	12.5	Atl.	23.9	1992	NFC
1992	AFC	Buff.	381	23.8	Buff.	350	Buff.	2436	152	Hou.	4.6	Buff.	18	Hou.	65.1	Hou.	4029	252	Mia.	6.73	Hou.	27	K.C.	12	K.C.	2.9	Hou.	45.2	Cin.	11.9	N.E.	21.5	1992	AFC
												S.D.	18																					
1993	NFC	S.F.	473	29.5	S.F.	372	NYG	2210	138	S.F.	4.6	S.F.	27	S.F.	67.6	S.F.	4302	269	S.F.	8.55	S.F.	29	Dall.	6	Dall.	1.3	Det.	44.5	N.O.	13.6	G.B.	24.7	1993	NFC
1993	AFC	Den.	373	23.3	Hou.	330	Sea.	2015	126	Hou.	4.4	K.C.	14	Den.	63.3	Mia.	4353	272	Mia.	7.86	Den.	27	Den.	10	Den.	1.8	Hou.	45.4	Cle.	13.4	Mia.	21.8	1993	AFC
												NYJ	14								Mia.	27	Mia.	10										
												S.D.	14																					

Bold-designates all-time leader

YEARLY TEAM LEADERS
DEFENSE

YEAR	LGUE	POINTS-PT/G			FIRST DOWNS		RUSH YARDS		YARDS GAME	RUSH AVERAGE		RUSH TD		PASS COMPLETION PECENTAGE		PASS YARDS		YARDS GAME	PASS YARDS/ ATTEMPT		PASS TD		MOST INT.		HIGHEST INT.%		PUNT RETURN AVERAGE		KICKOFF RETURN AVERAGE		TEAM	LGUE
1933	NFL	**Bkn.**	**54**	5.4																											1933	NFL
1934	NFL	Det	59	**4.5**																											1934	NFL
1935	NFL	G.B.	96	8.0										**ChiB**	**30.4**								ChiB	37	**ChiB**	**19.1**					1935	NFL
		NY G	96	8.0																												
1936	NFL	ChiB	94	7.8										Bos.	31.5								ChiB	35	ChiB	15.4					1936	NFL
1937	NFL	ChiB	100	9.1										Pit.	32.4								NY G	30	NY G	16.5					1937	NFL
1938	NFL	NY G	79	7.2										NY G	34.1								NY G	34	NY G	15.0					1938	NFL
1939	NFL	NY G	85	7.7										Was.	37.0								NY G	35	NY G	15.8					1939	NFL
1940	NFL	Bkn.	120	10.9										ChiC	37.1								G.B.	40	Det.	16.4					1940	NFL
1941	NFL	NY G	114	10.3	Bkn.	110	ChiB	1076	98	Was.	2.71	Bkn.	6	ChiB	40.0	Pit.	1168	106	ChiB	5.5	Bkn.	6	ChiB	34	NY G	13.3	Cle.	8.2	Was.	19.4	1941	NFL
					ChiC	110						ChiB	6								NY G	6										
1942	NFL	ChiB	84	7.6	ChiB	98	ChiB	519	**47**	ChiB	1.77	ChiB	3	Was.	37.5	Was.	1093	99	ChiB	4.2	NY G	4	ChiB	33	G.B.	13.6	Det.	10.2	Pit.	18.5	1942	NFL
																							G.B.	33								
1943	NFL	Was.	137	13.7	P-P	96	P-P	793	79	P-P	2.54	NY G	8	ChiB	31.5	ChiB	980	98	ChiB	4.8	ChiB	8	G.B.	42	G.B.	17.4	Was.	9.5	NY G	19.3	1943	NFL
1944	NFL	NY G	75	7.5	**Phi.**	**86**	**Phi.**	**558**	56	Phi.	1.74	NY G	6	ChiB	33.2	ChiB	1052	105	NY G	5.0	**NY G**	**3**	NY G	34	Phi.	14.3	C-P	9.9	Phi.	18.0	1944	NFL
1945	NFL	Was.	121	12.1	Phi.	104	Phi.	817	82	Det.	2.56	Det.	7	Cle.	39.1	Was.	1121	112	Was.	5.4	NY G	6	Bos.	30	Bos.	13.2	Det.	9.8	Det.	16.6	1945	NFL
1946	NFL	Pit.	117	10.6	ChiB	138	ChiB	1044	95	Phi.	2.69	Pit.	9	Pit.	39.5	**Pit.**	**939**	**85**	Pit.	5.8	G.B.	6	ChiB	27	Phi.	11.8	Pit.	7.7	ChiB	16.0	1946	NFL
																					Pit.	6										
1946	AAFC	Cle.	137	9.8	N.Y.	119	S.F.	873	62	S.F.	2.05	S.F.	7	Cle.	41.8	Cle.	1317	94	Cle.	4.4	Cle.	8	Cle.	41	Cle.	13.7	N.Y.	10.8	Mia.	18.5	1946	AAFC
1947	NFL	G.B.	210	17.5	Pit.	170	Phi.	1329	111	L.A.	3.41	ChiB	6	Pit.	40.2	G.B.	1790	149	G.B.	6.5	G.B.	14	G.B.	30	G.B.	10.8	ChiC	9.4	ChiB	17.5	1947	NFL
																					L.A.	14										
1947	AAFC	Cle.	185	13.2	N.Y.	140	N.Y.	1237	88	N.Y.	3.33	L.A.	9	Cle.	42.6	Cle.	1707	122	Cle.	5.6	Cle.	11	Cle.	32	Cle.	10.6	L.A.	10.8	Bal.	17.0	1947	AAFC
1948	NFL	ChiB	151	12.6	Phi.	158	Phi.	1209	101	Phi.	3.22	Phi.	5	Phi.	41.1	G.B.	1626	135	ChiB	4.9	ChiB	12	NY G	39	NY G	12.5	ChiB	9.2	Pit.	17.8	1948	NFL
1948	AAFC	Cle.	190	13.6	Cle.	171	Cle.	1519	108	Cle.	3.48	Cle.	10	Cle.	44.9	Bkn.	1985	142	Cle.	5.9	Cle.	14	S.F.	32	S.F.	8.6	Bal.	10.3	Chi.	17.5	1948	AAFC
1949	NFL	Phi.	134	11.2	Phi.	148	ChiB	1196	100	ChiB	2.79	Phi.	5	Phi.	39.9	Phi.	1607	134	Phi.	5.3	Pit.	9	ChiC	33	Det.	10.3	L.A.	8.3	Det.	18.7	1949	NFL
1949	AAFC	Cle.	171	14.2	N.Y.	129	N.Y.	1134	94	N.Y.	3.15	N.Y.	8	Cle.	39.5	Cle.	1677	140	Cle.	5.5	Cle.	9	S.F.	32	S.F.	10.1	N.Y.	11.0	L.A.	19.2	1949	AAFC
1950	NFL	Phi.	141	11.7	Phi.	141	Det.	1367	114	NY G	2.93	Phi.	5	Phi.	36.8	Cle.	1581	132	Cle.	5.4	Cle.	8	Bal.	34	Phi.	11.2	Cle.	6.6	Pit.	19.2	1950	NFL
1951	NFL	Cle.	152	12.7	NY G	174	NY G	913	76	NY G	2.33	Cle.	8	Phi.	41.5	Pit.	1687	141	Cle.	6.0	Cle.	10	NY G	41	NY G	10.9	S.F.	6.7	G.B.	18.5	1951	NFL
												NY G	8																			
1952	NFL	Det.	192	16.0	S.F.	167	Det.	1145	95	NY G	3.23	ChiC	8	Cle.	40.5	Was.	1817	151	S.F.	5.6	Was.	12	L.A.	38	L.A.	10.6	NY G	6.7	Pit.	18.3	1952	NFL
												Det.	8																			
												NY G	8																			
												Pit.	8																			
1953	NFL	Cle.	162	13.5	Pit.	184	Phi.	1117	93	Pit.	3.07	Phi.	6	Cle.	42.2	Was.	1950	162	Was.	5.6	Was.	8	Det.	38	Det.	10.7	ChiC	1.5	Pit.	16.3	1953	NFL
1954	NFL	Cle.	162	13.5	Cle.	147	Cle.	1050	88	Cle.	2.82	Cle.	4	Phi.	41.4	Cle.	1784	149	Phi.	5.9	Det.	10	NY G	33	Pit.	10.2	**ChiC**	**1.2**	G.B.	18.5	1954	NFL
1955	NFL	Cle.	218	18.2	Cle.	171	Cle.	1189	99	Was.	3.26	Was.	8	Cle.	39.0	Pit.	1530	127	Cle.	5.5	S.F.	10	G.B.	31	G.B.	12.0	Bal.	1.9	L.A.	19.7	1955	NFL
																							L.A.	31								
1956	NFL	Cle.	177	14.7	Pit.	167	NY G	1443	120	NY G	3.48	Det.	9	ChiC	44.9	Cle.	1215	101	Cle.	5.4	Cle.	7	ChiC	33	ChiC	11.5	S.F.	3.5	Pit.	19.0	1956	NFL
1957	NFL	Cle.	172	14.3	Pit.	156	Bal.	1174	98	Bal.	3.13	Pit.	7	Cle.	43.4	Cle.	1511	126	Cle.	6.2	Cle.	8	G.B.	30	G.B.	9.6	Det.	1.6	Pit.	20.1	1957	NFL
1958	NFL	NY G	183	15.2	ChiB	168	Bal.	1291	108	NY G	3.61	Cle.	6	NY G	45.7	NY G	2130	177	L.A.	6.0	Bal.	9	Bal.	35	Bal.	9.6	Cle.	2.5	S.F.	17.6	1958	NFL
1959	NFL	NY G	170	14.2	NY G	167	NY G	1261	105	NY G	3.33	NY G	6	Pit.	44.9	NY G	1811	151	NY G	6.0	NY G	11	Bal.	40	Bal.	11.4	Cle.	1.2	Pit.	17.5	1959	NFL
1960	NFL	S.F.	205	17.1	St.L.	158	St.L.	1212	101	NY G	3.20	G.B.	7	S.F.	47.8	Chi.	1808	151	Chi.	6.2	Bal.	8	Cle.	31	Phi.	10.6	Bal.	3.2	Was.	17.1	1960	NFL
1960	AFL	Dal.	253	18.1	Buf.	225	Dal.	980	70	Dal.	2.32	Hou.	6	Buf.	43.1	Buf.	2461	176	Buf.	5.7	Bos.	19	Buf.	33	Buf.	7.7	Dal.	5.8	Den.	20.1	1960	AFL
																					Buf.	19										
																					Dal.	19										
1961	NFL	NY G	220	15.7	NY G	212	Pit.	1463	104	St.L.	3.51	NY G	6	NY G	45.6	Bal.	2320	166	G.B.	6.4	Det.	11	NY G	33	NY G	8.5	Min.	6.0	St.L.	20.1	1961	NFL
1961	AFL	S.D.	219	15.6	Buf.	200	Bos.	1041	74	Bos.	2.97	S.D.	7	Hou.	43.0	S.D.	2736	195	Hou.	5.6	Hou.	13	**S.D.**	**49**	S.D.	10.1	Buf.	6.5	Den.	17.1	1961	AFL
1962	NFL	G.B.	148	10.6	Det.	180	Det.	1231	88	Det.	3.51	G.B.	4	Chi.	46.8	G.B.	2084	149	G.B.	5.9	G.B.	10	G.B.	31	G.B.	8.7	St.L.	4.7	G.B.	20.1	1962	NFL
1962	AFL	Dal.	233	16.6	Hou.	217	Dal.	1250	89	Dal.	3.56	Buf.	10	Hou.	43.8	Oak.	2517	180	Hou.	5.9	Dal.	13	Buf.	36	Buf.	8.2	Bos.	4.9	Hou.	21.0	1962	AFL
1963	NFL	Chi.	144	10.3	G.B.	193	Chi.	1442	103	Chi.	3.50	Chi.	7	Chi.	46.5	Chi.	2045	146	Chi.	5.8	G.B.	9	ChiB	36	ChiB	10.2	Dal.	4.9	G.B.	19.3	1963	NFL
1963	AFL	S.D.	256	18.3	N/A		N/A			N/A		N/A		N/A		N/A			N/A		N/A		N/A		N/A		N/A		N/A		1963	AFL
1964	NFL	Bal.	225	16.1	G.B.	197	L.A.	1501	107	Dal.	3.43	Dal.	6	Dal.	45.6	G.B.	1980	141	G.B.	6.2	G.B.	11	Was.	34	Was.	8.4	Dal.	2.7	Cle.	20.2	1964	NFL
1964	AFL	Buf.	242	17.3	Buf.	206	Buf.	913	65	Buf.	3.04	Buf.	4	Buf.	46.6	K.C.	2910	208	S.D.	6.0	Oak.	21	NY T	34	Den.	7.3	Oak.	6.6	Hou.	18.5	1964	AFL
1965	NFL	L.A.	224	16.0	L.A.	208	L.A.	1409	101	L.A.	3.38	Det.	9	Dal.	48.1	G.B.	2316	165	G.B.	6.0	G.B.	11	G.B.	27	Was.	8.5	Was.	4.6	Dal.	19.5	1965	NFL
																							Was.	27								
1965	AFL	Buf.	226	16.1	S.D.	190	S.D.	1094	78	Buf.	3.09	Buf.	5	Hou.	42.5	S.D.	2480	177	S.D.	5.2	Bos.	17	Buf.	32	Hou.	6.5	Bos.	7.0	Oak.	19.8	1965	AFL
1966	NFL	G.B.	163	11.6	L.A.	196	Dal.	1176	84	St.L.	3.16	Dal.	6	St.L.	44.5	G.B.	2316	165	G.B.	5.9	G.B.	7	Cle.	30	Cle.	7.4	Det.	3.6	St.L.	20.4	1966	NFL
1966	AFL	Buf.	255	18.2	Buf.	192	Buf.	1051	75	Buf.	3.06	Buf.	6	Buf.	44.0	S.D.	2386	170	K.C.	5.8	S.D.	13	K.C.	33	Mia.	7.3	NY J	5.0	Mia.	20.4	1966	AFL
1967	NFL	L.A.	196	14.0	G.B.	183	Dal.	1081	77	L.A.	3.10	Bal.	5	Chi.	42.7	G.B.	1644	117	G.B.	4.9	Det.	11	Bal.	32	Bal.	8.1	G.B.	1.7	Chi.	20.5	1967	NFL
																							L.A.	32								
1967	AFL	Hou.	199	14.2	Oak.	182	Oak.	1129	81	Oak.	3.21	Hou.	7	Oak.	41.2	Buf.	2191	156	Hou.	5.7	Hou.	10	K.C.	31	Mia.	8.0	Mia.	6.5	Hou.	18.6	1967	AFL
1968	NFL	Bal.	144	10.3	L.A.	190	Dal.	1195	85	Dal.	3.24	**Dal.**	**2**	N.O.	41.8	G.B.	2031	145	Bal.	5.6	Bal.	9	Cle.	32	Cle.	7.3	Bal.	3.3	Chi.	17.9	1968	NFL
1968	AFL	K.C.	170	12.1	N.Y.	178	NY J	1195	85	NY J	3.25	K.C.	4	Buf.	42.1	Hou.	2003	143	Hou.	5.6	Hou.	13	K.C.	37	K.C.	8.0	Oak.	5.3	K.C.	19.3	1968	AFL
1969	NFL	Min.	133	9.5	Min.	158	Dal.	1050	75	Min.	3.23	Dal.	3	L.A.	47.0	Min.	2035	145	Min.	5.0	Min.	8	Min.	30	Min.	7.3	G.B.	3.4	Dal.	19.4	1969	NFL
1969	AFL	K.C.	177	12.6	K.C.	181	K.C.	1091	78	K.C.	3.47	K.C.	6	Oak.	38.9	K.C.	2491	178	K.C.	5.8	K.C.	10	K.C.	32	K.C.	7.5	Oak.	4.1	Bos.	19.1	1969	AFL
1970	NFC	Min.	143	10.2	Min.	168	Det.	1152	82	Det.	3.18	Min.	4	St.L.	47.9	Min.	1798	128	Min.	4.9	Min.	6	Det.	28	Min.	7.6	NY G	2.9	L.A.	18.1	1970	NFC
																							Min.	28								
1970	AFC	Mia.	228	16.3	Den.	199	NY J	1283	92	NY J	3.14	Bal.	6	NY J	43.1	K.C.	2280	163	K.C.	5.6	S.D.	13	K.C.	31	K.C.	7.6	Cle.	3.6	Bos.	20.5	1970	AFC
1971	NFC	Min.	139	9.9	Min.	194	Dal.	1144	82	Dal.	3.24	**Min.**	**2**	S.F.	44.6	Atl.	1895	135	Min.	5.0	Atl.	9	Was.	29	Det.	7.2	S.F.	2.3	Was.	17.5	1971	NFC
1971	AFC	Bal.	140	10.0	Bal.	196	Bal.	1113	80	Bal.	3.16	Bal.	8	Den.	42.1	Bal.	2027	145	Bal.	5.6	Bal.	9	Bal.	28	Cin.	8.1	S.D.	2.0	Mia.	20.0	1971	AFC
1972	NFC	Was.	218	15.6	Min.	200	Dal.	1515	108	G.B.	3.42	Dal.	7	Atl.	45.5	Min.	1791	128	Min.	5.4	G.B.	7	Min.	26	Min.	7.9	Was.	2.1	L.A.	18.5	1972	NFC
1972	AFC	Mia.	171	12.2	Mia.	186	Mia.	1548	111	Oak.	3.76	Pit.	6	Buf.	42.5	Cle.	1994	142	Cin.	5.8	Pit.	9	Pit.	28	Buf.	7.5	Mia.	3.9	Hou.	19.5	1972	AFC
1973	NFC	Min.	168	12.0	L.A.	173	Dal.	1471	105	Was.	3.34	Dal.	5	Atl.	46.6	Atl.	1619	116	Atl.	5.0	Min.	8	Was.	26	NY G	7.3	Dal.	5.2	Min.	19.1	1973	NFC
												L.A.	5																			
												Min.	5																			
1973	AFC	Mia.	150	10.7	Min.	168	Oak.	1470	105	Oak.	3.38	Oak.	5	Buf.	45.1	N.E.	1600	114	Mia.	5.0	Mia.	6	Pit.	37	Pit.	10.3	Cin.	4.6	Den.	20.4	1973	AFC
1974	NFC	L.A.	181	12.9	L.A.	186	L.A.	1308	93	Dal.	3.23	L.A.	4	Atl.	45.0	Atl.	1847	132	Was.	5.3	Min.	8	Was.	25	Was.	6.4	Phi.	6.8	Min.	17.4	1974	NFC
1974	AFC	Pit.	189	13.5	Pit.	200	N.E.	1587	113	Pit.	3.41	Mia.	7	Pit.	43.4	Pit.	1872	134	Pit.	5.5	Buf.	11	K.C.	28	Cle.	7.8	Mia.	6.2	Mia.	19.1	1974	AFC
1975	NFC	L.A.	135	9.6	Min.	190	Min.	1532	109	S.F.	3.53	L.A.	4	Dal.	43.4	Min.	1994	142	L.A.	5.5	L.A.	11	Min.	28	Min.	7.8	G.B.	4.9	Min.	19.5	1975	NFC
1975	AFC	Pit.	162	11.6	Pit.	214	Hou.	1680	120	Hou.	3.38	Pit.	8	Oak.	43.0	Cin.	2001	143	Cin.	5.1	Mia.	9	Oak.	35	Oak.	8.8	Pit.	5.5	Oak.	18.6	1975	AFC
																					Pit.	9										

Bold - designates all-time leader

YEARLY TEAM LEADERS
DEFENSE

YEAR	LGUE	POINTS-PT/G	FIRST DOWNS	RUSH YARDS	YARDS GAME	RUSH AVERAGE	RUSH TD	PASS COMPLETION PECENTAGE	PASS YARDS	YARDS GAME	PASS YARDS/ ATTEMPT	PASS TD	MOST INT.	HIGHEST INT.%	PUNT RETURN AVERAGE	KICKOFF RETURN AVERAGE	TEAM	LGUE
1976	NFC	Min. 176 12.6	Det 191	L.A. 1564	112	L.A. 3.6	Chi. 10 S.F. 10	Was. 41.2	Min. 1575	113	Dal. 5.7	Min. 8	L.A. 32	L.A. 8.1	G.B. 5.6	Was. 16.4	1976	NFC
1976	AFC	Pit. 138 9.9	Pit. 182	Pit. 1457	104	Pit. 3.2	Pit. 5	Pit. 42.4	Cin. 1758	126	Den. 5.8	Den. 8	Cin. 26	Cin. 7.1	Pit. 5.7	Oak. 18.4	1976	AFC
1977	NFC	Atl. 129 9.2	Atl. 192	Dal. 1651	118	NY G 3.4	Atl. 5	Dal. 41.5	Atl. 1775	127	Dal. 5.4	Chi. 7	Atl. 26	Atl. 8.1	L.A. 4.0	Was. 19.1	1977	NFC
1977	AFC	Den. 148 10.6	Oak. 204	Den. 1531	109	Den. 3.3	Den. 5	Pit. 44.0	S.D. 2088	149	Mia. 5.8	Bal. 10 Mia. 10	Pit. 31	Pit. 8.7	Cin. 6.8	Oak. 15.8	1977	AFC
1978	NFC	Dal. 208 13.0	L.A. 229	Dal. 1721	108	T.B. 3.4	N.O. 9	Dal. 46.8	L.A. 2449	153	NY G 6.0	NY G 10	T.B. 29	L.A. 5.5	G.B. 5.6	Was 17.5	1978	NFC
1978	AFC	Pit. 195 12.2	Den. 251	Pit. 1774	111	Pit. 3.5	Pit. 11	Cin. 48.7	Buf. 2156	135	Den. 6.2	Den 9	Mia. 32	Mia. 7.3	Den. 4.7	Oak. 19.5	1978	AFC
1979	NFC	T.B. 237 4.8	T.B. 247	T.B. 1873	117	T.B. 3.5	Chi. 9	Dal 47.6	T.B. 2405	150	T.B. 5.5	Min. 14 T.B. 14	Chi. 29	Chi. 6.3	Was. 4.7	Was. 16.8	1979	NFC
1979	AFC	S.D. 246 15.4	Mia. 238	Den. 1693	106	Den. 3.4	K.C. 8	Pit. 47.1	Buf. 2713	170	Pit. 6.1	Den. 11 S.D. 11	Hou. 34	Hou. 7.3	Mia. 5.2	Sea. 17.7	1979	AFC
1980	NFC	Phi. 222 13.9	Det 265	Det 1599	100	Det 3.6	Atl. 8 Phi. 8	Was. 47.7	Was. 2504	157	Phi. 5.9	Det 14	Was. 33	Was. 8.4	Min. 6.2	Min. 16.9	1980	NFC
1980	AFC	Hou. 251 15.7	Buf. 251	Cin. 1680	105	Oak. 3.4	Hou. 8	Pit. 52.6	Buf. 2561	160	Buf. 5.9	Buf. 15	Oak. 35	Oak. 6.7	Buf. 6.0	**Cle. 14.3**	1980	AFC
1981	NFC	Phi. 221 13.9	Phi. 266	Det 1623	101	NY G 3.4	Atl. 10 NY G 10 S.F. 10	Chi. 44.4	Phi. 3050	191	Phi. 6.0	T.B. 10	Dal. 37	Dal. 7.2	Dal. 6.1	G.B. 16.9	1981	NFC
1981	AFC	Mia. 275 17.2	Den. 268	K.C. 1747	109	K.C. 3.4	Buf. 7	K.C. 51.3	N.E. 3052	191	Den. 6.4	Den. 13	Pit 30	Pit. 5.5	Sea 4.6	S.D. 17.4	1981	AFC
1982	NFC	Was. 128 14.2	N.O. 151 Was. 151	Det 854	95	Det 3.2	Chi. 4	Dal 52.6	T.B. 1384	154	G.B. 6.0	Was 8	Det 18	Det 6.3	Was. 3.5	Was. 17.3	1982	NFC
1982	AFC	Mia. 131 14.6	Mia. 147	Pit. 762	85	Den. 3.2 Pit. 3.2	NY J 5 Pit. 5	Buf. 44.5	Mia 1027	114	Buf. 5.4	Sea. 4	Mia. 19	Mia. 8.4	Buf 3.0	Sea. 15.0	1982	AFC
1983	NFC	Det 286 17.9	Chi. 286 Dal. 286 St.L. 286	Was. 1289	81	NY G 3.5	Was. 9	Chi. 50.8	N.O. 2691	168	N.O. 6.3	Chi. 15 T.B. 15	Was 34	Was 6.0	Atl. 5.3	Det 16.1	1983	NFC
1983	AFC	Mia. 250 15.6	Cin 276	Cin. 1499	94	Cin. 3.5	N.E. 9	K.C 52.2	Cin. 2828	179	Cin. 6.3	Cin 17	K.C 30	K.C. 6.0	Sea. 5.1	Sea. 16.1	1983	AFC
1984	NFC	S.F 227 14.2	Chi 216	Chi. 1377	86	Det 3.5	Dal 8	Chi 45.5	N.O. 2453	153	Dal. 6.1	Chi. 14 S.F. 14	Dal. 28	Dal 5.3	Dal. 4.2	G.B. 16.0	1984	NFC
1984	AFC	Den. 241 15.1	Cle. 270	Pit 1617	101	Ind. 3.6 Pit. 3.6	Cle. 10 Den. 10 K.C 10	Raid. 50.0	Cle 2696	169	Raid 6.4	Cin 15 Cle. 15	Sea 38	Sea 7.3	Sea. 6.4	Sea. 16.7	1984	AFC
1985	NFC	Chi 198 12.4	Chi. 236	Chi. 1319	82	NY G 3.5	Chi. 6	Chi. 47.7	Was. 2746	172	NY G 6.3	S.F. 11	Chi. 34	Chi. 6.5	Dal. 6.5	Atl. 18.3	1985	NFC
1985	AFC	NY J 264 16.5	Raid. 273 Pit. 273	NY J 1516	95	Raid 3.5 NY J 3.5	Raid 7	Raid. 49.1	Pit. 2783	174	Pit 6.4	N.E. 14	K.C. 27	Sea 4.8	Raid. 6.1	Cin. 17.3	1985	AFC
1986	NFC	Chi. 187 11.7	Chi. 241	NY G 1284	80	N.O. 3.2	Chi 4	Chi. 47.4	St.L. 2637	165	L.A. 5.5	Chi 12	S.F. 39	S.F. 6.5	Chi. 4.8	St.L. 17.7	1986	NFC
1986	AFC	Cle. 310 19.4	Raid. 283	Den. 1651	103	S.D. 3.5	Pit. 10	Hou. 46.5	N.E. 2978	186	K.C. 6.2	N.E. 15	K.C. 31	K.C. 5.4	NY J 4.6	Raid 16.9	1986	AFC
1987	NFC	S.F. 253 16.9	S.F. 250	Chi 1413	94	Chi 3.4	Chi. 5	S.F. 48.0	S.F. 2484	166	S.F 5.9	S.F. 13	N.O. 30	N.O. 6.1	Det 5.2	St.L. 18.0	1987	NFC
1987	AFC	Ind. 238 15.9	Cle. 251	Cle. 1433	96	Raid. 3.5	Ind. 6	Ind. 49.9	Raid 2727	182	Ind. 6.1	Cle. 15 Den 15	Den. 28	Den 6.1	NY J 4.9	Buf 15.8	1987	AFC
1988	NFC	Chi. 215 13.4	Min. 243	Chi. 1326	82.9	T.B. 3.2	Chi. 5	Chi 45.0	Min 2489	156	Min 4.8	G.B. 12 Min. 12	Min. 36	Min. 7.5	Atl 5.8	NYG 17.4	1988	NFC
1988	AFC	Buf. 237 14.8	N.E. 272	Hou. 1592	99.5	Pit. 3.6	Cle. 13	NYJ 51.3	K.C. 2434	152	Buf. 5.5	K.C. 12	NYJ 24	NYJ 5.0	Sea. 5.6	Buf. 16.2	1988	AFC
1989	NFC	NYG 252 15.8	Min. 266 NYG 266	N.O 1326	82.9	Det 3.5 NYG 3.5	Phil. 8	Phi 48.8	Min. 2501	156	Min. 4.5	S.F 15	Phi. 30	Phi. 5.7	Phi. 5.8	Det 16.0	1989	NFC
1989	AFC	Den. 226 14.1	Den. 246	Den. 1580	98.8	Den. 3.7	Cle. 8	Cle. 49.8	K.C. 2527	158	K.C. 5.0	Den. 13	Cle. 27	Cle. 5.0	Raid. 7.3	Buff. 15.8	1989	AFC
1990	NFC	NYG 211 13.2	NYG 245	Phi. 1169	73.1	Atl. 3.3	S.F. 7	Phi. 48.2	Dal. 2639	164.9	NYG 5.2 Dal. 5.2	Dal. 12 NYG 12	Chi. 31	Chi. 6.3	Phx. 6.3	N.O. 16.2	1990	NFC
1990	AFC	Pit. 240 15.0	Pit. 257	S.D. 1515	94.7	Pit. 3.6 S.D. 3.6	Raid. 4	Pit. 51.3	Pit. 2500	156.3	Pit. 5.1	Pit. 9	Pit. 24	Pit. 5.2	S.D. 4.7	Buf 15.5	1990	AFC
1991	NFC	N.O. 211 13.2	N.O. 214	Phil. 1136	71.0	Phil. 3.0	Phil 4	Phil. 44.1	Phil 2413	150.8	Phil. 4.6	N.O. 12 Phx. 12	N.O. 29	N.O. 5.9	Wash. 6.1	Dall 16.9	1991	NFC
1991	AFC	Den 235 14.7	Den. 242	NYJ 1442	98.7	N.E. 3.4 Pitt 3.4	Sea 4	Den 51.7	Den 2755	172.2	Den. 5.2	Buff 12 Den. 12	Buff 23 Den. 23	Den. 4.8	Buff. 3.5	NYJ 15.4	1991	AFC
1992	NFC	N.O. 202 12.6	Phil. 242	Dall. 1244	77.8	Dall. 3.6	Phil. 4	Phil. 50.9	N.O. 2470	154	N.O. 4.3	Minn 12	Minn. 28	Minn. 5.5	T.B 5.3	G.B 15.8	1992	NFC
1992	AFC	Pitt 225 14.1	Sea. 247	Buff. 1395 S.D. 1395	87.2 87.2	Buff. 3.3	Clev 5	Pitt 52.7	K.C 2507	159	K.C 5.0	Raid. 11 Sea. 11	S.D 25	K.C. 5.2	Ind 7.0	Hou. 15.7	1992	AFC
1993	NFC	NYG 205 12.8	Minn 259	Minn. 1534	95.9	G.B. 3.7 Minn. 3.7	G.B. 6 S.F. 6	Phil. 54.2	N.O. 2606	163	Dall 6.0	Minn 11	Minn. 24	Minn. 5.0	Chi. 5.2	Chi. 17.3	1993	NFC
1993	AFC	Hou. 238 14.8	NYJ 266	Hou 1273	79.6	S.D. 3.2	Den. 6 Pitt 6	Hou. 51.9	N.E. 2845	178	Clev 6.4	NYJ 15	Hou. 26	Pitt 4.6	NYJ 6.0	Ind. 14.9	1993	AFC

Bold-designatesall-timeleader

YEARLY PASSING LEADERS

		RANK		YARDS			COMPLETIONS			COMP. PCT.			TOUCHDOWNS			YARDS/ATT.			FEWEST PCT. INT.				
YEAR	LGUE	NAME	TEAM	NAME	TEAM		NAME	TEAM		NAME	TEAM		NAME	TEAM		NAME	TEAM		NAME	TEAM		YEAR	LGUE
1933	NFL	Friedman	Bkn.	Newman	NY G	973	Newman	NY G	53	Friedman	Bkn	52.5	Newman	NY G	9	Molesworth	ChiB	8.4	Monnett	G.B.	6.5	1933	NFL
1934	NFL	Herber	G.B.	Herber	G.B.	799	Herber	G.B.	42	Clark	Det	46.9	Herber	G.B.	8	Clark	Det	7.8	Newman	NY G	5.5	1934	NFL
1935	NFL	Danowski	NY G	Danowski	NY G	795	Danowski	NY G	57	Danowski	NY G	50.4	Danowski	NY G	11	Masterson	ChiB	10.4	N/A			1935	NFL
1938	NFL	Herber	G.B.	Herber	G.B.	1239	Herber	G.B.	77	Clark	Det	53.5	Herber	G.B.	11	Herber	G.B.	7.2	Monnett	G.B.	3.8	1936	NFL
1937	NFL	Monnett	G.B.	Baugh	Was.	1127	Baugh	Was.	81	Monnett	G.B.	50.7	Monnett	G.B.	9	Masterson	ChiB	8.5	Danowski	NY G	3.7	1937	NFL
1938	NFL	Monnett	G.B.	Parker	Bkn.	865	Danowski	NY G	70	Monnett	G.B.	54.4	Monnett	G.B	9	Monnett	G.B.	8.2	Parker	Bkn.	4.7	1938	NFL
1939	NFL	Filchock	Was.	O'Brien	Phi.	1324	Hall	Cle.	106	Filchock	Was.	61.8	Filchock	Was.	11	Filchock	Was.	12.3	Sloan	Det	2.8	1939	NFL
1940	NFL	Baugh	Was.	Baugh	Was.	1367	O'Brien	Phi.	124	Baugh	Was.	62.7	Baugh	Was.	12	Luckman	ChiB	9.0	Watkins	Phi.	3.5	1940	NFL
1941	NFL	Luckman	ChiB.	Isbell	G.B.	1479	Isbell	G.B.	117	Luckman	ChiB	57.1	Isbell	G.B.	15	Luckman	ChiB	9.9	Mallouf	ChiC	4.2	1941	NFL
1942	NFL	Baugh	Was.	Isbell	G.B	2021	Isbell	G.B.	146	Baugh	Was.	58.7	Isbell	G.B.	24	O'Rourke	ChiB	10.8	Baugh	Was.	4.9	1942	NFL
1943	NFL	Luckman	ChiB	Luckman	ChiB	2194	Baugh	Was	133	Baugh	Was.	56.2	Luckman	ChiB	28	Luckman	ChiB	10.9	Comp.	G.B.	4.3	1943	NFL
1944	NFL	Filchock	Was.	Comp	G.B.	1159	Filchock	Was.	84	Filchock	Was.	57.1	Filchock	Was.	13	Ronzani	ChiB	8.0	Baugh	Was.	5.5	1944	NFL
1945	NFL	Baugh	Was	Luckman	ChiB	1725	Baugh	Was	128	Baugh	Was.	70.3	Luckman	ChiB	14	Waterfield	Cle.	9.4	Baugh	Was.	2.2	1945	NFL
													Waterfield	Cle.	14								
1946	NFL	Luckman	ChiB	Luckman	ChiB	1826	Waterfield	L.A	127	Thompson	Phi.	55.3	Waterfield	L.A.	18	Luckman	ChiB	8.0	Governali	Bos.	5.2	1946	NFL
1946	AAFC	Graham	Cle.	Dobbs	Bkn.	1886	Dobbs	Bkn	135	O'Rourke	L.A.	57.7	Graham	Cle.	17	Graham	Cle.	10.5	Parker	N.Y	2.6	1946	AAFC
1947	NFL	Baugh	Was.	Baugh	Was	2938	Baugh	Was	210	Baugh	Was.	59.3	Baugh	Was.	25	Luckman	ChiB	8.4	Baugh	Was.	4.2	1947	NFL
1947	AAFC	Graham	Cle.	Graham	Cle	2753	Schwenk	Bal	168	Graham	Cle	60.6	Graham	Cle.	25	Graham	Cle.	10.2	Graham	Cle.	4.1	1947	AAFC
1948	NFL	Baugh	Was	Baugh	Was	2599	Baugh	Was.	185	Baugh	Was.	58.7	Thompson	Phi.	25	LeForce	Det	9.0	Hardy	L.A.	3.3	1948	NFL
1948	AAFC	Tittle	Bal.	Graham	Cle.	2713	Dobbs	L.A.	185	Albert	S.F.	58.3	Albert	S.F.	29	Tittle	Bal.	8.7	Tittle	Bal.	3.1	1948	AAFC
1949	NFL	Baugh	Was.	Lujack	ChiB	2658	Lujack	ChiB	162	Baugh	Was.	56.9	Lujack	ChiB	23	Lujack	ChiB	8.2	Enke	Det	3.5	1949	NFL
1949	AAFC	Graham	Cle.	Graham	Cle.	2785	Graham	Cle.	161	Ratterman	Buf.	57.9	Albert	S.F.	27	Graham	Cle	9.8	Graham	Cle.	3.5	1949	AAFC
1950	NFL	Van Brocklin	L.A.	Layne	Det	2323	Tittle	Bal.	161	Waterfield	L.A.	57.3	Ratterman	NY Y	22	Van Brocklin	L.A.	8.8	Conerly	NY G	5.3	1950	NFL
1951	NFL	Graham	Cle.	Layne	Det	2403	Layne	Det	152	Thomason	G.B.	56.6	Layne	Det	26	Waterfield	L.A.	8.9	Thomason	G.B.	4.1	1951	NFL
1952	NFL	Rote	G.B	Graham	Cle.	2816	Graham	Cle.	181	Van Brocklin	L.A	55.1	Finks	Pit	20	Van Brocklin	L.A.	8.5	Thomason	Phi.	4.2	1952	NFL
													Graham	Cle.	20								
1953	NFL	Graham	Cle.	Graham	Cle.	2722	Blanda	ChiB	169	Graham	Cle.	64.7	Thomason	Phi.	21	Graham	Cle.	10.6	Graham	Cle.	3.5	1953	NFL
1954	NFL	Layne	Det	Van Brocklin	L.A.	2637	Rote	G.B.	180	Graham	Cle.	59.2	Burk	Phi.	23	Van Brocklin	L.A.	10.1	Tittle	S.F.	3.1	1954	NFL
1955	NFL	Graham	Cle.	Finks	Pit.	2270	Finks	Pit.	165	Graham	Cle.	53.0	Rote	G.B.	17	Graham	Cle.	9.3	Gilmer	Det	3.3	1955	NFL
													Tittle	S.F.	17								
1956	NFL	Brown	ChiB	Rote	G.B.	2203	Rote	G.B.	146	Brown	ChiB	57.1	Rote	G.B.	18	Brown	ChiB	9.9	Conerly	NY G	4.0	1956	NFL
1957	NFL	Unitas	Bal.	Unitas	Bal	2550	Tittle	S.F.	176	Tittle	S.F	63.1	Unitas	Bal.	24	O'Connell	Cle.	11.2	Morrall	Pit.	4.2	1957	NFL
1958	NFL	Unitas	Bal.	Wade	L.A.	2875	Van Brocklin	Phi.	198	Brodie	S.F.	59.9	Unitas	Bal.	19	LeBaron	Was.	9.4	Unitas	Bal.	2.7	1958	NFL
1959	NFL	Conerly	NY G	Unitas	Bal.	2899	Unitas	Bal	193	Wade	L.A.	58.6	Unitas	Bal.	32	Conerly	NY G	8.8	Conerly	NY G	2.1	1959	NFL
1960	NFL	Plum	Cle.	Unitas	Bal	3099	Unitas	Bal.	190	Plum	Cle.	60.4	Unitas	Bal.	25	Plum	Cle	9.2	Plum	Cle.	2.0	1960	NFL
1960	AFL	Kemp	L.A.	Tripucka	Den.	3038	Tripucka	Den.	248	Flores	Oak.	54.0	Dorow	NY T	26	Kemp	L.A.	7.4	Songin	Bos.	3.8	1960	AFL
1961	NFL	Plum	Cle.	Jurgensen	Phi.	3723	Jurgensen	Phi.	235	Plum	Cle.	58.6	Jurgensen	Phi.	32	Brodie	S.F.	9.1	Plum	Cle.	3.3	1961	NFL
1961	AFL	Blanda	Hou.	Blanda	Hou.	3330	Dorow	NY T	197	Parilli	Bos.	52.5	Blanda	Hou.	36	Blanda	Hou.	9.2	Songin	Bos.	4.3	1961	AFL
1962	NFL	Starr	G.B.	Jurgensen	Phi.	3261	Wade	Chi.	225	Starr	G.B.	62.4	Tittle	NY G	33	Jurgensen	Phi.	8.9	Starr	G.B.	3.2	1962	NFL
1962	AFL	Dawson	Dal.	Tripucka	Den.	2917	Tripucka	Den.	240	Dawson	Dal.	61.0	Dawson	Dal.	29	Dawson	Dal.	8.9	Parilli	Bos	3.2	1962	AFL
1963	NFL	Tittle	NY G	Unitas	Bal.	3481	Unitas	Bal.	237	Tittle	NY G	60.2	Tittle	NY G	36	Tittle	NY G	8.6	Unitas	Bal.	2.9	1963	NFL
1963	AFL	Rote	S.D.	Blanda	Hou.	3003	Blanda	Hou.	224	Rote	S.D	59.4	Dawson	Dal.	26	Rote	S.D.	8.7	Wood	NY T	5.1	1963	AFL
1964	NFL	Starr	G.B.	Johnson	St.L.	3045	Johnson	St.L.	223	Bukich	Chi	61.9	Ryan	Cle.	25	Unitas	Bal.	9.3	Starr	G.B	1.5	1964	NFL
1964	AFL	Dawson	K.C.	Parilli	Bos.	3465	Blanda	Hou.	262	Dawson	K.C.	56.2	Parilli	Bos.	31	Kemp	Buf	8.5	Dawson	K.C	5.1	1964	AFL
1965	NFL	Bukich	ChiB	Brodie	S.F.	3112	Brodie	S.F.	242	Brodie	S.F.	61.9	Brodie	S.F.	30	Unitas	Bal.	9.0	Bukich	Chi.	2.9	1965	NFL
1965	AFL	Dawson	K.C.	Hadl	S.D.	2798	Blanda	Hou.	186	Dawson	K.C	53.4	Dawson	K.C.	21	Hadl	S.D.	8.0	Wood	Oak.	3.8	1965	AFL
1966	NFL	Starr	G.B.	Jurgensen	Was.	3209	Jurgensen	Was.	254	Starr	G.B.	62.2	Ryan	Cle.	29	Starr	G.B.	9.0	Starr	G.B.	1.2	1966	NFL
1966	AFL	Dawson	K.C.	Namath	NY J	3379	Namath	NY J	232	Dawson	K.C.	56.0	Dawson	K.C.	26	Dawson	K.C.	8.9	Trull	Hou.	2.9	1966	AFL
1967	NFL	Jurgensen	Was.	Jurgensen	Was.	3747	Jurgensen	Was.	288	Unitas	Bal.	58.5	Jurgensen	Was.	31	Starr	G.B.	8.7	Jurgensen	Was.	3.2	1967	NFL
1967	AFL	Lamonica	Oak.	Namath	NY J	4007	Namath	NY J	258	Dawson	K.C.	57.7	Lamonica	Oak.	30	Namath	NY J	8.2	Lamonica	Oak.	4.7	1967	AFL
1968	NFL	Morrall	Bal.	Brodie	S.F.	3020	Brodie	S.F.	234	Starr	G.B.	63.7	Morrall	Bal.	26	Starr	G.B.	9.5	Munson	Det	2.4	1968	NFL
1968	AFL	Dawson	K.C.	Hadl	S.D.	3473	Hadl	S.D.	208	Dawson	K.C.	58.5	Hadl	S.D.	27	Dawson	K.C.	9.4	Stc'a	Cin.	2.8	1968	AFL
1969	NFL	Jurgensen	Was.	Jurgensen	Was.	3102	Jurgensen	Was.	274	Starr	G.B.	62.2	Gabriel	L.A.	24	Horn	G.B.	9.0	Gabriel	L.A.	1.8	1969	NFL
1969	AFL	Cook	Cin.	Lamonica	Oak.	3302	Lamonica	Oak.	221	Dawson	K.C.	59.0	Lamonica	Oak.	34	Cook	Cin.	9.4	Hadl	S.D.	3.4	1969	AFL
1970	NFC	Brodie	S.F.	Brodie	S.F.	2941	Brodie	S.F.	223	Jurgensen	Was.	59.9	Brodie	S.F.	24	Morton	Dal.	8.8	Brodie	S.F.	2.7	1970	NFC
1970	AFC	Lamonica	Oak.	Lamonica	Oak.	2516	Lamonica	Oak.	179	Griese	Mia.	58.0	Hadl	S.D.	22	Griese	Mia.	8.2	Carter	Cin.	3.2	1970	AFC
													Lamonica	Oak.	22								
1971	NFC	Staubach	Dal.	Brodie	S.F	2642	Tarkenton	NY G	226	Berry	Atl.	60.2	Brodie	S.F	18	Staubach	Dal.	8.9	Staubach	Dal.	1.9	1971	NFC
1971	AFC	Griese	Mia.	Hadl	S.D.	3075	Hadl	S.D.	233	Carter	Cin.	62.2	Hadl	S.D.	21	Dawson	K.C.	8.3	Carter	Cin	3.2	1971	AFC
1972	NFC	Tarkenton	Min.	Manning	N.O.	2781	Manning	N.O.	230	Snead	NY G	60.3	Kilmer	Was.	19	Berry	Atl.	7.8	Tarkenton	Min.	3.4	1972	NFC
1972	AFC	Morrall	Mia.	Namath	NY J	2816	Hadl	S.D	190	Dawson	K.C.	57.4	Namath	NY J	19	Morrall	Mia.	9.1	Anderson	Cin.	2.3	1972	AFC
1973	NFC	Gabriel	Phi.	Gabriel	Phi	3219	Gabriel	Phi.	270	Staubach	Dal.	62.6	Gabriel	Phi.	23	Staubach	Dal	8.5	Tarkenton	Min	2.6	1973	NFC
													Staubach	Dal	23								
1973	AFC	Anderson	Cin.	Plunkett	N.E.	2550	Plunkett	N.E.	193	Stabler	Oak.	62.7	Johnson	Den.	20	Stabler	Oak.	7.7	Anderson	Cin	3.6	1973	AFC
1974	NFC	Jurgensen	Was.	Tarkenton	Min.	2598	Hart	St.L.	200	Jurgensen	Was.	64.1	Hart	St.L.	20	Harris	L.A	7.8	Hart	St.L	2.1	1974	NFC
1974	AFC	Anderson	Cin.	Anderson	Cin.	2667	Anderson	Cin	213	Anderson	Cin.	64.9	Stabler	Oak	26	Anderson	Cin.	8.1	Anderson	Cin	3.0	1974	AFC
1975	NFC	Tarkenton	Min	Tarkenton	Min	2994	Tarkenton	Cin.	273	Tarkenton	Min	64.2	Tarkenton	Min.	25	Staubach	Dal	7.7	Tarkenton	Min.	3.1	1975	NFC
1975	AFC	Anderson	Cin.	Anderson	Cin.	3169	Anderson	Cin	228	Dawson	K.C	66.4	Ferguson	Buf.	25	Griese	Mia.	8.9	Jones	Bal.	2.3	1975	AFC

YEARLY PASSING LEADERS

		RANK		YARDS			COMPLETIONS			COMP. PCT.			TOUCHDOWNS			YARDS/ATT.			FEWEST PCT. INT.				
YEAR	LGUE	NAME	TEAM	NAME	TEAM		NAME	TEAM		NAME	TEAM		NAME	TEAM		NAME	TEAM		NAME	TEAM		YEAR	LGUE
1976	NFC	Harris	L.A.	Tarkenton	Min.	2961	Tarkenton	Min.	255	Tarkenton	Min.	61.9	Hart	St.L.	18	Harris	L.A.	9.2	Tarkenton	Min.	1.9	1976	NFC
1976	AFC	Stabler	Oak.	Jones	Bal.	3014	Fouts	S.D.	208	Stabler	Oak.	66.7	Stabler	Oak.	27	Stabler	Oak.	9.4	Ferguson	Buf.	0.7	1976	AFC
1977	NFC	Staubach	Dal.	Staubach	Dal.	2620	Staubach	Dal.	210	Tarkenton	Min.	60.1	Jaworski	Phi.	18	Staubach	Dal.	7.3	Staubach	Dal.	2.5	1977	NFC
													Staubach	Dal.	18								
1977	AFC	Griese	Mia.	Ferguson	Buf.	2803	Jones	Bal.	224	Griese	Mia.	58.6	Griese	Mia.	22	Bradshaw	Pit.	8.0	Jones	Bal.	2.8	1977	AFC
1978	AFC	Bradshaw	Pit.	Zorn	Sea.	3283	Zorn	Sea.	248	Griese	Mia.	63.0	Bradshaw	Pit.	28	Bradshaw	Pit.	7.9	Morton	Den.	3.0	1978	AFC
1978	NFC	Staubach	Dal.	Tarkenton	Min.	3468	Tarkenton	Min.	345	Manning	N.O.	61.8	Staubach	Dal.	25	Staubach	Dal.	7.7	Manning	N.O.	3.4	1978	NFC
													Tarkenton	Min.	25								
1979	AFC	Fouts	S.D.	Fouts	S.D.	4082	Fouts	S.D.	332	Fouts	S.D	62.6	Grogan	N.E.	28	Todd	N.Y.J.	8.0	Anderson	Cin.	2.9	1979	AFC
													Sipe	Cle.	28								
1979	NFC	Staubach	Dal.	DeBerg	S.F.	3652	DeBerg	S.F.	347	DeBerg	S.F.	60.0	Staubach	Dal.	27	Staubach	Dal.	7.8	Staubach	Dal.	2.4	1979	NFC
1980	AFC	Sipe	Cle.	Fouts	S.D.	4715	Fouts	S.D.	348	Stabler	Hou.	64.1	Fouts	S.D.	30	Grogan	N.E.	8.1	Sipe	Cle.	2.5	1980	AFC
													Sipe	Cle.	30								
1980	NFC	Jaworski	Phi.	Manning	N.O.	3716	Manning	N.O.	309	Montana	S.F.	64.5	Bartkowski	Atl.	31	Ferragamo	L.A.	7.9	Danielson	Det.	2.6	1980	NFC
1981	AFC	Anderson	Cin.	Fouts	S.D.	4802	Fouts	S.D.	360	Anderson	Cin	62.6	Fouts	S.D.	33	Grogan	N.E.	8.6	Anderson	Cin.	2.1	1981	AFC
1981	NFC	Montana	S.F	Kramer	Min.	3912	Kramer	Min.	322	Montana	S.F	63.7	Bartkowski	Atl.	30	Hipple	Det.	8.5	Montana	S.F.	2.5	1981	NFC
1982	NFC	Theismann	Was.	Montana	S.F.	2613	Montana	S.F.	213	Theismann	Was.	63.9	Montana	S.F.	17	White	Dal.	8.4	Lomax	St.L.	2.9	1982	NFC
1982	AFC	Anderson	Cin.	Fouts	S.D.	2883	Anderson	Cin	218	Anderson	Cin.	70.6	Bradshaw	Pit.	17	Fouts	S.D.	8.7	Anderson	Cin.	2.9	1982	AFC
													Fouts	S.D.	17								
1983	NFC	Bartkowski	Atl.	Dickey	G.B.	4458	White	Dal.	334	Montana	S.F	64.5	Dickey	G.B.	32	Dickey	G.B.	9.2	Bartkowski	Atl.	1.2	1983	NFC
1983	AFC	Marino	Mia.	Kenney	K.C.	4348	Kenney	K.C.	346	Anderson	Cin	66.7	Ferguson	Buf.	26	Krieg	Sea.	8.8	Marino	Mia.	2.0	1983	AFC
													Sipe	Cle.	26								
1984	NFC	Montana	S.F	Lomax	St.L.	4614	Lomax	St.L.	345	Bartkowski	Atl.	67.3	Lomax	St.L.	28	Montana	S.F	8.4	Montana	S.F.	2.3	1984	NFC
													Montana	S.F.	28								
1984	AFC	Marino	Mia.	Marino	Mia.	5084	Marino	Mia.	362	Marino	Mia.	64.2	Marino	Mia.	48	Marino	Mia.	9.0	Eason	N.E.	1.9	1984	AFC
1985	NFC	Montana	S.F.	Simms	NY G	3829	Montana	S.F	303	Montana	S.F.	61.3	Montana	S.F.	27	Simms	NY G	7.7	Lomax	St.L.	2.5	1985	NFC
1985	AFC	O'Brien	NY J	Marino	Mia.	4137	Marino	Mia.	336	O'Brien	NY J	60.9	Marino	Mia.	30	Fouts	S.D.	8.5	O'Brien	NY J	1.6	1985	AFC
1986	NFC	Kramer	Min.	Schroeder	Was.	4109	Schroeder	Was.	276	Hipple	Det.	63.0	Kramer	Min.	24	Kramer	Min.	8.1	Jaworski	Phi.	2.4	1986	NFC
1986	AFC	Marino	Mia.	Marino	Mia.	4746	Marino	Mia.	378	O'Brien	NY J	62.2	Marino	Mia.	44	Esiason	Cin.	8.4	Kosar	Cle.	1.9	1986	AFC
1987	NFC	Montana	S.F.	Lomax	St.L.	3387	Lomax	St.L.	275	Montana	S.F	66.8	Montana	S.F.	31	Wilson	Min.	8.0	DeBerg	T.B.	2.5	1987	NFC
1987	AFC	Kosar	Cle.	Esiason	Cin.	3321	Marino	Mia.	263	Kosar	Cle.	62.0	Marino	Mia.	26	Elway	Den.	7.8	O'Brien	NY J	2.0	1987	AFC
1988	NFC	W. Wilson	Min.	Everett	L.A.	3964	Everett	L.A.	308	W. Wilson	Min.	61.4	Everett	L.A.	31	W. Wilson	Min.	8.3	Simms	NYG	2.3	1988	NFC
1988	AFC	Esiason	Cin.	Marino	Mia.	4434	Marino	Mia.	354	Kosar	Clev.	60.2	Esiason	Cin.	28	Esiason	Cin.	9.2	O'Brien	NYJ	1.7	1988	AFC
													Marino	Mia.	28								
1989	NFC	Montana	S.F.	Majkowski	G.B.	4318	Majkowski	G.B.	353	Montana	S.F.	70.2	Everett	L.A.	29	Montana	S.F.	9.1	Miller	Atl.	1.9	1989	NFC
1989	AFC	Esiason	Cin.	Marino	Mia.	3997	Marino	Mia.	308	DeBerg	K.C.	60.5	Esiason	Cin.	28	Kelly	Buff.	8.0	Esiason	Cin.	2.4	1989	AFC
1990	NFC	Simms	NYG	Everett	L.A.	3989	Montana	S.F.	321	Montana	S.F.	61.7	Cunningham	Phi.	30	Testaverde	T.B.	7.7	Simms	NYG	1.3	1990	NFC
1990	AFC	Kelly	Buf.	Moon	Hou.	4689	Moon	Hou.	362	Kelly	Buf.	63.3	Moon	Hou.	33	Schroeder	Raid.	8.5	DeBerg	K.C.	0.9	1990	AFC
1991	NFC	Young	S.F.	Rypien	Wash.	3564	Everett	L.A.	277	Aikman	Dall.	65.3	Rypien	Wash.	28	Young	S.F.	9.0	Hostetler	NYG	1.4	1991	NFC
1991	AFC	Kelly	Buf.	Moon	Hou.	4690	Moon	Hou.	404	Krieg	Sea.	65.6	Kelly	Buff.	33	Kelly	Buff.	8.1	Kosar	Clev.	1.8	1991	AFC
1992	NFC	Young	S.F.	Young	S.F.	3465	Aikman	Dall.	302	Young	S.F	66.7	Young	S.F	25	Young	S.F.	8.6	Young	S.F.	1.7	1992	NFC
							Favre	G.B.	302														
1992	AFC	Moon	Hou.	Marino	Mia	4116	Marino	Mia.	330	Carlson	Hou.	65.6	Marino	Mia.	24	Krieg	K.C	7.5	O'Donnell	Pitt.	2.9	1992	AFC
1993	NFC	Young	S.F.	Young	S.F	4023	Favre	G.B	318	Young	S.F.	68.0	Young	S.F	29	Young	S.F.	8.71	Aikman	Dali.	1.5	1993	NFC
1993	AFC	Elway	Den.	Elway	Den.	4030	Elway	Den	348	Elway	Den.	63.2	Elway	Den.	25	Testaverde	Clev.	7.81	O'Donnell	Pitt.	1.4	1993	AFC

YEARLY RUSHING LEADERS

		ATTEMPTS			YARDS			AVERAGE YARDS			TOUCHDOWNS				
YEAR	LGUE	NAME	TEAM		NAME	TEAM		NAME	TEAM		NAME	TEAM		YEAR	LGUE
1933	NFL	Jim Musick	Bos.	173	Jim Musick	Bos.	809	Kink Richards	NY	6.2	Glenn Presnell	Det.	6	1933	NFL
1934	NFL	Swede Hanson	Phi.	147	Beattie Feathers	ChiB	1004	Beattie Feathers	ChiB	9.9	Dutch Clark	Det.	8	1934	NFL
											Beattie Feathers	ChiB	8		
1935	NFL	Kink Richards	NY G	149	Doug Russell	ChiC	499	Ernie Caddel	Det.	5.2	Ernie Caddel	Det.	6	1935	NFL
1936	NFL	Tuffy Leemans	NY G	206	Tuffy Leemans	NY G	830	Ernie Caddel	Det.	6.4	Dutch Clark	Det.	7	1936	NFL
1937	NFL	Cliff Battles	Was.	216	Cliff Battles	Was.	874	Ernie Caddel	Det.	5.6	Cliff Battles	Was.	5	1937	NFL
											Dutch Clark	Det.	5		
											Clarke Hinkle	G.B.	5		
1938	NFL	Whizzer White	Pit.	152	Whizzer White	Pit.	567	Cecil Isbell	G.B.	5.2	Andy Farkas	Was.	6	1938	NFL
1939	NFL	Andy Farkas	Was.	139	Bill Osmanski	ChiB	699	Joe Maniaci	ChiB	7.1	Johnny Drake	Cle.	9	1939	NFL
1940	NFL	Whizzer White	Det.	146	Whizzer White	Det.	514	Banks McFadden	Bkn	6.3	Johnny Drake	Cle.	9	1940	NFL
1941	NFL	Clarke Hinkle	G.B.	129	Pug Manders	Bkn.	486	George McAfee	ChiB	7.3	Hugh Gallarneau	ChiB	8	1941	NFL
1942	NFL	Bill Dudley	Pit.	162	Bill Dudley	Pit.	696	Frank Maznicki	ChiB	6.4	Gary Famiglietti	ChiB	8	1942	NFL
1943	NFL	Bill Paschal	NY G	147	Bill Paschal	NY G	572	Ward Cuff	NY G	6.5	Bill Paschal	NY G	10	1943	NFL
1944	NFL	Bill Paschal	NY G	196	Bill Paschal	NY G	737	Al Grygo	ChiB	6.1	Bill Paschal	NY G	9	1944	NFL
1945	NFL	Frank Akins	Was.	147	Steve Van Buren	Phi.	832	Fred Gehrke	Cle.	6.3	Steve Van Buren	Phi.	15	1945	NFL
1946	NFL	Bill Dudley	Pit.	146	Bill Dudley	Pit.	604	Elmer Angsman	ChiC	6.8	Ted Fritsch	G.B.	9	1946	NFL
1946	AAFC	Spec Sanders	N.Y.	140	Spec Sanders	N.Y.	709	Chuck Fenenbock	L.A.	8.4	Len Eshmont	S.F.	6	1946	AAFC
											Don Greenwood	Cle.	6		
											John Kimbrough	L.A.	6		
											Spec Sanders	N.Y.	6		
1947	NFL	Steve Van Buren	Phi.	217	Steve Van Buren	Phi.	1008	Kenny Washington	L.A.	7.4	Steve Van Buren	Phi.	13	1947	NFL
1947	AAFC	Spec Sanders	N.Y.	231	Spec Sanders	N.Y.	1432	Special Delivery Jones	Cle.	7.0	Spec Sanders	N.Y.	18	1947	AAFC
1948	NFL	Steve Van Buren	Phi.	201	Steve Van Buren	Phi.	945	Charlie Trippi	ChiC	5.4	Steve Van Buren	Phi.	10	1948	NFL
1948	AAFC	Spec Sanders	N.Y.	169	Marion Motley	Cle.	964	Joe Perry	S.F.	7.3	Chet Mutryn	Buf.	10	1948	AAFC
											Joe Perry	S.F.	10		
1949	NFL	Steve Van Buren	Phi.	263	Steve Van Buren	Phi.	1146	Bosh Pritchard	Phi.	6.0	Steve Van Buren	Phi.	11	1949	NFL
1949	AAFC	Bob Hoernschemeyer	Chi.	133	Joe Perry	S.F.	783	Frankie Albert	S.F	7.1	Marion Motley	Cle.	8	1949	AAFC
											Joe Perry	S.F	8		
1950	NFL	Joe Geri	Pit.	188	Marion Motley	Cle.	810	Johnny Lujack	ChiB	6.3	Johnny Lujack	ChiB	11	1950	NFL
		Steve Van Buren	Phi.	188											
1951	NFL	Eddie Price	NY G	271	Eddie Price	NY G	971	Tobin Rote	G.B.	6.9	Rob Goode	Was.	9	1951	NFL
1952	NFL	Eddie Price	NY G	183	Dan Towler	L.A.	894	Hugh McElhenny	S.F.	7.0	Dan Towler	L.A	10	1952	NFL
1953	NFL	Joe Perry	S.F.	192	Joe Perry	S.F	1018	Skeets Quinlan	L.A	7.3	Joe Perry	S.F	10	1953	NFL
1954	NFL	Joe Perry	S.F.	173	Joe Perry	S.F.	1049	Hugh McElhenny	S.F.	8.0	Dan Towler	L.A.	11	1954	NFL
1955	NFL	Alan Ameche	Bal.	213	Alan Ameche	Bal.	961	Rick Casares	ChiB	5.4	Alan Ameche	Bal.	9	1955	NFL
1956	NFL	Rick Casares	ChiB	234	Rick Casares	ChiB	1126	Lenny Moore	Bal.	7.5	Rick Casares	ChiB	12	1956	NFL
1957	NFL	Rick Casares	ChiB	204	Jimmy Brown	Cle.	942	Lenny Moore	Bal.	5.0	Jimmy Brown	Cle.	9	1957	NFL
1958	NFL	Jimmy Brown	Cle.	257	Jimmy Brown	Cle.	1527	Lenny Moore	Bal.	7.3	Jimmy Brown	Cle.	17	1958	NFL
1959	NFL	Jimmy Brown	Cle.	290	Jimmy Brown	Cle.	1329	Johnny Olszewski	Was.	6.6	Jimmy Brown	Cle.	14	1959	NFL
1960	NFL	Jim Taylor	G.B.	230	Jimmy Brown	Cle.	1257	John David Crow	St.L.	5.9	Paul Hornung	G.B.	13	1960	NFL
1960	AFL	Abner Haynes	Dal.	156	Abner Haynes	Dal.	875	Paul Lowe	L.A.	6.3	Abner Haynes	Dal.	9	1960	AFL
											Paul Lowe	L.A.	9		
1961	NFL	Jimmy Brown	Cle.	305	Jimmy Brown	Cle.	1408	Lenny Moore	Bal.	7.0	Jim Taylor	G.B.	15	1961	NFL
1961	AFL	Bill Mathis	NY T	202	Billy Cannon	Hou.	948	Jack Spikes	Dal.	8.6	Abner Haynes	Dal.	9	1961	AFL
											Paul Lowe	L.A.	9		
1962	NFL	Jim Taylor	G.B.	272	Jim Taylor	G.B.	1474	Amos Marsh	Dal.	5.6	Jim Taylor	G.B.	19	1962	NFL
1962	AFL	Charley Tolar	Hou.	244	Cookie Gilchrist	Buf.	1096	Len Dawson	Dal.	6.6	Cookie Gilchrist	Buf.	13	1962	AFL
											Abner Haynes	Dal.	13		
1963	NFL	Jimmy Brown	Cle.	291	Jimmy Brown	Cle.	1863	Jimmy Brown	Cle.	6.4	Jimmy Brown	Cle.	12	1963	NFL
1963	AFL	Cookie Gilchrist	Buf.	232	Clem Daniels	Oak.	1099	Keith Lincoln	S.D.	6.5	Cookie Gilchrist	Buf.	12	1963	AFL
1964	NFL	Jimmy Brown	Cle.	280	Jimmy Brown	Cle.	1446	Jimmy Brown	Cle.	5.2	Lenny Moore	Bal.	16	1964	NFL
1964	AFL	Cookie Gilchrist	Buf.	230	Cookie Gilchrist	Buf.	981	Mack Lee Hill	K.C.	5.5	Sid Banks	Hou.	6	1964	AFL
											Cookie Gilchrist	Buf.	6		
											Daryle Lamonica	Buf.	6		
1965	NFL	Jimmy Brown	Cle.	289	Jimmy Brown	Cle.	1544	Timmy Brown	Phi.	5.4	Jimmy Brown	Cle.	17	1965	NFL
1965	AFL	Cookie Gilchrist	Buf.	252	Paul Lowe	S.D.	1121	Paul Lowe	S.D.	5.1	Paul Lowe	S.D.	7	1965	AFL
1966	NFL	Bill Brown	Min.	251	Gale Sayers	Chi.	1231	Leroy Kelly	Cle.	5.5	Leroy Kelly	Cle.	15	1966	NFL
1966	AFL	Jim Nance	Bos	299	Jim Nance	Bos	1458	Mike Garrett	K.C.	5.5	Jim Nance	Bos.	11	1966	AFL
1967	NFL	Leroy Kelly	Cle.	235	Leroy Kelly	Cle	1205	Leroy Kelly	Cle.	5.1	Leroy Kelly	Cle.	11	1967	NFL
1967	AFL	Jim Nance	Bos.	269	Jim Nance	Bos.	1216	Brad Hubbert	S.D.	5.5	Emerson Boozer	NY J	10	1967	AFL
1968	NFL	Leroy Kelly	Cle.	248	Leroy Kelly	Cle.	1239	Gale Sayers	Chi.	6.2	Leroy Kelly	Cle.	16	1968	NFL
1968	AFL	Paul Robinson	Cin.	238	Paul Robinson	Cin.	1023	Dickie Post	S.D.	5.0	Paul Robinson	Cin.	8	1968	AFL
1969	NFL	Gale Sayers	Chi	236	Gale Sayers	Chi.	1032	Tony Baker	N.O.	4.8	Tom Matte	Bal.	11	1969	NFL
1969	AFL	Jim Nance	Bos.	193	Dickie Post	S.D.	873	Carl Garrett	Bos	5.0	Jim Kiick	Mia.	9	1969	AFL
1970	NFC	Ron Johnson	NY G	263	Larry Brown	Was.	1125	Duane Thomas	Dal.	5.3	MacArthur Lane	St.L	11	1970	NFC
1970	AFC	Floyd Little	Den.	209	Floyd Little	Den.	901	John Fuqua	Pit	5.0	John Fuqua	Pit.	7	1970	AFC
											Jim Nance	Bos.	7		
											Bo Scott	Cle.	7		
1971	NFC	Larry Brown	Was.	253	John Brockington	G.B.	1105	John Brockington	G.B.	5.1	Duane Thomas	Dal	11	1971	NFC
1971	AFC	Floyd Little	Den	284	Floyd Little	Den.	1133	Larry Csonka	Mia	5.4	Leroy Kelly	Cle	10	1971	AFC
1972	NFC	Ron Johnson	NY G	298	Larry Brown	Was.	1216	Bobby Douglass	Chi.	6.9	Ron Johnson	NY G	9	1972	NFC
											Greg Landry	Det.	9		
1972	AFC	O.J. Simpson	Buf	292	O.J. Simpson	Buf.	1251	Franco Harris	Pit.	5.6	Mercury Morris	Mia.	12	1972	AFC
1973	NFC	Calvin Hill	Dal.	273	John Brockington	G.B.	1144	Bobby Douglass	Chi.	5.6	Donny Anderson	St.L.	10	1973	NFC
1973	AFC	O.J. Simpson	Buf	332	O.J. Simpson	Buf.	2003	Mercury Morris	Mia.	6.4	Floyd Little	Den.	12	1973	AFC
											O.J. Simpson	Buf.	12		
1974	NFC	John Brockington	G.B.	266	Lawrence McCutcheon	L.A.	1109	Terry Metcalf	St.L.	4.7	Tom Sullivan	Phi.	11	1974	NFC
1974	AFC	O.J. Simpson	Buf.	270	Otis Armstrong	Den.	1407	Otis Armstrong	Den	5.3	Jon Keyworth	Den	10	1974	AFC
1975	NFC	Chuck Foreman	Min.	280	Jim Otis	St.L.	1076	Del Williams	S.F.	5.4	Chuck Foreman	Min.	13	1975	NFC
1975	AFC	O.J. Simpson	Buf.	329	O.J. Simpson	Oak	1817	O.J. Simpson	Oak	5.5	Pete Banaszak	Oak.	16	1975	AFC
											O.J. Simpson	Buf.	16		
1976	NFC	Walter Payton	Chi.	311	Walter Payton	Chi.	1390	Delvin Williams	S.F	4.9	Chuck Foreman	Min.	13	1976	NFC
											Walter Payton	Chi.	13		
1976	AFC	O.J. Simpson	Buf.	290	O.J. Simpson	Buf.	1503	Don Calhoun	N.E.	5.6	Franco Harris	Pit	14	1976	AFC
1977	NFC	Walter Payton	Chi.	339	Walter Payton	Chi.	1852	Walter Payton	Chi	5.5	Walter Payton	Chi	14	1977	NFC
1977	AFC	Mark van Eeghen	Oak	324	Mark van Eeghen	Oak.	1273	Benny Malone	Mia.	4.8	Franco Harris	Pit	11	1977	AFC
1978	AFC	Franco Harris	Pit.	310	Earl Campbell	Hou.	1450	Ted McKnight	K.C	6.0	David Sims	Sea	14	1978	AFC
1978	NFC	Walter Payton	Chi	333	Walter Payton	Chi.	1395	Wilbert Montgomery	Phi	4.7	Terdell Middleton	G.B.	11	1978	NFC
											Walter Payton	Chi	11		
1979	AFC	Earl Campbell	Hou	368	Earl Campbell	Hou.	1697	Sidney Thornton	Pit	5.0	Earl Campbell	Hou	19	1979	AFC
1979	NFC	Walter Payton	Chi	369	Walter Payton	Chi.	1610	Wendell Tyler	L.A	5.1	Walter Payton	Chi	14	1979	NFC

YEARLY RUSHING LEADERS

		ATTEMPTS			YARDS			AVERAGE YARDS			TOUCHDOWNS				
YEAR	LGUE	NAME	TEAM		NAME	TEAM		NAME	TEAM		NAME	TEAM		YEAR	LGUE
1980	AFC	Earl Campbell	Hou.	373	Earl Campbell	Hou.	1934	Earl Campbell	Hou.	5.2	Earl Campbell	Hou.	13	1980	AFC
1980	NFC	Walter Payton	Chi.	317	Walter Payton	Chi.	1460	Dexter Bussey	Det.	5.0	Billy Sims	Det.	13	1980	NFC
1981	AFC	Earl Campbell	Hou.	361	Earl Campbell	Hou.	1376	Tony Nathan	Mia.	5.3	Chuck Muncie	N.O.	19	1981	AFC
1981	NFC	George Rogers	N.O.	378	George Rogers	N.O.	1674	Wilbert Montgomery	Phi.	4.9	John Riggins	Was.	13	1981	NFC
											George Rogers	N.O.	13		
											Billy Sims	Det.	13		
1982	AFC	Andra Franklin	Mia.	177	Freeman McNeil	NY J	786	Freeman McNeil	NY J	5.2	Marcus Allen	Raid.	11	1982	AFC
1982	NFC	Tony Dorsett	Dal.	177	Tony Dorsett	Dal.	745	Wilbert Montgomery	Phi.	4.5	Eddie Lee Ivery	G.B.	9	1982	NFC
		John Riggins	Was.	177							Wendell Tyler	L.A.	9		
1983	AFC	Curt Warner	Sea.	335	Curt Warner	Sea.	1449	Mosi Tatupu	N.E.	5.5	Pete Johnson	Cin.	24	1983	AFC
1983	NFC	Eric Dickerson	L.A.	390	Eric Dickerson	L.A.	1806	Gerry Ellis	G.B.	5.3	John Riggins	Was.	24	1983	NFC
1984	AFC	Earnest Jackson	S.D.	296	Earnest Jackson	S.D	1179	Joe Carter	Mia.	5.0	Marcus Allen	Raid.	13	1984	AFC
		Sammy Winder	Den.	296											
1984	NFC	James Wilder	T.B	407	Eric Dickerson	L.A.	2105	Hokie Gajan	N.O.	6.0	Eric Dickerson	L.A.	14	1984	NFC
											John Riggins	Was.	14		
1985	AFC	Marcus Allen	Raid.	380	Marcus Allen	Raid	1759	George Wonsley	Ind.	5.2	Marcus Allen	Raid.	11	1985	AFC
											Ron Davenport	Mia.	11		
1985	NFC	Gerald Riggs	Atl.	397	Gerald Riggs	Atl.	1719	Stump Mitchell	St.L.	5.5	Joe Morris	NY G	21	1985	NFC
1986	AFC	Curt Warner	Sea.	319	Curt Warner	Sea	1481	James Brooks	Cin.	5.3	Curt Warner	Sea	13	1986	AFC
1986	NFC	Eric Dickerson	L.A	404	Eric Dickerson	L.A	1821	Herschel Walker	Dal.	4.9	George Rogers	Was.	18	1986	NFC
1987	AFC	Eric Dickerson	L.A.-Ind.	283	Eric Dickerson	L.A.-Ind.	1288	Eric Dickerson	L.A.-Ind.	4.6	Johnny Hector	NY J	11	1987	AFC
1987	NFC	Charles White	L.A.	324	Charles White	L.A.	1374	Darrin Nelson	Min.	4.9	Charles White	L.A.	11	1987	NFC
1988	AFC	Eric Dickerson	Ind	388	Eric Dickerson	Ind.	1659	Ickey Woods	Cin.	5.3	Ickey Woods	Cin.	15	1988	AFC
1988	NFC	Herschel Walker	Dal.	361	Herschel Walker	Dal.	1514	Randall Cunningham	Phil.	6.7	Greg Bell	L.A.	16	1988	NFC
1989	NFC	Dalton Hilliard	N.O.	344	Barry Sanders	Det.	1470	Randall Cunningham	Phil.	6.0	Greg Bell	L.A. Rams	15	1989	NFC
1989	AFC	Christian Okoye	K.C.	370	Christian Okoye	K.C.	1480	James Brooks	Cin.	5.6	Christian Okoye	K.C.	12	1989	AFC
1990	NFC	Earnest Byner	Was.	297	Barry Sanders	Det.	1304	Randall Cunningham	Phil.	8.0	Cleveland Gary	L.A.	14	1990	NFC
1990	AFC	Bobby Humphrey	Den.	288	Thurman Thomas	Buf.	1297	Bo Jackson	Raid.	5.6	Derrick Fenner	Sea.	14	1990	NFC
1991	NFC	Emmitt Smith	Dall.	365	Emmitt Smith	Dall.	1563	Terry Allen	Minn.	4.7	Barry Sanders	Det.	16	1991	NFC
1991	AFC	Thurman Thomas	Buff.	288	Thurman Thomas	Buff.	1407	Thurman Thomas	Buff.	4.9	Brad Baxter	NYJ	11	1991	AFC
1992	NFC	Emmitt Smith	Dall.	373	Emmitt Smith	Dall.	1713	Heath Sherman	Phil.	5.2	Emmitt Smith	Dall.	18	1992	NFC
1992	AFC	Barry Foster	Pitt.	390	Barry Foster	Pitt.	1690	Thurman Thomas	Buff.	4.8	Barry Foster	Pitt.	11	1992	AFC
1993	NFC	Jerome Bettis	L.A.	294	Emmitt Smith	Dall.	1486	Steve Young	S.F.	5.9	Ricky Watters	S.F.	10	1993	NFC
1993	AFC	Thurman Thomas	Buff.	355	Thurman Thomas	Buff.	1315	Gary Brown	Hou.	5.1	Marcus Allen	K.C.	12	1993	AFC

YEARLY LEADERS

RECEIVING

INTERCEPTIONS

		RECEPTIONS			YARDS			AVERAGE YARDS			TOUCHDOWNS			INTERCEPTIONS				
YEAR	LGUE	NAME	TEAM		NAME	TEAM		NAME	TEAM		NAME	TEAM		NAME	TEAM		YEAR	LGUE
1933	NFL	Shipwreck Kelly	Bkn.	22	Paul Moss	Pit	383	Paul Moss	Pit.	29.5	5 tied with 3 each						1933	NFL
1934	NFL	Red Badgro	NY G	20	Harry Ebding	Det	257	Harry Ebding	Det	28.6	Bill Hewitt	ChiB	5				1934	NFL
1935	NFL	Tod Goodwin	NY G	26	Charley Malone	Bos	433	Joe Carter	Phi.	23.6	Don Hutson	G.B.	7				1935	NFL
1936	NFL	Don Hutson	G.B.	34	Don Hutson	G.B.	526	Bill Hewitt	ChiB	23.9	Don Hutson	G.B.	8				1936	NFL
1937	NFL	Don Hutson	G.B.	41	Gaynell Tinsley	ChiC	675	Jeff Barrett	Bkn.	23.1	Don Hutson	G.B.	7				1937	NFL
1938	NFL	Gaynell Tinsley	ChiC	41	Don Hutson	G.B.	548	Jim Benton	Cle.	19.9	Don Hutson	G.B.	9				1938	NFL
1939	NFL	Don Hutson	G.B	34	Don Hutson	G.B	846	Andy Farkas	Was.	27.3	Jim Benton	Cle.	7				1939	NFL
1940	NFL	Don Looney	Phi.	58	Don Looney	Phi.	707	Paul McDonough	Cle.	26.3	Don Hutson	G.B.	7	Don Hutson	G.B.	6	1940	NFL
														Ace Parker	Bkn.	6		
														Rip Ryan	Det.	6		
1941	NFL	Don Hutson	G.B.	58	Don Hutson	G.B.	738	Ken Kavanaugh	ChiB	28.5	Don Hutson	G.B.	10	Marshall Goldberg	ChiC	7	1941	NFL
														Art Jones	Pit.	7		
1942	NFL	Don Hutson	G.B.	74	Don Hutson	G.B.	1211	Ray McLean	ChiB	30.1	Don Hutson	G.B.	17	Bulldog Turner	ChiB	8	1942	NFL
1943	NFL	Don Hutson	G.B	47	Don Hutson	G.B.	776	Tony Bova	P-P	24.6	Don Hutson	G.B.	11	Sammy Baugh	Was.	11	1943	NFL
1944	NFL	Don Hutson	G.B.	58	Don Hutson	G.B	866	Mel Bleeker	Phi.	37.4	Don Hutson	G.B	9	Howie Livingston	NY G	9	1944	NFL
1945	NFL	Don Hutson	G.B.	47	Jim Benton	Cle.	1067	Frank Liebel	NY G	27.0	Frank Liebel	NY G	10	Roy Zimmerman	Phi.	7	1945	NFL
1946	NFL	Jim Benton	L.A	63	Jim Benton	L.A	981	Bill Dewell	ChiC	23.8	Bill Dewell	ChiC	7	Bill Dudley	Pit.	10	1946	NFL
1946	AAFC	Alyn Beals	S.F.	40	Dante Lavelli	Cle.	843	Jim McCarthy	Bkn	26.9	Alyn Beals	S.F.	10	Tom Colella	Cle.	10	1946	AAFC
		Dante Lavelli	Cle.	40														
1947	NFL	Jim Keane	ChiB	64	Mal Kutner	ChiC	944	Dan Currivan	Bos.	32.6	Ken Kavanaugh	ChiB	13	Frank Reagan	NY G	10	1947	NFL
														Frank Seno	Bos.	10		
1947	AAFC	Mac Speedie	Cle	67	Mac Speedie	Cle.	1146	Crazy Legs Hirsch	Chi.	28.2	Alyn Beals	S.F.	10	Tom Colella	Cle.	6	1947	AAFC
														Len Eshmont	S.F.	6		
														Bill Killagher	Chi.	6		
1948	NFL	Tom Fears	L.A.	51	Mal Kutner	ChiC	943	Frank Seno	Bos.	24.8	Mal Kutner	ChiC	14	Dan Sandifer	Was.	13	1948	NFL
1948	AAFC	Mac Speedie	Cle.	58	Billy Hillenbrand	Bal.	970	John North	Bal.	26.0	Alyn Beals	S.F.	14	Otto Schnellbacher	N.Y.	11	1948	AAFC
1949	NFL	Tom Fears	L.A	77	Bob Mann	Det.	1014	Elbie Nickel	Pit.	24.3	Tom Fears	L.A.	9	Bob Nussbaumer	ChiC	12	1949	NFL
											Ken Kavanaugh	ChiB	9					
											Hugh Taylor	Was.	9					
1949	AAFC	Mac Speedie	Cle	62	Mac Speedie	Cle.	1028	Bill Boedecker	Cle.	33.7	Alyn Beals	S.F	12	Jim Cason	S.F.	9	1949	AAFC
1950	NFL	Tom Fears	L.A	84	Tom Fears	L.A.	1116	Hugh Taylor	Was.	21.4	Bob Shaw	ChiC	12	Spec Sanders	NY Y	13	1950	NFL
1951	NFL	Crazy Legs Hirsch	L.A.	66	Crazy Legs Hirsch	L.A.	1495	Crazy Legs Hirsch	L.A.	22.7	Crazy Legs Hirsch	L.A.	17	Otto Schnellbacher	NY G	11	1951	NFL
1952	NFL	Mac Speedie	Cle	62	Billy Howton	G.B.	1231	Hugh Taylor	Was.	23.4	Cloyce Box	Det	15	Night Train Lane	L.A.	14	1952	NFL
1953	NFL	Pete Pihos	Phi.	63	Pete Pihos	Phi	1049	Bob Boyd	L.A	22.8	Pete Pihos	Phi.	10	Jack Christiansen	Det	12	1953	NFL
											Billy Wilson	S.F.	10					
1954	NFL	Pete Pihos	Phi.	60	Bob Boyd	L.A.	1212	Harlon Hill	ChiB	25.0	Harlon Hill	ChiB	12	Night Train Lane	ChiC	10	1954	NFL
1955	NFL	Pete Pihos	Phi	62	Pete Pihos	Phi	864	Ray Renfro	Cle.	20.8	Harlon Hill	ChiB	9	Will Sherman	L.A	11	1955	NFL
1956	NFL	Billy Wilson	S.F	60	Billy Howton	G.B	1188	Harlon Hill	ChiB	24.0	Billy Howton	G.B.	12	Linden Crow	ChiC	11	1956	NFL
1957	NFL	Billy Wilson	S.F.	52	Ray Berry	Bal.	800	Ray Renfro	Cle	28.0	Jim Mutscheller	Bal.	8	Jack Butler	Pit.	10	1957	NFL
														Jack Christiansen	Det.	10		
														Milt Davis	Bal.	10		
1958	NFL	Ray Berry	Bal.	56	Del Shofner	L.A.	1097	Jimmy Orr	Pit.	27.6	Ray Berry	Bal.	9	Jimmy Patton	NY G	11	1958	NFL
		Pete Retzlaff	Phi	56							Tommy McDonald	Phi.	9					
1959	NFL	Ray Berry	Bal	66	Ray Berry	Bal	959	Max McGee	G.B	23.2	Ray Berry	Bal.	14	Milt Davis	Bal.	7	1959	NFL
														Dean Derby	Pit.	7		
														Don Shinnick	Bal.	7		
1960	NFL	Ray Berry	Bal	74	Ray Berry	Bal	1298	Buddy Dial	Pit.	24.3	Sonny Randle	St.L.	15	Dave Baker	S.F.	10	1960	NFL
														Jerry Norton	St.L.	10		
1960	AFL	Lionel Taylor	Den.	92	Bill Groman	Hou.	1473	Bill Groman	Hou.	20.5	Art Powell	NY T	14	Goose Gonsoulin	Den.	11	1960	AFL
1961	NFL	Jim Phillips	L.A.	78	Tommy McDonald	Phi.	1144	Frank Clarke	Dal.	22.4	Tommy McDonald	Phi.	13	Dick Lynch	NY G	9	1961	NFL
1961	AFL	Lionel Taylor	Den.	100	Charley Hennigan	Hou.	1746	Bill Groman	Hou.	23.5	Bill Groman	Hou	17	Billy Atkins	Buf.	10	1961	AFL
1962	NFL	Bobby Mitchell	Was.	72	Bobby Mitchell	Was	1384	Frank Clarke	Dal.	22.2	Frank Clarke	Dal.	14	Willie Wood	G.B.	9	1962	NFL
1962	AFL	Lionel Taylor	Den.	77	Art Powell	NY T	1130	Jim Colclough	Bos.	21.7	Chris Burford	Dal.	12	Lee Riley	NY T	11	1962	AFL
1963	NFL	Bobby Joe Conrad	St.L.	73	Bobby Mitchell	Was.	1436	Buddy Dial	Pit	21.6	Terry Barr	Det.	13	Dick Lynch	NY G	9	1963	NFL
											Gary Collins	Cle.	13	Rosey Taylor	ChiB	9		
1963	AFL	Lionel Taylor	Den	78	Art Powell	Oak	1304	Clem Daniels	Oak	22.8	Art Powell	Oak.	16	Freddie Glick	Hou	12	1963	AFL
1964	NFL	Johnny Morris	Chi.	93	Johnny Morris	Chi	1200	Gary Ballman	Pit.	19.9	Bobby Mitchell	Was.	10	Paul Krause	Was	12	1964	NFL
											Johnny Morris	Chi.	10					
											Bucky Pope	L.A.	10					
1964	AFL	Charley Hennigan	Hou.	101	Charley Hennigan	Hou.	1546	Elbert Dubenion	Buf	27.1	Lance Alworth	S.D	13	Dainard Paulson	NY T	12	1964	AFL
1965	NFL	Dave Parks	S.F.	80	Dave Parks	S.F.	1344	Bob Hayes	Dal.	21.8	Bob Hayes	Dal	12	Bobby Boyd	Bal.	9	1965	NFL
											Dave Parks	S.F	12					
1965	AFL	Lionel Taylor	Den.	85	Lance Alworth	S.D.	1602	Lance Alworth	S.D.	23.2	Lance Alworth	S.D	14	W.K. Hicks	Hou.	9	1965	AFL
											Don Maynard	NY J	14					
1966	NFL	Charley Taylor	Was.	72	Pat Studstill	Det.	1266	Homer Jones	NY G	21.8	Bob Hayes	Dal	13	Larry Wilson	St.L.	10	1966	NFL
1966	AFL	Lance Alworth	S.D.	73	Lance Alworth	S.D.	1383	Otis Taylor	K.C.	22.4	Lance Alworth	S.D.	13	Bobby Hunt	K.C	10	1966	AFL
														Johnny Robinson	K.C.	10		
1967	NFL	Charley Taylor	Was	70	Ben Hawkins	Phi.	1265	Homer Jones	NY G	24.7	Homer Jones	NY G	13	Lem Barney	Det	10	1967	NFL
														Dave Whitsell	N.O.	10		
1967	AFL	George Sauer	NY J	75	Don Maynard	NY J	1434	Don Maynard	NY J	20.2	Al Denson	Den	11	Miller Farr	Hou	10	1967	AFL
											Otis Taylor	K.C	11	Tom Janik	Buf.	10		
														Dick Westmoreland	Mia	10		
1968	NFL	Clifton McNeil	S.F	71	Roy Jefferson	Pit	1074	Homer Jones	NY G	23.5	Paul Warfield	Cle.	12	Willie Williams	NY G	10	1968	NFL
1968	AFL	Lance Alworth	S.D	68	Lance Alworth	S.D	1312	Don Maynard	NY J	22.8	Warren Wells	Oak.	11	Dave Grayson	Oak.	10	1968	AFL
1969	NFL	Dan Abramowicz	N.O.	73	Harold Jackson	Phi	1116	Lance Rentzel	Dal.	22.3	Lance Rentzel	Dal.	12	Mel Renfro	Dal	10	1969	NFL
1969	AFL	Lance Alworth	S.D	64	Warren Wells	Oak	1260	Warren Wells	Oak	26.8	Warren Wells	Oak	14	Emmitt Thomas	K.C.	9	1969	AFL
1970	NFC	Dick Gordon	Chi	71	Gene Washington	S.F	1100	John Gilliam	St.L	21.2	Dick Gordon	Chi.	13	Dick LeBeau	Det	9	1970	NFC
1970	AFC	Marlin Briscoe	Buf.	57	Marlin Briscoe	Buf	1036	Gary Garrison	S.D	22.9	Gary Garrison	S.D	12	Johnny Robinson	K.C	10	1970	AFC
1971	NFC	Bob Tucker	NY G	59	Gene Washington	S.F	884	Bob Hayes	Dal	24.0	Bob Hayes	Dal	8	Bill Bradley	Phi.	11	1971	NFC
1971	AFC	Fred Biletnikoff	Oak.	61	Otis Taylor	K.C.	1110	Paul Warfield	Mia.	23.2	Paul Warfield	Mia.	11	Ken Houston	Hou	9	1971	AFC
1972	NFC	Harold Jackson	Phi	62	Harold Jackson	Phi.	1048	John Gilliam	Min.	22.0	Gene Washington	S.F.	12	Bill Bradley	Phi	9	1972	NFC
1972	AFC	Fred Biletnikoff	Oak.	58	Rich Caster	NY J	833	Rich Caster	NY J	21.4	Rich Caster	NY J	10	Mike Sensibaugh	K.C	8	1972	AFC
1973	NFC	Harold Carmichael	Phi.	67	Harold Carmichael	Phi	1116	Harold Jackson	L.A.	21.9	Harold Jackson	L.A.	13	Bobby Bryant	Min.	7	1973	NFC
1973	AFC	Fred Willis	Hou.	57	Isaac Curtis	Cin.	843	Isaac Curtis	Cin.	18.7	Paul Warfield	Mia.	11	Dick Anderson	Mia.	8	1973	AFC
														Mike Wagner	Pit	8		

YEARLY LEADERS

RECEIVING

INTERCEPTIONS

		RECEPTIONS			YARDS			AVERAGE YARDS			TOUCHDOWNS							
YEAR	LGUE	NAME	TEAM		NAME	TEAM		NAME	TEAM		NAME	TEAM		NAME	TEAM		YEAR	LGUE
1974	NFC	Charle Young	Phi.	63	Drew Pearson	Dal.	1087	Gene Washington	S.F.	21.2	Harold Carmichael	Phi.	8	Ray Brown	Atl.	8	1974	NFC
1974	AFC	Lydell Mitchell	Bal.	72	Cliff Branch	Oak.	1092	Isaac Curtis	Cin.	21.1	Cliff Branch	Oak.	13	Emmitt Thomas	K.C.	12	1974	AFC
1975	NFC	Chuck Foreman	Min.	73	Mel Gray	St.L.	996	Alfred Jenkins	Atl.	20.2	Mel Gray	St.L	11	Paul Krause	Min.	10	1975	NFC
1975	AFC	Lydell Mitchell	Bal.	60	Ken Burrough	Hou.	1063	Isaac Curtis	Cin.	21.2	Lynn Swann	Pit	11	Mel Blount	Pit.	11	1975	AFC
		Reggie Rucker	Cle.	60														
1976	NFC	Drew Pearson	Dal.	58	Sammy White	Min.	906	Ron Jessie	L.A.	22.9	Sammy White	Min.	10	Monte Jackson	L.A.	10	1976	NFC
1976	AFC	MacArthur Lane	K.C.	66	Roger Carr	Bal.	1112	Roger Carr	Bal.	25.9	Cliff Branch	Oak.	12	Ken Riley	Cin.	9	1976	AFC
1977	NFC	Ahmad Rashad	Min.	51	Drew Pearson	Dal.	870	Mel Gray	St.L.	20.6	Henry Childs	N.O.	9	Rolland Lawrence	Atl.	7	1977	NFC
											Sammy White	Min.	9					
1977	AFC	Lydell Mitchell	Bal.	71	Ken Burrough	Hou.	816	Wesley Walker	NY J	21.1	Nat Moore	Mia.	12	Lyle Blackwood	Bal.	10	1977	AFC
1978	AFC	Steve Largent	Sea.	71	Wesley Walker	NY J	1169	Wesley Walker	NY J	24.4	John Jefferson	S.D.	13	Thom Darden	Cle.	10	1978	AFC
1978	NFC	Rickey Young	Min.	88	Harold Carmichael	Phi.	1072	Morris Owens	T.B.	20.0	Billy Joe DuPree	Dal.	9	Willie Buchanon	G.B.	9	1978	NFC
											Sammy White	Min.	9	Ken Stone	St.L.	9		
1979	AFC	Joe Washington	Bal.	82	Steve Largent	Sea.	1237	Stanley Morgan	N.E.	22.8	Stanley Morgan	N.E.	12	Mike Reinfeldt	Hou.	12	1979	AFC
1979	NFC	Ahmad Rashad	Min.	80	Ahmad Rashad	Min.	1156	Drew Pearson	Dal.	18.7	Harold Carmichael	Phi.	11	Lemar Parrish	Was.	9	1979	NFC
1980	AFC	Kellen Winslow	S.D.	89	John Jefferson	S.D.	1340	Stanley Morgan	N.E.	22.0	John Jefferson	S.D.	13	Lester Hayes	Oak.	13	1980	AFC
1980	NFC	Earl Cooper	S.F.	83	James Lofton	G.B.	1226	James Scott	Chi.	19.3	Earnest Gray	NY G	10	Nolan Cromwell	L.A.	8	1980	NFC
1981	AFC	Kellen Winslow	S.D.	88	Frank Lewis	Buf.	1244	Stanley Morgan	N.E.	23.4	Steve Watson	Den	13	John Harris	Sea.	10	1981	AFC
					Steve Watson	Den.	1244											
1981	NFC	Dwight Clark	S.F.	85	Alfred Jenkins	Atl.	1358	Kevin House	T.B.	21.0	Alfred Jenkins	Atl.	13	Everson Walls	Dal.	11	1981	NFC
1982	AFC	Kellen Winslow	S.D.	54	Wes Chandler	S.D.	1032	Wes Chandler	S.D.	21.1	Wes Chandler	S.D	9	4 tied with 5 each			1982	AFC
1982	NFC	Dwight Clark	S.F.	60	Dwight Clark	S.F.	913	Charlie Brown	Was.	21.6	Charlie Brown	Was.	8	Everson Walls	Dal	7	1982	NFC
1983	AFC	Todd Christensen	Raid.	92	Carlos Carson	K.C.	1351	Mark Duper	Mia.	19.7	Todd Christensen	Raid	12	Vann McElroy	Raid.	8	1983	AFC
														Ken Riley	Cin.	8		
1983	NFC	Charlie Brown	Was.	78	Mike Quick	Phi.	1409	James Lofton	G.B.	22.4	Roy Green	St.L.	14	Mark Murphy	Was.	9	1983	NFC
		Earnest Gray	NY G	78														
		Roy Green	St.L.	78														
1984	AFC	Ozzie Newsome	Cle.	89	John Stallworth	Pit.	1395	Daryl Turner	Sea	20.4	Mark Clayton	Mia.	18	Kenny Easley	Sea	10	1984	AFC
1984	NFC	Art Monk	Was.	106	Roy Green	St.L	1555	James Lofton	G.B.	22.0	Roy Green	St.L.	12	Tom Flynn	G.B.	9	1984	NFC
1985	AFC	Lionel James	S.D.	86	Steve Largent	Sea.	1287	Stephone Paige	K.C.	21.9	Daryl Turner	Sea.	13	Eugene Daniel	Ind.	8	1985	AFC
														Albert Lewis	K.C.	8		
1985	NFC	Roger Craig	S.F.	92	Mike Quick	Phi.	1247	Willie Gault	Chi.	21.3	Mike Quick	Phi.	11	Everson Walls	Dal.	9	1985	NFC
1986	AFC	Todd Christensen	Raid.	95	Stanley Morgan	NE	1491	Chris Burkett	Buf.	22.9	Wesley Walker	NY J	12	Deron Cherry	K.C.	9	1986	AFC
1986	NFC	Jerry Rice	S.F.	86	Jerry Rice	S.F.	1570	Walter Stanley	G.B.	20.7	Jerry Rice	S.F.	15	Ronnie Lott	S.F.	10	1986	NFC
1987	AFC	Al Toon	NY J	68	Carlos Carson	K.C.	1044	James Lofton	Raid.	21.5	Steve Largent	Sea.	8	Mike Prior	Ind.	6	1987	AFC
											Mark Duper	Mia.	8	Mark Kelso	Buf.	6		
														Keith Bostic	Hou.	6		
1987	NFC	J.T. Smith	St.L.	91	J.T. Smith	St.L.	1117	Anthony Carter	Min.	24.3	Jerry Rice	S.F.	22	Barry Wilburn	Was.	9	1987	NFC
1988	AFC	Al Toon	NYJ	93	Eddie Brown	Cin.	1273	Eddie Brown	Cin.	24.0	Mark Clayton	Mia.	14	Erik McMillan	NYJ	8	1988	AFC
1988	NFC	Henry Ellard	L.A.	86	Henry Ellard	L.A.	1414	Jerry Rice	S.F.	20.4	Ricky Sanders	Was.	12	Scott Case	Atl.	10	1988	NFC
1989	NFC	Sterling Sharpe	G.B.	90	Jerry Rice	S.F.	1483	Willie Anderson	L.A.	26.0	Jerry Rice	S.F.	17	Eric Allen	Phi.	8	1989	NFC
1989	AFC	Andre Reed	Buf.	88	Andre Reed	Buf.	1312	Webster Slaughter	Cle.	19.0	Anthony Miller	S.D.	10	Felix Wright	Cle.	9	1989	AFC
1990	NFC	Jerry Rice	S.F.	100	Jerry Rice	S.F.	1502	Willie Anderson	L.A.	21.5	Jerry Rice	S.F.	13	Mark Carrier	Chi.	10	1990	NFC
1990	AFC	Drew Hill	Hou.	74	Haywood Jeffires	Hou	1048	James Lofton	Buf.	20.3	Eddie Brown	Cin.	9	Richard Johnson	Hou.	8	1990	Hou
		Haywood Jeffires	Hou.	74							Ernest Givins	Hou	9					
1991	NFC	Michael Irvin	Dall.	93	Michael Irvin	Dall.	1523	Michael Haynes	Atl.	22.4	Jerry Rice	S.F.	14	Ray Crockett	Det	6	1991	NFC
														Tim McKyer	Atl	6		
														Deion Sanders	Atl.	6		
														Aeneas Williams	Phx.	6		
1991	AFC	Haywood Jeffires	Hou.	100	Haywood Jeffires	Hou.	1181	Dwight Stone	Pitt.	20.3	Mark Clayton	Mia.	12	Ronnie Lott	Raid.	8	1001	AFC
1992	NFC	Sterling Sharpe	G.B.	108	Sterling Sharpe	G.B.	1461	Herman Moore	Det	18.9	Sterling Sharpe	G.B.	13	Audray McMillian	Minn.	8	1992	NFC
1992	AFC	Haywood Jeffires	Hou.	90	Anthony Miller	S.D.	1060	Willie Davis	K.C.	21.0	Ernest Givins	Hou	10	Henry Jones	Buff.	8	1992	AFC
1993	NFC	Sterling Sharpe	G.B.	112	Jerry Rice	S.F.	1503	Alvin Harper	Dall.	21.6	Jerry Rice	S.F.	15	Deion Sanders	Atl.	7	1993	NFC
											Andre Rison	Atl	15					
1993	AFC	Reggie Langhorne	Ind.	85	Tim Brown	L.A.	1180	James Lett	L.A.	23.4	Shannon Sharpe	Den.	9	Eugene Robinson	Sea.	9	1993	AFC
														Nate Odomes	Buff	9		

YEARLY LEADERS

YEAR	LGUE	PUNTING AVERAGE NAME	TEAM		FIELD GOALS MADE NAME	TEAM		FIELD GOALS PERCENTAGE NAME	TEAM		PAT'S MADE NAME	TEAM		POINTS SCORED NAME	TEAM		YEAR	LGUE
1933	NFL				Jack Manders	ChiB	5				Jack Manders	ChiB	14	Glenn Pressnell	Det	63	1933	NFL
					Glenn Pressnell	Det	5				Ken Strong	NY G	14					
					Ken Strong	NY G	5											
1934	NFL				Jack Manders	ChiB	10				Jack Manders	ChiB	31	Jack Manders	ChiB	79	1934	NFL
1935	NFL				Armand Niccolai	Pit.	6				Dutch Clark	Det	16	Dutch Clark	Det	55	1935	NFL
					Bill Smith	ChiC	6				Jack Manders	ChiB	16					
1936	NFL				Jack Manders	ChiB	7				Dutch Clark	Det	19	Dutch Clark	Det	73	1936	NFL
					Armand Niccolai	Pit.	7											
1937	NFL				Jack Manders	ChiB	8				Riley Smith	Was.	22	Jack Manders	ChiB	69	1937	NFL
1938	NFL				Ward Cuff	NY G	5	Regis Monohan	Det	.80	Ward Cuff	NY G	18	Clarke Hinkle	G.B.	58	1938	NFL
					Ralph Kercheval	Bkn.	5											
1939	NFL	George Faust	ChiC	44	Ward Cuff	NY G	7	Chuck Hanneman	Det	.80	Tiny Engebretsen	G.B.	18	Andy Farkas	Was.	68	1939	NFL
		Sid Luckman	ChiB	44														
1940	NFL	Sammy Baugh	Was.	51.3	Clarke Hinkle	G.B.	9	Clarke Hinkle	G.B.	.64	Ace Parker	Bkn	19	Don Hutson	G.B.	57	1940	NFL
1941	NFL	Sammy Baugh	Was.	48.7	Clarke Hinkle	G.B.	6	Andy Marefos	NY G	.80	Don Hutson	G.B.	20	Don Hutson	G.B.	95	1941	NFL
											Bob Snyder	ChiB	20					
1942	NFL	Sammy Baugh	Was.	46.6	Bill Daddio	ChiC	5	Ted Fritsch	G.B.	.80	Don Hutson	G.B.	33	Don Hutson	G.B.	138	1942	NFL
								Frank Maznicki	ChiB	.80								
1943	NFL	Sammy Baugh	Was.	45.9	Ward Cuff	NY G	3	Don Hutson	G.B.	.60	Bob Snyder	ChiB	39	Don Hutson	G.B.	117	1943	NFL
					Don Hutson	G.B.	3											
1944	NFL	Cecil Johnson	Bkn.	42.6	Ken Strong	NY G	6	Ken Strong	NY G	.50	Pete Gudauskas	ChiB	36	Don Hutson	G.B.	85	1944	NFL
1945	NFL	Sammy Baugh	Was.	43.3	Joe Aguirre	Was.	7	Ben Agajanian	Phi.+Pit.	1.00	Don Hutson	G.B.	31	Steve Van Buren	Phi.	110	1945	NFL
											Bob Waterfield	Cle.	31					
1946	NFL	Bob Cifers	Det.	45.6	Ted Fritsch	G.B.	9	Bob Waterfield	L.A.	.67	Bob Waterfield	L.A.	37	Ted Fritsch	G.B.	100	1946	NFL
1946	AAFC	Glenn Dobbs	Bkn.	47.8	Lou Groza	Cle.	13	Steve Nemeth	Chi.	.75	Lou Groza	Cle.	45	Lou Groza	Cle.	84	1946	AAFC
1947	NFL	George Gulyanics	ChiB	44.8	Ward Cuff	G.B.	7	Pat Harder	ChiC	.70	Ray McLean	ChiB	44	Pat Harder	ChiC	102	1947	NFL
					Pat Harder	ChiC	7											
					Bob Waterfield	L.A.	7											
1947	AAFC	Bob Reinhard	L.A.	45.7	Ben Agajanian	L.A.	15	Harvey Johnson	N.Y.	.88	Harvey Johnson	N.Y.	49	Spec Sanders	N.Y.	114	1947	AAFC
1948	NFL	Joe Muha	Phi	47.2	Cliff Patton	Phi	8	Dick Poillon	Was	.71	Pat Harder	ChiC	53	Pat Harder	ChiC	110	1948	NFL
1948	AAFC	Glenn Dobbs	L.A.	49.1	Rex Grossman	Bal	10	Joe Vetrano	S.F.	.63	Joe Vetrano	S.F.	62	Chet Mutryn	Buf.	96	1948	AAFC
1949	NFL	George Gulyanics	ChiB	47.2	Cliff Patton	Phi.	9	Vinnie Yablonski	ChiC	.83	Pat Harder	ChiC	45	Pat Harder	ChiC	102	1949	NFL
					Bob Waterfield	L.A.	9							Choo-Choo Roberts	NY G	102		
1949	AAFC	Frankie Albert	S.F	48.2	Harvey Johnson	N.Y	7	Rex Grossman	Bal.	.55	Joe Vetrano	S.F	56	Alyn Beals	S.F	73	1949	AAFC
1950	NFL	Curley Morrison	ChiB	43.3	Lou Groza	Cle.	13	Lou Groza	Cle.	.68	Bob Waterfield	L.A.	54	Doak Walker	Det	128	1950	NFL
1951	NFL	Horace Gillom	Cle.	45.5	Bob Waterfield	L.A.	13	Bill Dudley	Was.	.77	Lou Groza	Cle.	43	Elroy Hirsch	L.A.	102	1951	NFL
											Doak Walker	Det	43					
1952	NFL	Horace Gillom	Cle.	45.7	Lou Groza	Cle.	19	Bob Waterfield	L.A.	.61	Bob Waterfield	L.A.	44	Gordy Soltau	S.F	94	1952	NFL
1953	NFL	Pat Brady	Pit.	46.9	Lou Groza	Cle.	23	Lou Groza	Cle	.88	Gordy Soltau	S.F	48	Gordy Soltau	S.F	114	1953	NFL
1954	NFL	Pat Brady	Pit.	43.2	Lou Groza	Cle.	16	Lou Groza	Cle	.67	Doak Walker	Det	43	Bobby Walston	Phi	114	1954	NFL
1955	NFL	Norm Van Brocklin	L.A.	44.6	Fred Cone	G.B	16	Fred Cone	G.B	.67	Lou Groza	Cle.	44	Doak Walker	Det	96	1955	NFL
1956	NFL	Norm Van Brocklin	L.A.	43.1	Sam Baker	Was	17	Bobby Layne	Det	.80	George Blanda	ChiB	45	Bobby Layne	Det	99	1956	NFL
1957	NFL	Don Chandler	NY G	44.6	Lou Groza	Cle.	15	Bobby Walston	Phi	.75	Paige Cothren	L.A.	38	Sam Baker	Was.	77	1957	NFL
1958	NFL	Sam Baker	Was	45.4	Paige Cothren	L.A	14	Paige Cothren	L.A.	.56	Steve Myhra	Bal	48	Jim Brown	Cle.	108	1958	NFL
					Tom Miner	Pit	14											
1959	NFL	Yale Lary	Det	47.1	Pat Summerall	NY G	20	Pat Summerall	NY G	.69	Steve Myhra	Bal	50	Paul Hornung	G.B.	94	1959	NFL
1960	NFL	Jerry Norton	St.L.	45.6	Tommy Davis	S.F	19	Bobby Walston	Phi.	.70	Sam Baker	Cle	44	Paul Hornung	G.B.	176	1960	NFL
1960	AFL	Paul Maguire	L.A	40.5	Gene Mingo	Den	18	Gene Mingo	Den.	.64	Bill Shockley	NY T	47	Gene Mingo	Den.	123	1960	AFL
1961	NFL	Yale Lary	Det.	48.4	Steve Myhra	Bal.	21	Lou Groza	Cle.	.70	Pat Summerall	NY G	46	Paul Hornung	G.B	146	1961	NFL
1961	AFL	Billy Atkins	Buf	45.0	Gino Cappelletti	Bos	17	George Blanda	Hou.	.62	George Blanda	Hou	64	Gino Cappelletti	Bos.	147	1961	AFL
1962	NFL	Tommy Davis	S.F.	45.6	Lou Michaels	Pit.	26	Don Chandler	NY G	.68	Sam Baker	Dal	50	Jim Taylor	G.B.	114	1962	NFL
1962	AFL	Jim Fraser	Den	44.4	Gene Mingo	Den	27	George Blair	S.D.	.85	George Blanda	Hou.	48	Gene Mingo	Den.	137	1962	AFL
1963	NFL	Yale Lary	Det.	48.9	Jim Martin	Bal	24	Lou Groza	Cle	.65	Don Chandler	NY G	52	Don Chandler	NY G	106	1963	NFL
1963	AFL	Jim Fraser	Den	46.1	Gino Cappelletti	Bos.	22	George Blair	S.D.	.63	Mike Mercer	Oak.	47	Gino Cappelletti	Bos	113	1963	AFL
1964	NFL	Bobby Walden	Min.	46.4	Jim Bakken	St.L.	25	Bruce Gossett	L.A.	.75	Lou Michaels	Bal.	53	Lenny Moore	Bal.	120	1964	NFL
1964	AFL	Jim Fraser	Den.	44.7	Gino Cappelletti	Bos	25	Pete Gogolak	Buf	.66	Tommy Brooker	K.C.	46	Gino Cappelletti	Bos.	155	1964	AFL
1965	NFL	Gary Collins	Cle.	46.7	Fred Cox	Min	23	Jim Bakken	St.L.	.68	Tommy Davis	S.F.	52	Gale Sayers	ChiB	132	1965	NFL
											Roger Leclerc	ChiB	52					
1965	AFL	Jerrel Wilson	K.C.	46.1	Pete Gogolak	Buf.	28	Gino Cappelletti	Bos.	.63	Herb Travenio	S.D.	40	Gino Cappelletti	Bos	132	1965	AFL
1966	NFL	David Lee	Bal.	45.6	Bruce Gossett	L.A	28	Sam Baker	Phi.	.72	Danny Villanueva	Dal	56	Bruce Gossett	L.A.	113	1966	NFL
1966	AFL	Bob Scarpitto	Den.	45.8	Mike Mercer	Oak.+K.C.	21	Mike Mercer	Oak.+K.C.	.70	Booth Lusteg	Buf	41	Gino Cappelletti	Bos.	119	1966	AFL
1967	NFL	Billy Lothridge	Atl.	43.7	Jim Bakken	St.L	27	Jim Bakken	St.L.	.69	Bruce Gossett	L.A	48	Jim Bakken	St.L	117	1967	NFL
1967	AFL	Bob Scarpitto	Den.	44.9	Jan Stenerud	K.C.	21	George Blanda	Hou.	.67	George Blanda	Hou	56	George Blanda	Hou.	116	1967	AFL
1968	NFL	Billy Lothridge	Atl	44.3	Mac Percival	Chi.	25	Don Cockroft	Cle.	.75	Mike Clark	Dal	54	Leroy Kelly	Cle	120	1968	NFL
1968	AFL	Jerrel Wilson	K.C.	45.1	Jim Turner	NY J	34	Jan Stenerud	K.C	.75	George Blanda	Hou.	54	Jim Turner	NY J	145	1968	AFL
1969	NFL	David Lee	Bal.	45.3	Fred Cox	Min.	26	Fred Cox	Min	.70	Don Cockroft	Cle	45	Fred Cox	Min.	121	1969	NFL
1969	AFL	Dennis Partee	S.D.	44.6	Jim Turner	NY J	32	Jan Stenerud	K.C	.77	George Blanda	Oak	45	Jim Turner	NY J	129	1969	AFL
1970	NFC	Julian Fagan	N.O.	42.5	Fred Cox	Min	30	Curt Knight	Was	.74	Errol Mann	Det.	41	Fred Cox	Min	125	1970	NFC
1970	AFC	Dave Lewis	Cin.	46.2	Jan Stenerud	K.C	30	Garo Yepremian	Mia	.76	George Blanda	Oak	36	Jan Stenerud	K.C.	116	1970	AFC
											Jim O'Brien	Bal	36					
1971	NFC	Tom McNeill	Phi	42.0	Curt Knight	Was	29	Tom Dempsey	Phi.	.71	Mike Clark	Dal.	47	Curt Knight	Was	114	1971	NFC
1971	AFC	Dave Lewis	Cin.	44.8	Garo Yepremian	Mia	28	Garo Yepremian	Mia	.70	George Blanda	Oak	41	Garo Yepremian	Mia	117	1971	AFC
1972	NFC	Dave Chapple	L.A.	44.2	Chester Marcol	G.B.	33	Errol Mann	Det	.69	Bruce Gossett	S.F.	41	Chester Marcol	G.B.	128	1972	NFC
1972	AFC	Jerrel Wilson	K.C.	44.8	Roy Gerela	Pit.	28	Don Cockroft	Cle.	.82	George Blanda	Oak	44	Bobby Howfield	NY J	121	1972	AFC
1973	NFC	Tom Wittum	S.F	43.7	David Ray	L.A.	30	Bruce Gossett	S.F	.79	Toni Fritsch	Dal	43	David Ray	L.A.	130	1973	NFC
1973	AFC	Jerrel Wilson	K.C.	45.5	Roy Gerela	Pit	29	Don Cockroft	Cle	.71	Jim Turner	Den.	40	Roy Gerela	Pit	123	1973	AFC
1974	NFC	Tom Blanchard	N.O.	42.1	Chester Marcol	G.B	25	Errol Mann	Det.	.72	Efren Herrara	Dal	33	Chester Marcol	G.B.	94	1974	NFC
1974	AFC	Ray Guy	Oak.	42.2	Roy Gerela	Pit.	20	Don Cockroft	Cle.	.80	George Blanda	Oak	44	Roy Gerela	Pit	93	1974	AFC
1975	NFC	Herman Weaver	Det	42.0	Toni Fritsch	Dal	22	Tom Dempsey	L.A.	.81	Fred Cox	Min.	46	Chuck Foreman	Min	132	1975	NFC
1975	AFC	Ray Guy	Oak.	43.8	Jan Stenerud	K.C	22	Garo Yepremian	Mia	.81	John Leypoldt	Buf.	51	O.J. Simpson	Buf.	138	1975	AFC
											Toni Linhart	Bal	51					
1976	NFC	John James	Atl.	42.1	Mark Moseley	Was.	22	Efren Herrera	Dal	.78	Tom Dempsey	L.A.	36	Mark Moseley	Was	97	1976	NFC
								Rick Szaro	N.O	.78								
1976	AFC	Marv Bateman	Buf	42.8	Jan Stenerud	K.C.	21	Toni Linhart	Bal	.74	Toni Linhart	Bal.	49	Toni Linhart	Bal	109	1976	AFC
1977	NFC	Tom Blanchard	N.O.	42.4	Mark Moseley	Was.	21	Efren Herrera	Dal.	.62	Efren Herrera	Dal.	39	Walter Payton	Chi	96	1977	NFC
1977	AFC	Ray Guy	Oak	43.3	Errol Mann	Oak	20	Rolf Benirschke	S.D.	.74	Errol Mann	Oak	39	Errol Mann	Oak.	99	1977	AFC
								Don Cockroft	Cle	.74								

YEARLY LEADERS

		PUNTING AVERAGE			FIELD GOALS MADE			FIELD GOALS PERCENTAGE			PAT'S MADE			POINTS SCORED				
YEAR	LGUE	NAME	TEAM		NAME	TEAM		NAME	TEAM		NAME	TEAM		NAME	TEAM		YEAR	LGUE
1978	AFC	Pat McInally	Cin.	43.1	Pat Leahy	NY J	22	Garo Yepremian	Mia.	.826	Roy Gerela	Pit.	44	Pat Leahy	NY J	107	1978	AFC
1978	NFC	Tom Skladany	Det.	42.5	Frank Corral	L.A.	29	Tim Mazzetti	Atl.	.813	Rafael Septien	Dal.	46	Frank Corral	L.A.	118	1978	NFC
1979	AFC	Bob Grupp	K.C.	43.6	John Smith	N.E.	23	Toni Fritsch	Hou.	.840	Matt Bahr	Pit.	50	John Smith	N.E.	115	1979	AFC
1979	NFC	Dave Jennings	NY G	42.7	Mark Moseley	Was.	25	Ray Wersching	S.F.	.833	Rafael Septien	Dal.	40	Mark Moseley	Was.	114	1979	NFC
1980	AFC	Luke Prestridge	Den.	43.9	John Smith	N.E.	26	Toni Fritsch	Hou.	.792	John Smith	N.E.	51	John Smith	N.E.	124	1980	AFC
					Fred Steinfort	Den.	26											
1980	NFC	Dave Jennings	NY G	44.8	Ed Murray	Det.	27	Ray Wersching	S.F.	.789	Rafael Septien	Dal.	59	Ed Murray	Det.	116	1980	NFC
1981	AFC	Pat McInally	Cin.	45.4	Nick Lowery	K.C.	26	Uwe von Schamann	Mia.	.779	Rolf Benirschke	S.D.	55	Jim Breech	Cin.	115	1981	AFC
														Nick Lowery	K.C.	115		
1981	NFC	Tom Skladany	Det.	43.5	Rafael Septien	Dal.	27	Jan Stenerud	G.B.	.917	Mick Luckhurst	Atl.	51	Ed Murray	Det.	121	1981	NFC
														Rafael Septien	Dal.	121		
1982	AFC	Luke Prestridge	Den.	45.0	Nick Lowery	K.C.	19	Nick Lowery	K.C.	79.2	Pat Leahy	NY J	32	Marcus Allen	Raid.	84	1982	AFC
											Rolf Benirschke	S.D.	32					
1982	NFC	Carl Birdsong	St.L.	43.8	Mark Moseley	Was.	20	Mark Moseley	Was.	90.5	Rafael Septien	Dal.	28	Wendell Tyler	L.A.	78	1982	NFC
1983	AFC	Rohn Stark	Bal.	45.3	Raul Allegre	Bal.	30	Matt Bahr	Cle.	87.5	Chris Bahr	Raid.	51	Gary Anderson	Pit.	119	1983	AFC
1983	NFC	Frank Garcia	T.B.	42.2	Ali Haji-Sheikh	NY G	35	Ray Wersching	S.F.	83.3	Mark Moseley	Was.	62	John Riggins	Was.	144	1983	NFC
1984	AFC	Jim Arnold	K.C.	44.9	Gary Anderson	Pit.	24	Norm Johnson	Sea.	83.3	Uwe von Schamann	Mia.	66	Gary Anderson	Pit.	117	1984	AFC
1984	NFC	Brian Hansen	N.O.	43.8	Paul McFadden	Phi.	30	Jan Stenerud	Min.	87.0	Ray Wersching	S.F.	56	Ray Wersching	S.F.	131	1984	NFC
1985	AFC	Rohn Stark	Ind.	45.9	Gary Anderson	Pit.	31	Nick Lowery	K.C.	88.9	Bob Thomas	S.D.	51	Gary Anderson	Pit.	139	1985	AFC
1985	NFC	Rick Donnelly	Atl.	42.6	Kevin Butler	Chi.	33	Morten Andersen	N.O.	88.5	Ray Wersching	S.F.	52	Kevin Butler	Chi.	144	1985	NFC
1986	AFC	Rohn Stark	Ind.	45.2	Tony Franklin	N.E.	32	Matt Bahr	Cle.	76.9	Fuad Reveiz	Mia.	52	Tony Franklin	N.E.	140	1986	AFC
1986	NFC	Sean Landeta	NY G	44.8	Kevin Butler	Chi.	28	Morten Andersen	N.O.	86.7	Chuck Nelson	Min.	44	Kevin Butler	Chi.	120	1986	NFC
1987	AFC	Ralf Mojsiejenko	S.D.	42.9	Jim Breech	Cin.	24	Dean Biasucci	Ind.	88.9	Norm Johnson	Sea.	40	Jim Breech	Cin	97	1987	AFC
					Dean Biasucci	Ind.	24											
1987	NFC	Rick Donnelly	Atl.	44.0	Morten Andersen	N.O.	28	Roger Ruzek	Dal.	88.0	Ray Wersching	S.F.	44	Jerry Rice	S.F.	138	1987	NFC
1988	AFC	Mike Horan	Den	44.0	Scott Norwood	Buf.	32	Scott Norwood	Buf	86.5	Jim Breech	Cin.	56	Scott Norwood	Buf.	129	1988	AFC
1988	NFC	Jim Arnold	Det	42.4	Mike Cofer	S.F.	27	Eddie Murray	Det	95.2	Chuck Nelson	Min.	48	Mike Cofer	S.F.	121	1988	NFC
1989	NFC	Rich Camarillo	Phx.	43.4	Rich Karlis	Min.	31	Eddie Murray	Det	95.2	Mike Lansford	L.A.	51	Mike Cofer	S.F.	136	1989	NFC
1989	AFC	Greg Montgomery	Hou.	43.3	David Treadwell	Den.	27	Tony Zendejas	Hou.	87.6	Scott Norwood	Buf.	46	David Treadwell	Den.	120	1980	AFC
1990	NFC	Sean Landeta	NYG	44.1	Chip Lohmiller	Was.	30	Donald Igwebuike	Min.	87.5	Roger Ruzek	Phi.	45	Chip Lohmiller	Was	131	1990	NFC
1990	AFC	Mike Horan	Den.	44.4	Nick Lowery	K.C	34	Nick Lowery	K.C.	91.9	Scott Norwood	Buf.	50	Nick Lowery	K.C	139	1990	AFC
1991	NFC	Harry Newsome	Minn	45.5	Chip Lomiller	Wash	31	Tony Zendejas	L.A.	1.000	Chip Lohmiller	Wash.	56	Chip Lohmiller	Wash	149	1991	NFC
1991	AFC	Reggie Roby	Mia.	45.7	Pete Styanovich	Mia.	31	Jeff Jaeger	Raid.	85.3	Scott Norwood	Buff	56	Pete Stoyanovich	Mia.	121	1991	Mia.
1992	NFC	Harry Newsome	Minn.	45.0	Chip Lohmiller	Wash.	30	Morten Andersen	N.O.	85.3	Mike Cofer	S.F.	53	Morten Andersen	N.O.	120	1992	NFC
														Chip Lohmiller	Wash	120		
1992	AFC	Greg Montgomery	Hou.	46.9	Pete Stoyanovich	Mia.	30	Nick Lowery	K.C.	91.7	Steve Christie	Buff.	43	Pete Stoyanovich	Mia.	124	1992	AFC
1993	NFC	Jim Arnold	Det	44.5	Jason Hanson	Det	34	Norm Johnson	Atl.	96.3	Mike Cofer	S.F.	59	Jason Hanson	Det	130	1993	NFC
1993	AFC	Greg Montgomery	Hou.	45.6	Jeff Jaeger	L.A.Rd.	35	Gary Anderson	Pitt	93.3	Jason Elam	Den.	41	Jeff Jaeger	L.A.Rd.	132	1993	AFC

YEARLY RETURN LEADERS

		PUNT RETURNS — RETURNS			PUNT RETURNS — YARDS			PUNT RETURNS — AVERAGE YARDS			KICKOFF RETURNS — RETURNS			KICKOFF RETURNS — YARDS			KICKOFF RETURNS — AVERAGE YARDS				
YEAR	LGUE	NAME	TEAM		NAME	TEAM		NAME	TEAM		NAME	TEAM		NAME	TEAM		NAME	TEAM		YEAR	LGUE
1941	NFL	Whizzer White	Det	1[illegible]	Whizzer White	Det	262													1941	NFL
1942	NFL	Merl Condit	Bkn	21	Bill Dudley	Pit	271	Ernie Steele	Phi.	26.4	Marshall Goldberg	ChiC	15	Marshall Goldberg	ChiC	393	Bill Dudley	Pit	27.1	1942	NFL
1943	NFL	Andy Farkas	Was.	15	Frankie Sinkwich	Det	228	Frankie Sinkwich	Det	20.7	Ken Heineman	Bkn.	16	Ken Heineman	Bkn.	442	Ned Matthews	Det	35.1	1943	NFL
1944	NFL	Bob Davis	Bos.	22	Bob Davis	Bos.	271	Ernie Steele	Phi.	16.5	John Grigas	C-P	23	John Grigas	C-P	471	Steve Van Buren	Phi.	33.3	1944	NFL
1945	NFL	Steve Bagarus	Was.	21	Steve Bagarus	Was.	251	Fred Gehrke	Cle.	15.0	Frank Seno	ChiC	19	Frank Seno	ChiC	408	Ted Fritsch	G.B.	34.9	1945	NFL
1946	NFL	Bill Dudley	Pit.	27	Bill Dudley	Pit.	385	Gil Steinke	Phi.	14.5	Sonny Karnofsky	Bos.	21	Sonny Karnofsky	Bos.	599	Frank Seno	ChiC	31.4	1946	NFL
1946	AAFC	Ken Casanega	S.F.	18	Chuck Fenenbock	L.A.	299	Chuck Fenenbock	L.A.	18.7	Steve Juzwik	Buf	21	Chuck Fenenbock	L.A.	479	Monk Gafford	Bkn.-Mia.	31.4	1946	NFL
		Bob Seymour	L.A.	18																	
1947	NFL	Walt Slater	Pit.	28	Walt Slater	Pit.	435	Frank Seno	Bos.	17.8	Eddie Saenz	Was.	29	Eddie Saenz	Was.	797	Steve Van Buren	Phi.	29.4	1947	NFL
1947	AAFC	Glenn Dobbs	Bkn.-L.A.	19	Glenn Dobbs	Bkn-L.A.	215	Spec Sanders	N.Y.	27.3	Spec Sanders	N.Y.	22	Chet Mutryn	Buf.	691	Chet Mutryn	Buf.	32.9	1947	AAFC
1948	NFL	George McAfee	ChiB	30	George McAfee	ChiB	417	Jerry Davis	ChiC	20.9	Dan Sandifer	Was.	26	Dan Sandifer	Was.	594	Frank Minini	G.B.	30.8	1948	NFL
1948	AAFC	Cliff Lewis	Cle.	26	Herm Wedermeyer	L.A.	368	Tom Casey	N.Y.	25.4	Monk Gafford	Bkn.	23	Monk Gafford	Bkn.	559	Forrest Hall	S.F.	28.4	1948	AAFC
1949	NFL	Vitamin Smith	L.A.	27	Vitamin Smith	L.A.	427	Red Cochran	ChiC	20.9	Eddie Saenz	Was.	24	Don Doll	Det.	536	John Salscheider	NY G	31.6	1949	NFL
											Dan Sandifer	Was.	24								
1949	AAFC	Pete Layden	N.Y.	29	Jim Cason	S.F.	351	Buddy Young	N.Y.	19.0	Herm Wedermeyer	Bal.	30	Herm Wedermeyer	Bal	602	Ray Ramsey	Chi	29.2	1949	AAFC
1950	NFL	George McAfee	ChiB	33	Billy Grimes	G.B.	555	Herb Rich	Bal.	23.0	Don Paul	ChiC	28	Vitamin Smith	L.A.	742	Vitamin Smith	L.A	33.7	1950	NFL
1951	NFL	Em Tunnel	NY G	34	Em Tunnell	NY G	489	Buddy Young	NY Y	19.3	George Taliaferro	NY Y	27	George Taliaferro	NY Y	622	Lynn Chandnois	Pit.	32.5	1951	NFL
1952	NFL	Bibbles Bawel	Phi.	34	Em Tunnell	NY G	411	Jack Christiansen	Det.	21.5	Billy Baggett	Dal.	23	Buddy Young	Dal.	643	Lynn Chandnois	Pit.	35.2	1952	NFL
											Buddy Young	Dal	23								
1953	NFL	Em Tunnell	NY G	38	Woodley Lewis	L.A.	267	Charlie Trippi	ChiC	11.4	Woodley Lewis	L.A.	32	Woodley Lewis	L.A.	830	Joe Arenas	S.F.	34.4	1953	NFL
1954	NFL	Chet Hanulak	Cle.	27	Veryl Switzer	G.B.	306	Veryl Switzer	G.B.	12.8	Woodley Lewis	L.A.	34	Woodley Lewis	L.A.	836	Billy Reynolds	Cle.	29.5	1954	NFL
1955	NFL	Bert Rechichar	Bal.	30	Ollie Matson	ChiC	245	Ollie Matson	ChiC	18.8	Sid Watson	Pit.	27	Sid Watson	Pit.	716	Al Carmichael	G.B.	29.9	1955	NFL
1956	NFL	Carl Taseff	Bal.	27	Carl Taseff	Bal.	233	Kenny Konz	Cle.	14.4	Al Carmichael	G.B.	33	Al Carmichael	G.B.	927	Tom Wilson	L.A.	31.8	1956	NFL
1957	NFL	Tommy McDonald	Phi.	26	Bert Zagers	Was.	217	Bert Zagers	Was.	15.5	Al Carmichael	G.B.	31	Al Carmichael	G.B.	690	Jon Arnett	L.A.	28.0	1957	NFL
1958	NFL	Carl Taseff	Bal.	29	Jon Arnett	L.A.	223	Jon Arnett	L.A.	12.4	Jimmy Sears	ChiC	32	Jimmy Sears	ChiC	756	Ollie Matson	ChiC	35.5	1958	NFL
1959	NFL	Bill Stacy	ChiC	29	Bill Stacy	ChiC	281	Johnny Morris	ChiB	12.2	Lenny Lyles	S.F.	25	Lenny Lyles	S.F.	565	Abe Woodson	S.F.	29.4	1959	NFL
1960	NFL	Bill Stits	NY G	18	Abe Woodson	S.F.	174	Abe Woodson	S.F.	13.4	Ted Dean	Phi.	26	Ted Dean	Phi.	533	Tom Moore	G.B.	33.1	1960	NFL
											Tom Frankhouser	Dal.	26								
1960	AFL	Al Carmichael	Den.	15	Abner Haynes	Dal.	215	Abner Haynes	Dal.	15.4	Leon Burton	NY T	31	Leon Burton	NY T	897	Ken Hall	Hou.	31.3	1960	AFL
1961	NFL	Johnny Sample	Pit.	26	Johnny Sample	Pit.	283	Willie Wood	G.B.	16.1	Timmy Brown	Phi.	29	Timmy Brown	Phi.	811	Dick Bass	L.A.	30.3	1961	NFL
											Jim Steffen	Was.	29								
1961	AFL	Fred Bruney	Bos.	23	Dick Christy	NY T	383	Dick Christy	NY T	21.3	George Fleming	Oak.	29	Frank Jackson	Dal.	645	Dave Grayson	Oak.	28.3	1961	AFL
1962	NFL	Pat Studstill	Det	29	Pat Studstill	Det	457	Pat Studstill	Det	15.8	Abe Woodson	S.F.	37	Abe Woodson	S.F.	1157	Abe Woodson	S.F.	31.3	1962	NFL
1962	AFL	Leon Burton	Bos.	21	Dick Christy	NY T	250	Dick Christy	NY T	16.7	Dick Christy	NY T	38	Dick Christy	NY T	824	Bobby Jancik	Hou.	30.3	1962	AFL
1963	NFL	Tom Watkins	Det	32	Tom Watkins	Det	399	Dick James	Was.	13.4	Timmy Brown	Phi.	33	Timmy Brown	Phi.	945	Abe Woodson	S.F.	32.2	1963	NFL
											Bill Butler	Min.	33								
1963	AFL	Claude Gibson	Oak.	26	Claude Gibson	Oak.	307	Claud. Gibson	Oak.	11.8	Bobby Jancik	Hou	45	Bobby Jancik	Hou.	1317	Bobby Jancik	Hou.	29.3	1963	AFL
1964	NFL	Mel Renfro	Dal.	32	Mel Renfro	Dal.	418	Tom Watkins	Det	14.9	Mel Renfro	Dal	40	Mel Renfro	Dal.	1017	Clarence Childs	NY G	29.0	1964	NFL
1964	AFL	Hagood Clarke	Buf.	33	Claude Gibson	Oak.	419	Bobby Jancik	Hou.	18.3	Odell Barry	Den.	47	Odell Barry	Den.	1245	Bo Roberson	Oak.	27.1	1964	AFL
1965	NFL	Alvin Haymond	Bal.	41	Alvin Haymond	Bal.	403	Leroy Kelly	Cle.	15.6	Kermit Alexander	S.F.	32	Kermit Alexander	S.F.	741	Tom Watkins	Det	34.4	1965	AFL
1965	AFL	Claude Gibson	Oak.	31	Speedy Duncan	S.D.	464	Speedy Duncan	S.D.	15.5	Abner Haynes	Den.	34	Abner Haynes	Den.	901	Abner Haynes	Den.	26.5	1965	AFL
1966	NFL	Alvin Haymond	Bal.	40	Alvin Haymond	Bal.	347	Johnny Roland	St.L.	11.1	Ron Smith	Atl.	43	Ron Smith	Atl.	1013	Gale Sayers	Chi.	31.2	1966	NFL
1966	AFL	Rodger Bird	Oak.	37	Rodger Bird	Oak.	323	Speedy Duncan	S.D.	13.2	Bobby Jancik	Hou.	34	Bobby Jancik	Hou.	875	Goldie Sellers	Den	28.5	1966	AFL
1967	NFL	Doug Cunningham	S.F.	27	Bob Hayes	Dal.	276	Ben Davis	Cle.	12.7	Ron Smith	Atl.	39	Ron Smith	Atl.	976	Travis Williams	G.B.	41.1	1967	NFL
1967	AFL	Rodger Bird	Oak.	46	Rodger Bird	Oak.	612	Floyd Little	Den.	16.9	Noland Smith	K.C.	41	Noland Smith	K.C.	1148	Zeke Moore	Hou.	28.9	1967	AFL
1968	NFL	Roy Jefferson	Pit.	28	Chuck Latourette	St.L.	345	Bob Hayes	Dal	20.8	Chuck Latourette	St.L.	46	Chuck Latourette	St.L.	1237	Preston Pearson	Bal.	35.1	1968	NFL
		Chuck Latourette	St.L.	28																	
1968	AFL	Butch Atkinson	Oak.	36	Butch Atkinson	Oak.	490	Noland Smith	K.C.	15.0	Max Anderson	Buf	39	Max Anderson	Buf.	971	Butch Atkinson	Oak.	25.1	1968	AFL
1969	NFL	Charlie West	Min.	39	Alvin Haymond	L.A.	435	Alvin Haymond	L.A.	13.2	Preston Pearson	Bal.	31	Bo Scott	Cle.	722	Bobby Williams	Det	33.1	1969	NFL
1969	AFL	Jerry LeVias	Hou.	35	Jerry LeVias	Hou.	292	Bill Thompson	Den.	11.5	Mercury Morris	Mia.	43	Mercury Morris	Mia.	1136	Bill Thompson	Den.	28.5	1969	AFL
1970	NFC	Alvin Haymond	L.A.	53	Bruce Taylor	S.F.	516	Bruce Taylor	S.F.	12.0	Alvin Haymond	L.A.	35	Alvin Haymond	L.A.	1022	Cecil Turner	Chi.	32.7	1970	NFC
1970	AFC	Hubie Bryant	Pit.	37	Ron Gardin	Bal.	330	Ed Podolak	K.C.	13.5	Mike Battle	NY J	40	Mike Battle	NY J	891	Jim Duncan	Bal.	35.4	1970	AFC
1971	NFC	Bruce Taylor	S.F.	34	Bruce Taylor	S.F.	235	Speedy Duncan	Was.	10.6	Dave Hampton	G.B.	46	Dave Hampton	G.B.	1314	Travis Williams	L.A.	29.7	1971	NFC
1971	AFC	Jake Scott	Mia	33	Jake Scott	Mia.	318	Leroy Kelly	Cle.	9.7	Linzy Cole	Hou.	32	Linzy Cole	Hou	834	Mercury Morris	Mia.	28.2	1971	AFC
1972	NFC	Ron Smith	Chi.	26	Jim Bertelsen	L.A.	232	Ken Ellis	G.B.	15.4	Margene Adkins	N.O.	43	Margene Adkins	N.O.	1020	Ron Smith	Chi.	30.8	1972	NFC
1972	AFC	Bruce Laird	Bal.	34	Bruce Laird	Bal.	303	Chris Farasopoulos	NY J	10.5	Jesse Taylor	S.D.	31	Bruce Laird	Bal.	843	Bruce Laird	Bal.	29.1	1972	AFC
1973	NFC	Ray Brown	Atl.	40	Ray Brown	Atl.	360	Bruce Taylor	S.F.	13.8	Herb Mul-Key	Was.	36AFC	Herb Mul-Key	Was.	1011	Carl Garrett	Chi.	30.4	1973	NFC
		Butch Atkinson	Oak.	41	Bill Thompson	Den	366	Ron Smith	S.D.	13.0	Mack Herron	N.E.	41	Mack Herron	N.E.	1092	Wallace Francis	Buf.	29.9	1973	AFC
1974	NFC	Howard Stevens	N.O.	37	Howard Stevens	N.O.	376	Dick Jauron	Det	16.8	Jimmie Jones	Det	38	Jimmie Jones	Det	927	Terry Metcalf	St.L.	31.2	1974	NFC
1974	AFC	Donnie Walker	Buf.	43	Lynn Swann	Pit.	577	Lemar Parrish	Cin.	18.8	Lou Piccone	NY J	39	Lou Piccone	NY J	961	Greg Pruitt	Cle.	27.5	1974	AFC
1975	NFC	Larry Jones	Was.	53	Virgil Livers	Chi.	456	Terry Metcalf	St.L.	12.4	Larry Jones	Was.	47	Larry Jones	Was.	1086	Walter Payton	Chi.	31.7	1975	NFC
1975	AFC	Neal Colzie	Oak.	48	Neal Colzie	Oak.	655	Billy Johnson	Hou.	15.3	Rick Upchurch	Den	40	Rick Upchurch	Den	1084	Harold Hart	Oak.	30.5	1975	AFC
1976	NFC	Rolland Lawrence	Atl.	54	Eddie Brown	Was.	646	Eddie Brown	Was.	13.5	Eddie Brown	Was.	30	Brian Baschnagel	Chi.	754	Cullen Bryant	L.A.	28.7	1976	NFC
											Larry Marshall	Phi.	30								
											Oliver Ross	Sea.	30								
1976	AFC	Mike Haynes	N.E.	45	Mike Haynes	N.E.	608	Rick Upchurch	Den	13.7	Lou Piccone	NY J	31	Willie Shelby	Cin.	761	Duriel Harris	Mia.	32.9	1976	AFC
1977	NFC	Eddie Brown	Was	57	Larry Marshall	Phi.	489	Larry Marshall	Phi.	10.6	Paul Hofer	S.F.	36	Paul Hofer	S.F.	871	Wilbert Montgomery	Phi.	26.9	1977	NFC
1977	AFC	Rick Upchurch	Den.	51	Rick Upchurch	Den.	653	Billy Johnson	Hou.	15.4	Bruce Harper	NY J	42	Bruce Harper	NY J	1035	Ray Clayborn	N.E.	31.0	1977	AFC

YEARLY RETURN LEADERS

		PUNT RETURNS									KICKOFF RETURNS										
		RETURNS			YARDS			AVERAGE YARDS			RETURNS			YARDS			AVERAGE YARDS				
YEAR	LGUE	NAME	TEAM		NAME	TEAM		NAME	TEAM		NAME	TEAM		NAME	TEAM		NAME	TEAM		YEAR	LGUE
1978	AFC	Neal Colzie	Den.	47	Rick Upchurch	Den.	493	Rick Upchurch	Den.	13.7	Bruce Harper	NY J	55	Bruce Harper	NY J	1280	Keith Wright	Cle.	26.3	1978	AFC
1978	NFC	Jackie Wallace	L.A.	52	Jackie Wallace	L.A.	618	Jackie Wallace	L.A.	11.9	Kevin Miller	Min.	40	Tony Green	Was.	870	Steve Odom	G.B.	27.1	1978	NFC
1979	AFC	J.T. Smith	K.C.	58	J.T. Smith	K.C.	612	Tony Nathan	Mia.	10.9	Bruce Harper	NY J	55	Bruce Harper	NY J	1158	Larry Brunson	Oak.	25.9	1979	AFC
											David Turner	Cin.	55								
1979	NFC	Danny Reece	T.B.	70	Danny Reece	T.B.	431	John Sciarra	Phi.	11.4	Jimmy Edwards	Min.	40	Jimmy Edwards	Min.	1103	Jimmy Edwards	Min.	25.1	1979	NFC
											Steve Odom	GB-NYG	40								
1980	AFC	Ira Matthews	Oak.	48	J.T. Smith	K.C.	581	J.T. Smith	K.C.	14.5	Bruce Harper	NY J	49	Bruce Harper	NY J	1070	Horace Ivory	N.E.	27.6	1980	AFC
1980	NFC	Danny Reece	T.B.	57	James Jones	Dal.	548	Kenny Johnson	Atl.	12.2	Eddie Payton	Min.	53	Eddie Payton	Min.	1184	Rich Mauti	N.O.	25.7	1980	NFC
1981	AFC	J.T. Smith	K.C.	50	J.T. Smith	K.C.	528	James Brooks	S.D.	13.2	James Brooks	S.D.	40	James Brooks	S.D.	949	Carl Roaches	Hou.	27.5	1981	AFC
1981	NFC	Wally Henry	Phi.	54	LeRoy Irvin	L.A.	615	LeRoy Irvin	L.A.	13.4	Drew Hill	L.A.	60	Stump Mitchell	St.L.	1292	Mike Nelms	Was.	29.7	1981	NFC
1982	AFC	Greg Pruitt	Raid.	27	Rick Upchurch	Den.	242	Rick Upchurch	Den.	16.1	James Brooks	S.D.	33	James Brooks	S.D.	749	Mike Mosley	Buf.	27.1	1982	AFC
1982	NFC	Leon Bright	NY G	37	Leon Bright	NY G	325	Billy Johnson	Atl.	11.4	Wally Henry	Phil.	24	Mike Nelms	Was.	557	Alvin Hall	Det.	26.6	1982	NFC
											Reggie Brown	Atl.	24								
1983	AFC	Greg Pruitt	Raid.	58	Greg Pruitt	Raid.	666	Kirk Springs	NY J	13.6	Zachary Dixon	Bal.-Sea.	51	Zachary Dixon	Bal.-Sea.	1171	Fulton Walker	Mia.	26.7	1983	AFC
1983	NFC	Billy Johnson	Atl.	46	Billy Johnson	Atl.	489	Henry Ellard	L.A.	13.6	Ron Fellows	Dal.	43	Ron Fellows	Dal.	855	Darrin Nelson	Min.	24.7	1983	NFC
1984	AFC	Louis Lipps	Pit.	53	Louis Lipps	Pit.	656	Mike Martin	Cin.	15.7	Lionel James	S.D.	43	Lionel James	S.D.	959	Bobby Humphery	NY J	30.7	1984	AFC
		Greg Pruitt	Raid.	53																	
1984	NFC	Jeff Fisher	Chi.	57	Dana McLemore	S.F.	521	Henry Ellard	L.A.	13.4	Mike Nelms	Was.	42	Darrin Nelson	Min.	891	Barry Redden	L.A.	23.0	1984	AFC
1985	AFC	Fulton Walker	Raid.	62	Fulton Walker	Raid.	692	Irving Fryar	N.E.	14.1	Mike Martin	Cin.	48	Mike Martin	Cin.	1104	Glen Young	Cle.	25.7	1985	AFC
											Stephen Starring	N.E.	48								
1985	NFC	Phil McConkey	NY G	53	Henry Ellard	L.A.	501	Henry Ellard	L.A.	13.5	Buster Rhymes	Min.	48	Buster Rhymes	Min.	1345	Ron Brown	L.A.	32.8	1985	NFC
1986	AFC	Fulton Walker	Raid.	49	Gerald Wilhite	Den.	468	Bobby Joe Edmonds	Sea.	12.3	Ice Cube McNeil	Cle.	47	Tim McGee	Cin.	1007	Lupe Sanchez	Pit.	23.6	1986	AFC
1986	NFC	Lew Barnes	Chi.	57	Vai Sikahema	St.L.	522	Vai Sikahema	St.L.	12.1	Herman Hunter	Det.	49	Herman Hunter	Det.	1007	Dennis Gentry	Chi.	28.8	1986	NFC
1987	AFC	Ice Cube McNeil	Cle.	34	Lionel James	S.D.	400	Bobby Joe Edmonds	Sea.	12.6	Paul Palmer	K.C.	38	Paul Palmer	K.C.	923	Paul Palmer	K.C.	24.3	1987	AFC
1987	NFC	Vai Sikahema	St.L.	44	Vai Sikahema	St.L.	550	Mel Gray	N.O.	14.7	Neal Guggemos	Min.	36	Neal Guggemos	Min.	808	Sylvester Stamps	Atl.	27.5	1987	NFC
1988	AFC	Tim Brown	Raid.	49	Tim Brown	Raid.	444	JoJo Townsell	NYJ	11.7	Tim Brown	Raid.	41	Tim Brown	Raid.	1098	Tim Brown	Raid.	26.8	1988	AFC
1988	NFC	Leo Lewis	Min.	58	John Taylor	S.F.	556	John Taylor	S.F.	12.6	Daryl Harris	Min.	39	Daryl Harris	Min.	833	Donnie Elder	T.B.	22.7	1988	NFC
1989	NFC	Dave Meggett	NYG	46	Dave Meggett	NYG	582	Walter Stanley	Det.	13.8	James Dixon	Dall.	47	James Dixon	Dall.	1181	Mel Gray	Det	26.7	1989	NFC
											Ron Brown	L.A.	47								
1989	AFC	Gerald McNeil	Clev.	49	Gerald McNeil	Clev.	496	Clarence Verdin	Ind.	12.9	Rod Woodson	Pitt.	36	Rod Woodson	Pitt.	982	Rod Woodson	Pitt.	27.3	1989	AFC
1990	NFC	Dave Meggett	NYG	43	Dave Meggett	NYG	467	Johnny Bailey	Chi.	11.1	Herschel Walker	Min.	44	Herschel Walker	Min.	966	Dave Meggett	NYG	23.4	1990	NFC
1990	AFC	Rod Woodson	Pit.	38	Rod Woodson	Pit.	398	Clarence Verdin	Ind.	12.8	Eric Metcalf	Cle.	52	Eric Metcalf	Cle.	1052	Kevin Clark	Den.	25.3	1990	AFC
1991	NFC	Rod Harris	Phil.	53	Brian Mitchell	Wash.	600	Mel Gray	Det.	15.4	Dexter Carter	S.F.	37	Mel Gray	Det.	929	Mel Gray	Det.	25.8	1991	NFC
1991	AFC	Chris Warren	Sea.	32	Tim Brown	Raid.	330	Rod Woodson	Pitt.	11.4	Rod Woodson	Pitt.	44	Rod Woodson	Pitt.	880	Nate Lewis	S.D.	25.1	1991	AFC
1992	NFC	Kelvin Martin	Dall.	42	Kelvin Martin	Dall.	532	Johnny Bailey	Phx.	13.2	Mel Gray	Det.	42	Deion Sanders	Atl.	1067	Deion Sanders	Atl.	26.7	1992	NFC
1992	AFC	Eric Metcalf	Clev.	44	Eric Metcalf	Clev.	429	Rod Woodson	Pitt.	11.4	Clarence Verdin	Ind.	39	Clarence Verdin	Ind.	815	Jon Vaughn	N.E.	28.2	1992	AFC
1993	NFC	Kevin Williams	Dall.	38	Tyrone Hughes	N.O.	503	Tyrone Hughes	N.O.	13.6	Qadry Ismail	Minn.	42	Tony Smith	Atl.	948	Robert Brooks	G.B.	26.6	1993	NFC
1993	AFC	Patrick Robinson	Cin.	43	Tim Brown	L.A.Rd.	465	Eric Metcalf	Clev.	12.9	Clarence Verdin	Ind.	50	Clarence Verdin	Ind.	1050	Raghib Ismail	L.A.Rd.	24.2	1993	AFC

SINGLE SEASON LEADERS

PASSING

Note: (For all single season leaders)—Number after individual name indicates the number of times that individual appears within a specific category; the bold indicates the individual appearing most within a specific category.

COMPLETIONS

1	Warren Moon	Hou.	AFC	91	404
2	Dan Marino-1	Mia.	AFC	86	377
3	Dan Marino-2	Mia.	AFC	84	362
	Warren Moon-2	Hou.	AFC	90	362
5	Dan Fouts-1	S.D.	AFC	81	360
6	Dan Marino-3	Mia.	AFC	88	354
7	Don Majkowski-1	G.B.	NFC	89	353
8	Dan Fouts-2	S.D.	AFC	80	348
	John Elway-1	Den.	AFC	93	348
10	Steve DeBerg-1	S.F.	NFC	79	347
11	Bill Kenney	K.C.	AFC	83	346
12	Neil Lomax-1	St.L.	NFC	84	345
	Fran Tarkenton	Min.	NFC	78	345
14	Brian Sipe-1	Cle.	AFC	80	337
15	Dan Marino-4	Mia.	AFC	85	336
16	Danny White-1	Dal.	NFC	83	334
17	Dan Fouts-3	S.D.	AFC	80	332
	Joe Montana-1	S.F.	NFC	83	332
	Dan Marino-5	Mia.	AFC	92	332
20	John Elway-2	Den.	AFC	85	327
21	Tommy Kramer-1	Min.	NFC	81	322
22	Joe Montana-2	S.F.	NFC	90	321
23	Dan Marino-6	Mia.	AFC	91	318
	Brett Favre-1	G.B.	NFC	93	318
25	Dan Fouts-4	S.D.	AFC	83	317
26	Tommy Kramer-2	Min.	NFC	79	315
27	Steve Young	S.F.	NFC	93	314
28	Brian Sipe-2	Clev.	AFC	81	313
29	Joe Montana-2	S.F.	NFC	81	311
30	Bernie Kosar-1	Cle.	AFC	86	310
31	Archie Manning-1	N.O.	NFC	80	309
32	Richard Todd-1	NYJ	AFC	83	308
	Steve DeBerg-2	T.B.	NFC	84	308
	Jim Everett-1	L.A.	NFC	88	308
	Dan Marino-7	Mia.	AFC	89	308
36	Jim Everett-2	L.A.	NFC	90	307
	Bernie Kosar-2	Clev.	AFC	91	307
38	Dan Marino-8	Mia.	AFC	90	306
39	Ken Stabler-1	Oak.	AFC	79	304
	Jim Everett-3	L.A.	NFC	89	304
	Jim Kelly-1	Buff.	AFC	91	304
42	Joe Montana-4	S.F.	NFC	85	303
	Bernie Kosar-3	Clev.	AFC	89	303
	Warren Moon	Hou.	AFC	93	303
45	Troy Aikman	Dall.	NFC	92	302
	Brett Favre-2	G.B.	NFC	92	302
47	R. Cunningham-1	Phil.	NFC	88	301
48	Ken Anderson-1	Cin.	AFC	81	300
	Ken O'Brien-1	NYJ	AFC	86	300
50	Tommy Kramer-3	Min.	NFC	80	299
51	Steve Bartkowski	Atl.	NFC	81	297
	Ken O'Brien-2	NYJ	AFC	85	297
53	John Elway-3	Den	AFC	90	294
54	Ken Stabler-2	Hou.	AFC	80	293
	Joe Theismann-1	Was.	NFC	81	293
56	Jeff George	Ind.	AFC	91	292
57	Archie Manning-2	N.O.	NFC	78	291
	Brian Sipe-3	Cle.	AFC	83	291
59	R. Cunningham-2	Phil.	NFC	89	290
60	Lynn Dickey-1	G.B.	NFC	83	289
61	Sonny Jurgensen	Was.	NFL	67	288
	Ken O'Brien-3	NYJ	AFC	89	288
	Boomer Esiason	NYJ	AFC	93	288
	Jim Kelly-2	Buff.	AFC	93	288
65	Ken O'Brien-4	NYJ	AFC	91	287
66	Brian Sipe-4	Cle.	AFC	79	286
	Phil Simms-1	NYG	NFC	84	286
	Dave Krieg-1	Sea.	AFC	89	286
69	Jim Zorn	Sea.	AFC	85	285
	Dave Krieg-2	Sea.	AFC	85	285
	Jim Kelly-3	Buf.	AFC	86	285
72	Joe Theismann-2	Was.	NFC	84	283
73	Joe Theismann-3	Was.	NFC	80	282
74	Joe Ferguson	Buf.	AFC	83	281
	Jim Everett-4	L.A.	NFC	92	281
76	John Elway-4	Den.	AFC	86	280
	Bobby Hebert	N.O.	NFC	88	280
	Mark Rypien	Wash.	NFC	89	280
	Chris Miller	Atl.	NFC	89	280
	Warren Moon-4	Hous.	AFC	89	280
81	Richard Todd-2	NYJ	AFC	81	279
	Joe Montana-5	S.F.	NFC	84	279
83	Lynn Dickey-2	G.B.	NFC	80	278

COMPLETION PERCENTAGE

(Minimum 100 Attempts)

					Att.	Comp.	Pct.
1	Ken Anderson-1	Cin.	AFC	82	309	218	70.6
2	Sammy Baugh-1	Was.	NFL	45	182	128	70.3
3	Joe Montana-1	S.F.	NFC	89	386	271	70.2
4	Troy Aikman-1	Dall.	NFC	93	392	271	69.1
5	Steve Young-1	S.F.	NFC	93	462	314	68.0
6	Steve Bartkowski-1	Atl.	NFC	84	269	181	67.3
7	Joe Montana-2	S.F.	NFC	87	398	266	66.8
8	Ken Stabler-1	Oak.	AFC	76	291	194	66.7
	Ken Anderson-2	Cin	AFC	83	297	198	66.7
	Turk Schonert	Cin	AFC	84	117	78	66.7
	Steve Young-2	S.F.	NFC	92	402	268	66.7
12	Dave Krieg	Sea.	AFC	91	285	187	65.6
	Cody Carlson	Hou.	AFC	92	227	149	65.6
14	Len Dawson-1	K.C.	AFC	75	140	93	66.4
15	Len Dawson-2	K.C.	AFC	73	101	66	65.3
	Troy Aikman-2	Dall.	NFC	91	363	237	65.3
17	Ken Anderson-3	Cin.	AFC	74	328	213	64.9
18	Otto Graham	Cle.	NFL	53	258	167	64.7
	Warren Moon-1	Hou.	AFC	92	346	224	64.7
20	Joe Montana-3	S.F.	NFC	84	432	279	64.6
21	Joe Montana-4	S.F.	NFC	80	273	176	64.5
	Joe Montana-5	S.F.	NFC	83	515	332	64.5
	Steve Young-3	S.F.	NFC	91	279	180	64.5
24	Fran Tarkenton-1	Min.	NFC	75	475	273	64.2
	Dan Marino	Mia.	AFC	84	564	362	64.2
26	Ken Stabler-2	Hou.	AFC	80	457	293	64.1
	Sonny Jurgensen-1	Was.	NFC	74	167	107	64.1
	Jim Kelly-1	Buff.	AFC	91	474	304	64.1
	Troy Aikman	Dall.	NFC	92	473	302	64.1
30	Joe Theismann	Was.	NFC	82	252	161	63.9
31	Bart Starr-1	G.B.	NFL	68	171	109	63.7
	Joe Montana-6	S.F.	NFC	81	488	311	63.7
33	John Brodie-1	S.F.	NFC	72	110	70	63.6
	Ken Anderson-4	Cin.	AFC	84	275	175	63.6
35	Steve Bartkowski-2	Atl.	NFC	82	262	166	63.4
	Steve Bartkowski-3	Atl.	NFC	83	432	274	63.4
37	Jim Kelly-2	Buf.	AFC	90	346	219	63.3
38	Danny White-1	Dal.	NFC	82	247	156	63.2
	Dan Fouts	S.D.	AFC	83	340	215	63.2
	John Elway	Den.	AFC	93	551	348	63.2
41	Y.A. Tittle	S.F.	NFL	57	279	176	63.1
42	Bob Griese-1	Mia.	AFC	78	235	148	63.0
	Eric Hipple	Det.	NFC	86	305	192	63.0
44	Bobby Hebert	N.O.	NFC	89	353	222	62.9
45	Jeff Hostetler	NYG	NFC	91	285	179	62.8
46	Sammy Baugh-2	Was.	NFL	40	177	111	62.7
	Ken Stabler-3	Oak.	AFC	73	260	163	62.7
	Danny White-2	Dal.	NFC	83	533	334	62.7
49	Dan Fouts-2	S.D.	AFC	79	530	332	62.6
	Ken Anderson-5	Cin.	AFC	81	479	300	62.6
	Roger Staubach	Dal.	NFC	73	286	179	62.6
52	Bart Starr-2	G.B.	NFL	62	285	178	62.5
	Dan Fouts-3	S.D.	AFC	84	507	317	62.5
	Rodney Peete	Det.	NFC	93	252	157	62.3
55	Bart Starr-3	G.B.	NFL	69	148	92	62.2
	Virgil Carter	Chi.	NFC	71	222	138	62.2
	Bart Starr-4	G.B.	NFL	66	251	156	62.2
	Joe Montana-7	S.F.	NFC	86	307	191	62.2
59	Bernie Kosar-1	Clev.	AFC	91	494	307	62.1
60	Sonny Jurgensen-2	Was.	NFL	69	442	274	62.0
	Bernie Kosar-2	Cle.	AFC	87	389	241	62.0
	Warren Moon-2	Hou.	AFC	90	584	362	62.0
63	John Brodie-2	S.F.	NFL	65	391	242	61.9
	Fran Tarkenton-2	Min.	NFC	76	412	255	61.9
	Rudy Bukich	Chi.	NFL	64	160	99	61.9
	Ken Stabler-4	N.O.	NFC	82	189	117	61.9
67	Bob Griese-2	Mia.	AFC	76	191	118	61.8
	Archie Manning	N.O.	NFC	78	471	291	61.8
	Dan Fouts-4	S.D.	AFC	82	330	204	61.8
	Phil Simms	NYG	NFC	93	400	247	61.8
71	Fran Tarkenton-3	Min.	NFC	73	274	169	61.7
72	Joe Montana-8	S.F.	NFC	90	520	321	61.7
	Warren Moon-3	Hou.	AFC	91	655	404	61.7
	Steve Beuerlein	Phx.	NFC	93	418	258	61.7
75	Joe Montana-9	S.F.	NFC	82	346	213	61.6
	Neil Lomax	St.L.	NFC	84	560	345	61.6
	Tony Eason	N.E.	AFC	86	448	276	61.6
78	Gary Danielson	Det.	NFC	84	410	252	61.5
	Jim Harbaugh	Chi.	NFC	93	325	200	61.5
80	Wade Wilson	Minn.	NFC	88	332	204	61.4
81	Joe Montana-10	S.F.	NFC	85	303	494	61.3
	Jim Kelly-3	Buff.	AFC	93	470	288	61.3

YARDS PASSING

1	Dan Marino-1	Mia.	AFC	84	5084
2	Dan Fouts-1	S.D.	AFC	81	4802
3	Dan Marino-2	Mia.	AFC	86	4746
4	Dan Fouts-2	S.D.	AFC	80	4715
5	Warren Moon-1	Hou.	AFC	91	4690
6	Warren Moon-2	Hou.	AFC	90	4689
7	Neil Lomax-1	St.L.	NFC	84	4619
8	Lynn Dickey-1	G.B.	NFC	83	4458
9	Dan Marino-3	Mia.	AFC	88	4434
10	Bill Kenney	K.C.	AFC	83	4348
11	Don Majkowski	G.B.	NFC	89	4318
12	Jim Everett-1	L.A.	NFC	89	4310
13	Dan Marino-4	Mia.	AFC	85	4137
14	Brian Sipe-1	Cle.	AFC	80	4132
15	Dan Marino-5	Mia.	AFC	92	4116
16	Jay Schroeder	Was.	NFC	86	4109
17	Dan Fouts-3	S.D.	AFC	79	4082
18	Joe Namath	NYJ	AFL	67	4097
19	Phil Simms-1	NYG	NFC	84	4044
20	John Elway-1	Den	AFC	93	4030
21	Steve Young	S.F.	NFC	93	4023
22	Dan Marino-6	Mia.	AFC	89	3997
23	Jim Everett	L.A.	NFC	90	3989
24	Danny White	Dal	NFC	83	3980
25	Dan Marino-7	Mia.	AFC	91	3970
26	Jim Everett-3	L.A.	NFC	88	3964
27	Boomer Esiason-1	Cin.	AFC	86	3959
28	Joe Montana-1	S.F.	NFC	90	3944
29	Tommy Kramer-1	Min.	NFC	81	3912
30	Joe Montana-2	S.F.	NFC	83	3910
31	John Elway-2	Den.	AFC	85	3891
32	Ken O'Brien	NYJ	AFC	85	3888
33	Brian Sipe-2	Cle.	AFC	81	3876
34	Bernie Kosar	Cle.	AFC	86	3854
35	Jim Kelly	Buff.	AFC	91	3844
36	Steve Bartkowski-1	Atl.	NFC	81	3829
	Phil Simms-2	NYG	NFC	85	3829
38	R. Cunningham	Phil.	NFC	88	3808
39	Brian Sipe-3	Cle.	AFC	79	3793
40	Mark Rypien-1	Wash.	NFC	89	3768
41	Ken Anderson	Cin.	AFC	81	3754
42	Sonny Jurgensen	Was.	NFL	67	3747
43	Dan Fouts-4	S.D.	AFC	84	3740
44	Terry Bradshaw	Pit.	AFC	79	3724
45	Sonny Jurgensen-2	Phi	NFL	61	3723
46	Archie Manning	N.O.	NFC	80	3716
47	Joe Theismann-1	Was.	NFC	83	3714
48	Ken O'Brien-2	NYJ	AFC	86	3690
49	Dave Krieg-1	Sea.	AFC	84	3671
50	Jim Zorn	Sea.	AFC	79	3661
51	Joe Montana-3	S.F.	NFC	85	3653
52	Steve DeBerg-1	S.F.	NFC	79	3652
	Joe Ferguson	Buf.	AFC	81	3652
54	Dan Fouts-5	S.D.	AFC	85	3638
55	Warren Moon-3	Hous.	AFC	89	3631
56	Joe Montana-4	S.F.	NFC	84	3630
57	Ken Stabler	Oak	AFC	79	3615
58	Dave Krieg-2	Sea.	AFC	85	3602
59	Jim Kelly-2	Buf.	AFC	86	3593
60	Roger Staubach	Dal.	NFC	79	3586
61	Tommy Kramer-2	Min.	NFC	80	3582
62	Joe Ferguson-2	Buf.	AFC	79	3572
	Boomer Esiason-2	Cin.	AFC	88	3572
64	Joe Theismann-2	Was.	NFC	81	3568
65	Brian Sipe-4	Cle.	AFC	83	3566
66	Joe Montana-5	S.F.	NFC	81	3565
	Mark Rypien-2	Wash.	NFC	91	3564
68	Doug Williams	T.B.	NFC	81	3563
	Dan Marino-6	Mia.	AFC	90	3563
70	Steve DeBerg-2	T.B.	NFC	84	3554
71	Steve Bartkowski-2	Atl.	NFC	80	3544
72	Bernie Kosar	Clev.	AFC	89	3533
73	Lynn Dickey-2	G.B.	NFC	80	3529
74	John Elway-3	Den.	AFC	90	3526
75	Boomer Esiason-3	Cin.	AFC	89	3525
76	Tommy Kramer-3	Min.	NFC	85	3522
77	Joe Montana-6	S.F.	NFC	89	3521
78	Warren Moon-4	Hou.	AFC	86	3489
79	Phil Simms-3	NYG	NFC	86	3487
80	John Elway-4	Den.	AFC	86	3489

YARDS PASSING PER SCHEDULED GAME

1	Dan Fouts-1	S.D.	AFC	82	320
2	Dan Marino-1	Mia.	AFC	84	318
3	Dan Fouts-2	S.D.	AFC	81	300
4	Dan Marino-2	Mia.	AFC	86	297
5	Dan Fouts-3	S.D.	AFC	80	295
6	Warren Moon-1	Hou.	AFC	90	293
	Warren Moon-2	Hou.	AFC	91	293
8	Joe Montana-1	S.F.	NFC	82	290
9	Neil Lomax	St.L.	NFC	84	289
10	Joe Namath-1	NYJ	AFL	67	286
11	Lynn Dickey	G.B.	NFC	83	279
12	Ken Anderson	Cin.	AFC	82	278
13	Dan Marino-3	Mia.	AFC	88	277
14	Bill Kenney	K.C.	AFC	83	272
15	Don Majkowski	G.B.	NFC	89	270
16	Jim Everett-1	L.A.	NFC	89	269
17	Sonny Jurgensen-1	Was.	NFL	67	268
18	Sonny Jurgensen-2	Phi.	NFL	61	266
19	Dan Marino-4	Mia.	AFC	85	259
20	Johnny Unitas-1	Bal.	NFL	60	258
	Brian Sipe-1	Cle.	AFC	80	258
22	Dan Marino-5	Mia.	AFC	92	257
23	Dan Marino-6	Mia.	AFC	89	250
24	John Elway-1	Den.	AFC	93	252
25	Steve Young	S.F.	NFC	93	251
26	Jay Schroeder	Was.	NFC	86	247
27	Phil Simms-1	NYG	NFC	84	253
28	Dan Fouts-4	S.D.	AFC	79	252
29	Johnny Unitas-2	Bal.	NFL	63	249
	Danny White	Dal.	NFC	83	249
	Jim Everett-2	L.A.	NFC	90	249
32	John Hadl-1	S.D.	AFL	68	248
	Babe Parilli	Bos.	AFL	64	248
	Jim Everett-3	L.A.	NFC	88	248
	Dan Marino-7	Mia.	AFC	91	248
36	Boomer Esiason	Cin.	AFC	86	247
	Joe Montana-2	S.F.	NFC	90	247
38	Johnny Unitas-3	Bal.	NFL	67	245
	Sammy Baugh	Was.	NFL	47	245
	Tommy Kramer	Min.	NFC	81	245
41	Joe Montana-3	S.F.	NFC	83	244
42	Norm Snead	Phi.	NFL	67	243
	John Elway-2	Den.	AFC	85	243
	Ken O'Brien	NYJ	AFC	85	243
45	Brian Sipe-2	Cle.	AFC	81	242
	Johnny Unitas-4	Bal.	NFL	59	242
47	Joe Namath-2	NYJ	AFL	66	241
48	John Hadl-2	S.D.	AFL	67	240
	Bill Wade	L.A.	NFL	58	240
	Bernie Kosar	Cle.	AFC	86	240
	Jim Kelly	Buff.	AFC	91	240
52	Steve Bartkowski	Atl.	NFC	81	239
	Phil Simms-2	NYG	NFC	85	239
54	George Blanda	Hou.	AFL	61	238
55	Randall Cunningham	Phil.	NFC	88	238
56	Brian Sipe-3	Cle.	AFC	79	237

YARDS PER ATTEMPT

(Minimum 100 Attempts)

					Att.	Yards	Yd/A
1	Tom O'Connell	Cle.	NFL	57	110	1229	11.2
2	Sid Luckman-1	ChiB	NFL	43	202	2194	10.9
3	Otto Graham-1	Cle	NFL	53	258	2722	10.6
4	Otto Graham-2	Cle.	AAFC	46	174	1834	10.5
5	Otto Graham-3	Cle.	AAFC	47	269	2753	10.2
6	Norm Van Brocklin	L.A.	NFL	54	260	2637	10.1
7	Bill Neisen	Pit.	NFL	66	112	1122	10.0
8	Sid Luckman-2	ChiB	NFL	41	119	1181	9.9
	Ed Brown	ChiB	NFL	56	168	1667	9.9
10	Otto Graham-4	Cle.	AAFC	49	285	2785	9.8
11	Sid Luckman-3	ChiB	NFL	42	105	1023	9.7
12	Jacky Lee	Hou.	AFL	61	127	1205	9.5
13	Bart Starr	G.B.	NFL	68	171	1617	9.5
14	Len Dawson	K.C.	AFL	68	224	2109	9.4
	Eddie LeBaron	Was.	NFL	58	145	1365	9.4
	Greg Cook	Cin.	AFL	69	197	1854	9.4
	Bob Waterfield	Cle.	NFL	45	171	1609	9.4
	Ken Stabler	Oak.	AFC	76	291	2737	9.4
	Bob Berry	Atl.	NFL	68	153	1433	9.4
20	Otto Graham-5	Cle.	NFL	55	185	1721	9.3
	Johnny Unitas	Bal.	NFL	64	305	2824	9.3
22	James Harris	L.A.	NFC	76	158	1460	9.2
	George Blanda	Hou.	AFL	61	362	3330	9.2
	Milt Plum	Cle.	NFL	60	250	2297	9.2
	Earl Morrall	Bal.	NFL	68	317	2909	9.2
	Sammy Baugh	Was.	NFL	45	182	1669	9.2
	Lynn Dickey	G.B.	NFC	83	484	4458	9.2
	Boomer Esiason	Cin.	AFC	88	388	3572	9.2
29	John Brodie	S.F.	NFL	61	283	2588	9.1
	Earl Morrall-2	Mia.	AFC	72	150	1360	9.1
	Joe Montana	S.F.	NFC	89	386	3521	9.1

SINGLE SEASON LEADERS

PASSING

TOUCHDOWN PASSES

1	Dan Marino-1	Mia.	AFC	84	48
2	Dan Marino-2	Mia.	AFC	86	44
3	George Blanda	Hou.	AFL	61	36
	Y.A. Tittle-1	NYG	NFL	63	36
5	Daryle Lamonica-1	Oak.	AFL	69	34
6	Y.A. Tittle-2	NYG	NFL	62	33
	Dan Fouts-1	S.D.	AFC	81	33
	Warren Moon	Hou.	AFC	90	33
	Jim Kelly	Buff.	AFC	91	33
10	Johnny Unitas	Bal.	NFL	59	32
	Lynn Dickey	G.B.	NFC	83	32
	Dave Krieg-1	Sea.	AFC	84	32
13	Babe Parilli	Bos.	AFL	64	31
	Sonny Jurgensen-1	Was.	NFL	67	31
	Steve Bartkowski-1	Atl.	NFC	80	31
	Joe Montana-1	S.F.	NFC	87	31
	Jim Everett-1	L.A.	NFC	88	31
18	Len Dawson-1	K.C.	AFL	64	30
	John Brodie	S.F.	NFL	65	30
	Daryle Lamonica-2	Oak.	AFL	67	30
	Vince Ferragamo	L.A.	NFC	80	30
	Dan Fouts-2	S.D.	AFC	80	30
	Brian Sipe-1	Cle.	AFC	80	30
	Steve Bartkowski-2	Atl.	NFC	81	30
	Dan Marino-3	Mia.	AFC	85	30
	R. Cunningham	Phi.	NFC	90	30
27	Frankie Albert-1	S.F.	AAFC	48	29
	Len Dawson-2	Dal.	AFL	62	29
	Frank Ryan	Cle.	NFL	66	29
	Norm Snead	Phi.	NFL	67	29
	Fran Tarkenton	NYG	NFL	67	29
	Ken Anderson	Cin.	AFC	81	29
	Joe Theismann	Was.	NFC	83	29
	Danny White-1	Dal.	NFC	83	29
	Jim Everett-2	L.A.	NFC	89	29
	Steve Young	S.F.	NFC	93	29
37	Sid Luckman	ChiB	NFL	43	28
	Charley Johnson	St.L.	NFL	63	28
	Sonny Jurgensen-2	Was.	NFL	64	28
	Terry Bradshaw-1	Pit.	AFC	78	28
	Steve Grogan	N.E.	AFC	79	28
	Brian Sipe-2	Cle.	AFC	79	28
	Danny White-2	Dal.	NFC	80	28
	Neil Lomax	St.L.	NFC	84	28
	Joe Montana-2	S.F.	NFC	84	28
	Boomer Esiason-1	Cin.	AFC	88	28
	Dan Marino-4	Mia.	AFC	88	28
	Boomer Esiason-2	Cin.	AFC	89	28
	Mark Rypien	Wash.	NFC	91	28
50	Frankie Albert-2	S.F.	AAFC	47	27
	George Blanda-2	Hou.	AFL	62	27
	John Hadl	S.D.	AFL	68	27
	Ken Stabler-1	Oak.	AFC	76	27
	Roger Staubach	Dal.	NFC	79	27
	Ron Jaworski	Phi.	NFC	80	27
	Dave Krieg-2	Sea.	AFC	85	27
	Dan Fouts-3	S.D.	AFC	85	27
	Boomer Esiason-3	Cin.	AFC	85	27
	Joe Montana-3	S.F.	NFC	85	27
	Don Majkowski	G.B.	NFC	89	27
60	Bobby Layne	Det.	NFL	51	26
	Al Dorow	NYT	AFL	60	26
	Len Dawson-3	K.C.	AFL	63	26
	Len Dawson-4	K.C.	AFL	66	26
	Joe Namath	NYJ	AFL	67	26
	Earl Morrall	Bal.	NFL	68	26
	Ken Stabler-2	Oak.	AFC	74	26
	Terry Bradshaw-2	Pit.	AFC	79	26
	Ken Stabler-3	Oak.	AFC	79	26
	Tommy Kramer	Min.	NFC	81	26
	Joe Ferguson	Buf.	AFC	83	26
	Brian Sipe-3	Cle.	AFC	83	26
	Joe Montana-4	S.F.	NFC	83	26
	Dan Marino-5	Mia.	AFC	87	26
	Joe Montana-5	S.F.	NFC	90	26
	Chris Miller	Atl.	NFC	91	26

LOWEST PASS INTERCEPTION PERCENTAGE

(MINIMUM 100 ATTEMPTS)

					Att.	Int.	Pct.
1	Joe Ferguson	Buf.	AFC	76	151	1	0.662
2	Bill Nelsen	Pit.	NFL	66	112	1	0.893
3	Steve DeBerg	K.C.	AFC	90	444	4	0.900
4	Steve Bartkowski	Atl.	NFC	83	432	5	1.157
5	Bart Starr	G.B.	NFL	66	251	3	1.195
6	Phil Simms	N.Y.	NFC	90	311	4	1.286
7	Jim McMahon	Chi.	NFC	84	143	2	1.399
8	Jeff Hostetler	NYG	NFC	91	285	4	1.408
9	Neil O'Donnell	Pitt.	AFC	93	486	7	1.440
10	Bart Starr-2	G.B.	NFL	64	272	4	1.471
11	Jeff George	Ind.	AFC	93	407	6	1.474
12	Bob Berry	Atl.	NFL	69	124	2	1.612
13	Bubby Brister	Phil.	NFC	93	309	5	1.618
14	Ken O'Brien-1	NYJ	AFC	85	488	8	1.639
15	Ken O'Brien-2	NYJ	AFC	88	424	7	1.651
16	John Friesz	S.D.	AFC	93	238	4	1.681
17	Steve Bono	S.F.	NFC	91	237	4	1.688
18	Rich Gannon	Minn.	NFC	91	354	6	1.695
19	Joe Pisarcik	Phi.	NFC	84	176	3	1.705
20	Steve Young	S.F.	NFC	92	402	7	1.741
21	Roman Gabriel-1	L.A.	NFL	69	399	7	1.754
22	John Elway	Den.	AFC	93	551	10	1.814
23	Bernie Kosar-1	Clev.	AFC	91	494	9	1.821
24	Bill Munson-1	Det.	NFC	75	109	2	1.835
25	Tony Eason	N.E.	AFC	84	431	8	1.856
26	Bernie Kosar-2	Cle.	AFC	86	531	10	1.883
27	Roger Staubach-1	Dal.	NFC	71	211	4	1.895
28	Chris Miller	Atl.	NFC	89	526	10	1.901
29	Jim Harbaugh	Chi.	NFC	90	312	6	1.923
30	Fran Tarkenton-1	Min.	NFC	76	412	8	1.942
31	Fran Tarkenton-2	NYG	NFL	69	409	8	1.955
32	Steve Dils	Min.	NFC	81	101	2	1.961
33	Johnny Unitas	Bal.	NFL	64	305	6	1.967
34	Roman Gabriel-2	L.A.	NFL	62	101	2	1.980
	Steve Pelluer	Dal.	NFL	87	101	2	1.980
36	Scott Hunter	Atl.	NFC	77	151	3	1.987
	Ed Luther	S.D.	AFC	84	151	3	1.987
38	Milt Plum	Cle.	NFL	60	250	5	2.000
39	Dan Marino-1	Mia.	AFC	83	296	6	2.027
40	Ken O'Brien-3	NYJ	AFC	87	393	8	2.036
41	Charlie Conerly	NYG	NFL	59	194	4	2.062
	Jim Hart	St.L.	NFC	74	388	8	2.062
43	Dan Marino	Mia.	AFC	90	531	11	2.071
44	Joe Montana-1	S.F.	NFC	89	386	8	2.072
45	Ken Anderson-1	Cin.	AFC	81	479	10	2.088
46	Gary Wood	NYG	NFL	64	143	3	2.098
47	Sammy Baugh	Was.	NFL	45	182	4	2.198
48	Warren Moon	Hou.	AFC	90	584	13	2.222
49	Tony Eason	N.E.	AFC	86	448	10	2.232
50	Ken O'Brien-4	NYJ	AFC	91	489	11	2.249
51	Phil Simms-1	NYG	NFC	93	400	9	2.250
52	Jim Zorn	Sea.	AFC	81	397	7	2.267
53	Phil Simms-2	NYG	NFC	88	479	11	2.296
54	Bernie Kosar-3	Cle.	AFC	87	389	9	2.314
55	Joe Montana-2	S.F.	NFC	84	432	10	2.315
56	Ken Anderson-2	Cin.	AFC	72	301	7	2.325
57	Boomer Esiason-1	NYJ	AFC	93	473	11	2.235
58	Bert Jones	Bal.	AFC	75	344	8	2.326
59	Joe Montana-3	S.F.	NFC	83	515	12	2.330
60	Joe Montana-4	K.C.	AFC	93	298	7	2.349
61	Steve Walsh	N.O.	NFC	91	255	6	2.353
62	Y.A. Tittle	S.F.	NFL	60	127	3	2.362
	Don Majkowski	G.B.	NFC	87	127	3	2.362
64	Dan Marino-2	Mia.	AFC	91	549	13	2.368
65	Chris Miller-2	Atl.	NFC	92	253	6	2.371
66	Edd Hargett	N.O.	NFC	71	210	5	2.380
67	Roger Staubach-2	Dal.	NFC	79	461	11	2.386
68	Jeff Hostetler	Phx.	NFC	93	419	10	2.387
69	Bill Munson-2	Det.	NFC	74	292	7	2.397
	Joe Theismann	Was.	NFC	83	459	11	2.397
71	Boomer Esiason-2	Cin.	AFC	89	455	11	2.417
72	Jim McMahon	Minn.	NFC	93	331	8	2.417
73	Bill Munson	Det.	NFC	68	329	8	2.431
74	Ken O'Brien-5	N.Y.	AFC	90	411	10	2.433
75	Neil O'Donnell	Pitt.	AFC	91	286	7	2.447
76	Ron Jaworski	Phi.	NFC	86	245	6	2.449
77	Joe Montana-5	S.F.	NFC	81	488	12	2.459
78	Jeff Kemp	L.A.	NFC	84	284	7	2.465
79	Jeff George	Ind.	AFC	91	485	12	2.474
80	Neil Lomax	Phx.	NFC	88	443	11	2.483
81	Roger Staubach-3	Dal.	NFC	77	361	8	2.493
82	Joe Montana-6	S.F.	NFC	88	397	10	2.519
83	Brian Sipe	Cle.	AFC	80	554	14	2.527
84	Steve DeBerg	T.B.	NFC	87	275	7	2.545

INTERCEPTIONS

1	Night Train Lane-1	L.A.	NFL	62	14
2	Don Sandler	Was.	NFL	48	13
	Spec Sanders	NYY	NFL	50	13
	Lester Hayes	Oak.	AFC	80	13
5	Bob Nussbaumer	ChiC	NFL	49	12
	Don Doll-1	Det.	NFL	50	12
	Woodley Lewis	L.A.	NFL	50	12
	Jack Christiansen	Det.	NFL	53	12
	Fred Glick	Hou.	AFL	63	12
	Paul Krause-1	Min.	NFL	64	12
	Dainard Paulson	NYJ	AFL	64	12
	Emmitt Thomas	K.C.	AFC	74	12
	Mike Reinfeldt	Hou.	AFC	79	12
14	Sammy Baugh	Was.	NFL	43	11
	Don Doll-2	Det.	NFL	49	11
	O. Schnellbacher-1	N.Y.	AAFC	48	11
	O. Schnellbacher-2	NYG	NFL	51	11
	Tom Keane-1	Bal.	NFL	53	11
	Will Sherman	L.A.	NFL	55	11
	Lindon Crow	ChiC	NFL	56	11
	Jim Patton	NYG	NFL	58	11
	Goose Gonsoulin	Den.	AFL	60	11
	Lee Riley	NYT	AFL	62	11
	Ron Hall	Bos.	AFL	63	11
	Bill Bradley	Phi.	NFC	71	11
	Mel Blount	Pit.	AFC	75	11
	Everson Walls	Dal	NFC	81	11
28	Eddie Kotal	G.B.	NFL	28	10
	Irv Comp	G.B.	NFL	43	10
	Bill Dudley	Pit.	NFL	46	10
	Tom Colella	Cle.	AAFC	46	10
	Frank Seno	Bos.	NFL	47	10
	Frank Reagan	NYG	NFL	47	10
	Em Tunnell	NYG	NFL	49	10
	Howard Hartley	Pit.	NFL	51	10
	Tom Keane-2	Dal.	NFL	51	10
	Don Doll-3	Was.	NFL	53	10
	Ray Ramsey	ChiC	NFL	53	10
	Night Train Lane-2	ChiC	NFL	54	10
	Jack Butler	Pit.	NFL	57	10
	Jack Christiansen	Det.	NFL	57	10
	Milt Davis	Bal.	NFL	57	10
	Dave Baker	S.F.	NFL	60	10
	Jerry Norton	St.L.	NFL	60	10
	Billy Atkins	Buf.	AFL	61	10
	Tommy Morrow	Oak.	AFL	62	10
	Pat Fischer	St.L.	NFL	64	10
	Bobby Hunt	K.C.	AFL	66	10
	Larry Wilson	St.L.	NFL	66	10
	Johnny Robinson	K.C.	AFL	66	10
	Lem Barney	Det.	NFL	67	10
	Miller Farr	Hou.	AFL	67	10
	Tom Janik	Buf.	AFL	67	10
	Dick Westmoreland	Mia.	AFL	67	10
	Dave Whitsell	N.O.	NFL	67	10
	Dave Grayson	Oak.	AFL	68	10
	Willie Williams	NYG	NFL	68	10
	Mel Renfro	Dal.	NFL	69	10
	Johnny Robinson	K.C.	AFC	70	10
	Paul Krause-2	Min.	NFC	75	10
	Monte Jackson	L.A.	NFC	76	10
	Lyle Blackwood	Bal.	AFC	77	10
	Gary Barbaro	K.C.	AFC	80	10
	John Harris	Sea.	AFC	81	10
	Kenny Easley	Sea.	AFC	84	10
	Ronnie Lott	S.F.	NFC	86	10
	Scott Case	Atl.	NFC	88	10
	Mark Carrier	Chi.	NFC	90	10

PUNTING AVERAGE

(MINIMUM 30 PUNTS)

1	Sammy Baugh-1	Was.	NFL	40	51.3
2	Glenn Dobbs-1	L.A.	AAFC	48	49.1
3	Yale Lary-1	Det.	NFL	63	48.9
4	Sammy Baugh-2	Was.	NFL	41	48.7
5	Yale Lary-2	Det.	NFL	61	48.4
6	Frankie Albert	S.F.	AAFC	49	48.2
7	Glenn Dobbs-2	Bkn.	AAFC	46	47.8
8	Joe Muha	Phi.	NFL	48	47.2
9	Yale Lary-3	Det.	NFL	59	47.1
10	Bobby Joe Green-1	Pit.	NFL	61	47.0
11	Pat Brady	Pit.	NFL	53	46.9
	Greg Montgomery-1	Hou.	AFC	92	46.9
13	Gary Collins	Cle.	NFL	65	46.7
14	Sammy Baugh-3	Was.	NFL	42	46.6
16	Don Chandler-1	NYG	NFL	59	46.6
15	Bobby Joe Green-2	Chi.	NFL	63	46.5
17	Bobby Walden-1	Min.	NFL	64	46.4
18	Yale Lary-4	Det	NFL	64	46.3
19	Dave Lewis	Cin.	AFC	70	46.2
20	Jim Fraser	Den.	AFL	63	46.1
	Jerrel Wilson-1	K.C.	AFL	65	46.1
22	Sammy Baugh-4	Was.	NFL	43	45.9
	Rohn Stark-1	Ind.	AFC	85	45.9
24	Tommy Davis-1	S.F.	NFL	65	45.8
	Bob Scarpitto	Den.	AFL	66	45.8
26	Horace Gillom-1	Cle.	NFL	52	45.7
	Tommy Davis-2	S.F.	NFL	59	45.7
	Reggie Roby	Mia.	AFC	91	45.7
20	Bob Cifers	Det.	NFL	46	45.6
	Jerry Norton	St.L.	NFL	60	45.6
	Tommy Davis-3	S.F.	NFL	62	45.6
	Don Chandler-2	NYG	NFL	64	45.6
	Tommy Davis-4	S.F.	NFL	64	45.6
	David Lee-1	Bal.	NFL	66	45.6
	Greg Montgomery-2	Hou.	AFC	93	45.6
35	Horace Gillom-2	Cle.	NFL	51	45.5
	Sam Baker-1	Was.	NFL	59	45.5
	Danny Villanueva-1	L.A.	NFL	62	45.5
	Jerrel Wilson-2	K.C.	AFC	73	45.5
	Harry Newsome	Minn.	NFC	91	45.5
39	Bob Reinhard	L.A.	AAFC	46	45.4
	Sam Baker-2	Was.	NFL	58	45.4
	Tommy Davis-5	S.F.	NFL	61	45.4
	Sam Baker-3	Dal.	NFL	62	45.4
	Danny Villanueva-2	L.A.	NFL	63	45.4
	Tommy Davis-6	S.F.	NFL	63	45.4
	Pat McInally	Cin.	AFC	81	45.4
47	Yale Lary-5	Det.	NFL	62	45.3
	Curley Johnson	NYJ	AFL	65	45.3
	David Lee-2	Bal.	NFL	69	45.3
	Ray Guy	Oak.	AFC	73	45.3
	Rohn Stark-2	Bal.	AFC	83	45.3
	Rich Camarillo	Phx.	NFC	91	45.3
53	Bobby Walden-2	Pit.	AFC	70	45.2
	Rohn Stark	Ind.	AFC	83	45.2

SINGLE SEASON LEADERS
RUSHING

RUSHING ATTEMPTS

1	James Wilder-1	T.B.	NFC	84	407
2	Eric Dickerson-1	L.A.	NFC	86	404
3	Gerald Riggs-1	Atl.	NFC	85	397
4	Eric Dickerson-2	L.A.	NFC	83	390
	Barry Foster	Pitt.	AFC	92	390
6	Eric Dickerson-3	Ind.	AFC	88	388
7	Walter Payton-1	Chi.	NFC	83	381
8	Marcus Allen	L.A.	AFC	85	380
9	Eric Dickerson-4	L.A.	NFC	84	379
10	George Rogers-1	N.O.	NFC	81	378
11	John Riggins-1	Was.	NFC	83	375
12	Earl Campbell-1	Hou.	AFC	80	373
	Emmitt Smith-1	Dall.	NFC	92	373
14	Christian Okoye	K.C.	AFC	89	370
15	Walter Payton-2	Chi.	NFC	79	369
16	Earl Campbell	Hou.	AFC	79	368
17	James Wilder-2	T.B.	NFC	85	365
	Emmitt Smith-2	Dall.	NFC	91	365
19	Earl Campbell-3	Hou.	AFC	81	361
	Herschel Walker	Dal.	NFC	88	361
21	Thurman Thomas-1	Buff.	AFC	93	355
22	Gerald Riggs-2	Atl.	NFC	84	353
23	Dalton Hilliard	N.O.	NFC	89	344
24	Gerald Riggs-3	Atl.	NFC	86	343
25	Tony Dorsett-1	Dal.	NFC	81	342
	Barry Sanders-1	Det.	NFC	91	343
27	Joe Morris-1	NYG	NFC	86	341
28	Walter Payton-3	Chi.	NFC	77	339
	Walter Payton-4	Chi.	NFC	81	339
30	Wilb. Montgomery	Phi.	NFC	79	338
31	Curt Warner-1	Sea.	AFC	83	335
32	Walter Payton-5	Chi.	NFC	78	333
33	O.J. Simpson-1	Buf.	AFC	73	332
34	Ottis Anderson-1	St.L.	NFC	79	331
	William Andrews	Atl.	NFC	83	331
36	O.J. Simpson-2	Buf.	AFC	75	329
37	Ottis Anderson-2	St.L.	NFC	81	328
38	John Riggins-2	Was.	NFC	84	327
39	Ottis Anderson-3	NYG	NFC	89	325
40	Mark van Eeghen	Oak.	AFC	77	324
	Walter Payton-6	Chi.	NFC	85	324
	Charles White	L.A.	NFC	87	324
43	Earl Campbell-4	Hou.	AFC	83	322
44	Walter Payton-7	Chi.	NFC	86	321
45	Curt Warner-2	Sea.	AFC	86	319
46	Walter Payton-8	Chi.	NFC	80	317
47	Walter Payton-9	Chi.	NFC	83	314
	Eric Dickerson-5	Ind.	AFC	89	314
49	Billy Sims-1	Det.	NFC	80	313
50	Thurman Thomas-2	Buff.	AFC	92	312
	Barry Sanders-2	Det.	NFC	92	312
52	Walter Payton-10	Chi.	NFC	76	311
53	Franco Harris-1	Pit.	AFC	78	310
	Roger Craig	S.F.	NFC	88	310
	Reggie Cobb	T.B.	NFC	92	310
56	Joe Morris-2	NYG	NFC	88	307
57	Joe Cribbs	Buf.	AFC	80	306
58	Jim Brown-1	Cle.	NFL	61	305
	Tony Dorsett-2	Dal.	NFC	85	305
60	George Rogers-2	Was	NFC	86	303
61	Earl Campbell-5	Hou.	AFC	78	302
	Tony Dorsett-3	Dal.	NFC	84	302
63	Franco Harris-2	Pit.	AFC	77	301
	Ottis Anderson-4	St.L.	NFC	80	301
65	Lydell Mitchell	Bal.	AFC	77	300
	Leonard Russell	N.E.	AFC	93	300
67	Jim Nance	Bos.	AFL	66	299
68	Ron Johnson	NYG	NFC	72	298
	Thurman Thomas-3	Buff.	AFC	89	298
70	John Stephens	N.E.	AFC	88	297
	Earnest Byner	Was.	NFC	90	297
72	Billy Sims-2	Det.	NFC	81	296
	Ottis Anderson-5	St.L.	NFC	83	296
	Sammy Winder	Den.	AFC	84	296
	Earnest Jackson	S.D.	AFC	84	296
76	Law. McCutcheon-1	L.A.	NFC	77	294
	Freeman McNeil	NYJ	AFC	85	294
	Joe Morris-3	NYG	NFC	85	294
	Bobby Humphrey	Den.	AFC	89	294
	Jerome Bettis	L.A.	NFC	93	294
81	Mike Pruitt	Cle.	AFC	83	293
82	O.J. Simpson-3	Buf.	AFC	72	292
	Eric Dickerson-6	L.A.	NFC	85	292
	Eric Pegram	Atl.	NFC	93	292
	Rodney Hampton	NYG	NFC	93	292
86	Jim Brown-2	Cle.	NFL	63	291
	Law. McCutcheon-2	L.A.	NFC	76	291
	Curt Warner-3	Sea.	AFC	85	291
89	Jim Brown-3	Cle.	NFL	59	290
	O.J. Simpson-4	Buf.	AFC	76	290
	Tony Dorsett-4	Dal.	NFC	78	290

YARDS

1	Eric Dickerson-1	L.A.	NFC	84	2105
2	O.J. Simpson	Buf.	AFC	73	2003
3	Earl Campbell-1	Hou.	AFC	80	1934
4	Jim Brown-1	Cle.	NFL	63	1863
5	Walter Payton-1	Chi.	NFC	77	1852
6	Eric Dickerson-2	L.A.	NFC	86	1821
7	O.J. Simpson-2	Buf.	AFC	75	1817
8	Eric Dickerson-3	L.A.	NFC	83	1808
9	Marcus Allen	Raid.	AFC	85	1759
10	Gerald Riggs	Atl.	NFC	85	1719
11	Emmitt Smith-1	Dall.	NFC	92	1713
12	Earl Campbell-2	Hou.	AFC	79	1697
13	Barry Foster	Pitt.	AFC	92	1690
14	Walter Payton-2	Chi.	NFC	84	1684
15	George Rogers-1	N.O.	NFC	81	1674
16	Eric Dickerson-4	Ind.	AFC	88	1659
17	Tony Dorsett-1	Dal.	NFC	81	1646
18	Walter Payton-3	Chi.	NFC	79	1610
19	Ottis Anderson-1	St.L.	NFC	79	1605
20	William Andrews	Atl.	NFC	83	1567
21	Emmitt Smith-2	Dall.	NFC	91	1563
22	Walter Payton-4	Chi.	NFC	85	1551
23	Barry Sanders-1	Det.	NFC	91	1548
24	Jim Brown-2	Cle.	NFL	65	1544
	James Wilder-1	T.B.	NFC	84	1544
26	Jim Brown-3	Cle.	NFL	58	1527
27	Joe Morris	NYG	NFC	86	1516
28	Herschel Walker	Dall.	NFC	88	1514
29	Wilb. Montgomery-1	Phi.	NFC	79	1512
30	O.J. Simpson-3	Buff.	AFC	76	1503
31	Roger Craig	S.F.	NFC	88	1502
32	Thurman Thomas-1	Buff.	AFC	92	1487
33	Gerald Riggs	Atl.	NFC	84	1486
	Emmitt Smith	Dall.	NFC	93	1486
35	Curt Warner-1	Sea.	AFC	86	1481
36	Christian Okoye	K.C.	AFC	89	1480
37	Jim Taylor-1	G.B.	NFL	62	1474
38	Barry Sanders-2	Det.	NFC	89	1470
39	Walter Payton-5	Chi.	NFC	80	1460
40	Jim Nance	Bos.	AFL	66	1458
41	Earl Campbell-3	Hou.	AFC	78	1450
42	Curt Warner-2	Sea.	AFC	83	1449
43	Jim Brown-4	Cle.	NFL	64	1446
44	Billy Sims-1	Det.	NFC	81	1437
45	Spec Sanders	N.Y.	AAFC	47	1432
46	Jerome Bettis	L.A.	NFC	93	1429
47	Walter Payton-6	Chi.	NFC	83	1421
48	Jim Brown-5	Cle.	NFL	61	1408
49	Otis Armstrong	Den.	AFC	74	1407
	Thurman Thomas-2	Buff.	AFC	91	1407
51	Wilb. Montgomery-2	Phi.	NFC	81	1402
52	Walter Payton-7	Chi.	NFC	78	1395
53	Walter Payton-8	Chi.	NFC	76	1390
54	Ottis Anderson-2	St.L.	NFC	81	1376
	Earl Campbell-4	Hou.	AFC	81	1376
56	Charles White	L.A.	NFC	87	1374
57	Rueben Mayes	N.O.	NFC	86	1353
58	Ottis Anderson-3	St.L.	NFC	80	1352
	Barry Sanders-3	Det.	NFC	93	1352
60	John Riggins-1	Was.	NFC	83	1347
61	Joe Morris	NYG	NFC	85	1336
62	Walter Payton-9	Chi.	NFC	86	1333
63	Freeman McNeil	NYJ	AFC	85	1331
64	Jim Brown-6	Cle.	NFL	59	1329
65	Gerald Riggs-2	Atl.	NFC	86	1327
66	Tony Dorsett-2	Dal.	NFC	78	1325
67	Tony Dorsett-3	Dal.	NFC	83	1321
68	Thurman Thomas-3	Buff.	AFC	93	1315
69	Eric Dickerson-5	Ind.	AFC	89	1311
70	William Andrews-2	Atl.	NFC	80	1308
71	Jim Taylor-2	G.B.	NFL	61	1307
	Tony Dorsett-4	Dal.	NFC	85	1307
73	Barry Sanders-4	Det.	NFC	90	1304
74	Billy Sims-2	Det.	NFC	80	1303
75	Williams Andrews-3	Atl.	NFC	81	1301
	Earl Campbell-5	Hou.	AFC	83	1301
77	James Wilder-2	T.B.	NFC	85	1300
78	Thurman Thomas-4	Buf.	AFC	90	1297
79	Mike Pruitt	Cle.	AFC	79	1294
80	Eric Dickerson-6	L.A.-Ind.	N/AFC	87	1288
81	Neal Anderson	Chi.	NFC	89	1275
82	Mark van Eeghen	Oak.	AFC	77	1273
83	Ottis Anderson-4	St.L.	NFC	83	1270
84	Ricky Bell	T.B.	NFC	79	1263
85	Wendell Tyler	S.F.	NFC	84	1262
	Dalton Hilliard	N.O.	NFC	89	1262
87	Delvin Williams	Mia	AFC	78	1258
88	Jim Brown-7	Cle.	NFL	60	1257
89	O.J. Simpson-4	Buf.	AFC	72	1251
90	Franco Harris	Pit.	AFC	75	1246
91	Thurman Thomas-5	Buff.	AFC	89	1244
92	Leroy Kelly	Cle.	NFL	68	1239
	John Riggins-2	Was.	NFC	84	1239
	James Brooks	Cin.	AFC	89	1239
95	Law. McCutcheon	L.A.	NFC	77	1238
96	Eric Dickerson-6	L.A.	NFC	85	1234
97	Gale Sayers	Chi.	NFL	66	1231
98	Craig James	N.E.	AFC	85	1227
99	Lorenzo White	Hou.	AFC	92	1226
100	Marion Butts	S.D.	AFC	90	1225

YARDS PER SCHEDULED GAME

1	O.J. Simpson-1	Buf.	AFC	73	143
2	Jim Brown-1	Cle.	NFL	63	133
3	Walter Payton-1	Chi.	NFC	77	132
	Eric Dickerson-1	L.A.	NFC	84	132
5	O.J. Simpson-2	Buf.	AFC	75	130
6	Jim Brown-2	Cle.	NFL	58	127
7	Earl Campbell-1	Hou.	AFC	80	121
8	Eric Dickerson-2	L.A.	NFC	86	114
9	Eric Dickerson-3	L.A.	NFC	83	113
10	Jim Brown-3	Cle.	NFL	59	111
11	Jim Brown-4	Cle.	NFL	65	110
	Marcus Allen	Raid.	AFC	85	110
13	O.J. Simpson-3	Buf.	AFC	76	107
	Emmitt Smith-1	Dall.	NFC	92	107
15	Earl Campbell-2	Hou.	AFC	79	106
	Barry Foster	Pitt.	AFC	92	106
17	JimTaylor-1	G.B.	NFL	62	105
	Jim Brown-5	Cle.	NFL	60	105
	Walter Payton-2	Chi.	NFC	84	105
20	George Rogers	N.O.	NFC	81	104
	Jim Nance	Bos.	AFL	66	104
	Eric Dickerson-4	Ind.	AFC	88	104
23	Jim Brown-6	Cle.	NFL	64	103
	Tony Dorsett	Dal.	NFC	81	103
25	Spec Sanders	N.Y.	AAFC	47	102
26	Walter Payton-3	Chi.	NFC	79	101
	Jim Brown-7	Cle.	NFL	61	101
	Otis Armstrong	Den.	AFC	74	101
29	Ottis Anderson	St.L.	NFC	79	100
30	Walter Payton-4	Chi.	NFC	76	99
31	William Andrews	Atl.	NFC	83	98
	Emmitt Smith-2	Dall.	NFC	91	98
33	James Wilder	T.B.	NFC	84	97
	Walter Payton-5	Chi.	NFC	85	97
	Barry Sanders-1	Det.	NFC	91	97
36	Steve Van Buren	Phi.	NFL	48	96
37	Wilb. Montgomery-1	Phi.	NFC	79	95
	Joe Morris	NYG	NFC	86	95
	Herschel Walker	Dall.	NFC	88	95
40	Rick Casares	ChiB	NFL	56	94
	Roger Craig	S.F.	NFC	88	94
	Thurman Thomas	Buff.	AFC	92	94
43	Jim Taylor-2	G.B.	NFL	61	93
	Gerald Riggs	Atl.	NFC	84	93
	Curt Warner	Sea.	AFC	86	93
	Christian Okoye	K.C.	AFC	89	93
	Emmitt Smith-3	Dall.	NFC	93	93
47	Jim Taylor-3	G.B.	NFL	60	92
	Charles White	L.A.	NFC	87	92
	Barry Sanders-2	Det.	NFC	89	92
50	Walter Payton-6	Chi.	NFC	80	91
	Mark van Eeghen	Oak.	AFC	77	91
	Earl Campbell-3	Hou.	AFC	78	91
	Curt Warner-2	Sea.	AFC	83	91
54	Billy Sims	Det.	NFC	81	90

AVERAGE YARDS

(Minimum 100 Attempts)

					Att.	Yards	Avg.
1	Beattie Feathers	ChiB	NFL	34	101	1004	9.94
2	Randall Cunningham	Phi.	NFC	90	118	942	7.78
3	Bobby Douglass	Chi	NFC	72	141	948	6.87
4	Joe Perry-1	S.F.	AAFC	49	115	783	6.81
5	Dan Towler-1	L.A.	NFL	51	126	854	6.78
6	Johnny Strzykalski-1	S.F.	AAFC	48	141	915	6.46
7	Keith Lincoln	S.D.	NFL	63	128	826	6.45
8	Mercury Morris	Mia.	AFC	73	149	954	6.40
	Jim Brown-1	Cle.	NFL	63	291	1863	6.40
10	Johnny Strzykalski-2	S.F.	AAFC	47	143	906	6.34
11	Paul Lowe	L.A.	AFL	60	136	855	6.29
12	Dutch Clark	Det.	NFL	34	122	763	6.25
13	Gale Sayers	Chi.	NFL	68	138	856	6.20
	Chet Mutryn-1	Buf.	AAFC	47	140	868	6.20
	Spec Sanders	N.Y.	AAFC	47	231	1432	6.20
16	Marion Motley-1	Cle.	AAFC	48	157	964	6.14
	Buddy Young	N.Y.	AAFC	47	116	712	6.14
18	Marion Motley-2	Cle.	AAFC	47	146	889	6.09
19	Joe Perry-2	S.F.	NFL	58	125	758	6.06
	Joe Perry-3	S.F.	NFL	54	173	1049	6.06
21	O.J. Simpson-1	Buf.	AFC	73	322	2003	6.03
	Ted McKnight	K.C.	AFC	78	104	627	6.03
	Hokie Gajan	N.O.	NFC	84	102	615	6.03
24	Randall Cunningham	Phil.	NFC	89	104	621	5.97
25	Jim Brown-2	Cle.	NFL	60	215	1257	5.94
26	John David Crow	St.L.	NFL	60	183	1071	5.85
	Jim Brown-3	Cle.	NFL	60	215	1257	5.85
28	Steve Van Buren	Phi.	NFL	45	143	832	5.82
29	Marion Motley-3	Cle.	NFL	50	140	810	5.79
30	Dan Towler-2	L.A.	NFL	53	152	879	5.78
	Bill Osmanski	ChiB	NFL	39	121	699	5.78
32	Dan Towler-3	L.A.	NFL	52	156	894	5.73
33	Paul Lowe-2	S.D.	AFL	63	177	1010	5.71
34	Bobby Mitchell	Cle.	NFL	59	131	743	5.67
35	Franco Harris	Pit	AFC	72	188	1055	5.61
	Abner Haynes	Dal.	AFL	60	156	875	5.61
	James Brooks	Cin.	AFC	89	221	1239	5.61
38	Chet Mutryn-2	Buf.	AAFC	48	147	823	5.60
39	Don Calhoun	N.E.	AFC	76	129	721	5.59
40	Eddie Price	NYG	NFL	50	126	703	5.58
	Bo Jackson	L.A.	AFC	90	125	698	5.58
42	Amos Marsh	Dal.	NFL	62	114	802	5.57
43	Eric Dickerson	L.A.	NFC	84	379	2105	5.55
44	Brad Hubbert	S.D.	AFL	67	116	643	5.54
45	O.J. Simpson-2	Buf.	AFC	75	329	1817	5.52
46	Stump Mitchell	St.L.	NFC	85	183	1006	5.50
47	Mack Lee Hill	K.C.	AFL	64	105	576	5.49
	Gerry Ellis	G.B.	NFC	85	104	571	5.49
	Bo Jackson	L.A.	AFC	89	173	950	5.49
50	Swede Hansen	Phi.	NFL	34	147	805	5.48
51	Walter Payton	Chi	NFC	77	339	1852	5.46
	Leroy Kelly	Cle.	NFL	66	209	1141	5.46
53	Timmy Brown	Phi.	NFL	65	148	861	5.45
	Greg Pruitt	Cle.	AFC	78	176	960	5.45
	Mike Garrett	K.C.	AFL	66	147	801	5.45
	Mosi Tatupu	N.E.	AFC	83	106	578	5.45
57	Curtis McClinton	Dal.	AFL	62	111	604	5.44

TOUCHDOWNS

1	John Riggins-1	Was.	NFC	83	24
2	Joe Morris-1	NYG	NFC	85	21
3	Jim Taylor-1	G.B.	NFL	62	19
	Earl Campbell-1	Hou.	AFC	79	19
	Chuck Muncie-1	N.O.	NFC	81	19
6	Spec Sanders	N.Y.	AAFC	47	18
	Eric Dickerson-1	L.A.	NFC	83	18
	George Rogers-1	Was.	NFC	86	18
	Emmitt Smith	Dall.	NFC	92	18
10	Jim Brown-1	Cle.	NFL	58	17
	Jim Brown-2	Cle.	NFL	65	17
12	Lenny Moore	Bal.	NFL	64	16
	Leroy Kelly-1	Cle.	NFL	68	16
	O.J. Simpson-1	Buf.	AFC	75	16
	Pete Banaszek	Oak.	AFC	75	16
	Greg Bell	L.A.	NFC	88	16
	Barry Sanders-1	Det.	NFC	91	16
18	Steve Van Buren-1	Phi.	NFL	45	15
	Jim Taylor-2	G.B.	NFL	61	15
	Leroy Kelly-2	Cle.	NFL	66	15
	Pete Johnson-1	S.D.,Mia	AFC	84	15
	Marcus Allen-1	Raid.	NFC	84	15
	Ickey Woods	Cin.	AFC	88	15
	Greg Bell	L.A.	NFC	89	15
25	Jim Brown-3	Cle.	NFL	59	14
	John David Crow	St.L.	NFL	62	14
	Gale Sayers	Chi.	NFL	65	14
	Franco Harris-1	Pit.	AFC	76	14
	Walter Payton-1	Chi.	NFC	77	14
	David Sims	Sea.	AFC	78	14
	Pete Johnson-2	Cin.	AFC	79	14
	Walter Payton-2	Chi.	NFC	79	14
	Pete Johnson-3	Cin.	AFC	83	14
	John Riggins-2	Was.	NFC	84	14
	Eric Dickerson-2	L.A.	NFC	84	14
	Joe Morris-2	NYG	NFC	86	14
	Eric Dickerson-3	Ind.	AFC	88	14
	Barry Sanders-2	Det.	NFC	89	14
	Ottis Anderson	NYG	NFC	89	14
	Derrick Fenner	Sea.	AFC	90	14
	Cleveland Gary	L.A.	NFC	90	14
	Reggie Cobb	T.B.	NFC	92	14
43	Steve Van Buren-2	Phi.	NFL	47	13
	Paul Hornung	G.B.	NFL	60	13
	Jim Brown-4	Cle.	NFL	62	13
	Cookie Gilchrist-1	Buf.	AFL	62	13
	Abner Haynes	Dal.	AFL	62	13
	Chuck Foreman-1	Min.	NFC	75	13
	Chuck Foreman-2	Min.	NFC	76	13
	Walter Payton-3	Chi.	NFC	76	13
	Earl Campbell-2	Hou.	AFC	78	13
	Earl Campbell-3	Hou.	AFC	80	13
	Billy Sims	Det.	NFC	80	13
	John Riggins-3	Was.	NFC	81	13
	George Rogers-2	N.O.	NFC	81	13
	Billy Sims-2	Det.	NFC	81	13
	Curt Warner-1	Sea.	AFC	83	13
	James Wilder	T.B.	NFC	84	13
	Gerald Riggs	Atl.	NFC	84	13
	Curt Warner-2	Sea	AFC	86	13
	Dalton Hilliard	N.O.	NFC	89	13
	Barry Sanders-3	Det.	NFC	90	13
	Terry Allen	Minn.	NFC	92	13

SINGLE SEASON LEADERS
RECEIVING

RECEPTIONS

1	Sterling Sharpe-1	G.B.	NFC	93	112
2	Sterling Sharpe	G.B.	NFC	92	108
3	Art Monk-1	Was.	NFC	84	106
4	Charley Hennigan-1	Hou.	AFL	64	101
5	Lionel Taylor-1	Den.	AFL	61	100
	Jerry Rice-1	S.F.	NFC	90	100
	Haywood Jeffires-1	Hou.	AFC	91	100
8	Jerry Rice-2	S.F.	NFC	93	98
9	Todd Christensen-1	Raid.	AFC	86	95
10	Johnny Morris	Chi.	NFL	64	93
	Al Toon-1	NYJ	AFC	88	93
	Michael Irvin-1	Dall.	NFC	91	93
	Andre Rison-1	Atl.	NFC	92	93
14	Lionel Taylor-2	Den.	AFL	60	92
	Todd Christensen	Raid.	AFC	83	92
16	Art Monk-2	Was.	NFC	85	91
	J.T. Smith-1	St.L.	NFC	87	91
18	Sterling Sharpe-3	G.B.	NFC	89	90
	Drew Hill	Hou.	AFC	91	90
	Haywood Jeffires-2	Hou.	AFC	92	90
21	Kellen Winslow	S.D.	AFC	80	89
	Ozzie Newsome-1	Cle.	AFC	83	89
	Ozzie Newsome-2	Cle.	AFC	84	89
24	Rickey Young	Min.	NFC	78	88
	Kellen Winslow-2	S.D.	AFC	81	88
	Kellen Winslow-3	S.D.	AFC	83	88
	Andre Reed-1	Buff.	AFC	89	88
	Michael Irvin-2	Dall.	NFC	93	88
29	Lionel James	S.D.	AFC	85	86
	Jerry Rice-3	S.F.	NFC	86	86
	Mark Clayton	Mia.	AFC	88	86
	Henry Ellard	L.A.	NFC	88	86
	Mark Carrier	T.B.	NFC	89	86
	Art Monk-3	Wash.	NFC	89	86
	Andre Rison-2	Atl.	NFC	93	86
	Cris Carter	Minn.	NFC	93	86
37	Lionel Taylor-3	Den.	AFL	75	85
	Dwight Clark-1	S.F.	NFC	81	85
	James Wilder	T.B.	NFC	84	85
	Al Toon-2	NYJ	AFC	86	85
	Eric Martin	N.O.	NFC	88	85
	Reggie Langhorne	Ind.	AFC	93	85
43	Tom Fears	L.A.	NFL	50	84
	Stanley Morgan	N.E.	AFC	86	84
	Jerry Rice-4	S.F.	NFC	92	84
	Anthony Miller	S.D.	AFC	93	84
47	Earl Cooper	S.F.	NFC	80	83
	Ted Brown	Min.	NFC	81	83
	Tim Smith	Hou.	AFC	83	83
	J.T. Smith-2	Phx.	NFC	88	83
51	Charley Hennigan-2	Hou.	AFL	61	82
	Joe Washington	Bal.	AFC	79	82
	Dwight Clark-2	S.F.	NFC	80	82
	John Jefferson	S.D.	AFC	80	82
	Todd Christensen-3	Raid.	AFC	85	82
	Jerry Rice-5	S.F.	NFC	89	82
	Andre Rison-3	Atl.	NFC	90	82
	Marv Cook	N.E.	AFC	91	82
	Curtis Duncan	Hou.	AFC	92	82
60	Roger Craig-2	S.F.	NFC	86	81
	Keith Jackson	Phil.	NFC	88	81
	Keith Byars	Phi.	NFC	90	81
	Andre Rison-4	Atl.	NFC	91	81
	Andre Reed-2	Buff.	AFC	91	81
	Shannon Sharpe	Den.	AFC	93	81

YARDS

1	Charley Hennigan-1	Hou.	AFL	61	1746
2	Lance Alworth-1	S.D.	AFL	65	1602
3	Jerry Rice-1	S.F.	NFC	86	1570
4	Roy Green-1	St.L.	NFC	84	1555
5	Charley Hennigan-2	Hou.	AFL	64	1546
6	Michael Irvin-1	Dall.	NFC	91	1523
7	Jerry Rice-2	S.F.	NFC	93	1503
8	Jerry Rice-3	S.F.	NFC	90	1502
9	Crazy Legs Hirsch	L.A.	NFL	51	1495
10	Stanley Morgan	N.E.	AFC	86	1491
11	Jerry Rice-4	S.F.	NFC	89	1483
12	Bill Groman	Hou.	AFL	60	1473
13	Sterling Sharpe-1	G.B.	NFC	92	1461
14	Bobby Mitchell	Was.	NFL	63	1436
15	Don Maynard-1	NYJ	AFL	67	1434
16	Sterling Sharpe-2	G.B.	NFC	89	1423
17	Mark Carrier	T.B.	NFC	89	1422
18	Henry Ellard-1	L.A.	NFC	88	1414
19	Mike Quick	Phi.	NFC	83	1409
20	Michael Irvin-2	Dall.	NFC	92	1396
21	John Stallworth	Pit.	AFC	84	1395
22	Mark Clayton	Mia.	AFC	84	1389
23	Bobby Mitchell-2	Was.	NFL	62	1384
24	Lance Alworth-2	S.D.	AFL	66	1383
25	Henry Ellard-2	L.A.	NFC	89	1382
26	Art Monk-1	Was.	NFC	84	1372
27	Art Powell-1	Oak.	AFL	64	1361
	James Lofton-1	G.B.	NFC	84	1361
29	Alfred Jenkins	Atl.	NFC	81	1358
30	Carlos Carson	K.C.	AFC	83	1351
31	Dave Parks	S.F.	NFL	65	1344
32	John Jefferson	S.D.	AFC	80	1340
	Gary Clark-1	Wash.	NFC	91	1340
34	Michael Irvin-3	Dall.	NFC	93	1330
35	Mark Duper-1	Mia.	AFC	86	1313
36	Lance Alworth-3	S.D.	AFL	68	1312
	Andre Reed	Buff.	AFC	89	1312
38	Mark Duper-2	Mia.	AFC	84	1306
	Jerry Rice-5	S.F.	NFC	88	1306
40	Art Powell-2	Oak.	AFL	63	1304
41	James Lofton-2	G.B.	NFC	83	1300
42	Raymond Berry	Bal.	NFL	60	1298
43	Otis Taylor	K.C.	AFL	66	1297
	Don Maynard-2	NYJ	AFL	68	1297
45	Buddy Dial	Pit.	NFL	63	1295
46	James Lofton-3	G.B.	NFC	81	1294
	Henry Ellard-3	L.A.	NFC	90	1294
48	Kellen Winslow	S.D.	AFC	80	1290
49	Steve Largent-1	Sea.	AFC	85	1287
50	Sterling Sharpe-3	G.B.	NFC	93	1274
51	Eddie Brown	Cin.	AFC	88	1273
52	Pat Studstill	Det.	NFL	66	1266
53	Don Maynard-3	NYJ	AFL	60	1265
	Ben Hawkins	Phi.	NFL	67	1265
	Gary Clark-2	Was.	NFC	86	1265
56	Warren Wells	Oak.	AFL	69	1260
57	Anthony Miller	S.D.	AFC	89	1252
58	Todd Christensen	Raid.	AFC	83	1247
	Mike Quick	Phi.	NFC	85	1247
60	Frank Lewis	Buf.	AFC	81	1244
	Steve Watson	Den.	AFC	81	1244
62	Andre Rison-1	Atl.	NFC	93	1242
63	Steve Largent-2	Sea.	AFC	79	1237
64	Webster Slaughter	Clev.	AFC	89	1236
65	Lionel Taylor	Den.	AFL	60	1235
	Lance Alworth-4	S.D.	AFL	64	1235
67	Bob Hayes	Dal.	NFL	66	1232
68	Billy Howton-1	G.B.	NFL	52	1231
69	Gary Clark-3	Wash.	NFC	89	1229
70	Roy Green-2	St.L.	NFC	83	1227
71	James Lofton-4	G.B.	NFC	80	1226
	Art Monk-2	Was.	NFC	85	1226
73	Charlie Brown	Was.	NFC	83	1225
	Anthony Carter	Minn.	NFC	88	1225
75	Steve Largent-3	Sea.	AFC	79	1224
76	Don Maynard-4	NYJ	AFL	65	1218
77	Bob Boyd	L.A.	NFL	54	1212
78	Don Hutson	G.B.	NFL	42	1211
	Tim McGee	Cin.	AFC	89	1211
80	Homer Jones	NYG	NFL	67	1209
81	Andre Rison-2	Atl.	NFC	90	1208
83	Lance Alworth-5	S.D.	AFL	63	1206
	Jerry Rice-6	S.F.	NFC	91	1206
84	Jackie Smith	St.L.	NFL	67	1205
85	Jerry Rice-7	S.F.	NFC	92	1201
86	Johnny Morris	Chi	NFL	64	1200
87	Wes Chandler	S.D.	AFC	85	1199
88	Pete Retzlaff	Phi.	NFL	65	1190

YARDS PER SCHEDULED GAME

1	Charley Hennigan-1	Hou.	AFL	61	125
	Crazy Legs Hirsch	L.A.	NFL	51	125
3	Wes Chandler	S.D.	AFC	82	115
4	Lance Alworth-1	S.D.	AFL	65	114
5	Charley Hennigan-2	Hou.	AFL	64	110
	Don Hutson-1	G.B.	NFL	42	110
7	Raymond Berry	Bal.	NFL	60	108
8	Jim Benton-1	Cle.	NFL	45	107
9	Bill Groman-1	Hou.	AFL	60	105
10	Billy Howton-1	G.B.	NFL	52	103
	Bobby Mitchell-1	Was.	NFL	63	103
12	Don Maynard-1	NYJ	AFL	67	102
13	Bob Boyd	L.A.	NFL	54	101
	Dwight Clark	S.F.	NFC	54	101
15	Billy Howton-2	G.B.	NFL	56	99
	Bobby Mitchell-2	Was.	NFL	62	99
	Lance Alworth-2	S.D.	AFL	66	99
18	Jerry Rice-1	S.F.	NFC	86	98
19	Art Powell-1	Oak.	AFL	64	97
	Roy Green	St.L.	NFC	84	97
21	Dave Parks	S.F.	NFL	65	96
22	Michael Irvin-1	Dall.	NFC	91	95
23	Harlon Hill-1	ChiB	NFL	56	94
	Lance Alworth-3	S.D.	AFL	68	94
	Harlon Hill-2	ChiB	NFL	54	94
	Jerry Rice-2	S.F.	NFC	90	94
	Jerry Rice-3	S.F.	NFC	93	94
28	Art Powell	NYT	AFL	63	93
	Tom Fears-1	L.A.	NFL	50	93
	Otis Taylor	K.C.	AFL	66	93
	Don Maynard-2	NYJ	AFL	68	93
	Buddy Dial	Pit.	NFL	63	93
	Jerry Rice-4	S.F.	NFC	89	93
34	Del Shofner-1	L.A.	NFL	58	91
	Sterling Sharpe-1	G.B.	NFC	92	91
36	Pat Studstill	Det.	NFL	66	90
	Don Maynard-3	NYJ	AFL	60	90
	Ben Hawkins	Phi.	NFL	67	90
	Warren Wells	Oak.	AFL	69	90
40	Jim Benton-2	L.A.	NFL	46	89
	Sterling Sharpe-2	G.B.	NFC	89	89
	Mark Carrier	T.B.	NFC	89	89
43	Lionel Taylor-1	Den.	AFL	69	88
	Lance Alworth-4	S.D.	AFL	64	88
	Bob Hayes	Dal.	NFL	66	88
	Mike Quick	Phi.	NFC	83	88
	Henry Ellard	L.A.	NFC	88	88
48	Pete Pihos	Phi.	NFL	53	87
	Don Hutson-2	G.B.	NFL	44	87
	Don Maynard-4	NYJ	AFL	65	87
	Mark Clayton	Mia.	AFC	84	87
	John Stallworth	Pit.	AFC	84	87
	Michael Irvin-2	Dall.	NFC	92	87

AVERAGE YARDS

(Minimum 400 Yards)

					Rec.	Yards	Avg.
1	Don Currivan	Bos.	NFL	47	24	782	32.6
2	Bucky Pope	L.A.	NFL	64	25	786	31.4
3	Billy Cannon	Oak.	AFL	66	14	436	31.1
4	Ray McLean-1	ChiB	NFL	42	19	571	30.1
5	Mel Gray	St.L.	NFC	71	18	534	29.7
6	Bobby Duckworth	S.D.	AFC	84	25	715	28.6
7	Ray Renfro	Cle.	NFL	57	21	589	28.0
8	Jimmy Orr-1	Pit.	NFL	58	33	910	27.6
9	Jesse Hester	Raid.	AFC	86	23	632	27.5
10	Andy Farkas	Was.	NFL	39	16	437	27.3
	Homer Jones-1	NYG	NFL	65	26	709	27.3
12	Elbert Dubenion	Buf.	AFL	64	42	1139	27.1
13	Frank Liebel	NYG	NFL	45	22	593	27.0
14	Leonard Thompson	Det.	NFC	80	19	511	26.9
15	Warren Wells	Oak.	AFL	69	47	1260	26.8
	Buddy Dial-1	Pit.	NFL	69	16	428	26.8
17	Billy Van Heusen	Den.	AFC	74	16	421	26.3
	Earl McCullough	Det.	NFC	71	21	552	26.3
	Jack Snow	L.A.	NFL	67	28	735	26.3
20	Art Graham	Bos.	AFL	63	21	550	26.2
	Bob Hayes-1	Dal.	NFC	70	34	889	26.2
22	Ron Sellers	Bos.	AFL	69	27	705	26.1
23	Mervyn Fernandez	Raid.	AFC	88	31	805	26.0
	Willie Anderson	L.A.	NFC	89	44	1146	26.0
25	Roger Carr	Bal.	AFC	76	43	1112	25.9
26	Theo Bell	Pit.	AFC	80	29	748	25.8
27	Jimmy Orr-2	Bal.	NFL	68	29	743	25.6
	Ken Kavanaugh	ChiB	NFL	47	32	818	25.6
29	Cloyce Box	Det.	NFL	53	16	403	25.2
30	Paul Warfield	Mia.	AFC	70	28	703	25.1
31	Harlon Hill-1	ChiB	NFL	54	45	1124	25.0
32	Don Hutson	G.B.	NFL	39	34	846	24.9
33	Wesley Walker-1	NYJ	AFC	79	23	569	24.7
	Red Mack	Pit.	NFL	63	25	618	24.7
	Homer Jones-2	NYG	NFL	67	49	1209	24.7
36	Tony Bowa	P-P	NFL	43	17	419	24.6
37	Wesley Walker-2	NYJ	AFC	78	48	1169	24.4
38	Elbie Nickel-1	Pit.	NFL	49	26	633	24.3
	Walter White	K.C.	AFC	75	23	559	24.3
	Buddy Dial-2	Pit.	NFL	60	40	972	24.3
	Anthony Carter	Min.	NFC	87	38	922	24.3
42	Rick Upchurch	Den.	AFC	75	18	436	24.2
	Ray McLean-2	ChiB	NFL	43	18	435	24.2
	Cliff Branch	Oak.	AFC	76	46	1111	24.2
45	Roy Jefferson	Pit.	NFL	66	32	772	24.1
	Stanley Morgan	N.E.	AFC	78	34	820	24.1
	Rod Barksdale	Raid.	AFC	86	18	434	24.1
48	Harlon Hill-2	ChiB	NFL	56	47	1128	24.0
	Bob Hayes-2	Dal.	NFC	71	35	840	24.0
	Elbie Nickel-2	Pit.	NFL	50	22	527	24.0
	Eddie Brown	Cin.	AFC	88	53	1273	24.0

TOUCHDOWNS

1	Jerry Rice-1	S.F.	NFC	87	22
2	Mark Clayton-1	Mia.	AFC	84	18
3	Don Hutson	G.B.	NFL	42	17
	Crazy Legs Hirsch	L.A.	NFL	51	17
	Bill Groman	Hou.	AFL	61	17
	Jerry Rice-2	S.F.	NFC	89	17
7	Art Powell-1	NYT	AFL	63	16
8	Cloyce Box	Det.	NFL	52	15
	Sonny Randle	St.L.	NFL	60	15
	Jerry Rice-3	S.F.	NFC	86	15
	Jerry Rice-4	S.F.	NFC	93	15
	Andre Rison	Atl.	NFC	93	15
13	Mal Kutner	ChiC	NFL	48	14
	Alyn Beals	S.F.	AAFC	48	14
	Raymond Berry	Bal.	NFL	59	14
	Art Powell-2	NYT	AFL	60	14
	Frank Clarke	Dal.	NFL	62	14
	Lance Alworth-1	S.D.	AFL	65	14
	Don Maynard	NYJ	AFL	65	14
	Warren Wells	Oak.	AFL	69	14
	Roy Green	St.L.	NFC	83	14
	Mark Clayton-2	Mia.	AFC	88	14
	Jerry Rice-5	S.F.	NFC	91	14
24	Ken Kavanaugh	ChiB	NFL	47	13
	Billy Howton	G.B.	NFL	52	13
	Tommy McDonald-1	Phi.	NFL	60	13
	Tommy McDonald-2	Phi.	NFL	61	13
	Terry Barr	Det.	NFL	63	13
	Gary Collins	Cle.	NFL	63	13
	Lance Alworth-2	S.D.	AFL	64	13
	Lance Alworth-3	S.D.	AFL	66	13
	Bob Hayes	Dal.	NFL	66	13
	Homer Jones	NYG	NFL	67	13
	Dick Gordon	Chi	NFC	70	13
	Harold Jackson	L.A.	NFC	73	13
	Cliff Branch	Oak.	AFC	74	13
	John Jefferson-1	S.D.	AFC	78	13
	John Jefferson-2	S.D.	AFC	80	13
	Alfred Jenkins	Atl.	NFC	81	13
	Steve Watson	Den.	AFC	81	13
	Mike Quick	Phi.	NFC	83	13
	Jerry Rice-6	S.F.	NFC	90	13
	Sterling Sharpe	G.B.	NFC	92	13

SINGLE SEASON LEADERS

PUNT RETURNS

1	Danny Reece-1	T.B.	NFC	79	70
2	Fulton Walker-1	Raid.	AFC	85	62
3	Greg Pruitt-1	Raid.	AFC	83	58
	Leo Lewis	Min.	NFC	88	58
5	Eddie Brown-1	Was.	NFC	77	57
	Danny Reece-2	T.B.	NFC	80	57
	Jeff Fisher-1	Chi.	NFC	84	57
	Lew Barnes	Chi.	NFC	86	57
9	Eddie Brown-2	L.A.	NFC	79	56
10	Rolland Lawrence-1	Atl.	NFC	76	54
	James Jones	Dal.	NFC	80	54
	Wally Henry	Phi.	NFC	81	54
	Gary Allen	Dal.	NFC	84	54
14	Alvin Hammond-1	L.A.	NFC	70	53
	Larry Jones	Was.	NFC	75	53
	Louis Lipps	Pit.	AFC	84	53
	Greg Pruitt-2	Raid.	AFC	84	53
	Phil McConkey-1	NYG	NFC	85	53
19	Jackie Wallace	L.A.	NFC	78	52
	Leon Bright	NYG	NFC	81	52
	Bobby Martin	Det.	NFC	81	52
22	Rolland Lawrence-2	Atl.	NFC	77	51
	Rick Upchurch-1	Den.	AFC	77	51
	Butch Johnson-1	Dal.	NFC	78	51
25	Butch Johnson-2	Dal.	NFC	77	50
	J.T. Smith-1	K.C.	AFC	79	50
	J.T. Smith-2	K.C.	AFC	81	50
28	Mike Nelms-1	Was.	NFC	84	49
	Fulton Walker-2	Raid.	AFC	86	49
	Tim Brown	Raid.	AFC	88	49
	Gerald McNeil	Clev.	AFC	89	49
32	Neal Colzie-1	Oak.	AFC	75	48
	Eddie Brown-3	Was.	NFC	76	48
	Ira Matthews	Oak.	AFC	80	48
	Mike Nelms-2	Was.	NFC	80	48
36	Manfred Moore	Min.	NFC	77	47
	Neal Colzie-2	Oak.	AFC	78	47
	Carl Roaches	Hou.	AFC	80	47
39	Rodger Bird	Oak.	AFL	67	46
	Larry Marshall	Phi.	NFC	77	46
	Mike Fuller	S.D.	AFC	79	46
	LeRoy Irvin	L.A.	NFC	80	46
	Butch Johnson-3	Atl.	NFC	83	46
	Phil McConkey-2	NYG	NFC	84	46
	Dave Meggett	NYG	NFC	89	46
46	Mike Haynes	N.E.	AFC	76	45
	Butch Johnson-4	Dal.	NFC	76	45
	Theo Bell	Pit.	AFC	79	45
	Mike Nelms-3	Was.	NFC	81	45
	Dana McLemore	S.F.	NFC	84	45
	Brian Mitchell	Wash.	NFC	91	45
52	Nesby Glasgow	Bal.	AFC	79	44
	Danny Reese-3	T.B.	NFC	78	44
	Vai Sikahema-1	St.L.	NFC	87	44
	John Taylor	S.F.	NFC	88	44
	Kelvin Martin	Dal.	NFC	88	44
	Eric Metcalf	Clev.	AFC	92	44

YARDS

1	Fulton Walker	Raid.	AFC	85	692
2	Greg Pruitt-1	Raid.	AFC	83	666
3	Louis Lipps-1	Pit.	AFC	84	656
4	Neal Colzie-1	Oak.	AFC	75	655
5	Rick Upchurch-1	Den.	AFC	77	653
6	Eddie Brown-1	Was.	NFC	76	646
7	Jackie Wallace	L.A.	NFC	78	618
8	LeRoy Irvin	L.A.	NFC	81	615
9	Rodger Bird	Oak.	AFL	67	612
	J.T. Smith-1	K.C.	AFC	79	612
11	Billy Johnson-1	Hou.	AFC	75	610
12	Mike Haynes	N.E.	AFC	76	608
13	Brian Mitchell	Wash.	NFC	91	600
14	Charley Rogers-1	Fra.	NFL	27	589
15	Dave Meggett	NYG	NFC	89	582
16	J.T. Smith-2	K.C.	AFC	80	581
17	Lynn Swann	Pit.	AFC	74	577
18	John Taylor	S.F.	NFC	88	556
19	Billy Grimes	G.B.	NFL	50	555
20	Vai Sikahema-1	St.L.	NFC	87	550
	Leo Lewis	Min.	NFC	88	550
22	James Jones	Dal.	NFC	80	548
23	Billy Johnson-2	Hou.	AFC	77	539
24	Rick Upchurch-2	Den.	AFC	76	536
25	Kelvin Martin	Dall.	NFC	92	532
26	Charley Rogers-2	Fra.	NFL	28	528
	J.T. Smith-3	K.C.	AFC	81	528
28	Vai Sikahema-2	St.L.	NFC	86	522
29	Dana McLemore	S.F.	NFC	84	521
30	Irving Fryar	N.E.	AFC	85	520
31	Mack Herron	N.E.	AFC	74	517
32	Bruce Taylor	S.F.	NFC	70	516
33	Jeff Fisher-1	Chi.	NFC	81	509
34	Vai Sikahema-3	Phil.	NFC	92	503
35	Tyrone Hughes	N.O.	NFC	93	503
36	Henry Ellard	L.A.	NFC	85	501
37	Walter Stanley	Det.	NFC	89	496
	Gerald McNeil	Clev.	AFC	89	496
39	Rick Upchurch-3	Den.	AFC	78	493
40	Mike Nelms-1	Was.	NFC	81	492
	Jeff Fisher-2	Chi.	NFC	84	492
42	Butch Atkinson	Oak.	AFL	68	490
43	Emlen Tunnell	NYG	NFL	51	489
	Butch Johnson	Dal.	NFC	76	489
	Larry Marshall	Phi.	NFC	77	489
	Billy Johnson-3	Atl.	NFC	83	489
47	Mike Nelms-2	Was.	NFC	80	487
48	Ron Smith	Oak.	AFC	74	486
49	Lew Barnes	Chi.	NFC	86	482
50	Greg Pruitt-2	Raid.	AFC	84	473
51	Gerald Willhite	Den.	AFC	86	468
52	Dave Meggett	NYG	NFC	90	467
53	Tim Brown	L.A.Rd.	AFC	93	465
54	Speedy Duncan	S.D.	AFL	65	464
55	Eric Metcalf	Clev.	AFC	93	464
56	Pat Studstill	Det.	NFL	62	457
57	Virgil Livers	Chi.	NFC	75	456
58	Jack Ernst	Port.	NFL	26	453
59	Eddie Brown-2	Was.	NFC	77	452
60	Robbie Martin	Det.	NFC	81	450
61	Neal Colzie-2	Oak.	AFC	76	448
	Mike Fuller	S.D.	AFC	79	448
63	Gary Allen	Dal.	NFC	84	446
	Leo Lewis	Minn.	NFC	89	446
65	Stump Mitchell	St.L.	NFC	81	445
66	Tim Brown	Raid.	AFC	88	444
67	Tony Green	Was.	NFC	78	443
	Robbie Martin	Ind.	AFC	85	443
69	Phil McConkey	NYG	NFC	85	442
70	Fulton Walker-2	Raid.	AFC	86	440
71	Two Bits Homan	Fra.	NFL	29	439
72	Louis Lipps-2	Pit.	AFC	85	437

AVERAGE RETURNS

(Minimum — 1 Return per Game)

					Ret.	Yds.	Avg.
1	Ernie Steele	Phi.	NFL	42	10	264	26.40
2	Herb Rich	Bal.	NFL	50	12	276	23.00
3	Jack Christiansen-1	Det.	NFL	52	15	322	21.47
4	Dick Christy	NYT	AFL	61	18	383	21.28
5	Rex Baumgardner	Buf.	AAFC	48	16	336	21.00
6	Red Cochran	ChiC	NFL	49	15	314	20.93
7	Jerome Davis	ChiC	NFL	48	16	334	20.88
8	Bob Hayes	Dal.	NFL	68	15	312	20.80
9	Frank Sinkwich	Det.	NFL	43	11	228	20.73
10	Paddy Driscoll	ChiC	NFL	21	8	154	19.25
	Buddy Young	NYY	NFL	51	12	231	19.25
12	Billy Grimes	G.B.	NFL	50	29	555	19.14
13	Jack Christiansen-2	Det.	NFL	51	18	343	19.06
14	Ollie Matson	ChiC	NFL	55	13	245	18.85
15	Lemar Parrish	Cin.	AFC	74	18	338	18.78
16	Chuck Fenenbock	L.A.	AAFC	46	16	299	18.69
17	Woodley Lewis	L.A.	NFL	52	19	351	18.47
18	Frank Seno	Bos.	NFL	47	12	213	17.75

KICKOFF RETURNS

1	Drew Hill-1	L.A.	NFC	81	60
2	Bruce Harper-1	NYJ	AFC	78	55
	Bruce Harper-2	NYJ	AFC	79	55
	David Turner	Cin.	AFC	79	55
	Stump Mitchell	St.L.	NFC	81	55
6	Eddie Payton-1	Min.	NFC	80	53
	Buster Rhymes	Min.	NFC	85	53
8	Eric Metcalf	Cle.	AFC	90	52
9	Zachary Dixon	Sea.	AFC	83	51
10	Nesby Glasgow	Bal.	AFC	79	50
	Clarence Verdin	Ind.	AFC	93	50
12	Bruce Harper-3	NYJ	AFC	80	49
	Herman Hunter-1	Det.	NFC	86	49
14	Mike Martin	Cin.	AFC	85	48
	Stephen Starring	N.E.	AFC	85	48
	Phil Freeman	T.B.	NFC	85	48
	Herman Hunter-2	Phi.	NFC	85	48
18	Odell Barry	Den.	AFL	64	47
	Larry Jones	Was.	NFC	75	47
	Reggie Smith	Atl.	NFC	81	47
	Gerald McNeil	Cle.	AFC	86	47
	James Dixon	Dall.	NFC	89	47
	Ron Brown	L.A.	NFC	89	47
24	Chuck Latourette	St.L.	NFL	68	46
	Dave Hampton	G.B.	NFC	71	46
26	Bobby Jancik	Atl.	NFL	68	45
	Tony Nathan	Mia.	AFC	79	45
	Lorenzo Hampton	Mia.	AFC	86	45
29	Jimmy Edwards	Min.	NFC	79	44
	Steve Odom-1	GB,NYG	NFC	79	44
	Gary Davis	T.B.	NFC	80	44
	Cle Montgomery	Cin.	AFC	80	44
	Herschel Walker	Min.	NFC	90	44
	Rod Woodson	Pitt.	AFC	91	44
35	Ron Smith-1	Atl.	NFL	66	43
	Mercury Morris	Mia.	AFL	69	43
	Margene Adkins	N.O.	NFC	72	43
	Dino Hall	Cle.	AFC	79	43
	Drew Hill-2	L.A.	NFC	80	43
	Ron Fellows	Dal.	NFC	83	43
	Lionel James	S.D.	AFC	84	43
	Tim McGee	Cin.	AFC	86	43
	Terance Mathis	NYJ	AFC	90	43
44	Steve Odom-2	G.B.	NFC	75	42
	Bruce Harper-4	NYJ	AFC	77	42
	Ricky Smith	N.E.	AFC	83	42
	Mike Nelms	Was.	NFC	84	42
	Qadry Ismail	Minn.	NFC	93	42
49	Noland Smith	K.C.	AFL	67	41
	Mack Herron	N.E.	AFC	73	41
	Marshall Johnson	Bal.	AFC	78	41
	Roy Green	St.L.	NFC	79	41
	James Owens	S.F.	NFC	79	41
	Jimmy Rogers	N.O.	NFC	80	41
	Harlan Huckleby	G.B.	NFC	83	41
	Ken Jenkins	Was.	NFC	85	41
	Tim Brown	Raid.	AFC	88	41
	Mel Gray	Det.	NFC	90	41
	Dexter Carter	S.F.	NFC	90	41

YARDS

1	Buster Rhymes	Min.	NFC	85	1345
2	Bobby Jancik	Hou.	AFL	63	1317
3	Dave Hampton	G.B.	NFC	71	1314
4	Stump Mitchell	St.L.	NFC	81	1292
5	Bruce Harper-1	NYJ	AFC	78	1280
6	Odell Berry	Den.	AFL	64	1245
7	Chuck Latourette	St.L.	NFL	68	1237
8	Eddie Payton	Min.	NFC	80	1184
9	James Dixon	Dall.	NFC	89	1181
10	Zachary Dixon	Sea.	AFC	83	1171
11	Drew Hill	L.A.	NFC	81	1170
12	Bruce Harper-2	NYJ	AFC	79	1158
13	Abe Woodson	S.F.	NFL	62	1157
14	David Turner	Cin.	AFC	79	1149
15	Noland Smith	K.C.	AFL	67	1148
16	Reggie Smith	Atl.	NFC	81	1143
17	Mercury Morris	Mia.	AFC	69	1136
18	Nesby Glasgow	Bal.	AFC	79	1126
19	Mike Martin	Cin.	AFC	85	1104
20	Jimmy Edwards	Min.	NFC	79	1103
21	Mike Nelms	Was.	NFC	81	1099
22	Tim Brown	Raid.	AFC	88	1098
23	Mack Herron	N.E.	AFC	73	1092
24	Larry Jones	Was.	NFC	75	1086
25	Phil Freeman	T.B.	NFL	85	1085
26	Rick Upchurch	Den.	AFC	75	1084
27	Bruce Harper-3	NYJ	AFC	80	1070
28	Deion Sanders	Atl.	NFC	92	1067
29	Eric Metcalf	Cle.	AFC	90	1052
30	Clarence Verdin	Ind.	AFC	93	1050
31	Herman Hunter-1	Phi.	NFC	85	1047
32	Bruce Harper-4	NYJ	AFC	77	1035
33	Steve Odom-1	G.B.	NFC	75	1034
34	Alvin Haymond	L.A.	NFC	70	1022
35	Margene Adkins	N.O.	NFC	72	1020
	Lorenzo Hampton	Mia.	AFC	85	1020
37	Ken Jenkins	Was.	NFC	85	1018
38	Mel Renfro	Dal.	NFL	64	1017
39	Tony Nathan	Mia.	AFC	79	1016
40	Ron Smith-1	Atl.	NFL	66	1013
41	Stephen Starring	N.E.	AFC	85	1012
42	Herb Mul-Key	Was.	NFC	73	1011
43	Tim McGee	Cin	AFC	86	1007
	Herman Hunter-2	Det.	NFC	86	1007
45	Mel Gray	Det.	NFC	92	1006
46	Roy Green	St.L.	NFC	79	1005
47	James Owens	S.F.	NFC	79	1002
48	Horace Ivory	N.E.	AFC	80	992
49	Clarence Childs	NYG	NFL	64	987
50	Kermit Alexander	SF	NFL	66	984
51	Rod Woodson	Pitt.	AFC	89	982
52	Ron Smith-2	Atl.	NFL	67	976
53	Bo Roberson	Oak.	AFL	64	975
54	Max Anderson	Buf.	AFL	68	971
55	Ron Brown	L.A.	NFC	89	968
56	Herschel Walker	Min.	NFC	90	966
57	Fulton Walker	Mia.	AFC	83	962
58	Lou Piccone	NYJ	AFC	74	961
59	Terry Metcalf	St.L.	NFC	75	960
60	Lionel James	S.D.	AFC	84	959
61	Charley Mitchell	Den.	AFL	63	954
62	Gary Davis	T.B.	NFC	80	951
63	Steve Odom-2	GB,NYG	NFC	79	949
	James Brooks	S.D.	AFC	79	949

AVERAGE RETURNS

(Minimum — 1 Return per Game)

					Ret.	Yds.	Avg.
1	Travis Williams	G.B.	NFL	67	18	739	41.06
2	Gale Sayers-1	Chi.	NFL	67	16	603	37.69
3	Ollie Matson-1	ChiC	NFL	58	14	479	35.50
4	Speedy Duncan	Bal.	AFC	70	20	707	35.35
5	Lynn Chandnois-1	Pit	NFL	52	17	599	35.24
6	Preston Pearson	Bal.	NFL	68	15	527	35.13
7	Joe Arenas	S.F.	NFL	53	16	551	34.44
8	Tom Watkins	Det.	NFL	65	17	584	34.35
9	Vitamin Smith	L.A.	NFL	50	22	742	33.73
10	Bobby Williams	Det.	NFL	69	17	563	33.12
11	Tom Moore	G.B.	NFL	60	12	397	33.08
12	Chet Mutryn	Buf.	AAFC	47	21	691	32.90
13	Duriel Harris	Mia.	AFC	76	17	559	32.88
14	Ron Brown	L.A.	NFC	85	28	918	32.79
15	Cecil Turner	Chi.	NFC	70	23	752	32.70
16	Lynn Chandnois-2	Pit.	NFL	51	23	752	32.70
17	Abe Woodson-1	S.F.	NFL	63	29	935	32.24
18	Tom Willson	L.A.	NFL	56	15	477	31.80
19	Gary Ballman	Pit.	NFL	63	22	698	31.73
20	Walter Payton	Chi.	NFC	75	14	444	31.71
21	Jack Salscheider	NYG	NFL	49	15	474	31.60
22	Gale Sayers-2	Chi.	NFL	65	21	660	31.43
23	Frank Zeno	ChiC	NFL	46	13	408	31.38
24	Abe Woodson-2	S.F.	NFL	62	37	1157	31.27
25	Ron Hall	Hou.	AFL	60	19	594	31.26
26	Gale Sayers-3	Chi.	NFL	66	23	718	31.22
27	Ollie Matson-2	ChiC	NFL	52	20	624	31.20
28	Terry Metcalf	St.L.	NFC	74	20	623	31.15
29	Ray Clayborn	N.E.	AFC	77	28	869	31.04
30	Lenny Lyles	S.F.	NFL	60	19	526	30.94
31	Frank Minini	ChiB	NFL	48	12	370	30.83
32	Ron Smith	Chi.	NFC	72	30	924	30.80
33	Alvin Haymond	Bal.	NFL	65	20	614	30.70
34	Bobby Humphery	NYJ	AFC	84	22	675	30.68
35	Buddy Young	NYY	NFL	51	14	427	30.50
36	Harold Hart	Oak.	AFC	75	17	518	30.47
37	Carl Garrett	Chi.	NFC	73	16	486	30.38
38	Dick Bass	L.A.	NFL	61	23	698	30.35
39	Bobby Jancik	Hou.	AFL	62	24	726	30.25
40	Johnny Counts	NYG	NFL	62	26	784	30.15
41	Lemar Parrish	Cin.	AFC	70	16	482	30.13
42	John Gilliam	N.O.	NFL	67	16	431	30.01
43	Mel Renfro	Dal.	NFL	65	21	630	30.00

SINGLE SEASON LEADERS

POINTS

1	Paul Hornung-1	G.B.	NFL	60	176
2	Mark Moseley-1	Was.	NFC	83	161
3	Gino Cappelletti-1	Bos.	AFL	64	155
4	Chip Lohmiller-1	Wash.	NFC	91	149
5	Gino Cappelletti-2	Bos.	AFL	61	147
6	Paul Hornung-2	G.B.	NFL	61	146
7	Jim Turner-1	NY J	AFL	68	145
8	John Riggins	Was.	NFC	83	144
	Kevin Butler	Chi.	NFL	85	144
10	Tony Franklin	NE	AFC	85	140
11	Gary Anderson	Pit.	AFC	85	139
	Nick Lowery	K.C.	AFC	90	139
13	Don Hutson-1	G.B.	NFL	42	138
	O.J. Simpson	Buf.	AFC	75	138
	Jerry Rice	S.F.	NFC	87	138
16	Gene Mingo-1	Den.	AFL	62	137
17	Mike Cofer-1	S.F.	NFC	89	136
18	Gale Sayers	Chi.	NFL	65	132
	Gino Cappelletti-3	Bos.	AFL	65	132
	Chuck Foreman	Min.	NFC	75	132
	Jeff Jaeger	L.A.Rd.	AFC	93	132
22	Ray Wersching-1	S.F.	NFC	84	131
	Chip Lohmiller-2	Was.	NFC	90	131
24	Dave Ray-1	L.A.	NFC	73	130
	Jason Hanson	Det.	NFC	93	130
26	Jan Stenerud-1	K.C.	AFL	68	129
	Jim Turner-2	NY J	AFL	69	129
	John Smith-	NE	AFC	80	129
	Scott Norwood	Buf.	AFC	88	129
30	Doak Walker	Det.	NFL	50	128
	Gino Cappelletti-4	Bos.	AFL	62	128
	Cookie Gilchrist	Buf.	AFL	62	128
	Chester Marcol	G.B.	NFC	72	128
	Chip Lohmiller-2	Wash.	NFC	89	128
	Chris Jacke	G.B.	NFC	93	128
36	Ali Haji-Sheikh	NY G	NFC	83	127
37	Jimmy Brown	Cle.	NFL	65	126
	Ray Wersching-2	S.F.	NFC	83	126
	Joe Morris	NY G	NFC	85	126
	Al Del Greco	Hou.	AFC	93	126
41	Fred Cox-1	Min.	NFC	70	125
42	Pete Stoyanovich	Mia.	AFC	92	124
43	John Carney	S.D.	AFC	93	124
44	Gene Mingo-2	Den.	AFL	60	123
	Roy Gerela-1	Pit.	AFC	73	123
	Rafael Septien-1	Dal.	NFC	83	123
47	Eddie Murray-1	Dall.	NFC	93	122
48	Fred Cox-2	Min.	NFL	64	121
	Dave Ray-2	L.A.	NFC	70	121
	Bobby Howfield	NY J	AFC	72	121
	Eddie Murray-2	Det.	NFC	81	121
	Rafael Septien-2	Dal.	NFC	81	121
	Pat Leahy	NY J	AFC	85	121
	Morten Andersen-1	N.O.	NFC	87	121
	Mike Cofer-2	S.F.	NFC	88	121
	Pete Stoyanovich	Mia.	AFC	91	121
57	Lenny Moore	Bal.	NFL	64	120
	Leroy Kelly	Cle.	NFL	68	120
	Eric Dickerson	L.A.	NFC	83	120
	Mark Moseley-2	Was.	NFC	84	120
	Morten Andersen-2	N.O.	NFC	85	120
	Jim Breech	Cin.	AFC	85	120
	Kevin Butler-2	Chi.	NFC	86	120
	David Treadwell	Den.	AFC	89	120
	Rich Karlis	Minn.	NFC	89	120
	Mike Lansford-1	L.A.	NFC	89	120
	Chip Lohmiller-3	Wash.	NFC	92	120
	Morten Andersen-3	N.O.	NFC	92	120
69	Gino Cappelletti-5	Bos.	AFL	66	119
	Jan Stenerud-2	K.C.	AFL	66	119
	Roy Gerela-2	Pit.	AFC	72	119
	Gary Anderson-1	Pit.	AFC	83	119
	Lin Elliott	Dall.	NFC	92	119
	Jason Elam	Den.	AFC	93	119
75	Frank Corral	L.A.	NFC	78	118
	Rolf Benirschke	S.D.	AFC	80	118
	Gary Anderson	Pit.	AFC	88	118
	Ken Willis	Dall.	NFC	91	118
79	Don Hutson-2	G.B.	NFL	43	117
	Jim Bakken-	St.L.	NFL	67	117
	George Blanda-	Oak.	NFL	68	117
	Garo Yepremian	Mia.	AFC	71	117
	Gary Anderson-2	Pit.	AFC	84	117
	Neil O'Donoghue	St.L.	NFC	84	117
	Mike Lansford-2	L.A.	NFC	88	117

POINTS PER SCHEDULED GAME

1	Paul Hornung-1	G.B.	NFL	60	14.7
2	Don Hutson-1	G.B.	NFL	42	12.5
3	Don Hutson-2	G.B.	NFL	43	11.7
4	Gino Cappelletti-1	Bos.	AFL	64	11.1
5	Steve Van Buren	Phi.	NFL	45	11.0
6	Doak Walker-1	Det.	NFL	50	10.7
7	Gino Cappelletti-2	Bos.	AFL	61	10.5
8	Paul Hornung-2	G.B.	NFL	61	10.4
	Jim Turner-1	NY J	AFL	68	10.4
10	Mark Moseley	Was.	NFC	83	10.1
11	O.J. Simpson	Buf.	AFC	75	9.9
12	Gene Mingo-1	Den.	AFL	62	9.8
13	Don Hutson-3	G.B.	NFL	45	9.7
14	Gordon Soltau	S.F.	NFL	53	9.5
	Bobby Walston-1	Phi.	NFL	54	9.5
16	Gale Sayers	Chi.	NFL	65	9.4
	Gino Cappelletti-3	Bos.	AFL	65	9.4
	Chuck Foreman	Min.	NFC	75	9.4
19	Dave Ray-1	L.A.	NFC	73	9.3
	Marcus Allen	Raid.	AFC	82	9.3
	Chip Lohmiller	Wash.	NFC	91	9.3
22	Jan Stenerud-	K.C.	AFL	68	9.2
	Jim Turner-2	NY J	AFL	69	9.2
	Pat Harder	ChiC	NFL	48	9.2
	Jerry Rice	S.F.	NFC	87	9.2
26	Gino Cappelletti-4	Bos.	AFL	62	9.1
	Cookie Gilchrist	Buf.	AFL	62	9.1
	Chester Marcol	G.B.	NFC	72	9.1
	Johnny Lujack	ChiB	NFL	50	9.1
30	Lou Groza	Cle.	NFL	53	9.0
	Jimmy Brown-1	Cle.	NFL	58	9.0
	Jimmy Brown-2	Cle.	NFL	65	9.0
	John Riggins	Was.	NFC	83	9.0
	Kevin Butler	Chi.	NFC	85	9.0
35	Fred Cox-1	Min.	NFC	70	8.9
	Rolf Benirschke	S.D.	AFC	82	8.9
37	Doak Walker-2	Det.	NFL	54	8.8
	Gene Mingo-2	Den.	AFL	60	8.8
	Roy Gerela-	Pit.	AFC	73	8.8
	Bobby Walston-2	Phi.	NFL	60	8.8
	Tony Franklin	NE	AFC	86	8.8
42	Gary Anderson	Pit.	AFC	85	8.7
	Nick Lowery	K.C.	AFC	90	8.7
43	Fred Cox-2	Min.	NFL	69	8.6
	Dave Ray-2	L.A.	NFC	70	8.6
	Bobby Howfield	NY J	AFC	72	8.6
	Don Hutson-4	G.B.	NFL	41	8.6
	Lenny Moore	Bal.	NFL	64	8.6
	Leroy Kelly	Cle.	NFL	68	8.6

FIELD GOALS

1	Ali Haji-Sheikh	NY G	NFC	83	35
	Jeff Jaeger-1	L.A.Rd.	AFC	93	35
3	Jim Turner-1	NY J	AFL	68	34
	Nick Lowery-1	K.C.	AFC	90	34
	Jason Hanson	Det.	NFC	93	34
6	Chester Marcol-1	G.B.	NFC	72	33
	Mark Moseley-1	Was.	NFC	83	33
	Gary Anderson-1	Pit.	AFC	85	33
9	Jim Turner-2	NY J	AFL	69	32
	Tony Franklin	NE	AFC	86	32
	Scott Norwood	Buf.	AFC	88	32
12	Morten Andersen-1	N.O.	NFC	85	31
	Kevin Butler-1	Chi.	NFC	85	31
	Rich Karlis	Minn.	NFC	89	31
	Chip Lohmiller-1	Wash.	NFC	91	31
	Pete Stoyanovich-1	Mia.	AFC	91	31
	John Carney	S.D.	AFC	93	31
	Chris Jacke	G.B.	NFC	93	31
19	Jan Stenerud-1	K.C.	AFL	68	30
	Jan Stenerud-2	K.C.	AFC	70	30
	Fred Cox-	Min.	NFC	70	30
	Dave Ray-1	L.A.	NFC	73	30
	Raul Allegre	Bal.	AFC	83	30
	Paul McFadden-1	Phil.	NFC	84	30
	Chip Lohmiller-2	Wash.	NFC	90	30
	Chip Lohmiller-3	Wash.	NFC	92	30
	Pete Stoyanovich-2	Mia.	AFC	92	30
28	David Ray-2	L.A.	NFC	70	29
	Curt Knight	Was.	NFC	71	29
	Roy Gerela-1	Pitt.	AFC	73	29
	Frank Corral	L.A.	NFC	78	29
	Mike Cofer	S.F.	NFC	89	29
	Chip Lohmiller-4	Wash.	NFC	89	29
	Jeff Jaeger-2	L.A.	AFC	91	29
	Morten Andersen-2	N.O.	NFC	92	29
	Al Del Greco	Hou.	AFC	93	29
37	Pete Gogolak-1	Buf.	AFL	65	28
	Kevin Butler-2	Chi.	NFC	86	28
	Bruce Gossett-	L.A.	NFL	66	28
	Garo Yepremian-1	Mia.	AFC	71	28
	Roy Gerela-2	Pit.	AFC	72	28
	Morten Andersen-3	N.O.	NFC	87	28
	Gary Anderson-2	Pit.	AFC	88	28
	Roger Ruzek	Phil.	NFC	91	28
	Gary Anderson-3	Pitt.	AFC	92	28
	Gary Anderson-4	Pitt	AFC	93	28
	Eddie Murray-1	Dall.	NFC	93	28
	Morten Andersen-4	N.O.	NFC	93	28

PERCENTAGE—FIELD GOALS MADE

(Minimum Attempts: to 1949=5, 1950-59=10, 1960-91=20)

					Made	Att.	Pct.
1	Norm Johnson-1	Atl.	NFC	93	26	27	96.3
2	Mark Moseley-1	Was.	NFC	82	20	21	95.2
3	Eddie Murray-1	Det.	NFC	88	20	21	95.2
	Eddie Murray-2	Det.	NFC	89	20	21	95.2
5	Gary Anderson-1	Pitt.	AFC	93	28	30	93.3
6	Nick Lowery-1	K.C.	AFC	90	34	37	91.9
7	Jan Stenerud-1	G.B.	NFC	81	22	24	91.7
	Nick Lowery-2	K.C.	AFC	92	22	24	91.7
9	John Carney	S.D.	AFC	90	19	21	90.5
10	Nick Lowery-3	K.C.	AFC	85	24	27	88.9
	Dean Biasucci-1	Ind.	AFC	87	24	27	88.9
12	Morten Andersen-1	N.O.	NFC	85	31	35	88.6
13	Lou Groza	Cle.	NFL	53	23	26	88.5
	Pat Leahy-1	NYJ	AFC	90	23	26	88.5
15	Roger Ruzek	Dal.	NFC	87	22	25	88.0
16	Tony Zendejas	Hous.	AFC	89	25	27	87.6
17	Jack Manders	ChiB	NFL	36	7	8	87.5
	Matt Bahr-1	Cle.	AFC	83	21	24	87.5
19	Gary Anderson-2	Pit.	AFC	83	27	31	87.1
20	Jan Stenerud-2	Min.	NFC	84	20	23	87.0
21	Morten Andersen-2	N.O.	NFC	86	26	30	86.7
22	Scott Norwood	Buf.	AFC	88	32	37	86.5
23	David Treadwell-1	NYG	NFC	93	25	29	86.2
24	Raul Allegre	Bal.	AFC	83	30	35	85.7
25	Jeff Jaeger	L.A.	AFC	91	29	34	85.3
	Morten Andersen-3	N.O.	NFC	92	29	34	85.3
	Al Del Greco	Hou.	AFC	93	29	34	85.3
28	Steve Christie	T.B.	NFC	90	23	27	85.2
29	Roger Ruzek	Phil.	NFC	91	28	33	84.9
	Eddie Murray-3	Dall.	NFC	93	28	33	84.9
31	Nick Lowery-3	K.C.	AFC	88	27	32	84.4
232	Toni Fritsch-1	Hou.	AFC	79	21	25	84.0
	Rick Danmeier	Min.	NFC	81	21	25	84.0
	Rich Karlis-1	Den.	AFC	83	21	25	84.0
	Pete Stoyanovich-1	Mia.	AFC	90	21	25	84.0
36	Eddie Murray-4	Det.	NFC	85	26	31	83.9
	Dean Biasucci-2	Ind.	AFC	93	26	31	83.9
38	Kevin Butler	Chi.	NFC	85	31	37	83.8
	Pete Stoyanovich	Mia.	AFC	91	31	37	83.8
	Chris Jacke	G.B.	NFC	93	31	37	83.8
41	Ray Wersching-	S.F.	NFC	79	20	24	83.3
	Ali Haji-Sheikh	NY G	NFC	83	35	42	83.3
	Ray Wersching-2	S.F.	NFC	83	25	30	83.3
	Norm Johnson-2	Sea.	AFC	84	20	24	83.3
	Paul McFadden-1	Phi.	NFC	85	25	30	83.3
	Nick Lowery-5	K.C.	AFC	91	25	30	83.3
	David Treadwell-2	Den.	AFC	92	20	24	83.3
48	Matt Bahr-2	Clev.	AFC	88	24	29	82.8
49	Garo Yepremian	Mia.	AFC	78	19	23	82.6
	Efren Herrera	Sea.	AFC	79	19	23	82.6
	Nick Lowery-6	K.C.	AFC	87	19	23	82.6
	Norm Johnson-3	Atl.	NFC	91	19	23	82.6
53	Pat Leahy-2	NYJ	AFC	88	23	28	82.1
	John Kasay-1	Sea.	AFC	93	23	28	82.1
55	Rolf Benirschke	S.D.	AFC	78	18	22	81.8
	Pat Leahy-3	NYJ	AFC	87	18	22	81.8
	David Treadwell-3	Den.	AFC	89	27	33	81.8
	Norm Johnson-2	Atl.	NFC	92	18	22	81.8
59	Don Cockroft	Cle.	AFC	72	22	27	81.5
	Rafael Septien	Dal.	NFC	83	22	27	81.5
	Fuad Reveiz	Mia.	AFC	85	22	27	81.5
	Tony Zendejas-2	Hou.	AFC	86	22	27	81.5
	Gary Anderson-3	Pit.	AFC	87	22	27	81.5
64	John Carney	S.D.	AFC	92	26	32	81.3
65	Paul McFadden-2	Phi.	NFC	84	30	37	81.1
	Pete Stoyanovich-2	Mia.	AFC	92	30	37	81.1
67	Roy Gerela	Pit.	AFC	75	17	21	81.0
	Florian Kempf	Hou.	AFC	83	17	21	81.0
	Mike Lansford	L.A.	NFC	87	17	21	81.0
	Jim Breech	Cin.	AFC	90	17	21	81.0
71	Tom Dempsey	L.A.	NFC	75	21	26	80.8
	Jan Stenerud-3	G.B.	NFC	83	21	26	80.8
	Jason Hanson	Det.	NFC	92	21	26	80.8
	John Kasay-2	Sea.	AFC	91	25	31	80.7
75	Mike Cofer	S.F.	NFC	89	29	36	80.6

POINTS AFTER TOUCHDOWN

1	Uwe von Schamann	Mia.	AFC	84	66
2	George Blanda-1	Hou.	AFL	61	64
3	Joe Vetrano-1	S.F.	AAFC	48	62
	Mark Moseley-	Was.	NFC	83	62
5	Rafael Septien-1	Dal.	NFC	80	59
	Mike Cofer	S.F.	NFC	93	59
7	Rafael Septien-2	Dal.	NFC	83	57
8	Joe Vetrano-2	S.F.	AAFC	49	56
	Danny Villanueva	Dal.	NFL	66	56
	George Blanda-2	Oak.	AFL	67	56
	Ray Wersching-1	S.F.	NFC	84	56
	Jim Breech-1	Cin.	AFC	88	56
	Chip Lohmiller	Wash.	NFC	91	56
	Scott Norwood	Buff.	AFC	91	56
15	Rolf Benirschke	S.D.	AFC	81	55
16	Bob Waterfield	L.A.	NFL	50	54
	George Blanda-3	Oak.	AFL	68	54
	Mike Clark-1	Dal.	NFL	68	54
19	Pat Harder	ChiC	NFL	48	53
	Lou Michaels-	Bal.	NFL	64	53
	Mike Cofer	S.F.	NFC	92	53
22	Don Chandler-1	NY G	NFL	63	52
	Tommy Davis	S.F.	NFL	65	52
	Roger LeClerc	Chi.	NFL	65	52
	Jan Stenerud	G.B.	NFC	83	52
	Ray Wersching-2	S.F.	NFC	85	52
	Fuad Reveiz-1	Mia.	AFC	86	52
28	Lou Groza-1	Cle.	AAFC	48	51
	Lou Groza-2	Cle.	NFL	66	51
	John Leypoldt	Buf.	AFC	75	51
	Toni Linhart-1	Bal.	AFC	75	51
	Frank Corral	L.A.	NFC	80	51
	John Smith	NE	AFC	80	51
	Mick Luckhurst	Atl.	NFC	81	51
	Chris Bahr	Raid.	AFC	83	51
	Bob Thomas	S.D.	AFC	85	51
	Kevin Butler	Chi.	NFC	85	51
	Ray Wersching-3	S.F.	NFC	83	51
	Mike Lansford	L.A.	NFC	89	51
40	Cliff Patton	Phi.	NFL	48	50
	Steve Myrha-	Bal.	NFL	59	50
	Sam Baker	Dal.	NFL	62	50
	Matt Bahr	Pit	AFC	79	50
	Norm Johnson-1	Sea.	AFC	84	50
	Fuad Reveiz-2	Mia.	AFC	85	50
	Jim Breech-2	Cin.	AFC	86	50
	Scott Norwood	Buf.	AFC	90	50
47	Harvey Johnson	N.Y.	AAFC	47	49
	Lou Groza-3	Cle.	NFL	64	49
	Toni Linhart-2	Bal.	AFC	76	49
	Jim Breech-3	Cin.	AFC	81	49
	Norm Johnson-2	Sea.	AFC	83	49
	Mike Cofer-2	S.F.	NFC	89	49
	Mike Cofer-3	S.F.	NFC	91	49

MOST PAT'S—NO MISSES

1	Joe Vetrano	S.F.	AAFC	49	56
	Danny Villanueva	Dal.	NFL	66	56
	Ray Wersching-1	S.F.	NFC	84	56
4	George Blanda-1	Oak.	AFL	68	54
	Mike Clark-1	Dal.	NFL	68	54
6	Pat Harder	ChiC	NFL	48	53
7	Roger LeClerc	Chi.	NFL	65	52
	Jan Stenerud-1	G.B.	NFC	83	52
9	Mick Luckhurst	Atl.	NFC	81	51
	John Smith	NE	AFC	80	51
	Ray Wersching-2	S.F.	NFC	83	51
	Kevin Butler	Chi.	NFC	85	51
	Mike Lansford	L.A.	NFC	89	51
14	Cliff Paxton	Phi.	NFL	48	50
15	Jim Bakken-1	St.L.	NFL	65	48
	Bruce Gossett	L.A.	NFL	67	48
	Tony Franklin	Phi.	NFC	80	48
18	Mike Mercer	Oak.	AFL	63	47
	Mike Clark-2	Dal.	NFC	71	47
20	Pat Summerall	NYG	NFL	61	46
	Tom Brooker	K.C.	AFL	64	46
	Eddie Murray	Det.	NFC	81	46
23	Lou Groza-1	Cle.	NFL	65	45
	Sam Baker	Phi.	NFL	67	45
	Jan Stenerud-2	K.C.	AFL	67	45
	Dick Van Raaphorst	S.D.	AFL	67	45
	George Blanda-2	Oak.	AFL	69	45
	Don Cockroft	Cle.	NFL	69	45
	Gary Anderson-1	Pit.	AFC	84	45
	Fuad Reveiz	Minn.	NFC	92	45
31	Tommy Davis	S.F.	NFL	61	44
	Jim Bakken-2	St.L.	NFL	63	44
	Fred Cox-1	Min.	NFL	65	44
	George Blanda-3	Oak.	AFC	72	44
	Pat Leahy	NY J	AFC	86	44
36	Rex Grossan	Bal.	AAFC	48	43
	Lou Groza-2	Cle.	NFL	51	43
	Doak Walker	Det.	NFL	54	43
	Lou Groza-3	Cle.	NFL	67	43
	Jim Turner-1	NY J	AFL	68	43
	Rafael Septien-1	Dal.	NFC	86	43
	Nick Lowery	K.C.	AFC	86	43
	Fred Cox-2	Min.	NFC	69	43
	Toni Fritsch	Dal.	NFC	73	43
	Garo Yepremian	Mia.	AFC	74	43
	Pat Leahy	NYJ	AFC	88	43

LIFETIME LEADERS
PASSING

ATTEMPTS (1790)

1	Fran Tarkenton	1961-78	6467
2	Dan Fouts	1973-87	5604
3	**Dan Marino**	**1983-**	**5434**
4	Johnny Unitas	1956-73	5186
5	Jim Hart	1966-84	5076
6	**Steve DeBerg**	**1977-**	**4965**
7	**Joe Montana**	**1979-**	**4898**
8	**John Elway**	**1983-**	**4890**
9	John Hadl	1962-77	4687
10	**Phil Simms**	**1979-81,83-**	**4647**
11	**Warren Moon**	**1984-**	**4546**
12	Joe Ferguson	1973-90	4519
13	Roman Gabriel	1962-77	4498
14	John Brodie	1957-73	4491
15	Ken Anderson	1971-86	4475
16	Y. A. Tittle	1948-64	4395
17	Norm Snead	1961-76	4353
18	Sonny Jurgensen	1957-74	4262
19	**Dave Krieg**	**1980-**	**4178**
20	Ron Jaworski	1974-89	4117
21	George Blanda	1949-58,60-75	4007
22	Terry Bradshaw	1970-83	3901
23	**Boomer Esiason**	**1984-**	**3851**
24	Ken Stabler	1970-84	3793
25	Craig Morton	1965-82	3786
26	Joe Namath	1965-77	3762
27	Len Dawson	1957-75	3741
28	Jim Plunkett	1971-86	3701
29	Bobby Layne	1948-62	3700
30	Tommy Kramer	1977-90	3651
31	Archie Manning	1971-84	3642
32	Joe Theismann	1971-85	3602
	Ken O'Brien	**1983-**	**3602**
34	Steve Grogan	1975-90	3593
35	**Jim Kelly**	**1986-**	**3494**
36	Steve Bartkowski	1975-86	3456
37	Brian Sipe	1974-83	3439
38	Bob Griese	1967-80	3429
39	Charley Johnson	1961-75	3392
40	Babe Parilli	1952-53,56-58,60-69	3330
41	**Jim Everett**	**1986-**	**3277**
42	**Bernie Kosar**	**1985-**	**3213**
43	Neil Lomax	1981-88	3153
44	Bart Starr	1956-71	3149
	Jim Zorn	1976-85,87	3149
46	Lynn Dickey	1971-77,79-85	3125
47	Jack Kemp	1957,60-67,69	3073
48	Dan Pastorini	1971-83	3055
49	Sammy Baugh	1937-52	2995
50	Billy Kilmer	1961-62,64,66-78	2984
51	Richard Todd	1976-86	2967
52	Roger Staubach	1969-79	2958
53	Danny White	1976-88	2950
54	Tobin Rote	1950-59,63-64,66	2907
55	Norm Van Brocklin	1949-60	2895
56	Charlie Conerly	1948-61	2833
57	**R. Cunningham**	**1985-**	**2751**
58	Earl Morrall	1956-76	2689
59	Otto Graham	1946-55	2626
60	Daryle Lamonica	1963-74	2601
61	**Jay Schroeder**	**1984-**	**2569**
62	Bert Jones	1973-82	2551
63	**Jim McMahon**	**1982-**	**2525**
64	Billy Wade	1954-66	2523
65	Doug Williams	1978-82,86-89	2507
66	**Bobby Hebert**	**1985-89,91-**	**2485**
67	Bill Kenney	1979-88	2430
68	Milt Plum	1957-69	2419
69	**Vinny Testaverde**	**1987-**	**2390**
70	Don Meredith	1960-68	2308
71	Greg Landry	1968-81,84	2300
72	**Wade Wilson**	**1981-**	**2216**
73	**Mark Rypien**	**1987-**	**2207**
74	Frank Ryan	1958-70	2133
75	**Chris Miller**	**1987-**	**2089**
76	Marc Wilson	1980-87,89-90	2081
77	Ed Brown	1954-65	1987
78	Bill Munson	1964-79	1982
79	**Steve Young**	**1985-**	**1968**
80	Gary Danielson	1976-85,87-88	1932
81	**Troy Aikman**	**1989-**	**1920**
82	Bill Nelsen	1963-72	1905
83	Mike Phipps	1970-81	1799
84	Eddie LeBaron	1952-53,55-63	1796

COMPLETIONS (925)

1	Fran Tarkenton	1961-78	3686
2	Dan Fouts	1973-87	3297
3	**Dan Marino**	**1983-**	**3219**
4	**Joe Montana**	**1979-**	**3110**
5	**Steve DeBerg**	**1978-**	**2844**
6	Johnny Unitas	1956-73	2830
7	**John Elway**	**1983-**	**2723**
8	Ken Anderson	1971-84	2654
9	**Warren Moon**	**1984-**	**2632**
10	Jim Hart	1966-84	2593
11	**Phil Simms**	**1979-81,83-**	**2576**
12	John Brodie	1957-73	2469
13	Sonny Jurgensen	1957-74	2433
14	**Dave Krieg**	**1980-**	**2431**
15	Y. A. Tittle	1948-64	2427
16	Joe Ferguson	1973-90	2369
17	Roman Gabriel	1962-77	2366
18	John Hadl	1962-77	2363
19	Norm Snead	1961-76	2276
20	Ken Stabler	1970-84	2270
21	Ron Jaworski	1974-89	2187
22	**Boomer Esiason**	**1984-**	**2185**
23	Len Dawson	1957-75	2136
24	**Jim Kelly**	**1986-**	**2112**
25	**Ken O'Brien**	**1983-**	**2110**
26	Craig Morton	1965-82	2053
27	Joe Theismann	1974-85	2044
28	Terry Bradshaw	1970-83	2025
29	Tommy Kramer	1977-90	2012
30	Archie Manning	1971-75,77-84	2011
31	Brian Sipe	1974-83	1944
32	Jim Plunkett	1971-86	1943
33	Steve Bartkowski	1975-86	1932
34	Bob Griese	1967-80	1926
35	George Blanda	1949-58,60-75	1911
36	**Bernie Kosar**	**1985**	**1889**
37	Joe Namath	1965-77	1886
38	Steve Grogan	1975-90	1879
39	**Jim Everett**	**1986-**	**1847**
40	Neil Lomax	1981-88	1817
41	Bobby Layne	1948-62	1814
42	Bart Starr	1956-71	1808
43	Danny White	1976-88	1761
44	Lynn Dickey	1971-77,79-85	1747
45	Charley Johnson	1961-75	1737
46	Sammy Baugh	1937-52	1693
47	Roger Staubach	1969-79	1685
48	Jim Zorn	1976-85,87	1669
49	Richard Todd	1976-86	1610
50	Billy Kilmer	1961-62,64,66-78	1585
51	Dan Pastorini	1971-83	1556
52	Norm Van Brocklin	1949-60	1553
53	Babe Parilli	1952-53,56-58,60-69	1552
54	**R. Cunningham**	**1985-**	**1540**
55	**Jim McMahon**	**1982-**	**1465**
	Bobby Hebert	**1985-89,91**	**1465**
57	Otto Graham	1946-55	1464
58	Jack Kemp	1957,60-67,69	1436
59	Bert Jones	1973-82	1430
60	Charlie Conerly	1948-61	1418
61	Earl Morrall	1956-76	1379
62	Billy Wade	1954-66	1370
63	Bill Kenney	1979-88	1330
64	Tobin Rote	1950-52,63-64,66	1329
65	Milt Plum	1957-69	1306
66	**Jay Schroeder**	**1984-**	**1293**
67	Daryle Lamonica	1963-74	1288
68	Greg Landry	1968-81,84	1276
69	**Wade Wilson**	**1981-**	**1261**
70	**Vinny Testaverde**	**1987-**	**1256**
71	**Mark Rypien**	**1987-**	**1244**
72	Doug Williams	1978-82,86-89	1240
73	**Steve Young**	**1985-**	**1222**
74	**Troy Aikman**	**1989-**	**1191**
75	Don Meredith	1960-68	1170
76	**Chris Miller**	**1987-**	**1129**
77	Gary Danielson	1976-85,87-88	1105
78	Frank Ryan	1958-70	1090
79	Marc Wilson	1980-87,89-90	1085
80	Bill Munson	1964-79	1070
81	**Jim Harbaugh**	**1987-**	**1023**
82	Bill Nelson	1963-72	963
83	**Bubby Brister**	**1986-**	**957**
84	Ed Brown	1954-65	949

COMPLETION PERCENTAGE
(All with over 1790 Attempts)

		Att.	Comp.	Pct.
1	**Joe Montana**	**4898**	**3110**	**63.50**
2	**Steve Young**	**1968**	**1222**	**62.09**
3	**Troy Aikman**	**1920**	**1191**	**62.03**
4	**Jim Kelly**	**3494**	**2112**	**60.45**
5	Ken Stabler	3793	2270	59.85
6	Danny White	2950	1761	59.70
7	Ken Anderson	4475	2654	59.31
8	**Dan Marino**	**5434**	**3219**	**59.24**
9	**Bobby Hebert**	**2485**	**1465**	**58.95**
10	Dan Fouts	5604	3297	58.83
11	**Bernie Kosar**	**3213**	**1889**	**58.79**
12	**Ken O'Brien**	**3602**	**2110**	**58.58**
13	**Dave Krieg**	**4178**	**2431**	**58.19**
14	**Jim McMahon**	**2525**	**1465**	**58.02**
15	**Warren Moon**	**4546**	**2632**	**57.90**
16	Neil Lomax	3153	1817	57.63
17	Bart Starr	3149	1808	57.42
18	**Steve DeBerg**	**4965**	**2844**	**57.28**
19	Gary Danielson	1932	1105	57.19
20	Len Dawson	3741	2136	57.10
21	Sonny Jurgensen	4262	2433	57.09
22	Fran Tarkenton	6467	3686	57.00
23	Roger Staubach	2958	1685	56.96
24	**Wade Wilson**	**2216**	**1261**	**56.90**
25	Joe Theismann	3602	2044	56.75
26	**Boomer Esiason**	**3851**	**2185**	**56.74**
27	Brian Sipe	3439	1944	56.53
	Sammy Baugh	2995	1693	56.53
29	**Mark Rypien**	**2207**	**1244**	**56.37**
30	**Jim Everett**	**3277**	**1847**	**56.36**
31	Bob Griese	3429	1926	56.17
32	Bert Jones	2551	1430	56.06
33	**Randall Cunningham**	**2751**	**1540**	**55.98**
34	Lynn Dickey	3125	1747	55.90
	Steve Bartkowski	3456	1932	55.90
36	Otto Graham	2626	1464	55.75
37	**John Elway**	**4890**	**2723**	**55.69**
38	Greg Landry	2300	1276	55.48
39	**Phil Simms**	**4647**	**2576**	**55.43**
40	Y. A. Tittle	4395	2427	55.22
	Archie Manning	3642	2011	55.22
42	Tommy Kramer	3651	2012	55.10
43	John Brodie	4491	2469	54.98
44	Bill Kenney	2430	1330	54.73
45	Johnny Unitas	5186	2830	54.47
46	Billy Wade	2523	1370	54.30
47	Richard Todd	2967	1610	54.26
48	Craig Morton	3786	2053	54.23
49	**Chris Miller**	**2089**	**1129**	**54.04**
50	Milt Plum	2419	1306	53.99
	Bill Munson	1982	1070	53.99
52	Norm Van Brocklin	2895	1553	53.64
53	Billy Kilmer	2984	1585	53.12
	Ron Jaworski	4117	2187	53.12
55	Jim Zorn	3149	1669	53.00
56	Roman Gabriel	4498	2366	52.60
57	**Vinny Testaverde**	**2390**	**1256**	**52.55**
58	Jim Plunkett	3701	1943	52.50
59	Joe Ferguson	4511	2367	52.47
60	Steve Grogan	3593	1879	52.29
61	Norm Snead	4353	2373	52.21
62	Marc Wilson	2081	1085	52.13
63	Terry Bradshaw	3901	2025	51.91
64	Earl Morrall	2689	1379	51.28
65	Charley Johnson	3392	1737	51.21
66	Frank Ryan	2133	1090	51.10
67	Jim Hart	5076	2593	51.08
68	Dan Pastorini	3055	1556	50.93
69	Don Meredith	2308	1170	50.69
70	Bill Nelsen	1905	963	50.55
71	John Hadl	4687	2363	50.42
72	**Jay Schroeder**	**2569**	**1293**	**50.33**
73	Joe Namath	3762	1886	50.13
74	Charlie Conerly	2833	1418	50.05
75	Eddie LeBaron	1796	897	49.94
76	Daryle Lamonica	2601	1288	49.52
77	Doug Williams	2507	1240	49.46
78	Mike Phipps	1799	886	49.25
79	Bobby Layne	3700	1814	49.03
80	Ed Brown	1987	949	47.77
81	George Blanda	4007	1911	47.69
82	Jack Kemp	3073	1436	46.73
83	Babe Parilli	3330	1552	46.61
84	Tobin Rote	2907	1329	45.72

YARDS (11,700)

1	Fran Tarkenton	1961-78	47003
2	Dan Fouts	1973-87	43040
3	**Dan Marino**	**1983-**	**40720**
4	Johnny Unitas	1956-73	40239
5	**Joe Montana**	**1979-**	**37268**
6	Jim Hart	1966-84	34665
7	**John Elway**	**1983-**	**34246**
8	**Steve DeBerg**	**1978-**	**33872**
9	**Warren Moon**	**1984-**	**33685**
10	John Hadl	1962-77	33513
11	**Phil Simms**	**1979-**	**33462**
12	Y. A. Tittle	1948-64	33070
13	Ken Anderson	1971-84	32838
14	Sonny Jurgensen	1957-74	32224
15	John Brodie	1957-73	31548
16	Norm Snead	1961-76	30797
17	**Dave Krieg**	**1980-**	**30485**
18	Joe Ferguson	1973-89	29816
19	Roman Gabriel	1962-77	29444
20	**Boomer Esiason**	**1984-**	**29092**
21	Len Dawson	1957-75	28711
22	Ron Jaworski	1974-89	28190
23	Terry Bradshaw	1970-83	27989
24	Ken Stabler	1970-84	27938
25	Craig Morton	1965-82	27908
26	Joe Namath	1965-77	27663
27	George Blanda	1949-58,60-75	26920
28	Steve Grogan	1975-90	26886
29	**Jim Kelly**	**1986-**	**26413**
30	Bobby Layne	1948-62	25967
31	Jim Plunkett	1971-86	25882
32	Joe Theismann	1974-85	25206
33	**Ken O'Brien**	**1983-**	**25094**
34	Bob Griese	1967-80	25092
35	Tommy Kramer	1977-90	24776
36	Bart Starr	1956-71	24718
37	Charley Johnson	1961-75	24410
38	Steve Bartkowski	1975-86	24124
39	Archie Manning	1971-75,77-84	23911
40	**Jim Everett**	**1986-**	**23758**
41	Brian Sipe	1974-83	23713
42	Norm Van Brocklin	1949-60	23611
43	Otto Graham	1946-55	23584
44	Lynn Dickey	1971-77,79-85	23322
45	Neil Lomax	1981-88	22771
46	Roger Staubach	1969-79	22700
47	Babe Parilli	1952-53,56-58,60-69	22681
48	**Bernie Kosar**	**1985-**	**22314**
49	Danny White	1976-88	21959
50	Sammy Baugh	1937-52	21886
51	Jack Kemp	1957,60-67,69	21218
52	Jim Zorn	1976-85,87	21115
53	Earl Morrall	1956-76	20809
54	Richard Todd	1976-86	20610
55	Billy Kilmer	1961-62,64,66-78	20495
56	Charlie Conerly	1948-61	19488
57	Daryle Lamonica	1963-74	19154
58	**R. Cunningham**	**1985-**	**19040**
59	Tobin Rote	1950-59,63-64,66	18850
60	**Jay Schroeder**	**1984-**	**18553**
61	Billy Wade	1954-66	18530
62	Dan Pastorini	1971-83	18515
63	Bert Jones	1973-82	18190
64	**Jim McMahon**	**1982-**	**17833**
65	**Bobby Hebert**	**1985-89,91**	**17608**
66	Milt Plum	1957-69	17536
67	Bill Kenney	1980-88	17277
68	Don Meredith	1960-68	17199
69	Doug Williams	1978-82,86-89	16998
70	**Vinny Testaverde**	**1987-**	**16617**
71	Greg Landry	1968-81,84	16052
72	Frank Ryan	1958-70	16042
73	**Wade Wilson**	**1981-**	**15960**
74	**Mark Rypien**	**1987-**	**15928**
75	**Steve Young**	**12985-**	**15900**
76	Ed Brown	1954-65	15600
77	Sid Luckman	1939-50	14683
78	Marc Wilson	1980-87,89-90	14391
79	Bill Nelsen	1963-72	14165
80	**Chris Miller**	**1987-**	**14066**
81	Gary Danielson	1976-85,87-88	13764
82	**Troy Aikman**	**1989-**	**13627**
83	Eddie LeBaron	1952-53,55-63	13399
84	Bill Munson	1964-79	12896
85	**Bubby Brister**	**1986-**	**12009**
86	Tom Flores	1960-61,63-69	11959
87	Bob Waterfield	1945-52	11849
88	Cotton Davidson	1954-57,60-66,68	11760

Players active at the end of 1993 are shown in **bold face**.

LIFETIME LEADERS
PASSING

YARDS PER ATTEMPT

(All with over 1790 Attempts)

		Yards	Att.	Y/A
1	Otto Graham	23584	2626	8.98
2	Norm Van Brocklin	23611	2895	8.16
3	**Steve Young**	**15900**	**1968**	**8.08**
4	Ed Brown	15600	1987	7.85
	Bart Starr	24718	3149	7.85
6	Johnny Unitas	40239	5186	7.76
7	Earl Morrall	20809	2689	7.74
8	Len Dawson	28711	3741	7.68
	Dan Fouts	43040	5604	7.68
10	Roger Staubach	22700	2958	7.67
11	**Joe Montana**	**37628**	**4898**	**7.61**
12	**Jim Kelly**	**26413**	**3494**	**7.56**
	Sonny Jurgensen	32224	4262	7.56
14	**Boomer Esiason**	**28092**	**3851**	**7.55**
15	Y.A. Tittle	33070	4395	7.52
	Frank Ryan	16042	2133	7.52
17	**Dan Marino**	**40720**	**5434**	**7.49**
	Steve Grogan	26886	3593	7.48
19	Lynn Dickey	23322	3125	7.47
20	Eddie LeBaron	13399	1796	7.46
21	Don Meredith	17199	2308	7.45
22	Danny White	21959	2950	7.44
	Bill Nelson	14165	1905	7.44
24	**Warren Moon**	**33685**	**4546**	**7.41**
25	Craig Morton	27908	3786	7.37
	Ken Stabler	27938	3793	7.37
	Daryle Lamonica	19154	2601	7.36
28	Joe Namath	27663	3762	7.35
29	Ken Anderson	32838	4475	7.34
	Billy Wade	18530	2523	7.34
31	Bob Griese	25092	3426	7.32
32	Sammy Baugh	21886	2995	7.31
33	**Dave Krieg**	**30485**	**4178**	**7.30**
34	Fran Tarkenton	47003	6467	7.27
35	Milt Plum	17536	2419	7.25
	Jim Everett	**23758**	**3277**	**7.25**
37	Bobby Layne	25967	3700	7.24
38	Neil Lomax	22771	3153	7.22
39	**Mark Rypien**	**15928**	**2207**	**7.22**
	Jay Schroeder	**18553**	**2569**	**7.22**
41	Charley Johnson	24410	3392	7.20
	Wade Wilson	**15960**	**2216**	**7.20**
	Phil Simms	**33462**	**4647**	**7.20**
44	Terry Bradshaw	27989	3901	7.17
45	John Hadl	33503	4687	7.15
46	Bert Jones	18190	2551	7.13
47	Gary Danielson	13764	1932	7.12
48	Bill Kenney	17277	2430	7.11
49	**Troy Aikman**	**13627**	**1920**	**7.10**
50	**Jim McMahon**	**17883**	**2525**	**7.08**
51	Norm Snead	30797	4353	7.07
52	John Brodie	31548	4491	7.03
53	**John Elway**	**34246**	**4890**	**7.00**
	Joe Theismann	25206	3602	7.00
55	Jim Plunkett	25882	3701	6.99
56	Steve Bartkowski	24124	3456	6.98
57	**Ken O'Brien**	**25094**	**3602**	**6.97**
58	Greg Landry	15853	2280	6.95
	Richard Todd	20610	2967	6.95
	Vinny Testaverde	**16617**	**2390**	**6.95**
61	**Bernie Kosar**	**22314**	**3213**	**6.94**
62	**Randall Cunningham**	**19040**	**2751**	**6.92**
63	Marc Wilson	14391	2081	6.91
64	Brian Sipe	23713	3439	6.90
	Jack Kemp	21218	3073	6.90
66	Charlie Conerly	19488	2833	6.88
67	Billy Kilmer	20495	2984	6.87
	Bobby Hebert	**17068**	**2485**	**6.87**
69	Ron Jaworski	28190	4117	6.85
70	Jim Hart	34665	5076	6.83
71	**Steve DeBerg**	**33872**	**4965**	**6.82**
72	Babe Parilli	22681	3330	6.81
73	Tommy Kramer	24776	3651	6.78
	Doug Williams	16998	2507	6.78
75	**Chris Miller**	**14066**	**2089**	**6.73**
76	George Blanda	26920	4007	6.72
	Jim Zorn	21115	3149	6.71
78	Joe Ferguson	29816	4519	6.59
79	Archie Manning	23911	3642	6.57
80	Roman Gabriel	29444	4498	6.55
81	Bill Munson	12896	1982	6.51
82	Tobin Rote	18850	2907	6.45
83	Dan Pastorini	18515	3055	6.06
84	Mike Phipps	10506	1799	5.84

TOUCHDOWNS (125)

1	Fran Tarkenton	1961-78	342
2	**Dan Marino**	**1983-**	**298**
3	Johnny Unitas	1956-73	290
4	**Joe Montana**	**1979-**	**257**
5	Sonny Jurgensen	1957-74	255
6	Dan Fouts	1973-87	254
7	John Hadl	1962-77	244
8	Y.A. Tittle	1948-64	242
9	Len Dawson	1957-75	239
10	George Blanda	1948-58,60-75	236
11	**Dave Krieg**	**1980-**	**217**
12	John Brodie	1957-73	214
13	Terry Bradshaw	1970-83	212
14	Jim Hart	1966-84	209
15	Roman Gabriel	1962-77	201
16	**Phil Simms**	**1979-**	**199**
17	Ken Anderson	1971-84	197
18	Bobby Layne	1948-62	196
	Joe Ferguson	1973-90	196
	Warren Moon	**1984-**	**196**
	Norm Snead	1961-76	196
22	Ken Stabler	1970-84	194
23	**Steve DeBerg**	**1977-**	**193**
24	Bob Griese	1967-80	192
25	**Boomer Esiason**	**1984-**	**190**
26	Sammy Baugh	1937-52	186
27	**John Elway**	**1983-**	**183**
	Craig Morton	1965-82	183
29	Steve Grogan	1975-90	182
30	**Jim Kelly**	**1986-**	**179**
31	Babe Parilli	1952-53,56-58,60-69	178
32	Ron Jaworski	1974-89	179
33	Otto Graham	1946-55	174
34	Charlie Conerly	1948-81	173
	Norm Van Brocklin	1949-60	173
	Joe Namath	1965-77	173
37	Charley Johnson	1961-75	170
38	Daryle Lamonica	1963-74	164
	Jim Plunkett	1971-86	164
40	Earl Morrall	1956-76	161
41	Joe Theismann	1974-85	160
42	Tommy Kramer	1977-90	159
43	Steve Bartkowski	1975-86	156
44	Danny White	1976-88	155
45	Brian Sipe	1974-83	154
46	Roger Staubach	1969-79	153
47	Bart Starr	1956-71	152
	Billy Kilmer	1961-62,64,66-78	152
49	Frank Ryan	1958-70	149
50	Tobin Rote	1950-59,63,64,66	148
51	**Jim Everett**	**1986-**	**142**
52	Lynn Dickey	1971-85	141
53	Sid Luckman	1939-50	137
54	Neil Lomax	1981-88	136
55	Don Meredith	1960-68	135
56	**Randall Cunningham**	**1985-**	**131**
57	**Ken O'Brien**	**1983-**	**128**
58	Archie Manning	1971-75,77-84	125

INTERCEPTIONS (150)

1	George Blanda	1949-58,60-75	277
2	John Hadl	1962-77	268
3	Fran Tarkenton	1961-78	266
4	Norm Snead	1961-76	257
5	Johnny Unitas	1956-73	253
6	Y.A. Tittle	1948-64	248
7	Jim Hart	1966-84	247
8	Bobby Layne	1948-62	245
9	Dan Fouts	1973-87	242
10	John Brodie	1957-73	224
11	Ken Stabler	1970-84	222
12	Babe Parilli	1952-53,56-58,60-69	220
	Joe Namath	1965-77	220
14	Terry Bradshaw	1970-83	210
15	Joe Ferguson	1973-90	209
16	Steve Grogan	1975-90	208
17	Sammy Baugh	1937-52	203
18	**Steve DeBerg**	**1978-**	**203**
19	Jim Plunkett	1971-86	198
20	Tobin Rote	1950-59,63-64,66	191
21	Sonny Jurgensen	1957-74	189
22	Craig Morton	1965-82	187
23	Len Dawson	1957-75	183
	Jack Kemp	1957,60-67,69	183
25	Charley Johnson	1949-60	181
26	Lynn Dickey	1971-85	179
27	Norm Van Brocklin	1949-60	178
28	Archie Manning	1972-75,77-84	173
29	Bob Griese	1967-80	172
30	**Dan Marino**	**1983-**	**168**
31	Charlie Conerly	1948-61	167
	John Elway	**1983-**	**167**
33	**Warren Moon**	**1984-**	**166**
34	Ron Jaworski	1974-89	164
35	**Dave Krieg**	**1980-**	**163**
36	Dan Pastorini	1971-83	161
	Richard Todd	1976-86	161
38	Ken Anderson	1971-84	160
39	Tommy Kramer	1977-90	158

PERCENT INTERCEPTED

(All with over 1790 Attempts)

		Att.	Int.	Pct.
1	**Bernie Kosar**	**3213**	**81**	**2.52**
2	**Joe Montana**	**4898**	**130**	**2.65**
3	**Ken O'Brien**	**3602**	**98**	**2.72**
4	Neil Lomax	3153	90	2.85
5	**Steve Young**	**1968**	**58**	**2.95**
6	**Dan Marino**	**5434**	**168**	**3.09**
7	**Randall Cunningham**	**2751**	**87**	**3.16**
8	Roman Gabriel	4498	149	3.31
9	**Phil Simms**	**4647**	**157**	**3.38**
10	**Mark Rypien**	**2207**	**75**	**3.40**
11	**John Elway**	**4890**	**167**	**3.41**
12	**Jim McMahon**	**2525**	**87**	**3.44**
13	**Chris Miller**	**2089**	**72**	**3.45**
14	Bill Kenney	2430	86	3.54
15	Ken Anderson	4475	160	3.58
16	**Troy Aikman**	**1920**	**69**	**3.59**
17	**Jim Kelly**	**3494**	**126**	**3.61**
18	**Boomer Esiason**	**3851**	**140**	**3.63**
19	**Warren Moon**	**4546**	**166**	**3.65**
20	Roger Staubach	2958	109	3.68
21	**Bobby Hebert**	**2485**	**92**	**3.70**
22	Doug Williams	2507	93	3.71
23	**Jim Everett**	**3277**	**123**	**3.75**
24	Joe Theismann	3602	138	3.83
25	**Dave Krieg**	**4178**	**163**	**3.90**
26	**Jay Schroeder**	**2569**	**101**	**3.93**
27	Bert Jones	2551	101	3.96
28	Ron Jaworski	4117	164	3.98
29	Bill Munson	1982	80	4.04
30	Gary Danielson	1932	78	4.04
31	**Steve DeBerg**	**4965**	**203**	**4.09**
32	Fran Tarkenton	6467	266	4.11
33	Steve Bartkowski	3456	144	4.17
34	**Wade Wilson**	**2216**	**94**	**4.24**
35	Tommy Kramer	3051	158	4.32
	Dan Fouts	5604	242	4.32
37	Brian Sipe	3439	149	4.33
38	Bart Starr	3149	138	4.38
39	Greg Landry	2280	100	4.39
40	Sonny Jurgensen	4262	189	4.44
41	Danny White	2050	132	4.47
42	Jim Zorn	3149	141	4.48
43	Joe Ferguson	4519	209	4.62
44	Archie Manning	3642	173	4.75
45	Don Meredith	2308	111	4.81
46	Jim Hart	5076	247	4.87
47	Johnny Unitas	5186	253	4.88
48	Len Dawson	3741	183	4.89
	Billy Kilmer	2984	146	4.89
50	Marc Wilson	2081	102	4.90
51	Craig Morton	3786	187	4.94
52	John Brodie	4491	224	4.99
53	Bob Griese	3429	172	5.02
54	**Vinny Testaverde**	**2390**	**121**	**5.06**
55	Otto Graham	2626	135	5.14
56	Frank Ryan	2133	111	5.20
57	Milt Plum	2410	127	5.27
	Dan Pastorini	3055	161	5.27
59	Bill Nelson	1905	101	5.30
60	Daryle Lamonica	2601	138	5.31
	Billy Wade	2523	134	5.31
62	Charley Johnson	3392	181	5.34
63	Jim Plunkett	3701	198	5.35
64	Terry Bradshaw	3901	210	5.38
65	Richard Todd	2967	161	5.43
66	Earl Morrall	2689	148	5.50
67	Y.A. Tittle	4395	248	5.51
68	John Hadl	4687	268	5.72
69	Lynn Dickey	3125	179	5.73
70	Steve Grogan	3593	208	5.78
71	Joe Namath	3762	220	5.85
	Ken Stabler	3793	222	5.85
73	Charlie Conerly	2833	167	5.90
74	Norm Snead	4353	257	5.94
75	Mike Phipps	1799	108	6.00
76	Norm Van Brocklin	2895	178	6.15
77	Jack Kemp	2973	183	6.16
78	Bobby Layne	3700	243	6.57
	Tobin Rote	2907	191	6.57
80	Babe Parilli	3330	220	6.61
81	Sammy Baugh	2995	203	6.78
82	George Blanda	4057	277	6.91
83	Ed Brown	1987	138	6.94
84	Eddie LeBaron	1796	141	7.85

RANK

(All with over 1790 Attempts)

		Comp. Pct.	Yds./ Att.	Pct. Int.	Pct. TD Passes		Total
1	**Steve Young**	**2**	**3**	**5**	**18**	—	**28**
2	**Joe Montana**	**1**	**11**	**2**	**21**	—	**35**
3	**Dan Marino**	**8**	**17**	**6**	**16**	—	**47**
4	**Jim Kelly**	**4**	**12**	**17**	**28**	—	**61**
5	Roger Staubach	23	10	20	25	—	78
6	Len Dawson	20	8	48	3	—	79
7	Sonny Jurgensen	21	12	40	8	—	81
8	Bart Starr	17	4	38	29	—	88
9	Danny White	6	22	41	21	—	90
10	Boomer Esiason	26	14	18	36	—	94
	Otto Graham	36	1	55	2	—	94
12	**Dave Krieg**	**13**	**33**	**25**	**24**	—	**95**
13	Dan Fouts	10	8	35	44	—	97
14	Ken Anderson	7	29	15	53	—	104
15	Fran Tarkenton	22	34	32	20	—	108
16	Johnny Unitas	45	6	47	14	—	112
17	**Warren Moon**	**15**	**24**	**19**	**60**	—	**118**
	Neil Lomax	16	38	4	60	—	118
19	**Mark Rypien**	**29**	**39**	**10**	**43**	—	**121**
20	Bob Griese	31	31	53	13	—	128
21	Ken Stabler	5	25	71	29	—	130
22	**Jim McMahon**	**14**	**50**	**12**	**73**	—	**137**
	Y.A. Tittle	40	15	67	15	—	137
24	Norm Van Brocklin	52	2	76	8	—	138
	Frank Ryan	66	15	56	1	—	138
26	Bert Jones	32	46	27	38	—	143
	Randall Cunningham	**33**	**62**	**7**	**41**	—	**143**
28	Earl Morrall	64	7	66	7	—	144
29	Sammy Baugh	27	32	81	5	—	145
30	**Jim Everett**	**30**	**35**	**23**	**58**	—	**146**
	Don Meredith	69	21	45	11	—	146
32	**Troy Aikman**	**3**	**49**	**16**	**79**	—	**147**
33	**Bernie Kosar**	**11**	**61**	**1**	**77**	—	**150**
34	**Bobby Hebert**	**9**	**67**	**21**	**54**	—	**151**
35	**Ken O'Brien**	**12**	**57**	**3**	**80**	—	**152**
	Phil Simms	**39**	**41**	**9**	**63**	—	**152**
37	Joe Theismann	25	53	24	51	—	153
38	Gary Danielson	19	47	30	65	—	161
39	Craig Morton	48	25	51	39	—	163
40	Bill Kenney	44	48	14	59	—	165
	Daryle Lamonica	76	25	60	4	—	165
42	Lynn Dickey	34	19	69	46	—	168
43	Steve Bartkowski	34	56	33	46	—	169
44	**Wade Wilson**	**25**	**41**	**34**	**71**	—	**170**
45	Bill Wade	46	29	60	37	—	172
46	Milt Plum	50	35	57	34	—	176
47	Brian Sipe	27	64	37	49	—	177
	Bill Nelson	70	22	59	26	—	177
	John Elway	**37**	**53**	**11**	**76**	—	**177**
50	Steve Grogan	60	17	70	33	—	180
51	John Brodie	43	52	52	40	—	187
52	Eddie LeBaron	75	20	84	12	—	191
53	Roman Gabriel	56	80	8	50	—	194
	Steve DeBerg	**18**	**71**	**31**	**74**	—	**194**
	Ed Brown	80	4	83	27	—	194
56	Greg Landry	38	58	39	62	—	197
57	Bill Kilmer	53	67	48	31	—	199
58	**Jay Schroeder**	**72**	**39**	**26**	**63**	—	**200**
59	Charley Johnson	65	41	62	35	—	203
60	Ron Jaworski	53	69	28	55	—	205
	Tommy Kramer	42	73	35	55	—	205
	Chris Miller	**49**	**75**	**13**	**68**	—	**205**
63	John Hadl	71	45	68	23	—	207
64	Bobby Layne	79	37	78	19	—	213
65	Joe Namath	73	28	71	42	—	214
66	Terry Bradshaw	63	44	64	44	—	215
67	Charlie Conerly	74	66	73	6	—	219
68	Bill Munson	50	81	29	65	—	225
69	Jim Plunkett	58	55	63	52	—	228
70	Norm Snead	61	51	74	48	—	234
71	Joe Ferguson	59	78	43	57	—	237
	Richard Todd	47	58	65	67	—	237
73	Marc Wilson	62	63	50	69	—	244
	Doug Williams	77	73	22	72	—	244
	Vinny Testaverde	**57**	**58**	**54**	**75**	—	**244**
76	Archie Manning	40	79	44	82	—	245
77	George Blanda	81	76	82	10	—	249
78	Babe Parilli	83	72	80	17	—	252
79	Jim Hart	67	70	46	70	—	253
80	Jim Zorn	55	76	42	81	—	254
81	Tobin Rote	84	82	78	31	—	275
82	Dan Pastorini	68	83	57	83	—	291
83	Jack Kemp	82	64	77	78	—	301
84	Mike Phipps	78	84	75	84	—	321

Players Active at the end of 1993 are shown in **bold face**.

LIFETIME LEADERS
RUSHING

ATTEMPTS (1140)

1	Walter Payton	1975-87	3838
2	Eric Dickerson	1983-93	2996
3	Franco Harris	1972-84	2949
4	Tony Dorsett	1977-88	2936
5	John Riggins	1971-79, 81-85	2740
6	Ottis Anderson	1979-92	2562
7	O.J. Simpson	1969-79	2404
8	Jimmy Brown	1957-65	2359
9	**Marcus Allen**	**1982-**	**2296**
10	Earl Campbell	1978-85	2187
11	**Roger Craig**	**1983-**	**1991**
12	Gerald Riggs	1982-91	1989
13	Jim Taylor	1958-67	1941
14	Joe Perry	1948-63	1929
15	Larry Csonka	1968-74,76-79	1891
16	Mike Pruitt	1976-86	1846
17	Freeman McNeil	1981-92	1798
18	**Herschel Walker**	**1986-**	**1794**
19	**Thurman Thomas**	**1988-**	**1731**
20	Leroy Kelly	1964-73	1727
21	Curt Warner	1983-90	1698
22	George Rogers	1981-87	1692
23	James Brooks	1981-92	1685
24	Lydell Mitchell	1972-80	1675
25	**Ernest Byner**	**1984-**	**1662**
26	Mark van Eeghen	1974-83	1652
27	Bill Brown	1961-74	1649
28	Floyd Little	1967-75	1641
29	Ken Willard	1965-74	1622
30	James Wilder	1981-90	1586
31	John Henry Johnson	1954-66	1571
32	Chuck Muncie	1976-84	1561
33	Chuck Foreman	1973-80	1556
34	Wilbert Montgomery	1977-85	1540
35	Larry Brown	1969-76	1530
36	Lawrence McCutcheon	1972-81	1521
37	**Neal Anderson**	**1986-**	**1515**
38	Don Perkins	1961-68	1500
39	Sammy Winder	1982-90	1495
40	Pete Johnson	1977-84	1489
41	Calvin Hill	1969-74,76-81	1452
42	**Barry Sanders**	**1989-**	**1432**
43	Rick Casares	1955-66	1431
44	Sam Cunningham	1973-79,81-82	1385
45	John Brockington	1971-77	1347
46	Wendell Tyler	1977-86	1344
47	Jim Nance	1965-71,73	1341
48	Steve Van Buren	1944-51	1320
49	Joe Morris	1982-88,91	1411
50	William Andrews	1979-83,86	1315
51	Delvin Williams	1974-81	1312
52	Mike Garrett	1966-73	1308
53	Joe Cribbs	1980-83,85-88	1299
54	Emerson Boozer	1966-75	1291
	Kevin Mack	**1985-**	**1291**
56	**Emmitt Smith**	**1990-**	**1262**
57	Christian Okoye	1987-92	1246
58	Dick Bass	1960-69	1218
59	MacArthur Lane	1968-78	1206
60	Greg Bell	1984-90	1204
61	Ron Johnson	1969-75	1203
	Dexter Bussey	1974-84	1203
63	Tom Matte	1961-71	1200
64	Donny Anderson	1966-74	1197
65	Alex Webster	1955-64	1196
	Greg Pruitt	1973-84	1196
67	Joe Washington	1977-85	1195
68	Tony Collins	1981-87,90	1191
69	Dave Osborn	1965-76	1179
70	Rob Carpenter	1977-86	1172
71	Ollie Matson	1952, 54-66	1170
	Altie Taylor	1969-76	1170
73	Jim Otis	1970-78	1160
	Robert Newhouse	1972-83	1160
75	Mike Rozier	1985-91	1159
76	John David Crow	1958-68	1157
	Ed Podolak	1969-77	1157
78	Dave Hampton	1969-76	1148
	John L. Williams	**1986-**	**1148**
80	Clem Daniels	1960-68	1146

YARDS (3750)

1	Walter Payton	1975-87	16726
2	Eric Dickerson	1983-93	13259
3	Tony Dorsett	1977-88	12739
4	Jimmy Brown	1957-65	12312
5	Franco Harris	1972-84	12120
6	John Riggins	1974-79,81-85	11352
7	O.J. Simpson	1969-79	11236
8	Ottis Anderson	1979-92	10273
9	Joe Perry	1948-63	9723
10	Earl Campbell	1978-85	9407
11	**Marcus Allen**	**1982-**	**9309**
12	Jim Taylor	1958-67	8597
13	**Roger Craig**	**1983-**	**8189**
14	Gerald Riggs	1982-91	8188
15	Larry Csonka	1968-74,76-79	8081
16	Freeman McNeil	1981-92	8074
17	James Brooks	1981-92	7962
18	**Thurman Thomas**	**1988-**	**7631**
19	**Herschel Walker**	**1986-**	**7468**
20	Mike Pruitt	1976-86	7378
21	Leroy Kelly	1964-73	7274
22	George Rogers	1982-87	7176
23	Curt Warner	1983-90	6844
24	John Henry Johnson	1954-66	6803
25	**Barry Sanders**	**1989-**	**6789**
	Wilbert Montgomery	1977-85	6789
27	Chuck Muncie	1976-84	6702
28	**Ernest Byner**	**1984-**	**6663**
29	Mark van Eeghen	1974-83	6651
30	Lawrence McCutcheon	1972-81	6578
31	Lydell Mitchell	1972-80	6534
32	Wendell Tyler	1977-86	6378
33	Floyd Little	1965-75	6323
34	Don Perkins	1961-68	6217
35	**Neal Anderson**	**1986-**	**6166**
36	Ken Willard	1965-74	6105
37	Calvin Hill	1969-74,76-81	6083
38	James Wilder	1981-90	6008
39	William Andrews	1979-83,86	5986
40	Chuck Foreman	1973-80	5950
41	Larry Brown	1969-76	5875
42	Steve Van Buren	1944-51	5860
43	Bill Brown	1961-74	5838
44	Rick Casares	1955-66	5797
45	**Emmitt Smith**	**1990-**	**5699**
46	Greg Pruitt	1973-84	5672
47	Pete Johnson	1977-84	5626
48	Delvin Williams	1974-81	5598
49	Joe Morris	1982-88,91	5585
50	Mike Garrett	1966-73	5481
51	Sam Cunningham	1973-79,81-82	5453
52	Sammy Winder	1982-90	5427
53	Dick Bass	1960-69	5417
54	Jim Nance	1965-71,73	5401
55	Joe Cribbs	1980-83,85-88	5356
56	Hugh McElhenny	1952-64	5281
57	John Brockington	1971-77	5185
58	Lenny Moore	1956-67	5174
59	Ollie Matson	1952-66	5173
60	Clem Daniels	1960-68	5138
61	Emerson Boozer	1966-75	5135
62	**Kevin Mack**	**1985-**	**5123**
63	Billy Sims	1980-84	5106
64	Dexter Bussey	1974-84	5105
65	Paul Lowe	1960-61,63-69	4995
66	John David Crow	1958-68	4963
67	Greg Bell	1984-90	4959
68	Gale Sayers	1965-71	4956
69	Christian Okoye	1987-92	4897
70	Joe Washington	1977-85	4839
71	Robert Newhouse	1972-83	4784
72	Marion Motley	1946-53,55	4720
73	Donny Anderson	1966-74	4696
74	J.D. Smith	1955-66	4672
75	MacArthur Lane	1968-78	4656
76	Stump Mitchell	1981-89	4649
77	Tony Collins	1981-87,90	4647
78	Tom Matte	1961-71	4646
79	Alex Webster	1955-64	4638
80	Abner Haynes	1960-67	4630
81	**John L. Williams**	**1986-**	**4579**
82	Bob Hoernschemeyer	1946-55	4548
83	Ted Brown	1979-86	4546
84	Marv Hubbard	1969-75,77	4544
85	Dave Hampton	1969-76	4536
86	Mike Rozier	1985-91	4462
87	Otis Armstrong	1973-80	4453
88	Ed Podolak	1969-77	4451
89	Rob Carpenter	1977-86	4363
90	Jim Otis	1970-78	4350
91	Dave Osborn	1965-76	4336
92	Altie Taylor	1969-76	4308
93	Ron Johnson	1969-75	4307
94	Cookie Gilchrist	1962-67	4293
95	Matt Snell	1964-72	4285
96	Darrin Nelson	1982-92	4442
97	**Marion Butts**	**1989-**	**4297**
98	Johnny Hector	1983-92	4280
99	Tommy Mason	1961-71	4203
100	Tony Canadeo	1941-44,46-52	4197
	Carl Garrett	1969-77	4197
102	Mike Thomas	1975-80	4196
103	Earnest Jackson	1983-88	4167
104	**Dalton Hilliard**	**1986-**	**4164**
105	Mercury Morris	1969-76	4133
106	**Randall Cunningham**	**1985-**	**4096**
107	Tony Galbreath	1976-87	4072
108	Alan Ameche	1955-60	4045
109	Nick Pietrosante	1959-67	4026
110	Curtis Dickey	1980-86	4019
111	Frank Pollard	1980-88	3989
112	Dick Hoak	1961-70	3965
113	Walt Garrison	1966-74	3886
114	Randy McMillan	1981-86	3876
115	Rocky Bleier	1968-69,71-80	3864
116	Timmy Brown	1959-68	3862
117	Wilbur Jackson	1974-82	3852
118	Clarke Hinkle	1932-41	3850
119	Jon Arnett	1957-66	3833
120	Gerry Ellis	1980-86	3826

AVERAGE YARDS (4.21)

(Minimum 700 Rushes)

			Att.	Yards	Avg.
1	Marion Motley	1946-53,55	828	4720	5.70
2	Jimmy Brown	1957-65	2359	12312	5.22
3	Mercury Morris	1969-76	804	4133	5.14
4	Joe Perry	1948-63	1929	9723	5.04
5	Gale Sayers	1965-71	991	4956	5.00
6	Paul Lowe	1960-61,63-69	1026	4995	4.87
7	Lenny Moore	1956-67	1069	5174	4.84
8	Tony Nathan	1979-87	732	3543	4.84
9	Marv Hubbard	1965-75,77	951	4544	4.78
10	Wendell Tyler	1977-86	1344	6378	4.75
11	**Barry Sanders**	**1989-**	**1432**	**6789**	**4.74**
12	Greg Pruitt	1973-84	1196	5672	4.74
13	Tank Younger	1949-58	770	3640	4.73
	James Brooks	1981-92	1685	7962	4.73
15	Stump Mitchell	1981-89	986	4699	4.71
16	Hugh McElhenny	1952-64	1124	5281	4.70
17	O.J. Simpson	1969-79	2404	11236	4.67
18	Dutch Clark	1931-32,34-38	706	3272	4.63
19	Gerry Ellis	1980-86	836	3826	4.58
20	Terry Metcalf	1973-77,81	766	3498	4.57
21	William Andrews	1979-83,86-87	1315	5986	4.55
22	Bronko Nagurski	1930-37,43	738	3353	4.54
	Hoyle Granger	1966-72	805	3653	4.54
24	Clarence Davis	1971-78	804	3640	4.53
25	**Emmitt Smith**	**1990-**	**1262**	**5699**	**4.52**
26	Billy Sims	1980-84	1131	5106	4.51
	Freeman McNeil	1981-92	1798	8074	4.49
28	Clem Daniels	1960-68	1146	5138	4.48
	Essex Daniels	1968-76	722	3236	4.48
30	Abner Haynes	1960-67	1036	4630	4.47
31	Keith Lincoln	1961-68	758	3386	4.46
32	Dick Bass	1960-69	1218	5417	4.45
33	Steve Van Buren	1944-51	1320	5860	4.44
34	Jim Taylor	1958-67	1941	8597	4.43
	Eric Dickerson	1983-92	2996	13259	4.43
36	Ollie Matson	1952,54-66	1170	5173	4.42
37	**Thurman Thomas**	**1988-**	**1731**	**7631**	**4.41**
	Wilbert Montgomery	1977-85	1540	6789	4.41
39	Walter Payton	1975-87	3838	16726	4.36
40	Otis Armstrong	1973-80	1023	4453	4.35
	Darrin Nelson	1982-92	1020	4442	4.35
42	Tony Dorsett	1977-88	2936	12739	4.34
	Timmy Brown	1959-68	889	3862	4.34
44	John Henry Johnson	1954-66	1571	6803	4.33
45	Walt Garrison	1966-74	899	3886	4.32
	Lawrence McCutcheon	1972-81	1521	6578	4.32
47	Earl Campbell	1978-85	2187	9407	4.30
	Frank Gifford	1952-60,62-64	840	3609	4.30
	Amos Marsh	1961-67	750	3222	4.30
50	Bob Hoernschemeyer	1946-55	1059	4548	4.29
	John David Crow	1958-68	1157	4963	4.29
	Curtis Dickey	1980-86	937	4019	4.29
	Chuck Muncie	1976-84	1561	6702	4.29
54	Tom Woodeschick	1963-72	1836	3577	4.28
	Willie Ellison	1967-74	801	3426	4.28
56	Les Josephson	1964-67,69-74	797	3407	4.27
	Larry Csonka	1968-74,76-79	1891	8081	4.27
58	Cookie Gilchrist	1962-67	1010	4293	4.25
	J.D. Smith	1956-66	1100	4672	4.25
	Dexter Bussey	1974-84	1203	5105	4.25
61	George Rogers	1981-87	1692	7176	4.24
62	Nick Pietrosante	1959-67	955	4026	4.22
	John Fuqua	1969-76	719	3031	4.22
	Sherman Smith	1976-83	834	3520	4.22

TOUCHDOWNS (33)

1	Walter Payton	1975-87	110
2	Jimmy Brown	1957-65	106
3	John Riggins	1971-79,81-85	104
4	Franco Harris	1972-84	91
	Marcus Allen	**1982-**	**91**
6	Eric Dickerson	1983-93	90
7	Jim Taylor	1958-67	83
8	Ottis Anderson	1979-92	81
9	Tony Dorsett	1977-88	77
10	Pete Johnson	1977-84	76
11	Leroy Kelly	1964-73	74
	Earl Campbell	1978-85	74
13	Joe Perry	1948-53	71
	Chuck Muncie	1976-84	71
15	Steve Van Buren	1944-51	69
16	Gerald Riggs	1982-91	69
17	Larry Csonka	1968-74,76-79	64
18	Lenny Moore	1956-67	63
19	O.J. Simpson	1969-79	61
20	Curt Warner	1983-90	56
	Roger Craig	**1983-**	**56**
22	**Herschel Walker**	**1986-**	**55**
	Barry Sanders	**1989-**	**55**
24	George Rogers	1981-87	54
25	Chuck Foreman	1973-80	53
26	Bill Brown	1961-74	52
	Emerson Boozer	1966-75	52
28	Mike Pruitt	1976-86	51
	Greg Bell	1984-90	51
	Neal Anderson	**1986-**	**51**
31	Paul Hornung	1957-62,64-66	50
	Wendell Tyler	1977-86	50
	Joe Morris	1982-88,91	50
	Emmitt Smith	**1990-**	**50**
35	Rick Casares	1955-66	49
	James Brooks	1981-92	49
37	John Henry Johnson	1954-66	48
	Earnest Byner	**1984-**	**48**
39	Pete Banaszak	1966-78	47
40	Abner Haynes	1960-67	46
	Kevin Mack	**1985-**	**46**
42	Tom Matte	1961-72	45
	Jim Nance	1965-71,73	45
	Ken Willard	1965-74	45
	Wilbert Montgomery	1977-85	45
46	Otto Graham	1946-55	44
	Larry Kinnebrew	1983-87,89-90	44
48	Dan Towler	1950-55	43
	Floyd Little	1967-75	43
	Sam Cunningham	1973-79,81	43
51	Don Perkins	1961-68	42
	Calvin Hill	1969-74,76-81	42
	Billy Sims	1980-84	42
54	Donny Anderson	1966-74	41
	Johnny Hector	1983-92	41
	Thurman Thomas	**1988-**	**41**
57	Vern Lewellen	1924-32	40
	Alan Ameche	1955-60	40
	Ollie Matson	1952,54-66	40
	J.D. Smith	1955-66	40
	Jack Kemp	1957,60-67,69	40
	Paul Lowe	1960-61,63-69	40
	Ron Johnson	1969-75	40
	Ted Brown	1979-86	40
	Don McCauley	1971-81	40
	Christian Okoye	1987-92	40
67	Alex Webster	1955-64	39
	Gale Sayers	1965-71	39
	Y.A. Tittle	1948-64	39
	Sammy Winder	1982-90	39
	Dalton Hilliard	**1986-**	**39**
72	Hugh McElhenny	1952-64	38
	John David Crow	1958-68	38
	Freeman McNeil	1981-92	38
75	Ernie Nevers	1926-27,29-31	37
	Tobin Rote	1950-59,63-64,66	37
	Bill Mathis	1960-69	37
	Cookie Gilchrist	1962-67	37
	Mark van Eeghen	1974-83	37
	Wayne Morris	1976-84	37
	James Wilder	1981-90	37
82	Dutch Clark	1931-32,34-38	36
	Pug Manders	1939- 47	36
84	Clarke Hinkle	1932- 41	35
	Mike Garrett	1966-73	35
	Larry Brown	1969-76	35
	Steve Grogan	1975-90	35
88	Tank Younger	1949-58	34
	Frank Gifford	1952-60,62-64	34
	Dick Bass	1960-69	34
	Ed Podolak	1969-77	34
	Don Nottingham	1971-78	34
	Tony Galbreath	1976-87	34
94	Pat Harder	1946-53	33
	Spec Sanders	1946-48,50	33
	Delvin Williams	1974-81	33

Players active at the end of 1993 are shown in **bold face.**

LIFETIME LEADERS
RECEIVING

RECEPTIONS (385)

1	**Art Monk**	1980-	888
2	Steve Largent	1976-89	819
3	**James Lofton**	1978-	764
4	Charlie Joiner	1969-86	750
5	**Jerry Rice**	1985-	708
6	Ozzie Newsome	1978-90	662
7	Charley Taylor	1964-75,77	649
8	**Drew Hill**	1979-	634
9	Don Maynard	1958, 60-73	633
10	Raymond Berry	1955-67	631
11	**Gary Clark**	1985-	612
12	**Henry Ellard**	1983-	593
13	Harold Carmichael	1971-84	590
14	Fred Biletnikoff	1965-78	589
15	**Andre Reed**	1985-	586
16	**Mark Clayton**	1983-	582
17	Harold Jackson	1968-83	579
18	Lionel Taylor	1959-68	567
19	**Roger Craig**	1983-	566
20	Wes Chandler	1978-88	559
21	Roy Green	1979-92	559
22	Stanley Morgan	1977-90	557
23	J.T. Smith	1978-90	544
24	Lance Alworth	1962-72	542
25	Kellen Winslow	1979-87	541
26	John Stallworth	1974-87	537
27	**Eric Martin**	1985-	532
28	Bobby Mitchell	1958-68	521
29	Al Toon	1985-92	517
30	Mark Duper	1982-92	511
31	Nat Moore	1974-86	510
32	**Ernest Givins**	1986-	506
33	Dwight Clark	1979-87	506
34	Billy Howton	1952-63	503
35	**Sterling Sharpe**	1988-	501
	Cliff Branch	1972-85	501
37	Tommy McDonald	1957-68	495
	Ahmad Rashad	1972-74,76-82	495
	Steve Jordan	1982-	495
40	Walter Payton	1975-87	492
41	Tony Galbreath	1976-88	490
42	Drew Pearson	1973-83	489
43	Don Hutson	1935-45	488
44	Jackie Smith	1963-78	480
	Marcus Allen	1982-	480
46	Art Powell	1959-68	479
	Tony Hill	1977-86	479
	Anthony Carter	1985-	478
49	Boyd Dowler	1959-69,71	474
50	**John L. Williams**	1986-	471
51	**Bill Brooks**	1986-	471
52	Pat Tilley	1976-86	468
53	Mickey Shuler	1978-91	462
54	Todd Christensen	1979-88	461
55	Pete Retzlaff	1956-66	452
56	Roy Jefferson	1965-76	451
57	Haven Moses	1968-81	448
58	Reggie Rucker	1970-81	447
59	Carroll Dale	1960-73	438
	Wesley Walker	1977-89	438
61	**Keith Byars**	1986-	432
62	James Wilder	1981-90	431
63	Mike Ditka	1961-72	427
	Paul Warfield	1964-74,76-77	427
	Irving Fryar	1984-	427
66	Bobby Joe Conrad	1958-69	422
	Bob Tucker	1970-80	422
68	Jerry Smith	1965-77	421
	Ken Burrough	1970-82	421
	Webster Slaughter	1986-	421
	Ronnie Harmon	1986-	421
72	Charle Young	1973-85	418
73	Cris Collinsworth	1981-88	417
74	Isaac Curtis	1973-84	416
	Henry Marshall	1976-87	416
76	**Ricky Sanders**	1986-	414
77	**Reggie Langhorne**	1985-	411
78	Charley Hennigan	1960-66	410
	Herschel Walker	1986-	410
	Otis Taylor	1965-74	410
81	Rickey Young	1975-83	408
82	Billy Wilson	1951-60	407
83	Gary Garrison	1966-77	405
84	**Vance Johnson**	1985-	403
85	Jim Phillips	1958-67	401
86	Tom Fears	1948-56	400
	Jimmy Orr	1958-70	400
88	Tony Dorsett	1977-88	398
89	Frank Lewis	1971-83	397
90	Riley Odoms	1972-83	396
91	Joe Morrison	1959-72	395
	Joe Washington	1977-85	395
93	**Andre Rison**	1989-	394
94	Sammy White	1976-85	393
	Russ Francis	1975-80,82-88	393
96	Chris Burford	1960-67	391
97	**Earnest Byner**	1984-	389
98	Elroy Hirsch	1946-57	387
99	Dante Lavelli	1946-56	386
	Haywood Jeffires	1987-	386

YARDS (5900)

1	**James Lofton**	1978-	14004
2	Steve Largent	1976-89	13089
3	Charlie Joiner	1969-86	12146
4	**Art Monk**	1980-	12026
5	Don Maynard	1958,1960-73	11834
6	**Jerry Rice**	1985-	11776
7	Stanley Morgan	1977-90	10716
8	Harold Jackson	1968-83	10372
9	Lance Alworth	1962-72	10266
10	**Drew Hill**	1979-	9831
11	**Henry Ellard**	1983-	9761
12	**Gary Clark**	1985-	9560
13	Raymond Berry	1955-67	9275
14	Charley Taylor	1964-75, 77	9110
15	Harold Carmichael	1971-84	8985
16	Fred Biletnikoff	1965-78	8974
	Mark Clayton	1983-	8974
18	Wes Chandler	1978-88	8966
19	Roy Green	1979-92	8965
20	Mark Duper	1982-92	8869
21	John Stallworth	1974-87	8723
22	Cliff Branch	1972-85	8685
23	Paul Warfield	1964-74,76-77	8565
24	Billy Howton	1952-63	8459
25	Tommy McDonald	1957-68	8410
26	Wesley Walker	1977-89	8306
27	Carroll Dale	1960-73	8277
28	**Andre Reed**	1985-	8233
29	Haven Moses	1968-81	8091
30	Art Powell	1959-68	8046
31	Tony Hill	1977-86	7988
32	Don Hutson	1935-45	7981
33	Bobby Mitchell	1958-68	7954
34	Jimmy Orr	1958-70	7914
35	**Eric Martin**	1985-	7854
36	Drew Pearson	1973-83	7822
37	Ozzie Newsome	1978-90	7980
38	**Anthony Carter**	1985-	7635
39	Nat Moore	1974-86	7546
40	Roy Jefferson	1965-76	7539
41	Gary Garrison	1966-77	7538
42	Jackie Smith	1963-78	7418
43	Bob Hayes	1965-75	7414
	Ernest Givins	1986-	7414
45	Pete Retzlaff	1956-66	7412
46	Otis Taylor	1965-74	7306
47	Boyd Dowler	1959-69,71	7270
48	Lionel Taylor	1959-68	7195
49	Ken Burrough	1970-81	7102
50	Isaac Curtis	1973-84	7101
51	Reggie Rucker	1970-81	7065
52	John Gilliam	1967-77	7056
53	Elroy Hirsch	1946-57	7029
54	**Sterling Sharpe**	1988-	7015
55	Pat Tilley	1976-86	7005
56	J.T. Smith	1978-90	6974
57	Gene Washington	1968-77,79	6856
58	Ahmad Rashad	1972-74,76-82	6831
59	Charley Hennigan	1960-66	6823
60	Dwight Clark	1979-87	6750
61	Kellen Winslow	1979-87	6741
62	**Irving Fryar**	1984-	6736
63	Frank Lewis	1971-83	6724
64	Cris Collinsworth	1981-88	6698
65	Mel Gray	1971-82	6644
66	**Willie Gault**	1983-	6635
67	Al Toon	1985-92	6605
68	Henry Marshall	1976-87	6545
69	**Bill Brooks**	1986-	6532
70	Dante Lavelli	1946-56	6488
71	Del Shofner	1957-67	6470
72	Mike Quick	1982-90	6464
73	Sammy White	1976-85	6400
74	Carlos Carson	1980-89	6372
75	Max McGee	1954,57-67	6346
76	Stephone Paige	1983-91	6341
77	**Steve Jordan**	1982-	6284
78	Alfred Jenkins	1975-83	6258
79	**Webster Slaughter**	1986-	6224
80	Eddie Brown	1985-91	6134
81	Steve Watson	1979-88	6112
82	Jim Phillips	1958-67	6044
83	Lenny Moore	1956-76	6039
84	Louis Lipps	1984-92	6019
85	Jack Snow	1965-75	6012
86	Sonny Randle	1959-68	5996
87	Billy Wilson	1951-60	5902
	Bobby Joe Conrad	1958-69	5902

AVERAGE YARDS (16.25)

(Minimum 200 Receptions)

1	Homer Jones	1964-70	224	4986	22.26
2	Buddy Dial	1959-66	261	5436	20.83
3	Harlon Hill	1954-62	233	4717	20.25
4	**Willie Anderson**	1988-	213	4301	20.19
5	Paul Warfield	1964-74,76-77	427	8656	20.06
6	Bob Hayes	1965-75	371	7414	19.98
7	**Willie Gault**	1983-	333	6635	19.92
8	Jimmy Orr	1958-70	400	7914	19.79
9	Ray Renfro	1952-63	281	5508	19.60
10	Stanley Morgan	1977-90	557	10716	19.24
	Hugh Taylor	1947-54	272	5233	19.24
12	Wesley Walker	1977-89	438	8306	18.96
13	Lance Alworth	1962-72	542	10267	18.94
14	Mel Gray	1971-83	351	6644	18.93
15	Carroll Dale	1960-73	438	8277	18.90
16	Roger Carr	1974-84	254	4770	18.78
17	Don Maynard	1958,60-73	633	11834	18.70
18	Frank Clarke	1957-67	291	5426	18.65
19	Gary Garrison	1966-77	405	7538	18.61
20	Del Shofner	1957-67	349	6470	18.54
21	John Gilliam	1967-77	382	7056	18.47
22	Max McGee	1954,57-67	345	6346	18.39
23	**James Lofton**	1978-	764	14004	18.33
24	Ben Hawkins	1966-73	261	4764	18.25
25	Elroy Hirsch	1946-57	387	7029	18.16
26	Haven Moses	1968-81	448	8091	18.06
27	Carlos Carson	1980-89	353	6372	18.05
28	Lance Rentzel	1965-72,74	268	4826	18.01
29	Mervyn Fernandez	1987-92	209	3764	18.01
30	Elbert Dubenion	1960-68	295	5305	17.98
31	Harold Jackson	1968-83	579	10372	17.92
32	Darrell Brewster	1952-60	210	3798	17.90
33	Otis Taylor	1965-74	410	7302	17.82
34	Gene Washington	1968-77,79	385	6856	17.81
	Jack Snow	1965-75	340	6012	17.81
36	Mike Quick	1982-90	363	6464	17.80
37	Jim Colclough	1960-68	283	5001	17.67
38	Alfred Jenkins	1975-83	359	6258	17.43
39	Aaron Thomas	1961-70	262	4554	17.38
	Bob Schnelker	1953-61	211	3667	17.38
41	Mark Duper	1982-92	511	8869	17.36
42	Cliff Branch	1972-85	501	8685	17.34
43	Steve Watson	1979-87	353	6112	17.31
44	Jim Doran	1951-61	212	3667	17.30
45	Kevin House	1980-87	299	5169	17.29
46	Bobby Walston	1951-62	311	5363	17.24
47	Rich Caster	1970-81	322	5515	17.13
48	Ray Mathews	1951-60	233	3963	17.01
49	Tommy McDonald	1957-68	495	8410	16.99
50	Frank Lewis	1971-83	397	6724	16.94
51	Isaac Curtis	1973-84	420	7106	16.92
52	**John Taylor**	1987-	277	4680	16.90
	Leonard Thompson	1975-86	277	4682	16.90
	Eddie Brown	1985-	363	6134	16.90
	Michael Irvin	1988-	337	5694	16.90
56	**Ernie Jones**	1988-	215	3630	16.88
57	Ken Burrough	1970-81	421	7102	16.87
58	Billy Howton	1952-63	503	8549	16.82
	Stephone Paige	1983-91	377	6341	16.82
60	Dante Lavelli	1946-56	386	6488	16.81
61	Art Powell	1959-68	479	8046	16.80
	Lionel Manuel	1984-90	232	3898	16.80
63	Terry Barr	1957-65	227	3810	16.78
64	Louis Lipps	1984-92	359	6019	16.77
65	Jim Mutscheller	1954-61	220	3864	16.75
66	Duriel Harris	1976-84	302	5055	16.74
67	Roy Jefferson	1956-76	451	7539	16.72
68	**Hassan Jones**	1986-	229	3824	16.70
69	Tony Hill	1977-86	479	7988	16.68
70	Jim Benton	1938-40,42-47	288	4801	16.67
71	Charley Hennigan	1960-66	410	6823	16.64
	Lenny Moore	1956-67	363	6039	16.64
73	**Jerry Rice**	1985-	708	11776	16.63
74	Gary Ballman	1962-73	323	5366	16.61
75	Charley Frazier	1962-70	209	3461	16.56
76	Ray Butler	1980-88	239	3948	16.52
77	Jackie Smith	1963-78	480	7418	16.50
78	**Henry Ellard**	1983-	5593	9761	16.46
79	Stacey Bailey	1982-90	208	3422	16.45
80	Al Denson	1964-71	260	4278	16.44
81	Sonny Randle	1959-68	365	5996	16.43
	Dave Kocourek	1960-68	249	4090	16.43
83	Pete Retzlaff	1956-66	452	7412	16.40
84	Don Hutson	1935-45	488	7981	16.36
	Rick Upchurch	1975-83	267	4369	16.36
86	Clem Daniels	1960-68	203	3314	16.33
	Mark Jackson	1986-	334	5454	16.33
88	**Tim McGee**	1986-	308	5028	16.32
89	Jeff Chadwick	1983-90	241	3932	16.31
90	Freddie Scott	1974-83	257	4199	16.30
91	Sammy White	1976-85	393	6400	16.28
	John Jefferson	1978-85	351	5714	16.28
93	Lynn Swann	1974-82	336	5462	16.26

TOUCHDOWNS (48)

1	**Jerry Rice**	1985-	118
2	Don Hutson	1935-45	100
	Steve Largent	1976-89	100
4	Don Maynard	1958,60-73	88
5	Lance Alworth	1962-72	85
6	Paul Warfield	1964-74,76-77	85
7	Tommy McDonald	1957-68	84
8	Art Powell	1959-68	81
	Mark Clayton	1983-	84
10	Charley Taylor	1964-75,77	79
	Harold Carmichael	1971-84	79
12	Fred Biletnikoff	1965-78	76
	Harold Jackson	1968-83	76
14	**James Lofton**	1978-	75
15	Nat Moore	1974-86	74
16	Stanley Morgan	1977-90	72
17	Bob Hayes	1965-75	71
18	Wesley Walker	1977-89	71
19	Gary Collins	1962-71	70
20	Raymond Berry	1955-67	68
21	Cliff Branch	1972-85	67
22	Jimmy Orr	1958-70	66
23	Roy Green	1979-92	66
24	Bobby Mitchell	1958-68	65
	Sonny Randle	1959-68	65
	Charley Joiner	1969-86	65
	Art Monk	1980-	65
28	John Stallworth	1974-87	63
29	Dante Lavelli	1946-56	62
	Gary Clark	1985-	62
31	Pete Pihos	1947-55	61
	Billy Howton	1952-63	61
	Mike Quick	1982-90	61
34	Elroy Hirsch	1946-57	60
	Jerry Smith	1965-77	60
	Gene Washington	1969-77,79	60
	Drew Hill	1979-	60
38	Mark Duper	1982-92	59
39	Hugh Taylor	1947-54	58
	Gary Garrison	1966-77	58
	Andre Reed	1985-	58
42	Otis Taylor	1965-74	57
43	Haven Moses	1968-81	56
	Wes Chandler	1978-88	56
45	Chris Burford	1960-67	55
46	Isaac Curtis	1973-84	53
47	Carroll Dale	1960-73	52
	Roy Jefferson	1965-76	52
	Dave Casper	1974-84	52
	Andre Rison	1989-	52
	Anthony Carter	1985-	52
52	Del Shofner	1957-67	51
	Charley Hennigan	1960-66	51
	Lynn Swann	1974-82	51
	Tony Hill	1977-86	51
56	Ken Kavanaugh	1940-41, 45-50	50
	Ray Renfro	1952-63	50
	Max McGee	1954, 57-67	50
	Frank Clarke	1957-67	50
	Sammy White	1976-85	50
61	Alyn Beals	1946-51	49
	Billy Wilson	1951-60	49
	Ken Burrough	1970-81	49
	Stephone Paige	1983-91	49
65	Kyle Rote	1951-61	48
	Lenny Moore	1956-67	48
	John Gilliam	1967-77	48
	Bob Chandler	1971-82	48
	Ray Chester	1970-81	48
	Drew Pearson	1973-83	48
	Freddie Solomon	1975-85	48
	Dwight Clark	1979-87	48
	Henry Ellard	1983-	48
	Eric Martin	1985-	48

Players active at the end of 1993 are shown in **bold face.**

LIFETIME LEADERS
PUNT RETURNS

(141)

1	**Val Sikahema**	**1986-**	**292**
2	Billy Johnson	1974-87	282
3	J.T. Smith	1978-90	267
4	Emlen Tunnell	1948-61	258
5	Alvin Haymond	1964-73	253
6	Mike Fuller	1975-82	252
7	Rick Upchurch	1975-83	248
8	Ron Smith	1965-74	235
9	Danny Reece	1976-80	222
10	Phil McConkey	1984-89	218
11	**Rod Woodson**	**1987-**	**217**
12	Mike Nelms	1980-84	212
13	**Irving Fryar**	**1984-**	**206**
14	Speedy Duncan	1964-74	202
	Leo Lewis	1981-91	202
16	Greg Pruitt	1973-84	194
17	**Tim Brown**	**1988-**	**193**
18	**Willie Drewrey**	**1985-**	**192**
19	Gerald McNeil	1986-90	191
20	Theo Bell	1976-85	189
21	Willie Wood	1960-71	187
22	Bruce Harper	1977-84	183
23	**Dave Meggett**	**1989-**	**178**
24	Freddie Solomon	1975-85	177
25	Robbie Martin	1981-86	175
26	Walter Stanley	1985-90,92	175
27	Eddie Brown	1974-79	172
28	**Kelvin Martin**	**1987-**	**170**
29	Neal Colzie	1975-83	170
30	Pete Mandley	1984-90	165
31	Howard Stevens	1973-77	163
32	Larry Marshall	1972-78	162
33	**Mel Gray**	**1986**	**160**
34	Charlie West	1968-79	158
35	Bill Thompson	1969-81	157
36	Eddie Payton	1977-78,80-82	156
	Stump Mitchell	1981-89	156
38	**Clarence Verdin**	**1986-**	**155**
39	Carl Roaches	1980-85	155
40	Dana McLemore	1982-87	152
41	Butch Atkinson	1968-77,79	148
	Wally Henry	1977-82	148
43	Butch Johnson	1976-85	146
	LeRoy Irvin	1980-90	146
45	Fulton Walker	1981-86	145
46	Lem Barney	1967-77	143
47	Bruce Taylor	1970-77	142
48	Leon Bright	1981-85	141

YARDS (1250)

1	Billy Johnson	1974-88	3317
2	**Val Sikahema**	**1986-**	**3169**
3	Rick Upchurch	1975-83	3008
4	J.T. Smith	1978-90	2764
5	Mike Fuller	1975-82	2660
6	Emlen Tunnell	1948-61	2209
7	Speedy Duncan	1964-74	2201
8	Alvin Haymond	1964-73	2148
9	**Irving Fryar**	**1984-**	**2055**
10	**Rod Woodson**	**1987-**	**2043**
11	Greg Pruitt	1973-84	2007
12	**Tim Brown**	**1988-**	**1960**
13	Mike Nelms	1980-84	1948
14	**Dave Meggett**	**1989-**	**1907**
15	Leo Lewis	1981-91	1868
16	**Mel Gray**	**1986-**	**1851**
17	Phil McConkey	1984-89	1832
18	Bill Thompson	1969-81	1814
19	Ron Smith	1965-74	1788
20	Bruce Harper	1977-84	1784
21	Neal Colzie	1975-82	1759
22	Gerald McNeil	1986-90	1717
23	**Kelvin Martin**	**1987-**	**1700**
24	Robbie Martin	1981-86	1670
25	Walter Stanley	1985-90,92	1619
26	Freddie Solomon	1975-85	1614
27	Dana McLemore	1982-87	1598
28	**Willie Drewrey**	**1985-**	**1597**
29	Howard Stevens	1973-77	1559
30	Danny Reece	1976-80	1554
31	**ClarenceVerdin**	**1986-**	**1537**
32	**Henry Ellard**	**1983-**	**1527**
33	Bill Dudley	1942,45-51,53	1515
34	Pete Mandley	1984-90	1514
35	Eddie Brown	1974-79	1511
36	Theo Bell	1976,78-85	1511
37	Larry Marshall	1972-78	1466
38	**John Taylor**	**1987-**	**1461**
39	LeRoy Irvin	1980-90	1451
40	Fulton Walker	1981-86	1439
41	George McAfee	1940-41,45-50	1431
42	Willie Wood	1960-71	1391
43	Eddie Payton	1977-78,80-82	1387
44	Claude Gibson	1961-65	1381
	Mike Martin	1983-89	1381
46	Stump Mitchell	1981-89	1377
47	JoJo Townsell	1985-90	1360
48	Jake Scott	1970-78	1357
49	Curly Oden	1925-28,30-32	1336
50	Bruce Taylor	1970-77	1323
51	Butch Johnson	1976-85	1313
52	Lem Barney	1967-77	1312

AVERAGE RETURN (10.3)

(Minimum 75 Returns)

			Ret.	Yards	Avg.
1	Two Bits Homan	1925-30	76	1009	13.28
2	Charley Rogers	1927-29	92	1199	13.03
3	George McAfee	1940-41,45-50	112	1431	12.78
4	Jack Christiansen	1951-58	85	1084	12.75
5	Ken Strong	1929-35,39-44,47	88	1112	12.64
6	Claude Gibson	1961-65	110	1381	12.56
7	Bill Dudley	1942,45-51,53	124	1515	12.22
8	Rick Upchurch	1975-83	248	3008	12.13
9	Jack Ernst	1925-30	89	1060	11.91
10	Billy Johnson	1974-88	282	3317	11.76
11	Mack Herron	1973-75	84	982	11.69
12	**Mel Gray**	**1986-**	**160**	**1851**	**11.57**
13	Bill Thompson	1969-81	157	1814	11.55
14	**Henry Ellard**	**1983-**	**135**	**1527**	**11.31**
15	Rodger Bird	1961-68	94	1063	11.31
16	Bosh Pritchard	1942,46-49,51	95	1072	11.28
17	Bobby Joe Edmonds	1986-89	105	1178	11.22
18	Terry Metcalf	1973-77,81	84	936	11.14
19	Bob Hayes	1965-75	104	1158	11.13
20	Floyd Little	1967-75	81	893	11.02
	Louis Lipps	1984-92	112	1234	11.02
22	Speedy Duncan	1964-74	202	2201	10.90
23	Vitamin Smith	1949-53	75	814	10.85
24	**Val Sikahema**	**1986-**	**292**	**3169**	**10.85**
25	**Eric Metcalf**	**1989-**	**92**	**993**	**10.79**
26	**Dave Meggett**	**1989-**	**178**	**1907**	**10.71**
27	JoJo Townsell	1985-90	127	1360	10.71
28	**John Taylor**	**1987-**	**138**	**1461**	**10.59**
29	Mike Fuller	1975-82	252	2660	10.56
30	Leroy Kelly	1964-73	94	990	10.53
31	Tommy Vigorito	1981-83,85	79	830	10.51
32	Dana McLemore	1982-87	152	1598	10.51
33	Keith Moody	1976-80	88	920	10.45
34	Jake Scott	1970-78	130	1357	10.44
35	Gerald Wilhite	1982-88	101	1054	10.44
36	Mike Haynes	1976-88	112	1168	10.43
	Stanley Morgan	1977-90	92	960	10.43
38	Neal Colzie	1975-82	170	1759	10.35
	Greg Pruitt	1973-84	194	2007	10.35
	J.T. Smith	1978-90	267	2764	10.35

TOUCHDOWNS (3)

1	Jack Christiansen	1951-58	8
	Rick Upchurch	1975-83	8
3	Billy Johnson	1974-88	6
4	Em Tunnell	1948-61	5
	Clarence Verdin	**1986-**	**5**
6	Curly Oden	1925-28,30-32	4
	Speedy Duncan	1964-74	4
	Dick Christy	1958,60-62	4
	Lemar Parrish	1970-81	4
	Freddie Solomon	1975-85	4
	J.T. Smith	1978-90	4
	LeRoy Irvin	1980-90	4
	Dana McLemore	1982-87	4
	Henry Ellard	**1983-**	**4**
	Val Sikahema	**1986-**	**4**
	Dave Meggett	**1989-**	**4**
17	Dick Todd	1939-40,42,45-48	3
	Ray McLean	1940,42-47	3
	Bill Dudley	1942,45-51,53	3
	Woodley Lewis	1950-60	3
	Ray Mathews	1951-60	3
	Yale Lary	1952-53,56-64	3
	Ollie Matson	1952,54-66	3
	Bert Zagers	1955,57-58	3
	Bobby Mitchell	1958-68	3
	Claude Gibson	1961-65	3
	Tom Watkins	1961-65,67-68	3
	Leroy Kelly	1964-73	3
	Bob Hayes	1965-75	3
	Rickie Harris	1965-72	3
	Butch Atkinson	1968-77,79	3
	John Staggers	1970-75	3
	Steve Schubert	1974-79	3
	Keith Moody	1976-80	3
	Dennis McKinnon	1983-85,87-90	3
	Irving Fryar	**1984-**	**3**
	Louis Lipps	1984-92	3
	Mel Gray	**1986-**	**3**
	Kelvin Martin	**1987-**	**3**
	Brian Mitchell	**1990-**	**3**

KICKOFF RETURNS

(133)

1	Ron Smith	1965-74	275
2	**Mel Gray**	**1986-**	**264**
3	Bruce Harper	1977-84	243
4	**Val Sikahema**	**1986-**	**235**
5	**Clarence Verdin**	**1986-**	**209**
6	**Rod Woodson**	**1987-**	**205**
7	Ron Brown	1984-91	199
8	Steve Odom	1974-79	194
9	Abe Woodson	1958-68	193
10	Dennis Gentry	1982-92	192
11	Al Carmichael	1953-58,60-61	191
12	Dick James	1956-61	189
	Larry Anderson	1978-84	189
14	Timmy Brown	1959-68	184
15	Speedy Duncan	1964-74	180
16	Stump Mitchell	1981-89	177
17	Mike Nelms	1980-84	175
18	**Drew Hill**	**1979-**	**172**
19	Alvin Haymond	1963-73	170
20	Fulton Walker	1981-86	167
21	Darrin Nelson	1982-92	163
22	Eddie Payton	1977-78,80-82	156
23	Bobby Jancik	1962-67	158
24	Carl Garrett	1969-77	154
	Carl Roaches	1980-85	154
26	Kermit Alexander	1963-73	153
27	Bruce Laird	1972-83	152
28	Dino Hall	1979-83	151
29	Donnie Elder	1985-86,89-91	150
30	Albert Bentley	1985-92	149
31	Stanford Jennings	1984-92	148
32	**Deion Sanders**	**1989-**	**147**
33	Ollie Matson	1952,54-66	143
	Gary Anderson	**1985-88,90**	**143**
35	Joe Arenas	1951-57	139
36	Larry Marshall	1972-78	138
37	Woodley Lewis	1950-60	137
38	Clarence Childs	1964-68	134
39	Cannonball Butler	1965-72	133
	Jamie Holland	1987-92	133

YARDS (2806)

1	Ron Smith	1965-74	6922
2	**Mel Gray**	**1986-**	**6374**
3	Abe Woodson	1958-66	5538
4	Bruce Harper	1977-84	5407
5	**Val Sikahema**	**1986-**	**4933**
6	Al Carmichael	1953-58,60-61	4798
7	Timmy Brown	1959-68	4781
8	Dick James	1956-61	4676
9	Speedy Duncan	1964-74	4539
10	**Rod Woodson**	**1987-**	**4529**
11	Ron Brown	1981-91	4493
12	Alvin Haymond	1963-73	4438
13	Dennis Gentry	1982-92	4353
14	Steve Odom	1974-79	4251
15	**Clarence Verdin**	**1986-**	**4226**
16	Larry Anderson	1978-84	4217
17	Bobby Jancik	1962-67	4185
18	Mike Nelms	1980-84	4128
19	Stump Mitchell	1981-89	4007
20	Joe Arenas	1951-57	3798
21	Fulton Walker	1981-86	3769
22	Ollie Matson	1952, 54-66	3746
23	Bruce Laird	1972-83	3728
24	Carl Garrett	1969-77	3704
25	Darrin Nelson	1982-92	3659
26	Kermit Alexander	1963-73	3586
27	Buddy Young	1947-55	3465
28	**Drew Hill**	**1979-**	**3460**
29	Clarence Childs	1964-68	3454
30	Larry Marshall	1972-78	3396
31	**Deion Sanders**	**1989-**	**3390**
32	Carl Roaches	1980-85	3352
33	Vic Washington	1971-76	3341
34	Woodley Lewis	1950-60	3325
35	Dino Hall	1979-83	3185
36	Albert Bentley	1985-92	3192
37	Jon Arnett	1957-66	3110
38	Terry Metcalf	1973-77,81	3087
39	Herb Adderley	1961-72	3080
40	Bo Roberson	1961-66	3057
41	Donnie Elder	1985-86,89-91	3040
42	Abner Haynes	1960-67	3025
43	Bobby Humphery	1981-90	2974
44	Stanford Jennings	1984-92	2965
45	Mercury Morris	1969-76	2947
46	Billy Johnson	1974-88	2941
47	Cannonball Butler	1965-72	2931
48	Dave Hampton	1969-76	2923
49	Bill Butler	1959-64	2886
50	Rich Mauti	1977-84	2836
51	Alvin Hall	1981-85	2819
52	Jamie Holland	1987-92	2806

AVERAGE RETURNS (25.5)

(Minimum 75 Returns)

			Ret.	Yards	Avg.
1	Gale Sayers	1965-71	91	2781	30.56
2	Lynn Chandnois	1950-56	92	2720	29.57
3	Abe Woodson	1958-66	193	5538	28.69
4	Buddy Young	1947-55	125	3465	27.72
5	Travis Williams	1967-71	102	2801	27.46
6	Joe Arenas	1951-57	139	3798	27.32
7	Clarence Davis	1971-78	79	2140	27.09
8	Steve Van Buren	1944-51	76	2030	26.71
9	Lenny Lyles	1958-69	81	2161	26.68
10	Mercury Morris	1969-76	111	2947	26.55
11	Bobby Jancik	1962-67	158	4185	26.49
12	Mel Renfro	1964-77	85	2246	26.42
13	Bobby Mitchell	1958-68	102	2690	26.37
14	Ollie Matson	1952,54-66	143	3746	26.20
15	Alvin Haymond	1963-73	170	4438	26.11
16	Noland Smith	1967-69	82	2137	26.06
17	Al Nelson	1965-73	101	2625	25.99
18	Timmy Brown	1959-68	184	4781	25.98
19	Vic Washington	1971-76	129	3341	25.90
20	Dave Hampton	1966-76	113	2923	25.87
21	Larry Garron	1960-68	89	2299	25.83
22	Clarence Childs	1964-68	134	3454	25.78
23	Terry Metcalf	1973-77,81	120	3087	25.73
24	Herb Adderley	1961-72	120	3080	25.67
25	Pat Studstill	1961-62,64-72	75	1924	25.65
26	Walter Roberts	1964-67,69-70	107	2728	25.50

TOUCHDOWNS (3)

1	Ollie Matson	1952,54-66	6
	Gale Sayers	1965-71	6
	Travis Williams	1967-71	6
4	Bobby Mitchell	1958-68	5
	Abe Woodson	1958-66	5
	Timmy Brown	1959-68	5
7	Buddy Young	1947-55	4
	Cecil Turner	1968-73	4
	Steve Van Buren	1944-51	4
	Ron Brown	1984-91	4
11	Vitamin Smith	1949-53	3
	Lynn Chandnois	1950-56	3
	Lenny Lyles	1958-69	3
	Charley Warner	1963-66	3
	Ron Smith	1965-74	3
	Dave Hampton	1969-76	3
	Mercury Morris	1969-76	3
	Cullen Bryant	1969-76	3
	Ray Clayborn	**1977-88**	**3**
	Dave Williams	1977-81	3
	Dennis Gentry	1982-92	3
	Deion Sanders	**1989-**	**3**
	Mel Gray	**1986-**	**3**

Players active at the end of 1993 are shown in **bold face**.

LIFETIME LEADERS
POINTS AFTER TOUCHDOWNS

ATTEMPTS (276)

1	George Blanda	1949-58,60-75	959	13	**Matt Bahr**	1979-	471	25	Roy Gerela	1969-79	365	37	John Smith	1974-83	326
2	Lou Groza	1946-59,61-67	834	14	Garo Yepremian	1966-67,70-81	464	26	Tony Franklin	1979-88	355	38	**Al Del Greco**	1984-	324
3	Jan Stenerud	1967-85	601	15	Don Cockroft	1968-80	457	27	Pete Gogolak	1964-74	354	39	Mike Lansford	1982-90	315
4	Pat Leahy	1974-91	584	16	**Norm Johnson**	1982-	450	28	Gino Cappelletti	1960-70	353	40	**Fuad Reveiz**	1985-88,90-	304
5	Jim Bakken	1962-78	553	17	Sam Baker	1953,56-69	444		Rolf Benirschke	1977-86	353	41	**Mike Cofer**	1987-	303
6	Jim Turner	1964-79	544	18	**Eddie Murray**	1980-	437	30	Ben Agajanian	1945,47-49,53-57,60-62,64	351	42	Gordy Soltau	1945-52	302
7	Fred Cox	1963-77	539	19	Rafael Septien	1977-86	433	31	Tommy Davis	1959-69	350	43	Mike Mercer	1950-58	295
	Jim Breech	1979-92	539	20	Lou Michaels	1958-69,71	402	32	Mike Clark	1963-71,73	338	44	Rich Karlis	1982-90	294
9	Chris Bahr	1976-89	519	21	**Morten Andersen**	1982-	396	33	Bob Waterfield	1945-52	336	45	**Tony Zendejas**	1985-	293
10	Mark Moseley	1970-86	511	22	**Gary Anderson**	1982-	388	34	Errol Mann	1968-78	333	46	Toni Fritsch	1971-73,75-81	291
11	**Nick Lowery**	1978,80-	490	23	Bobby Walston	1951-62	384	35	Bob Thomas	1975-86	330	47	Tom Dempsey	1969-79	282
12	Ray Wersching	1973-87	477	24	Bruce Gossett	1964-74	383	36	**Kevin Butler**	1985-	328	48	Scott Norwood	1985-91	278

GOOD (257)

1	George Blanda	1949-58,60-75	943	13	Ray Wersching	1973-87	456	25	Roy Gerela	1969-79	351	37	Mike Lansford	1982-90	315
2	Lou Groza	1946-59,61-67	810	14	**Norm Johnson**	1982-	444	26	Tommy Davis	1959-69	348	38	John Smith	1974-83	308
3	Jan Stenerud	1967-85	580	15	Garo Yepremian	1966-67,70-81	444	27	Pete Gogolak	1964-74	344	39	Bob Thomas	1975-86	303
4	Pat Leahy	1974-91	558	16	**Eddie Murray**	1980-	432	28	Ben Agajanian	1945,47-49,53-57,60-62,64	343	40	**Mike Cofer**	1987-	294
5	Jim Bakken	1962-78	534		Don Cockroft	1968-80	432	29	Gino Cappelletti	1960-70	342	41	**Fuad Reveiz**	1985-88,90-	293
6	Jim Turner	1964-79	521	18	Sam Baker	1953,56-59	428	30	Tony Franklin	1979-88	341	42	Mike Mercer	1950-58	288
7	Fred Cox	1963-77	519	19	Rafael Septien	1977-86	420	31	Rolf Benirschke	1977-86	328	43	Gordy Soltau	1945-52	284
8	Jim Breech	1979-92	517	20	Lou Michaels	1958-69,71	386	32	Mike Clark	1968-71,73	325	44	**Tony Zendejas**	1985-	283
9	Mark Moseley	1970-86	511	21	**Gary Anderson**	1982-	384	33	**Kevin Butler**	1985-	318		Rich Karlis	1982-90	283
10	Chris Bahr	1976-89	490	22	**Morten Andersen**	1982	380	34	**Al Del Greco**	1984-	317	46	Toni Fritsch	1971-73,75-81	279
11	**Nick Lowery**	1978-	486	23	Bruce Gossett	1964-74	374	35	Bob Waterfield	1945-52	315	47	Scott Norwood	1985-91	271
12	**Matt Bahr**	1979-	459	24	Bobby Walston	1951-62	365		Errol Mann	1968-78	315	48	Pat Summerall	1952-61	257

PERCENT MADE (95.8)

(Minimum 200 Attempts)

			Good	Att.	Pct.				Good	Att.	Pct.				Good	Att.	Pct.
1	Tommy Davis	1959-69	348	350	99.43	16	**Dean Biasucci**	1984,86-	218	224	97.32	31	Gene Mingo	1960-67,69-70	215	223	96.41
2	**Nick Lowery**	1978-	486	490	99.18	17	**Al Del Greco**	1984-	317	324	97.24	32	Sam Baker	1953,56-59	428	444	96.39
3	**Gary Anderson**	1982	384	388	98.97	18	Pete Gogolak	1964-74	344	354	97.18	33	**Fuad Reveiz**	1985-8,90-91	293	304	96.38
4	**Eddie Murray**	1980-	432	437	98.86	19	Lou Groza	1946-59,61-69	810	834	97.12	34	Fred Cox	1963-77	519	539	96.28
5	**Chip Lohmiller**	1988-	232	235	98.72	20	Pat Harder	1946-53	198	204	97.05	35	Rich Karlis	1982-90	283	294	96.26
6	**Norm Johnson**	1982-	444	450	98.67	21	**Mike Cofer**	1987-	294	303	97.03	36	Roy Gerela	1969-79	351	365	96.16
7	Mick Luckhurst	1981-87	213	216	98.61	22	Rafael Septien	1977-86	420	433	97.00	37	Mike Clark	1963-71,73	325	338	96.15
8	**Morten Andersen**	1982-	380	386	98.45	23	Pat Summerall	1952-61	257	265	96.98	38	Don Chandler	1956-67	248	258	96.12
9	George Blanda	1949-58,60-75	943	959	98.33	24	**Kevin Butler**	1985-	318	328	96.95	39	Tony Franklin	1978-88	341	355	96.06
10	Danny Villanueva	1960-67	236	241	97.92	25	Mike Lansford	1982-90	315	325	96.92	40	Bobby Howfield	1968-74	193	201	96.02
11	Ben Agajanian	1945,47-49,53-57,60-62,64	343	351	97.72	26	Gino Cappelletti	1960-70	342	353	96.88	41	Lou Michaels	1958-69,71	386	402	96.01
12	Bruce Gossett	1964-74	374	383	97.65	27	**Tony Zendejas**	1985-	283	293	96.59	42	Joe Danelo	1975-84	240	250	96.00
13	Mike Mercer	1950-58	288	295	97.62	28	Nick Mike-Mayer	1973-82	226	234	96.58	43	Jim Breech	1979-92	517	539	95.92
14	Scott Norwood	1985-91	271	278	97.48	29	Jim Bakken	1962-78	534	553	96.56	44	Toni Fritsch	1971-73,75-81	279	291	95.88
15	**Matt Bahr**	1979-	459	471	97.45	30	Jan Stenerud	1967-85	580	601	96.51	45	John Smith	1974-82	302	315	95.87

FIELD GOALS

ATTEMPTS (160)

1	George Blanda	1949-58,60-75	638	18	Gino Cappelletti	1960-70	333	35	Mike Clark	1963-71,73	232	52	John Smith	1974-83	191
2	Jan Stenerud	1967-85	558	19	Ray Wersching	1973-87	329	36	Joe Danelo	1975-84	228	53	Mac Percival	1967-74	190
3	Jim Turner	1964-79	488	20	Don Cockroft	1968-80	328		**Al Del Greco**	1984-	228	54	Neil O' Donoghue	1977-85	189
4	Lou Groza	1946-59,61-67	481	21	Sam Baker	1953,56-69	316	38	**Dean Biasucci**	1984,86-	226	55	Raul Allegre	1983-91	186
5	Mark Moseley	1970-86	457	22	Garo Yepremian	1966-67,70-81	313	39	Toni Fritsch	1971-73,75-81	224	56	**Greg Davis**	1987-	185
6	Fred Cox	1963-77	455	23	Roy Gerela	1969-79	306	40	**Tony Zendejas**	1985-	223		**Fuad Reveiz**	1985-88,90-	185
7	Jim Bakken	1962-78	447	24	**Norm Johnson**	1982-	300	41	Gene Mingo	1960-67,69-70	219	58	Scott Norwood	1985-91	184
8	Pat Leahy	1974-91	426	25	Pete Gogolak	1964-74	294	42	**Chip Lohmiller**	1988-	217	59	**Jeff Jaeger**	1987,89-	180
9	**Nick Lowery**	1978-	411	26	Tommy Davis	1959-69	276		Mike Lansford	1982-90	217	60	David Ray	1969-74	178
10	Chris Bahr	1976-89	381		Errol Mann	1968-78	276	44	Pat Summerall	1952-61	212	61	Curt Knight	1969-73	175
11	**Eddie Murray**	1980-	367	28	**Kevin Butler**	1985-	273	45	Rolf Benirschke	1977-86	208	62	Efren Herrera	1974,76-82	171
12	**Gary Anderson**	1982-	364	29	Tony Franklin	1979-88	264	46	Ben Agajanian	1945,47-49,53-57,60-62,64	204	63	Bobby Howfield	1968-74	166
13	Bruce Gossett	1964-74	360	30	Tom Dempsey	1969-79	258		Nick Mike-Mayer	1973-82	204		**Roger Ruzek**	1987-	166
14	**Morten Andersen**	1982-	350	31	Rafael Septien	1977-86	256	48	Chester Marcol	1972-80	196	65	Mick Luckhurst	1981-87	164
15	**Matt Bahr**	1979-	348	32	Horst Muhlmann	1969-77	239	49	Mike Mercer	1961-70	193	66	Paul McFadden	1984-89	163
16	Lou Michaels	1958-69,71	341		Bob Thomas	1975-86	239	50	Jim Martin	1950-61,63-64	192	67	Don Chandler	1956-67	161
17	Jim Breech	1979-92	340		Rich Karlis	1982-90	239		**Mike Cofer**	1987-	192	68	Danny Villanueva	1960-67	160

GOOD (120)

1	Jan Stenerud	1967-85	373	15	Chris Bahr	1976-89	241	29	Pete Gogolak	1964-74	173		Joe Danelo	1975-84	133
2	George Blanda	1949-58,60-75	335	16	**Norm Johnson**	1982-	222	30	Rich Karlis	1982-90	172		Scott Norwood	1985-91	133
3	**Nick Lowery**	1978-	329		Ray Wersching	1973-87	222	31	**Tony Zendejas**	1985-	165	45	**Jeff Jaeger**	1987,89-91	131
4	Pat Leahy	1974-91	304	18	Bruce Gossett	1964-74	219	32	**Al Del Greco**	1984-	161	46	Tommy Davis	1959-69	130
	Jim Turner	1964-79	304	19	Don Cockroft	1968-80	216	33	**Dean Biasucci**	1984,86-	160	47	**Mike Cofer**	1987-	129
6	Mark Moseley	1970-86	300	20	Garo Yepremian	1966-67,70-81	210	34	Tom Dempsey	1968-79	159	48	**Fuad Reveiz**	1985-88,90	128
7	**Gary Anderson**	1982-	285	21	**Kevin Butler**	1985-	199	35	Mike Lansford	1982-90	158		John Smith	1974-83	128
8	Jim Bakken	1962-78	282	22	Lou Michaels	1958-69,71	187	36	**Chip Lohmiller**	1988-	155	50	**Pete Stoyanovich**	1989-	125
	Fred Cox	1963-77	282	23	Roy Gerela	1969-79	184	37	Horst Muhlmann	1969-77	154	51	**David Treadwell**	1989-	124
10	**Eddie Murray**	1980-	277	24	Rafael Septien	1977-86	180	38	Toni Fritsch	1971-73,75-81	153	52	**Greg Davis**	1987-	122
11	**Morten Andersen**	1982-	274	25	Sam Baker	1953,56-69	179	39	Bob Thomas	1975-86	151	53	Chester Marcol	1972-80	121
12	Lou Groza	1946-59,61-67	264	26	Errol Mann	1968-78	177	40	Rolf Benirschke	1977-86	146	54	Paul McFadden	1984-89	120
13	**Matt Bahr**	1979-	250		Tony Franklin	1979-88	177	41	Raul Allegre	1983-91	137		**Roger Ruzek**	1987-	120
14	Jim Breech	1979-92	243	28	Gino Cappelletti	1960-70	176	42	Mike Clark	1963-71,73	133				

PERCENT MADE (56.0)

(Minimum 100 Attempts)

			Good	Att.	Pct.				Good	Att.	Pct.				Good	Att.	Pct.
1	**Nick Lowery**	1978-	329	411	80.05	24	**Chip Lohmiller**	1988-	155	217	71.43	47	Errol Mann	1968-78	177	276	64.13
2	**Pete Stoyanovich**	1989-	125	157	79.62	25	Pat Leahy	1974-91	304	426	71.36	48	Chris Bahr	1976-89	241	381	63.25
3	**David Treadwell**	1989-	124	158	78.48	26	**Dean Biasucci**	1984,86-	160	226	70.80	49	Bob Thomas	1975-86	151	239	63.18
4	**Chris Jacke**	1989-	116	148	78.38	27	**Al Del Greco**	1984-	161	228	70.61	50	Jim Bakken	1962-78	282	447	63.09
5	**Gary Anderson**	1982-	285	364	78.30	28	Rafael Septien	1977-86	180	256	70.31	51	Jim Turner	1964-79	304	488	62.30
6	**Morten Andersen**	1982-	274	350	78.29	29	Rolf Benirschke	1977-86	146	208	70.19	52	Fred Cox	1963-77	282	455	61.98
7	**Steve Christie**	1990-	85	109	77.98	30	Mick Luckhurst	1981-87	115	164	70.12	53	David Ray	1969-74	110	178	61.80
8	**John Carney**	1988-	99	127	77.95	31	Ali Haji-Sheikh	1983-87	76	111	68.47	54	Chester Marcol	1972-80	121	196	61.73
9	Donald Igwebuike	1985-90	108	143	75.52	32	Toni Fritsch	1971-73,75-81	153	224	68.30	55	Tom Dempsey	1968-79	159	258	61.63
10	**Eddie Murray**	1980-	277	367	75.48	33	Efren Herrera	1974,76-82	116	171	67.84	56	Bruce Gossett	1964-74	219	360	60.83
11	**Norm Johnson**	1982-	222	300	74.00	34	Uwe von Schamann	1979-84	101	149	67.79	57	Frank Corral	1978-81	75	124	60.48
12	**Tony Zendejas**	1985-	165	223	73.99	35	Ray Wersching	1973-87	222	329	67.48	58	John Leypoldt	1971-78	93	154	60.39
13	Raul Allegre	1983-91	137	186	73.66	36	**Mike Cofer**	1987-	129	192	67.19	59	Roy Gerela	1969-79	184	306	60.13
14	Paul McFadden	1984-89	120	163	73.62	37	Garo Yepremian	1966-67,70-81	210	313	67.09	60	Neil O' Donoghue	1977-85	112	189	59.26
15	**Fuad Reveiz**	1985-88,90-	128	175	73.14	38	Tony Franklin	1979-88	177	264	67.05	61	Toni Linhart	1972,74-79	75	127	59.06
16	**Kevin Butler**	1985-	199	273	72.89	39	John Smith	1974-83	128	191	67.02	62	Bobby Howfield	1968-74	98	166	59.04
17	Mike Lansford	1982-90	158	217	72.81	40	Jan Stenerud	1967-85	373	558	66.85	63	Pete Gogolak	1964-74	173	294	58.84
18	**Jeff Jaeger**	1987,89-	131	180	72.78	41	**Greg Davis**	1987	122	185	65.95	64	Dennis Partee	1968-75	71	121	58.68
19	**Roger Ruzek**	1987-	120	166	72.29	42	Don Cockroft	1968-80	216	328	65.85	65	Don Chandler	1956-67	94	161	58.38
20	Scott Norwood	1985-91	133	184	72.28	43	Mark Moseley	1970-86	300	457	65.65	66	Joe Danelo	1975-84	133	228	58.33
21	Rich Karlis	1982-90	172	239	71.96	44	Rick Danmeier	1978-82	78	120	65.00	67	Fred Cone	1951-57,60	59	102	57.84
22	**Matt Bahr**	1979-	250	348	71.84	45	Benny Ricardo	1976-84	92	142	64.79	68	Curt Knight	1969-73	101	175	57.71
23	Jim Breech	1979-92	243	340	71.47	46	Horst Muhlmann	1969-77	154	239	64.44	69	Mike Clark	1963-71,73	133	232	57.32

Players active at the end of 1993 are shown in **bold face.**

LIFETIME LEADERS
POINTS

(378)

1	George Blanda	1949-58, 60-75	2002
2	Jan Stenerud	1967-85	1699
3	Lou Groza	1946-59, 61-67	1608
4	**Nick Lowery**	**1978-**	**1473**
5	Pat Leahy	1974-91	1470
6	Jim Turner	1964-79	1439
7	Mark Moseley	1970-86	1382
8	Jim Bakken	1962-78	1380
9	Fred Cox	1963-77	1365
10	**Eddie Murray**	**1980-**	**1264**
11	Jim Breech	1979-92	1246
12	**Gary Anderson**	**1982-**	**1239**
13	Chris Bahr	1976-89	1213
14	**Matt Bahr**	**1979-**	**1209**
15	**Morten Andersen**	**1982-**	**1202**
16	Gino Cappelletti	1960-70	1130
17	Ray Wersching	1973-87	1122
18	**Norm Johnson**	**1982-**	**1110**
19	Don Cockroft	1968-80	1080
20	Garo Yepremian	1966-67, 70-81	1074
21	Bruce Gossett	1964-74	1031
22	Sam Baker	1953, 56-69	977
23	Rafael Septien	1977-86	960
24	Lou Michaels	1958-69, 71	955
25	**Kevin Butler**	**1985-**	**915**
26	Roy Gerela	1969-79	903
27	Bobby Walston	1951-62	881
28	Tony Franklin	1979-88	872
29	Pete Gogolak	1964-74	863
30	Errol Mann	1968-78	846
31	Don Hutson	1935-45	823
32	**Al Del Greco**	**1984-**	**800**
33	Rich Karlis	1982-90	799
34	Mike Lansford	1982-90	789
35	**Tony Zendejas**	**1985-**	**778**
36	Rolf Benirschke	1977-86	766
37	Paul Hornung	1957-62, 64-66	760
38	Toni Fritsch	1971-73, 75-82	758
39	Jim Brown	1957-65	756
	Bob Thomas	1975-86	756
41	Walter Payton	1975-87	750
42	**Jerry Rice**	**1985-**	**744**
43	Tommy Davis	1959-69	738
44	Tom Dempsey	1969-79	729
45	Mike Clark	1963-71,73	724
46	Horst Muhlmann	1967-77	707
47	**Chip Lohmiller**	**1988-**	**697**
48	**Dean Biasucci**	**1984,86-**	**698**
49	John Riggins	1971-79,81-85	696
50	John Smith	1974-83	692
51	**Mike Cofer**	**1987-**	**690**
52	**Marcus Allen**	**1982-**	**678**
	Lenny Moore	1956-67	678
54	Scott Norwood	1985-91	670
55	**Fuad Reveiz**	**1985-88,90-**	**667**
56	Ben Agajanian	1945,47-49,53-57, 60-62,64	655
57	Gordy Soltau	1950-58	644
58	Joe Danelo	1975-84	639
59	Gene Mingo	1960-67,69-70	629
60	Steve Largent	1976-89	608
61	Efren Herrera	1974,76-82	604
62	Franco Harris	1972-84	600
63	Mike Mercer	1961-70	594
64	Raul Allegre	1983-91	594
65	**Jeff Jaeger**	**1987-**	**584**
66	Neil O'Donoghue	1977-85	576
	Eric Dickerson	1983-93	576
68	Bob Waterfield	1945-52	573
69	Nick Mike-Mayer	1973-82	571
70	**Roger Ruzek**	**1987-**	**566**
71	Pat Summerall	1952-61	563
72	Jim Taylor	1958-67	558
	Mick Luckhurst	1981-87	558
74	Tony Dorsett	1977-88	552
75	**Pete Stoyanovich**	**1989-**	**549**
76	**Greg Davis**	**1987-**	**547**
77	Bobby Mitchell	1958-68	546
78	Leroy Kelly	1964-73	540
	Charley Taylor	1964-75,77	540
	Uwe von Schamann	1979-84	540
81	Doak Walker	1950-55	534
82	**David Treadwell**	**1989-**	**532**
	Don Maynard	1958, 60-67	532
84	Chester Marcol	1972-80	525
85	Lance Alworth	1962-72	524
86	Paul McFadden	1984-89	520
87	Ottis Anderson	1979-92	518
88	Paul Warfield	1964-74, 76-77	516
89	**Chris Jacke**	**1989**	**514**
90	Joe Perry	1948-63	513
91	Tommy McDonald	1957-68	510
	Pete Johnson	1977-84	510
	Mark Clayton	**1983-**	**510**
94	David Ray	1969-74	497
95	Fred Cone	1951-57, 60	494
96	Art Powell	1959-67	492
97	Danny Villanueva	1960-67	491
98	Bobby Howfield	1968-74	487
99	Bill Dudley	1942, 45-51, 53	484
	Frank Gifford	1952-60, 62-64	484
101	John Leypoldt	1971-78	482
102	Ken Strong	1929-35, 39, 44-47	479
103	Donald Igwebuike	1985-90	477
104	Curt Knight	1969-73	475
105	Harold Carmichael	1971-84	474
	James Brooks	1981-92	474
107	Mac Percival	1967-74	466
108	Steve Van Buren	1944-51	464
109	Fred Biletnikoff	1965-78	462
110	Bill Brown	1961-74	456
	Bob Hayes	1965-75	456
	O.J. Simpson	1969-79	456
	Chuck Foreman	1973-80	456
	Harold Jackson	1968-83	456
	James Lofton	**1978-**	**456**
116	Nat Moore	1974-86	450
117	Benny Ricardo	1976, 78-84	447
118	John David Crow	1958-68	444
	Chuck Muncie	1976-84	444
	Earl Campbell	1978-85	444
121	Ollie Matson	1952, 54-66	438
	Stanley Morgan	1977-90	438
	Roger Craig	**1983-**	**438**
124	Jim Martin	1950-61, 63-64	434
	Herschel Walker	**1986-**	**432**
126	Wesley Walker	1977-89	428
	Neal Anderson	**1986-**	**426**
128	Toni Linhart	1972, 74-79	425
129	**John Carney**	**1988-**	**421**
130	Gary Collins	1962-71	420
131	Paddy Driscoll	1920-29	418
132	Ward Cuff	1937-47	417
133	Abner Haynes	1960-67	414
	Roy Green	1979-92	414
	Gerald Riggs	1982-91	414
136	Raymond Berry	1955-67	408
	Larry Csonka	1968-74, 76-79	408
138	Elroy Hirsch	1946-57	405
139	Cliff Branch	1972-85	402
140	Jimmy Orr	1958-70	396
	Wendell Tyler	1977-86	396
142	Billy Cannon	1960-70	392
143	Joe Morrison	1959-72	390
	Sonny Randle	1959-68	390
	Emerson Boozer	1966-75	390
	Calvin Hill	1969-74, 76-81	390
	Charlie Joiner	1969-86	390
	Art Monk	**1980-**	**390**
149	Bobby Joe Conrad	1958-69	389
150	Timmy Brown	1959-68	384
	John Stallworth	1974-87	384
152	**Steve Christie**	**1990-**	**383**
153	Roger LeClerc	1960-67	382
154	Ted Fritsch	1942-50	380
	Dennis Partee	1968-75	380

INTERCEPTIONS

(31)

1	Paul Krause	1964-79	81
2	Emlen Tunnell	1948-61	79
3	Night Train Lane	1952-65	68
4	Ken Riley	1969-83	65
5	**Ronnie Lott**	**1981-**	**63**
6	Dick LeBeau	1959-72	62
	Dave Brown	1975-89	62
8	Emmitt Thomas	1966-81	58
9	Bobby Boyd	1960-68	57
	Mel Blount	1970-83	57
	Everson Walls	**1981-**	**57**
12	Pat Fischer	1961-77	56
	Lem Barney	1967-77	56
14	Donnie Shell	1974-87	55
15	Willie Brown	1963-78	54
16	Jack Butler	1951-59	52
	Bobby Dillon	1952-59	52
	Jimmy Patton	1955-66	52
	Larry Wilson	1960-72	52
	Mel Renfro	1964-77	52
21	Bobby Bryant	1968-80	51
22	Yale Lary	1952-53, 56-64	50
	Don Burroughs	1955-64	50
	Deron Cherry	1981-91	50
25	Ken Houston	1967-80	49
	Jake Scott	1970-78	49
27	Richie Petitbon	1959-73	48
	Willie Wood	1960-70	48
	Herb Adderley	1961-72	48
	Dave Grayson	1961-70	48
	Dave Waymer	1980-92	48
32	Jimmy Johnson	1961-76	47
	Lemar Parrish	1970-82	47
	John Harris	1978-88	47
35	Jack Christiansen	1951-58	46
	Dave Whitsell	1958-69	46
	Ed Meador	1959-70	46
	Goose Gonsoulin	1960-67	46
	Mike Haynes	1976-89	46
40	Erich Barnes	1958-71	45
	Jim Norton	1960-68	45
	Thom Darden	1972-74, 76-81	45
43	Warren Lahr	1949-59	44
	Steve Foley	1976-86	44
45	Kermit Alexander	1963-73	43
46	Bobby Hunt	1962-69	42
	Gill Byrd	**1983-**	**42**
48	Don Doll	1949-54	41
	Johnny Sample	1958-68	41
	Spider Lockhart	1965-75	41
	Charlie Waters	1970-81	41
52	Tom Keane	1948-55	40
	Ed Sharockman	1962-72	40
	Butch Byrd	1964-71	40
	W.K. Hicks	1964-72	40
	Bill Thompson	1969-81	40
	Roger Wehrli	1969-82	40
58	Glen Edwards	1971-81	39
	Rolland Lawrence	1973-80	39
	Gary Barbaro	1976-82	39
	Clarence Scott	1971-83	39
	Lester Hayes	1977-87	39
	Mike Harden	1980-90	39
64	Linden Crow	1955-64	38
	Rick Volk	1965-78	38
	Ray Brown	1971-80	38
	Gary Fencik	1976-87	38
	Eugene Robinson	**1985-**	**38**
	Albert Lewis	**1983-**	**38**
70	Don Shinnick	1957-69	37
	Dick Lynch	1958-66	37
	Ken Reaves	1966-77	37
	Bob Howard	1967-79	37
	Tony Greene	1971-79	37
	Jack Tatum	1971-80	37
	Nolan Cromwell	1977-87	37
	Joey Browner	1983-91	37
	Dwayne Woodruff	1979-90	37
79	Jim David	1952-59	36
	Fred Williamson	1960-67	36
	Brig Owens	1966-77	36
	Mike Wagner	1971-80	36
	Tom Myers	1972-81	36
	Dennis Thurman	1978-86	36
	Raymond Clayborn	1977-91	36
86	Frank Reagan	1941,1946-51	35
	Ray Ramsey	1947-53	35
	Jerry Norton	1954-64	35
	Miller Farr	1965-73	35
	Willie Williams	1965-73	35
	Nate Wright	1969-80	35
	Ron Bolton	1972-82	35
	Lyle Blackwood	1973-86	35
	Michael Downs	1981-88	35
	LeRoy Irvin	1980-90	35
96	Tommy James	1947-56	34
	Jim Cason	1948-52, 54-56	34
	Otto Schnellbacher	1948-51	34
	Don Paul	1950-58	34
	Bill Baird	1963-69	34
	Jerry Logan	1963-72	34
	Cornell Green	1962-74	34
	Dick Anderson	1968-74, 76-77	34
	Bill Bradley	1969-77	34
	Clarence Scott	1971-81	34
	Stan White	1972-82	34
	Bill Simpson	1974-78, 80-82	34
108	Irv Comp	1943-49	33
	Jim Smith	1948-53	33
	Andy Nelson	1957-64	33
	Gary Green	1977-85	33
	Herman Edwards	1977-86	33
	Norm Thompson	1971-79	33
	Joe Lavender	1973-82	33
	Louis Breeden	1978-87	33
116	Lowell Wagner	1946-53, 55	32
	Tom Landry	1949-55	32
	Roosevelt Taylor	1961-72	32
	Nick Buoniconti	1962-64, 66-76	32
	Lee Roy Jordan	1963-75	32
	Charlie Stukes	1967-74	32
	Jack Ham	1971-82	32
	Dwight Hicks	1979-86	32
	Kenny Easley	1981-87	32
	Mark Lee	1980-91	32
126	Johnny Blood	1925-39	31
	Bert Rechichar	1952-61	31
	Bernie Parrish	1959-66	31
	Jim Allen	1974-81	31
	Vann McElroy	1982-90	31
	Terry Kinard	1983-90	31
	David Fulcher	**1986-**	**31**
	Eric Allen	**1988-**	**31**

PUNTING

PUNTS (365)

1	Dave Jennings	1974-87	1168
2	Jerrel Wilson	1963-78	1069
3	Ray Guy	1974-86	1052
4	John James	1972-83	995
5	Mike Bragg	1968-80	978
6	Bobby Walden	1964-77	974
7	Bobby Joe Green	1960-73	970
8	**Rohn Stark**	**1982-**	**918**
9	Bob Parsons	1972-83	884
10	**Rich Camarillo**	**1981-**	**859**
11	David Lee	1966-78	838
12	**Jim Arnold**	**1983-**	**825**
13	Greg Coleman	1977-88	823
14	Tom Blanchard	1971-81	819
15	Paul Maguire	1960-70	794
16	**Jeff Gossett**	**1981-83,85-**	**776**
17	**John Kidd**	**1984-**	**714**
18	Sam Baker	1953, 56-69	701
19	Pat McInally	1976-85	700
20	**Harry Newsome**	**1985-**	**697**
21	**Brian Hansen**	**1984-88,90-93**	**697**
22	Verne Lewellyn	1924-32	679
23	**Mike Saxon**	**1985-**	**671**
24	Max Runager	1979-89	668
25	Don Chandler	1956-67	660
26	Don Cockroft	1968-80	651
27	**Reggie Roby**	**1983-**	**636**
28	Herman Weaver	1970-80	635
29	Larry Seiple	1968-77	633
30	Jeff West	1975-79, 81-85	625
31	Danny White	1976-88	612
32	**Lee Johnson**	**1985-**	**609**
33	**Mike Horan**	**1984-**	**606**
34	Spike Jones	1970-77	592
35	Dave Beverly	1974-80	586
36	Maury Buford	1982-86,88-91	586
37	Bill Van Heusen	1968-76	574
38	**Sean Landeta**	**1985-**	**572**
39	Mike Eischeid	1966-74	564
40	Pat Studstill	1961-62, 64-72	560
41	Curley Johnson	1960-69	556
42	Chuck Ramsey	1977-84	553
43	Billy Lothridge	1964-72	532
44	Norm Van Brocklin	1949-60	523
45	Dennis Partee	1968-75	519
46	Jim Norton	1960-68	518
47	Tommy Davis	1959-69	511
48	Yale Lary	1952-53, 56-64	503
49	**Dale Hatcher**	**1985-89,91,93**	**494**
50	Ed Brown	1954-65	493
51	Horace Gillon	1947-56	492
52	Danny Villanueva	1960-67	488
53	**Jeff Feagles**	**1988-**	**482**
54	Adrian Burke	1950-56	474
55	**Don Bracken**	**1985-90,92**	**466**
56	Craig Colquitt	1978-84	429
57	Dave Green	1973-78	424
58	Luke Prestridge	1979-84	421
59	Ralf Mojsiejenko	1985-91	418
60	**Bryan Wagner**	**1987-**	**409**
61	Cliff Parsley	1977-81	407
62	Marv Bateman	1972-77	401
	Scott Fulhage	1987-92	401
64	Jug Girard	1948-57	397
65	Steve Cox	1981-88	393
66	Tom Landry	1949-55	389
	Tommy Barnhardt	**1987-**	**389**
68	Donny Anderson	1966-74	387
69	Frank Garcia	1981,83-87	384
70	Greg Cater	1980-83,86-87	379
71	Rick Donnelly	1985-88,91	377
72	Joe Prokop	1985,87-92	376
73	Tom Yewcic	1961-66	369
	Carl Birdsong	1981-85	369
75	King Hill	1958-69	368
	Ron Widby	1968-73	368

PUNTING AVERAGE (42.5)

(Minimum 250 Punts)

1	Sammy Baugh	1937-52	44.9
2	Tommy Davis	1959-69	44.7
3	Yale Lary	1952-53, 56-64	44.3
4	Bob Scarpitto	1961-68	44.0
5	Jerry Norton	1954-64	43.8
6	Dave Lewis	1960-73	43.7
	Rohn Stark	**1982-**	**43.7**
8	Don Chandler	1956-67	43.5
9	Jim Fraser	1962-66, 68	43.3
	Jerrel Wilson	1963-78	43.2
11	**Reggie Roby**	**1983-**	**43.2**
12	**Sean Landeta**	**1985-**	**43.1**
	Horace Gillom	1947-56	43.1
14	Frankie Albert	1946-52	43.0
	Rick Tuten	**1989-**	**43.0**
16	Norm Van Brocklin	1949-60	42.9
17	**Greg Montgomery**	**1988-**	**42.8**
18	Danny Villanueva	1960-67	42.7
	Rich Camarillo	**1981-**	**42.7**
20	Bobby Joe Green	1960-73	42.6
	Curley Johnson	1960-69	42.6
	Tommy Barnhardt	**1987-**	**42.6**

Players active at the end of 1993 are shown in bold face.

THE HALL OF FAME

1963

Sammy Baugh — Quarterback, Coach
Bert Bell — NFL Commissioner, Coach, Owner
Johnny Blood (McNally) — Halfback, Coach
Joe Carr — NFL President, Founder
Dutch Clark — Quarterback, Coach
Red Grange — Halfback
George Halas — End, Coach, Owner, Founder
Mel Hein — Center
Pete Henry — Tackle
Carl Hubbard — Tackle
Don Hutson — End
Curly Lambeau — Halfback, Coach, Founder
Tim Mara — Owner
George Preston Marshall — Owner
Bronko Nagurski — Fullback
Ernie Nevers — Fullback, Tailback, Coach
Jim Thorpe — Halfback, Coach, First NFL President

1964

Jimmy Conzelman — Quarterback, Coach, Owner
Ed Healey — Tackle
Clarke Hinkle — Fullback
Mike Michalske — Guard
Art Rooney — Owner
George Trafton — Center

1965

Guy Chamberlin — End, Coach
Paddy Driscoll — Quarterback
Danny Fortmann — Guard
Otto Graham — Quarterback
Sid Luckman — Quarterback
Steve Van Buren — Halfback
Bob Waterfield — Quarterback, Kicker

1966

Bill Dudley — Halfback, Tailback, Kicker
Joe Guyon — Fullback, Tailback
Arnie Herber — Quarterback
Walt Kiesling — Guard, Coach
George McAfee - Halfback
Steve Owen — Tackle, Coach
Shorty Ray — League Official

1967

Chuck Bednarik — Center, Linebacker
Charles Bidwell — Owner
Paul Brown — Coach, Owner
Bobby Layne — Quarterback
Dan Reeves — Owner
Ken Strong — Halfback, Kicker
Joe Stydahar — Tackle
Emlen Tunnell — Defensive Back

1968

Cliff Battles — Halfback, Tailback
Art Donovan — Defensive Tackle
Elroy "Crazy Legs" Hirsch — End
Wayne Millner — End
Marion Motley — Fullback
Charlie Trippi — Halfback, Quarterback
Alex Wojciechowicz — Center, Linebacker

1969

Turk Edwards — Tackle
Greasy Neale — Coach
Leo Nomellini — Defensive Tackle
Joe Perry — Fullback
Ernie Stautner — Defensive Tackle

1970

Jack Christiansen — Defensive Back
Tom Fears — End
Hugh McElhenny — Halfback
Pete Pihos — End

1971

Jim Brown — Fullback
Bill Hewitt — End
Bruiser Kinard — Tackle
Vince Lombardi — Coach
Andy Robustelli — Defensive End
Y.A. Tittle — Quarterback
Norm Van Brocklin — Quarterback

1972

Lamar Hunt — AFL Founder and Owner
Gino Marchetti — Defensive End
Ollie Matson — Halfback
Ace Parker — Tailback, Quarterback

1973

Raymond Berry — End
Jim Parker — Offensive Tackle, Offensive Guard
Joe Schmidt — Linebacker

1974

Tony Canadeo — Halfback, Fullback
Bill George — Guard, Linebacker, Tackle
Lou Groza — Kicker, Tackle
Dick "Night Train" Lane — Defensive Back

1975

Roosevelt Brown — Offensive Tackle
George Conner — Tackle, Guard, Linebacker
Dante Lavelli — End
Lenny Moore — Halfback, Flanker

1976

Ray Flaherty — End
Len Ford — End
Jim Taylor — Fullback

1977

Frank Gifford — Halfback, Flanker
Forrest Gregg — Offensive Tackle
Gale Sayers — Halfback
Bart Starr — Quarterback
Bill Willis — Guard

1978

Lance Alworth — Wide Receiver
Weeb Ewbank — Coach
Tuffy Leemans — Fullback
Ray Nitschke — Linebacker
Larry Wilson — Defensive Back

THE HALL OF FAME (Continued)

1979

Dick Butkus — Linebacker
Yale Lary — Defensive Back, Punter
Ron Mix — Offensive Tackle
Johnny Unitas — Quarterback

1980

Herb Adderley — Cornerback
Deacon Jones — Defensive End
Bob Lilly — Defensive Tackle
Jim Otto — Center

1981

Red Badgro — End
George Blanda — Quarterback, Kicker
Willie Davis — Defensive End
Jim Ringo — Center

1982

Doug Atkins — Defensive End
Sam Huff — Linebacker
George Musso — Tackle, Guard
Merlin Olsen — Defensive Tackle

1983

Bobby Bell — Linebacker
Sid Gillman — Coach
Sonny Jurgensen — Quarterback
Bobby Mitchell — Halfback, Wide Receiver
Paul Warfield — Wide Receiver

1984

Willie Brown — Safety
Mike McCormack — Tackle
Charley Taylor — Wide Receiver
Arnie Weinmeister — Defensive Tackle

1985

Frank Gatski — Center
Joe Namath — Quarterback
Pete Rozelle — Commissioner
O.J. Simpson — Running Back
Roger Staubach — Quarterback

1986

Paul Hornung — Halfback, Kicker
Ken Houston — Safety
Willie Lanier — Linebacker
Fran Tarkenton — Quarterback
Doak Walker — Halfback, Kicker

1987

Larry Csonka — Fullback
Len Dawson — Quarterback
Joe Greene — Defensive Tackle
John Henry Johnson — Fullback
Jim Langer — Center
Don Maynard — Wide Receiver
Gene Upshaw — Offensive Guard

1988

Fred Biletnikoff — Wide Receiver
Mike Ditka — Tight End, Coach
Jack Ham — Linebacker
Alan Page — Defensive Tackle

1989

Mel Blount — Cornerback
Terry Bradshaw — Quarterback
Art Shell — Offensive Tackle
Willie Wood — Safety

1990

Buck Buchanan — Defensive Tackle
Bob Griese — Quarterback
Franco Harris — Running Back
Ted Hendricks — Linebacker
Jack Lambert — Linebacker
Tom Landry — Defensive Back, Coach
Bob St. Clair — Offensive Tackle

1991

Earl Campbell — Running Back
John Hannah — Offensive Guard
Stan Jones — Offensive Guard, Defensive Tackle
Tex Schramm — General Manager
Jan Stenerud — Kicker

1992

Lem Barney — Cornerback
Al Davis — Coach, Owner, Commissioner
John Mackey — Tight End
John Riggins — Running Back

1993

Dan Fouts — Quarterback
Larry Little — Offensive Guard
Chuck Noll — Coach
Walter Payton — Running Back
Bill Walsh — Coach

1994

Tony Dorsett — Running Back
Bud Grant — Coach
Jimmy Johnson — Cornerback
Leroy Kelly — Running Back
Jackie Smith — Tight End
Randy White — Defensive Tackle

Pro Football's Offensive Formations

Single Wing

The single wing formation, which pre-dates pro football, derives its name from the fact that the right halfback acts as a wing back and is positioned just outside the end. This formation is basically executed by the ball being snapped under the center's legs directly to the tailback or the fullback.

The following are the strengths of the Single Wing:

. . . Two offensive men will be blocking each of the key defensive men on any particular play.

. . . More than normal amount of personnel on strong side where most of the running will take place.

. . . Effective ball-control type of offense.

. . . The biggest advantage is that the BB (Blocking Back), can be used as a blocker on running plays and does not hand off the football.

. . . It offers a deceptive offense in that many players are bunched and able to go in different directions.

. . . The defense is outnumbered at the point of the offensive attack.

. . . The defense cannot key directly to the strong side since the play can be run to the weak side.

The following are the weaknesses of the Single Wing:

. . . The plays are very slow in developing.

. . . Because of its slow development, there are seldom any long runs and long passes.

SINGLE WING — 1935 DETROIT

LE — Klewicki
LT — Johnson
C — Randolph
LG — Monahan
RG — Emerson
RT — G. Christensen
RE — Schneller
BB — F. Christensen
WB — Caddel
FB — Gutowski
TB — Clark

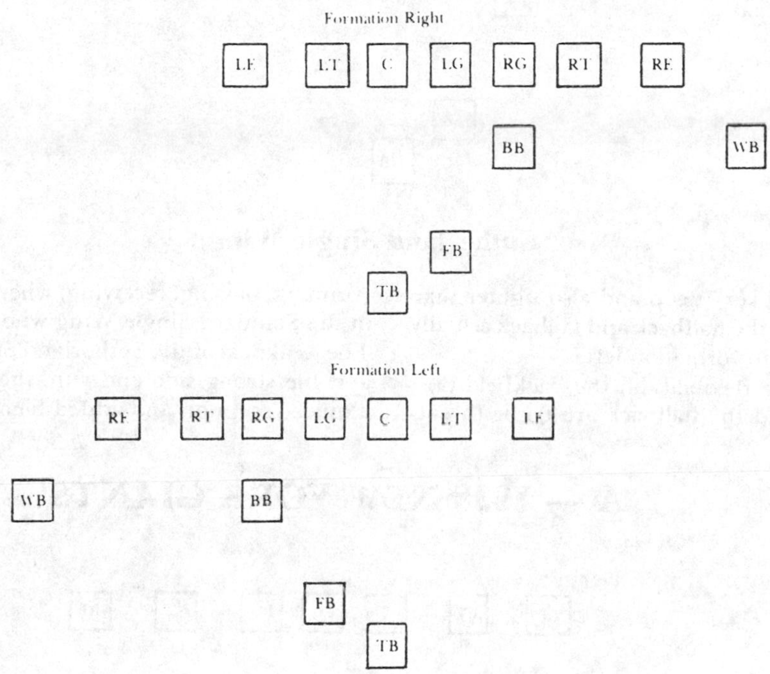

Standard Single Wing

In the Standard Single Wing the change from the formations lining up right to left, or vice versa, means that the backfield occupies the same exact position in relation to the line.

Multiple Offense

Most teams in the 1920's lined up in a tight T-formation and then shifted into a single wing or box. For most of these teams, the T-formation was just a device and they rarely snapped the ball in this line-up. Some teams, such as Buffalo, Dayton and the Chicago Cardinals, played true multiple offense football. Sometimes, they ran plays from the T-formation, sometimes they shifted into the Single Wing and sometimes they shifted into a Double Wing, Short Punt, or a combination or variation of any of these. This was very effective when the timing and execution was good, which was difficult in the days when teams could not practice regularly. This also put great pressure on the quarterback who had to be a T-formation signal caller, ball handler and passer and still be a Single Wing blocking back and receiver. Thus, teams tended to use this set-up only when they had versatile, outstanding quarterbacks such as Paddy Driscoll, Tommy Hughett, or Al Mahrt.

SUTHERLAND SINGLE WING — 1941 BROOKLYN

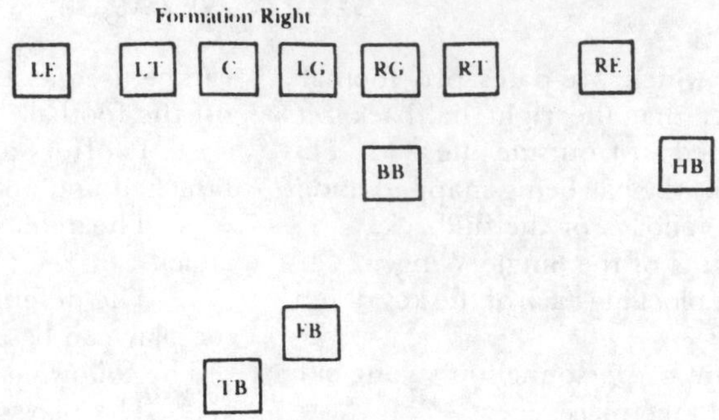

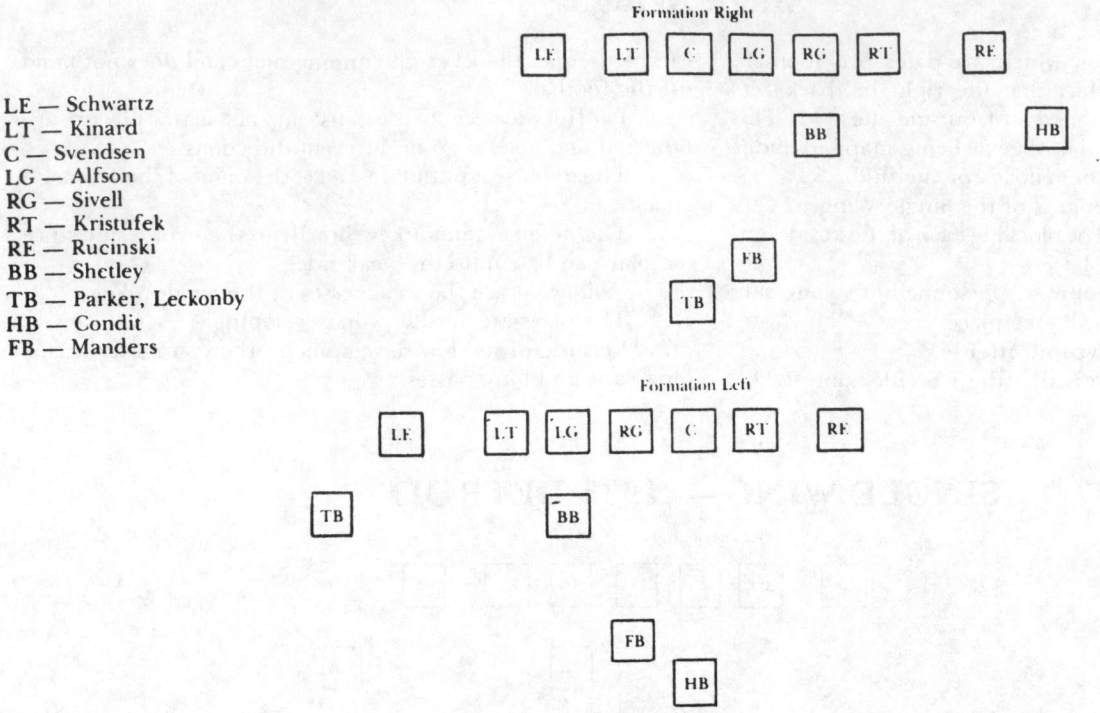

LE — Schwartz
LT — Kinard
C — Svendsen
LG — Alfson
RG — Sivell
RT — Kristufek
RE — Rucinski
BB — Shetley
TB — Parker, Leckonby
HB — Condit
FB — Manders

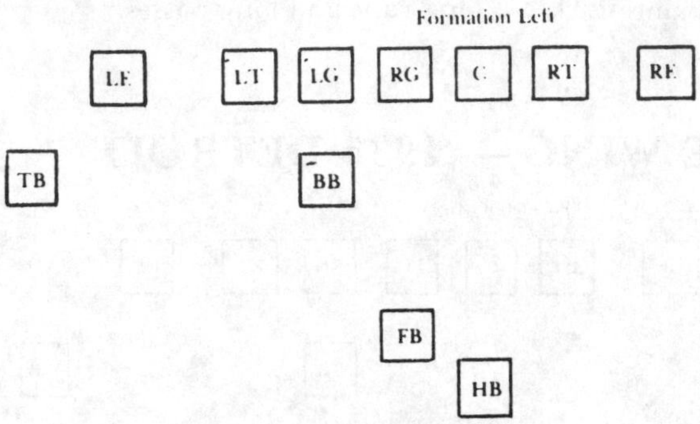

Sutherland Single Wing

The halfback is positioned very deep and also tighter than in the Standard Single Wing; the halfback and tailback actually switch positions when going to formation left.

This formation gives more flexibility in the backfield positions as both the tailback and the halfback are triple threats (running, passing, receiving) when compared to the wing back in the Standard Single Wing who is normally only a receiver. The weakness of the Sutherland Single Wing is that on passing and the strong side end run, the wing back is not there for a quick reception and added blocking.

A — 1938 NEW YORK GIANTS

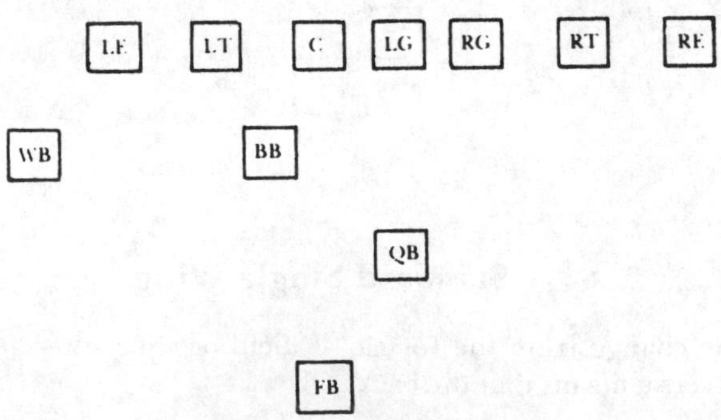

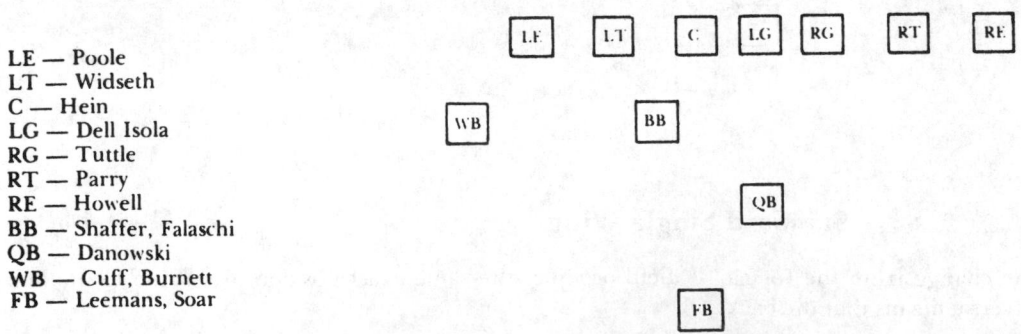

LE — Poole
LT — Widseth
C — Hein
LG — Dell Isola
RG — Tuttle
RT — Parry
RE — Howell
BB — Shaffer, Falaschi
QB — Danowski
WB — Cuff, Burnett
FB — Leemans, Soar

"A" Formation

This formation is quite unique in that a great center such as Mel Hein could snap to any of three men who had the option to go in either a left or right direction. This is also a great running formation designed to put pressure on the defensive tackle facing the strong side of the line.

The following are the differences from the Standard Single Wing:

. . . When the line forms right, the backs are strong left. When the line forms left, the backs form strong right.

. . . The quarterback, who is the primary passer, lines up closer to the line of scrimmage than the tailback in the Single Wing.

. . . The fullback is a potential passer.

The advantage of this formation is that because of its versatility in using any of three men, the defense is constantly off-balance. On the other hand, such a formation is a disadvantage in that it could not be effectively executed unless a team had a great center such as Hein. Perhaps for this reason the Giants were the only team to use this formation, giving them an advantage difficult to overcome.

NOTRE DAME BOX — 1939 GREEN BAY

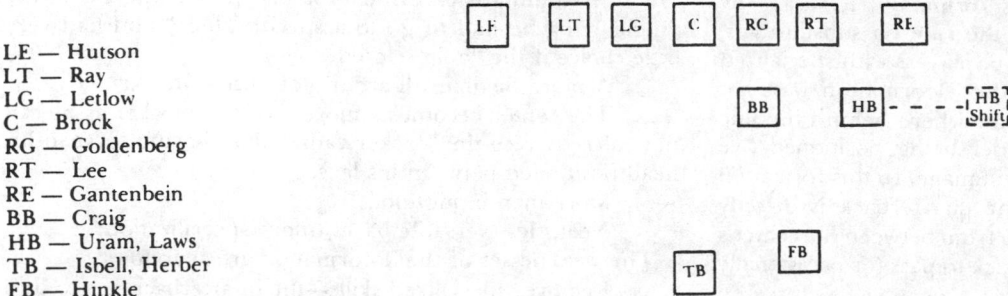

LE — Hutson
LT — Ray
LG — Letlow
C — Brock
RG — Goldenberg
RT — Lee
RE — Gantenbein
BB — Craig
HB — Uram, Laws
TB — Isbell, Herber
FB — Hinkle

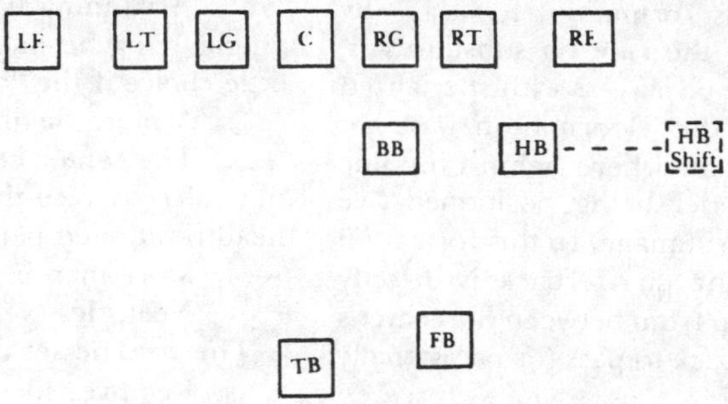

Notre Dame Box

The box formation originated about 1913. However, when Knute Rockne added the shift in the 1920's he exerted such an impact on the game that for the next two decades this formation was very popular.

Upon breaking the huddle the team lined up in a T-formation with the ends split. The quarterback was several feet behind the center; therefore, on the rare occasion when he received a direct snap, the ball had to be snapped back, it could not be handed.

On a cadence count the backs would take three quick steps either to the right or left to form the box. The ends would either move in or remain stationary.

This formation differs from the Standard Single Wing in that the line is balanced and the halfback frequently in tight between the tackle and the end.

The result of these two factors makes it easier to effect a running game to the weak side. Also, the halfback does more ball-carrying than the wing back in the Standard Single Wing.

DOUBLE WING — 1926 DULUTH ESKIMOS

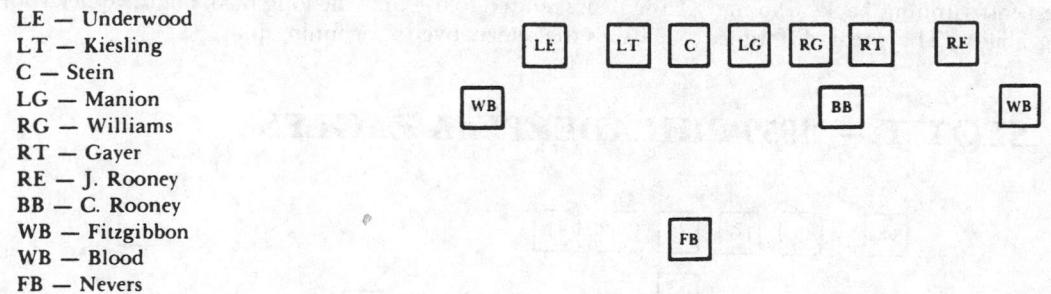

LE — Underwood
LT — Kiesling
C — Stein
LG — Manion
RG — Williams
RT — Gayer
RE — J. Rooney
BB — C. Rooney
WB — Fitzgibbon
WB — Blood
FB — Nevers

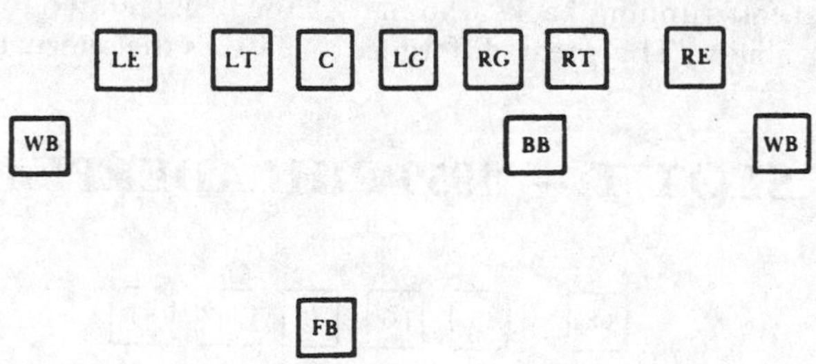

Double Wing

The great innovator, Pop Warner, is credited with developing the Double Wing formation when he was coaching Carlisle around 1912. As with many formations, the Double Wing was later used with several variations. Warner, himself, used three of these but this is his original or "A Set" line-up.

The Double Wing is the father of the modern "Shotgun". Five pass receivers can get downfield quickly and the passer (the Fullback in the Double Wing) has a clear view of the downfield action. The weakness of the formation is its dependence on one star to be passer, runner and kicker and to do it all with no deep back to block for him. Of course, Warner developed the Double Wing when he had Jim Thorpe at Carlisle and he later coached Ernie Nevers at Stanford.

T-Formations

The Chicago Bears first introduced the modern T-formation—a strategy which revolutionized pro football. Following the introduction of this formation, its usage by most clubs came about because of the rule on substitutions, permitting teams to take advantage of players with specialized talents. Another rule influencing the T-formation was that in 1940 passing was allowed from anywhere behind the line of scrimmage, rather that the passer being positioned five yards back behind the line of the scrimmage. In this formation the line is always balanced and the quarterback is directly behind the center and takes the snap from between the center's legs and either handoffs or drops back to pass (or occasionally runs).

The strengths of the T-formation are as follows:

. . . Allows for speed, with great fakes and maneuvers by the backs—a factor which is the key to this formation's success.

. . . The backs can be running at full speed or close to full speed when taking the handoff from the quarterback.

. . . Quick openers and fast development of plays.

. . . Because of speed, double blocking is no longer necessary.

. . . Provides a pocket for pass protection.

. . . A running back can choose his "hole", whereas in the Single Wing he had to go to a specific "hole" and had very little choice if the "hole" closed.

. . . A more flexible, all-around offensive attack.

. . . The center becomes a more effective blocker as he can now directly face the blocker rather than having to keep his head positioned between his legs.

. . . More men in motion.

. . . Needs less versatile backs (more specialization).

The weaknesses of the T-formation are as follows:

. . . Requires specialized skills—the quarterback has to be a good ball handler and a good passer.

. . . Lacks the power of the Single Wing on short yardage situations.

. . . The quarterback is no longer a blocker after he has made his handoff.

T — 1940 CHICAGO BEARS

LE — Kavanaugh, Nowaskey
LT — Stydahar
LG — Fortmann
C — Turner
RG — Musso
RT — Artoe
RE — Wilson, Manske
QB — Luckman
LHB — Nolting, Clark
FB — Osmanski, Maniaci
RHB — McAfee, McLean
MIM — Man-In-Motion

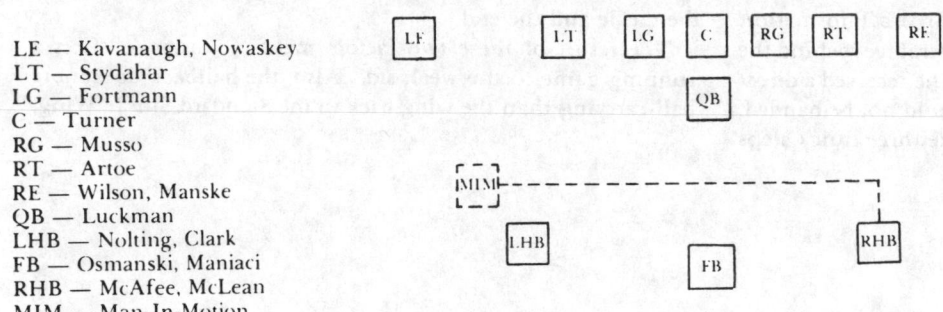

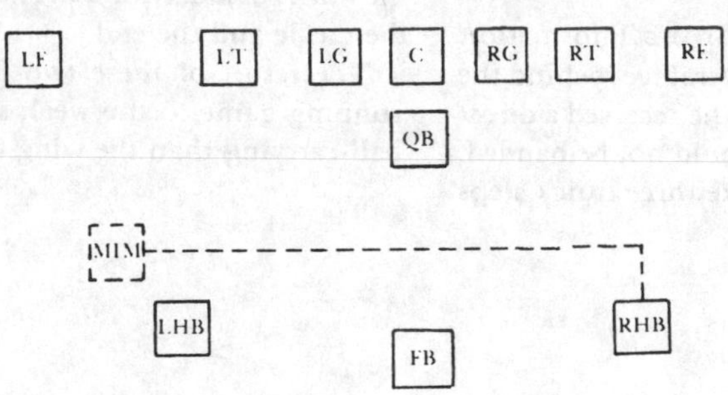

Chicago "T" (or Tight "T")

The Chicago "T", or Tight "T" as used by the Bears in the 1930's and 1940's employed fast running backs who had great faking and maneuvering ability. The great difference between the Chicago "T" and following T-formations was that the Bears tended to use only the long pass, not the quick short pass, as the alternative to a running play.

SLOT T — 1959 PHILADELPHIA EAGLES

LE — Retzlaff
LT — Smith
LG — Campbell
C — Bednarik
RG — Huth
RT — McCusker
RE — Walston
QB — Van Brocklin
FL — McDonald
HB — Barnes
FB — Peaks

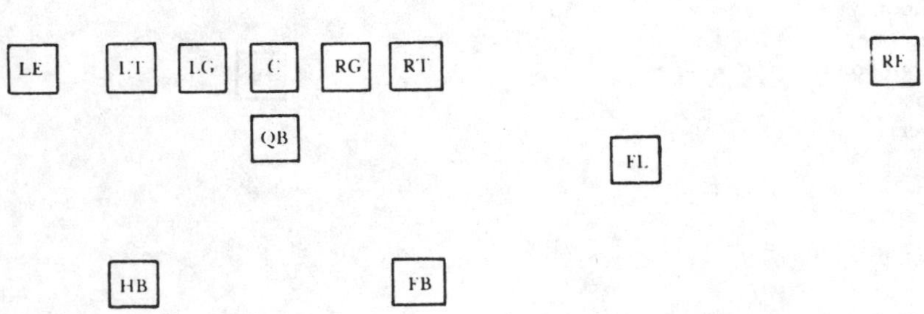

Slot T

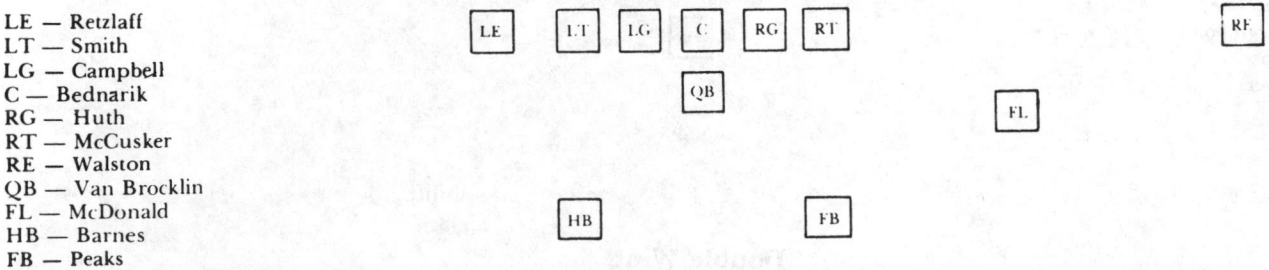

The major difference from the Tight T is splitting the right end eight to ten yards outside the tackle and placing the right halfback as a flanker in the "slot" between the right tackle and the split right end.

Neither the split end or the flanker needs to be a good blocker that the right end or halfback are in the Tight T. Both are exclusively used for their pass-catching ability. The advantage of this formation is that it spreads the defense and isolates the split end or flanker into a one-on-one situation with the defense, a goal of all receivers. The major disadvantage of this formation is basically that it is pass oriented and has limited running potential.

ONE-BACK OFFENSE — 1982 WASHINGTON REDSKINS

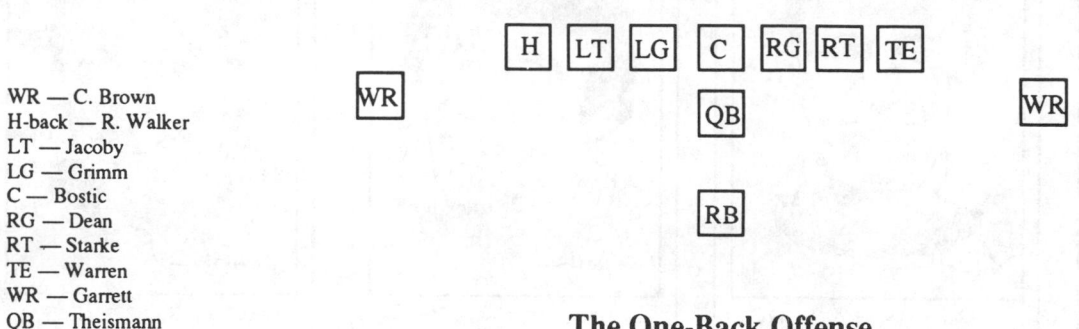

WR — C. Brown
H-back — R. Walker
LT — Jacoby
LG — Grimm
C — Bostic
RG — Dean
RT — Starke
TE — Warren
WR — Garrett
QB — Theismann
RB — Riggins

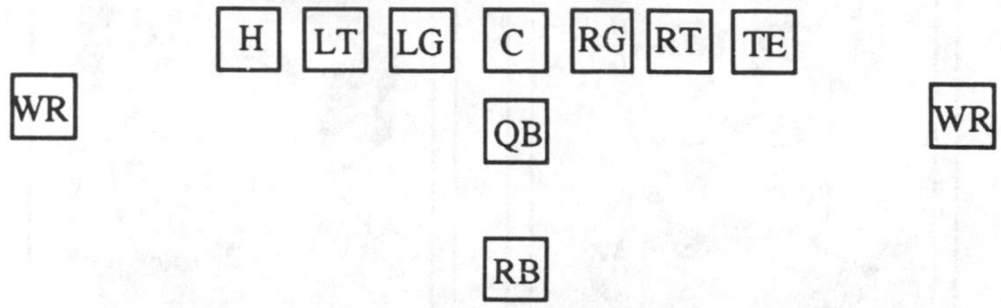

The One-Back Offense

The one-back offense, devised in the 1980s, uses two tight ends and only one running back. The second tight end is usually called the H-back, and is, in a sense, a relocated fullback.

The advantage are: another blocker is set closer to the line and a second tight end instead of a back can get downfield quicker for passes.

The one-back formation helps the running game by creating better running lanes, since the four receivers stretch the defense across the field. It also puts another good blocker on the line.

The Redskins started using the one-back offense in 1981 and they won the Super Bowl the next year.

If the second tight end is lined up next to the tackle, it is a variation of the old T-formation (the halfbacks have moved outside to become wide receivers. If the tight end moves away from the tackle, it is a variation of the I-formation (the blocking back has moved out from behind the quarterback to where he is a receiver).

RUN-AND-SHOOT — 1990 HOUSTON OILERS

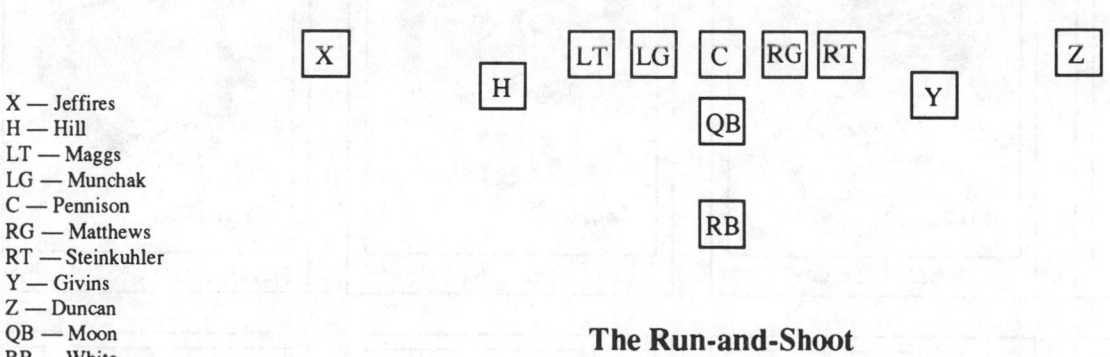

X — Jeffires
H — Hill
LT — Maggs
LG — Munchak
C — Pennison
RG — Matthews
RT — Steinkuhler
Y — Givins
Z — Duncan
QB — Moon
RB — White

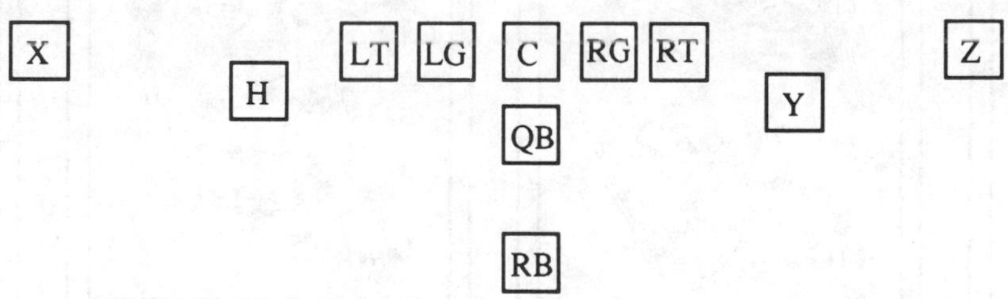

The Run-and-Shoot

The run-and-shoot offense was made popular in the NFL by the Detroit Lions and Houston Oilers.

The offensive features four wide receivers (two split wide, one in the slot and one in motion from the slot). There is no tight end. The quarterback usually takes the snap from under the center.

The Oilers designated their receivers as X (wide left), H (wing left), Y (wing right) and Z (wide right).

If it looks like a playground formation, that's because it virtually is. The four receivers run various routes but all develop on the receiver reacting to the defensive adjustment and the quarterbacks's ability to read his receivers' minds and moves. The quarterback can either drop straight back or do a half-roll behind the tackle.

If a defense overreacts to the pass, the running back is popped loose on draw plays and traps.

The weakness of the run-and-shoot is that, since teams lack a tight end and a true fullback, it is hard to score near the goal line because the receivers can't stretch the defense. Quarterbacks also take a pounding because there are fewer blockers, whether the passer is sacked or not.

Football Caricatures by Bob Carroll

Reprinted by Permission

JIM THORPE

SAMMY BAUGH

JOE NAMATH

PETE ROZELLE

EMLEN TUNNELL

GEORGE HALAS

MARION MOTLEY

SID LUCKMAN

BART STARR

BOB LILLY

WILLIE LANIER

TERRY BRADSHAW

SAM HUFF

FRANK GIFFORD

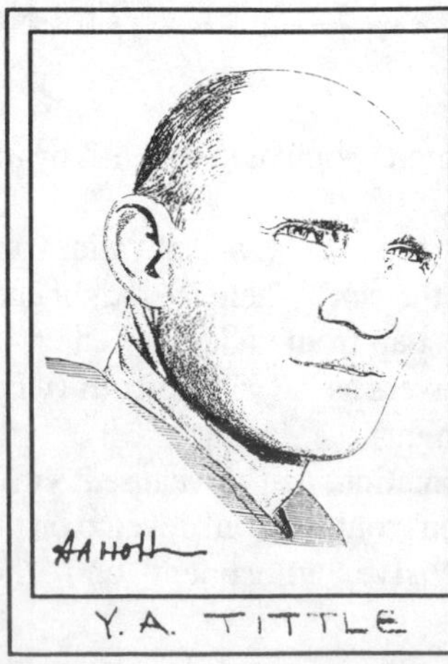
Y. A. TITTLE

LENNY MOORE

Football Caricatures by Bob Carroll

Reprinted by Permission

ROGER STAUBACH

ERNIE NEVERS

ART DONOVAN

PAUL BROWN

PADDY DRISCOLL

OTTO GRAHAM

ACE PARKER

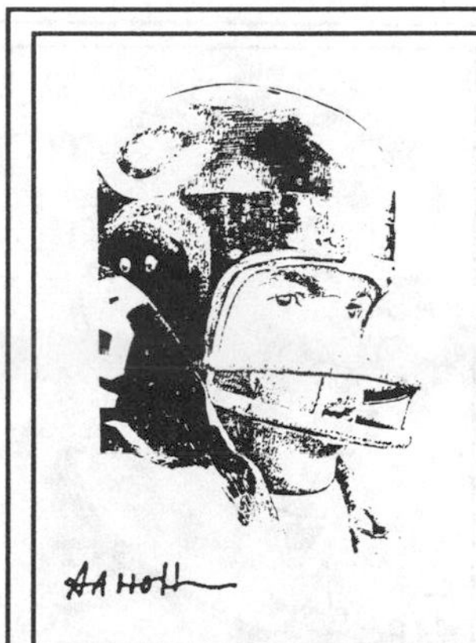
GALE SAYERS

GEORGE BLANDA

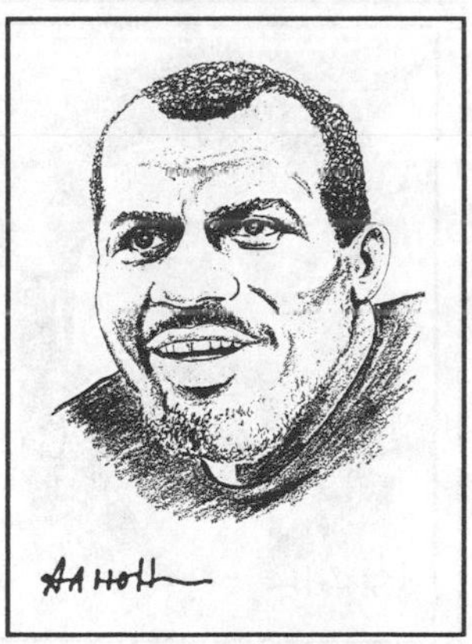
ALAN PAGE

BOBBY LAYNE

LARRY CSONKA

ART ROONEY

JOHNNY UNITAS

NORM BROCKLIN

DEACON JONES

Football Caricatures by Bob Carroll

Reprinted by Permission

DON HUTSON

RED GRANGE

JIM BROWN

CLIFF BATTLES

VINCE LOMBARDI

LOU GROZA

DICK BUTKUS

PAUL WARFIELD

O.J. SIMPSON

FRAN TARKENTON

FRANCO HARRIS

JIM TAYLOR

JACK HAM

WILLIE DAVIS

CLARKE HINKLE

JIM OTTO